2001 County and City Extra
Tenth Edition

2001 County and City Extra
Annual Metro, City, and County Data Book
Tenth Edition

Editors
Deirdre A. Gaquin
Katherine A. DeBrandt

BERNAN PRESS
Lanham, MD

© 2001 Bernan, a division of The Kraus Organization Limited.

No part of this publication may be reproduced, stored in a retrieval system, or transmitted, in any form or by any means, electronic, mechanical, photocopying, recording, or otherwise, without the prior written permission of the copyright holder. Bernan does not claim copyright in U.S. government information.

First edition 1992. Tenth edition 2001.

ISBN: 0-89059-287-X

ISSN: 1059-9096

Composed and printed by Automated Graphic Systems, Inc., White Plains, MD, on acid-free paper that meets the American National Standards Institute Z39-48 standard.

2002   2001   4 3 2 1

BERNAN
4611-F Assembly Drive
Lanham, MD 20706
800-274-4447
email: info@bernan.com
www.bernan.com

Contents

Page

xi   **Introduction**
New and Updated Information for the 2001 Edition
Subjects Covered and Volume Organization
Symbols and Terms
Sources

xiii   **Subjects Covered, by Type of Area**

xvii   **Column Headings for Tables**
States
States and Counties
Metropolitan Areas
Cities
Congressional Districts

1   **2001 Highlights**
Highlights for States, Counties, and Places at the
end of the Century
National Data Maps

23   **Area Rankings**

79   **Table A. States**

107   **Table B. States and Counties**

809   **Table C. Metropolitan Areas**

895   **Table D. Cities**

1083   **Table E. Congressional Districts**

Appendices
A-1   A. Geographic Concepts and Codes
B-1   B. Metropolitan Statistical Areas and Components
C-1   C. Metropolitan Statistical Areas and Components
by State
D-1   D. Maps of States and Congressional Districts
E-1   E. Cities by County
F-1   F. Source Notes and Explanations

Contents

Page

Introduction xi
  New and Updated Information for the 2001 Edition
  Subjects Covered and Volume Organization
  Symbols and Terms
  Sources

Subjects Covered by Type of Area xiii

Column Headings for Tables xvii
  States
  States and Counties
  Metropolitan Areas
  Cities
  Congressional Districts

2001 Highlights 1
  Highlights for States, Counties, and Places at the
    end of the Century
  National Data Maps

Area Rankings 23

Table A. States 79

Table B. States and Counties 107

Table C. Metropolitan Areas 809

Table D. Cities 895

Table E. Congressional Districts 1033

Appendices
  A. Geographic Concepts and Codes A-1
  B. Metropolitan Statistical Areas and Components . B-1
  C. Metropolitan Statistical Areas and Components
    by State C-1
  D. Maps of States and Congressional Districts ... D-1
  E. Cities by County E-1
  F. Source Notes and Explanations F-1

ABOUT THE EDITORS

Deirdre Gaquin has been a data use consultant to private organizations, government agencies, and universities for almost 20 years. Prior to that, she was Director of Data Access Services at Data Use & Access Laboratories, a pioneer in private sector distribution of federal statistical data. A former President of the Association of Public Data Users, Ms. Gaquin has served on numerous boards, panels, and task forces concerned with federal statistical data. She holds a Master of Urban Planning (MUP) degree from Hunter College.

Katherine A. DeBrandt is an editor with Bernan Associates. She received her B.A. in political science from Colgate University. She is also an editor of Education Statistics of the United States, Second Edition, 2000.

ACKNOWLEDGEMENTS

The editors of *2001 County and City Extra* extend their thanks to George Hall, Courtenay Slater, Richard Dodge, and Mark Littman, former editors and advisors whose contributions continue to enrich this book.

We are extremely grateful to Dan Parham who has ably shepherded this edition through the editorial and production process, allowing us, with tremendous support from Automated Graphic Systems, Inc., to meet many tight deadlines.

Lorrent Smith of Bernan Press prepared the text graphics and the color county maps were prepared by Bowring Cartographic.

As always we are especially grateful to the many federal agency personnel who assisted us in obtaining data in a timely manner and who responded patiently to our many queries about data availability, definitions, coverage, and numerous other matters.

INTRODUCTION

County and City Extra is an annual publication providing the most up-to-date statistical information available for every state, county, metropolitan area, congressional district, and for all cities in the United States with a 1990 population of 25,000 or more. Data for places including towns and cities under 25,000 population are published in a separate companion Bernan Press volume, *Places, Towns, and Townships*. These two volumes are designed to meet the needs of libraries, businesses, and other organizations or individuals who desire convenient and timely sources of the most frequently sought information about geographic entities within the United States. Annual updating of *County and City Extra* ensures its stature as a reliable and authoritative source for statistical information.

New and Updated Information for the 2001 Edition

As this edition went to press, release of the data from the 2000 Census was just beginning. The 2000 Census population for the states is included in Table A, but more details and additional geographic coverage will follow in a companion volume later in the year.

Since last year's edition, the release of the 1997 Economic Census was completed. This edition includes new Manufacturing and Construction data, as well as state-level comparisons with 1992 data based on the Standard Industrial Classification (SIC) codes which are no longer used for most of the 1997 Economic Census data.

Recently released government finance data from the 1997 Census of Governments is included for states, counties, metropolitan areas, and cities.

Results of the 2000 Presidential Election are included for all states and for counties in many of the states.

Updated data in this edition include 1999 population estimates by age and race for states, counties, and metropolitan areas as well as 1999 city population totals. Civilian labor force, crimes known to police, residential construction, and federal funds data have all been updated for cities, counties, metropolitan areas, and states. Vital statistics (births and deaths), income and poverty, educational expenditures, and employment and payroll have been updated for states, counties, and metropolitan areas.

Although some of the state data are also included in Table B (States and Counties), the separate state data table offers several important features:

- Additional data not available at the county level can be found. Examples include population projections, health insurance coverage, homeownership rates, number of immigrants, personal tax payments, information on health service firms not subject to federal tax, and exports by state of origin.

- Additional detail that exceeds the space limitations for counties can be found for states. Examples are age of householder, the more detailed information on employment in retail trade and services, and the expanded presentation of federal grants and payments to individuals by type.

- State totals can be found more quickly and compared more readily.

In addition to the new data and special features, users will find in this volume not only a careful selection of the most frequently used data from the 1990 Census, but also the latest available data for population estimates, education, vital statistics, employment and unemployment, production by industry, health resources, crime, the distribution of federal funds, city government finances, weather statistics, and many other topics.

Subjects Covered and Volume Organization

Immediately following this introduction (pages **xiii–xv**) is a chart summarizing the **subjects covered** in each of the five tables in this volume. Pages **xvii–xxxiv** show the complete column headings for each table.

The **colored map portfolio** begins on page **7**. **Rankings** of counties, cities, metropolitan areas, and congressional districts on a number of key demographic and economic characteristics begin on page **23**.

The main body of this volume contains five basic tables. **Table A**, which begins on page **79**, contains data for states. **Table B**, beginning on page **107**, contains information for states and counties, while **Table C**, beginning on page **809**, contains similar information for metropolitan areas. The county geography codes include *county typology* or *Beale* codes from the Economic Research Service of the Department of Agriculture. These codes characterize counties by size of the largest place as well as other criteria for nonmetropolitan counties (see

Appendix A for the definition of each code). Statistics for cities with a 1990 population of 25,000 or more can be found in **Table D**, which begins on page **895**. **Table E**, beginning on page **1083**, contains data for congressional districts of the 105th Congress. A contents page preceding each of tables B through E lists the page number where the data for a given geographic area begin. Counties and cities are listed alphabetically by state. Metropolitan areas are listed alphabetically, except that Primary Metropolitan Statistical Areas (PMSAs) are listed alphabetically within the Consolidated Metropolitan Statistical Area (CMSA) of which they are components. Congressional districts are listed in numeric order within state.

The Appendices include definitions of geographic concepts (**Appendix A**), sources and definitions of each data item included in this volume (**Appendix F**), a listing of metropolitan areas with their component counties delineated as of June 1999 listed alphabetically (**Appendix B**) and within state (**Appendix C**), a list of cities by county (**Appendix E**), and maps showing counties, metropolitan areas and selected places within each state (**Appendix D**).

Symbols and Terms

The following symbols are used in this volume:

D Indicates that a figure has been withheld to avoid disclosure of information pertaining to a specific organization or individual, or because it does not meet statistical standards for publication.

NA Indicates that data are not available.

X Indicates that data are not applicable or meaningful for this geographic unit.

Figures that are less than half of the unit of measure shown appear in this volume as zero.

Sources

The great majority of the data in this volume have been obtained from federal government sources. A few items are obtained from private sources that are widely recognized as reliable basic sources of those particular data items. Complete source notes for each item are included in **Appendix F**, beginning on page F-1. Data included in this volume meet the publication standards established by the Census Bureau and the other federal statistical agencies from which they were obtained. Every effort has been made to select data that are accurate, meaningful and useful. All data from censuses, surveys, and administrative records are subject to error arising from factors such as sampling variability, reporting errors, incomplete coverage, nonresponse, imputations, and processing error. Responsibility of the editors and publisher of this volume is limited to reasonable care in the reproduction and presentation of data obtained from sources believed to be reliable.

SUBJECTS COVERED, BY TYPE OF AREA

State data begin on page 79
County data begin on page 107
Metropolitan area data begin on page 809
City data begin on page 895
Congressional District data begin on page 1083

Subject	Column Number				
	Table A: States	Table B: States and Counties	Table C: Metropolitan Areas	Table D: Cities	Table E: Congressional Districts
Land area in 1990	1	1	1	1	1
Population:					
Total in 1980	29	21	21	7	
Total in 1990	30	20	20	5	2
Total in 1999	3	2	2	2	
Total in 2000	2				
Rank in 1999	4	3	3	3	
Per Square Kilometer	5	4	4	4	3
Race and Hispanic Origin in 1999	6-10	5-9	5-9		
Race and Hispanic Origin in 1990	38-43			9-14	4-9
Immigrants in 1996	28				
Foreign born population in 1990	44			15	10
Percent U.S. citizen					11
Age Distribution 1999	11-19	10-18	10-18		
Age Distribution 1990	45-53			16-24	12-20
Percent Female	20,54	19	19	25	21
Population Change 1990-1999	34	23	23	6	
Population Change 1980-1990	33	22	22	8	
Components of Population Change	35-37	24-26	24-26		
Projections to 2025	31-32				
Households:					
Number in 1998	21				
Number in 1990	55	27	27	26	22
Change	22,56	28	28	27	
Persons per Household	23,57	29	29	28	23
Age of Householder	24-27				
Female-family Householder	58	30	30	29	24
One-person	59	31	31	30	25
Vital Statistics:					
Births, birth rate	60-61	32-33	32-33		
Deaths, death rate	62,64	34,36	34,36		
Age adjusted death rate	65				
Infant deaths, infant death rate	63,66	35,37	35,37		
Health:					
Physicians	67-68	38-39	38-39		
Hospitals	69-71	40-42	40-42		
Total persons in group quarters				31	
Persons in mental hospitals				32	26
Persons in nursing homes				33	27
Persons identified as homeless				34	28
Medicare enrollees	72	43	43		
Percent lacking health insurance	96				
Percent of children lacking health insurance	97				
Crime:					
Serious	73-74	44-45	44-45	35-36	
Violent	75	46	46	37	
Property	76	47	47	38	

SUBJECTS COVERED, BY TYPE OF AREA - Continued

State data begin on page 79
County data begin on page 107
Metropolitan area data begin on page 809
City data begin on page 895
Congressional District data begin on page 1083

Subject	Table A: States	Table B: States and Counties	Table C: Metropolitan Areas	Table D: Cities	Table E: Congressional Districts
Education:					
Enrollment	77-78	48-49	48-49	39-40	29-30
Years of School/Degrees completed	79-82	50-51	50-51	41-42	31-32
Local Government Expenditures	83-84	52-53	52-53		
Income and Personal Taxes					
Money Income, Per capita and Household	85-90,98-101	54-58,62-65	54-57,62-65	43-46	33-35
Poverty	91-94	59	59	47-49	36-37
Children in poverty	95	60-61	60-61		
Personal Income by type	102-110	66-74	66-74		
Personal tax payments	111				
Disposable personal income	112-113				
Earnings by Industry	114-122	75-83	75-83		
Gross state product	123				
Transfer Payments by type	105-110	69-74	69-74		
Social Security recipients	138-139	84-85	84-85		
Supplemental Security Income recipients	140	86	86		
Construction and Housing:					
Housing units in 1998	124,126				
Housing units in 1990	128,130	87,89	87,89	50,52-53	38-39
Percent change in housing units	125,129	88	88	51	
Percent owner-occupied	127,131	90	90	54	40
Median Value, Owner costs	132-134	91-93	91-93	55-57	41-43
Median Gross Rent, rent/income ratio	135-136	94-95	94-95	58-59	44-45
Substandard units	137	96	96	60	46
Value of New Residential Construction	279-282	133-134	133-134	69-71	
Labor Force and Employment:					
Civilian labor force, change in labor force	144-146	97-98	97-98	61-62	47
Unemployment, unemployment rate	147-148	99-100	99-100	63-64	48-49
Employment in selected occupations	141-143	101-103	101-103	65-67	50-52
Work disabled persons				68	53
Nonfarm establishments		104	104		
Earnings and employment in manufacturing	151-153				
Employment by Industry	149-150,154-159	105-110	105-110		
Payroll		111-112	111-112		
Agriculture:					
Farms	160-162	113-115	113-115		
Farm Operators	163	116	116		
Acreage	164-168	117-121	117-121		
Value of land and buildings	169-170	122-123	122-123		
Value of machinery and equipment	171	124	124		
Value of agricultural sales	172-177	125-130	125-130		
Land and Water:					
Land owned by the Federal Government	178	131	131		
Developed land	179				
Water use	180	132	132		

SUBJECTS COVERED, BY TYPE OF AREA - Continued

State data begin on page 79
County data begin on page 107
Metropolitan area data begin on page 809
City data begin on page 895
Congressional District data begin on page 1083

Subject	Column Number				
	Table A: States	Table B: States and Counties	Table C: Metropolitan Areas	Table D: Cities	Table E: Congressional Districts
Manufacturing:	181-190 269-270	151-154	151-154	88-91	
Construction:	191-194 267-268				
Wholesale Trade:	195-198 271-272	135-138	135-138	72-75	
Retail Trade:	199-206 273-274	139-142	139-142	76-79	
Transportation and Warehousing:	207-210				
Finance and Insurance:	211-214 275-276				
Real Estate and Rental and Leasing:	215-218 275-276	143-146	143-146	80-83	
Information:	219-226				
Utilities:	227-230				
Professional, Scientific, and Technical Services:	231-238 277-278	147-150	147-150	84-87	
Arts, Entertainment, and Recreation:	239-242			96-99	
Health Care and Social Assistance:	243-254 277-278	159-162	159-162	100-103	
Accommodation and Food Services:	255-259	155-158	155-158	92-95	
Other Services:	260-266 277-278	163-166	163-166	104-107	
Export of goods produced	283-285				
Federal Funds and Grants:					
Payments to Individuals	290-296	168-170	168-170	115-116	
Total, salaries and wages	286-287	167,171	167,171		
Procurement contract awards	288-289	172-173	172-173	108-109	
Grants by purpose	297-302	174-177	174-177	110-114	
Government Finances:					
Revenue	303-310	178-179	178-179	117-119	
Taxes	307-310	180-182	180-182	120-123	
Expenditures	311-319	183-189	183-189	124-136	
Debt outstanding	320-321	190-191	190-191	137-139	
Government Employment:					
Federal civilian and military	322-323	192-193	192-193		
State and/or local	324	194	194	140	
Election results	325-327	195-197	195-197		
Climate				141-147	

COLUMN HEADINGS FOR STATES

Table A. States — **Land Area and Population**

STATE code	STATE	Land area, 1990[1] (sq km)	Population 2000	Population and population characteristics, 1999											
				Population			Race (percent)					Age (percent)			
				Total persons	Rank	Per square kilometer	White	Black	American Indian, Eskimo, Aleut	Asian and Pacific Islander	Hispanic[2] (percent)	Under 5 years	5 to 17 years	18 to 24 years	25 to 34 years
		1	2	3	4	5	6	7	8	9	10	11	12	13	14

1. Dry land or land partially or temporarily covered by water.   2. Hispanic persons may be of any race.

Table A. States — **Population and Households**

STATE	Population and population characteristics, 1999 (cont'd)						Households, 1998						
	Age (percent) (cont'd)									Age of householder (percent)			
	35 to 44 years	45 to 54 years	55 to 64 years	65 to 74 years	75 years and over	Percent female	Number	Percent change, 1990 to 1998	Persons per house-hold	Under 25 years	25 to 44 years	45 to 64 years	65 years and over
	15	16	17	18	19	20	21	22	23	24	25	26	27

Table A. States — **Immigration and Population Change**

STATE	Immigrants admitted to legal status, 1996	Population, 1980–2025				Population change, 1980–1999				
		Census counts		Projections		Percent change		Components of change, 1990–1999		
		1980	1990	2000	2025	1980–1990	1990–1999	Births	Deaths	Net migration
	28	29	30	31	32	33	34	35	36	37

Table A. States — **Population Characteristics, 1990**

STATE	Population characteristics, 1990 (percent)																
	Race							Age									
	White	Black	American Indian, Eskimo, Aleut	Asian and Pacific Islander	Other race	His-panic[1]	Foreign born	Under 5 years	5 to 17 years	18 to 24 years	25 to 34 years	35 to 44 years	45 to 54 years	55 to 64 years	65 to 74 years	75 years and over	Female
	38	39	40	41	42	43	44	45	46	47	48	49	50	51	52	53	54

1. Hispanic persons may be of any race.

COLUMN HEADINGS FOR STATES

Table A. States — Households 1990, Vital Statistics, and Health Resources

STATE	Households, 1990					Births, 1998		Deaths, 1998					Physicians 1998	
				Percent				Number		Rate				
										Total				
	Number	Percent change, 1980–1990	Persons per house-hold	Female family house-holder[1]	One person	Total	Rate[2]	Total	Infant[3]	Crude[2]	Age-adjusted	Infant[4]	Number	Rate[5]
	55	56	57	58	59	60	61	62	63	64	65	66	67	68

1. No spouse present.   2. Per 1,000 resident population.   3. Deaths of infants under 1 year old.   4. Deaths of infants under 1 year old per 1,000 live births.
5. Per 100,000 resident population as of July 1 of the year shown.

Table A. States — Health Resources, Crime, and Education

| STATE | Hospitals, 1998 | | | | Serious crimes known to police, 1999[2] | | | | Elementary and secondary school enrollment, 1997–1998 | | Educational attainment[4] (percent) | | | |
| | | Beds | | | | Total | | Rate[3] | | | 1990 | | 2000 | |
	Total	Number	Rate[1]	Medicare enrollees 1999	Number	Rate[3]	Violent	Property	Total (1,000)	Percent private	High school graduate or more	Bach-elor's degree or more	High school graduate or more	Bach-elor's degree or more
	69	70	71	72	73	74	75	76	77	78	79	80	81	82

1. Per 100,000 resident population as of July 1 of the year shown and over time.   3. Per 100,000 population estimated by the FBI.   2. Data for serious crimes have not been adjusted for underreporting; this may affect comparability between geographic areas   4. Persons 25 years old and older.

Table A. States — Education Expenditures, Income, Poverty, and Health Insurance

STATE	Local government expenditures for education, 1997–1998		Money income						Percent below poverty level						Average percent lacking health insurance, 1999
				1989						1989			1999		
				Households						Persons					
				Median											
	Total current expend-itures (mil dol)	Current expend-itures per student (dollars)	Per capita[1] (dollars)	Dollars	Percent change, 1979–1989 (constant 1989 dollars)	Percent with $100,000 or more	Median household income, 1997–1999 average (dollars)	Median income of family of four 1998	Total	Percent change in rate, 1979–1989	Families	Persons	Children under 18 years	Persons	Children under 18 years
	83	84	85	86	87	88	89	90	91	92	93	94	95	96	97

1. Based on population enumerated as of April 1, 1990.

Table A. States — Personal Income

STATE	Personal income, 1999												
								Sources of personal income (mil dol)					
										Transfer payments				
											Government payments to individuals			
	Total (mil dol)	Percent change, 1998–1999	Per capita[1]		Wages and salaries[2]	Propri-etors' income	Divi-dends, interest, and rent	Total	Total	Social Security	Medical payments	Income mainte-nance	Unemploy-ment insurance
			Dollars	Rank									
	98	99	100	101	102	103	104	105	106	107	108	109	110

1. Based on the resident population estimated as of July 1 of the year shown.   2. Includes other labor income.

COLUMN HEADINGS FOR STATES

Table A. States — **Personal Income and Earnings**

STATE	Personal tax payments 1999 (mil dol)	Disposable personal income, 1999		Earnings, 1999									Gross state product (mil dol) 1998
						Percent by selected industries							
								Goods-related[2]		Service-related and other[3]			
		Total (mil dol)	Per capita[1] (dollars)	Total (mil dol)	Farm	Total	Manu-facturing	Total	Retail trade	Finance, insurance, and real estate	Services	Government	
	111	112	113	114	115	116	117	118	119	120	121	122	123

1. Based on the resident population estimated as of July 1 of the year shown. 2. Includes mining, construction, and manufacturing. 3. Includes private sector earnings in agricultural services, forestry, and fisheries; transportation and public utilities; wholesale and retail trade; finance, insurance, and real estate; and services.

Table A. States — **Housing**

STATE	Housing units, 1998				Housing units, 1990									
			Occupied units				Occupied units							
									Owner-occupied				Renter-occupied	
											Owner cost as a percent of income				
	Total	Percent change 1990–1998	Total	Percent owner-occupied	Total	Percent change, 1980–1990	Total	Percent	Median value[1] (dollars)	With a mort-gage	Without a mort-gage	Median rent[2] (dollars)	Rent as a per-cent of income	Sub-standard units[3] (percent)
	124	125	126	127	128	129	130	131	132	133	134	135	136	137

1. Specified owner-occupied units. 2. Specified renter-occupied units. 3. Overcrowded or lacking complete plumbing facilities.

Table A. States — **Social Security, Employment, Unemployment, and Labor Force**

STATE	Social Security beneficiaries, December 1999		Supple-mental Security Income recipients, December 1999	Civilian employment and selected occupations, March 1999[2]			Civilian labor force annual average 1999				
					Percent					Unemployed	
	Number	Rate[1]		Total	Profes-sional, managerial, and technical	Precision production, craft, and repair	Total	Percent change, 1998–1999	Employed	Total	Rate[3]
	138	139	140	141	142	143	144	145	146	147	148

1. Per 1,000 resident population estimated as of July 1 of the year shown. 2. Persons 16 years and older. 3. Percent of civilian labor force.

Table A. States — **Nonfarm Employment and Earnings**

STATE	Private nonfarm employment and earnings, 1999										
	Employment		Manufacturing			Employment (1,000)					
				Average earnings of production workers							
	Total (1,000)	Percent change, 1998–1999	Employ-ment (1,000)	Hourly	Weekly	Con-struction	Trans-portation and public utilities	Whole-sale trade	Retail trade	Finance, insurance, and real estate	Services
	149	150	151	152	153	154	155	156	157	158	159

COLUMN HEADINGS FOR STATES

Table A. States — **Agriculture**

STATE	Agriculture, 1997										
	Farms				Land in farms					Value of land and buildings	
		Percent with —					Acres				
	Number	Less than 50 acres	500 acres and over	Farm operators whose principal occupation is farming (percent)	Acreage (1,000)	Percent change, 1992–1997	Average size of farm	Total irrigated (1,000)	Total cropland (1,000)	Average per farm ($1,000)	Average per acre (dollars)
	160	161	162	163	164	165	166	167	168	169	170

Table A. States — **Agriculture, Land, and Water**

STATE	Agriculture, 1997 (cont'd)							Land, 1997		
		Value of products sold				Percent of farms with sales of —				
				Percent from —						
	Value of machinery and equipment Average per farm ($1,000)	Total (mil dol)	Average per farm (dollars)	Crops	Livestock and poultry products	$10,000 or more	$100,000 or more	Owned by Federal Government (percent)	Developed (percent)	Water consumption (mil gal per day) 1995
	171	172	173	174	175	176	177	178	179	180

Table A. States — **Manufactures and Construction**

STATE	Manufactures, 1998										Construction, 1997			
	All employees			Production workers				Value added by manufacture (mil dol)	Value of shipments (mil dol)	Total capital expenditures (mil dol)				
						Wages								
	Number (1,000)	Percent change, 1997–1998	Annual Payroll (mil dol)	Number (1,000)	Work hours (millions)	Total (mil dol)	Average per worker (dollars)				Establishments	Value (mil dol)	Paid employees	Annual Payroll (mil dol)
	181	182	183	184	185	186	187	188	189	190	191	192	193	194

Table A. States — **Wholesale and Retail Trade**

STATE	Wholesale Trade, 1997				Retail Trade[1], 1997							
						Number of Employees						
	Number of Establishments	Number of Employees	Sales (mil dol)	Annual Payroll (mil dol)	Number of Establishments	Total	Motor Vehicle and Parts Dealers	Food and Beverage Stores	Clothing and Clothing Accessory Stores	General Merchandise Stores	Sales (mil dol)	Annual Payroll (mil dol)
	195	196	197	198	199	200	201	202	203	204	205	206

1. Establishments with payroll.

COLUMN HEADINGS FOR STATES

Table A. States — Transportation and Warehousing, Finance and Insurance, and Real Estate

STATE	Transportation and Warehousing, 1997				Finance and Insurance, 1997				Real Estate and Rental and Leasing, 1997			
	Number of Establishments	Number of Employees	Receipts (mil dol)	Annual Payroll (mil dol)	Number of Establishments	Number of Employees	Receipts (mil dol)	Annual Payroll (mil dol)	Number of Establishments	Number of Employees	Receipts (mil dol)	Annual Payroll (mil dol)
	207	208	209	210	211	212	213	214	215	216	217	218

Table A. States — Information and Utilities

STATE	Information, 1997								Utilities, 1997			
	Number of Establishments	Number of Employees					Receipts (mil dol)	Annual Payroll (mil dol)	Number of Establishments	Number of Employees	Receipts (mil dol)	Annual Payroll (mil dol)
		Total	Publishing	Motion Picture and Sound Recording	Broadcast and telecommunications	Information and Data Processing Services						
	219	220	221	222	223	224	225	226	227	228	229	230

Table A. States — Professional, Scientific, and Technical Services, and Arts, Entertainment, and Recreation

STATE	Professional, Scientific, and Technical Services,[1] 1997								Arts, Entertainment, and Recreation,[1] 1997			
	Number of Establishments	Number of Employees					Receipts (mil dol)	Annual Payroll (mil dol)	Number of Establishments	Number of Employees	Receipts (mil dol)	Annual Payroll (mil dol)
		Total	Legal Services	Accounting and Related Services	Architectural, Engineering, and Related Services	Computer Systems Design and Related Services						
	231	232	233	234	235	236	237	238	239	240	241	242

1. Firms subject to federal tax.

Table A. States — Health Care and Social Assistance

STATE	Health Care and Social Assistance, 1997											
	Subject to Federal Tax						Tax Exempt					
	Number of Establishments	Number of Employees			Receipts (mil dol)	Annual Payroll (mil dol)	Number of Establishments	Number of Employees			Receipts (mil dol)	Annual Payroll (mil dol)
		Total	Ambulatory Health Care Services	Hospitals				Total	Ambulatory Health Care Services	Hospitals		
	243	244	245	246	247	248	249	250	251	252	253	254

COLUMN HEADINGS FOR STATES

Table A. States — Accommodation and Food Services and Other Services

STATE	Accommodation and Food Services, 1997					Other Services						
		Number of Employees						Number of Employees				
	Number of Establish-ments	Total	Food Services and Drinking Places	Receipts (mil dol)	Annual Payroll (mil dol)	Number of Establish-ments[1]	Total[1]	Repair and Maintenance[1]	Personal and Laundry Services[1]	Religious, Civic, and Similar Services[2]	Receipts (mil dol)[1]	Annual Payroll (mil dol)[1]
	255	256	257	258	259	260	261	262	263	264	265	266

1. Firms subject to federal tax.

Table A. States — Economic Census by SIC Code

STATE	Construction		Manufacturing		Wholesale Trade		Retail Trade		Finance, Insurance, and Real Estate		Service industries, subject to federal tax	
	Paid Employees 1997	Percent change, 1992–1997	Paid Employees 1997	Percent change, 1992–1997	Paid Employees 1997	Percent change, 1992–1997	Paid Employees 1997	Percent change, 1992–1997	Paid Employees 1997	Percent change, 1992–1997	Paid Employees 1997	Percent change, 1992–1997
	267	268	269	270	271	272	273	274	275	276	277	278

Table A. States — Residential Construction, Exports, and Federal Funds

STATE	Value of residential construction authorized by building permits, 1999				Exports of goods by state of origin, 2000 (mil dol)			Federal funds and grants, fiscal 1999[1] (mil dol)				
											Procurement contract awards	
	New Construction ($1,000)	Number of housing units	Percent single family	Manufactured housing units put in place 1999 (1,000)	Total	Manufactured	Non-manufactured	Total	Salaries and wages		Defense	Other
	279	280	281	282	283	284	285	286	287		288	289

1. October 1, 1998–September 30, 1999.

Table A. States — Federal Funds

STATE	Federal funds and grants, fiscal 1999[1] (mil dol) (cont'd)											
	Direct payments for individuals							Grants				
	Total	Social Security and government retirement	Medicare	Food stamps	Supple-mental Security Income	Educational assistance	Housing assistance	Total[2]	Medicaid and other health-related	Nutrition and family welfare	Education	Housing and community devel-opment	Energy and environ-ment
	290	291	292	293	294	295	296	297	298	299	300	301	302

1. October 1, 1998 to September 30, 1999.   2. Includes program categories not shown separately.

COLUMN HEADINGS FOR STATES

Table A. States — **State Government Finances**

STATE	State government finances, fiscal 1998											
	General revenue (mil dol)								General expenditures (mil dol)			
	From federal government			From own sources							Direct general expenditures	
					Taxes		Taxes per capita[1] (dollars)					
	Total	Total	Per capita[1] (dollars)	Total	Total	Sales and gross receipts	Total	Sales and gross receipts	Total	To local govern-ments	Total	Per capita[1] (dollars)
	303	304	305	306	307	308	309	310	311	312	313	314

1. Based on the estimated population as of July 1 of the year shown.

Table A. States — **State Government Finances, Government Employment, and Elections**

STATE	State government finances, fiscal 1998 (cont'd)							Government employment, 1998			Presidential election, 2000 (percent of vote cast)		
	General expenditures (mil dol) (cont'd)					Debt outstanding							
	By selected function (mil dol)												
	Education	Health and hospitals	Highways	Public safety	Public welfare	Total (mil dol)	Per capita[1]	Federal civilian	Federal military	State and local	Demo-cratic	Repub-lican	All other
	315	316	317	318	319	320	321	322	323	324	325	326	327

1. Based on the estimated population as of July 1 of the year shown.

COLUMN HEADINGS FOR STATES AND COUNTIES

Table B. States and Counties — **Land Area and Population**

STATE/ County code	MSA/ PMSA/ NECMA code[1]	County Type[2]	STATE County	Land area,[3] (sq km) 1990	Population and population characteristics, 1999												
								Race (percent)					Age (percent)					
					Total persons	Rank	Per square kilometer	White	Black	Am. Indian, Eskimo, Aleut	Asian and Pacific Islander	Percent Hispanic[4]	Under 5 years	5 to 17 years	18 to 24 years	25 to 34 years	35 to 44 years	45 to 54 years
				1	2	3	4	5	6	7	8	9	10	11	12	13	14	15

1. MSA = Metropolitan Statistical Area. PMSA = Primary MSA. NECMA = New England County Metropolitan Area. See Appendix A for explanation of these concepts. See Appendix B for list of metropolitan areas identified by type, with component counties.   2. County typology code from the Economic Research Service of USDA. See Appendix A for definition.   3. Dry land or land partially or temporarily covered by water.   4. Hispanic persons may be of any race.

Table B. States and Counties — **Population and Households**

STATE County	Population, 1999 (cont'd)				Population — change and components of change, 1980–1999							Households, 1990				
	Age (percent) (cont'd)				Total persons		Percent change		Components of change, 1990–1999						Percent	
	55 to 64 years	65 to 74 years	75 years and over	Percent female	1990	1980	1980–1990	1990–1999	Births	Deaths	Net migration	Number	Percent change, 1980–1990	Persons per house-hold	Female family house-holder[1]	One person
	16	17	18	19	20	21	22	23	24	25	26	27	28	29	30	31

1. No spouse present.

COLUMN HEADINGS FOR STATES AND COUNTIES

Table B. States and Counties — **Vital Statistics, Health Resources, and Crime**

STATE County	Births, average 1996–1998		Deaths, average 1996–1998				Physicians,[4] 1998		Hospitals,[4] 1998			Medicare enrollees 1999	Serious crimes known to police, 1998[6]	
			Number		Rate					Beds			Total	
	Total	Rate[1]	Total	Infant[2]	Total[1]	Infant[3]	Number	Rate[5]	Number	Number	Rate[5]		Number	Rate[7]
	32	33	34	35	36	37	38	39	40	41	42	43	44	45

1. Per 1,000 estimated resident population, average 1996–1998.   2. Deaths of infants under 1 year old.   3. Deaths of infants under 1 year old per 1,000 live births.   4. Data subject to copyright.   5. Per 100,000 resident population as of July 1 of the year shown.   6. Data for serious crimes have not been adjusted for underreporting; this may affect comparability between geographic areas and over time.   7. Per 100,000 population estimated by the FBI.

Table B. States and Counties — **Crime, Education, Money Income, and Poverty**

STATE County	Serious crimes known to police, 1998[1] (cont'd)		Education							Money income				Income and poverty, 1997		
	Rate[2]		School enrollment and attainment, 1990					Local government expenditures, fiscal 1997[5]		1989				Percent below poverty level		
			Enrollment[3]		Attainment[4] (percent)						Households					
											Median					
	Violent	Property	Total	Percent private	High school graduate or more	Bachelor's degree or more	Total current expenditures (mil dol)	Current expenditures per student (dollars)	Per capita[6] (dollars)	Dollars	Percent change, 1979–1989 (constant 1989 dollars)	Percent with $100,000 or more	Median household income	All persons	Persons under 18	Persons 5–17 in families
	46	47	48	49	50	51	52	53	54	55	56	57	58	59	60	61

1. Data for serious crimes have not been adjusted for underreporting; this may affect comparability between geographic areas and over time.   2. Per 100,000 population estimated by the FBI.   3. All persons 3 years old and over enrolled in nursery school through college.   4. Persons 25 years old and over.   5. Elementary and secondary education expenditures, local government fiscal years ending between July 1, 1996 and June 30, 1997.   6. Based on population enumerated as of April 1, 1990.

Table B. States and Counties — **Personal Income**

STATE County	Personal income, 1998												
			Per capita[1]							Transfer payments			
											Government payments to individuals		
	Total (mil dol)	Percent change, 1997–1998	Dollars	Rank	Wages and salaries[2] (mil dol)	Proprietor's income (mil dol)	Dividends, interest, and rent (mil dol)	Total (mil dol)	Total (mil dol)	Social Security (mil dol)	Medical payments (mil dol)	Income mainte-nance (mil dol)	Unemploy-ment insurance (mil dol)
	62	63	64	65	66	67	68	69	70	71	72	73	74

1. Based on the resident population estimated as of July 1 of the year shown.   2. Includes other labor income.

Table B. States and Counties — **Earnings, Social Security, and Housing**

STATE County	Earnings, 1998									Social Security bene-ficiaries, December 1998		Supple-mental Security Income recipients, December 1998	Housing units, 1990	
			Percent by selected industries											
			Goods-related[1]		Service-related and other[2]									
	Total (mil dol)	Farm	Total	Manu-facturing	Total	Retail trade	Finance, insur-ance, and real estate	Services	Govern-ment	Number	Rate[3]		Total	Percent change, 1980–1990
	75	76	77	78	79	80	81	82	83	84	85	86	87	88

1. Covers mining, construction, and manufacturing.   2. Covers private sector earnings in agricultural services, forestry, and fisheries; transportation and public utilities; wholesale trade; retail trade; finance, insurance, and real estate; and services.   3. Per 1,000 resident population estimated as of July 1 of the year shown.

COLUMN HEADINGS FOR STATES AND COUNTIES

Table B. States and Counties — **Housing, Labor Force, and Employment**

STATE County	Housing units, 1990 (cont'd)								Civilian labor force, 1999				Civilian employment, 1990[5]		
	Occupied units										Unemployment			Percent	
		Owner-occupied				Renter-occupied									
				Owner cost as a percent of income											
	Total	Percent	Median value[1]	With a mortgage	Without a mortgage	Median rent[2]	Rent as percent of income	Sub-standard units[3] (percent)	Total	Percent change, 1998–1999	Total	Rate[4]	Total	Professional, managerial, and technical	Precision production, craft, and repair
	89	90	91	92	93	94	95	96	97	98	99	100	101	102	103

1. Specified owner-occupied units.   2. Specified renter-occupied units.   3. Overcrowded or lacking complete plumbing facilities.   4. Percent of civilian labor force.   5. Persons 16 years and older.

Table B. States and Counties — **Nonfarm Employment and Agriculture**

STATE County	Private nonfarm establishments, employment and payroll, 1998									Agriculture, 1997			Farm operators
		Employment						Annual payroll		Farms			
											Percent with—		
	Number of establishments	Total	Health Care and Social Assistance	Manufacturing	Retail trade	Finance and Insurance	Professional Scientific and Technical Services	Total (mil dol)	Average per employee (dollars)	Number	Less than 50 acres	500 acres and over	Whose principal occupation is farming (percent)
	104	105	106	107	108	109	110	111	112	113	114	115	116

Table B. States and Counties — **Agriculture, Land, and Water**

STATE County	Agriculture, 1997 (cont'd)															
	Land in farms					Value of land and buildings			Value of products sold				Percent of farms with sales of —			
			Acres								Percent from —					
	Acreage (1,000)	Percent change, 1992–1997	Average size of farm	Total irrigated (1,000)	Total cropland (1,000)	Average per farm ($1,000)	Average per acre (dollars)	Value of machinery and equipment Average per farm ($1,000)	Total (mil dol)	Average per farm (dollars)	Crops	Live-stock and poultry products	$10,000 or more	$100,000 or more	Percent of land owned by Fed. Gov. 1997	Water con-sumption 1995 (mil gal/ day)
	117	118	119	120	121	122	123	124	125	126	127	128	129	130	131	132

Table B. States and Counties — **Residential Construction, Wholesale and Retail Trade, and Real Estate**

STATE County	Value of Residential Construction Authorized by Building Permits, 1999		Wholesale Trade, 1997				Retail Trade[1], 1997				Real Estate and Rental and Leasing, 1997			
	New Construction ($1,000)	Number of Housing Units	Number of Establish-ments	Number of Employees	Sales (mil dol)	Annual Payroll (mil dol)	Number of Establish-ments	Number of Employees	Sales (mil dol)	Annual Payroll (mil dol)	Number of Establish-ments	Number of Employees	Receipts (mil dol)	Annual Payroll (mil dol)
	133	134	135	136	137	138	139	140	141	142	143	144	145	146

1. Establishments with payroll.

COLUMN HEADINGS FOR STATES AND COUNTIES

Table B. States and Counties — **Professional, Manufacturing, and Accommodation and Foodservices**

STATE County	Professional, Scientific, and Technical Services[1], 1997				Manufacturing, 1997				Accommodation and Foodservices, 1997			
	Number of Establishments	Number of Employees	Receipts (mil dol)	Annual Payroll (mil dol)	Number of Establishments	Number of Employees	Receipts (mil dol)	Annual Payroll (mil dol)	Number of Establishments	Number of Employees	Sales (mil dol)	Annual Payroll (mil dol)
	147	148	149	150	151	152	153	154	155	156	157	158

1. Firms subject to federal tax.

Table B. States and Counties — **Health and Other Services and Federal Funds**

STATE County	Health Care and Social Assistance[1], 1997				Other Services[1], 1997				Federal funds and grants, fiscal 1999[2]			
									Expenditures (mil dol)			
										Direct payments for individuals[3]		
	Number of Establishments	Number of Employees	Receipts (mil dol)	Annual Payroll (mil dol)	Number of Establishments	Number of Employees	Receipts (mil dol)	Annual Payroll (mil dol)	Total	Social Security and government retirement	Medicare	Food stamps and Supplemental Security Income
	159	160	161	162	163	164	165	166	167	168	169	170

1. Firms subject to federal tax.   2. October 1, 1998 to September 30, 1999.   3. State totals may include programs not allocated by county.

Table B. States and Counties — **Federal Funds and Local Government Finances**

STATE County	Federal funds and grants, fiscal 1999[1] (cont'd)							Local government finances, 1997				
	Expenditures (mil dol) (cont'd)							General revenue				
	Procurement contract awards			Grants[2]							Taxes	
												Per capita[3] (dollars)
	Salaries and wages	Defense	Other	Medicaid and other health-related	Nutrition and family welfare	Education	Other	Total (mil dol)	Intergovernmental (mil dol)	Total (mil dol)	Total	Property
	171	172	173	174	175	176	177	178	179	180	181	182

1. October 1, 1998 to September 30, 1999.   2. State totals may include programs not allocated by county.   3. Based on the resident population estimated as of July 1 of the year shown.

Table B. States and Counties — **Local Government Finances, Government Employment, and Elections**

STATE County	Local government finances, 1997 (cont'd)									Government employment, 1998			Presidential election, 2000		
	Direct general expenditure							Debt outstanding					Percent of vote cast —		
			Percent of total for —												
	Total (mil dol)	Per capita[1] (dollars)	Education	Health and hospitals	Police protection	Public welfare	Highways	Total (mil dol)	Per capita[1] (dollars)	Federal civilian	Federal military	State and local	Democratic	Republican	All other
	183	184	185	186	187	188	189	190	191	192	193	194	195	196	197

1. Based on the resident population estimated as of July 1 of the year shown.

COLUMN HEADINGS FOR METROPOLITAN AREAS

Table C. Metropolitan Areas — **Land Area and Population**

CMSA/ MSA/ PMSA/ NECMA code[1]	Area Name	Land area,[2] (sq km) 1990	Population and population characteristics, 1999													
						Race (percent)					Age (percent)					
			Total persons	Rank	Per square kilometer	White	Black	Am. Indian, Eskimo, Aleut	Asian and Pacific Islander	Percent Hispanic[3]	Under 5 years	5 to 17 years	18 to 24 years	25 to 34 years	35 to 44 years	45 to 54 years
		1	2	3	4	5	6	7	8	9	10	11	12	13	14	15

1. MSA = Metropolitan Statistical Area. CMSA = Consolidated MSA. PMSA = Primary MSA. NECMA = New England County Metropolitan Area. See Appendix A for explanation of these concepts. See Appendix B for list of metropolitan areas identified by type, with component counties.   2. Dry land or land partially or temporarily covered by water.   3. Hispanic persons may be of any race.

Table C. Metropolitan Areas — **Population and Households**

Area Name	Population, 1999 (cont'd)				Population — change and components of change, 1980–1999							Households, 1990				
	Age (percent) (cont'd)				Total persons		Percent change		Components of change, 1990–1999						Percent	
	55 to 64 years	65 to 74 years	75 years and over	Percent female	1990	1980	1980– 1990	1990– 1999	Births	Deaths	Net migration	Number	Percent change, 1980– 1990	Persons per house- hold	Female family house- holder[1]	One person
	16	17	18	19	20	21	22	23	24	25	26	27	28	29	30	31

1. No spouse present.

Table C. Metropolitan Areas — **Vital Statistics, Health Resources, and Crime**

Area Name	Births, average 1996–1998		Deaths, average 1996–1998				Physicians,[4] 1998		Hospitals,[4] 1998			Medicare enrollees 1999	Serious crimes known to police, 1998[6]	
			Number		Rate					Beds			Total	
	Total	Rate[1]	Total	Infant[2]	Total[1]	Infant[3]	Number	Rate[5]	Number	Number	Rate[5]		Number	Rate[7]
	32	33	34	35	36	37	38	39	40	41	42	43	44	45

1. Per 1,000 estimated resident population, average 1996–1998.   2. Deaths of infants under 1 year old.   3. Deaths of infants under 1 year old per 1,000 live births.   4. Data subject to copyright.   5. Per 100,000 resident population as of July 1 of the year shown.   6. Data for serious crimes have not been adjusted for underreporting; this may affect comparability between geographic areas and over time.   7. Per 100,000 population estimated by the FBI.

Table C. Metropolitan Areas — **Crime, Education, Money Income, and Poverty**

Area Name	Serious crimes known to police, 1998[1] (cont'd)		Education							Money income				Income and poverty, 1997		
	Rate[2]		School enrollment and attainment, 1990					Local government expenditures, fiscal 1997[5]		1989				Percent below poverty level		
			Enrollment[3]		Attainment[4] (percent)						Households					
											Median					
	Violent	Property	Total	Percent private	High school grad- uate or more	Bach- elor's degree or more	Total current expendi- tures (mil dol)	Current expendi- tures per student (dollars)	Per capita[6] (dollars)	Dollars	Percent change, 1979–1989 (constant 1989 dollars)	Percent with $100,000 or more	Median house- hold income	All persons	Persons under 18	Persons 5–17 in families
	46	47	48	49	50	51	52	53	54	55	56	57	58	59	60	61

1. Data for serious crimes have not been adjusted for underreporting; this may affect comparability between geographic areas and over time.   2. Per 100,000 population estimated by the FBI.   3. All persons 3 years old and over enrolled in nursery school through college.   4. Persons 25 years old and over.   5. Elementary and secondary education expenditures, local government fiscal years ending between July 1, 1996 and June 30, 1997.   6. Based on population enumerated as of April 1, 1990.

COLUMN HEADINGS FOR METROPOLITAN AREAS

Table C. Metropolitan Areas — **Personal Income**

Area Name	Personal income, 1998												
	Total (mil dol)	Per capita[1]			Wages and salaries[2] (mil dol)	Proprietor's income (mil dol)	Dividends, interest, and rent (mil dol)	Transfer payments		Government payments to individuals			
		Percent change, 1997–1998	Dollars	Rank				Total (mil dol)	Total (mil dol)	Social Security (mil dol)	Medical payments (mil dol)	Income mainte-nance (mil dol)	Unemploy-ment insurance (mil dol)
	62	63	64	65	66	67	68	69	70	71	72	73	74

1. Based on the resident population estimated as of July 1 of the year shown.   2. Includes other labor income.

Table C. Metropolitan Areas — **Earnings, Social Security, and Housing**

Area Name	Earnings, 1998									Social Security bene-ficiaries, December 1998			Housing units, 1990	
	Total (mil dol)	Percent by selected industries										Supple-mental Security Income recipients, December 1998	Total	Percent change, 1980–1990
		Goods-related[1]			Service-related and other[2]									
		Farm	Total	Manu-facturing	Total	Retail trade	Finance, insur-ance, and real estate	Services	Govern-ment	Number	Rate[3]			
	75	76	77	78	79	80	81	82	83	84	85	86	87	88

1. Covers mining, construction, and manufacturing.   2. Covers private sector earnings in agricultural services, forestry, and fisheries; transportation and public utilities; wholesale trade; retail trade; finance, insurance, and real estate; and services.   3. Per 1,000 resident population estimated as of July 1 of the year shown.

Table C. Metropolitan Areas — **Housing, Labor Force, and Employment**

Area Name	Housing units, 1990 (cont'd)									Civilian labor force, 1999				Civilian employment, 1990[5]		
	Total	Occupied units								Total	Percent change, 1998–1999	Unemployment		Total	Percent	
		Percent	Owner-occupied				Renter-occupied		Sub-stand-ard units[3] (percent)			Total	Rate[4]		Professional, managerial, and technical	Precision production, craft, and repair
			Median value[1]	Owner cost as a percent of income		Median rent[2]	Rent as per-cent of income									
				With a mort-gage	Without a mort-gage											
	89	90	91	92	93	94	95	96	97	98	99	100	101	102	103

1. Specified owner-occupied units.   2. Specified renter-occupied units.   3. Overcrowded or lacking complete plumbing facilities.   4. Percent of civilian labor force.   5. Persons 16 years and older.

Table C. Metropolitan Areas — **Nonfarm Employment and Agriculture**

Area Name	Private nonfarm establishments, employment and payroll, 1998									Agriculture, 1997			
	Number of establish-ments	Employment						Annual payroll		Farms			Farm operators
		Total	Health Care and Social Assistance	Manufac-turing	Retail trade	Finance and Insurance	Professional Scientific and Technical Services	Total (mil dol)	Average per employee (dollars)	Number	Percent with—		Whose principal occu-pation is farming (percent)
											Less than 50 acres	500 acres and over	
	104	105	106	107	108	109	110	111	112	113	114	115	116

COLUMN HEADINGS FOR METROPOLITAN AREAS

Table C. Metropolitan Areas — **Agriculture, Land, and Water**

Area Name	Agriculture, 1997 (cont'd)															
	Land in farms					Value of land and buildings		Value of products sold					Percent of farms with sales of —		Percent of land owned by Fed. Gov. 1997	Water consumption 1995 (mil gal/day)
			Acres								Percent from —					
	Acreage (1,000)	Percent change, 1992–1997	Average size of farm	Total irrigated (1,000)	Total cropland (1,000)	Average per farm ($1,000)	Average per acre (dollars)	Value of machinery and equipment Average per farm ($1,000)	Total (mil dol)	Average per farm (dollars)	Crops	Live-stock and poultry products	$10,000 or more	$100,000 or more		
	117	118	119	120	121	122	123	124	125	126	127	128	129	130	131	132

Table C. Metropolitan Areas — **Residential Construction, Wholesale and Retail Trade, and Real Estate**

Area Name	Value of Residential Construction Authorized by Building Permits, 1999		Wholesale Trade, 1997				Retail Trade[1], 1997				Real Estate and Rental and Leasing, 1997			
	New Construction ($1,000)	Number of Housing Units	Number of Establish-ments	Number of Employees	Sales (mil dol)	Annual Payroll (mil dol)	Number of Establish-ments	Number of Employees	Sales (mil dol)	Annual Payroll (mil dol)	Number of Establish-ments	Number of Employees	Receipts (mil dol)	Annual Payroll (mil dol)
	133	134	135	136	137	138	139	140	141	142	143	144	145	146

1. Establishments with payroll.

Table C. Metropolitan Areas — **Professional, Manufacturing, Accommodation and Foodservices, Finance and Insurance**

Area Name	Professional, Scientific, and Technical Services[1], 1997				Manufacturing, 1997				Accommodation and Foodservices, 1997			
	Number of Establish-ments	Number of Employees	Sales (mil dol)	Annual Payroll (mil dol)	Number of Establish-ments	Number of Employees	Sales (mil dol)	Annual Payroll (mil dol)	Number of Establish-ments	Number of Employees	Sales (mil dol)	Annual Payroll (mil dol)
	147	148	149	150	151	152	153	154	155	156	157	158

1. Firms subject to federal tax.

Table C. Metropolitan Areas — **Health and Other Services and Federal Funds**

Area Name	Health Care and Social Assistance[1], 1997				Other Services[1], 1997				Federal funds and grants, fiscal 1999[2]			
									Expenditures (mil dol)			
										Direct payments for individuals		
	Number of Establish-ments	Number of Employees	Receipts (mil dol)	Annual Payroll (mil dol)	Number of Establish-ments	Number of Employees	Receipts (mil dol)	Annual Payroll (mil dol)	Total	Social Security and government retirement	Medicare	Food stamps and Supplemental Security Income
	159	160	161	162	163	164	165	166	167	168	169	170

1. Firms subject to federal tax.   2. October 1, 1998 to September 30, 1999.

COLUMN HEADINGS FOR METROPOLITAN AREAS

Table C. Metropolitan Areas — Federal Funds and Local Government Finances

Area Name	Federal funds and grants, fiscal 1999[1] (cont'd)							Local government finances, 1997				
	Expenditures (mil dol) (cont'd)							General revenue				
	Procurement contract awards			Grants[2]							Taxes	
											Per capita[3] (dollars)	
	Salaries and wages	Defense	Other	Medicaid and other health-related	Nutrition and family welfare	Education	Other	Total (mil dol)	Intergovern-mental (mil dol)	Total (mil dol)	Total	Property
	171	172	173	174	175	176	177	178	179	180	181	182

1. October 1, 1998 to September 30, 1999. 2. State totals may include programs not allocated by county. 3. Based on the resident population estimated as of July 1 of the year shown.

Table C. Metropolitan Areas — Local Government Finances, Government Employment, and Elections

Area Name	Local government finances, 1997 (cont'd)									Government employment, 1998			Presidential election, 2000		
	Direct general expenditure							Debt outstanding					Percent of vote cast —		
			Percent of total for —												
	Total (mil dol)	Per capita[1] (dollars)	Educa-tion	Health and hospitals	Police protec-tion	Public welfare	High-ways	Total (mil dol)	Per capita[1] (dollars)	Federal civilian	Federal military	State and local	Demo-cratic	Republi-can	All other
	183	184	185	186	187	188	189	190	191	192	193	194	195	196	197

1. Based on the resident population estimated as of July 1 of the year shown.

COLUMN HEADINGS FOR CITIES

Table D. Cities — Land Area and Population

STATE Place code	City	Land area, 1990[1] (sq km)	Population, 1999			Population				Population characteristics, 1990						
										Percent						
										Race						
			Total persons	Rank	Per square kilo-meter	Total persons 1990	Percent change 1990–1999	Total persons 1980	Percent change 1980–1990	White	Black	Am. Indian, Eskimo, Aleut	Asian and Pacific Islander	Other race	His-panic[2]	Foreign born
		1	2	3	4	5	6	7	8	9	10	11	12	13	14	15

1. Dry land or land partially or temporarily covered by water. 2. Hispanic persons may be of any race.

Table D. Cities — Population and Households

City	Population characteristics, 1990 (cont'd)										Households, 1990				
	Age of population (percent)													Percent	
	Under 5 years	5 to 17 years	18 to 24 years	25 to 34 years	35 to 44 years	45 to 54 years	55 to 64 years	65 to 74 years	75 years and over	Percent female	Number	Percent change, 1980–1990	Persons per house-hold	Female family house-holder[1]	One-person
	16	17	18	19	20	21	22	23	24	25	26	27	28	29	30

1. No spouse present.

COLUMN HEADINGS FOR CITIES

Table D. Cities — **Group Quarters, Crime, Education, and Income**

City	Persons in group quarters, 1990				Serious crimes known to police, 1998[2]				Education, 1990				Money income, 1989		
					Total		Rate[3]		School enrollment		Attainment[4] (percent)			Households	
														Median	
	Total	Persons in mental hospitals	Persons in nursing homes	Persons identified as homeless[1]	Number	Rate[3]	Violent	Property	Public	Private	High school graduate or more	Bachelor's degree or more	Per capita (dollars)[5]	Dollars	Percent change, 1979–1989 (constant 1989 dollars)
	31	32	33	34	35	36	37	38	39	40	41	42	43	44	45

1. Persons in emergency shelters and persons visible in street locations.   2. Data for serious crimes have not been adjusted for underreporting. This may affect comparability between geographic areas and over time.   3. Per 100,000 population estimated by the FBI.   4. Persons 25 years old and older.   5. Based on population enumerated as of April 1, 1990.

Table D. Cities — **Income, Poverty, and Housing**

City	Money income, 1989 (cont'd)				Housing units, 1990										
	Households (cont'd)	Percent below poverty, 1989						Occupied units						
		Persons		Families					Owner-occupied units				Renter-occupied units	
											Owner cost as a percent of income				
	Percent with $100,000 or more	Total	Percent change in rate, 1979–1989	Total	Total	Percent change, 1980–1990	Vacant units for sale or rent[1]	Total	Percent	Median value[2] (dollars)	With a mortgage	Without a mortgage	Median rent[3] (dollars)	Rent as percent of income	Substandard units[4] (percent)
	46	47	48	49	50	51	52	53	54	55	56	57	58	59	60

1. Includes units rented or sold but not occupied.   2. Specified owner-occupied units.   3. Specified renter-occupied units.   4. Overcrowded or lacking complete plumbing facilities.

Table D. Cities — **Labor Force, Employment, Disability, and Construction**

City	Civilian labor force, 1999				Civilian employment, 1990[2]			Disability 1990	Value of residential construction authorized by building permits, 1999		
		Unemployment				Percent					
	Total	Percent change, 1998–1999	Total	Rate[1]	Total	Professional, managerial, and technical	Precision production, craft, and repair	Work disabled persons[3] (percent)	New construction ($1,000)	Number of housing units	Percent single family
	61	62	63	64	65	66	67	68	69	70	71

1. Percent of civilian labor force.   2. Persons 16 years and older.   3. Persons 16 to 64 years old.

Table D. Cities — **Wholesale Trade, Retail Trade, and Real Estate**

City	Wholesale Trade, 1997				Retail Trade[1], 1997				Real Estate and Rental and Leasing, 1997			
	Number of Establishments	Number of Employees	Sales (mil dol)	Annual Payroll (mil dol)	Number of Establishments	Number of Employees	Sales (mil dol)	Annual Payroll (mil dol)	Number of Establishments	Number of Employees	Receipts (mil dol)	Annual Payroll (mil dol)
	72	73	74	75	76	77	78	79	80	81	82	83

1. Establishments with payroll.

COLUMN HEADINGS FOR CITIES

Table D. Cities — Professional Services, Manufacturing, Accommodation and Foodservices

City	Professional, Scientific, and Technical Services, 1997[1]				Manufacturing, 1997				Accommodation and Foodservices, 1997			
	Number of Establishments	Number of Employees	Receipts (mil dol)	Annual Payroll (mil dol)	Number of Establishments	Number of Employees	Receipts (mil dol)	Annual Payroll (mil dol)	Number of Establishments	Number of Employees	Sales (mil dol)	Annual Payroll (mil dol)
	84	85	86	87	88	89	90	91	92	93	94	95

1. Firms subject to federal tax.

Table D. Cities — Entertainment, Health Care, and Other Services

City	Arts, Entertainment, and Recreation[1], 1997				Health Care and Social Assistance[1], 1997				Other Services[1], 1997			
	Number of Establishments	Number of Employees	Receipts (mil dol)	Annual Payroll (mil dol)	Number of Establishments	Number of Employees	Receipts (mil dol)	Annual Payroll (mil dol)	Number of Establishments	Number of Employees	Receipts (mil dol)	Annual Payroll (mil dol)
	96	97	98	99	100	101	102	103	104	105	106	107

1. Firms subject to federal tax.

Table D. Cities — Federal Funds and City Government Finances

City	Selected federal funds, fiscal 1999[1] (mil dol)										City government finances, 1997					
	Procurement contracts		Grants					Direct payments for individuals			General revenue					
											Intergovernmental			Taxes		
															Per capita[3] (dollars)	
	Defense	Other	Total[2]	Health and family welfare	Energy and environment	Education	Housing and community development	Educational assistance	Housing assistance	Total (mil dol)	Total (mil dol)	Percent from state government	Total (mil dol)	Total	Property	Sales and gross receipts
	108	109	110	111	112	113	114	115	116	117	118	119	120	121	122	123

1. October 1, 1998 to September 30, 1999.   2. Includes program categories not shown separately. State totals include additional categories not allocated by city.   3. Based on population estimated as of July 1 of the year shown.

Table D. Cities — City Government Finances

City	City government finances, 1997 (cont'd)												
	General expenditure												
	Per capita[1] (dollars)		Percent of total for —										
	Total (mil dol)	Total	Capital outlays	Public welfare	Highways	Parking facilities	Education	Health and hospitals	Police protection	Sewerage and sanitation	Parks and recreation	Housing and community development	Interest on debt
	124	125	126	127	128	129	130	131	132	133	134	135	136

1. Based on population estimated as of July 1 of the year shown.

COLUMN HEADINGS FOR CITIES

Table D. Cities — City Government Finances, City Government Employment, and Climate

City	City government finances, 1997 (cont'd)			City government employment, 1999	Climate[2]							
	Debt outstanding				Average daily temperature (degrees Fahrenheit)							
					Mean		Limits					
	Total (mil dol)	Per capita[1] (dollars)	Percent utility		January	July	January[3]	July[4]	Annual precipitation (inches)	Heating degree days	Cooling degree days
	137	138	139	140	141	142	143	144	145	146	147

1. Based on the population estimated as of July 1 of the year shown. 2. Represents normal values based on the 30-year period, 1961–1990. 3. Average daily minimum. 4. Average daily maximum.

COLUMN HEADINGS FOR CONGRESSIONAL DISTRICTS

Table E. Congressional Districts 105th Congress — Land Area and Population

STATE District	Land area, 1990[1] (sq km)	Population and population characteristics, 1990																
									Percent								
				Race								Age					
		Total persons	Per square kilometer	White	Black	Am. Indian, Eskimo, Aleut	Asian and Pacific Islander	Other race	Hispanic[2]	Foreign born	U.S. citizen	Under 5 years	5 to 17 years	18 to 24 years	25 to 34 years	35 to 44 years	45 to 54 years	55 to 64 years
	1	2	3	4	5	6	7	8	9	10	11	12	13	14	15	16	17	18

1. Dry land or land partially or temporarily covered by water. 2. Hispanic persons may be of any race.

Table E. Congressional Districts 105th Congress — Population, Households, Group Quarters, and Education

STATE District	Population and population characteristics, 1990 (cont'd)			Households, 1990				Persons in mental hospitals, 1990	Persons in nursing homes, 1990	Persons identified as homeless, 1990[2]	Education, 1990	
	Percent (cont'd)					Percent					School enrollment	
	Age (cont'd)											
	65 to 74 years	75 years and over	Percent female	Number	Persons per house-hold	Female family house-holder[1]	One person				Public	Private
	19	20	21	22	23	24	25	26	27	28	29	30

1. No spouse present. 2. Persons in emergency shelters and persons visible in street locations.

COLUMN HEADINGS FOR CONGRESSIONAL DISTRICTS

Table E. Congressional Districts 105th Congress — **Education, Money Income, Poverty, and Housing**

STATE District	Education, 1990 (cont'd)		Money income, 1989			Percent below poverty level, 1989			Housing units, 1990					
	Attainment[1] (percent)			Households		Persons	Families			Occupied units				
												Owner-occupied		
													Owner cost as a percent of income	
	High school graduate or more	Bachelor's degree or more	Per capita[2]	Median	Percent with $100,000 or more	Total	Total	Total	Total	Percent	Median value[3] (dollars)	With a mortgage	Without a mortgage
	31	32	33	34	35	36	37	38	39	40	41	42	43

1. Persons 25 years old and older.   2. Based on the population enumerated as of April 1, 1990.   3. Specified owner-occupied units.

Table E. Congressional Districts 105th Congress — **Housing, Labor Force, and Employment**

STATE District	Housing units, 1990 (cont'd)			Civilian labor force, 1990			Civilian employment, 1990[4]			Disability, 1990
	Occupied units (cont'd)				Unemployment			Percent		
	Renter-occupied									
	Median rent[1] (dollars)	Rent as a percent of income	Substandard units[2] (percent)	Total	Total	Rate[3]	Total	Professional, managerial, and technical	Precision production, craft, and repair	Work disabled persons[5] (percent)
	44	45	46	47	48	49	50	51	52	53

1. Specified renter-occupied units.   2. Overcrowded or lacking complete plumbing facilities.   3. Percent of total civilian labor force.   4. Persons 16 years old and older.   5. Persons 16 to 64 years of age.

2001
Highlights

Page

2   **Highlights for States, Counties, Cities, and Metropolitan Areas at the end of the Century**

Data Maps by County
7   Population Change 1990 to 1999
8   Population Density Per Square Kilometer in 1999
9   Percent of the Population That is Black in 1999
10   Percent of the Population That is of Hispanic Origin in 1999
11   Percent of the Population Under 18 Years Old in 1999
12   Percent of the Population 65 Years and Over in 1999
13   Educational Expenditures per Student 1997
14   Unemployment Rate in 1999
15   Median Household Income in 1997
16   Poverty Rate in 1997
17   Percent of Land Owned by Federal Government 1997
18   Percent of Land in Farms in 1997
19   Value of Agricultural Sales in 1997
20   Percent of Earnings from Manufacturing in 1998
21   Percent of Earnings from Services 1998
22   Physicians per 100,000 People in 1998

Highlights for States, Counties, Cities, and Metropolitan Areas at the End of the Century

This book contains data for a variety of geographic entities—cities of 25,000 or more population, counties (or their equivalents in states without counties), metropolitan areas (regardless of size), Congressional Districts, states, and the United States as a whole. Such geographic constructs are often the basic building blocks for several forms of government organization and community services. Often they also serve as the root of many social ties within the United States such as which schools our children attend or the boundaries of what we consider our neighborhood. The discussion that follows has been gleaned from data presented in *2001 County and City Extra*.

Population

There is no simple relationship between population size and land area for most of the geographic entities for which data are presented here. At the **state** level, for example, population in 2000 ranged from a high of 33.9 million for California that was almost 69 times the low of 494,000 for Wyoming. (The median population for states—with half having a larger and half a smaller populace—was about four million persons). While California is also one of our largest states in land area (ranking third), Alaska is by far the largest state in area, more than twice the size of Texas, even though its population rank is close to the bottom (48th). Texas is the 2nd largest state in both land area and total population. At the other end of the geographic size spectrum are many of the New England states (with Rhode Island the smallest), as well as Delaware and Hawaii. As a consequence of the differing area size and population rank, New Jersey is the most densely settled state, with about 424 persons per square kilometer of land, while Alaska is the least densely settled, with less than one person (.4) per square kilometer. California, which is the state with the largest population and third largest land area, ranks 13th in terms of population density (with 82 persons per square kilometer).

The population of the United States as a whole increased by 13.1 percent between 1990 and 2000, with 19 **states** exceeding this rate and the remainder growing more slowly. States with the fastest population growth in the 1990's were concentrated in the West, with seven out of the ten fastest growing states located in that region. Heading the list was Nevada, whose population increased by two-thirds during the decade. The big surprise of the early numbers from the 2000 Census was that the United States has about 6 million more people than the estimates predicted. Every state gained population during the decade, though 1999 estimates showed declines in three states and the District of Columbia. The census showed gains of less than 1 percent in West Virginia and North Dakota, but a population loss only in DC—a loss of 5.7 percent compared with a 1999 estimated loss of 14.5 percent.

Within states, the number and physical size of **counties** varies considerably; Delaware has 3 counties while Texas has over 250 counties. For the approximately 3,140 counties (and county equivalents—see Appendix A) in the United States, population in 1999 ranged from over 9 million in Los Angeles, CA, to 113 in Loving County, TX.

Other particularly large counties in terms of population include Cook County, IL (over 5 million population), and Harris county, TX (over 3 million); the former encompassing Chicago and its suburbs, the latter containing Houston. There were 33 counties with a population of 1,000,000 or more, which combined contain about one-fourth of the U.S. population. About half of the U.S. population lived in the 150 largest counties in 1999. At the other extreme, there were 29 counties with fewer than 1,000 people in 1999. The median county population size was about 24,000 in 1999.

The nation's fastest growing counties in the 1990's tended to be in or near metropolitan areas in the West or South regions. Douglas County, CO (near Denver), grew by 160 percent, while Forsyth County, GA (near Atlanta), grew by 119 percent. The five biggest *numeric* gainers of the decade were Maricopa (AZ), Clark (NV), Los Angeles (CA), Harris (TX), and Riverside (CA). Three more California counties (Orange, San Diego, and San Bernardino) and two Florida counties (Broward and Miami-Dade) complete the top-ten numeric gainers from 1990 to 1999. The largest numeric population losses occurred in the mid-Atlantic urban counties of Philadelphia, PA; Baltimore City, MD; and Washington, DC.

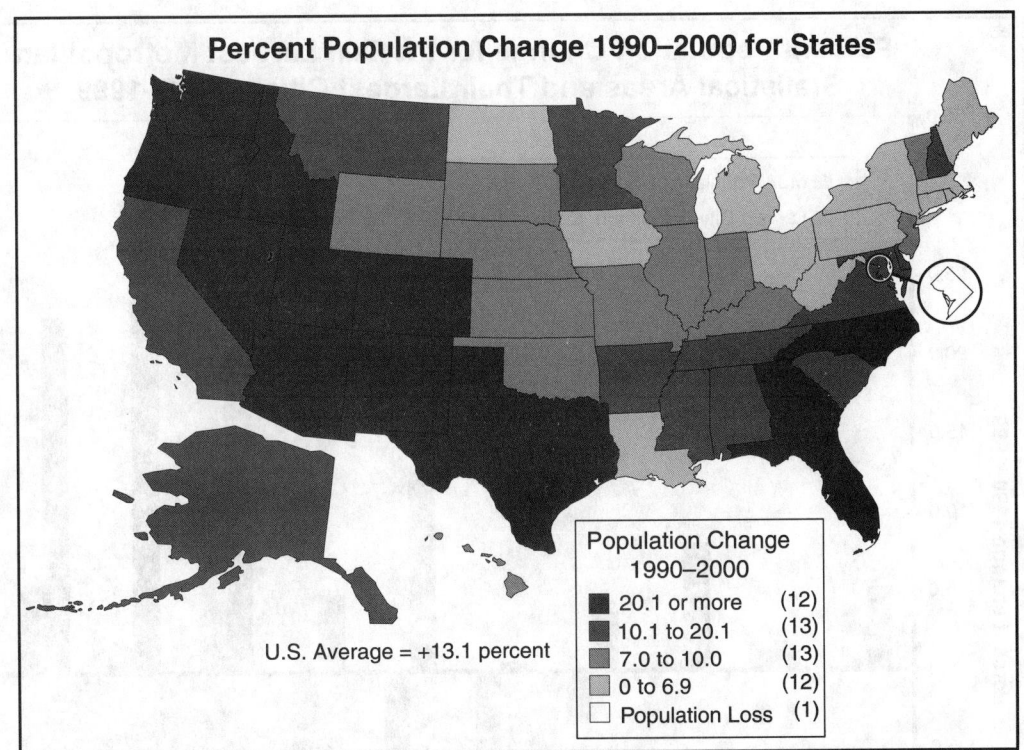

Percent Population Change 1990–2000 for States

Population Change 1990–2000

■ 20.1 or more (12)
■ 10.1 to 20.1 (13)
■ 7.0 to 10.0 (13)
■ 0 to 6.9 (12)
□ Population Loss (1)

U.S. Average = +13.1 percent

In terms of land area, counties range from the nearly 407,000 square kilometers of Yukon-Koyukuk (AK) to New York (NY) with 73 square kilometers, Arlington (VA) with 67 and Bristol (RI) with only 64 square kilometers.[1] Counties tend to be larger in the western United States (most of the largest 50 are in that region). The median land area for all U.S. counties was about 1,600 square kilometers in 1990.

While New York county (Manhattan) may have one of the smallest land areas, it had by far the highest population density among U.S. counties in 1999, with over 21,000 persons per square kilometer. No other county approached that density (although three other New York City boroughs were among the top-five counties in population density). Most of the high population density counties were components of cities (as illustrated by New York's boroughs) or areas in which large cities (e.g., Philadelphia, San Francisco, or Baltimore) were coextensive with or treated as a county equivalent. The median county only had about 16 persons per square kilometer, with only 100 counties having more than 500 persons per square kilometer. The Nation's largest county in terms of population (Los Angeles) had a population density of 887 persons per square kilometer, ranking only 46th among all U.S. counties.

The nation's 10 largest **cities** in 1999 all had populations over 1 million persons, topped by New York

City with 7.4 million, Los Angeles with 3.6 million, and Chicago with 2.8 million. California and Texas each have four cities among the Nation's 20 largest: Houston, San Antonio, Dallas, and El Paso in Texas, and Los Angeles, San Diego, San Jose, and San Francisco in California. No other state has more than one city among the 20 most populous in the country. While the majority of these large cities grew in the 1990's, Philadelphia lost 10.6 percent of its population and St. Louis lost 15.8 percent. Other major cities losing population in the 1990–99 period were Milwaukee, Memphis, Baltimore, Washington, and New Orleans. Large cities are not alone in losing population: about one out of four of the 1,100 U.S. cities with a population of 25,000 or more lost population between 1990 and 1999. The largest proportionate increase among large cities was in Phoenix, which grew by more than 22 percent in the 1990–99 period. This 1990's growth is dwarfed by the percentage increase in many smaller cities, with such places as Gilbert, AZ (1999 population of about 98,000), more than tripling during the 1990–99 period. Henderson, NV, was the fastest growing ''large'' city (with a population over 100,000), increasing its population by 156 percent between 1990 and 1999.

Juneau, AK, is the Nation's largest city in terms of land area, with over 6,700 square kilometers, an area 5.5 times the size of Los Angeles. Sixteen cities in the U.S. have land area larger than New York City (which has a land area of about 800 square kilometers). Cities with very

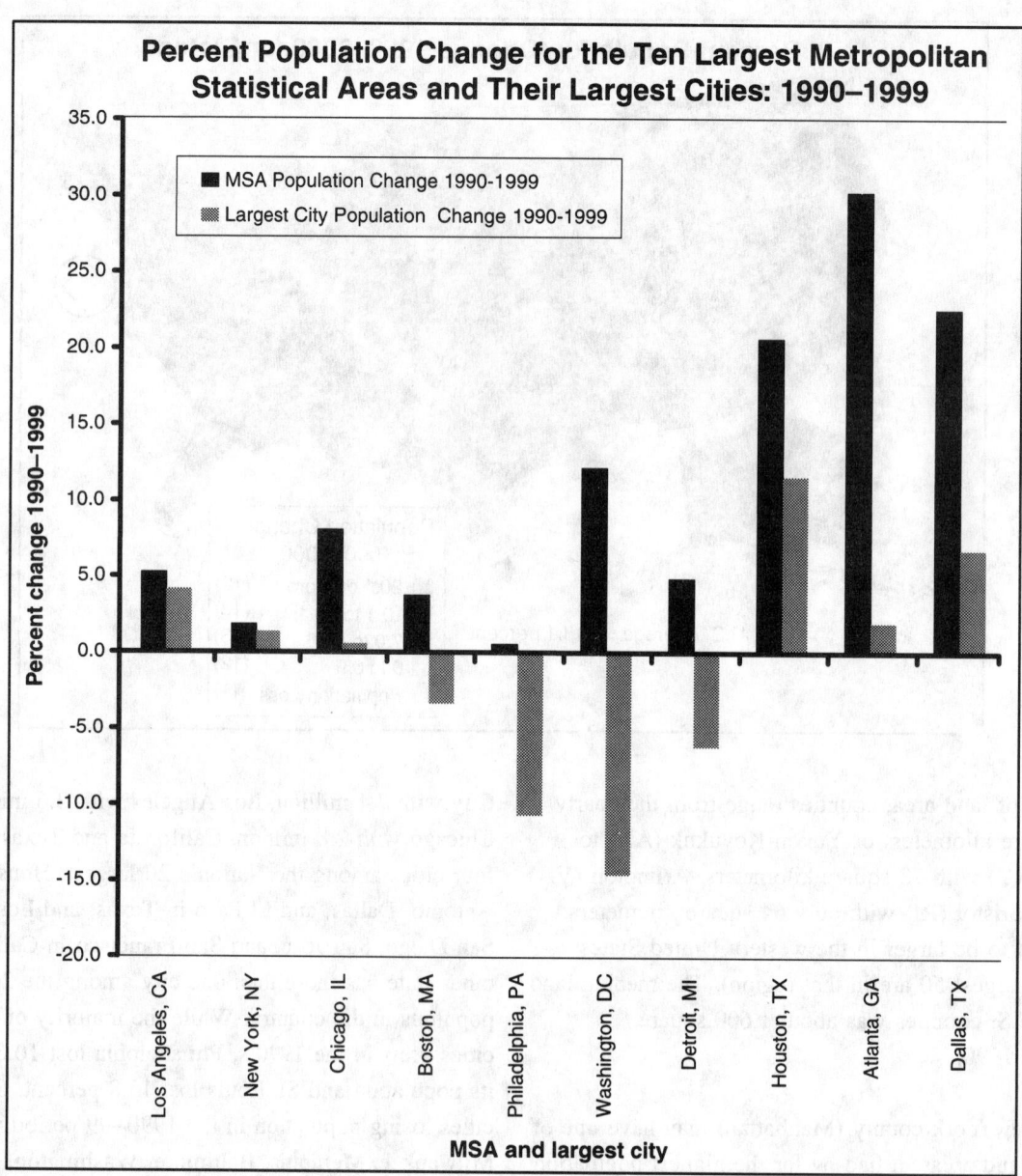

Percent Population Change for the Ten Largest Metropolitan Statistical Areas and Their Largest Cities: 1990–1999

- MSA Population Change 1990-1999
- Largest City Population Change 1990-1999

Percent change 1990–1999

MSA and largest city

large land area tend to be in the West, but some cities with boundaries coextensive with their respective counties (such as the Nashville-Davidson consolidated city in Tennessee or Indianapolis, IN) also have particularly large land area. The median land area for all places of 25,000 or more was about 48 square kilometers.

The growth (or declining population) of the largest city in a **metropolitan area** may not correspond to the growth of the metropolitan statistical area (MSA) as a whole. While, for example, Detroit city lost population during the decade, the metropolitan area grew by about 5 percent between 1990 and 1999. The population of the city of Washington, DC, decreased by about 14 percent while the metropolitan area as a whole grew by over 12 percent during this same period. It was, however, far from the fastest growing metropolitan area during the 1990's. That

distinction went to Las Vegas, Nevada-Arizona MSA, whose population increased by 62 percent between 1990 and 1999. The Atlanta metropolitan area was the fastest growing among the largest 10 metropolitan areas; after dropping 7 percent in the 1980's, the city's population grew by 2 percent in the 1990's, but the MSA as a whole had a population increase of over 30 percent between 1990 and 1999.

However, 34 MSAs did lose population during the decade, representing about one of every ten metropolitan areas in the United States. As a group those experiencing population loss are geographically dispersed, and tend to be relatively small metropolitan areas, although they may have been metropolitan for decades. They include Pine Bluff, AR; Alexandria, LA; Binghamton, NY; and Champaign-Urbana, IL, as well as larger metropolitan areas such as

Pittsburgh, Pennsylvania, and Hartford, Connecticut. None of the MSAs that lost population between 1990 and 1999 were in the West region, and about one-third of them were in the New England states or New York.

Labor Force

Often accompanying population growth is a surge in the labor force. Nevada had the highest recent population growth but, after several years of growing by more than 4 percent per year, Nevada's labor force increased by only 2.4 percent between 1998 and 1999. The District of Columbia led the states with a one-year growth of 4.8 percent in its labor force, its second year of growth after declining earlier in the decade. Arizona's labor force grew by 4.6 percent. Colorado's labor force, which had led the states in growth from 1997 to 1998, grew by only 1 percent from 1998 to 1999, less than the U.S. average of 1.2 percent. None of the states experienced declining labor forces between 1998 and 1999.

Proportionally large year-to-year labor force changes are not unusual for counties. Terrell and Delta Counties are nonmetropolitan counties in Texas with less than 5,000 people. Both experienced labor-force growth of nearly one-third between 1998 and 1999. The labor force of more than 1,300 counties shrank during the year. Though most of the decreases were small, 35 nonmetropolitan counties lost more than 10 percent of their labor force.

Seven MSAs experienced labor force increases of 5 percent or more, with the top three in Illinois (Bloomington-Normal, Champaign-Urbana, and Decatur). Five MSAs lost 3 percent or more or their labor force, three of them in Texas (Abilene, San Angelo, and Odessa-Midland).

The unemployment rate for the United States in 1998 was 4.2 percent. 24 states and the District of Columbia had higher unemployment rates, while lower rates occurred in 26 states. Iowa, New Hampshire, and Virginia were the states with the lowest unemployment rates. More than 1,500 counties had unemployment rates above the national average of 4.2 percent. Six counties had more than 20 percent unemployment, including three counties in Texas. Of the counties with high unemployment, Yuma (AZ) and Imperial (CA) had the largest labor forces. Only one metropolitan area (Yuma, AZ) had an unemployment rate of more than 20 percent, down from thirteen areas in 1998.

Seven metropolitan areas, all in Texas and California, had unemployment rates over 10 percent. Nine metropolitan areas, in different parts of the country, had unemployment rates of 2 percent or less.

The Economy

The 1997 Economic Census is the first major data source to use the new North American Industry Classification System (NAICS) which replaces the Standard Industrial Classification (SIC) system used for the past several decades. NAICS consistently classifies business establishments based on a single economic concept: economic units that use like processes to produce goods or services are grouped together—a "production-oriented" system. Developed with Canada and Mexico, NAICS seeks to reflect the structure of today's economy, including the emergence and growth of the service sector and new and advanced technologies.

The information sector is a new NAICS group that includes publishing, motion picture and sound recording, broadcast and telecommunications, and information and data processing services. Nearly 115,000 establishments in this sector reported receipts of $623 billion. California and New York accounted for 30 percent of these receipts, and 24 percent of the 3 million employees in this sector. In the Motion Picture and Sound Recording industry, however, more than 45 percent of employees worked in these two states.

Computer Systems Design and Related Services is an industry in the Professional, Scientific, and Technical Services sector. The 765,000 employees in this industry are more geographically dispersed than those in the Information sector, but Virginia, which ranked 12th in population, ranked second to California in Computer Systems employment. Los Angeles County, the most populous county, also had the highest employment (346,000) in the Professional, Scientific, and Technical Services sector. New York County (Manhattan), which was the 15th largest county in terms of population, was second in employment in this sector with 230,000 employees. Among the other top counties for Professional, Scientific, and Technical employment were Dallas County, TX; Washington, DC, and nearby Fairfax County, VA; Middlesex County, MA, near Boston; Santa Clara County, CA, which includes San Jose; and King County, WA, which includes Seattle.

Income and Poverty

The Census Bureau produced median household income and poverty estimates for all counties in 1997. Counties with high household income are scattered throughout the country. While they tend to be noncentral counties of large metropolitan areas, that is not universal. Douglas County, CO (part of the Denver metropolitan area), had the highest median household income at nearly $78,000 in 1997. Other counties with relatively high median household income included Los Alamos, NM; Hunterdon, Morris, and Somerset in New Jersey; Fairfax and Loudoun in Virginia; Fayette, GA; Hamilton, Indiana; and Howard County, MD. At the other end of the income spectrum, counties with low median household income in 1997 were virtually all nonmetropolitan and tended to be in the South. For example, counties with a 1997 median under $15,000 were East Carroll, LA; Starr, TX; and Owsley, KY. Nationally, about half the counties had median household income below $31,700 and half had a median above that figure in 1997.

Like those with low median household income, counties with the highest poverty rates also tended to be in the South and rural. But counties containing an Indian reservation were also among the poorest in 1997. Of the poorest 10 counties—which had poverty rates ranging from 40 to 47 percent—five were in Texas (Starr, Zavala, Dimmitt, Maverick, and Willacy), and three contained Indian Reservations in South Dakota (Shannon, Zeibach, and Todd). Large city poverty rates are typically lower than those in these extremely poor rural counties. The Bronx, for example, had a poverty rate of about 30 percent in 1997, ranking 80th among poor counties. The median county in the U.S. had a poverty rate of about 14 percent in 1997. The correlation is not perfect, but counties with high median income tended to have low poverty rates. Thus, Douglas county, CO, and Los Alamos, NM—top 10 counties in terms of median household income—had two of the lowest poverty rates for counties (about 2 percent) in 1997. Most of the counties with low poverty rates tended to be noncentral counties of metropolitan areas.

Agriculture

At the beginning of the 20th century, nearly 40 percent of Americans lived on farms. Today fewer than 2 percent of the U.S. population lives on farms. The number of farms has declined from about 2.7 million in 1969 to 1.9 million during the 1990's. While 86 percent of farms were still owned by individuals or families in 1997, farms have become larger on average and corporate or partnership farms now represent about 13 percent of farms. Corporation and partnership farms now account for about 37 percent of all land in farms and about 48 percent of the market value of agricultural products sold in the U.S.[2] Fewer than half of persons living on farms are employed in farm occupations, and only about a third of persons doing farm work actually live on farms.

As can be seen rather dramatically in the map on page 18, counties with high proportions of their total land area in farms are concentrated in the central third of the country as well as parts of the West. Over 700 counties have 50 percent or more of their land area in farms. Several counties in Texas and South Dakota have three-fourths or more of their land in farms (Midland, Wilbarger, Knox and Sterling in Texas; Dewey, Todd and Ziebach in South Dakota). While the total land area in farms declined 1.5 percent nationally between 1992 and 1997, that is not the case for all counties. The number of acres in farmland increased in about 1,430 counties and remained the same in 40 more. Noncentral counties of metropolitan areas typically experienced losses as suburban areas expanded. For example in the Washington, DC, metropolitan area, the land in farms declined 5 percent in Montgomery county and 12 percent in Prince George's county, MD, and by 23 percent in Fairfax county, VA, between 1992 and 1997.

About one of four farms sold under $2,500 worth of agricultural products in 1997 according to the Census, and half sold under $10,000 worth of agricultural products, making it difficult to sustain a family on the income derived from these sales alone. Farms are defined as places that produced or sold $1,000 worth of agricultural products in 1997, with no acreage limitation. Thus many farms were small, with about 30 percent under 50 acres and 60 percent under 180 acres. The average size of a farm in the median county was about 280 acres, ranging from 31,203 acres in Coconino, AZ, to less than an acre in Kings, NY, (a borough of New York City).

---

[1] Several independent cities in Virginia, which are treated as counties for tabulation purposes, were excluded here.

[2] U.S. Department of Agriculture, National Agricultural Statistics Service, 1997 Census of Agriculture, table 47, U.S. Summary.

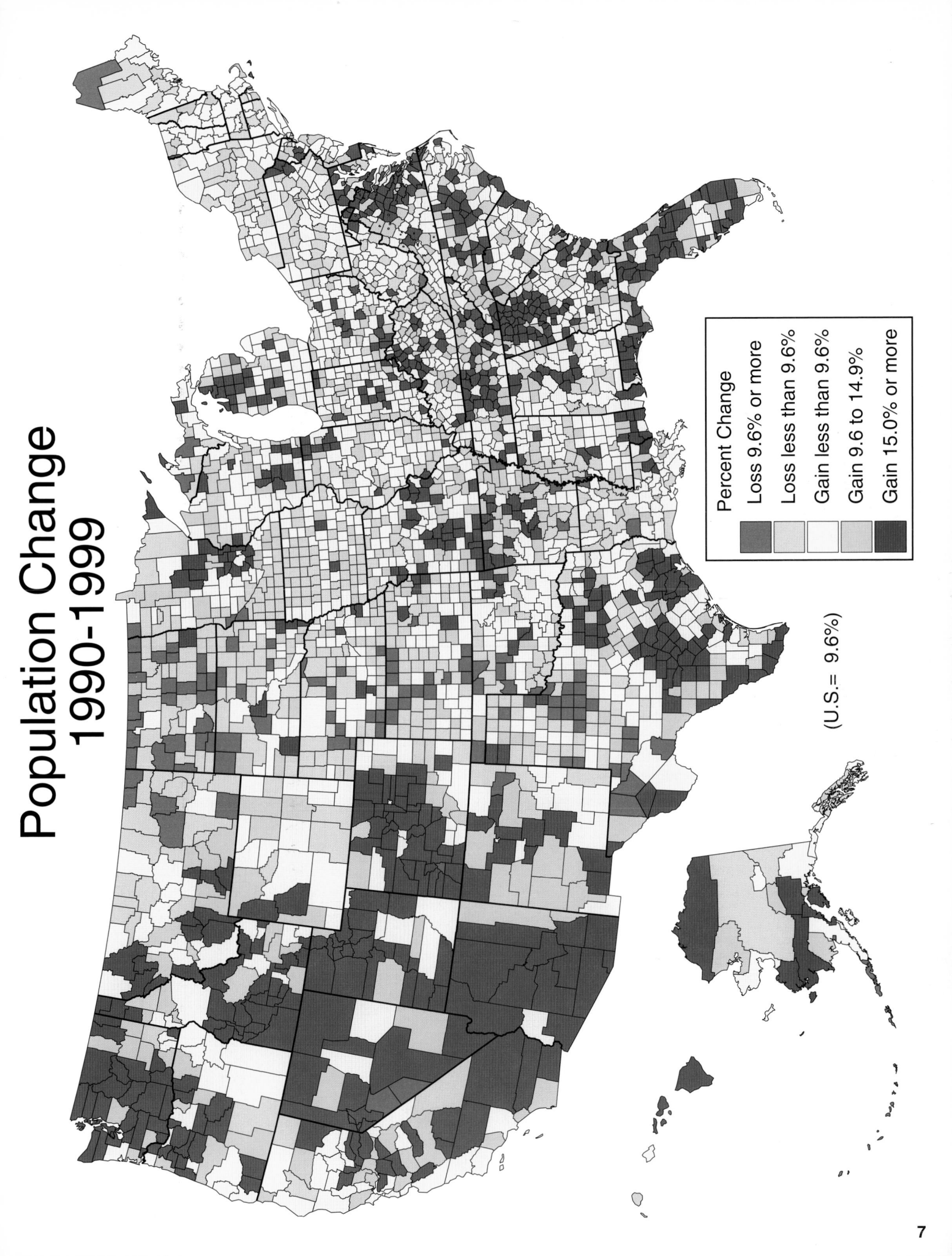

Population Change
1990-1999

Percent Change

	Loss 9.6% or more
	Loss less than 9.6%
	Gain less than 9.6%
	Gain 9.6 to 14.9%
	Gain 15.0% or more

(U.S.= 9.6%)

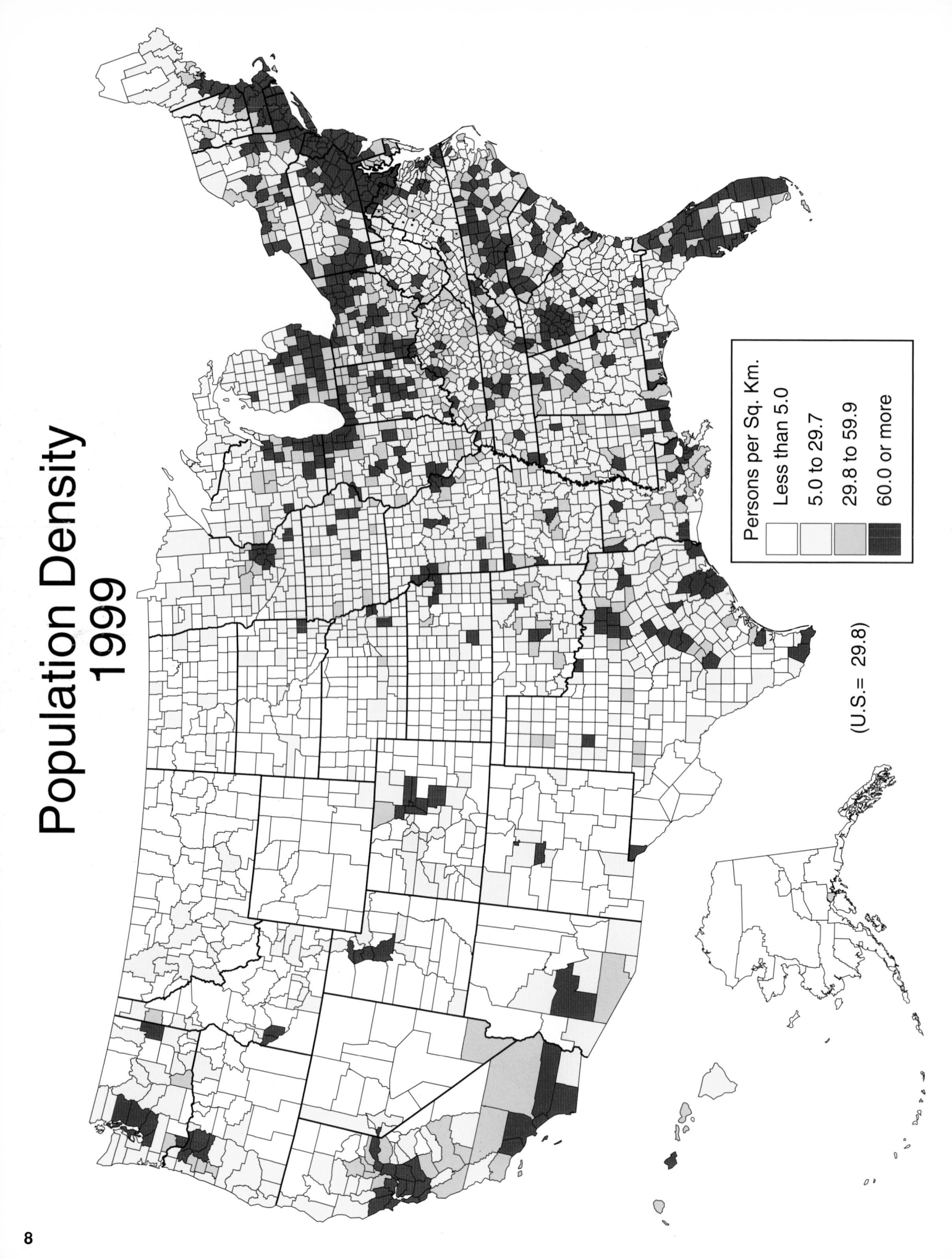

Population Density
1999

Persons per Sq. Km.

Less than 5.0

5.0 to 29.7

29.8 to 59.9

60.0 or more

(U.S. = 29.8)

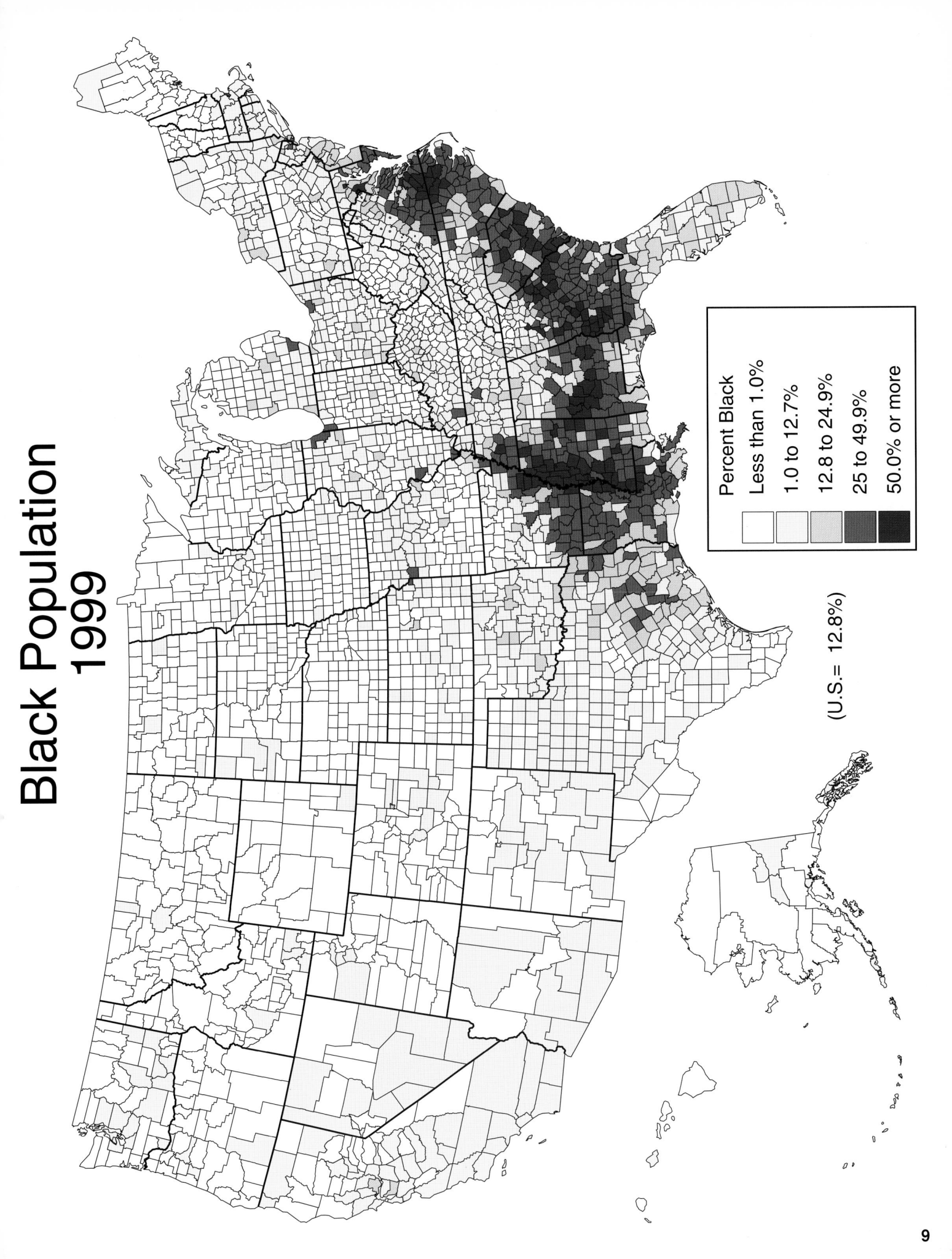

Black Population 1999

Percent Black

Less than 1.0%	
1.0 to 12.7%	
12.8 to 24.9%	
25 to 49.9%	
50.0% or more	

(U.S. = 12.8%)

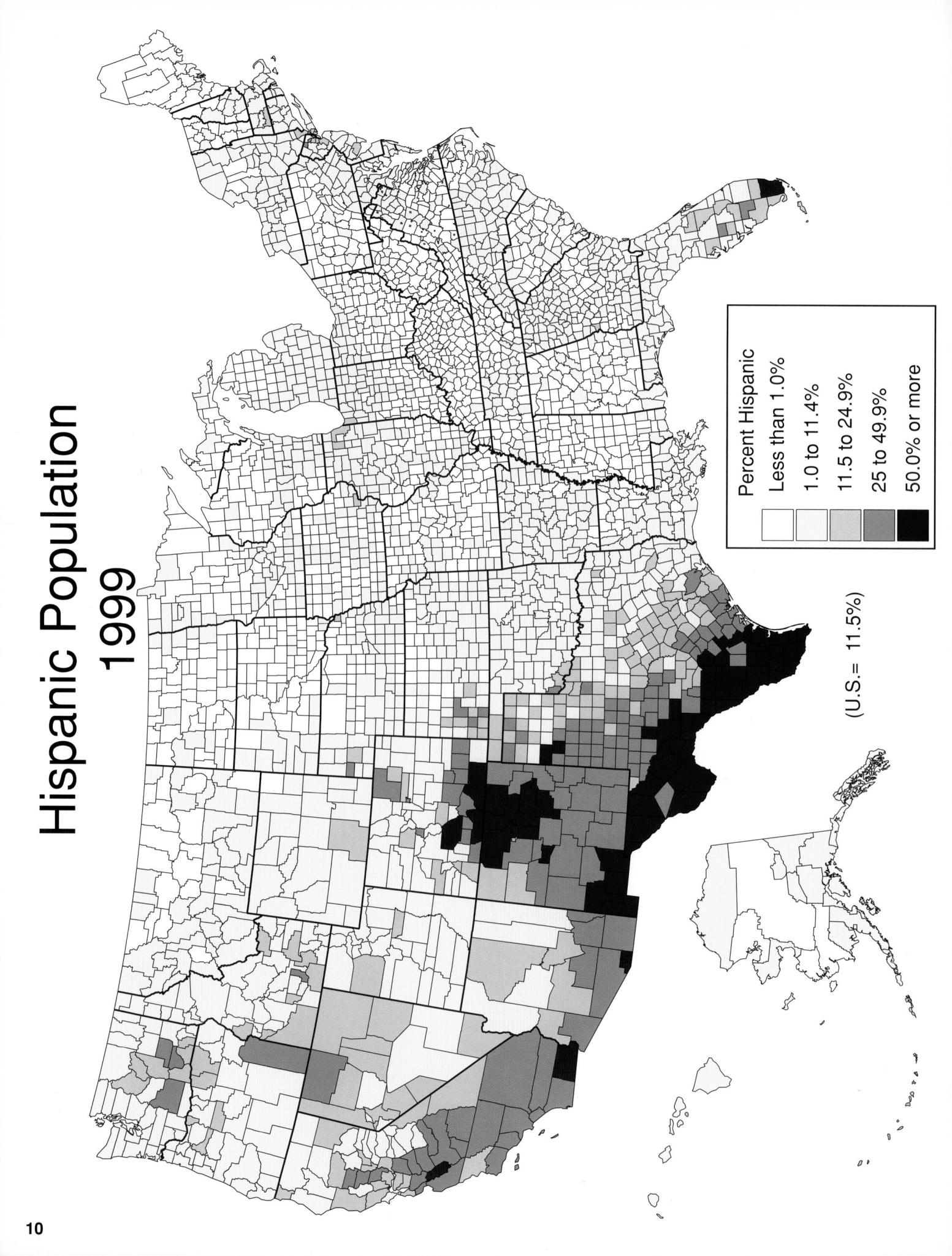

Hispanic Population
1999

Percent Hispanic

Less than 1.0%
1.0 to 11.4%
11.5 to 24.9%
25 to 49.9%
50.0% or more

(U.S. = 11.5%)

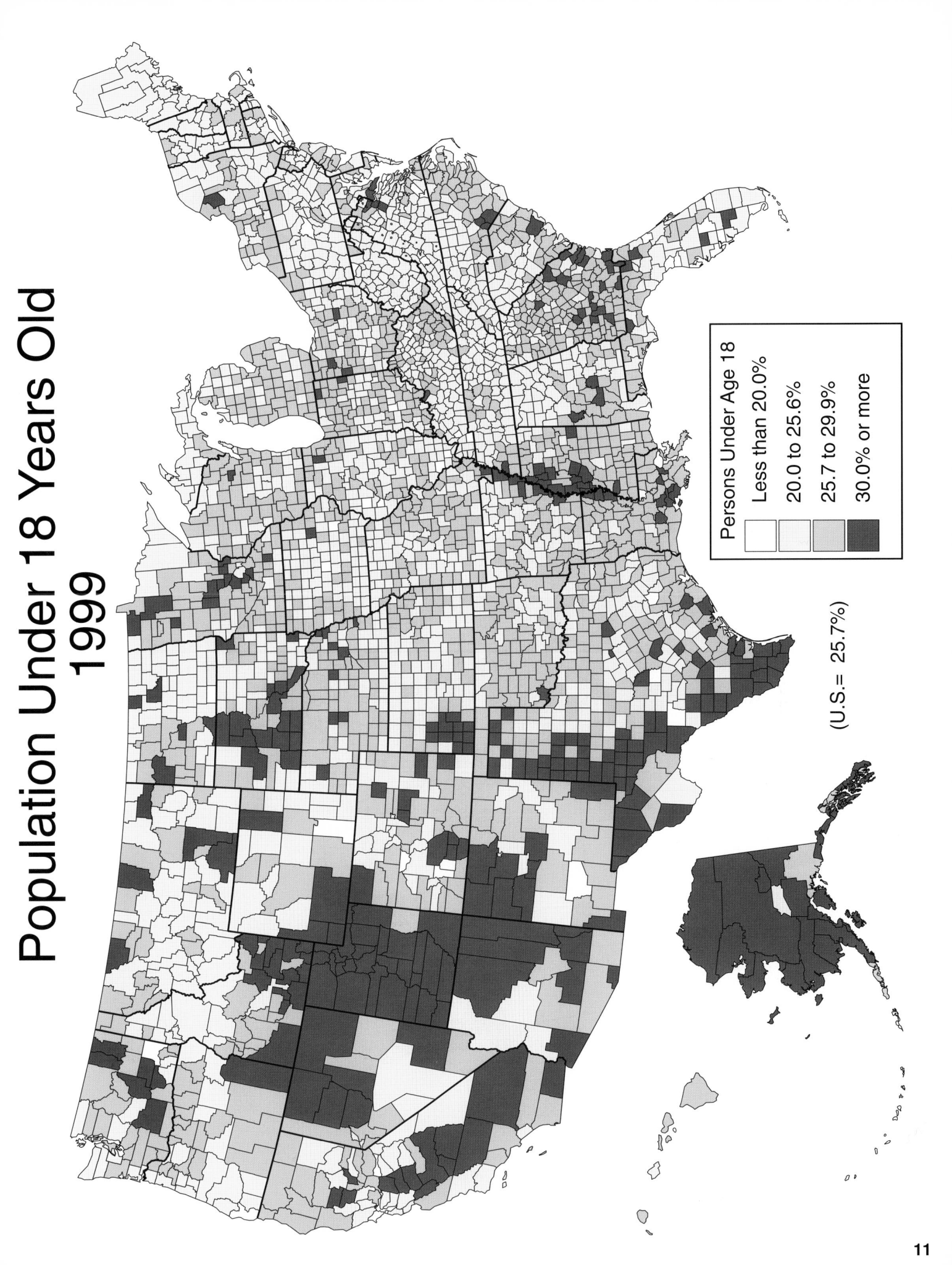

Population Under 18 Years Old
1999

Persons Under Age 18

- Less than 20.0%
- 20.0 to 25.6%
- 25.7 to 29.9%
- 30.0% or more

(U.S.= 25.7%)

Population 65 and Older
1999

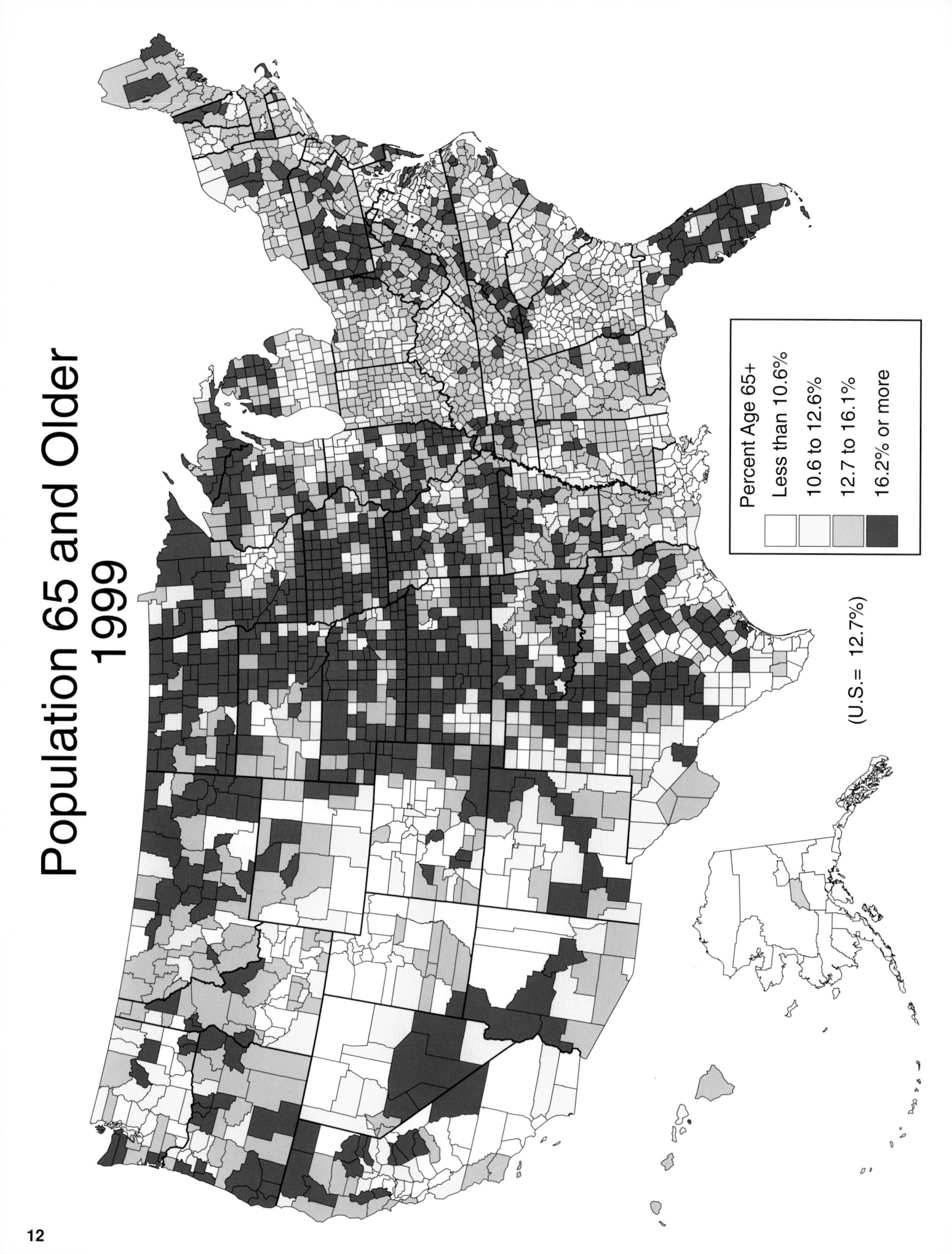

Percent Age 65+

Less than 10.6%
10.6 to 12.6%
12.7 to 16.1%
16.2% or more

(U.S. = 12.7%)

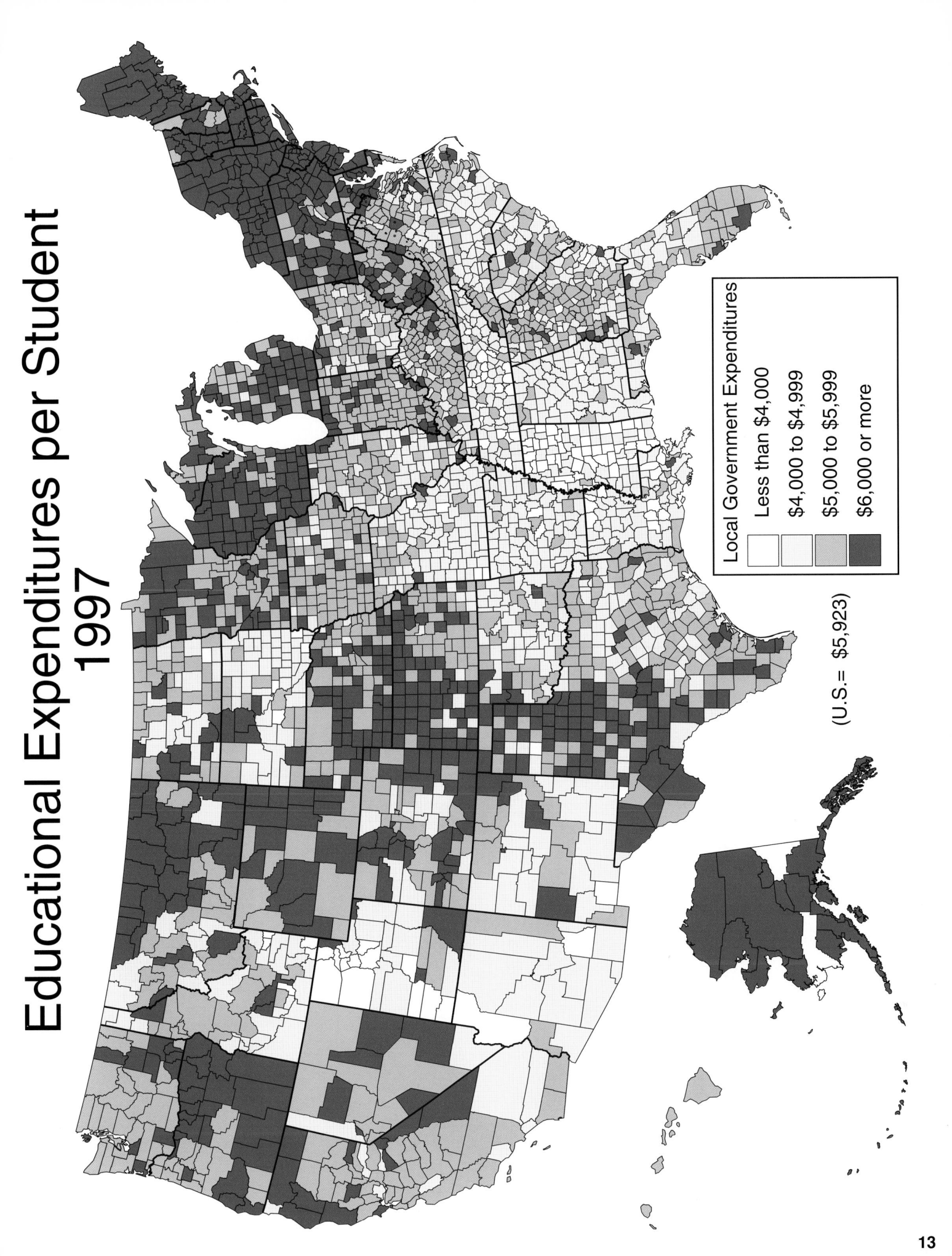

Educational Expenditures per Student
1997

Local Government Expenditures

Less than $4,000

$4,000 to $4,999

$5,000 to $5,999

$6,000 or more

(U.S.= $5,923)

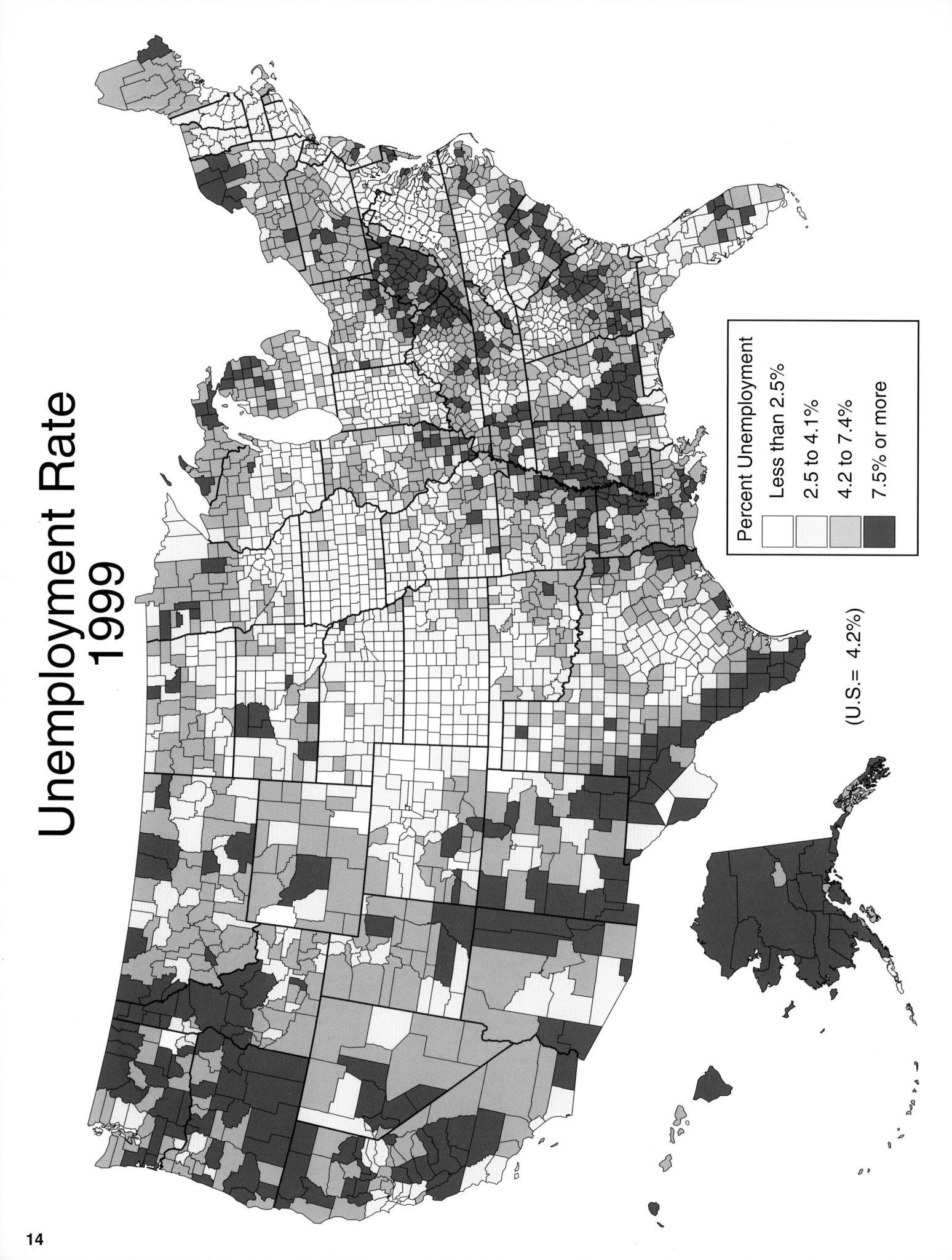

Unemployment Rate
1999

Percent Unemployment

Less than 2.5%

2.5 to 4.1%

4.2 to 7.4%

7.5% or more

(U.S.= 4.2%)

Median Household Income
1997

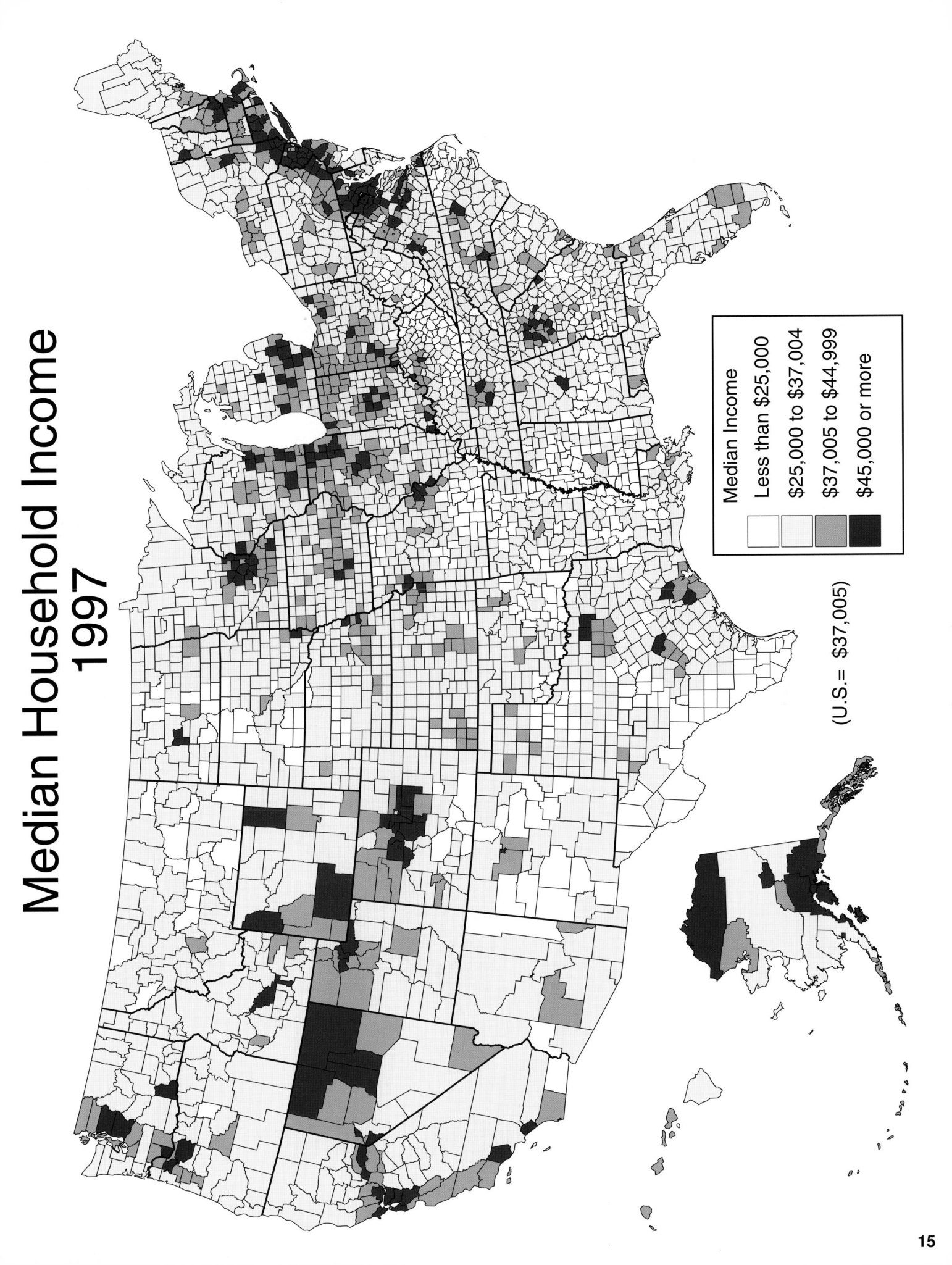

Median Income

- Less than $25,000
- $25,000 to $37,004
- $37,005 to $44,999
- $45,000 or more

(U.S.= $37,005)

15

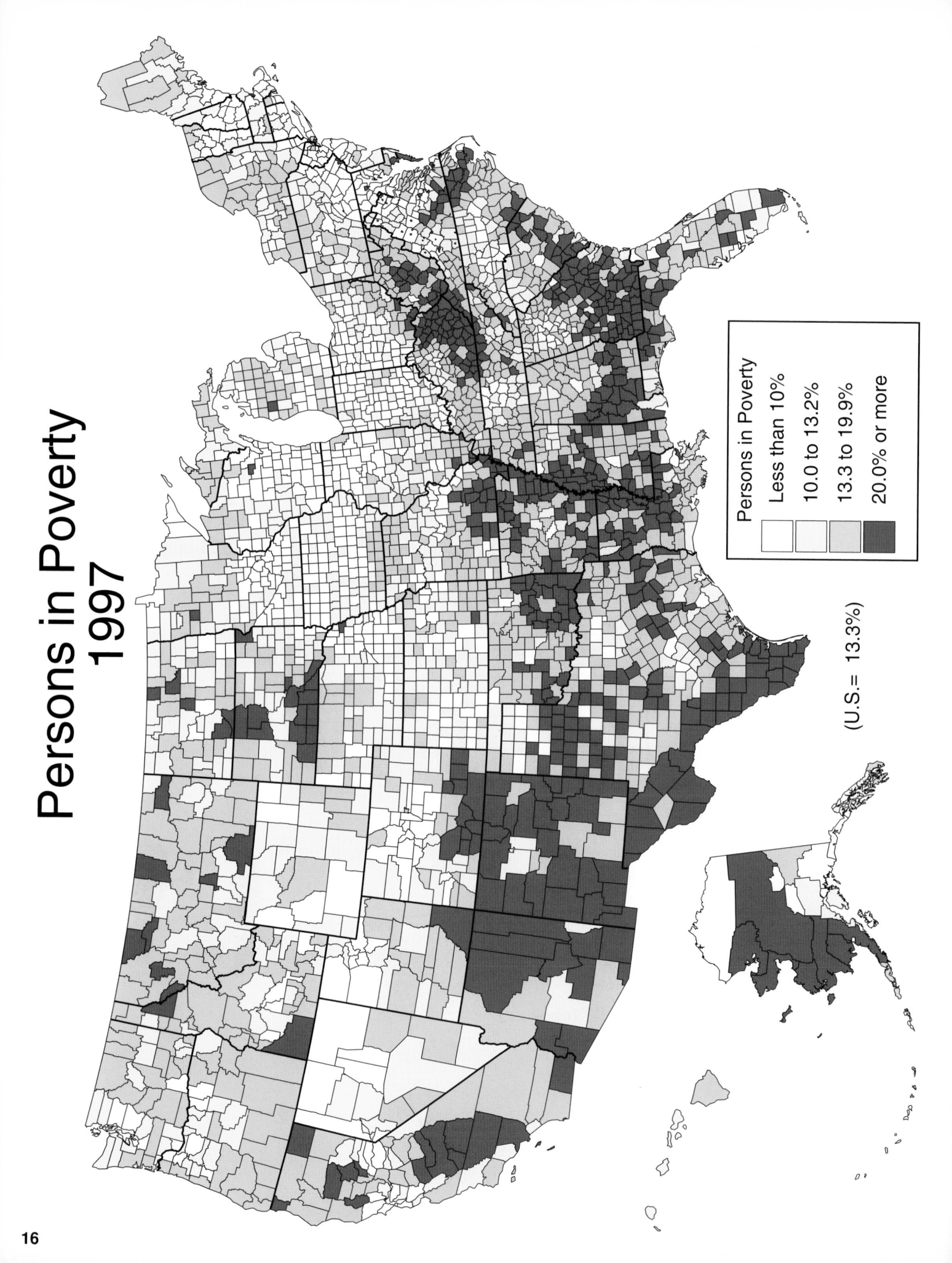

Persons in Poverty
1997

Persons in Poverty

Less than 10%
10.0 to 13.2%
13.3 to 19.9%
20.0% or more

(U.S. = 13.3%)

Land Owned by the Federal Government
1997

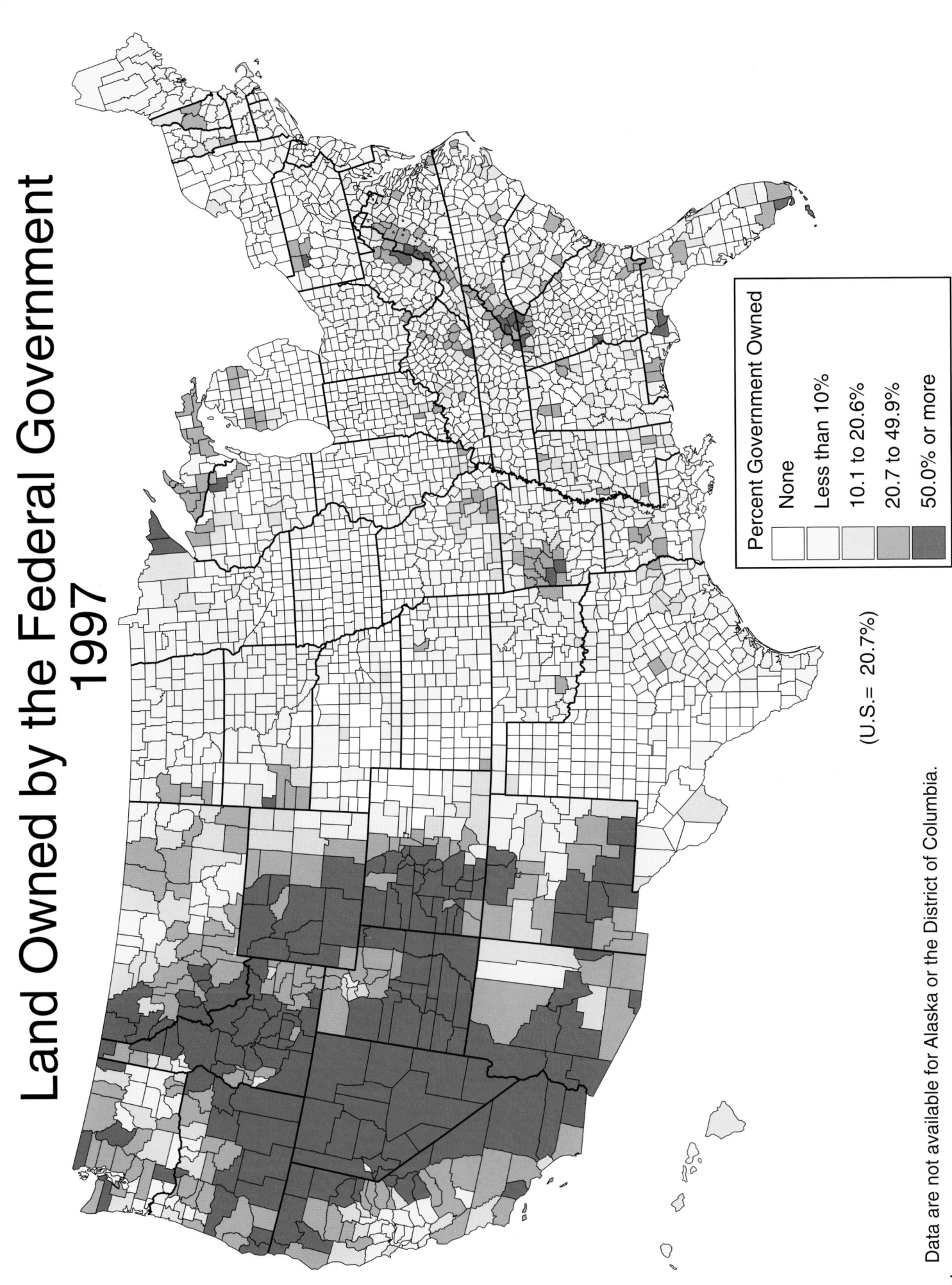

Percent Government Owned

- None
- Less than 10%
- 10.1 to 20.6%
- 20.7 to 49.9%
- 50.0% or more

(U.S.= 20.7%)

Data are not available for Alaska or the District of Columbia.

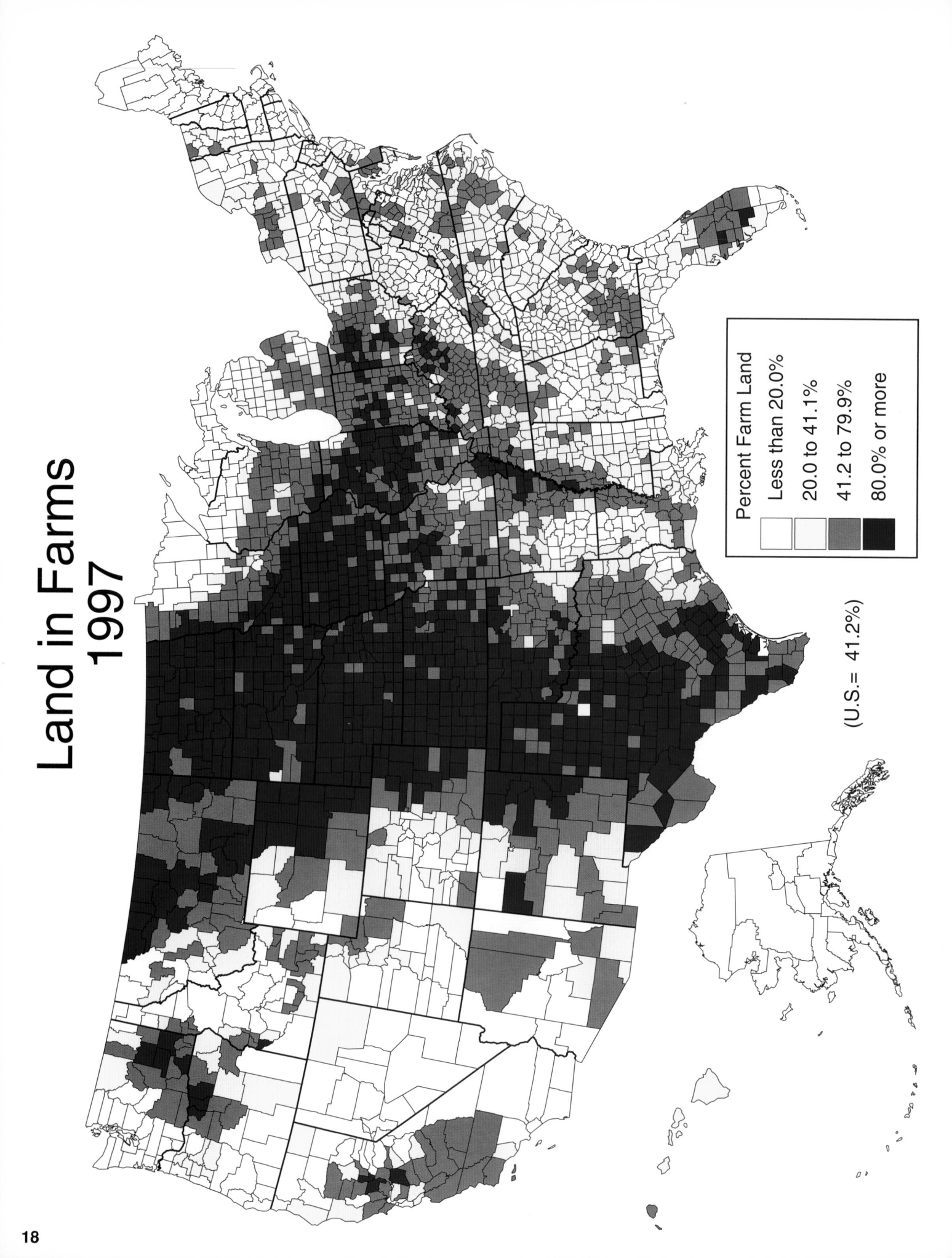

Land in Farms
1997

Percent Farm Land

Less than 20.0%
20.0 to 41.1%
41.2 to 79.9%
80.0% or more

(U.S. = 41.2%)

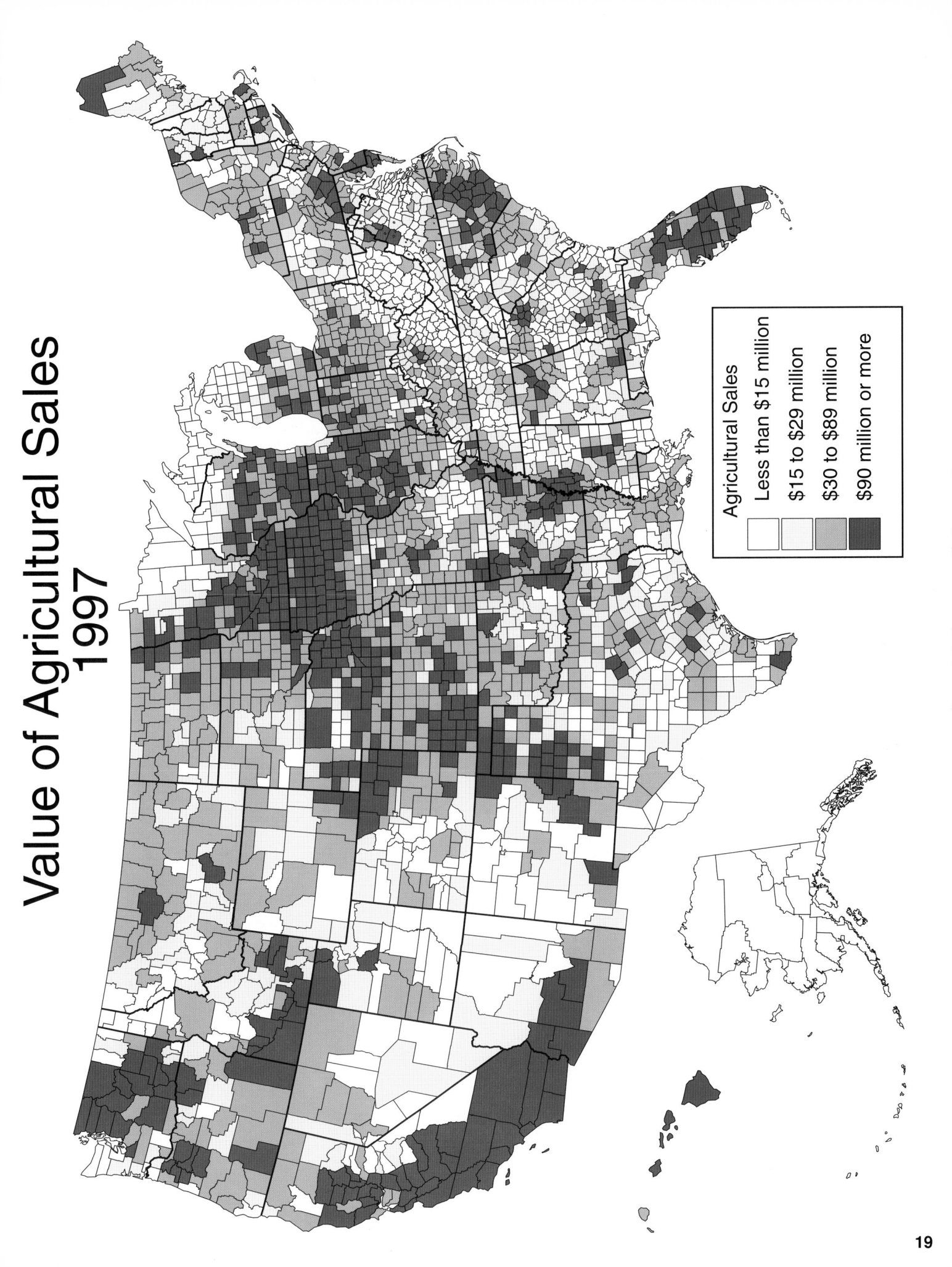

Value of Agricultural Sales
1997

Agricultural Sales

Less than $15 million

$15 to $29 million

$30 to $89 million

$90 million or more

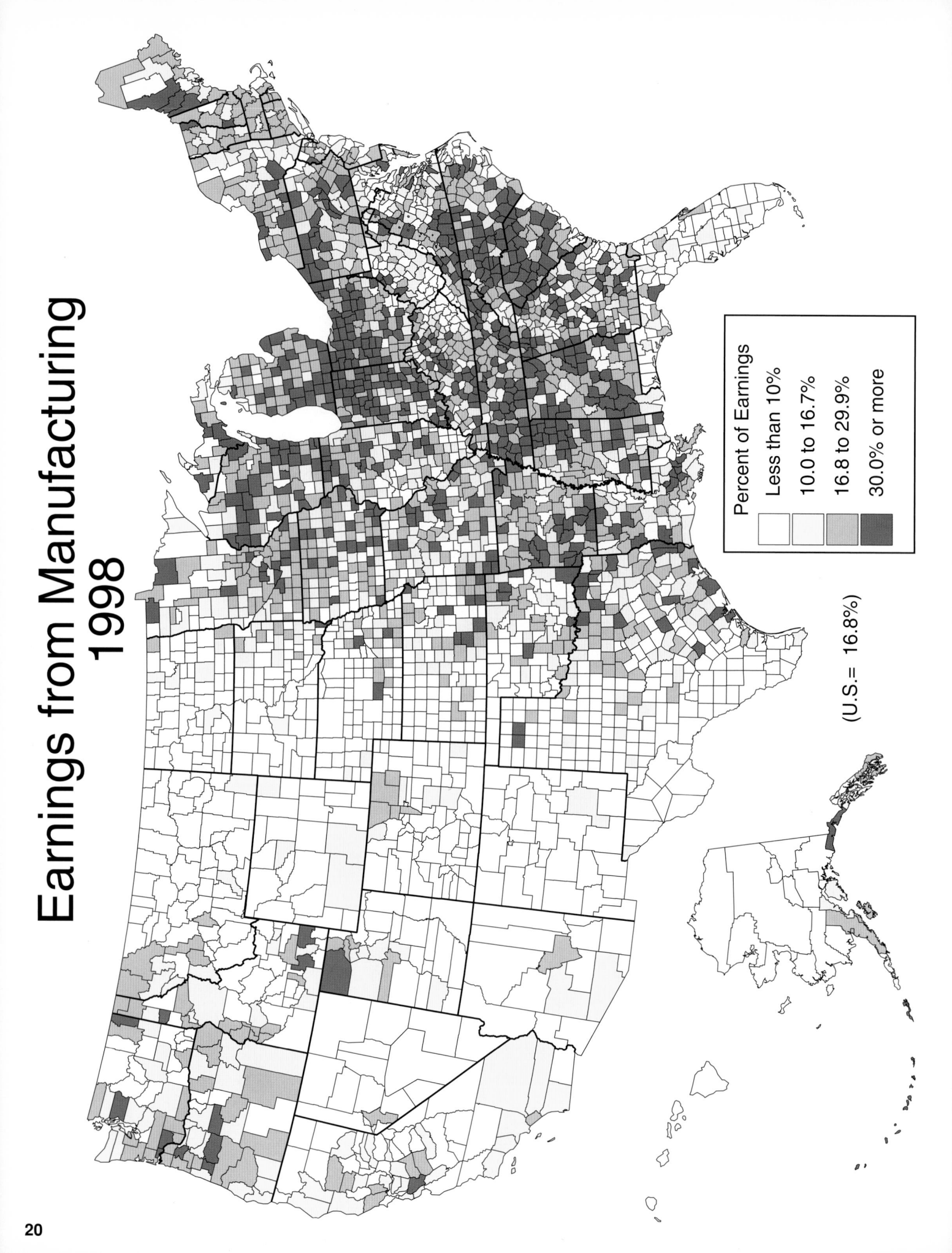

Earnings from Manufacturing
1998

Percent of Earnings

Less than 10%
10.0 to 16.7%
16.8 to 29.9%
30.0% or more

(U.S.= 16.8%)

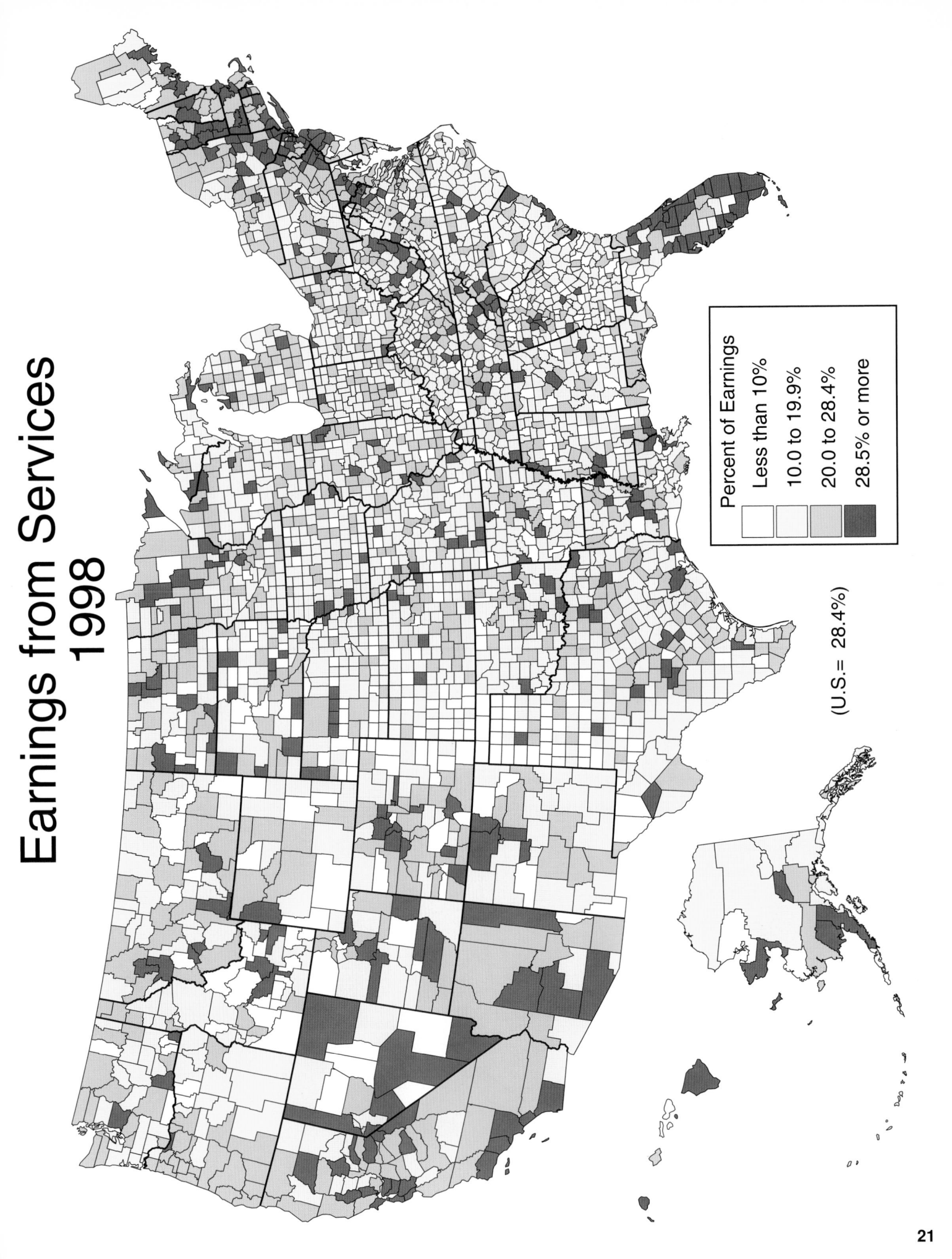

Earnings from Services
1998

Percent of Earnings

Less than 10%
10.0 to 19.9%
20.0 to 28.4%
28.5% or more

(U.S. = 28.4%)

21

Physicians per 100,000 People 1998

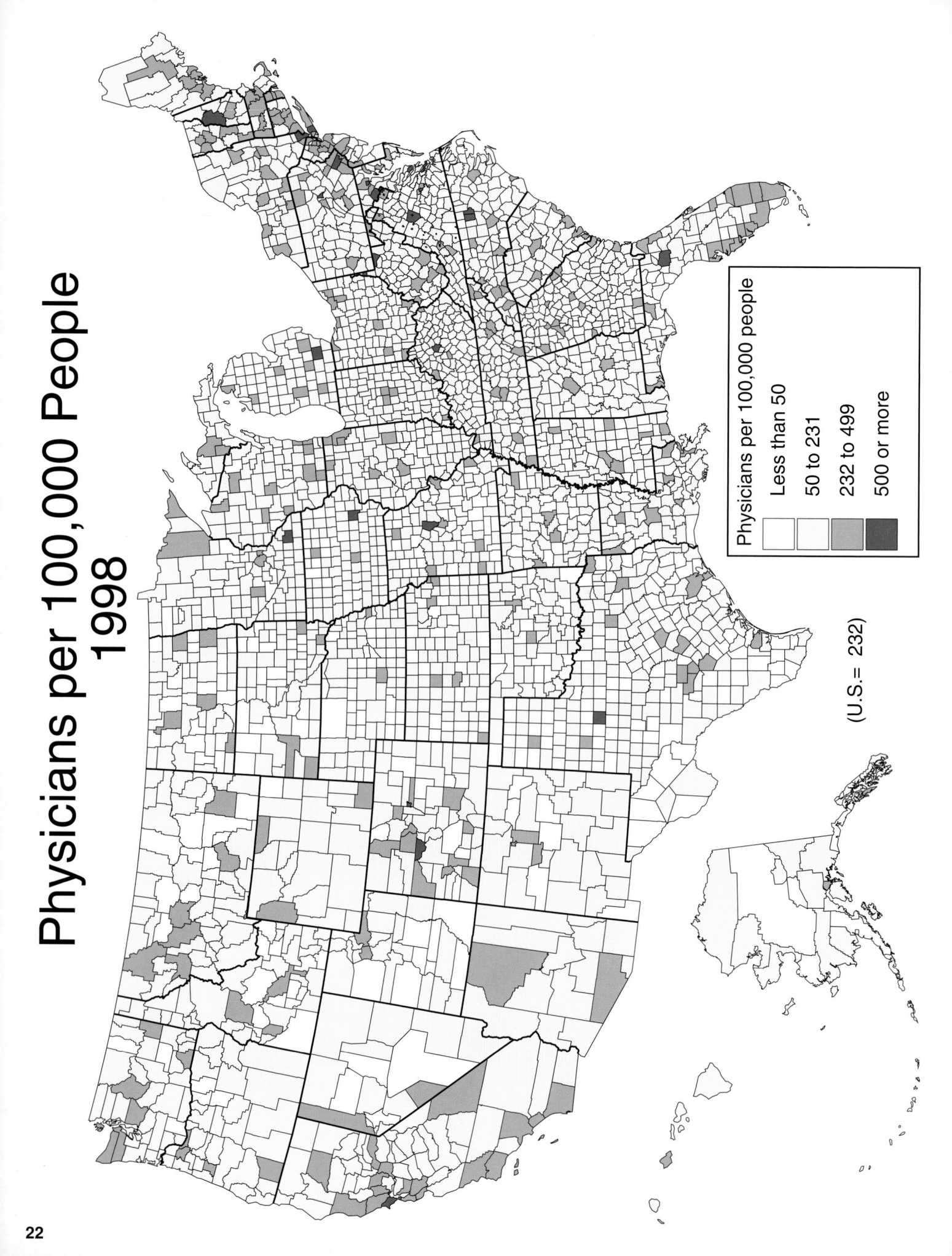

Physicians per 100,000 people

☐	Less than 50
☐	50 to 231
☐	232 to 499
■	500 or more

(U.S. = 232)

Area Rankings

Page

Table 1

27   Counties (rankings restricted to 75 largest counties by 1999 population)

27   Total Population 1999
27   Total Land Area 1990
27   Population Density 1999
28   Percent Population Change 1990-1999
28   Percent White 1999
28   Percent Black 1999
29   Percent American Indian 1999
29   Percent Asian and Pacific Islander 1999
29   Percent Hispanic 1999
30   Percent age 65 and over 1999
30   Percent under 18 years of age 1999
30   Percent Female-headed Family Household 1990
31   Birth rate per 1,000 population, 1996-1998
31   Infant deaths per 1,000 live births, 1996-1998
31   Percent college graduates 1990
32   Expenditures per student 1997
32   Per capita personal income 1998
32   Median household income 1997
33   Percent of persons below the poverty level 1997
33   Percent of persons under age 18 below the poverty level 1997
33   Median Value of owner-occupied units 1990
34   Median gross rent, 1990
34   Unemployment rate 1999
34   Employment in manufacturing as a percent of total nonfarm employment 1998
35   Employment in services as a percent of total nonfarm employment 1998
35   Employment in Finance and Insurance as a percent of total nonfarm employment 1998
35   Per capita taxes in 1997
36   Violent crime rate per 100,000 population 1998
36   Percent of Land owned by the Federal government 1997
36   Military as a percent of total Federal Employment 1998

Table 2

37   75 Counties with Highest Agricultural Sales, 1997

37   Value of agricultural sales (millions of '97 dollars)
37   Average agricultural sales per farm 1997
37   Number of farms 1997
38   Average size of farm (acres) 1997
38   Average value of land and buildings per farm, 1997
38   Average value of land and buildings per acre, 1997

Area Rankings

Page

Table 3

39 75 Largest Metropolitan Areas by 1999 Population

39 Largest total population 1999
39 Largest Total Land Area 1990
40 Population Density 1999
40 Percent Population Change 1990-1999
41 Percent White 1999
41 Percent Black 1999
42 Percent American Indian 1999
42 Percent Asian and Pacific Islander 1999
43 Percent Hispanic 1999
43 Percent age 65 and over 1999
44 Percent under 18 years of age 1999
44 Percent of Households with female householder 1990
45 Live Birth Rate per 1,000 population, 1996-1998
45 Infant deaths per 1,000 live births, 1996-1998
46 Percent college graduates 1990
46 Median household income 1989
47 Percent of persons below the poverty level 1997
47 Percent of persons under age 18 below the poverty level 1997
48 Median Value of owner-occupied units 1990
48 Median gross rent, 1990
49 Unemployment rate 1999
49 Employment in manufacturing as a percent of total nonfarm employment 1998
50 Employment in services as a percent of total nonfarm employment 1998
50 Employment in Finance and Insurance as a percent of total nonfarm employment 1998
51 Per capita taxes in 1997
51 Violent crime rate per 100,000 population 1998

Table 4

52 75 Metropolitan Areas with Highest Agricultural Sales

52 Value of agricultural sales 1997
52 Land in farms, 1997
53 Average value of land and buildings per acre, 1997
53 Number of farms 1997

Table 5

54 75 Largest Cities by 1999 Population

54 Total population 1999
54 Total Land Area 1990
54 Population Density 1999

Area Rankings

Page

55	Percent Population Change 1990-1999
55	Percent White 1990
55	Percent Black 1990
56	Percent Hispanic 1990
56	Percent Foreign Born 1990
56	Percent age 65 and over 1990
57	Percent under 18 years of age 1990
57	Percent of Households with female householder 1990
57	Percent of Households composed of one person 1990
58	Percent college graduates 1990
58	Median household income 1989
58	Persons poverty rate in 1989
59	Median Value of owner-occupied units 1990
59	Median gross rent, 1990
59	Ratio of gross rent to income 1990
60	Percent change in civilian labor force 1998-1999
60	Unemployment rate 1999
60	Per capita Local Government Taxes, 1997
61	Percent of City Expenditures for Police Protection 1997
61	Violent Crime Rate per 100,000 Population 1998
61	Average Annual Precipitation (1961-1990 average)

Table 6

62	States and the District of Columbia
62	Total population 2000
62	Total Land Area 1990
62	Population Density 1999
63	Percent Population Change 1990-1999
63	Projected state population in 2025
63	Percent White 1999
64	Percent Black 1999
64	Percent Hispanic 1999
64	Number of Immigrants by state of intended residence 1996
65	Percent age 65 and over 1999
65	Percent under 18 years of age 1999
65	Live Birth Rate per 1,000 Population 1998
66	Infant deaths per 1,000 Live Births, 1998
66	Percent college graduates 2000
66	Median household income 1997-1999 average
67	Percent of persons below the poverty level in 1999
67	Percent of persons under age 18 below the poverty level 1999
67	Percent of persons lacking health insurance coverage 1999
68	Percent of Occupied Units that were Owner-occupied 1998
68	Median Value of owner-occupied units 1990

Area Rankings

Page

68	Median gross rent, 1990	
69	Unemployment rate 1999	
69	Exports of Goods by State of Origin, 2000 (Millions of dollars)	
69	Residential Construction Authorized by Building Permits, 1999	
70	Value of Agricultural Products sold 1997	
70	Per capita state taxes, 1998	
70	Violent crime rate per 100,000 population 1999	

Table 7

71   Defense Procurement Contracts by Geographic Area, 1998 (For States and 75 Cities, Counties and Metro Areas with Largest contract amounts)

Table 8

72   Congressional Districts (105th Congress)

72	Districts with the largest population 1990
72	Districts with largest total land area 1990
72	Districts with highest population density 1990
73	Districts with the largest White population 1990
73	Districts with the largest Black population 1990
73	Districts with the largest American Indian population, 1990
74	Districts with the largest Asian population, 1990
74	Districts with the largest Hispanic population, 1990
74	Districts with the largest foreign born population, 1990
75	Districts with the largest percent of population age 65 and over, 1990
75	Districts with the largest percent of population under 18 years of age, 1990
75	Districts with the largest percent of households with female householder, 1990
76	Districts with the largest percent of households composed of one person, 1990
76	Districts with the highest percentage of college graduates, 1990
76	Districts with the highest median household income, 1989
77	Districts with the highest poverty rate for persons, 1989
77	Districts with the highest median value of owner-occupied housing units, 1990
77	Districts with the highest median gross rent for renter-occupied units, 1990

TABLE 1—75 Largest Counties by 1999 Population
Selected Rankings

Total Persons, 1999			Land Area (Square Kilometers), 1990				Population Density (per Square Kilometer), 1999			
Population Rank	County	[col 2] Population	Population Rank	Land Area Rank	County	[col 1] Land Area	Population Rank	Density Rank	County	[col 4] Density
1	Los Angeles, CA	9 329 989	12	1	San Bernardino, CA	51 960	15	1	New York, NY	21 258.1
2	Cook, IL	5 192 326	4	2	Maricopa, AZ	23 838	7	2	Kings, NY	12 395.1
3	Harris, TX	3 250 404	53	3	Pima, AZ	23 794	28	3	Bronx, NY	10 955.0
4	Maricopa, AZ	2 861 395	17	4	Clark, NV	20 489	11	4	Queens, NY	7 069.4
5	San Diego, CA	2 820 844	57	5	Riverside, CA	18 669	59	5	San Francisco, CA	6 171.7
6	Orange, CA	2 760 948	5	6	Fresno, CA	15 445	19	6	Philadelphia, PA	4 050.3
7	Kings, NY	2 268 297	1	7	San Diego, CA	10 890	58	7	Essex, NJ	2 285.5
8	Miami-Dade, FL	2 175 634	8	8	Los Angeles, CA	10 515	2	8	Cook, IL	2 120.2
9	Wayne, MI	2 106 495	13	9	King, WA	5 507	25	9	Nassau, NY	1 756.5
10	Dallas, TX	2 062 100	32	10	Palm Beach, FL	5 269	39	10	Milwaukee, WI	1 447.7
11	Queens, NY	2 000 642	8	11	Miami-Dade, FL	5 036	45	11	Bergen, NJ	1 411.9
12	San Bernardino, CA	1 669 934	60	12	Ventura, CA	4 781	6	12	Orange, CA	1 350.1
13	King, WA	1 664 846	3	13	Harris, TX	4 478	9	13	Wayne, MI	1 324.0
14	Santa Clara, CA	1 647 419	72	14	Pierce, WA	4 340	42	14	Pinellas, FL	1 210.1
15	New York, NY	1 551 844	62	15	Worcester, MA	3 919	24	15	Cuyahoga, OH	1 155.6
16	Broward, FL	1 535 468	14	16	Santa Clara, CA	3 344	41	16	Du Page, IL	1 030.7
17	Riverside, CA	1 530 653	23	17	Bexar, TX	3 230	35	17	Fairfax, VA	922.7
18	Middlesex, MA	1 426 606	16	18	Broward, FL	3 131	10	18	Dallas, TX	904.8
19	Philadelphia, PA	1 417 601	74	19	Jefferson, AL	2 882	67	19	Middlesex, NJ	891.9
20	Alameda, CA	1 415 582	36	20	Hillsborough, FL	2 722	1	20	Los Angeles, CA	887.3
21	Suffolk, NY	1 383 847	38	21	Erie, NY	2 706	40	21	Westchester, NY	807.8
22	Tarrant, TX	1 382 442	71	22	El Paso, TX	2 624	49	22	Hamilton, OH	796.6
23	Bexar, TX	1 372 867	64	23	Travis, TX	2 563	52	23	Marion, IN	789.6
24	Cuyahoga, OH	1 371 717	29	24	Sacramento, CA	2 501	34	24	St. Louis, MO	757.6
25	Nassau, NY	1 305 057	2	25	Cook, IL	2 449	20	25	Alameda, CA	741.1
26	Allegheny, PA	1 256 806	21	26	Suffolk, NY	2 360	31	26	Hennepin, MN	738.2
27	Clark, NV	1 217 155	51	27	Orange, FL	2 351	33	27	Franklin, OH	734.7
28	Bronx, NY	1 194 099	10	28	Dallas, TX	2 279	3	28	Harris, TX	725.9
29	Sacramento, CA	1 184 586	30	29	Oakland, MI	2 260	73	29	Jefferson, KY	674.9
30	Oakland, MI	1 179 978	22	30	Tarrant, TX	2 236	18	30	Middlesex, MA	668.8
31	Hennepin, MN	1 064 419	18	31	Middlesex, MA	2 133	46	31	Montgomery, MD	665.2
32	Palm Beach, FL	1 049 420	6	32	Orange, CA	2 045	26	32	Allegheny, PA	664.6
33	Franklin, OH	1 027 821	63	33	Duval, FL	2 004	55	33	Macomb, MI	636.7
34	St. Louis, MO	996 181	43	34	Shelby, TN	1 955	56	34	Prince George's, MD	620.5
35	Fairfax, VA	945 717	50	35	Salt Lake, UT	1 910	22	35	Tarrant, TX	618.3
36	Hillsborough, FL	940 484	20	36	Alameda, CA	1 910	70	36	San Mateo, CA	603.7
37	Contra Costa, CA	933 141	47	37	Hartford, CT	1 905	21	37	Suffolk, NY	586.4
38	Erie, NY	925 957	26	38	Allegheny, PA	1 891	65	38	Montgomery, PA	578.8
39	Milwaukee, WI	906 248	37	39	Contra Costa, CA	1 866	44	39	Honolulu, HI	556.4
40	Westchester, NY	905 572	68	40	Monroe, NY	1 708	69	40	Essex, MA	546.1
41	Du Page, IL	892 547	48	41	Fairfield, CT	1 621	61	41	Fulton, GA	544.1
42	Pinellas, FL	878 499	9	42	Wayne, MI	1 591	30	42	Oakland, MI	522.1
43	Shelby, TN	873 000	54	43	New Haven, CT	1 569	48	43	Fairfield, CT	519.0
44	Honolulu, HI	864 571	75	44	Jackson, MO	1 566	54	44	New Haven, CT	505.6
45	Bergen, NJ	857 052	44	45	Honolulu, HI	1 554	37	45	Contra Costa, CA	500.1
46	Montgomery, MD	852 174	66	46	Baltimore, MD	1 550	14	46	Santa Clara, CA	492.6
47	Salt Lake, UT	850 243	31	47	Hennepin, MN	1 442	16	47	Broward, FL	490.4
48	Fairfield, CT	841 334	33	48	Franklin, OH	1 399	29	48	Sacramento, CA	473.6
49	Hamilton, OH	840 443	61	49	Fulton, GA	1 369	66	49	Baltimore, MD	467.0
50	Hartford, CT	829 671	34	50	St. Louis, MO	1 315	43	50	Shelby, TN	446.5
51	Orange, FL	817 206	69	51	Essex, MA	1 290	47	51	Salt Lake, UT	445.2
52	Marion, IN	810 946	46	52	Montgomery, MD	1 281	50	52	Hartford, CT	435.5
53	Pima, AZ	803 618	56	53	Prince George's, MD	1 260	8	53	Miami-Dade, FL	432.0
54	New Haven, CT	793 208	65	54	Montgomery, PA	1 251	23	54	Bexar, TX	425.0
55	Macomb, MI	792 082	55	55	Macomb, MI	1 244	75	55	Jackson, MO	417.9
56	Prince George's, MD	781 781	24	56	Cuyahoga, OH	1 187	68	56	Monroe, NY	417.1
57	Fresno, CA	763 069	70	57	San Mateo, CA	1 163	63	57	Duval, FL	368.5
58	Essex, NJ	747 355	40	58	Westchester, NY	1 121	51	58	Orange, FL	347.6
59	San Francisco, CA	746 777	49	59	Hamilton, OH	1 055	36	59	Hillsborough, FL	345.5
60	Ventura, CA	745 063	52	60	Marion, IN	1 027	38	60	Erie, NY	342.2
61	Fulton, GA	744 827	35	61	Fairfax, VA	1 025	13	61	King, WA	302.3
62	Worcester, MA	738 629	73	62	Jefferson, KY	997	64	62	Travis, TX	283.7
63	Duval, FL	738 483	41	63	Du Page, IL	866	71	63	El Paso, TX	267.5
64	Travis, TX	727 022	67	64	Middlesex, NJ	805	5	64	San Diego, CA	259.0
65	Montgomery, PA	724 087	25	65	Nassau, NY	743	74	65	Jefferson, AL	228.1
66	Baltimore, MD	723 914	42	66	Pinellas, FL	726	32	66	Palm Beach, FL	199.2
67	Middlesex, NJ	717 949	39	67	Milwaukee, WI	626	62	67	Worcester, MA	188.5
68	Monroe, NY	712 419	45	68	Bergen, NJ	607	72	68	Pierce, WA	158.7
69	Essex, MA	704 407	19	69	Philadelphia, PA	350	60	69	Ventura, CA	155.8
70	San Mateo, CA	702 102	58	70	Essex, NJ	327	4	70	Maricopa, AZ	120.0
71	El Paso, TX	701 908	11	71	Queens, NY	283	17	71	Riverside, CA	82.0
72	Pierce, WA	688 807	7	72	Kings, NY	183	27	72	Clark, NV	59.4
73	Jefferson, KY	672 900	59	73	San Francisco, CA	121	57	73	Fresno, CA	49.4
74	Jefferson, AL	657 422	28	74	Bronx, NY	109	53	74	Pima, AZ	33.8
75	Jackson, MO	654 484	15	75	New York, NY	73	12	75	San Bernardino, CA	32.1

Note: Column numbers refer to Table B. States and Counties.

TABLE 1—75 Largest Counties by 1999 Population
Selected Rankings

Percent Population Change: 1990-1999

Population Rank	Percent Change Rank	County	[col 23] Percent Change
27	1	Clark, NV	64.2
4	2	Maricopa, AZ	34.8
17	3	Riverside, CA	30.8
64	4	Travis, TX	26.1
16	5	Broward, FL	22.3
32	6	Palm Beach, FL	21.5
51	7	Orange, FL	20.6
53	8	Pima, AZ	20.5
71	9	El Paso, TX	18.6
22	10	Tarrant, TX	18.1
12	11	San Bernardino, CA	17.7
72	12	Pierce, WA	17.5
47	13	Salt Lake, UT	17.1
37	14	Contra Costa, CA	16.1
23	15	Bexar, TX	15.8
35	16	Fairfax, VA	15.6
3	17	Harris, TX	15.3
61	18	Fulton, GA	14.8
6	19	Orange, CA	14.5
57	20	Fresno, CA	14.3
41	21	Du Page, IL	14.2
5	22	San Diego, CA	12.9
36	23	Hillsborough, FL	12.8
8	24	Miami-Dade, FL	12.3
46	25	Montgomery, MD	11.7
60	26	Ventura, CA	11.4
10	27	Dallas, TX	11.3
29	28	Sacramento, CA	11.0
13	29	King, WA	10.5
55	30	Macomb, MI	10.4
14	31	Santa Clara, CA	10.0
63	32	Duval, FL	9.7
30	33	Oakland, MI	8.9
20	34	Alameda, CA	8.5
56	35	Prince George's, MD	8.2
70	36	San Mateo, CA	8.1
33	37	Franklin, OH	6.9
67	37	Middlesex, NJ	6.9
65	39	Montgomery, PA	6.8
43	40	Shelby, TN	5.6
1	41	Los Angeles, CA	5.3
69	42	Essex, MA	5.1
21	43	Suffolk, NY	4.7
66	44	Baltimore, MD	4.6
15	45	New York, NY	4.3
62	46	Worcester, MA	4.1
45	47	Bergen, NJ	3.8
40	48	Westchester, NY	3.5
44	49	Honolulu, HI	3.4
75	49	Jackson, MO	3.4
42	51	Pinellas, FL	3.2
59	51	San Francisco, CA	3.2
31	53	Hennepin, MN	3.1
11	54	Queens, NY	2.5
18	55	Middlesex, MA	2.0
2	56	Cook, IL	1.7
48	56	Fairfield, CT	1.7
52	56	Marion, IN	1.7
25	59	Nassau, NY	1.3
73	60	Jefferson, KY	1.2
74	61	Jefferson, AL	0.9
34	62	St. Louis, MO	0.3
68	63	Monroe, NY	-0.2
9	63	Wayne, MI	-0.2
28	65	Bronx, NY	-0.8
7	66	Kings, NY	-1.4
54	66	New Haven, CT	-1.4
50	68	Hartford, CT	-2.6
24	69	Cuyahoga, OH	-2.9
49	70	Hamilton, OH	-3.0
58	71	Essex, NJ	-3.9
38	72	Erie, NY	-4.4
39	73	Milwaukee, WI	-5.5
26	74	Allegheny, PA	-6.0
19	75	Philadelphia, PA	-10.6

Percent White, 1999

Population Rank	White Rank	County	[col 5] Percent White
55	1	Macomb, MI	96.1
71	2	El Paso, TX	94.5
47	3	Salt Lake, UT	94.2
62	4	Worcester, MA	94.1
69	5	Essex, MA	92.4
4	6	Maricopa, AZ	91.3
23	7	Bexar, TX	90.6
41	8	Du Page, IL	90.6
18	9	Middlesex, MA	90.2
53	9	Pima, AZ	90.2
21	11	Suffolk, NY	89.9
60	12	Ventura, CA	89.8
65	13	Montgomery, PA	89.7
30	14	Oakland, MI	88.2
17	14	Riverside, CA	88.2
42	16	Pinellas, FL	88.1
54	17	New Haven, CT	86.1
50	18	Hartford, CT	85.4
26	19	Allegheny, PA	85.3
48	19	Fairfield, CT	85.3
31	21	Hennepin, MN	85.2
25	21	Nassau, NY	85.2
12	23	San Bernardino, CA	85.0
38	24	Erie, NY	84.7
6	25	Orange, CA	84.2
68	26	Monroe, NY	83.5
45	27	Bergen, NJ	83.3
32	27	Palm Beach, FL	83.3
72	27	Pierce, WA	83.3
64	27	Travis, TX	83.3
27	31	Clark, NV	83.1
57	32	Fresno, CA	82.8
22	33	Tarrant, TX	82.6
36	34	Hillsborough, FL	82.2
13	35	King, WA	81.8
5	35	San Diego, CA	81.8
34	37	St. Louis, MO	81.2
73	38	Jefferson, KY	81.0
66	39	Baltimore, MD	80.0
67	40	Middlesex, NJ	79.7
35	41	Fairfax, VA	79.5
33	42	Franklin, OH	79.0
16	43	Broward, FL	78.9
40	43	Westchester, NY	78.9
51	45	Orange, FL	78.2
8	46	Miami-Dade, FL	77.6
37	47	Contra Costa, CA	76.5
29	48	Sacramento, CA	75.5
49	49	Hamilton, OH	75.0
1	50	Los Angeles, CA	74.8
52	51	Marion, IN	74.3
10	52	Dallas, TX	74.0
3	53	Harris, TX	73.9
14	54	Santa Clara, CA	73.4
75	55	Jackson, MO	73.0
46	56	Montgomery, MD	72.8
70	57	San Mateo, CA	72.4
39	58	Milwaukee, WI	72.3
24	59	Cuyahoga, OH	70.6
63	60	Duval, FL	67.9
2	61	Cook, IL	67.8
15	62	New York, NY	62.2
74	63	Jefferson, AL	62.1
20	64	Alameda, CA	60.6
11	65	Queens, NY	59.5
9	66	Wayne, MI	55.4
28	67	Bronx, NY	52.9
19	68	Philadelphia, PA	52.2
59	68	San Francisco, CA	52.2
43	68	Shelby, TN	52.2
58	71	Essex, NJ	52.1
7	72	Kings, NY	51.6
61	73	Fulton, GA	42.5
56	74	Prince George's, MD	36.7
44	75	Honolulu, HI	30.9

Percent Black, 1999

Population Rank	Black Rank	County	[col 6] Percent Black
56	1	Prince George's, MD	58.2
61	2	Fulton, GA	55.3
43	3	Shelby, TN	46.2
19	4	Philadelphia, PA	43.6
58	5	Essex, NJ	43.3
9	6	Wayne, MI	42.7
28	7	Bronx, NY	42.3
7	8	Kings, NY	41.1
74	9	Jefferson, AL	37.2
63	10	Duval, FL	28.5
24	11	Cuyahoga, OH	27.4
2	12	Cook, IL	26.9
15	13	New York, NY	26.8
75	14	Jackson, MO	25.1
39	15	Milwaukee, WI	24.6
52	16	Marion, IN	24.1
49	17	Hamilton, OH	23.4
11	18	Queens, NY	23.0
10	19	Dallas, TX	21.0
8	20	Miami-Dade, FL	20.4
3	21	Harris, TX	19.8
20	22	Alameda, CA	19.0
16	23	Broward, FL	18.6
33	24	Franklin, OH	18.0
51	24	Orange, FL	18.0
73	26	Jefferson, KY	17.8
34	27	St. Louis, MO	16.7
66	28	Baltimore, MD	16.5
46	29	Montgomery, MD	15.7
36	30	Hillsborough, FL	15.3
40	31	Westchester, NY	15.2
32	32	Palm Beach, FL	14.8
68	33	Monroe, NY	13.4
26	34	Allegheny, PA	13.1
38	35	Erie, NY	13.0
22	35	Tarrant, TX	13.0
64	37	Travis, TX	12.1
50	38	Hartford, CT	11.8
54	39	New Haven, CT	11.6
1	40	Los Angeles, CA	11.2
48	41	Fairfield, CT	11.0
59	42	San Francisco, CA	10.7
27	43	Clark, NV	10.5
29	44	Sacramento, CA	10.1
25	45	Nassau, NY	9.8
37	46	Contra Costa, CA	9.7
42	46	Pinellas, FL	9.7
67	48	Middlesex, NJ	9.2
31	49	Hennepin, MN	8.7
12	50	San Bernardino, CA	8.3
35	51	Fairfax, VA	8.2
72	51	Pierce, WA	8.2
30	53	Oakland, MI	7.9
21	54	Suffolk, NY	7.2
23	55	Bexar, TX	7.0
65	56	Montgomery, PA	6.6
5	57	San Diego, CA	6.5
13	58	King, WA	6.0
17	59	Riverside, CA	5.8
45	60	Bergen, NJ	5.6
70	61	San Mateo, CA	5.5
57	62	Fresno, CA	5.2
69	63	Essex, MA	4.8
4	64	Maricopa, AZ	4.3
53	65	Pima, AZ	3.9
14	66	Santa Clara, CA	3.8
18	67	Middlesex, MA	3.7
44	68	Honolulu, HI	3.6
71	69	El Paso, TX	3.4
62	70	Worcester, MA	3.0
60	71	Ventura, CA	2.4
41	72	Du Page, IL	2.2
6	73	Orange, CA	1.8
55	74	Macomb, MI	1.6
47	75	Salt Lake, UT	1.2

Note: Column numbers refer to Table B. States and Counties.

TABLE 1—75 Largest Counties by 1999 Population
Selected Rankings

Percent American Indian, 1999				Percent Asian and Pacific Islander, 1999				Percent Hispanic, 1999			
Popu-lation Rank	American Indian Rank	County	[col 7] Percent American Indian	Popu-lation Rank	Asian & Pac. Is. Rank	County	[col 8] Percent Asian & Pac. Is.	Popu-lation Rank	Hispanic Rank	County	[col 9] Percent Hispanic
53	1	Pima, AZ	3.4	44	1	Honolulu, HI	65.0	71	1	El Paso, TX	75.4
4	2	Maricopa, AZ	2.0	59	2	San Francisco, CA	36.6	8	2	Miami-Dade, FL	57.4
31	3	Hennepin, MN	1.5	14	3	Santa Clara, CA	22.1	23	3	Bexar, TX	57.0
72	3	Pierce, WA	1.5	70	4	San Mateo, CA	21.7	28	4	Bronx, NY	48.6
29	5	Sacramento, CA	1.4	20	5	Alameda, CA	19.6	1	5	Los Angeles, CA	44.4
57	6	Fresno, CA	1.3	11	6	Queens, NY	17.0	57	6	Fresno, CA	43.1
13	7	King, WA	1.2	6	7	Orange, CA	13.5	12	7	San Bernardino, CA	34.3
17	7	Riverside, CA	1.2	1	8	Los Angeles, CA	13.4	17	8	Riverside, CA	33.8
12	9	San Bernardino, CA	1.1	37	9	Contra Costa, CA	13.1	60	9	Ventura, CA	33.4
27	10	Clark, NV	1.0	29	10	Sacramento, CA	12.9	15	10	New York, NY	30.7
47	11	Salt Lake, UT	0.9	35	11	Fairfax, VA	12.0	53	11	Pima, AZ	29.6
5	11	San Diego, CA	0.9	46	12	Montgomery, MD	11.1	6	12	Orange, CA	29.0
60	11	Ventura, CA	0.9	45	13	Bergen, NJ	11.0	3	13	Harris, TX	27.9
20	14	Alameda, CA	0.8	13	13	King, WA	11.0	64	14	Travis, TX	26.9
39	14	Milwaukee, WI	0.8	67	15	Middlesex, NJ	10.8	5	15	San Diego, CA	26.5
37	16	Contra Costa, CA	0.7	5	15	San Diego, CA	10.8	14	16	Santa Clara, CA	25.9
10	16	Dallas, TX	0.7	57	17	Fresno, CA	10.7	7	17	Kings, NY	23.8
38	16	Erie, NY	0.7	15	18	New York, NY	10.5	11	18	Queens, NY	22.6
14	16	Santa Clara, CA	0.7	41	19	Du Page, IL	7.1	70	19	San Mateo, CA	21.8
28	20	Bronx, NY	0.6	72	20	Pierce, WA	7.0	10	20	Dallas, TX	21.4
1	20	Los Angeles, CA	0.6	7	21	Kings, NY	6.9	4	21	Maricopa, AZ	20.4
6	20	Orange, CA	0.6	60	21	Ventura, CA	6.9	20	22	Alameda, CA	18.6
22	20	Tarrant, TX	0.6	3	23	Harris, TX	5.9	36	23	Hillsborough, FL	18.3
23	24	Bexar, TX	0.5	18	23	Middlesex, MA	5.9	27	24	Clark, NV	18.0
71	24	El Paso, TX	0.5	12	25	San Bernardino, CA	5.6	2	25	Cook, IL	17.9
44	24	Honolulu, HI	0.5	40	25	Westchester, NY	5.6	59	26	San Francisco, CA	16.9
75	24	Jackson, MO	0.5	27	27	Clark, NV	5.3	58	27	Essex, NJ	16.5
15	24	New York, NY	0.5	2	28	Cook, IL	5.1	29	28	Sacramento, CA	15.9
59	24	San Francisco, CA	0.5	25	29	Nassau, NY	4.8	22	29	Tarrant, TX	15.6
70	24	San Mateo, CA	0.5	56	29	Prince George's, MD	4.8	37	30	Contra Costa, CA	15.0
64	24	Travis, TX	0.5	17	29	Riverside, CA	4.8	51	31	Orange, FL	14.0
63	32	Duval, FL	0.4	31	32	Hennepin, MN	4.5	16	32	Broward, FL	12.8
3	32	Harris, TX	0.4	10	33	Dallas, TX	4.3	67	33	Middlesex, NJ	12.2
36	32	Hillsborough, FL	0.4	58	33	Essex, NJ	4.3	40	34	Westchester, NY	12.2
7	32	Kings, NY	0.4	28	35	Bronx, NY	4.2	48	35	Fairfield, CT	11.2
55	32	Macomb, MI	0.4	64	36	Travis, TX	4.1	32	35	Palm Beach, FL	11.2
30	32	Oakland, MI	0.4	19	37	Philadelphia, PA	3.9	50	37	Hartford, CT	11.0
51	32	Orange, FL	0.4	22	37	Tarrant, TX	3.9	46	38	Montgomery, MD	10.8
11	32	Queens, NY	0.4	47	39	Salt Lake, UT	3.7	69	39	Essex, MA	10.0
9	32	Wayne, MI	0.4	65	40	Montgomery, PA	3.6	35	40	Fairfax, VA	9.4
16	41	Broward, FL	0.3	48	41	Fairfield, CT	3.5	47	41	Salt Lake, UT	8.9
2	41	Cook, IL	0.3	30	41	Oakland, MI	3.5	21	42	Suffolk, NY	8.6
58	41	Essex, NJ	0.3	51	43	Orange, FL	3.3	45	43	Bergen, NJ	8.5
35	41	Fairfax, VA	0.3	66	44	Baltimore, MD	3.2	54	44	New Haven, CT	8.4
8	41	Miami-Dade, FL	0.3	63	44	Duval, FL	3.2	25	45	Nassau, NY	7.7
67	41	Middlesex, NJ	0.3	33	46	Franklin, OH	2.8	19	46	Philadelphia, PA	7.5
68	41	Monroe, NY	0.3	50	47	Hartford, CT	2.7	44	47	Honolulu, HI	7.4
46	41	Montgomery, MD	0.3	68	47	Monroe, NY	2.7	39	48	Milwaukee, WI	6.6
19	41	Philadelphia, PA	0.3	21	47	Suffolk, NY	2.7	62	49	Worcester, MA	6.4
42	41	Pinellas, FL	0.3	62	47	Worcester, MA	2.7	41	50	Du Page, IL	6.1
56	41	Prince George's, MD	0.3	69	51	Essex, MA	2.6	72	51	Pierce, WA	5.4
21	41	Suffolk, NY	0.3	4	52	Maricopa, AZ	2.5	56	52	Prince George's, MD	5.2
66	53	Baltimore, MD	0.2	53	53	Pima, AZ	2.4	68	53	Monroe, NY	4.8
45	53	Bergen, NJ	0.2	39	54	Milwaukee, WI	2.3	18	54	Middlesex, MA	4.6
24	53	Cuyahoga, OH	0.2	16	55	Broward, FL	2.2	13	55	King, WA	4.5
69	53	Essex, MA	0.2	61	56	Fulton, GA	2.1	75	56	Jackson, MO	4.1
48	53	Fairfield, CT	0.2	36	56	Hillsborough, FL	2.1	63	57	Duval, FL	3.9
33	53	Franklin, OH	0.2	54	56	New Haven, CT	2.1	42	58	Pinellas, FL	3.7
61	53	Fulton, GA	0.2	34	59	St. Louis, MO	2.0	61	59	Fulton, GA	3.4
50	53	Hartford, CT	0.2	23	60	Bexar, TX	1.9	38	60	Erie, NY	3.1
52	53	Marion, IN	0.2	55	60	Macomb, MI	1.9	9	61	Wayne, MI	3.0
18	53	Middlesex, MA	0.2	42	60	Pinellas, FL	1.9	24	62	Cuyahoga, OH	2.8
25	53	Nassau, NY	0.2	24	63	Cuyahoga, OH	1.8	30	63	Oakland, MI	2.4
54	53	New Haven, CT	0.2	8	63	Miami-Dade, FL	1.8	31	64	Hennepin, MN	2.1
32	53	Palm Beach, FL	0.2	38	65	Erie, NY	1.6	66	65	Baltimore, MD	1.9
43	53	Shelby, TN	0.2	32	65	Palm Beach, FL	1.6	65	66	Montgomery, PA	1.8
40	53	Westchester, NY	0.2	26	67	Allegheny, PA	1.5	52	67	Marion, IN	1.7
62	53	Worcester, MA	0.2	71	67	El Paso, TX	1.5	55	68	Macomb, MI	1.5
26	69	Allegheny, PA	0.1	49	67	Hamilton, OH	1.5	43	69	Shelby, TN	1.4
41	69	Du Page, IL	0.1	75	67	Jackson, MO	1.5	34	69	St. Louis, MO	1.4
49	69	Hamilton, OH	0.1	9	67	Wayne, MI	1.5	33	71	Franklin, OH	1.3
74	69	Jefferson, AL	0.1	52	72	Marion, IN	1.4	26	72	Allegheny, PA	1.0
73	69	Jefferson, KY	0.1	43	72	Shelby, TN	1.4	73	73	Jefferson, KY	1.0
65	69	Montgomery, PA	0.1	73	74	Jefferson, KY	1.0	49	74	Hamilton, OH	0.8
34	69	St. Louis, MO	0.1	74	75	Jefferson, AL	0.6	74	75	Jefferson, AL	0.7

Note: Column numbers refer to Table B. States and Counties.

TABLE 1—75 Largest Counties by 1999 Population
Selected Rankings

Percent Age 65 and Over, 1999				Percent Under 18 Years of Age, 1999				Percent Female-headed Family Household, 1990			
Population Rank	Age 65 and Over Rank	County	[cols 17 & 18] Percent Age 65 and Over	Population Rank	Under 18 Years of Age Rank	County	[cols 10 & 11] Percent Under 18 Years of Age	Population Rank	Female Households Rank	County	[col 30] Percent Female Households
32	1	Palm Beach, FL	24.2	71	1	El Paso, TX	32.4	28	1	Bronx, NY	28.0
42	2	Pinellas, FL	23.1	57	1	Fresno, CA	32.4	7	2	Kings, NY	21.5
26	3	Allegheny, PA	18.0	12	3	San Bernardino, CA	32.1	9	3	Wayne, MI	20.8
16	4	Broward, FL	16.8	47	4	Salt Lake, UT	31.9	19	4	Philadelphia, PA	20.3
65	5	Montgomery, PA	16.4	17	5	Riverside, CA	29.8	58	5	Essex, NJ	19.2
38	6	Erie, NY	16.0	23	6	Bexar, TX	29.4	43	6	Shelby, TN	18.6
24	7	Cuyahoga, OH	15.9	28	6	Bronx, NY	29.4	61	7	Fulton, GA	18.5
66	8	Baltimore, MD	15.8	3	8	Harris, TX	28.5	56	8	Prince George's, MD	16.3
45	9	Bergen, NJ	15.7	60	9	Ventura, CA	28.0	71	9	El Paso, TX	15.8
59	10	San Francisco, CA	15.3	63	10	Duval, FL	27.8	39	9	Milwaukee, WI	15.8
50	11	Hartford, CT	15.1	4	10	Maricopa, AZ	27.8	74	11	Jefferson, AL	15.7
25	12	Nassau, NY	15.0	22	12	Tarrant, TX	27.4	2	12	Cook, IL	15.4
54	12	New Haven, CT	15.0	7	13	Kings, NY	27.2	24	13	Cuyahoga, OH	14.9
19	14	Philadelphia, PA	14.6	27	14	Clark, NV	27.1	8	13	Miami-Dade, FL	14.9
40	15	Westchester, NY	14.5	43	14	Shelby, TN	27.1	23	15	Bexar, TX	14.5
53	16	Pima, AZ	14.4	1	16	Los Angeles, CA	27.0	73	15	Jefferson, KY	14.5
11	16	Queens, NY	14.4	72	16	Pierce, WA	27.0	11	17	Queens, NY	14.3
55	18	Macomb, MI	14.3	29	16	Sacramento, CA	27.0	49	18	Hamilton, OH	14.0
8	18	Miami-Dade, FL	14.3	10	19	Dallas, TX	26.9	57	19	Fresno, CA	13.9
34	18	St. Louis, MO	14.3	9	20	Wayne, MI	26.7	52	20	Marion, IN	13.8
69	21	Essex, MA	14.2	41	21	Du Page, IL	26.2	63	21	Duval, FL	13.7
74	22	Jefferson, AL	14.1	53	22	Pima, AZ	26.1	75	22	Jackson, MO	13.6
48	23	Fairfield, CT	13.9	51	23	Orange, CA	26.0	38	23	Erie, NY	13.3
49	23	Hamilton, OH	13.9	2	24	Cook, IL	25.9	1	24	Los Angeles, CA	13.1
44	23	Honolulu, HI	13.9	36	24	Hillsborough, FL	25.9	29	25	Sacramento, CA	13.0
73	23	Jefferson, KY	13.9	5	26	San Diego, CA	25.7	20	26	Alameda, CA	12.9
39	27	Milwaukee, WI	13.4	62	26	Worcester, MA	25.7	15	27	New York, NY	12.8
18	28	Middlesex, MA	13.3	49	28	Hamilton, OH	25.6	10	28	Dallas, TX	12.7
62	28	Worcester, MA	13.3	75	28	Jackson, MO	25.6	3	28	Harris, TX	12.7
70	30	San Mateo, CA	13.2	39	28	Milwaukee, WI	25.6	50	28	Hartford, CT	12.7
68	31	Monroe, NY	13.1	58	31	Essex, NJ	25.5	33	31	Franklin, OH	12.6
75	32	Jackson, MO	13.0	19	31	Philadelphia, PA	25.5	26	32	Allegheny, PA	12.5
67	33	Middlesex, NJ	12.9	56	31	Prince George's, MD	25.5	68	32	Monroe, NY	12.5
36	34	Hillsborough, FL	12.7	6	34	Orange, CA	25.4	54	32	New Haven, CT	12.5
9	34	Wayne, MI	12.7	52	35	Marion, IN	25.3	69	35	Essex, MA	12.4
15	36	New York, NY	12.6	54	35	New Haven, CT	25.3	12	36	San Bernardino, CA	12.1
7	37	Kings, NY	12.4	37	37	Contra Costa, CA	25.2	36	37	Hillsborough, FL	11.9
2	38	Cook, IL	12.3	68	37	Monroe, NY	25.2	51	38	Orange, FL	11.6
58	38	Essex, NJ	12.3	50	39	Hartford, CT	25.0	40	39	Westchester, NY	11.6
17	38	Riverside, CA	12.3	21	39	Suffolk, NY	25.0	48	40	Fairfield, CT	11.3
4	41	Maricopa, AZ	12.0	64	39	Travis, TX	25.0	27	41	Clark, NV	11.2
21	42	Suffolk, NY	11.8	69	42	Essex, MA	24.9	62	41	Worcester, MA	11.2
46	43	Montgomery, MD	11.6	48	42	Fairfield, CT	24.9	66	43	Baltimore, MD	11.1
37	44	Contra Costa, CA	11.5	8	44	Miami-Dade, FL	24.8	72	44	Pierce, WA	10.9
30	44	Oakland, MI	11.5	33	45	Franklin, OH	24.5	53	44	Pima, AZ	10.9
29	44	Sacramento, CA	11.5	20	46	Alameda, CA	24.4	37	46	Contra Costa, CA	10.8
5	44	San Diego, CA	11.5	14	46	Santa Clara, CA	24.4	5	46	San Diego, CA	10.8
52	48	Marion, IN	11.4	46	48	Montgomery, MD	24.3	22	46	Tarrant, TX	10.8
27	49	Clark, NV	11.2	61	49	Fulton, GA	24.2	34	49	St. Louis, MO	10.7
31	50	Hennepin, MN	11.1	35	50	Fairfax, VA	24.1	44	50	Honolulu, HI	10.5
13	51	King, WA	11.0	30	50	Oakland, MI	24.1	18	50	Middlesex, MA	10.5
28	52	Bronx, NY	10.9	34	52	St. Louis, MO	24.0	64	50	Travis, TX	10.5
51	53	Orange, FL	10.8	24	53	Cuyahoga, OH	23.8	21	53	Suffolk, NY	10.4
63	54	Duval, FL	10.6	38	54	Erie, NY	23.5	14	54	Santa Clara, CA	10.3
20	55	Alameda, CA	10.5	31	55	Hennepin, MN	23.4	4	55	Maricopa, AZ	10.2
23	55	Bexar, TX	10.5	44	55	Honolulu, HI	23.4	25	55	Nassau, NY	10.2
60	55	Ventura, CA	10.5	74	57	Jefferson, AL	23.0	55	57	Macomb, MI	10.1
1	58	Los Angeles, CA	10.4	55	57	Macomb, MI	23.0	47	57	Salt Lake, UT	10.1
72	58	Pierce, WA	10.4	16	59	Broward, FL	22.9	16	59	Broward, FL	10.0
57	60	Fresno, CA	10.3	67	59	Middlesex, NJ	22.9	31	59	Hennepin, MN	10.0
14	61	Santa Clara, CA	10.2	73	61	Jefferson, KY	22.8	67	59	Middlesex, NJ	10.0
33	63	Franklin, OH	10.1	66	62	Baltimore, MD	22.4	59	62	San Francisco, CA	9.9
6	62	Orange, CA	10.1	13	62	King, WA	22.4	70	63	San Mateo, CA	9.8
43	64	Shelby, TN	10.0	65	62	Montgomery, PA	22.4	60	63	Ventura, CA	9.8
71	65	El Paso, TX	9.5	40	62	Westchester, NY	22.4	6	65	Orange, CA	9.7
41	66	Du Page, IL	9.4	25	66	Nassau, NY	22.2	30	66	Oakland, MI	9.6
61	67	Fulton, GA	8.9	11	66	Queens, NY	22.2	17	66	Riverside, CA	9.6
12	68	San Bernardino, CA	8.7	70	66	San Mateo, CA	22.2	45	68	Bergen, NJ	9.4
10	69	Dallas, TX	8.6	18	69	Middlesex, MA	21.7	46	68	Montgomery, MD	9.4
22	70	Tarrant, TX	8.4	45	70	Bergen, NJ	21.4	42	68	Pinellas, FL	9.4
47	71	Salt Lake, UT	8.3	26	71	Allegheny, PA	21.3	13	71	King, WA	9.0
56	72	Prince George's, MD	7.9	32	72	Palm Beach, FL	21.1	32	72	Palm Beach, FL	8.6
35	73	Fairfax, VA	7.8	42	73	Pinellas, FL	19.8	35	73	Fairfax, VA	8.4
3	74	Harris, TX	7.7	15	74	New York, NY	18.2	65	74	Montgomery, PA	8.3
64	75	Travis, TX	7.3	59	75	San Francisco, CA	16.7	41	75	Du Page, IL	7.3

Note: Column numbers refer to Table B. States and Counties.

TABLE 1—75 Largest Counties by 1999 Population
Selected Rankings

Live Birth Rate per 1,000 Population, 1996-1998				Infant Deaths Per 1,000 Live Births, 1996-1998 Average				Percent College Graduates (16+ Years of Education), 1990			
Population Rank	Birth Rate Rank 1996-98	County	[col 33] Birth Rate 1996-98 Average	Population Rank	Infant Mortality Rate	County	[col 37] Infant Mortality Rate	Population Rank	Percent College Graduate Rank	County	[col 51] Percent College Grads
71	1	El Paso, TX	21.2	43	1	Shelby, TN	12.7	46	1	Montgomery, MD	49.9
47	2	Salt Lake, UT	20.1	56	2	Prince George's, MD	12.6	35	2	Fairfax, VA	49.0
28	3	Bronx, NY	19.2	19	3	Philadelphia, PA	12.4	15	3	New York, NY	42.2
10	3	Dallas, TX	19.2	74	4	Jefferson, AL	11.5	41	4	Du Page, IL	36.0
57	3	Fresno, CA	19.2	9	5	Wayne, MI	11.0	18	5	Middlesex, MA	35.4
3	6	Harris, TX	18.8	58	6	Essex, NJ	10.8	40	6	Westchester, NY	35.3
1	7	Los Angeles, CA	17.9	39	7	Milwaukee, WI	10.2	59	7	San Francisco, CA	35.0
12	8	San Bernardino, CA	17.8	2	8	Cook, IL	10.0	64	8	Travis, TX	34.7
7	9	Kings, NY	17.7	61	9	Fulton, GA	9.8	48	9	Fairfield, CT	34.2
4	9	Maricopa, AZ	17.7	24	10	Cuyahoga, OH	9.7	13	10	King, WA	32.8
6	11	Orange, CA	17.6	49	10	Hamilton, OH	9.7	14	11	Santa Clara, CA	32.6
23	12	Bexar, TX	17.3	52	10	Marion, IN	9.7	65	12	Montgomery, PA	32.1
64	12	Travis, TX	17.3	63	13	Duval, FL	9.1	45	13	Bergen, NJ	31.7
43	14	Shelby, TN	17.2	33	14	Franklin, OH	8.9	37	14	Contra Costa, CA	31.6
22	14	Tarrant, TX	17.2	75	15	Jackson, MO	8.8	61	14	Fulton, GA	31.6
61	16	Fulton, GA	17.1	38	16	Erie, NY	8.4	31	14	Hennepin, MN	31.6
52	16	Marion, IN	17.1	50	16	Hartford, CT	8.4	70	17	San Mateo, CA	31.3
27	18	Clark, NV	17.0	36	18	Hillsborough, FL	8.3	30	18	Oakland, MI	30.2
2	19	Cook, IL	16.6	7	19	Kings, NY	8.2	25	19	Nassau, NY	30.0
63	20	Duval, FL	16.4	73	20	Jefferson, KY	8.0	34	20	St. Louis, MO	29.2
14	20	Santa Clara, CA	16.4	42	20	Pinellas, FL	8.0	20	21	Alameda, CA	28.8
58	22	Essex, NJ	16.3	66	22	Baltimore, MD	7.9	6	22	Orange, CA	27.8
17	23	Riverside, CA	16.2	28	22	Bronx, NY	7.9	33	23	Franklin, OH	26.6
11	24	Queens, NY	16.1	68	24	Monroe, NY	7.7	67	24	Middlesex, NJ	26.5
5	24	San Diego, CA	16.1	12	24	San Bernardino, CA	7.7	10	25	Dallas, TX	26.3
39	26	Milwaukee, WI	15.9	34	24	St. Louis, MO	7.7	68	25	Monroe, NY	26.3
60	26	Ventura, CA	15.9	57	27	Fresno, CA	7.6	69	27	Essex, MA	25.9
33	28	Franklin, OH	15.8	26	28	Allegheny, PA	7.4	50	28	Hartford, CT	25.8
51	29	Orange, FL	15.7	23	28	Bexar, TX	7.4	56	29	Prince George's, MD	25.5
29	30	Sacramento, CA	15.6	4	28	Maricopa, AZ	7.4	3	30	Harris, TX	25.4
41	31	Du Page, IL	15.5	16	31	Broward, FL	7.0	5	31	San Diego, CA	25.3
56	31	Prince George's, MD	15.5	31	31	Hennepin, MN	7.0	66	32	Baltimore, MD	25.0
36	33	Hillsborough, FL	15.3	22	31	Tarrant, TX	7.0	44	33	Honolulu, HI	24.6
19	33	Philadelphia, PA	15.3	72	34	Pierce, WA	6.9	54	34	New Haven, CT	24.2
75	35	Jackson, MO	15.2	54	35	New Haven, CT	6.7	58	35	Essex, NJ	24.0
20	36	Alameda, CA	15.1	17	35	Riverside, CA	6.7	22	35	Tarrant, TX	24.0
48	37	Fairfield, CT	14.9	29	35	Sacramento, CA	6.7	47	37	Salt Lake, UT	23.8
44	37	Honolulu, HI	14.9	51	38	Orange, FL	6.6	49	38	Hamilton, OH	23.7
9	37	Wayne, MI	14.9	46	39	Montgomery, MD	6.5	53	39	Pima, AZ	23.3
8	40	Miami-Dade, FL	14.8	44	40	Honolulu, HI	6.4	29	40	Sacramento, CA	23.0
31	41	Hennepin, MN	14.6	53	40	Pima, AZ	6.4	21	40	Suffolk, NY	23.0
72	41	Pierce, WA	14.6	27	42	Clark, NV	6.3	60	40	Ventura, CA	23.0
53	41	Pima, AZ	14.6	3	42	Harris, TX	6.3	2	43	Cook, IL	22.8
21	41	Suffolk, NY	14.6	10	44	Dallas, TX	6.2	26	44	Allegheny, PA	22.6
73	45	Jefferson, KY	14.5	15	44	New York, NY	6.2	1	45	Los Angeles, CA	22.3
70	45	San Mateo, CA	14.5	32	44	Palm Beach, FL	6.2	62	46	Worcester, MA	22.2
35	47	Fairfax, VA	14.4	11	44	Queens, NY	6.2	4	47	Maricopa, AZ	22.1
46	47	Montgomery, MD	14.4	47	44	Salt Lake, UT	6.2	32	47	Palm Beach, FL	22.1
49	49	Hamilton, OH	14.3	41	49	Du Page, IL	6.1	52	49	Marion, IN	21.4
40	50	Westchester, NY	14.2	55	49	Macomb, MI	6.1	51	50	Orange, FL	21.2
67	51	Middlesex, NJ	14.1	69	51	Essex, MA	6.0	43	51	Shelby, TN	20.8
24	52	Cuyahoga, OH	14.0	48	51	Fairfield, CT	6.0	11	52	Queens, NY	20.6
74	52	Jefferson, AL	14.0	30	51	Oakland, MI	6.0	36	53	Hillsborough, FL	20.2
50	54	Hartford, CT	13.9	64	51	Travis, TX	6.0	24	54	Cuyahoga, OH	20.1
16	55	Broward, FL	13.8	60	51	Ventura, CA	6.0	38	55	Erie, NY	20.0
69	55	Essex, MA	13.8	1	56	Los Angeles, CA	5.9	75	55	Jackson, MO	20.0
37	57	Contra Costa, CA	13.7	8	57	Miami-Dade, FL	5.8	74	57	Jefferson, AL	19.9
30	58	Oakland, MI	13.6	62	57	Worcester, MA	5.8	23	58	Bexar, TX	19.7
18	59	Middlesex, MA	13.5	20	59	Alameda, CA	5.7	73	59	Jefferson, KY	19.3
68	59	Monroe, NY	13.5	65	60	Montgomery, PA	5.6	39	59	Milwaukee, WI	19.3
62	61	Worcester, MA	13.4	37	61	Contra Costa, CA	5.5	16	61	Broward, FL	18.8
13	62	King, WA	13.3	5	62	San Diego, CA	5.4	8	61	Miami-Dade, FL	18.8
25	62	Nassau, NY	13.3	67	63	Middlesex, NJ	5.3	42	63	Pinellas, FL	18.5
54	62	New Haven, CT	13.3	25	63	Nassau, NY	5.3	63	64	Duval, FL	18.4
65	65	Montgomery, PA	12.9	21	63	Suffolk, NY	5.3	72	65	Pierce, WA	17.5
34	65	St. Louis, MO	12.9	13	66	King, WA	5.2	57	66	Fresno, CA	16.9
15	67	New York, NY	12.7	71	67	El Paso, TX	5.1	7	67	Kings, NY	16.6
45	68	Bergen, NJ	12.6	35	67	Fairfax, VA	5.1	71	68	El Paso, TX	15.2
55	68	Macomb, MI	12.6	59	69	San Francisco, CA	4.9	19	68	Philadelphia, PA	15.2
32	68	Palm Beach, FL	12.6	14	69	Santa Clara, CA	4.9	12	70	San Bernardino, CA	14.9
38	71	Erie, NY	12.5	40	69	Westchester, NY	4.9	17	71	Riverside, CA	14.6
66	72	Baltimore, MD	12.4	6	72	Orange, CA	4.5	27	72	Clark, NV	13.8
26	73	Allegheny, PA	11.4	70	72	San Mateo, CA	4.5	9	73	Wayne, MI	13.7
59	74	San Francisco, CA	11.1	45	74	Bergen, NJ	4.2	55	74	Macomb, MI	13.5
42	75	Pinellas, FL	10.6	18	75	Middlesex, MA	4.1	28	75	Bronx, NY	12.2

Note: Column numbers refer to Table B. States and Counties.

TABLE 1—75 Largest Counties by 1999 Population
Selected Rankings

Expenditures Per Student, 1997				Per Capita Income, 1998				Median Household Income, 1997			
Population Rank	Expenditures Rank	County	[col 53] Expenditures Per Student (dollars)	Population Rank	Per Capita Income Rank	County	[col 64] Per Capita Income 1998 (dollars)	Population Rank	Median Income Rank	County	[col 58] Median Income 1997 (dollars)
40	1	Westchester, NY	11 744	15	1	New York, NY	72 194	35	1	Fairfax, VA	71 057
25	2	Nassau, NY	11 402	48	2	Fairfield, CT	51 866	41	2	Du Page, IL	62 825
21	3	Suffolk, NY	11 018	40	3	Westchester, NY	47 267	46	3	Montgomery, MD	62 130
58	4	Essex, NJ	10 612	45	4	Bergen, NJ	47 101	25	4	Nassau, NY	61 026
45	5	Bergen, NJ	10 419	59	5	San Francisco, CA	44 518	30	5	Oakland, MI	59 677
67	6	Middlesex, NJ	9 336	35	6	Fairfax, VA	44 303	14	6	Santa Clara, CA	59 639
65	7	Montgomery, PA	8 993	70	7	San Mateo, CA	43 338	45	7	Bergen, NJ	59 557
48	8	Fairfield, CT	8 802	65	8	Montgomery, PA	42 431	70	8	San Mateo, CA	57 267
26	9	Allegheny, PA	8 722	46	9	Montgomery, MD	42 393	48	9	Fairfield, CT	56 872
38	10	Erie, NY	8 390	30	10	Oakland, MI	42 378	65	10	Montgomery, PA	55 580
50	11	Hartford, CT	8 371	25	11	Nassau, NY	42 368	40	11	Westchester, NY	55 040
68	12	Monroe, NY	8 294	41	12	Du Page, IL	42 215	37	12	Contra Costa, CA	54 275
46	13	Montgomery, MD	8 223	61	13	Fulton, GA	41 325	21	13	Suffolk, NY	53 560
54	14	New Haven, CT	8 046	13	14	King, WA	40 905	18	14	Middlesex, MA	53 268
30	15	Oakland, MI	7 884	14	15	Santa Clara, CA	40 828	67	15	Middlesex, NJ	52 646
18	16	Middlesex, MA	7 748	31	16	Hennepin, MN	40 126	13	16	King, WA	51 300
31	17	Hennepin, MN	7 497	32	17	Palm Beach, FL	40 044	60	17	Ventura, CA	49 763
39	18	Milwaukee, WI	7 445	18	18	Middlesex, MA	39 857	55	18	Macomb, MI	49 601
28	19	Bronx, NY	7 414	34	19	St. Louis, MO	36 800	6	19	Orange, CA	49 583
7	19	Kings, NY	7 414	37	20	Contra Costa, CA	36 006	31	20	Hennepin, MN	48 054
15	19	New York, NY	7 414	50	21	Hartford, CT	34 544	56	21	Prince George's, MD	47 882
11	19	Queens, NY	7 414	10	22	Dallas, TX	33 617	34	22	St. Louis, MO	47 825
24	23	Cuyahoga, OH	7 374	67	23	Middlesex, NJ	33 289	20	23	Alameda, CA	46 795
55	24	Macomb, MI	7 132	58	24	Essex, NJ	33 102	50	24	Hartford, CT	46 011
19	25	Philadelphia, PA	7 123	69	25	Essex, MA	32 740	66	25	Baltimore, MD	44 715
9	26	Wayne, MI	7 102	21	26	Suffolk, NY	32 648	54	26	New Haven, CT	44 412
35	27	Fairfax, VA	7 076	6	27	Orange, CA	32 541	44	27	Honolulu, HI	44 310
69	28	Essex, MA	6 917	54	28	New Haven, CT	32 290	69	28	Essex, MA	44 187
52	29	Marion, IN	6 795	66	29	Baltimore, MD	32 269	47	29	Salt Lake, UT	44 118
66	30	Baltimore, MD	6 755	64	30	Travis, TX	32 148	59	30	San Francisco, CA	43 405
62	31	Worcester, MA	6 712	20	31	Alameda, CA	32 130	22	31	Tarrant, TX	42 927
56	32	Prince George's, MD	6 709	3	32	Harris, TX	32 052	68	32	Monroe, NY	41 954
61	33	Fulton, GA	6 644	2	33	Cook, IL	31 806	72	33	Pierce, WA	41 853
59	34	San Francisco, CA	6 631	49	34	Hamilton, OH	31 708	10	34	Dallas, TX	40 960
2	35	Cook, IL	6 538	26	35	Allegheny, PA	31 665	62	35	Worcester, MA	40 489
34	36	St. Louis, MO	6 478	24	36	Cuyahoga, OH	30 846	64	36	Travis, TX	40 250
49	37	Hamilton, OH	6 428	42	37	Pinellas, FL	30 633	2	37	Cook, IL	40 181
41	38	Du Page, IL	6 377	68	38	Monroe, NY	29 938	4	38	Maricopa, AZ	40 134
73	39	Jefferson, KY	6 343	73	39	Jefferson, KY	29 473	58	39	Essex, NJ	39 823
33	40	Franklin, OH	6 237	33	40	Franklin, OH	29 425	27	40	Clark, NV	39 586
75	41	Jackson, MO	6 121	43	41	Shelby, TN	28 984	33	41	Franklin, OH	39 498
13	42	King, WA	5 860	27	42	Clark, NV	28 884	29	42	Sacramento, CA	39 461
8	43	Miami-Dade, FL	5 845	52	43	Marion, IN	28 851	5	43	San Diego, CA	39 427
44	44	Honolulu, HI	5 774	60	44	Ventura, CA	28 711	61	44	Fulton, GA	39 047
72	45	Pierce, WA	5 704	44	45	Honolulu, HI	28 670	3	45	Harris, TX	39 037
70	46	San Mateo, CA	5 533	62	46	Worcester, MA	28 587	26	46	Allegheny, PA	38 893
14	47	Santa Clara, CA	5 425	16	47	Broward, FL	28 546	49	47	Hamilton, OH	38 763
23	48	Bexar, TX	5 408	11	48	Queens, NY	28 425	73	48	Jefferson, KY	38 733
1	49	Los Angeles, CA	5 398	55	49	Macomb, MI	28 283	15	49	New York, NY	38 224
32	50	Palm Beach, FL	5 333	56	50	Prince George's, MD	27 996	16	50	Broward, FL	37 832
42	50	Pinellas, FL	5 333	5	51	San Diego, CA	27 657	75	51	Jackson, MO	37 732
20	52	Alameda, CA	5 306	39	52	Milwaukee, WI	27 607	52	52	Marion, IN	37 686
5	53	San Diego, CA	5 252	22	53	Tarrant, TX	27 538	39	53	Milwaukee, WI	37 229
36	54	Hillsborough, FL	5 220	74	54	Jefferson, AL	27 272	32	54	Palm Beach, FL	37 045
16	55	Broward, FL	5 191	4	55	Maricopa, AZ	27 254	51	55	Orange, FL	36 979
29	56	Sacramento, CA	5 175	1	56	Los Angeles, CA	26 773	12	56	San Bernardino, CA	36 876
57	57	Fresno, CA	5 131	63	57	Duval, FL	26 637	24	57	Cuyahoga, OH	36 754
37	58	Contra Costa, CA	5 040	75	58	Jackson, MO	26 380	38	58	Erie, NY	36 711
64	59	Travis, TX	5 035	36	59	Hillsborough, FL	26 355	1	59	Los Angeles, CA	36 441
3	60	Harris, TX	5 016	29	60	Sacramento, CA	26 257	17	60	Riverside, CA	36 368
51	61	Orange, FL	5 005	51	61	Orange, FL	26 186	36	61	Hillsborough, FL	35 994
71	62	El Paso, TX	4 992	38	62	Erie, NY	26 183	63	62	Duval, FL	35 883
74	63	Jefferson, AL	4 963	47	63	Salt Lake, UT	26 100	11	63	Queens, NY	35 820
6	64	Orange, CA	4 944	9	64	Wayne, MI	25 065	74	64	Jefferson, AL	35 464
60	65	Ventura, CA	4 934	19	65	Philadelphia, PA	24 769	9	65	Wayne, MI	35 357
27	66	Clark, NV	4 903	72	66	Pierce, WA	24 500	43	66	Shelby, TN	34 583
12	67	San Bernardino, CA	4 899	7	67	Kings, NY	24 076	42	67	Pinellas, FL	32 816
10	68	Dallas, TX	4 896	8	68	Miami-Dade, FL	23 919	53	68	Pima, AZ	32 544
17	69	Riverside, CA	4 864	23	69	Bexar, TX	23 852	23	69	Bexar, TX	32 374
43	70	Shelby, TN	4 806	53	70	Pima, AZ	22 723	57	70	Fresno, CA	31 587
63	71	Duval, FL	4 725	17	71	Riverside, CA	22 451	8	71	Miami-Dade, FL	30 000
22	72	Tarrant, TX	4 702	57	72	Fresno, CA	20 333	19	72	Philadelphia, PA	28 897
53	73	Pima, AZ	4 491	12	73	San Bernardino, CA	20 258	7	73	Kings, NY	26 108
4	74	Maricopa, AZ	4 384	28	74	Bronx, NY	19 841	71	74	El Paso, TX	25 866
47	75	Salt Lake, UT	3 799	71	75	El Paso, TX	16 359	28	75	Bronx, NY	24 031

Note: Column numbers refer to Table B. States and Counties.

32

TABLE 1—75 Largest Counties by 1999 Population
Selected Rankings

Percent of Persons Below the Poverty Level, 1997				Percent of Persons Under Age 18 Below the Poverty Level, 1997				Median Value of Owner-Occupied Housing Units, 1990			
Population Rank	Poverty Rate Rank	County	[col 59] Poverty Rate for Persons 1997	Population Rank	Poverty Rate Rank for under 18 yrs.	County	[col 60] Poverty Rate in 1997 for under 18 yrs.	Population Rank	Median Value Rank	County	[col 91] Median Value 1990 (dollars)
28	1	Bronx, NY	30.2	28	1	Bronx, NY	41.9	15	1	New York, NY	487 300
71	2	El Paso, TX	27.8	7	2	Kings, NY	39.7	70	2	San Mateo, CA	343 900
7	3	Kings, NY	26.5	71	3	El Paso, TX	38.6	59	3	San Francisco, CA	298 900
57	4	Fresno, CA	25.6	15	4	New York, NY	38.4	14	4	Santa Clara, CA	289 400
19	5	Philadelphia, PA	21.7	57	5	Fresno, CA	38.0	44	5	Honolulu, HI	283 600
8	6	Miami-Dade, FL	21.1	19	6	Philadelphia, PA	32.8	40	6	Westchester, NY	283 500
15	7	New York, NY	20.7	1	7	Los Angeles, CA	30.5	6	7	Orange, CA	252 700
1	8	Los Angeles, CA	20.5	61	8	Fulton, GA	29.8	48	8	Fairfield, CT	249 800
23	9	Bexar, TX	18.5	8	9	Miami-Dade, FL	29.6	60	9	Ventura, CA	245 300
61	10	Fulton, GA	18.3	11	10	Queens, NY	29.3	45	10	Bergen, NJ	227 700
9	11	Wayne, MI	18.0	9	11	Wayne, MI	28.5	20	11	Alameda, CA	227 200
12	12	San Bernardino, CA	17.9	39	12	Milwaukee, WI	28.4	1	12	Los Angeles, CA	226 400
58	13	Essex, NJ	17.3	29	13	Sacramento, CA	27.3	37	13	Contra Costa, CA	219 400
29	14	Sacramento, CA	17.2	58	14	Essex, NJ	27.0	35	14	Fairfax, VA	213 800
11	15	Queens, NY	17.0	23	15	Bexar, TX	26.4	25	15	Nassau, NY	209 500
39	16	Milwaukee, WI	16.5	12	16	San Bernardino, CA	25.7	46	16	Montgomery, MD	200 800
43	17	Shelby, TN	16.3	53	17	Pima, AZ	24.4	58	17	Essex, NJ	196 100
53	18	Pima, AZ	16.2	2	18	Cook, IL	22.7	7	17	Kings, NY	196 100
3	19	Harris, TX	15.2	17	18	Riverside, CA	22.7	18	19	Middlesex, MA	192 800
36	20	Hillsborough, FL	15.0	43	20	Shelby, TN	22.1	11	20	Queens, NY	191 000
17	20	Riverside, CA	15.0	36	21	Hillsborough, FL	22.0	5	21	San Diego, CA	186 700
74	22	Jefferson, AL	14.5	5	21	San Diego, CA	22.0	69	22	Essex, MA	176 200
5	23	San Diego, CA	14.2	59	23	San Francisco, CA	21.7	28	23	Bronx, NY	173 900
2	24	Cook, IL	14.0	38	24	Erie, NY	21.5	50	24	Hartford, CT	168 900
38	25	Erie, NY	13.9	74	24	Jefferson, AL	21.5	21	25	Suffolk, NY	165 900
24	26	Cuyahoga, OH	13.6	24	26	Cuyahoga, OH	21.4	54	26	New Haven, CT	165 200
10	27	Dallas, TX	13.5	3	27	Harris, TX	20.9	67	27	Middlesex, NJ	164 700
63	28	Duval, FL	13.4	51	28	Orange, FL	20.2	65	28	Montgomery, PA	143 400
51	28	Orange, FL	13.4	10	29	Dallas, TX	19.9	13	29	King, WA	140 100
4	30	Maricopa, AZ	12.7	68	29	Monroe, NY	19.9	62	30	Worcester, MA	140 000
59	31	San Francisco, CA	12.6	52	31	Marion, IN	19.5	17	31	Riverside, CA	139 100
68	32	Monroe, NY	12.5	73	32	Jefferson, KY	19.4	41	32	Du Page, IL	137 100
75	33	Jackson, MO	12.2	42	32	Pinellas, FL	19.4	29	33	Sacramento, CA	129 800
73	33	Jefferson, KY	12.2	4	34	Maricopa, AZ	19.1	12	34	San Bernardino, CA	129 200
42	33	Pinellas, FL	12.2	63	35	Duval, FL	18.8	56	35	Prince George's, MD	122 600
52	36	Marion, IN	12.0	32	36	Palm Beach, FL	18.6	2	36	Cook, IL	102 100
20	37	Alameda, CA	11.8	75	37	Jackson, MO	18.4	66	37	Baltimore, MD	99 900
16	38	Broward, FL	11.7	54	38	New Haven, CT	18.0	32	38	Palm Beach, FL	98 400
64	38	Travis, TX	11.7	20	39	Alameda, CA	17.6	61	39	Fulton, GA	97 700
32	40	Palm Beach, FL	11.5	16	40	Broward, FL	17.5	30	40	Oakland, MI	95 400
22	40	Tarrant, TX	11.5	50	40	Hartford, CT	17.5	27	41	Clark, NV	93 300
49	42	Hamilton, OH	11.4	6	42	Orange, CA	17.4	16	42	Broward, FL	91 800
27	43	Clark, NV	11.1	26	43	Allegheny, PA	17.1	31	43	Hennepin, MN	91 000
33	43	Franklin, OH	11.1	33	43	Franklin, OH	17.1	68	44	Monroe, NY	90 700
62	43	Worcester, MA	11.1	69	45	Essex, MA	17.0	8	45	Miami-Dade, FL	86 500
6	46	Orange, CA	11.0	64	45	Travis, TX	17.0	4	46	Maricopa, AZ	85 300
72	46	Pierce, WA	11.0	22	47	Tarrant, TX	16.8	57	47	Fresno, CA	83 600
26	48	Allegheny, PA	10.9	62	47	Worcester, MA	16.8	34	48	St. Louis, MO	83 500
69	49	Essex, MA	10.6	49	49	Hamilton, OH	16.6	72	49	Pierce, WA	82 500
54	49	New Haven, CT	10.6	60	49	Ventura, CA	16.6	51	50	Orange, FL	81 400
50	51	Hartford, CT	10.4	27	51	Clark, NV	16.4	10	51	Dallas, TX	79 200
60	52	Ventura, CA	10.3	72	52	Pierce, WA	15.6	64	52	Travis, TX	78 300
44	53	Honolulu, HI	10.2	31	53	Hennepin, MN	15.5	55	53	Macomb, MI	76 800
31	54	Hennepin, MN	9.4	40	54	Westchester, NY	15.2	53	54	Pima, AZ	76 500
56	55	Prince George's, MD	9.3	56	55	Prince George's, MD	15.1	38	55	Erie, NY	74 000
40	55	Westchester, NY	9.3	44	56	Honolulu, HI	14.8	33	56	Franklin, OH	73 800
47	57	Salt Lake, UT	9.1	37	57	Contra Costa, CA	13.6	42	56	Pinellas, FL	73 800
14	58	Santa Clara, CA	9.0	14	57	Santa Clara, CA	13.6	36	58	Hillsborough, FL	73 100
37	59	Contra Costa, CA	8.7	48	59	Fairfield, CT	12.9	22	59	Tarrant, TX	72 900
13	60	King, WA	8.0	66	60	Baltimore, MD	12.8	49	60	Hamilton, OH	72 200
48	61	Fairfield, CT	7.9	13	61	King, WA	12.3	24	61	Cuyahoga, OH	72 100
66	62	Baltimore, MD	7.6	21	62	Suffolk, NY	11.9	47	62	Salt Lake, UT	71 000
21	62	Suffolk, NY	7.6	47	63	Salt Lake, UT	11.7	43	63	Shelby, TN	66 500
18	64	Middlesex, MA	7.3	34	64	St. Louis, MO	11.2	39	64	Milwaukee, WI	65 300
34	65	St. Louis, MO	7.2	18	65	Middlesex, MA	10.9	63	65	Duval, FL	64 000
67	66	Middlesex, NJ	6.8	67	66	Middlesex, NJ	10.7	3	66	Harris, TX	63 500
70	67	San Mateo, CA	6.6	25	67	Nassau, NY	9.6	52	67	Marion, IN	61 400
30	68	Oakland, MI	6.0	30	67	Oakland, MI	9.6	74	68	Jefferson, AL	58 700
55	69	Macomb, MI	5.9	70	69	San Mateo, CA	9.5	75	69	Jackson, MO	58 400
25	70	Nassau, NY	5.8	55	70	Macomb, MI	9.4	71	70	El Paso, TX	57 300
46	71	Montgomery, MD	5.6	46	71	Montgomery, MD	8.8	26	71	Allegheny, PA	57 100
45	72	Bergen, NJ	5.3	45	72	Bergen, NJ	8.1	73	72	Jefferson, KY	57 000
35	72	Fairfax, VA	5.3	35	73	Fairfax, VA	8.0	23	73	Bexar, TX	56 300
65	74	Montgomery, PA	4.8	65	74	Montgomery, PA	7.1	19	74	Philadelphia, PA	49 400
41	75	Du Page, IL	3.6	41	75	Du Page, IL	5.6	9	75	Wayne, MI	48 500

Note: Column numbers refer to Table B. States and Counties.

TABLE 1—75 Largest Counties by 1999 Population
Selected Rankings

Median Gross Rent of Renter-Occupied Housing Units, 1990

Population Rank	Median Rate Rank	County	[col 94] Median Rent in 1990 (dollars)
35	1	Fairfax, VA	834
21	2	Suffolk, NY	802
6	3	Orange, CA	790
14	4	Santa Clara, CA	773
70	5	San Mateo, CA	769
60	6	Ventura, CA	754
25	7	Nassau, NY	749
46	8	Montgomery, MD	740
48	9	Fairfield, CT	709
45	10	Bergen, NJ	689
37	11	Contra Costa, CA	675
18	12	Middlesex, MA	671
67	13	Middlesex, NJ	667
44	14	Honolulu, HI	663
59	15	San Francisco, CA	653
56	16	Prince George's, MD	642
20	17	Alameda, CA	626
1	17	Los Angeles, CA	626
41	19	Du Page, IL	625
5	20	San Diego, CA	611
40	21	Westchester, NY	600
69	22	Essex, MA	597
65	23	Montgomery, PA	593
32	24	Palm Beach, FL	587
54	25	New Haven, CT	585
16	26	Broward, FL	575
17	27	Riverside, CA	572
50	28	Hartford, CT	568
11	29	Queens, NY	560
30	30	Oakland, MI	557
12	31	San Bernardino, CA	556
66	32	Baltimore, MD	529
58	33	Essex, NJ	528
29	34	Sacramento, CA	527
62	35	Worcester, MA	522
51	36	Orange, FL	517
27	37	Clark, NV	516
15	38	New York, NY	513
13	39	King, WA	510
55	40	Macomb, MI	493
8	40	Miami-Dade, FL	493
31	42	Hennepin, MN	487
34	43	St. Louis, MO	482
61	44	Fulton, GA	479
2	45	Cook, IL	478
68	45	Monroe, NY	478
7	47	Kings, NY	477
4	48	Maricopa, AZ	466
42	49	Pinellas, FL	463
19	50	Philadelphia, PA	452
10	51	Dallas, TX	448
36	52	Hillsborough, FL	446
28	53	Bronx, NY	443
72	54	Pierce, WA	436
57	55	Fresno, CA	434
39	55	Milwaukee, WI	434
63	57	Duval, FL	431
33	58	Franklin, OH	430
22	58	Tarrant, TX	430
64	60	Travis, TX	416
52	61	Marion, IN	412
9	62	Wayne, MI	406
3	63	Harris, TX	405
75	64	Jackson, MO	402
24	65	Cuyahoga, OH	397
43	66	Shelby, TN	394
53	67	Pima, AZ	390
26	68	Allegheny, PA	389
38	69	Erie, NY	384
23	70	Bexar, TX	379
47	70	Salt Lake, UT	379
74	72	Jefferson, AL	358
49	73	Hamilton, OH	355
71	74	El Paso, TX	347
73	75	Jefferson, KY	346

Unemployment Rate, 1999

Population Rank	Unemployment Rate Rank	County	[col 100] Unemployment Rate 1999
57	1	Fresno, CA	13.5
71	2	El Paso, TX	9.4
28	3	Bronx, NY	8.1
7	4	Kings, NY	7.8
19	5	Philadelphia, PA	6.0
1	6	Los Angeles, CA	5.9
11	6	Queens, NY	5.9
8	8	Miami-Dade, FL	5.8
58	9	Essex, NJ	5.7
15	9	New York, NY	5.7
17	11	Riverside, CA	5.5
38	12	Erie, NY	5.2
32	13	Palm Beach, FL	5.0
44	14	Honolulu, HI	4.9
12	15	San Bernardino, CA	4.8
60	15	Ventura, CA	4.8
3	17	Harris, TX	4.7
24	18	Cuyahoga, OH	4.6
2	19	Cook, IL	4.5
72	19	Pierce, WA	4.5
27	21	Clark, NV	4.4
29	22	Sacramento, CA	4.2
9	22	Wayne, MI	4.2
16	24	Broward, FL	4.0
26	25	Allegheny, PA	3.9
68	25	Monroe, NY	3.9
61	27	Fulton, GA	3.8
67	27	Middlesex, NJ	3.8
39	27	Milwaukee, WI	3.8
66	30	Baltimore, MD	3.7
45	30	Bergen, NJ	3.7
73	30	Jefferson, KY	3.7
43	30	Shelby, TN	3.7
21	30	Suffolk, NY	3.7
10	35	Dallas, TX	3.5
69	35	Essex, MA	3.5
49	35	Hamilton, OH	3.5
50	35	Hartford, CT	3.5
75	35	Jackson, MO	3.5
56	35	Prince George's, MD	3.5
20	41	Alameda, CA	3.4
74	41	Jefferson, AL	3.4
54	41	New Haven, CT	3.4
47	41	Salt Lake, UT	3.4
40	41	Westchester, NY	3.4
62	41	Worcester, MA	3.4
23	47	Bexar, TX	3.2
13	47	King, WA	3.2
55	47	Macomb, MI	3.2
63	50	Duval, FL	3.1
53	50	Pima, AZ	3.1
5	50	San Diego, CA	3.1
22	50	Tarrant, TX	3.1
37	54	Contra Costa, CA	3.0
65	54	Montgomery, PA	3.0
25	54	Nassau, NY	3.0
59	54	San Francisco, CA	3.0
14	54	Santa Clara, CA	3.0
48	59	Fairfield, CT	2.9
4	59	Maricopa, AZ	2.9
52	61	Marion, IN	2.8
34	61	St. Louis, MO	2.8
41	63	Du Page, IL	2.7
51	63	Orange, FL	2.7
42	63	Pinellas, FL	2.7
36	66	Hillsborough, FL	2.6
6	66	Orange, CA	2.6
33	68	Franklin, OH	2.5
18	68	Middlesex, MA	2.5
30	68	Oakland, MI	2.5
64	71	Travis, TX	2.3
31	72	Hennepin, MN	2.2
70	73	San Mateo, CA	2.0
46	74	Montgomery, MD	1.8
35	75	Fairfax, VA	1.6

Manufacturing Employment as a Percent of Total Nonfarm Employment, 1998

Population Rank	Manufacturing Rank	County	[col 107/col 105] Percent employed in Mfg 1998
55	1	Macomb, MI	28.9
14	2	Santa Clara, CA	25.4
68	3	Monroe, NY	22.0
69	4	Essex, MA	21.7
62	5	Worcester, MA	21.0
71	6	El Paso, TX	19.0
39	7	Milwaukee, WI	18.4
6	8	Orange, CA	17.6
54	9	New Haven, CT	17.5
1	10	Los Angeles, CA	17.3
9	11	Wayne, MI	17.2
20	12	Alameda, CA	16.0
24	13	Cuyahoga, OH	15.8
12	14	San Bernardino, CA	15.7
22	14	Tarrant, TX	15.7
38	16	Erie, NY	15.6
50	17	Hartford, CT	15.4
60	18	Ventura, CA	15.3
13	19	King, WA	14.7
18	20	Middlesex, MA	14.6
2	21	Cook, IL	14.5
73	22	Jefferson, KY	14.4
17	23	Riverside, CA	14.3
34	24	St. Louis, MO	14.1
21	25	Suffolk, NY	14.0
49	26	Hamilton, OH	13.9
67	27	Middlesex, NJ	13.6
65	28	Montgomery, PA	13.4
57	29	Fresno, CA	13.1
48	30	Fairfield, CT	13.1
45	31	Bergen, NJ	12.9
31	32	Hennepin, MN	12.8
52	33	Marion, IN	12.6
5	34	San Diego, CA	12.5
64	35	Travis, TX	12.5
41	36	Du Page, IL	12.4
30	37	Oakland, MI	12.2
4	38	Maricopa, AZ	11.8
7	39	Kings, NY	11.7
47	40	Salt Lake, UT	11.6
10	41	Dallas, TX	11.5
72	42	Pierce, WA	11.3
75	43	Jackson, MO	10.9
58	43	Essex, NJ	10.9
11	43	Queens, NY	10.9
74	46	Jefferson, AL	10.8
53	47	Pima, AZ	10.6
42	48	Pinellas, FL	10.5
3	49	Harris, TX	10.3
66	50	Baltimore, MD	10.1
70	51	San Mateo, CA	9.5
43	52	Shelby, TN	9.2
33	53	Franklin, OH	8.6
26	54	Allegheny, PA	8.3
19	55	Philadelphia, PA	7.7
29	55	Sacramento, CA	7.7
8	57	Miami-Dade, FL	7.5
63	58	Duval, FL	7.4
23	59	Bexar, TX	7.1
25	59	Nassau, NY	7.1
37	61	Contra Costa, CA	6.9
32	62	Palm Beach, FL	6.5
16	63	Broward, FL	6.4
28	64	Bronx, NY	6.3
51	65	Orange, FL	6.2
36	66	Hillsborough, FL	6.0
61	67	Fulton, GA	5.7
40	68	Westchester, NY	5.1
56	69	Prince George's, MD	5.0
59	70	San Francisco, CA	4.4
46	71	Montgomery, MD	4.1
15	72	New York, NY	3.8
44	73	Honolulu, HI	3.4
27	74	Clark, NV	3.3
35	75	Fairfax, VA	2.9

Note: Column numbers refer to Table B. States and Counties.

TABLE 1—75 Largest Counties by 1999 Population
Selected Rankings

Employment in Professional, Scientific, and Technological Services as a Percent of Total Nonfarm Employment, 1998				Finance and Insurance as a Percent of Total Nonfarm Employment, 1998				Per Capita Local Government Taxes, 1997			
Population Rank	Services Rank	County	[col 110/col 105] Percent employed in Services 1998	Population Rank	FIRE Rank	County	[col 109/col 105] Percent FIRE Employment 1998	Population Rank	Local Taxes Rank	County	[col 181] Local Taxes Per Capita (Dollars)
35	1	Fairfax, VA	23.3	15	1	New York, NY	17.4	25	1	Nassau, NY	3 089
46	2	Montgomery, MD	14.9	50	2	Hartford, CT	14.0	40	2	Westchester, NY	2 843
15	3	New York, NY	13.2	59	3	San Francisco, CA	12.6	28	3	Bronx, NY	2 638
59	4	San Francisco, CA	12.9	63	4	Duval, FL	12.5	7	3	Kings, NY	2 638
18	5	Middlesex, MA	10.8	33	5	Franklin, OH	10.1	15	3	New York, NY	2 638
1	6	Los Angeles, CA	10.4	58	6	Essex, NJ	10.0	11	3	Queens, NY	2 638
56	7	Prince George's, MD	10.2	65	7	Montgomery, PA	9.2	21	7	Suffolk, NY	2 479
30	8	Oakland, MI	10.1	31	8	Hennepin, MN	8.7	61	8	Fulton, GA	2 127
61	9	Fulton, GA	9.8	25	9	Nassau, NY	8.3	45	9	Bergen, NJ	1 987
67	10	Middlesex, NJ	9.6	37	10	Contra Costa, CA	8.2	48	10	Fairfield, CT	1 878
19	11	Philadelphia, PA	9.4	39	11	Milwaukee, WI	8.1	46	11	Montgomery, MD	1 817
64	12	Travis, TX	9.2	19	12	Philadelphia, PA	8.0	59	12	San Francisco, CA	1 773
14	13	Santa Clara, CA	9.0	29	12	Sacramento, CA	8.0	2	13	Cook, IL	1 742
70	14	San Mateo, CA	8.0	75	14	Jackson, MO	7.9	35	14	Fairfax, VA	1 682
48	15	Fairfield, CT	7.9	61	15	Fulton, GA	7.8	68	15	Monroe, NY	1 681
5	15	San Diego, CA	7.9	2	16	Cook, IL	7.5	58	16	Essex, NJ	1 656
2	17	Cook, IL	7.8	48	16	Fairfield, CT	7.5	24	17	Cuyahoga, OH	1 632
42	17	Pinellas, FL	7.8	66	18	Baltimore, MD	7.1	67	18	Middlesex, NJ	1 605
31	19	Hennepin, MN	7.7	26	18	Allegheny, PA	7.1	19	19	Philadelphia, PA	1 591
37	20	Contra Costa, CA	7.6	74	20	Jefferson, AL	7.0	41	20	Du Page, IL	1 563
10	21	Dallas, TX	7.5	73	20	Jefferson, KY	7.0	33	21	Franklin, OH	1 531
26	21	Allegheny, PA	7.5	24	20	Cuyahoga, OH	7.0	50	22	Hartford, CT	1 526
3	23	Harris, TX	7.4	36	20	Hillsborough, FL	7.0	10	23	Dallas, TX	1 521
13	23	King, WA	7.4	52	24	Marion, IN	6.9	49	24	Hamilton, OH	1 506
65	25	Montgomery, PA	7.2	10	25	Dallas, TX	6.8	38	25	Erie, NY	1 496
41	25	Du Page, IL	7.2	23	26	Bexar, TX	6.5	32	26	Palm Beach, FL	1 495
36	25	Hillsborough, FL	7.2	30	26	Oakland, MI	6.5	64	27	Travis, TX	1 422
58	28	Essex, NJ	7.1	41	26	Du Page, IL	6.5	13	28	King, WA	1 399
6	29	Orange, CA	6.8	47	29	Salt Lake, UT	6.4	75	29	Jackson, MO	1 395
25	29	Nassau, NY	6.8	4	30	Maricopa, AZ	6.3	54	29	New Haven, CT	1 395
75	31	Jackson, MO	6.6	6	31	Orange, CA	6.2	65	31	Montgomery, PA	1 375
34	31	St. Louis, MO	6.6	67	32	Middlesex, NJ	6.0	31	32	Hennepin, MN	1 363
66	33	Baltimore, MD	6.5	16	33	Broward, FL	5.9	39	33	Milwaukee, WI	1 328
49	34	Hamilton, OH	6.4	42	33	Pinellas, FL	5.9	3	34	Harris, TX	1 317
29	34	Sacramento, CA	6.4	38	35	Erie, NY	5.8	26	35	Allegheny, PA	1 311
21	34	Suffolk, NY	6.4	34	35	St. Louis, MO	5.8	18	36	Middlesex, MA	1 301
4	37	Maricopa, AZ	6.2	44	37	Honolulu, HI	5.7	14	37	Santa Clara, CA	1 281
24	38	Cuyahoga, OH	6.1	40	38	Westchester, NY	5.6	20	38	Alameda, CA	1 271
32	38	Palm Beach, FL	6.1	49	38	Hamilton, OH	5.6	52	39	Marion, IN	1 268
45	40	Bergen, NJ	6.0	70	38	San Mateo, CA	5.6	70	40	San Mateo, CA	1 255
20	41	Alameda, CA	5.9	62	41	Worcester, MA	5.5	66	41	Baltimore, MD	1 207
40	41	Westchester, NY	5.9	64	42	Travis, TX	5.4	51	42	Orange, FL	1 190
33	43	Franklin, OH	5.8	46	42	Montgomery, MD	5.4	34	43	St. Louis, MO	1 185
23	44	Bexar, TX	5.7	8	42	Miami-Dade, FL	5.4	22	44	Tarrant, TX	1 182
16	45	Broward, FL	5.6	32	45	Palm Beach, FL	5.2	16	45	Broward, FL	1 166
60	45	Ventura, CA	5.6	13	45	King, WA	5.2	8	46	Miami-Dade, FL	1 151
51	47	Orange, FL	5.5	60	45	Ventura, CA	5.2	74	47	Jefferson, AL	1 109
47	47	Salt Lake, UT	5.5	21	48	Suffolk, NY	4.9	56	48	Prince George's, MD	1 093
8	49	Miami-Dade, FL	5.4	35	48	Fairfax, VA	4.9	30	49	Oakland, MI	1 044
53	49	Pima, AZ	5.4	1	50	Los Angeles, CA	4.8	69	50	Essex, MA	1 041
63	51	Duval, FL	5.3	45	51	Bergen, NJ	4.7	42	51	Pinellas, FL	1 016
52	52	Marion, IN	5.1	54	51	New Haven, CT	4.7	37	52	Contra Costa, CA	954
50	53	Hartford, CT	4.9	3	51	Harris, TX	4.7	36	53	Hillsborough, FL	936
68	53	Monroe, NY	4.9	5	51	San Diego, CA	4.7	27	54	Clark, NV	931
38	53	Erie, NY	4.9	57	55	Fresno, CA	4.6	43	55	Shelby, TN	929
39	53	Milwaukee, WI	4.9	43	56	Shelby, TN	4.5	73	56	Jefferson, KY	908
74	57	Jefferson, AL	4.8	9	56	Wayne, MI	4.5	6	57	Orange, CA	895
44	58	Honolulu, HI	4.7	69	58	Essex, MA	4.1	1	58	Los Angeles, CA	890
73	59	Jefferson, KY	4.4	72	58	Pierce, WA	4.1	9	59	Wayne, MI	868
27	60	Clark, NV	4.2	22	60	Tarrant, TX	3.9	60	60	Ventura, CA	865
55	60	Macomb, MI	4.2	51	60	Orange, FL	3.9	23	61	Bexar, TX	864
9	60	Wayne, MI	4.2	68	62	Monroe, NY	3.8	4	61	Maricopa, AZ	864
22	60	Tarrant, TX	4.2	56	63	Prince George's, MD	3.7	53	63	Pima, AZ	860
57	60	Fresno, CA	4.2	7	63	Kings, NY	3.7	47	64	Salt Lake, UT	857
69	65	Essex, MA	4.1	27	65	Clark, NV	3.6	63	65	Duval, FL	834
43	66	Shelby, TN	3.9	18	65	Middlesex, MA	3.6	62	66	Worcester, MA	830
54	67	New Haven, CT	3.8	20	67	Alameda, CA	3.4	29	67	Sacramento, CA	784
72	68	Pierce, WA	3.3	12	68	San Bernardino, CA	3.1	72	68	Pierce, WA	776
71	69	El Paso, TX	3.0	53	69	Pima, AZ	3.0	5	69	San Diego, CA	766
62	69	Worcester, MA	3.0	71	70	El Paso, TX	2.9	17	70	Riverside, CA	741
17	71	Riverside, CA	2.8	17	71	Riverside, CA	2.8	71	71	El Paso, TX	724
7	72	Kings, NY	2.7	11	72	Queens, NY	2.6	55	72	Macomb, MI	706
12	73	San Bernardino, CA	2.3	55	73	Macomb, MI	2.2	12	73	San Bernardino, CA	673
11	73	Queens, NY	2.3	14	74	Santa Clara, CA	2.1	57	74	Fresno, CA	640
28	75	Bronx, NY	1.9	28	75	Bronx, NY	1.5	44	75	Honolulu, HI	606

Note: Column numbers refer to Table B. States and Counties.

35

TABLE 1—75 Largest Counties by 1999 Population
Selected Rankings

Violent Crime Rate per 100,000 Population, 1998				Percent of County's Land Owned by Federal Government, 1997				Military as a Percent of All Federal Employment, 1998			
Population Rank	Crime Rate Rank	County	[col 46] Violent Crime Rate	Population Rank	Fed. Land Rank	County	[col 131] Percent Fed. Land	Population Rank	Military Rank	County	[col 193/col 192+193] Percent Fed. Employment Military
61	1	Fulton, GA	1 867	27	1	Clark, NV	88.3	5	1	San Diego, CA	70.9
8	2	Miami-Dade, FL	1 532	12	2	San Bernardino, CA	74.5	72	2	Pierce, WA	70.7
19	3	Philadelphia, PA	1 465	17	3	Riverside, CA	55.7	44	3	Honolulu, HI	64.9
9	4	Wayne, MI	1 379	4	4	Maricopa, AZ	53.2	63	4	Duval, FL	62.5
58	5	Essex, NJ	1 303	60	5	Ventura, CA	50.0	12	5	San Bernardino, CA	62.1
36	6	Hillsborough, FL	1 301	57	6	Fresno, CA	38.4	71	6	El Paso, TX	57.9
51	7	Orange, FL	1 285	8	7	Miami-Dade, FL	33.4	27	7	Clark, NV	51.5
75	8	Jackson, MO	1 179	1	8	Los Angeles, CA	29.6	23	8	Bexar, TX	49.8
15	9	New York, NY	1 167	53	9	Pima, AZ	29.0	53	9	Pima, AZ	47.3
63	10	Duval, FL	1 135	72	10	Pierce, WA	28.8	6	10	Orange, CA	46.8
43	11	Shelby, TN	1 114	13	11	King, WA	23.1	65	11	Montgomery, PA	44.7
52	12	Marion, IN	1 085	5	12	San Diego, CA	22.9	18	12	Middlesex, MA	44.3
1	13	Los Angeles, CA	1 017	47	13	Salt Lake, UT	20.4	60	13	Ventura, CA	44.2
56	14	Prince George's, MD	1 012	71	14	El Paso, TX	13.7	48	14	Fairfield, CT	43.4
59	15	San Francisco, CA	999	6	15	Orange, CA	13.1	26	15	Allegheny, PA	41.6
32	16	Palm Beach, FL	967	44	16	Honolulu, HI	12.5	36	16	Hillsborough, FL	40.6
42	17	Pinellas, FL	944	32	17	Palm Beach, FL	10.1	4	17	Maricopa, AZ	40.4
73	18	Jefferson, KY	913	59	18	San Francisco, CA	7.3	9	18	Wayne, MI	39.6
10	19	Dallas, TX	907	56	19	Prince George's, MD	7.1	47	19	Salt Lake, UT	36.4
57	20	Fresno, CA	903	35	20	Fairfax, VA	6.3	7	19	Kings, NY	36.4
20	21	Alameda, CA	857	23	21	Bexar, TX	6.1	67	21	Middlesex, NJ	35.3
66	22	Baltimore, MD	844	7	22	Kings, NY	5.4	16	22	Broward, FL	34.9
3	23	Harris, TX	841	63	23	Duval, FL	4.6	22	23	Tarrant, TX	34.5
27	24	Clark, NV	779	41	24	Du Page, IL	4.3	62	24	Worcester, MA	33.2
53	25	Pima, AZ	746	11	25	Queens, NY	4.0	68	24	Monroe, NY	33.2
74	26	Jefferson, AL	742	20	26	Alameda, CA	3.3	28	26	Bronx, NY	33.1
72	27	Pierce, WA	735	46	26	Montgomery, MD	3.3	50	27	Hartford, CT	32.8
16	28	Broward, FL	719	3	28	Harris, TX	2.6	17	28	Riverside, CA	32.5
17	29	Riverside, CA	696	10	29	Dallas, TX	2.3	2	29	Cook, IL	31.6
29	30	Sacramento, CA	685	37	30	Contra Costa, CA	2.0	73	30	Jefferson, KY	30.8
71	31	El Paso, TX	668	18	30	Middlesex, MA	2.0	64	31	Travis, TX	29.7
62	32	Worcester, MA	654	62	32	Worcester, MA	1.7	25	32	Nassau, NY	29.7
31	33	Hennepin, MN	653	29	33	Sacramento, CA	1.6	32	33	Palm Beach, FL	29.6
33	34	Franklin, OH	635	19	34	Philadelphia, PA	1.5	40	34	Westchester, NY	28.8
4	35	Maricopa, AZ	609	69	35	Essex, MA	1.4	3	35	Harris, TX	28.1
5	36	San Diego, CA	602	14	35	Santa Clara, CA	1.4	1	35	Los Angeles, CA	28.1
12	37	San Bernardino, CA	600	22	37	Tarrant, TX	1.3	56	37	Prince George's, MD	27.9
22	38	Tarrant, TX	573	33	38	Franklin, OH	1.2	41	38	Du Page, IL	27.8
37	39	Contra Costa, CA	558	65	39	Montgomery, PA	1.1	8	39	Miami-Dade, FL	27.7
47	40	Salt Lake, UT	518	24	40	Cuyahoga, OH	1.0	13	40	King, WA	26.4
64	41	Travis, TX	508	52	40	Marion, IN	1.0	14	41	Santa Clara, CA	26.3
14	42	Santa Clara, CA	496	15	40	New York, NY	1.0	31	41	Hennepin, MN	26.3
54	43	New Haven, CT	495	21	40	Suffolk, NY	1.0	38	43	Erie, NY	26.2
38	44	Erie, NY	479	55	44	Macomb, MI	0.9	37	44	Contra Costa, CA	26.2
13	45	King, WA	474	70	45	San Mateo, CA	0.8	75	45	Jackson, MO	26.0
23	46	Bexar, TX	458	61	46	Fulton, GA	0.7	69	46	Essex, MA	25.6
69	47	Essex, MA	452	36	46	Hillsborough, FL	0.7	29	47	Sacramento, CA	25.0
26	48	Allegheny, PA	422	43	46	Shelby, TN	0.7	51	48	Orange, FL	24.5
55	48	Macomb, MI	422	31	49	Hennepin, MN	0.5	54	49	New Haven, CT	24.3
30	50	Oakland, MI	416	64	49	Travis, TX	0.5	43	50	Shelby, TN	24.2
50	51	Hartford, CT	404	66	51	Baltimore, MD	0.4	11	50	Queens, NY	24.2
48	52	Fairfield, CT	375	48	52	Fairfield, CT	0.3	30	52	Oakland, MI	23.2
6	53	Orange, CA	351	49	52	Hamilton, OH	0.3	42	53	Pinellas, FL	22.8
70	54	San Mateo, CA	336	75	52	Jackson, MO	0.3	39	54	Milwaukee, WI	22.6
68	55	Monroe, NY	332	25	52	Nassau, NY	0.3	33	55	Franklin, OH	22.3
40	56	Westchester, NY	319	16	56	Broward, FL	0.2	15	56	New York, NY	21.7
60	57	Ventura, CA	316	54	56	New Haven, CT	0.2	45	57	Bergen, NJ	21.5
18	58	Middlesex, MA	283	26	58	Allegheny, PA	0.1	10	58	Dallas, TX	20.5
34	59	St. Louis, MO	275	58	58	Essex, NJ	0.1	74	59	Jefferson, AL	20.1
44	60	Honolulu, HI	268	51	58	Orange, FL	0.1	52	60	Marion, IN	19.7
67	61	Middlesex, NJ	267	45	61	Bergen, NJ	0.0	34	61	St. Louis, MO	19.6
46	62	Montgomery, MD	243	28	61	Bronx, NY	0.0	19	62	Philadelphia, PA	19.4
65	63	Montgomery, PA	219	2	61	Cook, IL	0.0	21	63	Suffolk, NY	19.2
25	64	Nassau, NY	150	38	61	Erie, NY	0.0	49	64	Hamilton, OH	19.0
45	65	Bergen, NJ	147	50	61	Hartford, CT	0.0	70	65	San Mateo, CA	18.8
35	66	Fairfax, VA	105	74	61	Jefferson, AL	0.0	35	66	Fairfax, VA	16.7
21	67	Suffolk, NY	83	73	61	Jefferson, KY	0.0	61	67	Fulton, GA	16.4
28	68	Bronx, NY	NA	67	61	Middlesex, NJ	0.0	58	68	Essex, NJ	16.2
2	68	Cook, IL	NA	39	61	Milwaukee, WI	0.0	20	69	Alameda, CA	15.7
24	68	Cuyahoga, OH	NA	68	61	Monroe, NY	0.0	66	70	Baltimore, MD	15.0
41	68	Du Page, IL	NA	30	61	Oakland, MI	0.0	46	71	Montgomery, MD	14.9
49	68	Hamilton, OH	NA	42	61	Pinellas, FL	0.0	57	72	Fresno, CA	14.5
7	68	Kings, NY	NA	34	61	St. Louis, MO	0.0	24	73	Cuyahoga, OH	13.3
39	68	Milwaukee, WI	NA	9	61	Wayne, MI	0.0	55	74	Macomb, MI	9.5
11	68	Queens, NY	NA	40	61	Westchester, NY	0.0	59	75	San Francisco, CA	8.2

Note: Column numbers refer to Table B. States and Counties.

TABLE 2—75 Counties with Highest Agricultural Sales, 1997
Selected Rankings

Value of Agricultural Sales, 1997			Average Agricultural Sales per Farm, 1997				Number of Farms, 1997			
Value of Sales Rank	County	[col 125] Value of Sales (Mil Dol)	Value of Sales Rank	Average Sales Rank	County	[col 126] Average Sales per Farm ($)	Value of Sales Rank	Number of Farms Rank	County	[col 113] Number of Farms
1	Fresno, CA	2 773	38	1	Haskell, KS	1 794 382	1	1	Fresno, CA	6 592
2	Kern, CA	1 969	12	2	Imperial, CA	1 526 662	24	2	San Diego, CA	5 925
3	Tulare, CA	1 921	4	3	Monterey, CA	1 447 268	3	3	Tulare, CA	5 446
4	Monterey, CA	1 750	47	4	Hartley, TX	1 428 449	15	4	Lancaster, PA	4 556
5	Weld, CO	1 287	20	5	Castro, TX	1 366 952	7	5	Stanislaus, CA	4 009
6	Merced, CA	1 273	35	6	Scott, KS	1 347 057	8	6	San Joaquin, CA	3 862
7	Stanislaus, CA	1 209	48	7	Hansford, TX	1 241 020	11	7	Yakima, WA	3 365
8	San Joaquin, CA	1 180	70	8	Grant, KS	1 133 381	9	8	Riverside, CA	3 048
9	Riverside, CA	1 048	28	9	Yuma, AZ	1 122 717	62	9	Stearns, MN	2 982
10	Palm Beach, FL	873	67	10	Moore, TX	1 118 443	5	10	Weld, CO	2 959
11	Yakima, WA	873	10	11	Palm Beach, FL	1 020 908	6	11	Merced, CA	2 831
12	Imperial, CA	850	23	12	Deaf Smith, TX	1 014 894	34	12	Sonoma, CA	2 745
13	Ventura, CA	846	66	13	Sherman, TX	1 006 870	55	13	Hillsborough, FL	2 639
14	Grant, WA	804	2	14	Kern, CA	985 735	74	14	Dane, WI	2 595
15	Lancaster, PA	767	33	15	Finney, KS	922 739	36	15	Marion, OR	2 546
16	Duplin, NC	746	27	16	Parmer, TX	919 706	45	16	Washington, AR	2 476
17	Sampson, NC	733	46	17	Dallam, TX	862 291	51	17	Benton, AR	2 323
18	Kings, CA	694	19	18	Texas, OK	850 985	13	18	Ventura, CA	2 214
19	Texas, OK	668	42	19	Gray, KS	810 604	54	19	Cullman, AL	2 151
20	Castro, TX	668	58	20	Hendry, FL	802 575	2	20	Kern, CA	1 997
21	Maricopa, AZ	664	43	21	Swisher, TX	688 268	73	21	Butte, CA	1 942
22	Santa Barbara, CA	660	44	22	Pinal, AZ	671 865	59	22	San Luis Obispo, CA	1 916
23	Deaf Smith, TX	657	18	23	Kings, CA	642 889	60	23	Canyon, ID	1 898
24	San Diego, CA	633	17	24	Sampson, NC	617 925	37	24	Rockingham, VA	1 834
25	Madera, CA	627	16	25	Duplin, NC	609 844	29	25	Sioux, IA	1 752
26	San Bernardino, CA	618	53	26	Phelps, NE	609 402	14	26	Grant, WA	1 699
27	Parmer, TX	551	32	27	Yuma, CO	537 247	25	27	Madera, CA	1 673
28	Yuma, AZ	522	40	28	Morgan, CO	534 842	21	28	Maricopa, AZ	1 643
29	Sioux, IA	508	30	29	Cuming, NE	509 501	68	29	Gonzales, TX	1 629
30	Cuming, NE	507	14	30	Grant, WA	473 368	39	30	Dade, FL	1 576
31	Sussex, DE	500	41	31	Dawson, NE	465 589	26	31	San Bernardino, CA	1 455
32	Yuma, CO	481	57	32	Cassia, ID	456 541	22	32	Santa Barbara, CA	1 451
33	Finney, KS	480	22	33	Santa Barbara, CA	454 680	50	33	Chester, PA	1 424
34	Sonoma, CA	464	6	34	Merced, CA	449 832	31	34	Sussex, DE	1 366
35	Scott, KS	451	61	35	Ford, KS	445 514	71	35	Custer, NE	1 307
36	Marion, OR	438	5	36	Weld, CO	434 821	65	36	Ottawa, MI	1 292
37	Rockingham, VA	438	26	37	San Bernardino, CA	424 628	72	37	Mercer, OH	1 255
38	Haskell, KS	432	1	38	Fresno, CA	420 629	16	38	Duplin, NC	1 224
39	Dade, FL	417	52	39	Wayne, NC	407 604	4	39	Monterey, CA	1 209
40	Morgan, CO	406	21	40	Maricopa, AZ	404 174	17	40	Sampson, NC	1 186
41	Dawson, NE	399	56	41	Franklin, WA	392 612	75	41	Union, NC	1 142
42	Gray, KS	374	13	42	Ventura, CA	381 939	64	42	Renville, MN	1 114
43	Swisher, TX	364	25	43	Madera, CA	374 901	18	43	Kings, CA	1 079
44	Pinal, AZ	363	49	44	Yolo, CA	373 666	63	44	Benton, WA	1 078
45	Washington, AR	359	31	45	Sussex, DE	366 149	30	45	Cuming, NE	995
46	Dallam, TX	357	3	46	Tulare, CA	352 806	49	46	Yolo, CA	923
47	Hartley, TX	350	9	47	Riverside, CA	343 676	32	47	Yuma, CO	896
48	Hansford, TX	346	69	48	Logan, CO	333 038	69	48	Logan, CO	879
49	Yolo, CA	345	8	49	San Joaquin, CA	305 465	41	49	Dawson, NE	858
50	Chester, PA	343	7	50	Stanislaus, CA	301 453	10	50	Palm Beach, FL	855
51	Benton, AR	338	29	51	Sioux, IA	289 932	56	51	Franklin, WA	848
52	Wayne, NC	337	63	52	Benton, WA	278 785	52	52	Wayne, NC	827
53	Phelps, NE	336	64	53	Renville, MN	269 849	19	53	Texas, OK	785
54	Cullman, AL	334	39	54	Dade, FL	264 278	40	54	Morgan, CO	759
55	Hillsborough, FL	333	11	55	Yakima, WA	259 582	57	55	Cassia, ID	729
56	Franklin, WA	333	75	56	Union, NC	248 304	61	56	Ford, KS	692
57	Cassia, ID	333	50	57	Chester, PA	240 778	23	57	Deaf Smith, TX	647
58	Hendry, FL	323	37	58	Rockingham, VA	238 879	27	58	Parmer, TX	599
59	San Luis Obispo, CA	313	65	59	Ottawa, MI	232 187	12	59	Imperial, CA	557
60	Canyon, ID	311	72	60	Mercer, OH	229 213	53	60	Phelps, NE	552
61	Ford, KS	308	71	61	Custer, NE	220 766	44	61	Pinal, AZ	541
62	Stearns, MN	302	68	62	Gonzales, TX	180 725	43	62	Swisher, TX	529
63	Benton, WA	301	36	63	Marion, OR	172 179	33	63	Finney, KS	520
64	Renville, MN	301	34	64	Sonoma, CA	168 895	20	64	Castro, TX	489
65	Ottawa, MI	300	15	65	Lancaster, PA	168 293	28	65	Yuma, AZ	465
66	Sherman, TX	295	60	66	Canyon, ID	164 066	42	66	Gray, KS	461
67	Moore, TX	294	59	67	San Luis Obispo, CA	163 335	46	67	Dallam, TX	414
68	Gonzales, TX	294	54	68	Cullman, AL	155 345	58	68	Hendry, FL	403
69	Logan, CO	293	73	69	Butte, CA	147 388	35	69	Scott, KS	335
70	Grant, KS	291	51	70	Benton, AR	145 296	66	70	Sherman, TX	293
71	Custer, NE	289	45	71	Washington, AR	145 163	48	71	Hansford, TX	279
72	Mercer, OH	288	55	72	Hillsborough, FL	126 084	67	72	Moore, TX	263
73	Butte, CA	286	74	73	Dane, WI	109 687	70	73	Grant, KS	257
74	Dane, WI	285	24	74	San Diego, CA	106 790	47	74	Hartley, TX	245
75	Union, NC	284	62	75	Stearns, MN	101 356	38	75	Haskell, KS	241

Note: Column numbers refer to Table B. States and Counties.

37

TABLE 2—75 Counties with Highest Agricultural Sales, 1997
Selected Rankings

	Average Size of Farm, 1997				Average Value of Lands and Buildings per Farm, 1997				Average Value of Land and Buildings per Acre, 1997		
Value of Sales Rank	Size of Farm Rank	County	[col 119] Average Size of Farm	Value of Sales Rank	Value of Land and Bldgs per Farm Rank	County	[col 122] Average Value per Farm ($1,000)	Value of Sales Rank	Value of Land and Bldgs per Acre Rank	County	[col 123] Average Value per Acre (Dollars)
47	1	Hartley, TX	3 359	58	1	Hendry, FL	4 289	39	1	Dade, FL	8 047
44	2	Pinal, AZ	2 409	4	2	Monterey, CA	2 685	13	2	Ventura, CA	6 860
46	3	Dallam, TX	2 250	12	3	Imperial, CA	2 614	50	3	Chester, PA	5 658
67	4	Moore, TX	2 112	10	4	Palm Beach, FL	2 398	15	4	Lancaster, PA	5 578
48	5	Hansford, TX	2 086	28	5	Yuma, AZ	2 266	24	5	San Diego, CA	5 504
66	6	Sherman, TX	2 072	2	6	Kern, CA	2 162	34	6	Sonoma, CA	5 211
38	7	Haskell, KS	1 530	44	7	Pinal, AZ	1 891	8	7	San Joaquin, CA	4 667
32	8	Yuma, CO	1 524	18	8	Kings, CA	1 602	9	8	Riverside, CA	4 618
58	9	Hendry, FL	1 500	49	9	Yolo, CA	1 420	7	9	Stanislaus, CA	4 508
33	10	Finney, KS	1 464	21	10	Maricopa, AZ	1 384	28	10	Yuma, AZ	4 496
2	11	Kern, CA	1 428	22	11	Santa Barbara, CA	1 378	36	11	Marion, OR	4 248
35	12	Scott, KS	1 422	38	12	Haskell, KS	1 321	55	12	Hillsborough, FL	4 234
19	13	Texas, OK	1 384	47	13	Hartley, TX	1 240	73	13	Butte, CA	3 589
23	14	Deaf Smith, TX	1 360	46	14	Dallam, TX	1 181	25	14	Madera, CA	3 537
70	15	Grant, KS	1 294	66	15	Sherman, TX	1 166	3	15	Tulare, CA	3 444
69	16	Logan, CO	1 284	25	16	Madera, CA	1 157	10	16	Palm Beach, FL	3 404
4	17	Monterey, CA	1 277	63	17	Benton, WA	1 122	1	17	Fresno, CA	3 334
42	18	Gray, KS	1 206	59	18	San Luis Obispo, CA	1 046	6	18	Merced, CA	3 149
71	19	Custer, NE	1 188	34	19	Sonoma, CA	1 025	37	19	Rockingham, VA	3 069
20	20	Castro, TX	1 142	8	20	San Joaquin, CA	1 017	12	20	Imperial, CA	3 068
40	21	Morgan, CO	976	14	21	Grant, WA	1 001	65	21	Ottawa, MI	3 066
43	22	Swisher, TX	975	1	22	Fresno, CA	971	21	22	Maricopa, AZ	2 944
61	23	Ford, KS	967	56	23	Franklin, WA	969	58	23	Hendry, FL	2 868
27	24	Parmer, TX	913	33	24	Finney, KS	951	72	24	Mercer, OH	2 812
57	25	Cassia, ID	901	6	25	Merced, CA	951	75	25	Union, NC	2 790
12	26	Imperial, CA	879	57	26	Cassia, ID	918	18	26	Kings, CA	2 732
41	27	Dawson, NE	757	64	27	Renville, MN	913	49	27	Yolo, CA	2 732
10	28	Palm Beach, FL	707	32	28	Yuma, CO	891	22	28	Santa Barbara, CA	2 716
53	29	Phelps, NE	686	70	29	Grant, KS	888	54	29	Cullman, AL	2 647
59	30	San Luis Obispo, CA	679	13	30	Ventura, CA	883	51	30	Benton, AR	2 549
56	31	Franklin, WA	665	53	31	Phelps, NE	876	29	31	Sioux, IA	2 445
5	32	Weld, CO	647	48	32	Hansford, TX	856	31	32	Sussex, DE	2 441
14	33	Grant, WA	645	3	33	Tulare, CA	835	4	33	Monterey, CA	2 358
26	34	San Bernardino, CA	635	67	34	Moore, TX	804	16	34	Duplin, NC	2 321
18	35	Kings, CA	609	42	35	Gray, KS	786	45	35	Washington, AR	2 230
49	36	Yolo, CA	581	7	36	Stanislaus, CA	779	60	36	Canyon, ID	2 225
63	37	Benton, WA	568	73	37	Butte, CA	754	63	37	Benton, WA	2 169
22	38	Santa Barbara, CA	563	9	38	Riverside, CA	749	52	38	Wayne, NC	2 025
64	39	Renville, MN	540	19	39	Texas, OK	718	17	39	Sampson, NC	1 971
28	40	Yuma, AZ	511	35	40	Scott, KS	694	74	40	Dane, WI	1 853
11	41	Yakima, WA	500	20	41	Castro, TX	676	64	41	Renville, MN	1 703
68	42	Gonzales, TX	436	50	42	Chester, PA	670	2	42	Kern, CA	1 605
21	43	Maricopa, AZ	431	29	43	Sioux, IA	662	14	43	Grant, WA	1 596
25	44	Madera, CA	383	41	44	Dawson, NE	625	59	44	San Luis Obispo, CA	1 591
30	45	Cuming, NE	361	23	45	Deaf Smith, TX	611	30	45	Cuming, NE	1 571
6	46	Merced, CA	311	11	46	Yakima, WA	605	56	46	Franklin, WA	1 469
1	47	Fresno, CA	285	40	47	Morgan, CO	604	53	47	Phelps, NE	1 376
29	48	Sioux, IA	282	72	48	Mercer, OH	582	11	48	Yakima, WA	1 220
52	49	Wayne, NC	277	5	49	Weld, CO	567	62	49	Stearns, MN	1 099
3	50	Tulare, CA	240	27	50	Parmer, TX	564	57	50	Cassia, ID	932
17	51	Sampson, NC	228	30	51	Cuming, NE	549	41	51	Dawson, NE	859
31	52	Sussex, DE	225	71	52	Custer, NE	547	38	52	Haskell, KS	828
62	53	Stearns, MN	217	52	53	Wayne, NC	542	5	53	Weld, CO	807
8	54	San Joaquin, CA	209	31	54	Sussex, DE	518	68	54	Gonzales, TX	797
34	55	Sonoma, CA	208	69	55	Logan, CO	511	44	55	Pinal, AZ	760
73	56	Butte, CA	208	36	56	Marion, OR	500	26	56	San Bernardino, CA	693
72	57	Mercer, OH	208	61	57	Ford, KS	483	42	57	Gray, KS	663
74	58	Dane, WI	198	15	58	Lancaster, PA	472	70	58	Grant, KS	660
16	59	Duplin, NC	195	26	59	San Bernardino, CA	470	40	59	Morgan, CO	649
60	60	Canyon, ID	187	17	60	Sampson, NC	464	27	60	Parmer, TX	621
7	61	Stanislaus, CA	183	16	61	Duplin, NC	457	33	61	Finney, KS	588
9	62	Riverside, CA	167	43	62	Swisher, TX	445	66	62	Sherman, TX	584
13	63	Ventura, CA	156	75	63	Union, NC	428	20	63	Castro, TX	578
75	64	Union, NC	156	39	64	Dade, FL	408	32	64	Yuma, CO	565
45	65	Washington, AR	135	24	65	San Diego, CA	407	46	65	Dallam, TX	516
65	66	Ottawa, MI	132	60	66	Canyon, ID	399	19	66	Texas, OK	511
51	67	Benton, AR	128	65	67	Ottawa, MI	396	35	67	Scott, KS	510
37	68	Rockingham, VA	126	55	68	Hillsborough, FL	391	61	68	Ford, KS	508
50	69	Chester, PA	123	37	69	Rockingham, VA	383	71	69	Custer, NE	444
36	70	Marion, OR	120	68	70	Gonzales, TX	381	43	70	Swisher, TX	437
55	71	Hillsborough, FL	94	74	71	Dane, WI	367	23	71	Deaf Smith, TX	430
54	72	Cullman, AL	94	45	72	Washington, AR	303	69	72	Logan, CO	427
15	73	Lancaster, PA	86	51	73	Benton, AR	300	48	73	Hansford, TX	424
24	74	San Diego, CA	80	54	74	Cullman, AL	253	67	74	Moore, TX	385
39	75	Dade, FL	54	62	75	Stearns, MN	227	47	75	Hartley, TX	367

Note: Column numbers refer to Table B. States and Counties.

TABLE 3—75 Largest Metropolitan Areas by 1999 Population
Selected Rankings

	Total Persons, 1999			Land Area (Square Kilometers), 1990		
Population Rank	Metropolitan Area	[col 2] Population	Population Rank	Land Area Rank	Metropolitan Area	[col 1] Land Area
1	Los Angeles-Long Beach, CA	9 329 989	43	1	Las Vegas, NV-AZ	101 969
2	New York, NY	8 712 600	11	2	Riverside-San Bernardino, CA	70 629
3	Chicago, IL	8 008 507	12	3	Phoenix-Mesa, AZ	37 746
4	Boston-Worcester-Lawrence-Lowell-Brockton, MA-NH	5 901 589	70	4	Tucson, AZ	23 794
5	Philadelphia, PA-NJ	4 949 867	67	5	Fresno, CA	20 984
6	Washington, DC-MD-VA-WV	4 739 999	6	6	Washington, DC-MD-VA-WV	16 863
7	Detroit, MI	4 474 614	4	7	Boston-Worcester-Lawrence-Lowell-Brockton, MA-NH	16 706
8	Houston, TX	4 010 969	17	8	St. Louis, MO-IL	16 556
9	Atlanta, GA	3 857 097	10	9	Dallas, TX	16 025
10	Dallas, TX	3 280 310	9	10	Atlanta, GA	15 867
11	Riverside-San Bernardino, CA	3 200 587	13	11	Minneapolis-St. Paul, MN-WI	15 709
12	Phoenix-Mesa, AZ	3 013 696	8	12	Houston, TX	15 335
13	Minneapolis-St. Paul, MN-WI	2 872 109	28	13	Kansas City, MO-KS	14 004
14	San Diego, CA	2 820 844	3	14	Chicago, IL	13 119
15	Orange County, CA	2 760 948	27	15	Portland-Vancouver, OR-WA	13 021
16	Nassau-Suffolk, NY	2 688 904	71	16	Tulsa, OK	12 988
17	St. Louis, MO-IL	2 569 029	21	17	Pittsburgh, PA	11 974
18	Baltimore, MD	2 491 254	20	18	Seattle-Bellevue-Everett, WA	11 461
19	Oakland, CA	2 348 723	60	19	Oklahoma City, OK	11 002
20	Seattle-Bellevue-Everett, WA	2 334 934	49	20	Austin-San Marcos, TX	10 946
21	Pittsburgh, PA	2 331 336	14	21	San Diego, CA	10 890
22	Tampa-St. Petersburg-Clearwater, FL	2 278 169	34	22	Sacramento, CA	10 571
23	Cleveland-Lorain-Elyria, OH	2 221 181	48	23	Nashville, TN	10 549
24	Miami, FL	2 175 634	1	24	Los Angeles-Long Beach, CA	10 515
25	Denver, CO	1 978 991	7	25	Detroit, MI	10 093
26	Newark, NJ	1 954 671	47	26	Greensboro—Winston-Salem—High Point, NC	10 056
27	Portland-Vancouver, OR-WA	1 845 840	5	27	Philadelphia, PA-NJ	9 986
28	Kansas City, MO-KS	1 755 899	25	28	Denver, CO	9 740
29	San Francisco, CA	1 685 647	37	29	Indianapolis, IN	9 126
30	San Jose, CA	1 647 419	39	30	Orlando, FL	9 042
31	New Haven-Bridgeport-Stamford-Danbury-Waterbury, CT	1 634 542	54	31	Raleigh-Durham-Chapel Hill, NC	9 041
32	Fort Worth-Arlington, TX	1 629 213	56	32	Rochester, NY	8 873
33	Cincinnati, OH-KY-IN	1 627 509	45	33	New Orleans, LA	8 806
34	Sacramento, CA	1 585 429	42	34	Charlotte-Gastonia-Rock Hill, NC-SC	8 751
35	San Antonio, TX	1 564 949	33	35	Cincinnati, OH-KY-IN	8 658
36	Norfolk-Virginia Beach-Newport News, VA-NC	1 562 635	35	36	San Antonio, TX	8 617
37	Indianapolis, IN	1 536 665	68	37	Albany-Schenectady-Troy, NY	8 347
38	Fort Lauderdale, FL	1 535 468	64	38	Greenville-Spartanburg-Anderson, SC	8 316
39	Orlando, FL	1 535 004	65	39	Birmingham, AL	8 255
40	Columbus, OH	1 489 487	40	40	Columbus, OH	8 139
41	Milwaukee-Waukesha, WI	1 462 422	73	41	Syracuse, NY	7 985
42	Charlotte-Gastonia-Rock Hill, NC-SC	1 417 217	55	42	Memphis, TN-AR-MS	7 790
43	Las Vegas, NV-AZ	1 381 086	62	43	Richmond-Petersburg, VA	7 628
44	Bergen-Passaic, NJ	1 342 116	32	44	Fort Worth-Arlington, TX	7 557
45	New Orleans, LA	1 305 479	58	45	Grand Rapids-Muskegon-Holland, MI	7 145
46	Salt Lake City-Ogden, UT	1 275 076	23	46	Cleveland-Lorain-Elyria, OH	7 013
47	Greensboro—Winston-Salem—High Point, NC	1 179 384	57	47	Jacksonville, FL	6 826
48	Nashville, TN	1 171 755	18	48	Baltimore, MD	6 757
49	Austin-San Marcos, TX	1 146 050	22	49	Tampa-St. Petersburg-Clearwater, FL	6 617
50	Buffalo-Niagara Falls, NY	1 142 121	75	50	Omaha, NE-IA	6 412
51	Middlesex-Somerset-Hunterdon, NJ	1 130 592	36	51	Norfolk-Virginia Beach-Newport News, VA-NC	6 082
52	Hartford, CT	1 113 800	61	52	Louisville, KY-IN	5 367
53	Monmouth-Ocean, NJ	1 108 977	59	53	West Palm Beach-Boca Raton, FL	5 269
54	Raleigh-Durham-Chapel Hill, NC	1 105 535	24	54	Miami, FL	5 036
55	Memphis, TN-AR-MS	1 105 058	72	55	Ventura, CA	4 781
56	Rochester, NY	1 079 073	63	56	Dayton-Springfield, OH	4 361
57	Jacksonville, FL	1 056 332	46	57	Salt Lake City-Ogden, UT	4 190
58	Grand Rapids-Muskegon-Holland, MI	1 052 092	26	58	Newark, NJ	4 087
59	West Palm Beach-Boca Raton, FL	1 049 420	50	59	Buffalo-Niagara Falls, NY	4 060
60	Oklahoma City, OK	1 046 283	52	60	Hartford, CT	3 923
61	Louisville, KY-IN	1 005 849	41	61	Milwaukee-Waukesha, WI	3 782
62	Richmond-Petersburg, VA	961 416	19	62	Oakland, CA	3 776
63	Dayton-Springfield, OH	958 698	30	63	San Jose, CA	3 344
64	Greenville-Spartanburg-Anderson, SC	929 565	31	64	New Haven-Bridgeport-Stamford-Danbury-Waterbury, CT	3 190
65	Birmingham, AL	915 077	38	65	Fort Lauderdale, FL	3 131
66	Providence-Warwick-Pawtucket, RI	907 795	16	66	Nassau-Suffolk, NY	3 103
67	Fresno, CA	879 829	2	67	New York, NY	2 972
68	Albany-Schenectady-Troy, NY	869 474	53	68	Monmouth-Ocean, NJ	2 870
69	Honolulu, HI	864 571	51	69	Middlesex-Somerset-Hunterdon, NJ	2 708
70	Tucson, AZ	803 618	29	70	San Francisco, CA	2 630
71	Tulsa, OK	786 117	74	71	El Paso, TX	2 624
72	Ventura, CA	745 063	66	72	Providence-Warwick-Pawtucket, RI	2 436
73	Syracuse, NY	732 920	15	73	Orange County, CA	2 045
74	El Paso, TX	701 908	69	74	Honolulu, HI	1 554
75	Omaha, NE-IA	698 875	44	75	Bergen-Passaic, NJ	1 086

Note: Column numbers refer to Table C. Metropolitan Areas.

TABLE 3—75 Largest Metropolitan Areas by 1999 Population
Selected Rankings

Population Density (per Square Kilometer), 1999				Percent Population Change, 1990-1999			
Population Rank	Density Rank	Metropolitan Area	[col 4] Density	Population Rank	Percent Change Rank	Metropolitan Area	[col 23] Percent Change
2	1	New York, NY	2 932	43	1	Las Vegas, NV-AZ	62.0
15	2	Orange County, CA	1 350	49	2	Austin-San Marcos, TX	35.4
44	3	Bergen-Passaic, NJ	1 236	12	3	Phoenix-Mesa, AZ	34.6
1	4	Los Angeles-Long Beach, CA	887	9	4	Atlanta, GA	30.3
16	5	Nassau-Suffolk, NY	867	54	5	Raleigh-Durham-Chapel Hill, NC	28.8
29	6	San Francisco, CA	641	39	6	Orlando, FL	25.3
19	7	Oakland, CA	622	11	7	Riverside-San Bernardino, CA	23.6
3	8	Chicago, IL	611	10	8	Dallas, TX	22.6
69	9	Honolulu, HI	556	38	9	Fort Lauderdale, FL	22.3
31	10	New Haven-Bridgeport-Stamford-Danbury-Waterbury, CT	512	42	10	Charlotte-Gastonia-Rock Hill, NC-SC	22.0
5	11	Philadelphia, PA-NJ	496	25	11	Denver, CO	21.9
30	12	San Jose, CA	493	27	12	Portland-Vancouver, OR-WA	21.8
38	13	Fort Lauderdale, FL	490	59	13	West Palm Beach-Boca Raton, FL	21.5
26	14	Newark, NJ	478	8	14	Houston, TX	20.7
7	15	Detroit, MI	443	70	15	Tucson, AZ	20.5
24	16	Miami, FL	432	32	16	Fort Worth-Arlington, TX	19.7
51	17	Middlesex-Somerset-Hunterdon, NJ	418	48	17	Nashville, TN	19.0
41	18	Milwaukee-Waukesha, WI	387	46	18	Salt Lake City-Ogden, UT	18.9
53	19	Monmouth-Ocean, NJ	386	74	19	El Paso, TX	18.6
66	20	Providence-Warwick-Pawtucket, RI	373	35	20	San Antonio, TX	18.1
18	21	Baltimore, MD	369	57	21	Jacksonville, FL	16.5
4	22	Boston-Worcester-Lawrence-Lowell-Brockton, MA-NH	353	67	22	Fresno, CA	16.4
22	23	Tampa-St. Petersburg-Clearwater, FL	344	34	23	Sacramento, CA	16.1
23	24	Cleveland-Lorain-Elyria, OH	317	20	24	Seattle-Bellevue-Everett, WA	14.8
46	25	Salt Lake City-Ogden, UT	304	15	25	Orange County, CA	14.5
52	26	Hartford, CT	284	13	26	Minneapolis-St. Paul, MN-WI	13.1
50	27	Buffalo-Niagara Falls, NY	281	14	27	San Diego, CA	12.9
6	28	Washington, DC-MD-VA-WV	281	53	28	Monmouth-Ocean, NJ	12.4
74	29	El Paso, TX	268	47	29	Greensboro—Winston-Salem—High Point, NC	12.3
8	30	Houston, TX	262	24	29	Miami, FL	12.3
14	31	San Diego, CA	259	58	31	Grand Rapids-Muskegon-Holland, MI	12.2
36	32	Norfolk-Virginia Beach-Newport News, VA-NC	257	6	31	Washington, DC-MD-VA-WV	12.2
9	33	Atlanta, GA	243	64	33	Greenville-Spartanburg-Anderson, SC	11.9
63	34	Dayton-Springfield, OH	220	19	34	Oakland, CA	11.4
32	35	Fort Worth-Arlington, TX	216	72	34	Ventura, CA	11.4
10	36	Dallas, TX	205	37	36	Indianapolis, IN	11.3
20	37	Seattle-Bellevue-Everett, WA	204	62	37	Richmond-Petersburg, VA	11.1
25	38	Denver, CO	203	28	38	Kansas City, MO-KS	10.9
59	39	West Palm Beach-Boca Raton, FL	199	51	38	Middlesex-Somerset-Hunterdon, NJ	10.9
21	40	Pittsburgh, PA	195	71	38	Tulsa, OK	10.9
33	41	Cincinnati, OH-KY-IN	188	40	41	Columbus, OH	10.7
61	42	Louisville, KY-IN	187	22	42	Tampa-St. Petersburg-Clearwater, FL	10.2
40	43	Columbus, OH	183	30	43	San Jose, CA	10.0
13	44	Minneapolis-St. Paul, MN-WI	183	55	44	Memphis, TN-AR-MS	9.7
35	45	San Antonio, TX	182	75	45	Omaha, NE-IA	9.3
39	46	Orlando, FL	170	60	46	Oklahoma City, OK	9.1
37	47	Indianapolis, IN	168	65	47	Birmingham, AL	8.9
42	48	Charlotte-Gastonia-Rock Hill, NC-SC	162	36	48	Norfolk-Virginia Beach-Newport News, VA-NC	8.2
72	49	Ventura, CA	156	3	49	Chicago, IL	8.1
17	50	St. Louis, MO-IL	155	33	50	Cincinnati, OH-KY-IN	6.6
57	51	Jacksonville, FL	155	61	51	Louisville, KY-IN	6.0
34	52	Sacramento, CA	150	1	52	Los Angeles-Long Beach, CA	5.3
45	53	New Orleans, LA	148	29	53	San Francisco, CA	5.1
58	54	Grand Rapids-Muskegon-Holland, MI	147	7	54	Detroit, MI	4.9
55	55	Memphis, TN-AR-MS	142	18	55	Baltimore, MD	4.6
27	56	Portland-Vancouver, OR-WA	142	4	56	Boston-Worcester-Lawrence-Lowell-Brockton, MA-NH	3.8
62	57	Richmond-Petersburg, VA	126	44	57	Bergen-Passaic, NJ	3.5
28	58	Kansas City, MO-KS	125	69	58	Honolulu, HI	3.4
54	59	Raleigh-Durham-Chapel Hill, NC	122	16	59	Nassau-Suffolk, NY	3.1
56	60	Rochester, NY	122	17	59	St. Louis, MO-IL	3.1
47	61	Greensboro—Winston-Salem—High Point, NC	117	41	61	Milwaukee-Waukesha, WI	2.1
64	62	Greenville-Spartanburg-Anderson, SC	112	26	62	Newark, NJ	2.0
48	63	Nashville, TN	111	2	63	New York, NY	1.9
65	64	Birmingham, AL	111	45	64	New Orleans, LA	1.6
75	65	Omaha, NE-IA	109	56	64	Rochester, NY	1.6
49	66	Austin-San Marcos, TX	105	68	66	Albany-Schenectady-Troy, NY	0.9
68	67	Albany-Schenectady-Troy, NY	104	23	66	Cleveland-Lorain-Elyria, OH	0.9
60	68	Oklahoma City, OK	95	63	68	Dayton-Springfield, OH	0.8
73	69	Syracuse, NY	92	5	69	Philadelphia, PA-NJ	0.6
12	70	Phoenix-Mesa, AZ	80	31	70	New Haven-Bridgeport-Stamford-Danbury-Waterbury, CT	0.2
71	71	Tulsa, OK	61	71	71	Hartford, CT	-0.9
11	72	Riverside-San Bernardino, CA	45	52	71	Providence-Warwick-Pawtucket, RI	-0.9
67	73	Fresno, CA	42	66	73	Syracuse, NY	-1.3
70	74	Tucson, AZ	34	21	74	Pittsburgh, PA	-2.7
43	75	Las Vegas, NV-AZ	14	50	75	Buffalo-Niagara Falls, NY	-4.0

Note: Column numbers refer to Table C. Metropolitan Areas.

TABLE 3—75 Largest Metropolitan Areas by 1999 Population
Selected Rankings

Percent White, 1999

Population Rank	White Rank	Metropolitan Area	[col 5] Percent White
46	1	Salt Lake City-Ogden, UT	94.6
74	2	El Paso, TX	94.5
68	3	Albany-Schenectady-Troy, NY	92.7
66	4	Providence-Warwick-Pawtucket, RI	91.9
27	5	Portland-Vancouver, OR-WA	91.3
73	5	Syracuse, NY	91.3
35	7	San Antonio, TX	91.2
12	8	Phoenix-Mesa, AZ	91.0
58	9	Grand Rapids-Muskegon-Holland, MI	90.5
13	10	Minneapolis-St. Paul, MN-WI	90.3
21	10	Pittsburgh, PA	90.3
70	12	Tucson, AZ	90.2
4	13	Boston-Worcester-Lawrence-Lowell-Brockton, MA-NH	89.9
25	14	Denver, CO	89.8
72	14	Ventura, CA	89.8
53	16	Monmouth-Ocean, NJ	89.5
75	17	Omaha, NE-IA	89.0
52	18	Hartford, CT	87.6
16	18	Nassau-Suffolk, NY	87.6
56	20	Rochester, NY	87.5
22	21	Tampa-St. Petersburg-Clearwater, FL	87.1
11	22	Riverside-San Bernardino, CA	86.5
49	23	Austin-San Marcos, TX	86.1
50	24	Buffalo-Niagara Falls, NY	86.1
33	25	Cincinnati, OH-KY-IN	86.0
61	26	Louisville, KY-IN	85.9
31	27	New Haven-Bridgeport-Stamford-Danbury-Waterbury, CT	85.7
37	28	Indianapolis, IN	85.0
32	29	Fort Worth-Arlington, TX	84.7
20	29	Seattle-Bellevue-Everett, WA	84.7
28	31	Kansas City, MO-KS	84.6
43	31	Las Vegas, NV-AZ	84.6
40	33	Columbus, OH	84.3
15	34	Orange County, CA	84.2
67	35	Fresno, CA	84.1
63	36	Dayton-Springfield, OH	83.7
71	37	Tulsa, OK	83.6
59	38	West Palm Beach-Boca Raton, FL	83.3
51	39	Middlesex-Somerset-Hunterdon, NJ	82.9
39	40	Orlando, FL	82.7
48	41	Nashville, TN	82.5
60	42	Oklahoma City, OK	82.2
41	43	Milwaukee-Waukesha, WI	82.1
14	44	San Diego, CA	81.8
64	45	Greenville-Spartanburg-Anderson, SC	81.1
17	46	St. Louis, MO-IL	80.8
44	47	Bergen-Passaic, NJ	80.7
34	48	Sacramento, CA	80.5
10	49	Dallas, TX	79.9
23	50	Cleveland-Lorain-Elyria, OH	79.8
47	51	Greensboro—Winston-Salem—High Point, NC	79.0
38	52	Fort Lauderdale, FL	78.9
24	53	Miami, FL	77.6
42	54	Charlotte-Gastonia-Rock Hill, NC-SC	77.4
5	55	Philadelphia, PA-NJ	76.5
3	56	Chicago, IL	75.8
8	57	Houston, TX	75.1
7	58	Detroit, MI	74.9
1	59	Los Angeles-Long Beach, CA	74.8
57	60	Jacksonville, FL	74.2
30	61	San Jose, CA	73.4
54	62	Raleigh-Durham-Chapel Hill, NC	72.9
26	63	Newark, NJ	72.3
9	64	Atlanta, GA	70.9
65	65	Birmingham, AL	70.4
18	66	Baltimore, MD	69.1
62	67	Richmond-Petersburg, VA	67.7
6	67	Washington, DC-MD-VA-WV	67.7
19	69	Oakland, CA	66.9
29	70	San Francisco, CA	65.9
36	71	Norfolk-Virginia Beach-Newport News, VA-NC	65.6
45	72	New Orleans, LA	62.6
2	73	New York, NY	61.3
55	74	Memphis, TN-AR-MS	56.3
69	75	Honolulu, HI	30.9

Percent Black, 1999

Population Rank	Black Rank	Metropolitan Area	[col 6] Percent Black
55	1	Memphis, TN-AR-MS	42.4
45	2	New Orleans, LA	34.9
36	3	Norfolk-Virginia Beach-Newport News, VA-NC	30.5
62	4	Richmond-Petersburg, VA	30.0
65	5	Birmingham, AL	28.9
2	5	New York, NY	28.9
18	7	Baltimore, MD	28.0
9	8	Atlanta, GA	25.9
6	9	Washington, DC-MD-VA-WV	25.3
54	10	Raleigh-Durham-Chapel Hill, NC	24.0
26	11	Newark, NJ	22.8
57	12	Jacksonville, FL	22.7
7	13	Detroit, MI	22.6
42	14	Charlotte-Gastonia-Rock Hill, NC-SC	20.5
24	15	Miami, FL	20.4
5	16	Philadelphia, PA-NJ	20.1
47	17	Greensboro—Winston-Salem—High Point, NC	19.5
3	18	Chicago, IL	19.3
8	19	Houston, TX	18.9
23	20	Cleveland-Lorain-Elyria, OH	18.6
38	20	Fort Lauderdale, FL	18.6
64	22	Greenville-Spartanburg-Anderson, SC	17.8
17	23	St. Louis, MO-IL	17.6
48	24	Nashville, TN	15.7
10	25	Dallas, TX	15.6
41	26	Milwaukee-Waukesha, WI	15.4
19	27	Oakland, CA	15.3
59	28	West Palm Beach-Boca Raton, FL	14.8
63	29	Dayton-Springfield, OH	14.7
39	30	Orlando, FL	14.2
37	31	Indianapolis, IN	13.7
28	32	Kansas City, MO-KS	13.4
40	33	Columbus, OH	13.3
61	34	Louisville, KY-IN	13.0
33	35	Cincinnati, OH-KY-IN	12.8
50	36	Buffalo-Niagara Falls, NY	11.7
32	37	Fort Worth-Arlington, TX	11.3
31	37	New Haven-Bridgeport-Stamford-Danbury-Waterbury, CT	11.3
1	39	Los Angeles-Long Beach, CA	11.2
60	40	Oklahoma City, OK	10.9
22	41	Tampa-St. Petersburg-Clearwater, FL	10.7
44	42	Bergen-Passaic, NJ	10.5
56	43	Rochester, NY	10.1
49	44	Austin-San Marcos, TX	10.0
52	45	Hartford, CT	9.7
43	46	Las Vegas, NV-AZ	9.3
75	47	Omaha, NE-IA	8.7
71	47	Tulsa, OK	8.7
21	49	Pittsburgh, PA	8.6
16	50	Nassau-Suffolk, NY	8.4
51	51	Middlesex-Somerset-Hunterdon, NJ	7.9
34	52	Sacramento, CA	7.7
58	53	Grand Rapids-Muskegon-Holland, MI	7.5
29	53	San Francisco, CA	7.5
11	55	Riverside-San Bernardino, CA	7.1
53	56	Monmouth-Ocean, NJ	7.0
35	57	San Antonio, TX	6.6
14	58	San Diego, CA	6.5
73	59	Syracuse, NY	6.4
25	60	Denver, CO	6.2
4	61	Boston-Worcester-Lawrence-Lowell-Brockton, MA-NH	6.0
68	62	Albany-Schenectady-Troy, NY	5.2
66	63	Providence-Warwick-Pawtucket, RI	5.1
67	64	Fresno, CA	5.0
13	65	Minneapolis-St. Paul, MN-WI	4.9
20	66	Seattle-Bellevue-Everett, WA	4.7
12	67	Phoenix-Mesa, AZ	4.2
70	68	Tucson, AZ	3.9
30	69	San Jose, CA	3.8
69	70	Honolulu, HI	3.6
74	71	El Paso, TX	3.4
27	72	Portland-Vancouver, OR-WA	3.1
72	73	Ventura, CA	2.4
15	74	Orange County, CA	1.8
46	75	Salt Lake City-Ogden, UT	1.4

Note: Column numbers refer to Table C. Metropolitan Areas.

TABLE 3—75 Largest Metropolitan Areas by 1999 Population
Selected Rankings

Population Rank	American Indian Rank	Metropolitan Area	[col 7] Percent American Indian	Population Rank	Asian & Pac. Is. Rank	Metropolitan Area	[col 8] Percent Asian & Pac. Is.
71	1	Tulsa, OK	6.6	69	1	Honolulu, HI	65.0
60	2	Oklahoma City, OK	4.6	29	2	San Francisco, CA	26.0
70	3	Tucson, AZ	3.4	30	3	San Jose, CA	22.1
12	4	Phoenix-Mesa, AZ	2.4	19	4	Oakland, CA	17.0
67	5	Fresno, CA	1.3	15	5	Orange County, CA	13.5
34	5	Sacramento, CA	1.3	1	6	Los Angeles-Long Beach, CA	13.4
20	5	Seattle-Bellevue-Everett, WA	1.3	14	7	San Diego, CA	10.8
43	8	Las Vegas, NV-AZ	1.2	34	8	Sacramento, CA	10.4
11	9	Riverside-San Bernardino, CA	1.1	67	9	Fresno, CA	9.6
13	10	Minneapolis-St. Paul, MN-WI	1.0	2	10	New York, NY	9.3
27	10	Portland-Vancouver, OR-WA	1.0	20	10	Seattle-Bellevue-Everett, WA	9.3
14	12	San Diego, CA	0.9	51	12	Middlesex-Somerset-Hunterdon, NJ	9.0
72	12	Ventura, CA	0.9	44	13	Bergen-Passaic, NJ	8.5
25	14	Denver, CO	0.8	72	14	Ventura, CA	6.9
19	14	Oakland, CA	0.8	6	15	Washington, DC-MD-VA-WV	6.7
46	14	Salt Lake City-Ogden, UT	0.8	8	16	Houston, TX	5.7
50	17	Buffalo-Niagara Falls, NY	0.7	11	17	Riverside-San Bernardino, CA	5.2
30	17	San Jose, CA	0.7	43	18	Las Vegas, NV-AZ	4.8
10	19	Dallas, TX	0.6	27	19	Portland-Vancouver, OR-WA	4.7
32	19	Fort Worth-Arlington, TX	0.6	3	20	Chicago, IL	4.6
58	19	Grand Rapids-Muskegon-Holland, MI	0.6	26	20	Newark, NJ	4.6
1	19	Los Angeles-Long Beach, CA	0.6	4	22	Boston-Worcester-Lawrence-Lowell-Brockton, MA-NH	3.9
41	19	Milwaukee-Waukesha, WI	0.6	10	22	Dallas, TX	3.9
75	19	Omaha, NE-IA	0.6	13	24	Minneapolis-St. Paul, MN-WI	3.8
15	19	Orange County, CA	0.6	16	25	Nassau-Suffolk, NY	3.7
73	19	Syracuse, NY	0.6	36	26	Norfolk-Virginia Beach-Newport News, VA-NC	3.6
49	27	Austin-San Marcos, TX	0.5	32	27	Fort Worth-Arlington, TX	3.4
74	27	El Paso, TX	0.5	53	28	Monmouth-Ocean, NJ	3.3
69	27	Honolulu, HI	0.5	49	29	Austin-San Marcos, TX	3.2
28	27	Kansas City, MO-KS	0.5	5	29	Philadelphia, PA-NJ	3.2
66	27	Providence-Warwick-Pawtucket, RI	0.5	46	29	Salt Lake City-Ogden, UT	3.2
29	27	San Francisco, CA	0.5	25	32	Denver, CO	3.1
42	33	Charlotte-Gastonia-Rock Hill, NC-SC	0.4	9	33	Atlanta, GA	2.9
7	33	Detroit, MI	0.4	57	34	Jacksonville, FL	2.8
47	33	Greensboro—Winston-Salem—High Point, NC	0.4	31	34	New Haven-Bridgeport-Stamford-Danbury-Waterbury, CT	2.8
8	33	Houston, TX	0.4	54	34	Raleigh-Durham-Chapel Hill, NC	2.8
57	33	Jacksonville, FL	0.4	39	37	Orlando, FL	2.7
2	33	New York, NY	0.4	18	38	Baltimore, MD	2.6
36	33	Norfolk-Virginia Beach-Newport News, VA-NC	0.4	52	38	Hartford, CT	2.6
39	33	Orlando, FL	0.4	12	40	Phoenix-Mesa, AZ	2.4
56	33	Rochester, NY	0.4	66	40	Providence-Warwick-Pawtucket, RI	2.4
35	33	San Antonio, TX	0.4	70	40	Tucson, AZ	2.4
22	33	Tampa-St. Petersburg-Clearwater, FL	0.4	60	43	Oklahoma City, OK	2.3
18	44	Baltimore, MD	0.3	38	44	Fort Lauderdale, FL	2.2
44	44	Bergen-Passaic, NJ	0.3	45	44	New Orleans, LA	2.2
38	44	Fort Lauderdale, FL	0.3	40	46	Columbus, OH	2.1
24	44	Miami, FL	0.3	56	46	Rochester, NY	2.1
45	44	New Orleans, LA	0.3	7	48	Detroit, MI	2.0
54	44	Raleigh-Durham-Chapel Hill, NC	0.3	62	48	Richmond-Petersburg, VA	2.0
62	44	Richmond-Petersburg, VA	0.3	68	50	Albany-Schenectady-Troy, NY	1.9
6	44	Washington, DC-MD-VA-WV	0.3	24	51	Miami, FL	1.8
68	52	Albany-Schenectady-Troy, NY	0.2	41	51	Milwaukee-Waukesha, WI	1.8
9	52	Atlanta, GA	0.2	35	51	San Antonio, TX	1.8
65	52	Birmingham, AL	0.2	22	51	Tampa-St. Petersburg-Clearwater, FL	1.8
4	52	Boston-Worcester-Lawrence-Lowell-Brockton, MA-NH	0.2	42	55	Charlotte-Gastonia-Rock Hill, NC-SC	1.7
3	52	Chicago, IL	0.2	75	55	Omaha, NE-IA	1.7
33	52	Cincinnati, OH-KY-IN	0.2	73	55	Syracuse, NY	1.7
23	52	Cleveland-Lorain-Elyria, OH	0.2	28	58	Kansas City, MO-KS	1.6
40	52	Columbus, OH	0.2	59	58	West Palm Beach-Boca Raton, FL	1.6
63	52	Dayton-Springfield, OH	0.2	74	60	El Paso, TX	1.5
64	52	Greenville-Spartanburg-Anderson, SC	0.2	48	60	Nashville, TN	1.5
52	52	Hartford, CT	0.2	50	62	Buffalo-Niagara Falls, NY	1.4
37	52	Indianapolis, IN	0.2	23	62	Cleveland-Lorain-Elyria, OH	1.4
61	52	Louisville, KY-IN	0.2	63	62	Dayton-Springfield, OH	1.4
55	52	Memphis, TN-AR-MS	0.2	58	62	Grand Rapids-Muskegon-Holland, MI	1.4
51	52	Middlesex-Somerset-Hunterdon, NJ	0.2	17	66	St. Louis, MO-IL	1.3
53	52	Monmouth-Ocean, NJ	0.2	55	67	Memphis, TN-AR-MS	1.2
48	52	Nashville, TN	0.2	71	67	Tulsa, OK	1.2
16	52	Nassau-Suffolk, NY	0.2	47	69	Greensboro—Winston-Salem—High Point, NC	1.1
31	52	New Haven-Bridgeport-Stamford-Danbury-Waterbury, CT	0.2	37	69	Indianapolis, IN	1.1
26	52	Newark, NJ	0.2	33	71	Cincinnati, OH-KY-IN	1.0
5	52	Philadelphia, PA-NJ	0.2	21	71	Pittsburgh, PA	1.0
17	52	St. Louis, MO-IL	0.2	64	73	Greenville-Spartanburg-Anderson, SC	0.9
59	52	West Palm Beach-Boca Raton, FL	0.2	61	73	Louisville, KY-IN	0.9
21	75	Pittsburgh, PA	0.1	65	75	Birmingham, AL	0.6

Note: Column numbers refer to Table C. Metropolitan Areas.

TABLE 3—75 Largest Metropolitan Areas by 1999 Population
Selected Rankings

	Percent Hispanic, 1999				Percent Age 65 and Over, 1999		
Population Rank	Hispanic Rank	Metropolitan Area	[col 9] Percent Hispanic	Population Rank	Age 65 and Over Rank	Metropolitan Area	[cols 17 & 18] Percent Age 65 and Over
74	1	El Paso, TX	75.4	59	1	West Palm Beach-Boca Raton, FL	24.2
24	2	Miami, FL	57.4	22	2	Tampa-St. Petersburg-Clearwater, FL	19.8
35	3	San Antonio, TX	54.2	21	3	Pittsburgh, PA	17.8
1	4	Los Angeles-Long Beach, CA	44.4	53	4	Monmouth-Ocean, NJ	17.2
67	5	Fresno, CA	43.1	38	5	Fort Lauderdale, FL	16.8
11	6	Riverside-San Bernardino, CA	34.1	50	6	Buffalo-Niagara Falls, NY	15.9
72	7	Ventura, CA	33.4	66	7	Providence-Warwick-Pawtucket, RI	15.6
70	8	Tucson, AZ	29.6	23	8	Cleveland-Lorain-Elyria, OH	14.7
15	9	Orange County, CA	29.0	68	9	Albany-Schenectady-Troy, NY	14.5
14	10	San Diego, CA	26.5	44	10	Bergen-Passaic, NJ	14.4
49	11	Austin-San Marcos, TX	26.2	31	10	New Haven-Bridgeport-Stamford-Danbury-Waterbury, CT	14.4
30	12	San Jose, CA	25.9	70	10	Tucson, AZ	14.4
8	13	Houston, TX	25.7	52	13	Hartford, CT	14.3
2	14	New York, NY	25.6	24	13	Miami, FL	14.3
12	15	Phoenix-Mesa, AZ	21.1	29	15	San Francisco, CA	14.2
29	16	San Francisco, CA	18.0	5	16	Philadelphia, PA-NJ	14.0
19	17	Oakland, CA	17.2	69	17	Honolulu, HI	13.9
10	18	Dallas, TX	17.0	63	18	Dayton-Springfield, OH	13.5
43	19	Las Vegas, NV-AZ	16.7	39	18	Orlando, FL	13.5
44	20	Bergen-Passaic, NJ	16.1	16	20	Nassau-Suffolk, NY	13.4
25	21	Denver, CO	14.9	73	21	Syracuse, NY	13.3
3	22	Chicago, IL	14.8	47	22	Greensboro—Winston-Salem—High Point, NC	13.2
34	23	Sacramento, CA	14.6	4	23	Boston-Worcester-Lawrence-Lowell-Brockton, MA-NH	13.0
32	24	Fort Worth-Arlington, TX	14.4	17	23	St. Louis, MO-IL	13.0
26	25	Newark, NJ	13.0	2	25	New York, NY	12.9
38	26	Fort Lauderdale, FL	12.8	56	25	Rochester, NY	12.9
39	27	Orlando, FL	12.0	65	27	Birmingham, AL	12.8
59	28	West Palm Beach-Boca Raton, FL	11.2	61	27	Louisville, KY-IN	12.8
22	29	Tampa-St. Petersburg-Clearwater, FL	10.0	41	27	Milwaukee-Waukesha, WI	12.8
31	30	New Haven-Bridgeport-Stamford-Danbury-Waterbury, CT	9.8	26	30	Newark, NJ	12.6
51	31	Middlesex-Somerset-Hunterdon, NJ	9.6	7	31	Detroit, MI	12.5
52	32	Hartford, CT	8.8	43	31	Las Vegas, NV-AZ	12.5
46	33	Salt Lake City-Ogden, UT	8.5	64	33	Greenville-Spartanburg-Anderson, SC	12.4
16	34	Nassau-Suffolk, NY	8.1	18	34	Baltimore, MD	12.3
6	35	Washington, DC-MD-VA-WV	7.6	51	35	Middlesex-Somerset-Hunterdon, NJ	12.2
69	36	Honolulu, HI	7.4	12	35	Phoenix-Mesa, AZ	12.2
66	37	Providence-Warwick-Pawtucket, RI	7.3	33	37	Cincinnati, OH-KY-IN	12.0
4	38	Boston-Worcester-Lawrence-Lowell-Brockton, MA-NH	5.7	71	37	Tulsa, OK	12.0
27	39	Portland-Vancouver, OR-WA	5.5	62	39	Richmond-Petersburg, VA	11.6
53	40	Monmouth-Ocean, NJ	5.4	34	39	Sacramento, CA	11.6
60	40	Oklahoma City, OK	5.4	28	41	Kansas City, MO-KS	11.5
45	42	New Orleans, LA	5.2	60	41	Oklahoma City, OK	11.5
75	42	Omaha, NE-IA	5.2	14	41	San Diego, CA	11.5
41	44	Milwaukee-Waukesha, WI	4.9	45	44	New Orleans, LA	11.4
5	45	Philadelphia, PA-NJ	4.7	57	45	Jacksonville, FL	11.3
20	46	Seattle-Bellevue-Everett, WA	4.3	3	46	Chicago, IL	11.2
58	47	Grand Rapids-Muskegon-Holland, MI	4.1	37	46	Indianapolis, IN	11.2
28	48	Kansas City, MO-KS	4.0	58	48	Grand Rapids-Muskegon-Holland, MI	11.0
56	48	Rochester, NY	4.0	19	49	Oakland, CA	10.9
57	50	Jacksonville, FL	3.8	75	49	Omaha, NE-IA	10.9
9	51	Atlanta, GA	3.6	35	49	San Antonio, TX	10.9
36	52	Norfolk-Virginia Beach-Newport News, VA-NC	3.3	27	52	Portland-Vancouver, OR-WA	10.8
71	53	Tulsa, OK	3.1	42	53	Charlotte-Gastonia-Rock Hill, NC-SC	10.7
23	54	Cleveland-Lorain-Elyria, OH	2.9	67	53	Fresno, CA	10.7
50	55	Buffalo-Niagara Falls, NY	2.7	20	53	Seattle-Bellevue-Everett, WA	10.7
54	56	Raleigh-Durham-Chapel Hill, NC	2.6	72	56	Ventura, CA	10.5
7	57	Detroit, MI	2.5	1	57	Los Angeles-Long Beach, CA	10.4
68	58	Albany-Schenectady-Troy, NY	2.3	11	57	Riverside-San Bernardino, CA	10.4
13	58	Minneapolis-St. Paul, MN-WI	2.3	48	59	Nashville, TN	10.3
18	60	Baltimore, MD	2.0	40	60	Columbus, OH	10.2
42	61	Charlotte-Gastonia-Rock Hill, NC-SC	2.0	36	60	Norfolk-Virginia Beach-Newport News, VA-NC	10.2
73	62	Syracuse, NY	1.8	30	60	San Jose, CA	10.2
47	63	Greensboro—Winston-Salem—High Point, NC	1.6	15	63	Orange County, CA	10.1
62	63	Richmond-Petersburg, VA	1.6	55	64	Memphis, TN-AR-MS	10.0
17	65	St. Louis, MO-IL	1.5	13	64	Minneapolis-St. Paul, MN-WI	10.0
48	66	Nashville, TN	1.4	25	66	Denver, CO	9.6
37	67	Indianapolis, IN	1.3	74	67	El Paso, TX	9.5
55	67	Memphis, TN-AR-MS	1.3	6	67	Washington, DC-MD-VA-WV	9.5
64	69	Greenville-Spartanburg-Anderson, SC	1.2	54	69	Raleigh-Durham-Chapel Hill, NC	9.2
40	70	Columbus, OH	1.1	32	70	Fort Worth-Arlington, TX	9.0
63	71	Dayton-Springfield, OH	1.0	46	71	Salt Lake City-Ogden, UT	8.5
61	72	Louisville, KY-IN	0.9	10	72	Dallas, TX	8.1
65	73	Birmingham, AL	0.8	8	73	Houston, TX	7.8
21	73	Pittsburgh, PA	0.8	9	74	Atlanta, GA	7.7
33	75	Cincinnati, OH-KY-IN	0.7	49	75	Austin-San Marcos, TX	7.5

Note: Column numbers refer to Table C. Metropolitan Areas.

43

TABLE 3—75 Largest Metropolitan Areas by 1999 Population
Selected Rankings

Percent Under 18 Years of Age, 1999				Percent of Female-headed Family Households, 1990			
Population Rank	Under 18 Years of Age Rank	Metropolitan Area	[cols 10 & 11] Percent Under 18 Years of Age	Population Rank	Female Households Rank	Metropolitan Area	[col 30] Percent Female Households
46	1	Salt Lake City-Ogden, UT	55.0	55	1	Memphis, TN-AR-MS	17.9
74	2	El Paso, TX	45.0	45	2	New Orleans, LA	17.5
67	3	Fresno, CA	2.0	2	3	New York, NY	17.1
11	4	Riverside-San Bernardino, CA	74.0	74	4	El Paso, TX	15.8
35	5	San Antonio, TX	7.0	7	5	Detroit, MI	15.3
8	6	Houston, TX	24.0	24	6	Miami, FL	14.9
12	7	Phoenix-Mesa, AZ	18.0	18	7	Baltimore, MD	14.6
58	8	Grand Rapids-Muskegon-Holland, MI	65.0	65	8	Birmingham, AL	14.1
10	9	Dallas, TX	35.0	35	9	San Antonio, TX	13.9
32	9	Fort Worth-Arlington, TX	26.0	26	10	Newark, NJ	13.8
72	11	Ventura, CA	5.0	5	11	Philadelphia, PA-NJ	13.7
55	12	Memphis, TN-AR-MS	67.0	67	12	Fresno, CA	13.6
57	13	Jacksonville, FL	62.0	62	12	Richmond-Petersburg, VA	13.6
1	13	Los Angeles-Long Beach, CA	61.0	61	14	Louisville, KY-IN	13.5
49	15	Austin-San Marcos, TX	3.0	3	15	Chicago, IL	13.3
75	16	Omaha, NE-IA	23.0	23	16	Cleveland-Lorain-Elyria, OH	13.2
3	17	Chicago, IL	1.0	1	17	Los Angeles-Long Beach, CA	13.1
43	18	Las Vegas, NV-AZ	41.0	41	18	Milwaukee-Waukesha, WI	13.0
36	19	Norfolk-Virginia Beach-Newport News, VA-NC	36.0	36	18	Norfolk-Virginia Beach-Newport News, VA-NC	13.0
34	20	Sacramento, CA	9.0	9	20	Atlanta, GA	12.9
70	20	Tucson, AZ	50.0	50	20	Buffalo-Niagara Falls, NY	12.9
33	22	Cincinnati, OH-KY-IN	57.0	57	22	Jacksonville, FL	12.6
13	23	Minneapolis-St. Paul, MN-WI	33.0	33	23	Cincinnati, OH-KY-IN	12.5
60	23	Oklahoma City, OK	17.0	17	23	St. Louis, MO-IL	12.5
9	25	Atlanta, GA	8.0	8	25	Houston, TX	12.3
25	25	Denver, CO	48.0	48	26	Nashville, TN	12.2
45	25	New Orleans, LA	64.0	64	27	Greenville-Spartanburg-Anderson, SC	12.1
71	25	Tulsa, OK	19.0	19	27	Oakland, CA	12.1
42	29	Charlotte-Gastonia-Rock Hill, NC-SC	42.0	42	29	Charlotte-Gastonia-Rock Hill, NC-SC	12.0
17	29	St. Louis, MO-IL	63.0	63	29	Dayton-Springfield, OH	12.0
37	31	Indianapolis, IN	34.0	34	29	Sacramento, CA	12.0
28	31	Kansas City, MO-KS	47.0	47	32	Greensboro—Winston-Salem—High Point, NC	11.9
14	33	San Diego, CA	31.0	31	32	New Haven-Bridgeport-Stamford-Danbury-Waterbury, CT	11.9
15	34	Orange County, CA	66.0	66	32	Providence-Warwick-Pawtucket, RI	11.9
73	35	Syracuse, NY	6.0	6	35	Washington, DC-MD-VA-WV	11.8
27	36	Portland-Vancouver, OR-WA	37.0	37	36	Indianapolis, IN	11.7
56	36	Rochester, NY	4.0	4	37	Boston-Worcester-Lawrence-Lowell-Brockton, MA-NH	11.6
39	38	Orlando, FL	40.0	40	37	Columbus, OH	11.6
41	39	Milwaukee-Waukesha, WI	52.0	52	37	Hartford, CT	11.6
7	40	Detroit, MI	21.0	21	40	Pittsburgh, PA	11.5
48	40	Nashville, TN	56.0	56	40	Rochester, NY	11.5
5	42	Philadelphia, PA-NJ	60.0	60	42	Oklahoma City, OK	11.4
18	42	Baltimore, MD	10.0	10	43	Dallas, TX	11.3
40	42	Columbus, OH	44.0	44	44	Bergen-Passaic, NJ	11.2
31	45	New Haven-Bridgeport-Stamford-Danbury-Waterbury, CT	28.0	28	44	Kansas City, MO-KS	11.2
24	45	Miami, FL	75.0	75	44	Omaha, NE-IA	11.2
53	47	Monmouth-Ocean, NJ	54.0	54	44	Raleigh-Durham-Chapel Hill, NC	11.2
26	47	Newark, NJ	73.0	73	44	Syracuse, NY	11.2
54	47	Raleigh-Durham-Chapel Hill, NC	11.0	11	49	Riverside-San Bernardino, CA	11.0
52	50	Hartford, CT	70.0	70	50	Tucson, AZ	10.9
19	50	Oakland, CA	58.0	58	51	Grand Rapids-Muskegon-Holland, MI	10.8
30	52	San Jose, CA	14.0	14	51	San Diego, CA	10.8
23	53	Cleveland-Lorain-Elyria, OH	68.0	68	53	Albany-Schenectady-Troy, NY	10.6
6	53	Washington, DC-MD-VA-WV	43.0	43	53	Las Vegas, NV-AZ	10.6
2	55	New York, NY	39.0	39	53	Orlando, FL	10.6
63	56	Dayton-Springfield, OH	25.0	25	56	Denver, CO	10.5
66	57	Providence-Warwick-Pawtucket, RI	69.0	69	56	Honolulu, HI	10.5
47	58	Greensboro—Winston-Salem—High Point, NC	32.0	32	58	Fort Worth-Arlington, TX	10.4
62	58	Richmond-Petersburg, VA	71.0	71	58	Tulsa, OK	10.4
65	60	Birmingham, AL	16.0	16	60	Nassau-Suffolk, NY	10.3
4	60	Boston-Worcester-Lawrence-Lowell-Brockton, MA-NH	30.0	30	60	San Jose, CA	10.3
20	62	Seattle-Bellevue-Everett, WA	49.0	49	62	Austin-San Marcos, TX	10.2
61	62	Louisville, KY-IN	12.0	12	62	Phoenix-Mesa, AZ	10.2
68	64	Albany-Schenectady-Troy, NY	38.0	38	64	Fort Lauderdale, FL	10.0
50	64	Buffalo-Niagara Falls, NY	46.0	46	64	Salt Lake City-Ogden, UT	10.0
69	66	Honolulu, HI	22.0	22	66	Tampa-St. Petersburg-Clearwater, FL	9.9
51	67	Middlesex-Somerset-Hunterdon, NJ	72.0	72	67	Ventura, CA	9.8
16	67	Nassau-Suffolk, NY	13.0	13	68	Minneapolis-St. Paul, MN-WI	9.7
44	69	Bergen-Passaic, NJ	15.0	15	68	Orange County, CA	9.7
38	70	Fort Lauderdale, FL	27.0	27	68	Portland-Vancouver, OR-WA	9.7
64	70	Greenville-Spartanburg-Anderson, SC	29.0	29	68	San Francisco, CA	9.7
22	72	Tampa-St. Petersburg-Clearwater, FL	53.0	53	72	Monmouth-Ocean, NJ	9.3
21	73	Pittsburgh, PA	51.0	51	73	Middlesex-Somerset-Hunterdon, NJ	9.2
59	74	West Palm Beach-Boca Raton, FL	20.0	20	74	Seattle-Bellevue-Everett, WA	8.9
29	75	San Francisco, CA	59.0	59	75	West Palm Beach-Boca Raton, FL	8.6

Note: Column numbers refer to Table C. Metropolitan Areas.

TABLE 3—75 Largest Metropolitan Areas by 1999 Population
Selected Rankings

Live Birth Rate per 1,000 Population, 1996-1998				Infant Deaths Per 1,000 Live Births, 1996-1998 Average			
Population Rank	Birth Rate Rank 1996-98	Metropolitan Area	[col 33] Birth Rate 1996-98 Average	Population Rank	Infant Mortality Rate	Metropolitan Area	[col 37] Infant Mortality Rate
74	1	El Paso, TX	21.2	55	1	Memphis, TN-AR-MS	12.3
46	2	Salt Lake City-Ogden, UT	20.1	65	2	Birmingham, AL	10.6
67	3	Fresno, CA	19.0	36	3	Norfolk-Virginia Beach-Newport News, VA-NC	10.4
10	4	Dallas, TX	18.1	47	4	Greensboro—Winston-Salem—High Point, NC	9.5
8	5	Houston, TX	18.0	60	5	Oklahoma City, OK	9.2
1	6	Los Angeles-Long Beach, CA	17.9	57	6	Jacksonville, FL	9.0
15	7	Orange County, CA	17.6	54	6	Raleigh-Durham-Chapel Hill, NC	9.0
12	8	Phoenix-Mesa, AZ	17.5	3	8	Chicago, IL	8.8
11	9	Riverside-San Bernardino, CA	17.1	37	8	Indianapolis, IN	8.8
55	10	Memphis, TN-AR-MS	16.9	23	10	Cleveland-Lorain-Elyria, OH	8.7
35	10	San Antonio, TX	16.9	41	10	Milwaukee-Waukesha, WI	8.7
49	12	Austin-San Marcos, TX	16.7	18	12	Baltimore, MD	8.6
32	13	Fort Worth-Arlington, TX	16.6	7	12	Detroit, MI	8.6
43	13	Las Vegas, NV-AZ	16.6	62	12	Richmond-Petersburg, VA	8.6
3	15	Chicago, IL	16.5	40	15	Columbus, OH	8.4
9	16	Atlanta, GA	16.4	17	15	St. Louis, MO-IL	8.4
30	16	San Jose, CA	16.4	5	17	Philadelphia, PA-NJ	8.3
14	18	San Diego, CA	16.1	50	18	Buffalo-Niagara Falls, NY	8.2
2	19	New York, NY	16.0	33	18	Cincinnati, OH-KY-IN	8.2
72	20	Ventura, CA	15.9	75	18	Omaha, NE-IA	8.2
58	21	Grand Rapids-Muskegon-Holland, MI	15.8	52	21	Hartford, CT	8.1
37	22	Indianapolis, IN	15.7	45	21	New Orleans, LA	8.1
25	23	Denver, CO	15.6	22	21	Tampa-St. Petersburg-Clearwater, FL	8.1
75	23	Omaha, NE-IA	15.6	6	21	Washington, DC-MD-VA-WV	8.1
57	25	Jacksonville, FL	15.2	9	25	Atlanta, GA	7.8
42	26	Charlotte-Gastonia-Rock Hill, NC-SC	15.1	64	25	Greenville-Spartanburg-Anderson, SC	7.8
40	26	Columbus, OH	15.1	56	27	Rochester, NY	7.7
54	26	Raleigh-Durham-Chapel Hill, NC	15.1	58	28	Grand Rapids-Muskegon-Holland, MI	7.6
45	29	New Orleans, LA	15.0	61	28	Louisville, KY-IN	7.6
26	29	Newark, NJ	15.0	26	28	Newark, NJ	7.6
36	29	Norfolk-Virginia Beach-Newport News, VA-NC	15.0	71	28	Tulsa, OK	7.6
60	29	Oklahoma City, OK	15.0	12	32	Phoenix-Mesa, AZ	7.5
71	29	Tulsa, OK	15.0	67	33	Fresno, CA	7.3
6	29	Washington, DC-MD-VA-WV	15.0	35	33	San Antonio, TX	7.3
69	35	Honolulu, HI	14.9	63	35	Dayton-Springfield, OH	7.2
13	35	Minneapolis-St. Paul, MN-WI	14.9	32	35	Fort Worth-Arlington, TX	7.2
28	37	Kansas City, MO-KS	14.8	28	35	Kansas City, MO-KS	7.2
24	37	Miami, FL	14.8	11	35	Riverside-San Bernardino, CA	7.2
48	37	Nashville, TN	14.8	42	39	Charlotte-Gastonia-Rock Hill, NC-SC	7.1
27	37	Portland-Vancouver, OR-WA	14.8	38	40	Fort Lauderdale, FL	7.0
19	41	Oakland, CA	14.6	48	41	Nashville, TN	6.9
34	41	Sacramento, CA	14.6	2	41	New York, NY	6.9
70	41	Tucson, AZ	14.6	21	43	Pittsburgh, PA	6.8
33	44	Cincinnati, OH-KY-IN	14.5	43	44	Las Vegas, NV-AZ	6.7
41	44	Milwaukee-Waukesha, WI	14.5	73	44	Syracuse, NY	6.7
39	46	Orlando, FL	14.3	25	46	Denver, CO	6.6
51	47	Middlesex-Somerset-Hunterdon, NJ	14.2	66	47	Providence-Warwick-Pawtucket, RI	6.5
65	48	Birmingham, AL	14.1	69	48	Honolulu, HI	6.4
31	48	New Haven-Bridgeport-Stamford-Danbury-Waterbury, CT	14.1	70	48	Tucson, AZ	6.4
7	50	Detroit, MI	14.0	8	50	Houston, TX	6.3
47	50	Greensboro—Winston-Salem—High Point, NC	14.0	31	50	New Haven-Bridgeport-Stamford-Danbury-Waterbury, CT	6.3
61	50	Louisville, KY-IN	14.0	39	50	Orlando, FL	6.3
16	50	Nassau-Suffolk, NY	14.0	68	53	Albany-Schenectady-Troy, NY	6.2
44	54	Bergen-Passaic, NJ	13.9	34	53	Sacramento, CA	6.2
17	54	St. Louis, MO-IL	13.9	59	53	West Palm Beach-Boca Raton, FL	6.2
18	56	Baltimore, MD	13.8	13	56	Minneapolis-St. Paul, MN-WI	6.1
38	56	Fort Lauderdale, FL	13.8	46	56	Salt Lake City-Ogden, UT	6.1
62	56	Richmond-Petersburg, VA	13.8	72	58	Ventura, CA	6.0
64	59	Greenville-Spartanburg-Anderson, SC	13.7	1	59	Los Angeles-Long Beach, CA	5.9
5	59	Philadelphia, PA-NJ	13.7	10	60	Dallas, TX	5.8
23	61	Cleveland-Lorain-Elyria, OH	13.6	24	60	Miami, FL	5.8
20	61	Seattle-Bellevue-Everett, WA	13.6	49	62	Austin-San Marcos, TX	5.7
4	63	Boston-Worcester-Lawrence-Lowell-Brockton, MA-NH	13.5	19	63	Oakland, CA	5.6
52	63	Hartford, CT	13.5	14	64	San Diego, CA	5.4
53	65	Monmouth-Ocean, NJ	13.4	20	64	Seattle-Bellevue-Everett, WA	5.4
63	66	Dayton-Springfield, OH	13.2	16	66	Nassau-Suffolk, NY	5.3
56	67	Rochester, NY	13.0	27	67	Portland-Vancouver, OR-WA	5.2
66	68	Providence-Warwick-Pawtucket, RI	12.8	74	68	El Paso, TX	5.1
73	69	Syracuse, NY	12.7	53	68	Monmouth-Ocean, NJ	5.1
59	70	West Palm Beach-Boca Raton, FL	12.6	44	70	Bergen-Passaic, NJ	4.9
29	71	San Francisco, CA	12.5	4	70	Boston-Worcester-Lawrence-Lowell-Brockton, MA-NH	4.9
50	72	Buffalo-Niagara Falls, NY	12.4	51	70	Middlesex-Somerset-Hunterdon, NJ	4.9
22	72	Tampa-St. Petersburg-Clearwater, FL	12.4	30	70	San Jose, CA	4.9
68	74	Albany-Schenectady-Troy, NY	11.9	15	74	Orange County, CA	4.5
21	75	Pittsburgh, PA	11.2	29	74	San Francisco, CA	4.5

Note: Column numbers refer to Table C. Metropolitan Areas.

45

TABLE 3—75 Largest Metropolitan Areas by 1999 Population
Selected Rankings

Percent College Graduates (16+ Years of Education), 1990				Median Household Income, 1989			
Population Rank	Percent College Graduate Rank	Metropolitan Area	[col 51] Percent College Grad	Population Rank	Median Income Rank	Metropolitan Area	[col 58] Median Income 1989 (dollars)
6	1	Washington, DC-MD-VA-WV	37.0	16	1	Nassau-Suffolk, NY	51 670
29	2	San Francisco, CA	34.9	51	2	Middlesex-Somerset-Hunterdon, NJ	48 701
30	3	San Jose, CA	32.6	30	3	San Jose, CA	48 115
54	4	Raleigh-Durham-Chapel Hill, NC	31.7	15	4	Orange County, CA	45 921
49	5	Austin-San Marcos, TX	30.7	6	5	Washington, DC-MD-VA-WV	45 900
51	6	Middlesex-Somerset-Hunterdon, NJ	30.2	72	6	Ventura, CA	45 612
19	7	Oakland, CA	29.9	44	7	Bergen-Passaic, NJ	45 039
20	8	Seattle-Bellevue-Everett, WA	29.5	31	8	New Haven-Bridgeport-Stamford-Danb	43 268
31	9	New Haven-Bridgeport-Stamford-Danb	29.3	26	9	Newark, NJ	42 174
25	10	Denver, CO	28.9	52	10	Hartford, CT	41 428
4	11	Boston-Worcester-Lawrence-Lowell-Bro	27.8	19	11	Oakland, CA	40 620
15	11	Orange County, CA	27.8	69	12	Honolulu, HI	40 580
44	13	Bergen-Passaic, NJ	27.3	29	13	San Francisco, CA	40 493
10	14	Dallas, TX	26.9	53	14	Monmouth-Ocean, NJ	39 830
13	14	Minneapolis-St. Paul, MN-WI	26.9	4	15	Boston-Worcester-Lawrence-Lowell-Bro	38 529
26	14	Newark, NJ	26.9	18	16	Baltimore, MD	36 549
52	17	Hartford, CT	26.5	13	17	Minneapolis-St. Paul, MN-WI	36 467
16	17	Nassau-Suffolk, NY	26.5	3	18	Chicago, IL	36 301
9	19	Atlanta, GA	26.1	20	19	Seattle-Bellevue-Everett, WA	36 126
14	20	San Diego, CA	25.3	9	20	Atlanta, GA	35 606
8	21	Houston, TX	25.0	5	21	Philadelphia, PA-NJ	35 406
69	22	Honolulu, HI	24.6	14	22	San Diego, CA	35 021
2	22	New York, NY	24.6	1	23	Los Angeles-Long Beach, CA	34 964
3	24	Chicago, IL	24.5	7	24	Detroit, MI	34 300
62	25	Richmond-Petersburg, VA	23.8	56	25	Rochester, NY	34 001
68	26	Albany-Schenectady-Troy, NY	23.6	62	26	Richmond-Petersburg, VA	33 488
40	27	Columbus, OH	23.3	11	27	Riverside-San Bernardino, CA	33 278
27	27	Portland-Vancouver, OR-WA	23.3	34	28	Sacramento, CA	33 195
70	27	Tucson, AZ	23.3	25	29	Denver, CO	32 851
28	30	Kansas City, MO-KS	23.2	10	30	Dallas, TX	32 667
18	31	Baltimore, MD	23.1	59	31	West Palm Beach-Boca Raton, FL	32 523
72	32	Ventura, CA	23.0	68	32	Albany-Schenectady-Troy, NY	32 427
56	33	Rochester, NY	22.9	41	33	Milwaukee-Waukesha, WI	32 315
46	33	Salt Lake City-Ogden, UT	22.9	32	34	Fort Worth-Arlington, TX	32 112
34	35	Sacramento, CA	22.7	54	35	Raleigh-Durham-Chapel Hill, NC	32 046
5	36	Philadelphia, PA-NJ	22.6	66	36	Providence-Warwick-Pawtucket, RI	31 908
53	37	Monmouth-Ocean, NJ	22.5	58	37	Grand Rapids-Muskegon-Holland, MI	31 796
75	37	Omaha, NE-IA	22.5	17	38	St. Louis, MO-IL	31 718
32	39	Fort Worth-Arlington, TX	22.4	2	39	New York, NY	31 658
1	40	Los Angeles-Long Beach, CA	22.3	28	40	Kansas City, MO-KS	31 559
59	41	West Palm Beach-Boca Raton, FL	22.1	8	41	Houston, TX	31 473
60	42	Oklahoma City, OK	21.6	37	42	Indianapolis, IN	31 314
48	43	Nashville, TN	21.4	42	43	Charlotte-Gastonia-Rock Hill, NC-SC	31 124
12	43	Phoenix-Mesa, AZ	21.4	27	44	Portland-Vancouver, OR-WA	31 037
41	45	Milwaukee-Waukesha, WI	21.3	46	45	Salt Lake City-Ogden, UT	30 881
73	46	Syracuse, NY	20.8	36	46	Norfolk-Virginia Beach-Newport News	30 766
17	47	St. Louis, MO-IL	20.5	73	47	Syracuse, NY	30 705
39	48	Orlando, FL	20.4	40	48	Columbus, OH	30 609
66	48	Providence-Warwick-Pawtucket, RI	20.4	38	49	Fort Lauderdale, FL	30 570
71	50	Tulsa, OK	20.3	63	50	Dayton-Springfield, OH	30 471
37	51	Indianapolis, IN	20.2	33	51	Cincinnati, OH-KY-IN	30 370
33	52	Cincinnati, OH-KY-IN	19.9	23	52	Cleveland-Lorain-Elyria, OH	30 350
36	53	Norfolk-Virginia Beach-Newport News	19.8	12	52	Phoenix-Mesa, AZ	30 350
65	54	Birmingham, AL	19.7	75	54	Omaha, NE-IA	30 258
42	55	Charlotte-Gastonia-Rock Hill, NC-SC	19.6	48	55	Nashville, TN	30 222
45	56	New Orleans, LA	19.3	39	56	Orlando, FL	30 211
35	56	San Antonio, TX	19.3	43	57	Las Vegas, NV-AZ	30 022
63	58	Dayton-Springfield, OH	19.1	57	58	Jacksonville, FL	29 513
50	59	Buffalo-Niagara Falls, NY	18.8	47	59	Greensboro—Winston-Salem—High Poin	29 043
38	59	Fort Lauderdale, FL	18.8	50	60	Buffalo-Niagara Falls, NY	28 083
24	59	Miami, FL	18.8	49	61	Austin-San Marcos, TX	27 956
47	62	Greensboro—Winston-Salem—High Poin	18.7	61	62	Louisville, KY-IN	27 435
55	62	Memphis, TN-AR-MS	18.7	64	63	Greenville-Spartanburg-Anderson, SC	27 236
21	62	Pittsburgh, PA	18.7	71	64	Tulsa, OK	26 990
57	65	Jacksonville, FL	18.6	24	65	Miami, FL	26 908
23	66	Cleveland-Lorain-Elyria, OH	18.5	55	66	Memphis, TN-AR-MS	26 899
58	67	Grand Rapids-Muskegon-Holland, MI	17.8	60	67	Oklahoma City, OK	26 882
7	68	Detroit, MI	17.7	21	68	Pittsburgh, PA	26 656
22	69	Tampa-St. Petersburg-Clearwater, FL	17.3	65	69	Birmingham, AL	26 613
61	70	Louisville, KY-IN	17.2	67	70	Fresno, CA	26 481
64	71	Greenville-Spartanburg-Anderson, SC	16.7	35	71	San Antonio, TX	26 048
67	72	Fresno, CA	16.3	22	72	Tampa-St. Petersburg-Clearwater, FL	26 035
74	73	El Paso, TX	15.2	70	73	Tucson, AZ	25 400
11	74	Riverside-San Bernardino, CA	14.8	45	74	New Orleans, LA	24 415
43	75	Las Vegas, NV-AZ	13.3	74	75	El Paso, TX	22 643

Note: Column numbers refer to Table C. Metropolitan Areas.

TABLE 3—75 Largest Metropolitan Areas by 1999 Population
Selected Rankings

Percent of Persons Below the Poverty Level, 1997				Percent of Persons Under Age 18 Below the Poverty Level, 1997			
Population Rank	Poverty Rate Rank	Metropolitan Area	[col 59] Poverty Rate for Persons 1997	Population Rank	Poverty Rate Rank for under 18 yrs.	Metropolitan Area	[col 60] Poverty Rate in 1997 for under 18 yrs.
74	1	El Paso, TX	27.8	74	1	El Paso, TX	38.6
67	2	Fresno, CA	25.2	67	2	Fresno, CA	37.7
24	3	Miami, FL	21.1	2	3	New York, NY	32.9
1	4	Los Angeles-Long Beach, CA	20.5	1	4	Los Angeles-Long Beach, CA	30.5
2	5	New York, NY	20.4	24	5	Miami, FL	29.6
45	6	New Orleans, LA	18.0	45	6	New Orleans, LA	26.4
35	7	San Antonio, TX	17.9	35	7	San Antonio, TX	25.5
11	8	Riverside-San Bernardino, CA	16.5	70	8	Tucson, AZ	24.4
70	9	Tucson, AZ	16.2	11	9	Riverside-San Bernardino, CA	24.3
55	10	Memphis, TN-AR-MS	15.7	34	10	Sacramento, CA	23.5
34	11	Sacramento, CA	14.9	14	11	San Diego, CA	22.0
60	12	Oklahoma City, OK	14.4	60	12	Oklahoma City, OK	21.5
8	13	Houston, TX	14.3	55	13	Memphis, TN-AR-MS	21.4
14	14	San Diego, CA	14.2	22	14	Tampa-St. Petersburg-Clearwater, FL	21.2
36	15	Norfolk-Virginia Beach-Newport News,	13.7	50	15	Buffalo-Niagara Falls, NY	21.0
50	16	Buffalo-Niagara Falls, NY	13.6	36	16	Norfolk-Virginia Beach-Newport News,	19.7
22	16	Tampa-St. Petersburg-Clearwater, FL	13.6	12	17	Phoenix-Mesa, AZ	19.6
65	18	Birmingham, AL	13.2	71	17	Tulsa, OK	19.6
12	19	Phoenix-Mesa, AZ	13.1	8	19	Houston, TX	19.5
71	19	Tulsa, OK	13.1	65	20	Birmingham, AL	19.4
73	21	Syracuse, NY	12.8	73	20	Syracuse, NY	19.4
39	22	Orlando, FL	12.5	41	22	Milwaukee-Waukesha, WI	19.2
57	23	Jacksonville, FL	12.0	39	22	Orlando, FL	19.2
7	24	Detroit, MI	11.8	7	24	Detroit, MI	19.1
43	24	Las Vegas, NV-AZ	11.8	59	25	West Palm Beach-Boca Raton, FL	18.6
56	24	Rochester, NY	11.8	56	26	Rochester, NY	18.5
38	27	Fort Lauderdale, FL	11.7	43	27	Las Vegas, NV-AZ	17.8
62	28	Richmond-Petersburg, VA	11.6	66	27	Providence-Warwick-Pawtucket, RI	17.8
23	29	Cleveland-Lorain-Elyria, OH	11.5	9	29	Atlanta, GA	17.7
66	29	Providence-Warwick-Pawtucket, RI	11.5	23	30	Cleveland-Lorain-Elyria, OH	17.5
59	29	West Palm Beach-Boca Raton, FL	11.5	38	30	Fort Lauderdale, FL	17.5
10	32	Dallas, TX	11.4	61	32	Louisville, KY-IN	17.4
41	32	Milwaukee-Waukesha, WI	11.4	15	32	Orange County, CA	17.4
32	34	Fort Worth-Arlington, TX	11.3	3	34	Chicago, IL	17.2
61	35	Louisville, KY-IN	11.2	5	35	Philadelphia, PA-NJ	17.1
5	35	Philadelphia, PA-NJ	11.2	21	35	Pittsburgh, PA	17.1
21	35	Pittsburgh, PA	11.2	64	37	Greenville-Spartanburg-Anderson, SC	17.0
49	38	Austin-San Marcos, TX	11.1	57	38	Jacksonville, FL	16.9
64	38	Greenville-Spartanburg-Anderson, SC	11.1	62	38	Richmond-Petersburg, VA	16.9
9	40	Atlanta, GA	11.0	68	40	Albany-Schenectady-Troy, NY	16.8
15	40	Orange County, CA	11.0	18	41	Baltimore, MD	16.6
3	42	Chicago, IL	10.9	32	41	Fort Worth-Arlington, TX	16.6
17	43	St. Louis, MO-IL	10.8	72	41	Ventura, CA	16.6
18	44	Baltimore, MD	10.7	10	44	Dallas, TX	16.4
68	45	Albany-Schenectady-Troy, NY	10.6	26	44	Newark, NJ	16.4
19	45	Oakland, CA	10.6	17	44	St. Louis, MO-IL	16.4
26	47	Newark, NJ	10.4	19	47	Oakland, CA	16.0
63	48	Dayton-Springfield, OH	10.3	47	48	Greensboro—Winston-Salem—High Poin	15.7
47	48	Greensboro—Winston-Salem—High Poin	10.3	42	49	Charlotte-Gastonia-Rock Hill, NC-SC	15.4
72	48	Ventura, CA	10.3	63	49	Dayton-Springfield, OH	15.4
42	51	Charlotte-Gastonia-Rock Hill, NC-SC	10.2	31	49	New Haven-Bridgeport-Stamford-Danb	15.4
69	51	Honolulu, HI	10.2	49	52	Austin-San Marcos, TX	15.3
40	53	Columbus, OH	10.1	4	53	Boston-Worcester-Lawrence-Lowell-Bro	15.2
33	54	Cincinnati, OH-KY-IN	9.9	40	54	Columbus, OH	15.1
48	54	Nashville, TN	9.9	52	54	Hartford, CT	15.1
4	56	Boston-Worcester-Lawrence-Lowell-Bro	9.8	69	56	Honolulu, HI	14.8
54	57	Raleigh-Durham-Chapel Hill, NC	9.6	37	57	Indianapolis, IN	14.3
37	58	Indianapolis, IN	9.3	33	58	Cincinnati, OH-KY-IN	14.2
28	58	Kansas City, MO-KS	9.3	29	58	San Francisco, CA	14.2
29	58	San Francisco, CA	9.3	54	60	Raleigh-Durham-Chapel Hill, NC	14.1
31	61	New Haven-Bridgeport-Stamford-Danb	9.2	48	61	Nashville, TN	13.8
27	61	Portland-Vancouver, OR-WA	9.2	28	62	Kansas City, MO-KS	13.6
52	63	Hartford, CT	9.1	30	62	San Jose, CA	13.6
25	64	Denver, CO	9.0	25	64	Denver, CO	13.4
30	64	San Jose, CA	9.0	44	65	Bergen-Passaic, NJ	13.0
75	66	Omaha, NE-IA	8.9	58	65	Grand Rapids-Muskegon-Holland, MI	13.0
46	66	Salt Lake City-Ogden, UT	8.9	27	67	Portland-Vancouver, OR-WA	12.9
58	68	Grand Rapids-Muskegon-Holland, MI	8.7	6	68	Washington, DC-MD-VA-WV	12.8
6	69	Washington, DC-MD-VA-WV	8.2	75	69	Omaha, NE-IA	12.3
44	70	Bergen-Passaic, NJ	7.9	13	70	Minneapolis-St. Paul, MN-WI	11.7
20	71	Seattle-Bellevue-Everett, WA	7.8	20	70	Seattle-Bellevue-Everett, WA	11.7
13	72	Minneapolis-St. Paul, MN-WI	7.7	53	72	Monmouth-Ocean, NJ	11.4
53	73	Monmouth-Ocean, NJ	7.1	46	72	Salt Lake City-Ogden, UT	11.4
16	74	Nassau-Suffolk, NY	6.7	16	74	Nassau-Suffolk, NY	10.9
51	75	Middlesex-Somerset-Hunterdon, NJ	5.7	51	75	Middlesex-Somerset-Hunterdon, NJ	8.9

Note: Column numbers refer to Table C. Metropolitan Areas.

TABLE 3—75 Largest Metropolitan Areas by 1999 Population
Selected Rankings

Median Value of Owner-Occupied Housing Units, 1990				Median Gross Rent of Renter-Occupied Housing Units, 1990			
Population Rank	Median Value Rank	Metropolitan Area	[col 91] Median Value 1990 (dollars)	Population Rank	Median Rent Rank	Metropolitan Area	[col 94] Median Rent in 1990 (dollars)
29	1	San Francisco, CA	332 400	15	1	Orange County, CA	789
30	2	San Jose, CA	289 400	16	2	Nassau-Suffolk, NY	777
69	3	Honolulu, HI	283 600	30	3	San Jose, CA	772
15	4	Orange County, CA	252 700	72	4	Ventura, CA	753
72	5	Ventura, CA	245 300	29	5	San Francisco, CA	708
1	6	Los Angeles-Long Beach, CA	226 400	51	6	Middlesex-Somerset-Hunterdon, NJ	679
19	7	Oakland, CA	224 400	69	7	Honolulu, HI	662
44	8	Bergen-Passaic, NJ	214 400	6	8	Washington, DC-MD-VA-WV	658
2	9	New York, NY	209 000	53	9	Monmouth-Ocean, NJ	647
31	10	New Haven-Bridgeport-Stamford-Danb	198 400	44	10	Bergen-Passaic, NJ	645
26	11	Newark, NJ	188 400	19	11	Oakland, CA	641
16	12	Nassau-Suffolk, NY	187 000	31	12	New Haven-Bridgeport-Stamford-Danb	630
14	13	San Diego, CA	186 700	1	13	Los Angeles-Long Beach, CA	625
51	14	Middlesex-Somerset-Hunterdon, NJ	173 500	14	14	San Diego, CA	610
52	15	Hartford, CT	169 300	4	15	Boston-Worcester-Lawrence-Lowell-Bro	595
4	16	Boston-Worcester-Lawrence-Lowell-Bro	165 200	59	16	West Palm Beach-Boca Raton, FL	586
6	17	Washington, DC-MD-VA-WV	160 939	26	17	Newark, NJ	581
53	18	Monmouth-Ocean, NJ	150 600	52	18	Hartford, CT	576
34	19	Sacramento, CA	136 700	38	19	Fort Lauderdale, FL	574
20	20	Seattle-Bellevue-Everett, WA	135 900	11	20	Riverside-San Bernardino, CA	561
11	21	Riverside-San Bernardino, CA	133 900	34	21	Sacramento, CA	532
66	22	Providence-Warwick-Pawtucket, RI	131 300	9	22	Atlanta, GA	524
3	23	Chicago, IL	109 900	39	23	Orlando, FL	515
18	24	Baltimore, MD	101 200	5	24	Philadelphia, PA-NJ	514
5	25	Philadelphia, PA-NJ	100 400	20	24	Seattle-Bellevue-Everett, WA	514
68	26	Albany-Schenectady-Troy, NY	99 000	43	26	Las Vegas, NV-AZ	511
59	27	West Palm Beach-Boca Raton, FL	98 400	2	27	New York, NY	502
38	28	Fort Lauderdale, FL	91 800	24	28	Miami, FL	492
43	29	Las Vegas, NV-AZ	91 500	3	29	Chicago, IL	491
54	30	Raleigh-Durham-Chapel Hill, NC	89 100	18	30	Baltimore, MD	489
9	31	Atlanta, GA	88 800	66	31	Providence-Warwick-Pawtucket, RI	480
13	32	Minneapolis-St. Paul, MN-WI	88 300	36	32	Norfolk-Virginia Beach-Newport News,	479
25	33	Denver, CO	87 800	13	33	Minneapolis-St. Paul, MN-WI	477
36	34	Norfolk-Virginia Beach-Newport News,	86 800	56	34	Rochester, NY	462
24	35	Miami, FL	86 500	12	35	Phoenix-Mesa, AZ	461
56	36	Rochester, NY	85 500	62	36	Richmond-Petersburg, VA	458
12	37	Phoenix-Mesa, AZ	84 200	68	37	Albany-Schenectady-Troy, NY	456
67	38	Fresno, CA	83 900	54	37	Raleigh-Durham-Chapel Hill, NC	456
39	39	Orlando, FL	82 500	10	39	Dallas, TX	453
10	40	Dallas, TX	81 500	7	39	Detroit, MI	453
62	41	Richmond-Petersburg, VA	79 300	22	41	Tampa-St. Petersburg-Clearwater, FL	447
41	42	Milwaukee-Waukesha, WI	76 900	41	42	Milwaukee-Waukesha, WI	446
70	43	Tucson, AZ	76 500	57	43	Jacksonville, FL	438
48	44	Nashville, TN	76 000	27	44	Portland-Vancouver, OR-WA	436
73	45	Syracuse, NY	75 300	67	45	Fresno, CA	432
49	46	Austin-San Marcos, TX	74 800	25	46	Denver, CO	431
27	47	Portland-Vancouver, OR-WA	72 400	32	47	Fort Worth-Arlington, TX	428
42	48	Charlotte-Gastonia-Rock Hill, NC-SC	72 300	73	48	Syracuse, NY	426
40	48	Columbus, OH	72 300	48	49	Nashville, TN	425
23	50	Cleveland-Lorain-Elyria, OH	72 100	42	50	Charlotte-Gastonia-Rock Hill, NC-SC	424
32	51	Fort Worth-Arlington, TX	72 000	28	50	Kansas City, MO-KS	424
50	52	Buffalo-Niagara Falls, NY	71 900	40	52	Columbus, OH	420
22	53	Tampa-St. Petersburg-Clearwater, FL	71 300	58	52	Grand Rapids-Muskegon-Holland, MI	420
46	54	Salt Lake City-Ogden, UT	71 000	49	54	Austin-San Marcos, TX	414
47	55	Greensboro—Winston-Salem—High Poin	70 700	17	55	St. Louis, MO-IL	413
33	56	Cincinnati, OH-KY-IN	70 400	37	56	Indianapolis, IN	407
45	57	New Orleans, LA	69 800	8	57	Houston, TX	406
17	57	St. Louis, MO-IL	69 800	23	58	Cleveland-Lorain-Elyria, OH	399
57	59	Jacksonville, FL	67 800	75	58	Omaha, NE-IA	399
7	60	Detroit, MI	67 600	63	60	Dayton-Springfield, OH	398
28	61	Kansas City, MO-KS	66 300	45	61	New Orleans, LA	396
58	62	Grand Rapids-Muskegon-Holland, MI	65 700	47	62	Greensboro—Winston-Salem—High Poin	390
63	63	Dayton-Springfield, OH	65 000	70	63	Tucson, AZ	389
55	64	Memphis, TN-AR-MS	64 600	55	64	Memphis, TN-AR-MS	388
8	65	Houston, TX	64 200	50	65	Buffalo-Niagara Falls, NY	380
37	66	Indianapolis, IN	64 100	35	66	San Antonio, TX	379
65	67	Birmingham, AL	60 600	46	67	Salt Lake City-Ogden, UT	377
75	68	Omaha, NE-IA	59 000	60	68	Oklahoma City, OK	368
71	69	Tulsa, OK	58 900	33	69	Cincinnati, OH-KY-IN	364
64	70	Greenville-Spartanburg-Anderson, SC	58 700	21	70	Pittsburgh, PA	362
74	71	El Paso, TX	57 300	65	71	Birmingham, AL	361
35	72	San Antonio, TX	57 200	71	72	Tulsa, OK	360
61	73	Louisville, KY-IN	56 100	64	73	Greenville-Spartanburg-Anderson, SC	358
21	74	Pittsburgh, PA	55 600	74	74	El Paso, TX	346
60	75	Oklahoma City, OK	54 500	61	75	Louisville, KY-IN	345

Note: Column numbers refer to Table C. Metropolitan Areas.

TABLE 3—75 Largest Metropolitan Areas by 1999 Population
Selected Rankings

Unemployment Rate, 1999				Manufacturing Employment as a Percent of Total Nonfarm Employment, 1998			
Population Rank	Unemployment Rate Rank	Metropolitan Area	[col 100] Unemployment Rate 1999	Population Rank	Manufacturing Rank	Metropolitan Area	[col 107/col 105] Percent employed in Mfg 1998
67	1	Fresno, CA	13.2	58	1	Grand Rapids-Muskegon-Holland, MI	29.8
74	2	El Paso, TX	9.4	64	2	Greenville-Spartanburg-Anderson, SC	25.5
2	3	New York, NY	6.2	30	3	San Jose, CA	25.4
1	4	Los Angeles-Long Beach, CA	5.9	47	4	Greensboro—Winston-Salem—High Poin	24.9
24	5	Miami, FL	5.8	56	5	Rochester, NY	22.5
50	6	Buffalo-Niagara Falls, NY	5.4	41	6	Milwaukee-Waukesha, WI	21.8
11	7	Riverside-San Bernardino, CA	5.1	63	7	Dayton-Springfield, OH	21.1
59	8	West Palm Beach-Boca Raton, FL	5.0	23	8	Cleveland-Lorain-Elyria, OH	19.4
69	9	Honolulu, HI	4.9	66	9	Providence-Warwick-Pawtucket, RI	19.1
72	10	Ventura, CA	4.8	74	10	El Paso, TX	19.0
44	11	Bergen-Passaic, NJ	4.5	42	11	Charlotte-Gastonia-Rock Hill, NC-SC	18.4
23	11	Cleveland-Lorain-Elyria, OH	4.5	7	12	Detroit, MI	17.7
8	11	Houston, TX	4.5	15	13	Orange County, CA	17.6
26	11	Newark, NJ	4.5	20	14	Seattle-Bellevue-Everett, WA	17.3
27	11	Portland-Vancouver, OR-WA	4.5	50	14	Buffalo-Niagara Falls, NY	17.3
43	16	Las Vegas, NV-AZ	4.4	1	14	Los Angeles-Long Beach, CA	17.3
45	16	New Orleans, LA	4.4	52	17	Hartford, CT	16.1
21	18	Pittsburgh, PA	4.3	61	17	Louisville, KY-IN	16.1
56	18	Rochester, NY	4.3	27	17	Portland-Vancouver, OR-WA	16.1
73	18	Syracuse, NY	4.3	32	20	Fort Worth-Arlington, TX	15.9
53	21	Monmouth-Ocean, NJ	4.2	3	21	Chicago, IL	15.8
66	22	Providence-Warwick-Pawtucket, RI	4.2	73	21	Syracuse, NY	15.8
3	23	Chicago, IL	4.1	72	23	Ventura, CA	15.3
5	23	Philadelphia, PA-NJ	4.1	33	24	Cincinnati, OH-KY-IN	15.2
18	25	Baltimore, MD	4.0	11	25	Riverside-San Bernardino, CA	15.1
38	25	Fort Lauderdale, FL	4.0	31	26	New Haven-Bridgeport-Stamford-Danb	15.0
34	25	Sacramento, CA	4.0	17	26	St. Louis, MO-IL	15.0
63	28	Dayton-Springfield, OH	3.8	44	28	Bergen-Passaic, NJ	14.9
17	29	St. Louis, MO-IL	3.7	13	29	Minneapolis-St. Paul, MN-WI	14.7
68	30	Albany-Schenectady-Troy, NY	3.6	71	29	Tulsa, OK	14.7
55	30	Memphis, TN-AR-MS	3.6	4	31	Boston-Worcester-Lawrence-Lowell-Bro	14.6
46	30	Salt Lake City-Ogden, UT	3.6	49	32	Austin-San Marcos, TX	14.2
33	33	Cincinnati, OH-KY-IN	3.5	37	33	Indianapolis, IN	14.1
7	33	Detroit, MI	3.5	67	34	Fresno, CA	13.7
61	35	Louisville, KY-IN	3.4	54	34	Raleigh-Durham-Chapel Hill, NC	13.7
36	35	Norfolk-Virginia Beach-Newport News,	3.4	48	36	Nashville, TN	13.5
20	35	Seattle-Bellevue-Everett, WA	3.4	46	37	Salt Lake City-Ogden, UT	13.3
64	38	Greenville-Spartanburg-Anderson, SC	3.3	19	38	Oakland, CA	13.0
16	38	Nassau-Suffolk, NY	3.3	26	39	Newark, NJ	12.9
19	38	Oakland, CA	3.3	10	39	Dallas, TX	12.9
58	41	Grand Rapids-Muskegon-Holland, MI	3.2	14	41	San Diego, CA	12.5
52	41	Hartford, CT	3.2	51	41	Middlesex-Somerset-Hunterdon, NJ	12.5
51	41	Middlesex-Somerset-Hunterdon, NJ	3.2	60	43	Oklahoma City, OK	12.2
71	41	Tulsa, OK	3.2	62	44	Richmond-Petersburg, VA	11.9
9	45	Atlanta, GA	3.1	12	44	Phoenix-Mesa, AZ	11.9
65	45	Birmingham, AL	3.1	21	44	Pittsburgh, PA	11.9
4	45	Boston-Worcester-Lawrence-Lowell-Bro	3.1	65	47	Birmingham, AL	11.8
10	45	Dallas, TX	3.1	5	48	Philadelphia, PA-NJ	11.6
32	45	Fort Worth-Arlington, TX	3.1	28	49	Kansas City, MO-KS	11.5
41	45	Milwaukee-Waukesha, WI	3.1	40	50	Columbus, OH	11.1
31	45	New Haven-Bridgeport-Stamford-Danb	3.1	55	51	Memphis, TN-AR-MS	10.8
35	45	San Antonio, TX	3.1	8	52	Houston, TX	10.6
14	45	San Diego, CA	3.1	70	52	Tucson, AZ	10.6
70	45	Tucson, AZ	3.1	16	54	Nassau-Suffolk, NY	10.4
57	55	Jacksonville, FL	3.0	75	55	Omaha, NE-IA	10.2
28	55	Kansas City, MO-KS	3.0	9	56	Atlanta, GA	10.1
12	55	Phoenix-Mesa, AZ	3.0	68	57	Albany-Schenectady-Troy, NY	9.9
30	55	San Jose, CA	3.0	36	58	Norfolk-Virginia Beach-Newport News,	9.5
48	59	Nashville, TN	2.7	18	59	Baltimore, MD	9.1
39	59	Orlando, FL	2.7	45	60	New Orleans, LA	8.6
22	59	Tampa-St. Petersburg-Clearwater, FL	2.7	35	60	San Antonio, TX	8.6
42	62	Charlotte-Gastonia-Rock Hill, NC-SC	2.6	34	62	Sacramento, CA	8.1
40	62	Columbus, OH	2.6	25	62	Denver, CO	8.1
60	62	Oklahoma City, OK	2.6	22	64	Tampa-St. Petersburg-Clearwater, FL	7.8
75	62	Omaha, NE-IA	2.6	24	65	Miami, FL	7.5
15	62	Orange County, CA	2.6	57	66	Jacksonville, FL	7.4
6	62	Washington, DC-MD-VA-WV	2.6	53	67	Monmouth-Ocean, NJ	6.5
25	68	Denver, CO	2.4	59	67	West Palm Beach-Boca Raton, FL	6.5
47	68	Greensboro—Winston-Salem—High Poin	2.4	38	69	Fort Lauderdale, FL	6.4
37	68	Indianapolis, IN	2.4	39	70	Orlando, FL	6.3
62	68	Richmond-Petersburg, VA	2.4	29	71	San Francisco, CA	6.2
29	68	San Francisco, CA	2.4	2	72	New York, NY	6.1
49	73	Austin-San Marcos, TX	2.2	6	73	Washington, DC-MD-VA-WV	3.9
13	73	Minneapolis-St. Paul, MN-WI	2.2	43	74	Las Vegas, NV-AZ	3.7
54	75	Raleigh-Durham-Chapel Hill, NC	1.6	69	75	Honolulu, HI	3.4

Note: Column numbers refer to Table C. Metropolitan Areas.

TABLE 3—75 Largest Metropolitan Areas by 1999 Population
Selected Rankings

Employment in Professional, Scientific, and Technical Services as a Percent of Total Nonfarm Employment, 1998				Finance and Insurance as a Percent of Total Nonfarm Employment, 1998			
Population Rank	Services Rank	Metropolitan Area	[col 110/col 105] Percent employed in Services 1998	Population Rank	F/I Rank	Metropolitan Area	[col 109/col 105] Percent F/I Employment 1998
6	1	Washington, DC-MD-VA-WV	16.2	52	1	Hartford, CT	13.0
29	2	San Francisco, CA	10.7	2	2	New York, NY	11.2
1	3	Los Angeles-Long Beach, CA	10.4	57	3	Jacksonville, FL	10.8
51	4	Middlesex-Somerset-Hunterdon, NJ	9.9	40	4	Columbus, OH	9.9
30	5	San Jose, CA	9.0	29	5	San Francisco, CA	9.6
2	6	New York, NY	8.8	62	6	Richmond-Petersburg, VA	9.2
49	7	Austin-San Marcos, TX	8.0	68	7	Albany-Schenectady-Troy, NY	7.6
14	8	San Diego, CA	7.9	75	8	Omaha, NE-IA	7.5
5	9	Philadelphia, PA-NJ	7.7	4	9	Boston-Worcester-Lawrence-Lowell-Brockton, MA-NH	7.2
18	10	Baltimore, MD	7.6	34	10	Sacramento, CA	7.0
26	11	Newark, NJ	7.5	25	10	Denver, CO	7.0
54	12	Raleigh-Durham-Chapel Hill, NC	7.3	65	10	Birmingham, AL	7.0
8	13	Houston, TX	7.2	26	13	Newark, NJ	6.9
3	13	Chicago, IL	7.2	3	13	Chicago, IL	6.9
25	13	Denver, CO	7.2	37	15	Indianapolis, IN	6.8
9	16	Atlanta, GA	7.1	13	15	Minneapolis-St. Paul, MN-WI	6.8
22	16	Tampa-St. Petersburg-Clearwater, FL	7.1	28	15	Kansas City, MO-KS	6.8
4	18	Boston-Worcester-Lawrence-Lowell-Brockton, MA-NH	7.0	51	15	Middlesex-Somerset-Hunterdon, NJ	6.8
10	19	Dallas, TX	6.8	41	19	Milwaukee-Waukesha, WI	6.7
15	19	Orange County, CA	6.8	16	19	Nassau-Suffolk, NY	6.7
16	21	Nassau-Suffolk, NY	6.6	5	19	Philadelphia, PA-NJ	6.7
20	21	Seattle-Bellevue-Everett, WA	6.6	10	22	Dallas, TX	6.3
53	23	Monmouth-Ocean, NJ	6.5	31	23	New Haven-Bridgeport-Stamford-Danbury-Waterbury, CT	6.2
19	23	Oakland, CA	6.5	22	23	Tampa-St. Petersburg-Clearwater, FL	6.2
68	25	Albany-Schenectady-Troy, NY	6.4	35	23	San Antonio, TX	6.2
7	25	Detroit, MI	6.4	66	23	Providence-Warwick-Pawtucket, RI	6.2
28	27	Kansas City, MO-KS	6.3	12	23	Phoenix-Mesa, AZ	6.2
36	28	Norfolk-Virginia Beach-Newport News, VA-NC	6.2	15	23	Orange County, CA	6.2
31	29	New Haven-Bridgeport-Stamford-Danbury-Waterbury, CT	6.1	61	29	Louisville, KY-IN	6.1
59	29	West Palm Beach-Boca Raton, FL	6.1	47	30	Greensboro—Winston-Salem—High Point, NC	6.0
12	29	Phoenix-Mesa, AZ	6.1	46	31	Salt Lake City-Ogden, UT	5.9
21	32	Pittsburgh, PA	6.0	38	31	Fort Lauderdale, FL	5.9
13	32	Minneapolis-St. Paul, MN-WI	6.0	23	33	Cleveland-Lorain-Elyria, OH	5.8
44	32	Bergen-Passaic, NJ	6.0	42	33	Charlotte-Gastonia-Rock Hill, NC-SC	5.8
34	35	Sacramento, CA	5.9	69	35	Honolulu, HI	5.7
38	36	Fort Lauderdale, FL	5.6	21	35	Pittsburgh, PA	5.7
72	36	Ventura, CA	5.6	18	35	Baltimore, MD	5.7
17	36	St. Louis, MO-IL	5.6	48	35	Nashville, TN	5.7
27	39	Portland-Vancouver, OR-WA	5.5	9	35	Atlanta, GA	5.7
33	40	Cincinnati, OH-KY-IN	5.4	71	40	Tulsa, OK	5.6
24	40	Miami, FL	5.4	49	41	Austin-San Marcos, TX	5.5
70	40	Tucson, AZ	5.4	17	41	St. Louis, MO-IL	5.5
35	40	San Antonio, TX	5.4	73	43	Syracuse, NY	5.4
40	44	Columbus, OH	5.3	24	43	Miami, FL	5.4
39	45	Orlando, FL	5.2	59	45	West Palm Beach-Boca Raton, FL	5.2
45	45	New Orleans, LA	5.2	50	45	Buffalo-Niagara Falls, NY	5.2
46	45	Salt Lake City-Ogden, UT	5.2	72	45	Ventura, CA	5.2
23	45	Cleveland-Lorain-Elyria, OH	5.2	27	45	Portland-Vancouver, OR-WA	5.2
63	49	Dayton-Springfield, OH	5.0	60	49	Oklahoma City, OK	5.0
57	49	Jacksonville, FL	5.0	33	49	Cincinnati, OH-KY-IN	5.0
42	49	Charlotte-Gastonia-Rock Hill, NC-SC	5.0	19	49	Oakland, CA	5.0
65	52	Birmingham, AL	4.9	20	49	Seattle-Bellevue-Everett, WA	5.0
75	53	Omaha, NE-IA	4.8	44	53	Bergen-Passaic, NJ	4.9
71	53	Tulsa, OK	4.8	1	54	Los Angeles-Long Beach, CA	4.8
41	53	Milwaukee-Waukesha, WI	4.8	7	54	Detroit, MI	4.8
62	53	Richmond-Petersburg, VA	4.8	14	56	San Diego, CA	4.7
69	57	Honolulu, HI	4.7	45	57	New Orleans, LA	4.6
37	57	Indianapolis, IN	4.7	6	58	Washington, DC-MD-VA-WV	4.5
52	57	Hartford, CT	4.7	8	58	Houston, TX	4.5
60	57	Oklahoma City, OK	4.7	67	60	Fresno, CA	4.4
73	61	Syracuse, NY	4.6	55	61	Memphis, TN-AR-MS	4.3
50	61	Buffalo-Niagara Falls, NY	4.6	36	61	Norfolk-Virginia Beach-Newport News, VA-NC	4.3
56	63	Rochester, NY	4.5	54	63	Raleigh-Durham-Chapel Hill, NC	4.1
48	64	Nashville, TN	4.3	53	64	Monmouth-Ocean, NJ	4.0
32	65	Fort Worth-Arlington, TX	4.1	39	64	Orlando, FL	4.0
43	65	Las Vegas, NV-AZ	4.1	32	66	Fort Worth-Arlington, TX	3.8
61	67	Louisville, KY-IN	4.0	43	67	Las Vegas, NV-AZ	3.6
67	68	Fresno, CA	3.9	56	68	Rochester, NY	3.5
55	69	Memphis, TN-AR-MS	3.8	63	68	Dayton-Springfield, OH	3.5
66	70	Providence-Warwick-Pawtucket, RI	3.7	58	68	Grand Rapids-Muskegon-Holland, MI	3.5
64	71	Greenville-Spartanburg-Anderson, SC	3.6	64	71	Greenville-Spartanburg-Anderson, SC	3.0
58	72	Grand Rapids-Muskegon-Holland, MI	3.4	11	71	Riverside-San Bernardino, CA	3.0
47	72	Greensboro—Winston-Salem—High Point, NC	3.4	70	71	Tucson, AZ	3.0
74	74	El Paso, TX	3.0	74	74	El Paso, TX	2.9
11	75	Riverside-San Bernardino, CA	2.5	30	75	San Jose, CA	2.1

Note: Column numbers refer to Table C. Metropolitan Areas.

TABLE 3—75 Largest Metropolitan Areas by 1999 Population
Selected Rankings

	Per Capita Local Government Taxes, 1997				Violent Crime Rate per 100,000 Population, 1998		
Population Rank	Local Taxes Rank	Metropolitan Area	[col 181] Local Taxes Per Capita (Dollars)	Population Rank	Crime Rate Rank	Metropolitan Area	[col 46] Violent Crime Rate
16	1	Nassau-Suffolk, NY	2 777	24	1	Miami, FL	1 532
2	2	New York, NY	2 657	55	2	Memphis, TN-AR-MS	1 081
6	3	Washington, DC-MD-VA-WV	1 840	48	3	Nashville, TN.	1 069
26	4	Newark, NJ	1 744	2	4	New York, NY	1 037
44	5	Bergen-Passaic, NJ	1 735	1	5	Los Angeles-Long Beach, CA	1 017
51	6	Middlesex-Somerset-Hunterdon, NJ	1 713	39	6	Orlando, FL	991
31	7	New Haven-Bridgeport-Stamford-Danb	1 643	22	7	Tampa-St. Petersburg-Clearwater, FL	990
3	8	Chicago, IL	1 632	59	8	West Palm Beach-Boca Raton, FL	967
53	9	Monmouth-Ocean, NJ	1 628	57	9	Jacksonville, FL	958
68	10	Albany-Schenectady-Troy, NY	1 562	42	10	Charlotte-Gastonia-Rock Hill, NC-SC	950
56	11	Rochester, NY	1 561	45	11	New Orleans, LA	918
59	12	West Palm Beach-Boca Raton, FL	1 495	67	12	Fresno, CA	872
50	13	Buffalo-Niagara Falls, NY	1 491	7	13	Detroit, MI	870
73	14	Syracuse, NY	1 483	64	14	Greenville-Spartanburg-Anderson, SC	850
29	15	San Francisco, CA	1 478	75	15	Omaha, NE-IA	830
52	16	Hartford, CT	1 463	37	16	Indianapolis, IN	809
23	17	Cleveland-Lorain-Elyria, OH	1 437	61	17	Louisville, KY-IN	791
5	18	Philadelphia, PA-NJ	1 354	8	18	Houston, TX	749
10	19	Dallas, TX	1 339	70	19	Tucson, AZ	746
25	20	Denver, CO	1 337	19	20	Oakland, CA	739
40	21	Columbus, OH	1 324	18	21	Baltimore, MD	730
41	22	Milwaukee-Waukesha, WI	1 321	43	21	Las Vegas, NV-AZ	730
30	23	San Jose, CA	1 281	10	23	Dallas, TX	723
8	24	Houston, TX	1 262	38	24	Fort Lauderdale, FL	719
49	25	Austin-San Marcos, TX	1 237	71	25	Tulsa, OK	712
66	26	Providence-Warwick-Pawtucket, RI	1 235	9	26	Atlanta, GA	689
20	27	Seattle-Bellevue-Everett, WA	1 224	26	27	Newark, NJ	670
9	28	Atlanta, GA	1 167	74	28	El Paso, TX	668
38	29	Fort Lauderdale, FL	1 166	5	29	Philadelphia, PA-NJ	667
33	30	Cincinnati, OH-KY-IN	1 162	11	30	Riverside-San Bernardino, CA	646
18	31	Baltimore, MD	1 161	29	31	San Francisco, CA	630
4	32	Boston-Worcester-Lawrence-Lowell-Bro	1 158	60	32	Oklahoma City, OK	614
24	33	Miami, FL	1 151	12	33	Phoenix-Mesa, AZ	613
28	34	Kansas City, MO-KS	1 147	14	34	San Diego, CA	602
63	35	Dayton-Springfield, OH	1 146	65	35	Sacramento, CA	589
19	36	Oakland, CA	1 145	47	36	Birmingham, AL	581
75	37	Omaha, NE-IA	1 134	34	37	Greensboro—Winston-Salem—High Point, NC	576
13	38	Minneapolis-St. Paul, MN-WI	1 113	27	38	Portland-Vancouver, OR-WA	567
27	39	Portland-Vancouver, OR-WA	1 107	54	39	Raleigh-Durham-Chapel Hill, NC	560
32	40	Fort Worth-Arlington, TX	1 101	40	40	Columbus, OH	537
62	41	Richmond-Petersburg, VA	1 092	6	40	Washington, DC-MD-VA-WV	537
45	42	New Orleans, LA	1 091	32	42	Fort Worth-Arlington, TX	520
37	43	Indianapolis, IN	1 086	62	43	Richmond-Petersburg, VA	506
21	44	Pittsburgh, PA	1 050	4	44	Boston-Worcester-Lawrence-Lowell-Brockton, MA-NH	505
39	45	Orlando, FL	1 024	30	45	San Jose, CA	496
36	46	Norfolk-Virginia Beach-Newport News,	1 003	58	46	Grand Rapids-Muskegon-Holland, MI	486
17	46	St. Louis, MO-IL	1 003	63	47	Dayton-Springfield, OH	474
48	48	Nashville, TN.	991	36	48	Norfolk-Virginia Beach-Newport News, VA-NC	459
65	49	Birmingham, AL	934	31	49	New Haven-Bridgeport-Stamford-Danbury-Waterbury, CT	432
43	50	Las Vegas, NV-AZ	929	35	50	San Antonio, TX.	431
22	51	Tampa-St. Petersburg-Clearwater, FL	919	50	51	Buffalo-Niagara Falls, NY	425
15	52	Orange County, CA	895	46	52	Salt Lake City-Ogden, UT	422
1	53	Los Angeles-Long Beach, CA	890	20	53	Seattle-Bellevue-Everett, WA	419
7	54	Detroit, MI	871	13	54	Minneapolis-St. Paul, MN-WI	414
72	55	Ventura, CA	865	49	55	Austin-San Marcos, TX	413
12	56	Phoenix-Mesa, AZ	864	25	56	Denver, CO	385
70	57	Tucson, AZ	860	52	57	Hartford, CT	360
35	58	San Antonio, TX	850	15	58	Orange County, CA	351
47	59	Greensboro—Winston-Salem—High Poin	840	21	59	Pittsburgh, PA	317
54	60	Raleigh-Durham-Chapel Hill, NC	838	72	60	Ventura, CA	316
42	61	Charlotte-Gastonia-Rock Hill, NC-SC	836	66	61	Providence-Warwick-Pawtucket, RI	304
55	62	Memphis, TN-AR-MS	834	73	62	Syracuse, NY	298
34	63	Sacramento, CA	831	68	63	Albany-Schenectady-Troy, NY	276
61	64	Louisville, KY-IN	808	56	63	Rochester, NY	276
57	65	Jacksonville, FL	796	69	65	Honolulu, HI	268
46	66	Salt Lake City-Ogden, UT	771	44	66	Bergen-Passaic, NJ	261
14	67	San Diego, CA	766	51	67	Middlesex-Somerset-Hunterdon, NJ	215
71	68	Tulsa, OK	746	53	68	Monmouth-Ocean, NJ	211
60	69	Oklahoma City, OK	735	16	69	Nassau-Suffolk, NY	116
74	70	El Paso, TX	724	3		Chicago, IL	NA
11	71	Riverside-San Bernardino, CA	705	33		Cincinnati, OH-KY-IN	NA
58	72	Grand Rapids-Muskegon-Holland, MI	683	23		Cleveland-Lorain-Elyria, OH	NA
64	73	Greenville-Spartanburg-Anderson, SC	631	28		Kansas City, MO-KS	NA
67	74	Fresno, CA	630	41		Milwaukee-Waukesha, WI	NA
69	75	Honolulu, HI	606	17		St. Louis, MO-IL	NA

Note: Column numbers refer to Table C. Metropolitan Areas.

TABLE 4—75 Metropolitan Areas with Highest Agricultural Sales, 1997
Selected Rankings

Value of Sales Rank	Metropolitan Area	[col 125] Sales (Mil Dollars)	Value of Sales Rank	Land in Farms Rank	Metropolitan Area	[col 117] Land in Farms (1000 acres)	[col 117 & col 1] Farm Land as % of Total Land
1	Fresno, CA	3 400	2	1	Bakersfield, CA	2 851	54.7
2	Bakersfield, CA	1 969	1	2	Fresno, CA	2 523	48.6
3	Visalia-Tulare-Porterville, CA	1 921	35	3	Kansas City, MO-KS	2 256	65.2
4	Salinas, CA	1 750	25	4	St. Louis, MO-IL	2 159	52.7
5	Riverside-San Bernardino, CA	1 665	10	5	Phoenix-Mesa, AZ	2 012	21.6
6	Greeley, CO	1 287	6	6	Greeley, CO	1 914	74.9
7	Merced, CA	1 273	17	7	Minneapolis-St. Paul, MN-WI	1 906	49.1
8	Modesto, CA	1 209	52	8	Grand Forks, ND-MN	1 827	83.7
9	Stockton-Lodi, CA	1 180	12	9	Yakima, WA	1 683	61.2
10	Phoenix-Mesa, AZ	1 028	57	10	Fargo-Moorhead, ND-MN	1 649	91.6
11	West Palm Beach-Boca Raton, FL	873	59	11	Wichita, KS	1 620	85.2
12	Yakima, WA	873	16	12	Chicago, IL	1 590	49.0
13	Ventura, CA	846	4	13	Salinas, CA	1 544	72.6
14	Lancaster, PA	767	5	14	Riverside-San Bernardino, CA	1 433	8.2
15	Portland-Vancouver, OR-WA	734	29	15	Indianapolis, IN	1 423	63.1
16	Chicago, IL	712	48	16	Washington, DC-MD-VA-WV	1 381	33.1
17	Minneapolis-St. Paul, MN-WI	701	3	17	Visalia-Tulare-Porterville, CA	1 310	42.4
18	Fayetteville-Springdale-Rogers, AR	697	55	18	San Luis Obispo-Atascadero-Paso Robles, CA	1 302	61.5
19	Philadelphia, PA-NJ	690	36	19	Omaha, NE-IA	1 271	80.2
20	Santa Barbara-Santa Maria-Lompoc, CA	660	38	20	Columbus, OH	1 204	59.8
21	Grand Rapids-Muskegon-Holland, MI	652	39	21	Fort Wayne, IN	1 193	76.1
22	San Diego, CA	633	23	22	Richland-Kennewick-Pasco, WA	1 176	62.4
23	Richland-Kennewick-Pasco, WA	633	24	23	Lexington, KY	1 058	86.1
24	Lexington, KY	556	27	24	Orlando, FL	1 008	45.1
25	St. Louis, MO-IL	555	30	25	Rochester, NY	968	44.1
26	Salem, OR	529	56	26	Peoria-Pekin, IL	895	77.8
27	Orlando, FL	525	7	27	Merced, CA	882	71.4
28	Yuma, AZ	522	51	28	Davenport-Moline-Rock Island, IA-IL	852	77.9
29	Indianapolis, IN	504	72	29	Des Moines, IA	849	76.7
30	Rochester, NY	478	43	30	St. Cloud, MN	822	73.3
31	Raleigh-Durham-Chapel Hill, NC	465	20	31	Santa Barbara-Santa Maria-Lompoc, CA	817	46.6
32	Santa Rosa, CA	464	9	32	Stockton-Lodi, CA	809	90.3
33	Atlanta, GA	455	45	33	Greensboro—Winston-Salem—High Point, NC	800	32.2
34	Tampa-St. Petersburg-Clearwater, FL	452	8	34	Modesto, CA	733	76.6
35	Kansas City, MO-KS	451	65	35	Rockford, IL	716	71.9
36	Omaha, NE-IA	451	58	36	Detroit, MI	704	28.2
37	Charlotte-Gastonia-Rock Hill, NC-SC	450	62	37	Syracuse, NY	687	34.8
38	Columbus, OH	435	15	38	Portland-Vancouver, OR-WA	670	20.8
39	Fort Wayne, IN	420	31	39	Raleigh-Durham-Chapel Hill, NC	669	29.9
40	Miami, FL	417	21	40	Grand Rapids-Muskegon-Holland, MI	667	37.8
41	Boise City, ID	405	33	41	Atlanta, GA	640	16.3
42	Vallejo-Fairfield-Napa, CA	400	18	42	Fayetteville-Springdale-Rogers, AR	631	54.9
43	St. Cloud, MN	392	71	43	Lakeland-Winter Haven, FL	621	51.7
44	Yuba City, CA	386	11	44	West Palm Beach-Boca Raton, FL	605	46.4
45	Greensboro—Winston-Salem—High Point, NC	370	37	45	Charlotte-Gastonia-Rock Hill, NC-SC	591	27.3
46	Harrisburg-Lebanon-Carlisle, PA	368	41	46	Boise City, ID	586	55.6
47	Boston-Worcester-Lawrence-Lowell-Brockton, MA-NH	348	75	47	Toledo, OH	581	66.5
48	Washington, DC-MD-VA-WV	346	42	48	Vallejo-Fairfield-Napa, CA	575	56.8
49	Yolo, CA	345	69	49	Baltimore, MD	573	34.3
50	Goldsboro, NC	337	32	50	Santa Rosa, CA	571	56.6
51	Davenport-Moline-Rock Island, IA-IL	324	19	51	Philadelphia, PA-NJ	569	23.0
52	Grand Forks, ND-MN	323	67	52	Kalamazoo-Battle Creek, MI	567	47.1
53	Fort Pierce-Port St. Lucie, FL	318	63	53	Appleton-Oshkosh-Neenah, WI	564	63.0
54	Rocky Mount, NC	317	44	54	Yuba City, CA	557	70.5
55	San Luis Obispo-Atascadero-Paso Robles, CA	313	66	55	Sacramento, CA	550	21.0
56	Peoria-Pekin, IL	308	49	56	Yolo, CA	537	82.8
57	Fargo-Moorhead, ND-MN	307	61	57	Madison, WI	513	66.6
58	Detroit, MI	289	26	58	Salem, OR	478	38.8
59	Wichita, KS	287	22	59	San Diego, CA	475	17.6
60	Chico-Paradise, CA	286	70	60	Cleveland-Lorain-Elyria, OH	467	26.9
61	Madison, WI	285	34	61	Tampa-St. Petersburg-Clearwater, FL	464	28.4
62	Syracuse, NY	284	46	62	Harrisburg-Lebanon-Carlisle, PA	455	35.7
63	Appleton-Oshkosh-Neenah, WI	280	53	63	Fort Pierce-Port St. Lucie, FL	411	56.9
64	Naples, FL	277	60	64	Chico-Paradise, CA	404	38.5
65	Rockford, IL	272	68	65	Sarasota-Bradenton, FL	397	47.2
66	Sacramento, CA	268	14	66	Lancaster, PA	392	64.5
67	Kalamazoo-Battle Creek, MI	267	47	67	Boston-Worcester-Lawrence-Lowell-Brockton, MA-NH	379	9.2
68	Sarasota-Bradenton, FL	264	54	68	Rocky Mount, NC	347	51.9
69	Baltimore, MD	262	13	69	Ventura, CA	346	29.3
70	Cleveland-Lorain-Elyria, OH	261	64	70	Naples, FL	277	21.4
71	Lakeland-Winter Haven, FL	253	28	71	Yuma, AZ	238	6.7
72	Des Moines, IA	248	50	72	Goldsboro, NC	229	64.7
73	Reading, PA	248	73	73	Reading, PA	222	40.4
74	Santa Cruz-Watsonville, CA	248	40	74	Miami, FL	85	6.8
75	Toledo, OH	245	74	75	Santa Cruz-Watsonville, CA	71	24.9

Note: Column numbers refer to Table C. Metropolitan Areas.

TABLE 4—75 Metropolitan Areas with Highest Agricultural Sales, 1997
Selected Rankings

Value of Sales Rank	Value per Acre Rank	Metropolitan Area (Value of Agricultural Land and Buildings, Average per Acre, 1997)	[col 123] Value per (1000 acres)	Value of Sales Rank	Number of Farms Rank	Metropolitan Area (Number of Farms, 1997)	[col 113] Number of Farms
40	1	Miami, FL	8 047	17	1	Minneapolis-St. Paul, MN-WI	10 460
13	2	Ventura, CA	6 860	35	2	Kansas City, MO-KS	9 774
74	3	Santa Cruz-Watsonville, CA	6 234	15	3	Portland-Vancouver, OR-WA	9 677
42	4	Vallejo-Fairfield-Napa, CA	5 909	25	4	St. Louis, MO-IL	8 702
15	5	Portland-Vancouver, OR-WA	5 804	1	5	Fresno, CA	8 265
47	6	Boston-Worcester-Lawrence-Lowell-Brockton, MA-NH	5 771	48	6	Washington, DC-MD-VA-WV	7 955
14	7	Lancaster, PA	5 578	45	7	Greensboro—Winston-Salem—High Point, NC	6 934
22	8	San Diego, CA	5 504	24	8	Lexington, KY	6 229
19	9	Philadelphia, PA-NJ	5 254	22	9	San Diego, CA	5 925
32	10	Santa Rosa, CA	5 211	33	10	Atlanta, GA	5 572
9	11	Stockton-Lodi, CA	4 667	3	11	Visalia-Tulare-Porterville, CA	5 446
8	12	Modesto, CA	4 508	39	12	Fort Wayne, IN	5 416
28	13	Yuma, AZ	4 496	29	13	Indianapolis, IN	5 113
69	14	Baltimore, MD	3 900	19	14	Philadelphia, PA-NJ	5 077
44	15	Yuba City, CA	3 882	16	15	Chicago, IL	4 878
26	16	Salem, OR	3 877	18	16	Fayetteville-Springdale-Rogers, AR	4 799
34	17	Tampa-St. Petersburg-Clearwater, FL	3 788	38	17	Columbus, OH	4 646
48	18	Washington, DC-MD-VA-WV	3 718	14	18	Lancaster, PA	4 556
16	19	Chicago, IL	3 681	5	19	Riverside-San Bernardino, CA	4 503
73	20	Reading, PA	3 673	47	20	Boston-Worcester-Lawrence-Lowell-Brockton, MA-NH	4 421
60	21	Chico-Paradise, CA	3 589	58	21	Detroit, MI	4 388
33	22	Atlanta, GA	3 514	37	22	Charlotte-Gastonia-Rock Hill, NC-SC	4 253
3	23	Visalia-Tulare-Porterville, CA	3 444	21	23	Grand Rapids-Muskegon-Holland, MI	4 175
11	24	West Palm Beach-Boca Raton, FL	3 404	34	24	Tampa-St. Petersburg-Clearwater, FL	4 151
1	25	Fresno, CA	3 386	31	25	Raleigh-Durham-Chapel Hill, NC	4 112
66	26	Sacramento, CA	3 336	8	26	Modesto, CA	4 009
7	27	Merced, CA	3 149	9	27	Stockton-Lodi, CA	3 862
70	28	Cleveland-Lorain-Elyria, OH	3 103	43	28	St. Cloud, MN	3 816
46	29	Harrisburg-Lebanon-Carlisle, PA	3 070	26	29	Salem, OR	3 693
37	30	Charlotte-Gastonia-Rock Hill, NC-SC	2 803	70	30	Cleveland-Lorain-Elyria, OH	3 675
58	31	Detroit, MI	2 790	69	31	Baltimore, MD	3 622
53	32	Fort Pierce-Port St. Lucie, FL	2 748	30	32	Rochester, NY	3 609
49	33	Yolo, CA	2 732	36	33	Omaha, NE-IA	3 446
45	34	Greensboro—Winston-Salem—High Point, NC	2 731	59	34	Wichita, KS	3 430
20	35	Santa Barbara-Santa Maria-Lompoc, CA	2 716	12	35	Yakima, WA	3 365
29	36	Indianapolis, IN	2 714	41	36	Boise City, ID	3 119
31	37	Raleigh-Durham-Chapel Hill, NC	2 712	46	37	Harrisburg-Lebanon-Carlisle, PA	3 098
56	38	Peoria-Pekin, IL	2 621	27	38	Orlando, FL	3 080
65	39	Rockford, IL	2 524	66	39	Sacramento, CA	3 048
24	40	Lexington, KY	2 469	6	40	Greeley, CO	2 959
68	41	Sarasota-Bradenton, FL	2 465	72	41	Des Moines, IA	2 932
21	42	Grand Rapids-Muskegon-Holland, MI	2 416	63	42	Appleton-Oshkosh-Neenah, WI	2 849
38	43	Columbus, OH	2 392	67	43	Kalamazoo-Battle Creek, MI	2 840
18	44	Fayetteville-Springdale-Rogers, AR	2 380	7	44	Merced, CA	2 831
4	45	Salinas, CA	2 358	51	45	Davenport-Moline-Rock Island, IA-IL	2 761
51	46	Davenport-Moline-Rock Island, IA-IL	2 324	56	46	Peoria-Pekin, IL	2 756
75	47	Toledo, OH	2 275	32	47	Santa Rosa, CA	2 745
39	48	Fort Wayne, IN	2 188	62	48	Syracuse, NY	2 745
71	49	Lakeland-Winter Haven, FL	2 110	61	49	Madison, WI	2 595
41	50	Boise City, ID	2 093	71	50	Lakeland-Winter Haven, FL	2 464
5	51	Riverside-San Bernardino, CA	2 087	65	51	Rockford, IL	2 276
27	52	Orlando, FL	2 037	13	52	Ventura, CA	2 214
50	53	Goldsboro, NC	2 025	75	53	Toledo, OH	2 194
72	54	Des Moines, IA	2 005	10	54	Phoenix-Mesa, AZ	2 184
17	55	Minneapolis-St. Paul, MN-WI	1 977	52	55	Grand Forks, ND-MN	2 134
25	56	St. Louis, MO-IL	1 951	42	56	Vallejo-Fairfield-Napa, CA	2 113
36	57	Omaha, NE-IA	1 943	44	57	Yuba City, CA	2 020
61	58	Madison, WI	1 853	2	58	Bakersfield, CA	1 997
23	59	Richland-Kennewick-Pasco, WA	1 833	60	59	Chico-Paradise, CA	1 942
64	60	Naples, FL	1 796	23	60	Richland-Kennewick-Pasco, WA	1 926
54	61	Rocky Mount, NC	1 746	55	61	San Luis Obispo-Atascadero-Paso Robles, CA	1 916
67	62	Kalamazoo-Battle Creek, MI	1 658	57	62	Fargo-Moorhead, ND-MN	1 806
2	63	Bakersfield, CA	1 605	73	63	Reading, PA	1 586
35	64	Kansas City, MO-KS	1 601	40	64	Miami, FL	1 576
55	65	San Luis Obispo-Atascadero-Paso Robles, CA	1 591	20	65	Santa Barbara-Santa Maria-Lompoc, CA	1 451
63	66	Appleton-Oshkosh-Neenah, WI	1 556	4	66	Salinas, CA	1 209
10	67	Phoenix-Mesa, AZ	1 529	68	67	Sarasota-Bradenton, FL	1 012
30	68	Rochester, NY	1 339	49	68	Yolo, CA	923
12	69	Yakima, WA	1 220	11	69	West Palm Beach-Boca Raton, FL	855
62	70	Syracuse, NY	1 099	50	70	Goldsboro, NC	827
43	71	St. Cloud, MN	1 075	53	71	Fort Pierce-Port St. Lucie, FL	805
59	72	Wichita, KS	976	54	72	Rocky Mount, NC	787
57	73	Fargo-Moorhead, ND-MN	900	74	73	Santa Cruz-Watsonville, CA	722
6	74	Greeley, CO	807	28	74	Yuma, AZ	465
52	75	Grand Forks, ND-MN	780	64	75	Naples, FL	235

Note: Column numbers refer to Table C. Metropolitan Areas.

TABLE 5—75 Largest Cities by 1999 Population
Selected Rankings

Total Persons, 1999			Land Area (Square Kilometers), 1990				Population Density (per Square Kilometer), 1999			
Population Rank	City	[col 2] Population	Population Rank	Land Area Rank	City	[col 1] Land Area	Population Rank	Density Rank	City	[col 4] Density
1	New York City, NY	7 428 162	63	1	Anchorage city, AK	4 396.9	1	1	New York City, NY	9 283
2	Los Angeles city, CA	3 633 591	14	2	Jacksonville consolidated city,FL	2 004.0	2	2	San Francisco city, CA	6 172
3	Chicago city, IL	2 799 050	30	3	Oklahoma City, OK	1 575.1	72	3	Jersey City, NJ	5 986
4	Houston city, TX	1 845 967	4	4	Houston city, TX	1 398.3	3	4	Chicago city, IL	4 756
5	Philadelphia city, PA	1 417 601	25	5	Nashville-Davidsn consol. city,TN	1 301.0	21	5	Boston city, MA	4 428
6	San Diego city, CA	1 238 974	2	6	Los Angeles city, CA	1 215.6	54	6	Santa Ana city, CA	4 406
7	Phoenix city, AZ	1 211 466	7	7	Phoenix city, AZ	1 087.6	61	7	Newark city, NJ	4 264
8	San Antonio city, TX	1 147 213	13	8	Indianapolis consolidated city,IN	950.0	5	8	Philadelphia city, PA	4 050
9	Dallas city, TX	1 076 214	9	9	Dallas city, TX	886.8	44	9	Miami city, FL	4 009
10	Detroit city, MI	965 084	8	10	San Antonio city, TX	862.6	34	10	Long Beach city, CA	3 359
11	San Jose city, CA	867 675	6	11	San Diego city, CA	839.2	24	11	Washington city, DC	3 262
12	San Francisco city, CA	746 777	33	12	Kansas City, MO	806.9	16	12	Baltimore city, MD	3 023
13	Indianapolis consolidated city,IN	738 907	1	13	New York City, NY	800.2	2	13	Los Angeles city, CA	2 989
14	Jacksonville consolidated city,FL	695 877	69	14	Lexington-Fayette, KY	736.9	57	14	Buffalo city, NY	2 810
15	Columbus city, OH	671 247	27	15	Fort Worth city, TX	728.0	10	15	Detroit city, MI	2 686
16	Baltimore city, MD	632 681	18	16	Memphis city, TN	663.2	56	16	Anaheim city, CA	2 621
17	El Paso city, TX	612 770	35	17	Virginia Beach city, VA	643.2	28	17	Cleveland city, OH	2 515
18	Memphis city, TN	606 109	17	18	El Paso city, TX	635.5	46	17	Oakland city, CA	2 515
19	Austin city, TX	587 873	3	19	Chicago city, IL	588.5	47	19	Minneapolis city, MN	2 483
20	Milwaukee city, WI	572 424	19	20	Austin city, TX	564.0	22	20	Seattle city, WA	2 472
21	Boston city, MA	555 249	15	21	Columbus city, OH	494.5	49	21	Pittsburgh city, PA	2 338
22	Seattle city, WA	537 150	43	22	Tulsa city, OK	475.3	20	22	Milwaukee city, WI	2 301
23	Charlotte city, NC	520 829	48	23	Colorado Springs city, CO	474.5	51	23	St. Louis city, MO	2 082
24	Washington city, DC	519 000	32	24	New Orleans city, LA	467.9	11	24	San Jose city, CA	1 956
25	Nashville-Davidsn consol. city,TN	506 385	23	25	Charlotte city, NC	451.3	37	25	Las Vegas city, NV	1 941
26	Portland city, OR	503 637	11	26	San Jose city, CA	443.6	64	26	St. Paul city, MN	1 874
27	Fort Worth city, TX	502 369	31	27	Tucson city, AZ	404.8	41	27	Honolulu CDP, HI	1 843
28	Cleveland city, OH	501 662	29	28	Denver city, CO	397.0	68	28	Stockton city, CA	1 799
29	Denver city, CO	499 775	67	29	Birmingham city, AL	384.6	52	29	Cincinnati city, OH	1 655
30	Oklahoma City, OK	475 322	10	30	Detroit city, MI	359.3	38	30	Sacramento city, CA	1 632
31	Tucson city, AZ	466 591	5	31	Philadelphia city, PA	350.0	73	31	Norfolk city, VA	1 623
32	New Orleans city, LA	460 913	59	32	Corpus Christi city, TX	349.6	39	32	Fresno city, CA	1 574
33	Kansas City, MO	437 764	66	33	Aurora city, CO	343.2	65	33	Louisville city, KY	1 573
34	Long Beach city, CA	435 027	36	34	Albuquerque city, NM	342.4	26	34	Portland city, OR	1 560
35	Virginia Beach city, VA	433 461	40	35	Atlanta city, GA	341.3	70	35	St. Petersburg city, FL	1 531
36	Albuquerque city, NM	420 578	26	36	Portland city, OR	322.9	42	36	Omaha city, NE	1 483
37	Las Vegas city, NV	418 658	50	37	Wichita city, KS	298.2	6	37	San Diego city, CA	1 476
38	Sacramento city, CA	406 899	58	38	Tampa city, FL	281.5	55	37	Toledo city, OH	1 476
39	Fresno city, CA	404 141	45	39	Mesa city, AZ	281.3	15	39	Columbus city, OH	1 357
40	Atlanta city, GA	401 726	42	40	Omaha city, NE	260.7	71	39	Plano city, TX	1 357
41	Honolulu CDP, HI	395 327	39	41	Fresno city, CA	256.8	8	41	San Antonio city, TX	1 330
42	Omaha city, NE	386 742	38	42	Sacramento city, CA	249.4	60	42	Riverside city, CA	1 321
43	Tulsa city, OK	381 579	20	43	Milwaukee city, WI	248.8	4	43	Houston city, TX	1 320
44	Miami city, FL	369 253	53	44	Arlington city, TX	240.9	75	44	Lincoln city, NE	1 317
45	Mesa city, AZ	368 811	74	45	Bakersfield city, CA	237.9	45	45	Mesa city, AZ	1 311
46	Oakland city, CA	365 210	62	46	Raleigh city, NC	228.3	53	46	Arlington city, TX	1 295
47	Minneapolis city, MN	353 395	22	47	Seattle city, WA	217.3	29	47	Denver city, CO	1 259
48	Colorado Springs city, CO	350 199	37	48	Las Vegas city, NV	215.7	36	48	Albuquerque city, NM	1 228
49	Pittsburgh city, PA	336 882	41	49	Honolulu CDP, HI	214.5	9	49	Dallas city, TX	1 214
50	Wichita city, KS	335 562	16	50	Baltimore city, MD	209.3	40	50	Atlanta city, GA	1 177
51	St. Louis city, MO	333 960	55	51	Toledo city, OH	208.7	23	51	Charlotte city, NC	1 154
52	Cincinnati city, OH	330 914	60	52	Riverside city, CA	201.2	31	52	Tucson city, AZ	1 153
53	Arlington city, TX	311 962	52	53	Cincinnati city, OH	200.0	62	53	Raleigh city, NC	1 144
54	Santa Ana city, CA	309 290	28	54	Cleveland city, OH	199.5	50	54	Wichita city, KS	1 125
55	Toledo city, OH	307 946	71	55	Plano city, TX	171.6	7	55	Phoenix city, AZ	1 114
56	Anaheim city, CA	300 650	75	56	Lincoln city, NE	163.9	19	56	Austin city, TX	1 042
57	Buffalo city, NY	295 619	65	57	Louisville city, KY	160.9	58	57	Tampa city, FL	1 034
58	Tampa city, FL	290 973	51	58	St. Louis city, MO	160.4	32	58	New Orleans city, LA	985
59	Corpus Christi city, TX	281 791	24	59	Washington city, DC	159.1	17	59	El Paso city, TX	964
60	Riverside city, CA	265 721	70	60	St. Petersburg city, FL	153.3	74	60	Bakersfield city, CA	935
61	Newark city, NJ	263 087	46	61	Oakland city, CA	145.2	18	61	Memphis city, TN	914
62	Raleigh city, NC	261 205	49	62	Pittsburgh city, PA	144.1	59	62	Corpus Christi city, TX	806
63	Anchorage city, AK	257 808	47	63	Minneapolis city, MN	142.3	43	63	Tulsa city, OK	803
64	St. Paul city, MN	256 213	73	64	Norfolk city, VA	139.2	13	64	Indianapolis consolidated city,IN	778
65	Louisville city, KY	253 128	64	65	St. Paul city, MN	136.7	48	65	Colorado Springs city, CO	738
66	Aurora city, CO	252 956	68	66	Stockton city, CA	136.2	66	66	Aurora city, CO	737
67	Birmingham city, AL	249 459	34	67	Long Beach city, CA	129.5	27	67	Fort Worth city, TX	690
68	Stockton city, CA	245 020	21	68	Boston city, MA	125.4	35	68	Virginia Beach city, VA	674
69	Lexington-Fayette, KY	243 785	12	69	San Francisco city, CA	121.0	67	69	Birmingham city, AL	649
70	St. Petersburg city, FL	234 647	56	70	Anaheim city, CA	114.7	33	70	Kansas City, MO	543
71	Plano city, TX	232 904	57	71	Buffalo city, NY	105.2	25	71	Nashville-Davidsn consol. city,TN	389
72	Jersey City, NJ	230 458	44	72	Miami city, FL	92.1	14	72	Jacksonville consolidated city,FL	347
73	Norfolk city, VA	225 875	54	73	Santa Ana city, CA	70.2	69	73	Lexington-Fayette, KY	331
74	Bakersfield city, CA	222 352	61	74	Newark city, NJ	61.7	30	74	Oklahoma City, OK	302
75	Lincoln city, NE	215 928	72	75	Jersey City, NJ	38.5	63	75	Anchorage city, AK	59

Note: Column numbers refer to Table D. Cities.

TABLE 5—75 Largest Cities by 1999 Population
Selected Rankings

Percent Population Change, 1990-1999

Population Rank	Percent Change Rank	City	[col 6] Percent Change
71	1	Plano city, TX	82.1
37	2	Las Vegas city, NV	61.7
45	3	Mesa city, AZ	27.5
74	4	Bakersfield city, CA	26.1
48	5	Colorado Springs city, CO	24.9
19	6	Austin city, TX	24.5
23	7	Charlotte city, NC	24.1
7	8	Phoenix city, AZ	22.6
62	9	Raleigh city, NC	19.3
53	10	Arlington city, TX	19.2
17	11	El Paso city, TX	18.9
8	12	San Antonio city, TX	17.5
60	13	Riverside city, CA	17.3
68	14	Stockton city, CA	16.2
39	15	Fresno city, CA	14.1
63	16	Anchorage city, AK	13.9
66	16	Aurora city, CO	13.9
56	18	Anaheim city, CA	12.9
75	19	Lincoln city, NE	12.5
42	20	Omaha city, NE	12.3
31	20	Tucson city, AZ	12.3
27	22	Fort Worth city, TX	12.2
4	23	Houston city, TX	11.6
6	23	San Diego city, CA	11.6
11	25	San Jose city, CA	10.9
50	26	Wichita city, KS	10.4
35	27	Virginia Beach city, VA	10.3
38	28	Sacramento city, CA	10.2
14	29	Jacksonville consolidated city,FL	9.6
59	30	Corpus Christi city, TX	9.5
36	31	Albuquerque city, NM	9.3
69	32	Lexington-Fayette, KY	8.2
29	33	Denver city, CO	6.9
30	33	Oklahoma City, OK	6.9
9	35	Dallas city, TX	6.8
15	36	Columbus city, OH	6.1
54	37	Santa Ana city, CA	5.3
41	38	Honolulu CDP, HI	4.8
2	39	Los Angeles city, CA	4.2
22	40	Seattle city, WA	4.0
58	41	Tampa city, FL	3.9
43	41	Tulsa city, OK	3.9
25	43	Nashville-Davidsn consol. city,TN	3.7
26	44	Portland city, OR	3.6
12	45	San Francisco city, CA	3.2
44	46	Miami city, FL	3.0
40	47	Atlanta city, GA	2.0
1	48	New York City, NY	1.4
34	49	Long Beach city, CA	1.3
13	50	Indianapolis consolidated city,IN	1.0
72	51	Jersey City, NY	0.8
33	52	Kansas City, MO	0.7
3	53	Chicago city, IL	0.6
28	54	Cleveland city, OH	-0.8
46	55	Oakland city, CA	-1.9
18	56	Memphis city, TN	-2.0
70	57	St. Petersburg city, FL	-2.4
21	58	Boston city, MA	-3.3
47	59	Minneapolis city, MN	-4.1
61	60	Newark city, NJ	-4.4
64	61	St. Paul city, MN	-5.9
67	62	Birmingham city, AL	-6.0
10	63	Detroit city, MI	-6.1
65	63	Louisville city, KY	-6.1
32	65	New Orleans city, LA	-7.2
55	66	Toledo city, OH	-7.5
20	67	Milwaukee city, WI	-8.9
49	67	Pittsburgh city, PA	-8.9
52	69	Cincinnati city, OH	-9.1
57	70	Buffalo city, NY	-9.9
5	71	Philadelphia city, PA	-10.6
73	72	Norfolk city, VA	-13.5
16	73	Baltimore city, MD	-14.0
24	74	Washington city, DC	-14.5
51	75	St. Louis city, MO	-15.8

Percent White, 1990

Population Rank	White Rank	City	[col 9] Percent White
75	1	Lincoln city, NE	94.5
45	2	Mesa city, AZ	90.1
71	3	Plano city, TX	88.5
48	4	Colorado Springs city, CO	85.9
26	5	Portland city, OR	84.6
69	6	Lexington-Fayette, KY	84.5
42	7	Omaha city, NE	83.9
53	8	Arlington city, TX	82.6
66	9	Aurora city, CO	82.4
64	10	St. Paul city, MN	82.3
50	10	Wichita city, KS	82.3
7	12	Phoenix city, AZ	81.7
63	13	Anchorage city, AK	80.7
35	14	Virginia Beach city, VA	80.5
43	15	Tulsa city, OK	79.3
37	16	Las Vegas city, NV	78.4
47	16	Minneapolis city, MN	78.4
36	18	Albuquerque city, NM	78.2
70	19	St. Petersburg city, FL	78.0
55	20	Toledo city, OH	77.0
17	21	El Paso city, TX	76.9
13	22	Indianapolis consolidated city,IN	76.2
59	23	Corpus Christi city, TX	76.1
22	24	Seattle city, WA	75.3
31	25	Tucson city, AZ	75.2
25	26	Nashville-Davidsn consol. city,TN	74.8
30	26	Oklahoma City, OK	74.8
15	28	Columbus city, OH	74.4
74	29	Bakersfield city, CA	72.7
14	29	Jacksonville consolidated city,FL	72.7
8	31	San Antonio city, TX	72.2
29	32	Denver city, CO	72.1
49	32	Pittsburgh city, PA	72.1
56	34	Anaheim city, CA	71.4
58	35	Tampa city, FL	70.9
60	36	Riverside city, CA	70.8
19	37	Austin city, TX	70.6
65	38	Louisville city, KY	69.2
62	38	Raleigh city, NC	69.2
54	40	Santa Ana city, CA	68.0
6	41	San Diego city, CA	67.1
33	42	Kansas City, MO	66.8
23	43	Charlotte city, NC	65.6
44	43	Miami city, FL	65.6
57	45	Buffalo city, NY	64.7
27	46	Fort Worth city, TX	63.8
20	47	Milwaukee city, WI	63.4
21	48	Boston city, MA	62.8
11	48	San Jose city, CA	62.8
52	50	Cincinnati city, OH	60.5
38	51	Sacramento city, CA	60.1
39	52	Fresno city, CA	59.2
34	53	Long Beach city, CA	58.4
68	54	Stockton city, CA	57.5
73	55	Norfolk city, VA	56.7
9	56	Dallas city, TX	55.3
12	57	San Francisco city, CA	53.6
5	58	Philadelphia city, PA	53.5
2	59	Los Angeles city, CA	52.8
4	60	Houston city, TX	52.7
1	61	New York City, NY	52.3
51	62	St. Louis city, MO	50.9
28	63	Cleveland city, OH	49.5
72	64	Jersey City, NJ	48.2
3	65	Chicago city, IL	45.4
18	66	Memphis city, TN	44.0
16	67	Baltimore city, MD	39.1
67	68	Birmingham city, AL	36.0
32	69	New Orleans city, LA	34.9
46	70	Oakland city, CA	32.5
40	71	Atlanta city, GA	31.0
24	72	Washington city, DC	29.6
61	73	Newark city, NJ	28.6
41	74	Honolulu CDP, HI	26.7
10	75	Detroit city, MI	21.6

Percent Black, 1990

Population Rank	Black Rank	City	[col 10] Percent Black
10	1	Detroit city, MI	75.7
40	2	Atlanta city, GA	67.1
24	3	Washington city, DC	65.8
67	4	Birmingham city, AL	63.3
32	5	New Orleans city, LA	61.9
16	6	Baltimore city, MD	59.2
61	7	Newark city, NJ	58.5
18	8	Memphis city, TN	54.8
51	9	St. Louis city, MO	47.5
28	10	Cleveland city, OH	46.6
46	11	Oakland city, CA	43.9
5	12	Philadelphia city, PA	39.9
13	13	Chicago city, IL	39.1
73	13	Norfolk city, VA	39.1
52	15	Cincinnati city, OH	37.9
23	16	Charlotte city, NC	31.8
57	17	Buffalo city, NY	30.7
20	18	Milwaukee city, WI	30.5
72	19	Jersey City, NJ	29.7
65	19	Louisville city, KY	29.7
33	21	Kansas City, MO	29.5
9	22	Dallas city, TX	29.5
1	23	New York City, NY	28.7
4	24	Houston city, TX	28.1
62	25	Raleigh city, NC	27.6
44	26	Miami city, FL	27.4
49	27	Pittsburgh city, PA	25.8
21	28	Boston city, MA	25.6
58	29	Tampa city, FL	25.0
14	30	Jacksonville consolidated city,FL	24.4
25	31	Nashville-Davidsn consol. city,TN	23.4
15	32	Columbus city, OH	22.6
13	33	Indianapolis consolidated city,IN	22.3
27	34	Fort Worth city, TX	22.0
55	35	Toledo city, OH	19.7
70	36	St. Petersburg city, FL	19.6
30	37	Oklahoma City, OK	16.0
38	38	Sacramento city, CA	15.3
2	39	Los Angeles city, CA	14.0
35	40	Virginia Beach city, VA	13.9
34	41	Long Beach city, CA	13.7
43	42	Tulsa city, OK	13.6
69	43	Lexington-Fayette, KY	13.4
42	44	Omaha city, NE	13.1
47	45	Minneapolis city, MN	13.0
29	46	Denver city, CO	12.8
19	47	Austin city, TX	12.4
66	48	Aurora city, CO	11.4
37	48	Las Vegas city, NV	11.4
50	50	Wichita city, KS	11.3
12	51	San Francisco city, CA	10.9
22	52	Seattle city, WA	10.1
68	53	Stockton city, CA	9.6
74	54	Bakersfield city, CA	9.4
6	54	San Diego city, CA	9.4
53	56	Arlington city, TX	8.4
39	57	Fresno city, CA	8.3
26	58	Portland city, OR	7.7
60	59	Riverside city, CA	7.4
64	60	St. Paul city, MN	7.4
48	60	Colorado Springs city, CO	7.0
8	61	San Antonio city, TX	7.0
63	63	Anchorage city, AK	6.4
7	64	Phoenix city, AZ	5.2
59	65	Corpus Christi city, TX	4.8
11	66	San Jose city, CA	4.7
31	67	Tucson city, AZ	4.3
71	68	Plano city, TX	4.1
17	69	El Paso city, TX	3.4
36	70	Albuquerque city, NM	3.0
54	71	Santa Ana city, CA	2.6
56	72	Anaheim city, CA	2.5
75	73	Lincoln city, NE	2.4
45	74	Mesa city, AZ	1.9
41	75	Honolulu CDP, HI	1.3

Note: Column numbers refer to Table D. Cities.

TABLE 5—75 Largest Cities by 1999 Population
Selected Rankings

Percent Hispanic, 1990				Percent Foreign Born, 1990				Percent Age 65 and Over, 1990			
Population Rank	Hispanic Rank	City	[col 14] Percent Hispanic	Population Rank	Foreign Born Rank	City	[col 15] Percent Foreign Born	Population Rank	Age 65 and Over Rank	City	[cols 23 & 24] Percent Age 65 and Over
17	1	El Paso city, TX	69.0	44	1	Miami city, FL	59.7	70	1	St. Petersburg city, FL	22.2
54	2	Santa Ana city, CA	65.2	54	2	Santa Ana city, CA	50.9	49	2	Pittsburgh city, PA	18.0
44	3	Miami city, FL	62.5	2	3	Los Angeles city, CA	38.4	44	3	Miami city, FL	16.8
8	4	San Antonio city, TX	55.6	12	4	San Francisco city, CA	34.0	51	4	St. Louis city, MO	16.7
59	5	Corpus Christi city, TX	50.4	56	5	Anaheim city, CA	28.4	65	5	Louisville city, KY	16.6
2	6	Los Angeles city, CA	39.9	1	5	New York City, NY	28.4	41	6	Honolulu CDP, HI	15.9
36	7	Albuquerque city, NM	34.5	11	7	San Jose city, CA	26.5	5	7	Philadelphia city, PA	15.2
56	8	Anaheim city, CA	31.4	72	8	Jersey City, NJ	24.6	22	7	Seattle city, WA	15.2
39	9	Fresno city, CA	29.9	34	9	Long Beach city, CA	24.3	57	9	Buffalo city, NY	14.9
31	10	Tucson city, AZ	29.3	17	10	El Paso city, TX	23.4	67	10	Birmingham city, AL	14.8
4	11	Houston city, TX	27.6	68	11	Stockton city, CA	22.6	58	11	Tampa city, FL	14.6
11	12	San Jose city, CA	26.6	41	12	Honolulu CDP, HI	21.4	12	11	San Francisco city, CA	14.6
61	13	Newark city, NJ	26.1	6	13	San Diego city, CA	20.9	26	13	Portland city, OR	14.5
60	14	Riverside city, CA	26.0	21	14	Boston city, MA	20.0	28	14	Cleveland city, OH	14.0
68	15	Stockton city, CA	25.0	46	15	Oakland city, CA	19.8	52	15	Cincinnati city, OH	13.9
1	16	New York City, NY	24.4	61	16	Newark city, NJ	18.7	64	16	St. Paul city, MN	13.8
72	17	Jersey City, NJ	24.2	4	17	Houston city, TX	17.8	29	17	Denver city, CO	13.7
34	18	Long Beach city, CA	23.6	39	18	Fresno city, CA	17.1	16	18	Baltimore city, MD	13.6
19	19	Austin city, TX	23.0	3	19	Chicago city, IL	16.9	55	18	Toledo city, OH	13.6
29	19	Denver city, CO	23.0	60	20	Riverside city, CA	15.5	33	20	Kansas City, MO	13.0
9	21	Dallas city, TX	20.9	38	21	Sacramento city, CA	13.7	32	20	New Orleans city, LA	13.0
6	22	San Diego city, CA	20.7	22	22	Seattle city, WA	13.1	1	20	New York City, NY	13.0
74	23	Bakersfield city, CA	20.5	9	23	Dallas city, TX	12.5	47	23	Minneapolis city, MN	12.9
7	24	Phoenix city, AZ	20.0	31	24	Tucson city, AZ	10.7	42	24	Omaha city, NE	12.8
3	25	Chicago city, IL	19.6	37	25	Las Vegas city, NV	10.3	24	24	Washington city, DC	12.8
27	26	Fort Worth city, TX	19.5	24	26	Washington city, DC	9.7	43	26	Tulsa city, OK	12.7
38	27	Sacramento city, CA	16.2	8	27	San Antonio city, TX	9.4	31	27	Tucson city, AZ	12.6
58	28	Tampa city, FL	15.0	27	28	Fort Worth city, TX	9.0	20	28	Milwaukee city, WI	12.4
46	29	Oakland city, CA	13.9	7	29	Phoenix city, AZ	8.6	45	28	Mesa city, AZ	12.4
12	29	San Francisco city, CA	13.9	19	30	Austin city, TX	8.5	50	28	Wichita city, KS	12.4
37	31	Las Vegas city, NV	12.5	74	31	Bakersfield city, CA	8.0	10	31	Detroit city, MI	12.2
45	32	Mesa city, AZ	10.9	58	31	Tampa city, FL	8.0	18	31	Memphis city, TN	12.2
21	33	Boston city, MA	10.8	26	33	Portland city, OR	7.7	46	31	Oakland city, CA	12.2
48	34	Colorado Springs city, CO	9.1	53	34	Arlington city, TX	7.6	38	34	Sacramento city, CA	12.0
53	35	Arlington city, TX	8.9	71	35	Plano city, TX	7.5	3	35	Chicago city, IL	11.9
66	36	Aurora city, CO	6.6	29	36	Denver city, CO	7.4	30	36	Oklahoma City, OK	11.8
20	37	Milwaukee city, WI	6.3	64	37	St. Paul city, MN	7.3	13	37	Indianapolis consolidated city,IN	11.6
71	38	Plano city, TX	6.2	70	38	St. Petersburg city, FL	7.2	25	37	Nashville-Davidsn consol. city,TN	11.6
5	39	Philadelphia city, PA	5.6	5	39	Philadelphia city, PA	6.6	21	39	Boston city, MA	11.5
24	40	Washington city, DC	5.4	47	40	Minneapolis city, MN	6.1	40	40	Atlanta city, GA	11.3
30	41	Oklahoma City, OK	5.0	63	41	Anchorage city, AK	5.9	27	41	Fort Worth city, TX	11.2
50	41	Wichita city, KS	5.0	66	42	Aurora city, CO	5.6	36	42	Albuquerque city, NM	11.1
57	43	Buffalo city, NY	4.9	36	43	Albuquerque city, NM	5.5	75	43	Lincoln city, NE	11.0
28	44	Cleveland city, OH	4.6	59	44	Corpus Christi city, TX	5.3	72	44	Jersey City, NJ	10.9
41	44	Honolulu CDP, HI	4.6	35	45	Virginia Beach city, VA	5.2	34	45	Long Beach city, CA	10.8
64	46	St. Paul city, MN	4.2	62	46	Raleigh city, NC	5.0	14	46	Jacksonville consolidated city,FL	10.7
63	47	Anchorage city, AK	4.1	45	47	Mesa city, AZ	4.9	68	47	Stockton city, CA	10.4
55	48	Toledo city, OH	4.0	48	48	Colorado Springs city, CO	4.7	73	47	Norfolk city, VA	10.4
33	49	Kansas City, MO	3.9	20	48	Milwaukee city, WI	4.7	8	47	San Antonio city, TX	10.4
22	50	Seattle city, WA	3.6	49	50	Pittsburgh city, PA	4.6	37	50	Las Vegas city, NV	10.3
32	51	New Orleans city, LA	3.5	57	51	Buffalo city, NY	4.5	6	51	San Diego city, CA	10.1
26	52	Portland city, OR	3.2	32	52	New Orleans city, LA	4.2	59	52	Corpus Christi city, TX	10.0
42	53	Omaha city, NE	3.1	30	52	Oklahoma City, OK	4.2	39	52	Fresno city, CA	10.0
35	53	Virginia Beach city, VA	3.1	28	54	Cleveland city, OH	4.1	69	54	Lexington-Fayette, KY	9.9
73	55	Norfolk city, VA	2.9	50	55	Wichita city, KS	4.0	2	54	Los Angeles city, CA	9.9
10	56	Detroit city, MI	2.8	23	56	Charlotte city, NC	3.8	23	56	Charlotte city, NC	9.7
70	57	St. Petersburg city, FL	2.6	15	57	Columbus city, OH	3.7	7	56	Phoenix city, AZ	9.7
43	57	Tulsa city, OK	2.6	73	57	Norfolk city, VA	3.7	9	58	Dallas city, TX	9.6
14	59	Jacksonville consolidated city,FL	2.4	14	59	Jacksonville consolidated city,FL	3.5	61	59	Newark city, NJ	9.3
47	60	Minneapolis city, MN	2.1	40	60	Atlanta city, GA	3.4	48	60	Colorado Springs city, CO	9.2
75	61	Lincoln city, NE	2.0	10	60	Detroit city, MI	3.4	74	61	Bakersfield city, CA	9.1
40	62	Atlanta city, GA	1.9	16	62	Baltimore city, MD	3.2	15	61	Columbus city, OH	9.1
23	63	Charlotte city, NC	1.4	43	63	Tulsa city, OK	3.0	60	63	Riverside city, CA	9.0
62	63	Raleigh city, NC	1.4	69	64	Lexington-Fayette, KY	2.9	62	64	Raleigh city, NC	8.8
51	65	St. Louis city, MO	1.3	52	65	Cincinnati city, OH	2.8	17	65	El Paso city, TX	8.7
15	66	Columbus city, OH	1.1	33	65	Kansas City, MO	2.8	4	66	Houston city, TX	8.2
69	66	Lexington-Fayette, KY	1.1	42	65	Omaha city, NE	2.8	56	67	Anaheim city, CA	8.1
16	68	Baltimore city, MD	1.0	55	65	Toledo city, OH	2.8	19	68	Austin city, TX	7.3
13	68	Indianapolis consolidated city,IN	1.0	75	69	Lincoln city, NE	2.7	11	69	San Jose city, CA	7.1
49	70	Pittsburgh city, PA	0.9	25	70	Nashville-Davidsn consol. city,TN	2.5	66	70	Aurora city, CO	6.6
25	71	Nashville-Davidsn consol. city,TN	0.8	51	70	St. Louis city, MO	2.5	35	71	Virginia Beach city, VA	5.9
52	72	Cincinnati city, OH	0.7	13	72	Indianapolis consolidated city,IN	1.9	54	72	Santa Ana city, CA	5.5
65	72	Louisville city, KY	0.7	65	73	Louisville city, KY	1.5	53	73	Arlington city, TX	4.9
18	72	Memphis city, TN	0.7	18	74	Memphis city, TN	1.4	63	74	Anchorage city, AK	3.6
67	75	Birmingham city, AL	0.4	67	75	Birmingham city, AL	1.2	71	74	Plano city, TX	3.6

Note: Column numbers refer to Table D. Cities.

TABLE 5—75 Largest Cities by 1999 Population
Selected Rankings

Percent Under 18 Years Old, 1990				Percent of Female-Headed Family Households, 1990				Percent of Households Composed of One Person, 1990			
Population Rank	Under 18 Rank	City	[cols 16 & 17] Percent Under 18 Years Old	Population Rank	Female House-holder Rank	City	[col 29] % with Female House-holder	Population Rank	One Person House-hold Rank	City	[col 30] % of All House-holds
17	1	El Paso city, TX	31.8	10	1	Detroit city, MI	30.3	24	1	Washington city, DC	41.5
39	2	Fresno city, CA	31.7	61	2	Newark city, NJ	28.6	29	2	Denver city, CO	40.4
68	2	Stockton city, CA	31.7	16	3	Baltimore city, MD	24.6	22	3	Seattle city, WA	39.8
74	4	Bakersfield city, CA	30.8	32	4	New Orleans city, LA	24.1	52	4	Cincinnati city, OH	39.5
54	5	Santa Ana city, CA	30.4	40	5	Atlanta city, GA	23.4	12	5	San Francisco city, CA	39.3
71	6	Plano city, TX	30.2	28	6	Cleveland city, OH	22.7	51	6	St. Louis city, MO	39.2
59	7	Corpus Christi city, TX	30.1	18	7	Memphis city, TN	21.9	47	7	Minneapolis city, MN	38.5
10	8	Detroit city, MI	29.4	67	8	Birmingham city, AL	21.7	49	8	Pittsburgh city, PA	36.2
63	9	Anchorage city, AK	29.3	51	9	St. Louis city, MO	20.5	57	9	Buffalo city, NY	35.6
8	10	San Antonio city, TX	29.1	72	10	Jersey City, NJ	20.4	21	10	Boston city, MA	35.5
60	11	Riverside city, CA	28.8	5	11	Philadelphia city, PA	20.3	70	11	St. Petersburg city, FL	35.1
61	12	Newark city, NJ	28.6	57	12	Buffalo city, NY	20.2	40	12	Atlanta city, GA	35.0
45	12	Mesa city, AZ	28.6	20	13	Milwaukee city, WI	19.8	65	12	Louisville city, KY	35.0
35	14	Virginia Beach city, VA	27.9	3	14	Chicago city, IL	19.6	26	14	Portland city, OR	34.9
32	15	New Orleans city, LA	27.5	24	15	Washington city, DC	19.5	64	15	St. Paul city, MN	34.7
66	16	Aurora city, CO	27.4	44	16	Miami city, FL	18.6	9	16	Dallas city, TX	34.2
20	16	Milwaukee city, WI	27.4	46	17	Oakland city, CA	18.5	19	17	Austin city, TX	34.1
7	18	Phoenix city, AZ	27.1	65	18	Louisville city, KY	18.3	28	18	Cleveland city, OH	33.5
53	19	Arlington city, TX	26.9	52	19	Cincinnati city, OH	18.2	46	19	Oakland city, CA	33.2
28	19	Cleveland city, OH	26.9	1	20	New York City, NY	18.0	1	20	New York City, NY	32.9
18	19	Memphis city, TN	26.9	49	21	Pittsburgh city, PA	17.2	43	21	Tulsa city, OK	32.7
48	22	Colorado Springs city, CO	26.8	21	22	Boston city, MA	16.8	33	22	Kansas City, MO	32.5
4	23	Houston city, TX	26.7	17	23	El Paso city, TX	16.4	58	23	Tampa city, FL	32.3
11	23	San Jose city, CA	26.7	39	24	Fresno city, CA	16.2	32	24	New Orleans city, LA	32.2
50	25	Wichita city, KS	26.6	73	25	Norfolk city, VA	16.1	62	25	Raleigh city, NC	32.2
27	26	Fort Worth city, TX	26.5	8	26	San Antonio city, TX	15.7	3	26	Chicago city, IL	32.1
38	27	Sacramento city, CA	26.1	55	26	Toledo city, OH	15.7	67	27	Birmingham city, AL	31.9
55	28	Toledo city, OH	26.1	68	28	Stockton city, CA	15.5	5	28	Philadelphia city, PA	31.6
3	29	Chicago city, IL	26.0	58	28	Tampa city, FL	15.5	15	29	Columbus city, OH	31.3
56	30	Anaheim city, CA	25.9	33	30	Kansas City, MO	15.1	31	29	Tucson city, AZ	31.3
14	30	Jacksonville consolidated city,FL	25.9	4	31	Houston city, TX	14.6	4	31	Houston city, TX	31.0
30	30	Oklahoma City, OK	25.9	38	32	Sacramento city, CA	14.3	38	32	Sacramento city, CA	30.9
13	33	Indianapolis consolidated city,IN	25.6	15	33	Columbus city, OH	14.2	34	33	Long Beach city, CA	30.8
42	34	Omaha city, NE	25.5	74	34	Bakersfield city, CA	14.0	42	34	Omaha city, NE	30.6
67	35	Birmingham city, AL	25.4	23	34	Charlotte city, NC	14.0	16	35	Baltimore city, MD	30.5
34	35	Long Beach city, CA	25.4	25	34	Nashville-Davidsn consol. city,TN	14.0	20	35	Milwaukee city, WI	30.5
51	37	St. Louis city, MO	25.3	9	37	Dallas city, TX	13.9	25	37	Nashville-Davidsn consol. city,TN	30.1
52	38	Cincinnati city, OH	25.1	59	38	Corpus Christi city, TX	13.6	30	38	Oklahoma City, OK	30.0
36	39	Albuquerque city, NM	25.0	13	39	Indianapolis consolidated city,IN	13.6	50	38	Wichita city, KS	30.0
9	39	Dallas city, TX	25.0	2	39	Los Angeles city, CA	13.6	10	40	Detroit city, MI	29.8
46	41	Oakland city, CA	24.9	14	41	Jacksonville consolidated city,FL	13.4	55	41	Toledo city, OH	29.7
33	42	Kansas City, MO	24.8	27	42	Fort Worth city, TX	13.3	13	42	Indianapolis consolidated city,IN	29.1
37	42	Las Vegas city, NV	24.8	42	42	Omaha city, NE	13.3	69	42	Lexington-Fayette, KY	29.1
2	44	Los Angeles city, CA	24.7	34	44	Long Beach city, CA	13.0	27	44	Fort Worth city, TX	29.0
64	45	St. Paul city, MN	24.5	64	44	St. Paul city, MN	13.0	44	45	Miami city, FL	28.9
72	46	Jersey City, NJ	24.4	47	46	Minneapolis city, MN	12.7	75	46	Lincoln city, NE	28.8
16	46	Baltimore city, MD	24.4	30	47	Oklahoma City, OK	12.6	72	47	Jersey City, NJ	28.7
31	46	Tucson city, AZ	24.4	60	48	Riverside city, CA	12.5	2	48	Los Angeles city, CA	28.5
57	49	Buffalo city, NY	24.3	70	49	St. Petersburg city, FL	12.4	18	49	Memphis city, TN	28.3
23	49	Charlotte city, NC	24.3	31	49	Tucson city, AZ	12.4	36	50	Albuquerque city, NM	28.2
43	49	Tulsa city, OK	24.3	69	51	Lexington-Fayette, KY	12.2	66	51	Aurora city, CO	28.1
40	52	Atlanta city, GA	24.1	36	52	Albuquerque city, NM	12.1	23	52	Charlotte city, NC	28.0
5	53	Philadelphia city, PA	23.9	37	53	Las Vegas city, NV	12.0	61	53	Newark city, NJ	27.5
15	54	Columbus city, OH	23.7	11	54	San Jose city, CA	11.9	41	54	Honolulu CDP, HI	27.4
65	55	Louisville city, KY	23.5	66	55	Aurora city, CO	11.8	73	55	Norfolk city, VA	26.8
75	56	Lincoln city, NE	23.4	7	55	Phoenix city, AZ	11.8	48	56	Colorado Springs city, CO	26.7
6	57	San Diego city, CA	23.2	54	55	Santa Ana city, CA	11.8	6	57	San Diego city, CA	26.3
19	58	Austin city, TX	23.1	43	55	Tulsa city, OK	11.8	37	58	Las Vegas city, NV	26.2
44	59	Miami city, FL	23.0	56	59	Anaheim city, CA	11.6	7	59	Phoenix city, AZ	26.1
1	59	New York City, NY	23.0	29	60	Denver city, CO	11.5	14	60	Jacksonville consolidated city,FL	25.3
73	59	Norfolk city, VA	23.0	62	61	Raleigh city, NC	11.3	8	61	San Antonio city, TX	25.0
58	62	Tampa city, FL	22.9	6	62	San Diego city, CA	11.2	53	62	Arlington city, TX	24.8
25	63	Nashville-Davidsn consol. city,TN	22.8	50	63	Wichita city, KS	11.1	39	63	Fresno city, CA	24.1
69	64	Lexington-Fayette, KY	22.3	19	64	Austin city, TX	11.0	45	64	Mesa city, AZ	24.0
26	65	Portland city, OR	22.0	41	64	Honolulu CDP, HI	11.0	68	65	Stockton city, CA	23.4
29	66	Denver city, CO	21.9	26	64	Portland city, OR	11.0	74	66	Bakersfield city, CA	23.0
47	67	Minneapolis city, MN	20.6	63	67	Anchorage city, AK	10.1	63	67	Anchorage city, AK	22.9
49	68	Pittsburgh city, PA	19.9	48	67	Colorado Springs city, CO	10.1	59	68	Corpus Christi city, TX	22.5
70	69	St. Petersburg city, FL	19.7	12	69	San Francisco city, CA	9.9	60	69	Riverside city, CA	20.6
62	70	Raleigh city, NC	19.6	35	70	Virginia Beach city, VA	9.5	56	70	Anaheim city, CA	19.9
24	71	Washington city, DC	19.2	53	71	Arlington city, TX	9.4	11	71	San Jose city, CA	18.4
41	72	Honolulu CDP, HI	19.1	45	72	Mesa city, AZ	9.3	17	72	El Paso city, TX	17.9
21	73	Boston city, MA	19.0	75	73	Lincoln city, NE	9.1	35	73	Virginia Beach city, VA	17.1
22	74	Seattle city, WA	16.3	22	74	Seattle city, WA	9.0	54	74	Santa Ana city, CA	16.6
12	75	San Francisco city, CA	16.2	71	75	Plano city, TX	7.6	71	75	Plano city, TX	15.7

Note: Column numbers refer to Table D. Cities.

TABLE 5—75 Largest Cities by 1999 Population
Selected Rankings

Percent College Graduates (16+ Years of Education), 1990				Median Household Income, 1989				Percent of Persons Below the Poverty Level, 1989			
Population Rank	% College Graduate Rank	City	[col 42] Percent College Grads	Population Rank	Median Income Rank	City	[col 44] Median Income 1989 (dollars)	Population Rank	Poverty Rate Rank	City	[col 47] Poverty Rate for Persons 1989
71	1	Plano city, TX	46.6	71	1	Plano city, TX	53 905	10	1	Detroit city, MI	32.4
62	2	Raleigh city, NC	40.6	11	2	San Jose city, CA	46 206	32	2	New Orleans city, LA	31.6
22	3	Seattle city, WA	37.9	63	3	Anchorage city, AK	43 946	44	3	Miami city, FL	31.2
12	4	San Francisco city, CA	35.0	56	4	Anaheim city, CA	39 620	28	4	Cleveland city, OH	28.7
19	5	Austin city, TX	34.4	41	5	Honolulu CDP, HI	37 190	40	5	Atlanta city, GA	27.3
24	6	Washington city, DC	33.3	35	6	Virginia Beach city, VA	36 271	61	6	Newark city, NJ	26.3
69	7	Lexington-Fayette, KY	30.6	54	7	Santa Ana city, CA	35 162	57	7	Buffalo city, NY	25.6
47	8	Minneapolis city, MN	30.3	53	8	Arlington city, TX	35 048	17	8	El Paso city, TX	25.3
53	9	Arlington city, TX	30.0	60	9	Riverside city, CA	34 801	67	9	Birmingham city, AL	24.8
21	10	Boston city, MA	30.0	6	10	San Diego city, CA	33 686	51	10	St. Louis city, MO	24.6
6	11	San Diego city, CA	29.8	12	11	San Francisco city, CA	33 414	52	11	Cincinnati city, OH	24.3
29	12	Denver city, CO	29.0	66	12	Aurora city, CO	33 214	39	12	Fresno city, CA	24.0
75	13	Lincoln city, NE	28.5	62	13	Raleigh city, NC	32 451	18	13	Memphis city, TN	23.0
36	14	Albuquerque city, NM	28.4	74	14	Bakersfield city, CA	32 154	65	14	Louisville city, KY	22.6
23	15	Charlotte city, NC	28.4	34	15	Long Beach city, CA	31 938	8	14	San Antonio city, TX	22.6
41	16	Honolulu CDP, HI	27.7	23	16	Charlotte city, NC	31 873	20	16	Milwaukee city, WI	22.2
48	17	Colorado Springs city, CO	27.5	2	17	Los Angeles city, CA	30 925	16	17	Baltimore city, MD	21.9
46	18	Oakland city, CA	27.2	24	18	Washington city, DC	30 727	3	18	Chicago city, IL	21.6
9	19	Dallas city, TX	27.1	37	19	Las Vegas city, NV	30 590	49	19	Pittsburgh city, PA	21.4
63	20	Anchorage city, AK	26.9	45	20	Mesa city, AZ	30 273	68	19	Stockton city, CA	21.4
40	21	Atlanta city, GA	26.6	1	21	New York City, NY	29 823	4	21	Houston city, TX	20.7
64	22	St. Paul city, MN	26.5	22	22	Seattle city, WA	29 353	5	22	Philadelphia city, PA	20.3
66	23	Aurora city, CO	26.3	7	23	Phoenix city, AZ	29 291	31	23	Tucson city, AZ	20.2
26	24	Portland city, OR	25.9	21	24	Boston city, MA	29 180	59	24	Corpus Christi city, TX	20.0
43	25	Tulsa city, OK	25.8	13	25	Indianapolis consolidated city, IN	29 083	58	25	Tampa city, FL	19.4
35	26	Virginia Beach city, VA	25.5	72	26	Jersey City, NJ	29 054	1	26	New York City, NY	19.3
11	27	San Jose city, CA	25.3	48	27	Colorado Springs city, CO	28 928	73	26	Norfolk city, VA	19.3
4	28	Houston city, TX	25.1	14	28	Jacksonville consolidated city, FL	28 513	55	28	Toledo city, OH	19.1
15	29	Columbus city, OH	24.6	25	29	Nashville-Davidsn consol. city, TN	28 377	72	29	Jersey City, NJ	18.9
25	30	Nashville-Davidsn consol. city, TN	24.4	38	30	Sacramento city, CA	28 183	2	29	Los Angeles city, CA	18.9
38	31	Sacramento city, CA	23.5	69	31	Lexington-Fayette, KY	28 056	46	31	Oakland city, CA	18.8
34	32	Long Beach city, CA	23.2	75	31	Lincoln city, NE	28 056	21	32	Boston city, MA	18.7
42	33	Omaha city, NE	23.1	50	33	Wichita city, KS	28 024	47	33	Minneapolis city, MN	18.5
2	34	Los Angeles city, CA	23.0	36	34	Albuquerque city, NM	27 555	54	34	Santa Ana city, CA	18.1
1	35	New York City, NY	23.0	9	35	Dallas city, TX	27 489	9	35	Dallas city, TX	18.0
50	36	Wichita city, KS	22.7	46	36	Oakland city, CA	27 095	19	36	Austin city, TX	17.9
32	37	New Orleans city, LA	22.4	42	37	Omaha city, NE	26 927	27	37	Fort Worth city, TX	17.4
52	38	Cincinnati city, OH	22.2	68	38	Stockton city, CA	26 876	15	38	Columbus city, OH	17.2
33	39	Kansas City, MO	22.0	33	39	Kansas City, MO	26 713	38	38	Sacramento city, CA	17.2
13	40	Indianapolis consolidated city, IN	21.9	15	40	Columbus city, OH	26 651	29	40	Denver city, CO	17.1
30	41	Oklahoma City, OK	21.6	27	41	Fort Worth city, TX	26 547	24	41	Washington city, DC	16.9
27	42	Fort Worth city, TX	21.5	64	42	St. Paul city, MN	26 498	34	42	Long Beach city, CA	16.8
72	43	Jersey City, NJ	21.4	3	43	Chicago city, IL	26 301	64	43	St. Paul city, MN	16.7
45	44	Mesa city, AZ	21.0	4	44	Houston city, TX	26 261	30	44	Oklahoma City, OK	15.9
31	45	Tucson city, AZ	20.7	59	45	Corpus Christi city, TX	25 773	33	45	Kansas City, MO	15.3
49	46	Pittsburgh city, PA	20.1	30	46	Oklahoma City, OK	25 741	74	46	Bakersfield city, CA	15.0
7	47	Phoenix city, AZ	19.9	43	47	Tulsa city, OK	25 708	43	46	Tulsa city, OK	15.0
74	48	Bakersfield city, CA	19.6	26	48	Portland city, OR	25 592	26	48	Portland city, OR	14.5
3	49	Chicago city, IL	19.5	19	49	Austin city, TX	25 414	7	49	Phoenix city, AZ	14.2
60	50	Riverside city, CA	19.3	47	50	Minneapolis city, MN	25 324	69	50	Lexington-Fayette, KY	14.1
39	51	Fresno city, CA	19.1	29	51	Denver city, CO	25 106	36	51	Albuquerque city, NM	14.0
56	52	Anaheim city, CA	18.8	39	52	Fresno city, CA	24 923	70	52	St. Petersburg city, FL	13.6
58	53	Tampa city, FL	18.7	55	53	Toledo city, OH	24 819	6	53	San Diego city, CA	13.4
70	54	St. Petersburg city, FL	18.6	5	54	Philadelphia city, PA	24 603	25	54	Nashville-Davidsn consol. city, TN	13.0
14	55	Jacksonville consolidated city, FL	18.4	16	55	Baltimore city, MD	24 045	14	55	Jacksonville consolidated city, FL	12.8
59	56	Corpus Christi city, TX	17.8	20	56	Milwaukee city, WI	23 627	12	56	San Francisco city, CA	12.7
8	57	San Antonio city, TX	17.8	8	57	San Antonio city, TX	23 584	42	57	Omaha city, NE	12.6
18	58	Memphis city, TN	17.5	70	58	St. Petersburg city, FL	23 577	13	58	Indianapolis consolidated city, IN	12.5
65	59	Louisville city, KY	17.2	73	59	Norfolk city, VA	23 563	50	58	Wichita city, KS	12.5
73	60	Norfolk city, VA	16.8	17	60	El Paso city, TX	23 460	22	60	Seattle city, WA	12.4
67	61	Birmingham city, AL	16.2	58	61	Tampa city, FL	22 772	60	61	Riverside city, CA	11.9
17	62	El Paso city, TX	16.2	18	62	Memphis city, TN	22 674	62	62	Raleigh city, NC	11.8
57	63	Buffalo city, NY	16.0	40	63	Atlanta city, GA	22 275	37	63	Las Vegas city, NV	11.5
16	64	Baltimore city, MD	15.5	31	64	Tucson city, AZ	21 748	75	64	Lincoln city, NE	11.3
51	65	St. Louis city, MO	15.3	61	65	Newark city, NJ	21 650	48	65	Colorado Springs city, CO	10.9
5	66	Philadelphia city, PA	15.2	52	66	Cincinnati city, OH	21 006	23	66	Charlotte city, NC	10.8
68	67	Stockton city, CA	15.0	49	67	Pittsburgh city, PA	20 747	56	67	Anaheim city, CA	10.6
20	68	Milwaukee city, WI	14.8	65	68	Louisville city, KY	20 141	45	68	Mesa city, AZ	9.5
55	69	Toledo city, OH	14.1	51	69	St. Louis city, MO	19 458	11	69	San Jose city, CA	9.3
37	70	Las Vegas city, NV	13.4	67	70	Birmingham city, AL	19 193	41	70	Honolulu CDP, HI	8.4
44	71	Miami city, FL	12.8	10	71	Detroit city, MI	18 742	53	71	Arlington city, TX	8.2
54	72	Santa Ana city, CA	10.6	57	72	Buffalo city, NY	18 482	66	72	Aurora city, CO	7.4
10	73	Detroit city, MI	9.6	32	73	New Orleans city, LA	18 477	63	73	Anchorage city, AK	7.1
61	74	Newark city, NJ	8.5	28	74	Cleveland city, OH	17 822	35	74	Virginia Beach city, VA	5.9
28	75	Cleveland city, OH	8.1	44	75	Miami city, FL	16 925	71	75	Plano city, TX	3.3

Note: Column numbers refer to Table D. Cities.

TABLE 5—75 Largest Cities by 1999 Population
Selected Rankings

Median Value of Owner-Occupied Housing Units, 1990				Median Gross Rent of Renter-Occupied Housing Units, 1990				Median Gross Rent as a Percent of Median Household Income for Renters, 1990			
Popu-lation Rank	Median Value Rank	City	[col 55] Median Value in 1990 (dollars)	Popu-lation Rank	Median Rent Rank	City	[col 58] Median Rent in 1990 (dollars)	Popu-lation Rank	Rent/ Income Rank	City	[col 59] Rent/ Income Ratio
41	1	Honolulu CDP, HI	353 900	11	1	San Jose city, CA	755	10	1	Detroit city, MI	35.1
12	2	San Francisco city, CA	298 900	54	2	Santa Ana city, CA	736	44	2	Miami city, FL	32.7
11	3	San Jose city, CA	259 100	56	3	Anaheim city, CA	712	57	3	Buffalo city, NY	31.8
2	4	Los Angeles city, CA	244 500	12	4	San Francisco city, CA	653	32	4	New Orleans city, LA	31.2
34	5	Long Beach city, CA	222 900	21	5	Boston city, MA	625	54	4	Santa Ana city, CA	31.2
56	6	Anaheim city, CA	218 700	41	6	Honolulu CDP, HI	623	46	6	Oakland city, CA	30.7
1	7	New York City, NY	189 600	34	7	Long Beach city, CA	605	2	7	Los Angeles city, CA	30.4
6	8	San Diego city, CA	189 400	6	8	San Diego city, CA	602	39	8	Fresno city, CA	30.1
54	9	Santa Ana city, CA	185 400	2	9	Los Angeles city, CA	600	34	9	Long Beach city, CA	30.0
46	10	Oakland city, CA	177 400	71	10	Plano city, TX	586	5	10	Philadelphia city, PA	29.8
21	11	Boston city, MA	161 400	35	11	Virginia Beach city, VA	577	6	10	San Diego city, CA	29.8
22	12	Seattle city, WA	137 900	60	12	Riverside city, CA	575	38	12	Sacramento city, CA	29.7
60	13	Riverside city, CA	134 800	63	13	Anchorage city, AK	564	60	13	Riverside city, CA	29.6
72	14	Jersey City, NJ	127 700	46	14	Oakland city, CA	538	31	13	Tucson city, AZ	29.6
24	15	Washington city, DC	123 900	72	15	Jersey City, NJ	527	68	15	Stockton city, CA	29.5
38	16	Sacramento city, CA	115 800	1	16	New York City, NY	496	56	16	Anaheim city, CA	29.3
71	17	Plano city, TX	114 100	38	17	Sacramento city, CA	495	28	16	Cleveland city, OH	29.3
61	18	Newark city, NJ	110 000	37	18	Las Vegas city, NV	490	11	18	San Jose city, CA	28.9
63	19	Anchorage city, AK	109 700	62	19	Raleigh city, NC	479	40	19	Atlanta city, GA	28.7
68	20	Stockton city, CA	107 200	24	19	Washington city, DC	479	49	19	Pittsburgh city, PA	28.7
62	21	Raleigh city, NC	96 600	68	21	Stockton city, CA	476	73	21	Norfolk city, VA	28.5
35	22	Virginia Beach city, VA	96 500	45	22	Mesa city, AZ	470	74	22	Bakersfield city, CA	28.4
74	23	Bakersfield city, CA	91 200	74	23	Bakersfield city, CA	468	21	22	Boston city, MA	28.4
37	24	Las Vegas city, NV	89 200	22	24	Seattle city, WA	463	47	22	Minneapolis city, MN	28.4
45	25	Mesa city, AZ	86 500	23	25	Charlotte city, NC	462	64	22	St. Paul city, MN	28.4
36	26	Albuquerque city, NM	85 900	66	26	Aurora city, CO	455	70	26	St. Petersburg city, FL	28.3
53	27	Arlington city, TX	82 800	5	27	Philadelphia city, PA	452	20	27	Milwaukee city, WI	28.0
48	28	Colorado Springs city, CO	81 900	3	28	Chicago city, IL	445	12	27	San Francisco city, CA	28.0
23	29	Charlotte city, NC	81 300	61	28	Newark city, NJ	445	51	29	St. Louis city, MO	27.9
39	30	Fresno city, CA	80 300	53	30	Arlington city, TX	444	36	30	Albuquerque city, NM	27.3
66	31	Aurora city, CO	80 200	7	31	Phoenix city, AZ	442	19	30	Austin city, TX	27.3
44	32	Miami city, FL	79 200	39	32	Fresno city, CA	441	16	30	Baltimore city, MD	27.3
29	33	Denver city, CO	79 000	73	33	Norfolk city, VA	438	3	30	Chicago city, IL	27.3
9	34	Dallas city, TX	78 800	25	34	Nashville-Davidsn consol. city,TN	433	37	30	Las Vegas city, NV	27.3
3	35	Chicago city, IL	78 700	14	35	Jacksonville consolidated city,FL	431	7	30	Phoenix city, AZ	27.3
7	36	Phoenix city, AZ	77 100	9	36	Dallas city, TX	426	58	36	Tampa city, FL	27.2
25	37	Nashville-Davidsn consol. city,TN	75 600	47	37	Minneapolis city, MN	424	55	36	Toledo city, OH	27.2
73	38	Norfolk city, VA	74 500	64	37	St. Paul city, MN	424	18	38	Memphis city, TN	27.1
69	39	Lexington-Fayette, KY	73 900	40	39	Atlanta city, GA	422	45	39	Mesa city, AZ	27.0
19	40	Austin city, TX	72 600	15	39	Columbus city, OH	422	35	39	Virginia Beach city, VA	27.0
47	41	Minneapolis city, MN	71 700	20	41	Milwaukee city, WI	418	41	41	Honolulu CDP, HI	26.9
40	42	Atlanta city, GA	71 200	70	42	St. Petersburg city, FL	417	61	41	Newark city, NJ	26.9
64	43	St. Paul city, MN	70 900	16	43	Baltimore city, MD	413	22	41	Seattle city, WA	26.9
32	44	New Orleans city, LA	69 600	48	43	Colorado Springs city, CO	413	65	44	Louisville city, KY	26.4
31	45	Tucson city, AZ	66 800	19	45	Austin city, TX	410	29	45	Denver city, CO	26.2
15	46	Columbus city, OH	66 000	13	46	Indianapolis consolidated city,IN	409	67	46	Birmingham city, AL	26.1
14	47	Jacksonville consolidated city,FL	63 400	58	47	Tampa city, FL	408	17	46	El Paso city, TX	26.1
70	48	St. Petersburg city, FL	63 000	33	48	Kansas City, MO	404	52	48	Cincinnati city, OH	25.8
52	49	Cincinnati city, OH	61 900	44	48	Miami city, FL	404	26	48	Portland city, OR	25.8
75	50	Lincoln city, NE	61 700	27	50	Fort Worth city, TX	403	48	50	Colorado Springs city, CO	25.7
43	51	Tulsa city, OK	60 500	36	51	Albuquerque city, NM	402	59	50	Corpus Christi city, TX	25.7
13	52	Indianapolis consolidated city,IN	60 400	26	52	Portland city, OR	397	75	50	Lincoln city, NE	25.7
27	53	Fort Worth city, TX	59 900	50	53	Wichita city, KS	395	1	50	New York City, NY	25.7
26	54	Portland city, OR	59 200	69	54	Lexington-Fayette, KY	394	14	54	Jacksonville consolidated city,FL	25.6
58	55	Tampa city, FL	59 000	4	55	Houston city, TX	390	72	54	Jersey City, NJ	25.6
17	56	El Paso city, TX	58 500	29	56	Denver city, CO	386	24	56	Washington city, DC	25.4
4	57	Houston city, TX	58 000	42	56	Omaha city, NE	386	50	56	Wichita city, KS	25.4
50	58	Wichita city, KS	56 700	75	58	Lincoln city, NE	379	25	58	Nashville-Davidsn consol. city,TN	25.3
59	59	Corpus Christi city, TX	56 500	32	58	New Orleans city, LA	379	8	58	San Antonio city, TX	25.3
33	60	Kansas City, MO	56 100	55	60	Toledo city, OH	378	30	60	Oklahoma City, OK	25.1
18	61	Memphis city, TN	55 700	31	61	Tucson city, AZ	377	42	60	Omaha city, NE	25.1
30	62	Oklahoma City, OK	54 900	59	62	Corpus Christi city, TX	373	15	62	Columbus city, OH	25.0
16	63	Baltimore city, MD	54 700	18	62	Memphis city, TN	373	33	62	Kansas City, MO	25.0
42	64	Omaha city, NE	54 600	10	64	Detroit city, MI	372	69	64	Lexington-Fayette, KY	24.9
20	65	Milwaukee city, WI	53 500	8	65	San Antonio city, TX	369	63	65	Anchorage city, AK	24.8
51	66	St. Louis city, MO	50 700	49	66	Pittsburgh city, PA	368	66	66	Aurora city, CO	24.7
8	67	San Antonio city, TX	49 700	30	67	Oklahoma City, OK	364	27	67	Fort Worth city, TX	24.6
5	68	Philadelphia city, PA	49 400	43	68	Tulsa city, OK	358	62	68	Raleigh city, NC	24.6
55	69	Toledo city, OH	48 900	57	69	Buffalo city, NY	352	43	69	Tulsa city, OK	24.4
57	70	Buffalo city, NY	46 700	17	70	El Paso city, TX	349	23	70	Charlotte city, NC	24.3
67	71	Birmingham city, AL	44 500	51	71	St. Louis city, MO	342	13	70	Indianapolis consolidated city,IN	24.3
65	72	Louisville city, KY	44 300	52	72	Cincinnati city, OH	329	9	72	Dallas city, TX	24.2
49	73	Pittsburgh city, PA	41 200	67	73	Birmingham city, AL	322	53	73	Arlington city, TX	23.7
28	74	Cleveland city, OH	40 900	28	73	Cleveland city, OH	322	4	74	Houston city, TX	23.6
10	75	Detroit city, MI	25 600	65	75	Louisville city, KY	308	71	75	Plano city, TX	23.3

Note: Column numbers refer to Table D. Cities.

TABLE 5—75 Largest Cities by 1999 Population
Selected Rankings

Percent Change in Civilian Labor Force, 1998-1999				Unemployment Rate, 1999				Per Capita Local Government Taxes, 1997			
Population Rank	Percent Change Rank	City	[col 62] Percent Change 1998-1999	Population Rank	Unemployment Rate Rank	City	[col 64] Unemployment Rate 1999	Population Rank	Local Taxes Rank	City	[col 121] Local Taxes Per Capita (Dollars)
71	1	Plano city, TX	6.6	39	1	Fresno city, CA	12.1	24	1	Washington city, DC	4 855
24	2	Washington city, DC	5.5	68	2	Stockton city, CA	10.3	1	2	New York City, NY	2 624
60	3	Riverside city, CA	4.7	61	3	Newark city, NJ	9.7	12	3	San Francisco city, CA	1 469
7	4	Phoenix city, AZ	4.5	17	4	El Paso city, TX	9.0	21	4	Boston city, MA	1 437
45	5	Mesa city, AZ	4.4	72	4	Jersey City, NJ	9.0	25	5	Nashville-Davidsn consol. city,TN	1 291
37	6	Las Vegas city, NV	4.3	57	6	Buffalo city, NY	8.8	41	6	Honolulu CDP, HI	1 244
23	7	Charlotte city, NC	4.1	28	6	Cleveland city, OH	8.8	5	7	Philadelphia city, PA	1 161
3	8	Chicago city, IL	3.6	74	8	Bakersfield city, CA	8.4	51	8	St. Louis city, MO	1 062
38	9	Sacramento city, CA	3.4	44	8	Miami city, FL	8.4	73	9	Norfolk city, VA	1 051
31	9	Tucson city, AZ	3.4	16	10	Baltimore city, MD	7.1	16	10	Baltimore city, MD	1 034
19	11	Austin city, TX	2.9	10	11	Detroit city, MI	7.0	35	11	Virginia Beach city, VA	1 017
6	11	San Diego city, CA	2.9	2	12	Los Angeles city, CA	6.7	29	12	Denver city, CO	1 007
58	11	Tampa city, FL	2.9	1	12	New York City, NY	6.7	63	13	Anchorage city, AK	937
40	14	Atlanta city, GA	2.7	59	14	Corpus Christi city, TX	6.5	33	14	Kansas City, MO	936
30	14	Oklahoma City, OK	2.7	51	14	St. Louis city, MO	6.5	22	15	Seattle city, WA	903
56	16	Anaheim city, CA	2.5	24	16	Washington city, DC	6.3	52	16	Cincinnati city, OH	827
62	17	Raleigh city, NC	2.3	55	17	Toledo city, OH	6.1	67	17	Birmingham city, AL	820
54	17	Santa Ana city, CA	2.3	5	18	Philadelphia city, PA	6.0	49	18	Pittsburgh city, PA	706
15	19	Columbus city, OH	2.0	4	19	Houston city, TX	5.5	32	19	New Orleans city, LA	698
53	20	Arlington city, TX	1.8	73	19	Norfolk city, VA	5.5	13	20	Indianapolis consolidated city,IN	688
27	21	Fort Worth city, TX	1.7	46	19	Oakland city, CA	5.5	28	21	Cleveland city, OH	679
70	21	St. Petersburg city, FL	1.7	26	19	Portland city, OR	5.5	26	22	Portland city, OR	667
48	23	Colorado Springs city, CO	1.5	3	23	Chicago city, IL	5.4	46	23	Oakland city, CA	655
25	23	Nashville-Davidsn consol. city,TN	1.5	34	23	Long Beach city, CA	5.4	65	24	Louisville city, KY	649
66	25	Aurora city, CO	1.3	60	23	Riverside city, CA	5.4	3	25	Chicago city, IL	640
9	25	Dallas city, TX	1.3	40	26	Atlanta city, GA	5.2	10	26	Detroit city, MI	636
18	25	Memphis city, TN	1.3	38	26	Sacramento city, CA	5.2	47	27	Minneapolis city, MN	628
46	25	Oakland city, CA	1.3	52	28	Cincinnati city, OH	5.1	30	28	Oklahoma City, OK	613
12	25	San Francisco city, CA	1.3	32	28	New Orleans city, LA	5.1	40	29	Atlanta city, GA	600
28	30	Cleveland city, OH	1.1	20	30	Milwaukee city, WI	5.0	15	30	Columbus city, OH	584
55	30	Toledo city, OH	1.1	67	31	Birmingham city, AL	4.9	61	31	Newark city, NJ	565
39	32	Fresno city, CA	1.0	41	31	Honolulu CDP, HI	4.9	2	32	Los Angeles city, CA	560
10	33	Detroit city, MI	0.9	54	33	Santa Ana city, CA	4.8	9	33	Dallas city, TX	546
61	33	Newark city, NJ	0.9	63	34	Anchorage city, AK	4.5	43	34	Tulsa city, OK	539
43	33	Tulsa city, OK	0.9	18	34	Memphis city, TN	4.5	44	35	Miami city, FL	529
22	36	Seattle city, WA	0.8	37	36	Las Vegas city, NV	4.4	14	36	Jacksonville consolidated city,FL	526
74	37	Bakersfield city, CA	0.7	49	37	Pittsburgh city, PA	4.3	55	37	Toledo city, OH	513
72	37	Jersey City, NJ	0.7	65	38	Louisville city, KY	4.2	4	38	Houston city, TX	511
68	37	Stockton city, CA	0.7	9	39	Dallas city, TX	4.1	72	38	Jersey City, NJ	511
8	40	San Antonio city, TX	0.6	27	39	Fort Worth city, TX	4.1	11	40	San Jose city, CA	506
50	40	Wichita city, KS	0.6	33	41	Kansas City, MO	3.9	71	41	Plano city, TX	504
4	42	Houston city, TX	0.5	22	42	Seattle city, WA	3.8	27	42	Fort Worth city, TX	500
34	43	Long Beach city, CA	0.4	36	43	Albuquerque city, NM	3.7	66	43	Aurora city, CO	495
44	43	Miami city, FL	0.4	50	43	Wichita city, KS	3.7	58	44	Tampa city, FL	495
2	45	Los Angeles city, CA	0.3	11	45	San Jose city, CA	3.6	38	45	Sacramento city, CA	486
65	46	Louisville city, KY	0.2	8	46	San Antonio city, TX	3.5	42	46	Omaha city, NE	483
52	47	Cincinnati city, OH	0.1	31	46	Tucson city, AZ	3.5	56	47	Anaheim city, CA	479
33	47	Kansas City, MO	0.1	43	46	Tulsa city, OK	3.5	23	48	Charlotte city, NC	471
5	47	Philadelphia city, PA	0.1	21	49	Boston city, MA	3.3	19	49	Austin city, TX	469
35	47	Virginia Beach city, VA	0.1	48	49	Colorado Springs city, CO	3.3	34	50	Long Beach city, CA	428
14	51	Jacksonville consolidated city,FL	0.0	7	49	Phoenix city, AZ	3.3	64	51	St. Paul city, MN	415
69	51	Lexington-Fayette, KY	0.0	58	49	Tampa city, FL	3.3	31	52	Tucson city, AZ	403
1	51	New York City, NY	0.0	14	53	Jacksonville consolidated city,FL	3.2	36	53	Albuquerque city, NM	401
11	51	San Jose city, CA	0.0	42	53	Omaha city, NE	3.2	62	54	Raleigh city, NC	400
63	55	Anchorage city, AK	-0.3	56	55	Anaheim city, CA	3.1	7	55	Phoenix city, AZ	398
75	56	Lincoln city, NE	-0.4	29	55	Denver city, CO	3.1	70	55	St. Petersburg city, FL	398
17	57	El Paso city, TX	-0.6	6	55	San Diego city, CA	3.1	18	57	Memphis city, TN	383
42	58	Omaha city, NE	-0.7	70	55	St. Petersburg city, FL	3.1	57	58	Buffalo city, NY	378
26	58	Portland city, OR	-0.7	12	59	San Francisco city, CA	3.0	6	58	San Diego city, CA	378
67	60	Birmingham city, AL	-0.8	15	60	Columbus city, OH	2.9	75	60	Lincoln city, NE	370
57	60	Buffalo city, NY	-0.8	64	60	St. Paul city, MN	2.9	54	61	Santa Ana city, CA	359
21	62	Boston city, MA	-1.0	13	62	Indianapolis consolidated city,IN	2.8	53	62	Arlington city, TX	350
49	62	Pittsburgh city, PA	-1.0	47	62	Minneapolis city, MN	2.8	59	63	Corpus Christi city, TX	322
59	64	Corpus Christi city, TX	-1.1	25	62	Nashville-Davidsn consol. city,TN	2.8	68	64	Stockton city, CA	312
41	64	Honolulu CDP, HI	-1.1	30	62	Oklahoma City, OK	2.8	74	65	Bakersfield city, CA	308
64	64	St. Paul city, MN	-1.1	53	66	Arlington city, TX	2.7	48	66	Colorado Springs city, CO	303
29	67	Denver city, CO	-1.2	35	67	Virginia Beach city, VA	2.6	17	67	El Paso city, TX	302
13	67	Indianapolis consolidated city,IN	-1.2	75	68	Lincoln city, NE	2.5	60	68	Riverside city, CA	299
47	69	Minneapolis city, MN	-1.8	45	68	Mesa city, AZ	2.5	8	69	San Antonio city, TX	297
51	70	St. Louis city, MO	-2.2	66	70	Aurora city, CO	2.4	39	70	Fresno city, CA	279
32	71	New Orleans city, LA	-2.3	19	70	Austin city, TX	2.4	20	70	Milwaukee city, WI	279
36	72	Albuquerque city, NM	-2.4	23	72	Charlotte city, NC	2.2	37	72	Las Vegas city, NV	271
20	73	Milwaukee city, WI	-2.7	69	73	Lexington-Fayette, KY	2.0	50	73	Wichita city, KS	251
16	74	Baltimore city, MD	-2.9	71	74	Plano city, TX	1.8	45	74	Mesa city, AZ	227
73	75	Norfolk city, VA	-7.3	62	75	Raleigh city, NC	1.6	69	75	Lexington-Fayette, KY	NA

Note: Column numbers refer to Table D. Cities.

TABLE 5—75 Largest Cities by 1999 Population
Selected Rankings

Percent of City Expenditures for Police Protection, 1997

Population Rank	Police Exp. Rank	City	[col 132] % of City Expenditures
54	1	Santa Ana city, CA	28.4
68	2	Stockton city, CA	25.2
44	3	Miami city, FL	23.9
58	3	Tampa city, FL	23.9
45	5	Mesa city, AZ	23.0
38	5	Sacramento city, CA	23.0
28	7	Cleveland city, OH	22.8
17	8	El Paso city, TX	22.7
66	9	Aurora city, CO	21.6
20	9	Milwaukee city, WI	21.6
59	11	Corpus Christi city, TX	21.5
53	12	Arlington city, TX	20.9
74	13	Bakersfield city, CA	20.8
3	14	Chicago city, IL	20.7
60	15	Riverside city, CA	20.6
15	16	Columbus city, OH	20.1
4	17	Houston city, TX	19.9
30	18	Oklahoma City, OK	19.8
70	18	St. Petersburg city, FL	19.8
27	20	Fort Worth city, TX	19.7
39	21	Fresno city, CA	19.6
55	22	Toledo city, OH	19.1
2	23	Los Angeles city, CA	18.1
8	24	San Antonio city, TX	17.8
51	25	St. Louis city, MO	17.6
61	26	Newark city, NJ	16.9
10	27	Detroit city, MI	16.8
42	27	Omaha city, NE	16.8
23	29	Charlotte city, NC	16.7
7	29	Phoenix city, AZ	16.7
11	31	San Jose city, CA	16.3
67	32	Birmingham city, AL	16.0
9	33	Dallas city, TX	15.7
69	34	Lexington-Fayette, KY	15.6
62	34	Raleigh city, NC	15.6
56	36	Anaheim city, CA	15.0
37	37	Las Vegas city, NV	14.9
31	38	Tucson city, AZ	14.8
65	39	Louisville city, KY	14.5
26	39	Portland city, OR	14.5
41	41	Honolulu CDP, HI	13.6
33	42	Kansas City, MO	13.4
71	43	Plano city, TX	13.0
6	43	San Diego city, CA	13.0
49	45	Pittsburgh city, PA	12.9
43	45	Tulsa city, OK	12.9
48	47	Colorado Springs city, CO	12.8
36	48	Albuquerque city, NM	12.7
46	49	Oakland city, CA	12.6
22	49	Seattle city, WA	12.6
72	51	Jersey City, NJ	12.4
34	52	Long Beach city, CA	12.3
19	53	Austin city, TX	12.2
5	54	Philadelphia city, PA	11.8
52	55	Cincinnati city, OH	11.7
50	56	Wichita city, KS	11.5
64	57	St. Paul city, MN	11.4
40	58	Atlanta city, GA	11.2
21	58	Boston city, MA	11.2
16	60	Baltimore city, MD	11.1
18	60	Memphis city, TN	11.1
47	62	Minneapolis city, MN	10.8
32	63	New Orleans city, LA	9.9
14	64	Jacksonville consolidated city, FL	9.8
13	65	Indianapolis consolidated city, IN	8.3
75	66	Lincoln city, NE	7.8
12	66	San Francisco city, CA	7.8
29	68	Denver city, CO	6.9
25	68	Nashville-Davidsn consol. city, TN	6.9
1	68	New York City, NY	6.9
73	71	Norfolk city, VA	6.3
24	72	Washington city, DC	6.2
57	73	Buffalo city, NY	6.1
35	74	Virginia Beach city, VA	5.6
63	75	Anchorage city, AK	5.1

Violent Crime Rate per 100,000 Population, 1998

Population Rank	Violent Crime Rate Rank	City	[col 37] Violent Crime Rate
51	1	St. Louis city, MO	2 571
58	2	Tampa city, FL	2 557
44	3	Miami city, FL	2 549
10	4	Detroit city, MI	2 443
16	5	Baltimore city, MD	2 420
3	6	Chicago city, IL	2 179
61	7	Newark city, NJ	2 094
70	8	St. Petersburg city, FL	1 937
46	9	Oakland city, CA	1 862
24	10	Washington city, DC	1 719
47	11	Minneapolis city, MN	1 525
18	12	Memphis city, TN	1 499
5	13	Philadelphia city, PA	1 464
32	14	New Orleans city, LA	1 462
23	15	Charlotte city, NC	1 455
72	16	Jersey City, NJ	1 418
2	17	Los Angeles city, CA	1 359
21	18	Boston city, MA	1 327
36	19	Albuquerque city, NM	1 317
42	20	Omaha city, NE	1 315
28	21	Cleveland city, OH	1 308
67	22	Birmingham city, AL	1 213
1	23	New York City, NY	1 167
57	24	Buffalo city, NY	1 129
68	24	Stockton city, CA	1 129
4	26	Houston city, TX	1 123
39	27	Fresno city, CA	1 052
31	28	Tucson city, AZ	1 034
20	29	Milwaukee city, WI	1 002
12	30	San Francisco city, CA	990
65	31	Louisville city, KY	943
64	32	St. Paul city, MN	909
55	33	Toledo city, OH	905
49	34	Pittsburgh city, PA	891
38	35	Sacramento city, CA	878
27	36	Fort Worth city, TX	870
34	37	Long Beach city, CA	860
60	38	Riverside city, CA	850
7	39	Phoenix city, AZ	832
22	39	Seattle city, WA	832
62	41	Raleigh city, NC	826
15	42	Columbus city, OH	817
59	43	Corpus Christi city, TX	729
6	44	San Diego city, CA	725
17	45	El Paso city, TX	700
73	46	Norfolk city, VA	678
50	47	Wichita city, KS	665
45	48	Mesa city, AZ	662
63	49	Anchorage city, AK	642
53	50	Arlington city, TX	608
11	51	San Jose city, CA	599
29	52	Denver city, CO	573
54	53	Santa Ana city, CA	554
75	54	Lincoln city, NE	549
19	55	Austin city, TX	541
48	56	Colorado Springs city, CO	540
56	57	Anaheim city, CA	508
74	58	Bakersfield city, CA	484
8	59	San Antonio city, TX	451
71	60	Plano city, TX	392
41	61	Honolulu CDP, HI	268
35	62	Virginia Beach city, VA	227
40		Atlanta city, GA	NA
66		Aurora city, CO	NA
52		Cincinnati city, OH	NA
9		Dallas city, TX	NA
13		Indianapolis consolidated city, IN	NA
14		Jacksonville consolidated city, FL	NA
33		Kansas City, MO	NA
37		Las Vegas city, NV	NA
69		Lexington-Fayette, KY	NA
25		Nashville-Davidsn consol. city, TN	NA
30		Oklahoma City, OK	NA
26		Portland city, OR	NA
43		Tulsa city, OK	NA

Average Annual Precipitation (in inches), 1961-1990

Population Rank	Precipitation Rank	City	[col 145] Annual Precipitation
32	1	New Orleans city, LA	61.88
44	2	Miami city, FL	55.91
67	3	Birmingham city, AL	54.58
18	4	Memphis city, TN	52.10
4	5	Houston city, TX	50.83
40	6	Atlanta city, GA	50.77
70	7	St. Petersburg city, FL	48.62
1	8	New York City, NY	47.25
62	9	Raleigh city, NC	44.97
73	10	Norfolk city, VA	44.64
35	10	Virginia Beach city, VA	44.64
69	12	Lexington-Fayette, KY	44.55
65	13	Louisville city, KY	44.39
61	14	Newark city, NJ	43.97
58	15	Tampa city, FL	43.92
72	16	Jersey City, NJ	43.50
23	17	Charlotte city, NC	43.09
21	18	Boston city, MA	41.51
5	19	Philadelphia city, PA	41.41
16	20	Baltimore city, MD	40.76
52	21	Cincinnati city, OH	40.70
43	22	Tulsa city, OK	40.59
24	23	Washington city, DC	38.63
57	24	Buffalo city, NY	38.58
15	25	Columbus city, OH	38.09
51	26	St. Louis city, MO	37.86
33	27	Kansas City, MO	37.62
3	28	Chicago city, IL	37.38
22	29	Seattle city, WA	37.19
49	30	Pittsburgh city, PA	36.85
28	31	Cleveland city, OH	36.63
26	32	Portland city, OR	36.30
9	33	Dallas city, TX	36.08
53	34	Arlington city, TX	33.70
27	34	Fort Worth city, TX	33.70
71	34	Plano city, TX	33.70
30	37	Oklahoma City, OK	33.36
55	38	Toledo city, OH	32.97
10	39	Detroit city, MI	32.09
19	40	Austin city, TX	31.88
20	41	Milwaukee city, WI	31.11
8	42	San Antonio city, TX	30.98
59	43	Corpus Christi city, TX	30.13
42	44	Omaha city, NE	29.86
50	45	Wichita city, KS	29.33
47	46	Minneapolis city, MN	28.32
64	47	St. Paul city, MN	28.32
75	48	Lincoln city, NE	28.26
46	49	Oakland city, CA	24.30
41	50	Honolulu CDP, HI	21.53
12	51	San Francisco city, CA	19.71
38	52	Sacramento city, CA	17.52
48	53	Colorado Springs city, CO	16.24
63	54	Anchorage city, AK	15.91
66	55	Aurora city, CO	15.40
29	55	Denver city, CO	15.40
2	57	Los Angeles city, CA	14.77
11	58	San Jose city, CA	14.42
68	59	Stockton city, CA	13.95
56	60	Anaheim city, CA	12.27
54	60	Santa Ana city, CA	12.27
31	62	Tucson city, AZ	12.00
34	63	Long Beach city, CA	11.80
39	64	Fresno city, CA	10.60
6	65	San Diego city, CA	9.90
60	66	Riverside city, CA	9.58
36	67	Albuquerque city, NM	8.88
17	68	El Paso city, TX	8.81
45	69	Mesa city, AZ	8.50
7	70	Phoenix city, AZ	7.66
74	71	Bakersfield city, CA	5.72
37	72	Las Vegas city, NV	4.13
13		Indianapolis consolidated city, IN	NA
14		Jacksonville consolidated city, FL	NA
25		Nashville-Davidsn consol. city, TN	NA

Note: Column numbers refer to Table D. Cities.

TABLE 6—States and the District of Columbia
Selected Rankings

Population, 2000			Total Land Area, (Square Kilometers), 1990				Population Density (per Square Kilometer), 1999			
Population Rank	State	[col 2] Population	Population Rank	Land Area Rank	State	[col 1] Land Area	Population Rank	Density Rank	State	[col 5] Density
X	United States	281 421 906	X	X	United States	9 159 127	X	X	United States	29.8
1	California	33 871 648	48	1	Alaska	1 477 268	50	1	District of Columbia	3 262.1
2	Texas	20 851 820	2	2	Texas	678 358	9	2	New Jersey	423.8
3	New York	18 976 457	1	3	California	403 971	43	3	Rhode Island	366.1
4	Florida	15 982 378	44	4	Montana	376 991	13	4	Massachusetts	304.2
5	Illinois	12 419 293	36	5	New Mexico	314 334	29	5	Connecticut	261.5
6	Pennsylvania	12 281 054	20	6	Arizona	294 333	19	6	Maryland	204.3
7	Ohio	11 353 140	35	7	Nevada	284 396	45	7	Delaware	148.8
8	Michigan	9 938 444	24	8	Colorado	268 658	3	8	New York	148.8
9	New Jersey	8 414 350	51	9	Wyoming	251 501	4	9	Florida	108.1
10	Georgia	8 186 453	28	10	Oregon	248 646	7	10	Ohio	106.1
11	North Carolina	8 049 313	39	11	Idaho	214 325	6	11	Pennsylvania	103.3
12	Virginia	7 078 515	34	12	Utah	212 816	5	12	Illinois	84.2
13	Massachusetts	6 349 097	32	13	Kansas	211 922	1	13	California	82.0
14	Indiana	6 080 485	21	14	Minnesota	206 207	42	14	Hawaii	71.3
15	Washington	5 894 121	38	15	Nebraska	199 113	8	15	Michigan	67.0
16	Tennessee	5 689 283	46	16	South Dakota	196 571	12	15	Virginia	67.0
17	Missouri	5 595 211	47	17	North Dakota	178 695	14	17	Indiana	64.0
18	Wisconsin	5 363 675	17	18	Missouri	178 446	11	18	North Carolina	60.6
19	Maryland	5 296 486	27	19	Oklahoma	177 877	10	19	Georgia	51.9
20	Arizona	5 130 632	15	20	Washington	172 445	41	20	New Hampshire	51.7
21	Minnesota	4 919 479	10	21	Georgia	150 010	16	21	Tennessee	51.4
22	Louisiana	4 468 976	8	22	Michigan	147 136	26	22	South Carolina	49.8
23	Alabama	4 447 100	30	23	Iowa	144 716	22	23	Louisiana	38.7
24	Colorado	4 301 261	5	24	Illinois	143 987	25	24	Kentucky	38.5
25	Kentucky	4 041 769	18	25	Wisconsin	140 672	18	25	Wisconsin	37.3
26	South Carolina	4 012 012	4	26	Florida	139 853	15	26	Washington	33.4
27	Oklahoma	3 450 654	33	27	Arkansas	134 875	23	27	Alabama	33.2
28	Oregon	3 421 399	23	28	Alabama	131 443	17	28	Missouri	30.6
29	Connecticut	3 405 565	11	29	North Carolina	126 180	2	29	Texas	29.5
30	Iowa	2 926 324	3	30	New York	122 310	37	30	West Virginia	29.0
31	Mississippi	2 844 658	31	31	Mississippi	121 506	49	31	Vermont	24.8
32	Kansas	2 688 418	6	32	Pennsylvania	116 083	21	32	Minnesota	23.2
33	Arkansas	2 673 400	22	33	Louisiana	112 836	31	33	Mississippi	22.8
34	Utah	2 233 169	16	34	Tennessee	106 759	30	34	Iowa	19.8
35	Nevada	1 998 257	7	35	Ohio	106 067	33	35	Arkansas	18.9
36	New Mexico	1 819 046	25	36	Kentucky	102 907	27	35	Oklahoma	18.9
37	West Virginia	1 808 344	12	37	Virginia	102 558	20	37	Arizona	16.2
38	Nebraska	1 711 263	14	38	Indiana	92 904	40	38	Maine	15.7
39	Idaho	1 293 953	40	39	Maine	79 939	24	39	Colorado	15.1
40	Maine	1 274 923	26	40	South Carolina	77 988	28	40	Oregon	13.3
41	New Hampshire	1 235 786	37	41	West Virginia	62 384	32	41	Kansas	12.5
42	Hawaii	1 211 537	19	42	Maryland	25 316	34	42	Utah	10.0
43	Rhode Island	1 048 319	49	43	Vermont	23 956	38	43	Nebraska	8.4
44	Montana	902 195	41	44	New Hampshire	23 231	35	44	Nevada	6.4
45	Delaware	783 600	13	45	Massachusetts	20 300	39	45	Idaho	5.8
46	South Dakota	754 844	9	46	New Jersey	19 215	36	46	New Mexico	5.5
47	North Dakota	642 200	42	47	Hawaii	16 637	46	47	South Dakota	3.7
48	Alaska	626 932	29	48	Connecticut	12 550	47	48	North Dakota	3.5
49	Vermont	608 827	45	49	Delaware	5 063	44	49	Montana	2.3
50	District of Columbia	572 059	43	50	Rhode Island	2 707	51	50	Wyoming	1.9
51	Wyoming	493 782	50	51	District of Columbia	159	48	51	Alaska	0.4

Note: Column numbers refer to Table A. States.

TABLE 6—States and the District of Columbia
Selected Rankings

Percent Population Change, 1990-1999				Projected State Population, 2025				Percent White, 1999			
Population Rank	Percent Change Rank	State	[col 34] Percent Change	1999 Population Rank	2025 Population Rank	State	[col 32] Projected Population 2025	Population Rank	White Rank	State	[col 6] Percent White
X	X	United States	9.6	X	X	United States	335 048 000	X	X	United States	82.4
35	1	Nevada	50.6	1	1	California	49 285 000	26	1	Vermont	98.4
20	2	Arizona	30.4	2	2	Texas	27 183 000	14	2	Maine	98.3
40	3	Idaho	24.3	4	3	Florida	20 710 000	2	3	New Hampshire	97.8
34	4	Utah	23.6	3	4	New York	19 830 000	44	4	Idaho	96.9
24	5	Colorado	23.1	5	5	Illinois	13 440 000	18	5	Iowa	96.4
10	6	Georgia	20.2	6	6	Pennsylvania	12 683 000	31	6	West Virginia	96.3
15	7	Washington	18.3	7	7	Ohio	11 744 000	42	7	Wyoming	96.0
2	8	Texas	18.0	8	8	Michigan	10 078 000	10	8	Utah	95.1
4	9	Florida	16.8	10	9	Georgia	9 869 000	16	9	North Dakota	93.7
28	10	Oregon	16.7	9	10	New Jersey	9 558 000	37	10	Nebraska	93.6
11	11	North Carolina	15.4	11	11	North Carolina	9 349 000	9	11	Oregon	93.4
37	12	New Mexico	14.8	12	12	Virginia	8 466 000	6	12	Minnesota	92.9
45	13	Delaware	13.1	15	13	Washington	7 808 000	7	13	Montana	92.5
48	14	Alaska	12.6	13	14	Massachusetts	6 902 000	36	14	Colorado	92.3
16	15	Tennessee	12.4	16	15	Tennessee	6 665 000	3	15	Rhode Island	92.1
26	16	South Carolina	11.5	14	16	Indiana	6 546 000	32	16	Kentucky	91.9
1	17	California	11.2	20	17	Arizona	6 412 000	50	16	Wisconsin	91.9
12	18	Virginia	11.0	19	18	Maryland	6 274 000	25	18	Kansas	91.4
44	19	Montana	10.5	17	19	Missouri	6 250 000	43	19	Indiana	90.4
21	20	Minnesota	9.1	18	20	Wisconsin	5 867 000	48	19	South Dakota	90.4
33	21	Arkansas	8.5	21	21	Minnesota	5 510 000	15	21	Massachusetts	89.4
41	22	New Hampshire	8.3	23	22	Alabama	5 224 000	41	22	Arizona	88.7
23	23	Alabama	8.2	24	23	Colorado	5 188 000	22	22	Washington	88.7
19	23	Maryland	8.2	22	24	Louisiana	5 133 000	45	24	Pennsylvania	88.4
31	25	Mississippi	7.5	26	25	South Carolina	4 645 000	51	25	Connecticut	87.8
25	26	Kentucky	7.4	28	26	Oregon	4 349 000	17	26	Missouri	87.2
18	27	Wisconsin	7.3	25	27	Kentucky	4 314 000	5	27	Ohio	87.0
14	28	Indiana	7.2	27	28	Oklahoma	4 057 000	27	28	New Mexico	86.3
32	29	Kansas	7.1	29	29	Connecticut	3 739 000	35	29	Nevada	85.6
42	30	Hawaii	7.0	31	30	Mississippi	3 142 000	23	30	Texas	84.3
17	31	Missouri	6.9	32	31	Kansas	3 108 000	20	31	Michigan	83.4
27	32	Oklahoma	6.8	33	32	Arkansas	3 055 000	1	32	Oklahoma	83.0
5	33	Illinois	6.1	30	33	Iowa	3 040 000	40	33	Arkansas	82.6
8	33	Michigan	6.1	34	34	Utah	2 883 000	47	34	Florida	82.3
51	35	Wyoming	5.7	36	35	New Mexico	2 612 000	11	35	Tennessee	82.1
38	36	Nebraska	5.6	35	36	Nevada	2 312 000	24	36	Illinois	81.1
49	37	Vermont	5.5	38	37	Nebraska	1 930 000	30	37	California	79.4
46	38	South Dakota	5.3	37	38	West Virginia	1 845 000	8	38	New Jersey	79.3
9	39	New Jersey	5.1	42	39	Hawaii	1 812 000	34	39	Delaware	77.7
7	40	Ohio	3.8	39	40	Idaho	1 739 000	33	40	New York	76.2
22	41	Louisiana	3.6	41	41	New Hampshire	1 439 000	19	41	Virginia	75.8
30	42	Iowa	3.3	40	42	Maine	1 423 000	4	42	North Carolina	75.3
13	43	Massachusetts	2.6	43	43	Rhode Island	1 141 000	39	43	Alaska	75.2
39	44	Maine	2.0	44	44	Montana	1 121 000	49	44	Alabama	73.0
3	45	New York	1.1	48	45	Alaska	885 000	12	45	South Carolina	69.1
6	46	Pennsylvania	0.9	46	46	South Dakota	866 000	28	46	Georgia	69.0
36	47	West Virginia	0.7	45	47	Delaware	861 000	13	47	Maryland	67.5
29	48	Connecticut	-0.2	47	48	North Dakota	729 000	46	48	Louisiana	65.9
47	49	North Dakota	-0.8	51	49	Wyoming	694 000	29	49	Mississippi	62.4
43	50	Rhode Island	-1.3	49	50	Vermont	678 000	38	50	District of Columbia	35.2
50	51	District of Columbia	-14.5	50	51	District of Columbia	655 000	21	51	Hawaii	33.0

Note: Column numbers refer to Table A. States.

TABLE 6—States and the District of Columbia
Selected Rankings

Percent Black, 1999				Percent Hispanic, 1999				Number of Immigrants, 1996			
Population Rank	Black Rank	State	[col 7] Percent Black	Population Rank	Hispanic Rank	State	[col 10] Percent Hispanic	Population Rank	Immigrant Rank	State	[col 28] Number of Immigrants
X	X	United States	12.8	X		United States	11.5	X	X	United States	915 900
50	1	District of Columbia	61.4	36	1	New Mexico	40.7	1	1	California	201 529
31	2	Mississippi	36.5	1	2	California	31.6	3	2	New York	154 095
22	3	Louisiana	32.4	2	3	Texas	30.2	2	3	Texas	83 385
26	4	South Carolina	29.8	20	4	Arizona	22.7	4	4	Florida	79 461
10	5	Georgia	28.7	35	5	Nevada	16.8	9	5	New Jersey	63 303
19	6	Maryland	28.1	4	6	Florida	15.4	5	6	Illinois	42 517
23	7	Alabama	26.1	24	7	Colorado	14.9	13	7	Massachusetts	23 085
11	8	North Carolina	22.0	3	8	New York	14.6	12	8	Virginia	21 375
12	9	Virginia	20.1	9	9	New Jersey	12.6	19	9	Maryland	20 732
45	10	Delaware	19.8	5	10	Illinois	10.5	15	10	Washington	18 833
3	11	New York	17.7	29	11	Connecticut	8.5	8	11	Michigan	17 253
16	12	Tennessee	16.6	42	12	Hawaii	8.1	6	12	Pennsylvania	16 938
33	13	Arkansas	16.1	50	13	District of Columbia	7.4	10	13	Georgia	12 608
4	14	Florida	15.4	39	13	Idaho	7.4	29	14	Connecticut	10 874
5	15	Illinois	15.3	34	15	Utah	7.1	7	15	Ohio	10 237
9	16	New Jersey	14.7	43	16	Rhode Island	6.9	21	16	Minnesota	8 977
8	17	Michigan	14.3	15	17	Washington	6.5	20	17	Arizona	8 900
2	18	Texas	12.3	28	18	Oregon	6.4	24	18	Colorado	8 895
7	19	Ohio	11.6	13	19	Massachusetts	6.3	42	19	Hawaii	8 436
17	20	Missouri	11.3	51	20	Wyoming	6.1	28	20	Oregon	7 554
6	21	Pennsylvania	9.8	32	21	Kansas	5.6	11	21	North Carolina	7 011
29	22	Connecticut	9.4	38	22	Nebraska	4.6	35	22	Nevada	5 874
14	23	Indiana	8.4	27	23	Oklahoma	4.1	36	23	New Mexico	5 780
27	24	Oklahoma	7.8	48	24	Alaska	4.0	17	24	Missouri	5 690
35	25	Nevada	7.7	19	25	Maryland	3.9	14	25	Indiana	4 692
1	26	California	7.5	12	25	Virginia	3.9	16	26	Tennessee	4 343
25	27	Kentucky	7.3	45	27	Delaware	3.7	32	27	Kansas	4 303
13	28	Massachusetts	6.6	10	28	Georgia	3.1	34	28	Utah	4 250
32	29	Kansas	5.9	8	29	Michigan	2.8	22	29	Louisiana	4 092
18	30	Wisconsin	5.6	22	30	Louisiana	2.7	50	30	District of Columbia	3 784
43	31	Rhode Island	5.1	6	30	Pennsylvania	2.7	18	31	Wisconsin	3 607
24	32	Colorado	4.3	18	30	Wisconsin	2.7	27	32	Oklahoma	3 511
38	33	Nebraska	4.1	14	33	Indiana	2.6	43	33	Rhode Island	3 098
48	34	Alaska	3.9	11	34	North Carolina	2.3	30	34	Iowa	3 037
20	35	Arizona	3.7	33	35	Arkansas	2.1	26	35	South Carolina	2 151
15	36	Washington	3.5	30	35	Iowa	2.1	38	36	Nebraska	2 150
21	37	Minnesota	3.1	21	37	Minnesota	1.9	25	37	Kentucky	2 019
37	37	West Virginia	3.1	44	38	Montana	1.8	39	38	Idaho	1 825
42	39	Hawaii	2.8	17	39	Missouri	1.7	23	39	Alabama	1 782
36	40	New Mexico	2.6	41	40	New Hampshire	1.6	41	40	New Hampshire	1 512
30	41	Iowa	2.0	7	40	Ohio	1.6	33	41	Arkansas	1 494
28	42	Oregon	1.9	26	42	South Carolina	1.4	45	42	Delaware	1 377
34	43	Utah	0.9	46	43	South Dakota	1.2	48	43	Alaska	1 280
51	43	Wyoming	0.9	16	43	Tennessee	1.2	31	44	Mississippi	1 073
41	45	New Hampshire	0.8	47	45	North Dakota	1.1	40	45	Maine	1 028
46	46	South Dakota	0.7	23	46	Alabama	1.0	49	46	Vermont	654
39	47	Idaho	0.6	25	47	Kentucky	0.9	47	47	North Dakota	606
47	47	North Dakota	0.6	31	47	Mississippi	0.9	37	48	West Virginia	583
40	49	Maine	0.5	49	47	Vermont	0.9	46	49	South Dakota	519
49	49	Vermont	0.5	40	50	Maine	0.7	44	50	Montana	449
44	51	Montana	0.4	37	51	West Virginia	0.6	51	51	Wyoming	280

Note: Column numbers refer to Table A. States.

TABLE 6—States and the District of Columbia
Selected Rankings

Percent Age 65 and Over, 1999				Percent Under 18 Years Old, 1999				Live Birth Rate Per 1,000 Population, 1998			
Popu-lation Rank	Age 65 and Over Rank	State	[cols 18 & 19] Percent Age 65 and Over	Popu-lation Rank	Under 18 Rank	State	[cols 11 & 12] Percent Under 18 Years Old	Popu-lation Rank	Birth Rate Rank	State	[col 61] Birth Rate 1998
X	X	United States	12.7	X	X	United States	25.7	X	X	United States	14.5
4	1	Florida	18.1	34	1	Utah	33.2	34	1	Utah	21.2
6	2	Pennsylvania	15.8	48	2	Alaska	31.8	20	2	Texas	17.1
43	3	Rhode Island	15.6	2	3	Texas	28.5	48	3	Arizona	16.4
37	4	West Virginia	15.1	36	3	New Mexico	28.5	35	4	Alaska	16.0
30	5	Iowa	14.9	39	5	Idaho	28.0	1	5	Nevada	15.9
47	6	North Dakota	14.6	20	6	Arizona	27.9	10	6	California	15.7
46	7	South Dakota	14.4	22	7	Louisiana	27.2	36	6	Georgia	15.7
29	8	Connecticut	14.3	31	7	Mississippi	27.2	31	6	New Mexico	15.7
33	9	Arkansas	14.2	35	7	Nevada	27.2		9	Mississippi	15.5
40	10	Maine	14.0	46	10	South Dakota	27.0	39	9	Idaho	15.5
13	11	Massachusetts	13.9	1	11	California	26.9	22	11	Louisiana	15.3
50	11	District of Columbia	13.9	38	12	Nebraska	26.6	5	12	Illinois	15.1
38	13	Nebraska	13.7	21	12	Minnesota	26.6	42	13	Hawaii	14.8
42	13	Hawaii	13.7	51	14	Wyoming	26.4	50	13	District of Columbia	14.8
17	15	Missouri	13.6	10	15	Georgia	26.4	27	15	Oklahoma	14.7
9	15	New Jersey	13.6	32	16	Kansas	26.3	24	15	Colorado	14.7
27	17	Oklahoma	13.4	24	17	Colorado	26.3	11	17	North Carolina	14.6
3	17	New York	13.4	27	17	Oklahoma	26.3	32	18	Kansas	14.5
32	19	Kansas	13.3	5	19	Illinois	26.2	33	19	Arkansas	14.4
7	19	Ohio	13.3	8	20	Michigan	26.0	14	20	Indiana	14.3
44	19	Montana	13.3	33	21	Arkansas	25.9	23	21	Alabama	14.2
18	22	Wisconsin	13.2	15	22	Washington	25.8	3	21	New York	14.2
20	22	Arizona	13.2	14	23	Indiana	25.7	38	23	Nebraska	14.1
28	24	Oregon	13.1	18	23	Wisconsin	25.7	16	23	Tennessee	14.1
45	25	Delaware	13.0	17	25	Missouri	25.6	9	23	New Jersey	14.1
23	25	Alabama	13.0	11	26	North Carolina	25.4	45	26	Delaware	14.0
14	27	Indiana	12.5	44	26	Montana	25.4	46	26	South Dakota	14.0
11	27	North Carolina	12.5	41	28	New Hampshire	25.3	19	28	Maryland	13.9
25	27	Kentucky	12.5	19	28	Maryland	25.3	26	28	South Carolina	13.9
16	30	Tennessee	12.4	7	28	Ohio	25.3	15	30	Washington	13.8
8	30	Michigan	12.4	47	28	North Dakota	25.3	17	30	Missouri	13.8
5	32	Illinois	12.3	29	32	Connecticut	25.2	12	32	Virginia	13.7
49	32	Vermont	12.3	30	33	Iowa	25.1	25	32	Kentucky	13.7
21	32	Minnesota	12.3	28	34	Oregon	25.0	21	32	Minnesota	13.7
26	35	South Carolina	12.2	26	35	South Carolina	24.6	28	32	Oregon	13.7
31	36	Mississippi	12.1	9	35	New Jersey	24.6	7	36	Ohio	13.6
41	37	New Hampshire	12.0	16	37	Tennessee	24.5	8	36	Michigan	13.6
51	38	Wyoming	11.6	42	38	Hawaii	24.4	29	38	Connecticut	13.4
19	39	Maryland	11.5	3	38	New York	24.4	13	39	Massachusetts	13.2
36	39	New Mexico	11.5	23	38	Alabama	24.4	51	40	Wyoming	13.0
22	39	Louisiana	11.5	25	38	Kentucky	24.4	30	40	Iowa	13.0
35	39	Nevada	11.5	43	42	Rhode Island	24.3	4	42	Florida	12.9
15	43	Washington	11.4	12	43	Virginia	24.2	18	43	Wisconsin	12.8
39	44	Idaho	11.3	45	43	Delaware	24.2	43	44	Rhode Island	12.7
12	44	Virginia	11.3	6	45	Pennsylvania	23.8	47	45	North Dakota	12.5
1	46	California	11.0	13	45	Massachusetts	23.8	44	46	Montana	12.2
2	47	Texas	10.1	4	47	Florida	23.6	6	46	Pennsylvania	12.2
24	47	Colorado	10.1	49	48	Vermont	23.5	41	48	New Hampshire	12.0
10	49	Georgia	9.8	40	49	Maine	23.2	37	49	West Virginia	11.5
34	50	Utah	8.7	37	50	West Virginia	22.3	49	50	Vermont	11.1
48	51	Alaska	5.6	50	51	District of Columbia	18.4	40	51	Maine	11.0

Note: Column numbers refer to Table A. States.

TABLE 6—States and the District of Columbia
Selected Rankings

Infant Deaths Per 1,000 Live Births, 1998

Population Rank	Infant Mortality Rate	State	[col 66] Infant Mortality Rank
X	X	United States	7.2
50	1	District of Columbia	12.5
23	2	Alabama	10.2
31	3	Mississippi	10.1
45	4	Delaware	9.6
26	4	South Carolina	9.6
11	6	North Carolina	9.3
22	7	Louisiana	9.1
46	7	South Dakota	9.1
33	9	Arkansas	8.9
19	10	Maryland	8.6
47	10	North Dakota	8.6
10	12	Georgia	8.5
27	12	Oklahoma	8.5
5	14	Illinois	8.4
8	15	Michigan	8.2
16	16	Tennessee	8.2
7	17	Ohio	8.0
37	17	West Virginia	8.0
17	19	Missouri	7.7
12	19	Virginia	7.7
14	21	Indiana	7.6
20	22	Arizona	7.5
25	22	Kentucky	7.5
44	24	Montana	7.4
38	25	Nebraska	7.3
4	26	Florida	7.2
39	26	Idaho	7.2
36	26	New Mexico	7.2
18	26	Wisconsin	7.2
51	26	Wyoming	7.2
6	31	Pennsylvania	7.1
29	32	Connecticut	7.0
32	32	Kansas	7.0
35	32	Nevada	7.0
43	32	Rhode Island	7.0
49	32	Vermont	7.0
42	37	Hawaii	6.9
24	38	Colorado	6.7
30	39	Iowa	6.6
9	40	New Jersey	6.4
2	40	Texas	6.4
40	42	Maine	6.3
3	42	New York	6.3
48	44	Alaska	5.9
21	44	Minnesota	5.9
1	46	California	5.8
15	47	Washington	5.7
34	48	Utah	5.6
28	49	Oregon	5.4
13	50	Massachusetts	5.1
41	51	New Hampshire	4.4

Percent College Graduates (Bachelor's or Higher Degree), 2000

Population Rank	Percent College Graduate Rank	State	[col 82] Percent College Grads
X	X	United States	25.6
50	1	District of Columbia	38.3
24	2	Colorado	34.6
13	3	Massachusetts	32.7
19	4	Maryland	32.3
12	5	Virginia	31.9
29	6	Connecticut	31.6
21	7	Minnesota	31.2
41	8	New Hampshire	30.1
9	8	New Jersey	30.1
49	10	Vermont	28.8
3	11	New York	28.7
15	12	Washington	28.6
48	13	Alaska	28.1
1	14	California	27.5
32	15	Kansas	27.3
28	16	Oregon	27.2
5	17	Illinois	27.1
43	18	Rhode Island	26.4
34	18	Utah	26.4
42	20	Hawaii	26.3
17	21	Missouri	26.2
46	22	South Dakota	25.7
30	23	Iowa	25.5
20	24	Arizona	24.6
38	24	Nebraska	24.6
7	24	Ohio	24.6
6	27	Pennsylvania	24.3
40	28	Maine	24.1
45	29	Delaware	24.0
2	30	Texas	23.9
44	31	Montana	23.8
18	31	Wisconsin	23.8
36	33	New Mexico	23.6
11	34	North Carolina	23.2
10	35	Georgia	23.1
8	36	Michigan	23.0
4	37	Florida	22.8
47	38	North Dakota	22.6
22	39	Louisiana	22.5
27	39	Oklahoma	22.5
16	41	Tennessee	22.0
51	42	Wyoming	20.6
25	43	Kentucky	20.5
23	44	Alabama	20.4
39	45	Idaho	20.0
35	46	Nevada	19.3
26	47	South Carolina	19.0
31	48	Mississippi	18.7
33	49	Arkansas	18.4
14	50	Indiana	17.1
37	51	West Virginia	15.3

Median Household Income, 1997-1999 average

Population Rank	Median Income Rank	State	[col 89] Median Income (dollars)
X	X	United States	39 657
48	1	Alaska	51 046
19	2	Maryland	50 630
9	3	New Jersey	50 234
29	4	Connecticut	47 997
24	5	Colorado	46 950
21	6	Minnesota	46 802
15	7	Washington	46 788
34	8	Utah	45 257
41	9	New Hampshire	44 891
12	10	Virginia	44 884
45	11	Delaware	44 627
5	12	Illinois	44 459
13	13	Massachusetts	43 697
8	14	Michigan	43 066
18	15	Wisconsin	43 055
42	16	Hawaii	42 864
1	17	California	42 262
35	18	Nevada	40 882
14	19	Indiana	40 635
43	20	Rhode Island	40 213
17	21	Missouri	40 166
28	22	Oregon	39 768
49	23	Vermont	39 419
10	24	Georgia	39 003
7	25	Ohio	38 970
6	26	Pennsylvania	38 938
3	27	New York	38 479
30	28	Iowa	38 047
32	29	Kansas	37 618
38	30	Nebraska	37 338
2	31	Texas	37 320
11	32	North Carolina	37 057
40	33	Maine	36 459
20	34	Arizona	36 337
51	35	Wyoming	36 039
39	36	Idaho	36 023
23	37	Alabama	35 478
26	38	South Carolina	35 376
50	39	District of Columbia	35 309
25	40	Kentucky	35 226
4	41	Florida	35 081
16	42	Tennessee	34 393
46	43	South Dakota	33 438
27	44	Oklahoma	33 311
22	45	Louisiana	33 218
47	46	North Dakota	32 238
36	47	New Mexico	31 981
44	48	Montana	31 280
31	49	Mississippi	30 628
37	50	West Virginia	28 420
33	51	Arkansas	28 398

Note: Column numbers refer to Table A. States.

TABLE 6—States and the District of Columbia
Selected Rankings

Percent of Persons Below the Poverty Level, 1999

Population Rank	Poverty Rate Rank	State	[col 94] Poverty Rate for Persons 1999
X		United States	13.3
50	1	District of Columbia	19.3
36	1	New Mexico	19.3
22	3	Louisiana	18.4
31	4	Mississippi	18.1
33	5	Arkansas	17.5
37	6	West Virginia	16.8
2	7	Texas	16.7
27	8	Oklahoma	16.3
23	9	Alabama	16.2
1	10	California	16.0
25	10	Kentucky	16.0
3	12	New York	15.6
20	13	Arizona	15.5
44	13	Montana	15.5
26	15	South Carolina	14.9
10	16	Georgia	14.7
4	17	Florida	14.4
46	18	South Dakota	14.0
16	19	Tennessee	13.6
39	20	Idaho	13.0
11	21	North Carolina	12.6
47	22	North Dakota	12.5
17	23	Missouri	12.2
51	24	Wyoming	12.0
28	25	Oregon	11.6
12	25	Virginia	11.6
8	27	Michigan	11.5
5	28	Illinois	11.3
48	29	Alaska	11.2
43	29	Rhode Island	11.2
42	31	Hawaii	11.1
7	32	Ohio	11.0
32	33	Kansas	10.9
6	33	Pennsylvania	10.9
40	35	Maine	10.7
13	35	Massachusetts	10.7
35	35	Nevada	10.7
24	38	Colorado	10.2
15	38	Washington	10.2
45	40	Delaware	10.0
34	40	Utah	10.0
14	42	Indiana	9.9
30	42	Iowa	9.9
49	44	Vermont	9.7
38	45	Nebraska	9.6
19	46	Maryland	9.5
9	47	New Jersey	9.3
18	48	Wisconsin	9.2
29	49	Connecticut	8.9
21	49	Minnesota	8.9
41	51	New Hampshire	7.5

Percent of Children Under 18 Years Old Below the Poverty Level, 1999

Population Rank	Poverty Rate Rank for Children Under 18 Years	State	[col 95] Poverty Rate in 1999 for Children Under 18 Years
X	X	United States	19.9
50	1	District of Columbia	33.7
36	2	New Mexico	27.5
22	3	Louisiana	26.0
33	4	Arkansas	25.0
3	5	New York	24.7
37	5	West Virginia	24.7
1	7	California	24.6
31	8	Mississippi	24.5
23	9	Alabama	23.8
27	10	Oklahoma	23.7
2	11	Texas	23.6
20	12	Arizona	23.2
25	13	Kentucky	23.1
26	14	South Carolina	23.0
10	15	Georgia	22.8
4	16	Florida	21.8
44	17	Montana	21.3
46	18	South Dakota	19.0
16	19	Tennessee	18.9
11	20	North Carolina	18.6
8	21	Michigan	18.0
17	22	Missouri	17.7
5	23	Illinois	17.5
39	24	Idaho	17.3
43	24	Rhode Island	17.3
13	26	Massachusetts	17.0
12	26	Virginia	17.0
47	28	North Dakota	16.8
6	29	Pennsylvania	16.6
28	30	Oregon	16.3
48	31	Alaska	16.2
42	31	Hawaii	16.2
7	33	Ohio	16.0
45	34	Delaware	15.4
32	34	Kansas	15.4
35	34	Nevada	15.4
51	37	Wyoming	15.3
15	38	Washington	15.2
40	39	Maine	14.9
19	39	Maryland	14.9
14	41	Indiana	14.8
9	41	New Jersey	14.8
29	43	Connecticut	14.7
24	44	Colorado	14.6
18	45	Wisconsin	14.3
30	46	Iowa	13.7
21	47	Minnesota	13.1
49	48	Vermont	12.7
38	49	Nebraska	12.6
34	50	Utah	12.5
41	51	New Hampshire	10.0

Average Percentage of Persons Lacking Health Insurance, 1999

Population Rank	% Lacking Health Insurance Rank	State	[col 96] % Lacking Health Insurance
X	X	United States	15.5
36	1	New Mexico	25.8
2	2	Texas	23.3
22	3	Louisiana	22.5
20	4	Arizona	21.2
35	5	Nevada	20.7
1	6	California	20.3
4	7	Florida	19.2
48	8	Alaska	19.1
39	8	Idaho	19.1
44	10	Montana	18.6
26	11	South Carolina	17.6
27	12	Oklahoma	17.5
37	13	West Virginia	17.1
24	14	Colorado	16.8
31	15	Mississippi	16.6
3	16	New York	16.4
10	17	Georgia	16.1
51	17	Wyoming	16.1
15	19	Washington	15.8
50	20	District of Columbia	15.4
11	20	North Carolina	15.4
33	22	Arkansas	14.7
28	23	Oregon	14.6
25	24	Kentucky	14.5
23	25	Alabama	14.3
34	26	Utah	14.2
5	27	Illinois	14.1
12	27	Virginia	14.1
9	29	New Jersey	13.4
49	30	Vermont	12.3
32	31	Kansas	12.1
40	32	Maine	11.9
19	33	Maryland	11.8
47	33	North Dakota	11.8
46	33	South Dakota	11.8
16	36	Tennessee	11.5
45	37	Delaware	11.4
8	38	Michigan	11.2
42	39	Hawaii	11.1
7	40	Ohio	11.0
18	40	Wisconsin	11.0
14	42	Indiana	10.8
38	42	Nebraska	10.8
13	44	Massachusetts	10.5
41	45	New Hampshire	10.2
29	46	Connecticut	9.8
6	47	Pennsylvania	9.4
17	48	Missouri	8.6
30	49	Iowa	8.3
21	50	Minnesota	8.0
43	51	Rhode Island	6.9

Note: Column numbers refer to Table A. States.

TABLE 6—States and the District of Columbia
Selected Rankings

Percent of Occupied Units that were Owner-Occupied, 1998				Median Value of Owner-Occupied Housing Units, 1990				Medium Gross Rent of Renter-Occupied Housing Units, 1990			
Population Rank	Rank of Percent Owner-Occupied	State	[col 127] Percent Owner-Occupied	Population Rank	Median Value Rank	State	[col 132] Median Value in 1990 (dollars)	Population Rank	Median Rent Rank	State	[col 135] Median Rent in 1990 (dollars)
X	X	United States	66.3	X	X	United States	79 100	X	X	United States	447
26	1	South Carolina	76.6	42	1	Hawaii	245 300	42	1	Hawaii	650
21	2	Minnesota	75.4	1	2	California	195 500	1	2	California	620
25	3	Kentucky	75.1	29	3	Connecticut	177 800	29	3	Connecticut	598
31	3	Mississippi	75.1	13	4	Massachusetts	162 800	9	4	New Jersey	592
36	5	West Virginia	74.8	9	5	New Jersey	162 300	13	5	Massachusetts	580
39	6	Maine	74.6	43	6	Rhode Island	133 500	48	6	Alaska	559
8	7	Michigan	74.4	3	7	New York	131 600	41	7	New Hampshire	549
6	8	Pennsylvania	73.9	41	8	New Hampshire	129 400	19	8	Maryland	548
34	9	Utah	73.7	50	9	District of Columbia	123 900	35	9	Nevada	509
23	10	Alabama	72.9	19	10	Maryland	116 500	45	10	Delaware	495
40	11	Idaho	72.6	45	11	Delaware	100 100	12	10	Virginia	495
14	11	Indiana	72.6	35	12	Nevada	95 700	43	12	Rhode Island	489
30	13	Iowa	72.1	49	13	Vermont	95 500	3	13	New York	486
37	14	New Mexico	71.3	48	14	Alaska	94 400	4	14	Florida	481
11	14	North Carolina	71.3	15	15	Washington	93 400	50	15	District of Columbia	479
16	14	Tennessee	71.3	12	16	Virginia	91 000	49	16	Vermont	446
10	17	Georgia	71.2	39	17	Maine	87 400	5	17	Illinois	445
45	18	Delaware	71.0	24	18	Colorado	82 700	15	17	Washington	445
17	19	Missouri	70.7	5	19	Illinois	80 900	20	19	Arizona	438
7	19	Ohio	70.7	20	20	Arizona	80 100	10	20	Georgia	433
18	21	Wisconsin	70.1	4	21	Florida	77 100	8	21	Michigan	423
51	22	Wyoming	70.0	21	22	Minnesota	74 000	21	22	Minnesota	422
38	23	Nebraska	69.9	10	23	Georgia	71 300	39	23	Maine	419
27	24	Oklahoma	69.7	37	24	New Mexico	70 100	24	24	Colorado	418
41	25	New Hampshire	69.6	6	25	Pennsylvania	69 700	28	25	Oregon	408
12	26	Virginia	69.4	34	26	Utah	68 900	6	26	Pennsylvania	404
29	27	Connecticut	69.3	28	27	Oregon	67 100	18	27	Wisconsin	399
49	28	Vermont	69.1	11	28	North Carolina	65 800	2	28	Texas	395
19	29	Maryland	68.7	7	29	Ohio	63 500	11	29	North Carolina	382
44	30	Montana	68.6	18	30	Wisconsin	62 500	7	30	Ohio	379
5	31	Illinois	68.0	51	31	Wyoming	61 600	26	31	South Carolina	376
47	31	North Dakota	68.0	26	32	South Carolina	61 100	14	32	Indiana	374
46	33	South Dakota	67.3	8	33	Michigan	60 600	32	33	Kansas	372
4	34	Florida	66.9	17	34	Missouri	59 800	37	33	New Mexico	372
33	35	Arkansas	66.7	2	35	Texas	59 600	34	35	Utah	369
32	35	Kansas	66.7	22	36	Louisiana	58 500	17	36	Missouri	368
22	37	Louisiana	66.6	16	37	Tennessee	58 400	16	37	Tennessee	357
48	38	Alaska	66.3	40	38	Idaho	58 200	22	38	Louisiana	352
24	39	Colorado	65.2	44	39	Montana	56 600	38	39	Nebraska	348
15	40	Washington	64.9	14	40	Indiana	53 900	27	40	Oklahoma	340
20	41	Arizona	64.3	23	41	Alabama	53 700	30	41	Iowa	336
28	42	Oregon	63.4	32	42	Kansas	52 200	51	42	Wyoming	333
9	43	New Jersey	63.1	47	43	North Dakota	50 800	40	43	Idaho	330
2	44	Texas	62.5	25	44	Kentucky	50 500	33	44	Arkansas	328
35	45	Nevada	61.4	38	45	Nebraska	50 400	23	45	Alabama	325
13	46	Massachusetts	61.3	27	46	Oklahoma	48 100	25	46	Kentucky	319
43	47	Rhode Island	59.8	36	47	West Virginia	47 900	47	47	North Dakota	313
1	48	California	56.0	33	48	Arkansas	46 300	44	48	Montana	311
42	49	Hawaii	52.8	30	49	Iowa	45 900	31	49	Mississippi	309
3	49	New York	52.8	31	50	Mississippi	45 600	46	50	South Dakota	306
50	51	District of Columbia	40.3	46	51	South Dakota	45 200	36	51	West Virginia	303

Note: Column numbers refer to Table A. States.

TABLE 6—States and the District of Columbia
Selected Rankings

	Unemployment Rate, 1999				Exports of Goods by State of Origin (mil dol), 2000				Value of Residential Construction Authorized by Building Permits, 1999		
Population Rank	Unemployment Rate Rank	State	[col 148] Unemployment Rate 1999	Population Rank	Export Rank	State	[col 283] Exports by State (mil dol)	Population Rank	Value Rank	State	[col 279] Value of Residential Construction ($1,000)
X	X	United States	4.2	X	X	United States	653 632	X	X	United States	181 439 531
37	1	West Virginia	6.6	1	1	California	111 476	1	1	California	21 030 600
48	2	Alaska	6.4	2	2	Texas	60 909	4	2	Florida	16 197 445
50	3	District of Columbia	6.3	8	3	Michigan	47 971	2	3	Texas	14 045 115
28	4	Oregon	5.7	3	4	New York	45 440	10	4	Georgia	8 749 615
42	5	Hawaii	5.6	15	5	Washington	32 385	11	5	North Carolina	8 616 858
36	5	New Mexico	5.6	5	6	Illinois	30 360	20	6	Arizona	7 350 364
1	7	California	5.2	7	7	Ohio	27 811	5	7	Illinois	6 537 643
39	7	Idaho	5.2	9	8	New Jersey	25 540	7	8	Ohio	6 401 999
44	7	Montana	5.2	6	9	Pennsylvania	22 530	8	9	Michigan	6 204 660
3	7	New York	5.2	4	10	Florida	22 244	24	10	Colorado	6 035 973
22	11	Louisiana	5.1	13	11	Massachusetts	18 155	12	11	Virginia	5 142 222
31	11	Mississippi	5.1	21	12	Minnesota	16 573	14	12	Indiana	4 786 192
51	13	Wyoming	4.9	11	13	North Carolina	14 009	6	13	Pennsylvania	4 634 786
23	14	Alabama	4.8	14	14	Indiana	13 419	15	14	Washington	4 588 556
15	15	Washington	4.7	29	15	Connecticut	12 659	3	15	New York	4 414 787
9	16	New Jersey	4.6	10	16	Georgia	10 628	21	16	Minnesota	4 052 938
2	16	Texas	4.6	18	17	Wisconsin	10 453	18	17	Wisconsin	3 868 481
33	18	Arkansas	4.5	16	18	Tennessee	10 331	16	18	Tennessee	3 836 987
25	18	Kentucky	4.5	12	19	Virginia	10 153	26	19	South Carolina	3 614 665
26	18	South Carolina	4.5	24	20	Colorado	9 869	9	20	New Jersey	3 162 436
20	21	Arizona	4.4	20	21	Arizona	9 129	19	21	Maryland	3 102 361
35	21	Nevada	4.4	28	22	Oregon	8 492	35	22	Nevada	2 976 683
6	21	Pennsylvania	4.4	25	23	Kentucky	7 854	17	23	Missouri	2 742 784
5	24	Illinois	4.3	17	24	Missouri	7 679	13	24	Massachusetts	2 666 006
7	24	Ohio	4.3	26	25	South Carolina	7 450	28	25	Oregon	2 652 791
40	26	Maine	4.1	45	26	Delaware	5 692	34	26	Utah	2 296 384
43	26	Rhode Island	4.1	23	27	Alabama	5 516	25	27	Kentucky	1 909 051
10	28	Georgia	4.0	32	28	Kansas	4 803	23	28	Alabama	1 883 871
16	28	Tennessee	4.0	19	29	Maryland	4 635	22	29	Louisiana	1 766 666
4	30	Florida	3.9	50	30	District of Columbia	4 454	32	30	Kansas	1 668 027
8	31	Michigan	3.8	22	31	Louisiana	3 786	29	31	Connecticut	1 466 185
34	32	Utah	3.7	30	32	Iowa	3 160	27	32	Oklahoma	1 430 600
45	33	Delaware	3.5	27	33	Oklahoma	3 139	30	33	Iowa	1 405 608
19	33	Maryland	3.5	38	34	Nebraska	3 097	39	34	Idaho	1 366 527
17	35	Missouri	3.4	34	35	Utah	2 603	36	35	New Mexico	1 079 858
47	35	North Dakota	3.4	39	36	Idaho	2 464	31	36	Mississippi	989 518
27	35	Oklahoma	3.4	41	37	New Hampshire	2 282	33	37	Arkansas	965 992
29	38	Connecticut	3.2	33	38	Arkansas	2 012	38	38	Nebraska	827 968
13	38	Massachusetts	3.2	49	39	Vermont	1 782	41	39	New Hampshire	781 944
11	38	North Carolina	3.2	31	40	Mississippi	1 696	42	40	Hawaii	632 743
14	41	Indiana	3.0	40	41	Maine	1 587	40	41	Maine	623 269
32	41	Kansas	3.0	37	42	West Virginia	1 421	45	42	Delaware	492 470
49	41	Vermont	3.0	35	43	Nevada	1 316	37	43	West Virginia	381 091
18	41	Wisconsin	3.0	43	44	Rhode Island	1 062	43	44	Rhode Island	336 166
24	45	Colorado	2.9	48	45	Alaska	948	46	45	South Dakota	329 767
38	45	Nebraska	2.9	47	46	North Dakota	693	48	46	Alaska	306 585
46	45	South Dakota	2.9	36	47	New Mexico	581	49	47	Vermont	304 942
21	48	Minnesota	2.8	44	48	Montana	531	51	48	Wyoming	278 559
12	48	Virginia	2.8	46	49	South Dakota	455	44	49	Montana	226 260
41	50	New Hampshire	2.7	42	50	Hawaii	268	47	50	North Dakota	223 249
30	51	Iowa	2.5	51	51	Wyoming	133	50	51	District of Columbia	53 284

Note: Column numbers refer to Table A. States.

TABLE 6—States and the District of Columbia
Selected Rankings

Value of Agricultural Products Sold (Millions of Dollars), 1997				Per Capita State Taxes, 1998				Violent Crime Rate, 1999 (Violent Crimes Known to Police per 100,000 Population)			
Population Rank	Agricultural Production Rank	State	[col 172] Value of Agricultural Products Sold	Population Rank	Taxes Rank	State	[col 309] State Taxes Per Capita (Dollars)	Population Rank	Crime Rate Rank	State	[col 75] Crime Rate per 100,000 Population
X	X	United States	196 865	X	X	United States	X	X	X	United States	525
1	1	California	23 032	23	1	Connecticut	2 869	50	1	District of Columbia	1 628
2	2	Texas	13 767	48	2	Delaware	2 665	4	2	Florida	854
30	3	Iowa	11 948	20	3	Hawaii	2 662	26	3	South Carolina	847
38	4	Nebraska	9 832	33	4	Minnesota	2 434	36	4	New Mexico	835
32	5	Kansas	9 207	1	5	Massachusetts	2 357	19	5	Maryland	743
5	6	Illinois	8 556	24	6	Michigan	2 161	45	6	Delaware	734
21	7	Minnesota	8 290	29	7	Wisconsin	2 135	22	7	Louisiana	733
11	8	North Carolina	7 677	45	8	Washington	2 075	5	7	Illinois	733
4	9	Florida	6 005	50	9	California	2 073	16	9	Tennessee	695
18	10	Wisconsin	5 580	4	10	New Mexico	2 058	48	10	Alaska	632
33	11	Arkansas	5 480	10	11	New York	1 989	1	11	California	627
17	12	Missouri	5 368	42	12	Alaska	1 932	3	12	New York	589
14	13	Indiana	5 230	39	13	New Jersey	1 923	8	13	Michigan	575
10	14	Georgia	4 993	5	14	Maine	1 905	35	14	Nevada	570
15	15	Washington	4 768	14	15	Rhode Island	1 843	2	15	Texas	560
7	16	Ohio	4 684	30	16	North Carolina	1 838	20	16	Arizona	551
24	17	Colorado	4 534	32	17	Kentucky	1 807	13	16	Massachusetts	551
27	18	Oklahoma	4 146	25	18	Maryland	1 790	11	18	North Carolina	542
6	19	Pennsylvania	3 998	22	19	Nevada	1 782	10	19	Georgia	534
46	20	South Dakota	3 570	40	20	Wyoming	1 779	27	20	Oklahoma	508
8	21	Michigan	3 568	19	21	Kansas	1 773	17	21	Missouri	500
40	22	Idaho	3 346	13	22	Pennsylvania	1 719	23	22	Alabama	490
31	23	Mississippi	3 127	8	23	North Dakota	1 690	38	23	Nebraska	430
23	24	Alabama	3 099	21	24	Iowa	1 678	33	24	Arkansas	425
25	25	Kentucky	3 064	31	25	Idaho	1 674	6	25	Pennsylvania	421
28	26	Oregon	2 969	17	26	Utah	1 667	9	26	New Jersey	412
47	27	North Dakota	2 869	44	27	West Virginia	1 663	32	27	Kansas	383
3	28	New York	2 835	38	28	Indiana	1 652	15	28	Washington	377
12	29	Virginia	2 344	35	29	Illinois	1 641	28	29	Oregon	375
16	30	Tennessee	2 178	41	30	Vermont	1 621	14	29	Indiana	375
22	31	Louisiana	2 031	9	31	Arkansas	1 598	37	31	West Virginia	351
20	32	Arizona	1 903	36	32	Oklahoma	1 584	31	32	Mississippi	349
44	33	Montana	1 871	3	32	Nebraska	1 584	29	33	Connecticut	346
37	34	New Mexico	1 618	11	34	Ohio	1 574	24	34	Colorado	341
26	35	South Carolina	1 588	47	35	Virginia	1 552	7	35	Ohio	316
19	36	Maryland	1 312	7	36	Mississippi	1 542	12	36	Virginia	315
51	37	Wyoming	899	27	37	Oregon	1 523	25	37	Kentucky	301
34	38	Utah	877	28	38	Georgia	1 517	43	38	Rhode Island	287
9	39	New Jersey	697	6	39	Missouri	1 512	30	39	Iowa	280
45	40	Delaware	691	43	40	Florida	1 510	34	40	Utah	276
42	41	Hawaii	497	26	41	Montana	1 508	21	41	Minnesota	274
49	42	Vermont	476	46	42	Arizona	1 489	18	42	Wisconsin	246
13	43	Massachusetts	454	16	43	Colorado	1 483	39	43	Idaho	245
36	44	West Virginia	447	2	44	South Carolina	1 482	42	44	Hawaii	235
39	45	Maine	439	34	45	Louisiana	1 392	51	45	Wyoming	232
29	46	Connecticut	422	49	46	Alabama	1 319	44	46	Montana	207
35	47	Nevada	357	12	47	Tennessee	1 288	46	47	South Dakota	167
41	48	New Hampshire	149	15	48	Texas	1 246	49	48	Vermont	114
43	49	Rhode Island	48	37	49	South Dakota	1 129	40	49	Maine	112
48	50	Alaska	25	18	50	New Hampshire	851	41	50	New Hampshire	97
50	51	District of Columbia		51	51	District of Columbia	X	47	51	North Dakota	67

Note: Column numbers refer to Table A. States.

70

TABLE 7—Defense Procurement Contracts by Geographic Areas, 1998—75 Cities, Counties, Metropolitan Areas and States with the Largest Contract Amounts

Defense Contracts Rank	City	[col 108] Defense Contracts (Mil. Dol.)	County	[col 172] Defense Contracts (Mil. Dol.)	Metropolitan Area	[col 172] Defense Contracts (Mil. Dol.)	State	[col 262] Defense Contracts (Mil. Dol.)
1	St. Louis city, MO	3 797.6	Los Angeles, CA	6 890.5	Washington, DC-MD-VA-WV	11 655.3	California	17 301
2	Marietta city, GA	2 510.2	Fairfax, VA	4 739.1	Los Angeles-Long Beach, CA	6 890.5	Virginia	12 628
3	Long Beach city, CA	2 249.6	St. Louis city, MO	3 797.6	Boston-Worcester-Lawrence-Lowell-Brockton, MA-NH	4 343.4	Texas	7 863
4	Sunnyvale city, CA	2 053.3	Santa Clara, CA	2 540.0	St. Louis, MO-IL	4 133.7	Florida	5 443
5	San Diego city, CA	1 975.3	Cobb, GA	2 528.8	Norfolk-Virginia Beach-Newport News, VA-NC	3 401.9	Maryland	5 186
6	Fort Worth city, TX	1 719.1	Middlesex, MA	2 427.9	Atlanta, GA	2 873.6	Missouri	4 334
7	Seattle city, WA	1 683.0	San Diego, CA	2 392.5	San Jose, CA	2 540.0	Massachusetts	4 209
8	Newport News city, VA	1 577.3	New London, CT	2 139.1	San Diego, CA	2 392.5	Georgia	3 679
9	Orlando city, FL	1 333.1	Tarrant, TX	1 898.0	Philadelphia, PA-NJ	2 329.7	Connecticut	3 365
10	Huntsville city, AL	1 295.6	King, WA	1 806.3	Dallas, TX	2 159.9	Pennsylvania	3 311
11	Washington city, DC	1 095.6	Maricopa, AZ	1 759.8	New London-Norwich, CT	2 139.1	New York	3 039
12	West Palm Beach city, FL	1 025.0	Newport News City, VA	1 645.5	Seattle-Bellevue-Everett, WA	1 969.2	Arizona	2 919
13	Norfolk city, VA	989.4	Orange, CA	1 432.0	Fort Worth-Arlington, TX	1 898.5	New Jersey	2 668
14	Louisville city, KY	971.9	Madison, AL	1 397.6	Baltimore, MD	1 892.2	Washington	2 596
15	Denver city, CO	937.7	Dallas, TX	1 387.8	Phoenix-Mesa, AZ	1 762.2	Ohio	2 469
16	Tucson city, AZ	830.5	Orange, FL	1 357.2	Denver, CO	1 453.9	Colorado	2 382
17	Alexandria city, VA	829.3	Arlington, VA	1 291.0	Orange County, CA	1 432.0	Alabama	2 200
18	Baltimore city, MD	792.3	St. Mary's, MD	1 263.4	Huntsville, AL	1 398.6	Indiana	1 629
19	New Orleans city, LA	751.5	Montgomery, MD	1 166.2	Orlando, FL	1 391.2	Kentucky	1 581
20	Pascagoula city, MS	732.3	Palm Beach, FL	1 143.5	West Palm Beach-Boca Raton, FL	1 143.5	Illinois	1 277
21	Cincinnati city, OH	721.9	District of Columbia	1 095.6	Minneapolis-St. Paul, MN-WI	1 129.5	Louisiana	1 223
22	Grand Prairie city, TX	703.5	Norfolk City, VA	993.5	Louisville, KY-IN	1 075.4	Mississippi	1 222
23	Phoenix city, AZ	674.7	Jefferson, KY	973.8	Houston, TX	941.0	Tennessee	1 210
24	Indianapolis consolidated city, IN	637.5	Denver, CO	948.2	Biloxi-Gulfport-Pascagoula, MS	909.8	Minnesota	1 165
25	Minneapolis city, MN	582.1	Harris, TX	915.3	Pittsburgh, PA	901.2	District of Columbia	1 096
26	Pico Rivera city, CA	553.2	Burlington, NJ	910.6	Melbourne-Titusville-Palm Bay, FL	899.3	Michigan	1 062
27	Wichita city, KS	550.6	Hennepin, MN	900.5	Nassau-Suffolk, NY	877.2	Kansas	1 004
28	Philadelphia city, PA	538.0	Brevard, FL	899.3	Tucson, AZ	861.9	North Carolina	992
29	Mesa city, AZ	537.2	Allegheny, PA	874.6	Sacramento, CA	861.2	South Carolina	949
30	Los Angeles city, CA	527.8	Pima, AZ	861.9	Dayton-Springfield, OH	847.9	Oklahoma	926
31	Redondo Beach city, CA	513.1	Sacramento, CA	845.5	Colorado Springs, CO	839.0	Hawaii	915
32	Houston city, TX	478.2	El Paso, CO	839.0	Honolulu, HI	835.8	Maine	893
33	Melbourne city, FL	454.4	Honolulu, HI	835.8	New Orleans, LA	834.5	Alaska	624
34	Manassas city, VA	447.8	Alexandria City, VA	835.5	New Haven-Bridgeport-Stamford-Danbury-Waterbury, CT	797.5	New Mexico	559
35	Colorado Springs city, CO	446.0	Baltimore city, MD	800.3	Cincinnati, OH-KY-IN	785.9	Wisconsin	549
36	Sacramento city, CA	430.0	Fairfield, CT	759.3	San Antonio, TX	745.5	Utah	465
37	Lynn city, MA	414.4	Sagadahoc, ME	757.6	New York, NY	730.4	Iowa	452
38	Sterling Heights city, MI	400.2	Orleans, LA	753.1	Detroit, MI	672.7	New Hampshire	423
39	Anaheim city, CA	381.5	Jackson, MS	737.0	Tampa-St. Petersburg-Clearwater, FL	667.5	Oregon	289
40	Fort Wayne city, IN	377.6	Essex, MA	736.8	Indianapolis, IN	646.9	Nebraska	232
41	Dallas city, TX	369.7	Bexar, TX	730.7	Oakland, CA	630.6	Nevada	221
42	Rockville city, MD	368.8	Hamilton, OH	726.1	Monmouth-Ocean, NJ	621.1	Arkansas	217
43	Lewisville city, TX	367.7	Prince George's, MD	677.4	Wichita, KS	616.1	Rhode Island	214
44	Downey city, CA	367.4	Marion, IN	642.7	Chicago, IL	602.3	Idaho	169
45	San Antonio city, TX	363.4	Sedgwick, KS	615.5	Oklahoma City, OK	545.1	North Dakota	140
46	Huntington Beach city, CA	339.4	Nassau, NY	613.4	Riverside-San Bernardino, CA	449.3	Montana	107
47	Cedar Rapids city, IA	336.7	Fairfax City, VA	598.3	Fort Wayne, IN	424.3	West Virginia	102
48	St. Petersburg city, FL	314.7	Macomb, MI	580.4	Ventura, CA	418.9	Vermont	92
49	York city, PA	311.0	Greene, OH	569.4	Santa Barbara-Santa Maria-Lompoc, CA	405.9	Delaware	87
50	Memphis city, TN	302.7	Philadelphia, PA	538.8	Hartford, CT	402.4	South Dakota	87
51	New York city, NY	299.6	Oklahoma, OK	512.9	San Francisco, CA	379.0	Wyoming	68
52	Littleton city, CO	297.7	Monmouth, NM	498.7	Bergen-Passaic, NJ	374.2		
53	Walnut Creek city, CA	297.6	Pinellas, FL	492.3	Memphis, TN-AR-MS	363.5		
54	Virginia Beach city, VA	270.7	Manassas City, VA	447.8	Salt Lake City-Ogden, UT	363.3		
55	Cambridge city, MA	261.0	Anne Arundel, MD	445.5	Charleston-North Charleston, SC	362.3		
56	Deer Park city, TX	254.6	Arapahoe, CO	431.5	Corpus Christi, TX	360.5		
57	Jacksonville city, FL	251.8	Contra Costa, CA	422.4	Fort Walton Beach, FL	357.8		
58	Corpus Christi city, TX	250.7	Ventura, CA	418.9	Binghamton, NY	353.3		
59	Schenectady city, NY	250.0	Montgomery, PA	414.3	York, PA	348.2		
60	Greenville city, SC	249.2	Santa Barbara, CA	405.9	Cedar Rapids, IA	336.8		
61	Nashua city, NH	242.5	Cook, IL	388.8	Jacksonville, FL	325.4		
62	MarlBorough city, MA	232.4	Hartford, CT	387.8	Kansas City, MO-KS	315.9		
63	Charleston city, SC	232.2	Denton, TX	382.4	Columbus, OH	308.7		
64	Dayton city, OH	223.7	Allen, IN	380.2	Newark, NJ	300.0		
65	Taunton city, MA	222.0	San Bernardino, CA	380.0	Albany-Schenectady-Troy, NY	292.1		
66	Annapolis city, MD	209.7	Okaloosa, FL	357.8	South Bend, IN	282.1		
67	Irvine city, CA	209.4	Charleston, SC	355.1	Albuquerque, NM	278.8		
68	Mishawaka city, IN	206.4	Shelby, TN	354.4	Austin-San Marcos, TX	267.9		
69	Syracuse city, NY	206.1	York, PA	348.2	Bakersfield, CA	266.9		
70	Richardson city, TX	202.2	Linn, IA	336.8	Greenville-Spartanburg-Anderson, SC	263.3		
71	Salt Lake City, UT	198.2	Norfolk, MA	335.1	El Paso, TX	263.0		
72	San Jose city, CA	194.3	Coffee, TN	332.9	Fayetteville, NC	248.6		
73	Albuquerque city, NM	192.3	Hillsborough, NH	327.2	Syracuse, NY	243.8		
74	Tempe city, AZ	189.4	Nueces, TX	317.5	Anchorage, AK	235.8		
75	Palmdale city, CA	187.8	Harford, MD	313.7	Macon, GA	224.8		

TABLE 8—Congressional Districts of the 105th Congress
Selected Rankings

Largest Population, 1990			Largest Total Land Area, 1990 (Square Kilometers)			Population Density, 1990 (Per Square Kilometer)		
Population Rank	State/Congressional District	[col 2] Population	Land Area Rank	State/Congressional District	[col 1] Land Area	Density Rank	State/Congressional District	[col 3] Population Density
1	MT At Large	799 065	1	AK At Large	1 477 268	1	NY District 11	22 392.1
2	SD At Large	696 004	2	MT At Large	376 991	2	NY District 15	20 568.4
3	DE At Large	666 168	3	NV District 2	283 798	3	NY District 14	16 756.3
4	ND At Large	638 800	4	WY At Large	251 501	4	NY District 12	16 276.5
5	KY District 5	624 837	5	SD At Large	196 571	5	NY District 16	14 504.8
6	KS District 3	619 439	6	OR District 2	182 842	6	NY District 8	14 349.5
7	KS District 2	619 391	7	ND At Large	178 695	7	NY District 10	13 266.0
8	KS District 4	619 374	8	NM District 2	174 423	8	NY District 17	10 392.9
9	KS District 1	619 370	9	NE District 3	162 857	9	NY District 7	8 679.6
10	KY District 6	614 901	10	TX District 23	151 286	10	CA District 8	6 432.2
11	KY District 2	614 794	11	CO District 3	147 743	11	NY District 6	5 970.5
12	KY District 1	614 265	12	KS District 1	145 674	12	NY District 9	5 970.2
13	ME District 2	613 967	13	NM District 3	127 709	13	CA District 30	5 935.1
14	ME District 1	613 961	14	UT District 3	123 348	14	IL District 4	5 586.7
15	KY District 3	613 603	15	ID District 2	111 884	15	MA District 8	5 224.2
16	AZ District 1	610 872	16	AZ District 3	107 783	16	CA District 35	5 061.5
17	AZ District 6	610 872	17	AZ District 6	106 765	17	PA District 2	4 807.7
18	AZ District 2	610 871	18	CO District 4	104 338	18	CA District 32	4 695.2
19	AZ District 5	610 871	19	ID District 1	102 441	19	CA District 33	4 609.9
20	AZ District 4	610 871	20	UT District 1	88 280	20	IL District 7	4 345.1
21	AZ District 3	610 871	21	TX District 13	82 250	21	IL District 5	4 181.4
22	DC Delegate	606 900	22	CA District 40	77 473	22	NJ District 10	4 179.6
23	LA District 5	602 933	23	CA District 2	73 595	23	PA District 1	4 175.2
24	KY District 4	602 896	24	TX District 17	72 894	24	IL District 9	4 106.4
25	LA District 2	602 877	25	ME District 2	70 572	25	NJ District 13	4 019.3
26	LA District 4	602 876	26	MN District 7	68 167	26	IL District 1	3 976.0
27	LA District 1	602 842	27	MN District 8	66 874	27	PA District 3	3 846.8
28	LA District 3	602 839	28	OK District 6	66 291	28	DC Delegate	3 815.7
29	LA District 7	602 832	29	WA District 4	61 396	29	CA District 46	3 510.2
30	LA District 6	602 774	30	MI District 1	58 963	30	NY District 13	3 440.1
31	MA District 8	601 643	31	TX District 19	52 286	31	CA District 26	3 158.7
32	MA District 9	601 643	32	AR District 4	46 733	32	CA District 37	3 059.7
33	MA District 5	601 643	33	OK District 3	46 526	33	CA District 9	3 037.3
34	MA District 6	601 643	34	IA District 5	46 106	34	CA District 38	2 977.6
35	MA District 1	601 643	35	AZ District 2	45 869	35	CA District 31	2 931.5
36	MA District 4	601 642	36	WA District 5	45 781	36	MI District 14	2 809.2
37	MA District 7	601 642	37	MO District 8	45 248	37	NY District 4	2 659.9
38	MA District 3	601 642	38	TX District 21	44 851	38	MI District 15	2 656.5
39	MA District 2	601 642	39	WI District 7	43 313	39	NJ District 9	2 481.0
40	MA District 10	601 642	40	AR District 1	42 989	40	CA District 34	2 448.6
41	NV District 1	600 957	41	MN District 2	42 187	41	CA District 45	2 411.9
42	NV District 2	600 876	42	OR District 4	41 649	42	NY District 18	2 384.1
43	WV District 1	598 056	43	TX District 14	39 829	43	NJ District 8	2 197.2
44	WV District 2	597 921	44	TX District 2	36 767	44	MD District 7	2 119.7
45	MD District 4	597 690	45	MO District 4	36 523	45	OH District 11	2 117.5
46	MD District 6	597 688	46	KS District 2	36 195	46	CA District 39	2 112.7
47	MD District 1	597 684	47	IA District 3	35 828	47	WI District 5	2 080.5
48	MD District 2	597 683	48	MO District 6	35 149	48	FL District 17	2 069.8
49	MD District 8	597 682	49	NE District 1	34 705	49	CA District 12	2 060.2
50	MD District 5	597 681	50	LA District 5	33 948	50	MN District 5	1 972.8
51	MD District 3	597 680	51	AZ District 5	32 870	51	FL District 18	1 887.6
52	MD District 7	597 680	52	NY District 24	32 098	52	CA District 49	1 874.1
53	WV District 3	597 500	53	IA District 2	31 757	53	CA District 29	1 871.4
54	NJ District 13	594 630	54	MS District 2	31 730	54	IL District 2	1 772.8
55	NJ District 9	594 630	55	TX District 28	31 540	55	IL District 3	1 744.3
56	NJ District 10	594 630	56	MO District 9	31 461	56	FL District 22	1 700.9
57	NJ District 6	594 630	57	FL District 2	30 610	57	WA District 7	1 653.1
58	NJ District 11	594 630	58	OK District 2	30 294	58	CA District 50	1 638.9
59	NJ District 5	594 630	59	TX District 1	29 959	59	MO District 1	1 506.3
60	NJ District 12	594 630	60	AR District 3	29 810	60	MI District 12	1 505.6
61	NJ District 4	594 630	61	GA District 8	29 791	61	NY District 5	1 475.9
62	NJ District 3	594 630	62	GA District 2	29 683	62	CA District 5	1 467.7
63	NJ District 2	594 630	63	TX District 11	29 262	63	NY District 3	1 448.1
64	NJ District 1	594 630	64	KY District 1	29 089	64	FL District 10	1 440.2
65	NJ District 8	594 629	65	CA District 4	27 990	65	OH District 10	1 416.0
66	NJ District 7	594 629	66	CA District 1	27 981	66	TX District 18	1 395.7
67	GA District 3	589 630	67	IL District 19	27 798	67	MA District 7	1 344.9
68	GA District 6	589 600	68	WI District 3	27 554	68	VA District 8	1 340.4
69	AR District 3	589 523	69	PA District 5	27 142	69	OH District 1	1 246.8
70	GA District 9	589 420	70	MS District 1	26 926	70	AZ District 4	1 220.2
71	GA District 7	589 405	71	KY District 5	26 746	71	IL District 6	1 198.8
72	GA District 11	589 398	72	LA District 4	26 407	72	MD District 4	1 196.0
73	GA District 5	589 359	73	AL District 2	26 241	73	NY District 2	1 181.9
74	GA District 4	589 322	74	KS District 4	26 036	74	HI District 1	1 178.6
75	AR District 1	588 588	75	MS District 3	25 910	75	MN District 4	1 148.6

Note: Column numbers refer to Table E. Congressional Districts.

TABLE 8—Congressional Districts of the 105th Congress
Selected Rankings

	Percent White, 1990			Percent Black, 1990			Percent American Indian and Alaska Native Population, 1990	
White Rank	State/Congressional District	[col 4] Percent White	Black Rank	State/Congressional District	[col 5] Percent Black	Native American Rank	State/Congressional District	[col 6] Percent Native American
1	KY District 5	98.7	1	NY District 11	74.0	1	AZ District 6	21.7
2	VT At Large	98.6	2	MD District 7	71.0	2	NM District 3	20.1
3	ME District 1	98.5	3	MI District 15	70.0	3	OK District 2	17.2
4	MN District 2	98.5	4	IL District 1	69.7	4	AK At Large	15.6
5	PA District 11	98.4	5	MI District 14	69.1	5	OK District 3	11.4
6	PA District 12	98.3	6	IL District 2	68.5	6	NC District 7	7.3
7	PA District 9	98.3	7	AL District 7	67.5	7	SD At Large	7.3
8	ME District 2	98.3	8	DC Delegate	65.8	8	MT At Large	6.0
9	WI District 9	98.1	9	IL District 7	65.6	9	OK District 1	5.1
10	PA District 10	98.1	10	VA District 3	64.4	10	OK District 6	4.9
11	NH District 2	98.1	11	MS District 2	63.0	11	OK District 4	4.8
12	WI District 6	98.1	12	SC District 6	62.2	12	OK District 5	4.6
13	NH District 1	98.0	13	PA District 2	62.2	13	AZ District 2	4.5
14	WI District 3	98.0	14	GA District 5	62.0	14	ND At Large	4.1
15	IA District 5	98.0	15	LA District 2	60.7	15	NM District 2	3.7
16	MN District 1	97.8	16	NY District 10	60.7	16	AZ District 3	3.3
17	PA District 5	97.8	17	NJ District 10	60.2	17	WA District 4	2.8
18	IN District 6	97.7	18	TN District 9	59.2	18	NM District 1	2.7
19	IN District 9	97.7	19	OH District 11	58.6	19	CA District 1	2.7
20	WV District 1	97.6	20	MD District 4	58.5	20	UT District 3	2.6
21	NE District 3	97.6	21	FL District 17	58.4	21	WI District 8	2.6
22	TN District 1	97.5	22	NC District 1	57.3	22	NC District 8	2.5
23	IA District 3	97.5	23	NC District 12	56.6	23	NV District 2	2.4
24	KY District 4	97.3	24	NY District 6	56.2	24	CA District 2	2.4
25	MO District 7	97.3	25	PA District 1	52.4	25	MN District 5	2.4
26	IA District 2	97.3	26	MO District 1	52.3	26	MI District 1	2.4
27	WI District 7	97.2	27	FL District 23	51.6	27	OR District 2	2.3
28	OH District 18	97.1	28	FL District 3	47.0	28	WA District 6	2.3
29	OH District 6	97.1	29	NY District 15	46.9	29	MN District 7	2.2
30	MI District 4	97.1	30	TX District 18	44.7	30	WY At Large	2.1
31	MN District 8	97.0	31	TX District 30	44.5	31	MN District 8	2.1
32	OH District 19	96.8	32	CA District 35	42.7	32	WA District 2	2.0
33	MN District 6	96.8	33	NY District 16	42.2	33	WA District 5	1.8
34	OH District 2	96.7	34	NY District 17	41.9	34	AZ District 1	1.7
35	IN District 5	96.7	35	MS District 4	40.7	35	CA District 21	1.5
36	MN District 7	96.7	36	CA District 32	40.3	36	CA District 40	1.5
37	MI District 16	96.6	37	GA District 2	39.2	37	WA District 9	1.5
38	NY District 22	96.6	38	GA District 10	37.5	38	LA District 3	1.5
39	VA District 9	96.6	39	GA District 4	36.6	39	WI District 7	1.5
40	MI District 10	96.5	40	WI District 5	35.2	40	CO District 3	1.4
41	MO District 6	96.5	41	CA District 37	33.6	41	CA District 3	1.4
42	NE District 1	96.4	42	LA District 4	32.5	42	ID District 2	1.4
43	MO District 3	96.3	43	VA District 4	32.1	43	WA District 7	1.4
44	PA District 4	96.3	44	LA District 6	31.8	44	OR District 4	1.4
45	IN District 7	96.3	45	CA District 9	31.8	45	NC District 11	1.4
46	PA District 20	96.2	46	MS District 3	31.3	46	CA District 19	1.3
47	OH District 8	96.2	47	LA District 5	31.1	47	CA District 4	1.3
48	MI District 1	96.2	48	GA District 8	31.1	48	ID District 1	1.3
49	WV District 2	96.0	49	SC District 5	30.8	49	WA District 3	1.3
50	WI District 8	96.0	50	GA District 1	30.6	50	CA District 5	1.2
51	OR District 4	96.0	51	OH District 1	30.1	51	AZ District 4	1.2
52	PA District 19	95.9	52	IN District 10	29.8	52	OR District 5	1.2
53	OH District 5	95.9	53	AL District 1	28.5	53	KS District 4	1.2
54	NY District 31	95.9	54	AR District 4	26.6	54	OR District 3	1.2
55	AR District 3	95.9	55	AL District 3	26.0	55	KS District 2	1.2
56	IN District 8	95.8	56	SC District 2	25.1	56	CA District 44	1.1
57	NY District 23	95.8	57	VA District 5	24.8	57	CA District 52	1.1
58	TN District 4	95.8	58	GA District 3	24.7	58	CO District 1	1.1
59	NY District 27	95.5	59	AL District 2	24.1	59	CA District 11	1.1
60	WI District 2	95.5	60	FL District 2	24.1	60	CA District 48	1.1
61	IL District 19	95.5	61	LA District 7	23.8	61	NE District 1	1.1
62	MN District 3	95.4	62	MO District 5	23.7	62	AR District 3	1.1
63	NY District 24	95.4	63	LA District 3	23.6	63	MS District 3	1.1
64	MO District 4	95.4	64	MA District 8	23.3	64	CA District 20	1.0
65	MA District 6	95.3	65	OH District 12	23.2	65	CA District 18	1.0
66	IA District 4	95.3	66	NC District 8	23.2	66	CA District 22	1.0
67	PA District 7	95.2	67	TX District 25	23.0	67	WA District 8	1.0
68	PA District 21	95.2	68	MS District 1	22.8	68	WA District 1	1.0
69	MA District 10	95.1	69	TN District 5	22.8	69	MO District 7	1.0
70	PA District 8	95.0	70	NC District 2	21.9	70	CA District 42	0.9
71	CT District 6	95.0	71	TX District 9	21.7	71	CA District 17	0.9
72	IN District 2	95.0	72	NC District 3	21.5	72	AZ District 5	0.9
73	IA District 1	95.0	73	SC District 3	21.1	73	UT District 1	0.9
74	WV District 3	95.0	74	IN District 1	21.1	74	MN District 4	0.9
75	IL District 20	21.6	75	TX District 24	20.4	75	FL District 1	0.9

Note: Column numbers refer to Table E. Congressional Districts.

TABLE 8—Congressional Districts of the 105th Congress
Selected Rankings

	Percent Asian Population, 1990			Percent Hispanic, 1990			Percent Foreign Born, 1990	
Asian Rank	State/Congressional District	[col 7] Percent Asian	Hispanic Rank	State/Congressional District	[col 9] Percent Hispanic	Foreign Born Rank	State/Congressional District	[col 10] Percent Foreign Born
1	HI District 1	66.6	1	CA District 33	83.7	1	CA District 30	58.5
2	HI District 2	57.1	2	TX District 15	74.5	2	FL District 18	56.8
3	CA District 8	27.8	3	TX District 16	70.4	3	CA District 33	56.0
4	CA District 12	25.7	4	FL District 21	69.6	4	FL District 21	55.8
5	CA District 31	22.8	5	FL District 18	66.7	5	CA District 31	45.2
6	CA District 30	21.3	6	TX District 27	66.2	6	NY District 12	42.7
7	CA District 16	21.1	7	IL District 4	65.0	7	CA District 46	42.7
8	NY District 12	19.7	8	TX District 23	62.5	8	CA District 26	42.2
9	CA District 13	19.4	9	CA District 34	62.3	9	NY District 11	39.6
10	CA District 9	15.7	10	CA District 30	61.5	10	NY District 7	36.0
11	CA District 50	14.8	11	TX District 20	60.7	11	CA District 8	33.7
12	CA District 7	14.4	12	TX District 28	60.4	12	CA District 35	32.8
13	CA District 39	13.8	13	NY District 16	60.2	13	CA District 37	32.5
14	CA District 5	13.2	14	CA District 31	58.5	14	NJ District 13	32.5
15	CA District 28	13.0	15	NY District 12	57.9	15	IL District 4	32.5
16	CA District 36	12.5	16	CA District 20	55.4	16	CA District 34	31.1
17	CA District 46	12.3	17	CA District 26	52.7	17	CA District 29	30.7
18	CA District 14	12.2	18	AZ District 2	50.5	18	CA District 27	30.5
19	WA District 7	11.6	19	CA District 46	50.0	19	CA District 16	30.4
20	CA District 11	11.5	20	NY District 15	46.4	20	CA District 50	30.1
21	NY District 7	11.5	21	CA District 37	45.1	21	CA District 32	30.1
22	CA District 15	11.3	22	TX District 29	45.1	22	CA District 12	29.8
23	CA District 45	11.0	23	CA District 35	43.1	23	NY District 15	29.6
24	CA District 37	10.8	24	NM District 2	42.1	24	FL District 17	29.5
25	NY District 5	10.6	25	NJ District 13	41.5	25	NY District 6	28.9
26	CA District 27	10.5	26	CA District 50	40.6	26	NY District 18	26.4
27	CA District 41	10.1	27	NM District 1	38.1	27	NY District 17	26.2
28	IL District 9	10.0	28	CA District 16	36.8	28	CA District 20	25.4
29	CA District 47	9.6	29	NM District 3	34.6	29	NY District 8	25.1
30	CA District 34	9.3	30	CA District 42	34.3	30	IL District 9	24.4
31	CA District 38	9.1	31	CA District 17	31.6	31	NY District 9	24.4
32	CA District 51	8.2	32	CA District 41	31.5	32	NY District 14	24.2
33	NY District 18	8.2	33	CA District 32	30.2	33	TX District 16	24.1
34	VA District 11	8.1	34	CA District 23	30.0	34	IL District 5	23.1
35	MD District 8	8.0	35	NY District 17	29.1	35	NJ District 9	22.4
36	CA District 32	7.9	36	CA District 44	28.1	36	CA District 24	22.4
37	CA District 29	7.7	37	CA District 18	26.0	37	NY District 5	22.3
38	CA District 19	7.4	38	CA District 38	25.7	38	CA District 41	21.9
39	CA District 26	7.3	39	CA District 43	25.0	39	CA District 39	21.8
40	TX District 22	6.9	40	CA District 28	24.1	40	CA District 13	21.5
41	VA District 8	6.7	41	TX District 14	23.6	41	CA District 38	21.5
42	CA District 49	6.6	42	CA District 19	23.6	42	MA District 8	21.3
43	NJ District 9	6.6	43	TX District 18	23.4	43	NY District 16	21.3
44	CA District 25	6.5	44	FL District 17	23.0	44	CA District 28	20.9
45	CA District 10	6.4	45	CA District 39	22.8	45	FL District 22	20.9
46	CA District 24	6.4	46	CA District 52	22.6	46	CA District 14	20.7
47	CA District 17	6.3	47	CO District 1	21.9	47	NY District 10	20.5
48	NY District 6	6.3	48	TX District 10	21.4	48	CA District 17	19.7
49	NY District 8	6.3	49	NY District 7	21.3	49	CA District 36	19.4
50	NY District 9	6.2	50	CA District 22	21.3	50	TX District 29	19.4
51	WA District 9	6.1	51	CA District 11	21.1	51	CA District 9	19.2
52	CA District 18	6.0	52	TX District 24	21.0	52	CA District 45	19.2
53	CA District 35	6.0	53	CA District 27	20.6	53	NJ District 8	18.4
54	IL District 5	5.9	54	CA District 21	20.3	54	HI District 1	18.1
55	MA District 8	5.6	55	NY District 10	19.7	55	FL District 23	18.1
56	NY District 14	5.6	56	TX District 19	19.6	56	TX District 15	18.0
57	CA District 3	5.5	57	TX District 13	19.4	57	CA District 23	17.8
58	CA District 20	5.5	58	TX District 25	18.6	58	CA District 47	17.7
59	TX District 7	5.5	59	TX District 30	18.4	59	AZ District 2	17.3
60	NY District 13	5.5	60	CA District 13	18.4	60	MD District 8	17.2
61	WA District 1	5.4	61	NJ District 8	17.8	61	VA District 8	16.7
62	CA District 23	5.2	62	CO District 3	17.4	62	NY District 13	16.6
63	IL District 6	4.9	63	CA District 48	17.2	63	TX District 23	16.4
64	NJ District 6	4.8	64	TX District 17	17.2	64	CA District 7	16.3
65	WA District 8	4.6	65	TX District 22	17.0	65	CA District 18	16.3
66	MN District 4	4.6	66	NY District 6	16.9	66	NJ District 10	16.2
67	NJ District 13	4.6	67	AZ District 5	16.5	67	CA District 44	16.0
68	MD District 4	4.6	68	TX District 7	16.4	68	TX District 7	15.9
69	NJ District 7	4.6	69	CA District 25	16.4	69	CA District 51	15.7
70	OR District 3	4.5	70	TX District 12	16.3	70	VA District 11	15.7
71	CA District 48	4.5	71	CA District 40	16.1	71	CA District 25	15.4
72	TX District 3	4.5	72	WA District 4	15.9	72	CA District 42	15.2
73	NJ District 5	4.5	73	CA District 8	15.7	73	CA District 11	15.1
74	NJ District 12	4.4	74	CA District 36	14.9	74	CA District 15	15.0
75	CA District 43	4.3	75	CA District 45	14.8	75	NY District 4	15.0

Note: Column numbers refer to Table E. Congressional Districts.

TABLE 8—Congressional Districts of the 105th Congress
Selected Rankings

Percent Age 65 and Over, 1990			Percent Under 18 Years Old, 1990			Percent of Households with Female Householder, 1990		
65 and Over Rank	State/Congressional District	[cols 19 & 20] Percent 65 and Over	Under Age 18 Rank	State/Congressional District	[cols 12 & 13] Percent Under 18 Years	Female House-holder Rank	State/Congressional District	[col 24] Percent with Female Householder
1	FL District 22	30.9	1	UT District 3	38.0	1	NY District 16	38.0
2	FL District 13	30.9	2	UT District 1	37.3	2	MI District 15	29.1
3	FL District 19	28.2	3	CA District 20	34.8	3	MI District 14	28.0
4	FL District 10	26.1	4	TX District 15	34.7	4	NY District 11	27.8
5	FL District 14	25.6	5	CA District 37	34.4	5	NY District 15	27.5
6	FL District 5	24.8	6	UT District 2	33.9	6	NY District 10	27.4
7	FL District 16	23.8	7	TX District 23	33.8	7	PA District 1	26.3
8	FL District 9	21.8	8	NY District 16	33.6	8	MD District 7	26.1
9	AZ District 3	19.8	9	CA District 42	33.4	9	IL District 7	25.8
10	NY District 9	19.7	10	IL District 4	32.9	10	IL District 2	25.6
11	PA District 11	18.7	11	MS District 2	32.8	11	IL District 1	25.6
12	PA District 18	18.6	12	TX District 27	32.8	12	NY District 12	25.0
13	FL District 15	18.6	13	CA District 33	32.8	13	AL District 7	24.4
14	FL District 6	18.4	14	ID District 2	32.5	14	LA District 2	24.3
15	CA District 44	18.2	15	TX District 29	32.5	15	FL District 17	23.4
16	IA District 5	18.2	16	TX District 28	32.4	16	MS District 2	23.3
17	PA District 3	17.8	17	TX District 16	32.4	17	NJ District 10	23.3
18	NC District 11	17.7	18	AZ District 2	32.2	18	VA District 3	23.0
19	NE District 3	17.6	19	CA District 35	31.8	19	TN District 9	22.8
20	PA District 14	17.5	20	CA District 18	31.5	20	NY District 17	22.8
21	IL District 19	17.4	21	NM District 3	31.5	21	CA District 35	22.5
22	FL District 18	17.3	22	LA District 3	31.4	22	SC District 6	21.9
23	FL District 12	17.2	23	AK At Large	31.4	23	PA District 2	21.9
24	KS District 1	17.2	24	MN District 6	31.1	24	OH District 11	21.7
25	NY District 7	17.1	25	NM District 2	30.5	25	CA District 37	21.6
26	NY District 18	17.0	26	FL District 17	30.5	26	NY District 6	21.5
27	PA District 12	17.0	27	CA District 50	30.5	27	GA District 5	21.5
28	PA District 6	16.9	28	AZ District 2	30.4	28	NC District 12	21.2
29	PA District 20	16.8	29	CA District 21	30.3	29	NC District 1	20.8
30	PA District 10	16.8	30	CA District 41	30.2	30	MO District 1	20.3
31	NJ District 4	16.7	31	TX District 24	30.1	31	FL District 3	19.8
32	IL District 17	16.6	32	LA District 7	30.1	32	TX District 30	19.5
33	IA District 3	16.5	33	WY At Large	29.9	33	DC Delegate	19.5
34	IL District 9	16.4	34	CA District 34	29.8	34	WI District 5	19.3
35	PA District 4	16.4	35	CA District 43	29.8	35	IL District 4	18.7
36	AR District 4	16.3	36	WA District 4	29.7	36	TX District 18	18.7
37	IA District 2	16.3	37	MI District 14	29.6	37	FL District 23	18.5
38	IL District 3	16.2	38	IL District 2	29.6	38	GA District 2	18.1
39	FL District 20	16.2	39	AL District 7	29.5	39	MD District 4	18.1
40	MO District 8	16.2	40	LA District 2	29.5	40	CA District 32	18.1
41	NJ District 9	16.1	41	TX District 20	29.5	41	NJ District 13	17.3
42	CA District 29	16.0	42	CA District 31	29.5	42	CA District 50	17.0
43	TX District 1	16.0	43	CA District 19	29.4	43	MS District 4	16.6
44	OK District 3	16.0	44	TX District 22	29.4	44	GA District 10	16.6
45	TX District 17	16.0	45	GA District 2	29.3	45	CA District 33	16.5
46	MA District 10	15.9	46	LA District 5	29.2	46	OH District 1	16.4
47	OH District 17	15.9	47	CA District 11	29.2	47	IN District 10	16.4
48	FL District 7	15.8	48	SC District 6	29.1	48	TX District 16	16.0
49	IL District 20	15.8	49	CA District 40	29.0	49	TX District 20	16.0
50	AR District 3	15.7	50	CA District 46	29.0	50	TX District 28	15.7
51	MI District 1	15.7	51	TX District 30	28.9	51	GA District 8	15.7
52	MN District 8	15.7	52	IL District 7	28.8	52	LA District 5	15.6
53	OR District 2	15.7	53	LA District 4	28.8	53	AZ District 2	15.5
54	NY District 14	15.6	54	TX District 19	28.8	54	CA District 20	15.4
55	WV District 1	15.6	55	ID District 1	28.7	55	CA District 31	15.4
56	RI District 1	15.6	56	MN District 2	28.7	56	LA District 4	15.4
57	MO District 7	15.6	57	IL District 14	28.7	57	CA District 9	15.4
58	MN District 2	15.6	58	MI District 2	28.6	58	MI District 9	15.3
59	NY District 21	15.4	59	SD At Large	28.5	59	MA District 8	15.3
60	CA District 2	15.4	60	IN District 4	28.5	60	AL District 1	15.1
61	NY District 5	15.4	61	HI District 2	28.5	61	CA District 30	15.1
62	PA District 13	15.4	62	NY District 10	28.5	62	SC District 5	15.0
63	OH District 19	15.3	63	LA District 6	28.5	63	NY District 30	15.0
64	PA District 9	15.3	64	NY District 11	28.5	64	IN District 1	14.8
65	KY District 1	15.3	65	TX District 3	28.5	65	KY District 3	14.8
66	NY District 8	15.2	66	MS District 4	28.4	66	LA District 6	14.7
67	IL District 5	15.2	67	MS District 5	28.4	67	PA District 14	14.7
68	OH District 10	15.2	68	CA District 16	28.4	68	TX District 27	14.6
69	AR District 1	15.2	69	MI District 3	28.3	69	CA District 34	14.6
70	MA District 7	15.1	70	CA District 26	28.3	70	TX District 29	14.5
71	NJ District 3	15.1	71	CO District 5	28.2	71	OH District 12	14.5
72	PA District 7	15.1	72	AL District 1	28.2	72	NJ District 1	14.4
73	OH District 18	15.1	73	MS District 3	28.1	73	MS District 3	14.3
74	WI District 7	15.1	74	WA District 8	28.1	74	CA District 42	14.2
75	PA District 15	15.0	75	KY District 5	28.1	75	TX District 24	14.2

Note: Column numbers refer to Table E. Congressional Districts.

TABLE 8—Congressional Districts of the 105th Congress
Selected Rankings

Percent of Households Composed of One Person, 1990			Percent College Graduates (16+ Years of Education), 1990			Median Household Income, 1989		
One Person House-hold Rank	State/Congressional District	[col 25] Percent of All Households	Percent College Gradu-ate Rank	State/Congressional District	[col 32] Percent of All Persons 25 Yrs. and Over	House-hold Income Rank	State/Congressional District	[col 34] Median Income (dollars)
1	NY District 14	52.3	1	NY District 14	51.4	1	NJ District 11	57 219
2	NY District 8	48.4	2	MD District 8	51.1	2	MD District 8	56 789
3	CA District 29	44.1	3	VA District 8	48.0	3	NY District 3	56 060
4	CA District 8	41.7	4	VA District 11	44.3	4	NJ District 12	54 630
5	DC Delegate	41.5	5	CA District 14	44.2	5	VA District 11	54 369
6	FL District 22	40.1	6	CA District 29	43.5	6	NJ District 5	53 433
7	CO District 1	38.9	7	NY District 8	42.1	7	CA District 10	52 378
8	WA District 7	38.9	8	TX District 26	40.8	8	CA District 47	51 554
9	IL District 9	38.2	9	TX District 7	40.6	9	NJ District 7	50 996
10	NY District 15	35.6	10	IL District 10	40.4	10	NY District 4	50 887
11	IL District 5	35.6	11	NJ District 12	39.7	11	CA District 15	50 823
12	PA District 2	35.3	12	GA District 6	39.5	12	IL District 10	50 355
13	MA District 8	35.3	13	NJ District 11	37.4	13	NY District 19	50 239
14	MN District 5	35.3	14	CA District 47	37.1	14	NY District 5	50 103
15	CA District 9	34.4	15	WA District 7	37.0	15	IL District 13	50 087
16	MI District 15	34.1	16	CA District 36	36.8	16	CA District 14	50 078
17	PA District 14	33.3	17	IL District 9	36.6	17	NY District 2	50 076
18	FL District 10	33.2	18	MA District 8	36.0	18	MI District 11	49 021
19	CA District 49	33.1	19	NC District 4	35.9	19	VA District 8	48 839
20	OH District 11	32.6	20	TX District 3	35.9	20	CA District 36	48 522
21	NY District 9	32.4	21	CA District 10	35.8	21	CA District 24	48 433
22	IL District 7	32.3	22	CA District 9	35.4	22	CT District 4	47 636
23	GA District 5	32.2	23	IL District 13	35.0	23	IL District 8	47 374
24	MO District 1	32.0	24	NY District 5	34.8	24	NY District 20	47 107
25	OH District 1	31.9	25	CA District 15	34.8	25	MD District 5	46 936
26	NY District 7	31.9	26	TX District 10	34.5	26	CA District 25	46 480
27	TX District 10	31.7	27	CA District 51	34.5	27	VA District 10	46 205
28	VA District 8	31.4	28	MI District 11	34.4	28	CA District 39	46 196
29	IL District 1	31.1	29	CT District 4	34.0	29	GA District 6	46 148
30	CA District 32	31.0	30	CA District 49	33.9	30	NY District 1	45 464
31	MO District 5	30.9	31	CA District 8	33.8	31	CA District 51	45 186
32	TX District 26	30.9	32	MO District 2	33.6	32	CA District 45	45 074
33	IN District 10	30.8	33	PA District 13	33.5	33	PA District 13	44 764
34	NY District 17	30.6	34	NY District 18	33.4	34	CA District 12	44 720
35	WI District 5	30.1	35	CO District 6	33.4	35	CA District 41	44 607
36	NY District 10	29.9	36	CA District 24	33.4	36	MN District 3	44 329
37	OH District 10	29.7	37	DC Delegate	33.3	37	IL District 6	44 216
38	TX District 18	29.6	38	GA District 4	33.1	38	CT District 5	44 056
39	TN District 5	29.6	39	CA District 6	33.0	39	MO District 2	43 957
40	NY District 21	29.4	40	MN District 3	32.9	40	CA District 13	43 877
41	PA District 1	29.2	41	TX District 6	32.6	41	NY District 18	43 754
42	NJ District 10	29.2	42	NJ District 5	32.6	42	CA District 28	43 508
43	TX District 5	29.2	43	NY District 19	32.4	43	PA District 8	43 483
44	PA District 3	29.1	44	NJ District 7	32.4	44	CA District 23	42 989
45	CA District 38	29.0	45	CA District 12	31.6	45	CT District 6	42 817
46	MN District 4	29.0	46	KS District 3	31.5	46	MA District 5	42 701
47	LA District 2	28.9	47	CA District 27	31.4	47	CA District 48	42 389
48	CA District 5	28.9	48	WA District 1	31.2	48	WA District 8	42 379
49	TX District 7	28.7	49	PA District 7	31.0	49	NJ District 6	42 309
50	TN District 9	28.6	50	MA District 4	30.9	50	CA District 16	42 223
51	MD District 8	28.5	51	OR District 1	30.8	51	NY District 14	42 184
52	OR District 3	28.5	52	MA District 7	30.6	52	MN District 6	42 161
53	KY District 3	28.4	53	VA District 7	30.5	53	PA District 7	41 710
54	FL District 11	28.4	54	MN District 5	30.3	54	TX District 3	41 683
55	PA District 18	28.4	55	VA District 10	30.3	55	AK At Large	41 408
56	TX District 25	28.3	56	IL District 8	30.2	56	MA District 7	41 318
57	OK District 1	28.3	57	CO District 5	30.1	57	NJ District 3	41 257
58	CA District 27	28.3	58	TX District 22	29.9	58	MD District 4	41 081
59	NJ District 9	28.0	59	NY District 3	29.9	59	TX District 6	40 930
60	MO District 3	28.0	60	NY District 20	29.6	60	MA District 6	40 836
61	CA District 36	28.0	61	CO District 2	29.5	61	NJ District 9	40 816
62	OH District 15	27.9	62	TX District 8	29.2	62	CA District 6	40 564
63	NY District 28	27.8	63	WA District 8	29.0	63	WA District 1	40 390
64	NY District 29	27.7	64	MA District 5	28.8	64	TX District 7	40 331
65	AZ District 1	27.6	65	IL District 6	28.6	65	TX District 26	40 269
66	OK District 5	27.6	66	MN District 4	28.1	66	HI District 1	40 257
67	NC District 12	27.5	67	TX District 21	28.0	67	TX District 22	40 160
68	NY District 18	27.5	68	MA District 9	27.8	68	MD District 2	40 120
69	NJ District 13	27.4	69	CA District 45	27.7	69	CT District 1	39 961
70	AZ District 5	27.3	70	MD District 4	27.7	70	NJ District 8	39 944
71	OR District 1	27.3	71	CA District 48	27.7	71	CT District 3	39 815
72	MA District 9	27.2	72	AZ District 1	27.6	72	IL District 14	39 815
73	CA District 14	27.2	73	NY District 28	27.4	73	MA District 4	39 005
74	NY District 30	27.1	74	MA District 6	27.4	74	VA District 7	38 865
75	OH District 3	27.1	75	MI District 13	27.3	75	MI District 12	38 760

Note: Column numbers refer to Table E. Congressional Districts.

TABLE 8—Congressional Districts of the 105th Congress
Selected Rankings

Poverty Rate Rank	Percent of Persons Below the Poverty Level, 1989 — State/Congressional District	[col 36] Poverty Rate for Persons 1989	Median Value Rank	Median Value of Owner-Occupied Housing Units, 1990 — State/Congressional District	[col 41] Median Value in 1990 (dollars)	Median Rent Rank	Median Gross Rent of Renter-Occupied Housing Units, 1990 — State/Congressional District	[col 44] Median Rent in 1990 (dollars)
1	NY District 16	41.8	1	CA District 29	500 001	1	CA District 47	845
2	MS District 2	37.7	2	CA District 14	404 400	2	NY District 2	817
3	TX District 15	37.5	3	CA District 36	371 100	3	CA District 45	815
4	MI District 15	36.6	4	CA District 12	324 100	4	CA District 36	812
5	NY District 15	33.0	5	HI District 1	311 200	5	NY District 3	811
6	KY District 5	32.7	6	CA District 24	305 700	6	VA District 11	797
7	AL District 7	31.2	7	CA District 27	296 000	7	CA District 15	794
8	LA District 2	31.0	8	CA District 15	291 500	8	NY District 1	782
9	NY District 12	30.4	9	NY District 18	288 500	9	CA District 12	780
10	TX District 27	29.7	10	CA District 47	280 800	10	CA District 24	779
11	IL District 7	29.5	11	CT District 4	277 400	11	CA District 14	777
12	TX District 23	29.5	12	CA District 10	275 100	12	MD District 8	777
13	NY District 10	28.3	13	CA District 8	274 700	13	CA District 10	746
14	TX District 28	28.2	14	CA District 45	266 300	14	CA District 39	736
15	CA District 33	28.0	15	CA District 6	257 400	15	CA District 23	733
16	PA District 1	28.0	16	NY District 5	256 900	16	CA District 51	730
17	CA District 20	27.9	17	CA District 39	239 000	17	NJ District 11	730
18	AZ District 2	27.9	18	CA District 48	237 300	18	VA District 8	729
19	LA District 5	27.9	19	NY District 14	235 700	19	CA District 13	726
20	TX District 16	27.0	20	CA District 23	235 600	20	CA District 46	719
21	SC District 6	27.0	21	CA District 32	234 800	21	CA District 16	718
22	TX District 18	26.7	22	CA District 16	234 500	22	NJ District 5	717
23	FL District 17	26.6	23	CA District 28	233 700	23	CA District 6	709
24	NC District 1	26.1	24	CA District 51	231 000	24	CT District 4	706
25	MS District 4	25.3	25	CA District 22	230 100	25	CA District 28	705
26	LA District 7	24.7	26	CA District 49	226 000	26	NY District 4	705
27	CA District 35	24.6	27	CA District 38	224 700	27	NJ District 7	699
28	MI District 14	24.6	28	CA District 9	223 900	28	CA District 48	696
29	AR District 1	24.6	29	CA District 13	223 700	29	NJ District 12	696
30	TX District 20	24.4	30	NY District 8	223 000	30	CA District 25	690
31	TN District 9	24.2	31	CA District 17	220 800	31	MA District 7	685
32	GA District 2	24.2	32	NJ District 11	215 600	32	CA District 29	678
33	CA District 30	24.1	33	NJ District 5	214 400	33	NY District 14	678
34	WV District 3	24.1	34	CA District 25	214 100	34	MD District 5	674
35	IL District 1	23.8	35	NY District 9	212 300	35	FL District 19	672
36	IL District 4	23.8	36	VA District 8	209 900	36	CA District 27	671
37	LA District 4	23.7	37	MD District 8	207 200	37	IL District 8	667
38	NM District 3	23.6	38	NY District 7	206 100	38	NY District 5	660
39	NM District 2	23.5	39	NJ District 12	205 700	39	HI District 1	659
40	CA District 37	23.3	40	NY District 3	205 300	40	NY District 20	659
41	LA District 3	22.6	41	CA District 41	204 600	41	VA District 10	657
42	AR District 4	22.4	42	NY District 19	199 200	42	CA District 41	656
43	OK District 3	22.4	43	NY District 4	197 800	43	NY District 19	653
44	MO District 8	22.4	44	NJ District 9	195 700	44	MA District 10	651
45	OH District 11	22.1	45	NY District 20	193 600	45	NJ District 3	651
46	GA District 5	22.0	46	NY District 6	193 600	46	NJ District 6	645
47	MS District 3	22.0	47	MA District 7	193 600	47	CA District 17	643
48	FL District 3	22.0	48	VA District 11	191 000	48	MD District 4	643
49	TX District 30	21.8	49	HI District 2	190 900	49	NJ District 9	640
50	TX District 29	21.8	50	NY District 13	190 700	50	MI District 11	638
51	VA District 3	21.8	51	MA District 8	189 700	51	CA District 34	637
52	NY District 11	21.7	52	CA District 30	189 000	52	CA District 38	636
53	FL District 23	21.5	53	CA District 46	188 500	53	MA District 8	636
54	MD District 7	21.4	54	NJ District 7	186 900	54	HI District 2	633
55	AZ District 6	21.3	55	CA District 26	186 600	55	CA District 8	631
56	TX District 13	21.3	56	NY District 15	186 600	56	CA District 7	625
57	WI District 5	21.0	57	CT District 5	183 900	57	CA District 26	624
58	PA District 2	20.9	58	NY District 11	183 900	58	FL District 20	624
59	AL District 1	20.9	59	IL District 10	181 400	59	CT District 3	623
60	MS District 5	20.8	60	MA District 6	181 100	60	CA District 31	622
61	TX District 2	20.5	61	CA District 31	180 100	61	CA District 22	621
62	OH District 6	20.1	62	NY District 17	176 400	62	IL District 13	619
63	TX District 1	20.1	63	NY District 12	176 300	63	MA District 6	617
64	MS District 1	20.1	64	CA District 34	174 400	64	MA District 9	616
65	LA District 6	20.0	65	MA District 5	174 200	65	PA District 8	608
66	TX District 14	20.0	66	CT District 3	173 800	66	CA District 49	607
67	OK District 2	19.7	67	MA District 9	172 800	67	IL District 10	605
68	FL District 2	19.5	68	CT District 1	172 000	68	IL District 6	605
69	GA District 8	19.3	69	MA District 4	170 600	69	MA District 5	603
70	AL District 3	19.3	70	CA District 7	168 100	70	PA District 13	600
71	CA District 32	19.2	71	NY District 10	167 900	71	GA District 6	598
72	MO District 1	19.1	72	CT District 6	166 400	72	NJ District 8	595
73	TX District 17	19.1	73	MA District 10	163 700	73	CA District 43	595
74	VA District 9	19.1	74	NJ District 6	160 600	74	NY District 18	594
75	KY District 1	19.0	75	NY District 2	159 600	75	CA District 32	592

Note: Column numbers refer to Table E. Congressional Districts.

States

(For explanation of symbols, see page xii)

Table A. States — **Land Area and Population**

STATE code	STATE	Land area, 1990[1] (sq km)	Population 2000	Population and population characteristics, 1999			Race (percent)					Age (percent)			
				Population											
				Total persons	Rank	Per square kilometer	White	Black	American Indian, Eskimo, Aleut	Asian and Pacific Islander	Hispanic[2] (percent)	Under 5 years	5 to 17 years	18 to 24 years	25 to 34 years
		1	2	3	4	5	6	7	8	9	10	11	12	13	14
00	UNITED STATES	9 159 127	281 421 906	272 690 813	X	29.8	82.4	12.8	0.9	4.0	11.5	6.9	18.8	9.5	13.9
01	ALABAMA........................	131 443	4 447 100	4 369 862	23	33.2	73.0	26.1	0.3	0.7	1.0	6.7	17.7	10.1	14.1
02	ALASKA..........................	1 477 268	626 932	619 500	48	0.4	75.2	3.9	16.4	4.5	4.0	8.0	23.7	11.4	11.7
04	ARIZONA.........................	294 333	5 130 632	4 778 332	20	16.2	88.7	3.7	5.5	2.1	22.7	8.1	19.9	9.6	13.2
05	ARKANSAS......................	134 875	2 673 400	2 551 373	33	18.9	82.6	16.1	0.5	0.7	2.1	7.0	18.9	9.9	12.8
06	CALIFORNIA.....................	403 971	33 871 648	33 145 121	1	82.0	79.4	7.5	0.9	12.2	31.6	7.5	19.4	10.0	15.4
08	COLORADO......................	268 658	4 301 261	4 056 133	24	15.1	92.3	4.3	0.9	2.5	14.9	7.1	19.2	9.7	12.9
09	CONNECTICUT..................	12 550	3 405 565	3 282 031	29	261.5	87.8	9.4	0.2	2.6	8.5	6.6	18.6	7.8	13.6
10	DELAWARE......................	5 063	783 600	753 538	45	148.8	77.7	19.8	0.3	2.1	3.7	6.7	17.6	9.2	15.0
11	DISTRICT OF COLUMBIA .	159	572 059	519 000	50	3 262.1	35.2	61.4	0.3	3.1	7.4	5.3	13.1	8.8	18.3
12	FLORIDA..........................	139 853	15 982 378	15 111 244	4	108.1	82.3	15.4	0.4	1.9	15.4	6.3	17.3	8.2	12.4
13	GEORGIA.........................	150 010	8 186 453	7 788 240	10	51.9	69.0	28.7	0.2	2.1	3.1	7.4	19.0	9.9	15.5
15	HAWAII............................	16 637	1 211 537	1 185 497	42	71.3	33.0	2.8	0.6	63.6	8.1	6.8	17.6	10.1	12.4
16	IDAHO.............................	214 325	1 293 953	1 251 700	40	5.8	96.9	0.6	1.3	1.2	7.4	7.4	20.6	11.5	12.3
17	ILLINOIS..........................	143 987	12 419 293	12 128 370	5	84.2	81.1	15.3	0.2	3.4	10.5	7.2	19.0	9.4	14.0
18	INDIANA..........................	92 904	6 080 485	5 942 901	14	64.0	90.4	8.4	0.3	1.0	2.6	7.0	18.8	9.7	13.9
19	IOWA..............................	144 716	2 926 324	2 869 413	30	19.8	96.4	2.0	0.3	1.3	2.1	6.4	18.7	9.8	12.4
20	KANSAS	211 922	2 688 418	2 654 052	32	12.5	91.4	5.9	0.9	1.8	5.6	6.9	19.4	10.2	12.8
21	KENTUCKY......................	102 907	4 041 769	3 960 825	25	38.5	91.9	7.3	0.1	0.7	0.9	6.5	17.8	10.2	13.7
22	LOUISIANA......................	112 836	4 468 976	4 372 035	22	38.7	65.9	32.4	0.4	1.3	2.7	7.2	20.0	11.0	13.1
23	MAINE............................	79 939	1 274 923	1 253 040	39	15.7	98.3	0.5	0.5	0.8	0.7	5.4	17.8	8.8	13.3
24	MARYLAND......................	25 316	5 296 486	5 171 634	19	204.3	67.5	28.1	0.3	4.0	3.9	6.7	18.6	8.5	14.7
25	MASSACHUSETTS...........	20 300	6 349 097	6 175 169	13	304.2	89.4	6.6	0.2	3.8	6.3	6.4	17.4	8.3	15.2
26	MICHIGAN.......................	147 136	9 938 444	9 863 775	8	67.0	83.4	14.3	0.6	1.7	2.8	6.6	19.3	9.4	13.8
27	MINNESOTA....................	206 207	4 919 479	4 775 508	21	23.2	92.9	3.1	1.2	2.7	1.9	6.7	19.9	9.5	13.2
28	MISSISSIPPI....................	121 506	2 844 658	2 768 619	31	22.8	62.4	36.5	0.4	0.7	0.9	7.3	19.9	10.9	13.7
29	MISSOURI.......................	178 446	5 595 211	5 468 338	17	30.6	87.2	11.3	0.4	1.1	1.7	6.6	19.0	9.5	13.2
30	MONTANA.......................	376 991	902 195	882 779	44	2.3	92.5	0.4	6.5	0.6	1.8	6.0	19.3	10.1	10.7
31	NEBRASKA......................	199 113	1 711 263	1 666 028	38	8.4	93.6	4.1	0.9	1.4	4.6	6.9	19.7	10.2	12.4
32	NEVADA.........................	284 396	1 998 257	1 809 253	35	6.4	85.6	7.7	1.8	4.9	16.8	7.9	19.3	8.6	13.7
33	NEW HAMPSHIRE............	23 231	1 235 786	1 201 134	41	51.7	97.8	0.8	0.2	1.2	1.6	6.2	19.2	8.2	14.8
34	NEW JERSEY	19 215	8 414 350	8 143 412	9	423.8	79.3	14.7	0.3	5.8	12.6	6.7	17.9	8.3	13.6
35	NEW MEXICO	314 334	1 819 046	1 739 844	37	5.7	86.3	2.6	9.5	1.5	40.7	7.6	20.9	10.1	12.1
36	NEW YORK	122 310	18 976 457	18 196 601	3	148.8	76.2	17.7	0.4	5.6	14.6	6.7	17.7	8.9	14.4
37	NORTH CAROLINA	126 180	8 049 313	7 650 789	11	60.6	75.3	22.0	1.3	1.4	2.3	7.0	18.4	9.3	14.5
38	NORTH DAKOTA	178 695	642 200	633 666	47	3.5	93.7	0.6	4.8	0.8	1.1	6.2	19.1	10.8	12.3
39	OHIO..............................	106 067	11 353 140	11 256 654	7	106.1	87.0	11.6	0.2	1.2	1.6	6.6	18.7	9.5	13.6
40	OKLAHOMA.....................	177 877	3 450 654	3 358 044	27	18.9	83.0	7.8	7.8	1.3	4.1	6.9	19.3	10.2	12.4
41	OREGON.........................	248 646	3 421 399	3 316 154	28	13.3	93.4	1.9	1.4	3.3	6.4	6.6	18.3	9.4	12.8
42	PENNSYLVANIA	116 083	12 281 054	11 994 016	6	103.3	88.4	9.8	0.2	1.7	2.7	5.9	17.8	8.5	13.1
44	RHODE ISLAND................	2 707	1 048 319	990 819	43	366.1	92.1	5.1	0.5	2.3	6.9	6.3	18.1	8.5	14.5
45	SOUTH CAROLINA	77 988	4 012 012	3 885 736	26	49.8	69.1	29.8	0.2	0.9	1.4	6.5	18.1	10.1	14.4
46	SOUTH DAKOTA	196 571	754 844	733 133	46	3.7	90.4	0.7	8.2	0.7	1.2	6.8	20.2	10.7	11.7
47	TENNESSEE	106 759	5 689 283	5 483 535	16	51.4	82.1	16.6	0.2	1.0	1.2	6.7	17.8	9.5	14.2
48	TEXAS............................	678 358	20 851 820	20 044 141	2	29.5	84.3	12.3	0.5	2.9	30.2	8.2	20.4	10.5	13.8
49	UTAH..............................	212 816	2 233 169	2 129 836	34	10.0	95.1	0.9	1.4	2.6	7.1	9.9	23.3	14.1	13.7
50	VERMONT........................	23 956	608 827	593 740	49	24.8	98.4	0.5	0.2	0.8	0.9	5.4	18.1	9.0	14.0
51	VIRGINIA.........................	102 558	7 078 515	6 872 912	12	67.0	75.8	20.1	0.3	3.8	3.9	6.6	17.7	9.8	15.2
53	WASHINGTON	172 445	5 894 121	5 756 361	15	33.4	88.7	3.5	1.8	6.0	6.5	6.8	19.0	9.7	13.7
54	WEST VIRGINIA	62 384	1 808 344	1 806 928	36	29.0	96.3	3.1	0.1	0.5	0.6	5.6	16.8	9.9	12.5
55	WISCONSIN.....................	140 672	5 363 675	5 250 446	18	37.3	91.9	5.6	0.9	1.6	2.7	6.3	19.4	9.7	13.1
56	WYOMING........................	251 501	493 782	479 602	51	1.9	96.0	0.9	2.3	0.9	6.1	6.3	20.1	11.2	11.0

1. Dry land or land partially or temporarily covered by water.   2. Hispanic persons may be of any race.

Table A. States — **Population and Households**

STATE	Population and population characteristics, 1999 (cont'd) Age (percent) (cont'd) 35 to 44 years	45 to 54 years	55 to 64 years	65 to 74 years	75 years and over	Percent female	Households, 1998 Number	Percent change, 1990 to 1998	Persons per house-hold	Age of householder (percent) Under 25 years	25 to 44 years	45 to 64 years	65 years and over
	15	16	17	18	19	20	21	22	23	24	25	26	27
UNITED STATES	16.4	13.1	8.6	6.7	6.0	51.1	101 041 243	9.9	2.61	5.2	40.9	32.4	21.5
ALABAMA	15.9	13.3	9.3	7.1	5.9	52.0	1 663 416	10.4	2.56	5.7	39.0	32.9	22.5
ALASKA	17.2	14.7	7.6	3.5	2.1	47.5	214 712	13.7	2.78	8.3	44.9	37.0	9.8
ARIZONA	15.4	12.3	8.4	7.1	6.0	50.5	1 761 567	28.7	2.60	6.7	40.2	31.2	21.9
ARKANSAS	14.8	12.8	9.6	7.5	6.7	51.7	970 386	8.9	2.56	6.1	36.9	32.6	24.3
CALIFORNIA	16.9	12.4	7.4	5.8	5.2	50.0	11 445 772	10.3	2.79	5.2	44.4	31.2	19.3
COLORADO	17.2	15.0	8.9	5.5	4.6	50.4	1 560 682	21.7	2.49	6.4	42.5	34.7	16.4
CONNECTICUT	17.2	13.3	8.6	7.1	7.2	51.5	1 238 314	0.6	2.57	3.4	40.9	32.7	23.1
DELAWARE	17.3	12.9	8.4	7.2	5.8	51.4	283 969	14.7	2.54	4.5	43.1	31.3	21.1
DISTRICT OF COLUMBIA	17.1	14.0	9.5	7.4	6.5	53.2	224 548	-10.0	2.15	3.7	42.3	32.5	21.5
FLORIDA	15.6	12.5	9.5	9.5	8.7	51.5	5 880 567	14.5	2.48	4.8	36.0	30.5	28.7
GEORGIA	17.2	13.1	8.1	5.4	4.4	51.3	2 842 557	20.1	2.63	5.8	44.7	32.6	16.9
HAWAII	16.7	14.0	8.8	7.4	6.2	50.1	400 927	12.5	2.87	4.2	38.3	34.8	22.8
IDAHO	14.9	13.0	8.9	5.9	5.5	50.1	448 341	24.3	2.69	8.2	38.9	33.0	19.8
ILLINOIS	16.5	12.9	8.5	6.4	6.0	51.2	4 437 969	5.6	2.65	4.6	41.5	32.4	21.3
INDIANA	16.2	13.2	8.8	6.6	5.9	51.3	2 230 739	8.0	2.57	5.4	40.9	32.4	21.3
IOWA	15.4	13.2	9.1	7.2	7.7	51.3	1 103 360	3.7	2.50	5.9	37.9	31.5	24.8
KANSAS	16.1	12.9	8.3	6.6	6.7	50.8	999 189	5.8	2.55	6.7	40.1	30.6	22.6
KENTUCKY	16.2	13.7	9.4	6.8	5.7	51.4	1 496 784	8.5	2.56	5.6	39.2	33.6	21.7
LOUISIANA	15.4	13.0	8.8	6.3	5.1	51.9	1 598 882	6.6	2.66	6.1	39.8	33.6	20.5
MAINE	17.4	14.4	8.9	7.4	6.6	51.2	489 811	5.3	2.48	4.9	40.1	32.5	22.4
MARYLAND	18.1	13.5	8.2	6.2	5.3	51.4	1 906 482	9.0	2.63	3.8	43.9	33.2	19.1
MASSACHUSETTS	17.1	13.4	8.3	7.0	7.0	51.8	2 348 519	4.5	2.52	3.5	42.0	31.7	22.8
MICHIGAN	16.5	13.3	8.5	6.5	5.9	51.3	3 693 285	8.0	2.60	4.9	41.2	32.6	21.2
MINNESOTA	17.0	13.1	8.3	6.1	6.2	50.7	1 790 648	8.7	2.58	5.6	42.4	31.3	20.6
MISSISSIPPI	15.1	12.4	8.7	6.6	5.5	52.1	997 464	9.4	2.68	5.6	39.5	32.5	22.4
MISSOURI	16.3	12.9	8.9	7.1	6.5	51.5	2 088 986	6.5	2.53	5.4	39.9	31.8	22.9
MONTANA	15.6	15.0	10.0	6.8	6.5	50.3	346 070	13.0	2.47	6.8	36.0	35.4	21.8
NEBRASKA	15.7	12.9	8.5	6.8	6.9	51.1	635 521	5.5	2.54	6.8	39.3	30.8	23.0
NEVADA	16.4	13.4	9.3	6.9	4.6	49.1	676 210	45.0	2.54	5.9	41.6	34.0	18.5
NEW HAMPSHIRE	18.6	13.4	7.7	6.4	5.7	50.8	450 302	9.5	2.56	4.2	45.6	31.0	19.3
NEW JERSEY	17.5	13.5	8.9	7.1	6.5	51.5	2 956 576	5.8	2.69	2.8	40.3	33.9	22.9
NEW MEXICO	16.0	13.2	8.6	6.4	5.1	50.2	632 316	16.5	2.70	6.3	39.9	33.6	20.2
NEW YORK	16.6	13.4	9.0	7.0	6.3	51.8	6 765 714	1.9	2.61	3.6	40.3	33.7	22.4
NORTH CAROLINA	16.2	13.2	9.0	6.9	5.6	51.5	2 882 737	14.5	2.54	5.3	41.1	32.5	21.0
NORTH DAKOTA	15.4	13.0	8.7	7.1	7.5	50.3	247 018	2.5	2.48	7.3	38.5	30.4	23.8
OHIO	16.2	13.3	8.8	7.0	6.3	51.7	4 284 963	4.8	2.55	5.1	40.0	32.5	22.4
OKLAHOMA	15.1	13.1	9.5	7.1	6.3	51.2	1 288 331	6.8	2.52	6.9	37.7	32.8	22.7
OREGON	15.9	14.7	9.1	6.6	6.5	50.6	1 285 885	16.5	2.50	6.2	38.6	33.9	21.4
PENNSYLVANIA	16.2	13.5	9.1	8.1	7.7	51.9	4 592 785	2.2	2.54	3.7	37.7	32.3	26.2
RHODE ISLAND	16.5	12.6	7.9	7.6	8.0	51.9	376 238	-0.5	2.53	3.8	40.7	30.2	25.3
SOUTH CAROLINA	16.2	13.5	9.0	6.9	5.3	51.7	1 441 217	14.6	2.58	5.2	40.3	33.5	21.0
SOUTH DAKOTA	15.3	12.6	8.3	7.0	7.3	50.8	276 736	6.8	2.55	7.2	38.2	30.1	24.5
TENNESSEE	16.4	13.7	9.4	6.8	5.7	51.7	2 099 672	13.3	2.52	5.3	40.1	33.7	20.9
TEXAS	16.3	12.7	8.1	5.5	4.5	50.7	7 112 985	17.2	2.71	6.8	43.2	32.2	17.8
UTAH	13.1	10.4	6.6	4.6	4.1	50.3	676 697	26.0	3.06	9.8	43.4	29.4	17.4
VERMONT	17.6	15.0	8.7	6.4	5.9	50.8	231 353	9.8	2.46	4.8	42.1	33.3	19.7
VIRGINIA	17.4	13.5	8.6	6.2	5.0	51.1	2 579 144	12.5	2.55	5.0	43.4	33.0	18.6
WASHINGTON	17.1	14.0	8.3	5.8	5.6	50.3	2 210 949	18.1	2.52	6.4	42.5	32.6	18.7
WEST VIRGINIA	14.9	14.7	10.5	8.1	7.0	51.8	715 831	4.0	2.48	5.1	34.2	34.9	25.8
WISCONSIN	16.5	13.3	8.6	6.7	6.5	50.9	1 973 057	8.3	2.58	5.4	40.8	31.8	22.0
WYOMING	15.5	14.8	9.5	6.3	5.3	49.8	185 060	9.6	2.54	8.0	37.5	34.7	19.7

Table A. States — Immigration and Population Change

STATE	Immigrants admitted to legal status, 1996	Population, 1980–2025 — Census counts		Projections		Population change, 1980–1999 — Percent change		Components of change, 1990–1999		
		1980	1990	2000	2025	1980–1990	1990–1999	Births	Deaths	Net migration
	28	29	30	31	32	33	34	35	36	37
UNITED STATES	915 900	226 542 204	248 790 925	274 635 000	335 048 000	9.8	9.6	36 820 132	20 934 303	7 478 078
ALABAMA	1 782	3 894 025	4 040 389	4 451 000	5 224 000	3.8	8.2	568 961	387 158	126 336
ALASKA	1 280	401 851	550 043	653 000	885 000	36.9	12.6	98 976	22 291	-15 046
ARIZONA	8 900	2 716 546	3 665 339	4 798 000	6 412 000	34.9	30.4	670 677	317 200	683 188
ARKANSAS	1 494	2 286 357	2 350 624	2 631 000	3 055 000	2.8	8.5	330 123	244 180	121 082
CALIFORNIA	201 529	23 667 765	29 811 427	32 521 000	49 285 000	25.7	11.2	5 227 258	2 039 044	109 564
COLORADO	8 895	2 889 735	3 294 473	4 168 000	5 188 000	14.0	23.1	513 908	225 699	468 212
CONNECTICUT	10 874	3 107 564	3 287 116	3 284 000	3 739 000	5.8	-0.2	423 922	268 842	- 152 981
DELAWARE	1 377	594 338	666 168	768 000	861 000	12.1	13.1	97 768	58 165	44 318
DISTRICT OF COLUMBIA	3 784	638 432	606 900	523 000	655 000	-4.9	-14.5	87 167	59 836	- 116 932
FLORIDA	79 461	9 746 961	12 938 071	15 233 000	20 710 000	32.7	16.8	1 781 648	1 370 234	1 748 623
GEORGIA	12 608	5 462 982	6 478 149	7 875 000	9 869 000	18.6	20.2	1 053 424	525 580	771 257
HAWAII	8 436	964 691	1 108 229	1 257 000	1 812 000	14.9	7.0	173 388	67 676	-45 144
IDAHO	1 825	944 127	1 006 734	1 347 000	1 739 000	6.6	24.3	166 298	77 951	154 383
ILLINOIS	42 517	11 427 409	11 430 602	12 051 000	13 440 000	0.0	6.1	1 735 493	971 944	- 175 977
INDIANA	4 692	5 490 214	5 544 156	6 045 000	6 546 000	1.0	7.2	779 368	482 740	111 727
IOWA	3 037	2 913 808	2 776 831	2 900 000	3 040 000	-4.7	3.3	349 191	256 794	5 609
KANSAS	4 303	2 364 236	2 477 588	2 668 000	3 108 000	4.8	7.1	348 226	215 686	12 009
KENTUCKY	2 019	3 660 324	3 686 892	3 995 000	4 314 000	0.7	7.4	494 758	340 897	113 050
LOUISIANA	4 092	4 206 116	4 221 826	4 425 000	5 133 000	0.3	3.6	629 286	362 228	- 113 794
MAINE	1 028	1 125 043	1 227 928	1 259 000	1 423 000	9.1	2.0	137 791	107 664	-3 452
MARYLAND	20 732	4 216 933	4 780 753	5 275 000	6 274 000	13.4	8.2	687 293	375 178	76 811
MASSACHUSETTS	23 085	5 737 093	6 016 425	6 199 000	6 902 000	4.9	2.6	778 803	506 880	-96 660
MICHIGAN	17 253	9 262 044	9 295 287	9 679 000	10 078 000	0.4	6.1	1 287 572	763 166	-99 730
MINNESOTA	8 977	4 075 970	4 375 665	4 830 000	5 510 000	7.4	9.1	603 264	338 093	142 020
MISSISSIPPI	1 073	2 520 770	2 575 475	2 816 000	3 142 000	2.2	7.5	389 349	246 225	51 526
MISSOURI	5 690	4 916 766	5 116 901	5 540 000	6 250 000	4.1	6.9	697 038	492 127	139 371
MONTANA	449	786 690	799 065	950 000	1 121 000	1.6	10.5	103 358	69 332	50 625
NEBRASKA	2 150	1 569 825	1 578 417	1 705 000	1 930 000	0.5	5.6	217 510	139 754	11 445
NEVADA	5 874	800 508	1 201 675	1 871 000	2 312 000	50.1	50.6	227 622	110 437	488 789
NEW HAMPSHIRE	1 512	920 610	1 109 252	1 224 000	1 439 000	20.5	8.3	142 027	83 680	36 602
NEW JERSEY	63 303	7 365 011	7 747 750	8 178 000	9 558 000	5.0	5.1	1 079 022	667 367	-665
NEW MEXICO	5 780	1 303 302	1 515 069	1 860 000	2 612 000	16.2	14.8	254 934	111 862	80 606
NEW YORK	154 095	17 558 165	17 990 778	18 146 000	19 830 000	2.5	1.1	2 539 280	1 519 562	- 781 122
NORTH CAROLINA	7 011	5 880 095	6 632 448	7 777 000	9 349 000	12.8	15.4	967 386	586 354	612 390
NORTH DAKOTA	606	652 717	638 800	662 000	729 000	-2.1	-0.8	78 833	54 150	-32 082
OHIO	10 237	10 797 603	10 847 115	11 319 000	11 744 000	0.5	3.8	1 454 713	957 171	- 113 278
OKLAHOMA	3 511	3 025 487	3 145 576	3 373 000	4 057 000	4.0	6.8	437 373	298 499	71 324
OREGON	7 554	2 633 156	2 842 337	3 397 000	4 349 000	7.9	16.7	399 411	255 204	337 146
PENNSYLVANIA	16 938	11 864 720	11 882 842	12 202 000	12 683 000	0.2	0.9	1 438 566	1 163 384	- 136 205
RHODE ISLAND	3 098	947 154	1 003 464	998 000	1 141 000	5.9	-1.3	125 103	89 187	-46 911
SOUTH CAROLINA	2 151	3 120 729	3 486 310	3 858 000	4 645 000	11.7	11.5	498 067	301 259	161 777
SOUTH DAKOTA	519	690 768	696 004	777 000	866 000	0.8	5.3	98 048	62 765	2 009
TENNESSEE	4 343	4 591 023	4 877 203	5 657 000	6 665 000	6.2	12.4	687 916	463 719	387 196
TEXAS	83 385	14 225 513	16 986 335	20 119 000	27 183 000	19.4	18.0	3 025 567	1 254 005	1 285 377
UTAH	4 250	1 461 037	1 722 850	2 207 000	2 883 000	17.9	23.6	369 419	98 393	103 356
VERMONT	654	511 456	562 758	617 000	678 000	10.0	5.5	67 101	44 797	10 574
VIRGINIA	21 375	5 346 797	6 189 197	6 997 000	8 466 000	15.8	11.0	872 681	477 233	242 295
WASHINGTON	18 833	4 132 353	4 866 669	5 858 000	7 808 000	17.8	18.3	729 025	372 964	528 382
WEST VIRGINIA	583	1 950 186	1 793 477	1 841 000	1 845 000	-8.0	0.7	198 388	184 750	5 547
WISCONSIN	3 607	4 705 642	4 891 954	5 326 000	5 867 000	4.0	7.3	637 733	412 353	115 193
WYOMING	280	469 557	453 589	525 000	694 000	-3.4	5.7	60 099	32 704	-1 662

STATE	Race					His-panic[1]	Foreign born	Age									Female
	White	Black	American Indian, Eskimo, Aleut	Asian and Pacific Islander	Other race			Under 5 years	5 to 17 years	18 to 24 years	25 to 34 years	35 to 44 years	45 to 54 years	55 to 64 years	65 to 74 years	75 years and over	
	38	39	40	41	42	43	44	45	46	47	48	49	50	51	52	53	54
UNITED STATES	80.3	12.1	0.8	2.9	3.9	9.0	7.9	7.4	18.2	10.8	17.4	15.1	10.1	8.5	7.3	5.3	51.3
ALABAMA	73.6	25.3	0.4	0.5	0.1	0.6	1.1	7.0	19.2	11.0	16.0	14.4	10.4	9.0	7.5	5.5	52.1
ALASKA	75.5	4.1	15.6	3.6	1.2	3.2	4.5	10.0	21.4	10.2	20.5	18.7	9.8	5.4	2.8	1.2	47.3
ARIZONA	80.8	3.0	5.6	1.5	9.1	18.8	7.6	8.0	18.8	10.7	17.3	14.4	9.5	8.2	7.9	5.1	50.6
ARKANSAS	82.7	15.9	0.5	0.5	0.3	0.8	1.1	7.0	19.4	10.1	15.3	13.9	10.4	9.1	8.3	6.6	51.8
CALIFORNIA	69.0	7.4	0.8	9.6	13.2	25.8	21.7	8.1	18.0	11.5	19.1	15.6	9.8	7.5	6.2	4.3	49.9
COLORADO	88.2	4.0	0.8	1.8	5.1	12.9	4.3	7.7	18.5	10.2	18.6	17.2	10.2	7.6	5.9	4.1	50.5
CONNECTICUT	87.0	8.3	0.2	1.5	2.9	6.5	8.5	6.9	15.9	10.5	17.8	15.5	10.8	9.0	7.8	5.8	51.5
DELAWARE	80.3	16.9	0.3	1.4	1.1	2.4	3.3	7.3	17.2	11.4	17.9	14.8	10.2	9.0	7.4	4.7	51.5
DISTRICT OF COLUMBIA	29.6	65.8	0.2	1.8	2.5	5.4	9.7	6.2	13.1	13.6	20.0	15.7	10.2	8.4	7.3	5.5	53.4
FLORIDA	83.1	13.6	0.3	1.2	1.8	12.2	12.9	6.6	15.6	9.4	16.4	14.0	10.0	9.8	10.6	7.7	51.6
GEORGIA	71.0	27.0	0.2	1.2	0.7	1.7	2.7	7.6	19.0	11.4	18.1	15.7	10.3	7.7	6.0	4.1	51.5
HAWAII	33.4	2.5	0.5	61.8	1.9	7.3	14.7	7.5	17.8	10.9	18.1	16.1	9.8	8.5	7.1	4.2	49.1
IDAHO	94.4	0.3	1.4	0.9	3.0	5.3	2.9	8.0	22.7	9.8	15.2	14.8	9.8	7.7	6.9	5.1	50.2
ILLINOIS	78.3	14.8	0.2	2.5	4.2	7.9	8.3	7.4	18.4	10.6	17.4	14.9	10.2	8.5	7.2	5.4	51.4
INDIANA	90.6	7.8	0.2	0.7	0.7	1.8	1.7	7.2	19.1	10.9	16.5	14.8	10.3	8.7	7.3	5.3	51.5
IOWA	96.6	1.7	0.3	0.9	0.5	1.2	1.6	7.0	18.9	10.2	15.4	14.2	9.9	9.0	8.2	7.2	51.6
KANSAS	90.1	5.8	0.9	1.3	2.0	3.8	2.5	7.6	19.1	10.3	16.7	14.6	9.5	8.4	7.5	6.4	51.0
KENTUCKY	92.0	7.1	0.2	0.5	0.2	0.6	0.9	6.8	19.1	10.9	16.6	14.9	10.4	8.8	7.3	5.4	51.6
LOUISIANA	67.3	30.8	0.4	1.0	0.5	2.2	2.1	7.9	21.2	11.0	16.7	14.4	9.6	8.1	6.5	4.6	51.9
MAINE	98.4	0.4	0.5	0.5	0.1	0.6	3.0	7.0	18.2	10.1	16.7	15.7	10.2	8.8	7.5	5.8	51.3
MARYLAND	71.0	24.9	0.3	2.9	0.9	2.6	6.6	7.5	16.8	10.6	18.8	16.3	10.9	8.3	6.6	4.2	51.5
MASSACHUSETTS	89.8	5.0	0.2	2.4	2.6	4.8	9.5	6.9	15.6	11.8	18.3	15.3	10.0	8.6	7.6	6.0	52.0
MICHIGAN	83.4	13.9	0.6	1.1	0.9	2.2	3.8	7.6	18.9	10.8	16.9	15.1	10.2	8.5	7.1	4.9	51.5
MINNESOTA	94.4	2.2	1.1	1.8	0.5	1.2	2.6	7.7	19.0	10.1	17.8	15.2	9.8	7.9	6.7	5.8	51.0
MISSISSIPPI	63.5	35.6	0.3	0.5	0.1	0.6	0.8	7.6	21.4	11.4	15.5	13.6	9.6	8.3	7.0	5.5	52.2
MISSOURI	87.7	10.7	0.4	0.8	0.4	1.2	1.6	7.2	18.5	10.1	16.7	14.4	10.2	8.9	7.7	6.3	51.8
MONTANA	92.7	0.3	6.0	0.5	0.5	1.5	1.7	7.4	20.4	8.8	15.4	15.9	10.3	8.6	7.6	5.7	50.5
NEBRASKA	93.8	3.6	0.8	0.8	1.0	2.3	1.8	7.6	19.6	9.9	16.3	14.5	9.5	8.6	7.5	6.7	51.3
NEVADA	84.3	6.6	1.6	3.2	4.4	10.4	8.7	7.7	17.0	9.9	18.5	16.0	11.3	9.0	7.1	3.5	49.1
NEW HAMPSHIRE	98.0	0.6	0.2	0.8	0.3	1.0	3.7	7.6	17.5	10.6	18.5	16.5	10.1	8.0	6.4	4.8	51.0
NEW JERSEY	79.3	13.4	0.2	3.5	3.6	9.6	12.5	6.9	16.4	10.1	17.6	15.5	10.9	9.3	7.9	5.5	51.7
NEW MEXICO	75.6	2.0	8.9	0.9	12.6	38.2	5.3	8.3	21.2	10.0	16.9	15.0	9.7	8.0	6.4	4.3	50.8
NEW YORK	74.4	15.9	0.3	3.9	5.5	12.3	15.9	7.0	16.7	10.9	17.4	15.1	10.6	9.1	7.5	5.6	52.1
NORTH CAROLINA	75.6	22.0	1.2	0.8	0.5	1.2	1.7	6.9	17.3	11.8	17.3	15.2	10.5	8.9	7.3	4.8	51.5
NORTH DAKOTA	94.6	0.6	4.1	0.5	0.3	0.7	1.5	7.5	20.0	10.6	16.3	14.1	8.9	8.4	7.4	6.8	50.2
OHIO	87.8	10.6	0.2	0.8	0.5	1.3	2.4	7.2	18.6	10.5	16.5	14.9	10.3	9.0	7.6	5.3	51.8
OKLAHOMA	82.1	7.4	8.0	1.1	1.3	2.7	2.1	7.2	19.4	10.2	16.2	14.4	10.3	8.9	7.5	6.0	51.3
OREGON	92.8	1.6	1.4	2.4	1.8	4.0	4.9	7.1	18.4	9.4	15.9	16.7	10.4	8.3	7.9	5.9	50.8
PENNSYLVANIA	88.5	9.2	0.1	1.2	1.0	2.0	3.1	6.7	16.8	10.3	16.1	14.7	10.2	9.8	9.0	6.4	52.1
RHODE ISLAND	91.4	3.9	0.4	1.8	2.5	4.6	9.5	6.7	15.8	12.0	17.3	14.7	9.6	8.9	8.5	6.5	52.0
SOUTH CAROLINA	69.0	29.8	0.2	0.6	0.3	0.9	1.4	7.4	19.0	11.7	17.0	15.0	10.2	8.4	7.1	4.3	51.6
SOUTH DAKOTA	91.6	0.5	7.3	0.4	0.2	0.8	1.1	7.8	20.7	9.8	15.7	13.7	9.0	8.6	7.8	6.9	50.8
TENNESSEE	83.0	16.0	0.2	0.7	0.2	0.7	1.2	6.8	18.1	10.8	16.7	15.2	10.8	8.9	7.3	5.4	51.8
TEXAS	75.2	11.9	0.4	1.9	10.6	25.5	9.0	8.2	20.3	11.1	18.2	14.9	9.6	7.6	5.9	4.2	50.7
UTAH	93.8	0.7	1.4	1.9	2.2	4.9	3.4	9.8	26.6	11.6	16.0	13.0	8.0	6.2	5.1	3.6	50.3
VERMONT	98.6	0.3	0.3	0.6	0.1	0.7	3.1	7.3	18.1	11.2	16.9	16.4	10.2	8.0	6.6	5.2	51.0
VIRGINIA	77.4	18.8	0.2	2.6	0.9	2.6	5.0	7.2	17.2	11.6	18.4	16.0	10.7	8.1	6.5	4.3	51.0
WASHINGTON	88.5	3.1	1.7	4.3	2.4	4.4	6.6	7.5	18.4	10.0	17.6	16.5	10.3	7.8	6.9	4.9	50.4
WEST VIRGINIA	96.2	3.1	0.1	0.4	0.1	0.5	0.9	5.9	18.8	10.0	14.6	15.1	10.7	9.9	8.7	6.3	52.0
WISCONSIN	92.2	5.0	0.8	1.1	0.9	1.9	2.5	7.4	19.0	10.5	16.8	14.8	9.8	8.5	7.3	6.0	51.1
WYOMING	94.2	0.8	2.1	0.6	2.3	5.7	1.7	7.7	22.2	9.1	16.4	16.4	10.0	7.8	6.1	4.3	50.0

1. Hispanic persons may be of any race.

Table A. States — Households 1990, Vital Statistics, and Health Resources

STATE	Households, 1990 Number	Percent change, 1980–1990	Persons per house-hold	Percent Female family house-holder[1]	One person	Births, 1998 Total	Rate[2]	Deaths, 1998 Number Total	Infant[3]	Crude[2]	Age-adjusted	Infant[4]	Physicians 1998 Number	Rate[5]
	55	56	57	58	59	60	61	62	63	64	65	66	67	68
UNITED STATES	91 947 410	14.4	2.63	11.6	24.6	3 941 553	14.5	2 337 256	28 371	8.6	4.7	7.2	626 947	232
ALABAMA	1 506 790	12.3	2.62	13.4	23.8	62 074	14.2	43 950	633	10.1	5.7	10.2	7 498	172
ALASKA	188 915	43.7	2.80	9.6	22.1	9 926	16.0	2 571	59	4.2	4.4	5.9	1 125	183
ARIZONA	1 368 843	43.0	2.62	10.4	24.7	78 243	16.4	38 300	590	8.2	4.6	7.5	10 161	218
ARKANSAS	891 179	9.2	2.57	11.1	24.0	36 865	14.4	27 510	329	10.8	5.5	8.9	4 351	171
CALIFORNIA	10 381 206	20.3	2.79	11.5	23.4	521 661	15.7	226 954	3 007	6.9	4.3	5.8	77 191	236
COLORADO	1 282 489	20.8	2.51	9.7	26.6	59 577	14.7	26 640	399	6.7	4.2	6.7	9 622	242
CONNECTICUT	1 230 479	12.5	2.59	11.4	24.2	43 820	13.4	29 710	307	9.1	4.3	7.0	10 407	318
DELAWARE	247 497	19.5	2.61	11.8	23.2	10 578	14.0	6 578	102	8.8	5.0	9.6	1 722	232
DISTRICT OF COLUMBIA	249 634	-1.4	2.26	19.5	41.5	7 686	14.8	6 054	96	11.6	6.8	12.5	3 117	596
FLORIDA	5 134 869	37.1	2.46	10.7	25.5	195 637	12.9	158 167	1 417	10.6	4.6	7.2	37 384	251
GEORGIA	2 366 615	26.4	2.66	13.9	22.7	122 368	15.7	60 428	1 035	7.9	5.4	8.5	14 636	192
HAWAII	356 267	21.2	3.01	10.5	19.4	17 583	14.8	8 091	121	6.8	3.7	6.9	3 189	267
IDAHO	360 723	11.3	2.73	8.0	22.4	19 391	15.5	9 155	140	7.5	4.2	7.2	1 965	160
ILLINOIS	4 202 240	3.9	2.65	12.0	25.7	182 588	15.1	104 480	1 539	8.7	4.8	8.4	26 650	221
INDIANA	2 065 355	7.2	2.61	10.5	24.1	85 122	14.3	53 477	649	9.1	5.0	7.6	10 510	178
IOWA	1 064 325	1.1	2.52	8.0	25.9	37 282	13.0	28 362	246	9.9	4.2	6.6	5 241	183
KANSAS	944 726	8.3	2.53	8.6	25.9	38 422	14.5	24 057	270	9.2	4.5	7.0	5 216	198
KENTUCKY	1 379 782	9.2	2.60	11.6	23.3	54 329	13.7	37 832	409	9.6	5.3	7.5	7 186	183
LOUISIANA	1 499 269	6.2	2.74	15.6	23.7	66 888	15.3	40 337	609	9.2	5.8	9.1	9 110	209
MAINE	465 312	17.7	2.56	9.5	23.3	13 733	11.0	12 135	87	9.8	4.6	6.3	2 950	237
MARYLAND	1 748 991	19.7	2.67	13.3	22.6	71 972	13.9	42 059	616	8.2	4.9	8.6	17 802	347
MASSACHUSETTS	2 247 110	10.5	2.58	12.1	25.8	81 411	13.2	55 237	416	9.0	4.2	5.1	21 233	345
MICHIGAN	3 419 331	7.0	2.66	12.9	23.7	133 666	13.6	85 160	1 098	8.7	4.8	8.2	21 525	219
MINNESOTA	1 647 853	14.0	2.58	8.6	25.1	65 202	13.7	37 195	386	7.9	3.9	5.9	10 190	216
MISSISSIPPI	911 374	10.2	2.75	15.9	23.4	42 939	15.5	27 847	435	10.1	6.1	10.1	4 204	153
MISSOURI	1 961 206	9.4	2.54	10.6	26.0	75 358	13.8	55 070	577	10.1	5.1	7.7	11 722	216
MONTANA	306 163	7.9	2.53	8.6	26.3	10 795	12.2	7 981	80	9.1	4.5	7.4	1 775	202
NEBRASKA	602 363	5.4	2.54	8.3	26.5	23 534	14.1	15 198	172	9.1	4.3	7.3	3 142	189
NEVADA	466 297	53.2	2.53	10.2	25.7	28 699	15.9	14 464	200	8.3	5.4	7.0	3 104	178
NEW HAMPSHIRE	411 186	27.1	2.62	8.5	22.0	14 429	12.0	9 495	63	8.0	4.4	4.4	2 700	228
NEW JERSEY	2 794 711	9.7	2.70	12.1	23.1	114 550	14.1	71 611	734	8.8	4.5	6.4	22 333	275
NEW MEXICO	542 709	22.9	2.74	11.9	23.0	27 318	15.7	12 907	197	7.4	4.6	7.2	3 684	212
NEW YORK	6 639 322	4.7	2.63	13.8	27.2	258 207	14.2	156 619	1 623	8.6	4.4	6.3	58 578	322
NORTH CAROLINA	2 517 026	23.2	2.54	12.3	23.7	111 688	14.6	67 993	1 038	9.0	5.2	9.3	15 823	210
NORTH DAKOTA	240 878	5.8	2.55	7.3	26.5	7 932	12.5	5 920	68	9.3	4.1	8.6	1 327	208
OHIO	4 087 546	6.6	2.59	11.7	25.0	152 794	13.6	105 891	1 221	9.4	4.9	8.0	24 240	216
OKLAHOMA	1 206 135	7.8	2.53	10.4	25.6	49 461	14.7	33 929	420	10.1	5.3	8.5	5 679	170
OREGON	1 103 313	11.3	2.52	9.2	25.3	45 273	13.7	29 383	245	9.0	4.5	5.4	7 552	230
PENNSYLVANIA	4 495 966	6.5	2.57	11.3	25.6	145 899	12.2	126 700	1 043	10.6	4.8	7.1	32 665	272
RHODE ISLAND	377 977	11.6	2.55	11.7	26.2	12 599	12.7	9 604	88	9.7	4.3	7.0	2 924	296
SOUTH CAROLINA	1 258 044	22.1	2.68	14.0	22.4	53 877	13.9	34 827	515	9.1	5.5	9.6	6 967	182
SOUTH DAKOTA	259 034	6.8	2.59	8.0	26.4	10 288	14.0	6 867	94	9.3	4.4	9.1	1 343	182
TENNESSEE	1 853 725	14.5	2.56	12.6	23.9	77 396	14.1	53 415	635	9.8	5.6	8.2	11 512	212
TEXAS	6 070 937	23.2	2.73	11.6	23.9	342 283	17.1	142 605	2 185	7.2	4.8	6.4	36 341	184
UTAH	537 273	19.8	3.15	9.1	18.9	45 165	21.2	11 824	255	5.6	4.0	5.6	3 744	178
VERMONT	210 650	18.1	2.57	9.2	23.4	6 582	11.1	4 948	46	8.4	4.3	7.0	1 651	279
VIRGINIA	2 291 830	23.0	2.61	11.1	22.9	94 351	13.7	54 446	722	8.0	4.8	7.7	15 118	223
WASHINGTON	1 872 431	21.5	2.53	9.4	25.4	79 663	13.8	42 706	455	7.5	4.2	5.7	13 390	235
WEST VIRGINIA	688 557	0.3	2.55	10.7	24.5	20 747	11.5	20 767	166	11.5	5.5	8.0	3 663	202
WISCONSIN	1 822 118	10.3	2.61	9.6	24.3	67 450	12.8	45 947	489	8.8	4.3	7.2	10 943	209
WYOMING	168 839	1.9	2.63	8.3	24.5	6 252	13.0	3 853	45	8.0	4.6	7.2	842	175

1. No spouse present. 2. Per 1,000 resident population. 3. Deaths of infants under 1 year old. 4. Deaths of infants under 1 year old per 1,000 live births.
5. Per 100,000 resident population as of July 1 of the year shown.

Table A. States — **Health Resources, Crime, and Education**

STATE	Hospitals, 1998 Total	Beds Number	Beds Rate[1]	Medicare enrollees 1999	Serious crimes known to police, 1999[2] Total Number	Total Rate[3]	Rate[3] Violent	Rate[3] Property	Elementary and secondary school enrollment, 1997–1998 Total (1,000)	Percent private	Educational attainment[4] (percent) 1990 High school graduate or more	1990 Bachelor's degree or more	2000 High school graduate or more	2000 Bachelor's degree or more
	69	70	71	72	73	74	75	76	77	78	79	80	81	82
UNITED STATES	5 214	895 681	331	38 283 375	11 635 149	4 267	525	3 742	51 203	9.9	75.2	20.3	84.1	25.6
ALABAMA	110	17 785	409	676 569	192 819	4 412	490	3 922	822	8.8	66.9	15.7	77.5	20.4
ALASKA	16	1 324	216	40 062	27 008	4 363	632	3 732	138	4.5	86.6	23.0	90.4	28.1
ARIZONA	61	10 161	218	658 193	281 735	5 897	551	5 345	859	5.2	78.7	20.3	85.1	24.6
ARKANSAS	80	10 107	398	435 880	103 131	4 043	425	3 618	483	5.5	66.3	13.3	81.7	18.4
CALIFORNIA	444	90 767	278	3 837 080	1 261 164	3 805	627	3 178	6 413	9.5	76.2	23.4	81.2	27.5
COLORADO	68	9 438	238	458 288	164 813	4 063	341	3 723	740	7.1	84.4	27.0	89.7	34.6
CONNECTICUT	35	7 782	238	511 611	111 236	3 389	346	3 044	604	11.5	79.2	27.2	88.2	31.6
DELAWARE	9	1 990	268	109 575	36 456	4 835	734	4 101	136	17.8	77.5	21.4	86.1	24.0
DISTRICT OF COLUMBIA	10	4 322	826	75 423	41 868	8 067	1 628	6 439	94	17.8	73.1	33.3	83.2	38.3
FLORIDA	214	51 241	344	2 770 576	937 718	6 206	854	5 352	2 568	10.7	74.4	18.3	84.0	22.8
GEORGIA	157	24 637	322	897 503	400 968	5 149	534	4 615	1 483	7.2	70.9	19.3	82.6	23.1
HAWAII	19	3 166	265	161 787	57 324	4 838	235	4 602	223	14.9	80.1	22.9	87.4	26.3
IDAHO	43	3 271	266	161 362	39 429	3 149	245	2 904	254	3.8	79.7	17.7	86.2	20.0
ILLINOIS	206	40 475	336	1 628 744	546 561	4 507	733	3 774	2 297	13.0	76.2	21.0	85.5	27.1
INDIANA	117	19 596	332	844 835	223 808	3 766	375	3 391	1 093	9.6	75.6	15.6	84.6	17.1
IOWA	120	13 473	471	474 846	92 497	3 224	280	2 944	551	9.1	80.1	16.9	89.7	25.5
KANSAS	132	11 383	433	389 103	117 803	4 439	383	4 056	509	8.0	81.3	21.1	88.1	27.3
KENTUCKY	105	16 966	431	615 436	114 003	2 878	301	2 578	740	9.6	64.6	13.6	78.7	20.5
LOUISIANA	133	18 314	419	597 485	251 252	5 747	733	5 014	918	15.4	68.3	16.1	80.8	22.5
MAINE	40	4 371	351	213 210	36 024	2 875	112	2 763	230	7.5	78.8	18.8	89.3	24.1
MARYLAND	48	13 611	265	634 527	254 420	4 919	743	4 176	961	13.5	78.4	26.5	85.7	32.3
MASSACHUSETTS	90	20 369	331	954 180	201 460	3 263	551	2 712	1 076	11.8	80.0	27.2	85.1	32.7
MICHIGAN	167	31 719	323	1 389 107	426 596	4 325	575	3 750	1 890	9.9	76.8	17.4	86.2	23.0
MINNESOTA	142	17 140	363	648 272	171 802	3 597	274	3 323	944	9.6	82.4	21.8	90.8	31.2
MISSISSIPPI	104	12 563	456	413 900	118 231	4 270	349	3 921	559	9.7	64.3	14.7	80.3	18.7
MISSOURI	134	21 768	400	854 472	250 363	4 579	500	4 079	1 030	11.6	73.9	17.8	86.6	26.2
MONTANA	54	4 084	464	135 415	35 937	4 070	207	3 863	171	4.9	81.0	19.8	89.6	23.8
NEBRASKA	89	7 870	473	252 231	68 444	4 108	430	3 678	334	12.3	81.8	18.9	90.4	24.6
NEVADA	23	3 716	213	228 631	84 185	4 654	570	4 084	309	4.2	78.8	15.3	82.8	19.3
NEW HAMPSHIRE	26	3 179	268	166 751	27 406	2 282	97	2 185	223	9.5	82.2	24.4	88.1	30.1
NEW JERSEY	94	30 258	373	1 194 539	276 873	3 400	412	2 988	1 455	14.1	76.7	24.9	87.3	30.1
NEW MEXICO	36	4 015	231	229 124	103 740	5 962	835	5 128	351	5.5	75.1	20.4	82.2	23.6
NEW YORK	235	73 682	405	2 694 015	596 743	3 279	589	2 691	3 329	14.0	74.8	23.1	82.5	28.7
NORTH CAROLINA	121	21 735	288	1 111 273	395 971	5 175	542	4 633	1 324	6.7	70.0	17.4	79.2	23.2
NORTH DAKOTA	46	4 304	674	103 066	15 172	2 393	67	2 326	126	5.8	76.7	18.1	85.5	22.6
OHIO	188	39 924	356	1 692 072	449 880	3 996	316	3 680	2 099	12.0	75.7	17.0	87.0	24.6
OKLAHOMA	110	11 495	343	503 506	157 286	4 684	508	4 176	651	4.2	74.6	17.8	86.1	22.5
OREGON	62	7 352	224	483 898	165 866	5 002	375	4 627	586	7.6	81.5	20.6	88.1	27.2
PENNSYLVANIA	214	46 466	387	2 088 116	373 452	3 114	421	2 693	2 158	15.9	74.7	17.9	85.7	24.3
RHODE ISLAND	10	2 814	285	170 331	35 497	3 582	287	3 295	179	14.3	72.0	21.3	81.3	26.4
SOUTH CAROLINA	64	11 249	293	555 082	206 907	5 324	847	4 477	715	7.9	68.3	16.6	83.0	19.0
SOUTH DAKOTA	51	4 195	568	118 979	19 386	2 645	167	2 477	152	6.4	77.1	17.2	91.8	25.7
TENNESSEE	135	21 953	404	815 231	257 413	4 694	695	3 999	978	8.7	67.1	16.0	79.9	22.0
TEXAS	406	55 695	282	2 223 175	1 008 567	5 032	560	4 472	4 115	5.4	72.1	20.3	79.2	23.9
UTAH	39	4 269	203	201 217	105 999	4 977	276	4 701	496	2.6	85.1	22.3	90.7	26.4
VERMONT	15	1 566	265	86 630	16 735	2 817	114	2 704	117	9.3	80.8	24.3	90.0	28.8
VIRGINIA	92	18 211	268	875 799	231 886	3 374	315	3 059	1 209	8.1	75.2	24.5	86.6	31.9
WASHINGTON	92	12 093	213	725 018	302 509	5 256	377	4 878	1 068	7.2	83.8	22.9	91.8	28.6
WEST VIRGINIA	56	8 397	464	335 529	49 161	2 721	351	2 370	316	4.6	66.0	12.3	77.1	15.3
WISCONSIN	126	17 111	328	777 273	173 062	3 296	246	3 051	1 025	14.0	78.6	17.7	86.7	23.8
WYOMING	26	2 309	480	64 448	16 583	3 455	232	3 223	100	2.6	83.0	18.8	90.0	20.6

1. Per 100,000 resident population as of July 1 of the year shown. and over time.   3. Per 100,000 population estimated by the FBI.   2. Data for serious crimes have not been adjusted for underreporting; this may affect comparability between geographic areas   4. Persons 25 years old and older.

Table A. States — Education Expenditures, Income, Poverty, and Health Insurance

STATE	Local government expenditures for education, 1997–1998		Money income						Percent below poverty level					Average percent lacking health insurance, 1999	
			1989						1989			1999			
			Households						Persons						
			Median												
	Total current expenditures (mil dol)	Current expenditures per student (dollars)	Per capita[1] (dollars)	Dollars	Percent change, 1979–1989 (constant 1989 dollars)	Percent with $100,000 or more	Median household income, 1997–1999 average (dollars)	Median income of family of four 1998	Total	Percent change in rate, 1979–1989	Families	Persons	Children under 18 years	Persons	Children under 18 years
	83	84	85	86	87	88	89	90	91	92	93	94	95	96	97
UNITED STATES	285 490	6 189	14 420	30 056	6.5	4.4	39 657	56 061	13.1	5.8	10.0	11.8	16.9	15.5	13.9
ALABAMA	3 633	4 849	11 486	23 597	3.0	2.3	35 478	51 156	18.3	-3.0	14.3	15.1	24.0	14.3	10.6
ALASKA	1 093	8 271	17 610	41 408	-2.8	7.7	51 046	59 726	9.0	-15.9	6.8	7.6	8.0	19.1	16.2
ARIZONA	3 741	4 595	13 461	27 540	-0.1	3.4	36 337	49 397	15.7	19.3	11.4	12.0	16.1	21.2	22.0
ARKANSAS	2 149	4 708	10 520	21 147	3.3	1.8	28 398	44 471	19.1	0.4	14.8	14.7	18.5	14.7	11.8
CALIFORNIA	32 759	5 644	16 409	35 798	17.1	7.1	42 262	55 209	12.5	9.7	9.3	13.8	20.3	20.3	18.3
COLORADO	3 887	5 656	14 821	30 140	-0.4	3.8	46 950	63 428	11.7	15.6	8.6	8.3	11.6	16.8	16.0
CONNECTICUT	4 765	8 904	20 189	41 721	24.0	9.2	47 997	75 534	6.8	-14.8	5.0	7.1	8.8	9.8	9.2
DELAWARE	831	7 420	15 854	34 875	16.6	4.5	44 627	65 157	8.7	-26.8	6.1	10.4	17.6	11.4	6.7
DISTRICT OF COLUMBIA	647	8 393	18 881	30 727	13.1	7.8	35 309	60 674	16.9	-9.3	13.3	14.9	24.5	15.4	17.2
FLORIDA	12 737	5 552	14 698	27 483	11.7	3.9	35 081	52 581	12.7	-6.0	9.0	12.4	18.4	19.2	16.5
GEORGIA	7 770	5 647	13 631	29 021	15.2	3.8	39 003	55 989	14.7	-11.7	11.5	12.9	19.5	16.1	12.6
HAWAII	1 112	5 858	15 770	38 829	13.2	7.1	42 864	61 838	8.3	-16.6	6.0	10.9	13.5	19.1	10.6
IDAHO	1 154	4 721	11 457	25 257	-1.4	2.1	36 023	49 174	13.3	5.2	9.7	13.9	21.9	19.1	20.5
ILLINOIS	12 473	6 242	15 201	32 252	-0.4	4.9	44 459	61 672	11.9	8.2	9.0	9.9	15.0	14.1	12.1
INDIANA	6 235	6 318	13 149	28 797	-2.3	2.5	40 635	55 284	10.7	10.1	7.9	6.7	8.5	10.8	8.9
IOWA	3 005	5 998	12 422	26 229	-6.8	2.1	38 047	53 230	11.5	13.7	8.4	7.5	9.9	8.3	6.2
KANSAS	2 684	5 727	13 300	27 291	-0.5	2.8	37 618	55 341	11.5	13.7	8.3	12.2	18.5	12.1	12.5
KENTUCKY	3 489	5 213	11 153	22 534	-3.7	2.0	35 226	49 108	19.0	8.1	16.0	12.1	16.7	14.5	13.7
LOUISIANA	4 030	5 188	10 635	21 949	-14.0	2.4	33 218	49 037	23.6	26.8	19.4	19.2	26.6	22.5	24.6
MAINE	1 433	6 742	12 957	27 854	20.3	2.4	36 459	51 059	10.8	-16.9	8.0	10.6	17.5	11.9	6.7
MARYLAND	5 844	7 034	17 730	39 386	15.9	6.9	50 630	71 404	8.3	-15.6	6.0	7.3	6.6	11.8	9.5
MASSACHUSETTS	7 382	7 778	17 224	36 952	25.4	6.7	43 697	68 958	8.9	-6.9	6.7	11.7	19.5	10.5	9.1
MICHIGAN	12 004	7 050	14 154	31 020	-3.7	3.8	43 066	59 019	13.1	26.1	10.2	9.7	14.1	11.2	9.7
MINNESOTA	5 453	6 388	14 389	30 909	3.8	3.6	46 802	67 140	10.2	7.6	7.3	7.2	7.9	8.0	7.4
MISSISSIPPI	2 165	4 288	9 648	20 136	-0.7	1.7	30 628	43 907	25.2	5.5	20.2	16.1	22.3	16.6	15.5
MISSOURI	5 068	5 565	12 989	26 362	1.0	2.8	40 166	54 190	13.3	9.3	10.1	11.6	18.2	8.6	5.4
MONTANA	929	5 724	11 213	22 988	-11.1	1.7	31 280	44 737	16.1	30.7	12.0	15.6	21.8	18.6	18.9
NEBRASKA	1 744	5 958	12 452	26 016	-2.5	2.2	37 338	56 692	11.1	4.2	8.0	10.9	11.5	10.8	8.9
NEVADA	1 571	5 295	15 214	31 011	1.6	3.8	40 882	53 054	10.2	16.7	7.3	11.3	17.3	20.7	22.1
NEW HAMPSHIRE	1 241	6 156	15 959	36 329	27.4	4.5	44 891	61 014	6.4	-24.4	4.4	7.7	8.1	10.2	5.9
NEW JERSEY	12 057	9 643	18 714	40 927	23.3	8.8	50 234	70 983	7.6	-20.2	5.6	7.8	10.1	13.4	9.8
NEW MEXICO	1 660	5 005	11 246	24 087	-1.9	2.5	31 981	43 829	20.6	17.1	16.5	20.7	29.7	25.8	27.7
NEW YORK	25 333	8 852	16 501	32 965	18.2	6.8	38 479	57 142	13.0	-2.8	10.0	14.1	21.8	16.4	11.5
NORTH CAROLINA	6 498	5 257	12 885	26 647	9.8	2.6	37 057	54 331	13.0	-12.3	9.9	13.5	18.5	15.4	12.4
NORTH DAKOTA	599	5 056	11 051	23 213	-9.4	1.6	32 238	51 002	14.4	14.1	10.9	13.0	19.2	11.8	10.4
OHIO	11 449	6 198	13 461	28 706	-3.5	2.9	38 970	60 169	12.5	21.7	9.7	12.0	17.6	11.0	8.9
OKLAHOMA	3 139	5 033	11 893	23 577	-4.6	2.3	33 311	47 436	16.7	24.7	13.0	12.7	16.7	17.5	17.0
OREGON	3 475	6 419	13 418	27 250	-3.1	2.8	39 768	55 892	12.4	16.1	8.7	12.6	17.0	14.6	13.2
PENNSYLVANIA	13 085	7 209	14 068	29 069	2.8	3.6	38 938	58 507	11.1	6.0	8.2	9.4	12.8	9.4	7.6
RHODE ISLAND	1 216	7 928	14 981	32 181	19.3	4.1	40 213	62 339	9.6	-6.7	6.8	9.9	14.3	6.9	6.9
SOUTH CAROLINA	3 507	5 320	11 897	26 256	6.5	2.3	35 376	52 111	15.4	-7.4	11.9	11.7	17.5	17.6	19.4
SOUTH DAKOTA	665	4 669	10 661	22 503	2.1	1.7	33 438	49 702	15.9	-6.2	11.6	7.7	7.3	11.8	9.1
TENNESSEE	4 409	4 937	12 255	24 807	4.7	2.6	34 393	50 310	15.7	-4.8	12.4	11.9	17.4	11.5	9.4
TEXAS	21 189	5 444	12 904	27 016	-3.5	3.7	37 320	51 148	18.1	23.1	14.1	15.0	22.1	23.3	24.1
UTAH	1 917	3 969	11 029	29 470	-0.5	2.5	45 257	54 946	11.4	10.3	8.6	5.7	7.1	14.2	11.4
VERMONT	750	7 075	13 527	29 792	20.2	2.8	39 419	53 691	9.9	-18.5	6.9	9.7	12.5	12.3	8.0
VIRGINIA	6 739	6 067	15 713	33 328	13.8	5.2	44 884	60 860	10.2	-13.2	7.7	7.9	10.9	14.1	14.1
WASHINGTON	5 987	6 040	14 923	31 183	1.3	3.7	46 788	61 059	10.9	11.5	7.8	9.5	10.7	15.8	13.3
WEST VIRGINIA	1 906	6 323	10 520	20 795	-14.8	1.5	28 420	43 239	19.7	31.1	16.0	15.7	22.6	17.1	13.8
WISCONSIN	6 281	7 123	13 276	29 442	-0.6	2.6	43 055	57 890	10.7	23.0	7.6	8.6	9.3	11.0	10.7
WYOMING	604	6 218	12 311	27 096	-19.1	2.0	36 039	50 989	11.9	50.1	9.3	11.6	14.8	16.1	14.5

1. Based on population enumerated as of April 1, 1990.

Table A. States — Personal Income

	Personal income, 1999												
	Total (mil dol)	Percent change, 1998–1999	Per capita[1] Dollars	Per capita[1] Rank	Sources of personal income (mil dol)			Transfer payments					
									Government payments to individuals				
STATE					Wages and salaries[2]	Propri-etors' income	Divi-dends, interest, and rent	Total	Total	Social Security	Medical payments	Income mainte-nance	Unemploy-ment insurance
	98	99	100	101	102	103	104	105	106	107	108	109	110
UNITED STATES	7 783 152	5.1	28 542	X	4 964 370	665 226	1 476 316	1 016 203	964 173	379 905	399 060	104 137	20 765
ALABAMA	100 452	4.2	22 987	42	62 508	7 072	17 908	16 519	15 723	6 554	6 116	1 812	215
ALASKA	17 704	3.0	28 577	17	11 752	1 610	3 185	2 669	2 573	423	592	249	123
ARIZONA	120 360	6.4	25 189	35	76 235	9 103	23 851	16 036	15 173	6 710	5 651	1 383	189
ARKANSAS	56 752	4.9	22 244	46	33 485	5 422	10 747	9 869	9 391	4 051	3 454	1 008	189
CALIFORNIA	991 382	6.8	29 910	13	627 943	108 272	183 792	114 051	107 700	35 972	42 783	18 996	2 734
COLORADO	127 955	7.4	31 546	6	84 864	13 459	23 770	11 224	10 509	4 428	4 226	945	156
CONNECTICUT	128 983	5.0	39 300	1	80 980	10 277	23 545	14 451	13 854	5 406	6 353	1 191	361
DELAWARE	23 192	5.1	30 778	11	16 562	1 319	4 642	2 692	2 532	1 192	944	207	55
DISTRICT OF COLUMBIA	20 686	4.9	39 858	X	41 277	2 605	4 192	2 607	2 529	556	1 338	420	63
FLORIDA	419 792	4.4	27 780	19	234 979	26 041	110 470	63 740	60 987	27 281	25 017	4 722	704
GEORGIA	212 929	6.3	27 340	22	145 289	18 522	35 610	23 558	21 888	8 894	8 554	2 747	302
HAWAII	32 653	2.6	27 544	20	21 112	2 551	6 355	3 933	3 753	1 518	1 293	616	135
IDAHO	28 582	5.6	22 835	45	16 827	3 439	5 493	3 671	3 459	1 594	1 145	275	113
ILLINOIS	377 744	4.2	31 145	7	246 163	31 288	75 426	42 054	39 567	16 726	15 610	4 286	1 176
INDIANA	155 365	4.2	26 143	30	101 111	9 408	28 922	20 001	18 844	8 926	7 254	1 469	266
IOWA	73 499	3.3	25 615	33	44 938	5 775	15 686	9 945	9 345	4 698	3 251	694	191
KANSAS	71 194	4.8	26 824	27	43 704	6 378	14 219	8 701	8 226	3 862	2 965	657	155
KENTUCKY	92 036	4.4	23 237	41	58 102	5 961	17 141	15 542	14 807	5 893	5 783	1 748	262
LOUISIANA	99 887	2.4	22 847	44	60 572	8 190	17 576	17 418	16 643	5 626	7 800	2 170	175
MAINE	30 828	4.8	24 603	37	18 364	2 443	5 854	5 153	4 932	1 966	2 057	497	92
MARYLAND	167 895	5.7	32 465	5	98 191	9 508	31 609	16 959	15 962	6 223	6 897	1 484	299
MASSACHUSETTS	219 533	6.5	35 551	2	148 237	17 549	39 712	27 328	26 204	9 230	12 974	2 133	832
MICHIGAN	277 296	5.1	28 113	18	184 774	16 099	50 792	37 166	35 272	15 103	14 516	3 521	877
MINNESOTA	147 050	5.2	30 793	10	98 281	9 710	31 033	15 951	14 978	6 273	6 082	1 342	359
MISSISSIPPI	57 278	3.9	20 688	50	33 778	4 459	9 512	10 630	10 075	3 863	4 102	1 381	118
MISSOURI	144 235	4.2	26 376	29	93 627	10 135	29 562	20 965	19 960	8 424	8 403	1 766	298
MONTANA	19 438	3.5	22 019	47	10 645	2 007	4 616	3 021	2 854	1 310	885	245	67
NEBRASKA	45 065	4.7	27 049	24	28 047	4 769	9 240	5 678	5 382	2 425	2 083	407	49
NEVADA	56 127	7.4	31 022	9	36 068	4 829	12 627	5 606	5 310	2 367	1 835	384	193
NEW HAMPSHIRE	37 372	5.8	31 114	8	21 774	2 947	7 107	3 977	3 749	1 729	1 528	228	31
NEW JERSEY	289 503	4.1	35 551	3	175 843	24 129	51 540	31 852	30 259	12 761	12 565	2 358	1 114
NEW MEXICO	38 020	3.4	21 853	48	23 171	2 993	7 380	5 892	5 570	2 164	2 026	766	92
NEW YORK	616 678	5.1	33 890	4	400 116	61 054	111 373	96 863	93 031	27 279	47 585	12 104	1 624
NORTH CAROLINA	198 943	3.5	26 003	31	132 959	13 514	35 327	27 201	25 828	10 942	10 427	2 654	455
NORTH DAKOTA	14 773	1.7	23 313	39	9 026	1 198	3 244	2 333	2 220	938	823	155	34
OHIO	305 643	3.8	27 152	23	198 077	18 615	60 248	42 788	40 367	16 976	15 657	3 592	665
OKLAHOMA	77 077	3.8	22 953	43	44 682	8 820	13 906	11 975	11 370	4 891	4 194	1 125	141
OREGON	89 614	4.9	27 023	25	56 233	6 952	20 159	12 038	11 443	4 956	3 976	994	450
PENNSYLVANIA	343 088	4.3	28 605	16	207 062	29 664	64 372	55 093	52 674	21 154	22 598	4 711	1 474
RHODE ISLAND	29 107	4.9	29 377	15	16 778	1 855	5 789	4 813	4 626	1 659	2 096	438	155
SOUTH CAROLINA	91 490	5.4	23 545	38	58 071	5 679	16 768	13 777	13 075	5 550	5 076	1 409	204
SOUTH DAKOTA	18 361	5.3	25 045	36	10 214	2 485	4 184	2 477	2 356	1 076	878	187	15
TENNESSEE	140 234	4.8	25 574	34	90 003	13 495	22 655	21 510	20 577	8 024	9 131	1 997	359
TEXAS	538 345	5.5	26 858	26	346 816	71 576	83 329	61 386	57 931	21 512	25 264	6 430	1 255
UTAH	49 600	5.6	23 288	40	34 012	4 005	8 711	5 040	4 665	2 025	1 692	393	103
VERMONT	15 371	4.7	25 889	32	9 251	1 352	3 139	2 195	2 060	873	809	230	46
VIRGINIA	204 736	6.0	29 789	14	136 829	11 388	37 972	19 671	18 386	8 481	6 521	1 717	180
WASHINGTON	174 948	6.9	30 392	12	114 499	13 398	32 515	20 437	19 244	7 460	6 838	1 708	983
WEST VIRGINIA	37 884	3.2	20 966	49	21 106	2 335	6 894	8 583	8 265	3 342	2 869	790	138
WISCONSIN	143 811	4.7	27 390	21	92 333	8 295	29 310	17 648	16 622	7 964	6 107	1 289	468
WYOMING	12 660	5.5	26 396	28	7 099	1 274	3 305	1 517	1 422	652	435	106	31

1. Based on the resident population estimated as of July 1 of the year shown.   2. Includes other labor income.

Table A. States — Personal Income and Earnings

STATE	Personal tax payments 1999 (mil dol)	Disposable personal income, 1999 Total (mil dol)	Per capita[1] (dollars)	Earnings, 1999 Total (mil dol)	Farm	Goods-related[2] Total	Manu-facturing	Service-related and other[3] Total	Retail trade	Finance, insurance, and real estate	Services	Government	Gross state product (mil dol) 1998
	111	112	113	114	115	116	117	118	119	120	121	122	123
UNITED STATES	1 150 799	6 632 353	24 322	5 629 596	0.8	22.8	16.1	60.6	8.9	9.1	28.9	15.8	8 745 219
ALABAMA	12 310	88 142	20 170	69 580	1.9	26.8	19.6	51.2	9.4	5.7	23.4	20.1	109 833
ALASKA	2 202	15 501	25 022	13 362	0.2	18.0	4.2	49.3	9.3	4.2	21.6	32.5	24 236
ARIZONA	16 571	103 789	21 721	85 339	0.9	21.0	12.6	62.3	10.5	9.7	29.3	15.7	133 801
ARKANSAS	6 918	49 834	19 532	38 907	4.4	27.5	21.2	51.5	11.4	4.8	21.3	16.6	61 628
CALIFORNIA	156 294	835 087	25 195	736 215	1.1	20.9	15.1	62.9	8.9	8.8	32.1	15.0	1 118 945
COLORADO	19 761	108 194	26 674	98 324	0.9	19.5	10.4	64.4	9.2	9.4	29.0	15.1	141 791
CONNECTICUT	24 953	104 030	31 697	91 257	0.3	24.6	19.5	63.5	7.9	14.4	29.7	11.6	142 099
DELAWARE	3 585	19 608	26 021	17 881	0.7	27.6	21.2	57.3	8.7	15.2	24.9	13.8	33 735
DISTRICT OF COLUMBIA	3 609	17 078	32 905	43 882	0.0	3.3	2.3	52.2	2.1	5.7	40.1	42.1	54 100
FLORIDA	57 416	362 376	23 981	261 020	1.3	13.9	7.8	68.1	11.1	9.8	33.4	16.7	418 851
GEORGIA	30 859	182 071	23 378	163 810	1.2	21.2	14.9	61.9	9.0	7.5	26.5	15.7	253 769
HAWAII	4 113	28 541	24 075	23 663	0.8	8.5	2.8	60.1	11.1	8.2	29.0	30.6	39 712
IDAHO	3 695	24 887	19 883	20 266	4.7	26.3	17.4	51.0	10.2	5.1	22.5	18.0	30 936
ILLINOIS	57 747	319 997	26 384	277 451	0.2	23.5	17.7	63.1	7.8	10.4	30.0	13.2	425 679
INDIANA	22 965	132 401	22 279	110 519	0.2	36.5	29.5	50.0	9.3	6.2	22.3	13.3	174 433
IOWA	9 522	63 977	22 296	50 713	2.1	26.9	20.2	54.9	9.5	7.8	23.0	16.1	84 628
KANSAS	9 763	61 430	23 146	50 082	2.6	24.3	17.5	55.8	9.6	6.1	23.2	17.2	76 991
KENTUCKY	12 688	79 348	20 033	64 063	0.8	28.8	20.7	52.0	10.1	5.0	23.0	18.4	107 152
LOUISIANA	11 697	88 190	20 171	68 762	0.8	25.0	13.0	55.1	9.3	5.3	26.9	19.1	129 251
MAINE	4 308	26 520	21 165	20 807	0.7	23.5	16.4	57.7	11.7	6.8	27.5	18.1	32 318
MARYLAND	27 659	140 236	27 116	107 700	0.3	15.1	8.1	61.3	8.9	8.2	32.5	23.3	164 798
MASSACHUSETTS	38 639	180 895	29 294	165 786	0.1	20.6	15.4	67.2	8.3	11.3	35.5	12.1	239 379
MICHIGAN	42 179	235 117	23 836	200 874	0.4	36.1	30.2	50.3	8.4	5.6	24.8	13.2	294 505
MINNESOTA	22 348	124 702	26 113	107 991	1.0	26.2	19.6	59.8	9.3	8.8	27.1	13.0	161 392
MISSISSIPPI	6 150	51 128	18 467	38 237	2.3	27.0	20.1	49.3	10.1	4.5	23.0	21.5	62 216
MISSOURI	19 858	124 377	22 745	103 762	0.1	24.1	17.1	60.5	9.6	8.1	27.2	15.3	162 772
MONTANA	2 397	17 041	19 303	12 652	2.9	17.1	7.3	58.5	11.8	5.9	27.0	21.6	19 861
NEBRASKA	6 129	38 936	23 370	32 816	4.5	19.7	13.2	59.2	8.8	7.6	25.5	16.6	51 737
NEVADA	7 847	48 280	26 685	40 897	0.2	17.1	4.4	68.4	9.7	8.7	39.4	14.4	63 044
NEW HAMPSHIRE	4 973	32 398	26 973	24 721	0.2	27.7	20.8	60.8	12.0	7.6	28.8	11.3	41 313
NEW JERSEY	47 786	241 717	29 683	199 972	0.1	18.9	14.2	66.9	7.8	9.8	31.8	14.1	319 201
NEW MEXICO	4 564	33 456	19 229	26 164	2.6	15.8	6.6	54.4	10.7	5.4	27.7	27.2	47 736
NEW YORK	106 810	509 868	28 020	461 170	0.2	14.7	10.9	70.8	6.6	21.3	31.3	14.3	706 886
NORTH CAROLINA	28 887	170 056	22 227	146 473	1.3	28.5	21.4	52.5	9.3	7.2	23.6	17.7	235 752
NORTH DAKOTA	1 661	13 112	20 692	10 225	2.0	17.3	8.1	59.2	9.9	5.9	26.2	21.4	17 214
OHIO	45 048	260 595	23 150	216 692	0.3	30.8	24.7	54.3	9.4	6.9	25.3	14.6	341 070
OKLAHOMA	9 839	67 239	20 023	53 502	1.9	25.6	15.5	52.1	9.6	5.2	24.2	20.5	81 655
OREGON	13 334	76 280	23 003	63 185	1.0	25.5	18.0	57.6	10.7	6.8	25.4	15.9	104 771
PENNSYLVANIA	49 763	293 326	24 456	236 726	0.3	26.5	20.1	60.1	8.9	8.1	30.1	13.1	364 039
RHODE ISLAND	3 998	25 109	25 342	18 633	0.1	22.1	16.6	59.9	9.5	7.9	31.6	18.0	30 443
SOUTH CAROLINA	11 618	79 872	20 555	63 750	0.6	28.2	21.0	51.3	10.9	6.1	22.3	19.9	100 350
SOUTH DAKOTA	1 893	16 468	22 463	12 699	7.9	20.4	13.9	54.9	10.1	7.2	24.3	16.8	21 224
TENNESSEE	15 902	124 332	22 674	103 499	0.0	26.3	19.7	60.1	10.7	7.0	27.7	13.6	159 575
TEXAS	66 435	471 910	23 544	418 392	1.1	24.2	13.3	60.2	9.2	7.6	26.7	14.5	645 596
UTAH	6 530	43 071	20 222	38 017	0.7	22.1	13.1	59.2	10.5	7.7	27.7	18.0	59 624
VERMONT	2 120	13 251	22 318	10 602	1.5	26.9	19.7	55.6	10.1	5.6	29.2	16.0	16 257
VIRGINIA	31 959	172 777	25 139	148 217	0.2	17.2	10.8	58.8	8.3	7.3	30.6	23.7	230 825
WASHINGTON	25 049	149 899	26 041	127 897	0.9	21.4	14.7	60.5	9.2	6.4	31.8	17.2	192 864
WEST VIRGINIA	4 458	33 425	18 498	23 441	-0.1	26.2	14.4	52.0	9.6	4.3	25.5	21.9	39 938
WISCONSIN	22 196	121 615	23 163	100 628	0.8	32.9	26.3	52.5	9.1	6.8	24.1	13.8	157 761
WYOMING	1 795	10 865	22 654	8 372	1.8	27.4	5.2	47.1	9.7	5.1	19.2	23.8	17 530

1. Based on the resident population estimated as of July 1 of the year shown.   2. Includes mining, construction, and manufacturing.   3. Includes private sector earnings in agricultural services, forestry, and fisheries; transportation and public utilities; wholesale and retail trade; finance, insurance, and real estate; and services.

Table A. States — Housing

STATE	Housing units, 1998 Total	Percent change 1990–1998	Occupied units Total	Percent owner-occupied	Housing units, 1990 Total	Percent change, 1980–1990	Owner-occupied Total	Percent	Median value[1] (dollars)	Owner cost as a percent of income With a mortgage	Owner cost as a percent of income Without a mortgage	Renter-occupied Median rent[2] (dollars)	Rent as a percent of income	Sub-standard units[3] (percent)
	124	125	126	127	128	129	130	131	132	133	134	135	136	137
UNITED STATES	112 498 582	10.0	101 041 243	66.3	102 263 678	15.7	91 947 410	64.2	79 100	21.0	12.9	447	26.4	5.3
ALABAMA	1 865 970	11.7	1 663 416	72.9	1 670 379	13.8	1 506 790	70.5	53 700	18.4	12.8	325	24.8	4.5
ALASKA	248 472	6.8	214 712	66.3	232 608	42.9	188 915	56.1	94 400	21.5	12.2	559	23.8	12.4
ARIZONA	2 005 552	20.9	1 761 567	64.3	1 659 430	49.4	1 368 843	64.2	80 100	22.8	12.4	438	27.5	7.8
ARKANSAS	1 092 343	9.2	970 386	66.7	1 000 667	11.4	891 179	69.6	46 300	20.0	13.4	328	26.5	4.9
CALIFORNIA	12 037 170	7.6	11 445 772	56.0	11 182 882	20.5	10 381 206	55.6	195 500	24.9	11.8	620	29.1	12.0
COLORADO	1 722 056	16.6	1 560 682	65.2	1 477 349	23.7	1 282 489	62.2	82 700	22.5	12.7	418	26.1	3.0
CONNECTICUT	1 379 006	4.4	1 238 314	69.3	1 320 850	14.0	1 230 479	65.6	177 800	22.9	13.7	598	26.6	2.5
DELAWARE	326 363	12.6	283 969	71.0	289 919	21.5	247 497	70.2	100 100	19.5	12.0	495	24.7	2.5
DISTRICT OF COLUMBIA	264 831	-4.9	224 548	40.3	278 489	0.5	249 634	38.9	123 900	20.5	12.8	479	25.4	8.3
FLORIDA	7 006 759	14.9	5 880 567	66.9	6 100 262	39.3	5 134 869	67.2	77 100	22.3	12.2	481	28.0	5.7
GEORGIA	3 184 246	20.7	2 842 557	71.2	2 638 418	30.1	2 366 615	64.9	71 300	20.9	12.8	433	25.8	4.7
HAWAII	440 044	12.9	400 927	52.8	389 810	16.6	356 267	53.9	245 300	21.4	10.8	650	27.4	15.6
IDAHO	503 455	21.8	448 341	72.6	413 327	10.2	360 723	70.1	58 200	19.3	11.8	330	23.8	4.5
ILLINOIS	4 776 992	6.0	4 437 969	68.0	4 506 275	4.3	4 202 240	64.2	80 900	20.2	12.7	445	25.9	4.2
INDIANA	2 502 753	11.4	2 230 739	72.6	2 246 046	7.4	2 065 355	70.2	53 900	16.7	12.3	374	24.3	2.6
IOWA	1 208 296	5.7	1 103 360	72.1	1 143 669	1.1	1 064 325	70.0	45 900	17.3	12.8	336	24.1	1.9
KANSAS	1 129 786	8.2	999 189	66.7	1 044 112	9.3	944 726	67.9	52 200	19.1	12.6	372	24.5	2.7
KENTUCKY	1 663 975	10.4	1 496 784	75.1	1 506 845	10.1	1 379 782	69.6	50 500	18.0	12.3	319	24.9	4.7
LOUISIANA	1 805 917	5.2	1 598 882	66.6	1 716 241	10.8	1 499 269	65.9	58 500	20.6	13.3	352	27.9	6.5
MAINE	626 434	6.7	489 811	74.6	587 045	17.2	465 312	70.5	87 400	21.4	13.4	419	26.8	3.1
MARYLAND	2 091 171	10.5	1 906 482	68.7	1 891 917	20.4	1 748 991	65.0	116 500	21.1	12.4	548	25.4	3.3
MASSACHUSETTS	2 568 415	3.9	2 348 519	61.3	2 472 711	12.0	2 247 110	59.3	162 800	22.3	13.8	580	26.8	2.7
MICHIGAN	4 167 866	8.3	3 693 285	74.4	3 847 926	7.2	3 419 331	71.0	60 600	18.0	13.5	423	27.2	2.9
MINNESOTA	2 020 508	9.3	1 790 648	75.4	1 848 445	14.6	1 647 853	71.8	74 000	20.4	12.4	422	26.7	2.4
MISSISSIPPI	1 106 487	9.5	997 464	75.1	1 010 423	10.8	911 374	71.5	45 600	20.8	13.5	309	27.1	7.2
MISSOURI	2 393 506	8.8	2 088 986	70.7	2 199 129	10.6	1 961 206	68.8	59 800	18.4	12.3	368	25.2	3.0
MONTANA	382 881	6.0	346 070	68.6	361 155	10.0	306 163	67.3	56 600	20.2	12.5	311	25.0	3.2
NEBRASKA	711 203	7.7	635 521	69.9	660 621	5.7	602 363	66.5	50 400	19.4	12.6	348	23.7	1.9
NEVADA	766 560	47.8	676 210	61.4	518 858	52.6	466 297	54.8	95 700	22.4	11.9	509	26.8	6.4
NEW HAMPSHIRE	539 112	7.0	450 302	69.6	503 904	30.4	411 186	68.2	129 400	24.4	14.7	549	26.4	2.1
NEW JERSEY	3 236 773	5.3	2 956 576	63.1	3 075 310	10.9	2 794 711	64.9	162 300	23.4	15.1	592	26.3	4.1
NEW MEXICO	746 634	18.1	632 316	71.3	632 058	24.5	542 709	67.4	70 100	21.6	12.5	372	26.5	8.8
NEW YORK	7 455 399	3.2	6 765 714	52.8	7 226 891	5.2	6 639 322	52.2	131 600	21.5	14.4	486	26.3	6.8
NORTH CAROLINA	3 366 723	19.5	2 882 737	71.3	2 818 193	23.9	2 517 026	68.0	65 800	20.5	12.9	382	24.4	3.9
NORTH DAKOTA	293 415	6.2	247 018	68.0	276 340	6.8	240 878	65.6	50 800	20.3	13.0	313	23.9	2.5
OHIO	4 681 506	7.1	4 284 963	70.7	4 371 945	6.4	4 087 546	67.5	63 500	18.2	12.5	379	25.3	2.2
OKLAHOMA	1 459 000	3.7	1 288 331	69.7	1 406 499	13.7	1 206 135	68.1	48 100	20.0	12.8	340	25.4	3.7
OREGON	1 400 764	17.4	1 285 885	63.4	1 193 567	10.2	1 103 313	63.1	67 100	20.4	13.4	408	25.5	3.9
PENNSYLVANIA	5 228 921	5.9	4 592 785	73.9	4 938 140	7.4	4 495 966	70.6	69 700	20.2	13.3	404	26.1	2.3
RHODE ISLAND	430 609	3.9	376 238	59.8	414 572	11.2	377 977	59.5	133 500	22.7	13.9	489	27.5	2.6
SOUTH CAROLINA	1 683 172	18.2	1 441 217	76.6	1 424 155	23.4	1 258 044	69.8	61 100	19.8	13.0	376	24.4	5.0
SOUTH DAKOTA	321 649	10.0	276 736	67.3	292 436	5.6	259 034	66.1	45 200	19.8	13.3	306	24.6	3.4
TENNESSEE	2 318 069	14.4	2 099 672	71.3	2 026 067	15.9	1 853 725	68.0	58 400	20.1	12.6	357	25.0	3.8
TEXAS	7 807 968	11.4	7 112 985	62.5	7 008 999	26.3	6 070 937	60.9	59 600	20.9	13.1	395	24.6	8.4
UTAH	730 847	22.1	676 697	73.7	598 388	22.1	537 273	68.1	68 900	20.9	12.1	369	23.8	5.4
VERMONT	288 739	6.5	231 353	69.1	271 214	21.5	210 650	69.0	95 500	21.9	14.7	446	27.1	2.5
VIRGINIA	2 836 783	13.6	2 579 144	69.4	2 496 334	23.5	2 291 830	66.3	91 000	21.9	12.5	495	25.8	4.1
WASHINGTON	2 386 485	17.4	2 210 949	64.9	2 032 378	20.3	1 872 431	62.6	93 400	20.4	11.8	445	25.7	4.0
WEST VIRGINIA	794 481	1.7	715 831	74.8	781 295	4.5	688 557	74.1	47 900	17.5	12.0	303	26.8	4.0
WISCONSIN	2 279 245	10.9	1 973 057	70.1	2 055 774	10.3	1 822 118	66.7	62 500	20.1	13.4	399	24.9	2.6
WYOMING	213 271	4.8	185 060	70.0	203 411	8.1	168 839	67.8	61 600	18.8	11.9	333	23.7	3.1

1. Specified owner-occupied units.   2. Specified renter-occupied units.   3. Overcrowded or lacking complete plumbing facilities.

Social Security, Employment, Unemployment, and Labor Force

STATE	Social Security beneficiaries, December 1999		Supplemental Security Income recipients, December 1999	Civilian employment and selected occupations, March 1999[2]			Civilian labor force annual average 1999			Unemployed	
					Percent						
	Number	Rate[1]		Total	Professional, managerial, and technical	Precision production, craft, and repair	Total	Percent change, 1998–1999	Employed	Total	Rate[3]
	138	139	140	141	142	143	144	145	146	147	148
UNITED STATES	44 595 202	164	6 556 634	131 806 148	33.3	10.9	139 368 000	1.2	133 488 000	5 880 000	4.2
ALABAMA	810 196	185	160 292	2 081 543	31.9	11.7	2 140 872	-0.7	2 038 912	101 960	4.8
ALASKA	51 320	83	8 165	284 571	34.8	8.0	318 882	0.4	298 577	20 305	6.4
ARIZONA	772 631	162	79 490	2 259 733	32.4	10.8	2 359 071	4.6	2 255 117	103 954	4.4
ARKANSAS	517 826	203	87 732	1 149 158	25.9	14.2	1 229 122	1.2	1 173 971	55 151	4.5
CALIFORNIA	4 105 728	124	1 065 323	15 507 925	34.9	10.1	16 596 485	1.6	15 731 727	864 758	5.2
COLORADO	522 116	129	54 685	2 230 245	41.5	10.2	2 264 105	1.0	2 198 147	65 958	2.9
CONNECTICUT	567 637	173	47 669	1 588 488	40.7	10.9	1 708 434	0.1	1 654 455	53 979	3.2
DELAWARE	128 935	171	11 849	381 091	31.1	10.7	389 642	-0.7	375 970	13 672	3.5
DISTRICT OF COLUMBIA	73 176	141	20 009	256 591	50.9	4.3	280 766	4.8	263 158	17 608	6.3
FLORIDA	3 139 437	208	366 966	6 895 579	30.4	11.2	7 360 875	1.8	7 076 924	283 951	3.9
GEORGIA	1 073 388	138	196 959	3 792 663	30.3	11.8	4 078 263	1.6	3 916 080	162 183	4.0
HAWAII	178 000	150	20 417	552 884	34.9	6.6	592 801	-0.3	559 587	33 214	5.6
IDAHO	190 674	152	17 813	606 899	28.6	11.7	651 090	-0.3	617 393	33 697	5.2
ILLINOIS	1 816 192	150	251 058	6 144 975	33.3	9.0	6 378 454	2.3	6 105 124	273 330	4.3
INDIANA	986 207	166	88 314	2 992 249	27.3	12.3	3 075 563	-0.4	2 982 597	92 966	3.0
IOWA	537 366	187	40 484	1 517 382	29.0	13.9	1 572 830	0.2	1 532 729	40 101	2.5
KANSAS	435 613	164	36 298	1 344 349	34.7	12.3	1 434 249	1.1	1 391 523	42 726	3.0
KENTUCKY	729 134	184	172 253	1 859 096	27.1	12.5	1 966 574	1.9	1 878 686	87 888	4.5
LOUISIANA	702 105	161	168 025	1 898 818	29.9	11.9	2 051 621	-0.2	1 947 655	103 966	5.1
MAINE	246 214	196	29 365	617 361	34.1	13.0	669 937	3.1	642 471	27 466	4.1
MARYLAND	704 867	136	86 748	2 624 269	43.5	7.7	2 774 718	0.8	2 676 488	98 230	3.5
MASSACHUSETTS	1 046 655	169	166 825	3 139 041	36.6	10.2	3 284 079	0.3	3 179 102	104 977	3.2
MICHIGAN	1 620 377	164	209 957	4 757 711	29.6	12.5	5 144 356	2.2	4 950 204	194 152	3.8
MINNESOTA	728 088	152	63 632	2 534 990	35.8	10.7	2 703 016	0.8	2 627 437	75 579	2.8
MISSISSIPPI	505 731	183	131 379	1 222 608	27.8	12.9	1 267 509	0.0	1 202 968	64 541	5.1
MISSOURI	993 174	182	111 040	2 763 077	32.3	11.6	2 841 203	-0.5	2 745 464	95 739	3.4
MONTANA	155 072	176	13 723	436 803	29.9	10.4	474 006	1.6	449 361	24 645	5.2
NEBRASKA	282 661	170	21 054	892 313	25.0	11.2	911 831	-0.5	885 755	26 076	2.9
NEVADA	271 205	150	24 395	873 519	28.0	9.9	941 600	2.4	899 737	41 863	4.4
NEW HAMPSHIRE	195 065	162	11 445	630 759	34.3	10.5	668 096	2.3	649 969	18 127	2.7
NEW JERSEY	1 322 550	162	145 376	4 003 478	39.9	8.2	4 205 456	1.5	4 012 218	193 238	4.6
NEW MEXICO	270 658	156	45 911	758 558	34.9	12.0	809 094	-2.6	763 609	45 485	5.6
NEW YORK	2 966 658	163	608 986	8 278 973	35.6	8.5	8 881 776	-0.1	8 422 650	459 126	5.2
NORTH CAROLINA	1 322 399	173	191 841	3 682 416	31.8	13.2	3 868 374	1.8	3 746 412	121 962	3.2
NORTH DAKOTA	114 171	180	8 264	315 408	28.1	9.5	336 822	-2.7	325 366	11 456	3.4
OHIO	1 893 896	168	242 752	5 485 155	34.8	11.7	5 753 779	1.1	5 507 825	245 954	4.3
OKLAHOMA	586 802	175	72 665	1 529 253	33.1	11.5	1 654 805	1.9	1 597 865	56 940	3.4
OREGON	553 547	167	50 623	1 633 034	32.1	11.8	1 761 124	-0.2	1 660 724	100 400	5.7
PENNSYLVANIA	2 332 589	194	277 998	5 855 737	33.5	9.5	5 976 070	0.7	5 713 423	262 647	4.4
RHODE ISLAND	190 681	192	26 837	499 374	36.0	9.7	504 450	1.3	483 532	20 918	4.1
SOUTH CAROLINA	672 353	173	108 198	1 849 355	28.9	14.8	1 963 273	0.0	1 875 433	87 840	4.5
SOUTH DAKOTA	135 165	184	12 756	380 739	26.5	10.0	399 704	1.2	388 072	11 632	2.9
TENNESSEE	970 895	177	166 435	2 709 103	26.8	11.8	2 815 538	2.0	2 702 168	113 370	4.0
TEXAS	2 575 745	129	408 084	9 678 132	31.8	11.9	10 219 113	1.2	9 746 879	472 234	4.6
UTAH	234 587	110	19 999	1 076 751	34.7	11.1	1 086 080	2.1	1 045 501	40 579	3.7
VERMONT	102 729	173	12 520	328 699	36.6	12.2	335 778	1.7	325 585	10 193	3.0
VIRGINIA	1 008 033	147	131 989	3 287 023	36.1	11.3	3 528 041	1.2	3 429 908	98 133	2.8
WASHINGTON	825 281	143	98 067	2 876 848	38.7	11.0	3 074 556	1.2	2 929 243	145 313	4.7
WEST VIRGINIA	390 558	216	70 972	736 065	33.6	10.6	816 445	2.4	746 787	53 872	6.6
WISCONSIN	890 588	170	86 544	2 762 280	30.2	11.7	2 889 812	-2.1	2 852 556	88 035	3.0
WYOMING	74 688	156	5 783	243 077	28.1	13.6	262 069	2.1	245 607	12 746	4.9

1. Per 1,000 resident population estimated as of July 1 of the year shown.   2. Persons 16 years and older.   3. Percent of civilian labor force.

STATE	Employment Total (1,000)	Percent change, 1998–1999	Manufacturing Employment (1,000)	Average earnings of production workers Hourly	Weekly	Construction	Transportation and public utilities	Wholesale trade	Retail trade	Finance, insurance, and real estate	Services
	149	150	151	152	153	154	155	156	157	158	159
UNITED STATES	108 616.0	2.4	18 543.0	13.91	580.05	6 404.0	6 826.0	6 924.0	22 788.0	7 569.0	39 027.0
ALABAMA	1 568.8	1.1	367.6	12.54	527.93	104.3	94.5	97.7	346.9	90.9	456.7
ALASKA	204.2	1.4	14.4	12.16	550.85	13.8	26.1	8.9	48.4	12.8	70.4
ARIZONA	1 809.0	4.4	211.7	12.70	513.08	154.7	104.2	109.4	400.2	139.6	677.8
ARKANSAS	954.3	1.8	252.1	11.55	481.64	50.5	69.2	51.7	210.2	45.8	271.3
CALIFORNIA	11 752.5	2.8	1 923.0	13.95	581.72	680.6	719.3	813.1	2 388.2	817.3	4 387.2
COLORADO	1 803.5	4.0	204.6	14.19	588.89	146.9	139.7	105.9	401.1	140.8	651.2
CONNECTICUT	1 434.0	1.3	268.4	15.33	649.99	61.4	77.5	81.5	277.6	140.0	526.4
DELAWARE	357.8	3.5	59.8	15.91	684.13	24.5	17.1	14.8	74.9	49.2	117.3
DISTRICT OF COLUMBIA	404.9	4.4	11.6	NA	NA	9.3	18.4	5.7	42.6	31.8	285.4
FLORIDA	5 861.4	3.2	487.7	11.83	494.49	367.6	348.8	365.8	1 347.8	443.7	2 493.7
GEORGIA	3 290.7	4.3	596.7	12.51	521.67	199.2	258.7	256.5	703.2	202.6	1 065.8
HAWAII	422.3	0.8	16.5	13.49	530.16	NA	41.2	21.1	112.0	34.8	174.9
IDAHO	433.7	3.5	76.3	13.42	528.75	34.9	26.8	32.1	104.1	23.6	133.2
ILLINOIS	5 132.7	1.0	954.9	14.05	588.70	253.4	347.8	358.4	986.8	404.2	1 816.7
INDIANA	2 567.3	2.0	690.2	15.26	654.65	149.5	147.6	144.2	555.6	142.3	730.9
IOWA	1 229.2	1.9	261.0	14.20	587.88	65.1	71.9	85.5	271.6	85.1	386.6
KANSAS	1 087.4	1.4	213.1	14.44	593.48	65.4	78.5	76.9	242.3	62.9	341.6
KENTUCKY	1 494.4	2.5	320.7	14.27	595.06	86.5	105.0	86.6	340.4	70.6	462.7
LOUISIANA	1 525.9	0.2	187.1	15.18	657.29	127.4	112.1	96.0	346.9	85.6	523.5
MAINE	489.6	3.2	86.2	13.94	568.75	28.0	24.1	27.0	119.0	31.4	173.9
MARYLAND	1 947.5	2.9	177.9	14.62	605.27	149.9	112.4	112.3	434.6	138.9	820.2
MASSACHUSETTS	2 819.4	1.9	433.6	14.24	598.08	119.2	139.7	175.6	559.3	226.3	1 163.9
MICHIGAN	3 914.4	1.6	981.8	18.38	812.40	196.5	178.9	234.9	840.0	208.0	1 267.2
MINNESOTA	2 225.6	2.4	439.0	14.34	590.81	111.4	132.0	153.6	467.0	160.1	755.3
MISSISSIPPI	926.2	1.7	243.9	11.17	461.32	55.5	55.7	47.2	206.9	42.8	268.8
MISSOURI	2 305.3	1.6	411.8	13.93	578.10	136.7	172.1	152.0	490.5	165.8	771.0
MONTANA	301.6	2.4	24.5	14.17	552.63	19.5	22.1	18.7	82.4	17.5	111.8
NEBRASKA	741.3	2.2	118.2	12.77	535.06	43.1	57.9	55.1	161.0	60.7	243.7
NEVADA	865.5	6.3	42.6	13.92	574.90	88.7	52.0	37.2	164.3	44.2	424.2
NEW HAMPSHIRE	524.3	3.0	106.6	13.17	534.70	24.2	21.4	31.7	128.4	32.5	178.7
NEW JERSEY	3 323.5	2.9	466.7	15.11	630.09	145.6	268.5	284.4	628.2	260.9	1 267.4
NEW MEXICO	549.4	1.5	42.4	12.53	488.67	43.6	35.4	27.6	143.6	32.8	210.0
NEW YORK	7 010.1	2.9	890.3	13.87	571.44	311.2	420.9	444.6	1 264.3	744.6	2 929.3
NORTH CAROLINA	3 266.2	2.7	801.9	12.32	505.12	225.7	176.5	199.5	678.5	185.5	994.3
NORTH DAKOTA	252.1	1.5	24.1	11.94	477.60	16.6	18.4	21.8	99.5	16.4	91.5
OHIO	4 791.3	1.5	1 090.4	16.26	697.55	240.4	246.7	298.8	1 041.2	306.1	1 554.8
OKLAHOMA	1 179.3	1.4	183.8	12.70	524.51	58.4	82.2	68.6	268.7	72.8	416.3
OREGON	1 313.7	1.3	242.2	14.61	590.24	83.3	77.8	93.5	294.5	95.1	425.6
PENNSYLVANIA	4 876.0	1.8	930.4	14.19	593.14	236.3	294.3	273.1	977.4	324.1	1 820.1
RHODE ISLAND	402.2	1.8	74.8	11.98	478.00	17.7	16.3	19.6	84.4	29.7	159.3
SOUTH CAROLINA	1 515.3	2.8	344.6	10.67	454.54	112.8	89.8	79.1	359.0	81.3	446.6
SOUTH DAKOTA	301.4	3.1	50.1	10.58	453.88	17.0	16.7	20.2	70.4	24.5	101.0
TENNESSEE	2 295.3	1.9	511.0	12.50	507.50	123.5	172.4	149.1	481.6	131.1	721.9
TEXAS	7 624.4	2.5	1 084.4	12.25	532.88	529.2	564.1	530.9	1 649.0	516.3	2 603.7
UTAH	869.1	2.7	132.0	13.39	535.60	72.3	59.3	50.9	197.4	56.6	292.7
VERMONT	243.7	2.1	47.9	13.65	539.18	14.4	12.2	12.4	54.3	12.5	89.0
VIRGINIA	2 801.1	3.1	395.7	13.37	566.89	197.9	178.4	147.2	602.6	184.4	1 084.8
WASHINGTON	2 174.4	2.1	364.2	16.14	660.13	153.9	139.8	154.1	482.0	137.6	739.7
WEST VIRGINIA	585.1	1.2	81.6	14.09	586.14	33.6	38.1	30.7	132.6	29.8	217.5
WISCONSIN	2 385.1	2.6	617.6	14.50	607.55	121.4	131.1	137.2	489.6	145.9	739.2
WYOMING	173.6	2.2	11.1	15.40	605.22	17.2	14.3	7.6	45.7	8.0	53.5

Private nonfarm employment and earnings, 1999

Table A. States — **Agriculture**

STATE	Farms Number	Farms Percent with — Less than 50 acres	Farms Percent with — 500 acres and over	Farm operators whose principal occupation is farming (percent)	Land in farms Acreage (1,000)	Percent change, 1992–1997	Acres Average size of farm	Total irrigated (1,000)	Total cropland (1,000)	Value of land and buildings Average per farm ($1,000)	Average per acre (dollars)
	160	161	162	163	164	165	166	167	168	169	170
UNITED STATES	1 911 859	29.5	18.4	50.3	931 795	-1.5	487	55 058	431 144	450	933
ALABAMA	41 384	33.8	9.2	37.6	8 704	3.0	210	77	4 198	298	1 442
ALASKA	548	35.4	16.4	55.8	881	-4.5	1 608	3	95	487	303
ARIZONA	6 135	44.8	27.1	53.0	26 867	-23.3	4 379	1 014	1 277	1 689	388
ARKANSAS	45 142	24.1	16.4	49.4	14 365	1.7	318	3 717	10 062	360	1 151
CALIFORNIA	74 126	60.6	11.7	53.0	27 699	-4.4	374	8 713	10 804	941	2 605
COLORADO	28 268	28.4	34.2	54.5	32 634	-4.0	1 154	3 430	10 509	707	618
CONNECTICUT	3 687	54.7	2.8	49.5	359	0.0	97	7	181	571	5 949
DELAWARE	2 460	47.6	11.9	60.9	580	-1.6	236	73	487	610	2 660
DISTRICT OF COLUMBIA	NA	NA	NA	NA	NA	NA	NA	NA	NA	NA	NA
FLORIDA	34 799	57.9	8.7	45.4	10 454	-2.9	300	1 862	3 640	663	2 241
GEORGIA	40 334	31.4	12.6	43.4	10 671	6.4	265	749	5 371	393	1 505
HAWAII	5 473	89.0	2.6	55.8	1 439	-9.4	263	77	292	632	2 405
IDAHO	22 314	39.0	22.6	54.0	11 830	-12.2	530	3 494	6 309	537	1 017
ILLINOIS	73 051	23.1	25.1	57.0	27 205	-0.2	372	350	23 921	773	2 126
INDIANA	57 916	31.4	15.1	46.6	15 111	-3.3	261	250	12 849	533	2 064
IOWA	90 792	18.3	22.8	62.0	31 167	-0.6	343	125	26 822	567	1 697
KANSAS	61 593	14.9	37.9	56.8	46 089	-1.2	748	2 707	30 021	431	577
KENTUCKY	82 273	33.9	5.9	41.1	13 334	-2.4	162	58	8 549	230	1 450
LOUISIANA	23 823	34.1	17.3	47.4	7 877	0.5	331	943	5 331	381	1 206
MAINE	5 810	29.6	9.3	49.4	1 212	-3.7	209	22	540	251	1 190
MARYLAND	12 084	43.3	8.2	51.6	2 155	-3.1	178	69	1 613	564	3 176
MASSACHUSETTS	5 574	56.0	2.7	52.5	518	-1.5	93	25	224	455	5 207
MICHIGAN	46 027	31.9	10.7	47.9	9 873	-2.1	215	393	7 892	358	1 671
MINNESOTA	73 367	18.0	20.8	60.0	25 995	1.3	354	380	21 492	408	1 164
MISSISSIPPI	31 318	22.3	14.5	40.7	10 125	-0.6	323	1 076	5 947	337	1 052
MISSOURI	98 860	20.1	15.5	45.3	28 826	1.0	292	882	19 229	309	1 069
MONTANA	24 279	18.4	53.0	64.7	58 608	-1.7	2 414	1 994	17 629	699	294
NEBRASKA	51 454	14.2	42.2	69.5	45 525	2.6	885	6 939	22 093	567	645
NEVADA	2 829	39.6	26.1	55.1	6 409	-30.8	2 266	765	847	876	388
NEW HAMPSHIRE	2 937	41.2	5.2	42.9	415	7.5	141	3	133	324	2 250
NEW JERSEY	9 101	66.5	3.8	43.1	833	-1.8	91	93	595	594	6 642
NEW MEXICO	14 094	37.0	35.5	51.1	45 787	-2.3	3 249	805	2 179	625	195
NEW YORK	31 757	24.3	10.7	58.0	7 254	-2.7	228	69	4 722	287	1 284
NORTH CAROLINA	49 406	39.6	8.2	49.3	9 122	2.1	185	156	5 608	376	2 081
NORTH DAKOTA	30 504	6.4	63.9	74.3	39 359	-0.2	1 290	180	27 025	513	401
OHIO	68 591	30.7	10.0	45.2	14 103	-1.0	206	34	11 341	415	2 039
OKLAHOMA	74 214	20.5	21.6	44.5	33 219	3.3	448	506	14 844	272	610
OREGON	34 030	56.3	12.9	46.0	17 449	-0.9	513	1 949	5 286	479	960
PENNSYLVANIA	45 457	29.2	5.4	56.4	7 168	-0.3	158	36	5 032	372	2 390
RHODE ISLAND	735	59.6	2.0	50.3	55	10.5	75	3	26	442	5 885
SOUTH CAROLINA	20 189	34.4	10.6	39.4	4 593	2.7	228	86	2 463	325	1 482
SOUTH DAKOTA	31 284	11.5	52.2	72.6	44 355	-1.1	1 418	344	19 355	487	348
TENNESSEE	76 818	39.5	5.0	36.0	11 122	-0.4	145	46	7 069	261	1 808
TEXAS	194 301	27.6	21.4	42.9	131 308	0.3	676	5 485	37 662	398	593
UTAH	14 181	46.3	16.4	42.2	12 025	24.9	848	1 212	2 070	486	575
VERMONT	5 828	25.0	10.0	56.6	1 262	-1.3	217	3	617	323	1 520
VIRGINIA	41 095	32.0	9.0	44.8	8 228	-0.8	200	85	4 322	385	1 920
WASHINGTON	29 011	51.4	16.2	53.3	15 180	-3.5	523	1 705	7 914	635	1 192
WEST VIRGINIA	17 772	21.1	7.5	40.2	3 456	5.8	194	3	1 337	213	1 090
WISCONSIN	65 602	19.5	9.2	59.5	14 900	-3.6	227	342	10 353	282	1 244
WYOMING	9 232	16.9	50.5	60.5	34 089	3.7	3 692	1 719	2 968	808	222

Agriculture, 1997

Table A. States — **Agriculture, Land, and Water**

STATE	Agriculture, 1997 (cont'd) Value of machinery and equipment Average per farm ($1,000)	Value of products sold Total (mil dol)	Average per farm (dollars)	Percent from — Crops	Livestock and poultry products	Percent of farms with sales of — $10,000 or more	$100,000 or more	Land, 1997 Owned by Federal Government (percent)	Developed (percent)	Water consumption (mil gal per day) 1995
	171	172	173	174	175	176	177	178	179	180
UNITED STATES...............	58	196 865	102 970	49.8	50.2	49.6	18.1	20.7	5.1	340 751.3
ALABAMA	36	3 099	74 884	20.4	79.6	31.1	11.3	3.0	6.7	7 088.0
ALASKA	53	25	44 982	64.8	35.2	40.1	8.6	NA	NA	211.1
ARIZONA	71	1 903	310 254	64.2	35.8	48.0	22.0	41.7	2.0	6 815.9
ARKANSAS........................	56	5 480	121 388	39.9	60.1	45.4	22.2	9.1	4.1	8 767.3
CALIFORNIA......................	70	23 032	310 718	74.0	26.0	56.2	26.6	45.9	5.4	36 297.8
COLORADO.......................	71	4 534	160 401	29.3	70.7	52.6	16.9	35.7	2.5	13 823.9
CONNECTICUT	41	422	114 361	62.6	37.4	39.8	12.6	0.5	27.4	1 275.1
DELAWARE	76	691	280 811	25.3	74.7	69.8	43.8	2.0	14.7	752.1
DISTRICT OF COLUMBIA ...	NA	NA	NA	NA	NA	NA	NA	NA	NA	10.2
FLORIDA	41	6 005	172 550	80.2	19.8	42.4	14.9	10.1	13.8	7 215.0
GEORGIA	44	4 993	123 789	38.5	61.5	39.5	17.8	5.6	10.5	5 754.0
HAWAII	39	497	90 798	80.8	19.2	41.9	8.2	8.7	4.3	1 012.4
IDAHO...............................	78	3 346	149 945	53.0	47.0	53.5	21.5	62.7	1.4	15 141.5
ILLINOIS	90	8 556	117 130	76.8	23.2	68.2	31.7	1.4	8.8	19 896.9
INDIANA............................	64	5 230	90 303	62.1	37.9	56.3	20.8	2.0	9.8	9 139.3
IOWA.................................	81	11 948	131 596	51.8	48.2	74.0	34.6	0.5	4.7	3 034.6
KANSAS............................	74	9 207	149 483	35.0	65.0	63.0	21.8	1.0	3.7	5 235.4
KENTUCKY........................	33	3 064	37 247	51.5	48.5	44.0	6.8	4.6	6.7	4 420.2
LOUISIANA........................	59	2 031	85 265	69.5	30.5	40.2	17.6	4.2	5.2	9 847.8
MAINE...............................	49	439	75 503	48.4	51.6	41.2	13.2	1.0	3.4	221.0
MARYLAND........................	60	1 312	108 580	35.0	65.0	50.2	21.5	2.1	15.7	1 452.2
MASSACHUSETTS	40	454	81 522	78.6	21.4	46.4	15.4	1.8	27.7	1 145.7
MICHIGAN	66	3 568	77 516	61.7	38.3	49.1	15.8	8.8	9.5	12 059.3
MINNESOTA......................	85	8 290	112 997	50.7	49.3	64.4	28.1	6.2	4.0	3 391.5
MISSISSIPPI......................	52	3 127	99 859	41.3	58.7	33.4	14.4	5.8	4.8	3 088.0
MISSOURI	41	5 368	54 297	43.0	57.0	44.4	10.8	4.3	5.6	7 029.0
MONTANA	78	1 871	77 051	48.3	51.7	61.6	22.1	28.8	1.1	8 847.2
NEBRASKA........................	85	9 832	191 074	38.6	61.4	77.6	35.4	1.3	2.4	10 543.2
NEVADA............................	70	357	126 039	42.5	57.5	51.8	18.0	84.6	0.5	2 259.3
NEW HAMPSHIRE	38	149	50 891	49.3	50.7	33.0	9.4	12.8	9.9	445.5
NEW JERSEY.....................	48	697	76 627	85.0	15.0	39.0	12.8	2.8	34.1	2 137.5
NEW MEXICO.....................	44	1 618	114 780	28.6	71.4	38.9	12.2	34.0	1.5	3 505.3
NEW YORK	60	2 835	89 256	35.3	64.7	54.0	21.6	0.7	10.2	10 277.6
NORTH CAROLINA..............	49	7 677	155 376	33.8	66.2	46.2	20.5	7.4	11.4	7 730.2
NORTH DAKOTA	112	2 869	94 064	76.5	23.5	75.1	28.4	3.9	2.2	1 122.4
OHIO.................................	58	4 684	68 293	60.4	39.6	52.3	15.7	1.4	13.7	10 523.3
OKLAHOMA	37	4 146	55 870	21.9	78.1	40.0	8.5	2.6	4.3	1 781.3
OREGON	55	2 969	87 252	71.2	28.8	38.2	13.4	50.3	2.0	7 906.0
PENNSYLVANIA.................	53	3 998	87 942	32.1	67.9	54.1	21.1	2.5	13.7	9 684.9
RHODE ISLAND	39	48	65 578	81.8	18.2	46.7	13.2	0.4	24.7	136.2
SOUTH CAROLINA.............	45	1 588	78 665	49.8	50.2	31.0	11.3	5.2	10.5	6 202.9
SOUTH DAKOTA	91	3 570	114 114	46.3	53.7	76.9	30.2	6.3	1.9	460.0
TENNESSEE......................	33	2 178	28 358	52.5	47.5	27.7	5.1	4.6	8.8	10 076.2
TEXAS	40	13 767	70 852	31.2	68.8	33.4	8.7	1.7	5.0	24 332.9
UTAH................................	51	877	61 864	28.2	71.8	43.6	11.5	63.1	1.2	4 301.4
VERMONT	49	476	81 734	12.5	87.5	50.9	22.9	6.4	5.2	565.3
VIRGINIA	42	2 344	57 027	33.3	66.7	39.3	10.0	9.8	9.7	5 466.9
WASHINGTON	70	4 768	164 342	68.2	31.8	48.5	23.3	27.1	4.7	8 822.5
WEST VIRGINIA.................	24	447	25 176	14.5	85.5	20.7	3.6	7.8	5.6	4 618.3
WISCONSIN	67	5 580	85 056	29.4	70.6	61.4	24.0	5.1	6.7	7 251.7
WYOMING	61	899	97 327	19.3	80.7	62.6	20.6	45.9	1.0	7 040.2

Table A. States — **Manufactures and Construction**

STATE	Manufactures, 1998										Construction, 1997			
	All employees			Production workers										
						Wages								
	Number (1,000)	Percent change, 1997–1998	Annual Payroll (mil dol)	Number (1,000)	Work hours (millions)	Total (mil dol)	Average per worker (dollars)	Value added by manu- facture (mil dol)	Value of ship- ments (mil dol)	Total capital expenditures (mil dol)	Estab- lishments	Value (mil dol)	Paid employees	Annual Payroll (mil dol)
	181	182	183	184	185	186	187	188	189	190	191	192	193	194
UNITED STATES	17 056.9	1.0	590 039	12 276	24 764	351 204	28 608	1 899 238	3 914 816	151 905	656 448	845 543.6	5 664 853	174 184.6
ALABAMA	351.4	-0.3	10 293	273	540	7 009	25 659	29 059	69 661	3 089	9 586	12 566.7	95 218	2 475.7
ALASKA	12.1	11.2	360	10	20	266	27 101	1 422	3 322	142	2 034	2 406.2	14 114	565.0
ARIZONA	198.3	2.3	7 034	124	250	3 309	26 658	28 006	43 511	1 537	11 058	18 866.5	131 871	3 621.2
ARKANSAS	235.0	2.2	6 135	192	385	4 447	23 125	20 763	46 602	1 582	5 457	5 143.1	42 033	982.8
CALIFORNIA	1 843.9	2.0	68 434	1 211	2 409	33 063	27 301	211 490	400 066	16 089	60 162	93 145.3	561 338	19 147.7
COLORADO	174.5	0.5	6 436	115	242	3 314	28 736	19 412	38 406	1 491	14 681	19 442.4	125 228	3 807.9
CONNECTICUT	252.7	0.2	10 509	155	324	5 124	33 013	28 416	48 637	1 901	9 057	9 729.3	63 935	2 246.7
DELAWARE	40.8	1.7	1 578	31	63	1 026	33 512	4 984	15 074	595	2 294	3 052.4	20 421	633.0
DISTRICT OF COLUMBIA	2.9	0.5	102	2	4	63	32 508	169	320	6	310	1 437.3	6 356	240.2
FLORIDA	431.2	0.1	13 461	291	579	7 046	24 247	41 432	79 281	3 267	36 608	50 173.8	324 844	8 802.5
GEORGIA	535.0	0.1	16 202	414	840	10 663	25 768	59 524	130 423	4 517	17 896	28 171.3	163 981	4 687.5
HAWAII	15.4	2.0	396	10	19	230	22 118	1 135	2 816	98	2 335	3 902.1	21 791	845.2
IDAHO	68.2	2.9	2 244	51	94	1 345	26 498	7 001	18 187	880	5 360	5 365.1	40 535	1 131.5
ILLINOIS	894.3	0.8	32 830	631	1 296	19 137	30 304	95 197	200 760	7 970	27 953	39 447.2	240 092	8 885.1
INDIANA	632.0	0.7	22 965	483	993	15 444	32 005	72 314	148 765	5 551	16 000	19 228.1	140 520	4 344.7
IOWA	244.2	3.4	8 144	184	378	5 211	28 362	28 428	63 491	2 011	7 941	7 941.4	62 146	1 734.1
KANSAS	202.4	4.3	6 819	149	302	4 281	28 795	20 120	48 495	1 814	7 115	8 762.2	61 915	1 755.6
KENTUCKY	289.9	0.4	9 571	226	455	6 462	28 602	39 834	91 174	3 292	8 878	9 754.4	76 876	2 000.7
LOUISIANA	166.7	0.6	6 258	124	258	4 114	33 055	31 441	77 248	3 582	7 812	11 330.6	107 773	3 033.2
MAINE	81.4	-1.1	2 640	62	121	1 730	27 819	6 802	14 226	904	4 249	2 812.3	25 157	662.4
MARYLAND	162.6	-0.8	6 172	111	219	3 462	31 120	19 454	37 841	1 461	14 525	20 880.7	141 469	4 367.5
MASSACHUSETTS	414.3	-0.5	16 611	256	508	7 938	31 059	45 599	79 375	3 554	14 959	20 413.4	107 813	3 868.8
MICHIGAN	836.7	0.6	34 728	634	1 313	23 410	36 940	91 407	215 237	9 887	25 399	30 400.1	187 135	6 280.5
MINNESOTA	389.7	1.9	13 714	264	533	7 609	28 772	38 619	79 052	3 371	12 993	18 125.1	103 200	3 603.8
MISSISSIPPI	234.1	2.7	5 915	191	375	4 152	21 720	17 186	39 722	1 552	4 824	5 978.2	47 695	1 155.5
MISSOURI	368.2	-0.4	11 951	268	534	7 394	27 547	47 537	95 027	2 743	15 020	18 772.4	130 555	3 978.1
MONTANA	20.6	4.6	602	16	30	421	26 664	1 960	4 851	159	3 452	2 209.0	18 096	445.6
NEBRASKA	111.6	4.4	3 234	87	181	2 247	25 912	10 874	28 594	727	5 198	5 388.6	40 363	1 148.2
NEVADA	39.5	4.2	1 241	27	54	707	25 954	3 625	6 751	230	4 436	11 696.5	70 168	2 313.4
NEW HAMPSHIRE	99.5	0.6	3 495	70	139	2 086	29 782	11 552	21 018	683	3 684	3 278.7	22 690	677.9
NEW JERSEY	404.5	-1.3	15 584	269	554	8 194	30 406	47 700	94 201	3 283	22 102	24 512.8	143 627	5 189.7
NEW MEXICO	39.6	-0.2	1 147	29	59	756	25 952	10 342	14 874	558	4 673	4 746.1	39 671	1 026.8
NEW YORK	785.8	0.1	26 560	541	1 082	14 904	27 565	79 736	148 193	5 884	36 806	43 890.8	275 501	9 670.0
NORTH CAROLINA	775.9	0.3	21 956	604	1 216	14 576	24 119	83 224	166 563	5 098	23 990	26 505.7	198 367	5 177.6
NORTH DAKOTA	22.9	4.0	631	17	33	400	23 353	2 234	5 780	216	2 034	1 802.1	15 782	408.4
OHIO	996.3	1.2	36 916	744	1 518	24 136	32 451	119 786	245 082	8 854	26 047	33 174.5	224 302	7 067.7
OKLAHOMA	166.0	1.2	5 140	124	250	3 388	27 352	16 924	37 917	1 479	6 751	6 502.3	50 556	1 256.4
OREGON	219.8	3.2	7 394	162	324	4 661	28 794	26 794	50 537	2 928	11 740	12 948.1	80 041	2 649.0
PENNSYLVANIA	831.3	0.8	28 350	605	1 216	17 500	28 924	89 746	176 743	6 794	27 563	33 423.0	230 026	7 275.8
RHODE ISLAND	78.2	3.4	2 415	55	108	1 360	24 950	5 799	10 797	390	3 060	3 689.8	17 070	551.8
SOUTH CAROLINA	339.7	-1.8	10 543	265	536	6 999	26 432	34 063	72 670	3 455	10 430	10 799.8	86 200	2 113.7
SOUTH DAKOTA	47.5	2.1	1 342	34	70	784	23 339	6 210	12 853	250	2 418	1 721.0	14 488	355.2
TENNESSEE	487.1	0.5	14 686	378	750	9 698	25 636	46 327	98 020	4 412	11 417	17 064.2	119 458	3 360.2
TEXAS	986.7	2.5	34 091	685	1 385	18 956	27 679	126 608	280 608	11 535	35 315	59 456.7	426 765	12 398.3
UTAH	122.0	-0.3	3 852	86	170	2 242	26 053	12 211	25 044	1 105	7 288	8 418.2	55 801	1 578.3
VERMONT	45.1	5.7	1 591	32	63	854	27 087	4 640	8 795	596	2 474	1 666.7	13 101	331.3
VIRGINIA	367.2	-1.0	12 033	277	559	7 580	27 369	46 457	87 032	2 591	19 537	22 796.8	179 909	4 837.4
WASHINGTON	336.2	2.2	13 320	218	428	7 003	32 148	37 148	87 655	2 605	19 867	21 433.5	138 194	4 528.5
WEST VIRGINIA	73.3	0.6	2 513	56	113	1 677	29 910	8 767	17 854	800	4 506	3 022.0	31 312	757.3
WISCONSIN	574.2	1.8	19 635	428	863	12 645	29 578	58 730	123 016	4 278	14 976	16 627.6	115 488	3 863.9
WYOMING	8.6	2.0	266	7	13	179	27 458	1 031	2 649	109	2 177	1 521.7	13 867	345.0

Table A. States — Wholesale and Retail Trade

STATE	Wholesale Trade, 1997				Retail Trade[1], 1997							
						Number of Employees						
	Number of Establishments	Number of Employees	Sales (mil dol)	Annual Payroll (mil dol)	Number of Establishments	Total	Motor Vehicle and Parts Dealers	Food and Beverage Stores	Clothing and Clothing Accessory Stores	General Merchandise Stores	Sales (mil dol)	Annual Payroll (mil dol)
	195	196	197	198	199	200	201	202	203	204	205	206
UNITED STATES	453 470	5 796 557	4 059 658	214 915.4	1 118 446	13 991 004	1 718 963	2 893 074	1 280 153	2 507 540	2 460 963.0	237 201.0
ALABAMA	6 315	79 229	40 986	2 394.7	20 163	231 665	28 935	47 883	20 397	47 697	36 623.3	3 381.7
ALASKA	784	6 860	2 990	256.8	2 866	32 502	3 965	7 622	2 463	6 912	6 251.4	670.5
ARIZONA	6 689	80 155	45 899	2 748.9	16 283	232 050	34 688	43 818	17 411	38 525	43 960.9	4 223.9
ARKANSAS	3 619	41 385	27 515	1 136.6	12 600	132 335	16 255	25 232	9 307	31 801	21 643.7	1 904.4
CALIFORNIA	57 841	757 294	548 865	29 875.0	106 357	1 354 797	174 669	268 874	144 936	215 325	263 118.3	26 362.7
COLORADO	7 383	88 364	60 310	3 282.0	18 299	225 647	28 164	41 242	19 259	37 873	40 536.0	4 163.3
CONNECTICUT	5 283	77 716	76 168	3 595.3	14 574	186 935	20 876	43 270	19 413	24 650	34 938.9	3 634.3
DELAWARE	906	13 509	12 586	619.5	3 736	47 116	6 082	9 605	4 082	8 412	8 237.0	798.7
DISTRICT OF COLUMBIA	348	5 008	3 919	223.0	2 075	19 608	482	5 572	3 469	1 452	2 788.8	351.5
FLORIDA	31 214	296 139	187 080	9 678.2	66 643	841 814	107 767	196 921	80 667	143 248	151 191.2	14 169.5
GEORGIA	13 978	191 087	163 783	7 519.7	33 073	420 676	52 692	92 982	38 596	74 468	72 212.5	6 943.6
HAWAII	1 872	18 532	7 148	576.0	5 088	64 218	5 739	12 269	11 409	12 586	11 317.8	1 161.8
IDAHO	1 980	22 828	10 128	628.0	5 848	63 732	9 894	10 998	3 936	11 112	11 649.6	1 079.7
ILLINOIS	21 951	325 752	275 968	13 324.5	44 568	610 790	69 604	109 745	60 545	113 502	108 002.2	10 596.0
INDIANA	8 896	112 705	66 350	3 737.8	24 954	337 867	40 300	59 909	23 949	73 621	57 241.7	5 273.8
IOWA	5 399	63 596	35 454	1 820.1	14 695	175 694	22 099	37 582	12 451	30 028	26 723.8	2 633.4
KANSAS	5 085	59 954	42 210	1 946.8	12 271	140 412	17 846	28 684	10 423	27 776	22 571.9	2 191.1
KENTUCKY	5 051	69 309	37 243	2 071.2	17 369	212 189	26 010	43 623	14 324	46 951	33 332.7	3 128.1
LOUISIANA	6 390	76 350	46 972	2 375.2	17 863	224 412	28 561	47 341	18 327	46 951	35 807.9	3 307.9
MAINE	1 726	19 932	7 306	616.2	7 074	72 897	8 930	16 636	5 547	11 281	12 737.1	1 164.2
MARYLAND	6 283	92 458	54 907	3 656.3	19 798	274 260	33 636	61 969	27 846	45 060	46 428.2	4 914.0
MASSACHUSETTS	9 993	146 827	112 792	6 484.8	26 209	335 736	34 301	86 377	36 560	45 293	58 578.0	5 894.8
MICHIGAN	13 936	189 057	158 757	7 629.6	39 564	529 441	64 429	96 770	44 447	116 058	93 706.1	8 922.3
MINNESOTA	9 348	131 787	99 445	5 024.0	20 883	282 282	31 889	54 634	20 926	50 297	48 077.7	4 525.7
MISSISSIPPI	3 173	36 520	18 445	1 012.1	12 791	138 372	16 921	30 128	10 476	32 314	20 774.5	1 935.3
MISSOURI	9 522	125 929	91 412	4 639.8	24 181	297 556	39 365	51 029	22 005	62 480	51 269.9	4 945.0
MONTANA	1 574	14 356	7 597	371.6	5 042	48 337	7 261	8 733	2 780	8 231	7 779.1	746.5
NEBRASKA	3 157	41 002	38 015	1 170.2	8 295	102 684	11 353	20 126	7 016	18 531	16 529.3	1 554.6
NEVADA	2 253	27 251	12 807	918.5	6 222	89 452	11 430	16 587	8 165	15 910	18 220.8	1 798.2
NEW HAMPSHIRE	2 033	22 631	11 371	875.0	6 645	84 170	10 384	18 316	7 444	14 470	15 890.1	1 428.2
NEW JERSEY	17 812	266 944	227 309	11 886.1	34 837	420 724	44 951	109 004	50 706	56 016	79 914.9	7 926.0
NEW MEXICO	2 182	21 344	7 398	601.1	7 421	86 300	11 470	14 352	6 777	15 779	14 984.5	1 455.5
NEW YORK	37 499	414 249	319 698	17 185.8	75 241	805 208	72 275	190 395	102 985	118 379	139 303.9	14 329.8
NORTH CAROLINA	12 284	157 774	98 080	5 574.1	35 563	416 287	54 750	83 706	38 088	74 486	72 356.8	6 697.4
NORTH DAKOTA	1 604	16 992	8 618	454.4	3 569	40 685	6 193	7 505	2 345	7 559	6 702.1	616.1
OHIO	17 322	254 226	160 416	9 192.2	44 521	630 098	75 633	125 217	46 151	129 491	102 938.8	9 924.5
OKLAHOMA	5 191	59 641	32 132	1 756.1	14 352	161 613	23 418	28 420	11 438	35 788	27 065.6	2 406.9
OREGON	5 943	74 790	53 679	2 578.7	14 467	178 349	25 422	33 345	14 650	33 171	33 396.8	3 308.8
PENNSYLVANIA	17 138	237 567	159 354	8 588.2	50 208	650 144	79 521	152 042	56 354	105 437	109 948.5	10 561.9
RHODE ISLAND	1 590	18 762	7 603	635.2	4 169	45 747	4 725	11 885	4 011	6 974	7 505.8	752.2
SOUTH CAROLINA	5 035	58 910	34 180	1 866.8	18 481	209 256	24 983	46 596	21 374	37 949	33 634.3	3 107.2
SOUTH DAKOTA	1 402	15 509	7 874	389.8	4 311	45 867	5 866	9 253	2 861	7 759	11 707.1	689.6
TENNESSEE	8 234	120 228	82 626	3 975.4	24 808	304 452	38 615	58 824	27 531	64 223	50 813.2	4 810.3
TEXAS	33 346	425 750	323 112	15 504.9	74 105	950 848	129 773	183 970	86 657	190 380	182 516.1	16 197.1
UTAH	3 277	44 312	21 272	1 420.4	7 656	114 474	14 590	20 592	9 189	21 022	19 964.6	1 856.9
VERMONT	941	10 987	4 731	330.6	4 093	36 306	4 453	9 342	2 727	3 420	5 898.6	603.3
VIRGINIA	7 868	106 365	61 047	3 784.4	29 032	379 039	47 195	73 141	36 212	65 241	62 569.9	6 202.6
WASHINGTON	10 039	118 810	75 398	4 376.0	22 841	283 653	37 408	55 974	24 915	46 693	52 472.9	5 385.9
WEST VIRGINIA	1 956	23 805	10 290	681.1	8 082	90 087	11 622	18 509	5 572	18 530	14 057.9	1 309.3
WISCONSIN	8 025	110 309	57 193	3 764.9	21 717	305 255	37 641	61 524	19 470	54 081	50 520.5	4 826.2
WYOMING	800	5 761	2 547	161.9	2 939	26 934	3 928	5 001	1 564	4 846	4 530.5	426.7

1. Establishments with payroll.

Table A. States — Transportation and Warehousing, Finance and Insurance, and Real Estate

STATE	Transportation and Warehousing, 1997				Finance and Insurance, 1997				Real Estate and Rental and Leasing, 1997			
	Number of Establishments	Number of Employees	Receipts (mil dol)	Annual Payroll (mil dol)	Number of Establishments	Number of Employees	Receipts (mil dol)	Annual Payroll (mil dol)	Number of Establishments	Number of Employees	Receipts (mil dol)	Annual Payroll (mil dol)
	207	208	209	210	211	212	213	214	215	216	217	218
UNITED STATES	178 025	2 920 777	318 245.0	82 346.2	395 203	5 835 214	2 197 808	264 551.4	288 273	1 702 420	240 917.6	41 590.7
ALABAMA	3 024	44 692	4 285.3	1 151.6	5 640	70 679	NA	2 323.1	3 664	20 629	2 130.3	396.7
ALASKA	940	13 562	3 346.9	576.6	666	6 728	NA	253.7	716	4 014	543.2	98.3
ARIZONA	2 257	45 233	4 086.2	1 107.2	6 568	84 970	NA	3 007.9	5 450	32 529	4 110.1	747.4
ARKANSAS	2 330	39 917	3 804.4	1 093.4	3 478	32 597	NA	1 000.8	2 269	9 761	1 001.6	163.2
CALIFORNIA	16 056	317 832	36 610.2	9 344.2	40 503	618 971	NA	29 660.2	37 243	243 168	37 937.4	6 563.7
COLORADO	2 411	38 399	3 626.9	1 017.5	7 400	86 239	NA	3 473.2	6 663	38 224	4 853.5	883.8
CONNECTICUT	1 568	28 540	3 266.1	859.0	5 550	117 684	NA	6 533.0	3 372	20 635	3 522.8	609.3
DELAWARE	585	7 258	594.1	179.6	1 619	44 780	NA	1 942.1	1 101	5 243	5 006.5	118.3
DISTRICT OF COLUMBIA	215	3 356	567.1	91.3	908	16 481	NA	1 318.7	934	7 725	1 354.2	275.4
FLORIDA	9 768	157 343	19 852.1	4 429.8	24 785	317 250	NA	11 928.3	20 388	118 086	15 360.4	2 652.2
GEORGIA	4 733	85 109	8 306.3	2 359.4	11 668	153 755	NA	6 005.3	7 794	47 669	6 912.9	1 308.8
HAWAII	686	16 684	1 249.3	427.7	1 573	21 757	NA	775.1	1 753	12 446	1 824.1	311.9
IDAHO	1 233	10 633	948.0	237.8	1 919	14 583	NA	454.9	1 236	4 870	450.3	73.9
ILLINOIS	8 559	153 788	16 521.6	4 377.2	20 195	334 241	NA	16 014.5	11 411	73 819	12 830.0	2 101.4
INDIANA	4 389	77 568	8 991.9	2 177.4	8 946	108 304	NA	3 727.5	5 427	28 948	3 269.1	572.6
IOWA	3 100	36 220	3 914.1	948.5	5 238	72 895	NA	2 509.3	2 518	12 619	1 457.5	249.0
KANSAS	2 332	32 051	3 220.1	870.2	4 973	53 304	NA	1 827.0	2 602	13 005	1 525.8	259.6
KENTUCKY	2 919	49 545	6 288.7	1 447.9	5 373	60 241	NA	1 860.0	3 227	16 284	1 961.6	314.3
LOUISIANA	3 715	64 767	7 889.9	1 875.5	6 968	66 707	NA	2 143.8	4 151	28 571	3 342.1	642.2
MAINE	1 232	9 199	934.6	223.5	1 657	22 211	NA	805.5	1 343	5 929	601.7	114.2
MARYLAND	3 136	46 415	4 023.3	1 259.6	7 064	103 894	NA	4 436.6	5 065	39 502	4 764.7	971.3
MASSACHUSETTS	3 283	53 297	4 704.3	1 391.8	8 875	212 188	NA	11 427.7	5 834	41 233	5 925.4	1 214.1
MICHIGAN	4 733	77 977	9 249.2	2 493.8	12 249	181 898	NA	6 598.9	8 302	50 941	6 492.7	1 126.2
MINNESOTA	3 810	53 811	5 662.8	1 375.1	7 969	124 827	NA	5 390.5	5 051	30 172	3 886.4	687.2
MISSISSIPPI	2 201	24 411	2 475.5	657.3	4 059	33 400	NA	979.8	2 125	8 354	794.2	132.1
MISSOURI	4 874	69 082	7 681.6	1 725.1	8 738	122 082	NA	4 474.4	5 500	31 301	3 991.1	698.1
MONTANA	967	8 758	948.9	196.2	1 553	12 581	NA	366.8	1 186	4 265	353.4	58.1
NEBRASKA	1 874	24 848	3 475.1	700.7	3 369	50 003	NA	1 576.2	1 587	8 240	891.1	160.8
NEVADA	830	18 368	1 410.5	419.0	2 799	27 162	NA	916.4	2 460	16 890	2 276.5	381.5
NEW HAMPSHIRE	733	13 714	933.3	332.7	1 646	23 143	NA	871.2	1 399	6 639	719.4	151.1
NEW JERSEY	6 632	131 171	14 404.7	4 053.0	10 567	208 318	NA	10 519.9	8 292	47 558	8 881.9	1 376.5
NEW MEXICO	1 009	11 841	1 392.3	293.6	2 453	22 936	NA	662.3	1 887	8 844	893.9	165.2
NEW YORK	10 485	178 698	17 635.2	4 848.9	24 691	611 857	NA	52 522.2	27 214	145 326	27 770.1	4 447.8
NORTH CAROLINA	5 077	77 841	6 625.9	2 123.9	10 831	142 234	NA	5 276.5	7 346	39 349	5 026.0	900.6
NORTH DAKOTA	913	8 297	862.5	191.5	1 364	11 790	NA	336.0	657	3 325	287.0	46.3
OHIO	6 709	117 984	11 722.3	3 531.0	16 208	251 657	NA	9 008.4	9 692	62 628	7 243.7	1 334.6
OKLAHOMA	2 112	30 145	4 590.4	868.8	5 587	54 064	NA	1 697.8	3 344	15 354	1 576.0	284.5
OREGON	2 610	38 544	3 771.3	1 163.5	5 172	63 386	NA	2 317.2	4 556	23 058	2 704.0	470.9
PENNSYLVANIA	6 379	126 839	11 540.6	3 400.0	16 601	287 143	NA	11 173.6	8 684	57 519	7 668.6	1 360.5
RHODE ISLAND	546	5 947	587.2	145.0	1 250	22 920	NA	812.9	922	4 649	573.4	105.4
SOUTH CAROLINA	2 126	35 301	3 303.1	913.0	5 596	57 283	NA	1 801.0	3 541	18 760	2 012.6	377.1
SOUTH DAKOTA	957	7 361	887.1	162.0	1 612	18 869	NA	508.3	719	2 951	245.7	45.1
TENNESSEE	3 945	73 973	7 083.4	2 244.3	8 345	102 124	NA	3 650.4	4 999	29 626	3 732.0	667.3
TEXAS	12 800	209 782	28 532.9	6 137.1	28 074	352 019	NA	13 833.6	20 753	128 915	15 957.4	3 119.2
UTAH	1 167	29 028	2 854.2	799.9	3 167	39 603	NA	1 228.8	2 169	12 318	1 342.6	236.0
VERMONT	512	4 856	390.5	111.8	897	9 228	NA	328.3	701	2 362	240.6	42.2
VIRGINIA	4 482	60 884	6 338.2	1 666.9	9 549	135 689	NA	5 064.4	6 717	43 976	5 749.2	1 028.4
WASHINGTON	3 984	61 576	7 289.5	1 933.2	8 332	91 844	NA	3 697.3	7 544	41 899	5 352.8	935.3
WEST VIRGINIA	1 439	14 526	1 979.3	419.9	2 115	21 144	NA	555.3	1 449	5 812	665.0	100.8
WISCONSIN	5 068	69 166	7 028.7	1 868.2	8 062	129 664	NA	4 785.4	4 598	23 924	2 637.5	464.1
WYOMING	580	4 640	557.5	123.9	782	5 885	NA	169.7	717	2 463	220.8	39.5

Table A. States — **Information and Utilities**

STATE	Information, 1997								Utilities, 1997			
	Number of Establishments	Number of Employees					Receipts (mil dol)	Annual Payroll (mil dol)	Number of Establishments	Number of Employees	Receipts (mil dol)	Annual Payroll (mil dol)
		Total	Publishing	Motion Picture and Sound Recording	Broadcast and telecommunications	Information and Data Processing Services						
	219	220	221	222	223	224	225	226	227	228	229	230
UNITED STATES	114 475	3 066 167	1 006 214	275 981	1 434 455	349 517	623 213.9	129 481.6	15 513	702 703	411 713.3	36 594.7
ALABAMA	1 430	35 476	8 863	1 302	22 528	2 783	6 477.5	1 320.1	455	14 286	6 607.8	798.7
ALASKA	353	5 209	1 247	352	3 439	171	1 038.6	203.1	85	1 670	598.4	102.6
ARIZONA	1 731	42 238	12 643	3 370	22 499	3 726	7 209.4	1 487.1	235	10 546	5 840.3	595.4
ARKANSAS	904	20 101	7 233	1 225	9 405	2 238	3 326.6	583.9	359	7 711	3 423.2	352.7
CALIFORNIA	16 302	450 511	154 837	98 151	163 482	34 041	108 719.1	22 868.5	894	52 662	27 017.6	3 090.5
COLORADO	2 653	76 024	21 109	3 881	43 139	7 895	12 743.0	3 306.3	317	9 771	5 205.7	467.7
CONNECTICUT	1 561	48 173	16 027	1 989	20 893	9 264	9 054.2	2 136.8	145	11 161	5 253.3	666.4
DELAWARE	275	8 701	1 571	316	5 093	1 721	1 652.6	310.0	27	D	D	D
DISTRICT OF COLUMBIA	632	23 787	9 456	1 396	9 880	3 055	6 351.0	1 363.0	33	D	D	D
FLORIDA	5 883	145 025	40 014	10 952	78 187	15 872	27 830.2	5 522.4	524	27 652	12 879.4	1 385.8
GEORGIA	3 163	100 656	24 347	4 781	61 056	10 472	18 939.2	4 176.5	498	21 420	10 729.9	1 053.0
HAWAII	458	8 996	2 066	1 496	5 100	334	1 464.2	318.7	43	D	D	D
IDAHO	526	9 017	3 229	697	4 540	551	1 313.6	257.5	169	3 216	1 261.2	153.9
ILLINOIS	4 994	129 204	50 296	10 037	58 436	10 435	26 496.6	5 488.0	390	33 717	15 364.5	1 989.6
INDIANA	2 032	43 961	16 597	3 273	19 353	4 738	8 130.9	1 406.6	418	18 511	9 070.3	867.6
IOWA	1 502	34 363	13 479	1 732	12 653	6 499	5 433.0	1 016.2	280	8 353	3 422.2	363.0
KANSAS	1 357	32 258	11 785	1 934	16 778	1 761	7 324.2	1 161.9	248	7 811	3 697.9	378.3
KENTUCKY	1 261	29 098	9 516	1 820	12 739	5 023	5 056.1	814.7	328	11 367	8 236.0	505.2
LOUISIANA	1 285	27 271	5 876	2 013	18 008	1 374	4 621.7	907.8	516	12 641	6 797.8	609.4
MAINE	647	9 693	3 503	438	4 753	999	1 303.0	297.4	105	3 766	1 687.8	170.7
MARYLAND	2 026	56 781	16 507	3 213	28 435	8 626	10 618.5	2 302.1	106	11 295	5 065.0	645.7
MASSACHUSETTS	3 282	113 698	57 901	4 921	36 815	14 061	20 548.9	5 395.7	222	15 931	12 081.6	942.2
MICHIGAN	3 273	90 178	26 353	6 184	34 788	22 853	18 878.4	3 362.4	385	25 464	15 044.2	1 486.1
MINNESOTA	2 430	58 855	23 652	4 308	24 185	6 710	9 660.3	2 111.5	240	13 205	4 441.1	675.6
MISSISSIPPI	880	14 259	3 257	683	9 693	626	2 480.8	466.6	617	8 307	3 085.6	340.4
MISSOURI	2 254	75 706	25 662	4 143	38 152	7 749	12 112.4	2 743.6	342	16 685	6 172.1	838.1
MONTANA	568	7 077	2 036	693	3 610	738	1 061.7	177.5	215	3 296	949.3	160.1
NEBRASKA	841	28 950	8 099	1 120	9 413	10 318	4 242.2	984.4	141	D	D	D
NEVADA	660	10 750	2 978	1 203	6 201	368	2 110.9	376.3	86	D	1 484.7	179.5
NEW HAMPSHIRE	669	11 602	6 004	644	4 217	737	1 839.2	483.7	104	3 222		
NEW JERSEY	3 384	131 970	38 059	6 283	78 402	9 226	21 004.9	6 833.3	294	21 147	11 626.2	1 254.4
NEW MEXICO	767	11 265	3 772	1 341	5 696	456	1 905.1	320.2	206	5 868	2 168.7	251.1
NEW YORK	9 454	287 054	99 892	27 891	119 678	39 593	83 185.9	14 837.6	371	59 255	23 107.7	3 019.2
NORTH CAROLINA	2 584	60 047	17 572	4 116	34 127	4 232	11 337.2	2 126.3	390	23 765	9 018.2	1 218.8
NORTH DAKOTA	382	7 710	2 627	332	3 357	1 394	921.6	206.8	129	3 303	1 158.0	154.9
OHIO	3 518	102 414	36 336	8 488	45 595	11 995	18 139.8	3 746.8	533	31 560	16 893.4	1 533.3
OKLAHOMA	1 338	28 871	6 708	1 730	17 353	3 080	5 281.8	926.9	362	9 128	5 170.3	401.9
OREGON	1 631	31 382	13 357	2 618	13 793	1 614	5 839.9	1 181.0	226	7 402	4 568.6	424.6
PENNSYLVANIA	4 168	118 315	44 615	6 468	53 020	14 212	21 854.5	4 272.8	606	38 952	39 604.0	2 080.8
RHODE ISLAND	359	10 611	3 773	444	4 014	2 380	1 441.0	363.7	27	1 963	1 038.7	99.6
SOUTH CAROLINA	1 099	25 054	7 287	1 485	13 414	2 868	4 714.5	845.3	267	12 209	4 353.9	600.1
SOUTH DAKOTA	466	6 243	2 058	421	3 673	91	916.1	155.5	137	2 153	619.7	84.0
TENNESSEE	2 101	45 015	14 213	4 366	23 518	2 918	7 949.7	1 511.9	162	3 771	1 815.0	155.0
TEXAS	7 520	210 654	49 949	15 791	114 361	30 553	40 363.2	8 605.6	1 816	57 717	74 102.3	2 817.5
UTAH	971	24 253	8 758	2 204	10 024	3 267	3 567.7	807.9	152	5 580	3 882.5	293.8
VERMONT	483	6 667	2 829	362	2 751	725	1 724.1	188.7	53	1 838	831.7	93.7
VIRGINIA	2 945	90 346	23 602	4 740	47 411	14 593	20 400.4	4 347.3	291	17 251	10 386.6	916.7
WASHINGTON	2 546	61 830	23 439	4 563	29 996	3 832	14 571.3	3 102.5	339	6 245	3 217.9	291.2
WEST VIRGINIA	605	11 862	3 135	490	7 649	588	1 773.5	305.8	240	7 767	3 263.4	353.8
WISCONSIN	2 009	43 546	16 920	3 227	17 343	6 056	7 733.9	1 362.9	253	13 762	5 486.6	716.3
WYOMING	313	3 440	1 170	354	1 810	106	549.9	82.6	132	2 767	1 012.4	137.9

Table A. States — Professional, Scientific, and Technical Services, and Arts, Entertainment, and Recreation

STATE	Professional, Scientific, and Technical Services,[1] 1997 — Number of Establishments	Number of Employees — Total	Legal Services	Accounting and Related Services	Architectural, Engineering, and Related Services	Computer Systems Design and Related Services	Receipts (mil dol)	Annual Payroll (mil dol)	Arts, Entertainment, and Recreation,[1] 1997 — Number of Establishments	Number of Employees	Receipts (mil dol)	Annual Payroll (mil dol)
	231	232	233	234	235	236	237	238	239	240	241	242
UNITED STATES	615 305	5 212 745	1 012 092	966 533	1 038 317	764 659	579 542.1	225 376.1	79 637	1 207 943	85 129.4	26 115.0
ALABAMA	7 076	54 413	12 773	8 097	14 353	7 904	5 295.6	2 051.4	791	9 381	435.7	105.0
ALASKA	1 437	7 892	2 030	1 146	3 027	418	945.9	370.8	320	3 055	168.3	34.9
ARIZONA	10 163	75 789	14 064	15 992	17 543	9 195	6 669.4	2 724.7	1 071	24 416	2 033.3	475.1
ARKANSAS	4 125	23 094	5 608	5 165	4 303	3 010	1 825.8	719.6	594	5 343	228.7	56.8
CALIFORNIA	78 635	805 856	124 890	242 857	129 826	101 494	89 555.7	35 258.6	12 015	182 004	15 913.8	6 296.6
COLORADO	14 315	103 008	15 384	12 498	23 939	27 261	12 887.7	4 625.1	1 494	30 541	1 909.6	625.0
CONNECTICUT	9 393	71 058	14 748	10 537	10 930	9 377	9 115.8	3 700.1	1 046	27 236	2 526.8	589.2
DELAWARE	1 717	12 382	3 859	1 753	2 548	1 609	1 430.4	553.4	216	4 074	240.1	62.0
DISTRICT OF COLUMBIA	3 760	61 123	28 841	5 430	3 785	4 188	10 365.2	3 935.5	171	1 564	161.9	56.1
FLORIDA	42 403	276 263	67 822	54 881	52 415	31 272	27 231.1	10 803.5	4 763	103 980	7 871.5	1 972.9
GEORGIA	17 810	138 198	23 148	26 704	24 718	27 116	15 266.4	5 908.8	1 653	23 437	1 533.7	408.9
HAWAII	2 480	15 743	4 325	3 155	3 735	906	1 574.0	606.5	386	6 925	409.6	116.6
IDAHO	2 364	19 669	3 386	2 308	10 225	1 009	2 046.1	756.2	457	4 425	174.1	45.2
ILLINOIS	30 378	274 714	51 486	44 700	40 670	41 999	33 855.1	13 105.4	3 097	46 972	3 640.3	1 040.6
INDIANA	9 795	69 393	14 161	15 664	14 409	8 216	5 974.2	2 207.5	1 500	24 903	1 918.3	516.1
IOWA	4 670	31 115	7 332	6 347	4 220	2 876	2 435.6	887.9	875	14 169	919.8	220.3
KANSAS	5 345	39 534	6 737	8 086	10 169	4 736	3 559.3	1 396.0	652	7 618	374.5	91.0
KENTUCKY	6 189	41 991	10 036	8 445	8 708	4 604	3 820.3	1 260.1	906	10 580	550.2	126.3
LOUISIANA	9 077	63 642	18 467	13 162	18 537	3 040	5 754.6	2 159.0	1 016	22 828	1 958.1	412.9
MAINE	2 552	13 747	3 918	2 633	3 654	742	1 215.6	474.8	524	5 456	254.4	64.0
MARYLAND	14 115	146 814	17 537	17 492	36 646	36 640	15 940.2	6 483.8	1 460	19 398	1 412.4	494.8
MASSACHUSETTS	18 086	177 345	28 887	21 727	38 025	32 595	22 744.1	9 261.4	1 781	22 598	1 578.5	518.6
MICHIGAN	18 614	162 971	27 677	28 444	42 085	19 296	16 231.7	6 882.9	2 693	34 161	2 202.8	664.6
MINNESOTA	12 391	96 677	18 545	13 690	15 041	19 384	10 447.9	4 091.8	1 593	27 958	1 469.7	477.9
MISSISSIPPI	3 627	21 671	6 814	4 702	5 444	1 046	1 761.6	662.1	483	21 239	1 394.0	371.7
MISSOURI	10 601	93 792	18 383	16 493	18 076	15 307	9 953.3	3 643.6	1 493	29 484	1 803.9	684.2
MONTANA	2 082	10 735	2 700	2 075	2 710	763	769.4	297.7	639	5 638	306.5	62.2
NEBRASKA	3 076	25 720	4 336	4 767	4 318	3 546	2 273.4	838.0	517	5 957	258.6	58.1
NEVADA	4 171	28 963	6 396	4 064	8 395	1 590	2 974.4	1 171.1	811	23 960	1 667.5	465.8
NEW HAMPSHIRE	3 341	18 268	4 469	4 008	3 214	2 685	1 626.6	713.1	460	6 545	365.0	99.6
NEW JERSEY	25 849	220 238	39 180	36 932	31 200	50 602	25 943.8	10 441.0	2 393	27 187	1 981.2	602.2
NEW MEXICO	3 702	31 535	5 450	3 477	7 147	2 078	3 243.4	1 307.3	440	8 679	520.4	115.4
NEW YORK	45 619	416 892	109 483	78 021	47 439	41 878	57 475.0	21 773.1	7 311	77 057	7 029.0	2 284.6
NORTH CAROLINA	14 351	101 610	17 536	18 315	21 380	14 218	9 760.9	3 693.5	2 090	23 481	1 632.6	470.5
NORTH DAKOTA	1 077	7 076	1 609	1 349	1 340	1 322	418.0	175.7	248	3 154	164.3	32.6
OHIO	21 182	182 805	33 925	29 820	37 298	26 134	18 294.7	6 948.0	2 902	37 210	2 308.6	706.6
OKLAHOMA	7 009	40 633	10 986	7 642	8 958	4 167	3 543.0	1 323.7	746	8 904	531.4	110.3
OREGON	8 117	52 514	10 464	10 662	10 806	6 861	4 734.6	1 925.0	968	16 098	875.8	260.6
PENNSYLVANIA	23 184	235 025	46 483	33 381	58 166	35 029	26 240.3	10 448.3	2 883	40 892	2 439.3	810.6
RHODE ISLAND	2 349	14 866	3 522	3 414	3 149	1 633	1 418.1	541.5	307	3 877	234.8	58.1
SOUTH CAROLINA	6 576	47 679	11 256	8 301	16 571	3 517	6 820.9	1 850.5	1 325	18 499	1 107.1	251.9
SOUTH DAKOTA	1 282	6 228	1 673	1 419	1 050	878	450.4	161.7	432	4 647	299.2	60.2
TENNESSEE	8 812	72 225	12 552	11 830	17 174	6 827	6 911.8	2 686.6	1 755	18 263	1 228.7	394.3
TEXAS	42 492	351 422	70 228	53 143	92 449	50 071	42 044.1	15 906.7	3 894	65 218	3 743.8	1 143.4
UTAH	4 282	36 468	5 861	6 511	8 211	6 730	3 306.1	1 303.1	480	9 444	412.4	137.7
VERMONT	1 622	7 792	1 988	1 051	1 596	1 302	719.1	279.0	293	5 450	226.9	61.4
VIRGINIA	17 539	212 632	21 082	19 896	52 792	66 065	24 151.7	9 729.8	1 613	26 624	1 397.9	392.9
WASHINGTON	13 411	101 848	19 122	14 797	26 137	13 232	10 564.8	4 247.3	1 680	27 971	1 620.1	544.6
WEST VIRGINIA	2 517	15 714	4 814	3 353	3 532	799	1 166.9	395.2	408	4 996	273.3	56.6
WISCONSIN	9 281	70 689	14 887	14 876	14 616	7 321	6 398.9	2 542.3	1 730	22 339	1 327.5	384.3
WYOMING	1 264	5 274	1 312	1 321	1 638	171	388.8	146.9	262	2 108	93.3	23.3

1. Firms subject to federal tax.

Table A. States — **Health Care and Social Assistance**

STATE	Health Care and Social Assistance, 1997											
	Subject to Federal Tax						Tax Exempt					
		Number of Employees						Number of Employees				
	Number of Establishments	Total	Ambulatory Health Care Services	Hospitals	Receipts (mil dol)	Annual Payroll (mil dol)	Number of Establishments	Total	Ambulatory Health Care Services	Hospitals	Receipts (mil dol)	Annual Payroll (mil dol)
	243	244	245	246	247	248	249	250	251	252	253	254
UNITED STATES	531 069	6 231 768	3 744 279	511 584	418 602.2	182 256.3	114 784	7 329 811	669 335	4 421 454	466 451.8	195 949.4
ALABAMA	7 121	104 492	55 516	16 915	7 116.7	3 104.8	1 375	93 858	8 567	68 868	6 075.5	2 463.9
ALASKA	1 143	8 156	6 222	790	758.1	309.4	427	18 858	1 444	10 400	1 283.2	583.6
ARIZONA	9 155	97 091	58 340	7 344	6 687.9	2 893.3	1 366	89 141	9 554	52 682	6 153.3	2 370.6
ARKANSAS	4 571	59 960	28 478	8 079	3 655.1	1 609.7	1 205	67 065	5 348	41 630	3 642.0	1 429.1
CALIFORNIA	69 857	664 539	422 929	59 673	51 968.0	20 619.3	10 715	586 414	49 193	357 559	48 778.8	17 749.8
COLORADO	8 611	85 370	54 140	3 412	5 790.8	2 538.1	1 709	91 319	9 636	54 858	5 866.8	2 392.0
CONNECTICUT	7 515	100 363	60 395	D	6 849.7	3 199.3	1 828	113 366	12 823	60 723	7 058.3	3 296.7
DELAWARE	1 465	15 980	10 043	D	1 131.6	526.4	365	23 991	2 276	14 149	1 500.3	662.3
DISTRICT OF COLUMBIA	1 464	13 692	8 294	904	1 054.8	476.7	655	45 837	1 645	30 712	3 826.3	1 651.4
FLORIDA	35 568	447 117	254 419	81 958	32 559.1	13 610.7	4 170	294 240	28 422	178 820	19 415.1	7 800.2
GEORGIA	13 960	173 768	96 547	18 587	12 065.1	5 158.0	2 028	161 127	14 284	116 039	11 646.5	4 477.7
HAWAII	2 360	18 221	13 828	D	1 646.3	730.8	581	29 344	3 172	17 876	2 329.1	886.9
IDAHO	2 551	26 365	15 393	2 197	1 548.3	680.1	519	22 760	797	15 906	1 287.2	547.3
ILLINOIS	21 122	248 667	150 878	12 907	16 870.2	7 441.8	4 920	355 013	20 457	221 511	22 905.3	9 350.5
INDIANA	10 236	132 416	77 163	5 945	8 132.3	3 675.3	2 565	167 894	11 713	106 580	9 910.6	4 061.4
IOWA	4 876	56 374	32 156	D	3 183.2	1 540.6	2 319	117 658	6 652	64 543	5 582.4	2 425.5
KANSAS	4 793	66 613	38 032	D	4 116.1	1 771.8	1 621	81 767	3 963	46 923	4 082.2	1 817.1
KENTUCKY	6 805	94 720	48 595	11 593	5 936.2	2 620.3	1 579	100 156	8 609	64 953	6 026.7	2 386.4
LOUISIANA	8 580	129 773	69 375	24 000	7 967.6	3 341.5	1 506	110 849	2 121	80 152	6 477.3	2 625.8
MAINE	2 727	28 944	14 464	D	1 608.4	766.3	1 074	47 404	6 469	23 258	2 641.0	1 119.8
MARYLAND	10 841	116 241	76 315	2 859	8 060.7	3 538.0	2 181	144 008	8 363	87 288	9 405.0	3 816.7
MASSACHUSETTS	11 887	182 902	102 893	8 984	11 361.4	5 310.5	4 537	266 968	37 592	139 988	16 091.6	7 410.6
MICHIGAN	18 943	186 954	128 354	1 638	11 811.5	5 696.8	4 684	301 078	27 857	189 916	19 458.5	8 309.7
MINNESOTA	8 033	106 839	66 962	D	5 864.5	2 946.0	2 929	191 473	32 851	83 648	10 965.0	4 893.3
MISSISSIPPI	4 139	55 529	29 916	7 299	3 632.3	1 547.0	847	68 886	3 245	54 786	4 249.0	1 660.9
MISSOURI	10 213	131 485	69 052	10 901	7 885.5	3 596.7	2 580	184 143	11 577	119 145	10 535.6	4 410.5
MONTANA	2 034	15 673	9 118	D	928.6	412.6	691	29 526	3 450	16 885	1 440.4	619.1
NEBRASKA	3 057	34 763	19 225	D	2 027.7	970.3	914	55 235	1 641	35 363	3 074.8	1 263.6
NEVADA	3 226	39 476	23 312	8 604	3 406.5	1 358.9	361	17 185	931	11 538	1 261.6	506.9
NEW HAMPSHIRE	2 373	28 889	15 341	2 228	1 734.1	836.3	834	37 674	8 075	18 197	2 246.2	878.2
NEW JERSEY	18 905	172 723	120 922	1 122	13 702.4	5 900.2	2 742	227 434	21 103	148 173	14 828.8	6 842.7
NEW MEXICO	2 923	32 824	21 144	3 138	2 057.3	864.3	778	43 501	4 479	25 609	2 412.3	1 089.3
NEW YORK	36 054	358 075	259 094	10 262	26 008.3	10 970.9	9 880	768 835	105 062	407 706	48 759.5	23 372.8
NORTH CAROLINA	12 582	173 770	94 102	8 741	10 708.8	4 859.6	2 794	187 651	13 552	129 016	12 400.3	5 006.8
NORTH DAKOTA	1 013	13 181	8 237	D	904.1	386.4	539	33 578	909	16 585	1 463.7	668.9
OHIO	20 399	261 520	156 386	2 579	15 440.1	7 477.0	4 779	352 454	26 617	214 539	21 423.5	9 093.7
OKLAHOMA	6 991	91 803	47 776	8 847	5 061.4	2 244.0	1 463	76 949	4 052	51 711	4 283.6	1 758.5
OREGON	7 328	68 285	42 060	1 410	4 431.4	1 899.6	1 788	82 517	7 491	45 158	4 869.2	2 097.6
PENNSYLVANIA	24 888	262 603	174 984	6 961	17 633.5	7 994.9	6 624	453 579	37 043	260 036	27 620.1	11 860.5
RHODE ISLAND	2 074	25 368	13 270	D	1 459.3	647.4	606	38 409	4 861	20 710	2 443.0	1 132.3
SOUTH CAROLINA	6 261	78 888	40 632	13 530	5 318.5	2 361.3	1 271	75 881	3 537	53 077	4 729.9	1 922.6
SOUTH DAKOTA	1 314	14 080	8 732	167	881.6	414.3	623	33 920	1 156	19 717	1 646.8	753.3
TENNESSEE	10 113	155 667	84 719	22 103	10 753.0	4 659.9	2 180	129 028	11 485	86 739	8 459.9	3 429.5
TEXAS	37 974	557 007	324 347	89 469	35 620.9	14 725.4	5 546	334 563	24 434	223 849	21 137.9	8 357.4
UTAH	3 851	46 989	27 659	5 700	2 988.8	1 226.7	521	33 973	1 583	23 515	2 070.3	859.6
VERMONT	1 262	11 481	6 146	D	631.6	273.9	592	20 697	4 672	9 772	1 129.0	496.6
VIRGINIA	12 014	150 797	89 453	17 193	9 859.6	4 417.9	2 143	135 917	7 245	87 411	8 975.6	3 539.8
WASHINGTON	12 310	122 813	73 402	2 089	7 797.7	3 390.2	2 575	140 792	21 340	78 274	8 982.2	4 039.8
WEST VIRGINIA	3 266	40 085	21 188	5 172	2 575.0	1 056.9	973	55 653	6 667	33 425	3 250.1	1 350.2
WISCONSIN	9 315	114 562	69 466	587	6 917.4	3 447.3	2 932	175 152	18 639	93 326	9 654.7	4 089.4
WYOMING	1 006	7 875	4 865	555	493.6	210.3	350	15 091	681	8 210	695.9	320.6

STATE	Accommodation and Food Services, 1997					Other Services						
	Number of Employees						Number of Employees					
	Number of Establishments	Total	Food Services and Drinking Places	Receipts (mil dol)	Annual Payroll (mil dol)	Number of Establishments[1]	Total[1]	Repair and Maintenance[1]	Personal and Laundry Services[1]	Religious, Civic, and Similar Services[2]	Receipts (mil dol)[1]	Annual Payroll (mil dol)[1]
	255	256	257	258	259	260	261	262	263	264	265	266
UNITED STATES	545 060	9 451 056	7 754 462	350 389.1	97 003.9	420 950	2 493 574	1 276 389	1 217 185	762 604	163 033.3	48 452.6
ALABAMA	6 955	134 719	120 455	3 881.8	1 059.6	6 329	37 061	19 092	17 969	5 480	2 241.7	659.3
ALASKA	1 763	20 587	15 108	1 065.5	301.5	852	4 364	2 489	1 875	2 127	331.0	93.4
ARIZONA	9 089	184 323	143 326	6 633.0	1 823.2	6 494	43 669	24 677	18 992	9 381	2 794.0	829.6
ARKANSAS	4 663	73 397	63 326	2 179.7	589.9	3 553	18 809	9 759	9 050	3 308	1 113.9	310.5
CALIFORNIA	62 532	1 052 715	866 573	42 261.1	11 437.2	44 642	282 762	158 338	124 424	71 943	20 521.5	5 852.2
COLORADO	10 064	195 126	152 323	6 705.5	1 937.4	6 793	39 363	21 585	17 778	13 958	2 571.1	770.0
CONNECTICUT	6 903	96 556	85 802	3 746.6	1 062.8	6 121	34 089	15 534	18 555	11 215	2 370.2	727.8
DELAWARE	1 605	26 969	24 532	1 009.0	280.8	1 198	7 006	3 349	3 657	3 096	420.5	140.7
DISTRICT OF COLUMBIA	1 700	42 650	27 281	2 263.5	701.4	6 218	9 197	951	5 267	36 416	404.8	111.1
FLORIDA	28 999	608 834	462 266	24 165.3	6 239.5	26 121	146 360	72 673	73 687	47 246	9 123.6	2 665.7
GEORGIA	13 829	274 322	229 132	9 689.9	2 695.1	11 482	69 422	35 701	33 721	13 418	4 580.7	1 407.5
HAWAII	3 081	88 083	47 978	5 007.9	1 507.5	1 476	10 375	3 941	6 434	7 096	683.2	206.4
IDAHO	2 978	42 067	33 222	1 232.5	345.7	1 858	9 461	5 979	3 482	2 562	550.6	151.7
ILLINOIS	23 984	397 300	345 271	14 826.8	4 018.7	18 806	118 317	61 653	56 664	47 363	8 296.8	2 503.0
INDIANA	11 705	215 710	192 910	6 646.3	1 865.3	9 243	60 711	32 426	28 285	15 556	3 701.4	1 127.8
IOWA	6 830	99 148	85 641	2 762.8	769.5	5 234	24 383	12 589	11 794	8 008	1 486.5	411.3
KANSAS	5 677	91 173	81 206	2 685.7	757.1	4 604	24 081	12 846	11 235	7 737	1 548.4	452.9
KENTUCKY	6 546	129 442	113 557	4 056.1	1 140.6	5 383	31 164	15 971	15 193	5 534	1 870.3	551.4
LOUISIANA	7 151	147 016	118 902	5 259.9	1 408.9	5 998	39 764	23 348	16 416	6 418	2 595.2	767.2
MAINE	3 714	39 624	32 211	1 509.3	428.8	1 923	8 820	4 687	4 133	3 201	612.3	169.6
MARYLAND	9 049	161 273	142 027	5 972.5	1 644.7	7 871	55 241	26 167	29 074	18 724	3 561.3	1 129.2
MASSACHUSETTS	14 800	227 476	198 069	9 269.9	2 575.6	10 806	61 557	28 744	32 813	18 807	4 359.8	1 338.6
MICHIGAN	18 958	320 014	287 623	10 158.7	2 835.8	14 705	93 792	50 987	42 805	22 180	6 159.1	1 893.8
MINNESOTA	9 982	179 487	149 584	5 934.2	1 688.8	7 614	55 723	27 703	28 020	21 512	3 394.6	1 103.6
MISSISSIPPI	4 050	84 834	61 742	3 064.8	814.5	3 491	17 449	9 171	8 278	3 701	1 057.1	299.6
MISSOURI	11 150	203 849	169 646	6 780.8	1 933.3	9 427	52 060	26 216	25 844	14 434	3 203.3	963.1
MONTANA	3 278	38 533	30 120	1 198.9	325.4	1 612	6 986	4 518	2 468	2 278	449.1	117.0
NEBRASKA	4 070	61 048	53 127	1 726.6	488.2	3 288	16 940	9 770	7 170	6 500	1 039.2	297.1
NEVADA	3 632	241 672	51 613	15 322.7	4 665.3	2 175	16 185	8 124	8 061	3 033	1 061.7	328.0
NEW HAMPSHIRE	3 029	43 942	36 251	1 543.5	449.8	2 159	11 379	5 720	5 659	3 271	794.5	236.6
NEW JERSEY	16 974	251 872	180 343	13 407.4	3 608.2	15 077	78 644	35 774	42 870	18 414	5 434.8	1 665.1
NEW MEXICO	3 825	67 134	52 969	2 144.9	599.1	2 318	13 448	7 651	5 797	3 814	759.1	227.2
NEW YORK	38 045	473 327	399 485	21 671.1	6 101.1	30 104	146 365	59 977	86 388	76 173	10 014.6	2 858.7
NORTH CAROLINA	14 579	262 848	229 210	8 625.0	2 393.2	11 483	64 802	33 418	31 384	14 644	4 060.6	1 204.0
NORTH DAKOTA	1 827	26 330	21 495	684.9	189.0	1 281	6 294	3 074	3 220	3 410	364.3	101.3
OHIO	22 631	401 206	365 806	12 411.0	3 444.2	17 314	116 165	58 331	57 834	29 986	7 087.5	2 165.7
OKLAHOMA	6 534	105 934	95 639	3 151.3	856.8	4 572	26 308	13 465	12 843	5 709	1 599.4	458.5
OREGON	8 363	124 425	105 930	4 385.7	1 236.6	4 794	28 185	16 554	11 631	7 463	1 897.5	561.9
PENNSYLVANIA	24 465	365 158	317 321	12 227.2	3 364.1	19 754	107 502	51 109	56 393	36 273	7 085.7	2 049.0
RHODE ISLAND	2 617	34 162	31 264	1 220.9	340.6	1 949	8 602	4 142	4 460	3 325	546.2	167.8
SOUTH CAROLINA	7 775	150 621	126 533	4 835.8	1 313.8	5 672	32 166	17 395	14 771	7 364	1 901.0	563.8
SOUTH DAKOTA	2 258	30 131	23 609	888.0	234.4	1 356	5 828	3 296	2 532	2 670	344.7	90.7
TENNESSEE	9 604	197 881	166 252	6 790.2	1 880.3	7 767	49 204	22 362	26 842	11 871	2 996.7	918.7
TEXAS	34 160	638 333	552 066	22 698.8	6 175.4	29 162	197 113	107 946	89 167	38 747	12 477.7	3 785.0
UTAH	3 780	74 390	58 884	2 309.0	648.8	2 728	17 612	10 403	7 209	3 284	1 090.5	312.6
VERMONT	1 932	27 088	18 000	910.2	277.2	1 171	4 490	2 263	2 227	2 859	304.7	76.4
VIRGINIA	12 343	233 639	192 645	8 281.2	2 320.7	11 301	68 807	33 111	35 696	27 818	4 397.2	1 360.3
WASHINGTON	13 105	194 955	169 685	6 995.1	1 962.9	8 771	49 756	27 517	22 239	14 138	3 492.0	1 033.0
WEST VIRGINIA	3 290	51 529	43 149	1 633.2	462.3	2 512	14 805	7 551	7 254	3 308	867.4	255.9
WISCONSIN	13 252	190 411	163 318	5 641.0	1 548.5	8 648	49 101	23 608	25 493	14 402	2 991.3	886.4
WYOMING	1 751	24 950	17 192	808.9	219.0	980	4 866	2 734	2 132	1 429	422.8	94.8

1. Firms subject to federal tax.

STATE	Construction		Manufacturing		Wholesale Trade		Retail Trade		Finance, Insurance, and Real Estate		Service industries, subject to federal tax	
	Paid Employees 1997	Percent change, 1992–1997	Paid Employees 1997	Percent change, 1992–1997	Paid Employees 1997	Percent change, 1992–1997	Paid Employees 1997	Percent change, 1992–1997	Paid Employees 1997	Percent change, 1992–1997	Paid Employees 1997	Percent change, 1992–1997
	267	268	269	270	271	272	273	274	275	276	277	278
UNITED STATES...............	5 567 052	19.3	17 557 008	3.6	6 509 333	12.4	21 165 862	15.0	7 314 321	12.4	25 278 399	31.0
ALABAMA	94 525	20.8	364 887	0.0	90 151	12.6	342 835	27.1	86 105	18.7	319 408	28.6
ALASKA	13 911	7.3	13 402	-13.4	D	D	46 235	17.1	9 842	8.0	38 822	21.7
ARIZONA	129 315	49.1	199 959	18.9	93 586	36.0	363 999	26.3	110 539	25.7	488 055	63.1
ARKANSAS	D	D	239 244	7.5	48 274	10.0	189 643	24.7	40 995	14.1	174 209	30.5
CALIFORNIA...................	548 028	7.2	1 867 099	1.1	D	D	366 950	29.5	820 011	6.7	3 285 881	24.2
COLORADO....................	122 733	46.5	186 156	7.0	101 918	21.3	366 950	29.5	119 331	20.6	457 757	43.5
CONNECTICUT	D	D	262 959	-9.3	D	D	264 497	9.8	137 061	-8.9	348 287	27.8
DELAWARE	20 070	13.5	41 969	-3.7	15 805	-1.7	69 887	16.1	52 071	35.5	70 912	30.9
DISTRICT OF COLUMBIA ...	D	D	11 906	0.4	D	D	26 621	-6.5	D	D	130 661	8.3
FLORIDA........................	D	D	463 791	2.3	333 153	18.6	1 274 403	15.6	190 856	15.4	1 745 657	37.0
GEORGIA.......................	160 111	29.2	552 706	6.1	214 242	19.4	630 376	23.8	190 856	15.4	755 082	50.5
HAWAII	20 985	-35.2	16 412	-17.8	20 809	-10.7	110 892	0.4	35 201	-5.4	120 784	2.4
IDAHO...........................	40 060	80.3	71 274	14.9	27 231	9.4	93 090	25.9	18 741	6.3	88 434	39.2
ILLINOIS........................	D	D	915 860	4.6	357 606	7.7	931 248	10.1	401 132	6.5	1 150 231	27.5
INDIANA........................	D	D	637 736	7.6	129 290	11.7	516 853	16.9	D	D	455 626	28.5
IOWA	D	D	244 994	10.4	75 462	8.8	250 724	10.9	82 571	16.9	210 117	29.3
KANSAS	61 345	28.0	203 303	11.9	68 008	10.1	214 819	15.6	64 496	8.7	220 599	36.2
KENTUCKY	76 131	19.4	296 956	11.7	80 672	14.8	315 734	20.9	71 664	14.7	279 646	32.7
LOUISIANA	106 314	15.7	173 489	0.5	87 291	7.4	333 931	15.6	81 495	8.3	391 385	32.0
MAINE	24 902	16.1	88 327	-2.1	23 360	6.8	102 614	14.0	26 289	9.9	87 636	28.8
MARYLAND	139 269	3.8	174 740	-3.4	105 973	5.4	404 802	10.4	140 830	6.7	557 370	33.2
MASSACHUSETTS	D	D	441 770	-0.7	161 894	14.4	522 783	11.3	247 837	14.4	703 699	29.0
MICHIGAN......................	D	D	850 368	8.6	213 537	15.3	796 730	12.7	226 680	18.8	819 080	33.4
MINNESOTA...................	D	D	399 756	15.3	147 559	19.8	419 310	12.7	152 750	22.4	468 166	34.1
MISSISSIPPI...................	47 242	36.7	234 764	-0.1	43 026	7.7	194 483	28.8	39 365	6.6	179 905	66.2
MISSOURI......................	129 183	33.1	391 945	4.6	144 328	11.3	451 894	15.4	149 584	14.3	478 052	28.0
MONTANA......................	17 987	34.5	22 526	5.1	17 417	6.2	75 840	17.8	D	D	33 381	13.8
NEBRASKA.....................	40 127	33.3	111 098	16.4	48 010	2.0	149 478	13.1	57 400	18.3	64 191	9.6
NEVADA	68 283	66.4	39 954	48.8	32 203	47.5	137 171	38.2	40 038	41.1	20 265	23.0
NEW HAMPSHIRE	22 371	30.4	102 193	14.4	26 379	28.9	117 518	21.0	28 719	-0.5	42 407	16.7
NEW JERSEY..................	140 900	7.2	432 049	-9.7	287 964	9.6	585 436	12.1	251 453	10.3	257 500	5.1
NEW MEXICO..................	38 990	26.2	42 254	9.4	26 259	16.2	135 164	20.3	30 150	16.8	49 430	15.1
NEW YORK	271 483	5.5	860 233	-10.0	450 559	3.9	1 181 372	8.5	771 470	4.8	900 533	3.4
NORTH CAROLINA...........	195 189	34.1	789 476	1.0	178 604	18.2	628 124	23.7	170 949	30.1	607 654	43.0
NORTH DAKOTA..............	15 693	33.0	23 218	26.8	20 321	10.1	59 130	14.3	14 314	16.6	46 358	42.3
OHIO.............................	221 240	16.2	1 009 620	5.5	D	D	971 264	15.9	303 503	22.0	950 157	25.3
OKLAHOMA	49 861	14.1	168 926	10.2	D	D	251 502	19.0	67 101	13.2	259 359	32.1
OREGON	78 985	48.4	226 715	12.6	D	D	274 347	21.0	83 852	29.1	275 689	41.1
PENNSYLVANIA...............	226 488	6.1	857 041	-0.8	269 103	5.8	940 957	9.2	342 807	13.8	978 912	22.8
RHODE ISLAND	16 820	20.3	78 452	-7.2	20 487	4.9	75 777	12.6	26 944	-2.1	84 785	31.6
SOUTH CAROLINA	83 661	20.1	353 858	-0.3	67 606	19.3	328 850	24.6	73 899	18.6	325 235	39.6
SOUTH DAKOTA..............	14 229	10.9	48 306	38.2	19 329	18.1	66 008	14.8	D	D	48 237	40.0
TENNESSEE...................	118 094	31.6	495 760	2.2	135 432	17.3	457 976	24.4	123 091	21.6	487 855	34.6
TEXAS	420 823	25.4	985 731	11.0	D	D	1 464 183	19.0	452 103	13.6	1 968 608	37.6
UTAH	54 881	57.0	122 200	20.2	50 823	28.3	167 441	32.6	48 569	34.2	207 939	50.1
VERMONT	12 967	9.2	44 648	0.8	D	D	52 529	14.5	D	D	46 922	26.4
VIRGINIA	176 432	22.8	387 576	0.4	125 191	8.1	555 088	17.0	173 123	13.0	716 667	36.3
WASHINGTON	D	D	347 549	5.4	134 842	10.1	D	D	127 681	10.9	461 505	30.0
WEST VIRGINIA...............	30 892	23.7	76 772	1.5	27 352	11.8	129 956	16.0	D	D	106 642	27.1
WISCONSIN...................	114 490	18.3	575 318	12.2	128 690	9.4	453 927	12.1	152 563	14.9	416 814	31.6
WYOMING	13 703	25.2	9 763	8.8	D	D	D	D	D	D	33 771	27.6

STATE	Value of residential construction authorized by building permits, 1999				Exports of goods by state of origin, 2000 (mil dol)			Federal funds and grants, fiscal 1999[1] (mil dol)		Procurement contract awards	
	New Construction ($1,000)	Number of housing units	Percent single family	Manufactured housing units put in place 1999 (1,000)	Total	Manufactured	Non-manufactured	Total	Salaries and wages	Defense	Other
	279	280	281	282	283	284	285	286	287	288	289
UNITED STATES	181 439 531	1 664 800	74.9	311.3	653 632	602 990	50 642	1 516 775	176 085	125 434	81 727
ALABAMA	1 883 871	19 037	78.4	16.6	5 516	5 111	405	26 776	2 798	2 679	1 017
ALASKA	306 585	2 211	69.6	D	948	294	655	5 279	1 272	612	233
ARIZONA	7 350 364	65 109	81.8	8.4	9 129	8 543	586	26 959	2 661	4 156	625
ARKANSAS	965 992	11 502	67.4	7.2	2 012	1 937	76	13 631	1 116	248	219
CALIFORNIA	21 030 600	138 039	74.4	6.7	111 476	103 617	7 858	166 050	17 733	17 370	8 424
COLORADO	6 035 973	49 313	77.9	4.2	9 869	9 648	221	21 755	3 499	2 443	1 999
CONNECTICUT	1 466 185	10 637	87.0	D	12 659	10 565	2 094	19 241	1 350	3 126	510
DELAWARE	492 470	5 285	91.2	1.9	5 692	5 608	84	3 766	406	92	129
DISTRICT OF COLUMBIA	53 284	683	46.7	D	4 454	3 841	613	27 034	11 975	1 344	5 059
FLORIDA	16 197 445	165 018	64.6	18.3	22 244	20 871	1 373	87 215	7 835	6 764	1 875
GEORGIA	8 749 615	89 600	79.9	17.1	10 628	10 011	617	39 215	6 292	4 095	1 054
HAWAII	632 743	4 211	79.8	D	268	210	58	8 568	2 436	992	149
IDAHO	1 366 527	12 309	86.3	1.8	2 464	2 313	151	6 165	693	156	714
ILLINOIS	6 537 643	53 974	72.7	3.5	30 360	27 698	2 662	55 836	6 000	1 310	2 170
INDIANA	4 786 192	41 844	80.7	7.9	13 419	13 143	276	26 828	1 972	1 643	578
IOWA	1 405 608	13 491	71.9	2.3	3 160	2 968	192	15 602	970	413	484
KANSAS	1 668 027	15 688	72.1	2.6	4 803	3 866	937	14 447	1 752	939	324
KENTUCKY	1 909 051	21 581	76.4	10.5	7 854	7 543	311	22 198	2 615	1 364	910
LOUISIANA	1 766 666	17 836	81.6	8.9	3 786	2 594	1 192	24 384	2 165	1 449	1 217
MAINE	623 269	5 695	94.5	1.4	1 587	1 233	354	7 281	795	681	121
MARYLAND	3 102 361	29 757	81.2	1.1	4 635	4 300	335	41 990	8 346	5 438	5 145
MASSACHUSETTS	2 666 006	18 967	81.5	0.3	18 155	17 395	761	37 803	2 919	4 449	1 303
MICHIGAN	6 204 660	54 257	83.7	11.2	47 971	47 297	674	43 872	2 932	1 167	897
MINNESOTA	4 052 938	33 344	80.0	2.8	16 573	11 746	4 827	21 666	1 778	1 198	609
MISSISSIPPI	989 518	12 871	74.5	10.0	1 696	1 565	131	16 488	1 699	1 528	411
MISSOURI	2 742 784	26 881	77.0	6.9	7 679	6 532	1 147	33 231	3 313	4 318	1 387
MONTANA	226 260	2 566	62.6	1.6	531	387	144	6 225	667	99	421
NEBRASKA	827 968	8 696	76.2	1.0	3 097	2 545	552	8 793	992	226	244
NEVADA	2 976 683	32 643	74.4	1.4	1 316	1 262	54	7 942	903	273	528
NEW HAMPSHIRE	781 944	6 326	90.0	0.9	2 282	2 131	150	5 301	453	359	122
NEW JERSEY	3 162 436	31 976	78.6	0.4	25 540	23 544	1 996	40 398	3 599	2 838	1 368
NEW MEXICO	1 079 858	9 716	88.5	4.9	581	530	51	13 580	1 646	615	3 316
NEW YORK	4 414 787	42 619	58.1	4.1	45 440	40 539	4 901	101 809	7 521	3 217	3 555
NORTH CAROLINA	8 616 858	84 754	75.6	26.0	14 009	13 483	526	37 228	5 275	1 045	1 004
NORTH DAKOTA	223 249	2 579	56.0	0.5	693	590	103	4 535	618	149	105
OHIO	6 401 999	55 888	71.6	7.7	27 811	26 883	928	53 262	4 341	2 596	1 911
OKLAHOMA	1 430 600	14 186	78.0	7.1	3 139	2 982	156	19 189	2 761	1 197	472
OREGON	2 652 791	23 249	71.4	4.0	8 492	6 982	1 510	15 592	1 506	303	462
PENNSYLVANIA	4 634 786	42 662	85.7	5.5	22 530	21 616	914	69 448	5 424	3 841	2 093
RHODE ISLAND	336 166	3 414	79.1	D	1 062	936	126	6 036	723	303	118
SOUTH CAROLINA	3 614 665	36 161	75.1	14.8	7 450	7 328	122	20 833	2 441	847	1 693
SOUTH DAKOTA	329 767	3 672	78.3	1.3	455	436	19	4 909	559	91	432
TENNESSEE	3 836 987	37 049	80.7	20.5	10 331	9 157	1 174	30 867	2 718	1 075	3 445
TEXAS	14 045 115	146 644	69.5	35.2	60 909	57 722	3 187	97 988	11 798	8 326	6 176
UTAH	2 296 384	20 547	81.4	1.3	2 603	2 414	189	9 239	1 469	548	720
VERMONT	304 942	2 600	84.1	0.6	1 782	1 737	45	3 114	301	213	62
VIRGINIA	5 142 222	53 151	79.1	5.6	10 153	8 836	1 317	57 842	12 050	12 388	6 656
WASHINGTON	4 588 556	42 809	65.8	5.1	32 385	28 949	3 436	31 993	4 869	2 296	2 318
WEST VIRGINIA	381 091	4 233	84.5	5.2	1 421	1 263	158	11 028	911	108	516
WISCONSIN	3 868 481	35 620	69.8	3.5	10 453	10 171	282	22 604	1 514	643	790
WYOMING	278 559	1 900	76.6	1.1	133	118	15	2 916	410	63	136

1. October 1, 1998–September 30, 1999.

Table A. States — **Federal Funds**

STATE	Federal funds and grants, fiscal 1999[1] (mil dol) (cont'd)												
	Direct payments for individuals							Grants					
	Total	Social Security and government retirement	Medicare	Food stamps	Supplemental Security Income	Educational assistance	Housing assistance	Total[2]	Medicaid and other health-related	Nutrition and family welfare	Education	Housing and community development	Energy and environment
	290	291	292	293	294	295	296	297	298	299	300	301	302
UNITED STATES	844 974	490 502	207 501	15 818	28 329	7 594	9 697	288 551	133 659	53 121	25 140	7 062	5 075
ALABAMA	15 650	9 223	3 714	347	665	121	164	4 632	2 092	650	434	114	107
ALASKA	1 232	755	161	49	32	6	55	1 929	593	196	222	21	94
ARIZONA	14 979	9 103	3 155	236	370	123	74	4 537	1 674	898	469	101	67
ARKANSAS	9 434	5 465	2 019	208	350	58	83	2 614	1 257	384	253	42	21
CALIFORNIA	86 152	46 584	23 935	1 837	4 102	858	874	36 370	15 258	8 676	3 009	860	292
COLORADO	10 368	6 633	2 104	145	244	88	90	3 446	1 306	577	297	67	106
CONNECTICUT	10 409	6 124	3 008	151	219	51	149	3 846	2 006	722	252	78	90
DELAWARE	2 314	1 486	532	32	52	11	31	825	309	125	82	11	62
DISTRICT OF COLUMBIA	3 362	1 625	586	80	92	33	149	5 293	1 550	1 197	347	96	55
FLORIDA	59 550	35 730	17 102	820	1 656	433	414	11 191	4 706	2 174	1 200	239	153
GEORGIA	21 022	12 422	4 752	530	824	147	312	6 752	2 978	1 323	641	160	106
HAWAII	3 656	2 340	658	180	91	17	40	1 335	417	278	163	44	33
IDAHO	3 425	2 159	601	45	79	26	13	1 177	431	165	115	18	59
ILLINOIS	35 769	19 736	9 183	773	1 282	245	502	10 586	4 708	2 194	1 027	320	142
INDIANA	17 929	10 634	4 116	256	421	166	199	4 706	2 245	785	430	132	72
IOWA	11 138	5 581	1 931	104	170	81	53	2 595	1 174	457	240	61	32
KANSAS	9 249	5 070	1 877	82	162	54	35	2 183	884	424	255	47	42
KENTUCKY	12 913	7 584	2 905	332	756	88	110	4 395	2 228	719	417	97	61
LOUISIANA	14 325	7 180	4 064	457	731	131	159	5 228	2 615	907	514	144	108
MAINE	4 020	2 642	852	90	116	42	6	1 664	883	243	131	29	22
MARYLAND	17 317	10 397	3 839	236	408	79	226	5 744	3 118	847	398	122	131
MASSACHUSETTS	20 293	11 063	6 284	206	670	230	335	8 838	4 774	1 159	554	210	408
MICHIGAN	29 110	17 110	7 716	516	1 031	180	290	9 764	4 394	2 096	899	281	235
MINNESOTA	13 582	7 557	2 700	175	290	141	145	4 499	2 218	838	354	92	86
MISSISSIPPI	9 463	5 118	2 160	234	538	102	122	3 387	1 579	600	327	69	56
MISSOURI	18 734	10 702	4 471	350	486	150	139	5 478	2 757	898	458	150	45
MONTANA	3 639	1 818	531	52	60	26	46	1 399	402	165	146	21	145
NEBRASKA	5 680	3 202	983	67	88	38	39	1 651	749	284	171	32	33
NEVADA	4 989	3 351	1 023	57	106	15	25	1 249	374	217	102	28	117
NEW HAMPSHIRE	3 246	2 250	689	31	51	31	36	1 120	508	145	86	25	28
NEW JERSEY	25 331	14 796	7 084	353	629	136	385	7 262	3 446	1 181	616	220	155
NEW MEXICO	5 253	3 327	901	145	193	55	71	2 750	991	451	344	44	123
NEW YORK	58 645	31 322	16 712	1 494	2 675	936	1 332	28 870	16 379	5 313	1 870	928	363
NORTH CAROLINA	22 295	14 121	4 770	392	764	147	200	7 608	3 992	1 306	599	126	98
NORTH DAKOTA	2 653	1 186	425	26	32	31	18	1 009	295	140	97	11	30
OHIO	34 159	20 419	8 676	544	1 226	359	529	10 254	4 956	2 305	911	293	94
OKLAHOMA	11 528	6 950	2 597	223	306	88	119	3 231	1 325	648	356	80	69
OREGON	9 803	6 295	1 970	192	228	71	61	3 518	1 629	575	309	68	45
PENNSYLVANIA	44 950	25 905	12 835	715	1 269	351	572	13 141	6 685	2 313	978	445	137
RHODE ISLAND	3 481	2 062	908	62	104	43	27	1 411	691	220	109	31	23
SOUTH CAROLINA	11 973	7 634	2 383	252	453	105	116	3 879	2 006	557	349	67	92
SOUTH DAKOTA	2 770	1 420	460	37	54	68	26	1 056	331	143	131	14	29
TENNESSEE	17 729	10 382	4 384	427	710	109	281	5 900	3 142	841	390	119	93
TEXAS	53 317	29 869	12 506	1 266	1 638	491	485	18 370	8 456	3 017	2 028	459	236
UTAH	4 508	3 071	796	73	91	70	22	1 994	713	334	189	31	49
VERMONT	1 654	1 060	353	34	45	32	6	883	380	135	79	17	35
VIRGINIA	21 999	14 903	3 855	281	562	436	180	4 749	1 780	823	522	115	94
WASHINGTON	16 790	10 612	3 161	270	461	110	157	5 720	2 710	1 052	455	108	90
WEST VIRGINIA	7 002	4 386	1 588	209	327	42	40	2 490	1 195	352	208	46	60
WISCONSIN	14 815	9 219	3 223	124	396	131	149	4 842	2 212	984	443	114	113
WYOMING	1 374	911	264	20	24	12	9	933	161	86	83	12	36

1. October 1, 1998 to September 30, 1999.   2. Includes program categories not shown separately.

Table A. States — **State Government Finances**

	State government finances, fiscal 1998											
	General revenue (mil dol)								General expenditures (mil dol)			
		From federal government		From own sources							Direct general expenditures	
					Taxes		Taxes per capita[1] (dollars)					
STATE	Total	Total	Per capita[1] (dollars)	Total	Total	Sales and gross receipts	Total	Sales and gross receipts	Total	To local govern-ments	Total	Per capita[1] (dollars)
	303	304	305	306	307	308	309	310	311	312	313	314
UNITED STATES	X	X	X	X	X	X	X	X	X	X	X	X
ALABAMA	12 433	4 021	924	8 412	5 739	3 428	1 319	788	13 728	3 420	10 309	2 369
ALASKA	7 973	1 080	1 759	6 894	1 186	211	1 932	344	5 803	983	4 820	7 850
ARIZONA	11 814	3 330	713	8 484	6 949	4 241	1 489	908	13 328	5 023	8 305	1 779
ARKANSAS	7 724	2 368	933	5 356	4 057	2 339	1 598	922	8 104	2 110	5 994	2 361
CALIFORNIA	111 088	30 894	946	80 194	67 714	29 647	2 073	908	120 330	51 053	69 276	2 121
COLORADO	10 953	2 789	702	8 165	5 890	2 596	1 483	654	11 278	3 159	8 118	2 044
CONNECTICUT	14 452	3 016	921	11 436	9 394	5 081	2 869	1 552	14 516	2 628	11 888	3 631
DELAWARE	3 883	725	975	3 158	1 981	904	2 665	1 216	3 465	591	2 874	3 865
DISTRICT OF COLUMBIA	X	X	X	X	X	X	X	X	X	X	X	X
FLORIDA	36 780	8 302	557	28 478	22 521	18 379	1 510	1 232	39 214	12 537	26 677	1 788
GEORGIA	20 165	5 676	743	14 488	11 589	5 389	1 517	705	21 735	6 311	15 425	2 018
HAWAII	5 474	1 176	985	4 298	3 176	2 004	2 662	1 680	5 860	147	5 713	4 789
IDAHO	3 592	863	702	2 729	2 057	1 149	1 674	935	3 786	1 104	2 681	2 182
ILLINOIS	33 787	8 959	744	24 828	19 771	10 319	1 641	857	35 685	9 862	25 823	2 144
INDIANA	17 113	3 943	668	13 170	9 747	4 625	1 652	784	17 223	5 883	11 340	1 922
IOWA	8 821	2 216	774	6 605	4 803	2 667	1 678	932	9 729	2 795	6 935	2 423
KANSAS	7 785	1 863	709	5 922	4 662	2 404	1 773	914	7 681	2 509	5 172	1 967
KENTUCKY	12 969	3 603	915	9 366	7 115	3 704	1 807	941	13 541	3 007	10 534	2 676
LOUISIANA	13 649	4 026	922	9 623	6 082	3 656	1 392	837	14 919	3 451	11 468	2 625
MAINE	4 567	1 411	1 134	3 156	2 370	1 259	1 905	1 012	4 606	852	3 755	3 018
MARYLAND	15 589	3 534	688	12 055	9 190	4 194	1 790	817	16 578	3 711	12 868	2 506
MASSACHUSETTS	25 801	6 458	1 051	19 343	14 488	4 821	2 357	784	27 194	6 215	20 979	3 413
MICHIGAN	36 085	8 557	872	27 528	21 216	10 606	2 161	1 080	37 410	15 430	21 979	2 239
MINNESOTA	17 856	3 938	833	13 918	11 504	5 808	2 434	1 229	18 418	6 022	12 396	2 623
MISSISSIPPI	8 400	2 947	1 071	5 453	4 243	3 098	1 542	1 126	9 336	2 876	6 460	2 347
MISSOURI	14 884	4 246	781	10 638	8 222	4 374	1 512	804	15 313	4 177	11 137	2 048
MONTANA	2 980	1 048	1 190	1 933	1 328	432	1 508	490	3 262	713	2 550	2 896
NEBRASKA	4 829	1 282	771	3 547	2 633	1 487	1 584	894	4 754	1 291	3 462	2 082
NEVADA	4 615	912	522	3 703	3 113	2 962	1 782	1 696	5 398	1 915	3 482	1 993
NEW HAMPSHIRE	2 968	1 024	864	1 945	1 009	623	851	525	3 477	455	3 022	2 551
NEW JERSEY	28 357	6 392	788	21 966	15 605	8 404	1 923	1 036	31 702	7 176	24 526	3 022
NEW MEXICO	7 127	1 846	1 063	5 281	3 575	2 139	2 058	1 231	7 540	2 187	5 353	3 082
NEW YORK	80 720	33 791	1 859	46 929	36 155	13 390	1 989	737	87 338	27 271	60 067	3 305
NORTH CAROLINA	23 950	6 817	903	17 133	13 869	6 577	1 838	872	24 605	7 928	16 676	2 210
NORTH DAKOTA	2 533	893	1 399	1 641	1 078	690	1 690	1 081	2 527	541	1 985	3 111
OHIO	32 300	8 953	799	23 347	17 643	9 768	1 574	871	39 209	11 214	27 995	2 497
OKLAHOMA	9 411	2 516	752	6 895	5 301	2 756	1 584	824	9 953	2 803	7 150	2 136
OREGON	11 273	3 365	1 025	7 909	4 999	1 177	1 523	359	13 466	3 707	9 759	2 973
PENNSYLVANIA	36 833	9 609	801	27 225	20 629	11 868	1 719	989	40 804	10 158	30 646	2 554
RHODE ISLAND	3 781	1 146	1 160	2 635	1 821	988	1 843	999	3 964	548	3 416	3 456
SOUTH CAROLINA	11 415	3 442	897	7 973	5 683	3 299	1 482	860	13 575	3 142	10 433	2 720
SOUTH DAKOTA	2 098	764	1 035	1 334	834	766	1 129	1 038	2 245	493	1 752	2 373
TENNESSEE	14 086	5 265	969	8 821	6 996	5 977	1 288	1 101	14 775	3 924	10 851	1 998
TEXAS	48 066	14 605	739	33 460	24 629	23 417	1 246	1 185	51 065	14 027	37 038	1 874
UTAH	6 627	1 690	805	4 938	3 501	1 893	1 667	902	7 470	1 717	5 753	2 740
VERMONT	2 196	730	1 235	1 467	958	490	1 621	829	2 295	356	1 940	3 283
VIRGINIA	19 268	3 781	557	15 487	10 543	4 367	1 552	643	20 529	5 660	14 869	2 189
WASHINGTON	19 079	4 247	747	14 832	11 806	9 212	2 075	1 619	22 880	6 048	16 832	2 959
WEST VIRGINIA	6 206	2 096	1 157	4 109	3 012	1 717	1 663	948	7 149	1 530	5 619	3 102
WISCONSIN	18 169	3 795	726	14 374	11 150	5 224	2 135	1 000	19 101	7 481	11 620	2 225
WYOMING	2 337	839	1 744	1 498	856	482	1 779	1 002	2 172	711	1 461	3 039

1. Based on the estimated population as of July 1 of the year shown.

Table A. States — State Government Finances, Government Employment, and Elections

STATE	State government finances, fiscal 1998 (cont'd) General expenditures (mil dol) (cont'd) By selected function (mil dol) — Education	Health and hospitals	Highways	Public safety	Public welfare	Debt outstanding Total (mil dol)	Per capita[1]	Government employment, 1998 Federal civilian	Federal military	State and local	Presidential election, 2000 (percent of vote cast) Democratic	Republican	All other
	315	316	317	318	319	320	321	322	323	324	325	326	327
UNITED STATES	X	X	X	X	X	X	X	2 808 000	2 098 000	17 042 000	48.4	47.9	3.7
ALABAMA	5 362	1 503	882	359	3 027	4 167	957	53 249	42 064	288 880	41.6	56.5	1.9
ALASKA	1 208	187	550	217	759	3 800	6 188	17 041	22 707	53 138	27.7	58.6	13.7
ARIZONA	4 393	719	1 192	852	2 648	2 807	601	44 070	32 672	266 516	44.7	51.0	4.2
ARKANSAS	3 019	643	779	269	1 797	2 384	939	20 728	19 178	158 504	45.9	51.3	2.8
CALIFORNIA	38 140	8 820	4 631	4 584	30 412	50 251	1 538	268 568	230 324	1 881 006	53.4	41.7	4.9
COLORADO	4 333	433	989	682	2 401	3 637	916	53 973	42 580	270 700	42.4	50.8	6.9
CONNECTICUT	3 143	1 457	686	595	3 036	17 727	5 414	22 175	16 986	185 623	55.9	38.4	5.6
DELAWARE	1 072	241	288	196	501	3 770	5 070	5 407	8 946	49 245	55.0	41.9	3.1
DISTRICT OF COLUMBIA	X	X	X	X	X	X	X	183 932	23 335	41 950	85.2	9.0	5.9
FLORIDA	12 595	2 342	3 254	2 270	8 160	16 969	1 138	119 348	111 309	823 269	48.8	48.8	2.3
GEORGIA	9 192	1 382	1 282	1 008	4 692	6 040	790	93 207	94 817	491 328	43.0	54.7	2.3
HAWAII	1 636	502	249	128	919	5 710	4 786	30 127	55 253	80 967	56.0	38.0	7.0
IDAHO	1 403	139	397	160	595	1 883	1 533	12 728	9 768	86 918	27.6	67.2	5.2
ILLINOIS	9 865	2 541	2 475	1 399	8 905	25 315	2 102	95 718	58 239	715 325	54.6	42.6	2.8
INDIANA	6 833	639	1 721	627	3 298	6 704	1 136	38 659	21 888	357 365	41.0	56.6	2.3
IOWA	3 744	732	1 056	293	1 937	2 029	709	20 040	13 979	212 503	48.5	48.2	3.2
KANSAS	3 237	579	937	300	1 093	1 411	537	26 060	29 108	215 634	37.2	58.0	4.7
KENTUCKY	4 574	763	1 172	434	3 291	6 814	1 731	36 894	47 221	245 003	41.4	56.5	2.1
LOUISIANA	4 828	1 593	981	655	2 958	7 093	1 624	35 309	41 812	324 870	44.9	52.6	2.6
MAINE	1 171	301	326	113	1 397	3 474	2 792	13 021	10 838	79 403	49.0	44.0	7.0
MARYLAND	4 770	1 110	1 198	1 016	3 255	10 536	2 052	153 567	51 984	303 307	57.0	40.0	3.0
MASSACHUSETTS	5 478	1 921	2 387	1 169	6 181	32 833	5 341	54 691	24 278	360 422	59.8	32.5	7.7
MICHIGAN	15 406	3 319	2 186	1 571	6 835	16 147	1 645	56 255	21 763	577 804	51.3	46.1	2.6
MINNESOTA	6 482	699	1 241	447	4 559	5 333	1 129	33 229	20 084	328 799	47.9	45.5	6.6
MISSISSIPPI	3 042	715	868	276	1 888	2 674	971	26 375	35 509	197 560	40.7	57.6	1.7
MISSOURI	5 451	1 064	1 278	616	3 301	8 091	1 488	58 899	37 557	351 621	47.0	50.0	3.0
MONTANA	1 059	229	349	122	466	2 259	2 565	12 647	8 474	61 856	33.4	58.4	8.2
NEBRASKA	1 683	358	573	166	1 108	1 908	1 148	15 840	15 873	129 070	33.3	62.2	4.5
NEVADA	1 835	175	389	249	723	2 881	1 649	14 155	11 329	96 433	46.0	49.5	4.5
NEW HAMPSHIRE	694	169	318	93	925	5 367	4 529	8 083	4 374	68 780	46.8	48.1	5.1
NEW JERSEY	8 460	1 835	1 865	1 320	5 235	27 214	3 353	65 637	30 205	491 838	56.1	40.3	3.6
NEW MEXICO	2 623	587	875	251	1 277	2 572	1 481	29 867	18 427	138 207	48.0	48.0	4.0
NEW YORK	17 403	5 698	2 772	2 791	28 538	73 254	4 030	138 893	57 885	1 242 103	60.2	35.2	4.6
NORTH CAROLINA	9 496	1 791	2 076	1 236	4 886	6 877	911	61 370	120 100	533 782	43.1	56.0	0.9
NORTH DAKOTA	810	91	322	42	462	857	1 343	8 985	13 097	49 267	33.1	60.7	6.3
OHIO	11 602	2 495	2 631	1 577	8 147	14 183	1 265	83 126	36 706	683 434	46.4	50.0	3.6
OKLAHOMA	3 922	598	862	443	1 749	3 951	1 181	44 493	41 819	227 140	38.4	60.3	1.3
OREGON	4 209	839	995	611	2 351	5 729	1 746	29 971	12 704	213 424	47.0	46.5	6.5
PENNSYLVANIA	11 013	2 899	3 069	1 933	10 516	16 394	1 366	111 517	45 066	601 726	50.6	46.4	3.0
RHODE ISLAND	982	208	190	152	1 017	5 352	5 414	10 591	9 676	54 934	61.0	32.0	7.0
SOUTH CAROLINA	4 209	1 335	711	593	2 955	5 191	1 353	29 258	56 340	278 278	40.9	56.8	2.3
SOUTH DAKOTA	643	100	347	75	410	2 068	2 802	10 767	8 260	50 252	37.6	60.3	2.1
TENNESSEE	4 920	1 078	1 374	545	4 197	3 192	588	50 308	23 782	329 985	47.3	51.1	1.6
TEXAS	19 770	3 755	3 520	2 889	10 833	14 408	729	184 577	165 408	1 308 218	38.0	59.3	2.7
UTAH	3 179	537	935	249	1 042	3 435	1 636	30 620	16 037	145 215	26.3	66.8	6.8
VERMONT	679	67	220	71	565	2 110	3 571	5 478	4 501	39 543	50.6	40.7	8.7
VIRGINIA	7 490	1 810	2 232	1 281	3 420	10 828	1 594	163 596	164 865	450 499	44.4	52.5	3.1
WASHINGTON	8 198	1 669	1 528	781	4 340	10 289	1 809	66 840	73 524	388 621	50.2	44.6	5.3
WEST VIRGINIA	2 301	210	807	164	1 648	3 433	1 896	21 583	9 662	118 538	45.6	51.9	2.5
WISCONSIN	6 595	1 012	1 352	716	3 007	10 721	2 052	29 494	19 338	344 990	47.8	47.6	4.6
WYOMING	663	107	301	55	264	1 043	2 170	7 034	6 349	48 207	27.7	67.8	4.5

1. Based on the estimated population as of July 1 of the year shown.

TABLE B:

States and Counties

(For explanation of symbols, see page xii)

Page

Page	
108	**AL**(Autauga)—**AL**(Walker)
122	**AL**(Washington)—**AR**(Columbia)
136	**AR**(Conway)—**CA**(Amador)
150	**CA**(Butte)—**CO**(Cheyenne)
164	**CO**(Clear Creek)—**CT**(Windham)
178	**DE**(Kent)—**FL**(Santa Rosa)
192	**FL**(Sarasota)—**GA**(Evans)
206	**GA**(Fannin)—**GA**(Randolph)
220	**GA**(Richmond)—**ID**(Clearwater)
234	**ID**(Custer)—**IL**(Iroquois)
248	**IL**(Jackson)—**IL**(Woodford)
262	**IN**(Adams)—**IN**(Pulaski)
276	**IN**(Putnam)—**IA**(Grundy)
290	**IA**(Guthrie)—**KS**(Atchison)
304	**KS**(Barber)—**KS**(Norton)
318	**KS**(Osage)—**KY**(Crittenden)
332	**KY**(Cumberland)—**KY**(Owen)
346	**KY**(Owsley)—**LA**(Plaquemines)
360	**LA**(Pointe Coupee)—**MD**(Talbot)
374	**MD**(Washington)—**MI**(Lapeer)
388	**MI**(Leelanau)—**MN**(Goodhue)
402	**MN**(Grant)—**MN**(Yellow Medicine)
416	**MS**(Adams)—**MS**(Stone)
430	**MS**(Sunflower)—**MO**(Jackson)
444	**MO**(Jasper)—**MO**(Wright)
458	**MO**(St. Louis City)—**NE**(Banner)
472	**NE**(Blaine)—**NE**(Pierce)
486	**NE**(Platte)—**NJ**(Hunterdon)
500	**NJ**(Mercer)—**NY**(Fulton)
514	**NY**(Genesee)—**NC**(Cherokee)
528	**NC**(Chowan)—**NC**(Surry)
542	**NC**(Swain)—**ND**(Walsh)
556	**ND**(Ward)—**OH**(Noble)
570	**OH**(Ottawa)—**OK**(Kingfisher)
584	**OK**(Kiowa)—**OR**(Marion)
598	**OR**(Morrow)—**PA**(Pike)
612	**PA**(Potter)—**SC**(Spartanburg)
626	**SC**(Sumter)—**SD**(Todd)
640	**SD**(Tripp)—**TN**(Marion)
654	**TN**(Marshall)—**TX**(Burnet)
668	**TX**(Caldwell)—**TX**(Grimes)
682	**TX**(Guadalupe)—**TX**(Martin)
696	**TX**(Mason)—**TX**(Titus)
710	**TX**(Tom Green)—**VT**(Caledonia)
724	**VT**(Chittenden)—**VA**(Loudoun)
738	**VA**(Louisa)—**VA**(Lynchburg City)
752	**VA**(Manassas City)—**WV**(Boone)
766	**WV**(Braxton)—**WI**(Crawford)
780	**WI**(Dane)—**WY**(Carbon)
794	**WY**(Converse)—**WY**(Weston)

Table B. States and Counties — Land Area and Population

STATE/County code	MSA/PMSA/NECMA code[1]	County Type[2]	STATE County	Land area[3] (sq km) 1990	Total persons	Rank	Per square kilometer	White	Black	Am. Indian, Eskimo, Aleut	Asian and Pacific Islander	Percent Hispanic[4]	Under 5 years	5 to 17 years	18 to 24 years	25 to 34 years	35 to 44 years	45 to 54 years
				1	2	3	4	5	6	7	8	9	10	11	12	13	14	15
00 000	...	X	UNITED STATES	9 159 127	272 690 813	X	29.8	82.4	12.8	0.9	4.0	11.5	6.9	18.8	9.5	13.9	16.4	13.1
01 000	...	X	ALABAMA	131 443	4 369 862	X	33.2	73.0	26.1	0.3	0.7	1.0	6.7	17.7	10.1	14.1	15.9	13.3
01 001	5240	2	Autauga	1 544	43 140	1 020	27.9	77.9	21.5	0.2	0.5	1.2	7.4	20.1	8.8	14.1	16.2	14.5
01 003	5160	2	Baldwin	4 135	135 820	387	32.8	85.4	13.8	0.5	0.3	1.8	6.6	17.7	7.6	12.8	15.6	13.7
01 005	...	6	Barbour	2 292	26 726	1 474	11.7	52.6	47.0	0.2	0.2	0.8	6.7	19.4	9.1	13.8	16.6	12.0
01 007	...	6	Bibb	1 612	19 601	1 784	12.2	77.1	22.6	0.1	0.1	0.4	6.8	20.5	10.0	13.2	15.4	13.6
01 009	1000	2	Blount	1 672	47 411	944	28.4	98.1	1.5	0.3	0.1	1.3	6.6	17.7	8.9	13.3	16.0	15.0
01 011	...	6	Bullock	1 619	11 343	2 317	7.0	26.6	73.2	0.1	0.1	0.9	7.8	20.0	9.7	14.6	15.5	12.1
01 013	...	7	Butler	2 012	21 522	1 683	10.7	57.6	42.2	0.1	0.1	0.5	7.1	21.1	8.2	12.2	14.2	12.2
01 015	0450	3	Calhoun	1 576	116 541	454	73.9	79.2	19.7	0.2	0.9	1.9	6.1	17.3	11.2	13.8	15.7	12.9
01 017	...	5	Chambers	1 547	36 369	1 182	23.5	61.8	38.0	0.1	0.0	0.5	6.2	18.1	9.6	12.5	14.9	13.0
01 019	...	6	Cherokee	1 433	21 894	1 663	15.3	92.3	7.3	0.2	0.1	0.5	5.4	16.7	8.5	12.1	15.5	14.7
01 021	...	6	Chilton	1 798	37 604	1 146	20.9	87.3	12.4	0.2	0.1	0.6	6.5	18.9	8.6	13.4	15.4	14.1
01 023	...	9	Choctaw	2 366	15 518	2 033	6.6	53.6	46.3	0.0	0.1	0.5	6.5	20.3	9.0	12.3	14.9	14.3
01 025	...	7	Clarke	3 208	28 756	1 420	9.0	55.0	44.8	0.1	0.1	0.5	6.7	21.0	9.9	13.0	14.3	13.8
01 027	...	9	Clay	1 567	14 012	2 138	8.9	81.9	17.8	0.2	0.1	0.5	5.8	17.4	9.1	12.0	14.2	14.2
01 029	...	6	Cleburne	1 451	14 456	2 102	10.0	94.5	5.2	0.2	0.1	0.6	6.6	18.0	9.0	13.4	15.0	14.7
01 031	...	4	Coffee	1 759	42 128	1 038	23.9	80.2	18.6	0.3	0.9	2.0	6.3	17.3	8.9	13.5	15.8	13.9
01 033	2650	3	Colbert	1 540	52 552	871	34.1	81.5	18.1	0.2	0.2	0.6	6.1	16.2	8.5	12.9	15.4	14.6
01 035	...	7	Conecuh	2 204	13 728	2 155	6.2	55.5	44.2	0.2	0.1	0.8	6.4	19.7	8.5	12.4	14.4	12.6
01 037	...	8	Coosa	1 690	11 712	2 294	6.9	63.0	36.8	0.2	0.0	0.2	6.4	16.9	9.8	13.6	14.0	13.4
01 039	...	7	Covington	2 680	37 587	1 148	14.0	85.5	14.2	0.2	0.1	0.6	6.1	17.6	8.1	12.3	14.4	13.5
01 041	...	6	Crenshaw	1 579	13 619	2 165	8.6	71.9	27.8	0.2	0.1	0.4	6.3	18.7	8.4	11.9	14.5	12.9
01 043	...	6	Cullman	1 913	75 661	656	39.6	98.6	1.0	0.2	0.2	0.8	6.4	17.4	8.6	13.2	15.3	14.1
01 045	2180	6	Dale	1 453	49 127	920	33.8	79.0	18.8	0.4	1.9	4.0	8.2	17.8	10.8	16.5	14.1	11.3
01 047	...	4	Dallas	2 540	46 669	955	18.4	40.0	59.7	0.1	0.3	0.4	7.5	21.5	9.7	12.7	14.3	12.5
01 049	...	6	De Kalb	2 015	58 948	802	29.3	97.0	2.1	0.7	0.2	0.8	6.0	18.0	8.5	13.1	15.6	14.1
01 051	5240	2	Elmore	1 610	63 488	753	39.4	75.5	23.9	0.2	0.3	0.9	6.6	18.2	9.9	15.0	16.9	14.0
01 053	...	6	Escambia	2 454	36 671	1 173	14.9	66.8	30.6	2.4	0.2	0.8	6.0	18.2	9.3	13.6	15.6	13.9
01 055	2880	3	Etowah	1 385	103 472	500	74.7	84.4	15.0	0.2	0.4	0.6	5.7	17.3	8.7	12.4	15.9	13.7
01 057	...	6	Fayette	1 626	18 103	1 866	11.1	86.5	13.3	0.0	0.1	0.8	5.8	18.3	8.7	12.3	15.2	14.2
01 059	...	6	Franklin	1 646	29 716	1 382	18.1	94.6	5.0	0.2	0.1	0.7	6.2	17.1	8.5	12.6	14.9	14.5
01 061	...	6	Geneva	1 493	24 968	1 532	16.7	86.6	13.0	0.4	0.1	0.9	6.1	17.4	8.6	12.0	14.8	14.2
01 063	...	8	Greene	1 673	9 756	2 451	5.8	18.6	81.3	0.1	0.1	0.3	7.1	23.0	8.9	12.5	13.8	11.5
01 065	...	6	Hale	1 667	16 870	1 934	10.1	38.5	61.3	0.1	0.1	0.5	7.5	22.1	9.2	12.9	14.0	12.0
01 067	...	6	Henry	1 455	15 787	2 016	10.9	62.5	37.3	0.2	0.1	0.9	6.1	18.3	8.8	11.5	15.3	13.4
01 069	2180	3	Houston	1 503	86 116	586	57.3	73.9	25.0	0.3	0.7	1.0	7.1	19.0	8.8	14.1	16.5	13.7
01 071	...	6	Jackson	2 794	51 535	887	18.4	93.6	4.6	1.6	0.2	0.7	6.0	17.8	8.5	13.0	16.1	15.1
01 073	1000	2	Jefferson	2 882	657 422	74	228.1	62.1	37.2	0.1	0.6	0.7	6.4	16.6	9.3	14.6	16.7	12.8
01 075	...	9	Lamar	1 567	16 034	2 002	10.2	86.9	12.9	0.1	0.1	0.8	6.0	17.5	8.6	12.4	14.5	13.9
01 077	2650	3	Lauderdale	1 734	84 327	599	48.6	89.0	10.5	0.2	0.3	0.7	6.1	16.2	9.9	13.0	15.2	14.1
01 079	2030	3	Lawrence	1 796	33 795	1 262	18.8	78.2	17.0	4.7	0.1	0.7	7.0	17.9	10.4	14.0	14.9	14.4
01 081	0580	4	Lee	1 577	102 164	508	64.8	72.0	25.8	0.1	2.1	1.1	6.1	15.1	23.2	14.0	14.2	11.5
01 083	3440	2	Limestone	1 471	63 037	761	42.9	84.8	14.6	0.3	0.4	0.9	6.5	17.0	9.7	16.0	16.3	14.1
01 085	...	8	Lowndes	1 860	13 029	2 214	7.0	23.8	76.1	0.1	0.0	0.6	8.4	23.9	10.9	13.3	13.4	11.6
01 087	...	6	Macon	1 581	22 993	1 612	14.5	12.7	86.7	0.1	0.5	0.6	6.4	17.5	19.7	11.1	13.3	10.8
01 089	3440	2	Madison	2 085	280 381	198	134.5	75.8	21.6	0.5	2.1	2.1	6.9	15.8	10.5	17.0	15.8	14.1
01 091	...	7	Marengo	2 531	23 158	1 609	9.1	47.0	52.8	0.1	0.1	0.5	7.1	20.9	9.3	12.2	14.6	12.9
01 093	...	7	Marion	1 920	30 464	1 363	15.9	95.9	3.8	0.2	0.2	0.4	6.0	17.0	8.8	12.6	15.0	14.8
01 095	...	4	Marshall	1 469	80 524	627	54.8	97.8	1.7	0.3	0.2	0.7	6.2	16.9	8.3	13.3	15.6	14.4
01 097	5160	2	Mobile	3 194	399 652	145	125.1	65.4	33.1	0.4	1.1	1.4	7.4	19.1	9.7	14.3	16.0	13.0
01 099	...	7	Monroe	2 657	23 960	1 580	9.0	57.9	41.1	0.7	0.3	0.7	7.2	21.2	9.6	12.7	14.7	12.6
01 101	5240	2	Montgomery	2 046	215 813	254	105.5	55.1	43.8	0.2	0.9	1.3	7.2	18.2	11.1	14.8	16.4	12.4
01 103	2030	3	Morgan	1 508	109 665	483	72.7	88.3	11.0	0.3	0.5	1.1	6.6	17.6	8.4	14.6	16.6	14.3
01 105	...	7	Perry	1 864	12 610	2 241	6.8	33.6	66.2	0.1	0.1	0.3	7.2	22.3	12.3	11.0	12.5	12.3
01 107	...	6	Pickens	2 283	21 028	1 715	9.2	56.1	43.6	0.1	0.2	0.4	6.8	19.8	8.6	12.0	13.5	13.3
01 109	...	6	Pike	1 738	28 469	1 428	16.4	62.2	37.0	0.4	0.3	0.6	6.5	17.4	16.9	12.1	13.6	12.2
01 111	...	7	Randolph	1 505	20 263	1 749	13.5	74.5	25.3	0.1	0.1	0.4	6.0	18.3	9.0	12.6	14.3	12.9
01 113	1800	2	Russell	1 661	50 071	906	30.1	58.6	41.0	0.2	0.3	1.0	7.1	17.4	9.9	13.8	15.2	14.0
01 115	1000	2	St. Clair	1 642	63 852	747	38.9	89.6	9.9	0.2	0.2	0.7	7.0	18.2	8.7	14.2	16.7	14.4
01 117	1000	2	Shelby	2 059	146 392	358	71.1	90.5	8.5	0.2	0.7	1.0	7.8	18.1	8.9	17.1	19.4	13.3
01 119	...	7	Sumter	2 344	15 615	2 025	6.7	27.9	71.9	0.0	0.2	0.7	7.3	21.6	13.7	13.0	13.0	10.5
01 121	...	4	Talladega	1 916	77 521	645	40.5	67.0	32.6	0.2	0.2	1.0	6.5	19.3	9.6	13.0	15.9	13.2
01 123	...	6	Tallapoosa	1 860	40 329	1 077	21.7	71.4	28.3	0.1	0.1	0.3	6.1	17.8	9.0	12.4	15.4	13.6
01 125	8600	3	Tuscaloosa	3 432	161 435	321	47.0	70.9	28.0	0.2	0.9	1.0	6.2	16.4	15.7	13.8	13.8	11.9
01 127	...	6	Walker	2 058	71 318	689	34.7	92.5	7.1	0.1	0.2	0.6	6.0	17.9	8.6	12.9	15.8	14.4

1. MSA = Metropolitan Statistical Area. PMSA = Primary MSA. NECMA = New England County Metropolitan Area. See Appendix A for explanation of these concepts. See Appendix B for list of metropolitan areas identified by type, with component counties.   2. County typology code from the Economic Research Service of USDA. See Appendix A for definition.   3. Dry land or land partially or temporarily covered by water.   4. Hispanic persons may be of any race.

Table B. States and Counties — **Population and Households**

STATE County	Population, 1999 (cont'd) Age (percent) (cont'd) 55 to 64 years	65 to 74 years	75 years and over	Percent female	Population — change and components of change, 1980-1999 Total persons 1990	1980	Percent change 1980-1990	1990-1999	Components of change, 1990-1999 Births	Deaths	Net migration	Households, 1990 Number	Percent change, 1980-1990	Persons per household	Percent Female family householder[1]	One person
	16	17	18	19	20	21	22	23	24	25	26	27	28	29	30	31
UNITED STATES	8.6	6.7	6.0	51.1	248 790 925	226 542 204	9.8	9.6	36 820 132	20 934 303	7 478 078	91 947 410	14.4	2.63	11.6	24.6
ALABAMA	9.3	7.1	5.9	52.0	4 040 389	3 894 025	3.8	8.2	568 961	387 158	126 336	1 506 790	12.3	2.62	13.4	23.8
Autauga	8.8	5.6	4.5	51.4	34 222	32 259	6.1	26.1	5 387	2 966	6 488	11 826	16.0	2.88	12.2	17.7
Baldwin	10.7	8.8	6.5	51.2	98 280	78 556	25.1	38.2	14 356	10 149	33 583	37 044	38.4	2.62	10.0	21.4
Barbour	8.6	7.4	6.5	50.7	25 417	24 756	2.7	5.2	3 451	2 531	455	9 218	10.1	2.70	16.5	25.4
Bibb	8.9	5.7	5.9	51.0	16 598	15 723	5.4	18.1	2 492	1 770	2 312	5 745	11.2	2.84	11.3	20.3
Blount	10.1	6.5	5.8	51.0	39 248	36 459	7.6	20.8	5 434	3 822	6 589	14 644	15.5	2.67	7.9	19.0
Bullock	7.4	6.6	6.4	49.9	11 042	10 596	4.2	2.7	1 648	1 253	-61	3 787	9.6	2.74	25.9	27.0
Butler	9.3	7.7	8.0	53.2	21 892	21 680	1.0	-1.7	2 723	2 623	-393	7 935	6.2	2.73	16.2	25.0
Calhoun	9.4	7.7	5.9	51.8	116 032	119 761	-3.1	0.4	15 230	11 208	-4 499	42 983	8.4	2.59	12.4	23.2
Chambers	9.7	8.2	7.8	52.7	36 876	39 191	-5.9	-1.4	4 847	4 341	-905	13 786	2.0	2.65	15.7	23.9
Cherokee	11.3	9.0	6.8	50.9	19 543	18 760	4.2	12.0	2 297	2 116	2 243	7 466	14.8	2.61	8.9	20.4
Chilton	10.2	6.7	6.1	51.3	32 458	30 612	6.0	15.9	4 409	3 305	4 104	12 114	12.8	2.66	10.1	21.1
Choctaw	9.1	6.9	6.7	52.5	16 018	16 839	-4.9	-3.1	2 097	1 597	-972	5 747	6.3	2.77	14.5	23.8
Clarke	8.8	6.4	6.1	52.2	27 240	27 702	-1.7	5.6	4 255	2 671	18	9 506	6.6	2.83	14.8	23.0
Clay	10.2	8.1	9.0	51.9	13 252	13 703	-3.3	5.7	1 628	1 471	651	5 003	5.0	2.62	9.9	23.0
Cleburne	10.4	6.9	6.0	50.7	12 730	12 595	1.1	13.6	1 515	1 324	1 560	4 776	9.2	2.65	8.1	20.0
Coffee	9.6	7.9	6.7	51.1	40 240	38 533	4.4	4.7	5 340	3 632	-131	15 260	13.6	2.61	10.7	21.7
Colbert	10.7	9.0	6.6	52.0	51 666	54 519	-5.2	1.7	6 437	5 173	-215	20 096	4.8	2.56	11.3	22.9
Conecuh	9.9	8.1	8.0	52.6	14 054	15 884	-11.5	-2.3	1 909	1 695	-490	5 259	-3.6	2.65	15.4	24.8
Coosa	10.4	8.2	7.0	50.1	11 063	11 377	-2.8	5.9	1 256	1 086	518	4 017	3.0	2.72	11.8	21.3
Covington	11.0	8.7	8.3	52.7	36 478	36 850	-1.0	3.0	4 681	4 274	819	14 444	5.1	2.50	11.3	25.7
Crenshaw	10.3	8.7	8.3	52.6	13 635	14 110	-3.4	0.1	1 627	1 598	-5	5 262	4.7	2.56	14.2	26.7
Cullman	10.6	7.7	6.7	51.3	67 613	61 642	9.7	11.9	8 434	6 905	6 688	25 605	17.7	2.61	8.2	20.6
Dale	7.4	7.8	6.2	50.7	49 633	47 821	3.8	-1.0	7 369	3 581	-5 418	17 574	15.9	2.69	11.7	21.1
Dallas	8.6	6.8	6.3	54.3	48 130	53 981	-10.8	-3.0	7 556	5 347	-3 564	17 033	-3.2	2.77	23.7	25.4
De Kalb	10.5	7.3	6.8	51.6	54 651	53 658	1.9	7.9	7 384	5 720	2 794	20 968	8.9	2.58	9.2	21.8
Elmore	9.0	5.7	4.8	49.4	49 210	43 390	13.4	29.0	7 704	4 623	11 168	16 532	17.9	2.77	11.2	19.4
Escambia	9.7	7.1	6.6	50.5	35 518	38 440	-7.6	3.2	4 629	3 729	359	12 899	1.9	2.65	14.3	24.2
Etowah	10.7	8.8	6.9	52.6	99 840	103 057	-3.1	3.6	12 188	11 522	850	38 675	4.9	2.55	11.8	24.3
Fayette	9.9	7.6	8.0	52.0	17 962	18 809	-4.5	0.8	2 077	2 068	193	6 859	2.2	2.59	9.7	23.1
Franklin	11.1	7.8	7.3	52.1	27 814	28 350	-1.9	6.8	3 728	3 287	1 575	10 850	6.3	2.53	9.0	23.3
Geneva	10.9	8.1	7.8	51.7	23 647	24 253	-2.5	5.6	2 826	2 749	1 306	9 231	7.7	2.55	9.9	24.2
Greene	8.7	6.7	7.9	54.3	10 153	11 021	-7.9	-3.9	1 644	1 165	-842	3 512	1.7	2.87	25.5	26.1
Hale	8.4	6.7	7.2	53.2	15 498	15 604	-0.7	8.9	2 463	1 784	748	5 397	11.3	2.82	20.3	24.4
Henry	9.8	8.9	8.0	52.8	15 374	15 302	0.5	2.7	1 959	1 695	193	5 769	9.7	2.65	13.5	23.3
Houston	9.3	6.4	5.1	52.5	81 331	74 632	9.0	5.9	11 413	7 091	825	30 844	17.8	2.61	13.3	24.1
Jackson	10.4	7.3	5.7	51.7	47 796	51 407	-7.0	7.8	6 196	4 935	2 618	18 020	1.9	2.63	9.3	20.7
Jefferson	9.3	7.6	6.5	53.3	651 520	671 371	-3.0	0.9	87 793	66 399	-24 237	251 479	3.0	2.54	15.7	26.5
Lamar	10.3	8.1	8.7	52.2	15 715	16 453	-4.5	2.0	1 804	1 787	164	6 005	3.8	2.59	9.5	23.6
Lauderdale	10.3	8.4	6.8	52.3	79 661	80 546	-1.1	5.9	9 799	7 729	2 843	30 905	9.5	2.53	10.1	23.4
Lawrence	9.4	6.7	5.4	50.8	31 513	30 170	4.5	7.2	4 142	2 809	1 046	11 410	16.3	2.75	10.4	19.5
Lee	7.2	4.9	3.8	50.5	87 146	76 283	14.2	17.2	12 445	5 963	8 636	33 097	22.7	2.50	11.1	26.1
Limestone	9.3	6.1	5.1	49.7	54 135	46 005	17.7	16.4	7 541	4 721	6 033	19 685	28.2	2.66	9.8	20.7
Lowndes	7.6	5.5	5.3	53.6	12 658	13 253	-4.5	2.9	2 027	1 253	-372	4 056	8.7	3.11	26.3	21.0
Macon	7.1	7.5	6.5	54.1	24 928	26 829	-7.1	-7.8	3 503	2 668	-2 711	8 483	2.5	2.67	24.2	29.3
Madison	9.1	6.6	4.4	51.0	238 912	196 966	21.3	17.4	36 365	16 774	10 285	91 208	36.0	2.56	10.5	24.0
Marengo	9.3	6.9	6.7	52.7	23 084	25 047	-7.8	0.3	3 435	2 492	-823	8 156	0.5	2.81	17.8	24.2
Marion	10.6	7.7	7.6	50.8	29 830	30 041	-0.7	2.1	3 312	3 167	562	11 521	6.8	2.54	8.8	23.0
Marshall	11.0	7.8	6.6	52.1	70 832	65 622	7.9	13.7	10 368	7 545	7 124	27 761	18.2	2.53	10.1	22.8
Mobile	8.6	6.8	5.1	52.6	378 643	364 980	3.7	5.5	59 505	33 653	-3 933	136 899	11.0	2.71	16.7	23.3
Monroe	8.7	6.7	6.7	51.8	23 968	22 651	5.8	0.0	3 731	2 168	-1 528	8 412	16.2	2.83	15.0	22.8
Montgomery	8.2	6.4	5.3	52.9	209 085	197 038	6.1	3.2	32 975	18 528	-8 360	77 173	12.7	2.61	17.2	26.7
Morgan	9.5	6.9	5.5	51.3	100 043	90 231	10.9	9.6	13 665	8 626	4 887	37 799	20.5	2.60	10.3	22.1
Perry	8.6	6.4	7.4	53.4	12 759	15 012	-15.0	-1.2	1 875	1 452	-540	4 201	-8.6	2.89	22.5	25.0
Pickens	10.6	7.6	7.7	53.3	20 699	21 481	-3.6	1.6	2 746	2 253	-76	7 568	8.2	2.70	16.3	24.1
Pike	8.2	6.6	6.6	53.0	27 595	28 050	-1.6	3.2	3 895	2 977	4	10 314	8.3	2.50	15.6	28.0
Randolph	10.5	8.5	8.0	51.8	19 881	20 075	-1.0	1.9	2 750	2 321	17	7 553	7.2	2.60	11.6	24.0
Russell	9.7	7.5	5.5	52.3	46 860	47 356	-1.0	6.9	6 467	5 022	1 792	17 499	7.7	2.65	17.4	24.5
St. Clair	9.9	6.3	4.6	49.7	49 811	41 205	20.9	28.2	7 110	4 554	11 519	17 666	27.6	2.74	9.0	18.5
Shelby	7.5	4.5	3.3	50.9	99 363	66 298	49.9	47.3	17 244	6 672	34 540	35 985	64.9	2.71	8.0	19.5
Sumter	7.8	6.4	6.6	53.8	16 174	16 908	-4.3	-3.5	2 391	1 626	-1 283	5 545	5.6	2.78	23.2	26.6
Talladega	9.6	7.2	5.7	51.6	74 109	73 826	0.4	4.6	9 996	7 668	1 283	26 448	9.9	2.71	14.2	21.9
Tallapoosa	10.6	8.1	7.1	52.8	38 826	38 766	0.2	3.9	5 405	4 500	742	14 700	10.7	2.60	13.9	23.4
Tuscaloosa	8.6	6.5	5.4	52.0	150 500	137 541	9.4	7.3	20 094	12 057	3 258	55 354	18.2	2.55	13.0	25.8
Walker	10.3	7.5	6.6	51.8	67 670	68 660	-1.4	5.4	8 631	7 498	2 756	25 554	7.3	2.62	10.7	21.9

1. No spouse present.

Table B. States and Counties — Vital Statistics, Health Resources, and Crime

STATE County	Births, average 1996–1998 Total	Rate[1]	Deaths, average 1996–1998 Number Total	Infant[2]	Rate Total[1]	Infant[3]	Physicians,[4] 1998 Number	Rate[5]	Hospitals,[4] 1998 Number	Beds Number	Rate[5]	Medicare enrollees 1999	Serious crimes known to police, 1998[6] Total Number	Rate[7]
	32	33	34	35	36	37	38	39	40	41	42	43	44	45
UNITED STATES	3 904 647	14.6	2 322 064	28 301	8.7	7.2	626 947	232	5 214	895 681	331	38 283 375	12 475 634	4 616
ALABAMA	61 159	14.1	43 345	616	10.0	10.1	7 498	172	110	17 785	409	676 569	200 065	4 597
Autauga	593	14.4	348	6	8.5	10.1	21	50	0	0	0	5 192	1 579	3 794
Baldwin	1 658	12.9	1 224	17	9.5	10.4	239	180	3	235	177	22 449	4 386	3 378
Barbour	348	13.0	280	2	10.4	6.7	20	74	1	52	193	4 389	NA	NA
Bibb	278	15.0	192	4	10.3	14.4	13	69	1	138	729	3 050	NA	NA
Blount	636	14.2	448	5	10.0	7.9	16	35	1	56	121	5 605	827	1 848
Bullock	172	15.2	134	1	11.9	7.8	8	71	1	62	548	1 945	50	440
Butler	289	13.3	268	1	12.3	4.6	12	55	2	91	419	4 015	1 069	4 891
Calhoun	1 626	13.9	1 256	21	10.7	12.9	176	150	3	366	313	20 378	6 902	5 850
Chambers	483	13.1	461	3	12.6	6.2	27	74	1	168	458	6 877	1 342	3 617
Cherokee	271	12.6	248	2	11.5	6.1	14	64	1	45	206	3 682	256	1 177
Chilton	502	13.8	389	4	10.7	7.3	13	35	1	25	68	5 500	826	2 306
Choctaw	228	14.3	174	2	10.9	8.8	7	44	0	0	0	2 775	82	530
Clarke	479	16.8	286	4	10.1	8.4	20	70	3	107	375	4 750	531	1 850
Clay	194	14.0	170	2	12.3	12.1	5	36	1	116	830	2 693	253	1 815
Cleburne	174	12.5	157	1	11.2	5.7	5	35	0	0	0	2 335	236	1 721
Coffee	559	13.2	437	7	10.3	13.1	52	123	2	229	540	6 899	919	2 204
Colbert	699	13.2	564	5	10.7	7.2	84	159	2	280	529	9 891	2 111	3 949
Conecuh	183	13.0	190	3	13.5	18.2	5	36	1	44	315	2 642	203	1 430
Coosa	134	11.6	114	2	9.8	12.4	3	17	0	0	0	2 041	398	3 419
Covington	489	13.1	457	4	12.2	7.5	33	88	3	177	473	7 755	868	2 435
Crenshaw	175	12.8	185	2	13.6	11.4	7	51	1	55	403	2 783	138	1 004
Cullman	949	12.8	764	8	10.3	8.4	79	105	2	215	287	12 788	2 111	2 822
Dale	771	15.7	403	10	8.2	13.0	113	231	1	79	162	9 130	1 088	2 279
Dallas	832	17.6	586	8	12.4	9.6	83	177	2	259	554	8 534	1 936	4 076
De Kalb	813	14.0	646	6	11.2	7.8	37	63	1	103	176	10 005	617	1 060
Elmore	867	14.4	539	8	8.9	8.8	36	58	1	138	223	8 668	1 730	2 849
Escambia	488	13.3	414	7	11.3	13.7	31	84	2	142	386	6 207	1 443	3 925
Etowah	1 337	12.9	1 293	12	12.5	9.2	164	158	2	538	517	19 168	6 371	6 061
Fayette	216	11.9	235	2	12.9	9.3	12	66	1	153	844	3 133	348	1 900
Franklin	416	14.0	369	3	12.5	6.4	6	20	2	133	448	5 935	269	910
Geneva	296	11.9	304	2	12.2	7.9	11	44	1	169	678	4 987	373	1 491
Greene	165	16.6	121	1	12.2	8.1	8	81	1	72	729	1 743	325	3 257
Hale	275	16.6	185	3	11.2	9.7	6	36	1	30	179	3 039	301	1 823
Henry	207	13.1	185	2	11.7	11.3	6	38	0	0	0	2 972	393	2 578
Houston	1 192	14.0	805	13	9.4	10.9	177	206	2	639	744	11 377	2 950	3 506
Jackson	671	13.2	537	5	10.5	8.0	46	90	2	191	372	8 904	1 283	2 543
Jefferson	9 242	14.0	7 259	106	11.0	11.5	2 616	397	13	4 650	705	110 187	42 238	6 379
Lamar	199	12.7	198	3	12.6	15.1	4	25	0	0	0	3 249	NA	NA
Lauderdale	1 035	12.3	861	8	10.2	8.1	148	176	2	627	744	15 255	2 345	2 779
Lawrence	411	12.4	323	4	9.7	8.9	28	84	1	51	152	4 287	186	563
Lee	1 389	14.1	682	12	6.9	8.4	137	136	1	289	288	10 319	6 532	6 581
Limestone	853	14.0	545	4	8.9	5.1	40	64	1	101	162	7 777	989	1 617
Lowndes	221	17.1	141	3	10.9	15.1	4	31	0	0	0	1 718	292	2 250
Macon	347	14.9	276	5	11.8	13.4	30	131	0	0	0	3 541	1 530	6 513
Madison	3 836	14.0	1 956	22	7.2	5.7	498	179	3	859	309	32 777	14 412	5 293
Marengo	334	14.3	254	2	10.8	5.0	14	60	1	99	423	3 532	NA	NA
Marion	367	11.9	366	3	11.8	9.1	30	97	2	189	610	5 528	453	1 556
Marshall	1 184	14.8	871	9	10.9	7.9	78	97	2	192	239	15 322	2 289	2 879
Mobile	6 285	15.8	3 853	78	9.7	12.4	844	211	6	1 762	441	56 706	26 905	6 771
Monroe	384	15.9	240	2	9.9	5.2	17	71	1	65	271	3 785	768	3 151
Montgomery	3 486	16.0	2 035	46	9.3	13.1	522	240	5	1 208	555	30 826	15 152	6 911
Morgan	1 468	13.5	970	17	8.9	11.3	154	141	3	446	408	16 700	4 715	4 388
Perry	195	15.4	151	2	12.0	8.5	7	55	1	76	600	2 033	NA	NA
Pickens	285	13.5	247	1	11.8	4.7	10	47	1	56	266	3 878	193	914
Pike	407	14.3	319	4	11.2	10.7	27	94	1	65	227	4 819	1 165	4 042
Randolph	280	14.0	244	2	12.2	8.3	10	50	2	90	452	4 038	425	2 176
Russell	706	13.9	564	9	11.1	12.3	30	60	1	120	238	8 213	1 880	3 679
St. Clair	780	12.9	537	5	8.9	6.8	33	53	1	72	116	7 486	1 151	1 960
Shelby	2 042	15.1	779	18	5.8	8.8	91	65	1	164	117	11 043	1 301	953
Sumter	230	14.4	179	2	11.2	7.2	7	44	1	33	209	2 447	NA	NA
Talladega	1 080	14.1	849	12	11.1	11.1	65	85	2	237	309	13 661	NA	NA
Tallapoosa	564	14.0	493	7	12.2	12.4	49	121	2	103	254	7 201	1 498	3 703
Tuscaloosa	2 175	13.6	1 336	21	8.3	9.8	333	207	2	680	423	22 174	14 889	9 191
Walker	946	13.4	841	13	11.9	13.4	51	72	1	267	376	14 047	1 504	2 224

1. Per 1,000 estimated resident population, average 1996–1998.   2. Deaths of infants under 1 year old.   3. Deaths of infants under 1 year old per 1,000 live births.   4. Data subject to copyright.   5. Per 100,000 resident population as of July 1 of the year shown.   6. Data for serious crimes have not been adjusted for underreporting; this may affect comparability between geographic areas and over time.   7. Per 100,000 population estimated by the FBI.

Table B. States and Counties — Crime, Education, Money Income, and Poverty

STATE County	Serious crimes known to police, 1998[1] (cont'd) Rate[2] Violent	Property	Education — School enrollment and attainment, 1990 — Enrollment[3] Total	Percent private	Attainment[4] (percent) High school graduate or more	Bach-elor's degree or more	Local government expenditures, fiscal 1997[5] Total current expenditures (mil dol)	Current expenditures per student (dollars)	Money income 1989 Per capita[6] (dollars)	Households Median Dollars	Percent change, 1979–1989 (constant 1989 dollars)	Percent with $100,000 or more	Income and poverty, 1997 Median household income	Percent below poverty level All persons	Persons under 18	Persons 5–17 in families
	46	47	48	49	50	51	52	53	54	55	56	57	58	59	60	61
UNITED STATES	566	4 050	64 987 101	15.6	75.2	20.3	270152.0	5 923	14 420	30 056	6.5	4.4	37 005	13.3	19.9	18.4
ALABAMA	512	4 085	1 056 402	11.0	66.9	15.7	3 436.0	4 595	11 486	23 597	3.0	2.3	30 790	16.2	23.8	22.1
Autauga	394	3 400	9 459	12.2	70.0	14.5	32.5	4 016	11 182	28 337	2.3	1.3	36 803	11.8	17.4	16.8
Baldwin	301	3 077	23 945	13.3	73.2	16.8	95.7	4 471	12 275	25 712	5.0	2.6	35 438	11.1	16.7	16.2
Barbour	NA	NA	6 710	10.2	55.6	11.8	23.1	4 521	9 515	19 389	15.0	2.1	25 925	23.8	32.8	30.7
Bibb	NA	NA	4 201	4.8	51.8	4.7	15.8	4 257	8 973	19 775	-4.1	0.8	28 039	17.4	24.8	24.0
Blount	152	1 696	8 631	4.4	60.5	7.0	31.7	4 050	10 168	22 382	5.5	1.1	32 676	13.3	20.1	19.0
Bullock	114	326	2 890	14.6	49.0	10.0	9.3	4 610	6 922	14 745	7.2	0.3	20 401	29.2	34.2	35.2
Butler	1 002	3 889	5 712	11.7	52.8	8.0	18.3	4 445	7 903	16 054	-6.1	1.0	22 813	23.4	30.8	30.2
Calhoun	795	5 055	30 580	7.5	67.4	14.2	85.0	4 311	10 704	23 802	3.9	1.2	30 432	16.2	24.5	21.4
Chambers	585	3 032	8 735	8.1	54.3	8.9	27.6	4 822	10 000	21 256	3.1	1.2	28 093	16.8	24.7	22.8
Cherokee	74	1 103	3 919	2.3	53.5	6.7	17.9	4 691	9 915	21 368	6.2	1.1	28 922	15.8	25.0	22.5
Chilton	586	1 720	7 600	4.5	56.6	7.5	27.2	4 283	9 826	21 627	8.6	1.0	30 539	16.3	24.2	22.5
Choctaw	78	452	4 178	13.5	54.3	8.5	12.9	4 913	9 622	17 115	0.8	1.1	24 714	22.3	29.6	29.1
Clarke	230	1 620	7 475	10.1	60.3	10.8	25.0	4 475	9 031	19 067	-5.9	1.7	26 898	21.8	29.9	27.5
Clay	122	1 693	2 835	2.5	53.8	7.3	12.5	4 813	9 533	19 252	4.6	1.1	26 809	14.8	21.8	20.6
Cleburne	44	1 677	2 845	2.4	49.8	6.5	10.8	4 258	9 876	21 158	-1.2	0.8	29 104	14.7	21.4	21.3
Coffee	192	2 012	10 543	4.9	67.2	16.5	38.6	4 576	11 286	23 905	0.8	1.6	31 316	14.9	23.1	21.9
Colbert	215	3 734	12 011	6.4	65.2	11.5	45.7	5 192	11 425	22 378	-13.6	2.0	31 413	13.5	21.0	19.9
Conecuh	169	1 261	3 345	7.6	52.7	6.4	10.6	4 555	7 953	15 992	3.6	0.7	22 643	27.4	39.2	35.9
Coosa	696	2 723	2 422	6.2	53.9	6.3	8.5	4 616	9 234	20 279	10.3	0.9	26 531	16.1	23.7	22.6
Covington	659	1 776	8 551	3.5	57.3	9.1	29.7	4 258	9 315	18 394	-2.1	1.0	25 691	19.5	28.3	26.8
Crenshaw	211	793	3 087	5.9	51.3	8.4	10.5	4 384	8 848	16 460	10.3	1.6	23 472	20.7	29.9	28.9
Cullman	235	2 587	15 330	4.7	58.8	7.8	51.5	4 290	10 447	21 672	6.7	1.6	30 705	13.0	18.9	18.2
Dale	268	2 011	13 525	6.1	74.2	13.5	37.2	4 767	10 580	24 091	13.8	1.1	30 476	17.3	26.2	25.8
Dallas	792	3 284	14 011	10.5	59.6	12.2	43.8	4 449	8 344	16 493	-6.9	1.7	23 379	29.7	39.2	37.2
De Kalb	21	1 039	11 794	2.3	53.0	7.1	42.5	4 188	9 604	20 135	4.7	1.2	27 948	15.5	23.4	20.6
Elmore	222	2 627	12 590	10.8	66.5	12.8	43.4	3 816	10 677	26 341	4.9	1.2	35 305	13.1	19.3	17.9
Escambia	862	3 063	8 834	6.0	59.9	7.6	30.5	4 679	8 858	18 472	-4.8	1.3	25 712	20.8	27.8	26.7
Etowah	979	5 082	23 854	8.5	64.1	10.2	77.0	4 638	10 997	22 314	0.0	1.5	28 747	16.9	25.5	22.7
Fayette	344	1 556	4 330	3.8	56.6	8.5	13.6	4 688	9 864	19 844	-0.3	1.2	28 717	15.6	22.3	20.7
Franklin	88	822	5 990	1.6	55.1	6.9	27.3	4 785	9 049	17 907	-11.8	1.1	26 592	16.6	24.5	22.9
Geneva	224	1 267	5 326	3.0	55.4	6.8	18.3	4 322	9 768	20 027	10.0	1.0	26 009	18.7	28.5	26.2
Greene	671	2 586	3 184	8.4	53.8	10.4	10.7	4 840	6 306	11 990	-3.4	0.6	17 602	35.5	44.6	42.3
Hale	412	1 411	4 166	6.0	54.4	8.9	16.2	4 744	8 164	14 508	5.1	1.1	20 704	26.6	34.1	33.3
Henry	269	2 309	3 713	7.7	58.5	8.2	13.3	4 661	9 909	22 130	13.6	1.1	28 276	18.1	28.6	26.2
Houston	308	3 198	21 193	10.3	68.3	15.0	72.5	4 971	12 118	24 813	5.2	2.3	32 086	16.4	24.4	22.8
Jackson	202	2 341	11 493	2.8	58.1	8.0	44.9	4 813	10 144	21 910	-5.1	1.2	30 791	14.7	21.7	20.1
Jefferson	742	5 637	164 480	14.5	73.8	19.9	562.2	4 963	13 277	25 858	-1.5	3.5	35 464	14.5	21.5	19.0
Lamar	NA	NA	3 432	1.5	52.9	6.2	12.5	4 268	9 945	20 618	-3.1	0.8	26 867	18.0	27.2	25.0
Lauderdale	249	2 530	19 867	9.7	67.9	16.4	68.6	5 065	11 685	23 690	-6.3	1.8	33 204	13.3	19.6	18.6
Lawrence	30	533	7 201	3.7	55.6	6.2	30.3	4 832	9 800	21 519	6.1	0.7	31 609	15.7	22.2	22.6
Lee	924	5 657	35 831	5.3	73.2	25.3	76.7	4 764	11 409	21 227	8.7	2.7	31 821	15.0	19.8	18.7
Limestone	142	1 475	12 671	7.4	63.1	13.8	51.5	4 906	11 696	26 875	12.7	1.7	35 981	13.5	20.0	18.1
Lowndes	601	1 649	3 682	10.2	56.7	8.2	14.2	4 793	6 848	15 584	10.9	0.8	20 285	31.5	39.4	39.9
Macon	673	5 840	8 607	30.8	61.9	18.0	19.0	4 558	7 534	15 642	5.5	0.9	21 469	31.9	40.4	39.7
Madison	538	4 755	65 156	13.1	80.2	30.1	209.3	4 879	15 443	33 048	16.3	4.0	43 239	11.0	17.6	16.0
Marengo	NA	NA	5 863	12.6	61.4	11.5	23.0	4 587	9 242	18 663	6.1	1.0	25 504	23.9	32.6	31.7
Marion	155	1 401	6 617	2.6	50.0	6.7	23.5	4 317	9 645	18 455	-8.0	1.2	26 919	16.0	22.5	22.1
Marshall	186	2 693	15 312	4.6	61.5	11.5	65.3	4 543	10 793	21 458	3.0	1.4	29 610	15.0	23.0	21.0
Mobile	703	6 068	104 729	18.3	70.1	15.5	273.8	4 223	11 158	22 994	-6.7	2.3	29 943	20.1	28.8	26.5
Monroe	858	2 293	6 774	9.7	59.2	10.8	22.0	4 320	9 299	21 140	8.8	1.0	28 061	21.6	30.5	28.8
Montgomery	743	6 168	60 057	17.0	75.3	24.2	153.8	4 425	12 806	26 551	6.5	3.1	34 569	17.6	26.2	23.6
Morgan	310	4 078	24 459	8.2	69.4	15.5	99.6	5 176	12 830	28 364	7.2	2.2	36 984	11.4	16.9	15.5
Perry	NA	NA	3 924	23.4	51.0	11.5	11.8	4 921	6 879	13 769	4.6	1.0	18 069	36.6	45.2	43.9
Pickens	128	786	5 247	10.5	56.2	6.6	18.6	4 751	8 564	17 879	2.2	0.6	24 567	23.5	32.9	31.6
Pike	465	3 577	8 613	6.9	59.0	14.3	24.1	5 045	9 423	17 312	6.0	2.1	23 915	24.6	34.4	32.5
Randolph	215	1 961	4 541	2.8	50.3	7.7	16.3	4 250	9 092	19 440	11.6	0.8	25 882	18.6	27.9	25.1
Russell	407	3 272	10 951	9.8	57.0	8.2	40.7	4 757	9 675	20 995	10.4	1.1	28 141	18.6	28.0	26.8
St. Clair	192	1 768	11 798	8.4	61.0	8.5	42.1	4 021	10 596	24 106	-0.7	1.7	33 812	13.9	20.2	19.7
Shelby	105	848	26 069	18.2	78.2	29.0	86.8	4 701	16 237	36 852	20.3	5.8	52 450	6.8	9.8	10.1
Sumter	NA	NA	5 119	9.7	52.4	11.1	14.2	5 072	8 031	12 811	-16.8	0.8	19 199	33.1	40.1	39.1
Talladega	NA	NA	18 839	7.5	60.7	10.2	64.9	4 678	9 700	21 378	1.0	1.1	27 147	19.4	27.6	25.7
Tallapoosa	376	3 327	9 364	3.7	57.8	11.5	31.4	4 404	10 878	22 020	5.3	1.8	27 804	16.9	26.0	23.6
Tuscaloosa	825	8 366	49 658	7.9	69.6	20.0	126.3	4 925	11 406	23 056	4.9	2.5	31 029	17.0	24.2	22.2
Walker	183	2 041	15 510	7.7	56.0	7.2	56.8	4 910	10 105	20 464	-7.4	1.2	28 254	14.4	21.2	20.5

1. Data for serious crimes have not been adjusted for underreporting; this may affect comparability between geographic areas and over time.　2. Per 100,000 population estimated by the FBI.　3. All persons 3 years old and over enrolled in nursery school through college.　4. Persons 25 years old and over.　5. Elementary and secondary education expenditures, local government fiscal years ending between July 1, 1996 and June 30, 1997.　6. Based on population enumerated as of April 1, 1990.

STATE County	Personal income, 1998 Total (mil dol)	Percent change, 1997–1998	Per capita[1] Dollars	Per capita[1] Rank	Wages and salaries[2] (mil dol)	Proprietor's income (mil dol)	Dividends, interest, and rent (mil dol)	Transfer payments Total (mil dol)	Government payments to individuals Total (mil dol)	Social Security (mil dol)	Medical payments (mil dol)	Income maintenance (mil dol)	Unemployment insurance (mil dol)
	62	63	64	65	66	67	68	69	70	71	72	73	74
UNITED STATES	7 351 547	5.9	27 203	X	4 695 309	606 757	1 382 416	983 530	933 859	369 366	384 716	100 887	20 232
ALABAMA	95 956	4.5	22 054	X	60 266	6 664	16 453	15 961	15 198	6 324	5 895	1 768	221
Autauga	890	6.3	21 093	1 355	286	51	128	119	111	49	39	13	2
Baldwin	3 203	8.5	24 109	620	1 143	222	700	440	417	220	141	27	4
Barbour	521	7.1	19 360	1 931	291	40	86	111	106	37	44	19	2
Bibb	346	5.9	18 214	2 291	114	19	42	73	69	27	29	9	1
Blount	917	7.5	19 813	1 776	234	80	119	144	136	64	48	14	2
Bullock	179	5.4	15 833	2 818	81	18	30	50	48	16	20	9	1
Butler	363	3.8	16 776	2 660	169	35	52	98	94	34	39	13	2
Calhoun	2 379	4.0	20 315	1 623	1 577	118	443	445	425	177	157	48	6
Chambers	692	3.3	18 864	2 102	372	34	98	144	138	64	51	15	2
Cherokee	387	2.7	17 749	2 420	114	46	66	81	78	37	28	8	1
Chilton	716	5.1	19 398	1 919	201	52	85	131	125	53	49	14	2
Choctaw	281	3.3	17 780	2 410	200	17	51	68	65	25	25	11	1
Clarke	522	1.3	18 309	2 261	275	35	80	120	115	43	45	19	3
Clay	273	5.0	19 550	1 870	129	27	39	57	54	23	23	5	1
Cleburne	257	4.6	17 968	2 352	85	32	31	47	45	21	17	5	1
Coffee	912	6.0	21 590	1 227	365	92	173	159	152	61	61	15	2
Colbert	1 160	0.3	21 911	1 126	761	68	204	217	207	101	72	18	5
Conecuh	251	2.7	18 104	2 320	137	20	34	68	65	24	25	12	1
Coosa	204	4.6	17 499	2 482	64	10	26	44	42	20	14	6	1
Covington	698	3.5	18 646	2 170	353	65	123	167	161	68	65	17	3
Crenshaw	260	8.3	19 114	2 018	89	49	38	61	59	21	25	9	1
Cullman	1 506	5.9	20 101	1 679	708	179	219	272	259	113	103	24	3
Dale	945	2.9	19 318	1 947	841	47	144	173	165	58	67	21	2
Dallas	827	2.7	17 675	2 445	459	53	135	231	223	69	89	49	4
De Kalb	1 172	5.1	20 118	1 674	594	148	165	221	211	96	79	23	3
Elmore	1 295	6.7	20 889	1 428	345	70	180	221	210	78	97	19	2
Escambia	648	2.4	17 654	2 451	386	49	108	144	138	58	53	17	2
Etowah	2 113	3.8	20 328	1 622	1 127	128	339	440	422	188	163	42	5
Fayette	331	-0.6	18 266	2 266	149	15	64	73	70	32	25	8	1
Franklin	580	2.9	19 553	1 869	287	52	96	130	124	51	53	12	3
Geneva	462	4.1	18 576	2 188	146	59	71	108	104	42	42	12	2
Greene	146	3.3	14 874	2 945	57	10	21	48	46	14	19	11	1
Hale	263	7.0	15 711	2 844	91	24	33	72	69	21	31	13	1
Henry	303	5.8	19 164	1 994	118	26	55	65	62	26	24	8	1
Houston	1 986	5.9	23 203	817	1 402	118	367	287	272	125	90	34	4
Jackson	1 024	3.9	19 952	1 728	510	68	142	181	172	77	64	19	4
Jefferson	18 001	3.7	27 272	282	14 532	1 539	3 439	2 626	2 510	1 077	985	254	28
Lamar	286	3.3	17 883	2 382	151	17	42	66	63	27	25	7	1
Lauderdale	1 727	0.5	20 515	1 549	829	118	347	321	306	149	106	27	7
Lawrence	640	7.7	19 127	2 012	266	61	68	105	99	44	36	14	2
Lee	1 892	3.7	18 831	2 116	1 134	113	350	254	236	106	78	28	4
Limestone	1 270	5.6	20 396	1 600	880	74	205	175	164	75	58	19	3
Lowndes	191	3.0	14 741	2 956	86	16	26	54	51	15	20	13	1
Macon	354	0.2	15 235	2 909	188	13	46	103	99	27	39	19	1
Madison	7 341	6.8	26 404	353	6 241	339	1 418	684	635	283	218	64	10
Marengo	443	4.7	18 959	2 074	228	41	73	99	95	34	39	17	2
Marion	585	4.8	18 961	2 071	364	37	91	123	118	49	48	12	2
Marshall	1 584	2.9	19 755	1 792	953	158	279	293	279	116	116	29	6
Mobile	7 997	3.0	20 048	1 697	5 723	441	1 315	1 476	1 406	552	560	186	21
Monroe	434	0.6	18 094	2 323	306	24	68	95	91	35	36	13	2
Montgomery	5 560	3.6	25 575	432	4 644	366	1 072	787	749	282	275	110	9
Morgan	2 608	3.7	23 882	667	1 590	141	429	401	382	156	174	28	5
Perry	180	4.0	14 190	2 991	72	11	25	64	62	17	27	15	1
Pickens	362	4.5	17 226	2 554	113	37	51	97	93	32	40	15	1
Pike	563	5.2	19 648	1 841	310	70	90	121	116	39	47	18	2
Randolph	363	3.0	18 119	2 317	142	34	56	87	83	35	33	10	1
Russell	945	4.6	18 756	2 139	399	53	117	182	174	71	60	26	2
St. Clair	1 222	6.7	19 698	1 818	345	86	151	182	171	80	63	16	2
Shelby	4 029	8.6	28 601	211	1 566	159	595	297	272	142	91	17	3
Sumter	238	3.8	15 071	2 925	124	20	30	68	65	19	25	15	1
Talladega	1 390	4.0	18 041	2 335	744	65	198	320	306	128	119	40	4
Tallapoosa	819	2.7	20 282	1 630	453	52	144	172	165	71	68	16	2
Tuscaloosa	3 547	4.3	22 063	1 081	2 451	199	602	625	597	219	269	61	6
Walker	1 408	5.0	19 828	1 770	535	124	205	328	316	129	129	28	4

1. Based on the resident population estimated as of July 1 of the year shown.   2. Includes other labor income.

STATE County	Earnings, 1998									Social Security beneficiaries, December 1998			Housing units, 1990	
			Percent by selected industries									Supplemental Security Income recipients, December 1998		
			Goods-related[1]		Service-related and other[2]									
	Total (mil dol)	Farm	Total	Manufacturing	Total	Retail trade	Finance, insurance, and real estate	Services	Government	Number	Rate[3]		Total	Percent change, 1980–1990
	75	76	77	78	79	80	81	82	83	84	85	86	87	88
UNITED STATES	5 302 066	0.8	23.4	16.8	59.7	8.8	9.0	28.4	16.0	43 185 679	160	6 562 639	102 263 678	15.7
ALABAMA	66 930	1.6	27.7	20.5	50.7	9.4	5.6	23.1	20.0	800 875	184	163 308	1 670 379	13.8
Autauga	336	2.3	D	30.3	D	15.2	4.3	15.3	17.3	6 434	153	1 233	12 732	16.1
Baldwin	1 365	0.9	22.4	12.8	58.8	15.7	9.9	23.3	17.8	26 190	197	2 667	50 933	53.1
Barbour	331	4.9	41.9	37.5	35.5	7.9	3.2	13.5	17.7	5 260	196	1 792	10 705	14.8
Bibb	132	2.5	D	19.8	D	8.8	D	14.1	24.5	3 659	193	947	6 404	11.2
Blount	313	13.1	29.7	18.8	40.6	9.7	4.6	15.2	16.5	8 150	176	1 141	15 790	14.0
Bullock	99	16.3	D	D	D	7.4	3.0	13.0	22.6	2 494	220	990	4 458	14.5
Butler	203	4.5	33.7	28.0	46.1	12.5	2.9	19.9	15.7	4 874	225	1 345	8 745	7.7
Calhoun	1 695	0.8	D	19.0	D	9.9	2.7	16.3	36.8	23 521	201	4 389	46 753	9.8
Chambers	406	0.8	51.0	46.3	36.4	10.4	1.7	14.5	11.7	7 892	215	1 422	14 910	3.3
Cherokee	160	13.7	D	19.0	43.6	12.1	6.8	12.6	18.9	4 862	223	688	9 379	14.4
Chilton	253	4.5	D	17.5	D	17.3	3.4	14.1	18.0	6 894	187	1 264	13 883	7.9
Choctaw	217	2.3	D	61.9	D	4.9	1.3	9.1	8.5	3 495	220	1 036	6 789	11.6
Clarke	309	0.3	41.7	37.1	39.3	11.5	4.8	13.1	18.6	5 855	205	1 785	10 853	8.3
Clay	156	9.3	49.8	46.7	22.5	5.1	1.8	8.7	18.4	3 215	230	544	5 608	5.3
Cleburne	116	14.4	D	30.0	D	8.0	1.7	7.4	19.1	2 829	198	504	5 232	9.0
Coffee	457	9.8	30.6	26.5	43.9	12.7	4.0	17.8	15.8	8 212	194	1 466	16 951	16.2
Colbert	829	1.1	33.6	24.9	39.0	8.9	2.6	15.7	26.4	12 055	228	1 824	21 812	4.9
Conecuh	158	3.8	D	20.0	D	5.4	D	12.2	17.2	3 373	241	954	6 207	3.5
Coosa	74	3.7	57.4	52.7	D	5.0	D	10.5	18.2	2 628	225	513	5 113	3.6
Covington	419	6.1	D	23.5	D	10.9	3.1	18.6	15.5	9 071	243	1 631	16 178	6.3
Crenshaw	138	20.0	D	14.2	D	6.3	2.6	14.3	13.7	3 146	231	874	5 938	7.9
Cullman	887	10.7	29.5	23.2	47.6	15.4	3.0	19.2	12.3	14 776	197	2 610	28 369	14.7
Dale	889	1.2	D	23.2	D	4.2	1.5	9.1	53.4	8 177	167	1 775	19 432	17.4
Dallas	512	2.8	31.7	27.1	47.6	10.9	3.4	22.9	17.9	9 964	213	4 880	19 045	-1.6
De Kalb	742	9.5	D	41.9	D	8.9	2.3	13.5	10.8	13 109	224	2 353	22 939	9.8
Elmore	415	0.7	D	21.2	D	11.9	3.5	16.8	24.7	10 071	162	1 877	19 497	13.3
Escambia	434	1.9	37.7	27.3	41.2	10.6	4.2	12.2	19.2	7 631	208	1 470	14 356	5.9
Etowah	1 255	1.6	D	28.9	D	11.3	3.6	25.7	13.4	23 147	223	4 299	41 787	4.8
Fayette	164	0.0	50.9	44.0	26.8	8.2	2.3	8.7	22.4	4 257	235	812	7 555	0.5
Franklin	340	5.6	D	39.0	D	9.6	2.7	17.0	16.7	6 732	227	1 287	11 772	4.7
Geneva	205	17.0	26.5	22.2	38.2	10.2	3.2	10.2	18.4	5 914	237	1 235	10 416	11.5
Greene	68	9.2	19.3	14.9	43.2	7.1	2.5	17.6	28.2	2 154	218	973	4 162	8.5
Hale	115	11.8	33.9	31.1	30.4	7.5	2.0	14.3	23.9	3 223	192	1 241	6 370	14.4
Henry	144	6.5	D	36.5	D	8.9	D	12.0	15.3	3 565	225	788	7 056	13.3
Houston	1 520	0.8	D	16.7	D	12.8	3.9	26.4	14.9	16 122	188	3 414	33 196	16.2
Jackson	578	3.2	D	40.4	D	8.7	2.6	10.4	20.4	9 997	195	1 963	19 768	0.8
Jefferson	16 071	0.0	17.6	10.0	67.9	8.4	10.0	30.7	14.5	125 037	190	22 194	273 097	5.1
Lamar	168	1.9	D	45.2	D	6.9	2.8	12.1	11.8	3 771	240	690	6 617	3.7
Lauderdale	947	0.8	D	21.9	D	13.0	5.3	22.7	21.1	17 808	211	2 554	33 522	9.7
Lawrence	327	11.8	D	D	D	6.4	1.6	8.7	13.7	5 819	174	1 287	12 212	11.4
Lee	1 248	0.6	D	20.3	D	11.6	4.0	16.8	32.9	13 099	130	2 643	36 636	23.5
Limestone	954	2.2	41.3	37.8	D	6.8	1.6	13.5	29.7	9 932	160	1 827	21 455	30.1
Lowndes	102	10.1	D	40.6	D	6.6	2.5	8.4	19.4	2 460	189	1 120	4 792	13.5
Macon	201	2.4	D	1.1	D	5.7	1.5	33.5	50.2	3 965	173	1 276	9 818	6.4
Madison	6 580	0.1	D	22.7	D	7.1	3.0	29.0	28.7	35 921	129	5 515	97 855	37.6
Marengo	269	3.7	38.3	32.3	39.4	8.8	3.2	11.4	18.7	4 562	195	1 541	9 144	2.6
Marion	401	2.4	D	49.4	D	6.6	2.8	13.6	11.6	6 477	209	1 114	12 597	8.6
Marshall	1 111	4.2	D	37.2	D	13.0	3.4	11.7	14.7	15 568	194	3 066	30 225	13.3
Mobile	6 164	0.4	26.1	16.3	57.0	10.1	5.0	27.3	16.5	68 044	170	14 227	151 220	14.6
Monroe	330	1.2	D	49.1	34.5	7.1	1.9	9.8	12.9	4 762	199	1 088	9 633	19.2
Montgomery	5 011	0.2	14.9	9.5	54.0	8.7	8.7	25.7	30.9	35 725	164	9 797	84 525	14.6
Morgan	1 731	1.0	45.6	36.5	40.4	9.5	4.2	16.7	13.1	19 100	175	3 078	40 419	19.5
Perry	83	8.1	D	30.0	D	6.9	3.6	20.5	22.7	2 740	216	1 235	4 807	-4.3
Pickens	149	13.0	26.6	21.2	41.0	7.5	3.4	20.9	19.4	4 520	214	1 474	8 379	7.5
Pike	379	8.2	24.4	18.5	48.2	10.3	3.8	14.7	19.2	5 427	189	1 852	11 506	12.8
Randolph	175	7.0	37.4	34.0	33.5	10.2	2.5	10.8	22.2	4 757	239	850	8 728	11.2
Russell	452	1.3	45.8	36.6	36.7	10.4	3.2	15.6	16.3	9 400	187	2 018	19 633	10.0
St. Clair	431	3.0	D	20.6	D	12.1	3.5	18.2	16.9	9 957	161	1 430	20 382	30.5
Shelby	1 725	0.5	31.5	19.0	58.6	7.8	7.1	21.3	9.4	16 084	114	1 349	39 201	59.1
Sumter	145	8.5	26.1	23.1	38.4	8.3	1.6	15.3	27.0	2 846	181	1 276	6 545	7.2
Talladega	809	1.4	41.8	34.5	36.7	9.5	2.7	18.0	20.1	16 621	217	3 963	29 861	14.6
Tallapoosa	505	0.6	47.6	42.6	39.2	8.4	3.7	21.3	12.5	9 016	222	1 689	17 312	12.8
Tuscaloosa	2 651	0.2	35.3	21.9	39.5	10.2	3.8	17.5	24.9	26 920	167	5 727	58 740	16.7
Walker	658	3.2	24.7	6.9	56.0	15.3	4.4	23.5	16.1	16 028	226	3 308	28 427	5.1

1. Covers mining, construction, and manufacturing.   2. Covers private sector earnings in agricultural services, forestry, and fisheries; transportation and public utilities; wholesale trade; retail trade; finance, insurance, and real estate; and services.   3. Per 1,000 resident population estimated as of July 1 of the year shown.

STATE County	Total	Percent	Median value[1]	With a mortgage	Without a mortgage	Median rent[2]	Rent as percent of income	Substandard units[3] (percent)	Total	Percent change, 1998–1999	Total	Rate[4]	Total	Professional, managerial, and technical	Precision production, craft, and repair
	89	90	91	92	93	94	95	96	97	98	99	100	101	102	103
UNITED STATES	91 947 410	64.2	79 100	21.0	12.9	447	26.4	5.3	139 368 000	1.2	5 880 000	4.2	115 681 202	30.1	11.3
ALABAMA	1 506 790	70.5	53 700	18.4	12.8	325	24.8	4.5	2 145 301	-0.3	102 171	4.8	1 741 794	26.1	13.0
Autauga	11 826	79.7	59 200	17.7	12.3	372	23.5	5.3	22 148	3.1	864	3.9	15 432	23.8	13.2
Baldwin	37 044	78.4	64 200	18.8	12.1	357	23.8	4.4	69 723	1.5	2 367	3.4	43 005	25.1	13.5
Barbour	9 218	70.4	41 400	18.2	13.7	227	21.8	9.7	13 400	5.0	651	4.9	10 313	20.9	13.3
Bibb	5 745	78.5	39 500	19.7	13.0	261	23.0	9.8	7 181	-10.0	495	6.9	6 725	14.4	15.3
Blount	14 644	81.8	46 500	19.1	12.4	258	23.9	4.2	23 640	0.8	675	2.9	17 568	17.2	20.6
Bullock	3 787	72.1	32 300	19.5	15.7	177	32.2	9.6	4 411	-2.9	449	10.2	3 753	18.8	12.1
Butler	7 935	72.9	34 000	19.4	13.5	225	24.7	9.7	9 768	-2.2	1 360	13.9	7 537	16.7	11.8
Calhoun	42 983	70.3	51 600	19.3	12.7	310	23.8	2.3	54 573	-0.3	2 795	5.1	46 899	23.6	14.0
Chambers	13 786	76.0	37 900	16.4	14.0	260	23.4	6.5	16 496	-2.9	782	4.7	16 376	17.3	14.7
Cherokee	7 466	79.8	44 700	20.3	12.6	253	21.5	4.6	10 168	-1.2	505	5.0	8 444	15.6	14.7
Chilton	12 114	81.2	42 800	20.2	13.4	268	24.4	4.7	18 494	0.9	715	3.9	13 648	18.8	19.2
Choctaw	5 747	84.8	37 200	16.5	14.3	182	26.6	13.7	5 929	7.2	537	9.1	5 659	15.9	14.3
Clarke	9 506	79.6	40 300	17.8	13.2	261	20.9	11.1	13 689	-0.9	1 179	8.6	10 305	21.6	13.7
Clay	5 003	75.6	35 500	20.3	12.5	180	17.8	6.7	6 662	-0.4	363	5.4	5 784	14.4	17.1
Cleburne	4 776	81.7	42 600	18.6	12.6	251	23.8	4.8	7 168	-0.8	313	4.4	5 741	15.5	16.7
Coffee	15 260	70.9	53 300	19.0	12.4	325	23.0	2.9	21 953	-0.5	1 036	4.7	16 963	26.2	13.6
Colbert	20 096	75.3	46 300	17.7	12.7	291	25.8	2.8	25 623	-3.2	1 831	7.1	22 098	21.8	16.3
Conecuh	5 259	80.1	33 300	22.1	13.8	203	28.2	11.6	5 878	-12.9	555	9.4	5 118	17.2	11.4
Coosa	4 017	82.7	35 600	19.7	12.2	241	21.7	7.0	5 292	-1.0	295	5.6	4 590	15.3	15.5
Covington	14 444	75.7	34 800	19.3	12.9	233	26.4	4.7	17 230	-1.3	1 408	8.2	15 388	20.4	12.8
Crenshaw	5 262	74.6	31 200	22.8	12.5	193	25.3	8.5	5 358	-5.0	600	11.2	5 479	17.4	11.7
Cullman	25 605	77.8	48 100	19.7	12.6	276	25.6	3.0	39 379	0.7	1 567	4.0	29 952	19.0	16.7
Dale	17 574	61.0	49 400	18.0	12.7	326	22.8	3.6	21 268	0.2	1 039	4.9	18 993	24.6	15.7
Dallas	17 033	62.2	43 800	17.1	13.8	253	29.9	11.2	19 599	-2.2	2 167	11.1	16 630	23.4	11.0
De Kalb	20 968	78.2	39 700	18.9	13.2	254	23.9	3.1	32 368	0.5	1 274	3.9	24 643	15.4	15.4
Elmore	16 532	80.3	58 100	17.7	12.3	309	21.9	5.7	30 140	3.7	1 027	3.4	20 610	24.2	14.2
Escambia	12 899	76.4	41 100	21.5	12.5	256	26.3	4.7	16 551	0.1	1 057	6.4	13 312	18.8	12.1
Etowah	38 675	74.0	42 700	17.8	12.9	281	24.0	2.6	49 625	-0.9	3 466	7.0	40 902	20.8	14.4
Fayette	6 859	76.8	36 800	17.9	12.4	230	23.6	5.8	7 948	-4.9	776	9.8	7 405	16.9	15.8
Franklin	10 850	75.1	38 300	21.0	13.6	233	24.7	2.9	16 849	-2.9	1 241	7.4	11 573	16.7	16.7
Geneva	9 231	78.1	35 800	18.0	12.7	214	22.5	3.9	10 714	-3.1	805	7.5	10 262	15.6	15.4
Greene	3 512	71.1	35 800	24.0	15.1	187	27.1	16.7	3 096	-6.0	385	12.4	3 246	21.0	10.4
Hale	5 397	79.1	34 900	21.3	13.8	164	25.7	14.3	7 016	-6.5	532	7.6	5 442	15.5	13.2
Henry	5 769	78.4	41 300	16.6	12.7	231	21.4	6.4	6 477	2.7	338	5.2	6 513	18.6	13.1
Houston	30 844	67.6	52 600	17.0	12.8	308	23.1	4.1	45 234	1.0	1 697	3.8	38 120	24.9	13.2
Jackson	18 020	76.7	43 200	18.2	12.7	277	23.2	4.0	25 406	-0.2	1 707	6.7	21 337	18.0	15.9
Jefferson	251 479	65.2	58 700	18.2	12.9	358	24.8	3.1	336 933	-1.0	11 517	3.4	289 888	30.9	10.1
Lamar	6 005	75.6	38 900	18.8	12.8	186	22.3	4.7	7 203	-7.0	686	9.5	6 975	13.7	15.8
Lauderdale	30 905	73.4	52 700	18.3	12.2	299	25.1	2.3	41 230	-2.6	2 615	6.3	34 721	23.9	16.1
Lawrence	11 410	80.8	44 300	18.9	13.5	244	23.7	5.0	16 495	0.0	995	6.0	13 646	13.3	19.9
Lee	33 097	58.1	64 900	16.9	12.4	339	35.1	3.7	48 931	-0.4	1 736	3.5	40 043	30.8	10.5
Limestone	19 685	76.2	56 300	17.1	12.4	305	21.8	4.1	28 900	0.0	1 065	3.7	24 389	24.0	16.8
Lowndes	4 056	80.5	34 800	24.7	13.6	195	29.3	16.5	4 128	1.3	526	12.7	4 200	15.3	12.9
Macon	8 483	66.9	43 400	21.7	13.7	285	33.5	8.7	7 667	-2.0	652	8.5	8 523	27.8	9.6
Madison	91 208	65.1	77 900	17.3	12.0	408	22.7	2.8	143 157	0.5	4 689	3.3	119 797	42.4	9.9
Marengo	8 156	77.1	41 800	18.2	13.3	199	27.3	12.5	11 103	1.2	586	5.3	8 768	20.2	14.0
Marion	11 521	75.3	38 300	19.4	12.5	208	23.5	3.0	16 171	-0.4	1 298	8.0	12 294	15.6	17.1
Marshall	27 761	74.2	48 100	19.6	12.6	290	25.3	2.7	40 297	0.2	2 490	6.2	31 405	21.5	16.5
Mobile	136 899	66.8	53 300	19.1	13.0	325	26.7	4.7	199 769	-1.0	10 204	5.1	155 065	27.7	12.8
Monroe	8 412	77.3	43 200	17.5	12.6	274	21.1	9.2	9 644	1.7	1 158	12.0	9 428	17.9	15.4
Montgomery	77 173	62.3	62 600	19.8	12.7	379	24.9	5.3	112 331	0.8	4 209	3.7	92 614	31.9	8.6
Morgan	37 799	71.8	60 900	17.1	12.0	341	22.3	2.9	56 675	0.5	2 437	4.3	46 358	27.0	16.1
Perry	4 201	70.1	31 600	21.7	14.6	188	28.8	14.8	4 568	1.3	429	9.4	4 254	19.3	11.5
Pickens	7 568	76.9	38 000	20.3	13.2	175	26.6	9.9	8 517	-1.7	903	10.6	7 676	17.2	13.4
Pike	10 314	66.4	43 500	17.0	13.3	246	28.6	5.8	13 642	3.9	748	5.5	11 441	22.2	12.6
Randolph	7 553	79.0	36 500	19.6	13.9	239	23.5	6.4	9 405	-3.7	561	6.0	8 546	14.5	14.2
Russell	17 499	65.0	46 200	19.1	12.9	294	25.8	6.9	25 972	0.9	1 254	4.8	19 698	17.7	16.6
St. Clair	17 666	83.1	53 400	19.0	12.5	316	24.3	4.1	30 903	1.2	1 097	3.5	21 593	19.1	19.1
Shelby	35 985	75.6	88 300	18.7	12.1	457	20.8	4.1	80 290	2.6	1 381	1.7	50 246	36.5	10.4
Sumter	5 545	71.0	34 700	23.0	14.3	196	29.4	13.6	5 537	-2.4	601	10.9	5 308	18.6	10.9
Talladega	26 448	75.2	44 800	17.6	13.0	261	26.5	5.4	34 205	-2.8	2 082	6.1	30 069	21.3	14.7
Tallapoosa	14 700	75.1	43 200	17.7	13.0	254	21.6	5.5	20 170	-1.4	1 043	5.2	17 702	20.4	13.0
Tuscaloosa	55 354	61.5	62 100	18.5	12.7	344	29.5	3.8	83 975	0.5	2 492	3.0	65 917	29.2	12.5
Walker	25 554	79.3	42 100	18.3	12.9	282	25.9	3.6	28 774	-3.8	1 802	6.3	26 620	17.6	19.5

1. Specified owner-occupied units. 2. Specified renter-occupied units. 3. Overcrowded or lacking complete plumbing facilities. 4. Percent of civilian labor force. 5. Persons 16 years and older.

Table B. States and Counties — Nonfarm Employment and Agriculture

| | Private nonfarm establishments, employment and payroll, 1998 | | | | | | | | Agriculture, 1997 | | | |
STATE County	Number of establishments	Total	Health Care and Social Assistance	Manufacturing	Retail trade	Finance and Insurance	Professional Scientific and Technical Services	Total (mil dol)	Average per employee (dollars)	Number	Less than 50 acres	500 acres and over	Whose principal occupation is farming (percent)
	104	105	106	107	108	109	110	111	112	113	114	115	116
UNITED STATES	6 941 822	108 117 731	13 757 996	16 945 834	14 240 726	5 770 209	6 051 636	3 309 406	30 609	1 911 859	29.5	18.4	50.3
ALABAMA	100 316	1 604 110	201 111	352 422	226 485	67 933	65 195	40 331	25 142	41 384	33.8	9.2	37.6
Autauga	754	8 100	569	1 803	1 961	256	192	173	21 341	348	26.1	12.4	48.0
Baldwin	3 760	39 662	4 658	5 751	8 018	1 049	1 342	786	19 825	977	45.8	8.4	42.2
Barbour	605	9 773	840	4 098	1 161	276	122	211	21 634	417	14.9	20.1	40.0
Bibb	340	3 636	400	932	565	111	38	74	20 225	177	21.5	15.8	32.8
Blount	716	7 670	848	2 605	1 235	298	149	150	19 608	1 191	39.0	2.7	38.2
Bullock	147	2 414	322	D	281	74	8	45	18 578	277	12.6	33.2	44.4
Butler	525	5 925	655	1 723	968	191	66	117	19 738	440	22.5	7.5	37.0
Calhoun	2 549	39 928	5 189	11 407	6 418	1 045	892	824	20 645	629	39.1	3.8	35.3
Chambers	653	11 930	1 192	5 575	1 436	200	107	269	22 537	324	22.2	15.7	36.4
Cherokee	365	3 520	283	1 193	788	152	32	61	17 497	494	24.7	10.7	38.9
Chilton	774	6 471	626	1 234	1 492	260	87	122	18 889	663	34.5	5.0	35.1
Choctaw	315	3 984	260	D	433	92	62	126	31 526	225	29.8	14.2	33.3
Clarke	747	8 337	821	2 788	1 420	380	117	177	21 199	248	25.4	11.3	25.0
Clay	231	4 461	597	2 564	384	82	32	86	19 269	397	20.9	6.3	42.1
Cleburne	193	2 280	104	1 033	245	53	68	49	21 605	340	27.9	3.8	47.9
Coffee	982	13 006	1 463	4 717	2 250	493	387	236	18 178	788	26.5	10.7	47.5
Colbert	1 376	18 467	2 065	4 805	2 841	476	278	438	23 694	557	37.3	8.4	31.6
Conecuh	266	3 773	330	739	292	69	22	82	21 644	366	22.1	8.5	32.0
Coosa	134	1 773	67	1 209	160	11	10	37	20 746	213	16.9	8.0	32.9
Covington	912	12 157	1 515	4 133	1 985	357	241	240	19 757	899	26.1	7.3	38.9
Crenshaw	272	2 806	333	816	374	81	32	48	17 200	488	19.5	12.9	43.2
Cullman	1 730	22 680	2 567	6 852	3 220	625	390	503	22 197	2 151	47.8	1.8	43.3
Dale	876	10 421	1 238	1 286	1 363	339	227	238	22 807	422	22.5	15.4	42.4
Dallas	984	15 011	2 334	5 042	2 374	451	409	320	21 305	435	25.5	29.4	43.0
De Kalb	1 228	20 861	1 536	11 910	2 425	440	469	418	20 024	2 080	42.9	2.9	38.7
Elmore	1 065	9 782	1 160	2 243	1 768	276	267	182	18 613	560	28.2	10.4	36.6
Escambia	864	11 719	1 161	3 089	1 853	408	163	249	21 224	380	35.0	11.6	40.3
Etowah	2 197	33 001	5 097	8 914	4 886	1 017	656	764	23 145	904	47.3	3.1	31.9
Fayette	355	5 164	757	2 044	682	91	D	110	21 382	305	21.6	8.5	32.8
Franklin	621	11 134	1 200	6 097	989	333	68	204	18 356	833	26.2	5.0	36.9
Geneva	460	5 014	626	1 910	775	175	111	83	16 618	872	26.5	11.2	51.8
Greene	136	1 309	193	348	207	D	D	23	17 747	261	13.8	30.3	38.3
Hale	229	3 140	D	1 602	345	81	31	56	17 702	411	16.3	18.0	39.9
Henry	331	4 046	366	1 489	521	93	68	82	20 159	334	19.8	28.1	49.4
Houston	2 822	46 545	7 397	9 725	7 977	·1 147	982	1 118	24 011	690	31.9	16.2	47.7
Jackson	903	12 829	1 548	6 094	1 783	418	202	296	23 069	1 296	37.8	7.5	35.0
Jefferson	17 672	354 243	51 974	38 118	42 759	24 909	16 910	10 570	29 839	426	52.3	3.1	30.8
Lamar	289	5 004	D	2 481	494	135	42	125	25 026	387	31.0	8.5	29.5
Lauderdale	2 089	30 630	4 332	7 266	5 623	990	914	596	19 456	1 355	40.5	6.0	31.0
Lawrence	418	5 828	706	D	745	206	45	196	33 585	1 287	40.0	4.7	33.1
Lee	2 008	30 235	4 098	6 598	5 836	832	722	633	20 943	347	32.9	10.7	31.7
Limestone	1 087	16 425	1 613	6 672	2 611	346	609	505	30 731	1 127	39.5	10.3	33.3
Lowndes	152	1 602	60	769	222	49	40	50	30 917	330	20.3	30.0	40.3
Macon	255	6 429	D	84	467	85	61	143	22 181	300	16.7	22.7	31.3
Madison	6 996	119 763	12 566	26 727	16 605	3 018	15 643	3 405	28 428	973	40.8	9.5	38.1
Marengo	514	6 375	731	1 686	989	270	68	162	25 429	464	19.4	21.1	35.3
Marion	698	10 627	1 444	5 498	1 081	361	96	236	22 251	677	26.7	3.5	29.7
Marshall	2 004	33 753	3 074	15 185	5 157	809	452	677	20 048	1 583	51.0	1.8	36.9
Mobile	9 380	160 695	21 865	21 861	21 948	5 483	7 054	4 001	24 900	755	55.2	7.8	39.6
Monroe	452	8 786	513	4 282	1 032	175	62	220	25 083	422	27.3	14.0	39.3
Montgomery	6 115	104 467	13 025	10 728	15 405	7 510	5 484	2 636	25 237	654	25.2	20.9	36.5
Morgan	2 808	45 996	4 433	14 697	6 432	1 588	1 100	1 154	25 084	1 214	41.8	4.1	30.1
Perry	157	1 963	288	556	256	66	D	34	17 439	340	19.1	19.4	40.3
Pickens	356	3 320	710	964	649	207	48	63	18 942	454	21.6	12.6	37.9
Pike	678	9 389	853	2 564	1 574	352	124	189	20 120	580	19.5	19.1	43.3
Randolph	400	4 843	639	2 224	699	138	53	86	17 759	599	22.5	7.2	39.9
Russell	882	10 868	1 164	3 454	1 830	318	201	258	23 735	246	27.2	21.5	38.2
St. Clair	1 119	11 944	1 236	3 273	1 667	337	258	250	20 950	594	37.5	3.2	37.4
Shelby	3 449	49 635	3 030	6 140	5 727	3 908	3 460	1 507	30 352	435	38.2	7.1	35.6
Sumter	265	3 402	336	761	486	77	16	69	20 212	369	19.0	26.6	38.2
Talladega	1 386	20 878	2 362	7 490	3 235	621	283	481	23 025	523	29.3	9.2	37.3
Tallapoosa	843	22 801	2 009	5 920	1 785	357	233	514	22 549	344	23.5	7.8	27.6
Tuscaloosa	3 973	65 228	10 317	11 593	10 399	1 790	2 176	1 641	25 164	510	30.8	10.0	37.3
Walker	1 451	16 159	3 351	1 883	3 500	640	501	347	21 450	470	44.3	4.3	34.7

Table B. States and Counties — **Agriculture, Land, and Water**

STATE County	Land in farms Acreage (1,000)	Percent change, 1992–1997	Acres Average size of farm	Total irrigated (1,000)	Total cropland (1,000)	Value of land and buildings Average per farm ($1,000)	Average per acre (dollars)	Value of machinery and equipment Average per farm ($1,000)	Value of products sold Total (mil dol)	Average per farm (dollars)	Percent from — Crops	Live-stock and poultry products	Percent of farms with sales of — $10,000 or more	$100,000 or more	Percent of land owned by Fed. Gov. 1997	Water consumption 1995 (mil gal/day)
	117	118	119	120	121	122	123	124	125	126	127	128	129	130	131	132
UNITED STATES	931 795	-1.5	487	55 058	431 144	450	933	58	196 865	102 970	49.8	50.2	49.6	18.1	20.7	340 751.3
ALABAMA	8 704	3.0	210	77	4 198	298	1 442	36	3 099	74 884	20.4	79.6	31.1	11.3	3.0	7 088.0
Autauga	105	-2.1	301	0	46	374	1 289	36	11	32 108	62.0	38.0	29.9	7.5	0.3	40.3
Baldwin	166	-1.4	169	8	117	425	2 534	44	62	63 757	76.7	23.3	32.9	9.5	1.4	41.9
Barbour	154	-13.1	369	1	63	308	934	48	24	58 180	51.8	48.2	42.7	12.2	0.7	15.0
Bibb	47	-2.3	265	D	16	313	1 403	31	2	12 149	11.5	88.5	19.8	1.7	15.1	3.3
Blount	139	1.1	116	0	73	244	2 137	29	138	115 854	3.7	96.3	32.2	15.8	0.0	51.3
Bullock	169	16.4	609	D	59	568	938	39	25	89 138	65.4	34.6	38.6	10.5	0.0	4.8
Butler	97	1.4	221	0	36	204	1 016	32	31	69 940	10.7	89.3	28.9	9.5	0.0	3.7
Calhoun	77	4.6	123	1	39	260	1 896	32	54	85 667	12.5	87.5	22.9	7.6	21.3	26.3
Chambers	94	-14.3	291	0	28	275	921	27	4	13 176	27.8	72.2	23.8	2.8	1.3	12.6
Cherokee	123	0.9	249	1	69	302	1 328	44	49	99 847	47.9	52.1	34.8	11.5	2.2	6.4
Chilton	99	-0.3	149	1	44	231	1 596	33	9	14 252	62.2	37.8	24.1	3.0	5.1	5.6
Choctaw	65	-4.4	289		16	240	811	32	7	29 641	8.5	91.5	19.6	3.6	0.5	50.8
Clarke	61	0.7	248	0	17	186	910	24	2	8 055	32.4	67.6	17.3	1.2	0.2	25.6
Clay	75	10.7	190	0	32	225	1 245	27	25	62 290	1.7	98.3	31.5	11.1	16.6	2.7
Cleburne	51	8.0	149	D	21	261	1 485	32	46	134 864	3.6	96.4	38.5	19.4	27.0	2.6
Coffee	187	6.8	237	2	95	282	1 319	46	136	172 947	13.2	86.8	47.8	20.8	3.7	16.3
Colbert	116	-16.3	207	2	70	304	1 464	35	33	58 509	36.1	63.9	26.8	9.3	6.5	91.1
Conecuh	88	7.7	241	0	33	257	1 008	21	6	15 599	35.3	64.7	24.0	3.6	0.0	2.2
Coosa	42	1.7	196	0	15	257	1 356	28	1	6 210	19.6	80.4	16.4	0.0	0.0	0.9
Covington	180	8.5	200	D	81	276	1 342	38	66	73 120	29.7	70.3	30.7	12.9	8.1	12.4
Crenshaw	129	16.6	265	2	51	237	1 077	34	54	110 790	9.3	90.7	39.3	17.4	0.0	2.5
Cullman	203	3.0	94	1	115	253	2 647	32	334	155 345	2.6	97.4	39.7	22.6	0.0	20.3
Dale	131	-3.0	310	1	63	365	1 141	57	34	81 371	33.2	66.8	39.8	14.0	12.4	13.8
Dallas	249	6.7	572	1	98	565	969	50	30	68 537	51.8	48.2	36.6	11.5	0.4	57.2
De Kalb	224	6.0	108	1	130	221	1 973	30	234	112 633	4.7	95.3	32.7	16.5	0.0	9.8
Elmore	124	19.5	222	1	62	378	1 649	35	19	34 677	68.9	31.1	24.6	7.3	0.0	6.3
Escambia	87	1.2	229	1	52	256	1 121	53	18	48 285	80.3	19.7	36.3	11.1	4.6	47.0
Etowah	95	10.4	105	0	47	207	2 253	28	55	60 779	6.2	93.8	25.3	9.4	0.0	264.5
Fayette	63	-3.1	206	D	26	219	1 039	38	8	26 719	23.8	76.2	22.0	5.6	0.0	3.1
Franklin	128	-1.2	154	0	61	196	1 167	25	90	108 477	1.2	98.8	30.3	15.0	0.3	5.3
Geneva	207	5.4	237	2	120	288	1 221	45	108	124 033	25.9	74.1	47.5	21.6	0.1	3.9
Greene	123	-3.7	472	D	47	314	795	50	12	44 137	13.1	86.9	32.6	9.6	1.6	320.4
Hale	158	-6.1	384	0	54	369	947	72	32	78 399	6.3	93.7	40.9	16.3	6.7	39.2
Henry	154	-8.1	460	3	90	442	842	69	27	81 435	85.4	14.6	50.0	20.7	0.4	9.5
Houston	198	3.2	287	10	137	340	1 145	62	56	81 579	67.9	32.1	48.7	15.9	0.1	120.0
Jackson	221	8.4	171	1	131	255	1 529	30	64	49 504	20.6	79.4	28.5	9.3	0.1	1 301.6
Jefferson	41	14.8	97	0	19	289	3 009	27	16	37 673	19.4	80.6	17.1	1.6	0.0	90.6
Lamar	71	27.4	184	1	27	244	1 236	27	5	13 926	20.0	80.0	18.6	2.8	0.0	4.2
Lauderdale	212	4.7	156	0	134	227	1 431	27	29	21 461	48.6	51.4	20.5	5.5	0.5	16.1
Lawrence	205	18.5	159	1	139	261	1 578	33	80	62 090	18.6	81.4	26.1	9.1	21.8	62.1
Lee	76	11.5	218	1	22	409	1 847	47	20	57 226	86.4	13.6	30.5	3.5	0.0	18.9
Limestone	254	22.7	225	5	181	480	2 090	47	53	47 051	43.6	56.4	26.4	8.0	3.1	792.3
Lowndes	173	-13.5	524	1	63	515	1 038	40	31	94 012	17.1	82.9	43.9	14.5	2.5	8.5
Macon	127	-7.7	424	2	43	446	1 077	46	10	31 923	70.0	30.0	27.0	5.7	3.1	6.8
Madison	210	-6.0	216	3	158	452	2 114	37	29	29 969	59.6	40.4	29.8	6.1	7.7	54.0
Marengo	198	-0.3	428	0	68	325	877	45	15	32 044	13.5	86.5	34.9	5.8	0.1	31.9
Marion	98	10.2	145	0	44	148	1 144	32	26	38 616	6.8	93.2	21.7	6.5	0.0	6.6
Marshall	146	2.2	92	0	85	205	2 344	29	201	126 742	2.4	97.6	27.9	13.8	0.0	22.4
Mobile	121	16.7	161	2	61	297	2 108	38	63	82 994	84.5	15.5	30.6	9.9	1.2	1 104.5
Monroe	135	22.3	319	2	57	350	1 253	64	23	54 245	77.8	22.2	40.8	12.1	0.2	63.8
Montgomery	241	4.3	368	1	102	582	1 673	44	33	50 633	29.1	70.9	37.2	7.3	0.6	60.0
Morgan	159	1.7	131	0	95	266	2 112	23	78	64 403	7.4	92.6	25.5	9.1	2.7	140.1
Perry	145	0.4	425	D	58	363	795	28	10	30 040	23.8	76.2	29.4	8.2	6.9	8.3
Pickens	123	16.2	271	1	45	309	1 109	39	61	133 424	4.6	95.4	37.4	23.3	0.7	6.2
Pike	174	-3.1	299	3	80	302	1 142	42	61	104 719	21.7	78.3	44.0	17.1	0.0	11.8
Randolph	108	12.6	181	0	43	215	1 092	32	54	90 670	1.2	98.8	30.1	12.9	0.0	2.2
Russell	96	-15.0	391	2	33	448	1 267	40	8	30 799	74.1	25.9	27.6	5.7	2.8	34.1
St. Clair	77	-1.5	129	2	37	281	2 307	31	52	87 084	12.1	87.9	23.9	10.9	0.0	8.7
Shelby	68	-5.0	157	1	39	449	2 594	34	11	25 784	66.6	33.4	23.9	4.6	0.0	719.9
Sumter	175	4.0	474	0	59	389	834	27	11	30 454	7.9	92.1	31.4	6.2	1.0	9.6
Talladega	110	5.3	209	1	60	297	1 555	42	40	77 134	14.9	85.1	31.4	8.4	9.5	77.2
Tallapoosa	78	-1.0	227	0	27	315	1 216	31	7	21 609	17.2	82.7	20.6	3.5	0.4	13.1
Tuscaloosa	100	4.0	196	1	43	294	1 569	29	21	40 254	30.1	69.9	25.1	6.7	1.5	35.3
Walker	55	9.9	117	D	27	262	1 999	26	55	116 522	1.5	98.5	23.6	11.7	0.0	906.7

STATE County	Value of Residential Construction Authorized by Building Permits, 1999		Wholesale Trade, 1997				Retail Trade[1], 1997				Real Estate and Rental and Leasing, 1997			
	New Construction ($1,000)	Number of Housing Units	Number of Establishments	Number of Employees	Sales (mil dol)	Annual Payroll (mil dol)	Number of Establishments	Number of Employees	Sales (mil dol)	Annual Payroll (mil dol)	Number of Establishments	Number of Employees	Receipts (mil dol)	Annual Payroll (mil dol)
	133	134	135	136	137	138	139	140	141	142	143	144	145	146
UNITED STATES	181 439 531	1 664 800	453 471	5 794 312	4 058 480.1	214 915.5	1 118 446	13 991 004	2 460 963.0	237 201.0	288 274	1 702 540	241 268.5	41 597.5
ALABAMA	1 883 871	19 037	6 315	79 229	40 986.3	2 394.7	20 163	231 665	36 623.3	3 381.7	3 664	20 629	2 130.3	396.7
Autauga	13 598	253	29	81	39.7	2.1	161	2 200	367.3	32.1	21	D	D	D
Baldwin	315 758	2 556	151	1 248	493.5	42.9	801	7 850	1 215.3	114.8	195	1 139	81.8	19.6
Barbour	2 873	38	32	228	79.6	4.2	129	1 076	163.2	15.0	14	29	2.1	0.4
Bibb	220	4	15	82	53.2	1.9	60	527	77.2	6.7	9	31	2.5	0.2
Blount	11 039	111	51	D	D	D	143	1 328	202.0	17.8	14	42	2.4	0.4
Bullock	53	1	10	D	D	D	38	289	40.3	3.8	3	13	0.7	0.3
Butler	6 680	142	23	148	58.1	3.6	122	1 023	144.2	13.9	16	35	2.0	0.4
Calhoun	29 152	422	130	1 688	890.9	47.0	578	6 747	982.0	92.5	73	298	24.5	4.4
Chambers	2 018	18	23	158	89.3	3.9	131	1 502	216.0	19.7	20	58	4.0	0.7
Cherokee	2 120	43	22	161	65.2	4.0	88	678	123.1	9.0	10	31	2.8	0.3
Chilton	5 076	41	29	193	64.2	3.8	180	1 510	246.6	21.8	21	37	3.1	0.4
Choctaw	100	1	19	191	108.0	5.7	76	386	69.1	6.1	9	34	1.0	0.2
Clarke	3 545	63	23	125	34.3	2.4	188	1 669	233.2	21.4	30	83	5.0	1.1
Clay	328	6	4	D	D	D	49	376	45.7	4.6	6	22	1.1	0.1
Cleburne	2 945	36	13	D	D	D	47	262	54.0	3.6	1	D	D	D
Coffee	13 404	180	47	259	141.0	5.8	223	2 405	411.0	34.6	23	111	7.0	1.4
Colbert	10 702	142	109	1 173	404.3	30.4	273	2 915	527.5	45.0	42	140	14.5	1.8
Conecuh	725	9	14	102	57.4	2.3	49	275	39.1	3.8	6	10	1.1	0.1
Coosa	45	1	6	D	D	D	28	130	15.3	1.8	5	8	0.7	0.1
Covington	1 770	19	49	585	223.1	12.2	239	1 974	287.9	27.8	23	70	4.8	0.7
Crenshaw	720	6	15	D	D	D	54	444	56.6	5.3	5	24	1.1	0.2
Cullman	10 512	203	95	637	256.1	16.2	360	3 334	650.9	52.1	51	205	20.1	3.6
Dale	5 826	82	37	537	118.6	8.1	182	1 402	201.8	18.1	33	152	9.0	2.4
Dallas	3 967	58	52	517	213.2	12.0	232	2 430	339.0	31.9	41	110	10.0	1.6
De Kalb	3 656	36	62	602	309.6	12.4	269	2 576	343.0	31.3	42	144	10.2	2.1
Elmore	31 795	464	47	309	116.6	7.1	199	1 780	296.8	23.7	35	D	D	D
Escambia	14 351	89	53	532	117.8	11.6	210	2 097	295.1	28.0	15	85	5.2	1.4
Etowah	16 091	195	135	D	D	D	452	4 935	737.8	65.9	68	273	23.9	4.4
Fayette	840	7	11	D	D	D	82	709	111.1	9.4	6	34	0.7	0.2
Franklin	3 773	64	27	287	99.8	6.0	144	1 167	184.5	15.5	17	35	1.8	0.4
Geneva	1 810	26	28	D	D	D	124	813	108.5	10.5	15	29	2.5	0.3
Greene	459	8	10	D	D	D	34	232	31.3	2.7	4	6	0.6	0.1
Hale	2 710	28	5	D	D	D	45	322	52.8	4.1	7	23	3.1	0.4
Henry	3 029	24	15	323	68.0	6.4	81	524	84.6	7.9	8	D	D	D
Houston	25 135	452	206	2 149	705.0	54.8	656	7 801	1 288.2	124.6	94	344	34.4	6.2
Jackson	5 491	58	47	630	203.2	12.8	218	1 849	299.8	25.7	31	94	5.6	1.2
Jefferson	452 641	3 660	1 480	23 438	14 471.2	824.1	3 020	44 165	7 636.8	705.6	650	5 558	811.3	132.8
Lamar	60	2	10	D	D	D	69	445	65.0	5.4	8	15	0.7	0.1
Lauderdale	15 922	171	100	1 959	368.9	45.4	462	5 546	780.8	74.9	79	294	27.4	5.7
Lawrence	656	27	19	D	D	D	100	721	116.6	9.6	4	11	1.0	0.1
Lee	58 936	557	86	727	308.0	18.6	425	5 437	774.4	73.7	84	464	35.0	6.9
Limestone	16 237	169	49	D	D	D	255	2 539	404.6	37.8	34	112	10.5	1.6
Lowndes	412	4	8	82	26.6	1.7	29	215	34.7	3.7	5	10	0.6	0.1
Macon	3 253	78	8	D	D	D	66	437	64.1	6.0	9	D	D	D
Madison	55 614	1 019	471	D	D	D	1 224	17 275	2 610.7	253.6	332	1 623	167.7	30.1
Marengo	1 915	20	25	229	91.8	5.0	140	1 060	143.5	13.6	15	42	4.9	0.7
Marion	3 534	37	44	387	243.7	10.8	138	1 063	167.6	14.2	15	48	2.5	0.4
Marshall	24 712	248	115	1 424	858.8	39.0	560	5 254	1 008.2	73.6	72	390	32.5	6.4
Mobile	166 715	2 111	699	8 647	3 332.9	252.1	1 681	22 860	3 404.5	338.1	380	2 170	228.7	43.3
Monroe	730	8	25	267	85.0	7.1	120	1 086	170.4	15.2	13	58	5.1	1.0
Montgomery	101 262	1 127	392	5 460	2 938.8	157.0	1 144	15 998	2 482.8	237.8	294	2 189	179.1	39.9
Morgan	39 842	413	180	D	D	D	583	6 426	1 136.5	95.5	100	454	40.3	8.2
Perry	530	11	4	D	D	D	41	249	31.7	3.7	5	5	0.4	0.0
Pickens	1 048	15	16	67	33.8	1.5	96	654	130.6	9.0	10	21	1.1	0.2
Pike	9 197	167	44	472	177.5	9.6	145	1 559	223.2	19.9	22	87	8.8	1.0
Randolph	0	0	14	74	30.6	0.9	89	722	89.4	9.3	10	33	2.9	0.4
Russell	16 656	204	23	D	D	D	168	1 797	229.6	23.1	38	120	13.2	1.5
St. Clair	19 149	207	68	D	D	D	205	1 724	270.6	21.5	37	125	8.7	1.4
Shelby	244 143	1 980	372	5 413	3 529.0	186.1	476	5 173	891.3	85.2	114	1 194	122.9	34.2
Sumter	533	8	15	162	47.0	2.9	66	511	69.3	6.0	8	16	1.1	0.2
Talladega	9 655	78	57	618	183.0	17.0	348	3 236	474.7	43.5	51	183	10.5	2.1
Tallapoosa	3 874	46	37	D	D	D	196	1 800	239.0	24.1	32	127	9.1	2.4
Tuscaloosa	78 356	728	185	1 981	858.1	61.1	790	10 852	1 543.2	151.0	161	1 079	82.6	13.7
Walker	4 844	45	69	677	210.8	12.4	359	3 923	679.0	54.7	44	150	11.3	2.2

1. Establishments with payroll.

STATE County	Professional, Scientific, and Technical Services[1], 1997				Manufacturing, 1997				Accommodation and Foodservices, 1997			
	Number of Establishments	Number of Employees	Receipts (mil dol)	Annual Payroll (mil dol)	Number of Establishments	Number of Employees	Receipts (mil dol)	Annual Payroll (mil dol)	Number of Establishments	Number of Employees	Sales (mil dol)	Annual Payroll (mil dol)
	147	148	149	150	151	152	153	154	155	156	157	158
UNITED STATES	615 305	5 212 745	579 542.1	225 376.0	363 753	16 888 016	3 842 061.4	572 101.1	545 060	9 451 056	350 389.1	97 003.9
ALABAMA	7 076	54 413	5 295.6	2 051.4	5 444	352 618	67 970.1	10 187.8	6 955	134 719	3 881.8	1 059.6
Autauga	38	140	13.2	3.2	38	2 130	366.4	69.2	50	1 036	28.0	8.7
Baldwin	225	981	69.6	29.2	138	5 150	809.5	127.1	303	6 337	224.3	61.0
Barbour	40	110	9.8	2.5	41	3 680	689.7	93.0	42	600	17.3	4.3
Bibb	8	32	2.1	0.8	27	1 218	244.3	23.9	12	D	D	D
Blount	34	137	8.3	3.6	60	2 742	403.5	49.5	42	461	13.7	3.3
Bullock	3	D	D	D	6	D	D	D	12	D	D	D
Butler	21	53	2.7	0.7	27	2 044	305.5	41.9	31	595	17.2	4.8
Calhoun	149	702	45.2	13.2	149	10 841	1 504.5	257.8	185	4 262	114.4	31.3
Chambers	23	80	6.5	1.6	40	5 612	765.8	147.2	44	671	18.3	4.6
Cherokee	15	34	2.3	0.6	21	1 194	121.2	25.4	26	251	6.9	1.8
Chilton	25	58	3.2	0.8	54	1 488	162.1	30.3	50	744	18.4	5.0
Choctaw	21	68	4.6	0.8	12	D	D	D	15	233	5.6	1.5
Clarke	29	96	7.4	1.4	32	2 888	540.1	82.7	41	665	17.2	4.2
Clay	9	26	0.8	0.2	15	2 789	212.4	49.6	11	171	3.2	0.8
Cleburne	9	41	1.3	0.3	10	1 108	175.1	19.9	11	D	D	D
Coffee	49	286	17.4	5.3	39	4 725	679.8	89.8	63	1 092	26.9	7.2
Colbert	77	223	17.4	5.3	118	5 581	1 491.6	205.8	103	1 766	46.3	12.3
Conecuh	7	13	1.6	0.3	21	821	98.8	17.0	17	279	6.1	1.4
Coosa	4	D	D	D	11	978	123.1	22.3	3	D	D	D
Covington	56	250	13.9	5.0	30	3 872	388.0	83.5	58	830	20.1	5.0
Crenshaw	8	31	1.8	0.9	15	830	26.1	9.6	11	138	3.8	0.6
Cullman	82	286	17.4	5.0	123	5 994	964.1	147.4	94	1 980	52.8	14.4
Dale	55	209	12.7	4.2	26	1 254	70.0	23.0	82	1 204	26.9	7.0
Dallas	50	355	15.9	7.2	53	5 336	1 064.8	137.6	63	887	26.0	6.3
De Kalb	65	338	25.4	11.6	216	11 774	1 286.0	237.3	100	1 419	40.8	10.7
Elmore	55	193	14.4	4.8	51	2 340	280.3	57.1	62	1 117	33.1	9.1
Escambia	41	122	9.6	2.6	53	3 145	689.5	79.5	56	905	24.0	6.0
Etowah	122	621	36.6	13.7	136	8 775	1 577.0	277.0	169	3 223	85.0	23.6
Fayette	9	20	4.1	0.3	33	2 617	372.0	55.9	18	D	D	D
Franklin	22	66	3.8	0.9	64	5 348	645.8	97.0	44	529	12.7	3.3
Geneva	20	41	3.3	0.9	26	2 123	171.1	34.1	31	343	6.1	1.7
Greene	6	17	0.7	0.2	NA	NA	NA	NA	5	105	1.3	0.5
Hale	10	24	1.1	0.2	16	1 443	210.0	28.4	12	D	D	D
Henry	15	52	3.6	0.9	18	1 410	382.5	33.9	12	D	D	D
Houston	169	1 171	71.3	26.7	125	9 233	1 457.7	231.9	198	3 945	121.6	31.4
Jackson	49	213	17.5	5.8	83	6 557	1 253.5	182.4	70	848	25.9	6.9
Jefferson	1 631	14 700	1 504.0	603.6	817	35 972	7 475.6	1 168.7	1 197	25 250	796.1	225.2
Lamar	12	40	1.7	0.6	22	2 589	313.4	61.3	17	106	3.5	0.9
Lauderdale	148	740	50.3	17.2	115	7 545	885.1	169.9	146	2 558	67.2	19.5
Lawrence	24	35	3.0	0.6	29	D	D	D	33	524	13.5	3.6
Lee	129	589	50.6	16.3	88	7 016	1 232.9	194.9	199	4 165	110.3	29.6
Limestone	62	444	38.7	21.5	69	6 780	1 321.0	309.0	71	1 759	45.9	12.8
Lowndes	7	38	3.9	1.2	10	D	D	D	4	D	D	D
Macon	19	65	3.8	2.7	NA	NA	NA	NA	21	393	9.9	2.3
Madison	773	13 046	1 591.0	598.1	335	28 280	6 991.7	1 079.1	513	11 052	345.9	94.6
Marengo	21	57	4.1	0.8	18	1 701	404.8	54.1	34	465	12.6	3.2
Marion	27	79	7.2	2.2	53	6 423	964.2	154.8	41	D	D	D
Marshall	98	371	25.0	7.7	152	15 773	2 616.7	338.5	157	2 732	70.7	17.9
Mobile	769	5 949	518.6	205.9	445	22 130	5 494.8	835.3	649	12 767	370.1	102.2
Monroe	17	42	3.3	0.7	28	4 748	1 094.0	165.0	34	591	15.2	3.5
Montgomery	553	4 447	418.0	193.5	214	11 343	2 024.6	299.4	422	10 064	279.5	77.1
Morgan	169	949	71.4	28.3	214	D	D	D	185	3 752	101.1	29.0
Perry	7	17	1.2	0.2	8	926	96.9	21.7	11	178	3.0	0.8
Pickens	12	44	2.9	0.6	21	1 051	113.7	18.3	14	D	D	D
Pike	27	105	5.8	2.1	32	2 302	356.1	47.1	58	1 135	25.8	7.2
Randolph	16	36	2.2	0.9	28	2 322	218.5	39.0	27	335	8.0	2.2
Russell	41	126	10.2	2.7	49	3 295	1 000.4	107.8	71	938	32.2	8.3
St. Clair	68	181	11.5	4.0	85	3 180	480.2	85.1	78	1 170	31.3	8.4
Shelby	340	2 445	289.2	105.0	158	6 076	876.6	174.8	188	3 762	120.1	32.5
Sumter	5	15	1.0	0.5	15	832	89.4	17.4	21	327	7.0	2.0
Talladega	69	283	20.3	5.5	100	7 160	1 420.6	201.1	94	1 504	37.9	10.0
Tallapoosa	35	129	14.8	3.8	53	5 868	1 074.8	112.8	51	788	21.4	5.7
Tuscaloosa	257	1 733	134.0	51.6	160	10 738	2 557.9	378.9	317	7 396	202.5	55.6
Walker	76	472	26.2	9.1	72	1 709	381.3	32.8	93	1 650	43.5	10.8

1. Firms subject to federal tax.

Table B. States and Counties — **Health and Other Services and Federal Funds**

STATE County	Health Care and Social Assistance[1], 1997				Other Services[1], 1997				Federal funds and grants, fiscal 1999[2]			
									Expenditures (mil dol)			
										Direct payments for individuals[3]		
	Number of Establish-ments	Number of Employees	Receipts (mil dol)	Annual Payroll (mil dol)	Number of Establish-ments	Number of Employees	Receipts (mil dol)	Annual Payroll (mil dol)	Total	Social Security and government retirement	Medicare	Food stamps and Supplemental Security Income
	159	160	161	162	163	164	165	166	167	168	169	170
UNITED STATES............	531 069	6 231 768	418 602.2	182 256.3	420 950	2 493 574	163 033.3	48 452.6	1 516 775.0	490 502.1	207 501.2	44 147.1
ALABAMA	7 121	104 492	7 116.7	3 104.8	6 329	37 061	2 241.7	659.3	26 775.6	9 222.9	3 713.8	1 011.7
Autauga...........................	43	572	32.7	12.7	43	233	12.2	3.7	154.7	90.7	23.9	7.3
Baldwin............................	222	1 901	105.5	51.8	190	809	49.4	14.7	563.3	331.8	103.7	14.5
Barbour............................	42	446	19.7	7.7	26	93	6.1	1.3	130.2	49.7	28.5	8.9
Bibb.................................	16	140	7.0	2.7	20	194	13.5	3.6	81.9	36.7	19.3	4.7
Blount..............................	30	603	23.3	12.5	62	271	18.0	4.6	138.6	66.8	34.4	6.5
Bullock............................	12	280	12.0	5.3	5	12	0.7	0.1	61.1	19.9	11.1	5.7
Butler..............................	37	669	39.9	14.0	30	144	6.9	1.7	121.7	43.8	24.8	7.8
Calhoun...........................	212	2 824	185.1	81.1	206	855	45.3	15.1	865.7	350.2	102.3	29.3
Chambers........................	53	511	29.3	12.0	39	208	9.2	2.3	157.7	78.7	36.8	9.4
Cherokee.........................	16	110	9.3	4.3	23	61	5.3	1.0	92.4	43.8	19.2	3.7
Chilton............................	32	524	29.8	9.9	44	130	9.6	2.2	142.4	66.5	35.5	7.4
Choctaw...........................	17	234	9.8	3.6	20	60	2.9	0.8	78.9	30.2	15.8	5.1
Clarke..............................	42	557	31.5	11.2	47	169	13.5	3.1	144.7	54.8	25.6	9.8
Clay.................................	17	204	8.6	3.7	14	49	2.2	0.6	64.3	31.3	14.1	2.5
Cleburne.........................	7	45	2.5	1.0	9	49	3.1	1.0	58.0	28.3	9.9	2.0
Coffee.............................	67	415	26.5	10.2	70	324	14.7	3.9	405.2	115.8	36.8	6.8
Colbert............................	101	1 401	99.5	44.4	103	587	33.5	9.3	367.6	143.2	51.1	9.5
Conecuh..........................	14	320	14.7	6.1	21	65	6.0	1.1	76.7	29.9	17.1	5.7
Coosa..............................	7	96	4.0	1.8	4	8	1.3	0.2	46.9	24.4	8.8	2.9
Covington.........................	57	1 086	64.5	24.8	56	271	12.7	3.4	196.5	90.0	43.1	8.8
Crenshaw.........................	12	191	8.9	3.5	13	34	2.3	0.5	77.6	30.1	14.8	4.3
Cullman...........................	120	1 694	110.0	44.5	109	462	27.6	7.0	306.0	157.5	69.9	11.7
Dale.................................	60	649	28.4	12.7	63	226	8.9	2.4	455.5	141.9	41.2	11.7
Dallas..............................	80	1 394	90.6	35.1	62	281	17.2	4.4	314.8	97.3	50.2	30.3
De Kalb...........................	72	986	42.2	19.9	62	213	11.8	2.9	236.5	107.1	48.4	11.5
Elmore.............................	74	829	37.2	15.2	70	235	12.7	3.3	236.5	139.6	40.4	11.4
Escambia.........................	41	537	24.0	10.2	50	171	10.5	2.2	175.1	75.4	34.7	10.5
Etowah............................	199	4 291	312.8	127.9	132	570	34.8	9.5	481.9	236.2	112.4	24.6
Fayette............................	21	81	6.0	2.8	22	58	3.3	0.9	74.4	34.3	16.0	4.2
Franklin...........................	63	929	50.4	20.0	47	152	8.9	2.6	148.4	64.5	33.2	6.4
Geneva............................	25	194	9.0	3.3	27	59	4.1	0.8	136.9	63.2	26.9	6.9
Greene............................	4	34	2.3	0.9	9	43	2.7	0.7	68.6	17.2	9.7	6.2
Hale.................................	10	256	8.6	4.0	11	30	2.9	0.5	86.6	32.9	17.4	6.9
Henry..............................	11	101	3.9	1.7	18	56	4.3	1.4	92.1	36.0	15.4	3.4
Houston...........................	223	4 564	374.4	171.6	183	1 047	56.9	17.2	386.3	183.9	59.8	20.7
Jackson...........................	75	743	36.1	15.2	49	157	10.8	2.6	348.7	109.9	44.3	10.9
Jefferson.........................	1 364	24 333	1 989.4	863.5	1 185	9 418	641.5	191.2	3 775.1	1 459.4	701.5	151.0
Lamar..............................	13	282	11.1	5.4	13	43	3.5	0.6	74.7	34.7	15.4	3.7
Lauderdale.......................	194	2 206	156.7	66.0	131	780	38.0	11.8	364.1	198.5	69.1	14.1
Lawrence.........................	19	308	13.3	6.4	25	107	5.1	1.1	123.9	47.5	22.4	7.0
Lee..................................	133	1 478	104.9	51.3	125	661	35.6	10.2	329.9	144.2	47.2	16.6
Limestone........................	76	797	43.0	15.9	84	347	16.2	5.0	212.9	103.1	37.5	8.8
Lowndes..........................	3	D	D	D	6	10	1.1	0.1	71.1	18.8	9.3	6.8
Macon..............................	18	299	12.9	5.1	21	80	4.3	1.3	196.8	53.0	18.6	10.8
Madison...........................	582	6 750	496.1	209.8	446	2 526	136.6	45.8	3 958.8	633.6	135.2	41.0
Marengo...........................	31	264	15.0	5.3	33	111	5.6	1.6	114.1	39.1	22.3	8.6
Marion.............................	59	498	27.8	12.7	36	106	7.6	1.7	155.1	61.2	29.9	5.6
Marshall...........................	143	1 600	74.9	31.4	107	519	24.9	6.4	358.2	182.2	74.1	14.1
Mobile.............................	561	10 565	742.2	347.1	648	4 775	305.4	91.0	1 900.4	769.8	351.5	114.8
Monroe............................	26	257	12.0	5.6	24	85	4.6	1.3	108.0	42.0	21.9	6.7
Montgomery	537	8 911	638.5	262.8	386	2 760	143.3	44.8	2 514.5	563.4	160.6	66.4
Morgan............................	243	2 955	184.3	85.7	172	1 310	69.3	22.4	489.1	218.5	81.2	15.5
Perry...............................	8	125	4.0	2.0	8	37	2.7	0.4	70.8	21.1	13.5	8.3
Pickens...........................	20	219	9.5	4.3	15	44	3.1	0.8	109.5	42.5	24.0	8.0
Pike.................................	38	702	42.2	16.8	43	136	6.9	2.1	162.5	54.0	29.0	11.0
Randolph..........................	34	353	14.1	6.4	23	66	3.6	0.8	101.4	45.0	20.0	4.6
Russell............................	40	740	35.7	11.7	75	357	20.0	5.9	230.9	125.1	37.9	13.4
St. Clair...........................	59	722	27.4	13.6	64	409	36.7	9.0	185.8	102.1	43.8	9.0
Shelby.............................	191	1 886	113.7	50.7	177	1 096	71.3	22.2	270.5	147.4	62.4	10.1
Sumter............................	7	49	2.7	1.2	10	62	2.2	0.6	81.0	24.8	12.4	8.6
Talladega.........................	90	1 150	68.2	29.3	90	454	31.6	9.0	394.1	167.7	77.4	23.5
Tallapoosa.......................	66	869	43.7	22.0	42	170	12.1	2.9	178.7	86.7	38.1	9.6
Tuscaloosa.......................	274	3 580	223.9	116.2	248	1 481	79.3	25.1	697.6	277.8	120.2	35.1
Walker.............................	118	1 521	81.2	36.1	84	598	36.9	10.0	404.3	179.9	84.2	16.5

1. Firms subject to federal tax.   2. October 1, 1998 to September 30, 1999.   3. State totals may include programs not allocated by county.

	Federal funds and grants, fiscal 1999[1] (cont'd)							Local government finances, 1997				
	Expenditures (mil dol) (cont'd)							General revenue				
	Procurement contract awards			Grants[2]							Taxes	
STATE County											Per capita[3] (dollars)	
	Salaries and wages	Defense	Other	Medicaid and other health-related	Nutrition and family welfare	Education	Other	Total (mil dol)	Intergovern-mental (mil dol)	Total (mil dol)	Total	Property
	171	172	173	174	175	176	177	178	179	180	181	182
UNITED STATES...........	176 085.0	125 433.9	81 726.8	133 659.3	53 120.8	25 139.6	76 631.1	X	X	X	X	X
ALABAMA	2 797.8	2 679.0	1 017.5	2 091.5	650.0	434.1	1 456.1	X	X	X	X	X
Autauga............................	5.2	0.0	1.3	15.1	3.1	1.9	2.2	58.0	33.7	13.8	333	84
Baldwin............................	14.3	5.6	3.1	22.6	7.9	4.2	12.1	282.3	88.5	71.8	557	210
Barbour............................	3.9	0.4	0.7	20.2	3.7	2.5	5.5	55.0	35.2	10.1	376	118
Bibb..................................	3.5	0.0	0.8	9.0	1.9	1.4	4.1	39.0	18.7	4.3	232	80
Blount..............................	4.4	0.3	0.9	15.0	2.3	1.6	4.4	67.7	35.3	10.4	231	150
Bullock............................	1.9	0.0	0.4	14.4	2.6	1.0	2.8	18.0	13.4	3.0	262	117
Butler..............................	2.6	0.0	0.6	16.5	3.5	1.8	18.1	37.8	25.6	7.6	352	124
Calhoun...........................	146.0	151.2	6.7	43.3	9.8	6.3	9.2	301.6	98.5	51.1	436	125
Chambers.........................	3.5	0.1	2.2	17.0	4.1	1.9	2.2	46.6	27.9	11.1	301	101
Cherokee..........................	2.6	6.3	0.6	8.2	1.5	1.0	2.5	30.7	18.7	7.3	336	156
Chilton............................	3.6	0.0	0.9	15.0	2.4	1.6	8.1	45.7	27.5	11.7	321	164
Choctaw...........................	2.0	3.6	0.6	14.1	2.7	1.2	3.5	25.4	16.3	4.1	256	158
Clarke..............................	5.1	1.6	0.7	19.1	4.3	2.0	21.2	50.5	27.0	11.9	416	132
Clay.................................	3.0	0.0	0.5	7.7	1.0	0.6	2.5	46.2	16.6	2.3	167	72
Cleburne..........................	3.3	0.0	0.6	6.6	0.9	0.5	5.2	22.7	15.0	2.8	200	129
Coffee..............................	12.7	192.8	3.3	17.9	3.2	2.6	1.9	69.3	40.2	19.5	464	161
Colbert............................	78.7	3.8	30.9	21.4	3.9	3.9	11.4	146.0	52.8	23.5	443	142
Conecuh...........................	2.2	0.1	0.5	13.8	2.0	1.0	1.9	17.2	12.0	3.2	229	159
Coosa..............................	1.6	0.7	0.4	5.0	1.2	0.5	1.1	13.5	9.9	2.3	201	109
Covington........................	7.4	0.9	1.3	21.9	2.9	3.4	9.9	61.5	36.4	13.5	361	116
Crenshaw.........................	2.9	2.8	0.5	13.9	1.6	0.9	3.3	17.9	12.5	2.3	170	92
Cullman...........................	11.5	0.3	2.1	30.4	4.1	3.4	8.4	144.3	58.0	24.8	334	102
Dale.................................	206.2	14.0	3.9	17.4	3.6	2.4	5.3	75.6	44.3	18.5	376	134
Dallas..............................	8.5	14.8	32.1	45.4	13.9	7.1	4.7	83.2	49.4	25.8	548	195
De Kalb............................	8.0	0.1	1.8	32.1	5.9	2.7	14.7	84.9	47.6	18.5	321	104
Elmore..............................	8.3	0.1	1.8	17.6	5.9	2.4	4.5	87.0	49.7	13.9	231	85
Escambia	4.3	0.0	0.9	19.4	4.0	3.2	10.2	79.3	32.9	11.8	323	118
Etowah............................	16.0	2.3	4.5	50.1	9.0	6.4	11.1	184.1	91.8	58.4	560	152
Fayette............................	2.9	0.0	0.6	10.0	1.3	1.3	2.5	29.0	15.6	3.5	194	75
Franklin...........................	4.2	0.0	0.9	20.1	2.2	1.3	12.9	54.7	37.7	7.8	263	136
Geneva............................	4.6	0.2	0.9	16.0	2.3	1.0	4.2	34.7	21.2	5.8	232	94
Greene.............................	1.9	0.0	0.4	21.1	3.1	1.3	6.0	21.0	13.2	2.5	250	117
Hale.................................	3.0	0.5	0.5	15.4	3.7	1.6	1.5	27.2	19.4	2.6	159	77
Henry...............................	2.6	8.6	3.9	10.9	2.0	0.8	2.1	31.3	17.3	3.9	250	101
Houston...........................	15.4	20.9	12.0	36.3	9.2	5.7	9.8	312.7	73.7	54.4	639	210
Jackson............................	33.6	0.1	98.5	29.6	3.7	2.1	10.4	126.1	47.7	17.7	348	120
Jefferson..........................	464.4	141.1	126.1	406.2	70.7	36.3	138.9	1 671.5	584.3	730.5	1 109	421
Lamar...............................	3.4	0.0	2.1	10.5	1.1	0.8	1.7	30.3	16.4	5.0	318	116
Lauderdale........................	16.1	0.4	3.4	30.7	6.0	3.2	10.6	261.0	65.4	59.4	705	436
Lawrence..........................	4.9	0.3	0.8	18.5	2.7	2.0	7.6	55.9	31.8	5.5	164	79
Lee..................................	21.0	1.3	7.3	28.2	9.7	4.7	38.5	272.4	66.3	53.8	546	170
Limestone.........................	7.1	0.0	5.5	21.5	2.8	1.9	9.2	106.2	45.1	14.3	236	70
Lowndes...........................	2.0	1.4	0.3	12.4	5.3	1.7	10.7	22.1	17.9	2.5	193	87
Macon..............................	45.9	0.8	2.5	29.0	6.9	5.5	16.1	40.5	26.1	10.8	464	161
Madison............................	725.3	1 695.8	519.5	61.6	14.5	16.7	83.3	501.6	180.1	183.1	672	261
Marengo...........................	4.2	4.4	0.6	20.5	4.3	1.8	5.2	61.0	28.2	9.9	421	206
Marion..............................	4.5	0.1	2.3	15.5	1.8	1.4	29.8	45.9	27.8	9.7	314	96
Marshall...........................	15.9	0.1	13.7	36.0	4.5	2.7	7.9	132.7	67.7	33.7	427	119
Mobile..............................	147.6	103.9	30.1	144.1	53.5	28.5	78.8	758.5	332.6	278.8	700	208
Monroe............................	3.0	0.0	0.6	17.7	3.1	3.0	2.2	41.6	29.2	6.9	284	132
Montgomery	435.6	233.2	36.8	160.3	219.2	141.8	464.6	379.7	177.8	151.6	697	169
Morgan............................	91.7	2.3	6.6	35.0	11.4	4.3	11.3	286.2	87.3	56.4	521	231
Perry................................	2.3	0.1	0.3	13.6	4.6	1.6	1.3	23.1	16.3	2.7	215	104
Pickens............................	3.3	0.0	0.6	20.0	4.7	1.6	3.0	41.2	23.1	4.9	235	108
Pike.................................	5.6	12.0	2.1	22.8	8.0	2.1	3.2	43.8	24.6	11.2	393	115
Randolph..........................	2.5	6.2	1.3	13.5	1.9	0.9	2.8	32.5	17.8	6.6	331	208
Russell.............................	5.3	0.1	1.3	26.0	6.5	2.8	7.3	107.8	51.5	24.0	473	160
St. Clair...........................	6.1	0.2	1.7	13.7	4.3	2.3	2.0	78.5	45.4	21.0	346	121
Shelby.............................	16.1	0.4	4.1	13.8	4.4	3.3	5.5	190.1	76.1	79.1	584	238
Sumter.............................	2.6	0.0	1.1	16.1	5.9	2.2	3.5	28.5	18.3	6.7	420	217
Talladega..........................	28.0	20.2	3.8	40.9	13.6	5.8	6.3	116.1	69.1	25.1	326	115
Tallapoosa........................	5.0	0.1	2.4	18.3	5.8	2.7	6.3	74.7	42.5	16.0	399	155
Tuscaloosa.......................	65.1	21.4	13.8	59.5	17.7	11.1	57.0	476.7	141.7	64.7	402	206
Walker.............................	10.8	0.0	2.5	31.5	6.4	4.4	61.9	100.8	59.9	26.4	373	111

1. October 1, 1998 to September 30, 1999.   2. State totals may include programs not allocated by county.   3. Based on the resident population estimated as of July 1 of the year shown.

Table B. States and Counties — Local Government Finances, Government Employment, and Elections

STATE County	Direct general expenditure — Total (mil dol)	Per capita[1] (dollars)	Education	Health and hospitals	Police protection	Public welfare	Highways	Debt outstanding — Total (mil dol)	Per capita[1] (dollars)	Federal civilian	Federal military	State and local	Demo-cratic	Republi-can	All other
	183	184	185	186	187	188	189	190	191	192	193	194	195	196	197
UNITED STATES	X	X	X	X	X	X	X	X	X	2 808 000	2 098 000	17 042 000	48.4	47.9	3.7
ALABAMA	X	X	X	X	X	X	X	X	X	53 249	42 064	288 880	41.6	56.5	1.9
Autauga	75.3	1 822	73.0	0.2	4.8	0.4	4.7	67.7	1 638	86	261	1 786	28.7	69.7	1.6
Baldwin	310.0	2 406	37.2	23.2	4.1	0.1	8.3	265.3	2 059	265	841	7 663	24.8	72.4	2.9
Barbour	52.7	1 967	49.7	12.9	5.8	0.3	6.8	34.0	1 270	62	177	1 999	53.4	45.2	1.4
Bibb	38.3	2 062	46.2	32.0	3.4	0.3	4.8	14.9	801	76	117	1 026	38.2	60.2	1.7
Blount	67.3	1 494	56.6	17.8	3.3	0.4	7.2	42.9	951	94	287	1 581	27.7	70.5	1.8
Bullock	15.5	1 376	63.8	11.8	1.2	0.8	9.0	12.5	1 112	42	70	726	69.2	29.2	1.5
Butler	38.2	1 762	55.6	12.0	4.6	0.0	8.4	9.8	450	45	135	1 073	46.2	52.9	0.9
Calhoun	295.2	2 521	33.0	36.3	3.6	0.0	3.0	131.3	1 121	4 953	3 881	7 422	40.6	57.3	2.1
Chambers	58.6	1 592	56.4	0.8	6.5	0.2	7.2	34.7	944	58	228	1 532	47.5	51.0	1.5
Cherokee	31.0	1 434	66.3	0.4	3.4	0.1	10.2	3.8	177	48	135	1 020	44.7	53.1	2.2
Chilton	53.2	1 464	60.3	1.5	4.9	0.1	15.4	24.8	682	66	229	1 465	31.8	66.7	1.5
Choctaw	26.1	1 642	53.7	3.7	4.0	0.0	13.7	23.4	1 474	32	99	620	50.3	48.8	0.9
Clarke	48.8	1 711	61.1	8.5	5.9	0.1	5.3	25.0	876	94	177	1 876	43.5	55.7	0.8
Clay	36.6	2 649	38.9	36.0	5.1	0.1	5.9	10.1	727	46	87	1 041	34.8	63.2	2.0
Cleburne	21.7	1 543	53.7	9.5	2.0	0.1	12.2	3.7	264	80	89	693	32.7	65.5	1.9
Coffee	66.4	1 582	63.8	0.6	6.0	0.7	7.3	20.2	481	148	263	2 218	33.8	64.4	1.8
Colbert	152.8	2 881	34.0	39.1	3.5	0.1	4.5	84.6	1 595	1 457	328	4 014	49.0	48.8	2.2
Conecuh	17.1	1 215	67.4	0.2	6.3	0.0	8.9	10.8	766	45	94	842	50.1	48.6	1.2
Coosa	12.9	1 116	71.9	0.0	3.3	0.3	9.4	0.4	37	25	72	433	46.1	52.2	1.8
Covington	64.0	1 712	53.5	0.4	5.9	0.2	11.6	34.5	925	147	234	2 063	32.6	65.8	1.6
Crenshaw	19.7	1 444	60.3	1.0	4.8	0.1	12.4	5.2	380	46	85	599	40.3	58.2	1.4
Cullman	135.2	1 821	47.0	26.8	4.4	0.1	8.0	138.1	1 860	257	465	3 453	33.0	64.9	2.1
Dale	78.7	1 603	53.0	4.1	6.6	0.2	7.5	40.9	832	3 004	4 343	2 791	31.0	67.0	1.9
Dallas	75.5	1 601	64.5	0.4	4.9	0.1	3.6	28.0	595	159	290	3 014	59.4	39.9	0.7
De Kalb	85.1	1 473	61.4	2.7	5.5	0.6	6.7	81.9	1 418	171	362	2 571	34.8	63.2	2.0
Elmore	89.2	1 481	55.3	16.2	4.7	0.7	7.2	21.3	354	131	384	3 143	27.9	70.5	1.6
Escambia	75.4	2 065	47.6	27.3	4.2	0.5	6.1	20.0	547	75	236	2 774	38.8	59.8	1.4
Etowah	177.1	1 698	49.6	1.9	7.7	0.3	6.0	79.1	758	308	646	5 086	44.3	53.6	2.1
Fayette	31.5	1 732	52.8	17.0	3.2	0.4	3.7	18.6	1 022	51	112	1 312	39.2	58.7	2.1
Franklin	45.3	1 531	64.2	0.1	4.3	0.2	11.1	22.2	749	93	184	1 791	43.2	55.1	1.7
Geneva	38.1	1 534	60.1	7.2	4.4	0.2	8.7	11.4	458	72	155	1 359	29.0	68.9	2.1
Greene	19.7	1 987	58.6	18.0	2.4	0.4	4.7	5.7	573	33	61	731	79.7	19.3	1.0
Hale	28.3	1 724	65.0	12.3	3.2	0.1	9.9	1.8	108	60	104	907	60.2	38.6	1.2
Henry	32.8	2 097	50.4	0.1	4.9	13.5	7.6	10.6	677	50	98	756	40.1	58.5	1.4
Houston	316.3	3 715	24.9	45.5	3.1	0.3	3.1	317.2	3 725	344	534	6 690	29.4	69.1	1.5
Jackson	122.7	2 417	40.9	33.3	4.2	0.5	5.0	88.3	1 739	458	318	3 244	50.6	47.3	2.0
Jefferson	1 657.6	2 517	36.9	8.9	6.7	1.2	4.4	2 297.0	3 487	9 305	4 536	49 243	47.4	50.6	2.0
Lamar	29.0	1 842	47.9	14.8	3.8	0.1	9.2	17.2	1 090	45	98	615	36.6	61.7	1.7
Lauderdale	243.7	2 893	36.7	36.1	3.1	0.0	3.8	90.7	1 076	324	531	5 999	43.2	54.4	2.4
Lawrence	56.8	1 702	57.1	0.6	3.6	0.4	5.9	188.8	5 656	90	207	1 384	51.7	46.5	1.8
Lee	269.9	2 741	40.6	31.9	3.5	0.0	3.9	317.7	3 225	331	726	12 233	38.1	58.6	3.3
Limestone	117.9	1 943	48.4	28.7	3.9	0.4	4.5	85.6	1 409	1 448	386	4 143	38.0	60.1	1.9
Lowndes	20.2	1 571	76.9	0.2	5.0	0.1	6.2	4.5	348	28	81	718	73.0	26.2	0.8
Macon	39.8	1 706	55.9	0.8	6.6	0.4	9.6	26.7	1 144	1 287	156	1 232	86.8	12.4	0.8
Madison	575.0	2 112	41.6	1.9	5.3	0.1	5.0	799.8	2 937	13 817	3 131	19 355	42.5	54.8	2.6
Marengo	71.8	3 055	38.0	36.2	2.6	0.3	4.5	27.0	1 147	78	162	1 728	50.4	48.8	0.8
Marion	42.8	1 390	64.1	0.2	4.1	0.2	6.5	26.7	867	75	192	1 502	39.1	58.8	2.1
Marshall	124.8	1 581	56.8	3.8	6.0	0.2	5.8	110.0	1 395	340	498	4 971	37.1	61.0	1.9
Mobile	725.5	1 822	44.1	4.7	6.0	0.3	6.7	958.2	2 406	2 477	3 261	24 677	42.0	55.9	2.1
Monroe	46.1	1 907	52.6	10.4	4.7	0.0	14.3	18.8	778	57	149	1 437	41.8	57.6	0.6
Montgomery	367.4	1 689	48.2	2.1	8.5	0.2	8.5	365.4	1 679	6 832	6 363	24 329	50.3	48.3	1.4
Morgan	297.4	2 746	36.8	34.7	4.1	0.1	2.9	240.5	2 221	289	679	6 691	37.6	60.4	2.0
Perry	22.7	1 794	58.5	19.8	2.8	0.1	7.7	5.8	461	30	87	616	69.5	29.9	0.6
Pickens	41.0	1 955	51.5	2.6	3.1	0.0	9.4	83.1	3 963	58	131	946	48.5	50.4	1.1
Pike	51.9	1 813	52.5	2.0	5.2	0.2	10.0	37.8	1 323	93	183	2 385	41.3	57.5	1.2
Randolph	33.2	1 668	56.4	13.2	4.7	0.1	7.4	13.1	659	48	124	1 388	39.1	58.9	2.0
Russell	97.2	1 917	46.0	15.7	4.8	0.1	4.4	47.5	936	97	312	2 367	56.8	41.9	1.2
St. Clair	76.9	1 264	69.8	0.4	5.0	0.0	5.7	36.2	595	104	384	2 165	26.9	71.1	2.0
Shelby	175.6	1 296	55.9	2.4	7.0	0.3	6.2	147.5	1 089	257	872	4 830	21.2	76.7	2.1
Sumter	28.3	1 768	53.7	0.9	6.4	0.5	10.3	16.3	1 018	43	98	1 410	72.5	26.8	0.7
Talladega	122.2	1 590	59.2	4.0	4.4	0.1	5.7	87.5	1 138	527	475	4 628	44.3	54.2	1.5
Tallapoosa	75.1	1 871	51.3	13.4	5.1	0.2	4.3	83.0	2 068	98	252	1 933	38.0	60.3	1.6
Tuscaloosa	431.2	2 682	35.6	32.7	3.9	0.0	4.1	333.6	2 075	1 477	1 025	18 547	40.9	56.6	2.5
Walker	104.2	1 473	58.7	0.3	4.8	0.0	7.6	62.4	882	197	440	3 277	45.3	52.6	2.1

1. Based on the resident population estimated as of July 1 of the year shown.

Table B. States and Counties — Land Area and Population

STATE/ County code	MSA/ PMSA/ NECMA code[1]	County Type[2]	STATE County	Land area,[3] (sq km) 1990	Total persons	Rank	Per square kilometer	White	Black	Am. Indian, Eskimo, Aleut	Asian and Pacific Islander	Percent Hispanic[4]	Under 5 years	5 to 17 years	18 to 24 years	25 to 34 years	35 to 44 years	45 to 54 years
					1	2	3	4	5	6	7	8	9	10	11	12	13	14	15
			ALABAMA—Cont'd															
01 129	...	8	Washington	2 799	17 742	1 884	6.3	64.9	30.0	5.0	0.1	0.5	6.9	20.6	9.6	13.3	14.8	13.6
01 131	...	9	Wilcox	2 302	13 414	2 182	5.8	29.6	70.4	0.0	0.0	0.4	7.4	24.4	9.4	11.7	13.2	11.7
01 133	...	6	Winston	1 592	24 459	1 553	15.4	99.2	0.4	0.2	0.2	0.6	6.1	16.9	8.6	12.8	15.6	15.1
02 000	...	X	ALASKA	1 477 268	619 500	X	0.4	75.2	3.9	16.4	4.5	4.0	8.0	23.7	11.4	11.7	17.2	14.7
02 013	...	NA	Aleutians East Borough	18 091	2 179	3 050	0.1	33.3	1.1	47.0	18.5	7.2	7.0	19.6	14.9	18.7	17.6	13.1
02 016	...	NA	Aleutians West Census Area	11 401	3 913	2 922	0.3	61.5	4.4	15.1	19.0	13.1	6.0	12.3	19.2	23.8	19.3	10.6
02 020	0380	3	Anchorage	4 397	257 808	210	58.6	80.2	6.3	7.1	6.4	5.2	7.5	21.4	12.7	12.3	17.4	15.6
02 050	...	7	Bethel	106 416	16 215	1 993	0.2	14.1	0.5	84.6	0.8	0.9	11.5	31.7	11.6	10.4	13.1	10.4
02 060	...	NA	Bristol Bay	1 345	1 061	3 110	0.8	54.9	0.2	43.9	1.0	2.4	9.1	27.2	8.3	11.2	16.7	15.3
02 068	...	NA	Denali Borough	33 414	1 883	3 069	0.1	90.4	1.6	7.0	1.0	2.3	5.7	18.9	4.8	10.5	19.0	18.7
02 070	...	NA	Dillingham	47 829	4 565	2 866	0.1	23.4	0.2	75.6	0.9	1.1	12.2	29.6	9.5	10.9	14.7	11.1
02 090	...	5	Fairbanks North Star	19 069	84 366	598	4.4	82.1	6.7	7.8	3.4	4.9	8.5	23.0	14.4	13.1	16.7	13.1
02 100	...	9	Haines	6 105	2 288	3 034	0.4	84.7	0.0	14.2	1.1	1.5	5.6	21.9	7.4	9.0	17.6	17.7
02 110	...	5	Juneau	6 717	30 192	1 370	4.5	79.1	1.1	14.2	5.6	3.3	7.4	22.1	9.8	10.9	19.4	16.7
02 122	...	5	Kenai Peninsula	41 644	48 993	925	1.2	90.1	0.5	8.0	1.4	2.4	7.1	24.7	9.0	10.0	17.9	15.4
02 130	...	7	Ketchikan Gateway	3 159	14 097	2 125	4.5	80.2	0.4	14.8	4.7	2.3	6.9	22.8	10.1	10.2	16.6	17.1
02 150	...	7	Kodiak Island	16 738	14 350	2 108	0.9	66.0	0.9	18.3	14.8	5.6	9.2	23.8	11.6	13.4	18.1	12.9
02 164	...	NA	Lake and Peninsula Borough	61 208	1 748	3 080	0.0	21.2	0.3	78.0	0.6	1.7	11.2	30.8	8.2	11.2	13.4	10.5
02 170	...	6	Matanuska-Susitna	63 957	57 945	812	0.9	92.5	0.9	5.6	1.0	2.5	7.6	27.3	7.5	9.9	18.3	15.1
02 180	...	7	Nome	59 603	8 908	2 515	0.1	22.4	0.1	76.8	0.7	1.3	11.2	31.4	10.1	10.5	14.9	10.7
02 185	...	NA	North Slope	227 559	7 089	2 671	0.0	19.3	0.7	74.3	5.6	2.4	12.2	29.8	10.3	11.1	14.4	12.4
02 188	...	NA	Northwest Arctic Borough	92 884	6 720	2 706	0.1	12.4	0.2	86.4	1.0	0.8	13.6	34.3	10.9	9.9	11.9	8.3
02 201	...	NA	Prince of Wales-Outer Ketchikan	18 970	6 694	2 710	0.4	56.9	0.1	42.4	0.5	2.2	8.1	27.1	9.0	9.9	17.4	15.8
02 220	...	NA	Sitka	7 463	8 193	2 577	1.1	72.0	0.4	22.8	4.7	2.4	7.0	24.2	10.3	10.8	15.7	16.0
02 232	...	NA	Skagway-Hoonah-Angoon	20 660	3 489	2 952	0.2	57.9	0.1	41.3	0.7	1.5	7.8	28.9	6.8	9.8	17.6	15.0
02 240	...	NA	Southeast Fairbanks	67 325	5 852	2 782	0.1	78.6	4.1	15.6	1.7	3.2	7.8	27.8	9.1	10.4	16.8	15.2
02 261	...	7	Valdez-Cordova	95 688	10 229	2 403	0.1	81.5	0.6	13.8	4.2	3.3	7.1	22.6	9.6	10.6	18.9	16.7
02 270	...	9	Wade Hampton	44 351	6 963	2 680	0.2	5.4	0.2	93.8	0.5	0.6	14.9	34.8	11.8	8.9	10.6	7.9
02 280	...	7	Wrangell-Petersburg	15 044	6 802	2 697	0.5	76.8	0.1	21.2	1.8	2.1	7.6	23.6	8.5	10.2	16.9	15.1
02 282	...	NA	Yakutat Borough	17 586	770	3 125	0.0	50.6	0.0	46.5	2.9	1.4	6.8	26.9	9.2	11.8	16.9	14.5
02 290	...	NA	Yukon-Koyukuk	406 944	6 188	2 757	0.0	25.5	0.2	73.5	0.7	0.8	9.7	31.1	6.8	9.0	15.4	11.6
04 000	...	X	ARIZONA	294 333	4 778 332	X	16.2	88.7	3.7	5.5	2.1	22.7	8.1	19.9	9.6	13.2	15.4	12.3
04 001	...	5	Apache	29 023	68 562	710	2.4	21.9	0.2	77.7	0.2	5.1	9.8	30.7	9.8	12.3	13.6	10.0
04 003	...	4	Cochise	15 980	112 754	467	7.1	90.6	5.5	0.9	3.1	34.5	7.7	21.0	8.8	11.7	14.5	12.7
04 005	2620	5	Coconino	48 224	114 498	461	2.4	66.9	1.9	30.0	1.2	12.6	8.1	23.7	15.1	13.4	16.4	11.0
04 007	...	4	Gila	12 349	49 051	923	4.0	86.4	0.3	12.8	0.5	22.6	6.7	19.9	6.1	8.7	13.7	13.4
04 009	...	7	Graham	11 991	31 998	1 314	2.7	83.0	2.0	14.5	0.5	30.1	8.6	25.6	9.6	11.1	13.7	11.1
04 011	...	7	Greenlee	4 784	9 018	2 505	1.9	96.7	0.4	2.6	0.3	49.7	7.9	27.7	5.6	10.8	15.3	13.2
04 012	...	7	La Paz	11 654	14 867	2 074	1.3	81.3	1.1	16.5	1.1	24.0	6.9	17.3	6.2	8.9	11.8	11.0
04 013	6200	0	Maricopa	23 838	2 861 395	4	120.0	91.3	4.3	2.0	2.5	20.4	8.3	19.5	9.7	14.0	15.9	12.6
04 015	4120	2	Mohave	34 479	134 222	391	3.9	96.2	0.4	2.4	1.0	6.7	6.3	16.4	5.8	9.5	13.1	14.1
04 017	...	5	Navajo	25 780	98 327	524	3.8	46.2	1.1	52.2	0.5	8.9	9.4	28.5	8.7	11.9	14.1	11.1
04 019	8520	2	Pima	23 794	803 618	53	33.8	90.2	3.9	3.4	2.4	29.6	7.7	18.4	10.5	13.0	15.6	11.9
04 021	6200	1	Pinal	13 908	152 301	337	11.0	85.6	3.6	10.1	0.7	34.2	8.4	21.7	8.1	11.4	14.2	11.8
04 023	...	6	Santa Cruz	3 206	39 150	1 108	12.2	98.4	0.7	0.2	0.7	81.9	10.5	25.3	8.8	11.8	14.6	10.9
04 025	...	4	Yavapai	21 040	152 957	335	7.3	97.3	0.3	1.7	0.6	8.1	5.5	16.6	6.1	8.4	14.2	13.5
04 027	9360	3	Yuma	14 282	135 614	388	9.5	93.0	3.5	1.6	1.9	46.4	9.0	22.0	10.2	12.3	13.1	12.1
05 000	...	X	ARKANSAS	134 875	2 551 373	X	18.9	82.6	16.1	0.5	0.7	2.1	7.0	18.9	9.9	12.8	14.8	12.8
05 001	...	7	Arkansas	2 560	20 717	1 727	8.1	75.1	24.5	0.2	0.2	0.7	6.6	20.2	7.7	11.8	15.1	12.6
05 003	...	7	Ashley	2 386	24 287	1 563	10.2	69.3	30.2	0.2	0.3	2.2	7.0	20.5	9.3	11.6	14.7	13.6
05 005	...	7	Baxter	1 436	36 664	1 174	25.5	99.3	0.1	0.4	0.3	1.4	4.7	14.6	5.7	8.8	12.6	12.4
05 007	2580	3	Benton	2 184	138 424	380	63.4	97.8	0.2	1.4	0.7	3.5	7.1	18.3	8.6	13.0	14.5	12.4
05 009	...	7	Boone	1 531	31 846	1 320	20.8	99.1	0.1	0.6	0.3	1.6	6.5	17.9	8.3	11.9	14.2	13.3
05 011	...	7	Bradley	1 685	11 409	2 311	6.8	65.9	33.9	0.2	0.0	3.8	6.6	18.9	9.0	11.0	13.6	13.1
05 013	...	9	Calhoun	1 627	5 657	2 795	3.5	71.3	28.4	0.1	0.2	1.3	7.0	19.5	9.2	12.5	14.5	12.8
05 015	...	7	Carroll	1 642	22 516	1 633	13.7	98.7	0.2	0.7	0.4	2.7	6.4	17.7	7.4	11.4	15.1	13.5
05 017	...	7	Chicot	1 668	14 858	2 076	8.9	40.3	59.1	0.2	0.2	2.5	7.4	22.5	10.2	11.0	12.7	12.2
05 019	...	7	Clark	2 242	21 403	1 686	9.5	73.4	25.9	0.2	0.4	1.4	6.0	16.3	17.3	11.0	12.8	11.8
05 021	...	7	Clay	1 656	17 025	1 928	10.3	99.5	0.1	0.3	0.1	1.1	5.8	16.8	7.8	11.0	13.0	13.8
05 023	...	6	Cleburne	1 433	23 296	1 603	16.3	99.4	0.1	0.4	0.2	1.3	5.2	15.8	6.4	10.7	12.6	14.5
05 025	...	8	Cleveland	1 548	8 558	2 547	5.5	84.1	15.5	0.2	0.2	1.5	6.3	19.3	9.1	11.4	15.0	14.7
05 027	...	7	Columbia	1 984	24 686	1 542	12.4	60.9	38.6	0.2	0.3	0.7	6.7	18.4	12.2	11.8	13.0	12.1

1. MSA = Metropolitan Statistical Area. PMSA = Primary MSA. NECMA = New England County Metropolitan Area. See Appendix A for explanation of these concepts. See Appendix B for list of metropolitan areas identified by type, with component counties. 2. County typology code from the Economic Research Service of USDA. See Appendix A for definition. 3. Dry land or land partially or temporarily covered by water. 4. Hispanic persons may be of any race.

Table B. States and Counties — **Population and Households**

STATE County	55 to 64 years (16)	65 to 74 years (17)	75 years and over (18)	Percent female (19)	1990 (20)	1980 (21)	1980–1990 (22)	1990–1999 (23)	Births (24)	Deaths (25)	Net migration (26)	Number (27)	Percent change, 1980–1990 (28)	Persons per household (29)	Female family householder[1] (30)	One person (31)
ALABAMA—Cont'd																
Washington	9.0	6.5	5.7	51.3	16 694	16 821	-0.8	6.3	2 493	1 644	255	5 709	8.3	2.91	12.7	19.2
Wilcox	8.3	7.0	6.8	53.3	13 568	14 755	-8.0	-1.1	2 142	1 524	-726	4 415	1.2	3.02	23.4	23.9
Winston	10.9	7.6	6.4	51.0	22 053	21 953	0.5	10.9	2 743	2 302	2 017	8 544	10.7	2.55	8.3	21.5
ALASKA	7.6	3.5	2.1	47.5	550 043	401 851	36.9	12.6	98 976	22 291	-15 046	188 915	43.7	2.80	9.6	22.1
Aleutians East Borough	6.5	2.2	0.4	36.4	2 464	1 643	50.0	-11.6	241	55	-470	533	0.0	2.97	9.6	22.5
Aleutians West Census Area	4.0	3.3	1.5	32.7	9 478	6 125	54.7	-58.7	816	126	-7 301	1 845	0.0	3.02	5.1	14.3
Anchorage	7.8	3.4	1.9	48.7	226 338	174 431	29.8	13.9	41 771	8 469	-5 075	82 702	36.8	2.68	10.1	22.9
Bethel	5.7	3.5	2.0	47.7	13 660	10 999	24.2	18.7	3 734	690	-483	3 605	34.3	3.72	14.7	18.2
Bristol Bay	7.4	3.3	1.5	45.9	1 410	1 094	28.9	-24.8	180	27	-591	407	65.4	2.81	6.1	27.0
Denali Borough	6.9	11.9	3.6	41.6	1 682	NA	NA	12.0	210	39	9	NA	NA	NA	NA	NA
Dillingham	6.6	3.1	2.3	48.1	4 010	3 232	24.1	13.8	1 051	206	-277	1 215	0.1	3.30	13.3	18.6
Fairbanks North Star	6.7	2.8	1.7	47.0	77 720	53 983	44.0	8.6	14 480	2 738	-7 685	26 693	46.5	2.76	8.1	22.4
Haines	10.1	6.8	3.8	46.8	2 117	1 680	26.0	8.1	216	126	86	791	38.3	2.59	5.1	24.4
Juneau	7.7	3.4	2.6	48.7	26 752	19 528	37.0	12.9	4 075	1 051	392	9 902	40.8	2.66	10.2	23.6
Kenai Peninsula	8.9	4.8	2.3	46.5	40 802	25 282	61.4	20.1	6 463	1 876	3 669	14 250	66.7	2.79	8.4	21.8
Ketchikan Gateway	8.9	4.1	3.4	47.0	13 828	11 316	22.2	1.9	2 132	752	-1 160	5 030	26.2	2.70	9.2	24.0
Kodiak Island	6.2	2.9	1.8	45.2	13 309	9 939	33.9	7.8	2 605	442	-1 496	4 083	34.9	3.03	8.1	18.4
Lake and Peninsula Borough	7.0	5.0	2.7	45.3	1 666	1 384	20.5	4.9	372	97	-182	509	0.0	3.22	11.0	21.6
Matanuska-Susitna	8.6	3.5	2.1	47.4	39 683	17 816	122.7	46.0	6 574	1 868	13 454	13 394	135.0	2.92	8.7	19.0
Nome	6.0	2.9	2.4	45.7	8 288	6 537	26.8	7.5	2 040	504	-929	2 371	36.2	3.41	14.6	21.7
North Slope	6.0	2.4	1.5	46.3	5 986	4 199	42.4	18.4	1 385	303	33	1 673	70.7	3.44	14.8	20.8
Northwest Arctic Borough	5.8	2.9	2.4	47.1	6 106	4 831	26.5	10.1	1 635	327	-695	1 526	0.0	3.96	17.8	17.6
Prince of Wales-Outer Ketchikan	7.1	3.6	1.9	44.6	6 278	3 822	64.3	6.6	929	235	-269	2 061	83.9	2.92	9.1	21.4
Sitka	7.9	4.3	3.8	46.8	8 588	7 803	10.1	-4.6	1 275	440	-1 303	2 939	20.5	2.81	9.1	20.9
Skagway-Hoonah-Angoon	7.9	3.8	2.4	46.1	3 679	NA	NA	-5.2	360	151	-386	NA	NA	NA	NA	NA
Southeast Fairbanks	6.9	3.9	2.2	46.2	5 925	5 676	4.2	-1.2	1 025	250	-1 015	1 909	14.6	2.96	7.0	19.7
Valdez-Cordova	8.6	3.6	2.3	45.4	9 920	8 348	19.2	3.1	1 261	416	-558	3 425	27.4	2.73	7.5	24.2
Wade Hampton	5.4	3.8	1.8	48.3	5 789	4 665	24.1	20.3	2 097	279	-645	1 368	44.5	4.23	15.8	16.9
Wrangell-Petersburg	8.9	5.2	4.0	46.5	7 042	6 167	14.2	-3.4	888	401	-737	2 514	21.3	2.73	7.6	22.9
Yakutat Borough	7.1	4.4	2.3	44.8	725	NA	NA	6.2	95	37	-13	NA	NA	NA	NA	NA
Yukon-Koyukuk	7.2	5.4	3.9	45.0	6 798	7 873	-14.7	-9.0	1 066	386	-1 419	2 748	20.5	2.88	12.6	27.7
ARIZONA	8.4	7.1	6.0	50.5	3 665 339	2 716 546	34.9	30.4	670 677	317 200	683 188	1 368 843	43.0	2.62	10.4	24.7
Apache	6.3	4.5	3.1	50.7	61 591	52 108	18.2	11.3	13 738	3 409	-3 271	15 981	26.5	3.80	20.4	16.8
Cochise	9.2	8.3	6.0	49.4	97 624	85 686	13.9	15.5	15 742	8 423	5 900	34 546	19.2	2.68	10.2	23.3
Coconino	6.2	3.7	2.5	50.9	96 591	75 008	28.8	18.5	17 067	4 101	5 043	29 918	36.7	2.99	11.5	19.9
Gila	11.7	11.3	8.6	50.9	40 216	37 080	8.5	22.0	6 251	5 083	7 821	15 438	20.2	2.56	8.8	24.3
Graham	8.4	6.1	5.7	48.9	26 554	22 862	16.1	20.5	4 204	2 202	3 526	7 930	20.4	3.09	12.2	19.9
Greenlee	9.6	5.8	4.0	49.0	8 008	11 406	-29.8	12.6	1 462	577	128	2 809	-22.1	2.85	8.0	22.7
La Paz	9.9	16.1	11.9	48.2	13 844	12 557	10.2	7.4	1 428	1 246	949	5 348	0.0	2.56	9.5	25.0
Maricopa	8.0	6.3	5.7	50.6	2 122 101	1 509 175	40.6	34.8	405 257	175 848	430 870	807 560	48.2	2.59	10.2	25.0
Mohave	13.3	13.4	8.2	49.9	93 497	55 865	67.4	43.6	16 169	13 611	38 620	36 801	74.3	2.47	7.5	21.8
Navajo	7.6	5.4	3.4	50.2	77 674	67 629	14.9	26.6	16 258	5 458	9 370	22 189	21.2	3.44	15.3	16.8
Pima	8.4	7.7	6.7	51.1	666 957	531 443	25.5	20.5	105 788	60 931	90 365	261 792	33.9	2.49	10.9	27.8
Pinal	9.2	8.9	6.4	48.9	116 397	90 918	28.0	30.8	19 600	11 325	27 231	39 154	37.8	2.83	11.4	19.9
Santa Cruz	7.7	6.3	4.2	52.5	29 676	20 459	45.1	31.9	7 469	1 801	3 892	8 808	46.8	3.35	14.9	16.6
Yavapai	12.9	13.1	9.8	50.8	107 714	68 145	58.1	42.0	13 224	14 857	46 327	44 778	68.3	2.35	7.0	24.9
Yuma	8.1	8.8	6.3	49.3	106 895	76 205	40.3	26.9	27 020	8 328	16 417	35 791	19.9	2.87	9.4	19.0
ARKANSAS	9.6	7.5	6.7	51.7	2 350 624	2 286 357	2.8	8.5	330 123	244 180	121 082	891 179	9.2	2.57	11.1	24.0
Arkansas	10.0	8.1	8.0	52.7	21 653	24 175	-10.4	-4.3	2 616	2 504	-938	8 389	-5.8	2.54	12.1	25.8
Ashley	9.4	7.2	6.7	52.1	24 319	26 538	-8.4	0.1	3 269	2 555	-630	8 890	-1.9	2.70	11.9	21.9
Baxter	13.9	14.4	12.9	52.1	31 186	27 409	13.8	17.6	2 933	5 119	8 175	13 486	20.6	2.28	6.1	24.5
Benton	11.1	8.6	6.3	51.0	97 530	78 115	24.8	46.3	16 314	10 121	34 360	37 555	31.2	2.55	6.9	20.0
Boone	11.2	8.3	8.4	52.1	28 297	26 067	8.6	12.5	3 906	3 245	3 334	11 131	13.8	2.50	7.9	23.2
Bradley	10.2	8.5	9.1	52.4	11 793	13 803	-14.6	-3.3	1 379	1 674	-33	4 545	-9.8	2.54	13.3	25.2
Calhoun	9.7	7.4	7.4	52.1	5 826	6 079	-4.2	-2.9	607	696	-46	2 185	3.0	2.63	10.5	24.0
Carroll	11.5	8.8	8.1	51.6	18 623	16 203	15.1	20.9	2 641	2 074	3 432	7 550	17.4	2.45	8.4	24.4
Chicot	8.7	7.6	7.8	52.6	15 713	17 793	-11.7	-5.4	2 067	1 849	-1 012	5 557	-7.3	2.81	21.7	26.8
Clark	9.2	7.8	8.0	52.0	21 437	23 326	-8.1	-0.2	2 566	2 352	-157	7 907	-2.8	2.42	11.2	27.4
Clay	12.4	9.6	9.9	52.0	18 107	20 616	-12.2	-6.0	1 968	2 476	-467	7 504	-5.1	2.38	7.7	26.5
Cleburne	13.9	11.6	9.2	51.5	19 411	16 909	14.8	20.0	1 951	2 460	4 447	7 926	23.7	2.41	6.7	22.0
Cleveland	10.3	6.8	6.9	51.4	7 781	7 868	-1.1	10.0	898	749	664	2 868	3.6	2.69	9.5	19.5
Columbia	9.6	7.7	8.5	53.3	25 691	26 644	-3.6	-3.9	3 205	2 983	-1 092	9 638	1.1	2.57	13.8	26.8

1. No spouse present.

Table B. States and Counties — **Vital Statistics, Health Resources, and Crime**

STATE County	Births, average 1996–1998 Total	Rate[1]	Deaths, average 1996–1998 Number Total	Infant[2]	Rate Total[1]	Infant[3]	Physicians,[4] 1998 Number	Rate[5]	Hospitals,[4] 1998 Number	Beds Number	Rate[5]	Medicare enrollees 1999	Serious crimes known to police, 1998[6] Total Number	Rate[7]
	32	33	34	35	36	37	38	39	40	41	42	43	44	45
ALABAMA—Cont'd														
Washington	238	13.5	182	2	10.3	9.8	9	51	1	100	566	2 739	107	603
Wilcox	229	16.9	172	2	12.7	10.2	5	37	1	32	238	2 467	70	621
Winston	294	12.3	255	2	10.7	6.8	13	54	1	45	186	4 475	272	1 161
ALASKA	9 970	16.4	2 576	69	4.2	6.9	1 125	183	16	1 324	216	40 062	29 331	4 777
Aleutians East Borough	NA	NA	NA	NA	NA	NA	NA	NA	0	0	0	NA	NA	NA
Aleutians West Census Area	NA	NA	NA	NA	NA	NA	NA	NA	0	0	0	NA	NA	NA
Anchorage	NA	NA	NA	NA	NA	NA	655	257	2	603	236	16 091	NA	NA
Bethel	NA	NA	NA	NA	NA	NA	22	138	0	0	0	692	NA	NA
Bristol Bay	NA	NA	NA	NA	NA	NA	NA	NA	0	0	0	595	NA	NA
Denali Borough	NA	NA	NA	NA	NA	NA	NA	NA	0	0	0	NA	NA	NA
Dillingham	NA	NA	NA	NA	NA	NA	8	176	0	0	0	NA	NA	NA
Fairbanks North Star	NA	NA	NA	NA	NA	NA	162	192	1	224	266	4 631	NA	NA
Haines	NA	NA	NA	NA	NA	NA	NA	NA	0	0	0	297	NA	NA
Juneau	NA	NA	NA	NA	NA	NA	57	189	1	59	195	2 414	NA	NA
Kenai Peninsula	NA	NA	NA	NA	NA	NA	53	110	3	128	267	3 755	NA	NA
Ketchikan Gateway	NA	NA	NA	NA	NA	NA	28	208	1	71	528	1 233	NA	NA
Kodiak Island	NA	NA	NA	NA	NA	NA	19	131	1	49	337	413	NA	NA
Lake and Peninsula Borough	NA	NA	NA	NA	NA	NA	NA	NA	0	0	0	NA	NA	NA
Matanuska-Susitna	NA	NA	NA	NA	NA	NA	50	89	1	36	64	NA	NA	NA
Nome	NA	NA	NA	NA	NA	NA	9	100	1	35	388	536	NA	NA
North Slope	NA	NA	NA	NA	NA	NA	5	70	0	0	0	NA	NA	NA
Northwest Arctic Borough	NA	NA	NA	NA	NA	NA	4	59	0	0	0	NA	NA	NA
Prince of Wales-Outer Ketchikan	NA	NA	NA	NA	NA	NA	4	57	0	0	0	384	NA	NA
Sitka	NA	NA	NA	NA	NA	NA	27	324	1	28	336	724	NA	NA
Skagway-Hoonah-Angoon	NA	NA	NA	NA	NA	NA	NA	NA	0	0	0	328	NA	NA
Southeast Fairbanks	NA	NA	NA	NA	NA	NA	4	70	0	0	0	437	NA	NA
Valdez-Cordova	NA	NA	NA	NA	NA	NA	12	117	2	43	418	NA	NA	NA
Wade Hampton	NA	NA	NA	NA	NA	NA	NA	NA	0	0	0	384	NA	NA
Wrangell-Petersburg	NA	NA	NA	NA	NA	NA	6	88	2	48	704	662	NA	NA
Yakutat Borough	NA	NA	NA	NA	NA	NA	NA	NA	0	0	0	NA	NA	NA
Yukon-Koyukuk	NA	NA	NA	NA	NA	NA	NA	NA	0	0	0	335	NA	NA
ARIZONA	76 421	16.8	37 319	567	8.2	7.4	10 161	218	61	10 161	218	658 193	306 985	6 575
Apache	1 320	19.2	423	9	6.1	7.1	70	102	2	50	73	6 250	488	685
Cochise	1 668	15.0	984	12	8.8	7.2	137	122	5	250	222	17 627	5 016	4 360
Coconino	1 816	16.0	495	17	4.4	9.4	277	243	2	141	123	12 388	6 648	5 916
Gila	683	14.2	583	6	12.1	8.3	72	147	2	93	190	10 930	1 950	3 932
Graham	483	15.5	259	5	8.3	9.7	23	73	1	42	133	4 170	860	2 698
Greenlee	158	16.8	62	1	6.6	4.2	5	54	0	0	0	1 049	NA	NA
La Paz	[7]NA	[7]NA	[7]NA	[7]NA	[7]NA	[7]NA	21	141	1	39	262	3 455	548	2 969
Maricopa	47 680	17.7	20 697	355	7.7	7.4	6 302	226	27	6 245	224	355 749	197 329	7 140
Mohave	1 867	14.5	1 705	20	13.3	10.5	170	130	4	283	217	31 913	7 117	5 387
Navajo	1 710	18.1	645	17	6.8	9.8	106	109	2	83	86	10 686	2 920	3 001
Pima	11 377	14.6	6 979	73	9.0	6.4	2 446	309	9	2 078	263	123 255	60 504	7 566
Pinal	2 165	15.1	1 361	18	9.5	8.5	90	61	2	316	215	24 042	NA	NA
Santa Cruz	784	21.1	205	3	5.5	4.2	27	71	1	80	210	4 600	1 369	3 622
Yavapai	1 607	11.1	1 793	13	12.4	8.1	261	176	2	186	125	34 156	6 106	4 416
Yuma	[7]3 104	[7]21.5	[7]1 127	[7]19	[7]7.8	[7]6.1	154	116	1	275	208	17 758	NA	NA
ARKANSAS	36 571	14.5	27 296	327	10.8	9.0	4 351	171	80	10 107	398	435 880	108 713	4 283
Arkansas	278	13.4	270	2	13.0	7.2	17	82	2	187	900	3 906	774	3 700
Ashley	342	14.0	281	3	11.5	8.8	14	57	1	28	115	4 186	716	2 915
Baxter	330	9.1	599	0	16.5	1.0	73	201	1	207	569	11 184	586	1 593
Benton	2 039	15.6	1 184	20	9.1	9.7	173	129	4	316	236	23 410	3 415	2 611
Boone	445	14.0	357	2	11.2	4.5	53	166	1	125	392	6 993	711	2 210
Bradley	145	12.6	176	1	15.3	4.6	9	79	1	60	525	2 489	296	2 546
Calhoun	63	11.0	79	1	13.8	21.3	1	17	0	0	0	893	67	1 159
Carroll	321	14.3	228	3	10.1	10.4	22	98	2	60	266	4 234	640	2 846
Chicot	212	14.1	194	3	12.9	12.6	12	81	1	35	236	2 688	748	4 917
Clark	291	13.2	251	2	11.4	5.7	17	78	1	57	260	4 079	568	2 553
Clay	209	12.0	271	3	15.6	12.8	3	17	1	35	203	4 033	354	2 023
Cleburne	221	9.8	273	0	12.1	1.5	21	92	1	49	214	5 493	573	2 537
Cleveland	100	12.0	97	1	11.6	0.0	1	12	0	0	0	1 358	69	824
Columbia	340	13.5	327	3	13.0	7.8	14	56	1	71	283	4 933	1 053	4 152

1. Per 1,000 estimated resident population, average 1996–1998.   2. Deaths of infants under 1 year old.   3. Deaths of infants under 1 year old per 1,000 live births.   4. Data subject to copyright.   5. Per 100,000 resident population as of July 1 of the year shown.   6. Data for serious crimes have not been adjusted for underreporting; this may affect comparability between geographic areas and over time.   7. Per 100,000 population estimated by the FBI.   7. La Paz County included with Yuma County.

Table B. States and Counties — Crime, Education, Money Income, and Poverty

STATE County	Serious crimes known to police, 1998[1] (cont'd) Rate[2] Violent	Property	Education — School enrollment and attainment, 1990 — Enrollment[3] Total	Percent private	Attainment[4] (percent) High school graduate or more	Bachelor's degree or more	Local government expenditures, fiscal 1997[5] Total current expenditures (mil dol)	Current expenditures per student (dollars)	Money income 1989 Per capita[6] (dollars)	Households Median Dollars	Percent change, 1979–1989 (constant 1989 dollars)	Percent with $100,000 or more	Income and poverty, 1997 Median household income	Percent below poverty level All persons	Persons under 18	Persons 5–17 in families
	46	47	48	49	50	51	52	53	54	55	56	57	58	59	60	61
ALABAMA—Cont'd																
Washington	90	513	4 370	5.0	58.2	6.7	17.8	4 693	8 340	20 082	-6.0	0.4	28 549	19.0	25.4	24.5
Wilcox	186	435	4 120	16.1	51.1	10.3	13.7	5 248	6 552	12 437	-10.2	1.5	17 822	36.1	44.0	42.1
Winston	94	1 067	4 534	2.3	48.8	5.4	20.6	4 484	9 349	17 936	-10.8	1.3	25 418	16.8	23.5	24.1
ALASKA	654	4 123	156 357	9.2	86.6	23.0	1 069.0	8 231	17 610	41 408	-2.8	7.7	43 657	11.2	16.2	15.1
Aleutians East Borough	NA	NA	476	1.5	66.4	12.9	5.8	14 246	17 242	42 384	NA	10.9	42 714	14.2	20.8	20.4
Aleutians West Census Area	NA	NA	1 636	3.9	85.8	14.8	4.6	10 730	15 035	35 187	NA	5.1	44 745	6.7	8.2	10.1
Anchorage	NA	NA	63 357	11.5	90.4	26.9	307.4	6 390	19 620	43 946	-4.2	9.3	54 245	9.1	13.2	11.9
Bethel	NA	NA	4 156	1.4	62.3	13.1	0.0	0	8 833	25 402	11.0	3.1	29 628	33.1	40.5	38.9
Bristol Bay	NA	NA	395	4.1	89.8	18.9	4.1	11 553	19 123	51 112	-9.0	8.4	56 570	8.4	12.8	12.0
Denali Borough	NA	NA	NA	NA	NA	NA	4.2	10 858	NA	NA	NA	NA	44 065	6.1	10.1	10.3
Dillingham	NA	NA	1 119	1.7	69.8	15.3	6.7	12 278	12 782	28 779	NA	6.2	35 094	28.1	38.0	38.0
Fairbanks North Star	NA	NA	23 206	8.5	89.8	25.2	118.1	7 229	15 914	37 468	-5.5	5.0	46 944	9.1	12.5	12.0
Haines	NA	NA	518	7.1	78.5	17.6	4.0	9 038	16 204	36 048	2.9	5.6	37 631	11.5	17.2	16.7
Juneau	NA	NA	7 638	10.6	89.9	30.7	42.1	7 385	19 920	47 924	-7.3	8.6	57 809	6.5	8.7	8.4
Kenai Peninsula	NA	NA	11 757	9.4	87.2	17.9	82.1	7 739	18 173	42 403	6.9	8.3	47 189	11.4	16.6	14.7
Ketchikan Gateway	NA	NA	3 737	10.0	85.4	20.2	20.0	6 889	18 789	45 172	-0.2	6.9	53 502	8.2	12.3	10.6
Kodiak Island	NA	NA	3 454	10.9	84.7	21.5	23.7	8 239	19 979	44 815	1.2	10.9	46 673	9.2	14.0	12.2
Lake and Peninsula Borough	NA	NA	459	2.8	60.7	14.4	9.7	17 815	11 560	25 231	NA	6.1	27 016	27.4	33.9	34.6
Matanuska-Susitna	NA	NA	12 099	8.4	87.8	18.1	93.7	7 508	15 898	40 745	3.5	5.6	50 273	11.6	16.0	14.5
Nome	NA	NA	2 573	1.2	65.0	13.8	8.0	10 313	10 701	30 144	23.6	4.0	36 633	24.2	29.7	29.5
North Slope	NA	NA	1 843	1.4	68.5	14.1	45.9	20 637	18 231	50 473	NA	13.4	56 915	5.8	6.2	7.6
Northwest Arctic Borough	NA	NA	1 940	1.6	63.8	11.9	26.7	12 321	10 040	33 313	NA	3.8	39 119	21.0	25.0	26.3
Prince of Wales-Outer Ketchikan	NA	NA	1 635	3.4	77.5	11.4	7.9	10 598	15 510	39 495	7.4	3.9	42 226	14.1	17.4	18.1
Sitka	NA	NA	2 538	15.4	87.0	21.4	13.1	7 339	16 962	43 337	-16.9	4.0	50 166	8.5	11.6	10.4
Skagway-Hoonah-Angoon	NA	NA	NA	NA	NA	15.8	NA	NA	15 463	38 583	7.6	2.8	NA	NA	NA	NA
Southeast Fairbanks	NA	NA	1 949	13.1	85.9	19.0	0.0	0	12 505	30 222	13.4	2.7	36 982	18.4	27.3	25.7
Valdez-Cordova	NA	NA	2 516	8.2	83.9	18.5	12.7	8 939	22 772	47 500	3.2	14.2	50 526	9.8	12.9	12.7
Wade Hampton	NA	NA	1 964	1.4	57.8	10.2	1.5	10 556	6 519	20 586	8.0	2.2	23 796	39.4	48.3	47.5
Wrangell-Petersburg	NA	NA	1 776	5.8	81.0	19.8	12.8	8 516	19 012	42 020	2.7	9.2	44 826	10.2	14.8	14.3
Yakutat Borough	NA	NA	NA	NA	NA	NA	2.2	13 054	NA	NA	NA	NA	41 252	7.9	14.3	15.0
Yukon-Koyukuk	NA	NA	2 424	2.5	73.2	13.8	7.2	16 038	11 554	23 945	15.5	2.8	30 532	24.2	27.1	28.8
ARIZONA	578	5 997	991 122	9.6	78.7	20.3	3 527.0	4 413	13 461	27 540	-0.1	3.4	34 751	15.5	23.2	22.1
Apache	52	633	21 515	5.9	54.7	8.5	104.5	5 773	5 399	14 100	-23.9	0.5	20 260	39.7	45.4	43.2
Cochise	288	4 072	26 371	6.3	75.7	16.1	90.5	4 249	10 716	22 425	-2.1	1.4	29 295	21.7	31.8	30.4
Coconino	413	5 503	37 122	5.9	79.0	24.6	94.2	4 725	10 580	26 112	-2.4	2.4	33 747	20.0	25.7	25.0
Gila	399	3 533	9 215	6.6	68.1	9.7	42.7	4 420	10 297	20 964	-9.5	1.9	27 960	20.2	32.8	29.9
Graham	210	2 488	8 843	3.4	67.6	11.3	24.3	3 926	8 955	18 455	-11.8	0.9	27 564	22.8	26.4	27.7
Greenlee	NA	NA	2 519	4.8	74.2	10.4	9.7	4 306	9 794	27 491	-23.3	0.3	43 696	10.3	12.6	12.9
La Paz	190	2 779	3 464	2.6	63.0	8.5	15.4	5 060	9 240	16 555	NA	1.5	23 534	24.3	36.3	37.7
Maricopa	609	6 531	557 988	10.9	81.5	22.1	1 984.7	4 384	14 970	30 797	3.7	4.2	40 134	12.7	19.1	17.9
Mohave	393	4 994	18 422	6.3	72.8	10.3	81.4	3 775	11 933	24 002	1.1	1.8	28 250	17.6	32.5	29.1
Navajo	282	2 719	25 979	5.1	64.6	10.0	99.2	4 698	7 586	19 452	-14.6	1.1	25 913	28.4	34.1	33.6
Pima	746	6 820	188 199	9.8	80.5	23.3	556.1	4 491	13 177	25 401	-4.1	3.1	32 544	16.2	24.4	23.4
Pinal	NA	NA	30 776	4.9	65.5	8.2	113.1	4 383	9 228	21 301	-12.2	1.1	28 003	20.0	27.9	28.5
Santa Cruz	294	3 328	8 566	5.1	57.2	10.8	40.5	4 488	9 007	22 066	-9.7	2.2	26 515	25.8	36.4	35.6
Yavapai	491	3 925	23 789	13.4	78.9	17.7	85.8	4 062	12 657	22 060	0.7	2.0	30 230	13.8	23.2	21.4
Yuma	NA	NA	28 755	5.9	64.9	12.7	121.5	4 368	10 428	23 635	NA	1.8	27 227	25.3	40.3	35.1
ARKANSAS	490	3 793	582 405	9.0	66.3	13.3	2 074.0	4 535	10 520	21 147	3.3	1.8	27 875	17.5	25.0	22.7
Arkansas	502	3 198	5 510	7.0	61.1	10.3	17.9	4 479	11 169	19 516	-4.5	2.3	28 742	18.9	26.8	24.4
Ashley	273	2 642	6 176	4.8	62.8	9.3	21.6	4 435	9 696	20 609	-3.2	1.5	30 040	20.0	28.3	25.7
Baxter	82	1 511	5 352	5.3	67.9	10.4	21.2	4 175	10 648	18 826	-1.7	1.5	26 352	14.6	25.2	22.7
Benton	205	2 406	21 018	11.7	74.8	14.4	94.8	4 238	12 274	26 021	11.5	2.0	36 004	10.1	16.3	13.9
Boone	227	1 983	6 278	7.1	67.6	10.7	24.8	4 199	10 129	20 656	8.7	1.6	28 336	16.6	25.6	21.6
Bradley	172	2 374	2 532	2.8	56.1	9.8	11.0	4 829	8 824	17 259	2.7	0.7	24 482	21.4	30.1	27.6
Calhoun	121	1 038	1 345	2.5	63.3	7.4	4.0	4 332	9 464	21 198	28.8	1.5	27 092	16.5	23.8	22.2
Carroll	333	2 513	3 778	5.8	68.4	11.6	15.5	4 243	10 176	20 623	12.9	1.5	26 411	17.2	26.7	24.0
Chicot	776	4 141	4 522	8.8	51.2	8.3	16.1	5 200	7 452	12 680	1.5	1.6	19 604	33.8	40.8	39.5
Clark	153	2 400	7 008	19.9	64.9	17.9	16.7	5 023	9 001	18 068	-6.1	1.1	26 783	18.9	24.6	22.7
Clay	149	1 874	3 384	2.5	47.9	5.2	12.2	4 022	9 018	16 219	3.4	1.3	24 735	18.0	25.9	23.5
Cleburne	173	2 364	3 542	3.4	61.0	9.4	14.4	4 067	10 039	19 438	6.5	1.1	27 223	15.8	25.4	21.8
Cleveland	24	800	1 990	2.4	59.9	7.8	6.9	4 423	9 025	19 703	5.8	0.6	29 956	16.8	23.5	21.3
Columbia	489	3 663	6 843	4.0	64.3	13.1	20.8	4 279	9 425	18 470	-2.9	1.5	26 826	21.9	30.7	27.3

1. Data for serious crimes have not been adjusted for underreporting; this may affect comparability between geographic areas and over time.   2. Per 100,000 population estimated by the FBI.   3. All persons 3 years old and over enrolled in nursery school through college.   4. Persons 25 years old and over.   5. Elementary and secondary education expenditures, local government fiscal years ending between July 1, 1996 and June 30, 1997.   6. Based on population enumerated as of April 1, 1990.

STATE County	Total (mil dol)	Percent change, 1997–1998	Per capita[1] Dollars	Per capita[1] Rank	Wages and salaries[2] (mil dol)	Proprietor's income (mil dol)	Dividends, interest, and rent (mil dol)	Total (mil dol)	Government payments to individuals Total (mil dol)	Social Security (mil dol)	Medical payments (mil dol)	Income maintenance (mil dol)	Unemployment insurance (mil dol)
	62	63	64	65	66	67	68	69	70	71	72	73	74
ALABAMA—Cont'd													
Washington	316	5.7	17 912	2 374	225	11	42	69	66	26	25	10	2
Wilcox	185	3.6	13 728	3 031	119	16	29	68	66	19	26	18	1
Winston	462	3.5	19 141	2 004	296	52	63	103	99	37	46	9	2
ALASKA	17 124	4.2	27 835	X	11 706	1 406	3 069	2 441	2 346	396	544	249	111
Aleutians East Borough	53	0.2	24 069	629	49	2	6	6	6	1	1	0	0
Aleutians West Census Area	112	-0.4	28 356	221	131	7	14	12	11	1	2	1	1
Anchorage	8 348	5.0	32 659	95	5 814	672	1 474	989	950	159	219	96	36
Bethel	280	4.5	17 524	2 478	177	9	27	79	76	6	25	17	3
Bristol Bay	47	-0.8	43 439	15	39	8	7	5	5	1	1	0	0
Denali Borough	62	9.0	32 152	109	73	2	12	12	12	1	1	0	0
Dillingham	112	4.4	25 046	485	75	14	13	19	19	2	5	3	1
Fairbanks North Star	2 135	4.2	25 341	456	1 536	124	384	314	301	49	69	29	15
Haines	70	3.8	30 059	162	27	12	16	11	11	3	3	1	1
Juneau	1 010	2.8	33 516	76	662	70	220	110	106	21	20	8	5
Kenai Peninsula	1 214	4.2	25 120	476	599	145	235	205	198	42	43	16	12
Ketchikan Gateway	452	0.2	31 803	116	284	47	91	61	59	14	14	6	3
Kodiak Island	350	1.4	24 166	614	237	45	71	47	44	7	8	4	3
Lake and Peninsula Borough	32	4.9	18 419	2 234	17	5	4	8	7	1	2	1	0
Matanuska-Susitna	1 046	6.1	18 752	2 141	383	102	194	199	191	40	31	13	12
Nome	185	2.6	20 508	1 554	118	8	22	47	46	5	15	9	2
North Slope	205	2.8	29 271	189	599	8	34	25	24	4	5	2	1
Northwest Arctic Borough	140	5.2	20 700	1 489	126	3	13	37	36	3	14	7	1
Prince of Wales-Outer Ketchikan	125	-1.4	18 278	2 270	76	10	20	25	23	3	4	2	2
Sitka	237	3.9	28 480	216	142	29	57	34	32	8	7	2	2
Skagway-Hoonah-Angoon	NA	NA	NA	0	NA	NA	NA	NA	NA	NA	NA	NA	NA
Southeast Fairbanks	129	2.3	21 614	1 217	72	9	20	27	26	5	6	3	2
Valdez-Cordova	290	3.1	28 256	228	215	28	52	37	36	7	6	3	2
Wade Hampton	87	3.2	12 684	3 076	43	3	7	39	38	3	15	8	2
Wrangell-Petersburg	177	1.5	25 983	400	87	29	36	31	30	7	7	3	2
Yakutat Borough	22	-1.9	27 352	276	15	2	5	3	3	0	1	0	0
Yukon-Koyukuk	114	1.7	18 005	2 342	66	8	17	41	40	3	16	9	2
ARIZONA	112 974	8.7	24 206	X	71 151	8 005	23 077	15 261	14 447	6 423	5 268	1 332	176
Apache	812	3.9	11 809	3 088	504	22	74	305	293	44	139	76	6
Cochise	2 051	5.0	18 249	2 281	1 161	123	417	421	403	155	149	46	6
Coconino	2 284	6.2	20 020	1 704	1 368	185	529	314	294	89	109	46	8
Gila	888	6.2	18 178	2 303	393	66	203	254	245	108	96	25	4
Graham	448	4.2	14 115	2 999	192	37	68	120	114	39	49	15	2
Greenlee	180	-1.3	19 305	1 953	176	10	17	30	28	11	12	3	1
La Paz	321	5.4	21 612	1 218	136	36	46	74	71	32	26	7	1
Maricopa	75 869	9.7	27 254	284	51 232	5 383	14 725	8 237	7 750	3 580	2 804	607	73
Mohave	2 487	7.5	19 039	2 041	934	169	530	585	562	318	166	42	2
Navajo	1 253	4.6	12 940	3 065	704	76	175	354	337	92	127	72	10
Pima	17 959	6.9	22 723	915	10 144	1 068	4 441	2 804	2 666	1 173	1 014	237	19
Pinal	2 341	4.3	15 930	2 804	1 268	162	367	629	603	236	261	62	3
Santa Cruz	600	7.7	15 725	2 840	347	54	137	100	94	36	36	14	3
Yavapai	3 071	7.8	20 643	1 510	1 164	269	982	611	585	356	146	33	5
Yuma	2 411	9.6	18 277	2 272	1 427	345	367	425	402	153	136	47	34
ARKANSAS	53 725	4.6	21 167	X	31 983	5 084	9 670	9 607	9 162	3 949	3 356	969	209
Arkansas	456	3.5	22 097	1 067	274	58	84	87	83	36	32	9	2
Ashley	493	2.3	20 245	1 638	342	39	68	101	97	40	36	13	3
Baxter	797	5.3	21 937	1 118	345	68	263	194	187	109	56	8	3
Benton	3 353	9.8	25 044	486	2 051	312	746	414	391	229	111	21	6
Boone	655	6.7	20 594	1 532	364	78	139	129	124	61	41	10	3
Bradley	236	2.8	20 716	1 482	108	25	38	63	61	23	27	7	2
Calhoun	90	3.4	15 764	2 832	106	7	12	22	21	10	7	2	1
Carroll	425	4.6	18 961	2 072	206	83	89	78	74	38	24	6	2
Chicot	240	0.6	15 975	2 797	106	26	36	69	66	21	27	14	1
Clark	416	3.0	19 277	1 964	242	31	75	93	89	36	36	7	1
Clay	305	0.2	17 820	2 402	140	32	53	79	76	33	28	8	2
Cleburne	441	6.5	19 252	1 973	152	56	110	100	96	50	30	7	2
Cleveland	156	5.3	18 510	2 206	24	20	18	30	28	12	10	3	1
Columbia	519	4.7	20 686	1 493	285	59	110	109	105	47	36	14	2

1. Based on the resident population estimated as of July 1 of the year shown.   2. Includes other labor income.

Table B. States and Counties — Earnings, Social Security, and Housing

STATE County	Earnings, 1998									Social Security beneficiaries, December 1998		Housing units, 1990		
				Percent by selected industries										
			Goods-related[1]		Service-related and other[2]									
	Total (mil dol)	Farm	Total	Manu-facturing	Total	Retail trade	Finance, insurance, and real estate	Services	Govern-ment	Number	Rate[3]	Supplemental Security Income recipients, December 1998	Total	Percent change, 1980–1990
	75	76	77	78	79	80	81	82	83	84	85	86	87	88

ALABAMA—Cont'd														
Washington	236	0.1	D	59.2	D	3.3	1.5	5.5	11.4	3 525	199	937	6 625	12.0
Wilcox	135	4.8	49.4	45.8	26.8	5.8	1.8	10.6	19.1	2 987	222	1 883	5 119	1.6
Winston	347	5.7	D	51.1	D	6.5	2.1	11.0	9.5	5 033	208	1 115	10 254	17.9
ALASKA	13 112	0.1	D	4.3	48.1	8.9	4.0	20.8	33.1	49 452	81	7 891	232 608	42.9
Aleutians East Borough	51	0.0	D	D	D	2.7	1.6	D	16.5	NA	NA	NA	693	NA
Aleutians West Census Area	138	0.1	45.8	44.3	37.4	6.3	2.8	14.2	16.7	NA	NA	NA	2 051	NA
Anchorage	6 486	0.0	15.4	1.5	54.2	9.4	5.3	23.9	30.4	19 039	75	3 549	94 153	33.8
Bethel	186	0.0	D	D	D	5.7	4.3	27.1	42.3	1 163	73	379	4 362	32.3
Bristol Bay	47	0.0	24.0	19.4	D	5.2	D	10.1	34.0	NA	NA	NA	596	61.5
Denali Borough	75	0.0	D	0.0	D	3.0	D	37.4	29.5	NA	NA	NA	NA	NA
Dillingham	89	0.0	D	D	D	6.2	3.2	35.6	25.3	NA	NA	NA	1 691	-13.4
Fairbanks North Star	1 660	0.0	10.6	1.9	41.1	9.0	2.4	18.3	48.3	5 781	69	862	31 823	40.1
Haines	39	0.0	D	D	D	13.7	D	20.5	19.0	338	152	23	1 112	49.7
Juneau	732	0.1	D	2.1	D	8.6	4.7	15.3	49.4	2 594	86	331	10 638	38.9
Kenai Peninsula	744	0.1	29.2	11.1	45.0	10.9	1.9	16.7	25.7	NA	NA	NA	19 364	64.9
Ketchikan Gateway	331	0.0	22.5	13.4	48.5	10.7	3.3	20.0	29.0	1 519	113	158	5 463	23.3
Kodiak Island	282	0.0	25.3	20.5	40.1	6.4	2.4	14.5	34.7	833	57	110	4 885	37.3
Lake and Peninsula Borough	21	0.0	D	23.9	D	5.4	0.3	29.9	23.5	NA	NA	NA	991	NA
Matanuska-Susitna	484	3.6	D	1.2	D	13.8	3.2	24.8	26.8	5 040	90	554	20 953	107.5
Nome	126	0.0	D	1.1	51.4	7.7	5.6	29.9	42.1	821	91	171	3 684	41.3
North Slope	607	0.0	D	D	D	3.8	D	10.0	16.9	NA	NA	NA	2 153	85.9
Northwest Arctic Borough	129	0.0	D	0.2	D	5.6	4.7	D	25.8	NA	NA	NA	1 998	NA
Prince of Wales-Outer Ketchikan	86	0.0	D	25.7	D	8.6	4.6	10.1	32.1	NA	NA	NA	2 543	83.6
Sitka	170	0.0	D	5.0	D	9.6	2.1	26.1	33.8	866	104	69	3 222	19.6
Skagway-Hoonah-Angoon	NA	NA	NA	NA	NA	NA	NA	NA	NA	NA	NA	NA	2 102	35.4
Southeast Fairbanks	80	0.0	D	D	D	9.8	0.5	11.9	61.7	603	106	113	3 149	28.5
Valdez-Cordova	243	0.0	19.9	7.0	56.5	5.6	2.3	12.6	23.6	NA	NA	NA	5 196	25.4
Wade Hampton	46	0.0	D	1.1	D	7.6	3.5	9.7	63.9	647	95	176	1 882	60.4
Wrangell-Petersburg	116	0.0	23.3	17.8	D	8.5	3.0	7.6	33.9	822	121	45	3 005	27.2
Yakutat Borough	16	0.0	38.3	33.3	D	6.8	D	17.9	25.7	NA	NA	NA	NA	NA
Yukon-Koyukuk	74	0.0	D	2.0	D	9.1	1.4	13.9	51.1	685	115	95	4 899	53.5
ARIZONA	79 155	1.0	21.8	13.5	61.3	10.4	9.5	28.6	15.9	755 158	162	77 846	1 659 430	49.4
Apache	525	-0.3	D	1.7	D	5.6	D	35.9	41.8	7 621	111	4 311	26 731	41.6
Cochise	1 285	2.8	7.3	2.3	D	8.3	D	20.6	51.7	20 566	183	2 237	40 238	23.6
Coconino	1 553	0.2	14.3	7.5	52.5	13.3	4.3	27.6	32.9	11 672	102	2 897	42 914	41.8
Gila	459	0.1	D	17.3	49.9	11.1	4.7	26.3	21.0	12 777	261	1 118	22 961	22.4
Graham	228	5.5	D	2.9	D	14.4	2.1	20.5	42.3	4 908	155	806	9 112	23.1
Greenlee	186	2.7	D	0.3	D	2.1	0.4	2.0	9.1	1 328	143	106	3 582	-17.5
La Paz	172	12.9	D	6.0	D	15.3	3.9	24.4	20.3	4 030	271	340	10 182	NA
Maricopa	56 615	0.6	23.0	15.2	64.5	10.2	11.2	29.1	11.9	408 182	147	36 791	952 041	55.9
Mohave	1 102	0.4	19.8	8.9	61.6	16.6	5.9	28.1	18.2	37 180	285	2 141	50 822	76.4
Navajo	780	0.2	D	5.9	53.3	11.3	2.3	23.0	26.6	12 886	133	4 090	38 967	37.2
Pima	11 212	0.1	19.9	12.4	57.3	10.5	6.4	31.5	22.7	137 510	174	13 733	298 207	36.4
Pinal	1 430	8.1	27.1	7.6	37.4	9.7	2.4	18.9	27.4	29 080	198	3 287	52 732	54.7
Santa Cruz	402	0.1	D	7.7	D	12.3	2.9	15.4	28.0	5 112	134	1 177	9 595	49.9
Yavapai	1 433	0.6	22.5	7.7	58.5	13.6	6.7	29.3	18.4	41 854	282	2 208	54 805	62.3
Yuma	1 771	14.6	D	3.8	D	8.9	D	17.0	28.4	20 439	155	2 269	46 541	24.1
ARKANSAS	37 067	4.1	28.0	21.9	51.3	10.9	4.9	21.5	16.5	515 948	203	89 969	1 000 667	11.4
Arkansas	332	10.5	33.2	28.8	44.9	8.1	3.0	12.2	11.4	4 597	221	788	9 575	-3.0
Ashley	381	3.6	D	48.8	D	6.3	2.1	D	9.2	5 050	207	1 075	9 820	0.5
Baxter	412	1.7	D	25.4	D	12.4	4.8	31.8	11.2	12 986	357	748	15 549	20.3
Benton	2 363	4.1	D	21.8	D	30.0	4.2	D	7.6	27 670	206	1 764	41 444	28.7
Boone	442	4.1	D	23.9	D	10.6	4.2	14.7	17.9	8 174	256	978	12 380	15.8
Bradley	134	6.5	D	40.6	D	7.1	2.7	16.1	15.4	2 949	258	521	5 092	-8.9
Calhoun	112	0.3	D	69.6	D	2.0	D	3.2	13.4	1 305	228	197	2 437	2.7
Carroll	289	14.5	D	D	D	11.4	3.4	19.8	10.1	4 984	221	432	8 740	19.0
Chicot	132	16.4	D	D	D	7.5	3.8	12.7	25.1	3 132	211	1 211	6 191	-6.0
Clark	273	3.3	34.0	32.0	42.0	10.3	3.7	19.6	20.7	4 694	214	653	8 807	-0.2
Clay	172	11.1	39.6	35.5	D	7.5	D	8.7	14.3	4 630	269	835	8 362	-3.8
Cleburne	208	6.5	33.3	24.7	48.0	12.3	3.5	20.0	12.1	6 495	283	639	10 802	25.8
Cleveland	45	30.4	D	13.1	D	4.9	D	9.8	21.4	1 618	191	247	3 322	7.9
Columbia	344	5.2	45.3	35.7	34.3	8.1	3.3	12.4	15.2	6 051	241	1 269	10 690	2.3

1. Covers mining, construction, and manufacturing. 2. Covers private sector earnings in agricultural services, forestry, and fisheries; transportation and public utilities; wholesale trade; retail trade; finance, insurance, and real estate; and services. 3. Per 1,000 resident population estimated as of July 1 of the year shown.

Table B. States and Counties — Housing, Labor Force, and Employment

STATE County	Housing units, 1990 (cont'd)								Civilian labor force, 1999				Civilian employment, 1990[5]		
	Occupied units										Unemployment			Percent	
		Owner-occupied				Renter-occupied									
				Owner cost as a percent of income											
	Total	Percent	Median value[1]	With a mortgage	Without a mortgage	Median rent[2]	Rent as percent of income	Substandard units[3] (percent)	Total	Percent change, 1998–1999	Total	Rate[4]	Total	Professional, managerial, and technical	Precision production, craft, and repair
	89	90	91	92	93	94	95	96	97	98	99	100	101	102	103
ALABAMA—Cont'd															
Washington	5 709	87.2	34 300	19.8	13.3	230	22.0	8.9	5 956	-5.3	729	12.2	5 954	16.3	18.4
Wilcox	4 415	77.1	34 000	23.0	14.4	179	28.9	19.6	3 808	0.7	546	14.3	3 672	21.4	11.4
Winston	8 544	79.9	37 700	19.4	12.2	212	22.5	3.5	12 496	-1.3	791	6.3	9 219	15.3	15.4
ALASKA	188 915	56.1	94 400	21.5	12.2	559	23.8	12.4	315 209	-0.5	20 072	6.4	245 379	34.3	11.2
Aleutians East Borough	533	61.4	85 700	13.5	11.6	602	14.5	6.2	1 548	-2.5	55	3.6	1 432	13.5	14.5
Aleutians West Census Area	1 845	17.9	80 100	20.0	13.9	441	16.0	6.8	1 941	-16.2	134	6.9	3 870	18.8	14.0
Anchorage	82 702	52.8	109 700	22.6	11.4	564	24.8	4.3	141 119	-0.3	6 360	4.5	111 242	37.5	9.5
Bethel	3 605	58.8	51 900	21.6	15.8	534	20.7	68.2	6 008	2.0	528	8.8	4 109	37.3	8.0
Bristol Bay	407	48.6	102 000	17.7	11.0	549	14.6	8.9	605	1.7	46	7.6	510	42.4	15.5
Denali Borough	NA	NA	NA	NA	NA	NA	NA	NA	1 192	-2.1	96	8.1	NA	NA	NA
Dillingham	1 215	63.2	63 300	16.5	13.8	592	20.5	38.9	1 733	2.5	130	7.5	1 243	42.6	7.8
Fairbanks North Star	26 693	49.0	87 300	21.4	11.3	534	26.2	10.3	43 359	0.1	2 572	5.9	31 379	35.4	12.0
Haines	791	65.0	81 000	18.1	12.4	470	17.8	23.1	1 198	2.4	133	11.1	1 031	25.9	13.9
Juneau	9 902	58.2	113 500	20.3	11.6	653	23.9	6.3	16 898	-0.6	844	5.0	14 482	42.0	8.3
Kenai Peninsula	14 250	67.9	85 100	19.2	11.4	479	20.3	11.5	21 574	-0.2	2 378	11.0	17 137	26.5	16.3
Ketchikan Gateway	5 030	56.0	112 600	20.6	11.5	614	21.6	8.9	7 167	-3.4	537	7.5	6 943	30.9	13.0
Kodiak Island	4 083	50.0	111 500	20.5	13.2	676	23.5	11.9	6 900	-4.8	484	7.0	6 178	25.8	12.0
Lake and Peninsula Borough	509	69.5	67 100	16.7	12.9	535	22.0	48.1	572	-4.0	45	7.9	454	35.5	9.9
Matanuska-Susitna	13 394	73.3	71 500	21.8	11.5	508	23.9	12.2	29 699	2.5	2 406	8.1	15 714	29.5	15.6
Nome	2 371	56.8	56 700	23.8	15.3	698	22.4	51.8	3 150	-7.1	359	11.4	2 700	38.1	9.2
North Slope	1 673	40.0	80 700	15.4	12.6	724	15.8	66.9	3 109	-8.5	242	7.8	2 522	29.8	15.7
Northwest Arctic Borough	1 526	57.9	62 800	17.8	13.9	762	24.8	65.7	2 042	-6.0	276	13.5	1 681	35.3	10.1
Prince of Wales-Outer Ketchikan	2 061	60.5	63 300	15.3	12.1	457	15.5	18.7	3 308	-1.5	425	12.8	2 618	20.1	12.5
Sitka	2 939	55.9	120 000	18.7	10.2	610	23.5	8.9	4 332	-2.5	224	5.2	4 307	27.8	12.8
Skagway-Hoonah-Angoon	1 422	54.2	65 200	14.7	11.8	398	15.4	23.7	NA	NA	NA	NA	NA	NA	NA
Southeast Fairbanks	1 909	60.8	54 900	20.1	12.2	489	19.6	28.7	2 508	3.0	257	10.2	1 943	29.4	12.7
Valdez-Cordova	3 425	64.5	97 100	14.6	13.0	564	19.7	21.4	5 100	-2.9	450	8.8	4 730	27.7	13.1
Wade Hampton	1 368	67.9	42 400	18.0	13.2	443	15.9	74.9	2 080	2.2	314	15.1	1 316	39.0	6.7
Wrangell-Petersburg	2 514	66.7	91 700	14.8	10.9	520	19.5	14.0	3 497	-2.9	310	8.9	3 352	24.9	10.8
Yakutat Borough	NA	NA	NA	NA	NA	NA	NA	NA	309	-0.3	26	8.4	NA	NA	NA
Yukon-Koyukuk	2 748	71.1	31 800	16.2	14.1	418	17.4	59.6	2 027	0.1	290	14.3	2 451	35.3	12.4
ARIZONA	1 368 843	64.2	80 100	22.8	12.4	438	27.5	7.8	2 363 705	4.0	104 158	4.4	1 603 896	30.8	11.4
Apache	15 981	73.2	19 400	17.7	12.7	243	15.5	51.8	22 171	8.6	3 049	13.8	14 039	26.2	14.9
Cochise	34 546	63.6	60 600	21.4	12.7	356	26.1	5.3	39 994	2.8	2 271	5.7	33 766	30.5	10.9
Coconino	29 918	60.5	82 800	20.8	12.2	431	24.9	19.2	59 098	2.9	4 003	6.8	41 990	28.5	11.7
Gila	15 438	77.4	58 300	19.4	12.7	346	24.0	7.8	17 882	-2.5	1 283	7.2	13 601	22.7	15.9
Graham	7 930	73.7	51 300	21.4	13.1	303	29.7	13.2	10 730	5.3	905	8.4	7 701	24.1	11.1
Greenlee	2 809	49.7	40 900	17.5	13.1	295	12.8	5.8	4 165	-8.4	365	8.8	2 829	16.2	24.7
La Paz	5 348	72.5	57 000	21.1	14.4	337	25.3	12.9	6 821	2.8	554	8.1	5 215	17.8	10.2
Maricopa	807 560	63.3	85 300	23.2	12.3	466	27.5	6.1	1 514 859	4.5	44 687	2.9	1 005 925	32.1	11.0
Mohave	36 801	72.1	75 600	21.9	11.9	468	27.4	5.6	63 861	4.4	2 905	4.5	37 191	20.8	15.8
Navajo	22 189	74.5	51 900	19.9	12.4	292	21.6	30.9	31 358	2.8	4 211	13.4	22 424	25.1	13.5
Pima	261 792	60.9	76 500	22.2	12.0	390	28.7	6.5	384 579	3.4	12 066	3.1	290 058	33.1	10.8
Pinal	39 154	72.0	53 200	21.5	13.4	376	27.0	11.0	60 032	4.9	3 324	5.5	40 326	19.7	16.3
Santa Cruz	8 808	66.0	71 500	23.1	13.9	366	29.1	16.7	13 396	-1.7	2 286	17.1	11 286	22.3	9.7
Yavapai	44 778	72.1	84 500	24.4	12.4	416	28.7	4.2	67 989	2.8	2 293	3.4	40 356	27.0	14.5
Yuma	35 791	66.0	64 000	21.3	13.5	436	27.7	14.6	66 773	2.3	19 957	29.9	37 189	24.2	10.2
ARKANSAS	891 179	69.6	46 300	20.0	13.4	328	26.5	4.9	1 222 213	0.6	54 841	4.5	994 289	23.3	12.5
Arkansas	8 389	67.0	40 600	20.8	14.1	293	26.5	4.2	10 548	2.0	521	4.9	9 228	21.7	10.4
Ashley	8 890	77.0	39 200	19.3	13.9	291	25.9	5.9	10 795	-3.0	871	8.1	9 632	19.7	13.4
Baxter	13 486	80.5	51 800	22.1	12.4	344	28.0	3.1	14 103	0.0	543	3.9	10 621	23.3	13.3
Benton	37 555	73.1	58 700	19.5	11.8	369	23.9	3.7	67 738	4.3	1 474	2.2	44 371	21.6	13.7
Boone	11 131	76.1	45 900	21.4	12.9	327	26.9	4.2	14 469	-1.0	801	5.5	12 534	21.4	11.4
Bradley	4 545	74.9	30 500	19.1	13.4	217	25.2	6.0	4 383	-7.5	391	8.9	4 410	20.0	13.2
Calhoun	2 185	81.2	34 400	16.7	14.5	288	20.3	7.8	2 228	-3.3	205	9.2	2 249	16.6	12.4
Carroll	7 550	75.6	47 700	23.3	12.7	301	24.1	4.9	11 557	0.3	515	4.5	8 312	18.8	14.8
Chicot	5 557	69.2	28 700	24.6	17.7	266	31.9	9.1	6 212	0.1	569	9.2	5 004	17.7	8.6
Clark	7 907	68.8	40 000	17.4	13.5	274	28.2	4.1	11 576	0.6	338	2.9	8 992	26.5	8.8
Clay	7 504	74.0	28 900	20.1	14.1	235	22.8	3.5	7 971	-1.6	509	6.4	7 198	16.4	14.6
Cleburne	7 926	81.3	50 700	24.7	12.2	319	26.3	3.5	9 377	0.4	365	3.9	7 510	17.5	16.4
Cleveland	2 868	83.1	33 900	18.8	14.4	238	27.6	5.8	3 801	6.2	208	5.5	3 104	16.0	15.5
Columbia	9 638	71.9	39 200	21.1	14.4	282	28.3	8.3	11 278	0.6	685	6.1	10 347	21.0	13.7

1. Specified owner-occupied units.   2. Specified renter-occupied units.   3. Overcrowded or lacking complete plumbing facilities.   4. Percent of civilian labor force.   5. Persons 16 years and older.

STATE County	Private nonfarm establishments, employment and payroll, 1998									Agriculture, 1997			
		Employment						Annual payroll		Farms			Farm operators
											Percent with—		
	Number of establish-ments	Total	Health Care and Social Assistance	Manufac-turing	Retail trade	Finance and Insurance	Professional Scientific and Technical Services	Total (mil dol)	Average per employee (dollars)	Number	Less than 50 acres	500 acres and over	Whose principal occu-pation is farming (percent)
	104	105	106	107	108	109	110	111	112	113	114	115	116

STATE County	104	105	106	107	108	109	110	111	112	113	114	115	116
ALABAMA—Cont'd													
Washington	261	3 664	283	D	332	95	50	149	40 765	397	27.2	9.3	37.0
Wilcox	227	2 527	228	D	338	97	24	78	30 712	248	19.0	32.7	34.3
Winston	481	10 381	478	6 932	727	217	57	234	22 537	582	38.7	1.7	33.8
ALASKA	18 212	196 135	28 919	12 117	32 186	6 956	9 497	6 884	35 098	548	35.4	16.4	55.8
Aleutians East Borough	49	1 995	D	D	55	D	0	32	16 083	NA	NA	NA	NA
Aleutians West Census Area	112	4 375	63	2 924	198	14	0	82	18 836	NA	NA	NA	NA
Anchorage	7 786	107 084	15 075	1 718	14 906	4 830	6 892	4 182	39 054	NA	NA	NA	NA
Bethel	210	2 657	D	D	707	37	12	66	24 785	NA	NA	NA	NA
Bristol Bay	73	572	D	209	90	D	D	22	37 628	NA	NA	NA	NA
Denali Borough	70	346	D	0	31	0	D	21	61 032	NA	NA	NA	NA
Dillingham	89	1 213	D	D	167	26	0	39	31 751	NA	NA	NA	NA
Fairbanks North Star	2 173	21 009	3 771	441	4 839	662	849	656	31 213	NA	NA	NA	NA
Haines	130	500	D	D	105	D	D	13	26 272	NA	NA	NA	NA
Juneau	1 125	9 730	1 718	180	1 837	297	487	306	31 411	NA	NA	NA	NA
Kenai Peninsula	1 703	11 104	1 692	1 274	2 303	257	296	336	30 276	89	38.2	12.4	51.7
Ketchikan Gateway	582	4 982	606	225	1 091	193	94	176	35 357	NA	NA	NA	NA
Kodiak Island	455	4 217	436	1 612	512	104	55	110	26 022	NA	NA	NA	NA
Lake and Peninsula Bor-ough	56	181	0	D	21	0	0	8	45 453	NA	NA	NA	NA
Matanuska-Susitna	1 333	8 609	1 359	126	2 174	259	320	236	27 399	NA	NA	NA	NA
Nome	183	1 931	D	D	360	41	26	51	26 421	NA	NA	NA	NA
North Slope	137	1 698	D	25	304	D	D	82	48 403	NA	NA	NA	NA
Northwest Arctic Borough	84	1 541	D	D	232	D	D	74	47 817	NA	NA	NA	NA
Prince of Wales-Outer Ket-chikan	175	1 349	55	402	149	D	D	40	29 307	NA	NA	NA	NA
Sitka	387	2 787	749	189	495	66	61	74	26 483	NA	NA	NA	NA
Skagway-Hoonah-Angoon	161	650	7	40	132	10	D	19	29 069	NA	NA	NA	NA
Southeast Fairbanks	142	572	78	9	159	15	8	13	22 080	NA	NA	NA	NA
Valdez-Cordova	464	2 249	247	361	414	D	51	72	31 907	NA	NA	NA	NA
Wade Hampton	64	698	40	D	306	D	D	8	11 216	NA	NA	NA	NA
Wrangell-Petersburg	285	1 718	191	252	426	41	21	47	27 222	NA	NA	NA	NA
Yakutat Borough	34	274	D	D	29	D	0	7	27 354	NA	NA	NA	NA
Yukon-Koyukuk	133	522	18	D	144	D	D	12	23 774	NA	NA	NA	NA
ARIZONA	110 245	1 763 508	190 110	199 616	241 092	92 132	98 547	49 052	27 815	6 135	44.8	27.1	53.0
Apache	508	7 141	1 617	323	1 197	105	171	138	19 284	288	30.9	34.7	43.8
Cochise	2 169	21 008	3 679	832	4 777	473	1 761	445	21 168	824	23.7	38.3	57.8
Coconino	3 341	36 979	4 372	2 253	7 133	636	1 012	781	21 107	199	37.2	33.2	43.2
Gila	1 110	13 714	1 864	2 469	2 014	193	241	348	25 405	148	45.9	18.2	56.8
Graham	497	4 817	811	D	1 381	127	115	79	16 472	281	41.3	28.1	54.1
Greenlee	104	3 643	111	D	145	D	D	124	33 940	99	37.4	14.1	59.6
La Paz	357	3 695	437	329	830	D	D	63	17 006	97	24.7	44.3	69.1
Maricopa	68 955	1 246 448	118 231	147 574	153 238	78 148	76 896	37 009	29 692	1 643	67.4	12.5	47.2
Mohave	3 212	31 142	4 105	3 568	6 908	1 049	688	641	20 586	212	34.4	41.5	50.5
Navajo	1 622	15 462	1 857	1 297	3 543	D	238	353	22 807	310	37.7	32.3	42.6
Pima	18 247	268 142	39 133	28 391	39 354	7 942	14 457	6 699	24 982	419	60.1	22.0	45.6
Pinal	1 988	27 851	2 937	4 326	4 526	594	741	688	24 713	541	26.1	44.7	68.2
Santa Cruz	1 070	10 403	608	1 428	2 181	192	192	214	20 555	156	19.2	34.0	57.7
Yavapai	4 603	41 861	6 169	3 501	7 557	1 282	1 219	853	20 366	453	47.5	26.3	57.2
Yuma	2 443	30 497	4 179	3 082	6 308	934	717	595	19 515	465	44.7	25.6	59.4
ARKANSAS	62 353	944 935	130 129	232 671	134 134	32 334	27 689	21 765	23 033	45 142	24.1	16.4	49.4
Arkansas	587	8 404	904	2 975	1 099	267	78	193	22 953	518	7.9	58.5	78.4
Ashley	515	8 602	631	3 828	930	225	74	246	28 637	299	23.7	31.8	53.8
Baxter	1 034	11 273	2 161	3 062	1 812	347	325	245	21 728	492	22.8	9.8	38.8
Benton	3 393	57 907	4 621	13 561	6 054	1 745	1 676	1 581	27 305	2 323	44.2	3.9	45.7
Boone	908	13 275	1 630	3 217	2 263	346	195	291	21 932	1 259	25.3	8.7	40.9
Bradley	293	3 015	568	436	392	139	29	50	16 484	249	29.3	2.8	42.2
Calhoun	103	974	90	372	79	D	D	20	20 633	112	23.2	3.6	29.5
Carroll	767	7 904	634	3 497	1 205	234	105	146	18 446	1 032	20.7	10.7	48.9
Chicot	280	3 116	484	1 050	613	143	65	50	16 117	361	8.3	47.4	76.7
Clark	588	8 204	863	3 076	1 010	302	171	153	18 633	376	19.1	14.1	41.0
Clay	356	5 276	483	2 775	590	123	38	91	17 272	611	16.9	36.7	61.2
Cleburne	562	5 745	635	1 994	898	183	78	103	17 962	710	24.4	4.9	43.8
Cleveland	111	718	D	117	88	D	5	11	15 826	222	31.5	4.1	45.9
Columbia	652	8 533	1 055	2 998	1 208	258	194	188	22 016	313	24.0	7.0	46.6

Table B. States and Counties — Agriculture, Land, and Water

STATE County	Land in farms Acreage (1,000) [117]	Percent change, 1992–1997 [118]	Acres Average size of farm [119]	Total irrigated (1,000) [120]	Total cropland (1,000) [121]	Value of land and buildings Average per farm ($1,000) [122]	Average per acre (dollars) [123]	Value of machinery and equipment Average per farm ($1,000) [124]	Value of products sold Total (mil dol) [125]	Average per farm (dollars) [126]	Percent from Crops [127]	Live-stock and poultry products [128]	Percent of farms with sales of $10,000 or more [129]	$100,000 or more [130]	Percent of land owned by Fed. Gov. 1997 [131]	Water consumption 1995 (mil gal/day) [132]
ALABAMA—Cont'd																
Washington	87	2.5	220	0	26	274	1 329	31	22	55 127	10.1	89.9	32.2	10.8	0.1	86.4
Wilcox	154	9.3	621	0	39	564	914	43	7	29 106	34.5	65.5	30.2	5.2	0.3	43.0
Winston	59	3.7	102	0	29	181	1 731	28	59	101 564	0.5	99.5	32.1	18.4	23.3	2.7
ALASKA	881	-4.5	1 608	3	95	487	303	53	25	44 982	64.8	35.2	40.1	8.6	NA	211.1
Aleutians East Borough	NA	NA	NA	NA	NA	NA	NA	NA	NA	NA	NA	NA	NA	NA	NA	1.7
Aleutians West Census Area	NA	NA	NA	NA	NA	NA	NA	NA	NA	NA	NA	NA	NA	NA	NA	3.3
Anchorage	NA	NA	NA	NA	NA	NA	NA	NA	NA	NA	NA	NA	NA	NA	NA	45.2
Bethel	NA	NA	NA	NA	NA	NA	NA	NA	NA	NA	NA	NA	NA	NA	NA	0.4
Bristol Bay	NA	NA	NA	NA	NA	NA	NA	NA	NA	NA	NA	NA	NA	NA	NA	0.1
Denali Borough	NA	NA	NA	NA	NA	NA	NA	NA	NA	NA	NA	NA	NA	NA	NA	0.1
Dillingham	NA	NA	NA	NA	NA	NA	NA	NA	NA	NA	NA	NA	NA	NA	NA	0.0
Fairbanks North Star	NA	NA	NA	NA	NA	NA	NA	NA	NA	NA	NA	NA	NA	NA	NA	32.0
Haines	NA	NA	NA	NA	NA	NA	NA	NA	NA	NA	NA	NA	NA	NA	NA	0.5
Juneau	NA	NA	NA	NA	NA	NA	NA	NA	NA	NA	NA	NA	NA	NA	NA	0.7
Kenai Peninsula	56	10.7	635	0	8	477	752	37	1	14 151	71.8	28.2	23.6	2.2	NA	4.7
Ketchikan Gateway	NA	NA	NA	NA	NA	NA	NA	NA	NA	NA	NA	NA	NA	NA	NA	8.6
Kodiak Island	NA	NA	NA	NA	NA	NA	NA	NA	NA	NA	NA	NA	NA	NA	NA	54.1
Lake and Peninsula Borough	NA	NA	NA	NA	NA	NA	NA	NA	NA	NA	NA	NA	NA	NA	NA	5.3
Matanuska-Susitna	NA	NA	NA	NA	NA	NA	NA	NA	NA	NA	NA	NA	NA	NA	NA	5.7
Nome	NA	NA	NA	NA	NA	NA	NA	NA	NA	NA	NA	NA	NA	NA	NA	1.3
North Slope	NA	NA	NA	NA	NA	NA	NA	NA	NA	NA	NA	NA	NA	NA	NA	0.9
Northwest Arctic Borough	NA	NA	NA	NA	NA	NA	NA	NA	NA	NA	NA	NA	NA	NA	NA	6.4
Prince of Wales-Outer Ketchikan	NA	NA	NA	NA	NA	NA	NA	NA	NA	NA	NA	NA	NA	NA	NA	1.5
Sitka	NA	NA	NA	NA	NA	NA	NA	NA	NA	NA	NA	NA	NA	NA	NA	5.1
Skagway-Hoonah-Angoon	NA	NA	NA	NA	NA	NA	NA	NA	NA	NA	NA	NA	NA	NA	NA	0.0
Southeast Fairbanks	NA	NA	NA	NA	NA	NA	NA	NA	NA	NA	NA	NA	NA	NA	NA	2.7
Valdez-Cordova	NA	NA	NA	NA	NA	NA	NA	NA	NA	NA	NA	NA	NA	NA	NA	4.5
Wade Hampton	NA	NA	NA	NA	NA	NA	NA	NA	NA	NA	NA	NA	NA	NA	NA	0.2
Wrangell-Petersburg	NA	NA	NA	NA	NA	NA	NA	NA	NA	NA	NA	NA	NA	NA	NA	2.0
Yakutat Borough	NA	NA	NA	NA	NA	NA	NA	NA	NA	NA	NA	NA	NA	NA	NA	0.0
Yukon-Koyukuk	NA	NA	NA	NA	NA	NA	NA	NA	NA	NA	NA	NA	NA	NA	NA	7.7
ARIZONA	26 867	-23.3	4 379	1 014	1 277	1 689	388	71	1 903	310 254	64.2	35.8	48.0	22.0	41.7	6 815.9
Apache	D	D	D	11	17	2 813	D	18	7	23 375	3.9	96.1	30.2	5.2	10.7	39.0
Cochise	1 260	-33.4	1 529	63	116	546	348	41	60	73 003	68.2	31.8	52.2	15.7	25.3	234.0
Coconino	6 209	3.7	31 203	3	D	4 416	142	33	11	53 702	3.8	96.2	32.7	10.6	38.9	47.3
Gila	D	D	D	1	8	2 777	D	27	3	19 775	2.6	97.4	36.5	2.7	57.2	40.6
Graham	1 245	-32.6	4 430	40	D	1 648	377	92	56	199 306	90.0	10.0	58.0	23.1	37.8	176.4
Greenlee	29	-78.7	297	5	8	210	749	41	5	47 921	30.5	69.5	43.4	9.1	77.0	36.8
La Paz	279	13.4	2 875	101	D	4 311	1 512	176	95	975 925	99.2	0.8	77.3	54.6	77.6	628.6
Maricopa	709	-2.9	431	298	341	1 384	2 944	79	664	404 174	57.6	42.4	44.9	25.9	53.2	2 392.0
Mohave	997	-49.7	4 704	13	19	1 237	257	51	15	70 674	54.5	45.5	39.2	11.3	68.4	140.3
Navajo	3 903	-46.0	12 589	10	19	2 703	219	49	26	82 894	4.1	95.9	28.7	6.5	9.5	63.7
Pima	2 914	-16.1	6 954	29	D	2 346	340	38	47	111 841	80.6	19.4	41.1	13.6	29.0	263.8
Pinal	1 303	-31.5	2 409	228	D	1 891	760	145	363	671 865	52.3	47.7	70.6	51.9	20.6	1 257.1
Santa Cruz	265	-20.6	1 701	6	11	1 352	838	20	4	23 758	D	D	42.3	4.5	54.6	15.4
Yavapai	772	-63.4	1 703	9	24	592	359	37	27	58 825	8.5	91.5	39.3	8.2	50.0	82.4
Yuma	238	3.8	511	196	215	2 266	4 496	145	522	1 122 717	D	D	68.4	43.0	81.5	1 398.6
ARKANSAS	14 365	1.7	318	3 717	10 062	360	1 151	56	5 480	121 388	39.9	60.1	45.4	22.2	9.1	8 767.3
Arkansas	426	3.7	823	309	376	896	1 136	176	142	274 913	99.4	0.6	78.4	63.5	8.5	820.6
Ashley	166	9.8	555	91	138	550	1 078	95	59	198 590	86.4	13.6	51.8	33.8	4.2	134.8
Baxter	105	13.3	214	0	40	239	1 081	25	21	42 776	1.2	98.8	31.3	6.5	18.5	5.5
Benton	297	0.9	128	1	168	300	2 549	34	338	145 296	1.4	98.6	41.5	20.5	3.8	336.3
Boone	258	2.7	205	0	116	251	1 397	26	60	47 583	1.2	98.8	36.6	7.7	0.6	4.6
Bradley	29	-3.7	116	1	15	194	1 690	32	14	57 871	23.5	76.5	35.7	14.5	4.1	1.5
Calhoun	18	-7.3	157	0	10	145	1 069	29	2	15 307	11.0	89.1	25.9	4.5	0.0	1.1
Carroll	242	-1.4	235	0	105	283	1 186	33	146	141 837	0.5	99.5	51.0	22.6	0.9	7.3
Chicot	288	7.0	798	116	254	704	912	156	101	280 472	74.8	25.2	80.9	55.7	0.0	233.5
Clark	96	-2.7	256	2	51	252	965	30	19	49 801	15.4	84.6	34.6	9.6	0.8	5.2
Clay	324	3.1	530	176	296	676	1 351	106	88	144 183	98.0	2.0	66.1	37.8	0.7	176.1
Cleburne	117	8.7	165	0	55	169	1 167	31	46	65 474	1.4	98.6	36.1	15.9	1.6	6.7
Cleveland	33	-3.5	148	0	14	224	1 381	36	51	228 476	0.3	99.7	42.8	28.4	0.0	1.3
Columbia	58	1.2	184	0	26	217	1 327	27	41	130 548	8.0	92.0	35.8	18.5	0.0	6.3

Table B. States and Counties — Residential Construction, Wholesale and Retail Trade, and Real Estate

STATE County	Value of Residential Construction Authorized by Building Permits, 1999		Wholesale Trade, 1997				Retail Trade[1], 1997				Real Estate and Rental and Leasing, 1997			
	New Construction ($1,000)	Number of Housing Units	Number of Establishments	Number of Employees	Sales (mil dol)	Annual Payroll (mil dol)	Number of Establishments	Number of Employees	Sales (mil dol)	Annual Payroll (mil dol)	Number of Establishments	Number of Employees	Receipts (mil dol)	Annual Payroll (mil dol)
	133	134	135	136	137	138	139	140	141	142	143	144	145	146
ALABAMA—Cont'd														
Washington	239	2	11	D	D	D	53	319	52.1	4.2	2	D	D	D
Wilcox	0	0	8	36	18.3	0.7	62	331	53.0	5.0	7	9	0.4	0.0
Winston	892	9	37	560	127.2	11.6	108	751	103.8	10.8	16	37	2.8	0.4
ALASKA	306 585	2 211	784	6 860	2 989.8	256.8	2 866	32 502	6 251.4	670.5	716	4 014	543.2	98.3
Aleutians East Borough	0	0	2	D	D	D	6	56	7.2	1.0	2	D	D	D
Aleutians West Census Area	0	0	14	110	61.4	3.2	20	197	41.2	4.2	4	55	9.5	2.2
Anchorage	205 251	1 265	434	4 748	1 989.1	181.4	1 001	15 115	3 114.9	319.3	356	2 145	322.2	56.8
Bethel	5 387	42	3	9	1.1	0.2	59	829	77.2	8.5	7	33	5.3	0.7
Bristol Bay	904	7	2	D	D	D	13	91	12.8	2.1	3	15	1.4	0.2
Denali Borough	NA	NA	2	D	D	D	7	D	D	D	1	D	D	D
Dillingham	0	0	4	10	4.7	0.5	16	220	33.1	3.6	4	15	1.9	0.5
Fairbanks North Star	16 028	179	75	737	266.0	27.7	359	4 431	927.9	99.5	91	687	79.1	17.3
Haines	919	12	3	D	D	D	26	98	13.1	2.0	4	15	1.1	0.2
Juneau	14 888	177	33	196	96.3	8.2	173	1 807	312.7	37.2	49	249	38.3	4.0
Kenai Peninsula	9 814	177	70	337	242.0	12.6	292	2 219	426.5	45.1	49	219	21.9	4.0
Ketchikan Gateway	6 465	57	31	190	78.8	4.7	119	1 164	205.1	28.6	27	110	13.5	2.9
Kodiak Island	6 794	59	35	87	50.8	4.4	67	590	102.9	11.9	16	49	7.6	0.9
Lake and Peninsula Borough	NA	NA	NA	NA	NA	NA	10	D	D	D	3	6	0.3	0.0
Matanuska-Susitna	7 440	66	22	D	D	D	201	2 149	477.3	46.6	35	169	13.7	2.0
Nome	1 154	9	1	D	D	D	41	442	57.0	5.8	8	D	D	D
North Slope	8 479	85	4	26	42.5	2.0	22	293	45.0	7.4	3	D	D	D
Northwest Arctic Borough	NA	NA	NA	NA	NA	NA	30	286	40.8	5.4	1	D	D	D
Prince of Wales-Outer Ketchikan	387	3	6	32	21.6	1.0	40	158	26.0	2.7	4	D	D	D
Sitka	3 572	42	9	D	D	D	75	534	78.2	10.3	17	44	4.0	0.8
Skagway-Hoonah-Angoon	423	9	2	D	D	D	45	208	25.3	3.2	3	2	0.2	0.1
Southeast Fairbanks	NA	NA	3	D	D	D	30	193	28.4	2.9	4	10	0.4	0.1
Valdez-Cordova	3 824	31	20	D	D	D	78	417	81.7	8.2	15	23	3.8	0.7
Wade Hampton	NA	NA	1	D	D	D	29	353	27.3	3.1	NA	NA	NA	NA
Wrangell-Petersburg	1 727	15	7	D	D	D	61	406	54.1	8.2	5	10	0.6	0.1
Yakutat Borough	585	4	1	D	D	D	6	30	5.3	0.8	1	D	D	D
Yukon-Koyukuk	NA	NA	NA	NA	NA	NA	40	147	22.3	2.1	4	20	1.9	0.3
ARIZONA	7 350 364	65 109	6 689	80 155	45 763.9	2 748.9	16 283	232 050	43 960.9	4 223.9	5 450	32 529	4 110.1	747.4
Apache	8 112	89	9	D	D	D	126	1 242	170.0	17.0	13	56	6.5	0.8
Cochise	51 827	660	68	468	132.3	11.4	421	4 557	712.1	68.1	96	330	27.9	4.7
Coconino	111 062	949	112	D	D	D	653	7 217	1 081.2	112.1	175	662	75.3	13.0
Gila	42 577	380	42	220	60.7	6.4	176	2 040	329.6	32.9	50	111	16.5	2.1
Graham	8 640	92	25	193	59.1	3.9	110	1 377	205.4	19.4	18	47	4.0	0.7
Greenlee	122	2	7	D	D	D	22	146	20.8	1.8	1	D	D	D
La Paz	3 177	36	14	183	56.4	3.9	79	830	177.5	10.8	14	D	D	D
Maricopa	5 150 729	44 156	4 752	61 594	39 518.5	2 265.9	9 214	144 912	29 331.0	2 792.4	3 391	22 214	3 047.6	553.6
Mohave	168 781	1 944	106	D	D	D	578	6 944	1 236.9	111.1	148	486	50.0	7.6
Navajo	66 847	605	50	266	98.7	7.3	296	3 667	602.7	55.2	67	273	21.6	4.6
Pima	1 039 225	8 734	929	9 257	2 759.8	266.0	2 785	39 285	6 853.8	693.4	978	6 631	676.6	130.5
Pinal	319 997	3 557	88	690	206.4	18.1	404	4 355	680.8	63.9	111	337	32.3	4.6
Santa Cruz	31 361	374	205	1 859	1 124.9	49.9	207	2 169	320.3	30.7	49	113	11.6	1.9
Yavapai	269 099	2 484	150	1 134	480.6	29.1	757	7 325	1 203.1	120.8	226	737	88.2	15.6
Yuma	78 808	1 047	132	2 376	512.9	41.3	455	5 984	1 035.7	94.5	113	485	48.4	7.0
ARKANSAS	965 992	11 502	3 619	41 385	27 515.4	1 136.6	12 600	132 335	21 643.7	1 904.4	2 269	9 761	1 001.6	163.2
Arkansas	1 991	16	39	485	233.0	15.1	143	1 190	201.1	17.7	12	26	1.9	0.4
Ashley	1 309	18	28	D	D	D	117	961	133.8	12.3	12	43	1.8	0.5
Baxter	5 386	81	27	130	22.9	2.8	227	1 713	298.2	27.1	41	116	13.6	2.0
Benton	113 835	1 160	167	1 886	2 480.5	52.6	548	6 217	1 015.6	93.2	138	523	51.1	8.1
Boone	15 760	154	45	D	D	D	194	2 205	368.9	30.4	44	130	9.9	2.0
Bradley	356	5	11	37	25.6	1.0	62	385	65.1	4.9	5	14	0.5	0.1
Calhoun	40	1	2	D	D	D	22	91	13.3	1.1	1	D	D	D
Carroll	2 120	22	26	126	25.6	3.0	202	1 204	174.9	17.3	23	46	3.9	0.6
Chicot	544	11	23	216	87.6	5.7	80	627	87.1	7.1	10	D	D	D
Clark	3 496	43	25	128	39.1	3.4	116	1 100	171.3	14.8	26	70	3.9	0.6
Clay	5 409	30	23	350	98.8	7.4	86	632	106.2	8.1	10	19	1.6	0.2
Cleburne	3 017	38	33	255	63.9	5.3	111	982	135.7	12.4	20	44	4.1	0.8
Cleveland	0	0	6	D	D	D	19	94	9.2	0.8	2	D	D	D
Columbia	1 447	10	30	177	47.1	3.7	136	1 205	157.8	14.9	25	94	7.9	1.3

1. Establishments with payroll.

Table B. States and Counties — Professional, Manufacturing, and Accommodation and Foodservices

STATE County	Professional, Scientific, and Technical Services¹, 1997				Manufacturing, 1997				Accommodation and Foodservices, 1997			
	Number of Establishments	Number of Employees	Receipts (mil dol)	Annual Payroll (mil dol)	Number of Establishments	Number of Employees	Receipts (mil dol)	Annual Payroll (mil dol)	Number of Establishments	Number of Employees	Sales (mil dol)	Annual Payroll (mil dol)
	147	148	149	150	151	152	153	154	155	156	157	158
ALABAMA—Cont'd												
Washington	11	39	3.1	1.8	12	D	D	D	13	D	D	D
Wilcox	8	13	1.0	0.1	12	D	D	D	17	178	4.5	1.1
Winston	25	71	5.0	1.4	87	6 573	838.7	135.8	33	426	11.1	2.7
ALASKA	1 437	7 892	945.9	370.8	488	10 770	3 305.0	331.2	1 763	20 587	1 065.5	301.5
Aleutians East Borough	NA	NA	NA	NA	2	D	D	D	8	D	D	D
Aleutians West Census Area	1	D	D	D	8	D	D	D	11	165	7.6	3.4
Anchorage	907	5 939	767.2	301.3	187	2 022	322.3	62.9	640	11 364	574.0	165.8
Bethel	4	11	1.3	0.6	NA	NA	NA	NA	12	44	3.2	0.6
Bristol Bay	2	D	D	D	NA	NA	NA	NA	12	71	4.5	1.3
Denali Borough	NA	NA	NA	NA	NA	NA	NA	NA	18	80	8.7	2.6
Dillingham	NA	NA	NA	NA	NA	NA	NA	NA	18	73	8.9	2.2
Fairbanks North Star	167	784	70.5	28.1	NA	NA	NA	NA	184	2 488	112.1	29.4
Haines	4	8	0.5	0.3	NA	NA	NA	NA	19	84	5.3	1.4
Juneau	96	415	44.9	18.5	NA	NA	NA	NA	94	1 117	57.7	16.1
Kenai Peninsula	80	211	19.6	6.6	56	1 246	1 027.0	56.7	213	1 251	65.2	16.2
Ketchikan Gateway	25	84	9.8	3.4	18	762	131.3	31.1	57	476	25.2	7.1
Kodiak Island	20	48	3.4	1.5	25	1 576	204.3	35.4	41	378	18.4	5.3
Lake and Peninsula Borough	NA	NA	NA	NA	NA	NA	NA	NA	16	D	D	D
Matanuska-Susitna	78	251	17.2	7.0	NA	NA	NA	NA	126	928	43.9	10.2
Nome	2	D	D	D	NA	NA	NA	NA	20	215	6.6	2.1
North Slope	3	D	D	D	NA	NA	NA	NA	31	313	32.4	12.0
Northwest Arctic Borough	1	D	D	D	NA	NA	NA	NA	13	159	11.1	4.2
Prince of Wales-Outer Ketchikan	3	D	D	D	NA	NA	NA	NA	25	135	8.2	2.4
Sitka	13	34	2.6	0.6	NA	NA	NA	NA	32	331	15.5	4.4
Skagway-Hoonah-Angoon	1	D	D	D	NA	NA	NA	NA	39	120	9.4	2.7
Southeast Fairbanks	4	D	D	D	NA	NA	NA	NA	28	140	6.6	1.8
Valdez-Cordova	15	39	3.2	0.9	NA	NA	NA	NA	58	315	19.8	4.9
Wade Hampton	NA	NA	NA	NA	NA	NA	NA	NA	2	D	D	D
Wrangell-Petersburg	9	19	0.9	0.2	NA	NA	NA	NA	23	120	6.3	1.7
Yakutat Borough	NA	NA	NA	NA	NA	NA	NA	NA	6	75	2.8	0.9
Yukon-Koyukuk	2	D	D	D	NA	NA	NA	NA	17	38	4.4	0.7
ARIZONA	10 163	75 789	6 669.4	2 724.7	4 917	193 616	43 030.3	6 753.6	9 089	184 323	6 633.0	1 823.2
Apache	26	99	5.6	1.5	NA	NA	NA	NA	65	1 310	37.7	10.0
Cochise	127	1 731	148.2	61.9	53	921	153.8	20.9	270	3 310	94.2	23.9
Coconino	181	777	58.8	21.6	95	D	D	D	477	9 409	407.7	105.8
Gila	63	191	12.8	4.4	34	D	D	D	147	1 660	55.9	14.5
Graham	21	71	3.0	1.2	NA	NA	NA	NA	59	734	19.0	4.8
Greenlee	3	13	0.4	0.1	NA	NA	NA	NA	15	180	3.9	1.1
La Paz	12	39	2.3	0.7	NA	NA	NA	NA	76	795	23.2	6.5
Maricopa	7 158	57 583	5 115.0	2 134.1	3 364	143 683	32 782.1	5 045.0	4 901	112 073	4 196.1	1 170.4
Mohave	138	517	33.0	10.0	156	3 807	760.4	85.2	324	4 516	144.6	39.3
Navajo	59	234	16.2	4.4	45	1 346	275.9	44.2	222	2 890	118.5	26.2
Pima	1 811	12 214	1 124.2	430.9	764	26 746	4 455.2	1 064.7	1 524	32 305	1 041.9	292.2
Pinal	70	468	21.8	7.4	74	4 594	2 530.6	154.8	233	3 995	139.6	36.8
Santa Cruz	42	143	8.9	3.8	35	D	D	D	87	1 374	40.3	11.7
Yavapai	304	1 043	71.1	25.4	189	3 511	445.8	91.3	444	5 614	180.4	48.6
Yuma	148	666	48.1	17.3	66	3 041	389.5	54.6	245	4 158	130.0	31.3
ARKANSAS	4 125	23 094	1 825.8	719.6	3 316	230 153	45 186.0	5 778.4	4 663	73 397	2 179.7	589.9
Arkansas	25	63	3.2	0.9	28	2 768	916.2	66.4	43	340	10.5	2.8
Ashley	25	83	4.5	1.3	24	3 792	921.4	141.7	24	280	9.9	2.3
Baxter	65	312	17.1	6.4	56	3 185	350.8	74.1	106	1 060	32.3	9.1
Benton	250	1 239	155.5	46.2	194	14 220	2 491.8	346.5	230	3 585	98.9	26.9
Boone	54	137	6.8	2.2	67	2 808	495.0	70.4	65	1 015	26.7	7.0
Bradley	16	62	2.6	0.9	9	594	90.0	12.5	16	193	5.0	1.3
Calhoun	2	D	D	D	NA	NA	NA	NA	4	13	0.4	0.1
Carroll	27	76	3.4	1.3	41	3 408	426.5	62.8	157	1 117	41.3	10.9
Chicot	15	49	2.5	1.0	11	1 019	67.1	12.8	23	124	4.0	1.0
Clark	28	140	6.9	2.8	31	2 960	401.1	64.2	45	862	23.3	6.6
Clay	17	27	1.1	0.5	23	2 475	188.6	42.0	17	D	D	D
Cleburne	25	64	4.4	1.5	34	1 687	367.0	39.1	49	735	21.0	6.2
Cleveland	4	D	D	D	NA	NA	NA	NA	2	D	D	D
Columbia	40	153	7.5	3.1	39	2 957	602.3	96.6	50	755	19.5	4.8

1. Firms subject to federal tax.

STATE County	Health Care and Social Assistance[1], 1997				Other Services[1], 1997				Federal funds and grants, fiscal 1999[2] Expenditures (mil dol)			
										Direct payments for individuals[3]		
	Number of Establish-ments	Number of Employees	Receipts (mil dol)	Annual Payroll (mil dol)	Number of Establish-ments	Number of Employees	Receipts (mil dol)	Annual Payroll (mil dol)	Total	Social Security and government retirement	Medicare	Food stamps and Supplemental Security Income
	159	160	161	162	163	164	165	166	167	168	169	170
ALABAMA—Cont'd												
Washington	7	D	D	D	7	12	0.6	0.1	78.7	32.7	14.6	5.8
Wilcox	8	144	5.3	2.2	9	25	1.6	0.4	81.9	24.3	12.4	11.4
Winston	25	452	20.6	7.7	33	90	4.5	1.3	107.9	49.8	29.4	5.2
ALASKA	1 143	8 156	758.1	309.4	852	4 364	331.0	93.4	5 278.7	754.9	161.3	81.3
Aleutians East Borough	8	D	D	D	NA	NA	NA	NA	19.4	3.8	0.1	0.2
Aleutians West Census Area	5	22	1.6	0.5	5	42	7.8	2.2	68.6	1.5	0.5	0.1
Anchorage	599	5 053	508.6	203.9	393	2 576	185.8	54.8	1 961.4	338.5	63.5	30.8
Bethel	5	47	2.1	0.6	7	23	2.5	0.4	185.2	8.2	3.2	6.6
Bristol Bay	1	D	D	D	NA	NA	NA	NA	22.0	3.0	0.8	0.0
Denali Borough	1	D	D	D	NA	NA	NA	NA	23.3	0.9	0.0	0.0
Dillingham	1	D	D	D	4	8	0.9	0.1	50.5	6.1	0.0	1.6
Fairbanks North Star	146	1 007	96.4	45.9	129	658	52.2	14.6	760.0	96.3	21.0	7.5
Haines	3	D	D	D	4	5	0.7	0.2	21.1	4.0	1.2	0.3
Juneau	81	437	40.1	16.6	56	240	15.8	4.5	440.5	41.2	10.1	2.5
Kenai Peninsula	97	543	37.3	12.8	80	266	20.1	5.3	196.4	64.5	19.2	5.0
Ketchikan Gateway	24	130	9.9	3.6	21	76	6.6	1.7	101.1	17.2	6.4	1.2
Kodiak Island	14	78	6.7	3.1	20	79	6.7	1.8	136.4	7.0	1.7	1.5
Lake and Peninsula Borough	NA	NA	NA	NA	NA	NA	NA	NA	11.2	1.8	1.2	0.5
Matanuska-Susitna	95	484	33.5	13.6	78	270	20.6	5.5	188.0	70.1	14.8	5.5
Nome	5	27	1.3	0.7	5	14	2.1	0.3	89.9	7.1	1.7	3.0
North Slope	3	11	0.4	0.1	1	D	D	D	48.5	5.2	1.1	0.3
Northwest Arctic Borough	NA	NA	NA	NA	NA	NA	NA	NA	65.7	4.5	1.2	2.4
Prince of Wales-Outer Ketchikan	4	18	1.3	0.3	5	16	1.2	0.3	37.2	4.9	0.7	0.7
Sitka	14	76	5.2	2.3	15	41	2.5	0.6	79.4	12.3	3.7	0.8
Skagway-Hoonah-Angoon	NA	NA	NA	NA	4	3	0.2	0.0	21.0	4.9	0.0	0.4
Southeast Fairbanks	8	46	2.9	1.6	3	D	D	D	63.1	8.7	1.6	1.1
Valdez-Cordova	18	85	4.0	1.5	15	35	3.4	0.7	84.5	9.7	2.3	0.9
Wade Hampton	1	D	D	D	NA	NA	NA	NA	56.5	3.9	1.3	4.9
Wrangell-Petersburg	8	19	1.7	0.3	7	9	1.1	0.2	43.2	9.8	3.3	0.5
Yakutat Borough	NA	NA	NA	NA	NA	NA	NA	NA	4.6	0.0	0.0	0.0
Yukon-Koyukuk	2	D	D	D	NA	NA	NA	NA	121.1	8.3	0.6	2.8
ARIZONA	9 155	97 091	6 687.9	2 893.3	6 494	43 669	2 794.0	829.6	26 959.3	9 102.8	3 155.3	606.7
Apache	24	180	8.1	3.7	18	67	3.6	0.9	538.5	81.1	22.7	29.0
Cochise	145	1 432	79.1	30.7	122	514	25.0	6.7	1 086.7	338.7	70.1	18.1
Coconino	240	1 627	107.5	45.8	183	899	54.7	14.2	552.4	167.7	47.1	20.4
Gila	76	666	37.1	14.8	54	184	10.7	2.6	275.8	139.9	51.3	8.8
Graham	53	501	26.7	10.1	32	210	12.2	3.6	142.4	53.5	17.3	5.7
Greenlee	6	20	1.0	0.3	5	8	0.5	0.2	26.5	13.2	4.5	0.9
La Paz	20	100	7.9	3.8	19	80	5.0	0.8	118.0	43.1	0.0	3.1
Maricopa	5 848	63 697	4 532.2	1 979.0	4 060	30 024	2 012.8	597.3	12 976.7	4 813.7	1 832.2	300.7
Mohave	258	1 950	134.6	55.3	194	1 039	67.4	18.7	665.4	409.8	133.9	18.1
Navajo	108	675	43.0	16.3	91	424	24.5	6.3	447.6	148.1	39.4	29.9
Pima	1 614	19 280	1 283.3	563.9	1 171	7 575	437.9	138.1	5 700.9	1 777.2	593.1	104.5
Pinal	132	1 395	86.4	37.1	108	656	27.7	9.0	717.0	304.4	120.5	24.4
Santa Cruz	30	126	19.5	5.7	48	130	6.4	1.6	165.6	49.2	16.4	7.4
Yavapai	377	3 014	167.5	66.8	231	1 004	59.1	16.1	732.7	463.8	110.0	15.1
Yuma	224	2 428	154.1	60.1	158	855	46.5	13.6	775.0	276.7	96.8	20.8
ARKANSAS	4 571	59 960	3 655.1	1 609.7	3 553	18 809	1 113.9	310.5	13 630.8	5 465.0	2 018.9	557.5
Arkansas	31	362	13.8	6.2	38	138	7.5	1.5	148.0	45.0	21.0	4.5
Ashley	23	325	13.8	6.2	25	103	6.5	1.9	129.7	49.1	23.2	7.3
Baxter	99	796	62.0	28.1	83	466	25.3	8.1	213.7	139.5	42.3	4.6
Benton	207	2 285	121.6	60.2	193	1 162	72.4	22.3	448.5	292.9	77.3	10.2
Boone	64	535	32.5	12.8	54	226	12.6	3.5	147.9	83.3	25.4	5.5
Bradley	19	265	11.1	4.4	23	58	5.0	1.1	70.4	28.5	14.4	2.9
Calhoun	3	D	D	D	3	D	D	D	29.7	10.2	3.8	1.1
Carroll	35	256	12.3	4.8	34	88	5.0	1.2	86.8	50.5	17.1	2.4
Chicot	16	167	7.4	3.2	17	61	2.7	0.8	103.3	27.6	15.0	7.9
Clark	40	380	15.3	6.4	29	115	5.6	1.5	99.3	47.1	20.2	3.9
Clay	18	265	10.1	4.5	20	55	3.3	0.8	118.6	42.4	19.8	3.8
Cleburne	28	304	12.1	5.2	28	138	7.0	2.0	114.2	70.8	21.3	3.5
Cleveland	3	D	D	D	5	10	0.9	0.3	31.9	16.9	6.2	1.4
Columbia	45	375	15.7	7.0	40	165	9.1	2.8	123.4	55.5	23.1	8.6

1. Firms subject to federal tax.　　2. October 1, 1998 to September 30, 1999.　　3. State totals may include programs not allocated by county.

Table B. States and Counties — Federal Funds and Local Government Finances

	Federal funds and grants, fiscal 1999[1] (cont'd)							Local government finances, 1997				
	Expenditures (mil dol) (cont'd)							General revenue				
	Procurement contract awards			Grants[2]							Taxes	
STATE / County												Per capita[3] (dollars)
	Salaries and wages	Defense	Other	Medicaid and other health-related	Nutrition and family welfare	Education	Other	Total (mil dol)	Intergovern-mental (mil dol)	Total (mil dol)	Total	Property
	171	172	173	174	175	176	177	178	179	180	181	182
ALABAMA—Cont'd												
Washington	2.1	0.0	0.5	12.1	2.3	1.1	6.4	35.3	18.1	7.3	412	314
Wilcox	3.9	0.1	0.6	21.2	4.2	1.7	0.7	31.2	16.1	3.4	250	95
Winston	5.1	0.6	0.9	11.4	1.5	1.0	2.1	43.1	31.1	5.7	239	97
ALASKA	1 271.8	612.1	233.4	593.4	195.8	222.1	918.0	X	X	X	X	X
Aleutians East Borough	1.2	6.3	0.5	3.8	0.6	2.4	0.0	16.3	8.3	5.0	2 142	410
Aleutians West Census Area	2.3	57.9	1.8	0.6	0.6	1.9	1.3	34.0	8.4	14.6	3 121	934
Anchorage	708.2	277.1	81.6	179.3	56.7	25.0	171.4	747.0	306.7	234.7	935	835
Bethel	8.3	1.6	2.6	101.5	11.5	22.3	12.0	35.6	26.1	3.4	212	0
Bristol Bay	2.7	3.3	0.6	8.5	0.1	2.4	0.2	10.6	6.1	2.7	2 022	1 081
Denali Borough	5.9	16.0	0.2	0.0	0.1	0.2	0.0	6.0	4.1	1.7	849	100
Dillingham	2.7	3.1	3.1	20.5	3.3	5.3	4.4	13.4	7.2	1.8	406	0
Fairbanks North Star	322.7	113.7	26.7	56.2	21.8	13.1	69.5	261.4	141.8	58.7	697	631
Haines	0.6	1.1	0.2	1.3	0.1	0.2	12.2	10.5	3.3	4.2	1 909	875
Juneau	51.7	0.3	6.5	36.5	61.4	67.4	153.1	160.4	54.3	50.1	1 671	771
Kenai Peninsula	20.9	1.9	4.9	17.3	4.5	3.9	49.6	181.6	89.3	62.9	1 322	800
Ketchikan Gateway	19.4	8.8	9.3	7.8	2.8	1.2	26.7	90.1	37.3	22.2	1 606	765
Kodiak Island	41.4	10.7	44.5	9.0	2.8	1.8	15.6	60.0	31.3	13.1	882	424
Lake and Peninsula Borough	1.5	0.1	0.3	0.0	0.4	0.2	5.2	17.8	11.5	4.3	2 443	809
Matanuska-Susitna	7.1	0.0	15.7	6.5	6.9	4.5	56.3	147.2	90.7	41.0	755	613
Nome	5.3	11.9	1.8	14.2	6.4	17.1	16.4	34.0	21.8	4.1	463	147
North Slope	1.5	7.0	1.2	5.4	1.1	8.4	13.8	335.6	43.5	224.1	31 157	31 139
Northwest Arctic Borough	4.0	2.4	1.3	35.1	2.2	5.8	6.5	47.9	36.3	1.9	288	0
Prince of Wales-Outer Ketchikan	3.9	2.4	5.4	3.9	0.9	3.5	9.7	20.6	13.0	2.1	289	46
Sitka	15.0	0.0	5.8	34.3	1.7	1.1	3.0	45.5	21.3	9.1	1 070	375
Skagway-Hoonah-Angoon	5.1	1.5	2.1	2.2	0.3	2.0	2.5	12.3	7.2	2.8	730	282
Southeast Fairbanks	15.9	7.8	4.7	6.7	0.9	2.2	13.4	0.2	0.2	0.0	1	1
Valdez-Cordova	8.0	26.6	3.2	4.9	1.3	0.8	26.2	112.3	11.6	19.7	1 895	1 677
Wade Hampton	2.0	0.3	0.6	14.4	1.9	11.3	15.9	6.4	2.9	0.6	91	14
Wrangell-Petersburg	7.8	7.2	5.5	2.2	1.2	1.2	3.2	39.0	17.4	6.5	935	337
Yakutat Borough	0.7	2.9	0.2	0.3	0.2	0.2	0.1	5.0	3.6	0.5	572	159
Yukon-Koyukuk	6.1	40.3	3.2	17.2	3.1	7.3	31.7	13.9	9.3	0.8	125	39
ARIZONA	2 661.3	4 156.8	624.8	1 674.2	897.7	469.2	1 496.1	X	X	X	X	X
Apache	76.0	0.1	33.1	111.2	71.6	65.4	34.8	174.4	115.8	33.5	481	430
Cochise	311.3	199.8	14.2	46.2	17.6	14.4	40.8	259.3	137.4	71.2	635	533
Coconino	111.3	3.5	33.5	61.2	25.5	21.9	50.1	277.5	122.9	94.2	828	569
Gila	19.2	0.1	5.2	23.7	10.2	3.5	12.5	116.4	59.1	41.0	847	667
Graham	16.5	1.4	5.3	17.3	6.5	2.7	10.8	76.4	51.6	12.6	404	260
Greenlee	1.5	0.0	0.3	2.8	1.4	0.4	1.2	29.5	12.4	8.2	875	782
La Paz	6.0	44.4	6.6	0.1	3.5	1.6	3.3	47.5	24.1	10.6	710	597
Maricopa	1 141.7	2 203.0	361.9	763.0	505.2	230.4	615.2	6 771.3	2 846.3	2 329.4	864	588
Mohave	22.8	1.5	7.0	15.3	10.1	5.3	38.5	283.3	104.9	121.7	944	765
Navajo	59.7	0.0	9.9	78.2	28.5	22.2	19.7	237.3	151.0	54.4	573	430
Pima	576.0	1 658.5	91.8	353.7	106.4	62.5	327.3	1 850.7	837.9	671.3	860	654
Pinal	35.8	1.8	26.5	83.7	37.5	13.9	32.5	371.0	165.3	123.1	859	700
Santa Cruz	43.2	0.7	2.3	25.2	6.3	5.5	7.9	87.4	48.5	24.6	649	543
Yavapai	50.5	3.0	9.1	27.0	9.7	7.1	33.1	322.9	131.7	135.5	939	677
Yuma	189.7	38.9	17.9	37.8	26.0	11.3	40.6	336.4	182.6	93.8	721	481
ARKANSAS	1 115.6	248.0	218.8	1 256.8	384.3	253.4	719.7	X	X	X	X	X
Arkansas	7.7	0.6	12.4	13.6	2.2	1.1	3.3	40.3	16.2	11.7	564	293
Ashley	3.9	0.0	0.8	17.9	2.5	1.3	10.1	43.2	19.1	12.3	503	292
Baxter	7.8	0.9	2.2	7.4	1.2	1.3	5.4	40.7	17.0	16.8	460	288
Benton	19.5	0.4	14.4	17.2	5.5	2.6	3.3	204.5	71.8	79.9	614	356
Boone	9.9	1.5	2.5	11.0	3.2	1.9	-0.9	82.3	24.7	14.1	442	237
Bradley	2.2	0.0	0.4	8.1	3.0	0.7	8.2	33.8	11.2	7.2	623	466
Calhoun	0.7	6.8	0.2	5.8	0.5	0.2	0.1	9.2	3.8	4.2	723	657
Carroll	6.4	0.5	1.1	5.5	0.7	0.7	0.6	39.4	12.7	12.4	554	315
Chicot	1.5	0.0	0.3	23.1	3.9	1.9	1.4	35.9	15.8	6.0	396	292
Clark	4.9	0.1	0.7	11.1	2.2	2.6	0.6	32.5	15.9	11.5	519	253
Clay	3.4	0.0	0.8	16.2	1.3	0.8	2.1	23.4	12.5	5.6	323	233
Cleburne	4.7	0.1	1.0	8.1	1.0	1.1	1.6	25.0	12.4	8.1	359	271
Cleveland	0.9	0.0	0.2	4.4	1.1	0.4	0.3	9.9	7.0	1.9	232	187
Columbia	3.0	4.8	0.9	17.7	2.9	2.2	1.4	44.7	21.1	7.3	289	231

1. October 1, 1998 to September 30, 1999. 2. State totals may include programs not allocated by county. 3. Based on the resident population estimated as of July 1 of the year shown.

Table B. States and Counties — Local Government Finances, Government Employment, and Elections

STATE County	Direct general expenditure — Total (mil dol)	Per capita[1] (dollars)	Percent of total for — Education	Health and hospitals	Police protection	Public welfare	Highways	Debt outstanding — Total (mil dol)	Per capita[1] (dollars)	Govt employment — Federal civilian	Federal military	State and local	Presidential election 2000 — Democratic	Republican	All other
	183	184	185	186	187	188	189	190	191	192	193	194	195	196	197
ALABAMA—Cont'd															
Washington	35.6	2 019	55.0	15.9	3.3	0.1	6.8	15.6	888	40	110	989	44.6	54.2	1.2
Wilcox	38.3	2 830	54.0	5.1	1.8	0.1	4.0	93.9	6 934	85	84	796	67.2	32.4	0.4
Winston	44.5	1 859	51.7	21.1	4.2	0.1	8.5	15.8	660	91	150	1 032	28.9	68.8	2.3
ALASKA	X	X	X	X	X	X	X	X	X	17 041	22 707	53 138	27.7	58.6	13.7
Aleutians East Borough	15.0	6 467	42.2	3.4	3.3	0.0	3.5	6.6	2 834	20	17	220	NA	NA	NA
Aleutians West Census Area	32.5	6 923	14.8	0.7	8.5	0.2	12.8	16.9	3 601	55	56	422	NA	NA	NA
Anchorage	796.1	3 171	47.4	3.8	5.0	1.1	7.7	1 314.8	5 237	9 954	10 753	17 745	NA	NA	NA
Bethel	33.6	2 122	0.0	1.0	4.7	0.2	5.7	70.2	4 442	124	120	2 138	NA	NA	NA
Bristol Bay	10.9	8 125	38.7	6.5	7.1	0.0	2.9	1.1	806	46	10	315	NA	NA	NA
Denali Borough	5.2	2 620	92.2	0.4	0.0	0.0	1.0	0.0	0	189	134	115	NA	NA	NA
Dillingham	15.3	3 433	47.5	0.6	6.8	0.0	1.8	0.0	0	51	34	534	NA	NA	NA
Fairbanks North Star	268.4	3 184	53.7	0.3	2.2	0.0	3.7	146.4	1 737	3 302	7 723	6 504	NA	NA	NA
Haines	9.6	4 422	44.1	1.8	10.9	0.1	3.5	3.9	1 783	12	17	166	NA	NA	NA
Juneau	148.3	4 944	35.8	21.0	4.7	1.4	4.7	58.6	1 954	840	428	5 841	NA	NA	NA
Kenai Peninsula	177.8	3 738	50.9	4.9	2.9	0.0	3.5	84.6	1 778	401	456	3 767	NA	NA	NA
Ketchikan Gateway	63.0	4 566	32.4	4.9	4.0	0.1	4.6	44.8	3 246	273	313	1 504	NA	NA	NA
Kodiak Island	58.6	3 944	41.1	4.9	4.4	0.6	2.6	50.9	3 421	169	976	947	NA	NA	NA
Lake and Peninsula Borough	20.5	11 550	63.1	0.3	0.6	0.0	1.9	8.5	4 798	48	13	115	NA	NA	NA
Matanuska-Susitna	135.8	2 496	71.2	5.0	2.1	0.0	3.7	30.0	551	136	424	2 761	NA	NA	NA
Nome	40.1	4 512	21.2	0.6	3.5	0.0	2.8	1.1	125	80	91	1 271	NA	NA	NA
North Slope	325.0	45 193	14.3	3.5	5.2	1.9	4.7	893.1	124 196	28	54	1 921	NA	NA	NA
Northwest Arctic Borough	45.0	6 788	74.9	0.2	1.8	0.0	0.5	39.1	5 899	59	51	849	NA	NA	NA
Prince of Wales-Outer Ketchikan	20.4	2 852	39.5	0.6	1.3	0.0	1.0	29.6	4 131	98	53	643	NA	NA	NA
Sitka	35.8	4 227	38.6	17.1	6.6	0.7	2.3	73.4	8 661	204	244	842	NA	NA	NA
Skagway-Hoonah-Angoon	13.5	3 561	60.4	1.5	5.0	0.3	2.9	2.6	693	157	29	342	NA	NA	NA
Southeast Fairbanks	0.2	36	0.0	19.4	0.0	0.0	9.5	0.0	0	325	352	369	NA	NA	NA
Valdez-Cordova	114.5	11 009	11.8	6.1	1.9	0.1	1.9	874.1	84 056	130	180	1 032	NA	NA	NA
Wade Hampton	6.8	998	25.4	4.1	11.0	2.1	1.5	0.0	0	34	51	1 058	NA	NA	NA
Wrangell-Petersburg	41.7	5 995	31.7	21.2	2.6	0.1	3.1	9.9	1 422	190	77	649	NA	NA	NA
Yakutat Borough	5.5	6 358	40.2	0.4	5.3	0.0	3.3	0.0	0	19	0	75	NA	NA	NA
Yukon-Koyukuk	14.3	2 370	54.0	5.5	4.3	0.0	1.6	1.2	205	97	45	993	NA	NA	NA
ARIZONA	X	X	X	X	X	X	X	X	X	44 070	32 672	266 516	44.7	51.0	4.2
Apache	164.2	2 362	72.4	1.2	2.4	0.8	4.0	351.4	5 053	2 060	169	3 549	67.0	30.6	2.4
Cochise	241.3	2 150	46.6	1.4	6.6	6.7	5.3	172.7	1 538	3 933	5 868	5 713	40.2	54.8	5.0
Coconino	262.4	2 307	44.3	1.6	6.3	6.2	5.4	373.3	3 283	2 787	295	11 154	49.6	43.0	7.4
Gila	101.1	2 089	51.0	1.8	5.3	2.7	6.9	42.9	887	472	121	2 589	43.4	51.6	5.0
Graham	81.0	2 605	69.3	1.8	3.6	2.1	4.6	5.6	179	322	78	2 648	34.7	62.2	3.1
Greenlee	30.5	3 242	37.8	3.0	6.2	2.7	5.3	81.9	8 719	39	23	544	41.1	54.7	4.2
La Paz	44.9	3 008	40.0	3.5	8.6	0.4	8.9	23.7	1 587	140	37	924	39.5	56.7	3.8
Maricopa	6 755.5	2 506	36.9	3.4	7.2	7.7	4.2	13 875.8	5 146	18 714	12 677	144 715	43.0	53.3	3.7
Mohave	272.6	2 115	38.6	1.4	7.6	1.1	8.0	363.9	2 823	478	321	5 543	39.6	55.2	5.2
Navajo	229.0	2 412	64.2	2.2	3.4	1.1	5.0	205.3	2 163	1 356	238	5 089	46.9	49.3	3.8
Pima	2 026.7	2 598	36.8	5.1	5.5	7.0	3.9	2 077.0	2 662	8 619	7 728	56 163	51.3	43.3	5.3
Pinal	369.7	2 579	49.1	3.5	5.4	5.8	5.7	338.8	2 364	778	361	12 443	47.6	48.7	3.7
Santa Cruz	100.4	2 652	46.7	1.0	5.6	7.2	8.3	84.4	2 229	834	94	1 894	58.8	37.6	3.6
Yavapai	307.7	2 133	42.8	1.1	6.4	2.3	8.5	247.2	1 713	1 139	375	6 812	35.3	59.0	5.7
Yuma	334.0	2 569	46.4	1.4	6.7	2.1	7.3	266.5	2 049	2 399	4 287	6 736	42.1	54.8	3.1
ARKANSAS	X	X	X	X	X	X	X	X	X	20 728	19 178	158 504	45.9	51.3	2.8
Arkansas	39.9	1 921	46.9	9.6	5.8	0.0	7.9	40.0	1 923	175	117	1 182	45.2	52.6	2.2
Ashley	43.6	1 784	53.2	0.2	3.7	0.0	6.6	90.9	3 721	84	138	1 212	51.4	46.9	1.7
Baxter	45.2	1 237	60.5	0.3	4.3	3.7	10.3	31.9	872	164	205	1 312	39.0	57.1	3.9
Benton	195.6	1 505	55.8	5.9	6.1	0.0	5.0	213.8	1 644	393	757	5 309	32.2	64.9	2.9
Boone	74.6	2 332	34.5	42.9	2.5	0.0	5.0	19.5	609	234	180	2 342	33.0	62.8	4.2
Bradley	30.0	2 597	39.2	41.5	2.9	0.0	4.2	6.4	552	36	65	734	53.3	45.1	1.6
Calhoun	8.0	1 391	61.1	0.0	4.6	0.1	9.9	1.2	205	12	32	604	46.5	51.6	1.8
Carroll	42.3	1 893	40.9	17.5	5.5	0.1	7.7	29.4	1 315	109	127	902	37.5	57.9	4.6
Chicot	34.3	2 267	50.7	26.1	3.8	0.0	4.8	16.8	1 110	44	84	1 193	63.3	35.1	1.5
Clark	30.5	1 381	57.2	0.2	5.6	0.1	9.8	18.8	851	103	124	1 986	54.0	43.8	2.2
Clay	20.9	1 200	62.8	0.3	4.6	0.3	11.4	11.0	631	66	97	857	59.8	38.2	2.0
Cleburne	24.3	1 081	69.4	0.1	5.3	0.4	4.7	21.9	975	107	129	756	40.4	56.1	3.5
Cleveland	10.1	1 214	77.2	0.4	3.3	0.0	7.6	2.5	296	17	48	353	44.5	52.8	2.8
Columbia	47.5	1 884	46.2	24.5	3.1	0.0	3.8	18.6	737	56	141	1 794	43.0	53.9	3.1

1. Based on the resident population estimated as of July 1 of the year shown.

Table B. States and Counties — **Land Area and Population**

STATE/ County code	MSA/ PMSA/ NECMA code[1]	County Type[2]	STATE County	Land area[3] (sq km) 1990	Total persons	Rank	Per square kilometer	White	Black	Am. Indian, Eskimo, Aleut	Asian and Pacific Islander	Percent Hispanic[4]	Under 5 years	5 to 17 years	18 to 24 years	25 to 34 years	35 to 44 years	45 to 54 years
				1	2	3	4	5	6	7	8	9	10	11	12	13	14	15
			ARKANSAS—Cont'd															
05 029	...	6	Conway	1 441	19 856	1 769	13.8	82.5	16.9	0.4	0.2	1.5	6.8	19.0	8.2	11.8	13.1	12.6
05 031	3700	5	Craighead	1 841	77 668	643	42.2	92.5	6.5	0.3	0.7	1.4	7.0	17.5	13.9	13.6	14.8	12.6
05 033	2720	3	Crawford	1 542	51 409	889	33.3	96.0	1.2	1.5	1.3	2.8	7.7	21.2	8.4	13.4	15.2	13.6
05 035	4920	1	Crittenden	1 581	50 138	902	31.7	52.8	46.5	0.2	0.5	1.7	8.6	22.2	10.5	13.5	14.7	12.5
05 037	...	6	Cross	1 595	19 302	1 799	12.1	71.4	28.2	0.2	0.3	1.5	7.4	22.2	9.4	12.0	14.4	12.9
05 039	...	7	Dallas	1 729	8 920	2 514	5.2	57.8	41.9	0.1	0.1	0.8	6.4	19.1	8.4	11.2	15.1	13.0
05 041	...	7	Desha	1 981	14 855	2 077	7.5	53.6	45.9	0.2	0.1	2.1	7.8	22.8	9.4	11.9	13.9	11.8
05 043	...	7	Drew	2 145	17 449	1 905	8.1	68.8	30.9	0.2	0.2	1.3	7.0	20.4	12.0	12.4	14.8	12.8
05 045	4400	2	Faulkner	1 677	80 034	630	47.7	90.0	9.1	0.4	0.5	1.4	7.2	18.7	15.0	14.1	15.1	11.9
05 047	...	6	Franklin	1 579	16 801	1 943	10.6	98.3	0.7	0.7	0.3	2.7	6.6	20.2	8.8	12.0	14.4	13.5
05 049	...	9	Fulton	1 601	11 019	2 344	6.9	99.2	0.2	0.4	0.1	0.7	5.6	16.7	6.7	9.5	13.4	13.1
05 051	...	4	Garland	1 756	84 475	597	48.1	90.3	8.6	0.6	0.4	2.5	5.7	15.2	7.2	10.7	13.5	12.7
05 053	...	6	Grant	1 636	15 984	2 005	9.8	96.3	3.2	0.3	0.2	1.5	6.7	19.5	8.5	12.6	15.8	15.0
05 055	...	7	Greene	1 496	36 395	1 181	24.3	99.3	0.2	0.3	0.3	1.5	6.7	18.2	9.5	12.6	14.9	14.1
05 057	...	6	Hempstead	1 888	22 093	1 654	11.7	66.2	33.2	0.3	0.3	2.9	7.0	20.2	8.8	12.2	14.2	12.9
05 059	...	6	Hot Spring	1 593	29 154	1 406	18.3	86.8	12.6	0.4	0.2	1.2	6.4	19.0	8.1	11.3	15.2	13.4
05 061	...	7	Howard	1 522	13 681	2 159	9.0	74.6	24.3	0.4	0.6	1.7	6.9	20.3	9.1	11.9	14.0	13.0
05 063	...	7	Independence	1 978	33 066	1 283	16.7	96.8	2.4	0.3	0.6	1.5	6.5	19.3	8.8	12.4	15.3	13.3
05 065	...	9	Izard	1 504	13 112	2 203	8.7	97.2	1.9	0.6	0.3	1.5	5.6	15.8	7.1	10.6	13.0	13.7
05 067	...	7	Jackson	1 641	17 516	1 899	10.7	83.2	16.3	0.3	0.2	0.8	5.8	18.1	7.4	11.2	13.8	12.3
05 069	6240	3	Jefferson	2 292	80 785	625	35.2	52.4	46.8	0.2	0.5	1.1	7.1	20.0	12.1	12.7	14.8	12.3
05 071	...	7	Johnson	1 715	21 358	1 689	12.5	96.6	2.2	0.6	0.5	2.8	6.5	18.3	10.8	12.1	13.7	12.8
05 073	...	8	Lafayette	1 364	8 846	2 518	6.5	57.2	42.4	0.2	0.2	0.9	6.5	20.1	9.5	10.8	13.4	13.7
05 075	...	7	Lawrence	1 519	17 342	1 910	11.4	98.4	0.7	0.7	0.2	1.0	6.3	17.9	9.1	11.4	13.5	13.3
05 077	...	6	Lee	1 558	12 699	2 234	8.2	40.2	59.0	0.3	0.5	3.1	6.9	22.4	10.5	11.7	14.4	11.7
05 079	...	8	Lincoln	1 454	14 372	2 107	9.9	61.1	38.1	0.5	0.2	2.1	6.1	17.3	11.0	18.1	16.7	12.0
05 081	...	6	Little River	1 377	13 065	2 209	9.5	75.2	23.8	0.8	0.2	2.4	6.4	20.3	9.1	11.7	14.6	13.6
05 083	...	6	Logan	1 839	21 134	1 708	11.5	97.6	1.6	0.6	0.2	1.6	6.8	19.8	8.1	11.7	14.0	13.3
05 085	4400	2	Lonoke	1 983	51 447	888	25.9	88.8	10.4	0.4	0.4	1.6	7.1	22.1	8.4	13.6	16.1	14.0
05 087	...	8	Madison	2 168	13 313	2 190	6.1	98.9	0.1	1.1	0.2	2.6	7.0	19.6	7.7	11.4	14.9	13.5
05 089	...	9	Marion	1 548	14 902	2 069	9.6	99.2	0.1	0.4	0.3	1.0	5.2	16.6	6.3	9.7	13.8	14.1
05 091	8360	3	Miller	1 616	39 377	1 101	24.4	73.8	25.4	0.3	0.5	2.0	7.4	20.5	9.6	12.8	14.7	12.6
05 093	...	4	Mississippi	2 327	49 920	909	21.5	68.2	30.7	0.3	0.8	3.1	8.9	22.1	10.3	13.7	14.0	11.0
05 095	...	7	Monroe	1 571	9 990	2 426	6.4	56.8	42.7	0.2	0.3	0.6	7.6	21.3	8.3	10.7	13.0	12.6
05 097	...	9	Montgomery	2 023	8 740	2 531	4.3	98.5	0.2	1.1	0.2	1.8	5.6	16.8	7.3	10.7	13.1	14.2
05 099	...	7	Nevada	1 606	10 024	2 421	6.2	64.4	35.2	0.3	0.1	1.6	6.4	20.6	8.9	11.3	15.0	13.1
05 101	...	9	Newton	2 132	8 226	2 575	3.9	98.9	0.0	0.6	0.4	1.4	6.5	20.9	7.2	10.9	14.8	14.9
05 103	...	7	Ouachita	1 897	27 487	1 450	14.5	61.1	38.5	0.1	0.3	1.0	6.6	18.9	8.1	11.9	14.9	12.4
05 105	...	8	Perry	1 427	9 678	2 455	6.8	97.5	1.7	0.6	0.2	1.5	6.4	18.7	8.5	11.5	14.4	13.7
05 107	...	7	Phillips	1 794	27 049	1 464	15.1	41.8	57.7	0.1	0.4	2.0	8.8	24.7	9.0	10.7	12.9	12.2
05 109	...	9	Pike	1 562	10 451	2 384	6.7	94.8	4.5	0.6	0.1	1.5	6.5	19.3	8.0	11.4	13.7	13.6
05 111	...	6	Poinsett	1 963	24 592	1 546	12.5	91.3	8.3	0.2	0.3	1.3	7.1	19.2	8.9	12.2	14.0	14.1
05 113	...	7	Polk	2 226	19 607	1 782	8.8	98.6	0.1	1.1	0.3	4.4	6.7	19.2	7.7	10.5	13.7	13.7
05 115	...	5	Pope	2 103	52 598	868	25.0	95.8	2.9	0.7	0.6	2.3	7.5	18.9	12.0	13.5	15.2	12.5
05 117	...	8	Prairie	1 673	9 284	2 486	5.5	84.1	15.4	0.5	0.1	1.0	6.6	18.3	8.2	11.7	13.9	13.2
05 119	4400	2	Pulaski	1 997	349 232	163	174.9	69.1	29.6	0.3	1.1	2.2	7.4	18.2	10.0	15.3	16.8	12.4
05 121	...	7	Randolph	1 688	17 904	1 876	10.6	98.4	1.1	0.3	0.2	1.3	6.4	18.6	7.8	11.2	13.6	13.5
05 123	...	6	St. Francis	1 642	27 766	1 441	16.9	48.4	50.8	0.1	0.6	1.7	8.3	23.8	9.2	11.7	14.3	12.0
05 125	4400	2	Saline	1 877	78 361	640	41.7	96.6	2.4	0.4	0.5	1.5	6.8	19.9	8.4	13.6	16.4	14.0
05 127	...	6	Scott	2 315	10 644	2 364	4.6	98.2	0.1	1.0	0.8	1.2	7.1	18.0	8.4	12.0	12.9	14.7
05 129	...	9	Searcy	1 728	7 791	2 622	4.5	98.8	0.1	0.8	0.3	1.1	5.9	18.0	6.9	9.9	14.3	13.6
05 131	2720	3	Sebastian	1 389	106 252	491	76.5	87.6	6.6	1.3	4.5	3.4	7.6	18.6	9.2	13.9	15.6	12.9
05 133	...	6	Sevier	1 461	14 671	2 090	10.0	90.8	6.7	2.3	0.1	10.5	6.8	19.9	9.2	13.6	14.3	12.6
05 135	...	7	Sharp	1 565	17 092	1 924	10.9	98.3	0.7	0.7	0.3	1.0	5.1	17.1	6.6	9.3	12.5	12.6
05 137	...	9	Stone	1 571	11 220	2 331	7.1	99.1	0.1	0.5	0.3	1.1	5.5	17.7	6.1	10.4	14.3	14.7
05 139	...	5	Union	2 691	44 967	986	16.7	66.1	33.5	0.2	0.3	1.1	7.1	19.6	8.5	12.5	15.1	12.4
05 141	...	8	Van Buren	1 843	15 677	2 022	8.5	98.9	0.4	0.5	0.3	1.8	5.2	16.6	6.2	9.1	12.2	12.5
05 143	2580	3	Washington	2 461	146 593	357	59.6	95.8	1.8	1.2	1.2	3.4	7.2	17.8	14.4	14.4	15.4	12.0
05 145	...	4	White	2 678	65 081	733	24.3	95.6	3.7	0.4	0.3	1.5	6.5	18.3	12.8	11.9	14.1	12.9
05 147	...	7	Woodruff	1 519	8 710	2 534	5.7	65.1	34.6	0.1	0.1	0.5	7.1	21.1	8.8	11.2	14.4	11.8
05 149	...	7	Yell	2 403	18 853	1 825	7.8	96.3	2.5	0.4	0.8	2.4	7.0	18.4	8.7	12.2	13.5	13.7
06 000	...	X	**CALIFORNIA**	403 970	33 145 121	X	82.0	79.4	7.5	0.9	12.2	31.6	7.5	19.4	10.0	15.4	16.9	12.4
06 001	5775	0	Alameda	1 910	1 415 582	20	741.1	60.6	19.0	0.8	19.6	18.6	6.7	17.7	9.8	15.8	18.6	13.3
06 003	...	9	Alpine	1 913	1 161	3 105	0.6	74.0	0.5	24.7	0.8	8.6	6.3	17.9	8.8	14.9	20.7	16.8
06 005	...	6	Amador	1 535	34 153	1 252	22.2	92.0	5.1	1.8	1.1	9.9	4.4	15.0	8.9	12.0	16.8	14.0

1. MSA = Metropolitan Statistical Area. PMSA = Primary MSA. NECMA = New England County Metropolitan Area. See Appendix A for explanation of these concepts. See Appendix B for list of metropolitan areas identified by type, with component counties. 2. County typology code from the Economic Research Service of USDA. See Appendix A for definition. 3. Dry land or land partially or temporarily covered by water. 4. Hispanic persons may be of any race.

STATE County	Population, 1999 (cont'd) Age (percent) (cont'd)				Population — change and components of change, 1980–1999 Total persons		Percent change		Components of change, 1990–1999			Households, 1990			Percent	
	55 to 64 years	65 to 74 years	75 years and over	Percent female	1990	1980	1980– 1990	1990– 1999	Births	Deaths	Net migration	Number	Percent change, 1980– 1990	Persons per house-hold	Female family house-holder[1]	One person
	16	17	18	19	20	21	22	23	24	25	26	27	28	29	30	31
ARKANSAS—Cont'd																
Conway	10.0	10.0	8.7	52.4	19 151	19 505	-1.8	3.7	2 382	2 127	589	7 179	5.6	2.62	10.9	23.5
Craighead	9.1	6.1	5.5	51.9	68 956	63 239	9.0	12.6	9 879	6 148	6 126	26 285	17.7	2.53	10.5	23.5
Crawford	9.1	6.1	5.3	50.9	42 493	36 892	15.2	21.0	6 450	4 022	6 686	15 251	21.4	2.75	9.9	17.9
Crittenden	7.8	5.8	4.3	52.9	49 939	49 499	0.9	0.4	8 270	4 521	-3 302	17 120	9.0	2.89	18.7	21.3
Cross	8.7	6.7	6.4	52.0	19 225	20 434	-5.9	0.4	2 707	2 045	-476	6 754	1.9	2.81	12.8	20.8
Dallas	9.9	8.4	8.4	51.9	9 614	10 515	-8.6	-7.2	1 141	1 257	-537	3 600	-3.6	2.61	11.6	25.3
Desha	7.8	7.1	7.5	53.6	16 798	19 760	-15.0	-11.6	2 404	1 808	-2 487	5 957	-10.3	2.78	17.5	24.3
Drew	8.6	6.0	6.1	51.9	17 369	17 910	-3.0	0.5	2 355	1 779	-413	6 342	2.3	2.63	13.6	23.7
Faulkner	8.1	5.3	4.5	51.5	60 006	46 192	29.9	33.4	9 072	4 687	15 764	21 325	37.7	2.65	9.3	20.5
Franklin	10.4	7.0	7.1	50.1	14 897	14 705	1.3	12.8	2 073	1 791	1 688	5 578	8.0	2.58	8.0	22.2
Fulton	12.9	12.1	10.1	51.8	10 037	9 975	0.6	9.8	1 090	1 265	1 187	4 010	6.5	2.47	7.0	23.3
Garland	12.2	12.7	10.2	52.3	73 397	70 531	4.1	15.1	8 734	10 477	13 191	30 836	9.5	2.32	9.5	27.6
Grant	9.5	6.4	5.9	50.7	13 948	13 008	7.2	14.6	1 729	1 238	1 620	5 118	13.6	2.70	7.2	19.1
Greene	10.8	7.2	6.8	51.5	31 804	30 744	3.4	14.4	4 170	3 478	4 037	12 325	9.8	2.54	8.5	22.0
Hempstead	9.5	6.9	7.7	52.3	21 621	23 635	-8.5	2.2	3 031	2 430	2	8 212	-4.3	2.58	13.4	25.0
Hot Spring	10.9	8.6	7.1	51.6	26 115	26 819	-2.6	11.6	3 317	2 854	2 539	10 115	4.5	2.55	10.0	23.2
Howard	9.3	7.4	8.1	51.7	13 569	13 459	0.8	0.8	1 823	1 685	53	4 975	3.3	2.65	11.5	23.4
Independence	10.3	7.2	7.0	51.3	31 192	30 147	3.5	6.0	3 792	3 206	1 476	11 846	8.7	2.58	8.2	22.8
Izard	12.8	10.9	10.4	50.4	11 364	10 768	5.5	15.4	1 218	1 758	2 333	4 684	9.3	2.37	6.9	24.2
Jackson	10.2	10.4	10.3	52.5	18 944	21 646	-12.5	-7.5	2 176	2 373	-1 137	7 361	-5.5	2.54	12.2	25.0
Jefferson	8.3	6.8	5.9	51.9	85 487	90 718	-5.8	-5.5	12 364	8 714	-8 036	30 001	-1.9	2.70	16.0	24.2
Johnson	10.9	7.4	7.6	50.9	18 221	17 423	4.6	17.2	2 521	2 069	2 765	7 059	10.4	2.50	8.6	24.4
Lafayette	9.1	8.4	8.6	52.5	9 643	10 213	-5.6	-8.3	1 186	1 111	-825	3 584	-0.1	2.66	13.9	26.6
Lawrence	10.9	8.4	9.2	51.8	17 455	18 447	-5.4	-0.6	2 131	2 167	6	6 857	0.9	2.49	9.3	24.9
Lee	8.4	7.3	6.8	48.4	13 053	15 539	-16.0	-2.7	1 763	1 426	-640	4 578	-7.4	2.82	20.1	25.6
Lincoln	8.0	5.1	5.6	41.9	13 690	13 369	2.4	5.0	1 455	1 160	453	3 796	-3.1	2.76	14.0	23.4
Little River	9.3	7.8	7.3	51.4	13 966	13 952	0.1	-6.5	1 719	1 350	-1 202	5 150	8.8	2.68	11.5	22.1
Logan	10.1	7.9	8.2	50.5	20 557	20 144	2.1	2.8	2 566	2 369	488	7 628	8.1	2.60	8.6	23.6
Lonoke	8.6	5.3	4.8	50.7	39 268	34 518	13.8	31.0	5 646	3 575	10 149	13 866	21.5	2.80	9.4	18.5
Madison	10.7	7.9	7.3	50.7	11 618	11 373	2.2	14.6	1 581	1 257	1 438	4 392	7.3	2.63	6.2	20.7
Marion	14.1	11.2	9.0	51.0	12 001	11 334	5.9	24.2	1 289	1 567	3 103	4 970	15.3	2.40	6.8	23.3
Miller	9.1	7.0	6.3	52.3	38 467	37 766	1.9	2.4	5 243	3 756	-357	14 273	5.9	2.64	14.9	23.7
Mississippi	7.9	6.4	5.6	52.4	57 525	59 517	-3.3	-13.2	8 901	5 283	-11 494	20 420	3.4	2.76	15.3	22.4
Monroe	10.0	8.4	8.1	53.2	11 333	14 052	-19.3	-11.9	1 580	1 378	-1 504	4 361	-11.4	2.57	15.8	28.7
Montgomery	12.7	10.4	9.2	50.7	7 841	7 771	0.9	11.5	840	921	1 009	3 062	4.8	2.46	6.9	23.2
Nevada	9.3	7.5	7.9	51.9	10 101	11 097	-9.0	-0.8	1 148	1 235	63	3 798	-4.6	2.60	12.3	26.0
Newton	10.4	7.9	6.6	49.9	7 666	7 756	-1.2	7.3	828	710	376	2 818	3.7	2.70	6.1	20.5
Ouachita	10.1	8.9	8.3	52.9	30 574	30 541	0.1	-10.1	3 789	3 680	-3 070	11 712	4.6	2.57	13.0	25.8
Perry	11.7	8.8	6.5	50.8	7 969	7 266	9.7	21.4	1 069	995	1 661	3 055	19.1	2.58	6.9	22.8
Phillips	8.6	6.8	6.3	54.3	28 830	34 772	-17.1	-6.2	5 098	3 656	-3 140	10 183	-10.9	2.80	22.1	26.8
Pike	10.2	8.9	8.5	51.0	10 086	10 373	-2.8	3.6	1 296	1 163	280	3 855	0.4	2.57	6.8	22.5
Poinsett	10.2	7.5	6.8	51.9	24 664	27 032	-8.8	-0.3	3 321	2 859	-399	9 368	-1.0	2.60	11.4	23.1
Polk	11.3	8.5	8.6	51.0	17 347	17 007	2.0	13.0	2 497	2 195	2 046	6 827	8.1	2.51	7.5	24.0
Pope	9.1	5.9	5.4	50.5	45 883	38 964	17.8	14.6	6 739	3 954	4 185	16 828	23.6	2.61	8.7	21.8
Prairie	10.7	9.3	8.2	51.1	9 518	10 140	-6.1	-2.5	1 091	1 071	-207	3 661	0.1	2.58	8.9	24.1
Pulaski	8.1	6.4	5.3	52.6	349 569	340 597	2.6	0.1	52 944	29 488	-23 299	137 209	10.2	2.49	13.5	27.5
Randolph	11.6	8.9	8.4	51.5	16 558	16 834	-1.6	8.1	1 947	1 834	1 328	6 445	6.0	2.54	8.5	23.1
St. Francis	8.3	6.6	5.8	53.6	28 497	30 858	-7.7	-2.6	4 732	3 054	-679	9 958	0.3	2.83	19.2	23.8
Saline	9.6	6.4	4.8	50.5	64 183	53 156	20.7	22.1	8 455	5 461	11 471	23 037	31.1	2.73	8.1	17.6
Scott	11.5	7.5	7.9	50.8	10 205	9 685	5.4	4.3	1 235	1 155	401	3 957	12.0	2.55	8.1	22.0
Searcy	12.7	9.5	9.2	51.0	7 841	8 847	-11.4	-0.6	761	1 022	256	3 117	-4.3	2.49	5.5	23.6
Sebastian	9.0	6.9	6.3	51.6	99 590	95 172	4.6	6.7	15 389	9 780	1 467	39 298	9.8	2.49	9.8	26.7
Sevier	9.5	6.9	7.2	49.3	13 637	14 060	-3.0	7.6	2 108	1 632	632	5 118	1.2	2.62	8.8	23.2
Sharp	14.1	12.1	10.5	52.0	14 109	14 607	-3.4	21.1	1 515	2 121	3 620	5 819	3.1	2.39	6.5	24.0
Stone	12.8	9.9	8.5	51.0	9 775	9 022	8.3	14.8	1 049	1 196	1 657	3 866	17.9	2.50	7.0	22.0
Union	9.2	8.1	7.6	52.8	46 719	48 573	-3.8	-3.8	6 147	5 398	-2 299	17 819	-1.4	2.57	13.0	25.8
Van Buren	14.3	14.5	9.5	50.7	14 008	13 357	4.9	11.9	1 452	1 871	2 164	5 698	13.6	2.43	6.5	22.8
Washington	8.4	5.5	4.9	50.5	113 409	100 494	12.9	29.3	19 340	9 518	19 208	43 372	20.2	2.52	8.1	24.4
White	9.8	7.0	6.7	51.3	54 676	50 835	7.6	19.0	7 565	5 898	8 988	19 823	13.8	2.60	8.5	21.4
Woodruff	9.0	8.4	8.2	52.9	9 520	11 222	-15.2	-8.5	1 171	1 213	-736	3 630	-9.6	2.59	16.3	26.8
Yell	10.8	8.2	7.5	51.3	17 759	17 026	4.3	6.2	2 519	2 112	779	6 907	11.1	2.55	8.4	22.8
CALIFORNIA	7.4	5.8	5.2	50.0	29 811 427	23 667 765	25.7	11.2	5 227 258	2 039 044	109 564	10 381 206	20.3	2.79	11.5	23.4
Alameda	7.5	5.5	5.0	50.7	1 304 347	1 105 379	15.5	8.5	199 318	89 976	2 481	479 518	12.5	2.59	12.9	26.8
Alpine	9.7	2.4	2.5	46.9	1 113	1 097	1.5	4.3	92	47	2	450	16.6	2.47	10.2	29.8
Amador	10.8	9.8	8.3	44.2	30 039	19 314	55.5	13.7	2 594	3 052	4 627	10 518	40.8	2.41	6.0	22.3

1. No spouse present.

Table B. States and Counties — Vital Statistics, Health Resources, and Crime

STATE County	Births, average 1996–1998 Total	Rate[1]	Deaths, average 1996–1998 Number Total	Infant[2]	Rate Total[1]	Infant[3]	Physicians,[4] 1998 Number	Rate[5]	Hospitals,[4] 1998 Number	Beds Number	Rate[5]	Medicare enrollees 1999	Serious crimes known to police, 1998[6] Total Number	Rate[7]
	32	33	34	35	36	37	38	39	40	41	42	43	44	45
ARKANSAS—Cont'd														
Conway	258	13.0	238	2	12.0	9.0	7	35	1	60	301	4 628	496	2 465
Craighead	1 109	14.5	709	9	9.3	8.1	214	276	2	425	548	11 220	3 508	4 533
Crawford	737	14.9	470	5	9.5	7.2	38	75	1	66	131	7 815	1 473	2 955
Crittenden	874	17.6	500	11	10.1	12.2	40	80	1	122	244	6 108	2 804	5 610
Cross	283	14.5	233	3	12.0	10.6	8	41	1	59	302	3 111	741	3 781
Dallas	126	13.7	135	2	14.7	18.5	7	77	1	54	596	1 912	415	4 496
Desha	247	16.2	169	1	11.1	5.4	12	79	2	79	523	2 579	602	3 923
Drew	260	14.7	188	2	10.6	9.0	16	91	1	50	284	2 589	317	1 776
Faulkner	1 110	14.5	550	6	7.2	5.7	89	114	1	116	148	9 379	3 030	3 933
Franklin	244	14.6	196	1	11.7	5.5	5	30	1	39	230	3 135	229	1 382
Fulton	119	11.0	134	1	12.4	5.6	10	92	1	39	358	2 713	171	1 551
Garland	1 000	12.0	1 185	7	14.3	6.7	226	269	2	441	525	22 373	3 943	4 711
Grant	193	12.4	148	2	9.5	8.6	7	44	0	0	0	2 219	202	1 280
Greene	463	13.0	403	5	11.3	11.5	38	105	1	129	356	6 078	1 091	3 052
Hempstead	338	15.3	264	4	11.9	12.8	21	95	1	75	339	3 600	1 131	5 123
Hot Spring	378	13.2	314	3	10.9	8.8	13	45	1	77	265	5 266	1 075	3 741
Howard	197	14.3	187	1	13.5	6.8	10	73	1	50	364	2 653	276	1 979
Independence	440	13.3	359	2	10.9	5.3	44	133	1	146	442	6 107	1 111	3 356
Izard	131	10.2	207	2	16.1	12.7	8	61	1	27	206	3 311	76	585
Jackson	236	13.1	253	2	14.0	9.9	27	152	2	174	978	5 201	795	4 452
Jefferson	1 290	15.7	957	17	11.6	12.9	146	179	2	484	593	12 901	6 180	7 468
Johnson	296	14.0	242	2	11.4	5.6	20	93	1	68	318	3 941	521	2 447
Lafayette	118	13.0	117	1	13.0	8.5	3	34	0	0	0	1 642	86	1 260
Lawrence	223	12.8	241	3	13.9	13.4	8	46	1	202	1 167	4 035	311	1 771
Lee	169	13.5	147	3	11.8	15.8	8	64	0	0	0	2 043	433	3 445
Lincoln	160	11.2	130	2	9.1	10.4	3	21	0	0	0	1 819	137	949
Little River	191	14.3	148	1	11.2	7.0	8	61	1	42	318	2 283	355	2 672
Logan	303	14.3	251	1	11.8	4.4	18	85	2	42	198	4 498	368	1 722
Lonoke	666	13.6	423	7	8.6	10.5	20	40	0	0	0	6 266	1 206	2 433
Madison	171	13.1	137	1	10.4	5.8	6	45	0	0	0	2 392	122	924
Marion	138	9.4	171	1	11.7	9.7	12	80	0	0	0	3 270	319	2 199
Miller	599	15.1	409	5	10.3	8.9	9	23	0	0	0	5 809	2 526	6 324
Mississippi	931	18.4	596	9	11.8	9.3	42	83	2	270	533	7 728	3 721	7 324
Monroe	152	14.7	138	2	13.4	11.0	12	118	0	0	0	2 025	244	2 341
Montgomery	105	12.2	110	0	12.9	3.2	4	46	0	0	0	1 790	60	702
Nevada	124	12.4	140	2	13.9	13.4	3	30	1	49	488	1 853	120	1 189
Newton	91	11.2	80	1	9.8	10.9	4	49	0	0	0	1 547	92	1 128
Ouachita	371	13.2	405	7	14.4	19.8	16	57	1	118	423	5 997	1 408	4 978
Perry	118	12.5	119	1	12.6	8.5	2	21	0	0	0	1 894	201	2 113
Phillips	526	19.1	371	7	13.4	13.9	22	80	1	125	457	4 783	749	2 695
Pike	149	14.1	129	1	12.2	4.5	8	76	1	41	387	2 048	64	607
Poinsett	348	14.1	311	3	12.6	9.6	11	44	0	0	0	4 623	548	2 214
Polk	293	15.0	260	2	13.3	6.8	27	137	1	38	193	3 949	310	1 569
Pope	743	14.4	472	6	9.2	7.6	83	159	1	157	302	7 815	2 001	3 884
Prairie	116	12.4	119	2	12.7	20.1	3	32	0	0	0	1 753	172	1 842
Pulaski	5 565	15.9	3 247	58	9.3	10.4	1 631	466	8	2 569	733	50 088	30 256	8 579
Randolph	213	12.0	208	2	11.8	10.9	12	67	1	50	281	3 528	218	1 224
St. Francis	501	17.7	308	4	10.9	7.3	17	60	1	90	320	4 606	2 058	7 207
Saline	969	12.8	667	5	8.8	5.2	52	67	1	120	155	7 712	2 730	3 575
Scott	138	12.8	128	2	11.9	12.1	4	37	1	24	225	2 067	129	1 182
Searcy	89	11.4	115	1	14.9	15.0	6	77	0	0	0	2 046	100	1 277
Sebastian	1 713	16.2	1 093	12	10.3	7.2	320	301	2	722	680	17 274	5 623	5 275
Sevier	247	16.9	183	2	12.5	9.5	16	109	1	77	527	2 379	428	2 875
Sharp	168	10.1	246	1	14.7	5.9	11	65	1	34	200	4 752	224	1 338
Stone	118	10.7	132	1	12.0	8.5	12	108	1	48	430	2 436	137	1 245
Union	641	14.1	559	5	12.3	7.8	94	207	2	378	834	8 795	1 908	4 170
Van Buren	158	10.2	219	1	14.2	6.3	9	58	1	144	926	3 904	193	1 234
Washington	2 324	16.9	1 099	20	8.0	8.5	310	224	2	419	303	18 676	5 269	3 824
White	856	13.5	687	9	10.8	10.1	69	107	2	253	392	11 054	2 108	3 413
Woodruff	122	13.6	122	0	13.6	2.7	5	56	0	0	0	1 794	53	588
Yell	285	14.9	227	1	11.9	4.7	15	78	2	85	445	4 083	441	2 297
CALIFORNIA	528 645	16.4	224 998	3 105	7.0	5.9	77 191	236	444	90 767	278	3 837 080	1 418 674	4 343
Alameda	20 806	15.1	9 722	119	7.0	5.7	3 394	242	17	3 748	268	156 177	87 960	6 337
Alpine	13	10.7	10	0	8.0	25.6	1	83	0	0	0	124	180	14 754
Amador	274	8.2	353	1	10.6	2.4	63	189	1	89	267	6 660	828	2 430

1. Per 1,000 estimated resident population, average 1996–1998.   2. Deaths of infants under 1 year old.   3. Deaths of infants under 1 year old per 1,000 live births.   4. Data subject to copyright.   5. Per 100,000 resident population as of July 1 of the year shown.   6. Data for serious crimes have not been adjusted for underreporting; this may affect comparability between geographic areas and over time.   7. Per 100,000 population estimated by the FBI.

Table B. States and Counties — Crime, Education, Money Income, and Poverty

STATE County	Serious crimes known to police, 1998[1] (cont'd) Rate[2] Violent	Property	Education — School enrollment and attainment, 1990 Enrollment[3] Total	Percent private	Attainment[4] (percent) High school graduate or more	Bachelor's degree or more	Local government expenditures, fiscal 1997[5] Total current expenditures (mil dol)	Current expenditures per student (dollars)	Money income 1989 Per capita[6] (dollars)	Households Median Dollars	Percent change, 1979–1989 (constant 1989 dollars)	Percent with $100,000 or more	Income and poverty, 1997 Median household income	Percent below poverty level All persons	Persons under 18	Persons 5–17 in families
	46	47	48	49	50	51	52	53	54	55	56	57	58	59	60	61
ARKANSAS—Cont'd																
Conway	80	2 385	4 477	9.4	64.5	9.8	20.6	5 759	9 126	20 538	4.9	0.5	28 503	17.1	24.0	22.4
Craighead	341	4 192	19 048	5.2	67.5	16.4	56.5	4 247	11 301	22 150	1.3	2.2	31 515	16.6	22.9	20.3
Crawford	251	2 704	10 569	6.4	63.8	7.6	44.0	4 270	9 689	21 574	-0.5	1.4	30 400	16.1	23.0	20.7
Crittenden	1 174	4 436	13 573	8.1	57.6	9.8	46.4	4 272	9 334	20 948	6.9	1.3	27 549	24.9	33.0	30.4
Cross	908	2 873	5 029	3.3	55.8	8.0	18.2	4 393	8 897	19 049	-6.6	1.5	26 344	22.4	29.4	27.5
Dallas	1 105	3 391	2 169	3.0	59.2	8.8	8.3	4 632	9 101	17 651	-8.2	1.0	24 786	20.9	28.1	27.4
Desha	652	3 271	4 633	4.3	56.5	10.4	18.5	4 700	8 428	15 719	-7.8	2.1	23 361	27.5	34.5	33.0
Drew	196	1 580	4 807	2.4	63.1	13.9	17.9	5 298	9 114	18 906	-5.3	1.2	27 738	19.9	26.4	25.6
Faulkner	405	3 528	18 315	11.6	72.4	17.9	56.9	4 207	10 141	23 663	4.6	1.3	35 722	10.9	15.1	13.0
Franklin	115	1 267	3 319	4.0	60.1	8.8	16.5	4 577	8 877	18 408	-4.2	0.9	27 300	17.3	23.4	21.7
Fulton	118	1 433	1 956	1.0	54.9	5.4	7.8	4 602	8 240	14 950	-5.6	1.7	20 848	25.2	36.6	34.0
Garland	471	4 240	14 792	8.6	70.2	14.2	54.9	4 385	11 873	20 260	-0.4	1.8	28 140	16.3	27.2	24.2
Grant	76	1 204	3 230	4.3	68.9	9.3	18.0	4 080	10 344	24 278	1.8	0.5	35 486	11.5	16.6	15.0
Greene	375	2 677	7 058	8.0	58.5	9.1	28.1	4 444	9 757	19 940	3.4	1.2	29 904	14.9	21.7	19.8
Hempstead	403	4 720	5 090	8.3	62.0	9.3	19.6	4 471	8 583	16 986	-9.2	1.0	24 690	21.4	29.3	26.2
Hot Spring	491	3 250	5 961	3.5	64.5	9.0	27.0	4 763	9 164	19 355	-7.0	0.7	27 757	16.9	23.6	21.6
Howard	29	1 950	3 132	5.1	61.8	8.3	13.6	4 375	9 563	21 277	9.5	1.3	27 782	18.6	25.3	23.2
Independence	97	3 259	7 325	11.2	63.1	10.3	29.0	4 884	10 493	20 208	2.5	2.2	28 864	16.7	23.7	20.6
Izard	0	585	2 026	2.8	61.1	9.4	10.7	5 242	8 852	16 910	4.9	0.8	22 868	22.4	34.1	31.5
Jackson	717	3 735	4 099	3.4	51.6	6.7	14.0	4 744	8 984	16 641	-9.4	1.2	23 942	23.6	33.8	30.8
Jefferson	1 796	5 672	23 015	6.0	65.9	14.6	77.7	4 797	9 852	21 322	-0.3	1.6	27 363	24.9	33.3	29.2
Johnson	56	2 391	4 347	12.9	63.3	12.0	15.7	4 032	8 924	18 225	3.0	1.2	25 612	19.0	28.6	25.4
Lafayette	88	1 172	2 466	1.1	51.6	6.9	8.7	4 784	7 573	13 849	-10.5	0.7	21 324	28.2	33.7	35.3
Lawrence	222	1 549	3 945	10.6	53.3	6.1	17.2	5 021	8 231	15 337	-5.5	0.8	23 133	22.1	31.3	28.1
Lee	302	3 143	3 903	9.8	44.2	7.4	11.2	5 407	6 582	11 949	-3.3	1.4	19 194	38.0	43.6	41.3
Lincoln	97	852	3 065	7.3	58.5	5.6	9.7	4 374	7 899	18 457	6.1	1.5	26 071	27.9	30.9	29.1
Little River	241	2 431	3 468	3.9	64.6	8.1	11.4	4 836	9 942	21 791	-3.8	0.7	28 739	18.2	24.3	22.8
Logan	220	1 502	4 835	8.1	58.1	6.8	15.4	4 090	8 283	18 992	13.1	0.4	26 233	18.4	25.3	23.3
Lonoke	258	2 175	10 228	6.2	67.1	10.0	41.0	3 974	10 273	23 831	5.4	1.9	35 825	12.3	16.5	14.9
Madison	53	871	2 459	5.7	59.6	8.2	10.8	4 068	8 548	18 392	7.9	0.8	26 499	18.9	26.7	24.3
Marion	358	1 841	2 240	4.5	64.2	8.0	10.2	4 225	9 339	17 220	3.4	1.2	23 450	19.4	31.8	27.0
Miller	801	5 523	9 781	6.0	63.9	9.5	34.5	4 813	9 663	20 232	-3.6	1.5	28 034	21.3	29.6	27.7
Mississippi	890	6 434	15 874	5.1	60.0	10.5	47.0	4 371	8 691	18 522	-1.4	1.3	26 528	23.5	30.9	29.3
Monroe	393	1 948	2 955	8.9	52.9	8.4	9.6	4 463	7 587	13 633	-4.5	1.1	20 702	30.6	40.1	38.5
Montgomery	187	515	1 601	2.7	60.1	7.0	6.4	4 339	8 343	16 503	0.0	0.8	23 928	21.3	30.5	30.1
Nevada	20	1 169	2 384	1.2	60.6	9.8	9.1	4 515	9 666	18 919	8.7	1.3	25 561	19.7	26.2	24.3
Newton	135	993	1 878	2.3	58.1	6.8	7.1	4 850	7 114	15 139	15.1	0.4	21 621	25.2	34.5	32.3
Ouachita	562	4 416	7 568	4.4	64.8	12.2	29.3	4 847	9 974	21 056	11.1	1.0	27 593	21.1	30.4	26.6
Perry	473	1 640	1 683	5.4	61.1	6.2	8.5	4 493	8 848	17 626	-8.4	0.9	26 507	15.3	22.1	20.6
Phillips	356	2 339	8 596	8.5	51.5	9.2	29.8	4 737	6 692	13 071	-9.1	0.7	18 898	37.5	45.8	42.9
Pike	104	503	2 203	5.6	61.1	8.5	10.0	4 449	9 220	19 240	3.8	1.7	26 974	18.1	26.0	23.8
Poinsett	105	2 109	5 483	2.0	48.9	5.6	24.1	4 696	8 792	16 858	-10.2	1.1	25 052	22.6	31.1	28.8
Polk	238	1 331	3 999	4.1	62.4	9.9	15.8	4 161	8 884	17 789	5.5	1.0	23 934	21.1	31.5	27.9
Pope	233	3 651	12 350	4.3	66.5	14.7	42.5	4 425	10 347	22 326	4.1	1.7	31 290	15.7	22.0	19.3
Prairie	310	1 532	2 121	4.0	56.3	7.2	7.0	4 321	8 642	17 044	0.8	0.8	26 039	18.4	25.3	24.6
Pulaski	891	7 688	89 508	18.1	79.0	23.5	309.2	5 692	13 760	26 883	2.5	3.3	34 727	14.3	21.3	19.0
Randolph	101	1 123	3 724	9.4	54.4	7.9	13.2	4 393	8 219	16 719	-7.5	0.9	24 454	20.5	30.1	26.7
St. Francis	1 170	6 037	8 461	3.8	55.1	8.5	30.0	4 696	7 194	15 029	-7.1	0.6	22 001	30.5	37.8	35.4
Saline	303	3 272	15 304	8.2	72.9	11.9	47.8	3 993	11 677	28 262	-3.8	1.7	39 001	9.6	13.2	12.6
Scott	55	1 127	2 101	3.7	53.8	5.9	7.0	4 109	8 360	16 470	7.9	1.0	24 049	22.4	33.4	30.8
Searcy	166	1 111	1 711	2.3	52.6	7.5	6.6	4 498	7 209	13 221	3.8	1.5	19 091	27.4	38.7	36.7
Sebastian	470	4 805	23 363	10.4	71.7	14.6	86.5	4 611	12 361	24 037	4.2	2.7	32 360	14.4	21.6	18.7
Sevier	309	2 566	3 185	4.8	59.0	7.2	14.3	4 806	9 060	19 208	-4.4	1.2	26 121	18.9	27.4	24.5
Sharp	78	1 260	2 724	4.8	64.5	8.7	13.8	4 367	8 578	17 362	4.2	0.8	22 433	21.2	32.5	30.4
Stone	82	1 163	2 077	5.7	59.6	9.4	8.0	4 350	7 679	15 655	13.6	0.2	21 846	23.2	33.6	31.4
Union	643	3 527	11 170	6.8	65.9	12.7	39.9	4 420	10 617	21 041	4.5	1.9	29 359	18.7	25.6	23.6
Van Buren	38	1 196	2 765	4.6	62.6	10.5	10.5	4 308	8 706	17 103	-4.3	0.2	23 828	20.1	31.3	28.4
Washington	401	3 423	33 005	5.9	73.2	20.0	109.2	4 485	11 625	23 124	7.8	2.2	32 188	13.5	19.1	17.2
White	376	3 037	14 775	24.3	62.6	10.9	50.0	4 310	9 902	19 722	4.6	1.5	28 513	17.4	23.7	21.0
Woodruff	0	588	2 437	2.8	48.7	7.5	7.7	4 513	7 583	14 024	-8.1	1.0	20 623	30.9	39.2	38.7
Yell	469	1 828	3 762	3.8	57.2	7.4	16.0	4 090	9 400	19 647	11.6	1.3	25 751	16.8	25.0	22.7
CALIFORNIA	704	3 639	8 300 046	13.5	76.2	23.4	29 909.0	5 260	16 409	35 798	17.1	7.1	39 595	16.0	24.6	23.6
Alameda	857	5 480	351 410	14.5	81.4	28.8	1 089.7	5 306	17 547	37 544	19.8	6.7	46 795	11.8	17.6	17.4
Alpine	2 213	12 541	257	7.8	87.6	24.0	2.1	12 860	13 799	24 929	-6.5	2.4	31 080	17.5	30.6	36.2
Amador	320	2 110	6 355	11.2	82.5	14.0	22.6	4 673	14 282	30 265	17.5	3.2	37 829	11.4	17.1	17.2

1. Data for serious crimes have not been adjusted for underreporting; this may affect comparability between geographic areas and over time. 2. Per 100,000 population estimated by the FBI. 3. All persons 3 years old and over enrolled in nursery school through college. 4. Persons 25 years old and over. 5. Elementary and secondary education expenditures, local government fiscal years ending between July 1, 1996 and June 30, 1997. 6. Based on population enumerated as of April 1, 1990.

Table B. States and Counties — Personal Income

	Personal income, 1998												
			Per capita[1]						Transfer payments				
										Government payments to individuals			
STATE County	Total (mil dol)	Percent change, 1997–1998	Dollars	Rank	Wages and salaries[2] (mil dol)	Proprietor's income (mil dol)	Dividends, interest, and rent (mil dol)	Total (mil dol)	Total (mil dol)	Social Security (mil dol)	Medical payments (mil dol)	Income mainte-nance (mil dol)	Unemploy-ment insurance (mil dol)
	62	63	64	65	66	67	68	69	70	71	72	73	74
ARKANSAS—Cont'd													
Conway	398	4.0	20 053	1 695	195	53	55	85	81	35	32	8	2
Craighead	1 604	3.9	20 771	1 463	1 071	135	271	253	239	101	90	25	5
Crawford	869	6.7	17 286	2 536	404	75	117	167	158	70	56	16	5
Crittenden	986	5.3	19 811	1 777	453	68	109	167	158	56	59	34	2
Cross	332	1.8	17 126	2 579	152	38	50	73	70	27	27	10	2
Dallas	180	2.7	19 835	1 765	89	25	26	47	45	17	21	4	1
Desha	258	1.0	17 142	2 574	156	30	39	65	62	21	25	10	2
Drew	329	4.8	18 852	2 107	180	31	50	66	63	24	24	8	3
Faulkner	1 829	9.6	23 381	772	896	104	264	251	237	88	105	14	6
Franklin	301	4.1	17 917	2 372	120	45	51	65	62	27	24	6	1
Fulton	153	3.9	13 972	3 009	39	18	27	47	45	20	16	5	0
Garland	2 000	4.8	23 900	662	886	137	620	424	410	201	153	26	6
Grant	312	5.2	19 691	1 823	107	19	42	47	45	21	15	4	1
Greene	652	4.6	18 112	2 319	366	62	107	127	120	55	41	12	4
Hempstead	412	1.3	18 675	2 161	226	59	63	86	82	33	33	10	2
Hot Spring	488	4.8	16 900	2 629	198	35	80	116	111	50	41	10	3
Howard	292	1.6	21 348	1 281	197	63	42	56	54	22	23	5	1
Independence	663	5.7	20 142	1 668	428	71	110	130	124	54	46	11	4
Izard	211	6.2	16 070	2 785	70	24	44	64	61	29	21	5	1
Jackson	347	7.5	19 597	1 857	160	43	51	98	94	32	44	10	3
Jefferson	1 579	3.2	19 357	1 933	1 092	79	260	319	305	106	106	49	7
Johnson	376	4.3	17 537	2 477	186	47	65	80	76	35	25	8	1
Lafayette	145	2.8	16 261	2 748	48	26	21	38	36	13	15	6	1
Lawrence	292	1.5	16 950	2 623	117	41	47	79	76	31	29	9	2
Lee	176	2.4	13 620	3 036	62	22	28	54	52	15	20	13	2
Lincoln	199	3.6	13 858	3 020	88	31	22	44	41	15	16	7	1
Little River	272	1.8	20 648	1 505	173	36	35	50	48	20	17	5	1
Logan	395	1.0	18 714	2 153	152	58	63	99	95	38	40	9	2
Lonoke	1 046	6.6	20 925	1 412	252	78	134	149	140	53	59	12	2
Madison	243	5.0	18 380	2 243	60	58	38	44	42	20	12	5	1
Marion	240	4.1	16 172	2 768	82	23	60	64	61	31	19	6	1
Miller	724	2.7	18 321	2 258	362	92	118	143	136	53	57	19	1
Mississippi	955	0.6	18 899	2 090	659	75	124	197	188	67	68	34	9
Monroe	175	0.9	17 300	2 530	67	23	29	51	49	17	20	9	1
Montgomery	144	3.2	16 679	2 681	37	30	27	37	35	15	13	4	1
Nevada	173	3.3	17 369	2 512	62	22	27	44	43	16	19	5	1
Newton	109	4.9	13 388	3 051	23	9	18	33	31	13	10	5	1
Ouachita	521	3.2	18 752	2 140	220	37	90	129	124	54	45	16	3
Perry	149	3.6	15 422	2 887	27	24	21	36	34	16	12	3	1
Phillips	413	0.6	15 140	2 917	205	30	57	137	132	39	52	33	3
Pike	201	2.1	19 021	2 048	70	40	30	42	40	19	15	3	1
Poinsett	439	1.0	17 804	2 406	171	63	64	102	97	39	37	14	3
Polk	345	4.8	17 577	2 472	146	69	58	80	77	35	26	8	1
Pope	1 050	4.5	20 174	1 661	704	99	168	177	168	74	58	16	4
Prairie	160	0.7	17 137	2 576	45	26	27	39	37	16	14	4	1
Pulaski	9 922	3.9	28 445	217	8 633	713	1 850	1 231	1 171	470	446	113	24
Randolph	280	1.9	15 754	2 836	122	30	46	73	70	32	23	7	3
St. Francis	478	4.6	17 010	2 612	268	40	62	121	116	37	43	26	4
Saline	1 670	6.0	21 645	1 206	471	69	199	250	237	112	97	11	4
Scott	202	6.3	19 075	2 033	73	53	31	43	41	20	14	5	1
Searcy	123	4.9	15 935	2 803	33	20	20	38	37	15	13	5	1
Sebastian	2 612	5.1	24 664	532	2 130	292	493	380	361	165	130	31	9
Sevier	282	3.2	19 334	1 942	134	58	34	52	50	21	19	4	1
Sharp	278	4.2	16 448	2 715	81	30	68	90	87	44	30	7	1
Stone	185	5.2	16 721	2 673	58	34	31	52	50	22	18	6	1
Union	1 057	4.9	23 373	778	619	109	230	194	186	86	66	21	5
Van Buren	255	4.4	16 397	2 722	74	24	63	76	74	37	24	6	2
Washington	3 032	4.6	20 910	1 420	2 211	286	590	389	365	170	111	29	10
White	1 128	5.9	17 452	2 494	601	95	184	225	214	94	76	20	5
Woodruff	151	-0.9	17 123	2 580	71	15	21	45	43	14	19	7	1
Yell	349	3.9	18 399	2 238	158	51	54	78	74	34	28	7	1
CALIFORNIA	920 452	6.7	28 163	X	579 301	97 916	172 732	109 388	103 313	34 948	40 768	17 933	2 681
Alameda	44 887	7.9	32 130	111	30 041	3 688	7 705	4 763	4 501	1 411	1 845	809	94
Alpine	27	4.8	22 688	926	20	4	4	6	6	1	2	2	0
Amador	692	5.3	20 721	1 476	275	87	187	134	128	66	42	10	2

1. Based on the resident population estimated as of July 1 of the year shown. 2. Includes other labor income.

Table B. States and Counties — Earnings, Social Security, and Housing

STATE County	Earnings, 1998									Social Security beneficiaries, December 1998			Housing units, 1990	
			Percent by selected industries											
			Goods-related[1]		Service-related and other[2]							Supplemental Security Income recipients, December 1998		
	Total (mil dol)	Farm	Total	Manufacturing	Total	Retail trade	Finance, insurance, and real estate	Services	Government	Number	Rate[3]		Total	Percent change, 1980-1990
	75	76	77	78	79	80	81	82	83	84	85	86	87	88
ARKANSAS—Cont'd														
Conway	248	10.5	D	26.7	D	9.4	2.0	15.9	12.8	4 680	235	897	8 009	7.4
Craighead	1 205	2.6	D	22.2	54.1	10.8	4.4	27.2	14.9	12 995	168	2 584	28 434	17.8
Crawford	478	4.0	D	22.1	D	9.1	2.7	16.6	12.2	9 637	191	1 535	16 711	21.4
Crittenden	521	3.1	D	14.5	D	15.1	3.7	22.7	15.1	7 873	158	2 895	18 875	11.2
Cross	191	12.9	27.7	23.0	41.9	10.5	3.9	12.9	17.6	3 739	191	1 055	7 254	0.9
Dallas	115	1.5	47.0	41.5	40.2	9.6	2.2	18.0	11.3	2 306	255	586	4 049	-4.4
Desha	186	13.2	D	24.8	D	8.5	3.1	12.2	18.1	3 059	202	886	6 706	-7.7
Drew	211	6.1	31.7	29.3	38.8	10.3	4.6	13.7	23.4	3 196	182	669	7 159	7.7
Faulkner	1 000	0.7	D	23.7	D	9.7	3.6	29.3	16.9	11 191	143	1 492	23 397	39.2
Franklin	165	16.3	D	17.2	32.7	6.9	3.9	11.7	24.8	3 741	221	556	6 228	9.5
Fulton	57	8.8	21.0	13.0	D	9.5	D	19.6	24.7	3 000	275	467	4 839	11.0
Garland	1 022	1.5	23.0	12.6	62.1	13.8	5.4	33.2	13.4	24 112	287	2 562	37 966	11.3
Grant	126	1.5	D	43.8	D	7.4	2.2	9.8	18.0	2 665	168	304	5 540	13.0
Greene	427	5.1	D	44.0	D	9.9	2.4	17.2	11.1	7 559	209	1 247	13 216	10.6
Hempstead	285	14.4	D	33.1	D	7.3	2.6	16.1	15.8	4 304	195	820	9 690	-0.1
Hot Spring	233	1.8	40.6	32.1	37.1	9.7	3.6	13.1	20.5	6 395	220	812	11 378	6.3
Howard	260	15.9	49.0	46.7	25.9	5.9	1.6	9.5	9.1	2 977	217	450	5 600	8.9
Independence	498	3.4	38.3	33.5	47.3	8.7	2.4	20.8	11.0	7 354	222	1 189	12 838	10.4
Izard	94	7.8	D	20.3	D	11.6	4.9	17.0	24.3	3 872	296	455	5 535	9.1
Jackson	204	13.4	D	23.1	D	8.9	D	24.4	12.0	4 385	247	917	8 086	-2.6
Jefferson	1 171	1.3	27.3	24.0	46.8	9.1	3.7	21.0	24.5	14 396	177	3 965	33 311	0.8
Johnson	233	9.4	D	36.3	D	15.4	3.0	15.3	12.7	4 852	227	863	7 984	11.2
Lafayette	74	24.7	28.8	20.3	29.2	6.4	3.9	9.0	17.3	1 778	199	623	4 523	0.5
Lawrence	158	12.6	28.2	21.8	39.0	10.6	2.6	11.9	20.3	4 528	262	949	7 692	2.8
Lee	84	23.8	D	8.8	D	8.5	2.5	15.0	29.8	2 495	201	1 177	5 085	-3.5
Lincoln	119	24.2	D	14.1	D	4.5	1.7	8.7	32.8	2 212	155	618	4 295	1.6
Little River	208	7.0	D	50.4	D	4.8	1.8	5.3	10.8	2 693	204	476	6 171	7.7
Logan	210	13.9	D	33.1	D	9.0	2.8	12.7	17.5	5 339	252	822	8 539	8.1
Lonoke	330	10.7	27.3	18.0	D	12.5	4.3	16.4	17.6	7 070	141	1 092	15 009	20.6
Madison	118	31.8	27.9	21.2	26.3	6.3	2.3	10.8	14.0	3 044	230	400	5 182	9.2
Marion	105	5.9	D	39.7	D	8.7	4.3	14.6	15.5	4 047	271	459	6 139	13.9
Miller	454	3.1	36.2	27.6	47.8	11.1	3.4	17.7	12.9	6 948	174	1 538	16 172	10.1
Mississippi	734	3.0	D	45.6	D	7.7	3.0	13.8	11.6	9 588	189	3 412	22 232	3.1
Monroe	90	16.9	D	10.5	D	12.9	4.1	14.7	17.4	2 409	236	782	5 063	-11.7
Montgomery	66	23.3	D	19.9	D	7.6	3.4	11.5	20.5	2 136	247	284	4 269	18.6
Nevada	84	15.7	D	D	D	7.1	1.9	12.1	17.2	2 217	221	488	4 287	-3.4
Newton	32	1.0	D	13.1	D	8.6	D	16.1	41.7	2 031	248	477	3 439	11.6
Ouachita	257	1.2	31.3	25.7	48.9	11.6	3.7	20.5	18.6	6 975	250	1 476	13 204	9.0
Perry	51	21.5	D	7.6	D	8.3	D	15.7	24.1	2 210	229	398	3 702	16.6
Phillips	234	4.0	D	14.9	D	10.2	3.8	23.2	21.7	6 005	219	2 835	11 094	-10.5
Pike	109	20.0	24.4	18.1	38.6	10.8	4.2	10.4	17.0	2 521	238	318	4 550	7.0
Poinsett	234	17.0	D	26.2	37.7	7.5	4.3	10.6	15.1	5 478	221	1 489	10 271	0.6
Polk	215	19.0	31.8	27.7	35.2	8.8	2.8	15.1	13.9	4 805	244	615	7 732	10.5
Pope	803	3.5	D	21.1	D	9.5	3.0	18.2	12.9	9 981	192	1 796	18 430	23.7
Prairie	71	30.1	14.3	9.9	38.7	8.1	2.0	12.5	16.9	2 117	225	345	4 340	6.9
Pulaski	9 346	0.1	13.9	9.0	63.7	8.4	8.6	27.1	22.4	57 741	165	10 428	151 538	14.1
Randolph	152	7.6	36.0	30.2	40.0	9.8	3.7	17.3	16.4	4 384	246	661	7 343	9.3
St. Francis	308	4.7	D	22.7	D	9.5	2.8	16.9	25.5	5 430	193	957	10 958	2.8
Saline	541	0.3	D	17.1	D	16.9	4.0	21.4	21.1	13 212	171	390	24 602	30.5
Scott	126	30.4	34.2	31.9	24.4	6.7	1.8	9.0	11.0	2 837	265	556	4 485	16.8
Searcy	53	4.7	D	15.7	D	10.7	D	16.3	25.9	2 328	300	2 860	3 739	1.5
Sebastian	2 422	0.6	37.4	31.0	53.2	8.7	3.9	29.7	8.8	20 513	193	349	43 621	11.5
Sevier	192	20.5	D	32.0	31.8	6.7	2.2	13.5	12.7	2 845	195	692	5 880	6.4
Sharp	111	11.5	D	8.0	D	14.7	5.6	20.5	19.0	5 678	334	2 447	7 617	5.7
Stone	92	17.2	25.5	20.7	39.3	13.2	2.7	17.0	18.0	3 232	290	606	4 548	17.9
Union	728	1.9	45.9	31.2	41.7	8.5	3.7	17.2	10.5	10 498	232	1 974	20 276	2.8
Van Buren	98	6.2	23.9	17.2	51.5	13.3	6.3	20.5	18.4	4 874	313	510	7 580	25.1
Washington	2 496	3.5	28.9	22.6	50.4	10.2	4.5	19.7	17.1	21 732	157	2 616	47 349	23.0
White	695	2.4	D	21.0	D	17.9	2.8	25.3	11.8	12 584	195	1 902	21 658	17.2
Woodruff	86	16.9	D	20.5	D	5.3	2.6	8.4	17.1	2 040	230	625	4 169	-7.0
Yell	210	12.9	D	36.0	D	6.4	3.4	9.5	18.0	4 752	249	809	7 868	14.4
CALIFORNIA	677 217	1.2	20.8	15.2	62.4	8.8	8.9	31.6	15.6	4 060 885	124	1 042 002	11 182 882	20.5
Alameda	33 728	0.0	22.9	16.3	59.5	8.7	5.4	29.7	17.6	162 133	116	47 328	504 109	13.4
Alpine	24	0.0	D	D	D	2.9	D	61.8	19.9	135	112	170	1 319	41.4
Amador	362	0.6	16.9	10.1	56.3	14.1	3.8	27.0	26.2	7 547	226	578	12 814	35.7

1. Covers mining, construction, and manufacturing.   2. Covers private sector earnings in agricultural services, forestry, and fisheries; transportation and public utilities; wholesale trade; retail trade; finance, insurance, and real estate; and services.   3. Per 1,000 resident population estimated as of July 1 of the year shown.

Table B. States and Counties — Housing, Labor Force, and Employment

	Housing units, 1990 (cont'd)								Civilian labor force, 1999				Civilian employment, 1990[5]		
	Occupied units										Unemployment			Percent	
	Owner-occupied					Renter-occupied									
				Owner cost as a percent of income											
STATE County	Total	Percent	Median value[1]	With a mortgage	Without a mortgage	Median rent[2]	Rent as percent of income	Substandard units[3] (percent)	Total	Percent change, 1998–1999	Total	Rate[4]	Total	Professional, managerial, and technical	Precision production, craft, and repair
	89	90	91	92	93	94	95	96	97	98	99	100	101	102	103
ARKANSAS—Cont'd															
Conway	7 179	76.4	38 200	19.8	13.6	299	27.5	5.2	9 154	-5.2	623	6.8	7 821	17.3	14.0
Craighead	26 285	65.4	50 200	19.3	13.1	335	26.8	2.2	42 053	2.1	1 371	3.3	32 772	23.6	11.2
Crawford	15 251	76.4	43 500	21.1	12.8	298	25.3	5.4	24 132	2.5	858	3.6	18 095	17.7	15.0
Crittenden	17 120	61.0	48 900	20.7	14.6	338	28.6	9.9	22 444	-0.2	972	4.3	20 049	20.9	11.6
Cross	6 754	69.7	39 100	20.9	14.6	297	26.9	6.1	7 992	-1.4	520	6.5	7 393	16.9	12.1
Dallas	3 600	77.9	33 600	20.1	13.3	265	28.8	6.5	3 512	-2.7	273	7.8	3 757	15.2	12.7
Desha	5 957	66.0	36 700	20.2	14.9	249	34.5	8.5	6 991	-0.8	649	9.3	5 758	19.6	10.6
Drew	6 342	72.0	38 700	18.8	13.8	281	28.5	5.3	9 686	0.1	653	6.7	7 414	20.9	10.9
Faulkner	21 325	70.5	55 400	20.6	13.0	351	27.3	4.3	41 448	1.5	1 301	3.1	27 806	25.9	13.3
Franklin	5 578	79.0	36 600	22.8	12.6	268	23.5	5.5	7 517	-2.3	259	3.4	6 161	17.9	16.3
Fulton	4 010	81.7	34 000	22.6	13.5	248	29.1	6.3	4 116	-2.7	160	3.9	3 557	16.9	14.0
Garland	30 836	70.8	53 500	21.2	13.3	327	28.4	2.8	35 497	0.3	1 585	4.5	29 450	25.1	11.4
Grant	5 118	82.9	43 000	17.3	13.9	312	24.2	4.2	7 344	-3.0	319	4.3	6 269	21.0	16.7
Greene	12 325	73.0	39 400	18.0	12.3	274	25.1	3.1	18 167	0.2	878	4.8	13 831	16.9	14.8
Hempstead	8 212	73.6	34 900	20.3	13.9	288	28.4	6.7	11 273	0.1	628	5.6	8 839	18.1	15.6
Hot Spring	10 115	77.7	39 200	20.9	13.4	297	24.9	4.5	12 008	-0.4	523	4.4	10 264	19.9	14.3
Howard	4 975	73.6	36 200	19.2	13.3	270	21.7	6.0	6 747	-3.0	358	5.3	5 873	14.8	15.6
Independence	11 846	75.3	40 600	19.2	13.5	300	23.7	4.4	16 864	1.7	789	4.7	13 650	20.7	15.2
Izard	4 684	79.8	37 300	22.5	12.9	249	25.4	4.8	4 260	3.0	175	4.1	3 986	18.4	14.8
Jackson	7 361	68.6	34 100	20.6	13.9	271	27.5	4.8	7 832	-2.2	751	9.6	7 153	19.6	11.3
Jefferson	30 001	67.1	43 300	17.0	15.0	337	28.1	5.7	35 997	-0.3	2 709	7.5	33 236	25.2	11.6
Johnson	7 059	75.2	38 200	18.5	12.6	267	24.6	5.6	10 500	0.7	380	3.6	7 155	20.8	15.1
Lafayette	3 584	76.3	24 300	20.9	14.6	263	29.4	9.6	3 381	0.1	252	7.5	3 315	18.2	13.4
Lawrence	6 857	75.1	31 000	20.9	14.0	268	28.4	2.7	7 258	-4.0	472	6.5	6 710	16.5	13.1
Lee	4 578	62.8	31 500	22.2	15.8	234	35.1	13.0	4 477	5.0	335	7.5	3 853	17.8	9.8
Lincoln	3 796	75.5	30 300	18.7	15.3	253	26.5	9.5	5 237	0.1	273	5.2	4 045	18.2	11.3
Little River	5 150	76.6	40 100	16.7	12.8	288	25.6	6.4	5 416	-0.3	301	5.6	6 046	19.7	14.7
Logan	7 628	78.2	34 200	19.5	13.1	256	26.5	5.0	9 466	-4.0	492	5.2	8 222	17.8	16.6
Lonoke	13 866	74.4	52 700	22.1	13.8	341	25.9	4.8	25 184	1.6	635	2.5	17 388	19.5	14.4
Madison	4 392	80.0	34 800	21.5	12.9	265	24.4	8.6	6 566	2.8	228	3.5	5 090	16.0	15.1
Marion	4 970	80.4	41 800	23.1	13.1	287	30.1	4.6	6 124	3.6	192	3.1	4 363	20.6	12.9
Miller	14 273	68.3	43 200	17.5	14.1	328	26.3	5.5	17 075	1.5	750	4.4	15 440	20.8	14.3
Mississippi	20 420	54.4	41 800	20.6	15.2	315	26.2	7.1	26 392	-0.2	2 859	10.8	20 907	19.8	13.0
Monroe	4 361	63.1	32 300	23.1	15.5	247	29.6	9.2	4 000	-1.3	275	6.9	3 871	19.1	10.4
Montgomery	3 062	82.5	32 600	23.6	13.6	254	29.0	5.9	3 890	-0.3	141	3.6	3 090	14.5	14.4
Nevada	3 798	76.3	30 000	19.9	13.2	245	25.1	7.5	4 887	-0.2	291	6.0	3 929	16.4	12.9
Newton	2 818	83.2	32 200	17.8	13.3	207	23.4	16.2	2 883	-1.2	171	5.9	2 625	16.8	13.3
Ouachita	11 712	73.2	38 900	17.7	13.9	286	26.4	5.8	11 209	-4.3	990	8.8	12 234	23.9	13.4
Perry	3 055	83.6	34 800	23.5	13.3	248	23.0	7.1	3 522	1.0	216	6.1	3 277	11.0	16.1
Phillips	10 183	53.7	36 900	18.6	16.1	253	34.1	9.2	9 423	-2.5	723	7.7	9 188	21.6	11.8
Pike	3 855	79.9	32 800	22.0	13.3	243	25.0	4.5	4 840	-0.9	228	4.7	4 083	16.7	14.0
Poinsett	9 368	65.2	34 500	19.7	13.9	233	27.6	4.9	10 491	-0.2	627	6.0	9 626	14.7	14.2
Polk	6 827	76.2	36 300	23.1	13.1	255	25.7	5.5	9 127	1.5	349	3.8	6 841	21.0	15.8
Pope	16 828	70.8	48 000	20.9	13.4	328	25.3	3.0	26 584	1.0	1 160	4.4	20 347	23.4	14.3
Prairie	3 661	73.2	35 200	19.5	15.9	248	23.4	4.8	3 838	2.4	218	5.7	3 906	14.5	11.9
Pulaski	137 209	60.3	61 300	19.6	13.1	403	26.4	3.5	190 959	0.2	6 467	3.4	166 541	32.9	8.9
Randolph	6 445	74.9	31 300	18.4	13.2	262	26.1	5.8	7 734	-0.7	525	6.8	6 339	17.7	16.2
St. Francis	9 958	61.1	38 600	22.4	17.3	270	32.6	10.0	12 179	-4.3	1 095	9.0	9 665	20.8	12.4
Saline	23 037	80.6	59 000	18.6	12.5	373	24.4	3.7	40 899	2.3	1 055	2.6	29 887	24.7	15.4
Scott	3 957	78.0	34 100	23.1	13.2	241	23.2	5.9	4 882	1.6	129	2.6	4 179	14.2	11.6
Searcy	3 117	79.6	29 400	19.4	14.2	234	31.4	11.9	2 902	-1.8	216	7.4	2 803	16.3	14.6
Sebastian	39 298	65.2	48 600	18.2	12.4	316	23.7	3.5	55 374	1.2	1 859	3.4	46 226	24.6	13.8
Sevier	5 118	76.3	35 000	19.1	13.1	264	23.2	5.8	6 789	-2.0	303	4.5	5 926	16.4	15.8
Sharp	5 819	82.5	37 100	22.0	13.7	282	25.8	4.9	6 123	2.8	309	5.0	4 344	20.6	12.9
Stone	3 866	78.5	36 900	23.1	13.2	238	31.9	8.5	5 086	4.3	245	4.8	3 788	20.9	11.5
Union	17 819	73.8	40 500	19.2	13.8	311	27.5	5.7	20 516	0.2	1 231	6.0	18 506	24.1	13.5
Van Buren	5 698	82.3	44 300	25.4	13.1	288	26.2	6.9	6 047	-1.6	346	5.7	4 735	19.2	12.4
Washington	43 372	61.6	56 500	19.8	12.4	352	25.8	3.5	75 560	1.9	1 935	2.6	55 567	26.9	11.6
White	19 823	73.3	43 200	20.6	14.0	300	27.7	3.7	31 162	2.6	1 465	4.7	22 651	21.8	14.3
Woodruff	3 630	63.2	29 700	22.5	15.1	236	28.7	6.2	3 832	-4.6	395	10.3	3 364	15.5	10.3
Yell	6 907	73.5	37 000	21.3	13.5	280	24.4	4.2	9 335	-0.4	363	3.9	7 571	15.0	15.8
CALIFORNIA	10 381 206	55.6	195 500	24.9	11.8	620	29.1	12.0	16 585 881	1.6	864 205	5.2	13 996 309	32.3	11.1
Alameda	479 518	53.3	227 200	25.3	11.9	626	28.6	8.2	722 322	1.7	24 852	3.4	635 840	37.2	10.1
Alpine	450	57.3	113 200	29.2	14.0	413	16.7	7.0	502	1.0	45	9.0	514	31.1	16.7
Amador	10 518	74.6	118 500	23.9	12.2	494	26.1	3.2	13 609	0.6	628	4.6	10 623	25.5	13.1

1. Specified owner-occupied units. 2. Specified renter-occupied units. 3. Overcrowded or lacking complete plumbing facilities. 4. Percent of civilian labor force. 5. Persons 16 years and older.

Table B. States and Counties — Nonfarm Employment and Agriculture

| | Private nonfarm establishments, employment and payroll, 1998 | | | | | | | | Agriculture, 1997 | | | |
| | Employment | | | | | | Annual payroll | | Farms | | | Farm operators |
STATE County	Number of establishments	Total	Health Care and Social Assistance	Manufacturing	Retail trade	Finance and Insurance	Professional Scientific and Technical Services	Total (mil dol)	Average per employee (dollars)	Number	Percent with— Less than 50 acres	Percent with— 500 acres and over	Whose principal occupation is farming (percent)
	104	105	106	107	108	109	110	111	112	113	114	115	116
ARKANSAS—Cont'd													
Conway	405	7 672	1 518	1 991	937	106	147	141	18 364	729	19.6	8.0	49.7
Craighead	2 289	32 834	5 648	7 187	5 603	1 095	809	755	22 999	754	21.6	33.8	63.8
Crawford	916	13 681	1 298	3 650	1 717	288	1 352	291	21 241	806	35.7	7.6	40.3
Crittenden	965	15 699	2 225	2 111	2 994	161	344	323	20 549	259	11.2	62.5	77.2
Cross	375	4 722	580	1 740	757	180	43	92	19 461	382	15.2	50.3	74.9
Dallas	263	2 996	755	824	475	90	38	63	21 025	121	15.7	9.9	33.9
Desha	409	5 005	999	1 557	917	165	72	108	21 530	302	12.6	55.0	81.1
Drew	462	6 923	621	2 309	956	153	88	132	19 037	342	23.1	20.2	51.2
Faulkner	1 620	26 766	2 877	7 433	3 879	687	565	631	23 563	1 111	29.3	8.8	34.1
Franklin	285	3 475	502	1 216	502	143	45	62	17 831	783	22.1	9.6	45.3
Fulton	174	1 368	300	353	171	56	34	22	16 417	737	12.2	17.0	41.7
Garland	2 582	30 382	6 112	3 886	5 737	898	885	603	19 853	360	36.1	3.1	33.6
Grant	277	3 616	176	1 988	410	150	41	77	21 244	215	38.6	2.8	30.7
Greene	771	13 141	1 233	6 606	1 690	237	322	255	19 381	733	22.6	23.2	52.0
Hempstead	451	7 694	1 033	3 916	927	173	62	152	19 813	752	24.2	14.6	52.1
Hot Spring	556	5 805	738	1 890	849	257	73	119	20 567	447	25.1	5.4	41.4
Howard	319	7 199	692	4 897	583	120	61	132	18 334	656	30.5	6.7	54.6
Independence	815	13 925	2 501	4 697	1 691	264	200	291	20 870	1 044	21.6	13.8	41.9
Izard	246	2 238	437	584	407	97	25	39	17 505	703	16.6	13.7	41.4
Jackson	444	4 709	1 091	1 164	872	141	113	99	21 026	461	11.3	38.8	64.9
Jefferson	1 640	26 837	4 359	8 004	4 544	828	631	610	22 729	362	25.7	37.0	60.2
Johnson	402	7 385	644	3 384	888	189	69	132	17 907	606	23.8	6.6	46.5
Lafayette	154	1 447	222	473	177	71	20	28	19 105	261	24.1	19.2	64.0
Lawrence	380	4 180	399	1 495	717	117	51	74	17 674	661	12.7	30.4	62.8
Lee	157	1 285	236	235	272	57	59	23	18 076	273	13.2	47.3	74.7
Lincoln	155	1 632	234	637	229	54	14	31	19 161	292	19.2	34.6	64.0
Little River	244	3 565	323	D	381	100	45	114	32 082	381	19.4	16.0	42.8
Logan	391	5 200	644	2 654	665	174	52	93	17 932	953	23.0	8.6	42.0
Lonoke	868	8 228	1 036	1 688	1 758	307	209	151	18 317	869	22.8	28.2	55.2
Madison	182	1 641	149	769	273	73	38	33	20 347	1 203	16.0	11.0	50.5
Marion	236	3 194	294	1 893	371	93	28	52	16 435	495	16.2	14.5	45.5
Miller	719	10 320	1 032	2 291	1 608	337	201	232	22 501	502	25.7	14.1	44.8
Mississippi	1 002	18 275	1 580	7 411	2 366	401	206	437	23 920	462	14.5	57.8	80.1
Monroe	263	2 088	264	308	470	87	44	32	15 203	245	12.7	58.0	78.0
Montgomery	188	1 121	D	265	141	D	D	18	15 660	417	20.1	6.2	59.0
Nevada	151	1 787	327	642	282	D	24	39	21 792	372	23.1	7.8	44.1
Newton	109	566	D	106	118	D	9	8	13 717	521	15.2	7.9	35.7
Ouachita	637	7 894	1 145	2 592	1 348	164	105	188	23 756	177	35.0	8.5	39.0
Perry	114	595	102	D	177	D	10	10	16 176	391	24.0	7.2	45.8
Phillips	553	5 939	1 150	992	1 264	209	84	113	19 104	323	13.6	50.5	74.6
Pike	261	2 390	244	632	448	112	92	41	16 955	406	26.1	7.4	47.5
Poinsett	436	4 600	516	1 870	753	226	37	89	19 336	570	9.6	54.2	80.5
Polk	488	5 334	653	2 073	840	164	170	99	18 577	850	34.2	6.2	50.6
Pope	1 460	21 162	2 248	4 701	3 530	550	421	480	22 700	917	31.0	5.6	44.2
Prairie	194	1 205	212	207	259	D	22	20	16 890	420	11.2	48.1	71.4
Pulaski	11 744	216 792	36 417	19 866	27 560	11 785	11 741	5 820	26 848	421	40.1	12.6	34.7
Randolph	328	4 396	620	1 692	672	128	55	78	17 701	694	13.3	21.9	47.4
St. Francis	621	7 597	1 177	1 948	1 439	301	144	142	18 740	328	12.5	45.7	63.7
Saline	1 325	14 865	2 090	2 102	3 373	428	299	312	20 977	329	38.0	5.8	33.7
Scott	180	2 576	260	1 401	310	65	21	48	18 594	655	24.4	6.3	51.8
Searcy	120	1 193	240	283	236	D	18	14	11 965	614	15.3	16.1	43.8
Sebastian	3 427	70 368	9 605	22 575	8 083	1 664	1 295	1 654	23 508	724	33.8	6.9	39.6
Sevier	297	4 748	638	2 179	606	105	58	79	16 706	588	27.9	8.2	55.1
Sharp	369	3 057	372	402	659	167	63	48	15 753	618	13.4	12.5	40.0
Stone	234	2 096	310	663	442	67	37	35	16 465	601	19.5	12.3	50.4
Union	1 267	18 396	2 003	5 717	2 442	701	345	458	24 885	281	43.4	3.9	41.3
Van Buren	315	2 780	445	654	509	83	39	44	15 893	578	15.2	10.7	45.3
Washington	4 039	65 847	8 050	14 821	9 640	1 836	2 001	1 516	23 022	2 476	38.1	4.8	44.7
White	1 388	20 657	2 702	4 892	3 142	476	281	439	21 269	1 667	26.3	11.0	37.9
Woodruff	160	1 981	188	729	292	D	D	35	17 758	239	12.1	61.9	76.2
Yell	351	5 749	700	2 944	535	136	240	103	17 962	826	22.3	10.0	48.9
CALIFORNIA	773 925	12 026 989	1 269 893	1 827 350	1 382 460	599 859	923 030	406 481	33 797	74 126	60.6	11.7	53.0
Alameda	35 137	598 220	66 829	95 527	61 181	20 469	35 372	22 237	37 172	458	49.6	16.8	41.0
Alpine	57	D	D	0	D	0	D	D	D	12	58.3	25.0	33.3
Amador	819	7 377	1 243	761	1 599	238	282	152	20 620	360	41.1	14.2	41.9

Table B. States and Counties — Agriculture, Land, and Water

	Agriculture, 1997 (cont'd)														
STATE County	Land in farms				Value of land and buildings		Value of machinery and equipment Average per farm ($1,000)	Value of products sold		Percent from —		Percent of farms with sales of —		Percent of land owned by Fed. Gov. 1997	Water consumption 1995 (mil gal/day)
	Acreage (1,000)	Percent change, 1992–1997	Acres			Average per farm ($1,000)	Average per acre (dollars)		Total (mil dol)	Average per farm (dollars)	Crops	Livestock and poultry products	$10,000 or more	$100,000 or more		
			Average size of farm	Total irrigated (1,000)	Total cropland (1,000)											
	117	118	119	120	121	122	123	124	125	126	127	128	129	130	131	132

STATE County	117	118	119	120	121	122	123	124	125	126	127	128	129	130	131	132
ARKANSAS—Cont'd																
Conway	163	-3.1	223	7	96	237	1 099	46	83	114 397	6.6	93.4	46.5	25.2	2.0	28.5
Craighead	363	3.8	482	222	335	612	1 365	119	123	162 763	98.3	1.7	68.4	41.4	0.6	349.6
Crawford	139	-4.9	172	4	78	259	1 617	33	60	74 461	17.5	82.5	32.9	14.3	23.1	15.9
Crittenden	320	-2.2	1 235	96	304	1 239	1 059	216	82	318 153	99.7	0.3	82.2	61.4	1.2	112.4
Cross	344	5.7	900	223	317	922	1 082	203	103	269 240	98.5	1.5	75.9	53.4	0.0	299.2
Dallas	23	10.6	192	0	9	187	1 017	27	2	16 119	33.2	66.8	22.3	2.5	0.0	1.2
Desha	276	5.3	914	159	257	798	930	177	101	334 018	92.9	7.1	83.1	60.9	5.3	330.3
Drew	123	11.4	358	49	94	333	1 157	93	36	104 704	78.4	21.6	47.4	23.7	0.0	71.0
Faulkner	211	0.2	190	3	120	291	1 425	29	21	18 955	27.2	72.8	26.7	4.6	1.9	11.9
Franklin	171	1.4	219	0	86	283	1 357	33	100	127 355	1.7	98.3	42.7	16.3	29.6	12.6
Fulton	228	1.7	309	0	92	238	735	19	15	20 605	4.2	95.8	35.0	5.3	0.2	73.8
Garland	43	1.1	121	0	21	222	1 816	25	25	70 772	6.3	93.7	22.8	5.6	26.1	266.3
Grant	33	-14.4	151	0	16	217	1 314	32	5	21 881	3.0	97.0	23.7	4.2	0.0	2.3
Greene	263	4.3	359	116	230	394	1 184	64	64	87 297	93.6	6.4	49.5	23.5	0.0	153.7
Hempstead	189	12.1	252	1	90	270	924	38	142	188 922	1.1	98.9	50.3	25.3	0.0	9.4
Hot Spring	75	-3.5	168	1	37	190	1 083	25	10	22 673	9.8	90.2	25.3	4.5	0.9	8.1
Howard	108	1.9	165	2	54	241	1 277	47	129	195 924	0.4	99.6	62.0	38.3	2.2	5.9
Independence	283	7.7	271	15	154	254	914	37	73	69 454	18.0	82.0	35.2	10.3	0.0	36.6
Izard	188	2.1	267	0	80	197	735	26	28	39 801	1.5	98.5	30.3	5.8	0.0	2.9
Jackson	335	-8.9	727	155	295	629	966	106	80	173 952	97.3	2.7	71.8	42.3	0.7	298.3
Jefferson	289	2.4	797	147	258	761	976	155	95	263 117	85.0	15.0	60.5	40.3	2.5	454.5
Johnson	115	5.1	189	2	66	264	1 370	37	82	135 766	3.7	96.3	35.5	18.5	40.5	4.2
Lafayette	98	-9.5	374	10	67	357	948	56	72	275 575	13.3	86.7	64.0	41.8	0.3	32.7
Lawrence	294	4.1	444	112	238	440	1 000	78	75	113 296	85.3	14.7	60.4	33.3	0.0	281.4
Lee	280	-6.5	1 024	102	263	856	865	175	80	294 530	98.0	2.0	75.1	49.1	2.8	167.1
Lincoln	184	-1.5	631	98	156	589	989	138	110	375 933	47.6	52.4	61.6	45.5	0.3	151.4
Little River	146	2.3	384	1	83	333	859	41	37	97 454	17.5	82.5	45.9	16.8	0.5	5.0
Logan	199	6.6	209	1	107	229	1 135	30	93	97 184	3.3	96.7	37.8	15.8	23.7	4.9
Lonoke	391	2.0	450	210	327	585	1 305	97	126	144 990	78.9	21.1	50.6	31.2	0.0	372.9
Madison	282	5.3	235	0	125	248	1 176	30	105	86 989	0.8	99.2	44.2	17.2	9.0	3.7
Marion	140	-2.4	282	0	53	238	832	26	22	43 743	1.6	98.4	36.6	5.3	9.0	1.7
Miller	154	-11.4	307	8	105	266	932	43	47	92 816	24.3	75.7	43.4	18.1	0.0	100.4
Mississippi	489	0.9	1 059	163	480	1 287	1 233	236	167	361 061	99.4	0.6	86.6	59.7	2.1	152.8
Monroe	236	7.7	962	128	211	879	918	172	63	257 924	96.9	3.1	77.1	57.6	6.2	194.0
Montgomery	74	-7.2	178	0	36	228	1 201	31	43	103 499	1.0	99.0	49.2	24.2	66.2	1.7
Nevada	73	5.5	196	0	37	213	1 066	32	33	89 393	1.3	98.7	39.8	16.9	0.0	1.7
Newton	109	5.5	209	0	37	214	1 157	19	10	19 057	2.2	97.8	26.7	1.9	46.2	1.0
Ouachita	29	-8.0	166	D	13	179	1 158	28	7	37 807	5.8	94.2	28.8	6.8	0.0	36.4
Perry	73	8.5	186	5	45	286	1 500	34	37	94 079	14.0	86.0	42.7	18.9	26.2	4.4
Phillips	361	1.2	1 118	131	346	1 034	933	163	114	352 013	99.4	0.6	77.4	54.5	4.0	313.7
Pike	73	3.1	180	1	33	217	1 126	33	57	140 568	1.0	99.0	50.5	25.6	1.9	1.9
Poinsett	401	-0.9	704	274	375	786	1 217	168	140	245 117	98.6	1.4	84.7	63.9	1.4	500.5
Polk	133	8.3	157	1	61	205	1 343	26	99	116 782	0.3	99.7	46.2	27.2	35.9	4.9
Pope	152	-2.5	166	2	85	229	1 482	33	110	120 358	2.5	97.5	41.3	19.3	35.9	980.3
Prairie	302	-3.6	719	179	257	780	1 117	149	90	214 481	93.2	6.8	71.7	51.0	0.9	297.1
Pulaski	111	-1.0	263	20	77	334	1 187	40	25	58 816	55.1	44.9	30.2	10.5	1.9	86.3
Randolph	266	4.6	383	47	163	320	837	43	44	63 562	64.1	35.9	40.8	12.7	0.0	80.4
St. Francis	290	-5.0	884	103	244	899	1 006	131	69	210 138	96.0	4.0	70.7	45.4	0.0	201.0
Saline	50	9.2	153	0	26	262	1 956	29	4	12 308	40.1	59.9	24.0	1.2	11.5	9.7
Scott	116	0.6	177	D	56	206	1 196	31	89	135 790	0.4	99.6	44.6	22.0	62.7	2.7
Searcy	188	-3.9	307	0	69	215	653	26	10	16 690	3.1	96.9	31.3	4.2	12.9	1.8
Sebastian	115	0.0	159	0	64	253	1 537	23	37	50 903	4.8	95.2	30.9	8.1	23.2	32.4
Sevier	133	1.9	227	1	63	243	1 005	40	129	218 576	0.4	99.6	54.6	35.5	0.4	4.4
Sharp	174	9.2	281	1	69	220	733	22	33	53 544	2.6	97.4	31.2	8.6	0.0	2.0
Stone	142	4.7	237	0	56	211	765	27	37	62 122	2.0	98.0	43.6	17.3	15.7	1.8
Union	34	10.2	122	D	14	206	1 632	30	50	176 908	0.5	99.5	33.8	23.5	3.1	15.9
Van Buren	132	10.3	229	0	62	234	829	34	20	34 366	2.8	97.2	36.2	9.3	7.3	2.5
Washington	335	-4.9	135	1	175	303	2 230	31	359	145 163	1.1	98.9	38.4	18.6	3.8	27.4
White	394	9.8	237	51	268	289	1 207	38	63	37 689	49.8	50.2	30.2	8.6	2.0	114.0
Woodruff	285	3.5	1 191	159	255	1 128	998	221	74	309 958	98.3	1.7	76.6	60.3	2.9	274.7
Yell	188	-0.8	228	5	107	274	1 086	37	113	137 176	3.5	96.5	49.9	24.3	38.0	9.7
CALIFORNIA	27 699	-4.4	374	8 713	10 804	941	2 605	70	23 032	310 718	74.0	26.0	56.2	26.6	45.9	36 297.8
Alameda	258	-9.8	563	10	42	758	1 504	35	42	91 496	70.4	29.6	46.5	12.9	3.3	237.0
Alpine	4	-21.2	329	3	3	802	2 442	16	0	25 588	D	D	41.7	8.3	90.4	23.7
Amador	204	-13.4	568	12	25	756	1 500	21	21	58 713	44.3	55.7	44.7	7.2	22.1	26.8

STATE County	New Construction ($1,000)	Number of Housing Units	Number of Establishments	Number of Employees	Sales (mil dol)	Annual Payroll (mil dol)	Number of Establishments	Number of Employees	Sales (mil dol)	Annual Payroll (mil dol)	Number of Establishments	Number of Employees	Receipts (mil dol)	Annual Payroll (mil dol)
	Value of Residential Construction Authorized by Building Permits, 1999		Wholesale Trade, 1997				Retail Trade[1], 1997				Real Estate and Rental and Leasing, 1997			
	133	134	135	136	137	138	139	140	141	142	143	144	145	146
ARKANSAS—Cont'd														
Conway	860	10	23	D	D	D	91	948	157.1	12.3	8	28	1.6	0.3
Craighead	53 189	843	140	1 548	509.7	35.6	480	5 589	854.3	80.8	86	349	41.5	5.9
Crawford	12 326	134	58	373	170.1	9.3	171	1 599	268.5	22.8	38	114	9.9	1.6
Crittenden	25 770	282	64	D	D	D	206	2 722	496.9	33.1	38	137	15.1	2.4
Cross	1 681	25	22	344	102.7	7.1	80	720	129.8	10.5	10	27	2.4	0.2
Dallas	345	7	13	D	D	D	63	480	63.3	6.1	5	D	D	D
Desha	1 385	22	23	D	D	D	99	859	159.4	12.2	15	48	2.3	0.6
Drew	2 575	32	21	170	78.4	4.8	102	952	153.7	12.3	17	87	6.6	1.2
Faulkner	84 626	1 021	76	826	242.0	17.0	309	3 423	571.2	51.5	66	145	18.6	2.3
Franklin	899	17	8	D	D	D	63	461	71.2	5.9	6	21	0.6	0.2
Fulton	722	7	8	D	D	D	40	184	21.8	1.9	6	6	1.5	0.2
Garland	12 845	122	110	898	966.5	25.5	498	5 023	875.8	74.8	106	285	33.9	5.7
Grant	1 468	20	14	113	28.7	2.2	54	450	58.5	6.0	6	8	0.9	0.2
Greene	22 540	484	55	571	115.5	9.9	183	1 649	263.2	22.0	22	43	7.2	0.8
Hempstead	879	15	17	D	D	D	111	925	134.4	12.0	19	69	4.7	1.0
Hot Spring	1 423	16	28	170	54.0	4.1	99	787	144.6	11.1	10	36	2.0	0.6
Howard	1 576	21	14	44	12.7	0.7	73	634	88.2	8.0	7	26	0.8	0.1
Independence	2 204	18	50	624	172.5	12.6	195	1 741	284.2	23.2	26	66	5.5	0.9
Izard	1 141	15	9	D	D	D	57	374	71.0	4.8	12	49	2.8	0.4
Jackson	1 705	30	29	D	D	D	108	862	152.4	12.0	15	51	4.7	1.0
Jefferson	10 606	174	77	780	309.8	18.9	393	4 785	726.6	71.8	58	368	23.8	5.8
Johnson	2 621	46	9	D	D	D	104	988	155.5	13.4	16	41	4.0	0.9
Lafayette	1 260	26	2	D	D	D	40	216	22.1	2.1	8	15	1.5	0.2
Lawrence	2 415	23	21	173	85.2	3.7	88	710	122.0	9.5	8	20	0.6	0.1
Lee	1 250	40	10	95	63.7	2.3	39	273	40.8	3.6	5	11	0.4	0.1
Lincoln	1 052	11	7	D	D	D	28	228	30.6	2.9	4	11	0.7	0.1
Little River	463	8	16	76	22.5	2.2	57	396	77.4	5.2	10	26	1.3	0.2
Logan	1 235	18	17	D	D	D	94	707	119.5	9.5	10	14	1.4	0.1
Lonoke	33 467	378	37	321	144.4	7.3	178	1 622	269.1	23.3	27	75	3.8	0.8
Madison	0	0	2	D	D	D	41	282	47.7	4.0	3	10	0.2	0.1
Marion	11 280	194	8	D	D	D	39	360	46.2	4.5	10	D	D	D
Miller	13 803	243	49	D	D	D	167	1 512	254.1	21.0	24	75	4.9	0.8
Mississippi	4 250	99	60	457	237.9	13.1	261	2 117	361.8	29.1	33	138	9.7	1.7
Monroe	754	12	13	65	33.6	1.7	72	488	89.8	7.2	3	D	D	D
Montgomery	NA	NA	12	34	16.6	0.6	36	174	20.9	2.4	9	10	0.9	0.2
Nevada	239	5	5	21	18.2	0.9	40	261	37.0	3.1	NA	NA	NA	NA
Newton	0	0	7	D	D	D	16	121	15.1	1.5	3	10	0.5	0.1
Ouachita	2 564	14	31	264	121.0	6.8	148	1 380	198.2	19.3	22	156	16.0	3.5
Perry	150	1	3	D	D	D	27	154	19.0	1.7	2	D	D	D
Phillips	2 552	39	30	D	D	D	151	1 310	187.6	16.9	18	127	9.1	2.2
Pike	NA	NA	13	107	45.5	1.6	60	441	72.7	5.2	5	36	1.0	0.4
Poinsett	5 721	58	24	267	179.0	7.7	111	760	118.1	10.0	14	52	4.3	0.8
Polk	1 600	22	18	65	10.1	0.8	99	828	121.3	10.2	19	50	2.5	0.5
Pope	8 571	125	81	543	193.9	16.6	302	3 168	502.4	45.4	52	177	10.9	2.3
Prairie	557	8	8	53	18.5	1.3	54	246	36.6	3.1	4	8	0.4	0.0
Pulaski	208 771	1 912	882	14 654	9 759.8	455.7	1 847	26 898	4 584.4	415.1	472	3 405	394.4	64.1
Randolph	1 305	44	16	95	28.5	2.2	73	705	96.1	9.1	8	16	0.8	0.1
St. Francis	1 681	24	36	392	303.7	9.1	144	1 485	259.3	21.3	14	29	2.3	0.3
Saline	55 777	539	78	514	204.2	14.1	250	2 860	793.4	51.9	53	125	13.7	1.7
Scott	563	10	8	84	39.4	1.2	40	343	42.2	4.1	4	7	0.6	0.1
Searcy	128	3	7	D	D	D	40	253	31.4	2.6	2	D	D	D
Sebastian	50 050	462	245	2 101	708.5	56.8	659	8 721	1 360.6	128.1	135	670	81.6	12.4
Sevier	358	9	12	88	39.7	3.1	70	710	86.4	8.1	8	18	2.4	0.4
Sharp	0	0	11	D	D	D	91	778	112.6	8.6	17	D	D	D
Stone	746	12	11	D	D	D	63	470	66.3	6.4	3	4	0.2	0.0
Union	2 001	17	78	511	119.7	12.3	263	2 603	408.6	36.5	38	234	20.3	3.8
Van Buren	0	0	9	17	4.2	0.2	78	536	71.7	6.5	5	53	5.0	1.8
Washington	130 340	1 745	278	3 203	6 815.1	101.4	762	9 555	1 444.9	141.6	184	687	90.7	11.5
White	21 874	427	85	624	243.0	14.2	312	2 997	509.0	42.5	53	162	15.1	2.1
Woodruff	392	11	17	163	112.0	5.3	48	268	34.1	3.2	4	9	0.6	0.1
Yell	726	13	19	68	17.0	1.3	70	638	93.2	7.3	15	46	3.0	0.5
CALIFORNIA	21 030 600	138 039	57 842	755 513	551 230.6	29 900.2	106 357	1 354 797	263 118.3	26 362.7	37 244	243 288	38 288.4	6 570.5
Alameda	857 783	6 397	3 232	51 312	47 790.8	2 155.3	4 363	59 289	12 404.9	1 227.8	1 665	10 321	1 645.6	266.1
Alpine	18 789	59	NA	NA	NA	NA	7	28	2.3	0.2	5	18	1.6	0.2
Amador	21 710	203	28	D	D	D	158	1 570	475.0	25.7	36	155	16.8	2.2

1. Establishments with payroll.

STATE County	Professional, Scientific, and Technical Services[1], 1997				Manufacturing, 1997				Accommodation and Foodservices, 1997			
	Number of Establishments	Number of Employees	Receipts (mil dol)	Annual Payroll (mil dol)	Number of Establishments	Number of Employees	Receipts (mil dol)	Annual Payroll (mil dol)	Number of Establishments	Number of Employees	Sales (mil dol)	Annual Payroll (mil dol)
	147	148	149	150	151	152	153	154	155	156	157	158
ARKANSAS—Cont'd												
Conway	26	60	3.3	1.0	23	2 108	334.8	49.4	29	342	10.4	2.6
Craighead	148	675	53.4	19.3	122	6 886	1 257.6	184.9	133	2 720	80.2	21.6
Crawford	51	827	26.2	17.3	62	D	D	D	65	961	32.5	7.9
Crittenden	50	300	14.1	4.8	45	2 323	620.6	56.2	84	1 561	51.1	13.3
Cross	19	55	2.3	0.6	17	1 698	286.0	37.8	21	412	8.3	2.3
Dallas	9	31	1.3	0.4	15	786	131.3	21.9	10	D	D	D
Desha	24	57	3.2	0.9	16	1 611	319.2	45.1	35	263	8.0	1.7
Drew	21	72	4.3	1.4	33	2 429	222.0	51.2	31	507	15.3	3.7
Faulkner	81	520	42.6	12.3	93	7 556	1 230.5	189.0	112	2 389	69.3	19.0
Franklin	11	30	1.7	0.5	16	1 284	216.0	24.2	27	211	5.9	1.5
Fulton	10	23	0.7	0.3	NA	NA	NA	NA	17	106	3.4	1.0
Garland	167	673	46.3	17.4	108	3 827	795.5	100.0	222	4 005	120.2	36.8
Grant	14	49	3.5	1.4	25	1 481	314.6	42.0	11	D	D	D
Greene	45	269	12.1	6.8	47	5 223	961.3	126.6	54	768	20.8	5.9
Hempstead	22	66	2.8	0.8	32	3 565	558.9	75.9	34	519	14.9	3.8
Hot Spring	29	82	3.5	1.0	47	1 764	315.2	45.3	33	454	13.5	3.6
Howard	14	34	1.8	0.6	26	5 067	1 120.2	94.5	18	224	6.7	1.8
Independence	50	157	11.6	3.3	54	5 168	1 013.3	123.3	48	812	22.6	5.8
Izard	7	7	0.4	0.1	NA	NA	NA	NA	20	88	2.1	0.6
Jackson	30	82	5.2	1.6	23	1 129	199.9	31.5	28	284	8.6	2.3
Jefferson	85	619	38.1	14.5	84	7 774	1 741.5	218.8	131	2 049	57.9	15.0
Johnson	22	58	3.2	0.9	39	3 318	409.4	65.1	36	456	13.7	3.4
Lafayette	7	27	0.7	0.2	NA	NA	NA	NA	9	61	1.6	0.4
Lawrence	18	42	1.9	0.5	37	1 615	215.5	31.2	28	284	7.7	2.1
Lee	9	70	2.6	0.7	NA	NA	NA	NA	8	D	D	D
Lincoln	4	6	0.6	0.1	8	D	D	D	7	63	1.9	0.4
Little River	11	41	2.3	0.8	16	D	D	D	23	D	D	D
Logan	19	36	2.2	0.5	36	2 569	393.0	44.8	33	335	8.7	2.2
Lonoke	57	204	10.7	3.7	39	1 739	269.8	45.4	53	728	21.3	5.3
Madison	12	32	1.8	0.5	19	738	170.7	12.8	9	79	2.1	0.6
Marion	10	22	1.4	0.5	23	1 847	133.7	29.5	30	191	6.1	1.6
Miller	38	167	12.7	4.2	25	2 274	495.6	99.7	79	1 363	45.8	11.6
Mississippi	45	125	8.0	2.7	62	7 644	2 801.7	252.7	74	1 254	36.2	8.6
Monroe	13	55	3.1	1.0	NA	NA	NA	NA	24	430	12.0	2.9
Montgomery	9	18	0.9	0.3	NA	NA	NA	NA	14	148	9.4	2.0
Nevada	8	26	1.4	0.4	8	D	D	D	9	113	3.8	1.2
Newton	3	D	D	D	NA	NA	NA	NA	10	69	1.9	0.5
Ouachita	18	99	6.5	2.6	33	2 961	854.3	96.0	40	626	18.0	4.4
Perry	6	11	0.8	0.2	NA	NA	NA	NA	8	31	1.0	0.2
Phillips	33	94	6.6	1.4	19	983	411.8	24.1	39	369	9.4	2.5
Pike	6	16	0.5	0.2	13	596	121.5	12.0	26	205	4.8	1.3
Poinsett	19	40	2.1	0.5	27	1 895	367.1	42.5	34	249	9.5	2.0
Polk	27	131	14.5	6.0	29	1 933	322.2	38.2	34	435	14.5	3.6
Pope	82	355	19.5	7.4	82	4 940	1 222.1	118.4	106	2 025	50.5	13.8
Prairie	8	20	1.1	0.3	NA	NA	NA	NA	17	132	3.5	0.8
Pulaski	1 217	9 974	918.2	406.5	431	20 557	4 342.4	572.8	801	16 728	508.0	144.7
Randolph	18	59	2.9	0.8	32	1 688	190.5	37.6	27	D	D	D
St. Francis	30	119	7.9	2.4	27	1 606	628.2	41.1	54	822	24.2	6.4
Saline	78	224	19.6	6.3	72	1 827	352.7	56.8	83	1 368	46.3	12.2
Scott	8	14	0.6	0.2	19	1 367	220.7	27.1	17	D	D	D
Searcy	4	13	0.5	0.2	NA	NA	NA	NA	10	88	2.1	0.7
Sebastian	227	1 262	101.0	29.4	233	22 891	4 319.3	582.0	257	4 669	138.9	38.1
Sevier	20	35	1.9	0.7	15	1 985	402.0	37.3	22	D	D	D
Sharp	17	35	1.9	0.7	NA	NA	NA	NA	41	379	10.1	2.6
Stone	12	37	1.5	0.5	26	602	39.8	10.4	21	278	7.6	1.9
Union	67	371	22.8	8.1	63	5 443	2 082.2	158.1	68	1 007	28.1	6.6
Van Buren	15	38	2.0	0.7	15	638	111.5	12.5	27	336	8.9	2.4
Washington	336	1 629	121.3	44.1	193	14 795	2 388.9	357.1	372	6 181	183.4	50.9
White	65	263	16.0	5.5	75	4 149	646.5	103.3	95	1 323	48.1	11.0
Woodruff	6	13	0.5	0.2	9	796	78.4	14.0	6	34	0.9	0.2
Yell	15	185	4.1	2.7	22	2 880	337.7	52.4	18	D	D	D
CALIFORNIA	78 635	805 856	89 555.7	35 258.6	49 418	1 809 667	379 612.4	65 762.8	62 532	1 052 715	42 261.1	11 437.2
Alameda	3 667	30 441	3 875.3	1 498.3	2 507	93 809	22 337.8	3 803.0	2 773	38 360	1 573.2	417.8
Alpine	1	D	D	D	NA	NA	NA	NA	16	148	6.0	1.4
Amador	50	119	9.3	2.7	51	732	136.8	19.5	105	910	29.5	8.1

1. Firms subject to federal tax.

Table B. States and Counties — **Health and Other Services and Federal Funds**

STATE County	Health Care and Social Assistance[1], 1997				Other Services[1], 1997				Federal funds and grants, fiscal 1999[2] — Expenditures (mil dol)			
										Direct payments for individuals[3]		
	Number of Establishments	Number of Employees	Receipts (mil dol)	Annual Payroll (mil dol)	Number of Establishments	Number of Employees	Receipts (mil dol)	Annual Payroll (mil dol)	Total	Social Security and government retirement	Medicare	Food stamps and Supplemental Security Income
	159	160	161	162	163	164	165	166	167	168	169	170
ARKANSAS—Cont'd												
Conway	28	745	21.8	9.7	15	75	4.2	1.3	98.3	50.3	18.4	5.1
Craighead	214	3 357	245.4	115.8	118	623	39.5	10.0	301.2	130.9	47.2	12.8
Crawford	51	957	52.0	21.2	64	364	30.8	6.5	177.2	97.2	33.1	9.1
Crittenden	66	768	42.0	16.7	64	439	25.7	7.3	234.3	70.2	36.4	20.2
Cross	26	299	12.3	5.8	21	74	4.3	1.0	116.6	33.6	14.7	6.1
Dallas	14	707	23.6	11.6	13	56	2.9	0.8	45.6	21.1	11.4	1.6
Desha	21	499	22.0	11.1	17	59	2.6	0.7	130.3	27.9	15.8	5.7
Drew	29	281	14.4	5.2	27	114	7.7	1.4	92.0	30.0	14.0	5.0
Faulkner	137	1 330	74.4	34.5	82	520	27.4	8.1	256.7	127.1	39.0	8.1
Franklin	18	243	9.6	4.8	14	100	3.3	1.2	85.6	38.8	13.9	3.4
Fulton	8	153	5.3	1.7	12	26	1.4	0.3	51.6	29.3	10.1	2.3
Garland	202	3 342	226.8	93.7	133	670	31.1	10.0	490.6	287.3	107.0	16.3
Grant	14	154	6.7	2.6	15	35	2.3	0.5	53.6	29.1	9.4	1.8
Greene	65	421	28.4	10.9	46	202	10.7	2.8	149.9	68.4	25.5	6.7
Hempstead	49	848	38.5	16.9	32	178	12.0	3.2	94.6	40.4	22.2	5.6
Hot Spring	32	331	14.0	5.8	26	78	5.1	1.3	134.7	63.5	27.1	5.5
Howard	31	404	11.8	4.8	17	74	3.9	0.9	61.1	29.3	14.9	2.6
Independence	71	792	41.5	19.2	45	182	12.5	3.3	162.6	69.9	27.4	6.0
Izard	9	336	6.8	2.6	15	25	2.5	0.5	75.6	39.7	13.1	2.4
Jackson	45	922	62.3	18.6	29	97	5.8	1.5	132.0	37.2	32.5	5.0
Jefferson	191	1 709	110.3	48.3	110	750	40.7	12.6	536.5	172.1	62.4	29.8
Johnson	24	278	12.2	5.3	28	99	6.5	1.3	97.9	46.2	15.9	4.4
Lafayette	6	109	4.4	1.8	7	32	1.7	0.5	56.8	17.4	10.5	3.6
Lawrence	16	122	6.4	2.5	26	88	5.7	1.1	124.6	42.0	18.7	5.1
Lee	11	135	4.3	1.5	11	18	1.2	0.2	89.9	18.9	10.3	7.8
Lincoln	9	206	5.2	2.4	11	54	6.3	2.0	63.7	19.9	8.8	3.5
Little River	14	155	4.5	2.0	11	34	2.6	0.7	62.4	31.5	11.2	3.0
Logan	22	238	10.5	4.5	24	100	5.8	1.3	98.6	53.8	17.1	4.7
Lonoke	51	800	29.5	13.9	50	152	8.8	2.2	197.6	100.6	31.6	5.4
Madison	10	47	2.4	1.0	8	30	4.1	1.3	48.0	26.7	7.9	2.2
Marion	8	102	4.0	1.2	12	23	2.4	0.4	65.3	41.8	11.5	2.9
Miller	34	573	23.9	8.9	41	298	14.2	4.5	196.8	67.6	40.3	11.8
Mississippi	72	731	31.3	14.0	51	341	28.0	7.8	272.3	91.3	38.8	20.5
Monroe	11	174	5.4	2.1	15	47	3.7	0.7	90.5	20.8	11.0	5.0
Montgomery	7	19	1.0	0.2	6	13	0.6	0.2	41.0	22.4	8.4	1.4
Nevada	7	193	6.6	3.2	9	33	2.2	0.6	47.4	20.5	12.0	2.7
Newton	1	D	D	D	3	3	0.2	0.0	37.5	17.1	5.0	2.6
Ouachita	40	632	28.3	10.6	37	181	10.2	2.9	172.6	70.0	29.2	10.7
Perry	9	102	3.2	1.4	2	D	D	D	51.3	23.2	8.0	1.9
Phillips	45	449	19.0	7.8	24	86	5.7	1.2	195.1	48.2	25.8	19.6
Pike	11	156	4.5	2.0	5	34	1.8	0.5	45.3	23.5	9.9	1.6
Poinsett	20	315	9.1	4.1	25	49	3.7	0.8	153.3	48.6	23.3	8.5
Polk	36	341	14.4	4.9	33	92	5.6	1.1	91.7	50.1	18.5	3.9
Pope	107	1 999	139.8	54.3	93	458	23.2	6.6	198.0	97.5	30.0	10.3
Prairie	12	207	6.6	3.0	15	48	3.6	0.5	70.7	19.2	10.0	1.8
Pulaski	1 002	12 393	955.6	448.5	698	4 422	273.2	78.7	2 595.2	827.8	263.6	72.2
Randolph	21	293	16.0	6.1	20	47	3.3	0.8	82.0	38.8	13.9	6.1
St. Francis	35	412	19.6	7.5	29	148	7.4	2.1	183.6	47.3	22.3	16.3
Saline	87	1 069	55.0	24.5	83	403	24.3	7.2	175.1	103.4	36.4	7.0
Scott	5	24	1.3	0.7	5	17	1.4	0.3	49.4	24.4	8.3	2.2
Searcy	6	145	3.0	1.2	1	D	D	D	49.8	21.4	7.4	2.6
Sebastian	288	4 698	337.1	152.7	192	1 278	74.3	20.6	448.5	224.8	80.0	18.1
Sevier	27	442	24.3	9.0	22	89	5.3	1.3	56.6	29.1	12.6	2.4
Sharp	21	172	6.6	2.8	15	39	1.8	0.4	96.0	57.1	19.5	4.2
Stone	13	286	19.3	4.9	7	19	1.3	0.3	58.0	29.2	10.6	3.0
Union	95	1 607	100.9	37.0	74	391	25.2	6.1	208.6	103.7	43.3	12.6
Van Buren	11	49	2.7	0.9	15	38	2.5	0.4	78.8	48.4	15.7	3.4
Washington	290	2 938	192.9	92.0	232	1 421	71.8	22.1	501.1	236.9	69.4	15.9
White	97	1 798	122.5	47.4	85	549	28.4	7.8	252.0	133.6	46.9	10.4
Woodruff	10	94	4.6	2.3	5	16	0.9	0.2	89.0	18.2	12.7	3.6
Yell	28	406	16.2	7.4	16	62	3.5	0.7	104.1	47.2	16.7	3.9
CALIFORNIA	69 857	664 539	51 968.0	20 619.3	44 642	282 762	20 521.5	5 852.2	166 049.7	46 584.1	23 935.2	5 939.3
Alameda	3 124	32 552	2 698.7	1 066.4	2 164	14 520	1 186.7	346.2	8 052.8	1 948.6	1 037.4	268.9
Alpine	2	D	D	D	1	D	D	D	9.1	3.6	0.7	0.1
Amador	70	631	26.6	8.9	32	98	8.1	1.6	149.5	85.1	35.2	2.2

1. Firms subject to federal tax. 2. October 1, 1998 to September 30, 1999. 3. State totals may include programs not allocated by county.

STATE County	Federal funds and grants, fiscal 1999[1] (cont'd)							Local government finances, 1997				
	Expenditures (mil dol) (cont'd)							General revenue				
	Procurement contract awards			Grants[2]							Taxes	
											Per capita[3] (dollars)	
	Salaries and wages	Defense	Other	Medicaid and other health-related	Nutrition and family welfare	Education	Other	Total (mil dol)	Intergovern-mental (mil dol)	Total (mil dol)	Total	Property
	171	172	173	174	175	176	177	178	179	180	181	182
ARKANSAS—Cont'd												
Conway	3.4	0.1	0.7	12.8	1.8	0.9	1.5	52.2	17.3	31.6	1 581	1 424
Craighead	22.6	0.7	4.0	26.9	10.0	7.0	5.1	110.0	53.7	36.3	471	305
Crawford	5.2	1.8	1.3	13.6	4.6	2.3	6.2	70.4	42.1	15.7	317	239
Crittenden	5.7	0.0	1.4	44.4	7.0	4.6	21.0	90.2	47.5	25.3	509	217
Cross	2.8	12.1	0.6	12.4	2.6	1.4	5.3	35.2	17.2	7.1	366	259
Dallas	2.1	0.0	0.3	6.5	1.2	0.6	0.5	13.9	8.4	3.2	350	266
Desha	5.3	30.8	0.5	15.4	3.1	1.6	2.3	40.0	18.9	8.2	538	393
Drew	4.0	0.7	1.5	9.8	1.6	2.1	13.3	43.9	19.1	7.9	443	240
Faulkner	10.1	6.1	2.1	14.1	7.1	1.8	32.9	99.6	51.6	27.8	363	275
Franklin	11.3	7.7	0.7	5.7	0.8	0.9	0.7	24.3	15.7	5.8	351	307
Fulton	1.5	0.0	0.4	5.7	0.6	0.5	0.5	17.2	8.7	3.0	273	183
Garland	27.6	5.8	4.5	25.5	5.5	4.4	3.2	123.7	45.1	48.8	586	322
Grant	2.1	0.0	0.5	4.0	0.6	0.7	5.1	26.3	17.1	5.9	376	358
Greene	4.9	1.2	1.1	16.7	2.0	1.4	2.5	52.3	27.1	13.7	385	162
Hempstead	4.7	0.0	0.7	11.4	2.3	1.9	2.1	31.5	19.7	7.3	332	193
Hot Spring	4.4	0.0	1.6	9.6	2.0	1.3	17.6	59.5	23.3	10.8	377	254
Howard	3.1	0.1	0.5	6.6	1.0	1.1	0.7	23.9	13.5	7.3	527	304
Independence	10.5	1.3	8.4	20.5	3.1	2.0	7.1	65.8	29.5	17.5	532	371
Izard	1.7	0.8	0.4	6.8	0.7	0.8	7.7	16.1	10.3	3.9	301	234
Jackson	3.0	0.3	0.7	18.5	2.1	1.3	1.2	29.6	12.4	8.4	473	277
Jefferson	65.0	43.6	18.7	57.9	12.9	8.4	30.2	148.9	72.7	47.6	579	343
Johnson	5.0	0.2	1.1	9.3	1.2	1.1	12.6	42.2	24.4	10.2	482	302
Lafayette	1.7	0.0	0.4	9.0	1.3	0.9	6.5	16.0	10.1	3.7	409	296
Lawrence	3.7	0.0	0.8	13.9	1.4	1.0	18.1	35.3	16.3	5.6	322	173
Lee	2.7	0.1	0.5	20.8	3.6	1.7	1.6	18.7	12.7	4.4	352	225
Lincoln	1.0	1.0	0.2	11.5	1.5	0.6	0.4	15.3	10.1	2.8	194	140
Little River	1.9	0.3	0.6	6.6	1.0	0.7	2.2	25.5	7.4	9.0	678	383
Logan	6.1	0.0	1.2	10.8	1.4	0.9	0.8	26.3	15.6	6.2	290	197
Lonoke	5.3	1.1	3.5	12.7	2.3	3.6	4.4	69.3	42.6	17.7	359	206
Madison	2.4	0.0	1.2	6.0	0.7	0.5	-0.5	19.4	12.4	4.8	366	207
Marion	1.4	0.3	0.3	4.8	0.8	0.5	0.1	17.8	10.8	5.0	349	234
Miller	2.7	2.2	1.3	19.3	5.7	2.7	30.7	68.8	33.7	19.3	487	305
Mississippi	6.8	8.7	2.0	41.2	11.1	5.2	3.0	100.3	54.5	25.7	509	206
Monroe	1.8	0.0	0.6	15.6	2.2	1.3	15.0	17.8	10.7	4.3	419	271
Montgomery	2.4	0.0	0.9	3.8	0.4	0.4	0.3	12.2	8.4	2.5	291	187
Nevada	2.1	0.0	0.6	6.3	1.1	0.5	0.9	19.7	8.8	4.0	399	267
Newton	2.3	0.0	0.3	7.3	0.8	0.5	0.8	10.7	7.6	1.7	206	121
Ouachita	7.5	23.9	1.5	21.0	3.2	1.7	1.5	64.3	28.2	10.6	376	272
Perry	2.1	0.2	0.8	4.7	0.5	0.4	8.4	25.2	10.0	9.4	991	160
Phillips	3.9	1.7	0.9	43.2	10.7	3.9	9.7	51.8	33.3	11.9	431	261
Pike	3.0	0.1	0.4	4.4	0.6	0.5	0.7	18.2	9.1	4.5	428	304
Poinsett	3.6	1.4	1.0	23.4	2.8	1.4	3.7	39.4	24.0	9.4	381	230
Polk	4.5	0.0	1.4	6.4	1.3	1.1	3.0	26.7	16.7	6.0	306	183
Pope	13.8	0.4	6.6	18.8	8.0	2.1	5.6	85.0	32.2	35.4	691	333
Prairie	2.3	0.7	0.4	5.8	0.8	0.5	4.9	12.6	6.8	3.8	406	279
Pulaski	566.5	49.2	54.7	190.2	174.2	94.4	253.7	775.2	262.0	288.0	822	477
Randolph	1.8	0.0	0.5	9.7	2.6	0.7	0.6	20.7	12.8	5.1	287	163
St. Francis	20.3	0.1	7.0	36.1	6.5	3.3	5.1	46.8	29.3	11.0	387	199
Saline	5.1	0.5	1.2	9.3	3.4	1.8	5.8	154.3	60.3	26.7	352	250
Scott	3.3	0.0	0.9	4.7	0.6	0.5	4.0	19.4	9.4	2.0	184	123
Searcy	2.2	0.1	0.3	9.5	0.6	0.4	3.8	10.7	7.0	2.8	357	291
Sebastian	54.7	3.8	11.3	23.8	4.2	4.5	14.7	194.1	72.8	82.5	778	405
Sevier	4.0	0.1	0.6	4.2	0.7	0.7	1.4	21.6	13.5	5.0	337	223
Sharp	3.2	0.0	0.8	8.1	1.3	0.7	0.6	23.5	12.4	6.3	377	249
Stone	2.3	0.0	0.3	8.7	0.8	0.5	1.8	15.1	8.3	5.3	481	334
Union	9.2	0.1	1.9	27.7	7.7	3.0	-6.2	72.3	33.8	24.8	545	272
Van Buren	2.4	0.0	0.5	7.4	0.9	0.6	-1.1	16.8	10.4	4.3	280	217
Washington	55.8	12.8	15.8	21.8	6.4	7.7	44.9	243.4	104.0	87.7	640	383
White	9.2	1.2	2.0	25.3	3.3	3.2	3.0	112.4	48.1	23.8	376	227
Woodruff	2.0	0.3	0.5	10.6	1.5	0.9	15.9	15.4	10.8	2.9	319	226
Yell	6.6	8.1	3.6	10.1	1.0	0.8	3.1	36.8	18.6	5.9	309	271
CALIFORNIA	17 733.2	17 370.6	8 424.5	15 257.9	8 675.6	3 008.9	9 427.4	X	X	X	X	X
Alameda	752.3	196.3	1 945.0	927.5	272.8	90.3	488.8	5 667.1	2 317.1	1 742.3	1 271	757
Alpine	0.3	0.1	1.5	0.5	0.3	0.3	1.4	12.2	5.2	3.1	2 579	1 881
Amador	4.4	0.0	1.2	6.2	4.4	0.4	8.8	69.6	32.7	25.4	735	619

1. October 1, 1998 to September 30, 1999.   2. State totals may include programs not allocated by county.   3. Based on the resident population estimated as of July 1 of the year shown.

Table B. States and Counties — Local Government Finances, Government Employment, and Elections

	Local government finances, 1997 (cont'd)									Government employment, 1998			Presidential election, 2000		
	Direct general expenditure							Debt outstanding					Percent of vote cast —		
			Percent of total for —												
STATE County	Total (mil dol)	Per capita[1] (dollars)	Education	Health and hospitals	Police protection	Public welfare	High-ways	Total (mil dol)	Per capita[1] (dollars)	Federal civilian	Federal military	State and local	Demo-cratic	Republi-can	All other
	183	184	185	186	187	188	189	190	191	192	193	194	195	196	197
ARKANSAS—Cont'd															
Conway	30.7	1 535	68.3	0.2	4.2	0.0	5.6	24.6	1 230	66	112	1 123	48.3	49.0	2.7
Craighead	111.5	1 449	60.6	0.5	4.6	0.0	6.7	139.4	1 812	437	444	5 252	49.2	48.3	2.5
Crawford	71.2	1 437	74.0	0.0	4.5	0.0	4.2	58.5	1 180	89	284	1 788	35.7	61.3	3.0
Crittenden	84.3	1 697	56.4	2.1	7.0	0.1	3.9	57.4	1 156	113	282	2 531	54.6	44.3	1.2
Cross	32.9	1 688	57.1	19.8	4.7	0.0	4.8	17.1	878	61	110	1 113	49.8	48.8	1.4
Dallas	14.4	1 572	60.6	0.1	5.5	0.0	8.4	7.1	778	26	51	477	51.4	47.2	1.3
Desha	38.3	2 512	51.1	19.9	5.4	0.0	3.9	30.2	1 979	102	85	1 177	61.8	35.7	2.6
Drew	41.7	2 349	55.5	24.2	3.0	0.2	2.2	20.5	1 156	100	99	1 609	51.7	46.5	1.8
Faulkner	107.8	1 407	65.4	0.1	4.5	0.3	3.7	155.2	2 026	202	448	5 086	40.9	55.0	4.1
Franklin	22.3	1 355	77.6	1.6	2.5	0.1	6.6	16.4	995	164	273	807	43.6	53.4	3.1
Fulton	16.3	1 487	51.2	16.2	2.9	0.1	6.6	7.8	713	37	62	499	48.1	49.6	2.3
Garland	117.1	1 407	53.8	0.3	9.4	0.2	4.7	132.0	1 586	590	476	3 442	44.1	53.1	2.8
Grant	25.0	1 592	81.7	0.1	1.9	0.0	4.3	15.9	1 017	34	90	815	42.2	54.6	3.2
Greene	50.4	1 419	58.1	0.3	4.2	0.0	7.5	64.8	1 822	85	204	1 514	50.6	46.7	2.7
Hempstead	30.8	1 405	66.0	0.2	4.9	0.0	9.2	21.6	983	106	125	1 473	54.0	44.7	1.3
Hot Spring	57.2	2 003	51.3	21.9	2.7	0.2	3.4	79.3	2 776	65	164	1 666	50.3	45.9	3.8
Howard	21.2	1 525	67.6	0.1	3.5	0.0	6.3	19.1	1 379	70	77	750	46.3	52.2	1.6
Independence	65.1	1 978	47.5	0.2	3.6	0.7	5.9	144.6	4 393	213	187	1 657	44.4	53.0	2.6
Izard	16.7	1 295	76.1	0.7	4.5	0.2	6.1	8.7	670	37	74	810	51.4	45.7	2.9
Jackson	25.2	1 421	56.2	1.0	5.3	0.1	7.0	18.6	1 048	56	100	911	60.1	37.5	2.3
Jefferson	150.9	1 835	53.0	0.3	7.5	0.0	4.3	109.7	1 334	1 609	516	6 134	65.1	32.2	2.6
Johnson	41.4	1 957	45.2	28.7	2.6	0.0	7.7	16.3	771	110	121	854	45.7	51.1	3.3
Lafayette	14.1	1 548	63.5	0.2	4.5	0.0	9.4	3.4	370	36	50	482	53.4	45.5	1.2
Lawrence	34.0	1 947	53.0	19.6	4.4	4.7	5.2	9.0	513	75	98	1 200	53.9	43.5	2.6
Lee	17.2	1 376	66.3	3.1	5.8	0.2	8.8	4.9	392	56	70	891	66.2	32.8	1.0
Lincoln	15.6	1 089	68.4	1.7	4.2	0.2	7.4	4.8	331	31	81	1 255	55.2	43.0	1.8
Little River	31.4	2 374	36.6	36.9	2.3	0.0	5.9	100.6	7 616	50	75	816	54.8	43.4	1.8
Logan	28.8	1 356	68.2	3.0	4.9	0.0	8.2	12.1	570	134	119	1 172	40.6	55.4	4.0
Lonoke	67.3	1 366	69.8	0.5	4.4	0.0	6.1	35.9	728	103	283	1 894	38.2	59.1	2.7
Madison	25.8	1 965	47.4	1.5	28.2	0.1	12.1	7.7	586	55	75	516	36.5	60.2	3.3
Marion	16.6	1 154	67.8	3.2	5.4	0.2	11.4	10.8	747	39	84	547	37.1	56.6	6.3
Miller	67.1	1 689	54.7	0.9	7.7	0.2	5.7	90.8	2 288	79	226	1 892	45.7	52.9	1.4
Mississippi	90.7	1 795	55.1	0.1	5.8	0.0	4.3	79.9	1 582	140	287	3 000	56.5	41.3	2.2
Monroe	15.6	1 506	63.7	0.3	5.4	0.1	8.8	8.1	780	45	58	555	58.0	40.4	1.6
Montgomery	9.9	1 169	66.9	0.2	3.7	0.1	9.0	4.5	526	68	49	438	38.5	56.9	4.6
Nevada	19.6	1 958	53.9	16.8	2.6	0.1	5.9	16.2	1 618	33	57	535	49.9	48.0	2.0
Newton	9.9	1 217	78.1	1.5	2.0	0.2	4.6	3.7	462	58	46	455	30.7	64.4	4.9
Ouachita	60.3	2 145	52.3	26.4	3.3	0.1	3.5	35.1	1 250	151	158	1 452	52.6	45.6	1.8
Perry	22.4	2 363	42.0	1.7	9.9	0.0	10.1	57.6	6 091	39	54	432	41.1	52.8	6.1
Phillips	48.5	1 756	67.3	3.9	5.1	0.1	4.0	29.3	1 062	76	154	1 879	64.6	33.9	1.5
Pike	20.9	1 993	70.9	8.0	2.0	0.1	3.9	9.2	880	79	60	640	40.4	57.3	2.3
Poinsett	36.3	1 475	69.9	0.5	5.0	0.0	4.9	21.4	869	73	140	1 269	56.7	41.3	2.0
Polk	28.1	1 428	71.8	0.1	3.8	0.0	8.1	9.6	487	102	111	990	32.2	64.0	3.9
Pope	72.9	1 422	60.2	1.1	4.1	0.0	5.6	121.0	2 363	321	299	2 886	36.2	61.0	2.8
Prairie	12.3	1 323	63.2	1.4	6.0	0.0	11.1	6.5	695	40	53	403	44.6	53.1	2.3
Pulaski	779.3	2 224	41.2	6.3	7.1	0.0	5.7	844.4	2 410	9 094	6 553	37 793	53.7	43.9	2.3
Randolph	21.6	1 222	67.5	0.1	6.3	0.2	5.0	17.2	974	41	100	892	51.4	45.5	3.1
St. Francis	48.8	1 720	62.8	0.5	4.3	0.0	4.9	11.5	406	441	159	1 944	58.7	40.2	1.1
Saline	121.4	1 599	43.0	25.9	3.5	0.0	3.9	81.2	1 070	83	437	3 724	39.2	57.5	3.3
Scott	17.0	1 564	43.1	30.5	4.8	0.1	7.5	5.5	504	79	60	384	36.3	60.3	3.5
Searcy	9.3	1 199	75.2	0.2	3.1	0.0	7.2	3.0	387	42	44	471	30.3	64.3	5.4
Sebastian	174.2	1 644	54.0	0.3	5.4	0.0	11.4	104.2	984	1 059	601	4 818	38.7	58.5	2.8
Sevier	21.6	1 456	72.7	0.3	4.7	0.1	6.4	5.0	340	79	83	796	48.8	49.2	2.0
Sharp	22.7	1 366	64.7	0.2	3.6	0.1	8.9	6.2	370	54	96	763	45.4	51.9	2.7
Stone	15.8	1 448	53.2	0.1	3.4	0.2	9.3	3.8	351	65	63	598	42.0	54.0	4.0
Union	68.9	1 515	59.9	0.1	5.9	0.0	7.5	47.5	1 044	200	257	2 414	40.1	55.4	4.5
Van Buren	16.4	1 053	69.3	0.5	4.7	0.4	7.6	6.2	399	48	88	635	45.8	49.9	4.3
Washington	254.3	1 857	48.9	0.4	4.9	0.1	5.0	141.5	1 033	1 214	800	11 280	41.6	54.9	3.5
White	107.5	1 699	50.0	22.5	3.4	0.2	4.3	84.4	1 333	161	364	2 720	37.7	59.5	2.9
Woodruff	15.5	1 735	53.4	0.7	4.9	17.3	8.3	7.0	786	44	50	538	64.1	33.9	2.0
Yell	36.1	1 889	49.0	25.8	3.2	0.0	4.0	18.7	980	169	108	1 111	47.3	49.7	3.0
CALIFORNIA	X	X	X	X	X	X	X	X	X	268 568	230 324	1 881 006	53.4	41.7	4.9
Alameda	5 455.9	3 979	25.9	11.8	5.4	8.6	3.4	7 320.1	5 339	12 755	4 491	103 466	69.4	24.2	6.4
Alpine	12.1	10 029	24.3	5.0	7.0	6.8	16.2	1.2	1 030	12	0	156	45.3	48.0	6.7
Amador	66.4	1 924	35.6	3.9	7.0	8.2	6.6	18.4	533	99	67	2 534	38.2	56.7	5.1

1. Based on the resident population estimated as of July 1 of the year shown.

Table B. States and Counties — **Land Area and Population**

STATE/ County code	MSA/ PMSA/ NECMA code[1]	County Type[2]	STATE County	Land area[3] (sq km) 1990	Total persons	Rank	Per square kilometer	White	Black	Am. Indian, Eskimo, Aleut	Asian and Pacific Islander	Percent Hispanic[4]	Under 5 years	5 to 17 years	18 to 24 years	25 to 34 years	35 to 44 years	45 to 54 years
					1	2	3	4	5	6	7	8	9	10	11	12	13	14	15

Population and population characteristics, 1999 — Race (percent): White, Black, Am. Indian Eskimo Aleut, Asian and Pacific Islander. Age (percent): Under 5 to 45 to 54 years.

STATE/ County code	MSA code[1]	Type[2]	STATE County	Land area (sq km) 1990 (1)	Total persons (2)	Rank (3)	Per square kilometer (4)	White (5)	Black (6)	Am. Indian, Eskimo, Aleut (7)	Asian and Pacific Islander (8)	Percent Hispanic[4] (9)	Under 5 years (10)	5 to 17 years (11)	18 to 24 years (12)	25 to 34 years (13)	35 to 44 years (14)	45 to 54 years (15)
			CALIFORNIA--Cont'd															
06 007	1620	3	Butte	4 247	195 220	277	46.0	92.6	1.5	2.0	4.0	10.5	6.3	18.6	12.3	11.3	15.1	11.6
06 009	...	6	Calaveras	2 642	40 051	1 088	15.2	96.1	0.7	2.3	0.9	7.7	5.7	19.1	4.4	9.4	16.8	15.3
06 011	...	6	Colusa	2 981	18 844	1 828	6.3	94.1	0.8	2.2	2.9	41.5	8.0	24.2	8.1	12.6	15.6	11.9
06 013	5775	0	Contra Costa	1 866	933 141	37	500.1	76.5	9.7	0.7	13.1	15.0	6.6	18.6	7.7	13.7	18.7	15.1
06 015	...	7	Del Norte	2 610	26 477	1 480	10.1	86.9	4.1	6.3	2.7	13.2	6.6	20.8	8.4	15.5	15.7	12.3
06 017	6920	1	El Dorado	4 433	161 358	322	36.4	95.5	0.5	1.2	2.8	9.7	6.6	20.0	6.0	12.3	19.8	14.0
06 019	2840	2	Fresno	15 445	763 069	57	49.4	82.8	5.2	1.3	10.7	43.1	9.0	23.4	9.9	14.2	15.4	11.0
06 021	...	6	Glenn	3 406	26 328	1 483	7.7	92.6	0.6	2.4	4.4	26.1	8.2	23.8	7.6	12.2	14.9	12.2
06 023	...	5	Humboldt	9 254	121 358	435	13.1	90.7	0.9	5.7	2.7	5.9	6.3	19.7	9.9	12.6	18.0	12.7
06 025	...	4	Imperial	10 813	145 287	361	13.4	93.0	2.9	1.6	2.6	73.8	8.2	24.8	9.5	14.7	15.4	10.2
06 027	...	7	Inyo	26 397	17 958	1 870	0.7	88.0	0.5	10.1	1.4	11.5	5.6	18.4	5.0	10.5	16.9	14.6
06 029	0680	2	Kern	21 087	642 495	78	30.5	87.0	6.6	1.8	4.7	35.9	8.9	23.0	9.2	15.4	15.8	11.3
06 031	...	4	Kings	3 599	123 241	428	34.2	83.7	10.3	1.4	4.6	42.2	8.4	21.7	11.4	18.9	16.4	10.2
06 033	...	6	Lake	3 259	55 405	835	17.0	93.7	2.1	2.7	1.4	10.1	6.2	18.8	5.1	9.9	15.7	13.2
06 035	...	6	Lassen	11 804	33 028	1 284	2.8	85.9	9.6	2.9	1.5	15.3	5.1	17.5	11.9	19.3	18.7	11.5
06 037	4480	0	Los Angeles	10 515	9 329 989	1	887.3	74.8	11.2	0.6	13.4	44.4	7.9	19.1	10.8	16.3	16.6	11.9
06 039	2840	2	Madera	5 539	116 760	451	21.1	92.5	3.6	2.0	1.9	43.1	7.4	22.1	9.6	13.1	15.8	11.6
06 041	7360	0	Marin	1 346	236 768	236	175.9	89.9	3.9	0.4	5.8	10.3	5.1	13.6	6.6	13.0	21.3	17.6
06 043	...	8	Mariposa	3 759	15 605	2 027	4.2	93.1	0.8	4.8	1.3	6.9	5.4	17.1	5.6	10.9	16.0	15.1
06 045	...	4	Mendocino	9 089	84 085	603	9.3	93.4	0.7	4.3	1.6	13.7	6.6	21.0	6.7	11.0	18.7	13.9
06 047	4940	3	Merced	4 996	200 746	270	40.2	83.4	4.8	1.1	10.7	40.3	9.9	25.8	9.2	14.2	14.6	10.5
06 049	...	7	Modoc	10 216	9 210	2 490	0.9	94.2	0.8	4.4	0.6	9.8	5.7	21.5	5.3	10.1	16.0	13.7
06 051	...	7	Mono	7 885	10 512	2 376	1.3	93.8	0.7	3.6	1.8	14.9	7.4	17.2	9.3	17.7	20.8	13.3
06 053	7120	2	Monterey	8 604	371 756	153	43.2	82.1	6.4	1.0	10.5	41.1	8.3	20.5	10.4	16.2	16.1	10.6
06 055	8720	0	Napa	1 953	120 962	437	61.9	93.7	1.1	0.8	4.4	19.1	6.2	17.6	8.1	11.9	16.8	13.9
06 057	...	4	Nevada	2 480	92 014	548	37.1	97.4	0.3	1.2	1.2	6.0	5.4	18.9	4.8	9.2	19.2	14.0
06 059	5945	0	Orange	2 045	2 760 948	6	1 350.1	84.2	1.8	0.6	13.5	29.0	7.3	18.1	11.0	16.1	16.7	13.5
06 061	6920	1	Placer	3 637	239 485	231	65.8	95.0	0.7	1.2	3.2	11.3	6.5	20.0	6.7	12.0	19.2	15.0
06 063	...	6	Plumas	6 615	20 370	1 745	3.1	95.2	0.8	3.2	0.8	6.6	5.6	19.8	4.5	9.3	17.4	14.7
06 065	6780	0	Riverside	18 669	1 530 653	17	82.0	88.2	5.8	1.2	4.8	33.8	8.5	21.3	8.9	14.8	15.5	11.1
06 067	6920	0	Sacramento	2 501	1 184 586	29	473.6	75.5	10.1	1.4	12.9	15.9	7.2	19.8	9.1	15.1	17.0	12.5
06 069	...	6	San Benito	3 598	51 276	892	14.3	95.0	0.6	1.3	3.0	55.2	8.6	24.0	8.9	14.5	16.9	11.6
06 071	6780	0	San Bernardino	51 960	1 669 934	12	32.1	85.0	8.3	1.1	5.6	34.3	9.1	23.0	9.5	15.5	16.6	11.1
06 073	7320	0	San Diego	10 890	2 820 844	5	259.0	81.8	6.5	0.9	10.8	26.5	7.3	18.4	11.5	16.0	16.6	11.6
06 075	7360	0	San Francisco	121	746 777	59	6 171.7	52.2	10.7	0.5	36.6	16.9	4.5	12.2	9.0	17.4	18.9	13.5
06 077	8120	2	San Joaquin	3 625	563 183	92	155.4	77.2	5.7	1.1	16.0	29.4	8.4	22.5	9.1	14.0	16.1	11.9
06 079	7460	3	San Luis Obispo	8 559	236 953	234	27.7	92.1	2.8	1.2	3.9	17.6	5.9	16.8	12.7	13.2	16.9	11.6
06 081	7360	0	San Mateo	1 163	702 102	70	603.7	72.4	5.5	0.5	21.7	21.8	6.3	15.9	8.3	15.2	17.9	14.5
06 083	7480	2	Santa Barbara	7 093	391 071	148	55.1	89.7	3.1	1.2	6.0	33.6	7.0	17.4	12.8	14.7	15.6	11.7
06 085	7400	0	Santa Clara	3 344	1 647 419	14	492.6	73.4	3.8	0.7	22.1	25.9	6.9	17.5	9.8	17.0	17.3	13.7
06 087	7485	0	Santa Cruz	1 155	245 201	222	212.3	92.5	1.4	1.0	5.2	26.8	6.9	18.4	11.2	14.3	19.9	12.3
06 089	6690	3	Shasta	9 805	164 530	317	16.8	93.8	0.8	2.8	2.5	5.5	6.7	21.0	6.9	10.9	16.4	14.3
06 091	...	8	Sierra	2 469	3 334	2 969	1.4	96.9	0.2	2.4	0.5	8.1	6.1	20.0	4.1	9.0	17.5	16.0
06 093	...	7	Siskiyou	16 284	43 570	1 008	2.7	92.9	1.7	4.2	1.2	8.1	5.8	20.9	5.7	9.5	17.1	13.7
06 095	8720	0	Solano	2 145	385 723	149	179.8	67.6	13.9	1.0	17.5	17.2	7.7	21.3	8.5	15.2	18.7	12.5
06 097	7500	0	Sonoma	4 082	439 970	130	107.8	93.2	1.6	1.3	3.9	14.5	6.7	18.8	8.1	13.0	19.5	13.5
06 099	5170	2	Stanislaus	3 871	436 790	133	112.8	90.0	1.9	1.2	7.0	28.5	8.7	23.3	8.6	14.0	15.8	11.9
06 101	9340	3	Sutter	1 561	78 423	639	50.2	83.4	1.9	1.8	12.8	21.2	7.6	21.5	8.2	12.7	15.3	13.8
06 103	...	6	Tehama	7 643	54 012	852	7.1	96.0	0.6	2.3	1.0	14.2	6.8	21.4	6.5	10.8	14.6	13.9
06 105	...	6	Trinity	8 233	12 927	2 219	1.6	93.6	0.4	5.0	1.0	4.6	5.7	20.1	5.0	9.3	18.4	14.1
06 107	8780	2	Tulare	12 495	358 470	158	28.7	90.7	1.7	1.7	6.0	47.2	9.2	25.6	9.0	13.3	14.9	11.2
06 109	...	6	Tuolumne	5 790	53 764	856	9.3	93.1	3.5	2.2	1.2	10.1	4.9	17.3	6.9	12.6	17.4	13.1
06 111	8735	0	Ventura	4 781	745 063	60	155.8	89.8	2.4	0.9	6.9	33.4	7.5	20.5	9.3	14.3	17.4	13.3
06 113	9270	0	Yolo	2 622	155 573	331	59.3	85.3	2.5	1.6	10.6	26.2	7.1	18.4	16.1	14.4	15.5	11.6
06 115	9340	3	Yuba	1 633	59 607	798	36.5	81.2	4.3	3.1	11.4	15.6	9.7	23.2	9.1	13.5	14.1	11.6
08 000	...	X	**COLORADO**	268 660	4 056 133	X	15.1	92.3	4.3	0.9	2.5	14.9	7.1	19.2	9.7	12.9	17.2	15.0
08 001	2080	0	Adams	3 087	331 045	172	107.2	91.8	3.6	1.0	3.5	22.3	8.2	21.2	9.7	13.8	15.8	14.5
08 003	...	7	Alamosa	1 872	14 595	2 094	7.8	97.0	0.6	1.0	1.4	44.3	8.8	21.7	14.3	11.3	14.6	12.7
08 005	2080	0	Arapahoe	2 080	482 089	113	231.8	89.1	6.4	0.6	3.9	6.8	6.8	19.5	8.3	13.2	18.7	16.1
08 007	...	9	Archuleta	3 495	9 604	2 463	2.7	97.0	0.3	1.9	0.7	27.8	7.6	21.5	5.4	9.4	16.6	15.3
08 009	...	9	Baca	6 620	4 319	2 882	0.7	97.8	0.0	1.6	0.6	6.6	5.6	18.0	5.1	8.4	13.3	14.7
08 011	...	9	Bent	3 921	5 799	2 786	1.5	94.6	3.3	1.3	0.8	33.4	5.4	20.3	7.7	10.9	15.1	13.3
08 013	1125	0	Boulder	1 923	273 112	201	142.0	95.1	1.0	0.6	3.2	8.3	6.4	16.6	13.6	13.6	18.5	15.2
08 015	...	7	Chaffee	2 625	15 601	2 028	5.9	97.1	1.4	1.0	0.5	11.2	4.8	17.2	7.6	10.6	15.1	15.3
08 017	...	9	Cheyenne	4 614	2 229	3 043	0.5	99.5	0.0	0.4	0.1	4.0	8.2	22.6	5.9	11.9	13.6	12.2

1. MSA = Metropolitan Statistical Area. PMSA = Primary MSA. NECMA = New England County Metropolitan Area. See Appendix A for explanation of these concepts. See Appendix B for list of metropolitan areas identified by type, with component counties. 2. County typology code from the Economic Research Service of USDA. See Appendix A for definition. 3. Dry land or land partially or temporarily covered by water. 4. Hispanic persons may be of any race.

STATE County	55 to 64 years	65 to 74 years	75 years and over	Percent female	Total persons 1990	Total persons 1980	Percent change 1980–1990	Percent change 1990–1999	Births	Deaths	Net migration	Number	Percent change, 1980–1990	Persons per household	Female family householder[1]	One person
	16	17	18	19	20	21	22	23	24	25	26	27	28	29	30	31
CALIFORNIA—Cont'd																
Butte	8.5	8.2	8.1	50.3	182 120	143 851	26.6	7.2	23 083	19 097	9 724	71 665	25.9	2.48	9.7	25.4
Calaveras	11.9	10.2	7.3	49.6	31 998	20 710	54.5	25.2	3 312	3 274	8 073	12 649	58.0	2.50	7.1	21.2
Colusa	8.1	6.2	5.3	48.1	16 275	12 791	27.2	15.8	2 867	1 312	1 063	5 612	19.7	2.84	9.3	22.5
Contra Costa	8.1	6.2	5.3	50.9	803 731	656 331	22.5	16.1	116 698	56 777	70 782	300 288	24.3	2.64	10.8	22.3
Del Norte	8.1	6.8	5.7	44.8	23 460	18 217	28.8	12.9	3 206	2 156	1 968	7 987	17.6	2.63	10.8	23.0
El Dorado	8.9	7.2	5.2	49.4	125 995	85 812	46.8	28.1	16 360	8 911	28 107	46 845	44.1	2.66	7.8	18.3
Fresno	6.8	5.4	4.9	49.9	667 479	514 621	29.7	14.3	141 269	47 612	3 182	220 933	23.8	2.96	13.9	21.0
Glenn	8.0	6.5	6.7	49.4	24 798	21 350	16.1	6.2	4 164	2 117	-423	8 821	14.5	2.77	10.0	23.2
Humboldt	8.1	6.5	6.2	49.8	119 118	108 525	9.8	1.9	14 680	10 357	-2 027	46 420	11.7	2.49	10.6	26.2
Imperial	7.3	5.7	4.1	48.6	109 303	92 110	18.7	32.9	24 737	7 607	18 937	32 842	16.6	3.26	15.0	18.0
Inyo	10.9	8.9	9.2	50.4	18 281	17 895	2.2	-1.8	2 062	1 946	-330	7 565	4.9	2.35	8.7	29.0
Kern	7.0	5.1	4.3	48.3	544 981	403 089	35.2	17.9	112 484	39 666	24 885	181 480	29.8	2.92	12.3	20.3
Kings	5.8	3.8	3.4	45.0	101 469	73 738	37.6	21.5	20 577	6 089	5 942	29 082	23.8	3.08	12.9	17.4
Lake	11.3	10.6	9.2	50.1	50 631	36 366	39.2	9.4	6 019	7 122	6 102	20 805	36.9	2.38	9.5	21.3
Lassen	7.4	4.9	3.8	36.7	27 598	21 661	27.4	19.7	2 906	1 617	4 031	8 543	15.4	2.66	9.5	21.3
Los Angeles	7.0	5.5	4.9	50.5	8 863 052	7 477 239	18.5	5.3	1 676 786	563 984	-658 590	2 989 552	9.5	2.91	13.1	25.0
Madera	7.4	7.0	5.9	46.7	88 090	63 116	39.6	32.5	18 398	7 024	17 679	28 370	35.4	3.05	10.9	17.0
Marin	9.0	7.2	6.6	50.2	230 096	222 592	3.4	2.9	25 563	16 884	-1 916	95 006	7.1	2.33	8.5	28.4
Mariposa	11.7	10.2	8.0	48.9	14 302	11 108	28.8	9.1	1 505	1 436	1 275	5 604	35.6	2.42	7.1	23.9
Mendocino	8.4	7.1	6.7	49.5	80 345	66 738	20.4	4.7	10 193	7 383	1 204	30 419	21.3	2.57	10.7	24.6
Merced	6.9	5.0	4.0	49.5	178 403	134 558	32.6	12.5	37 222	11 419	-4 519	55 331	24.2	3.17	12.5	17.7
Modoc	10.2	9.1	8.4	48.2	9 678	8 610	12.4	-4.8	1 032	949	-519	3 711	16.0	2.49	8.0	25.1
Mono	7.2	4.2	2.9	44.6	9 956	8 577	16.1	5.6	1 234	318	-380	3 961	14.7	2.48	6.1	25.0
Monterey	6.8	5.8	5.1	48.6	355 660	290 444	22.5	4.5	67 026	20 869	-35 893	112 965	18.0	2.96	10.4	20.4
Napa	8.6	8.0	8.0	50.0	110 765	99 199	11.7	9.2	14 068	11 414	8 036	41 312	12.8	2.54	9.2	24.7
Nevada	10.2	10.2	8.0	50.2	78 510	51 645	52.0	17.2	7 874	7 124	12 892	30 758	53.7	2.51	7.6	20.8
Orange	7.3	5.3	4.8	49.8	2 410 668	1 932 921	24.7	14.5	458 127	142 260	37 150	827 066	20.5	2.87	9.7	20.7
Placer	8.5	6.4	5.6	49.9	172 796	117 247	47.4	38.6	24 995	13 871	55 699	64 101	50.0	2.66	8.7	19.5
Plumas	11.6	9.7	7.3	49.4	19 739	17 340	13.8	3.2	1 588	1 787	952	8 125	22.4	2.41	8.1	24.1
Riverside	7.4	6.5	5.8	49.6	1 170 413	663 199	76.5	30.8	225 623	98 826	233 948	402 067	65.5	2.85	9.6	20.6
Sacramento	7.8	6.3	5.2	51.0	1 066 789	783 381	32.9	11.0	171 604	76 162	23 123	394 530	31.6	2.58	13.0	25.3
San Benito	7.2	4.5	3.9	49.3	36 697	25 005	46.8	39.7	7 386	2 224	9 415	11 422	44.9	3.15	9.8	16.0
San Bernardino	6.5	4.7	4.0	49.4	1 418 380	895 016	58.5	17.7	285 899	94 567	57 217	464 737	50.6	2.97	12.1	19.0
San Diego	7.1	6.1	5.4	49.6	2 498 016	1 861 846	34.2	12.9	434 438	167 684	28 193	887 403	32.4	2.69	10.8	22.9
San Francisco	9.2	7.5	7.8	50.5	723 959	678 974	6.6	3.2	82 279	70 269	11 242	305 584	2.2	2.29	9.9	39.3
San Joaquin	7.3	5.6	5.1	49.2	480 628	347 342	38.4	17.2	84 945	36 647	35 370	158 156	26.9	2.94	12.7	20.9
San Luis Obispo	7.8	7.8	7.2	48.0	217 162	155 435	39.7	9.1	24 733	17 104	12 677	80 281	37.9	2.53	8.5	23.8
San Mateo	8.6	7.0	6.2	50.9	649 623	587 329	10.6	8.1	94 992	45 441	4 623	241 914	7.4	2.64	9.8	25.1
Santa Barbara	7.6	6.5	6.7	49.6	369 608	298 694	23.7	5.8	57 628	25 612	-11 003	129 802	18.7	2.73	9.3	23.0
Santa Clara	7.4	5.6	4.6	49.6	1 497 577	1 295 071	15.6	10.0	248 056	79 991	-16 874	520 180	13.4	2.81	10.3	21.7
Santa Cruz	6.6	4.9	5.6	49.8	229 734	188 141	22.1	6.7	34 730	15 587	-3 155	83 566	16.4	2.66	9.6	24.1
Shasta	9.1	7.9	6.8	50.4	147 036	115 613	27.2	11.9	19 602	14 308	12 637	55 966	30.1	2.58	11.0	22.3
Sierra	9.4	9.3	8.6	49.1	3 318	3 073	8.0	0.5	174	271	128	1 336	4.9	2.45	5.7	26.3
Siskiyou	10.1	9.0	8.3	50.1	43 531	39 732	9.6	0.1	4 492	4 458	174	17 306	14.5	2.48	9.6	25.7
Solano	6.9	5.3	4.0	49.2	339 469	235 203	44.3	13.6	55 200	20 818	8 969	113 429	41.0	2.88	11.5	18.5
Sonoma	7.4	6.3	6.7	50.4	388 222	299 681	29.5	13.3	52 221	32 871	33 316	149 011	30.2	2.55	9.8	24.6
Stanislaus	7.1	5.5	5.1	50.4	370 522	265 900	39.3	17.9	67 833	28 402	27 664	125 375	32.4	2.91	11.5	19.9
Sutter	8.9	6.3	5.7	50.1	64 409	52 246	23.3	21.8	11 053	5 423	8 479	23 111	22.9	2.75	10.9	21.6
Tehama	10.1	8.3	7.7	50.0	49 625	38 888	27.6	8.8	6 632	5 279	3 225	18 704	28.7	2.60	9.9	22.3
Trinity	11.0	9.4	7.1	48.2	13 063	11 858	10.2	-1.0	1 247	1 328	4	5 156	14.6	2.49	8.4	24.6
Tulare	6.9	5.1	4.9	49.8	311 932	245 738	26.9	14.9	66 772	23 528	3 888	97 861	21.3	3.12	12.8	18.1
Tuolumne	10.2	10.1	7.6	47.2	48 456	33 928	42.8	11.0	4 554	4 417	5 320	17 959	39.6	2.46	8.5	22.5
Ventura	7.2	5.5	5.0	49.6	669 016	529 174	26.4	11.4	111 208	38 503	3 539	217 298	25.8	3.02	9.8	17.5
Yolo	6.9	5.2	4.8	50.0	141 212	113 374	24.6	10.2	20 833	9 323	3 311	50 972	23.4	2.63	10.2	23.1
Yuba	8.0	5.8	4.9	49.9	58 234	49 733	17.1	2.4	11 085	4 544	-6 062	19 776	13.0	2.85	12.8	20.6
COLORADO	8.9	5.5	4.6	50.4	3 294 473	2 889 735	14.0	23.1	513 908	225 699	468 212	1 282 489	20.8	2.51	9.7	26.6
Adams	9.1	4.6	3.2	50.5	265 038	245 944	7.8	24.9	45 486	15 802	36 341	96 353	14.4	2.72	12.2	21.7
Alamosa	7.8	4.2	4.7	50.8	13 617	11 799	15.4	7.2	2 275	1 010	-262	4 721	20.4	2.67	12.3	24.7
Arapahoe	8.1	5.5	3.7	51.4	391 572	293 300	33.5	23.1	58 098	20 194	52 279	154 710	45.9	2.51	10.1	26.3
Archuleta	12.7	7.3	4.2	48.7	5 345	3 664	45.9	79.7	751	349	3 824	2 010	62.0	2.66	8.0	19.8
Baca	12.2	11.3	11.4	50.8	4 556	5 419	-15.9	-5.2	391	534	-83	1 872	-8.5	2.39	5.0	28.4
Bent	10.7	8.0	8.7	44.7	5 048	5 945	-15.1	14.9	564	592	788	1 865	-6.7	2.51	8.7	28.6
Boulder	7.5	4.3	4.2	50.0	225 339	189 625	18.8	21.2	30 200	11 546	29 761	88 402	28.2	2.45	7.9	26.3
Chaffee	12.2	9.1	8.0	46.8	12 684	13 227	-4.1	23.0	1 171	1 346	3 124	4 848	1.9	2.38	7.2	27.5
Cheyenne	9.2	6.7	9.8	48.8	2 397	2 153	11.3	-7.0	264	209	-216	904	11.2	2.60	5.1	29.0

1. No spouse present.

Table B. States and Counties — **Vital Statistics, Health Resources, and Crime**

STATE County	Births, average 1996–1998 Total	Rate[1]	Deaths, average 1996–1998 Number Total	Infant[2]	Rate Total[1]	Infant[3]	Physicians,[4] 1998 Number	Rate[5]	Hospitals,[4] 1998 Number	Beds Number	Rate[5]	Medicare enrollees 1999	Serious crimes known to police, 1998[6] Total Number	Rate[7]
	32	33	34	35	36	37	38	39	40	41	42	43	44	45
CALIFORNIA—Cont'd														
Butte	2 334	12.1	2 156	17	11.2	7.1	383	197	5	661	340	35 957	8 690	4 421
Calaveras	312	8.0	376	1	9.6	2.1	40	100	1	49	123	7 838	1 245	3 084
Colusa	308	16.8	145	2	7.9	5.4	8	43	1	56	302	2 486	463	2 435
Contra Costa	12 362	13.7	6 489	68	7.2	5.5	2 123	231	10	2 081	227	114 456	45 664	5 016
Del Norte	324	12.0	255	2	9.4	7.2	40	148	1	47	174	4 231	1 206	4 212
El Dorado	1 670	10.8	1 057	6	6.8	3.8	240	151	2	188	119	24 293	3 830	2 431
Fresno	14 374	19.2	5 285	109	7.0	7.6	1 405	186	14	2 118	280	88 668	47 113	6 169
Glenn	416	15.9	222	2	8.5	5.6	13	50	1	28	107	4 024	918	3 440
Humboldt	1 477	12.1	1 142	9	9.3	5.9	281	230	5	332	272	19 004	6 069	4 859
Imperial	2 531	17.8	892	12	6.3	4.9	100	69	3	221	153	17 201	7 094	4 876
Inyo	207	11.3	232	2	12.7	8.1	46	254	2	69	381	3 832	614	3 314
Kern	11 459	18.3	4 513	90	7.2	7.8	868	137	11	1 649	261	72 391	30 539	4 899
Kings	2 169	18.8	723	18	6.2	8.4	115	97	3	175	147	10 468	4 054	3 467
Lake	571	10.4	765	5	13.9	8.2	73	132	2	115	209	12 988	2 666	4 760
Lassen	351	10.7	207	1	6.3	2.9	32	96	1	59	177	3 792	703	2 046
Los Angeles	163 301	17.9	59 857	965	6.5	5.9	22 895	248	114	30 364	330	975 304	400 975	4 331
Madera	2 023	18.0	792	11	7.0	5.6	87	76	2	124	108	17 437	5 075	4 386
Marin	2 623	11.2	1 861	9	7.9	3.4	1 361	575	3	417	176	34 192	6 712	2 813
Mariposa	141	9.0	166	1	10.5	4.7	23	145	1	34	214	3 035	549	3 443
Mendocino	1 042	12.5	819	7	9.8	6.7	205	245	4	209	250	13 747	2 670	3 129
Merced	3 623	18.7	1 336	25	6.9	6.8	208	105	4	402	203	19 515	10 159	5 117
Modoc	103	10.8	120	1	12.5	12.9	9	96	2	113	1 202	1 716	208	2 028
Mono	138	13.3	46	0	4.5	0.0	22	214	1	15	146	807	535	5 016
Monterey	6 659	18.6	2 286	39	6.4	5.9	743	203	4	675	185	42 526	14 601	3 985
Napa	1 495	12.7	1 286	6	10.9	3.8	413	346	3	1 429	1 198	21 676	4 021	3 330
Nevada	798	8.9	823	6	9.2	7.5	199	218	2	193	211	16 213	2 748	2 997
Orange	47 032	17.6	16 114	210	6.0	4.5	6 940	255	37	6 889	253	282 452	82 556	3 050
Placer	2 706	12.2	1 650	11	7.5	4.2	532	232	2	310	135	30 818	7 058	3 148
Plumas	170	8.4	219	2	10.8	11.7	29	142	4	108	530	3 873	751	3 546
Riverside	23 359	16.2	11 425	155	7.9	6.7	2 007	136	16	3 009	203	196 148	64 767	4 419
Sacramento	17 652	15.6	8 666	118	7.7	6.7	2 677	234	11	3 174	277	147 960	69 580	6 104
San Benito	860	18.5	259	5	5.6	5.4	32	66	1	101	207	4 468	1 371	2 956
San Bernardino	28 686	17.8	10 597	221	6.6	7.7	2 703	165	19	3 704	227	164 919	73 693	4 505
San Diego	43 942	16.1	18 713	236	6.9	5.4	7 405	266	25	6 828	246	336 516	108 908	3 951
San Francisco	8 247	11.1	6 994	40	9.4	4.9	4 336	581	11	4 155	557	117 217	47 303	6 381
San Joaquin	8 719	16.1	4 099	61	7.6	7.0	750	136	8	1 140	207	66 446	31 889	5 806
San Luis Obispo	2 453	10.6	1 946	13	8.4	5.4	619	264	6	636	271	38 602	7 357	3 115
San Mateo	10 077	14.5	4 950	45	7.1	4.5	2 357	336	8	2 036	291	91 684	21 760	3 097
Santa Barbara	5 849	15.1	2 825	27	7.3	4.7	1 083	278	8	1 314	337	54 627	12 393	3 137
Santa Clara	26 600	16.4	8 922	129	5.5	4.9	4 356	265	15	4 488	273	164 906	55 571	3 411
Santa Cruz	3 540	14.8	1 679	19	7.0	5.5	564	232	2	395	163	28 364	9 985	4 101
Shasta	1 999	12.3	1 674	13	10.3	6.3	399	243	5	656	399	30 619	7 327	4 435
Sierra	28	8.3	34	0	10.1	0.0	2	59	1	40	1 183	706	65	1 868
Siskiyou	471	10.7	495	2	11.2	5.0	65	148	2	137	311	9 467	1 331	2 971
Solano	5 597	15.1	2 370	38	6.4	6.8	635	168	4	522	138	37 967	17 699	4 712
Sonoma	5 462	12.8	3 713	25	8.7	4.6	1 142	264	8	889	205	62 630	17 232	3 971
Stanislaus	6 970	16.6	3 277	48	7.8	6.9	642	151	7	1 478	347	53 593	26 165	6 127
Sutter	1 172	15.4	615	9	8.1	7.4	151	196	1	132	171	10 665	2 854	3 626
Tehama	875	16.2	571	3	10.5	3.4	52	96	1	76	141	9 265	2 312	4 230
Trinity	122	9.2	156	1	11.8	8.2	10	76	1	65	496	2 587	333	2 493
Tulare	7 011	20.0	2 581	44	7.3	6.3	421	119	7	854	240	40 519	17 579	4 917
Tuolumne	453	8.6	533	4	10.1	8.8	97	182	3	223	419	10 849	2 048	3 791
Ventura	11 509	15.9	4 466	69	6.2	6.0	1 221	167	8	1 451	198	82 821	19 971	2 717
Yolo	2 137	14.1	1 038	14	6.8	6.4	505	328	2	169	110	17 016	6 712	4 339
Yuba	1 041	17.3	482	8	8.0	8.0	69	115	1	128	213	8 076	3 028	4 859
COLORADO	57 306	14.7	25 996	388	6.7	6.8	9 622	242	68	9 438	238	458 288	178 197	4 488
Adams	5 093	16.1	1 861	35	5.9	6.9	239	74	4	539	166	37 603	18 006	5 585
Alamosa	232	16.1	114	4	8.0	17.3	38	263	1	70	484	1 690	616	4 201
Arapahoe	6 297	13.6	2 455	45	5.3	7.1	1 166	246	3	605	128	41 533	20 461	4 462
Archuleta	86	10.2	47	1	5.5	11.6	15	165	0	0		1 268	299	3 442
Baca	38	8.6	62	0	14.2	8.8	4	92	1	65	1 489	1 059	22	490
Bent	62	11.3	71	0	12.9	0.0	9	164	0	0		976	140	2 504
Boulder	3 326	12.7	1 348	15	5.2	4.6	754	282	3	360	135	27 015	11 522	4 339
Chaffee	131	8.8	143	1	9.6	5.1	20	133	1	38	252	2 997	486	3 633
Cheyenne	25	10.9	25	0	10.7	0.0	2	85	1	32	1 364	371	43	1 851

1. Per 1,000 estimated resident population, average 1996–1998.   2. Deaths of infants under 1 year old.   3. Deaths of infants under 1 year old per 1,000 live births.   4. Data subject to copyright.   5. Per 100,000 resident population as of July 1 of the year shown.   6. Data for serious crimes have not been adjusted for underreporting; this may affect comparability between geographic areas and over time.   7. Per 100,000 population estimated by the FBI.

Table B. States and Counties — Crime, Education, Money Income, and Poverty

STATE County	Serious crimes known to police, 1998[1] (cont'd) Rate[2] Violent	Property	Education — School enrollment and attainment, 1990 — Enrollment[3] Total	Percent private	Attainment[4] (percent) High school graduate or more	Bachelor's degree or more	Local government expenditures, fiscal 1997[5] Total current expenditures (mil dol)	Current expenditures per student (dollars)	Money income 1989 Per capita[6] (dollars)	Households Median Dollars	Percent change, 1979–1989 (constant 1989 dollars)	Percent with $100,000 or more	Income and poverty, 1997 Percent below poverty level Median household income	All persons	Persons under 18	Persons 5–17 in families
	46	47	48	49	50	51	52	53	54	55	56	57	58	59	60	61
CALIFORNIA—Cont'd																
Butte	336	4 085	56 394	5.7	77.6	19.5	196.9	5 598	12 083	22 776	4.4	2.4	29 367	20.9	30.9	30.8
Calaveras	275	2 809	7 030	7.6	81.6	14.4	46.0	6 156	13 497	27 645	8.0	2.7	34 672	13.0	20.8	21.3
Colusa	352	2 083	4 654	3.8	62.9	11.1	27.0	6 339	12 402	24 912	-3.3	3.5	30 464	18.1	29.4	28.6
Contra Costa	558	4 458	213 707	15.2	86.5	31.6	741.0	5 040	20 748	45 087	17.6	10.3	54 275	8.7	13.6	13.1
Del Norte	583	3 629	5 940	9.3	70.9	10.0	27.0	4 935	10 625	22 917	-0.8	2.2	29 044	22.9	31.8	33.0
El Dorado	380	2 051	32 520	7.9	85.9	20.8	148.4	5 101	15 703	35 058	19.4	4.7	44 954	8.8	13.2	13.4
Fresno	903	5 266	204 179	6.6	66.2	16.9	898.2	5 131	11 824	26 377	0.1	3.6	31 587	25.6	38.0	36.5
Glenn	483	2 957	6 553	6.3	66.9	9.4	37.0	5 957	10 677	22 831	-7.1	1.8	28 649	19.9	29.2	31.1
Humboldt	454	4 405	36 198	6.0	80.5	20.0	120.8	6 380	12 436	23 586	-4.7	2.2	30 426	18.5	26.0	26.8
Imperial	534	4 342	36 361	5.2	53.2	9.7	174.3	5 407	9 208	22 442	-8.7	2.5	23 359	30.3	43.8	37.6
Inyo	696	2 618	4 093	6.3	81.7	13.5	25.3	7 193	13 397	24 386	-0.2	2.2	32 871	14.0	21.5	22.0
Kern	599	4 300	153 512	7.7	67.6	13.3	744.5	5 316	12 154	28 634	4.4	3.2	30 577	21.0	30.2	29.2
Kings	380	3 087	28 156	8.1	65.6	9.0	128.1	5 259	10 035	25 507	4.8	2.3	30 577	23.6	31.3	31.7
Lake	657	4 103	11 069	7.6	70.9	10.7	56.7	5 568	11 705	21 794	16.4	1.4	27 295	20.1	33.2	33.4
Lassen	259	1 787	7 124	5.7	72.8	11.7	33.7	5 984	12 626	26 764	2.4	1.4	36 819	19.4	22.9	22.7
Los Angeles	1 017	3 314	2 521 219	15.9	70.0	22.3	8 295.3	5 398	16 149	34 965	18.9	7.9	36 441	20.5	30.5	28.7
Madera	671	3 715	24 840	6.1	63.4	11.7	123.3	5 337	10 856	27 370	6.5	2.2	30 804	22.8	35.5	32.9
Marin	349	2 464	51 962	23.9	91.9	44.0	187.1	6 753	28 381	48 544	18.0	17.0	60 967	7.0	9.5	10.4
Mariposa	928	2 515	2 883	5.5	77.8	16.8	15.4	5 537	13 074	25 272	13.2	2.4	31 178	15.3	27.1	26.6
Mendocino	566	2 563	22 123	9.1	78.7	17.8	100.5	6 294	12 776	26 443	5.1	2.7	32 306	18.1	28.5	28.4
Merced	703	4 414	56 282	6.6	63.1	12.0	261.0	5 406	10 606	25 548	3.9	2.7	29 178	25.4	37.4	37.3
Modoc	497	1 531	2 344	6.8	72.2	11.2	17.0	7 314	10 971	22 029	-1.9	1.6	28 174	21.1	33.3	35.2
Mono	609	4 407	2 096	9.2	87.8	21.9	13.7	7 073	16 120	31 924	12.5	5.1	36 276	11.2	17.8	20.1
Monterey	574	3 411	97 096	10.0	72.9	21.5	357.4	5 384	14 578	33 520	13.3	5.3	38 341	15.4	24.1	24.0
Napa	335	2 995	28 565	16.9	80.7	22.3	100.6	5 375	17 640	36 773	16.2	6.2	44 667	8.8	14.4	14.1
Nevada	515	2 482	18 382	9.1	86.3	22.1	70.3	5 149	15 760	32 200	19.1	4.3	40 347	9.6	15.3	15.0
Orange	351	2 699	666 355	13.5	81.2	27.8	2 189.7	4 944	19 890	45 922	21.5	11.2	49 583	11.0	17.4	16.2
Placer	249	2 899	45 465	12.3	85.1	22.7	227.3	4 856	17 311	37 601	20.1	6.2	49 638	7.7	11.0	11.2
Plumas	335	3 211	5 037	5.8	82.7	15.1	21.0	5 674	12 952	24 299	-4.6	1.8	35 154	13.1	20.1	21.6
Riverside	696	3 723	307 709	10.9	74.1	14.6	1 348.8	4 864	14 510	33 081	23.1	4.7	36 368	15.0	22.7	22.1
Sacramento	685	5 419	289 451	11.4	82.2	23.0	1 037.5	5 175	15 265	32 297	10.8	3.9	39 461	17.2	27.3	26.2
San Benito	390	2 566	10 792	10.8	68.4	14.4	49.9	4 993	13 933	36 473	28.0	4.8	42 578	11.4	17.9	18.2
San Bernardino	600	3 905	405 639	11.7	75.4	14.9	1 700.2	4 899	13 358	33 443	14.3	3.9	36 876	17.9	25.7	24.4
San Diego	602	3 349	678 445	12.5	81.9	25.3	2 360.8	5 252	16 220	35 022	22.2	6.0	39 427	14.2	22.0	21.0
San Francisco	999	5 382	179 009	22.3	78.0	35.0	412.1	6 631	19 695	33 414	25.7	7.4	43 405	12.6	21.7	21.9
San Joaquin	751	5 055	137 025	11.3	68.6	13.2	547.5	5 046	12 705	30 635	13.7	3.5	35 629	18.8	27.3	27.5
San Luis Obispo	348	2 767	65 365	9.3	83.3	22.9	192.3	5 325	15 237	31 164	25.6	4.4	38 597	12.9	18.5	18.7
San Mateo	336	2 761	164 491	19.4	84.1	31.3	508.8	5 533	22 430	46 437	19.6	11.9	57 267	6.6	9.5	9.9
Santa Barbara	474	2 663	109 709	11.8	80.0	26.6	328.9	5 287	17 155	35 677	18.5	7.3	40 232	14.6	22.5	22.4
Santa Clara	496	2 915	429 640	17.4	82.0	32.6	1 347.6	5 425	20 423	48 115	22.8	11.4	59 639	9.0	13.6	13.5
Santa Cruz	573	3 528	67 978	10.7	81.9	29.7	206.4	5 259	17 347	37 112	31.2	7.4	44 607	13.1	21.3	20.7
Shasta	679	3 756	39 216	9.9	78.4	13.7	171.3	5 571	12 381	25 581	3.8	2.4	32 109	18.1	28.2	27.8
Sierra	172	1 696	728	4.3	75.5	15.9	6.8	7 852	13 731	23 657	-2.4	1.3	34 941	11.6	15.2	16.9
Siskiyou	270	2 701	11 087	4.2	77.4	14.2	51.7	6 021	11 610	21 921	-9.6	2.3	28 178	19.0	30.1	29.6
Solano	749	3 963	94 781	11.2	82.7	18.7	334.2	4 832	14 833	39 113	21.1	3.8	46 115	11.3	17.0	16.3
Sonoma	357	3 614	101 892	11.3	84.4	24.5	383.4	5 466	17 239	36 299	22.1	5.2	43 770	9.1	13.6	13.2
Stanislaus	760	5 367	102 957	7.8	68.4	13.0	455.5	5 075	12 731	29 793	10.6	3.5	35 913	18.4	27.2	26.6
Sutter	304	3 322	17 917	7.4	72.3	15.4	81.3	5 311	12 763	27 096	3.1	3.4	33 775	17.2	26.5	27.0
Tehama	660	3 570	12 493	6.2	72.2	10.2	62.6	5 607	10 990	22 436	-0.3	1.6	28 030	20.0	30.9	32.1
Trinity	337	2 156	3 276	7.1	74.2	12.9	19.9	8 093	10 781	20 494	-13.7	1.8	27 042	19.4	28.2	31.6
Tulare	719	4 198	92 825	5.7	60.2	11.8	452.2	5 407	10 302	24 450	3.1	2.6	27 622	27.9	39.9	38.5
Tuolumne	535	3 256	11 301	11.2	80.0	14.7	41.9	5 167	13 224	27 030	13.8	3.2	33 810	14.8	23.6	22.6
Ventura	316	2 401	188 292	14.7	79.4	23.0	629.0	4 934	17 861	45 612	28.2	9.3	49 763	10.3	16.6	15.7
Yolo	720	3 619	51 330	7.6	79.1	30.3	134.3	5 178	13 861	28 866	11.9	4.2	38 751	15.8	23.6	23.8
Yuba	682	4 177	16 537	4.8	68.5	9.5	70.0	5 113	9 874	21 523	6.7	1.3	26 842	25.5	38.1	41.8
COLORADO	378	4 110	896 144	11.9	84.4	27.0	3 577.0	5 312	14 821	30 140	-0.4	3.8	40 853	10.2	14.6	13.3
Adams	462	5 123	69 822	10.3	78.8	13.0	268.4	4 934	12 615	30 522	-6.7	1.5	40 802	10.4	15.7	13.8
Alamosa	382	3 819	4 883	4.1	76.9	24.1	16.9	6 026	9 286	20 265	1.2	1.0	28 204	23.0	29.4	29.1
Arapahoe	403	4 059	107 390	14.7	91.5	35.2	488.8	5 500	18 777	37 234	-6.9	6.5	50 748	6.4	9.6	8.3
Archuleta	23	3 419	1 292	5.0	80.9	19.7	7.0	4 743	10 913	22 894	4.4	2.3	30 518	13.7	20.1	20.3
Baca	156	334	1 031	2.1	72.0	13.6	6.5	7 451	9 571	18 602	0.5	0.5	26 731	19.1	28.1	25.5
Bent	322	2 182	1 099	2.6	72.7	14.6	5.8	5 728	9 170	18 977	-12.8	1.0	26 427	24.5	36.5	33.1
Boulder	263	4 076	72 000	9.7	91.3	42.1	215.8	5 006	17 359	35 322	6.6	5.5	50 245	7.8	9.9	8.9
Chaffee	232	3 401	3 630	9.7	81.0	15.2	13.1	5 765	10 788	21 174	-16.9	1.0	30 881	13.1	18.4	16.8
Cheyenne	258	1 593	635	0.0	80.8	11.9	3.5	7 142	11 382	24 341	23.8	2.7	34 746	10.8	13.6	14.4

1. Data for serious crimes have not been adjusted for underreporting; this may affect comparability between geographic areas and over time.   2. Per 100,000 population estimated by the FBI.   3. All persons 3 years old and over enrolled in nursery school through college.   4. Persons 25 years old and over.   5. Elementary and secondary education expenditures, local government fiscal years ending between July 1, 1996 and June 30, 1997.   6. Based on population enumerated as of April 1, 1990.

Table B. States and Counties — **Personal Income**

	Personal income, 1998												
			Per capita[1]					Transfer payments	Government payments to individuals				
STATE County	Total (mil dol)	Percent change, 1997–1998	Dollars	Rank	Wages and salaries[2] (mil dol)	Proprietor's income (mil dol)	Dividends, interest, and rent (mil dol)	Total (mil dol)	Total (mil dol)	Social Security (mil dol)	Medical payments (mil dol)	Income mainte- nance (mil dol)	Unemploy- ment insurance (mil dol)
	62	63	64	65	66	67	68	69	70	71	72	73	74
CALIFORNIA—Cont'd													
Butte	4 050	4.0	20 838	1 446	1 897	402	911	888	852	336	298	142	19
Calaveras	800	4.9	20 172	1 663	191	109	202	174	166	80	57	16	4
Colusa	377	-4.3	20 287	1 629	188	68	74	65	61	24	22	8	5
Contra Costa	33 052	6.0	36 006	60	14 313	3 178	6 680	2 967	2 795	1 129	1 058	355	59
Del Norte	442	5.0	16 385	2 724	210	56	84	119	114	39	44	22	3
El Dorado	4 282	6.9	27 046	299	1 218	470	784	493	463	211	165	42	13
Fresno	15 352	3.7	20 333	1 620	8 897	1 747	2 586	2 880	2 738	772	1 045	594	152
Glenn	442	-5.7	16 882	2 636	223	43	95	101	96	37	35	16	4
Humboldt	2 696	5.1	22 066	1 079	1 402	327	577	528	505	182	183	86	14
Imperial	2 494	7.6	17 353	2 515	1 326	502	291	511	484	143	169	111	36
Inyo	424	3.4	23 468	752	213	34	114	81	78	34	28	10	2
Kern	12 407	4.3	19 643	1 842	7 673	1 369	1 896	2 146	2 029	674	723	407	98
Kings	1 838	-0.7	15 492	2 879	1 192	138	270	343	321	94	125	65	17
Lake	1 195	5.5	21 696	1 195	340	106	241	320	310	125	117	46	7
Lassen	555	2.8	16 667	2 687	313	47	97	105	99	32	38	18	3
Los Angeles	246 949	5.9	26 773	322	171 990	28 857	44 226	32 721	30 999	8 515	13 588	6 535	670
Madera	1 993	4.4	17 403	2 505	988	196	348	409	388	140	137	69	19
Marin	12 497	5.4	52 869	3	4 732	1 454	3 592	737	692	349	219	60	11
Mariposa	335	5.6	21 231	1 315	141	30	81	72	69	32	25	7	2
Mendocino	1 904	3.4	22 728	910	851	254	480	371	355	129	138	55	12
Merced	3 498	4.1	17 732	2 432	1 684	495	514	756	719	192	295	153	38
Modoc	187	3.1	20 005	1 708	71	27	41	46	45	17	16	8	2
Mono	258	7.1	25 020	490	158	41	56	22	20	9	5	3	2
Monterey	10 333	5.8	28 185	230	5 250	1 852	2 316	1 133	1 065	390	379	150	60
Napa	3 903	6.6	32 649	96	1 891	422	931	453	431	182	172	35	10
Nevada	2 282	7.1	25 051	484	754	283	686	346	329	173	104	25	8
Orange	88 634	8.2	32 541	100	55 033	10 248	16 433	7 140	6 633	2 735	2 455	812	120
Placer	7 408	11.1	32 319	104	3 234	803	1 303	723	681	303	223	67	15
Plumas	484	2.5	23 783	683	201	72	123	95	91	39	32	10	3
Riverside	33 244	8.8	22 451	987	13 346	2 987	5 965	4 920	4 644	1 892	1 714	626	127
Sacramento	30 634	7.0	26 257	369	22 015	2 420	5 238	4 552	4 339	1 268	1 785	871	96
San Benito	1 033	6.0	21 088	1 359	412	152	184	119	110	43	37	16	8
San Bernardino	33 142	6.3	20 258	1 635	16 712	2 820	4 444	5 154	4 851	1 548	1 873	955	123
San Diego	76 502	7.6	27 657	255	47 165	7 219	16 001	8 697	8 196	3 031	3 180	1 174	135
San Francisco	33 199	8.5	44 518	12	32 273	5 191	6 716	3 098	2 959	913	1 161	627	54
San Joaquin	11 440	3.9	20 813	1 454	6 035	1 132	1 925	2 154	2 051	600	867	399	71
San Luis Obispo	5 807	5.7	24 807	514	2 746	783	1 551	792	748	364	225	81	16
San Mateo	30 384	5.1	43 338	16	18 457	3 198	6 964	1 947	1 816	890	572	179	33
Santa Barbara	11 177	5.2	28 698	206	5 947	1 356	3 193	1 199	1 127	516	355	137	25
Santa Clara	67 034	8.9	40 828	28	57 686	4 843	11 327	4 383	4 076	1 527	1 513	586	92
Santa Cruz	7 613	5.9	31 302	131	3 435	764	1 598	722	677	264	238	85	32
Shasta	3 609	4.1	21 986	1 107	1 744	505	711	779	748	282	281	116	21
Sierra	78	2.9	23 175	825	37	5	17	14	13	6	4	2	1
Siskiyou	901	3.0	20 474	1 568	381	120	212	226	218	85	77	33	7
Solano	8 938	7.0	23 724	695	3 995	494	1 374	1 060	991	340	344	165	39
Sonoma	13 408	7.8	30 911	136	6 488	1 362	3 163	1 436	1 355	608	478	139	29
Stanislaus	9 022	6.4	21 136	1 348	4 689	1 027	1 474	1 546	1 466	489	558	263	71
Sutter	1 693	5.9	21 965	1 111	639	237	302	290	276	96	99	41	16
Tehama	951	3.9	17 600	2 466	407	81	190	237	227	95	77	36	6
Trinity	244	3.4	18 704	2 156	80	23	59	67	65	25	25	9	2
Tulare	6 698	6.6	18 893	2 092	3 259	1 181	978	1 331	1 265	361	493	268	79
Tuolumne	1 065	4.6	20 082	1 684	413	100	294	233	223	111	72	23	5
Ventura	21 020	6.1	28 711	205	10 310	2 032	3 979	2 007	1 871	778	666	215	71
Yolo	3 954	2.7	25 791	412	3 058	418	803	484	455	155	168	78	14
Yuba	984	3.2	16 405	2 720	660	57	142	290	279	71	118	61	8
COLORADO	119 044	9.0	29 994	X	78 460	11 780	22 578	11 098	10 421	4 267	3 995	917	152
Adams	7 611	9.7	23 533	737	4 699	433	941	916	860	321	367	80	13
Alamosa	289	7.7	19 858	1 759	184	27	48	56	53	13	22	9	1
Arapahoe	18 116	9.3	38 333	42	11 814	2 173	3 191	986	905	438	269	60	15
Archuleta	155	9.2	16 919	2 627	64	23	46	23	21	12	5	2	1
Baca	113	23.0	26 120	386	30	42	24	18	18	9	6	2	0
Bent	98	1.5	16 894	2 631	57	5	19	23	22	7	10	3	0
Boulder	9 619	10.0	36 071	58	7 029	711	2 136	556	510	238	161	34	9
Chaffee	298	6.8	19 655	1 836	139	23	88	56	54	26	20	3	1
Cheyenne	58	15.9	25 031	488	24	16	14	9	8	3	4	1	0

1. Based on the resident population estimated as of July 1 of the year shown.   2. Includes other labor income.

Table B. States and Counties — **Earnings, Social Security, and Housing**

STATE County	Earnings, 1998 Total (mil dol)	Farm	Goods-related[1] Total	Manu-facturing	Service-related and other[2] Total	Retail trade	Finance, insurance, and real estate	Services	Govern-ment	Social Security beneficiaries, December 1998 Number	Rate[3]	Supplemental Security Income recipients, December 1998	Housing units, 1990 Total	Percent change, 1980–1990
	75	76	77	78	79	80	81	82	83	84	85	86	87	88
CALIFORNIA—Cont'd														
Butte	2 299	1.4	14.4	8.1	62.5	13.0	6.1	32.3	21.7	40 494	208	8 507	76 115	24.0
Calaveras	300	-1.4	D	5.1	D	11.5	7.5	26.5	25.3	9 262	233	927	19 153	50.3
Colusa	256	29.5	13.0	10.2	41.0	10.1	1.9	10.9	16.5	2 865	154	520	6 295	18.0
Contra Costa	17 491	0.1	21.0	12.1	67.2	9.7	12.4	31.4	11.7	122 758	134	21 057	316 170	25.5
Del Norte	266	5.1	10.8	6.3	44.8	10.4	2.2	21.7	39.3	5 055	187	1 583	9 091	19.9
El Dorado	1 688	0.0	19.6	6.1	62.1	12.3	6.3	35.6	18.2	24 717	156	2 367	61 451	36.6
Fresno	10 644	5.2	15.9	9.5	58.2	10.0	6.6	24.2	20.7	97 859	129	35 083	235 563	21.6
Glenn	266	4.7	28.1	17.3	40.8	8.2	2.1	13.1	26.4	4 635	177	895	9 329	10.7
Humboldt	1 728	1.6	D	14.8	D	12.4	5.1	25.2	22.1	21 876	179	5 460	51 134	12.7
Imperial	1 828	22.5	D	3.2	D	9.1	D	12.2	30.5	20 783	144	8 015	36 559	13.9
Inyo	247	-1.3	12.9	3.6	53.5	15.5	2.5	25.8	34.9	4 154	229	511	8 712	2.7
Kern	9 041	4.3	19.4	5.3	50.6	8.8	4.0	20.1	25.7	84 862	134	24 526	198 636	27.6
Kings	1 331	7.4	D	9.5	D	9.1	D	14.3	43.3	12 576	106	3 794	30 843	20.0
Lake	446	2.1	D	4.0	D	13.8	4.9	30.0	24.1	15 108	274	3 246	28 822	25.3
Lassen	360	0.4	D	7.6	D	8.9	D	14.3	54.4	4 141	124	942	10 358	16.4
Los Angeles	200 847	0.1	18.8	15.0	68.2	8.2	9.6	36.5	12.9	971 134	105	343 335	3 163 343	10.8
Madera	1 184	8.1	D	11.7	D	9.7	D	22.5	22.5	17 748	155	4 101	30 831	25.3
Marin	6 187	0.2	D	4.6	D	10.8	14.8	44.0	9.8	35 618	150	3 464	99 757	7.7
Mariposa	171	-2.7	D	3.7	D	8.5	2.7	38.5	39.4	3 852	243	270	7 700	33.6
Mendocino	1 105	2.7	D	16.5	D	14.4	3.6	25.4	18.4	15 796	189	3 458	33 649	16.0
Merced	2 179	14.6	22.1	17.6	44.2	10.5	3.7	16.4	19.2	25 466	129	8 448	58 410	16.7
Modoc	97	12.8	D	D	D	8.9	3.0	13.6	43.5	2 147	228	354	4 672	25.0
Mono	198	-0.7	10.7	0.9	62.2	16.9	6.6	35.4	27.8	1 019	99	117	10 664	27.0
Monterey	7 102	15.5	10.2	5.3	53.0	8.8	6.4	22.4	21.3	47 704	130	8 522	121 224	17.1
Napa	2 313	2.6	D	18.8	D	9.6	6.0	28.6	15.1	21 462	180	2 064	44 199	10.4
Nevada	1 037	-0.2	24.7	11.8	58.2	14.2	7.2	29.7	17.2	20 005	219	1 613	37 352	50.9
Orange	65 282	0.3	24.0	18.0	66.0	9.3	12.1	30.0	9.6	293 473	108	52 070	875 072	21.3
Placer	4 037	0.0	27.3	15.5	60.3	13.6	8.6	26.1	12.4	35 302	154	3 898	77 879	44.2
Plumas	273	5.2	21.8	13.9	45.1	10.8	4.5	15.7	27.9	4 681	230	674	11 942	26.4
Riverside	16 333	2.9	22.7	12.0	54.4	12.0	5.8	26.5	20.0	218 916	148	37 743	483 847	64.0
Sacramento	24 435	0.3	13.6	7.7	52.5	8.0	9.3	26.2	33.6	156 775	137	47 312	417 574	29.0
San Benito	565	13.0	D	13.2	D	10.9	3.9	15.0	17.6	5 242	107	842	12 230	39.8
San Bernardino	19 532	1.4	19.8	12.4	55.9	11.7	5.3	24.2	22.9	189 863	116	50 032	542 332	46.5
San Diego	54 385	0.6	17.8	12.0	57.6	9.4	8.2	30.7	23.9	359 709	129	74 347	946 240	31.4
San Francisco	37 464	0.0	7.8	4.8	78.7	6.7	21.8	37.1	13.5	105 155	141	46 036	328 471	3.7
San Joaquin	7 166	4.6	20.5	13.6	55.5	10.6	6.6	21.7	19.4	73 894	134	23 644	166 274	22.3
San Luis Obispo	3 529	3.2	17.3	8.1	57.7	13.0	6.1	25.8	21.9	42 674	182	4 990	90 200	35.1
San Mateo	21 655	0.3	18.3	12.3	74.6	9.0	9.7	36.5	6.8	92 737	132	12 994	251 782	8.0
Santa Barbara	7 304	4.6	18.4	11.6	57.9	10.2	6.7	31.4	19.1	59 571	153	8 654	138 149	20.2
Santa Clara	62 530	0.2	40.4	35.9	52.1	5.9	4.0	32.3	7.3	165 361	101	40 213	540 240	14.0
Santa Cruz	4 200	5.4	21.4	14.5	57.8	11.6	5.1	30.5	15.4	31 012	128	5 354	91 878	13.6
Shasta	2 250	0.5	D	9.2	D	12.5	4.0	30.3	19.2	34 394	209	7 813	60 552	27.6
Sierra	41	-4.7	D	D	D	5.6	D	10.3	51.6	747	221	83	2 166	14.4
Siskiyou	501	3.9	D	9.5	53.1	12.7	3.8	21.0	27.8	10 554	240	2 131	20 141	15.1
Solano	4 489	0.6	20.6	10.5	48.2	12.7	3.6	22.4	30.6	43 039	114	9 834	119 533	41.8
Sonoma	7 850	1.5	27.2	17.9	57.6	11.0	8.4	27.3	13.7	68 926	159	9 453	161 062	29.7
Stanislaus	5 716	6.1	D	19.2	D	10.9	4.2	23.0	16.6	60 448	142	17 431	132 027	28.8
Sutter	876	8.9	16.6	8.7	57.2	13.7	4.9	24.6	17.3	12 102	157	2 933	24 163	18.3
Tehama	489	2.9	23.9	18.6	51.4	17.1	4.4	20.2	21.8	11 711	217	2 285	20 403	23.2
Trinity	103	0.3	D	12.1	D	10.6	2.9	16.8	44.2	3 111	237	566	7 540	18.7
Tulare	4 440	14.7	14.3	9.3	50.5	10.8	4.0	15.8	20.5	47 853	135	15 272	105 013	18.3
Tuolumne	513	-0.6	18.6	8.9	52.5	14.3	4.1	27.3	29.6	12 684	238	1 473	25 175	30.0
Ventura	12 342	3.5	20.2	13.3	58.4	9.9	6.6	30.3	17.9	89 870	123	13 522	228 478	24.6
Yolo	3 476	3.4	14.6	8.3	51.1	10.7	4.5	16.8	30.9	18 727	122	4 439	53 000	21.5
Yuba	717	2.9	12.9	6.6	33.8	6.6	2.1	16.3	50.4	9 359	156	3 404	21 245	10.4
COLORADO	90 240	0.8	20.3	11.0	62.8	9.0	9.0	28.6	16.0	515 291	130	56 204	1 477 349	23.7
Adams	5 132	0.4	28.0	15.8	57.2	11.5	3.9	16.3	14.4	38 423	119	5 167	106 947	19.8
Alamosa	211	6.5	D	1.1	D	13.0	4.4	27.3	29.0	1 997	138	552	5 254	18.5
Arapahoe	13 987	0.0	14.1	5.2	77.5	8.2	13.7	33.2	8.4	49 347	104	3 445	168 665	49.0
Archuleta	87	-1.6	21.4	2.1	62.7	17.3	14.7	22.6	17.5	1 511	166	106	3 951	93.3
Baca	72	46.5	D	0.8	D	6.9	1.5	5.8	23.0	1 132	259	134	2 434	-1.9
Bent	62	5.9	D	D	D	4.3	2.8	D	60.9	1 059	193	219	2 332	-1.5
Boulder	7 740	0.1	28.9	23.2	58.0	7.7	4.9	37.0	12.9	26 998	101	2 339	94 621	26.8
Chaffee	162	-0.5	D	4.7	D	16.8	7.2	20.7	31.4	3 312	220	200	6 547	13.3
Cheyenne	40	31.8	D	D	D	4.6	D	5.5	21.0	421	179	15	1 083	13.0

1. Covers mining, construction, and manufacturing. 2. Covers private sector earnings in agricultural services, forestry, and fisheries; transportation and public utilities; wholesale trade; retail trade; finance, insurance, and real estate; and services. 3. Per 1,000 resident population estimated as of July 1 of the year shown.

STATE County	Housing units, 1990 (cont'd)								Civilian labor force, 1999				Civilian employment, 1990[5]		
	Occupied units										Unemployment			Percent	
		Owner-occupied				Renter-occupied									
				Owner cost as a percent of income											
	Total	Percent	Median value[1]	With a mortgage	Without a mortgage	Median rent[2]	Rent as percent of income	Substandard units[3] (percent)	Total	Percent change, 1998–1999	Total	Rate[4]	Total	Professional, managerial, and technical	Precision production, craft, and repair
	89	90	91	92	93	94	95	96	97	98	99	100	101	102	103
CALIFORNIA—Cont'd															
Butte	71 665	60.9	94 000	22.4	11.9	439	32.6	5.1	85 763	-0.7	5 830	6.8	70 880	29.6	11.0
Calaveras	12 649	76.1	113 700	24.7	12.8	476	29.3	5.6	14 564	2.6	1 012	6.9	12 114	24.2	17.8
Colusa	5 612	63.5	68 900	21.2	11.5	354	22.6	12.7	8 888	4.1	1 395	15.7	6 653	17.0	8.1
Contra Costa	300 288	67.6	219 400	25.3	11.7	675	28.5	4.9	489 320	1.8	14 820	3.0	406 507	38.6	10.3
Del Norte	7 987	65.4	84 600	21.1	11.6	422	28.3	6.9	9 837	-2.1	791	8.0	7 858	22.2	11.4
El Dorado	46 845	70.4	155 000	25.7	12.6	569	29.2	5.0	81 227	3.6	3 098	3.8	58 893	30.0	12.4
Fresno	220 933	54.3	83 600	22.3	12.2	434	29.2	13.7	379 628	0.9	51 091	13.5	269 826	27.3	9.7
Glenn	8 821	61.8	67 400	20.9	12.7	355	26.5	9.6	10 741	2.4	1 173	10.9	9 896	17.3	11.6
Humboldt	46 420	58.8	88 000	20.8	11.9	409	29.8	6.0	60 208	-1.9	3 869	6.4	50 831	26.6	11.1
Imperial	32 842	57.6	72 500	21.6	12.6	394	28.9	21.1	55 815	-1.5	12 974	23.2	36 412	22.4	10.4
Inyo	7 565	66.3	115 800	21.4	12.6	412	24.4	5.3	7 246	-0.3	409	5.6	7 800	25.8	12.7
Kern	181 480	59.3	82 800	22.5	12.4	440	27.4	10.9	280 491	0.4	31 866	11.4	214 668	26.2	13.3
Kings	29 082	52.9	70 700	21.8	12.2	411	25.8	12.9	43 486	-1.2	5 650	13.0	33 037	19.9	10.9
Lake	20 805	71.2	93 300	24.7	13.5	460	30.7	5.2	23 947	-0.4	1 838	7.7	17 143	25.5	15.3
Lassen	8 543	69.4	70 400	20.6	12.4	412	25.2	5.9	11 179	-2.9	783	7.0	8 843	26.0	8.9
Los Angeles	2 989 552	48.2	226 400	25.2	11.6	626	29.5	18.9	4 658 630	0.4	272 818	5.9	4 203 792	30.9	11.0
Madera	28 370	64.9	86 500	23.5	12.5	423	27.9	12.0	52 733	0.7	6 136	11.6	33 263	20.8	11.8
Marin	95 006	62.1	354 200	25.5	11.8	824	29.8	3.0	135 751	0.2	2 616	1.9	125 886	46.0	7.5
Mariposa	5 604	69.3	99 800	25.4	11.3	392	25.0	5.0	6 705	-2.3	495	7.4	5 908	28.1	13.5
Mendocino	30 419	62.1	123 900	24.3	12.0	471	28.4	9.4	41 963	-1.3	2 823	6.7	34 983	25.9	12.0
Merced	55 331	54.4	90 800	22.7	12.1	430	28.2	15.6	84 759	-0.9	11 238	13.3	66 116	21.7	11.5
Modoc	3 711	69.6	49 600	20.1	12.2	328	23.8	5.3	4 027	0.1	343	8.5	3 535	20.4	11.4
Mono	3 961	51.9	159 900	25.1	13.4	550	23.4	8.0	6 283	0.6	412	6.6	5 642	29.3	12.2
Monterey	112 965	50.6	198 200	24.8	11.4	625	28.5	14.5	191 707	3.7	18 137	9.5	146 885	26.8	8.7
Napa	41 312	64.5	183 600	24.4	11.5	632	29.2	5.3	63 067	3.0	2 055	3.3	52 533	31.7	11.7
Nevada	30 758	74.4	154 700	26.0	12.4	598	30.0	3.8	43 644	3.3	1 778	4.1	33 210	32.1	14.0
Orange	827 066	60.1	252 700	25.2	11.4	790	29.0	10.7	1 471 602	2.5	38 932	2.6	1 292 472	35.0	10.3
Placer	64 101	70.7	169 000	25.0	11.9	575	28.8	4.1	119 898	5.5	3 883	3.2	82 920	32.5	12.8
Plumas	8 125	67.5	89 900	22.0	13.0	366	28.9	3.5	9 466	-4.3	856	9.0	7 783	25.2	12.7
Riverside	402 067	67.4	139 100	26.6	12.3	572	29.9	9.7	687 847	4.6	37 724	5.5	488 257	26.1	14.4
Sacramento	394 530	56.6	129 800	22.9	11.5	527	29.2	6.1	586 755	3.6	24 644	4.2	485 063	33.3	10.1
San Benito	11 422	61.1	206 600	26.7	12.3	547	25.2	13.0	26 411	-0.7	2 123	8.0	16 800	23.6	13.6
San Bernardino	464 737	63.3	129 200	25.1	12.1	556	29.5	9.9	754 716	4.1	36 240	4.8	591 371	27.0	14.4
San Diego	887 403	53.8	186 700	25.9	11.5	611	29.8	9.1	1 358 210	2.9	41 932	3.1	1 145 266	34.5	11.1
San Francisco	305 584	34.5	298 900	24.6	11.8	653	28.0	11.4	422 030	1.3	12 793	3.0	386 530	38.5	6.3
San Joaquin	158 156	57.6	121 700	23.3	11.8	489	28.2	12.4	252 954	1.0	22 127	8.7	195 575	24.2	12.5
San Luis Obispo	80 281	59.8	215 300	27.4	11.3	573	31.8	5.7	110 612	1.8	3 615	3.3	97 417	29.3	12.3
San Mateo	241 914	60.2	343 900	26.0	11.6	769	27.6	8.9	399 144	0.6	7 817	2.0	352 964	35.6	9.8
Santa Barbara	129 802	54.7	250 000	25.0	11.3	654	31.3	9.6	199 462	1.9	7 713	3.9	180 217	32.7	10.7
Santa Clara	520 180	59.1	289 400	24.9	11.5	773	27.4	10.5	962 821	0.0	29 227	3.0	806 917	41.1	10.6
Santa Cruz	83 566	59.9	256 100	27.2	11.7	713	31.4	9.4	140 849	-0.6	8 852	6.3	117 904	36.3	10.7
Shasta	55 966	64.5	91 300	21.7	11.9	432	29.2	5.1	72 922	1.2	5 113	7.0	58 578	26.8	12.6
Sierra	1 336	68.1	79 300	23.5	15.0	423	25.2	5.5	1 581	-2.3	150	9.5	1 333	29.4	9.7
Siskiyou	17 306	67.2	68 300	21.9	12.6	366	27.7	4.9	17 767	-3.8	1 829	10.3	16 505	25.0	10.4
Solano	113 429	62.9	147 300	25.4	12.0	590	27.6	6.6	190 135	4.5	8 720	4.6	151 310	28.4	14.0
Sonoma	149 011	62.9	201 400	26.2	11.7	645	29.5	4.6	251 168	1.4	6 735	2.7	193 296	31.7	12.3
Stanislaus	125 375	60.7	124 300	23.3	11.7	482	28.9	10.4	203 050	0.4	21 435	10.6	151 010	23.8	14.0
Sutter	23 111	58.7	91 900	21.5	12.3	387	27.0	8.9	35 804	1.3	4 663	13.0	26 359	27.1	12.5
Tehama	18 704	68.6	68 700	22.2	12.2	366	27.8	6.9	24 234	0.3	1 632	6.7	17 898	19.8	13.1
Trinity	5 156	69.6	81 800	23.5	13.6	367	29.3	10.5	4 885	-5.0	563	11.5	4 547	25.6	11.0
Tulare	97 861	60.1	73 900	22.6	12.1	403	29.2	14.5	166 552	1.7	27 308	16.4	118 964	21.8	9.6
Tuolumne	17 959	70.6	120 400	24.4	12.8	500	27.5	4.5	19 886	0.2	1 304	6.6	17 601	26.4	13.7
Ventura	217 298	65.5	245 300	26.2	11.4	754	29.3	10.2	395 788	2.2	18 930	4.8	336 772	33.1	11.7
Yolo	50 972	51.9	137 800	22.2	11.6	510	31.2	7.8	90 200	3.4	3 969	4.4	66 260	37.1	8.8
Yuba	19 776	52.8	67 600	21.6	11.6	383	28.5	9.7	21 093	0.5	2 400	11.4	18 329	20.7	13.9
COLORADO	1 282 489	62.2	82 700	22.5	12.7	418	26.1	3.0	2 264 105	0.8	65 958	2.9	1 633 281	34.3	9.8
Adams	96 353	65.5	71 500	22.9	12.6	434	26.4	3.6	182 040	1.3	4 860	2.7	132 884	23.5	13.4
Alamosa	4 721	62.5	48 100	21.3	12.8	291	31.5	6.4	8 104	-3.9	411	5.1	6 068	29.9	8.3
Arapahoe	154 710	63.6	93 000	22.3	11.8	463	24.6	2.1	284 243	1.4	6 066	2.1	210 935	39.4	7.4
Archuleta	2 010	70.7	79 600	30.6	14.0	385	25.9	7.6	4 561	6.6	177	3.9	2 210	25.3	11.4
Baca	1 872	72.9	31 100	22.1	14.7	235	22.7	3.1	2 360	-1.7	57	2.4	1 903	18.6	6.8
Bent	1 865	69.3	24 300	17.9	14.7	296	23.9	2.1	2 157	-3.5	72	3.3	1 729	28.3	7.4
Boulder	88 402	61.1	102 800	22.3	12.3	502	28.7	2.4	175 656	1.8	4 662	2.7	124 542	45.0	8.1
Chaffee	4 848	70.9	62 900	22.8	11.9	336	26.2	2.8	7 708	0.5	243	3.2	4 950	25.6	11.1
Cheyenne	904	70.0	38 200	19.0	13.1	297	17.6	2.8	1 290	-9.5	45	3.5	1 122	16.9	12.1

1. Specified owner-occupied units. 2. Specified renter-occupied units. 3. Overcrowded or lacking complete plumbing facilities. 4. Percent of civilian labor force. 5. Persons 16 years and older.

Table B. States and Counties — Nonfarm Employment and Agriculture

| | Private nonfarm establishments, employment and payroll, 1998 | | | | | | | | | Agriculture, 1997 | | | |
| | | Employment | | | | | | Annual payroll | | Farms | | | Farm operators |
STATE County	Number of establishments	Total	Health Care and Social Assistance	Manufacturing	Retail trade	Finance and Insurance	Professional Scientific and Technical Services	Total (mil dol)	Average per employee (dollars)	Number	Percent with— Less than 50 acres	500 acres and over	Whose principal occupation is farming (percent)
	104	105	106	107	108	109	110	111	112	113	114	115	116
CALIFORNIA—Cont'd													
Butte	4 494	49 894	9 863	5 139	9 021	1 700	2 214	1 062	21 294	1 942	58.7	9.4	54.8
Calaveras	930	5 337	964	425	967	238	229	111	20 854	457	45.1	23.0	45.5
Colusa	365	3 273	274	655	520	106	D	84	25 690	810	25.7	27.5	64.9
Contra Costa	21 674	288 747	34 080	19 873	38 106	23 670	21 948	10 793	37 377	587	64.6	11.6	49.2
Del Norte	493	4 159	1 012	225	874	100	143	79	19 031	66	45.5	7.6	50.0
El Dorado	3 703	33 891	3 998	1 912	5 095	944	1 930	821	24 219	763	74.2	2.8	41.9
Fresno	15 130	205 823	29 050	26 971	30 737	9 515	8 599	5 247	25 492	6 592	58.6	11.2	62.3
Glenn	504	4 422	399	780	681	145	124	114	25 852	1 189	44.6	16.0	63.4
Humboldt	3 590	37 239	6 973	5 211	7 289	1 291	1 377	808	21 693	792	40.9	20.2	52.7
Imperial	2 230	23 205	3 131	1 359	6 269	755	627	481	20 724	557	24.6	37.7	75.4
Inyo	609	6 338	890	249	1 095	100	120	106	16 758	82	37.8	34.1	53.7
Kern	10 709	142 507	19 216	13 257	23 794	6 615	6 948	3 763	26 406	1 997	35.1	33.8	63.8
Kings	1 493	17 632	2 975	2 572	3 562	577	388	395	22 421	1 079	50.6	18.9	62.2
Lake	1 069	9 241	1 895	287	1 977	446	261	180	19 459	776	66.2	5.4	42.4
Lassen	533	4 167	779	336	1 040	143	83	86	20 662	365	32.1	33.4	51.5
Los Angeles	219 933	3 693 537	360 703	638 389	349 666	177 067	383 371	123 783	33 513	1 226	84.7	4.7	39.9
Madera	1 811	22 178	2 613	4 271	3 129	405	383	451	20 349	1 673	44.6	13.8	58.4
Marin	10 031	97 596	14 026	4 731	14 412	6 879	8 112	3 566	36 542	276	34.1	34.1	62.3
Mariposa	359	3 388	385	100	465	73	D	65	19 147	252	38.9	27.8	49.6
Mendocino	2 754	24 475	3 703	4 329	4 548	586	685	533	21 773	1 092	45.1	19.3	51.6
Merced	2 898	37 537	5 122	8 269	6 471	1 777	725	830	22 112	2 831	52.5	10.8	61.9
Modoc	195	1 447	447	D	D	D	D	27	18 982	440	16.1	41.8	64.8
Mono	530	5 547	192	D	720	D	139	90	16 251	63	27.0	39.7	61.9
Monterey	8 457	101 381	12 257	7 403	16 661	5 001	3 479	2 786	27 478	1 209	40.7	29.9	66.3
Napa	3 537	47 205	9 027	9 173	5 609	1 451	1 733	1 375	29 132	1 318	68.2	6.6	44.8
Nevada	2 800	23 644	3 455	2 860	4 269	966	840	543	22 945	412	70.1	8.0	45.6
Orange	75 154	1 274 074	105 147	224 709	129 105	78 537	87 038	43 261	33 955	349	74.8	3.2	49.3
Placer	6 562	81 772	8 357	9 340	12 684	3 430	2 958	2 390	29 233	997	71.8	6.9	43.8
Plumas	696	4 451	909	652	758	183	154	105	23 578	117	32.5	29.9	53.8
Riverside	24 817	341 885	40 108	49 013	55 859	9 510	9 614	8 481	24 807	3 048	79.3	4.8	44.0
Sacramento	25 062	388 764	52 027	29 752	52 616	31 120	24 901	11 752	30 229	1 288	63.0	11.3	51.5
San Benito	890	10 122	972	2 242	1 704	341	205	246	24 337	562	48.0	24.9	55.2
San Bernardino	26 132	425 068	54 033	66 832	60 145	13 333	9 929	10 829	25 475	1 455	78.9	3.2	45.6
San Diego	64 413	961 014	103 808	120 081	121 465	44 864	75 483	29 596	30 797	5 925	90.2	2.0	37.2
San Francisco	31 632	531 023	48 294	23 518	39 227	66 697	68 508	23 635	44 509	9	100.0	0.0	22.2
San Joaquin	9 830	143 285	19 747	22 561	20 891	6 333	3 798	3 785	26 417	3 862	62.6	8.3	59.3
San Luis Obispo	6 557	69 698	11 648	6 770	11 348	2 087	2 822	1 609	23 085	1 916	49.3	19.7	48.4
San Mateo	20 014	333 418	24 713	31 634	35 628	18 598	26 680	14 608	43 812	240	60.8	8.3	55.0
Santa Barbara	10 535	129 260	15 493	15 729	19 489	4 941	7 333	3 708	28 688	1 451	59.0	16.1	52.0
Santa Clara	44 204	946 363	69 613	240 608	81 748	19 746	85 359	47 589	50 287	985	74.5	7.8	47.6
Santa Cruz	6 737	74 213	9 655	8 824	12 368	2 242	4 163	2 113	28 473	722	75.8	3.5	59.8
Shasta	4 380	44 494	9 019	3 601	8 382	1 371	1 798	1 074	24 136	850	61.3	14.0	41.6
Sierra	89	D	D	D	D	D	D	D	D	47	14.9	31.9	57.4
Siskiyou	1 261	9 380	1 544	826	1 796	378	D	183	19 557	733	32.5	27.3	61.0
Solano	6 242	85 967	13 095	9 177	15 492	2 637	2 711	2 309	26 856	795	57.7	15.5	50.7
Sonoma	13 017	154 187	21 527	25 915	23 550	9 819	6 684	4 637	30 071	2 745	66.3	7.3	49.0
Stanislaus	8 027	113 536	17 086	22 882	17 944	3 504	3 485	2 938	25 876	4 009	65.5	6.5	55.8
Sutter	1 616	16 850	3 735	1 528	3 653	605	450	390	23 119	1 314	45.7	12.8	64.6
Tehama	1 014	11 518	1 665	2 262	1 860	607	284	259	22 462	1 362	57.3	13.1	51.0
Trinity	316	1 811	434	179	299	55	53	35	19 437	116	41.4	19.8	43.1
Tulare	5 812	73 205	10 342	11 806	12 637	2 881	1 910	1 672	22 844	5 446	59.7	8.2	55.5
Tuolumne	1 405	11 852	2 222	1 066	2 309	463	304	250	21 091	264	43.2	23.5	43.2
Ventura	16 463	217 737	22 731	33 356	31 841	11 283	12 201	6 343	29 133	2 214	73.3	5.6	46.5
Yolo	3 340	53 870	4 651	6 030	6 058	2 651	2 364	1 532	28 436	923	45.6	21.1	56.4
Yuba	807	8 807	1 704	1 135	1 470	287	189	191	21 677	706	49.3	11.2	48.2
COLORADO	130 354	1 757 628	180 801	173 403	232 581	97 679	117 740	53 791	30 604	28 268	28.4	34.2	54.5
Adams	7 008	117 241	7 226	12 822	15 080	2 654	2 837	3 431	29 266	696	36.1	29.2	50.0
Alamosa	525	4 920	962	129	1 082	278	191	91	18 426	306	14.7	35.3	62.1
Arapahoe	16 039	271 272	21 052	19 595	31 178	30 547	20 636	10 260	37 822	258	34.5	30.2	45.3
Archuleta	410	2 400	122	43	428	60	67	41	17 157	206	26.2	21.4	44.2
Baca	114	650	D	D	155	49	D	10	16 088	608	3.0	67.6	63.5
Bent	75	1 076	D	D	95	45	D	33	30 714	270	13.7	49.3	70.0
Boulder	10 464	136 146	12 030	26 368	17 624	3 645	17 000	4 827	35 454	657	60.4	6.7	42.0
Chaffee	667	4 398	466	155	877	229	175	83	18 777	189	21.7	19.6	46.6
Cheyenne	66	478	D	D	83	D	D	11	22 983	333	3.0	73.0	69.4

Table B. States and Counties — Agriculture, Land, and Water

Agriculture, 1997 (cont'd)

STATE County	Land in farms: Acreage (1,000) [117]	Land in farms: Percent change 1992–1997 [118]	Acres: Average size of farm [119]	Acres: Total irrigated (1,000) [120]	Acres: Total cropland (1,000) [121]	Value of land and buildings: Average per farm ($1,000) [122]	Value of land and buildings: Average per acre (dollars) [123]	Value of machinery and equipment: Average per farm ($1,000) [124]	Value of products sold: Total (mil dol) [125]	Value of products sold: Average per farm (dollars) [126]	Percent from: Crops [127]	Percent from: Livestock and poultry products [128]	Percent of farms with sales of $10,000 or more [129]	Percent of farms with sales of $100,000 or more [130]	Percent of land owned by Fed. Gov. 1997 [131]	Water consumption 1995 (mil gal/day) [132]
CALIFORNIA—Cont'd																
Butte	404	-10.6	208	224	247	754	3 589	73	286	147 388	96.9	3.1	57.3	26.7	14.1	957.7
Calaveras	245	-0.4	536	7	21	722	1 320	20	10	21 535	17.9	82.1	34.6	4.4	19.9	14.7
Colusa	431	-4.2	532	277	317	1 305	2 426	125	277	341 405	97.8	2.2	80.5	53.6	15.0	1 049.1
Contra Costa	148	-9.3	252	30	44	1 046	3 339	29	67	114 256	78.1	21.9	40.7	13.1	2.0	521.0
Del Norte	13	2.3	202	6	8	702	3 480	69	21	315 112	51.9	48.1	40.9	18.2	66.8	19.7
El Dorado	103	0.7	135	5	13	363	2 926	19	13	17 666	74.9	25.1	25.4	3.9	45.2	73.8
Fresno	1 881	6.0	285	1 154	1 251	971	3 334	78	2 773	420 629	76.3	23.7	72.4	35.2	38.4	3 547.7
Glenn	483	1.8	406	220	256	799	2 083	85	228	191 944	78.7	21.3	66.5	34.3	25.6	848.4
Humboldt	585	-2.3	738	18	51	705	1 118	33	75	95 297	32.9	67.1	48.9	17.3	20.8	123.5
Imperial	490	-8.1	879	438	459	2 614	3 068	195	850	1 526 662	69.4	30.6	82.9	62.1	56.8	2 607.7
Inyo	199	-19.9	2 423	19	D	1 975	815	38	5	61 444	20.1	79.9	51.2	19.5	92.1	149.4
Kern	2 851	0.4	1 428	913	1 054	2 162	1 605	189	1 969	985 735	90.8	9.2	66.8	45.6	27.9	2 462.7
Kings	657	-15.3	609	421	526	1 602	2 732	148	694	642 889	53.2	46.8	69.3	43.7	3.2	1 413.4
Lake	138	-15.6	178	17	33	450	2 563	31	40	52 018	95.1	4.9	32.1	11.5	45.0	57.1
Lassen	454	-6.8	1 243	68	118	937	686	79	26	72 325	55.8	44.2	50.7	14.8	56.8	300.9
Los Angeles	131	-28.9	107	27	49	507	4 475	39	238	193 854	94.3	5.7	37.1	14.1	29.6	1 683.0
Madera	642	-14.3	383	309	333	1 157	3 537	76	627	374 901	81.0	19.0	71.4	42.5	36.2	981.0
Marin	150	-11.4	542	1	28	1 315	1 900	44	54	195 212	6.6	93.4	62.0	26.1	20.5	41.0
Mariposa	198	-3.8	787	3	9	598	871	30	6	22 284	6.6	93.4	34.1	6.0	51.8	8.3
Mendocino	639	-11.9	585	25	66	930	1 728	46	117	107 014	87.7	12.3	44.2	15.4	13.3	52.6
Merced	882	-9.9	311	493	532	951	3 149	96	1 273	449 832	45.4	54.6	72.3	38.6	1.9	1 688.4
Modoc	663	-3.5	1 507	159	183	1 055	861	110	64	144 993	63.8	36.2	69.3	28.4	61.8	429.0
Mono	69	-33.2	1 092	31	D	1 119	1 024	67	7	103 208	49.8	50.2	58.7	28.6	85.5	221.4
Monterey	1 544	12.5	1 277	260	389	2 685	2 358	226	1 750	1 447 268	98.0	2.0	69.9	44.4	27.5	632.6
Napa	212	-9.6	161	46	75	1 537	11 629	52	239	181 104	98.0	2.0	65.2	28.8	8.8	67.3
Nevada	63	-12.8	152	7	15	297	3 591	23	4	9 647	45.9	54.1	21.1	0.7	30.4	40.8
Orange	58	-4.7	167	13	17	871	6 010	90	229	655 818	98.6	1.4	53.0	29.2	13.1	517.3
Placer	140	1.2	140	35	62	567	4 765	30	37	37 097	68.4	31.6	25.8	6.4	37.7	200.2
Plumas	109	-9.3	931	29	43	994	1 284	40	23	197 650	70.8	29.2	49.6	12.0	70.3	127.1
Riverside	509	20.1	167	220	280	749	4 618	63	1 048	343 676	55.0	45.0	48.0	19.4	55.7	1 432.3
Sacramento	308	-18.7	239	123	159	718	2 825	52	218	169 272	62.3	37.7	44.5	20.4	1.6	876.1
San Benito	512	-14.7	910	36	73	1 124	1 193	55	157	278 838	84.8	15.2	55.7	21.5	14.3	87.5
San Bernardino	924	-28.2	635	41	58	470	693	63	618	424 628	12.0	88.0	44.1	23.4	74.5	578.1
San Diego	475	-8.3	80	70	113	407	5 504	23	633	106 790	86.6	13.4	34.7	10.9	22.9	776.5
San Francisco	0	0.0	2	0	D	110	46 991	25	1	97 753	100.0	0.0	88.9	33.3	7.3	101.9
San Joaquin	809	3.2	209	519	559	1 017	4 667	82	1 180	305 465	73.4	26.6	65.3	33.6	0.3	1 816.8
San Luis Obispo	1 302	-1.7	679	61	281	1 046	1 591	49	313	163 335	89.5	10.5	47.2	17.6	16.7	188.4
San Mateo	45	-21.8	186	4	15	808	5 653	69	139	577 787	99.1	0.9	60.4	25.0	0.8	111.4
Santa Barbara	817	-2.4	563	104	157	1 378	2 716	82	660	454 680	94.3	5.7	52.9	27.0	49.5	322.2
Santa Clara	319	-7.1	324	19	32	606	2 425	50	188	191 355	89.6	10.4	41.5	13.6	1.4	350.3
Santa Cruz	71	34.2	98	21	28	573	6 234	67	248	343 234	94.9	5.1	57.9	29.8	0.1	72.2
Shasta	317	-18.4	373	39	59	420	1 021	22	31	36 881	58.6	41.4	29.1	5.1	38.0	310.8
Sierra	46	-15.7	986	10	15	1 095	1 110	38	1	27 755	23.9	76.1	55.3	4.3	68.8	40.6
Siskiyou	629	-2.8	858	140	182	1 070	1 139	73	74	101 288	70.3	29.7	55.0	18.0	61.9	474.6
Solano	362	6.5	455	162	210	1 224	2 554	83	161	203 042	83.8	16.2	49.3	25.0	2.6	526.5
Sonoma	571	10.4	208	57	145	1 025	5 211	47	464	168 895	69.1	30.9	53.3	23.8	2.5	126.1
Stanislaus	733	-3.6	183	359	382	779	4 508	61	1 209	301 453	45.5	54.5	63.5	29.4	0.3	1 437.9
Sutter	348	9.5	265	242	297	1 203	4 532	115	280	212 826	97.5	2.5	69.6	37.4	0.7	1 053.9
Tehama	885	-12.9	650	86	127	772	1 106	39	107	78 636	62.4	37.6	49.1	14.2	23.6	399.8
Trinity	118	1.9	1 019	2	7	413	460	24	2	15 494	D	D	21.6	2.6	74.4	25.5
Tulare	1 310	-3.3	240	625	703	835	3 444	68	1 921	352 806	58.4	41.6	67.4	35.7	48.5	2 208.7
Tuolumne	152	10.4	577	3	13	736	1 029	23	19	72 640	6.3	93.7	32.2	8.7	74.0	37.9
Ventura	346	7.9	156	111	132	883	6 860	46	846	381 939	98.0	2.0	57.3	27.5	50.0	372.7
Yolo	537	3.4	581	294	381	1 420	2 732	126	345	373 666	96.9	3.1	62.1	30.6	4.1	1 090.1
Yuba	208	-11.3	295	85	97	763	2 797	63	107	150 972	86.8	13.2	48.2	24.1	17.0	354.7
COLORADO	32 634	-4.0	1 154	3 430	10 509	707	618	71	4 534	160 401	29.3	70.7	52.6	16.9	35.7	13 823.9
Adams	674	-1.8	968	27	530	654	784	67	88	126 062	78.1	21.9	51.0	17.2	(1)2.3	132.2
Alamosa	190	-8.2	621	106	103	763	1 164	166	57	186 912	90.4	9.6	66.7	28.4	19.4	413.8
Arapahoe	333	3.1	1 290	4	169	1 181		59	24	91 519	61.7	38.3	43.8	9.7	1.5	86.5
Archuleta	113	-27.3	547	17	18	855	1 654	27	6	29 850	6.4	93.6	36.4	7.3	51.3	48.2
Baca	1 142	-9.1	1 879	65	633	748	427	83	77	127 252	36.1	63.9	61.7	21.7	12.5	105.8
Bent	784	-1.6	2 905	63	D	900	283	78	51	188 798	24.6	75.4	69.3	25.6	1.2	426.0
Boulder	128	-18.4	195	39	59	534	2 054	55	44	66 471	63.9	36.1	34.7	7.8	35.0	173.6
Chaffee	86	1.9	453	24	24	850	1 747	39	5	27 308	40.3	59.7	45.0	6.3	76.9	56.7
Cheyenne	796	-12.9	2 390	21	434	586	237	111	34	101 035	57.0	43.0	71.2	26.4	0.0	26.4

1. Denver County included with Adams County.

STATE County	Value of Residential Construction Authorized by Building Permits, 1999		Wholesale Trade, 1997				Retail Trade[1], 1997				Real Estate and Rental and Leasing, 1997			
	New Construction ($1,000)	Number of Housing Units	Number of Establishments	Number of Employees	Sales (mil dol)	Annual Payroll (mil dol)	Number of Establishments	Number of Employees	Sales (mil dol)	Annual Payroll (mil dol)	Number of Establishments	Number of Employees	Receipts (mil dol)	Annual Payroll (mil dol)
	133	134	135	136	137	138	139	140	141	142	143	144	145	146
CALIFORNIA—Cont'd														
Butte	117 290	1 028	179	1 792	637.9	56.9	777	9 004	1 502.6	154.0	212	1 012	80.5	13.4
Calaveras	55 098	302	27	D	D	D	136	862	135.5	14.0	36	100	10.4	1.6
Colusa	6 148	48	25	318	152.3	8.3	67	545	121.7	10.8	19	49	4.8	0.7
Contra Costa	852 256	4 413	1 159	11 092	14 968.0	518.5	2 705	37 550	7 376.8	752.8	1 056	6 172	972.6	172.2
Del Norte	3 630	34	15	D	D	D	88	982	123.1	12.5	20	58	4.9	0.8
El Dorado	272 413	1 372	108	684	249.7	19.3	546	4 894	926.8	91.1	180	781	68.6	9.9
Fresno	364 305	2 971	971	13 004	5 845.2	415.5	2 492	30 231	5 574.6	548.9	593	3 496	376.5	67.3
Glenn	4 967	51	36	298	125.8	8.6	79	720	98.9	10.5	18	149	7.1	1.4
Humboldt	40 332	497	128	1 306	493.6	37.1	668	6 816	1 024.0	108.7	141	494	47.1	7.9
Imperial	38 499	339	189	1 951	673.7	41.0	521	5 991	989.4	98.8	86	408	33.2	6.5
Inyo	3 729	18	24	D	D	D	145	1 092	171.1	17.8	18	59	4.3	1.1
Kern	335 609	3 118	612	7 930	4 313.9	256.4	1 918	22 792	4 224.4	412.1	419	2 479	220.5	43.8
Kings	60 018	539	60	623	411.6	15.8	316	3 690	629.3	60.0	66	235	20.8	3.3
Lake	28 245	182	39	D	D	D	197	1 954	309.3	30.7	41	89	7.0	1.0
Lassen	12 341	138	11	D	D	D	106	1 032	159.2	15.5	16	56	3.9	0.6
Los Angeles	1 900 284	14 060	21 474	259 217	177 244.9	9 450.4	27 577	343 656	69 534.2	6 769.0	10 932	76 904	13 608.6	2 256.3
Madera	47 722	607	87	623	265.8	18.8	313	3 173	527.3	53.0	60	217	22.3	3.8
Marin	184 274	818	570	4 167	2 414.8	170.4	1 291	14 793	2 775.7	322.0	537	2 978	556.7	91.0
Mariposa	10 716	74	7	D	D	D	78	397	57.4	6.3	14	68	4.3	1.0
Mendocino	21 349	266	108	1 095	308.7	27.0	490	4 572	711.4	76.8	109	445	35.7	5.8
Merced	122 639	1 001	117	1 333	699.9	36.4	551	6 122	1 102.1	108.0	121	461	46.0	5.7
Modoc	0	0	11	D	D	D	46	256	34.3	3.5	6	D	D	D
Mono	34 382	207	2	D	D	D	79	683	84.0	10.2	37	269	13.8	3.4
Monterey	335 614	2 058	473	7 530	4 747.4	267.9	1 558	16 413	3 035.9	327.9	386	1 837	236.4	38.9
Napa	150 050	713	153	1 296	533.0	46.4	525	5 292	952.6	102.8	153	1 068	84.2	15.7
Nevada	119 950	817	90	453	118.7	13.1	430	3 914	654.8	73.7	115	449	57.7	8.2
Orange	2 013 489	12 239	7 029	103 113	94 403.4	3 999.6	9 084	126 575	26 172.8	2 572.0	3 537	29 156	4 714.8	939.1
Placer	784 768	4 899	283	3 888	1 792.6	147.7	875	11 769	2 666.6	254.7	302	2 158	204.0	40.7
Plumas	10 243	101	12	D	D	D	119	829	127.5	16.1	26	60	4.8	0.9
Riverside	2 329 165	14 154	1 200	12 649	6 715.6	416.6	4 030	54 433	10 609.0	1 028.9	1 190	6 164	698.6	126.9
Sacramento	896 084	6 748	1 287	18 090	8 555.8	626.7	3 587	51 962	9 502.3	990.0	1 180	8 334	909.1	185.4
San Benito	52 215	422	43	752	211.1	21.6	117	1 731	276.8	30.9	34	95	14.5	1.4
San Bernardino	1 166 691	6 767	1 747	24 756	14 254.1	805.8	4 372	60 940	11 342.8	1 100.5	1 134	6 103	753.5	126.0
San Diego	2 668 332	16 295	4 159	53 589	26 543.9	2 273.7	9 109	119 022	22 215.3	2 241.1	3 742	23 069	3 250.0	573.9
San Francisco	342 967	2 694	1 900	17 677	12 219.1	779.8	3 841	39 693	6 795.0	830.6	1 627	14 492	2 721.2	472.9
San Joaquin	595 595	4 203	560	9 751	7 651.7	319.3	1 594	19 957	3 679.6	364.7	436	2 602	257.7	52.3
San Luis Obispo	244 914	1 648	244	1 904	561.5	46.8	1 132	10 917	1 780.7	182.4	319	1 243	149.7	20.9
San Mateo	231 101	880	1 687	21 640	14 662.6	1 088.3	2 285	33 757	7 335.4	735.4	1 003	8 940	1 496.0	270.8
Santa Barbara	166 817	810	469	4 282	1 636.0	137.5	1 653	19 187	3 183.5	354.0	558	2 733	708.8	71.0
Santa Clara	993 444	6 880	3 468	66 542	68 095.4	3 891.8	5 278	79 921	16 673.6	1 696.7	1 968	12 585	2 456.4	372.8
Santa Cruz	94 804	465	342	4 472	1 541.8	140.3	986	11 794	1 970.2	215.5	314	1 649	166.5	27.1
Shasta	103 983	804	217	1 786	566.6	51.9	713	8 113	1 354.5	140.3	199	878	80.3	14.6
Sierra	1 793	17	NA	NA	NA	NA	13	64	8.8	0.9	1	D	D	D
Siskiyou	22 353	150	35	D	D	D	233	1 770	256.1	25.4	42	89	6.6	1.0
Solano	295 707	2 011	262	3 909	2 170.1	145.7	1 116	15 046	2 789.4	281.0	321	1 344	164.9	24.5
Sonoma	408 199	3 036	619	7 430	3 069.7	259.4	1 808	22 190	4 146.2	443.7	576	2 394	329.3	48.5
Stanislaus	282 965	2 183	417	5 118	2 264.4	159.1	1 368	17 706	3 282.2	319.2	340	2 033	244.5	42.4
Sutter	27 562	180	90	D	D	D	291	3 604	606.7	61.1	85	488	40.7	6.1
Tehama	19 055	156	40	D	D	D	176	1 953	360.6	33.0	42	149	9.6	1.5
Trinity	4 786	40	6	D	D	D	54	334	38.9	4.6	7	18	0.6	0.2
Tulare	163 030	1 636	343	5 120	2 527.7	135.1	1 107	12 742	2 135.7	211.8	206	809	97.7	12.6
Tuolumne	22 735	198	37	280	96.2	8.8	228	2 343	341.4	38.0	64	198	18.0	2.6
Ventura	866 340	4 418	1 088	13 811	10 402.7	522.6	2 348	30 831	6 476.6	608.7	672	3 254	409.0	73.4
Yolo	183 892	1 456	282	7 829	5 000.2	257.8	458	5 776	1 026.7	110.6	189	1 305	177.9	30.0
Yuba	17 431	219	40	D	D	D	155	1 525	244.6	25.6	33	104	11.2	1.3
COLORADO	6 035 973	49 313	7 383	88 364	60 310.4	3 282.0	18 299	225 647	40 536.0	4 163.3	6 663	38 224	4 853.5	883.8
Adams	355 782	3 730	732	12 884	7 044.5	443.5	952	14 489	2 859.1	308.8	323	2 677	289.6	69.1
Alamosa	5 538	78	30	225	68.8	5.3	97	1 090	167.2	17.2	18	48	4.6	0.8
Arapahoe	616 155	5 799	1 156	15 912	22 395.3	813.5	2 003	30 860	6 353.6	603.5	859	5 109	766.1	157.8
Archuleta	49 610	271	9	13	10.2	0.6	67	370	54.6	5.9	25	109	19.0	4.1
Baca	475	10	11	51	24.1	1.0	27	127	18.6	1.7	3	6	0.3	0.1
Bent	437	14	2	D	D	D	16	94	11.6	1.1	3	6	0.3	0.1
Boulder	368 516	2 992	539	5 558	3 906.0	234.9	1 275	17 269	2 915.0	309.9	486	2 189	287.9	49.2
Chaffee	18 568	218	25	130	37.4	2.1	112	928	124.4	14.0	31	124	10.0	1.7
Cheyenne	220	3	5	43	39.7	1.1	13	68	11.4	0.9	2	D	D	D

1. Establishments with payroll.

Table B. States and Counties — Professional, Manufacturing, and Accommodation and Foodservices

STATE County	Professional, Scientific, and Technical Services[1], 1997 Number of Establishments	Number of Employees	Receipts (mil dol)	Annual Payroll (mil dol)	Manufacturing, 1997 Number of Establishments	Number of Employees	Receipts (mil dol)	Annual Payroll (mil dol)	Accommodation and Foodservices, 1997 Number of Establishments	Number of Employees	Sales (mil dol)	Annual Payroll (mil dol)
	147	148	149	150	151	152	153	154	155	156	157	158
CALIFORNIA—Cont'd												
Butte	308	1 513	130.7	45.0	232	4 944	771.6	128.4	380	5 920	156.2	43.3
Calaveras	55	177	13.1	4.5	NA	NA	NA	NA	95	753	21.4	5.7
Colusa	19	37	2.6	0.6	20	651	265.8	20.8	43	508	17.1	4.9
Contra Costa	2 678	19 116	2 487.5	1 020.1	723	19 366	11 644.8	889.0	1 515	23 374	902.1	238.4
Del Norte	33	88	6.0	1.8	NA	NA	NA	NA	82	710	24.1	5.8
El Dorado	262	1 478	165.9	74.4	144	1 775	287.9	56.4	410	5 539	209.0	55.3
Fresno	1 184	11 156	584.1	234.3	696	27 552	5 667.6	704.3	1 256	19 886	631.9	169.6
Glenn	32	108	6.2	1.6	29	946	290.6	29.2	50	549	17.8	4.3
Humboldt	205	981	65.9	23.5	178	5 540	1 041.9	161.4	371	4 312	134.2	36.4
Imperial	113	519	46.2	15.8	61	1 481	241.6	40.6	238	2 723	89.3	23.0
Inyo	32	101	5.8	2.0	NA	NA	NA	NA	100	1 248	54.4	13.5
Kern	753	6 296	525.7	224.6	390	14 306	2 824.6	379.2	1 013	14 724	493.2	129.1
Kings	74	358	26.8	8.6	65	2 796	748.7	90.6	156	2 037	65.1	16.2
Lake	58	159	10.6	3.4	NA	NA	NA	NA	132	978	29.1	6.9
Lassen	22	89	4.9	1.5	NA	NA	NA	NA	68	733	25.8	7.0
Los Angeles	22 194	346 290	31 678.8	12 767.4	17 915	622 302	106 706.4	20 311.3	15 718	267 157	11 074.3	2 991.3
Madera	81	364	42.3	10.7	94	3 913	952.3	120.8	162	2 136	73.0	18.7
Marin	1 495	7 487	881.8	344.4	341	4 605	656.2	160.0	680	10 183	414.7	119.8
Mariposa	19	32	2.9	0.9	NA	NA	NA	NA	56	1 112	80.9	14.8
Mendocino	169	477	33.7	11.6	160	4 287	769.3	124.1	321	3 626	124.6	33.4
Merced	138	668	41.0	15.8	123	8 381	2 431.5	198.2	269	3 265	108.4	27.2
Modoc	6	23	0.9	0.3	NA	NA	NA	NA	27	178	4.9	1.1
Mono	26	115	10.0	3.7	NA	NA	NA	NA	133	3 192	113.3	35.1
Monterey	694	2 998	293.1	109.2	302	7 070	1 329.4	223.7	905	16 869	835.3	226.0
Napa	268	1 752	301.7	132.2	277	8 466	2 139.7	320.7	347	6 250	287.1	80.3
Nevada	220	724	60.3	21.4	174	2 311	372.9	74.1	229	3 968	117.5	33.3
Orange	8 838	75 635	9 728.8	3 540.6	5 767	215 936	39 134.1	7 643.6	5 397	105 298	4 241.7	1 133.2
Placer	526	2 488	260.0	95.9	260	9 244	3 808.4	403.4	546	10 083	334.1	94.0
Plumas	44	102	7.3	1.9	23	643	176.7	21.9	116	512	23.5	5.6
Riverside	1 642	8 798	904.9	277.4	1 420	46 134	7 736.0	1 329.1	2 159	41 940	1 619.4	447.9
Sacramento	2 731	21 959	2 343.5	892.2	910	30 493	8 939.6	1 017.0	2 185	36 413	1 195.3	320.1
San Benito	51	151	13.8	5.2	75	2 160	365.3	64.2	80	962	30.0	7.9
San Bernardino	1 482	8 262	743.8	259.7	1 992	63 448	11 618.7	1 830.4	2 323	37 291	1 279.7	335.0
San Diego	7 144	59 761	7 072.3	2 725.7	3 407	118 868	22 233.6	4 223.5	5 426	105 069	4 237.9	1 157.4
San Francisco	4 984	58 942	9 016.6	3 517.4	1 247	25 037	3 978.9	642.4	3 258	60 113	3 281.1	955.7
San Joaquin	575	3 531	277.7	111.2	553	24 646	5 879.1	749.6	826	11 413	376.9	96.5
San Luis Obispo	529	2 292	212.2	76.7	323	6 322	1 156.3	182.3	674	10 534	382.5	101.7
San Mateo	2 370	21 418	3 235.2	1 313.0	1 019	34 438	6 690.1	1 649.6	1 495	27 990	1 379.0	385.8
Santa Barbara	981	6 344	711.2	270.6	502	14 985	2 770.4	584.2	952	17 195	633.1	177.1
Santa Clara	6 338	71 612	10 440.6	4 424.1	3 464	249 947	72 528.3	13 094.0	3 495	60 330	2 590.7	677.7
Santa Cruz	678	3 073	384.1	132.1	387	10 011	2 135.0	315.2	591	8 223	305.5	80.8
Shasta	304	1 636	127.0	51.6	177	3 526	635.0	118.7	402	5 070	161.7	41.7
Sierra	4	D	D	D	NA	NA	NA	NA	22	86	5.4	1.2
Siskiyou	65	168	12.0	3.0	41	1 016	207.3	30.1	160	1 396	46.9	12.4
Solano	391	2 149	179.3	66.2	277	9 175	3 496.4	331.0	568	8 747	291.1	73.8
Sonoma	1 171	5 682	565.8	239.1	793	24 209	5 119.8	968.8	1 005	13 993	490.2	132.2
Stanislaus	478	2 974	232.5	81.3	435	25 056	6 886.6	823.1	676	9 877	312.7	80.4
Sutter	102	436	26.6	10.4	70	1 589	354.0	49.3	102	1 443	44.9	12.8
Tehama	52	194	17.7	3.8	48	2 228	455.2	62.9	102	1 128	36.7	9.2
Trinity	17	38	1.9	0.6	NA	NA	NA	NA	57	296	11.1	2.5
Tulare	335	1 788	265.6	45.0	282	11 439	3 167.3	314.5	510	7 020	232.3	56.8
Tuolumne	78	240	17.3	5.2	65	880	155.2	22.5	168	1 747	58.4	15.2
Ventura	1 597	10 829	1 229.3	464.9	1 008	33 562	6 163.4	1 136.3	1 200	21 879	775.3	209.4
Yolo	231	1 541	204.1	59.4	175	6 178	1 514.9	212.0	302	4 379	140.1	36.2
Yuba	41	136	10.7	3.9	44	1 203	248.2	26.8	85	940	31.0	9.1
COLORADO	14 315	103 008	12 887.7	4 625.1	5 480	173 069	40 012.8	6 176.8	10 064	195 126	6 705.5	1 937.4
Adams	386	2 568	205.6	86.4	436	13 151	3 045.1	428.4	512	8 990	288.8	79.3
Alamosa	43	157	8.5	3.5	NA	NA	NA	NA	49	938	20.7	5.8
Arapahoe	2 105	19 081	2 225.0	905.6	549	18 852	5 017.3	798.0	914	19 366	683.7	188.7
Archuleta	27	57	5.2	1.6	NA	NA	NA	NA	56	530	15.1	4.4
Baca	3	6	0.3	0.1	NA	NA	NA	NA	7	41	1.3	0.3
Bent	2	D	D	D	NA	NA	NA	NA	8	83	2.2	0.6
Boulder	1 612	15 458	3 081.9	760.2	686	26 225	5 196.3	1 052.1	708	13 824	453.1	131.0
Chaffee	42	178	7.7	2.7	NA	NA	NA	NA	100	969	30.9	8.6
Cheyenne	1	D	D	D	NA	NA	NA	NA	4	D	D	D

1. Firms subject to federal tax.

STATE County	Health Care and Social Assistance[1], 1997				Other Services[1], 1997				Federal funds and grants, fiscal 1999[2] Expenditures (mil dol)			
										Direct payments for individuals[3]		
	Number of Establishments	Number of Employees	Receipts (mil dol)	Annual Payroll (mil dol)	Number of Establishments	Number of Employees	Receipts (mil dol)	Annual Payroll (mil dol)	Total	Social Security and government retirement	Medicare	Food stamps and Supplemental Security Income
	159	160	161	162	163	164	165	166	167	168	169	170
CALIFORNIA—Cont'd												
Butte	553	5 261	299.4	114.3	261	1 454	147.1	25.3	935.2	421.3	195.2	44.9
Calaveras	57	435	22.4	9.5	41	112	22.6	3.2	185.7	100.6	39.7	4.5
Colusa	23	132	7.5	2.6	24	109	6.5	1.8	120.2	28.4	16.0	2.1
Contra Costa	2 034	18 842	1 446.1	631.4	1 201	7 107	526.0	157.5	3 329.3	1 420.9	675.8	119.5
Del Norte	43	369	23.3	7.8	20	56	6.0	1.3	120.2	50.4	21.2	8.9
El Dorado	314	1 781	127.5	47.2	174	692	53.4	13.1	522.5	278.1	119.0	12.3
Fresno	1 614	15 504	1 103.7	463.9	947	6 026	458.9	120.0	3 028.3	984.8	396.5	208.2
Glenn	28	236	11.4	4.3	22	68	6.1	1.2	154.7	44.2	22.4	4.1
Humboldt	325	3 003	174.8	68.8	187	828	57.9	14.7	591.9	228.2	98.2	28.5
Imperial	172	1 665	103.7	40.8	107	506	34.5	9.4	585.1	171.0	92.6	34.6
Inyo	46	333	18.5	8.1	33	116	9.9	2.3	259.8	47.7	19.2	2.5
Kern	938	9 631	755.0	278.5	694	4 192	348.6	92.2	3 150.3	913.6	452.9	139.9
Kings	142	1 544	99.7	40.9	88	331	25.4	5.8	631.7	141.1	57.9	19.9
Lake	98	759	54.0	18.8	52	150	11.0	2.6	332.5	156.3	87.4	13.9
Lassen	43	348	19.3	5.8	28	78	5.7	1.1	145.6	54.3	18.0	5.0
Los Angeles	20 278	196 543	15 709.6	6 162.8	13 134	86 614	6 086.4	1 734.3	43 465.6	10 026.1	7 475.1	2 066.9
Madera	155	1 238	69.8	26.0	95	386	27.8	7.0	417.7	170.3	77.9	18.1
Marin	841	7 043	494.2	219.1	496	2 608	208.2	62.8	859.1	446.7	189.4	17.0
Mariposa	17	148	7.2	2.6	7	57	6.0	1.6	118.8	40.0	15.5	2.0
Mendocino	202	1 310	78.1	30.2	113	429	32.6	7.3	465.2	162.1	75.1	17.0
Merced	323	2 668	167.8	64.2	171	813	49.2	14.3	734.8	281.5	111.4	52.8
Modoc	7	59	2.5	1.2	8	D	D	D	58.4	20.6	8.0	1.6
Mono	15	46	5.7	2.4	10	50	3.3	0.8	36.1	10.7	3.3	0.4
Monterey	708	5 613	430.5	177.7	445	2 416	172.1	48.0	1 670.5	635.3	242.6	44.3
Napa	357	3 272	229.2	90.5	165	916	60.2	17.1	518.0	258.2	138.2	10.4
Nevada	252	1 691	100.9	37.5	107	409	33.0	8.8	450.0	208.1	76.6	7.4
Orange	6 986	66 269	5 571.4	2 170.8	4 249	28 174	2 101.9	600.0	9 292.5	3 335.9	1 833.9	298.5
Placer	585	4 845	380.4	142.6	305	3 164	239.5	83.7	836.2	490.7	134.5	18.4
Plumas	44	269	12.6	5.1	26	99	7.9	1.9	110.9	51.4	21.3	2.6
Riverside	2 307	24 783	1 905.2	707.4	1 499	9 119	620.7	173.1	5 154.1	2 425.2	1 203.0	198.2
Sacramento	2 383	24 874	2 014.7	870.2	1 549	10 484	731.1	214.1	12 388.6	2 446.2	794.5	293.4
San Benito	64	389	20.1	7.7	46	189	17.8	3.1	142.5	51.2	22.1	4.1
San Bernardino	2 314	26 710	2 051.5	798.4	1 720	12 182	804.8	232.9	5 898.9	2 107.8	1 028.0	320.0
San Diego	5 508	53 541	4 232.7	1 656.5	3 811	24 273	1 648.1	466.0	17 857.4	4 914.6	2 013.7	409.8
San Francisco	2 260	14 360	1 209.7	478.5	1 477	8 794	634.9	179.0	5 673.6	1 174.3	759.2	233.2
San Joaquin	949	9 252	664.0	273.5	690	3 838	265.3	74.2	2 126.5	797.5	349.0	137.9
San Luis Obispo	599	5 083	375.3	161.3	294	1 446	96.2	25.9	882.9	451.4	180.1	23.2
San Mateo	1 597	14 194	1 166.2	495.9	1 178	7 290	582.9	172.6	2 612.7	1 106.3	476.4	55.5
Santa Barbara	934	6 609	516.9	199.8	536	3 054	192.1	57.4	2 097.6	689.2	266.4	44.1
Santa Clara	3 742	38 283	3 032.2	1 240.9	2 471	16 850	1 352.9	400.5	8 637.6	1 903.9	881.6	236.4
Santa Cruz	631	4 739	309.8	121.7	330	1 614	112.1	31.3	808.1	325.7	167.1	26.4
Shasta	487	5 441	387.9	156.8	241	1 289	86.4	22.8	845.6	375.9	153.9	41.3
Sierra	2	D	D	D	NA	NA	NA	NA	22.7	8.2	4.0	0.2
Siskiyou	86	668	32.0	13.0	57	146	11.7	2.7	275.3	116.2	43.1	9.7
Solano	628	6 046	480.3	199.2	446	3 104	210.4	70.1	1 885.2	777.4	173.1	56.8
Sonoma	1 241	11 357	766.6	319.5	676	3 604	252.0	74.0	1 630.5	781.4	350.1	44.4
Stanislaus	805	9 346	656.1	253.2	538	3 154	210.7	58.7	1 539.1	607.0	297.2	93.9
Sutter	199	1 999	209.0	61.5	105	589	36.9	10.3	333.5	145.6	54.8	13.7
Tehama	89	705	37.3	14.5	62	315	21.3	5.5	243.0	111.0	46.2	11.7
Trinity	18	93	4.5	1.7	18	60	4.0	0.8	79.2	34.9	13.1	1.8
Tulare	588	5 102	334.0	127.8	308	1 544	115.2	28.7	1 317.8	427.2	209.9	85.8
Tuolumne	119	648	47.4	19.8	56	257	16.8	4.4	246.1	134.8	49.2	8.0
Ventura	1 591	13 110	1 086.6	413.1	875	5 577	442.5	126.7	3 190.8	1 081.6	476.1	67.6
Yolo	267	2 432	136.7	58.6	209	1 141	92.3	25.4	798.0	203.3	88.1	24.4
Yuba	53	703	39.1	17.5	43	232	17.0	4.0	457.2	115.8	47.2	20.5
COLORADO	8 611	85 370	5 790.8	2 538.1	6 793	39 363	2 571.1	770.0	21 755.4	6 633.3	2 103.7	388.2
Adams	377	4 049	262.0	117.3	505	3 508	240.0	72.5	1 126.3	453.2	182.1	33.0
Alamosa	27	213	15.8	6.3	34	168	7.6	2.2	63.1	18.7	6.6	3.1
Arapahoe	1 244	15 685	1 250.8	511.9	851	5 400	354.3	110.7	1 978.7	734.7	180.7	30.0
Archuleta	13	34	2.3	0.7	8	36	1.4	0.4	28.0	17.9	2.5	0.7
Baca	4	17	0.6	0.1	13	30	2.2	0.5	47.5	10.6	4.3	0.6
Bent	6	22	0.8	0.2	1	D	D	D	50.7	16.4	3.6	1.5
Boulder	715	6 087	405.5	170.7	482	2 945	192.2	60.9	1 348.3	354.2	117.6	15.6
Chaffee	28	290	11.4	5.2	28	90	6.4	1.3	61.7	36.9	9.4	1.3
Cheyenne	1	D	D	D	3	13	0.8	0.2	25.9	4.0	2.9	0.1

1. Firms subject to federal tax.   2. October 1, 1998 to September 30, 1999.   3. State totals may include programs not allocated by county.

Table B. States and Counties — Federal Funds and Local Government Finances

STATE County	Federal funds and grants, fiscal 1999[1] (cont'd)							Local government finances, 1997				
	Expenditures (mil dol) (cont'd)							General revenue				
	Procurement contract awards		Grants[2]							Taxes		
											Per capita[3] (dollars)	
	Salaries and wages	Defense	Other	Medicaid and other health-related	Nutrition and family welfare	Education	Other	Total (mil dol)	Intergovern-mental (mil dol)	Total (mil dol)	Total	Property
	171	172	173	174	175	176	177	178	179	180	181	182
CALIFORNIA—Cont'd												
Butte	26.9	2.4	18.9	99.7	38.6	11.4	25.0	568.4	340.3	112.7	580	416
Calaveras	5.6	5.9	1.8	9.9	6.2	3.4	4.8	102.5	52.1	31.4	788	696
Colusa	2.9	0.8	3.0	7.1	4.6	0.9	9.0	72.1	37.4	16.7	891	727
Contra Costa	330.6	104.1	86.2	284.3	123.1	31.6	95.6	3 041.2	1 150.9	858.2	954	714
Del Norte	6.5	0.0	2.0	10.8	6.6	1.4	11.9	88.1	58.0	13.5	476	347
El Dorado	30.6	3.6	11.6	23.3	17.7	5.0	16.9	454.4	206.7	126.7	814	661
Fresno	395.7	9.7	86.5	373.8	229.5	72.3	133.1	2 675.7	1 509.5	482.9	640	661
Glenn	11.4	3.9	4.5	10.5	6.4	1.8	7.8	99.2	57.8	16.7	632	501
Humboldt	44.7	13.2	11.0	61.6	32.7	11.2	31.6	377.2	231.6	81.9	664	506
Imperial	87.4	16.9	10.5	74.0	36.5	17.9	22.7	519.5	281.7	81.0	564	422
Inyo	12.3	132.6	6.1	9.9	4.5	2.8	21.8	101.1	32.0	34.0	1 857	1 243
Kern	651.1	267.5	63.5	264.7	144.8	45.1	121.9	2 258.4	1 111.7	475.7	757	618
Kings	205.3	65.2	1.9	48.0	30.1	11.9	16.6	325.1	203.7	53.7	465	334
Lake	7.2	1.6	3.3	34.5	12.8	3.1	11.0	170.7	87.5	35.9	649	544
Lassen	30.1	10.3	4.3	12.8	5.6	1.9	0.5	95.0	63.6	17.7	522	427
Los Angeles	2 959.5	7 329.3	2 757.9	5 062.7	2 440.9	632.2	2 108.6	33 598.5	18 386.9	8 143.3	890	573
Madera	12.4	0.1	10.9	53.9	23.7	6.7	22.7	295.4	170.8	64.8	567	457
Marin	58.5	10.4	30.2	52.8	15.8	5.4	19.2	673.8	220.0	287.2	1 218	923
Mariposa	20.4	22.8	1.7	4.0	3.6	0.6	7.1	53.9	25.5	16.4	1 041	624
Mendocino	14.6	1.3	51.6	48.0	34.8	9.6	46.2	313.8	151.2	72.7	863	667
Merced	21.9	10.7	16.3	94.9	62.5	17.1	30.4	764.1	458.6	102.0	520	413
Modoc	10.1	0.0	3.1	4.7	3.3	1.3	2.0	51.5	28.6	7.6	748	648
Mono	11.7	5.1	1.1	1.2	1.3	0.6	0.6	59.3	16.9	26.8	2 547	1 794
Monterey	376.2	77.0	15.5	106.6	68.1	23.3	66.2	1 447.7	558.4	319.6	883	585
Napa	15.7	2.1	4.0	38.4	18.7	4.4	23.8	325.9	138.7	130.8	1 097	821
Nevada	17.6	42.8	13.1	20.2	8.3	2.4	51.4	263.4	93.2	73.1	807	667
Orange	709.3	1 149.1	541.8	599.5	261.8	104.6	342.2	7 098.7	2 844.4	2 392.0	895	637
Placer	40.5	14.7	15.6	54.3	22.6	5.4	23.1	710.8	253.5	240.0	1 084	778
Plumas	13.0	0.3	6.2	7.1	5.2	1.6	1.3	98.0	40.5	20.4	974	834
Riverside	342.5	91.7	67.8	359.1	210.8	66.5	133.1	4 524.7	2 359.5	1 073.4	741	549
Sacramento	683.1	752.5	228.5	948.1	2 541.7	942.7	2 533.7	3 850.7	1 849.5	882.2	784	512
San Benito	6.4	23.6	7.1	9.9	6.8	2.5	6.7	245.9	68.3	42.2	887	627
San Bernardino	825.6	352.6	103.9	466.3	305.6	93.9	227.4	5 012.4	2 909.5	1 086.7	673	492
San Diego	4 797.3	2 409.3	680.4	1 338.9	441.6	173.5	497.0	8 204.5	3 812.5	2 084.2	766	544
San Francisco	1 024.9	217.9	283.0	1 122.6	124.7	40.2	497.4	4 194.8	1 591.1	1 298.5	1 773	927
San Joaquin	152.7	35.7	51.0	275.7	145.4	31.3	83.8	1 709.9	922.8	354.1	653	458
San Luis Obispo	37.9	7.6	7.8	64.2	36.0	8.1	48.5	676.0	233.4	248.9	1 067	849
San Mateo	289.8	137.0	112.4	217.5	47.3	20.4	126.0	2 114.5	623.0	870.7	1 255	872
Santa Barbara	276.9	430.2	53.1	120.7	48.6	21.7	120.6	1 210.2	497.5	347.8	891	672
Santa Clara	615.8	2 770.8	776.3	683.3	203.1	67.4	392.5	5 453.7	2 104.5	2 060.5	1 281	826
Santa Cruz	29.0	9.6	26.9	93.0	31.5	15.8	63.7	804.9	339.1	228.5	950	629
Shasta	58.6	3.8	23.1	75.1	42.5	8.8	53.6	535.3	281.8	115.6	709	548
Sierra	2.7	0.0	0.7	2.2	0.6	0.1	4.1	27.0	13.0	4.7	1 363	1 214
Siskiyou	27.4	0.7	7.8	22.6	10.9	3.1	27.5	155.6	104.0	26.8	604	467
Solano	420.5	194.5	22.9	97.4	48.0	17.5	49.5	1 155.2	600.9	277.3	748	517
Sonoma	116.3	15.9	31.1	133.7	54.5	15.8	64.7	1 276.7	511.5	384.6	897	665
Stanislaus	60.5	2.4	72.6	200.1	107.3	23.7	36.5	1 342.0	740.0	254.6	604	412
Sutter	9.3	1.8	3.0	27.4	15.0	4.3	10.2	212.9	116.9	49.4	635	492
Tehama	10.8	0.0	4.9	23.2	13.7	5.9	6.4	147.6	94.4	30.6	566	438
Trinity	7.2	0.1	2.2	4.6	3.3	1.0	10.7	63.9	36.5	6.5	490	416
Tulare	50.6	5.1	28.8	213.1	111.2	32.0	70.7	1 468.0	786.8	190.2	539	364
Tuolumne	17.3	1.4	6.0	13.8	8.0	1.1	4.3	152.5	63.3	37.7	706	570
Ventura	691.2	390.8	46.9	164.9	84.4	28.9	134.0	2 111.5	858.6	628.3	865	668
Yolo	140.1	9.6	39.3	125.8	26.2	9.5	84.2	445.1	218.9	121.8	797	490
Yuba	152.6	6.1	5.3	47.1	22.7	8.8	6.4	193.2	130.6	38.0	617	524
COLORADO	3 499.1	2 443.1	1 999.4	1 305.9	576.9	296.9	1 266.0	X	X	X	X	X
Adams	165.8	86.3	34.0	74.9	35.9	14.5	21.0	774.2	274.9	329.1	1 041	644
Alamosa	6.8	0.3	2.3	13.8	4.3	2.2	1.6	43.6	22.9	12.7	883	530
Arapahoe	174.9	446.9	176.5	151.6	23.6	13.8	32.8	1 242.0	356.3	615.4	1 329	924
Archuleta	2.3	0.0	0.5	1.9	0.7	0.3	0.4	29.8	7.4	12.8	1 503	967
Baca	1.5	0.0	0.4	2.6	0.7	0.2	0.0	18.8	7.8	4.9	1 122	1 003
Bent	15.6	1.6	0.3	3.9	1.3	0.3	3.2	22.5	13.7	3.9	707	666
Boulder	178.2	77.8	262.9	64.5	14.8	10.3	237.9	657.8	156.2	368.1	1 407	666
Chaffee	4.3	0.1	1.1	5.3	2.1	0.4	0.3	42.8	11.1	14.9	994	893
Cheyenne	0.7	0.0	0.2	0.9	0.3	0.1	0.1	14.0	3.9	4.5	1 974	1 828

1. October 1, 1998 to September 30, 1999.   2. State totals may include programs not allocated by county.   3. Based on the resident population estimated as of July 1 of the year shown.

Table B. States and Counties — Local Government Finances, Government Employment, and Elections

STATE County	Total (mil dol)	Per capita[1] (dollars)	Educa-tion	Health and hospitals	Police protec-tion	Public welfare	High-ways	Total (mil dol)	Per capita[1] (dollars)	Federal civilian	Federal military	State and local	Demo-cratic	Republi-can	All other
	183	184	185	186	187	188	189	190	191	192	193	194	195	196	197
CALIFORNIA—Cont'd															
Butte	588.4	3 031	43.5	4.7	3.8	14.3	2.4	196.0	1 010	555	395	13 192	37.5	54.5	8.0
Calaveras	93.3	2 340	52.7	4.7	3.9	10.6	4.8	72.3	1 814	135	80	2 050	37.6	56.2	6.2
Colusa	68.9	3 666	42.1	4.4	5.6	7.1	5.1	22.7	1 208	71	37	1 262	31.3	65.0	3.7
Contra Costa	3 068.2	3 412	31.4	16.1	5.5	7.1	4.6	3 045.8	3 387	6 389	2 264	36 847	58.9	37.1	4.0
Del Norte	79.8	2 822	38.4	6.6	3.6	13.8	3.5	11.2	394	145	66	2 807	37.6	54.6	7.8
El Dorado	456.2	2 931	39.4	3.9	4.6	6.2	5.0	451.9	2 904	743	317	7 410	36.4	58.3	5.3
Fresno	2 616.2	3 468	40.0	10.8	4.7	13.5	2.8	1 746.2	2 315	9 446	1 597	45 727	43.1	53.2	3.7
Glenn	95.5	3 622	43.7	5.5	3.6	10.3	4.9	33.8	1 283	273	53	1 741	28.7	66.6	4.7
Humboldt	386.9	3 136	40.9	6.2	4.2	13.0	4.5	122.2	990	842	440	9 523	44.4	41.5	14.1
Imperial	510.7	3 554	42.5	19.2	3.9	10.2	3.4	368.8	2 566	1 603	553	11 701	53.6	43.3	3.1
Inyo	105.8	5 783	26.1	37.4	4.1	7.1	3.7	2.7	149	340	36	1 910	34.0	60.4	5.6
Kern	2 097.2	3 336	42.5	10.0	3.9	11.5	2.4	1 046.2	1 664	9 314	5 637	38 818	36.3	60.8	2.9
Kings	318.2	2 755	44.7	7.5	4.3	11.9	2.5	124.5	1 078	1 133	4 927	8 139	39.0	57.8	3.2
Lake	174.2	3 149	36.5	14.0	4.1	14.4	2.7	35.9	649	142	117	3 102	51.3	41.6	7.1
Lassen	91.0	2 681	56.8	2.9	3.3	11.5	5.2	29.9	883	925	90	4 192	28.2	66.9	4.9
Los Angeles	31 842.4	3 482	30.2	8.3	8.9	12.9	2.3	36 250.4	3 964	55 490	21 671	485 747	63.5	32.4	4.1
Madera	294.4	2 576	47.0	6.0	3.6	10.9	3.8	85.5	748	322	230	7 025	34.9	60.8	4.3
Marin	738.4	3 133	32.8	6.6	5.7	5.2	4.3	304.1	1 290	1 037	702	12 348	64.3	28.4	7.3
Mariposa	56.1	3 558	35.1	16.7	5.1	10.6	7.0	9.9	626	586	32	1 019	34.9	58.6	6.5
Mendocino	319.7	3 793	42.8	10.5	3.6	10.5	2.6	176.1	2 089	285	194	5 419	48.4	35.7	15.9
Merced	735.8	3 752	44.4	12.9	3.2	14.4	1.7	149.4	762	447	397	11 662	45.1	51.8	3.1
Modoc	51.6	5 095	37.7	23.7	2.7	8.1	10.0	7.2	714	248	19	1 129	23.1	72.3	4.6
Mono	54.9	5 211	27.9	19.1	6.0	3.3	9.3	27.5	2 614	174	266	1 006	41.0	52.6	6.4
Monterey	1 453.5	4 016	30.8	26.3	4.2	6.0	3.2	538.4	1 488	5 214	6 018	23 061	57.6	37.3	5.1
Napa	328.8	2 757	40.8	5.6	5.8	7.6	3.5	94.8	795	473	239	8 173	54.4	39.9	5.7
Nevada	235.6	2 601	31.9	19.0	5.5	6.4	8.0	154.5	1 705	466	183	4 343	37.3	54.8	7.9
Orange	6 992.4	2 615	37.4	3.2	8.2	7.5	4.5	9 731.1	3 639	13 070	11 475	122 560	40.4	55.8	3.8
Placer	669.7	3 024	39.8	3.8	7.7	6.5	4.9	588.0	2 655	603	470	12 620	36.1	59.3	4.6
Plumas	98.0	4 686	31.9	31.1	3.8	5.8	7.8	6.6	318	381	41	1 926	33.3	61.0	5.7
Riverside	4 415.1	3 050	36.9	8.4	6.1	10.6	4.2	5 007.8	3 459	6 393	3 084	72 301	45.0	51.5	3.5
Sacramento	3 829.3	3 401	36.5	3.6	4.2	13.7	4.3	8 229.3	7 309	15 379	5 132	150 261	49.4	45.4	5.2
San Benito	228.0	4 796	26.8	11.3	2.0	5.7	1.6	122.2	2 569	143	98	2 386	54.3	41.7	4.0
San Bernardino	5 308.7	3 285	38.2	9.1	6.0	12.4	3.0	6 150.8	3 807	10 993	18 034	79 192	47.3	48.8	3.9
San Diego	8 408.2	3 088	34.2	7.9	5.3	9.5	3.2	7 951.5	2 920	42 919	104 495	150 058	45.7	49.7	4.6
San Francisco	4 362.5	5 957	14.1	18.5	6.4	8.3	1.7	5 560.1	7 593	19 698	1 766	70 081	75.6	16.2	8.2
San Joaquin	1 703.2	3 139	38.6	10.0	5.4	13.2	3.4	1 050.8	1 937	4 283	1 141	29 290	47.8	48.9	3.3
San Luis Obispo	664.8	2 850	39.4	8.4	4.8	8.4	4.4	258.3	1 107	656	490	18 268	40.9	52.3	6.8
San Mateo	1 918.8	2 765	29.7	10.5	7.0	7.0	4.5	1 345.0	1 938	3 670	1 552	25 686	64.3	31.0	4.7
Santa Barbara	1 179.2	3 022	36.8	8.6	6.4	7.4	3.8	516.1	1 323	3 944	4 093	26 460	47.4	46.2	6.4
Santa Clara	5 376.2	3 341	32.6	8.6	5.5	9.2	3.5	4 548.0	2 827	12 508	4 466	75 306	60.7	34.5	4.8
Santa Cruz	812.3	3 378	33.2	9.6	5.4	6.7	3.1	432.9	1 800	538	488	16 185	61.5	27.4	11.1
Shasta	520.3	3 189	42.7	6.9	4.7	11.6	4.8	456.1	2 795	1 194	330	10 104	30.3	65.1	4.6
Sierra	24.8	7 213	28.5	31.3	4.9	5.6	10.0	3.5	1 014	86	0	531	29.3	63.5	7.2
Siskiyou	152.4	3 443	46.5	4.1	5.6	10.9	8.3	14.2	321	721	88	3 320	32.0	61.6	6.4
Solano	1 133.1	3 054	35.3	4.6	7.2	10.7	4.4	1 217.8	3 282	4 172	8 157	19 746	57.1	39.2	3.7
Sonoma	1 357.0	3 166	40.4	10.0	5.3	5.9	4.8	947.4	2 210	1 821	1 424	24 012	59.6	32.3	8.1
Stanislaus	1 293.6	3 067	42.7	12.1	4.9	11.6	2.2	1 786.6	4 235	1 241	856	22 055	44.1	52.4	3.5
Sutter	219.7	2 826	39.8	7.2	4.3	7.9	4.6	26.4	340	179	155	3 911	31.7	65.4	2.9
Tehama	145.6	2 697	47.3	7.8	4.7	15.7	4.9	17.8	329	249	108	2 936	31.3	63.7	5.0
Trinity	64.9	4 918	37.8	22.3	2.8	8.1	8.8	20.4	1 549	226	26	1 127	33.4	57.7	8.9
Tulare	1 436.4	4 067	38.3	20.1	3.0	12.0	1.5	565.2	1 600	1 196	713	23 673	36.8	60.2	3.0
Tuolumne	147.0	2 755	33.0	27.4	4.2	8.7	3.7	81.0	1 518	365	107	3 877	39.5	55.6	4.9
Ventura	2 081.2	2 867	37.2	8.8	7.1	6.5	3.7	1 336.7	1 841	8 700	6 883	31 576	47.2	48.2	4.6
Yolo	462.2	3 025	31.9	4.5	5.4	11.7	7.6	253.1	1 657	2 341	320	21 673	55.0	37.6	7.4
Yuba	191.1	3 104	53.8	1.1	3.5	17.6	2.9	123.0	1 998	1 235	3 205	4 376	34.4	61.1	4.5
COLORADO	X	X	X	X	X	X	X	X	X	53 973	42 580	270 700	42.4	50.8	6.9
Adams	712.3	2 254	41.7	0.3	5.8	7.9	6.6	1 298.6	4 109	3 373	1 474	14 830	50.2	44.1	5.7
Alamosa	51.3	3 566	55.7	6.5	4.8	10.7	6.4	15.3	1 064	150	44	1 831	43.4	50.5	6.1
Arapahoe	1 426.5	3 080	41.2	1.4	5.6	3.0	14.6	1 899.4	4 101	2 564	2 367	25 364	43.5	51.5	5.0
Archuleta	25.5	2 990	33.6	21.3	3.1	2.3	13.7	22.6	2 650	49	27	441	30.1	62.8	7.1
Baca	22.1	5 026	32.2	31.5	2.4	11.0	10.0	9.0	2 048	43	13	742	23.3	73.0	3.7
Bent	21.6	3 942	28.9	3.0	2.8	17.4	7.0	14.1	2 580	512	17	469	39.9	55.8	4.3
Boulder	681.5	2 605	38.9	1.0	6.3	3.5	7.7	620.6	2 372	2 649	915	22 832	50.1	36.4	13.4
Chaffee	40.3	2 683	36.9	26.6	3.8	3.8	6.1	20.1	1 338	98	45	1 401	36.4	56.5	7.1
Cheyenne	13.2	5 804	29.8	19.4	2.6	17.3	15.8	0.8	348	20	0	306	17.2	79.0	3.8

1. Based on the resident population estimated as of July 1 of the year shown.

Table B. States and Counties — Land Area and Population

| STATE/ County code | MSA/ PMSA/ NECMA code[1] | County Type[2] | STATE County | Land area[3] (sq km) 1990 | Population and population characteristics, 1999 | | | Race (percent) | | | | | Age (percent) | | | | | |
| | | | | | Total persons | Rank | Per square kilometer | White | Black | Am. Indian, Eskimo, Aleut | Asian and Pacific Islander | Percent Hispanic[4] | Under 5 years | 5 to 17 years | 18 to 24 years | 25 to 34 years | 35 to 44 years | 45 to 54 years |
				1	2	3	4	5	6	7	8	9	10	11	12	13	14	15
			COLORADO—Cont'd															
08 019	...	8	Clear Creek	1 024	9 167	2 496	9.0	98.5	0.3	0.5	0.7	4.1	6.1	19.2	5.6	10.9	23.6	19.0
08 021	...	9	Conejos	3 334	8 077	2 589	2.4	99.0	0.2	0.4	0.4	65.7	8.4	26.1	7.1	9.1	12.5	12.4
08 023	...	9	Costilla	3 178	3 575	2 946	1.1	97.5	0.4	0.6	1.5	80.3	7.6	21.4	7.5	9.1	12.7	14.0
08 025	...	8	Crowley	2 044	4 428	2 875	2.2	90.9	5.8	2.1	1.2	27.7	5.8	17.1	8.7	16.7	17.2	12.7
08 027	...	8	Custer	1 914	3 596	2 941	1.9	98.1	0.0	1.7	0.2	3.6	5.0	20.7	3.6	8.3	15.0	19.9
08 029	...	7	Delta	2 958	27 197	1 455	9.2	98.3	0.5	0.8	0.4	11.3	5.3	19.1	6.1	8.3	13.8	15.8
08 031	2080	0	Denver	397	499 775	107	1 258.9	80.4	15.0	1.4	3.3	27.8	7.4	16.1	9.7	14.7	17.0	13.4
08 033	...	9	Dolores	2 764	1 876	3 070	0.7	96.9	0.0	3.0	0.1	4.0	5.8	20.6	6.3	9.2	13.5	16.4
08 035	2080	1	Douglas	2 176	156 860	329	72.1	97.5	0.8	0.5	1.2	4.0	8.5	22.1	5.6	13.8	22.1	17.6
08 037	...	7	Eagle	4 372	34 950	1 227	8.0	98.5	0.3	0.6	0.6	16.7	8.9	17.9	10.3	19.7	22.3	12.6
08 039	...	8	Elbert	4 794	19 757	1 775	4.1	97.9	0.7	0.8	0.7	2.7	6.4	24.3	5.4	11.2	21.3	17.3
08 041	1720	2	El Paso	5 508	499 994	106	90.8	87.7	7.9	0.9	3.5	11.0	7.6	19.8	11.5	13.7	16.1	14.1
08 043	...	6	Fremont	3 971	44 699	990	11.3	94.3	4.0	1.2	0.5	12.3	4.7	16.5	8.1	13.7	16.8	14.8
08 045	...	7	Garfield	7 634	40 671	1 070	5.3	98.4	0.3	0.8	0.6	6.9	7.5	20.2	8.5	12.9	18.5	14.6
08 047	...	8	Gilpin	388	4 474	2 873	11.5	97.5	0.6	1.3	0.6	4.8	5.8	18.5	4.9	12.7	26.0	18.7
08 049	...	9	Grand	4 791	10 474	2 382	2.2	98.7	0.3	0.4	0.7	3.9	5.9	19.4	8.1	14.0	19.5	14.0
08 051	...	7	Gunnison	8 389	12 576	2 244	1.5	98.0	0.7	0.7	0.6	4.7	6.1	15.2	21.6	12.9	16.9	13.1
08 053	...	9	Hinsdale	2 895	740	3 127	0.3	98.6	0.3	0.7	0.4	1.5	2.7	13.8	4.6	10.1	19.9	16.5
08 055	...	6	Huerfano	4 121	6 802	2 697	1.7	97.9	0.5	1.3	0.2	46.0	5.9	20.6	5.9	8.1	13.2	15.3
08 057	...	9	Jackson	4 178	1 540	3 092	0.4	97.9	0.0	2.0	0.1	8.1	6.2	18.1	7.1	10.3	15.5	17.3
08 059	2080	0	Jefferson	2 000	509 222	104	254.6	96.2	0.8	0.6	2.4	8.5	6.6	18.7	7.9	12.2	18.0	16.9
08 061	...	9	Kiowa	4 587	1 634	3 088	0.4	99.4	0.0	0.6	0.0	3.9	5.4	23.4	4.3	9.4	14.7	15.7
08 063	...	7	Kit Carson	5 597	7 411	2 647	1.3	99.1	0.2	0.4	0.2	8.1	7.0	21.7	5.7	10.4	13.4	15.4
08 065	...	7	Lake	976	6 385	2 744	6.5	98.3	0.3	1.0	0.5	28.5	8.3	20.3	9.9	13.4	17.0	14.6
08 067	...	7	La Plata	4 383	41 148	1 058	9.4	93.8	0.3	5.2	0.7	13.7	6.4	19.3	13.4	10.8	17.5	14.2
08 069	2670	3	Larimer	6 738	236 849	235	35.2	96.6	0.7	0.7	2.0	8.2	6.7	18.7	13.3	12.5	16.8	14.1
08 071	...	7	Las Animas	12 362	14 712	2 087	1.2	98.0	0.2	1.2	0.6	50.2	6.5	19.9	8.2	8.5	14.0	13.9
08 073	...	8	Lincoln	6 698	5 672	2 792	0.8	94.9	3.5	1.2	0.4	8.6	5.5	16.3	8.2	14.0	14.9	15.8
08 075	...	9	Logan	4 762	17 932	1 872	3.8	99.2	0.2	0.3	0.3	9.9	6.0	19.6	9.2	10.0	13.0	14.7
08 077	2995	5	Mesa	8 619	115 147	459	13.4	97.8	0.5	0.8	1.0	10.0	6.3	19.9	8.4	10.1	15.1	14.7
08 079	...	9	Mineral	2 268	727	3 128	0.3	98.9	0.0	1.0	0.1	5.6	7.2	11.8	3.7	11.7	13.1	18.0
08 081	...	7	Moffat	12 283	12 714	2 231	1.0	98.6	0.1	0.8	0.5	7.7	7.5	23.7	6.6	11.5	16.9	15.0
08 083	...	7	Montezuma	5 276	22 672	1 626	4.3	88.8	0.1	10.8	0.4	10.5	7.2	22.6	6.6	9.9	14.5	14.5
08 085	...	7	Montrose	5 804	31 432	1 334	5.4	98.5	0.4	0.6	0.5	13.5	5.9	20.9	5.9	8.8	14.8	16.6
08 087	...	6	Morgan	3 329	25 393	1 517	7.6	98.1	0.5	0.9	0.6	22.1	8.3	22.2	7.9	11.0	13.2	13.6
08 089	...	6	Otero	3 271	20 612	1 735	6.3	97.1	0.8	1.3	0.9	40.2	7.3	22.1	8.1	9.2	13.0	14.0
08 091	...	9	Ouray	1 404	3 475	2 954	2.5	99.2	0.0	0.6	0.1	5.4	4.9	18.6	4.0	8.2	18.0	21.4
08 093	...	8	Park	5 700	14 218	2 119	2.5	98.2	0.7	0.8	0.3	3.6	5.9	20.8	4.1	11.6	22.3	19.0
08 095	...	9	Phillips	1 781	4 226	2 893	2.4	99.6	0.0	0.1	0.3	4.9	5.8	20.0	5.1	9.2	12.8	14.6
08 097	...	7	Pitkin	2 514	13 332	2 188	5.3	97.7	0.4	0.4	1.5	4.4	5.0	11.3	8.8	16.7	25.5	18.7
08 099	...	7	Prowers	4 249	13 781	2 150	3.2	98.5	0.4	0.8	0.3	27.4	7.8	23.5	8.3	10.2	14.3	13.3
08 101	6560	3	Pueblo	6 187	136 987	385	22.1	96.0	2.3	0.9	0.8	41.1	6.8	20.0	8.8	10.3	14.3	13.6
08 103	...	9	Rio Blanco	8 343	6 203	2 756	0.7	98.5	0.2	0.8	0.5	5.0	6.3	22.3	9.4	10.5	15.5	16.2
08 105	...	7	Rio Grande	2 364	11 508	2 307	4.9	98.8	0.1	0.8	0.2	45.5	7.8	22.8	7.3	9.8	13.5	14.1
08 107	...	7	Routt	6 117	17 941	1 871	2.9	99.0	0.1	0.5	0.4	3.3	6.5	18.9	10.3	14.6	23.6	14.6
08 109	...	9	Saguache	8 207	6 176	2 758	0.8	96.4	0.3	3.0	0.4	51.7	8.8	24.8	8.0	11.1	15.4	13.5
08 111	...	9	San Juan	1 003	522	3 135	0.5	99.0	0.2	0.4	0.4	20.7	5.4	24.5	6.3	10.3	21.8	14.6
08 113	...	9	San Miguel	3 332	5 464	2 808	1.6	99.1	0.1	0.4	0.4	3.6	6.4	16.3	9.1	16.1	26.3	16.1
08 115	...	9	Sedgwick	1 420	2 587	3 017	1.8	97.6	0.5	0.5	1.3	10.3	4.2	19.0	5.1	7.7	13.2	14.5
08 117	...	9	Summit	1 575	19 610	1 781	12.5	98.0	0.3	0.6	1.1	3.2	6.9	14.2	13.1	22.1	21.6	12.3
08 119	...	6	Teller	1 443	21 228	1 695	14.7	98.3	0.2	0.9	0.6	3.2	6.7	21.5	5.0	11.4	22.0	17.1
08 121	...	9	Washington	6 530	4 357	2 881	0.7	99.5	0.0	0.3	0.2	3.4	5.6	19.9	5.6	9.0	12.5	15.3
08 123	3060	3	Weld	10 341	165 805	316	16.0	97.5	0.6	0.7	1.2	25.1	7.8	21.2	12.5	11.5	15.2	14.0
08 125	...	7	Yuma	6 128	9 430	2 478	1.5	99.3	0.0	0.5	0.2	3.8	5.9	22.2	5.8	9.3	13.8	15.4
09 000	...	X	CONNECTICUT	12 550	3 282 031	X	261.5	87.8	9.4	0.2	2.6	8.5	6.6	18.6	7.8	13.6	17.2	13.3
09 001	5483	2	Fairfield	1 621	841 334	48	519.0	85.3	11.0	0.2	3.5	11.2	6.6	18.3	6.9	13.2	17.3	14.5
09 003	3283	0	Hartford	1 905	829 671	50	435.5	85.4	11.8	0.2	2.7	11.0	6.6	18.4	7.7	13.7	16.8	12.9
09 005	...	4	Litchfield	2 383	182 399	291	76.5	97.3	1.1	0.2	1.4	1.5	6.5	19.4	6.2	12.6	18.7	14.1
09 007	3283	1	Middlesex	956	151 461	340	158.4	93.3	4.7	0.2	1.7	2.7	6.3	18.1	7.4	13.9	18.7	13.9
09 009	5483	2	New Haven	1 569	793 208	54	505.6	86.1	11.6	0.2	2.1	8.4	6.8	18.5	8.3	13.9	16.8	12.4
09 011	5523	2	New London	1 725	246 049	218	142.6	91.5	5.5	0.6	2.3	4.6	7.0	19.1	8.6	14.6	16.5	12.4
09 013	3283	1	Tolland	1 062	132 668	394	124.9	94.7	2.2	0.2	2.9	2.3	6.5	18.7	11.7	13.5	18.3	13.3
09 015	...	4	Windham	1 328	105 241	493	79.2	97.0	1.3	0.4	1.2	5.6	7.1	21.8	8.4	13.2	16.8	12.6

1. MSA = Metropolitan Statistical Area. PMSA = Primary MSA. NECMA = New England County Metropolitan Area. See Appendix A for explanation of these concepts. See Appendix B for list of metropolitan areas identified by type, with component counties.   2. County typology code from the Economic Research Service of USDA. See Appendix A for definition.   3. Dry land or land partially or temporarily covered by water.   4. Hispanic persons may be of any race.

Table B. States and Counties — **Population and Households**

STATE County	55 to 64 years	65 to 74 years	75 years and over	Percent female	1990	1980	1980–1990	1990–1999	Births	Deaths	Net migration	Number	Percent change, 1980–1990	Persons per house-hold	Female family house-holder[1]	One person
	16	17	18	19	20	21	22	23	24	25	26	27	28	29	30	31
COLORADO—Cont'd																
Clear Creek	9.0	3.8	2.8	47.7	7 619	7 308	4.3	20.3	945	352	982	3 153	11.2	2.40	6.2	27.5
Conejos	10.5	7.4	6.6	50.0	7 453	7 794	-4.4	8.4	1 135	646	160	2 492	5.8	2.98	10.6	21.6
Costilla	11.9	8.2	7.6	50.1	3 190	3 071	3.9	12.1	418	335	309	1 192	16.3	2.67	11.9	23.9
Crowley	10.2	5.4	6.3	38.5	3 946	2 988	32.1	12.2	416	386	470	1 165	3.1	2.50	9.0	27.0
Custer	15.1	6.8	5.5	49.3	1 926	1 528	26.0	86.7	265	142	1 538	770	34.6	2.50	5.5	23.4
Delta	12.8	9.1	9.6	49.8	20 980	21 225	-1.2	29.6	2 704	2 728	6 297	8 372	5.7	2.45	6.7	24.5
Denver	9.7	5.9	6.0	51.3	467 549	492 686	-5.1	6.9	83 705	44 498	-6 213	210 952	-0.3	2.17	11.5	40.4
Dolores	14.0	7.8	6.4	49.0	1 504	1 658	-9.3	24.7	174	132	332	581	-0.5	2.59	3.1	24.3
Douglas	6.8	2.1	1.2	49.4	60 391	25 153	140.1	159.7	16 834	2 339	80 842	20 844	165.3	2.89	5.5	12.4
Eagle	4.9	2.2	1.3	47.3	21 928	13 320	64.6	59.4	4 618	527	8 945	8 354	59.9	2.61	7.0	22.0
Elbert	8.6	2.7	2.8	49.6	9 646	6 850	40.8	104.8	1 568	570	9 038	3 377	48.3	2.84	4.9	14.7
El Paso	8.4	5.1	3.7	50.3	397 014	309 424	28.3	25.9	71 062	22 983	45 852	146 965	36.3	2.60	9.8	23.7
Fremont	11.3	6.7	7.4	44.6	32 273	28 676	12.5	38.5	3 750	4 089	12 892	11 713	16.5	2.42	9.5	26.4
Garfield	8.7	4.8	4.4	49.0	29 974	22 514	33.1	35.7	4 976	2 087	7 816	11 266	38.6	2.60	7.6	22.3
Gilpin	9.1	2.5	1.8	46.5	3 070	2 441	25.8	45.7	362	141	1 172	1 308	36.5	2.35	5.4	27.2
Grand	10.7	5.1	3.4	46.8	7 966	7 475	6.6	31.5	1 004	364	1 878	3 168	13.3	2.49	5.1	23.9
Gunnison	7.6	3.6	3.0	47.1	10 273	10 689	-3.9	22.4	1 130	496	1 691	3 855	1.9	2.38	5.7	26.8
Hinsdale	15.5	10.0	6.9	47.3	467	408	14.5	58.5	44	26	256	214	31.3	2.18	2.8	28.5
Huerfano	12.5	9.0	9.6	50.9	6 009	6 440	-6.7	13.2	579	767	990	2 446	1.8	2.41	11.2	30.2
Jackson	11.9	5.8	6.9	45.8	1 605	1 863	-13.8	-4.0	161	109	-115	632	-4.5	2.52	4.6	25.0
Jefferson	8.9	6.2	4.5	50.8	438 430	371 753	17.9	16.1	60 432	25 243	37 297	166 545	28.3	2.59	9.2	22.1
Kiowa	10.1	8.3	8.7	50.4	1 688	1 936	-12.8	-3.2	149	183	-14	657	-8.5	2.50	5.5	26.9
Kit Carson	11.1	7.3	8.1	50.5	7 140	7 599	-6.0	3.8	807	623	110	2 785	0.7	2.54	6.2	25.7
Lake	9.1	4.0	3.3	48.3	6 007	8 830	-32.0	6.3	953	300	-250	2 382	-20.6	2.51	8.4	27.5
La Plata	9.0	5.1	4.3	49.6	32 284	27 195	18.7	27.5	4 099	2 118	6 950	11 976	30.2	2.56	8.8	23.6
Larimer	7.9	5.2	4.8	50.5	186 136	149 184	24.8	27.2	25 881	11 288	36 630	70 472	30.3	2.55	7.6	23.0
Las Animas	11.3	8.1	9.6	50.9	13 765	14 897	-7.6	6.9	1 561	1 665	1 086	5 421	1.0	2.47	12.2	29.3
Lincoln	10.6	7.1	7.7	44.0	4 529	4 663	-2.9	25.2	527	545	1 172	1 817	-0.3	2.43	6.4	28.5
Logan	11.2	7.7	8.5	51.5	17 567	19 800	-11.3	2.1	2 264	1 657	-199	6 978	-2.4	2.46	7.4	27.5
Mesa	10.6	8.0	7.0	51.4	93 145	81 530	14.2	23.6	12 467	8 831	18 664	36 250	22.2	2.50	9.8	24.8
Mineral	12.4	13.5	8.7	49.5	558	804	-30.6	30.3	66	49	156	247	-21.3	2.26	5.7	30.4
Moffat	8.8	5.2	4.8	49.2	11 357	13 133	-13.5	11.9	1 413	724	703	4 178	-8.7	2.69	7.4	23.5
Montezuma	10.9	7.7	6.2	51.2	18 672	16 510	13.1	21.4	2 879	1 711	2 909	6 762	19.4	2.74	10.4	21.5
Montrose	11.5	8.2	7.3	50.9	24 423	24 352	0.3	28.7	3 757	2 465	5 799	9 405	11.6	2.55	8.1	22.5
Morgan	10.6	6.0	7.2	50.8	21 939	22 513	-2.5	15.7	4 107	2 169	1 593	8 139	2.0	2.64	7.9	24.6
Otero	10.7	7.3	8.4	51.5	20 185	22 567	-10.6	2.1	2 809	2 315	-70	7 593	-4.3	2.59	11.7	25.7
Ouray	12.5	7.2	5.2	49.4	2 295	1 925	19.2	51.4	252	151	1 081	947	31.0	2.42	5.2	24.3
Park	10.0	4.2	2.0	48.4	7 174	5 333	34.5	98.2	1 107	348	6 225	2 775	49.4	2.59	4.0	19.9
Phillips	12.8	8.0	11.6	52.4	4 189	4 542	-7.8	0.9	511	535	72	1 712	-2.3	2.41	6.5	28.9
Pitkin	7.3	4.3	2.5	47.3	12 661	10 338	22.5	5.3	1 373	312	-365	5 877	30.1	2.13	5.4	35.4
Prowers	9.7	6.5	6.3	51.1	13 347	13 070	2.1	3.3	2 021	1 056	-487	4 984	7.0	2.64	10.6	25.7
Pueblo	11.1	8.1	7.1	51.5	123 051	125 972	-2.3	11.3	16 439	12 006	9 730	47 057	4.4	2.55	13.7	25.8
Rio Blanco	9.1	5.6	5.1	48.9	6 051	6 255	-3.3	2.5	652	391	-99	2 181	3.7	2.67	5.9	22.1
Rio Grande	10.2	7.4	7.2	50.9	10 770	10 511	2.5	6.9	1 490	1 085	372	3 930	11.6	2.69	10.8	21.8
Routt	6.3	3.0	2.3	46.5	14 088	13 404	5.1	27.3	1 704	567	2 746	5 483	11.1	2.54	6.5	23.3
Saguache	8.9	5.1	4.4	48.7	4 619	3 935	17.4	33.7	808	312	1 064	1 643	20.8	2.76	11.0	23.4
San Juan	8.8	6.9	1.3	44.8	745	833	-10.6	-29.9	71	37	-251	287	-9.7	2.60	7.7	26.1
San Miguel	6.1	1.8	1.8	46.4	3 653	3 192	14.4	49.6	509	116	1 426	1 489	19.1	2.42	6.4	26.5
Sedgwick	13.4	10.2	12.7	51.2	2 690	3 266	-17.6	-3.8	270	353	-8	1 141	-9.4	2.33	5.2	28.7
Summit	6.1	2.6	1.1	45.6	12 881	8 848	45.6	52.2	2 029	263	4 962	5 295	48.3	2.42	4.6	23.7
Teller	9.3	4.5	2.6	48.6	12 468	8 034	55.2	70.3	1 815	632	7 534	4 720	63.8	2.63	6.6	19.3
Washington	12.9	9.6	9.5	50.1	4 812	5 304	-9.3	-9.5	534	504	-461	1 915	-5.1	2.50	4.8	26.1
Weld	8.4	4.7	4.6	50.3	131 821	123 438	6.8	25.8	22 018	8 899	21 075	47 470	11.0	2.69	9.1	22.3
Yuma	11.1	7.6	8.8	50.7	8 954	9 682	-7.5	5.3	1 084	947	372	3 472	-3.7	2.54	5.6	26.9
CONNECTICUT	8.6	7.1	7.2	51.5	3 287 116	3 107 564	5.8	-0.2	423 922	268 782	-152 981	1 230 479	12.5	2.59	11.4	24.2
Fairfield	9.4	7.0	6.9	51.7	827 645	807 143	2.5	1.7	116 049	65 605	-33 835	305 011	8.7	2.66	11.3	22.9
Hartford	8.8	7.5	7.6	51.9	851 783	807 766	5.4	-2.6	109 356	73 275	-55 812	324 691	12.1	2.55	12.7	25.0
Litchfield	8.4	6.8	7.5	50.7	174 092	156 769	11.1	4.8	19 786	14 366	3 404	66 371	19.2	2.59	8.4	23.1
Middlesex	8.2	6.4	7.1	50.9	143 196	129 017	11.0	5.8	18 236	11 506	2 001	54 651	19.0	2.51	9.0	24.4
New Haven	8.4	7.3	7.7	51.8	804 219	761 325	5.6	-1.4	103 285	70 403	-41 329	304 730	12.2	2.55	12.5	25.9
New London	8.2	7.0	6.7	49.9	254 957	238 409	6.9	-3.5	30 049	17 906	-23 335	93 245	14.0	2.59	9.6	23.1
Tolland	7.1	5.7	5.2	49.9	128 699	114 823	12.1	3.1	14 615	7 448	-2 801	44 309	22.2	2.66	7.6	20.1
Windham	7.5	6.0	6.6	50.9	102 525	92 312	11.1	2.6	12 546	8 273	-1 274	37 471	16.3	2.66	10.8	22.2

1. No spouse present.

Table B. States and Counties — Vital Statistics, Health Resources, and Crime

STATE County	Births, average 1996–1998 Total	Rate[1]	Deaths, average 1996–1998 Number Total	Number Infant[2]	Rate Total[1]	Rate Infant[3]	Physicians,[4] 1998 Number	Rate[5]	Hospitals,[4] 1998 Number	Beds Number	Beds Rate[5]	Medicare enrollees 1999	Serious crimes known to police, 1998[6] Total Number	Rate[7]
	32	33	34	35	36	37	38	39	40	41	42	43	44	45
COLORADO—Cont'd														
Clear Creek	92	10.4	36	0	4.1	3.6	5	56	0	0	0	560	371	4 079
Conejos	127	16.1	72	1	9.2	7.9	4	50	1	49	615	1 389	NA	NA
Costilla	44	12.3	42	0	11.6	7.5	3	82	0	0	0	784	NA	NA
Crowley	48	11.1	44	1	10.3	13.9	1	23	0	0	0	694	4	92
Custer	35	10.7	16	0	5.0	9.5	2	58	0	0	0	550	67	1 995
Delta	315	12.1	311	3	11.9	8.5	36	135	1	44	165	5 900	553	2 178
Denver	9 442	18.9	4 797	71	9.6	7.5	2 863	574	8	2 845	570	71 414	27 471	5 393
Dolores	18	10.5	13	0	7.7	0.0	0	0	0	0	0	378	30	1 724
Douglas	2 409	19.0	344	10	2.7	4.0	218	155	0	0	0	4 600	2 948	2 289
Eagle	594	18.6	61	3	1.9	4.5	98	292	1	49	146	1 225	1 975	6 295
Elbert	204	11.7	68	1	3.9	4.9	9	48	0	0	0	1 116	NA	NA
El Paso	7 748	16.1	2 693	59	5.6	7.6	1 016	207	4	1 008	206	50 821	24 219	5 088
Fremont	433	10.1	468	3	10.9	6.2	47	107	1	277	631	7 322	1 196	2 730
Garfield	613	16.2	247	5	6.5	7.6	69	176	2	140	356	4 254	1 247	3 370
Gilpin	42	10.7	14	0	3.6	0.0	2	48	0	0	0	165	300	7 415
Grand	126	12.9	44	0	4.5	0.0	13	129	1	21	209	1 017	NA	NA
Gunnison	125	10.2	45	1	3.7	5.3	21	169	1	24	193	997	631	5 072
Hinsdale	7	9.9	2	0	2.8	0.0	3	407	0	0	0	86	20	2 809
Huerfano	62	9.3	95	0	14.1	5.4	9	132	1	38	558	1 514	133	1 940
Jackson	15	10.1	11	0	7.5	0.0	0	0	0	0	0	228	23	1 471
Jefferson	6 369	12.8	2 983	34	6.0	5.3	971	194	1	322	64	52 499	NA	NA
Kiowa	16	9.7	19	0	11.6	20.8	2	122	1	42	2 572	320	4	235
Kit Carson	79	11.0	77	1	10.7	8.4	5	68	1	24	328	1 283	NA	NA
Lake	114	18.1	33	2	5.2	14.6	4	63	1	22	344	567	189	2 930
La Plata	445	11.1	245	4	6.1	8.2	140	346	1	96	238	4 433	1 580	3 858
Larimer	2 825	12.5	1 332	17	5.9	6.1	442	191	3	375	162	25 902	9 017	3 911
Las Animas	153	10.6	170	1	11.7	4.4	15	103	1	32	220	3 095	386	2 612
Lincoln	57	10.0	60	0	10.6	0.0	5	87	1	56	977	841	NA	NA
Logan	237	13.2	185	2	10.3	9.8	26	145	1	50	279	3 379	NA	NA
Mesa	1 411	12.8	1 030	13	9.3	9.0	312	276	3	422	374	19 622	5 292	4 687
Mineral	5	7.9	5	0	7.9	0.0	0	0	0	0	0	115	NA	NA
Moffat	160	13.0	77	1	6.2	4.2	16	128	1	27	215	1 524	452	3 714
Montezuma	312	14.0	204	3	9.2	8.6	43	191	1	137	610	3 658	732	3 223
Montrose	445	14.7	305	3	10.1	6.7	57	185	1	75	244	5 466	1 091	3 532
Morgan	484	19.4	228	4	9.1	8.3	24	96	2	69	275	3 675	NA	NA
Otero	270	13.0	245	2	11.8	7.4	35	169	1	206	997	4 073	NA	NA
Ouray	30	9.4	17	0	5.2	0.0	12	362	0	0	0	426	46	1 409
Park	145	11.5	44	1	3.5	6.9	9	67	0	0	0	1 035	275	2 258
Phillips	64	14.7	58	1	13.3	15.7	7	162	2	66	1 526	955	NA	NA
Pitkin	139	10.3	34	0	2.5	2.4	81	603	1	49	365	816	905	6 535
Prowers	215	15.7	124	2	9.1	7.8	9	66	1	40	291	2 092	585	4 373
Pueblo	1 795	13.5	1 339	14	10.1	8.0	324	240	2	563	417	24 749	7 844	5 786
Rio Blanco	66	10.5	49	1	7.8	10.2	8	128	2	67	1 069	752	NA	NA
Rio Grande	156	13.7	118	1	10.4	4.3	11	96	0	0	0	1 958	256	2 201
Routt	188	10.9	67	1	3.9	7.1	47	268	1	71	405	1 079	351	2 283
Saguache	92	15.6	37	0	6.3	0.0	2	33	0	0	0	750	72	1 195
San Juan	6	10.9	5	0	9.1	0.0	1	189	0	0	0	62	39	6 866
San Miguel	60	11.3	11	0	2.1	0.0	6	110	0	0	0	250	306	5 636
Sedgwick	32	12.1	40	0	15.2	10.5	4	157	1	58	2 277	695	NA	NA
Summit	235	12.9	35	2	1.9	8.5	58	309	0	0	0	836	2 104	11 169
Teller	205	10.4	75	1	3.8	6.5	21	102	0	0	0	1 821	573	2 838
Washington	55	11.9	58	0	12.6	6.1	0	0	0	0	0	881	NA	NA
Weld	2 529	16.3	1 029	19	6.6	7.5	247	155	1	326	204	17 509	6 663	4 557
Yuma	123	13.1	108	1	11.6	5.4	12	128	2	39	415	1 644	148	1 548
CONNECTICUT	43 799	13.4	29 562	301	9.0	6.9	10 407	318	35	7 782	238	511 611	123 971	3 787
Fairfield	12 469	14.9	7 093	75	8.5	6.0	2 769	330	8	1 965	234	123 398	28 568	3 515
Hartford	11 568	13.9	8 143	97	9.8	8.4	2 628	317	9	2 395	289	138 705	35 937	4 439
Litchfield	1 978	11.0	1 630	7	9.0	3.4	358	197	3	279	154	28 108	NA	NA
Middlesex	1 877	12.6	1 305	12	8.8	6.6	376	251	1	158	105	22 400	NA	NA
New Haven	10 549	13.3	7 676	71	9.7	6.7	3 246	409	8	2 268	286	130 932	37 953	5 059
New London	2 595	10.5	1 896	17	7.7	6.7	568	231	8	428	174	37 856	NA	NA
Tolland	1 488	11.4	889	12	6.8	8.3	318	241	2	137	104	14 553	NA	NA
Windham	1 275	12.2	930	10	8.9	7.8	144	137	2	152	145	15 589	NA	NA

1. Per 1,000 estimated resident population, average 1996–1998. 2. Deaths of infants under 1 year old. 3. Deaths of infants under 1 year old per 1,000 live births. 4. Data subject to copyright. 5. Per 100,000 resident population as of July 1 of the year shown. 6. Data for serious crimes have not been adjusted for underreporting; this may affect comparability between geographic areas and over time. 7. Per 100,000 population estimated by the FBI.

Table B. States and Counties — Crime, Education, Money Income, and Poverty

STATE County	Serious crimes known to police, 1998[1] (cont'd) Rate[2] Violent	Property	Education School enrollment and attainment, 1990 Enrollment[3] Total	Percent private	Attainment[4] (percent) High school graduate or more	Bachelor's degree or more	Local government expenditures, fiscal 1997[5] Total current expenditures (mil dol)	Current expenditures per student (dollars)	Money income 1989 Per capita[6] (dollars)	Households Median Dollars	Percent change, 1979–1989 (constant 1989 dollars)	Percent with $100,000 or more	Income and poverty, 1997 Median house-hold income	Percent below poverty level All persons	Persons under 18	Persons 5–17 in families
	46	47	48	49	50	51	52	53	54	55	56	57	58	59	60	61
COLORADO—Cont'd																
Clear Creek	418	3 661	1 859	13.0	91.8	31.2	7.6	5 243	16 196	33 149	-6.3	2.8	56 537	5.2	7.9	6.6
Conejos	NA	NA	2 149	1.2	63.7	10.7	10.6	5 127	6 664	14 188	-7.7	0.3	20 708	28.6	35.8	33.9
Costilla	NA	NA	776	2.1	60.5	10.5	4.9	6 326	7 057	13 057	5.9	0.5	18 700	33.5	46.8	45.1
Crowley	69	23	973	8.7	70.3	8.0	3.1	4 852	6 978	16 088	-3.8	0.8	23 524	32.2	40.0	37.0
Custer	89	1 906	441	4.3	83.8	19.2	2.3	5 170	11 309	20 000	-1.4	2.1	29 797	14.5	22.7	21.2
Delta	130	2 048	4 404	6.2	73.0	13.6	27.3	5 847	9 586	18 532	-2.8	0.9	27 418	16.2	23.9	21.0
Denver	574	4 819	108 999	21.1	79.2	29.0	377.7	5 694	15 590	25 106	-3.4	3.9	35 616	16.4	26.6	25.3
Dolores	172	1 552	328	0.9	71.8	9.8	2.1	5 505	9 784	19 952	-9.6	1.0	25 826	14.0	19.8	18.1
Douglas	108	2 181	16 990	11.7	94.8	40.7	120.6	4 924	21 002	51 718	8.7	11.5	77 513	1.9	2.2	2.3
Eagle	424	5 871	5 173	13.0	89.8	33.0	26.3	6 653	18 202	36 931	3.3	6.0	50 000	4.3	6.1	7.1
Elbert	NA	NA	2 680	6.9	84.2	17.6	17.6	5 145	14 566	36 273	19.3	4.8	52 636	5.6	7.4	6.8
El Paso	479	4 609	109 787	14.5	88.3	25.8	427.5	4 948	13 664	29 604	8.8	2.9	42 023	9.5	13.8	12.2
Fremont	132	2 598	7 678	10.3	75.4	11.8	31.0	4 856	9 971	19 988	-8.2	1.3	29 939	17.2	22.5	19.4
Garfield	257	3 113	7 740	8.9	85.2	21.6	40.7	4 706	13 086	29 176	-6.9	2.6	40 923	8.9	12.9	12.2
Gilpin	272	7 143	732	6.1	93.0	29.5	2.4	6 550	15 267	31 898	-2.1	1.7	51 044	5.2	8.0	7.6
Grand	NA	NA	1 706	4.8	87.4	30.2	11.2	6 075	13 457	29 991	-3.5	2.0	38 865	6.6	9.1	9.0
Gunnison	88	4 984	3 687	6.7	90.6	36.9	8.7	5 284	11 516	23 013	-10.3	2.2	32 300	11.8	13.4	14.2
Hinsdale	0	2 809	75	17.3	93.0	32.0	0.6	16 216	12 978	26 250	1.2	1.4	32 993	10.8	20.8	19.6
Huerfano	131	1 809	1 479	15.8	65.0	12.6	6.7	5 444	8 212	14 730	-14.5	0.6	21 389	23.4	34.3	32.1
Jackson	0	1 471	379	1.1	82.1	15.3	2.0	6 370	10 858	20 938	-25.9	1.4	29 031	13.3	21.0	19.2
Jefferson	NA	NA	117 385	13.3	89.8	30.7	451.6	5 211	17 310	39 084	-3.0	4.9	54 175	5.4	7.3	6.7
Kiowa	59	176	455	1.3	69.8	9.1	2.8	7 335	10 305	21 417	-6.0	1.7	32 455	14.0	19.1	16.9
Kit Carson	NA	NA	1 681	2.9	73.5	15.8	10.4	6 076	11 385	23 125	0.7	2.3	32 964	12.9	17.0	16.7
Lake	78	2 852	1 566	1.5	81.7	16.2	12.5	9 368	11 269	24 708	-33.6	1.3	34 986	9.5	12.8	14.3
La Plata	222	3 636	10 161	6.8	85.7	28.1	40.9	5 933	12 163	25 759	0.8	2.9	36 822	11.5	14.6	14.2
Larimer	298	3 613	62 261	7.4	88.6	32.3	177.8	4 799	13 968	29 686	3.2	3.0	43 853	8.5	10.3	9.5
Las Animas	460	2 152	3 691	8.9	67.6	12.7	14.8	6 016	8 934	16 286	-13.5	0.7	22 682	23.8	33.9	31.1
Lincoln	NA	NA	956	3.6	74.5	12.9	7.6	7 648	10 052	20 595	-4.1	1.0	29 117	17.4	21.7	21.5
Logan	NA	NA	4 906	5.8	79.1	14.2	19.7	5 675	10 899	22 065	-13.9	1.4	33 076	13.4	18.8	17.1
Mesa	325	4 362	24 299	7.4	79.5	17.4	94.7	4 789	11 850	23 698	-14.8	1.8	33 519	13.0	18.3	16.5
Mineral	NA	NA	94	2.1	84.8	17.9	1.2	8 307	11 082	19 830	-22.5	2.8	29 810	12.9	21.2	23.5
Moffat	378	3 336	3 118	6.1	79.9	16.4	14.4	5 087	12 354	31 615	-10.9	2.0	42 476	11.4	15.5	14.5
Montezuma	75	3 148	4 827	4.4	74.8	15.9	25.0	5 245	10 176	22 491	-3.9	2.0	30 882	17.8	24.7	23.1
Montrose	210	3 322	5 584	6.1	74.5	15.4	30.2	5 121	11 092	22 610	-11.7	2.1	32 312	13.2	19.8	17.2
Morgan	NA	NA	5 683	3.5	67.6	11.7	28.8	5 376	10 928	22 849	-9.1	2.6	31 197	14.4	19.5	18.3
Otero	NA	NA	5 508	3.4	69.4	13.0	27.6	6 238	9 573	18 178	-6.5	2.3	25 143	22.8	32.1	29.8
Ouray	123	1 286	496	2.8	87.5	27.9	3.6	6 300	13 208	27 500	15.3	2.9	38 465	7.2	10.7	10.8
Park	148	2 110	1 765	8.0	91.1	22.4	11.7	5 205	14 325	32 102	6.1	2.5	46 090	6.8	9.5	9.2
Phillips	NA	NA	981	6.3	79.0	14.2	8.0	8 088	10 444	21 484	2.3	0.7	32 863	10.5	13.4	13.6
Pitkin	310	6 225	2 430	19.9	94.7	49.8	8.0	6 401	26 755	39 991	13.7	12.6	52 744	5.2	7.7	8.7
Prowers	135	4 238	3 828	3.7	70.2	12.2	19.1	6 405	9 662	20 625	-3.6	1.9	28 881	20.4	27.9	26.1
Pueblo	875	4 911	32 691	6.1	73.9	14.0	113.5	4 805	10 347	21 553	-16.9	1.3	29 112	18.1	25.8	23.1
Rio Blanco	NA	NA	1 935	4.1	81.2	15.4	10.0	6 152	12 357	29 243	-16.3	1.8	40 921	10.3	12.4	12.3
Rio Grande	241	1 960	2 929	3.1	69.7	17.5	13.7	5 083	9 582	19 193	-12.0	2.4	25 808	23.4	35.1	29.6
Routt	111	2 172	3 779	8.8	91.7	34.7	20.1	6 755	15 429	31 409	-12.8	4.4	42 799	6.8	7.8	8.4
Saguache	216	979	1 296	3.3	65.9	14.4	7.1	6 078	8 630	15 853	-4.1	2.6	22 419	26.1	35.9	33.7
San Juan	352	6 514	195	6.7	82.7	24.0	1.1	9 706	11 029	26 167	6.3	1.0	27 635	19.8	27.1	26.0
San Miguel	166	5 470	665	11.7	93.5	40.3	5.3	6 349	16 454	30 578	34.1	4.4	42 160	8.5	12.7	14.0
Sedgwick	NA	NA	583	1.5	70.9	8.6	3.5	7 123	9 901	19 335	-10.3	0.0	28 209	14.2	23.2	19.8
Summit	234	10 935	2 648	10.5	95.5	39.7	16.1	6 776	17 400	35 229	-1.8	4.8	45 857	4.5	5.9	7.1
Teller	238	2 600	3 243	12.0	92.1	26.4	17.9	4 640	13 698	32 209	13.8	1.9	45 552	8.4	12.2	11.5
Washington	NA	NA	1 075	1.8	75.9	11.8	7.8	7 349	10 473	20 637	-9.8	1.2	29 870	12.2	15.8	16.4
Weld	674	3 883	41 250	6.0	74.9	18.4	142.6	5 329	11 350	25 642	-3.2	2.0	35 351	12.5	16.8	15.0
Yuma	52	1 496	2 354	3.5	78.5	13.4	10.7	5 305	10 713	22 249	12.2	2.2	31 639	12.0	16.1	15.0
CONNECTICUT	366	3 421	805 486	22.2	79.2	27.2	4 523.0	8 580	20 189	41 721	24.0	9.2	46 648	8.9	14.7	13.9
Fairfield	375	3 140	197 636	27.1	81.0	34.2	1 119.2	8 802	26 161	49 891	29.6	17.3	56 872	7.9	12.9	12.2
Hartford	404	4 035	207 561	19.0	77.7	25.8	1 115.9	8 371	18 983	40 609	20.3	7.4	46 011	10.4	17.5	16.4
Litchfield	NA	NA	40 320	16.6	80.9	25.0	217.4	7 852	19 971	42 565	28.2	7.5	50 589	5.3	8.3	8.0
Middlesex	NA	NA	34 794	24.9	82.6	28.2	178.8	8 205	19 660	43 212	26.7	6.3	53 624	5.2	8.6	8.5
New Haven	495	4 564	197 532	25.9	77.5	24.2	971.3	8 046	17 666	38 471	24.6	6.3	44 412	10.6	18.0	16.7
New London	NA	NA	61 393	19.8	80.9	21.8	316.7	8 198	16 702	37 488	23.4	4.7	44 566	8.1	12.4	12.5
Tolland	NA	NA	39 989	9.6	84.7	29.2	165.5	7 786	17 849	45 019	26.1	6.1	55 223	5.4	7.5	7.4
Windham	NA	NA	26 261	13.2	71.1	16.8	131.2	7 593	14 520	33 851	24.8	3.0	41 108	9.8	16.1	15.7

1. Data for serious crimes have not been adjusted for underreporting; this may affect comparability between geographic areas and over time.   2. Per 100,000 population estimated by the FBI.   3. All persons 3 years old and over enrolled in nursery school through college.   4. Persons 25 years old and over.   5. Elementary and secondary education expenditures, local government fiscal years ending between July 1, 1996 and June 30, 1997.   6. Based on population enumerated as of April 1, 1990.

Table B. States and Counties — **Personal Income**

						Personal income, 1998						
		Per capita[1]					Transfer payments					
								Government payments to individuals				
STATE County	Total (mil dol)	Percent change, 1997– 1998	Dollars	Rank	Wages and salaries[2] (mil dol)	Proprietor's income (mil dol)	Dividends, interest, and rent (mil dol)	Total (mil dol)	Total (mil dol)	Social Security (mil dol)	Medical payments (mil dol)	Income mainte- nance (mil dol)	Unemploy- ment insurance (mil dol)
	62	63	64	65	66	67	68	69	70	71	72	73	74
COLORADO—Cont'd													
Clear Creek	262	9.7	29 018	194	93	15	33	18	16	8	5	1	0
Conejos	111	2.1	13 880	3 017	39	11	15	36	35	10	16	7	0
Costilla	57	4.3	15 662	2 857	17	3	9	19	18	6	7	4	0
Crowley	72	10.2	16 713	2 676	27	24	12	17	17	5	8	3	0
Custer	63	5.2	18 336	2 254	18	6	17	10	10	5	2	1	0
Delta	487	6.4	18 270	2 275	178	40	138	115	110	51	43	8	1
Denver	18 775	7.0	37 670	45	19 927	3 066	3 702	2 085	2 000	657	931	227	24
Dolores	33	5.3	18 363	2 247	9	7	7	7	7	3	2	1	0
Douglas	4 822	17.6	34 088	71	1 476	171	722	161	136	77	24	4	2
Eagle	1 247	10.7	37 000	49	857	199	263	35	29	14	6	2	2
Elbert	452	17.2	24 311	588	69	22	52	38	35	12	8	9	1
El Paso	12 873	8.6	26 270	368	8 953	795	2 428	1 256	1 177	461	431	101	18
Fremont	745	6.7	16 837	2 649	389	56	156	150	143	64	52	13	2
Garfield	945	9.7	24 011	641	543	104	196	88	82	41	25	5	2
Gilpin	124	10.1	29 565	179	136	8	27	7	6	3	1	0	0
Grand	258	9.0	25 504	439	144	34	63	21	19	10	6	1	0
Gunnison	268	8.0	21 572	1 233	183	26	71	23	20	9	5	2	0
Hinsdale	16	6.3	21 807	1 158	5	3	6	2	2	1	0	0	0
Huerfano	127	8.3	18 739	2 146	52	10	26	38	37	12	16	5	0
Jackson	28	0.5	18 477	2 220	12	2	9	5	4	2	1	0	0
Jefferson	16 701	9.0	33 348	80	7 808	1 255	3 122	1 109	1 023	530	306	53	15
Kiowa	57	21.8	34 789	66	18	26	9	6	6	3	2	1	0
Kit Carson	194	17.8	26 550	338	69	58	48	25	24	12	8	2	0
Lake	152	7.5	23 898	663	54	8	23	16	15	6	6	1	0
La Plata	1 023	6.7	25 241	464	560	121	264	100	93	41	33	7	2
Larimer	6 380	9.7	27 607	260	3 857	482	1 280	559	519	240	179	34	8
Las Animas	255	7.2	17 561	2 474	129	13	53	80	78	24	33	10	1
Lincoln	99	8.3	17 395	2 506	55	7	24	17	16	7	6	1	0
Logan	447	5.8	24 969	495	204	90	97	66	63	31	22	5	1
Mesa	2 539	7.0	22 491	980	1 405	194	573	410	390	175	144	28	5
Mineral	15	5.6	21 595	1 224	8	2	4	2	2	1	1	0	0
Moffat	266	2.9	21 179	1 336	158	19	42	34	32	14	13	3	1
Montezuma	458	8.4	20 464	1 572	237	45	94	76	72	33	26	7	1
Montrose	644	5.5	20 924	1 413	332	73	156	104	99	49	34	8	2
Morgan	544	6.7	21 699	1 192	295	89	101	83	78	34	32	7	1
Otero	408	4.6	19 729	1 804	190	33	72	114	111	30	55	14	1
Ouray	76	6.0	22 932	864	27	10	26	8	8	4	2	0	0
Park	309	14.2	23 081	841	50	22	45	23	21	11	4	2	0
Phillips	104	3.5	24 075	628	38	29	22	17	16	7	7	1	0
Pitkin	789	8.4	59 123	2	527	116	303	20	18	10	4	1	1
Prowers	313	11.5	22 853	880	143	73	53	55	52	18	24	6	1
Pueblo	2 884	6.2	21 379	1 272	1 588	135	515	722	699	206	357	75	7
Rio Blanco	139	2.8	22 236	1 030	78	36	26	17	16	7	6	1	0
Rio Grande	235	9.5	20 450	1 576	106	39	55	46	44	18	17	7	1
Routt	556	9.9	31 795	117	365	64	147	27	24	11	7	1	1
Saguache	86	13.3	14 257	2 989	38	15	14	17	16	4	7	4	0
San Juan	12	6.7	22 141	1 050	6	3	2	2	2	1	1	0	0
San Miguel	175	10.4	32 069	112	123	31	47	7	6	3	2	1	0
Sedgwick	65	14.0	25 505	438	22	16	15	13	13	6	5	1	0
Summit	686	9.8	36 508	52	482	96	149	21	17	9	4	1	1
Teller	502	6.4	24 415	575	162	44	95	40	36	19	9	3	1
Washington	109	5.5	23 977	647	37	29	25	17	16	8	6	2	0
Weld	3 478	9.4	21 803	1 159	2 036	398	562	439	412	163	170	39	6
Yuma	222	5.6	23 546	733	86	58	55	32	30	16	10	3	0
CONNECTICUT	122 191	4.9	37 338	X	77 040	9 081	22 216	14 122	13 558	5 301	6 169	1 199	330
Fairfield	43 437	5.2	51 866	5	26 122	4 072	8 530	3 529	3 384	1 310	1 554	294	79
Hartford	28 593	5.5	34 544	68	22 806	1 822	5 073	3 884	3 741	1 418	1 743	363	87
Litchfield	5 786	4.9	31 914	114	2 406	495	1 128	627	596	298	226	31	17
Middlesex	4 995	4.2	33 298	81	2 688	318	887	513	487	238	180	30	15
New Haven	25 602	5.0	32 290	105	15 142	1 542	4 335	3 777	3 640	1 334	1 732	344	79
New London	7 392	1.9	29 933	167	5 308	439	1 341	979	938	380	410	78	29
Tolland	3 730	4.3	28 393	220	1 350	234	555	376	353	165	135	21	10
Windham	2 656	3.3	25 328	457	1 219	159	367	437	418	159	190	39	15

1. Based on the resident population estimated as of July 1 of the year shown. 2. Includes other labor income.

Table B. States and Counties — Earnings, Social Security, and Housing

STATE County	Earnings, 1998 Total (mil dol)	Farm	Goods-related[1] Total	Manu-facturing	Service-related and other[2] Total	Retail trade	Finance, insur-ance, and real estate	Services	Govern-ment	Social Security beneficiaries, December 1998 Number	Rate[3]	Supple-mental Security Income recipients, December 1998	Housing units, 1990 Total	Percent change, 1980–1990
	75	76	77	78	79	80	81	82	83	84	85	86	87	88
COLORADO—Cont'd														
Clear Creek	108	0.0	D	1.2	D	11.3	3.3	D	19.8	929	103	49	4 811	14.6
Conejos	49	3.8	D	4.2	D	8.8	2.5	23.1	32.9	1 562	196	467	3 574	14.7
Costilla	20	20.6	D	1.6	D	5.3	D	8.2	42.5	987	271	282	1 743	21.3
Crowley	51	44.6	D	0.0	D	4.2	D	9.3	35.8	777	180	171	1 415	4.0
Custer	24	-8.3	33.0	2.8	D	12.6	6.1	17.9	25.1	662	192	39	2 216	100.0
Delta	217	4.5	D	6.0	D	12.7	4.8	20.8	27.5	6 602	248	530	10 082	9.1
Denver	22 992	0.0	14.4	6.4	71.2	6.0	11.9	30.4	14.4	77 613	156	14 276	239 636	5.2
Dolores	17	15.8	D	D	D	7.0	D	5.4	23.8	445	244	36	947	3.8
Douglas	1 647	0.1	21.2	6.0	66.2	17.3	9.4	23.9	12.7	8 435	60	154	22 291	157.0
Eagle	1 056	0.1	D	2.9	D	14.9	17.8	32.1	7.9	1 524	45	85	15 226	37.7
Elbert	91	-5.1	D	3.3	D	8.6	6.8	19.7	26.5	1 518	82	5 908	3 997	46.8
El Paso	9 748	0.0	18.6	11.6	52.9	8.4	6.1	27.9	28.5	58 499	119	42	165 056	40.4
Fremont	445	0.3	16.9	7.6	35.8	9.0	3.0	17.8	47.0	8 476	193	866	13 683	19.1
Garfield	647	0.1	26.1	2.7	56.7	14.8	7.4	25.3	17.1	4 907	125	342	12 517	33.9
Gilpin	143	0.0	D	D	D	1.8	0.4	84.5	8.4	404	96	9	2 438	21.2
Grand	178	-0.5	16.0	2.1	D	14.4	12.9	31.8	18.6	1 189	118	42	9 985	38.5
Gunnison	209	-1.2	26.1	1.5	52.0	15.9	8.3	23.1	23.1	1 147	92	55	7 294	27.2
Hinsdale	8	-3.8	D	D	D	19.2	11.9	25.3	21.2	113	153	8	1 254	79.9
Huerfano	62	-3.0	D	6.2	D	12.3	4.9	36.9	20.9	1 707	251	321	3 913	12.9
Jackson	14	-8.9	D	10.8	D	15.7	D	12.0	36.7	273	178	17	1 326	25.0
Jefferson	9 063	0.1	26.0	16.9	57.9	10.9	7.5	27.7	16.1	59 682	119	3 180	178 611	28.9
Kiowa	44	65.5	D	D	D	2.4	D	3.4	14.6	343	210	22	878	5.1
Kit Carson	126	38.9	D	4.1	37.9	8.9	3.1	10.5	15.5	1 474	202	88	3 224	-2.0
Lake	63	0.0	D	1.7	D	11.8	4.0	24.0	31.9	715	112	404	3 527	-6.0
La Plata	681	-0.3	18.6	3.5	63.7	13.1	7.6	33.6	18.0	5 076	126	40	15 412	26.8
Larimer	4 339	0.5	35.2	25.4	44.7	10.8	5.5	22.1	19.6	28 846	125	1 920	77 811	25.1
Las Animas	142	-3.0	14.5	2.7	55.8	11.4	5.0	20.5	32.7	3 330	229	701	6 975	8.5
Lincoln	62	4.0	3.9	0.9	44.7	14.2	3.9	13.3	47.4	986	172	81	2 204	2.8
Logan	293	12.7	14.1	5.1	56.1	10.5	4.5	20.9	17.1	3 788	212	323	7 824	0.1
Mesa	1 599	0.7	19.9	8.3	60.7	13.5	6.0	28.2	18.7	21 705	192	2 130	39 208	20.4
Mineral	11	-1.0	D	D	D	9.7	D	46.7	24.0	142	205	8	1 201	72.3
Moffat	177	-0.6	26.3	1.3	50.8	11.5	2.2	16.1	23.6	1 654	132	152	5 235	-0.6
Montezuma	282	0.7	D	4.3	D	12.7	4.1	25.5	20.0	4 219	188	429	8 050	23.9
Montrose	405	0.9	24.2	9.8	52.5	13.3	4.6	19.6	22.3	6 191	201	556	10 353	10.4
Morgan	384	12.6	29.3	22.0	41.5	7.1	4.5	15.7	16.5	4 223	168	367	9 230	2.3
Otero	223	4.9	13.1	9.5	57.3	10.3	4.1	23.4	24.7	4 260	206	967	8 739	-1.2
Ouray	37	-1.2	D	3.0	D	14.3	7.7	22.8	21.3	507	153	24	1 507	26.7
Park	71	-0.9	25.4	1.6	45.7	8.5	5.8	21.9	29.8	1 314	98	42	7 247	48.7
Phillips	67	38.7	7.3	1.3	D	5.8	3.0	D	19.2	841	194	58	1 960	-2.7
Pitkin	643	-0.2	D	1.8	D	16.4	15.6	38.5	10.2	1 017	76	35	9 837	15.7
Prowers	216	25.1	17.8	12.6	35.7	9.9	3.5	11.4	21.5	2 395	174	393	5 855	7.4
Pueblo	1 723	0.1	20.6	12.0	56.9	13.7	7.0	26.0	22.5	27 238	202	4 956	50 872	3.6
Rio Blanco	114	-3.4	54.3	0.7	D	4.4	2.1	9.2	25.9	917	146	52	2 803	11.1
Rio Grande	145	15.6	11.8	6.7	51.9	7.6	4.6	13.1	20.7	2 504	219	378	5 277	18.8
Routt	428	-1.0	31.3	1.6	57.9	12.5	8.9	26.7	11.8	1 318	75	66	9 252	27.1
Saguache	52	23.7	D	1.7	D	6.2	2.0	7.6	30.4	599	99	170	2 306	22.4
San Juan	8	0.0	D	D	D	30.5	D	7.3	27.2	79	149	5	481	1.3
San Miguel	154	-0.5	D	3.0	D	13.1	21.4	28.4	13.7	313	58	8	2 635	51.5
Sedgwick	38	43.4	D	D	D	8.3	2.7	8.6	21.0	744	292	39	1 414	-2.3
Summit	578	0.1	D	1.3	D	17.7	13.9	36.8	10.0	1 000	53	29	17 091	66.6
Teller	207	-0.2	D	4.2	D	8.6	7.8	41.0	16.6	2 276	110	84	7 565	48.3
Washington	66	32.9	D	3.3	D	7.0	2.5	5.6	19.9	975	213	54	2 307	-4.4
Weld	2 433	7.7	31.1	20.3	46.3	8.3	7.1	18.7	14.9	20 564	129	2 338	51 138	10.0
Yuma	144	39.8	D	1.8	D	6.8	4.3	9.4	17.3	2 046	218	124	4 082	-1.8
CONNECTICUT	86 121	0.2	25.1	20.1	62.8	7.5	13.7	29.5	11.9	566 055	173	46 972	1 320 850	14.0
Fairfield	30 194	0.0	D	20.8	D	7.0	18.5	29.8	6.8	133 741	160	10 236	324 355	9.9
Hartford	24 628	0.2	D	17.9	D	7.0	18.1	27.1	13.4	153 038	185	15 521	341 812	13.7
Litchfield	2 901	0.8	38.4	27.7	49.6	9.8	3.9	28.0	11.3	31 588	174	1 187	74 274	20.2
Middlesex	3 006	0.4	29.3	23.4	55.6	8.0	12.5	26.3	14.6	25 031	167	1 199	61 593	20.3
New Haven	16 683	0.1	D	19.6	D	8.4	6.1	33.0	13.0	144 392	182	13 422	327 079	13.9
New London	5 748	0.6	27.1	22.0	52.5	7.4	2.7	33.6	19.9	42 358	172	3 005	104 461	15.7
Tolland	1 584	1.3	20.4	12.1	42.9	9.2	3.9	23.9	35.3	17 614	134	525	46 677	22.7
Windham	1 378	1.0	34.9	28.5	45.8	10.8	3.4	23.8	18.3	18 270	174	1 759	40 599	17.2

1. Covers mining, construction, and manufacturing. 2. Covers private sector earnings in agricultural services, forestry, and fisheries; transportation and public utilities; wholesale trade; retail trade; finance, insurance, and real estate; and services. 3. Per 1,000 resident population estimated as of July 1 of the year shown.

Table B. States and Counties — Housing, Labor Force, and Employment

	Housing units, 1990 (cont'd)								Civilian labor force, 1999				Civilian employment, 1990[5]		
STATE County	Occupied units														
	Owner-occupied					Renter-occupied		Sub-stand-ard units[3] (percent)		Percent change, 1998–1999	Unemployment			Percent	
				Owner cost as a percent of income											
	Total	Percent	Median value[1]	With a mort-gage	Without a mort-gage	Median rent[2]	Rent as per-cent of income		Total		Total	Rate[4]	Total	Professional, managerial, and technical	Precision production, craft, and repair
	89	90	91	92	93	94	95	96	97	98	99	100	101	102	103
COLORADO—Cont'd															
Clear Creek	3 153	71.9	90 800	22.7	13.2	407	25.0	2.8	5 253	-2.1	148	2.8	4 311	36.4	12.9
Conejos	2 492	79.2	35 400	23.7	14.2	224	26.5	9.3	3 661	-3.4	259	7.1	2 662	21.0	11.2
Costilla	1 192	77.3	35 400	28.6	18.9	187	25.2	5.4	1 362	-8.1	153	11.2	1 054	16.1	14.0
Crowley	1 165	69.9	26 500	23.9	14.6	272	28.4	3.5	1 306	0.0	57	4.4	1 067	17.1	7.7
Custer	770	73.9	58 900	27.4	15.8	332	26.1	6.9	1 798	-3.7	43	2.4	771	23.0	12.6
Delta	8 372	74.5	51 200	23.2	14.1	305	28.7	2.7	10 901	-0.5	493	4.5	7 440	23.8	13.0
Denver	210 952	49.2	79 000	22.4	13.2	386	26.2	4.2	280 667	-1.2	8 620	3.1	233 602	35.4	7.2
Dolores	581	80.0	40 400	18.8	12.7	312	30.7	6.9	720	9.9	57	7.9	610	18.7	18.9
Douglas	20 844	85.2	119 500	24.4	11.6	597	24.4	1.0	85 174	11.0	1 260	1.5	32 943	45.7	7.7
Eagle	8 354	57.5	135 900	24.2	13.2	620	24.3	5.0	20 734	4.8	527	2.5	13 645	29.8	12.8
Elbert	3 377	82.9	92 400	27.4	15.4	434	25.1	2.5	12 230	11.8	337	2.8	4 961	27.3	15.0
El Paso	146 965	57.4	81 700	22.8	12.2	419	26.0	2.8	258 699	1.5	8 588	3.3	172 530	34.8	10.0
Fremont	11 713	72.9	57 900	21.4	12.9	330	29.0	3.2	17 593	-0.6	679	3.9	11 173	26.5	11.6
Garfield	11 266	57.9	90 400	21.4	12.8	407	24.5	3.5	22 975	3.5	638	2.8	15 266	27.7	15.9
Gilpin	1 308	75.5	74 600	24.0	12.0	469	31.1	6.5	3 315	7.1	71	2.1	1 655	36.2	10.9
Grand	3 168	57.7	81 400	21.8	12.7	457	23.7	3.5	5 944	0.1	135	2.3	4 681	29.5	11.7
Gunnison	3 855	51.3	79 000	22.0	12.7	373	29.0	3.9	7 880	-4.0	379	4.8	5 497	32.7	8.8
Hinsdale	214	59.3	84 200	24.4	15.9	335	20.4	4.7	598	-2.0	14	2.3	274	31.0	12.4
Huerfano	2 446	70.0	36 100	24.2	15.1	240	27.9	4.9	3 743	-8.9	198	5.3	2 071	21.6	9.6
Jackson	632	65.3	49 800	22.9	12.3	292	17.5	4.3	917	-1.5	44	4.8	814	20.1	6.5
Jefferson	166 545	70.1	93 600	22.5	12.0	476	24.9	1.5	307 416	0.2	6 664	2.2	240 911	38.8	9.9
Kiowa	657	68.9	31 300	22.4	16.4	271	18.3	1.2	841	-4.8	34	4.0	745	16.4	7.9
Kit Carson	2 785	71.2	46 700	18.8	13.3	290	20.5	3.5	3 789	3.4	82	2.2	3 330	20.1	8.7
Lake	2 382	64.4	48 700	17.8	12.8	373	22.9	4.1	3 270	0.6	157	4.8	3 022	25.9	18.4
La Plata	11 976	65.3	85 100	22.5	12.5	425	27.6	4.2	24 175	-1.6	926	3.8	15 601	30.4	11.5
Larimer	70 472	62.9	83 900	22.0	12.5	420	28.4	2.4	140 955	0.1	4 336	3.1	94 102	36.6	10.4
Las Animas	5 421	67.0	44 700	23.1	14.2	247	28.5	5.8	6 625	-3.7	343	5.2	5 023	24.9	11.0
Lincoln	1 817	70.2	43 800	23.5	12.6	302	24.1	3.1	2 670	2.3	39	1.5	2 120	17.5	9.9
Logan	6 978	66.7	43 200	21.0	13.7	279	23.3	3.2	10 009	0.0	326	3.3	8 532	21.1	10.1
Mesa	36 250	64.9	62 700	21.3	12.2	333	25.4	2.7	58 927	0.4	2 208	3.7	41 219	28.1	11.5
Mineral	247	70.4	53 800	24.0	12.7	293	25.4	1.2	419	-5.8	12	2.9	247	27.1	22.7
Moffat	4 178	66.7	52 900	16.1	11.7	299	19.0	3.2	6 341	-1.8	344	5.4	5 349	21.8	19.7
Montezuma	6 762	74.2	58 100	21.9	13.8	331	26.2	7.0	11 834	2.2	583	4.9	7 687	27.6	11.9
Montrose	9 405	72.0	60 000	21.6	12.7	338	26.7	3.0	15 548	-0.8	818	5.3	10 488	26.2	12.9
Morgan	8 139	62.5	52 000	20.0	13.1	321	24.4	4.6	12 897	-4.0	394	3.1	9 808	19.9	16.1
Otero	7 593	66.9	38 200	21.6	13.7	288	26.3	4.4	8 818	-2.9	414	4.7	7 656	26.1	8.6
Ouray	947	74.6	91 800	25.4	14.3	401	23.0	3.7	1 780	0.6	66	3.7	1 065	29.8	14.0
Park	2 775	80.6	80 100	25.4	12.1	513	32.5	6.0	7 927	0.0	239	3.0	3 587	27.5	14.8
Phillips	1 712	72.3	41 600	20.7	12.7	252	18.8	2.3	2 083	1.6	34	1.6	1 824	19.4	11.5
Pitkin	5 877	52.4	452 800	26.5	13.1	732	28.8	4.4	8 986	-4.5	298	3.3	8 567	36.6	8.8
Prowers	4 984	65.5	39 400	19.9	13.4	269	21.8	4.7	7 140	0.8	207	2.9	5 868	21.8	11.1
Pueblo	47 057	67.9	51 300	21.1	12.7	308	27.7	3.7	60 282	-3.6	2 894	4.8	47 431	26.7	10.7
Rio Blanco	2 181	66.1	57 400	21.0	12.6	329	23.0	1.8	3 044	-4.7	120	3.9	2 827	22.5	17.9
Rio Grande	3 930	68.3	47 400	22.7	13.7	291	24.6	5.9	5 051	-5.6	349	6.9	4 333	23.8	7.4
Routt	5 483	61.2	94 900	22.8	13.4	492	25.9	3.6	11 314	3.0	307	2.7	8 435	27.9	13.0
Saguache	1 643	67.1	39 000	23.3	14.4	261	29.0	9.2	2 768	-3.4	230	8.3	1 891	17.0	8.1
San Juan	287	61.7	51 000	21.1	14.8	370	23.1	4.8	282	-2.1	33	11.7	353	24.4	25.8
San Miguel	1 489	55.5	151 800	22.9	12.5	538	26.6	6.1	4 593	3.5	193	4.2	2 269	30.6	12.4
Sedgwick	1 141	71.1	29 200	19.3	12.1	207	17.6	3.2	1 217	-3.1	30	2.5	1 256	14.7	9.3
Summit	5 295	48.2	121 500	23.6	12.5	553	24.1	4.5	12 705	1.7	281	2.2	8 815	31.7	9.8
Teller	4 720	77.1	83 300	27.0	14.6	495	28.4	2.4	13 715	-0.2	456	3.3	6 262	37.6	13.5
Washington	1 915	72.2	37 100	23.2	14.0	240	20.0	3.2	2 401	-2.2	58	2.4	2 168	16.1	8.5
Weld	47 470	61.2	67 500	22.2	13.0	357	26.6	4.2	86 145	1.8	3 083	3.6	63 113	24.3	12.5
Yuma	3 472	70.2	47 000	19.6	14.1	302	22.7	1.6	4 549	0.0	108	2.4	4 007	16.6	9.5
CONNECTICUT	1 230 479	65.6	177 800	22.9	13.7	598	26.6	2.5	1 691 552	-1.0	53 446	3.2	1 692 874	35.5	11.2
Fairfield	305 011	68.2	249 800	23.2	14.4	709	27.3	3.1	440 910	-1.4	12 635	2.9	430 443	39.5	9.5
Hartford	324 691	62.7	168 900	22.4	13.3	568	26.2	2.8	410 615	-1.3	14 260	3.5	441 123	35.0	10.5
Litchfield	66 371	73.2	166 300	23.3	13.6	575	24.8	1.4	99 344	-0.4	2 616	2.6	93 697	33.4	14.0
Middlesex	54 651	70.4	175 100	22.9	13.1	619	25.1	1.3	80 887	0.3	2 222	2.7	78 790	36.5	12.6
New Haven	304 730	62.8	165 200	23.2	14.2	585	27.3	2.4	406 609	-0.9	13 759	3.4	407 425	33.6	11.8
New London	93 245	64.7	149 200	23.3	13.0	572	25.8	1.9	129 942	-1.6	4 274	3.3	120 161	33.0	13.6
Tolland	44 309	72.0	165 000	22.4	12.6	598	25.4	1.5	68 705	0.1	1 648	2.4	70 822	36.7	11.7
Windham	37 471	66.6	126 800	22.9	13.2	488	26.0	2.4	54 540	-0.2	2 034	3.7	50 413	27.4	13.9

1. Specified owner-occupied units.   2. Specified renter-occupied units.   3. Overcrowded or lacking complete plumbing facilities.   4. Percent of civilian labor force.   5. Persons 16 years and older.

STATE County		Private nonfarm establishments, employment and payroll, 1998								Agriculture, 1997			
		Employment						Annual payroll		Farms			Farm operators
											Percent with—		
	Number of establishments	Total	Health Care and Social Assistance	Manufacturing	Retail trade	Finance and Insurance	Professional Scientific and Technical Services	Total (mil dol)	Average per employee (dollars)	Number	Less than 50 acres	500 acres and over	Whose principal occupation is farming (percent)
	104	105	106	107	108	109	110	111	112	113	114	115	116
COLORADO—Cont'd													
Clear Creek	318	2 646	71	52	271	D	54	64	24 101	12	58.3	25.0	33.3
Conejos	113	940	D	88	166	D	4	15	16 205	429	16.3	30.5	63.9
Costilla	48	162	D	0	30	D	5	2	13 994	171	20.5	29.8	50.3
Crowley	46	255	64	0	83	D	D	5	19 455	203	14.8	42.9	63.5
Custer	124	515	D	26	112	27	D	10	19 130	152	15.1	36.8	53.9
Delta	697	5 267	1 074	420	1 000	211	172	96	18 204	1 041	51.7	9.3	53.1
Denver	21 317	384 052	47 898	25 577	30 845	25 787	30 223	13 481	35 102	16	100.0	0.0	37.5
Dolores	44	192	D	D	32	D	D	4	22 276	160	8.8	49.4	68.1
Douglas	3 572	29 453	1 638	1 903	8 161	806	1 539	743	25 236	574	42.9	16.4	36.4
Eagle	2 564	26 617	1 044	407	3 824	496	1 084	649	24 388	124	27.4	33.9	51.6
Elbert	382	1 668	133	71	273	54	85	37	21 938	822	23.5	38.4	44.2
El Paso	13 057	194 751	21 712	22 293	28 112	10 350	13 975	5 447	27 969	851	32.2	32.0	42.0
Fremont	853	7 920	1 611	894	1 445	281	200	149	18 813	561	62.9	16.0	38.5
Garfield	1 807	13 416	1 400	261	2 830	656	599	345	25 711	475	36.2	27.6	53.1
Gilpin	90	3 352	D	D	D	D	D	13	25 606	11	27.3	27.3	45.5
Grand	692	6 081	166	45	732	144	126	93	15 357	161	26.5	50.9	57.1
Gunnison	785	6 785	281	113	1 118	172	163	108	15 971	187	19.3	37.4	55.6
Hinsdale	74	174	11	D	23	D	D	3	17 517	14	0.0	57.1	57.1
Huerfano	206	1 425	421	D	219	68	D	25	17 831	273	14.3	52.7	52.7
Jackson	57	213	D	D	51	D	3	5	22 005	126	15.1	70.6	70.6
Jefferson	15 132	167 896	16 179	18 740	29 285	7 834	14 238	5 090	30 317	377	67.1	11.1	39.5
Kiowa	45	255	D	9	52	D	4	4	17 600	339	0.9	72.0	64.3
Kit Carson	283	1 901	256	D	447	106	45	35	18 441	718	7.8	66.6	67.7
Lake	210	1 480	207	D	206	61	D	27	18 576	20	30.0	45.0	20.0
La Plata	1 886	16 444	2 143	1 116	2 973	500	764	359	21 813	781	33.5	16.6	43.4
Larimer	7 586	87 930	9 003	14 121	14 193	2 752	5 014	2 235	25 421	1 298	50.5	13.0	39.3
Las Animas	370	2 890	513	143	572	136	83	48	16 728	485	10.5	60.4	61.6
Lincoln	129	1 216	212	D	311	47	20	24	19 425	467	6.9	75.4	70.4
Logan	625	5 836	1 013	448	1 167	228	425	113	19 346	879	9.0	53.2	67.6
Mesa	3 528	39 408	6 474	3 884	6 634	1 225	1 901	937	23 768	1 489	64.1	8.3	44.3
Mineral	50	143	D	D	38	10	D	3	17 874	10	20.0	30.0	20.0
Moffat	355	3 253	446	63	749	68	83	91	27 961	389	18.0	44.0	47.3
Montezuma	754	6 302	903	383	1 320	218	256	134	21 242	718	34.8	18.1	46.4
Montrose	1 077	9 349	1 168	1 487	1 555	314	350	200	21 365	866	38.8	14.9	52.9
Morgan	663	8 166	1 172	2 853	1 003	238	129	178	21 753	759	12.1	38.3	69.7
Otero	536	5 133	1 262	490	933	215	86	94	18 318	512	33.2	23.2	56.4
Ouray	216	711	D	D	100	47	36	15	20 567	79	19.0	43.0	60.8
Park	354	1 215	100	D	154	33	69	25	20 383	183	16.9	44.3	45.4
Phillips	150	977	249	D	155	53	19	19	19 042	344	7.6	61.6	75.3
Pitkin	1 527	16 543	752	289	2 094	283	816	374	22 612	70	20.0	20.0	42.9
Prowers	450	4 309	503	876	948	232	106	80	18 591	522	12.6	53.3	65.3
Pueblo	3 178	45 760	9 348	4 362	7 032	1 429	1 189	1 012	22 116	664	31.3	34.2	48.3
Rio Blanco	214	1 407	230	D	180	54	30	36	25 777	255	22.0	43.1	56.1
Rio Grande	372	2 859	317	331	518	133	65	55	19 337	348	14.9	37.9	67.8
Routt	1 204	14 730	781	211	1 488	252	397	353	23 971	494	25.9	35.8	44.5
Saguache	113	604	D	93	124	13	8	10	16 925	248	9.7	56.9	74.2
San Juan	46	67	0	0	D	0	D	2	25 388	4	50.0	50.0	25.0
San Miguel	485	4 307	74	125	514	86	151	81	18 809	83	24.1	39.8	50.6
Sedgwick	91	541	135	D	115	35	10	8	15 074	215	4.2	58.6	77.2
Summit	1 683	18 787	442	147	3 290	266	567	340	18 085	35	17.1	40.0	54.3
Teller	605	5 364	219	87	634	149	224	103	19 179	84	35.7	34.5	32.1
Washington	119	759	37	91	158	D	18	14	18 810	792	7.7	62.1	65.0
Weld	3 707	52 895	5 566	11 260	7 135	3 704	1 213	1 421	26 855	2 959	28.6	24.6	57.4
Yuma	342	2 116	455	107	506	135	69	39	18 419	896	8.5	60.3	69.3
CONNECTICUT	92 362	1 493 964	211 359	246 125	189 957	122 463	78 060	58 226	38 974	3 687	54.7	2.8	49.5
Fairfield	28 438	424 846	48 890	55 613	53 977	31 759	33 757	21 548	50 719	255	71.8	0.0	49.4
Hartford	23 275	459 632	61 484	70 785	51 456	64 223	22 552	17 360	37 770	627	58.4	1.9	55.5
Litchfield	5 146	56 331	8 656	15 578	8 076	1 667	1 412	1 713	30 418	689	48.5	4.6	45.3
Middlesex	4 180	59 152	10 254	12 967	7 951	5 667	2 045	1 922	32 498	288	64.2	1.4	43.1
New Haven	20 937	334 737	58 033	58 533	45 332	15 695	12 724	10 982	32 808	423	68.8	1.2	53.7
New London	5 715	103 413	14 053	19 975	13 539	1 995	4 016	3 212	31 058	610	45.4	3.1	51.0
Tolland	2 500	26 462	4 833	4 222	5 090	818	1 080	701	26 475	355	51.8	3.7	46.5
Windham	2 171	29 391	5 156	8 452	4 536	639	474	788	26 803	440	44.8	4.5	48.0

Table B. States and Counties — Agriculture, Land, and Water

	Agriculture, 1997 (cont'd)															
	Land in farms					Value of land and buildings			Value of products sold				Percent of farms with sales of —			
			Acres					Value of machinery and equipment			Percent from —					
STATE County	Acreage (1,000)	Percent change, 1992–1997	Average size of farm	Total irrigated (1,000)	Total cropland (1,000)	Average per farm ($1,000)	Average per acre (dollars)	Average per farm ($1,000)	Total (mil dol)	Average per farm (dollars)	Crops	Live-stock and poultry products	$10,000 or more	$100,000 or more	Percent of land owned by Fed. Gov. 1997	Water con-sump-tion 1995 (mil gal/ day)
	117	118	119	120	121	122	123	124	125	126	127	128	129	130	131	132
COLORADO—Cont'd																
Clear Creek	5	-26.9	426	D	D	1 442	3 383	17	0	2 490	0.0	100.0	8.3	0.0	69.3	7.4
Conejos	285	-6.7	664	131	135	450	656	72	25	59 411	54.6	45.4	60.8	15.4	58.6	731.6
Costilla	363	9.7	2 124	44	D	733	345	96	16	93 441	83.7	16.3	55.0	15.2	0.1	196.8
Crowley	390	-8.1	1 920	22	54	1 110	575	53	73	362 007	6.4	93.6	62.6	19.2	0.7	64.8
Custer	144	-8.1	949	20	24	613	561	43	5	31 681	40.6	59.4	48.7	8.6	37.2	41.6
Delta	282	8.0	271	71	75	483	1 925	46	39	37 544	38.8	61.2	39.2	7.5	54.0	704.3
Denver	74	D	5	0	D	D	D	74	2	135 888	99.6	0.4	56.2	25.0	(1)NA	122.5
Dolores	156	-6.7	973	8	68	634	567	63	9	53 753	57.1	42.9	51.9	11.2	60.9	28.5
Douglas	204	-11.5	356	4	40	795	2 126	28	17	29 823	56.5	43.5	25.6	4.4	26.1	28.7
Eagle	185	-13.1	1 492	17	19	1 901	1 356	50	7	59 784	9.6	90.4	41.9	12.9	78.3	137.6
Elbert	1 095	-1.0	1 332	6	179	700	539	43	31	38 016	14.1	85.9	41.7	7.8	0.0	33.8
El Paso	867	1.2	1 019	15	78	410	443	27	30	35 641	41.5	58.5	36.1	6.2	14.9	134.7
Fremont	283	-14.6	505	19	19	730	895	26	12	21 615	28.7	71.3	20.5	2.9	44.9	158.9
Garfield	427	-3.1	899	51	63	970	1 137	48	23	48 035	40.1	59.9	46.9	10.1	62.2	562.6
Gilpin	9	-32.5	797	D	D	1 084	1 360	15	D	D	D		45.5	0.0	41.9	0.5
Grand	251	-16.0	1 560	40	38	1 269	995	51	9	54 861	18.5	81.5	53.4	12.4	67.0	204.2
Gunnison	195	10.2	1 043	51	38	1 436	1 154	70	8	45 114	10.9	89.1	56.1	12.3	77.6	286.4
Hinsdale	9	-1.8	631	2	2	872	1 383	32	0	26 955	D	D	64.3	0.0	94.9	13.2
Huerfano	641	-0.1	2 348	16	28	854	346	41	10	35 461	9.0	91.0	48.0	6.6	20.8	91.3
Jackson	477	1.1	3 786	124	86	2 095	613	104	16	123 754	17.4	82.6	73.0	34.1	52.0	400.6
Jefferson	98	-5.2	259	3	15	615	2 266	35	19	51 655	89.3	10.7	29.2	7.2	21.7	96.7
Kiowa	914	4.1	2 696	6	494	657	264	96	62	182 077	27.8	72.2	69.0	19.5	0.2	14.8
Kit Carson	1 346	0.3	1 874	146	839	754	413	111	177	246 646	39.6	60.4	72.3	35.4	0.0	166.4
Lake	17	22.8	859	4	D	839	976	38	1	25 655	4.1	95.9	35.0	5.0	70.7	26.2
La Plata	580	-1.2	743	72	91	685	1 018	42	16	20 227	31.3	68.7	37.6	3.6	38.6	378.2
Larimer	542	0.4	418	78	127	657	1 602	49	100	77 414	38.1	61.9	37.1	10.2	46.9	270.2
Las Animas	2 215	-3.1	4 567	24	77	886	196	58	20	41 930	10.1	89.9	53.0	9.3	10.4	120.9
Lincoln	1 648	-0.7	3 530	5	D	617	173	86	45	95 873	33.4	66.6	68.1	22.5	0.1	17.6
Logan	1 129	5.9	1 284	109	524	511	427	99	293	333 038	16.8	83.2	74.7	28.1	0.0	335.2
Mesa	417	-0.8	280	88	92	487	2 045	30	50	33 882	39.9	60.1	33.2	5.9	72.1	972.9
Mineral	D	D	D	0	0	460	1 139	28	0	14 551	D	D	50.0	0.0	93.4	2.1
Moffat	1 031	-11.1	2 651	30	104	1 790	668	37	19	48 683	15.4	84.6	46.3	10.3	56.9	206.8
Montezuma	935	12.1	1 303	61	103	576	441	40	22	30 465	59.0	41.0	41.2	6.0	37.5	314.0
Montrose	372	-16.8	429	85	89	508	1 382	53	88	101 933	22.3	77.7	51.3	11.0	67.6	644.2
Morgan	741	-1.5	976	142	342	604	649	99	406	534 842	18.9	81.1	75.8	35.6	0.1	335.5
Otero	580	-8.4	1 132	63	65	473	405	66	100	195 731	21.2	78.8	63.5	21.3	20.3	424.6
Ouray	117	-1.8	1 480	18	15	2 180	1 473	55	3	40 980	17.9	82.1	54.4	11.4	43.9	58.0
Park	311	-20.0	1 700	18	25	936	516	30	4	19 795	20.9	79.1	36.1	3.8	50.8	8.7
Phillips	463	0.7	1 347	88	389	841	625	183	117	340 302	45.8	54.2	77.3	45.9	0.0	86.2
Pitkin	25	-21.2	360	10	10	839	2 329	68	2	21 812	39.5	60.5	50.0	2.9	82.5	46.6
Prowers	863	-14.0	1 653	111	445	679	427	102	151	288 652	28.2	71.8	68.8	28.0	0.1	695.3
Pueblo	823	-8.3	1 239	36	90	533	471	38	34	50 666	42.3	57.7	45.6	10.5	7.9	246.1
Rio Blanco	466	-14.8	1 829	36	56	885	531	52	14	55 239	8.7	91.3	62.4	15.7	73.4	122.8
Rio Grande	232	5.3	666	136	134	908	1 266	144	73	209 246	92.7	7.3	69.8	33.6	58.1	405.4
Routt	521	-9.6	1 054	50	102	935	966	60	23	46 271	15.4	84.6	46.0	10.1	44.3	307.0
Saguache	482	4.2	1 942	207	140	1 242	644	146	50	202 844	81.3	18.7	73.8	35.5	66.2	425.7
San Juan	D	D	D	D	D	D	D	13	D	D	D	D	25.0	0.0	88.3	0.3
San Miguel	162	-19.4	1 951	12	28	1 340	687	51	3	34 907	16.4	83.6	48.2	7.2	58.8	63.0
Sedgwick	294	-5.1	1 368	52	197	744	545	162	55	254 654	45.2	54.8	79.5	41.9	0.0	94.6
Summit	35	-9.1	987	11	7	1 164	1 180	69	2	43 166	52.5	47.5	45.7	11.4	77.5	29.2
Teller	83	-19.8	993	2	5	1 006	1 012	29	1	15 207	21.6	78.4	33.3	3.6	43.8	9.2
Washington	1 394	4.5	1 760	56	853	684	399	106	98	123 608	52.2	47.8	70.2	24.9	0.0	46.1
Weld	1 914	-8.3	647	393	882	567	807	95	1 287	434 821	16.3	83.7	59.8	23.7	8.1	1 161.9
Yuma	1 365	-4.7	1 524	274	633	891	565	161	481	537 247	24.8	75.2	75.6	39.6	0.0	272.7
CONNECTICUT	359	0.0	97	7	181	571	5 949	41	422	114 361	62.6	37.4	39.8	12.6	0.5	1 275.1
Fairfield	12	19.4	47	0	6	636	15 558	31	17	66 026	64.7	35.3	39.6	9.8	0.3	128.0
Hartford	53	-7.2	84	4	33	675	7 695	47	112	178 929	91.3	8.7	50.1	17.9	0.0	93.7
Litchfield	91	4.1	131	0	45	700	5 467	39	27	39 856	38.2	61.8	40.1	9.1	1.2	93.0
Middlesex	19	-6.6	65	1	8	366	7 248	35	34	117 861	92.6	7.4	28.5	6.2	0.1	626.2
New Haven	25	-5.5	58	1	13	643	8 904	39	43	102 326	85.1	14.9	43.0	13.0	0.2	261.0
New London	68	2.9	111	0	30	445	4 220	41	126	206 237	43.8	56.2	34.9	12.5	0.3	41.2
Tolland	36	-7.1	102	0	17	471	4 852	44	27	76 811	39.2	60.8	33.5	10.4	0.5	17.0
Windham	57	2.8	128	0	29	504	3 926	46	35	79 230	16.9	83.1	40.9	17.7	0.7	15.0

1. Denver County included with Adams County.

Table B. States and Counties — **Residential Construction, Wholesale and Retail Trade, and Real Estate**

STATE County	Value of Residential Construction Authorized by Building Permits, 1999		Wholesale Trade, 1997				Retail Trade[1], 1997				Real Estate and Rental and Leasing, 1997			
	New Construction ($1,000)	Number of Housing Units	Number of Establishments	Number of Employees	Sales (mil dol)	Annual Payroll (mil dol)	Number of Establishments	Number of Employees	Sales (mil dol)	Annual Payroll (mil dol)	Number of Establishments	Number of Employees	Receipts (mil dol)	Annual Payroll (mil dol)
	133	134	135	136	137	138	139	140	141	142	143	144	145	146
COLORADO—Cont'd														
Clear Creek	15 383	88	17	97	30.7	2.7	50	299	39.3	3.9	16	107	3.8	0.7
Conejos	4 628	181	6	57	11.4	0.9	22	139	22.5	2.0	3	9	0.3	0.1
Costilla	NA	NA	NA	NA	NA	NA	11	24	3.6	0.3	2	D	D	D
Crowley	320	4	NA	NA	NA	NA	10	87	12.6	1.3	3	6	0.2	0.1
Custer	8 894	90	4	8	1.6	0.1	21	100	13.9	1.4	12	29	1.6	0.4
Delta	7 476	94	26	272	40.8	4.9	129	957	156.8	15.0	24	54	5.5	1.0
Denver	299 673	3 379	1 681	26 604	16 177.1	972.8	2 410	30 080	5 600.9	628.0	1 201	11 339	1 771.9	287.0
Dolores	705	6	6	45	23.7	0.9	6	34	4.5	0.4	5	3	0.4	0.0
Douglas	1 051 255	7 164	198	967	943.9	34.5	500	8 052	1 212.0	123.5	157	397	69.9	9.6
Eagle	275 465	881	62	242	189.0	8.5	367	3 313	497.2	67.3	175	989	84.8	19.3
Elbert	39 635	291	18	60	39.3	2.8	40	188	34.9	2.8	7	8	0.9	0.2
El Paso	565 268	5 537	498	6 513	1 417.9	213.3	1 901	27 806	5 015.1	503.6	735	3 064	362.3	62.8
Fremont	30 975	416	28	120	42.8	3.0	143	1 311	203.8	21.6	30	101	10.7	1.4
Garfield	85 759	635	52	379	112.8	8.7	277	2 635	552.5	55.7	87	387	30.4	5.9
Gilpin	8 985	81	1	D	D	D	7	27	2.8	0.4	4	30	2.0	0.6
Grand	68 881	485	10	52	12.9	1.0	116	706	95.6	10.5	56	607	34.8	7.5
Gunnison	49 431	309	9	40	9.1	0.7	139	969	135.6	13.6	46	359	15.8	4.1
Hinsdale	1 674	13	1	D	D	D	14	15	5.1	0.5	6	11	1.9	0.2
Huerfano	8 128	115	7	26	2.9	0.6	39	211	33.0	3.3	10	14	1.6	0.1
Jackson	1 186	16	3	25	3.6	0.6	6	50	6.2	0.6	NA	NA	NA	NA
Jefferson	319 126	2 763	771	4 994	2 805.6	178.2	1 986	28 098	5 114.8	509.2	726	3 214	359.1	66.4
Kiowa	70	1	6	16	8.0	0.3	8	52	4.4	0.5	NA	NA	NA	NA
Kit Carson	4 015	57	28	241	122.5	4.8	64	462	100.1	7.6	4	11	1.6	0.2
Lake	5 270	43	4	D	D	D	33	202	25.9	2.7	12	56	4.4	0.7
La Plata	49 914	401	71	511	119.4	15.4	317	2 848	440.6	49.5	108	325	33.0	6.4
Larimer	403 100	3 591	311	2 630	805.6	75.9	1 201	13 810	2 440.5	234.2	360	1 497	190.0	27.8
Las Animas	9 171	89	17	117	33.8	3.3	54	576	84.8	8.0	8	28	4.8	0.5
Lincoln	1 251	13	9	61	20.6	0.9	36	320	58.3	5.1	4	D	D	D
Logan	6 036	55	32	338	97.4	6.4	115	1 149	199.5	16.5	22	61	3.2	0.8
Mesa	127 412	1 362	198	1 461	531.1	42.8	600	6 409	1 152.7	115.0	133	658	62.6	11.6
Mineral	141	13	NA	NA	NA	NA	10	34	3.7	0.5	4	D	D	D
Moffat	4 439	44	28	123	35.6	3.3	77	706	117.4	12.1	11	23	1.9	0.3
Montezuma	1 760	23	23	112	18.4	2.0	136	1 302	228.6	22.4	27	94	6.1	1.4
Montrose	27 076	320	44	377	88.7	6.7	171	1 710	304.1	31.3	44	176	11.4	2.5
Morgan	9 485	108	41	403	416.9	9.0	119	996	157.6	15.0	23	78	4.3	0.8
Otero	2 415	29	34	286	118.9	6.1	101	932	141.2	13.6	17	61	4.1	0.8
Ouray	16 833	68	2	D	D	D	41	99	11.9	1.4	12	25	2.7	0.3
Park	42 142	388	15	D	D	D	35	175	28.2	3.1	13	18	1.9	0.6
Phillips	1 895	20	15	170	142.3	4.7	23	165	28.4	2.4	3	D	D	D
Pitkin	152 955	263	26	204	79.0	9.3	265	2 264	288.9	41.0	144	644	82.0	18.2
Prowers	6 030	93	25	403	82.0	7.4	93	826	112.9	11.4	17	42	2.0	0.3
Pueblo	135 434	1 437	113	1 101	390.3	27.5	600	7 040	1 180.7	121.7	131	486	58.8	8.2
Rio Blanco	1 214	18	6	23	6.6	0.5	36	201	21.5	2.2	7	10	0.8	0.1
Rio Grande	11 495	94	31	564	98.1	9.1	77	476	96.8	8.6	14	29	3.0	0.5
Routt	103 940	480	31	185	51.4	5.3	184	1 484	190.3	22.5	86	633	33.9	9.1
Saguache	5 370	119	8	92	8.7	1.1	24	118	30.1	2.4	4	D	D	D
San Juan	503	4	NA	NA	NA	NA	18	39	5.1	0.8	1	D	D	D
San Miguel	81 001	145	5	28	2.2	0.6	76	524	44.6	6.5	44	159	17.4	3.4
Sedgwick	187	2	10	71	36.9	1.7	24	129	25.6	2.0	2	D	D	D
Summit	101 943	488	41	191	58.5	4.5	339	2 801	387.9	45.8	156	1 295	100.3	26.4
Teller	35 341	303	15	57	19.5	2.3	72	516	77.6	8.6	42	182	18.3	2.5
Washington	714	8	8	147	53.1	3.4	21	162	23.0	2.1	1	D	D	D
Weld	428 133	3 557	247	2 829	1 334.6	84.9	505	6 195	1 155.5	109.2	154	576	65.4	9.5
Yuma	1 140	14	30	239	112.4	4.8	68	529	89.4	8.6	1	D	D	D
CONNECTICUT	1 466 185	10 637	5 283	77 716	75 821.6	3 595.3	14 574	186 935	34 938.9	3 634.3	3 372	20 635	3 522.8	609.3
Fairfield	474 661	2 343	1 768	28 573	48 325.4	1 559.1	4 008	54 012	11 563.9	1 218.0	1 098	7 639	1 748.1	288.2
Hartford	273 106	2 182	1 369	25 741	16 831.0	1 108.2	3 683	51 121	8 829.0	943.6	874	6 243	996.4	181.9
Litchfield	127 814	846	240	2 203	779.0	90.7	816	8 193	1 611.0	158.0	141	409	48.2	9.1
Middlesex	98 720	869	218	2 045	823.0	74.2	742	8 050	1 345.0	143.1	142	765	96.3	14.8
New Haven	249 257	2 334	1 316	15 458	8 028.3	633.3	3 335	41 942	7 725.2	775.9	761	4 030	477.5	89.0
New London	107 116	879	201	2 279	801.6	81.9	1 182	13 923	2 405.0	240.3	188	723	82.4	13.8
Tolland	98 988	792	89	602	246.5	23.2	428	5 028	763.9	81.8	86	484	49.8	8.7
Windham	36 524	392	82	815	333.1	24.7	380	4 666	695.8	73.6	82	342	24.1	3.8

1. Establishments with payroll.

STATE County	Professional, Scientific, and Technical Services[1], 1997				Manufacturing, 1997				Accommodation and Foodservices, 1997			
	Number of Establishments	Number of Employees	Receipts (mil dol)	Annual Payroll (mil dol)	Number of Establishments	Number of Employees	Receipts (mil dol)	Annual Payroll (mil dol)	Number of Establishments	Number of Employees	Sales (mil dol)	Annual Payroll (mil dol)
	147	148	149	150	151	152	153	154	155	156	157	158
COLORADO—Cont'd												
Clear Creek	31	47	5.1	1.9	NA	NA	NA	NA	48	539	18.8	5.2
Conejos	3	8	0.2	0.1	NA	NA	NA	NA	14	44	1.9	0.5
Costilla	3	4	0.3	0.1	NA	NA	NA	NA	7	D	D	D
Crowley	NA	NA	NA	NA	NA	NA	NA	NA	5	D	D	D
Custer	9	59	2.8	0.7	NA	NA	NA	NA	14	103	4.2	1.0
Delta	43	126	5.6	2.1	NA	NA	NA	NA	68	559	15.2	4.2
Denver	3 147	29 056	3 640.3	1 455.0	976	26 320	4 867.8	816.2	1 564	33 749	1 335.2	386.0
Dolores	2	D	D	D	NA	NA	NA	NA	7	D	D	D
Douglas	459	1 143	166.7	43.0	119	1 941	289.7	58.8	178	3 593	109.1	32.1
Eagle	191	755	87.3	34.2	43	502	85.3	14.9	223	7 181	288.1	100.3
Elbert	36	46	4.1	1.7	NA	NA	NA	NA	11	73	2.4	0.7
El Paso	1 384	10 515	1 199.2	467.1	499	21 593	5 698.9	700.6	998	21 480	771.9	216.9
Fremont	37	118	6.6	2.3	47	950	146.9	26.8	82	1 008	29.8	7.6
Garfield	144	508	45.5	17.1	NA	NA	NA	NA	155	1 906	72.6	21.3
Gilpin	8	111	2.5	1.0	NA	NA	NA	NA	9	647	61.1	11.4
Grand	42	99	6.9	2.4	NA	NA	NA	NA	127	1 531	51.9	15.5
Gunnison	45	144	10.4	3.6	NA	NA	NA	NA	114	2 765	84.3	22.6
Hinsdale	4	4	0.6	0.1	NA	NA	NA	NA	18	71	3.7	0.8
Huerfano	13	23	1.3	0.4	NA	NA	NA	NA	28	201	5.9	1.7
Jackson	1	D	D	D	NA	NA	NA	NA	7	48	0.9	0.3
Jefferson	1 979	11 633	1 284.3	490.7	559	17 871	3 711.2	803.0	967	18 968	585.7	172.5
Kiowa	3	4	0.3	0.1	NA	NA	NA	NA	5	D	D	D
Kit Carson	15	42	2.3	0.9	NA	NA	NA	NA	20	360	9.8	2.6
Lake	13	22	1.8	0.9	NA	NA	NA	NA	44	342	8.4	2.1
La Plata	171	639	57.9	22.1	66	752	51.8	19.3	169	4 281	143.2	44.1
Larimer	711	3 815	336.3	134.2	384	15 840	3 890.7	645.0	647	10 779	343.6	95.0
Las Animas	19	83	3.4	1.6	NA	NA	NA	NA	42	462	13.6	3.4
Lincoln	5	16	0.5	0.2	NA	NA	NA	NA	25	238	8.0	2.2
Logan	33	376	17.1	6.8	19	736	163.2	15.2	51	769	20.4	5.8
Mesa	275	1 283	91.3	39.2	167	3 605	484.2	99.2	247	4 555	124.7	36.3
Mineral	NA	NA	NA	NA	NA	NA	NA	NA	11	19	2.0	0.6
Moffat	28	55	3.3	0.9	NA	NA	NA	NA	27	372	12.0	3.4
Montezuma	50	158	11.0	3.3	NA	NA	NA	NA	82	987	27.8	7.8
Montrose	80	259	18.8	7.4	64	1 540	156.0	31.5	76	825	29.3	7.3
Morgan	33	90	5.9	1.6	25	D	D	D	63	789	19.6	5.4
Otero	24	73	4.1	1.1	17	534	36.2	10.7	63	618	15.9	3.8
Ouray	12	30	2.0	0.9	NA	NA	NA	NA	45	223	10.9	2.8
Park	21	49	3.6	1.3	NA	NA	NA	NA	38	270	9.9	2.8
Phillips	8	15	1.2	0.2	NA	NA	NA	NA	10	D	D	D
Pitkin	184	661	81.0	27.3	NA	NA	NA	NA	189	5 720	228.3	81.8
Prowers	28	111	6.5	2.5	20	D	D	D	40	470	12.3	3.5
Pueblo	192	981	49.7	19.3	107	4 688	1 021.3	147.0	321	4 969	142.4	38.1
Rio Blanco	14	37	2.4	0.9	NA	NA	NA	NA	25	182	7.5	2.3
Rio Grande	18	62	3.7	1.7	NA	NA	NA	NA	41	353	10.9	3.0
Routt	102	394	30.8	10.5	NA	NA	NA	NA	108	3 225	98.1	28.1
Saguache	6	11	0.7	0.2	NA	NA	NA	NA	10	D	D	D
San Juan	1	D	D	D	NA	NA	NA	NA	15	6	2.0	0.5
San Miguel	44	110	9.8	3.7	NA	NA	NA	NA	59	848	25.1	8.8
Sedgwick	3	D	D	D	NA	NA	NA	NA	11	D	D	D
Summit	129	531	45.2	18.3	NA	NA	NA	NA	204	7 781	226.6	67.6
Teller	50	155	16.4	5.1	NA	NA	NA	NA	68	1 848	94.8	26.0
Washington	5	16	0.8	0.2	NA	NA	NA	NA	11	D	D	D
Weld	221	964	72.2	27.9	208	10 773	4 338.5	345.4	271	4 047	106.8	29.4
Yuma	15	46	3.1	1.0	NA	NA	NA	NA	24	211	4.6	1.3
CONNECTICUT	9 393	71 058	9 115.8	3 700.1	5 844	252 330	46 938.2	10 452.1	6 903	96 556	3 746.6	1 062.8
Fairfield	3 834	31 051	4 658.6	1 932.2	1 316	57 560	12 115.5	2 495.9	1 772	24 643	1 113.3	311.3
Hartford	2 188	20 638	2 471.2	978.9	1 592	71 982	11 319.8	3 113.1	1 778	28 579	995.4	289.1
Litchfield	381	1 150	133.8	42.5	448	17 288	3 246.8	589.8	369	3 709	150.6	43.2
Middlesex	332	1 747	211.6	76.0	309	13 132	2 999.3	513.5	355	4 231	172.0	49.3
New Haven	1 885	11 285	1 191.0	466.6	1 592	59 380	12 073.9	2 285.0	1 644	21 581	804.7	221.4
New London	463	3 944	338.9	162.2	237	19 888	2 962.8	1 035.1	590	8 652	333.0	95.7
Tolland	200	883	78.1	31.5	152	4 487	739.2	145.8	208	3 148	101.4	32.6
Windham	110	360	32.6	10.2	198	8 613	1 480.9	273.8	187	2 013	76.2	20.2

1. Firms subject to federal tax.

STATE County	Health Care and Social Assistance[1], 1997				Other Services[1], 1997				Federal funds and grants, fiscal 1999[2]			
									Expenditures (mil dol)			
										Direct payments for individuals[3]		
	Number of Establishments	Number of Employees	Receipts (mil dol)	Annual Payroll (mil dol)	Number of Establishments	Number of Employees	Receipts (mil dol)	Annual Payroll (mil dol)	Total	Social Security and government retirement	Medicare	Food stamps and Supplemental Security Income
	159	160	161	162	163	164	165	166	167	168	169	170
COLORADO—Cont'd												
Clear Creek	7	24	1.5	0.6	9	25	1.8	0.5	18.2	8.1	3.0	0.4
Conejos	4	27	0.9	0.4	5	26	1.0	0.4	43.0	12.9	5.3	2.6
Costilla	NA	NA	NA	NA	1	D	D	D	25.2	9.6	2.7	1.7
Crowley	2	D	D	D	4	7	0.2	0.0	19.8	8.0	2.8	1.0
Custer	2	D	D	D	3	10	0.5	0.1	12.7	8.4	1.4	0.3
Delta	50	551	19.0	8.8	28	91	6.2	1.5	124.1	69.0	23.4	3.4
Denver	1 478	15 938	1 197.2	562.3	1 101	8 212	604.5	172.8	5 019.2	1 036.4	460.7	104.9
Dolores	1	D	D	D	NA	NA	NA	NA	9.4	4.4	1.1	0.2
Douglas	168	1 175	75.0	38.1	169	854	56.7	17.3	141.2	102.1	14.3	1.0
Eagle	79	471	41.5	18.8	78	431	25.0	8.6	51.9	17.5	4.0	0.6
Elbert	11	65	2.9	1.1	20	44	3.5	0.9	55.0	20.5	4.9	0.4
El Paso	1 134	10 522	710.1	311.1	754	4 558	264.9	89.7	3 753.9	1 127.3	210.2	45.0
Fremont	71	771	29.7	13.5	39	158	8.3	2.4	218.4	95.2	27.3	5.2
Garfield	83	686	49.7	21.2	84	479	26.8	8.6	103.1	55.6	16.2	2.3
Gilpin	2	D	D	D	5	D	D	D	5.0	2.6	0.7	0.1
Grand	11	54	3.5	1.2	15	46	3.7	1.4	28.5	14.6	5.2	0.3
Gunnison	29	102	7.0	2.4	25	94	6.3	1.7	75.3	12.6	3.0	0.5
Hinsdale	2	D	D	D	1	D	D	D	2.3	1.2	0.3	0.0
Huerfano	13	117	4.3	1.7	9	18	0.9	0.3	42.5	18.7	10.1	1.9
Jackson	1	D	D	D	2	D	D	D	5.6	2.8	0.7	0.1
Jefferson	1 065	10 148	623.1	271.6	876	4 665	284.7	88.1	2 491.2	652.0	217.5	18.8
Kiowa	1	D	D	D	2	D	D	D	26.1	3.4	2.0	0.1
Kit Carson	11	97	4.5	1.5	15	32	2.5	0.5	72.5	14.1	6.2	0.6
Lake	5	34	2.0	0.6	6	21	1.0	0.2	17.2	7.9	3.3	0.3
La Plata	109	604	46.5	19.9	74	324	19.9	5.1	129.1	57.2	20.0	2.6
Larimer	530	4 957	296.2	133.5	384	2 151	127.6	39.0	751.9	331.3	107.4	13.4
Las Animas	25	137	6.7	2.4	27	80	5.2	1.2	95.0	37.2	13.2	4.1
Lincoln	8	112	4.3	1.7	5	19	1.4	0.5	34.7	9.6	5.1	0.5
Logan	40	416	20.5	9.2	47	200	15.9	3.8	88.4	35.8	15.0	2.1
Mesa	264	2 504	150.7	69.9	188	1 018	73.9	19.1	539.4	246.5	73.4	13.0
Mineral	NA	NA	NA	NA	1	D	D	D	2.0	1.4	0.2	0.0
Moffat	23	263	10.9	4.1	26	67	5.5	1.1	44.2	18.2	7.1	1.1
Montezuma	44	373	19.1	7.6	43	196	12.2	2.7	100.1	43.8	13.9	2.1
Montrose	79	517	30.4	11.3	45	141	10.1	2.6	127.6	66.8	21.1	2.8
Morgan	41	728	44.0	16.0	40	120	7.6	1.8	106.8	39.0	18.1	2.6
Otero	45	239	11.8	5.2	31	126	7.2	1.7	121.3	49.2	19.5	5.7
Ouray	4	3	0.4	0.1	2	D	D	D	9.2	5.2	1.4	0.1
Park	6	16	1.0	0.7	15	31	3.2	0.6	25.8	18.4	2.5	0.4
Phillips	7	79	2.2	1.0	9	19	1.5	0.3	40.0	10.1	5.5	0.1
Pitkin	48	235	20.4	8.1	43	116	9.6	2.6	23.7	9.9	2.6	0.1
Prowers	22	198	9.3	3.7	30	75	6.9	1.5	67.6	22.5	9.3	2.5
Pueblo	299	3 459	203.9	98.4	194	912	47.5	13.9	695.5	327.3	112.2	34.5
Rio Blanco	4	12	1.0	0.2	13	34	2.4	0.6	24.5	9.1	3.9	0.3
Rio Grande	19	198	6.8	2.7	20	62	3.3	0.6	52.7	21.3	6.3	2.4
Routt	44	199	15.2	6.9	43	125	9.0	2.6	-18.1	15.7	4.9	0.5
Saguache	NA	NA	NA	NA	2	D	D	D	24.9	8.2	2.6	1.5
San Juan	NA	NA	NA	NA	NA	NA	NA	NA	1.6	0.9	0.2	0.0
San Miguel	11	39	2.3	0.6	8	57	1.9	0.7	10.6	3.6	0.9	0.1
Sedgwick	4	22	0.5	0.2	7	14	1.1	0.2	27.0	7.5	3.9	0.3
Summit	36	168	9.9	4.1	49	200	12.8	3.5	25.8	15.5	1.9	0.2
Teller	26	125	5.8	2.2	28	70	5.5	1.1	46.3	34.8	4.8	1.0
Washington	3	13	0.5	0.2	3	9	0.5	0.1	56.2	10.1	4.2	0.4
Weld	209	2 279	138.2	56.5	215	1 130	67.8	17.9	486.7	206.4	79.9	15.8
Yuma	16	220	8.7	3.4	25	66	4.8	1.0	73.8	16.9	6.9	0.7
CONNECTICUT	7 515	100 363	6 849.7	3 199.3	6 121	34 089	2 370.2	727.8	19 240.5	6 124.4	3 007.7	370.3
Fairfield	2 124	25 229	1 915.4	900.3	1 497	8 289	596.6	192.2	4 108.8	1 442.2	753.6	78.5
Hartford	1 970	28 270	1 925.8	936.4	1 656	10 183	698.7	220.5	5 087.3	1 644.4	800.4	125.9
Litchfield	388	4 258	226.1	97.0	319	1 347	97.5	26.1	642.8	331.5	155.6	8.0
Middlesex	332	4 839	298.1	139.8	297	1 339	111.8	30.9	526.1	267.5	109.5	8.6
New Haven	1 855	26 597	1 750.3	800.2	1 634	9 237	633.4	191.6	4 007.1	1 532.9	822.5	109.8
New London	490	7 493	521.3	227.8	391	2 113	137.6	37.8	3 278.2	529.6	200.6	22.3
Tolland	188	1 657	100.0	41.5	183	1 030	61.4	18.4	384.5	181.3	75.1	3.9
Windham	168	2 020	112.6	56.3	144	551	33.3	10.4	438.9	186.2	90.4	13.3

1. Firms subject to federal tax.   2. October 1, 1998 to September 30, 1999.   3. State totals may include programs not allocated by county.

Table B. States and Counties — Federal Funds and Local Government Finances

	Federal funds and grants, fiscal 1999[1] (cont'd)							Local government finances, 1997				
	Expenditures (mil dol) (cont'd)							General revenue				
	Procurement contract awards			Grants[2]							Taxes		
STATE County	Salaries and wages	Defense	Other	Medicaid and other health-related	Nutrition and family welfare	Education	Other	Total (mil dol)	Intergovern-mental (mil dol)	Total (mil dol)	Per capita[3] (dollars) Total	Property
	171	172	173	174	175	176	177	178	179	180	181	182
COLORADO—Cont'd												
Clear Creek	1.6	0.0	0.3	0.8	0.4	0.3	3.3	23.0	6.0	14.1	1 577	1 315
Conejos	1.7	0.0	1.7	13.0	3.0	0.8	0.9	22.9	16.1	4.1	530	436
Costilla	0.8	0.0	0.1	7.8	1.1	0.3	0.0	14.0	7.6	4.4	1 215	1 132
Crowley	0.8	0.0	0.2	2.6	0.9	0.2	1.9	7.9	4.4	2.5	594	387
Custer	0.6	0.0	0.2	0.9	0.3	0.1	0.3	6.5	2.2	3.0	906	729
Delta	8.6	0.1	1.3	11.9	3.6	1.3	0.0	71.5	26.2	17.9	694	434
Denver	813.0	910.5	294.9	422.0	261.3	126.8	479.4	2 460.9	611.0	947.2	1 898	752
Dolores	0.5	0.0	0.1	0.9	0.3	0.1	0.0	6.0	3.5	1.7	994	955
Douglas	8.7	6.0	2.5	2.1	1.3	1.1	1.1	351.9	71.6	153.4	1 215	870
Eagle	7.4	0.1	2.4	1.3	1.1	0.4	15.8	149.6	17.9	92.1	2 882	1 718
Elbert	1.4	0.4	0.4	1.3	0.5	0.3	22.0	32.5	16.8	12.0	684	628
El Paso	1 194.3	875.0	93.6	82.4	44.5	22.3	29.1	1 187.2	404.2	379.5	791	492
Fremont	60.4	0.0	2.0	15.0	5.9	1.3	4.3	68.5	36.8	22.7	528	341
Garfield	13.7	0.2	2.8	4.6	2.3	1.3	1.8	104.7	34.3	50.9	1 354	962
Gilpin	0.4	0.0	0.2	0.8	0.2	0.1	0.0	32.7	11.5	17.7	4 471	2 192
Grand	4.3	0.0	1.1	0.6	0.5	0.3	1.6	45.7	8.2	23.1	2 349	1 552
Gunnison	5.4	0.0	44.9	1.1	0.5	0.3	5.8	42.2	6.9	22.7	1 859	1 119
Hinsdale	0.2	0.0	0.0	0.2	0.0	0.0	0.3	3.4	1.2	1.7	2 479	1 434
Huerfano	0.9	0.0	0.2	8.1	1.7	0.5	0.1	23.1	12.4	8.0	1 185	1 026
Jackson	1.2	0.0	0.3	0.2	0.1	0.1	0.0	5.4	2.6	2.0	1 272	1 034
Jefferson	490.3	12.9	964.0	49.2	24.1	13.8	37.0	1 002.1	321.0	496.0	999	746
Kiowa	0.7	0.0	0.2	0.6	0.2	0.1	1.8	12.8	2.9	4.3	2 553	2 418
Kit Carson	1.9	0.0	0.6	2.7	0.9	0.4	2.7	25.4	10.2	7.9	1 101	913
Lake	2.1	0.1	0.3	0.9	1.0	0.5	0.2	55.7	18.9	19.8	3 137	2 882
La Plata	16.9	0.9	4.6	10.3	5.3	2.7	4.0	102.8	26.8	57.5	1 432	943
Larimer	102.6	4.3	23.4	59.1	16.0	8.3	66.8	708.1	144.5	250.2	1 107	741
Las Animas	3.4	1.7	0.7	17.4	4.0	2.4	6.9	38.2	21.6	10.1	700	522
Lincoln	1.3	0.0	0.3	1.8	1.1	0.2	2.4	25.0	12.6	5.9	1 055	757
Logan	3.6	0.0	2.8	6.8	2.5	1.1	0.3	59.7	26.5	19.7	1 087	766
Mesa	53.5	4.3	79.6	34.6	10.9	5.4	7.8	248.0	103.1	97.9	884	501
Mineral	0.2	0.0	0.0	0.0	0.0	0.0	0.0	4.6	1.6	2.3	3 447	1 705
Moffat	5.9	0.0	1.7	1.8	1.3	0.5	2.2	66.7	7.9	25.9	2 106	1 621
Montezuma	11.6	0.7	2.8	9.5	3.9	1.9	8.1	74.2	28.0	20.4	916	662
Montrose	13.6	0.1	4.8	10.2	3.1	1.3	1.9	107.6	34.1	28.8	950	581
Morgan	6.0	0.0	5.1	8.7	4.6	1.3	0.5	71.4	26.2	28.7	1 141	921
Otero	5.3	0.0	1.3	18.8	10.3	1.8	0.7	58.2	35.5	11.7	559	306
Ouray	0.5	0.0	0.1	0.2	0.2	0.1	1.3	11.7	3.0	5.1	1 581	1 104
Park	2.2	0.1	0.7	0.4	0.6	0.3	0.3	29.2	11.2	12.6	991	947
Phillips	1.2	0.0	0.3	1.6	0.5	0.2	2.7	16.8	6.4	4.2	972	850
Pitkin	4.4	0.1	1.1	0.4	0.1	0.1	4.7	113.0	4.4	63.0	4 640	2 325
Prowers	2.2	0.0	0.5	7.4	3.0	1.2	0.8	39.7	22.1	10.3	753	451
Pueblo	35.9	8.6	12.6	90.7	39.0	10.0	10.8	303.9	144.2	112.1	844	517
Rio Blanco	2.9	0.0	0.6	1.0	0.5	0.3	5.3	40.6	11.9	16.0	2 547	2 326
Rio Grande	4.7	0.0	1.3	8.3	3.1	0.9	1.3	35.5	16.7	11.5	1 011	590
Routt	5.9	0.0	-50.2	1.5	0.6	0.5	1.3	66.3	9.5	40.4	2 343	1 455
Saguache	1.8	0.0	0.7	4.2	2.2	0.5	0.0	21.0	12.9	4.0	683	622
San Juan	0.1	0.0	0.1	0.1	0.1	0.0	0.2	3.9	1.3	2.0	3 544	1 785
San Miguel	1.5	0.0	0.8	0.8	0.3	0.1	2.4	36.5	7.0	22.2	4 163	2 898
Sedgwick	0.9	0.0	0.3	1.6	0.4	0.1	0.8	11.3	3.7	3.4	1 309	1 139
Summit	2.9	1.0	0.8	0.7	0.3	0.4	1.7	107.0	9.3	73.2	3 966	1 772
Teller	2.1	0.4	0.6	0.8	1.1	0.4	0.2	50.4	19.0	21.9	1 107	650
Washington	2.2	0.0	0.4	1.8	1.0	0.2	7.1	16.0	8.1	6.3	1 358	1 285
Weld	30.9	2.6	8.7	52.4	20.2	10.6	18.2	385.0	149.5	154.2	991	735
Yuma	2.2	0.0	0.6	2.9	1.5	0.4	0.8	29.8	9.1	13.4	1 433	1 313
CONNECTICUT	1 349.6	3 126.8	509.6	2 005.7	722.3	251.6	866.1	X	X	X	X	X
Fairfield	227.7	764.8	147.1	386.2	101.2	33.4	121.9	2 356.2	502.0	1 564.8	1 878	1 852
Hartford	371.7	322.3	191.3	611.8	399.7	120.4	383.0	2 202.7	715.6	1 259.4	1 526	1 510
Litchfield	26.7	19.4	11.7	50.0	9.7	4.4	19.6	398.3	104.7	255.6	1 411	1 394
Middlesex	22.3	9.1	8.2	59.4	9.7	4.5	17.5	358.1	94.4	216.6	1 454	1 440
New Haven	304.6	51.2	97.5	692.1	123.8	47.8	149.9	2 067.5	761.1	1 105.2	1 395	1 378
New London	363.0	1 943.2	35.3	103.2	24.9	11.3	25.0	663.2	233.3	332.3	1 314	1 285
Tolland	17.6	11.9	14.1	25.5	6.5	7.8	34.4	270.4	106.6	141.3	1 078	1 067
Windham	16.0	4.9	4.3	60.7	16.8	5.0	25.7	241.0	131.5	90.3	859	849

1. October 1, 1998 to September 30, 1999. 2. State totals may include programs not allocated by county. 3. Based on the resident population estimated as of July 1 of the year shown.

STATE County	Local government finances, 1997 (cont'd)									Government employment, 1998			Presidential election, 2000		
	Direct general expenditure							Debt outstanding					Percent of vote cast —		
					Percent of total for —										
	Total (mil dol)	Per capita[1] (dollars)	Educa-tion	Health and hospitals	Police protec-tion	Public welfare	High-ways	Total (mil dol)	Per capita[1] (dollars)	Federal civilian	Federal military	State and local	Demo-cratic	Republi-can	All other
	183	184	185	186	187	188	189	190	191	192	193	194	195	196	197
COLORADO—Cont'd															
Clear Creek	23.1	2 593	34.5	2.8	6.8	4.1	14.2	12.7	1 428	39	27	587	44.4	45.6	9.9
Conejos	21.8	2 786	52.3	5.1	2.3	10.6	8.3	5.8	744	45	24	581	47.6	48.3	4.1
Costilla	14.9	4 090	45.3	7.0	4.4	13.2	7.6	4.7	1 284	14	11	396	64.0	30.6	5.5
Crowley	8.0	1 886	53.1	0.8	3.2	11.3	12.1	0.9	213	15	13	509	35.4	59.2	5.5
Custer	6.6	2 014	39.1	17.2	1.1	8.2	10.3	1.2	350	13	10	208	24.0	68.7	7.2
Delta	71.1	2 755	44.4	20.2	3.1	5.8	6.1	29.2	1 131	194	80	1 689	25.7	66.0	8.3
Denver	2 235.7	4 481	17.5	10.2	5.1	8.3	2.6	5 696.5	11 416	15 836	2 863	51 732	61.9	30.9	7.3
Dolores	5.8	3 377	39.6	2.4	5.1	5.1	26.9	0.3	147	12	0	170	25.8	65.3	8.8
Douglas	368.8	2 921	45.5	0.2	2.5	0.6	7.2	756.2	5 990	155	425	5 632	31.4	65.0	3.6
Eagle	152.0	4 756	25.0	2.0	4.8	1.1	8.7	261.8	8 195	140	101	2 218	44.6	47.2	8.2
Elbert	31.2	1 778	68.5	0.3	2.3	3.0	10.2	8.4	481	34	56	800	25.9	68.6	5.4
El Paso	1 144.8	2 385	46.6	14.3	5.3	5.0	5.4	1 299.3	2 707	10 213	29 134	26 203	30.8	63.9	5.3
Fremont	66.4	1 545	52.0	2.7	5.9	6.8	6.3	24.0	558	1 183	132	3 819	33.0	61.7	5.3
Garfield	112.3	2 984	50.1	2.7	3.2	4.1	5.5	177.5	4 716	296	118	2 825	35.6	53.2	11.2
Gilpin	26.8	6 764	10.4	0.6	11.5	2.2	14.9	40.7	10 266	0	13	322	44.6	40.8	14.6
Grand	42.7	4 343	28.9	10.7	6.0	1.9	15.2	23.2	2 360	119	30	903	36.3	56.2	7.5
Gunnison	60.6	4 972	47.4	9.7	3.9	1.1	10.8	39.5	3 240	160	38	1 396	42.3	43.2	14.5
Hinsdale	3.0	4 319	21.7	1.7	6.5	0.1	34.9	0.6	881	0	0	62	33.2	55.8	11.0
Huerfano	21.7	3 223	32.5	1.3	6.3	15.0	15.0	7.1	1 051	19	21	434	47.1	46.2	6.7
Jackson	5.5	3 572	42.6	4.8	3.9	3.6	17.5	4.6	2 985	33	0	151	18.7	73.7	7.6
Jefferson	1 026.6	2 067	49.9	1.1	7.3	3.9	6.2	930.6	1 874	8 884	1 522	22 700	42.9	51.0	6.1
Kiowa	12.3	7 399	24.9	23.6	1.8	24.6	12.2	0.8	453	17	0	240	21.8	75.2	3.0
Kit Carson	27.1	3 782	43.1	15.9	3.3	2.8	13.7	1.8	251	46	22	747	23.4	73.5	3.1
Lake	65.8	10 404	84.8	3.7	1.3	1.0	2.5	1.1	174	54	19	620	49.3	40.2	10.5
La Plata	104.2	2 596	49.5	0.3	4.7	4.2	8.8	62.7	1 561	371	122	3 258	38.4	48.8	12.9
Larimer	577.9	2 557	34.1	17.4	4.7	4.2	8.5	1 031.1	4 562	2 069	728	20 876	38.9	52.7	8.5
Las Animas	40.5	2 792	46.8	2.2	4.5	13.2	7.4	8.1	561	72	44	1 618	53.2	42.2	4.6
Lincoln	22.3	3 972	37.3	11.7	4.5	4.3	24.6	6.7	1 191	30	17	857	23.2	74.1	2.7
Logan	64.4	3 556	57.9	0.5	3.0	5.7	10.3	20.0	1 107	74	54	1 797	28.4	68.3	3.3
Mesa	237.6	2 147	45.0	1.3	6.4	8.4	7.7	240.6	2 174	1 170	341	6 556	30.3	63.5	6.3
Mineral	4.4	6 529	36.2	1.6	7.9	0.0	28.7	0.1	133	0	0	85	34.6	60.5	4.9
Moffat	65.0	5 287	23.0	14.4	3.8	2.4	8.4	245.2	19 948	148	38	1 045	22.9	72.0	5.1
Montezuma	70.2	3 151	42.3	20.9	4.8	4.6	4.5	29.5	1 325	339	68	1 445	27.2	65.6	7.1
Montrose	104.3	3 445	31.4	25.3	3.5	5.4	4.7	58.2	1 922	290	93	2 245	28.4	65.2	6.4
Morgan	77.5	3 081	49.4	0.9	4.3	6.3	8.5	60.1	2 391	133	76	2 119	32.1	63.6	4.3
Otero	65.1	3 123	55.2	1.5	2.9	12.5	5.1	17.5	841	117	62	1 877	40.5	55.8	3.7
Ouray	11.7	3 647	51.8	1.5	6.1	3.5	8.7	4.2	1 313	0	10	271	31.6	57.3	11.2
Park	34.0	2 667	45.3	1.8	3.6	2.7	11.1	13.1	1 032	60	40	644	35.9	55.2	8.9
Phillips	16.9	3 910	50.5	19.3	3.9	2.9	9.7	1.4	316	29	13	482	25.4	70.9	3.7
Pitkin	93.8	6 911	11.5	22.5	6.3	5.3	8.2	89.5	6 590	95	40	1 543	53.0	32.9	14.1
Prowers	39.0	2 858	53.6	1.3	3.6	6.3	7.9	9.5	699	54	41	1 491	30.1	66.9	3.0
Pueblo	298.9	2 249	43.8	1.9	4.8	12.0	5.9	413.0	3 107	706	408	10 269	53.5	42.3	4.1
Rio Blanco	40.0	6 368	51.8	19.0	4.0	3.0	7.6	7.5	1 198	73	19	952	19.0	76.5	4.4
Rio Grande	34.7	3 041	50.6	1.5	4.3	10.0	8.1	7.2	630	118	34	821	33.6	61.3	5.1
Routt	62.9	3 653	36.5	5.7	6.3	2.1	9.0	39.3	2 283	129	53	1 413	43.7	46.4	9.9
Saguache	18.1	3 062	46.2	4.8	3.1	8.3	13.9	3.8	635	62	18	568	45.3	42.6	12.1
San Juan	4.0	7 111	30.9	2.9	7.4	0.8	11.3	0.6	1 048	0	0	71	34.2	48.2	17.7
San Miguel	38.8	7 287	15.2	3.5	7.1	1.4	12.3	55.7	10 469	31	16	540	49.1	32.0	18.9
Sedgwick	13.1	5 036	30.7	33.9	2.4	3.5	6.6	6.5	2 484	19	0	302	29.5	67.3	3.2
Summit	109.1	5 909	36.3	2.5	4.2	0.9	10.7	124.4	6 734	70	56	1 536	47.9	40.6	11.4
Teller	47.5	2 402	40.9	4.2	8.6	7.4	8.3	34.3	1 736	44	62	974	27.9	65.8	6.3
Washington	16.1	3 472	55.0	0.9	3.6	4.0	15.0	0.4	88	61	14	418	19.5	76.8	3.7
Weld	387.6	2 491	51.6	2.0	5.2	5.1	6.7	205.5	1 321	547	488	10 606	36.3	58.0	5.7
Yuma	31.5	3 364	37.8	21.1	4.9	1.4	15.7	13.1	1 393	51	28	861	24.8	72.4	2.8
CONNECTICUT	X	X	X	X	X	X	X	X	X	22 175	16 986	185 623	55.9	38.4	5.6
Fairfield	2 334.9	2 802	48.1	1.5	5.9	2.2	4.0	1 042.3	1 251	4 483	2 069	38 097	NA	NA	NA
Hartford	2 189.0	2 653	51.8	0.9	6.4	1.8	3.9	1 032.5	1 251	7 385	2 155	58 715	NA	NA	NA
Litchfield	417.6	2 306	63.8	0.7	3.6	0.3	6.3	186.6	1 031	389	444	7 371	NA	NA	NA
Middlesex	385.6	2 588	60.8	1.0	3.9	0.6	5.6	297.4	1 996	324	368	8 707	NA	NA	NA
New Haven	2 132.3	2 692	52.4	1.0	5.9	1.9	3.3	1 353.4	1 708	6 543	2 095	39 880	NA	NA	NA
New London	673.9	2 664	55.5	0.8	5.8	1.1	5.7	441.4	1 745	2 625	9 258	13 885	NA	NA	NA
Tolland	277.7	2 120	64.2	0.4	2.5	0.8	4.6	127.8	976	208	338	12 730	NA	NA	NA
Windham	232.0	2 207	64.3	0.5	1.8	1.0	4.9	128.1	1 218	218	259	6 238	NA	NA	NA

1. Based on the resident population estimated as of July 1 of the year shown.

Table B. States and Counties — Land Area and Population

Population and population characteristics, 1999

STATE/County code	MSA/PMSA/NECMA code[1]	County Type[2]	STATE County	Land area[3] (sq km) 1990	Total persons	Rank	Per square kilometer	White	Black	Am. Indian, Eskimo, Aleut	Asian and Pacific Islander	Percent Hispanic[4]	Under 5 years	5 to 17 years	18 to 24 years	25 to 34 years	35 to 44 years	45 to 54 years
				1	2	3	4	5	6	7	8	9	10	11	12	13	14	15
10 000	...	X	DELAWARE	5 062	753 538	X	148.9	77.7	19.8	0.3	2.1	3.7	6.7	17.6	9.2	15.0	17.3	12.9
10 001	2190	3	Kent	1 530	126 048	415	82.4	75.8	21.6	0.6	2.1	3.6	7.6	19.2	9.5	14.9	16.6	12.9
10 003	9160	2	New Castle	1 104	487 182	110	441.3	77.9	19.4	0.2	2.5	4.2	6.6	17.3	9.8	15.7	17.8	13.0
10 005	...	6	Sussex	2 429	140 308	378	57.8	79.0	19.5	0.6	0.9	2.1	6.0	17.0	6.7	12.8	16.1	12.5
11 000	...	X	DISTRICT OF COLUMBIA	159	519 000	X	3 264.2	35.2	61.4	0.3	3.1	7.4	5.3	13.1	8.8	18.3	17.1	14.0
11 001	8840	0	District of Columbia	159	519 000	103	3 264.2	35.2	61.4	0.3	3.1	7.4	5.3	13.1	8.8	18.3	17.1	14.0
12 000	...	X	FLORIDA	139 852	15 111 244	X	108.1	82.3	15.4	0.4	1.9	15.4	6.3	17.3	8.2	12.4	15.6	12.5
12 001	2900	3	Alachua	2 264	198 484	273	87.7	73.3	22.7	0.3	3.7	5.3	6.3	17.2	19.5	14.0	15.9	10.6
12 003	...	6	Baker	1 516	21 181	1 701	14.0	81.6	17.5	0.4	0.5	1.9	7.2	24.7	8.8	13.7	16.8	12.7
12 005	6015	3	Bay	1 978	147 958	351	74.8	83.3	13.0	1.0	2.8	2.8	6.8	20.0	8.2	13.0	15.8	13.6
12 007	...	6	Bradford	759	24 872	1 536	32.8	75.4	23.4	0.5	0.7	3.3	5.7	19.1	8.1	15.2	17.3	13.9
12 009	4900	2	Brevard	2 638	470 365	118	178.3	87.9	9.5	0.5	2.1	4.7	6.0	16.5	7.2	12.4	14.5	13.1
12 011	2680	0	Broward	3 131	1 535 468	16	490.4	78.9	18.6	0.3	2.2	12.8	6.3	16.6	7.6	13.7	17.3	12.9
12 013	...	8	Calhoun	1 470	12 436	2 253	8.5	80.0	18.3	1.5	0.2	1.9	6.3	20.8	9.3	12.9	15.1	13.9
12 015	6580	3	Charlotte	1 797	136 992	384	76.2	93.8	4.7	0.3	1.2	4.0	4.1	12.6	4.8	7.8	11.3	11.3
12 017	...	4	Citrus	1 512	116 111	455	76.8	95.9	2.9	0.4	0.7	2.9	4.5	14.2	4.6	7.6	11.8	12.5
12 019	3600	2	Clay	1 557	141 353	377	90.8	90.4	6.3	0.5	2.9	4.2	7.0	23.1	7.9	12.1	18.7	14.6
12 021	5345	3	Collier	5 246	207 029	261	39.5	93.1	5.7	0.5	0.7	18.6	6.0	15.2	6.6	10.6	13.5	11.8
12 023	...	6	Columbia	2 065	53 738	857	26.0	76.3	22.3	0.3	1.0	2.2	6.5	21.8	8.1	11.7	15.6	13.1
12 027	...	6	De Soto	1 651	24 636	1 544	14.9	80.4	18.2	0.7	0.8	13.4	6.6	18.7	8.5	11.6	13.6	11.7
12 029	...	9	Dixie	1 824	12 919	2 220	7.1	89.8	9.4	0.4	0.3	1.4	6.1	19.3	7.3	9.6	14.4	14.9
12 031	3600	2	Duval	2 004	738 483	63	368.5	67.9	28.5	0.4	3.2	3.9	7.7	20.1	9.5	14.7	17.1	12.4
12 033	6080	2	Escambia	1 719	282 432	195	164.3	72.3	23.4	1.2	3.1	3.0	6.7	19.4	10.8	12.7	15.1	13.0
12 035	2020	2	Flagler	1 256	49 110	921	39.1	88.0	10.1	0.3	1.6	6.7	4.5	14.4	4.9	7.6	12.1	11.5
12 037	...	7	Franklin	1 383	9 978	2 428	7.2	83.6	15.2	0.7	0.4	1.7	5.7	18.5	6.6	10.0	14.0	15.9
12 039	8240	3	Gadsden	1 337	44 077	1 001	33.0	36.3	63.0	0.3	0.4	3.3	6.8	23.4	9.9	12.9	15.4	11.8
12 041	...	8	Gilchrist	904	14 056	2 130	15.5	90.1	9.3	0.4	0.3	2.4	6.2	20.2	11.7	9.9	14.8	13.5
12 043	...	8	Glades	2 003	8 693	2 536	4.3	76.5	17.0	6.1	0.4	11.8	5.6	18.0	7.5	10.9	14.0	13.6
12 045	...	6	Gulf	1 463	13 562	2 170	9.3	72.8	26.2	0.6	0.4	1.4	5.2	18.3	8.9	14.0	13.6	13.0
12 047	...	9	Hamilton	1 334	12 785	2 227	9.6	55.1	44.2	0.4	0.3	4.3	6.5	22.7	10.8	14.0	16.0	11.9
12 049	...	6	Hardee	1 651	21 017	1 717	12.7	91.3	7.7	0.7	0.4	30.7	7.5	22.5	10.0	12.2	13.8	10.9
12 051	...	6	Hendry	2 985	29 463	1 393	9.9	78.0	18.8	2.5	0.7	29.0	8.8	23.8	9.3	12.3	13.9	11.8
12 053	8280	0	Hernando	1 239	128 482	407	103.7	94.3	4.7	0.3	0.7	4.6	4.6	14.7	4.9	7.5	11.8	11.4
12 055	...	6	Highlands	2 664	74 795	663	28.1	87.0	11.6	0.4	0.9	7.4	4.8	14.5	4.8	7.7	10.2	9.9
12 057	8280	0	Hillsborough	2 722	940 484	36	345.5	82.2	15.3	0.4	2.1	18.3	7.0	18.9	9.2	14.0	17.0	12.9
12 059	...	7	Holmes	1 250	18 761	1 834	15.0	91.7	6.3	1.5	0.6	2.1	5.7	20.6	8.1	11.4	15.5	14.9
12 061	...	4	Indian River	1 303	100 253	517	76.9	88.7	10.2	0.2	0.9	4.5	5.1	15.1	5.9	9.4	12.9	11.4
12 063	...	6	Jackson	2 372	44 549	991	18.8	68.8	30.3	0.6	0.3	4.2	5.3	20.5	9.9	12.0	15.9	13.1
12 065	...	6	Jefferson	1 548	13 090	2 207	8.5	50.7	48.8	0.2	0.3	2.7	6.0	22.2	9.3	11.8	16.5	12.3
12 067	...	9	Lafayette	1 406	6 477	2 735	4.6	81.8	17.6	0.4	0.3	6.0	5.2	19.4	9.7	17.1	16.4	12.6
12 069	5960	1	Lake	2 469	209 812	258	85.0	87.6	11.4	0.4	0.6	4.4	5.3	15.7	5.8	9.0	12.5	12.1
12 071	2700	2	Lee	2 081	400 542	144	192.5	90.7	8.1	0.3	1.0	6.8	5.7	15.2	6.3	10.3	13.6	12.0
12 073	8240	3	Leon	1 727	215 926	253	125.0	69.2	28.3	0.4	2.2	3.4	6.1	18.2	17.9	13.7	17.5	11.5
12 075	...	8	Levy	2 897	32 386	1 300	11.2	83.9	14.5	0.6	1.0	3.1	5.8	19.4	6.6	9.6	14.0	13.6
12 077	...	8	Liberty	2 165	6 703	2 709	3.1	77.2	21.7	0.7	0.4	3.8	5.2	19.3	10.6	16.7	17.6	11.9
12 079	...	7	Madison	1 792	17 919	1 875	10.0	53.0	46.6	0.4	0.1	2.1	7.0	21.1	10.0	12.8	14.6	12.4
12 081	7510	2	Manatee	1 920	243 531	225	126.8	89.1	9.6	0.4	1.0	6.8	5.8	15.5	6.5	10.5	13.6	11.5
12 083	5790	3	Marion	4 090	245 975	219	60.1	83.9	14.9	0.4	0.8	4.6	5.7	16.9	6.3	9.7	13.2	12.0
12 085	2710	2	Martin	1 439	118 117	446	82.1	91.5	7.0	0.6	1.0	7.0	5.0	13.6	5.9	9.9	13.6	11.9
12 086	5000	0	Miami-Dade	5 036	2 175 634	8	432.0	77.6	20.4	0.3	1.8	57.4	6.9	17.9	9.0	13.8	16.3	12.6
12 087	...	4	Monroe	2 583	79 941	632	30.9	92.0	6.4	0.5	1.2	18.0	5.6	12.9	6.2	12.9	18.3	14.8
12 089	3600	2	Nassau	1 688	56 811	818	33.7	86.5	12.6	0.4	0.5	1.8	6.6	21.0	7.5	11.6	16.6	14.7
12 091	2750	3	Okaloosa	2 424	170 049	311	70.2	84.7	10.5	0.7	4.1	4.8	7.3	19.8	8.8	14.4	15.9	13.0
12 093	...	6	Okeechobee	2 006	32 386	1 300	16.1	88.9	9.6	0.7	0.8	16.4	7.5	22.4	8.2	11.2	13.3	11.3
12 095	5960	0	Orange	2 351	817 206	51	347.6	78.2	18.0	0.4	3.3	14.0	7.2	18.8	11.0	15.6	16.8	12.1
12 097	5960	1	Osceola	3 424	150 596	346	44.0	90.2	6.9	0.5	2.5	17.6	7.2	20.1	8.5	12.7	16.5	12.9
12 099	8960	2	Palm Beach	5 269	1 049 420	32	199.2	83.3	14.8	0.2	1.6	11.2	6.0	15.1	6.7	11.9	15.1	11.7
12 101	8280	0	Pasco	1 930	330 704	173	171.3	96.0	2.6	0.4	1.0	5.4	5.4	15.5	6.0	9.5	13.1	12.0
12 103	8280	0	Pinellas	726	878 499	42	1 210.1	88.1	9.7	0.3	1.9	3.7	5.2	14.6	6.7	11.4	15.5	12.9
12 105	3980	2	Polk	4 856	457 347	122	94.2	82.7	15.9	0.4	1.0	6.1	6.6	18.9	7.8	10.8	14.3	12.6
12 107	...	6	Putnam	1 870	70 215	701	37.5	77.4	21.5	0.3	0.8	4.0	6.3	20.1	6.8	9.9	13.9	12.5
12 109	3600	2	St. Johns	1 577	119 685	442	75.9	88.1	10.6	0.3	1.0	3.5	6.0	17.5	7.4	11.3	16.9	13.7
12 111	2710	2	St. Lucie	1 483	181 850	293	122.6	79.2	19.4	0.3	1.1	5.9	6.5	17.4	6.5	11.1	13.6	11.2
12 113	6080	2	Santa Rosa	2 631	120 952	438	46.0	92.1	4.8	1.1	2.0	2.4	7.2	21.1	7.5	13.0	16.6	14.8

1. MSA = Metropolitan Statistical Area. PMSA = Primary MSA. NECMA = New England County Metropolitan Area. See Appendix A for explanation of these concepts. See Appendix B for list of metropolitan areas identified by type, with component counties.   2. County typology code from the Economic Research Service of USDA. See Appendix A for definition.   3. Dry land or land partially or temporarily covered by water.   4. Hispanic persons may be of any race.

Table B. States and Counties — **Population and Households**

STATE County	55 to 64 years (16)	65 to 74 years (17)	75 years and over (18)	Percent female (19)	1990 (20)	1980 (21)	1980–1990 (22)	1990–1999 (23)	Births (24)	Deaths (25)	Net migration (26)	Number (27)	Percent change, 1980–1990 (28)	Persons per house-hold (29)	Female family house-holder[1] (30)	One person (31)
DELAWARE	8.4	7.2	5.8	51.4	666 168	594 338	12.1	13.1	97 768	58 165	44 318	247 497	19.5	2.61	11.8	23.2
Kent	8.0	6.1	5.3	51.3	110 993	98 219	13.0	13.6	17 410	9 006	5 822	39 655	21.1	2.70	11.9	21.2
New Castle	8.0	6.5	5.3	51.4	441 946	398 115	11.0	10.2	63 837	35 504	13 832	164 161	18.1	2.61	12.1	24.0
Sussex	9.9	10.8	8.0	51.3	113 229	98 004	15.5	23.9	16 521	13 655	24 664	43 681	23.4	2.54	10.9	22.3
DISTRICT OF COLUMBIA	9.5	7.4	6.5	53.2	606 900	638 432	-4.9	-14.5	87 167	59 836	-116 932	249 634	-1.4	2.26	19.5	41.5
District of Columbia	9.5	7.4	6.5	53.2	606 900	638 432	-4.9	-14.5	87 167	59 836	-116 932	249 634	-1.4	2.26	19.5	41.5
FLORIDA	9.5	9.5	8.7	51.5	12 938 071	9 746 961	32.7	16.8	1 781 648	1 370 234	1 748 623	5 134 869	37.1	2.46	10.7	25.5
Alachua	6.4	5.4	4.7	51.0	181 596	151 369	20.0	9.3	23 901	12 754	6 115	71 258	30.5	2.40	12.0	28.1
Baker	7.4	4.6	4.0	47.4	18 486	15 289	20.9	14.6	2 727	1 399	1 367	5 554	30.9	3.00	12.4	15.8
Bay	9.3	7.8	5.6	50.9	126 994	97 740	29.9	16.5	18 904	11 158	11 949	48 938	40.8	2.54	11.8	23.0
Bradford	8.5	6.5	5.5	44.1	22 515	20 023	12.4	10.5	2 946	2 322	1 763	7 193	14.2	2.68	12.3	20.4
Brevard	10.3	11.6	8.3	50.8	398 978	272 959	46.2	17.9	48 165	38 835	62 789	161 365	58.5	2.43	9.1	23.7
Broward	8.8	7.5	9.3	51.7	1 255 531	1 018 257	23.3	22.3	180 561	145 429	242 062	528 442	26.6	2.35	10.0	29.5
Calhoun	8.4	6.2	7.1	46.9	11 011	9 294	18.5	12.9	1 333	1 298	1 413	3 793	17.8	2.64	13.3	24.3
Charlotte	14.2	18.4	15.4	51.8	110 975	58 460	89.8	23.4	9 177	17 013	34 069	48 433	86.8	2.23	6.0	23.0
Citrus	13.8	17.4	13.6	51.9	93 513	54 703	70.9	24.2	8 034	14 942	29 617	40 573	76.5	2.27	6.8	23.1
Clay	7.2	5.3	4.2	50.7	105 986	67 052	58.1	33.4	15 464	7 776	26 547	36 663	69.4	2.86	9.1	15.2
Collier	10.6	14.4	11.2	50.3	152 099	85 971	76.9	36.1	23 017	16 606	49 196	61 703	81.7	2.41	7.1	22.6
Columbia	9.1	8.2	5.9	49.9	42 613	35 399	20.4	26.1	6 346	4 464	9 382	15 611	28.1	2.67	13.0	22.7
De Soto	9.1	11.0	9.2	47.5	23 865	19 039	25.3	3.2	3 540	2 661	-32	8 222	31.4	2.62	10.9	22.1
Dixie	11.9	9.7	6.8	48.7	10 585	7 751	36.6	22.1	1 389	1 086	2 041	3 916	47.1	2.56	10.0	22.4
Duval	8.0	5.9	4.7	51.8	672 971	571 003	17.9	9.7	112 299	56 509	3 740	257 245	23.5	2.54	13.7	26.0
Escambia	8.7	7.7	5.9	51.4	262 445	233 794	12.4	7.6	37 958	23 005	2 019	98 608	21.6	2.57	14.2	23.6
Flagler	14.1	21.4	9.5	51.7	28 701	10 913	163.0	71.1	2 796	4 004	21 771	11 880	172.5	2.40	7.1	18.9
Franklin	11.2	9.4	8.7	50.4	8 967	7 661	17.0	11.3	976	1 136	1 207	3 628	31.2	2.42	9.6	25.4
Gadsden	8.0	6.3	5.4	52.8	41 116	41 674	-1.3	7.2	6 687	4 003	400	13 405	10.9	2.90	22.5	21.5
Gilchrist	10.1	8.0	5.5	47.0	9 667	5 767	67.6	45.4	1 338	1 168	4 236	3 284	63.7	2.65	9.4	19.0
Glades	10.9	11.6	7.8	45.9	7 591	5 992	26.7	14.5	788	840	1 172	2 885	29.7	2.57	7.0	22.1
Gulf	10.1	8.6	7.2	46.0	11 504	10 658	7.9	17.9	1 375	1 343	2 070	4 324	17.4	2.56	11.1	22.6
Hamilton	7.2	5.7	5.2	45.8	10 930	8 761	24.8	17.0	1 444	1 038	1 463	3 488	20.1	2.81	18.4	22.2
Hardee	7.6	8.5	6.9	46.5	19 499	20 357	-4.2	7.8	4 098	1 760	-768	6 391	2.2	2.95	10.4	17.6
Hendry	7.6	7.1	5.3	48.6	25 773	18 599	38.6	14.3	5 600	2 191	309	8 402	41.0	2.99	12.1	17.6
Hernando	13.4	19.7	12.1	51.7	101 115	44 469	127.4	27.1	9 290	15 633	34 064	42 300	138.5	2.37	6.9	19.7
Highlands	11.9	19.6	16.5	52.2	68 432	47 526	44.0	9.3	7 764	10 721	9 617	29 544	55.8	2.28	7.0	24.2
Hillsborough	8.3	7.0	5.7	51.3	834 054	646 939	28.9	12.8	128 478	71 647	49 726	324 872	36.5	2.51	11.9	25.3
Holmes	9.5	7.2	7.1	48.1	15 778	14 723	7.2	18.9	1 956	1 936	3 015	5 800	10.6	2.56	11.2	23.6
Indian River	11.5	16.0	12.8	51.5	90 208	59 896	50.6	11.1	9 260	11 657	12 771	38 057	63.1	2.33	7.8	23.9
Jackson	9.0	7.1	7.2	48.7	41 375	39 154	5.7	7.7	5 032	4 305	2 599	14 465	8.5	2.56	12.9	25.3
Jefferson	8.3	7.1	6.5	49.2	11 296	10 703	5.5	15.9	1 510	1 191	1 496	3 982	14.2	2.79	16.7	22.1
Lafayette	8.4	6.2	4.9	40.4	5 578	4 035	38.2	16.1	653	406	660	1 721	21.8	2.74	10.7	19.6
Lake	11.6	14.5	13.5	51.8	152 104	104 870	45.0	37.9	18 559	21 937	61 911	63 616	52.7	2.35	8.0	23.8
Lee	11.3	14.0	11.6	51.5	335 113	205 266	63.3	19.5	40 776	40 166	65 644	140 124	69.8	2.35	8.2	23.0
Leon	6.3	4.9	3.9	52.0	192 493	148 655	29.5	12.2	25 775	11 775	9 871	74 828	38.3	2.43	12.3	27.0
Levy	11.0	11.7	8.3	52.0	25 912	19 870	30.4	25.0	3 262	3 227	6 453	10 079	38.7	2.52	11.1	22.4
Liberty	8.5	5.5	4.7	40.7	5 569	4 260	30.7	20.4	686	458	928	1 706	14.9	2.69	11.3	21.9
Madison	8.4	6.9	6.9	48.1	16 569	14 894	11.2	8.1	2 044	1 567	921	5 522	11.0	2.75	17.1	22.9
Manatee	10.7	12.3	13.4	52.3	211 707	148 445	42.6	15.0	26 236	28 287	34 508	91 060	46.9	2.29	8.4	27.0
Marion	10.9	14.9	10.4	51.5	194 835	122 488	59.1	26.2	24 659	25 011	52 288	78 177	72.0	2.44	10.3	22.9
Martin	11.1	15.5	13.6	50.7	100 900	64 014	57.6	17.1	10 923	13 004	19 713	43 022	66.3	2.28	6.5	25.0
Miami-Dade	9.3	7.5	6.8	52.4	1 937 194	1 625 509	19.2	12.3	301 761	172 737	101 096	692 355	13.5	2.75	14.9	24.9
Monroe	11.2	10.9	7.4	47.9	78 024	63 188	23.5	2.5	8 430	6 570	-552	33 583	27.5	2.24	6.4	27.8
Nassau	8.9	7.6	5.6	50.6	43 941	32 894	33.6	29.3	6 467	3 701	10 176	16 192	47.5	2.68	9.5	21.2
Okaloosa	8.9	7.3	4.6	50.1	143 777	109 920	30.8	18.3	22 365	9 964	10 239	53 313	42.0	2.60	9.5	20.9
Okeechobee	9.2	9.9	6.8	46.5	29 627	20 264	46.2	9.3	4 773	3 105	1 192	10 214	46.3	2.75	9.3	19.1
Orange	7.9	6.0	4.8	50.7	677 491	470 865	43.9	20.6	111 054	50 571	76 772	254 852	49.3	2.56	11.6	23.7
Osceola	8.6	7.2	6.2	51.0	107 728	49 287	118.6	39.8	18 505	10 004	34 540	39 150	110.3	2.68	9.5	19.2
Palm Beach	9.2	11.7	12.5	51.7	863 503	576 758	49.7	21.5	116 406	106 994	176 334	365 558	56.0	2.32	8.6	27.5
Pasco	12.2	13.5	12.9	52.0	281 131	193 661	45.2	17.6	29 619	43 885	64 369	121 674	49.6	2.26	7.3	25.7
Pinellas	10.5	10.1	13.0	52.9	851 659	728 531	16.9	3.2	88 393	116 209	57 694	380 635	19.1	2.18	9.4	31.9
Polk	9.7	10.3	8.9	51.3	405 382	321 652	26.0	12.8	58 365	42 914	37 696	155 969	36.3	2.53	10.8	22.4
Putnam	11.0	11.4	8.0	51.1	65 070	50 549	28.7	7.9	8 800	7 499	4 102	25 070	36.3	2.55	11.8	23.1
St. Johns	10.0	9.7	7.3	51.4	83 829	51 303	63.4	42.8	10 693	8 830	33 977	33 426	79.5	2.44	9.3	24.1
St. Lucie	10.2	13.8	9.6	50.8	150 171	87 182	72.3	21.1	20 805	17 342	28 867	58 174	79.0	2.54	9.9	20.3
Santa Rosa	8.8	6.4	4.6	50.3	81 961	55 988	45.8	47.6	12 760	6 234	31 707	29 900	60.8	2.68	9.8	18.3

1. No spouse present.

Table B. States and Counties — **Vital Statistics, Health Resources, and Crime**

STATE County	Births, average 1996–1998 Total	Rate[1]	Deaths, average 1996–1998 Number Total	Infant[2]	Deaths Rate Total[1]	Infant[3]	Physicians,[4] 1998 Number	Rate[5]	Hospitals,[4] 1998 Number	Beds Number	Beds Rate[5]	Medicare enrollees 1999	Serious crimes known to police, 1998[6] Total Number	Rate[7]
	32	33	34	35	36	37	38	39	40	41	42	43	44	45
DELAWARE	10 329	14.0	6 530	86	8.9	8.4	1 722	232	9	1 990	268	109 575	39 902	5 363
Kent...........................	1 821	14.8	996	16	8.1	9.0	181	146	1	190	153	15 837	6 325	5 071
New Castle.....................	6 704	14.0	3 979	53	8.3	8.0	1 256	260	5	1 423	295	63 288	27 198	5 630
Sussex.........................	1 804	13.5	1 555	17	11.6	9.2	285	208	3	377	276	30 338	6 190	4 544
DISTRICT OF COLUMBIA	8 001	15.0	6 269	109	11.8	13.6	3 117	596	10	4 322	826	75 423	46 210	8 836
District of Columbia............	8 001	15.0	6 269	109	11.8	13.6	3 117	596	10	4 322	826	75 423	46 210	8 836
FLORIDA	192 471	13.1	155 369	1 398	10.6	7.3	37 384	251	214	51 241	344	2 770 576	1 027 123	6 886
Alachua	2 471	12.5	1 476	27	7.5	10.8	1 325	667	3	1 057	532	25 051	19 116	9 469
Baker...........................	307	14.7	165	3	7.9	9.8	14	66	1	93	441	2 481	636	3 010
Bay.............................	1 996	13.7	1 298	19	8.9	9.7	256	174	2	478	325	22 484	8 666	5 822
Bradford	319	13.0	267	5	10.9	15.7	9	36	1	23	93	3 309	980	3 954
Brevard........................	4 871	10.6	4 600	24	10.0	5.0	872	187	5	1 190	255	93 639	23 708	5 053
Broward........................	20 333	13.8	15 819	142	10.7	7.0	3 758	250	20	5 538	368	251 056	95 761	6 397
Calhoun........................	154	12.4	135	1	10.9	8.7	8	64	1	36	290	1 949	308	2 453
Charlotte.......................	1 005	7.6	1 998	5	15.1	5.0	401	297	3	652	483	38 452	3 920	2 881
Citrus..........................	840	7.5	1 830	6	16.4	6.8	203	178	2	299	262	35 083	3 253	2 842
Clay...........................	1 746	13.1	942	14	7.1	7.8	262	191	2	284	207	14 621	5 017	3 646
Collier.........................	2 574	13.4	2 053	19	10.7	7.5	772	387	2	500	251	47 572	10 495	5 268
Columbia.......................	729	14.1	544	8	10.5	10.5	104	196	2	145	274	8 816	3 356	6 238
De Soto........................	377	15.2	278	4	11.2	10.6	35	141	1	82	330	5 084	1 534	5 739
Dixie...........................	154	12.2	132	2	10.4	13.0	4	31	0	0	0	2 514	567	4 434
Duval..........................	11 999	16.4	6 279	109	8.6	9.1	1 771	241	7	2 615	355	92 737	57 799	7 750
Escambia.......................	3 918	14.0	2 650	35	9.5	8.9	690	244	3	1 555	551	42 825	16 146	5 613
Flagler.........................	336	7.5	541	2	12.1	6.9	56	118	1	81	171	13 493	1 395	2 971
Franklin........................	113	11.2	119	4	11.8	35.4	9	89	1	29	288	1 833	498	5 506
Gadsden........................	679	15.4	434	8	9.8	11.8	44	100	0	0	0	6 808	2 338	5 055
Gilchrist........................	160	12.0	135	2	10.1	10.4	3	22	0	0	0	2 042	292	2 146
Glades.........................	89	10.5	98	1	11.6	15.0	2	24	0	0	0	900	382	3 870
Gulf............................	149	11.1	159	1	11.8	6.7	15	111	1	45	334	2 457	421	2 970
Hamilton........................	158	12.6	120	1	9.6	6.3	5	40	1	42	332	1 848	541	4 506
Hardee.........................	450	21.2	209	2	9.9	5.2	9	43	1	50	238	3 373	1 134	5 038
Hendry.........................	619	21.2	247	3	8.5	4.8	22	75	1	66	225	3 575	2 208	6 857
Hernando.......................	1 049	8.4	1 899	8	15.3	7.3	158	124	3	316	248	41 011	4 500	3 522
Highlands	859	11.4	1 202	6	16.0	6.6	150	199	3	327	435	25 438	4 497	5 749
Hillsborough	13 957	15.3	8 061	116	8.9	8.3	2 572	278	10	2 943	318	132 602	75 803	8 189
Holmes.........................	205	11.2	229	2	12.5	11.4	9	48	1	34	183	3 304	336	1 796
Indian River....................	1 017	10.4	1 393	5	14.2	5.2	317	320	2	480	484	31 587	5 541	5 487
Jackson.........................	547	12.0	504	5	11.0	9.1	43	94	2	129	283	8 267	1 142	2 504
Jefferson.......................	149	11.7	131	2	10.3	13.4	4	31	0	0	0	2 062	552	4 098
Lafayette.......................	78	12.3	52	1	8.2	12.9	2	32	0	0	0	686	34	531
Lake...........................	2 071	10.6	2 582	16	13.3	7.7	316	156	4	706	349	58 936	8 493	4 281
Lee............................	4 526	11.7	4 674	36	12.1	8.0	1 026	261	6	1 707	434	99 107	20 757	5 268
Leon...........................	2 894	13.4	1 348	24	6.2	8.3	529	244	2	812	374	21 392	18 265	8 340
Levy...........................	373	12.0	370	3	11.9	8.9	20	63	1	25	79	6 550	1 808	5 507
Liberty.........................	81	12.1	53	1	7.9	12.3	1	15	0	0	0	883	131	1 920
Madison........................	214	12.2	185	2	10.6	10.9	8	45	1	57	323	3 070	1 007	5 635
Manatee........................	2 866	12.2	3 175	15	13.5	5.2	574	239	2	903	377	53 829	13 995	5 798
Marion.........................	2 652	11.2	3 013	21	12.8	7.9	385	159	2	534	221	66 595	11 781	4 877
Martin..........................	1 118	9.8	1 516	7	13.3	6.3	410	354	2	307	265	33 507	4 891	4 139
Miami-Dade.....................	31 593	14.8	18 508	183	8.7	5.8	6 847	318	25	8 657	402	304 339	213 401	10 323
Monroe.........................	794	9.8	722	3	8.9	4.2	256	315	4	342	421	11 092	6 286	7 539
Nassau.........................	712	13.2	434	4	8.1	6.1	62	112	1	48	87	7 730	2 188	3 974
Okaloosa.......................	2 327	13.9	1 175	22	7.0	9.4	356	210	3	433	256	23 429	6 254	3 666
Okeechobee.....................	477	15.4	386	3	12.5	7.0	41	132	1	101	324	6 715	NA	NA
Orange.........................	12 344	15.7	5 761	81	7.3	6.6	1 739	216	9	2 816	349	103 228	71 846	9 003
Osceola........................	2 143	15.2	1 205	14	8.6	6.4	165	113	3	365	251	21 110	10 743	7 426
Palm Beach.....................	12 736	12.6	12 402	79	12.2	6.2	3 403	330	14	3 294	319	239 091	86 639	8 357
Pasco..........................	3 331	10.5	5 021	27	15.8	8.1	468	144	5	941	289	84 944	15 113	4 636
Pinellas........................	9 294	10.6	12 615	74	14.4	8.0	2 564	292	15	3 931	448	205 973	56 120	6 336
Polk...........................	6 392	14.3	4 932	55	11.0	8.6	725	160	5	1 430	316	88 530	36 322	7 954
Putnam.........................	904	12.9	837	8	11.9	9.2	59	84	1	161	229	13 759	4 226	5 895
St. Johns.......................	1 183	10.6	1 055	13	9.5	11.0	386	332	2	230	198	20 484	4 650	4 053
St. Lucie........................	2 190	12.4	2 072	21	11.7	9.6	261	146	2	485	271	39 972	10 031	5 488
Santa Rosa.....................	1 473	13.1	788	10	7.0	6.8	155	132	3	237	202	14 316	4 014	3 445

1. Per 1,000 estimated resident population, average 1996–1998. 2. Deaths of infants under 1 year old. 3. Deaths of infants under 1 year old per 1,000 live births. 4. Data subject to copyright. 5. Per 100,000 resident population as of July 1 of the year shown. 6. Data for serious crimes have not been adjusted for underreporting; this may affect comparability between geographic areas and over time. 7. Per 100,000 population estimated by the FBI.

Table B. States and Counties — **Crime, Education, Money Income, and Poverty**

STATE County	Serious crimes known to police, 1998[1] (cont'd) Rate[2]		Education School enrollment and attainment, 1990 Enrollment[3]		Attainment[4] (percent)		Local government expenditures, fiscal 1997[5]		Money income 1989	Households Median			Income and poverty, 1997 Percent below poverty level		
	Violent	Property	Total	Percent private	High school graduate or more	Bachelor's degree or more	Total current expenditures (mil dol)	Current expenditures per student (dollars)	Per capita[6] (dollars)	Dollars	Percent change, 1979–1989 (constant 1989 dollars)	Percent with $100,000 or more	Median household income	All persons	Persons under 18	Persons 5–17 in families
	46	47	48	49	50	51	52	53	54	55	56	57	58	59	60	61
DELAWARE	762	4 601	171 219	20.9	77.5	21.4	789.0	7 135	15 854	34 875	16.6	4.5	41 315	10.0	15.4	13.8
Kent	701	4 370	29 454	13.8	73.1	15.0	138.8	6 637	12 726	29 497	14.7	2.4	36 555	12.1	17.7	16.8
New Castle	709	4 921	117 099	25.3	80.6	25.2	475.3	7 356	17 442	38 617	17.2	5.6	47 819	8.7	13.1	11.6
Sussex	737	3 807	24 666	9.0	69.7	13.0	168.3	6 807	12 723	26 904	10.8	2.4	33 281	12.7	21.5	18.4
DISTRICT OF COLUMBIA	1 719	7 117	151 248	35.8	73.1	33.3	633.0	8 048	18 881	30 727	13.1	7.8	34 980	19.3	33.7	33.9
District of Columbia	1 719	7 117	151 248	35.8	73.1	33.3	633.0	8 048	18 881	30 727	13.1	7.8	34 980	19.3	33.7	33.9
FLORIDA	939	5 947	2 926 662	16.0	74.4	18.3	12 019.0	5 360	14 698	27 483	11.7	3.9	32 877	14.4	21.8	20.0
Alachua	1 246	8 223	71 842	7.3	82.7	34.6	146.6	4 943	12 252	22 084	6.7	3.0	31 382	18.3	23.0	22.3
Baker	587	2 423	4 783	3.7	64.1	5.7	22.6	4 884	9 417	25 816	7.0	1.4	32 377	16.9	20.7	20.3
Bay	566	5 256	32 011	9.5	74.7	15.7	130.8	5 098	12 225	24 684	11.0	2.0	32 047	15.1	22.4	21.4
Bradford	633	3 321	4 932	4.8	65.0	8.1	20.8	4 951	10 287	24 625	24.3	1.1	30 033	22.2	28.0	27.2
Brevard	712	4 341	90 909	17.5	82.3	20.4	312.6	4 690	15 093	30 534	8.1	2.8	36 353	11.3	17.6	16.2
Broward	719	5 678	263 345	20.1	76.8	18.8	1 134.9	5 191	16 883	30 571	10.0	4.7	37 832	11.7	17.5	15.9
Calhoun	366	2 087	2 864	5.4	55.9	8.2	11.1	4 844	8 867	18 615	4.2	2.3	25 362	23.0	28.2	28.0
Charlotte	205	2 676	16 107	11.9	75.7	13.4	83.4	5 182	14 431	25 746	16.5	2.6	32 211	9.5	17.8	16.9
Citrus	401	2 441	14 735	8.1	68.6	10.4	72.8	5 130	12 151	21 285	12.8	1.4	26 883	14.5	25.6	23.8
Clay	426	3 220	29 105	11.6	81.2	17.9	115.6	4 456	13 945	34 860	13.0	2.8	42 729	7.7	10.6	10.0
Collier	600	4 668	27 492	11.9	79.0	22.3	170.2	6 039	21 386	34 001	22.1	9.1	41 000	11.2	20.5	19.3
Columbia	1 020	5 218	10 868	8.3	69.0	11.0	43.9	4 737	10 324	21 961	2.4	1.7	28 521	19.7	28.0	27.4
De Soto	947	4 792	4 711	7.5	54.5	7.6	24.4	5 277	10 286	20 962	10.8	1.7	25 525	23.4	35.1	32.9
Dixie	735	3 699	2 000	4.5	57.7	6.2	12.5	5 394	8 527	15 380	-4.7	1.5	21 982	23.9	32.9	33.8
Duval	1 135	6 615	163 788	16.6	76.9	18.4	595.9	4 725	13 857	28 513	13.9	2.9	35 883	13.4	18.8	17.6
Escambia	913	4 700	68 858	13.8	76.2	18.2	232.4	5 081	12 161	25 158	3.9	2.2	31 069	17.8	24.9	23.4
Flagler	309	2 662	5 340	10.3	78.7	17.3	32.1	5 655	15 124	28 628	17.3	3.2	34 675	10.5	20.2	18.3
Franklin	498	5 008	1 895	7.7	59.5	12.4	9.5	5 989	9 954	17 247	9.0	2.1	24 088	19.0	25.2	27.2
Gadsden	1 053	4 002	11 311	9.7	59.9	11.2	45.9	5 376	8 597	19 985	7.3	1.3	24 881	25.9	32.3	30.7
Gilchrist	220	1 926	2 140	7.9	63.0	7.4	13.8	5 187	9 690	20 632	14.2	0.4	27 483	18.4	25.0	25.3
Glades	446	3 424	1 577	11.7	57.4	7.1	6.1	5 324	10 719	20 687	22.5	1.2	26 336	18.1	28.0	26.4
Gulf	508	2 462	2 611	4.7	66.4	9.2	12.8	5 447	10 028	21 866	7.9	0.4	28 605	19.8	27.4	26.5
Hamilton	900	3 606	2 774	3.1	58.4	7.0	14.7	6 307	8 851	18 709	5.7	1.2	24 174	26.2	30.5	31.3
Hardee	484	4 554	4 510	3.3	54.8	8.6	27.1	5 041	9 411	22 065	9.5	2.3	25 482	27.8	38.6	35.0
Hendry	1 102	5 755	6 790	7.3	56.6	10.0	40.0	5 505	10 035	24 904	2.0	2.1	28 325	22.8	33.0	30.4
Hernando	441	3 081	16 891	9.5	70.5	9.7	75.3	4 750	11 864	22 741	9.7	1.4	27 740	13.8	23.9	22.2
Highlands	741	5 008	11 006	9.8	68.2	10.9	61.2	5 544	12 112	21 146	11.8	1.9	26 006	16.4	29.0	26.5
Hillsborough	1 301	6 888	203 572	16.9	75.6	20.2	771.6	5 220	14 203	28 477	14.3	3.5	35 994	15.0	22.0	19.9
Holmes	353	1 443	3 607	3.7	57.1	7.4	19.3	5 040	8 609	17 241	4.1	0.9	23 416	24.7	33.6	31.2
Indian River	474	5 013	16 602	15.1	76.5	19.1	75.7	5 414	17 825	28 961	14.4	5.8	35 895	11.2	20.3	18.4
Jackson	524	1 980	10 802	6.4	61.6	10.9	43.3	5 345	9 654	19 471	9.2	1.3	25 953	20.8	27.0	25.4
Jefferson	1 314	2 784	3 014	9.0	64.1	14.7	11.5	5 412	9 744	21 782	32.8	2.6	27 788	22.0	28.9	27.8
Lafayette	359	172	1 255	0.7	58.2	5.2	5.6	5 011	8 966	20 744	11.6	1.3	27 354	24.1	25.7	28.1
Lake	725	3 556	26 991	12.8	70.6	12.7	118.8	4 546	12 450	23 395	11.8	1.9	30 768	12.8	22.7	20.3
Lee	614	4 654	59 636	13.1	76.9	16.4	296.8	5 673	15 623	28 448	16.2	4.0	34 117	11.5	19.9	18.6
Leon	1 136	7 204	71 666	9.8	84.9	37.1	169.2	5 362	14 088	27 323	13.5	3.5	37 832	13.8	17.4	16.0
Levy	1 258	4 249	5 434	6.1	62.8	8.3	30.6	5 178	9 386	18 807	5.0	1.1	24 838	19.8	29.0	27.4
Liberty	264	1 656	1 167	2.3	56.7	7.3	6.2	4 945	11 500	22 253	26.0	0.7	27 178	22.3	27.0	26.0
Madison	750	4 885	3 999	7.1	56.5	9.7	17.8	5 112	9 727	18 153	6.5	1.7	24 980	23.2	27.9	29.0
Manatee	865	4 933	37 553	11.6	75.6	15.5	174.1	5 308	14 444	25 951	14.1	2.9	35 063	11.7	18.9	19.5
Marion	747	4 130	37 941	11.7	69.6	11.5	173.9	4 798	11 782	22 452	13.6	2.0	28 244	16.4	26.7	24.3
Martin	484	3 655	17 470	19.1	79.7	20.3	81.4	5 490	20 328	31 760	20.3	7.6	40 161	10.1	17.9	16.5
Miami-Dade	1 532	8 791	515 611	20.8	65.0	18.8	1 993.8	5 845	13 686	26 909	3.1	4.9	30 000	21.1	29.6	26.3
Monroe	693	6 846	13 043	13.9	79.7	20.3	53.9	5 752	18 869	29 351	27.7	6.4	36 353	11.5	18.3	19.6
Nassau	601	3 373	10 571	11.0	71.2	12.5	46.1	4 505	13 288	30 233	6.4	2.6	40 128	9.7	13.7	13.6
Okaloosa	539	3 127	37 715	7.7	83.8	21.0	138.0	4 591	13 147	27 941	10.0	2.0	36 788	10.5	14.7	14.3
Okeechobee	NA	NA	6 842	8.1	59.1	9.8	34.7	5 253	9 792	21 427	5.9	1.5	26 129	20.0	28.5	30.6
Orange	1 285	7 718	161 178	15.1	78.8	21.2	646.4	5 005	14 570	30 252	18.0	3.5	36 979	13.4	20.2	17.9
Osceola	791	6 635	24 293	12.1	73.7	11.2	132.0	4 823	12 268	27 260	25.3	1.6	32 552	13.4	21.8	18.8
Palm Beach	967	7 390	171 097	20.2	78.8	22.1	733.8	5 333	19 937	32 524	16.4	7.2	37 045	11.5	18.6	17.2
Pasco	444	4 192	46 760	11.9	66.9	9.1	221.0	5 086	11 732	21 480	10.1	1.2	28 202	13.5	21.8	20.2
Pinellas	944	5 392	157 458	17.2	78.1	18.5	571.0	5 333	15 712	26 296	17.1	3.4	32 816	12.2	19.4	17.5
Polk	829	7 125	89 009	13.4	68.0	12.9	370.6	4 954	12 392	25 216	5.6	2.4	31 030	16.9	25.4	22.7
Putnam	1 011	4 884	14 792	7.0	64.3	8.3	63.8	4 802	10 079	20 155	5.1	1.4	25 318	22.1	31.5	30.5
St. Johns	617	3 436	18 876	19.9	79.9	23.6	82.3	5 026	17 113	29 926	25.6	6.2	42 857	9.4	14.1	14.6
St. Lucie	1 021	4 467	31 850	14.0	71.7	13.1	147.7	5 336	13 387	27 710	19.1	2.5	30 788	15.1	23.9	22.9
Santa Rosa	516	2 929	21 043	7.4	78.5	18.6	95.6	4 624	12 656	27 584	9.1	2.6	37 201	11.8	16.1	16.1

1. Data for serious crimes have not been adjusted for underreporting; this may affect comparability between geographic areas and over time.   2. Per 100,000 population estimated by the FBI.   3. All persons 3 years old and over enrolled in nursery school through college.   4. Persons 25 years old and over.   5. Elementary and secondary education expenditures, local government fiscal years ending between July 1, 1996 and June 30, 1997.   6. Based on population enumerated as of April 1, 1990.

	Personal income, 1998												
			Per capita[1]						Transfer payments				
										Government payments to individuals			
STATE County	Total (mil dol)	Percent change, 1997–1998	Dollars	Rank	Wages and salaries[2] (mil dol)	Proprietor's income (mil dol)	Dividends, interest, and rent (mil dol)	Total (mil dol)	Total (mil dol)	Social Security (mil dol)	Medical payments (mil dol)	Income mainte-nance (mil dol)	Unemploy-ment insurance (mil dol)
	62	63	64	65	66	67	68	69	70	71	72	73	74
DELAWARE	21 863	7.7	29 383	X	15 715	1 232	4 266	2 552	2 407	1 150	863	199	67
Kent	2 757	6.0	22 178	1 042	1 794	144	455	399	375	159	145	29	15
New Castle	15 983	8.2	33 121	83	12 308	843	3 110	1 540	1 446	689	498	141	41
Sussex	3 123	7.2	22 766	900	1 614	245	701	613	586	303	220	30	11
DISTRICT OF COLUMBIA	18 988	1.9	36 415	X	38 391	2 262	3 343	2 584	2 508	552	1 317	400	71
District of Columbia	18 988	1.9	36 415	55	38 391	2 262	3 343	2 584	2 508	552	1 317	400	71
FLORIDA	400 209	6.3	26 845	X	224 007	24 366	103 922	62 523	59 885	26 498	24 674	4 806	730
Alachua	4 887	7.0	24 656	534	3 493	207	949	693	657	223	277	80	8
Baker	383	7.2	18 191	2 297	142	24	46	70	66	23	27	8	1
Bay	3 252	4.3	22 163	1 046	1 985	228	651	548	522	205	209	50	10
Bradford	420	4.0	16 893	2 632	183	20	57	87	83	24	38	13	1
Brevard	11 043	4.9	23 758	686	6 385	405	2 707	1 937	1 854	928	676	102	22
Broward	43 041	5.9	28 546	213	22 379	1 846	11 427	5 935	5 667	2 539	2 473	332	99
Calhoun	191	4.7	15 380	2 892	88	15	27	52	50	16	24	7	1
Charlotte	3 201	5.2	23 752	689	958	152	1 295	791	767	437	270	20	3
Citrus	2 259	4.7	19 878	1 752	746	106	745	663	642	365	227	27	6
Clay	3 236	7.8	23 519	742	938	138	515	344	320	151	104	21	4
Collier	8 553	5.8	42 813	18	2 991	751	4 087	882	846	500	283	34	7
Columbia	1 006	5.7	19 004	2 056	555	43	169	217	208	79	86	28	2
De Soto	533	7.2	21 560	1 238	236	78	104	124	119	48	54	12	1
Dixie	190	6.6	14 726	2 957	70	16	35	58	55	23	20	8	1
Duval	19 569	5.4	26 637	331	17 162	1 298	3 173	2 438	2 313	853	951	265	27
Escambia	6 160	3.5	21 682	1 198	4 524	285	1 207	1 046	998	378	390	127	8
Flagler	1 007	7.2	21 413	1 263	310	21	329	226	217	142	61	7	1
Franklin	192	4.4	18 988	2 061	64	22	42	50	48	17	22	6	0
Gadsden	782	6.0	17 771	2 415	378	55	100	182	174	57	70	38	2
Gilchrist	214	6.5	15 450	2 883	62	27	30	48	45	19	18	4	0
Glades	147	7.4	17 139	2 575	33	15	37	28	27	15	7	3	1
Gulf	226	0.1	16 754	2 665	109	13	44	64	62	24	27	6	1
Hamilton	177	3.4	13 967	3 010	140	10	26	48	45	15	19	8	0
Hardee	423	6.1	20 081	1 686	189	70	63	88	84	30	35	14	2
Hendry	652	9.0	22 193	1 039	344	116	88	104	99	37	42	13	4
Hernando	2 733	5.3	21 587	1 228	751	100	802	774	751	409	274	27	4
Highlands	1 661	4.3	22 175	1 044	559	139	539	480	467	240	173	27	4
Hillsborough	24 389	6.1	26 355	357	19 948	1 544	4 598	3 260	3 096	1 248	1 208	344	39
Holmes	282	3.6	15 149	2 916	83	30	43	87	83	29	36	12	1
Indian River	3 618	5.1	36 501	54	1 217	202	1 745	578	561	303	208	21	7
Jackson	775	3.7	17 425	2 503	370	43	127	210	202	67	95	25	2
Jefferson	254	6.1	19 228	1 979	70	18	44	50	48	18	18	9	0
Lafayette	105	6.6	16 675	2 682	38	26	13	20	18	8	6	3	0
Lake	4 498	6.6	22 256	1 024	1 641	269	1 348	1 033	997	522	376	52	6
Lee	10 860	6.0	27 640	256	4 719	744	3 928	1 919	1 849	984	690	79	11
Leon	5 690	6.7	26 453	346	4 582	271	932	569	531	205	185	67	6
Levy	560	5.4	17 668	2 449	178	57	113	145	139	65	51	14	1
Liberty	102	1.6	15 139	2 918	48	5	12	21	20	8	8	3	0
Madison	283	3.2	15 959	2 799	127	22	43	78	75	25	31	14	1
Manatee	7 294	5.7	30 440	155	3 236	576	2 300	1 103	1 060	584	363	55	7
Marion	5 195	7.1	21 533	1 246	2 288	356	1 293	1 201	1 158	629	400	85	8
Martin	4 653	5.6	40 133	29	1 527	221	2 335	631	610	337	222	23	6
Miami-Dade	51 448	5.7	23 919	659	35 782	3 681	9 488	8 987	8 605	2 364	4 594	1 223	163
Monroe	2 628	5.8	32 501	102	1 138	182	1 035	267	252	113	100	20	2
Nassau	1 450	7.6	26 175	380	508	76	294	169	159	79	56	11	2
Okaloosa	4 155	5.6	24 655	535	2 826	233	1 000	525	497	201	186	35	5
Okeechobee	599	5.3	18 725	2 151	250	74	107	153	148	57	70	12	2
Orange	21 066	8.6	26 186	378	20 081	1 682	3 394	2 511	2 368	943	999	238	27
Osceola	2 801	8.1	19 216	1 981	1 279	140	436	474	448	203	195	33	5
Palm Beach	41 361	6.5	40 044	31	17 206	3 142	16 414	5 083	4 900	2 500	1 964	202	71
Pasco	7 378	7.8	22 691	925	2 013	247	1 730	1 789	1 731	877	674	83	11
Pinellas	26 874	7.0	30 633	148	14 053	1 306	7 278	4 359	4 203	1 958	1 761	218	37
Polk	10 234	8.2	22 609	950	5 586	812	2 076	1 862	1 782	865	623	171	21
Putnam	1 223	4.7	17 393	2 507	535	37	227	325	312	133	124	41	3
St. Johns	4 180	12.9	36 014	59	1 132	149	1 048	424	403	201	152	22	3
St. Lucie	3 831	5.5	21 362	1 278	1 452	185	1 073	916	884	424	343	62	18
Santa Rosa	2 566	7.9	21 808	1 157	791	144	441	332	312	138	113	29	4

1. Based on the resident population estimated as of July 1 of the year shown.   2. Includes other labor income.

Table B. States and Counties — Earnings, Social Security, and Housing

STATE County	Earnings, 1998									Social Security beneficiaries, December 1998			Housing units, 1990	
	Total (mil dol)	Farm	Percent by selected industries							Number	Rate[3]	Supplemental Security Income recipients, December 1998	Total	Percent change, 1980–1990
			Goods-related[1]		Service-related and other[2]									
			Total	Manu-facturing	Total	Retail trade	Finance, insurance, and real estate	Services	Govern-ment					
	75	76	77	78	79	80	81	82	83	84	85	86	87	88
DELAWARE	16 947	0.7	28.7	22.7	56.6	8.4	14.9	24.5	14.0	126 520	170	11 796	289 919	21.5
Kent	1 938	1.4	D	12.8	D	10.5	4.1	18.4	39.4	18 937	153	2 490	42 106	19.1
New Castle	13 151	0.1	D	24.5	D	7.1	17.4	25.8	10.4	73 085	151	6 846	173 560	16.8
Sussex	1 859	4.4	29.0	19.9	54.1	14.7	8.8	21.5	12.5	34 489	252	2 413	74 253	35.8
DISTRICT OF COLUMBIA	40 653	0.0	D	2.3	53.0	2.2	5.7	39.4	43.6	73 860	141	19 711	278 489	0.5
District of Columbia	40 653	0.0	D	2.3	53.0	2.2	5.7	39.4	43.6	73 860	141	19 711	278 489	0.5
FLORIDA	248 372	1.0	14.4	8.2	67.7	11.0	9.9	33.0	17.0	3 109 035	208	361 892	6 100 262	39.3
Alachua	3 701	0.5	D	5.2	D	9.3	6.5	30.4	38.0	27 353	138	4 752	79 022	34.1
Baker	166	6.0	10.8	5.6	31.9	9.4	2.8	11.6	51.4	3 082	146	495	5 975	31.4
Bay	2 214	0.1	16.2	6.9	55.5	12.7	5.7	26.9	28.3	26 367	179	3 419	65 999	53.8
Bradford	203	2.6	13.9	10.1	D	10.6	2.9	D	40.2	3 194	129	733	8 099	11.7
Brevard	6 790	0.2	D	19.9	D	9.6	4.1	35.9	17.9	108 141	232	7 381	185 150	62.6
Broward	24 225	0.1	13.6	7.3	71.4	12.8	10.9	33.2	14.9	279 948	186	25 076	628 660	29.3
Calhoun	103	3.3	17.3	8.0	49.5	9.9	2.2	25.9	29.9	2 327	187	500	4 468	25.4
Charlotte	1 110	1.1	D	2.7	D	16.9	6.7	38.4	16.7	49 396	366	1 370	64 641	85.8
Citrus	853	0.2	D	4.2	D	13.5	6.3	33.6	15.5	42 361	371	1 597	49 854	70.8
Clay	1 076	0.9	D	6.8	D	19.3	4.1	31.8	17.3	18 693	136	1 208	40 249	65.4
Collier	3 743	3.9	14.8	2.8	71.8	12.7	14.7	35.9	9.5	52 833	265	1 900	94 165	85.6
Columbia	598	0.6	18.6	11.2	48.8	13.9	2.9	20.4	31.9	10 494	198	2 110	17 818	30.7
De Soto	314	21.4	D	2.7	D	7.5	1.9	12.5	30.0	6 043	243	720	10 310	38.2
Dixie	86	2.0	D	D	D	9.6	1.5	11.1	37.4	3 128	241	543	6 445	60.7
Duval	18 460	0.1	12.9	7.3	67.4	8.3	16.8	26.6	19.7	105 051	143	17 806	284 673	25.4
Escambia	4 809	0.1	D	8.7	D	10.1	4.2	27.0	33.1	49 532	175	8 319	112 230	26.6
Flagler	331	2.8	D	16.6	D	12.5	6.2	32.1	17.9	15 802	333	469	15 215	158.3
Franklin	86	0.0	D	5.3	D	15.4	6.5	21.1	24.3	2 216	220	433	5 891	31.0
Gadsden	433	10.7	D	12.2	D	7.4	1.9	10.1	40.7	8 360	190	2 698	14 859	11.2
Gilchrist	88	18.4	11.1	7.0	32.6	5.9	1.5	13.8	37.9	2 547	185	394	4 071	53.8
Glades	49	27.2	D	D	D	7.3	D	11.5	23.0	1 767	208	116	4 624	33.1
Gulf	121	0.0	30.9	25.6	39.7	7.0	3.0	17.4	29.4	2 863	212	373	6 339	33.7
Hamilton	150	2.2	D	D	D	3.8	0.6	6.9	30.6	2 179	172	610	4 119	23.2
Hardee	258	24.2	D	3.4	42.2	6.8	3.1	14.8	22.8	4 065	193	869	7 941	12.5
Hendry	460	28.9	D	11.2	D	7.3	1.7	9.7	18.4	4 765	162	672	9 945	41.4
Hernando	851	0.9	14.9	5.6	63.1	15.5	6.0	31.6	21.1	47 171	371	1 839	50 018	121.9
Highlands	699	10.3	D	6.3	D	13.0	3.7	28.1	18.0	28 716	382	1 954	40 114	54.3
Hillsborough	21 492	0.9	12.2	6.7	72.3	9.8	10.6	35.6	14.7	152 215	165	25 031	367 740	39.5
Holmes	113	12.3	13.8	7.8	D	9.7	2.2	19.5	36.2	4 326	232	763	6 785	18.0
Indian River	1 420	2.4	D	7.4	D	14.2	9.9	32.8	13.2	33 400	337	1 397	47 128	60.2
Jackson	413	1.9	D	8.8	D	12.3	3.0	13.3	46.6	9 542	209	2 076	16 320	11.9
Jefferson	88	9.2	14.0	6.5	42.6	9.1	5.6	17.3	34.2	2 428	187	660	4 395	14.4
Lafayette	63	32.3	D	6.0	D	4.1	1.4	6.3	32.0	1 068	169	131	2 266	28.5
Lake	1 910	3.3	20.6	7.3	60.6	13.4	7.3	29.6	15.5	60 890	301	3 659	75 707	49.9
Lee	5 463	0.8	14.6	4.5	66.7	15.0	9.2	31.5	17.9	110 604	282	5 683	189 051	70.3
Leon	4 853	0.0	D	2.4	D	8.3	5.7	29.7	42.4	24 314	112	3 834	81 325	36.6
Levy	235	13.9	D	4.9	D	13.3	3.5	15.9	24.3	8 344	262	965	12 307	35.7
Liberty	54	0.7	D	14.8	D	4.6	D	11.3	45.8	1 070	158	238	2 157	6.4
Madison	148	6.9	23.1	21.7	37.9	8.8	1.7	19.2	32.1	3 599	204	1 158	6 275	12.9
Manatee	3 812	3.5	D	13.6	D	10.2	4.5	44.0	11.2	66 077	276	3 331	115 245	37.9
Marion	2 644	2.7	23.2	14.6	56.2	13.7	6.1	24.7	17.9	74 980	310	5 824	94 567	70.9
Martin	1 747	2.9	D	8.6	D	12.6	10.4	35.5	10.8	36 239	313	1 288	54 199	59.4
Miami-Dade	39 463	0.4	10.4	6.7	72.9	9.7	10.4	32.2	16.3	307 785	143	112 354	771 288	15.9
Monroe	1 320	0.0	D	1.4	D	17.4	6.4	36.0	23.4	13 045	161	1 130	46 215	21.3
Nassau	583	2.7	24.5	18.6	47.8	11.1	5.0	21.7	25.0	9 255	167	784	18 726	40.8
Okaloosa	3 059	0.0	9.3	4.2	45.9	10.4	6.1	24.0	44.8	26 049	154	2 376	62 569	45.2
Okeechobee	323	19.7	6.8	1.9	53.5	12.5	2.6	26.5	20.0	7 181	230	908	13 266	38.1
Orange	21 763	0.5	14.3	8.5	74.2	10.0	8.6	41.0	11.1	115 415	143	19 274	282 686	53.0
Osceola	1 419	2.0	12.1	5.4	67.6	17.7	6.8	35.2	18.3	25 374	174	2 262	47 959	101.3
Palm Beach	20 348	1.7	14.9	9.1	72.1	10.0	16.0	34.6	11.3	259 559	251	13 253	461 665	56.1
Pasco	2 261	1.3	13.5	5.1	66.6	15.1	5.4	37.1	18.6	103 141	317	5 820	148 965	47.7
Pinellas	15 359	0.0	D	11.7	D	11.0	10.9	37.5	11.7	225 889	257	14 981	458 341	21.6
Polk	6 398	2.0	23.0	14.0	61.0	14.5	5.8	26.1	14.0	104 308	230	12 100	186 225	38.1
Putnam	572	2.8	30.1	23.9	39.8	11.0	2.6	18.8	27.4	16 943	241	2 532	31 840	34.7
St. Johns	1 280	1.0	D	12.8	D	12.8	6.9	35.3	16.1	23 027	198	1 764	40 712	78.1
St. Lucie	1 637	2.4	11.7	4.8	64.6	12.6	5.7	28.7	21.3	49 250	275	4 415	73 843	80.5
Santa Rosa	935	0.8	22.0	8.6	47.9	9.8	4.3	25.9	29.3	17 465	149	1 528	32 831	61.3

1. Covers mining, construction, and manufacturing.   2. Covers private sector earnings in agricultural services, forestry, and fisheries; transportation and public utilities; wholesale trade; retail trade; finance, insurance, and real estate; and services.   3. Per 1,000 resident population estimated as of July 1 of the year shown.

	Housing units, 1990 (cont'd)							Civilian labor force, 1999				Civilian employment, 1990[5]		
										Unemployment		Percent		
STATE County	Occupied units													
	Owner-occupied				Renter-occupied									
				Owner cost as a percent of income										
	Total	Percent	Median value[1]	With a mortgage	Without a mortgage	Median rent[2]	Rent as percent of income	Substandard units[3] (percent)	Total	Percent change, 1998–1999	Total	Rate[4]	Total	Professional, managerial, and technical	Precision production, craft, and repair
	89	90	91	92	93	94	95	96	97	98	99	100	101	102	103
DELAWARE	247 497	70.2	100 100	19.5	12.0	495	24.7	2.5	388 971	-0.8	13 648	3.5	335 147	31.0	11.9
Kent	39 655	69.2	80 800	18.8	12.1	422	24.6	3.4	68 139	-0.5	2 601	3.8	51 615	25.9	14.0
New Castle	164 161	68.3	110 900	19.8	11.9	524	24.8	2.0	251 065	-0.8	8 031	3.2	230 822	34.2	10.4
Sussex	43 681	78.6	79 800	18.8	12.3	383	24.5	3.5	69 768	-1.2	3 017	4.3	52 710	22.1	15.9
DISTRICT OF COLUMBIA	249 634	38.9	123 900	20.5	12.8	479	25.4	8.3	282 119	5.5	17 692	6.3	303 994	44.0	4.5
District of Columbia	249 634	38.9	123 900	20.5	12.8	479	25.4	8.3	282 119	5.5	17 692	6.3	303 994	44.0	4.5
FLORIDA	5 134 869	67.2	77 100	22.3	12.2	481	28.0	5.7	7 366 498	1.9	284 168	3.9	5 810 467	28.8	11.5
Alachua	71 258	54.1	66 000	20.3	12.4	396	32.8	4.7	105 303	2.6	2 248	2.1	85 785	41.8	7.6
Baker	5 554	79.3	53 400	18.5	12.2	342	26.7	6.7	8 618	4.2	287	3.3	7 130	19.2	15.3
Bay	48 938	65.5	61 600	20.0	12.3	370	25.2	2.9	65 935	0.4	4 037	6.1	53 222	28.3	11.4
Bradford	7 193	77.0	49 300	18.0	12.8	320	26.0	4.2	9 613	1.4	320	3.3	8 251	21.5	14.0
Brevard	161 365	69.2	75 200	21.0	11.5	483	26.2	2.2	206 340	1.0	8 019	3.9	183 692	34.7	12.8
Broward	528 442	68.0	91 800	23.6	13.1	575	29.0	5.2	770 374	1.7	31 157	4.0	599 119	29.9	11.7
Calhoun	3 793	79.4	33 200	21.6	14.1	244	25.1	6.1	4 884	-14.6	316	6.5	3 865	19.2	11.9
Charlotte	48 433	79.6	77 200	23.7	11.9	500	25.8	2.1	46 899	5.1	1 509	3.2	38 468	26.2	13.8
Citrus	40 573	83.2	66 100	22.5	11.4	382	26.6	2.1	35 214	0.2	1 667	4.7	29 904	24.8	14.9
Clay	36 663	73.4	82 100	21.6	11.1	494	25.7	2.9	69 673	1.9	1 824	2.6	48 601	28.9	12.4
Collier	61 703	70.2	121 400	22.7	11.7	572	26.5	5.5	93 644	2.0	3 530	3.8	68 449	25.9	12.9
Columbia	15 611	73.7	47 300	19.7	12.7	312	26.8	6.2	24 443	-1.3	1 060	4.3	17 569	23.5	14.3
De Soto	8 222	74.0	49 600	20.0	11.6	353	25.0	7.2	8 590	-5.4	565	6.6	8 770	17.7	12.0
Dixie	3 916	82.6	37 500	21.6	13.2	264	27.3	6.2	3 729	1.2	192	5.1	3 335	18.2	10.8
Duval	257 245	62.0	64 000	20.6	12.4	431	25.6	4.4	381 867	0.6	11 837	3.1	314 432	28.9	11.1
Escambia	98 608	64.7	57 800	19.9	12.5	387	26.3	3.8	120 859	-0.4	4 270	3.5	108 456	28.9	12.9
Flagler	11 880	76.5	97 500	25.3	11.3	551	26.8	2.4	17 144	3.6	562	3.3	10 542	27.3	12.8
Franklin	3 628	80.5	51 700	26.4	13.3	317	26.4	8.1	4 776	7.2	210	4.4	3 324	21.3	8.2
Gadsden	13 405	75.6	39 500	18.0	13.2	261	24.9	11.6	19 615	-1.3	703	3.6	16 215	22.8	9.6
Gilchrist	3 284	85.4	45 900	20.0	12.1	293	26.0	6.6	4 446	-2.6	173	3.9	3 572	21.4	16.1
Glades	2 885	78.2	57 200	18.7	11.4	361	28.4	7.5	3 728	-9.6	275	7.4	2 823	21.3	11.2
Gulf	4 324	78.5	43 200	16.9	11.3	301	27.5	3.7	5 467	4.5	721	13.2	4 531	21.3	16.3
Hamilton	3 488	76.2	36 300	16.3	12.9	242	29.9	9.7	3 365	-2.5	220	6.5	3 807	16.6	14.1
Hardee	6 391	75.8	40 300	16.5	12.5	358	27.9	9.2	9 148	-7.2	943	10.3	7 773	19.3	11.7
Hendry	8 402	70.8	61 200	17.8	13.7	403	27.0	12.2	15 558	-3.6	1 895	12.2	10 971	20.5	12.7
Hernando	42 300	84.5	71 200	24.1	11.4	426	29.3	2.4	47 777	2.2	1 588	3.3	31 552	22.6	15.8
Highlands	29 544	78.0	58 500	21.3	11.4	371	26.9	3.7	25 869	-2.7	1 753	6.8	22 212	23.2	11.3
Hillsborough	324 872	63.1	73 100	22.2	12.5	446	26.4	4.7	546 338	3.0	14 326	2.6	412 188	30.0	10.0
Holmes	5 800	80.8	36 200	20.9	13.0	262	29.9	5.1	6 627	2.2	358	5.4	6 113	19.6	14.4
Indian River	38 057	75.0	78 800	22.0	11.8	505	27.3	2.7	45 043	0.1	3 375	7.5	35 215	27.3	11.9
Jackson	14 465	77.0	41 400	18.3	13.2	257	25.6	4.5	17 677	-1.4	1 133	6.4	16 422	23.5	9.2
Jefferson	3 982	76.7	43 900	16.0	12.1	311	26.0	10.3	4 904	-1.7	204	4.2	4 734	27.6	11.0
Lafayette	1 721	80.7	43 700	19.3	14.3	255	18.6	5.0	3 030	11.6	66	2.2	2 121	16.3	8.2
Lake	63 616	78.3	67 800	21.6	11.5	387	24.9	2.9	90 483	4.9	2 329	2.6	57 965	22.5	13.1
Lee	140 124	72.1	84 300	22.6	11.8	504	26.2	3.0	179 970	3.2	4 598	2.6	144 465	25.7	13.3
Leon	74 828	56.9	75 200	20.0	12.3	445	30.0	3.9	129 722	3.2	3 187	2.5	103 094	41.2	6.8
Levy	10 079	81.8	49 100	22.4	12.7	297	27.4	5.7	12 530	-2.6	405	3.2	9 649	21.6	14.6
Liberty	1 706	80.8	39 600	16.7	11.6	240	22.0	6.3	2 254	-6.4	109	4.8	2 024	23.5	10.1
Madison	5 522	76.0	38 800	19.5	15.2	249	27.8	8.9	7 168	1.2	266	3.7	6 124	20.2	12.1
Manatee	91 060	70.9	79 400	23.1	12.0	488	27.8	3.1	121 309	5.4	2 663	2.2	87 581	25.5	13.3
Marion	78 177	75.6	61 800	22.0	11.7	386	25.4	4.2	98 169	2.1	3 566	3.6	74 958	23.8	12.9
Martin	43 022	76.9	112 700	22.1	11.5	525	25.4	2.9	48 074	3.8	2 392	5.0	41 198	28.9	14.2
Miami-Dade	692 355	54.3	86 500	23.1	13.0	493	31.3	17.6	1 045 018	0.7	60 550	5.8	901 828	27.8	10.7
Monroe	33 583	62.1	151 200	26.1	12.5	589	29.5	6.6	46 109	1.7	1 024	2.2	38 900	27.3	12.1
Nassau	16 192	78.5	72 600	19.1	12.5	415	24.4	4.2	28 258	2.7	954	3.4	20 137	23.5	15.7
Okaloosa	53 313	62.2	70 600	21.6	11.5	413	25.6	2.8	80 527	0.5	2 636	3.3	58 554	31.7	11.4
Okeechobee	10 214	72.4	55 600	20.6	12.9	393	26.4	8.4	15 819	-1.9	1 185	7.5	12 087	18.1	14.9
Orange	254 852	59.3	81 400	22.5	12.0	517	27.4	4.8	490 919	5.0	13 377	2.7	350 953	29.0	10.6
Osceola	39 150	65.7	75 700	22.8	11.8	526	27.8	5.2	83 411	4.6	2 271	2.7	52 455	21.7	12.9
Palm Beach	365 558	71.9	98 400	23.4	12.4	587	28.1	4.3	506 543	-0.2	25 472	5.0	387 274	31.4	11.2
Pasco	121 674	80.9	59 000	23.3	11.6	397	28.1	2.2	135 965	2.5	4 249	3.1	97 682	23.7	14.7
Pinellas	380 635	69.2	73 800	22.6	12.3	463	27.7	2.1	471 280	1.7	12 698	2.7	382 230	30.6	10.8
Polk	155 969	70.5	61 000	19.7	11.9	386	25.4	4.4	200 286	1.4	9 711	4.8	171 677	23.2	13.3
Putnam	25 070	79.0	49 900	18.6	12.3	296	25.8	5.6	27 928	2.1	1 395	5.0	23 383	20.8	15.8
St. Johns	33 426	70.4	85 800	21.7	12.2	487	25.5	3.3	60 016	3.3	1 476	2.5	39 251	32.2	11.5
St. Lucie	58 174	71.9	73 400	21.6	11.9	512	27.0	4.3	77 502	3.1	6 993	9.0	61 238	23.1	14.8
Santa Rosa	29 900	75.3	65 900	20.8	11.7	367	23.6	3.2	52 227	2.4	2 067	4.0	34 866	29.4	15.5

1. Specified owner-occupied units. 2. Specified renter-occupied units. 3. Overcrowded or lacking complete plumbing facilities. 4. Percent of civilian labor force. 5. Persons 16 years and older.

Table B. States and Counties — Nonfarm Employment and Agriculture

| | Private nonfarm establishments, employment and payroll, 1998 | | | | | | | | Agriculture, 1997 | | | |
| | Employment | | | | | | Annual payroll | | Farms | | | Farm operators |
STATE County	Number of establish-ments	Total	Health Care and Social Assistance	Manufac-turing	Retail trade	Finance and Insurance	Professional Scientific and Technical Services	Total (mil dol)	Average per employee (dollars)	Number	Percent with— Less than 50 acres	500 acres and over	Whose principal occu-pation is farming (percent)
	104	105	106	107	108	109	110	111	112	113	114	115	116
DELAWARE	22 871	354 643	41 202	43 511	47 631	41 611	17 043	11 831	33 361	2 460	47.6	11.9	60.9
Kent	2 966	42 453	5 809	7 256	7 871	2 660	1 387	964	22 716	767	40.3	12.0	59.8
New Castle	15 490	265 039	28 691	25 316	30 661	37 261	14 695	9 795	36 958	327	46.8	13.1	51.7
Sussex	4 415	47 151	6 702	10 939	9 099	1 690	961	1 071	22 721	1 366	51.9	11.5	63.6
DISTRICT OF COLUMBIA	19 571	402 070	58 820	2 991	18 727	16 671	71 140	17 358	43 172	NA	NA	NA	NA
District of Columbia	19 571	402 070	58 820	2 991	18 727	16 671	71 140	17 358	43 172	NA	NA	NA	NA
FLORIDA	420 638	5 756 353	740 828	428 642	872 391	302 704	318 814	149 937	26 047	34 799	57.9	8.7	45.4
Alachua	5 124	75 584	16 212	5 370	13 469	2 495	4 385	1 771	23 426	1 086	57.9	6.2	40.8
Baker	277	3 589	1 642	208	599	76	D	73	20 419	157	66.2	3.8	45.2
Bay	4 220	54 230	7 311	3 799	9 774	2 836	3 585	1 106	20 390	70	60.0	4.3	40.0
Bradford	385	4 042	797	711	902	101	96	69	17 002	274	55.8	4.0	40.5
Brevard	11 330	154 136	21 088	20 143	24 865	3 828	13 109	4 171	27 059	470	74.9	8.7	36.2
Broward	49 026	585 668	75 472	37 674	94 524	34 526	32 995	16 037	27 382	347	86.2	2.3	55.6
Calhoun	237	2 069	468	188	452	71	40	39	18 997	130	33.1	16.2	53.1
Charlotte	2 900	30 868	7 036	623	7 115	1 189	1 210	643	20 826	209	47.8	22.0	47.4
Citrus	2 271	22 282	4 767	1 311	5 010	669	527	491	22 014	294	56.8	8.5	39.8
Clay	2 779	29 361	4 752	1 669	7 031	594	1 091	594	20 236	211	64.0	6.6	44.1
Collier	7 959	82 383	9 837	2 613	16 562	3 141	3 617	2 054	24 938	235	53.6	23.0	46.8
Columbia	1 149	15 306	3 215	1 909	3 109	366	337	339	22 143	600	48.3	6.8	40.2
De Soto	397	4 786	1 803	172	978	163	104	102	21 280	715	53.1	11.9	46.2
Dixie	183	1 341	110	366	278	D	D	23	17 242	155	51.0	10.3	34.8
Duval	20 774	381 829	44 460	28 281	45 871	47 730	20 284	10 724	28 085	320	70.3	6.6	45.9
Escambia	6 728	107 234	18 281	7 443	16 309	3 402	6 099	2 489	23 211	466	59.0	4.5	42.1
Flagler	955	9 356	1 025	1 613	1 712	250	305	184	19 620	91	39.6	28.6	53.8
Franklin	287	1 910	142	73	415	122	57	31	16 112	19	57.9	10.5	47.4
Gadsden	594	9 075	3 141	1 487	1 182	229	194	226	24 915	290	37.9	10.3	39.7
Gilchrist	179	1 057	307	91	242	D	26	17	16 433	365	40.0	10.1	45.5
Glades	153	1 409	134	D	342	52	31	30	21 065	188	39.4	28.7	62.8
Gulf	265	2 408	485	662	399	107	49	56	23 402	33	54.5	9.1	27.3
Hamilton	181	2 515	329	D	333	D	D	80	31 738	256	26.2	12.1	39.1
Hardee	357	3 229	756	D	773	175	138	69	21 343	1 045	51.8	9.8	46.5
Hendry	489	4 972	882	714	1 139	205	88	100	20 108	403	40.0	24.8	51.9
Hernando	2 258	23 665	4 482	1 222	5 460	814	582	477	20 154	432	62.7	6.5	39.4
Highlands	1 749	29 231	4 061	1 104	3 886	484	531	509	17 416	779	53.8	13.7	44.4
Hillsborough	26 125	493 710	51 804	29 467	57 866	34 351	35 316	14 011	28 379	2 639	75.8	3.3	45.8
Holmes	256	2 257	549	346	320	54	64	34	14 957	578	28.2	4.5	44.8
Indian River	3 474	37 569	5 749	2 326	8 285	1 366	1 520	819	21 787	437	58.6	10.8	58.6
Jackson	802	8 776	1 353	1 127	2 205	438	197	148	16 879	844	25.5	14.6	52.6
Jefferson	238	1 685	257	56	381	96	57	31	18 173	342	35.7	13.7	36.8
Lafayette	98	747	120	79	68	27	26	15	19 444	221	27.1	14.0	50.7
Lake	4 354	47 696	8 392	3 589	9 755	1 545	1 673	1 021	21 397	1 389	68.5	6.2	39.8
Lee	11 616	134 701	16 880	5 473	26 249	4 494	8 196	3 144	23 341	509	70.9	10.0	40.3
Leon	6 269	85 703	12 748	2 474	15 825	4 065	7 308	2 032	23 709	243	51.9	6.2	28.8
Levy	623	5 704	673	245	1 494	241	146	96	16 803	549	43.4	13.5	42.3
Liberty	88	778	164	D	D	D	D	15	19 172	47	46.8	4.3	36.2
Madison	308	3 424	550	1 033	599	61	76	59	17 184	486	20.0	11.1	46.7
Manatee	5 441	106 633	10 721	11 383	11 827	2 185	2 342	2 309	21 652	697	54.1	13.5	51.8
Marion	5 383	69 245	10 059	9 922	13 567	2 118	2 354	1 478	21 345	1 669	62.1	5.0	47.0
Martin	4 181	44 730	6 504	3 091	8 702	1 703	2 227	1 109	24 801	305	59.0	19.0	46.9
Miami-Dade	67 042	835 903	101 798	62 468	114 044	44 730	45 105	23 873	28 560	1 576	87.2	2.9	52.7
Monroe	3 762	32 132	2 385	403	6 846	954	1 083	633	19 697	13	61.5	0.0	38.5
Nassau	1 138	12 551	1 278	1 676	2 315	270	376	316	25 181	238	55.5	5.0	39.9
Okaloosa	4 779	55 450	7 054	3 634	10 844	2 112	3 343	1 153	20 799	342	37.1	6.4	36.5
Okeechobee	685	6 403	1 344	155	1 647	209	117	121	18 821	459	35.9	23.1	41.4
Orange	25 218	528 249	43 659	32 716	58 136	20 527	29 133	14 383	27 228	862	77.0	7.0	55.3
Osceola	3 191	47 905	5 136	1 511	8 962	803	858	929	19 394	485	55.9	15.3	49.3
Palm Beach	35 287	414 845	59 208	26 764	65 074	21 779	25 345	12 129	29 237	855	76.0	10.4	57.0
Pasco	6 068	63 316	12 784	3 884	14 563	2 509	2 373	1 303	20 572	951	65.0	6.6	43.2
Pinellas	26 243	396 192	55 913	41 578	54 874	23 332	30 842	10 342	26 103	129	91.5	0.0	41.1
Polk	9 625	151 889	18 119	19 335	22 298	8 922	4 620	3 845	25 316	2 464	62.3	8.6	39.3
Putnam	1 228	12 991	2 167	2 407	2 745	449	257	289	22 244	391	57.0	8.7	46.3
St. Johns	3 211	35 718	3 808	2 334	5 937	939	1 409	779	21 823	149	55.0	21.5	61.1
St. Lucie	3 752	40 612	8 082	2 521	7 598	1 504	1 981	893	21 977	500	50.8	13.8	49.6
Santa Rosa	1 901	18 733	2 634	2 011	3 657	505	700	359	19 167	438	43.6	11.6	49.5

Table B. States and Counties — Agriculture, Land, and Water

Agriculture, 1997 (cont'd)

STATE County	Land in farms — Acreage (1,000) [117]	Percent change, 1992–1997 [118]	Acres — Average size of farm [119]	Acres — Total irrigated (1,000) [120]	Acres — Total cropland (1,000) [121]	Value of land and buildings — Average per farm ($1,000) [122]	Value of land and buildings — Average per acre (dollars) [123]	Value of machinery and equipment Average per farm ($1,000) [124]	Value of products sold — Total (mil dol) [125]	Value of products sold — Average per farm (dollars) [126]	Percent from — Crops [127]	Percent from — Livestock and poultry products [128]	Percent of farms with sales of — $10,000 or more [129]	Percent of farms with sales of — $100,000 or more [130]	Percent of land owned by Fed. Gov. 1997 [131]	Water consumption 1995 (mil gal/day) [132]
DELAWARE	580	-1.6	236	73	487	610	2 660	76	691	280 811	25.3	74.7	69.8	43.8	2.0	752.1
Kent	195	-1.2	254	21	168	647	2 556	74	154	200 379	40.7	59.3	64.4	29.9	3.7	33.9
New Castle	77	-11.1	236	3	67	908	3 708	84	37	112 976	71.3	28.7	52.0	20.8	0.9	624.7
Sussex	308	0.9	225	49	253	518	2 441	75	500	366 149	17.2	82.8	77.1	57.2	1.3	93.4
DISTRICT OF COLUMBIA	NA	NA	NA	NA	NA	NA	NA	NA	NA	NA	NA	NA	NA	NA	NA	10.2
District of Columbia	NA	NA	NA	NA	NA	NA	NA	NA	NA	NA	NA	NA	NA	NA	NA	10.2
FLORIDA	10 454	-2.9	300	1 862	3 640	663	2 241	41	6 005	172 550	80.2	19.8	42.4	14.9	10.1	7 215.0
Alachua	198	3.8	182	8	75	361	2 209	22	50	46 276	61.9	38.1	32.5	7.7	0.0	48.3
Baker	13	-45.7	83	1	5	247	2 689	37	25	160 535	38.6	61.4	29.3	15.3	22.4	5.4
Bay	7	-25.2	96	0	3	179	1 858	23	3	38 176	91.8	8.2	24.3	4.3	5.1	58.9
Bradford	44	21.1	159	0	10	262	1 680	26	17	63 509	6.7	93.3	27.4	8.0	0.0	7.5
Brevard	277	38.3	588	31	27	909	1 474	33	38	80 758	85.6	14.4	36.0	9.8	12.7	135.5
Broward	31	28.7	89	2	7	414	4 791	33	49	141 280	85.8	14.2	57.6	21.3	0.2	287.3
Calhoun	44	1.9	337	1	27	395	1 298	35	16	124 592	89.5	10.5	47.7	17.7	0.0	4.2
Charlotte	290	27.9	1 389	26	45	1 878	1 359	45	50	240 010	89.4	10.6	51.2	22.0	0.0	49.9
Citrus	49	-30.7	167	1	21	340	2 726	21	6	20 992	59.8	40.2	29.9	4.8	2.2	30.0
Clay	71	-17.6	336	1	8	623	1 992	31	30	142 739	10.9	89.1	22.3	9.5	16.5	21.5
Collier	277	-8.2	1 180	53	69	2 152	1 796	166	277	1 178 401	96.7	3.3	66.8	34.0	35.5	208.2
Columbia	97	0.1	162	3	46	349	1 885	28	22	36 767	46.4	53.6	27.2	5.7	15.8	16.7
De Soto	322	-3.8	451	73	127	1 134	2 510	59	181	253 123	87.6	12.4	52.3	18.9	0.0	70.9
Dixie	34	4.7	216	1	6	211	1 121	17	5	29 844	34.2	65.8	27.1	5.8	6.1	3.4
Duval	36	-11.2	111	1	11	390	3 310	27	26	82 697	36.9	63.1	31.2	8.1	4.6	145.1
Escambia	55	-4.2	117	1	35	248	2 044	36	16	34 727	58.3	41.7	27.0	9.2	3.0	269.6
Flagler	88	68.7	964	8	13	1 236	1 282	84	28	305 906	95.6	4.4	49.5	29.7	0.0	14.2
Franklin	5	0.0	270	0	D	358	1 328	26	D	D	D		52.6	0.0	7.1	2.9
Gadsden	58	-0.1	200	5	24	546	2 521	63	93	319 421	92.2	7.8	36.9	12.1	0.0	16.4
Gilchrist	78	10.0	214	6	44	429	1 911	44	52	142 583	15.0	85.0	38.4	10.7	0.0	9.4
Glades	380	2.8	2 023	26	41	1 663	835	38	59	311 642	64.7	35.3	48.9	23.4	0.0	99.6
Gulf	4	-72.7	116	0	1	132	1 136	16	0	10 876	13.1	86.9	27.3	3.0	0.3	31.1
Hamilton	66	-3.8	259	4	25	303	1 129	30	13	51 094	52.6	47.4	36.3	10.5	0.0	46.2
Hardee	346	5.4	331	54	106	860	2 880	32	155	148 170	75.9	24.1	59.2	18.3	0.0	51.0
Hendry	605	14.1	1 500	184	205	4 289	2 868	178	323	802 575	95.4	4.6	62.3	31.5	0.0	557.0
Hernando	53	-13.1	123	1	21	416	2 963	18	23	53 267	27.6	72.4	28.5	4.6	3.6	41.6
Highlands	490	1.2	628	88	122	1 191	1 909	55	203	260 414	82.4	17.6	54.7	22.7	7.7	119.5
Hillsborough	248	-6.6	94	46	103	391	4 234	31	333	126 084	79.3	20.7	41.0	14.6	0.7	246.3
Holmes	88	0.7	152	0	41	218	1 476	20	32	54 557	16.5	83.5	33.4	13.3	0.0	7.2
Indian River	168	-3.8	385	77	86	1 243	3 169	94	95	217 722	94.7	5.3	59.7	23.6	0.1	212.9
Jackson	245	0.2	290	18	136	300	1 104	41	51	60 965	74.6	25.4	46.6	13.4	0.5	81.1
Jefferson	127	7.3	370	1	33	499	1 429	24	18	52 779	77.4	22.6	35.4	7.6	2.1	11.6
Lafayette	93	-2.7	423	4	22	547	1 207	52	54	245 800	10.8	89.2	54.3	34.8	0.0	7.5
Lake	185	-6.9	133	26	80	407	2 990	27	168	121 049	85.7	14.3	42.4	12.2	12.3	83.1
Lee	129	20.6	253	26	34	724	2 664	38	116	228 678	98.0	2.0	39.9	10.6	0.6	134.0
Leon	68	-33.1	278	3	16	456	1 575	26	3	14 252	38.8	61.2	24.3	1.6	23.4	39.3
Levy	157	-17.6	287	13	68	365	1 325	32	52	94 393	32.0	68.0	43.9	10.6	3.1	23.4
Liberty	7	-39.7	154	0	1	227	1 475	22	1	11 733	7.6	92.6	34.0	0.0	53.2	1.6
Madison	132	-0.3	271	4	54	381	1 397	45	32	65 827	36.5	63.5	31.5	11.3	0.0	9.3
Manatee	268	-10.7	384	58	106	922	2 524	71	240	343 793	91.6	8.4	49.1	17.9	0.0	122.7
Marion	266	-10.3	159	6	100	491	3 094	27	102	60 833	22.6	77.4	31.3	9.3	28.3	52.1
Martin	184	-3.8	602	62	75	1 618	2 704	106	145	475 486	80.5	19.5	53.1	26.2	0.2	170.0
Miami-Dade	85	1.3	54	58	68	408	8 047	49	417	264 278	98.2	1.8	51.2	23.2	33.4	569.3
Monroe	1	0.0	95	0	D	296	3 104	11	D	D	D		7.7	7.7	78.0	1.8
Nassau	35	-21.9	148	0	6	276	2 068	22	28	115 849	2.0	98.0	26.1	12.6	0.0	44.7
Okaloosa	51	-10.8	149	0	21	249	1 608	25	9	25 470	60.9	39.1	21.3	3.8	38.8	29.9
Okeechobee	392	11.3	854	35	73	1 227	1 506	55	138	300 666	24.1	75.9	46.6	17.6	0.0	41.2
Orange	175	26.8	203	25	44	604	3 334	62	248	287 423	98.6	1.4	55.5	27.7	0.1	259.6
Osceola	611	-14.8	1 259	58	51	1 647	1 325	45	89	183 061	68.1	31.9	45.8	16.9	0.0	81.5
Palm Beach	605	-5.2	707	417	529	2 398	3 404	84	873	1 020 908	99.5	0.5	64.1	33.9	10.1	959.8
Pasco	162	-26.7	170	13	58	500	3 149	29	84	88 644	35.8	64.2	35.9	9.1	0.0	141.8
Pinellas	2	-52.6	15	0	1	284	23 143	26	12	91 994	98.7	1.3	41.9	9.3	0.0	44.8
Polk	621	1.7	252	118	187	532	2 110	31	253	102 865	80.5	19.5	48.0	12.5	2.5	391.9
Putnam	86	-19.1	219	7	17	467	2 440	28	34	87 017	89.8	10.2	37.1	11.5	5.1	88.4
St. Johns	50	1.3	333	20	25	749	2 256	141	46	309 042	95.6	4.4	55.0	33.6	0.0	46.4
St. Lucie	227	-24.4	455	139	136	1 183	2 783	60	173	346 274	94.2	5.8	62.4	22.0	0.0	309.9
Santa Rosa	88	11.4	201	5	59	297	1 586	50	30	68 426	93.1	6.9	41.1	17.8	9.9	23.3

STATE County	Value of Residential Construction Authorized by Building Permits, 1999		Wholesale Trade, 1997				Retail Trade[1], 1997				Real Estate and Rental and Leasing, 1997			
	New Construction ($1,000)	Number of Housing Units	Number of Establishments	Number of Employees	Sales (mil dol)	Annual Payroll (mil dol)	Number of Establishments	Number of Employees	Sales (mil dol)	Annual Payroll (mil dol)	Number of Establishments	Number of Employees	Receipts (mil dol)	Annual Payroll (mil dol)
	133	134	135	136	137	138	139	140	141	142	143	144	145	146
DELAWARE	492 470	5 285	906	13 509	12 585.5	619.5	3 736	47 116	8 237.0	798.7	1 101	5 243	5 006.5	118.3
Kent	81 008	866	110	D	D	D	594	7 864	1 325.4	128.3	128	506	49.4	8.0
New Castle	195 084	2 575	637	D	D	D	2 079	30 375	5 367.0	523.1	767	3 712	4 824.3	90.1
Sussex	216 378	1 844	159	1 435	481.2	35.9	1 063	8 877	1 544.5	147.4	206	1 025	132.7	20.1
DISTRICT OF COLUMBIA	53 284	683	348	5 008	3 918.6	223.0	2 075	19 608	2 788.8	351.5	934	7 725	1 354.2	275.4
District of Columbia	53 284	683	348	5 008	3 918.6	223.0	2 075	19 608	2 788.8	351.5	934	7 725	1 354.2	275.4
FLORIDA	16 197 445	165 018	31 214	296 139	187 079.9	9 678.2	66 643	841 814	151 191.2	14 169.5	20 388	118 086	15 360.4	2 652.2
Alachua	181 650	2 728	224	1 824	738.0	54.5	923	12 726	1 934.5	186.2	279	1 630	155.2	28.2
Baker	6 196	97	7	D	D	D	61	630	95.7	7.3	6	26	0.7	0.1
Bay	98 590	1 044	173	1 406	422.1	34.2	832	9 558	1 496.8	148.1	229	1 018	76.8	15.6
Bradford	3 974	62	20	78	31.1	1.7	94	930	151.7	12.7	13	38	3.5	0.4
Brevard	496 714	4 659	577	4 389	1 362.4	136.2	1 856	23 867	3 900.5	370.3	525	2 443	220.0	45.3
Broward	1 409 811	12 013	4 359	38 614	26 122.2	1 414.7	6 804	89 290	17 979.8	1 639.9	2 263	14 394	2 196.6	351.6
Calhoun	1 350	22	13	D	D	D	49	478	81.0	6.4	3	13	0.9	0.1
Charlotte	149 416	1 418	103	446	117.2	11.2	515	6 840	1 063.3	100.4	167	601	60.7	10.1
Citrus	66 890	1 086	88	383	90.4	7.1	429	5 049	800.6	71.8	107	343	33.6	5.7
Clay	154 884	1 522	104	503	220.6	12.7	516	6 956	1 100.5	106.0	114	561	62.3	11.5
Collier	931 569	7 542	350	2 076	813.8	63.0	1 343	15 366	2 627.1	274.1	509	2 874	305.2	66.0
Columbia	17 083	279	87	859	286.7	21.6	239	3 132	556.0	49.0	38	94	10.1	1.3
De Soto	15 186	238	19	D	D	D	81	937	197.0	14.9	20	61	5.7	0.8
Dixie	2 197	33	4	D	D	D	42	271	39.2	3.6	6	18	0.6	0.2
Duval	581 098	6 411	1 394	21 860	16 590.0	760.3	3 134	44 276	8 034.1	761.4	886	6 374	918.5	158.4
Escambia	148 272	1 926	388	4 769	1 616.0	128.3	1 301	16 602	2 874.7	261.4	292	1 292	131.8	22.7
Flagler	97 987	1 407	39	272	94.6	7.9	119	1 608	244.1	22.2	53	184	28.3	3.6
Franklin	18 060	103	26	309	64.1	4.4	69	389	57.0	5.6	14	85	6.5	1.4
Gadsden	11 823	100	21	D	D	D	157	1 228	179.8	16.2	15	59	4.0	0.8
Gilchrist	5 612	66	11	D	D	D	34	206	29.9	2.8	6	15	1.0	0.4
Glades	2 582	31	4	D	D	D	27	211	35.2	2.7	11	14	2.7	0.2
Gulf	14 657	114	8	24	28.2	0.6	60	404	48.9	4.7	8	18	1.5	0.2
Hamilton	2 354	29	5	D	D	D	55	393	53.6	4.3	3	33	0.5	0.3
Hardee	3 699	38	21	164	92.4	5.1	79	721	116.8	10.6	9	22	2.5	0.3
Hendry	4 042	45	23	D	D	D	104	1 030	202.6	16.8	22	50	6.8	0.7
Hernando	111 942	1 254	98	513	142.3	13.8	371	5 270	821.5	74.3	97	248	24.2	3.4
Highlands	55 381	667	85	618	184.1	13.1	349	4 035	618.2	57.1	75	249	25.0	3.8
Hillsborough	1 094 231	14 665	2 233	33 851	23 668.5	1 151.4	3 821	57 038	10 931.6	1 001.4	1 164	8 336	1 034.2	190.0
Holmes	5 215	62	11	D	D	D	55	327	46.3	3.9	6	13	0.9	0.2
Indian River	253 200	1 318	147	D	D	D	667	7 793	1 143.9	121.5	170	714	76.5	12.9
Jackson	9 259	136	42	301	86.0	7.1	221	2 289	376.9	31.6	27	48	4.5	0.7
Jefferson	6 985	72	10	D	D	D	55	426	51.5	4.3	5	19	1.1	0.2
Lafayette	2 230	25	9	D	D	D	17	93	10.0	1.2	2	D	D	D
Lake	326 044	4 146	229	2 137	680.2	48.2	760	9 663	1 514.3	148.2	217	930	82.0	17.3
Lee	1 021 861	8 816	586	4 593	1 450.3	135.3	1 924	25 417	4 367.0	430.5	642	3 328	461.1	72.2
Leon	193 615	2 129	260	D	D	D	1 038	15 478	2 244.4	229.7	301	1 835	202.3	33.1
Levy	15 745	155	21	141	37.7	2.2	132	1 455	234.5	19.2	24	61	4.1	0.8
Liberty	1 208	12	1	D	D	D	17	83	11.9	1.2	1	D	D	D
Madison	4 636	63	15	128	60.9	2.3	72	567	64.1	6.6	8	25	1.7	0.4
Manatee	330 514	2 863	270	2 348	1 087.6	76.5	938	12 165	2 141.0	194.4	265	1 002	158.6	19.4
Marion	273 830	2 759	309	3 219	999.6	80.0	1 014	13 159	2 221.4	202.1	244	786	88.4	13.8
Martin	228 252	1 114	174	695	423.8	23.7	712	8 425	1 454.0	147.5	211	986	118.6	27.7
Miami-Dade	1 181 263	14 067	8 935	70 050	43 604.4	2 235.9	9 814	110 292	20 720.6	1 995.8	3 378	19 793	2 853.9	465.8
Monroe	47 642	407	131	870	217.5	19.5	707	6 246	914.2	99.5	254	952	108.4	16.1
Nassau	69 141	651	40	238	158.4	8.9	215	2 172	332.2	28.6	43	130	28.0	2.7
Okaloosa	187 696	1 807	139	959	248.3	23.9	931	11 322	1 754.9	165.7	280	1 582	140.3	29.0
Okeechobee	11 944	143	31	D	D	D	149	1 657	270.1	23.6	29	70	8.2	1.5
Orange	1 164 945	15 500	1 931	25 730	24 089.1	868.5	3 911	53 854	10 450.9	913.6	1 309	14 060	1 952.2	345.5
Osceola	441 144	4 717	108	1 499	1 070.1	41.3	612	8 289	1 349.7	124.8	234	2 884	274.7	60.4
Palm Beach	1 111 405	10 008	2 187	17 864	11 544.5	707.0	4 967	61 563	11 731.2	1 126.1	1 716	9 409	1 323.8	248.3
Pasco	331 259	3 824	243	1 378	351.6	34.1	1 055	14 200	2 247.1	212.5	260	979	116.1	16.9
Pinellas	425 872	3 237	1 730	17 616	11 558.7	609.3	3 895	51 843	10 183.9	911.4	1 238	5 676	630.5	112.9
Polk	284 802	3 879	639	8 329	4 176.2	212.7	1 816	22 751	3 844.3	360.9	431	2 001	217.3	39.8
Putnam	15 268	211	56	D	D	D	250	2 395	397.7	36.1	45	151	12.4	1.9
St. Johns	411 308	3 020	179	1 050	428.0	31.1	549	5 640	862.5	81.0	153	505	83.4	9.6
St. Lucie	217 037	2 233	198	2 262	581.5	53.8	610	7 644	1 387.2	125.1	178	652	85.9	12.1
Santa Rosa	107 114	988	82	296	103.1	7.1	319	3 615	561.1	44.2	97	333	27.6	5.1

1. Establishments with payroll.

Table B. States and Counties — Professional, Manufacturing, and Accommodation and Foodservices

STATE County	Professional, Scientific, and Technical Services[1], 1997				Manufacturing, 1997				Accommodation and Foodservices, 1997			
	Number of Establishments	Number of Employees	Receipts (mil dol)	Annual Payroll (mil dol)	Number of Establishments	Number of Employees	Receipts (mil dol)	Annual Payroll (mil dol)	Number of Establishments	Number of Employees	Sales (mil dol)	Annual Payroll (mil dol)
	147	148	149	150	151	152	153	154	155	156	157	158
DELAWARE	1 717	12 382	1 430.4	553.4	675	41 084	13 397.3	1 474.3	1 605	26 969	1 009.0	280.8
Kent	155	1 091	69.4	30.3	82	7 985	1 965.5	209.8	234	3 796	118.4	31.9
New Castle	1 368	10 597	1 314.2	503.2	458	22 610	8 735.0	1 000.1	929	17 837	656.1	187.4
Sussex	194	694	46.8	20.0	135	10 489	2 696.8	264.4	442	5 336	234.5	61.5
DISTRICT OF COLUMBIA	3 760	61 123	10 365.2	3 935.5	200	2 858	320.2	101.1	1 700	42 650	2 263.5	701.4
District of Columbia	3 760	61 123	10 365.2	3 935.5	200	2 858	320.2	101.1	1 700	42 650	2 263.5	701.4
FLORIDA	42 403	276 263	27 231.1	10 803.5	15 992	433 149	77 477.5	13 185.1	28 999	608 834	24 165.3	6 239.5
Alachua	570	3 788	292.8	126.4	151	5 251	1 010.3	157.1	431	8 981	263.0	67.8
Baker	8	32	1.0	0.4	NA	NA	NA	NA	18	380	9.8	2.4
Bay	268	1 730	138.9	56.1	136	3 492	719.0	108.7	483	9 268	336.3	84.8
Bradford	22	72	4.8	1.9	15	698	44.1	10.7	28	698	17.3	4.8
Brevard	1 073	11 192	1 195.6	455.0	494	20 832	3 450.7	753.9	860	16 207	495.3	136.3
Broward	5 625	27 496	2 940.7	1 103.7	1 967	37 134	5 788.3	1 115.4	3 206	61 243	2 474.5	615.5
Calhoun	11	34	1.5	0.5	NA	NA	NA	NA	13	120	4.1	1.1
Charlotte	194	1 083	73.3	37.3	74	587	77.7	13.8	218	3 935	123.5	31.9
Citrus	136	602	38.8	16.0	58	1 025	92.4	18.2	166	2 393	66.3	19.0
Clay	188	685	51.8	19.8	74	1 579	247.2	43.7	195	3 990	114.6	32.7
Collier	743	3 074	414.1	196.5	205	2 305	259.0	62.4	518	11 599	536.7	140.9
Columbia	67	287	21.3	7.8	35	1 798	244.5	46.3	99	2 118	54.1	14.8
De Soto	21	83	4.1	2.0	NA	NA	NA	NA	33	412	12.4	3.0
Dixie	8	14	0.9	0.2	NA	NA	NA	NA	22	152	3.5	0.9
Duval	1 959	17 491	1 552.9	690.0	754	28 237	7 231.0	944.1	1 420	28 354	917.2	244.2
Escambia	547	3 956	306.0	132.3	236	7 526	2 214.1	294.6	493	11 101	350.9	92.3
Flagler	70	242	20.1	7.5	42	1 560	260.7	45.9	88	1 465	42.4	12.8
Franklin	14	48	2.4	0.8	NA	NA	NA	NA	43	393	14.9	3.4
Gadsden	39	133	8.1	2.4	32	1 399	187.8	32.3	39	321	10.7	2.6
Gilchrist	10	38	1.8	0.7	NA	NA	NA	NA	16	D	D	D
Glades	9	34	2.2	0.7	NA	NA	NA	NA	20	129	4.7	1.0
Gulf	15	147	7.5	2.8	12	D	D	D	21	155	4.6	1.2
Hamilton	7	D	D	D	4	D	D	D	13	161	3.7	0.9
Hardee	22	69	3.1	1.4	NA	NA	NA	NA	17	225	7.4	1.6
Hendry	23	71	3.9	1.8	22	724	437.7	26.8	48	644	18.4	5.0
Hernando	132	523	33.0	11.4	72	1 192	235.2	29.4	184	2 772	74.0	19.9
Highlands	106	410	23.4	9.8	54	1 199	191.6	27.0	118	1 817	52.3	13.8
Hillsborough	3 050	34 249	3 859.1	1 403.9	960	30 861	6 019.8	859.3	1 552	34 618	1 248.3	330.4
Holmes	14	53	2.6	0.9	NA	NA	NA	NA	13	160	4.5	1.2
Indian River	281	1 296	103.1	43.3	116	1 825	219.8	55.4	204	3 527	112.4	31.6
Jackson	35	177	11.6	4.6	26	1 344	182.1	27.3	58	931	26.0	7.6
Jefferson	16	36	2.7	0.6	NA	NA	NA	NA	13	121	3.4	0.9
Lafayette	6	D	D	D	NA	NA	NA	NA	13	94	3.1	0.7
Lake	313	1 397	87.7	37.2	164	3 730	578.5	90.2	291	5 161	154.6	42.4
Lee	997	6 053	458.2	197.4	357	5 363	741.8	141.1	824	17 424	699.1	175.2
Leon	838	6 865	702.3	292.9	127	2 676	557.6	68.0	456	9 884	296.8	77.1
Levy	30	104	5.9	2.1	NA	NA	NA	NA	57	809	19.5	5.1
Liberty	1	D	D	D	NA	NA	NA	NA	3	D	D	D
Madison	13	64	3.3	1.2	11	1 114	270.3	25.8	29	433	9.9	2.4
Manatee	445	1 884	147.8	56.1	284	11 156	2 115.7	348.4	390	7 480	241.5	64.5
Marion	361	1 882	132.9	52.8	215	9 620	1 287.8	238.0	363	6 558	200.9	54.1
Martin	409	1 598	141.8	55.5	172	3 274	555.2	101.7	258	4 676	167.8	46.4
Miami-Dade	7 821	42 781	4 640.0	1 856.0	3 031	66 391	8 523.9	1 663.8	3 835	75 597	3 199.5	878.5
Monroe	262	835	72.1	26.6	NA	NA	NA	NA	567	10 939	569.1	151.3
Nassau	65	256	25.9	11.7	34	1 790	630.6	77.3	100	3 102	143.3	37.4
Okaloosa	417	3 181	264.0	113.5	133	3 448	296.5	81.5	401	8 450	261.7	73.0
Okeechobee	28	142	5.9	2.2	NA	NA	NA	NA	60	988	34.8	8.9
Orange	2 878	25 810	2 679.2	1 077.7	889	32 437	5 786.6	1 213.4	1 720	73 124	4 058.7	962.7
Osceola	172	758	50.3	18.8	77	1 295	379.9	37.1	423	12 152	763.0	152.2
Palm Beach	4 211	21 787	2 352.0	985.5	1 051	26 262	6 344.5	1 138.1	2 087	41 031	1 659.8	440.9
Pasco	417	1 931	107.1	41.6	213	4 091	713.3	100.7	437	7 654	246.3	62.6
Pinellas	2 799	26 125	2 187.0	861.6	1 335	40 954	5 732.8	1 256.8	1 965	36 685	1 383.4	367.6
Polk	712	4 006	347.6	135.4	480	20 627	5 999.9	633.5	711	13 383	419.3	113.2
Putnam	67	171	10.8	3.5	48	2 556	730.2	88.9	88	1 318	37.5	9.8
St. Johns	294	961	96.9	34.7	88	2 277	299.6	53.8	332	6 999	263.6	71.1
St. Lucie	257	1 442	91.6	38.6	124	2 230	542.7	60.1	245	3 959	147.6	36.6
Santa Rosa	122	490	34.0	11.4	59	1 895	427.7	41.6	119	1 970	53.8	14.6

1. Firms subject to federal tax.

STATE County	Health Care and Social Assistance[1], 1997				Other Services[1], 1997				Federal funds and grants, fiscal 1999[2] Expenditures (mil dol)			
										Direct payments for individuals[3]		
	Number of Establishments	Number of Employees	Receipts (mil dol)	Annual Payroll (mil dol)	Number of Establishments	Number of Employees	Receipts (mil dol)	Annual Payroll (mil dol)	Total	Social Security and government retirement	Medicare	Food stamps and Supplemental Security Income
	159	160	161	162	163	164	165	166	167	168	169	170
DELAWARE	1 465	15 980	1 131.6	526.4	1 198	7 006	420.5	140.7	3 765.7	1 485.6	531.5	84.4
Kent	192	2 157	137.6	59.6	215	1 016	56.0	16.8	902.6	274.0	65.3	16.1
New Castle	1 016	11 380	846.6	398.1	768	5 051	311.5	108.2	2 002.3	815.9	331.8	52.0
Sussex	257	2 443	147.4	68.6	215	939	53.0	15.7	702.8	394.0	134.3	16.3
DISTRICT OF COLUMBIA	1 464	13 692	1 054.8	476.7	978	6 218	404.8	111.1	27 033.7	1 625.4	585.7	172.1
District of Columbia	1 464	13 692	1 054.8	476.7	978	6 218	404.8	111.1	27 033.7	1 625.4	585.7	172.1
FLORIDA	35 568	447 117	32 559.1	13 610.7	26 121	146 360	9 123.6	2 665.7	87 214.9	35 729.8	17 101.9	2 476.6
Alachua	502	6 499	435.3	201.2	318	1 631	94.1	28.0	1 038.6	349.5	133.0	34.9
Baker	21	299	12.4	4.9	19	57	3.9	0.8	73.4	37.5	12.7	4.3
Bay	317	4 398	315.8	131.2	246	1 569	85.5	27.6	1 211.3	426.2	119.4	23.4
Bradford	27	609	22.2	9.6	17	116	7.4	1.8	96.3	46.9	20.7	3.7
Brevard	1 017	10 631	783.2	358.0	728	3 778	206.4	63.8	4 132.0	1 520.3	458.9	54.4
Broward	4 226	51 708	3 879.0	1 603.0	3 246	19 188	1 397.3	373.4	6 375.8	2 995.4	2 064.7	178.8
Calhoun	13	49	3.0	1.0	8	32	1.6	0.4	56.5	22.4	11.1	3.1
Charlotte	305	4 286	306.9	134.7	189	674	37.4	10.2	776.7	505.8	217.8	9.7
Citrus	228	3 228	205.1	85.0	150	525	29.0	7.5	635.8	413.0	170.5	12.5
Clay	250	3 913	260.4	97.6	193	970	47.8	14.3	467.3	339.9	67.2	8.1
Collier	492	5 124	404.9	175.0	431	2 035	109.6	34.8	893.2	551.2	203.7	15.8
Columbia	108	1 406	88.1	35.3	59	227	15.9	3.7	272.4	122.8	44.2	12.7
De Soto	37	253	14.8	5.2	26	100	5.1	1.2	118.1	54.4	36.3	5.8
Dixie	6	60	2.2	1.0	7	31	2.0	0.5	67.1	41.3	11.6	4.4
Duval	1 579	23 107	1 729.8	810.5	1 448	9 054	604.7	184.3	4 901.5	1 493.5	570.6	126.0
Escambia	535	9 282	658.6	301.3	437	3 132	176.5	64.3	2 190.0	829.3	223.1	59.0
Flagler	62	305	21.3	9.8	47	167	10.0	2.2	246.4	178.2	43.2	4.2
Franklin	15	279	8.9	4.0	8	15	1.1	0.2	51.0	23.7	13.7	2.0
Gadsden	26	156	11.5	3.8	37	149	7.3	2.3	215.2	74.0	34.6	16.9
Gilchrist	7	21	1.3	0.4	3	D	D	D	45.7	26.2	9.2	2.0
Glades	2	D	D	D	7	24	2.2	0.9	28.0	17.1	5.6	0.4
Gulf	16	370	20.3	8.3	19	46	3.0	0.5	75.0	34.8	17.8	2.4
Hamilton	14	188	9.0	4.3	12	28	1.9	0.3	52.4	22.3	9.2	3.5
Hardee	27	554	21.9	10.7	22	70	4.0	1.0	84.9	36.5	18.9	6.3
Hendry	28	311	12.7	5.5	29	179	7.4	3.0	105.7	43.8	21.2	6.2
Hernando	252	2 630	181.1	84.2	193	756	38.6	10.8	845.3	535.6	225.7	15.8
Highlands	184	1 759	134.0	47.2	110	431	21.1	5.4	505.0	299.9	136.2	12.5
Hillsborough	2 233	29 728	2 295.7	905.7	1 590	10 820	700.2	209.4	4 436.3	1 800.8	759.3	175.9
Holmes	16	367	25.3	7.2	8	38	2.7	0.8	104.8	43.3	19.5	6.0
Indian River	287	3 388	263.7	96.4	206	944	45.4	13.7	645.9	389.7	179.7	8.8
Jackson	62	701	36.8	14.0	51	218	13.1	3.4	264.5	96.7	41.7	10.0
Jefferson	12	77	3.8	1.2	11	30	1.0	0.2	80.2	23.3	9.6	4.0
Lafayette	4	D	D	D	5	31	2.3	0.4	22.1	8.9	3.7	0.4
Lake	376	3 834	244.4	107.5	300	1 353	71.9	21.3	1 145.8	742.1	266.7	25.8
Lee	825	12 968	954.5	408.4	695	3 599	224.9	68.5	2 031.6	1 228.5	505.3	42.9
Leon	441	6 479	459.0	210.2	390	2 563	144.2	46.7	2 974.3	407.8	98.1	29.7
Levy	33	534	23.8	7.8	32	108	5.9	1.5	148.3	83.3	30.1	6.6
Liberty	8	156	4.5	2.2	2	D	D	D	30.5	10.7	4.5	0.8
Madison	16	179	6.9	3.2	22	93	4.8	1.5	97.3	33.9	16.0	5.8
Manatee	472	9 114	634.7	243.7	316	1 565	84.9	25.8	1 143.7	678.3	285.5	23.2
Marion	466	6 512	466.6	185.9	369	1 680	93.9	29.4	1 325.7	787.4	272.6	38.6
Martin	317	3 142	231.3	101.1	244	1 045	63.9	18.9	658.3	413.9	173.1	8.2
Miami-Dade	6 157	60 718	4 782.5	1 877.5	3 901	22 435	1 391.0	385.8	10 358.7	2 748.9	2 725.7	733.6
Monroe	162	1 416	105.1	40.0	183	674	46.5	11.3	480.6	165.0	70.8	7.9
Nassau	56	683	38.0	16.4	79	321	19.9	6.2	244.4	121.7	34.9	4.9
Okaloosa	356	5 134	412.2	142.7	313	1 531	86.3	25.5	1 764.4	633.9	102.5	14.3
Okeechobee	68	1 153	75.0	27.1	46	184	13.2	3.2	162.0	81.0	50.0	6.4
Orange	1 792	22 044	1 627.8	774.0	1 494	11 286	713.7	216.5	4 791.7	1 443.5	608.2	133.5
Osceola	252	4 024	241.3	103.8	207	923	55.6	16.4	480.5	260.5	120.7	16.8
Palm Beach	3 280	39 623	2 981.7	1 257.5	2 113	11 678	726.5	209.6	6 887.8	2 847.6	1 554.2	97.5
Pasco	676	12 112	849.4	342.5	443	2 124	112.6	31.9	1 695.5	927.5	550.2	36.8
Pinellas	2 633	36 006	2 496.2	1 052.0	1 746	9 799	614.7	189.1	5 493.9	2 681.9	1 406.8	107.9
Polk	643	9 886	657.7	279.4	611	3 224	199.6	60.6	1 983.0	1 094.6	405.6	84.6
Putnam	93	1 961	120.3	47.7	74	342	21.5	5.8	347.0	168.1	75.3	18.5
St. Johns	249	2 057	152.3	66.9	139	658	42.5	12.3	559.0	293.6	97.6	10.7
St. Lucie	360	7 250	525.1	193.7	273	1 181	74.2	19.9	945.1	559.5	235.4	33.9
Santa Rosa	127	1 881	90.2	42.8	120	540	33.9	9.3	560.8	303.1	63.3	10.3

1. Firms subject to federal tax.   2. October 1, 1998 to September 30, 1999.   3. State totals may include programs not allocated by county.

Table B. States and Counties — **Federal Funds and Local Government Finances**

	Federal funds and grants, fiscal 1999[1] (cont'd)							Local government finances, 1997				
	Expenditures (mil dol) (cont'd)							General revenue				
	Procurement contract awards			Grants[2]						Taxes		
											Per capita[3] (dollars)	
STATE County	Salaries and wages	Defense	Other	Medicaid and other health-related	Nutrition and family welfare	Education	Other	Total (mil dol)	Intergovernmental (mil dol)	Total (mil dol)	Total	Property
	171	172	173	174	175	176	177	178	179	180	181	182
DELAWARE	405.9	92.7	128.5	308.9	125.0	82.5	308.8	X	X	X	X	X
Kent	203.0	64.3	4.5	61.9	34.1	39.4	122.0	220.2	144.7	37.8	308	280
New Castle	178.2	26.2	117.7	187.5	68.4	24.3	166.0	942.9	402.1	306.6	646	525
Sussex	24.6	2.3	6.4	59.5	10.5	10.8	20.1	271.1	155.1	68.1	508	433
DISTRICT OF COLUMBIA	11 975.2	1 344.1	5 059.3	1 550.3	1 197.4	347.2	2 197.9	X	X	X	X	X
District of Columbia	11 975.2	1 344.1	5 059.3	1 550.3	1 197.4	347.2	2 197.9	5 279.0	1 994.5	2 637.4	4 986	1 322
FLORIDA	7 834.9	6 764.2	1 875.1	4 705.7	2 173.5	1 199.7	3 112.0	X	X	X	X	X
Alachua	143.5	6.1	49.6	132.8	29.8	15.2	99.8	469.0	198.4	135.7	684	581
Baker	2.5	0.0	0.6	4.8	2.7	1.4	6.1	52.2	26.0	8.7	420	296
Bay	277.6	129.8	26.1	34.2	18.5	8.5	5.5	460.6	158.6	108.1	739	475
Bradford	7.0	0.3	0.5	10.4	3.3	1.1	0.5	49.8	31.1	9.1	370	247
Brevard	333.1	1 101.5	514.9	48.7	31.6	16.5	31.6	992.6	322.6	330.2	716	569
Broward	386.6	77.6	113.6	199.1	97.0	51.8	128.7	4 746.9	1 168.5	1 714.5	1 166	921
Calhoun	1.1	0.0	0.4	9.1	2.5	0.9	3.8	22.5	16.3	4.3	351	241
Charlotte	13.5	1.8	3.7	5.2	7.2	2.9	6.6	268.9	54.4	131.5	984	744
Citrus	10.4	0.0	3.0	10.8	6.7	3.7	1.9	196.8	55.8	83.4	742	682
Clay	18.2	5.2	2.8	10.1	6.1	4.0	1.7	245.5	112.9	71.6	529	398
Collier	30.4	0.3	8.9	22.9	20.9	6.1	26.5	502.7	92.3	285.7	1 459	1 257
Columbia	41.5	3.7	2.8	22.9	8.0	3.3	6.5	116.0	63.4	26.8	507	320
De Soto	3.0	0.0	0.6	7.8	4.1	2.0	3.5	53.3	26.8	15.3	583	442
Dixie	1.0	0.0	0.2	4.2	2.2	1.0	0.3	25.1	15.5	5.3	421	326
Duval	1 415.3	478.3	178.5	239.2	104.3	45.4	94.9	1 764.1	657.0	611.2	834	628
Escambia	655.1	145.7	25.7	97.4	46.6	19.2	47.4	659.9	309.9	178.9	633	398
Flagler	5.4	0.0	5.7	2.2	2.4	1.1	3.4	90.5	26.0	44.0	955	859
Franklin	1.2	0.0	0.3	5.9	1.7	0.7	-0.2	23.5	9.3	11.0	1 085	963
Gadsden	6.0	2.2	0.9	33.8	15.5	6.0	16.6	78.6	51.5	15.9	349	261
Gilchrist	1.2	0.0	0.3	2.9	1.3	0.5	0.3	28.1	14.9	5.0	376	298
Glades	0.5	0.9	0.1	0.8	0.8	0.4	1.2	16.5	7.1	6.8	697	628
Gulf	0.8	0.0	0.2	6.5	1.9	0.7	8.5	33.3	12.0	11.6	836	761
Hamilton	1.5	0.0	0.4	8.5	2.8	1.5	1.2	56.8	18.9	27.8	2 224	969
Hardee	2.7	0.0	0.6	9.2	4.6	1.7	2.5	54.0	27.3	17.8	806	666
Hendry	4.2	1.1	0.5	7.0	5.3	1.9	10.3	101.2	40.3	29.4	931	771
Hernando	15.6	0.7	4.1	11.7	9.6	4.1	20.4	311.5	97.6	134.6	1 072	1 010
Highlands	13.0	1.9	3.1	16.2	7.5	5.4	5.7	156.3	67.6	55.9	727	565
Hillsborough	684.8	190.6	117.6	291.3	113.2	56.7	168.5	2 752.7	1 022.1	851.5	936	726
Holmes	2.9	1.0	0.6	14.4	4.8	1.2	8.1	35.3	26.3	5.1	277	188
Indian River	18.4	8.6	4.3	11.9	8.6	3.6	10.7	350.9	51.9	133.0	1 340	1 093
Jackson	27.9	0.3	2.2	40.8	7.7	2.6	20.1	125.3	58.2	18.7	410	228
Jefferson	1.5	0.1	0.4	12.1	2.9	1.1	21.7	24.3	15.0	6.1	464	340
Lafayette	0.7	2.5	0.2	1.8	0.8	0.4	1.9	12.8	8.8	2.3	369	329
Lake	25.5	3.7	10.2	26.7	15.7	8.7	13.5	348.0	127.2	129.1	658	484
Lee	96.0	6.4	22.9	45.9	29.4	17.4	20.6	1 548.2	259.2	458.5	1 184	1 041
Leon	90.9	19.7	27.3	321.6	688.7	377.4	833.4	585.2	208.8	191.1	888	598
Levy	4.2	0.1	1.0	10.0	4.2	2.8	1.3	61.0	32.1	18.0	558	431
Liberty	1.6	0.4	0.2	3.9	1.0	0.4	7.0	12.0	8.5	2.3	343	260
Madison	2.2	0.0	0.5	17.5	4.1	2.0	12.6	43.3	26.9	7.6	434	276
Manatee	56.9	10.4	15.2	30.6	19.3	8.4	8.1	586.6	167.7	222.9	940	788
Marion	33.9	8.6	40.1	51.8	28.7	11.1	36.1	411.8	199.1	119.9	505	446
Martin	14.5	14.1	4.9	10.0	7.3	3.4	7.4	296.6	53.6	161.0	1 387	1 231
Miami-Dade	1 017.9	101.4	214.7	1 847.6	315.7	139.3	343.2	7 614.5	2 402.8	2 454.4	1 151	869
Monroe	92.7	60.5	8.0	19.6	6.0	2.7	2.2	297.6	58.9	141.3	1 724	1 327
Nassau	52.8	6.2	2.2	11.0	4.7	1.9	3.1	115.4	43.2	41.7	771	633
Okaloosa	480.4	444.5	12.9	26.7	14.5	7.1	12.2	354.9	167.7	108.4	647	548
Okeechobee	3.7	1.4	1.0	9.3	4.6	2.3	1.4	65.2	34.7	20.6	623	444
Orange	376.1	1 654.5	106.0	145.2	71.7	35.6	165.8	2 574.5	678.8	932.6	1 190	901
Osceola	14.3	6.3	4.0	9.4	9.3	4.8	30.3	372.6	119.5	143.3	1 008	695
Palm Beach	290.3	1 501.3	116.2	133.2	72.3	34.2	205.5	3 140.0	632.2	1 523.2	1 495	1 256
Pasco	37.0	1.1	10.5	36.9	25.7	10.4	45.4	549.0	226.7	174.7	545	488
Pinellas	323.8	542.3	96.3	124.8	65.2	40.5	64.1	2 106.4	566.2	886.1	1 016	764
Polk	72.5	19.7	17.5	97.3	55.4	24.0	90.8	896.4	388.5	274.6	612	505
Putnam	7.0	0.2	1.7	28.2	14.0	5.3	21.7	240.0	95.3	98.9	1 404	1 312
St. Johns	22.6	62.4	8.6	19.3	7.4	4.2	27.3	243.8	69.7	99.4	882	769
St. Lucie	26.4	7.5	6.6	27.3	18.4	10.9	14.1	471.1	163.9	182.2	1 015	911
Santa Rosa	58.5	37.3	5.4	18.8	10.7	5.0	37.3	201.0	101.1	59.2	517	404

1. October 1, 1998 to September 30, 1999.   2. State totals may include programs not allocated by county.   3. Based on the resident population estimated as of July 1 of the year shown.

	Local government finances, 1997 (cont'd)									Government employment, 1998			Presidential election, 2000		
STATE County	Direct general expenditure							Debt outstanding					Percent of vote cast —		
			Percent of total for —												
	Total (mil dol)	Per capita[1] (dollars)	Educa- tion	Health and hospitals	Police protec- tion	Public welfare	High- ways	Total (mil dol)	Per capita[1] (dollars)	Federal civilian	Federal military	State and local	Demo- cratic	Republi- can	All other
	183	184	185	186	187	188	189	190	191	192	193	194	195	196	197
DELAWARE	X	X	X	X	X	X	X	X	X	5 407	8 946	49 245	55.0	41.9	3.1
Kent	218.1	1 778	71.3	0.0	5.3	0.2	1.7	105.5	860	1 733	4 558	13 462	47.2	49.9	2.9
New Castle	938.9	1 977	56.5	0.6	6.4	0.1	7.0	968.3	2 039	3 215	3 424	29 705	59.9	36.9	3.2
Sussex	269.8	2 013	65.3	1.2	3.7	0.1	1.7	237.3	1 770	459	964	6 078	44.9	52.2	2.9
DISTRICT OF COLUMBIA	X	X	X	X	X	X	X	X	X	183 932	23 335	41 950	85.2	9.0	5.9
District of Columbia	4 335.8	8 197	15.5	10.2	6.5	27.4	2.7	4 274.6	8 081	183 932	23 335	41 950	85.2	9.0	5.9
FLORIDA	X	X	X	X	X	X	X	X	X	119 348	111 309	823 269	48.8	48.8	2.3
Alachua	479.9	2 420	47.0	1.5	8.0	0.1	2.6	1 023.6	5 161	2 937	632	36 357	55.2	39.8	4.9
Baker	50.2	2 420	49.6	23.3	4.3	0.1	4.0	5.2	253	71	48	2 591	29.3	68.8	1.9
Bay	472.5	3 232	38.8	23.9	6.6	0.0	3.4	247.6	1 693	3 030	4 452	6 836	32.1	65.7	2.2
Bradford	43.3	1 756	65.9	2.0	5.3	0.2	4.7	17.5	712	37	56	2 447	35.5	62.4	2.1
Brevard	964.9	2 093	45.0	7.6	6.9	0.5	4.7	1 111.7	2 412	5 541	3 574	19 592	44.6	52.7	2.7
Broward	4 649.6	3 161	31.9	22.2	8.4	0.6	1.9	4 913.8	3 341	7 008	3 749	73 771	67.4	30.9	1.7
Calhoun	23.3	1 890	50.5	0.8	5.0	1.1	9.2	0.7	58	24	28	952	41.7	55.5	2.8
Charlotte	239.6	1 792	40.7	3.4	7.5	1.5	8.7	365.3	2 732	259	305	4 839	44.3	53.0	2.7
Citrus	199.0	1 770	43.6	1.7	6.9	0.3	6.4	407.5	3 624	194	257	3 632	44.6	52.0	3.3
Clay	234.9	1 737	54.9	1.0	6.7	0.5	6.0	164.6	1 217	324	313	4 575	25.5	72.8	1.7
Collier	530.4	2 710	46.9	2.9	7.6	0.6	6.7	559.5	2 859	579	451	8 491	32.5	65.6	1.9
Columbia	113.0	2 139	58.3	3.0	5.0	0.1	5.4	49.3	933	1 050	119	3 913	38.1	59.2	2.7
De Soto	51.6	1 963	51.9	1.8	11.0	0.0	7.4	8.7	333	55	56	2 883	42.5	54.5	3.0
Dixie	24.5	1 953	55.0	3.4	4.5	0.1	4.5	1.1	89	17	29	1 041	39.1	57.8	3.1
Duval	1 821.6	2 486	42.8	2.8	6.0	0.5	2.3	5 216.9	7 121	17 172	28 570	33 558	40.8	57.5	1.8
Escambia	636.3	2 251	49.3	1.5	6.0	0.8	5.4	1 111.8	3 934	7 004	14 190	16 195	35.1	62.6	2.3
Flagler	78.7	1 706	49.1	3.2	6.7	0.3	9.0	71.7	1 555	90	107	1 889	51.3	46.5	2.2
Franklin	22.7	2 236	45.3	1.7	12.2	0.2	6.7	3.9	387	23	23	656	44.1	52.8	3.1
Gadsden	88.0	1 937	56.8	2.7	9.9	0.1	7.0	24.6	541	117	99	5 668	66.1	32.4	1.5
Gilchrist	28.1	2 102	55.7	17.6	3.7	0.5	3.1	3.8	286	28	31	1 064	35.4	61.2	3.4
Glades	16.4	1 686	45.0	7.3	9.3	0.7	7.9	0.4	40	11	19	364	42.9	54.7	2.4
Gulf	32.7	2 348	41.1	1.8	5.9	0.5	11.0	13.1	940	15	30	1 148	39.0	57.8	3.2
Hamilton	63.3	5 059	25.7	8.8	2.9	0.0	3.4	20.5	1 640	33	29	1 397	43.4	54.1	2.4
Hardee	51.6	2 332	58.3	2.8	6.2	0.1	6.6	14.8	668	50	47	1 733	37.5	60.4	2.1
Hendry	105.5	3 336	50.7	13.1	6.6	0.4	4.3	43.2	1 366	110	66	2 388	39.8	58.3	1.9
Hernando	298.2	2 375	28.6	0.9	4.4	0.1	3.5	726.8	5 790	291	288	4 836	50.1	47.0	3.0
Highlands	152.4	1 983	55.7	2.8	6.7	0.6	6.3	80.2	1 043	292	170	3 576	40.3	57.5	2.2
Hillsborough	2 698.4	2 967	38.0	12.8	6.7	2.2	3.4	3 520.6	3 871	11 153	7 614	57 304	47.1	50.2	2.8
Holmes	33.5	1 821	59.5	3.1	2.3	0.1	7.2	2.5	137	61	42	1 280	29.4	67.8	2.8
Indian River	324.1	3 266	26.7	31.6	6.3	0.9	4.6	440.3	4 438	342	224	4 468	39.8	57.7	2.5
Jackson	124.3	2 720	50.8	24.1	3.0	3.9	4.5	21.5	471	495	109	5 547	42.1	56.1	1.8
Jefferson	24.0	1 813	53.9	2.5	8.3	0.0	7.7	1.8	135	29	29	936	53.9	43.9	2.2
Lafayette	13.0	2 071	65.7	2.4	2.9	0.3	6.2	0.4	65	15	14	637	31.5	66.7	1.8
Lake	327.7	1 670	47.4	2.6	7.6	0.5	4.9	264.3	1 347	502	492	8 139	41.3	56.4	2.3
Lee	1 485.2	3 837	25.8	15.4	3.9	0.4	7.9	2 032.5	5 251	1 821	942	23 544	39.9	57.6	2.5
Leon	579.3	2 693	41.7	0.2	7.8	0.3	4.8	1 208.2	5 615	1 693	628	52 108	59.6	37.9	2.6
Levy	57.1	1 769	57.5	3.0	7.4	0.9	5.8	17.1	530	76	97	1 742	42.4	53.9	3.7
Liberty	11.9	1 771	57.6	1.5	3.6	5.4	9.8	0.8	123	49	15	729	42.2	54.6	3.2
Madison	41.6	2 368	62.6	2.3	4.7	0.6	7.1	13.6	772	50	40	1 459	48.9	49.3	1.8
Manatee	589.2	2 485	48.8	2.4	6.6	0.5	3.9	655.1	2 763	1 143	569	9 924	44.6	52.6	2.8
Marion	416.0	1 753	51.9	0.8	8.5	0.4	9.1	334.0	1 408	649	549	13 640	43.4	53.6	3.1
Martin	284.9	2 454	33.5	2.9	9.1	0.8	5.0	424.6	3 657	281	265	4 751	42.9	54.8	2.3
Miami-Dade	7 843.1	3 679	34.1	9.4	7.5	0.8	1.9	9 180.4	4 306	18 213	6 970	118 867	52.6	46.3	1.1
Monroe	270.0	3 296	30.9	4.5	15.3	1.2	2.6	250.8	3 062	1 268	1 555	4 779	48.6	47.4	4.0
Nassau	106.0	1 960	50.7	3.9	5.8	0.1	5.5	52.5	971	602	125	2 428	29.2	69.0	1.8
Okaloosa	346.9	2 070	61.9	2.2	5.0	0.4	4.2	155.5	928	6 513	15 163	7 276	24.0	73.7	2.3
Okeechobee	66.1	1 996	55.4	1.0	7.4	0.4	6.1	25.9	783	75	70	1 745	46.6	51.3	2.1
Orange	2 576.3	3 286	34.0	2.5	6.3	0.9	6.2	7 335.1	9 356	7 316	5 218	48 715	50.1	48.0	1.9
Osceola	404.5	2 846	46.4	0.7	6.4	1.1	8.2	658.4	4 632	254	328	6 882	50.6	47.1	2.3
Palm Beach	3 052.6	2 997	32.4	4.1	8.0	0.7	3.8	3 439.3	3 377	5 731	2 409	47 726	62.3	35.3	2.4
Pasco	525.8	1 642	52.8	1.7	6.1	2.3	4.9	587.9	1 836	652	736	11 419	48.7	48.0	3.2
Pinellas	2 047.5	2 349	37.7	3.2	8.4	1.6	4.7	2 116.7	2 428	6 027	2 983	35 840	50.3	46.4	3.3
Polk	895.2	1 995	48.6	2.8	7.8	1.0	4.2	1 182.9	2 637	1 409	1 030	25 237	44.6	53.6	1.8
Putnam	154.0	2 187	54.1	2.4	5.9	0.1	5.3	294.1	4 176	158	159	4 477	46.2	51.3	2.6
St. Johns	231.9	2 057	42.9	4.1	6.8	0.6	4.5	292.5	2 595	404	270	5 421	32.1	65.1	2.8
St. Lucie	505.8	2 817	48.7	0.6	7.0	0.8	3.1	931.4	5 187	483	460	8 809	53.3	44.5	2.2
Santa Rosa	199.4	1 741	56.2	1.3	9.1	0.1	4.4	134.8	1 178	783	1 564	4 576	25.4	72.1	2.5

1. Based on the resident population estimated as of July 1 of the year shown.

Table B. States and Counties — Land Area and Population

STATE/ County code	MSA/ PMSA/ NECMA code[1]	County Type[2]	STATE County	Land area[3] (sq km) 1990	Total persons	Rank	Per square kilometer	White	Black	Am. Indian, Eskimo, Aleut	Asian and Pacific Islander	Percent Hispanic[4]	Under 5 years	5 to 17 years	18 to 24 years	25 to 34 years	35 to 44 years	45 to 54 years
				1	2	3	4	5	6	7	8	9	10	11	12	13	14	15
			FLORIDA—Cont'd															
12 115	7510	2	Sarasota	1 481	306 546	182	207.0	93.6	5.3	0.2	0.9	3.3	4.3	12.5	5.2	8.8	13.2	12.1
12 117	5960	0	Seminole	798	357 390	161	447.9	86.8	10.2	0.4	2.7	9.7	6.5	20.2	8.1	13.4	18.8	13.9
12 119	...	6	Sumter	1 413	42 754	1 029	30.3	77.1	21.9	0.6	0.3	4.4	5.4	17.6	9.2	11.9	13.4	12.7
12 121	...	7	Suwannee	1 781	32 972	1 285	18.5	81.5	17.5	0.5	0.4	2.3	5.7	22.0	7.2	9.5	14.4	13.8
12 123	...	7	Taylor	2 699	19 049	1 818	7.1	75.4	23.1	1.1	0.4	2.9	6.8	21.2	8.2	12.4	15.6	13.1
12 125	...	8	Union	622	12 720	2 230	20.5	70.9	27.8	0.7	0.6	6.2	5.7	19.2	8.1	20.0	20.6	12.4
12 127	2020	2	Volusia	2 864	425 601	137	148.6	87.5	10.9	0.3	1.2	5.7	5.5	15.7	8.2	11.0	14.4	12.1
12 129	...	8	Wakulla	1 571	19 179	1 810	12.2	83.1	15.6	0.9	0.4	0.9	6.4	23.0	6.9	10.7	17.7	14.3
12 131	...	6	Walton	2 739	38 124	1 134	13.9	88.4	9.0	1.9	0.8	1.4	5.6	18.9	7.2	10.9	15.2	14.7
12 133	...	6	Washington	1 502	20 614	1 734	13.7	77.8	19.4	2.0	0.8	1.8	5.7	19.9	8.5	11.9	14.6	13.6
13 000	...	X	**GEORGIA**	150 010	7 788 240	X	51.9	69.0	28.7	0.2	2.1	3.1	7.4	19.0	9.9	15.5	17.2	13.1
13 001	...	7	Appling	1 318	16 675	1 955	12.7	74.2	25.2	0.1	0.5	1.7	6.4	22.2	8.5	12.6	15.7	13.2
13 003	...	9	Atkinson	876	7 295	2 653	8.3	67.9	31.9	0.0	0.1	4.6	8.1	22.4	9.7	13.3	14.3	13.7
13 005	...	7	Bacon	738	10 365	2 392	14.0	80.5	18.8	0.2	0.1	1.8	7.3	22.5	9.2	12.2	15.2	12.7
13 007	...	8	Baker	889	3 617	2 940	4.1	42.2	57.7	0.0	0.1	0.7	6.8	22.2	9.1	12.3	15.3	12.1
13 009	...	4	Baldwin	669	42 181	1 037	63.1	51.8	46.9	0.1	1.2	1.5	5.7	17.1	12.0	16.0	16.6	13.0
13 011	...	8	Banks	605	13 166	2 199	21.8	94.5	4.7	0.2	0.5	1.1	6.5	19.5	9.0	13.3	16.9	14.3
13 013	0520	1	Barrow	420	41 891	1 043	99.7	83.9	14.4	0.3	1.5	1.7	8.4	19.7	9.3	16.1	15.6	13.1
13 015	0520	1	Bartow	1 191	74 607	664	62.6	87.8	11.4	0.3	0.5	1.9	8.0	19.1	9.5	14.9	16.4	13.7
13 017	...	7	Ben Hill	652	17 474	1 902	26.8	62.8	36.7	0.1	0.4	0.9	7.7	22.7	7.9	12.5	15.4	12.3
13 019	...	7	Berrien	1 172	16 529	1 968	14.1	84.7	14.5	0.2	0.5	2.6	7.4	20.0	8.8	12.8	15.0	14.1
13 021	4680	2	Bibb	648	155 441	332	239.9	51.5	47.4	0.2	0.9	1.1	7.1	18.9	9.7	14.1	16.0	12.4
13 023	...	6	Bleckley	563	11 314	2 324	20.1	72.0	26.6	0.1	1.4	0.8	6.7	19.2	11.1	12.1	14.4	13.5
13 025	...	9	Brantley	1 151	13 895	2 143	12.1	92.7	6.9	0.3	0.1	0.7	7.4	22.0	8.8	12.9	16.2	13.6
13 027	...	7	Brooks	1 279	16 122	1 997	12.6	52.4	47.1	0.2	0.3	2.5	8.1	21.8	9.1	12.2	13.9	12.1
13 029	7520	6	Bryan	1 144	24 394	1 558	21.3	80.6	18.3	0.2	0.9	1.8	8.2	23.8	8.2	14.6	18.6	12.4
13 031	...	6	Bulloch	1 768	50 777	896	28.7	67.6	31.4	0.2	0.8	1.4	6.4	17.2	22.4	12.1	13.6	11.2
13 033	...	6	Burke	2 151	23 217	1 606	10.8	41.6	58.1	0.1	0.3	0.6	8.8	24.1	9.0	13.6	14.9	11.6
13 035	...	6	Butts	483	18 380	1 849	38.1	59.0	40.2	0.3	0.5	1.3	6.7	19.0	9.6	14.7	16.6	13.4
13 037	...	8	Calhoun	726	4 936	2 844	6.8	35.2	64.5	0.2	0.0	0.2	6.8	22.2	8.2	12.8	14.7	11.3
13 039	...	6	Camden	1 632	47 032	947	28.8	73.2	23.8	0.6	2.4	4.0	10.3	20.2	12.9	21.0	16.1	9.5
13 043	...	7	Candler	640	8 953	2 512	14.0	63.5	36.1	0.1	0.3	3.4	7.3	20.2	9.0	11.3	15.4	13.2
13 045	0520	1	Carroll	1 293	84 765	594	65.6	79.9	19.3	0.2	0.6	1.7	7.2	19.4	12.3	13.9	15.7	13.5
13 047	1560	2	Catoosa	420	52 100	876	124.0	97.9	1.1	0.3	0.7	1.1	6.5	18.7	8.1	13.3	16.6	15.1
13 049	...	8	Charlton	2 022	9 462	2 476	4.7	66.5	32.8	0.5	0.3	0.9	8.7	22.0	9.1	13.9	13.6	13.8
13 051	7520	2	Chatham	1 141	225 662	246	197.8	54.5	43.4	0.2	1.9	2.3	7.5	18.5	9.8	14.5	15.6	12.2
13 053	1800	2	Chattahoochee	644	16 654	1 956	25.9	62.8	31.9	0.7	4.6	18.5	8.0	21.2	29.6	22.0	13.2	3.2
13 055	...	7	Chattooga	813	22 858	1 618	28.1	88.4	11.1	0.2	0.2	0.7	6.6	18.2	8.7	12.0	14.6	14.0
13 057	0520	1	Cherokee	1 098	141 686	375	129.0	96.6	2.4	0.3	0.6	2.6	9.1	18.8	8.0	18.4	19.2	13.0
13 059	0500	3	Clarke	313	90 638	555	289.6	64.6	31.1	0.2	4.1	3.1	6.1	14.7	25.2	15.0	13.8	9.9
13 061	...	9	Clay	506	3 524	2 949	7.0	33.9	65.7	0.2	0.1	0.9	6.6	21.6	7.9	11.5	14.5	10.8
13 063	0520	0	Clayton	369	213 252	255	579.2	67.5	27.3	0.3	4.9	3.9	8.1	19.6	10.2	17.7	18.0	13.1
13 065	...	7	Clinch	2 096	6 677	2 711	3.2	67.6	32.1	0.2	0.2	1.2	7.6	22.2	8.8	12.7	15.4	13.0
13 067	0520	0	Cobb	881	583 541	89	662.4	84.8	11.8	0.2	3.2	4.2	7.4	17.5	9.0	18.0	20.2	13.7
13 069	...	7	Coffee	1 552	34 958	1 226	22.5	69.0	30.2	0.1	0.7	3.2	8.0	21.9	9.8	13.9	15.3	13.0
13 071	...	7	Colquitt	1 430	40 724	1 065	28.5	70.8	28.8	0.2	0.2	5.2	7.4	21.5	9.3	12.4	15.0	13.1
13 073	0600	2	Columbia	751	93 312	541	124.3	82.0	13.4	0.2	4.3	2.9	7.8	21.4	7.3	14.7	20.0	13.6
13 075	...	7	Cook	593	15 197	2 054	25.6	64.0	35.3	0.2	0.5	2.1	7.6	20.9	9.5	12.1	14.3	13.6
13 077	0520	1	Coweta	1 148	89 401	562	77.9	71.9	27.4	0.2	0.5	1.5	8.2	20.1	8.7	14.4	17.1	14.5
13 079	...	8	Crawford	842	10 414	2 388	12.4	62.7	36.6	0.4	0.3	2.4	7.5	20.4	8.8	15.0	16.3	14.9
13 081	...	6	Crisp	709	20 637	1 730	29.1	53.2	46.4	0.2	0.2	0.5	7.4	22.2	8.1	12.0	15.3	12.5
13 083	1560	2	Dade	450	15 344	2 047	34.1	98.1	1.2	0.4	0.4	1.0	6.4	18.5	9.8	12.8	15.6	14.5
13 085	...	8	Dawson	547	15 945	2 009	29.1	98.4	0.2	1.2	0.2	1.2	7.6	19.4	8.0	15.7	16.4	14.6
13 087	...	6	Decatur	1 546	27 128	1 457	17.5	54.3	45.1	0.3	0.3	2.4	7.2	22.4	9.0	13.2	15.0	12.0
13 089	0520	0	De Kalb	695	596 853	85	858.8	48.4	46.5	0.2	4.9	4.9	6.8	17.0	10.6	17.9	18.9	13.2
13 091	...	7	Dodge	1 297	18 146	1 861	14.0	67.3	32.1	0.1	0.4	1.5	6.7	18.8	9.5	12.9	15.2	13.8
13 093	...	6	Dooly	1 018	10 433	2 386	10.2	44.4	54.7	0.0	0.8	1.4	7.2	22.9	8.3	12.0	14.7	12.9
13 095	0120	3	Dougherty	854	94 080	536	110.2	43.6	55.4	0.3	0.8	1.5	7.7	21.6	10.6	12.8	15.5	11.9
13 097	0520	0	Douglas	516	91 175	554	176.7	88.8	9.9	0.3	1.0	2.2	7.7	20.0	8.9	15.6	18.6	14.2
13 099	...	6	Early	1 324	12 127	2 271	9.2	49.9	49.6	0.3	0.2	0.6	7.3	22.5	8.1	11.2	14.7	12.3
13 101	...	9	Echols	1 047	2 534	3 020	2.4	83.5	14.7	1.6	0.2	3.1	7.4	23.1	9.1	14.0	15.1	13.6
13 103	7520	2	Effingham	1 242	38 370	1 124	30.9	81.7	17.6	0.2	0.5	1.4	7.7	22.8	8.6	14.8	16.8	13.6
13 105	...	6	Elbert	955	19 363	1 796	20.3	64.0	35.4	0.1	0.5	1.4	6.8	19.2	8.1	12.2	16.8	13.6
13 107	...	7	Emanuel	1 777	21 042	1 714	11.8	61.4	38.1	0.1	0.4	0.7	7.4	22.6	8.0	12.1	14.7	12.5
13 109	...	8	Evans	479	10 089	2 415	21.1	60.5	39.0	0.0	0.4	2.1	7.5	21.7	8.5	13.2	14.0	12.4

1. MSA = Metropolitan Statistical Area. PMSA = Primary MSA. NECMA = New England County Metropolitan Area. See Appendix A for explanation of these concepts. See Appendix B for list of metropolitan areas identified by type, with component counties. 2. County typology code from the Economic Research Service of USDA. See Appendix B for list of metropolitan areas identified by type, with component counties. 2. County typology code from the Economic Research Service of USDA. See Appendix A for definition. 3. Dry land or land partially or temporarily covered by water. 4. Hispanic persons may be of any race.

Table B. States and Counties — Population and Households

STATE County	55 to 64 years (16)	65 to 74 years (17)	75 years and over (18)	Percent female (19)	Total persons 1990 (20)	Total persons 1980 (21)	Percent change 1980–1990 (22)	Percent change 1990–1999 (23)	Births (24)	Deaths (25)	Net migration (26)	Number (27)	Percent change, 1980–1990 (28)	Persons per household (29)	Female family householder[1] (30)	One person (31)
FLORIDA—Cont'd																
Sarasota	11.7	15.4	16.7	52.9	277 776	202 251	37.3	10.4	24 168	41 142	46 815	125 493	41.4	2.18	7.3	27.7
Seminole	7.8	6.2	5.1	51.2	287 521	179 752	60.0	24.3	40 679	19 845	49 627	107 657	70.2	2.64	10.1	21.2
Sumter	11.3	10.8	7.6	46.0	31 577	24 272	30.1	35.4	3 930	4 144	11 302	12 119	41.2	2.46	10.9	23.4
Suwannee	10.2	8.4	8.9	51.6	26 780	22 287	20.2	23.1	3 394	3 509	6 378	10 034	29.7	2.61	11.3	23.2
Taylor	9.5	7.2	6.0	48.9	17 111	16 532	3.5	11.3	2 264	1 816	1 509	6 401	9.9	2.67	12.2	21.4
Union	6.8	4.2	3.0	35.2	10 252	10 166	0.8	24.1	1 155	1 038	2 359	2 658	25.4	2.91	12.4	18.7
Volusia	10.5	11.5	11.0	51.6	370 737	258 762	43.3	14.8	41 404	48 058	62 556	153 416	45.0	2.33	9.5	26.4
Wakulla	8.7	6.6	5.8	50.7	14 202	10 887	30.4	35.0	1 937	1 254	4 338	5 210	39.7	2.70	12.5	19.0
Walton	11.9	8.7	6.9	49.3	27 759	21 300	30.3	37.3	3 549	3 232	10 024	11 294	40.4	2.44	10.1	24.5
Washington	10.2	7.8	7.7	48.9	16 919	14 509	16.6	21.8	2 246	1 969	3 424	6 443	23.1	2.55	11.1	23.2
GEORGIA	8.1	5.4	4.4	51.3	6 478 149	5 462 982	18.6	20.2	1 053 424	525 580	771 257	2 366 615	26.4	2.66	13.9	22.7
Appling	8.9	6.6	5.9	51.6	15 744	15 565	1.2	5.9	2 343	1 459	113	5 834	14.0	2.67	11.8	24.6
Atkinson	8.6	5.6	4.2	50.8	6 213	6 141	1.2	17.4	1 323	658	433	2 210	10.0	2.81	12.1	23.4
Bacon	9.4	6.3	5.2	52.5	9 566	9 379	2.0	8.4	1 316	1 070	597	3 442	10.5	2.74	15.7	21.6
Baker	9.2	6.6	6.4	53.9	3 615	3 808	-5.1	0.1	383	312	-51	1 300	7.6	2.78	16.9	25.1
Baldwin	8.2	6.3	5.0	48.7	39 530	34 686	14.0	6.7	4 993	3 174	964	12 165	19.8	2.65	17.9	22.8
Banks	9.2	6.1	5.2	49.5	10 308	8 702	18.5	27.7	1 373	892	2 377	3 775	24.4	2.73	7.5	19.2
Barrow	8.7	4.7	4.5	50.8	29 721	21 354	39.2	40.9	5 948	2 609	8 835	10 676	46.0	2.76	10.8	18.9
Bartow	8.9	5.3	4.2	50.5	55 915	40 760	37.2	33.4	10 111	4 884	13 406	20 091	45.5	2.76	10.7	19.2
Ben Hill	8.9	6.8	6.0	54.1	16 245	16 000	1.5	7.6	2 469	1 814	631	5 972	5.3	2.67	16.9	25.2
Berrien	10.2	6.1	5.6	51.2	14 153	13 525	4.6	16.8	2 061	1 461	1 765	5 149	10.7	2.69	11.1	21.5
Bibb	9.0	7.0	5.8	53.6	150 137	150 256	0.0	3.5	23 612	15 404	-2 619	56 307	7.1	2.58	19.1	26.4
Bleckley	9.7	7.2	6.2	52.0	10 430	10 767	-3.1	8.5	1 472	1 094	522	3 816	7.4	2.62	14.0	23.2
Brantley	9.3	5.5	4.3	50.1	11 077	8 701	27.3	25.4	1 280	944	2 503	3 811	36.9	2.90	10.1	16.5
Brooks	9.2	6.6	6.9	52.8	15 398	15 255	0.9	4.7	2 051	1 803	516	5 392	8.1	2.79	18.1	22.7
Bryan	7.5	4.1	2.7	50.6	15 438	10 175	51.7	58.0	3 145	1 119	6 804	5 070	57.7	3.02	10.9	14.5
Bulloch	7.7	5.0	4.4	51.3	43 125	35 785	20.5	17.7	5 678	3 326	5 419	14 984	32.1	2.63	11.9	23.3
Burke	8.1	5.2	4.6	52.7	20 579	19 349	6.4	12.8	3 437	2 093	1 343	7 037	13.3	2.89	21.9	22.4
Butts	8.6	6.0	5.5	47.9	15 326	13 665	12.2	19.9	2 048	1 499	2 526	4 696	17.8	2.89	14.6	18.6
Calhoun	9.6	6.5	7.9	54.3	5 013	5 717	-12.3	-1.5	717	680	-98	1 794	-2.1	2.74	20.4	27.4
Camden	5.3	2.7	1.9	46.7	30 167	13 371	125.6	55.9	7 040	1 504	9 485	9 459	115.6	2.89	10.6	17.0
Candler	9.5	7.1	7.0	52.3	7 744	7 518	3.0	15.6	1 236	1 018	1 005	2 828	11.9	2.63	14.7	25.4
Carroll	8.1	5.2	4.7	51.4	71 422	56 346	26.8	18.7	11 242	5 834	8 103	25 370	33.5	2.71	11.7	21.1
Catoosa	10.5	6.3	4.9	51.5	42 464	36 991	14.8	22.7	5 675	3 435	7 486	15 745	24.5	2.67	10.3	19.3
Charlton	9.0	5.2	4.9	51.4	8 496	7 343	15.7	11.4	1 302	842	524	2 911	30.8	2.88	14.0	19.7
Chatham	8.8	7.4	5.7	52.3	216 774	202 226	7.2	4.1	34 709	19 473	-7 288	81 111	13.7	2.59	16.0	25.9
Chattahoochee	1.4	0.9	0.6	34.8	16 934	21 732	-22.1	-1.7	2 178	302	-4 944	2 884	-4.2	3.68	7.4	7.5
Chattooga	11.0	8.3	6.8	51.9	22 236	21 856	1.8	2.8	2 803	2 565	448	8 467	9.5	2.61	12.6	22.6
Cherokee	6.7	3.7	3.0	49.4	90 204	51 699	74.5	57.1	17 996	5 306	38 604	31 309	85.8	2.86	7.4	14.1
Clarke	6.2	4.8	4.3	52.3	87 594	74 498	17.6	3.5	10 863	5 178	-2 566	33 170	24.8	2.40	13.3	28.8
Clay	9.5	9.2	8.5	54.8	3 364	3 553	-5.3	4.8	511	407	74	1 210	1.4	2.72	21.3	26.3
Clayton	7.0	3.8	2.5	51.3	181 436	150 357	20.7	17.8	32 776	10 383	9 884	65 523	29.9	2.75	14.1	19.9
Clinch	9.2	6.0	5.1	51.6	6 160	6 660	-7.5	8.4	995	652	187	2 173	2.5	2.78	14.4	21.9
Cobb	7.0	4.3	2.9	50.8	447 745	297 718	50.4	30.3	74 529	23 800	85 503	171 288	60.7	2.60	9.1	22.5
Coffee	8.1	5.4	4.5	51.7	29 592	26 894	10.0	18.1	5 488	2 677	2 634	10 541	18.4	2.75	15.3	22.0
Colquitt	9.1	6.5	5.8	51.4	36 645	35 376	3.6	11.1	5 738	3 896	2 112	12 980	6.8	2.69	16.0	22.8
Columbia	6.9	5.3	3.1	50.4	66 031	40 118	64.6	41.3	10 456	3 736	20 572	21 841	70.2	2.97	9.4	13.5
Cook	9.6	6.5	6.0	52.0	13 456	13 490	-0.3	12.9	2 106	1 428	1 084	4 825	7.8	2.73	13.5	23.1
Coweta	8.8	4.4	3.7	51.5	53 853	39 268	37.1	66.0	11 110	4 675	29 047	18 930	42.3	2.82	13.1	17.9
Crawford	8.2	4.5	4.4	50.5	8 991	7 684	17.0	15.8	1 155	700	967	3 069	30.2	2.87	12.9	18.8
Crisp	9.3	6.8	6.5	54.0	20 011	19 489	2.7	3.1	3 262	2 247	-321	7 287	11.1	2.69	20.5	24.8
Dade	9.4	7.4	5.7	51.0	13 183	12 318	6.7	16.4	1 774	1 062	1 482	4 661	16.6	2.70	9.2	18.4
Dawson	9.3	5.7	3.2	49.2	9 429	4 774	97.5	69.1	1 692	711	5 493	3 360	102.0	2.79	8.0	16.0
Decatur	9.0	6.7	5.6	52.3	25 517	25 495	0.0	6.3	4 057	2 708	312	8 962	7.8	2.76	18.2	23.2
De Kalb	7.6	4.5	3.5	52.0	546 174	483 024	13.1	9.3	88 061	35 895	267	208 690	20.7	2.57	15.0	25.2
Dodge	9.6	7.1	6.4	50.9	17 607	16 955	3.8	3.1	2 248	1 921	267	6 387	8.9	2.60	14.9	25.2
Dooly	8.9	6.5	6.5	54.4	9 901	10 826	-8.5	5.4	1 522	1 180	225	3 557	0.8	2.74	19.5	25.7
Dougherty	8.1	6.6	5.0	53.4	96 321	100 710	-4.4	-2.3	15 415	7 840	-10 124	34 163	3.4	2.72	22.0	23.3
Douglas	7.4	4.2	3.3	50.3	71 120	54 573	30.3	28.2	11 642	4 708	13 261	24 277	43.6	2.90	9.9	15.0
Early	9.4	6.9	7.7	54.0	11 854	13 158	-9.9	2.3	1 814	1 374	-120	4 263	-0.9	2.73	17.4	25.0
Echols	10.3	4.1	3.4	48.6	2 334	2 297	1.6	8.6	227	197	164	816	11.0	2.84	9.6	18.8
Effingham	7.8	4.7	3.2	49.7	25 687	18 327	40.2	49.4	4 098	1 768	10 305	8 759	51.4	2.93	10.6	16.2
Elbert	9.6	7.8	7.8	52.5	18 949	18 758	1.0	2.2	2 574	2 057	-38	7 115	8.6	2.62	14.2	23.6
Emanuel	8.9	7.3	6.4	52.4	20 546	20 795	-1.2	2.4	3 014	2 270	-181	7 420	6.1	2.72	16.2	24.2
Evans	9.0	7.0	6.7	51.5	8 724	8 428	3.5	15.6	1 266	940	1 076	3 144	10.0	2.66	16.3	24.8

1. No spouse present.

Table B. States and Counties — **Vital Statistics, Health Resources, and Crime**

STATE County	Births, average 1996–1998 Total	Rate[1]	Deaths, average 1996–1998 Number Total	Number Infant[2]	Rate Total[1]	Rate Infant[3]	Physicians,[4] 1998 Number	Rate[5]	Hospitals,[4] 1998 Number	Beds Number	Beds Rate[5]	Medicare enrollees 1999	Serious crimes known to police, 1998[6] Total Number	Rate[7]
	32	33	34	35	36	37	38	39	40	41	42	43	44	45
FLORIDA—Cont'd														
Sarasota	2 554	8.5	4 701	14	15.7	5.6	1 149	379	4	1 272	419	103 102	14 197	4 624
Seminole	4 354	12.7	2 324	20	6.8	4.7	705	201	3	706	201	37 978	15 371	4 381
Sumter	402	10.2	483	3	12.3	8.3	13	32	0	0	0	8 367	1 466	3 733
Suwannee	416	13.1	414	6	13.0	14.4	14	43	1	16	49	6 812	1 570	4 663
Taylor	234	12.5	200	2	10.7	7.1	18	95	1	48	255	3 142	922	4 839
Union	136	11.0	167	1	13.5	9.8	11	89	0	0	0	1 159	168	1 335
Volusia	4 398	10.5	5 495	29	13.2	6.5	774	183	8	1 493	353	100 263	25 974	6 079
Wakulla	236	12.8	152	2	8.3	8.5	12	64	0	0	0	2 520	734	3 761
Walton	404	11.1	391	2	10.8	5.0	16	43	1	50	134	5 358	1 207	3 128
Washington	244	12.1	217	1	10.8	4.1	12	59	1	45	222	3 805	106	642
GEORGIA	118 211	15.8	59 511	1 036	7.9	8.8	14 636	192	157	24 637	322	897 503	417 479	5 463
Appling	265	16.1	165	2	10.0	8.8	11	67	1	43	261	2 371	NA	NA
Atkinson	163	22.9	69	1	9.7	4.1	1	14	0	0	0	1 028	38	526
Bacon	146	14.2	123	0	11.9	2.3	9	87	1	38	366	1 480	165	1 562
Baker	39	10.7	26	0	7.0	0.0	0	0	0	0	0	447	36	945
Baldwin	484	11.6	349	8	8.3	17.2	113	269	1	145	346	5 760	1 838	4 293
Banks	163	13.2	102	1	8.2	4.1	5	39	0	0	0	1 410	492	3 877
Barrow	716	18.4	304	3	7.8	4.7	17	42	1	60	149	4 998	1 543	3 879
Bartow	1 235	17.8	589	8	8.5	6.2	56	78	1	81	113	8 475	1 931	2 789
Ben Hill	276	15.9	199	4	11.4	13.3	12	69	1	60	343	2 959	1 101	6 221
Berrien	240	15.0	162	2	10.1	8.3	9	55	1	167	1 021	2 464	370	2 270
Bibb	2 461	15.8	1 621	37	10.4	15.2	527	338	4	964	618	25 953	15 082	9 491
Bleckley	148	13.4	115	2	10.4	13.5	7	63	1	45	402	1 897	402	3 533
Brantley	102	7.7	112	2	8.5	16.4	0	0	0	0	0	1 747	276	2 021
Brooks	196	12.4	191	1	12.1	6.8	7	44	1	25	156	2 318	145	879
Bryan	380	16.6	143	2	6.2	5.3	27	115	0	0	0	2 378	511	2 168
Bulloch	639	12.8	374	7	7.5	10.4	71	140	1	130	257	5 305	1 921	3 823
Burke	356	16.0	235	4	10.5	12.2	9	39	1	40	175	2 937	1 417	6 278
Butts	242	14.0	157	3	9.1	11.0	6	34	1	28	157	2 699	616	3 507
Calhoun	94	18.6	77	0	15.2	3.6	2	40	1	24	475	1 150	131	2 530
Camden	759	16.9	184	4	4.1	4.8	37	78	1	30	63	2 619	1 535	3 433
Candler	144	16.2	113	2	12.7	13.9	7	77	1	49	540	1 518	NA	NA
Carroll	1 241	15.3	686	8	8.4	6.2	103	124	3	260	313	11 201	3 876	4 664
Catoosa	627	12.7	379	3	7.7	5.3	44	87	1	272	538	4 898	1 835	3 626
Charlton	135	14.5	97	1	10.4	9.8	7	74	1	50	530	1 292	266	2 810
Chatham	3 498	15.5	2 130	32	9.4	9.1	638	283	3	1 159	514	33 435	16 384	7 104
Chattahoochee	225	13.6	29	3	1.7	11.8	19	114	0	0	0	315	98	588
Chattooga	320	14.0	272	2	11.9	7.3	7	31	1	166	728	4 344	189	845
Cherokee	2 071	16.3	690	12	5.4	5.6	73	54	1	84	62	9 286	2 017	1 558
Clarke	1 185	13.1	584	9	6.5	7.9	248	274	2	486	536	9 990	8 009	8 617
Clay	68	19.7	44	0	12.8	4.9	3	87	0	0	0	636	49	1 387
Clayton	3 745	18.2	1 205	34	5.9	9.1	241	115	1	317	152	17 193	14 469	6 941
Clinch	113	17.1	73	2	11.0	14.7	3	45	1	48	721	1 023	244	3 599
Cobb	8 611	15.6	2 877	63	5.2	7.3	984	174	4	1 016	179	48 046	21 679	3 854
Coffee	619	18.3	295	4	8.7	7.0	45	131	1	114	332	4 521	2 383	7 163
Colquitt	650	16.4	410	7	10.4	10.3	46	115	1	155	386	6 180	2 040	5 181
Columbia	1 139	12.9	451	9	5.1	7.9	386	424	0	0	0	7 905	2 174	2 398
Cook	236	16.1	165	2	11.3	8.5	9	60	1	155	1 033	2 321	NA	NA
Coweta	1 366	16.9	552	6	6.8	4.4	80	94	2	253	298	8 690	2 779	3 429
Crawford	132	12.5	73	2	6.9	15.2	1	9	0	0	0	860	92	816
Crisp	343	16.6	246	5	11.9	15.5	26	125	1	65	314	3 302	1 331	6 453
Dade	183	12.4	128	1	8.7	7.3	12	80	1	13	86	2 226	243	1 623
Dawson	220	15.7	81	1	5.8	6.1	7	47	0	0	0	1 697	408	2 998
Decatur	453	16.9	281	4	10.5	8.1	31	115	1	187	692	4 167	1 608	5 984
De Kalb	10 020	16.9	3 960	90	6.7	9.0	2 521	425	5	1 398	235	58 382	48 984	8 293
Dodge	230	12.7	214	2	11.9	7.2	23	127	1	95	525	2 816	679	3 826
Dooly	179	17.2	124	2	11.9	13.0	6	58	2	93	895	1 664	263	2 474
Dougherty	1 633	17.0	853	20	8.9	12.2	219	230	2	601	631	13 562	7 081	7 241
Douglas	1 297	14.9	545	10	6.3	7.7	80	89	2	315	351	8 074	4 068	4 599
Early	192	15.8	151	2	12.4	10.4	10	82	1	176	1 443	2 040	131	1 056
Echols	22	9.1	20	0	8.3	15.4	0	0	0	0	0	162	75	3 034
Effingham	474	13.6	215	2	6.2	4.2	8	22	1	97	266	3 142	644	1 799
Elbert	265	13.8	234	1	12.2	5.0	11	57	1	52	269	3 817	711	3 640
Emanuel	322	15.3	250	3	11.9	8.3	19	90	1	119	566	3 788	NA	NA
Evans	152	15.6	103	1	10.6	8.8	8	80	1	36	362	1 576	NA	NA

1. Per 1,000 estimated resident population, average 1996–1998.   2. Deaths of infants under 1 year old.   3. Deaths of infants under 1 year old per 1,000 live births.   4. Data subject to copyright.   5. Per 100,000 resident population as of July 1 of the year shown.   6. Data for serious crimes have not been adjusted for underreporting; this may affect comparability between geographic areas and over time.   7. Per 100,000 population estimated by the FBI.

Table B. States and Counties — Crime, Education, Money Income, and Poverty

STATE County	Violent (46)	Property (47)	Enrollment Total (48)	Percent private (49)	High school graduate or more (50)	Bachelor's degree or more (51)	Total current expenditures (mil dol) (52)	Current expenditures per student (dollars) (53)	Per capita (dollars) (54)	Median Households Dollars (55)	Percent change 1979–1989 (constant 1989 dollars) (56)	Percent with $100,000 or more (57)	Median household income (58)	All persons (59)	Persons under 18 (60)	Persons 5–17 in families (61)
FLORIDA—Cont'd																
Sarasota	453	4 171	44 114	15.2	81.3	21.9	199.3	6 237	18 441	29 919	18.5	5.2	37 660	8.7	15.3	14.2
Seminole	554	3 827	74 824	15.0	84.6	26.3	259.7	4 640	16 644	35 637	16.3	5.2	43 061	9.8	14.2	13.0
Sumter	817	2 916	6 319	4.5	64.3	7.8	30.2	5 099	9 920	19 584	4.0	1.1	25 601	21.4	32.6	32.0
Suwannee	734	3 929	6 695	6.2	63.8	8.2	28.4	4 859	9 768	19 775	7.6	1.6	26 070	18.2	25.6	24.5
Taylor	924	3 915	4 095	7.4	62.1	9.8	20.6	5 369	10 331	21 380	3.8	1.5	27 354	22.0	28.7	29.4
Union	485	850	2 459	4.9	67.7	7.9	11.7	5 054	9 648	22 831	10.6	0.5	29 968	23.2	23.2	23.2
Volusia	807	5 272	78 296	20.9	75.4	14.8	285.3	4 918	13 288	24 818	19.5	2.4	29 843	14.2	22.3	20.5
Wakulla	748	3 013	3 744	4.9	71.6	10.1	21.5	4 832	10 858	25 019	22.8	2.1	34 492	13.7	19.8	18.5
Walton	332	2 796	5 988	4.3	66.5	11.9	27.3	4 996	11 290	21 297	18.9	2.1	27 211	18.8	27.2	27.7
Washington	127	515	4 086	3.2	60.9	7.4	20.4	6 294	8 794	18 266	8.7	0.6	25 224	22.5	30.0	29.8
GEORGIA	573	4 890	1 643 859	12.8	70.9	19.3	7 230.0	5 369	13 631	29 021	15.2	3.8	36 372	14.7	22.8	21.8
Appling	NA	NA	4 088	3.6	57.2	8.2	19.6	5 606	9 901	22 271	24.5	1.0	28 620	19.9	29.2	28.7
Atkinson	152	374	1 544	1.6	51.5	6.4	7.4	4 733	7 902	17 685	12.3	0.7	24 493	22.8	32.7	33.3
Bacon	161	1 401	2 370	1.6	58.1	6.6	10.4	4 939	9 137	19 118	4.2	1.7	25 594	22.5	32.3	32.6
Baker	52	893	974	12.3	53.6	9.4	3.6	8 332	8 667	18 489	0.9	1.5	25 261	24.6	36.6	35.7
Baldwin	434	3 859	11 002	12.1	64.7	13.3	32.3	5 090	10 358	25 513	2.6	2.5	31 153	18.4	25.2	23.8
Banks	528	3 349	2 452	3.9	56.6	6.4	8.7	4 282	10 741	24 220	9.2	1.4	33 061	14.4	23.7	21.9
Barrow	493	3 386	6 544	8.4	58.8	9.2	36.3	5 002	11 156	27 538	16.9	1.6	37 258	12.4	18.6	19.1
Bartow	248	2 541	12 761	6.0	58.7	9.0	73.0	5 392	11 748	27 554	13.4	2.0	37 469	11.5	18.7	17.8
Ben Hill	768	5 453	4 047	2.9	56.8	7.6	18.4	4 997	9 300	19 106	7.7	0.9	26 126	21.2	30.7	30.1
Berrien	368	1 902	3 407	5.3	57.5	7.5	15.3	5 097	9 403	20 979	2.5	1.1	27 848	19.5	30.6	30.4
Bibb	717	8 774	39 211	23.4	68.2	17.0	133.7	5 384	13 017	25 813	7.3	3.4	32 553	20.9	33.0	30.3
Bleckley	439	3 094	2 812	3.9	60.3	10.3	11.3	4 918	10 775	22 690	-0.9	2.2	31 756	17.9	28.0	26.7
Brantley	205	1 816	2 809	2.4	64.1	5.8	13.3	4 480	9 089	22 087	4.6	0.9	29 430	18.8	30.1	27.8
Brooks	133	746	3 821	5.7	58.7	9.1	13.0	4 713	8 522	19 474	22.4	0.9	26 002	23.7	36.6	34.0
Bryan	161	2 007	4 330	8.1	68.5	11.8	22.6	4 394	11 083	28 623	25.3	2.5	39 198	12.2	18.2	17.5
Bulloch	173	3 650	16 551	14.2	67.6	19.9	45.7	5 421	9 635	20 640	-1.3	1.9	30 483	20.7	28.2	28.0
Burke	1 998	4 280	5 564	11.1	55.3	9.6	25.1	5 050	8 185	17 667	-0.3	0.8	23 787	25.3	34.4	33.9
Butts	233	3 274	3 340	4.9	58.4	7.2	15.0	4 926	10 321	24 420	4.5	1.9	32 153	16.3	24.0	23.3
Calhoun	579	1 951	1 427	4.8	52.2	10.1	7.5	8 213	8 244	15 640	-7.9	1.3	21 573	28.4	42.3	39.9
Camden	286	3 147	7 445	7.4	79.5	13.5	39.6	4 351	11 710	28 212	24.9	1.1	37 797	11.1	15.1	16.3
Candler	NA	NA	1 748	5.1	53.2	9.9	9.1	4 991	9 293	19 375	16.9	2.0	25 017	23.0	34.9	34.1
Carroll	351	4 313	19 132	3.9	60.5	12.0	79.3	5 253	11 239	25 607	9.3	1.6	34 061	14.7	23.4	22.0
Catoosa	215	3 411	9 674	8.8	63.8	8.1	40.3	4 604	11 059	25 581	-4.7	1.2	35 597	11.6	17.7	17.1
Charlton	254	2 556	2 031	5.9	56.2	6.4	9.5	4 705	8 894	22 328	1.3	0.5	27 357	20.6	29.5	30.7
Chatham	688	6 416	55 327	20.7	73.7	18.6	190.3	5 230	12 983	26 721	11.9	3.1	33 639	19.0	29.8	28.2
Chattahoochee	72	516	4 671	9.7	88.5	20.2	2.8	6 077	8 673	25 305	12.1	0.1	36 899	14.2	14.7	16.4
Chattooga	22	823	4 728	6.0	50.1	5.9	21.6	5 085	9 281	20 335	-6.0	0.7	27 909	14.9	22.9	22.4
Cherokee	119	1 439	20 407	13.8	75.2	18.4	112.5	5 068	14 849	39 052	31.5	2.9	54 423	5.9	9.0	9.3
Clarke	554	8 063	37 672	6.5	77.1	37.5	75.5	6 589	11 604	20 806	0.3	3.4	30 664	19.4	26.7	26.7
Clay	255	1 132	827	13.8	51.4	11.2	2.5	6 443	7 678	13 709	11.5	1.6	20 277	32.3	47.2	46.9
Clayton	449	6 492	45 352	10.6	77.2	14.7	216.8	5 205	13 577	33 472	0.1	1.9	38 366	13.5	22.8	20.0
Clinch	1 490	2 109	1 622	2.5	46.2	6.7	8.3	5 371	8 354	18 098	-1.8	1.2	25 828	23.1	32.3	32.9
Cobb	274	3 580	112 101	15.8	85.8	33.0	474.8	5 153	19 166	41 297	15.0	7.3	52 924	6.6	10.6	9.8
Coffee	550	6 613	7 665	4.2	58.0	11.1	37.7	5 078	10 170	20 651	13.6	2.9	28 484	20.6	29.4	29.1
Colquitt	698	4 483	8 833	4.3	57.0	10.0	41.5	4 982	9 878	20 331	2.2	1.6	26 039	23.5	34.9	33.5
Columbia	131	2 267	18 757	12.2	81.1	23.9	82.2	4 584	15 372	40 122	30.4	5.5	50 345	7.7	11.7	10.9
Cook	NA	NA	3 277	3.4	55.2	6.5	14.8	5 032	8 870	19 858	0.7	0.9	26 448	20.6	30.8	30.4
Coweta	280	3 149	12 712	9.0	67.4	13.3	70.8	4 927	13 708	31 925	24.3	3.5	44 493	10.4	16.2	16.1
Crawford	195	621	2 263	11.2	60.2	5.7	9.8	5 171	10 003	25 799	4.6	0.5	33 827	15.0	22.4	22.2
Crisp	591	5 862	4 770	6.8	56.2	10.0	24.9	5 458	9 248	17 797	-9.0	1.3	23 859	28.6	42.4	40.0
Dade	160	1 463	3 390	21.5	55.3	8.0	12.5	4 942	9 360	20 176	-8.2	1.2	30 079	15.0	22.2	21.8
Dawson	169	2 829	2 053	3.4	60.1	8.6	12.1	5 596	12 198	28 380	38.4	2.6	40 128	11.0	17.5	18.2
Decatur	737	5 247	6 826	2.7	59.8	11.7	28.2	4 709	9 246	20 854	5.0	1.4	26 377	24.9	36.7	34.4
De Kalb	734	7 559	141 313	20.5	83.9	32.7	552.2	5 920	17 115	35 721	7.3	5.6	42 767	13.2	22.9	20.1
Dodge	518	3 308	4 227	6.2	56.8	8.0	19.2	5 423	8 643	18 244	3.8	0.6	25 409	22.7	32.7	32.6
Dooly	320	2 154	2 538	19.2	54.7	9.5	10.8	5 640	8 413	16 326	-5.6	1.4	22 555	27.9	39.2	37.0
Dougherty	643	6 598	28 313	11.3	67.5	17.0	104.2	5 855	10 888	23 587	-7.9	2.5	29 658	24.8	36.4	34.3
Douglas	292	4 307	17 511	11.6	72.3	12.0	80.4	5 019	14 096	37 138	10.5	2.9	46 284	9.1	14.7	13.8
Early	306	750	2 877	5.7	54.1	9.4	13.8	4 973	8 280	16 421	-1.5	1.1	22 525	29.9	43.5	42.2
Echols	688	2 346	574	4.5	61.0	4.7	3.6	5 359	8 915	21 574	11.6	0.6	30 080	20.0	31.6	30.8
Effingham	84	1 715	6 663	5.7	66.0	7.6	34.9	4 610	10 865	29 443	12.9	0.6	41 511	11.5	16.4	16.5
Elbert	466	3 174	4 411	5.4	54.3	8.0	20.0	5 128	9 288	20 501	0.9	1.0	27 555	19.1	28.9	27.7
Emanuel	NA	NA	5 319	5.4	52.6	9.1	25.0	4 901	8 535	17 891	0.7	0.9	22 876	26.4	39.1	36.6
Evans	NA	NA	2 105	6.7	58.5	8.6	9.1	4 818	9 792	19 972	9.7	1.0	25 659	24.6	36.6	36.7

1. Data for serious crimes have not been adjusted for underreporting; this may affect comparability between geographic areas and over time.   2. Per 100,000 population estimated by the FBI.   3. All persons 3 years old and over enrolled in nursery school through college.   4. Persons 25 years old and over.   5. Elementary and secondary education expenditures, local government fiscal years ending between July 1, 1996 and June 30, 1997.   6. Based on population enumerated as of April 1, 1990.

Table B. States and Counties — **Personal Income**

196 FL(Sarasota)—GA(Evans)

STATE County	Total (mil dol)	Percent change, 1997–1998	Per capita Dollars	Per capita Rank	Wages and salaries[2] (mil dol)	Proprietor's income (mil dol)	Dividends, interest, and rent (mil dol)	Transfer payments Total (mil dol)	Government payments to individuals Total (mil dol)	Social Security (mil dol)	Medical payments (mil dol)	Income maintenance (mil dol)	Unemployment insurance (mil dol)
	62	63	64	65	66	67	68	69	70	71	72	73	74
FLORIDA—Cont'd													
Sarasota	11 263	4.8	37 131	48	4 101	589	4 843	1 768	1 714	934	657	48	8
Seminole	10 041	9.7	28 647	208	4 254	422	1 593	960	898	423	309	62	13
Sumter	687	5.9	16 549	2 703	244	42	155	196	189	82	66	18	1
Suwannee	617	6.3	18 972	2 067	227	102	103	153	147	60	62	16	1
Taylor	333	4.5	17 669	2 448	204	19	52	83	80	31	32	12	1
Union	153	3.9	12 194	3 082	118	10	22	29	27	10	11	4	0
Volusia	9 221	4.5	21 920	1 121	3 844	408	2 705	1 986	1 910	962	717	119	14
Wakulla	450	10.1	24 169	613	118	29	57	61	58	23	23	7	0
Walton	624	6.3	16 664	2 688	256	50	134	138	132	57	47	14	1
Washington	332	5.5	16 381	2 726	164	19	52	94	90	31	40	11	1
GEORGIA	197 319	7.2	25 839	X	135 375	16 381	32 030	22 734	21 187	8 530	8 331	2 707	282
Appling	285	1.5	17 250	2 544	208	30	44	63	59	21	25	10	1
Atkinson	138	7.6	19 326	1 943	52	35	15	27	26	8	11	5	1
Bacon	187	4.2	18 061	2 330	91	21	25	44	42	13	20	7	1
Baker	68	-0.6	18 790	2 124	17	10	10	14	13	5	5	3	0
Baldwin	857	5.2	20 456	1 574	530	58	164	192	183	53	103	14	2
Banks	247	6.8	19 269	1 966	64	48	34	34	32	16	10	3	0
Barrow	808	8.1	19 971	1 722	327	70	116	114	106	43	47	12	1
Bartow	1 545	8.5	21 479	1 255	836	103	212	189	175	87	62	15	2
Ben Hill	361	7.9	20 634	1 517	239	40	56	73	70	24	30	10	1
Berrien	285	2.7	17 490	2 488	133	23	47	62	58	21	26	8	0
Bibb	3 933	4.8	25 222	467	2 992	259	721	663	631	222	268	97	8
Bleckley	235	5.0	21 078	1 366	102	11	43	44	41	14	18	6	0
Brantley	226	8.3	16 698	2 679	48	17	25	49	46	17	19	5	1
Brooks	268	-0.4	16 839	2 647	79	26	51	65	61	23	23	12	1
Bryan	467	9.4	19 976	1 721	94	34	57	59	54	22	21	6	1
Bulloch	924	4.0	18 279	2 269	544	65	168	145	135	51	51	20	1
Burke	356	3.0	15 607	2 863	192	10	50	87	82	26	34	16	2
Butts	340	6.3	19 079	2 031	139	20	49	62	58	23	26	6	1
Calhoun	96	2.2	19 214	1 982	39	16	16	25	24	7	11	5	0
Camden	765	5.4	16 159	2 769	709	26	106	78	69	28	26	8	1
Candler	169	0.7	18 628	2 175	65	19	28	42	40	13	20	6	0
Carroll	1 676	7.6	20 221	1 645	928	133	260	260	243	104	98	26	2
Catoosa	960	6.3	18 922	2 084	368	74	114	139	129	69	39	10	2
Charlton	149	5.5	15 804	2 827	51	9	19	35	33	12	14	4	0
Chatham	5 944	4.9	26 384	355	4 246	432	1 211	856	810	325	307	108	9
Chattahoochee	374	8.6	22 790	891	572	2	29	13	11	2	3	3	0
Chattooga	429	4.3	18 866	2 101	213	28	54	92	87	39	35	9	1
Cherokee	3 485	16.1	25 941	405	894	227	445	236	209	107	74	13	2
Clarke	2 106	5.2	23 270	802	1 986	117	464	246	228	92	83	31	2
Clay	55	0.7	15 703	2 847	18	5	11	16	15	5	6	4	0
Clayton	4 571	8.8	21 872	1 135	4 508	159	546	497	455	174	182	58	7
Clinch	123	6.2	18 506	2 207	85	8	14	31	29	9	15	5	0
Cobb	19 460	10.3	34 377	70	12 046	1 685	2 953	1 101	986	485	363	62	14
Coffee	710	8.5	20 740	1 472	457	93	90	122	115	39	49	18	2
Colquitt	738	4.4	18 345	2 252	371	86	112	151	143	54	57	22	2
Columbia	2 043	8.5	22 488	981	536	88	383	186	168	76	56	14	2
Cook	258	4.8	17 246	2 546	127	24	37	59	56	20	24	8	1
Coweta	1 953	10.7	22 941	863	735	93	269	210	193	87	77	18	2
Crawford	180	1.6	16 880	2 637	31	6	28	28	26	9	10	4	0
Crisp	392	3.1	18 963	2 070	223	32	66	95	90	28	40	18	1
Dade	260	6.2	17 297	2 531	79	21	35	46	43	19	16	5	1
Dawson	338	12.0	22 709	918	86	36	45	35	32	14	13	3	0
Decatur	514	3.4	19 020	2 049	316	48	83	114	109	36	48	19	1
De Kalb	18 824	4.2	31 751	119	13 335	1 988	3 283	1 570	1 449	598	560	166	24
Dodge	318	4.8	17 543	2 476	142	17	56	74	70	24	31	12	1
Dooly	188	2.1	18 090	2 324	97	20	32	46	44	15	19	8	1
Dougherty	2 102	2.2	22 122	1 061	1 814	146	364	382	363	118	140	72	7
Douglas	2 085	8.2	23 319	790	770	101	237	205	187	83	76	15	2
Early	228	1.4	18 762	2 133	150	27	42	54	51	17	21	11	1
Echols	43	4.8	18 101	2 321	8	5	5	7	6	2	2	1	0
Effingham	758	11.1	20 743	1 471	196	34	74	86	78	35	27	9	1
Elbert	380	5.2	19 641	1 843	180	37	75	86	82	34	33	11	1
Emanuel	368	2.7	17 498	2 483	179	23	66	99	95	32	42	16	1
Evans	190	5.6	19 161	1 995	107	15	31	39	37	14	15	6	0

1. Based on the resident population estimated as of July 1 of the year shown.   2. Includes other labor income.

Table B. States and Counties — Earnings, Social Security, and Housing

STATE County	Earnings, 1998 Total (mil dol)	Farm	Goods-related[1] Total	Manu-facturing	Service-related and other[2] Total	Retail trade	Finance, insur-ance, and real estate	Services	Govern-ment	Social Security beneficiaries, December 1998 Number	Rate[3]	Supple-mental Security Income recipients, December 1998	Housing units, 1990 Total	Percent change, 1980–1990
	75	76	77	78	79	80	81	82	83	84	85	86	87	88
FLORIDA—Cont'd														
Sarasota	4 691	0.3	14.8	6.7	74.4	14.5	11.9	39.6	10.5	102 046	336	3 183	157 055	38.6
Seminole	4 676	0.2	D	8.5	D	14.7	8.0	30.2	11.7	49 923	142	4 356	117 845	72.9
Sumter	286	3.9	16.0	8.7	40.4	10.2	2.3	12.9	39.6	14 448	357	1 284	15 298	38.0
Suwannee	329	14.7	D	D	D	12.1	3.4	17.4	17.4	7 902	242	1 109	11 699	33.5
Taylor	223	0.9	D	35.9	D	8.3	2.0	D	20.7	3 964	210	760	7 908	13.3
Union	128	2.2	D	7.7	D	3.4	0.6	10.6	63.8	1 433	115	307	2 975	27.7
Volusia	4 253	1.4	D	9.1	D	14.5	6.4	35.5	17.5	113 077	267	8 097	180 972	45.4
Wakulla	148	1.6	37.5	26.1	33.5	7.8	3.9	15.2	27.3	3 092	166	500	6 587	29.9
Walton	306	2.0	D	8.6	D	14.4	5.5	26.8	24.0	7 581	203	899	18 728	71.5
Washington	182	1.0	D	12.5	D	9.3	1.8	12.7	42.3	4 355	215	840	7 703	28.8
GEORGIA	151 756	1.2	21.5	15.6	61.1	8.8	7.8	26.0	16.2	1 056 394	138	199 408	2 638 418	30.1
Appling	239	6.6	22.5	17.2	56.7	6.6	2.5	7.6	14.2	2 960	179	793	6 629	14.1
Atkinson	87	35.6	D	34.9	D	4.3	2.0	4.6	11.5	1 207	169	470	2 449	5.7
Bacon	112	10.5	37.0	34.4	37.9	8.9	3.3	12.1	14.7	1 930	186	571	3 859	13.0
Baker	27	39.0	7.2	2.1	D	3.9	D	20.2	20.7	696	189	223	1 499	17.7
Baldwin	588	0.2	D	20.0	D	9.9	3.1	14.3	44.3	6 589	157	1 463	14 200	16.1
Banks	112	35.5	D	22.5	D	9.0	D	7.0	12.3	2 160	169	266	4 193	27.8
Barrow	398	5.3	D	31.6	D	12.0	3.2	14.5	15.2	5 473	136	1 231	11 812	51.9
Bartow	939	1.8	44.0	35.6	40.6	9.8	3.6	14.2	13.6	10 581	147	1 408	21 757	46.7
Ben Hill	280	5.7	49.6	45.7	29.4	7.5	3.0	10.3	15.3	3 298	189	855	6 875	10.9
Berrien	156	6.5	D	34.2	D	15.2	5.8	12.5	13.8	2 922	179	696	5 858	14.4
Bibb	3 251	0.1	D	20.0	D	9.8	9.3	31.7	12.3	28 815	185	7 054	61 462	10.6
Bleckley	114	2.9	D	D	D	7.9	2.5	11.2	24.1	2 115	189	452	4 268	8.8
Brantley	65	9.7	22.5	13.4	39.9	7.3	1.5	10.0	27.8	2 349	173	489	4 404	39.7
Brooks	105	20.2	25.1	21.4	34.6	6.1	3.1	12.5	20.0	3 214	201	810	5 972	11.4
Bryan	128	-0.3	25.2	13.2	49.4	14.9	7.4	17.7	25.7	2 720	116	535	5 549	58.0
Bulloch	609	1.8	D	16.5	D	13.7	4.0	18.8	28.7	6 683	132	1 510	16 541	30.4
Burke	203	-0.8	D	11.8	D	6.8	2.2	12.4	20.3	3 728	163	1 155	8 329	22.3
Butts	159	1.4	D	19.8	D	9.4	4.5	15.8	24.4	2 941	165	523	5 536	11.3
Calhoun	54	24.8	D	D	D	5.4	2.5	7.6	35.7	1 129	223	459	2 061	5.0
Camden	736	0.1	17.3	14.4	21.0	5.8	1.4	11.5	61.6	3 483	73	566	10 885	102.3
Candler	84	4.2	18.7	14.0	55.7	12.6	7.4	19.9	21.3	1 817	200	570	3 203	12.7
Carroll	1 061	3.1	D	32.3	D	9.4	4.3	19.5	15.4	12 966	156	2 331	27 736	36.5
Catoosa	442	2.6	D	26.2	D	13.6	4.2	24.7	12.6	8 061	159	679	16 762	25.1
Charlton	60	2.3	29.2	20.4	39.0	12.0	2.2	15.6	29.5	1 577	167	375	3 222	28.6
Chatham	4 678	0.0	D	18.4	D	9.7	4.7	30.1	18.3	38 120	169	6 853	91 178	17.7
Chattahoochee	574	0.0	D	D	D	1.8	D	1.9	95.1	370	22	128	3 108	-2.9
Chattooga	241	0.6	D	50.6	D	9.9	2.1	10.8	18.1	4 928	216	811	9 142	10.3
Cherokee	1 121	1.8	D	10.9	D	12.0	8.2	24.0	14.0	12 400	92	891	33 840	89.1
Clarke	2 103	0.2	D	16.3	D	10.2	4.2	23.8	33.3	11 015	122	2 363	35 971	30.3
Clay	22	14.2	D	D	D	8.2	1.5	9.6	42.8	805	233	244	1 586	18.4
Clayton	4 667	0.0	D	6.0	D	9.8	2.6	17.0	10.4	21 089	101	3 541	71 926	35.7
Clinch	93	1.7	45.2	44.2	36.1	15.0	2.1	9.9	17.0	1 273	191	472	2 423	3.0
Cobb	13 731	0.0	17.8	10.4	72.6	11.1	9.2	29.6	9.6	52 461	93	5 226	189 872	67.6
Coffee	550	9.7	34.5	29.8	43.9	17.5	2.2	15.3	11.9	5 468	159	1 555	11 650	19.0
Colquitt	457	10.2	27.1	21.1	42.2	9.9	4.1	15.1	20.5	7 348	183	1 886	14 350	10.8
Columbia	624	0.6	D	22.4	D	11.3	5.9	24.7	15.3	9 169	101	832	23 745	68.4
Cook	150	9.3	37.8	32.7	38.6	10.0	3.1	14.7	14.3	2 837	189	712	5 340	9.9
Coweta	828	0.3	D	27.0	D	15.3	3.7	22.2	14.0	10 354	122	1 500	20 413	44.6
Crawford	37	9.3	D	9.0	D	5.3	D	14.2	31.3	1 338	125	316	3 279	27.4
Crisp	255	5.2	25.1	18.8	51.8	15.1	4.4	18.6	17.9	3 897	188	1 264	8 318	12.7
Dade	99	3.3	37.5	31.3	D	14.8	3.9	18.7	16.3	2 480	165	386	4 998	16.4
Dawson	122	9.4	29.6	11.2	46.7	17.0	5.3	18.0	14.4	1 780	120	300	4 321	80.0
Decatur	364	7.0	D	27.9	D	9.6	3.1	12.0	20.0	5 002	185	1 415	10 120	11.6
De Kalb	15 323	0.0	14.6	9.3	73.9	7.9	8.7	33.9	11.5	67 944	114	11 744	231 520	27.3
Dodge	159	2.8	22.2	16.7	39.8	10.7	3.4	16.9	35.2	3 559	197	983	7 094	10.9
Dooly	117	11.0	30.5	28.8	34.8	6.0	3.9	9.3	23.7	2 203	212	622	4 003	6.1
Dougherty	1 961	0.5	26.4	20.4	50.9	8.4	3.7	25.8	22.2	15 481	162	4 926	37 373	7.6
Douglas	871	0.0	D	9.2	D	17.4	4.0	25.0	15.5	9 792	109	1 056	26 495	49.2
Early	177	13.6	40.0	37.9	33.4	4.8	5.0	10.3	12.9	2 465	202	758	4 714	0.7
Echols	13	27.6	D	9.9	D	2.5	D	6.5	30.0	264	110	71	942	13.9
Effingham	230	0.3	47.4	35.5	31.2	10.6	2.7	9.7	21.1	4 315	118	566	9 492	50.1
Elbert	217	2.3	40.1	33.7	36.7	8.7	3.9	14.5	20.9	4 426	229	1 031	7 891	11.9
Emanuel	202	1.1	29.0	25.3	40.1	10.3	2.8	15.4	29.8	4 650	221	1 570	8 344	6.9
Evans	122	4.0	D	D	D	9.2	2.7	15.2	15.9	1 983	199	516	3 512	10.1

1. Covers mining, construction, and manufacturing. 2. Covers private sector earnings in agricultural services, forestry, and fisheries; transportation and public utilities; wholesale trade; retail trade; finance, insurance, and real estate; and services. 3. Per 1,000 resident population estimated as of July 1 of the year shown.

Table B. States and Counties — **Housing, Labor Force, and Employment**

STATE County	Occupied units - Owner-occupied - Total	Percent	Median value[1]	Owner cost as a percent of income - With a mortgage	Without a mortgage	Renter-occupied - Median rent[2]	Rent as percent of income	Sub-standard units[3] (percent)	Civilian labor force, 1999 - Total	Percent change, 1998–1999	Unemployment - Total	Rate[4]	Civilian employment, 1990[5] - Total	Percent - Professional, managerial, and technical	Precision production, craft, and repair
	89	90	91	92	93	94	95	96	97	98	99	100	101	102	103
FLORIDA—Cont'd															
Sarasota	125 493	76.2	87 200	23.2	11.7	543	28.0	1.6	152 524	5.0	3 247	2.1	114 217	29.8	11.8
Seminole	107 657	66.9	91 500	22.0	11.9	548	26.1	2.7	217 115	4.2	5 794	2.7	151 377	35.3	9.8
Sumter	12 119	80.1	49 900	19.6	12.9	315	25.8	5.1	14 360	4.2	392	2.7	11 081	19.1	13.2
Suwannee	10 034	79.2	45 100	19.6	12.8	277	27.3	5.6	13 462	3.4	520	3.9	10 429	18.0	14.6
Taylor	6 401	78.5	43 600	16.5	12.6	281	25.1	7.5	7 326	0.7	525	7.2	6 850	21.6	16.3
Union	2 658	69.9	43 800	17.5	13.0	219	19.0	10.0	3 481	-4.1	90	2.6	3 332	18.5	8.4
Volusia	153 416	71.9	69 400	23.2	12.2	464	29.2	2.4	174 365	1.0	5 382	3.1	155 529	27.4	12.7
Wakulla	5 210	83.4	51 800	19.7	13.0	331	25.7	8.2	10 953	3.0	331	3.0	7 001	25.6	16.6
Walton	11 294	78.4	49 700	22.8	12.4	324	23.1	3.9	15 315	2.2	579	3.8	11 498	22.5	14.1
Washington	6 443	80.5	40 100	22.0	12.0	269	27.3	6.0	9 617	10.7	393	4.1	6 417	21.5	12.7
GEORGIA	2 366 615	64.9	71 300	20.9	12.8	433	25.8	4.7	4 088 008	1.7	162 571	4.0	3 090 276	28.2	11.9
Appling	5 834	76.6	39 200	16.2	13.4	264	23.6	7.8	8 323	-6.3	814	9.8	6 553	18.1	17.3
Atkinson	2 210	72.9	30 300	18.6	14.9	218	22.8	10.0	3 339	2.8	206	6.2	2 523	15.7	14.5
Bacon	3 442	71.8	40 500	19.8	12.3	219	27.2	5.6	4 247	-4.6	308	7.3	4 138	16.3	18.8
Baker	1 300	73.0	36 600	23.1	12.4	213	24.8	11.0	1 579	-0.8	113	7.2	1 498	17.3	13.0
Baldwin	12 165	68.3	54 900	20.1	12.8	334	24.1	4.2	17 663	-3.5	1 057	6.0	15 901	28.4	12.1
Banks	3 775	81.2	51 100	20.8	13.0	297	23.7	4.7	6 209	1.9	237	3.8	5 060	14.0	18.4
Barrow	10 676	72.3	64 000	22.5	12.1	392	24.5	3.8	20 962	3.3	629	3.0	13 875	18.4	17.5
Bartow	20 091	71.7	63 100	20.6	12.5	410	24.7	4.7	39 597	4.5	1 576	4.0	27 377	18.2	16.2
Ben Hill	5 972	66.3	42 300	21.4	13.4	265	27.1	5.1	9 259	-1.7	600	6.5	6 678	17.1	12.9
Berrien	5 149	73.9	40 400	19.3	13.2	259	23.2	5.6	7 043	-0.7	458	6.5	6 438	16.6	15.3
Bibb	56 307	57.6	57 900	18.4	12.7	352	26.7	4.3	73 844	-1.1	3 710	5.0	65 754	28.3	11.2
Bleckley	3 816	75.1	41 000	17.7	13.3	225	21.8	4.7	5 657	-1.2	252	4.5	4 644	22.0	15.3
Brantley	3 811	84.6	36 400	19.9	12.1	285	27.5	5.9	5 808	-3.7	407	7.0	4 504	16.6	22.9
Brooks	5 392	72.0	42 200	23.4	14.1	255	25.0	8.8	7 585	-7.7	342	4.5	6 185	18.1	10.6
Bryan	5 070	79.8	70 200	22.9	12.5	328	24.0	5.7	10 876	3.0	366	3.4	6 582	25.2	16.2
Bulloch	14 984	60.1	59 900	18.3	12.7	330	34.8	6.1	26 859	2.8	681	2.5	18 839	26.3	11.7
Burke	7 037	70.8	43 500	19.5	13.6	197	29.2	10.8	8 514	0.9	837	9.8	7 905	20.0	13.3
Butts	4 696	71.8	55 500	20.2	12.5	348	24.6	8.5	8 354	-6.3	361	4.3	6 122	15.0	13.9
Calhoun	1 794	69.1	29 400	16.6	14.2	169	22.2	15.2	2 271	-0.7	214	9.4	1 932	17.2	9.0
Camden	9 459	63.0	66 700	22.8	12.8	416	24.5	6.2	16 833	-3.9	625	3.7	10 805	25.0	14.1
Candler	2 828	71.7	44 700	21.1	15.4	253	20.6	7.3	3 995	-2.5	225	5.6	3 266	20.6	11.5
Carroll	25 370	69.4	60 300	20.7	12.3	351	26.0	4.5	44 914	2.9	2 010	4.5	34 189	21.0	15.6
Catoosa	15 745	75.9	56 500	18.5	12.3	358	24.8	3.6	25 953	3.6	855	3.3	20 146	20.4	13.3
Charlton	2 911	78.8	41 200	20.5	13.1	290	29.3	8.2	3 776	-6.8	176	4.7	3 396	13.3	15.0
Chatham	81 111	58.8	63 300	21.2	13.2	406	27.2	4.2	107 346	0.7	4 710	4.4	93 969	29.0	11.7
Chattahoochee	2 884	20.2	42 600	22.1	11.2	414	20.2	2.8	2 431	3.4	167	6.9	2 047	28.9	9.4
Chattooga	8 467	74.7	34 700	16.7	12.5	278	24.0	4.9	11 875	-1.8	481	4.1	9 868	14.7	16.3
Cherokee	31 309	82.5	86 600	22.3	12.7	534	26.2	2.8	79 287	6.8	1 639	2.1	48 237	27.9	15.7
Clarke	33 170	44.2	73 200	20.0	13.2	389	31.1	3.6	46 998	-0.6	1 307	2.8	40 991	37.0	7.5
Clay	1 210	66.4	31 300	19.1	13.1	210	23.2	11.6	1 498	-9.7	100	6.7	1 230	20.8	7.2
Clayton	65 523	58.8	70 100	20.8	12.2	532	26.0	3.5	124 459	3.0	4 352	3.5	96 580	23.3	13.8
Clinch	2 173	68.2	33 600	17.5	13.1	190	22.6	7.7	3 562	-16.7	127	3.6	2 404	15.3	11.8
Cobb	171 288	64.6	97 700	21.0	12.0	575	24.5	1.9	354 677	3.6	9 145	2.6	253 096	38.0	9.0
Coffee	10 541	72.6	45 600	18.5	14.9	273	25.8	6.8	20 560	9.2	1 009	4.9	13 229	16.2	13.9
Colquitt	12 980	68.5	40 700	19.1	13.4	266	27.5	5.5	19 355	-3.2	1 211	6.3	15 776	19.8	12.2
Columbia	21 804	79.3	83 700	21.0	11.9	442	23.6	3.2	44 240	4.3	1 405	3.2	32 628	36.9	13.2
Cook	4 825	75.0	39 500	16.7	13.4	276	24.6	5.9	7 735	-2.0	385	5.0	5 987	15.7	12.2
Coweta	18 930	72.8	68 700	21.0	12.4	415	26.5	5.3	44 971	5.8	1 280	2.8	25 632	23.4	16.2
Crawford	3 069	81.3	49 500	20.3	12.5	252	21.1	10.0	5 484	3.4	246	4.5	4 113	14.8	18.6
Crisp	7 287	61.1	47 100	19.1	13.6	268	29.6	5.1	9 685	-1.5	578	6.0	8 068	21.4	10.8
Dade	4 661	79.1	45 100	19.1	12.7	301	26.4	4.0	7 291	4.4	278	3.8	5 851	16.2	15.5
Dawson	3 360	85.2	80 900	26.6	12.1	390	23.2	3.9	14 752	7.8	321	2.2	4 719	18.2	19.1
Decatur	8 962	72.0	42 700	20.1	14.6	259	25.9	7.4	11 803	-7.4	665	5.6	10 438	21.2	12.3
De Kalb	208 690	57.8	91 600	21.3	12.3	552	26.6	4.1	366 054	1.7	14 076	3.8	299 852	36.9	7.5
Dodge	6 387	74.3	33 700	18.5	13.9	224	25.0	6.7	9 651	-2.6	501	5.2	7 070	19.9	12.8
Dooly	3 557	68.7	39 200	18.3	13.5	215	30.6	9.6	4 553	-1.6	307	6.7	3 713	18.1	10.8
Dougherty	34 163	52.3	57 500	18.5	13.1	334	26.5	6.9	45 624	-1.6	3 754	8.2	38 922	27.4	11.4
Douglas	24 277	77.8	73 400	20.5	12.3	549	25.7	2.8	52 552	4.4	1 503	2.9	37 431	25.7	15.0
Early	4 263	69.2	40 100	18.9	13.5	232	24.3	10.9	4 648	-5.9	415	8.9	4 751	16.1	12.3
Echols	816	81.4	40 000	17.0	13.6	244	19.8	6.8	1 195	-2.7	56	4.7	983	12.8	13.5
Effingham	8 759	78.8	61 300	19.3	12.1	365	21.8	8.0	17 740	4.8	601	3.4	11 495	19.0	19.3
Elbert	7 115	73.2	44 600	20.4	13.8	253	25.6	6.5	8 715	-1.9	648	7.3	8 182	19.3	16.9
Emanuel	7 420	69.9	35 200	18.1	13.2	230	25.6	7.7	8 653	-1.4	912	10.5	8 263	18.9	13.1
Evans	3 144	67.6	44 100	21.4	14.1	268	25.9	6.5	4 840	-2.2	191	3.9	3 663	17.6	14.4

1. Specified owner-occupied units. 2. Specified renter-occupied units. 3. Overcrowded or lacking complete plumbing facilities. 4. Percent of civilian labor force. 5. Persons 16 years and older.

Table B. States and Counties — Nonfarm Employment and Agriculture

| | Private nonfarm establishments, employment and payroll, 1998 | | | | | | | | Agriculture, 1997 | | | |
| | Employment | | | | | | Annual payroll | | Farms | | | Farm operators |
STATE County	Number of establishments	Total	Health Care and Social Assistance	Manufacturing	Retail trade	Finance and Insurance	Professional Scientific and Technical Services	Total (mil dol)	Average per employee (dollars)	Number	Percent with— Less than 50 acres	500 acres and over	Whose principal occupation is farming (percent)
	104	105	106	107	108	109	110	111	112	113	114	115	116
FLORIDA—Cont'd													
Sarasota	10 839	132 105	20 049	8 011	20 892	5 032	7 133	3 239	24 516	315	70.5	9.2	37.1
Seminole	10 272	122 055	10 694	9 295	22 368	6 594	7 415	3 225	26 423	344	83.1	2.6	44.2
Sumter	514	5 051	448	851	1 189	99	82	92	18 274	718	49.7	7.9	41.5
Suwannee	614	7 098	1 236	1 649	1 428	226	137	129	18 238	840	37.5	8.1	50.0
Taylor	404	4 836	566	1 812	909	134	107	122	25 258	126	38.1	12.7	38.1
Union	117	1 480	484	D	211	D	23	36	24 050	213	45.1	8.5	36.6
Volusia	10 713	125 059	20 735	10 149	22 937	4 128	4 916	2 561	20 477	910	73.0	4.0	49.7
Wakulla	318	2 362	244	475	449	148	96	47	19 915	88	58.0	8.0	38.6
Walton	884	9 208	648	1 002	1 839	156	190	164	17 796	476	30.7	5.7	39.5
Washington	335	3 886	837	730	688	82	74	72	18 561	322	28.0	6.8	40.4
GEORGIA	194 213	3 198 950	331 889	535 051	431 806	154 798	166 535	94 687	29 599	40 334	31.4	12.6	43.4
Appling	393	5 724	441	1 159	D	114	55	193	33 661	494	32.8	10.5	40.3
Atkinson	87	1 627	17	1 181	148	57	3	33	20 140	196	20.9	20.4	56.6
Bacon	198	2 870	296	1 180	398	117	D	61	21 158	324	29.3	8.3	46.6
Baker	21	232	D	0	D	D	D	5	21 940	131	21.4	40.5	64.9
Baldwin	824	14 982	5 240	3 176	2 337	373	189	329	21 980	137	24.8	14.6	37.2
Banks	210	2 782	29	878	590	D	28	50	17 950	446	40.8	2.5	48.4
Barrow	770	8 958	857	2 624	1 805	256	202	207	23 148	361	46.0	3.0	46.5
Bartow	1 514	24 318	1 488	8 930	3 256	458	385	629	25 847	400	35.2	7.8	38.2
Ben Hill	380	6 927	531	3 837	929	198	80	156	22 478	159	28.9	16.4	57.9
Berrien	280	4 003	451	1 838	460	233	33	89	22 269	399	19.3	19.0	56.9
Bibb	4 635	84 294	14 243	12 967	12 452	6 996	3 127	2 288	27 141	149	34.9	4.7	30.2
Bleckley	208	3 070	424	D	363	83	42	62	20 245	221	23.5	18.1	43.0
Brantley	170	1 166	107	143	232	D	D	23	20 065	207	31.4	4.3	37.7
Brooks	203	2 378	515	903	311	103	D	45	19 026	430	20.0	22.6	47.7
Bryan	361	2 717	297	298	526	149	90	51	18 913	61	44.3	16.4	54.1
Bulloch	1 188	15 335	1 866	2 974	3 164	546	651	305	19 886	524	26.1	21.2	51.5
Burke	320	4 486	560	977	648	123	D	130	29 066	346	17.9	30.9	41.3
Butts	321	3 915	340	1 118	598	110	53	84	21 525	148	31.1	6.8	37.2
Calhoun	101	941	154	257	150	36	D	13	13 953	122	13.1	50.0	58.2
Camden	677	7 849	838	1 327	1 804	252	182	165	20 993	46	43.5	17.4	37.0
Candler	197	2 005	381	265	358	110	75	40	19 746	264	15.5	16.7	41.7
Carroll	1 739	26 389	2 815	9 601	3 714	788	524	650	24 631	702	34.0	3.1	42.0
Catoosa	739	10 393	1 978	2 021	2 452	313	267	226	21 780	215	42.8	2.3	37.7
Charlton	175	1 239	226	268	212	42	12	25	19 967	75	36.0	9.3	28.0
Chatham	6 575	104 569	14 833	14 113	15 776	3 107	3 593	2 815	26 923	42	45.2	11.9	50.0
Chattahoochee	60	1 404	D	D	D	D	37	39	28 067	13	23.1	15.4	23.1
Chattooga	322	6 088	247	3 845	895	140	47	130	21 363	278	24.8	8.3	32.0
Cherokee	2 839	24 992	2 161	4 044	5 917	1 020	1 194	583	23 313	493	64.9	0.6	41.4
Clarke	2 529	40 179	6 342	7 276	7 544	1 133	1 160	926	23 042	80	43.8	7.5	31.2
Clay	50	434	120	D	107	D	0	7	16 240	56	10.7	44.6	64.3
Clayton	4 344	83 840	5 969	5 849	14 551	2 223	1 700	2 228	26 577	54	50.0	0.0	35.2
Clinch	148	2 607	255	898	166	D	130	44	17 046	93	52.7	8.6	34.4
Cobb	17 181	275 497	18 052	25 412	38 921	14 008	20 583	9 448	34 296	128	63.3	3.1	39.8
Coffee	828	14 798	1 130	5 947	2 103	373	217	323	21 801	656	22.1	7.0	52.7
Colquitt	908	11 501	1 656	3 761	2 122	333	178	232	20 170	634	23.2	20.0	51.4
Columbia	1 810	25 338	5 273	5 219	3 734	704	792	602	23 750	169	42.6	7.7	26.0
Cook	329	4 126	562	1 626	723	115	56	90	21 918	226	31.0	16.8	43.8
Coweta	1 527	21 784	2 398	5 520	3 573	591	440	513	23 568	316	40.2	4.1	38.0
Crawford	78	531	112	126	85	10	D	9	16 831	123	28.5	13.0	44.7
Crisp	556	7 417	1 018	1 793	1 701	301	103	148	20 001	213	20.7	31.9	59.2
Dade	212	2 404	151	940	450	72	24	46	19 173	175	37.1	5.7	29.7
Dawson	400	2 989	145	422	1 051	94	97	64	21 485	160	53.8	7.5	43.8
Decatur	616	9 459	890	3 754	1 609	393	85	204	21 565	335	20.0	22.4	51.6
De Kalb	17 013	314 225	36 161	24 642	34 189	17 060	21 602	10 350	32 938	46	78.3	2.2	34.8
Dodge	374	4 034	957	850	712	140	80	71	17 697	491	17.3	12.2	36.3
Dooly	191	2 753	240	1 559	306	117	7	53	19 413	259	18.9	34.4	62.9
Dougherty	2 632	45 671	7 244	8 401	7 175	1 636	1 328	1 147	25 108	139	43.9	25.9	47.5
Douglas	1 911	24 789	3 043	2 488	5 118	641	737	558	22 506	107	57.9	1.9	29.0
Early	247	2 969	312	1 082	432	88	60	83	27 998	279	16.1	31.5	55.9
Echols	12	12	D	0	D	0	D	0	26 417	67	34.3	9.0	43.3
Effingham	471	4 794	382	1 561	1 120	107	77	135	28 155	203	30.0	12.8	36.0
Elbert	536	5 848	671	2 816	741	101	113	117	20 030	320	20.3	6.2	39.7
Emanuel	424	5 401	802	2 272	869	167	126	93	17 226	441	16.3	19.7	37.2
Evans	224	3 507	396	1 669	482	85	48	71	20 333	183	28.4	14.2	38.3

Table B. States and Counties — Agriculture, Land, and Water

STATE County	Land in farms — Acreage (1,000) [117]	Percent change, 1992–1997 [118]	Acres — Average size of farm [119]	Total irrigated (1,000) [120]	Total cropland (1,000) [121]	Value of land and buildings — Average per farm ($1,000) [122]	Average per acre (dollars) [123]	Value of machinery and equipment Average per farm ($1,000) [124]	Value of products sold — Total (mil dol) [125]	Average per farm (dollars) [126]	Percent from — Crops [127]	Livestock and poultry products [128]	Percent of farms with sales of — $10,000 or more [129]	$100,000 or more [130]	Percent of land owned by Fed. Gov. 1997 [131]	Water consumption 1995 (mil gal/day) [132]
FLORIDA—Cont'd																
Sarasota	129	-14.8	408	5	19	900	2 342	27	24	76 657	70.6	29.4	37.1	12.1	0.0	47.9
Seminole	37	-38.0	108	4	7	332	2 870	14	20	58 040	91.3	8.7	35.8	9.3	0.7	69.8
Sumter	183	-27.5	255	2	55	468	1 733	22	34	47 970	27.5	72.5	26.6	7.0	0.0	66.1
Suwannee	158	-2.2	189	15	87	290	1 547	37	121	144 230	33.4	66.6	40.6	19.5	0.0	142.5
Taylor	57	0.0	451	0	6	396	950	15	4	34 226	19.6	80.4	25.4	3.2	0.1	53.1
Union	63	30.2	293	2	16	409	1 347	26	11	51 687	34.2	65.8	30.0	6.6	0.0	2.7
Volusia	112	-19.2	123	10	30	447	4 060	30	120	132 261	94.7	5.3	46.7	18.2	3.2	156.6
Wakulla	11	27.0	130	0	4	223	1 720	30	3	34 798	16.3	83.7	36.4	3.4	61.3	72.5
Walton	79	-18.7	166	1	35	203	1 329	24	20	41 529	24.0	76.0	25.4	8.6	21.0	11.8
Washington	55	22.8	172	0	26	229	1 204	28	9	29 042	38.8	61.2	30.4	6.2	0.0	4.6
GEORGIA	10 671	6.4	265	749	5 371	393	1 505	44	4 993	123 789	38.5	61.5	39.5	17.8	5.6	5 754.0
Appling	108	1.5	218	2	52	298	1 244	42	46	93 875	45.4	54.6	39.7	15.6	0.0	62.9
Atkinson	63	-19.5	320	4	31	304	1 054	50	59	298 910	27.1	72.9	62.8	31.1	0.0	3.0
Bacon	70	-10.8	217	1	25	256	1 245	34	35	107 729	31.9	68.1	50.0	17.3	0.0	3.0
Baker	119	9.4	910	25	63	1 139	1 237	151	39	295 922	69.8	30.2	68.7	42.7	0.0	24.1
Baldwin	30	-8.0	221	0	12	244	1 343	27	3	23 741	7.8	92.2	20.4	4.4	0.0	7.2
Banks	47	-3.2	106	0	21	327	2 829	35	103	231 898	2.6	97.4	48.0	33.0	1.1	2.3
Barrow	41	14.5	114	0	20	369	3 092	25	52	145 011	1.1	98.9	38.8	20.8	0.0	5.7
Bartow	84	-0.8	211	1	36	363	1 855	38	44	111 073	11.5	88.5	35.8	17.8	3.7	58.0
Ben Hill	53	13.5	335	10	34	361	1 160	51	16	103 025	76.3	23.7	56.0	22.0	0.0	17.3
Berrien	131	1.5	328	11	66	410	1 296	48	39	98 642	78.2	21.8	55.4	26.6	0.0	12.9
Bibb	22	29.8	148	0	9	241	1 807	25	5	36 637	18.4	81.6	25.5	5.4	0.5	107.0
Bleckley	71	12.5	321	6	45	325	964	48	12	52 390	89.8	10.2	38.9	14.9	0.0	9.1
Brantley	28	-0.8	134	0	10	177	1 234	18	13	64 950	17.8	82.2	31.9	7.2	0.0	2.5
Brooks	189	12.1	440	14	96	582	1 458	64	59	137 345	73.0	27.0	51.2	23.5	0.0	6.3
Bryan	25	59.2	418	D	6	520	1 246	55	2	29 210	92.1	7.9	31.1	6.6	37.5	2.0
Bulloch	200	-6.6	382	9	132	405	1 149	55	73	138 397	84.1	15.9	53.2	25.6	0.0	17.2
Burke	210	25.6	606	12	119	436	702	71	42	121 948	75.6	24.4	43.6	22.5	0.0	75.5
Butts	27	-5.2	186	0	11	323	1 755	24	3	20 754	20.6	79.4	20.3	3.4	0.1	5.6
Calhoun	129	12.8	1 054	21	65	1 074	1 025	226	40	329 422	71.0	29.0	73.8	45.1	0.0	18.8
Camden	19	5.4	412	D	1	557	1 350	18	1	14 197	88.5	11.5	23.9	2.2	8.6	40.9
Candler	78	37.5	297	2	34	267	938	36	19	70 690	68.6	31.4	37.9	16.7	0.0	3.2
Carroll	78	-6.1	111	1	41	307	2 690	30	90	128 592	3.5	96.5	29.8	14.0	0.0	13.7
Catoosa	22	-24.6	102	0	13	311	2 766	25	25	115 203	7.7	92.3	29.8	14.0	5.5	10.7
Charlton	20	-7.4	271	0	4	563	2 072	28	3	39 187	25.3	74.7	24.0	4.0	35.8	1.8
Chatham	9	-3.4	207	0	2	338	1 635	58	3	69 871	94.3	5.7	42.9	9.5	6.9	605.7
Chattahoochee	4	-32.2	313		1	214	682	33	0	6 083	D	D	23.1	0.0	73.8	13.8
Chattooga	55	4.4	199	D	23	273	1 419	24	5	17 561	16.4	83.6	26.6	0.0	9.7	4.9
Cherokee	32	-5.4	65	0	13	369	5 898	21	55	110 819	10.7	89.3	32.0	17.2	4.5	13.9
Clarke	13	5.5	158	0	5	570	3 601	30	11	142 862	27.6	72.4	30.0	11.2	0.0	18.1
Clay	44	3.0	791	4	24	731	924	122	10	179 821	84.2	15.8	73.2	37.5	3.0	5.6
Clayton	5	-1.6	91	D	3	376	4 126	28	1	14 312	44.2	55.8	25.9	3.7	1.6	25.6
Clinch	16	15.5	174	0	4	356	2 045	39	4	47 149	48.8	51.2	41.9	11.8	3.3	1.3
Cobb	10	-0.9	77	0	4	419	4 227	16	5	38 956	64.7	35.3	18.8	3.1	4.8	440.1
Coffee	204	14.1	311	11	104	448	1 499	48	141	215 585	39.5	60.5	55.6	24.5	0.0	13.2
Colquitt	229	15.8	362	35	136	456	1 373	79	122	192 429	76.3	23.7	57.4	29.0	0.0	39.8
Columbia	29	7.9	172	0	9	472	2 643	25	3	19 836	35.4	64.6	21.9	4.7	1.7	11.9
Cook	84	14.8	371	13	53	443	1 373	82	47	209 607	95.4	4.6	54.9	22.1	0.0	11.9
Coweta	43	1.4	135	0	19	328	3 263	27	7	21 318	65.0	35.0	19.0	2.2	0.0	352.5
Crawford	37	-1.6	304	3	18	357	1 118	54	15	121 089	62.7	37.3	33.3	17.1	0.0	5.9
Crisp	115	4.9	542	15	75	546	1 090	120	43	202 592	75.3	24.7	65.3	35.7	0.0	19.0
Dade	26	-1.1	147	D	11	255	1 668	24	9	51 626	0.9	99.1	28.0	7.4	0.7	1.7
Dawson	19	0.7	120	D	9	460	3 479	25	30	185 252	2.2	97.8	51.9	37.5	5.6	1.5
Decatur	164	-2.7	491	41	102	679	1 454	87	76	227 280	86.8	13.2	53.7	25.7	2.0	64.8
De Kalb	6	106.1	134	0	1	229	1 704	35	2	41 422	50.5	49.6	30.4	8.7	0.0	85.8
Dodge	156	60.5	317	10	64	256	867	42	18	37 089	82.8	17.2	33.2	7.5	0.0	7.5
Dooly	165	4.9	636	15	122	608	1 053	105	55	210 696	79.9	20.1	69.5	42.1	0.0	12.8
Dougherty	83	17.3	599	13	44	738	1 307	142	27	191 552	91.8	8.2	41.7	22.3	1.7	134.1
Douglas	10	22.2	91	0	3	399	3 809	23	1	11 860	44.1	55.9	9.3	2.8	0.5	7.6
Early	173	-6.1	619	31	107	777	1 174	95	45	162 830	94.0	6.0	62.7	32.6	0.1	142.0
Echols	18	11.9	267	1	4	330	1 235	48	5	75 507	93.9	6.1	40.3	16.4	0.0	2.9
Effingham	52	19.3	259	0	25	317	1 340	39	8	40 495	70.4	29.6	30.0	9.4	0.1	145.5
Elbert	57	5.6	178	0	28	256	1 574	26	14	44 989	16.7	83.3	22.5	8.1	5.0	2.8
Emanuel	153	23.6	347	4	61	320	887	97	23	51 078	77.5	22.6	31.3	13.2	0.0	5.6
Evans	43	5.7	237	2	22	346	1 212	45	21	116 048	39.6	60.4	41.0	19.1	14.3	3.3

STATE County	Value of Residential Construction Authorized by Building Permits, 1999		Wholesale Trade, 1997				Retail Trade[1], 1997				Real Estate and Rental and Leasing, 1997			
	New Construction ($1,000)	Number of Housing Units	Number of Establishments	Number of Employees	Sales (mil dol)	Annual Payroll (mil dol)	Number of Establishments	Number of Employees	Sales (mil dol)	Annual Payroll (mil dol)	Number of Establishments	Number of Employees	Receipts (mil dol)	Annual Payroll (mil dol)
	133	134	135	136	137	138	139	140	141	142	143	144	145	146
FLORIDA—Cont'd														
Sarasota	438 920	4 145	527	3 122	1 035.9	86.2	1 669	20 311	3 606.6	343.8	571	2 320	290.4	48.9
Seminole	680 140	5 230	881	7 301	3 669.7	242.9	1 512	21 219	3 550.1	352.1	440	2 090	338.2	50.4
Sumter	77 300	1 576	18	236	84.4	4.5	111	1 192	185.3	14.8	22	51	6.4	0.8
Suwannee	10 088	111	35	D	D	D	137	1 333	205.0	19.2	20	64	5.3	0.7
Taylor	4 950	69	16	D	D	D	97	945	144.2	12.6	12	40	2.4	0.5
Union	3 360	41	3	D	D	D	28	180	27.2	2.8	2	D	D	D
Volusia	385 018	3 858	488	4 314	1 629.7	105.4	1 865	23 251	3 887.6	360.5	546	2 856	277.6	49.8
Wakulla	25 824	379	15	D	D	D	53	418	57.6	5.0	10	14	2.0	0.3
Walton	197 864	1 554	29	283	98.2	6.6	215	1 959	262.6	27.0	55	588	52.2	10.9
Washington	6 296	94	5	D	D	D	70	742	104.4	9.1	8	34	3.3	0.3
GEORGIA	8 749 615	89 600	13 978	191 078	163 647.5	7 519.7	33 073	420 676	72 212.5	6 943.6	7 794	47 669	6 912.9	1 308.8
Appling	350	5	14	92	41.0	2.8	88	616	116.9	9.7	7	11	1.2	0.2
Atkinson	NA	NA	9	67	11.9	0.9	30	154	20.9	1.9	3	D	D	D
Bacon	0	0	10	141	40.4	2.4	37	291	47.1	4.1	4	D	D	D
Baker	NA	NA	1	D	D	D	5	45	4.4	0.4	NA	NA	NA	NA
Baldwin	14 125	152	23	169	57.6	3.8	218	2 407	372.0	34.3	20	65	6.0	1.0
Banks	11 463	118	12	331	44.6	8.5	69	560	75.7	7.1	2	D	D	D
Barrow	55 644	808	30	223	73.8	5.6	145	1 798	344.8	30.8	23	65	7.7	1.0
Bartow	135 210	1 453	92	814	258.2	23.1	246	3 219	580.0	53.3	56	265	22.4	3.5
Ben Hill	3 378	46	20	D	D	D	93	884	144.0	12.3	13	44	2.5	0.6
Berrien	927	18	24	110	40.5	2.4	62	471	79.3	8.1	9	15	1.0	0.2
Bibb	56 418	575	272	3 545	1 511.7	110.7	912	12 885	1 977.3	194.2	185	1 062	148.8	26.2
Bleckley	3 834	37	4	D	D	D	53	392	59.0	4.8	3	6	0.6	0.1
Brantley	525	4	7	44	6.5	1.2	32	180	26.4	2.1	5	16	0.8	0.1
Brooks	3 604	49	9	36	5.8	0.5	57	349	63.5	5.3	2	D	D	D
Bryan	40 003	335	14	D	D	D	61	537	85.3	7.4	11	D	D	D
Bulloch	34 382	445	54	582	333.4	13.9	259	3 386	471.9	44.0	45	208	15.4	2.4
Burke	6 562	76	19	208	128.0	6.1	81	700	118.6	10.6	8	D	D	D
Butts	15 048	225	12	169	143.4	6.7	71	613	111.9	8.3	15	24	2.5	0.2
Calhoun	76	1	6	44	18.8	1.1	25	212	29.0	2.6	2	D	D	D
Camden	35 137	489	9	63	12.5	1.0	143	1 687	275.7	21.7	28	143	14.0	2.7
Candler	174	3	16	146	54.3	3.2	50	388	74.6	5.5	4	8	0.8	0.1
Carroll	101 917	1 486	84	1 232	1 286.3	48.2	348	3 505	574.5	53.2	62	232	24.1	3.7
Catoosa	46 652	502	39	638	747.7	15.7	172	2 524	406.2	35.4	30	91	8.2	1.6
Charlton	3 048	31	8	37	85.0	0.9	49	201	31.8	3.1	4	12	0.6	0.1
Chatham	160 091	1 679	348	4 347	2 445.1	142.9	1 261	15 625	2 466.9	244.0	280	1 470	195.9	36.0
Chattahoochee	760	20	1	D	D	D	6	26	4.2	0.4	1	D	D	D
Chattooga	727	12	12	54	12.4	1.0	82	922	122.5	11.9	9	13	1.0	0.2
Cherokee	343 091	3 380	201	1 103	490.8	34.7	351	5 202	968.9	86.7	93	276	33.6	5.4
Clarke	56 921	1 024	81	D	D	D	540	7 760	1 118.8	110.3	131	524	55.8	9.5
Clay	0	0	5	16	3.8	0.3	17	123	10.5	1.2	NA	NA	NA	NA
Clayton	245 751	2 261	316	6 142	3 345.2	217.5	832	16 204	2 731.7	285.3	197	1 326	185.6	30.9
Clinch	997	17	8	60	11.7	1.2	32	220	25.1	2.5	3	4	0.3	0.0
Cobb	928 236	8 008	1 632	24 859	23 231.5	1 270.8	2 234	37 323	6 971.6	663.6	785	5 612	989.9	183.8
Coffee	11 549	125	55	469	183.3	11.2	210	2 120	389.9	33.0	23	112	7.3	1.4
Colquitt	920	10	53	436	156.4	9.8	214	2 026	326.0	29.4	29	102	9.0	1.3
Columbia	128 624	1 184	91	D	D	D	247	3 731	613.0	60.0	68	285	33.0	6.3
Cook	3 836	52	20	231	86.0	3.9	89	824	121.1	10.7	7	12	0.9	0.1
Coweta	175 781	1 808	79	735	513.5	16.8	259	3 728	550.0	52.7	53	155	21.4	3.2
Crawford	25 368	246	2	D	D	D	14	84	11.2	1.2	NA	NA	NA	NA
Crisp	3 357	49	29	483	266.8	12.5	158	1 859	234.5	23.7	22	96	8.3	1.2
Dade	400	5	8	D	D	D	54	476	92.3	5.9	7	44	3.1	0.6
Dawson	53 573	414	19	56	71.0	2.1	106	704	119.4	12.2	7	10	1.0	0.2
Decatur	7 201	85	35	452	341.1	11.0	172	1 656	243.6	21.7	22	90	4.9	1.0
De Kalb	819 878	6 851	1 518	23 560	19 215.9	964.4	2 407	34 901	6 229.3	635.7	867	7 216	906.7	188.1
Dodge	3 194	47	20	D	D	D	84	799	102.4	9.0	8	161	9.3	1.6
Dooly	225	3	15	120	56.7	3.2	51	336	65.7	4.8	3	D	D	D
Dougherty	38 022	350	184	D	D	D	574	7 707	1 154.7	113.9	128	629	82.5	12.4
Douglas	67 161	1 306	105	1 492	1 100.1	43.7	312	4 781	974.7	82.6	61	263	37.5	5.6
Early	407	6	19	277	133.3	5.7	68	519	69.9	6.4	5	27	1.2	0.4
Echols	NA	NA	1	D	D	D	3	D	D	D	1	D	D	D
Effingham	46 863	461	12	D	D	D	91	1 193	165.8	15.7	21	D	D	D
Elbert	537	20	50	294	68.2	6.6	85	726	130.7	10.5	12	28	1.5	0.4
Emanuel	137	2	25	239	126.3	4.0	102	902	139.6	12.0	9	42	1.7	0.5
Evans	1 977	16	10	74	35.0	1.3	60	444	85.8	7.1	5	15	0.9	0.2

1. Establishments with payroll.

Table B. States and Counties — Professional, Manufacturing, and Accommodation and Foodservices

STATE County	Professional, Scientific, and Technical Services[1], 1997 Number of Establishments	Number of Employees	Receipts (mil dol)	Annual Payroll (mil dol)	Manufacturing, 1997 Number of Establishments	Number of Employees	Receipts (mil dol)	Annual Payroll (mil dol)	Accommodation and Foodservices, 1997 Number of Establishments	Number of Employees	Sales (mil dol)	Annual Payroll (mil dol)
	147	148	149	150	151	152	153	154	155	156	157	158
FLORIDA—Cont'd												
Sarasota	1 070	5 780	515.2	207.0	379	7 809	872.6	222.9	687	13 051	481.8	132.1
Seminole	1 102	6 182	561.6	210.7	434	9 624	1 582.2	287.1	579	12 966	423.1	117.3
Sumter	21	60	3.1	1.1	30	907	200.9	19.6	48	661	23.6	5.7
Suwannee	35	94	5.4	1.7	19	D	D	D	32	512	15.5	3.7
Taylor	18	61	3.2	1.4	20	1 594	496.1	58.0	36	364	11.9	3.0
Union	3	12	0.5	0.2	NA	NA	NA	NA	5	D	D	D
Volusia	844	4 048	346.4	120.7	392	10 216	1 212.6	263.2	1 051	19 758	635.6	167.0
Wakulla	19	72	3.7	1.4	NA	NA	NA	NA	28	293	9.8	2.3
Walton	54	162	16.4	4.6	35	937	108.7	12.5	87	2 446	107.2	29.4
Washington	19	80	3.5	1.2	14	754	85.8	15.7	22	317	8.8	2.6
GEORGIA	17 810	138 198	15 266.4	5 908.8	9 083	533 830	124 526.8	15 534.1	13 829	274 322	9 689.9	2 695.1
Appling	12	44	2.5	0.8	25	1 160	432.9	28.7	29	350	10.5	2.9
Atkinson	3	3	0.3	0.0	13	1 081	123.8	24.1	7	69	1.7	0.5
Bacon	12	39	2.1	0.7	14	1 373	210.9	27.8	17	D	D	D
Baker	1	D	D	D	NA	NA	NA	NA	3	7	0.2	0.0
Baldwin	52	172	8.1	2.4	20	3 454	624.9	91.2	66	1 507	37.8	9.8
Banks	7	15	1.0	0.2	14	D	D	D	22	372	16.7	4.6
Barrow	39	142	9.7	3.7	64	2 217	509.9	64.0	47	642	24.1	5.7
Bartow	81	315	19.5	8.2	126	10 115	2 918.4	303.1	123	1 827	65.3	17.7
Ben Hill	15	70	4.3	1.4	34	3 621	641.5	93.6	26	D	D	D
Berrien	13	30	1.6	0.5	17	1 987	231.6	45.0	15	169	5.5	1.3
Bibb	358	2 139	190.7	63.0	179	D	D	D	340	7 265	229.8	62.1
Bleckley	14	42	2.3	0.9	6	D	D	D	15	176	5.4	1.5
Brantley	2	D	D	D	NA	NA	NA	NA	10	59	2.1	0.5
Brooks	12	28	1.5	0.6	12	1 077	106.3	17.4	13	D	D	D
Bryan	23	52	4.2	1.2	NA	NA	NA	NA	29	D	D	D
Bulloch	76	353	22.7	7.9	41	3 210	493.4	84.3	99	1 894	52.5	13.5
Burke	11	36	1.2	0.5	16	1 035	84.4	21.3	21	283	7.4	1.9
Butts	13	22	1.4	0.5	18	1 127	181.4	22.3	28	272	10.5	2.8
Calhoun	1	D	D	D	3	D	D	D	8	D	D	D
Camden	41	163	10.6	3.7	21	1 364	528.8	52.7	68	1 220	35.3	9.9
Candler	15	73	3.9	1.4	NA	NA	NA	NA	17	262	7.7	2.0
Carroll	88	429	27.6	11.0	121	9 590	2 156.7	229.6	124	2 196	63.1	16.8
Catoosa	36	130	7.4	2.4	64	2 291	458.5	56.2	57	920	34.3	8.3
Charlton	4	7	0.6	0.1	NA	NA	NA	NA	11	104	3.8	1.1
Chatham	479	2 779	216.1	86.0	207	D	D	D	581	12 599	427.6	116.4
Chattahoochee	4	26	3.0	1.4	NA	NA	NA	NA	2	D	D	D
Chattooga	13	40	4.0	0.8	23	3 996	873.6	91.0	31	378	10.1	2.6
Cherokee	257	893	75.7	32.5	152	3 886	656.7	100.5	139	2 314	75.2	21.0
Clarke	156	943	54.9	22.8	90	9 388	1 368.5	234.9	240	4 371	125.5	33.8
Clay	NA	NA	NA	NA	NA	NA	NA	NA	2	D	D	D
Clayton	227	1 521	118.1	45.0	167	5 901	1 641.6	184.1	376	10 412	422.9	123.2
Clinch	8	35	3.1	1.1	11	918	148.9	18.8	8	D	D	D
Cobb	2 217	17 016	1 854.5	739.9	604	24 499	4 134.7	980.2	1 098	23 334	847.3	236.3
Coffee	52	214	12.1	3.9	45	5 377	773.8	116.1	47	810	26.1	6.5
Colquitt	44	128	9.8	3.5	55	3 503	452.2	67.1	52	754	23.3	6.4
Columbia	147	723	52.1	18.6	77	5 323	1 356.1	154.3	100	1 813	63.3	16.2
Cook	12	49	2.1	0.9	35	1 582	227.4	34.1	30	278	9.7	2.7
Coweta	85	286	22.5	8.7	76	5 589	1 093.2	147.8	103	1 880	58.5	15.2
Crawford	1	D	D	D	NA	NA	NA	NA	2	D	D	D
Crisp	25	76	4.9	1.7	27	2 067	340.5	53.1	51	913	26.2	8.0
Dade	8	30	0.7	0.2	22	907	98.5	19.9	22	319	10.5	2.5
Dawson	15	54	4.5	1.8	NA	NA	NA	NA	16	D	D	D
Decatur	21	64	5.2	1.4	35	3 538	632.8	84.2	30	455	14.0	3.2
De Kalb	2 188	19 674	1 972.8	856.4	697	24 358	8 018.5	942.8	1 232	21 365	809.7	215.4
Dodge	21	79	4.5	1.8	16	867	155.0	17.5	22	324	8.4	2.3
Dooly	5	11	1.6	0.2	12	1 521	186.8	30.4	16	89	3.2	0.8
Dougherty	172	1 327	98.1	37.8	90	8 627	4 275.5	312.0	192	3 736	118.1	31.6
Douglas	127	438	37.7	14.7	95	2 211	371.2	54.5	127	3 049	96.8	25.5
Early	11	31	2.9	1.0	12	1 071	475.2	45.0	17	D	D	D
Echols	1	D	D	D	NA	NA	NA	NA	NA	NA	NA	NA
Effingham	26	77	4.3	1.1	11	D	D	D	31	D	D	D
Elbert	29	103	5.7	1.6	112	2 954	441.7	64.6	34	396	11.6	2.7
Emanuel	22	93	5.9	2.2	36	2 191	253.5	38.4	26	310	9.5	2.5
Evans	13	39	2.6	1.0	14	1 677	184.9	34.2	19	174	6.4	1.8

1. Firms subject to federal tax.

STATE County	Health Care and Social Assistance[1], 1997				Other Services[1], 1997				Federal funds and grants, fiscal 1999[2] Expenditures (mil dol)			
										Direct payments for individuals[3]		
	Number of Establishments	Number of Employees	Receipts (mil dol)	Annual Payroll (mil dol)	Number of Establishments	Number of Employees	Receipts (mil dol)	Annual Payroll (mil dol)	Total	Social Security and government retirement	Medicare	Food stamps and Supplemental Security Income
	159	160	161	162	163	164	165	166	167	168	169	170
FLORIDA—Cont'd												
Sarasota	1 032	12 069	878.3	369.5	623	3 136	174.8	56.1	1 986.0	1 260.6	551.8	20.3
Seminole	716	8 306	632.6	254.9	625	3 331	198.9	60.5	1 087.3	602.1	205.9	31.5
Sumter	23	332	14.4	6.5	32	116	7.7	1.7	242.3	114.2	45.7	8.1
Suwannee	27	382	21.2	7.4	37	142	13.3	2.5	163.7	87.0	34.4	7.3
Taylor	24	325	16.1	7.8	32	222	12.5	3.2	107.9	39.4	19.3	5.0
Union	6	46	2.8	0.9	6	28	1.4	0.3	33.0	14.8	6.3	1.7
Volusia	906	10 079	596.8	253.3	707	3 094	163.6	47.8	2 169.6	1 243.4	511.4	56.7
Wakulla	8	171	5.8	2.9	14	56	4.6	0.9	64.9	34.9	11.2	2.8
Walton	31	505	27.7	11.1	35	177	9.8	3.4	396.5	89.5	25.0	5.8
Washington	27	289	12.1	5.1	18	77	4.5	1.1	114.3	48.6	23.4	4.4
GEORGIA	13 960	173 768	12 065.1	5 158.0	11 482	69 422	4 580.7	1 407.5	39 215.0	12 422.5	4 751.6	1 354.1
Appling	16	75	3.6	1.4	23	97	6.0	1.5	72.5	26.7	15.1	4.1
Atkinson	6	31	1.1	0.4	2	D	D	D	40.3	10.6	7.5	2.5
Bacon	11	71	3.3	1.1	14	53	3.1	0.7	58.5	15.8	10.5	3.6
Baker	NA	NA	NA	NA	NA	NA	NA	NA	17.6	4.6	2.7	1.4
Baldwin	101	1 868	86.1	35.0	51	329	19.6	5.6	157.1	69.6	30.3	8.4
Banks	7	32	1.3	0.6	5	22	1.8	0.4	33.5	16.5	6.6	1.2
Barrow	43	771	39.7	16.7	47	157	10.0	2.8	123.2	58.5	27.1	6.9
Bartow	98	1 471	105.2	36.6	82	514	36.9	10.0	200.3	108.3	35.8	8.7
Ben Hill	27	227	12.5	5.4	30	85	6.0	1.3	77.6	33.7	16.5	4.7
Berrien	23	505	21.0	10.2	13	40	2.3	0.6	70.8	31.3	15.4	4.2
Bibb	471	8 277	650.9	257.8	305	1 738	105.8	33.4	915.5	358.9	160.5	48.4
Bleckley	19	193	7.2	2.9	11	45	2.7	0.6	60.8	29.6	11.5	4.0
Brantley	8	108	5.2	1.8	9	20	1.0	0.2	48.5	25.9	10.2	3.1
Brooks	10	102	5.0	1.9	17	77	3.2	1.1	72.8	25.1	13.3	4.8
Bryan	19	238	11.8	4.7	19	54	3.2	0.9	619.0	40.4	11.9	3.3
Bulloch	97	1 668	110.2	40.7	68	289	14.6	3.7	160.1	64.7	26.0	9.3
Burke	25	364	16.4	7.3	18	53	2.6	0.6	99.4	34.5	16.1	7.3
Butts	24	419	18.7	7.9	19	112	4.3	1.3	70.0	34.5	14.2	3.5
Calhoun	5	69	2.9	1.2	5	16	0.5	0.2	35.6	11.5	6.9	2.3
Camden	63	425	25.0	9.7	37	199	9.1	2.5	450.4	56.6	13.4	4.0
Candler	10	223	6.5	2.9	8	35	2.1	0.6	40.9	15.2	9.3	1.8
Carroll	137	1 800	106.7	47.8	121	484	30.1	7.6	273.2	134.7	62.4	14.3
Catoosa	55	709	43.6	21.7	49	228	14.6	4.5	117.1	64.7	24.3	5.8
Charlton	10	39	1.8	0.6	6	10	0.9	0.1	41.6	17.5	8.6	2.4
Chatham	452	6 348	466.1	235.6	395	2 731	168.6	57.6	1 389.8	473.8	196.8	50.7
Chattahoochee	1	D	D	D	6	100	3.7	1.6	128.6	7.0	1.4	0.4
Chattooga	20	226	12.0	5.2	9	39	2.8	0.6	99.0	48.2	22.1	4.1
Cherokee	152	1 980	126.4	48.4	166	631	47.9	12.2	243.0	131.5	43.6	5.1
Clarke	260	2 017	184.6	91.6	140	817	37.2	12.0	431.3	128.9	47.6	16.0
Clay	4	D	D	D	1	D	D	D	24.1	6.5	2.4	1.6
Clayton	369	4 290	294.0	134.7	312	1 842	131.7	39.4	571.1	284.4	98.7	30.5
Clinch	11	128	5.6	1.9	3	11	0.4	0.2	35.5	11.0	8.3	2.6
Cobb	1 082	12 012	893.9	380.1	1 061	6 802	446.1	154.3	3 973.5	691.9	224.9	36.7
Coffee	61	481	29.4	11.7	52	238	12.9	3.2	135.5	51.0	26.6	8.0
Colquitt	73	616	34.5	15.0	54	321	17.3	5.4	181.1	70.8	32.9	11.8
Columbia	129	1 206	66.0	29.5	142	799	47.1	15.6	550.9	123.4	26.1	5.3
Cook	24	545	19.5	8.5	18	61	3.3	1.0	63.0	26.8	12.5	3.6
Coweta	100	1 638	119.6	53.0	72	284	19.4	5.2	227.0	120.2	48.3	9.2
Crawford	6	127	5.7	1.7	6	33	2.5	0.6	26.0	11.6	5.7	1.8
Crisp	34	293	14.1	5.8	35	118	7.3	1.9	103.2	36.0	20.8	8.4
Dade	12	243	12.2	5.0	10	25	3.0	0.5	48.4	25.3	11.1	2.2
Dawson	18	121	4.6	2.1	13	59	6.7	1.4	38.3	19.9	7.9	1.3
Decatur	44	304	17.7	7.0	41	162	7.5	1.9	115.9	45.7	18.3	9.0
De Kalb	1 360	16 256	1 184.2	486.4	1 101	7 551	535.5	175.6	1 992.5	631.3	342.4	75.7
Dodge	44	484	20.6	8.9	23	65	4.5	0.9	90.6	37.3	18.3	5.2
Dooly	13	170	7.1	2.9	8	42	1.8	0.7	67.6	19.5	10.3	3.6
Dougherty	250	3 277	239.3	110.3	169	1 163	71.1	22.5	661.9	196.7	71.6	36.2
Douglas	139	2 277	125.8	52.9	150	965	63.7	20.4	201.6	116.3	45.4	7.7
Early	10	47	1.8	0.8	10	35	1.2	0.4	63.8	21.4	9.9	4.5
Echols	NA	NA	NA	NA	NA	NA	NA	NA	6.3	2.2	1.2	0.4
Effingham	22	147	9.3	2.9	25	136	12.3	2.6	90.7	47.7	14.4	4.6
Elbert	31	375	19.0	7.7	25	64	4.8	1.0	97.6	42.8	19.9	6.0
Emanuel	40	357	16.2	6.1	24	86	4.8	1.1	116.5	40.0	20.0	8.7
Evans	15	343	17.4	6.4	8	82	5.0	1.8	45.6	19.0	8.4	3.0

1. Firms subject to federal tax.   2. October 1, 1998 to September 30, 1999.   3. State totals may include programs not allocated by county.

STATE County	Federal funds and grants, fiscal 1999[1] (cont'd)							Local government finances, 1997				
	Expenditures (mil dol) (cont'd)							General revenue				
	Procurement contract awards			Grants[2]							Taxes	
											Per capita[3] (dollars)	
	Salaries and wages	Defense	Other	Medicaid and other health-related	Nutrition and family welfare	Education	Other	Total (mil dol)	Intergovern-mental (mil dol)	Total (mil dol)	Total	Property
	171	172	173	174	175	176	177	178	179	180	181	182
FLORIDA—Cont'd												
Sarasota	46.7	7.4	12.4	26.9	14.3	7.3	32.9	970.3	116.4	328.7	1 090	862
Seminole	80.5	15.6	23.7	39.0	17.5	12.6	44.4	709.8	249.9	297.4	863	620
Sumter	41.7	2.1	7.8	11.7	5.1	2.1	0.6	66.2	32.4	18.6	472	311
Suwannee	6.4	0.0	1.3	14.4	4.3	2.1	2.8	58.1	33.4	14.7	443	311
Taylor	1.9	23.2	0.5	10.5	4.1	1.6	0.8	44.9	20.3	16.3	870	610
Union	1.0	0.2	0.3	4.6	1.6	0.6	1.0	28.3	21.8	2.9	233	161
Volusia	69.2	44.7	19.0	73.3	31.3	20.4	73.5	1 122.4	316.8	362.7	864	693
Wakulla	3.2	0.1	1.2	4.7	2.4	1.0	1.0	40.0	25.7	8.2	426	328
Walton	252.0	0.8	0.9	14.0	4.2	2.1	-3.5	82.1	27.8	42.0	1 107	870
Washington	2.4	0.0	0.5	17.0	2.8	3.8	9.7	61.9	35.3	8.1	403	295
GEORGIA	6 291.7	4 095.8	1 054.3	2 977.6	1 323.4	640.7	1 809.8	X	X	X	X	X
Appling	2.5	0.3	0.5	12.5	2.7	1.9	1.1	55.1	12.8	18.1	1 105	773
Atkinson	0.9	0.0	0.2	6.9	1.5	0.5	7.0	11.8	6.7	4.2	598	362
Bacon	1.3	0.1	0.4	6.0	2.3	0.7	14.6	31.5	13.0	6.7	647	395
Baker	0.3	0.0	0.1	3.4	0.6	0.3	0.0	6.5	3.5	2.4	651	535
Baldwin	4.5	3.8	0.8	17.0	6.5	2.0	7.8	144.5	42.0	29.3	698	366
Banks	0.8	0.0	0.2	4.4	0.7	0.4	2.4	17.7	6.9	9.2	739	390
Barrow	8.7	2.0	1.0	12.1	2.4	1.5	1.9	65.9	27.8	28.2	724	474
Bartow	8.3	2.6	3.0	13.6	8.3	2.5	5.6	141.5	56.8	55.7	805	572
Ben Hill	1.7	0.0	0.5	12.5	2.9	1.3	1.1	51.0	16.3	13.5	781	464
Berrien	1.6	0.0	0.4	8.1	1.9	0.6	0.2	28.2	14.9	10.4	652	380
Bibb	87.8	7.5	23.8	82.8	28.5	11.3	82.0	377.6	142.4	168.9	1 083	648
Bleckley	1.1	0.0	0.3	6.5	1.6	0.5	0.6	26.3	11.0	6.4	578	348
Brantley	1.3	0.0	0.4	4.8	1.3	0.9	0.2	19.7	11.8	6.7	497	359
Brooks	1.5	0.0	0.4	11.0	3.5	1.3	0.8	24.1	13.3	7.8	468	329
Bryan	476.9	71.1	1.2	5.6	2.2	1.0	4.9	38.9	19.3	16.0	691	470
Bulloch	8.2	0.4	1.4	18.7	6.1	3.4	2.7	101.1	53.7	30.1	603	361
Burke	2.9	0.1	1.0	18.3	5.7	2.0	0.2	148.0	12.0	35.1	1 544	1 314
Butts	2.6	0.0	0.5	7.5	5.1	0.7	0.7	31.1	13.4	13.8	803	519
Calhoun	0.9	0.1	0.3	6.9	1.1	0.5	0.3	13.1	7.3	3.6	702	463
Camden	269.1	56.5	1.1	5.6	3.7	5.0	34.4	83.1	38.0	31.7	701	423
Candler	1.0	0.0	0.3	6.7	1.5	0.6	0.8	29.5	10.2	5.7	641	369
Carroll	11.0	0.1	3.9	25.2	6.4	3.9	5.9	134.7	67.1	47.6	585	310
Catoosa	3.4	0.2	2.9	8.2	3.3	1.7	1.0	138.6	32.0	22.9	462	300
Charlton	2.0	0.0	0.6	4.4	1.8	0.8	3.1	25.6	8.2	6.9	739	554
Chatham	248.2	188.5	19.5	93.3	44.3	16.1	18.1	663.3	215.9	301.0	1 332	863
Chattahoochee	0.4	114.6	0.3	1.7	0.4	0.5	1.5	5.9	3.4	1.6	101	32
Chattooga	2.0	0.1	0.5	11.8	3.1	1.0	4.4	38.0	19.2	11.9	518	323
Cherokee	13.3	0.5	3.7	12.2	3.4	2.2	25.8	211.7	81.1	78.8	621	463
Clarke	72.8	2.9	17.9	43.9	17.3	8.1	58.7	367.0	75.0	85.3	937	620
Clay	2.0	1.3	0.1	4.0	1.2	0.5	3.1	5.8	2.8	2.5	711	427
Clayton	64.4	17.5	5.5	22.4	13.0	9.3	3.4	419.5	154.8	178.2	872	579
Clinch	1.0	4.1	0.3	4.9	1.6	0.5	0.5	21.8	8.4	6.7	1 007	755
Cobb	167.1	2 675.9	51.4	37.1	16.2	12.9	45.5	1 114.2	322.0	556.0	1 009	730
Coffee	5.1	0.0	1.7	18.0	5.3	2.5	8.5	65.6	32.0	24.8	731	399
Colquitt	4.8	0.1	1.1	24.3	14.7	2.7	1.4	111.9	40.7	22.0	554	355
Columbia	295.9	82.4	1.5	9.4	3.7	1.7	0.0	141.7	57.8	59.6	671	459
Cook	1.5	0.0	0.4	8.3	2.1	1.3	1.5	25.7	12.8	9.3	634	350
Coweta	9.8	1.4	3.1	17.7	5.9	2.7	2.6	143.8	52.0	69.9	866	559
Crawford	0.6	0.0	0.2	3.3	1.0	0.5	0.6	15.4	8.7	5.6	507	392
Crisp	2.8	0.0	0.7	16.9	5.1	2.2	2.2	49.2	22.0	18.7	905	495
Dade	1.2	0.0	1.0	5.6	1.3	0.6	0.0	20.3	10.5	8.6	584	291
Dawson	1.6	0.0	0.5	3.8	0.8	0.3	2.1	27.6	12.2	12.7	912	637
Decatur	3.1	0.0	1.8	16.9	5.4	2.1	3.9	86.9	36.2	22.3	839	415
De Kalb	619.8	6.8	39.2	100.7	45.1	26.0	67.7	1 883.8	540.6	632.1	1 075	823
Dodge	2.2	0.0	0.5	15.0	3.7	1.0	0.6	43.9	18.3	7.5	409	262
Dooly	1.9	0.0	0.4	10.3	3.1	0.9	3.2	23.3	10.5	8.9	856	622
Dougherty	146.3	76.7	15.3	54.4	28.3	10.1	7.2	263.8	112.2	97.5	1 017	584
Douglas	9.5	0.1	2.6	10.9	3.9	2.4	1.9	155.3	62.3	72.7	839	545
Early	1.9	0.1	1.7	11.9	3.4	1.1	0.0	26.1	12.0	9.0	738	430
Echols	0.1	0.0	0.0	1.4	0.4	0.2	0.0	5.0	2.9	1.9	773	668
Effingham	3.3	0.0	0.8	6.7	2.4	1.1	8.2	67.7	29.8	22.1	630	453
Elbert	7.2	1.0	1.2	13.7	3.2	1.1	0.1	46.2	16.4	11.1	582	365
Emanuel	4.9	0.1	1.0	21.5	5.9	1.6	5.9	60.1	38.2	12.6	599	353
Evans	2.3	0.0	0.3	6.7	1.8	0.7	2.1	20.7	8.8	6.5	664	355

1. October 1, 1998 to September 30, 1999.   2. State totals may include programs not allocated by county.   3. Based on the resident population estimated as of July 1 of the year shown.

Table B. States and Counties — Local Government Finances, Government Employment, and Elections

STATE County	Direct general expenditure Total (mil dol)	Per capita[1] (dollars)	Percent of total for — Education	Health and hospitals	Police protection	Public welfare	Highways	Debt outstanding Total (mil dol)	Per capita[1] (dollars)	Government employment, 1998 Federal civilian	Federal military	State and local	Presidential election, 2000 Percent of vote cast — Democratic	Republican	All other
	183	184	185	186	187	188	189	190	191	192	193	194	195	196	197
FLORIDA—Cont'd															
Sarasota	919.7	3 049	26.1	29.4	5.9	0.3	5.5	856.0	2 838	838	695	11 286	45.3	51.6	3.1
Seminole	721.8	2 094	52.5	0.7	6.5	0.1	9.8	595.0	1 726	1 400	792	12 689	43.0	55.0	2.0
Sumter	72.6	1 842	46.9	0.4	5.9	1.4	5.7	81.3	2 063	776	91	2 055	43.3	54.5	2.2
Suwannee	57.2	1 730	55.6	1.9	5.9	1.0	5.7	21.5	649	120	74	1 538	32.7	64.3	3.0
Taylor	46.4	2 477	51.6	1.5	9.0	0.6	4.9	41.9	2 241	36	42	1 451	38.9	59.6	1.5
Union	25.0	2 025	70.9	1.1	2.5	0.2	4.5	3.6	293	19	28	2 401	36.8	61.0	2.3
Volusia	1 078.3	2 569	35.4	22.7	6.4	0.4	4.3	987.1	2 351	1 262	976	19 576	53.0	44.8	2.2
Wakulla	43.1	2 247	63.2	2.2	5.9	0.1	3.4	15.3	800	74	42	1 244	44.7	52.5	2.8
Walton	79.6	2 099	44.0	5.0	5.7	0.4	18.3	24.5	646	170	116	2 038	30.8	66.5	2.7
Washington	57.0	2 817	45.7	16.7	2.9	0.6	5.6	17.1	843	44	46	2 194	34.9	62.2	2.9
GEORGIA	X	X	X	X	X	X	X	X	X	93 207	94 817	491 328	43.0	54.7	2.3
Appling	52.5	3 202	37.7	29.4	2.6	0.1	4.3	90.4	5 513	46	64	1 190	NA	NA	NA
Atkinson	11.2	1 588	66.9	1.1	4.5	0.9	6.4	0.8	110	19	28	380	NA	NA	NA
Bacon	32.6	3 153	32.9	42.5	2.9	0.2	2.8	9.1	884	30	40	572	NA	NA	NA
Baker	6.7	1 783	56.6	2.4	4.3	0.2	4.2	0.1	22	11	14	203	NA	NA	NA
Baldwin	125.3	2 988	27.6	44.8	3.7	0.6	2.5	40.7	970	70	171	8 286	NA	NA	NA
Banks	16.8	1 354	59.7	1.6	5.4	0.4	8.8	9.5	767	15	49	474	NA	NA	NA
Barrow	69.9	1 794	61.8	0.6	4.4	0.6	7.8	58.8	1 508	126	156	1 977	NA	NA	NA
Bartow	157.5	2 277	58.3	0.4	6.1	0.4	4.7	254.9	3 685	171	277	3 827	NA	NA	NA
Ben Hill	49.6	2 861	39.7	25.1	3.6	0.4	3.6	22.6	1 302	36	67	1 490	NA	NA	NA
Berrien	27.3	1 709	57.9	0.8	4.3	2.2	15.2	4.2	264	42	63	741	NA	NA	NA
Bibb	369.6	2 369	41.4	8.2	6.5	0.5	5.3	293.9	1 884	1 475	739	9 930	NA	NA	NA
Bleckley	25.1	2 247	55.4	21.0	6.3	0.6	3.6	2.8	253	32	43	942	NA	NA	NA
Brantley	19.4	1 447	71.6	0.7	2.9	0.5	5.0	5.4	400	26	69	658	NA	NA	NA
Brooks	25.0	1 501	58.0	1.2	5.0	7.5	4.4	5.5	328	38	62	841	NA	NA	NA
Bryan	36.9	1 598	64.0	0.7	6.1	1.0	3.8	3.3	144	45	91	1 213	NA	NA	NA
Bulloch	112.1	2 247	49.2	13.7	3.8	0.1	5.9	33.5	671	141	205	4 836	NA	NA	NA
Burke	145.5	6 401	18.3	6.3	1.7	0.3	2.5	1 117.1	49 157	60	88	1 485	NA	NA	NA
Butts	29.9	1 738	52.3	6.8	7.5	0.2	3.6	9.6	560	38	69	1 212	NA	NA	NA
Calhoun	13.6	2 689	59.7	9.3	4.9	1.4	6.1	1.7	336	22	19	733	NA	NA	NA
Camden	82.5	1 826	53.8	4.7	5.3	0.3	4.2	32.8	726	2 590	5 820	2 239	NA	NA	NA
Candler	25.6	2 873	35.7	32.9	3.3	0.1	5.1	7.3	815	24	35	659	NA	NA	NA
Carroll	138.5	1 702	63.2	0.9	5.4	0.2	8.6	47.0	577	209	322	5 147	NA	NA	NA
Catoosa	149.2	3 011	28.0	56.1	2.5	0.3	3.3	53.4	1 077	72	195	1 814	NA	NA	NA
Charlton	22.2	2 392	45.2	31.7	3.9	0.3	4.4	6.3	681	48	51	562	NA	NA	NA
Chatham	642.5	2 844	38.2	5.2	6.8	0.3	7.0	569.2	2 519	2 664	5 077	14 464	NA	NA	NA
Chattahoochee	5.3	327	55.0	1.5	4.4	0.2	5.3	1.3	81	0	13 328	193	NA	NA	NA
Chattooga	45.3	1 975	53.4	0.7	5.4	0.2	6.7	8.3	362	36	88	1 496	NA	NA	NA
Cherokee	217.0	1 710	62.8	10.6	3.9	0.2	3.9	176.4	1 391	232	519	4 441	NA	NA	NA
Clarke	325.7	3 578	23.7	39.8	5.6	0.8	1.9	212.9	2 339	1 551	673	15 226	NA	NA	NA
Clay	5.6	1 629	49.5	2.5	6.3	0.6	8.0	1.6	458	69	13	245	NA	NA	NA
Clayton	424.7	2 080	54.2	4.6	6.1	0.7	3.0	270.2	1 323	2 093	840	11 642	NA	NA	NA
Clinch	20.0	3 008	44.6	25.1	3.1	0.2	5.1	3.8	579	19	26	580	NA	NA	NA
Cobb	1 260.2	2 287	48.6	2.4	5.4	0.8	10.1	1 600.0	2 904	2 633	3 359	30 180	NA	NA	NA
Coffee	66.3	1 955	59.8	1.8	5.3	0.4	10.6	17.1	503	115	132	2 135	NA	NA	NA
Colquitt	113.8	2 872	40.3	34.6	2.4	0.1	2.7	19.6	496	104	155	3 205	NA	NA	NA
Columbia	136.8	1 540	64.2	0.8	6.9	0.3	5.7	124.6	1 403	90	351	2 839	NA	NA	NA
Cook	27.2	1 861	57.7	1.2	5.4	5.3	6.5	14.5	991	32	58	803	NA	NA	NA
Coweta	141.6	1 755	52.6	2.7	4.0	0.1	6.9	91.5	1 135	182	328	3 223	NA	NA	NA
Crawford	14.8	1 342	66.6	1.3	4.4	0.2	8.1	2.1	191	11	41	454	NA	NA	NA
Crisp	45.0	2 179	57.6	1.1	6.9	0.2	5.8	36.7	1 775	58	80	1 499	NA	NA	NA
Dade	19.3	1 317	65.2	1.1	5.3	0.3	6.3	7.6	517	19	58	568	NA	NA	NA
Dawson	26.8	1 928	69.5	0.8	4.2	0.1	4.4	21.2	1 524	27	57	629	NA	NA	NA
Decatur	80.3	3 018	37.7	40.2	4.5	0.2	3.0	19.5	732	63	104	2 512	NA	NA	NA
De Kalb	1 661.5	2 827	34.6	40.1	4.0	0.3	1.2	1 039.2	1 768	10 767	2 920	29 116	NA	NA	NA
Dodge	44.4	2 439	45.2	36.5	2.8	1.0	3.8	4.3	238	46	70	1 926	NA	NA	NA
Dooly	22.8	2 187	48.9	11.2	4.8	0.1	8.7	7.9	762	52	40	960	NA	NA	NA
Dougherty	262.3	2 738	41.2	13.6	5.2	0.2	1.5	83.0	867	2 839	1 109	8 157	NA	NA	NA
Douglas	157.1	1 812	59.6	4.9	5.1	0.3	2.9	129.8	1 498	156	346	3 626	NA	NA	NA
Early	28.2	2 318	58.0	12.0	4.3	0.1	3.9	6.2	514	49	47	751	NA	NA	NA
Echols	4.9	2 014	77.6	1.6	3.3	0.2	3.9	0.0	7	0	0	170	NA	NA	NA
Effingham	72.3	2 063	55.2	13.7	2.8	0.7	8.0	50.1	1 429	58	141	1 825	NA	NA	NA
Elbert	44.2	2 311	45.8	29.9	4.4	0.5	2.8	7.4	384	147	75	1 435	NA	NA	NA
Emanuel	62.5	2 974	54.3	22.8	2.5	0.2	5.5	12.7	605	98	81	1 946	NA	NA	NA
Evans	21.0	2 151	44.8	22.2	4.2	0.1	6.0	2.4	247	57	38	619	NA	NA	NA

1. Based on the resident population estimated as of July 1 of the year shown.

Table B. States and Counties — **Land Area and Population**

Population and population characteristics, 1999 — Race (percent), Age (percent)

STATE/County code	MSA/PMSA/NECMA code[1]	County Type[2]	STATE County	Land area,[3] (sq km) 1990	Total persons	Rank	Per square kilometer	White	Black	Am. Indian, Eskimo, Aleut	Asian and Pacific Islander	Percent Hispanic[4]	Under 5 years	5 to 17 years	18 to 24 years	25 to 34 years	35 to 44 years	45 to 54 years
				1	2	3	4	5	6	7	8	9	10	11	12	13	14	15
			GEORGIA—Cont'd															
13 111	...	9	Fannin	999	18 945	1 819	19.0	99.4	0.1	0.3	0.2	0.9	5.6	16.4	6.5	10.8	14.6	13.8
13 113	0520	1	Fayette	511	92 378	546	180.8	90.0	6.8	0.2	3.1	3.4	6.7	21.0	6.6	11.6	21.6	16.6
13 115	...	4	Floyd	1 329	85 512	587	64.3	82.2	16.7	0.2	0.9	2.0	6.5	17.1	10.0	12.8	15.2	13.5
13 117	0520	1	Forsyth	585	96 686	530	165.3	99.3	0.0	0.3	0.4	2.9	7.8	18.1	8.6	16.0	18.4	15.3
13 119	...	8	Franklin	682	19 311	1 798	28.3	86.9	12.6	0.2	0.3	1.0	6.1	16.9	9.2	11.8	14.5	14.4
13 121	0520	0	Fulton	1 369	744 827	61	544.1	42.5	55.3	0.2	2.1	3.4	7.1	17.1	11.0	16.7	18.6	13.4
13 123	...	8	Gilmer	1 105	19 766	1 773	17.9	99.3	0.3	0.1	0.3	1.7	6.3	17.7	7.9	11.6	14.8	14.4
13 125	...	9	Glascock	373	2 544	3 019	6.8	84.5	15.4	0.1	0.0	0.6	5.4	17.8	7.6	11.7	14.4	14.7
13 127	...	5	Glynn	1 094	67 945	713	62.1	68.9	30.0	0.2	0.9	1.8	7.0	18.2	8.3	13.1	15.5	13.5
13 129	...	6	Gordon	920	41 966	1 041	45.6	94.2	4.8	0.3	0.7	1.2	7.0	19.4	8.9	13.9	16.0	14.7
13 131	...	6	Grady	1 187	21 600	1 676	18.2	62.5	36.8	0.5	0.2	2.5	7.0	20.9	8.7	12.9	14.7	13.0
13 133	...	6	Greene	1 006	14 094	2 126	14.0	44.2	55.7	0.1	0.0	1.5	7.1	23.1	8.5	11.6	14.8	12.9
13 135	0520	0	Gwinnett	1 121	545 632	96	486.7	88.4	6.1	0.2	5.3	4.9	8.6	19.1	8.3	19.4	20.5	12.6
13 137	...	7	Habersham	721	32 530	1 295	45.1	90.5	5.9	0.3	3.3	2.4	6.2	17.0	11.7	12.5	14.6	13.2
13 139	...	6	Hall	1 020	123 290	427	120.9	88.0	10.4	0.2	1.4	8.9	7.7	18.2	10.1	15.1	16.2	13.5
13 141	...	9	Hancock	1 226	9 046	2 503	7.4	18.0	81.9	0.1	0.0	1.0	6.9	22.7	9.0	12.1	14.9	11.7
13 143	...	6	Haralson	731	25 070	1 528	34.3	91.1	8.3	0.2	0.4	0.9	7.3	18.8	8.8	12.9	15.1	14.3
13 145	1800	2	Harris	1 201	22 634	1 628	18.8	68.7	30.6	0.3	0.4	1.1	6.0	18.6	7.7	12.7	17.5	14.7
13 147	...	6	Hart	601	22 124	1 652	36.8	75.0	24.5	0.1	0.3	0.7	6.4	17.8	8.6	12.3	14.5	13.8
13 149	...	8	Heard	767	10 490	2 379	13.7	82.6	16.8	0.2	0.5	1.8	7.1	21.2	8.8	13.4	15.5	14.4
13 151	0520	1	Henry	836	113 443	462	135.7	85.7	13.1	0.2	1.1	1.7	7.8	19.4	8.3	15.8	17.7	14.8
13 153	4680	2	Houston	976	107 644	487	110.3	71.9	25.7	0.3	2.1	3.2	7.8	19.6	8.6	15.7	16.4	13.8
13 155	...	7	Irwin	924	9 181	2 494	9.9	63.9	35.7	0.1	0.3	1.1	7.4	21.3	8.5	11.9	13.7	13.6
13 157	...	6	Jackson	887	39 057	1 109	44.0	87.2	12.3	0.2	0.3	1.1	7.1	19.2	8.8	14.1	16.2	14.7
13 159	...	8	Jasper	960	10 589	2 371	11.0	59.5	40.1	0.2	0.2	1.4	7.3	20.3	7.9	12.9	16.9	12.6
13 161	...	7	Jeff Davis	864	12 714	2 231	14.7	80.6	18.8	0.1	0.4	2.2	7.1	20.3	9.7	13.1	15.8	13.4
13 163	...	8	Jefferson	1 367	17 858	1 879	13.1	38.3	61.4	0.1	0.2	0.4	7.5	22.1	9.9	12.1	15.0	11.7
13 165	...	7	Jenkins	906	8 401	2 559	9.3	52.6	47.0	0.1	0.3	0.3	7.6	20.8	8.5	12.3	14.8	12.7
13 167	...	9	Johnson	788	8 293	2 568	10.5	60.3	39.4	0.0	0.2	0.7	7.4	21.4	8.4	12.4	13.3	12.3
13 169	4680	2	Jones	1 020	23 307	1 601	22.9	68.1	31.3	0.2	0.4	0.7	7.1	19.9	8.4	14.5	17.4	15.0
13 171	...	6	Lamar	479	15 010	2 063	31.3	60.1	39.6	0.1	0.2	0.8	6.6	19.0	9.8	12.7	15.5	13.5
13 173	...	9	Lanier	484	6 959	2 681	14.4	66.6	32.1	0.7	0.7	2.2	7.8	21.6	9.4	13.8	15.3	13.6
13 175	...	6	Laurens	2 105	43 927	1 002	20.9	60.3	38.9	0.1	0.6	0.9	7.1	20.7	8.7	12.9	15.5	12.9
13 177	0120	3	Lee	922	23 341	1 600	25.3	76.8	22.5	0.3	0.5	1.3	7.5	24.6	8.3	15.5	19.7	11.8
13 179	...	4	Liberty	1 345	59 694	797	44.4	52.8	42.8	0.5	3.9	10.5	11.8	20.2	19.7	20.8	12.8	6.8
13 181	...	8	Lincoln	547	8 339	2 564	15.2	56.1	43.5	0.0	0.3	1.4	6.2	19.7	8.6	12.5	15.0	13.5
13 183	...	9	Long	1 039	8 709	2 535	8.4	72.7	25.7	0.4	1.2	5.2	10.4	20.8	13.9	14.3	14.5	11.2
13 185	...	5	Lowndes	1 306	85 413	589	65.4	61.1	37.0	0.3	1.5	2.3	7.9	20.1	13.0	15.0	15.5	11.6
13 187	...	7	Lumpkin	737	19 772	1 772	26.8	82.6	2.1	1.8	0.6	3.0	6.9	17.8	13.4	14.5	14.8	13.2
13 189	0600	2	McDuffie	673	21 814	1 666	32.4	57.3	42.3	0.2	0.2	0.8	7.5	21.2	8.5	13.2	16.5	12.9
13 191	...	9	McIntosh	1 123	10 114	2 411	9.0	50.6	49.0	0.2	0.2	1.4	7.1	20.2	8.4	13.0	15.1	13.7
13 193	...	6	Macon	1 045	13 126	2 202	12.6	35.2	64.3	0.1	0.3	0.7	7.3	23.5	8.8	12.7	15.0	12.6
13 195	0500	3	Madison	737	25 208	1 523	34.2	87.9	11.4	0.2	0.5	1.6	7.0	19.1	8.7	14.1	16.8	14.5
13 197	...	8	Marion	951	6 779	2 702	7.1	51.9	47.5	0.3	0.3	0.8	7.6	21.1	9.1	14.1	15.7	14.1
13 199	...	6	Meriwether	1 304	23 043	1 611	17.7	49.0	50.7	0.1	0.1	0.9	7.4	21.1	9.6	12.7	14.7	13.0
13 201	...	9	Miller	733	6 318	2 749	8.6	67.7	32.1	0.1	0.1	0.7	6.3	20.7	8.3	11.3	13.3	13.9
13 205	...	6	Mitchell	1 326	21 219	1 696	16.0	46.2	53.4	0.3	0.2	1.9	7.4	23.9	9.3	12.2	14.1	12.5
13 207	...	6	Monroe	1 025	20 032	1 760	19.5	61.9	37.4	0.2	0.4	1.0	6.5	19.6	9.0	13.5	17.5	14.2
13 209	...	9	Montgomery	635	7 854	2 618	12.4	64.9	34.4	0.2	0.5	3.5	6.4	20.0	14.0	13.7	14.5	12.3
13 211	...	6	Morgan	906	15 437	2 040	17.0	59.2	40.4	0.1	0.4	1.7	7.2	19.9	8.7	13.9	15.4	13.7
13 213	...	7	Murray	892	33 922	1 257	38.0	99.0	0.3	0.2	0.5	1.2	7.8	20.4	9.6	15.6	15.9	14.1
13 215	1800	2	Muscogee	560	182 058	292	325.1	54.5	42.7	0.4	2.4	5.2	7.8	18.7	11.0	15.2	15.1	11.6
13 217	0520	1	Newton	716	60 583	787	84.6	72.0	27.4	0.2	0.4	1.8	7.9	19.8	10.2	14.1	15.6	14.0
13 219	0500	3	Oconee	481	24 526	1 550	51.0	89.3	9.6	0.2	1.0	2.1	7.7	20.4	7.7	14.0	19.5	14.1
13 221	...	8	Oglethorpe	1 143	11 564	2 304	10.1	69.5	30.1	0.2	0.1	1.2	7.1	18.8	8.7	13.9	16.4	15.0
13 223	0520	1	Paulding	812	79 587	634	98.0	94.2	5.1	0.3	0.3	1.5	9.4	20.2	9.5	18.2	17.1	12.7
13 225	4680	2	Peach	391	24 996	1 531	63.9	46.3	52.7	0.4	0.6	2.6	6.6	19.9	13.5	12.7	15.2	12.9
13 227	0520	1	Pickens	601	21 024	1 716	35.0	97.1	2.3	0.3	0.3	0.7	7.0	17.7	8.7	13.2	15.5	14.7
13 229	...	7	Pierce	888	15 804	2 014	17.8	85.0	14.7	0.2	0.1	1.7	6.4	21.1	8.3	12.4	16.1	14.4
13 231	...	8	Pike	566	13 104	2 206	23.2	74.6	24.6	0.2	0.4	1.0	7.2	19.3	8.3	13.3	16.0	14.9
13 233	...	6	Polk	806	36 627	1 176	45.4	81.9	17.4	0.2	0.5	2.8	7.0	19.1	8.9	12.7	14.6	13.9
13 235	...	6	Pulaski	641	8 359	2 561	13.0	61.7	37.7	0.1	0.5	1.8	6.5	19.8	7.8	11.8	14.5	14.2
13 237	...	6	Putnam	892	18 199	1 858	20.4	60.8	38.6	0.1	0.5	1.2	6.4	18.5	8.4	13.0	14.8	14.4
13 239	...	9	Quitman	393	2 449	3 024	6.2	44.7	54.7	0.3	0.3	0.2	6.8	18.3	8.7	10.5	13.8	12.9
13 241	...	9	Rabun	961	13 687	2 157	14.2	98.9	0.5	0.3	0.3	1.1	5.5	15.5	7.1	10.7	15.2	14.9
13 243	...	7	Randolph	1 112	8 012	2 597	7.2	36.1	63.1	0.0	0.7	0.6	6.7	22.7	10.8	11.4	13.4	10.9

1. MSA = Metropolitan Statistical Area. PMSA = Primary MSA. NECMA = New England County Metropolitan Area. See Appendix A for explanation of these concepts. See Appendix B for list of metropolitan areas identified by type, with component counties.   2. County typology code from the Economic Research Service of USDA. See Appendix A for definition.   3. Dry land or land partially or temporarily covered by water.   4. Hispanic persons may be of any race.

Table B. States and Counties — **Population and Households**

	Population, 1999 (cont'd) Age (percent) (cont'd)				Population — change and components of change, 1980–1999							Households, 1990				
					Total persons		Percent change		Components of change, 1990–1999						Percent	
STATE County	55 to 64 years	65 to 74 years	75 years and over	Percent female	1990	1980	1980–1990	1990–1999	Births	Deaths	Net migration	Number	Percent change, 1980–1990	Persons per house-hold	Female family house-holder[1]	One person
	16	17	18	19	20	21	22	23	24	25	26	27	28	29	30	31
GEORGIA—Cont'd																
Fannin	13.5	10.5	8.2	51.6	15 992	14 748	8.4	18.5	1 818	1 796	2 959	6 334	14.7	2.50	8.3	22.1
Fayette	7.1	5.3	3.6	50.4	62 415	29 043	114.9	48.0	7 494	3 572	26 032	21 054	128.6	2.96	6.8	12.5
Floyd	10.4	7.6	6.8	52.4	81 251	79 800	1.8	5.2	11 015	8 499	2 009	30 518	7.2	2.55	12.6	23.6
Forsyth	9.0	4.0	3.0	49.3	44 083	27 958	57.7	119.3	9 641	3 213	45 576	15 938	69.6	2.75	7.0	16.3
Franklin	11.4	8.5	7.1	52.0	16 650	15 185	9.6	16.0	2 397	1 943	2 254	6 365	18.7	2.56	9.9	23.3
Fulton	7.3	4.6	4.3	52.3	648 776	589 904	10.0	14.8	111 115	56 630	43 146	257 140	14.1	2.44	18.5	31.0
Gilmer	11.8	8.4	7.1	50.9	13 368	11 110	20.3	47.9	2 277	1 475	5 629	5 072	28.8	2.60	9.0	20.4
Glascock	10.7	7.6	10.1	53.1	2 357	2 382	-1.0	7.9	292	306	216	867	3.7	2.59	9.7	22.6
Glynn	9.5	8.3	6.5	52.5	62 496	54 981	13.7	8.7	8 490	5 884	2 961	23 947	20.8	2.57	14.0	23.6
Gordon	9.4	5.8	4.9	50.7	35 067	30 070	16.6	19.7	5 367	3 128	4 717	12 778	24.3	2.72	10.3	19.8
Grady	9.1	6.8	7.0	52.4	20 279	19 845	2.2	6.5	2 807	2 121	706	7 354	11.1	2.72	15.2	22.3
Greene	8.9	6.9	6.3	53.3	11 793	11 391	3.5	19.5	1 805	1 380	1 908	4 083	8.7	2.86	19.4	23.9
Gwinnett	5.7	3.5	2.4	50.2	352 910	166 808	111.6	54.6	66 898	15 856	141 978	126 971	129.9	2.77	8.3	17.7
Habersham	10.6	7.6	6.5	48.9	27 622	25 020	10.4	17.8	3 698	2 500	3 791	9 966	18.7	2.59	8.5	21.2
Hall	8.8	5.7	4.7	50.3	95 434	75 649	26.2	29.2	17 880	7 755	17 841	34 721	33.2	2.70	11.1	20.0
Hancock	8.4	7.4	6.8	54.6	8 908	9 466	-5.9	1.5	1 271	913	-199	2 969	6.4	2.95	26.5	24.4
Haralson	10.1	6.5	6.2	51.8	21 966	18 422	19.2	14.1	2 926	2 251	2 476	8 248	26.8	2.63	10.9	22.2
Harris	10.7	7.0	5.0	50.3	17 788	15 464	15.0	27.2	2 556	1 641	3 968	6 454	23.3	2.73	11.1	19.1
Hart	11.0	8.4	7.3	51.8	19 712	18 585	6.1	12.2	2 317	2 052	2 189	7 459	18.7	2.60	12.1	22.0
Heard	8.9	5.6	5.1	51.0	8 628	6 520	32.3	21.6	1 224	846	1 484	3 093	40.3	2.75	11.8	19.8
Henry	8.8	4.2	3.1	50.3	58 741	36 309	61.8	93.1	12 675	4 650	46 335	20 012	72.1	2.91	8.9	13.2
Houston	8.8	6.0	3.4	51.3	89 208	77 605	15.0	20.7	13 819	5 929	9 462	32 433	27.1	2.71	12.3	20.6
Irwin	9.7	6.9	7.2	52.6	8 649	8 988	-3.8	6.2	1 082	1 052	531	3 142	4.3	2.71	15.6	23.9
Jackson	9.3	5.6	5.0	50.3	30 005	25 343	18.4	30.2	4 893	2 834	7 012	10 721	24.4	2.73	10.2	19.5
Jasper	9.7	6.6	5.9	51.6	8 453	7 553	11.9	25.3	1 090	841	1 884	3 036	18.9	2.76	14.1	21.2
Jeff Davis	9.4	6.2	4.9	50.7	12 032	11 473	4.9	5.7	1 737	1 169	160	4 357	15.5	2.74	13.6	20.0
Jefferson	8.1	6.7	6.8	53.9	17 408	18 403	-5.4	2.6	2 674	1 968	-201	6 093	2.5	2.79	22.2	24.6
Jenkins	9.6	7.5	6.0	52.8	8 247	8 841	-6.7	1.9	1 195	920	-98	2 951	1.5	2.75	17.8	23.4
Johnson	9.8	7.7	7.4	53.5	8 329	8 660	-3.8	-0.4	1 194	907	-292	3 010	1.9	2.71	17.1	24.8
Jones	8.2	5.5	4.0	51.3	20 739	16 579	25.1	12.4	2 437	1 437	1 593	7 300	38.5	2.81	12.8	18.4
Lamar	9.5	7.1	6.2	52.7	13 038	12 215	6.7	15.1	1 818	1 322	1 510	4 669	16.4	2.73	15.1	21.4
Lanier	9.3	4.5	4.7	50.8	5 531	5 654	-2.2	25.8	783	622	1 257	1 965	7.8	2.78	15.1	21.3
Laurens	9.4	7.0	5.7	52.3	39 988	36 990	8.1	9.9	5 867	4 128	2 324	14 514	16.6	2.68	15.8	23.2
Lee	6.7	3.6	2.4	49.6	16 250	11 684	39.1	43.6	2 323	815	5 565	5 199	42.8	3.00	13.2	15.0
Liberty	3.5	2.6	1.9	46.3	52 745	37 583	40.3	13.2	13 674	2 041	-9 642	15 136	57.2	2.99	12.1	14.8
Lincoln	10.2	8.3	6.0	51.7	7 442	6 716	10.8	12.1	894	767	791	2 702	23.7	2.74	14.1	21.9
Long	7.2	4.6	3.1	49.9	6 202	4 524	37.1	40.4	1 394	434	1 445	2 196	43.0	2.79	9.9	20.4
Lowndes	7.5	5.2	4.4	51.3	75 981	67 972	11.8	12.4	13 032	5 921	1 572	26 311	16.4	2.72	15.2	21.8
Lumpkin	9.3	5.4	4.8	50.1	14 573	10 762	35.4	35.7	1 943	1 203	4 384	4 976	46.9	2.68	8.8	19.3
McDuffie	8.8	6.4	5.0	52.8	20 119	18 546	8.5	8.4	2 894	1 961	798	7 270	15.9	2.73	17.7	21.4
McIntosh	10.0	6.8	5.6	51.8	8 634	8 046	7.3	17.1	1 369	917	1 040	3 186	21.1	2.71	16.9	22.9
Macon	8.1	6.1	5.9	53.4	13 114	14 003	-6.3	0.1	1 954	1 523	-388	4 388	0.4	2.92	23.8	22.6
Madison	9.0	5.6	5.2	50.8	21 050	17 747	18.6	19.8	3 184	1 818	2 820	7 740	26.4	2.70	9.7	18.9
Marion	8.4	5.3	4.6	51.8	5 590	5 297	5.5	21.3	830	551	919	1 962	16.3	2.81	16.2	20.0
Meriwether	8.9	6.6	6.0	52.1	22 411	21 229	-5.6	2.8	2 998	2 391	92	7 637	11.1	2.87	17.8	22.1
Miller	10.0	7.9	8.2	52.5	6 280	7 038	-10.8	0.6	755	693	2	2 336	-2.9	2.65	13.7	23.7
Mitchell	8.4	6.3	6.0	53.1	20 275	21 114	-4.0	4.7	3 162	2 131	-35	6 798	4.8	2.94	21.4	20.8
Monroe	9.0	5.6	5.0	50.9	17 113	14 610	17.1	17.1	2 417	1 647	2 160	5 838	25.1	2.83	13.7	19.4
Montgomery	8.3	5.5	5.4	49.3	7 379	7 011	5.2	6.4	995	634	132	2 493	12.6	2.69	13.0	24.0
Morgan	8.7	6.5	6.0	51.8	12 883	11 572	11.3	19.8	1 883	1 166	1 858	4 399	20.1	2.89	15.5	19.4
Murray	8.4	4.5	3.7	50.2	26 147	19 685	32.8	29.7	4 321	1 855	5 341	9 363	43.2	2.77	9.5	17.4
Muscogee	8.8	6.6	5.1	51.8	179 280	170 108	5.4	1.5	30 117	15 967	-14 888	65 858	11.4	2.61	17.9	24.5
Newton	8.8	5.1	4.5	52.0	41 808	34 666	20.6	44.9	8 010	3 845	14 602	14 401	31.2	2.85	13.3	18.3
Oconee	7.5	4.6	4.5	50.8	17 618	12 427	41.8	39.2	2 490	1 196	5 612	6 156	45.3	2.84	9.0	16.0
Oglethorpe	9.7	5.3	5.1	51.6	9 763	8 929	9.3	18.4	1 277	860	1 414	3 581	21.5	2.70	12.5	20.6
Paulding	7.8	2.9	2.3	49.7	41 611	26 110	59.4	91.3	9 287	2 908	31 307	14 326	63.8	2.88	8.5	13.7
Peach	8.5	6.1	4.6	52.5	21 189	19 151	10.6	18.0	3 108	1 630	2 366	7 142	15.6	2.79	19.4	20.0
Pickens	10.8	6.8	5.6	50.7	14 432	11 652	23.9	45.7	2 031	1 525	6 054	5 386	29.4	2.65	8.4	19.5
Pierce	9.8	6.5	5.2	51.3	13 328	11 897	12.0	18.6	1 925	1 275	1 860	4 807	22.4	2.76	10.5	20.4
Pike	9.7	5.8	5.4	50.1	10 224	8 937	14.4	28.2	1 441	1 000	2 430	3 526	24.1	2.86	9.0	18.3
Polk	10.2	7.0	6.6	51.8	33 815	32 382	4.4	8.3	5 072	3 810	1 670	12 519	9.7	2.67	13.0	22.6
Pulaski	10.3	7.6	7.4	53.4	8 108	8 950	-9.4	3.1	1 048	1 001	235	3 098	1.0	2.58	16.3	27.2
Putnam	10.8	8.1	5.6	51.1	14 137	10 295	37.3	28.7	1 821	1 388	3 631	5 229	53.9	2.65	13.4	21.4
Quitman	10.7	11.2	7.1	53.8	2 210	2 357	-6.2	10.8	324	312	238	857	11.0	2.57	19.5	25.0
Rabun	12.7	9.6	8.7	51.2	11 648	10 466	11.3	17.5	1 468	1 438	2 018	4 630	19.0	2.48	8.9	22.4
Randolph	9.0	7.9	7.2	54.3	8 023	9 599	-16.4	0.1	1 140	971	-150	2 815	-9.9	2.73	21.1	27.5

1. No spouse present.

Table B. States and Counties — **Vital Statistics, Health Resources, and Crime**

STATE County	Births, average 1996–1998 Total	Births, average 1996–1998 Rate[1]	Deaths, average 1996–1998 Number Total	Deaths, average 1996–1998 Number Infant[2]	Deaths, average 1996–1998 Rate Total[1]	Deaths, average 1996–1998 Rate Infant[3]	Physicians,[4] 1998 Number	Physicians,[4] 1998 Rate[5]	Hospitals,[4] 1998 Number	Beds Number	Beds Rate[5]	Medicare enrollees 1999	Serious crimes known to police, 1998[6] Total Number	Serious crimes known to police, 1998[6] Total Rate[7]
	32	33	34	35	36	37	38	39	40	41	42	43	44	45
GEORGIA—Cont'd														
Fannin	211	11.6	212	2	11.7	9.5	13	70	1	51	274	4 042	178	964
Fayette	849	10.0	462	7	5.4	8.6	139	157	0	0	0	8 017	1 572	1 811
Floyd	1 179	13.9	920	9	10.8	7.9	252	296	2	505	593	14 631	4 691	5 429
Forsyth	1 411	18.2	417	7	5.4	4.7	49	57	1	28	33	5 903	3 026	3 913
Franklin	256	13.7	225	3	12.1	13.0	10	52	1	333	1 745	4 009	641	3 392
Fulton	12 482	17.1	6 291	122	8.6	9.8	2 814	381	13	4 287	580	80 069	79 299	10 755
Gilmer	298	16.6	174	2	9.7	5.6	16	86	1	50	268	3 709	195	1 089
Glascock	34	13.5	27	0	10.8	0.0	0	0	0	0	0	543	16	629
Glynn	878	13.2	665	8	10.0	8.7	185	275	1	337	501	10 937	5 310	7 804
Gordon	620	15.4	359	4	8.9	6.5	43	105	1	50	122	5 707	1 750	4 255
Grady	310	14.4	233	3	10.8	10.8	16	74	1	49	228	3 368	953	4 340
Greene	206	15.4	140	2	10.5	9.7	13	95	1	58	425	2 369	570	4 389
Gwinnett	8 069	16.2	2 002	46	4.0	5.7	630	121	3	428	82	30 227	19 241	3 872
Habersham	435	13.9	312	3	10.0	6.9	28	88	1	137	430	5 463	901	2 941
Hall	2 195	18.9	906	10	7.8	4.7	212	178	2	447	375	15 261	5 344	4 511
Hancock	130	14.4	103	1	11.4	10.3	5	55	1	52	569	1 519	66	719
Haralson	334	13.8	268	2	11.1	5.0	5	20	1	59	239	3 935	376	1 525
Harris	275	12.5	198	3	9.0	9.7	14	63	0	0	0	2 679	268	1 181
Hart	244	11.4	227	2	10.6	8.2	16	73	1	41	188	3 309	NA	NA
Heard	144	14.5	92	2	9.2	11.6	3	30	0	0	0	1 236	129	1 268
Henry	1 655	16.9	591	12	6.0	7.0	90	86	1	119	114	9 744	3 583	3 796
Houston	1 497	14.5	674	12	6.5	8.2	125	118	2	236	223	11 274	5 991	5 879
Irwin	111	12.5	114	1	12.9	6.0	17	189	1	34	379	1 301	NA	NA
Jackson	597	16.3	336	6	9.2	10.0	15	40	1	233	619	5 390	1 411	3 789
Jasper	121	12.3	99	2	10.1	16.5	3	30	1	68	670	1 332	215	2 133
Jeff Davis	204	16.1	130	2	10.2	9.8	9	71	1	50	392	1 964	426	3 308
Jefferson	272	15.3	199	3	11.2	9.8	8	45	1	37	208	3 122	NA	NA
Jenkins	125	14.8	91	0	10.8	0.0	5	59	1	38	450	1 408	185	2 154
Johnson	133	15.9	97	1	11.7	7.5	3	36	0	0	0	1 417	86	1 010
Jones	266	11.8	162	2	7.2	7.5	9	39	0	0	0	1 754	496	2 147
Lamar	201	14.0	147	2	10.2	8.3	7	48	0	0	0	2 323	501	3 345
Lanier	80	11.9	71	1	10.5	8.3	3	43	1	40	573	805	41	589
Laurens	618	14.2	453	9	10.4	14.0	94	215	1	190	434	6 929	1 853	4 173
Lee	288	13.3	97	2	4.4	6.9	7	31	0	0	0	1 556	670	3 000
Liberty	1 517	25.5	233	15	3.9	9.7	53	90	1	49	83	2 972	1 444	2 396
Lincoln	83	10.2	91	0	11.2	4.0	5	60	0	0	0	1 368	103	1 246
Long	162	19.6	52	2	6.2	10.3	0	0	0	0	0	567	184	2 160
Lowndes	1 440	17.0	647	20	7.6	14.1	169	198	2	359	421	10 354	6 669	7 779
Lumpkin	219	12.1	159	1	8.8	6.1	15	79	1	52	274	2 097	141	762
McDuffie	311	14.4	230	3	10.6	10.7	15	69	1	47	216	3 017	685	3 108
McIntosh	141	14.4	100	1	10.2	9.5	6	60	0	0	0	1 499	406	4 003
Macon	203	15.3	164	2	12.4	11.5	8	60	0	0	0	1 844	357	2 757
Madison	343	14.2	213	2	8.8	4.9	4	16	0	0	0	3 606	NA	NA
Marion	95	14.5	69	3	10.6	28.1	4	60	0	0	0	727	145	2 176
Meriwether	297	13.0	256	2	11.2	7.8	10	43	1	96	415	3 322	627	2 681
Miller	83	13.1	66	1	10.5	12.1	5	78	1	135	2 106	1 107	182	2 839
Mitchell	356	16.8	231	4	11.0	12.2	13	61	1	26	123	3 219	614	2 853
Monroe	259	13.3	197	3	10.1	11.6	7	36	1	40	204	2 358	573	2 913
Montgomery	113	14.6	71	1	9.2	8.8	0	0	0	0	0	1 165	NA	NA
Morgan	191	13.1	147	1	10.1	3.5	8	53	1	26	172	2 172	379	2 677
Murray	516	16.2	236	6	7.4	11.0	10	31	1	42	129	3 538	713	2 186
Muscogee	3 035	16.6	1 742	50	9.5	16.6	444	243	3	871	477	25 378	12 107	6 509
Newton	959	17.3	457	7	8.2	7.3	34	59	1	90	156	7 469	1 986	3 528
Oconee	276	12.0	151	1	6.6	3.6	31	131	0	0	0	2 387	399	1 695
Oglethorpe	133	11.9	94	0	8.4	0.0	3	26	0	0	0	1 131	241	2 100
Paulding	1 152	16.8	366	6	5.3	5.5	15	20	1	175	238	4 276	1 790	2 543
Peach	342	14.3	185	5	7.8	13.6	12	49	1	36	147	3 453	1 013	4 126
Pickens	236	12.7	172	1	9.3	2.8	20	102	1	91	462	2 888	293	1 545
Pierce	229	14.7	143	1	9.2	5.8	10	63	0	0	0	2 504	NA	NA
Pike	175	14.4	121	1	9.9	3.8	2	16	0	0	0	1 786	189	1 496
Polk	577	16.1	403	4	11.2	7.5	19	52	1	35	96	6 500	1 500	4 103
Pulaski	121	14.5	99	2	11.9	16.6	14	167	1	55	655	1 512	221	2 597
Putnam	219	12.9	162	3	9.5	15.2	14	80	1	50	285	2 620	435	2 527
Quitman	32	13.0	29	0	11.8	0.0	0	0	0	0	0	615	120	4 810
Rabun	172	12.9	169	0	12.8	1.9	30	224	2	66	492	2 817	278	2 364
Randolph	127	16.0	107	2	13.4	13.1	5	63	1	120	1 523	1 419	NA	NA

1. Per 1,000 estimated resident population, average 1996–1998.   2. Deaths of infants under 1 year old.   3. Deaths of infants under 1 year old per 1,000 live births.   4. Data subject to copyright.   5. Per 100,000 resident population as of July 1 of the year shown.   6. Data for serious crimes have not been adjusted for underreporting; this may affect comparability between geographic areas and over time.   7. Per 100,000 population estimated by the FBI.

Table B. States and Counties — Crime, Education, Money Income, and Poverty

STATE County	Serious crimes known to police, 1998[1] (cont'd) Rate[2] Violent	Property	Education — School enrollment and attainment, 1990 Enrollment[3] Total	Percent private	Attainment[4] (percent) High school graduate or more	Bachelor's degree or more	Local government expenditures, fiscal 1997[5] Total current expenditures (mil dol)	Current expenditures per student (dollars)	Money income — 1989 Per capita[6] (dollars)	Households Median Dollars	Percent change, 1979–1989 (constant 1989 dollars)	Percent with $100,000 or more	Income and poverty, 1997 Percent below poverty level Median household income	All persons	Persons under 18	Persons 5–17 in families
	46	47	48	49	50	51	52	53	54	55	56	57	58	59	60	61
GEORGIA—Cont'd																
Fannin	70	894	3 164	5.0	55.8	7.8	15.7	5 223	9 430	19 023	14.4	0.9	26 062	16.5	26.9	26.5
Fayette	56	1 755	17 522	12.0	86.5	25.8	86.9	4 997	19 025	50 167	17.0	8.3	69 309	4.0	6.0	5.4
Floyd	845	4 584	19 579	20.0	63.9	13.7	84.0	5 553	12 121	25 536	3.8	2.3	33 584	15.7	25.3	23.5
Forsyth	445	3 468	9 689	8.0	67.6	15.6	59.1	5 134	15 763	36 642	29.8	5.2	60 250	5.1	8.2	8.1
Franklin	608	2 784	3 421	13.5	54.1	9.5	16.7	4 901	10 390	21 663	10.3	1.3	28 909	16.6	25.9	25.3
Fulton	1 867	8 888	166 389	20.6	77.8	31.6	797.4	6 644	18 452	29 978	27.9	8.7	39 047	18.3	29.8	27.5
Gilmer	84	1 005	2 677	4.3	52.3	8.6	19.2	5 900	9 676	21 410	14.0	0.8	28 607	14.5	24.7	23.6
Glascock	118	511	471	2.1	50.3	5.3	2.3	4 646	9 585	21 806	12.5	0.7	28 625	15.0	23.8	22.3
Glynn	1 024	6 780	14 394	10.8	74.3	19.9	68.6	6 027	14 055	27 887	10.1	3.3	35 077	16.1	26.5	26.0
Gordon	107	4 148	7 907	8.0	58.4	9.2	39.3	4 966	11 587	26 981	14.4	2.0	33 828	12.7	20.7	19.4
Grady	597	3 743	5 070	7.8	54.9	7.7	22.9	4 834	9 200	19 507	9.2	0.8	25 527	21.8	34.2	31.0
Greene	354	4 035	3 118	10.1	51.2	8.8	13.9	5 634	9 390	20 264	11.8	2.0	27 011	21.6	32.4	31.9
Gwinnett	240	3 632	90 473	12.7	86.7	29.6	506.9	5 591	17 881	43 518	15.0	5.5	56 082	5.6	8.8	8.2
Habersham	353	2 588	6 369	9.7	59.0	12.0	29.1	5 274	10 950	24 386	14.6	1.5	33 582	11.2	17.2	16.7
Hall	316	4 195	21 551	9.8	65.1	15.4	106.1	5 068	13 356	29 774	12.2	3.4	38 435	11.9	20.0	18.6
Hancock	251	468	2 381	8.7	49.5	6.8	9.9	5 555	7 345	17 825	8.4	0.6	23 230	28.3	38.5	37.4
Haralson	89	1 436	4 872	4.6	56.0	7.5	23.2	4 910	9 939	22 775	4.9	0.5	30 043	16.7	26.6	25.9
Harris	128	1 053	4 129	13.9	65.0	13.6	17.7	4 694	13 135	27 616	8.0	4.3	40 645	10.6	16.2	15.2
Hart	NA	NA	4 089	5.6	56.9	9.1	18.1	5 145	11 187	24 333	19.0	2.0	30 794	15.9	25.2	25.2
Heard	236	1 032	1 918	2.6	49.1	5.7	9.8	5 120	9 218	21 513	0.8	1.4	30 441	17.3	25.0	25.3
Henry	239	3 557	14 087	13.0	72.9	10.7	83.4	4 840	14 167	37 550	18.6	2.4	49 548	6.4	10.5	9.8
Houston	414	5 465	23 336	11.8	79.5	16.0	102.7	5 146	12 939	31 229	0.2	1.6	41 188	11.8	19.0	18.0
Irwin	NA	NA	2 272	4.8	53.1	8.3	10.3	5 114	10 057	20 169	12.7	1.6	26 957	21.9	29.2	29.8
Jackson	639	3 150	6 627	5.2	54.5	9.0	34.8	5 001	10 885	25 418	12.5	1.2	34 033	14.4	22.5	21.7
Jasper	169	1 964	1 868	8.2	64.6	10.8	10.0	5 619	10 761	25 736	20.1	1.6	34 164	16.6	26.5	25.6
Jeff Davis	272	3 036	2 853	6.3	55.2	8.3	12.7	4 766	9 632	21 470	-2.5	1.6	28 010	19.1	28.8	27.9
Jefferson	NA	NA	4 470	11.7	49.7	6.2	18.6	4 834	8 317	17 076	5.7	1.1	23 243	26.6	37.0	36.3
Jenkins	547	1 607	2 014	2.5	49.9	7.7	8.5	4 821	8 391	16 967	11.1	0.0	22 686	26.0	36.6	37.4
Johnson	153	857	1 900	4.3	52.0	4.9	7.9	5 299	8 550	18 064	1.9	1.1	24 315	24.8	36.4	36.3
Jones	195	1 952	5 387	13.6	70.2	12.0	17.7	3 934	13 543	31 934	15.1	3.8	39 176	12.2	17.6	17.8
Lamar	668	2 677	3 206	10.0	58.0	10.0	12.3	4 800	10 198	23 336	2.8	1.1	30 332	17.0	26.5	25.3
Lanier	172	417	1 381	2.0	51.2	5.4	7.3	5 071	8 319	17 618	1.9	1.6	24 428	22.4	32.7	34.1
Laurens	432	3 741	9 841	6.0	61.0	12.0	48.4	5 273	10 423	21 788	5.0	2.0	28 950	20.1	30.4	28.5
Lee	242	2 758	5 023	10.7	69.8	13.7	22.1	4 358	11 106	30 974	4.1	1.4	44 326	10.8	14.4	14.3
Liberty	224	2 172	12 587	6.8	82.1	13.4	49.1	4 389	8 986	21 596	10.4	0.8	29 508	18.8	25.6	27.5
Lincoln	97	1 149	1 774	6.8	59.2	8.2	8.0	5 044	9 628	21 472	-3.7	1.4	27 034	18.8	29.1	27.9
Long	164	1 996	1 413	5.2	63.6	5.2	6.7	3 756	8 815	18 802	3.1	0.6	27 388	21.7	33.3	36.7
Lowndes	639	7 140	22 514	8.2	69.8	16.3	77.7	4 937	10 919	23 295	8.9	2.3	30 296	20.5	29.4	29.0
Lumpkin	92	670	4 125	4.0	60.2	11.1	15.0	5 052	10 814	26 116	28.4	1.5	35 598	14.4	21.5	22.1
McDuffie	236	2 872	4 949	9.6	56.1	10.4	23.6	5 224	10 274	21 292	3.1	1.3	28 268	20.3	29.7	29.2
McIntosh	414	3 589	2 000	8.1	56.9	8.7	8.9	4 820	8 878	19 182	11.4	1.1	24 357	22.2	35.1	34.5
Macon	317	2 440	3 650	11.0	53.7	10.1	12.6	5 044	8 101	17 526	2.3	1.2	24 175	29.0	38.7	37.1
Madison	NA	NA	4 555	7.8	59.7	9.7	19.8	4 532	10 997	25 092	17.1	1.3	33 855	14.4	21.6	21.3
Marion	570	1 606	1 418	4.2	54.5	4.6	8.2	4 439	9 779	18 343	3.3	2.0	25 355	22.0	32.1	33.5
Meriwether	312	2 369	5 319	8.3	51.6	6.7	22.8	5 369	8 660	20 212	-1.2	1.1	27 349	21.1	30.1	31.1
Miller	312	2 527	1 496	5.7	57.4	8.2	6.9	5 264	11 096	20 488	13.9	2.7	26 289	23.4	35.1	34.8
Mitchell	372	2 481	5 577	10.3	54.9	7.8	23.0	4 984	8 327	18 926	-3.4	1.5	24 688	26.3	36.6	35.8
Monroe	259	2 654	4 123	16.4	66.2	12.9	18.8	5 078	11 348	27 770	17.8	2.4	34 310	14.8	22.6	21.5
Montgomery	NA	NA	1 940	20.2	57.4	10.1	6.4	4 935	9 283	20 054	17.8	1.8	24 936	23.3	33.4	33.3
Morgan	162	2 515	3 154	8.0	59.6	11.0	15.3	5 504	10 713	26 018	19.6	2.4	33 165	16.2	24.8	24.3
Murray	49	2 137	6 044	5.1	52.1	5.5	28.4	4 579	10 575	26 517	7.2	1.2	33 175	12.1	19.2	18.8
Muscogee	426	6 083	44 639	10.8	71.5	16.6	177.9	5 294	11 949	24 056	7.6	2.6	31 349	19.3	29.5	27.8
Newton	229	3 299	9 963	12.1	59.7	9.5	48.8	4 999	11 641	27 992	7.6	2.4	37 415	13.1	21.0	20.0
Oconee	110	1 585	4 936	11.8	77.1	28.4	22.2	4 718	15 164	34 566	19.7	4.5	47 659	8.2	11.5	12.0
Oglethorpe	627	1 473	2 216	8.5	61.8	12.8	10.2	5 108	10 064	24 667	13.8	0.9	33 398	15.0	22.1	22.6
Paulding	246	2 297	9 143	8.9	64.1	7.6	55.7	4 562	12 322	33 085	28.0	1.4	44 575	7.7	12.1	12.7
Peach	896	3 230	6 679	7.8	67.5	15.2	23.4	5 169	10 989	25 604	18.8	2.3	29 557	25.6	37.6	36.3
Pickens	132	1 413	2 874	6.5	56.8	9.0	18.3	5 393	11 442	25 248	20.4	3.1	36 883	12.2	21.2	21.4
Pierce	NA	NA	3 259	3.2	60.0	6.3	14.6	4 726	9 858	20 499	4.7	1.3	28 318	19.9	30.3	29.0
Pike	95	1 401	2 264	12.7	64.9	9.3	9.5	3 940	11 593	27 733	8.1	2.8	35 062	11.8	18.2	18.3
Polk	320	3 783	7 728	6.0	51.8	6.8	32.4	4 723	10 184	22 326	2.5	1.6	29 437	17.0	26.1	25.3
Pulaski	893	1 704	1 996	4.0	60.6	10.7	9.3	5 518	11 265	21 376	5.2	2.1	29 139	20.4	30.4	29.5
Putnam	372	2 155	3 277	11.3	61.8	11.7	13.3	5 304	11 951	24 325	4.6	2.3	32 956	16.3	26.5	25.4
Quitman	240	4 570	498	6.4	49.5	7.3	1.8	6 718	8 820	15 972	14.6	1.6	20 838	28.2	44.2	47.4
Rabun	536	1 828	2 100	8.2	62.7	11.6	10.3	5 359	11 161	21 177	9.5	2.8	29 803	13.9	23.0	22.3
Randolph	NA	NA	2 212	18.3	49.3	6.0	11.3	5 982	6 991	13 972	-7.1	0.9	20 461	32.2	43.2	43.3

1. Data for serious crimes have not been adjusted for underreporting; this may affect comparability between geographic areas and over time.   2. Per 100,000 population estimated by the FBI.   3. All persons 3 years old and over enrolled in nursery school through college.   4. Persons 25 years old and over.   5. Elementary and secondary education expenditures, local government fiscal years ending between July 1, 1996 and June 30, 1997.   6. Based on population enumerated as of April 1, 1990.

Table B. States and Counties — Personal Income

STATE County	Personal income, 1998 Total (mil dol)	Percent change, 1997–1998	Per capita[1] Dollars	Rank	Wages and salaries[2] (mil dol)	Proprietor's income (mil dol)	Dividends, interest, and rent (mil dol)	Transfer payments Total (mil dol)	Government payments to individuals Total (mil dol)	Social Security (mil dol)	Medical payments (mil dol)	Income mainte- nance (mil dol)	Unemploy- ment insurance (mil dol)
	62	63	64	65	66	67	68	69	70	71	72	73	74
GEORGIA—Cont'd													
Fannin	327	5.8	17 598	2 467	107	39	62	86	82	38	32	8	1
Fayette	2 684	8.3	30 247	159	894	145	448	175	157	89	49	6	1
Floyd	1 957	3.4	22 987	856	1 244	103	352	335	318	147	125	31	3
Forsyth	2 565	12.6	29 687	176	965	160	383	146	128	68	47	8	1
Franklin	412	6.8	21 590	1 226	185	85	59	78	75	32	31	8	1
Fulton	30 466	8.3	41 325	26	35 182	3 937	5 681	2 338	2 187	756	872	384	28
Gilmer	362	8.2	19 294	1 956	160	56	63	77	73	31	33	6	1
Glascock	49	3.2	19 572	1 864	15	1	8	13	13	4	7	1	0
Glynn	1 756	4.7	26 129	383	1 053	109	451	269	255	112	105	24	2
Gordon	846	7.6	20 601	1 528	584	70	117	125	116	54	45	11	2
Grady	372	2.9	17 392	2 508	146	38	65	79	75	30	27	14	1
Greene	264	7.7	19 315	1 948	131	26	52	56	53	22	21	8	1
Gwinnett	16 024	10.8	30 657	147	10 386	947	1 935	776	670	354	230	39	11
Habersham	712	8.7	22 445	989	383	96	136	110	103	49	39	8	1
Hall	2 863	8.2	23 991	644	1 840	236	507	337	313	150	119	26	2
Hancock	151	4.4	16 547	2 705	42	7	21	46	44	13	20	9	1
Haralson	461	6.1	18 747	2 142	161	49	75	89	84	37	34	8	1
Harris	550	8.6	24 672	531	110	35	103	61	57	28	17	6	0
Hart	435	7.7	19 955	1 726	209	38	83	82	78	38	29	8	1
Heard	169	6.1	16 772	2 661	76	20	18	32	30	13	13	3	0
Henry	2 289	12.4	21 819	1 154	775	116	300	222	200	100	75	12	2
Houston	2 315	4.0	21 914	1 123	1 786	112	401	258	237	86	98	29	4
Irwin	173	3.6	19 159	1 998	63	13	30	36	34	13	14	5	0
Jackson	854	8.4	22 634	942	391	152	102	121	113	49	47	11	1
Jasper	211	7.4	20 749	1 470	71	16	40	33	31	14	11	4	0
Jeff Davis	228	3.3	17 946	2 362	143	21	37	46	43	18	17	5	1
Jefferson	296	0.3	16 580	2 697	159	13	48	83	79	25	34	15	2
Jenkins	142	0.9	16 812	2 655	69	10	23	37	35	11	16	7	0
Johnson	148	4.0	17 822	2 400	53	12	20	39	37	12	17	6	1
Jones	482	3.4	20 964	1 405	77	24	59	54	50	20	19	6	1
Lamar	270	4.9	18 393	2 241	107	21	43	52	49	22	18	5	0
Lanier	114	6.5	16 365	2 732	28	9	17	25	24	8	11	4	0
Laurens	884	3.6	20 239	1 641	564	56	146	165	156	58	63	23	3
Lee	444	6.9	19 522	1 879	86	29	46	43	38	16	14	5	1
Liberty	944	3.4	15 985	2 796	1 043	40	135	110	101	27	40	19	2
Lincoln	148	5.2	17 970	2 350	41	12	22	30	29	13	11	3	0
Long	114	5.2	13 245	3 058	15	5	16	20	18	6	7	4	0
Lowndes	1 817	5.5	21 366	1 277	1 325	109	302	282	265	90	106	40	4
Lumpkin	409	10.8	21 539	1 243	162	48	67	52	48	22	18	5	0
McDuffie	419	3.8	19 293	1 959	209	26	77	79	75	27	31	12	1
McIntosh	156	6.9	15 557	2 871	48	10	25	40	38	14	17	6	0
Macon	247	5.9	18 734	2 147	124	41	36	56	54	14	26	11	1
Madison	518	7.8	21 217	1 325	85	71	67	78	73	32	29	8	1
Marion	104	5.6	15 476	2 880	51	12	15	21	20	7	8	4	0
Meriwether	416	6.0	18 007	2 341	165	55	57	86	81	31	31	12	1
Miller	127	2.9	19 952	1 727	38	14	25	26	25	9	10	5	0
Mitchell	415	5.7	19 596	1 859	192	62	61	84	80	27	33	16	1
Monroe	397	5.5	20 241	1 639	146	27	62	61	57	25	23	6	1
Montgomery	132	4.0	17 082	2 592	50	9	20	30	28	10	10	4	0
Morgan	342	8.1	22 658	936	169	36	67	50	47	21	18	5	1
Murray	579	6.7	17 710	2 437	341	36	63	83	76	34	30	8	1
Muscogee	4 222	4.6	23 145	828	3 224	219	754	668	630	232	219	96	9
Newton	1 140	8.5	19 702	1 814	524	72	154	172	160	71	66	17	1
Oconee	587	8.2	24 744	524	145	53	92	51	46	23	16	4	0
Oglethorpe	221	6.5	19 318	1 946	38	32	26	32	30	14	11	4	0
Paulding	1 226	11.5	16 593	2 694	288	76	110	127	112	54	40	10	1
Peach	471	3.8	19 245	1 974	235	29	70	88	83	27	30	15	1
Pickens	490	12.8	24 845	507	158	53	89	70	66	32	25	5	1
Pierce	298	6.7	18 913	2 086	83	27	41	61	57	20	22	8	1
Pike	248	6.9	19 587	1 862	48	23	37	36	34	16	13	3	0
Polk	676	5.6	18 625	2 178	255	48	98	149	141	59	56	15	1
Pulaski	187	3.2	22 197	1 038	89	14	35	36	34	12	15	6	0
Putnam	373	6.9	21 228	1 317	182	24	76	63	60	27	23	6	1
Quitman	43	7.4	17 261	2 542	7	2	6	12	12	4	4	2	0
Rabun	276	4.3	20 609	1 526	132	22	76	58	55	25	22	4	0
Randolph	134	1.1	16 838	2 648	61	14	23	36	35	11	13	8	1

1. Based on the resident population estimated as of July 1 of the year shown. 2. Includes other labor income.

Table B. States and Counties — Earnings, Social Security, and Housing

	Earnings, 1998									Social Security beneficiaries, December 1998			Housing units, 1990	
		Percent by selected industries												
		Goods-related[1]		Service-related and other[2]										
STATE County	Total (mil dol)	Farm	Total	Manufacturing	Total	Retail trade	Finance, insurance, and real estate	Services	Government	Number	Rate[3]	Supplemental Security Income recipients, December 1998	Total	Percent change, 1980–1990
	75	76	77	78	79	80	81	82	83	84	85	86	87	88

GEORGIA—Cont'd														
Fannin	145	2.7	24.3	16.8	D	19.8	D	21.3	16.8	4 784	257	762	8 363	24.3
Fayette	1 039	0.3	D	20.2	D	11.0	7.8	22.5	12.9	9 575	108	383	22 428	133.2
Floyd	1 347	0.6	D	27.2	D	9.3	4.0	28.5	15.0	17 464	205	2 657	32 821	8.5
Forsyth	1 125	2.4	D	21.8	D	8.1	4.0	18.5	8.5	7 667	89	572	17 869	62.9
Franklin	270	20.9	D	22.8	D	14.1	2.3	16.3	9.9	4 262	223	748	7 613	23.0
Fulton	39 119	0.0	11.4	8.5	76.6	5.9	13.1	33.7	12.0	88 408	120	21 433	297 503	20.7
Gilmer	216	14.2	D	33.8	D	10.3	3.9	D	12.3	4 006	215	616	6 986	57.9
Glascock	16	-3.8	D	D	D	5.7	D	D	23.9	606	241	116	1 036	13.8
Glynn	1 163	0.0	22.0	14.7	53.7	12.1	6.2	27.8	24.2	12 909	192	1 771	27 724	24.0
Gordon	654	4.5	54.8	50.7	31.1	7.8	1.9	11.7	9.5	6 826	166	949	13 777	26.0
Grady	184	8.9	29.1	23.2	42.8	11.3	3.7	15.7	19.2	4 161	194	1 076	8 129	14.1
Greene	157	5.9	D	32.0	D	7.5	13.1	11.7	16.1	2 885	211	588	4 699	13.3
Gwinnett	11 333	0.0	D	16.5	D	10.7	7.7	24.5	7.8	39 253	75	3 164	137 608	136.7
Habersham	479	9.4	D	30.8	D	9.5	4.7	14.0	16.6	6 152	193	861	11 076	24.0
Hall	2 076	2.1	35.9	28.8	50.0	9.2	6.1	23.2	12.0	18 002	151	2 144	38 315	37.1
Hancock	49	5.1	D	8.7	D	6.3	3.6	20.5	48.8	1 859	204	568	3 396	7.4
Haralson	210	2.8	38.7	28.2	40.2	10.3	2.5	16.8	18.3	4 740	192	776	9 016	29.0
Harris	145	1.1	31.5	22.0	48.8	10.9	3.7	28.7	18.5	3 556	159	439	7 814	29.1
Hart	247	6.5	D	43.7	D	7.2	D	14.0	13.0	4 708	216	609	8 942	18.8
Heard	96	9.3	D	39.8	D	2.3	1.1	4.8	15.3	1 717	170	329	3 536	43.8
Henry	891	0.2	D	11.7	D	13.4	5.9	20.5	22.9	11 625	111	1 135	21 275	73.3
Houston	1 899	0.2	12.0	8.5	28.3	7.5	2.5	14.5	59.5	12 594	119	2 214	34 785	26.8
Irwin	76	9.7	D	18.1	D	4.5	3.4	19.7	24.3	1 848	206	422	3 479	4.1
Jackson	543	19.1	D	27.9	D	9.8	4.4	8.5	11.5	6 240	166	1 147	11 775	29.3
Jasper	86	7.5	D	38.9	D	5.1	1.9	11.3	20.2	1 889	186	270	3 637	18.0
Jeff Davis	164	6.5	43.3	40.5	36.4	10.1	1.6	8.1	13.8	2 427	190	502	4 792	18.4
Jefferson	172	1.7	D	38.3	D	7.4	3.0	9.2	17.3	3 609	203	1 261	7 065	8.4
Jenkins	79	3.6	48.8	46.7	29.5	5.9	2.5	10.1	18.2	1 617	191	534	3 365	0.6
Johnson	65	8.7	22.5	17.4	36.4	4.8	1.6	12.7	32.4	1 726	208	499	3 389	1.9
Jones	100	3.3	D	7.6	D	7.1	3.5	19.0	23.2	2 520	109	376	7 722	32.4
Lamar	128	5.1	36.8	32.7	D	9.3	5.7	D	20.5	2 759	188	413	5 066	16.9
Lanier	36	6.3	21.0	8.6	D	10.1	D	22.1	27.7	1 116	160	290	2 202	8.2
Laurens	620	1.3	D	26.6	D	11.9	3.2	18.4	23.0	8 086	185	1 998	16 504	22.4
Lee	116	12.4	D	3.2	D	5.7	D	16.1	29.0	2 104	92	329	5 537	42.8
Liberty	1 082	0.0	D	3.7	D	3.9	1.7	4.7	81.9	3 944	67	1 007	16 776	55.3
Lincoln	52	2.2	38.0	30.6	D	8.6	2.1	12.5	22.8	1 699	205	283	3 870	25.3
Long	20	9.0	D	D	D	6.1	1.8	10.3	49.5	873	102	170	2 638	52.1
Lowndes	1 434	0.6	D	14.0	D	13.0	3.5	17.7	33.7	11 827	139	2 915	28 906	18.8
Lumpkin	210	8.4	D	15.9	D	10.4	5.3	18.2	26.2	2 744	145	430	5 729	49.4
McDuffie	235	2.9	D	27.1	D	15.4	3.4	16.6	18.9	3 657	168	806	8 043	16.6
McIntosh	58	0.0	9.3	4.7	61.0	19.0	6.1	15.9	29.7	1 918	191	806	4 276	17.4
Macon	164	21.5	37.4	34.1	24.3	5.4	1.3	11.8	16.8	2 059	155	290	4 848	3.7
Madison	156	25.8	D	13.2	D	6.1	2.2	13.8	16.6	4 213	173	886	8 428	30.1
Marion	64	11.5	D	D	D	4.7	1.7	8.6	17.7	963	143	423	2 152	16.9
Meriwether	220	1.5	33.8	27.2	41.5	9.0	7.9	15.3	23.3	4 111	178	997	8 409	10.6
Miller	52	21.5	6.2	1.7	46.1	9.5	6.8	13.3	26.2	1 327	207	331	2 602	1.6
Mitchell	254	18.1	29.4	25.8	30.4	6.4	2.9	9.9	22.1	3 963	187	1 233	7 443	5.6
Monroe	173	4.3	D	10.8	D	7.2	1.8	14.5	26.2	3 231	164	474	6 401	28.1
Montgomery	59	5.7	26.4	14.3	46.7	10.2	6.2	18.2	21.1	1 409	182	387	2 885	13.6
Morgan	205	8.4	35.7	30.2	43.4	13.1	3.7	10.6	12.4	2 670	177	403	4 814	22.9
Murray	377	3.2	D	60.0	D	5.2	1.8	9.7	10.8	4 513	138	810	10 207	47.0
Muscogee	3 443	0.0	D	17.2	D	9.6	11.6	25.9	23.2	29 545	162	5 641	70 902	11.1
Newton	596	0.2	D	32.6	D	9.1	3.2	17.6	13.5	8 589	148	1 515	15 494	28.6
Oconee	198	7.2	30.5	19.5	46.1	9.9	6.7	20.8	16.2	2 809	118	314	6 561	45.8
Oglethorpe	70	36.1	21.2	4.9	25.2	5.4	2.2	11.4	17.6	1 892	166	325	3 936	25.0
Paulding	364	0.1	D	11.7	D	14.3	3.9	13.6	23.4	6 491	88	695	15 237	66.2
Peach	264	4.3	D	38.1	D	9.2	3.4	9.2	26.2	3 843	157	887	7 537	13.5
Pickens	211	9.4	D	13.7	44.2	10.2	9.9	15.8	14.3	3 803	193	416	6 403	32.5
Pierce	110	11.0	22.6	13.6	48.5	10.9	5.1	15.3	17.8	2 830	179	678	5 271	22.7
Pike	71	12.3	D	19.9	D	4.7	3.8	15.4	22.3	2 111	167	302	3 797	22.6
Polk	304	2.2	D	28.3	D	10.5	3.5	16.4	18.7	7 450	205	1 409	13 585	12.6
Pulaski	103	5.9	D	14.3	D	8.6	3.3	30.2	23.0	1 769	211	431	3 470	1.9
Putnam	206	3.3	41.3	34.6	40.2	5.7	3.8	9.4	15.2	3 305	188	402	7 113	35.3
Quitman	9	0.6	D	21.3	D	13.4	D	9.2	37.9	616	248	179	1 346	38.1
Rabun	154	3.0	D	31.6	D	10.6	4.7	22.7	14.4	3 254	243	456	7 883	27.9
Randolph	76	7.8	30.8	26.3	34.6	7.2	2.3	12.9	26.8	1 680	213	535	3 225	-9.4

1. Covers mining, construction, and manufacturing. 2. Covers private sector earnings in agricultural services, forestry, and fisheries; transportation and public utilities; wholesale trade; retail trade; finance, insurance, and real estate; and services. 3. Per 1,000 resident population estimated as of July 1 of the year shown.

Items 75—88

Table B. States and Counties — Housing, Labor Force, and Employment

STATE County	Housing units, 1990 (cont'd)								Civilian labor force, 1999				Civilian employment, 1990[5]		
	Occupied units										Unemployment		Percent		
	Owner-occupied					Renter-occupied									
				Owner cost as a percent of income											
	Total	Percent	Median value[1]	With a mortgage	Without a mortgage	Median rent[2]	Rent as percent of income	Substandard units[3] (percent)	Total	Percent change, 1998–1999	Total	Rate[4]	Total	Professional, managerial, and technical	Precision production, craft, and repair
	89	90	91	92	93	94	95	96	97	98	99	100	101	102	103
GEORGIA—Cont'd															
Fannin	6 334	83.8	48 000	25.4	12.6	253	25.0	4.2	8 806	-0.8	396	4.5	6 461	19.3	14.7
Fayette	21 054	86.1	116 700	22.3	11.9	598	24.3	1.7	49 734	4.7	927	1.9	31 844	36.2	11.2
Floyd	30 518	66.1	50 100	17.5	13.3	325	23.6	2.8	44 666	-4.1	2 174	4.9	38 308	25.5	13.0
Forsyth	15 938	81.9	96 200	22.6	13.0	497	25.0	3.1	49 945	14.5	870	1.7	23 266	26.2	16.0
Franklin	6 365	78.0	49 500	20.7	12.3	245	27.3	5.0	10 135	-1.4	342	3.4	7 635	16.3	15.9
Fulton	257 140	49.5	97 700	22.6	13.6	479	27.3	5.0	409 362	3.0	15 471	3.8	320 149	35.5	6.6
Gilmer	5 072	80.4	56 800	23.4	13.1	295	25.8	5.7	8 343	-1.2	310	3.7	6 073	16.5	17.2
Glascock	867	77.9	30 700	18.5	12.3	200	21.4	4.9	977	-7.0	69	7.1	1 041	13.4	16.5
Glynn	23 947	65.1	67 200	20.1	12.4	407	26.2	3.5	34 848	-4.0	1 160	3.3	29 437	29.5	11.2
Gordon	12 778	72.1	53 100	16.4	12.0	350	21.9	4.3	22 199	0.6	1 137	5.1	17 439	18.2	13.3
Grady	7 354	73.0	41 400	20.5	14.1	270	26.8	6.4	9 668	-1.9	847	8.8	8 852	19.0	13.5
Greene	4 083	77.2	38 800	22.1	13.8	258	21.8	11.0	5 820	-0.7	351	6.0	4 863	15.6	12.0
Gwinnett	126 971	68.4	95 900	22.2	12.0	577	23.8	2.2	332 809	5.1	7 969	2.4	203 387	36.2	10.6
Habersham	9 966	76.7	57 800	20.6	13.2	316	22.5	3.5	16 140	-1.4	569	3.5	13 384	20.1	15.5
Hall	34 721	69.4	75 400	21.2	12.3	424	23.8	4.1	71 026	-2.5	1 856	2.6	49 052	23.3	15.2
Hancock	2 969	77.1	29 200	18.9	14.3	195	26.4	16.4	3 981	-3.4	502	12.6	3 426	16.0	10.6
Haralson	8 248	76.2	47 100	20.0	13.5	299	25.4	4.4	9 496	-2.1	467	4.9	9 769	17.0	19.3
Harris	6 454	82.4	64 500	19.6	12.7	311	22.7	5.8	11 960	2.2	334	2.8	8 253	24.4	14.6
Hart	7 459	79.3	51 700	20.7	12.1	269	25.0	4.5	9 232	4.3	391	4.2	9 091	15.1	17.4
Heard	3 093	78.9	43 900	19.7	13.0	263	23.1	8.1	4 829	-5.2	317	6.6	3 702	12.3	22.5
Henry	20 012	83.4	81 200	22.0	12.1	531	25.1	3.4	59 288	7.3	1 246	2.1	30 173	24.1	16.2
Houston	32 433	65.1	62 100	17.6	11.9	396	22.9	3.4	51 637	2.0	2 004	3.9	40 787	30.3	15.8
Irwin	3 142	73.3	40 900	19.2	14.5	227	27.2	6.1	4 748	-3.4	228	4.8	3 615	20.4	12.4
Jackson	10 721	75.1	55 300	20.4	12.4	326	24.5	4.8	22 709	0.4	811	3.6	14 303	19.0	18.3
Jasper	3 036	76.5	51 100	21.8	12.7	284	20.7	7.6	4 757	-3.5	187	3.9	3 669	18.1	14.3
Jeff Davis	4 357	73.1	39 200	18.4	12.6	269	24.1	5.9	5 345	-8.9	377	7.1	5 529	17.5	13.9
Jefferson	6 093	69.1	38 300	18.6	13.9	218	28.6	10.0	7 534	-6.2	1 005	13.3	6 780	15.3	12.7
Jenkins	2 951	71.1	39 500	19.5	18.4	224	30.8	12.3	4 353	-8.0	209	4.8	3 344	17.7	14.7
Johnson	3 010	78.0	31 600	17.3	14.3	193	22.8	8.4	3 546	-4.6	308	8.7	3 486	13.3	16.2
Jones	7 300	83.7	63 500	17.4	12.9	337	23.5	4.6	12 046	1.1	500	4.2	10 139	25.0	17.6
Lamar	4 669	70.0	47 600	22.1	13.7	319	25.8	8.0	6 927	-7.6	405	5.8	5 829	18.9	14.3
Lanier	1 965	71.5	37 500	18.5	12.7	294	22.4	5.4	3 554	0.9	145	4.1	2 395	16.2	13.7
Laurens	14 514	70.9	46 500	19.0	12.6	282	27.4	5.3	22 628	-5.6	1 786	7.9	17 535	22.0	13.6
Lee	5 199	77.9	65 300	19.7	14.3	389	21.7	4.8	11 754	3.0	545	4.6	7 359	28.8	14.5
Liberty	15 136	43.5	60 400	24.5	13.5	399	26.0	6.8	16 849	-3.8	1 067	6.3	12 969	24.5	11.3
Lincoln	2 702	80.3	46 000	20.1	13.1	237	22.5	13.2	3 671	1.4	380	10.4	3 151	16.9	17.2
Long	2 196	67.1	40 500	23.4	14.8	362	29.3	7.1	3 571	0.6	108	3.0	2 306	21.9	15.5
Lowndes	26 311	59.7	60 800	20.2	13.3	356	25.6	5.3	42 850	-0.9	1 887	4.4	32 401	26.0	10.9
Lumpkin	4 976	76.0	66 400	21.8	12.8	371	24.6	5.3	10 707	6.6	236	2.2	6 838	20.7	16.6
McDuffie	7 270	68.6	48 000	18.3	12.1	275	27.3	6.9	9 790	1.4	659	6.7	8 869	21.9	15.7
McIntosh	3 186	83.5	37 500	23.6	15.2	280	24.9	7.9	4 668	0.4	195	4.2	3 541	19.5	15.1
Macon	4 388	68.7	35 900	18.1	14.1	238	30.6	9.0	5 316	-4.4	475	8.9	5 187	20.5	11.8
Madison	7 740	82.1	53 900	18.3	11.4	322	22.8	5.4	13 385	-0.3	421	3.1	10 419	17.4	20.3
Marion	1 962	78.8	38 400	17.5	13.5	205	27.6	12.2	3 307	-1.2	173	5.2	2 075	19.3	15.4
Meriwether	7 637	74.8	39 900	19.0	13.0	290	26.0	10.0	8 959	-5.9	517	5.8	8 800	15.7	14.3
Miller	2 336	75.7	41 200	19.0	12.7	214	24.9	7.3	3 146	3.1	154	4.9	2 581	20.8	11.9
Mitchell	6 798	70.1	40 800	19.7	13.8	237	25.2	10.8	11 645	-0.7	929	8.0	8 248	17.3	11.2
Monroe	5 838	74.6	62 400	18.8	14.4	324	20.8	7.4	7 427	-5.2	424	5.7	7 792	24.4	16.8
Montgomery	2 493	74.1	40 100	20.5	14.0	215	23.9	6.1	3 832	-1.4	385	10.0	3 113	18.6	13.8
Morgan	4 399	76.4	55 000	20.9	13.8	319	20.1	8.0	6 971	-9.5	274	3.9	5 851	18.2	13.8
Murray	9 363	75.0	52 000	17.0	12.1	332	21.8	4.9	18 575	2.4	607	3.3	13 247	13.4	16.0
Muscogee	65 858	53.9	58 900	19.8	12.2	358	25.5	4.5	87 085	2.0	4 756	5.5	71 922	28.4	10.9
Newton	14 401	70.9	65 400	21.9	12.7	423	27.6	6.1	29 655	5.2	1 025	3.5	19 166	20.7	16.6
Oconee	6 156	77.5	77 900	20.7	12.7	436	24.6	2.8	13 280	2.9	200	1.5	9 012	35.1	12.3
Oglethorpe	3 581	82.3	52 500	22.5	11.7	261	29.0	7.6	6 035	4.2	192	3.2	4 739	19.8	15.3
Paulding	14 326	81.5	68 600	21.8	11.8	442	27.6	3.7	40 430	7.4	877	2.2	20 732	18.9	20.4
Peach	7 142	69.1	56 700	19.2	12.7	303	30.2	6.7	11 152	0.7	646	5.8	8 870	27.8	11.2
Pickens	5 386	80.2	59 500	23.2	12.2	341	24.8	5.2	10 593	6.6	284	2.7	7 003	18.9	17.0
Pierce	4 807	80.0	41 700	19.4	13.3	254	23.7	4.8	7 379	-2.4	388	5.3	5 863	17.9	16.7
Pike	3 526	80.7	51 600	19.8	12.5	300	24.4	6.1	6 674	3.7	267	4.0	4 578	20.4	16.3
Polk	12 519	72.4	41 600	19.2	12.8	316	26.0	4.7	16 024	0.9	947	5.9	14 385	16.5	15.1
Pulaski	3 098	70.5	44 900	20.7	14.2	235	27.0	8.7	4 488	-8.1	225	5.0	3 340	23.7	14.9
Putnam	5 229	74.9	59 000	19.2	12.0	296	24.2	7.0	9 373	2.5	326	3.5	6 558	20.0	14.9
Quitman	857	73.5	36 400	20.4	14.4	183	25.7	13.5	1 267	-6.4	48	3.8	813	18.2	10.9
Rabun	4 630	81.5	65 900	23.7	12.8	292	23.6	4.1	7 130	-0.7	205	2.9	5 478	19.1	20.1
Randolph	2 815	66.7	33 000	25.3	13.7	205	25.7	13.0	3 079	-13.5	286	9.3	2 830	16.3	8.0

1. Specified owner-occupied units.   2. Specified renter-occupied units.   3. Overcrowded or lacking complete plumbing facilities.   4. Percent of civilian labor force.   5. Persons 16 years and older.

Table B. States and Counties — Nonfarm Employment and Agriculture

	Private nonfarm establishments, employment and payroll, 1998								Agriculture, 1997			
		Employment					Annual payroll		Farms			Farm operators
										Percent with—		
STATE County	Number of establishments	Total	Health Care and Social Assistance	Manufacturing	Retail trade	Finance and Insurance	Professional Scientific and Technical Services	Total (mil dol)	Average per employee (dollars)	Number	Less than 50 acres	500 acres and over	Whose principal occupation is farming (percent)
	104	105	106	107	108	109	110	111	112	113	114	115	116
GEORGIA—Cont'd													
Fannin	417	3 844	591	971	834	164	87	69	18 068	151	37.1	0.7	40.4
Fayette	2 223	26 498	1 938	4 786	5 034	966	962	677	25 538	184	44.6	2.7	34.8
Floyd	1 993	37 430	6 583	10 437	4 973	1 238	844	876	23 406	437	29.1	5.7	34.6
Forsyth	2 190	26 936	1 186	4 792	3 829	490	1 074	735	27 299	434	60.1	1.6	43.3
Franklin	443	6 313	583	1 750	1 227	265	74	124	19 574	699	36.3	2.3	48.5
Fulton	29 887	678 327	56 063	38 518	55 392	52 577	66 578	26 477	39 033	257	56.0	3.9	35.8
Gilmer	426	5 758	410	2 864	772	169	132	114	19 824	267	51.3	1.1	58.4
Glascock	25	200	D	0	D	D	D	3	14 940	76	15.8	14.5	42.1
Glynn	2 392	29 800	4 250	3 653	4 854	971	780	654	21 948	36	55.6	16.7	38.9
Gordon	907	19 580	1 000	10 031	2 372	278	285	443	22 607	535	43.7	4.5	41.3
Grady	418	4 078	349	1 254	836	168	58	79	19 334	462	28.6	13.9	54.5
Greene	318	3 873	358	1 533	D	285	65	83	21 557	198	27.8	14.6	53.0
Gwinnett	16 423	251 369	13 178	28 362	36 333	13 459	15 624	8 355	33 239	303	57.4	2.3	35.0
Habersham	776	11 724	647	4 814	1 705	388	143	265	22 616	407	55.5	1.0	51.1
Hall	3 209	51 461	5 802	17 063	6 737	1 803	1 201	1 352	26 276	666	53.5	1.2	45.6
Hancock	91	881	366	D	199	D	17	13	14 991	103	11.7	14.6	31.1
Haralson	423	5 481	481	2 244	860	119	73	110	20 113	260	36.9	3.5	34.2
Harris	413	3 996	225	1 158	276	73	104	73	18 311	207	33.8	10.6	37.7
Hart	375	5 446	521	2 599	767	113	68	129	23 726	460	33.9	4.8	43.7
Heard	106	1 136	107	551	165	D	15	21	18 120	160	21.2	5.6	40.6
Henry	1 978	23 373	2 125	3 282	3 729	657	748	535	22 879	327	45.6	5.5	34.9
Houston	1 963	24 998	3 917	2 472	5 472	902	2 073	532	21 286	249	39.4	16.1	36.5
Irwin	142	2 065	342	830	172	51	D	34	16 669	288	14.9	26.7	63.9
Jackson	883	13 412	701	5 438	1 848	280	167	314	23 447	719	47.8	3.2	45.2
Jasper	158	1 592	129	763	156	55	21	39	24 242	185	15.7	11.9	36.8
Jeff Davis	309	5 115	285	2 299	698	102	53	100	19 527	220	25.0	16.8	45.9
Jefferson	351	4 974	522	1 910	670	163	50	117	23 595	356	14.6	19.1	43.3
Jenkins	148	2 459	269	1 382	247	56	17	44	17 917	248	12.9	21.4	44.0
Johnson	129	1 411	136	485	186	37	23	27	19 147	288	15.6	13.9	37.8
Jones	245	1 845	301	240	220	69	21	39	21 149	157	27.4	8.3	34.4
Lamar	225	3 303	242	1 488	394	98	40	61	18 429	188	30.9	8.0	37.8
Lanier	104	745	291	56	120	83	14	14	19 342	92	25.0	22.8	42.4
Laurens	1 045	17 544	3 142	5 740	2 841	468	217	401	22 852	688	23.0	12.8	34.0
Lee	195	1 768	272	313	348	36	26	34	19 010	157	29.9	38.9	48.4
Liberty	712	8 370	1 496	917	1 808	349	229	164	19 606	43	25.6	25.6	37.2
Lincoln	151	1 514	63	683	130	38	27	25	16 617	163	27.0	9.2	29.4
Long	52	225	D	D	D	D	D	3	12 284	64	26.6	18.8	29.7
Lowndes	2 360	33 989	4 970	6 004	6 815	875	922	711	20 929	373	40.5	10.2	38.1
Lumpkin	353	3 658	604	830	776	125	71	78	21 352	198	35.4	5.1	43.4
McDuffie	460	6 836	1 147	1 831	1 460	233	211	147	21 490	217	33.2	10.6	34.1
McIntosh	240	1 966	214	90	801	81	11	30	15 087	24	33.3	8.3	25.0
Macon	232	2 692	431	1 000	407	77	30	72	26 585	282	19.9	23.4	59.2
Madison	528	6 964	294	2 939	608	251	255	158	22 752	622	38.3	2.4	44.5
Marion	80	2 116	150	D	190	D	4	36	16 933	147	12.2	19.0	38.8
Meriwether	337	4 895	957	2 251	579	151	55	107	21 819	257	24.9	13.6	39.7
Miller	142	1 009	211	8	268	37	11	16	15 916	251	16.3	27.9	64.1
Mitchell	416	3 631	417	504	885	194	111	63	17 402	464	22.4	25.4	53.2
Monroe	367	3 293	444	355	524	84	67	75	22 917	179	25.7	19.0	35.2
Montgomery	112	1 214	D	188	149	71	14	24	19 781	252	20.6	19.8	34.1
Morgan	376	5 579	283	1 563	921	126	81	128	23 027	390	27.2	13.1	40.3
Murray	479	8 836	327	5 615	761	162	123	206	23 304	238	42.9	5.0	33.6
Muscogee	4 328	84 737	9 130	17 064	12 399	6 155	2 085	2 137	25 221	39	43.6	10.3	28.2
Newton	1 101	13 521	1 376	4 127	2 284	413	208	324	23 993	260	40.4	7.7	36.9
Oconee	494	4 331	317	728	972	162	268	97	22 327	305	35.1	8.5	42.3
Oglethorpe	154	848	95	103	138	26	61	14	16 669	319	27.0	8.8	42.3
Paulding	869	7 989	714	1 204	2 006	231	186	168	21 034	218	50.9	0.5	35.3
Peach	448	6 263	370	2 895	882	190	65	142	22 696	157	35.0	15.9	40.8
Pickens	442	4 692	730	1 215	709	156	73	106	22 656	194	49.5	0.5	37.6
Pierce	317	2 445	105	464	D	135	D	46	18 907	379	27.2	13.2	50.7
Pike	171	1 149	163	163	122	D	27	24	21 199	252	30.2	9.5	35.3
Polk	595	7 674	744	2 505	1 295	214	155	163	21 272	344	38.4	4.4	32.0
Pulaski	222	2 518	571	599	321	108	50	52	20 631	161	23.6	30.4	46.0
Putnam	314	4 375	306	1 938	683	114	72	112	25 657	152	27.0	8.6	54.6
Quitman	39	212	D	14	D	D	D	4	18 986	17	11.8	47.1	64.7
Rabun	466	4 921	542	1 844	625	146	84	100	20 322	122	51.6	2.5	41.8
Randolph	170	1 606	147	458	225	63	36	30	18 465	119	10.9	47.9	67.2

Table B. States and Counties — Agriculture, Land, and Water

STATE County	Acreage (1,000) [117]	Percent change, 1992–1997 [118]	Average size of farm [119]	Total irrigated (1,000) [120]	Total cropland (1,000) [121]	Average per farm ($1,000) [122]	Average per acre (dollars) [123]	Value of machinery and equipment Average per farm ($1,000) [124]	Total (mil dol) [125]	Average per farm (dollars) [126]	Crops [127]	Livestock and poultry products [128]	$10,000 or more [129]	$100,000 or more [130]	Percent of land owned by Fed. Gov. 1997 [131]	Water consumption 1995 (mil gal/day) [132]
GEORGIA—Cont'd																
Fannin	15	-5.9	100	0	6	308	3 284	29	10	66 368	13.9	86.1	26.5	9.9	53.7	1.9
Fayette	18	-16.6	100	0	9	406	4 117	19	4	21 898	62.9	37.1	24.5	4.3	0.0	13.9
Floyd	83	12.7	191	1	36	388	2 092	31	31	70 958	9.6	90.4	23.1	7.6	2.0	452.3
Forsyth	31	-14.1	71	0	13	406	6 966	23	62	143 406	9.0	91.0	37.8	23.0	2.8	13.7
Franklin	77	3.1	111	0	40	280	2 467	28	148	211 306	0.9	99.1	40.9	24.2	1.0	3.8
Fulton	27	23.5	106	0	10	380	3 642	17	4	15 939	71.2	28.8	17.5	3.5	0.7	226.0
Gilmer	23	-7.8	86	0	9	329	3 745	33	77	288 985	1.6	98.4	54.3	40.4	16.8	3.3
Glascock	20	-30.3	266	0	8	258	969	30	1	12 239	48.8	51.2	26.3	3.9	0.0	0.4
Glynn	8	-22.6	215	0	1	311	1 446	24	0	10 404	30.1	69.6	19.4	2.8	0.1	67.1
Gordon	69	-7.0	129	1	41	376	2 602	34	88	165 101	4.9	95.1	41.5	23.2	3.5	18.1
Grady	127	-7.6	276	6	72	401	1 487	61	70	151 887	77.1	22.9	53.5	18.8	0.0	12.1
Greene	52	11.5	265	D	22	335	1 494	49	29	147 763	D	D	37.9	19.2	10.0	5.1
Gwinnett	31	30.7	103	0	9	546	4 796	34	11	35 021	51.6	48.4	18.8	7.3	0.7	71.8
Habersham	31	-13.1	77	0	15	313	4 146	35	114	279 810	0.8	99.2	54.3	36.1	28.2	10.1
Hall	51	-5.4	77	0	25	409	4 487	28	138	207 017	0.9	99.1	39.3	25.8	4.0	19.8
Hancock	34	-3.8	327	D	7	237	769	21	3	31 777	4.6	95.4	20.4	3.9	0.0	1.1
Haralson	31	-4.0	118	0	14	250	1 820	29	17	63 979	2.7	97.3	22.3	6.9	0.0	2.1
Harris	47	51.4	227	0	13	363	1 483	22	3	14 590	50.4	49.6	22.2	4.3	0.0	10.3
Hart	58	-1.9	126	1	36	274	1 931	33	56	121 576	3.8	96.2	30.0	15.7	3.2	4.2
Heard	28	15.2	173	D	12	254	1 612	37	21	131 628	0.6	99.4	28.8	10.6	3.9	1.1
Henry	45	-2.9	137	0	20	401	3 817	23	7	20 337	72.1	27.9	24.8	3.4	0.0	7.1
Houston	87	19.3	350	6	49	498	1 467	88	28	111 785	57.8	42.2	39.4	16.5	2.5	29.1
Irwin	132	-2.4	457	15	82	480	1 096	84	41	142 154	87.6	12.4	72.9	33.3	0.0	9.8
Jackson	77	-6.6	108	1	38	383	3 134	31	191	265 459	1.3	98.7	44.1	25.7	0.0	6.4
Jasper	52	-14.8	281	0	20	365	1 381	29	14	76 168	3.4	96.6	31.9	8.6	16.9	1.7
Jeff Davis	71	-2.5	324	4	36	380	1 159	39	23	106 017	70.7	29.3	46.8	25.0	0.0	5.0
Jefferson	142	4.4	399	14	84	331	787	56	24	68 524	75.9	24.1	43.0	18.3	1.2	15.5
Jenkins	93	19.4	375	3	44	287	768	41	20	81 249	52.4	47.6	37.1	18.1	0.0	5.5
Johnson	96	35.4	334	1	40	334	984	24	6	22 509	72.8	27.2	29.2	4.5	0.0	3.1
Jones	31	-0.3	197	0	11	301	1 453	32	7	47 187	7.6	92.4	26.8	7.6	17.8	2.4
Lamar	38	-5.3	202	D	20	276	1 642	30	15	78 634	13.7	86.3	30.3	9.6	0.0	4.7
Lanier	43	4.6	466	1	15	470	987	39	7	79 245	90.2	9.8	54.3	20.7	3.0	3.3
Laurens	198	18.1	288	7	85	319	1 137	32	24	34 531	79.7	20.3	27.8	7.8	0.0	32.9
Lee	138	31.4	879	16	76	1 399	1 491	97	38	241 076	79.5	20.5	56.7	32.5	0.0	26.2
Liberty	21	31.2	488	0	2	419	858	32	1	21 222	78.5	21.5	30.2	4.7	33.8	17.5
Lincoln	31	-5.5	191	0	12	283	1 554	31	2	11 155	4.5	95.5	23.3	1.2	6.7	1.2
Long	19	57.3	295	D	4	285	967	28	6	94 750	13.7	86.3	29.7	14.1	11.2	0.8
Lowndes	72	-1.2	193	3	38	304	1 624	37	23	61 445	88.9	11.1	36.7	12.1	1.3	28.1
Lumpkin	25	9.7	127	0	10	308	2 991	39	64	325 481	1.8	98.2	39.4	28.3	31.7	3.1
McDuffie	41	21.0	190	1	18	277	1 362	29	16	75 097	D	D	25.3	6.5	4.8	3.7
McIntosh	4	-47.4	175	0	1	221	1 261	19	0	6 614	46.5	53.5	16.7	0.0	4.3	1.4
Macon	119	-1.8	421	19	69	386	987	78	99	351 448	24.8	75.2	61.0	35.5	0.2	23.6
Madison	70	12.4	112	0	34	245	2 093	27	107	172 699	1.7	98.3	37.5	20.7	0.0	3.1
Marion	52	14.8	351	1	18	369	976	37	34	228 854	10.3	89.7	42.2	17.7	0.0	3.2
Meriwether	69	-0.2	268	1	22	370	1 270	28	6	24 848	32.7	67.3	29.6	4.3	0.0	5.7
Miller	116	-4.9	462	26	79	478	1 076	85	38	152 124	82.1	17.9	70.5	34.7	0.0	28.8
Mitchell	221	7.3	477	41	135	590	1 288	88	141	304 636	49.0	51.0	56.7	33.8	0.0	32.5
Monroe	57	26.2	317	0	15	491	1 570	36	28	158 360	1.7	98.3	33.5	15.6	0.0	34.8
Montgomery	75	15.5	298	2	22	357	1 143	35	9	36 745	64.4	35.6	25.0	6.7	0.0	4.4
Morgan	88	-5.8	225	1	43	471	2 200	36	43	109 218	5.5	94.5	44.6	21.5	0.1	2.9
Murray	35	5.5	146	0	21	300	2 181	30	44	183 629	3.1	96.9	34.9	16.0	24.1	4.1
Muscogee	8	70.0	218	0	2	347	1 592	19	0	4 824	68.6	31.4	7.7	0.0	35.7	39.5
Newton	46	-0.9	175	0	17	486	3 184	25	10	37 424	9.7	90.3	24.6	5.4	0.0	4.1
Oconee	51	-1.4	168	0	21	406	2 434	32	44	144 348	14.5	85.5	38.4	17.4	1.1	3.1
Oglethorpe	63	13.8	196	0	27	337	2 154	28	57	178 063	2.4	97.6	35.1	16.9	1.3	1.7
Paulding	18	-3.3	84	0	8	347	4 609	19	11	51 241	5.9	94.1	18.8	5.0	0.0	3.5
Peach	51	15.8	325	5	35	499	1 584	66	31	194 444	83.1	16.9	43.3	16.6	1.7	6.8
Pickens	16	-11.5	82	0	7	251	3 921	22	54	278 414	0.3	99.7	37.6	25.8	0.0	2.9
Pierce	100	24.0	265	6	41	364	1 362	40	30	78 211	69.2	30.8	44.6	17.4	0.0	5.8
Pike	48	6.6	190	1	24	425	2 952	26	19	76 138	11.5	88.5	29.4	7.5	0.0	3.1
Polk	50	9.6	147	0	23	190	1 685	25	19	54 281	8.8	91.2	24.4	7.6	0.0	10.6
Pulaski	92	15.5	574	14	64	691	1 223	80	28	171 595	83.2	16.8	49.1	29.8	0.0	12.2
Putnam	31	-10.6	206	0	14	347	1 611	45	21	141 178	1.5	98.5	44.1	27.6	20.4	1 010.5
Quitman	11	-5.4	668	D	6	520	779	80	1	85 914	91.2	8.8	70.6	23.5	0.9	1.9
Rabun	11	-16.4	89	0	5	280	4 198	24	13	106 515	18.0	82.0	32.0	14.8	73.0	4.1
Randolph	94	-1.8	792	15	64	703	897	105	20	171 588	86.0	14.0	61.3	37.8	0.0	10.6

Table B. States and Counties — Residential Construction, Wholesale and Retail Trade, and Real Estate

STATE County	Value of Residential Construction Authorized by Building Permits, 1999		Wholesale Trade, 1997				Retail Trade[1], 1997				Real Estate and Rental and Leasing, 1997			
	New Construction ($1,000)	Number of Housing Units	Number of Establishments	Number of Employees	Sales (mil dol)	Annual Payroll (mil dol)	Number of Establishments	Number of Employees	Sales (mil dol)	Annual Payroll (mil dol)	Number of Establishments	Number of Employees	Receipts (mil dol)	Annual Payroll (mil dol)
	133	134	135	136	137	138	139	140	141	142	143	144	145	146
GEORGIA—Cont'd														
Fannin	67 444	663	16	56	21.1	1.4	103	779	126.7	10.7	12	15	2.0	0.2
Fayette	197 595	1 250	135	1 236	545.5	42.3	298	4 697	677.6	69.9	91	287	42.0	6.2
Floyd	51 607	479	112	1 163	523.3	35.8	442	4 991	808.1	75.0	56	313	26.8	5.2
Forsyth	321 250	2 929	228	3 138	1 140.8	110.0	255	3 503	653.9	63.5	88	208	44.8	6.5
Franklin	2 179	28	32	208	56.5	3.9	92	937	202.3	15.2	16	43	3.6	0.8
Fulton	895 953	9 157	2 462	40 435	55 915.1	1 823.9	3 569	51 556	9 248.2	990.1	1 496	14 372	2 523.5	516.3
Gilmer	44 705	596	17	170	44.4	2.9	89	778	136.1	11.9	18	69	4.4	0.6
Glascock	60	1	NA	NA	NA	NA	7	30	2.9	0.3	NA	NA	NA	NA
Glynn	110 251	880	118	903	461.5	30.7	504	4 847	716.1	69.6	122	622	51.4	9.9
Gordon	33 541	434	57	675	150.6	16.5	241	2 260	360.1	33.9	24	84	8.1	2.0
Grady	6 534	71	24	272	125.3	5.7	111	824	130.1	12.2	16	33	3.2	0.5
Greene	54 440	224	16	90	102.0	2.2	56	465	66.8	6.2	14	37	5.6	0.7
Gwinnett	885 045	9 731	1 959	31 305	29 114.6	1 365.0	2 013	33 639	6 829.0	632.5	580	3 193	492.4	89.2
Habersham	36 267	402	34	203	35.1	4.8	153	1 677	256.3	24.1	21	71	9.7	1.6
Hall	253 106	2 624	238	3 407	1 777.8	100.6	548	6 357	1 240.8	114.6	105	398	44.3	9.0
Hancock	4 690	86	3	D	D	D	24	149	17.0	2.0	1	D	D	D
Haralson	14 670	144	16	121	50.8	4.3	98	845	145.7	11.3	5	21	1.1	0.1
Harris	49 164	303	9	D	D	D	59	259	31.3	3.2	8	D	D	D
Hart	950	10	25	113	35.6	2.6	78	778	96.9	9.6	7	24	1.1	0.2
Heard	4 240	48	2	D	D	D	21	117	17.2	1.7	2	D	D	D
Henry	303 493	3 443	84	1 136	377.1	29.1	300	3 580	660.7	58.9	77	313	33.3	4.7
Houston	89 563	1 337	54	454	236.5	14.7	403	5 818	941.2	86.6	88	347	43.4	5.1
Irwin	0	0	10	54	13.3	1.1	31	226	28.3	3.1	2	D	D	D
Jackson	89 318	636	48	867	502.2	25.4	218	1 673	288.4	25.5	24	49	5.4	0.9
Jasper	14 559	150	3	D	D	D	21	148	19.9	2.0	3	12	0.3	0.1
Jeff Davis	0	0	23	228	177.9	6.1	79	660	127.9	9.2	4	19	1.7	0.3
Jefferson	1 624	19	19	188	59.8	3.1	83	681	94.3	10.2	6	33	0.9	0.4
Jenkins	0	0	8	44	10.9	0.7	34	235	38.0	3.2	2	D	D	D
Johnson	65	1	13	56	25.4	0.9	29	250	27.3	2.9	1	D	D	D
Jones	23 434	221	15	D	D	D	36	249	37.7	3.6	8	D	D	D
Lamar	7 894	116	6	63	10.0	1.2	51	440	74.1	6.8	5	6	0.3	0.1
Lanier	1 933	30	3	D	D	D	29	167	24.0	2.3	3	10	0.9	0.1
Laurens	5 021	95	64	390	125.3	9.5	265	2 872	417.5	38.4	35	149	14.8	2.3
Lee	32 572	286	7	D	D	D	39	362	54.0	4.4	5	7	0.9	0.1
Liberty	23 797	316	14	D	D	D	165	1 762	255.0	22.2	39	261	24.7	4.4
Lincoln	2 990	39	6	33	4.1	0.6	21	118	15.9	1.4	1	D	D	D
Long	NA	NA	1	D	D	D	9	37	7.1	0.4	1	D	D	D
Lowndes	38 888	571	135	1 155	452.9	31.5	533	6 187	1 008.5	91.3	88	517	52.4	8.2
Lumpkin	39 847	347	10	42	8.1	0.7	64	740	120.1	11.8	14	34	4.3	0.4
McDuffie	5 906	72	12	D	D	D	112	1 382	312.3	25.0	12	42	2.5	0.5
McIntosh	16 176	145	7	D	D	D	106	732	104.9	9.1	5	D	D	D
Macon	729	12	15	129	63.6	2.6	52	409	57.7	5.5	6	39	1.3	0.2
Madison	20 111	184	47	1 146	514.3	39.3	74	453	76.4	5.9	19	51	4.6	0.8
Marion	NA	NA	4	11	1.2	0.1	23	181	30.1	2.7	3	2	0.2	0.1
Meriwether	10 188	106	8	21	3.1	0.3	85	556	99.4	9.4	8	27	1.9	0.2
Miller	285	3	7	D	D	D	43	286	39.2	3.4	1	D	D	D
Mitchell	3 588	45	39	408	148.5	8.2	107	897	122.3	12.1	12	51	2.8	1.0
Monroe	22 864	194	13	59	26.4	1.0	75	503	70.3	6.7	7	13	1.4	0.2
Montgomery	3 375	45	5	106	36.5	2.7	29	138	20.2	1.9	1	D	D	D
Morgan	18 862	190	17	186	66.7	4.2	71	886	166.3	15.6	6	18	3.2	0.7
Murray	22 889	237	33	320	537.2	10.5	108	743	166.9	13.6	15	45	2.7	0.4
Muscogee	83 992	1 022	208	2 884	1 316.5	91.3	845	11 718	1 950.9	186.6	224	1 197	142.7	27.3
Newton	206 090	1 829	52	D	D	D	173	2 023	319.8	32.4	33	114	16.1	2.8
Oconee	51 689	299	22	D	D	D	55	799	166.6	14.7	18	86	10.8	1.2
Oglethorpe	NA	NA	10	84	6.3	1.2	25	140	27.9	1.9	2	D	D	D
Paulding	141 181	2 088	45	260	98.6	7.4	124	2 137	390.8	31.4	18	48	3.2	0.7
Peach	12 018	175	18	D	D	D	110	862	146.7	11.5	15	45	7.4	0.9
Pickens	72 702	559	23	D	D	D	74	694	238.5	12.9	22	33	4.8	0.7
Pierce	5 070	126	15	D	D	D	69	417	68.6	6.5	7	15	2.1	0.1
Pike	18 208	169	13	44	14.4	1.4	23	109	15.9	1.4	2	D	D	D
Polk	23 494	358	20	318	121.5	9.5	146	1 377	183.9	18.3	26	90	6.8	1.4
Pulaski	2 756	37	16	215	162.7	5.5	53	319	48.8	4.6	3	6	0.3	0.0
Putnam	30 205	203	8	88	63.7	2.6	56	490	83.7	8.3	8	21	0.9	0.3
Quitman	0	0	2	D	D	D	6	30	4.1	0.4	1	D	D	D
Rabun	20 301	320	8	D	D	D	91	561	97.6	8.7	22	63	7.7	1.2
Randolph	0	0	10	54	33.5	1.2	40	261	27.5	3.3	5	4	0.6	0.2

1. Establishments with payroll.

Table B. States and Counties — Professional, Manufacturing, and Accommodation and Foodservices

STATE County	Professional, Scientific, and Technical Services[1], 1997				Manufacturing, 1997				Accommodation and Foodservices, 1997			
	Number of Establishments	Number of Employees	Receipts (mil dol)	Annual Payroll (mil dol)	Number of Establishments	Number of Employees	Receipts (mil dol)	Annual Payroll (mil dol)	Number of Establishments	Number of Employees	Sales (mil dol)	Annual Payroll (mil dol)
	147	148	149	150	151	152	153	154	155	156	157	158
GEORGIA—Cont'd												
Fannin	26	76	3.0	1.2	28	922	146.6	15.7	35	431	11.3	3.3
Fayette	212	719	69.7	27.1	85	5 595	1 345.1	170.2	118	2 750	102.3	27.6
Floyd	131	650	61.6	19.7	120	9 583	1 892.4	280.0	151	2 572	87.8	22.9
Forsyth	206	824	83.2	30.1	129	4 337	701.3	127.7	89	1 523	54.5	15.0
Franklin	18	53	3.3	0.9	46	1 852	281.1	43.2	35	621	16.8	4.3
Fulton	4 614	56 202	7 607.2	2 846.1	897	37 948	14 240.9	1 283.6	2 292	57 973	2 364.4	682.1
Gilmer	28	90	4.4	1.7	34	3 404	303.0	52.3	30	428	11.1	2.9
Glascock	1	D	D	D	NA	NA	NA	NA	2	D	D	D
Glynn	179	579	43.4	16.6	71	3 784	993.6	124.9	214	7 051	251.5	84.3
Gordon	34	235	10.8	4.6	102	10 527	2 419.0	255.4	76	1 201	40.8	11.3
Grady	13	45	2.9	0.8	19	1 402	153.7	29.6	26	300	8.2	2.0
Greene	25	51	3.1	1.3	19	1 533	448.4	33.1	19	208	6.3	1.6
Gwinnett	1 939	12 871	1 326.6	534.3	737	29 121	6 241.7	1 071.3	896	19 623	720.4	199.8
Habersham	37	112	9.8	2.5	69	4 354	681.2	111.8	64	879	26.0	7.3
Hall	217	972	91.6	32.0	226	16 519	4 293.7	443.1	202	4 192	148.5	41.6
Hancock	5	13	2.2	0.3	NA	NA	NA	NA	5	46	1.2	0.3
Haralson	19	75	4.7	1.3	35	2 552	340.0	59.4	31	D	D	D
Harris	16	82	3.9	1.7	19	D	D	D	35	D	D	D
Hart	22	55	4.0	1.5	36	2 540	465.6	61.1	22	268	9.0	2.4
Heard	4	22	0.6	0.2	9	550	77.6	12.8	5	D	D	D
Henry	122	499	48.5	15.4	68	3 392	854.8	106.1	139	2 485	74.5	20.0
Houston	135	1 504	111.5	44.5	66	D	D	D	183	3 753	102.5	28.4
Irwin	5	25	2.0	0.9	7	746	38.5	13.7	9	70	2.0	0.5
Jackson	33	95	8.5	2.0	65	5 896	1 204.5	135.8	53	1 318	65.3	16.7
Jasper	6	19	1.4	0.4	19	737	176.7	21.4	7	78	2.2	0.6
Jeff Davis	15	49	2.4	0.8	23	2 493	304.4	49.0	20	D	D	D
Jefferson	11	36	2.0	1.1	28	1 999	294.2	51.9	17	207	6.4	1.5
Jenkins	7	15	0.7	0.1	4	1 294	154.3	25.0	12	D	D	D
Johnson	4	16	0.8	0.3	8	762	34.9	8.8	7	D	D	D
Jones	12	24	1.4	0.5	NA	NA	NA	NA	8	D	D	D
Lamar	16	27	1.7	0.5	13	1 605	190.9	35.1	18	217	6.6	1.6
Lanier	6	13	0.8	0.1	NA	NA	NA	NA	5	D	D	D
Laurens	44	197	12.4	5.1	43	5 703	888.6	134.2	76	1 448	40.9	10.0
Lee	7	7	0.7	0.1	NA	NA	NA	NA	9	94	2.4	0.8
Liberty	30	182	18.3	3.0	14	1 020	319.0	33.9	65	1 209	35.8	9.0
Lincoln	4	10	0.4	0.2	7	688	55.8	10.9	12	D	D	D
Long	2	D	D	D	NA	NA	NA	NA	6	39	1.1	0.3
Lowndes	132	738	46.2	18.5	98	5 492	1 468.9	146.7	194	3 700	109.3	30.8
Lumpkin	16	34	3.4	1.1	17	879	85.9	21.0	34	465	16.5	4.0
McDuffie	24	105	10.4	4.0	26	1 677	297.8	41.7	34	572	17.8	4.8
McIntosh	6	16	0.7	0.1	NA	NA	NA	NA	23	332	9.0	2.7
Macon	5	17	1.8	0.6	14	1 624	369.0	46.7	15	D	D	D
Madison	58	332	45.7	31.2	31	826	69.0	18.9	50	1 032	33.4	9.8
Marion	2	D	D	D	5	D	D	D	5	D	D	D
Meriwether	15	47	3.4	0.8	22	2 105	273.7	46.1	29	269	9.0	2.5
Miller	7	25	1.2	0.4	NA	NA	NA	NA	7	121	2.7	0.7
Mitchell	21	103	5.1	1.9	17	1 016	72.2	15.4	30	292	11.6	4.0
Monroe	23	63	3.8	1.1	21	515	57.1	10.7	33	616	21.6	4.7
Montgomery	5	13	0.4	0.2	NA	NA	NA	NA	7	90	2.0	0.5
Morgan	21	58	6.3	2.3	20	1 512	262.1	39.8	37	574	16.8	4.4
Murray	19	140	3.9	1.8	100	5 321	1 201.9	121.8	39	493	20.0	5.1
Muscogee	264	1 607	146.2	43.6	158	D	D	D	365	D	D	D
Newton	62	169	13.9	4.0	62	3 976	1 348.8	146.4	58	1 074	30.9	8.2
Oconee	44	158	15.7	5.3	30	746	208.8	20.8	13	134	3.5	0.8
Oglethorpe	10	20	1.4	0.8	NA	NA	NA	NA	8	59	1.4	0.4
Paulding	45	176	10.6	3.8	38	1 161	137.3	26.0	51	D	D	D
Peach	21	63	3.6	1.2	32	D	D	D	44	D	D	D
Pickens	30	69	5.2	2.0	35	1 155	135.8	26.7	25	331	11.3	3.0
Pierce	12	32	2.3	0.8	17	521	77.2	9.1	21	229	5.6	1.8
Pike	13	23	3.2	0.6	NA	NA	NA	NA	10	77	2.1	0.7
Polk	25	110	7.6	2.9	35	2 273	423.1	62.1	43	D	D	D
Pulaski	13	31	2.5	1.1	11	D	D	D	16	326	5.6	1.9
Putnam	21	48	3.4	0.7	24	2 030	424.8	56.8	22	191	6.1	1.3
Quitman	1	D	D	D	NA	NA	NA	NA	1	D	D	D
Rabun	25	72	4.2	1.5	27	1 870	316.0	44.1	47	573	19.0	5.3
Randolph	10	35	3.1	0.9	NA	NA	NA	NA	14	88	2.6	0.6

1. Firms subject to federal tax.

Table B. States and Counties — Health and Other Services and Federal Funds

STATE County	Health Care and Social Assistance[1], 1997				Other Services[1], 1997				Federal funds and grants, fiscal 1999[2] Expenditures (mil dol)			
										Direct payments for individuals[3]		
	Number of Establishments	Number of Employees	Receipts (mil dol)	Annual Payroll (mil dol)	Number of Establishments	Number of Employees	Receipts (mil dol)	Annual Payroll (mil dol)	Total	Social Security and government retirement	Medicare	Food stamps and Supplemental Security Income
	159	160	161	162	163	164	165	166	167	168	169	170
GEORGIA—Cont'd												
Fannin	32	418	29.7	9.2	12	39	2.5	0.6	93.7	49.7	21.3	4.0
Fayette	150	1 197	86.9	37.1	129	777	41.6	13.2	203.0	145.7	30.5	2.1
Floyd	165	4 018	345.6	131.4	95	721	41.6	14.1	332.2	170.7	70.9	14.2
Forsyth	90	1 115	50.4	22.3	105	607	34.8	10.9	126.1	72.5	25.7	4.0
Franklin	20	177	10.4	4.5	33	222	18.2	4.6	85.8	42.3	19.4	4.3
Fulton	2 252	26 639	2 258.3	1 009.7	1 543	12 781	928.9	270.3	6 801.8	1 397.9	526.8	215.5
Gilmer	22	437	23.5	8.8	18	87	6.2	1.7	80.9	42.9	17.9	4.4
Glascock	2	D	D	D	1	D	D	D	13.1	5.9	3.1	0.3
Glynn	205	2 257	149.3	60.7	123	557	36.0	10.5	412.2	155.9	65.7	12.0
Gordon	42	373	26.1	9.9	37	174	12.3	3.1	132.5	66.4	26.9	5.5
Grady	24	263	11.0	4.0	17	84	6.2	1.3	86.6	37.6	14.2	7.1
Greene	13	139	7.3	3.2	15	70	4.1	1.0	61.7	29.0	11.7	3.4
Gwinnett	927	9 585	656.4	265.8	1 032	7 165	510.3	173.4	926.6	383.7	123.5	20.8
Habersham	60	488	26.5	10.7	42	149	10.8	2.8	117.6	63.3	25.3	4.9
Hall	245	2 626	230.0	95.8	184	860	56.2	15.3	372.8	187.4	72.5	13.8
Hancock	12	267	8.2	3.3	9	11	1.1	0.2	52.7	20.9	11.1	2.9
Haralson	28	319	12.8	5.3	25	100	8.0	1.7	99.5	45.4	20.3	4.6
Harris	9	D	D	D	13	27	1.9	0.4	73.0	42.5	9.6	2.5
Hart	27	509	24.8	9.2	22	110	8.9	1.8	90.9	39.0	16.7	3.1
Heard	8	111	3.1	1.6	6	12	0.8	0.2	30.3	14.1	6.5	1.7
Henry	127	1 299	66.8	31.8	120	586	34.0	10.3	311.5	164.3	44.7	7.2
Houston	181	1 927	125.5	52.7	162	744	38.3	11.3	1 214.2	287.0	52.5	16.0
Irwin	8	146	4.2	2.1	11	29	1.7	0.3	41.9	14.3	7.1	2.2
Jackson	39	317	19.5	11.1	43	185	10.8	2.8	131.3	62.7	25.9	5.8
Jasper	7	37	1.5	0.5	11	21	1.7	0.3	35.7	17.7	6.3	1.7
Jeff Davis	11	61	2.9	0.8	20	67	4.5	0.9	49.7	22.2	10.3	2.9
Jefferson	22	248	9.7	3.5	19	61	2.8	0.8	95.7	34.2	18.0	6.3
Jenkins	8	60	3.4	1.2	8	20	1.0	0.2	44.6	14.6	8.8	2.8
Johnson	5	136	6.9	3.0	9	21	1.4	0.3	42.7	16.0	9.5	3.3
Jones	16	335	14.8	6.7	15	48	2.3	0.5	61.5	32.2	10.9	2.2
Lamar	16	186	6.8	2.4	14	84	8.1	1.9	61.4	33.7	11.1	2.6
Lanier	8	128	2.7	1.3	5	13	1.1	0.2	27.9	10.8	6.5	1.7
Laurens	96	1 855	135.5	48.9	54	212	11.1	2.9	230.9	88.7	33.7	11.7
Lee	7	142	3.9	1.6	16	51	3.5	1.1	46.8	24.2	6.6	2.0
Liberty	45	586	25.5	9.2	60	379	16.7	5.2	231.0	85.7	15.1	8.1
Lincoln	10	44	3.0	1.3	14	31	2.4	0.4	38.9	17.5	8.4	1.5
Long	3	16	0.2	0.1	2	D	D	D	29.6	10.4	3.0	1.3
Lowndes	185	2 740	162.4	76.4	142	695	37.7	10.6	532.8	154.9	55.1	20.5
Lumpkin	28	456	30.7	9.5	15	69	4.0	0.8	58.5	26.5	8.9	1.5
McDuffie	41	873	29.9	17.2	38	110	7.4	1.6	89.4	40.6	18.1	5.8
McIntosh	5	40	2.3	0.9	13	26	1.4	0.4	59.6	20.4	9.7	3.1
Macon	20	417	22.7	9.0	10	53	4.9	1.5	68.9	21.0	14.0	4.4
Madison	33	311	16.5	7.3	31	256	22.7	4.7	83.0	42.6	16.2	5.3
Marion	5	38	1.8	0.6	2	D	D	D	27.7	8.8	3.5	2.1
Meriwether	24	203	7.4	3.7	15	56	3.7	0.8	89.7	40.1	16.4	5.7
Miller	9	46	1.8	0.7	12	24	1.8	0.5	33.1	11.3	5.5	2.1
Mitchell	14	160	8.6	3.0	26	118	6.1	1.7	101.8	34.6	16.5	7.8
Monroe	20	256	9.8	4.0	20	74	6.8	1.4	57.9	29.6	11.6	3.0
Montgomery	4	12	0.5	0.1	2	D	D	D	34.0	12.8	6.6	2.9
Morgan	16	169	7.9	2.5	12	52	2.5	0.7	52.8	25.9	11.4	2.5
Murray	17	248	17.3	5.8	14	59	4.1	1.4	77.7	40.3	16.6	4.5
Muscogee	343	5 225	439.9	171.5	305	2 004	104.6	35.8	1 586.7	475.8	119.1	47.0
Newton	80	747	40.7	17.9	61	248	19.3	5.8	178.7	86.8	38.7	10.9
Oconee	34	202	11.4	4.9	32	260	12.3	4.9	57.8	33.3	10.5	2.3
Oglethorpe	9	97	4.6	1.8	6	9	0.7	0.1	31.8	13.0	6.2	1.5
Paulding	39	339	13.2	5.5	58	226	14.5	4.7	120.1	63.6	20.5	5.5
Peach	22	196	9.9	3.9	27	122	8.3	1.7	138.4	70.1	16.5	6.9
Pickens	22	476	24.6	9.5	12	30	1.9	0.4	90.6	40.9	13.7	2.4
Pierce	13	106	4.3	2.3	20	61	2.8	0.6	64.6	31.3	11.5	4.0
Pike	5	102	3.3	1.6	4	7	0.6	0.1	47.3	22.4	8.0	1.4
Polk	42	505	24.8	8.8	42	312	24.4	5.3	169.5	79.8	34.5	8.4
Pulaski	18	333	12.5	5.4	10	35	1.6	0.4	50.8	21.7	8.9	2.5
Putnam	14	243	10.8	4.2	14	43	2.6	0.7	67.4	37.3	13.0	2.7
Quitman	1	D	D	D	1	D	D	D	17.4	6.7	2.8	1.1
Rabun	27	276	14.7	5.9	18	41	3.5	0.8	64.9	33.2	15.5	1.8
Randolph	3	27	0.7	0.5	13	34	1.9	0.4	45.7	14.5	7.0	4.1

1. Firms subject to federal tax. 2. October 1, 1998 to September 30, 1999. 3. State totals may include programs not allocated by county.

Table B. States and Counties — Federal Funds and Local Government Finances

	Federal funds and grants, fiscal 1999[1] (cont'd)							Local government finances, 1997				
	Expenditures (mil dol) (cont'd)							General revenue				
	Procurement contract awards			Grants[2]							Taxes	
STATE County											Per capita[3] (dollars)	
	Salaries and wages	Defense	Other	Medicaid and other health-related	Nutrition and family welfare	Education	Other	Total (mil dol)	Intergovern-mental (mil dol)	Total (mil dol)	Total	Property
	171	172	173	174	175	176	177	178	179	180	181	182
GEORGIA—Cont'd												
Fannin	2.5	0.0	0.5	10.0	1.8	0.8	2.1	28.5	14.0	11.0	605	334
Fayette	11.7	1.8	2.5	3.2	2.0	1.0	1.3	165.5	59.4	86.5	1 017	808
Floyd	11.3	0.2	4.8	30.6	11.1	3.6	6.4	319.2	89.7	79.3	937	553
Forsyth	7.6	0.1	1.9	8.7	1.8	1.2	2.2	134.6	42.9	74.7	986	635
Franklin	2.6	0.0	0.7	11.2	1.4	0.9	1.4	56.4	14.7	13.2	711	384
Fulton	1 213.8	356.5	563.5	754.2	546.2	243.2	796.0	3 275.8	972.5	1 537.1	2 127	1 387
Gilmer	3.2	0.0	0.6	7.2	1.4	0.7	2.1	32.3	16.2	12.1	675	492
Glascock	0.6	0.0	0.2	2.4	0.2	0.1	0.1	4.0	2.0	1.5	600	484
Glynn	82.4	2.8	44.6	17.9	12.3	3.2	11.2	283.1	67.1	78.6	1 179	745
Gordon	5.6	0.7	1.5	8.8	2.9	1.6	9.6	78.0	38.4	22.5	559	342
Grady	1.7	0.0	0.5	11.8	2.9	1.6	2.0	38.3	21.5	11.7	545	362
Greene	2.5	0.0	0.5	8.4	2.3	1.2	1.6	26.5	11.2	12.2	914	621
Gwinnett	167.6	76.0	73.4	21.8	10.3	8.0	32.8	1 219.1	341.7	493.6	986	833
Habersham	5.6	0.0	1.2	10.7	1.7	0.6	2.4	76.7	20.7	19.6	627	427
Hall	21.9	12.2	5.9	26.8	20.3	3.8	2.3	258.8	98.1	115.0	991	609
Hancock	0.8	0.0	0.2	10.6	3.9	0.8	0.8	32.1	11.6	8.1	905	771
Haralson	2.8	0.0	0.8	9.1	2.4	1.1	12.6	50.5	22.7	13.7	566	354
Harris	2.5	0.1	0.5	8.0	1.8	0.8	3.9	41.5	20.1	16.8	756	536
Hart	4.3	5.5	0.6	11.8	1.9	0.9	5.8	40.1	19.3	12.2	566	389
Heard	0.8	0.0	0.2	4.0	1.3	0.5	0.7	20.6	8.1	7.8	785	570
Henry	64.0	0.5	4.6	10.6	3.7	1.4	9.0	158.7	53.2	84.1	857	640
Houston	603.4	201.9	6.1	20.0	13.9	2.8	2.2	255.6	83.8	54.7	528	423
Irwin	1.7	0.0	0.3	6.8	1.6	0.7	0.2	16.1	8.7	5.9	658	509
Jackson	5.4	0.0	7.1	14.8	2.5	1.5	4.6	83.6	31.7	26.3	722	432
Jasper	1.1	0.0	0.3	4.5	1.9	0.4	1.3	18.5	8.2	7.8	792	588
Jeff Davis	1.3	0.0	0.4	7.2	1.8	0.6	0.1	33.8	15.3	9.1	722	346
Jefferson	2.2	0.0	0.5	20.4	4.8	1.7	0.7	36.7	17.4	10.1	566	411
Jenkins	1.0	0.0	0.3	9.1	2.1	1.0	0.0	18.7	8.4	5.1	602	363
Johnson	0.9	0.0	0.3	8.2	1.6	0.6	0.1	13.3	7.8	4.1	494	324
Jones	1.5	0.2	0.3	5.6	1.9	0.9	5.2	30.8	16.8	10.8	475	313
Lamar	2.3	0.0	0.5	5.9	1.8	0.6	0.9	24.0	10.2	8.7	590	437
Lanier	0.7	0.0	0.2	4.6	1.2	0.5	0.1	10.5	6.3	3.2	467	302
Laurens	36.1	1.9	4.8	28.3	7.1	2.8	5.7	94.1	56.3	24.0	551	333
Lee	1.5	0.0	0.4	4.3	1.5	0.7	0.2	36.4	20.0	12.1	554	412
Liberty	64.9	0.3	1.8	9.5	7.2	9.9	26.3	111.4	47.3	40.1	668	330
Lincoln	0.9	0.0	4.1	4.4	1.1	0.7	-0.2	13.3	7.3	4.4	537	362
Long	0.5	0.0	0.1	2.7	0.8	0.4	9.7	11.5	7.0	3.9	464	392
Lowndes	157.3	72.7	2.8	31.2	15.7	5.6	4.3	298.0	91.2	68.8	819	343
Lumpkin	10.0	0.1	0.5	6.5	1.2	0.4	1.7	30.3	11.0	13.5	743	512
McDuffie	3.7	0.0	0.5	12.7	3.4	2.0	2.0	56.8	23.0	14.5	673	363
McIntosh	1.2	0.0	0.3	5.4	1.8	0.6	17.1	16.4	7.6	7.4	747	441
Macon	1.6	0.0	0.3	12.7	4.3	1.5	1.7	29.5	13.7	10.4	781	522
Madison	3.0	0.0	0.9	10.8	1.9	1.1	0.3	30.4	16.7	10.7	438	291
Marion	1.3	0.0	0.1	5.8	1.1	0.5	3.3	13.2	8.0	3.3	498	322
Meriwether	2.3	0.1	0.7	15.1	4.0	1.6	2.0	40.6	20.6	14.6	638	429
Miller	0.9	0.0	0.2	4.5	1.1	0.4	0.6	11.1	5.9	4.2	671	514
Mitchell	3.2	0.2	0.6	18.6	5.7	2.0	0.4	46.9	27.4	11.4	542	395
Monroe	2.5	0.3	0.5	5.7	1.2	0.7	1.5	61.9	11.6	23.0	1 194	834
Montgomery	1.1	0.0	0.3	6.9	1.1	0.5	0.0	9.7	5.6	3.2	414	253
Morgan	1.9	0.0	0.5	6.7	1.8	0.6	0.2	34.3	12.9	13.6	931	620
Murray	4.3	0.5	0.8	5.8	2.0	1.0	1.4	50.7	25.9	18.0	563	339
Muscogee	778.8	1.2	9.4	67.8	33.2	13.6	22.0	420.3	171.7	182.5	999	589
Newton	7.1	1.0	2.2	14.4	5.7	2.4	8.8	133.1	44.7	40.4	732	484
Oconee	4.3	0.1	0.9	3.8	0.9	0.5	0.1	37.2	16.6	16.9	735	541
Oglethorpe	0.9	0.0	1.7	5.6	1.4	0.5	0.2	17.8	10.8	5.7	506	377
Paulding	5.0	0.1	1.4	8.4	2.8	1.2	10.9	123.4	46.4	39.7	576	386
Peach	4.9	2.5	0.7	10.6	6.6	4.2	7.5	49.7	19.1	16.3	678	414
Pickens	2.6	0.0	3.1	5.7	1.8	0.6	19.2	33.6	17.9	12.4	666	486
Pierce	2.0	0.0	0.9	7.0	1.7	0.8	0.8	24.4	13.9	8.4	546	350
Pike	5.6	0.0	0.5	4.5	0.9	0.5	2.6	16.3	8.9	6.1	492	347
Polk	4.0	7.3	3.6	17.8	4.6	1.6	6.0	63.0	28.4	22.9	639	405
Pulaski	1.0	0.0	0.2	7.5	1.7	0.5	0.0	15.9	8.4	5.5	659	475
Putnam	2.7	0.1	0.5	5.6	3.3	0.7	0.5	45.5	13.8	16.7	990	658
Quitman	0.5	0.0	0.2	2.9	0.6	0.2	2.1	4.8	2.9	1.4	578	466
Rabun	2.5	0.1	0.6	8.3	0.8	0.3	1.3	27.6	7.4	12.3	928	735
Randolph	0.9	0.1	0.2	9.1	2.9	2.0	1.5	25.7	12.3	4.3	542	322

1. October 1, 1998 to September 30, 1999. 2. State totals may include programs not allocated by county. 3. Based on the resident population estimated as of July 1 of the year shown.

Table B. States and Counties — Local Government Finances, Government Employment, and Elections

STATE County	Local government finances, 1997 (cont'd)									Government employment, 1998			Presidential election, 2000		
	Direct general expenditure							Debt outstanding					Percent of vote cast —		
			Percent of total for —												
	Total (mil dol)	Per capita¹ (dollars)	Education	Health and hospitals	Police protection	Public welfare	Highways	Total (mil dol)	Per capita¹ (dollars)	Federal civilian	Federal military	State and local	Democratic	Republican	All other
	183	184	185	186	187	188	189	190	191	192	193	194	195	196	197
GEORGIA—Cont'd															
Fannin	26.3	1 454	65.2	0.7	4.0	0.1	8.6	6.0	330	67	72	789	NA	NA	NA
Fayette	180.3	2 120	65.0	0.4	5.3	0.1	4.5	161.5	1 899	182	342	3 728	NA	NA	NA
Floyd	303.5	3 586	29.1	41.9	3.5	0.1	3.6	141.5	1 672	240	341	5 971	NA	NA	NA
Forsyth	154.7	2 042	65.5	0.6	3.3	0.4	3.9	158.5	2 092	138	332	2 628	NA	NA	NA
Franklin	55.5	2 999	30.8	42.1	4.1	0.9	4.3	14.3	771	48	74	945	NA	NA	NA
Fulton	2 693.7	3 728	33.2	6.7	5.8	1.6	2.6	7 810.4	10 810	23 204	4 555	77 637	NA	NA	NA
Gilmer	31.0	1 734	62.6	0.7	4.0	0.0	5.0	9.7	544	75	72	867	NA	NA	NA
Glascock	3.9	1 582	61.6	1.8	3.5	1.1	10.4	0.4	151	11	10	157	NA	NA	NA
Glynn	273.2	4 099	30.3	44.0	4.0	0.3	2.1	141.7	2 126	1 168	278	5 804	NA	NA	NA
Gordon	78.4	1 947	53.9	4.1	3.7	0.3	3.4	31.1	772	93	158	1 992	NA	NA	NA
Grady	41.0	1 906	65.7	1.2	3.6	0.1	4.6	7.3	341	41	83	1 191	NA	NA	NA
Greene	25.2	1 878	55.9	4.7	6.7	1.2	5.4	8.2	612	38	53	866	NA	NA	NA
Gwinnett	1 234.1	2 464	50.5	15.2	3.7	0.4	6.5	1 006.1	2 009	3 626	2 018	18 497	NA	NA	NA
Habersham	75.6	2 424	39.4	32.5	3.0	0.1	4.2	32.5	1 042	132	123	2 481	NA	NA	NA
Hall	262.2	2 259	47.4	8.4	4.2	0.9	2.6	234.4	2 019	456	461	6 953	NA	NA	NA
Hancock	26.2	2 917	38.7	30.3	3.1	0.7	4.6	14.3	1 594	15	35	889	NA	NA	NA
Haralson	53.6	2 220	49.1	18.8	4.5	0.2	4.5	12.7	525	51	95	1 361	NA	NA	NA
Harris	38.7	1 742	67.1	0.9	3.6	1.4	3.3	24.2	1 088	56	86	931	NA	NA	NA
Hart	39.2	1 824	46.6	27.3	3.7	0.2	2.2	12.4	576	99	84	985	NA	NA	NA
Heard	20.7	2 080	52.8	0.6	4.1	3.7	7.5	27.5	2 760	15	39	543	NA	NA	NA
Henry	163.7	1 669	59.4	5.0	5.4	0.6	4.5	216.7	2 208	404	3 713	NA	NA	NA	
Houston	256.3	2 476	41.7	32.6	4.6	0.0	2.2	107.8	1 041	11 505	4 671	6 254	NA	NA	NA
Irwin	16.0	1 781	66.3	1.2	4.9	0.5	5.8	2.9	324	29	35	679	NA	NA	NA
Jackson	89.9	2 464	50.1	17.1	3.4	0.4	8.0	57.7	1 581	107	145	2 026	NA	NA	NA
Jasper	17.7	1 789	57.5	3.1	7.5	0.2	6.5	7.6	766	23	39	664	NA	NA	NA
Jeff Davis	33.6	2 664	46.0	21.7	3.5	0.2	6.5	5.9	470	30	49	768	NA	NA	NA
Jefferson	38.0	2 128	49.9	19.1	4.7	0.7	3.7	14.2	794	46	69	1 058	NA	NA	NA
Jenkins	19.0	2 262	45.3	22.2	3.7	0.5	10.1	2.5	303	25	33	576	NA	NA	NA
Johnson	14.4	1 731	61.5	1.1	3.5	0.6	7.6	1.2	144	17	32	739	NA	NA	NA
Jones	31.1	1 376	69.9	0.8	5.0	0.0	6.1	20.3	899	30	89	787	NA	NA	NA
Lamar	25.3	1 722	55.7	0.8	4.6	0.1	6.8	15.9	1 086	37	57	866	NA	NA	NA
Lanier	10.5	1 545	71.3	0.9	4.4	0.1	5.2	2.2	324	13	27	344	NA	NA	NA
Laurens	118.2	2 718	44.3	14.7	3.5	0.4	5.2	34.7	797	906	169	3 042	NA	NA	NA
Lee	39.4	1 803	65.5	0.6	3.6	0.2	6.7	18.4	840	37	88	1 110	NA	NA	NA
Liberty	92.2	1 536	55.0	13.7	5.5	0.4	2.4	21.6	360	3 226	15 923	2 656	NA	NA	NA
Lincoln	14.3	1 769	58.1	1.1	3.1	0.9	6.6	7.2	886	19	32	441	NA	NA	NA
Long	10.7	1 288	69.8	1.0	5.9	2.1	5.3	2.5	303	11	33	410	NA	NA	NA
Lowndes	290.3	3 456	27.7	48.8	3.5	0.1	6.1	52.7	628	975	4 097	8 132	NA	NA	NA
Lumpkin	33.3	1 837	48.0	0.8	4.4	0.2	4.4	17.2	946	73	275	1 263	NA	NA	NA
McDuffie	50.3	2 330	47.6	19.3	2.8	1.0	3.6	11.4	528	43	127	1 417	NA	NA	NA
McIntosh	17.7	1 785	57.9	3.7	7.0	0.2	10.5	1.8	185	25	39	675	NA	NA	NA
Macon	30.7	2 320	55.7	1.0	4.6	0.2	3.5	34.8	2 625	31	51	945	NA	NA	NA
Madison	32.1	1 315	62.5	1.1	2.7	0.4	7.5	7.5	305	46	94	890	NA	NA	NA
Marion	14.4	2 201	73.2	1.1	2.3	0.4	7.9	6.4	983	36	26	408	NA	NA	NA
Meriwether	38.4	1 676	63.3	1.5	4.9	0.5	3.5	29.9	1 304	47	89	1 736	NA	NA	NA
Miller	11.1	1 775	65.3	1.6	5.2	0.3	4.7	2.6	409	24	25	449	NA	NA	NA
Mitchell	52.6	2 494	53.3	6.3	4.8	0.1	4.7	23.1	1 095	77	82	1 960	NA	NA	NA
Monroe	59.8	3 104	32.7	12.3	5.0	0.2	3.0	248.2	12 883	44	76	1 449	NA	NA	NA
Montgomery	9.5	1 232	68.2	1.3	3.0	1.5	6.2	1.9	242	25	30	410	NA	NA	NA
Morgan	34.6	2 378	49.5	12.9	3.3	0.8	12.3	9.7	663	40	58	870	NA	NA	NA
Murray	53.0	1 659	63.4	2.0	3.0	0.3	8.4	42.5	1 331	100	126	1 234	NA	NA	NA
Muscogee	403.1	2 205	45.6	8.8	6.3	0.2	2.8	423.9	2 319	5 769	4 761	11 932	NA	NA	NA
Newton	134.3	2 436	47.3	20.7	4.8	0.3	3.3	83.7	1 518	120	224	2 531	NA	NA	NA
Oconee	43.5	1 886	65.7	1.0	3.2	0.8	6.6	32.8	1 423	90	92	1 064	NA	NA	NA
Oglethorpe	17.6	1 565	72.2	0.9	2.6	0.8	5.9	0.1	12	15	44	435	NA	NA	NA
Paulding	125.9	1 825	56.0	19.3	3.2	0.3	4.1	104.7	1 518	81	284	2 677	NA	NA	NA
Peach	49.6	2 061	54.6	15.0	5.7	0.2	2.6	16.4	682	94	102	1 949	NA	NA	NA
Pickens	37.6	2 026	71.3	1.3	3.5	0.1	3.6	19.6	1 056	50	76	969	NA	NA	NA
Pierce	26.2	1 691	66.5	0.8	3.6	0.1	10.4	6.3	407	46	61	737	NA	NA	NA
Pike	15.6	1 258	65.2	4.1	3.9	0.2	6.3	10.6	860	29	49	542	NA	NA	NA
Polk	62.4	1 741	54.1	8.6	5.5	0.2	4.4	22.0	613	72	140	1 752	NA	NA	NA
Pulaski	17.2	2 059	57.9	1.0	6.8	0.2	6.2	5.3	641	17	32	827	NA	NA	NA
Putnam	50.7	3 007	47.1	14.9	5.0	0.4	3.3	109.8	6 515	79	68	1 007	NA	NA	NA
Quitman	4.5	1 824	60.6	2.0	4.6	0.2	6.4	2.0	822	0	10	119	NA	NA	NA
Rabun	29.3	2 213	35.9	17.7	5.5	0.4	11.4	4.5	342	63	52	751	NA	NA	NA
Randolph	26.6	3 362	47.3	27.9	2.3	0.1	6.0	2.0	257	26	30	783	NA	NA	NA

1. Based on the resident population estimated as of July 1 of the year shown.

STATE/County code	MSA/PMSA/NECMA code[1]	County Type[2]	STATE County	Land area,[3] (sq km) 1990	Total persons	Rank	Per square kilometer	White	Black	Am. Indian, Eskimo, Aleut	Asian and Pacific Islander	Percent Hispanic[4]	Under 5 years	5 to 17 years	18 to 24 years	25 to 34 years	35 to 44 years	45 to 54 years
				1	2	3	4	5	6	7	8	9	10	11	12	13	14	15
			GEORGIA—Cont'd															
13 245	0600	2	Richmond	839	190 310	283	226.8	49.9	46.8	0.3	3.0	3.6	7.4	18.8	12.0	15.5	15.6	11.7
13 247	0520	1	Rockdale	339	68 968	707	203.4	88.0	10.0	0.2	1.8	2.2	7.3	20.0	8.2	14.1	18.1	14.8
13 249	...	9	Schley	434	3 949	2 918	9.1	59.9	39.8	0.3	0.0	3.2	7.7	21.2	10.3	11.8	14.7	15.1
13 251	...	6	Screven	1 680	14 463	2 101	8.6	48.9	50.8	0.1	0.2	0.7	7.3	21.1	8.1	12.7	15.6	12.0
13 253	...	6	Seminole	617	9 803	2 445	15.9	61.5	38.0	0.3	0.2	5.8	6.5	20.0	9.5	12.7	13.8	12.8
13 255	0520	1	Spalding	513	57 825	813	112.7	65.0	34.1	0.2	0.8	1.2	7.6	20.1	9.0	13.9	15.9	13.4
13 257	...	7	Stephens	464	25 332	1 521	54.6	84.2	14.9	0.2	0.8	1.2	6.3	16.9	10.0	11.8	15.1	13.7
13 259	...	8	Stewart	1 188	5 374	2 816	4.5	31.1	68.0	0.4	0.5	0.8	6.2	20.2	9.4	11.8	14.2	12.4
13 261	...	6	Sumter	1 257	31 362	1 337	24.9	47.0	52.1	0.3	0.6	1.1	7.5	21.5	11.4	12.8	14.8	11.8
13 263	...	8	Talbot	1 019	6 969	2 679	6.8	32.4	67.3	0.2	0.1	1.3	6.2	19.9	8.3	13.4	16.2	13.3
13 265	...	9	Taliaferro	506	1 924	3 065	3.8	33.1	66.6	0.1	0.3	1.4	6.4	20.5	7.6	11.3	13.2	14.3
13 267	...	7	Tattnall	1 253	19 171	1 811	15.3	66.3	32.9	0.2	0.6	5.1	6.7	18.0	9.1	15.9	15.6	13.3
13 269	...	8	Taylor	978	8 287	2 570	8.5	50.5	49.2	0.0	0.3	1.2	6.7	20.7	9.5	13.0	13.6	13.9
13 271	...	7	Telfair	1 143	11 406	2 312	10.0	59.9	40.0	0.1	0.1	0.6	6.7	21.1	8.6	12.5	14.7	11.5
13 273	...	6	Terrell	869	11 205	2 334	12.9	34.3	65.4	0.1	0.3	0.6	7.3	22.0	8.4	12.1	14.4	13.5
13 275	...	6	Thomas	1 420	42 896	1 026	30.2	55.9	43.5	0.3	0.3	1.3	7.2	20.8	8.1	12.7	15.1	13.4
13 277	...	7	Tift	687	36 975	1 159	53.8	67.8	31.1	0.1	0.9	5.4	7.8	20.8	10.9	13.4	15.4	12.0
13 279	...	7	Toombs	950	25 990	1 495	27.4	70.4	27.8	0.3	1.4	6.4	7.8	22.0	8.2	13.2	15.2	13.1
13 281	...	9	Towns	431	8 800	2 521	20.4	99.7	0.0	0.2	0.1	0.6	4.2	11.8	8.9	9.2	12.0	12.0
13 283	...	7	Treutlen	520	5 933	2 777	11.4	61.4	38.5	0.0	0.0	0.5	7.0	21.1	9.5	11.7	14.2	13.0
13 285	...	4	Troup	1 072	58 801	805	54.9	63.5	35.5	0.1	0.9	1.0	7.5	20.2	9.3	13.5	15.9	12.1
13 287	...	7	Turner	741	9 249	2 489	12.5	53.5	45.9	0.2	0.4	0.7	7.8	23.1	9.4	11.0	14.0	12.3
13 289	4680	2	Twiggs	933	10 198	2 406	10.9	47.9	51.9	0.1	0.1	0.7	7.3	22.1	8.8	13.6	14.6	13.1
13 291	...	9	Union	836	17 234	1 915	20.6	99.2	0.2	0.3	0.3	0.9	5.5	15.6	6.8	10.3	13.9	13.7
13 293	...	7	Upson	843	27 079	1 461	32.1	66.5	32.8	0.1	0.5	0.8	6.5	18.6	8.7	13.0	14.8	13.9
13 295	1560	2	Walker	1 156	62 963	765	54.5	94.4	4.8	0.3	0.4	0.8	6.4	18.6	7.8	12.9	15.6	14.5
13 297	0520	1	Walton	853	58 498	807	68.6	76.5	22.5	0.3	0.7	1.7	7.6	20.0	9.4	14.3	16.0	14.3
13 299	...	7	Ware	2 338	35 232	1 217	15.1	68.6	30.5	0.2	0.7	1.0	6.6	19.4	8.1	12.2	15.5	12.4
13 301	...	8	Warren	740	6 075	2 766	8.2	34.8	65.0	0.0	0.2	0.1	7.4	19.7	8.6	12.3	14.5	11.8
13 303	...	7	Washington	1 762	20 198	1 752	11.5	42.3	57.4	0.0	0.2	0.6	7.4	21.1	8.5	13.8	15.4	12.3
13 305	...	7	Wayne	1 670	25 610	1 510	15.3	76.0	23.5	0.2	0.4	1.5	7.4	21.0	8.1	12.8	16.0	13.3
13 307	...	8	Webster	543	2 203	3 046	4.1	44.3	55.5	0.2	0.0	0.1	6.2	19.9	8.8	12.6	15.1	11.8
13 309	...	9	Wheeler	771	4 864	2 850	6.3	64.4	35.4	0.1	0.2	3.3	7.5	21.3	8.8	10.8	15.0	13.5
13 311	...	9	White	626	18 195	1 859	29.1	95.2	3.5	0.3	1.0	1.5	5.7	16.4	8.3	11.5	15.3	15.1
13 313	...	4	Whitfield	751	83 220	610	110.8	93.7	5.1	0.4	0.8	6.3	7.3	18.8	9.7	14.3	16.2	14.2
13 315	...	9	Wilcox	985	7 419	2 646	7.5	62.4	37.4	0.1	0.1	0.8	7.1	21.1	8.1	11.1	15.0	13.2
13 317	...	6	Wilkes	1 221	10 556	2 373	8.6	47.4	52.3	0.2	0.2	0.6	6.0	19.3	7.5	12.4	15.0	13.5
13 319	...	8	Wilkinson	1 157	10 908	2 352	9.4	51.7	48.1	0.1	0.1	0.5	7.3	21.5	9.6	13.9	14.4	13.0
13 321	...	6	Worth	1 476	22 483	1 637	15.2	63.2	36.1	0.3	0.4	1.8	8.0	22.0	9.1	12.8	15.7	13.1
15 000	...	X	HAWAII	16 636	1 185 497	X	71.3	33.0	2.8	0.6	63.6	8.1	6.8	17.6	10.1	12.4	16.7	14.0
15 001	...	5	Hawaii	10 433	142 390	373	13.6	40.0	0.9	0.9	58.3	10.0	7.2	20.5	7.4	10.4	17.7	14.1
15 003	3320	2	Honolulu	1 554	864 571	44	556.4	30.9	3.6	0.5	65.0	7.4	6.6	16.8	11.0	12.8	16.3	13.9
15 005	...	NA	Kalawao	34	58	3 141	1.7	22.4	12.1	19.0	46.6	19.0	3.4	5.2	10.3	17.2	13.8	1.7
15 007	...	5	Kauai	1 612	56 539	824	35.1	35.0	0.7	0.4	63.9	11.4	7.3	19.6	7.9	10.9	17.4	14.1
15 009	...	5	Maui	3 002	121 939	433	40.6	39.3	0.9	0.7	59.2	8.8	7.4	19.0	8.2	12.2	18.2	14.5
16 000	...	X	IDAHO	214 325	1 251 700	X	5.8	96.9	0.6	1.3	1.2	7.4	7.4	20.6	11.5	12.3	14.9	13.0
16 001	1080	2	Ada	2 733	283 402	194	103.7	97.0	0.7	0.7	1.7	4.0	7.2	18.8	11.9	14.3	16.9	13.4
16 003	...	9	Adams	3 535	3 787	2 930	1.1	98.3	0.5	1.1	0.1	2.1	6.4	18.5	6.9	10.5	15.2	15.2
16 005	6340	5	Bannock	2 883	74 881	662	26.0	94.7	1.2	2.7	1.4	6.2	7.6	21.8	13.0	12.8	14.7	12.0
16 007	...	7	Bear Lake	2 516	6 561	2 724	2.6	98.8	0.5	0.4	0.3	3.8	8.1	26.0	7.3	10.3	11.7	12.1
16 009	...	8	Benewah	2 010	9 066	2 500	4.5	92.2	0.2	7.2	0.4	2.3	6.5	20.1	8.8	10.5	15.8	14.6
16 011	...	7	Bingham	5 426	42 127	1 039	7.8	91.9	0.4	6.8	0.9	13.1	8.7	26.8	9.4	11.7	12.9	11.9
16 013	...	7	Blaine	6 850	17 326	1 911	2.5	98.3	0.3	0.4	1.0	4.3	7.0	17.0	8.9	15.9	21.3	14.9
16 015	...	8	Boise	4 927	5 311	2 819	1.1	97.8	0.4	1.2	0.6	4.0	6.6	19.1	7.8	11.0	17.9	15.6
16 017	...	6	Bonner	4 500	36 071	1 191	8.0	98.4	0.4	0.8	0.4	2.2	6.5	19.4	7.3	10.4	17.4	14.7
16 019	...	5	Bonneville	4 840	81 536	623	16.8	97.6	0.7	0.6	1.2	6.0	8.6	23.1	11.0	12.8	13.9	12.5
16 021	...	9	Boundary	3 286	9 977	2 429	3.0	97.6	0.3	1.7	0.4	4.4	7.0	22.2	8.6	10.5	15.6	12.6
16 023	...	9	Butte	5 783	3 012	2 987	0.5	98.7	0.4	0.7	0.2	4.8	6.9	24.6	6.6	9.4	14.8	13.7
16 025	...	9	Camas	2 784	865	3 118	0.3	97.6	0.6	1.3	0.6	1.0	6.8	20.6	6.4	10.6	15.5	19.1
16 027	1080	2	Canyon	1 527	124 442	420	81.5	97.4	0.4	0.8	1.4	18.5	8.2	21.4	11.7	11.8	14.1	12.6
16 029	...	7	Caribou	4 574	7 273	2 656	1.6	98.0	1.5	0.3	0.2	5.1	7.4	26.4	7.6	10.3	13.3	12.7
16 031	...	7	Cassia	6 647	21 573	1 677	3.2	98.4	0.0	1.0	0.6	18.3	8.9	25.3	9.7	10.8	12.9	11.3
16 033	...	9	Clark	4 571	913	3 115	0.2	99.2	0.0	0.8	0.0	12.2	6.6	21.7	8.9	13.6	13.8	16.8
16 035	...	7	Clearwater	6 375	9 359	2 482	1.5	97.2	0.4	2.1	0.4	2.3	4.7	17.9	6.9	11.4	15.5	16.6

1. MSA = Metropolitan Statistical Area. PMSA = Primary MSA. NECMA = New England County Metropolitan Area. See Appendix A for explanation of these concepts. See Appendix B for list of metropolitan areas identified by type, with component counties. 2. County typology code from the Economic Research Service of USDA. See Appendix A for definition. 3. Dry land or land partially or temporarily covered by water. 4. Hispanic persons may be of any race.

STATE County	55 to 64 years	65 to 74 years	75 years and over	Percent female	Total persons 1990	Total persons 1980	Percent change 1980–1990	Percent change 1990–1999	Births	Deaths	Net migration	Number	Percent change, 1980–1990	Persons per house-hold	Female family house-holder[1]	One person
	16	17	18	19	20	21	22	23	24	25	26	27	28	29	30	31
GEORGIA—Cont'd																
Richmond	8.1	6.1	4.7	51.5	189 719	181 629	4.5	0.3	31 034	17 081	-16 253	68 675	15.4	2.61	18.0	26.1
Rockdale	8.1	5.5	4.0	50.6	54 091	36 570	47.9	27.5	7 684	3 678	11 077	18 337	58.2	2.92	9.9	14.4
Schley	8.0	6.1	5.1	51.8	3 590	3 433	4.6	10.0	529	362	206	1 315	16.9	2.72	13.5	24.6
Screven	8.6	7.6	7.0	52.8	13 842	14 043	-1.4	4.5	2 011	1 600	251	5 048	5.9	2.70	17.1	24.5
Seminole	10.7	7.7	6.3	50.7	9 010	9 057	-0.5	8.8	1 213	989	545	3 137	2.8	2.68	16.5	23.8
Spalding	8.8	6.1	5.3	52.0	54 457	47 899	13.7	6.2	8 241	5 077	346	19 426	20.1	2.76	16.6	19.9
Stephens	9.8	8.9	7.4	51.8	23 436	21 761	7.7	8.1	3 200	2 399	1 181	8 949	14.9	2.54	10.7	23.8
Stewart	9.2	8.7	7.9	51.8	5 654	5 896	-4.1	-5.0	702	739	-231	1 982	4.8	2.80	21.4	25.5
Sumter	7.8	5.8	6.5	53.8	30 232	29 360	3.0	3.7	4 969	3 126	-642	10 484	10.8	2.75	21.7	24.3
Talbot	9.6	6.3	6.9	52.5	6 524	6 536	-0.2	6.8	859	697	298	2 345	12.4	2.78	20.2	23.2
Taliaferro	9.0	9.0	8.6	52.6	1 915	2 032	-5.8	0.5	226	239	32	727	-4.1	2.63	16.4	31.6
Tattnall	9.1	6.6	5.8	46.6	17 722	18 134	-2.3	8.2	2 811	1 845	494	5 845	4.6	2.61	14.1	24.6
Taylor	9.2	7.3	6.0	53.1	7 642	7 902	-3.3	8.4	1 240	890	320	2 804	5.7	2.72	18.9	24.1
Telfair	9.7	7.3	7.9	53.7	11 000	11 445	-3.9	3.7	1 460	1 497	487	4 017	2.8	2.65	17.1	26.0
Terrell	9.2	6.6	6.5	54.0	10 653	12 017	-11.4	5.2	1 701	1 177	65	3 738	-2.6	2.81	21.5	23.7
Thomas	9.3	7.2	6.3	53.3	38 943	38 098	2.2	10.2	5 926	4 033	2 139	14 323	12.0	2.68	17.9	23.3
Tift	8.1	6.1	5.4	51.4	34 998	32 862	6.5	5.6	5 879	3 162	-693	12 184	13.5	2.75	15.7	22.4
Toombs	8.3	6.5	5.7	52.4	24 072	22 592	6.6	8.0	4 021	2 411	379	8 804	14.8	2.69	15.4	24.8
Towns	14.7	14.3	13.0	51.1	6 754	5 638	19.8	30.3	618	859	2 321	2 812	38.9	2.26	6.5	25.3
Treutlen	9.6	6.7	7.1	53.8	5 994	6 087	-1.5	-1.0	836	663	-214	2 158	4.1	2.74	17.0	23.8
Troup	9.2	6.4	6.0	52.7	55 532	50 003	11.1	5.9	8 824	6 033	645	20 371	16.7	2.68	16.2	23.1
Turner	8.6	7.0	6.6	53.1	8 703	9 510	-8.5	6.3	1 439	977	116	3 043	-1.1	2.82	18.9	22.1
Twiggs	8.7	6.5	5.1	52.0	9 806	9 354	4.8	4.0	1 246	910	69	3 296	17.2	2.93	16.8	20.2
Union	13.8	10.9	9.5	50.4	11 993	9 390	27.7	43.7	1 377	1 363	5 266	4 709	39.8	2.50	7.5	20.8
Upson	10.1	7.3	7.1	52.6	26 300	25 998	1.2	3.0	3 420	2 989	439	9 911	8.1	2.61	15.5	24.0
Walker	10.6	7.4	6.2	51.3	58 310	56 470	3.3	8.0	7 671	5 793	2 970	21 697	10.5	2.65	10.8	20.1
Walton	8.5	5.3	4.6	51.5	38 586	31 211	23.6	51.6	7 324	3 433	15 968	13 433	34.2	2.85	12.0	17.4
Ware	10.2	8.2	7.4	51.7	35 471	37 180	-4.6	-0.7	4 698	3 955	-872	13 046	2.0	2.59	14.9	25.4
Warren	9.1	7.9	8.8	54.7	6 078	6 583	-7.7	0.0	748	670	-59	2 130	0.9	2.80	21.9	22.9
Washington	8.5	6.5	6.6	53.1	19 112	18 842	1.4	5.7	2 763	1 938	333	6 739	10.9	2.79	19.7	23.8
Wayne	9.6	6.2	5.5	51.4	22 356	20 750	7.7	14.6	3 194	2 213	2 319	7 922	15.2	2.75	13.3	21.1
Webster	10.0	9.1	6.5	52.8	2 263	2 341	-3.3	-2.7	262	217	-101	798	5.6	2.84	16.4	21.6
Wheeler	8.7	7.4	7.0	51.2	4 903	5 155	-4.9	-0.8	620	563	-85	1 786	3.1	2.70	13.2	24.7
White	11.7	8.8	7.2	51.2	13 006	10 120	28.5	39.9	1 842	1 305	4 662	4 907	40.2	2.55	7.8	20.8
Whitfield	9.2	5.7	4.7	50.5	72 462	65 775	10.2	14.8	12 722	5 764	4 034	26 859	19.6	2.67	10.9	20.3
Wilcox	9.6	7.9	6.9	52.4	7 008	7 682	-8.8	5.9	1 037	817	214	2 511	-3.3	2.71	14.3	25.5
Wilkes	9.8	8.7	7.8	52.0	10 597	10 951	-3.2	-0.4	1 319	1 306	-24	4 022	3.7	2.61	16.1	25.1
Wilkinson	9.0	6.0	5.3	52.5	10 228	10 368	-1.4	6.6	1 437	968	244	3 619	8.0	2.81	17.0	21.8
Worth	8.6	6.0	4.7	51.8	19 744	18 064	9.3	13.9	2 854	1 724	1 665	6 895	18.7	2.85	15.3	19.5
HAWAII	8.8	7.4	6.2	50.1	1 108 229	964 691	14.9	7.0	173 388	67 676	-45 144	356 267	21.2	3.01	10.5	19.4
Hawaii	9.3	7.2	6.2	50.1	120 317	92 053	30.7	18.3	19 008	9 084	12 514	41 461	41.8	2.86	11.5	20.6
Honolulu	8.7	7.6	6.3	50.2	836 231	762 565	9.7	3.4	129 486	48 642	-69 992	265 304	15.2	3.02	10.5	19.2
Kalawao	3.4	15.5	29.3	34.5	130	144	-9.7	-55.4	2	26	-43	62	-12.7	1.37	0.0	62.9
Kauai	8.7	7.1	7.0	49.9	51 177	39 082	30.9	10.5	7 983	3 512	985	16 295	35.6	3.10	9.8	17.4
Maui	8.5	6.4	5.6	49.5	100 374	70 847	41.7	21.5	16 909	6 412	11 392	33 145	47.2	2.99	9.9	19.8
IDAHO	8.9	5.9	5.5	50.1	1 006 734	944 127	6.6	24.3	166 298	77 951	154 383	360 723	11.3	2.73	8.0	22.4
Ada	8.0	4.9	4.5	50.6	205 775	173 125	18.9	37.7	35 228	14 038	56 671	77 471	22.7	2.60	9.2	23.6
Adams	11.7	8.0	7.6	48.0	3 254	3 347	-2.8	16.4	341	305	513	1 251	3.2	2.59	4.9	20.5
Bannock	7.8	5.3	4.9	50.3	66 026	65 421	0.9	13.4	11 749	4 546	798	23 412	4.1	2.78	8.8	23.9
Bear Lake	10.5	7.0	7.0	50.5	6 084	6 931	-12.2	7.8	793	553	251	2 005	-9.3	3.01	4.4	22.1
Benewah	10.5	6.5	6.7	49.2	7 937	8 292	-4.3	14.2	1 092	805	873	2 991	2.0	2.63	7.8	21.8
Bingham	8.4	5.3	4.9	50.0	37 583	36 489	3.0	12.1	6 515	2 501	594	11 513	6.9	3.23	9.2	16.5
Blaine	7.3	4.5	3.2	48.0	13 552	9 841	37.7	27.8	2 014	568	2 357	5 506	38.4	2.43	7.2	28.0
Boise	11.7	6.4	3.9	47.1	3 509	2 999	17.0	51.4	600	270	1 485	1 357	22.6	2.59	5.2	22.5
Bonner	11.0	7.3	6.0	49.9	26 622	24 163	10.2	35.5	3 447	2 443	8 492	10 269	16.5	2.58	7.2	23.2
Bonneville	8.2	5.5	4.6	49.6	72 207	65 980	9.4	12.9	12 723	4 382	833	24 289	14.0	2.94	7.8	20.3
Boundary	10.4	6.4	6.7	49.0	8 332	7 289	14.3	19.7	1 124	658	1 206	2 857	15.2	2.78	7.4	21.0
Butte	11.1	6.5	6.4	49.9	2 918	3 342	-12.7	3.2	411	270	-38	997	-7.0	2.87	6.5	22.6
Camas	11.4	4.9	4.7	46.0	727	818	-11.1	19.0	64	53	126	275	-5.5	2.64	4.0	20.7
Canyon	8.7	5.6	5.8	50.7	90 076	83 756	7.5	38.2	17 765	7 838	24 556	31 288	9.9	2.79	9.3	21.2
Caribou	9.4	6.4	4.5	49.5	6 963	8 695	-19.9	4.5	972	522	-122	2 262	-15.4	3.06	3.7	19.7
Cassia	9.0	6.4	5.7	49.8	19 532	19 427	0.5	10.4	3 616	1 406	-123	6 373	4.2	3.04	7.2	20.4
Clark	10.4	4.6	3.7	44.9	762	798	-4.5	19.8	142	47	57	277	5.7	2.67	4.7	26.0
Clearwater	12.2	7.9	6.8	47.5	8 505	10 390	-18.1	10.0	910	749	720	3 213	-11.6	2.51	6.6	21.6

1. No spouse present.

Table B. States and Counties — Vital Statistics, Health Resources, and Crime

STATE County	Births, average 1996–1998 Total	Rate[1]	Deaths, average 1996–1998 Number Total	Infant[2]	Deaths Rate Total[1]	Infant[3]	Physicians,[4] 1998 Number	Rate[5]	Hospitals,[4] 1998 Number	Beds Number	Rate[5]	Medicare enrollees 1999	Serious crimes known to police, 1998[6] Total Number	Rate[7]
	32	33	34	35	36	37	38	39	40	41	42	43	44	45
GEORGIA—Cont'd														
Richmond	3 124	16.3	1 861	36	9.7	11.5	904	472	4	1 571	821	25 910	15 175	7 698
Rockdale	845	12.7	445	8	6.7	9.1	86	126	1	107	157	6 979	3 109	4 542
Schley	66	17.0	42	0	10.8	5.1	1	25	0	0	0	495	46	1 175
Screven	207	14.4	178	1	12.4	6.5	5	35	1	40	277	2 445	410	2 789
Seminole	138	14.4	98	0	10.2	0.0	9	92	1	62	633	1 719	347	3 460
Spalding	879	15.3	547	10	9.5	11.0	75	130	1	160	278	8 516	4 239	7 289
Stephens	350	13.8	271	2	10.7	5.7	42	165	1	96	378	5 273	828	3 214
Stewart	70	12.8	75	1	13.7	14.3	3	55	1	32	585	980	103	1 899
Sumter	537	17.0	336	7	10.7	12.4	45	144	1	152	485	4 525	1 424	4 403
Talbot	83	12.2	84	2	12.3	24.0	1	14	0	0	0	1 071	115	1 634
Taliaferro	27	14.4	28	0	14.9	12.2	0	0	0	0	0	423	NA	NA
Tattnall	346	18.2	211	3	11.1	7.7	10	53	1	40	211	3 085	497	2 602
Taylor	123	15.0	94	1	11.4	10.8	3	36	0	0	0	1 490	103	1 228
Telfair	144	12.5	164	1	14.2	9.2	6	52	1	52	450	2 240	317	2 708
Terrell	176	15.8	121	3	10.9	17.1	7	63	0	0	0	1 707	460	4 254
Thomas	660	15.5	448	5	10.5	7.1	117	272	1	264	615	7 640	2 252	5 357
Tift	653	17.8	345	10	9.4	14.8	80	218	1	168	458	5 371	2 359	6 264
Toombs	433	16.9	276	4	10.7	8.5	34	132	1	122	472	4 107	965	4 511
Towns	76	9.2	102	0	12.4	0.0	10	117	1	101	1 184	2 465	18	233
Treutlen	88	14.8	78	1	13.1	11.3	3	50	0	0	0	974	36	592
Troup	910	15.6	673	11	11.5	12.4	97	165	1	364	619	9 343	4 143	6 932
Turner	151	16.6	116	2	12.7	13.2	3	33	0	0	0	1 564	232	2 484
Twiggs	126	12.8	104	1	10.5	10.6	3	30	0	0	0	1 358	77	764
Union	151	9.6	176	1	11.2	4.4	13	79	1	145	878	3 784	247	1 544
Upson	348	12.9	335	3	12.4	8.6	38	140	1	119	440	4 726	1 005	3 615
Walker	832	13.4	665	5	10.7	5.6	20	32	0	0	0	11 069	1 948	3 105
Walton	901	17.4	409	7	7.9	7.4	31	57	1	135	248	6 956	2 234	4 246
Ware	503	14.2	418	6	11.8	11.9	59	167	1	125	353	7 018	1 752	4 792
Warren	71	11.9	81	1	13.5	14.0	2	33	0	0	0	1 087	110	1 785
Washington	268	13.4	211	4	10.6	14.9	16	80	1	114	569	3 129	496	2 459
Wayne	345	13.8	252	2	10.1	5.8	35	138	1	123	484	3 712	1 030	4 176
Webster	30	13.3	21	1	9.4	22.5	0	0	0	0	0	317	8	348
Wheeler	69	14.0	53	0	10.8	4.8	1	21	1	40	821	906	42	831
White	227	13.5	150	2	8.9	10.3	11	63	0	0	0	3 149	521	3 033
Whitfield	1 506	18.5	635	8	7.8	5.3	142	173	1	282	344	10 693	4 103	5 028
Wilcox	120	16.4	92	1	12.5	5.5	4	54	0	0	0	1 356	12	161
Wilkes	137	13.0	140	1	13.2	7.3	12	114	1	44	416	2 163	225	2 089
Wilkinson	153	14.1	98	3	9.1	21.8	3	28	0	0	0	1 701	460	4 379
Worth	287	12.9	195	3	8.8	9.3	11	49	1	50	222	2 449	456	2 020
HAWAII	17 792	14.9	7 977	114	6.7	6.4	3 189	267	19	3 166	265	161 787	63 623	5 333
Hawaii	2 180	15.4	1 186	15	8.4	7.0	298	208	5	435	304	20 924	6 757	4 753
Honolulu	13 057	14.9	5 632	84	6.4	6.4	2 526	290	10	2 316	265	117 980	47 453	5 425
Kalawao	(8)NA	(8)NA	(8)NA	(8)NA	(8)NA	(8)NA	NA	NA	NA	NA	NA	70	NA	NA
Kauai	770	13.6	415	5	7.3	6.5	108	191	2	240	424	8 101	2 263	3 991
Maui	(8)1 786	(8)15.0	(8)743	(8)10	(8)6.2	(8)5.6	257	213	2	175	145	14 623	7 150	5 989
IDAHO	18 866	15.6	8 948	135	7.4	7.1	1 965	160	43	3 271	266	161 362	45 653	3 715
Ada	4 220	15.7	1 627	20	6.1	4.7	653	237	3	596	216	29 756	11 897	4 388
Adams	27	7.2	34	0	9.0	12.2	3	79	1	26	683	698	92	2 347
Bannock	1 318	17.7	554	10	7.5	7.8	146	195	2	248	331	8 935	2 961	3 947
Bear Lake	81	12.5	68	0	10.4	4.1	4	61	1	58	887	1 090	56	838
Benewah	110	12.2	85	1	9.5	6.1	7	77	1	33	362	1 535	192	2 108
Bingham	705	17.0	282	6	6.8	9.0	22	53	1	120	287	4 912	936	2 214
Blaine	222	13.0	67	1	3.9	6.0	83	483	2	88	512	1 457	492	2 814
Boise	76	15.1	34	1	6.8	8.7	0	0	0	0	0	673	98	1 920
Bonner	377	10.9	282	3	8.2	8.0	53	150	1	62	176	5 314	1 036	2 933
Bonneville	1 348	16.9	521	9	6.5	6.4	153	190	1	270	335	9 500	3 966	4 863
Boundary	121	12.4	81	0	8.3	2.8	10	102	1	62	633	1 581	190	1 893
Butte	38	12.3	31	1	10.1	17.7	3	99	1	43	1 418	514	26	815
Camas	9	11.0	3	0	3.9	0.0	0	0	0	0	0	134	9	1 051
Canyon	2 147	18.4	906	15	7.8	7.0	148	123	2	274	228	15 984	5 165	4 358
Caribou	92	12.5	58	1	7.9	7.2	5	67	1	65	875	1 071	108	1 441
Cassia	386	18.1	160	2	7.5	4.3	36	169	1	70	328	2 881	945	4 339
Clark	16	19.4	7	0	8.3	0.0	0	0	0	0	0	99	16	1 882
Clearwater	93	9.9	81	0	8.6	0.0	11	118	1	22	236	1 583	129	1 343

1. Per 1,000 estimated resident population, average 1996–1998. 2. Deaths of infants under 1 year old. 3. Deaths of infants under 1 year old per 1,000 live births. 4. Data subject to copyright. 5. Per 100,000 resident population as of July 1 of the year shown. 6. Data for serious crimes have not been adjusted for underreporting; this may affect comparability between geographic areas and over time. 7. Per 100,000 population estimated by the FBI. 8. Kalawao County included with Maui County.

Table B. States and Counties — Crime, Education, Money Income, and Poverty

STATE County	Serious crimes known to police, 1998[1] (cont'd) Rate[2] Violent	Serious crimes known to police, 1998[1] (cont'd) Rate[2] Property	Education School enrollment and attainment, 1990 Enrollment[3] Total	Education School enrollment and attainment, 1990 Enrollment[3] Percent private	Education School enrollment and attainment, 1990 Attainment[4] (percent) High school graduate or more	Education School enrollment and attainment, 1990 Attainment[4] (percent) Bachelor's degree or more	Education Local government expenditures, fiscal 1997[5] Total current expenditures (mil dol)	Education Local government expenditures, fiscal 1997[5] Current expenditures per student (dollars)	Money income 1989 Per capita[6] (dollars)	Money income 1989 Households Median Dollars	Money income 1989 Households Median Percent change, 1979–1989 (constant 1989 dollars)	Money income 1989 Households Percent with $100,000 or more	Income and poverty, 1997 Median household income	Income and poverty, 1997 Percent below poverty level All persons	Income and poverty, 1997 Percent below poverty level Persons under 18	Income and poverty, 1997 Percent below poverty level Persons 5–17 in families
	46	47	48	49	50	51	52	53	54	55	56	57	58	59	60	61
GEORGIA—Cont'd																
Richmond	480	7 218	49 505	12.7	70.9	17.3	185.8	5 046	11 799	25 265	10.6	2.3	30 339	21.9	32.5	30.3
Rockdale	533	4 009	13 798	11.6	77.7	18.1	70.8	5 507	15 710	39 389	12.7	4.4	48 632	8.7	14.3	13.4
Schley	128	1 047	907	11.9	56.4	8.0	2.8	5 373	9 747	21 417	11.2	1.6	28 479	19.8	28.7	30.7
Screven	299	2 490	3 535	5.3	58.9	8.6	16.1	4 934	9 269	20 531	30.2	1.1	26 631	22.3	32.4	31.9
Seminole	1 047	2 413	2 021	6.3	52.7	7.8	10.2	5 052	9 270	18 438	-0.6	1.2	24 521	26.6	39.8	39.3
Spalding	1 047	6 242	13 169	9.3	60.0	11.1	57.2	5 452	11 073	25 634	12.5	1.3	33 073	16.6	25.4	24.6
Stephens	256	2 958	5 414	19.3	60.1	13.1	22.5	5 386	10 531	22 204	5.3	1.4	29 980	16.5	26.2	26.0
Stewart	295	1 604	1 349	12.5	51.4	8.0	5.6	6 242	7 772	15 606	12.1	1.1	21 518	27.2	37.4	38.0
Sumter	390	4 013	8 591	14.2	62.8	15.9	30.9	5 450	9 600	20 957	4.5	1.3	28 247	25.0	35.1	33.8
Talbot	142	1 492	1 497	7.5	56.2	7.1	5.4	5 709	8 728	20 489	2.2	0.3	25 356	22.2	32.0	34.1
Taliaferro	NA	NA	467	12.6	48.6	5.6	1.2	7 228	7 624	14 700	-1.2	0.4	20 700	29.0	43.4	45.4
Tattnall	471	2 131	3 926	7.1	57.4	6.5	15.8	4 560	9 286	20 293	27.7	1.1	26 649	25.6	37.3	34.6
Taylor	250	978	1 908	3.9	51.2	7.1	8.6	4 713	9 182	16 210	-15.6	1.9	22 906	26.3	38.4	38.2
Telfair	444	2 264	2 630	7.3	52.1	8.6	11.6	5 328	8 452	16 573	-1.1	1.2	22 159	25.7	35.8	35.2
Terrell	878	3 376	2 779	16.1	52.4	9.2	11.5	5 509	8 524	18 036	1.2	1.1	23 292	27.5	39.3	38.7
Thomas	457	4 900	9 870	8.5	63.3	13.4	47.1	5 269	10 293	20 901	0.8	2.3	27 741	21.2	29.9	30.8
Tift	943	5 321	9 644	5.7	61.3	14.0	35.4	4 639	10 612	22 421	10.9	2.4	29 926	21.3	31.0	30.4
Toombs	594	3 917	6 003	12.3	59.0	11.4	26.9	5 142	9 775	19 473	7.5	1.8	24 964	24.9	36.3	35.4
Towns	0	233	1 429	23.7	58.2	11.4	4.8	5 066	10 777	19 356	21.8	1.7	28 110	13.7	25.2	23.2
Treutlen	197	395	1 355	6.9	52.7	6.3	6.3	4 726	7 865	17 391	1.0	0.8	23 362	26.3	38.8	37.5
Troup	331	6 601	13 802	14.7	60.8	13.6	63.4	5 591	11 581	24 788	13.5	2.2	32 523	16.3	24.2	23.7
Turner	343	2 141	2 389	4.3	55.3	7.2	11.1	5 434	7 953	17 766	-2.3	0.5	22 686	27.4	38.0	38.6
Twiggs	20	744	2 477	11.3	48.4	4.8	10.5	5 233	8 510	19 213	-10.6	0.8	26 941	22.2	29.3	32.4
Union	44	1 500	2 194	2.8	58.7	10.1	12.2	4 906	10 975	20 275	30.9	2.3	28 294	14.1	22.5	23.4
Upson	381	3 234	5 938	7.9	54.6	9.0	23.8	4 844	10 554	22 747	5.3	1.5	28 680	16.5	24.8	24.6
Walker	155	2 950	12 824	7.8	58.3	8.4	49.3	4 967	10 575	24 068	3.8	1.1	30 675	13.6	20.6	19.6
Walton	608	3 638	8 993	7.8	57.9	9.4	44.1	4 518	11 932	28 198	21.8	2.2	36 324	13.6	20.8	21.5
Ware	380	4 412	8 784	4.1	61.1	10.4	37.8	5 594	9 712	20 426	2.1	1.3	25 866	23.9	34.9	33.7
Warren	211	1 574	1 381	9.2	42.8	4.2	5.7	5 193	7 864	17 284	-2.5	0.5	22 520	27.1	38.3	39.9
Washington	248	2 211	4 901	13.9	58.1	9.8	21.9	5 531	9 917	21 460	13.0	2.0	28 092	23.0	34.2	32.9
Wayne	430	3 746	5 675	6.0	62.9	9.6	24.5	4 922	9 856	23 311	14.8	1.1	30 376	21.6	31.7	31.5
Webster	130	218	544	15.6	50.4	5.5	2.1	5 514	9 202	19 028	17.0	1.5	26 651	18.5	26.7	27.2
Wheeler	99	732	1 331	8.6	56.7	8.6	5.7	5 362	9 522	16 585	16.3	1.1	22 855	26.3	36.1	37.9
White	250	2 783	2 787	16.5	62.9	13.6	21.2	7 188	11 277	24 234	12.4	1.7	32 377	12.4	20.6	19.6
Whitfield	420	4 608	16 160	8.2	59.8	12.0	88.7	5 774	13 324	27 797	2.7	2.9	35 754	11.9	19.4	18.0
Wilcox	67	94	1 678	6.2	52.8	7.6	7.3	5 362	8 733	16 333	-8.8	1.0	23 291	26.6	39.0	38.9
Wilkes	362	1 727	2 460	11.1	56.6	10.4	11.2	5 344	10 752	18 629	-2.2	2.7	26 224	20.7	31.2	29.4
Wilkinson	1 352	3 027	2 548	8.6	62.0	8.8	11.4	5 714	10 415	25 166	7.6	0.8	30 950	17.4	25.6	27.1
Worth	142	1 878	5 148	5.3	58.1	6.3	22.2	4 655	9 469	21 312	-2.4	1.6	28 921	22.5	31.6	33.0
HAWAII	247	5 086	290 578	19.5	80.1	22.9	1 057.0	5 633	15 770	38 829	13.2	7.1	43 627	11.1	16.2	14.6
Hawaii	179	4 574	31 939	12.3	77.7	18.5	0.0	0	13 169	29 712	4.4	3.9	34 557	16.6	23.4	21.8
Honolulu	268	5 157	221 821	21.6	81.2	24.6	1 083.5	5 774	16 256	40 581	14.9	7.9	44 310	10.2	14.8	13.1
Kalawao	NA	NA	6	0.0	51.5	4.6	0.0	0	11 281	10 000	3.8	0.0	9 213	0.0	0.0	0.0
Kauai	106	3 885	13 229	11.3	73.1	16.3	0.0	0	14 254	37 425	17.1	5.2	38 877	12.1	18.6	16.5
Maui	242	5 747	23 583	13.8	77.0	17.8	0.0	0	15 616	38 771	14.3	6.0	40 647	10.8	15.8	14.5
IDAHO	282	3 433	295 638	9.2	79.7	17.7	1 091.0	4 447	11 457	25 257	-1.4	2.1	33 612	13.0	17.3	14.9
Ada	293	4 095	57 564	9.4	87.2	24.9	219.6	4 473	14 268	30 246	3.1	3.2	43 321	8.9	12.0	10.0
Adams	383	1 964	718	4.7	75.3	10.8	7.2	5 731	13 732	22 455	-9.4	2.3	28 944	14.6	21.2	19.3
Bannock	309	3 638	23 087	4.3	82.9	19.8	64.7	4 253	10 976	26 275	-10.2	1.6	35 382	13.9	17.1	14.5
Bear Lake	30	808	1 879	0.9	79.8	11.4	7.2	3 907	8 989	21 646	-17.2	0.7	32 181	13.4	15.8	13.9
Benewah	187	1 921	1 956	7.7	74.2	8.8	10.3	5 447	9 921	21 508	-24.4	1.2	31 728	14.4	19.1	16.9
Bingham	173	2 041	12 432	3.4	76.8	13.1	46.9	4 135	9 474	25 158	-2.3	1.5	34 488	14.7	18.1	15.3
Blaine	206	2 608	3 007	13.1	91.7	33.0	17.1	6 046	19 979	31 199	27.4	7.0	45 504	7.5	10.9	10.3
Boise	255	1 665	873	12.6	80.0	14.4	6.0	5 291	11 747	26 048	0.1	2.6	34 807	11.3	15.8	15.7
Bonner	275	2 658	6 325	10.3	78.2	15.2	25.9	4 199	10 527	21 465	5.0	1.8	30 311	15.2	21.2	18.1
Bonneville	430	4 433	22 449	7.4	84.0	23.2	78.7	4 146	12 123	30 462	0.0	2.3	39 962	12.2	15.7	13.3
Boundary	90	1 803	2 187	13.4	74.6	13.3	8.0	4 478	9 054	21 662	3.7	0.5	29 732	16.5	23.1	19.8
Butte	31	784	831	3.1	80.4	13.5	3.4	5 166	10 257	26 292	15.4	1.9	31 780	15.4	19.0	17.6
Camas	117	934	183	5.5	81.8	15.0	1.3	6 227	11 373	24 440	10.5	3.3	35 445	7.4	7.5	8.6
Canyon	347	4 011	24 516	12.6	71.0	12.0	93.2	4 218	9 916	22 979	-0.9	1.6	31 558	16.0	21.6	18.4
Caribou	67	1 374	2 324	1.1	84.3	11.8	10.3	4 895	10 808	29 979	1.1	1.7	42 574	9.6	12.0	10.1
Cassia	312	4 027	6 118	4.0	72.7	14.0	23.2	4 287	9 726	23 381	1.5	2.4	32 175	15.4	20.4	17.1
Clark	0	1 882	244	0.0	74.7	14.1	1.3	5 259	10 608	24 583	28.0	0.7	30 827	12.4	18.1	14.4
Clearwater	198	1 145	1 997	5.6	73.4	11.4	9.2	5 264	11 234	23 925	-17.3	1.5	32 881	14.9	20.8	17.6

1. Data for serious crimes have not been adjusted for underreporting; this may affect comparability between geographic areas and over time. 2. Per 100,000 population estimated by the FBI. 3. All persons 3 years old and over enrolled in nursery school through college. 4. Persons 25 years old and over. 5. Elementary and secondary education expenditures, local government fiscal years ending between July 1, 1996 and June 30, 1997. 6. Based on population enumerated as of April 1, 1990.

Table B. States and Counties — **Personal Income**

STATE County	Personal income, 1998 Total (mil dol)	Percent change, 1997–1998	Per capita[1] Dollars	Per capita[1] Rank	Wages and salaries[2] (mil dol)	Proprietor's income (mil dol)	Dividends, interest, and rent (mil dol)	Transfer payments Total (mil dol)	Government payments to individuals Total (mil dol)	Social Security (mil dol)	Medical payments (mil dol)	Income maintenance (mil dol)	Unemployment insurance (mil dol)
	62	63	64	65	66	67	68	69	70	71	72	73	74
GEORGIA—Cont'd													
Richmond	4 375	3.3	22 861	878	3 916	159	734	776	739	242	300	116	12
Rockdale	1 706	5.9	24 989	492	982	96	268	160	147	74	52	11	1
Schley	71	6.1	18 073	2 326	31	8	8	13	12	4	5	2	0
Screven	256	0.3	17 687	2 440	106	14	44	61	58	20	23	11	1
Seminole	170	2.2	17 444	2 497	62	17	28	43	41	15	17	7	0
Spalding	1 233	4.6	21 401	1 264	627	65	201	204	192	82	76	24	2
Stephens	528	3.0	20 824	1 453	296	51	93	108	103	46	40	10	2
Stewart	97	4.2	17 844	2 394	32	5	14	26	25	7	12	5	0
Sumter	652	2.4	20 841	1 444	398	69	117	127	121	39	48	23	2
Talbot	104	5.7	14 838	2 949	22	16	16	25	23	9	8	4	0
Taliaferro	32	5.8	16 455	2 714	4	3	6	9	9	3	4	2	0
Tattnall	363	2.1	19 068	2 036	151	77	52	75	72	23	32	12	1
Taylor	146	6.2	17 805	2 404	56	19	20	36	34	11	14	7	0
Telfair	201	3.5	17 450	2 495	112	17	34	59	56	18	27	8	1
Terrell	172	1.6	15 405	2 888	65	14	35	46	44	14	17	10	1
Thomas	905	2.5	21 089	1 358	575	75	168	180	171	64	72	25	3
Tift	802	4.6	21 799	1 161	584	65	134	128	120	45	48	19	2
Toombs	473	3.5	18 321	2 257	254	35	83	108	102	35	44	18	2
Towns	176	7.5	20 708	1 486	58	16	48	45	43	22	15	3	0
Treutlen	96	3.1	16 043	2 788	27	9	15	25	24	8	10	4	0
Troup	1 318	5.6	22 499	978	997	61	223	211	199	86	73	24	2
Turner	154	4.4	16 814	2 654	59	18	25	37	35	11	15	7	1
Twiggs	161	5.2	15 908	2 806	79	11	18	36	34	14	13	5	0
Union	308	8.8	18 644	2 172	106	35	71	72	69	34	25	5	0
Upson	518	4.6	19 157	1 999	273	40	74	105	99	46	37	11	1
Walker	1 169	4.1	18 641	2 173	396	80	169	234	221	98	92	19	3
Walton	1 042	8.8	19 076	2 032	358	73	133	157	146	60	62	17	1
Ware	671	4.4	18 948	2 076	472	46	113	177	170	51	67	24	2
Warren	103	4.6	16 926	2 625	52	4	15	30	29	9	13	5	1
Washington	436	4.9	21 731	1 179	298	18	84	84	79	27	34	14	2
Wayne	464	3.9	19 110	2 264	259	35	68	98	93	35	40	12	1
Webster	42	0.7	18 266	2 021	11	5	9	8	7	3	3	1	0
Wheeler	87	2.7	17 671	2 446	23	11	11	23	22	7	10	4	0
White	378	4.8	21 642	1 208	146	51	84	62	59	29	21	4	1
Whitfield	2 037	6.2	24 834	509	1 863	109	372	234	218	104	84	19	3
Wilcox	137	3.3	18 670	2 163	36	19	22	35	34	9	17	6	0
Wilkes	216	3.1	20 397	1 598	114	17	41	47	45	18	19	6	1
Wilkinson	198	3.6	18 266	2 279	115	10	25	39	37	15	14	5	1
Worth	406	4.0	18 088	2 325	88	36	53	71	66	26	25	12	1
HAWAII	31 856	1.8	26 759	X	20 833	2 476	6 019	3 794	3 619	1 455	1 241	591	154
Hawaii	2 792	2.6	19 686	1 825	1 567	202	572	551	529	203	159	115	30
Honolulu	24 994	1.7	28 670	207	16 730	1 889	4 707	2 646	2 520	1 031	847	403	100
Kalawao	[3]2 815	[3]2.4	[3]23 325	[3]787	[3]1 791	[3]262	[3]505	[3]390	[3]371	[3]144	[3]161	[3]45	[3]11
Kauai	1 256	1.2	22 340	1 008	745	123	235	207	198	78	74	27	14
Maui	[3]	[3]	[3]	[3]	[3]	[3]	[3]	[3]	[3]	[3]	[3]	[3]	[3]
IDAHO	27 177	6.8	22 079	X	15 765	3 176	5 460	3 552	3 351	1 534	1 111	254	120
Ada	8 332	8.0	30 230	160	5 531	1 129	1 654	695	650	290	212	42	20
Adams	68	4.0	17 955	2 358	24	8	23	14	13	7	4	1	1
Bannock	1 468	4.6	19 759	1 791	856	87	237	218	206	78	63	17	6
Bear Lake	100	5.0	15 378	2 893	33	9	18	21	20	9	6	1	0
Benewah	168	0.9	18 440	2 231	99	22	31	31	29	14	9	2	2
Bingham	704	6.3	16 837	2 650	344	64	116	115	108	48	39	10	4
Blaine	674	5.1	39 186	38	322	93	264	33	30	15	8	1	3
Boise	102	6.1	19 944	1 730	31	8	14	14	13	7	3	1	1
Bonner	644	7.1	18 232	2 287	292	71	173	113	107	53	32	9	5
Bonneville	1 744	4.5	21 608	1 220	1 099	139	334	221	208	95	77	15	6
Boundary	164	6.4	16 669	2 684	89	19	32	31	29	14	8	3	2
Butte	57	5.9	18 886	2 094	322	6	11	10	10	5	4	1	0
Camas	18	6.6	21 698	1 193	6	3	4	2	2	1	0	0	0
Canyon	2 147	7.7	17 833	2 397	1 200	195	360	371	351	143	136	31	13
Caribou	144	-0.4	19 484	1 899	120	18	27	19	18	11	4	1	1
Cassia	425	8.4	19 923	1 736	210	80	91	62	59	27	21	5	3
Clark	17	3.3	19 145	2 001	13	3	3	2	2	1	1	0	0
Clearwater	172	2.1	18 377	2 244	95	12	37	36	34	16	10	3	3

1. Based on the resident population estimated as of July 1 of the year shown.   2. Includes other labor income.   3. Kalawao County included with Maui County.

Table B. States and Counties — Earnings, Social Security, and Housing

STATE County	Earnings, 1998									Social Security beneficiaries, December 1998			Housing units, 1990	
				Percent by selected industries										
			Goods-related[1]		Service-related and other[2]							Supplemental Security Income recipients, December 1998		
	Total (mil dol)	Farm	Total	Manufacturing	Total	Retail trade	Finance, insurance, and real estate	Services	Government	Number	Rate[3]		Total	Percent change, 1980–1990
	75	76	77	78	79	80	81	82	83	84	85	86	87	88
GEORGIA—Cont'd														
Richmond	4 075	0.0	18.9	13.8	44.1	9.0	5.1	22.9	37.0	31 128	163	6 939	77 288	19.2
Rockdale	1 078	0.0	D	24.3	D	11.3	3.7	19.2	9.0	8 306	122	864	19 963	64.1
Schley	39	10.8	53.5	50.4	D	4.4	D	6.0	11.4	606	154	150	1 447	16.2
Screven	120	2.0	41.6	37.1	D	9.2	2.9	10.7	23.1	2 883	200	887	5 861	6.4
Seminole	79	12.3	D	8.4	58.0	11.2	5.0	21.1	18.6	2 038	208	538	3 962	2.8
Spalding	692	0.1	D	30.2	D	11.9	3.7	20.8	18.1	10 237	178	2 010	20 702	21.5
Stephens	346	4.2	D	37.9	D	9.8	4.6	17.2	14.2	5 760	227	1 015	10 254	19.6
Stewart	37	4.1	D	35.1	D	11.2	2.8	18.3	21.6	1 101	201	383	2 156	3.2
Sumter	466	8.2	D	25.1	D	8.8	2.4	19.2	18.6	5 260	168	1 455	11 726	15.3
Talbot	29	2.8	D	D	D	6.5	3.3	13.1	29.0	1 282	185	375	2 645	10.8
Taliaferro	7	16.6	D	D	D	8.9	D	9.9	35.4	448	235	127	886	1.7
Tattnall	229	27.7	11.7	8.2	26.9	5.8	2.6	8.6	33.8	3 435	181	1 074	6 756	6.4
Taylor	75	16.0	D	5.7	50.7	9.1	3.7	11.5	20.3	1 587	191	564	3 162	10.4
Telfair	130	2.6	43.2	42.2	31.7	6.7	3.0	12.8	22.4	2 544	220	653	4 756	8.5
Terrell	80	10.9	20.3	18.3	44.7	8.6	4.8	14.5	24.2	2 037	183	713	4 069	-1.9
Thomas	650	1.6	D	26.0	D	10.2	3.8	27.7	17.8	8 366	195	2 194	15 936	15.5
Tift	648	4.2	26.5	20.4	49.5	14.0	3.2	19.0	19.8	6 039	165	1 471	13 359	21.4
Toombs	289	5.5	24.5	18.0	55.7	12.6	3.5	21.9	14.3	4 801	186	1 539	9 952	17.2
Towns	74	-0.2	D	1.6	D	12.0	7.7	36.5	12.7	2 659	312	269	4 577	34.0
Treutlen	35	8.2	26.4	17.2	35.2	9.5	3.6	13.3	30.1	1 250	208	386	2 437	3.9
Troup	1 058	0.1	D	40.2	D	8.7	3.5	14.7	15.2	10 608	180	2 335	22 426	22.2
Turner	77	15.9	21.3	17.2	42.1	10.5	4.9	9.7	20.7	1 722	188	499	3 426	6.8
Twiggs	91	5.8	62.4	3.1	D	2.9	1.1	8.0	14.0	1 997	197	450	3 648	16.0
Union	141	5.5	D	7.0	D	10.9	10.2	14.8	23.0	4 385	265	495	6 624	50.9
Upson	313	0.8	47.4	42.8	35.8	8.5	3.2	21.1	16.0	5 779	213	836	10 667	9.5
Walker	475	1.8	D	38.9	D	9.5	2.9	15.8	17.8	11 847	188	1 700	23 347	11.6
Walton	431	2.8	37.6	24.4	38.9	10.8	5.0	14.7	20.7	7 339	135	1 341	14 514	39.0
Ware	519	1.3	22.5	14.1	56.4	12.7	2.8	22.5	19.8	6 904	195	1 984	14 628	6.0
Warren	57	4.6	D	51.0	26.1	4.9	1.4	11.4	13.9	1 323	218	339	2 443	5.1
Washington	316	1.3	45.2	10.4	33.5	6.6	1.7	11.2	20.0	3 739	187	1 039	7 416	11.9
Wayne	294	1.4	39.5	32.0	31.4	11.0	1.7	11.3	27.7	4 442	175	943	8 812	15.3
Webster	16	25.6	27.1	26.7	D	3.8	D	D	21.6	421	192	98	898	8.2
Wheeler	34	16.7	15.9	13.8	D	4.2	D	16.3	25.5	1 092	224	355	2 148	11.8
White	197	11.3	28.5	18.4	45.4	14.8	4.3	17.9	14.8	3 603	206	394	6 082	48.7
Whitfield	1 973	0.7	D	51.3	D	7.3	2.4	13.3	8.4	12 532	153	1 758	28 832	20.9
Wilcox	56	30.2	D	5.2	D	5.6	3.1	11.0	32.8	1 496	203	470	2 865	2.5
Wilkes	131	3.9	D	37.2	D	7.1	3.2	13.0	18.4	2 397	227	549	4 548	8.4
Wilkinson	125	0.4	63.0	48.8	25.1	3.6	1.4	5.9	11.5	1 908	176	354	4 151	9.2
Worth	124	19.3	15.2	10.8	41.6	10.7	3.4	16.4	24.0	3 644	162	775	7 597	18.7
HAWAII	23 309	0.7	8.8	3.1	60.0	10.8	8.5	28.7	30.5	174 520	146	19 648	389 810	16.6
Hawaii	1 769	2.4	D	2.7	D	11.9	7.6	33.2	24.7	24 736	173	2 781	48 253	41.0
Honolulu	18 619	0.3	8.7	3.1	57.9	10.1	8.6	26.9	33.1	123 553	142	14 760	281 683	11.8
Kalawao	(4)2 053	(4)2.4	(4)D	(4)3.3	(4)D	(4)15.1	(4)9.5	(4)37.5	(4)16.1	4	54	1	101	-16.5
Kauai	868	2.0	(4)	1.7	(4)	14.2	7.0	38.9	20.7	9 311	164	775	17 613	18.8
Maui	(4)	(4)	(4)	(4)	(4)	(4)	(4)	(4)	(4)	16 911	140	1 274	42 160	27.6
IDAHO	18 941	4.6	D	17.1	D	10.1	5.2	22.3	18.2	186 926	152	17 489	413 327	10.2
Ada	6 659	0.5	32.1	21.9	53.1	9.4	7.3	22.3	14.4	33 955	123	3 355	80 849	19.2
Adams	32	-0.3	D	22.8	D	8.9	2.4	7.1	37.9	850	223	47	1 778	12.5
Bannock	944	0.4	D	11.1	D	11.9	5.2	19.5	27.0	9 368	125	1 273	25 694	3.5
Bear Lake	42	9.2	9.2	5.2	D	16.0	3.9	D	34.9	1 203	184	74	2 934	5.1
Benewah	121	0.7	D	32.8	D	9.0	1.5	15.0	17.0	1 780	195	167	3 731	6.6
Bingham	409	10.5	D	18.3	D	8.3	D	13.6	24.2	5 993	143	601	12 664	4.8
Blaine	415	1.4	22.1	4.5	66.2	13.4	10.7	33.3	10.3	1 696	99	55	9 500	29.8
Boise	39	0.6	25.5	15.0	D	7.1	D	20.2	38.1	844	165	45	2 894	22.0
Bonner	363	0.5	27.2	18.2	54.4	17.9	5.6	20.0	17.8	6 579	187	496	15 152	16.1
Bonneville	1 238	1.4	D	4.9	D	11.3	3.9	39.2	15.0	11 131	138	1 162	26 049	10.9
Boundary	108	6.8	D	22.1	D	9.0	D	20.9	22.5	1 812	185	146	3 242	17.7
Butte	328	1.2	0.6	0.1	D	0.9	0.2	94.4	2.2	556	183	56	1 265	-1.2
Camas	9	25.1	D	D	D	8.3	D	9.5	32.1	156	184	7	481	-8.7
Canyon	1 396	6.4	35.9	27.1	44.7	9.8	3.3	18.9	13.1	18 068	150	2 334	33 137	8.2
Caribou	138	5.8	62.1	40.0	19.6	4.3	1.2	5.0	12.5	1 236	166	58	2 867	-7.7
Cassia	290	23.3	D	12.5	D	11.0	3.6	14.5	15.6	3 373	158	303	7 212	2.9
Clark	16	21.6	D	D	D	3.2	3.4	1.4	26.6	115	132	11	502	12.8
Clearwater	107	0.0	33.2	27.7	D	7.7	D	11.5	37.2	2 007	216	178	3 805	-7.5

1. Covers mining, construction, and manufacturing. 2. Covers private sector earnings in agricultural services, forestry, and fisheries; transportation and public utilities; wholesale trade; retail trade; finance, insurance, and real estate; and services. 3. Per 1,000 resident population estimated as of July 1 of the year shown. 4. Kalawao County included with Maui County.

STATE County	Housing units, 1990 (cont'd)								Civilian labor force, 1999				Civilian employment, 1990[5]		
	Occupied units										Unemployment			Percent	
	Owner-occupied					Renter-occupied									
				Owner cost as a percent of income											
	Total	Percent	Median value[1]	With a mortgage	Without a mortgage	Median rent[2]	Rent as percent of income	Substandard units[3] (percent)	Total	Percent change, 1998–1999	Total	Rate[4]	Total	Professional, managerial, and technical	Precision production, craft, and repair
	89	90	91	92	93	94	95	96	97	98	99	100	101	102	103
GEORGIA—Cont'd															
Richmond	68 675	56.4	58 500	20.1	12.6	390	26.3	5.0	81 275	0.1	5 110	6.3	79 382	29.1	12.0
Rockdale	18 337	75.2	86 200	21.4	11.5	555	26.2	2.4	39 755	2.4	985	2.5	28 439	28.5	14.3
Schley	1 315	72.2	40 400	18.9	14.4	246	25.5	8.3	1 757	-6.2	83	4.7	1 504	20.7	14.2
Screven	5 048	73.5	41 800	18.9	13.5	257	27.4	9.5	5 979	-7.3	435	7.3	5 626	16.2	15.2
Seminole	3 137	78.6	42 800	18.6	14.3	239	24.7	8.2	4 449	-2.6	212	4.8	3 855	17.3	15.2
Spalding	19 426	61.4	57 700	19.9	12.7	365	26.1	5.0	29 788	1.7	1 210	4.1	25 015	20.7	14.1
Stephens	8 949	72.9	49 900	18.8	12.8	292	26.0	3.0	12 101	-6.9	589	4.9	11 097	19.8	15.7
Stewart	1 982	70.8	30 400	21.1	12.7	196	22.6	14.9	2 279	-13.4	139	6.1	2 029	18.2	16.3
Sumter	10 484	64.1	45 300	18.1	12.9	273	26.6	8.1	15 435	-2.5	952	6.2	12 375	25.6	12.1
Talbot	2 345	77.8	35 100	23.9	14.7	180	22.9	12.9	2 896	3.3	183	6.3	2 706	15.1	14.1
Taliaferro	727	79.4	28 600	20.2	13.7	159	23.3	16.6	692	-3.6	42	6.1	726	13.5	11.3
Tattnall	5 845	68.9	43 500	18.4	12.9	244	26.2	4.9	7 242	1.0	427	5.9	6 620	17.6	12.4
Taylor	2 804	73.2	35 800	16.8	14.5	229	29.6	9.2	3 904	6.9	243	6.2	2 935	15.9	15.5
Telfair	4 017	76.5	31 100	18.3	13.0	232	25.8	6.2	5 324	1.7	599	11.3	4 410	18.4	10.4
Terrell	3 738	63.6	41 200	18.8	12.4	241	28.5	12.5	3 867	-5.5	393	10.2	4 143	17.2	9.6
Thomas	14 323	68.5	46 400	20.2	14.0	317	25.8	6.0	21 978	0.1	1 145	5.2	17 173	25.0	10.9
Tift	12 184	66.2	51 600	19.8	12.9	300	24.6	5.8	20 574	-5.9	1 023	5.0	16 075	24.0	12.1
Toombs	8 804	64.6	49 100	16.6	14.1	276	24.4	5.6	12 682	-1.1	1 269	10.0	10 080	23.2	12.1
Towns	2 812	87.6	69 400	27.4	12.7	276	23.8	2.2	3 737	-3.6	159	4.3	2 666	22.2	15.1
Treutlen	2 158	72.6	33 300	22.8	13.8	203	22.2	9.2	2 984	2.1	374	12.5	2 469	16.5	17.6
Troup	20 371	64.1	54 600	20.6	13.3	348	24.7	4.5	30 250	0.4	1 468	4.9	25 071	23.0	14.5
Turner	3 043	66.4	37 000	18.8	15.6	238	27.3	7.9	4 267	-7.2	439	10.3	3 197	18.8	9.2
Twiggs	3 296	80.0	37 300	20.2	14.0	251	23.5	12.1	4 275	1.6	284	6.6	3 767	14.1	18.2
Union	4 709	82.6	58 300	21.9	11.9	313	28.6	3.8	7 627	5.2	256	3.4	4 963	21.5	14.7
Upson	9 911	70.5	41 300	17.1	13.0	272	25.3	5.9	13 318	-1.6	961	7.2	11 748	18.0	15.6
Walker	21 697	77.3	45 800	18.0	12.8	332	23.6	3.3	31 327	3.7	1 258	4.0	26 571	18.6	14.9
Walton	13 433	70.6	66 700	20.6	12.8	386	25.9	6.3	28 563	6.8	977	3.4	18 096	18.5	19.3
Ware	13 046	69.7	41 200	20.2	13.2	287	28.2	4.5	15 752	-2.4	815	5.2	13 787	23.0	12.7
Warren	2 130	74.3	33 200	20.5	13.1	224	22.0	11.6	2 776	-15.4	280	10.1	2 409	13.8	13.8
Washington	6 739	72.0	39 600	18.1	13.5	237	21.2	10.9	9 716	-3.5	729	7.5	8 053	21.5	13.3
Wayne	7 922	72.3	44 500	16.9	13.5	264	23.1	6.4	11 503	-1.5	755	6.6	9 387	21.7	17.3
Webster	798	79.8	30 900	21.0	12.8	223	23.3	13.8	1 074	-5.5	60	5.6	951	14.4	16.1
Wheeler	1 786	75.9	29 700	20.1	15.1	177	23.5	7.3	2 193	-1.2	240	10.9	1 926	14.8	12.3
White	4 907	82.0	69 700	21.5	13.0	350	26.2	4.3	9 250	2.2	421	4.6	6 367	23.0	12.8
Whitfield	26 859	66.9	61 200	17.5	12.0	365	21.3	4.6	45 724	-6.8	1 209	2.6	37 932	20.8	12.1
Wilcox	2 511	76.3	32 000	18.7	14.3	220	24.3	5.9	3 315	-1.1	190	5.7	2 728	18.4	12.0
Wilkes	4 022	77.4	42 200	21.4	14.6	221	21.6	8.8	5 637	-4.4	324	5.7	4 509	20.7	10.6
Wilkinson	3 619	81.1	40 000	19.4	12.2	262	23.6	9.4	4 604	-2.9	427	9.3	4 464	20.5	18.0
Worth	6 895	73.9	45 700	19.8	13.3	276	28.6	8.1	9 350	-1.8	705	7.5	8 475	18.9	14.3
HAWAII	356 267	53.9	245 300	21.4	10.8	650	27.4	15.6	594 810	-0.4	33 326	5.6	529 059	29.9	10.5
Hawaii	41 461	61.1	113 000	20.5	10.9	490	27.0	13.2	69 921	1.8	6 068	8.7	54 348	26.0	12.0
Honolulu	265 304	52.0	283 600	21.5	10.7	663	27.6	15.9	424 230	-1.1	20 947	4.9	395 811	31.5	9.9
Kalawao	62	0.0	0	0.0	0.0	125	10.0	0.0	NA	NA	NA	NA	41	34.1	0.0
Kauai	16 295	58.8	171 500	21.2	10.9	618	24.1	14.3	29 011	-0.2	2 228	7.7	25 241	25.1	12.2
Maui	33 145	57.6	202 100	22.3	11.1	722	27.1	16.7	71 647	2.1	4 082	5.7	53 618	23.5	12.4
IDAHO	360 723	70.1	58 200	19.3	11.8	330	23.8	4.5	655 272	0.3	33 913	5.2	443 703	27.1	11.3
Ada	77 471	69.1	70 500	20.2	11.5	401	24.9	2.6	166 712	3.4	5 424	3.3	104 423	34.3	10.0
Adams	1 251	75.3	43 900	18.6	11.4	254	15.0	4.5	1 639	-9.0	245	14.9	1 293	21.3	11.1
Bannock	23 412	68.7	53 300	18.5	11.6	294	24.3	3.8	40 279	-0.3	2 086	5.2	29 061	30.2	11.0
Bear Lake	2 005	83.2	38 700	17.5	13.1	276	22.0	4.6	3 038	-0.2	137	4.5	2 081	21.8	14.4
Benewah	2 991	76.4	44 500	17.1	12.7	246	19.8	8.1	4 578	0.9	566	12.4	3 044	17.9	11.8
Bingham	11 513	76.7	50 700	17.6	11.7	284	23.0	7.8	22 125	2.2	1 114	5.0	15 003	23.0	12.2
Blaine	5 506	64.2	127 400	22.1	13.7	474	23.1	3.8	11 047	0.5	418	3.8	7 800	30.9	17.4
Boise	1 357	79.2	59 700	18.8	11.0	306	18.0	8.3	2 596	4.4	190	7.3	1 438	27.3	15.2
Bonner	10 269	75.8	60 500	22.5	12.7	318	24.6	7.0	17 533	1.3	1 676	9.6	10 445	23.1	12.9
Bonneville	24 289	71.5	63 700	17.4	11.7	366	23.0	4.1	46 706	2.1	1 688	3.6	32 016	36.7	10.4
Boundary	2 857	78.3	49 500	20.0	12.1	296	21.0	10.0	4 522	-2.0	414	9.2	3 045	19.0	11.1
Butte	997	74.6	41 400	15.4	12.0	243	17.0	5.4	1 631	-2.0	64	3.9	1 198	20.7	11.3
Camas	275	75.6	35 500	15.0	11.8	235	20.0	3.3	425	-1.6	18	4.2	326	18.4	14.4
Canyon	31 288	68.7	51 900	20.1	11.5	306	23.5	6.2	63 371	3.0	3 061	4.8	39 181	21.8	12.6
Caribou	2 262	80.2	48 200	17.9	12.0	249	15.6	3.9	3 135	-7.0	189	6.0	2 625	22.4	12.8
Cassia	6 373	71.4	46 100	16.3	12.2	274	21.1	7.0	9 537	-3.7	654	6.9	7 708	21.2	11.2
Clark	277	62.8	37 300	14.3	12.8	281	14.6	6.0	559	-15.6	19	3.4	416	17.8	8.2
Clearwater	3 213	74.3	43 000	14.4	11.2	268	17.2	2.2	4 104	-7.3	554	13.5	3 061	23.1	10.9

1. Specified owner-occupied units.   2. Specified renter-occupied units.   3. Overcrowded or lacking complete plumbing facilities.   4. Percent of civilian labor force.   5. Persons 16 years and older.

Table B. States and Counties — Nonfarm Employment and Agriculture

	Private nonfarm establishments, employment and payroll, 1998									Agriculture, 1997			
		Employment						Annual payroll		Farms			Farm operators
											Percent with—		
STATE County	Number of establishments	Total	Health Care and Social Assistance	Manufacturing	Retail trade	Finance and Insurance	Professional Scientific and Technical Services	Total (mil dol)	Average per employee (dollars)	Number	Less than 50 acres	500 acres and over	Whose principal occupation is farming (percent)
	104	105	106	107	108	109	110	111	112	113	114	115	116
GEORGIA—Cont'd													
Richmond	4 513	79 530	15 522	12 105	12 382	2 763	2 270	2 037	25 614	106	49.1	3.8	37.7
Rockdale	1 903	29 133	2 546	6 421	4 771	521	875	799	27 432	102	64.7	6.9	35.3
Schley	71	1 003	D	627	83	D	D	22	21 851	91	19.8	22.0	49.5
Screven	236	2 863	367	1 269	460	105	24	61	21 324	325	14.2	27.4	42.5
Seminole	192	1 424	344	82	379	84	35	26	17 911	183	24.6	28.4	54.6
Spalding	1 187	18 880	2 317	6 474	3 276	525	317	421	22 291	193	40.4	5.2	32.6
Stephens	570	9 749	1 007	3 957	1 173	199	144	198	20 284	188	38.8	2.7	43.1
Stewart	93	913	226	D	123	34	D	19	20 501	77	13.0	33.8	46.8
Sumter	701	11 997	2 391	3 037	2 129	294	166	257	21 432	314	16.9	31.5	57.3
Talbot	67	446	D	D	69	D	9	10	22 457	111	16.2	20.7	36.0
Taliaferro	25	96	12	D	D	D	0	2	16 156	55	12.7	18.2	40.0
Tattnall	306	3 284	519	606	598	172	42	52	15 927	589	31.2	10.5	49.4
Taylor	143	1 112	95	151	216	54	23	25	22 602	196	11.2	20.9	37.8
Telfair	239	3 935	480	2 246	477	125	30	66	16 890	271	13.7	16.2	51.3
Terrell	188	2 013	198	875	319	86	D	36	17 798	174	17.2	43.1	51.7
Thomas	1 107	18 085	2 697	4 986	2 491	567	263	381	21 068	421	31.8	20.9	49.6
Tift	1 107	17 387	2 329	4 266	2 543	531	426	384	22 113	359	30.9	16.7	50.4
Toombs	706	9 956	1 461	2 377	1 531	287	191	196	19 689	401	21.4	13.2	39.2
Towns	243	1 966	328	82	365	110	41	37	18 989	121	45.5	0.0	47.1
Treutlen	99	812	129	296	103	D	D	11	13 767	157	17.8	11.5	29.3
Troup	1 400	28 425	2 833	9 681	3 628	775	359	752	26 448	230	12.2	26.5	30.8
Turner	189	1 860	110	596	290	95	14	33	17 581	98	28.6	14.3	66.1
Twiggs	88	1 441	166	D	135	D	D	55	38 187	98	28.6	14.3	43.9
Union	436	3 277	614	450	635	187	91	60	18 271	256	53.5	2.3	35.5
Upson	530	9 406	1 207	4 586	1 033	210	72	192	20 438	185	22.7	8.6	27.6
Walker	865	14 831	1 318	6 667	1 655	363	991	331	22 338	478	34.3	6.3	34.3
Walton	1 070	9 326	958	2 290	1 645	385	246	219	23 497	493	42.6	4.3	33.1
Ware	976	12 660	2 751	2 289	2 621	406	202	259	20 447	274	34.3	11.3	40.9
Warren	84	1 418	212	815	154	26	4	32	22 434	134	17.2	17.9	46.3
Washington	418	6 965	915	654	992	166	144	218	31 341	327	17.1	19.3	38.8
Wayne	509	7 735	1 903	1 809	1 427	129	94	151	19 488	276	30.8	10.9	41.3
Webster	23	267	D	D	D	0	0	7	24 573	76	10.5	34.2	59.2
Wheeler	75	544	183	13	59	D	D	12	22 096	176	9.1	22.2	36.9
White	522	4 774	406	934	979	150	73	91	19 161	284	51.8	2.1	45.1
Whitfield	2 563	55 338	2 878	27 231	6 948	910	1 013	1 470	26 567	325	42.2	4.3	34.5
Wilcox	103	668	200	121	155	51	D	12	17 786	273	16.1	25.3	54.9
Wilkes	274	3 585	454	1 551	405	86	45	79	22 052	298	15.8	14.4	29.2
Wilkinson	160	2 733	91	1 266	226	57	24	83	30 393	88	11.4	18.2	39.8
Worth	291	2 518	355	660	492	103	D	47	18 522	406	24.6	30.0	59.9
HAWAII	29 603	416 571	47 389	14 535	60 620	20 050	17 140	11 292	27 107	5 473	89.0	2.6	55.8
Hawaii	3 552	38 917	5 135	1 653	7 583	966	1 243	923	23 727	3 319	89.0	2.6	55.1
Honolulu	20 675	309 487	35 818	10 652	41 597	17 786	14 659	8 744	28 253	880	93.2	1.7	67.6
Kalawao	NA	NA	NA	NA	NA	NA	NA	NA	NA	NA	NA	NA	NA
Kauai	1 630	19 400	2 253	411	3 441	459	398	432	22 275	468	84.8	3.0	54.5
Maui	3 746	48 767	4 183	1 819	7 999	839	840	1 193	24 454	806	87.0	3.5	46.1
IDAHO	35 961	423 615	50 674	66 719	65 665	16 285	22 338	10 595	25 012	22 314	39.0	22.6	54.0
Ada	9 377	140 801	15 706	20 083	17 474	7 788	7 112	4 280	30 396	1 221	70.7	5.7	38.2
Adams	109	793	75	D	79	D	D	14	17 687	279	40.9	27.6	48.4
Bannock	1 822	23 376	3 299	4 153	4 343	1 403	988	522	22 345	664	44.0	20.6	40.5
Bear Lake	112	837	184	80	267	40	4	15	17 552	410	20.2	28.5	47.1
Benewah	297	2 525	292	595	296	45	68	60	23 701	226	26.1	31.4	47.8
Bingham	722	8 956	1 160	2 420	1 564	208	190	186	20 721	1 168	44.6	22.9	52.0
Blaine	1 252	9 714	496	224	1 295	208	623	231	23 779	195	31.3	31.3	57.9
Boise	124	488	D	D	62	D	5	8	17 107	78	25.6	24.4	46.2
Bonner	1 233	10 236	962	1 955	2 418	198	287	210	20 521	501	43.3	8.8	43.3
Bonneville	2 535	36 220	4 254	2 704	5 626	1 051	8 166	1 033	28 520	787	44.0	23.8	51.1
Boundary	354	2 240	214	265	362	55	42	46	20 396	312	37.2	11.9	45.2
Butte	63	336	D	D	89	29	11	6	17 759	207	21.3	31.9	63.3
Camas	25	D	D	D	13	D	0	D	D	98	10.2	55.1	70.4
Canyon	2 773	35 885	4 408	10 798	4 819	720	660	838	23 354	1 898	56.4	7.5	51.1
Caribou	193	2 112	191	D	340	D	D	72	33 932	427	15.2	46.6	57.8
Cassia	586	5 732	800	1 093	1 212	179	155	113	19 770	729	30.6	35.9	66.9
Clark	16	99	D	0	36	D	D	1	13 273	83	8.4	59.0	63.9
Clearwater	275	2 163	433	459	305	55	57	48	22 358	210	24.3	20.5	46.7

Table B. States and Counties — Agriculture, Land, and Water

STATE County	Acreage (1,000) [117]	Percent change 1992–1997 [118]	Average size of farm [119]	Total irrigated (1,000) [120]	Total cropland (1,000) [121]	Average per farm ($1,000) [122]	Average per acre (dollars) [123]	Value of machinery and equipment Average per farm ($1,000) [124]	Total (mil dol) [125]	Average per farm (dollars) [126]	Crops [127]	Livestock and poultry products [128]	$10,000 or more [129]	$100,000 or more [130]	Percent of land owned by Fed. Gov. 1997 [131]	Water consumption 1995 (mil gal/day) [132]
GEORGIA—Cont'd																
Richmond	15	-7.7	139	D	10	194	1 388	25	4	38 749	59.6	40.5	30.2	5.7	21.2	127.3
Rockdale	12	-7.7	118	0	4	418	3 226	22	1	11 825	47.4	52.6	19.6	2.0	0.0	2.3
Schley	41	7.6	449	1	16	703	1 565	50	12	132 136	24.8	75.2	41.8	23.1	0.0	1.8
Screven	165	18.5	507	10	90	497	1 016	59	30	91 820	86.9	13.1	46.5	16.3	0.0	8.1
Seminole	107	-1.5	587	29	68	714	1 227	118	40	217 821	92.3	7.7	66.7	30.1	3.7	23.7
Spalding	27	11.2	138	D	13	405	2 688	20	5	26 127	21.9	78.1	19.7	5.2	0.0	10.1
Stephens	20	22.5	104	D	10	258	2 508	25	41	219 608	1.2	98.8	29.8	16.5	20.3	3.1
Stewart	56	14.7	730	3	17	601	823	62	6	81 196	60.0	40.0	45.5	16.9	0.4	3.5
Sumter	186	9.7	594	30	122	576	1 060	88	92	291 658	80.8	19.2	54.5	30.6	0.0	28.4
Talbot	36	-4.0	329	D	11	415	992	20	2	16 468	10.0	90.0	23.4	1.8	0.0	2.9
Taliaferro	16	-13.9	297		5	279	939	31	3	56 425	2.3	97.7	40.0	12.7	0.0	0.2
Tattnall	137	14.1	232	11	66	301	1 540	37	144	244 885	42.5	57.5	47.7	27.5	2.1	18.4
Taylor	70	28.9	355	1	27	345	948	48	29	148 537	24.7	75.3	37.8	13.3	0.0	2.1
Telfair	86	21.4	318	7	32	345	1 147	41	10	38 349	79.5	20.5	39.5	11.4	0.0	10.4
Terrell	139	-3.1	797	15	88	750	969	83	28	159 838	97.1	2.9	62.6	37.9	0.0	20.8
Thomas	180	3.3	427	5	79	662	1 560	59	38	89 419	87.0	13.0	46.6	22.6	0.0	12.7
Tift	106	-6.9	296	17	67	548	1 704	61	54	149 897	93.8	6.2	57.7	20.9	0.0	34.5
Toombs	100	12.3	249	9	42	269	1 108	35	29	73 244	87.5	12.5	31.7	13.5	0.0	7.0
Towns	9	-12.9	72	D	5	224	2 907	26	1	8 329	15.2	84.7	12.4	1.7	60.4	2.0
Treutlen	42	27.4	268	1	12	198	722	23	3	18 474	88.8	11.2	17.2	4.5	0.0	1.7
Troup	43	4.9	195	D	20	283	1 566	18	4	19 573	24.3	75.7	27.6	4.1	8.0	13.3
Turner	98	-0.8	427	9	63	540	1 320	92	35	150 149	80.3	19.7	74.3	33.5	0.0	19.1
Twiggs	26	-15.5	267	1	11	368	1 029	39	4	37 612	76.9	23.1	31.6	7.1	0.1	23.3
Union	22	0.7	87	0	11	384	4 730	46	17	66 255	D	D	26.6	4.7	46.5	1.4
Upson	38	13.7	203	0	15	269	1 491	27	10	53 462	9.4	90.6	20.5	7.0	0.0	11.1
Walker	86	-3.8	179	D	39	304	1 644	21	28	58 935	4.4	95.6	26.2	6.7	7.3	10.9
Walton	60	6.8	121	1	31	449	3 393	25	29	59 281	26.1	73.9	24.5	8.1	0.0	5.8
Ware	64	19.1	235	2	20	289	1 147	30	18	65 522	57.1	42.9	37.2	13.5	31.4	5.9
Warren	44	-5.4	332	D	15	271	821	29	4	32 791	10.3	89.7	30.6	8.2	0.1	5.0
Washington	111	-1.1	339	5	56	318	876	30	12	35 497	72.2	27.8	34.6	9.8	0.0	24.4
Wayne	65	20.8	236	5	33	407	1 730	44	17	61 724	80.9	19.1	37.7	14.5	0.1	66.0
Webster	58	8.6	758	3	29	810	1 070	90	9	118 219	94.1	5.9	56.6	35.5	0.0	5.4
Wheeler	71	45.5	405	3	20	320	720	42	9	50 299	91.5	8.5	34.7	8.5	0.0	3.1
White	26	9.6	93	0	12	367	3 834	25	53	187 285	1.7	98.3	39.1	23.9	27.5	5.9
Whitfield	39	-0.6	119	0	20	361	2 602	36	46	141 679	2.4	97.6	30.5	13.8	6.1	38.9
Wilcox	123	6.2	451	17	73	382	826	70	52	190 286	47.4	52.6	62.6	27.8	0.0	15.3
Wilkes	95	2.1	319	D	32	325	925	27	22	73 937	4.2	95.8	28.9	6.4	2.1	4.1
Wilkinson	28	-14.0	313		8	233	746	29	1	14 454	45.0	55.0	31.8	2.3	0.0	23.4
Worth	191	-4.6	470	21	122	577	1 215	92	65	159 241	87.2	12.8	62.8	35.5	0.0	29.1
HAWAII	1 439	-9.4	263	77	292	632	2 405	39	497	90 798	80.8	19.2	41.9	8.2	8.7	1 012.4
Hawaii	870	-6.1	262	7	103	574	2 192	22	168	50 651	76.7	23.3	40.7	6.4	10.3	115.8
Honolulu	80	-13.1	91	16	29	565	6 225	33	143	162 460	72.4	27.6	57.5	14.5	12.5	278.9
Kalawao	NA	NA	NA	NA	NA	NA	NA	NA	NA	NA	NA	NA	NA	NA	NA	0.0
Kauai	197	-7.9	421	18	D	848	2 013	81	57	122 808	91.9	8.1	30.8	4.9	0.7	243.8
Maui	292	-18.0	362	35	D	818	2 258	89	128	159 287	90.4	9.6	36.4	10.3	5.3	373.9
IDAHO	11 830	-12.2	530	3 494	6 309	537	1 017	78	3 346	149 945	53.0	47.0	53.5	21.5	62.7	15 141.5
Ada	231	-0.8	189	78	90	362	1 891	40	94	76 756	38.8	61.2	33.8	11.2	42.6	1 098.3
Adams	200	-9.3	719	28	48	535	651	33	8	29 890	13.4	86.6	42.7	6.1	63.9	63.7
Bannock	309	-4.8	466	42	167	257	658	43	25	37 699	62.3	37.7	35.7	8.1	27.4	313.5
Bear Lake	222	-17.6	541	50	121	341	634	34	15	36 284	23.1	76.9	54.6	11.7	44.2	117.3
Benewah	126	12.5	557	0	77	507	960	60	11	50 595	91.9	8.1	31.0	14.2	10.1	8.0
Bingham	796	-42.0	682	322	378	651	932	105	225	193 059	75.0	25.0	55.7	26.2	26.8	1 093.7
Blaine	215	-19.2	1 102	57	70	1 446	1 361	70	24	120 943	53.8	46.2	42.6	25.6	77.0	160.2
Boise	45	-43.2	583	3	7	519	891	34	2	28 885	52.6	47.4	41.0	5.1	73.3	15.2
Bonner	99	-34.2	197	2	37	357	1 781	26	7	14 509	55.4	44.6	24.0	2.8	40.2	35.2
Bonneville	449	-1.0	571	154	312	504	800	85	91	115 106	79.7	20.3	51.0	19.8	47.8	644.9
Boundary	73	-0.4	233	3	51	400	1 892	37	14	43 401	86.5	13.5	43.6	11.2	58.9	2.3
Butte	130	-18.5	626	62	70	492	775	85	22	103 932	69.3	30.7	71.0	28.5	86.8	167.6
Camas	128	-1.2	1 301	12	80	832	639	73	9	89 944	77.3	22.7	73.5	25.5	64.0	27.0
Canyon	355	-9.2	187	221	235	399	2 225	65	311	164 066	50.2	49.8	51.6	21.3	3.4	639.0
Caribou	469	-20.2	1 099	81	265	663	578	76	43	100 510	68.6	31.4	59.5	26.0	40.3	225.4
Cassia	657	-1.4	901	266	378	918	932	155	333	456 541	42.8	57.2	70.4	37.2	53.0	585.5
Clark	215	-25.0	2 594	56	D	1 370	528	159	32	385 897	74.9	25.1	74.7	43.4	65.1	105.8
Clearwater	73	-29.0	348	0	42	310	1 198	30	5	23 091	79.8	20.2	34.3	5.2	51.5	36.4

Table B. States and Counties — Residential Construction, Wholesale and Retail Trade, and Real Estate

STATE County	Value of Residential Construction Authorized by Building Permits, 1999		Wholesale Trade, 1997				Retail Trade[1], 1997				Real Estate and Rental and Leasing, 1997			
	New Construction ($1,000)	Number of Housing Units	Number of Establishments	Number of Employees	Sales (mil dol)	Annual Payroll (mil dol)	Number of Establishments	Number of Employees	Sales (mil dol)	Annual Payroll (mil dol)	Number of Establishments	Number of Employees	Receipts (mil dol)	Annual Payroll (mil dol)
	133	134	135	136	137	138	139	140	141	142	143	144	145	146
GEORGIA—Cont'd														
Richmond	51 914	1 168	245	2 262	756.9	68.8	912	12 332	1 909.9	189.3	223	1 064	114.0	20.4
Rockdale	73 017	915	124	1 267	1 230.4	47.3	281	4 411	766.0	71.4	58	250	36.6	4.9
Schley	0	0	9	57	21.5	1.5	14	96	9.9	1.1	1	D	D	D
Screven	513	8	8	41	9.8	0.7	56	483	82.1	7.0	7	7	0.6	0.1
Seminole	1 469	17	14	182	83.0	2.0	61	413	71.5	5.4	5	13	1.0	0.1
Spalding	35 312	462	49	611	338.5	18.4	248	3 119	521.5	52.1	47	170	13.9	2.5
Stephens	12 886	130	28	222	50.8	5.1	121	1 247	203.9	17.8	14	31	4.7	0.5
Stewart	0	0	5	39	9.7	1.2	26	133	14.5	1.3	2	D	D	D
Sumter	4 021	86	42	430	168.9	11.0	162	1 984	283.9	28.1	23	62	6.3	1.0
Talbot	235	19	2	D	D	D	13	68	7.1	0.7	NA	NA	NA	NA
Taliaferro	NA	NA	2	D	D	D	4	D	D	D	1	D	D	D
Tattnall	653	7	19	389	58.4	7.3	78	581	76.2	6.7	6	10	1.0	0.1
Taylor	887	16	7	D	D	D	36	227	36.5	2.8	4	3	0.4	0.0
Telfair	60	2	14	237	53.6	4.5	60	407	49.5	4.9	3	7	0.8	0.1
Terrell	2 221	54	17	198	125.8	4.3	57	321	55.3	4.2	2	D	D	D
Thomas	21 283	177	64	701	293.0	21.0	256	2 661	395.8	39.0	32	135	15.9	2.6
Tift	13 695	161	88	1 117	459.4	26.6	260	2 500	440.4	36.1	37	127	11.4	1.7
Toombs	1 661	16	39	333	203.6	8.4	152	1 706	253.7	23.1	17	67	5.7	0.9
Towns	22 412	221	7	D	D	D	52	289	42.4	3.9	13	22	2.6	0.3
Treutlen	387	6	2	D	D	D	23	111	14.2	1.3	3	5	0.2	0.0
Troup	40 212	561	69	681	270.8	22.6	293	3 500	526.0	52.7	45	175	18.9	3.4
Turner	285	4	16	230	203.8	5.8	54	316	58.3	4.4	6	40	4.4	0.6
Twiggs	2 600	29	3	D	D	D	14	116	17.2	1.6	2	D	D	D
Union	39 190	387	15	92	37.3	2.1	75	592	101.8	8.2	16	22	3.7	0.3
Upson	7 565	90	17	112	17.0	1.4	121	1 119	174.5	14.5	12	39	3.3	0.5
Walker	22 400	303	58	D	D	D	180	1 515	240.1	22.4	22	67	4.5	0.9
Walton	120 185	1 322	45	322	239.9	10.4	162	1 567	247.6	25.0	35	108	12.7	1.4
Ware	6 583	76	62	493	169.4	10.4	226	2 628	390.1	35.8	26	131	14.9	2.1
Warren	0	0	3	6	0.8	0.1	22	128	12.5	1.9	1	D	D	D
Washington	814	15	24	157	37.8	4.0	108	925	139.3	13.2	12	26	3.4	0.4
Wayne	1 246	13	17	159	50.7	3.9	125	1 145	172.5	16.6	9	57	2.6	0.5
Webster	NA	NA	2	D	D	D	8	80	7.6	0.8	NA	NA	NA	NA
Wheeler	0	0	3	D	D	D	13	64	11.1	0.7	1	D	D	D
White	32 881	340	12	110	23.6	1.8	139	1 028	230.4	18.3	20	36	4.4	0.5
Whitfield	27 185	481	340	4 254	3 475.7	122.9	508	5 908	1 068.1	103.7	87	365	61.3	8.2
Wilcox	0	0	5	D	D	D	30	138	20.1	1.8	2	D	D	D
Wilkes	3 271	67	18	138	61.5	3.1	65	414	56.3	5.2	3	6	0.5	0.1
Wilkinson	NA	NA	7	125	24.8	3.3	29	190	29.5	2.3	NA	NA	NA	NA
Worth	7 144	63	32	308	118.7	7.9	62	461	101.5	8.1	10	24	2.2	0.3
HAWAII	632 743	4 211	1 872	18 532	7 147.5	576.0	5 088	64 218	11 317.8	1 161.8	1 753	12 446	1 824.1	311.9
Hawaii	167 982	1 098	179	1 362	457.3	35.9	688	7 587	1 183.1	128.5	211	1 838	196.9	39.0
Honolulu	260 117	1 928	1 463	15 423	6 079.9	487.0	3 269	44 960	8 264.7	823.6	1 221	7 746	1 219.9	208.4
Kalawao	NA	NA	NA	NA	NA	NA	NA	NA	NA	NA	NA	NA	NA	NA
Kauai	81 955	291	64	423	176.7	11.9	326	3 427	510.7	59.0	108	1 166	131.7	24.8
Maui	122 689	894	166	1 324	433.6	41.2	805	8 244	1 359.3	150.7	213	1 696	275.6	39.7
IDAHO	1 366 527	12 309	1 980	22 828	10 127.8	628.0	5 848	63 732	11 649.6	1 079.7	1 236	4 870	450.3	73.9
Ada	556 933	4 480	578	7 610	5 362.7	273.5	1 264	16 663	3 163.2	300.9	379	1 860	197.1	33.5
Adams	6 302	56	1	D	D	D	16	81	13.4	0.9	1	D	D	D
Bannock	26 622	308	104	935	282.6	25.2	343	4 177	705.7	65.1	64	255	23.5	3.5
Bear Lake	8 191	91	3	88	20.2	1.5	34	271	40.2	3.3	7	60	1.2	0.4
Benewah	2 516	31	8	52	17.6	1.2	41	313	50.2	4.9	4	17	0.9	0.3
Bingham	16 928	185	54	974	189.4	18.0	125	1 363	243.8	22.0	14	44	1.8	0.4
Blaine	93 297	332	41	301	172.3	12.3	189	1 372	226.9	26.3	73	292	31.0	4.9
Boise	12 029	134	NA	NA	NA	NA	18	65	6.6	0.5	NA	NA	NA	NA
Bonner	5 967	73	37	256	69.8	6.2	200	2 325	573.8	41.5	46	170	14.4	2.9
Bonneville	62 347	893	181	2 484	808.0	63.2	480	5 615	933.4	90.1	69	368	19.2	3.6
Boundary	7 230	65	12	89	16.7	2.9	54	373	61.6	6.1	8	22	1.8	0.3
Butte	182	3	3	D	D	D	15	81	10.6	0.9	NA	NA	NA	NA
Camas	1 788	19	1	D	D	D	4	11	3.0	0.1	NA	NA	NA	NA
Canyon	214 277	2 117	157	1 512	555.2	38.4	429	4 724	1 014.1	88.9	88	268	22.9	3.6
Caribou	2 455	23	15	64	25.3	1.6	42	301	57.8	4.5	3	7	0.3	0.1
Cassia	5 940	61	40	271	218.6	6.3	116	1 144	193.0	19.2	17	39	3.0	0.6
Clark	351	5	1	D	D	D	4	40	4.5	0.3	NA	NA	NA	NA
Clearwater	431	15	5	D	D	D	45	331	56.8	5.0	6	D	D	D

1. Establishments with payroll.

STATE County	Professional, Scientific, and Technical Services[1], 1997				Manufacturing, 1997				Accommodation and Foodservices, 1997			
	Number of Establishments	Number of Employees	Receipts (mil dol)	Annual Payroll (mil dol)	Number of Establishments	Number of Employees	Receipts (mil dol)	Annual Payroll (mil dol)	Number of Establishments	Number of Employees	Sales (mil dol)	Annual Payroll (mil dol)
	147	148	149	150	151	152	153	154	155	156	157	158
GEORGIA—Cont'd												
Richmond	324	1 931	147.2	58.3	134	12 084	4 092.6	423.4	400	8 301	255.6	70.4
Rockdale	141	777	55.7	22.2	116	6 730	1 625.1	200.0	122	2 657	86.6	23.5
Schley	2	D	D	D	9	589	115.4	14.6	4	6	0.3	0.1
Screven	12	28	1.2	0.4	13	1 289	127.8	33.9	18	89	4.0	0.9
Seminole	8	30	1.5	0.5	NA	NA	NA	NA	10	82	2.9	0.6
Spalding	65	302	23.2	8.0	70	6 328	1 118.8	150.7	92	1 524	46.7	12.6
Stephens	33	111	7.9	2.4	64	3 970	634.8	88.4	44	844	21.3	5.7
Stewart	1	D	D	D	NA	NA	NA	NA	6	30	1.7	0.4
Sumter	31	136	9.5	3.3	38	3 163	475.4	71.3	51	770	23.5	6.2
Talbot	3	7	0.3	0.1	NA	NA	NA	NA	6	D	D	D
Taliaferro	NA	NA	NA	NA	NA	NA	NA	NA	1	D	D	D
Tattnall	12	51	2.4	0.8	12	762	62.9	8.4	19	241	6.6	1.6
Taylor	8	21	1.0	0.4	NA	NA	NA	NA	6	48	1.3	0.3
Telfair	12	19	1.0	0.3	14	1 946	566.3	37.0	19	175	4.9	1.1
Terrell	5	41	2.1	0.8	13	786	141.6	15.1	9	D	D	D
Thomas	45	221	18.1	6.6	72	4 926	933.7	108.6	64	1 100	36.9	9.6
Tift	55	297	25.1	8.6	51	4 449	613.3	103.7	80	1 434	44.3	12.8
Toombs	39	174	13.5	4.5	38	2 516	169.3	41.6	60	814	22.8	5.7
Towns	9	34	1.5	0.7	NA	NA	NA	NA	24	381	14.8	4.8
Treutlen	4	12	0.5	0.2	NA	NA	NA	NA	8	131	2.3	0.7
Troup	71	301	21.0	8.6	101	9 369	1 807.7	284.2	111	1 757	50.6	12.8
Turner	7	16	0.7	0.2	10	686	66.1	11.8	16	194	6.0	0.9
Twiggs	4	7	0.4	0.2	NA	NA	NA	NA	4	D	D	D
Union	25	69	3.9	1.8	NA	NA	NA	NA	27	272	8.4	2.3
Upson	24	57	4.0	0.9	26	4 241	555.1	82.9	46	502	14.6	3.8
Walker	46	197	12.7	4.6	77	6 555	1 207.7	159.9	51	658	20.0	5.1
Walton	62	160	10.9	3.7	55	2 611	441.5	70.4	45	D	D	D
Ware	55	161	10.2	3.5	42	2 121	287.4	55.8	63	1 180	34.4	9.9
Warren	2	D	D	D	6	798	131.0	20.0	1	D	D	D
Washington	18	132	6.0	2.9	18	917	131.7	22.3	20	D	D	D
Wayne	25	74	4.1	1.4	23	1 816	460.6	56.0	34	555	15.7	4.1
Webster	NA	NA	NA	NA	NA	NA	NA	NA	NA	NA	NA	NA
Wheeler	2	D	D	D	NA	NA	NA	NA	3	8	0.4	0.0
White	20	49	2.7	0.7	28	952	172.8	27.0	73	666	25.3	6.6
Whitfield	144	856	64.4	29.3	379	27 373	6 166.5	687.5	143	2 565	92.0	25.4
Wilcox	NA	NA	NA	NA	NA	NA	NA	NA	1	D	D	D
Wilkes	10	35	1.6	0.3	23	1 584	315.4	36.8	13	D	D	D
Wilkinson	6	15	1.0	0.3	14	1 307	391.2	49.7	8	D	D	D
Worth	10	26	1.4	0.5	NA	NA	NA	NA	18	D	D	D
HAWAII	2 480	15 743	1 574.0	606.5	921	15 109	3 192.5	405.0	3 081	88 083	5 007.9	1 507.5
Hawaii	246	933	73.3	24.9	106	1 588	192.5	37.5	326	10 441	546.6	188.1
Honolulu	1 917	13 729	1 400.6	546.8	685	11 161	2 692.2	300.9	2 125	53 916	3 036.8	852.8
Kalawao	NA	NA	NA	NA	NA	NA	NA	NA	NA	NA	NA	NA
Kauai	90	327	25.0	9.0	NA	NA	NA	NA	210	5 775	293.8	102.3
Maui	227	754	75.2	25.7	100	1 919	259.6	51.3	420	17 951	1 130.7	364.4
IDAHO	2 364	19 669	2 046.1	756.2	1 647	66 184	16 952.9	2 099.8	2 978	42 067	1 232.5	345.7
Ada	805	6 419	903.2	264.2	395	20 850	6 318.4	862.6	648	12 105	370.1	103.9
Adams	2	D	D	D	NA	NA	NA	NA	14	134	3.4	1.7
Bannock	108	934	47.4	22.5	62	3 482	775.1	119.2	188	2 792	75.3	20.5
Bear Lake	2	D	D	D	NA	NA	NA	NA	13	90	2.8	0.7
Benewah	13	44	1.6	0.7	8	586	141.8	20.2	26	181	4.2	1.3
Bingham	26	110	6.4	2.6	44	2 413	366.1	64.2	51	583	12.6	3.7
Blaine	102	524	55.0	19.2	NA	NA	NA	NA	131	3 365	115.3	34.3
Boise	5	13	1.5	0.4	NA	NA	NA	NA	23	110	3.1	0.7
Bonner	86	214	13.6	5.5	86	1 898	382.1	56.8	115	1 385	33.6	11.1
Bonneville	210	7 327	748.5	338.6	115	2 550	267.9	55.8	180	3 381	90.3	25.9
Boundary	11	31	1.3	0.5	NA	NA	NA	NA	24	276	13.3	2.5
Butte	1	D	D	D	NA	NA	NA	NA	9	50	1.5	0.3
Camas	NA	NA	NA	NA	NA	NA	NA	NA	5	D	D	D
Canyon	128	553	35.4	12.7	176	9 817	3 581.7	268.2	188	2 619	71.4	19.1
Caribou	14	26	1.2	0.3	7	D	D	D	16	129	2.7	0.7
Cassia	30	D	D	D	24	D	D	D	48	653	17.9	4.8
Clark	NA	NA	NA	NA	NA	NA	NA	NA	3	D	D	D
Clearwater	9	40	1.7	0.6	NA	NA	NA	NA	31	186	4.7	1.3

1. Firms subject to federal tax.

Table B. States and Counties — Health and Other Services and Federal Funds

STATE County	Health Care and Social Assistance[1], 1997				Other Services[1], 1997				Federal funds and grants, fiscal 1999[2] Expenditures (mil dol)	Direct payments for individuals[3]		
	Number of Establishments	Number of Employees	Receipts (mil dol)	Annual Payroll (mil dol)	Number of Establishments	Number of Employees	Receipts (mil dol)	Annual Payroll (mil dol)	Total	Social Security and government retirement	Medicare	Food stamps and Supplemental Security Income
	159	160	161	162	163	164	165	166	167	168	169	170
GEORGIA—Cont'd												
Richmond	500	5 944	498.0	212.2	282	1 997	102.3	33.3	1 142.2	513.5	135.0	54.9
Rockdale	127	1 615	94.8	43.0	109	518	35.0	9.4	147.1	88.6	31.3	4.3
Schley	2	D	D	D	2	D	D	D	14.5	5.4	2.9	0.6
Screven	13	173	6.4	2.9	13	36	2.9	0.7	70.1	26.3	13.8	4.6
Seminole	15	95	5.8	2.8	17	60	3.6	1.0	48.0	20.0	8.4	3.7
Spalding	103	1 979	107.0	45.3	71	438	28.3	8.5	228.5	111.1	44.5	13.6
Stephens	36	531	32.4	10.2	38	116	8.7	1.8	111.4	58.6	24.9	4.6
Stewart	3	140	6.9	2.2	4	9	0.8	0.1	34.1	10.7	6.6	2.0
Sumter	64	787	38.5	17.5	39	195	10.8	3.0	142.0	51.3	23.6	10.1
Talbot	3	19	1.7	0.6	5	12	0.4	0.1	32.8	16.3	4.4	2.0
Taliaferro	2	D	D	D	2	D	D	D	19.4	4.5	2.8	0.6
Tattnall	19	518	17.2	7.5	18	52	3.7	0.8	89.5	40.3	16.5	5.9
Taylor	1	D	D	D	10	22	1.7	0.3	46.4	19.1	7.6	3.1
Telfair	16	464	19.3	8.3	14	62	4.4	1.1	71.2	30.2	15.2	3.2
Terrell	13	127	4.7	1.7	15	52	2.8	0.6	61.3	18.4	9.9	3.9
Thomas	86	960	70.2	33.6	74	282	17.6	4.6	200.9	87.4	35.8	12.5
Tift	83	1 157	69.5	37.1	57	584	43.3	12.3	143.6	60.7	26.2	9.1
Toombs	67	804	35.1	15.7	37	263	10.6	4.1	108.4	45.0	21.1	6.8
Towns	14	284	14.6	6.3	8	18	0.9	0.2	48.6	29.6	8.8	0.8
Treutlen	9	79	2.8	1.2	4	D	D	D	28.5	10.2	5.0	2.1
Troup	91	1 173	73.7	36.9	94	410	26.5	8.1	230.5	109.8	44.2	13.5
Turner	6	104	3.7	1.5	13	34	2.8	0.5	48.3	16.3	9.4	3.0
Twiggs	5	143	5.2	2.1	7	8	0.9	0.1	38.9	17.2	7.1	2.4
Union	30	171	9.4	4.5	19	59	6.3	1.0	80.1	45.4	15.3	2.2
Upson	48	515	26.9	11.9	39	140	9.6	2.5	110.4	54.4	22.5	5.2
Walker	52	507	25.5	11.2	64	377	22.6	6.3	240.3	129.6	60.2	9.7
Walton	59	639	28.4	12.2	49	152	12.0	3.2	157.2	82.1	35.9	8.5
Ware	90	1 100	62.7	29.8	60	292	16.6	4.4	193.5	88.2	38.0	13.4
Warren	7	234	6.0	3.5	6	19	0.9	0.1	34.0	11.5	7.6	2.2
Washington	41	508	20.6	9.3	30	95	5.9	1.4	91.7	34.4	20.0	5.6
Wayne	46	530	30.1	11.9	26	118	8.3	2.4	138.6	46.5	23.8	5.8
Webster	NA	NA	NA	NA	1	D	D	D	9.8	3.5	1.9	0.5
Wheeler	6	164	9.7	3.3	2	D	D	D	26.4	8.9	5.5	1.4
White	24	269	14.5	4.6	20	69	4.8	1.0	64.2	38.5	11.7	1.8
Whitfield	129	1 442	114.0	52.5	123	672	47.2	14.6	242.9	121.8	52.1	10.0
Wilcox	5	208	6.4	3.0	8	18	0.7	0.2	45.1	17.2	8.4	2.6
Wilkes	22	159	8.6	3.4	21	64	5.4	1.6	53.8	23.3	13.0	2.6
Wilkinson	6	108	4.6	1.6	8	30	1.9	0.5	47.1	22.6	9.5	2.4
Worth	21	316	15.4	5.8	16	51	3.1	0.9	80.7	31.0	12.8	5.2
HAWAII	2 360	18 221	1 646.3	730.8	1 476	10 375	683.2	206.4	8 568.2	2 340.0	658.3	270.0
Hawaii	321	2 441	224.8	76.2	157	808	50.3	14.5	597.0	268.1	78.3	53.0
Honolulu	1 730	13 474	1 231.7	563.1	1 097	8 402	560.8	170.7	6 944.7	1 793.4	486.3	184.7
Kalawao	NA	NA	NA	NA	NA	NA	NA	NA	NA	NA	NA	NA
Kauai	79	745	51.4	27.6	59	281	17.9	5.1	253.7	96.3	34.6	12.2
Maui	230	1 561	138.4	63.9	163	884	54.2	16.2	393.1	175.7	58.6	20.1
IDAHO	2 551	26 365	1 548.3	680.1	1 858	9 461	550.6	151.7	6 164.7	2 159.3	600.8	124.4
Ada	711	6 993	484.7	228.8	462	3 185	171.1	51.3	1 304.4	456.6	110.1	22.4
Adams	2	D	D	D	1	D	D	D	28.9	10.0	2.0	0.4
Bannock	157	1 421	79.8	39.1	108	564	33.5	9.5	272.1	125.9	32.3	10.5
Bear Lake	7	33	1.6	0.6	6	10	1.3	0.2	30.9	13.6	3.6	0.5
Benewah	9	9	1.4	0.4	15	136	7.2	2.0	46.4	19.8	7.1	1.3
Bingham	51	391	17.2	7.9	39	215	15.7	4.2	151.9	58.5	16.0	4.4
Blaine	52	239	21.1	10.0	44	188	11.8	3.3	40.1	19.4	5.2	0.4
Boise	NA	NA	NA	NA	3	D	D	D	28.6	10.4	2.2	0.1
Bonner	70	535	26.3	10.0	54	166	11.4	3.0	131.1	75.0	18.8	3.9
Bonneville	241	3 151	229.1	91.6	140	709	49.5	13.0	808.4	125.0	38.5	8.7
Boundary	16	48	2.2	0.6	17	43	4.1	0.9	45.7	20.0	4.1	1.2
Butte	3	27	1.0	0.3	3	17	1.3	0.2	26.1	6.1	2.3	0.2
Camas	1	D	D	D	NA	NA	NA	NA	5.4	1.9	0.3	0.0
Canyon	182	2 692	161.3	74.9	158	697	39.0	10.9	433.4	192.5	59.7	16.0
Caribou	14	76	3.5	1.2	13	37	1.9	0.4	33.9	13.0	3.1	0.3
Cassia	56	421	20.6	6.4	44	176	10.7	2.7	85.3	30.4	11.5	1.9
Clark	2	D	D	D	NA	NA	NA	NA	13.8	1.4	0.4	0.0
Clearwater	9	94	3.9	1.3	13	39	2.6	0.8	52.3	21.4	6.3	1.3

1. Firms subject to federal tax.   2. October 1, 1998 to September 30, 1999.   3. State totals may include programs not allocated by county.

STATE County	Federal funds and grants, fiscal 1999[1] (cont'd)							Local government finances, 1997				
	Expenditures (mil dol) (cont'd)							General revenue				
	Procurement contract awards			Grants[2]						Taxes		
											Per capita[3] (dollars)	
	Salaries and wages	Defense	Other	Medicaid and other health-related	Nutrition and family welfare	Education	Other	Total (mil dol)	Intergovern-mental (mil dol)	Total (mil dol)	Total	Property
	171	172	173	174	175	176	177	178	179	180	181	182
GEORGIA—Cont'd												
Richmond	197.9	7.6	25.2	103.1	40.5	12.2	29.5	431.8	189.9	153.7	796	401
Rockdale	6.6	0.0	1.9	6.9	2.9	1.6	1.9	137.6	45.8	65.7	980	763
Schley	0.4	0.0	0.1	2.6	0.6	0.3	0.9	6.2	2.5	2.0	530	420
Screven	1.9	0.0	0.5	12.3	3.1	1.0	1.7	32.0	14.8	9.4	652	449
Seminole	1.0	0.0	0.3	6.9	1.8	0.6	0.6	16.3	9.2	5.4	548	321
Spalding	6.8	1.6	1.4	25.5	7.5	3.5	5.7	127.7	58.6	45.9	805	490
Stephens	3.9	0.2	0.8	12.0	2.3	1.2	0.1	45.4	17.2	19.6	776	504
Stewart	0.8	0.0	0.2	7.4	1.9	0.5	2.8	10.3	5.6	3.1	572	459
Sumter	6.4	0.0	1.4	19.9	7.3	2.9	5.0	120.4	49.6	23.0	726	413
Talbot	0.8	0.1	0.2	4.7	1.4	0.5	2.0	10.6	4.9	4.3	622	483
Taliaferro	0.4	0.0	0.1	2.8	0.5	0.1	7.2	2.9	1.1	1.6	844	728
Tattnall	2.1	0.1	0.5	14.5	3.8	0.9	1.9	31.5	15.9	10.7	559	364
Taylor	1.1	0.0	0.3	7.7	1.9	0.7	3.6	15.4	9.3	4.3	529	311
Telfair	1.6	0.1	0.4	11.5	2.7	0.9	2.3	25.8	11.4	7.8	680	399
Terrell	3.2	0.2	4.6	11.2	2.8	1.0	0.7	22.3	12.7	7.1	638	374
Thomas	9.0	0.0	1.4	27.7	6.9	4.1	3.5	90.8	48.5	19.5	457	261
Tift	9.8	0.0	1.2	18.4	5.3	2.7	2.4	144.2	41.1	27.3	741	389
Toombs	3.7	0.0	0.8	17.1	4.6	1.7	2.8	54.5	25.0	14.3	560	212
Towns	1.3	0.0	0.1	4.1	0.5	0.1	3.0	9.7	4.5	3.7	456	280
Treutlen	0.7	0.0	0.2	6.7	1.3	0.4	1.1	10.5	6.3	2.4	402	285
Troup	6.9	2.0	3.1	28.1	11.0	3.2	4.7	196.3	59.3	44.5	761	538
Turner	1.3	0.0	0.3	6.7	2.4	0.9	1.6	19.8	10.3	7.0	762	505
Twiggs	0.6	0.0	0.2	5.9	2.2	0.8	1.7	16.5	8.7	6.9	702	511
Union	3.0	0.0	0.8	7.6	1.0	0.4	4.1	38.2	10.3	9.4	601	355
Upson	2.8	0.0	1.4	13.4	4.3	1.3	1.6	41.5	20.0	15.9	585	415
Walker	6.3	0.0	1.5	18.5	8.6	2.8	0.6	95.5	52.2	29.0	469	286
Walton	6.8	0.0	1.7	14.0	3.7	1.9	0.8	107.5	36.3	34.5	670	521
Ware	7.7	0.0	1.7	25.6	10.7	2.9	0.6	90.9	51.4	28.6	799	417
Warren	1.0	0.0	0.6	7.9	1.5	0.6	0.0	12.0	5.5	4.4	726	502
Washington	2.6	0.0	0.9	16.3	5.7	1.3	0.6	57.0	17.1	18.3	916	594
Wayne	20.0	16.7	1.8	14.2	3.8	1.5	1.1	89.1	20.3	17.7	704	531
Webster	0.5	0.0	0.1	1.8	0.5	0.1	-0.4	4.0	2.3	1.3	578	517
Wheeler	0.6	0.0	0.2	5.7	1.4	0.4	0.5	8.5	5.8	2.1	421	259
White	2.1	0.0	0.8	5.0	0.8	1.8	0.8	37.2	16.1	16.5	981	606
Whitfield	9.1	1.0	5.6	20.9	6.3	3.8	8.1	314.5	75.0	85.5	1 051	795
Wilcox	1.0	0.0	0.3	7.4	1.4	0.6	0.2	13.3	8.4	4.0	550	394
Wilkes	1.7	0.0	0.3	8.6	2.2	0.6	0.0	34.3	9.1	8.5	806	542
Wilkinson	1.1	0.0	0.3	5.7	2.0	0.7	2.4	19.4	7.9	9.8	898	580
Worth	1.8	0.0	0.4	10.4	4.1	1.8	0.7	35.4	20.3	11.2	499	336
HAWAII	2 436.1	992.7	148.6	417.4	277.8	162.7	476.6	X	X	X	X	X
Hawaii	41.8	8.3	6.5	40.3	30.2	15.3	44.3	178.0	56.7	102.2	723	611
Honolulu	2 345.6	925.5	114.3	329.4	193.8	123.1	383.8	996.0	150.0	526.9	606	476
Kalawao	NA	NA	NA	NA	NA	NA	NA	NA	NA	NA	NA	NA
Kauai	24.8	34.1	7.8	17.9	7.5	0.9	15.9	94.0	42.2	39.8	705	581
Maui	24.0	24.8	20.1	22.9	15.6	1.4	24.4	181.1	48.6	91.9	773	624
IDAHO	692.8	156.3	713.8	430.9	165.4	114.8	465.7	X	X	X	X	X
Ada	225.8	49.1	49.9	80.5	60.2	43.5	188.6	529.1	198.1	205.2	768	709
Adams	3.2	0.0	0.8	0.9	1.6	0.1	9.9	10.4	5.1	2.0	524	502
Bannock	23.0	0.1	12.6	29.9	5.0	3.4	16.1	177.4	69.3	39.1	530	505
Bear Lake	1.7	0.0	0.6	2.4	3.8	0.1	1.3	19.5	8.6	4.3	655	631
Benewah	2.7	0.1	0.6	3.9	2.9	0.7	2.9	26.0	9.1	5.6	627	604
Bingham	10.2	2.4	4.9	20.0	4.9	3.9	6.4	90.8	49.1	18.8	451	433
Blaine	3.9	0.0	1.2	1.3	0.8	0.1	6.2	65.8	13.5	27.5	1 595	1 356
Boise	3.9	1.0	2.4	0.9	0.7	0.1	6.7	15.5	6.7	3.9	768	749
Bonner	9.4	1.2	1.7	11.4	1.6	0.9	6.7	62.4	24.6	20.5	589	564
Bonneville	42.0	4.3	537.5	21.8	6.4	1.6	7.9	154.0	83.7	45.4	565	541
Boundary	4.6	0.0	1.8	3.8	0.8	0.2	6.5	24.7	9.2	4.3	436	430
Butte	6.9	0.0	0.2	3.0	4.8	0.1	0.1	12.3	4.1	2.7	851	849
Camas	0.7	0.0	0.2	0.3	0.8	0.0	0.1	2.7	1.8	0.7	808	778
Canyon	16.7	27.2	10.7	60.1	11.5	3.8	20.5	187.4	99.0	53.7	461	431
Caribou	1.6	0.0	0.7	0.9	1.5	0.1	3.8	24.7	11.5	6.9	934	864
Cassia	6.8	0.0	1.2	6.4	2.0	0.7	4.3	46.5	24.1	12.1	563	537
Clark	1.4	0.0	0.2	0.0	6.8	0.0	1.7	3.6	1.9	0.9	1 016	962
Clearwater	9.6	1.2	2.9	6.3	0.7	0.2	1.4	30.2	13.6	5.6	591	570

1. October 1, 1998 to September 30, 1999. 2. State totals may include programs not allocated by county. 3. Based on the resident population estimated as of July 1 of the year shown.

Table B. States and Counties — Local Government Finances, Government Employment, and Elections

STATE County	Local government finances, 1997 (cont'd) Direct general expenditure Total (mil dol)	Per capita[1] (dollars)	Percent of total for — Education	Health and hospitals	Police protection	Public welfare	Highways	Debt outstanding Total (mil dol)	Per capita[1] (dollars)	Government employment, 1998 Federal civilian	Federal military	State and local	Presidential election, 2000 Percent of vote cast — Demo-cratic	Republi-can	All other
	183	184	185	186	187	188	189	190	191	192	193	194	195	196	197
GEORGIA—Cont'd															
Richmond	445.7	2 308	45.6	8.0	5.4	0.2	3.7	402.2	2 083	5 976	10 102	22 142	NA	NA	NA
Rockdale	176.1	2 627	47.6	0.4	3.1	0.5	9.1	247.8	3 696	132	263	2 976	NA	NA	NA
Schley	6.5	1 705	65.6	1.4	5.0	0.3	4.4	3.6	944	0	15	168	NA	NA	NA
Screven	32.3	2 241	56.9	14.3	3.8	0.5	3.9	9.4	655	43	56	954	NA	NA	NA
Seminole	16.8	1 713	64.6	1.1	3.4	2.2	4.1	0.3	30	25	38	490	NA	NA	NA
Spalding	130.8	2 295	46.6	11.0	9.4	0.3	2.8	107.3	1 883	128	222	3 847	NA	NA	NA
Stephens	48.3	1 916	48.9	10.6	4.0	0.3	4.3	9.8	387	69	98	1 606	NA	NA	NA
Stewart	10.6	1 951	54.7	1.0	5.9	0.2	3.3	1.6	290	13	21	304	NA	NA	NA
Sumter	115.6	3 648	27.8	42.0	3.5	0.2	1.5	29.7	938	133	121	3 055	NA	NA	NA
Talbot	10.4	1 507	54.3	1.0	4.5	1.0	12.3	4.1	587	16	27	305	NA	NA	NA
Taliaferro	2.3	1 251	51.7	5.1	6.4	2.7	6.8	0.1	52	0	0	100	NA	NA	NA
Tattnall	32.0	1 681	50.7	9.0	2.7	1.6	6.2	9.9	521	31	73	2 561	NA	NA	NA
Taylor	15.5	1 889	56.7	1.3	5.4	0.5	5.9	4.1	497	24	32	530	NA	NA	NA
Telfair	22.9	1 995	51.9	16.2	5.5	0.8	4.0	6.6	576	40	45	1 006	NA	NA	NA
Terrell	22.3	2 011	54.4	1.3	5.1	0.3	6.2	3.1	277	72	43	555	NA	NA	NA
Thomas	96.0	2 255	50.0	14.0	4.2	0.1	4.4	7.1	168	191	167	3 672	NA	NA	NA
Tift	164.7	4 464	29.6	46.7	2.3	0.1	2.2	46.3	1 256	196	141	3 979	NA	NA	NA
Toombs	53.8	2 100	58.1	1.9	5.1	0.1	3.5	16.5	643	68	100	1 320	NA	NA	NA
Towns	10.4	1 279	53.7	6.5	4.5	3.3	8.6	4.5	551	21	33	342	NA	NA	NA
Treutlen	10.4	1 746	60.8	1.5	6.6	0.8	7.0	0.2	31	14	23	372	NA	NA	NA
Troup	204.2	3 488	35.6	38.8	3.6	0.1	2.2	73.9	1 263	151	227	4 989	NA	NA	NA
Turner	19.5	2 136	59.4	1.0	5.0	0.3	8.8	11.2	1 225	30	35	476	NA	NA	NA
Twiggs	15.7	1 587	69.6	1.5	4.5	1.0	5.1	1.7	174	11	39	526	NA	NA	NA
Union	38.1	2 428	34.0	43.7	1.9	0.0	5.7	2.1	131	75	64	1 115	NA	NA	NA
Upson	42.4	1 559	57.8	2.4	5.7	0.2	5.8	19.7	724	52	104	1 644	NA	NA	NA
Walker	92.8	1 501	61.5	11.2	5.7	0.2	4.9	38.1	617	142	243	2 698	NA	NA	NA
Walton	105.9	2 056	49.6	19.0	3.7	0.4	4.3	41.5	805	113	210	2 680	NA	NA	NA
Ware	93.6	2 614	42.4	20.8	4.4	0.1	9.6	28.5	797	151	136	3 313	NA	NA	NA
Warren	11.1	1 846	54.0	1.1	3.9	0.9	6.7	9.5	1 566	18	23	295	NA	NA	NA
Washington	64.9	3 244	44.5	31.2	3.3	0.1	6.7	22.3	1 113	51	77	2 196	NA	NA	NA
Wayne	66.6	2 656	38.1	37.5	3.6	0.1	4.8	25.0	997	370	98	2 198	NA	NA	NA
Webster	3.9	1 743	55.5	2.0	4.2	0.4	17.9	0.2	100	12	0	138	NA	NA	NA
Wheeler	9.2	1 866	63.4	1.3	3.9	4.4	4.5	0.6	114	12	19	332	NA	NA	NA
White	46.2	2 743	52.9	0.9	4.0	0.1	22.8	13.6	806	40	67	878	NA	NA	NA
Whitfield	271.3	3 336	35.1	41.0	2.6	0.2	3.8	100.5	1 235	180	316	4 846	NA	NA	NA
Wilcox	14.5	1 982	70.2	0.9	4.5	0.8	5.0	2.7	368	29	28	640	NA	NA	NA
Wilkes	32.9	3 115	34.8	40.2	4.1	0.5	3.1	4.7	448	41	41	855	NA	NA	NA
Wilkinson	18.4	1 697	63.6	2.2	6.3	0.5	7.5	1.5	135	20	42	545	NA	NA	NA
Worth	36.7	1 643	66.9	0.7	4.0	0.2	10.6	7.2	324	43	87	1 143	NA	NA	NA
HAWAII	X	X	X	X	X	X	X	X	X	30 127	55 253	80 967	56.0	38.0	7.0
Hawaii	195.8	1 384	0.1	4.1	14.3	0.0	7.1	168.0	1 187	961	1 339	9 511	56.0	33.0	11.0
Honolulu	972.6	1 118	0.0	1.3	13.4	0.0	2.6	1 698.5	1 953	28 274	52 170	60 501	54.0	39.0	7.0
Kalawao	NA	NA	NA	NA	NA	NA	NA	NA	NA	(3)507	(3)1 116	(3)7 281	NA	NA	NA
Kauai	84.6	1 499	0.0	0.0	10.5	0.0	7.9	51.9	920	385	628	3 674	61.0	30.0	10.0
Maui	187.5	1 578	0.0	0.4	12.0	6.7	15.1	208.2	1 753	(3)	(3)	(3)	59.0	33.0	8.0
IDAHO	X	X	X	X	X	X	X	X	X	12 728	9 768	86 918	27.6	67.2	5.2
Ada	561.7	2 102	48.4	1.7	6.5	0.9	6.2	227.5	852	4 475	1 321	20 636	32.9	60.8	6.3
Adams	9.0	2 344	43.6	22.2	4.9	0.9	9.8	0.8	217	119	17	270	17.6	77.3	5.1
Bannock	171.1	2 317	40.7	26.7	5.0	0.7	4.2	43.1	584	520	340	7 800	35.3	59.1	5.6
Bear Lake	18.4	2 796	40.9	28.1	3.5	0.2	4.3	1.0	149	50	29	520	17.8	79.2	3.0
Benewah	24.5	2 730	43.7	27.8	2.5	0.5	4.6	6.2	693	73	41	645	24.3	70.7	5.0
Bingham	91.4	2 195	58.2	15.0	4.2	0.4	5.4	20.9	501	311	186	2 879	22.9	73.5	3.6
Blaine	66.3	3 854	32.9	25.0	4.1	0.5	6.1	28.4	1 649	90	77	1 184	47.2	44.4	8.3
Boise	15.6	3 101	41.8	28.4	4.5	0.7	9.5	4.9	974	152	23	335	24.4	66.1	9.5
Bonner	63.9	1 837	43.5	0.9	5.8	1.6	12.8	19.6	562	272	157	1 859	29.7	61.5	8.8
Bonneville	156.7	1 952	54.1	3.7	6.4	0.5	3.9	106.6	1 328	722	360	4 397	21.6	74.5	4.0
Boundary	22.0	2 223	39.2	22.3	6.5	4.0	10.1	6.5	659	128	44	688	21.4	72.0	6.6
Butte	11.7	3 722	31.4	36.1	2.7	0.7	7.0	0.6	183	51	15	201	24.2	72.2	3.6
Camas	3.0	3 550	50.1	1.0	4.7	0.7	18.7	0.8	940	20	0	87	22.3	70.8	6.9
Canyon	210.3	1 802	59.5	1.8	4.3	0.9	5.5	103.5	887	341	535	5 569	24.6	71.1	4.3
Caribou	26.3	3 568	47.7	14.4	5.3	0.6	11.5	10.1	1 375	45	33	570	15.0	81.9	3.2
Cassia	51.2	2 387	61.4	0.4	5.2	0.7	7.9	34.3	1 599	159	95	1 343	14.9	82.2	2.9
Clark	3.6	4 266	39.4	1.6	4.3	0.3	17.4	0.8	976	40	0	124	16.5	81.4	2.1
Clearwater	31.4	3 322	31.0	18.9	4.0	0.5	24.0	8.8	935	269	41	961	21.6	74.1	4.4

1. Based on the resident population estimated as of July 1 of the year shown.   3. Kalawao County included with Maui County.

Table B. States and Counties — **Land Area and Population**

STATE/ County code	MSA/ PMSA/ NECMA code[1]	County Type[2]	STATE County	Land area,[3] (sq km) 1990	Total persons	Rank	Per square kilometer	White	Black	Am. Indian, Eskimo, Aleut	Asian and Pacific Islander	Percent Hispanic[4]	Under 5 years	5 to 17 years	18 to 24 years	25 to 34 years	35 to 44 years	45 to 54 years
				1	2	3	4	5	6	7	8	9	10	11	12	13	14	15
			IDAHO—Cont'd															
16 037	...	9	Custer	12 757	4 089	2 909	0.3	97.9	0.6	0.9	0.6	3.7	6.8	20.0	6.8	11.2	16.8	14.6
16 039	...	6	Elmore	7 971	25 627	1 509	3.2	91.9	4.6	0.9	2.6	10.6	9.7	19.5	14.1	17.7	13.7	10.7
16 041	...	7	Franklin	1 724	11 350	2 314	6.6	99.0	0.3	0.4	0.2	4.1	8.9	28.1	9.8	10.1	11.5	11.5
16 043	...	7	Fremont	4 835	11 890	2 283	2.5	98.4	0.2	0.9	0.6	9.7	7.9	26.1	10.2	10.6	12.0	11.7
16 045	...	6	Gem	1 457	15 145	2 056	10.4	95.8	0.1	1.5	0.6	6.9	6.7	19.2	9.0	10.6	13.4	14.6
16 047	...	7	Gooding	1 893	13 743	2 153	7.3	99.1	0.1	0.5	0.3	12.3	7.0	21.1	8.4	10.8	13.2	13.6
16 049	...	7	Idaho	21 977	15 030	2 060	0.7	97.2	0.2	2.4	0.3	1.5	5.8	19.3	7.4	10.8	15.0	14.9
16 051	...	7	Jefferson	2 836	19 949	1 764	7.0	98.2	0.7	0.8	0.3	10.1	9.4	28.0	9.5	11.0	13.0	12.0
16 053	...	7	Jerome	1 554	18 110	1 864	11.7	98.7	0.1	0.7	0.5	9.4	7.9	22.3	8.9	12.1	13.7	12.9
16 055	...	4	Kootenai	3 225	104 807	495	32.5	98.3	0.2	0.9	0.6	2.2	6.5	18.1	10.2	11.5	16.4	15.0
16 057	...	7	Latah	2 789	32 509	1 297	11.7	95.8	0.8	0.7	2.8	2.2	6.0	14.6	24.8	13.7	13.5	11.0
16 059	...	7	Lemhi	11 822	7 978	2 600	0.7	98.4	0.4	0.8	0.4	3.3	6.3	18.8	6.5	9.2	15.0	15.7
16 061	...	9	Lewis	1 241	3 943	2 919	3.2	94.5	0.4	4.4	0.8	2.1	6.5	18.8	7.2	10.3	13.4	14.7
16 063	...	9	Lincoln	3 122	3 839	2 928	1.2	98.1	0.1	1.3	0.5	8.3	6.8	22.3	9.5	9.9	14.7	12.8
16 065	...	7	Madison	1 221	24 806	1 540	20.3	97.6	0.5	0.4	1.4	4.5	7.2	20.9	37.9	7.9	7.7	7.4
16 067	...	7	Minidoka	1 968	20 284	1 748	10.3	96.0	1.9	1.2	0.9	26.6	8.1	24.8	9.1	11.8	13.0	12.0
16 069	...	5	Nez Perce	2 199	36 913	1 164	16.8	94.3	0.3	4.7	0.7	1.8	5.6	16.2	10.9	11.6	14.2	13.7
16 071	...	9	Oneida	3 109	4 062	2 911	1.3	97.9	1.0	0.5	0.6	3.5	8.9	25.1	6.9	10.7	11.7	11.9
16 073	...	8	Owyhee	19 887	10 406	2 389	0.5	95.3	0.2	3.4	1.1	22.4	8.3	23.1	11.2	11.1	13.0	12.4
16 075	...	7	Payette	1 055	20 846	1 723	19.8	97.6	0.2	1.1	1.1	10.5	7.7	20.9	9.7	10.9	13.7	14.4
16 077	...	7	Power	3 641	8 404	2 558	2.3	96.0	0.2	2.8	1.0	18.0	8.5	24.8	9.2	11.6	15.2	12.2
16 079	...	7	Shoshone	6 822	13 654	2 162	2.0	98.1	0.2	1.3	0.4	2.5	5.1	18.2	8.5	10.2	15.2	12.2
16 081	...	9	Teton	1 167	5 708	2 791	4.9	99.4	0.2	0.4	0.1	9.4	9.4	22.7	11.3	12.9	15.2	12.2
16 083	...	5	Twin Falls	4 986	62 970	764	12.6	97.9	0.3	0.7	1.2	8.2	7.2	20.5	10.2	11.5	14.1	12.9
16 085	...	9	Valley	9 527	7 858	2 616	0.8	97.4	0.7	1.2	0.8	3.4	6.3	18.5	6.1	10.3	18.4	15.4
16 087	...	7	Washington	3 772	10 298	2 397	2.7	97.5	0.2	0.5	1.8	15.3	6.9	20.6	7.8	9.6	13.1	12.9
17 000	...	X	ILLINOIS	143 987	12 128 370	X	84.2	81.1	15.3	0.2	3.4	10.5	7.2	19.0	9.4	14.0	16.5	12.9
17 001	...	5	Adams	2 219	66 951	723	30.2	96.3	3.0	0.1	0.5	0.6	6.4	19.1	8.2	11.3	15.1	12.8
17 003	...	7	Alexander	612	9 919	2 435	16.2	62.2	36.9	0.2	0.6	1.3	7.7	20.9	7.8	11.9	14.1	12.3
17 005	...	6	Bond	985	17 155	1 920	17.4	91.3	8.3	0.3	0.1	2.2	5.3	17.1	13.0	12.9	15.7	11.6
17 007	6880	2	Boone	729	39 560	1 098	54.3	98.6	0.6	0.2	0.7	9.4	7.3	20.9	8.5	12.4	17.2	14.8
17 009	...	9	Brown	792	6 918	2 685	8.7	83.2	16.3	0.3	0.1	3.5	4.5	15.2	12.2	19.9	17.0	11.3
17 011	...	7	Bureau	2 250	35 355	1 211	15.7	98.7	0.3	0.2	0.8	4.1	6.2	20.1	7.0	10.8	15.4	13.4
17 013	...	8	Calhoun	657	4 862	2 851	7.4	99.5	0.0	0.1	0.3	0.4	5.9	18.1	7.2	10.3	13.7	14.3
17 015	...	7	Carroll	1 151	16 691	1 953	14.5	98.6	0.8	0.2	0.5	2.6	5.9	18.8	6.5	10.5	15.1	13.6
17 017	...	6	Cass	974	13 256	2 195	13.6	99.4	0.3	0.1	0.2	0.6	6.0	19.7	7.6	11.4	15.6	13.6
17 019	1400	3	Champaign	2 583	170 272	310	65.9	82.8	10.8	0.2	6.3	2.4	6.6	15.5	21.1	15.3	14.8	10.1
17 021	...	6	Christian	1 836	35 797	1 199	19.5	97.0	2.5	0.2	0.4	1.0	6.1	18.2	8.0	12.0	15.4	13.5
17 023	...	6	Clark	1 299	16 551	1 965	12.7	99.3	0.2	0.2	0.3	0.4	6.1	18.6	7.3	11.5	14.8	13.4
17 025	...	7	Clay	1 215	14 315	2 111	11.8	99.5	0.1	0.1	0.3	0.6	5.8	19.6	6.9	11.3	15.0	13.3
17 027	7040	1	Clinton	1 228	35 682	1 201	29.1	95.6	3.8	0.2	0.4	1.6	6.3	20.1	8.8	13.7	15.6	12.3
17 029	...	5	Coles	1 317	51 806	882	39.3	96.8	2.1	0.2	0.9	1.1	5.1	15.5	22.0	10.7	13.8	11.2
17 031	1600	0	Cook	2 449	5 192 326	2	2 120.2	67.8	26.9	0.3	5.1	17.9	7.5	18.4	9.5	15.1	16.0	12.6
17 033	...	7	Crawford	1 149	20 854	1 722	18.1	95.5	4.0	0.2	0.4	1.4	5.6	18.0	8.0	12.6	15.9	13.3
17 035	...	9	Cumberland	896	11 101	2 341	12.4	99.5	0.0	0.1	0.4	0.6	7.0	21.0	7.9	11.7	14.8	13.2
17 037	1600	1	De Kalb	1 643	86 993	579	52.9	93.9	2.9	0.2	3.0	4.1	6.1	15.8	22.7	12.8	14.3	11.1
17 039	...	6	De Witt	1 030	16 676	1 954	16.2	99.1	0.3	0.3	0.4	0.7	6.2	19.4	7.1	12.2	15.3	14.3
17 041	...	6	Douglas	1 080	19 872	1 768	18.4	99.4	0.2	0.1	0.3	2.2	6.7	21.0	6.6	11.8	14.8	12.9
17 043	1600	0	Du Page	866	892 547	41	1 030.7	90.6	2.2	0.1	7.1	6.1	7.7	18.5	8.4	15.4	18.9	14.1
17 045	...	6	Edgar	1 615	19 528	1 788	12.1	98.6	1.1	0.1	0.1	0.5	5.9	19.5	7.0	11.0	15.5	13.9
17 047	...	9	Edwards	576	6 874	2 689	11.9	99.4	0.1	0.1	0.3	0.5	5.8	18.6	7.0	10.8	15.4	13.2
17 049	...	7	Effingham	1 240	33 786	1 264	27.2	99.2	0.2	0.2	0.5	0.6	8.0	21.7	7.5	12.8	15.1	12.3
17 051	...	6	Fayette	1 856	22 022	1 657	11.9	95.2	4.2	0.3	0.3	1.2	6.1	18.8	8.3	13.6	15.3	13.2
17 053	...	6	Ford	1 259	14 045	2 133	11.2	99.1	0.4	0.1	0.4	0.8	6.1	19.6	6.2	11.3	14.8	13.6
17 055	...	7	Franklin	1 067	40 365	1 076	37.8	99.3	0.2	0.3	0.3	0.4	5.7	18.5	7.7	10.6	15.5	14.0
17 057	...	6	Fulton	2 242	38 679	1 119	17.3	96.2	3.2	0.3	0.4	1.1	5.2	18.6	8.0	12.1	15.7	12.8
17 059	...	8	Gallatin	838	6 586	2 721	7.9	99.1	0.6	0.1	0.2	0.3	5.6	17.9	7.8	9.7	15.2	15.7
17 061	...	6	Greene	1 407	15 737	2 021	11.2	98.6	0.8	0.4	0.2	0.6	6.5	19.8	7.7	11.3	14.2	12.9
17 063	1600	1	Grundy	1 088	37 181	1 156	34.2	99.1	0.2	0.2	0.5	3.3	6.7	21.0	7.9	13.0	17.0	13.7
17 065	...	7	Hamilton	1 127	8 583	2 545	7.6	99.4	0.0	0.2	0.4	0.5	5.6	18.8	6.4	10.9	14.7	13.9
17 067	...	7	Hancock	2 058	20 965	1 718	10.2	99.4	0.2	0.1	0.2	0.4	5.8	19.6	6.4	10.9	14.4	13.1
17 069	...	9	Hardin	462	4 907	2 848	10.6	97.0	2.3	0.4	0.3	0.9	4.9	18.1	8.1	11.0	15.6	13.5
17 071	...	9	Henderson	981	8 593	2 544	8.8	99.3	0.1	0.4	0.2	1.1	5.9	19.5	6.1	11.0	15.5	15.8
17 073	1960	2	Henry	2 132	51 862	881	24.3	97.9	1.6	0.2	0.4	2.3	6.2	20.4	6.9	10.7	16.1	14.0
17 075	...	6	Iroquois	2 892	31 196	1 345	10.8	98.8	0.7	0.2	0.3	3.1	6.1	19.5	6.4	10.9	14.7	13.6

1. MSA = Metropolitan Statistical Area. PMSA = Primary MSA. NECMA = New England County Metropolitan Area. See Appendix A for explanation of these concepts. See Appendix B for list of metropolitan areas identified by type, with component counties. 2. County typology code from the Economic Research Service of USDA. See Appendix A for definition. 3. Dry land or land partially or temporarily covered by water. 4. Hispanic persons may be of any race.

Table B. States and Counties — Population and Households

STATE County	Population, 1999 (cont'd) — Age (percent) (cont'd) 55 to 64 years	65 to 74 years	75 years and over	Percent female	Population — change and components of change, 1980–1999 — Total persons 1990	1980	Percent change 1980–1990	1990–1999	Components of change, 1990–1999 Births	Deaths	Net migration	Households, 1990 Number	Percent change, 1980–1990	Persons per household	Percent Female family householder[1]	One person
	16	17	18	19	20	21	22	23	24	25	26	27	28	29	30	31
IDAHO—Cont'd																
Custer	9.6	7.9	6.2	48.1	4 133	3 385	22.1	-1.1	501	318	-217	1 561	26.2	2.63	4.9	24.1
Elmore	6.8	4.4	3.5	48.4	21 205	21 565	-1.7	20.9	4 506	1 268	348	7 136	4.4	2.81	6.3	18.6
Franklin	8.4	5.3	6.5	49.3	9 232	8 895	3.8	22.9	1 801	818	1 165	2 824	6.1	3.25	4.9	18.5
Fremont	9.3	6.5	5.7	48.6	10 937	10 813	1.1	8.7	1 807	692	-135	3 453	5.4	3.12	6.5	19.5
Gem	11.0	8.1	7.2	49.6	11 844	11 972	-1.1	27.9	1 690	1 285	2 934	4 424	4.9	2.64	7.8	22.0
Gooding	10.8	7.2	7.8	49.5	11 633	11 874	-2.0	18.1	1 817	1 197	1 541	4 320	4.3	2.63	6.6	24.7
Idaho	12.1	7.3	7.4	48.8	13 768	14 769	-6.8	9.2	1 553	1 328	1 099	5 187	0.7	2.57	5.4	24.0
Jefferson	7.9	4.8	4.5	48.8	16 543	15 304	8.1	20.6	3 210	1 002	908	4 871	9.8	3.38	6.6	15.4
Jerome	10.1	6.4	5.6	49.8	15 138	14 840	2.0	19.6	2 579	1 259	1 684	5 325	4.7	2.79	7.2	21.0
Kootenai	10.3	6.5	5.5	50.5	69 795	59 770	16.8	50.2	11 260	6 233	30 095	26 942	25.9	2.57	8.5	23.0
Latah	6.8	4.3	5.3	48.9	30 617	28 749	6.5	6.2	4 061	1 892	-444	11 229	9.5	2.45	6.1	25.6
Lemhi	11.4	9.5	7.6	50.2	6 899	7 460	-7.5	15.6	891	707	905	2 769	3.3	2.47	6.9	26.4
Lewis	11.9	8.8	8.4	48.9	3 516	4 118	-14.6	12.1	390	369	425	1 393	-7.7	2.51	6.2	25.8
Lincoln	10.8	6.7	6.4	48.3	3 308	3 436	-3.7	16.1	448	314	409	1 191	0.5	2.75	4.3	24.5
Madison	4.3	3.4	3.4	52.9	23 674	19 480	21.5	4.8	4 151	940	-3 575	5 801	15.8	3.84	5.5	11.5
Minidoka	8.5	7.4	5.3	50.1	19 361	19 718	-1.8	4.8	3 360	1 372	-1 019	6 472	4.5	2.96	7.7	19.0
Nez Perce	10.5	8.6	8.7	51.0	33 754	33 220	1.6	9.4	4 245	3 229	2 293	13 618	9.0	2.43	8.3	26.7
Oneida	9.4	7.4	8.1	50.0	3 492	3 258	7.2	16.3	427	310	458	1 159	5.9	2.97	4.2	23.0
Owyhee	9.5	5.8	5.8	47.5	8 392	8 272	1.5	24.0	1 524	703	1 227	2 820	6.6	2.84	7.7	23.5
Payette	9.8	6.2	6.7	50.6	16 434	15 825	3.8	26.8	2 724	1 665	3 408	6 040	8.3	2.70	9.0	21.9
Power	8.5	5.2	4.8	50.0	7 086	6 844	3.5	18.6	1 223	488	449	2 370	8.0	2.97	7.4	19.2
Shoshone	11.1	8.9	8.3	50.1	13 931	19 226	-27.5	-2.0	1 587	1 638	-179	5 691	-17.2	2.42	8.9	27.4
Teton	8.6	4.3	3.6	46.9	3 439	2 897	18.7	66.0	763	214	1 723	1 123	26.0	3.03	3.7	20.4
Twin Falls	9.5	6.9	7.1	50.6	53 580	52 927	1.2	17.5	8 250	5 167	6 506	19 737	4.5	2.66	8.0	23.4
Valley	11.3	8.6	5.0	49.0	6 109	5 604	9.0	28.6	784	562	1 545	2 404	16.5	2.51	6.1	22.5
Washington	11.6	8.2	9.2	51.4	8 550	8 803	-2.9	20.4	1 240	1 027	1 581	3 257	2.9	2.59	7.0	24.6
ILLINOIS	8.5	6.4	6.0	51.2	11 430 602	11 427 409	0.0	6.1	1 735 493	971 944	-175 977	4 202 240	3.9	2.65	12.0	25.7
Adams	9.7	7.9	9.3	52.0	66 090	71 622	-7.7	1.3	8 098	7 350	315	25 515	-3.4	2.50	9.3	27.7
Alexander	9.7	7.1	8.4	51.0	10 626	12 264	-13.4	-6.7	1 429	1 294	-779	4 234	-10.9	2.46	18.0	29.9
Bond	9.2	6.9	8.3	47.6	14 991	16 224	-7.6	14.4	1 824	1 668	2 035	5 652	-3.2	2.53	7.7	25.1
Boone	8.2	5.3	5.4	50.1	30 806	28 630	7.6	28.4	4 741	2 426	6 522	10 950	12.7	2.78	8.3	18.7
Brown	7.2	5.3	7.4	37.9	5 836	5 411	7.9	18.5	579	570	1 080	1 991	-5.1	2.45	6.1	29.2
Bureau	9.5	8.3	9.4	51.7	35 688	39 114	-8.8	-0.9	3 871	3 674	-406	13 790	-3.2	2.55	7.6	25.8
Calhoun	11.1	8.5	11.0	49.7	5 322	5 867	-9.3	-8.6	458	585	-305	2 048	-2.2	2.56	5.2	24.5
Carroll	10.6	9.2	9.9	51.1	16 805	18 779	-10.5	-0.7	1 714	1 971	197	6 638	-4.6	2.49	7.2	25.4
Cass	9.8	7.5	8.8	50.7	13 437	15 084	-10.9	-1.3	1 628	1 569	-189	5 195	-8.2	2.53	8.3	25.6
Champaign	6.6	5.1	4.9	50.0	173 025	168 392	2.8	-1.6	21 446	9 900	-15 734	63 900	9.4	2.43	8.4	28.7
Christian	9.8	7.8	9.3	50.9	34 418	36 446	-5.6	4.0	4 116	3 824	1 203	13 591	-0.7	2.49	8.4	27.0
Clark	10.3	8.2	9.7	51.5	15 921	16 913	-5.9	4.0	1 768	1 831	752	6 394	-1.4	2.45	7.6	26.3
Clay	9.8	8.0	10.1	52.2	14 460	15 283	-5.4	-1.0	1 633	1 748	13	5 708	-1.6	2.47	7.9	26.1
Clinton	8.9	7.0	7.4	48.3	33 944	32 617	4.1	5.1	3 963	2 727	559	11 583	7.6	2.76	8.0	22.2
Coles	8.1	6.4	7.2	52.5	51 644	52 260	-1.2	0.3	5 469	4 655	-518	18 957	1.8	2.41	8.1	28.2
Cook	8.7	6.6	5.7	52.0	5 105 044	5 253 628	-2.8	1.7	844 323	443 014	-411 471	1 879 488	0.0	2.67	15.4	28.2
Crawford	10.2	7.6	8.8	48.7	19 464	20 818	-6.5	7.1	2 073	2 299	1 693	7 792	-3.2	2.46	7.4	26.3
Cumberland	9.5	7.4	7.5	50.1	10 670	11 062	-3.5	4.0	1 307	1 005	173	4 029	0.7	2.63	7.4	24.1
De Kalb	6.9	5.0	5.2	50.4	77 932	74 628	4.4	11.6	9 296	5 146	5 102	26 413	8.5	2.56	7.3	25.2
De Witt	9.5	7.8	8.2	50.6	16 516	18 108	-8.8	1.0	1 936	1 729	11	6 488	-5.2	2.51	8.0	25.6
Douglas	10.3	7.9	7.9	51.4	19 464	19 774	-1.6	2.1	2 575	1 780	-312	7 206	0.2	2.66	7.0	23.0
Du Page	7.6	5.1	4.3	50.6	781 689	658 858	18.6	14.2	128 286	45 796	27 364	279 344	25.8	2.76	7.3	20.4
Edgar	9.8	8.0	9.2	51.5	19 595	21 725	-9.8	-0.3	2 056	2 407	334	7 859	-5.7	2.45	8.9	27.8
Edwards	9.5	9.0	10.8	51.8	7 440	7 961	-6.5	-7.6	673	814	-406	3 016	-2.9	2.44	6.4	26.7
Effingham	8.3	6.7	7.5	50.8	31 704	30 944	2.5	6.6	4 609	2 814	382	11 465	7.8	2.73	8.4	23.8
Fayette	9.7	6.9	8.2	47.6	20 893	22 167	-5.7	5.4	2 413	2 268	1 037	7 719	-3.4	2.53	7.7	26.1
Ford	10.4	8.3	10.5	51.8	14 275	15 265	-6.5	-1.6	1 615	1 777	-30	5 602	-2.4	2.49	7.1	26.7
Franklin	9.7	8.7	9.5	51.9	40 319	43 201	-6.7	0.1	4 379	5 243	1 041	16 564	-2.4	2.40	9.2	28.9
Fulton	9.9	8.2	9.7	49.4	38 080	43 687	-12.8	1.6	3 887	4 291	1 123	14 893	-8.5	2.45	8.9	26.8
Gallatin	10.6	7.8	9.8	51.8	6 909	7 590	-9.0	-4.7	675	906	-69	2 784	-1.6	2.42	8.9	26.8
Greene	10.2	7.9	9.4	50.4	15 317	16 661	-8.1	2.7	1 781	1 831	532	5 910	-4.6	2.56	8.2	25.8
Grundy	8.3	6.2	6.2	50.0	32 337	30 582	5.7	15.0	4 380	2 614	3 176	11 979	11.2	2.67	6.8	22.8
Hamilton	10.7	8.7	10.4	52.0	8 499	9 172	-7.3	1.0	871	1 056	307	3 476	-4.5	2.41	7.2	27.8
Hancock	10.6	8.5	9.7	51.8	21 373	23 877	-10.5	-1.9	2 194	2 291	-408	8 409	-5.3	2.50	7.2	25.7
Hardin	10.9	9.1	8.7	49.0	5 189	5 383	-3.6	-5.4	461	646	-77	2 049	-1.5	2.43	10.2	27.7
Henderson	11.0	7.9	7.5	50.5	8 096	9 114	-11.2	6.1	815	811	513	3 237	-4.1	2.49	6.3	26.1
Henry	9.6	7.6	8.5	50.8	51 159	57 968	-11.7	1.4	5 496	5 084	452	19 514	-4.9	2.59	7.9	24.0
Iroquois	10.2	8.9	9.7	51.2	30 787	32 976	-6.6	1.3	3 334	3 438	610	11 788	-2.3	2.56	7.2	24.1

1. No spouse present.

STATE County	Births, average 1996–1998 Total	Rate[1]	Deaths, average 1996–1998 Number Total	Infant[2]	Rate Total[1]	Infant[3]	Physicians,[4] 1998 Number	Rate[5]	Hospitals,[4] 1998 Number	Beds Number	Rate[5]	Medicare enrollees 1999	Serious crimes known to police, 1998[6] Total Number	Rate[7]
	32	33	34	35	36	37	38	39	40	41	42	43	44	45
IDAHO—Cont'd														
Custer	52	12.3	35	1	8.2	12.8	2	49	0	0	0	678	58	1 346
Elmore	507	20.7	140	4	5.7	7.9	26	103	1	78	310	2 225	636	2 517
Franklin	221	20.3	97	3	8.9	15.1	3	27	1	65	585	1 438	202	1 839
Fremont	190	16.3	75	2	6.4	8.8	5	42	0	0	0	1 700	176	1 466
Gem	198	13.7	148	1	10.2	6.7	6	40	1	24	162	2 516	215	1 464
Gooding	220	16.3	129	2	9.5	10.6	6	44	1	27	198	2 314	325	2 359
Idaho	155	10.3	152	2	10.1	10.8	12	80	2	41	272	2 730	275	1 795
Jefferson	341	18.0	112	3	5.9	7.8	3	16	0	0	0	2 086	265	1 377
Jerome	299	16.9	133	3	7.5	10.0	12	67	1	73	406	2 455	742	4 136
Kootenai	1 346	13.7	749	11	7.6	8.4	169	167	1	187	184	14 906	4 594	4 579
Latah	437	13.5	214	3	6.6	6.9	41	128	1	40	125	3 627	895	2 709
Lemhi	88	11.0	73	0	9.1	0.0	6	75	1	28	349	1 536	NA	NA
Lewis	40	9.9	43	1	10.8	16.8	2	50	0	0	0	1 166	30	726
Lincoln	50	13.2	37	0	9.8	6.7	0	0	0	0	0	534	28	724
Madison	446	19.0	109	3	4.7	6.7	28	119	1	52	221	1 748	526	2 203
Minidoka	374	18.3	162	3	7.9	8.9	14	69	1	103	510	2 968	567	2 703
Nez Perce	454	12.3	369	4	10.0	8.8	83	225	1	120	326	6 715	1 647	4 404
Oneida	54	13.7	33	0	8.4	6.2	2	49	1	52	1 284	676	87	2 135
Owyhee	170	16.9	78	3	7.7	15.7	0	0	0	0	0	1 214	256	2 464
Payette	302	15.0	187	2	9.3	6.6	6	29	0	0	0	3 032	673	3 277
Power	131	15.9	50	1	6.0	5.1	4	48	1	41	493	814	277	3 288
Shoshone	164	11.8	169	1	12.2	6.1	18	130	2	69	497	2 940	622	4 380
Teton	98	18.5	19	0	3.6	3.4	6	109	1	13	237	547	86	1 595
Twin Falls	933	15.2	581	11	9.5	11.4	142	228	2	171	275	9 732	3 385	5 437
Valley	75	9.4	63	1	7.9	8.8	24	300	2	23	287	1 369	265	3 221
Washington	133	13.3	107	0	10.7	0.0	8	79	1	27	265	1 930	159	1 552
ILLINOIS	182 190	15.2	104 495	1 548	8.7	8.5	26 650	221	206	40 475	336	1 628 744	586 923	4 873
Adams	835	12.4	773	6	11.5	6.8	125	186	2	500	745	12 659	NA	NA
Alexander	139	14.1	134	2	13.6	16.8	4	41	0	0	0	1 962	NA	NA
Bond	194	12.3	175	1	11.0	5.2	9	57	1	50	315	2 810	NA	NA
Boone	537	14.2	275	5	7.2	9.3	43	111	2	129	333	4 551	NA	NA
Brown	54	8.3	56	0	8.6	0.0	1	15	0	0	0	972	NA	NA
Bureau	407	11.4	390	4	10.9	9.0	36	101	2	214	602	6 741	NA	NA
Calhoun	48	9.5	66	1	13.2	14.0	4	80	0	0	0	1 031	NA	NA
Carroll	174	10.3	210	2	12.4	11.5	10	59	0	0	0	3 478	NA	NA
Cass	175	13.2	164	0	12.3	1.9	7	53	0	0	0	2 465	NA	NA
Champaign	2 209	13.1	1 074	14	6.4	6.3	437	260	2	555	331	18 628	NA	NA
Christian	421	12.2	411	4	11.9	8.7	23	67	2	165	478	6 708	NA	NA
Clark	196	11.9	204	1	12.4	6.8	9	54	0	0	0	3 350	NA	NA
Clay	174	12.1	200	1	13.8	7.7	10	69	1	40	276	2 996	NA	NA
Clinton	402	11.4	310	1	8.8	3.3	20	56	1	54	152	4 864	NA	NA
Coles	593	11.6	480	5	9.4	7.9	86	168	1	176	344	7 880	NA	NA
Cook	86 461	16.6	46 407	865	8.9	10.0	14 826	286	63	19 465	375	673 286	NA	NA
Crawford	218	10.4	246	2	11.7	7.7	18	86	1	102	487	3 900	NA	NA
Cumberland	132	11.8	122	1	10.9	10.1	1	9	0	0	0	1 835	NA	NA
De Kalb	1 054	12.6	559	5	6.7	5.1	88	105	3	221	263	9 923	NA	NA
De Witt	199	11.8	176	0	10.5	1.7	13	77	1	36	214	3 003	NA	NA
Douglas	287	14.4	197	1	9.9	4.7	13	65	0	0	0	2 869	NA	NA
Du Page	13 469	15.5	5 176	82	6.0	6.1	2 865	325	8	1 880	214	92 890	NA	NA
Edgar	226	11.4	257	2	13.0	8.9	9	46	1	49	249	3 757	NA	NA
Edwards	73	10.4	89	1	12.7	9.1	0	0	0	0	0	1 319	NA	NA
Effingham	476	14.3	306	1	9.2	2.8	65	194	1	143	427	5 474	NA	NA
Fayette	266	12.3	243	2	11.2	8.8	10	46	1	170	774	3 725	NA	NA
Ford	176	12.4	192	2	13.6	9.5	13	92	1	56	398	2 756	NA	NA
Franklin	448	11.0	565	2	13.9	5.2	21	52	2	150	371	8 672	NA	NA
Fulton	414	10.7	461	2	11.9	4.8	30	77	1	124	320	7 696	NA	NA
Gallatin	61	9.1	93	0	14.0	5.5	4	60	0	0	0	1 380	NA	NA
Greene	188	12.1	189	2	12.2	8.9	8	51	1	73	469	3 040	NA	NA
Grundy	470	13.0	302	4	8.4	7.8	34	93	1	82	224	5 105	NA	NA
Hamilton	83	9.7	117	0	13.6	4.0	7	81	1	91	1 057	1 822	NA	NA
Hancock	209	9.9	236	1	11.1	6.4	15	71	1	67	318	4 175	NA	NA
Hardin	48	9.7	71	0	14.2	0.0	3	61	1	48	979	959	NA	NA
Henderson	84	9.8	93	0	10.9	4.0	6	70	0	0	0	1 372	NA	NA
Henry	564	10.9	528	4	10.2	6.5	34	66	2	168	326	8 832	NA	NA
Iroquois	353	11.2	383	2	12.2	6.6	20	64	2	99	317	6 228	NA	NA

1. Per 1,000 estimated resident population, average 1996–1998.   2. Deaths of infants under 1 year old.   3. Deaths of infants under 1 year old per 1,000 live births.   4. Data subject to copyright.   5. Per 100,000 resident population as of July 1 of the year shown.   6. Data for serious crimes have not been adjusted for underreporting; this may affect comparability between geographic areas and over time.   7. Per 100,000 population estimated by the FBI.

Table B. States and Counties — Crime, Education, Money Income, and Poverty

STATE County	Serious crimes known to police, 1998[1] (cont'd) Rate[2] Violent	Property	Education — School enrollment and attainment, 1990 Enrollment[3] Total	Percent private	Attainment[4] (percent) High school graduate or more	Bachelor's degree or more	Local government expenditures, fiscal 1997[5] Total current expenditures (mil dol)	Current expenditures per student (dollars)	Money income — 1989 Per capita[6] (dollars)	Households Median Dollars	Percent change, 1979–1989 (constant 1989 dollars)	Percent with $100,000 or more	Income and poverty, 1997 Median household income	Percent below poverty level All persons	Persons under 18	Persons 5–17 in families
	46	47	48	49	50	51	52	53	54	55	56	57	58	59	60	61
IDAHO—Cont'd																
Custer	186	1 160	1 036	5.3	81.7	15.6	5.3	5 355	11 607	24 393	23.9	1.8	34 460	12.1	14.9	14.6
Elmore	281	2 236	5 856	5.8	83.1	15.8	22.5	4 393	9 981	23 750	6.2	0.6	32 486	12.7	17.6	16.8
Franklin	82	1 757	3 106	2.4	82.2	14.3	11.1	3 752	8 532	25 446	5.2	1.2	33 892	12.5	15.4	13.1
Fremont	158	1 308	3 460	7.5	75.6	11.1	11.6	4 388	8 674	23 498	6.2	1.3	30 579	14.4	17.9	15.7
Gem	170	1 294	2 867	6.2	70.1	8.6	12.1	4 074	10 450	21 495	-3.9	1.6	30 132	15.4	21.0	18.8
Gooding	218	2 141	3 143	3.1	72.5	13.3	13.0	4 345	9 625	19 823	-1.9	1.6	28 957	14.8	19.6	17.8
Idaho	163	1 632	3 312	5.7	75.1	12.7	13.3	5 026	10 527	22 093	-9.0	1.4	29 674	17.6	25.2	20.5
Jefferson	172	1 205	5 708	6.3	77.6	11.8	23.0	4 103	9 055	24 421	2.8	1.9	34 390	13.1	15.8	14.3
Jerome	474	3 662	4 158	3.7	72.4	11.0	15.5	4 001	9 727	21 209	-8.2	2.4	30 938	15.4	20.5	18.1
Kootenai	376	4 203	18 166	9.4	81.1	16.0	68.7	4 097	12 330	25 593	0.8	2.2	36 123	11.5	16.6	13.7
Latah	94	2 615	13 452	6.2	86.6	35.8	26.6	5 524	10 892	22 635	-3.7	1.4	35 005	13.5	15.1	14.1
Lemhi	NA	NA	1 590	5.0	73.9	11.8	6.7	4 346	10 624	19 697	-6.1	1.0	28 159	15.8	20.7	19.7
Lewis	48	678	786	0.8	78.8	13.2	7.1	5 890	9 780	20 926	-11.7	1.1	28 202	15.2	22.2	20.2
Lincoln	26	698	885	2.7	79.8	11.9	4.8	5 478	9 339	21 640	7.5	0.7	30 036	13.0	18.7	15.8
Madison	113	2 090	12 995	51.1	87.6	19.2	23.0	3 934	7 385	23 000	5.2	2.1	35 718	15.3	14.4	13.0
Minidoka	281	2 422	5 728	3.6	68.5	9.0	20.3	3 892	10 110	23 327	-5.0	2.3	30 598	16.3	20.6	18.8
Nez Perce	120	4 284	8 769	6.3	79.9	15.6	33.5	5 642	12 476	25 219	-5.1	1.9	34 963	12.8	18.3	15.7
Oneida	196	1 939	1 031	3.5	78.7	12.9	4.3	4 235	8 824	22 582	17.6	0.4	33 141	12.8	15.3	14.7
Owyhee	279	2 185	2 293	6.7	62.0	8.7	12.1	4 610	9 786	18 595	4.8	1.5	26 702	21.4	28.2	26.8
Payette	180	3 097	4 226	7.1	67.4	9.8	17.7	4 130	9 400	20 367	4.3	1.5	29 849	17.2	23.4	20.8
Power	249	3 039	2 305	5.2	72.1	11.1	10.4	5 351	9 951	24 771	-5.8	1.2	32 719	17.8	23.9	21.4
Shoshone	493	3 887	3 222	4.0	70.1	9.0	16.0	6 058	10 373	20 980	-25.8	0.6	27 555	20.1	29.5	24.4
Teton	93	1 502	907	4.1	80.2	17.4	5.0	3 996	8 983	22 799	17.6	1.1	31 680	9.7	11.7	12.3
Twin Falls	408	5 029	14 332	5.9	75.4	13.3	51.4	4 142	11 096	23 520	-3.4	2.2	32 169	14.1	18.9	16.1
Valley	316	2 905	1 432	5.4	83.8	19.4	8.6	5 185	12 344	24 232	-8.5	3.3	33 587	13.8	20.6	17.9
Washington	146	1 406	2 183	6.1	72.7	10.3	9.6	4 603	9 088	17 917	-1.3	0.8	26 134	18.4	24.4	21.8
ILLINOIS	808	4 065	3 031 673	19.5	76.2	21.0	11 720.0	5 940	15 201	32 252	-0.4	4.9	41 179	11.3	17.5	16.2
Adams	NA	NA	16 253	23.2	75.1	13.7	56.1	5 102	11 601	23 317	-9.8	2.1	34 425	12.2	17.3	16.9
Alexander	NA	NA	2 677	4.6	59.7	7.8	11.1	6 199	8 846	14 786	-7.8	1.4	20 807	30.1	43.9	45.5
Bond	NA	NA	3 862	17.1	69.3	12.7	10.5	4 256	10 407	23 756	-0.2	0.7	33 762	12.5	17.0	16.4
Boone	NA	NA	7 840	15.1	75.5	12.0	30.7	4 522	14 355	35 103	1.0	3.8	49 782	6.1	9.4	9.2
Brown	NA	NA	1 400	16.4	68.9	9.8	3.6	4 494	8 894	20 445	3.2	1.2	31 633	14.8	16.7	16.7
Bureau	NA	NA	8 505	9.0	76.6	12.5	35.2	5 323	11 915	26 248	-9.5	1.1	36 572	8.7	12.2	12.4
Calhoun	NA	NA	1 196	25.4	62.8	7.0	4.0	5 174	9 815	21 163	1.5	0.9	32 469	12.1	16.3	16.0
Carroll	NA	NA	3 865	3.7	76.0	10.6	16.2	4 734	12 358	25 758	-2.4	2.0	34 934	10.3	15.7	15.8
Cass	NA	NA	3 230	8.5	72.3	10.6	11.0	4 874	10 850	23 642	-13.2	1.4	32 897	11.2	16.4	16.5
Champaign	NA	NA	67 446	5.9	87.5	34.1	127.5	5 309	13 130	26 541	-3.7	3.0	38 245	12.1	16.8	16.7
Christian	NA	NA	7 710	9.1	73.1	9.3	37.0	5 345	11 676	24 506	-8.1	1.3	34 836	10.7	16.1	15.4
Clark	NA	NA	3 450	2.7	71.3	9.2	13.4	4 586	11 176	23 281	-1.3	0.9	32 800	11.0	17.3	16.8
Clay	NA	NA	3 279	4.4	65.6	7.6	12.9	4 686	9 590	20 006	-1.8	1.1	29 330	12.5	17.5	17.5
Clinton	NA	NA	8 786	16.7	67.2	9.2	24.1	4 235	11 422	29 890	5.5	1.0	39 651	8.6	12.0	11.9
Coles	NA	NA	18 652	2.9	76.1	18.7	43.5	5 806	11 315	24 153	-4.6	1.9	35 093	13.7	18.8	17.7
Cook	NA	NA	1 324 299	25.6	73.4	22.8	5 069.4	6 538	15 697	32 673	1.6	5.5	40 181	14.0	22.7	20.4
Crawford	NA	NA	4 506	4.1	76.0	9.5	17.4	4 617	11 768	23 912	-8.5	1.8	32 516	12.0	18.0	17.1
Cumberland	NA	NA	2 695	3.9	72.2	8.2	8.4	3 937	10 486	23 623	-3.5	1.2	33 612	11.4	17.2	16.6
De Kalb	NA	NA	31 177	5.7	83.9	26.1	82.9	5 666	12 657	30 864	0.4	2.5	44 758	8.1	10.1	9.8
De Witt	NA	NA	3 822	6.0	74.6	11.8	19.3	5 642	12 833	27 196	-8.0	2.4	38 385	10.4	16.1	15.7
Douglas	NA	NA	4 509	5.9	74.0	11.4	14.9	4 575	11 461	26 758	-11.4	1.1	36 640	9.4	15.0	14.6
Du Page	NA	NA	210 271	23.5	88.6	36.0	925.1	6 377	21 155	48 876	6.0	10.2	62 825	3.6	5.6	5.4
Edgar	NA	NA	4 570	5.2	73.5	11.0	19.0	4 895	11 190	21 657	-7.0	1.2	31 089	13.4	20.1	19.8
Edwards	NA	NA	1 782	3.3	69.7	8.4	4.7	4 246	10 713	21 238	-7.9	1.2	30 874	11.0	16.2	15.9
Effingham	NA	NA	7 923	13.1	75.0	13.0	27.2	4 200	11 977	27 245	-4.3	1.7	37 864	8.9	12.5	12.6
Fayette	NA	NA	4 674	6.7	68.8	8.5	16.4	4 891	10 496	22 029	-2.7	1.3	30 256	14.3	21.0	20.2
Ford	NA	NA	3 390	5.2	77.2	12.1	17.1	6 622	11 895	25 801	-9.4	1.2	36 681	8.6	12.9	12.8
Franklin	NA	NA	9 597	4.0	66.7	8.2	37.4	5 471	10 204	18 698	-11.6	0.9	25 665	17.9	28.2	26.9
Fulton	NA	NA	8 982	4.3	73.8	9.5	40.6	5 281	10 720	21 701	-20.7	0.8	30 723	13.2	20.0	19.2
Gallatin	NA	NA	1 507	3.5	58.4	7.4	5.5	5 150	10 367	19 105	-5.3	1.3	26 278	19.1	29.6	30.0
Greene	NA	NA	3 350	8.2	69.0	9.0	12.5	4 718	9 884	20 752	-3.2	0.6	29 129	13.9	20.6	20.7
Grundy	NA	NA	8 101	9.7	79.0	12.5	43.8	5 413	14 474	35 728	-1.7	2.4	50 255	5.5	7.8	7.5
Hamilton	NA	NA	1 888	1.3	60.0	7.6	7.6	4 954	9 984	18 274	-5.9	1.4	27 994	14.7	21.9	21.6
Hancock	NA	NA	5 060	7.6	77.5	14.4	19.6	4 673	11 358	24 036	-5.3	1.7	35 162	10.3	14.4	14.2
Hardin	NA	NA	1 226	0.8	59.7	7.0	5.1	6 089	8 314	15 498	-11.1	0.9	24 285	20.0	28.5	30.1
Henderson	NA	NA	1 828	5.5	73.3	9.5	6.5	4 790	10 638	22 165	-17.2	0.7	33 363	11.0	16.5	16.5
Henry	NA	NA	13 143	8.5	77.2	11.8	46.3	4 619	12 260	26 198	-17.5	1.7	38 644	8.5	12.7	12.5
Iroquois	NA	NA	7 066	8.2	73.4	10.1	27.8	4 749	11 653	25 435	-7.4	1.4	34 287	9.5	15.2	14.2

1. Data for serious crimes have not been adjusted for underreporting; this may affect comparability between geographic areas and over time.   2. Per 100,000 population estimated by the FBI.   3. All persons 3 years old and over enrolled in nursery school through college.   4. Persons 25 years old and over.   5. Elementary and secondary education expenditures, local government fiscal years ending between July 1, 1996 and June 30, 1997.   6. Based on population enumerated as of April 1, 1990.

Table B. States and Counties — **Personal Income**

STATE County	Personal income, 1998 Total (mil dol)	Percent change, 1997–1998	Per capita[1] Dollars	Per capita[1] Rank	Wages and salaries[2] (mil dol)	Proprietor's income (mil dol)	Dividends, interest, and rent (mil dol)	Transfer payments Total (mil dol)	Government payments to individuals Total (mil dol)	Social Security (mil dol)	Medical payments (mil dol)	Income maintenance (mil dol)	Unemployment insurance (mil dol)
	62	63	64	65	66	67	68	69	70	71	72	73	74
IDAHO—Cont'd													
Custer	93	2.4	22 666	934	41	12	24	12	12	6	3	1	1
Elmore	524	6.1	20 679	1 494	349	38	77	50	46	20	12	4	2
Franklin	169	10.1	15 230	2 911	54	33	28	26	24	14	7	2	0
Fremont	179	3.4	14 979	2 930	72	21	40	31	29	16	8	3	1
Gem	260	6.2	17 516	2 480	84	16	50	51	48	24	16	4	2
Gooding	328	19.3	24 032	637	115	110	51	44	42	21	14	3	1
Idaho	259	5.1	17 226	2 552	117	20	74	56	53	27	16	5	3
Jefferson	324	7.0	16 564	2 701	102	39	49	44	41	20	13	4	2
Jerome	408	16.6	22 702	921	152	130	55	53	50	23	19	4	2
Kootenai	2 233	6.6	22 038	1 092	1 068	207	469	317	301	146	96	18	13
Latah	681	6.1	20 846	1 440	363	43	164	86	81	36	23	5	2
Lemhi	150	4.0	18 671	2 162	67	15	42	31	30	14	10	2	1
Lewis	73	7.3	18 269	2 277	26	6	24	19	18	9	7	2	1
Lincoln	71	8.7	18 854	2 106	30	12	15	12	11	6	3	1	0
Madison	341	5.8	13 553	3 040	217	49	62	40	37	17	14	3	1
Minidoka	337	5.4	16 669	2 685	198	38	53	59	56	25	20	5	3
Nez Perce	873	5.2	23 707	702	629	68	181	148	142	67	49	10	3
Oneida	61	3.8	15 260	2 905	19	6	12	13	12	6	5	1	0
Owyhee	168	8.1	16 370	2 730	58	30	26	28	26	11	10	3	0
Payette	350	8.6	17 096	2 588	141	38	63	62	58	29	18	6	1
Power	147	3.5	17 427	2 502	130	20	24	20	18	9	6	2	1
Shoshone	267	5.1	19 296	1 955	139	20	52	67	65	31	22	6	3
Teton	81	10.7	14 826	2 950	31	9	20	11	11	5	4	1	0
Twin Falls	1 307	6.2	21 008	1 387	722	192	280	196	186	91	62	13	5
Valley	185	3.8	23 100	834	80	23	59	29	28	13	7	1	2
Washington	161	4.6	15 761	2 834	75	18	36	37	35	18	11	3	1
ILLINOIS	360 317	5.4	29 853	X	234 566	28 832	71 536	41 566	39 199	16 413	15 459	4 520	1 119
Adams	1 607	3.7	23 869	669	925	134	404	251	237	120	77	23	5
Alexander	160	2.2	15 868	2 815	66	9	24	53	51	17	20	11	1
Bond	349	5.7	20 168	1 664	120	36	69	59	56	26	20	5	2
Boone	1 063	8.4	27 446	268	572	59	194	100	92	51	29	6	4
Brown	117	9.7	17 070	2 594	68	18	21	19	18	9	6	2	0
Bureau	772	0.1	21 750	1 173	333	42	189	128	121	66	40	7	4
Calhoun	106	-0.5	21 569	1 234	24	13	22	20	19	9	7	2	1
Carroll	402	10.0	23 795	682	153	66	91	65	61	30	20	4	2
Cass	298	4.9	22 430	992	151	35	63	52	50	23	19	4	2
Champaign	4 034	3.7	23 753	688	2 840	187	981	410	377	164	123	46	13
Christian	797	0.4	22 253	1 025	312	58	179	154	147	72	53	10	4
Clark	333	1.4	20 142	1 669	129	26	74	65	61	31	21	5	2
Clay	301	3.0	20 788	1 459	158	25	60	67	64	27	28	5	2
Clinton	806	5.8	22 582	959	288	66	161	121	114	51	48	7	3
Coles	1 151	3.2	22 148	1 048	837	72	237	181	171	72	67	14	4
Cook	165 150	4.9	31 806	115	123 080	15 299	33 209	20 183	19 161	6 837	8 399	2 754	512
Crawford	402	2.3	19 174	1 989	217	33	98	77	73	38	23	5	2
Cumberland	235	4.0	21 102	1 353	45	24	43	37	35	17	12	3	1
De Kalb	2 137	7.8	24 882	502	987	126	442	214	197	94	69	13	5
De Witt	390	3.6	23 276	799	297	20	75	65	61	28	20	5	2
Douglas	434	2.2	21 820	1 153	228	36	94	67	63	34	20	4	2
Du Page	37 191	6.6	42 215	24	25 733	3 669	7 038	2 143	1 969	1 067	674	96	59
Edgar	437	10.0	22 094	1 068	161	79	87	78	74	36	27	7	1
Edwards	137	-6.2	19 679	1 827	85	12	37	25	24	13	7	2	1
Effingham	803	6.2	23 939	656	553	71	186	106	100	49	35	7	4
Fayette	398	3.6	17 997	2 345	157	42	86	83	78	35	29	7	3
Ford	330	0.5	23 483	750	118	33	81	54	51	27	18	3	1
Franklin	697	2.6	17 232	2 549	270	45	148	196	188	81	65	20	7
Fulton	768	2.3	19 849	1 762	217	36	163	168	160	75	63	12	4
Gallatin	123	-3.0	18 605	2 182	51	8	29	32	30	13	12	4	1
Greene	256	3.1	16 268	2 747	66	25	57	60	57	27	19	6	1
Grundy	1 039	6.0	28 277	226	559	38	203	112	105	54	36	5	7
Hamilton	148	-1.8	17 206	2 557	35	15	32	39	37	16	14	4	1
Hancock	462	2.9	21 864	1 137	150	52	101	76	72	37	22	6	1
Hardin	81	2.1	16 407	2 719	29	7	16	25	24	10	10	3	1
Henderson	166	1.2	19 235	1 978	27	11	31	28	26	14	7	3	0
Henry	1 205	4.9	23 384	771	374	77	264	171	161	88	51	12	4
Iroquois	652	0.6	20 863	1 436	223	67	161	125	119	61	42	8	3

1. Based on the resident population estimated as of July 1 of the year shown. 2. Includes other labor income.

Table B. States and Counties — Earnings, Social Security, and Housing

STATE County	Earnings, 1998									Social Security beneficiaries, December 1998		Housing units, 1990	
			Percent by selected industries										
			Goods-related[1]		Service-related and other[2]							Supplemental Security Income recipients, December 1998		
	Total (mil dol)	Farm	Total	Manufacturing	Total	Retail trade	Finance, insurance, and real estate	Services	Government	Number	Rate[3]		Total	Percent change, 1980–1990
	75	76	77	78	79	80	81	82	83	84	85	86	87	88
IDAHO—Cont'd														
Custer	54	5.7	D	2.6	D	9.6	2.0	D	25.6	822	200	56	2 437	16.0
Elmore	386	7.8	5.1	2.5	18.2	6.1	1.6	6.6	68.9	2 690	107	224	8 430	4.7
Franklin	86	28.0	D	8.8	D	10.0	D	11.7	21.3	1 709	154	102	3 240	6.3
Fremont	93	15.1	D	2.9	D	8.8	D	11.1	33.0	2 023	170	123	5 961	10.9
Gem	100	4.3	D	23.4	D	9.2	D	15.2	23.5	2 976	201	207	4 725	3.2
Gooding	226	54.2	10.1	7.0	24.2	4.3	1.5	5.8	11.6	2 691	197	203	4 800	4.6
Idaho	137	-1.0	D	16.2	D	9.9	3.9	14.3	34.7	3 422	227	321	6 346	0.0
Jefferson	140	17.2	D	12.1	D	7.7	D	7.7	20.9	2 572	135	173	5 353	7.2
Jerome	282	39.6	11.6	7.7	40.5	6.7	1.4	10.4	8.3	2 884	161	281	5 886	6.4
Kootenai	1 275	0.1	26.1	14.3	55.7	14.0	6.0	23.5	18.2	17 470	172	1 422	31 964	18.6
Latah	405	0.6	D	6.6	D	11.2	2.7	18.9	47.8	4 083	127	235	11 870	7.8
Lemhi	82	0.5	D	6.6	D	13.0	2.4	D	35.2	1 831	228	131	3 752	8.7
Lewis	32	-3.3	D	14.1	D	13.4	2.8	10.4	32.9	1 068	267	130	1 681	-7.0
Lincoln	42	26.5	D	D	D	3.2	D	D	35.2	787	208	44	1 386	3.2
Madison	267	5.9	D	10.9	D	10.1	6.1	34.7	15.1	2 069	88	151	6 133	10.8
Minidoka	236	13.9	D	27.4	D	5.6	D	9.7	16.1	3 183	158	296	7 044	2.4
Nez Perce	697	0.3	D	25.6	D	11.2	7.2	23.9	14.0	7 737	210	713	14 463	7.1
Oneida	25	10.4	D	5.9	D	8.1	5.4	10.6	37.3	782	193	54	1 496	1.4
Owyhee	88	33.0	D	4.3	D	6.6	D	5.9	18.0	1 575	153	137	3 332	10.5
Payette	180	12.4	D	24.2	D	7.8	D	13.7	15.3	3 682	179	346	6 520	6.6
Power	149	12.8	52.6	49.7	23.0	3.0	1.3	3.7	11.6	1 020	123	63	2 701	5.6
Shoshone	160	0.1	38.6	5.4	38.2	14.7	2.5	15.6	23.3	3 539	255	383	6 923	-9.8
Teton	40	13.1	14.9	1.9	45.3	14.6	4.7	15.2	26.7	664	121	25	1 645	32.1
Twin Falls	913	9.9	18.1	11.2	55.3	13.4	5.2	20.9	16.8	10 968	176	980	21 158	3.1
Valley	103	2.0	17.9	6.3	45.9	13.9	6.3	17.6	34.1	1 627	203	77	6 640	30.0
Washington	93	10.6	24.4	18.0	44.9	8.4	4.2	12.1	20.1	2 324	228	202	3 685	2.2
ILLINOIS	263 398	0.4	24.2	18.6	62.2	7.7	10.3	29.3	13.2	1 817 522	151	255 099	4 506 275	4.3
Adams	1 059	2.0	D	26.4	D	11.0	3.9	24.6	12.7	14 124	210	1 177	28 021	-2.0
Alexander	76	0.3	D	16.7	D	7.0	2.1	17.8	27.2	2 269	233	747	4 902	-6.9
Bond	156	11.8	19.3	15.7	43.6	6.7	3.3	18.5	25.3	3 245	205	251	6 136	-3.8
Boone	632	1.9	64.1	53.2	26.3	6.9	2.2	10.4	7.7	5 575	144	206	11 477	14.1
Brown	86	12.2	D	D	D	4.2	2.8	8.5	21.0	1 074	157	101	2 357	-1.2
Bureau	375	2.3	D	22.5	D	8.7	4.5	21.3	18.2	7 373	208	281	14 762	-2.6
Calhoun	37	14.5	D	D	D	14.2	5.6	16.8	20.2	1 214	244	111	2 951	-2.5
Carroll	219	17.7	21.8	15.7	39.3	6.5	3.2	10.0	21.1	3 700	218	191	7 481	-1.8
Cass	186	11.8	D	D	D	6.5	2.8	13.0	12.3	2 729	206	219	5 698	-6.3
Champaign	3 027	0.4	18.3	12.7	45.6	8.5	4.8	24.6	35.7	20 244	121	2 204	68 416	9.4
Christian	371	5.0	30.2	16.9	D	10.9	D	20.0	14.2	8 135	236	592	14 640	0.3
Clark	155	0.8	44.0	36.5	41.5	9.7	3.9	12.8	13.7	3 817	231	262	7 115	-1.8
Clay	183	3.1	D	44.8	D	6.3	3.0	11.9	14.3	3 400	235	367	6 270	-3.3
Clinton	354	8.8	21.6	10.3	47.8	12.6	3.3	18.7	21.8	6 343	178	336	12 746	7.1
Coles	909	0.6	31.8	27.1	47.0	8.4	2.7	25.6	20.7	8 649	169	1 014	20 329	1.3
Cook	138 378	0.0	20.8	16.5	67.5	6.6	13.4	32.0	11.8	743 330	143	158 266	2 021 833	1.4
Crawford	250	-1.1	D	40.5	D	8.9	4.1	15.6	15.0	4 394	210	292	8 464	-2.7
Cumberland	69	13.3	D	8.7	D	16.2	3.3	17.0	20.3	2 124	191	186	4 448	0.9
De Kalb	1 113	2.6	27.0	19.4	40.0	8.4	4.2	18.4	30.4	10 490	125	421	27 351	8.1
De Witt	317	-0.2	27.4	16.2	D	6.2	D	15.5	11.6	3 234	193	220	6 942	-5.3
Douglas	264	1.8	D	39.1	D	13.3	3.4	9.6	9.8	3 830	192	182	7 607	-1.7
Du Page	29 402	0.0	20.2	14.0	73.3	9.0	8.1	36.1	6.5	107 674	122	5 238	292 537	24.6
Edgar	240	24.3	D	15.3	D	6.6	3.9	15.2	17.1	4 260	217	423	8 733	-4.3
Edwards	97	2.3	D	D	D	5.2	2.2	6.6	8.5	1 599	230	72	3 260	-4.2
Effingham	624	1.8	38.7	31.6	49.2	11.7	3.3	22.4	10.2	5 975	178	382	12 189	4.3
Fayette	200	7.0	28.5	22.1	44.5	12.7	3.0	16.8	20.0	4 428	202	480	8 551	-4.2
Ford	151	6.8	23.9	15.8	54.1	10.7	3.3	19.3	15.2	3 106	221	144	6 118	-3.3
Franklin	315	0.3	D	16.0	47.9	13.4	2.4	22.2	22.4	9 782	242	1 318	18 430	-2.7
Fulton	253	1.5	10.8	4.7	60.4	15.1	3.8	25.6	27.3	8 709	225	612	16 480	-6.0
Gallatin	59	4.4	D	5.2	D	7.9	D	12.5	15.4	1 575	237	286	3 197	0.2
Greene	91	15.2	D	10.3	D	11.5	5.7	17.1	23.5	3 438	221	386	6 575	-3.5
Grundy	597	-0.7	25.1	17.5	D	7.7	2.2	D	11.0	5 781	158	127	12 652	9.7
Hamilton	50	9.3	10.3	4.6	45.1	12.1	3.4	15.4	35.2	2 099	244	250	4 013	-3.9
Hancock	202	12.8	D	D	D	6.2	3.4	14.5	15.1	4 479	212	271	9 692	-3.1
Hardin	35	3.8	D	D	D	5.7	D	21.4	26.4	1 220	249	157	2 403	-2.9
Henderson	38	14.8	D	D	D	9.4	5.1	15.3	32.1	1 651	192	122	4 089	-3.9
Henry	451	3.8	D	15.2	D	14.7	4.7	16.1	19.7	10 069	195	437	20 881	-3.6
Iroquois	290	10.9	D	14.6	D	8.6	5.4	21.4	14.4	7 021	225	339	12 819	-4.9

1. Covers mining, construction, and manufacturing. 2. Covers private sector earnings in agricultural services, forestry, and fisheries; transportation and public utilities; wholesale trade; retail trade; finance, insurance, and real estate; and services. 3. Per 1,000 resident population estimated as of July 1 of the year shown.

	Housing units, 1990 (cont'd)								Civilian labor force, 1999				Civilian employment, 1990[5]		
	Occupied units														
	Owner-occupied					Renter-occupied					Unemployment			Percent	
				Owner cost as a percent of income											
STATE County	Total	Percent	Median value[1]	With a mortgage	Without a mortgage	Median rent[2]	Rent as percent of income	Substandard units[3] (percent)	Total	Percent change, 1998–1999	Total	Rate[4]	Total	Professional, managerial, and technical	Precision production, craft, and repair
	89	90	91	92	93	94	95	96	97	98	99	100	101	102	103
IDAHO—Cont'd															
Custer	1 561	71.0	49 800	14.9	13.3	317	17.7	3.4	2 000	-17.0	164	8.2	1 861	25.3	14.5
Elmore	7 136	54.4	57 900	21.9	11.4	295	22.5	3.8	9 267	-0.7	604	6.5	7 373	26.2	13.4
Franklin	2 824	80.2	46 800	18.5	12.4	309	15.7	5.4	4 618	-6.6	163	3.5	3 375	17.1	14.4
Fremont	3 453	80.2	46 200	20.9	12.6	273	21.7	6.2	4 844	1.3	333	6.9	4 317	20.2	8.1
Gem	4 424	77.7	46 700	20.0	12.3	265	21.8	5.3	6 304	-3.3	436	6.9	4 757	17.0	13.9
Gooding	4 320	69.9	40 600	20.0	12.2	257	20.2	4.0	6 629	-8.1	239	3.6	5 033	17.7	10.2
Idaho	5 187	75.5	45 700	17.1	11.4	267	19.7	5.8	6 282	-3.9	678	10.8	5 272	22.6	12.4
Jefferson	4 871	80.5	54 300	18.8	12.8	314	21.5	10.0	10 039	2.7	455	4.5	6 589	22.6	10.5
Jerome	5 325	70.4	42 100	20.0	12.9	275	21.5	4.8	8 972	-6.8	406	4.5	6 660	17.5	10.2
Kootenai	26 942	71.3	64 800	21.4	11.8	368	26.5	3.2	55 639	1.3	4 481	8.1	30 695	26.4	13.1
Latah	11 229	56.4	63 500	16.3	11.1	314	27.7	2.8	14 987	-1.5	492	3.3	14 060	36.7	6.7
Lemhi	2 769	73.6	47 500	20.0	13.0	258	21.2	4.2	3 929	-9.1	311	7.9	2 776	20.9	14.0
Lewis	1 393	71.2	38 500	18.1	11.3	232	19.9	2.0	1 560	-6.2	104	6.7	1 315	21.7	10.0
Lincoln	1 191	72.0	37 000	17.5	11.3	238	18.4	5.3	1 919	-11.8	103	5.4	1 587	17.1	9.8
Madison	5 801	59.9	68 500	20.6	11.7	299	26.1	15.0	10 539	2.2	269	2.6	8 592	24.0	7.1
Minidoka	6 472	74.5	41 400	16.8	11.9	269	20.3	6.6	9 746	-5.5	742	7.6	8 186	16.4	12.0
Nez Perce	13 618	66.2	56 700	16.5	11.6	304	22.9	1.4	23 485	0.4	925	3.9	15 295	25.1	13.0
Oneida	1 159	81.8	43 100	18.3	12.7	319	23.0	5.6	1 654	-15.0	67	4.1	1 327	20.0	12.4
Owyhee	2 820	68.4	39 900	22.5	12.4	244	19.3	8.2	4 460	-5.6	193	4.3	3 602	14.4	10.3
Payette	6 040	70.9	43 800	18.8	12.4	280	24.3	6.3	10 390	1.3	760	7.3	6 802	18.3	12.5
Power	2 370	73.8	50 400	20.8	11.9	267	20.2	6.8	3 514	0.2	252	7.2	3 029	14.5	9.8
Shoshone	5 691	70.9	32 500	13.5	11.9	240	21.5	3.2	6 836	-1.9	770	11.3	5 310	20.6	23.2
Teton	1 123	74.0	59 000	17.7	13.9	333	23.1	8.0	3 114	5.5	110	3.5	1 596	17.9	14.3
Twin Falls	19 737	67.8	50 700	18.0	11.7	307	22.9	3.6	32 252	-6.7	1 567	4.9	24 359	21.2	10.6
Valley	2 404	70.6	70 700	20.4	12.2	326	24.1	5.3	4 022	-3.9	381	9.5	2 548	28.8	13.8
Washington	3 257	72.5	43 700	20.1	12.2	256	26.7	3.9	4 737	1.3	390	8.2	3 223	22.8	9.1
ILLINOIS	4 202 240	64.2	80 900	20.2	12.7	445	25.9	4.2	6 385 420	2.6	273 628	4.3	5 417 967	30.0	10.7
Adams	25 515	71.1	43 400	17.1	12.4	275	24.2	2.2	36 117	1.8	1 318	3.6	30 089	24.8	11.2
Alexander	4 234	68.4	23 900	21.2	13.8	174	29.1	4.7	3 936	-2.3	301	7.6	3 418	21.1	8.7
Bond	5 652	77.8	40 400	19.3	14.0	271	25.9	2.5	7 992	3.2	343	4.3	6 640	19.5	12.1
Boone	10 950	72.3	67 900	17.6	11.8	378	21.9	3.0	21 865	4.0	982	4.5	15 239	20.9	16.2
Brown	1 991	73.7	30 600	16.8	14.0	251	22.3	1.1	2 968	11.5	102	3.4	2 152	19.3	9.9
Bureau	13 790	72.7	41 800	16.3	13.1	326	22.2	1.4	18 607	2.6	902	4.8	16 211	20.3	11.9
Calhoun	2 048	80.2	35 000	18.2	14.6	246	24.5	4.7	3 050	5.3	159	5.2	1 954	18.1	14.3
Carroll	6 638	71.8	38 300	16.4	12.4	286	20.7	1.9	8 631	3.2	530	6.1	7 667	19.2	12.9
Cass	5 195	74.1	32 900	16.3	12.6	294	22.2	2.1	7 321	4.2	395	5.4	6 007	18.8	15.3
Champaign	63 900	54.5	67 700	20.1	12.2	411	29.6	2.6	98 270	5.5	2 473	2.5	87 114	39.0	7.4
Christian	13 591	73.9	37 400	16.4	12.9	313	24.5	2.5	19 017	1.3	1 051	5.5	15 021	20.2	13.8
Clark	6 394	78.2	34 200	16.2	12.1	264	23.4	1.7	10 112	6.7	397	3.9	7 026	17.5	14.0
Clay	5 708	78.9	31 900	20.8	13.2	246	25.8	2.9	7 241	2.0	584	8.1	5 903	18.7	15.4
Clinton	11 583	79.5	55 000	20.4	12.3	330	22.5	3.1	17 575	2.3	684	3.9	15 025	20.0	12.6
Coles	18 957	64.7	44 600	17.6	12.7	332	26.8	2.2	27 141	1.3	931	3.4	24 092	24.9	9.5
Cook	1 879 488	55.5	102 100	20.9	12.8	478	26.6	6.4	2 711 723	2.5	122 645	4.5	2 414 964	31.0	9.6
Crawford	7 792	78.4	36 700	15.3	11.9	282	23.5	2.4	9 540	1.2	635	6.7	8 092	17.8	15.0
Cumberland	4 029	80.7	37 700	17.0	12.8	268	23.3	4.7	5 586	1.0	229	4.1	4 674	16.3	12.7
De Kalb	26 413	58.1	81 200	20.2	12.8	424	27.4	2.5	47 324	1.2	1 627	3.4	40 120	29.4	11.3
De Witt	6 488	70.9	43 700	16.2	12.5	305	22.1	1.0	8 592	-4.4	499	5.8	7 461	20.8	13.0
Douglas	7 206	74.5	44 000	16.0	12.3	309	22.2	3.8	11 647	0.1	416	3.6	9 069	18.7	13.6
Du Page	279 344	74.4	137 100	22.4	12.6	625	24.6	1.9	528 237	1.7	14 193	2.7	432 730	39.9	9.2
Edgar	7 859	72.8	33 200	18.4	13.4	282	26.0	2.1	10 078	1.8	427	4.2	8 307	21.8	12.4
Edwards	3 016	81.2	32 000	20.2	12.6	245	23.9	1.8	3 729	1.8	249	6.7	3 220	16.1	13.3
Effingham	11 465	76.5	54 400	17.4	12.0	299	20.9	3.0	18 231	2.4	809	4.4	14 996	20.3	11.6
Fayette	7 719	77.3	34 600	17.6	12.9	279	24.5	3.7	10 496	2.5	705	6.7	8 285	17.3	11.4
Ford	5 602	73.3	42 500	17.4	11.8	296	22.9	1.7	6 443	5.3	263	4.1	6 560	21.7	11.8
Franklin	16 564	76.4	30 000	19.1	14.0	295	29.0	2.5	16 480	1.4	1 339	8.1	14 305	21.4	17.7
Fulton	14 893	72.2	31 100	16.3	12.7	296	25.8	1.6	14 297	6.5	1 028	7.2	14 595	21.1	13.3
Gallatin	2 784	78.8	32 600	19.6	13.7	237	31.9	3.2	2 732	2.1	190	7.0	2 644	15.8	14.3
Greene	5 910	74.2	29 000	16.9	13.5	248	24.3	3.4	6 988	4.3	350	5.0	6 314	19.1	13.2
Grundy	11 979	69.8	71 900	16.5	12.1	410	20.9	1.7	19 314	1.7	1 217	6.3	15 126	24.6	17.1
Hamilton	3 476	79.4	29 400	19.4	13.4	231	29.3	4.8	3 784	3.5	272	7.2	3 086	22.1	12.8
Hancock	8 409	76.2	34 500	16.5	12.6	276	20.5	1.4	12 266	3.4	458	3.7	9 868	21.2	12.7
Hardin	2 049	78.4	25 100	21.0	12.5	214	30.1	6.6	1 794	2.4	129	7.2	1 762	19.8	18.4
Henderson	3 237	76.3	32 900	14.8	12.4	273	25.6	1.9	4 543	3.7	185	4.1	3 740	17.3	13.1
Henry	19 514	75.1	40 500	16.8	12.9	315	23.7	1.5	27 689	4.9	1 424	5.1	23 243	20.7	13.0
Iroquois	11 788	73.8	40 100	15.6	11.9	306	21.3	1.7	15 821	3.6	802	5.1	14 212	19.0	12.4

1. Specified owner-occupied units.　2. Specified renter-occupied units.　3. Overcrowded or lacking complete plumbing facilities.　4. Percent of civilian labor force.　5. Persons 16 years and older.

	Private nonfarm establishments, employment and payroll, 1998									Agriculture, 1997			Farm operators
		Employment						Annual payroll		Farms			
											Percent with—		
STATE County	Number of establish-ments	Total	Health Care and Social Assistance	Manufac-turing	Retail trade	Finance and Insurance	Professional Scientific and Technical Services	Total (mil dol)	Average per employee (dollars)	Number	Less than 50 acres	500 acres and over	Whose principal occu-pation is farming (percent)
	104	105	106	107	108	109	110	111	112	113	114	115	116

IDAHO—Cont'd

STATE County	104	105	106	107	108	109	110	111	112	113	114	115	116
Custer	150	950	82	D	120	27	D	21	21 993	268	26.5	32.8	54.1
Elmore	400	3 769	828	412	938	155	50	69	18 239	301	34.6	32.6	56.8
Franklin	231	1 574	274	215	389	61	18	26	16 535	655	31.1	22.0	49.9
Fremont	269	1 523	176	D	291	82	D	28	18 277	493	32.3	30.6	58.0
Gem	298	2 191	354	462	373	64	41	46	20 821	552	50.5	10.7	48.4
Gooding	325	3 907	326	234	468	75	65	61	15 513	675	44.7	13.0	59.6
Idaho	445	2 605	403	294	550	87	81	52	19 774	661	20.9	42.4	58.9
Jefferson	334	2 685	158	685	443	61	50	48	18 061	773	41.9	19.9	50.6
Jerome	406	3 702	419	706	667	62	80	76	20 659	683	41.7	15.4	62.1
Kootenai	3 556	33 622	4 306	4 432	5 920	941	1 296	746	22 174	598	48.0	13.0	46.3
Latah	904	7 655	1 170	430	1 869	219	283	135	17 647	659	26.6	29.1	47.5
Lemhi	284	1 633	271	122	369	40	57	32	19 641	308	33.8	33.4	61.4
Lewis	133	702	18	205	140	D	13	16	22 202	182	12.6	52.7	64.8
Lincoln	69	488	107	D	65	9	D	9	18 840	281	18.5	24.9	69.0
Madison	503	9 644	818	1 528	1 342	128	152	144	14 924	470	40.2	23.4	50.2
Minidoka	374	5 043	520	1 650	717	56	103	107	21 182	674	42.4	18.2	64.7
Nez Perce	1 224	16 063	2 465	3 171	2 814	962	406	415	25 836	383	27.2	43.9	59.5
Oneida	70	523	126	D	108	D	D	9	16 444	387	19.4	39.3	54.5
Owyhee	150	1 715	111	593	197	D	18	40	23 373	570	29.5	28.6	68.4
Payette	427	3 869	348	1 260	580	106	104	74	19 076	564	55.0	7.3	52.1
Power	161	2 120	144	829	245	37	30	42	19 865	323	17.3	55.7	65.6
Shoshone	409	3 745	612	172	712	115	204	89	23 687	44	50.0	2.3	50.0
Teton	194	845	148	D	226	24	D	16	18 411	270	22.2	28.9	57.8
Twin Falls	2 076	25 929	3 374	3 142	4 701	693	655	532	20 502	1 439	38.3	15.6	60.9
Valley	467	2 332	266	121	499	55	72	38	16 344	119	36.1	32.8	51.3
Washington	229	2 010	247	364	322	67	75	39	19 424	489	36.8	29.4	59.3
ILLINOIS	304 533	5 221 782	612 855	883 472	632 626	338 042	311 731	175 704	33 648	73 051	23.1	25.1	57.0
Adams	1 867	29 994	4 482	6 894	4 603	D	689	734	24 471	1 415	20.8	20.4	54.3
Alexander	173	1 673	268	369	225	D	D	35	20 919	166	16.9	22.9	51.2
Bond	348	3 747	492	707	511	125	68	75	19 886	616	27.8	19.8	49.0
Boone	708	11 626	705	5 594	1 184	363	96	421	36 236	490	35.1	19.6	54.1
Brown	121	1 781	175	D	129	69	D	43	24 034	377	19.1	24.4	47.5
Bureau	872	10 210	2 046	2 621	1 312	535	260	242	23 712	1 155	15.3	31.6	63.1
Calhoun	120	723	86	D	131	D	D	12	16 620	433	22.4	10.6	43.9
Carroll	447	3 702	460	956	475	216	57	85	22 955	625	18.6	24.8	67.0
Cass	308	4 566	407	2 218	479	165	59	96	21 001	417	21.8	32.6	61.6
Champaign	4 065	67 242	9 642	9 776	10 959	2 902	2 981	1 554	23 114	1 371	17.4	31.1	63.8
Christian	807	10 430	1 853	1 953	1 591	459	165	218	20 859	820	23.3	34.9	64.9
Clark	379	4 542	331	2 032	553	166	65	95	20 909	603	25.2	31.3	54.9
Clay	396	5 190	562	2 384	515	161	65	109	20 994	627	21.2	26.6	52.6
Clinton	810	7 681	1 253	1 103	1 356	319	233	150	19 546	860	23.1	14.2	55.5
Coles	1 278	20 024	2 729	5 491	D	678	705	474	23 666	681	26.6	28.3	56.5
Cook	127 124	2 446 113	288 812	353 633	253 390	184 420	191 594	91 486	37 401	237	53.6	11.0	43.5
Crawford	472	6 854	696	2 495	867	302	140	200	29 116	473	24.5	30.4	55.0
Cumberland	186	1 391	347	322	263	D	D	23	16 572	547	23.9	21.4	49.9
De Kalb	1 915	24 294	3 347	6 908	3 886	927	436	595	24 496	828	19.4	30.6	68.1
De Witt	405	5 357	442	1 347	723	179	87	177	32 970	463	23.3	33.3	62.9
Douglas	627	7 193	388	2 918	1 401	227	79	167	23 235	630	27.0	29.8	67.6
Du Page	31 672	586 425	40 532	72 710	68 348	37 911	42 024	22 129	37 735	93	59.1	10.8	41.9
Edgar	412	4 710	821	1 542	681	D	126	97	20 607	766	17.2	33.7	64.1
Edwards	175	2 998	90	D	167	72	D	64	21 200	329	24.3	23.1	52.0
Effingham	1 110	19 080	2 537	5 511	3 031	452	615	425	22 257	1 035	25.1	13.9	47.7
Fayette	477	5 063	755	1 544	918	180	116	98	19 271	1 119	26.1	18.4	45.6
Ford	416	4 071	638	890	691	148	73	84	20 522	550	11.1	43.8	67.6
Franklin	893	8 468	1 610	1 413	1 587	256	164	182	21 461	658	33.6	13.8	40.0
Fulton	722	7 219	1 884	346	1 634	366	119	126	17 500	1 101	20.8	26.2	56.0
Gallatin	142	1 220	169	76	142	D	D	31	25 477	238	20.2	39.9	65.1
Greene	309	1 990	360	286	484	133	72	33	16 444	720	20.6	28.6	61.1
Grundy	901	10 864	1 333	1 772	D	422	278	333	30 653	463	17.5	30.9	61.3
Hamilton	189	1 123	359	63	196	69	D	19	16 551	563	22.6	20.2	45.6
Hancock	510	4 754	589	D	620	236	65	100	21 135	1 137	17.2	28.2	63.1
Hardin	74	795	341	D	64	D	D	15	19 293	172	16.9	7.0	32.6
Henderson	126	596	105	D	134	75	D	9	15 230	414	16.7	36.7	70.8
Henry	1 161	13 728	1 336	4 419	D	566	287	282	20 552	1 344	21.6	24.0	63.8
Iroquois	731	7 467	1 296	1 992	1 058	362	79	148	19 878	1 393	14.0	37.6	69.2

STATE County	Agriculture, 1997 (cont'd)															
	Land in farms					Value of land and buildings		Value of machinery and equipment Average per farm ($1,000)	Value of products sold			Percent from —		Percent of farms with sales of —		Percent of land owned by Fed. Gov. 1997	Water consumption 1995 (mil gal/day)
			Acres														
	Acreage (1,000)	Percent change, 1992–1997	Average size of farm	Total irrigated (1,000)	Total cropland (1,000)	Average per farm ($1,000)	Average per acre (dollars)		Total (mil dol)	Average per farm (dollars)	Crops	Live-stock and poultry products	$10,000 or more	$100,000 or more		
	117	118	119	120	121	122	123	124	125	126	127	128	129	130	131	132
IDAHO—Cont'd																
Custer	148	4.9	552	62	68	596	1 155	48	18	65 511	20.6	79.4	56.7	19.8	92.3	141.8
Elmore	356	0.4	1 181	91	127	682	626	142	220	731 298	D	D	51.8	28.2	69.7	327.4
Franklin	246	7.0	376	55	148	289	869	64	57	87 346	19.3	80.7	56.0	19.7	32.2	177.7
Fremont	334	-12.3	678	119	193	568	882	112	81	164 308	85.9	14.1	57.8	27.4	57.9	338.4
Gem	183	-7.1	331	37	48	382	910	38	30	53 634	38.2	61.8	44.9	9.4	36.9	135.6
Gooding	220	-2.9	326	113	D	496	1 567	101	249	369 535	20.7	79.3	64.6	30.4	57.0	1 288.6
Idaho	650	-12.7	983	2	226	625	686	55	33	49 248	58.2	41.8	54.3	16.3	83.2	30.3
Jefferson	333	6.9	430	208	234	513	1 186	87	136	176 108	61.8	38.2	59.4	23.4	49.8	1 544.1
Jerome	194	-6.8	284	152	160	566	1 915	124	250	366 580	33.3	66.7	68.5	34.4	37.6	1 108.5
Kootenai	131	-0.1	219	16	77	406	2 203	45	14	22 711	80.9	19.1	25.9	5.2	30.5	47.1
Latah	325	-6.2	494	0	238	512	955	58	38	56 967	91.5	8.5	39.6	17.0	15.8	11.7
Lemhi	197	1.3	638	82	84	512	830	56	19	60 981	8.6	91.4	61.0	19.8	90.3	123.7
Lewis	194	-8.3	1 064	D	140	822	781	100	20	110 753	93.5	6.5	67.6	38.5	2.5	1.1
Lincoln	131	-0.4	468	73	D	430	1 030	88	44	156 215	61.1	38.9	69.0	26.3	75.8	420.6
Madison	223	-0.5	474	129	174	949	1 824	118	80	171 223	90.9	9.1	58.5	28.1	19.4	295.3
Minidoka	207	-0.5	307	181	D	538	1 856	129	152	225 836	75.4	24.6	66.2	37.2	50.2	526.8
Nez Perce	339	-29.0	886	0	208	877	901	114	38	98 580	87.7	12.3	55.9	27.7	3.7	18.6
Oneida	271	0.0	701	33	188	439	638	53	15	39 183	60.1	39.9	56.1	10.1	52.8	103.3
Owyhee	683	-9.2	1 198	132	158	705	623	71	103	180 656	45.6	54.4	65.8	30.7	78.4	474.0
Payette	148	-0.4	263	53	D	315	1 153	54	49	86 526	55.6	44.4	50.4	17.4	25.6	254.1
Power	424	-2.5	1 313	118	354	1 069	916	246	121	374 535	72.0	28.0	67.8	39.9	30.1	305.5
Shoshone	4	2.5	93	D	2	326	3 499	18	0	8 809	D	D	6.8	2.3	74.5	9.9
Teton	133	-1.7	491	57	102	822	1 631	75	23	84 682	74.1	25.9	60.4	19.3	33.2	116.3
Twin Falls	456	-6.9	317	276	308	494	1 548	78	239	166 372	56.3	43.7	66.2	28.2	50.1	1 890.6
Valley	64	-18.6	540	24	23	729	1 513	38	8	63 931	17.1	82.9	44.5	10.1	84.7	28.1
Washington	443	-20.3	906	45	107	504	550	62	39	79 379	60.8	39.2	53.8	18.2	37.4	83.4
ILLINOIS	27 205	-0.2	372	350	23 921	773	2 126	90	8 556	117 130	76.8	23.2	68.2	31.7	1.4	19 896.9
Adams	442	-4.9	312	2	340	440	1 428	62	121	85 362	61.6	38.4	64.5	24.1	1.8	23.5
Alexander	71	3.3	429	3	58	544	1 121	99	13	79 596	95.8	4.2	48.2	19.9	16.4	2.5
Bond	180	-1.6	292	0	156	423	1 729	58	46	74 326	73.5	26.5	56.0	24.7	0.0	2.4
Boone	141	4.8	289	2	130	651	2 825	68	54	109 577	75.2	24.8	64.3	30.4	0.0	6.3
Brown	152	5.7	404	D	101	447	1 189	57	30	80 520	69.6	30.4	53.8	20.2	0.0	0.4
Bureau	484	0.4	419	5	441	924	2 252	111	199	172 197	82.2	17.8	82.9	43.8	0.0	8.1
Calhoun	99	-0.5	230	0	59	236	1 383	31	19	42 765	70.6	29.4	43.2	8.1	5.5	8.3
Carroll	243	1.8	389	9	214	802	2 152	103	123	196 895	49.7	50.3	74.6	44.0	1.1	8.5
Cass	192	-8.1	461	9	160	862	1 857	106	74	177 869	56.1	43.9	67.4	37.9	0.4	9.5
Champaign	568	-0.8	414	6	549	1 201	2 940	117	190	138 614	96.2	3.8	85.7	42.0	0.3	36.1
Christian	390	0.0	476	D	366	1 172	2 530	113	123	150 070	93.7	6.3	75.7	42.6	0.0	775.6
Clark	269	3.4	446	6	225	651	1 499	116	63	104 874	87.2	12.8	62.0	30.8	0.0	4.2
Clay	239	6.6	381	D	207	508	1 407	90	49	78 538	87.2	12.8	60.9	23.9	0.0	1.7
Clinton	234	2.0	272	1	211	476	1 646	87	107	124 038	38.5	61.5	74.9	29.0	1.7	7.5
Coles	257	-2.3	377	D	237	892	2 373	92	73	107 021	93.5	6.5	66.7	33.9	0.0	7.7
Cook	39	-3.9	166	0	30	549	3 791	43	21	90 238	97.2	2.8	41.8	17.3	0.0	1 691.5
Crawford	209	-6.7	442	6	183	623	1 417	97	52	109 948	81.6	18.4	67.9	32.8	0.0	57.6
Cumberland	170	-3.5	310	0	148	597	1 822	73	54	98 472	67.1	32.9	69.3	28.3	0.0	1.9
De Kalb	368	-2.6	445	1	355	1 440	3 369	123	183	221 493	61.7	38.3	84.2	48.2	0.0	12.0
De Witt	205	-0.5	443	1	197	1 082	2 417	105	69	148 660	93.8	6.2	77.3	44.7	0.0	712.0
Douglas	250	-3.6	396	0	239	1 101	2 831	97	80	127 598	89.2	10.8	76.7	39.2	0.0	5.7
Du Page	17	-5.0	184	0	14	766	4 164	85	18	189 644	96.7	3.3	54.8	25.8	4.3	18.3
Edgar	352	-0.5	460	D	322	1 093	2 390	110	165	215 908	54.5	45.5	74.9	37.6	0.0	2.8
Edwards	113	-2.7	343	0	95	483	1 408	74	28	84 218	67.4	32.6	60.8	26.1	0.0	1.2
Effingham	257	-0.5	248	D	222	497	2 085	62	79	76 363	57.1	42.9	68.4	22.6	0.0	5.9
Fayette	333	-2.3	298	0	276	395	1 412	52	72	64 320	85.1	14.9	52.1	18.8	1.3	5.7
Ford	315	4.9	572	1	300	1 257	2 300	128	100	181 983	89.7	10.3	89.3	50.7	0.0	3.9
Franklin	180	11.5	273	D	152	297	1 112	54	32	48 082	78.4	21.6	38.4	13.1	4.1	15.5
Fulton	425	-1.4	386	0	319	584	1 534	81	99	89 785	80.9	19.1	67.9	25.7	0.0	273.4
Gallatin	191	11.1	803	19	165	1 271	1 441	165	45	189 965	94.1	5.9	69.3	39.1	5.0	10.0
Greene	328	7.8	455	1	261	690	1 575	85	106	146 875	62.3	37.7	68.3	33.2	0.3	3.1
Grundy	201	-10.9	435	0	190	1 317	2 974	117	59	127 933	93.7	6.3	84.0	40.8	0.0	2 560.5
Hamilton	215	6.3	381	D	181	393	1 109	63	39	68 934	93.5	6.5	45.3	17.6	0.0	0.5
Hancock	438	1.2	386	2	354	616	1 644	87	126	110 764	74.3	25.7	71.2	33.2	0.0	3.2
Hardin	39	3.3	228		24	224	961	24	3	18 372	34.4	65.6	23.3	2.3	23.1	2.8
Henderson	202	-0.9	488	10	169	866	1 835	97	60	145 435	81.1	18.9	82.1	44.9	0.5	15.1
Henry	457	0.6	340	5	413	712	2 246	96	179	133 231	57.8	42.2	77.2	37.4	0.0	9.1
Iroquois	667	0.6	479	4	634	1 109	2 309	123	240	172 320	81.1	18.9	87.4	49.6	0.0	4.4

Table B. States and Counties — **Residential Construction, Wholesale and Retail Trade, and Real Estate**

STATE County	Value of Residential Construction Authorized by Building Permits, 1999		Wholesale Trade, 1997				Retail Trade[1], 1997				Real Estate and Rental and Leasing, 1997			
	New Construction ($1,000)	Number of Housing Units	Number of Establish-ments	Number of Employees	Sales (mil dol)	Annual Payroll (mil dol)	Number of Establish-ments	Number of Employees	Sales (mil dol)	Annual Payroll (mil dol)	Number of Establish-ments	Number of Employees	Receipts (mil dol)	Annual Payroll (mil dol)
	133	134	135	136	137	138	139	140	141	142	143	144	145	146
IDAHO—Cont'd														
Custer	731	9	3	D	D	D	25	106	14.7	1.2	4	D	D	D
Elmore	10 598	148	11	64	20.1	1.6	84	894	231.0	17.3	10	43	3.7	0.5
Franklin	7 410	77	19	122	30.1	2.9	45	383	55.1	4.8	5	13	0.6	0.1
Fremont	9 391	69	17	235	83.0	4.2	50	285	53.0	4.2	4	D	D	D
Gem	9 017	87	18	155	35.7	3.0	42	326	49.5	5.4	9	22	1.2	0.2
Gooding	9 293	96	13	197	58.5	3.3	54	480	66.8	6.5	10	31	0.9	0.3
Idaho	578	6	15	168	38.6	2.8	81	540	75.2	8.0	7	16	0.6	0.2
Jefferson	10 950	105	30	511	101.2	8.0	48	438	59.9	5.7	7	8	0.7	0.1
Jerome	6 806	69	37	312	251.9	6.1	57	624	107.6	10.3	4	4	0.6	0.1
Kootenai	138 533	1 367	121	1 171	402.9	35.7	545	5 590	1 022.7	100.5	143	379	47.7	6.1
Latah	10 067	91	44	255	111.6	6.0	176	1 982	253.8	26.7	39	185	12.8	2.4
Lemhi	2 050	29	10	28	8.0	0.6	54	384	54.5	5.1	8	12	1.7	0.2
Lewis	300	4	8	87	27.2	1.8	27	137	21.0	2.5	3	16	0.9	0.2
Lincoln	1 053	14	1	D	D	D	12	57	11.2	0.7	1	D	D	D
Madison	11 851	149	40	605	94.3	8.4	93	1 286	211.9	18.9	19	80	5.6	0.6
Minidoka	4 183	39	42	776	158.4	16.8	76	775	130.4	12.1	6	22	1.3	0.3
Nez Perce	11 848	103	66	725	214.1	16.9	231	2 832	464.3	48.7	39	178	11.5	2.5
Oneida	1 809	22	1	D	D	D	11	78	10.3	0.9	3	11	0.4	0.1
Owyhee	3 852	44	13	161	40.6	4.0	33	202	31.6	2.9	4	D	D	D
Payette	14 798	173	25	308	58.0	5.0	66	490	89.5	8.8	10	18	2.0	0.3
Power	3 602	49	11	143	72.9	3.2	23	191	35.9	3.1	1	D	D	D
Shoshone	1 595	21	13	95	33.1	2.6	76	687	243.5	12.8	16	58	3.3	0.5
Teton	15 450	137	4	6	0.5	0.1	37	217	34.7	3.0	8	16	2.1	0.1
Twin Falls	32 388	341	159	1 600	450.7	37.9	378	4 721	837.9	76.8	65	241	25.9	4.0
Valley	21 390	142	9	21	3.8	0.9	65	436	66.2	6.7	25	49	5.5	0.6
Washington	3 198	27	9	322	46.7	4.2	40	341	58.7	5.5	7	22	1.1	0.2
ILLINOIS	6 537 643	53 974	21 956	325 847	275 978.4	13 325.5	44 568	610 790	108 002.2	10 596.0	11 411	73 819	12 830.0	2 101.4
Adams	12 717	92	127	1 650	686.7	45.7	341	4 752	669.5	68.2	60	256	25.3	3.7
Alexander	60	2	10	D	D	D	35	237	29.1	2.9	5	14	1.0	0.3
Bond	5 802	61	19	264	143.4	6.5	60	496	97.7	7.1	12	20	1.8	0.2
Boone	49 237	403	43	D	D	D	91	1 156	198.7	19.4	34	86	10.9	1.5
Brown	210	3	11	D	D	D	21	138	16.5	1.5	5	14	0.4	0.2
Bureau	6 519	58	58	D	D	D	145	1 379	229.5	20.7	16	41	3.3	0.5
Calhoun	2 645	26	4	D	D	D	24	134	26.8	2.0	4	D	D	D
Carroll	10 226	79	26	190	111.6	5.0	72	560	81.4	7.1	9	24	1.4	0.2
Cass	1 080	15	20	193	240.0	5.4	59	520	68.3	6.3	5	18	1.7	0.4
Champaign	97 651	999	199	3 737	2 419.0	111.5	675	10 654	1 556.7	151.9	203	1 356	179.7	27.3
Christian	8 684	111	51	482	363.6	15.0	156	1 644	283.1	24.7	20	67	5.9	0.9
Clark	1 076	19	22	199	104.8	4.6	77	627	106.7	8.5	6	14	0.5	0.1
Clay	1 490	17	31	316	84.2	6.1	66	662	92.1	7.4	9	38	1.7	0.5
Clinton	11 103	95	54	D	D	D	136	1 373	243.8	30.9	18	136	9.7	3.2
Coles	6 033	109	67	663	327.2	15.4	233	3 210	526.5	46.2	49	195	14.3	2.6
Cook	1 365 797	11 008	9 574	149 994	120 551.8	6 467.2	17 318	240 539	42 547.2	4 369.9	5 614	42 649	8 711.0	1 393.7
Crawford	1 965	17	24	151	246.8	3.4	93	907	136.4	12.5	16	30	2.5	0.3
Cumberland	779	10	16	87	48.7	1.9	42	253	37.2	3.3	4	9	0.5	0.0
De Kalb	61 628	631	75	835	871.8	32.2	309	4 008	642.3	63.1	63	275	34.4	3.9
De Witt	7 002	53	22	127	138.0	5.5	70	756	142.0	12.4	9	16	1.0	0.1
Douglas	4 290	34	33	370	203.4	8.6	165	1 299	185.8	16.7	10	46	4.1	0.6
Du Page	726 916	4 694	3 351	64 415	74 318.8	2 918.5	3 625	64 962	12 825.3	1 231.1	1 134	9 484	1 480.5	293.4
Edgar	3 512	40	31	260	163.8	5.4	68	721	108.3	9.8	12	33	1.4	0.2
Edwards	NA	NA	15	188	105.7	6.1	34	235	28.4	2.4	2	D	D	D
Effingham	8 430	83	58	879	265.9	29.6	236	3 205	561.3	50.2	27	119	8.6	1.3
Fayette	1 180	12	27	372	186.3	8.8	103	933	153.3	12.7	12	24	1.7	0.3
Ford	2 808	35	33	335	298.9	11.4	93	716	120.2	9.6	12	13	1.2	0.1
Franklin	4 253	59	47	258	72.6	6.1	192	1 707	276.9	27.1	22	62	9.1	0.8
Fulton	6 469	87	36	235	95.4	5.0	156	1 718	248.4	24.8	21	52	3.3	0.5
Gallatin	0	0	8	D	D	D	29	144	23.4	2.0	NA	NA	NA	NA
Greene	737	8	22	108	70.1	2.4	70	480	71.1	6.6	5	D	D	D
Grundy	31 400	249	40	347	387.3	12.3	137	1 604	288.0	27.2	39	199	16.7	4.2
Hamilton	NA	NA	13	68	54.3	1.4	37	207	37.7	2.7	2	D	D	D
Hancock	1 302	22	32	220	211.9	5.1	101	601	101.5	8.8	7	33	4.0	1.1
Hardin	162	2	NA	NA	NA	NA	15	60	8.6	0.8	1	D	D	D
Henderson	1 429	20	10	40	21.6	0.7	23	125	21.0	1.7	2	D	D	D
Henry	12 678	107	81	775	521.6	19.9	217	2 583	371.9	37.1	28	83	4.9	1.3
Iroquois	7 000	78	65	524	405.3	12.8	118	1 139	176.1	17.2	11	25	2.5	0.3

1. Establishments with payroll.

Table B. States and Counties — **Professional, Manufacturing, and Accommodation and Foodservices**

STATE County	Professional, Scientific, and Technical Services[1], 1997				Manufacturing, 1997				Accommodation and Foodservices, 1997			
	Number of Establishments	Number of Employees	Receipts (mil dol)	Annual Payroll (mil dol)	Number of Establishments	Number of Employees	Receipts (mil dol)	Annual Payroll (mil dol)	Number of Establishments	Number of Employees	Sales (mil dol)	Annual Payroll (mil dol)
	147	148	149	150	151	152	153	154	155	156	157	158
IDAHO—Cont'd												
Custer	8	18	0.9	0.2	NA	NA	NA	NA	26	131	5.8	1.7
Elmore	11	40	1.8	0.7	NA	NA	NA	NA	53	479	13.5	3.9
Franklin	9	16	0.7	0.1	NA	NA	NA	NA	14	171	3.3	0.9
Fremont	5	10	0.4	0.0	NA	NA	NA	NA	32	172	8.6	2.0
Gem	16	50	1.8	0.5	NA	NA	NA	NA	22	189	5.4	1.2
Gooding	13	45	2.6	1.0	NA	NA	NA	NA	28	254	5.0	1.5
Idaho	21	70	3.1	1.0	NA	NA	NA	NA	56	323	9.7	2.5
Jefferson	16	39	2.0	0.6	17	664	94.4	11.9	18	D	D	D
Jerome	17	54	3.9	1.4	19	803	176.3	15.9	30	210	6.9	1.7
Kootenai	245	1 121	81.8	32.8	195	4 472	592.1	116.9	298	4 086	137.7	37.9
Latah	69	230	13.3	5.2	NA	NA	NA	NA	91	1 348	33.5	8.6
Lemhi	21	45	2.6	0.7	NA	NA	NA	NA	36	209	6.5	2.0
Lewis	5	13	0.6	0.2	NA	NA	NA	NA	18	109	4.2	1.2
Lincoln	1	D	D	D	NA	NA	NA	NA	7	63	1.5	0.4
Madison	23	158	10.7	5.2	21	1 326	141.4	25.5	40	D	D	D
Minidoka	16	69	3.5	1.1	18	1 638	425.7	44.3	25	274	5.7	1.9
Nez Perce	69	349	24.0	9.4	55	3 263	769.1	128.0	103	1 439	43.0	12.5
Oneida	1	D	D	D	NA	NA	NA	NA	7	D	D	D
Owyhee	4	15	0.7	0.2	5	613	225.2	12.2	18	107	2.4	0.7
Payette	27	90	5.8	1.9	24	D	D	D	25	208	4.7	1.1
Power	6	17	0.6	0.2	8	889	155.3	21.3	16	76	2.3	0.6
Shoshone	24	132	9.2	4.2	NA	NA	NA	NA	49	326	8.1	2.3
Teton	11	33	4.1	0.8	NA	NA	NA	NA	19	104	4.1	1.1
Twin Falls	140	574	41.2	16.7	95	3 588	723.3	82.9	148	2 303	62.7	18.1
Valley	22	61	3.7	1.4	NA	NA	NA	NA	65	484	13.9	3.9
Washington	12	39	2.0	0.6	NA	NA	NA	NA	21	D	D	D
ILLINOIS	30 378	274 714	33 855.1	13 105.4	17 953	887 350	200 020.0	31 837.9	23 984	397 300	14 826.8	4 018.7
Adams	112	504	42.2	13.9	85	5 707	1 868.3	190.4	139	2 204	65.9	18.2
Alexander	11	35	1.6	0.7	NA	NA	NA	NA	23	130	4.3	1.0
Bond	14	51	2.3	0.8	16	695	166.0	19.2	36	407	11.0	3.1
Boone	34	D	D	D	63	5 846	2 300.0	283.9	53	556	18.6	4.7
Brown	7	15	0.6	0.1	NA	NA	NA	NA	12	77	1.8	0.5
Bureau	39	198	9.8	3.9	41	2 499	413.7	72.0	86	766	20.7	5.4
Calhoun	6	9	0.4	0.1	NA	NA	NA	NA	18	96	3.6	0.8
Carroll	18	42	2.2	0.6	33	1 015	235.2	27.0	55	317	9.0	2.1
Cass	16	44	2.4	0.5	13	D	D	D	36	237	7.7	1.8
Champaign	336	2 660	263.2	91.6	152	10 857	2 689.5	292.4	449	8 944	248.6	70.6
Christian	35	140	6.9	2.3	30	1 388	479.3	53.2	76	763	21.6	5.4
Clark	20	61	3.6	1.4	24	1 682	435.5	44.6	40	530	12.4	3.2
Clay	18	60	5.2	1.6	23	2 453	480.1	62.8	30	216	5.8	1.6
Clinton	34	197	8.6	3.7	39	963	175.9	22.4	92	D	D	D
Coles	77	387	37.5	12.2	57	5 754	1 455.6	182.9	136	2 058	59.8	15.4
Cook	15 689	178 223	23 915.1	9 267.6	7 966	362 364	74 563.3	13 032.0	9 912	177 351	7 770.0	2 092.4
Crawford	27	108	8.4	2.5	20	2 547	2 175.4	90.4	34	D	D	D
Cumberland	6	11	0.9	0.2	NA	NA	NA	NA	14	D	D	D
De Kalb	106	321	28.2	7.8	137	6 957	1 511.7	207.7	190	2 664	73.2	17.8
De Witt	21	63	4.5	1.5	15	1 300	267.1	39.6	42	384	11.1	2.9
Douglas	23	58	3.3	1.1	65	2 711	481.7	79.2	47	692	17.3	4.8
Du Page	4 099	32 018	4 200.8	1 475.6	2 033	71 351	11 938.5	2 503.0	1 698	37 452	1 495.4	405.7
Edgar	29	127	7.4	2.2	27	1 539	248.7	36.9	31	264	6.1	1.6
Edwards	8	15	0.7	0.1	8	D	D	D	7	D	D	D
Effingham	47	560	72.5	15.4	59	5 660	978.7	148.7	90	2 061	59.2	15.8
Fayette	18	93	4.0	1.8	22	1 529	277.9	37.8	39	477	12.5	3.5
Ford	21	52	3.1	1.0	22	951	322.4	23.7	32	290	7.5	2.0
Franklin	40	133	8.9	2.3	43	1 632	233.7	36.6	82	983	26.7	7.5
Fulton	25	90	5.2	1.8	NA	NA	NA	NA	81	837	20.4	5.8
Gallatin	7	14	0.7	0.3	NA	NA	NA	NA	8	45	1.3	0.3
Greene	14	56	2.0	0.8	NA	NA	NA	NA	31	D	D	D
Grundy	53	194	17.3	6.6	33	2 015	875.4	87.8	72	999	32.8	8.4
Hamilton	10	23	1.3	0.3	NA	NA	NA	NA	7	88	2.1	0.5
Hancock	14	43	2.9	0.7	28	1 862	193.2	42.5	44	321	7.8	2.0
Hardin	5	9	0.3	0.1	NA	NA	NA	NA	6	D	D	D
Henderson	5	15	0.7	0.1	NA	NA	NA	NA	12	83	2.0	0.3
Henry	52	185	11.0	4.0	53	4 019	1 288.0	124.3	113	1 309	32.9	9.1
Iroquois	27	68	5.1	1.4	30	1 723	296.9	43.0	67	435	14.5	3.3

1. Firms subject to federal tax.

Table B. States and Counties — Health and Other Services and Federal Funds

STATE County	Health Care and Social Assistance[1], 1997				Other Services[1], 1997				Federal funds and grants, fiscal 1999[2] Expenditures (mil dol)			
									Total	Direct payments for individuals[3]		
	Number of Establishments	Number of Employees	Receipts (mil dol)	Annual Payroll (mil dol)	Number of Establishments	Number of Employees	Receipts (mil dol)	Annual Payroll (mil dol)		Social Security and government retirement	Medicare	Food stamps and Supplemental Security Income
	159	160	161	162	163	164	165	166	167	168	169	170
IDAHO—Cont'd												
Custer	8	62	1.2	0.6	3	5	0.3	0.1	20.4	8.3	2.9	0.3
Elmore	27	195	8.7	3.0	35	152	7.9	1.9	288.0	53.3	7.9	1.4
Franklin	11	86	3.1	1.1	10	33	2.1	0.3	33.8	17.2	4.9	0.8
Fremont	16	78	4.0	1.8	9	20	1.5	0.3	50.5	20.4	5.4	0.9
Gem	19	293	9.0	4.1	22	76	3.6	1.0	57.2	31.9	8.7	1.3
Gooding	19	207	6.9	3.1	17	69	4.0	0.9	53.9	27.2	8.5	1.2
Idaho	26	147	6.7	1.9	21	62	4.4	0.8	91.0	32.7	10.2	2.2
Jefferson	19	127	4.7	1.8	12	26	2.2	0.4	55.8	25.8	7.8	1.2
Jerome	15	102	5.4	2.8	23	83	4.8	1.3	61.1	28.1	9.4	1.7
Kootenai	267	2 561	137.1	55.6	176	836	47.5	12.9	376.4	206.8	54.0	9.7
Latah	57	389	22.8	10.9	38	201	13.6	3.8	140.4	49.1	12.4	1.8
Lemhi	20	162	6.3	2.7	14	39	2.8	0.6	45.5	20.3	7.4	0.7
Lewis	6	8	0.7	0.1	2	D	D	D	37.2	14.2	3.5	0.9
Lincoln	5	63	3.4	1.3	2	D	D	D	16.2	6.6	1.9	0.3
Madison	49	463	21.9	7.3	27	109	5.2	1.2	49.8	20.9	6.4	1.4
Minidoka	26	185	7.8	3.2	23	117	11.5	2.2	72.7	35.1	12.3	2.2
Nez Perce	111	1 454	82.2	34.0	87	534	28.4	8.1	210.1	84.5	29.2	5.5
Oneida	5	35	1.3	0.5	5	7	0.9	0.1	20.7	7.9	2.6	0.4
Owyhee	5	180	4.2	2.4	6	6	0.6	0.1	32.9	13.6	3.8	1.2
Payette	33	466	12.4	4.5	18	67	3.1	0.7	98.3	36.1	10.5	2.8
Power	7	29	1.7	0.7	15	64	3.3	1.0	36.3	9.7	2.8	0.7
Shoshone	25	308	11.1	4.8	26	56	3.7	1.0	101.4	38.6	13.8	3.6
Teton	7	15	1.4	0.4	4	7	0.8	0.1	18.8	6.6	2.7	0.1
Twin Falls	154	2 301	116.0	52.5	114	630	31.9	9.3	253.8	115.8	36.6	6.3
Valley	19	130	6.3	2.5	20	41	2.8	0.7	53.9	23.6	5.4	0.7
Washington	12	178	7.7	3.1	9	32	2.4	0.6	49.8	23.7	6.6	1.5
ILLINOIS	21 122	248 667	16 870.2	7 441.8	18 806	118 317	8 296.8	2 503.0	55 836.0	19 736.2	9 183.5	2 054.9
Adams	122	1 605	96.3	50.9	146	749	43.3	13.2	290.3	140.4	52.6	9.2
Alexander	2	D	D	D	5	16	0.9	0.2	68.6	21.8	11.1	5.6
Bond	20	217	7.2	3.7	32	79	5.9	1.4	85.4	31.4	13.0	1.8
Boone	34	535	21.9	10.1	53	248	17.6	6.1	95.6	54.9	18.0	2.2
Brown	4	109	3.0	1.7	10	23	1.2	0.3	26.3	10.0	3.8	0.8
Bureau	54	629	30.7	15.4	57	197	10.4	2.5	150.8	75.6	31.0	2.2
Calhoun	5	72	3.8	1.1	5	38	1.8	1.0	27.0	11.0	5.2	0.6
Carroll	20	159	5.2	2.6	30	101	6.2	1.4	107.7	43.0	14.7	1.7
Cass	20	283	7.7	4.0	20	87	4.5	1.2	63.0	28.6	12.0	1.6
Champaign	204	4 973	367.9	182.4	244	1 241	65.0	21.0	772.7	231.8	70.9	16.7
Christian	45	798	30.5	11.8	63	195	12.4	2.7	162.9	78.9	36.1	4.2
Clark	17	102	5.3	1.8	27	74	4.2	0.8	83.3	37.4	15.5	1.9
Clay	23	249	12.6	3.9	24	67	5.8	1.3	70.2	31.9	14.8	1.8
Clinton	51	699	27.3	11.1	47	147	10.9	2.6	125.9	67.1	26.2	1.9
Coles	90	1 224	61.2	27.9	85	428	25.7	6.9	185.2	86.2	36.9	6.3
Cook	9 558	108 873	7 974.7	3 416.1	7 707	55 223	4 042.9	1 211.5	24 312.3	7 884.1	4 670.2	1 319.4
Crawford	37	354	14.6	5.5	33	117	6.6	2.0	92.3	45.1	16.8	2.0
Cumberland	5	84	2.5	1.5	13	35	2.4	0.4	46.5	20.1	8.1	1.5
De Kalb	104	1 453	87.5	40.2	131	495	31.6	8.4	226.5	112.8	43.9	3.3
De Witt	23	218	9.9	4.9	22	65	5.8	1.3	78.8	36.5	13.9	1.9
Douglas	30	399	12.7	5.2	26	117	11.4	2.7	76.7	33.9	12.3	1.3
Du Page	2 117	23 540	1 852.3	807.3	1 706	12 714	931.0	310.5	2 301.6	1 167.3	462.2	31.1
Edgar	24	270	11.5	4.6	22	64	4.5	0.9	98.5	43.4	17.6	2.8
Edwards	10	88	2.5	1.2	16	27	1.6	0.3	29.1	14.3	5.8	0.5
Effingham	90	895	63.5	25.7	70	426	26.4	6.1	130.2	60.3	23.7	2.3
Fayette	33	321	11.7	5.1	31	129	17.7	2.6	90.2	40.6	17.2	3.2
Ford	20	271	12.5	5.0	20	64	4.3	1.0	72.6	34.7	11.6	1.1
Franklin	63	474	19.2	7.1	55	168	11.2	2.8	246.7	108.1	42.0	9.6
Fulton	44	1 104	43.1	21.8	38	154	9.7	2.2	174.9	86.3	41.8	5.0
Gallatin	3	148	2.7	1.4	3	D	D	D	41.5	15.7	7.2	1.8
Greene	21	172	5.1	2.3	18	35	2.4	0.4	81.3	33.5	14.7	2.4
Grundy	62	670	34.5	15.0	58	300	21.1	5.2	124.6	64.1	26.8	1.3
Hamilton	8	70	3.2	1.5	11	28	2.5	0.3	47.4	19.3	8.5	1.4
Hancock	30	238	10.8	4.4	25	52	4.0	0.8	96.0	46.2	16.2	2.0
Hardin	8	76	2.2	0.8	2	D	D	D	25.9	11.4	6.0	1.1
Henderson	7	29	1.5	0.8	7	20	0.6	0.3	38.3	16.4	5.6	0.7
Henry	50	399	16.7	6.2	84	273	19.3	4.2	195.5	104.4	38.0	3.9
Iroquois	35	208	13.3	6.2	45	129	10.7	2.4	154.5	70.5	26.2	2.7

1. Firms subject to federal tax.   2. October 1, 1998 to September 30, 1999.   3. State totals may include programs not allocated by county.

STATE County	Federal funds and grants, fiscal 1999[1] (cont'd)							Local government finances, 1997				
	Expenditures (mil dol) (cont'd)							General revenue				
	Procurement contract awards			Grants[2]							Taxes	
											Per capita[3] (dollars)	
	Salaries and wages	Defense	Other	Medicaid and other health-related	Nutrition and family welfare	Education	Other	Total (mil dol)	Intergovern-mental (mil dol)	Total (mil dol)	Total	Property
	171	172	173	174	175	176	177	178	179	180	181	182
IDAHO—Cont'd												
Custer	3.5	0.0	1.0	0.9	0.8	0.1	1.9	9.6	5.3	2.8	667	640
Elmore	161.6	33.9	2.2	4.2	1.8	2.9	14.2	44.0	25.2	9.8	396	378
Franklin	2.3	0.0	0.5	2.1	0.7	0.2	0.5	21.3	12.3	3.8	354	344
Fremont	5.2	0.0	1.4	3.3	0.8	0.3	3.5	26.0	13.7	7.4	624	586
Gem	3.8	0.0	0.7	5.7	1.4	0.5	0.8	23.7	12.4	5.7	391	334
Gooding	2.5	0.0	0.7	6.9	1.0	0.5	1.3	28.0	14.3	7.3	541	529
Idaho	15.1	0.0	5.9	7.5	1.3	0.3	8.8	31.5	19.5	5.8	382	365
Jefferson	2.4	0.0	1.4	3.7	1.6	0.6	2.9	34.4	23.9	7.6	403	379
Jerome	2.5	0.0	0.9	7.4	1.2	0.6	2.9	30.7	17.6	7.8	442	431
Kootenai	30.7	7.3	9.8	29.5	5.7	1.8	13.1	212.8	76.2	73.7	746	685
Latah	11.1	0.8	7.2	7.0	4.0	5.4	23.0	64.2	24.8	20.3	624	606
Lemhi	9.3	0.0	2.4	3.0	0.6	0.4	1.2	18.6	7.8	3.1	388	371
Lewis	1.4	0.0	0.5	5.7	2.2	0.2	0.6	13.6	7.8	3.1	754	746
Lincoln	3.2	0.0	0.4	0.6	0.4	0.1	0.4	9.6	5.9	2.5	647	618
Madison	2.5	0.0	0.7	2.5	1.6	0.5	2.2	52.2	25.6	8.7	372	352
Minidoka	3.2	0.0	1.3	5.7	1.6	0.7	0.4	60.6	22.1	8.8	426	414
Nez Perce	9.7	0.3	15.8	22.1	5.8	2.8	18.9	77.1	27.1	32.8	892	848
Oneida	0.9	0.0	0.2	0.9	1.5	0.1	0.1	11.5	5.5	2.7	672	613
Owyhee	2.2	0.5	1.4	4.2	0.9	0.7	1.0	21.0	13.3	3.9	384	374
Payette	1.7	0.0	4.3	10.5	4.0	0.7	21.9	33.8	18.2	9.7	481	437
Power	1.1	0.0	0.3	1.6	0.5	0.5	1.1	25.3	10.0	8.3	999	990
Shoshone	3.6	26.5	4.7	7.2	0.7	0.5	1.8	34.8	17.4	8.5	610	595
Teton	1.1	0.0	0.4	3.0	0.5	0.1	0.9	12.2	4.4	2.7	515	484
Twin Falls	26.4	0.0	13.1	25.1	6.8	1.9	7.2	186.4	75.2	36.0	588	554
Valley	9.4	0.0	6.1	1.5	0.6	0.2	6.2	37.0	11.7	10.3	1 270	1 218
Washington	2.1	0.0	0.4	5.1	0.8	0.3	6.3	28.0	12.3	6.1	608	591
ILLINOIS	6 000.0	1 310.5	2 169.8	4 707.8	2 194.0	1 027.0	2 657.5	X	X	X	X	X
Adams	16.0	3.8	3.6	29.1	6.4	2.4	10.5	134.8	68.6	39.8	587	507
Alexander	1.9	0.0	0.4	17.8	2.7	0.9	3.5	21.6	12.9	4.6	456	315
Bond	18.5	0.0	1.5	5.3	1.1	0.3	2.8	23.8	12.6	6.9	403	378
Boone	4.0	0.0	1.1	3.5	1.4	0.5	1.9	67.9	21.9	32.7	862	832
Brown	1.6	0.0	0.4	1.3	1.9	0.1	1.2	10.2	4.9	3.1	490	437
Bureau	7.7	0.0	1.5	4.4	1.8	0.7	1.6	92.2	33.8	27.1	760	744
Calhoun	1.3	1.1	1.1	2.4	0.4	0.1	0.2	13.7	10.2	2.1	417	386
Carroll	11.6	14.5	1.9	3.2	1.1	0.4	3.4	30.7	13.4	13.3	784	739
Cass	4.1	0.3	0.8	3.7	1.0	0.4	0.1	26.5	14.1	9.2	698	588
Champaign	71.6	36.9	14.9	71.3	14.9	14.0	176.4	372.4	147.4	150.3	892	780
Christian	4.6	0.0	1.5	9.4	2.2	0.7	3.0	69.8	36.4	22.3	644	635
Clark	2.7	0.2	0.7	4.3	0.9	0.4	6.6	29.2	14.3	9.2	524	459
Clay	2.7	0.0	0.7	7.7	1.1	0.5	0.8	29.8	14.2	6.6	455	429
Clinton	4.6	5.2	1.1	4.5	1.7	0.6	2.5	47.9	23.6	16.4	463	411
Coles	7.7	0.0	1.9	13.8	2.8	1.2	9.5	117.9	54.0	37.7	735	679
Cook	2 575.7	494.9	1 237.9	3 010.6	840.6	308.4	1 268.4	17 600.0	5 704.9	8 846.2	1 742	1 284
Crawford	3.1	0.2	1.0	5.3	1.1	0.3	1.9	48.6	15.3	12.3	582	576
Cumberland	1.7	0.0	0.4	2.7	3.0	0.2	1.1	20.6	10.8	6.5	581	572
De Kalb	11.5	0.1	2.8	9.9	2.7	3.2	6.2	194.4	58.2	98.2	1 175	993
De Witt	2.9	0.0	0.7	3.3	0.9	0.3	5.5	49.7	11.4	25.5	1 522	1 512
Douglas	3.2	0.0	7.8	2.7	0.9	0.4	1.7	32.5	12.6	15.5	783	649
Du Page	307.3	73.2	104.7	58.3	14.1	9.7	27.0	2 338.6	494.5	1 360.3	1 563	1 383
Edgar	3.7	0.0	1.3	5.7	1.5	0.8	3.6	37.3	17.5	12.5	630	597
Edwards	1.3	0.0	0.4	1.4	0.5	0.1	1.0	11.4	5.9	2.8	392	367
Effingham	8.7	0.3	2.1	6.8	4.0	0.5	10.4	59.3	33.9	18.7	561	551
Fayette	3.4	0.1	0.9	7.0	1.5	0.5	2.6	33.2	18.1	9.3	429	423
Ford	2.7	0.0	0.7	1.9	0.8	0.3	3.7	35.9	16.2	13.1	936	830
Franklin	10.1	0.4	28.6	19.5	4.2	3.0	13.3	70.0	42.0	15.1	371	356
Fulton	6.7	3.7	2.1	7.9	3.4	1.4	1.2	85.0	46.8	24.2	631	600
Gallatin	1.4	0.0	-1.9	4.9	0.8	0.3	0.4	12.5	7.0	3.4	507	459
Greene	2.9	0.0	0.8	7.3	1.4	0.5	6.4	26.2	14.7	6.8	436	398
Grundy	6.0	0.0	1.4	2.1	1.0	0.3	8.0	92.9	18.9	56.0	1 545	1 481
Hamilton	1.7	0.0	0.4	4.6	0.7	0.3	0.8	23.7	10.3	4.0	462	381
Hancock	4.4	1.2	1.1	4.8	1.3	0.6	1.2	42.0	20.1	15.0	711	685
Hardin	0.9	0.0	0.2	4.1	0.6	0.3	0.4	7.9	6.0	0.9	177	172
Henderson	1.8	0.4	0.4	2.0	0.6	0.2	1.4	15.3	8.4	5.0	575	557
Henry	8.7	0.3	1.8	5.4	2.8	1.1	3.0	114.1	47.7	32.2	626	589
Iroquois	5.9	0.0	1.5	3.5	1.6	0.5	11.8	57.8	25.2	23.5	748	731

1. October 1, 1998 to September 30, 1999.   2. State totals may include programs not allocated by county.   3. Based on the resident population estimated as of July 1 of the year shown.

Table B. States and Counties — Local Government Finances, Government Employment, and Elections

STATE County	Total (mil dol)	Per capita[1] (dollars)	Education	Health and hospitals	Police protec-tion	Public welfare	High-ways	Total (mil dol)	Per capita[1] (dollars)	Federal civilian	Federal military	State and local	Demo-cratic	Republi-can	All other
	183	184	185	186	187	188	189	190	191	192	193	194	195	196	197
IDAHO—Cont'd															
Custer	9.0	2 131	62.5	3.2	3.8	2.7	10.0	2.2	519	127	18	324	17.9	77.0	5.2
Elmore	50.2	2 018	58.8	10.9	3.8	1.1	7.2	16.3	656	1 029	4 257	1 236	26.4	70.2	3.4
Franklin	23.8	2 200	63.2	14.2	2.5	1.8	5.4	6.3	584	35	49	719	12.1	84.7	3.2
Fremont	29.8	2 524	59.7	1.7	2.7	4.9	6.9	25.5	2 157	132	53	838	13.7	83.4	2.9
Gem	23.9	1 653	53.1	15.9	6.0	1.1	5.8	4.1	280	91	66	676	22.5	73.1	4.4
Gooding	26.5	1 953	54.0	1.9	2.8	2.8	10.2	20.7	1 524	61	61	954	25.5	69.7	4.8
Idaho	33.1	2 193	42.6	0.2	4.5	3.7	23.0	11.5	764	467	67	931	15.9	77.9	6.2
Jefferson	34.0	1 794	77.8	0.3	2.7	0.6	5.6	9.9	523	49	85	1 010	14.0	82.7	3.3
Jerome	28.9	1 634	57.3	0.4	5.1	2.3	10.3	10.5	594	54	80	819	22.6	73.5	3.8
Kootenai	205.4	2 079	49.7	3.3	5.2	0.6	7.9	84.1	851	651	453	6 466	30.8	64.3	4.9
Latah	65.6	2 016	44.7	6.9	5.6	9.3	12.2	8.2	252	234	189	6 173	37.0	53.3	9.7
Lemhi	17.2	2 127	41.3	18.9	4.2	1.8	7.9	9.8	1 214	269	36	541	18.1	78.5	3.4
Lewis	15.5	3 799	62.3	0.6	4.1	2.3	15.9	3.0	737	38	18	366	19.8	76.7	3.4
Lincoln	9.1	2 385	59.0	0.2	3.4	1.3	13.0	3.5	926	98	17	376	27.8	66.6	5.6
Madison	51.7	2 200	47.6	24.5	3.0	0.3	5.3	16.6	705	51	105	1 453	9.1	88.5	2.4
Minidoka	61.6	2 983	35.5	32.2	4.6	5.9	4.5	10.9	528	74	90	1 320	20.6	75.3	4.1
Nez Perce	81.4	2 212	44.5	0.3	5.5	0.6	9.5	44.6	1 212	200	165	2 872	31.2	66.0	2.8
Oneida	13.4	3 347	54.2	13.4	3.8	0.1	6.7	5.1	1 269	31	18	366	17.1	79.3	3.6
Owyhee	20.4	1 995	63.4	0.3	3.1	0.0	8.0	8.9	871	31	46	589	19.5	76.9	3.6
Payette	31.8	1 573	62.0	0.9	5.1	1.0	5.6	16.2	800	46	91	993	24.0	72.3	3.7
Power	26.0	3 130	41.8	16.7	3.8	0.6	10.1	13.7	1 657	29	37	644	27.9	69.1	3.0
Shoshone	36.2	2 587	46.3	1.9	5.3	1.8	11.4	9.1	653	131	62	1 115	41.3	53.5	5.2
Teton	13.0	2 444	50.5	28.8	1.8	0.1	4.1	10.5	1 986	41	24	358	27.0	65.3	7.7
Twin Falls	194.3	3 170	47.0	27.8	2.9	0.9	6.2	41.3	674	579	278	4 327	25.6	70.1	4.3
Valley	35.7	4 409	27.7	20.4	14.0	1.0	10.2	17.9	2 215	286	36	744	28.4	64.1	7.6
Washington	27.8	2 758	38.4	14.9	5.4	0.9	7.3	6.1	604	57	45	640	24.1	71.2	4.7
ILLINOIS	X	X	X	X	X	X	X	X	X	95 718	58 239	715 325	54.6	42.6	2.8
Adams	130.3	1 921	53.1	1.9	5.1	0.2	9.6	78.8	1 161	314	153	4 128	40.5	57.6	1.9
Alexander	19.1	1 908	58.6	0.7	11.5	3.2	7.3	2.3	228	39	22	583	58.6	39.5	1.9
Bond	24.4	1 428	49.2	7.3	4.7	0.1	12.1	16.7	978	351	36	635	43.5	54.1	2.4
Boone	62.3	1 643	52.5	1.0	4.5	3.9	7.7	35.8	943	75	88	1 459	41.8	55.5	2.7
Brown	9.4	1 482	40.1	3.3	5.3	0.2	22.9	2.3	360	38	15	494	40.5	57.5	2.0
Bureau	92.1	2 587	43.7	24.7	3.0	3.7	7.6	24.5	688	149	80	2 303	46.1	50.7	3.2
Calhoun	13.3	2 672	31.0	0.0	2.1	5.3	21.3	0.2	46	31	11	257	50.3	47.2	2.4
Carroll	28.1	1 659	61.3	1.0	4.1	0.1	12.2	13.4	788	419	40	827	43.4	53.4	3.2
Cass	24.6	1 857	46.4	6.6	3.7	0.2	16.4	8.2	620	77	30	799	47.3	50.3	2.4
Champaign	353.7	2 099	49.8	0.6	5.7	2.7	6.9	124.5	739	1 356	453	30 021	47.8	46.6	5.6
Christian	68.2	1 972	55.2	3.5	3.6	0.3	9.1	12.7	366	95	78	1 745	46.0	51.0	2.9
Clark	28.2	1 608	50.7	2.6	6.5	0.2	16.8	5.4	308	55	37	792	39.0	58.5	2.4
Clay	28.5	1 972	48.6	16.8	3.9	0.2	7.9	6.3	439	57	33	859	36.1	61.8	2.2
Clinton	44.7	1 263	55.9	1.4	5.6	0.4	11.9	31.1	878	112	80	2 275	41.7	55.7	2.6
Coles	110.0	2 144	62.1	1.4	6.1	0.3	4.8	42.2	822	143	122	6 122	44.3	52.2	3.5
Cook	16 158.6	3 183	36.8	5.1	8.1	1.1	4.4	18 276.7	3 600	49 579	12 108	292 547	68.6	28.6	2.7
Crawford	46.2	2 193	39.5	32.4	2.7	0.2	10.7	5.6	265	64	47	1 335	39.2	58.5	2.3
Cumberland	26.2	2 344	32.8	3.2	2.4	0.2	12.4	7.0	623	35	25	483	37.6	59.6	2.8
De Kalb	183.3	2 192	47.9	1.3	5.1	4.4	8.9	100.7	1 204	226	197	10 860	44.5	51.6	3.9
De Witt	44.7	2 664	44.3	13.4	6.2	5.0	9.9	4.8	283	54	38	1 237	40.7	56.3	3.0
Douglas	30.0	1 518	53.7	0.3	5.7	1.9	11.3	15.9	805	66	45	811	39.4	58.1	2.5
Du Page	2 228.8	2 561	50.8	1.2	5.6	1.6	6.9	1 945.5	2 235	5 208	2 001	40 591	41.9	55.2	3.0
Edgar	35.4	1 778	56.0	5.0	4.1	0.2	9.5	11.3	568	70	44	1 143	39.1	58.7	2.2
Edwards	9.8	1 392	48.8	0.0	3.4	0.4	5.1	6.8	969	24	16	268	30.0	67.9	2.1
Effingham	58.5	1 757	55.3	0.3	4.4	1.2	14.9	36.9	1 108	178	77	1 794	29.2	68.0	2.8
Fayette	29.3	1 357	51.3	5.0	4.5	1.9	15.6	9.1	423	74	50	1 267	41.6	55.7	2.7
Ford	34.9	2 484	49.5	1.1	4.0	5.2	10.1	3.5	251	55	32	738	34.0	63.2	2.8
Franklin	67.7	1 665	56.3	5.3	6.1	1.3	6.5	35.6	876	239	91	1 910	53.1	44.2	2.7
Fulton	79.5	2 070	62.3	3.3	3.8	1.8	8.5	17.2	448	112	88	2 415	54.9	42.6	2.5
Gallatin	11.6	1 735	46.8	0.2	4.1	3.0	19.4	7.6	1 143	29	15	296	52.8	44.7	2.5
Greene	24.9	1 593	50.9	8.7	3.0	0.4	12.9	4.8	306	60	35	723	43.2	54.3	2.6
Grundy	93.3	2 574	60.3	0.9	4.5	4.6	8.0	42.9	1 183	112	83	1 803	45.3	52.5	2.2
Hamilton	22.0	2 552	37.3	33.3	1.0	0.5	11.9	6.3	726	40	19	625	42.4	54.9	2.7
Hancock	41.4	1 960	51.2	4.2	3.3	1.1	12.3	14.2	671	90	48	1 186	43.9	53.0	3.1
Hardin	7.4	1 498	67.5	1.5	2.8	1.6	10.5	2.4	478	12	11	303	44.9	51.8	3.3
Henderson	15.2	1 758	42.5	7.2	3.1	0.2	20.8	5.6	647	44	19	441	52.5	44.2	3.3
Henry	107.2	2 084	45.5	14.6	4.0	4.4	8.3	34.7	675	162	117	3 104	50.8	46.4	2.8
Iroquois	57.4	1 827	50.3	4.8	3.6	0.9	13.2	16.5	527	117	71	1 431	32.8	64.7	2.5

1. Based on the resident population estimated as of July 1 of the year shown.

Table B. States and Counties — **Land Area and Population**

STATE/ County code	MSA/ PMSA/ NECMA code[1]	County Type[2]	STATE County	Land area,[3] (sq km) 1990	Population and population characteristics, 1999			Race (percent)					Age (percent)					
					Total persons	Rank	Per square kilometer	White	Black	Am. Indian, Eskimo, Aleut	Asian and Pacific Islander	Percent Hispanic[4]	Under 5 years	5 to 17 years	18 to 24 years	25 to 34 years	35 to 44 years	45 to 54 years
				1	2	3	4	5	6	7	8	9	10	11	12	13	14	15
			ILLINOIS—Cont'd															
17 077	...	5	Jackson	1 523	60 651	785	39.8	83.4	11.6	0.2	4.7	2.4	5.4	14.3	26.0	13.4	13.5	9.9
17 079	...	7	Jasper	1 281	10 571	2 372	8.3	99.6	0.0	0.1	0.2	0.5	6.8	21.7	6.8	11.8	14.6	12.8
17 081	...	7	Jefferson	1 479	39 188	1 106	26.5	91.0	8.3	0.2	0.5	1.4	6.5	19.4	8.3	12.6	16.5	12.8
17 083	7040	1	Jersey	956	21 573	1 677	22.6	99.1	0.5	0.2	0.2	0.8	6.5	20.1	9.7	11.9	15.2	13.5
17 085	...	6	Jo Daviess	1 557	21 562	1 680	13.8	99.6	0.1	0.1	0.2	0.6	5.8	19.4	6.7	10.8	15.0	13.7
17 087	...	9	Johnson	896	13 598	2 168	15.2	87.8	11.8	0.3	0.2	2.5	4.3	14.9	9.9	16.6	17.9	14.5
17 089	1600	0	Kane	1 349	402 622	143	298.5	91.2	6.6	0.2	2.0	18.7	8.8	22.0	8.9	14.6	17.9	12.6
17 091	3740	3	Kankakee	1 755	102 720	505	58.5	82.2	16.6	0.2	1.0	2.9	7.3	21.3	8.9	12.1	15.8	12.8
17 093	1600	1	Kendall	830	53 659	859	64.6	98.2	0.7	0.3	0.8	6.4	7.1	22.5	8.0	12.6	18.5	15.6
17 095	...	4	Knox	1 855	55 373	836	29.9	92.9	6.2	0.1	0.8	3.7	5.5	17.7	8.8	11.4	16.1	13.1
17 097	1600	0	Lake	1 160	617 975	83	532.7	89.0	7.3	0.3	3.4	10.3	8.1	19.6	9.2	14.4	18.6	13.6
17 099	...	4	La Salle	2 940	110 248	478	37.5	97.7	1.4	0.2	0.7	4.5	6.3	19.1	8.2	11.8	15.0	13.2
17 101	...	7	Lawrence	963	15 149	2 055	15.7	98.5	1.0	0.2	0.2	0.5	5.6	18.3	6.9	11.3	14.9	13.0
17 103	...	7	Lee	1 879	35 734	1 200	19.0	94.5	4.4	0.3	0.8	3.1	6.3	19.1	7.8	13.5	16.5	13.0
17 105	...	6	Livingston	2 703	39 639	1 096	14.7	94.4	4.8	0.2	0.5	2.8	6.4	18.9	7.8	13.9	16.1	12.9
17 107	...	6	Logan	1 601	31 733	1 324	19.8	92.8	6.4	0.1	0.6	1.9	5.6	16.9	10.9	14.0	15.9	12.9
17 109	...	5	McDonough	1 526	35 228	1 219	23.1	92.7	4.0	0.2	3.1	1.4	4.6	13.7	27.5	10.4	12.3	10.4
17 111	1600	0	McHenry	1 565	246 812	217	157.7	98.6	0.2	0.2	1.0	4.6	8.2	21.0	7.5	14.3	19.4	14.0
17 113	1040	3	McLean	3 066	145 477	360	47.4	93.2	4.8	0.2	1.8	1.9	6.4	17.4	18.3	13.2	16.0	11.4
17 115	2040	3	Macon	1 504	113 219	463	75.3	85.9	13.3	0.1	0.6	0.7	6.2	19.2	8.4	11.4	16.3	13.5
17 117	...	6	Macoupin	2 237	49 020	924	21.9	98.6	0.9	0.2	0.3	0.6	6.0	19.9	7.8	11.0	15.2	12.9
17 119	7040	0	Madison	1 878	259 434	208	138.1	91.6	7.3	0.3	0.8	1.6	6.7	18.8	8.6	12.9	16.0	13.3
17 121	...	7	Marion	1 482	41 813	1 046	28.2	94.7	4.2	0.3	0.8	0.9	6.5	20.1	7.4	11.7	15.2	13.4
17 123	...	6	Marshall	1 000	12 974	2 218	13.0	99.2	0.2	0.3	0.3	0.9	5.4	19.3	6.9	10.2	15.5	13.6
17 125	...	6	Mason	1 396	16 797	1 944	12.0	99.4	0.1	0.2	0.4	0.5	6.1	19.7	7.1	10.7	15.5	14.1
17 127	...	7	Massac	619	15 414	2 043	24.9	92.7	6.7	0.3	0.4	0.5	5.4	18.7	7.2	11.5	14.6	14.5
17 129	7880	3	Menard	814	12 724	2 229	15.6	99.4	0.1	0.3	0.2	0.6	6.4	21.1	6.4	11.9	17.6	14.6
17 131	...	6	Mercer	1 453	17 644	1 894	12.1	99.3	0.3	0.2	0.3	1.0	6.0	20.4	6.8	10.9	16.0	15.0
17 133	7040	1	Monroe	1 006	27 289	1 453	27.1	99.2	0.1	0.3	0.4	1.1	6.8	19.7	7.4	13.2	16.1	13.8
17 135	...	6	Montgomery	1 823	31 318	1 342	17.2	96.4	3.1	0.2	0.3	1.4	6.1	18.8	7.9	13.3	15.5	12.3
17 137	...	4	Morgan	1 473	35 158	1 222	23.9	94.2	5.1	0.2	0.5	1.2	5.8	17.9	10.2	12.6	15.4	13.0
17 139	...	6	Moultrie	869	14 573	2 096	16.8	99.6	0.1	0.2	0.1	0.5	6.3	20.2	6.4	11.1	15.6	13.6
17 141	6880	2	Ogle	1 966	50 954	893	25.9	99.1	0.2	0.2	0.5	4.3	6.8	20.6	7.3	12.4	16.2	14.0
17 143	6120	2	Peoria	1 605	181 126	294	112.9	83.1	15.0	0.2	1.7	2.1	6.6	19.4	9.7	12.0	16.2	13.0
17 145	...	7	Perry	1 142	21 330	1 691	18.7	96.7	2.7	0.1	0.4	0.9	6.1	19.5	7.7	11.2	15.7	12.7
17 147	...	6	Piatt	1 140	16 623	1 961	14.6	99.7	0.1	0.1	0.1	0.4	5.8	19.5	6.4	11.7	16.6	14.9
17 149	...	7	Pike	2 151	17 220	1 917	8.0	99.6	0.1	0.1	0.2	0.6	5.9	19.0	7.0	10.3	15.1	13.1
17 151	...	9	Pope	961	4 811	2 854	5.0	92.7	6.7	0.4	0.2	1.9	4.7	18.7	11.2	11.2	14.6	14.5
17 153	...	9	Pulaski	520	7 304	2 651	14.0	63.7	36.1	0.1	0.1	0.5	6.8	22.6	6.9	10.9	12.9	12.3
17 155	...	9	Putnam	414	5 853	2 781	14.1	99.4	0.3	0.2	0.2	3.5	6.4	19.1	6.9	11.2	15.4	15.4
17 157	...	6	Randolph	1 498	33 600	1 268	22.4	90.8	8.7	0.2	0.3	1.3	5.7	18.5	8.8	14.2	16.2	12.7
17 159	...	7	Richland	933	16 654	1 956	17.8	99.3	0.1	0.2	0.4	0.7	6.3	19.4	7.2	11.8	14.4	13.7
17 161	1960	2	Rock Island	1 105	147 522	353	133.5	90.9	7.9	0.3	1.0	7.8	6.5	18.9	8.6	11.9	16.0	13.4
17 163	7040	0	St. Clair	1 719	260 050	206	151.3	69.0	29.7	0.2	1.1	2.1	7.5	21.1	8.8	13.4	15.7	11.7
17 165	...	7	Saline	993	26 044	1 492	26.2	95.5	4.0	0.3	0.2	0.7	5.7	18.6	7.2	10.7	14.9	13.9
17 167	7880	3	Sangamon	2 249	191 306	281	85.1	89.6	9.0	0.2	1.1	1.1	6.7	18.8	7.7	13.5	17.8	13.2
17 169	...	7	Schuyler	1 133	7 496	2 639	6.6	99.6	0.2	0.1	0.1	0.1	5.4	19.4	6.9	11.1	15.3	13.4
17 171	...	9	Scott	650	5 614	2 798	8.6	99.8	0.0	0.1	0.1	0.4	6.3	19.9	7.0	11.7	14.9	13.8
17 173	...	6	Shelby	1 965	22 505	1 635	11.5	99.6	0.1	0.1	0.2	0.3	6.2	19.5	7.2	11.3	14.6	13.7
17 175	...	8	Stark	746	6 282	2 753	8.4	99.3	0.2	0.1	0.4	0.6	5.7	19.3	6.4	10.3	14.9	13.8
17 177	...	4	Stephenson	1 461	48 778	927	33.4	91.7	7.2	0.1	0.9	0.9	6.5	19.0	7.7	12.1	15.6	13.6
17 179	6120	2	Tazewell	1 681	129 801	402	77.2	98.6	0.7	0.2	0.5	1.1	6.1	19.2	7.7	11.8	16.8	13.8
17 181	...	7	Union	1 078	18 023	1 869	16.7	98.5	0.7	0.3	0.4	1.5	5.8	17.8	7.2	11.1	15.7	15.3
17 183	...	4	Vermilion	2 329	83 813	604	36.0	88.7	10.2	0.2	0.9	2.4	6.2	19.4	7.5	11.9	15.9	13.4
17 185	...	7	Wabash	579	12 513	2 247	21.6	98.8	0.4	0.1	0.7	0.8	5.8	19.6	7.9	11.6	15.6	12.6
17 187	...	7	Warren	1 405	18 931	1 821	13.5	96.9	2.4	0.1	0.6	1.6	5.8	19.5	11.4	10.3	15.0	12.7
17 189	...	6	Washington	1 457	15 200	2 053	10.4	99.2	0.4	0.2	0.2	0.5	6.3	20.2	6.7	11.7	15.2	13.3
17 191	...	7	Wayne	1 849	16 967	1 930	9.2	99.3	0.2	0.2	0.4	0.6	5.8	18.6	7.5	10.9	14.2	14.2
17 193	...	6	White	1 282	15 566	2 031	12.1	99.0	0.5	0.2	0.3	0.5	5.6	17.8	6.3	11.2	14.7	13.4
17 195	...	4	Whiteside	1 774	59 606	799	33.6	98.5	0.9	0.1	0.4	10.5	6.5	20.0	7.4	11.5	15.7	13.2
17 197	1600	0	Will	2 169	478 392	116	220.6	86.2	11.7	0.2	1.9	7.8	7.8	22.0	8.8	13.7	18.5	13.4
17 199	...	5	Williamson	1 099	61 550	776	56.0	96.6	2.6	0.2	0.7	1.3	5.9	17.9	8.0	12.3	16.3	14.5
17 201	6880	2	Winnebago	1 331	268 126	205	201.4	87.8	10.2	0.3	1.7	4.4	7.1	19.1	8.4	13.4	16.8	13.4
17 203	6120	2	Woodford	1 368	35 553	1 204	26.0	98.9	0.4	0.2	0.5	1.0	6.6	21.7	7.5	10.9	17.2	13.4

1. MSA = Metropolitan Statistical Area. PMSA = Primary MSA. NECMA = New England County Metropolitan Area. See Appendix A for explanation of these concepts. See Appendix B for list of metropolitan areas identified by type, with component counties.   2. County typology code from the Economic Research Service of USDA. See Appendix A for definition.   3. Dry land or land partially or temporarily covered by water.   4. Hispanic persons may be of any race.

Table B. States and Counties — **Population and Households**

STATE County	55 to 64 years	65 to 74 years	75 years and over	Percent female	1990	1980	1980–1990	1990–1999	Births	Deaths	Net migration	Number	Percent change, 1980–1990	Persons per house-hold	Female family house-holder[1]	One person
	16	17	18	19	20	21	22	23	24	25	26	27	28	29	30	31
ILLINOIS—Cont'd																
Jackson	6.7	5.1	5.7	48.6	61 067	61 649	-0.9	-0.7	6 406	4 304	-2 385	23 466	4.0	2.30	8.9	32.1
Jasper	9.4	7.3	8.7	50.7	10 609	11 318	-6.3	-0.4	1 213	1 042	-167	3 962	-0.9	2.66	6.2	22.8
Jefferson	8.8	7.3	7.8	49.7	37 020	36 558	1.3	5.9	4 600	3 871	1 572	14 606	4.6	2.51	10.1	26.3
Jersey	9.4	6.9	6.8	50.7	20 539	20 538	0.0	5.0	2 320	2 003	784	7 344	7.7	2.68	8.1	22.0
Jo Daviess	10.1	9.4	9.0	50.6	21 821	23 520	-7.2	-1.2	2 300	1 987	-490	8 371	0.5	2.59	7.0	23.9
Johnson	9.4	6.1	6.5	39.7	11 347	9 624	17.9	19.8	1 015	1 061	2 309	3 725	12.8	2.48	6.7	24.1
Kane	7.0	4.2	4.0	50.2	317 471	278 405	14.0	26.8	61 120	21 489	44 480	107 176	14.3	2.90	9.9	19.9
Kankakee	8.7	6.7	6.3	51.3	96 255	102 926	-6.5	6.7	14 762	9 809	1 820	34 623	-0.9	2.68	12.5	24.3
Kendall	7.2	4.7	3.8	49.7	39 413	37 202	5.9	36.1	6 116	2 362	10 535	13 301	10.5	2.94	7.0	16.1
Knox	9.9	8.1	9.2	50.3	56 393	61 607	-8.5	-1.8	5 935	5 964	-831	21 909	-4.1	2.42	9.6	28.3
Lake	7.5	4.9	4.0	49.6	516 418	440 388	17.3	19.7	92 023	30 276	32 952	173 966	24.5	2.85	8.7	18.5
La Salle	9.7	8.1	8.6	50.5	106 033	112 033	-4.6	3.1	12 584	11 231	2 373	41 284	0.8	2.53	8.7	26.4
Lawrence	10.5	7.9	11.6	52.7	15 972	17 807	-10.3	-5.2	1 586	2 335	-14	6 320	-6.4	2.43	9.0	27.4
Lee	9.2	7.0	7.6	49.0	34 392	36 328	-5.3	3.9	3 928	3 313	830	12 475	-1.4	2.59	8.0	25.1
Livingston	9.1	6.7	8.3	50.0	39 301	41 381	-5.0	0.9	4 438	3 998	5	13 737	-2.4	2.58	7.8	24.7
Logan	8.5	6.8	8.4	48.0	30 798	31 802	-3.2	3.0	3 238	3 059	827	11 033	-2.3	2.49	8.6	26.9
McDonough	7.5	6.1	7.5	49.9	35 244	37 467	-5.9	0.0	2 907	2 886	72	12 255	-2.1	2.35	7.5	29.6
McHenry	7.2	4.3	4.1	49.6	183 241	147 897	23.9	34.7	33 731	12 588	42 780	62 940	28.2	2.89	7.1	16.9
McLean	7.3	4.8	5.2	51.8	129 180	119 149	8.4	12.6	17 454	8 667	7 383	46 796	12.2	2.52	8.3	26.1
Macon	9.5	7.7	7.7	52.2	117 206	131 375	-10.8	-3.4	15 070	11 085	-7 708	45 996	-4.8	2.49	11.4	26.4
Macoupin	10.1	8.0	9.2	51.6	47 679	49 384	-3.5	2.8	5 089	5 485	1 899	18 176	0.0	2.56	8.9	24.3
Madison	9.6	7.2	6.9	51.8	249 238	247 661	0.6	4.1	32 138	23 486	685	94 857	6.6	2.59	11.2	23.9
Marion	9.4	7.5	8.8	52.0	41 561	43 523	-4.5	0.6	5 427	4 764	-262	16 272	-1.0	2.51	10.7	26.7
Marshall	9.8	9.1	10.2	51.0	12 846	14 479	-11.3	1.0	1 384	1 454	248	4 900	-5.4	2.57	6.0	23.6
Mason	10.0	8.1	8.7	50.8	16 269	19 492	-16.5	3.2	1 852	1 768	504	6 342	-12.0	2.54	7.9	24.2
Massac	10.8	8.0	9.2	52.4	14 752	14 990	-1.6	4.5	1 611	1 925	1 027	5 908	3.1	2.44	10.2	26.7
Menard	8.9	5.8	7.3	51.6	11 164	11 700	-4.6	14.0	1 413	1 059	1 237	4 199	0.0	2.61	8.0	22.0
Mercer	9.4	7.4	8.1	50.9	17 290	19 286	-10.3	2.0	1 677	1 634	376	6 572	-3.2	2.60	6.8	22.8
Monroe	9.6	6.4	7.1	50.3	22 422	20 117	11.5	21.7	2 808	2 099	4 207	8 189	16.8	2.70	6.4	21.0
Montgomery	9.3	7.7	9.2	48.6	30 728	31 686	-3.0	1.9	3 323	3 431	804	11 480	-4.0	2.53	8.0	25.8
Morgan	9.2	7.2	8.0	50.7	36 397	37 502	-2.9	-3.4	3 946	3 716	-1 372	13 678	0.4	2.44	8.8	28.6
Moultrie	9.6	6.9	10.3	51.7	13 930	14 546	-4.2	4.6	1 696	1 894	917	5 122	-0.5	2.61	7.0	23.0
Ogle	9.0	6.5	7.1	50.7	45 957	46 338	-0.8	10.9	5 806	3 954	3 302	17 132	5.0	2.65	7.1	22.2
Peoria	8.9	7.0	7.3	51.8	182 827	200 466	-8.8	-0.9	25 239	16 030	-10 336	70 797	-3.5	2.49	12.3	28.1
Perry	9.3	8.4	9.4	51.1	21 412	21 714	-1.4	-0.4	2 349	2 354	-4	8 306	2.1	2.54	9.1	25.5
Piatt	9.9	7.6	7.8	51.0	15 548	16 581	-6.2	6.9	1 775	1 496	846	5 934	-0.1	2.58	6.5	21.7
Pike	10.4	8.5	10.6	51.2	17 577	18 896	-7.0	-2.0	1 869	2 089	-56	7 016	-4.1	2.47	6.9	26.5
Pope	9.7	7.2	8.2	45.9	4 373	4 404	-0.7	10.0	369	430	516	1 611	4.0	2.45	7.3	26.3
Pulaski	9.8	8.2	9.6	53.3	7 523	8 840	-14.9	-2.9	1 001	1 043	-158	2 957	-10.7	2.52	14.1	29.4
Putnam	9.6	8.4	7.7	49.5	5 730	6 085	-5.8	2.1	614	494	19	2 204	2.3	2.60	6.8	22.9
Randolph	8.6	6.9	8.4	46.3	34 583	35 652	-3.0	-2.8	3 436	3 298	-1 021	11 949	1.0	2.57	8.3	25.3
Richland	10.0	7.6	9.5	51.8	16 545	17 587	-5.9	0.7	1 938	1 774	-6	6 503	-3.2	2.49	8.1	26.0
Rock Island	9.4	7.7	7.5	51.6	148 723	166 759	-10.8	-0.8	18 581	14 315	-5 120	59 317	-2.8	2.44	11.5	28.6
St. Clair	8.9	6.6	6.3	52.2	262 852	267 531	-1.7	-1.1	38 132	24 539	-18 140	95 333	4.8	2.71	16.4	24.4
Saline	10.3	8.4	10.3	52.1	26 551	28 448	-6.7	-1.9	2 890	3 805	499	10 839	-3.7	2.36	10.0	30.1
Sangamon	8.8	6.6	7.0	52.6	178 386	176 070	1.3	7.2	23 930	16 015	-1 599	72 146	6.1	2.43	11.3	29.4
Schuyler	10.5	8.1	9.8	50.5	7 498	8 365	-10.4	0.0	783	844	88	3 002	-5.7	2.46	7.0	25.1
Scott	10.1	6.9	9.4	51.9	5 644	6 142	-8.1	-0.5	621	593	-41	2 190	-4.9	2.55	8.4	24.3
Shelby	10.4	8.1	9.0	50.4	22 261	23 923	-6.9	1.1	2 578	2 357	95	8 563	-1.7	2.58	6.1	22.7
Stark	9.7	9.2	10.7	51.4	6 534	7 389	-11.6	-3.9	736	799	-168	2 512	-5.3	2.55	6.2	25.3
Stephenson	9.3	7.9	8.2	51.4	48 052	49 536	-3.0	1.5	5 897	4 512	-500	18 920	2.6	2.50	8.3	26.0
Tazewell	9.8	7.4	7.4	50.7	123 692	132 078	-6.3	4.9	15 094	10 798	2 197	47 171	1.7	2.59	8.3	22.8
Union	10.2	7.7	9.2	50.9	17 619	17 765	-0.8	2.1	1 990	2 183	657	6 838	2.9	2.43	8.0	27.0
Vermilion	9.7	8.1	7.9	50.8	88 257	95 222	-7.3	-5.0	11 078	9 111	-6 218	34 072	-3.7	2.50	11.2	27.0
Wabash	9.7	8.4	8.9	51.8	13 111	13 713	-4.4	-4.6	1 305	1 289	-575	5 032	-2.5	2.56	7.9	25.3
Warren	9.0	7.5	8.8	51.3	19 181	21 943	-12.6	-1.3	2 102	2 092	-203	7 393	-6.3	2.48	8.4	27.5
Washington	9.5	7.9	9.3	50.8	14 965	15 472	-3.3	1.6	1 534	1 535	290	5 658	0.9	2.59	5.8	25.3
Wayne	10.3	8.3	10.0	51.5	17 241	18 059	-4.5	-1.6	1 749	1 874	-81	6 935	-0.6	2.46	7.1	25.4
White	10.6	9.1	11.2	52.4	16 522	17 864	-7.5	-5.8	1 616	2 145	-363	6 845	-2.9	2.36	7.3	28.0
Whiteside	9.5	8.1	8.0	51.1	60 186	65 970	-8.8	-1.0	7 292	5 640	-2 210	22 740	-2.0	2.60	8.3	23.6
Will	7.0	4.7	4.0	50.0	357 313	324 460	10.1	33.9	59 066	23 304	83 896	116 933	13.4	2.98	9.9	17.7
Williamson	9.3	7.8	8.0	51.0	57 733	56 538	2.1	6.6	6 459	6 426	3 971	23 120	5.9	2.44	9.4	27.5
Winnebago	8.8	6.9	6.2	51.3	252 913	250 884	0.8	6.0	36 487	21 076	-689	96 727	8.2	2.57	10.9	24.5
Woodford	8.6	6.6	7.4	50.6	32 653	33 320	-2.0	8.9	3 895	2 833	1 916	11 395	3.1	2.78	6.0	19.5

1. No spouse present.

Table B. States and Counties — **Vital Statistics, Health Resources, and Crime**

STATE County	Births, average 1996–1998 Total	Rate[1]	Deaths, average 1996–1998 Number Total	Infant[2]	Rate Total[1]	Infant[3]	Physicians,[4] 1998 Number	Rate[5]	Hospitals,[4] 1998 Number	Beds Number	Rate[5]	Medicare enrollees 1999	Serious crimes known to police, 1998[6] Total Number	Rate[7]
	32	33	34	35	36	37	38	39	40	41	42	43	44	45
ILLINOIS—Cont'd														
Jackson	668	11.0	470	7	7.7	11.0	137	227	2	192	318	7 642	NA	NA
Jasper	120	11.3	102	1	9.6	8.3	1	9	0	0	0	1 767	NA	NA
Jefferson	453	12.1	423	3	11.3	5.9	57	153	2	207	554	6 612	NA	NA
Jersey	249	11.7	224	1	10.5	4.0	15	70	1	67	313	2 895	NA	NA
Jo Daviess	239	11.0	218	1	10.1	2.8	14	65	1	85	396	4 271	NA	NA
Johnson	105	8.1	124	1	9.5	9.5	3	23	0	0	0	2 219	NA	NA
Kane	6 988	18.3	2 397	53	6.3	7.6	496	127	4	850	217	39 171	NA	NA
Kankakee	1 521	14.9	1 059	12	10.4	8.1	158	155	2	482	472	16 174	NA	NA
Kendall	728	14.6	283	5	5.7	6.4	22	42	0	0	0	3 903	NA	NA
Knox	641	11.5	640	4	11.5	6.2	86	155	2	330	594	10 856	NA	NA
Lake	10 219	17.2	3 434	57	5.8	5.5	1 498	248	7	1 473	243	58 885	NA	NA
La Salle	1 372	12.5	1 212	9	11.0	6.8	124	113	4	466	423	20 214	NA	NA
Lawrence	157	10.1	258	3	16.6	16.9	11	72	1	59	385	3 337	NA	NA
Lee	397	11.1	373	3	10.4	8.4	39	108	1	101	280	6 053	NA	NA
Livingston	449	11.2	429	3	10.7	5.9	26	65	1	84	212	6 178	NA	NA
Logan	336	10.7	328	3	10.5	7.9	18	58	1	66	211	5 346	NA	NA
McDonough	293	8.6	307	2	9.0	8.0	59	174	1	144	425	4 989	NA	NA
McHenry	3 853	16.3	1 461	21	6.2	5.4	248	103	3	378	157	23 204	NA	NA
McLean	1 937	13.7	944	16	6.7	8.4	264	185	2	322	226	16 265	NA	NA
Macon	1 542	13.5	1 212	15	10.6	9.5	198	174	2	581	511	20 007	NA	NA
Macoupin	520	10.6	588	2	12.0	3.9	18	37	2	90	184	9 723	NA	NA
Madison	3 334	12.9	2 637	29	10.2	8.7	297	115	6	961	371	42 267	NA	NA
Marion	547	13.0	521	5	12.4	8.5	57	136	2	324	774	8 755	NA	NA
Marshall	148	11.5	159	2	12.4	11.3	9	70	0	0	0	2 406	NA	NA
Mason	188	11.2	192	2	11.4	10.6	14	83	1	36	214	3 319	NA	NA
Massac	181	11.7	211	0	13.6	0.0	8	51	1	53	340	2 998	NA	NA
Menard	144	11.6	112	1	9.0	6.9	4	32	0	0	0	1 777	NA	NA
Mercer	179	10.2	179	2	10.2	9.3	5	28	1	45	255	2 774	NA	NA
Monroe	307	11.8	226	2	8.7	5.4	16	60	0	0	0	3 818	NA	NA
Montgomery	339	10.9	370	2	11.9	6.9	21	67	2	189	602	5 916	NA	NA
Morgan	407	11.4	394	5	11.0	11.5	50	141	1	159	450	6 475	NA	NA
Moultrie	177	12.3	206	1	14.3	3.8	7	49	0	0	0	3 017	NA	NA
Ogle	592	11.8	442	3	8.8	4.5	28	55	1	42	83	7 137	NA	NA
Peoria	2 649	14.5	1 743	24	9.6	9.2	606	334	3	1 074	591	29 533	NA	NA
Perry	244	11.5	257	1	12.2	5.5	14	67	2	125	594	4 181	NA	NA
Piatt	194	11.8	157	0	9.6	1.7	11	67	1	18	110	2 891	NA	NA
Pike	197	11.4	220	1	12.7	3.4	10	58	1	59	340	3 676	NA	NA
Pope	48	10.1	45	0	9.5	6.9	1	21	0	0	0	745	NA	NA
Pulaski	95	13.2	107	1	14.7	7.0	0	0	0	0	0	1 524	NA	NA
Putnam	62	10.8	54	1	9.3	10.7	0	0	0	0	0	1 052	NA	NA
Randolph	365	10.8	370	3	10.9	8.2	31	93	3	199	594	5 943	NA	NA
Richland	215	12.8	189	2	11.3	7.8	38	227	1	134	799	3 211	NA	NA
Rock Island	1 949	13.2	1 523	18	10.3	9.1	243	165	3	648	439	25 303	NA	NA
St. Clair	3 801	14.4	2 561	39	9.7	10.3	390	149	4	965	368	38 345	NA	NA
Saline	304	11.6	404	1	15.4	4.4	30	115	2	130	497	5 786	NA	NA
Sangamon	2 502	13.1	1 776	22	9.3	8.9	670	350	3	1 336	698	28 798	NA	NA
Schuyler	84	11.0	91	1	11.9	7.9	4	52	1	53	694	1 392	NA	NA
Scott	66	11.8	62	0	11.1	5.0	1	18	0	0	0	923	NA	NA
Shelby	263	11.6	249	1	11.0	5.1	6	26	1	53	233	4 291	NA	NA
Stark	80	12.6	89	1	14.1	8.3	1	16	0	0	0	1 297	NA	NA
Stephenson	623	12.7	497	3	10.1	4.8	78	159	1	166	339	9 041	NA	NA
Tazewell	1 566	12.3	1 181	11	9.2	7.0	111	87	2	154	120	21 219	NA	NA
Union	206	11.4	238	1	13.2	6.5	26	144	1	94	522	3 587	NA	NA
Vermilion	1 152	13.6	977	7	11.5	6.4	143	170	2	233	277	15 699	NA	NA
Wabash	137	10.8	141	2	11.2	14.6	7	55	1	56	443	2 377	NA	NA
Warren	226	12.0	208	1	11.0	3.0	13	69	1	77	409	3 326	NA	NA
Washington	157	10.3	159	1	10.4	6.4	6	39	1	61	397	2 691	NA	NA
Wayne	190	11.2	208	1	12.2	3.5	8	47	1	81	477	3 382	NA	NA
White	156	9.9	237	0	15.1	2.1	11	70	1	126	805	3 793	NA	NA
Whiteside	793	13.2	623	5	10.4	5.9	62	104	2	182	305	11 059	NA	NA
Will	7 027	15.8	2 682	58	6.0	8.2	429	93	2	646	141	42 570	NA	NA
Williamson	697	11.5	700	6	11.6	9.1	103	169	2	181	298	10 772	NA	NA
Winnebago	3 884	14.6	2 360	29	8.8	7.5	639	239	3	897	335	39 761	NA	NA
Woodford	413	11.8	326	4	9.3	8.9	23	65	1	34	97	4 769	NA	NA

1. Per 1,000 estimated resident population, average 1996–1998.   2. Deaths of infants under 1 year old.   3. Deaths of infants under 1 year old per 1,000 live births.   4. Data subject to copyright.   5. Per 100,000 resident population as of July 1 of the year shown.   6. Data for serious crimes have not been adjusted for underreporting; this may affect comparability between geographic areas and over time.   7. Per 100,000 population estimated by the FBI.

STATE County	Serious crimes known to police, 1998[1] (cont'd) Rate[2] Violent	Property	Education School enrollment and attainment, 1990 Enrollment[3] Total	Percent private	Attainment[4] (percent) High school graduate or more	Bachelor's degree or more	Local government expenditures, fiscal 1997[5] Total current expenditures (mil dol)	Current expenditures per student (dollars)	Money income 1989 Per capita[6] (dollars)	Households Median Dollars	Percent change, 1979-1989 (constant 1989 dollars)	Percent with $100,000 or more	Income and poverty, 1997 Median household income	Percent below poverty level All persons	Persons under 18	Persons 5-17 in families
	46	47	48	49	50	51	52	53	54	55	56	57	58	59	60	61
ILLINOIS—Cont'd																
Jackson	NA	NA	27 965	4.2	78.8	29.5	45.9	5 697	10 003	17 567	-10.9	1.6	27 109	21.0	28.3	27.8
Jasper	NA	NA	2 505	7.9	69.7	8.1	12.2	6 118	10 298	22 751	-7.1	1.1	32 578	11.9	17.7	17.9
Jefferson	NA	NA	8 735	4.5	69.9	11.3	33.8	4 831	11 279	22 397	-9.5	1.8	31 850	17.0	25.1	23.9
Jersey	NA	NA	5 603	25.3	71.9	9.3	14.3	4 329	11 132	27 126	-6.7	1.0	37 772	10.1	15.1	13.9
Jo Daviess	NA	NA	5 216	15.6	74.1	12.1	19.0	4 922	12 497	26 882	-4.5	2.0	37 575	7.8	11.6	11.3
Johnson	NA	NA	2 650	4.2	66.2	9.1	8.7	4 589	9 170	21 953	5.3	0.5	30 621	16.5	22.5	21.3
Kane	NA	NA	88 277	18.4	77.7	21.4	455.5	5 153	15 890	40 080	8.2	5.9	53 337	6.8	9.8	10.1
Kankakee	NA	NA	26 064	17.1	73.1	11.9	102.2	5 580	12 142	28 284	-2.9	1.8	37 436	12.9	19.5	18.6
Kendall	NA	NA	11 335	11.9	83.7	17.8	46.8	5 067	16 115	42 834	4.3	4.4	58 694	3.8	5.3	5.2
Knox	NA	NA	13 887	13.8	76.6	12.7	45.6	5 290	11 973	24 523	-14.4	1.7	33 536	12.7	19.0	18.2
Lake	NA	NA	138 258	19.6	84.7	32.0	738.6	6 712	21 765	46 047	9.0	13.7	63 354	5.9	8.9	8.6
La Salle	NA	NA	25 539	13.5	73.1	10.5	101.6	5 836	12 337	27 093	-13.1	1.8	37 439	9.9	14.3	14.1
Lawrence	NA	NA	3 490	3.9	69.2	6.3	13.6	5 030	10 120	19 688	-16.3	0.5	28 505	14.7	21.3	22.3
Lee	NA	NA	8 623	10.4	76.3	11.8	29.7	5 081	12 050	28 284	-9.0	1.8	38 947	8.7	12.4	12.1
Livingston	NA	NA	8 930	8.5	74.1	9.4	42.0	5 271	12 124	29 848	-7.5	1.5	41 414	9.7	13.5	13.4
Logan	NA	NA	7 413	22.3	75.9	12.5	22.6	5 434	11 576	27 528	-4.5	0.8	37 223	11.6	16.1	15.5
McDonough	NA	NA	15 236	3.3	80.3	23.2	25.5	5 673	10 089	21 774	-8.0	1.5	32 790	15.6	19.6	18.7
McHenry	NA	NA	48 681	13.5	84.5	21.0	201.8	5 147	17 271	43 471	10.5	6.4	59 162	3.5	4.8	4.9
McLean	NA	NA	45 875	11.4	84.7	29.0	114.8	5 191	14 138	31 366	0.9	3.2	46 615	8.8	12.2	11.6
Macon	NA	NA	29 951	15.7	76.2	14.8	98.9	5 127	13 762	28 598	-8.7	2.5	38 653	14.0	23.2	21.1
Macoupin	NA	NA	11 697	9.9	72.8	9.2	47.1	4 631	11 365	23 913	-8.4	1.1	33 934	12.1	17.9	17.4
Madison	NA	NA	64 379	14.0	75.8	14.4	214.9	4 927	13 272	29 861	-3.0	2.3	39 405	11.0	17.3	16.0
Marion	NA	NA	9 961	7.2	70.1	9.6	46.8	5 513	11 500	22 813	-6.3	1.7	30 867	15.4	23.0	22.0
Marshall	NA	NA	3 053	5.4	77.8	10.3	8.9	5 145	12 109	26 450	-14.2	1.3	38 347	9.0	13.3	12.4
Mason	NA	NA	3 920	4.1	72.6	8.8	18.6	5 072	11 036	22 434	-19.7	0.8	33 274	12.1	18.3	18.1
Massac	NA	NA	3 279	3.8	65.3	8.0	12.6	4 788	10 136	19 632	-10.9	0.8	29 159	15.1	24.9	23.6
Menard	NA	NA	2 703	3.4	77.3	13.8	11.6	4 133	12 954	29 326	-7.1	1.9	42 678	9.0	14.1	13.7
Mercer	NA	NA	4 198	5.7	77.4	11.3	16.2	4 383	12 058	26 606	-11.6	1.7	38 584	9.3	14.1	13.2
Monroe	NA	NA	5 594	20.5	75.9	13.7	19.1	4 554	13 886	35 086	4.4	1.8	49 620	4.7	6.8	6.8
Montgomery	NA	NA	7 352	8.0	72.2	8.1	25.6	4 496	10 724	23 879	-3.8	1.4	33 368	13.7	19.7	18.9
Morgan	NA	NA	8 978	23.3	75.9	16.0	31.2	5 262	12 372	26 403	-2.8	2.3	36 018	11.9	18.1	17.0
Moultrie	NA	NA	3 174	8.8	70.3	9.5	8.7	4 446	11 840	26 852	-7.6	1.6	37 859	8.3	11.5	12.5
Ogle	NA	NA	11 394	5.9	77.6	12.1	57.4	5 610	12 880	30 958	-3.6	1.3	42 064	7.0	9.9	9.6
Peoria	NA	NA	50 947	23.7	77.9	19.5	155.9	5 546	13 924	28 193	-13.3	3.3	39 579	13.5	22.1	20.6
Perry	NA	NA	5 263	12.2	67.8	7.3	15.4	4 866	10 751	22 979	-15.5	0.8	30 674	13.9	20.5	20.2
Piatt	NA	NA	3 825	5.8	83.0	15.9	18.2	5 217	13 690	31 369	-3.7	2.1	43 109	6.7	9.6	9.4
Pike	NA	NA	3 853	5.8	69.9	8.1	16.3	5 198	10 200	20 527	-1.2	1.1	29 308	14.2	20.4	20.6
Pope	NA	NA	1 161	2.0	65.2	6.3	3.6	5 152	8 977	19 031	-5.3	0.7	28 308	17.3	24.0	28.0
Pulaski	NA	NA	2 178	2.5	59.8	6.1	12.3	7 081	8 479	15 625	-1.1	0.8	22 768	25.9	39.8	38.8
Putnam	NA	NA	1 361	10.8	75.8	9.8	5.0	4 709	13 672	30 136	-11.1	2.1	42 300	7.0	9.7	10.7
Randolph	NA	NA	8 187	14.1	64.2	8.3	25.4	5 077	11 155	25 859	-12.6	1.1	33 754	12.0	16.7	16.3
Richland	NA	NA	4 117	12.5	73.5	11.9	13.6	4 661	11 692	23 013	-4.8	2.0	31 468	12.9	19.6	19.2
Rock Island	NA	NA	38 550	17.5	77.4	15.0	126.9	5 366	13 214	26 803	-19.8	2.2	37 213	11.8	19.2	18.4
St. Clair	NA	NA	73 302	15.6	72.6	14.7	241.2	5 145	11 916	26 813	-0.7	2.2	35 439	16.1	24.7	23.5
Saline	NA	NA	6 041	2.4	63.2	9.4	22.2	4 817	10 066	18 349	-11.7	1.3	25 876	18.7	29.5	28.2
Sangamon	NA	NA	44 847	17.9	81.8	22.4	162.6	5 653	14 947	30 350	0.1	2.8	40 851	10.0	16.8	15.7
Schuyler	NA	NA	1 704	3.9	69.4	10.7	6.0	4 960	10 080	21 080	-11.4	0.7	30 794	11.4	15.7	17.1
Scott	NA	NA	1 205	7.8	73.6	9.2	5.4	4 999	10 505	23 642	-4.0	1.0	33 609	11.1	16.2	17.3
Shelby	NA	NA	5 209	6.1	72.7	9.8	15.4	4 463	11 608	26 040	-2.2	1.5	34 827	10.0	14.6	14.9
Stark	NA	NA	1 592	3.2	77.0	10.8	7.1	5 625	11 241	25 130	-12.7	0.9	35 747	9.8	14.1	14.6
Stephenson	NA	NA	11 418	9.3	76.7	13.6	40.4	4 957	13 156	28 340	-4.0	2.1	38 935	9.5	14.5	14.0
Tazewell	NA	NA	31 276	10.7	78.6	13.6	106.1	5 153	13 681	30 933	-12.7	2.1	42 860	8.4	12.6	11.9
Union	NA	NA	4 006	3.4	64.2	10.9	17.2	4 854	10 180	20 173	-11.0	1.3	28 982	16.8	26.8	25.7
Vermilion	NA	NA	21 697	9.4	72.8	11.1	78.8	5 334	11 771	23 841	-12.2	1.6	31 903	15.1	23.0	22.0
Wabash	NA	NA	3 324	8.8	74.9	12.6	10.8	4 674	12 072	26 021	-4.8	2.4	32 639	12.3	18.7	18.3
Warren	NA	NA	5 154	19.0	76.3	14.5	15.9	4 869	10 591	22 259	-16.8	1.1	31 412	13.3	18.3	19.1
Washington	NA	NA	3 459	14.9	65.7	8.7	10.6	4 368	11 539	25 387	-3.2	1.7	36 681	8.1	11.0	11.1
Wayne	NA	NA	3 946	5.6	63.1	8.7	14.6	4 846	10 139	20 659	-5.2	1.1	30 246	12.0	17.0	17.7
White	NA	NA	3 693	3.1	66.2	9.5	19.7	6 588	11 332	20 662	-10.8	1.5	29 569	15.3	23.7	23.9
Whiteside	NA	NA	15 402	10.9	73.3	9.9	59.1	5 421	12 245	27 085	-19.6	1.4	37 453	9.2	13.6	13.5
Will	NA	NA	101 606	18.6	80.4	18.0	365.2	5 245	15 186	41 195	5.4	4.5	54 061	6.5	9.3	9.0
Williamson	NA	NA	14 003	4.9	71.8	14.2	52.0	5 355	11 254	22 043	-8.1	1.1	31 147	14.9	23.7	22.6
Winnebago	NA	NA	62 777	18.5	76.3	16.7	264.6	6 065	14 516	31 336	-7.5	3.0	41 000	10.4	16.7	15.8
Woodford	NA	NA	9 138	12.8	80.0	15.4	38.4	4 930	13 516	34 375	-3.4	2.5	49 396	6.3	8.1	8.7

1. Data for serious crimes have not been adjusted for underreporting; this may affect comparability between geographic areas and over time. 2. Per 100,000 population estimated by the FBI. 3. All persons 3 years old and over enrolled in nursery school through college. 4. Persons 25 years old and over. 5. Elementary and secondary education expenditures, local government fiscal years ending between July 1, 1996 and June 30, 1997. 6. Based on population enumerated as of April 1, 1990.

Table B. States and Counties — **Personal Income**

STATE County	Personal income, 1998												
			Per capita[1]					Transfer payments					
									Government payments to individuals				
	Total (mil dol)	Percent change, 1997–1998	Dollars	Rank	Wages and salaries[2] (mil dol)	Proprietor's income (mil dol)	Dividends, interest, and rent (mil dol)	Total (mil dol)	Total (mil dol)	Social Security (mil dol)	Medical payments (mil dol)	Income mainte-nance (mil dol)	Unemploy-ment insurance (mil dol)
	62	63	64	65	66	67	68	69	70	71	72	73	74
ILLINOIS—Cont'd													
Jackson	1 174	4.6	19 294	1 957	791	79	236	200	188	63	62	27	6
Jasper	202	-4.9	18 958	2 075	81	25	52	35	33	17	10	3	2
Jefferson	820	5.3	20 999	1 391	528	79	160	158	151	62	58	17	5
Jersey	452	3.0	21 021	1 382	118	18	94	72	68	35	23	5	2
Jo Daviess	590	8.2	27 442	269	214	75	165	72	68	41	20	4	2
Johnson	186	4.3	13 767	3 028	64	17	39	42	39	19	12	4	1
Kane	10 864	7.3	27 736	249	6 360	451	1 830	862	785	340	306	73	33
Kankakee	2 312	3.3	22 596	953	1 314	104	425	409	389	159	155	45	13
Kendall	1 452	9.5	28 026	237	587	50	220	98	88	54	20	5	3
Knox	1 269	4.9	22 830	883	761	89	251	250	239	100	95	18	5
Lake	26 265	7.4	43 174	17	14 213	2 138	5 441	1 383	1 269	635	458	92	37
La Salle	2 510	4.2	22 782	894	1 375	162	566	409	388	211	122	23	17
Lawrence	348	6.8	22 699	924	125	33	95	77	74	31	33	6	2
Lee	758	0.7	21 083	1 363	393	37	184	125	117	60	43	7	3
Livingston	895	0.9	22 575	962	481	55	188	132	125	67	44	8	3
Logan	617	-0.3	19 358	1 932	305	30	141	113	107	52	40	7	2
McDonough	677	2.3	19 080	2 030	434	49	149	106	99	49	30	10	2
McHenry	7 646	11.0	31 721	121	2 825	319	1 161	503	455	250	145	23	21
McLean	3 908	5.8	27 260	283	2 973	199	715	353	325	164	96	28	10
Macon	2 918	4.3	25 674	419	2 062	160	579	455	433	200	140	52	12
Macoupin	1 100	4.0	22 561	968	311	84	222	198	189	91	69	15	4
Madison	6 354	4.3	24 514	557	3 103	297	1 202	984	933	422	348	89	19
Marion	911	3.4	21 728	1 183	499	71	186	210	202	69	91	17	6
Marshall	294	2.0	22 828	886	95	22	76	50	47	26	16	3	1
Mason	358	5.8	21 261	1 304	109	35	76	71	68	33	24	6	2
Massac	303	4.3	19 486	1 897	158	17	60	70	67	29	27	7	1
Menard	315	5.3	25 142	475	57	28	57	38	36	19	12	3	1
Mercer	397	3.9	22 538	969	83	30	75	57	54	30	17	4	2
Monroe	705	8.4	26 474	344	180	35	155	79	74	38	26	3	1
Montgomery	629	0.6	20 014	1 705	293	49	149	128	122	56	45	10	6
Morgan	797	1.7	22 511	976	442	52	185	138	131	63	47	12	3
Moultrie	297	2.2	20 524	1 548	101	27	56	54	51	26	19	3	1
Ogle	1 181	5.2	23 377	776	567	79	226	144	134	76	40	9	5
Peoria	5 016	5.4	27 638	257	3 632	235	1 113	676	640	300	219	81	14
Perry	393	2.3	18 470	2 221	164	23	88	91	87	39	30	7	3
Piatt	406	1.4	24 681	530	97	42	74	53	50	26	18	3	1
Pike	328	6.7	19 002	2 058	109	47	73	71	68	33	25	6	2
Pope	71	4.2	14 966	2 931	25	7	12	18	17	7	6	2	1
Pulaski	123	2.5	16 860	2 642	57	7	20	37	36	13	13	7	1
Putnam	143	-1.1	24 600	546	94	6	30	19	18	10	5	1	1
Randolph	632	4.1	18 781	2 125	360	40	148	125	118	57	42	9	3
Richland	371	1.5	22 115	1 062	206	33	84	67	64	30	22	6	2
Rock Island	3 952	4.6	26 719	327	3 182	270	867	526	497	250	161	48	12
St. Clair	5 897	3.0	22 527	971	3 230	223	1 176	1 042	992	363	378	159	21
Saline	501	2.8	19 145	2 002	259	38	109	137	132	54	51	14	3
Sangamon	5 237	4.2	27 351	277	3 764	368	1 084	646	609	288	208	64	19
Schuyler	144	5.2	19 019	2 051	49	16	31	26	25	13	8	2	1
Scott	100	1.2	17 804	2 405	66	8	21	20	19	10	6	2	1
Shelby	453	4.1	19 979	1 719	149	53	89	81	77	36	29	6	2
Stark	137	0.3	21 709	1 189	35	16	34	28	26	14	10	2	0
Stephenson	1 303	7.4	26 666	330	763	113	298	174	164	87	52	13	4
Tazewell	3 358	6.2	25 966	401	2 283	216	691	446	421	217	142	28	17
Union	348	4.1	19 353	1 935	146	24	71	84	81	30	36	9	3
Vermilion	1 726	2.0	20 436	1 581	1 049	79	348	348	331	150	107	40	11
Wabash	242	-0.2	19 237	1 977	119	15	65	50	47	23	16	4	1
Warren	340	0.7	17 979	2 348	135	34	73	65	61	29	22	6	1
Washington	369	5.7	24 087	623	183	46	81	61	58	26	24	3	1
Wayne	338	2.7	19 932	1 734	128	43	78	70	67	32	24	6	2
White	335	0.1	21 496	1 252	131	41	86	76	73	34	28	6	2
Whiteside	1 422	4.2	23 761	685	748	88	307	231	219	110	84	14	4
Will	12 018	8.9	26 114	388	4 728	511	1 740	1 071	980	447	357	83	42
Williamson	1 298	4.9	21 165	1 341	643	106	251	248	236	106	78	24	10
Winnebago	7 014	4.5	26 203	375	5 114	360	1 360	895	842	423	286	86	25
Woodford	857	3.3	24 352	582	276	53	169	100	93	52	31	5	2

1. Based on the resident population estimated as of July 1 of the year shown.   2. Includes other labor income.

Table B. States and Counties — Earnings, Social Security, and Housing

STATE County	Earnings, 1998 Total (mil dol)	Farm	Goods-related[1] Total	Manu-facturing	Service-related and other[2] Total	Retail trade	Finance, insurance, and real estate	Services	Govern-ment	Social Security beneficiaries, December 1998 Number	Rate[3]	Supplemental Security Income recipients, December 1998	Housing units, 1990 Total	Percent change, 1980–1990
	75	76	77	78	79	80	81	82	83	84	85	86	87	88
ILLINOIS—Cont'd														
Jackson	870	1.1	D	4.3	D	10.1	3.2	23.8	45.4	8 135	135	1 427	25 539	4.3
Jasper	106	13.2	16.9	10.9	50.5	7.9	3.4	8.7	19.3	2 146	202	172	4 297	-3.1
Jefferson	607	1.2	31.4	21.4	55.4	12.6	4.7	25.0	11.9	7 489	200	919	16 075	4.6
Jersey	136	-0.8	8.2	2.2	65.8	16.1	3.7	32.0	26.8	4 081	191	252	8 216	3.4
Jo Daviess	289	6.7	D	24.7	D	10.7	3.4	21.8	11.3	4 870	227	167	10 757	11.2
Johnson	81	3.7	D	2.2	D	8.2	3.7	13.6	49.2	2 414	182	305	4 671	11.6
Kane	6 811	0.2	32.2	24.8	53.5	7.9	6.6	27.7	14.2	35 532	91	3 594	111 496	13.1
Kankakee	1 418	1.2	D	24.7	D	11.1	4.4	24.1	15.5	18 258	179	2 725	37 001	-1.6
Kendall	637	0.3	D	48.3	D	8.6	3.5	9.7	10.7	5 629	109	105	13 747	9.8
Knox	850	3.7	29.6	24.2	54.1	9.2	2.6	24.6	12.6	11 507	207	1 125	23 722	-3.7
Lake	16 352	0.0	D	22.8	D	8.1	9.2	25.1	15.6	65 450	108	4 339	183 283	21.8
La Salle	1 537	0.6	27.7	20.1	58.4	11.2	4.5	19.9	13.4	23 097	210	1 085	43 827	0.8
Lawrence	159	4.1	D	3.8	D	7.1	9.6	17.6	16.5	3 822	249	362	6 980	-5.1
Lee	430	0.4	34.7	29.6	44.6	8.1	3.8	23.0	20.4	6 802	189	482	13 314	-0.3
Livingston	536	1.7	42.6	36.3	36.3	7.5	3.1	14.9	19.4	7 398	186	478	14 365	-4.1
Logan	335	-0.8	D	18.4	D	11.7	4.1	18.0	26.0	5 949	190	424	11 638	-3.4
McDonough	483	3.0	19.5	15.3	41.4	19.7	3.0	12.3	36.0	5 964	176	512	13 257	-4.9
McHenry	3 144	0.3	44.0	31.8	44.6	8.5	4.0	20.1	11.1	26 111	108	933	65 985	24.6
McLean	3 172	0.1	18.7	13.4	68.3	7.9	28.9	21.9	13.1	18 142	127	1 336	49 164	8.3
Macon	2 222	0.2	41.8	32.9	49.0	8.7	3.2	20.6	9.1	22 232	195	3 043	50 049	-3.0
Macoupin	394	2.6	29.4	14.0	50.5	9.9	4.0	18.7	17.5	10 664	218	869	20 068	-0.1
Madison	3 401	0.2	36.9	29.0	46.8	9.4	3.9	22.9	16.1	47 837	184	4 625	101 098	7.9
Marion	570	3.1	36.2	30.8	46.4	7.2	2.6	22.2	14.3	8 510	203	1 052	18 123	1.7
Marshall	117	7.5	D	33.2	D	8.5	4.3	18.6	9.7	2 894	225	102	5 317	-6.5
Mason	145	15.8	D	12.9	45.2	10.0	3.0	14.0	22.4	3 832	228	306	7 684	-9.3
Massac	175	1.7	D	22.8	D	7.9	3.1	25.3	14.8	3 582	230	477	6 446	3.7
Menard	85	12.2	D	2.0	D	10.6	5.5	16.6	23.1	2 125	170	124	4 650	0.9
Mercer	112	11.7	20.5	13.3	38.7	8.1	3.5	13.3	29.2	3 517	199	143	7 244	-4.7
Monroe	216	5.8	20.4	4.1	56.5	14.0	4.7	22.2	17.3	4 314	162	137	8 774	17.8
Montgomery	343	4.2	23.6	16.3	53.2	9.3	4.1	22.6	19.0	6 663	212	571	12 456	-3.6
Morgan	494	0.9	D	27.1	D	9.4	4.6	24.5	16.2	7 350	208	853	14 724	1.1
Moultrie	128	1.8	36.3	24.1	48.2	10.0	3.4	18.2	13.7	2 979	207	136	5 384	-1.9
Ogle	645	2.3	36.7	31.4	48.0	6.3	3.1	14.8	13.0	8 539	169	270	18 052	4.4
Peoria	3 866	0.3	23.8	17.9	64.8	9.4	6.1	38.4	11.1	33 112	182	4 900	75 211	-5.2
Perry	187	2.2	D	27.1	D	9.3	3.4	D	21.5	4 534	215	405	9 235	2.5
Piatt	139	2.6	D	11.5	D	10.1	4.7	29.3	18.2	2 948	180	126	6 227	-1.4
Pike	156	20.3	D	5.4	D	12.4	4.2	17.3	17.7	4 115	237	385	8 057	-2.6
Pope	32	1.7	D	3.8	D	5.4	1.0		42.8	961	200	119	2 154	11.5
Pulaski	64	2.3	26.1	4.7	32.8	4.6	1.5	15.8	38.8	1 762	245	407	3 410	-6.8
Putnam	101	1.2	65.1	55.4	D	3.8	2.4	D	6.7	1 153	198	57	2 600	5.6
Randolph	400	2.5	D	21.9	38.7	9.4	3.5	13.5	27.4	6 675	199	424	13 179	2.0
Richland	239	4.1	D	22.6	44.9	12.4	4.6	15.5	21.5	3 751	224	361	7 142	-4.0
Rock Island	3 452	0.2	31.1	25.1	47.8	7.2	5.2	21.2	20.9	28 345	192	2 670	63 327	-0.3
St. Clair	3 453	0.3	15.6	9.4	54.0	10.1	5.3	26.5	30.2	43 273	165	8 815	103 432	6.1
Saline	297	1.5	31.1	3.7	46.6	9.8	3.4	21.7	20.7	6 619	253	1 205	12 350	0.2
Sangamon	4 132	0.5	9.3	4.0	59.5	7.3	8.9	32.4	30.7	34 039	178	4 321	76 873	5.5
Schuyler	65	9.0	25.1	4.2	44.3	10.1	2.7	17.7	21.7	1 631	214	111	3 329	-7.7
Scott	74	4.9	50.0	2.2	D	3.4	2.3	D	12.3	1 148	205	84	2 442	-3.7
Shelby	202	8.0	D	22.4	D	9.0	3.7	19.3	15.8	4 351	191	301	9 329	-5.6
Stark	51	21.8	D	11.9	D	6.6	5.0	14.1	17.9	1 570	250	66	2 716	-5.5
Stephenson	876	6.1	47.9	39.0	36.7	5.9	8.9	15.9	9.3	9 942	203	755	20 378	5.5
Tazewell	2 500	1.3	54.3	47.3	36.0	6.8	3.4	11.4	8.4	23 650	185	1 543	49 315	0.9
Union	170	2.0	D	12.3	D	9.4	2.6	19.8	37.6	4 035	224	730	7 408	4.8
Vermilion	1 127	0.1	32.0	26.6	47.4	9.6	4.5	19.0	20.5	17 747	211	2 689	37 061	-3.4
Wabash	134	-2.3	44.0	21.3	40.7	8.9	4.4	16.7	17.6	2 674	212	221	5 572	-2.4
Warren	169	8.2	D	21.9	D	10.1	4.3	21.8	18.0	3 324	177	308	8 229	-4.0
Washington	229	10.7	D	24.8	D	9.2	3.1	10.8	10.8	3 144	205	117	6 261	-0.1
Wayne	171	6.4	34.5	24.6	44.5	9.5	4.8	16.2	14.6	3 901	230	260	7 622	-2.2
White	173	5.0	27.0	5.0	48.3	12.3	4.0	17.8	19.6	4 157	266	422	7 797	-0.6
Whiteside	836	2.3	D	37.6	D	8.8	4.1	16.1	14.3	12 366	207	859	24 000	-0.4
Will	5 239	0.4	31.2	18.1	53.0	8.9	4.5	25.1	15.4	48 328	105	3 408	122 870	12.0
Williamson	749	0.0	19.7	11.3	54.5	15.7	6.6	20.2	25.7	12 737	209	1 374	25 183	3.7
Winnebago	5 474	0.2	42.1	36.7	48.1	7.8	5.7	23.4	9.5	45 806	171	5 044	101 666	9.1
Woodford	329	3.3	35.8	27.8	45.2	8.9	2.5	17.4	15.7	5 725	163	156	11 932	1.1

1. Covers mining, construction, and manufacturing. 2. Covers private sector earnings in agricultural services, forestry, and fisheries; transportation and public utilities; wholesale trade; retail trade; finance, insurance, and real estate; and services. 3. Per 1,000 resident population estimated as of July 1 of the year shown.

STATE County	Housing units, 1990 (cont'd)								Civilian labor force, 1999				Civilian employment, 1990[5]		
	Occupied units										Unemployment			Percent	
	Owner-occupied					Renter-occupied									
				Owner cost as a percent of income											
	Total	Percent	Median value[1]	With a mortgage	Without a mortgage	Median rent[2]	Rent as percent of income	Substandard units[3] (percent)	Total	Percent change, 1998–1999	Total	Rate[4]	Total	Professional, managerial, and technical	Precision production, craft, and repair
	89	90	91	92	93	94	95	96	97	98	99	100	101	102	103
ILLINOIS—Cont'd															
Jackson	23 466	52.7	47 100	19.7	13.1	314	35.1	3.6	29 207	3.2	1 199	4.1	26 855	34.0	7.3
Jasper	3 962	82.6	39 400	16.3	12.8	259	25.2	2.9	3 848	1.9	309	8.0	4 600	16.3	13.2
Jefferson	14 606	73.0	41 500	20.3	14.8	300	26.6	3.6	18 163	2.0	1 114	6.1	15 038	23.9	13.0
Jersey	7 344	76.1	45 400	18.5	12.9	318	24.0	3.1	10 731	2.8	535	5.0	9 139	21.1	14.0
Jo Daviess	8 371	74.9	48 700	17.3	12.6	306	22.3	2.1	12 439	7.8	557	4.5	10 768	17.9	13.4
Johnson	3 725	81.7	36 800	20.2	13.6	235	22.3	3.3	4 800	3.4	309	6.4	3 639	23.9	10.0
Kane	107 176	69.5	102 500	21.5	12.8	508	24.4	5.0	217 482	3.2	8 304	3.8	160 944	29.0	12.7
Kankakee	34 623	66.8	54 700	16.9	12.8	376	24.2	3.3	52 498	0.1	2 853	5.4	42 205	25.2	12.1
Kendall	13 301	76.9	99 700	19.8	11.9	495	22.3	2.1	29 605	4.4	833	2.8	20 751	26.1	14.5
Knox	21 909	69.1	37 100	16.5	12.9	298	26.1	1.3	28 929	1.5	1 162	4.0	25 053	22.7	11.8
Lake	173 966	74.2	136 700	22.3	13.1	558	25.7	2.9	329 923	1.9	11 096	3.4	258 003	37.3	10.2
La Salle	41 284	73.2	50 500	16.6	12.4	324	23.3	1.6	55 590	3.2	3 651	6.6	45 938	22.2	13.5
Lawrence	6 320	76.5	32 800	18.5	12.2	275	27.8	2.7	6 555	2.5	499	7.6	6 134	19.0	12.8
Lee	12 475	69.6	46 600	16.3	12.3	331	21.5	1.4	17 846	2.5	741	4.2	15 232	22.0	12.7
Livingston	13 737	70.9	46 700	16.6	11.8	340	23.6	1.6	19 858	4.7	667	3.4	16 800	18.5	12.0
Logan	11 033	67.8	48 700	17.7	12.5	327	21.2	1.2	12 333	1.7	507	4.1	13 884	23.4	9.9
McDonough	12 255	62.2	36 000	16.4	12.6	289	29.5	2.1	19 237	5.2	436	2.3	15 637	27.0	9.2
McHenry	62 940	79.9	111 000	22.7	12.9	537	24.3	1.8	137 209	2.0	4 450	3.2	95 736	30.5	14.9
McLean	46 796	63.5	65 900	17.3	11.8	387	24.8	1.5	91 763	7.5	2 027	2.2	68 058	29.5	8.4
Macon	45 996	70.2	45 400	15.5	12.5	340	25.0	1.6	60 905	5.5	2 940	4.8	52 639	26.3	11.7
Macoupin	18 176	77.4	39 700	18.1	12.9	322	26.2	2.4	22 674	2.7	1 194	5.3	20 253	19.5	14.9
Madison	94 857	72.0	51 400	17.2	12.8	384	26.4	2.6	132 013	2.4	5 850	4.4	113 082	27.3	12.4
Marion	16 272	76.2	36 000	18.8	13.5	295	27.1	2.8	20 662	2.3	1 341	6.5	17 481	21.6	11.2
Marshall	4 900	76.1	44 000	16.1	12.0	297	23.4	1.5	6 388	1.7	285	4.5	5 811	18.8	13.1
Mason	6 342	73.8	35 800	16.8	13.1	298	23.9	2.4	8 034	3.1	549	6.8	6 702	19.1	11.4
Massac	5 908	77.6	35 700	19.5	13.0	271	30.7	2.1	7 972	3.7	374	4.7	5 757	20.9	13.0
Menard	4 199	76.6	51 500	18.6	12.2	320	23.6	2.2	6 232	2.6	228	3.7	5 383	25.7	11.3
Mercer	6 572	74.7	34 900	17.5	12.1	304	23.0	1.3	8 832	3.4	627	7.1	7 721	20.2	12.5
Monroe	8 189	78.6	72 100	18.2	12.5	376	19.4	2.7	14 237	4.6	422	3.0	10 867	23.0	13.8
Montgomery	11 480	76.6	35 300	17.3	13.3	302	25.3	2.2	15 176	3.6	1 022	6.7	12 425	18.7	13.0
Morgan	13 678	67.7	47 700	17.7	12.7	321	24.3	2.0	17 912	3.0	719	4.0	17 096	26.3	10.8
Moultrie	5 122	75.8	41 200	16.1	13.2	315	20.2	2.4	8 224	7.4	243	3.0	6 157	19.3	13.7
Ogle	17 132	71.2	57 200	17.1	12.0	343	20.1	2.0	28 168	3.0	1 166	4.1	22 541	21.1	14.2
Peoria	70 797	64.0	49 100	16.0	12.6	359	23.8	2.0	97 010	1.4	4 091	4.2	81 671	31.3	9.7
Perry	8 306	78.1	40 400	19.4	12.9	272	26.3	3.0	8 669	7.3	760	8.8	8 414	17.4	16.9
Piatt	5 934	76.5	51 200	19.6	12.0	350	22.7	1.6	8 351	10.5	293	3.5	7 600	25.8	12.7
Pike	7 016	73.7	28 500	17.3	12.8	230	22.2	3.0	8 982	3.3	473	5.3	7 572	18.4	12.2
Pope	1 611	75.5	29 700	21.4	12.4	194	29.6	4.5	1 722	4.7	139	8.1	1 440	19.1	16.5
Pulaski	2 957	75.8	24 000	19.2	14.3	212	30.2	7.3	2 970	0.4	268	9.0	2 434	19.7	11.6
Putnam	2 204	77.5	48 400	15.4	11.7	310	22.1	2.3	3 113	1.8	161	5.2	2 647	17.0	17.9
Randolph	11 949	78.5	45 000	19.6	12.4	306	23.8	2.6	14 051	3.0	729	5.2	13 735	19.0	15.1
Richland	6 503	76.6	35 800	18.1	12.1	261	26.6	3.7	10 077	3.2	643	6.4	7 378	24.6	12.0
Rock Island	59 317	66.9	47 800	16.2	12.3	331	24.9	1.8	78 111	4.6	4 413	5.6	66 235	25.6	11.3
St. Clair	95 333	64.7	55 500	19.3	13.3	399	28.6	4.4	119 326	1.3	6 556	5.5	105 544	26.6	10.9
Saline	10 839	75.2	33 400	20.0	13.7	269	33.5	2.5	10 178	2.2	798	7.8	9 523	23.7	16.2
Sangamon	72 146	66.5	60 900	16.6	12.0	382	23.4	1.8	102 202	1.3	3 690	3.6	91 949	34.9	8.5
Schuyler	3 002	76.0	35 100	17.2	13.7	265	28.7	4.1	4 180	10.9	212	5.1	3 219	17.5	12.7
Scott	2 190	73.9	32 800	15.8	12.6	249	20.7	3.1	2 761	5.2	152	5.5	2 534	16.8	14.2
Shelby	8 563	78.9	39 100	15.9	12.6	296	22.9	2.4	11 553	3.6	621	5.4	9 737	16.8	15.0
Stark	2 512	74.2	31 200	16.2	12.7	299	20.3	2.2	2 815	4.2	154	5.5	2 795	18.2	11.7
Stephenson	18 920	71.2	50 700	18.3	12.1	321	23.5	1.2	24 901	2.6	1 435	5.8	23 202	21.7	14.4
Tazewell	47 171	71.6	48 700	14.8	12.2	337	22.0	1.7	71 421	1.8	2 890	4.0	57 839	25.9	12.5
Union	6 838	72.2	36 700	17.5	13.9	251	26.7	2.5	8 223	3.9	619	7.5	7 061	26.1	10.1
Vermilion	34 072	71.2	38 700	16.6	12.9	324	27.1	2.2	38 711	0.1	2 313	6.0	37 147	23.1	12.3
Wabash	5 032	75.8	42 200	17.6	12.0	266	25.2	2.9	4 875	4.2	468	9.6	5 721	25.0	16.0
Warren	7 393	69.4	33 700	19.8	12.5	295	25.0	1.3	9 860	1.8	355	3.6	8 604	21.8	12.3
Washington	5 658	80.2	46 000	19.1	14.3	329	20.4	3.0	9 037	5.4	333	3.7	6 746	20.6	12.9
Wayne	6 935	79.1	34 500	20.6	12.4	248	27.6	2.3	8 016	-0.9	599	7.5	7 247	18.4	15.5
White	6 845	74.8	34 500	18.0	13.1	265	26.3	2.3	7 197	0.5	488	6.8	6 390	20.7	15.5
Whiteside	22 740	71.7	44 400	15.3	12.1	335	23.6	1.9	31 859	3.4	1 388	4.4	27 655	20.3	14.1
Will	116 933	77.4	89 900	21.4	12.6	453	24.4	2.8	244 440	3.7	9 892	4.0	173 060	28.0	13.8
Williamson	23 120	73.7	40 800	19.1	13.2	300	27.2	2.1	27 583	1.5	1 719	6.2	23 287	26.8	14.1
Winnebago	96 727	68.0	60 600	17.4	12.8	377	23.8	2.4	151 135	2.4	6 951	4.6	125 014	27.3	13.1
Woodford	11 395	78.3	57 700	15.3	11.7	337	21.2	1.3	19 481	3.3	575	3.0	15 307	25.6	13.0

1. Specified owner-occupied units.   2. Specified renter-occupied units.   3. Overcrowded or lacking complete plumbing facilities.   4. Percent of civilian labor force.   5. Persons 16 years and older.

Table B. States and Counties — Nonfarm Employment and Agriculture

STATE County	Private nonfarm establishments, employment and payroll, 1998									Agriculture, 1997			
	Number of establish-ments	Employment						Annual payroll		Farms			Farm operators
		Total	Health Care and Social Assistance	Manufac-turing	Retail trade	Finance and Insurance	Professional Scientific and Technical Services	Total (mil dol)	Average per employee (dollars)	Number	Percent with—		Whose principal occu-pation is farming (percent)
											Less than 50 acres	500 acres and over	
	104	105	106	107	108	109	110	111	112	113	114	115	116
ILLINOIS—Cont'd													
Jackson	1 411	17 365	3 632	905	D	706	766	347	19 965	680	24.0	14.3	42.6
Jasper	271	3 182	112	964	327	124	75	79	24 816	729	22.2	27.8	57.8
Jefferson	1 074	15 673	2 572	2 705	D	456	380	373	23 808	962	28.4	11.5	37.5
Jersey	424	4 591	747	94	928	209	121	75	16 283	481	24.7	22.7	48.9
Jo Daviess	746	7 757	436	1 848	811	238	172	158	20 368	941	18.5	15.0	57.6
Johnson	192	983	124	D	245	78	68	18	18 128	515	21.2	8.2	32.8
Kane	9 916	162 347	15 776	40 954	20 595	9 105	9 039	4 990	30 739	650	36.3	21.5	58.3
Kankakee	2 304	57 571	5 788	7 214	5 752	1 438	691	1 430	24 833	831	21.8	31.0	61.1
Kendall	1 069	10 793	568	2 105	D	498	231	277	25 655	441	23.4	25.9	62.1
Knox	1 311	22 401	4 340	5 422	3 765	544	325	487	21 751	928	22.2	27.4	62.4
Lake	17 633	291 924	26 317	60 828	40 927	19 195	16 994	11 251	38 541	335	65.4	6.6	39.7
La Salle	2 924	37 258	4 975	6 623	6 818	1 420	978	934	25 072	1 581	17.0	26.2	60.2
Lawrence	371	4 285	1 000	220	482	499	89	92	21 418	376	25.5	31.1	58.5
Lee	785	11 043	1 949	3 868	1 385	305	205	269	24 322	904	16.2	30.3	61.7
Livingston	947	12 167	1 601	4 495	D	533	205	338	27 790	1 380	12.3	36.9	66.4
Logan	733	8 765	1 542	1 591	1 185	347	140	187	21 369	739	15.3	40.5	69.1
McDonough	798	10 198	1 622	2 133	1 849	330	198	192	18 853	824	22.5	28.4	58.4
McHenry	6 503	83 558	6 659	26 697	11 388	2 250	2 767	2 442	29 225	921	42.6	14.8	54.0
McLean	3 523	76 943	7 327	8 323	9 142	19 323	2 050	2 368	30 775	1 475	18.0	35.5	66.0
Macon	2 802	54 225	6 854	10 621	7 048	D	1 105	1 579	29 116	665	24.7	36.7	62.1
Macoupin	1 067	9 918	1 639	643	1 690	469	328	209	21 109	1 206	24.3	22.3	56.5
Madison	5 914	82 009	13 002	17 855	11 727	2 975	2 470	2 161	26 350	1 195	34.9	14.6	45.0
Marion	1 172	15 658	3 084	5 457	D	361	287	364	23 216	882	24.5	17.6	45.0
Marshall	306	2 835	314	906	450	126	D	64	22 631	494	12.3	30.6	64.4
Mason	357	2 762	434	477	544	201	D	56	20 144	486	15.4	45.5	71.0
Massac	285	4 525	702	735	431	158	53	121	26 646	400	27.5	13.0	49.0
Menard	274	1 409	158	D	299	101	52	30	21 539	352	21.3	34.1	60.5
Mercer	339	2 478	402	477	580	150	D	45	18 345	754	21.9	28.5	61.9
Monroe	598	5 356	567	219	876	254	356	122	22 857	556	29.0	21.0	53.6
Montgomery	778	8 639	1 473	1 702	1 295	392	231	182	21 033	980	19.6	27.3	58.1
Morgan	933	14 867	2 624	3 650	D	598	276	338	22 740	780	21.5	27.7	63.1
Moultrie	318	3 317	740	900	318	132	D	63	18 943	464	29.1	25.6	59.5
Ogle	1 004	15 456	1 200	5 807	1 415	499	216	411	26 572	1 099	24.1	23.1	56.7
Peoria	4 866	107 509	17 710	14 049	12 044	4 410	5 342	3 443	32 022	924	28.8	19.2	49.9
Perry	458	5 030	908	1 536	759	171	92	96	19 088	551	25.2	21.1	49.9
Piatt	359	2 553	273	419	426	184	95	57	22 246	448	14.1	44.9	71.2
Pike	398	3 310	652	257	733	202	83	59	17 860	1 028	16.4	26.4	55.5
Pope	67	D	105	D	D	D	D	D	D	282	13.1	12.1	40.8
Pulaski	132	1 363	257	141	142	D	D	37	27 408	239	18.4	19.2	47.3
Putnam	134	1 738	24	963	134	D	D	65	37 262	190	18.9	29.5	60.5
Randolph	770	10 720	2 334	2 394	1 590	339	121	244	22 720	843	23.5	18.4	53.9
Richland	502	6 921	1 138	1 764	943	208	81	132	19 008	495	24.8	26.7	53.1
Rock Island	3 676	67 400	7 863	10 796	9 053	3 298	2 342	2 093	31 046	618	32.7	18.3	51.5
St. Clair	5 503	74 339	12 754	7 136	12 996	3 065	3 583	1 762	23 701	844	29.1	18.5	49.6
Saline	701	8 178	2 384	438	1 418	342	164	158	19 370	441	32.9	16.8	44.9
Sangamon	5 357	80 769	17 277	3 987	12 268	6 974	3 835	2 076	25 707	993	31.4	31.1	60.4
Schuyler	167	1 326	262	128	278	D	55	27	20 333	477	13.2	28.9	57.2
Scott	108	886	8	D	134	D	D	43	48 843	327	24.5	30.3	63.9
Shelby	498	4 793	730	1 435	563	227	105	100	20 859	1 250	23.9	21.9	55.3
Stark	135	968	170	247	142	80	59	19	19 205	354	17.8	39.0	77.1
Stephenson	1 122	21 597	2 408	8 136	D	D	318	619	28 679	1 081	24.4	15.1	66.9
Tazewell	2 783	41 640	4 340	6 820	6 801	1 805	841	1 211	29 085	909	26.2	27.0	57.5
Union	364	4 770	2 111	616	657	146	75	97	20 393	591	23.0	11.7	37.1
Vermilion	1 853	29 209	4 603	7 237	4 214	1 499	440	751	25 724	984	22.1	36.1	63.3
Wabash	325	3 838	802	508	513	164	106	78	20 399	212	28.3	40.6	64.2
Warren	378	4 383	760	1 088	623	222	78	81	18 396	710	16.5	34.2	67.7
Washington	415	5 733	800	2 263	701	174	81	148	25 854	777	16.6	25.6	58.6
Wayne	399	3 719	513	D	681	186	84	79	21 222	972	22.4	20.0	47.7
White	432	3 630	620	369	664	172	93	73	20 006	432	22.5	29.4	55.6
Whiteside	1 442	21 890	3 465	7 281	3 535	702	303	539	24 627	1 039	22.7	24.4	65.4
Will	9 348	124 757	12 014	24 899	18 343	4 295	4 692	3 941	31 590	910	32.7	20.7	55.6
Williamson	1 531	20 365	3 540	2 514	D	D	464	414	20 314	585	33.3	6.0	32.1
Winnebago	7 031	132 076	16 322	39 702	16 489	4 606	4 832	3 820	28 924	687	35.1	18.0	54.0
Woodford	718	8 309	1 150	2 372	991	242	197	196	23 546	923	22.5	22.2	56.3

Table B. States and Counties — Agriculture, Land, and Water

STATE County	Agriculture, 1997 (cont'd)															
	Land in farms				Value of land and buildings		Value of machinery and equipment Average per farm ($1,000)	Value of products sold				Percent of farms with sales of —		Percent of land owned by Fed. Gov. 1997	Water consumption 1995 (mil gal/day)
	Acreage (1,000)	Percent change, 1992–1997	Average size of farm	Total irrigated (1,000)	Total cropland (1,000)	Average per farm ($1,000)	Average per acre (dollars)		Total (mil dol)	Average per farm (dollars)	Crops	Livestock and poultry products	$10,000 or more	$100,000 or more		
	117	118	119	120	121	122	123	124	125	126	127	128	129	130	131	132
ILLINOIS—Cont'd																
Jackson	203	8.9	298	0	161	393	1 452	61	37	54 434	74.7	25.3	41.2	12.9	12.9	190.9
Jasper	252	-2.2	346	0	225	687	1 881	100	86	117 947	61.3	38.7	73.4	32.9	0.0	531.1
Jefferson	230	5.8	239	0	184	285	1 075	61	35	36 608	80.0	20.0	39.6	9.8	0.8	2.8
Jersey	164	-9.3	341	0	131	579	1 711	69	40	83 817	80.1	19.9	61.1	24.5	1.6	7.3
Jo Daviess	276	-4.9	293	0	189	408	1 399	75	73	77 131	37.9	62.1	64.5	24.9	3.5	8.6
Johnson	104	9.8	203	D	70	196	953	33	11	20 815	56.9	43.1	26.4	4.7	8.7	2.0
Kane	210	2.9	323	2	197	1 259	4 023	117	123	188 822	84.7	15.3	69.8	36.6	0.4	53.4
Kankakee	352	-2.1	423	14	338	1 102	2 759	132	133	159 906	89.0	11.0	82.6	40.2	0.0	29.0
Kendall	167	-5.9	380	0	158	1 561	3 994	120	59	133 238	85.6	14.4	79.4	35.1	0.0	5.5
Knox	390	1.0	420	0	318	737	1 923	91	130	140 413	69.6	30.4	71.7	35.3	0.0	8.7
Lake	51	-30.3	152	0	42	723	3 993	79	32	96 256	87.1	12.9	46.6	19.1	0.5	2 449.3
La Salle	588	-4.0	372	1	552	1 013	2 855	99	183	115 843	90.1	9.9	81.2	36.7	0.0	888.2
Lawrence	183	8.0	485	7	162	621	1 210	94	55	146 824	66.1	33.9	62.5	32.2	0.0	6.7
Lee	393	-5.1	435	13	369	947	2 313	107	136	150 681	81.9	18.1	84.4	43.1	0.0	15.6
Livingston	614	-3.8	445	0	589	1 111	2 554	109	214	154 814	77.5	22.5	88.8	50.3	0.0	7.2
Logan	381	3.0	515	1	361	1 372	2 663	135	133	180 310	84.1	15.9	85.8	51.8	0.0	4.8
McDonough	340	-1.4	413	0	292	759	1 878	91	97	117 497	84.1	15.9	72.0	35.2	0.0	4.6
McHenry	242	-2.6	263	8	220	1 038	4 072	96	109	118 509	71.4	28.6	60.2	28.0	0.0	39.8
McLean	697	-1.8	472	1	666	1 278	2 657	130	238	161 521	89.0	11.0	81.9	46.8	0.0	17.0
Macon	323	3.8	486	D	303	1 354	2 803	125	106	158 998	96.0	4.0	74.3	44.1	0.0	46.6
Macoupin	396	-1.6	328	1	336	645	2 028	79	121	100 092	71.2	28.8	65.7	27.4	0.0	10.5
Madison	284	-5.5	237	2	248	510	2 155	70	86	72 054	79.0	21.0	55.4	18.3	0.7	308.1
Marion	249	-1.8	283	0	203	298	1 193	54	56	63 037	65.3	34.7	50.6	16.3	0.0	5.7
Marshall	228	11.5	461	4	197	1 000	2 193	103	68	136 931	88.7	11.3	82.4	44.3	0.4	4.4
Mason	292	3.4	600	85	264	1 054	1 912	145	84	173 629	90.9	9.1	75.9	47.5	0.3	119.0
Massac	104	4.8	259	4	84	280	1 238	46	20	49 797	69.5	30.5	46.8	13.8	1.6	592.2
Menard	170	3.8	484	1	153	963	2 112	95	52	148 808	81.4	18.6	74.1	42.3	0.0	1.9
Mercer	310	-0.8	411	4	261	661	1 693	89	92	122 212	76.2	23.8	69.0	34.0	0.8	4.6
Monroe	187	-0.1	336	2	154	632	1 943	105	49	88 821	65.3	34.7	61.2	24.5	0.0	2.8
Montgomery	361	-3.0	368	0	324	686	1 985	82	109	111 381	78.2	21.8	71.9	34.4	0.0	333.7
Morgan	306	-1.7	392	2	267	887	2 319	101	96	123 266	78.0	21.9	74.7	33.1	0.3	159.1
Moultrie	173	-6.7	372	0	165	1 149	2 909	111	56	120 583	86.9	13.1	72.0	33.0	6.3	2.6
Ogle	379	-3.5	345	1	343	834	2 458	89	149	135 493	65.9	34.1	72.4	36.8	0.0	30.8
Peoria	267	2.4	289	3	224	609	2 253	64	77	83 538	86.3	13.7	62.8	23.3	0.0	110.4
Perry	172	2.4	312	0	145	310	1 056	69	29	51 756	81.0	19.0	58.1	15.8	0.0	11.3
Piatt	253	0.9	565	0	245	1 579	2 905	163	83	186 248	93.7	6.3	87.7	51.8	0.0	3.3
Pike	461	4.1	449	1	342	645	1 394	82	124	120 469	65.2	34.8	64.3	27.2	1.1	23.4
Pope	72	6.2	256	0	43	202	834	26	5	16 738	60.7	39.3	27.3	3.5	38.9	0.5
Pulaski	83	1.4	348	D	71	400	1 257	56	15	64 134	83.7	16.3	51.0	16.7	4.4	1.3
Putnam	77	-1.3	405	D	65	1 126	2 428	151	42	220 931	89.8	10.2	80.5	40.5	0.0	166.7
Randolph	262	-3.1	311	0	208	450	1 529	69	50	59 596	70.5	29.5	58.5	17.2	0.0	1 179.4
Richland	197	4.4	398	D	175	614	1 566	98	59	120 024	65.5	34.5	66.1	29.5	0.0	2.3
Rock Island	170	-3.4	275	4	135	499	1 907	58	50	80 565	72.9	27.1	59.9	22.7	2.4	924.9
St. Clair	265	0.2	313	1	239	669	2 228	83	78	92 646	81.5	18.5	66.2	23.3	0.6	46.8
Saline	131	-8.0	296	0	115	301	1 084	67	33	75 091	62.8	37.2	45.4	19.3	5.9	0.5
Sangamon	467	4.5	470	0	436	1 165	2 570	118	163	163 710	88.6	11.4	66.2	37.6	0.0	336.9
Schuyler	209	0.9	438	D	144	432	993	66	40	83 327	79.0	21.0	63.9	22.6	0.0	2.2
Scott	146	12.8	445	4	117	694	1 663	69	35	106 817	84.3	15.7	63.9	32.4	0.0	6.3
Shelby	419	4.2	335	0	376	651	2 061	74	112	89 973	78.1	21.9	65.1	27.0	2.3	4.4
Stark	180	5.7	508	D	165	1 113	2 433	95	65	184 888	84.8	15.2	83.1	52.8	0.0	1.4
Stephenson	309	-2.0	285	0	277	547	1 978	86	142	131 374	41.6	58.4	73.2	39.2	0.0	10.9
Tazewell	328	-2.3	361	30	305	1 006	2 824	94	123	135 493	76.0	24.0	73.3	36.7	0.1	798.5
Union	136	14.3	230	1	95	341	1 229	48	21	35 059	77.8	22.2	33.5	6.1	16.0	3.8
Vermilion	485	-0.6	493	0	458	1 183	2 397	146	140	142 438	95.7	4.3	75.2	41.4	0.1	16.3
Wabash	122	4.9	574	D	112	1 200	1 856	162	31	145 209	91.9	8.1	69.3	42.5	0.0	6.6
Warren	315	-0.6	444	D	278	1 041	2 345	97	105	148 004	80.0	20.0	82.3	42.3	0.0	3.6
Washington	309	3.9	397	1	279	629	1 630	99	88	113 197	62.7	37.3	76.3	31.5	0.0	2.8
Wayne	321	-3.7	330	D	274	325	994	58	71	72 963	70.0	30.0	52.6	18.0	0.0	3.7
White	256	9.1	594	6	224	809	1 409	113	61	141 834	86.9	13.1	60.9	28.2	0.0	4.0
Whiteside	385	-3.6	370	34	353	784	2 125	99	157	151 099	64.4	35.6	77.3	41.2	0.2	33.0
Will	294	-9.7	323	4	275	1 091	3 714	80	107	117 724	92.0	8.0	69.9	28.8	4.9	3 907.9
Williamson	92	2.5	158	0	67	214	1 476	40	11	19 524	70.0	30.0	27.9	5.0	12.3	13.7
Winnebago	196	-3.6	285	1	178	585	2 435	70	69	100 297	73.1	26.9	62.7	28.8	0.0	46.6
Woodford	300	1.3	325	0	275	954	2 728	99	107	116 202	78.6	21.4	75.9	33.0	0.0	10.8

STATE County	Value of Residential Construction Authorized by Building Permits, 1999		Wholesale Trade, 1997				Retail Trade[1], 1997				Real Estate and Rental and Leasing, 1997			
	New Construction ($1,000)	Number of Housing Units	Number of Establishments	Number of Employees	Sales (mil dol)	Annual Payroll (mil dol)	Number of Establishments	Number of Employees	Sales (mil dol)	Annual Payroll (mil dol)	Number of Establishments	Number of Employees	Receipts (mil dol)	Annual Payroll (mil dol)
	133	134	135	136	137	138	139	140	141	142	143	144	145	146
ILLINOIS—Cont'd														
Jackson	7 935	138	45	289	78.4	7.6	287	3 992	551.9	60.7	81	414	29.2	5.3
Jasper	0	0	22	206	120.1	5.1	45	366	78.5	5.9	6	D	D	D
Jefferson	3 552	30	64	667	362.9	18.5	216	2 678	385.2	36.8	31	98	6.4	1.1
Jersey	14 251	122	28	D	D	D	82	1 031	171.0	14.2	3	4	0.3	0.0
Jo Daviess	21 235	147	31	176	130.4	5.5	144	897	150.2	12.4	24	64	8.9	1.2
Johnson	NA	NA	12	90	38.5	1.7	34	235	42.8	4.1	2	D	D	D
Kane	751 421	5 787	787	9 948	8 557.1	392.4	1 353	19 688	3 116.6	331.1	318	1 620	212.1	35.8
Kankakee	47 125	376	126	1 628	809.3	47.2	388	5 594	907.0	88.5	85	348	34.9	5.9
Kendall	86 369	691	61	585	348.0	18.6	118	1 755	371.0	36.6	34	127	15.1	2.0
Knox	11 103	111	75	933	381.7	25.2	252	3 785	489.9	52.5	40	164	12.6	2.0
Lake	732 325	4 933	1 411	20 149	19 079.1	932.4	2 391	38 002	8 562.3	785.9	626	3 563	725.4	95.7
La Salle	40 945	436	168	1 729	1 292.6	55.8	502	6 352	1 047.7	96.8	72	296	23.3	4.0
Lawrence	0	0	16	248	64.0	6.7	63	535	71.8	6.9	4	D	D	D
Lee	11 352	104	55	525	248.5	14.7	138	1 379	234.8	23.6	28	133	7.1	1.5
Livingston	8 294	76	48	431	255.6	11.1	186	1 909	336.3	28.7	20	72	3.1	0.6
Logan	1 778	38	45	433	252.3	12.2	140	1 283	238.0	20.3	33	87	8.6	0.9
McDonough	2 989	39	37	233	164.8	5.6	167	1 870	246.6	24.8	29	205	9.5	2.6
McHenry	459 951	3 730	497	5 381	2 874.1	210.7	813	10 457	2 034.6	188.3	184	807	106.8	15.2
McLean	109 580	1 342	212	2 268	1 348.4	87.1	632	9 242	1 474.6	142.3	134	704	99.8	14.6
Macon	38 489	265	158	1 815	3 249.3	57.4	506	6 967	1 129.6	110.4	98	515	39.9	8.5
Macoupin	3 039	32	76	749	238.9	19.6	188	1 695	309.4	26.0	27	68	5.7	0.9
Madison	145 587	1 361	259	2 860	2 264.4	91.6	969	11 722	2 057.0	181.4	190	885	106.9	14.0
Marion	3 161	35	53	474	166.7	11.8	226	2 119	309.4	30.2	28	153	8.1	1.4
Marshall	1 788	18	16	127	232.5	3.9	49	395	68.7	6.4	10	16	0.9	0.1
Mason	3 471	35	32	225	305.2	5.6	59	601	98.4	9.5	4	D	D	D
Massac	165	1	6	D	D	D	55	414	79.7	6.4	7	19	1.1	0.2
Menard	8 673	77	15	104	74.7	2.7	41	320	58.3	4.6	11	48	2.2	0.4
Mercer	4 579	46	21	103	102.2	3.1	57	586	88.5	8.6	7	12	0.3	0.2
Monroe	33 737	256	29	D	D	D	85	858	175.2	15.4	22	56	5.1	0.8
Montgomery	1 223	15	46	351	215.1	9.0	142	1 344	236.6	19.3	17	37	2.3	0.3
Morgan	2 301	27	45	D	D	D	192	2 207	344.7	31.9	20	65	6.0	1.0
Moultrie	5 551	77	28	211	103.2	5.1	46	303	42.5	3.9	6	16	0.8	0.1
Ogle	32 164	248	54	D	D	D	150	1 491	268.3	24.0	35	80	8.3	0.9
Peoria	89 939	815	299	4 755	5 876.5	171.6	801	11 817	1 847.4	182.6	192	1 163	115.3	20.6
Perry	NA	NA	14	D	D	D	98	789	113.8	14.3	9	22	1.1	0.2
Piatt	6 976	55	29	335	332.4	7.6	55	432	99.4	7.8	8	37	2.0	0.4
Pike	3 380	52	37	319	175.1	8.0	85	725	119.9	10.6	6	17	1.1	0.2
Pope	50	1	2	D	D	D	12	36	7.5	0.5	3	5	0.2	0.0
Pulaski	0	0	9	D	D	D	27	127	15.5	1.4	3	4	0.4	0.0
Putnam	3 615	41	7	D	D	D	22	126	23.4	1.9	2	D	D	D
Randolph	8 008	77	32	D	D	D	140	1 601	261.7	27.3	17	45	2.4	0.3
Richland	3 378	25	38	641	266.2	14.0	94	940	149.0	13.8	10	45	1.1	0.3
Rock Island	40 599	367	239	4 530	2 042.8	148.4	623	8 593	1 427.4	142.2	136	650	81.8	13.6
St. Clair	121 908	1 109	214	2 169	1 615.1	64.2	965	12 887	2 048.5	197.7	207	961	90.5	18.9
Saline	0	0	26	D	D	D	154	1 404	232.5	32.3	14	56	2.7	0.5
Sangamon	97 810	1 069	259	3 517	1 513.4	119.7	836	12 054	1 991.9	187.0	204	837	85.3	14.3
Schuyler	NA	NA	8	93	62.5	2.3	37	303	45.5	4.3	6	22	0.5	0.1
Scott	0	0	13	123	152.5	3.4	13	113	20.5	1.5	2	D	D	D
Shelby	5 572	58	37	237	153.1	5.6	86	554	123.9	7.7	9	22	0.8	0.2
Stark	1 984	19	12	73	52.0	1.6	23	124	27.4	2.4	1	D	D	D
Stephenson	19 220	164	54	429	129.6	10.0	191	2 522	414.6	40.3	30	111	9.7	1.7
Tazewell	56 618	490	140	D	D	D	473	6 813	1 275.2	112.1	82	419	45.2	9.6
Union	2 635	29	14	93	25.0	2.6	66	641	96.8	9.4	12	30	1.9	0.5
Vermilion	13 041	193	102	2 221	1 257.5	68.5	351	4 505	639.2	64.4	63	265	17.6	4.2
Wabash	1 392	13	21	116	52.3	2.8	49	508	75.6	6.7	6	16	1.0	0.2
Warren	3 835	26	23	274	164.4	7.3	67	632	97.7	9.1	7	31	1.7	0.4
Washington	5 334	53	27	245	128.9	6.9	83	662	157.1	13.0	5	16	1.0	0.1
Wayne	525	6	32	176	113.3	4.2	80	703	103.6	9.9	10	17	1.1	0.1
White	234	5	33	152	104.7	3.7	84	644	109.7	9.3	10	22	1.2	0.2
Whiteside	18 606	177	75	522	481.9	15.3	241	3 303	515.4	54.1	55	181	13.3	2.4
Will	841 371	7 368	577	6 563	3 946.2	230.2	1 157	17 267	3 286.2	301.3	287	1 191	129.0	23.0
Williamson	18 018	237	80	629	189.3	15.0	306	3 405	576.2	51.1	39	185	16.3	2.4
Winnebago	94 446	1 405	510	6 308	2 530.0	216.5	1 090	17 044	2 754.5	270.3	217	1 169	160.4	24.2
Woodford	20 744	189	55	D	D	D	101	1 009	229.4	16.8	15	66	3.5	1.1

1. Establishments with payroll.

Table B. States and Counties — **Professional, Manufacturing, and Accommodation and Foodservices**

STATE County	Professional, Scientific, and Technical Services[1], 1997				Manufacturing, 1997				Accommodation and Foodservices, 1997			
	Number of Establishments	Number of Employees	Receipts (mil dol)	Annual Payroll (mil dol)	Number of Establishments	Number of Employees	Receipts (mil dol)	Annual Payroll (mil dol)	Number of Establishments	Number of Employees	Sales (mil dol)	Annual Payroll (mil dol)
	147	148	149	150	151	152	153	154	155	156	157	158
ILLINOIS—Cont'd												
Jackson	96	664	37.2	14.6	35	1 062	151.8	29.0	156	2 379	65.4	17.8
Jasper	9	72	2.7	1.7	15	874	66.4	15.2	18	87	2.3	0.5
Jefferson	61	386	29.1	12.2	44	2 922	743.1	104.5	72	1 270	41.9	11.3
Jersey	20	85	6.3	3.1	NA	NA	NA	NA	50	612	16.0	4.6
Jo Daviess	46	116	14.0	4.0	33	1 590	312.6	46.2	101	1 755	61.8	16.0
Johnson	12	55	3.1	0.9	NA	NA	NA	NA	15	111	3.6	1.1
Kane	955	6 298	541.4	225.7	877	40 200	8 226.1	1 443.8	633	11 078	367.0	106.3
Kankakee	132	507	32.7	12.7	116	6 937	2 253.2	263.8	229	3 563	100.4	27.4
Kendall	48	135	7.6	2.8	66	2 303	369.6	69.5	76	869	28.2	6.6
Knox	52	263	19.6	7.1	56	5 528	1 058.8	165.0	132	1 863	54.5	14.8
Lake	2 204	14 385	1 676.3	697.1	969	62 535	13 686.2	2 660.2	1 245	20 090	775.8	210.3
La Salle	154	877	56.0	24.0	152	6 752	1 732.6	232.1	332	3 830	109.7	30.8
Lawrence	20	75	4.8	1.9	NA	NA	NA	NA	24	199	5.6	1.5
Lee	35	186	14.5	6.2	35	3 798	739.4	115.3	68	638	20.1	5.0
Livingston	49	154	10.5	4.0	51	4 573	1 055.8	170.5	86	1 001	26.5	7.2
Logan	32	101	7.6	2.0	24	1 401	318.2	44.9	77	864	24.0	6.4
McDonough	39	169	10.1	2.6	30	1 956	255.9	61.2	78	1 303	29.8	8.1
McHenry	594	2 115	176.6	65.5	583	22 949	3 930.4	760.4	409	5 347	175.8	46.4
McLean	234	1 382	111.6	57.9	112	8 388	3 870.3	357.7	336	7 104	200.5	58.3
Macon	156	1 101	90.0	36.1	134	11 616	6 114.2	479.4	233	4 105	123.6	35.7
Macoupin	46	254	23.3	7.0	35	697	156.5	18.9	90	783	24.7	5.7
Madison	392	2 162	167.1	73.2	224	19 074	7 676.5	743.8	537	8 326	253.8	68.1
Marion	56	238	18.4	5.3	65	5 220	768.3	152.6	95	1 056	31.4	8.5
Marshall	16	56	3.9	1.4	18	921	179.6	28.2	31	422	7.7	2.1
Mason	13	33	2.1	0.6	NA	NA	NA	NA	48	294	8.3	2.1
Massac	13	57	2.1	0.9	12	732	191.5	31.2	38	343	10.3	2.6
Menard	18	40	3.2	1.2	NA	NA	NA	NA	24	D	D	D
Mercer	14	29	1.7	0.4	NA	NA	NA	NA	34	215	5.6	1.5
Monroe	42	245	18.1	9.1	NA	NA	NA	NA	51	D	D	D
Montgomery	41	203	12.1	5.1	37	1 752	300.7	48.3	77	924	25.7	6.5
Morgan	42	223	15.4	7.4	36	3 566	1 213.4	110.6	78	1 165	34.0	9.5
Moultrie	20	57	4.1	0.9	20	796	210.8	19.8	27	283	6.2	1.9
Ogle	52	D	D	D	70	5 859	1 020.5	166.2	93	999	27.6	7.2
Peoria	361	4 635	378.4	167.7	177	14 351	4 392.7	610.6	494	8 204	246.3	70.7
Perry	24	77	3.7	1.2	22	1 481	262.3	35.3	34	428	10.4	2.9
Piatt	25	90	4.6	2.2	NA	NA	NA	NA	28	D	D	D
Pike	16	52	2.0	0.8	NA	NA	NA	NA	39	389	9.3	2.4
Pope	3	D	D	D	NA	NA	NA	NA	8	36	1.8	0.4
Pulaski	4	D	D	D	NA	NA	NA	NA	10	64	1.6	0.4
Putnam	5	22	1.0	0.3	9	D	D	D	11	D	D	D
Randolph	33	99	6.0	2.2	32	2 353	398.6	51.8	75	749	20.4	5.3
Richland	24	67	3.9	1.4	34	1 814	218.3	37.0	34	439	12.9	3.4
Rock Island	238	2 124	164.9	72.3	197	10 675	3 508.8	493.8	373	5 780	161.4	43.9
St. Clair	395	3 109	284.7	119.2	198	7 123	1 763.5	249.3	477	8 481	245.0	66.7
Saline	39	134	11.2	2.9	NA	NA	NA	NA	58	709	19.7	5.1
Sangamon	471	3 283	277.1	117.6	134	D	D	D	497	D	D	D
Schuyler	9	56	3.6	1.8	NA	NA	NA	NA	15	D	D	D
Scott	6	15	0.6	0.1	NA	NA	NA	NA	9	90	1.2	0.3
Shelby	24	97	5.7	2.0	14	1 191	205.7	32.4	40	473	15.4	4.2
Stark	7	64	1.8	0.7	NA	NA	NA	NA	6	D	D	D
Stephenson	62	243	17.5	6.8	62	8 386	1 239.2	300.3	103	1 259	37.1	8.7
Tazewell	153	731	53.9	26.7	118	7 015	2 512.9	311.1	265	4 329	115.8	33.7
Union	17	65	3.8	1.5	11	616	132.2	17.0	26	D	D	D
Vermilion	94	331	27.9	8.6	104	7 055	1 696.1	228.9	185	2 570	68.5	20.0
Wabash	22	93	7.3	2.4	15	611	55.8	20.5	24	367	7.9	2.4
Warren	17	42	2.7	0.6	19	D	D	D	37	334	9.8	2.7
Washington	14	63	3.7	1.7	16	1 397	222.4	44.5	43	380	10.9	2.6
Wayne	23	77	4.6	1.4	20	D	D	D	20	D	D	D
White	20	80	3.4	1.1	NA	NA	NA	NA	28	404	10.7	3.3
Whiteside	56	236	19.2	7.6	102	7 374	1 381.8	245.0	112	1 567	42.9	10.9
Will	689	2 966	285.4	113.7	527	24 090	7 594.7	988.2	646	9 054	291.6	75.2
Williamson	89	381	29.5	8.6	51	2 551	425.1	69.2	135	2 155	68.1	18.1
Winnebago	567	5 447	327.5	128.6	779	39 740	6 608.4	1 483.6	556	9 693	306.3	84.1
Woodford	35	144	14.6	6.1	55	2 272	644.9	74.7	63	789	18.8	4.7

1. Firms subject to federal tax.

Table B. States and Counties — Health and Other Services and Federal Funds

STATE County	Health Care and Social Assistance[1], 1997				Other Services[1], 1997				Federal funds and grants, fiscal 1999[2]			
										Expenditures (mil dol)		
									Total	Direct payments for individuals[3]		
	Number of Establish-ments	Number of Employees	Receipts (mil dol)	Annual Payroll (mil dol)	Number of Establish-ments	Number of Employees	Receipts (mil dol)	Annual Payroll (mil dol)		Social Security and government retirement	Medicare	Food stamps and Supplemental Security Income
	159	160	161	162	163	164	165	166	167	168	169	170
ILLINOIS—Cont'd												
Jackson	118	1 698	96.9	46.9	85	338	20.3	4.7	223.6	87.7	33.7	11.3
Jasper	8	109	3.6	1.7	21	62	4.7	0.8	47.5	18.4	7.4	1.1
Jefferson	92	1 088	69.7	23.8	64	384	24.9	7.7	171.2	76.2	37.6	8.6
Jersey	28	387	15.4	6.1	28	63	4.4	0.9	69.8	35.0	15.0	1.9
Jo Daviess	26	224	9.6	4.6	41	130	11.6	1.9	96.0	49.5	16.1	1.2
Johnson	12	112	3.7	1.5	8	21	2.2	0.4	52.0	25.8	9.0	2.1
Kane	620	6 731	522.4	241.2	604	3 897	259.3	84.5	1 290.3	481.6	195.4	31.1
Kankakee	168	1 730	107.6	53.0	162	954	59.8	18.3	420.4	187.6	93.7	20.3
Kendall	43	464	20.9	8.9	69	391	26.3	7.1	96.2	51.8	15.7	1.0
Knox	72	1 213	71.7	27.1	86	390	24.4	6.4	251.0	130.2	52.2	7.8
Lake	1 210	12 163	896.3	414.7	975	5 862	468.9	140.9	2 776.5	807.7	285.4	33.8
La Salle	199	1 663	93.8	38.9	208	933	65.7	16.9	432.4	235.0	87.6	9.0
Lawrence	31	533	18.9	7.4	20	58	4.4	1.0	84.3	37.2	17.1	2.4
Lee	47	537	39.8	16.5	56	245	15.0	3.9	139.0	67.9	25.5	3.0
Livingston	41	265	15.3	7.0	59	206	14.1	3.7	156.1	69.8	30.2	3.3
Logan	31	366	17.4	5.8	37	133	7.7	1.9	134.7	60.6	24.6	2.7
McDonough	58	480	25.5	12.4	64	230	12.6	3.2	118.0	51.2	21.4	3.6
McHenry	410	4 539	226.2	108.2	401	2 001	126.7	38.8	506.8	290.3	108.4	6.3
McLean	228	2 901	190.8	91.6	226	1 433	85.6	26.8	457.0	192.7	64.6	10.2
Macon	204	2 546	155.6	70.3	189	1 456	86.0	28.7	508.4	240.7	85.9	23.5
Macoupin	65	943	29.1	12.4	65	208	13.4	3.1	221.5	115.2	49.0	6.3
Madison	501	5 457	307.2	141.5	438	2 526	158.9	45.8	1 101.7	549.3	221.6	41.2
Marion	96	1 070	62.4	23.6	71	242	13.3	3.5	222.3	105.9	53.5	8.2
Marshall	19	255	9.8	4.7	14	33	1.7	0.3	56.3	27.7	10.4	0.9
Mason	20	157	6.7	2.2	21	54	3.9	0.9	83.5	37.7	18.0	2.5
Massac	23	320	11.7	5.6	18	61	3.9	1.0	119.2	34.6	16.8	2.8
Menard	14	146	4.3	2.1	15	67	3.9	1.0	46.8	22.5	8.3	1.0
Mercer	15	132	5.5	2.6	21	66	3.8	0.8	69.2	34.2	12.0	1.4
Monroe	34	366	14.5	6.7	48	297	13.7	4.8	85.0	49.1	15.8	0.8
Montgomery	47	634	27.8	10.9	48	188	14.8	2.9	146.4	66.9	27.6	4.4
Morgan	75	792	33.0	14.7	58	246	15.6	4.5	165.5	72.3	28.9	5.4
Moultrie	16	195	8.2	2.8	15	49	3.5	0.7	65.5	34.0	12.6	0.9
Ogle	58	564	22.9	9.2	75	264	16.6	4.3	160.8	81.4	27.8	2.2
Peoria	365	4 477	369.3	193.7	291	2 391	172.4	56.2	902.8	359.9	139.5	40.4
Perry	35	368	13.4	5.1	31	106	7.0	1.7	93.8	50.9	19.7	3.1
Piatt	14	159	6.5	2.8	20	66	4.5	1.3	67.8	35.0	12.3	0.9
Pike	20	348	11.8	5.2	28	67	4.8	1.1	96.7	38.5	16.6	2.4
Pope	2	D	D	D	2	D	D	D	26.4	9.1	4.2	1.0
Pulaski	2	D	D	D	9	19	1.5	0.3	53.8	17.0	7.9	2.8
Putnam	4	13	0.5	0.1	6	8	0.7	0.1	23.5	12.4	4.4	0.3
Randolph	53	608	22.8	9.8	57	170	10.3	2.7	138.1	71.6	29.3	3.3
Richland	24	403	19.8	9.9	37	124	8.3	1.7	73.3	35.1	13.1	2.3
Rock Island	290	3 073	192.2	87.6	255	1 782	114.3	31.9	891.6	336.0	112.5	22.3
St. Clair	469	6 013	346.2	156.5	423	2 147	124.4	40.7	1 653.4	583.4	219.0	76.6
Saline	55	1 048	42.5	19.7	42	100	7.2	1.7	163.4	69.0	26.0	8.2
Sangamon	356	7 594	478.1	204.4	347	2 285	142.3	46.4	2 412.4	483.8	145.3	28.6
Schuyler	9	129	4.2	1.8	9	11	1.6	0.1	38.1	15.1	5.5	0.8
Scott	3	6	0.2	0.1	6	12	2.1	0.1	28.6	11.1	4.4	0.4
Shelby	26	337	14.9	5.8	33	123	9.5	2.1	104.7	48.3	21.1	1.9
Stark	5	25	0.6	0.2	4	14	1.3	0.2	36.5	14.1	7.1	0.5
Stephenson	67	713	37.8	19.4	86	395	21.8	6.4	192.8	100.4	33.8	5.7
Tazewell	152	1 931	88.1	40.6	221	1 122	72.3	22.3	452.4	239.5	91.1	9.6
Union	35	930	22.9	9.6	16	66	4.7	1.0	87.3	37.9	15.8	3.9
Vermilion	103	1 343	83.4	38.6	133	627	33.3	9.9	476.2	201.9	68.9	21.1
Wabash	22	499	9.3	3.9	19	91	6.0	1.5	53.6	27.4	10.3	1.7
Warren	17	331	10.0	3.9	23	83	4.1	0.9	87.8	37.8	15.0	2.5
Washington	17	295	10.9	4.6	29	94	5.4	1.3	70.4	32.0	16.2	0.9
Wayne	20	129	5.5	2.1	22	72	4.9	1.1	82.2	36.8	16.7	1.8
White	24	265	8.2	3.7	19	59	5.2	0.8	108.7	41.6	17.5	2.8
Whiteside	71	1 087	66.0	27.2	135	691	37.5	10.1	239.2	127.3	48.4	6.4
Will	558	5 682	377.4	173.6	617	3 523	251.6	76.8	980.4	548.2	206.2	29.7
Williamson	122	2 043	123.4	38.9	59	430	25.3	6.4	380.1	138.1	49.4	10.5
Winnebago	433	5 688	458.3	222.2	479	3 651	225.9	72.3	943.0	464.8	158.5	38.8
Woodford	27	265	10.3	4.8	47	159	10.5	2.8	109.1	53.5	20.5	1.2

1. Firms subject to federal tax.   2. October 1, 1998 to September 30, 1999.   3. State totals may include programs not allocated by county.

STATE County	Federal funds and grants, fiscal 1999[1] (cont'd)							Local government finances, 1997				
	Expenditures (mil dol) (cont'd)							General revenue				
	Procurement contract awards			Grants[2]							Taxes	
											Per capita[3] (dollars)	
	Salaries and wages	Defense	Other	Medicaid and other health-related	Nutrition and family welfare	Education	Other	Total (mil dol)	Intergovern-mental (mil dol)	Total (mil dol)	Total	Property
	171	172	173	174	175	176	177	178	179	180	181	182
ILLINOIS—Cont'd												
Jackson	17.0	3.6	4.2	26.3	7.4	4.1	8.0	114.5	57.6	30.6	504	429
Jasper	2.1	0.1	0.9	2.7	0.6	0.3	3.2	21.3	10.3	8.7	824	739
Jefferson	9.0	0.4	1.7	17.0	4.4	2.2	4.8	92.2	49.7	27.6	708	525
Jersey	2.4	0.0	0.6	5.8	1.0	0.3	0.9	45.8	19.9	7.9	372	335
Jo Daviess	4.2	0.0	2.8	3.0	0.9	0.3	8.0	48.9	14.9	21.4	988	885
Johnson	3.7	0.0	0.7	5.1	0.8	0.3	1.7	14.4	9.6	3.0	231	231
Kane	124.0	14.9	314.3	48.1	22.8	7.6	20.5	1 062.1	293.5	569.6	1 496	1 399
Kankakee	21.4	2.6	3.7	37.9	14.1	4.0	10.5	227.2	107.0	80.9	793	721
Kendall	12.5	0.4	1.2	1.4	0.7	0.3	1.3	89.6	27.2	52.4	1 051	977
Knox	11.1	0.0	2.7	14.5	4.4	2.3	7.9	121.3	57.7	36.1	650	517
Lake	1 255.7	178.4	62.2	66.8	25.0	17.7	23.1	1 662.8	363.7	967.2	1 626	1 500
La Salle	19.1	0.2	4.9	20.7	5.5	2.3	12.9	224.1	88.5	98.0	895	860
Lawrence	2.7	0.0	0.5	6.2	1.2	0.8	2.4	24.1	15.0	5.5	354	328
Lee	5.5	0.0	1.6	6.3	1.6	0.7	2.0	78.0	32.5	29.3	819	783
Livingston	6.1	0.0	1.5	4.7	2.0	0.7	3.1	89.0	37.7	36.4	903	891
Logan	6.0	0.0	1.3	5.8	3.3	1.2	6.7	56.6	20.7	24.3	776	769
McDonough	5.7	0.9	1.3	6.1	2.0	3.6	1.9	95.6	27.9	20.1	589	580
McHenry	29.3	5.4	9.2	12.9	5.0	1.2	26.5	488.0	118.1	268.3	1 132	1 042
McLean	40.5	1.3	8.0	22.1	7.0	4.6	30.4	287.4	91.3	149.2	1 060	903
Macon	21.0	9.2	20.8	42.1	12.5	4.9	23.3	270.8	134.0	79.6	697	658
Macoupin	7.4	0.5	1.9	10.4	4.8	1.4	3.7	81.4	47.0	26.3	535	434
Madison	39.0	29.7	43.7	85.8	33.9	12.2	18.9	536.5	250.4	179.6	695	619
Marion	11.2	0.2	2.9	17.4	5.9	1.8	3.3	120.6	53.0	25.1	596	542
Marshall	2.1	0.0	0.7	1.4	0.6	0.2	1.0	19.8	8.8	8.6	666	646
Mason	3.0	0.1	0.8	4.3	1.6	0.7	1.5	49.0	18.4	16.2	958	886
Massac	2.1	41.0	1.9	8.8	1.5	0.5	4.9	32.6	13.4	7.1	459	434
Menard	1.1	0.0	0.3	3.7	0.7	0.2	0.2	25.3	12.0	8.0	644	639
Mercer	3.1	0.2	0.7	2.2	1.1	0.2	0.6	41.0	17.9	10.6	604	583
Monroe	3.2	2.2	0.9	5.0	0.6	0.2	0.0	47.0	19.8	15.2	585	509
Montgomery	6.3	0.2	1.3	8.5	2.1	0.8	10.5	56.7	27.2	20.2	651	570
Morgan	5.7	0.3	1.7	17.5	2.4	0.6	13.3	58.4	26.5	21.7	601	541
Moultrie	2.1	0.1	0.4	2.2	0.5	0.3	0.7	20.7	9.0	8.9	617	615
Ogle	7.9	3.5	6.1	5.1	1.9	0.6	1.9	122.7	38.8	63.6	1 268	1 217
Peoria	127.4	40.8	30.6	52.1	22.5	7.5	46.9	395.6	173.7	146.4	801	619
Perry	2.7	0.0	0.7	6.3	1.6	0.7	2.0	30.1	19.3	6.6	308	283
Piatt	2.5	0.0	0.7	2.0	0.7	0.1	0.3	36.6	16.2	14.7	893	870
Pike	3.6	0.0	4.8	6.6	1.4	0.7	5.6	32.3	17.2	9.9	573	526
Pope	3.0	0.0	0.8	2.1	0.5	0.2	3.6	5.9	3.6	1.6	346	326
Pulaski	2.9	2.4	0.4	10.5	4.5	0.9	0.4	16.2	12.1	2.1	295	268
Putnam	0.8	0.0	0.2	0.3	0.3	0.1	0.1	10.3	5.0	3.9	662	653
Randolph	6.0	0.1	4.5	7.5	2.9	0.6	4.0	76.1	26.3	15.4	451	372
Richland	3.1	0.0	0.8	6.3	1.2	1.1	1.8	75.3	31.5	8.0	473	463
Rock Island	253.0	71.2	10.6	33.8	16.3	4.7	12.8	338.4	141.7	119.4	805	718
St. Clair	358.6	105.1	17.2	169.7	44.1	13.8	30.4	607.9	328.6	164.8	624	488
Saline	6.2	4.7	15.2	19.4	2.5	1.2	3.2	59.5	33.5	15.1	572	565
Sangamon	110.2	2.7	18.7	226.6	807.2	249.4	296.6	397.2	159.8	166.8	871	763
Schuyler	1.4	0.1	0.4	2.6	0.5	0.3	4.8	20.5	5.8	5.3	691	621
Scott	0.9	0.6	0.3	2.6	0.4	0.1	1.0	11.6	5.8	3.3	588	567
Shelby	4.5	1.1	0.9	6.1	1.2	0.4	0.3	36.8	16.2	15.2	674	600
Stark	1.3	0.1	0.6	1.3	0.4	0.2	1.1	14.7	5.5	7.0	1 108	1 087
Stephenson	7.8	0.4	2.0	11.8	3.5	1.3	9.1	104.9	45.0	37.5	760	737
Tazewell	27.8	1.3	3.5	21.4	8.5	3.0	25.7	289.5	124.2	105.4	820	753
Union	2.8	0.0	0.7	14.6	1.5	0.6	5.1	45.6	23.1	7.2	399	393
Vermilion	57.1	3.0	48.6	30.7	10.8	3.6	4.8	190.2	95.3	51.5	606	572
Wabash	1.7	0.0	0.5	3.5	0.9	0.3	1.6	40.5	11.4	9.5	747	679
Warren	3.7	0.0	2.6	5.7	3.2	0.6	0.6	44.7	16.6	12.9	685	645
Washington	3.0	0.0	0.7	3.4	0.8	0.2	0.2	31.6	12.2	9.3	606	525
Wayne	3.2	0.0	0.8	6.4	1.2	0.5	2.5	28.8	16.5	8.0	471	411
White	2.9	0.0	15.3	8.5	4.3	0.7	3.0	40.4	20.7	8.9	569	453
Whiteside	9.4	2.2	3.1	10.2	7.0	1.2	4.9	194.4	51.4	43.1	633	592
Will	46.7	12.2	13.4	44.2	21.7	6.9	30.7	915.2	273.2	465.8	1 048	892
Williamson	54.3	77.7	6.6	26.5	4.1	2.0	3.3	154.5	67.1	36.2	591	496
Winnebago	58.2	52.6	20.4	70.4	21.2	7.0	22.5	617.9	241.2	271.4	1 018	973
Woodford	3.7	0.0	6.4	3.0	1.4	0.5	2.1	68.3	30.1	30.9	888	850

1. October 1, 1998 to September 30, 1999.   2. State totals may include programs not allocated by county.   3. Based on the resident population estimated as of July 1 of the year shown.

Table B. States and Counties — **Local Government Finances, Government Employment, and Elections**

STATE County	Local government finances, 1997 (cont'd)									Government employment, 1998			Presidential election, 2000		
	Direct general expenditure							Debt outstanding					Percent of vote cast —		
			Percent of total for —												
	Total (mil dol)	Per capita[1] (dollars)	Education	Health and hospitals	Police protec-tion	Public welfare	High-ways	Total (mil dol)	Per capita[1] (dollars)	Federal civilian	Federal military	State and local	Demo-cratic	Republi-can	All other
	183	184	185	186	187	188	189	190	191	192	193	194	195	196	197
ILLINOIS—Cont'd															
Jackson	106.6	1 756	45.7	4.3	6.1	6.6	4.7	78.7	1 296	334	156	12 478	51.0	42.5	6.5
Jasper	23.2	2 196	53.8	5.7	4.2	0.9	17.6	3.7	347	46	24	674	36.1	62.1	1.7
Jefferson	79.4	2 036	62.0	0.0	4.7	0.3	11.2	17.4	447	165	85	2 015	43.5	54.4	2.0
Jersey	42.8	2 014	34.3	31.0	4.0	0.1	3.9	3.0	141	52	48	1 082	46.3	49.9	3.8
Jo Daviess	46.5	2 146	49.4	11.7	4.1	0.2	11.9	10.1	465	83	49	1 141	44.4	51.4	4.2
Johnson	13.4	1 022	67.1	0.0	3.7	0.3	10.5	6.5	499	81	30	978	36.0	61.3	2.8
Kane	1 114.6	2 927	55.4	0.5	6.5	0.2	6.0	1 084.3	2 847	1 829	886	21 576	42.5	54.5	3.0
Kankakee	215.3	2 111	58.1	1.3	6.2	0.4	8.2	128.2	1 257	337	231	6 035	47.7	49.9	2.4
Kendall	91.0	1 824	63.6	0.0	2.1	2.5	4.9	60.5	1 214	85	117	1 903	37.1	60.1	2.8
Knox	123.9	2 230	49.0	0.0	5.6	6.3	7.1	56.5	1 017	209	125	3 273	54.3	42.8	3.0
Lake	1 651.8	2 777	56.9	0.0	5.5	1.1	5.1	1 373.3	2 309	6 292	25 792	28 836	47.5	50.0	2.5
La Salle	217.5	1 986	58.6	1.4	4.7	2.2	8.6	129.4	1 181	361	249	5 864	50.8	46.2	3.0
Lawrence	22.5	1 442	61.5	0.1	4.3	0.3	13.9	4.4	280	52	35	974	42.9	54.6	2.5
Lee	73.7	2 061	59.8	1.6	4.9	3.5	8.5	21.3	595	99	81	2 433	41.8	55.2	3.0
Livingston	90.9	2 255	56.1	4.0	3.5	0.9	8.5	34.7	861	116	90	3 012	37.8	59.6	2.6
Logan	49.4	1 577	46.6	4.2	5.5	0.1	9.4	9.0	288	116	71	2 271	35.2	62.3	2.5
McDonough	88.4	2 593	30.3	36.0	2.8	3.4	6.7	32.9	967	107	82	6 390	46.7	49.7	3.6
McHenry	525.3	2 217	55.4	2.0	5.5	0.9	6.5	417.5	1 762	555	545	9 844	38.3	58.5	3.2
McLean	271.8	1 931	47.3	1.5	6.8	1.7	7.9	221.9	1 576	935	330	12 380	40.9	55.8	3.2
Macon	264.6	2 316	45.5	2.0	5.7	0.6	6.7	167.2	1 463	354	269	6 064	49.0	48.1	2.8
Macoupin	76.9	1 562	61.8	1.4	6.1	0.3	10.2	31.4	637	152	110	2 437	51.5	45.6	2.9
Madison	521.0	2 014	53.5	3.6	5.4	2.6	5.4	255.0	986	783	613	15 561	53.2	43.9	2.9
Marion	114.5	2 724	53.8	12.2	3.1	0.3	4.2	33.7	801	213	95	2 403	48.4	49.5	2.1
Marshall	18.5	1 442	50.8	0.9	5.0	1.0	15.2	11.5	893	43	29	400	43.5	53.2	3.3
Mason	49.1	2 909	42.0	20.2	2.4	0.3	7.9	21.6	1 277	65	38	1 124	47.1	50.4	2.5
Massac	30.9	2 004	42.6	26.6	4.1	1.1	5.1	8.1	523	51	35	869	43.2	54.5	2.3
Menard	24.3	1 966	60.8	2.2	5.9	9.2	4.2	19.2	1 551	37	28	737	34.9	62.3	2.8
Mercer	37.5	2 138	44.5	22.5	3.1	0.1	9.4	7.5	425	73	40	1 180	52.9	44.3	2.8
Monroe	43.6	1 681	46.7	1.6	4.8	8.4	6.0	17.7	684	62	60	1 201	42.0	55.3	2.7
Montgomery	53.5	1 726	57.7	1.9	5.5	0.1	8.3	25.0	805	117	71	1 907	50.0	47.6	2.5
Morgan	56.5	1 566	56.8	1.3	5.7	1.7	7.6	16.7	462	111	80	2 340	41.2	56.2	2.6
Moultrie	20.8	1 444	47.0	1.3	2.2	0.1	16.2	7.3	503	40	33	596	44.2	53.4	2.4
Ogle	121.6	2 422	62.8	1.1	3.7	0.5	7.1	57.7	1 150	160	114	2 416	37.2	59.8	2.9
Peoria	382.4	2 094	41.8	1.9	5.1	2.3	6.9	229.8	1 258	1 584	453	9 068	50.3	47.4	2.4
Perry	28.4	1 329	58.3	4.3	4.3	0.2	6.5	11.3	527	56	48	1 176	48.9	48.3	2.8
Piatt	35.9	2 175	51.4	0.7	3.9	9.9	11.1	16.3	987	55	37	897	41.6	55.1	3.3
Pike	32.9	1 903	57.3	6.4	2.9	1.4	8.7	14.1	817	76	39	938	39.4	58.0	2.6
Pope	5.7	1 221	61.7	1.1	4.0	0.3	4.1	3.7	781	97	12	286	39.8	57.8	2.4
Pulaski	17.2	2 380	69.9	1.8	2.5	0.6	7.6	1.7	237	69	16	807	50.3	47.4	2.3
Putnam	10.0	1 709	56.7	0.7	5.8	0.1	13.3	2.6	437	25	13	296	52.1	45.2	2.7
Randolph	69.4	2 036	38.0	29.1	3.8	4.1	8.3	24.4	715	108	76	2 877	47.6	49.9	2.6
Richland	76.7	4 554	49.8	30.4	1.1	0.0	7.0	4.6	273	67	38	1 840	33.5	63.5	2.9
Rock Island	311.1	2 098	53.0	1.0	6.6	2.6	4.9	180.0	1 214	6 388	507	8 700	58.3	38.7	3.0
St. Clair	575.1	2 179	52.8	1.8	4.9	1.1	4.8	387.0	1 467	4 599	6 368	11 852	55.7	42.1	2.1
Saline	57.7	2 191	59.1	4.0	3.9	1.0	7.3	24.8	941	133	59	1 888	46.6	50.9	2.5
Sangamon	382.5	1 997	50.5	1.3	7.9	0.4	6.5	439.7	2 295	2 153	452	27 077	42.0	55.1	2.9
Schuyler	20.7	2 714	39.3	35.4	1.0	0.1	5.7	5.0	655	31	17	502	42.1	55.1	2.9
Scott	12.0	2 139	48.3	0.0	3.6	12.8	10.0	1.1	201	21	13	347	38.6	59.1	2.3
Shelby	35.1	1 552	44.8	2.1	3.9	0.1	18.0	5.8	255	111	51	1 044	39.5	57.6	2.9
Stark	14.5	2 288	51.0	0.4	2.6	0.2	10.6	1.7	275	33	14	309	40.5	56.7	2.8
Stephenson	114.7	2 324	60.1	0.9	3.6	4.6	5.8	41.0	831	142	112	2 570	41.6	55.3	3.1
Tazewell	272.1	2 117	60.9	0.9	4.5	0.1	5.3	142.8	1 111	519	289	6 245	43.5	54.0	2.5
Union	44.1	2 443	62.2	21.6	2.0	0.8	3.0	14.7	813	65	41	1 990	46.0	50.8	3.2
Vermilion	174.4	2 049	55.7	1.9	5.7	4.4	5.7	72.5	852	1 576	191	4 479	48.0	49.2	2.8
Wabash	37.3	2 926	28.9	40.6	3.2	1.2	3.3	10.1	792	38	29	771	36.1	61.8	2.1
Warren	38.8	2 065	41.3	21.3	3.8	0.1	10.1	18.0	956	78	43	984	46.2	51.1	2.7
Washington	26.6	1 739	41.0	26.0	3.5	0.0	7.9	10.0	655	63	35	933	37.0	61.0	2.1
Wayne	27.0	1 590	58.1	1.2	4.0	1.2	13.8	3.0	179	70	38	830	28.7	69.5	1.8
White	39.6	2 528	51.7	18.8	3.4	0.7	10.7	6.6	423	65	35	1 141	38.7	59.2	2.1
Whiteside	192.3	2 824	32.8	40.0	2.8	1.0	4.8	52.8	776	191	136	3 579	51.9	45.3	2.8
Will	926.1	2 084	50.8	1.8	6.1	1.0	6.2	729.6	1 642	814	1 055	20 751	47.4	50.0	2.6
Williamson	150.3	2 458	50.4	18.7	3.0	0.6	4.8	68.2	1 115	1 196	137	3 901	45.3	52.0	2.7
Winnebago	617.2	2 315	49.7	1.1	7.1	2.7	5.7	433.9	1 627	1 143	609	12 612	47.6	49.2	3.2
Woodford	59.4	1 709	67.7	0.4	4.0	0.8	9.6	13.4	385	76	80	1 631	32.9	64.9	2.1

1. Based on the resident population estimated as of July 1 of the year shown.

Table B. States and Counties — Land Area and Population

STATE/ County code	MSA/ PMSA/ NECMA code[1]	County Type[2]	STATE County	Land area,[3] (sq km) 1990	Population and population characteristics, 1999			Race (percent)				Percent Hispanic[4]	Age (percent)					
					Total persons	Rank	Per square kilometer	White	Black	Am. Indian, Eskimo, Aleut	Asian and Pacific Islander		Under 5 years	5 to 17 years	18 to 24 years	25 to 34 years	35 to 44 years	45 to 54 years
				1	2	3	4	5	6	7	8	9	10	11	12	13	14	15
18 000	...	X	INDIANA	92 904	5 942 901	X	64.0	90.4	8.4	0.3	1.0	2.6	7.0	18.8	9.7	13.9	16.2	13.2
18 001	2760	2	Adams	879	33 168	1 280	37.7	99.3	0.2	0.2	0.3	4.0	8.5	22.7	8.7	12.7	14.8	11.8
18 003	2760	2	Allen	1 702	316 471	177	185.9	86.8	11.6	0.3	1.3	3.0	7.6	19.5	8.9	14.7	17.0	12.4
18 005	...	4	Bartholomew	1 054	69 714	703	66.1	96.5	1.9	0.2	1.4	1.1	6.8	18.1	8.1	13.2	17.1	15.5
18 007	...	8	Benton	1 052	9 776	2 447	9.3	99.7	0.1	0.2	0.0	1.8	7.2	20.7	6.8	12.4	14.8	13.2
18 009	...	6	Blackford	428	13 927	2 141	32.5	99.5	0.1	0.3	0.1	0.9	6.6	17.9	7.6	12.2	15.4	14.9
18 011	3480	1	Boone	1 095	44 835	988	40.9	99.1	0.3	0.3	0.4	1.1	7.2	19.5	6.6	13.5	17.7	14.9
18 013	...	8	Brown	809	15 992	2 004	19.8	99.1	0.2	0.4	0.2	1.1	5.9	17.9	6.8	12.2	17.8	16.2
18 015	...	6	Carroll	964	20 004	1 761	20.8	99.7	0.1	0.1	0.0	1.0	6.8	19.2	7.3	12.8	15.9	14.4
18 017	...	6	Cass	1 069	38 964	1 112	36.4	98.2	0.9	0.4	0.5	0.9	6.5	19.3	7.1	12.6	15.8	13.8
18 019	4520	2	Clark	972	95 121	532	97.9	92.9	6.2	0.3	0.6	1.0	6.2	18.6	8.3	14.0	17.1	13.9
18 021	8320	3	Clay	926	26 903	1 469	29.1	99.2	0.5	0.2	0.1	0.4	6.7	19.3	7.5	12.8	15.0	13.4
18 023	3920	3	Clinton	1 049	32 964	1 286	31.4	99.2	0.3	0.2	0.3	2.3	7.3	20.0	7.4	13.0	15.5	13.1
18 025	...	8	Crawford	792	10 739	2 361	13.6	99.5	0.1	0.3	0.2	0.3	6.7	20.2	8.1	12.4	15.5	13.8
18 027	...	7	Daviess	1 116	29 084	1 408	26.1	99.3	0.5	0.1	0.1	0.5	7.8	20.9	7.5	12.4	15.2	12.5
18 029	1640	1	Dearborn	791	48 011	936	60.7	98.8	0.8	0.2	0.3	0.5	7.3	20.8	7.7	13.1	17.2	13.9
18 031	...	6	Decatur	965	25 704	1 505	26.6	99.0	0.1	0.1	0.8	0.6	7.1	21.2	8.1	13.4	15.2	13.3
18 033	2760	2	De Kalb	940	39 683	1 094	42.2	99.2	0.1	0.3	0.4	1.4	7.6	21.0	8.1	14.3	16.2	12.9
18 035	5280	3	Delaware	1 019	115 472	457	113.3	92.0	7.0	0.3	0.8	1.1	5.8	15.6	16.9	11.5	14.2	13.4
18 037	...	7	Dubois	1 114	40 093	1 087	36.0	99.6	0.1	0.1	0.2	1.0	7.8	19.7	8.1	14.9	15.7	12.7
18 039	2330	3	Elkhart	1 201	174 680	304	145.4	93.5	5.2	0.3	1.0	2.9	8.2	19.6	9.1	14.0	16.6	13.1
18 041	...	7	Fayette	557	25 860	1 501	46.4	97.5	1.9	0.2	0.4	0.5	5.9	19.7	8.0	11.4	16.3	13.9
18 043	4520	2	Floyd	383	72 243	679	188.6	94.7	4.7	0.1	0.4	0.6	6.7	19.2	8.0	13.4	17.6	13.9
18 045	...	6	Fountain	1 025	18 374	1 850	17.9	99.5	0.1	0.1	0.3	0.8	6.6	18.7	7.3	12.0	14.5	14.9
18 047	...	6	Franklin	1 000	22 120	1 653	22.1	99.5	0.1	0.2	0.2	0.4	7.1	21.6	7.9	12.7	15.9	13.1
18 049	...	7	Fulton	954	20 893	1 721	21.9	98.4	0.9	0.3	0.4	1.2	6.8	19.4	6.6	12.9	14.9	14.0
18 051	...	6	Gibson	1 266	32 230	1 307	25.5	97.2	2.2	0.1	0.5	0.6	6.3	18.6	7.7	12.9	15.4	13.4
18 053	...	4	Grant	1 072	72 082	680	67.2	91.0	7.7	0.4	0.8	3.1	6.0	17.3	11.0	11.5	14.9	14.3
18 055	...	6	Greene	1 404	33 158	1 281	23.6	99.4	0.1	0.2	0.4	0.8	6.3	18.7	7.5	12.4	15.6	14.4
18 057	3480	0	Hamilton	1 031	172 094	306	166.9	97.4	0.7	0.2	1.7	1.1	7.9	20.3	6.5	14.6	20.1	15.0
18 059	3480	1	Hancock	793	55 617	832	70.1	99.1	0.1	0.2	0.6	1.1	6.2	20.1	7.4	12.3	18.3	15.9
18 061	4520	2	Harrison	1 257	35 376	1 210	28.1	99.1	0.5	0.2	0.2	0.7	6.6	20.9	7.6	13.3	17.5	13.8
18 063	3480	1	Hendricks	1 058	98 826	521	93.4	98.2	1.0	0.3	0.6	0.8	6.6	20.0	7.6	13.7	18.3	15.3
18 065	...	6	Henry	1 018	48 377	931	47.5	98.5	1.1	0.2	0.2	0.7	5.8	17.8	7.6	12.1	16.0	14.8
18 067	3850	3	Howard	759	83 736	605	110.3	92.5	6.3	0.3	0.8	2.0	6.7	18.8	7.8	12.8	16.2	15.2
18 069	2760	2	Huntington	991	37 377	1 152	37.7	98.7	0.3	0.4	0.6	1.2	7.3	19.9	8.9	13.5	15.3	12.6
18 071	...	7	Jackson	1 319	41 319	1 055	31.3	98.5	0.5	0.2	0.8	0.5	6.8	19.7	8.1	13.5	15.6	13.9
18 073	...	6	Jasper	1 450	29 462	1 394	20.3	99.2	0.3	0.3	0.2	1.9	7.0	21.3	9.4	12.2	15.8	13.9
18 075	...	6	Jay	994	21 686	1 672	21.8	99.2	0.2	0.1	0.5	1.1	6.6	19.2	7.9	12.0	14.9	14.6
18 077	...	6	Jefferson	936	31 813	1 321	34.0	97.7	1.5	0.2	0.6	0.7	6.3	18.3	10.5	12.9	15.9	14.2
18 079	...	7	Jennings	977	28 106	1 435	28.8	98.5	1.0	0.2	0.4	0.6	7.0	19.8	8.5	13.4	16.1	14.9
18 081	3480	0	Johnson	829	112 724	468	136.0	98.0	0.9	0.2	0.9	1.1	6.8	19.5	8.9	13.9	17.9	14.3
18 083	...	5	Knox	1 336	39 051	1 110	29.2	97.9	1.4	0.2	0.6	0.8	6.0	16.8	12.9	11.9	14.3	12.7
18 085	...	6	Kosciusko	1 392	71 336	688	51.2	98.5	0.6	0.2	0.7	3.0	7.9	20.0	8.5	13.6	15.9	13.2
18 087	...	8	Lagrange	983	33 997	1 255	34.6	99.0	0.2	0.3	0.5	1.9	9.6	24.6	9.1	12.3	14.3	11.9
18 089	2960	0	Lake	1 287	480 619	114	373.4	72.3	26.6	0.2	0.8	13.3	6.9	20.4	8.5	13.5	15.8	12.9
18 091	...	4	La Porte	1 550	109 939	480	70.9	89.0	10.1	0.3	0.6	2.3	6.4	18.1	8.4	13.9	17.1	13.4
18 093	...	6	Lawrence	1 163	45 752	974	39.3	99.2	0.3	0.2	0.3	0.5	6.3	18.5	7.8	12.3	16.0	14.7
18 095	3480	3	Madison	1 171	130 990	397	111.9	90.7	8.6	0.3	0.5	1.0	6.1	17.7	9.1	12.6	16.1	14.1
18 097	3480	0	Marion	1 027	810 946	52	789.6	74.3	24.1	0.2	1.4	1.7	7.7	17.6	9.6	17.1	16.2	12.1
18 099	...	6	Marshall	1 151	46 129	965	40.1	98.9	0.3	0.2	0.6	3.0	7.6	20.3	7.6	13.1	15.9	12.9
18 101	...	7	Martin	871	10 379	2 390	11.9	99.5	0.1	0.1	0.2	0.3	6.5	19.4	7.9	12.5	15.6	13.8
18 103	...	6	Miami	973	33 605	1 267	34.5	94.2	3.3	1.6	0.9	2.2	7.6	20.0	8.1	13.9	15.6	12.5
18 105	1020	3	Monroe	1 021	116 923	450	114.5	93.4	3.0	0.2	3.3	1.9	5.4	12.9	26.3	14.6	14.1	10.3
18 107	...	6	Montgomery	1 307	36 583	1 177	28.0	98.5	0.7	0.2	0.6	0.7	6.7	17.9	9.3	13.3	15.1	14.0
18 109	3480	1	Morgan	1 053	67 003	722	63.6	99.4	0.0	0.3	0.3	0.6	6.8	20.1	8.2	13.3	16.9	15.1
18 111	...	8	Newton	1 041	14 844	2 078	14.3	99.3	0.1	0.3	0.3	2.0	6.9	21.8	7.0	12.8	16.1	14.4
18 113	...	6	Noble	1 065	43 241	1 017	40.6	99.2	0.2	0.2	0.4	2.5	8.0	21.0	8.6	13.6	16.1	12.9
18 115	1640	1	Ohio	225	5 457	2 809	24.3	98.8	0.8	0.1	0.3	0.2	6.3	18.9	7.7	13.7	15.1	14.3
18 117	...	7	Orange	1 035	19 835	1 770	19.2	98.9	0.7	0.2	0.2	0.5	6.8	19.6	7.6	12.9	15.7	13.6
18 119	...	6	Owen	998	20 619	1 733	20.7	99.2	0.3	0.3	0.2	0.5	6.7	19.3	7.6	12.3	16.0	14.5
18 121	...	6	Parke	1 152	16 908	1 932	14.7	98.1	1.5	0.3	0.2	0.9	6.3	17.6	7.9	13.0	15.7	14.7
18 123	...	7	Perry	988	19 091	1 815	19.3	98.2	1.4	0.2	0.2	0.5	6.1	19.2	8.8	14.3	15.5	12.6
18 125	...	8	Pike	871	13 021	2 216	14.9	99.6	0.0	0.1	0.2	0.5	6.1	17.8	7.4	12.6	15.6	15.0
18 127	2960	1	Porter	1 083	147 758	352	136.4	98.3	0.4	0.2	1.1	4.6	6.6	20.1	9.3	13.0	18.2	14.1
18 129	2440	2	Posey	1 058	26 292	1 486	24.9	98.3	1.3	0.2	0.2	0.6	7.3	19.9	7.2	13.9	17.2	13.6
18 131	...	9	Pulaski	1 123	13 527	2 174	12.0	98.7	0.8	0.2	0.3	1.4	7.4	20.5	7.5	12.6	14.6	12.6

1. MSA = Metropolitan Statistical Area. PMSA = Primary MSA. NECMA = New England County Metropolitan Area. See Appendix A for explanation of these concepts. See Appendix B for list of metropolitan areas identified by type, with component counties.   2. County typology code from the Economic Research Service of USDA. See Appendix A for definition.   3. Dry land or land partially or temporarily covered by water.   4. Hispanic persons may be of any race.

Table B. States and Counties — **Population and Households**

STATE County	Population, 1999 (cont'd) Age (percent) (cont'd)				Population — change and components of change, 1980–1999 Total persons		Percent change		Components of change, 1990–1999			Households, 1990			Percent	
	55 to 64 years	65 to 74 years	75 years and over	Percent female	1990	1980	1980–1990	1990–1999	Births	Deaths	Net migration	Number	Percent change, 1980–1990	Persons per household	Female family householder[1]	One person
	16	17	18	19	20	21	22	23	24	25	26	27	28	29	30	31
INDIANA	8.8	6.6	5.9	51.3	5 544 156	5 490 214	1.0	7.2	779 368	482 740	111 727	2 065 355	7.2	2.61	10.5	24.1
Adams	7.7	6.3	6.7	50.7	31 095	29 619	5.0	6.7	5 417	2 505	-732	10 470	8.8	2.92	7.6	20.9
Allen	8.1	6.2	5.5	51.5	300 836	294 335	2.2	5.2	46 643	23 085	-6 982	113 333	8.6	2.61	10.9	24.9
Bartholomew	9.2	6.4	5.6	51.2	63 657	65 088	-2.2	9.5	9 406	5 255	2 102	24 192	6.1	2.60	9.2	21.7
Benton	9.7	7.6	7.6	50.9	9 441	10 218	-7.6	3.5	1 404	901	-136	3 524	-3.5	2.65	7.3	23.9
Blackford	10.2	7.9	7.5	51.4	14 067	15 570	-9.7	-1.0	1 722	1 465	-357	5 436	-2.5	2.56	8.6	23.2
Boone	8.6	5.8	6.3	51.6	38 147	36 446	4.7	17.5	5 373	3 510	4 946	13 922	10.1	2.69	6.9	19.7
Brown	10.5	7.2	5.4	49.8	14 080	12 377	13.8	13.6	1 329	1 038	1 668	5 370	21.2	2.61	5.7	20.4
Carroll	9.7	7.3	6.6	50.8	18 809	19 722	-4.6	6.4	2 325	1 636	595	7 067	1.1	2.63	6.1	21.4
Cass	9.7	8.2	7.1	51.9	38 413	40 936	-6.2	1.4	4 846	3 772	-412	14 659	-0.4	2.55	9.7	24.5
Clark	9.2	6.8	5.9	52.2	87 774	88 838	-1.2	8.4	11 649	8 488	4 416	33 292	7.3	2.59	12.2	23.3
Clay	10.0	7.4	7.9	51.8	24 705	24 862	-0.6	8.9	3 156	2 727	1 850	9 382	1.6	2.60	8.6	24.0
Clinton	9.2	7.1	7.4	51.4	30 974	31 545	-1.8	6.4	4 436	3 340	1 016	11 450	1.1	2.65	8.4	22.1
Crawford	9.6	6.6	7.2	50.2	9 914	9 820	1.0	8.3	1 134	993	717	3 660	5.7	2.69	8.1	22.4
Daviess	9.4	7.1	7.3	51.4	27 533	27 836	-1.1	5.6	4 149	2 763	259	10 012	1.4	2.70	8.3	24.2
Dearborn	9.0	5.9	5.1	50.7	38 835	34 291	13.3	23.6	5 270	3 302	7 288	13 642	18.8	2.81	9.1	19.2
Decatur	8.9	6.3	6.5	50.5	23 645	23 841	-0.8	8.7	3 294	2 146	1 003	8 427	4.4	2.77	8.6	20.9
De Kalb	8.4	5.8	5.7	50.9	35 324	33 606	5.1	12.3	5 286	2 911	2 092	12 725	11.3	2.75	8.3	21.3
Delaware	9.0	7.1	6.6	52.5	119 659	128 587	-6.9	-3.5	13 523	10 483	-6 965	45 177	1.1	2.47	10.6	25.9
Dubois	8.5	6.1	6.4	50.8	36 616	34 238	6.9	9.5	5 291	2 999	1 302	13 023	16.3	2.75	6.7	21.9
Elkhart	8.2	5.8	5.4	50.9	156 198	137 330	13.7	11.8	25 457	11 873	5 434	56 713	17.8	2.71	9.1	21.6
Fayette	9.7	7.9	7.1	51.5	26 015	28 272	-8.0	-0.6	3 281	2 580	-786	9 945	-0.2	2.58	11.0	24.1
Floyd	9.0	6.4	5.8	52.1	64 404	61 205	5.2	12.2	8 677	5 757	5 098	24 085	12.2	2.63	12.6	21.9
Fountain	10.1	8.0	7.8	51.5	17 808	19 033	-6.4	3.2	2 180	1 929	379	6 858	-1.6	2.57	7.3	23.8
Franklin	9.1	6.3	6.3	50.2	19 580	19 612	-0.2	13.0	2 574	1 480	1 486	6 636	8.1	2.90	6.8	18.2
Fulton	10.4	7.7	7.3	51.3	18 840	19 335	-2.6	10.9	2 517	1 935	1 523	7 345	2.0	2.54	7.6	24.2
Gibson	10.0	7.6	8.0	51.8	31 913	33 156	-3.7	1.0	3 715	3 177	-103	12 299	1.0	2.56	7.9	24.5
Grant	10.0	8.0	6.9	51.7	74 169	80 934	-8.4	-2.8	9 134	7 133	-3 869	27 701	-0.9	2.56	11.4	23.7
Greene	10.0	7.5	7.6	51.2	30 410	30 416	0.0	9.0	3 554	3 091	2 371	11 910	3.4	2.52	8.2	24.8
Hamilton	7.7	4.4	3.4	50.9	108 936	82 027	32.8	58.0	20 364	6 740	49 389	38 834	42.4	2.78	6.9	17.0
Hancock	8.7	6.0	5.1	50.7	45 527	43 939	3.6	22.2	5 994	3 578	7 775	15 959	10.3	2.82	6.8	17.0
Harrison	8.9	5.9	5.6	50.3	29 890	27 276	9.6	18.4	3 664	2 268	4 141	10 618	16.9	2.79	8.3	18.2
Hendricks	8.3	5.8	4.4	49.5	75 717	69 804	8.5	30.5	10 138	5 431	18 523	26 109	15.1	2.81	7.1	16.4
Henry	10.2	8.1	7.5	51.9	48 139	53 336	-9.7	0.5	5 695	4 775	-531	18 642	-0.8	2.55	9.3	22.8
Howard	9.6	7.1	5.9	52.2	80 827	86 896	-7.0	3.6	11 341	6 830	-1 394	31 523	1.5	2.54	11.3	25.0
Huntington	8.6	6.8	7.1	51.3	35 427	35 596	-0.5	5.5	4 729	3 349	693	12 830	3.8	2.68	8.1	21.9
Jackson	9.3	6.4	6.8	51.4	37 730	36 523	3.3	9.5	5 301	3 577	1 998	14 032	8.3	2.66	9.1	21.2
Jasper	8.5	6.4	5.6	50.6	24 823	26 138	-4.5	18.7	3 368	2 091	3 461	8 527	2.9	2.80	7.5	19.1
Jay	9.8	7.7	7.2	51.2	21 512	23 239	-7.4	0.8	3 065	2 131	-671	8 161	-2.4	2.61	8.4	23.7
Jefferson	9.2	6.7	6.1	50.9	29 797	30 419	-2.0	6.8	3 750	2 946	1 304	10 897	5.9	2.57	10.5	23.4
Jennings	9.2	5.8	5.2	50.5	23 661	22 854	3.5	18.8	3 570	2 079	3 008	8 351	14.2	2.75	8.7	20.0
Johnson	8.1	5.4	5.2	51.3	88 109	77 240	14.1	27.9	12 916	7 492	19 450	31 354	23.7	2.71	8.6	19.3
Knox	9.7	7.4	8.3	51.3	39 884	41 838	-4.7	-2.1	4 432	4 298	-877	15 145	-2.2	2.45	9.5	27.9
Kosciusko	8.6	6.5	5.7	50.8	65 294	59 555	9.6	9.3	10 107	5 058	1 213	23 449	12.4	2.74	7.2	20.1
Lagrange	7.7	5.6	4.8	49.9	29 477	25 550	15.4	15.3	6 045	1 859	433	9 209	18.5	3.15	5.7	16.6
Lake	8.9	7.6	5.4	52.0	475 594	522 917	-9.0	1.1	67 859	42 847	-21 629	170 748	-2.5	2.76	15.9	23.2
La Porte	9.2	7.4	6.1	48.8	107 066	108 632	-1.4	2.7	13 588	9 393	-923	38 488	2.9	2.63	10.9	23.6
Lawrence	9.8	7.3	7.3	51.4	42 836	42 472	0.9	6.8	5 519	4 475	2 018	16 235	4.6	2.60	8.3	22.5
Madison	9.6	7.7	6.8	51.0	130 669	139 336	-6.2	0.2	15 943	12 532	-2 761	49 804	-0.4	2.52	11.4	24.9
Marion	8.5	6.1	5.3	52.5	797 159	765 233	4.2	1.7	132 708	69 011	-48 260	319 471	12.1	2.45	13.8	29.3
Marshall	9.2	6.7	6.6	50.7	42 182	39 155	7.7	9.4	5 949	3 578	1 708	15 146	11.0	2.74	7.5	21.0
Martin	9.7	8.1	6.4	50.6	10 369	11 001	-5.7	0.1	1 408	968	-403	3 836	1.1	2.64	7.9	23.9
Miami	8.5	7.3	6.4	51.3	36 897	39 820	-7.3	-8.9	4 694	2 896	-5 323	13 484	-1.5	2.68	8.6	21.2
Monroe	6.7	5.0	4.6	51.6	108 978	98 787	10.3	7.3	11 123	6 030	3 170	39 351	15.9	2.39	8.3	28.5
Montgomery	9.6	6.9	7.0	50.2	34 436	35 501	-3.0	6.2	4 819	3 458	887	13 235	2.1	2.51	7.8	24.4
Morgan	8.9	5.8	4.8	50.8	55 920	51 999	7.5	19.8	8 064	4 441	7 564	19 600	14.2	2.83	8.4	16.2
Newton	9.0	6.0	6.1	50.5	13 551	14 844	-8.7	9.5	1 577	1 234	993	4 839	-4.3	2.77	7.5	20.4
Noble	8.5	5.9	5.5	50.5	37 877	35 443	6.9	14.2	6 135	3 156	2 495	13 418	11.2	2.78	8.1	19.8
Ohio	9.7	7.0	7.3	51.2	5 315	5 114	3.9	2.7	568	516	114	1 980	8.9	2.66	7.6	21.6
Orange	9.9	7.4	6.7	51.1	18 409	18 677	-1.4	7.7	2 319	1 868	1 032	6 950	3.5	2.61	8.8	22.8
Owen	10.5	6.8	6.4	50.5	17 281	15 841	9.1	19.3	2 279	1 580	2 685	6 394	13.5	2.68	7.5	19.6
Parke	10.7	7.0	7.2	52.3	15 410	16 372	-5.9	9.7	1 688	1 606	1 459	5 845	-1.8	2.55	8.3	23.6
Perry	9.4	7.3	7.0	49.0	19 107	19 346	-1.2	0.1	1 898	1 767	-89	6 845	1.3	2.66	9.1	23.0
Pike	10.6	7.3	7.6	50.5	12 509	13 465	-7.1	4.1	1 444	1 269	386	4 925	-2.5	2.52	7.5	23.5
Porter	8.1	6.0	4.6	50.9	128 932	119 816	7.6	14.6	15 590	9 097	12 634	45 159	15.4	2.77	8.4	19.6
Posey	8.8	6.2	6.0	50.3	25 968	26 414	-1.7	1.2	3 032	2 060	-562	9 508	4.8	2.71	7.2	20.4
Pulaski	9.8	7.7	7.2	50.0	12 780	13 258	-4.6	5.8	1 701	1 346	446	4 722	0.7	2.65	6.4	23.8

1. No spouse present.

Table B. States and Counties — **Vital Statistics, Health Resources, and Crime**

STATE County	Births, average 1996–1998 Total	Rate[1]	Deaths, average 1996–1998 Number Total	Number Infant[2]	Rate Total[1]	Rate Infant[3]	Physicians,[4] 1998 Number	Rate[5]	Hospitals,[4] 1998 Number	Beds Number	Beds Rate[5]	Medicare enrollees 1999	Serious crimes known to police, 1998[6] Total Number	Rate[7]
	32	33	34	35	36	37	38	39	40	41	42	43	44	45
INDIANA	84 024	14.3	53 192	686	9.1	8.2	10 510	178	117	19 596	332	844 835	245 952	4 169
Adams	600	18.3	275	5	8.4	8.3	17	51	1	87	263	4 563	NA	NA
Allen	4 977	15.9	2 499	38	8.0	7.7	703	224	3	1 042	332	42 156	17 150	5 463
Bartholomew	1 054	15.3	590	8	8.5	7.3	159	229	1	237	341	9 684	NA	NA
Benton	156	16.2	98	0	10.1	2.1	5	51	0	0	0	1 740	49	510
Blackford	182	13.0	165	2	11.8	11.0	8	58	1	28	201	2 412	261	1 851
Boone	580	13.5	399	3	9.3	5.7	160	365	1	49	112	5 468	NA	NA
Brown	128	8.2	122	1	7.8	7.8	11	69	0	0	0	1 302	NA	NA
Carroll	244	12.3	186	2	9.4	6.8	8	40	0	0	0	2 596	NA	NA
Cass	566	14.6	402	4	10.4	7.1	56	145	1	112	290	6 689	NA	NA
Clark	1 283	13.8	937	12	10.0	9.3	116	124	2	376	401	14 185	NA	NA
Clay	337	12.7	285	2	10.7	5.0	14	53	1	55	206	4 952	NA	NA
Clinton	488	14.8	376	4	11.4	8.9	20	60	1	53	160	5 231	NA	NA
Crawford	121	11.6	104	0	10.0	2.8	1	9	0	0	0	1 848	NA	NA
Daviess	424	14.7	301	6	10.4	13.3	20	69	1	85	293	4 435	NA	NA
Dearborn	611	13.2	352	3	7.6	4.9	42	89	1	76	161	6 042	620	1 463
Decatur	364	14.3	233	4	9.2	11.9	20	78	1	73	286	3 763	NA	NA
De Kalb	594	15.3	337	4	8.7	6.2	38	97	1	45	114	5 085	NA	NA
Delaware	1 430	12.2	1 144	13	9.7	9.3	255	218	1	428	366	18 131	NA	NA
Dubois	541	13.8	332	2	8.5	3.1	48	121	2	191	481	5 553	NA	NA
Elkhart	2 876	16.9	1 333	22	7.8	7.7	228	132	2	476	276	21 856	8 634	5 027
Fayette	358	13.7	289	3	11.1	8.4	18	69	1	140	539	4 619	NA	NA
Floyd	884	12.4	630	5	8.8	5.3	116	161	1	174	242	10 054	NA	NA
Fountain	239	13.1	229	3	12.6	12.6	7	38	0	0	0	3 503	NA	NA
Franklin	267	12.4	180	4	8.4	13.7	38	174	0	0	0	2 747	NA	NA
Fulton	269	13.2	210	2	10.3	7.4	17	82	1	49	238	3 409	NA	NA
Gibson	396	12.4	333	3	10.4	6.7	24	75	2	135	420	5 599	NA	NA
Grant	917	12.6	790	9	10.8	9.8	116	160	1	212	292	12 581	3 288	4 489
Greene	365	11.0	346	4	10.5	11.0	19	57	1	76	227	5 598	NA	NA
Hamilton	2 531	16.3	792	18	5.1	7.0	661	407	2	199	122	13 100	3 304	2 122
Hancock	712	13.4	427	4	8.0	5.2	67	123	1	70	128	6 537	608	1 139
Harrison	405	11.9	262	4	7.7	9.1	21	60	1	45	130	4 752	665	1 944
Hendricks	1 184	12.8	645	8	7.0	6.8	115	121	1	127	133	10 005	NA	NA
Henry	605	12.4	530	6	10.8	10.5	42	86	1	107	219	8 818	2 197	4 469
Howard	1 191	14.2	758	9	9.0	7.8	129	155	2	300	359	13 208	3 486	4 146
Huntington	503	13.6	371	4	10.0	8.0	33	89	1	75	201	6 092	752	2 013
Jackson	594	14.6	406	6	9.9	9.5	35	85	1	107	261	6 544	NA	NA
Jasper	364	12.7	241	2	8.4	6.4	14	48	1	69	236	4 240	NA	NA
Jay	328	15.1	238	2	10.9	6.1	16	74	1	71	327	3 819	NA	NA
Jefferson	402	12.9	312	3	10.0	8.3	43	137	1	119	378	4 946	616	1 957
Jennings	408	15.0	240	5	8.8	12.2	10	36	1	34	122	3 802	540	1 972
Johnson	1 489	13.9	862	8	8.1	5.2	168	154	2	180	165	13 651	NA	NA
Knox	470	11.9	462	3	11.7	5.7	76	193	1	301	764	7 034	NA	NA
Kosciusko	1 099	15.6	573	9	8.1	7.9	70	98	1	113	159	9 657	NA	NA
Lagrange	689	21.0	207	6	6.3	8.7	12	36	1	62	185	3 402	NA	NA
Lake	7 066	14.8	4 592	73	9.6	10.3	760	159	8	2 289	479	71 745	20 592	5 180
La Porte	1 433	13.1	1 024	10	9.4	7.2	154	141	3	468	428	16 247	5 554	5 407
Lawrence	602	13.2	487	4	10.7	6.7	41	90	2	245	537	7 459	1 062	2 603
Madison	1 735	13.1	1 388	22	10.5	12.5	146	111	3	659	502	22 359	NA	NA
Marion	13 925	17.1	7 603	136	9.3	9.7	2 718	334	11	4 037	496	112 170	50 878	6 217
Marshall	671	14.8	385	5	8.5	7.0	55	121	2	63	139	6 504	NA	NA
Martin	158	14.9	106	1	10.0	6.3	3	28	0	0	0	1 851	NA	NA
Miami	449	13.6	320	1	9.7	3.0	30	89	1	135	402	5 274	NA	NA
Monroe	1 241	10.7	683	10	5.9	8.3	239	208	1	265	230	12 352	3 965	3 379
Montgomery	499	13.7	373	3	10.3	6.7	45	124	1	120	330	5 768	945	2 589
Morgan	903	14.0	496	6	7.7	6.7	54	82	2	191	292	7 907	NA	NA
Newton	165	11.3	124	0	8.5	2.0	7	48	0	0	0	1 852	200	1 354
Noble	698	16.6	359	3	8.5	4.8	27	63	1	51	120	5 552	893	2 321
Ohio	59	10.8	64	1	11.9	22.7	3	55	0	0	0	758	NA	NA
Orange	255	13.2	208	4	10.7	14.4	16	82	1	37	189	3 196	NA	NA
Owen	234	11.6	187	1	9.2	4.3	4	20	0	0	0	2 736	NA	NA
Parke	173	10.5	160	2	9.7	9.7	11	66	0	0	0	2 772	NA	NA
Perry	199	10.4	191	1	9.9	6.7	6	31	1	44	227	3 184	NA	NA
Pike	156	12.3	139	1	10.9	8.5	5	39	0	0	0	2 178	NA	NA
Porter	1 712	11.9	1 061	13	7.4	7.8	240	165	1	367	252	16 740	4 029	2 780
Posey	287	10.9	227	2	8.6	7.0	12	45	0	0	0	3 605	NA	NA
Pulaski	169	12.8	142	1	10.8	7.9	7	53	1	47	355	2 285	150	1 129

1. Per 1,000 estimated resident population, average 1996–1998. 2. Deaths of infants under 1 year old. 3. Deaths of infants under 1 year old per 1,000 live births. 4. Data subject to copyright. 5. Per 100,000 resident population as of July 1 of the year shown. 6. Data for serious crimes have not been adjusted for underreporting; this may affect comparability between geographic areas and over time. 7. Per 100,000 population estimated by the FBI.

264 IN(Adams)—IN(Pulaski)

STATE County	Serious crimes known to police, 1998[1] (cont'd) Rate[2] Violent	Property	Education — School enrollment and attainment, 1990 Enrollment[3] Total	Percent private	Attainment[4] (percent) High school graduate or more	Bachelor's degree or more	Local government expenditures, fiscal 1997[5] Total current expenditures (mil dol)	Current expenditures per student (dollars)	Money income 1989 Per capita[6] (dollars)	Households Median Dollars	Percent change, 1979–1989 (constant 1989 dollars)	Percent with $100,000 or more	Income and poverty, 1997 Median household income	Percent below poverty level All persons	Persons under 18	Persons 5–17 in families
	46	47	48	49	50	51	52	53	54	55	56	57	58	59	60	61
INDIANA	431	3 738	1 436 188	14.1	75.6	15.6	6 055.0	6 161	13 149	28 797	-2.3	2.5	37 909	9.9	14.8	13.4
Adams	NA	NA	7 979	17.4	74.4	10.7	28.5	5 277	11 655	28 792	-2.3	2.2	38 587	9.5	14.4	14.1
Allen	324	5 139	80 225	21.1	81.2	19.0	318.5	6 347	14 631	31 835	-0.5	3.1	42 631	8.9	14.1	12.1
Bartholomew	NA	NA	15 078	10.7	76.9	16.9	67.9	5 818	14 216	30 971	-5.3	3.0	43 444	7.7	11.7	10.7
Benton	52	458	2 279	8.3	77.1	9.2	13.5	6 454	12 024	26 860	-3.0	2.0	36 927	8.2	12.6	11.6
Blackford	92	1 759	3 103	6.7	73.0	8.9	14.0	5 794	11 151	25 523	-2.9	0.8	35 048	10.0	16.3	14.1
Boone	NA	NA	9 325	9.0	82.5	22.2	41.1	5 166	16 674	34 652	6.4	6.0	51 856	5.1	7.0	6.8
Brown	NA	NA	2 780	9.2	76.4	15.2	13.8	5 484	13 048	29 425	6.5	1.5	42 891	7.6	13.1	11.4
Carroll	NA	NA	4 493	6.4	76.2	10.0	15.2	5 212	12 165	28 506	-1.8	1.2	40 352	6.9	11.0	10.0
Cass	NA	NA	8 934	6.6	75.9	9.0	44.3	6 521	11 860	25 963	-11.8	1.6	35 029	9.9	14.7	13.6
Clark	NA	NA	21 453	9.8	72.8	11.2	87.9	6 111	12 068	27 386	-4.0	1.3	36 729	9.7	15.5	13.8
Clay	NA	NA	5 854	5.6	75.9	9.8	25.7	5 446	10 538	23 470	-5.9	1.1	32 919	10.5	15.9	14.1
Clinton	NA	NA	7 223	7.0	76.2	11.0	35.2	5 465	11 849	26 148	-3.4	1.6	38 044	8.9	13.1	12.2
Crawford	NA	NA	2 224	6.5	59.6	5.7	10.2	5 350	8 837	20 367	3.5	0.4	28 679	15.4	23.4	22.7
Daviess	NA	NA	6 186	16.6	66.2	7.6	25.6	5 634	10 176	22 801	8.2	1.2	31 238	13.3	20.1	19.0
Dearborn	116	1 347	9 677	11.0	73.5	10.7	48.6	5 619	12 542	31 398	5.8	2.1	43 559	7.1	10.0	9.4
Decatur	NA	NA	5 816	8.2	72.3	9.7	25.5	5 820	11 930	27 701	5.2	2.1	39 954	8.4	12.1	11.0
De Kalb	NA	NA	8 630	7.5	77.5	9.9	42.8	5 783	12 665	30 970	1.4	2.2	42 612	5.6	7.7	7.6
Delaware	NA	NA	37 870	5.0	74.5	16.5	110.2	6 424	12 168	24 436	-11.4	2.0	34 155	13.8	20.0	17.9
Dubois	NA	NA	8 723	10.3	72.2	10.9	43.4	6 016	12 942	31 227	5.5	2.8	44 242	4.6	5.6	5.7
Elkhart	239	4 788	36 915	15.3	72.8	14.2	188.0	6 054	13 825	30 973	5.0	3.2	40 332	8.7	14.1	12.6
Fayette	NA	NA	6 278	7.5	63.9	8.1	34.1	7 701	11 577	25 565	0.9	1.1	34 737	11.0	15.3	14.2
Floyd	NA	NA	16 375	10.0	73.2	15.1	72.2	6 278	13 203	28 460	-1.8	2.2	38 808	9.6	14.4	13.4
Fountain	NA	NA	3 891	4.9	73.0	7.6	18.2	5 414	11 470	24 772	-7.0	1.3	34 593	8.9	12.8	12.1
Franklin	NA	NA	4 932	15.0	65.3	8.2	14.8	5 234	11 295	27 734	5.7	2.0	39 604	7.6	11.0	9.7
Fulton	NA	NA	4 208	6.0	75.3	9.4	14.2	5 042	11 164	26 141	-1.4	0.9	35 666	9.3	14.1	13.1
Gibson	NA	NA	7 666	13.6	72.8	9.1	34.4	6 498	11 615	25 985	-5.8	1.1	35 762	8.6	11.9	10.9
Grant	218	4 271	18 682	18.8	71.8	11.2	73.8	6 195	12 308	26 248	-8.0	1.7	34 274	13.2	20.6	18.2
Greene	NA	NA	7 097	4.8	71.6	9.9	35.5	5 924	10 798	23 139	4.2	0.5	32 293	10.8	15.9	15.2
Hamilton	210	1 912	29 183	15.8	88.7	36.2	161.0	5 706	20 426	45 748	11.8	10.3	68 017	3.2	4.3	4.0
Hancock	43	1 096	11 722	8.7	80.1	14.9	55.0	5 603	15 059	37 333	2.5	3.6	52 055	4.7	6.7	6.0
Harrison	82	1 862	7 389	8.5	71.1	8.4	33.4	5 405	11 159	27 238	0.3	1.1	38 204	9.2	13.1	12.2
Hendricks	NA	NA	19 683	12.9	84.1	18.2	87.0	5 235	15 526	39 892	5.0	3.8	55 548	4.3	6.4	5.7
Henry	67	4 402	10 733	4.9	71.4	9.2	54.2	6 223	11 914	25 668	-5.3	0.9	35 458	10.4	15.4	13.9
Howard	249	3 897	20 658	9.9	78.5	14.3	96.2	6 474	14 346	31 511	-2.2	2.2	43 491	9.7	15.1	13.9
Huntington	412	1 601	8 791	14.5	78.6	11.8	37.6	5 511	12 509	29 681	3.9	1.3	39 793	7.1	10.2	9.5
Jackson	NA	NA	8 630	9.8	69.3	8.7	34.0	5 162	11 562	25 767	-2.4	1.4	35 440	9.4	13.4	13.1
Jasper	NA	NA	7 012	22.0	75.5	10.8	26.6	5 465	11 256	28 546	-9.5	1.4	40 978	7.6	10.6	9.6
Jay	NA	NA	4 734	4.7	68.9	8.2	22.9	5 705	10 331	23 705	-3.4	0.7	32 147	10.4	16.2	14.1
Jefferson	314	1 643	7 804	20.8	70.3	13.3	34.4	6 917	11 631	24 820	0.6	1.7	33 630	11.6	17.6	16.1
Jennings	201	1 771	5 283	7.4	64.1	6.5	22.5	4 754	10 333	24 617	-7.9	0.9	32 121	9.8	13.8	13.5
Johnson	NA	NA	22 431	14.1	80.4	16.7	106.7	5 589	14 992	35 035	0.5	3.6	48 879	5.8	8.0	7.5
Knox	NA	NA	11 715	6.8	74.5	11.1	36.2	5 716	11 077	21 550	-2.5	2.2	30 709	14.5	20.6	18.9
Kosciusko	NA	NA	16 151	14.0	77.5	14.4	83.9	5 812	13 323	31 666	12.8	2.7	41 989	6.0	8.6	8.4
Lagrange	NA	NA	7 151	23.1	56.7	7.3	34.2	5 353	10 011	27 296	4.3	1.4	38 566	8.0	11.8	12.5
Lake	699	4 481	130 444	15.0	73.5	12.8	548.7	6 389	12 663	30 439	-14.8	2.1	38 205	13.0	20.0	17.5
La Porte	398	5 009	25 986	12.3	73.1	11.7	110.2	6 051	12 973	28 469	-9.2	2.3	38 753	10.4	15.5	13.8
Lawrence	127	2 476	9 248	6.7	69.7	9.4	45.4	5 984	11 492	25 764	4.2	0.6	35 933	9.4	14.2	12.7
Madison	NA	NA	31 071	14.2	73.5	11.7	123.9	5 999	12 811	27 435	-8.5	1.8	36 035	11.1	17.0	15.5
Marion	1 085	5 132	188 566	18.8	76.8	21.4	847.1	6 795	14 614	29 152	0.0	3.1	37 686	12.0	19.5	17.4
Marshall	NA	NA	10 517	10.1	74.0	12.3	47.3	5 963	12 428	28 311	2.3	1.8	39 179	7.3	10.3	9.9
Martin	NA	NA	2 466	7.0	64.4	8.6	10.2	5 249	10 177	23 344	0.0	0.4	33 765	11.3	16.9	16.4
Miami	NA	NA	9 139	6.6	76.4	9.7	41.9	5 378	10 862	24 441	-6.8	0.8	34 795	10.9	16.2	15.6
Monroe	150	3 229	47 386	4.6	82.1	32.9	77.7	5 827	12 017	24 781	7.8	2.9	35 366	12.0	14.1	13.5
Montgomery	101	2 488	8 081	15.3	80.0	12.8	39.2	5 949	12 419	28 020	-0.2	1.4	38 831	8.8	12.5	12.1
Morgan	NA	NA	13 660	7.8	73.6	10.0	57.9	5 125	13 068	32 762	-1.0	1.7	44 120	7.8	11.4	10.5
Newton	95	1 259	3 399	8.9	72.4	8.1	16.4	5 677	11 925	28 624	-5.3	1.8	36 875	9.8	14.0	14.1
Noble	143	2 178	9 306	6.7	72.1	8.0	41.9	5 366	11 772	29 845	8.2	1.3	40 449	6.4	9.1	9.2
Ohio	NA	NA	1 285	3.3	67.7	6.0	4.9	4 802	10 786	26 237	2.2	0.3	38 937	6.5	8.9	8.9
Orange	NA	NA	4 123	4.1	64.9	6.0	19.1	5 527	9 222	21 015	2.1	0.5	29 491	13.2	19.0	18.5
Owen	NA	NA	3 883	5.4	66.3	7.1	16.4	5 101	10 572	23 404	-0.3	0.7	32 835	11.8	16.9	17.2
Parke	NA	NA	3 391	7.0	76.7	10.1	14.4	5 349	11 058	24 514	-1.1	1.7	33 022	12.4	19.4	17.8
Perry	NA	NA	4 152	4.6	65.4	6.8	18.4	5 313	10 567	24 158	-4.6	0.8	34 365	9.4	11.3	11.3
Pike	NA	NA	2 784	4.8	65.5	8.5	12.5	5 740	10 934	23 096	-7.2	1.2	32 424	11.1	16.3	16.3
Porter	206	2 574	36 980	19.7	82.4	18.5	156.8	6 135	15 059	37 142	-8.4	3.7	50 493	6.2	8.3	7.7
Posey	NA	NA	6 522	14.6	76.3	11.0	32.1	6 611	12 879	31 530	0.1	1.8	45 011	8.0	11.1	10.2
Pulaski	143	986	3 124	4.2	71.9	8.9	14.1	5 278	11 107	25 418	1.4	1.5	35 837	10.5	14.9	14.4

1. Data for serious crimes have not been adjusted for underreporting; this may affect comparability between geographic areas and over time. 2. Per 100,000 population estimated by the FBI. 3. All persons 3 years old and over enrolled in nursery school through college. 4. Persons 25 years old and over. 5. Elementary and secondary education expenditures, local government fiscal years ending between July 1, 1996 and June 30, 1997. 6. Based on population enumerated as of April 1, 1990.

Table B. States and Counties — **Personal Income**

STATE County	Personal income, 1998 Total (mil dol)	Percent change, 1997–1998	Per capita[1] Dollars	Per capita Rank	Wages and salaries[2] (mil dol)	Proprietor's income (mil dol)	Dividends, interest, and rent (mil dol)	Transfer payments Total (mil dol)	Government payments to individuals Total (mil dol)	Social Security (mil dol)	Medical payments (mil dol)	Income mainte-nance (mil dol)	Unemploy-ment insurance (mil dol)
	62	63	64	65	66	67	68	69	70	71	72	73	74
INDIANA	148 651	5.9	25 163	X	97 168	8 881	27 038	19 383	18 279	8 710	7 000	1 397	267
Adams	748	8.2	22 653	938	433	43	139	91	85	48	30	5	1
Allen	8 852	5.2	28 153	231	6 748	550	1 788	965	906	447	339	68	11
Bartholomew	1 947	5.1	28 046	235	1 642	104	403	210	197	103	73	14	1
Benton	207	-3.9	21 189	1 334	66	8	45	32	30	17	10	2	0
Blackford	273	0.3	19 599	1 856	124	11	51	52	49	26	17	3	1
Boone	1 437	7.3	32 762	91	400	87	309	121	113	62	41	5	1
Brown	384	7.3	24 054	630	62	25	77	41	38	23	10	5	1
Carroll	460	3.6	22 992	854	151	34	95	58	54	32	17	2	1
Cass	882	4.3	22 725	914	498	45	156	151	143	65	59	8	1
Clark	2 314	9.4	24 615	544	1 325	125	375	332	314	139	131	23	5
Clay	515	4.0	19 263	1 969	210	31	98	101	96	46	37	7	1
Clinton	731	1.7	22 011	1 103	347	37	132	110	104	51	38	6	1
Crawford	182	6.5	17 226	2 553	42	14	24	41	39	16	16	4	1
Daviess	569	4.1	19 641	1 844	246	52	120	103	97	38	42	8	2
Dearborn	1 106	7.8	23 447	757	414	67	169	134	125	65	46	7	2
Decatur	598	3.8	23 381	773	381	27	116	77	72	37	27	5	1
De Kalb	954	5.9	24 258	599	750	52	155	108	101	52	38	4	1
Delaware	2 739	4.6	23 545	734	1 741	146	478	434	412	192	149	38	7
Dubois	1 113	7.5	28 079	234	869	60	281	116	109	55	44	4	1
Elkhart	4 409	7.3	25 527	435	3 965	254	841	482	450	228	162	33	8
Fayette	552	2.4	21 218	1 323	391	28	101	108	103	48	43	8	2
Floyd	1 871	8.6	26 052	393	791	99	331	240	226	100	90	18	4
Fountain	362	5.3	19 763	1 790	161	23	66	66	62	33	22	3	1
Franklin	451	4.7	20 660	1 499	100	27	103	66	62	37	18	4	1
Fulton	422	3.3	20 398	1 596	209	39	81	68	64	35	22	4	1
Gibson	754	13.5	23 432	760	330	39	153	117	111	55	40	6	2
Grant	1 554	1.3	21 391	1 268	1 013	72	287	295	282	131	113	22	3
Greene	613	2.7	18 391	2 242	213	31	117	114	108	50	40	8	3
Hamilton	6 396	10.7	39 295	37	2 762	496	1 241	316	285	156	105	10	3
Hancock	1 544	11.0	28 337	222	530	86	259	144	134	70	50	6	2
Harrison	768	12.4	22 182	1 040	247	39	115	100	94	45	35	7	2
Hendricks	2 653	9.2	27 775	246	799	139	402	224	206	111	74	7	2
Henry	1 113	2.6	22 868	877	503	49	180	195	186	91	76	13	2
Howard	2 230	4.5	26 732	325	2 177	89	373	298	282	141	109	21	2
Huntington	885	3.6	23 725	693	471	40	159	116	109	58	36	5	2
Jackson	861	5.3	20 988	1 395	587	39	136	132	125	63	47	9	1
Jasper	578	4.1	19 896	1 748	296	49	116	87	82	43	28	5	2
Jay	402	2.1	18 499	2 211	203	35	63	77	73	37	27	5	1
Jefferson	614	3.7	19 521	1 880	360	44	124	118	112	48	49	8	2
Jennings	566	8.4	20 395	1 601	228	35	62	117	112	37	65	9	1
Johnson	2 993	8.4	27 357	274	1 042	187	492	285	264	140	97	12	3
Knox	852	2.5	21 704	1 190	469	57	176	173	166	67	73	14	3
Kosciusko	1 783	6.9	25 055	483	1 166	95	372	200	186	102	64	9	4
Lagrange	613	5.6	18 344	2 253	379	48	108	73	67	36	22	5	2
Lake	11 903	5.7	24 749	523	7 430	591	1 951	1 867	1 778	775	701	203	27
La Porte	2 536	4.2	23 084	839	1 427	145	495	375	354	173	136	24	5
Lawrence	962	3.3	21 056	1 374	502	60	161	165	157	71	65	10	4
Madison	3 047	5.5	23 220	812	1 634	147	517	507	483	239	186	36	7
Marion	23 446	5.4	28 851	200	23 839	1 509	4 209	2 808	2 656	1 136	1 060	255	40
Marshall	1 028	5.9	22 564	965	576	68	202	129	121	66	42	6	2
Martin	208	2.9	19 845	1 763	352	13	43	34	32	14	13	3	1
Miami	672	4.2	20 061	1 691	311	33	114	118	112	48	41	9	2
Monroe	2 639	6.2	22 636	941	1 845	150	544	292	270	128	97	20	5
Montgomery	830	2.8	22 767	898	580	53	157	124	117	59	47	6	2
Morgan	1 530	8.0	23 337	784	409	72	182	178	166	83	62	11	3
Newton	272	4.0	18 408	2 236	108	20	41	44	42	21	15	3	1
Noble	968	5.8	22 720	916	624	48	140	118	110	59	40	6	1
Ohio	120	6.2	22 065	1 080	59	8	17	16	15	7	6	1	0
Orange	364	6.2	18 593	2 185	180	32	59	73	70	29	30	6	2
Owen	350	3.9	17 146	2 572	100	28	48	62	58	29	20	5	2
Parke	328	6.2	19 473	1 901	81	20	55	59	56	28	20	5	2
Perry	378	6.9	19 563	1 866	165	18	78	64	61	31	22	4	1
Pike	266	6.3	20 588	1 533	111	12	45	51	48	21	20	3	1
Porter	4 060	7.0	27 758	248	1 996	211	653	397	370	194	134	17	7
Posey	671	4.2	25 357	453	379	32	137	81	76	38	28	6	1
Pulaski	290	1.9	21 566	1 236	136	35	63	45	43	23	14	3	1

1. Based on the resident population estimated as of July 1 of the year shown. 2. Includes other labor income.

Table B. States and Counties — Earnings, Social Security, and Housing

STATE County	Earnings, 1998 Total (mil dol)	Farm	Goods-related[1] Total	Manufacturing	Service-related and other[2] Total	Retail trade	Finance, insurance, and real estate	Services	Government	Social Security beneficiaries, December 1998 Number	Rate[3]	Supplemental Security Income recipients, December 1998	Housing units, 1990 Total	Percent change, 1980–1990
	75	76	77	78	79	80	81	82	83	84	85	86	87	88
INDIANA	106 049	0.5	37.1	30.1	49.3	9.1	6.2	21.8	13.1	982 167	166	89 541	2 246 046	7.4
Adams	476	1.1	D	55.0	D	9.0	2.4	9.2	11.1	5 223	158	230	10 931	7.2
Allen	7 298	0.1	34.2	27.7	57.0	8.1	9.3	23.5	8.7	48 882	156	4 315	122 923	11.0
Bartholomew	1 746	0.1	55.5	50.4	34.4	6.8	6.3	13.7	10.0	11 467	165	981	25 432	6.0
Benton	74	-3.2	D	21.6	D	9.4	5.6	17.7	24.5	1 907	196	94	3 833	-3.1
Blackford	136	-0.2	D	47.7	D	8.0	3.2	11.7	17.0	2 974	214	180	5 856	-3.6
Boone	486	2.6	D	16.4	D	9.4	4.8	21.7	14.2	6 721	153	283	14 516	7.7
Brown	87	0.4	20.8	9.1	D	15.9	4.2	28.7	23.8	2 657	166	84	6 997	16.0
Carroll	185	7.6	D	39.7	D	6.7	3.3	11.5	13.2	3 563	178	109	8 431	0.4
Cass	543	1.9	D	38.3	D	8.9	3.0	12.1	19.8	7 400	191	628	15 633	-0.9
Clark	1 450	0.2	27.1	19.0	54.9	13.1	3.2	19.5	17.8	16 392	175	1 689	35 313	6.7
Clay	241	0.6	D	38.0	36.1	11.6	3.3	12.2	16.2	5 435	204	516	10 606	3.1
Clinton	383	2.7	52.9	46.9	31.1	7.2	2.5	14.8	13.3	5 772	174	382	12 100	-0.5
Crawford	56	0.3	D	D	D	12.8	4.0	D	25.4	2 180	206	317	4 374	6.0
Daviess	299	3.2	34.1	16.4	D	11.1	D	14.7	17.1	5 031	174	433	10 985	4.1
Dearborn	481	0.4	31.5	21.6	52.8	10.2	4.1	26.4	15.4	7 352	156	317	14 532	17.1
Decatur	408	0.5	D	51.5	D	7.5	2.7	14.6	10.2	4 373	171	452	9 098	4.0
De Kalb	802	1.2	66.9	62.4	24.6	5.5	1.9	10.1	7.3	5 857	149	306	13 601	10.7
Delaware	1 887	0.7	D	26.2	D	9.8	4.3	25.6	17.8	21 374	183	2 699	48 793	2.5
Dubois	929	1.4	55.5	49.9	36.2	8.6	2.9	13.3	6.9	6 350	160	267	13 964	18.2
Elkhart	4 220	0.3	D	55.6	D	6.3	2.9	13.6	6.0	24 921	145	2 059	60 182	16.0
Fayette	418	0.1	D	57.7	D	7.0	1.8	15.4	11.5	5 413	208	531	10 525	-1.0
Floyd	891	0.1	D	27.6	D	8.7	5.0	21.6	18.4	11 689	162	1 281	25 238	10.8
Fountain	184	-2.4	D	49.8	D	8.7	3.2	11.0	14.4	3 837	209	270	7 344	-5.0
Franklin	126	-1.6	D	13.7	D	11.1	5.2	25.5	21.4	3 969	182	251	7 176	7.5
Fulton	248	3.1	D	40.8	D	9.9	4.2	11.9	14.2	4 060	197	190	8 656	0.3
Gibson	369	2.2	41.0	32.8	46.0	10.5	2.5	15.0	10.8	6 387	199	388	13 454	3.0
Grant	1 085	0.2	D	40.3	D	9.5	3.8	20.4	15.1	14 856	205	1 515	29 904	-0.9
Greene	243	-1.4	35.6	10.4	41.9	11.0	3.3	16.1	23.9	6 460	193	569	13 337	5.6
Hamilton	3 258	0.3	24.2	14.4	67.3	11.5	20.1	22.7	8.2	16 142	99	623	41 074	41.3
Hancock	616	0.4	D	33.3	D	8.8	4.1	15.4	16.3	7 746	142	262	16 495	8.8
Harrison	286	1.5	36.5	29.2	43.8	11.1	3.6	18.9	18.2	5 671	163	453	11 456	14.9
Hendricks	938	0.2	D	7.3	D	14.1	5.2	20.6	19.7	11 826	124	346	26 962	14.1
Henry	552	0.9	D	42.6	D	10.3	3.3	14.0	17.5	10 389	213	794	19 835	-0.8
Howard	2 266	0.4	D	63.5	D	6.6	2.7	11.1	8.3	15 220	182	1 524	33 820	2.7
Huntington	510	1.5	D	45.7	D	9.5	3.5	13.6	12.8	6 644	178	327	13 629	2.6
Jackson	626	0.9	D	40.0	D	15.6	3.4	11.9	12.0	7 535	184	672	14 820	6.7
Jasper	344	4.0	27.3	16.3	54.3	11.0	2.6	13.7	14.4	4 848	166	244	8 984	2.7
Jay	238	3.9	D	45.8	D	8.9	3.0	13.6	15.1	4 322	199	306	8 905	-1.8
Jefferson	404	0.9	D	30.6	48.0	11.5	2.8	24.6	16.1	5 845	186	681	11 921	6.8
Jennings	263	0.7	D	29.8	D	13.0	2.0	15.4	22.6	4 618	166	511	9 129	16.8
Johnson	1 229	0.2	30.8	20.8	54.6	16.6	5.7	24.8	14.4	15 174	139	723	33 289	22.3
Knox	526	3.1	17.5	11.5	49.5	10.9	5.7	19.4	29.8	8 179	208	991	16 730	1.9
Kosciusko	1 260	1.7	D	56.4	D	7.4	2.9	13.2	7.2	11 424	160	519	30 516	4.0
Lagrange	427	4.0	D	54.1	D	8.0	2.2	10.2	9.7	4 126	123	1 452	12 218	15.5
Lake	8 021	0.1	37.3	27.3	50.4	8.6	4.3	25.7	12.2	84 426	177	162	183 014	-1.8
La Porte	1 572	1.0	35.8	29.3	47.9	10.4	2.9	22.3	15.3	18 843	172	10 569	42 268	4.2
Lawrence	562	0.1	49.4	43.1	36.1	10.5	2.6	16.7	14.4	8 739	192	802	17 587	6.1
Madison	1 780	0.5	D	39.3	D	9.8	4.0	22.6	12.9	26 206	199	2 560	53 353	0.0
Marion	25 348	0.1	26.6	21.3	61.3	8.8	9.6	26.7	12.0	127 658	157	16 848	349 403	12.9
Marshall	644	2.1	49.9	45.4	37.5	8.2	4.0	15.0	10.5	7 507	165	313	16 820	9.4
Martin	365	0.8	D	6.1	D	2.0	0.8	3.8	75.0	1 996	190	226	4 116	0.0
Miami	344	1.6	D	28.5	D	9.1	2.6	11.4	29.9	5 850	174	568	14 639	0.2
Monroe	1 996	0.1	25.9	19.6	43.6	9.7	5.0	21.2	30.5	14 170	123	1 255	41 948	15.8
Montgomery	633	2.0	D	51.1	D	7.9	2.5	16.5	9.2	6 698	184	497	13 957	1.4
Morgan	481	0.0	33.3	19.4	48.4	12.5	4.6	20.3	18.3	9 455	144	629	20 500	12.3
Newton	128	3.2	D	37.2	D	6.3	3.7	8.5	17.6	2 367	161	130	5 276	-4.1
Noble	672	1.4	D	61.1	D	6.0	1.6	10.1	9.9	6 814	160	382	15 516	7.6
Ohio	66	1.8	D	D	D	3.6	1.4	D	12.6	885	163	53	2 161	-0.4
Orange	212	1.8	48.4	33.0	33.7	9.0	2.8	14.2	16.1	3 887	198	439	7 732	3.8
Owen	128	-1.1	D	34.1	D	8.8	4.5	13.2	18.5	3 536	173	222	8 011	14.8
Parke	100	0.0	D	19.9	D	10.3	3.5	20.9	30.3	3 277	196	315	7 189	-3.5
Perry	184	-0.2	D	34.3	D	9.3	4.2	13.7	25.1	3 735	193	287	7 404	0.9
Pike	123	1.6	33.4	5.6	50.5	5.2	2.4	9.5	14.5	2 591	201	276	5 487	0.9
Porter	2 207	0.4	D	34.4	D	8.7	3.6	19.4	12.6	20 416	140	1 040	47 240	13.8
Posey	411	-0.4	D	50.6	D	4.6	1.5	11.1	10.1	4 385	165	336	10 401	4.7
Pulaski	171	11.3	D	33.8	D	6.8	3.5	10.6	17.5	2 715	205	159	5 541	2.3

1. Covers mining, construction, and manufacturing. 2. Covers private sector earnings in agricultural services, forestry, and fisheries; transportation and public utilities; wholesale trade; retail trade; finance, insurance, and real estate; and services. 3. Per 1,000 resident population estimated as of July 1 of the year shown.

STATE County	Housing units, 1990 (cont'd) Occupied units								Civilian labor force, 1999				Civilian employment, 1990[5]		
		Owner-occupied				Renter-occupied					Unemployment			Percent	
				Owner cost as a percent of income											
	Total	Percent	Median value[1]	With a mortgage	Without a mortgage	Median rent[2]	Rent as percent of income	Substandard units[3] (percent)	Total	Percent change, 1998–1999	Total	Rate[4]	Total	Professional, managerial, and technical	Precision production, craft, and repair
	89	90	91	92	93	94	95	96	97	98	99	100	101	102	103
INDIANA	2 065 355	70.2	53 900	16.7	12.3	374	24.3	2.6	3 077 612	-0.3	93 028	3.0	2 628 695	25.6	12.9
Adams	10 470	78.4	51 100	15.6	11.2	319	22.3	6.0	16 306	-0.8	361	2.2	14 121	18.9	15.4
Allen	113 333	70.2	59 900	16.2	11.7	393	23.7	2.1	173 970	-0.8	5 138	3.0	152 304	29.8	11.4
Bartholomew	24 192	73.2	57 200	16.6	11.8	396	24.0	1.9	39 473	0.1	822	2.1	31 464	28.4	13.2
Benton	3 524	72.9	38 100	16.9	13.9	316	18.7	1.3	5 385	9.7	168	3.1	4 429	18.1	13.0
Blackford	5 436	77.3	32 300	14.2	13.7	283	20.6	2.6	6 328	-3.6	282	4.5	6 431	18.2	12.2
Boone	13 922	76.2	71 100	17.6	11.8	388	23.7	1.7	24 347	1.0	419	1.7	19 550	29.4	12.4
Brown	5 370	82.6	64 900	20.3	12.2	378	21.5	5.9	8 845	1.9	205	2.3	6 773	24.9	17.5
Carroll	7 067	78.0	45 400	15.2	12.2	307	21.1	2.6	12 602	5.5	267	2.1	9 012	19.2	14.7
Cass	14 659	74.4	40 300	15.4	12.0	299	22.2	1.5	19 854	-0.6	632	3.2	17 360	19.4	16.0
Clark	33 292	68.4	50 000	17.4	12.4	362	25.0	2.4	52 170	0.3	1 440	2.8	42 447	22.3	12.0
Clay	9 382	79.3	35 500	15.7	13.4	295	26.3	3.5	12 065	-1.0	507	4.2	10 495	19.3	13.8
Clinton	11 450	72.0	40 900	15.1	12.8	326	23.3	2.4	16 170	-0.4	395	2.4	13 916	19.7	15.6
Crawford	3 660	85.2	31 800	22.2	13.3	241	29.5	7.2	5 339	10.1	304	5.7	3 905	14.8	17.4
Daviess	10 012	78.0	40 600	16.7	13.0	277	22.6	4.2	13 751	1.2	447	3.3	11 734	18.7	15.0
Dearborn	13 642	78.3	59 900	17.2	12.2	321	22.9	3.4	23 326	0.0	760	3.3	17 649	23.3	16.2
Decatur	8 427	75.6	44 900	15.8	12.5	357	21.6	3.7	16 422	3.1	316	1.9	11 214	17.3	14.7
De Kalb	12 725	81.2	49 700	16.0	12.2	345	21.0	1.8	21 647	0.5	676	3.1	17 747	17.7	15.2
Delaware	45 177	66.8	42 300	15.5	12.7	334	27.5	2.0	61 515	0.0	2 042	3.3	55 097	25.1	12.0
Dubois	13 023	78.7	58 000	17.1	11.8	316	18.1	2.7	22 982	2.1	481	2.1	19 280	19.0	14.5
Elkhart	56 713	71.8	62 300	17.0	11.6	405	23.3	2.3	96 605	1.7	2 090	2.2	80 588	22.6	13.8
Fayette	9 945	69.9	41 100	14.3	12.4	304	23.7	3.1	11 003	-2.3	556	5.1	11 315	18.1	14.3
Floyd	24 085	71.8	57 600	17.6	12.5	349	25.1	2.3	38 784	0.3	901	2.3	30 306	28.1	12.9
Fountain	6 858	76.7	37 000	16.2	12.4	290	19.9	2.5	8 397	-1.7	338	4.0	7 881	18.0	15.4
Franklin	6 636	79.5	53 300	18.0	11.4	284	23.9	4.8	10 984	2.7	368	3.4	8 857	16.4	15.6
Fulton	7 345	77.3	42 200	15.6	12.7	325	23.0	1.9	9 931	-2.0	390	3.9	8 754	16.3	15.6
Gibson	12 299	78.6	44 400	16.6	12.4	294	23.7	2.3	16 378	1.6	737	4.5	14 674	19.6	16.9
Grant	27 701	71.3	40 400	15.6	12.2	318	25.1	2.3	32 751	-1.4	1 310	4.0	33 810	21.5	14.1
Greene	11 910	80.4	36 800	15.5	12.4	274	23.2	2.8	14 249	-0.6	876	6.1	12 920	22.6	16.0
Hamilton	38 834	76.9	106 500	19.2	12.0	505	22.3	1.1	93 338	4.0	1 168	1.3	57 985	38.8	8.9
Hancock	15 959	80.0	72 000	16.1	11.8	386	22.6	2.2	30 068	1.6	591	2.0	23 112	27.7	14.7
Harrison	10 618	85.3	51 800	18.2	12.0	314	20.8	4.4	18 593	1.5	488	2.6	13 934	18.8	15.2
Hendricks	26 109	82.4	75 700	16.9	11.5	428	22.9	1.6	52 656	2.2	864	1.6	38 702	30.6	14.8
Henry	18 642	75.2	36 800	15.1	12.8	301	23.8	1.7	24 169	-2.3	991	4.1	21 215	21.4	14.2
Howard	31 523	72.1	51 700	14.6	12.2	364	25.0	1.8	41 681	-1.5	1 108	2.7	37 041	23.9	16.1
Huntington	12 830	76.7	44 200	16.2	11.6	344	23.6	1.9	20 274	-2.1	606	3.0	17 621	20.4	14.7
Jackson	14 032	77.1	43 900	16.0	12.7	333	23.1	3.5	21 443	3.4	512	2.4	17 331	19.2	12.8
Jasper	8 527	75.4	55 100	16.5	12.0	326	21.0	2.2	14 296	1.5	580	4.1	11 217	19.4	15.8
Jay	8 161	77.6	32 400	15.8	12.8	281	20.0	2.6	10 770	-3.7	443	4.1	9 999	16.1	15.6
Jefferson	10 897	73.2	44 900	19.3	12.2	295	22.1	3.9	13 733	-0.7	483	3.5	13 710	24.1	14.4
Jennings	8 351	80.0	43 700	16.0	12.7	322	27.4	4.2	14 537	0.9	328	2.3	10 765	17.5	17.1
Johnson	31 354	74.0	72 200	18.6	11.8	414	24.2	1.6	61 375	1.2	1 136	1.9	45 570	27.0	13.9
Knox	15 145	70.6	39 800	17.1	13.4	310	28.4	1.7	18 907	-2.7	636	3.4	17 167	22.9	11.0
Kosciusko	23 449	79.0	60 600	16.3	11.8	378	22.2	3.3	37 754	0.3	874	2.3	32 789	20.9	14.3
Lagrange	9 209	81.4	55 100	17.2	12.7	338	19.6	6.8	17 435	1.2	447	2.6	13 200	13.8	16.1
Lake	170 748	67.8	54 800	16.7	13.3	393	25.0	4.2	223 391	-2.3	9 501	4.3	203 966	24.4	14.0
La Porte	38 488	73.1	52 700	16.6	13.4	368	23.3	2.4	53 216	-0.9	1 884	3.5	48 306	22.1	13.7
Lawrence	16 235	79.7	42 000	16.6	12.3	311	23.7	2.9	22 390	-4.4	1 166	5.2	19 193	22.5	15.3
Madison	49 804	73.1	43 700	14.9	12.2	339	24.9	1.8	65 305	-2.0	2 091	3.2	59 046	21.2	13.4
Marion	319 471	57.0	61 400	17.6	12.3	412	24.2	2.5	448 235	-1.2	12 349	2.8	401 124	30.9	9.9
Marshall	15 146	76.7	49 600	17.1	12.3	362	22.0	2.0	24 348	-1.0	632	2.6	20 824	21.1	13.3
Martin	3 836	81.7	38 700	16.6	12.3	264	24.6	5.7	5 201	0.9	201	3.9	4 572	19.9	15.8
Miami	13 484	70.6	40 300	16.3	11.9	318	22.2	1.7	15 545	0.7	580	3.7	14 893	18.2	15.7
Monroe	39 351	54.8	66 600	18.5	12.0	401	32.2	2.5	60 866	0.2	1 411	2.3	52 564	36.6	9.2
Montgomery	13 235	72.2	48 100	15.2	12.0	323	23.9	1.9	17 931	-3.5	573	3.2	16 682	20.0	13.8
Morgan	19 600	78.9	59 700	16.8	11.9	380	23.0	3.4	35 063	-0.3	872	2.5	27 409	20.8	18.4
Newton	4 839	76.9	44 300	17.0	13.0	322	18.6	2.8	6 435	-5.2	236	3.7	6 073	18.3	15.6
Noble	13 418	78.1	49 100	15.3	11.4	332	21.8	3.2	24 293	-1.5	847	3.5	18 504	17.1	16.0
Ohio	1 980	78.6	45 400	17.5	13.3	272	20.9	3.7	2 645	-1.9	86	3.3	2 385	17.2	20.9
Orange	6 950	81.1	37 400	20.0	13.2	273	24.2	5.2	8 790	-3.4	612	7.0	7 783	17.1	14.4
Owen	6 394	83.0	43 000	16.0	12.9	322	25.7	5.9	10 899	3.0	398	3.7	7 587	17.3	19.4
Parke	5 845	79.0	37 900	16.6	12.8	278	21.2	4.4	7 685	1.0	261	3.4	6 594	19.2	14.3
Perry	6 845	79.8	42 600	16.5	11.9	260	21.8	3.4	9 027	3.3	521	5.8	7 809	14.3	16.1
Pike	4 925	82.6	35 700	16.1	12.6	277	23.0	2.7	6 318	2.0	244	3.9	5 477	18.1	16.6
Porter	45 159	75.2	69 600	15.8	12.0	431	23.6	1.6	75 143	-0.8	2 285	3.0	61 823	28.6	16.1
Posey	9 508	80.3	58 800	17.1	11.9	309	22.5	2.7	13 925	-0.5	404	2.9	12 058	24.7	14.8
Pulaski	4 722	77.5	40 300	16.5	13.3	306	21.3	1.7	6 329	3.0	423	6.7	5 500	15.7	13.5

1. Specified owner-occupied units. 2. Specified renter-occupied units. 3. Overcrowded or lacking complete plumbing facilities. 4. Percent of civilian labor force. 5. Persons 16 years and older.

Table B. States and Counties — Nonfarm Employment and Agriculture

STATE County	Private nonfarm establishments, employment and payroll, 1998									Agriculture, 1997			
	Number of establishments	Employment						Annual payroll		Farms	Percent with—		Farm operators
		Total	Health Care and Social Assistance	Manufacturing	Retail trade	Finance and Insurance	Professional Scientific and Technical Services	Total (mil dol)	Average per employee (dollars)	Number	Less than 50 acres	500 acres and over	Whose principal occupation is farming (percent)
	104	105	106	107	108	109	110	111	112	113	114	115	116
INDIANA	146 197	2 540 866	313 865	635 658	344 444	110 993	81 704	71 436	28 115	57 916	31.4	15.1	46.6
Adams	762	13 634	1 121	6 991	1 805	278	136	336	24 671	1 093	41.6	10.4	45.3
Allen	8 813	178 109	21 055	36 343	22 404	10 593	7 654	5 133	28 822	1 440	36.4	9.5	41.4
Bartholomew	2 019	36 972	3 811	13 471	4 402	1 459	921	999	27 032	577	33.6	19.1	48.7
Benton	268	2 023	220	D	427	109	D	40	19 679	433	10.2	42.0	73.7
Blackford	293	3 816	396	1 860	478	153	31	86	22 589	303	36.3	14.5	42.2
Boone	1 214	11 516	1 416	2 295	1 710	246	350	264	22 890	611	33.6	25.4	53.5
Brown	386	2 191	231	164	428	50	107	33	15 226	173	34.7	1.7	31.8
Carroll	429	4 605	335	2 195	569	142	89	101	21 837	563	28.8	24.9	58.4
Cass	870	16 482	2 620	7 226	2 043	325	201	377	22 859	700	34.6	17.7	47.6
Clark	2 427	39 066	4 663	6 405	7 860	657	703	979	25 061	647	33.1	7.3	43.0
Clay	543	5 610	539	1 612	1 150	218	110	111	19 732	520	26.9	20.8	51.0
Clinton	717	10 910	1 323	5 035	1 215	272	119	252	23 083	585	25.6	26.8	59.7
Crawford	159	1 305	150	D	318	54	D	22	16 934	410	19.8	3.9	31.7
Daviess	750	8 955	1 529	1 989	1 514	231	149	169	18 873	1 101	41.9	10.9	47.5
Dearborn	982	12 648	1 446	2 308	2 020	410	229	312	24 659	679	24.0	2.2	33.0
Decatur	622	11 852	911	5 659	1 397	201	791	295	24 909	654	24.0	19.9	59.3
De Kalb	986	21 324	1 311	13 218	1 733	305	376	652	30 581	785	27.3	9.8	36.6
Delaware	2 762	49 162	7 355	9 357	7 518	1 570	1 421	1 201	24 430	635	38.0	13.7	47.7
Dubois	1 226	27 299	2 454	13 176	3 063	569	303	749	27 454	812	22.2	11.3	49.5
Elkhart	5 030	109 830	7 545	57 042	11 050	1 729	1 675	3 033	27 618	1 335	45.9	6.2	46.7
Fayette	554	10 103	1 449	4 679	1 254	200	133	312	30 919	420	29.8	15.0	47.4
Floyd	1 747	25 635	3 691	7 166	3 570	653	879	576	22 464	310	47.1	3.2	36.5
Fountain	383	4 886	434	2 307	678	183	79	112	22 852	550	23.8	26.5	53.8
Franklin	355	3 687	491	780	442	132	54	79	21 405	776	23.3	7.2	43.2
Fulton	511	6 608	648	2 889	877	185	78	155	23 485	622	29.4	17.7	48.9
Gibson	756	10 281	1 231	2 262	1 638	226	220	247	24 057	579	27.8	25.4	54.2
Grant	1 565	30 690	4 630	9 481	3 721	707	458	776	25 296	575	28.9	23.5	52.7
Greene	640	5 899	1 003	1 108	1 211	257	216	107	18 058	878	25.1	11.3	37.9
Hamilton	5 000	72 679	6 446	5 923	10 243	10 562	4 742	2 557	35 183	591	47.9	14.6	42.5
Hancock	1 219	12 918	1 862	2 686	1 608	321	310	369	28 548	549	39.5	17.1	49.2
Harrison	649	7 731	860	2 476	1 459	270	148	156	20 149	1 108	32.5	4.9	37.1
Hendricks	2 061	22 967	3 330	1 717	4 543	673	602	535	23 316	631	38.0	13.5	50.4
Henry	951	12 480	1 978	3 545	2 099	426	283	358	28 699	770	39.6	13.8	41.4
Howard	1 997	43 994	4 654	19 735	5 851	1 145	513	1 682	38 243	486	28.4	19.5	55.1
Huntington	905	15 804	1 517	6 723	1 925	309	273	368	23 288	651	29.5	18.7	49.0
Jackson	1 100	18 245	2 234	6 357	2 436	498	313	448	24 542	809	30.7	15.9	49.4
Jasper	752	8 709	774	1 484	1 548	215	139	208	23 855	618	24.4	34.3	65.0
Jay	449	7 372	848	3 865	727	189	133	147	19 897	839	32.9	10.8	40.0
Jefferson	742	11 885	2 182	3 466	1 901	247	164	282	23 690	796	33.3	5.0	36.1
Jennings	428	7 527	1 672	2 642	729	143	78	176	23 360	605	33.7	10.4	40.3
Johnson	2 684	37 074	4 913	6 548	7 576	1 498	981	829	22 362	526	41.4	17.7	47.1
Knox	1 052	14 476	3 579	1 474	2 643	563	272	307	21 217	584	22.3	27.6	64.0
Kosciusko	1 896	31 645	2 398	15 952	3 558	825	474	969	30 610	1 130	35.8	12.0	40.6
Lagrange	685	10 000	579	5 110	1 291	222	167	257	25 661	1 392	38.2	5.3	48.2
Lake	10 186	175 897	26 087	36 252	26 585	5 767	5 708	5 236	29 769	442	32.6	20.1	49.5
La Porte	2 692	40 123	5 246	10 808	6 622	847	907	991	24 689	749	30.4	21.8	53.7
Lawrence	890	13 990	1 953	5 317	2 225	400	219	348	24 860	875	26.1	8.3	33.8
Madison	2 780	43 904	5 968	11 429	6 685	1 387	1 282	1 185	26 993	738	37.1	19.9	48.6
Marion	24 348	534 151	72 922	67 493	60 719	36 880	27 313	17 667	33 074	225	62.2	8.0	40.4
Marshall	1 133	18 712	1 611	8 384	2 103	361	279	446	23 825	865	31.9	11.9	46.8
Martin	227	2 244	164	762	347	94	105	51	22 528	335	28.7	9.6	42.7
Miami	686	7 892	956	2 435	1 098	267	101	170	21 558	678	27.4	18.0	51.3
Monroe	2 874	45 630	6 228	9 088	7 353	1 590	1 622	1 063	23 285	473	33.4	5.5	35.1
Montgomery	923	16 042	1 509	7 416	1 910	388	195	440	27 438	681	28.5	27.5	55.9
Morgan	1 293	12 549	1 752	2 795	2 251	365	245	287	22 836	601	41.9	12.5	41.8
Newton	289	3 135	120	1 546	426	94	43	67	21 263	381	20.5	36.7	63.0
Noble	943	18 396	1 210	11 204	1 609	238	295	524	28 489	942	31.7	10.1	38.7
Ohio	74	2 011	77	D	143	D	D	35	17 585	252	27.0	1.6	31.0
Orange	387	6 966	942	2 832	766	146	52	147	21 162	531	21.3	12.6	42.6
Owen	313	3 282	298	1 295	508	137	64	64	19 400	569	27.8	8.8	38.3
Parke	293	2 295	339	675	360	114	50	41	17 839	471	26.3	23.1	51.6
Perry	412	4 652	624	1 428	876	281	72	101	21 777	484	19.8	5.4	35.1
Pike	199	2 058	311	D	234	84	D	58	28 332	288	26.0	18.1	46.2
Porter	3 247	49 032	5 060	12 410	6 666	1 289	1 326	1 497	30 522	476	31.5	19.7	49.4
Posey	554	7 248	541	2 623	934	200	257	233	32 189	437	25.9	27.5	61.8
Pulaski	341	3 700	526	1 402	457	143	66	95	25 584	531	21.5	29.2	63.1

Items 104—116

Table B. States and Counties — Agriculture, Land, and Water

STATE County	Acreage (1,000)	Percent change, 1992–1997	Average size of farm	Total irrigated (1,000)	Total cropland (1,000)	Average per farm ($1,000)	Average per acre (dollars)	Value of machinery and equipment Average per farm ($1,000)	Total (mil dol)	Average per farm (dollars)	Crops	Livestock and poultry products	$10,000 or more	$100,000 or more	Percent of land owned by Fed. Gov. 1997	Water consumption 1995 (mil gal/ day)
	117	118	119	120	121	122	123	124	125	126	127	128	129	130	131	132
INDIANA	15 111	-3.3	261	250	12 849	533	2 064	64	5 230	90 303	62.1	37.9	56.3	20.8	2.0	9 139.3
Adams	209	5.4	191	0	191	387	2 290	56	95	87 134	48.0	52.0	66.6	23.6	0.0	7.4
Allen	276	-3.4	192	1	247	487	2 699	50	90	62 414	69.3	30.7	56.0	16.7	0.0	54.8
Bartholomew	167	1.0	289	6	146	674	2 355	79	47	80 939	82.0	18.0	56.3	23.1	10.2	21.8
Benton	257	-5.2	593	D	248	1 378	2 394	151	79	183 310	95.7	4.3	88.5	56.6	0.0	1.9
Blackford	86	-1.2	284	0	77	475	1 839	60	25	83 481	72.4	27.6	55.1	19.8	0.0	2.2
Boone	228	2.4	374	D	212	912	2 519	83	82	133 419	74.0	26.0	66.0	31.3	0.0	5.4
Brown	22	-5.6	125	0	10	287	2 390	25	2	12 733	52.0	48.0	24.3	1.2	13.0	0.6
Carroll	218	-0.8	388	1	198	892	2 282	94	117	207 704	52.1	47.9	74.2	39.1	0.0	4.7
Cass	205	-9.9	293	2	179	609	2 088	62	78	110 799	69.0	31.0	62.0	25.0	0.1	29.2
Clark	109	2.6	168	0	76	378	2 458	33	22	33 815	71.2	28.8	40.2	9.0	5.1	31.2
Clay	159	-1.6	307	D	135	489	1 625	66	43	81 824	71.6	28.4	61.2	23.5	0.0	2.1
Clinton	236	0.1	404	0	223	878	2 178	113	106	181 203	60.5	39.5	79.1	42.4	0.0	6.5
Crawford	61	2.2	150	0	30	219	1 471	21	4	8 541	31.1	68.9	16.8	1.0	16.7	6.3
Daviess	217	-2.2	197	2	189	362	1 973	59	118	107 075	34.0	66.0	59.9	21.7	0.0	9.0
Dearborn	81	-5.4	120	0	45	315	2 725	25	9	13 203	58.3	41.7	23.3	2.1	0.0	621.8
Decatur	199	-1.7	304	0	171	687	2 343	82	83	126 719	52.8	47.2	70.6	30.1	0.0	4.4
De Kalb	163	6.5	208	1	135	355	1 739	43	39	49 261	65.9	34.1	43.7	11.7	0.0	7.5
Delaware	173	2.6	273	0	160	585	2 219	65	53	82 874	84.3	15.7	57.2	19.8	0.0	18.8
Dubois	191	-1.0	235	0	138	393	1 686	61	144	177 526	15.5	84.5	61.5	28.8	1.7	9.5
Elkhart	183	-4.8	137	24	160	376	2 738	48	124	92 912	28.0	72.0	64.6	24.7	0.0	43.4
Fayette	107	-4.7	254	D	85	455	1 858	53	26	62 903	64.9	35.1	59.0	19.5	0.0	4.5
Floyd	29	-4.3	93	0	18	345	5 019	30	4	11 986	71.7	28.3	20.6	2.3	0.0	271.5
Fountain	205	-10.7	372	0	177	756	1 882	99	49	89 765	85.9	14.1	61.1	27.1	0.0	3.7
Franklin	139	-7.0	179	0	92	351	2 085	47	31	40 253	48.1	51.9	50.6	11.2	2.0	2.7
Fulton	171	-12.0	274	10	151	415	1 532	68	55	89 151	70.8	29.2	68.0	23.6	0.0	8.2
Gibson	233	-3.4	402	2	212	745	1 910	103	69	119 268	81.3	18.7	71.5	31.1	0.0	49.1
Grant	192	-2.4	334	0	178	767	2 224	98	63	108 781	83.2	16.8	62.6	30.6	0.7	13.6
Greene	206	-1.1	234	1	147	327	1 360	47	77	88 249	30.3	69.7	39.7	11.5	0.9	24.2
Hamilton	141	-13.6	238	1	127	788	3 478	62	59	100 662	87.2	12.8	57.2	18.6	0.0	76.1
Hancock	164	0.4	298	1	155	820	2 670	88	56	101 634	79.8	20.2	59.4	25.0	0.0	5.5
Harrison	161	-0.4	146	0	110	247	1 744	37	46	41 561	30.0	70.0	31.7	6.0	0.0	2.8
Hendricks	167	-10.6	265	0	150	757	2 770	67	49	77 899	81.7	18.3	55.2	18.9	0.0	9.9
Henry	178	-7.0	231	1	161	434	1 915	47	52	67 763	81.0	19.0	55.8	19.1	0.0	11.8
Howard	148	-0.8	304	0	138	773	2 657	81	63	128 779	69.2	30.8	71.6	35.0	0.0	22.9
Huntington	184	-2.1	283	0	169	517	1 861	80	70	107 146	63.6	36.4	66.1	25.0	5.3	5.2
Jackson	201	-1.0	248	1	157	442	1 728	65	93	114 599	35.5	64.5	56.7	20.1	8.5	10.0
Jasper	283	-6.3	458	17	258	812	1 872	95	111	179 636	66.9	33.1	76.7	42.7	0.0	31.0
Jay	180	-1.8	214	0	157	388	1 902	46	83	99 215	42.4	57.6	54.7	20.4	0.0	3.9
Jefferson	126	-3.5	159	0	81	233	1 628	35	23	29 453	76.9	23.1	43.7	6.5	7.4	1 317.8
Jennings	130	4.3	215	1	91	323	1 535	64	45	74 734	43.6	56.4	39.5	10.9	4.9	4.0
Johnson	136	-3.2	258	1	121	724	2 896	66	46	88 103	80.7	19.3	55.1	21.5	2.6	13.1
Knox	281	-8.3	481	14	256	945	1 923	112	101	173 280	70.7	29.3	76.4	35.8	0.0	61.0
Kosciusko	247	-2.0	219	12	210	402	1 870	50	146	129 259	33.4	66.6	56.0	20.0	0.0	23.1
Lagrange	190	1.0	136	23	156	332	2 418	36	103	74 194	36.2	63.8	66.9	13.2	0.0	11.7
Lake	149	3.4	337	6	139	937	2 716	65	48	108 206	89.4	10.6	62.4	26.5	0.2	2 173.7
La Porte	248	-7.6	331	27	227	736	2 069	91	96	127 922	71.0	29.0	65.6	29.2	0.3	85.5
Lawrence	171	7.4	195	3	100	258	1 478	40	22	25 506	46.7	53.3	31.8	4.3	4.3	8.8
Madison	224	0.3	303	1	209	744	2 423	82	78	105 030	88.0	12.0	62.2	24.8	0.0	21.6
Marion	29	-25.6	129	0	24	679	4 369	42	33	145 247	59.5	40.5	47.1	17.8	1.0	318.5
Marshall	202	-7.9	233	5	177	439	1 992	51	62	71 892	69.6	30.4	60.8	19.0	0.0	7.5
Martin	70	-2.6	209	0	46	316	1 421	40	24	71 632	26.6	73.4	37.9	14.6	31.9	2.9
Miami	197	4.3	291	2	175	551	1 926	65	75	110 270	58.4	41.6	64.5	27.3	1.3	7.4
Monroe	62	5.3	131	0	36	296	2 344	27	8	17 771	58.5	41.5	25.8	4.4	8.7	14.6
Montgomery	273	-3.4	401	1	244	782	2 005	88	85	124 935	73.1	26.9	67.7	30.8	0.0	6.6
Morgan	134	-4.3	223	0	111	556	2 567	54	34	57 096	82.1	17.9	43.6	14.0	0.0	151.2
Newton	207	0.2	544	7	193	1 056	1 946	126	84	221 262	68.4	31.6	78.5	44.9	0.0	4.4
Noble	182	-1.1	193	4	147	355	1 886	45	59	62 464	51.8	48.2	50.2	15.1	0.0	10.0
Ohio	30	-6.6	119	0	16	236	2 118	21	4	14 935	71.8	28.2	27.8	2.0	0.0	0.7
Orange	123	6.3	232	D	78	262	1 288	43	22	41 700	44.2	55.8	32.2	7.9	14.5	2.8
Owen	107	-5.1	189	0	70	325	1 457	34	16	28 853	62.2	37.8	32.9	6.3	1.2	2.2
Parke	189	3.7	401	1	146	691	1 600	73	43	92 110	79.8	20.2	59.2	24.2	0.2	1.9
Perry	84	5.3	174	0	44	230	1 214	35	13	27 240	28.0	72.0	31.4	5.4	23.5	2.4
Pike	84	-0.9	292	D	70	377	1 455	59	20	69 620	68.8	31.2	52.8	20.5	0.0	472.6
Porter	135	-5.3	283	7	123	651	2 344	71	42	88 712	86.3	13.7	61.1	28.4	4.8	678.9
Posey	195	-11.6	447	3	180	740	1 718	139	60	136 774	84.3	15.7	73.9	35.9	0.7	19.5
Pulaski	236	-2.7	445	11	216	727	1 591	96	98	184 665	62.4	37.6	77.0	37.7	0.0	9.9

Table B. States and Counties — Residential Construction, Wholesale and Retail Trade, and Real Estate

STATE County	Value of Residential Construction Authorized by Building Permits, 1999		Wholesale Trade, 1997				Retail Trade[1], 1997				Real Estate and Rental and Leasing, 1997			
	New Construction ($1,000)	Number of Housing Units	Number of Establishments	Number of Employees	Sales (mil dol)	Annual Payroll (mil dol)	Number of Establishments	Number of Employees	Sales (mil dol)	Annual Payroll (mil dol)	Number of Establishments	Number of Employees	Receipts (mil dol)	Annual Payroll (mil dol)
	133	134	135	136	137	138	139	140	141	142	143	144	145	146
INDIANA	4 786 192	41 844	8 896	112 705	66 350.1	3 737.8	24 954	337 867	57 241.6	5 273.8	5 427	28 948	3 269.1	572.6
Adams	17 012	196	43	314	151.3	7.5	172	1 824	344.6	27.9	14	54	5.3	0.9
Allen	350 933	2 667	686	10 861	6 586.2	357.8	1 320	21 917	3 534.6	351.1	336	1 988	254.8	43.2
Bartholomew	41 723	300	114	910	714.3	29.8	397	4 658	680.6	66.1	68	268	37.2	5.8
Benton	1 470	27	27	181	109.0	4.3	59	413	70.0	7.0	6	D	D	D
Blackford	4 142	48	15	110	20.8	2.9	56	515	82.9	6.8	14	29	2.5	0.4
Boone	108 515	549	94	629	500.9	18.8	173	1 632	261.0	25.3	33	135	11.2	2.0
Brown	11 194	172	9	D	D	D	102	432	42.1	5.3	9	34	2.8	0.6
Carroll	7 120	100	33	224	145.8	6.4	61	574	90.9	8.8	17	47	2.7	0.5
Cass	9 116	92	49	453	220.0	13.7	169	2 046	339.1	31.5	22	76	4.4	0.9
Clark	75 188	820	128	1 486	686.5	37.8	471	7 887	1 261.0	114.9	98	477	59.4	8.2
Clay	5 979	83	18	D	D	D	105	1 076	190.1	16.1	16	42	4.5	0.5
Clinton	8 701	84	47	D	D	D	126	1 200	193.5	18.8	23	70	5.8	1.1
Crawford	481	7	4	D	D	D	36	322	36.3	4.0	6	8	1.1	0.3
Daviess	4 477	26	22	233	76.6	6.0	145	1 490	260.5	21.4	15	60	4.3	0.7
Dearborn	48 579	455	37	D	D	D	158	1 896	344.3	29.0	37	D	D	D
Decatur	12 591	130	36	423	231.2	10.4	128	1 414	230.9	20.2	19	46	4.6	0.8
De Kalb	28 937	236	49	413	254.5	15.6	152	1 667	291.8	25.1	27	112	10.4	2.3
Delaware	43 611	365	119	1 501	653.4	45.8	548	7 340	1 118.7	105.4	119	433	46.9	8.4
Dubois	31 052	218	72	1 417	781.8	52.1	231	2 951	551.7	50.7	36	184	9.8	2.2
Elkhart	124 346	1 127	382	5 031	2 246.1	160.0	751	10 866	1 973.6	179.6	171	884	78.1	13.9
Fayette	6 769	94	19	227	69.5	6.2	94	1 202	193.4	16.8	24	83	4.9	1.0
Floyd	67 155	542	97	1 076	298.0	30.1	231	2 366	331.0	36.8	54	233	20.7	3.7
Fountain	370	8	22	D	D	D	75	675	120.4	8.9	9	30	1.0	0.2
Franklin	15 718	122	14	81	28.1	2.1	63	443	66.5	6.5	7	23	1.5	0.4
Fulton	3 029	31	35	175	70.0	4.0	91	936	143.8	11.6	15	39	2.5	0.9
Gibson	10 641	240	38	D	D	D	148	1 694	252.0	21.9	12	33	3.3	0.4
Grant	26 310	377	72	770	200.2	20.4	318	3 864	629.5	54.8	56	284	24.9	4.9
Greene	0	0	30	145	89.2	3.1	135	1 252	178.5	16.7	19	66	2.4	0.4
Hamilton	640 832	3 907	508	5 552	5 171.0	223.2	574	9 896	1 786.5	176.8	168	1 267	172.7	29.9
Hancock	79 042	671	62	665	258.7	17.9	149	1 639	341.4	25.4	39	121	12.5	2.1
Harrison	31 295	321	27	264	70.9	6.0	133	1 540	234.9	20.6	24	54	5.8	0.8
Hendricks	232 054	1 891	100	725	263.9	23.2	289	4 363	756.5	65.5	72	348	27.7	4.6
Henry	21 543	244	46	498	197.3	13.8	189	2 107	426.6	33.4	24	63	6.9	0.9
Howard	58 839	521	110	D	D	D	409	6 078	959.6	89.1	84	306	38.5	5.4
Huntington	20 579	160	54	485	265.1	12.9	169	1 943	312.8	28.1	28	86	7.2	1.3
Jackson	21 442	281	46	553	206.0	14.7	242	2 444	389.5	36.6	41	115	9.9	1.8
Jasper	23 183	250	43	299	283.7	8.6	149	1 718	278.5	24.7	20	113	29.2	2.6
Jay	6 394	78	21	231	122.7	5.2	82	707	115.0	17.0	20	99	3.4	0.6
Jefferson	17 814	232	27	226	40.3	4.8	167	1 766	281.2	24.5	24	76	7.8	1.1
Jennings	13 686	212	16	115	39.9	2.7	72	764	136.0	12.1	18	37	3.4	0.4
Johnson	232 208	1 529	113	788	659.9	26.6	490	7 338	1 171.2	109.2	99	362	42.1	6.1
Knox	8 749	150	68	842	373.7	19.3	234	2 668	399.9	36.7	28	120	10.9	1.7
Kosciusko	51 494	501	105	737	372.3	22.4	333	3 460	551.9	55.3	64	169	18.0	2.7
Lagrange	16 929	218	31	479	132.4	9.6	145	1 184	203.9	17.6	16	44	3.0	0.6
Lake	259 335	2 200	547	7 094	3 876.3	249.7	1 736	25 503	4 380.6	398.6	403	2 001	240.6	44.1
La Porte	53 928	544	135	1 525	658.5	44.6	552	6 312	1 041.7	95.7	95	313	31.0	4.9
Lawrence	5 336	102	26	228	54.7	5.3	207	2 108	372.1	31.6	24	179	22.3	4.2
Madison	47 230	413	105	1 157	428.6	31.3	521	6 790	1 123.4	101.3	112	439	35.0	7.0
Marion	653 516	6 098	1 953	32 619	21 284.8	1 245.4	3 654	59 830	10 757.4	1 038.3	1 106	9 086	1 137.7	212.1
Marshall	23 001	320	71	696	265.5	18.4	202	2 103	367.9	31.2	38	149	15.8	3.4
Martin	364	6	6	D	D	D	52	385	58.6	4.7	7	D	D	D
Miami	12 681	144	41	564	270.9	16.4	121	1 068	205.0	17.9	24	52	3.6	0.5
Monroe	99 399	1 013	102	D	D	D	514	6 846	1 073.7	97.5	162	869	83.1	15.3
Montgomery	12 256	192	56	271	176.4	8.9	167	1 947	293.8	27.2	30	97	8.8	1.2
Morgan	68 138	601	56	303	150.5	8.8	207	2 372	432.9	35.7	52	185	16.9	2.8
Newton	6 757	78	24	131	82.4	4.1	53	418	70.6	5.7	6	12	2.3	0.3
Noble	23 131	208	39	392	208.3	13.0	157	1 642	258.3	23.5	23	73	4.0	0.7
Ohio	5 496	60	NA	NA	NA	NA	12	108	13.7	1.4	2	D	D	D
Orange	1 017	31	19	109	33.4	2.0	89	574	103.2	9.0	6	47	2.9	0.5
Owen	570	8	15	60	13.0	1.4	59	510	71.3	6.1	8	D	D	D
Parke	4 166	47	12	67	21.0	1.1	50	367	48.8	4.8	8	33	3.2	0.6
Perry	4 411	46	15	178	77.3	5.8	85	974	131.2	11.7	16	35	4.3	0.5
Pike	6 500	82	12	113	37.1	3.2	38	266	41.1	3.1	1	D	D	D
Porter	156 737	1 325	174	1 823	941.7	56.1	436	6 231	1 040.3	98.6	133	593	74.4	10.2
Posey	18 228	140	30	D	D	D	95	906	151.5	13.9	8	27	1.5	0.2
Pulaski	6 890	64	36	356	167.3	9.7	58	419	73.9	6.9	15	36	1.5	0.3

1. Establishments with payroll.

STATE County	Professional, Scientific, and Technical Services[1], 1997				Manufacturing, 1997				Accommodation and Foodservices, 1997			
	Number of Establishments	Number of Employees	Receipts (mil dol)	Annual Payroll (mil dol)	Number of Establishments	Number of Employees	Receipts (mil dol)	Annual Payroll (mil dol)	Number of Establishments	Number of Employees	Sales (mil dol)	Annual Payroll (mil dol)
	147	148	149	150	151	152	153	154	155	156	157	158
INDIANA	9 795	69 393	5 974.2	2 207.5	9 303	625 692	142 270.7	22 121.4	11 705	215 710	6 646.3	1 865.3
Adams	39	115	6.7	2.1	67	6 536	1 428.9	189.6	61	1 103	27.4	7.9
Allen	658	5 508	463.9	162.4	576	36 585	9 182.2	1 362.0	626	13 472	414.0	122.2
Bartholomew	152	777	58.5	24.7	145	13 311	3 096.7	412.1	135	3 114	102.4	28.4
Benton	14	37	1.6	0.6	16	562	58.8	12.6	19	D	D	D
Blackford	14	32	2.0	0.5	28	2 081	299.2	58.6	21	D	D	D
Boone	76	245	26.4	7.7	73	1 769	190.9	48.5	85	1 303	37.5	11.0
Brown	36	107	5.8	2.5	NA	NA	NA	NA	46	623	18.4	6.1
Carroll	21	73	3.9	1.1	33	2 191	500.8	50.3	26	339	9.8	3.0
Cass	35	141	10.8	3.2	60	6 129	994.3	157.9	88	1 125	30.7	9.0
Clark	138	563	43.5	12.8	163	D	D	D	192	3 876	121.7	34.8
Clay	24	105	4.0	1.7	34	D	D	D	50	516	13.7	3.8
Clinton	35	104	6.0	1.6	49	4 959	1 565.1	148.1	63	753	19.4	5.2
Crawford	8	13	0.7	0.2	NA	NA	NA	NA	18	D	D	D
Daviess	30	127	6.1	1.8	51	1 947	350.0	37.4	59	899	20.4	5.6
Dearborn	46	149	8.8	2.9	39	D	D	D	79	1 068	31.7	8.6
Decatur	26	486	11.8	7.9	52	4 926	847.9	155.6	47	765	19.6	5.7
De Kalb	52	255	12.2	4.0	119	11 000	2 040.2	364.3	78	1 008	34.0	8.8
Delaware	153	1 691	87.8	37.3	176	9 972	1 764.5	402.6	228	4 981	126.7	35.6
Dubois	61	236	16.1	6.1	114	12 450	1 637.0	327.9	91	1 480	39.4	11.5
Elkhart	246	1 465	111.6	36.0	894	56 087	8 999.9	1 610.8	354	6 202	189.4	51.7
Fayette	32	132	6.7	2.8	36	4 809	1 254.3	217.0	49	759	22.0	5.9
Floyd	146	975	77.7	28.3	135	7 499	1 243.2	204.0	107	1 830	54.9	15.8
Fountain	12	47	2.6	0.7	22	2 616	282.8	67.8	48	546	16.4	5.1
Franklin	18	45	3.8	0.9	19	812	134.5	23.3	38	554	12.6	3.5
Fulton	23	56	4.6	1.0	52	3 004	424.4	79.1	46	551	14.2	3.9
Gibson	37	193	11.6	5.2	42	2 142	336.1	54.3	62	894	21.0	6.3
Grant	66	360	16.0	5.6	80	9 375	1 784.4	395.2	140	2 579	74.3	20.2
Greene	31	343	21.1	9.0	26	1 136	171.7	18.5	49	D	D	D
Hamilton	515	4 169	435.2	168.7	191	5 687	836.3	185.8	252	5 154	165.6	49.2
Hancock	81	247	21.9	6.9	66	2 564	712.9	88.4	79	1 470	41.5	11.0
Harrison	24	92	4.2	1.7	38	D	D	D	44	690	21.4	5.5
Hendricks	148	507	33.2	12.1	80	1 537	248.4	48.5	127	2 581	72.2	20.9
Henry	46	205	15.1	4.3	57	3 516	688.7	164.8	68	1 082	30.4	8.3
Howard	98	410	30.8	10.3	80	20 018	4 732.2	1 077.9	182	3 913	115.1	31.7
Huntington	33	239	14.3	6.7	78	7 451	1 245.5	207.8	85	1 260	32.3	9.0
Jackson	43	284	15.8	6.1	90	5 848	1 182.7	179.4	72	1 042	35.3	10.1
Jasper	28	107	5.8	1.6	33	1 479	279.4	35.2	57	810	24.1	6.6
Jay	19	99	3.7	1.2	39	3 751	539.1	86.6	41	528	14.4	3.8
Jefferson	29	124	7.9	2.4	51	3 655	548.9	97.3	77	1 068	29.6	8.7
Jennings	12	54	2.2	0.7	42	2 410	263.2	55.7	31	392	10.0	2.7
Johnson	187	890	54.9	22.1	126	6 486	1 305.5	204.6	214	4 190	121.6	34.9
Knox	47	189	12.1	3.6	44	1 715	289.1	46.2	80	1 375	36.1	10.3
Kosciusko	96	395	27.1	8.3	186	14 949	2 969.2	514.1	152	2 116	58.7	16.6
Lagrange	38	97	5.1	1.6	77	4 765	887.4	154.3	60	702	24.0	6.9
Lake	728	5 402	455.5	154.3	423	37 109	14 297.9	1 748.3	931	15 407	463.1	126.0
La Porte	145	707	40.1	13.9	189	10 835	2 007.9	351.2	234	3 394	106.1	29.0
Lawrence	37	175	9.6	3.6	75	5 322	1 063.0	195.0	74	1 321	38.0	10.5
Madison	187	1 152	62.2	31.9	133	12 144	2 256.8	534.3	244	4 794	139.8	38.4
Marion	2 264	23 108	2 423.6	899.9	1 194	66 571	19 561.3	2 898.6	1 893	43 946	1 523.7	432.4
Marshall	51	250	13.2	4.6	143	8 588	1 516.0	230.2	97	1 418	37.1	10.0
Martin	13	87	5.5	2.7	9	575	133.4	17.7	21	D	D	D
Miami	27	94	5.0	1.4	50	2 491	385.9	64.0	58	706	18.2	5.1
Monroe	196	1 360	97.0	34.0	122	8 817	2 444.2	302.6	302	6 312	176.6	48.8
Montgomery	44	137	9.5	3.5	67	7 634	1 878.7	264.1	88	1 054	33.7	8.6
Morgan	61	193	12.5	4.7	65	2 869	472.3	78.7	80	1 411	45.1	13.3
Newton	11	33	1.4	0.4	29	1 474	176.5	34.4	28	D	D	D
Noble	45	243	19.9	4.5	143	10 818	1 821.7	309.2	69	961	29.8	7.7
Ohio	3	8	0.3	0.2	NA	NA	NA	NA	9	D	D	D
Orange	22	39	2.3	0.7	34	2 478	296.4	55.3	35	610	10.0	3.1
Owen	15	55	2.2	0.7	24	1 242	109.2	31.5	20	D	D	D
Parke	16	48	2.5	0.9	17	641	92.1	13.7	34	D	D	D
Perry	19	55	2.8	0.7	27	1 211	141.1	33.6	44	465	14.1	3.6
Pike	9	30	1.2	0.4	NA	NA	NA	NA	12	D	D	D
Porter	237	1 217	109.8	42.1	146	12 353	4 353.6	624.5	259	4 385	126.5	35.9
Posey	35	247	18.0	9.3	31	D	D	D	35	D	D	D
Pulaski	25	82	3.3	0.8	20	1 353	218.1	41.1	22	D	D	D

1. Firms subject to federal tax.

Table B. States and Counties — **Health and Other Services and Federal Funds**

STATE County	Health Care and Social Assistance[1], 1997				Other Services[1], 1997				Federal funds and grants, fiscal 1999[2] Expenditures (mil dol)			
									Total	Direct payments for individuals[3]		
	Number of Establishments	Number of Employees	Receipts (mil dol)	Annual Payroll (mil dol)	Number of Establishments	Number of Employees	Receipts (mil dol)	Annual Payroll (mil dol)		Social Security and government retirement	Medicare	Food stamps and Supplemental Security Income
	159	160	161	162	163	164	165	166	167	168	169	170
INDIANA	10 236	132 416	8 132.3	3 675.3	9 243	60 711	3 701.4	1 127.8	26 828.1	10 634.4	4 116.3	676.6
Adams	35	238	14.6	6.5	58	223	12.9	3.2	111.3	51.8	20.7	2.0
Allen	580	9 292	618.5	281.0	584	4 490	272.7	86.3	1 284.4	518.4	179.3	35.0
Bartholomew	142	1 633	106.6	57.3	101	703	39.4	13.8	264.3	117.1	44.6	6.1
Benton	11	191	5.5	2.8	10	43	2.4	0.7	51.4	19.8	7.4	0.6
Blackford	18	209	10.7	3.5	18	54	3.0	1.0	51.9	29.2	10.5	1.5
Boone	71	686	40.3	19.1	67	303	26.2	6.2	122.9	68.1	27.0	1.9
Brown	12	177	6.4	3.2	8	18	1.1	0.2	27.9	17.0	4.9	0.7
Carroll	23	194	8.1	3.0	20	50	3.8	1.1	64.5	31.2	10.9	0.7
Cass	56	777	36.0	18.5	58	226	11.3	3.3	156.0	83.7	31.3	4.4
Clark	155	2 188	119.7	52.0	157	1 165	63.3	21.3	441.2	189.5	77.8	11.7
Clay	34	257	10.7	3.8	40	132	6.6	1.9	114.2	60.5	23.7	2.9
Clinton	31	237	12.8	4.7	46	176	11.4	3.0	122.4	63.1	24.1	2.8
Crawford	5	90	3.4	1.4	5	18	1.3	0.4	46.0	22.0	8.8	2.1
Daviess	59	700	31.5	12.9	52	257	42.4	6.9	117.0	59.4	22.8	2.8
Dearborn	66	759	38.1	17.2	62	182	13.5	3.1	132.2	74.7	27.3	3.3
Decatur	29	406	14.3	6.5	39	153	8.7	2.6	89.7	44.2	16.2	2.2
De Kalb	55	695	37.3	15.6	51	208	12.0	3.7	112.7	61.0	20.7	2.1
Delaware	223	3 304	200.9	94.2	186	1 530	98.7	24.4	445.9	218.3	82.1	19.5
Dubois	86	798	49.6	18.1	69	341	27.5	6.4	153.0	64.3	25.0	1.2
Elkhart	233	3 281	187.7	78.0	345	2 427	164.1	47.3	462.3	260.0	83.8	14.6
Fayette	55	667	27.4	12.4	42	214	11.5	3.4	105.4	53.9	22.6	4.3
Floyd	154	1 835	109.0	45.7	108	628	35.9	11.6	256.5	130.9	53.0	8.6
Fountain	19	298	9.5	4.1	24	81	7.4	1.2	91.3	43.4	15.0	1.6
Franklin	22	230	8.7	3.7	16	70	3.1	1.4	60.3	29.8	10.7	1.7
Fulton	22	133	9.7	3.4	34	104	6.5	2.2	76.3	40.3	14.8	1.5
Gibson	54	556	23.7	9.0	40	153	8.2	2.5	137.2	67.6	27.0	2.5
Grant	124	1 834	80.6	37.2	106	573	32.6	9.2	361.0	164.6	57.7	11.4
Greene	52	739	19.0	7.6	41	101	6.9	1.5	152.3	80.1	24.5	2.4
Hamilton	341	3 816	244.6	108.6	245	1 499	100.2	30.5	298.5	184.5	51.9	3.2
Hancock	78	849	43.8	20.0	80	398	21.4	6.2	148.9	92.4	28.3	1.4
Harrison	40	341	16.0	6.7	24	93	5.9	1.6	109.7	60.1	20.5	2.8
Hendricks	149	1 959	101.8	48.7	131	610	36.0	11.3	246.2	134.9	43.6	2.0
Henry	70	986	43.0	23.3	61	264	13.8	3.9	199.1	104.1	39.9	6.2
Howard	162	1 947	115.9	53.3	131	961	44.4	14.1	327.1	171.4	66.4	11.0
Huntington	46	604	25.0	10.8	58	247	12.2	3.5	136.6	72.2	21.6	2.2
Jackson	59	598	34.0	15.7	64	304	19.0	5.0	143.7	76.7	25.9	5.0
Jasper	33	161	10.9	4.2	40	205	10.9	3.1	101.6	51.3	19.2	1.9
Jay	24	397	18.1	7.0	28	79	4.8	1.4	88.1	42.8	17.5	2.0
Jefferson	51	671	38.8	16.7	36	183	8.5	2.5	132.0	62.6	25.1	4.3
Jennings	23	255	10.8	5.1	21	67	6.8	1.1	86.3	45.9	14.6	2.6
Johnson	158	2 065	123.1	53.3	174	1 031	62.3	20.2	309.2	178.9	57.7	5.4
Knox	81	1 315	65.7	31.0	63	404	24.0	7.2	199.0	85.3	39.7	6.5
Kosciusko	79	851	48.9	22.4	138	708	44.6	13.5	193.4	114.1	35.6	3.4
Lagrange	26	468	24.9	9.2	41	151	14.3	2.7	70.2	40.2	13.3	1.0
Lake	1 013	10 528	697.3	317.5	740	6 006	373.9	123.8	2 086.1	898.8	445.6	97.0
La Porte	181	1 995	137.2	64.5	189	929	49.9	17.3	385.6	198.6	84.5	12.7
Lawrence	73	627	28.5	12.6	58	252	14.2	4.5	197.4	98.9	35.6	4.8
Madison	206	2 232	119.4	53.5	199	1 133	60.5	19.2	566.8	294.8	117.6	20.2
Marion	1 847	27 477	1 891.6	876.8	1 442	12 491	742.6	236.4	5 623.1	1 563.5	652.8	138.4
Marshall	53	775	37.0	14.3	65	301	19.5	5.7	138.8	74.4	23.8	2.2
Martin	19	145	5.0	2.0	14	29	1.8	0.3	295.8	29.1	8.1	1.2
Miami	39	352	16.1	6.5	40	162	6.8	1.8	171.2	73.6	24.6	4.2
Monroe	243	2 384	162.1	76.2	160	1 124	64.3	20.0	457.9	158.1	50.7	9.1
Montgomery	61	1 161	70.6	26.5	67	540	37.3	10.8	140.9	67.8	26.6	3.2
Morgan	86	877	48.2	23.3	94	472	26.7	7.8	188.1	103.3	37.3	4.2
Newton	6	44	1.7	0.7	11	26	1.9	0.3	50.0	21.6	9.5	1.1
Noble	50	392	21.4	8.9	71	258	16.9	4.8	114.8	64.4	24.5	2.2
Ohio	3	60	3.0	1.0	6	20	0.7	0.2	16.9	9.1	3.6	0.3
Orange	28	431	15.5	6.5	17	54	3.7	0.5	77.5	38.1	14.8	2.9
Owen	14	212	9.1	4.4	24	92	6.0	1.3	60.1	34.2	10.3	1.9
Parke	20	323	12.2	5.7	18	50	8.5	0.9	69.5	33.4	11.5	1.9
Perry	21	216	10.2	4.3	24	72	4.9	1.1	75.7	35.9	14.4	1.7
Pike	14	188	6.7	3.1	14	44	3.6	0.6	53.8	27.2	11.6	1.8
Porter	263	2 434	158.6	74.5	239	1 330	77.3	24.2	387.7	217.0	84.6	7.9
Posey	25	317	13.4	4.6	31	90	4.9	1.2	88.4	42.5	18.2	1.6
Pulaski	18	137	5.3	2.6	24	76	9.1	1.4	55.0	26.8	9.8	0.9

1. Firms subject to federal tax.   2. October 1, 1998 to September 30, 1999.   3. State totals may include programs not allocated by county.

	Federal funds and grants, fiscal 1999[1] (cont'd)							Local government finances, 1997				
	Expenditures (mil dol) (cont'd)							General revenue				
	Procurement contract awards			Grants[2]						Taxes		
											Per capita[3] (dollars)	
STATE County	Salaries and wages	Defense	Other	Medicaid and other health-related	Nutrition and family welfare	Education	Other	Total (mil dol)	Intergovern-mental (mil dol)	Total (mil dol)	Total	Property
	171	172	173	174	175	176	177	178	179	180	181	182
INDIANA	1 971.7	1 643.8	578.0	2 245.1	785.0	429.9	1 245.8	X	X	X	X	X
Adams	3.3	0.0	0.9	12.8	1.3	1.0	7.5	81.1	25.2	23.3	710	663
Allen	119.0	199.2	70.9	87.1	28.7	6.9	14.8	673.0	233.8	326.6	1 046	965
Bartholomew	18.3	13.6	5.2	23.9	8.1	1.1	14.4	252.6	52.2	78.7	1 145	1 010
Benton	1.6	0.0	0.4	2.1	0.3	0.1	5.6	23.6	9.1	11.2	1 172	1 092
Blackford	1.6	0.0	0.5	4.3	1.1	0.2	0.6	43.6	21.1	11.8	840	757
Boone	5.1	0.4	1.4	4.8	1.2	0.4	1.3	117.4	32.3	44.9	1 044	846
Brown	0.9	0.0	0.3	2.1	0.8	0.2	0.7	28.0	11.6	12.7	812	685
Carroll	3.2	0.0	0.7	3.5	0.9	0.2	2.2	41.9	14.4	21.6	1 082	988
Cass	6.0	4.1	1.2	12.2	5.3	0.8	-3.5	104.6	33.9	29.4	762	671
Clark	91.6	4.1	5.0	33.5	9.9	3.1	6.1	259.1	78.3	77.2	828	815
Clay	4.5	0.0	1.1	13.3	1.6	0.5	0.1	59.3	22.3	19.3	727	649
Clinton	4.2	0.0	1.1	8.8	2.2	0.5	1.9	83.8	29.0	27.3	821	732
Crawford	1.8	0.0	0.5	8.0	0.8	0.4	0.6	19.8	11.8	5.7	541	533
Daviess	4.3	0.0	0.9	10.4	1.9	1.0	2.2	65.0	22.6	16.5	571	485
Dearborn	4.0	0.0	1.1	11.7	4.3	0.7	3.8	127.3	45.8	37.3	800	731
Decatur	3.0	0.0	0.8	8.2	1.5	0.4	1.8	60.2	19.3	19.3	759	673
De Kalb	4.3	14.7	1.0	6.4	2.0	0.4	-8.4	108.4	33.8	36.1	933	825
Delaware	21.8	0.2	5.9	55.2	13.9	3.8	7.8	214.2	97.2	86.0	731	670
Dubois	6.2	7.3	15.7	4.5	2.0	0.3	18.3	78.6	30.7	34.0	868	783
Elkhart	15.6	3.5	11.0	36.7	9.0	2.6	11.9	350.5	135.9	161.4	946	814
Fayette	2.8	0.0	0.7	12.8	3.6	0.7	0.2	59.2	27.5	25.4	971	747
Floyd	9.4	0.7	4.3	32.2	7.0	1.5	5.2	194.3	54.5	45.4	635	617
Fountain	3.0	0.0	0.8	5.3	2.3	0.3	9.4	33.9	15.4	13.6	744	660
Franklin	2.2	0.0	0.6	8.0	0.8	0.4	2.3	31.3	15.6	11.1	515	422
Fulton	2.6	0.0	0.7	3.5	1.0	0.3	2.8	50.2	14.9	15.6	769	694
Gibson	4.1	0.0	3.5	9.7	2.0	1.1	4.0	62.5	25.0	25.5	799	794
Grant	39.6	0.0	5.1	32.8	8.7	2.5	21.7	150.9	66.8	65.1	895	774
Greene	4.8	17.6	1.1	12.0	1.7	0.9	1.9	71.8	29.6	19.9	601	503
Hamilton	19.7	0.4	7.0	14.4	2.8	0.7	4.4	406.0	106.0	189.8	1 226	997
Hancock	5.9	0.0	1.7	5.8	1.6	0.4	4.6	138.9	40.8	40.5	764	647
Harrison	5.4	0.0	1.2	10.1	2.1	0.6	3.4	61.8	27.1	18.0	529	476
Hendricks	9.4	3.9	2.5	8.0	2.1	0.5	31.3	241.4	64.0	82.7	896	757
Henry	5.5	0.1	1.4	21.3	5.4	1.1	5.5	127.6	44.6	34.4	704	599
Howard	17.3	0.0	4.3	29.0	8.9	2.1	7.2	282.0	77.9	104.5	1 250	1 151
Huntington	4.8	0.7	1.3	5.6	1.8	0.4	17.7	66.7	29.3	26.2	704	614
Jackson	5.7	0.0	1.9	14.3	2.9	0.7	1.3	108.9	30.0	32.8	803	709
Jasper	4.3	0.0	1.1	5.0	1.3	0.4	2.0	81.0	19.7	30.0	1 047	964
Jay	2.4	0.0	0.7	8.2	3.1	0.4	0.6	52.9	20.3	14.8	682	595
Jefferson	5.2	5.8	1.0	16.2	3.9	0.7	3.6	62.3	27.3	23.2	742	734
Jennings	3.0	0.0	0.7	11.2	1.3	0.6	2.0	38.7	22.0	11.3	414	346
Johnson	15.6	0.3	18.0	18.9	3.5	1.1	2.6	213.2	74.2	80.1	750	640
Knox	8.4	1.0	1.5	21.3	6.2	2.7	3.1	159.7	32.9	27.0	681	677
Kosciusko	10.1	0.2	2.8	8.0	4.4	0.9	1.6	190.2	57.4	69.2	984	897
Lagrange	3.3	0.0	0.9	3.5	0.6	0.9	1.8	61.9	25.5	29.1	888	797
Lake	110.6	23.2	28.0	254.9	91.1	19.8	83.6	1 398.6	542.2	639.6	1 334	1 315
La Porte	13.2	2.0	3.9	30.8	10.7	2.8	5.8	268.9	94.5	117.3	1 076	963
Lawrence	7.6	3.2	1.5	19.1	4.2	0.7	16.1	160.2	38.1	33.6	739	633
Madison	17.3	0.0	9.9	56.9	13.2	4.0	15.7	244.0	118.1	93.9	712	629
Marion	679.2	909.7	155.7	460.8	344.4	153.2	416.1	2 332.3	829.0	1 031.6	1 268	1 127
Marshall	5.3	1.0	1.3	6.9	3.1	0.5	11.5	91.4	35.5	40.8	900	814
Martin	201.1	42.6	1.8	6.1	1.0	0.4	2.6	20.7	10.3	8.2	779	687
Miami	42.6	0.3	1.1	9.3	2.5	1.0	2.7	92.6	39.5	28.2	848	779
Monroe	21.9	1.6	12.1	116.3	7.0	7.2	42.7	209.9	67.1	83.6	716	589
Montgomery	6.1	0.5	1.8	9.8	1.6	0.5	7.6	89.3	29.9	47.4	1 307	1 178
Morgan	6.8	3.1	1.7	16.5	3.0	0.7	4.3	119.7	49.8	39.1	604	505
Newton	2.2	0.0	0.6	2.1	0.8	0.3	1.3	32.1	13.6	13.0	883	805
Noble	4.5	0.2	1.1	7.2	1.3	0.7	3.1	107.7	37.7	36.6	872	774
Ohio	0.8	0.0	0.2	2.1	0.3	0.1	0.0	12.2	5.6	3.5	635	390
Orange	1.7	0.0	0.6	11.2	1.5	0.6	1.8	44.0	16.9	10.6	547	476
Owen	2.4	0.1	0.9	6.1	1.0	0.5	0.4	31.2	16.3	11.8	582	508
Parke	2.9	0.0	0.8	6.4	3.7	0.2	1.9	30.1	15.0	12.2	742	664
Perry	3.6	1.3	0.8	8.5	2.5	0.6	5.2	47.2	18.8	13.1	678	533
Pike	1.8	0.0	0.5	5.8	0.8	0.4	0.1	33.4	8.9	10.6	829	822
Porter	21.1	1.0	7.3	19.9	6.4	1.4	12.3	433.4	109.3	146.2	1 015	971
Posey	3.7	0.3	0.9	6.6	1.6	0.3	0.9	62.1	18.3	32.4	1 218	1 215
Pulaski	2.0	0.0	0.5	3.5	0.7	0.3	-0.4	39.9	13.7	13.3	1 008	923

1. October 1, 1998 to September 30, 1999. 2. State totals may include programs not allocated by county. 3. Based on the resident population estimated as of July 1 of the year shown.

Table B. States and Counties — Local Government Finances, Government Employment, and Elections

STATE County	Direct general expenditure Total (mil dol)	Per capita[1] (dollars)	Education tion	Health and hospitals	Police protection	Public welfare	High- ways	Debt outstanding Total (mil dol)	Per capita[1] (dollars)	Federal civilian	Federal military	State and local	Demo- cratic	Republi- can	All other
	183	184	185	186	187	188	189	190	191	192	193	194	195	196	197
INDIANA	X	X	X	X	X	X	X	X	X	38 659	21 888	357 365	41.0	56.6	2.3
Adams	78.0	2 375	39.4	25.1	2.0	2.9	4.2	21.2	646	71	116	1 840	30.1	68.2	1.7
Allen	624.2	2 000	54.5	1.6	5.3	4.2	4.0	251.6	806	2 243	1 114	15 540	36.6	61.9	1.5
Bartholomew	239.0	3 477	35.6	36.9	2.1	1.8	2.8	127.2	1 851	231	245	5 077	35.2	63.3	1.5
Benton	22.9	2 395	61.7	0.3	2.1	4.2	9.1	3.7	386	33	34	594	34.5	63.3	2.2
Blackford	31.9	2 277	44.0	19.7	3.0	3.4	4.4	9.8	701	31	49	750	43.1	55.4	1.5
Boone	104.5	2 432	47.6	17.4	3.1	1.8	4.5	69.0	1 604	98	153	1 954	26.2	72.3	1.5
Brown	25.4	1 626	58.7	1.5	2.0	2.0	7.5	14.6	938	18	56	717	39.5	58.7	1.8
Carroll	46.0	2 301	53.5	1.2	2.0	1.7	6.7	29.0	1 449	68	70	767	36.3	62.4	1.3
Cass	105.3	2 729	45.0	25.9	2.6	2.1	3.4	55.7	1 444	117	135	3 354	35.9	61.7	2.3
Clark	238.3	2 556	39.3	33.3	3.0	1.9	2.4	85.3	915	2 569	330	5 201	46.8	52.3	0.9
Clay	66.9	2 523	56.2	14.3	1.4	1.2	3.6	16.3	615	83	93	1 214	35.6	63.1	1.4
Clinton	84.5	2 543	44.2	17.7	2.8	3.0	5.3	45.4	1 367	78	116	1 484	33.3	65.2	1.5
Crawford	18.2	1 732	64.9	0.6	0.8	1.8	7.8	3.3	312	32	37	474	43.3	55.5	1.1
Daviess	69.4	2 405	44.1	28.5	1.6	2.6	6.6	32.7	1 133	87	101	1 483	27.8	70.8	1.5
Dearborn	119.3	2 562	43.8	26.0	2.1	1.4	3.0	86.4	1 855	80	165	2 054	34.1	64.9	1.0
Decatur	56.0	2 206	45.6	24.9	2.1	2.5	5.4	23.3	918	70	89	1 215	31.5	66.8	1.7
De Kalb	107.1	2 767	46.1	21.0	2.6	2.1	4.2	49.0	1 266	88	138	1 718	34.8	63.5	1.7
Delaware	213.6	1 816	55.4	1.0	4.1	6.3	4.1	77.7	660	418	418	9 633	47.7	50.5	1.8
Dubois	81.5	2 083	58.2	0.7	2.5	1.2	7.3	51.3	1 312	110	139	1 790	32.9	65.5	1.5
Elkhart	364.3	2 134	60.9	1.3	4.8	4.8	3.5	157.6	923	292	604	6 815	30.5	68.3	1.2
Fayette	61.7	2 362	56.9	1.4	2.8	5.8	6.4	4.3	165	55	91	1 382	39.6	58.7	1.6
Floyd	195.5	2 736	43.2	34.8	2.7	1.7	1.8	53.1	743	169	252	4 968	44.1	55.0	0.9
Fountain	32.9	1 802	58.1	0.8	2.3	2.5	9.0	18.7	1 025	60	64	831	37.4	60.7	1.9
Franklin	28.5	1 321	58.4	0.5	1.2	2.8	11.7	30.2	1 398	49	76	837	31.2	67.2	1.6
Fulton	47.1	2 316	36.5	30.5	3.1	2.7	6.2	28.3	1 393	53	72	1 068	35.7	62.9	1.4
Gibson	67.8	2 121	57.9	1.3	2.1	2.5	6.2	140.1	4 385	87	113	1 087	42.4	56.5	1.1
Grant	135.6	1 862	55.3	0.5	5.3	5.1	4.8	38.9	534	1 067	255	3 224	36.9	61.4	1.6
Greene	71.1	2 149	50.6	17.7	1.7	3.5	5.1	33.5	1 013	83	117	1 817	39.0	59.3	1.7
Hamilton	397.1	2 565	50.1	12.6	3.5	0.7	6.9	216.0	1 395	342	569	7 180	23.9	74.9	1.1
Hancock	152.1	2 865	49.4	29.4	1.7	1.0	4.9	37.9	713	105	191	2 942	28.5	69.9	1.6
Harrison	62.8	1 848	58.4	18.7	1.6	2.1	5.5	40.1	1 178	116	122	1 549	39.7	58.9	1.4
Hendricks	225.3	2 441	52.3	21.4	2.6	1.4	2.7	113.7	1 232	158	333	5 398	26.9	71.5	1.5
Henry	125.6	2 570	45.9	23.7	1.7	1.4	4.3	74.9	1 533	102	171	3 195	41.8	56.4	1.8
Howard	241.9	2 895	40.9	22.3	4.3	2.2	3.7	116.8	1 397	321	293	5 361	38.2	60.3	1.5
Huntington	66.9	1 801	58.7	0.3	3.2	3.5	6.6	28.2	760	86	130	1 857	28.5	69.9	1.6
Jackson	105.1	2 571	43.3	30.7	2.3	1.6	3.1	47.5	1 161	110	143	2 151	36.6	62.1	1.3
Jasper	74.5	2 597	39.3	22.2	3.0	1.5	3.8	140.0	4 878	78	102	1 619	33.8	65.0	1.2
Jay	55.3	2 547	42.4	21.7	2.5	3.2	7.3	10.9	504	46	76	1 119	39.5	58.5	2.0
Jefferson	61.2	1 956	59.9	0.9	2.7	2.4	4.9	34.5	1 103	93	110	2 213	43.2	55.6	1.2
Jennings	37.4	1 375	63.9	1.5	2.9	3.9	6.9	11.9	438	61	97	1 931	37.6	60.7	1.8
Johnson	236.1	2 209	56.6	14.9	2.8	0.7	3.4	193.4	1 809	340	383	4 973	28.4	69.8	1.8
Knox	172.9	4 356	22.5	51.4	1.2	1.4	2.0	37.7	951	182	139	5 166	42.1	56.6	1.3
Kosciusko	188.8	2 683	50.4	21.7	2.2	0.8	3.6	119.8	1 702	181	249	2 631	23.0	75.6	1.4
Lagrange	56.6	1 730	68.2	0.5	1.2	2.9	5.4	46.9	1 434	63	117	1 223	33.0	65.7	1.3
Lake	1 347.7	2 812	46.5	0.9	4.4	10.4	2.7	693.3	1 446	2 117	1 685	26 306	62.6	36.4	1.1
La Porte	247.9	2 273	56.6	1.8	3.0	5.1	3.6	119.9	1 099	223	399	7 378	50.2	48.3	1.5
Lawrence	137.1	3 011	36.1	43.3	2.1	0.4	4.0	40.8	896	157	160	2 351	31.6	66.6	1.8
Madison	263.9	2 002	52.5	0.7	4.6	3.8	4.0	78.7	597	314	461	6 371	44.8	53.5	1.6
Marion	2 401.0	2 951	40.3	11.2	4.5	3.8	2.8	3 747.8	4 606	13 234	3 803	59 052	48.5	49.8	1.7
Marshall	92.5	2 039	59.4	1.2	3.5	3.2	4.5	44.3	978	97	159	2 039	34.5	64.0	1.5
Martin	17.3	1 644	61.4	0.7	2.4	3.5	8.7	4.8	461	3 862	99	475	33.0	65.5	1.5
Miami	88.2	2 656	52.7	18.7	1.7	2.6	3.2	21.7	652	789	123	1 814	32.2	65.2	2.5
Monroe	196.8	1 687	48.0	1.2	3.0	4.3	4.4	139.5	1 196	406	420	19 245	47.1	51.4	1.5
Montgomery	74.2	2 044	60.7	0.5	2.6	2.5	6.9	54.1	1 492	104	127	1 804	30.1	68.6	1.4
Morgan	121.6	1 877	53.3	18.0	2.5	1.6	4.0	64.4	994	122	229	2 520	28.5	69.9	1.7
Newton	31.9	2 175	62.3	0.6	1.8	3.6	7.5	9.9	673	42	52	742	38.3	59.3	2.4
Noble	97.6	2 327	48.2	20.9	2.8	1.3	5.2	51.3	1 225	88	149	2 051	34.1	64.3	1.6
Ohio	12.4	2 271	39.7	0.8	3.5	2.0	8.0	0.3	60	14	19	296	38.3	60.9	0.8
Orange	44.5	2 296	45.8	25.5	1.5	1.3	5.7	20.4	1 051	47	69	1 040	35.1	63.2	1.7
Owen	28.9	1 427	61.4	1.9	1.6	3.2	7.9	5.0	247	41	71	819	35.1	62.6	2.3
Parke	26.6	1 615	59.8	1.6	2.0	1.9	10.1	10.2	621	60	59	1 102	38.6	59.8	1.6
Perry	43.8	2 267	42.7	23.1	1.8	1.3	4.7	31.1	1 609	83	68	1 442	51.9	47.0	1.0
Pike	31.1	2 440	39.2	1.3	1.2	3.4	5.0	135.3	10 603	38	45	606	41.4	56.6	2.0
Porter	418.3	2 903	40.9	29.5	2.1	0.9	3.5	222.0	1 540	463	512	7 953	45.6	53.0	1.4
Posey	64.4	2 417	56.4	1.4	1.8	2.9	6.6	114.4	4 296	81	94	1 172	40.1	58.8	1.2
Pulaski	40.3	3 050	37.1	24.0	1.9	2.6	5.3	11.4	860	46	46	941	34.9	63.6	1.5

1. Based on the resident population estimated as of July 1 of the year shown.

Table B. States and Counties — Land Area and Population

STATE/ County code	MSA/ PMSA/ NECMA code[1]	County Type[2]	STATE County	Land area,[3] (sq km) 1990	Total persons	Rank	Per square kilometer	White	Black	Am. Indian, Eskimo, Aleut	Asian and Pacific Islander	Percent Hispanic[4]	Under 5 years	5 to 17 years	18 to 24 years	25 to 34 years	35 to 44 years	45 to 54 years
					1	2	3	4	5	6	7	8	9	10	11	12	13	14	15
			INDIANA—Cont'd															
18 133	...	6	Putnam	1 244	34 788	1 234	28.0	96.1	2.8	0.3	0.7	0.9	6.0	17.1	13.7	12.9	15.0	13.4
18 135	...	6	Randolph	1 173	27 417	1 451	23.4	99.3	0.2	0.2	0.2	1.1	6.3	18.9	7.7	12.0	15.4	14.1
18 137	...	6	Ripley	1 156	27 660	1 445	23.9	99.5	0.1	0.2	0.2	0.4	7.2	21.0	8.1	13.1	15.5	13.2
18 139	...	6	Rush	1 058	18 208	1 857	17.2	98.5	1.0	0.1	0.5	0.5	6.6	20.8	7.9	12.5	15.0	13.0
18 141	7800	3	St. Joseph	1 185	258 537	209	218.2	87.0	11.2	0.4	1.5	3.2	7.1	17.9	11.4	13.4	15.9	11.7
18 143	4520	2	Scott	493	23 433	1 595	47.5	99.4	0.1	0.1	0.4	1.2	7.0	20.2	8.7	13.3	15.9	14.8
18 145	3480	1	Shelby	1 069	43 630	1 007	40.8	98.3	1.0	0.2	0.5	0.5	7.1	19.5	7.9	13.9	16.2	13.8
18 147	...	8	Spencer	1 033	21 178	1 702	20.5	98.9	0.6	0.2	0.3	0.7	6.8	20.1	7.4	13.8	16.1	14.2
18 149	...	6	Starke	801	23 597	1 589	29.5	98.9	0.3	0.4	0.3	2.4	7.2	20.3	8.0	12.9	14.1	13.3
18 151	...	6	Steuben	800	31 742	1 323	39.7	98.9	0.2	0.3	0.7	1.1	7.2	18.7	9.6	13.0	16.1	13.9
18 153	...	6	Sullivan	1 158	21 535	1 682	18.6	95.6	4.0	0.3	0.1	1.3	5.6	17.6	8.6	13.2	17.7	13.7
18 155	...	8	Switzerland	573	8 961	2 509	15.6	99.3	0.2	0.3	0.2	0.5	6.6	20.4	7.1	12.2	15.3	15.0
18 157	3920	3	Tippecanoe	1 295	142 475	372	110.0	92.5	2.3	0.3	4.9	2.4	6.3	14.6	24.2	14.2	14.1	10.5
18 159	3850	3	Tipton	674	16 641	1 958	24.7	99.3	0.1	0.1	0.5	1.1	6.0	19.2	7.5	12.2	16.4	14.9
18 161	...	8	Union	418	7 297	2 652	17.5	99.0	0.4	0.2	0.4	0.6	6.5	20.4	7.8	12.1	16.3	13.8
18 163	2440	2	Vanderburgh	608	167 922	314	276.2	90.4	8.6	0.2	0.8	0.9	6.6	16.5	10.0	14.0	15.3	12.5
18 165	8320	3	Vermillion	665	16 954	1 931	25.5	99.4	0.2	0.2	0.3	0.5	5.9	18.7	7.5	11.9	16.3	14.5
18 167	8320	3	Vigo	1 045	104 349	496	99.9	92.0	6.1	0.3	1.5	1.3	6.1	16.7	13.8	13.0	15.2	12.1
18 169	...	7	Wabash	1 070	34 538	1 238	32.3	98.2	0.5	0.8	0.5	1.4	6.4	19.0	9.6	12.2	15.0	13.1
18 171	...	8	Warren	945	8 349	2 563	8.8	99.5	0.0	0.2	0.3	0.4	6.9	18.6	7.3	11.7	16.1	15.5
18 173	2440	2	Warrick	995	52 557	870	52.8	98.2	1.0	0.2	0.6	0.7	6.6	20.7	7.4	13.2	18.9	13.0
18 175	...	6	Washington	1 332	28 233	1 433	21.2	99.6	0.2	0.1	0.1	0.7	6.7	20.6	8.3	13.6	16.0	14.0
18 177	...	5	Wayne	1 045	71 134	693	68.1	93.0	6.1	0.2	0.6	0.8	6.3	18.2	8.9	12.1	15.0	13.7
18 179	2760	2	Wells	958	26 810	1 472	28.0	99.6	0.0	0.2	0.2	1.5	7.5	20.1	7.4	13.7	15.6	13.1
18 181	...	6	White	1 309	25 522	1 512	19.5	99.4	0.0	0.2	0.3	1.2	6.5	19.9	6.9	12.4	16.1	12.8
18 183	2760	2	Whitley	869	30 811	1 353	35.5	99.4	0.1	0.3	0.2	0.7	7.3	20.3	7.6	13.2	16.8	12.4
19 000	...	X	IOWA	144 716	2 869 413	X	19.8	96.4	2.0	0.3	1.3	2.1	6.4	18.7	9.8	12.4	15.4	13.2
19 001	...	8	Adair	1 475	8 066	2 590	5.5	99.6	0.0	0.0	0.4	0.8	5.9	18.6	6.1	10.3	12.9	13.5
19 003	...	9	Adams	1 097	4 405	2 878	4.0	99.7	0.1	0.2	0.1	0.5	6.1	17.1	5.6	10.1	13.2	14.5
19 005	...	7	Allamakee	1 657	14 068	2 128	8.5	99.1	0.4	0.2	0.4	0.6	6.4	19.7	6.6	11.2	13.9	13.1
19 007	...	7	Appanoose	1 285	13 446	2 179	10.5	98.8	0.6	0.2	0.3	0.9	5.8	18.9	7.3	10.8	13.8	13.3
19 009	...	7	Audubon	1 148	6 802	2 697	5.9	99.8	0.1	0.0	0.1	0.6	6.1	18.0	5.3	9.4	12.8	13.6
19 011	...	6	Benton	1 856	25 798	1 502	13.9	99.4	0.1	0.1	0.2	0.3	6.8	20.4	7.2	12.3	14.8	13.8
19 013	8920	3	Black Hawk	1 469	119 959	441	81.7	91.1	7.6	0.2	1.1	1.3	6.0	18.4	12.7	11.2	15.6	13.1
19 015	...	6	Boone	1 480	26 300	1 485	17.8	99.2	0.2	0.1	0.5	0.7	6.2	18.0	7.5	12.1	16.2	13.8
19 017	...	6	Bremer	1 134	23 440	1 593	20.7	98.8	0.3	0.1	0.8	0.6	5.3	18.7	11.8	9.8	14.8	14.8
19 019	...	6	Buchanan	1 480	21 160	1 704	14.3	99.4	0.2	0.1	0.3	1.0	7.2	22.8	7.1	11.3	14.8	13.5
19 021	...	7	Buena Vista	1 489	19 404	1 794	13.0	96.8	0.3	0.1	2.8	1.4	6.4	18.4	12.0	11.5	13.4	10.8
19 023	...	8	Butler	1 503	15 499	2 035	10.3	99.6	0.0	0.1	0.2	0.5	5.6	19.7	6.3	10.1	14.7	13.2
19 025	...	9	Calhoun	1 477	11 319	2 323	7.7	98.8	0.9	0.1	0.3	0.7	5.5	18.4	5.9	10.8	14.2	13.0
19 027	...	7	Carroll	1 475	21 518	1 684	14.6	99.3	0.1	0.1	0.4	0.6	7.2	21.4	6.7	11.5	13.3	12.2
19 029	...	6	Cass	1 462	14 512	2 099	9.9	99.7	0.1	0.1	0.1	0.5	5.8	18.8	5.8	10.7	14.1	13.4
19 031	...	6	Cedar	1 501	18 056	1 868	12.0	99.4	0.1	0.1	0.4	1.2	5.9	19.8	6.6	11.6	15.9	13.9
19 033	...	5	Cerro Gordo	1 472	45 669	976	31.0	98.4	0.7	0.1	0.8	3.7	6.1	17.5	8.5	12.4	15.0	12.7
19 035	...	7	Cherokee	1 495	13 060	2 210	8.7	99.3	0.1	0.1	0.3	0.6	6.1	19.5	5.8	10.3	14.3	12.9
19 037	...	7	Chickasaw	1 307	13 423	2 181	10.3	99.7	0.0	0.0	0.2	0.6	6.2	21.1	6.3	11.1	14.3	14.2
19 039	...	6	Clarke	1 117	8 273	2 571	7.4	99.5	0.0	0.1	0.3	0.4	6.2	19.2	6.6	11.1	14.8	13.9
19 041	...	7	Clay	1 474	17 245	1 914	11.7	99.0	0.1	0.2	0.7	0.5	6.4	19.5	7.1	11.7	15.3	12.6
19 043	...	9	Clayton	2 017	18 582	1 842	9.2	99.7	0.0	0.1	0.2	0.6	6.3	20.7	6.4	11.1	14.0	13.1
19 045	...	4	Clinton	1 800	49 612	915	27.6	97.5	1.6	0.3	0.6	1.0	6.3	19.3	7.9	11.8	15.2	14.0
19 047	...	7	Crawford	1 850	16 427	1 976	8.9	98.7	0.4	0.2	0.7	1.0	6.4	20.3	7.4	11.2	13.9	13.4
19 049	2120	2	Dallas	1 519	38 210	1 130	25.2	99.2	0.2	0.2	0.4	1.1	6.6	20.9	7.0	12.8	17.5	14.4
19 051	...	7	Davis	1 304	8 517	2 551	6.5	99.3	0.0	0.3	0.4	0.9	6.6	20.0	7.2	11.1	14.1	14.1
19 053	...	9	Decatur	1 379	8 319	2 566	6.0	98.0	0.5	0.2	1.3	1.0	5.6	16.9	14.9	9.4	12.4	12.3
19 055	...	6	Delaware	1 497	18 482	1 847	12.3	99.4	0.1	0.1	0.3	0.9	7.0	22.4	7.2	12.3	13.7	13.0
19 057	...	5	Des Moines	1 078	41 955	1 042	38.9	95.6	3.5	0.2	0.7	2.1	6.0	18.6	8.0	11.3	16.0	14.2
19 059	...	7	Dickinson	987	16 285	1 985	16.5	99.4	0.1	0.2	0.3	0.7	5.0	17.5	5.8	9.9	15.7	13.8
19 061	2200	3	Dubuque	1 575	88 112	570	55.9	98.7	0.5	0.1	0.7	0.9	6.3	19.5	10.4	11.9	15.0	13.2
19 063	...	9	Emmet	1 025	10 638	2 365	10.4	99.3	0.2	0.1	0.3	1.0	5.4	19.8	8.9	9.6	14.1	12.1
19 065	...	6	Fayette	1 893	21 566	1 679	11.4	99.2	0.4	0.1	0.3	1.6	6.2	19.2	8.3	10.7	13.8	13.3
19 067	...	7	Floyd	1 297	16 256	1 988	12.5	99.5	0.1	0.1	0.1	0.9	5.8	19.0	7.0	9.7	14.1	14.8
19 069	...	7	Franklin	1 509	10 781	2 358	7.1	99.6	0.1	0.1	0.2	2.4	5.9	18.9	6.0	10.6	14.9	13.5
19 071	...	9	Fremont	1 324	7 706	2 625	5.8	99.6	0.1	0.1	0.2	1.2	5.7	19.9	6.2	9.7	14.7	13.3
19 073	...	7	Greene	1 472	10 020	2 422	6.8	99.7	0.1	0.1	0.4	0.6	5.6	18.2	5.8	10.1	13.9	13.2
19 075	...	8	Grundy	1 302	12 284	2 264	9.4	99.6	0.1	0.1	0.3	0.5	5.8	18.9	5.6	10.2	14.9	14.9

1. MSA = Metropolitan Statistical Area. PMSA = Primary MSA. NECMA = New England County Metropolitan Area. See Appendix A for explanation of these concepts. See Appendix B for list of metropolitan areas identified by type, with component counties. 2. County typology code from the Economic Research Service of USDA. See Appendix A for definition. 3. Dry land or land partially or temporarily covered by water. 4. Hispanic persons may be of any race.

Table B. States and Counties — **Population and Households**

STATE County	Age (percent) (cont'd)				Population — change and components of change, 1980–1999							Households, 1990				
					Total persons		Percent change		Components of change, 1990–1999						Percent	
	55 to 64 years	65 to 74 years	75 years and over	Percent female	1990	1980	1980–1990	1990–1999	Births	Deaths	Net migration	Number	Percent change, 1980–1990	Persons per house-hold	Female family house-holder[1]	One person
	16	17	18	19	20	21	22	23	24	25	26	27	28	29	30	31
INDIANA—Cont'd																
Putnam	9.7	6.1	6.0	48.6	30 315	29 163	4.0	14.8	3 813	2 546	3 281	9 996	6.3	2.62	6.9	21.7
Randolph	10.5	7.7	7.6	51.4	27 148	29 997	-9.5	1.0	3 307	2 751	-182	10 451	-2.4	2.57	8.4	22.9
Ripley	9.2	6.0	6.7	50.7	24 616	24 398	0.9	12.4	3 739	2 264	1 648	8 778	7.0	2.76	7.6	22.2
Rush	9.4	7.5	7.3	51.5	18 129	19 604	-7.5	0.4	2 422	1 740	-541	6 504	-2.1	2.71	8.2	21.1
St. Joseph	8.9	7.1	6.7	51.7	247 052	241 617	2.2	4.6	35 286	21 753	-1 061	92 365	7.1	2.54	11.4	26.4
Scott	8.8	5.6	5.7	51.2	20 991	20 422	2.8	11.6	2 964	2 078	1 622	7 593	12.9	2.73	11.2	20.1
Shelby	9.1	6.5	6.1	51.2	40 307	39 887	1.1	8.2	5 388	3 416	1 466	14 761	6.8	2.70	8.2	21.0
Spencer	9.3	6.1	6.2	50.0	19 490	19 361	0.7	8.7	2 543	1 765	981	6 962	8.5	2.72	6.7	20.8
Starke	9.8	7.5	7.0	50.6	22 747	21 997	3.4	3.7	2 864	2 279	308	8 141	9.1	2.75	9.2	21.1
Steuben	9.5	6.4	5.6	50.0	27 446	24 694	11.1	15.7	3 960	2 377	2 779	10 194	16.4	2.62	6.9	22.8
Sullivan	9.5	6.9	7.2	47.2	18 993	21 107	-10.0	13.4	2 277	2 430	2 742	7 364	-7.3	2.54	7.5	25.6
Switzerland	10.4	6.4	6.6	50.7	7 738	7 153	8.2	15.8	870	798	1 171	2 839	11.5	2.69	7.0	23.0
Tippecanoe	6.7	4.8	4.5	49.3	130 598	121 702	7.3	9.1	16 838	8 624	1 584	45 618	12.1	2.50	7.9	25.4
Tipton	9.0	7.3	7.7	51.2	16 119	16 819	-4.2	3.2	1 859	1 448	171	6 026	0.6	2.64	7.7	21.8
Union	8.5	6.9	7.6	51.2	6 976	6 860	1.7	4.6	887	605	69	2 576	6.9	2.67	8.7	21.2
Vanderburgh	9.5	7.9	7.6	52.8	165 058	167 515	-1.5	1.7	21 143	17 161	-574	66 780	4.3	2.40	11.4	29.2
Vermillion	9.5	7.4	8.1	52.1	16 773	18 229	-8.0	1.1	2 041	2 021	214	6 638	-4.1	2.49	8.8	27.2
Vigo	8.9	7.2	7.0	51.1	106 107	112 385	-5.6	-1.7	13 357	10 804	-4 045	39 804	-1.2	2.45	10.7	28.3
Wabash	9.2	7.4	8.0	51.4	35 069	36 640	-4.3	-1.5	3 948	3 436	-939	12 630	0.3	2.62	7.6	22.4
Warren	10.3	7.1	6.5	50.4	8 176	8 976	-8.9	2.1	870	767	108	3 015	-2.5	2.68	6.0	19.1
Warrick	7.9	5.5	4.8	50.6	44 920	41 474	8.3	17.0	5 898	3 267	5 138	15 817	15.2	2.80	7.7	16.8
Washington	9.2	5.9	5.7	50.0	23 717	21 932	8.1	19.0	3 028	2 298	3 824	8 664	14.7	2.70	9.0	21.2
Wayne	10.0	8.1	7.8	52.1	71 951	76 058	-5.4	-1.1	8 634	7 162	-2 062	27 587	0.6	2.52	11.3	24.9
Wells	8.6	7.0	7.0	51.3	25 948	25 401	2.2	3.3	3 391	2 340	-107	9 438	6.7	2.70	7.5	20.9
White	10.1	8.1	7.2	51.4	23 265	23 867	-2.5	9.7	3 086	2 279	1 531	8 926	1.5	2.58	7.1	23.5
Whitley	9.0	6.7	6.8	50.8	27 651	26 215	5.5	11.4	3 829	2 427	1 842	10 010	10.4	2.72	6.8	20.3
IOWA	9.1	7.2	7.7	51.3	2 776 831	2 913 808	-4.7	3.3	349 191	256 794	5 609	1 064 325	1.1	2.52	8.0	25.9
Adair	10.6	9.2	12.8	51.5	8 409	9 509	-11.6	-4.1	739	1 108	65	3 419	-5.4	2.41	4.8	27.6
Adams	10.9	10.3	12.2	50.8	4 866	5 731	-15.1	-9.5	452	572	-321	2 005	-9.5	2.37	4.5	28.5
Allamakee	10.0	8.8	10.3	50.7	13 855	15 108	-8.3	1.5	1 612	1 592	243	5 268	1.0	2.55	5.7	27.1
Appanoose	10.2	9.1	10.8	52.0	13 743	15 511	-11.4	-2.2	1 462	1 768	62	5 609	-6.7	2.41	8.5	28.8
Audubon	11.3	10.6	12.9	51.9	7 334	8 559	-14.3	-7.3	717	886	-331	2 936	-8.0	2.43	4.5	26.8
Benton	9.7	7.2	7.7	50.7	22 429	23 649	-5.2	15.0	2 729	1 961	2 389	8 518	-0.5	2.59	6.8	23.5
Black Hawk	8.8	7.3	6.8	52.2	123 798	137 961	-10.3	-3.1	15 140	10 822	-7 793	46 932	-2.6	2.51	10.4	25.6
Boone	10.1	7.1	9.0	51.9	25 186	26 184	-3.8	4.4	2 794	2 746	1 134	9 827	1.0	2.46	7.2	25.8
Bremer	8.8	7.4	8.7	51.1	22 813	24 820	-8.1	2.7	2 222	2 073	560	8 394	-0.7	2.55	5.0	24.0
Buchanan	8.8	7.4	7.1	50.7	20 844	22 900	-9.0	1.5	2 736	1 960	-380	7 506	-2.2	2.71	7.4	23.6
Buena Vista	9.5	8.4	9.5	51.3	19 965	20 774	-3.9	-2.8	2 277	1 959	-796	7 515	-2.1	2.49	5.4	27.5
Butler	10.1	9.5	10.9	50.8	15 731	17 668	-11.0	-1.5	1 479	1 772	120	6 036	-5.0	2.55	5.4	23.8
Calhoun	10.6	10.0	11.6	50.5	11 508	13 542	-15.0	-1.6	1 008	1 531	389	4 684	-8.4	2.36	5.1	30.8
Carroll	9.7	8.6	9.5	51.6	21 423	22 951	-6.7	0.4	2 440	2 139	-126	7 964	1.2	2.63	6.3	27.0
Cass	10.2	9.0	11.8	52.1	15 128	16 932	-10.7	-4.1	1 539	1 858	-246	6 177	-5.3	2.39	5.5	29.6
Cedar	9.8	8.0	8.6	51.0	17 444	18 635	-6.4	3.5	1 878	1 562	366	6 684	-1.3	2.57	6.1	23.2
Cerro Gordo	9.8	8.8	9.1	52.7	46 733	48 458	-3.6	-2.3	5 462	4 654	-1 738	19 061	2.0	2.37	8.5	29.3
Cherokee	11.0	9.2	10.7	51.9	14 098	16 238	-13.2	-7.4	1 342	1 565	-775	5 514	-8.1	2.48	6.0	27.8
Chickasaw	9.4	8.1	9.2	50.2	13 295	15 437	-13.9	1.0	1 471	1 352	70	5 040	-6.0	2.59	5.8	24.9
Clarke	10.3	7.3	10.6	52.2	8 287	8 612	-3.8	-0.2	858	913	70	3 343	-0.4	2.45	6.8	26.8
Clay	9.9	8.5	8.8	52.2	17 585	19 576	-10.2	-1.9	1 965	1 628	-616	7 074	-4.1	2.45	6.7	27.9
Clayton	10.5	8.4	9.6	50.6	19 054	21 098	-9.7	-2.5	1 980	1 994	-385	7 218	-3.6	2.59	5.2	25.2
Clinton	9.5	8.1	7.9	51.8	51 040	57 122	-10.6	-2.8	6 066	5 149	-2 190	19 757	-2.9	2.53	9.2	25.6
Crawford	9.9	8.3	8.9	51.0	16 775	18 935	-11.4	-2.1	1 931	1 597	-626	6 397	-4.0	2.54	6.2	27.2
Dallas	8.9	5.7	6.2	50.6	29 755	29 513	0.8	28.4	4 284	2 729	6 354	11 204	4.8	2.61	7.7	22.1
Davis	10.0	7.2	9.6	50.9	8 312	9 104	-8.7	2.5	1 107	914	42	3 093	-5.6	2.63	5.6	23.3
Decatur	9.8	8.2	10.6	51.3	8 338	9 794	-14.9	-0.2	902	1 074	176	3 207	-7.3	2.38	5.6	29.8
Delaware	9.5	7.7	7.3	50.7	18 035	18 933	-4.7	2.5	2 271	1 508	-249	6 389	2.7	2.78	6.3	21.8
Des Moines	9.5	8.0	8.4	52.1	42 614	46 203	-7.8	-1.5	5 173	4 141	-1 541	16 874	-2.7	2.48	9.9	27.0
Dickinson	11.7	10.7	9.9	51.8	14 909	15 629	-4.6	9.2	1 391	1 608	1 641	6 160	2.1	2.34	6.1	27.7
Dubuque	8.9	7.3	7.4	51.5	86 403	93 745	-7.8	2.0	11 161	7 731	-1 783	30 799	2.6	2.67	8.5	24.4
Emmet	10.1	9.3	10.8	51.7	11 569	13 336	-13.2	-8.0	1 171	1 314	-745	4 461	-7.9	2.49	6.9	26.7
Fayette	10.1	8.6	9.6	51.1	21 843	25 488	-14.3	-1.3	2 506	2 379	-332	8 490	-6.6	2.50	5.9	27.4
Floyd	10.2	9.2	10.1	52.2	17 058	19 597	-13.0	-4.7	1 883	1 962	-655	6 721	-5.1	2.46	6.7	26.6
Franklin	10.7	8.8	10.7	51.5	11 364	13 036	-12.8	-5.1	1 173	1 239	-466	4 579	-8.6	2.44	5.7	27.7
Fremont	10.9	9.1	10.5	52.3	8 226	9 401	-12.5	-6.3	799	1 113	-169	3 217	-10.3	2.50	6.5	26.1
Greene	11.1	9.6	12.4	51.9	10 045	12 119	-17.1	-0.2	1 100	1 286	199	4 195	-10.4	2.36	6.0	29.4
Grundy	10.4	9.3	10.0	51.7	12 029	14 366	-16.3	2.1	1 165	1 197	333	4 776	-8.6	2.48	4.7	24.8

1. No spouse present.

STATE County	Births, average 1996–1998 Total	Rate¹	Deaths, average 1996–1998 Number Total	Number Infant²	Rate Total¹	Rate Infant³	Physicians⁴ 1998 Number	Rate⁵	Hospitals⁴ 1998 Number	Beds Number	Beds Rate⁵	Medicare enrollees 1999	Serious crimes known to police, 1998⁶ Total Number	Rate⁷
	32	33	34	35	36	37	38	39	40	41	42	43	44	45
INDIANA—Cont'd														
Putnam	427	12.6	275	2	8.1	3.9	21	61	1	85	247	4 673	NA	NA
Randolph	354	12.8	297	3	10.8	9.4	17	62	1	27	98	4 872	460	1 664
Ripley	397	14.7	259	2	9.6	5.9	3	11	1	73	268	4 411	NA	NA
Rush	260	14.2	201	1	10.9	3.9	8	44	1	44	240	2 914	NA	NA
St. Joseph	3 847	14.9	2 412	31	9.3	8.2	564	219	4	836	324	40 741	16 159	6 225
Scott	332	14.6	222	3	9.8	10.1	10	44	1	46	201	3 598	NA	NA
Shelby	610	14.1	371	5	8.6	8.2	24	55	1	59	136	5 563	NA	NA
Spencer	278	13.4	173	0	8.3	1.2	8	38	0	0	0	2 996	NA	NA
Starke	288	12.2	251	2	10.7	5.8	10	42	1	35	146	3 598	NA	NA
Steuben	440	14.2	277	2	8.9	4.5	24	76	1	57	181	4 691	1 162	3 714
Sullivan	243	12.6	261	2	13.5	6.8	11	57	1	53	275	3 646	NA	NA
Switzerland	100	11.5	88	1	10.2	10.0	2	22	0	0	0	1 219	NA	NA
Tippecanoe	1 772	12.8	910	9	6.6	4.9	299	215	2	477	343	14 876	5 241	3 767
Tipton	207	12.5	159	1	9.6	6.5	12	72	1	116	694	2 475	NA	NA
Union	96	13.1	64	0	8.7	3.5	1	14	0	0	0	1 087	NA	NA
Vanderburgh	2 232	13.3	1 881	20	11.2	9.1	490	291	3	1 127	670	30 275	9 142	5 447
Vermillion	222	13.1	204	1	12.1	4.5	7	41	1	56	331	2 924	NA	NA
Vigo	1 392	13.2	1 149	13	10.9	9.6	236	225	2	550	523	17 229	NA	NA
Wabash	405	11.7	370	3	10.7	8.2	43	125	1	69	200	6 061	NA	NA
Warren	94	11.6	83	0	10.2	0.0	2	24	1	35	424	1 021	NA	NA
Warrick	640	12.6	381	5	7.5	7.3	113	219	1	34	66	5 986	841	1 645
Washington	338	12.4	256	1	9.4	3.0	14	50	1	68	244	3 745	NA	NA
Wayne	911	12.7	773	7	10.8	8.1	137	192	1	250	351	13 179	NA	NA
Wells	357	13.4	255	1	9.6	2.8	40	149	2	144	536	3 759	371	1 377
White	346	13.7	237	2	9.4	4.8	15	59	1	59	233	4 673	192	977
Whitley	426	14.1	263	2	8.7	3.9	20	66	1	100	328	4 644	NA	NA
IOWA	37 027	13.0	27 965	245	9.8	6.6	5 241	183	120	13 473	471	474 846	100 188	3 501
Adair	68	8.4	116	0	14.3	0.0	6	74	1	34	422	1 609	58	702
Adams	43	9.8	60	0	13.7	7.8	5	115	1	22	506	0	62	1 398
Allamakee	170	12.1	171	1	12.2	7.8	9	64	0	0	0	2 855	NA	NA
Appanoose	154	11.4	179	1	13.2	6.5	10	74	1	60	441	3 082	666	4 912
Audubon	72	10.6	84	0	12.4	0.0	3	44	1	29	427	1 647	NA	NA
Benton	290	11.6	216	2	8.7	8.0	8	31	1	116	456	4 010	196	886
Black Hawk	1 609	13.2	1 155	11	9.5	7.0	272	225	3	609	503	19 923	6 305	5 171
Boone	295	11.3	309	1	11.8	4.5	19	72	1	65	248	4 417	514	2 121
Bremer	221	9.5	220	1	9.4	4.5	14	60	2	74	316	4 108	288	1 232
Buchanan	293	13.8	214	2	10.1	6.8	18	85	1	109	514	3 403	438	2 065
Buena Vista	241	12.3	217	1	11.1	5.5	18	93	1	41	211	3 846	613	3 122
Butler	157	10.0	186	0	11.9	0.0	1	6	0	0	0	3 387	85	540
Calhoun	109	9.5	161	0	14.1	0.0	9	79	1	49	431	2 650	225	1 962
Carroll	248	11.5	246	1	11.4	5.4	28	129	2	181	834	4 399	391	1 795
Cass	153	10.4	197	1	13.4	4.4	14	96	1	71	487	3 368	335	2 264
Cedar	193	10.8	185	1	10.3	6.9	10	56	0	0	0	2 930	244	1 353
Cerro Gordo	550	11.9	530	4	11.5	6.7	144	312	1	285	617	9 214	2 569	5 521
Cherokee	129	9.7	175	0	13.2	2.6	16	121	1	67	508	2 828	179	1 329
Chickasaw	136	10.1	133	0	9.9	2.5	5	37	1	55	409	2 536	NA	NA
Clarke	90	10.9	96	0	11.6	3.7	6	72	1	48	574	1 580	281	3 399
Clay	188	10.7	178	1	10.2	5.3	29	165	1	86	491	3 268	338	1 914
Clayton	193	10.3	223	1	11.9	3.5	9	48	2	54	288	3 766	9	48
Clinton	636	12.7	557	4	11.1	6.3	64	128	2	250	501	8 877	NA	NA
Crawford	210	12.7	174	1	10.6	4.8	8	49	1	72	438	3 176	217	1 319
Dallas	503	14.1	306	3	8.6	6.0	30	81	1	53	144	5 129	434	1 209
Davis	117	13.9	98	0	11.7	2.9	9	107	1	80	952	1 534	63	746
Decatur	96	11.6	111	1	13.5	7.0	8	97	1	50	608	1 746	NA	NA
Delaware	230	12.4	150	1	8.1	4.3	9	48	1	49	264	2 757	187	1 010
Des Moines	543	12.9	443	3	10.5	5.5	76	181	1	388	925	7 722	2 062	4 878
Dickinson	164	10.3	183	0	11.4	0.0	29	179	1	49	302	3 629	NA	NA
Dubuque	1 164	13.2	828	5	9.4	4.6	187	213	3	670	763	14 454	2 595	2 936
Emmet	127	11.6	139	0	12.7	2.6	11	101	1	58	533	2 332	242	2 206
Fayette	249	11.4	263	1	12.0	5.4	16	74	3	119	547	4 310	NA	NA
Floyd	200	12.1	207	1	12.6	3.3	11	67	1	20	122	3 537	218	1 319
Franklin	123	11.2	135	0	12.4	2.7	5	46	1	92	847	2 134	133	1 219
Fremont	81	10.4	120	1	15.4	8.2	4	52	1	36	465	1 670	73	928
Greene	113	11.2	144	1	14.3	11.8	11	109	1	115	1 143	2 369	NA	NA
Grundy	129	10.6	140	0	11.4	2.6	5	41	1	88	722	2 426	117	949

1. Per 1,000 estimated resident population, average 1996–1998. 2. Deaths of infants under 1 year old. 3. Deaths of infants under 1 year old per 1,000 live births. 4. Data subject to copyright. 5. Per 100,000 resident population as of July 1 of the year shown. 6. Data for serious crimes have not been adjusted for underreporting; this may affect comparability between geographic areas and over time. 7. Per 100,000 population estimated by the FBI.

Table B. States and Counties — Crime, Education, Money Income, and Poverty

STATE County	Serious crimes known to police, 1998¹ (cont'd) Rate² Violent	Property	School enrollment and attainment, 1990 — Enrollment³ Total	Percent private	Attainment⁴ (percent) High school graduate or more	Bachelor's degree or more	Local government expenditures, fiscal 1997⁵ Total current expenditures (mil dol)	Current expenditures per student (dollars)	Money income 1989 Per capita⁶ (dollars)	Households Median Dollars	Percent change, 1979–1989 (constant 1989 dollars)	Percent with $100,000 or more	Income and poverty, 1997 Median household income	Percent below poverty level All persons	Persons under 18	Persons 5–17 in families
	46	47	48	49	50	51	52	53	54	55	56	57	58	59	60	61
INDIANA—Cont'd																
Putnam	NA	NA	8 429	30.4	76.1	11.3	39.7	5 866	11 154	27 708	-4.5	1.7	37 804	9.0	12.4	11.6
Randolph	210	1 454	6 227	4.9	71.9	8.6	28.6	5 603	11 241	24 773	-5.6	1.0	33 264	12.1	17.9	16.4
Ripley	NA	NA	6 002	11.5	68.8	9.8	30.5	5 787	11 563	26 608	7.6	1.7	36 854	9.7	11.9	13.4
Rush	NA	NA	4 417	9.6	73.6	8.7	15.5	5 335	10 869	25 111	-3.4	1.6	35 434	9.3	12.3	12.4
St. Joseph	637	5 588	67 863	31.6	76.1	19.2	240.6	6 170	13 277	28 235	-4.1	2.6	37 482	11.0	16.9	14.8
Scott	NA	NA	4 895	3.6	60.0	6.6	22.6	5 484	9 766	21 723	-11.0	0.9	31 306	14.1	20.4	20.1
Shelby	NA	NA	9 626	8.6	74.1	9.9	41.6	5 345	12 935	30 366	0.5	1.8	40 915	7.5	10.5	10.3
Spencer	NA	NA	4 562	8.5	71.9	9.2	20.6	5 312	11 462	28 777	4.5	1.4	38 960	8.8	12.4	11.6
Starke	NA	NA	5 310	6.2	59.9	6.0	23.6	5 168	9 980	22 784	-8.7	1.0	29 349	13.9	22.0	19.7
Steuben	157	3 557	6 899	14.5	79.0	12.5	28.5	5 807	12 399	29 203	6.4	1.2	39 664	7.1	11.0	9.9
Sullivan	NA	NA	4 456	5.6	74.1	10.0	21.2	5 860	10 668	22 940	-4.4	0.9	31 067	14.1	19.9	17.8
Switzerland	NA	NA	1 741	6.0	65.8	5.6	8.4	5 171	10 201	23 871	18.1	0.5	31 355	12.9	18.5	18.2
Tippecanoe	242	3 525	53 925	7.1	85.2	30.7	110.0	5 974	12 570	27 630	0.4	3.0	40 042	10.1	12.2	11.5
Tipton	NA	NA	4 027	8.7	77.0	9.8	16.5	5 602	13 669	31 198	-0.9	1.9	43 258	7.0	9.7	9.4
Union	NA	NA	1 810	7.6	71.3	8.4	8.1	5 053	10 700	24 635	-0.2	1.6	35 644	10.5	14.5	15.4
Vanderburgh	415	5 032	39 087	23.2	75.2	16.0	150.1	6 315	13 434	25 798	-4.2	2.8	35 327	12.0	18.7	16.9
Vermillion	NA	NA	3 947	5.4	72.1	7.8	18.4	6 120	11 217	22 339	-5.6	1.1	33 002	10.4	15.5	14.4
Vigo	NA	NA	30 437	10.5	76.0	18.1	94.7	5 600	11 973	23 505	-7.9	2.1	32 007	14.6	21.1	18.9
Wabash	NA	NA	8 643	18.1	74.4	11.7	39.8	6 179	11 511	26 724	-3.2	1.5	36 878	8.4	11.2	10.8
Warren	NA	NA	1 787	3.8	71.6	9.4	7.5	5 614	10 911	25 680	-10.8	1.0	36 143	7.6	10.7	11.3
Warrick	37	1 608	11 956	12.1	80.1	16.2	47.0	5 226	14 037	34 069	-4.9	3.0	47 588	6.6	9.2	8.6
Washington	NA	NA	5 588	3.2	66.2	6.8	27.3	5 750	10 187	22 897	-0.3	1.2	31 668	11.9	17.4	16.4
Wayne	NA	NA	17 529	12.6	71.2	11.3	71.1	5 822	11 535	23 475	-10.5	1.9	33 379	13.5	20.2	18.3
Wells	71	1 306	6 281	6.3	79.0	12.1	30.6	5 758	12 765	31 261	2.1	1.6	42 291	5.8	8.0	8.0
White	137	840	5 459	6.2	77.9	10.7	29.3	5 266	12 111	26 610	-3.7	1.3	35 583	9.2	13.6	12.5
Whitley	NA	NA	6 806	8.1	78.9	8.8	28.4	5 622	12 605	31 128	1.5	1.4	43 494	5.3	7.2	7.2
IOWA	312	3 189	737 729	15.0	80.1	16.9	2 886.0	5 738	12 422	26 229	-6.8	2.1	35 427	9.9	13.7	12.1
Adair	0	702	1 858	3.2	77.5	9.8	6.9	5 406	10 565	21 426	2.1	1.2	32 245	10.8	13.6	12.8
Adams	113	1 285	1 068	3.6	77.1	9.4	4.2	5 599	10 110	20 570	-4.4	1.5	29 334	14.5	21.2	19.1
Allamakee	NA	NA	3 255	8.9	75.9	8.9	14.1	5 092	10 232	21 098	-3.9	1.7	30 475	11.1	15.4	13.7
Appanoose	243	4 669	3 307	7.4	72.1	11.5	13.7	5 460	9 748	17 833	-6.3	1.0	26 547	17.7	24.9	22.0
Audubon	NA	NA	1 612	6.6	71.7	9.8	6.7	5 577	11 210	21 501	-6.5	1.6	31 376	11.2	16.5	14.8
Benton	5	881	5 494	7.5	78.2	9.6	21.6	4 998	11 373	25 959	-7.5	0.9	39 886	7.6	9.7	9.0
Black Hawk	386	4 785	37 637	12.4	80.4	17.3	132.1	7 725	12 321	25 683	-21.4	2.0	35 644	12.8	18.0	15.9
Boone	103	2 018	5 989	9.0	80.8	13.7	22.6	5 356	12 031	26 110	-5.4	1.5	37 774	7.9	11.5	9.8
Bremer	77	1 155	6 448	24.0	78.5	15.1	27.1	4 727	11 626	27 326	-9.9	1.4	41 445	7.2	8.8	8.0
Buchanan	71	1 994	5 437	12.2	78.4	11.2	16.7	4 881	10 925	23 386	-13.1	1.4	35 939	10.6	14.3	13.2
Buena Vista	178	2 944	5 334	27.1	82.1	15.2	20.8	5 377	11 423	25 311	-6.9	1.8	35 545	9.8	13.9	12.1
Butler	32	508	3 861	4.0	71.8	9.4	11.3	5 024	10 803	23 292	-11.5	1.2	35 469	8.3	11.2	10.0
Calhoun	44	1 918	2 613	6.8	78.9	11.6	14.9	5 666	11 405	22 496	-10.7	1.6	32 924	11.2	15.3	13.4
Carroll	32	1 763	5 492	35.3	74.6	11.3	17.6	5 154	11 301	24 391	-9.7	1.8	36 859	8.8	11.3	10.2
Cass	142	2 122	3 420	5.9	80.7	12.5	16.9	5 281	11 059	21 801	-8.0	1.4	31 513	11.2	15.0	13.7
Cedar	78	1 275	4 343	5.6	79.3	12.8	18.9	5 043	12 113	27 713	-4.4	1.6	40 666	7.8	10.5	9.1
Cerro Gordo	475	5 046	11 418	11.2	81.3	15.5	48.2	6 462	12 304	25 116	-8.9	1.6	35 631	9.5	13.8	11.7
Cherokee	37	1 292	3 260	4.6	81.3	10.8	12.9	5 386	10 909	22 967	-12.2	1.4	34 690	8.9	11.6	10.7
Chickasaw	NA	NA	3 312	10.6	75.2	9.9	12.1	4 945	10 919	24 656	-5.3	0.9	36 314	8.7	11.2	10.2
Clarke	157	3 242	1 890	4.6	77.6	8.8	9.2	5 022	11 380	21 735	6.7	1.9	30 831	13.1	19.4	17.2
Clay	34	1 880	4 328	10.8	84.8	14.5	15.9	5 230	12 314	25 028	-7.9	2.2	37 019	8.4	11.0	10.1
Clayton	21	27	4 674	10.8	74.5	9.0	32.1	8 573	9 813	21 406	-4.4	1.1	31 594	10.0	12.9	11.7
Clinton	NA	NA	13 116	11.4	77.4	12.9	48.9	5 426	11 795	25 410	-18.1	1.0	35 978	11.1	15.9	13.4
Crawford	128	1 191	3 998	10.3	72.5	9.8	14.5	5 498	10 056	22 209	-15.2	0.6	32 555	12.3	16.6	15.1
Dallas	114	1 095	7 613	10.4	83.6	16.3	39.7	5 069	13 364	28 874	-7.7	2.2	45 825	5.9	8.1	7.0
Davis	12	734	2 005	9.1	71.9	10.5	6.8	5 089	9 965	20 054	-8.1	0.4	30 349	13.9	19.2	18.4
Decatur	NA	NA	2 334	32.3	71.8	12.3	8.3	5 944	8 918	18 105	-2.5	0.5	25 535	19.5	25.6	22.8
Delaware	124	886	4 577	11.9	78.3	11.0	18.6	4 859	11 515	25 757	-3.9	2.6	36 963	10.3	13.6	12.3
Des Moines	487	4 391	10 650	8.5	78.9	12.7	44.9	5 970	12 246	26 536	-8.2	1.3	37 294	11.4	17.2	14.8
Dickinson	NA	NA	3 341	6.3	84.1	17.5	14.9	5 098	13 639	25 211	-6.2	3.5	36 739	8.0	11.7	10.5
Dubuque	176	2 760	23 997	41.1	77.7	16.8	69.2	5 474	12 331	28 276	-13.0	2.4	38 998	9.1	12.1	10.3
Emmet	91	2 115	3 096	4.7	78.3	11.0	11.6	5 542	10 402	22 790	-16.8	1.1	32 841	10.8	15.4	13.7
Fayette	NA	NA	5 282	14.6	76.6	11.8	24.1	5 443	10 226	21 109	-15.0	1.5	31 301	12.3	16.6	15.0
Floyd	115	1 204	4 123	7.4	79.0	12.2	16.9	5 375	11 307	23 344	-13.1	1.7	32 486	12.1	17.6	15.8
Franklin	18	1 201	2 599	3.7	79.4	12.3	10.9	4 919	11 691	23 741	-7.8	1.3	34 741	9.8	13.9	12.1
Fremont	216	712	1 969	4.9	77.7	11.3	8.9	5 335	10 674	22 948	3.7	1.2	33 034	11.8	17.2	14.4
Greene	NA	NA	2 318	6.0	81.2	13.7	11.6	5 585	11 164	22 320	-7.9	1.0	33 384	10.5	15.3	13.7
Grundy	24	925	2 815	5.0	79.5	12.3	16.1	5 314	12 898	26 314	-12.8	1.5	40 457	6.9	9.0	8.3

1. Data for serious crimes have not been adjusted for underreporting; this may affect comparability between geographic areas and over time. 2. Per 100,000 population estimated by the FBI. 3. All persons 3 years old and over enrolled in nursery school through college. 4. Persons 25 years old and over. 5. Elementary and secondary education expenditures, local government fiscal years ending between July 1, 1996 and June 30, 1997. 6. Based on population enumerated as of April 1, 1990.

STATE County	Total (mil dol)	Percent change, 1997–1998	Per capita[1] Dollars	Per capita[1] Rank	Wages and salaries[2] (mil dol)	Proprietor's income (mil dol)	Dividends, interest, and rent (mil dol)	Transfer payments Total (mil dol)	Government payments to individuals Total (mil dol)	Social Security (mil dol)	Medical payments (mil dol)	Income mainte- nance (mil dol)	Unemploy- ment insurance (mil dol)
	62	63	64	65	66	67	68	69	70	71	72	73	74
INDIANA—Cont'd													
Putnam	679	5.8	19 653	1 838	321	40	120	99	93	50	32	5	1
Randolph	576	4.9	20 945	1 408	214	46	98	99	94	49	33	7	2
Ripley	635	9.2	23 311	791	406	40	109	78	73	32	32	5	1
Rush	387	5.2	21 228	1 318	163	20	58	63	59	29	24	4	1
St. Joseph	6 657	4.9	25 782	415	4 254	446	1 309	884	836	414	317	68	9
Scott	441	5.9	19 139	2 007	187	23	57	82	77	34	32	8	1
Shelby	1 032	4.9	23 817	679	539	44	144	131	123	60	50	7	2
Spencer	431	5.8	20 509	1 552	242	26	75	62	58	29	22	4	1
Starke	388	3.0	16 222	2 757	116	33	58	81	76	38	26	6	1
Steuben	761	6.2	24 192	608	514	54	132	95	89	47	33	5	1
Sullivan	404	4.2	18 912	2 087	155	29	72	84	81	36	34	6	2
Switzerland	145	4.6	16 415	2 718	39	13	17	28	27	12	11	2	1
Tippecanoe	3 337	5.9	23 617	719	2 677	157	659	341	315	154	100	21	4
Tipton	414	3.2	24 874	503	125	24	61	55	52	28	19	2	1
Union	132	1.2	18 276	2 273	36	12	19	22	20	9	8	2	0
Vanderburgh	4 536	5.4	27 042	300	3 569	345	1 027	691	659	303	259	52	9
Vermillion	354	5.2	20 884	1 430	195	20	60	63	60	29	22	4	1
Vigo	2 276	4.6	21 679	1 200	1 564	123	486	417	398	170	155	32	6
Wabash	775	3.5	22 406	1 000	424	73	153	125	118	62	44	6	1
Warren	159	4.4	19 116	2 017	42	14	26	25	23	13	7	1	0
Warrick	1 309	7.3	25 385	448	468	67	221	139	129	65	49	7	2
Washington	531	8.6	19 087	2 027	175	35	70	86	81	38	31	7	1
Wayne	1 641	4.0	22 968	858	1 079	115	300	286	272	132	103	22	3
Wells	664	3.4	24 744	525	335	48	113	76	71	41	25	3	1
White	544	7.0	21 459	1 257	281	39	98	88	84	43	32	4	1
Whitley	727	5.4	23 948	652	368	33	120	89	83	45	30	3	1
IOWA	70 797	3.9	24 745	X	43 050	6 091	14 609	9 742	9 153	4 603	3 248	642	163
Adair	173	3.2	21 382	1 271	70	16	46	30	29	15	10	2	0
Adams	91	-2.7	20 639	1 514	36	13	23	19	18	9	7	1	0
Allamakee	287	5.2	20 441	1 578	117	56	68	49	46	24	16	3	1
Appanoose	259	3.3	19 096	2 024	120	24	58	61	58	26	19	7	1
Audubon	143	-7.5	20 984	1 397	43	25	41	28	27	14	10	1	0
Benton	579	5.6	22 814	889	140	51	122	77	72	40	23	4	1
Black Hawk	2 961	4.2	24 484	562	2 179	166	584	467	442	203	162	41	10
Boone	641	1.7	24 554	552	258	42	137	120	114	46	56	5	1
Bremer	567	3.9	24 275	597	254	56	121	79	74	38	28	3	2
Buchanan	445	2.2	21 050	1 375	172	52	97	66	62	32	21	5	2
Buena Vista	450	-1.7	23 184	822	238	65	105	73	69	36	25	3	1
Butler	324	1.1	20 699	1 490	82	51	73	57	54	30	19	3	1
Calhoun	227	-5.5	20 002	1 710	73	25	64	49	47	25	17	2	0
Carroll	531	1.2	24 548	553	289	68	135	78	74	39	28	3	1
Cass	320	3.5	21 883	1 131	159	40	80	62	59	30	22	4	1
Cedar	439	2.4	24 460	566	123	44	122	55	51	30	16	3	1
Cerro Gordo	1 147	4.1	24 902	499	712	94	254	182	172	90	59	10	3
Cherokee	291	-1.8	22 044	1 089	143	38	73	52	49	28	17	2	1
Chickasaw	300	1.6	22 320	1 013	137	50	65	46	43	24	15	2	1
Clarke	165	6.0	19 891	1 749	86	17	32	31	30	14	11	2	1
Clay	434	1.6	24 817	511	238	68	95	60	56	32	18	3	1
Clayton	408	3.0	21 796	1 163	175	59	106	69	65	33	24	4	2
Clinton	1 151	3.1	23 062	846	624	90	223	193	183	88	67	14	3
Crawford	335	-0.7	20 342	1 617	177	42	76	61	57	29	22	4	1
Dallas	995	7.3	26 996	303	355	73	175	99	91	49	31	5	2
Davis	151	0.3	17 879	2 384	56	19	32	29	28	13	11	3	1
Decatur	129	-2.4	15 654	2 858	55	10	27	33	31	15	11	3	1
Delaware	380	0.4	20 487	1 563	148	66	84	53	49	26	17	4	2
Des Moines	1 036	4.6	24 637	541	749	66	221	166	157	77	53	13	3
Dickinson	440	4.7	27 155	289	205	55	121	63	60	35	19	2	1
Dubuque	2 153	4.8	24 499	561	1 525	169	500	293	275	141	99	17	6
Emmet	253	3.3	23 283	796	120	37	50	48	46	22	18	2	1
Fayette	439	0.9	20 122	1 672	185	66	98	82	78	39	26	5	2
Floyd	361	1.9	22 025	1 097	139	39	95	71	68	35	26	4	1
Franklin	245	0.2	22 567	964	101	37	59	44	41	22	15	2	1
Fremont	158	-4.9	20 392	1 603	86	11	46	33	31	16	11	3	0
Greene	212	-2.6	21 010	1 386	83	22	59	41	39	22	12	3	1
Grundy	313	-1.7	25 595	429	99	45	75	42	40	25	12	1	1

1. Based on the resident population estimated as of July 1 of the year shown.   2. Includes other labor income.

Table B. States and Counties — Earnings, Social Security, and Housing

STATE County	Earnings, 1998									Social Security beneficiaries, December 1998		Supplemental Security Income recipients, December 1998	Housing units, 1990	
	Total (mil dol)	Percent by selected industries								Number	Rate³		Total	Percent change, 1980–1990
		Farm	Goods-related¹		Service-related and other²									
			Total	Manu-facturing	Total	Retail trade	Finance, insur-ance, and real estate	Services	Govern-ment					
	75	76	77	78	79	80	81	82	83	84	85	86	87	88
INDIANA—Cont'd														
Putnam	361	0.6	31.9	25.6	46.0	14.3	3.1	20.0	21.5	5 636	164	392	10 981	7.1
Randolph	260	2.3	D	39.4	D	7.7	2.5	11.5	17.6	5 694	206	345	11 327	-1.8
Ripley	446	-0.2	D	51.1	D	6.7	5.3	15.1	9.1	4 396	162	339	9 587	4.4
Rush	183	0.4	D	34.1	D	8.4	D	16.5	19.3	3 394	185	212	7 014	-1.7
St. Joseph	4 699	0.3	D	21.7	D	9.2	6.1	32.3	10.1	45 266	175	3 971	97 956	7.4
Scott	209	-0.2	D	40.3	D	11.5	2.7	15.3	18.3	4 314	188	715	8 078	11.0
Shelby	583	0.5	53.8	45.8	33.1	7.5	2.1	13.5	12.6	6 915	159	468	15 654	4.8
Spencer	268	1.1	32.0	25.2	56.0	5.4	3.7	16.8	11.0	3 505	167	221	7 636	9.5
Starke	149	7.6	D	23.7	D	11.7	2.7	19.5	19.3	4 616	193	433	9 888	7.0
Steuben	569	0.9	D	47.1	D	10.4	2.7	13.4	8.0	5 312	169	267	15 768	5.1
Sullivan	185	4.8	18.4	9.3	44.3	8.3	4.4	13.6	32.5	4 294	223	357	8 487	-3.8
Switzerland	52	4.0	D	29.0	D	7.0	3.2	14.5	24.7	1 528	172	168	3 732	16.5
Tippecanoe	2 834	0.1	D	31.4	D	8.2	5.5	19.4	23.8	16 874	121	1 245	48 134	11.6
Tipton	149	4.6	30.0	23.4	42.3	10.4	2.6	14.1	23.1	3 053	183	144	6 427	-0.2
Union	49	1.2	D	13.2	D	15.6	6.9	13.7	22.6	1 138	157	107	2 813	7.1
Vanderburgh	3 915	0.1	34.0	20.9	57.0	10.1	6.5	28.4	9.0	34 253	204	3 754	72 637	7.6
Vermillion	215	-0.2	D	D	D	9.1	1.8	17.5	10.6	3 517	208	271	7 288	-2.4
Vigo	1 687	0.1	27.6	20.5	54.2	14.1	4.0	25.8	18.2	19 907	189	2 492	44 203	2.6
Wabash	497	1.4	D	45.3	D	8.3	3.2	14.7	12.7	7 035	204	407	13 394	-0.5
Warren	56	14.1	D	17.3	41.7	5.2	2.8	16.4	20.4	1 532	186	87	3 275	-3.7
Warrick	535	-0.4	52.1	38.7	36.7	6.5	3.9	16.2	11.5	7 256	141	465	16 926	14.7
Washington	210	2.6	D	39.4	D	10.0	3.1	12.0	19.5	4 759	171	537	9 520	11.8
Wayne	1 193	-0.2	D	32.1	D	10.1	4.0	23.0	12.5	15 106	212	1 639	29 586	1.0
Wells	382	3.5	D	35.2	D	13.3	2.4	18.1	12.5	4 497	168	129	9 928	4.5
White	319	3.7	D	38.2	D	9.9	D	12.2	14.0	4 896	193	234	11 875	6.4
Whitley	401	1.2	54.2	48.3	33.2	8.3	2.8	15.6	11.4	5 097	167	160	10 852	6.2
IOWA	49 142	3.4	27.5	21.1	53.2	9.2	7.7	22.3	15.8	537 341	188	40 815	1 143 669	1.1
Adair	87	10.2	D	22.4	D	8.3	3.9	D	16.4	1 915	237	87	3 714	-6.3
Adams	49	9.7	D	19.2	D	7.2	3.6	26.2	15.5	1 192	274	120	2 234	-9.8
Allamakee	173	13.8	D	21.5	D	10.1	3.7	13.3	14.8	3 199	229	195	6 603	0.4
Appanoose	144	1.1	D	32.2	D	10.7	3.2	17.9	17.0	3 418	251	413	6 402	-4.5
Audubon	68	16.4	D	7.9	D	8.9	4.3	17.3	18.5	1 869	276	90	3 247	-7.9
Benton	191	8.4	D	14.3	D	9.4	5.1	12.8	22.3	4 688	184	218	9 125	0.4
Black Hawk	2 345	1.3	D	30.5	D	9.1	5.0	23.5	15.9	22 831	188	2 806	49 688	-1.2
Boone	300	4.3	D	9.7	57.5	14.3	2.9	16.2	22.7	5 291	202	305	10 371	-0.5
Bremer	310	9.3	D	24.1	D	7.4	13.5	18.3	12.3	4 389	187	216	8 847	0.4
Buchanan	224	9.9	D	22.2	D	10.1	4.1	10.7	22.0	3 824	180	274	8 272	0.6
Buena Vista	303	12.2	30.4	25.6	43.7	10.0	4.3	17.4	13.7	4 174	215	239	8 140	-0.7
Butler	133	21.3	D	14.2	43.8	7.5	3.7	14.2	14.8	3 673	234	156	6 483	-4.4
Calhoun	98	10.6	D	7.2	D	8.3	5.4	25.7	24.0	3 039	267	153	5 362	-7.3
Carroll	356	6.2	D	13.3	D	10.0	7.6	20.8	10.0	4 788	221	265	8 356	-0.3
Cass	198	5.9	D	18.9	D	8.9	4.2	18.8	20.1	3 685	253	291	7 146	-3.4
Cedar	167	13.2	D	15.3	D	9.8	4.1	16.8	17.6	3 505	195	114	7 146	-2.3
Cerro Gordo	806	3.2	D	19.0	D	11.2	6.4	30.6	12.0	10 247	222	736	20 954	0.1
Cherokee	181	11.7	D	20.3	D	13.5	3.6	15.6	18.2	3 258	247	132	5 973	-7.8
Chickasaw	187	13.8	D	33.6	D	6.8	3.2	13.8	10.4	2 954	220	156	5 486	-3.8
Clarke	103	6.4	D	36.8	D	8.9	3.5	13.9	18.7	1 913	229	152	3 599	-3.1
Clay	307	8.3	D	15.7	D	12.1	4.0	19.5	14.2	3 726	213	201	7 659	-4.8
Clayton	233	15.3	D	16.7	D	7.9	D	17.4	16.5	4 328	231	323	8 344	-2.5
Clinton	714	3.5	D	31.9	D	9.1	3.6	23.2	11.3	10 144	203	915	21 296	-0.3
Crawford	219	5.4	D	29.9	D	9.0	3.1	15.2	15.8	3 637	221	235	6 920	-2.5
Dallas	429	6.7	D	17.4	D	7.4	D	21.5	13.3	5 526	150	280	11 812	2.2
Davis	75	4.4	D	20.4	D	8.9	3.4	17.1	22.6	1 666	198	149	3 365	-6.0
Decatur	64	-0.2	D	11.6	D	7.3	D	30.5	26.1	1 929	235	228	3 692	-7.1
Delaware	213	16.5	D	23.9	D	8.2	4.2	12.0	15.8	3 292	177	260	7 408	13.2
Des Moines	815	0.8	D	36.4	D	10.0	3.0	19.4	10.3	8 569	204	799	18 248	-1.7
Dickinson	260	4.4	35.5	27.4	48.5	13.6	6.2	20.3	11.6	4 085	252	161	9 723	-4.6
Dubuque	1 694	2.0	36.4	30.5	54.0	8.7	4.2	28.8	7.6	16 279	185	1 294	32 053	1.7
Emmet	156	12.4	D	19.0	D	8.1	3.1	18.8	16.0	2 525	232	147	4 914	-6.7
Fayette	251	17.2	D	15.0	D	8.7	3.8	21.6	14.7	4 905	225	357	9 262	-4.7
Floyd	178	11.2	27.6	19.5	44.1	10.1	4.3	18.7	17.1	4 126	252	307	7 233	-4.7
Franklin	138	15.8	D	23.4	D	6.4	3.2	16.3	14.5	2 652	244	121	5 018	-7.4
Fremont	97	7.1	D	42.0	D	6.4	3.9	13.6	13.3	1 936	250	132	3 607	-10.2
Greene	105	11.3	D	17.7	D	8.4	4.9	14.1	23.0	2 651	263	163	4 707	-6.2
Grundy	145	21.9	23.2	12.7	41.8	6.1	5.2	15.1	13.0	2 868	235	55	5 158	-5.9

1. Covers mining, construction, and manufacturing. 2. Covers private sector earnings in agricultural services, forestry, and fisheries; transportation and public utilities; wholesale trade; retail trade; finance, insurance, and real estate; and services. 3. Per 1,000 resident population estimated as of July 1 of the year shown.

Table B. States and Counties — Housing, Labor Force, and Employment

	Housing units, 1990 (cont'd)								Civilian labor force, 1999				Civilian employment, 1990[5]		
STATE County	Occupied units										Unemployment			Percent	
	Owner-occupied				Renter-occupied										
				Owner cost as a percent of income											
	Total	Percent	Median value[1]	With a mortgage	Without a mortgage	Median rent[2]	Rent as percent of income	Substandard units[3] (percent)	Total	Percent change, 1998–1999	Total	Rate[4]	Total	Professional, managerial, and technical	Precision production, craft, and repair
	89	90	91	92	93	94	95	96	97	98	99	100	101	102	103

INDIANA—Cont'd

Putnam	9 996	75.9	51 600	18.2	11.7	345	23.8	3.0	16 461	1.3	325	2.0	12 988	22.6	13.3
Randolph	10 451	75.6	35 500	15.2	12.0	279	23.5	2.3	11 469	1.1	749	6.5	12 023	18.7	14.4
Ripley	8 778	75.9	49 000	17.1	12.1	299	20.2	3.9	13 570	1.5	441	3.2	11 039	18.4	15.7
Rush	6 504	71.9	41 200	15.2	13.3	297	19.8	2.3	10 122	1.3	289	2.9	8 314	18.3	12.9
St. Joseph	92 365	72.0	50 800	17.1	12.4	402	25.3	2.2	134 879	-1.0	4 164	3.1	117 132	28.9	10.8
Scott	7 593	77.2	38 000	18.9	13.2	301	29.9	4.5	10 903	-0.2	334	3.1	8 648	15.7	14.7
Shelby	14 761	73.5	51 300	15.2	12.0	369	23.1	2.5	23 461	0.1	702	3.0	19 825	19.9	15.2
Spencer	6 962	81.3	47 000	16.4	11.6	284	21.2	2.8	11 933	-0.7	473	4.0	8 858	17.2	16.2
Starke	8 141	77.9	40 900	18.4	12.8	329	23.2	2.8	10 919	0.1	508	4.7	9 346	16.6	15.6
Steuben	10 194	79.0	59 800	16.8	11.9	359	21.2	2.6	17 777	-2.1	511	2.9	13 642	20.5	12.7
Sullivan	7 364	80.0	32 300	15.9	13.7	261	21.6	2.7	9 342	-4.0	513	5.5	7 810	21.7	16.8
Switzerland	2 839	79.1	37 700	15.8	14.7	260	23.0	7.1	3 661	0.3	154	4.2	3 349	15.9	18.3
Tippecanoe	45 618	57.1	66 000	17.6	11.7	401	27.1	3.4	73 683	0.9	1 584	2.1	64 082	35.2	9.1
Tipton	6 026	76.9	50 900	15.0	11.7	325	21.0	2.0	8 763	0.8	199	2.3	7 780	22.5	15.4
Union	2 576	72.3	41 800	17.8	11.9	289	21.8	2.0	3 884	-2.2	120	3.1	3 198	19.0	13.5
Vanderburgh	66 780	64.8	52 100	17.6	12.5	343	25.5	1.9	90 676	0.4	2 837	3.1	78 494	27.6	11.1
Vermillion	6 638	80.2	32 300	14.5	13.2	305	27.4	3.1	7 562	-2.8	404	5.3	6 952	20.6	14.5
Vigo	39 804	69.3	40 000	15.8	12.5	308	25.9	2.6	48 858	-1.6	2 128	4.4	46 198	28.0	11.1
Wabash	12 630	74.3	43 400	15.3	12.1	303	22.6	1.8	17 462	-0.3	544	3.1	16 882	18.2	13.9
Warren	3 015	78.6	39 700	16.7	12.6	273	18.8	2.3	3 775	-0.6	114	3.0	3 655	16.8	14.7
Warrick	15 817	81.7	64 800	17.5	11.8	362	23.4	2.5	28 568	1.1	810	2.8	21 998	25.5	15.3
Washington	8 664	80.0	40 000	18.3	13.2	302	25.5	3.7	11 754	-0.8	540	4.6	10 651	15.1	15.1
Wayne	27 587	67.6	42 400	15.8	12.6	300	24.5	1.8	37 895	-2.8	1 321	3.5	32 650	23.9	12.3
Wells	9 438	78.9	53 000	15.3	11.9	323	20.8	1.9	14 550	-1.5	342	2.4	12 941	20.5	13.6
White	8 926	76.0	46 900	17.2	12.8	335	21.7	1.9	13 666	-0.9	452	3.3	10 969	20.9	14.0
Whitley	10 010	82.5	57 300	16.1	11.8	321	21.0	1.5	16 445	0.2	419	2.5	13 708	19.0	16.5
IOWA	1 064 325	70.0	45 900	17.3	12.8	336	24.1	1.9	1 574 269	0.3	40 138	2.5	1 340 242	25.3	10.5
Adair	3 419	73.5	29 400	16.1	12.0	240	21.6	1.3	4 445	6.7	105	2.4	3 847	17.6	8.9
Adams	2 005	72.5	28 700	16.0	12.2	239	21.8	1.5	2 271	5.0	56	2.5	2 314	17.0	7.4
Allamakee	5 268	75.8	39 700	18.7	14.2	243	18.5	2.1	7 429	1.3	288	3.9	6 500	16.7	12.1
Appanoose	5 609	74.5	25 600	19.9	13.6	254	27.9	3.8	6 733	0.4	269	4.0	5 657	22.1	10.4
Audubon	2 936	76.1	25 300	17.6	13.6	254	22.5	0.8	3 528	3.0	85	2.4	3 391	17.3	7.1
Benton	8 518	74.8	38 600	16.2	13.1	281	22.7	1.8	11 732	0.4	312	2.7	10 265	18.0	13.5
Black Hawk	46 932	67.3	44 100	15.6	12.9	326	26.2	2.2	67 372	-3.3	2 621	3.9	56 595	26.2	11.0
Boone	9 827	71.9	40 300	16.4	13.0	301	22.6	1.5	14 129	0.2	286	2.0	11 815	21.7	12.2
Bremer	8 394	75.0	45 900	15.6	13.0	288	21.6	1.3	12 363	-2.4	351	2.8	10 809	24.1	12.1
Buchanan	7 506	75.0	36 300	15.8	12.2	271	24.3	3.7	11 022	-0.4	406	3.7	8 746	20.5	13.8
Buena Vista	7 515	67.8	41 400	17.3	12.8	298	20.2	1.8	11 060	3.3	228	2.1	9 575	21.3	14.2
Butler	6 036	77.6	31 600	15.2	13.2	279	21.8	2.1	7 679	1.1	343	4.5	6 902	17.4	11.0
Calhoun	4 684	71.7	26 700	17.6	13.5	255	20.5	1.6	4 886	1.8	137	2.8	4 764	21.6	10.0
Carroll	7 964	73.4	42 000	17.2	13.1	283	21.9	1.2	12 531	-0.9	276	2.2	9 818	20.3	10.4
Cass	6 177	71.8	34 700	17.8	12.4	273	22.1	1.4	7 560	1.8	241	3.2	6 845	22.3	10.8
Cedar	6 684	73.1	45 700	17.1	12.7	316	21.4	1.3	9 392	0.6	227	2.4	8 510	19.3	10.7
Cerro Gordo	19 061	68.8	45 400	17.6	13.0	321	24.2	1.1	26 040	-1.9	668	2.6	22 847	25.9	9.3
Cherokee	5 514	72.3	32 500	16.0	12.9	247	18.8	1.0	6 975	3.6	152	2.2	6 374	18.5	11.3
Chickasaw	5 040	78.4	37 200	18.3	13.1	262	18.7	2.6	7 780	4.1	256	3.3	6 100	17.7	11.8
Clarke	3 343	72.4	36 400	17.0	13.2	286	23.9	2.3	4 566	4.8	156	3.4	3 839	18.1	12.5
Clay	7 074	65.4	41 000	16.6	12.4	265	21.7	1.4	9 807	-1.3	223	2.3	8 506	21.6	11.1
Clayton	7 218	74.9	37 200	17.2	13.0	241	20.9	1.9	10 399	1.3	448	4.3	8 566	15.9	12.2
Clinton	19 757	71.2	39 100	15.3	12.7	306	23.7	1.7	26 687	-1.1	932	3.5	23 025	20.6	12.5
Crawford	6 397	71.5	33 900	17.3	12.6	272	20.1	1.9	8 810	0.5	199	2.3	7 732	18.1	11.5
Dallas	11 204	74.4	50 100	18.7	13.6	336	22.9	1.5	20 093	0.8	332	1.7	14 965	24.2	10.4
Davis	3 093	77.6	28 900	20.7	13.3	275	22.5	5.8	4 164	-0.8	151	3.6	3 591	18.4	10.2
Decatur	3 207	70.8	22 700	18.9	13.9	220	24.2	3.2	3 630	-3.6	157	4.3	3 680	21.8	8.9
Delaware	6 389	75.7	44 600	18.2	12.5	283	21.4	1.6	9 609	2.3	370	3.9	8 158	16.2	12.5
Des Moines	16 874	72.8	41 600	15.8	12.4	321	23.6	1.9	23 141	-1.8	715	3.1	20 136	24.0	13.9
Dickinson	6 160	75.8	49 400	17.3	12.3	292	22.3	1.2	9 610	-0.4	235	2.4	7 049	24.0	11.3
Dubuque	30 799	71.2	53 600	16.2	12.1	315	23.8	1.7	48 523	-0.3	1 309	2.7	42 025	25.3	10.5
Emmet	4 461	72.0	27 800	15.6	12.3	247	23.7	1.6	5 620	-1.7	184	3.3	5 084	20.8	10.4
Fayette	8 490	74.4	30 100	15.2	13.2	250	22.7	1.4	11 171	1.5	392	3.5	9 631	19.5	10.7
Floyd	6 721	73.2	36 200	17.7	12.8	265	23.8	1.4	7 717	2.0	272	3.5	7 886	22.7	9.2
Franklin	4 579	72.0	30 500	15.2	14.3	280	22.1	1.3	5 932	0.4	187	3.2	5 204	20.7	8.5
Fremont	3 217	72.3	32 000	15.6	13.5	262	22.6	1.7	3 799	5.1	79	2.1	3 555	19.8	12.3
Greene	4 195	71.7	27 200	16.1	12.7	265	20.9	1.6	5 089	3.9	146	2.9	4 551	22.7	9.9
Grundy	4 776	74.4	38 100	15.0	13.4	271	20.4	0.4	6 211	2.0	158	2.5	5 420	21.4	10.5

1. Specified owner-occupied units. 2. Specified renter-occupied units. 3. Overcrowded or lacking complete plumbing facilities. 4. Percent of civilian labor force. 5. Persons 16 years and older.

Table B. States and Counties — Nonfarm Employment and Agriculture

| | Private nonfarm establishments, employment and payroll, 1998 | | | | | | | | | Agriculture, 1997 | | | |
| | | Employment | | | | | | Annual payroll | | Farms | | | Farm operators |
STATE County	Number of establishments	Total	Health Care and Social Assistance	Manufacturing	Retail trade	Finance and Insurance	Professional Scientific and Technical Services	Total (mil dol)	Average per employee (dollars)	Number	Percent with— Less than 50 acres	500 acres and over	Whose principal occupation is farming (percent)
	104	105	106	107	108	109	110	111	112	113	114	115	116
INDIANA—Cont'd													
Putnam	674	10 414	1 214	2 427	1 237	276	146	204	19 612	794	34.0	14.4	42.9
Randolph	552	6 184	518	2 877	896	215	96	142	22 964	851	29.8	16.2	45.8
Ripley	727	10 596	1 116	3 628	1 195	546	150	327	30 864	821	28.7	8.4	43.1
Rush	421	4 650	730	1 250	713	147	97	95	20 344	663	22.5	24.6	64.6
St. Joseph	6 597	120 449	13 954	20 972	17 523	5 338	4 969	3 226	26 787	666	41.3	13.7	45.6
Scott	444	5 935	690	2 297	1 078	147	60	130	21 913	348	40.2	6.9	35.1
Shelby	938	15 042	1 425	6 682	1 542	250	225	404	26 858	641	34.9	20.7	52.4
Spencer	428	5 710	316	1 618	698	108	62	154	26 906	638	27.3	13.0	41.5
Starke	356	3 698	594	1 403	754	82	39	71	19 270	410	30.5	19.5	49.8
Steuben	1 020	22 240	983	7 702	2 437	219	207	534	24 013	581	24.3	9.1	34.6
Sullivan	400	4 165	658	630	701	215	91	101	24 176	473	28.5	21.6	47.6
Switzerland	111	1 235	124	573	138	38	15	22	17 936	541	34.9	2.6	35.9
Tippecanoe	3 100	61 322	6 982	16 381	9 629	3 652	1 585	1 709	27 864	665	35.8	23.9	46.2
Tipton	333	3 834	562	1 052	516	133	90	94	24 592	415	28.4	25.1	59.3
Union	135	929	D	80	203	86	16	18	18 916	268	17.9	23.1	56.0
Vanderburgh	5 347	105 914	16 189	18 419	14 605	4 022	3 921	2 845	26 857	271	36.5	14.0	48.0
Vermillion	288	4 563	607	1 627	696	108	D	150	32 765	249	18.9	29.3	56.2
Vigo	2 678	45 531	6 916	7 404	9 694	1 653	1 029	1 072	23 544	455	40.2	14.9	46.6
Wabash	833	12 851	1 713	5 492	1 922	316	180	301	23 422	762	27.0	14.3	50.3
Warren	116	977	D	320	101	36	D	21	21 850	378	22.2	31.7	54.5
Warrick	1 010	11 105	1 448	D	1 417	312	284	297	26 723	356	28.7	16.0	46.1
Washington	468	5 878	649	2 869	722	124	86	123	20 864	914	25.3	9.4	42.2
Wayne	1 748	31 912	4 657	9 294	4 527	969	481	762	23 880	814	29.2	12.2	43.7
Wells	638	10 510	1 536	3 553	1 199	203	141	249	23 665	660	28.9	19.5	48.5
White	717	9 298	718	4 279	1 187	207	145	207	22 311	620	26.5	31.6	57.7
Whitley	674	10 845	1 035	4 467	1 605	274	134	265	24 427	787	32.9	9.5	36.5
IOWA	80 838	1 213 285	172 793	245 282	177 723	73 746	37 298	30 410	25 064	90 792	18.3	22.8	62.0
Adair	212	2 064	410	491	302	79	D	46	22 119	792	13.0	26.2	62.9
Adams	128	945	286	162	D	56	23	18	19 044	573	14.0	27.6	60.6
Allamakee	439	4 526	781	1 539	645	148	86	78	17 290	958	15.0	18.6	63.7
Appanoose	346	3 571	524	1 030	710	121	55	68	18 944	797	17.4	19.4	50.4
Audubon	230	1 432	325	198	239	64	48	24	16 794	649	15.9	28.5	69.0
Benton	611	4 421	618	506	785	239	96	95	21 574	1 210	20.0	24.0	60.8
Black Hawk	3 210	58 478	8 764	13 683	9 021	2 756	1 760	1 490	25 485	1 002	25.1	18.2	52.5
Boone	574	6 785	1 780	897	1 104	187	135	147	21 635	863	22.4	27.0	62.2
Bremer	631	7 938	1 137	2 001	1 027	961	138	181	22 858	982	24.5	13.2	54.1
Buchanan	547	5 210	888	1 313	906	241	86	118	22 572	1 136	21.3	19.1	63.6
Buena Vista	627	8 282	1 119	2 676	1 386	308	158	164	19 861	867	15.3	31.3	75.9
Butler	389	2 270	364	437	415	128	71	39	17 253	1 085	21.4	16.8	60.2
Calhoun	317	2 444	936	155	508	135	40	39	15 992	793	16.0	33.5	70.0
Carroll	842	10 289	1 673	1 523	1 701	810	177	208	20 172	1 102	17.1	20.4	69.4
Cass	502	5 519	1 075	1 205	926	218	107	120	21 790	804	16.4	32.7	66.8
Cedar	496	3 896	492	790	635	165	211	72	18 475	965	19.4	24.8	64.6
Cerro Gordo	1 480	22 580	4 846	3 778	3 805	1 231	495	496	21 988	822	22.7	26.5	64.5
Cherokee	391	4 283	946	835	793	165	72	95	22 227	890	14.8	26.5	69.9
Chickasaw	399	4 156	513	1 700	477	151	64	93	22 298	926	19.3	18.6	67.0
Clarke	237	3 008	380	1 216	412	86	36	60	19 957	678	14.6	18.6	52.2
Clay	625	8 347	1 228	1 225	1 654	268	162	172	20 647	668	15.9	32.8	68.6
Clayton	571	5 519	867	1 475	711	221	106	110	19 958	1 638	14.2	14.7	64.5
Clinton	1 319	19 264	2 784	4 903	2 822	718	227	427	22 144	1 268	20.0	19.7	59.2
Crawford	477	5 508	841	1 767	865	181	121	104	18 952	1 107	18.8	26.4	64.0
Dallas	828	9 216	1 387	2 393	1 342	401	182	225	24 438	918	28.0	24.2	53.7
Davis	179	1 654	423	366	321	52	66	31	18 629	884	16.1	17.3	48.4
Decatur	174	2 402	330	324	238	D	30	34	13 954	730	17.1	22.5	49.6
Delaware	455	4 351	550	1 328	837	177	90	93	21 273	1 278	14.7	11.0	72.9
Des Moines	1 231	20 967	2 821	6 815	3 431	478	288	509	24 272	650	22.3	18.8	53.5
Dickinson	728	7 040	667	2 313	1 058	162	149	155	21 996	512	16.8	29.1	67.2
Dubuque	2 599	47 588	6 439	11 250	6 668	1 527	952	1 184	24 888	1 579	17.9	7.3	64.1
Emmet	305	3 510	804	806	573	120	71	73	20 700	519	15.2	36.2	72.6
Fayette	654	7 177	1 206	1 494	1 136	227	154	136	18 884	1 295	18.0	18.5	67.5
Floyd	462	4 416	982	919	825	182	78	87	19 598	850	19.5	24.7	63.1
Franklin	342	3 034	467	887	431	107	64	67	22 194	856	16.1	30.8	70.4
Fremont	187	1 497	349	242	302	99	75	30	19 971	568	10.9	38.7	68.1
Greene	313	2 578	487	607	315	133	76	52	20 232	763	14.7	35.1	69.1
Grundy	321	2 619	345	494	404	162	58	64	24 295	754	18.0	27.9	68.3

Table B. States and Counties — **Agriculture, Land, and Water**

	Agriculture, 1997 (cont'd)															
STATE County	Land in farms				Value of land and buildings		Value of machinery and equipment	Value of products sold				Percent of farms with sales of —		Percent of land owned by Fed. Gov. 1997	Water consumption 1995 (mil gal/day)
			Acres							Percent from —					
	Acreage (1,000)	Percent change, 1992–1997	Average size of farm	Total irrigated (1,000)	Total cropland (1,000)	Average per farm ($1,000)	Average per acre (dollars)	Value of machinery and equipment Average per farm ($1,000)	Total (mil dol)	Average per farm (dollars)	Crops	Live-stock and poultry products	$10,000 or more	$100,000 or more	Percent of land owned by Fed. Gov. 1997	Water consumption 1995 (mil gal/day)
	117	118	119	120	121	122	123	124	125	126	127	128	129	130	131	132
INDIANA—Cont'd																
Putnam	195	-4.2	246	0	153	518	2 131	48	49	61 427	70.0	30.0	47.0	16.2	0.9	8.0
Randolph	224	-5.2	263	0	202	486	1 784	67	68	79 631	70.2	29.8	63.9	20.8	0.0	4.2
Ripley	159	-2.8	194	0	124	347	1 802	48	57	69 317	46.9	53.1	50.9	11.0	9.3	4.1
Rush	228	-2.2	344	D	207	836	2 441	85	86	129 605	65.4	34.6	76.3	35.4	0.0	3.3
St. Joseph	154	-10.4	231	13	140	537	2 258	68	55	82 849	72.6	27.4	56.5	18.8	0.0	94.3
Scott	57	-8.9	165	0	41	299	1 624	35	9	26 388	83.8	16.2	35.3	6.0	0.0	4.2
Shelby	201	-7.5	313	2	186	794	2 451	92	67	104 425	78.8	21.2	64.0	27.8	0.0	8.5
Spencer	173	-1.3	271	0	142	411	1 615	69	52	81 341	56.5	43.5	53.8	19.1	0.0	31.6
Starke	136	0.5	331	11	116	522	1 519	78	33	80 825	96.2	3.8	51.2	20.5	0.0	7.3
Steuben	124	1.6	213	1	99	380	1 692	41	26	44 133	65.4	34.6	44.6	12.9	0.0	4.3
Sullivan	177	-2.3	374	6	154	603	1 636	90	44	92 614	87.2	12.8	63.2	25.4	0.0	450.3
Switzerland	68	-14.1	125	0	34	238	1 817	25	13	24 641	70.2	29.8	44.0	3.7	0.0	4.3
Tippecanoe	242	-6.0	363	4	221	955	2 595	74	80	119 552	77.1	22.9	64.5	27.7	0.0	44.8
Tipton	158	-1.6	382	D	148	1 093	2 895	115	66	158 646	79.7	20.3	77.1	36.6	0.0	2.2
Union	82	3.1	308	0	69	563	2 018	80	26	95 929	68.9	31.1	69.8	29.5	5.2	0.9
Vanderburgh	72	-11.0	266	D	67	662	2 533	80	21	77 030	88.9	11.1	58.3	22.5	0.0	29.5
Vermillion	118	-0.8	474	D	101	728	1 524	110	30	122 449	73.6	26.4	64.3	26.1	5.0	469.7
Vigo	115	-20.8	253	0	99	532	2 006	67	26	57 180	87.1	12.9	50.3	14.9	0.4	328.0
Wabash	188	-4.9	247	1	163	546	2 285	89	98	128 276	42.7	57.3	62.2	24.3	4.1	10.4
Warren	185	-8.6	489	D	162	937	1 914	108	58	153 429	70.8	29.2	67.2	32.8	0.0	6.2
Warrick	99	2.7	277	0	81	495	1 616	71	24	66 491	80.9	19.1	50.8	21.1	0.0	709.0
Washington	181	-4.1	198	0	125	270	1 462	41	40	43 894	41.2	58.8	40.8	10.3	0.0	4.3
Wayne	173	-8.5	212	0	142	412	1 939	54	51	62 680	63.7	36.3	54.8	17.8	0.0	16.2
Wells	196	-1.6	297	0	182	651	2 193	88	74	112 567	67.3	32.7	72.7	30.3	0.5	4.1
White	272	-4.5	439	2	253	957	2 227	102	119	191 296	62.0	38.0	75.6	40.6	0.0	6.4
Whitley	165	1.9	210	1	139	394	2 004	49	52	65 985	59.0	41.0	50.2	16.5	0.0	4.0
IOWA	31 167	-0.6	343	125	26 822	567	1 697	81	11 948	131 596	51.8	48.2	74.0	34.6	0.5	3 034.6
Adair	336	2.1	424	D	284	380	1 003	68	83	104 223	51.9	48.1	74.9	29.8	0.0	2.0
Adams	235	-1.9	411	D	185	380	905	68	50	86 635	51.8	48.2	66.3	23.9	0.0	1.7
Allamakee	296	-8.1	309	D	180	296	974	69	81	84 370	26.7	73.3	67.7	27.6	1.4	212.4
Appanoose	241	0.9	303	D	176	193	649	45	29	36 082	53.8	46.2	54.0	8.0	1.4	5.4
Audubon	272	1.2	420		248	651	1 587	88	114	175 824	46.0	54.0	79.2	39.8	0.0	1.8
Benton	418	-2.0	346	0	376	707	1 999	91	158	130 559	65.1	34.9	76.6	38.0	1.4	3.5
Black Hawk	286	-4.7	285	1	263	622	2 321	82	128	127 636	60.4	39.6	76.6	35.9	0.0	57.3
Boone	329	-0.3	381	0	297	771	2 160	97	120	139 045	71.4	28.6	75.0	38.0	2.1	3.4
Bremer	239	0.6	243	0	211	480	2 094	73	102	103 437	55.1	44.9	75.4	30.1	0.0	4.8
Buchanan	337	1.2	297	D	304	513	1 839	77	137	120 747	57.7	42.3	81.2	35.4	0.0	3.8
Buena Vista	357	4.3	411	D	326	846	2 242	99	210	242 317	43.4	56.6	90.4	53.7	0.0	5.4
Butler	324	2.9	299	0	295	519	1 781	68	131	121 174	56.2	43.8	75.8	34.4	0.0	7.8
Calhoun	337	-2.7	424	D	317	1 005	2 426	116	140	176 853	63.7	36.3	87.1	49.6	0.0	2.3
Carroll	353	-2.0	320	1	324	604	1 814	104	221	200 960	35.1	64.9	87.8	44.7	0.0	5.5
Cass	331	-4.5	412	D	288	518	1 318	74	94	117 040	56.4	43.6	75.6	33.7	0.0	3.6
Cedar	326	-3.9	338	D	292	696	2 071	97	129	133 229	61.9	38.1	76.0	39.6	0.0	3.0
Cerro Gordo	301	-2.3	366	0	282	680	1 946	96	121	146 739	67.5	32.5	74.3	42.5	0.6	9.4
Cherokee	330	-1.7	371		287	687	1 922	90	146	163 881	48.9	51.1	87.1	46.2	0.0	4.7
Chickasaw	272	-1.0	294	1	243	446	1 515	82	122	131 891	46.6	53.4	77.9	37.6	0.0	2.7
Clarke	222	-6.0	327	0	151	251	711	43	39	56 835	33.8	66.2	55.9	10.8	0.0	1.6
Clay	286	-9.3	428	1	263	794	1 927	110	121	180 574	56.5	43.5	82.3	45.7	0.2	3.3
Clayton	452	-1.1	276	0	337	386	1 457	69	171	104 665	31.4	68.6	70.8	32.5	1.3	5.1
Clinton	368	0.0	290	0	325	495	1 788	72	148	117 025	57.9	42.1	74.8	34.4	1.3	279.1
Crawford	432	4.0	390	0	375	560	1 500	89	143	129 188	56.4	43.6	77.2	35.0	0.0	3.7
Dallas	324	3.7	353	1	288	841	2 418	85	118	128 128	65.8	34.2	66.1	29.5	0.8	6.1
Davis	267	-3.1	301	D	189	254	838	39	56	63 178	33.1	66.9	57.0	11.8	0.0	1.3
Decatur	262	0.4	359	0	171	208	608	43	54	74 450	26.5	73.5	52.5	11.4	0.0	1.7
Delaware	326	-2.9	255	0	287	451	1 824	91	196	153 300	26.3	73.7	83.7	49.7	0.0	5.7
Des Moines	192	0.0	296	2	156	455	1 584	70	70	107 337	62.2	37.8	66.8	28.8	7.0	115.2
Dickinson	201	-0.4	393	D	181	667	1 744	81	73	142 294	57.1	42.9	74.6	38.3	1.4	3.0
Dubuque	336	-2.2	213	0	258	336	1 623	69	172	108 709	18.0	82.0	76.0	34.6	0.4	81.5
Emmet	220	-2.1	424	D	205	728	1 744	108	91	176 009	59.0	41.0	78.6	48.2	0.5	2.4
Fayette	404	0.6	312	1	344	469	1 536	86	181	139 874	42.4	57.6	78.5	39.8	0.0	4.9
Floyd	300	4.3	353	2	274	629	1 784	91	114	133 569	67.8	32.2	77.3	38.7	0.0	3.7
Franklin	344	0.4	402	D	316	754	2 014	105	180	210 504	48.0	52.0	84.2	46.1	0.0	2.5
Fremont	318	5.4	560	2	268	721	1 293	93	88	155 256	74.3	25.7	78.5	42.3	0.0	6.3
Greene	343	-6.4	450	1	317	852	2 024	94	122	160 203	71.3	28.7	83.4	49.8	0.1	2.1
Grundy	321	1.4	426	D	299	967	2 289	123	149	197 769	61.5	38.5	86.3	51.5	0.0	2.2

Table B. States and Counties — Residential Construction, Wholesale and Retail Trade, and Real Estate

STATE County	Value of Residential Construction Authorized by Building Permits, 1999		Wholesale Trade, 1997				Retail Trade[1], 1997				Real Estate and Rental and Leasing, 1997			
	New Construction ($1,000)	Number of Housing Units	Number of Establishments	Number of Employees	Sales (mil dol)	Annual Payroll (mil dol)	Number of Establishments	Number of Employees	Sales (mil dol)	Annual Payroll (mil dol)	Number of Establishments	Number of Employees	Receipts (mil dol)	Annual Payroll (mil dol)
	133	134	135	136	137	138	139	140	141	142	143	144	145	146
INDIANA—Cont'd														
Putnam	40 923	402	24	110	39.2	2.7	126	1 278	186.0	18.4	30	65	4.6	0.9
Randolph	8 192	87	21	120	76.5	3.1	111	978	152.2	13.7	8	19	1.0	0.1
Ripley	15 171	185	34	532	108.0	25.5	130	1 124	197.4	18.4	23	104	4.3	1.3
Rush	5 449	55	30	189	119.0	3.9	75	678	114.8	10.3	12	30	4.6	0.4
St. Joseph	149 681	1 397	472	7 080	3 389.0	230.7	1 069	16 822	2 782.9	249.0	215	1 274	127.8	25.5
Scott	12 587	230	15	83	13.9	1.8	105	1 134	168.2	15.9	11	52	5.9	1.0
Shelby	23 032	203	49	530	215.6	18.4	146	1 577	310.8	26.3	34	89	11.8	1.2
Spencer	16 072	179	24	308	217.5	8.4	80	661	94.6	9.7	13	49	2.1	0.6
Starke	7 611	138	20	127	75.8	3.2	95	812	110.3	11.2	13	54	3.7	1.0
Steuben	41 221	347	39	252	98.7	5.9	238	2 280	397.5	35.5	31	87	14.7	1.5
Sullivan	750	44	23	155	113.6	3.7	68	648	95.3	8.6	10	D	D	D
Switzerland	7 225	124	3	D	D	D	20	125	17.1	1.4	1	D	D	D
Tippecanoe	126 181	1 493	117	D	D	D	564	9 688	1 479.8	137.8	148	748	81.0	12.0
Tipton	6 643	46	20	D	D	D	52	478	118.1	7.3	11	23	1.2	0.2
Union	5 864	68	10	94	44.9	1.7	31	221	28.9	3.5	3	D	D	D
Vanderburgh	71 938	740	352	D	D	D	932	14 807	2 282.8	229.6	222	1 495	170.5	27.2
Vermillion	3 409	36	15	D	D	D	61	726	123.8	9.4	3	23	1.0	0.2
Vigo	39 727	377	143	1 646	682.4	43.0	509	9 685	2 321.3	158.4	87	480	39.5	8.6
Wabash	10 128	102	38	233	86.4	6.0	169	1 853	289.8	27.5	43	136	13.0	1.8
Warren	5 040	72	12	129	74.8	3.5	16	101	19.8	1.4	4	6	0.7	0.0
Warrick	61 118	521	48	D	D	D	170	1 438	219.1	20.2	33	139	14.7	2.0
Washington	3 938	45	16	D	D	D	88	731	176.1	11.8	15	47	5.2	0.6
Wayne	17 674	163	96	1 657	1 256.3	53.8	338	4 233	690.6	64.3	61	226	23.1	4.1
Wells	20 748	195	38	1 735	455.3	37.9	116	1 113	164.0	16.1	29	97	15.9	1.5
White	15 448	145	46	358	196.7	8.5	131	1 173	209.7	19.6	16	64	4.0	0.8
Whitley	60 093	446	29	240	168.0	6.1	108	1 657	221.0	22.8	21	66	9.1	1.3
IOWA	1 405 608	13 491	5 399	63 596	35 453.7	1 820.1	14 695	175 694	26 723.8	2 633.4	2 518	12 619	1 457.5	249.0
Adair	2 153	14	16	142	83.1	3.7	49	320	46.2	3.7	1	D	D	D
Adams	355	4	9	52	18.5	0.9	22	131	16.0	1.5	1	D	D	D
Allamakee	4 849	85	34	512	158.2	9.8	95	652	101.2	8.1	9	24	1.5	0.1
Appanoose	773	15	12	65	25.7	1.0	73	702	92.4	9.4	7	57	1.3	0.6
Audubon	497	5	24	169	76.2	3.5	34	254	51.9	4.0	3	11	0.7	0.1
Benton	12 421	100	40	506	186.3	12.5	101	789	144.1	12.2	11	39	1.3	0.4
Black Hawk	32 586	220	169	2 690	952.7	77.0	598	9 386	1 344.8	139.3	126	549	60.9	10.3
Boone	10 326	103	25	216	155.2	5.2	98	1 134	173.2	15.5	11	23	2.6	0.3
Bremer	10 514	80	42	293	151.8	6.0	115	1 037	144.7	13.7	14	26	2.9	0.5
Buchanan	4 625	50	38	311	222.7	8.4	106	911	154.9	13.8	16	32	1.3	0.2
Buena Vista	4 695	69	42	392	287.3	11.3	122	1 450	192.1	20.1	18	45	2.5	0.6
Butler	4 112	62	42	257	158.5	6.1	86	428	67.6	5.5	2	D	D	D
Calhoun	1 538	14	15	222	184.9	6.3	71	484	81.3	6.1	8	32	1.3	0.4
Carroll	11 914	135	53	868	354.5	21.4	176	1 706	226.0	22.9	23	122	10.9	1.9
Cass	1 009	11	41	D	D	D	99	927	122.3	11.9	11	21	2.8	0.4
Cedar	5 960	49	39	370	137.8	8.3	85	689	100.8	8.6	11	24	1.0	0.2
Cerro Gordo	9 948	80	85	875	489.6	24.5	292	3 995	609.9	54.9	52	164	16.2	2.3
Cherokee	1 127	10	22	184	59.1	3.9	83	787	107.7	10.3	5	7	0.9	0.1
Chickasaw	2 425	21	32	362	179.2	9.6	62	480	73.4	6.4	6	D	D	D
Clarke	2 050	25	8	D	D	D	39	402	51.3	5.3	7	9	2.2	0.2
Clay	7 407	82	58	612	246.8	14.8	141	1 529	215.0	25.7	19	69	4.8	0.8
Clayton	7 097	95	52	335	269.9	7.1	120	670	133.4	10.4	11	20	1.1	0.3
Clinton	14 806	134	68	492	217.7	12.1	227	2 523	418.3	43.3	50	177	12.2	1.9
Crawford	3 502	41	27	309	191.4	6.0	97	919	111.7	9.9	9	14	0.9	0.1
Dallas	53 688	378	53	D	D	D	134	1 371	220.7	21.1	10	20	1.8	0.3
Davis	510	8	15	136	62.6	2.4	42	294	43.4	4.2	5	12	0.7	0.1
Decatur	1 887	20	11	129	68.3	2.0	35	205	24.8	2.4	1	D	D	D
Delaware	3 057	40	39	444	250.5	10.0	80	726	110.8	10.7	2	D	D	D
Des Moines	4 934	50	67	618	375.8	14.5	238	3 724	499.9	51.7	43	422	48.5	10.2
Dickinson	20 246	154	26	738	176.1	17.6	143	1 087	172.2	17.0	38	236	21.5	4.7
Dubuque	42 725	320	157	1 845	926.5	50.8	525	6 583	935.5	100.2	89	341	32.8	4.9
Emmet	1 242	12	14	260	56.8	4.5	61	550	79.2	7.7	1	D	D	D
Fayette	3 702	40	41	D	D	D	133	1 089	174.3	16.6	10	39	1.3	0.3
Floyd	4 435	64	31	258	112.2	5.3	95	839	119.3	10.5	12	33	3.9	0.3
Franklin	692	6	24	241	144.8	5.2	65	459	61.1	5.8	15	27	2.1	0.2
Fremont	731	10	15	108	97.4	3.6	32	212	26.8	2.5	2	D	D	D
Greene	2 413	25	19	207	116.8	4.7	47	381	53.1	4.8	5	17	2.7	0.3
Grundy	3 636	35	20	231	171.9	8.2	49	377	61.4	5.3	7	37	9.3	2.2

1. Establishments with payroll.

STATE County	Professional, Scientific, and Technical Services[1], 1997				Manufacturing, 1997				Accommodation and Foodservices, 1997			
	Number of Establishments	Number of Employees	Receipts (mil dol)	Annual Payroll (mil dol)	Number of Establishments	Number of Employees	Receipts (mil dol)	Annual Payroll (mil dol)	Number of Establishments	Number of Employees	Sales (mil dol)	Annual Payroll (mil dol)
	147	148	149	150	151	152	153	154	155	156	157	158
INDIANA—Cont'd												
Putnam	34	123	7.3	2.8	25	2 482	421.7	64.8	75	1 022	27.8	7.5
Randolph	25	79	3.6	1.1	54	3 080	361.0	86.5	44	438	11.9	3.1
Ripley	27	117	7.5	2.6	35	3 168	755.2	109.9	58	787	19.8	5.2
Rush	22	81	3.8	1.2	32	1 081	289.1	32.4	30	D	D	D
St. Joseph	520	4 003	369.9	154.8	457	20 435	4 149.7	698.9	537	10 620	305.2	86.9
Scott	20	51	2.7	0.9	34	D	D	D	38	716	19.6	5.9
Shelby	63	228	15.3	5.3	86	6 656	1 188.8	218.5	57	1 059	31.2	9.3
Spencer	15	54	3.0	0.9	19	1 369	134.0	36.3	28	D	D	D
Starke	13	40	1.8	0.5	19	1 357	143.3	29.7	37	D	D	D
Steuben	47	172	10.0	2.8	110	6 774	1 056.5	189.0	88	1 300	41.6	11.8
Sullivan	24	88	4.4	1.4	18	579	73.0	14.3	28	D	D	D
Switzerland	4	11	0.6	0.1	6	619	58.7	10.7	9	D	D	D
Tippecanoe	207	1 232	104.4	36.5	113	16 695	7 519.0	692.2	312	6 722	194.3	56.0
Tipton	24	93	4.6	1.4	22	954	199.3	30.5	25	319	9.2	2.5
Union	4	6	0.3	0.1	NA	NA	NA	NA	10	D	D	D
Vanderburgh	404	3 594	258.6	99.3	271	17 536	3 824.6	607.7	426	8 841	267.3	78.5
Vermillion	9	12	1.0	0.2	10	D	D	D	35	463	13.7	3.4
Vigo	160	955	70.4	21.3	137	7 464	1 891.8	255.2	268	5 027	148.9	42.7
Wabash	39	130	10.0	3.2	77	5 300	812.8	156.3	71	D	D	D
Warren	6	14	0.7	0.2	NA	NA	NA	NA	7	D	D	D
Warrick	67	254	12.3	4.3	53	D	D	D	68	D	D	D
Washington	26	81	4.3	1.4	40	2 824	298.7	66.9	31	D	D	D
Wayne	76	420	26.5	11.8	132	8 940	1 598.7	270.0	145	2 808	83.7	24.2
Wells	24	127	8.8	2.8	49	3 615	490.2	106.2	36	597	15.3	4.4
White	40	126	16.8	4.8	56	3 402	638.0	90.6	66	459	17.2	4.6
Whitley	32	92	6.1	2.1	66	4 327	908.8	117.3	61	871	23.3	6.6
IOWA	4 670	31 115	2 435.6	887.9	3 749	235 880	62 413.7	7 573.3	6 830	99 148	2 762.8	769.5
Adair	13	39	1.9	0.7	8	527	101.9	15.1	19	246	5.4	1.4
Adams	5	19	0.7	0.2	NA	NA	NA	NA	9	55	1.2	0.3
Allamakee	20	62	2.3	0.9	26	1 505	209.7	27.4	42	293	6.1	1.5
Appanoose	16	43	1.9	0.6	15	1 070	156.5	30.1	35	284	7.4	1.8
Audubon	10	23	1.4	0.4	NA	NA	NA	NA	16	D	D	D
Benton	24	64	3.0	1.1	NA	NA	NA	NA	43	249	6.1	1.6
Black Hawk	193	1 530	100.9	44.9	165	13 542	5 133.1	555.7	293	5 544	135.8	39.2
Boone	27	92	8.1	2.4	26	914	131.9	22.5	48	574	15.1	4.4
Bremer	35	82	6.3	1.7	39	1 993	446.3	58.6	47	578	13.6	4.0
Buchanan	22	66	4.1	1.4	35	1 230	277.7	31.7	38	D	D	D
Buena Vista	34	147	9.3	3.7	28	2 546	688.6	55.2	47	604	15.0	4.0
Butler	19	51	2.6	0.6	23	601	70.7	16.3	29	D	D	D
Calhoun	10	20	1.1	0.2	NA	NA	NA	NA	17	D	D	D
Carroll	37	124	7.6	2.3	39	1 588	423.8	41.7	64	785	19.3	4.9
Cass	20	86	5.6	2.3	25	1 112	150.7	29.8	43	443	10.2	2.8
Cedar	21	211	7.2	3.3	25	810	122.3	19.4	37	375	8.1	1.9
Cerro Gordo	78	376	27.5	10.5	61	3 703	719.8	98.9	139	2 286	61.0	16.7
Cherokee	15	58	2.9	1.1	15	904	188.5	24.6	35	350	8.3	2.2
Chickasaw	16	43	3.0	0.7	25	1 674	414.4	42.2	33	D	D	D
Clarke	12	30	1.4	0.4	19	1 152	209.4	21.4	26	399	12.2	2.8
Clay	28	145	11.1	3.1	28	1 180	202.3	34.9	53	682	17.2	4.8
Clayton	22	66	3.9	1.4	31	1 538	184.6	28.6	51	266	7.2	1.5
Clinton	57	183	12.3	3.8	59	5 148	2 106.9	175.6	132	1 516	39.3	10.9
Crawford	19	120	6.7	2.8	22	1 879	908.9	49.5	49	477	11.4	2.9
Dallas	38	135	8.5	2.8	41	2 489	451.2	59.7	55	596	13.1	3.9
Davis	8	62	2.2	1.0	NA	NA	NA	NA	13	126	2.6	0.7
Decatur	8	22	0.7	0.2	NA	NA	NA	NA	16	110	2.2	0.6
Delaware	19	68	3.8	1.7	34	1 144	327.5	33.7	34	269	5.6	1.3
Des Moines	61	240	16.7	5.2	66	6 772	1 320.8	228.8	109	1 841	47.8	13.4
Dickinson	33	145	10.1	3.0	31	2 386	353.4	60.3	98	857	29.1	8.3
Dubuque	117	802	56.4	23.5	133	10 687	3 074.9	386.9	233	3 838	94.7	27.4
Emmet	18	76	4.9	1.7	15	752	115.8	18.2	25	218	5.5	1.4
Fayette	34	120	6.1	2.1	24	1 539	262.4	38.9	50	504	10.8	3.0
Floyd	24	75	3.9	1.1	17	591	94.5	16.6	37	368	8.9	2.0
Franklin	14	63	2.7	1.2	22	790	83.9	21.6	19	164	3.1	0.9
Fremont	9	58	2.0	0.7	NA	NA	NA	NA	18	83	2.6	0.6
Greene	12	67	3.2	1.4	17	525	83.4	14.4	22	D	D	D
Grundy	15	50	3.2	1.2	NA	NA	NA	NA	23	D	D	D

1. Firms subject to federal tax.

Table B. States and Counties — Health and Other Services and Federal Funds

STATE County	Health Care and Social Assistance[1], 1997				Other Services[1], 1997				Federal funds and grants, fiscal 1999[2] Expenditures (mil dol)		Direct payments for individuals[3]	
	Number of Establishments	Number of Employees	Receipts (mil dol)	Annual Payroll (mil dol)	Number of Establishments	Number of Employees	Receipts (mil dol)	Annual Payroll (mil dol)	Total	Social Security and government retirement	Medicare	Food stamps and Supplemental Security Income
	159	160	161	162	163	164	165	166	167	168	169	170
INDIANA—Cont'd												
Putnam	40	436	17.7	7.6	37	149	10.4	2.4	105.0	57.8	19.9	2.4
Randolph	23	241	9.2	4.1	34	124	8.4	1.8	112.2	57.1	20.9	2.6
Ripley	56	501	21.8	10.7	53	177	11.0	2.8	100.2	51.1	20.3	3.3
Rush	26	442	15.2	6.4	20	75	5.8	1.4	78.0	33.6	14.8	1.5
St. Joseph	496	5 999	458.0	212.7	452	3 851	256.3	81.0	1 363.3	481.5	186.4	32.3
Scott	28	224	11.7	4.6	25	76	5.4	1.3	96.5	43.9	19.2	4.0
Shelby	61	830	39.5	18.4	57	387	18.6	5.5	142.1	71.1	29.2	3.1
Spencer	14	245	9.8	4.2	21	54	3.7	1.0	72.3	35.2	13.2	1.5
Starke	16	176	6.8	2.9	18	41	2.9	0.8	83.2	42.7	13.8	2.9
Steuben	57	454	25.4	9.7	50	381	15.7	5.6	101.6	55.7	20.6	1.9
Sullivan	25	369	15.4	6.3	27	66	4.1	0.9	97.3	45.1	21.3	3.0
Switzerland	6	D	D	D	4	D	D	D	31.0	14.9	6.2	0.9
Tippecanoe	181	2 830	217.1	103.0	227	1 619	102.3	30.6	497.4	188.0	60.1	9.3
Tipton	27	216	11.6	4.2	21	129	6.8	2.3	62.6	30.6	13.2	1.0
Union	8	100	3.0	1.4	9	23	1.4	0.3	27.8	12.9	4.5	0.8
Vanderburgh	396	7 805	496.6	237.0	338	2 995	179.7	56.2	798.7	359.9	146.7	29.3
Vermillion	19	304	10.5	4.7	12	33	1.4	0.4	72.1	36.8	13.3	1.8
Vigo	249	3 340	243.7	76.8	170	1 395	66.2	20.2	527.1	209.9	98.2	17.1
Wabash	44	712	28.5	11.8	53	170	10.6	3.4	160.2	70.7	21.1	2.4
Warren	4	D	D	D	4	D	D	D	32.8	12.3	5.3	0.5
Warrick	73	931	44.7	18.5	57	275	16.6	5.2	133.4	77.2	25.9	2.4
Washington	31	335	12.9	4.8	33	98	4.5	1.1	90.4	44.7	16.4	3.6
Wayne	134	1 754	95.8	47.4	118	564	29.2	9.3	334.8	153.2	56.4	12.0
Wells	28	484	33.4	17.5	53	237	17.2	4.9	81.7	43.3	15.9	0.8
White	35	285	9.4	3.6	35	89	6.6	1.3	114.4	55.4	20.0	1.7
Whitley	30	314	16.1	7.1	46	302	16.4	6.0	94.8	55.7	18.1	0.8
IOWA	4 876	56 374	3 183.2	1 540.6	5 234	24 383	1 486.5	411.3	15 601.5	5 580.6	1 931.3	273.6
Adair	14	208	5.6	2.9	16	31	1.8	0.4	42.8	16.4	6.2	0.6
Adams	7	92	1.9	1.0	8	16	1.3	0.2	25.7	10.2	4.2	0.5
Allamakee	22	159	6.7	2.8	34	82	6.8	1.1	59.2	28.3	8.3	1.0
Appanoose	18	155	8.3	3.0	26	80	4.7	1.0	75.5	33.6	11.8	2.8
Audubon	8	117	3.5	1.7	20	50	2.9	0.6	42.8	15.8	6.4	0.4
Benton	23	150	5.5	2.3	43	99	6.3	1.3	104.4	44.5	15.6	1.5
Black Hawk	228	2 173	167.9	83.0	213	1 513	80.2	25.9	511.8	236.5	89.9	20.0
Boone	32	287	13.9	6.9	38	122	6.8	1.9	106.0	53.6	17.1	1.7
Bremer	41	333	16.1	7.0	59	153	10.1	2.3	95.8	45.9	16.8	1.4
Buchanan	20	235	8.9	3.5	40	115	7.8	1.7	86.0	38.5	14.6	1.8
Buena Vista	28	397	16.5	8.0	45	145	8.3	1.8	94.3	40.9	15.4	1.4
Butler	19	317	9.1	4.5	25	61	4.5	0.9	77.0	34.6	14.1	0.9
Calhoun	16	272	8.6	4.2	19	58	2.5	0.5	64.7	28.7	10.8	0.7
Carroll	44	305	20.6	8.4	47	174	11.1	2.3	96.7	45.2	15.9	1.5
Cass	27	294	13.5	5.5	43	102	7.3	1.4	75.2	35.3	14.5	1.5
Cedar	31	114	5.1	2.0	29	70	6.7	1.5	72.0	31.9	11.4	0.8
Cerro Gordo	80	1 328	81.5	50.1	97	437	20.3	6.6	220.6	104.3	35.5	4.7
Cherokee	25	250	8.8	4.6	28	53	4.4	1.0	66.6	31.3	10.7	0.6
Chickasaw	17	349	11.6	4.5	38	79	6.9	1.2	118.8	26.6	9.8	0.7
Clarke	12	46	3.9	1.5	18	36	2.4	0.5	37.1	16.0	6.4	1.0
Clay	31	315	24.1	11.4	37	224	11.6	3.4	89.9	35.7	11.5	1.2
Clayton	25	195	9.1	4.3	39	78	4.8	1.0	87.4	38.0	14.1	1.5
Clinton	95	922	46.4	18.0	97	374	21.8	6.1	203.3	105.2	41.0	6.7
Crawford	25	362	14.8	6.7	34	79	5.7	1.1	86.2	32.7	13.3	1.5
Dallas	61	693	39.5	21.5	50	130	10.2	1.7	127.7	61.5	20.8	1.7
Davis	18	210	8.4	3.3	7	20	1.2	0.3	40.1	16.2	5.8	0.9
Decatur	10	136	4.9	2.0	5	11	1.5	0.5	43.8	17.3	5.6	1.3
Delaware	20	127	7.0	2.7	39	96	5.4	1.2	69.9	28.6	9.7	1.4
Des Moines	100	910	54.1	24.0	62	345	16.6	4.5	202.3	92.7	32.9	5.6
Dickinson	37	373	17.5	8.6	37	116	6.5	1.6	77.6	40.2	11.9	0.9
Dubuque	124	2 376	185.8	89.3	172	889	51.2	14.9	322.2	165.7	61.2	7.5
Emmet	27	360	13.3	6.4	20	63	3.3	0.9	61.7	26.0	9.9	0.7
Fayette	44	534	17.8	8.2	50	180	12.7	3.4	103.5	45.7	16.9	2.4
Floyd	30	394	16.5	8.1	34	137	9.0	2.0	120.0	40.7	15.0	1.6
Franklin	16	166	6.0	2.9	23	67	7.4	1.7	59.6	22.8	7.9	0.5
Fremont	13	267	9.5	5.2	12	27	2.3	0.4	48.5	18.9	8.2	0.8
Greene	15	137	7.6	3.1	26	68	4.5	0.8	58.6	25.3	8.1	1.0
Grundy	15	181	6.3	2.6	26	55	4.8	0.8	60.6	26.7	9.2	0.4

1. Firms subject to federal tax.   2. October 1, 1998 to September 30, 1999.   3. State totals may include programs not allocated by county.

STATE County	Salaries and wages	Defense	Other	Medicaid and other health-related	Nutrition and family welfare	Education	Other	Total (mil dol)	Intergovernmental (mil dol)	Total (mil dol)	Per capita[3] (dollars) Total	Per capita[3] (dollars) Property
	171	172	173	174	175	176	177	178	179	180	181	182
INDIANA—Cont'd												
Putnam	4.0	0.0	0.9	7.7	1.5	0.4	1.7	81.8	31.2	28.5	847	761
Randolph	4.3	0.4	1.1	9.6	2.3	0.7	4.1	62.2	26.3	18.3	664	553
Ripley	4.2	0.7	2.3	10.4	1.7	0.5	0.4	53.5	24.0	22.0	811	689
Rush	2.8	0.0	0.8	6.1	1.0	0.3	5.4	41.4	14.1	14.3	783	698
St. Joseph	61.5	289.2	103.2	91.6	22.8	6.6	56.8	544.7	219.9	204.9	794	776
Scott	3.1	1.8	0.6	14.9	2.9	1.0	2.9	51.1	22.0	14.7	644	491
Shelby	9.7	1.7	1.2	11.4	2.0	0.5	1.9	110.6	37.3	29.5	683	587
Spencer	3.4	0.0	0.8	6.6	0.8	0.3	3.7	44.7	15.6	23.9	1 153	1 135
Starke	2.7	0.0	0.7	8.2	2.2	0.7	3.0	56.5	22.9	14.6	613	579
Steuben	4.6	0.4	1.1	5.3	1.9	0.3	3.5	64.8	21.7	31.4	1 009	908
Sullivan	3.7	0.6	0.8	9.0	1.1	0.5	2.5	56.5	16.7	17.0	840	837
Switzerland	1.3	0.0	0.3	5.6	0.3	0.2	0.0	14.5	8.7	4.6	532	485
Tippecanoe	28.4	3.0	7.9	47.6	7.5	4.7	107.5	242.6	92.4	112.5	813	713
Tipton	2.1	2.2	0.7	3.7	0.6	0.2	0.5	51.0	13.1	14.5	883	770
Union	0.9	0.0	0.2	2.1	0.9	0.1	1.0	16.9	7.4	7.3	1 000	913
Vanderburgh	50.5	54.2	10.6	84.4	21.1	4.1	16.4	367.0	142.9	153.0	917	775
Vermillion	2.7	1.5	1.3	6.1	1.3	0.4	2.8	35.8	13.1	18.4	1 084	1 081
Vigo	73.7	15.0	8.3	57.4	11.9	4.1	15.7	178.1	80.8	74.8	712	703
Wabash	4.3	0.6	1.1	12.0	2.1	0.5	35.6	87.3	30.5	25.4	735	632
Warren	1.1	0.0	0.3	1.9	0.5	0.1	0.8	16.7	7.2	7.1	868	742
Warrick	6.1	0.0	1.5	10.6	2.4	0.6	2.2	101.5	34.1	51.1	1 005	924
Washington	3.3	0.0	1.5	12.2	2.1	0.7	0.1	56.8	24.4	13.9	511	417
Wayne	9.1	0.8	4.5	41.7	11.0	2.3	28.7	148.3	67.4	61.3	854	758
Wells	3.3	0.0	0.8	4.5	1.5	0.3	1.6	64.3	23.8	19.8	740	647
White	3.7	0.0	1.0	5.0	2.1	0.3	11.1	72.7	21.6	32.0	1 276	1 160
Whitley	3.7	3.5	1.0	4.0	0.9	0.3	0.2	59.5	23.5	27.2	908	813
IOWA	970.0	413.9	484.0	1 173.8	457.4	239.8	724.3	X	X	X	X	X
Adair	1.4	0.0	0.3	5.3	0.7	0.3	1.6	16.5	8.0	6.5	787	762
Adams	1.4	0.0	0.3	1.6	0.4	0.2	0.0	8.7	4.1	3.6	805	801
Allamakee	3.0	0.1	1.3	5.3	1.2	0.3	0.5	34.6	14.4	11.3	805	752
Appanoose	3.9	0.0	0.8	12.0	2.2	0.9	2.8	28.4	16.4	8.9	659	644
Audubon	1.5	0.0	0.4	1.6	0.5	0.3	5.5	15.1	7.1	6.0	880	869
Benton	3.5	0.0	7.2	4.9	1.8	0.6	1.7	44.7	22.8	16.1	642	638
Black Hawk	32.1	4.6	6.2	56.3	20.1	10.5	9.5	351.5	147.2	104.2	857	735
Boone	7.5	0.0	1.1	7.0	2.1	0.5	0.7	59.1	20.3	18.8	720	611
Bremer	2.8	0.2	0.9	4.7	1.5	0.5	7.0	60.2	24.3	18.6	798	755
Buchanan	3.2	0.0	0.8	5.6	1.9	1.6	0.6	42.2	17.3	13.7	647	603
Buena Vista	5.8	0.3	3.2	5.6	1.5	0.7	0.5	57.3	19.8	16.9	861	793
Butler	2.4	0.0	0.6	6.0	1.1	0.6	0.9	25.8	11.6	10.2	647	622
Calhoun	2.2	0.0	0.6	3.7	0.9	0.3	0.0	29.4	14.1	11.3	989	987
Carroll	5.1	0.0	1.4	7.9	2.6	0.4	1.4	43.4	16.4	17.1	789	774
Cass	3.7	0.0	0.7	5.1	1.5	0.5	0.0	50.6	15.9	13.4	912	895
Cedar	4.6	0.0	0.7	3.7	1.1	0.4	0.2	37.9	16.8	15.0	836	807
Cerro Gordo	9.3	0.6	4.3	18.9	5.5	1.6	18.3	119.0	50.1	41.9	903	772
Cherokee	2.6	0.1	0.6	4.7	1.0	0.6	0.0	32.5	16.3	10.8	802	766
Chickasaw	2.5	0.0	60.9	3.7	0.9	0.4	0.5	26.3	12.7	9.3	691	684
Clarke	1.5	0.0	0.4	3.5	1.0	0.3	0.3	24.4	10.3	7.7	929	921
Clay	4.1	0.0	0.8	6.5	1.6	0.4	1.1	64.4	17.9	14.2	804	786
Clayton	4.4	0.1	0.9	9.0	1.6	0.5	0.0	45.4	23.1	15.2	810	722
Clinton	7.2	0.0	1.8	13.5	5.3	1.6	1.2	110.7	49.9	43.4	863	736
Crawford	4.7	0.0	7.2	6.7	1.6	0.7	2.5	40.6	15.4	12.2	747	727
Dallas	5.2	0.0	1.4	5.8	2.4	0.6	15.6	82.9	33.6	31.3	875	856
Davis	1.7	0.0	0.4	4.2	0.7	0.5	3.3	23.8	8.1	5.0	594	586
Decatur	1.9	0.0	0.5	5.6	2.4	1.6	0.4	21.4	9.2	5.7	696	671
Delaware	2.8	0.1	0.7	5.3	1.5	0.5	1.2	48.2	19.1	14.5	788	718
Des Moines	9.7	22.8	3.5	14.4	6.4	2.1	2.4	108.7	49.8	35.6	846	739
Dickinson	2.4	0.0	0.6	4.2	1.1	0.3	7.0	43.2	11.5	16.9	1 057	1 019
Dubuque	17.1	0.4	5.2	30.8	8.7	2.2	6.6	195.7	82.2	72.6	824	688
Emmet	2.4	0.0	3.7	3.9	1.2	1.5	0.5	43.0	21.4	8.1	743	706
Fayette	4.7	0.2	1.0	7.9	2.2	1.0	0.4	44.7	21.9	16.2	738	685
Floyd	2.8	0.0	1.5	10.1	1.7	0.5	32.4	46.2	17.2	13.3	807	781
Franklin	2.1	0.0	0.5	3.9	0.8	0.3	4.1	28.1	10.5	10.2	939	855
Fremont	1.6	0.5	0.4	3.9	0.8	0.2	1.3	18.9	9.3	7.5	952	888
Greene	2.3	0.0	0.5	4.6	0.9	0.3	0.7	32.3	10.8	9.7	966	942
Grundy	1.8	0.0	0.5	2.1	0.6	0.3	3.9	36.9	15.4	12.7	1 036	1 001

1. October 1, 1998 to September 30, 1999.   2. State totals may include programs not allocated by county.   3. Based on the resident population estimated as of July 1 of the year shown.

Table B. States and Counties — Local Government Finances, Government Employment, and Elections

STATE County	Local government finances, 1997 (cont'd)									Government employment, 1998			Presidential election, 2000		
	Direct general expenditure							Debt outstanding					Percent of vote cast —		
			Percent of total for —												
	Total (mil dol)	Per capita[1] (dollars)	Educa-tion	Health and hospitals	Police protec-tion	Public welfare	High-ways	Total (mil dol)	Per capita[1] (dollars)	Federal civilian	Federal military	State and local	Demo-cratic	Republi-can	All other
	183	184	185	186	187	188	189	190	191	192	193	194	195	196	197
INDIANA—Cont'd															
Putnam	86.8	2 574	49.8	21.2	1.1	1.7	5.5	75.2	2 231	83	121	2 490	35.2	62.7	2.1
Randolph	62.2	2 265	46.8	19.4	2.0	3.7	6.4	22.0	801	82	97	1 496	38.6	59.5	1.8
Ripley	48.3	1 777	68.5	0.4	1.9	1.2	6.8	28.9	1 062	83	95	1 199	32.8	65.6	1.6
Rush	38.0	2 083	43.2	24.8	3.6	2.0	7.2	3.4	189	57	64	1 182	32.6	65.4	2.0
St. Joseph	554.5	2 149	48.9	1.0	4.1	4.8	4.3	394.6	1 529	1 160	959	12 676	49.4	49.3	1.3
Scott	49.9	2 189	46.8	22.1	3.1	1.6	3.6	16.7	730	60	80	1 189	50.2	48.2	1.7
Shelby	107.6	2 494	51.6	19.6	2.9	1.5	3.2	31.3	726	140	152	2 064	35.3	62.9	1.8
Spencer	38.0	1 836	60.9	0.5	2.0	2.5	7.5	28.7	1 387	79	73	901	41.9	57.0	1.1
Starke	52.7	2 219	50.2	24.2	1.7	1.1	5.0	19.8	834	55	84	929	47.7	50.1	2.2
Steuben	60.9	1 957	56.3	1.7	2.9	3.5	5.1	37.8	1 215	74	110	1 478	36.5	61.9	1.6
Sullivan	57.9	2 856	41.8	0.2	0.8	2.0	5.4	249.9	12 323	69	67	2 073	46.4	52.3	1.3
Switzerland	14.9	1 726	71.6	2.4	1.3	1.6	6.4	10.2	1 180	28	31	399	41.5	56.8	1.7
Tippecanoe	238.3	1 723	56.1	0.5	5.0	6.7	4.3	75.1	543	523	526	19 356	40.3	57.7	2.0
Tipton	49.8	3 035	35.9	36.2	1.6	1.2	5.3	9.5	577	36	59	1 119	32.7	65.4	1.8
Union	15.1	2 075	59.6	0.9	2.5	2.2	8.0	12.8	1 765	16	25	402	32.9	65.3	1.8
Vanderburgh	352.1	2 110	45.8	1.7	7.1	3.7	4.1	115.3	691	919	601	8 707	44.4	54.4	1.2
Vermillion	34.3	2 016	61.1	0.3	1.1	1.6	5.6	28.3	1 664	51	67	686	50.9	47.3	1.8
Vigo	206.6	1 969	65.8	0.8	2.9	2.3	3.3	91.4	871	1 222	391	7 854	48.7	50.0	1.3
Wabash	91.8	2 658	46.8	23.2	2.5	2.4	3.6	51.0	1 477	87	121	1 955	33.5	65.2	1.2
Warren	15.5	1 892	57.1	2.4	1.7	2.5	11.0	6.5	796	24	29	353	39.3	59.2	1.5
Warrick	94.8	1 866	57.0	1.4	2.6	2.0	4.2	102.5	2 016	125	181	1 607	39.4	59.5	1.1
Washington	54.7	2 014	50.4	18.0	1.4	1.5	7.3	18.0	665	59	98	1 317	37.7	60.2	2.1
Wayne	142.3	1 982	53.3	1.0	4.4	2.9	4.9	38.6	537	165	251	4 754	41.2	57.2	1.6
Wells	69.2	2 586	46.9	18.3	2.4	2.7	5.1	34.1	1 275	61	94	1 491	29.5	69.0	1.5
White	71.9	2 873	61.6	15.1	1.1	1.1	4.8	27.0	1 077	74	89	1 430	37.1	61.2	1.8
Whitley	51.3	1 711	60.0	2.2	2.8	2.5	5.7	17.9	598	80	107	1 343	33.1	65.2	1.7
IOWA	X	X	X	X	X	X	X	X	X	20 040	13 979	212 503	48.5	48.2	3.2
Adair	17.0	2 065	43.8	7.6	4.2	0.3	25.1	7.5	914	35	38	537	42.5	55.2	2.3
Adams	8.3	1 882	52.4	6.2	4.6	0.8	15.1	1.2	268	30	21	258	41.8	54.5	3.6
Allamakee	32.0	2 287	45.9	20.1	3.5	1.1	11.1	7.9	568	75	66	934	44.6	50.7	4.7
Appanoose	27.8	2 059	55.9	6.8	5.6	0.9	12.9	9.3	688	78	64	699	44.9	52.5	2.7
Audubon	15.6	2 282	48.8	6.4	2.8	0.3	20.4	3.8	564	37	32	446	47.0	50.4	2.5
Benton	42.2	1 688	53.9	4.2	3.9	0.7	15.1	26.4	1 055	73	120	1 409	50.3	46.5	3.3
Black Hawk	380.5	3 131	44.8	7.7	4.1	4.2	7.8	232.1	1 910	561	593	10 899	54.7	42.6	2.7
Boone	57.7	2 206	41.9	27.4	3.3	1.2	9.2	41.2	1 574	112	124	2 044	51.2	45.9	2.9
Bremer	55.9	2 397	51.5	18.1	4.1	0.7	8.7	22.5	964	66	110	1 321	46.3	50.8	3.0
Buchanan	39.0	1 843	45.8	17.4	5.0	0.2	13.7	8.3	394	118	100	1 520	53.6	43.5	2.9
Buena Vista	57.4	2 933	45.5	23.9	5.6	0.2	7.8	22.9	1 173	79	92	1 469	41.3	54.6	4.1
Butler	25.0	1 592	52.2	5.5	4.4	0.1	15.4	9.0	575	57	74	708	40.7	57.1	2.3
Calhoun	28.1	2 462	57.6	8.3	3.9	4.2	12.7	3.9	340	50	54	808	42.3	55.1	2.6
Carroll	44.6	2 053	48.3	4.5	4.9	5.1	13.1	25.3	1 166	99	102	1 154	46.6	51.0	2.4
Cass	53.5	3 631	34.7	39.5	2.8	0.4	11.6	23.8	1 616	84	69	1 266	36.1	61.1	2.8
Cedar	37.3	2 076	53.8	5.8	3.3	1.8	15.3	10.2	569	119	85	913	48.3	48.3	3.4
Cerro Gordo	125.8	2 713	58.1	1.7	4.1	2.4	6.6	67.3	1 452	180	219	2 820	55.0	42.4	2.6
Cherokee	31.1	2 315	44.7	3.4	3.5	1.7	16.7	8.4	623	58	62	1 042	43.2	52.5	4.3
Chickasaw	25.7	1 912	50.8	5.7	3.3	1.3	15.5	4.7	351	58	63	668	52.2	44.6	3.2
Clarke	24.6	2 984	39.1	27.1	3.3	1.1	10.7	9.4	1 145	37	39	645	49.8	47.5	2.7
Clay	60.7	3 451	28.1	37.7	2.6	4.2	8.4	7.2	407	83	83	1 319	43.5	52.7	3.9
Clayton	53.3	2 838	64.1	2.6	2.6	2.2	10.3	17.0	904	112	88	1 146	49.4	47.1	3.5
Clinton	110.1	2 192	50.5	5.4	6.3	0.7	12.7	88.7	1 766	143	235	2 645	55.3	41.6	3.0
Crawford	40.4	2 462	38.0	22.5	3.5	0.8	15.9	8.2	499	100	78	1 041	43.3	53.1	3.6
Dallas	90.6	2 533	57.4	14.0	3.6	0.9	8.4	57.7	1 612	105	174	1 873	44.3	53.3	2.4
Davis	23.9	2 841	30.2	41.1	2.0	0.4	11.0	6.4	757	41	40	577	45.0	52.0	3.0
Decatur	21.3	2 596	42.5	26.5	2.4	1.2	12.6	5.7	702	46	39	618	45.1	51.3	3.6
Delaware	49.4	2 679	39.9	26.1	2.8	0.4	14.8	13.2	717	65	88	1 055	45.6	51.2	3.2
Des Moines	111.8	2 653	61.6	3.2	4.6	1.2	7.7	46.5	1 104	201	202	2 343	58.6	38.1	3.2
Dickinson	42.4	2 650	37.6	26.5	3.3	0.6	14.6	26.0	1 624	59	77	1 008	45.1	52.0	2.9
Dubuque	191.6	2 175	38.1	5.8	4.4	5.3	10.5	52.5	596	297	440	3 440	55.4	40.8	3.8
Emmet	44.2	4 041	72.5	3.5	2.9	0.5	7.6	8.8	804	49	51	815	46.8	50.3	2.9
Fayette	43.6	1 981	57.9	6.5	3.3	1.4	5.2	10.4	472	92	103	1 220	48.2	49.3	2.4
Floyd	41.1	2 498	43.4	24.6	4.1	1.2	8.4	10.0	606	61	77	1 012	52.9	44.1	3.0
Franklin	28.4	2 609	40.3	21.3	3.9	3.0	12.6	5.3	484	49	51	716	43.0	53.8	3.2
Fremont	17.4	2 220	53.9	4.9	1.8	1.0	17.6	6.4	820	39	37	453	40.3	57.2	2.4
Greene	33.0	3 283	37.4	24.9	3.2	6.0	12.3	14.6	1 459	44	47	880	48.8	48.4	2.9
Grundy	35.2	2 870	50.6	12.6	3.1	3.2	12.8	7.6	616	42	57	685	35.0	63.0	2.0

1. Based on the resident population estimated as of July 1 of the year shown.

Table B. States and Counties — Land Area and Population

STATE/ County code	MSA/ PMSA/ NECMA code[1]	County Type[2]	STATE County	Land area,[3] (sq km) 1990	Population and population characteristics, 1999			Race (percent)					Age (percent)					
					Total persons	Rank	Per square kilometer	White	Black	Am. Indian, Eskimo, Aleut	Asian and Pacific Islander	Percent Hispanic[4]	Under 5 years	5 to 17 years	18 to 24 years	25 to 34 years	35 to 44 years	45 to 54 years
				1	2	3	4	5	6	7	8	9	10	11	12	13	14	15
			IOWA—Cont'd															
19 077	...	8	Guthrie	1 530	11 591	2 302	7.6	99.4	0.1	0.2	0.3	0.6	5.2	19.0	5.8	9.8	14.4	14.7
19 079	...	7	Hamilton	1 494	15 905	2 011	10.6	98.9	0.1	0.1	0.8	1.3	6.0	18.7	6.5	11.6	14.9	13.6
19 081	...	7	Hancock	1 479	12 037	2 274	8.1	99.6	0.0	0.1	0.3	1.9	6.4	20.8	6.2	11.6	14.7	12.8
19 083	...	7	Hardin	1 475	18 159	1 860	12.3	98.9	0.5	0.1	0.4	0.9	5.3	18.7	7.3	10.1	13.8	12.8
19 085	...	6	Harrison	1 805	15 216	2 052	8.4	99.3	0.1	0.1	0.5	0.6	6.4	20.1	6.8	11.4	13.7	13.6
19 087	...	7	Henry	1 125	20 139	1 756	17.9	96.8	1.4	0.3	1.5	1.2	6.0	18.4	9.8	12.6	16.1	13.5
19 089	...	7	Howard	1 226	9 574	2 466	7.8	99.6	0.1	0.1	0.3	0.5	6.2	20.1	5.7	11.0	12.9	13.0
19 091	...	7	Humboldt	1 125	10 224	2 404	9.1	99.4	0.1	0.1	0.3	0.6	5.9	18.8	5.8	10.6	13.9	13.4
19 093	...	8	Ida	1 118	7 930	2 608	7.1	99.6	0.1	0.1	0.3	0.6	6.6	20.1	5.4	10.9	13.7	11.6
19 095	...	8	Iowa	1 519	15 667	2 024	10.3	99.5	0.1	0.1	0.3	0.5	6.7	18.5	6.4	12.4	14.7	13.8
19 097	...	6	Jackson	1 648	20 157	1 755	12.2	99.6	0.1	0.1	0.2	0.8	6.4	20.4	7.3	11.2	13.8	13.9
19 099	...	6	Jasper	1 891	36 659	1 175	19.4	98.5	0.6	0.2	0.7	1.0	5.6	18.4	7.7	12.4	15.7	14.2
19 101	...	7	Jefferson	1 128	16 762	1 947	14.9	90.8	0.7	0.2	1.2	1.4	5.9	18.0	6.7	11.6	23.0	13.5
19 103	3500	3	Johnson	1 592	103 813	497	65.2	92.2	2.4	0.2	5.1	2.7	6.1	13.7	23.5	17.2	15.8	10.3
19 105	...	6	Jones	1 490	20 075	1 758	13.5	98.0	1.6	0.2	0.2	0.9	5.9	18.9	8.3	12.6	15.4	13.5
19 107	...	9	Keokuk	1 500	11 340	2 318	7.6	99.5	0.1	0.2	0.3	0.3	5.9	19.4	6.5	11.4	13.3	13.1
19 109	...	7	Kossuth	2 520	17 630	1 895	7.0	99.5	0.1	0.0	0.4	0.9	6.2	20.7	5.5	10.7	14.0	13.4
19 111	...	5	Lee	1 340	38 309	1 125	28.6	95.8	3.5	0.2	0.5	3.4	6.0	18.9	7.6	12.1	15.8	13.9
19 113	1360	3	Linn	1 858	184 891	289	99.5	96.3	2.3	0.2	1.2	1.7	6.4	17.9	10.4	13.5	16.6	14.1
19 115	...	8	Louisa	1 041	11 945	2 279	11.5	98.8	0.6	0.3	0.3	6.3	6.3	20.4	8.5	12.4	15.1	13.7
19 117	...	6	Lucas	1 115	9 131	2 498	8.2	99.5	0.1	0.2	0.3	1.1	5.6	17.8	6.7	10.2	13.8	14.4
19 119	...	6	Lyon	1 522	12 030	2 275	7.9	99.3	0.1	0.2	0.5	0.3	7.1	21.8	6.5	10.3	13.6	11.6
19 121	...	6	Madison	1 453	14 105	2 124	9.7	99.3	0.1	0.4	0.2	1.0	6.3	21.1	7.1	11.0	16.0	14.4
19 123	...	7	Mahaska	1 479	21 954	1 659	14.8	98.5	0.2	0.1	1.2	0.7	6.6	19.1	9.0	11.9	14.8	12.6
19 125	...	6	Marion	1 436	31 529	1 327	22.0	98.2	0.3	0.1	1.3	1.0	6.1	19.1	10.5	11.3	14.9	13.4
19 127	...	5	Marshall	1 482	38 782	1 117	26.2	97.8	0.8	0.3	1.1	1.4	5.9	18.4	7.7	11.3	16.1	14.5
19 129	...	6	Mills	1 131	14 705	2 088	13.0	99.4	0.2	0.3	0.2	1.0	5.9	21.3	7.0	12.0	17.8	14.5
19 131	...	7	Mitchell	1 215	11 106	2 339	9.1	99.6	0.0	0.0	0.3	0.8	6.0	19.3	6.3	10.2	13.0	13.4
19 133	...	6	Monona	1 795	10 089	2 415	5.6	99.4	0.0	0.3	0.2	0.6	5.3	18.4	5.5	9.8	13.1	14.1
19 135	...	7	Monroe	1 123	8 017	2 596	7.1	99.0	0.3	0.2	0.5	0.4	5.7	19.2	6.9	10.9	13.8	13.4
19 137	...	6	Montgomery	1 098	11 707	2 295	10.7	99.7	0.1	0.1	0.2	0.8	5.6	18.6	6.5	10.8	14.9	12.7
19 139	...	4	Muscatine	1 136	41 195	1 057	36.3	97.9	0.8	0.3	1.0	12.5	7.0	20.6	8.8	13.2	15.7	13.2
19 141	...	7	O'Brien	1 484	14 621	2 091	9.9	99.3	0.1	0.2	0.4	0.4	5.9	19.7	6.4	10.7	13.4	12.2
19 143	...	7	Osceola	1 033	6 914	2 686	6.7	99.6	0.0	0.1	0.2	0.4	6.5	19.8	6.8	11.3	13.2	12.5
19 145	...	7	Page	1 385	17 139	1 921	12.4	97.5	1.5	0.4	0.6	2.1	5.1	18.1	7.8	11.6	15.1	12.7
19 147	...	7	Palo Alto	1 460	9 917	2 436	6.8	99.5	0.1	0.2	0.2	0.2	5.6	19.9	7.2	9.8	12.5	12.4
19 149	...	6	Plymouth	2 237	24 819	1 538	11.1	99.4	0.1	0.1	0.4	0.5	6.7	21.7	7.4	11.0	14.5	12.7
19 151	...	9	Pocahontas	1 496	8 774	2 526	5.9	99.6	0.0	0.1	0.2	0.6	6.2	18.8	4.8	10.3	13.2	14.3
19 153	2120	2	Polk	1 475	364 672	156	247.2	91.9	5.2	0.3	2.6	3.5	7.0	17.5	10.4	15.2	16.9	13.5
19 155	5920	2	Pottawattamie	2 472	86 425	584	35.0	98.5	0.7	0.3	0.5	3.3	6.9	19.4	8.7	12.9	15.1	13.6
19 157	...	7	Poweshiek	1 515	18 693	1 838	12.3	98.1	0.5	0.1	1.3	0.6	5.6	17.9	12.0	10.6	14.1	13.2
19 159	...	9	Ringgold	1 393	5 361	2 817	3.8	99.3	0.0	0.2	0.5	0.5	4.9	17.9	5.3	9.4	13.0	13.1
19 161	...	9	Sac	1 491	11 761	2 292	7.9	99.7	0.0	0.1	0.2	0.6	6.2	19.5	5.7	10.3	13.4	12.3
19 163	1960	2	Scott	1 186	159 458	325	134.5	92.4	6.0	0.4	1.3	5.1	7.1	20.0	9.4	13.4	16.7	13.7
19 165	...	6	Shelby	1 530	12 781	2 228	8.4	99.6	0.0	0.2	0.2	0.6	6.0	19.8	6.1	10.5	13.6	12.9
19 167	...	7	Sioux	1 989	31 355	1 339	15.8	98.7	0.1	0.1	1.1	0.5	6.9	21.4	13.7	10.2	13.0	11.5
19 169	...	4	Story	1 484	75 373	657	50.8	92.1	1.8	0.1	6.0	1.9	5.6	14.0	26.6	13.6	13.2	10.3
19 171	...	6	Tama	1 868	17 788	1 882	9.5	94.4	0.2	4.9	0.5	1.2	6.0	19.1	6.8	10.7	13.5	14.2
19 173	...	9	Taylor	1 383	7 025	2 675	5.1	99.4	0.0	0.2	0.4	1.2	5.5	19.7	6.0	9.4	13.9	13.0
19 175	...	7	Union	1 099	12 611	2 240	11.5	99.2	0.1	0.2	0.5	0.7	5.7	19.6	8.3	10.8	15.2	13.1
19 177	...	9	Van Buren	1 257	7 873	2 615	6.3	99.4	0.1	0.1	0.3	0.6	6.5	18.8	6.6	10.4	13.4	13.9
19 179	...	5	Wapello	1 118	35 458	1 207	31.7	98.2	0.9	0.3	0.7	1.1	5.9	17.4	8.7	11.1	15.1	13.3
19 181	2120	2	Warren	1 481	40 614	1 071	27.4	98.9	0.3	0.2	0.6	1.4	6.4	20.4	10.1	11.7	16.9	15.1
19 183	...	6	Washington	1 473	21 147	1 706	14.4	99.0	0.4	0.1	0.4	1.8	6.8	19.3	7.0	12.1	14.9	13.0
19 185	...	9	Wayne	1 361	6 581	2 722	4.8	99.6	0.0	0.1	0.3	0.7	5.8	17.4	5.6	10.0	14.2	13.0
19 187	...	5	Webster	1 853	38 832	1 115	21.0	96.4	2.7	0.3	0.6	2.2	6.5	18.4	8.7	11.7	14.5	12.8
19 189	...	7	Winnebago	1 037	11 971	2 278	11.5	98.5	0.3	0.2	1.0	1.5	6.0	18.5	9.2	10.7	14.6	12.5
19 191	...	7	Winneshiek	1 786	20 917	1 719	11.7	98.4	0.3	0.0	1.3	0.5	6.0	17.3	16.7	11.0	12.6	11.8
19 193	7720	3	Woodbury	2 260	101 437	512	44.9	90.3	2.2	2.1	1.8	4.8	7.3	20.5	9.4	12.9	15.4	12.0
19 195	...	9	Worth	1 036	7 657	2 629	7.4	99.6	0.2	0.0	0.2	2.1	5.9	18.5	6.6	11.0	14.3	14.1
19 197	...	7	Wright	1 504	13 892	2 145	9.2	99.4	0.1	0.1	0.4	1.2	6.1	17.6	6.2	10.4	14.4	12.9
20 000	...	X	**KANSAS**	211 922	2 654 052	X	12.5	91.4	5.9	0.9	1.8	5.6	6.9	19.4	10.2	12.8	16.1	12.9
20 001	...	7	Allen	1 303	14 435	2 104	11.1	96.9	2.0	0.7	0.4	2.7	6.2	20.6	8.5	10.3	14.2	12.8
20 003	...	6	Anderson	1 510	8 119	2 585	5.4	98.4	0.5	0.9	0.2	1.1	6.1	20.3	7.3	9.8	13.2	14.3
20 005	...	6	Atchison	1 120	16 856	1 938	15.1	92.4	6.1	0.5	0.9	3.0	6.3	21.0	11.0	10.7	13.1	13.0

1. MSA = Metropolitan Statistical Area. PMSA = Primary MSA. NECMA = New England County Metropolitan Area. See Appendix A for explanation of these concepts. See Appendix B for list of metropolitan areas identified by type, with component counties.   2. County typology code from the Economic Research Service of USDA. See Appendix A for definition.   3. Dry land or land partially or temporarily covered by water.   4. Hispanic persons may be of any race.

Table B. States and Counties — **Population and Households**

STATE County	Age (percent) (cont'd) 55 to 64 years	65 to 74 years	75 years and over	Percent female	Total persons 1990	1980	1980–1990	1990–1999	Births	Deaths	Net migration	Number	Percent change, 1980–1990	Persons per house-hold	Female family house-holder[1]	One person
	16	17	18	19	20	21	22	23	24	25	26	27	28	29	30	31
IOWA—Cont'd																
Guthrie	12.0	9.1	10.1	51.7	10 935	11 983	-8.7	6.0	1 187	1 253	761	4 407	-3.6	2.42	6.0	26.1
Hamilton	10.8	8.9	9.1	51.4	16 071	17 862	-10.0	-1.0	1 876	1 678	-307	6 358	-4.0	2.49	6.8	25.0
Hancock	9.6	8.3	9.6	51.0	12 638	13 833	-8.6	-4.8	1 239	1 219	-585	4 867	-2.7	2.55	5.6	24.9
Hardin	10.3	9.7	11.9	51.4	19 094	21 776	-12.3	-4.9	1 909	2 261	-532	7 611	-6.7	2.38	5.5	28.0
Harrison	10.4	7.8	9.7	51.5	14 730	16 348	-9.9	3.3	1 667	1 889	757	5 656	-5.1	2.55	6.8	25.7
Henry	8.5	6.8	8.2	49.0	19 226	18 890	1.8	4.7	2 257	1 843	567	7 089	5.7	2.51	7.0	25.8
Howard	10.9	8.6	11.5	51.0	9 809	11 114	-11.7	-2.4	1 006	1 198	-2	3 856	-3.9	2.48	5.1	28.5
Humboldt	11.3	10.0	10.3	51.3	10 756	12 246	-12.2	-4.9	1 053	1 217	-322	4 339	-6.1	2.44	5.4	26.6
Ida	10.6	9.7	11.5	51.5	8 365	8 908	-6.1	-5.2	884	986	-307	3 222	-4.4	2.53	4.3	26.4
Iowa	10.3	8.1	9.1	51.3	14 630	15 429	-5.2	7.1	1 872	1 580	791	5 713	2.1	2.51	6.0	24.9
Jackson	10.2	8.1	8.8	50.7	19 950	22 503	-11.3	1.0	2 375	2 135	-61	7 527	-1.4	2.61	7.5	24.8
Jasper	10.4	7.8	7.9	49.8	34 795	36 425	-4.5	5.4	4 031	3 292	1 245	13 632	0.5	2.50	6.6	23.7
Jefferson	8.2	5.9	7.1	50.9	16 310	16 316	0.0	2.8	1 598	1 471	368	6 309	10.4	2.42	7.4	28.2
Johnson	5.6	3.9	3.9	50.2	96 119	81 717	17.6	8.0	12 184	4 336	89	36 067	19.3	2.41	6.7	27.8
Jones	9.4	7.7	8.2	50.4	19 444	20 401	-4.7	3.2	2 147	1 646	197	6 917	-0.2	2.60	7.1	23.6
Keokuk	10.7	8.7	11.1	51.1	11 624	12 921	-10.0	-2.4	1 317	1 329	-220	4 573	-6.4	2.50	6.3	25.9
Kossuth	10.6	8.7	10.2	51.2	18 591	21 891	-15.1	-5.2	1 794	1 941	-744	7 194	-7.8	2.53	5.1	27.3
Lee	9.7	8.0	8.0	50.6	38 687	43 106	-10.3	-1.0	4 511	4 107	-658	14 936	-4.4	2.49	9.7	26.8
Linn	8.7	6.3	6.0	51.3	168 767	169 775	-0.6	9.6	24 182	12 254	3 832	65 501	6.0	2.51	8.5	25.0
Louisa	9.2	6.7	7.8	49.6	11 592	12 055	-3.8	3.0	1 535	1 073	-62	4 296	1.8	2.65	7.3	22.0
Lucas	11.2	9.0	11.3	52.1	9 070	10 313	-12.1	0.7	1 025	1 066	147	3 766	-6.9	2.35	6.6	29.9
Lyon	10.7	8.6	9.8	50.9	11 952	12 896	-7.3	0.7	1 434	1 169	-142	4 289	-4.4	2.74	4.0	22.4
Madison	9.4	6.6	8.1	50.8	12 483	12 597	-0.9	13.0	1 492	1 448	1 608	4 715	3.1	2.59	6.4	23.6
Mahaska	9.4	8.1	8.4	51.1	21 532	22 867	-5.8	2.0	2 532	2 124	87	8 306	-3.5	2.51	6.9	25.0
Marion	9.2	7.4	8.1	50.3	30 001	29 669	1.1	5.1	3 465	2 949	1 106	10 815	4.8	2.55	6.5	24.7
Marshall	9.7	7.9	8.5	50.8	38 276	41 652	-8.1	1.3	4 670	4 681	707	14 890	-3.4	2.47	8.3	26.0
Mills	9.0	6.0	6.6	50.3	13 202	13 406	-1.5	11.4	1 520	1 206	1 217	4 665	2.8	2.65	8.9	22.7
Mitchell	10.8	9.2	11.9	51.4	10 928	12 329	-11.4	1.6	1 282	1 383	331	4 253	-4.0	2.48	4.7	26.7
Monona	11.1	9.8	12.8	52.2	10 034	11 692	-14.2	0.5	1 086	1 431	315	4 098	-8.3	2.38	6.6	28.7
Monroe	10.8	9.1	10.3	51.6	8 114	9 209	-11.9	-1.2	933	980	-5	3 196	-8.9	2.48	7.6	27.9
Montgomery	10.6	8.4	11.8	52.4	12 076	13 413	-10.0	-3.1	1 371	1 674	-11	4 955	-6.0	2.37	7.4	29.0
Muscatine	8.0	6.6	6.9	50.8	39 907	40 436	-1.3	3.2	5 818	3 433	-993	14 806	4.2	2.65	9.2	23.0
O'Brien	10.6	9.4	11.9	51.8	15 444	16 972	-9.0	-5.3	1 762	1 777	-774	5 980	-4.4	2.49	4.6	27.1
Osceola	10.8	8.4	10.7	51.2	7 267	8 371	-13.2	-4.9	782	780	-329	2 817	-7.6	2.54	4.5	26.6
Page	10.0	8.8	10.8	48.8	16 870	19 063	-11.5	1.6	1 643	2 148	838	6 687	-8.6	2.41	7.3	28.7
Palo Alto	11.4	9.1	12.0	51.5	10 669	12 721	-16.1	-7.0	990	1 337	-377	4 183	-9.5	2.48	5.1	29.5
Plymouth	10.2	7.3	8.5	50.8	23 388	24 743	-5.5	6.1	2 943	2 204	546	8 417	-0.1	2.70	5.6	23.6
Pocahontas	10.9	10.0	11.6	51.4	9 525	11 369	-16.2	-7.9	787	1 148	-353	3 820	-10.5	2.44	4.4	27.9
Polk	8.3	5.8	5.4	52.1	327 140	303 170	7.9	11.5	51 994	24 621	10 319	129 237	12.6	2.47	10.2	27.0
Pottawattamie	9.9	7.2	6.4	51.8	82 628	86 561	-4.5	4.6	11 076	7 159	175	31 262	1.5	2.60	11.2	23.3
Poweshiek	9.2	8.2	9.2	51.8	19 033	19 306	-1.4	-1.8	1 934	1 877	-325	7 158	4.3	2.48	6.4	25.9
Ringgold	12.4	10.8	13.2	52.3	5 420	6 112	-11.3	-1.1	467	751	253	2 218	-7.9	2.38	5.0	27.6
Sac	11.0	9.7	11.9	51.1	12 324	14 118	-12.7	-4.6	1 278	1 544	-255	4 914	-8.2	2.46	5.4	28.1
Scott	8.1	6.2	5.4	51.4	150 973	160 022	-5.7	5.6	21 575	11 514	-1 352	57 438	1.3	2.58	11.1	24.9
Shelby	10.5	9.4	11.1	51.0	13 230	15 043	-12.1	-3.4	1 376	1 505	-273	5 024	-3.7	2.56	5.4	24.7
Sioux	8.4	7.4	7.6	51.3	29 903	30 813	-3.0	4.9	3 856	2 206	-108	9 925	0.1	2.80	3.7	22.0
Story	6.3	4.9	5.4	48.4	74 252	72 326	2.7	1.5	8 017	3 884	-2 810	25 941	9.6	2.45	5.8	25.4
Tama	10.5	8.7	10.5	51.4	17 419	19 533	-10.8	2.1	2 078	2 011	373	6 768	-4.5	2.51	6.6	24.8
Taylor	11.1	9.4	12.0	52.2	7 114	8 353	-14.8	-1.3	685	938	186	2 859	-12.9	2.42	5.6	27.7
Union	9.5	7.8	9.8	52.5	12 750	13 858	-8.0	-1.1	1 343	1 525	98	5 173	-2.7	2.41	8.5	28.9
Van Buren	10.5	8.8	10.5	50.3	7 676	8 626	-11.0	2.6	829	921	316	3 056	-4.4	2.47	5.7	27.0
Wapello	10.6	8.5	9.4	52.0	35 696	40 241	-11.3	-0.7	4 086	4 166	-29	14 555	-5.7	2.40	9.4	27.1
Warren	8.0	5.6	5.7	51.1	36 033	34 878	3.3	12.7	4 610	2 690	2 789	12 659	10.0	2.75	8.0	18.3
Washington	9.4	7.8	9.6	51.5	19 612	20 141	-2.6	7.8	2 699	2 131	1 069	7 454	3.3	2.55	6.4	25.9
Wayne	11.5	10.6	13.4	52.3	7 067	8 199	-13.8	-6.9	660	1 036	-75	2 953	-10.9	2.35	4.7	28.5
Webster	10.2	8.1	9.2	51.8	40 342	45 953	-12.2	-3.7	4 914	4 583	-1 717	15 963	-5.5	2.44	9.1	27.9
Winnebago	9.3	8.1	11.1	51.3	12 122	13 010	-6.8	-1.2	1 265	1 347	-20	4 704	-2.9	2.43	6.0	28.2
Winneshiek	8.9	7.5	8.1	51.1	20 847	21 876	-4.7	0.3	2 126	1 707	-267	7 256	2.7	2.58	5.1	25.6
Woodbury	9.0	6.8	6.8	51.3	98 276	100 884	-2.6	3.2	15 395	8 907	-3 184	36 899	0.7	2.59	10.5	25.9
Worth	10.4	8.1	11.1	51.3	7 991	9 075	-11.9	-4.2	808	961	-138	3 239	-6.2	2.43	5.8	27.2
Wright	10.8	9.9	11.6	52.2	14 269	16 319	-12.6	-2.6	1 576	1 808	-91	5 899	-5.5	2.37	5.6	28.3
KANSAS	8.3	6.6	6.7	50.8	2 477 588	2 364 236	4.8	7.1	348 226	215 686	12 009	944 726	8.3	2.53	8.6	25.9
Allen	9.4	8.1	9.9	51.5	14 638	15 654	-6.5	-1.4	1 648	1 708	-101	5 705	-4.9	2.50	7.7	27.3
Anderson	9.8	8.4	10.9	51.2	7 803	8 749	-10.8	4.0	841	1 001	509	3 067	-7.5	2.50	6.6	26.3
Atchison	9.2	7.2	8.5	51.0	16 932	18 397	-8.0	-0.4	1 972	1 750	-240	6 129	-1.5	2.56	9.4	26.3

1. No spouse present.

Table B. States and Counties — **Vital Statistics, Health Resources, and Crime**

STATE County	Births, average 1996–1998		Deaths, average 1996–1998				Physicians,[4] 1998		Hospitals,[4] 1998			Medicare enrollees 1999	Serious crimes known to police, 1998[6]	
			Number		Rate					Beds			Total	
	Total	Rate[1]	Total	Infant[2]	Total[1]	Infant[3]	Number	Rate[5]	Number	Number	Rate[5]		Number	Rate[7]
	32	33	34	35	36	37	38	39	40	41	42	43	44	45
IOWA—Cont'd														
Guthrie	126	11.0	138	0	12.0	0.0	7	60	1	26	225	2 564	100	872
Hamilton	203	12.7	177	2	11.0	8.2	13	81	1	42	262	3 118	465	2 886
Hancock	128	10.6	125	0	10.4	2.6	3	25	1	26	216	2 266	139	1 151
Hardin	204	11.0	261	1	14.0	4.9	14	76	2	76	412	4 331	375	2 019
Harrison	172	11.2	203	1	13.3	5.8	9	59	1	37	241	2 967	278	1 805
Henry	231	11.6	189	2	9.5	8.7	19	95	1	61	305	3 369	354	1 768
Howard	110	11.3	136	1	14.1	9.1	6	62	1	32	330	2 025	174	1 786
Humboldt	109	10.5	120	0	11.6	0.0	6	58	1	49	475	2 258	122	1 169
Ida	96	12.0	99	1	12.4	13.9	2	25	1	36	455	1 748	93	1 168
Iowa	186	12.1	171	1	11.1	7.2	9	58	1	44	283	2 760	81	522
Jackson	238	11.9	234	1	11.6	5.6	18	90	1	67	334	3 761	397	1 969
Jasper	427	11.9	341	3	9.6	7.0	29	81	1	61	170	6 246	299	835
Jefferson	168	9.9	160	1	9.4	6.0	21	123	1	83	485	2 322	573	3 355
Johnson	1 274	12.5	486	10	4.8	7.6	1 063	1 035	2	1 002	975	9 007	3 960	3 857
Jones	203	10.0	178	1	8.8	6.6	10	49	1	38	187	3 327	204	1 002
Keokuk	134	11.7	140	0	12.1	2.5	3	26	1	33	287	2 653	72	624
Kossuth	174	9.8	207	1	11.6	5.7	8	45	1	24	135	3 616	210	1 169
Lee	458	11.8	427	3	11.1	7.3	48	125	2	155	403	6 787	1 438	3 707
Linn	2 586	14.3	1 355	16	7.5	6.2	354	194	2	877	480	26 037	NA	NA
Louisa	174	14.6	107	1	9.0	7.7	2	17	0	0	0	1 821	164	1 369
Lucas	111	12.2	121	1	13.2	6.0	5	55	1	83	907	2 040	253	2 781
Lyon	148	12.4	119	1	10.0	4.5	3	25	1	30	250	2 284	107	892
Madison	162	11.8	164	2	11.9	10.3	8	58	1	23	166	2 213	162	1 176
Mahaska	268	12.3	214	1	9.8	3.7	12	55	1	53	242	3 905	485	2 215
Marion	372	11.9	333	2	10.7	4.5	44	140	2	215	686	5 356	490	1 562
Marshall	512	13.2	511	4	13.2	7.8	65	168	1	158	408	7 145	1 392	3 576
Mills	176	12.3	132	0	9.2	1.9	9	62	0	0	0	2 312	NA	NA
Mitchell	129	11.6	149	2	13.5	12.9	4	36	1	30	272	2 554	92	829
Monona	101	10.0	159	0	15.7	0.0	10	99	1	48	475	2 410	291	2 900
Monroe	90	11.1	98	0	12.1	3.7	6	75	1	46	572	1 670	131	1 623
Montgomery	141	11.9	184	2	15.4	11.8	12	101	1	40	336	2 605	361	3 021
Muscatine	592	14.4	355	2	8.7	2.8	30	73	1	80	195	6 260	1 503	3 634
O'Brien	181	12.1	189	1	12.6	7.4	8	54	2	121	812	3 415	273	1 823
Osceola	81	11.6	86	1	12.2	16.4	5	72	1	32	458	1 415	62	883
Page	185	10.7	232	3	13.5	16.2	18	104	2	137	793	3 714	453	2 635
Palo Alto	110	10.9	144	1	14.3	9.1	8	80	1	54	539	2 345	221	2 186
Plymouth	315	12.7	244	2	9.8	5.3	14	56	1	44	177	4 228	392	1 585
Pocahontas	72	8.2	119	0	13.5	4.6	2	23	1	20	228	2 074	41	462
Polk	5 791	16.2	2 769	41	7.8	7.1	1 029	286	6	1 879	522	46 194	20 065	5 651
Pottawattamie	1 151	13.5	807	10	9.4	9.0	126	146	2	545	632	13 755	NA	NA
Poweshiek	194	10.2	221	1	11.7	3.4	23	122	1	46	244	3 484	155	813
Ringgold	52	9.8	79	0	14.8	6.4	6	112	1	36	672	1 313	58	1 083
Sac	134	11.2	170	1	14.3	5.0	10	84	1	54	453	2 727	112	939
Scott	2 273	14.4	1 255	15	8.0	6.8	347	219	3	660	416	21 039	8 570	5 425
Shelby	132	10.2	160	2	12.3	12.6	5	39	1	52	401	2 740	161	1 223
Sioux	396	12.7	251	2	8.1	5.0	23	74	4	295	943	5 034	NA	NA
Story	870	11.6	441	5	5.9	6.1	159	211	2	338	449	8 538	1 929	2 577
Tama	233	13.2	206	2	11.6	10.0	7	39	0	0	0	3 632	301	1 701
Taylor	74	10.3	105	1	14.7	13.6	2	28	0	0	0	1 664	51	895
Union	152	12.1	157	1	12.5	6.6	8	64	1	53	422	2 687	NA	NA
Van Buren	91	11.6	101	1	12.9	11.0	7	89	1	40	507	1 776	117	1 490
Wapello	422	11.9	444	3	12.5	7.9	60	169	1	137	387	7 498	1 026	2 892
Warren	500	12.6	320	5	8.0	10.7	27	67	0	0	0	4 775	774	1 942
Washington	289	13.8	233	4	11.2	12.7	16	76	1	83	396	4 035	251	1 199
Wayne	59	8.8	119	0	17.7	0.0	3	45	1	28	420	1 729	112	1 636
Webster	510	13.1	479	3	12.3	5.2	76	196	1	182	470	7 869	2 123	5 479
Winnebago	135	11.3	144	1	12.0	7.4	6	50	0	0	0	2 496	86	711
Winneshiek	207	9.9	181	2	8.7	8.1	23	110	1	83	396	3 409	205	978
Woodbury	1 685	16.5	962	15	9.4	9.1	222	218	2	681	670	16 024	6 791	6 629
Worth	85	10.9	102	1	13.0	15.6	3	39	0	0	0	1 555	125	1 604
Wright	158	11.2	196	1	13.9	4.2	10	71	2	54	386	3 279	201	1 413
KANSAS	37 454	14.4	23 903	284	9.2	7.6	5 216	198	132	11 383	433	389 103	127 737	4 859
Allen	173	11.9	183	0	12.6	1.9	11	76	1	40	275	2 839	NA	NA
Anderson	95	11.9	102	0	12.7	3.5	6	74	1	60	744	1 795	NA	NA
Atchison	214	13.0	186	1	11.3	3.1	16	95	1	160	946	2 925	NA	NA

1. Per 1,000 estimated resident population, average 1996–1998. 2. Deaths of infants under 1 year old. 3. Deaths of infants under 1 year old per 1,000 live births. 4. Data subject to copyright. 5. Per 100,000 resident population as of July 1 of the year shown. 6. Data for serious crimes have not been adjusted for underreporting; this may affect comparability between geographic areas and over time. 7. Per 100,000 population estimated by the FBI.

STATE County	Serious crimes known to police, 1998[1] (cont'd) Rate[2] Violent	Property	Education — School enrollment and attainment, 1990 Enrollment[3] Total	Percent private	High school grad-uate or more	Bach-elor's degree or more	Local government expenditures, fiscal 1997[5] Total current expendi-tures (mil dol)	Current expendi-tures per student (dollars)	Money income 1989 Per capita[6] (dollars)	Households Median Dollars	Percent change, 1979–1989 (constant 1989 dollars)	Percent with $100,000 or more	Income and poverty, 1997 Median house-hold income	Percent below poverty level All persons	Persons under 18	Persons 5–17 in families
	46	47	48	49	50	51	52	53	54	55	56	57	58	59	60	61
IOWA—Cont'd																
Guthrie	0	872	2 355	3.4	78.0	9.9	12.5	5 334	11 201	23 356	4.4	1.2	33 467	10.0	14.0	12.2
Hamilton	112	2 774	3 761	6.0	79.5	12.8	16.3	5 301	11 879	25 847	-5.4	1.2	37 073	8.5	12.4	10.6
Hancock	33	1 118	3 238	8.6	78.4	10.3	11.8	5 435	11 064	25 445	-4.9	1.4	36 048	8.0	10.3	9.6
Hardin	43	1 976	4 727	6.3	78.5	12.4	20.4	5 565	11 356	23 457	-9.9	1.4	34 846	10.2	13.9	12.5
Harrison	117	1 688	3 461	6.3	76.2	9.1	17.1	5 080	10 411	22 258	-4.4	1.0	33 746	11.2	15.0	13.4
Henry	165	1 603	4 878	16.1	79.1	14.5	19.5	5 150	11 355	24 952	-4.9	1.6	37 047	10.1	13.2	11.4
Howard	103	1 683	2 177	14.3	72.9	8.2	11.8	5 473	9 960	21 913	-5.2	1.7	32 052	11.2	15.1	12.9
Humboldt	0	1 169	2 445	5.8	80.0	11.6	10.2	5 267	12 167	24 557	-7.5	2.1	37 018	8.1	11.0	10.0
Ida	0	1 168	1 931	4.5	75.9	11.0	8.2	5 245	10 993	22 859	0.1	1.9	34 459	10.3	13.8	12.9
Iowa	71	451	3 338	7.9	76.4	11.1	14.4	5 180	12 139	26 579	-7.1	1.6	40 002	7.1	9.1	8.5
Jackson	5	1 964	4 859	16.3	72.2	10.0	20.1	5 424	10 467	22 487	-17.7	0.9	32 214	11.3	14.1	13.0
Jasper	50	785	7 863	9.7	77.6	12.7	34.3	5 335	12 872	28 702	0.8	1.6	41 892	7.4	10.4	8.8
Jefferson	246	3 109	4 385	33.7	82.3	26.5	11.6	5 572	11 664	22 630	-4.7	2.0	34 196	12.7	16.1	14.3
Johnson	547	3 310	40 420	6.1	90.6	44.0	71.7	5 572	14 113	27 862	2.3	4.6	41 678	9.2	9.5	9.0
Jones	54	948	4 755	14.9	78.7	10.6	18.5	5 239	10 403	24 480	-10.4	1.3	34 772	9.9	12.6	11.7
Keokuk	26	598	2 663	4.8	76.8	9.4	13.1	5 139	10 427	22 234	-1.7	0.9	31 979	12.7	18.0	15.8
Kossuth	50	1 119	4 756	21.1	79.1	11.8	15.8	5 684	11 247	23 321	-9.5	1.5	34 492	9.5	12.6	11.4
Lee	379	3 328	8 965	16.8	77.5	10.7	34.1	5 342	11 488	24 671	-11.3	1.4	34 966	12.3	17.5	15.2
Linn	NA	NA	44 286	18.3	84.9	21.5	166.3	5 217	14 902	32 137	-4.5	2.9	44 748	7.8	11.2	9.6
Louisa	50	1 319	2 840	3.3	76.3	9.2	16.2	5 283	11 226	25 590	-8.4	1.3	35 652	11.2	17.6	14.3
Lucas	99	2 682	1 830	3.7	77.1	9.5	8.4	5 117	11 048	21 316	5.3	1.4	30 683	13.7	18.9	16.7
Lyon	75	817	2 951	16.2	70.4	10.2	11.8	5 279	9 871	22 676	-8.4	1.0	35 180	8.9	11.7	11.2
Madison	65	1 111	2 899	7.5	81.6	12.0	15.9	5 507	11 620	26 644	2.0	1.2	39 187	7.7	9.0	8.7
Mahaska	151	2 064	5 385	21.5	74.8	13.1	16.8	4 912	10 819	23 115	-3.2	1.4	35 589	11.4	14.8	13.2
Marion	131	1 431	8 069	30.1	73.7	12.9	29.2	5 038	11 945	27 991	0.9	2.0	41 988	8.2	10.1	9.2
Marshall	655	2 921	9 378	7.8	81.8	15.8	45.1	6 413	13 231	28 333	-5.3	1.7	37 314	10.5	16.2	13.0
Mills	NA	NA	3 421	5.7	76.1	12.6	14.8	5 392	11 140	27 420	-0.3	1.0	37 113	9.1	12.8	11.0
Mitchell	27	802	2 417	11.3	76.0	11.1	10.1	5 236	11 035	24 519	1.2	0.7	35 524	8.7	12.3	11.4
Monona	209	2 691	2 139	5.6	73.0	10.3	9.8	5 413	10 584	20 714	-8.0	2.2	30 266	12.6	17.5	16.0
Monroe	50	1 573	1 844	3.3	75.6	8.0	7.0	5 292	10 046	20 745	-6.2	1.1	29 870	13.9	18.2	16.5
Montgomery	151	2 870	2 619	4.9	80.0	12.8	11.0	5 098	11 595	23 312	-6.2	1.4	32 264	11.5	17.6	14.9
Muscatine	438	3 196	10 320	7.6	75.0	12.8	41.0	5 272	12 802	29 786	-2.5	1.8	40 800	11.2	15.5	13.8
O'Brien	80	1 743	3 759	21.6	73.5	12.6	15.2	5 019	10 842	23 125	-6.3	1.0	35 048	8.5	10.9	10.3
Osceola	0	883	1 647	11.5	72.1	10.0	5.1	4 859	11 508	23 037	-9.7	1.8	34 804	8.9	12.7	12.1
Page	116	2 519	4 041	6.6	78.2	13.5	17.1	5 272	11 122	22 050	-4.7	1.3	33 727	12.3	15.4	14.1
Palo Alto	138	2 048	2 758	13.7	76.9	12.8	15.6	7 740	10 749	21 223	-13.2	1.3	32 669	10.5	13.1	12.4
Plymouth	65	1 520	6 229	25.5	78.0	15.0	22.3	4 890	11 507	26 796	0.6	2.0	40 109	7.2	8.6	7.9
Pocahontas	11	451	2 136	11.5	80.1	12.8	7.8	5 452	11 531	23 517	-4.0	1.2	34 867	9.5	13.2	12.2
Polk	356	5 295	82 174	19.7	85.4	23.9	378.9	6 373	15 365	31 221	-1.2	3.6	42 975	8.7	13.0	11.1
Pottawattamie	NA	NA	20 448	10.3	77.1	11.0	97.4	5 624	11 734	26 639	-6.1	1.5	35 851	11.2	17.1	14.4
Poweshiek	42	771	5 224	26.2	81.6	16.2	17.0	5 143	12 066	26 063	-0.1	2.1	38 079	9.2	12.0	11.0
Ringgold	56	1 027	1 250	1.0	78.0	10.3	6.6	6 379	9 773	20 761	23.7	1.3	27 802	16.0	22.6	19.9
Sac	34	905	2 856	5.7	77.3	12.7	12.3	5 249	10 852	21 818	-11.9	1.4	32 612	10.5	14.7	13.6
Scott	953	4 472	41 790	18.7	81.4	21.9	173.6	6 101	13 625	29 979	-13.9	2.5	40 920	11.5	16.6	14.2
Shelby	175	1 048	3 235	14.9	79.0	12.8	13.5	5 158	10 720	22 702	-11.0	2.2	34 588	9.0	12.4	10.9
Sioux	NA	NA	9 408	50.6	71.7	14.4	29.4	6 639	10 411	25 692	-5.2	2.3	40 895	7.0	8.5	8.0
Story	73	2 504	33 981	3.6	91.0	38.4	61.0	5 490	11 958	26 668	-6.4	2.5	40 851	9.1	8.9	8.5
Tama	379	1 322	4 196	4.7	75.8	11.2	19.5	4 974	11 362	24 297	-6.2	1.5	34 794	9.2	12.4	11.5
Taylor	18	877	1 666	2.5	75.0	8.7	7.6	5 649	8 834	18 641	-5.3	0.2	27 341	15.7	21.5	19.2
Union	NA	NA	3 306	7.6	79.0	12.8	16.8	7 439	10 247	21 550	-5.9	0.8	29 928	12.8	16.9	15.8
Van Buren	64	1 426	1 682	7.9	74.7	9.6	7.7	5 323	9 348	19 244	-0.8	0.7	29 383	13.4	19.5	18.8
Wapello	279	2 613	8 262	5.9	74.2	11.0	44.3	6 599	11 055	21 060	-15.8	1.4	29 856	14.5	21.5	19.5
Warren	100	1 842	10 075	15.2	87.0	16.2	39.2	5 082	12 732	32 452	-3.6	2.0	46 404	6.3	7.7	6.9
Washington	124	1 075	4 417	11.6	76.9	11.7	19.1	5 376	11 387	25 822	2.4	1.2	36 470	9.3	14.2	12.6
Wayne	131	1 505	1 416	3.3	71.7	8.4	6.4	4 993	9 225	17 599	-3.0	0.3	25 699	15.6	22.3	20.3
Webster	511	4 968	9 603	16.6	78.4	13.7	44.0	7 002	11 358	23 692	-13.6	1.1	34 353	12.2	17.3	15.2
Winnebago	83	628	3 185	18.3	78.6	14.0	16.2	5 502	10 775	23 480	-5.8	1.4	34 048	9.5	12.1	11.0
Winneshiek	67	911	6 499	43.6	76.4	17.1	15.3	5 206	10 503	24 383	6.1	1.6	35 955	9.7	10.1	10.0
Woodbury	615	6 014	26 130	23.1	78.4	16.7	110.2	5 879	12 218	25 186	-6.4	2.6	36 357	10.7	14.9	13.2
Worth	128	1 476	1 901	7.5	77.9	10.9	6.1	5 232	11 443	22 902	-12.5	1.5	34 024	8.5	11.4	10.8
Wright	77	1 336	3 197	4.8	77.6	11.3	17.3	5 411	11 969	24 582	-6.2	1.7	35 533	8.8	12.5	11.5
KANSAS	397	4 462	668 365	11.2	81.3	21.1	2 569.0	5 508	13 300	27 291	-0.5	2.8	36 488	10.9	15.4	14.2
Allen	NA	NA	3 995	4.4	74.2	12.4	14.7	5 173	9 889	20 774	-3.7	1.2	30 171	15.0	21.4	19.8
Anderson	NA	NA	1 725	17.6	70.2	8.1	8.3	5 478	10 190	21 956	6.3	1.2	30 776	12.9	18.9	17.0
Atchison	NA	NA	4 474	25.7	77.5	13.3	15.4	6 230	10 144	22 339	-6.9	1.4	32 515	14.6	21.4	19.9

1. Data for serious crimes have not been adjusted for underreporting; this may affect comparability between geographic areas and over time.   2. Per 100,000 population estimated by the FBI.   3. All persons 3 years old and over enrolled in nursery school through college.   4. Persons 25 years old and over.   5. Elementary and secondary education expenditures, local government fiscal years ending between July 1, 1996 and June 30, 1997.   6. Based on population enumerated as of April 1, 1990.

STATE County	Personal income, 1998												
			Per capita[1]					Transfer payments					
									Government payments to individuals				
	Total (mil dol)	Percent change, 1997–1998	Dollars	Rank	Wages and salaries[2] (mil dol)	Proprietor's income (mil dol)	Dividends, interest, and rent (mil dol)	Total (mil dol)	Total (mil dol)	Social Security (mil dol)	Medical payments (mil dol)	Income mainte-nance (mil dol)	Unemploy-ment insurance (mil dol)
	62	63	64	65	66	67	68	69	70	71	72	73	74
IOWA—Cont'd													
Guthrie	243	2.5	21 154	1 345	68	23	54	46	44	24	15	2	1
Hamilton	397	-1.4	24 769	520	211	52	87	58	55	31	18	3	1
Hancock	262	-1.1	21 716	1 186	196	32	61	42	39	22	13	2	0
Hardin	440	1.4	23 994	643	221	60	96	77	73	40	25	4	1
Harrison	303	-1.8	19 748	1 795	95	24	56	61	58	26	23	4	1
Henry	443	3.4	22 130	1 057	310	25	90	63	59	32	19	4	2
Howard	222	3.3	22 942	862	105	34	57	36	34	19	12	2	1
Humboldt	243	-2.7	23 572	728	106	31	60	42	40	23	14	2	0
Ida	180	-1.3	22 784	893	97	29	45	29	27	16	9	2	0
Iowa	418	2.9	26 943	309	317	41	93	49	46	27	15	2	1
Jackson	395	3.2	19 630	1 849	138	37	93	75	71	34	28	5	2
Jasper	908	4.8	24 848	506	476	67	178	124	117	65	40	6	2
Jefferson	383	1.0	22 494	979	275	42	94	49	46	23	16	4	1
Johnson	2 850	6.4	27 785	245	2 063	194	563	209	188	95	59	13	3
Jones	377	2.3	18 715	2 152	148	41	84	61	57	33	18	3	1
Keokuk	221	-4.9	19 268	1 967	66	21	62	46	44	22	16	3	1
Kossuth	385	-2.5	21 726	1 185	152	70	99	64	61	36	19	4	1
Lee	874	3.8	22 701	922	576	84	189	148	140	66	50	11	3
Linn	5 421	8.8	29 656	178	4 148	340	1 034	551	513	272	171	34	9
Louisa	240	0.1	20 149	1 667	87	26	44	38	35	18	12	3	1
Lucas	180	2.7	19 817	1 775	83	11	45	37	36	17	12	3	1
Lyon	239	-4.1	19 871	1 754	78	46	56	39	37	21	13	2	0
Madison	314	4.6	22 594	954	89	19	56	44	41	22	15	2	1
Mahaska	497	3.8	22 684	928	214	43	105	78	73	37	24	6	1
Marion	759	4.3	24 242	600	553	40	161	99	92	50	28	5	1
Marshall	937	2.8	24 177	611	572	69	198	155	147	71	52	9	2
Mills	374	2.0	25 837	409	97	22	54	98	95	21	66	3	0
Mitchell	259	-2.8	23 495	748	92	46	67	40	38	21	13	2	1
Monona	200	-3.9	19 829	1 768	79	20	46	48	46	22	19	3	1
Monroe	175	3.7	21 754	1 171	90	15	36	36	34	15	13	2	1
Montgomery	273	1.2	23 007	852	133	32	64	53	50	24	20	3	1
Muscatine	1 047	6.7	25 531	434	774	49	231	125	117	62	39	10	2
O'Brien	347	-1.5	23 291	793	143	63	85	60	57	31	20	3	1
Osceola	152	-2.8	21 841	1 149	55	32	35	23	22	13	6	1	0
Page	374	0.5	21 674	1 201	188	43	86	71	67	34	25	5	1
Palo Alto	219	-5.4	21 743	1 174	87	38	46	41	39	21	14	2	1
Plymouth	559	0.9	22 728	911	243	82	131	73	68	41	19	4	1
Pocahontas	197	-3.5	22 353	1 007	81	39	46	37	35	19	13	2	0
Polk	10 960	6.5	30 468	153	9 191	718	1 948	1 078	1 004	476	370	81	20
Pottawattamie	1 927	3.8	22 356	1 006	952	94	318	304	286	124	99	24	3
Poweshiek	456	2.8	24 333	585	282	49	103	64	60	34	20	3	1
Ringgold	99	-3.9	18 447	2 229	35	11	25	23	22	11	8	2	0
Sac	236	-8.8	19 832	1 766	85	27	65	44	42	25	13	2	1
Scott	4 146	5.3	26 186	377	2 747	278	824	475	443	213	152	47	7
Shelby	280	-3.3	21 664	1 203	110	37	77	51	48	26	18	3	1
Sioux	706	-0.9	22 476	983	380	123	163	88	82	46	26	4	1
Story	1 894	5.3	25 296	461	1 291	119	397	189	173	86	56	9	2
Tama	377	1.2	21 216	1 326	148	47	80	63	59	33	20	3	1
Taylor	126	-1.4	17 676	2 444	40	19	29	28	27	14	10	2	0
Union	256	3.8	20 473	1 569	151	24	54	49	47	22	16	4	1
Van Buren	150	-0.6	19 023	2 046	53	10	31	30	29	15	10	2	0
Wapello	749	3.8	21 168	1 339	426	44	147	159	152	69	53	15	3
Warren	942	5.8	23 426	761	207	53	132	105	97	52	33	5	2
Washington	484	-0.8	23 140	829	170	65	119	75	70	38	25	4	1
Wayne	113	-4.8	16 868	2 640	42	11	28	31	29	14	11	3	0
Webster	908	1.9	23 285	795	553	58	199	162	154	78	54	11	2
Winnebago	267	4.9	22 368	1 004	128	43	56	41	39	22	13	2	2
Winneshiek	462	5.2	22 032	1 093	259	57	100	62	57	30	18	3	2
Woodbury	2 525	4.6	24 863	504	1 538	189	465	344	323	153	117	27	5
Worth	167	-2.1	21 624	1 214	48	31	37	27	26	14	8	1	1
Wright	327	-4.2	23 265	804	163	33	88	61	58	31	21	3	1
KANSAS	67 383	5.5	25 537	X	41 616	5 796	13 145	8 467	8 013	3 781	2 934	572	135
Allen	284	1.8	19 513	1 884	158	24	58	57	54	26	20	4	1
Anderson	137	-6.0	17 069	2 595	45	15	34	31	30	15	10	2	1
Atchison	327	5.2	19 386	1 920	184	22	65	60	57	26	22	5	1

1. Based on the resident population estimated as of July 1 of the year shown.   2. Includes other labor income.

Table B. States and Counties — Earnings, Social Security, and Housing

STATE County	Earnings, 1998									Social Security bene-ficiaries, December 1998			Housing units, 1990	
					Percent by selected industries									
			Goods-related[1]		Service-related and other[2]							Supplemental Security Income recipients, December 1998		Percent change, 1980–1990
	Total (mil dol)	Farm	Total	Manu-facturing	Total	Retail trade	Finance, insurance, and real estate	Services	Govern-ment	Number	Rate[3]		Total	
	75	76	77	78	79	80	81	82	83	84	85	86	87	88
IOWA—Cont'd														
Guthrie	91	8.4	D	2.8	D	10.5	7.2	16.7	22.2	2 959	256	136	5 179	-2.0
Hamilton	263	12.9	D	34.4	D	6.4	3.0	10.8	13.5	3 613	226	208	6 879	-3.7
Hancock	229	8.3	D	60.0	D	4.0	2.0	6.3	9.0	2 616	217	126	5 236	-3.2
Hardin	281	12.4	26.6	13.1	43.3	7.6	3.5	12.7	17.7	4 602	249	225	8 419	-4.3
Harrison	119	5.6	D	7.5	D	13.8	3.6	19.9	21.3	3 277	213	239	6 175	-2.9
Henry	335	1.0	D	32.1	D	19.7	2.3	16.3	16.6	3 728	187	214	7 507	3.7
Howard	139	12.6	40.5	36.5	32.5	8.1	3.4	9.8	14.4	2 478	256	138	4 155	-2.7
Humboldt	137	9.9	D	23.9	D	6.6	D	11.1	14.7	2 581	250	129	4 670	-6.9
Ida	126	12.9	38.6	30.1	D	6.6	3.6	12.7	10.3	1 971	249	65	3 473	-4.4
Iowa	358	4.4	48.6	44.5	D	9.1	2.3	8.1	7.1	3 193	205	108	6 003	2.2
Jackson	175	3.8	30.0	20.9	45.7	12.0	4.6	17.9	20.6	4 257	212	340	8 426	-1.6
Jasper	542	5.4	D	43.7	D	9.3	2.5	11.3	14.9	7 383	205	405	14 338	-0.8
Jefferson	317	2.7	D	23.3	D	7.9	4.2	20.9	10.6	2 692	157	221	6 739	11.7
Johnson	2 256	0.4	D	8.8	D	8.4	4.3	19.6	45.7	10 195	99	863	37 210	17.8
Jones	189	9.0	D	19.8	D	10.4	3.7	14.0	22.2	3 940	194	185	7 366	0.2
Keokuk	87	1.9	D	16.9	51.5	8.6	5.0	14.4	18.1	2 769	241	190	5 024	-6.9
Kossuth	222	14.8	D	17.9	D	9.6	6.3	16.6	13.8	4 304	243	210	7 765	-5.8
Lee	659	0.6	D	38.0	D	8.1	2.4	19.7	12.1	7 632	198	693	16 443	-1.4
Linn	4 488	0.3	32.6	25.9	58.0	8.5	7.8	25.9	9.1	29 616	162	2 219	68 357	5.5
Louisa	113	11.3	D	D	D	5.9	2.9	8.9	18.8	2 152	180	127	5 044	4.5
Lucas	94	-1.7	14.2	9.1	D	39.5	4.9	D	20.8	2 225	243	214	4 179	-7.2
Lyon	125	22.0	D	15.9	D	6.5	3.9	15.0	13.4	2 572	214	75	4 561	-4.5
Madison	108	-0.6	D	17.7	D	10.0	8.2	17.8	22.4	2 572	185	131	4 995	0.6
Mahaska	257	6.9	D	16.7	D	9.6	4.2	18.4	13.7	4 571	209	397	8 977	-3.7
Marion	593	0.5	D	50.8	D	5.3	2.0	14.4	15.7	6 042	193	348	11 420	3.6
Marshall	641	3.4	D	35.7	D	8.4	3.2	18.0	15.4	8 007	207	500	15 862	-2.9
Mills	120	3.1	D	2.9	D	8.8	5.2	19.8	42.7	2 613	180	305	5 004	3.6
Mitchell	138	21.0	D	20.7	D	7.4	3.9	15.5	13.6	2 608	237	103	4 514	-4.7
Monona	99	6.0	13.0	5.6	63.1	11.5	4.5	32.5	17.9	2 702	267	188	4 555	-6.6
Monroe	106	2.0	52.0	42.4	D	7.1	2.3	13.4	13.6	1 958	244	178	3 740	-2.1
Montgomery	165	6.6	D	21.8	D	7.7	D	15.7	16.8	2 961	249	195	5 363	-7.5
Muscatine	822	1.1	55.9	49.1	31.3	5.9	3.1	14.1	11.7	7 014	171	451	16 044	5.2
O'Brien	206	17.1	D	11.2	D	8.4	4.5	19.7	14.4	3 768	253	218	6 476	-2.7
Osceola	88	29.2	D	19.4	D	5.6	D	11.6	11.5	1 607	230	70	2 998	-8.2
Page	231	2.4	D	27.6	D	14.8	2.9	16.9	19.8	4 160	241	347	7 339	-9.1
Palo Alto	125	19.6	D	15.0	D	8.1	4.1	15.9	21.6	2 533	253	179	4 826	-8.0
Plymouth	325	14.5	D	D	D	8.2	4.9	12.5	11.5	4 875	196	190	8 806	-0.6
Pocahontas	120	21.2	D	22.6	D	5.4	3.4	12.5	14.7	2 277	259	116	4 193	-10.0
Polk	9 909	0.1	15.7	10.0	70.9	8.9	20.1	25.2	13.2	52 223	145	5 112	135 979	11.3
Pottawattamie	1 047	0.9	D	11.8	D	13.0	5.1	32.4	15.9	14 860	172	1 434	32 831	1.3
Poweshiek	331	5.7	D	21.0	D	7.1	9.4	26.5	8.2	3 829	203	158	8 199	1.5
Ringgold	46	7.0	D	7.9	D	10.2	D	18.4	28.6	1 445	270	126	2 713	-8.8
Sac	112	12.8	16.0	8.2	53.3	9.1	5.0	19.4	18.0	3 029	254	119	5 648	-7.0
Scott	3 025	0.4	30.5	22.8	59.2	10.9	4.5	29.3	9.9	24 122	152	2 781	61 379	2.7
Shelby	147	10.3	15.2	5.9	56.8	11.1	4.8	20.5	17.7	3 106	239	169	5 430	-3.2
Sioux	502	14.8	D	27.3	D	7.9	3.6	15.1	10.0	5 652	181	249	10 333	-0.8
Story	1 410	1.5	D	13.3	D	7.9	3.2	16.2	46.0	9 290	123	475	26 847	6.7
Tama	195	10.5	20.4	15.8	53.0	7.3	3.6	26.5	16.0	3 989	225	180	7 417	-3.9
Taylor	59	18.6	D	D	D	7.4	3.2	12.4	20.5	1 835	257	125	3 307	-10.2
Union	174	1.7	D	25.2	D	10.5	3.3	18.0	21.5	2 799	223	309	5 622	-2.2
Van Buren	63	2.8	D	30.2	D	5.6	3.9	10.0	25.6	1 947	247	164	3 529	1.3
Wapello	471	0.4	31.3	25.0	50.5	11.5	2.7	24.9	17.8	8 354	236	1 104	15 640	-4.3
Warren	260	1.0	D	7.4	D	13.4	5.0	26.9	21.1	5 848	145	203	13 157	8.0
Washington	235	9.7	D	18.5	D	9.6	3.6	16.9	15.2	4 557	217	235	7 866	2.2
Wayne	53	1.6	25.9	22.5	45.3	8.4	3.4	16.4	27.1	1 928	290	161	3 334	-13.4
Webster	611	1.4	D	20.7	D	10.7	3.6	25.2	15.6	8 961	232	763	17 063	-4.1
Winnebago	171	10.2	D	25.4	D	8.4	3.8	17.4	12.7	2 733	229	124	5 030	-4.2
Winneshiek	315	8.2	32.6	19.4	43.3	8.7	3.1	22.2	15.9	3 850	184	174	7 726	4.1
Woodbury	1 727	0.7	D	16.2	D	10.2	4.8	31.8	13.3	17 909	176	1 836	39 071	0.1
Worth	79	27.6	D	24.0	D	4.7	3.6	10.8	13.7	1 787	230	82	3 443	-7.5
Wright	196	11.1	D	25.6	D	10.9	D	11.7	14.4	3 564	255	190	6 636	-4.4
KANSAS	47 412	2.5	25.3	18.3	55.0	9.6	6.1	23.4	17.2	434 972	165	36 507	1 044 112	9.3
Allen	182	-1.8	36.5	29.6	45.5	17.0	4.4	15.7	19.8	3 307	227	286	6 454	-5.6
Anderson	60	5.5	D	9.5	D	10.2	5.2	19.6	22.8	1 922	238	100	3 514	-3.1
Atchison	205	2.9	33.9	28.2	46.2	9.4	2.8	20.5	17.0	3 239	192	300	6 691	-3.2

1. Covers mining, construction, and manufacturing. 2. Covers private sector earnings in agricultural services, forestry, and fisheries; transportation and public utilities; wholesale trade; retail trade; finance, insurance, and real estate; and services. 3. Per 1,000 resident population estimated as of July 1 of the year shown.

Table B. States and Counties — Housing, Labor Force, and Employment

STATE County	Housing units, 1990 (cont'd) Occupied units — Owner-occupied Total	Percent	Median value[1]	Owner cost as a percent of income — With a mortgage	Without a mortgage	Renter-occupied — Median rent[2]	Rent as percent of income	Sub-standard units[3] (percent)	Civilian labor force, 1999 Total	Percent change, 1998–1999	Unemployment Total	Rate[4]	Civilian employment, 1990[5] Total	Percent — Professional, managerial, and technical	Precision production, craft, and repair
	89	90	91	92	93	94	95	96	97	98	99	100	101	102	103
IOWA—Cont'd															
Guthrie	4 407	75.5	29 200	17.0	13.2	289	25.8	2.2	6 034	1.5	130	2.2	4 933	19.2	13.1
Hamilton	6 358	71.0	39 900	17.9	12.8	295	23.9	1.1	8 553	4.2	179	2.1	7 715	19.4	11.2
Hancock	4 867	73.0	36 800	18.8	14.0	291	18.6	1.8	9 720	6.1	142	1.5	5 777	19.4	10.7
Hardin	7 611	71.9	33 800	16.1	13.0	287	22.8	0.5	9 440	-0.5	274	2.9	8 505	22.5	10.4
Harrison	5 656	74.5	33 600	18.8	13.5	277	24.5	2.3	7 906	5.1	184	2.3	6 680	19.0	11.2
Henry	7 089	73.5	43 800	16.9	12.5	308	22.5	1.7	10 904	-0.5	301	2.8	9 134	20.3	11.7
Howard	3 856	78.0	30 400	17.7	13.3	233	21.5	2.4	5 553	0.6	146	2.6	4 296	17.6	9.5
Humboldt	4 339	72.8	34 600	16.5	12.0	270	22.4	1.0	5 485	-0.5	106	1.9	4 616	20.0	11.9
Ida	3 222	71.7	29 900	16.5	12.7	268	21.0	1.1	4 137	4.2	86	2.1	3 682	20.4	10.9
Iowa	5 713	76.1	43 600	16.5	13.6	295	19.2	1.5	9 335	2.1	155	1.7	7 463	19.6	12.2
Jackson	7 527	73.7	41 200	17.1	13.5	272	22.0	2.1	10 539	1.8	399	3.8	9 030	17.4	14.4
Jasper	13 632	74.6	46 000	15.4	12.2	305	20.0	1.6	19 106	2.3	372	1.9	16 785	20.2	13.8
Jefferson	6 309	66.7	47 000	18.8	14.2	339	25.9	2.2	9 623	-5.7	305	3.2	7 949	30.8	11.8
Johnson	36 067	52.7	76 900	19.0	12.2	412	28.3	2.9	67 137	2.5	1 363	2.0	54 591	40.8	6.3
Jones	6 917	73.6	40 800	14.6	13.5	278	18.5	1.9	9 874	3.6	261	2.6	8 678	18.2	12.2
Keokuk	4 573	78.0	23 900	15.4	12.2	250	23.0	2.3	5 183	-1.6	226	4.4	4 930	17.3	12.2
Kossuth	7 194	73.1	33 900	16.5	12.3	260	22.7	1.6	8 874	0.5	254	2.9	8 153	19.1	9.3
Lee	14 936	74.1	36 300	16.9	13.3	293	25.9	1.8	18 942	-1.6	733	3.9	17 072	19.7	12.3
Linn	65 501	70.4	58 500	16.5	12.1	369	23.2	1.4	112 571	1.8	2 047	1.8	87 606	30.8	10.8
Louisa	4 296	74.5	39 400	16.5	13.0	304	19.8	2.5	5 410	3.4	182	3.4	5 382	16.8	14.7
Lucas	3 766	74.3	30 200	16.5	12.6	258	22.6	2.0	4 055	0.4	132	3.3	3 941	17.4	8.8
Lyon	4 289	77.1	31 800	16.5	12.6	252	18.1	1.8	5 564	-1.3	99	1.8	5 356	18.4	9.6
Madison	4 715	73.5	42 800	17.7	12.4	294	22.2	2.1	7 636	0.9	238	3.1	5 945	21.4	13.4
Mahaska	8 306	70.0	36 400	17.4	12.8	289	24.4	1.0	11 215	-1.3	259	2.3	9 896	21.3	10.2
Marion	10 815	73.9	48 200	17.1	12.1	323	23.9	2.0	18 120	1.4	387	2.1	14 449	23.4	9.9
Marshall	14 890	71.2	42 100	16.5	12.6	321	23.0	1.3	20 279	-1.2	453	2.2	18 622	25.3	11.8
Mills	4 665	74.8	47 000	16.6	13.0	319	23.9	1.9	6 293	5.6	118	1.9	6 037	23.6	11.4
Mitchell	4 253	78.3	34 700	14.2	12.6	232	20.9	2.3	5 506	1.1	161	2.9	4 877	17.5	10.9
Monona	4 098	74.2	27 400	19.6	13.1	243	23.7	1.2	4 960	-1.9	155	3.1	4 193	20.6	10.6
Monroe	3 196	76.9	27 800	18.3	13.0	272	27.5	3.4	4 087	-0.4	122	3.0	3 366	17.0	12.4
Montgomery	4 955	71.7	35 200	18.2	12.7	254	20.6	0.7	5 895	-2.0	184	3.1	5 682	21.5	10.6
Muscatine	14 806	72.0	50 600	16.8	12.5	343	22.0	2.4	21 378	-1.2	589	2.8	19 093	20.6	12.8
O'Brien	5 980	75.0	32 700	15.3	12.5	249	22.5	1.2	7 912	2.4	169	2.1	6 953	21.7	10.4
Osceola	2 817	74.7	28 000	13.0	12.4	262	18.8	2.4	3 912	8.3	91	2.3	3 327	19.1	9.3
Page	6 687	70.6	33 700	15.8	13.4	253	23.4	1.2	8 978	1.2	217	2.4	7 658	21.3	10.9
Palo Alto	4 183	70.9	28 000	17.6	12.5	245	23.5	3.0	5 387	2.9	131	2.4	4 609	18.7	10.1
Plymouth	8 417	74.8	48 800	16.6	13.2	298	21.7	1.5	13 014	4.0	314	2.4	10 990	20.5	10.1
Pocahontas	3 820	74.3	27 000	14.5	12.2	246	18.8	0.8	4 090	-0.7	137	3.3	4 153	19.5	9.3
Polk	129 237	65.2	59 700	19.8	13.3	437	25.0	2.4	210 719	-0.8	4 016	1.9	176 499	31.5	8.2
Pottawattamie	31 262	71.1	46 900	18.9	13.4	371	24.7	2.2	47 517	0.1	945	2.0	40 343	21.8	11.7
Poweshiek	7 158	70.5	47 500	18.1	13.1	303	21.7	1.3	10 236	1.3	283	2.8	9 299	23.3	10.8
Ringgold	2 218	75.4	22 000	17.1	13.3	262	24.4	2.6	2 645	6.3	71	2.7	2 374	20.3	10.2
Sac	4 914	72.5	27 100	16.4	12.3	250	22.1	1.2	5 878	-1.1	152	2.6	5 452	18.7	10.9
Scott	57 438	66.4	54 400	17.5	12.8	361	25.0	1.6	84 852	0.4	2 578	3.0	72 497	29.1	10.8
Shelby	5 024	73.8	36 500	17.9	13.0	261	23.0	0.9	6 871	2.3	162	2.4	5 972	19.8	9.5
Sioux	9 925	78.2	44 700	17.1	12.1	268	21.4	1.7	17 493	-0.5	426	2.4	14 668	20.9	10.0
Story	25 941	56.0	63 900	18.4	12.2	392	28.2	2.3	45 870	0.7	960	2.1	39 384	39.9	6.8
Tama	6 768	75.2	32 100	16.5	13.7	304	22.0	3.0	9 378	4.2	266	2.8	7 694	18.4	12.5
Taylor	2 859	75.6	23 000	15.5	13.4	235	27.2	1.8	3 390	6.6	105	3.1	2 952	15.0	10.8
Union	5 173	68.7	32 900	15.4	13.4	291	25.4	1.5	6 606	2.1	239	3.6	5 655	22.5	11.5
Van Buren	3 056	77.7	21 300	18.3	13.2	240	21.6	4.3	4 030	-5.5	121	3.0	3 406	17.8	14.5
Wapello	14 555	75.6	27 000	15.5	12.0	276	26.6	1.8	17 499	-0.8	661	3.8	15 340	21.1	12.3
Warren	12 659	76.8	59 300	17.7	12.4	348	22.2	1.9	23 019	-1.2	402	1.7	19 042	24.7	10.9
Washington	7 454	71.8	43 000	16.8	12.1	297	20.5	2.5	11 241	-0.2	268	2.4	9 612	18.8	10.8
Wayne	2 953	75.8	19 900	18.0	13.9	233	26.1	1.6	3 017	0.5	86	2.9	3 014	19.1	9.2
Webster	15 963	68.9	37 000	17.4	12.5	296	24.2	1.3	20 325	1.2	554	2.7	18 044	23.9	11.3
Winnebago	4 704	74.6	39 300	16.9	12.8	271	21.2	0.9	4 674	-1.1	108	2.3	5 596	23.7	9.8
Winneshiek	7 256	71.0	49 700	18.7	13.2	276	20.4	2.6	12 244	7.9	393	3.2	10 489	21.0	9.7
Woodbury	36 899	68.5	41 000	17.4	13.1	325	25.1	2.6	53 805	-1.9	1 321	2.5	46 324	25.6	12.3
Worth	3 239	76.3	33 500	16.4	13.2	254	20.1	1.0	4 075	-1.3	111	2.7	3 622	16.5	10.8
Wright	5 899	72.2	32 700	16.0	12.6	282	24.1	1.1	6 781	-2.4	157	2.3	6 563	19.2	10.0
KANSAS	944 726	67.9	52 200	19.1	12.6	372	24.5	2.7	1 434 249	1.7	42 726	3.0	1 172 214	28.7	11.5
Allen	5 705	75.1	27 600	15.8	12.8	251	25.8	3.4	7 358	7.1	333	4.5	6 381	22.8	13.4
Anderson	3 067	77.9	27 200	15.0	12.7	256	24.5	2.7	4 005	4.9	175	4.4	3 409	15.9	10.7
Atchison	6 129	73.1	32 400	17.3	12.3	285	25.2	2.2	9 151	14.2	349	3.8	7 295	23.9	11.6

1. Specified owner-occupied units. 2. Specified renter-occupied units. 3. Overcrowded or lacking complete plumbing facilities. 4. Percent of civilian labor force. 5. Persons 16 years and older.

	Private nonfarm establishments, employment and payroll, 1998									Agriculture, 1997			
		Employment						Annual payroll		Farms			Farm operators
											Percent with—		
STATE County	Number of establishments	Total	Health Care and Social Assistance	Manufacturing	Retail trade	Finance and Insurance	Professional Scientific and Technical Services	Total (mil dol)	Average per employee (dollars)	Number	Less than 50 acres	500 acres and over	Whose principal occupation is farming (percent)
	104	105	106	107	108	109	110	111	112	113	114	115	116
IOWA—Cont'd													
Guthrie	291	1 841	364	183	364	133	60	31	16 714	847	17.7	24.0	58.1
Hamilton	454	6 423	689	2 466	783	183	106	150	23 290	790	16.8	32.2	70.3
Hancock	331	3 033	377	1 247	426	118	46	64	21 195	849	14.7	29.6	70.0
Hardin	656	7 088	1 080	1 628	1 044	261	140	147	20 797	857	20.8	29.6	68.7
Harrison	365	2 958	677	259	673	136	58	53	17 913	876	17.0	30.8	63.4
Henry	539	11 127	1 007	2 699	967	184	116	255	22 909	835	18.4	17.2	53.5
Howard	293	3 449	496	1 614	342	95	53	74	21 337	862	16.1	17.3	67.1
Humboldt	315	3 944	458	1 596	460	113	54	78	19 655	600	12.3	33.3	71.5
Ida	267	3 285	421	1 109	381	128	39	75	22 751	637	17.3	27.5	70.5
Iowa	519	9 196	521	5 172	1 243	116	57	241	26 227	976	17.2	18.8	55.6
Jackson	575	5 119	913	1 277	917	227	90	85	16 558	1 280	17.0	13.4	56.3
Jasper	852	13 041	1 467	4 812	1 757	321	597	324	24 818	1 204	21.3	25.4	60.4
Jefferson	685	8 048	714	1 973	1 363	270	620	215	26 736	765	16.3	17.1	55.0
Johnson	2 607	45 266	12 326	3 733	7 536	1 266	1 374	1 073	23 694	1 261	24.0	13.3	55.7
Jones	502	4 142	504	899	822	160	109	76	18 406	1 029	18.8	20.9	61.6
Keokuk	272	1 921	352	308	394	106	44	36	18 828	968	15.4	22.4	56.3
Kossuth	566	5 379	745	1 246	925	398	130	106	19 716	1 404	11.8	29.6	73.9
Lee	1 062	16 666	1 985	6 104	2 172	417	208	408	24 474	861	19.0	20.6	52.6
Linn	5 297	110 504	10 971	25 138	13 505	6 171	3 708	3 436	31 095	1 480	28.9	11.6	51.8
Louisa	222	2 586	263	1 269	232	90	46	53	20 341	593	16.9	23.3	56.0
Lucas	209	2 603	429	222	384	111	D	60	23 231	706	16.6	18.3	49.7
Lyon	354	2 473	395	422	464	116	93	42	17 135	1 149	20.5	18.9	68.8
Madison	337	2 705	619	468	477	131	95	50	18 450	986	18.6	19.3	46.2
Mahaska	594	6 375	752	986	1 199	230	107	126	19 798	1 022	15.2	21.4	61.9
Marion	778	15 918	2 360	7 144	1 538	245	162	424	26 640	971	20.2	18.3	45.5
Marshall	928	15 521	2 101	5 414	2 416	421	221	386	24 850	912	21.3	24.7	60.3
Mills	241	2 707	1 402	41	347	72	48	63	23 094	496	15.3	34.5	63.9
Mitchell	348	3 212	544	992	494	129	55	62	19 201	824	21.7	22.8	64.9
Monona	288	2 736	752	149	555	125	62	47	17 262	697	11.5	36.3	67.9
Monroe	212	2 655	486	1 054	356	D	31	58	21 791	691	12.4	19.0	50.9
Montgomery	349	4 664	788	1 416	591	213	77	92	19 672	577	13.0	31.2	68.8
Muscatine	996	19 834	1 726	7 508	2 265	389	856	584	29 441	783	25.4	17.9	55.6
O'Brien	559	5 264	1 181	817	977	221	112	94	17 905	977	13.8	26.4	73.1
Osceola	213	1 825	327	503	179	87	D	35	19 127	649	14.6	26.7	71.6
Page	507	6 714	1 218	2 325	1 043	161	146	151	22 514	845	16.1	26.7	58.1
Palo Alto	333	2 687	566	668	524	124	43	43	15 978	787	13.6	32.7	70.8
Plymouth	682	8 024	878	1 448	1 074	333	131	199	24 791	1 490	18.5	22.6	67.9
Pocahontas	278	2 424	409	765	278	103	65	48	19 965	778	9.8	37.1	77.1
Polk	11 307	229 586	28 006	19 757	29 468	36 579	11 667	6 936	30 211	800	36.9	18.0	46.4
Pottawattamie	1 896	28 219	3 656	3 833	5 784	593	796	622	22 056	1 325	21.2	30.6	67.4
Poweshiek	578	8 729	1 042	1 678	1 018	821	192	201	23 073	934	15.8	25.5	54.5
Ringgold	135	999	296	143	221	38	20	19	18 694	671	13.3	24.6	60.1
Sac	387	2 651	654	232	497	130	75	44	16 484	813	15.0	28.3	69.9
Scott	4 523	78 006	8 959	13 226	11 716	2 548	2 583	2 078	26 638	799	24.8	18.4	61.1
Shelby	411	4 457	828	402	660	176	107	79	17 797	921	14.0	26.6	75.0
Sioux	1 095	15 280	1 356	4 843	1 680	459	289	289	18 938	1 752	24.2	16.7	67.1
Story	1 842	26 903	3 996	3 894	5 008	765	2 065	611	22 714	946	23.4	25.4	56.7
Tama	400	4 689	451	974	641	141	60	90	19 253	1 152	18.1	22.3	60.5
Taylor	174	961	179	102	178	59	40	16	16 320	746	11.1	23.1	55.2
Union	354	4 530	924	972	833	137	93	89	19 723	671	19.8	21.0	50.5
Van Buren	179	1 590	327	684	168	67	43	33	20 795	807	13.8	19.2	48.5
Wapello	883	12 664	2 227	2 820	2 502	318	216	289	22 821	781	20.2	16.4	47.4
Warren	765	6 911	1 020	425	1 334	212	152	124	18 004	1 214	27.5	13.3	44.6
Washington	686	5 971	1 185	1 394	1 043	211	142	125	20 988	1 061	19.4	19.0	65.8
Wayne	197	1 508	320	444	240	61	46	25	16 768	729	12.2	27.2	56.5
Webster	1 219	16 687	2 617	2 106	3 249	536	375	398	23 866	937	15.3	30.5	71.0
Winnebago	354	7 342	594	4 095	548	166	62	180	24 499	607	20.8	28.2	65.1
Winneshiek	597	8 975	1 285	1 577	1 088	242	136	175	19 547	1 450	18.3	12.6	60.5
Woodbury	2 949	48 205	7 952	6 919	7 701	1 558	1 045	1 106	22 938	1 306	20.8	24.2	60.0
Worth	191	1 579	212	686	197	69	23	30	18 900	608	20.1	30.1	65.8
Wright	453	4 571	610	1 259	615	181	195	100	21 783	717	14.6	39.2	71.5
KANSAS	74 019	1 081 941	154 002	196 519	149 270	52 839	49 417	28 748	26 570	61 593	14.9	37.9	56.8
Allen	410	4 872	659	1 839	600	126	99	103	21 206	604	17.1	25.3	52.2
Anderson	241	1 515	300	228	234	99	38	24	15 556	688	15.4	33.3	55.8
Atchison	392	5 485	953	1 700	638	147	74	128	23 277	632	16.6	21.8	53.5

Table B. States and Counties — **Agriculture, Land, and Water**

STATE County	Land in farms — Acreage (1,000) [117]	Percent change, 1992–1997 [118]	Acres — Average size of farm [119]	Acres — Total irrigated (1,000) [120]	Acres — Total cropland (1,000) [121]	Value of land and buildings — Average per farm ($1,000) [122]	Value of land and buildings — Average per acre (dollars) [123]	Value of machinery and equipment Average per farm ($1,000) [124]	Value of products sold — Total (mil dol) [125]	Value of products sold — Average per farm (dollars) [126]	Percent from — Crops [127]	Percent from — Livestock and poultry products [128]	Percent of farms with sales of — $10,000 or more [129]	Percent of farms with sales of — $100,000 or more [130]	Percent of land owned by Fed. Gov. 1997 [131]	Water consumption 1995 (mil gal/day) [132]
IOWA—Cont'd																
Guthrie	304	-7.5	359	D	242	481	1 281	67	96	113 080	46.3	53.7	66.5	24.9	0.1	2.2
Hamilton	349	5.0	441	D	330	949	2 373	121	227	287 619	42.2	57.8	85.9	49.7	0.0	3.1
Hancock	334	1.5	393	0	315	829	2 121	107	141	165 679	61.2	38.8	84.3	46.4	0.1	3.6
Hardin	340	2.4	397	D	314	777	1 990	95	202	235 563	43.0	57.0	82.5	44.5	0.0	5.0
Harrison	393	-1.6	448	21	342	635	1 508	102	113	128 974	72.3	27.7	76.8	36.5	0.8	11.7
Henry	245	8.3	293	D	201	482	1 570	76	77	92 319	60.1	39.9	63.5	26.2	0.0	2.6
Howard	270	3.4	313	D	241	432	1 414	74	95	110 359	57.8	42.2	75.5	32.0	0.0	2.0
Humboldt	257	-8.4	429	D	245	924	2 284	137	101	167 533	72.2	27.8	89.3	50.8	0.0	3.6
Ida	253	-7.2	398	D	231	658	1 745	89	96	150 212	57.8	42.2	83.5	43.2	0.0	1.8
Iowa	332	3.4	340	0	272	472	1 406	73	105	107 443	51.0	49.0	67.1	28.2	2.8	3.4
Jackson	335	-3.5	262	0	234	297	1 254	57	97	75 515	27.7	72.3	66.2	22.7	1.6	8.5
Jasper	421	-2.4	349	D	366	540	1 605	73	154	127 776	58.0	42.0	73.3	36.2	0.9	7.5
Jefferson	228	0.4	298	D	178	328	1 175	51	58	75 190	60.9	39.1	59.6	20.8	0.0	2.5
Johnson	288	1.1	229	1	249	416	1 816	56	100	79 613	50.6	49.4	64.0	24.0	4.0	62.9
Jones	322	0.0	313	D	267	484	1 607	76	137	133 077	44.3	55.7	76.8	35.8	0.4	4.0
Keokuk	323	0.3	334	1	263	523	1 535	75	97	99 932	52.9	47.1	65.2	28.1	0.0	2.5
Kossuth	581	-5.5	414	1	548	885	2 216	109	243	172 917	62.9	37.1	91.2	51.7	0.2	3.4
Lee	257	-3.5	298	1	190	381	1 332	71	77	89 847	54.1	45.9	60.3	25.0	0.0	18.5
Linn	339	-2.8	229	0	292	526	2 347	60	113	76 662	66.2	33.8	60.6	20.8	0.0	259.9
Louisa	201	5.4	340	5	168	482	1 516	86	81	137 093	52.1	47.9	68.1	31.4	2.2	10.2
Lucas	227	3.7	322	D	157	246	732	43	29	41 602	46.1	53.9	51.3	10.3	1.6	1.4
Lyon	348	0.1	303	1	315	566	1 923	78	199	173 016	35.5	64.5	86.2	45.4	0.0	4.4
Madison	317	3.5	321	0	229	427	1 251	55	74	74 594	48.8	51.2	57.4	15.7	0.0	2.2
Mahaska	329	4.5	322	D	274	466	1 606	74	157	153 348	38.3	61.7	71.8	34.5	0.0	3.7
Marion	286	6.2	294	0	219	408	1 435	55	73	75 298	60.9	39.1	56.1	20.9	2.6	5.7
Marshall	319	2.0	350	0	290	663	2 029	82	118	128 992	67.6	32.4	71.9	34.9	0.0	11.1
Mills	232	-2.5	468	D	205	685	1 588	84	59	119 334	84.5	15.5	75.2	42.3	0.0	2.5
Mitchell	265	0.8	322	0	243	574	1 874	84	161	194 868	38.3	61.7	81.9	45.4	0.0	2.3
Monona	368	-6.5	527	41	317	692	1 317	89	101	144 267	67.1	32.9	80.5	40.7	0.0	12.2
Monroe	217	-3.0	314	D	151	254	827	43	39	56 907	37.0	63.0	60.1	12.4	0.0	1.3
Montgomery	243	1.1	421	D	209	535	1 227	93	83	143 157	56.9	43.1	72.6	34.5	0.0	1.9
Muscatine	219	-0.5	280	6	190	444	1 711	86	74	94 298	63.8	36.2	67.3	26.6	0.3	270.1
O'Brien	358	-1.0	367	D	330	795	2 253	109	180	184 274	49.7	50.3	93.9	51.2	0.0	3.7
Osceola	241	-7.8	371	1	222	729	1 829	102	140	215 627	39.9	60.1	90.4	47.5	0.0	2.8
Page	309	-3.1	366	0	260	402	1 150	69	79	93 986	65.7	34.3	72.2	30.5	0.0	3.1
Palo Alto	328	-3.3	416	4	306	791	1 962	91	156	197 925	52.5	47.5	84.5	48.9	0.1	2.9
Plymouth	512	-1.2	344	2	456	638	1 950	79	238	159 994	41.4	58.6	80.2	41.1	0.0	6.4
Pocahontas	357	-0.6	459	0	339	990	2 288	128	139	178 147	71.9	28.1	92.4	55.9	0.0	1.7
Polk	226	-1.9	282	0	201	603	2 052	74	71	89 026	86.2	13.8	57.9	24.2	3.6	56.5
Pottawattamie	537	-1.2	405	2	483	732	1 946	89	190	143 397	65.1	34.9	76.0	39.2	0.2	468.8
Poweshiek	335	-1.7	359	0	293	498	1 433	73	107	114 963	59.0	41.0	68.3	32.0	0.0	3.0
Ringgold	264	-10.0	393	D	210	274	741	55	49	72 526	38.2	61.8	60.4	14.3	0.0	1.3
Sac	345	-5.2	424	1	312	841	2 125	102	191	234 870	43.1	56.9	88.8	49.3	0.0	3.5
Scott	225	-3.3	282	1	206	852	2 797	102	95	119 029	64.9	35.1	74.8	34.3	0.9	100.8
Shelby	342	-3.3	372	0	315	609	1 627	80	133	144 237	57.5	42.5	87.6	42.9	0.0	2.6
Sioux	494	-0.5	282	8	453	662	2 445	93	508	289 932	21.7	78.3	89.6	53.3	0.0	15.6
Story	341	3.0	360	0	317	801	2 234	98	131	138 300	71.7	28.3	77.4	36.5	0.2	12.8
Tama	396	-1.4	344	0	348	609	1 911	77	128	110 952	67.5	32.5	72.7	32.7	1.1	4.8
Taylor	291	4.5	391	0	229	354	957	40	62	83 378	49.0	51.0	65.7	17.3	0.0	1.4
Union	225	-4.6	336	0	169	311	909	47	39	58 169	51.1	48.9	59.8	15.8	0.0	3.3
Van Buren	257	6.7	319	0	172	240	851	50	43	53 318	57.5	42.5	54.8	14.6	0.0	1.8
Wapello	208	6.8	267	0	160	355	1 392	63	45	57 112	65.0	35.0	46.0	16.1	0.0	20.2
Warren	300	-0.7	247	0	220	352	1 523	49	60	49 106	64.3	35.7	48.6	12.6	1.5	7.5
Washington	318	2.5	299	D	274	546	1 777	83	174	164 171	33.7	66.3	76.0	39.2	0.0	3.9
Wayne	286	1.2	393	D	219	253	630	48	37	50 157	59.3	40.7	62.0	14.4	1.0	0.9
Webster	413	1.1	440	0	386	1 070	2 330	112	166	177 436	68.0	32.0	85.9	45.1	0.0	8.8
Winnebago	242	4.1	398	0	227	718	1 814	109	78	129 088	81.7	18.3	77.1	43.0	0.1	1.9
Winneshiek	361	0.8	249	0	287	321	1 358	61	131	90 559	32.7	67.3	69.3	28.3	0.0	5.4
Woodbury	497	12.5	381	8	428	507	1 332	79	151	115 869	59.3	40.7	68.8	30.9	0.5	672.2
Worth	228	1.3	375	0	209	640	1 645	100	77	126 030	75.0	25.0	77.6	42.9	0.2	5.3
Wright	350	-1.2	488	D	330	1 056	2 226	137	175	244 136	54.7	45.3	85.4	51.6	0.2	3.3
KANSAS	46 089	-1.2	748	2 707	30 021	431	577	74	9 207	149 483	35.0	65.0	63.0	21.8	1.0	5 235.4
Allen	271	-4.2	449	D	182	316	698	51	33	54 688	65.7	34.3	54.8	12.9	0.0	2.9
Anderson	367	-3.2	533	1	242	312	558	59	53	77 407	57.1	42.9	62.1	19.3	0.0	1.7
Atchison	242	-1.2	383	D	178	342	932	54	36	56 420	66.5	33.5	62.3	15.5	0.0	5.9

Table B. States and Counties — Residential Construction, Wholesale and Retail Trade, and Real Estate

STATE County	Value of Residential Construction Authorized by Building Permits, 1999		Wholesale Trade, 1997				Retail Trade[1], 1997				Real Estate and Rental and Leasing, 1997			
	New Construction ($1,000)	Number of Housing Units	Number of Establishments	Number of Employees	Sales (mil dol)	Annual Payroll (mil dol)	Number of Establishments	Number of Employees	Sales (mil dol)	Annual Payroll (mil dol)	Number of Establishments	Number of Employees	Receipts (mil dol)	Annual Payroll (mil dol)
	133	134	135	136	137	138	139	140	141	142	143	144	145	146
IOWA—Cont'd														
Guthrie	7 051	68	14	121	70.6	2.1	53	359	57.9	5.0	11	31	2.1	0.4
Hamilton	1 985	27	36	D	D	D	82	747	90.8	9.0	11	28	1.3	0.2
Hancock	2 425	24	30	285	179.8	6.7	55	425	55.4	4.4	9	30	1.5	0.2
Hardin	4 921	66	63	1 095	554.5	31.5	114	1 097	151.0	13.6	14	46	2.3	0.5
Harrison	11 146	88	26	228	106.5	5.1	78	647	166.9	11.5	14	42	2.3	0.3
Henry	8 016	71	34	246	93.6	5.4	88	970	161.8	13.5	18	82	5.8	1.3
Howard	1 620	17	22	159	102.6	3.9	54	361	54.4	4.0	8	D	D	D
Humboldt	3 348	31	37	285	199.0	7.7	56	496	71.3	7.3	8	19	1.7	0.4
Ida	490	4	23	166	211.1	5.0	44	389	52.8	4.6	9	20	1.5	0.3
Iowa	3 680	53	28	217	112.4	4.8	164	1 250	153.6	14.7	4	3	0.8	0.1
Jackson	6 945	67	35	197	73.7	4.3	110	889	165.5	12.0	13	32	1.8	0.2
Jasper	14 625	114	47	465	465.2	11.3	175	1 703	232.3	25.2	21	73	4.5	0.6
Jefferson	7 590	132	50	275	78.3	6.6	107	1 165	279.2	38.5	14	29	1.9	0.4
Johnson	122 029	1 072	89	D	D	D	467	6 924	990.9	104.7	120	566	66.7	10.2
Jones	2 470	27	34	236	101.6	5.6	90	771	124.4	11.4	10	12	1.1	0.1
Keokuk	1 229	14	21	178	90.8	3.9	55	449	94.3	6.6	5	D	D	D
Kossuth	3 534	24	32	279	176.3	6.7	118	1 091	152.2	13.6	15	28	2.2	0.3
Lee	2 275	30	50	486	178.8	11.9	194	2 166	344.2	34.0	37	101	5.5	1.1
Linn	129 371	1 689	375	5 653	2 324.1	166.0	874	13 337	2 040.9	213.9	199	1 135	128.8	25.6
Louisa	3 084	36	14	185	70.9	5.1	39	256	45.7	3.6	6	D	D	D
Lucas	565	7	14	134	35.0	2.8	45	399	50.2	4.8	3	4	0.4	0.0
Lyon	3 901	34	24	243	133.7	5.7	62	476	63.8	5.5	3	D	D	D
Madison	14 413	152	15	89	62.8	2.3	61	522	82.8	7.1	11	26	1.7	0.2
Mahaska	5 167	91	43	374	192.8	10.3	114	1 246	190.8	17.1	21	57	3.8	0.5
Marion	31 104	321	42	510	98.6	7.2	156	1 519	243.1	22.4	23	78	5.4	0.9
Marshall	7 883	78	58	488	227.6	16.6	182	2 457	319.9	33.9	32	247	20.6	6.1
Mills	1 706	17	15	110	51.1	2.8	41	322	52.8	4.4	5	19	4.1	0.2
Mitchell	1 090	10	24	D	D	D	91	541	71.0	6.0	3	7	0.2	0.0
Monona	4 168	43	22	159	88.1	4.3	61	576	95.4	8.4	6	15	0.8	0.1
Monroe	1 918	20	11	73	20.9	1.4	43	363	51.7	4.7	1	D	D	D
Montgomery	1 841	14	30	214	151.3	5.1	68	581	82.8	7.4	6	14	0.7	0.2
Muscatine	11 845	141	63	381	264.1	10.1	177	2 390	337.6	34.5	36	140	11.4	2.4
O'Brien	2 306	18	41	367	201.1	8.9	111	976	169.5	14.0	7	28	3.1	0.6
Osceola	1 686	30	13	128	65.8	4.8	36	211	32.0	2.6	4	7	0.3	0.0
Page	843	9	26	223	87.4	5.0	108	1 185	148.5	14.3	11	42	6.8	1.0
Palo Alto	1 971	36	22	172	164.6	4.2	60	479	75.4	6.5	7	8	0.9	0.2
Plymouth	12 925	104	39	938	401.8	27.2	118	1 052	194.9	16.2	17	63	6.3	0.7
Pocahontas	1 571	32	18	277	197.4	6.8	46	301	43.4	3.4	5	9	0.5	0.1
Polk	362 814	2 977	901	D	D	D	1 680	28 123	4 454.0	461.4	456	3 433	584.7	84.4
Pottawattamie	40 318	406	101	D	D	D	382	5 742	978.5	87.1	63	D	D	D
Poweshiek	8 714	85	36	298	124.9	8.0	103	1 122	190.6	15.4	20	38	2.7	0.4
Ringgold	316	7	8	35	19.6	0.9	28	214	38.2	2.7	2	D	D	D
Sac	1 327	14	37	230	144.5	6.6	76	491	83.7	6.2	6	12	0.8	0.1
Scott	85 300	702	389	4 535	3 366.3	151.6	747	11 397	1 831.5	187.3	165	1 424	144.1	33.3
Shelby	3 653	33	27	D	D	D	80	645	117.4	9.6	5	18	0.9	0.1
Sioux	12 872	113	92	1 144	470.8	27.7	182	1 557	285.2	21.4	19	49	4.2	0.8
Story	53 115	837	95	772	321.2	21.7	359	4 729	631.3	65.8	68	366	24.4	5.6
Tama	3 294	32	31	221	215.9	4.9	90	646	90.8	8.1	8	22	1.3	0.2
Taylor	245	4	15	72	26.2	1.4	34	193	24.8	2.3	2	D	D	D
Union	362	4	24	318	108.9	5.6	72	800	114.6	11.5	22	63	5.3	1.1
Van Buren	581	10	8	69	35.2	0.5	34	154	19.8	1.9	3	5	0.4	0.1
Wapello	5 437	57	38	321	140.6	9.1	185	2 538	330.9	32.7	31	79	11.8	0.9
Warren	30 372	281	54	D	D	D	113	1 314	244.8	20.8	22	47	5.0	0.7
Washington	2 799	29	40	298	134.2	6.5	128	1 036	155.6	16.2	16	28	1.3	0.2
Wayne		0	17	130	53.5	2.2	38	252	31.6	3.5	1	D	D	D
Webster	7 553	76	71	885	710.2	31.4	252	3 142	438.7	44.9	47	168	13.3	2.4
Winnebago	6 015	70	17	D	D	D	74	573	81.6	6.2	7	15	1.0	0.1
Winneshiek	6 240	46	39	449	131.4	10.5	124	1 113	180.1	15.0	10	16	3.0	0.4
Woodbury	23 950	197	209	2 476	1 222.1	70.5	523	7 771	1 143.5	116.0	111	D	D	D
Worth	668	6	17	97	85.6	2.6	41	213	28.8	2.3	3	9	0.1	0.0
Wright	4 340	28	28	D	D	D	83	639	73.9	7.8	13	49	2.0	0.4
KANSAS	1 668 027	15 688	5 085	59 954	42 209.9	1 946.8	12 271	140 412	22 571.9	2 191.1	2 602	13 005	1 525.8	259.6
Allen	1 889	24	18	186	35.5	3.2	83	590	85.3	8.1	7	20	1.3	0.0
Anderson	2 030	14	12	77	48.4	1.4	38	207	43.0	2.9	3	9	0.3	0.0
Atchison	1 431	14	17	449	270.8	9.9	68	659	86.1	7.9	14	45	3.5	0.6

1. Establishments with payroll.

Table B. States and Counties — **Professional, Manufacturing, and Accommodation and Foodservices**

STATE County	Professional, Scientific, and Technical Services[1], 1997				Manufacturing, 1997				Accommodation and Foodservices, 1997			
	Number of Establishments	Number of Employees	Receipts (mil dol)	Annual Payroll (mil dol)	Number of Establishments	Number of Employees	Receipts (mil dol)	Annual Payroll (mil dol)	Number of Establishments	Number of Employees	Sales (mil dol)	Annual Payroll (mil dol)
	147	148	149	150	151	152	153	154	155	156	157	158
IOWA—Cont'd												
Guthrie	11	58	1.7	0.5	NA	NA	NA	NA	30	158	5.8	1.4
Hamilton	24	103	4.8	1.7	30	2 861	472.0	75.8	35	311	8.4	2.2
Hancock	12	33	1.5	0.4	27	1 126	221.2	29.7	22	199	3.9	0.9
Hardin	27	111	5.5	2.0	39	1 580	375.8	34.8	43	371	9.4	2.4
Harrison	12	36	1.5	0.6	NA	NA	NA	NA	30	318	8.6	2.5
Henry	24	94	4.5	2.0	34	2 839	717.4	85.2	44	612	16.7	4.5
Howard	15	45	2.5	0.9	20	1 405	177.7	29.2	29	D	D	D
Humboldt	13	40	2.5	0.7	28	1 257	159.7	31.8	21	210	4.5	1.3
Ida	12	28	1.8	0.5	9	1 112	165.0	32.5	22	D	D	D
Iowa	18	40	4.9	0.9	31	4 698	678.8	144.7	54	999	30.4	8.5
Jackson	26	74	3.6	0.9	34	1 208	194.5	25.7	58	515	11.4	2.6
Jasper	41	586	124.4	13.1	46	3 702	740.0	132.4	74	961	25.9	7.3
Jefferson	122	538	51.0	20.9	37	1 751	256.6	56.4	41	365	10.7	2.7
Johnson	164	1 085	81.9	29.3	89	3 639	2 510.4	121.1	271	5 496	144.3	40.8
Jones	21	78	4.5	1.5	23	889	170.1	23.5	37	366	7.7	1.9
Keokuk	7	25	0.8	0.3	NA	NA	NA	NA	20	86	1.7	0.5
Kossuth	23	89	5.6	1.3	30	1 126	207.3	33.7	42	417	9.2	2.2
Lee	50	182	11.7	3.4	70	6 397	1 671.5	209.0	108	1 257	33.0	8.8
Linn	369	2 936	268.6	106.7	239	22 877	6 376.1	935.0	439	7 853	240.1	68.2
Louisa	10	40	1.5	0.5	11	D	D	D	27	191	4.0	1.0
Lucas	9	23	1.0	0.3	NA	NA	NA	NA	18	148	3.5	0.8
Lyon	15	80	5.8	2.6	NA	NA	NA	NA	26	D	D	D
Madison	19	65	3.8	1.5	NA	NA	NA	NA	21	154	4.8	1.3
Mahaska	24	98	6.5	2.9	26	1 020	230.6	26.3	43	656	15.6	4.3
Marion	35	144	7.9	3.1	44	6 687	1 388.5	229.8	59	900	20.5	5.4
Marshall	50	201	13.4	4.9	44	5 363	1 413.2	174.0	86	1 070	29.7	8.4
Mills	9	43	2.1	0.8	NA	NA	NA	NA	23	221	5.7	1.6
Mitchell	7	37	1.7	0.6	16	1 021	186.3	27.4	21	D	D	D
Monona	15	53	3.5	1.1	NA	NA	NA	NA	36	267	6.4	1.6
Monroe	11	26	1.5	0.3	18	863	593.2	32.8	18	D	D	D
Montgomery	19	48	2.7	1.1	11	1 365	185.0	32.4	32	291	7.0	1.8
Muscatine	53	1 020	75.8	22.7	70	6 523	2 631.1	252.7	85	1 057	29.3	8.0
O'Brien	25	76	5.1	1.4	NA	NA	NA	NA	44	392	8.1	1.9
Osceola	7	35	1.7	0.3	NA	NA	NA	NA	14	117	2.3	0.5
Page	19	143	3.7	1.5	27	2 271	477.3	78.0	41	466	10.1	3.1
Palo Alto	12	31	2.1	0.5	NA	NA	NA	NA	30	D	D	D
Plymouth	29	108	5.6	2.0	26	D	D	D	57	D	D	D
Pocahontas	19	46	2.4	0.7	19	821	91.8	20.3	25	179	3.0	0.8
Polk	954	10 594	845.8	346.1	410	19 790	5 054.9	688.6	897	17 068	534.4	156.1
Pottawattamie	99	656	47.0	16.4	59	4 109	888.7	113.2	197	3 782	186.1	48.4
Poweshiek	33	115	7.2	2.0	32	1 533	226.6	42.7	43	677	13.2	4.1
Ringgold	3	10	0.3	0.1	NA	NA	NA	NA	9	64	1.3	0.3
Sac	20	65	3.3	1.0	NA	NA	NA	NA	25	207	3.9	1.1
Scott	315	1 999	177.4	58.0	210	11 845	4 614.8	478.3	378	8 050	234.2	70.0
Shelby	19	80	3.8	1.5	NA	NA	NA	NA	34	343	7.4	2.1
Sioux	43	192	12.7	4.2	67	4 610	822.0	104.6	71	1 098	19.8	5.0
Story	148	970	97.9	34.7	75	3 577	988.6	108.4	202	3 598	89.1	24.5
Tama	15	48	2.4	0.5	14	911	236.1	22.5	33	311	7.8	1.8
Taylor	10	26	1.1	0.4	NA	NA	NA	NA	11	77	1.4	0.3
Union	18	64	3.2	1.6	19	1 031	113.2	24.6	28	379	10.0	2.7
Van Buren	11	31	1.4	0.7	14	653	54.4	14.8	10	83	2.0	0.3
Wapello	45	206	12.9	4.2	22	2 701	741.8	92.5	85	1 076	29.8	7.8
Warren	35	108	6.2	2.0	NA	NA	NA	NA	58	809	18.3	5.1
Washington	33	133	5.8	1.7	32	1 441	196.2	41.2	42	506	10.8	3.1
Wayne	8	28	2.2	0.3	13	D	D	D	17	99	1.7	0.4
Webster	69	319	22.8	8.5	60	2 554	1 110.9	81.7	93	1 322	37.1	10.5
Winnebago	19	83	4.8	1.4	13	4 006	640.5	105.5	28	259	6.2	1.4
Winneshiek	21	90	5.6	2.6	29	1 453	215.0	38.0	51	573	14.5	4.0
Woodbury	178	946	73.6	23.9	113	D	D	D	246	3 812	109.2	29.9
Worth	6	18	0.8	0.1	12	596	49.2	12.5	9	D	D	D
Wright	27	173	8.8	2.5	25	1 318	546.5	39.2	40	292	7.3	1.8
KANSAS	5 345	39 534	3 559.3	1 396.0	3 309	193 742	46 296.4	6 532.5	5 677	91 173	2 685.7	757.1
Allen	25	94	4.5	1.8	28	1 722	277.3	45.7	38	534	13.7	4.1
Anderson	12	28	1.9	0.4	NA	NA	NA	NA	22	206	4.9	1.1
Atchison	16	48	2.7	1.0	24	1 753	360.1	53.7	32	340	8.2	2.2

1. Firms subject to federal tax.

Table B. States and Counties — Health and Other Services and Federal Funds

STATE County	Health Care and Social Assistance[1], 1997				Other Services[1], 1997				Federal funds and grants, fiscal 1999[2] Expenditures (mil dol)			
									Total	Direct payments for individuals[3]		
	Number of Establishments	Number of Employees	Receipts (mil dol)	Annual Payroll (mil dol)	Number of Establishments	Number of Employees	Receipts (mil dol)	Annual Payroll (mil dol)		Social Security and government retirement	Medicare	Food stamps and Supplemental Security Income
	159	160	161	162	163	164	165	166	167	168	169	170
IOWA—Cont'd												
Guthrie	17	36	2.6	0.6	13	36	2.2	0.5	57.7	26.9	9.2	0.8
Hamilton	30	292	14.8	7.3	23	86	5.9	1.2	76.5	34.4	14.3	1.3
Hancock	11	244	7.8	3.7	29	71	4.2	1.1	56.9	25.2	8.6	0.6
Hardin	24	257	8.9	4.0	41	103	7.0	1.5	103.8	47.3	16.6	1.6
Harrison	14	289	10.0	5.4	23	49	4.2	0.8	79.7	34.4	13.5	1.5
Henry	38	487	18.0	8.1	31	93	6.8	1.1	90.8	38.0	11.8	1.6
Howard	13	182	5.0	2.9	16	32	3.6	0.5	48.3	19.9	7.7	0.7
Humboldt	14	199	6.9	2.9	21	52	4.9	1.0	55.6	25.0	9.1	0.8
Ida	15	192	7.0	3.0	18	50	2.4	0.6	41.7	18.1	6.3	0.3
Iowa	22	244	8.4	4.1	22	73	4.2	1.2	65.4	30.2	10.2	0.6
Jackson	34	424	14.4	6.7	43	114	9.4	1.6	95.4	41.3	15.9	2.0
Jasper	42	664	22.5	12.4	58	198	11.9	3.1	140.7	72.0	25.3	2.5
Jefferson	37	466	17.7	8.4	30	78	5.5	1.2	60.5	25.3	9.9	1.8
Johnson	181	1 907	97.5	41.4	152	767	43.3	12.5	532.8	115.3	33.6	5.0
Jones	22	299	12.1	5.0	34	91	5.7	1.2	75.5	35.7	11.8	1.0
Keokuk	12	201	5.5	2.7	15	29	2.4	0.4	69.2	27.7	10.7	1.0
Kossuth	24	321	7.9	2.7	43	106	6.6	1.4	95.5	38.9	12.8	1.4
Lee	87	1 008	40.8	18.4	68	308	18.4	4.6	157.2	79.3	32.6	4.3
Linn	340	3 925	267.5	138.3	350	2 296	143.5	43.3	962.9	320.4	95.0	15.7
Louisa	10	193	5.6	2.7	11	31	1.7	0.3	51.3	21.4	6.4	0.9
Lucas	15	78	4.0	1.8	5	15	1.3	0.3	47.6	22.1	7.6	1.4
Lyon	16	113	4.6	1.8	26	59	4.6	1.0	51.3	22.9	7.7	0.4
Madison	17	305	8.4	4.4	24	53	3.0	0.7	52.2	25.2	10.3	0.8
Mahaska	28	249	11.2	5.5	46	143	10.3	2.0	95.7	42.3	14.9	2.4
Marion	41	479	16.6	7.6	56	208	10.5	2.9	155.4	72.5	20.0	2.4
Marshall	60	612	35.9	17.4	57	250	15.0	3.9	190.5	87.2	25.1	4.4
Mills	14	452	8.5	5.6	29	163	9.4	2.8	67.1	29.1	10.8	1.3
Mitchell	15	97	6.0	2.6	26	95	5.1	1.2	55.7	26.6	9.6	0.5
Monona	17	448	13.9	7.4	21	51	3.9	0.8	66.1	25.7	12.3	1.2
Monroe	12	144	4.2	2.0	10	29	1.6	0.4	43.1	19.7	8.5	0.9
Montgomery	18	231	12.9	4.5	31	76	6.0	1.2	60.6	28.3	12.7	0.7
Muscatine	60	606	28.7	14.8	61	296	17.6	5.5	147.3	73.5	22.0	4.4
O'Brien	33	275	11.2	4.8	45	146	8.5	1.9	78.9	35.4	12.7	0.9
Osceola	11	150	4.4	1.9	14	41	2.6	0.5	35.5	14.7	5.5	0.3
Page	33	569	26.0	10.3	41	105	7.7	1.7	82.5	40.2	14.5	1.9
Palo Alto	24	304	10.3	4.7	16	31	1.8	0.5	63.9	24.8	9.2	0.9
Plymouth	35	436	15.6	7.5	48	176	12.5	2.5	97.8	44.3	15.3	1.1
Pocahontas	17	190	6.1	2.9	17	26	1.8	0.4	56.0	22.4	9.1	0.7
Polk	766	9 160	632.7	311.0	674	4 664	294.6	90.9	3 064.3	631.8	208.3	39.5
Pottawattamie	103	1 322	74.8	41.9	142	684	43.8	12.5	791.2	176.4	60.3	10.9
Poweshiek	39	328	18.8	8.1	30	91	6.1	1.6	78.7	38.8	13.9	1.2
Ringgold	7	149	4.4	1.8	9	23	1.9	0.4	32.0	12.4	4.7	0.7
Sac	14	178	6.6	3.0	27	75	4.2	1.1	61.9	28.7	10.2	0.7
Scott	324	3 126	236.5	111.7	296	2 042	115.7	37.8	610.1	309.1	83.5	23.8
Shelby	19	218	6.7	3.1	29	79	5.4	0.9	72.6	28.6	13.7	1.5
Sioux	50	356	16.7	7.4	75	233	18.9	3.9	117.4	50.9	17.7	1.3
Story	91	1 545	88.0	47.2	107	617	33.9	9.3	359.5	108.0	35.7	3.5
Tama	18	247	7.9	3.8	27	93	6.1	0.9	86.6	38.0	13.5	1.1
Taylor	7	107	2.6	1.2	10	26	1.4	0.3	41.2	16.2	6.1	0.7
Union	17	283	11.1	5.7	20	86	8.3	1.8	63.7	28.9	10.1	1.7
Van Buren	5	9	0.5	0.1	10	13	1.8	0.2	38.8	18.0	6.8	0.9
Wapello	66	723	45.9	22.9	62	284	15.7	4.0	182.3	87.2	32.5	7.3
Warren	49	532	22.3	8.9	48	140	9.1	2.0	109.5	60.1	18.6	1.7
Washington	39	486	16.6	7.8	36	120	11.3	2.0	88.4	44.0	14.8	1.6
Wayne	7	82	2.9	1.3	14	38	2.2	0.6	45.2	17.0	7.7	0.9
Webster	85	809	53.3	25.5	80	448	24.0	7.2	199.8	90.9	35.1	5.1
Winnebago	22	236	8.6	3.8	18	37	3.2	0.6	57.1	25.7	9.1	0.6
Winneshiek	28	219	13.0	5.2	40	102	6.5	1.5	82.5	33.9	11.7	0.9
Woodbury	223	2 111	186.1	89.6	181	1 319	66.4	21.2	443.9	190.2	70.9	11.6
Worth	6	31	1.4	0.9	7	17	1.7	0.3	38.8	16.7	6.2	0.5
Wright	20	310	10.2	4.5	22	91	3.5	0.8	81.6	36.3	13.3	1.0
KANSAS	4 793	66 613	4 116.1	1 771.8	4 604	24 081	1 548.4	452.9	14 447.0	5 069.9	1 876.8	243.5
Allen	28	312	9.1	4.4	24	94	6.3	1.6	68.8	32.0	12.1	1.9
Anderson	14	152	4.7	2.2	14	31	2.4	0.4	37.9	19.9	7.7	0.4
Atchison	35	230	12.8	5.9	23	82	4.7	1.5	74.2	34.3	14.4	2.0

1. Firms subject to federal tax.　　2. October 1, 1998 to September 30, 1999.　　3. State totals may include programs not allocated by county.

STATE County	Federal funds and grants, fiscal 1999[1] (cont'd)							Local government finances, 1997				
	Expenditures (mil dol) (cont'd)							General revenue				
	Procurement contract awards			Grants[2]							Taxes	
											Per capita[3] (dollars)	
	Salaries and wages	Defense	Other	Medicaid and other health-related	Nutrition and family welfare	Education	Other	Total (mil dol)	Intergovern-mental (mil dol)	Total (mil dol)	Total	Property
	171	172	173	174	175	176	177	178	179	180	181	182
IOWA—Cont'd												
Guthrie	2.6	0.1	0.6	4.4	1.0	0.3	0.2	28.5	11.9	10.3	897	881
Hamilton	2.7	0.0	0.7	4.9	1.2	0.3	1.1	50.9	15.6	15.9	988	953
Hancock	2.4	0.0	0.6	2.1	0.8	0.2	0.0	30.7	12.6	11.1	922	853
Hardin	4.2	0.0	8.0	6.3	1.7	0.5	1.0	53.1	18.2	17.5	946	860
Harrison	4.0	0.0	0.8	6.0	1.5	0.5	3.3	47.1	17.9	14.6	949	893
Henry	3.5	0.0	0.9	5.6	1.3	0.7	14.6	54.3	19.3	15.2	760	667
Howard	1.7	0.4	0.4	4.8	0.9	0.3	0.0	27.8	11.5	9.5	975	865
Humboldt	2.7	0.0	0.6	3.2	0.8	0.4	0.4	27.2	9.4	9.4	905	888
Ida	1.7	0.0	0.4	2.3	0.6	0.2	0.3	16.8	7.6	6.5	816	793
Iowa	3.3	0.0	0.8	3.0	0.8	0.2	1.9	35.0	13.8	13.3	860	697
Jackson	3.6	0.0	0.8	9.0	2.0	0.7	7.4	48.1	19.0	13.8	688	598
Jasper	5.4	0.5	1.5	9.7	2.8	0.6	2.1	101.0	37.4	30.0	840	794
Jefferson	4.6	0.1	0.8	6.5	1.1	0.4	0.4	35.6	11.4	10.6	621	589
Johnson	63.8	1.0	112.8	137.9	4.6	5.3	29.6	199.1	69.1	84.8	829	768
Jones	2.7	0.0	1.1	5.2	1.6	0.5	1.0	34.1	16.2	13.0	639	612
Keokuk	3.0	0.0	0.8	5.1	0.9	0.4	3.0	26.7	12.4	9.6	834	808
Kossuth	4.1	0.0	1.2	6.5	1.0	0.5	0.4	43.5	14.6	15.0	837	788
Lee	6.5	0.4	1.4	13.0	4.2	1.6	5.3	83.1	39.5	30.9	798	670
Linn	55.1	308.2	38.5	51.7	19.4	5.2	27.8	464.3	173.9	175.0	963	924
Louisa	2.5	0.1	4.6	4.2	1.3	0.3	0.1	38.9	15.2	11.4	959	945
Lucas	2.1	0.0	0.4	6.0	1.2	0.4	0.6	25.6	8.5	6.6	727	701
Lyon	1.7	0.1	0.5	3.0	0.7	0.4	0.2	24.8	11.8	8.8	739	687
Madison	2.2	0.0	0.5	4.6	1.0	0.4	0.1	34.5	13.7	10.1	733	710
Mahaska	3.8	0.0	1.0	9.5	2.1	0.5	4.2	52.4	18.5	17.2	787	709
Marion	30.8	1.9	1.5	10.0	2.2	1.6	2.5	56.2	26.6	21.2	679	649
Marshall	6.6	0.3	21.2	14.3	3.4	1.3	10.4	104.6	47.9	35.0	903	888
Mills	2.8	0.0	0.7	6.9	1.2	0.3	4.6	27.8	13.9	10.9	757	744
Mitchell	2.0	0.0	0.5	3.0	0.6	0.4	0.0	31.2	10.1	9.3	838	760
Monona	2.5	0.0	0.6	6.7	1.2	0.5	0.8	22.8	10.9	9.0	901	811
Monroe	1.5	0.0	0.3	5.3	1.0	0.4	0.5	20.7	8.4	5.4	676	669
Montgomery	3.0	0.0	0.6	4.6	1.1	0.3	0.4	38.9	12.0	9.9	829	807
Muscatine	6.1	6.9	3.2	10.2	5.0	1.4	4.1	119.7	37.6	37.2	903	782
O'Brien	3.4	0.0	0.8	7.4	0.9	0.5	0.9	43.0	18.0	13.9	930	865
Osceola	1.4	0.0	0.3	1.9	0.4	0.2	0.1	13.1	5.8	5.3	756	727
Page	3.6	0.0	0.9	8.5	1.7	0.8	0.7	42.1	16.9	13.6	794	713
Palo Alto	2.1	0.0	0.5	6.5	3.2	0.4	1.3	32.0	12.3	9.7	964	936
Plymouth	4.9	0.7	0.9	5.4	2.7	0.6	1.8	55.5	20.8	17.3	702	688
Pocahontas	2.2	0.0	0.5	3.0	0.7	0.3	0.3	21.4	8.1	7.2	817	804
Polk	300.9	22.8	75.8	174.3	177.6	93.1	289.7	1 055.8	352.4	401.6	1 134	1 079
Pottawattamie	11.9	0.0	2.6	39.6	10.0	3.2	10.9	214.5	94.2	76.5	896	754
Poweshiek	2.7	0.0	0.7	4.2	1.2	0.4	0.5	35.1	15.2	12.8	672	661
Ringgold	1.6	0.0	0.4	3.0	0.7	0.3	0.3	19.8	8.5	5.1	960	950
Sac	2.3	0.1	0.5	3.0	1.0	0.4	0.0	24.8	12.1	9.6	811	805
Scott	55.3	15.1	12.7	51.1	22.3	6.0	7.4	405.3	165.7	152.0	966	831
Shelby	2.6	0.0	0.6	6.0	3.3	0.4	0.6	41.0	14.8	12.1	922	903
Sioux	4.7	0.0	2.7	12.7	1.4	0.6	0.8	66.1	21.7	20.4	657	598
Story	43.4	6.6	32.4	19.7	5.6	3.9	71.8	229.1	55.9	62.2	834	724
Tama	4.0	0.0	0.9	6.3	1.6	0.6	1.9	37.9	19.4	13.7	779	754
Taylor	1.9	0.0	0.5	3.9	1.0	0.4	1.0	16.1	8.7	5.0	695	647
Union	4.0	0.0	0.8	7.6	2.3	0.8	0.3	53.8	23.2	10.5	846	838
Van Buren	2.0	0.0	0.5	2.9	0.7	0.5	0.2	22.0	9.4	5.2	659	633
Wapello	7.1	0.0	3.0	25.6	6.6	2.0	2.2	108.1	51.1	30.0	849	831
Warren	5.4	0.0	1.2	7.7	2.4	0.8	0.8	72.8	35.8	25.8	649	631
Washington	3.6	0.0	0.8	5.7	1.3	0.5	0.8	50.8	18.7	15.9	763	737
Wayne	2.0	0.0	0.5	6.2	1.0	0.4	0.8	18.8	7.9	4.4	643	625
Webster	15.9	3.5	2.4	17.5	5.6	1.6	0.7	101.2	45.7	34.9	904	883
Winnebago	2.3	0.0	0.6	4.9	0.8	0.3	0.1	30.4	14.1	11.3	938	877
Winneshiek	4.1	0.1	0.8	4.8	3.0	1.4	3.5	67.1	24.1	17.1	819	720
Woodbury	44.9	15.0	6.4	42.1	14.7	5.4	18.3	261.2	120.8	90.1	882	809
Worth	1.7	0.0	0.5	2.3	0.5	0.2	0.2	14.2	6.3	6.3	809	799
Wright	4.1	0.0	0.9	4.9	1.2	0.3	2.2	42.9	15.6	16.2	1 144	1 123
KANSAS	1 752.4	939.3	323.9	884.4	424.1	254.8	619.4	X	X	X	X	X
Allen	3.4	0.0	0.5	9.5	1.6	0.6	1.1	34.1	16.2	11.4	786	637
Anderson	1.8	0.0	0.4	1.8	0.6	0.2	0.1	16.3	7.1	6.5	812	758
Atchison	2.7	1.8	1.0	6.1	2.2	1.0	1.5	32.0	14.6	12.0	734	565

1. October 1, 1998 to September 30, 1999. 2. State totals may include programs not allocated by county. 3. Based on the resident population estimated as of July 1 of the year shown.

Table B. States and Counties — Local Government Finances, Government Employment, and Elections

STATE County	Local government finances, 1997 (cont'd)									Government employment, 1998			Presidential election, 2000		
	Direct general expenditure							Debt outstanding					Percent of vote cast —		
			Percent of total for —												
	Total (mil dol)	Per capita[1] (dollars)	Education	Health and hospitals	Police protection	Public welfare	Highways	Total (mil dol)	Per capita[1] (dollars)	Federal civilian	Federal military	State and local	Democratic	Republican	All other
	183	184	185	186	187	188	189	190	191	192	193	194	195	196	197
IOWA—Cont'd															
Guthrie	28.3	2 474	48.7	17.0	2.7	1.9	12.2	12.3	1 079	63	55	739	45.6	51.9	2.5
Hamilton	53.6	3 337	43.7	26.5	3.1	0.7	8.3	21.7	1 354	61	75	1 221	45.0	52.4	2.6
Hancock	29.6	2 461	43.7	18.4	4.3	2.5	13.8	7.1	593	53	57	706	41.9	54.9	3.1
Hardin	52.9	2 857	42.4	20.7	2.9	0.3	9.6	18.5	1 000	82	87	1 726	44.3	53.2	2.5
Harrison	46.9	3 056	43.9	24.0	2.9	1.0	9.9	19.9	1 297	85	72	810	39.0	58.1	2.9
Henry	54.3	2 721	40.1	28.7	3.2	0.4	9.1	29.3	1 469	71	94	1 699	45.1	51.6	3.3
Howard	27.3	2 813	45.4	21.6	2.9	0.3	11.6	9.1	934	39	46	759	54.0	42.8	3.2
Humboldt	26.7	2 569	42.2	25.1	3.7	0.5	12.2	3.7	355	62	49	688	39.5	57.6	2.9
Ida	18.9	2 379	52.7	3.0	5.3	3.0	17.0	5.9	747	40	37	441	40.4	56.4	3.2
Iowa	33.9	2 189	47.2	17.3	4.2	1.9	15.3	15.5	999	69	73	884	43.6	52.5	3.9
Jackson	47.0	2 339	45.6	23.9	3.2	1.0	7.9	10.2	505	87	95	1 160	54.7	41.7	3.5
Jasper	99.0	2 772	37.1	30.4	3.5	2.5	7.5	40.3	1 130	111	169	2 515	48.8	48.9	2.3
Jefferson	34.9	2 053	36.7	33.6	4.4	0.4	9.4	9.7	567	86	81	1 019	37.9	43.0	19.0
Johnson	217.3	2 124	38.7	3.8	4.5	3.4	13.1	200.7	1 961	1 585	507	25 901	59.1	33.9	7.0
Jones	35.5	1 751	58.2	7.5	3.2	1.7	11.2	23.3	1 148	61	96	1 297	51.3	45.9	2.8
Keokuk	25.4	2 208	56.5	11.8	2.7	0.2	13.7	10.2	884	64	54	543	44.1	52.0	3.9
Kossuth	42.7	2 386	39.3	24.2	3.1	1.9	15.2	6.3	352	81	84	1 092	44.6	51.9	3.4
Lee	76.9	1 991	48.1	9.2	5.8	1.4	11.0	47.9	1 240	111	217	2 255	58.1	38.3	3.6
Linn	450.7	2 480	51.4	4.5	6.3	1.2	6.9	272.4	1 499	1 099	869	10 292	53.1	43.9	3.0
Louisa	38.2	3 202	45.1	4.9	3.0	0.6	7.7	129.1	10 815	61	56	670	49.5	47.6	2.9
Lucas	24.9	2 750	34.9	36.1	2.9	0.6	10.8	12.5	1 377	40	43	689	44.9	52.6	2.5
Lyon	28.6	2 391	62.3	2.9	1.7	0.2	14.9	7.6	635	45	57	566	24.6	73.3	2.1
Madison	35.7	2 598	49.1	24.6	3.0	0.4	9.4	24.3	1 769	52	65	783	44.4	52.5	3.1
Mahaska	54.6	2 503	34.2	25.1	2.6	1.1	11.3	29.5	1 354	78	103	1 106	35.3	62.6	2.1
Marion	60.8	1 946	62.0	3.5	4.6	0.7	10.4	46.2	1 477	897	148	1 462	39.8	58.0	2.1
Marshall	105.8	2 727	63.1	1.7	3.9	5.5	6.7	46.3	1 194	138	183	3 080	47.2	49.8	2.9
Mills	26.0	1 807	59.5	6.5	4.1	0.9	10.8	4.8	334	53	68	1 555	34.5	62.3	3.2
Mitchell	29.3	2 649	38.6	28.1	3.7	1.2	11.5	6.6	601	50	52	639	51.3	46.3	2.4
Monona	22.6	2 260	46.2	3.7	4.6	0.4	17.9	2.4	235	55	48	609	45.7	50.5	3.7
Monroe	20.3	2 525	36.3	27.8	3.7	0.8	16.1	10.0	1 244	35	38	493	46.6	50.9	2.5
Montgomery	35.1	2 949	33.2	35.3	3.0	0.1	12.1	11.3	950	60	56	925	34.1	63.3	2.6
Muscatine	110.6	2 685	40.5	24.4	4.4	0.9	4.7	177.0	4 296	124	194	2 819	50.1	46.5	3.3
O'Brien	41.1	2 756	58.7	9.0	2.0	0.4	11.8	12.9	865	65	70	1 085	30.8	66.4	2.8
Osceola	12.8	1 823	43.7	4.6	7.9	0.5	17.3	2.3	332	31	33	323	29.8	67.4	2.8
Page	45.6	2 664	43.1	18.0	4.0	0.3	10.8	19.4	1 131	73	81	1 425	32.5	65.0	2.5
Palo Alto	37.4	3 715	47.1	18.3	2.3	0.6	17.4	5.7	569	51	47	1 000	48.2	48.5	3.2
Plymouth	58.3	2 366	43.5	19.1	2.7	3.0	12.4	25.7	1 041	80	117	1 253	34.6	61.2	4.2
Pocahontas	21.7	2 460	41.5	21.5	4.2	1.2	13.4	4.6	522	46	41	641	41.9	54.1	3.9
Polk	1 021.4	2 884	46.5	10.4	4.8	1.3	5.0	904.5	2 553	5 867	2 015	25 390	51.5	45.9	2.6
Pottawattamie	228.0	2 670	61.2	2.5	4.4	0.3	6.8	107.5	1 258	222	407	4 751	42.7	54.5	2.8
Poweshiek	35.8	1 884	55.1	4.0	3.9	0.8	13.6	19.9	1 050	65	89	921	47.0	49.0	4.0
Ringgold	19.4	3 634	36.4	28.8	1.5	0.4	14.7	2.0	370	36	25	455	46.3	50.9	2.9
Sac	23.0	1 933	58.4	7.6	4.2	0.3	14.4	4.5	376	54	56	707	41.7	55.2	3.1
Scott	413.7	2 628	55.2	3.5	2.9	0.8	9.0	317.1	2 014	1 057	749	7 476	50.8	46.5	2.7
Shelby	40.9	3 121	38.8	26.5	2.7	0.2	12.7	22.6	1 726	59	61	909	36.3	60.8	2.9
Sioux	72.0	2 316	44.3	22.3	2.9	0.3	9.6	38.2	1 230	106	147	1 711	14.6	83.3	2.1
Story	220.0	2 950	31.5	38.3	3.4	0.7	7.2	136.1	1 825	974	389	17 987	49.4	45.9	4.7
Tama	37.3	2 116	56.4	5.5	4.5	0.5	17.2	9.8	554	88	84	944	48.6	48.5	2.8
Taylor	15.9	2 229	51.0	3.2	3.5	4.6	18.1	4.7	659	47	34	445	40.3	57.2	2.6
Union	56.8	4 554	46.9	26.1	2.3	0.1	5.5	12.4	992	88	59	1 182	44.3	52.3	3.4
Van Buren	24.6	3 141	33.9	39.8	2.3	0.8	11.7	4.8	611	45	37	600	40.4	56.6	2.9
Wapello	117.1	3 311	64.1	4.7	2.4	0.3	6.3	74.5	2 106	145	167	2 615	55.2	41.7	3.1
Warren	76.7	1 932	61.3	3.8	3.6	0.7	8.7	48.5	1 222	116	189	1 727	48.4	49.0	2.6
Washington	48.0	2 302	43.7	26.1	3.4	0.4	10.7	15.8	758	74	99	1 238	43.2	53.1	3.7
Wayne	19.5	2 855	40.5	28.9	2.5	0.2	12.3	6.1	896	44	31	506	43.0	55.1	1.8
Webster	107.2	2 777	63.7	5.9	3.0	0.9	7.6	31.6	818	296	184	2 586	49.7	47.9	2.3
Winnebago	28.5	2 360	60.5	4.6	5.2	1.7	10.2	15.8	1 312	53	56	734	48.7	48.2	3.1
Winneshiek	68.2	3 266	53.5	20.7	2.2	0.5	10.7	24.5	1 173	91	99	1 703	46.1	49.3	4.6
Woodbury	273.1	2 675	50.4	2.3	4.5	0.9	6.8	169.0	1 656	820	488	5 350	46.7	49.8	3.5
Worth	13.9	1 787	46.6	5.9	3.3	3.4	26.5	6.5	840	39	37	346	55.1	41.4	3.4
Wright	42.0	2 963	45.4	18.4	2.9	0.2	13.2	13.0	916	76	66	944	44.1	53.4	2.5
KANSAS	X	X	X	X	X	X	X	X	X	26 060	29 108	215 634	37.2	58.0	4.7
Allen	32.7	2 263	64.3	1.6	2.3	0.0	5.2	17.9	1 236	65	71	1 494	37.0	58.6	4.4
Anderson	15.3	1 904	55.9	1.9	3.6	0.0	9.8	16.3	2 032	38	39	550	38.2	57.0	4.8
Atchison	31.2	1 909	52.5	5.8	5.2	0.0	7.9	19.8	1 216	56	83	1 157	46.0	49.0	5.1

1. Based on the resident population estimated as of July 1 of the year shown.

STATE/ County code	MSA/ PMSA/ NECMA code[1]	County Type[2]	STATE County	Land area,[3] (sq km) 1990	Population and population characteristics, 1999													
								Race (percent)					Age (percent)					
					Total persons	Rank	Per square kilometer	White	Black	Am. Indian, Eskimo, Aleut	Asian and Pacific Islander	Percent Hispanic[4]	Under 5 years	5 to 17 years	18 to 24 years	25 to 34 years	35 to 44 years	45 to 54 years
				1	2	3	4	5	6	7	8	9	10	11	12	13	14	15
			KANSAS—Cont'd															
20 007	...	9	Barber	2 938	5 240	2 822	1.8	99.3	0.2	0.5	0.1	1.8	6.0	20.1	5.6	10.5	14.1	12.1
20 009	...	7	Barton	2 316	28 658	1 424	12.4	97.8	1.3	0.5	0.5	4.2	6.8	19.4	7.8	11.5	14.3	12.5
20 011	...	7	Bourbon	1 650	14 980	2 065	9.1	96.1	3.3	0.4	0.2	0.9	6.5	19.1	9.1	9.9	14.4	12.8
20 013	...	7	Brown	1 478	10 930	2 350	7.4	92.1	1.4	6.2	0.2	2.5	6.6	20.9	7.0	10.7	13.9	12.5
20 015	9040	2	Butler	3 699	62 769	766	17.0	97.5	1.2	0.9	0.5	2.3	6.7	21.2	8.1	12.1	17.0	13.2
20 017	...	9	Chase	2 010	2 855	3 000	1.4	99.3	0.2	0.4	0.0	2.2	6.2	19.2	6.3	10.3	14.8	13.4
20 019	...	9	Chautauqua	1 662	4 273	2 890	2.6	95.9	0.4	3.3	0.5	1.6	5.6	17.8	5.8	8.9	12.9	15.7
20 021	...	6	Cherokee	1 521	22 401	1 644	14.7	95.9	0.6	3.4	0.2	1.3	6.0	20.4	9.3	10.4	14.8	14.9
20 023	...	9	Cheyenne	2 642	3 225	2 975	1.2	99.4	0.2	0.0	0.3	1.1	5.6	18.4	4.6	8.4	14.9	11.8
20 025	...	9	Clark	2 525	2 342	3 029	0.9	98.5	0.0	1.1	0.4	2.6	5.4	19.8	5.3	9.6	15.1	13.4
20 027	...	7	Clay	1 668	8 971	2 507	5.4	99.0	0.3	0.3	0.4	0.6	5.9	19.7	6.5	9.5	15.0	13.1
20 029	...	7	Cloud	1 854	10 007	2 424	5.4	99.3	0.5	0.2	0.1	0.9	5.3	17.0	10.2	8.9	12.9	13.1
20 031	...	7	Coffey	1 632	8 741	2 530	5.4	98.8	0.1	0.7	0.4	1.3	6.1	21.5	6.8	11.1	16.2	13.6
20 033	...	9	Comanche	2 042	1 954	3 064	1.0	99.2	0.3	0.6	0.0	0.7	5.8	17.8	5.6	9.1	13.3	13.3
20 035	...	4	Cowley	2 917	36 948	1 162	12.7	93.5	3.3	2.0	1.2	4.5	6.4	19.6	9.5	11.0	14.9	13.7
20 037	...	4	Crawford	1 536	36 347	1 183	23.7	96.1	1.5	0.9	1.5	1.4	5.6	17.7	14.3	11.3	13.9	12.5
20 039	...	9	Decatur	2 314	3 370	2 962	1.5	99.6	0.1	0.2	0.1	0.6	6.0	18.5	4.1	10.1	12.0	11.4
20 041	...	7	Dickinson	2 197	19 645	1 779	8.9	98.5	0.7	0.4	0.4	2.8	6.2	19.6	7.0	10.5	14.4	13.8
20 043	...	8	Doniphan	1 016	7 954	2 603	7.8	96.2	2.2	1.3	0.3	0.9	5.9	19.3	11.9	10.0	14.6	12.6
20 045	4150	3	Douglas	1 184	98 343	523	83.1	89.2	4.4	2.5	3.9	3.8	5.9	14.6	26.5	14.0	14.6	10.2
20 047	...	9	Edwards	1 611	3 275	2 971	2.0	99.0	0.3	0.4	0.3	7.5	5.6	19.2	5.7	10.4	13.7	13.0
20 049	...	8	Elk	1 678	3 384	2 961	2.0	97.9	0.4	1.7	0.1	2.9	5.9	16.2	6.2	7.6	12.1	15.1
20 051	...	7	Ellis	2 331	26 338	1 482	11.3	98.6	0.4	0.2	0.8	1.2	6.0	18.8	15.2	11.5	14.9	11.2
20 053	...	9	Ellsworth	1 854	6 220	2 755	3.4	96.4	2.9	0.4	0.2	4.5	4.9	17.6	7.7	12.3	14.5	12.9
20 055	...	5	Finney	3 367	37 409	1 151	11.1	93.1	1.5	0.7	4.6	33.6	10.7	24.1	11.4	15.3	14.5	10.0
20 057	...	5	Ford	2 845	29 587	1 390	10.4	94.0	2.1	0.7	3.1	20.7	8.9	20.8	12.0	13.3	14.3	11.7
20 059	...	6	Franklin	1 486	25 136	1 526	16.9	97.0	1.5	1.0	0.6	3.3	7.3	20.7	9.3	11.9	14.7	13.6
20 061	...	5	Geary	995	24 911	1 533	25.0	69.5	24.0	0.7	5.8	9.0	9.6	18.2	17.1	15.5	13.6	9.5
20 063	...	9	Gove	2 775	3 028	2 982	1.1	99.7	0.1	0.1	0.1	0.4	5.8	19.6	5.5	9.4	13.5	12.8
20 065	...	9	Graham	2 327	3 118	2 980	1.3	95.9	3.3	0.4	0.5	1.0	5.1	19.6	4.7	10.0	12.9	14.6
20 067	...	7	Grant	1 489	7 885	2 613	5.3	97.0	0.7	1.3	1.1	29.6	8.6	26.0	8.3	13.0	15.4	11.8
20 069	...	9	Gray	2 251	5 579	2 800	2.5	99.1	0.3	0.5	0.1	6.7	7.6	24.2	7.6	11.3	16.5	12.5
20 071	...	9	Greeley	2 015	1 648	3 086	0.8	97.1	2.0	0.2	0.7	10.1	7.9	21.7	6.1	12.5	14.1	11.2
20 073	...	6	Greenwood	2 952	7 961	2 602	2.7	98.9	0.2	1.0	0.0	2.0	5.7	18.5	6.8	9.3	13.7	13.0
20 075	...	9	Hamilton	2 581	2 374	3 027	0.9	97.8	0.3	0.3	1.6	8.2	6.2	19.1	5.3	10.5	14.3	13.9
20 077	...	7	Harper	2 076	6 305	2 750	3.0	99.2	0.2	0.5	0.1	2.1	5.8	18.6	5.8	9.6	13.5	13.0
20 079	9040	2	Harvey	1 397	34 261	1 248	24.5	96.6	2.1	0.5	0.9	8.0	6.1	19.5	9.4	10.8	15.4	12.9
20 081	...	9	Haskell	1 495	4 042	2 913	2.7	98.9	0.0	0.7	0.3	19.9	8.4	23.7	8.3	13.4	14.8	12.8
20 083	...	9	Hodgeman	2 227	2 235	3 042	1.0	98.7	1.1	0.1	0.0	2.5	6.9	20.6	5.0	11.4	13.2	14.1
20 085	...	6	Jackson	1 701	12 177	2 267	7.2	93.6	0.5	5.8	0.1	1.5	6.5	21.2	7.7	10.4	15.6	14.6
20 087	...	8	Jefferson	1 389	18 146	1 861	13.1	98.2	0.5	0.8	0.6	1.3	6.2	20.7	7.2	11.3	16.3	15.9
20 089	...	9	Jewell	2 355	3 787	2 930	1.6	99.6	0.0	0.3	0.2	0.3	5.2	17.7	4.5	8.2	13.4	12.9
20 091	3760	0	Johnson	1 235	440 198	129	356.4	95.2	2.1	0.3	2.3	3.1	7.0	19.0	8.2	14.3	19.6	14.5
20 093	...	9	Kearny	2 253	4 137	2 905	1.8	99.1	0.1	0.7	0.1	23.7	8.9	24.0	8.0	12.5	15.5	11.5
20 095	...	6	Kingman	2 237	8 651	2 541	3.9	99.3	0.2	0.3	0.2	1.5	6.6	20.4	6.1	10.3	14.1	13.6
20 097	...	9	Kiowa	1 871	3 351	2 965	1.8	98.6	0.6	0.5	0.4	1.6	5.8	19.3	6.8	9.7	14.5	11.8
20 099	...	7	Labette	1 681	22 941	1 615	13.6	93.2	4.7	1.5	0.6	3.4	6.4	19.9	9.2	10.9	14.5	13.0
20 101	...	9	Lane	1 858	2 174	3 053	1.2	99.7	0.0	0.3	0.0	2.8	6.2	19.7	5.7	9.4	13.7	13.9
20 103	3760	1	Leavenworth	1 200	71 766	683	59.8	85.8	11.4	0.7	2.1	5.1	6.4	20.1	8.0	15.0	21.5	13.0
20 105	...	9	Lincoln	1 862	3 338	2 967	1.8	99.5	0.1	0.4	0.1	0.7	5.1	18.8	4.3	8.7	14.5	12.2
20 107	...	8	Linn	1 551	9 296	2 485	6.0	98.8	0.5	0.6	0.1	0.7	5.8	20.1	6.9	9.3	13.9	14.4
20 109	...	9	Logan	2 779	2 938	2 993	1.1	99.2	0.5	0.2	0.1	1.4	5.9	19.7	5.9	9.8	13.6	12.8
20 111	...	5	Lyon	2 204	33 794	1 263	15.3	94.2	2.3	0.6	2.8	9.2	7.4	19.7	16.0	12.9	14.7	11.0
20 113	...	7	McPherson	2 331	28 815	1 417	12.4	98.0	0.9	0.4	0.7	1.8	6.3	19.2	10.0	10.8	15.1	12.6
20 115	...	6	Marion	2 443	13 544	2 173	5.5	98.6	0.7	0.3	0.3	1.4	5.2	17.9	8.5	9.2	13.5	13.2
20 117	...	7	Marshall	2 338	10 908	2 352	4.7	99.5	0.1	0.3	0.2	0.7	6.5	19.6	5.7	10.5	13.0	12.9
20 119	...	9	Meade	2 534	4 407	2 877	1.7	99.4	0.0	0.2	0.4	7.1	6.8	20.4	6.4	10.8	14.0	12.8
20 121	3760	1	Miami	1 494	27 083	1 460	18.1	96.8	2.4	0.6	0.2	1.9	6.6	21.0	7.9	11.8	16.3	15.2
20 123	...	7	Mitchell	1 813	6 957	2 682	3.8	98.8	0.7	0.4	0.2	0.6	5.8	20.5	7.2	9.4	14.5	12.3
20 125	...	5	Montgomery	1 671	36 773	1 170	22.0	90.4	6.9	2.2	0.5	3.0	6.3	18.9	8.6	10.2	14.2	14.0
20 127	...	9	Morris	1 806	6 173	2 759	3.4	98.8	0.4	0.5	0.3	2.3	6.0	19.1	6.0	10.0	13.9	13.2
20 129	...	9	Morton	1 891	3 489	2 952	1.8	97.3	0.2	1.1	1.4	14.6	6.7	23.3	7.2	11.9	14.6	12.9
20 131	...	9	Nemaha	1 862	10 182	2 407	5.5	99.3	0.4	0.1	0.2	0.3	7.0	21.0	6.7	10.5	12.7	11.6
20 133	...	7	Neosho	1 481	16 641	1 958	11.2	97.8	1.2	0.7	0.3	3.4	6.3	19.1	8.1	10.8	14.6	13.4
20 135	...	9	Ness	2 784	3 564	2 947	1.3	99.6	0.0	0.1	0.2	0.8	5.1	20.0	4.3	10.5	14.0	11.8
20 137	...	7	Norton	2 274	5 635	2 796	2.5	96.1	3.2	0.3	0.5	2.0	5.1	16.6	8.1	11.6	14.5	13.7

1. MSA = Metropolitan Statistical Area. PMSA = Primary MSA. NECMA = New England County Metropolitan Area. See Appendix A for explanation of these concepts. See Appendix B for list of metropolitan areas identified by type, with component counties. 2. County typology code from the Economic Research Service of USDA. See Appendix A for definition. 3. Dry land or land partially or temporarily covered by water. 4. Hispanic persons may be of any race.

Table B. States and Counties — **Population and Households**

STATE County	55 to 64 years	65 to 74 years	75 years and over	Percent female	1990	1980	1980–1990	1990–1999	Births	Deaths	Net migration	Number	Percent change, 1980–1990	Persons per household	Female family householder[1]	One person
	16	17	18	19	20	21	22	23	24	25	26	27	28	29	30	31
KANSAS—Cont'd																
Barber	10.3	10.2	11.2	51.7	5 874	6 548	-10.3	-10.8	543	790	-373	2 358	-10.3	2.44	4.9	27.9
Barton	9.6	8.9	9.2	51.5	29 382	31 343	-6.3	-2.5	3 598	2 872	-2 778	11 561	-2.0	2.48	7.7	27.3
Bourbon	9.6	8.1	10.5	52.4	14 966	15 969	-6.3	0.1	1 856	1 966	160	5 897	-7.7	2.46	8.4	28.3
Brown	9.4	7.9	11.2	51.7	11 128	11 955	-6.9	-1.8	1 338	1 444	-66	4 347	-5.7	2.50	6.1	29.1
Butler	8.9	6.3	6.5	49.9	50 580	44 782	12.9	24.1	6 814	4 282	9 267	18 488	14.9	2.69	7.5	20.5
Chase	10.4	8.6	11.0	49.6	3 021	3 309	-8.7	-5.5	386	368	-171	1 214	-6.8	2.43	5.4	26.9
Chautauqua	10.4	10.6	12.3	51.2	4 407	5 016	-12.1	-3.0	309	614	192	1 835	-9.8	2.32	6.7	30.9
Cherokee	9.4	7.1	7.7	51.9	21 374	22 304	-4.2	4.8	2 759	2 668	1 009	8 396	-1.8	2.51	9.6	26.3
Cheyenne	13.0	11.3	12.1	51.5	3 243	3 678	-11.8	-0.6	269	411	134	1 389	-8.4	2.30	4.8	30.5
Clark	10.6	8.4	12.5	51.2	2 418	2 599	-7.0	-3.1	237	362	64	1 006	-4.1	2.34	3.7	31.4
Clay	10.3	8.2	11.7	51.3	9 158	9 802	-6.6	-2.0	888	1 192	125	3 641	-4.9	2.45	4.8	27.0
Cloud	9.5	8.9	14.3	52.5	11 023	12 494	-11.8	-9.2	972	1 650	-295	4 483	-5.8	2.36	5.5	29.9
Coffey	8.5	6.7	9.6	50.0	8 404	9 370	-10.3	4.0	959	970	379	3 311	-6.1	2.49	5.6	26.0
Comanche	10.7	9.8	14.7	51.3	2 313	2 554	-9.4	-15.5	205	399	-161	950	-5.1	2.33	5.4	30.5
Cowley	9.2	7.1	8.7	51.1	36 915	36 824	0.2	0.1	4 519	3 843	-1 032	14 047	1.1	2.50	8.8	26.2
Crawford	8.3	7.1	9.2	51.3	35 582	37 916	-6.2	2.1	4 428	4 372	295	14 606	-4.0	2.34	8.4	31.7
Decatur	11.1	11.0	15.9	51.2	4 021	4 509	-10.8	-16.2	348	591	-394	1 651	-8.0	2.35	5.2	30.5
Dickinson	10.1	7.9	10.5	51.4	18 958	20 175	-6.0	3.6	2 177	2 196	704	7 542	-2.3	2.46	6.5	27.0
Doniphan	9.0	7.8	8.9	50.5	8 134	9 268	-12.2	-2.2	904	815	-234	3 074	-8.4	2.56	7.7	25.5
Douglas	5.7	4.3	4.2	50.4	81 798	67 640	20.9	20.2	9 909	4 324	7 630	30 138	26.5	2.42	7.6	27.0
Edwards	10.1	10.1	12.1	51.5	3 787	4 271	-11.3	-13.5	349	527	-326	1 585	-8.1	2.33	4.9	30.9
Elk	12.3	9.8	14.8	51.4	3 327	3 918	-15.1	1.7	263	523	328	1 436	-12.4	2.25	5.2	31.5
Ellis	7.8	7.4	7.3	50.8	26 004	26 098	-0.4	1.3	2 965	2 026	-560	10 096	9.7	2.46	7.7	29.0
Ellsworth	9.1	8.2	12.8	46.7	6 586	6 640	-0.8	-5.6	513	879	21	2 522	-3.8	2.35	5.5	31.7
Finney	5.2	4.6	4.1	49.2	33 070	23 825	38.8	13.1	7 853	1 801	-1 666	10 836	33.7	3.01	9.3	19.4
Ford	7.3	5.9	5.8	49.2	27 463	24 315	12.9	7.7	5 488	2 273	-1 056	9 872	12.5	2.69	8.2	24.4
Franklin	9.0	5.9	7.6	51.1	21 994	22 062	-0.3	14.3	3 074	2 302	1 938	8 308	2.0	2.58	7.6	24.2
Geary	6.1	6.0	4.5	49.1	30 453	29 852	2.0	-18.2	7 009	1 801	-12 524	10 676	6.0	2.71	10.2	19.6
Gove	10.7	10.3	12.4	50.1	3 231	3 726	-13.3	-6.3	346	340	-200	1 284	-6.8	2.48	3.7	27.3
Graham	11.4	9.1	12.6	50.7	3 543	3 995	-11.3	-12.0	261	401	-268	1 435	-5.2	2.43	5.1	28.2
Grant	7.0	5.3	4.5	50.4	7 159	6 977	2.6	10.1	1 326	461	-126	2 393	2.7	2.96	6.9	17.8
Gray	7.8	5.7	6.9	50.3	5 396	5 138	5.0	3.4	774	438	-135	1 913	7.2	2.77	5.2	22.5
Greeley	9.3	8.6	8.6	50.6	1 774	1 845	-3.8	-7.1	183	175	-130	656	-2.1	2.65	4.6	24.2
Greenwood	11.1	9.5	12.2	51.0	7 847	8 764	-10.5	1.5	738	1 101	501	3 285	-8.1	2.33	6.1	31.1
Hamilton	10.6	8.3	11.9	52.3	2 388	2 514	-5.0	-0.6	268	268	-6	986	1.2	2.36	7.3	32.4
Harper	10.2	9.8	13.8	51.4	7 124	7 778	-8.4	-11.5	657	1 006	-432	3 007	-7.0	2.32	6.1	31.3
Harvey	8.8	7.7	9.5	51.3	31 028	30 531	1.6	10.4	3 704	2 961	926	11 581	5.8	2.54	7.0	25.2
Haskell	7.2	6.0	5.4	49.9	3 886	3 814	1.9	4.0	700	214	-319	1 372	6.2	2.81	4.3	21.1
Hodgeman	10.7	7.8	10.4	50.2	2 177	2 269	-4.1	2.7	207	227	87	826	-4.3	2.58	3.4	23.8
Jackson	8.7	6.8	8.6	50.6	11 525	11 644	-1.0	5.7	1 509	1 159	326	4 277	3.1	2.66	6.3	23.2
Jefferson	9.0	6.5	6.9	49.3	15 905	15 207	4.6	14.1	1 832	1 501	1 947	5 778	9.1	2.68	5.2	20.1
Jewell	12.5	11.1	14.4	50.4	4 251	5 241	-18.9	-10.9	327	537	-239	1 806	-14.3	2.34	4.5	28.5
Johnson	7.5	5.7	4.3	51.5	355 021	270 269	31.4	24.0	55 077	20 414	49 848	136 433	40.8	2.58	7.8	23.0
Kearny	7.3	6.1	6.1	48.9	4 027	3 435	17.2	2.7	649	296	-239	1 379	17.2	2.89	7.5	20.2
Kingman	10.1	8.8	9.9	50.9	8 292	8 960	-7.5	4.3	899	957	454	3 175	-5.6	2.55	6.0	25.1
Kiowa	11.2	9.8	11.2	50.9	3 660	4 046	-9.5	-8.4	385	350	-334	1 466	-7.0	2.39	5.1	29.4
Labette	8.9	7.8	9.4	51.9	23 693	25 682	-7.7	-3.2	2 740	2 784	-1 010	9 377	-3.3	2.44	9.3	29.0
Lane	9.8	10.0	11.7	49.4	2 375	2 472	-3.9	-8.5	222	213	-209	966	-0.5	2.41	5.1	29.6
Leavenworth	6.9	4.7	4.2	45.5	64 371	54 809	17.4	11.5	8 065	4 494	2 438	19 715	15.8	2.79	9.0	20.2
Lincoln	11.9	9.3	15.2	51.8	3 653	4 145	-11.9	-8.6	284	537	-43	1 531	-10.6	2.33	4.2	29.7
Linn	11.0	8.9	9.8	50.5	8 254	8 234	0.2	12.6	868	1 166	1 357	3 215	1.9	2.51	5.6	24.1
Logan	11.3	10.4	10.7	50.4	3 081	3 478	-11.4	-4.6	322	372	-80	1 221	-9.0	2.47	5.2	28.3
Lyon	6.6	5.2	6.7	50.8	34 732	35 108	-1.1	-2.7	4 777	2 730	-2 923	13 059	0.4	2.51	7.7	28.3
McPherson	8.9	7.5	9.5	51.0	27 268	26 855	1.5	5.7	3 129	2 784	1 317	10 230	4.3	2.51	5.3	25.5
Marion	10.4	9.3	12.8	51.5	12 888	13 522	-4.7	5.1	1 334	1 734	631	4 975	-3.2	2.43	4.9	26.6
Marshall	10.5	8.6	12.7	50.5	11 705	12 787	-8.5	-6.8	1 024	1 530	-244	4 689	-7.2	2.43	4.9	29.8
Meade	10.6	7.7	10.3	50.6	4 247	4 788	-11.3	3.8	613	486	47	1 667	-8.1	2.49	3.8	27.6
Miami	9.1	5.6	6.5	50.6	23 466	21 618	8.5	15.4	3 007	2 218	2 888	8 402	11.0	2.67	7.3	21.8
Mitchell	9.2	7.8	13.3	51.4	7 203	8 117	-11.3	-3.4	697	967	60	2 846	-9.6	2.41	4.5	30.5
Montgomery	9.5	8.5	9.8	52.5	38 816	42 281	-8.2	-5.3	4 189	4 470	-1 639	15 670	-4.4	2.42	9.2	28.9
Morris	11.1	9.4	11.4	50.9	6 198	6 419	-3.4	-0.4	706	718	-3	2 528	-1.2	2.41	5.6	26.4
Morton	9.1	7.1	7.1	49.8	3 480	3 454	0.8	0.3	490	293	-253	1 290	4.6	2.65	5.3	23.8
Nemaha	9.9	8.8	11.7	50.4	10 446	11 211	-6.8	-2.5	1 260	1 404	-83	3 996	-0.6	2.59	4.3	28.1
Neosho	9.8	8.1	9.8	51.6	17 035	18 967	-10.2	-2.3	1 928	1 976	-285	6 748	-8.0	2.45	7.2	27.3
Ness	10.2	10.1	14.0	50.8	4 033	4 498	-10.3	-11.6	351	506	-306	1 670	-6.7	2.38	4.7	30.3
Norton	9.9	8.3	12.3	46.8	5 947	6 689	-11.1	-5.2	517	706	-98	2 330	-10.0	2.31	5.0	31.3

1. No spouse present.

STATE County	Births, average 1996–1998		Deaths, average 1996–1998				Physicians,[4] 1998		Hospitals,[4] 1998			Medicare enrollees 1999	Serious crimes known to police, 1998[6] Total	
			Number		Rate					Beds				
	Total	Rate[1]	Total	Infant[2]	Total[1]	Infant[3]	Number	Rate[5]	Number	Number	Rate[5]		Number	Rate[7]
	32	33	34	35	36	37	38	39	40	41	42	43	44	45
KANSAS—Cont'd														
Barber	53	9.8	93	0	17.2	0.0	6	112	2	66	1 235	1 268	NA	NA
Barton	368	13.2	308	4	11.1	11.8	41	148	3	238	861	5 415	NA	NA
Bourbon	199	13.0	216	2	14.2	8.4	23	151	1	114	747	3 097	NA	NA
Brown	136	12.3	160	2	14.5	17.2	10	90	2	70	632	2 271	NA	NA
Butler	761	12.5	480	7	7.9	9.6	44	71	2	234	378	7 664	NA	NA
Chase	54	18.5	43	0	14.8	6.1	0	0	0	0	0	565	NA	NA
Chautauqua	34	7.9	70	1	16.1	29.1	4	92	2	73	1 674	1 054	NA	NA
Cherokee	295	13.1	278	2	12.3	5.7	8	35	1	39	173	3 838	NA	NA
Cheyenne	30	9.4	41	0	12.8	11.1	2	63	1	23	725	836	NA	NA
Clark	24	10.0	41	0	17.2	13.9	2	85	2	63	2 668	547	NA	NA
Clay	90	9.8	127	1	13.8	11.1	8	87	1	32	350	1 919	NA	NA
Cloud	99	9.7	163	1	16.1	6.8	23	229	1	39	389	2 576	NA	NA
Coffey	100	11.4	99	1	11.4	6.7	5	57	1	26	299	1 564	NA	NA
Comanche	22	10.6	36	0	17.5	0.0	3	149	1	14	696	531	NA	NA
Cowley	439	12.0	407	2	11.1	5.3	34	94	2	178	490	6 493	NA	NA
Crawford	515	14.1	474	2	12.9	4.5	48	132	2	175	481	6 784	NA	NA
Decatur	31	9.0	61	0	17.5	10.6	5	145	1	74	2 141	921	NA	NA
Dickinson	215	10.9	241	1	12.2	3.1	9	46	2	102	517	3 937	NA	NA
Doniphan	102	13.2	85	0	10.9	3.3	5	64	0	0	0	1 432	NA	NA
Douglas	1 085	11.9	492	8	5.4	7.4	152	163	1	167	179	8 802	NA	NA
Edwards	38	11.2	55	0	16.2	0.0	4	121	1	49	1 479	788	NA	NA
Elk	28	8.3	52	0	15.6	0.0	0	0	0	0	0	859	NA	NA
Ellis	317	12.1	237	3	9.1	9.5	72	274	1	104	395	4 244	NA	NA
Ellsworth	53	8.4	91	1	14.4	12.7	6	95	1	22	350	1 351	NA	NA
Finney	909	25.2	203	7	5.6	7.3	46	126	1	93	255	3 536	NA	NA
Ford	621	21.2	251	4	8.6	7.0	35	119	1	105	357	3 790	NA	NA
Franklin	343	14.1	277	3	11.4	9.7	13	52	1	45	182	3 937	NA	NA
Geary	620	24.2	199	11	7.8	18.3	27	106	1	49	193	2 919	NA	NA
Gove	33	10.7	42	0	13.6	0.0	6	196	1	123	4 028	717	NA	NA
Graham	24	7.5	42	0	13.1	0.0	2	62	1	42	1 311	714	NA	NA
Grant	153	19.5	55	1	7.0	8.7	5	62	1	45	562	820	NA	NA
Gray	92	16.7	48	0	8.7	3.6	3	54	0	0	0	824	NA	NA
Greeley	21	12.2	24	0	14.0	0.0	2	117	1	50	2 934	290	NA	NA
Greenwood	80	9.9	133	2	16.4	20.8	6	74	1	46	565	1 988	NA	NA
Hamilton	31	13.7	29	0	12.5	10.6	3	128	1	77	3 286	523	NA	NA
Harper	63	9.7	102	0	15.7	0.0	9	140	2	50	778	1 556	NA	NA
Harvey	389	11.6	337	3	10.0	8.6	79	230	2	221	643	5 963	NA	NA
Haskell	77	19.3	22	0	5.5	4.3	2	50	1	42	1 056	466	NA	NA
Hodgeman	18	8.1	26	0	11.6	18.5	1	45	1	54	2 445	396	NA	NA
Jackson	162	13.4	135	0	11.2	0.0	5	41	1	17	140	2 026	NA	NA
Jefferson	209	11.7	151	3	8.4	14.3	10	55	1	118	647	2 657	NA	NA
Jewell	30	7.6	56	0	14.2	11.1	1	26	1	57	1 474	1 036	NA	NA
Johnson	6 222	14.8	2 388	35	5.7	5.6	1 737	404	4	849	198	46 546	NA	NA
Kearny	69	16.5	33	0	8.0	4.8	2	48	1	20	479	526	NA	NA
Kingman	91	10.7	97	1	11.4	7.3	7	82	1	49	574	1 719	NA	NA
Kiowa	40	11.3	34	0	9.7	8.4	3	86	1	24	692	785	NA	NA
Labette	276	11.9	305	1	13.2	4.8	32	139	2	91	395	4 462	NA	NA
Lane	24	10.6	18	0	8.2	0.0	2	88	1	31	1 369	490	NA	NA
Leavenworth	847	12.0	499	7	7.1	7.9	73	102	2	136	191	6 827	NA	NA
Lincoln	28	8.4	51	0	15.2	0.0	3	90	1	34	1 019	858	NA	NA
Linn	96	10.6	124	1	13.7	6.9	2	22	0	0	0	1 951	NA	NA
Logan	32	10.7	39	0	13.0	10.3	1	33	1	51	1 707	720	NA	NA
Lyon	494	14.5	307	4	9.0	8.1	41	121	1	152	448	4 686	NA	NA
McPherson	345	12.4	317	2	11.4	4.8	27	94	3	83	290	5 364	NA	NA
Marion	141	10.5	177	0	13.1	2.4	13	96	2	152	1 118	2 929	NA	NA
Marshall	106	9.5	170	1	15.3	9.4	9	82	1	55	500	2 592	NA	NA
Meade	65	14.8	57	1	13.0	15.3	2	45	1	26	588	863	NA	NA
Miami	334	12.7	242	2	9.2	6.0	25	94	1	22	83	3 547	NA	NA
Mitchell	70	10.0	114	1	16.4	9.6	8	115	1	89	1 283	1 594	NA	NA
Montgomery	455	12.2	490	4	13.2	8.1	49	132	2	182	491	7 678	NA	NA
Morris	71	11.4	84	1	13.4	9.3	6	97	1	22	357	1 328	NA	NA
Morton	53	15.3	33	0	9.6	0.0	8	233	1	100	2 907	515	NA	NA
Nemaha	151	14.7	152	2	14.8	11.1	8	79	2	51	503	2 315	NA	NA
Neosho	198	11.8	204	1	12.1	3.4	17	101	1	60	358	3 382	NA	NA
Ness	36	9.9	54	0	15.0	0.0	4	111	2	104	2 883	912	NA	NA
Norton	54	9.3	79	0	13.7	0.0	5	87	1	43	748	1 289	NA	NA

1. Per 1,000 estimated resident population, average 1996–1998.   2. Deaths of infants under 1 year old.   3. Deaths of infants under 1 year old per 1,000 live births.   4. Data subject to copyright.   5. Per 100,000 resident population as of July 1 of the year shown.   6. Data for serious crimes have not been adjusted for underreporting; this may affect comparability between geographic areas and over time.   7. Per 100,000 population estimated by the FBI.

Table B. States and Counties — Crime, Education, Money Income, and Poverty

STATE County	Serious crimes known to police, 1998[1] (cont'd) Rate[2] Violent	Serious crimes known to police, 1998[1] (cont'd) Rate[2] Property	Education — School enrollment and attainment, 1990 — Enrollment[3] Total	Enrollment[3] Percent private	Attainment[4] (percent) High school graduate or more	Attainment[4] (percent) Bachelor's degree or more	Local government expenditures, fiscal 1997[5] Total current expenditures (mil dol)	Local government expenditures, fiscal 1997[5] Current expenditures per student (dollars)	Money income 1989 Per capita[6] (dollars)	Money income 1989 Households Median Dollars	Households Median Percent change, 1979–1989 (constant 1989 dollars)	Percent with $100,000 or more	Income and poverty, 1997 Median household income	Percent below poverty level All persons	Percent below poverty level Persons under 18	Percent below poverty level Persons 5–17 in families
	46	47	48	49	50	51	52	53	54	55	56	57	58	59	60	61
KANSAS—Cont'd																
Barber	NA	NA	1 446	3.9	79.4	12.9	6.6	5 614	10 664	21 476	-12.1	1.4	30 317	12.4	17.3	15.8
Barton	NA	NA	7 878	7.0	78.0	13.6	28.5	5 479	11 394	23 432	-14.2	1.3	33 079	12.5	17.8	16.7
Bourbon	NA	NA	3 757	7.5	73.9	14.0	13.0	4 750	9 958	20 367	0.2	1.5	28 362	17.6	25.7	23.5
Brown	NA	NA	2 694	2.3	78.4	12.5	11.0	5 329	10 299	20 392	-1.3	1.6	30 260	15.3	22.0	20.0
Butler	NA	NA	13 618	7.6	81.0	17.0	65.6	5 059	13 260	31 012	0.3	2.0	44 998	8.1	11.2	10.2
Chase	NA	NA	677	3.4	77.9	13.6	3.6	6 557	10 258	20 128	-10.8	0.7	29 129	16.0	23.5	22.6
Chautauqua	NA	NA	942	3.5	70.5	10.6	4.5	5 910	9 043	17 067	-10.1	0.6	24 358	18.6	28.1	25.5
Cherokee	NA	NA	5 256	2.4	70.2	10.3	21.7	5 361	9 705	19 001	-6.5	0.7	27 729	17.2	25.0	22.7
Cheyenne	NA	NA	694	2.7	74.2	13.3	4.5	6 775	11 165	21 750	0.0	0.5	29 484	11.4	15.4	15.9
Clark	NA	NA	565	9.7	83.5	17.5	3.9	7 027	11 804	24 003	-2.4	0.4	33 987	9.7	16.0	12.8
Clay	NA	NA	2 135	6.5	77.8	13.3	10.1	5 762	11 431	21 896	1.3	2.1	33 910	11.4	16.8	15.7
Cloud	NA	NA	2 678	2.8	76.0	13.8	11.5	6 760	10 853	20 782	2.8	0.6	29 851	13.4	18.9	17.1
Coffey	NA	NA	2 041	6.1	76.9	13.5	13.7	6 902	11 451	24 435	4.8	1.3	34 411	10.8	15.2	13.1
Comanche	NA	NA	497	3.6	78.0	14.9	4.0	10 109	10 587	19 421	-18.8	1.3	27 139	12.6	15.5	17.1
Cowley	NA	NA	9 487	10.8	76.9	14.9	38.3	5 527	11 624	25 047	-0.3	1.4	33 933	12.8	18.5	16.6
Crawford	NA	NA	10 622	6.3	74.7	18.7	38.1	6 226	10 507	19 616	1.9	1.2	28 442	16.9	22.9	21.0
Decatur	NA	NA	913	4.4	78.5	13.6	4.5	6 259	10 609	20 131	-11.2	1.4	28 427	13.3	18.9	19.0
Dickinson	NA	NA	4 503	7.1	79.7	11.9	22.8	5 288	11 407	22 953	0.2	0.7	33 975	9.9	13.4	12.7
Doniphan	NA	NA	2 046	4.2	73.0	9.7	10.5	6 249	9 465	22 102	-0.1	1.2	32 077	15.1	19.7	18.7
Douglas	NA	NA	36 059	6.7	88.8	38.4	70.1	5 643	12 003	25 244	6.4	2.7	37 248	11.9	14.1	13.5
Edwards	NA	NA	909	5.3	76.3	13.1	4.1	6 664	11 895	21 904	1.1	2.3	31 082	12.1	17.1	16.5
Elk	NA	NA	639	2.3	67.3	10.5	6.3	7 648	10 390	17 730	2.9	1.2	23 604	20.1	31.0	29.7
Ellis	NA	NA	8 919	8.4	80.6	23.4	26.5	6 040	11 459	22 466	-14.2	1.7	33 279	11.2	13.7	12.7
Ellsworth	NA	NA	1 438	3.4	76.6	12.8	9.1	6 337	9 801	20 064	-3.1	0.8	31 314	11.5	13.8	13.2
Finney	NA	NA	10 118	7.3	70.9	14.4	40.4	4 895	11 278	27 645	-5.8	2.7	36 823	10.8	15.4	15.0
Ford	NA	NA	7 587	15.9	76.6	18.1	25.0	4 245	11 114	25 041	-9.5	2.0	34 434	12.0	17.8	17.0
Franklin	NA	NA	5 561	12.4	77.1	12.9	24.8	5 081	11 483	24 981	4.8	1.6	34 879	11.8	16.0	16.0
Geary	NA	NA	7 197	7.7	83.4	14.6	32.3	4 972	9 996	21 905	2.4	1.0	28 857	16.7	26.2	24.5
Gove	NA	NA	709	3.7	79.1	13.6	5.5	7 232	10 859	23 377	13.6	0.5	30 725	9.5	12.7	12.2
Graham	NA	NA	873	1.1	77.5	14.2	4.2	7 017	11 472	22 047	5.3	1.9	29 829	13.5	19.2	17.9
Grant	NA	NA	2 058	4.4	75.1	13.6	9.7	5 331	10 757	30 173	-0.3	0.9	43 557	9.9	12.6	13.3
Gray	NA	NA	1 407	10.6	69.4	12.6	8.1	6 349	11 669	25 872	-5.8	3.1	39 728	8.6	11.3	11.1
Greeley	NA	NA	465	2.8	82.4	16.8	2.3	6 228	11 641	25 709	-4.0	2.5	34 125	8.0	10.1	10.8
Greenwood	NA	NA	1 695	3.9	75.1	10.4	8.3	6 252	10 694	19 481	-3.8	1.0	27 401	15.5	22.8	20.9
Hamilton	NA	NA	525	8.2	73.4	12.9	3.1	6 787	12 366	22 500	-1.0	1.8	33 413	12.4	19.6	18.1
Harper	NA	NA	1 560	2.3	78.2	10.9	7.2	5 529	10 717	21 226	-7.2	1.0	30 760	12.9	18.6	17.7
Harvey	NA	NA	8 200	21.3	81.2	20.3	32.5	5 408	12 725	27 539	-2.3	2.0	39 525	9.3	12.9	11.7
Haskell	NA	NA	1 055	10.0	76.1	13.4	6.1	6 554	10 990	26 761	-2.7	1.7	42 694	9.4	13.4	13.1
Hodgeman	NA	NA	516	3.3	84.9	17.3	3.2	6 460	10 347	23 788	-7.5	0.5	34 381	9.2	11.5	12.6
Jackson	NA	NA	2 859	3.3	80.8	10.4	15.6	6 461	10 891	25 398	-3.6	1.4	35 498	11.7	16.7	14.6
Jefferson	NA	NA	3 857	3.3	81.0	13.5	24.7	5 562	12 267	29 048	0.6	2.0	41 130	8.4	11.2	10.9
Jewell	NA	NA	843	2.0	80.8	11.7	4.9	7 162	9 698	18 839	-1.6	0.6	28 555	12.2	17.6	16.4
Johnson	NA	NA	94 579	18.5	92.9	40.5	389.5	5 543	20 592	42 741	1.3	8.7	59 870	4.1	5.4	4.9
Kearny	NA	NA	1 100	1.9	73.8	12.5	7.6	6 289	11 412	29 303	2.5	2.0	38 950	11.5	16.5	16.2
Kingman	NA	NA	2 066	10.2	77.5	11.9	8.6	5 269	10 676	22 763	-8.8	0.8	35 312	10.6	14.8	13.8
Kiowa	NA	NA	866	11.4	78.0	14.6	4.8	7 581	10 607	22 628	-5.2	0.8	32 148	10.4	13.4	13.9
Labette	NA	NA	6 316	4.4	74.2	12.1	21.8	4 830	10 815	21 871	-2.1	1.1	29 369	15.6	22.2	20.5
Lane	NA	NA	576	3.5	81.1	17.8	3.4	6 834	12 159	23 532	0.3	2.0	31 953	10.9	14.8	14.7
Leavenworth	NA	NA	17 505	13.8	84.5	23.9	61.0	5 001	12 822	32 500	4.8	1.6	44 056	9.5	12.1	10.7
Lincoln	NA	NA	798	6.5	77.6	11.6	3.9	6 344	9 668	18 652	-6.0	0.8	28 563	11.8	15.7	14.9
Linn	NA	NA	1 841	1.2	73.9	10.4	13.1	6 327	11 001	21 287	4.5	1.5	29 802	14.0	20.2	18.6
Logan	NA	NA	727	11.1	78.3	15.9	5.1	7 760	10 878	22 126	-6.1	1.6	32 148	11.8	17.5	16.5
Lyon	NA	NA	11 506	5.0	81.9	21.4	36.3	5 844	11 251	24 050	-9.9	1.6	33 688	13.5	17.8	16.8
McPherson	NA	NA	7 272	23.4	78.2	17.4	30.4	5 665	11 970	27 003	-0.3	1.1	40 361	6.4	8.1	7.9
Marion	NA	NA	2 966	20.5	73.8	14.9	15.1	5 700	10 428	21 725	-3.4	1.3	32 643	10.5	14.1	12.9
Marshall	NA	NA	2 683	10.8	77.5	10.2	15.8	6 130	10 166	20 597	-2.5	1.0	32 432	13.8	19.5	17.8
Meade	NA	NA	921	3.0	79.5	17.1	4.4	6 898	10 887	23 403	1.1	1.2	34 411	8.2	10.8	11.2
Miami	NA	NA	5 983	11.0	78.5	13.2	27.2	5 893	12 563	29 259	4.8	2.3	40 625	9.1	12.2	11.3
Mitchell	NA	NA	1 689	12.1	82.6	15.8	11.1	7 531	10 465	22 159	0.2	1.6	33 611	10.0	12.8	12.2
Montgomery	NA	NA	9 686	7.8	73.0	13.6	28.9	4 428	10 837	20 864	-9.5	1.2	29 277	15.9	23.2	21.0
Morris	NA	NA	1 349	1.0	80.8	12.5	5.7	5 074	11 451	22 202	8.7	1.6	31 810	11.4	15.6	15.4
Morton	NA	NA	871	2.5	75.8	16.2	5.8	7 676	12 669	25 659	-6.5	2.6	38 752	11.5	15.9	16.6
Nemaha	NA	NA	2 489	9.5	75.7	12.3	12.0	6 135	10 738	22 144	7.4	1.8	34 266	10.0	12.3	12.9
Neosho	NA	NA	4 379	4.0	77.2	11.5	15.4	4 650	10 402	22 299	-4.4	0.7	30 890	13.8	19.0	17.7
Ness	NA	NA	939	15.7	78.0	12.3	5.3	7 459	11 034	23 594	5.1	1.1	33 244	9.3	12.3	12.4
Norton	NA	NA	1 179	6.1	76.9	12.8	6.8	6 139	10 912	21 259	7.9	1.5	31 013	13.3	18.5	16.9

1. Data for serious crimes have not been adjusted for underreporting; this may affect comparability between geographic areas and over time.   2. Per 100,000 population estimated by the FBI.   3. All persons 3 years old and over enrolled in nursery school through college.   4. Persons 25 years old and over.   5. Elementary and secondary education expenditures, local government fiscal years ending between July 1, 1996 and June 30, 1997.   6. Based on population enumerated as of April 1, 1990.

Table B. States and Counties — Personal Income

STATE County	Total (mil dol)	Percent change, 1997–1998	Per capita Dollars	Per capita Rank	Wages and salaries[2] (mil dol)	Proprietor's income (mil dol)	Dividends, interest, and rent (mil dol)	Transfer payments Total (mil dol)	Government payments to individuals Total (mil dol)	Social Security (mil dol)	Medical payments (mil dol)	Income mainte-nance (mil dol)	Unemploy-ment insurance (mil dol)
	62	63	64	65	66	67	68	69	70	71	72	73	74
KANSAS—Cont'd													
Barber	105	-1.0	19 714	1 805	47	7	30	26	25	12	10	1	0
Barton	634	3.1	21 922	1 120	344	59	155	108	103	54	36	7	2
Bourbon	311	2.2	20 535	1 544	162	26	68	66	63	29	24	5	1
Brown	233	4.3	21 092	1 356	117	29	53	46	44	20	18	4	1
Butler	1 418	4.7	22 909	869	414	101	212	168	157	82	54	9	3
Chase	70	10.3	23 693	705	17	18	17	12	12	5	4	1	0
Chautauqua	75	3.6	17 247	2 545	22	7	22	22	21	10	9	2	0
Cherokee	404	2.3	17 942	2 364	169	31	70	90	86	37	34	9	1
Cheyenne	69	10.3	21 943	1 114	24	16	20	14	14	8	5	1	0
Clark	58	3.1	24 641	540	23	5	17	10	9	5	4	0	0
Clay	201	-1.1	22 083	1 074	69	34	51	34	33	17	11	2	1
Cloud	214	1.7	21 316	1 291	88	24	58	48	46	23	18	2	1
Coffey	182	-0.2	21 007	1 388	136	14	47	33	31	15	12	2	1
Comanche	41	0.4	20 418	1 589	14	4	13	10	9	5	4	0	0
Cowley	733	2.8	19 754	1 794	394	54	139	141	135	63	50	10	3
Crawford	753	2.4	20 703	1 487	430	35	162	157	150	61	60	12	2
Decatur	83	4.2	23 957	651	24	14	28	16	15	8	6	1	0
Dickinson	406	3.2	20 719	1 478	172	40	90	72	69	34	22	4	1
Doniphan	163	6.3	20 650	1 504	86	22	27	31	30	14	11	3	1
Douglas	1 993	5.7	20 645	1 507	1 217	101	408	208	192	87	67	14	4
Edwards	87	11.3	26 611	334	30	23	19	16	16	7	7	1	0
Elk	58	0.8	17 060	2 598	13	6	13	17	17	8	7	1	0
Ellis	626	4.2	23 539	736	364	67	124	88	84	39	31	4	1
Ellsworth	129	4.6	20 617	1 521	59	14	33	28	27	13	12	1	0
Finney	772	4.8	21 087	1 360	530	99	116	77	71	32	27	6	2
Ford	657	5.3	22 305	1 015	438	68	123	83	78	38	28	6	1
Franklin	498	4.2	20 040	1 701	222	30	84	81	77	37	28	6	2
Geary	524	2.5	20 771	1 464	747	29	106	72	69	25	22	10	1
Gove	73	17.6	24 041	634	28	18	18	13	13	6	5	1	0
Graham	73	14.3	22 779	895	25	18	15	15	14	7	6	1	0
Grant	171	-3.8	21 344	1 283	113	25	32	19	18	9	7	2	0
Gray	152	17.6	27 196	287	61	53	23	15	14	8	5	1	0
Greeley	46	29.7	26 995	304	17	18	8	6	6	3	2	0	0
Greenwood	150	4.3	18 499	2 212	41	19	38	38	36	18	14	3	0
Hamilton	73	18.4	30 771	141	24	27	14	10	10	5	4	0	0
Harper	142	-1.3	22 133	1 055	53	18	36	31	30	15	12	2	0
Harvey	827	3.7	24 204	605	393	92	139	117	111	51	41	5	1
Haskell	132	11.4	33 412	78	40	62	19	10	10	5	3	1	0
Hodgeman	50	2.4	22 465	985	14	15	12	8	8	4	3	0	0
Jackson	259	6.1	21 416	1 261	88	17	44	40	38	20	12	2	1
Jefferson	396	7.1	21 788	1 165	81	25	59	53	50	26	16	3	1
Jewell	87	6.1	22 450	988	22	23	22	17	16	9	5	1	0
Johnson	16 909	9.3	39 355	36	10 043	1 365	3 432	987	913	492	309	30	16
Kearny	97	1.2	23 508	743	32	21	21	12	11	5	4	1	0
Kingman	176	-4.1	20 598	1 531	65	14	41	35	33	17	13	2	0
Kiowa	77	4.3	22 513	975	27	11	22	16	15	8	6	1	0
Labette	437	2.8	18 976	2 066	263	34	81	96	92	39	36	8	1
Lane	61	22.3	27 155	290	20	17	16	9	9	5	3	0	0
Leavenworth	1 422	3.8	19 980	1 717	868	77	268	170	158	67	60	11	3
Lincoln	70	6.2	21 083	1 364	20	11	20	15	14	8	5	1	0
Linn	162	1.3	17 637	2 456	63	9	35	38	37	18	13	2	1
Logan	68	12.3	22 632	944	27	12	18	12	12	6	4	1	0
Lyon	723	3.9	21 390	1 269	471	45	143	108	102	42	37	8	2
McPherson	678	0.7	23 753	687	377	82	138	102	97	55	32	3	1
Marion	242	-0.6	17 781	2 408	88	23	55	51	49	27	16	2	0
Marshall	269	2.2	24 445	568	125	34	66	54	52	21	23	4	1
Meade	115	21.1	25 993	399	38	32	23	17	16	8	6	1	0
Miami	598	5.1	22 586	958	212	30	94	85	81	35	34	4	1
Mitchell	165	3.3	23 724	694	92	26	36	28	27	15	10	1	0
Montgomery	736	2.9	19 854	1 760	434	49	147	161	155	72	58	13	2
Morris	118	2.4	19 097	2 023	39	14	28	26	24	12	8	2	0
Morton	75	-3.0	22 017	1 100	50	5	18	12	11	5	5	1	0
Nemaha	247	-1.2	24 192	607	108	34	73	39	37	20	13	2	1
Neosho	345	1.3	20 658	1 500	191	28	67	72	69	30	29	5	1
Ness	86	2.1	23 717	699	32	15	24	16	16	8	6	1	0
Norton	130	5.9	22 705	919	61	18	33	24	23	12	9	1	0

1. Based on the resident population estimated as of July 1 of the year shown. 2. Includes other labor income.

Table B. States and Counties — Earnings, Social Security, and Housing

STATE County	Total (mil dol)	Farm	Goods-related[1] Total	Manu-facturing	Service-related and other[2] Total	Retail trade	Finance, insur-ance, and real estate	Services	Govern-ment	Number	Rate[3]	Supple-mental Security Income recipients, December 1998	Total	Percent change, 1980–1990
	75	76	77	78	79	80	81	82	83	84	85	86	87	88
KANSAS—Cont'd														
Barber	54	-3.5	D	D	D	9.4	5.8	13.9	28.3	1 388	260	71	3 120	2.9
Barton	403	3.8	26.8	12.4	D	11.6	6.0	25.5	14.5	5 998	217	375	13 144	2.1
Bourbon	188	0.0	D	21.8	D	14.5	10.3	22.0	15.9	3 672	241	363	6 920	-3.8
Brown	145	12.2	D	15.2	D	7.0	3.1	34.7	15.8	2 535	229	218	4 890	-6.4
Butler	515	0.1	28.5	16.3	48.3	12.1	4.3	21.2	23.3	9 186	148	403	20 072	16.4
Chase	35	33.1	D	1.6	D	8.1	4.8	11.6	18.3	687	233	44	1 547	-1.3
Chautauqua	28	3.1	D	3.4	D	8.5	3.5	29.8	23.7	1 266	290	100	2 249	-3.1
Cherokee	200	5.4	D	32.6	D	7.7	3.1	13.1	17.1	4 650	206	620	9 428	1.2
Cheyenne	40	27.6	D	D	D	8.2	4.3	15.7	15.9	910	287	34	1 687	-5.3
Clark	28	25.2	10.7	1.9	D	8.5	6.7	8.7	31.6	563	238	29	1 327	3.8
Clay	103	16.2	21.1	12.4	43.6	10.4	4.1	13.7	19.1	2 128	233	108	4 138	-2.6
Cloud	113	9.4	D	10.0	53.3	11.4	4.3	22.7	20.0	2 827	282	159	5 198	-5.4
Coffey	150	1.1	D	6.4	D	5.7	2.7	6.6	18.4	1 911	220	146	3 712	-3.9
Comanche	18	4.2	D	7.7	D	8.8	7.5	20.0	33.4	565	281	23	1 256	7.3
Cowley	448	1.6	38.8	32.4	39.2	9.4	3.8	17.0	20.4	7 271	200	710	15 569	2.9
Crawford	466	0.9	24.6	20.3	49.8	11.4	3.5	21.9	24.7	7 457	205	862	16 526	-1.8
Decatur	39	27.6	8.4	2.6	45.7	6.3	4.5	21.8	18.3	1 009	292	40	2 063	-4.2
Dickinson	212	8.9	D	15.8	D	15.5	3.9	12.9	18.0	4 240	215	258	8 415	-3.1
Doniphan	108	12.8	D	34.7	D	4.7	3.2	8.2	16.7	1 712	218	152	3 337	-12.3
Douglas	1 318	0.2	21.6	14.4	48.2	12.1	5.9	22.0	30.0	9 703	104	935	31 782	24.7
Edwards	52	36.7	D	13.5	D	4.8	1.8	12.6	13.3	886	268	41	1 867	-6.2
Elk	19	2.1	D	D	D	9.2	3.6	10.4	48.5	1 042	311	79	1 743	-11.7
Ellis	431	1.6	D	8.3	D	12.3	4.4	33.0	20.6	4 697	179	352	11 115	8.5
Ellsworth	73	10.3	D	14.1	D	6.3	4.6	17.7	27.5	1 514	241	61	3 317	1.4
Finney	629	5.5	33.8	23.1	47.0	9.9	3.7	19.9	13.6	3 750	103	432	11 696	30.0
Ford	506	4.8	D	29.5	D	11.7	3.7	18.3	13.9	4 244	144	356	10 842	10.3
Franklin	252	1.1	D	13.9	D	27.3	3.2	15.9	19.3	4 506	182	426	8 926	1.9
Geary	775	0.2	5.2	2.7	19.9	7.4	1.9	6.8	74.7	3 441	136	470	11 952	7.8
Gove	46	28.4	D	5.9	D	9.8	3.1	13.4	20.7	774	253	18	1 494	-6.4
Graham	43	26.9	D	D	D	7.5	4.0	13.7	22.9	886	277	48	1 753	-3.1
Grant	139	12.1	30.1	5.7	43.7	6.4	3.3	15.7	14.2	963	120	83	2 599	-0.1
Gray	113	42.0	11.1	2.1	31.6	3.3	4.4	7.3	15.3	839	150	34	2 114	5.2
Greeley	34	54.6	D	0.7	D	4.1	D	10.9	12.0	322	189	8	801	-1.7
Greenwood	60	8.3	22.2	2.9	47.2	10.9	3.9	22.0	22.3	2 197	270	190	4 243	-4.7
Hamilton	51	54.9	D	D	D	3.7	4.3	4.9	15.8	557	238	23	1 214	-4.6
Harper	70	10.2	D	14.1	D	10.0	4.6	10.6	27.8	1 713	266	89	3 481	-2.3
Harvey	485	2.8	40.1	32.0	46.9	8.8	2.8	25.1	10.2	5 801	169	294	12 290	6.3
Haskell	102	60.5	5.8	1.9	22.0	2.5	2.5	5.2	11.7	591	149	29	1 586	6.1
Hodgeman	29	39.6	D	D	D	6.0	3.0	6.4	24.3	467	211	10	1 022	-3.0
Jackson	105	-3.1	D	9.2	D	11.9	5.1	37.7	23.6	2 491	205	98	4 564	1.6
Jefferson	105	3.8	D	3.3	D	8.1	4.0	16.7	33.3	3 154	173	112	6 314	8.5
Jewell	45	40.2	D	D	D	5.7	5.2	7.5	24.0	1 182	306	57	2 409	-13.7
Johnson	11 408	0.1	14.8	8.7	76.9	10.8	11.3	31.4	8.3	50 087	117	1 990	144 155	40.2
Kearny	53	40.4	D	D	28.6	3.1	3.0	5.3	27.3	611	146	43	1 561	10.8
Kingman	80	3.6	32.5	13.7	45.5	9.1	6.4	20.2	18.4	2 018	236	103	3 645	-1.0
Kiowa	38	17.1	D	0.9	D	7.9	3.6	17.7	23.1	851	245	48	1 738	1.5
Labette	297	1.3	D	28.6	D	9.6	3.8	16.9	25.2	4 933	214	596	10 641	0.2
Lane	38	42.1	D	0.4	D	4.8	D	5.4	17.6	547	242	19	1 117	-6.4
Leavenworth	945	0.3	12.5	5.4	29.2	5.8	4.2	16.1	58.0	8 418	118	496	21 264	15.3
Lincoln	32	22.5	D	D	D	8.5	4.8	9.8	31.6	984	295	31	1 864	-11.7
Linn	72	2.0	18.6	4.4	D	7.1	5.5	D	23.8	2 276	249	147	4 811	21.0
Logan	38	18.9	D	1.2	D	10.8	5.5	12.0	25.0	751	251	31	1 466	-9.3
Lyon	515	0.7	38.0	34.0	39.5	9.3	2.6	15.9	21.8	4 968	146	469	14 346	2.6
McPherson	459	4.4	D	28.7	D	7.7	5.4	18.8	11.0	6 132	214	236	10 941	4.6
Marion	111	6.4	16.3	9.8	55.2	10.1	5.1	25.1	22.1	3 251	239	146	5 659	-3.5
Marshall	159	12.7	D	18.8	D	8.2	5.9	14.5	12.1	2 716	247	172	5 269	-5.6
Meade	70	46.7	D	1.0	D	4.1	2.7	8.1	16.7	933	211	33	2 049	0.0
Miami	243	0.1	24.7	10.3	52.6	10.5	5.7	17.6	22.7	4 182	157	355	8 971	6.1
Mitchell	118	13.8	17.0	13.6	50.9	8.6	2.9	18.3	18.3	1 727	249	71	3 359	-4.3
Montgomery	483	1.4	40.5	35.6	43.8	9.5	3.1	20.7	14.4	8 690	234	968	17 920	-1.3
Morris	53	9.6	D	11.7	D	11.2	D	14.7	23.2	1 540	250	79	3 149	-1.2
Morton	55	7.4	D	D	D	6.0	3.7	D	29.2	600	174	31	1 515	4.2
Nemaha	142	16.7	22.6	18.3	46.9	7.8	3.9	17.7	13.8	2 510	248	127	4 319	-2.5
Neosho	219	-0.5	36.8	28.7	43.4	9.7	4.0	17.1	20.3	3 724	222	341	7 726	-2.0
Ness	46	8.3	D	2.0	D	8.4	5.0	11.2	25.8	975	270	35	2 048	-2.8
Norton	78	14.6	D	6.6	D	7.5	5.5	14.4	29.3	1 403	244	61	2 798	-6.2

1. Covers mining, construction, and manufacturing.　　2. Covers private sector earnings in agricultural services, forestry, and fisheries; transportation and public utilities; wholesale trade; retail trade; finance, insurance, and real estate; and services.　　3. Per 1,000 resident population estimated as of July 1 of the year shown.

Table B. States and Counties — Housing, Labor Force, and Employment

STATE County	Housing units, 1990 (cont'd) Occupied units Owner-occupied Total	Percent	Median value[1]	Owner cost as a percent of income With a mortgage	Without a mortgage	Renter-occupied Median rent[2]	Rent as percent of income	Substandard units[3] (percent)	Civilian labor force, 1999 Total	Percent change, 1998–1999	Unemployment Total	Rate[4]	Civilian employment, 1990[5] Total	Percent Professional, managerial, and technical	Precision production, craft, and repair
	89	90	91	92	93	94	95	96	97	98	99	100	101	102	103
KANSAS—Cont'd															
Barber	2 358	75.1	28 400	20.7	13.1	276	21.2	1.7	2 441	1.9	54	2.2	2 645	17.4	11.2
Barton	11 561	72.3	37 700	18.2	12.4	299	21.9	2.2	14 974	-0.4	449	3.0	14 001	22.5	14.6
Bourbon	5 897	73.8	29 800	21.0	13.8	264	25.9	3.2	7 025	-1.1	285	4.1	6 172	23.8	9.3
Brown	4 347	70.6	28 000	15.1	12.3	240	22.0	1.7	6 090	-0.5	408	6.7	4 737	23.7	10.0
Butler	18 488	75.4	51 800	18.6	12.7	352	22.5	2.9	31 994	0.8	914	2.9	24 054	27.8	17.1
Chase	1 214	75.6	22 400	19.4	12.1	247	23.3	1.0	1 521	1.1	50	3.3	1 274	22.2	10.5
Chautauqua	1 835	79.9	18 900	20.6	14.0	263	22.8	4.1	1 768	-2.0	82	4.6	1 606	21.3	11.5
Cherokee	8 396	76.5	27 000	18.0	12.3	260	27.7	3.5	10 242	-0.6	423	4.1	8 740	20.6	14.3
Cheyenne	1 389	75.6	31 900	18.7	12.8	224	19.7	5.3	1 595	-9.6	24	1.5	1 425	16.6	8.6
Clark	1 006	75.3	29 500	14.4	13.2	288	18.7	2.0	1 345	1.1	20	1.5	1 204	17.0	11.0
Clay	3 641	73.4	33 800	20.7	11.9	231	21.3	2.5	4 986	1.3	135	2.7	3 984	19.6	13.2
Cloud	4 483	72.4	25 600	14.2	12.3	230	18.9	1.5	4 984	-1.8	139	2.8	5 001	22.7	10.0
Coffey	3 311	77.3	34 800	18.2	12.1	288	20.1	2.6	4 221	4.3	180	4.3	3 867	21.2	13.2
Comanche	950	71.8	24 300	16.1	12.5	227	21.2	2.9	1 053	4.9	13	1.2	1 044	16.7	9.5
Cowley	14 047	71.2	37 500	18.2	12.7	321	23.3	2.0	17 888	-3.6	656	3.7	16 476	23.4	15.0
Crawford	14 606	67.5	30 700	18.3	13.0	299	29.6	2.1	18 670	3.0	606	3.2	14 905	26.8	11.2
Decatur	1 651	75.1	28 800	17.8	14.6	249	21.9	1.6	1 729	1.4	32	1.9	1 854	18.4	8.4
Dickinson	7 542	73.5	35 600	19.0	12.3	280	22.5	1.4	10 448	0.2	293	2.8	8 579	21.8	11.3
Doniphan	3 074	75.4	29 200	16.6	13.2	260	21.8	3.8	4 561	6.9	215	4.7	3 467	18.4	10.9
Douglas	30 138	52.5	68 000	19.7	12.3	413	33.8	3.0	55 730	1.9	1 789	3.2	41 086	35.1	8.1
Edwards	1 585	75.3	24 900	16.4	13.1	242	18.9	1.4	1 739	4.6	39	2.2	1 714	19.7	11.4
Elk	1 436	80.0	14 999	19.3	13.4	188	25.4	2.3	1 400	0.1	52	3.7	1 354	19.7	12.4
Ellis	10 096	64.4	49 600	19.9	12.9	291	25.3	1.2	17 173	-0.6	378	2.2	13 255	27.1	10.3
Ellsworth	2 522	77.4	28 300	16.4	13.6	258	18.6	1.6	2 985	0.8	59	2.0	2 688	23.6	11.5
Finney	10 836	61.5	50 800	18.7	12.8	383	22.6	7.9	19 919	1.8	499	2.5	16 424	20.1	20.3
Ford	9 872	64.9	48 900	19.0	12.5	337	23.8	5.1	15 885	0.5	300	1.9	13 258	23.8	14.4
Franklin	8 308	72.7	37 700	18.1	12.7	311	23.9	2.2	13 279	-6.8	431	3.2	10 075	22.7	13.9
Geary	10 676	45.5	55 400	20.4	12.6	366	26.6	4.4	10 357	-1.2	609	5.9	9 714	26.0	10.2
Gove	1 284	79.7	30 300	18.8	12.4	246	13.9	1.4	1 543	6.6	24	1.6	1 404	19.2	10.1
Graham	1 435	76.8	24 900	16.2	13.2	245	18.0	2.5	1 577	3.2	33	2.1	1 631	20.7	11.6
Grant	2 393	69.2	53 200	18.3	11.3	319	22.8	4.4	3 877	-5.6	136	3.5	3 425	16.9	17.8
Gray	1 913	72.4	45 500	18.9	11.6	287	17.0	4.1	3 451	1.5	60	1.7	2 487	15.4	11.5
Greeley	656	70.1	39 500	23.1	14.5	297	17.2	3.2	817	0.2	21	2.6	868	18.5	9.4
Greenwood	3 285	74.2	21 900	16.8	13.2	265	25.6	1.6	3 254	-1.0	149	4.6	3 250	17.9	12.9
Hamilton	986	70.8	37 800	17.6	13.5	268	21.5	2.0	1 284	10.3	16	1.2	1 175	17.7	9.8
Harper	3 007	73.3	32 300	17.6	13.0	264	24.4	1.4	2 975	-1.0	84	2.8	3 125	18.7	14.0
Harvey	11 581	68.4	47 100	17.7	12.4	326	22.8	2.3	17 997	6.8	469	2.6	14 999	27.5	13.3
Haskell	1 372	70.0	45 900	17.6	12.3	330	19.4	5.1	2 196	5.8	42	1.9	1 887	14.9	10.3
Hodgeman	826	81.0	26 800	14.9	12.3	252	17.5	2.9	1 105	14.2	20	1.8	900	22.8	7.2
Jackson	4 277	81.4	34 300	17.1	13.2	249	26.5	4.7	8 915	22.5	247	2.8	5 250	21.5	12.9
Jefferson	5 778	83.9	47 100	16.6	13.2	327	22.5	4.4	9 937	-7.5	299	3.0	7 528	23.0	12.7
Jewell	1 806	78.7	14 999	15.3	12.9	201	18.0	1.3	2 132	6.6	33	1.5	1 948	18.1	10.3
Johnson	136 433	69.4	91 500	20.2	11.8	515	23.5	1.1	269 615	4.0	5 057	1.9	196 066	42.2	6.8
Kearny	1 379	69.4	45 900	18.8	12.4	341	20.5	6.3	2 176	-0.4	49	2.3	1 915	18.2	16.1
Kingman	3 175	75.6	34 600	17.9	13.5	287	19.0	1.4	4 237	-1.8	124	2.9	3 651	19.1	13.3
Kiowa	1 466	71.6	33 600	16.5	12.4	256	21.5	1.1	1 689	10.2	27	1.6	1 650	19.4	10.2
Labette	9 377	73.3	29 000	16.8	13.3	290	23.4	2.4	11 882	6.8	466	3.9	10 421	24.9	11.1
Lane	966	74.9	32 600	18.0	13.8	249	16.5	0.7	1 124	11.2	31	2.8	1 050	19.6	9.5
Leavenworth	19 715	65.2	64 000	20.8	12.8	426	22.2	2.7	29 659	2.1	943	3.2	23 248	28.8	11.7
Lincoln	1 531	78.8	17 200	17.8	12.9	195	20.2	1.8	1 882	5.0	33	1.8	1 673	20.6	7.2
Linn	3 215	80.2	26 800	16.9	13.5	256	25.9	3.8	3 215	-2.1	202	6.3	3 046	21.2	18.9
Logan	1 221	76.7	30 800	16.9	12.8	238	19.8	2.3	1 623	-6.2	28	1.7	1 472	16.8	8.9
Lyon	13 059	61.3	45 800	18.5	13.1	301	25.8	3.4	19 920	-0.6	619	3.1	16 719	23.1	15.2
McPherson	10 230	73.1	47 900	18.0	12.2	300	21.1	1.7	16 296	1.6	328	2.0	13 640	23.4	13.2
Marion	4 975	79.1	30 700	17.3	11.9	261	21.9	2.0	7 003	-1.0	152	2.2	5 896	20.2	11.9
Marshall	4 689	78.0	26 300	16.0	12.4	241	22.7	2.7	6 142	2.2	140	2.3	5 033	19.9	10.5
Meade	1 667	72.5	35 900	15.9	12.4	280	18.0	2.7	2 230	-4.1	43	1.9	2 065	23.2	10.3
Miami	8 402	77.1	47 700	18.9	13.0	328	23.7	2.9	14 416	2.4	395	2.7	11 093	22.5	15.8
Mitchell	2 846	74.0	28 800	16.5	13.1	257	22.7	1.5	3 778	9.0	62	1.6	3 251	22.3	9.2
Montgomery	15 670	72.3	29 400	19.0	13.4	290	24.6	1.9	18 875	7.7	826	4.4	16 545	23.4	15.2
Morris	2 528	75.8	33 500	16.7	12.4	259	21.3	2.2	3 171	2.4	87	2.7	2 770	20.4	10.4
Morton	1 290	72.7	44 700	17.0	12.4	300	21.3	3.7	1 749	-2.1	37	2.1	1 547	20.7	11.4
Nemaha	3 996	80.6	35 400	19.1	13.0	241	21.8	3.4	5 592	-6.5	132	2.4	4 820	21.3	10.5
Neosho	6 748	74.8	28 600	17.9	13.0	273	23.2	1.9	8 883	0.9	359	4.0	7 553	22.7	13.2
Ness	1 670	80.0	29 900	17.4	13.6	249	17.6	0.7	1 846	3.5	41	2.2	1 882	20.6	9.9
Norton	2 330	74.9	25 700	12.8	12.4	242	19.6	1.3	3 224	1.4	42	1.3	2 715	23.7	9.9

1. Specified owner-occupied units. 2. Specified renter-occupied units. 3. Overcrowded or lacking complete plumbing facilities. 4. Percent of civilian labor force. 5. Persons 16 years and older.

Table B. States and Counties — Nonfarm Employment and Agriculture

STATE County	Private nonfarm establishments, employment and payroll, 1998									Agriculture, 1997			
	Number of establishments	Employment						Annual payroll		Farms			Farm operators
		Total	Health Care and Social Assistance	Manufacturing	Retail trade	Finance and Insurance	Professional Scientific and Technical Services	Total (mil dol)	Average per employee (dollars)	Number	Percent with—		Whose principal occupation is farming (percent)
											Less than 50 acres	500 acres and over	
	104	105	106	107	108	109	110	111	112	113	114	115	116
KANSAS—Cont'd													
Barber	209	1 377	254	D	320	76	32	29	21 126	433	8.5	54.7	64.9
Barton	1 070	10 939	1 718	1 672	1 824	377	609	228	20 840	742	10.9	44.9	64.3
Bourbon	429	6 522	1 097	1 343	661	737	147	134	20 551	805	14.8	24.1	45.7
Brown	293	3 818	723	660	424	135	87	70	18 242	599	15.5	33.6	62.3
Butler	1 219	11 075	1 695	1 837	1 908	444	324	244	22 028	1 256	20.9	26.7	45.0
Chase	67	406	D	D	100	32	11	6	15 150	285	11.6	48.8	58.6
Chautauqua	99	614	225	D	90	37	6	8	12 993	376	12.2	43.1	55.9
Cherokee	401	5 343	703	2 334	597	134	106	117	21 943	725	26.3	19.0	49.5
Cheyenne	109	572	140	D	127	28	18	9	15 885	398	4.8	61.1	70.1
Clark	82	468	154	D	66	44	19	9	19 996	260	7.3	56.5	65.0
Clay	304	2 501	479	414	516	115	48	44	17 485	546	11.5	44.0	67.2
Cloud	356	3 057	694	348	555	166	70	56	18 170	545	14.3	44.0	60.0
Coffey	266	2 935	425	D	435	107	D	93	31 856	555	11.0	32.1	54.2
Comanche	79	431	132	62	68	36	D	6	14 961	256	5.5	65.6	74.2
Cowley	853	11 845	2 286	3 244	1 949	358	169	258	21 803	962	16.5	27.3	50.4
Crawford	1 006	13 684	2 137	3 457	1 882	424	402	278	20 301	787	21.9	21.0	48.2
Decatur	122	815	239	D	100	33	71	12	14 811	396	10.1	60.1	70.2
Dickinson	547	5 613	785	1 240	820	202	121	105	18 679	893	13.0	38.1	60.2
Doniphan	165	2 191	170	D	278	70	D	55	25 079	507	17.6	29.4	57.8
Douglas	2 590	35 809	4 527	4 640	6 189	1 357	1 753	731	20 407	839	30.3	13.8	42.9
Edwards	102	806	157	287	66	33	9	16	19 294	302	3.0	59.9	72.2
Elk	63	233	D	D	D	20	D	3	13 489	383	12.0	41.0	53.8
Ellis	1 029	12 378	3 058	1 159	2 201	367	881	231	18 661	674	8.2	42.4	54.5
Ellsworth	190	1 618	398	300	246	66	77	33	20 637	520	6.6	50.9	64.4
Finney	1 002	15 887	1 624	5 724	2 468	432	454	355	22 343	692	11.1	49.3	58.1
Ford	837	12 682	1 323	4 445	2 048	292	477	292	23 059	792	7.8	48.8	52.3
Franklin	584	7 173	963	751	1 060	209	151	156	21 707	956	22.7	16.9	42.9
Geary	576	7 531	1 154	343	1 164	252	220	140	18 613	223	17.5	41.7	60.1
Gove	134	793	206	131	178	49	9	14	17 723	439	5.9	62.0	74.7
Graham	113	710	224	D	150	51	13	11	15 777	382	6.5	56.0	64.1
Grant	253	2 414	187	215	430	116	29	59	24 500	257	6.2	62.6	70.0
Gray	202	1 206	133	38	160	114	37	27	22 631	461	5.4	66.4	74.8
Greeley	64	340	D	D	58	16	3	6	18 379	273	2.9	62.3	66.7
Greenwood	255	1 600	405	113	257	69	30	27	16 914	593	11.1	39.0	56.3
Hamilton	86	593	D	0	93	39	14	11	17 789	267	4.1	70.0	68.2
Harper	231	1 622	295	313	276	93	33	29	17 803	529	9.6	46.3	61.6
Harvey	826	12 256	2 732	3 139	1 694	286	189	276	22 491	779	23.2	27.5	56.5
Haskell	119	758	D	D	79	48	7	6	21 001	241	3.3	70.5	78.8
Hodgeman	46	292	D	D	54	D	7	6	18 911	359	4.5	67.7	67.7
Jackson	270	2 899	391	194	430	91	47	50	17 412	1 050	18.1	17.1	41.3
Jefferson	345	2 019	401	176	346	97	67	39	19 364	1 018	22.1	13.6	41.2
Jewell	121	567	D	D	96	73	11	8	13 457	579	7.4	47.5	73.2
Johnson	14 971	253 795	21 215	21 658	36 425	19 802	21 145	8 097	31 905	604	41.6	11.9	37.7
Kearny	90	504	90	0	62	39	9	12	23 464	271	2.6	66.8	76.0
Kingman	221	1 995	469	392	264	113	46	39	19 642	759	11.7	40.8	58.1
Kiowa	117	937	220	D	159	41	9	17	17 670	318	3.8	58.2	62.3
Labette	528	7 603	1 619	2 432	1 006	286	135	167	21 907	901	17.8	22.3	46.1
Lane	92	406	D	8	60	32	9	8	18 490	287	5.9	65.5	67.6
Leavenworth	1 089	14 079	3 054	766	2 026	751	772	325	23 095	1 046	33.0	8.3	41.1
Lincoln	116	721	182	D	111	36	18	11	15 193	454	8.1	51.8	70.0
Linn	199	1 287	127	143	208	71	22	35	27 453	757	16.0	21.4	45.6
Logan	136	748	143	D	159	49	39	13	17 733	326	5.5	66.6	69.3
Lyon	917	15 129	1 742	6 431	1 936	328	240	327	21 644	855	15.3	29.2	49.1
McPherson	942	12 640	1 866	3 811	1 377	599	197	290	22 925	1 163	16.2	30.8	56.7
Marion	348	3 214	723	405	551	127	98	54	16 876	968	16.2	36.3	60.6
Marshall	403	3 558	628	894	492	248	165	70	19 648	922	13.8	40.3	66.4
Meade	155	857	157	D	164	44	21	16	19 092	416	6.5	62.0	63.9
Miami	610	6 146	1 712	642	1 255	267	148	132	21 425	1 245	33.5	10.5	34.9
Mitchell	279	2 580	478	435	443	118	48	48	18 747	487	11.5	54.2	72.7
Montgomery	1 069	15 075	2 224	5 547	1 941	389	238	321	21 321	964	19.7	16.2	40.9
Morris	167	1 238	213	279	249	59	66	21	16 752	489	13.3	41.3	61.1
Morton	127	929	D	D	82	45	20	22	23 384	233	3.4	59.2	67.0
Nemaha	390	3 960	822	1 096	495	145	102	81	20 521	1 007	12.3	28.6	63.0
Neosho	545	6 748	1 225	2 210	923	280	137	129	19 158	722	18.8	26.0	47.2
Ness	153	1 005	230	33	105	57	29	18	17 442	516	3.1	62.6	69.0
Norton	215	1 666	372	128	253	92	62	33	19 530	399	10.5	56.6	63.7

Table B. States and Counties — Agriculture, Land, and Water

	Agriculture, 1997 (cont'd)														
STATE County	Land in farms				Value of land and buildings		Value of machinery and equipment Average per farm ($1,000)	Value of products sold		Percent from —		Percent of farms with sales of —		Percent of land owned by Fed. Gov. 1997	Water consumption 1995 (mil gal/day)
	Acreage (1,000)	Percent change, 1992–1997	Acres			Average per farm ($1,000)	Average per acre (dollars)		Total (mil dol)	Average per farm (dollars)	Crops	Livestock and poultry products	$10,000 or more	$100,000 or more		
			Average size of farm	Total irrigated (1,000)	Total cropland (1,000)											
	117	118	119	120	121	122	123	124	125	126	127	128	129	130	131	132

KANSAS—Cont'd

County	117	118	119	120	121	122	123	124	125	126	127	128	129	130	131	132
Barber	595	-6.9	1 374	5	194	484	353	75	48	111 277	34.9	65.1	73.0	27.3	0.0	4.7
Barton	613	5.6	826	43	488	465	573	84	186	250 210	28.5	71.5	73.2	25.1	0.0	38.2
Bourbon	329	-2.2	409	D	158	212	493	36	30	36 775	42.0	58.0	49.2	8.7	0.0	3.3
Brown	333	-1.8	556	D	267	538	961	104	70	117 284	67.0	33.0	75.0	29.4	0.0	2.1
Butler	759	-0.9	604	1	314	420	715	42	133	106 255	21.7	78.3	49.1	15.4	0.3	12.8
Chase	409	16.3	1 436	D	88	671	490	65	65	227 296	11.7	88.3	72.3	29.1	0.0	0.9
Chautauqua	391	1.1	1 041	D	61	439	414	33	29	77 171	23.5	76.5	54.5	15.4	0.4	1.2
Cherokee	269	-0.6	371	D	208	284	752	66	52	71 982	57.0	43.0	50.6	15.2	0.0	92.3
Cheyenne	562	-5.0	1 413	46	368	675	473	100	54	134 530	54.3	45.7	75.1	28.9	0.0	38.0
Clark	546	-3.4	2 098	17	196	1 059	499	84	105	405 162	12.0	88.0	73.1	28.8	0.0	5.3
Clay	369	-3.3	675	15	258	383	608	85	64	117 455	51.8	48.2	74.7	30.6	2.2	14.5
Cloud	393	-3.4	722	15	280	401	570	82	46	84 095	73.3	26.7	67.7	26.6	0.0	15.2
Coffey	307	-13.1	553	0	201	334	610	70	39	70 825	59.4	40.6	63.6	19.6	3.3	23.5
Comanche	504	3.5	1 969	6	168	805	390	66	29	113 712	40.0	60.0	78.9	32.4	0.0	7.7
Cowley	643	2.3	668	2	276	354	540	45	68	70 197	34.5	65.5	57.5	14.1	0.6	9.6
Crawford	291	-4.1	369	1	189	221	638	47	35	44 735	66.0	34.0	50.1	11.9	0.0	6.8
Decatur	515	-2.1	1 301	12	322	558	434	101	68	170 679	37.8	62.2	81.6	31.3	0.0	13.2
Dickinson	514	0.0	576	3	381	373	638	79	92	102 847	47.3	52.7	68.2	25.3	0.3	5.2
Doniphan	222	9.9	438	1	174	458	1 161	73	47	92 913	84.6	15.4	67.9	27.2	0.0	0.9
Douglas	219	-1.6	260	2	147	297	1 135	53	39	46 347	55.6	44.4	39.8	10.1	3.1	21.6
Edwards	357	-11.5	1 181	77	283	671	495	123	82	271 217	50.2	49.8	77.8	42.4	0.0	95.5
Elk	331	2.1	864	0	78	368	428	31	21	53 571	20.4	79.6	55.1	13.1	0.0	1.4
Ellis	507	-7.3	753	2	313	320	403	63	50	74 479	30.9	69.1	63.1	10.8	0.0	4.9
Ellsworth	376	-15.0	886	1	234	344	432	71	29	68 823	62.4	37.6	74.5	24.3	2.2	2.8
Finney	761	2.2	1 464	230	631	951	588	195	480	922 739	21.7	78.3	77.1	49.8	0.0	295.3
Ford	669	-0.3	967	70	524	483	508	130	308	445 514	15.8	84.2	70.2	29.6	0.0	103.7
Franklin	303	-4.1	317	1	193	317	975	38	47	49 466	51.0	49.0	45.5	11.1	0.0	3.2
Geary	154	-6.1	690	3	74	375	517	51	19	85 257	36.9	63.1	59.6	20.2	8.2	8.5
Gove	649	-3.5	1 478	14	389	682	477	116	122	277 233	24.2	75.8	81.5	34.9	0.0	20.1
Graham	486	-5.3	1 271	9	304	458	333	79	42	109 256	45.2	54.8	72.3	22.0	0.0	10.8
Grant	333	-2.7	1 294	109	277	888	660	175	291	1 133 381	14.8	85.2	76.7	49.4	0.0	173.0
Gray	556	7.3	1 206	165	469	786	663	172	374	810 604	20.8	79.2	84.2	55.5	0.0	225.6
Greeley	442	4.2	1 618	18	399	720	444	119	123	449 010	21.0	79.0	72.2	32.6	0.0	26.4
Greenwood	634	5.0	1 069	0	153	516	475	54	58	97 740	14.8	85.2	58.0	18.5	2.1	2.0
Hamilton	528	-1.0	1 976	22	397	711	353	117	176	658 671	12.5	87.5	68.9	36.3	0.0	47.4
Harper	461	-7.6	871	1	319	459	494	65	55	104 318	56.9	43.1	72.8	29.1	0.0	3.1
Harvey	321	0.3	412	28	282	449	1 001	85	71	91 652	58.4	41.6	63.4	24.6	0.0	41.9
Haskell	369	0.5	1 530	176	327	1 321	828	241	432	1 794 382	17.4	82.6	83.0	66.0	0.0	291.1
Hodgeman	485	1.0	1 351	24	344	536	423	89	96	268 587	20.2	79.8	77.2	30.4	0.0	32.8
Jackson	321	-5.5	306	D	190	206	660	31	29	27 536	47.9	52.1	47.0	7.2	0.0	2.0
Jefferson	269	-1.1	264	2	176	239	844	38	35	34 126	55.4	44.6	39.1	9.2	4.6	3.1
Jewell	459	-5.3	793	8	315	418	541	89	51	88 470	62.6	37.4	76.2	26.8	0.4	78.1
Johnson	136	-3.7	225	1	88	488	2 349	37	37	61 808	39.7	60.3	37.7	9.6	3.2	12.3
Kearny	526	1.7	1 940	80	381	890	468	148	185	681 602	24.5	75.5	75.3	42.4	0.0	192.3
Kingman	521	-4.3	686	12	351	366	532	72	56	73 880	61.4	38.6	68.5	22.5	0.1	16.4
Kiowa	442	10.5	1 390	40	268	640	446	91	47	149 012	57.5	42.5	72.0	28.0	0.0	51.2
Labette	331	-4.5	368	D	212	229	628	48	59	64 989	35.4	64.6	49.1	10.9	3.3	4.6
Lane	435	3.9	1 517	14	321	595	410	97	134	468 159	16.2	83.8	81.9	36.2	0.0	20.5
Leavenworth	202	-2.5	193	0	126	335	1 724	31	42	40 615	66.2	33.8	36.6	5.9	2.2	9.7
Lincoln	428	-11.3	942	1	248	481	514	60	34	75 796	67.8	32.2	74.9	24.2	0.3	1.3
Linn	278	1.5	367	0	157	217	669	31	30	39 646	46.9	53.1	41.9	8.9	1.6	727.2
Logan	628	4.1	1 926	16	362	647	341	86	36	111 259	62.9	37.1	78.8	28.8	0.0	8.0
Lyon	496	2.0	580	D	257	333	573	61	77	90 555	30.8	69.2	59.6	13.5	1.0	8.9
McPherson	523	-2.8	449	29	412	346	847	64	113	97 196	53.4	46.6	73.0	23.5	0.1	29.9
Marion	563	-4.3	582	2	368	394	717	70	81	83 990	45.6	54.4	70.8	22.6	0.8	3.3
Marshall	514	-10.3	558	1	358	401	718	70	70	76 208	63.1	36.9	72.5	24.6	1.0	3.1
Meade	555	-7.0	1 333	115	349	606	470	124	113	270 837	45.9	54.1	77.4	38.5	0.0	157.5
Miami	280	-2.5	225	1	175	321	1 440	41	40	32 050	45.2	54.8	34.4	5.9	1.3	4.0
Mitchell	455	-5.1	933	5	357	533	598	116	87	177 710	49.3	50.7	78.4	36.6	2.7	12.2
Montgomery	328	1.3	341	1	184	217	627	53	46	47 225	37.3	62.7	37.8	7.0	2.8	8.7
Morris	396	-3.4	810	0	186	386	516	71	47	96 583	37.1	62.9	71.4	21.1	0.5	1.8
Morton	422	-1.1	1 813	42	268	653	374	178	58	247 839	35.4	64.6	68.2	29.6	22.0	55.6
Nemaha	418	-5.3	415	0	305	301	738	60	91	89 977	37.0	63.0	73.9	23.7	0.0	3.0
Neosho	345	5.5	478	D	221	272	536	53	38	52 556	52.3	47.7	47.5	13.0	0.0	3.2
Ness	623	-6.7	1 208	3	414	380	334	73	34	66 584	56.2	43.8	78.9	20.0	0.0	5.6
Norton	479	2.7	1 200	8	289	621	432	81	42	104 447	50.0	50.0	73.7	30.3	0.9	12.2

Table B. States and Counties — Residential Construction, Wholesale and Retail Trade, and Real Estate

STATE County	Value of Residential Construction Authorized by Building Permits, 1999		Wholesale Trade, 1997				Retail Trade[1], 1997				Real Estate and Rental and Leasing, 1997			
	New Construction ($1,000)	Number of Housing Units	Number of Establishments	Number of Employees	Sales (mil dol)	Annual Payroll (mil dol)	Number of Establishments	Number of Employees	Sales (mil dol)	Annual Payroll (mil dol)	Number of Establishments	Number of Employees	Receipts (mil dol)	Annual Payroll (mil dol)
	133	134	135	136	137	138	139	140	141	142	143	144	145	146
KANSAS—Cont'd														
Barber	0	0	12	97	35.7	2.0	39	271	35.1	3.9	2	D	D	D
Barton	3 764	54	92	737	206.2	18.2	185	1 803	282.8	28.7	17	48	3.4	1.0
Bourbon	883	19	24	475	233.2	9.8	69	606	95.2	8.8	11	38	2.4	0.6
Brown	1 027	12	27	152	73.6	3.7	51	407	67.1	5.4	5	12	1.0	0.2
Butler	57 499	559	67	368	136.2	8.8	194	1 875	350.3	29.3	38	96	7.0	1.4
Chase	0	0	2	D	D	D	14	103	8.3	0.8	NA	NA	NA	NA
Chautauqua	NA	NA	7	39	9.3	0.8	19	98	10.9	0.9	NA	NA	NA	NA
Cherokee	514	19	18	134	210.5	3.4	91	621	93.2	7.8	9	26	0.8	0.2
Cheyenne	80	1	11	118	57.8	2.7	30	125	17.7	1.4	3	4	0.3	0.1
Clark	100	1	5	D	D	D	19	62	7.6	0.8	NA	NA	NA	NA
Clay	863	12	18	140	55.4	3.2	61	487	63.4	6.3	5	12	1.1	0.1
Cloud	647	6	22	238	110.5	5.5	71	608	83.2	7.7	8	D	D	D
Coffey	2 880	32	9	76	38.5	2.1	50	418	58.8	5.2	6	11	0.4	0.1
Comanche	0	0	4	D	D	D	14	71	8.4	0.8	NA	NA	NA	NA
Cowley	4 294	37	38	343	118.9	8.9	173	1 682	255.5	24.2	22	67	4.7	1.5
Crawford	8 336	91	53	624	173.3	17.0	180	2 132	296.5	27.7	29	112	9.2	1.5
Decatur	223	4	15	144	74.3	2.9	23	108	10.2	1.1	5	3	1.4	0.2
Dickinson	3 909	33	25	365	220.6	8.8	110	900	125.0	11.4	10	D	D	D
Doniphan	3 139	38	11	D	D	D	27	322	43.2	4.0	4	7	0.6	0.0
Douglas	89 030	896	88	777	248.8	21.0	453	5 664	758.5	80.3	122	434	46.4	6.6
Edwards	0	0	8	87	57.6	2.6	15	64	7.6	0.7	NA	NA	NA	NA
Elk	NA	NA	6	18	10.9	0.4	8	30	3.7	0.2	2	D	D	D
Ellis	3 796	47	46	411	93.1	8.3	216	2 207	326.7	32.3	36	122	10.3	1.8
Ellsworth	470	4	12	D	D	D	41	242	30.3	2.5	3	3	0.1	0.0
Finney	4 008	65	84	791	495.5	26.2	186	2 502	405.0	38.3	45	147	16.2	3.1
Ford	7 238	85	55	607	347.8	17.3	169	2 016	367.4	31.9	37	114	11.0	1.7
Franklin	10 896	152	29	487	298.4	11.4	89	1 114	167.2	15.3	16	47	2.5	0.5
Geary	2 772	25	18	153	60.1	2.7	99	1 174	181.1	17.9	33	121	10.7	1.6
Gove	100	1	11	74	31.8	1.7	22	122	19.3	1.4	1	D	D	D
Graham	0	0	9	39	16.9	1.0	21	133	25.3	2.1	NA	NA	NA	NA
Grant	2 378	22	20	165	97.8	4.9	39	371	60.1	6.1	5	26	1.8	0.3
Gray	627	7	23	189	126.5	6.0	28	163	33.2	2.7	2	D	D	D
Greeley	370	3	3	D	D	D	11	59	9.2	0.9	2	D	D	D
Greenwood	0	0	14	70	6.2	0.7	41	215	36.6	2.9	5	10	0.3	0.0
Hamilton	402	6	11	136	53.8	3.0	16	81	14.3	1.0	2	D	D	D
Harper	232	3	18	168	76.8	3.8	39	266	38.7	2.9	3	8	0.2	0.1
Harvey	20 006	166	35	280	181.2	7.7	156	1 608	185.8	19.1	27	56	4.7	0.7
Haskell	93	5	13	146	92.3	4.7	15	84	10.6	0.9	NA	NA	NA	NA
Hodgeman	NA	NA	4	D	D	D	9	55	11.3	0.6	NA	NA	NA	NA
Jackson	6 201	76	12	45	25.0	0.8	50	489	73.9	6.4	6	D	D	D
Jefferson	9 574	115	10	30	9.6	0.5	60	353	51.4	4.2	8	D	D	D
Jewell	0	0	8	76	50.2	1.2	27	89	9.3	0.9	1	D	D	D
Johnson	834 626	7 377	1 502	19 597	21 107.6	789.6	1 903	30 545	5 418.8	543.2	646	4 947	681.3	119.5
Kearny	1 165	19	7	35	24.1	1.0	14	69	5.8	0.6	1	D	D	D
Kingman	5 856	58	15	129	51.6	3.7	41	290	36.2	3.6	4	12	0.4	0.1
Kiowa	0	0	7	50	30.2	1.4	21	176	20.2	1.9	NA	NA	NA	NA
Labette	1 125	18	29	214	81.7	4.6	120	1 021	147.5	14.1	10	37	3.4	0.6
Lane	0	0	9	69	36.0	1.6	17	62	8.9	0.8	NA	NA	NA	NA
Leavenworth	49 121	492	24	D	D	D	178	2 081	359.2	31.6	39	152	16.0	2.2
Lincoln	265	2	15	93	37.5	1.4	22	104	14.6	1.2	1	D	D	D
Linn	3 680	29	6	24	8.6	0.4	34	241	30.1	2.7	2	D	D	D
Logan	509	5	8	72	30.6	1.5	28	249	43.9	3.1	NA	NA	NA	NA
Lyon	8 463	164	41	571	197.3	14.0	172	1 982	285.5	29.3	32	118	7.7	1.6
McPherson	10 208	96	52	337	165.6	9.4	155	1 378	213.7	19.4	20	50	3.8	0.7
Marion	4 521	44	17	215	79.0	4.6	80	482	97.3	7.8	5	12	0.8	0.1
Marshall	95	1	24	206	115.2	5.6	74	490	76.5	6.0	5	5	0.2	0.0
Meade	200	2	10	87	66.8	2.4	32	171	21.3	2.0	3	D	D	D
Miami	30 608	223	21	D	D	D	91	1 163	170.6	16.3	17	65	6.2	0.9
Mitchell	713	6	25	247	133.5	6.1	61	448	79.7	6.7	3	11	0.3	0.0
Montgomery	2 224	22	52	472	124.4	10.9	223	2 013	264.2	25.4	36	130	7.0	1.7
Morris	297	3	6	24	8.0	0.5	39	239	40.1	2.9	3	9	0.5	0.1
Morton	0	0	13	146	78.8	3.7	19	84	10.8	1.2	NA	NA	NA	NA
Nemaha	3 203	22	21	135	58.5	3.0	82	490	88.1	6.5	5	D	D	D
Neosho	1 836	37	37	297	125.2	8.2	107	925	149.1	12.7	8	18	1.2	0.2
Ness	0	0	18	118	39.4	2.9	25	103	13.3	1.2	1	D	D	D
Norton	115	2	15	92	66.1	1.5	37	263	32.7	2.8	2	D	D	D

1. Establishments with payroll.

STATE County	Professional, Scientific, and Technical Services[1], 1997				Manufacturing, 1997				Accommodation and Foodservices, 1997			
	Number of Establishments	Number of Employees	Receipts (mil dol)	Annual Payroll (mil dol)	Number of Establishments	Number of Employees	Receipts (mil dol)	Annual Payroll (mil dol)	Number of Establishments	Number of Employees	Sales (mil dol)	Annual Payroll (mil dol)
	147	148	149	150	151	152	153	154	155	156	157	158
KANSAS—Cont'd												
Barber	7	27	1.7	0.4	NA	NA	NA	NA	16	121	2.4	0.7
Barton	65	699	26.0	13.5	45	1 608	308.1	34.0	71	959	26.8	7.2
Bourbon	23	111	7.0	3.4	29	1 295	149.0	29.4	60	D	D	D
Brown	12	70	4.3	1.8	18	820	75.8	18.0	20	248	5.4	1.4
Butler	63	198	11.2	3.9	52	1 704	1 132.7	58.8	96	1 400	37.6	10.6
Chase	4	9	0.4	0.1	NA	NA	NA	NA	8	D	D	D
Chautauqua	5	6	0.3	0.1	NA	NA	NA	NA	10	58	1.0	0.2
Cherokee	21	86	8.2	1.8	44	2 291	343.5	59.6	29	285	7.3	2.0
Cheyenne	4	11	0.7	0.2	NA	NA	NA	NA	9	51	1.2	0.3
Clark	5	12	0.4	0.2	NA	NA	NA	NA	6	D	D	D
Clay	10	41	1.6	0.7	NA	NA	NA	NA	21	256	4.6	1.3
Cloud	9	55	2.3	1.2	NA	NA	NA	NA	28	314	7.9	2.0
Coffey	11	20	0.8	0.3	NA	NA	NA	NA	21	172	4.6	1.2
Comanche	3	4	0.1	0.0	NA	NA	NA	NA	10	32	1.0	0.2
Cowley	36	148	8.2	3.2	47	3 793	1 176.7	107.3	74	1 002	25.6	6.5
Crawford	53	354	18.1	7.2	74	3 206	519.3	77.2	96	1 623	50.7	14.0
Decatur	7	43	1.9	0.7	NA	NA	NA	NA	7	D	D	D
Dickinson	24	95	7.9	1.7	25	1 161	160.9	24.6	49	494	12.6	3.6
Doniphan	7	24	0.7	0.2	8	D	D	D	10	51	1.3	0.4
Douglas	192	1 280	84.5	33.1	76	4 240	728.8	120.0	240	4 627	120.7	34.2
Edwards	5	14	0.4	0.1	NA	NA	NA	NA	11	D	D	D
Elk	4	4	0.2	0.1	NA	NA	NA	NA	8	D	D	D
Ellis	58	262	17.7	6.3	28	1 061	95.1	20.6	89	1 717	43.6	11.8
Ellsworth	8	77	4.7	2.1	NA	NA	NA	NA	16	122	3.5	0.9
Finney	59	450	22.3	9.2	38	5 416	2 420.2	123.4	68	1 310	40.2	11.1
Ford	49	439	27.6	12.5	29	D	D	D	69	1 102	35.4	9.6
Franklin	31	123	7.1	2.4	25	806	151.0	22.0	43	603	17.1	4.7
Geary	23	136	7.6	2.8	NA	NA	NA	NA	77	1 128	28.7	9.5
Gove	4	4	0.2	0.0	NA	NA	NA	NA	7	D	D	D
Graham	4	13	0.4	0.2	NA	NA	NA	NA	10	108	1.4	0.3
Grant	10	26	1.9	0.4	NA	NA	NA	NA	23	243	7.0	1.6
Gray	12	41	1.7	0.6	NA	NA	NA	NA	9	44	1.0	0.3
Greeley	2	D	D	D	NA	NA	NA	NA	5	30	0.5	0.1
Greenwood	13	29	1.0	0.3	NA	NA	NA	NA	27	D	D	D
Hamilton	7	18	0.9	0.2	NA	NA	NA	NA	7	59	1.2	0.3
Harper	12	33	1.3	0.4	NA	NA	NA	NA	22	172	4.4	1.1
Harvey	40	140	9.4	3.8	55	2 855	446.6	87.9	65	942	25.5	7.5
Haskell	3	11	0.7	0.3	NA	NA	NA	NA	8	51	1.2	0.3
Hodgeman	3	5	0.1	0.0	NA	NA	NA	NA	4	D	D	D
Jackson	11	39	1.4	0.4	NA	NA	NA	NA	20	271	5.8	1.6
Jefferson	16	35	1.5	0.5	NA	NA	NA	NA	33	148	4.2	0.7
Jewell	4	11	0.6	0.2	NA	NA	NA	NA	11	75	1.2	0.4
Johnson	1 780	18 416	2 032.6	810.1	551	20 590	3 659.3	662.8	827	19 029	636.3	188.5
Kearny	2	D	D	D	NA	NA	NA	NA	6	47	1.1	0.2
Kingman	12	44	1.9	0.8	NA	NA	NA	NA	18	197	4.4	1.2
Kiowa	5	9	0.3	0.1	NA	NA	NA	NA	11	89	1.8	0.6
Labette	23	103	5.6	2.6	40	2 298	254.5	64.4	45	548	13.3	3.7
Lane	4	9	0.4	0.1	NA	NA	NA	NA	4	D	D	D
Leavenworth	71	680	75.5	20.2	36	645	62.3	16.2	85	1 409	37.4	10.8
Lincoln	7	18	0.6	0.2	NA	NA	NA	NA	7	62	1.0	0.2
Linn	12	21	1.0	0.4	NA	NA	NA	NA	12	54	1.8	0.4
Logan	5	8	0.3	0.1	NA	NA	NA	NA	11	77	2.1	0.5
Lyon	38	200	9.6	4.3	40	6 478	2 054.1	167.1	104	1 633	37.3	10.0
McPherson	47	154	9.3	2.6	68	3 845	1 633.5	131.2	64	992	22.9	6.3
Marion	17	81	19.7	1.8	NA	NA	NA	NA	34	264	5.4	1.5
Marshall	10	37	1.7	0.6	21	880	106.8	23.0	36	257	6.1	1.5
Meade	6	20	0.8	0.2	NA	NA	NA	NA	8	62	1.4	0.3
Miami	32	95	6.9	2.0	31	682	58.2	19.1	36	456	11.2	3.3
Mitchell	12	35	2.3	0.6	NA	NA	NA	NA	24	274	5.1	1.5
Montgomery	59	209	12.7	4.4	61	4 590	1 482.9	121.6	87	1 164	30.3	8.5
Morris	8	51	2.4	0.6	NA	NA	NA	NA	10	D	D	D
Morton	6	19	1.0	0.3	NA	NA	NA	NA	10	90	2.4	0.6
Nemaha	20	62	3.9	1.7	19	1 047	209.5	30.3	31	256	5.0	1.4
Neosho	30	119	5.8	2.2	40	2 281	289.0	53.7	41	497	11.1	3.0
Ness	7	24	1.1	0.3	NA	NA	NA	NA	14	D	D	D
Norton	11	41	2.3	0.6	NA	NA	NA	NA	14	157	4.0	0.9

1. Firms subject to federal tax.

Table B. States and Counties — **Health and Other Services and Federal Funds**

	Health Care and Social Assistance[1], 1997				Other Services[1], 1997				Federal funds and grants, fiscal 1999[2]			
									Expenditures (mil dol)			
										Direct payments for individuals[3]		
STATE County	Number of Establishments	Number of Employees	Receipts (mil dol)	Annual Payroll (mil dol)	Number of Establishments	Number of Employees	Receipts (mil dol)	Annual Payroll (mil dol)	Total	Social Security and government retirement	Medicare	Food stamps and Supplemental Security Income
	159	160	161	162	163	164	165	166	167	168	169	170
KANSAS—Cont'd												
Barber	8	87	2.5	1.2	13	28	2.3	0.4	35.4	14.5	6.7	0.4
Barton	72	723	38.8	18.6	66	275	19.3	5.2	126.8	61.9	25.5	3.0
Bourbon	32	509	20.9	11.7	19	52	3.8	0.7	78.1	35.3	16.6	2.2
Brown	18	226	9.0	4.4	20	41	3.7	0.7	65.1	25.1	10.2	1.3
Butler	82	966	45.9	19.3	81	263	17.3	3.9	178.7	100.0	31.6	3.1
Chase	2	D	D	D	5	8	0.7	0.1	17.4	6.5	3.1	0.3
Chautauqua	8	165	3.9	2.2	2	D	D	D	24.6	11.9	5.3	0.5
Cherokee	21	290	9.2	4.1	14	37	2.4	0.6	102.7	45.7	20.8	4.1
Cheyenne	7	27	1.2	0.5	3	3	0.4	0.0	33.6	8.6	4.2	0.1
Clark	4	D	D	D	6	18	0.8	0.2	17.0	6.2	3.2	0.1
Clay	14	191	6.4	3.4	22	65	3.9	0.7	49.2	23.0	8.9	0.7
Cloud	23	149	7.5	3.6	19	93	6.6	2.0	66.5	27.6	13.0	0.9
Coffey	13	125	3.6	1.5	15	25	2.3	0.4	42.7	18.0	9.1	0.7
Comanche	5	D	D	D	5	31	1.1	0.3	16.1	6.2	2.5	0.1
Cowley	57	801	34.7	14.6	52	197	11.2	2.5	161.3	79.2	27.9	4.5
Crawford	82	1 022	38.8	17.0	59	519	48.0	12.7	175.3	82.4	35.1	5.3
Decatur	6	37	2.1	1.0	4	5	0.8	0.2	30.6	9.9	4.2	0.2
Dickinson	35	237	8.5	3.8	37	115	10.9	1.5	101.3	52.8	16.1	1.7
Doniphan	8	129	2.6	1.6	10	26	2.3	0.5	41.6	16.2	6.7	1.0
Douglas	175	1 648	88.7	41.8	132	782	42.5	13.5	290.4	116.1	34.5	5.8
Edwards	7	72	3.6	1.3	9	20	1.2	0.3	35.0	8.7	4.8	0.2
Elk	NA	NA	NA	NA	5	13	0.8	0.2	19.8	9.5	4.2	0.4
Ellis	70	623	42.9	19.4	71	302	23.1	5.2	105.6	47.4	21.2	1.8
Ellsworth	10	145	6.7	3.0	11	27	1.9	0.3	36.0	14.8	8.3	0.3
Finney	48	576	40.4	19.0	75	399	23.1	6.8	110.9	41.7	14.9	3.0
Ford	60	774	65.7	24.5	51	227	13.6	3.6	114.6	46.2	17.2	2.6
Franklin	41	417	17.7	8.4	33	126	8.8	2.1	94.5	46.2	20.1	2.4
Geary	39	283	13.0	5.4	54	529	20.8	10.3	566.8	72.4	8.5	3.9
Gove	2	D	D	D	13	30	2.6	0.4	29.5	7.2	3.8	0.1
Graham	7	25	2.1	0.5	6	15	1.2	0.2	26.8	8.1	3.9	0.3
Grant	9	35	3.3	1.1	15	59	5.3	1.1	31.5	9.9	3.8	0.6
Gray	5	D	D	D	11	22	2.9	0.4	43.6	9.1	3.2	0.1
Greeley	2	D	D	D	6	19	1.7	0.3	23.8	3.7	1.0	0.0
Greenwood	8	186	6.7	3.2	16	32	2.4	0.4	43.8	22.3	9.9	1.0
Hamilton	2	D	D	D	9	23	1.4	0.2	24.7	5.6	3.0	0.1
Harper	11	66	2.6	1.0	17	35	2.0	0.5	46.4	17.7	8.1	0.5
Harvey	51	1 052	66.3	33.2	45	205	12.4	3.7	150.1	71.1	26.4	2.2
Haskell	6	9	0.6	0.0	8	26	3.2	0.4	36.2	5.7	2.1	0.2
Hodgeman	1	D	D	D	3	6	0.2	0.1	19.8	4.6	2.5	0.0
Jackson	16	148	4.0	2.0	23	92	6.5	1.2	49.5	24.8	7.5	0.8
Jefferson	18	231	6.8	3.0	22	63	4.6	1.2	61.2	36.8	10.1	1.0
Jewell	2	D	D	D	10	27	1.7	0.3	34.5	10.8	3.7	0.3
Johnson	1 050	14 539	1 046.2	449.9	765	5 116	347.7	107.9	1 491.7	632.6	225.2	13.2
Kearny	5	17	1.2	0.4	8	16	1.2	0.2	30.3	6.2	2.7	0.3
Kingman	10	189	4.6	2.2	11	24	1.5	0.2	51.5	19.7	9.0	0.5
Kiowa	3	60	1.6	0.7	7	17	1.0	0.2	27.9	8.7	4.5	0.2
Labette	37	430	20.8	8.8	31	262	15.9	4.8	113.6	51.5	23.0	3.5
Lane	3	D	D	D	5	7	0.5	0.1	24.2	5.8	2.6	0.1
Leavenworth	87	906	44.8	20.7	82	545	22.7	7.4	558.3	159.6	36.6	4.6
Lincoln	7	71	1.6	0.8	5	12	0.6	0.1	26.0	9.2	3.5	0.1
Linn	14	127	2.8	1.1	9	18	1.9	0.3	48.1	22.6	10.2	1.0
Logan	5	55	2.6	1.1	9	50	2.4	0.6	26.5	7.9	3.3	0.1
Lyon	67	754	33.8	17.2	64	289	14.5	4.2	112.3	57.2	20.4	3.4
McPherson	47	489	19.7	8.2	70	297	21.6	5.7	121.7	60.8	21.3	1.3
Marion	20	193	7.4	3.3	19	47	2.9	0.5	67.6	31.1	12.6	0.6
Marshall	28	190	8.6	4.1	33	74	5.0	0.9	73.4	28.5	10.9	0.9
Meade	3	18	1.1	0.3	9	14	1.2	0.2	32.7	9.7	4.7	0.1
Miami	39	623	22.0	9.7	41	112	7.7	1.8	87.5	45.0	19.7	1.9
Mitchell	12	235	6.6	3.5	19	81	3.6	1.1	47.7	17.5	7.4	0.4
Montgomery	80	1 233	49.5	22.8	58	211	11.6	3.3	182.9	89.5	36.4	5.9
Morris	9	109	4.4	1.5	15	23	1.9	0.3	34.3	17.1	5.8	0.4
Morton	6	17	1.1	0.5	8	13	1.2	0.2	25.2	6.2	3.3	0.2
Nemaha	25	367	8.3	3.2	24	75	5.4	1.1	59.8	23.5	9.4	0.4
Neosho	32	513	21.5	8.7	33	132	9.5	2.3	77.6	39.2	15.3	2.3
Ness	6	18	0.9	0.4	10	28	2.1	0.4	36.3	9.5	5.5	0.1
Norton	14	76	4.1	1.4	14	32	3.5	0.6	43.2	14.2	5.8	0.3

1. Firms subject to federal tax.   2. October 1, 1998 to September 30, 1999.   3. State totals may include programs not allocated by county.

STATE County	Federal funds and grants, fiscal 1999[1] (cont'd)							Local government finances, 1997				
	Expenditures (mil dol) (cont'd)							General revenue				
	Procurement contract awards			Grants[2]							Taxes	
											Per capita[3] (dollars)	
	Salaries and wages	Defense	Other	Medicaid and other health-related	Nutrition and family welfare	Education	Other	Total (mil dol)	Intergovern-mental (mil dol)	Total (mil dol)	Total	Property
	171	172	173	174	175	176	177	178	179	180	181	182
KANSAS—Cont'd												
Barber	1.4	0.0	0.4	1.4	0.3	0.1	0.3	19.7	7.4	7.6	1 411	1 302
Barton	4.8	0.0	2.0	4.8	2.9	1.8	0.4	69.9	27.6	27.0	968	780
Bourbon	4.5	0.0	1.1	7.7	1.7	0.8	2.7	33.4	17.0	10.4	684	579
Brown	3.7	0.0	0.7	4.5	4.4	0.9	2.5	24.1	12.5	8.2	744	631
Butler	7.1	0.6	1.7	9.7	4.8	0.9	3.0	140.2	68.7	43.0	715	643
Chase	1.1	0.0	0.2	0.9	0.3	0.1	2.9	7.3	3.5	3.1	1 064	1 023
Chautauqua	1.0	0.0	0.3	2.5	0.5	0.2	1.0	9.4	4.7	3.5	802	725
Cherokee	3.0	0.8	0.8	16.1	3.4	1.2	0.6	37.9	20.5	10.1	447	364
Cheyenne	0.7	0.0	0.2	1.1	0.2	0.1	0.0	7.5	3.3	3.1	962	870
Clark	0.5	0.0	0.1	0.5	0.1	0.0	0.0	12.8	2.7	4.6	1 898	1 748
Clay	1.8	0.0	0.4	2.3	1.8	0.3	0.4	29.6	11.5	7.0	758	620
Cloud	2.4	0.0	0.6	6.1	0.8	0.3	2.4	31.9	16.0	9.7	955	824
Coffey	2.1	1.5	0.4	1.8	0.6	0.2	2.6	61.1	9.4	39.6	4 536	4 520
Comanche	0.4	0.0	0.1	0.7	0.1	0.1	0.0	7.8	2.3	3.3	1 644	1 598
Cowley	5.0	3.1	5.1	13.1	4.2	3.5	2.9	112.9	36.5	29.1	792	679
Crawford	6.9	0.2	2.1	23.2	7.5	2.1	2.1	76.2	34.0	26.1	724	479
Decatur	1.0	0.0	0.3	0.9	0.2	0.1	0.2	9.4	3.8	3.9	1 116	983
Dickinson	4.9	0.8	1.3	6.3	1.9	0.5	1.2	46.1	21.1	13.9	705	563
Doniphan	1.8	0.4	0.4	4.4	0.9	0.5	0.7	26.1	13.7	6.4	836	734
Douglas	26.4	4.6	7.2	30.2	6.9	25.4	19.9	214.2	55.5	76.4	839	656
Edwards	1.1	0.0	0.9	2.0	0.3	0.1	0.2	9.6	3.6	4.9	1 433	1 372
Elk	1.1	0.0	0.3	2.0	0.4	0.1	0.2	17.6	9.4	3.0	885	825
Ellis	8.4	0.0	1.3	7.3	2.0	1.5	1.2	50.2	19.0	22.6	858	747
Ellsworth	1.1	0.0	0.4	1.1	0.4	0.1	0.7	20.2	10.5	7.7	1 222	1 133
Finney	7.2	0.0	0.8	8.6	3.5	2.9	2.1	99.9	35.5	44.0	1 224	991
Ford	10.7	0.0	1.3	5.7	4.3	1.7	2.1	76.8	30.0	31.3	1 070	821
Franklin	4.6	0.2	0.9	8.4	3.9	0.7	1.4	60.8	22.6	17.2	724	565
Geary	381.5	72.7	0.9	9.3	5.8	7.1	1.4	75.8	31.1	17.7	701	493
Gove	0.9	0.0	0.2	0.5	0.1	0.1	0.5	14.7	7.2	3.7	1 206	1 114
Graham	0.8	0.0	0.3	1.4	0.3	0.1	0.1	13.0	3.6	4.9	1 502	1 490
Grant	1.0	0.0	0.2	0.7	0.7	0.4	0.0	33.3	2.8	24.3	3 078	2 973
Gray	0.9	0.0	0.2	1.4	0.3	0.1	0.1	15.4	6.9	6.8	1 239	1 169
Greeley	0.3	0.0	0.1	0.9	0.1	0.0	0.0	5.4	1.6	3.2	1 870	1 795
Greenwood	2.3	0.2	0.6	4.1	0.8	0.3	0.4	16.9	8.1	6.8	851	769
Hamilton	0.5	0.0	0.1	0.5	0.2	0.1	0.0	8.8	2.3	5.7	2 483	2 359
Harper	1.7	0.0	0.4	1.8	0.5	0.2	0.1	26.0	7.1	7.5	1 147	1 072
Harvey	3.7	0.0	1.1	4.8	2.7	0.6	22.9	69.7	27.8	24.8	784	612
Haskell	0.7	0.0	0.1	0.7	0.3	0.1	0.3	19.8	2.4	10.4	2 593	2 515
Hodgeman	0.6	0.0	0.2	0.5	0.1	0.1	0.0	10.1	3.0	3.5	1 564	1 436
Jackson	3.0	0.0	0.7	3.5	1.6	0.4	2.2	27.7	15.3	7.0	579	518
Jefferson	3.2	0.2	0.7	2.5	1.2	0.5	0.3	39.7	23.9	12.0	668	584
Jewell	1.7	0.0	0.4	2.3	0.3	0.1	1.3	10.2	4.6	4.1	1 022	960
Johnson	199.3	25.7	104.8	34.1	27.1	3.1	35.1	1 046.2	249.2	541.1	1 297	1 029
Kearny	0.5	0.0	0.1	1.1	0.4	0.1	0.9	22.9	2.0	16.4	3 905	3 863
Kingman	2.1	0.0	0.5	1.6	0.6	0.2	0.2	16.4	6.5	8.0	936	919
Kiowa	1.0	0.0	0.3	0.9	0.3	0.1	0.8	9.7	3.2	5.2	1 522	1 456
Labette	4.5	1.3	0.9	15.0	2.9	1.8	1.7	68.3	24.3	12.0	523	455
Lane	0.4	0.0	0.1	1.6	0.1	0.1	0.6	7.5	2.6	3.6	1 634	1 558
Leavenworth	234.0	80.5	12.4	13.4	4.9	4.7	3.4	113.8	61.0	34.7	495	419
Lincoln	1.4	0.0	0.3	0.9	0.2	0.1	0.9	11.7	4.0	4.0	1 194	1 128
Linn	1.8	0.3	0.5	4.8	0.9	0.3	1.1	25.3	7.7	13.9	1 532	1 495
Logan	0.6	0.0	0.1	0.5	1.2	0.1	0.0	11.5	3.8	4.0	1 312	1 242
Lyon	7.4	0.5	1.1	6.4	2.7	2.5	0.8	108.2	32.5	24.5	717	590
McPherson	4.5	1.9	1.1	4.3	2.2	0.6	1.2	63.5	24.4	26.2	950	820
Marion	3.1	0.3	0.8	3.2	0.8	0.2	0.9	26.3	14.0	8.0	619	540
Marshall	3.4	0.1	0.8	4.8	0.9	0.3	6.8	27.0	14.7	9.0	805	780
Meade	0.6	0.0	0.1	1.1	0.2	0.1	0.2	22.2	3.5	7.7	1 746	1 653
Miami	3.6	0.1	0.9	6.8	1.7	0.4	3.6	49.1	20.8	14.8	564	429
Mitchell	1.7	0.0	0.4	2.3	0.6	0.2	2.7	20.0	8.9	6.7	959	813
Montgomery	7.8	0.2	2.9	22.9	5.0	2.2	3.2	99.2	31.5	31.7	854	640
Morris	1.6	0.6	0.3	1.8	0.5	0.2	0.4	11.3	5.3	4.4	705	630
Morton	0.7	0.0	0.1	0.5	0.3	0.2	0.2	25.2	3.0	12.6	3 743	3 590
Nemaha	3.0	0.0	0.7	3.2	0.7	0.4	5.3	21.9	11.1	7.5	736	660
Neosho	3.0	0.6	0.7	6.6	1.8	1.2	0.2	57.6	16.3	12.4	732	613
Ness	1.3	0.0	0.3	0.7	0.2	0.1	6.8	16.0	3.8	6.0	1 645	1 613
Norton	1.5	0.0	0.3	1.4	0.4	0.1	8.5	18.8	6.9	5.4	920	857

1. October 1, 1998 to September 30, 1999. 2. State totals may include programs not allocated by county. 3. Based on the resident population estimated as of July 1 of the year shown.

STATE County	Total (mil dol) [183]	Per capita[1] (dollars) [184]	Education [185]	Health and hospitals [186]	Police protection [187]	Public welfare [188]	Highways [189]	Total (mil dol) [190]	Per capita[1] (dollars) [191]	Federal civilian [192]	Federal military [193]	State and local [194]	Democratic [195]	Republican [196]	All other [197]
KANSAS—Cont'd															
Barber	20.7	3 816	34.6	25.8	3.9	0.0	11.1	1.8	337	29	26	680	25.5	70.3	4.2
Barton	71.0	2 540	63.9	1.9	4.6	0.0	6.1	34.9	1 248	93	135	2 317	29.6	66.7	3.8
Bourbon	33.5	2 197	63.7	0.7	3.5	0.0	7.0	14.1	923	102	75	1 126	35.1	61.1	3.9
Brown	22.1	2 005	51.4	1.9	2.7	0.0	7.4	12.4	1 125	69	54	855	32.2	63.6	4.1
Butler	138.1	2 293	68.5	1.4	2.9	0.0	5.8	138.6	2 300	127	303	4 555	32.2	63.7	4.1
Chase	7.1	2 458	50.6	2.3	3.4	0.0	10.2	4.8	1 653	29	14	268	29.7	64.4	5.9
Chautauqua	9.6	2 173	59.9	4.0	3.4	0.0	11.8	1.9	428	19	21	288	23.6	71.6	4.8
Cherokee	37.2	1 648	63.8	9.3	4.0	0.0	3.2	10.4	461	58	110	1 284	41.4	54.9	3.6
Cheyenne	7.3	2 262	64.4	0.3	3.5	0.0	10.9	0.2	55	19	16	298	20.3	76.0	3.8
Clark	12.1	4 971	34.3	39.4	2.9	0.0	6.8	1.6	667	15	12	404	23.2	73.4	3.4
Clay	29.6	3 212	35.8	22.0	2.5	0.0	8.9	13.5	1 465	38	45	838	23.3	73.3	3.4
Cloud	34.5	3 382	66.4	2.3	3.2	0.0	5.6	7.8	765	69	49	907	29.2	64.8	6.0
Coffey	59.7	6 826	50.8	13.6	1.6	0.0	12.4	17.7	2 029	43	43	1 226	29.6	66.8	3.6
Comanche	8.8	4 350	48.0	18.9	3.4	0.0	9.2	1.5	749	0	10	315	21.0	75.5	3.5
Cowley	111.9	3 048	46.2	26.4	3.1	0.0	4.2	52.2	1 422	104	178	3 332	39.0	56.9	4.2
Crawford	74.7	2 076	53.1	12.5	4.6	0.0	5.5	38.6	1 072	127	183	4 560	47.1	47.6	5.3
Decatur	8.9	2 509	52.5	3.8	2.9	0.6	11.5	2.1	583	26	17	315	24.1	71.3	4.5
Dickinson	45.8	2 324	54.6	13.4	3.6	0.0	8.3	16.1	817	111	97	1 507	29.8	64.8	5.4
Doniphan	25.9	3 374	75.8	1.9	1.4	0.0	5.6	7.1	924	39	38	757	31.1	64.4	4.5
Douglas	204.5	2 245	35.9	26.7	5.0	0.3	4.5	182.6	2 004	561	497	14 074	45.8	42.8	11.4
Edwards	9.9	2 880	43.8	6.6	4.4	0.0	11.8	1.6	454	25	16	292	28.6	67.9	3.5
Elk	17.4	5 176	38.0	5.9	1.4	0.0	5.0	11.8	3 501	23	16	435	25.9	69.7	4.4
Ellis	49.2	1 867	55.8	3.1	4.8	0.0	8.3	23.2	880	157	129	3 328	35.2	58.4	6.4
Ellsworth	19.7	3 140	47.5	2.6	3.0	0.0	4.1	18.6	2 966	29	31	810	29.1	65.0	6.0
Finney	100.2	2 789	58.0	2.0	5.4	0.0	5.3	80.2	2 232	161	179	2 705	26.6	70.4	3.0
Ford	71.0	2 427	59.6	2.1	4.5	0.0	4.5	49.2	1 682	217	144	2 312	28.8	67.8	3.4
Franklin	58.8	2 473	46.6	25.8	2.8	2.5	1.6	37.7	1 586	92	121	1 700	34.4	61.3	4.3
Geary	81.2	3 207	40.1	20.0	5.5	0.0	3.3	66.2	2 615	1 948	10 229	2 250	38.7	57.9	3.3
Gove	13.8	4 457	42.1	17.3	1.3	0.0	6.6	1.7	559	21	15	435	19.8	75.1	5.2
Graham	12.9	3 976	34.5	31.6	2.7	0.0	11.8	3.6	1 098	27	16	419	23.5	71.8	4.7
Grant	30.5	3 860	48.1	8.7	3.2	0.0	14.8	1.6	206	28	39	783	23.9	74.4	1.6
Gray	15.5	2 817	61.2	1.6	3.1	0.0	11.6	6.6	1 207	22	27	784	22.3	75.5	2.2
Greeley	5.4	3 097	44.5	4.2	4.5	0.0	15.0	2.5	1 473	12	0	199	17.8	78.2	4.0
Greenwood	15.7	1 953	56.1	1.6	5.6	0.0	12.8	2.8	343	51	40	521	28.8	67.2	4.0
Hamilton	8.5	3 728	38.8	2.6	10.6	0.0	13.9	1.0	435	13	11	347	22.1	75.6	2.3
Harper	24.2	3 732	30.7	44.3	2.1	0.0	8.4	0.6	94	39	31	895	28.4	68.0	3.6
Harvey	67.6	2 138	52.5	2.3	4.0	0.0	7.8	86.2	2 729	82	168	1 760	33.6	60.4	6.0
Haskell	18.3	4 564	46.1	23.4	0.8	0.0	11.6	1.2	302	19	19	472	16.3	81.9	1.9
Hodgeman	9.9	4 454	35.3	29.8	1.9	3.0	9.1	1.2	532	15	11	334	19.9	76.7	3.3
Jackson	28.4	2 362	58.3	9.9	2.5	0.0	8.5	13.7	1 141	62	59	914	37.9	57.2	4.9
Jefferson	38.3	2 135	67.7	4.1	4.7	0.0	7.9	20.2	1 129	72	89	1 345	38.1	56.2	5.8
Jewell	9.5	2 388	54.8	3.1	2.4	0.0	14.8	2.9	726	36	19	478	20.2	74.6	5.2
Johnson	1 079.0	2 585	44.8	2.8	8.0	1.1	8.9	1 773.0	4 248	4 029	2 107	20 814	36.4	59.7	3.9
Kearny	20.8	4 950	52.0	14.2	4.0	0.0	8.5	5.3	1 268	19	20	626	22.3	75.5	2.2
Kingman	16.3	1 915	57.1	3.4	4.3	0.0	14.0	9.7	1 136	45	42	591	26.0	70.2	3.8
Kiowa	9.5	2 767	53.9	5.1	4.0	0.0	13.2	1.0	289	22	17	403	18.3	78.5	3.2
Labette	62.6	2 738	46.3	22.8	3.4	0.0	5.2	17.3	759	89	113	2 787	43.9	52.4	3.7
Lane	7.4	3 382	52.8	2.5	3.9	0.0	9.0	1.6	740	13	11	329	22.2	74.7	3.1
Leavenworth	115.2	1 642	57.3	2.3	5.0	2.8	8.3	52.6	750	3 155	3 555	3 642	41.8	54.1	4.1
Lincoln	11.6	3 474	42.1	7.4	1.9	13.9	11.9	4.2	1 256	36	16	436	24.8	68.5	6.7
Linn	25.1	2 765	58.2	0.7	3.1	0.0	8.3	38.6	4 256	40	45	714	37.3	59.0	3.7
Logan	12.7	4 163	40.6	21.4	2.2	0.0	12.4	0.7	213	23	15	396	16.5	77.9	5.6
Lyon	103.6	3 039	37.6	29.4	3.7	2.7	5.7	59.2	1 738	147	166	4 240	41.7	53.4	4.9
McPherson	68.8	2 491	47.1	2.2	3.6	0.0	13.1	104.6	3 790	96	140	1 793	25.0	70.4	4.6
Marion	25.2	1 952	63.9	1.4	2.9	0.0	4.3	24.0	1 860	69	66	1 079	35.8	59.9	4.3
Marshall	27.3	2 450	61.3	1.3	2.7	0.0	11.6	11.4	1 025	69	54	808	26.3	68.2	5.5
Meade	16.7	3 808	28.6	32.6	2.8	0.0	11.1	4.1	932	14	22	529	19.5	78.1	2.4
Miami	45.6	1 742	62.5	12.0	4.9	0.0	2.1	40.7	1 555	75	130	1 894	39.2	57.0	3.8
Mitchell	19.9	2 846	56.7	4.6	3.3	0.0	9.1	10.3	1 467	40	34	794	23.0	72.0	5.1
Montgomery	94.9	2 554	49.6	22.7	3.1	0.0	4.6	39.5	1 062	154	181	2 512	34.7	61.8	3.5
Morris	11.2	1 814	53.3	1.5	1.4	0.0	14.6	4.6	743	36	30	507	33.4	60.5	6.1
Morton	22.9	6 782	36.9	26.2	1.9	7.2	9.6	4.1	1 210	20	17	630	20.6	77.3	2.1
Nemaha	21.5	2 099	56.7	1.1	3.3	0.0	13.5	12.0	1 170	66	50	716	28.2	67.6	4.1
Neosho	56.7	3 348	41.6	30.0	2.1	0.0	4.1	47.9	2 824	63	82	1 571	37.6	58.3	4.1
Ness	16.1	4 419	36.6	35.6	1.4	0.0	11.4	4.0	1 107	35	18	526	20.4	75.7	3.9
Norton	17.9	3 084	41.2	27.5	2.3	0.0	6.5	3.1	525	33	28	911	24.4	71.2	4.4

1. Based on the resident population estimated as of July 1 of the year shown.

STATE/ County code	MSA/ PMSA/ NECMA code[1]	County Type[2]	STATE County	Land area,[3] (sq km) 1990	Total persons	Rank	Per square kilometer	White	Black	Am. Indian, Eskimo, Aleut	Asian and Pacific Islander	Percent Hispanic[4]	Under 5 years	5 to 17 years	18 to 24 years	25 to 34 years	35 to 44 years	45 to 54 years
				1	2	3	4	5	6	7	8	9	10	11	12	13	14	15
			KANSAS—Cont'd															
20 139	...	6	Osage	1 822	17 199	1 918	9.4	98.9	0.3	0.6	0.2	2.0	6.2	20.8	6.8	11.3	15.3	14.1
20 141	...	9	Osborne	2 312	4 589	2 864	2.0	99.3	0.1	0.4	0.2	0.6	6.2	17.6	5.3	9.0	12.2	13.1
20 143	...	9	Ottawa	1 868	5 889	2 778	3.2	99.4	0.1	0.3	0.2	1.1	6.0	19.9	5.6	10.7	14.9	14.4
20 145	...	7	Pawnee	1 953	7 207	2 662	3.7	93.9	4.4	0.5	1.1	5.7	5.4	19.3	6.4	10.8	15.9	14.5
20 147	...	7	Phillips	2 295	5 958	2 776	2.6	99.0	0.3	0.2	0.6	0.7	5.9	18.4	5.2	9.3	14.8	13.6
20 149	...	6	Pottawatomie	2 187	18 942	1 820	8.7	98.1	0.6	0.8	0.6	2.3	7.5	21.9	8.4	12.4	16.1	12.8
20 151	...	7	Pratt	1 904	9 517	2 471	5.0	97.5	1.4	0.6	0.4	3.0	5.8	19.6	7.7	10.3	14.8	13.2
20 153	...	9	Rawlins	2 770	3 016	2 985	1.1	99.4	0.1	0.2	0.3	1.1	5.2	19.5	4.8	9.1	13.3	12.6
20 155	...	4	Reno	3 249	63 702	750	19.6	95.8	3.1	0.6	0.5	6.1	6.3	18.6	8.8	11.8	15.5	13.6
20 157	...	7	Republic	1 856	5 975	2 773	3.2	99.5	0.0	0.2	0.3	0.3	5.5	17.3	4.5	9.0	13.2	13.6
20 159	...	7	Rice	1 882	10 233	2 400	5.4	97.8	1.4	0.5	0.3	4.0	6.4	19.2	9.4	9.9	13.1	13.1
20 161	...	5	Riley	1 579	63 708	749	40.3	84.3	10.2	0.8	4.8	6.2	6.9	14.7	31.7	15.9	12.1	7.1
20 163	...	9	Rooks	2 301	5 626	2 797	2.4	98.9	0.7	0.3	0.1	0.7	6.3	19.8	6.0	10.3	13.4	12.7
20 165	...	9	Rush	1 860	3 365	2 964	1.8	99.6	0.1	0.1	0.2	1.2	5.1	16.5	4.5	9.3	12.6	12.6
20 167	...	7	Russell	2 291	7 459	2 641	3.3	98.7	0.7	0.5	0.1	0.9	4.9	17.2	5.6	9.8	14.0	13.3
20 169	...	5	Saline	1 864	51 379	890	27.6	94.5	3.4	0.5	1.5	3.9	6.7	19.0	9.4	12.8	15.8	13.5
20 171	...	7	Scott	1 859	4 941	2 842	2.7	99.0	0.1	0.2	0.6	4.2	7.4	23.4	7.2	11.7	17.2	14.5
20 173	9040	2	Sedgwick	2 591	451 684	125	174.3	86.3	9.6	1.1	2.9	6.6	7.8	19.6	9.8	14.3	16.4	12.5
20 175	...	7	Seward	1 656	20 115	1 757	12.1	89.9	6.1	0.8	3.2	26.4	9.4	22.8	11.5	14.8	14.1	11.0
20 177	8440	3	Shawnee	1 424	170 773	308	119.9	88.7	9.0	1.1	1.1	7.4	6.5	18.8	9.1	12.7	16.8	13.6
20 179	...	9	Sheridan	2 322	2 674	3 014	1.2	99.4	0.0	0.3	0.3	1.2	6.3	21.1	4.6	9.2	14.0	13.4
20 181	...	7	Sherman	2 735	6 523	2 730	2.4	98.8	0.6	0.2	0.4	10.0	7.0	18.8	9.1	10.1	13.5	14.7
20 183	...	9	Smith	2 319	4 575	2 865	2.0	99.7	0.1	0.2	0.1	0.2	4.8	17.1	4.1	8.8	12.9	12.9
20 185	...	9	Stafford	2 052	4 996	2 836	2.4	98.9	0.3	0.5	0.2	3.5	6.8	19.2	6.0	10.2	14.4	13.0
20 187	...	9	Stanton	1 761	2 225	3 044	1.3	98.0	0.1	0.7	1.2	23.2	9.0	22.2	8.0	13.3	12.3	12.8
20 189	...	7	Stevens	1 884	5 400	2 812	2.9	97.9	0.5	1.0	0.6	15.9	8.2	22.9	7.1	12.4	14.2	13.3
20 191	...	6	Sumner	3 061	27 173	1 456	8.9	97.9	0.7	1.0	0.4	5.3	7.0	21.9	6.8	11.0	15.3	13.2
20 193	...	7	Thomas	2 784	7 965	2 601	2.9	98.8	0.4	0.3	0.6	2.0	6.8	20.9	11.8	11.0	14.8	12.0
20 195	...	9	Trego	2 301	3 261	2 973	1.4	99.0	0.1	0.2	0.7	0.4	5.3	20.0	4.4	9.7	13.8	12.2
20 197	...	8	Wabaunsee	2 065	6 578	2 723	3.2	98.8	0.7	0.4	0.2	2.7	6.3	20.3	7.2	10.7	14.9	14.0
20 199	...	9	Wallace	2 367	1 801	3 074	0.8	99.1	0.3	0.3	0.3	6.4	7.0	21.2	8.5	9.5	15.1	11.0
20 201	...	9	Washington	2 327	6 473	2 736	2.8	99.8	0.1	0.1	0.0	0.5	5.4	19.3	5.7	8.8	12.3	13.0
20 203	...	9	Wichita	1 861	2 578	3 018	1.4	98.8	0.1	0.7	0.5	17.4	7.4	23.6	6.4	10.8	14.9	12.9
20 205	...	7	Wilson	1 486	10 339	2 395	7.0	98.6	0.3	0.8	0.3	1.3	6.0	19.6	6.5	9.2	14.4	13.8
20 207	...	9	Woodson	1 297	3 911	2 923	3.0	98.7	0.4	0.7	0.2	1.0	5.5	18.5	5.4	9.2	14.5	11.2
20 209	3760	0	Wyandotte	392	151 379	342	386.2	69.0	28.7	0.7	1.6	10.1	7.5	20.7	9.9	13.5	15.3	12.4
21 000	...	X	**KENTUCKY**	102 907	3 960 825	X	38.5	91.9	7.3	0.1	0.7	0.9	6.5	17.8	10.2	13.7	16.2	13.7
21 001	...	7	Adair	1 054	16 462	1 973	15.6	96.5	3.2	0.1	0.2	0.9	5.7	17.5	10.6	11.9	14.6	14.6
21 003	...	7	Allen	897	16 854	1 939	18.8	98.7	1.2	0.1	0.1	0.3	6.9	18.3	8.6	11.9	14.8	14.9
21 005	...	6	Anderson	525	18 807	1 832	35.8	96.6	3.2	0.0	0.2	0.8	6.9	18.3	8.8	14.1	17.5	14.6
21 007	...	9	Ballard	651	8 516	2 552	13.1	96.5	3.2	0.2	0.1	0.9	5.4	16.9	8.1	11.6	15.9	15.8
21 009	...	7	Barren	1 272	37 355	1 153	29.4	94.5	5.1	0.1	0.3	0.4	6.2	17.2	8.3	12.7	15.2	14.5
21 011	...	8	Bath	724	10 741	2 360	14.8	96.7	3.1	0.1	0.1	0.6	6.3	17.5	8.8	12.9	15.6	13.9
21 013	...	7	Bell	934	29 028	1 411	31.1	96.8	2.8	0.1	0.4	0.3	6.4	19.1	9.9	12.7	15.5	13.7
21 015	1640	0	Boone	638	83 356	609	130.7	98.3	0.7	0.1	0.9	0.8	7.9	19.7	8.9	15.2	18.0	13.7
21 017	4280	2	Bourbon	755	19 363	1 796	25.6	90.7	9.0	0.1	0.2	0.6	6.6	18.1	8.8	12.8	16.5	14.5
21 019	3400	2	Boyd	415	48 843	926	117.7	97.2	2.2	0.2	0.4	1.3	5.5	16.0	7.8	12.7	16.2	15.0
21 021	...	7	Boyle	470	27 358	1 452	58.2	89.5	10.0	0.1	0.5	0.7	5.7	17.0	10.2	12.0	16.2	13.9
21 023	...	8	Bracken	526	8 478	2 554	16.1	99.3	0.6	0.1	0.0	0.2	6.4	18.4	8.9	12.6	14.8	14.3
21 025	...	9	Breathitt	1 283	15 771	2 017	12.3	99.6	0.2	0.0	0.2	0.3	6.5	20.5	10.4	12.9	16.3	13.5
21 027	...	9	Breckinridge	1 483	17 728	1 885	12.0	95.9	3.7	0.1	0.1	0.4	6.1	18.4	7.7	11.7	15.4	14.6
21 029	4520	2	Bullitt	775	60 955	782	78.7	99.0	0.5	0.2	0.3	0.6	6.9	20.4	9.9	14.3	17.9	15.4
21 031	...	9	Butler	1 109	12 019	2 276	10.8	99.2	0.5	0.1	0.2	0.5	6.3	18.9	8.7	12.6	15.4	15.2
21 033	...	6	Caldwell	899	13 366	2 185	14.9	93.7	5.9	0.2	0.1	0.3	5.7	16.6	8.1	11.1	15.2	14.4
21 035	...	7	Calloway	1 000	33 293	1 276	33.3	96.0	3.3	0.1	0.6	0.8	5.2	13.5	18.9	11.1	13.7	13.1
21 037	1640	0	Campbell	393	87 203	578	221.9	98.3	1.1	0.1	0.5	0.6	7.5	17.8	9.8	14.5	15.4	12.6
21 039	...	9	Carlisle	499	5 386	2 814	10.8	98.6	1.1	0.2	0.1	0.5	5.6	17.0	8.4	10.4	14.5	14.3
21 041	...	6	Carroll	337	9 775	2 448	29.0	97.3	2.3	0.2	0.2	0.3	6.6	19.0	8.7	13.1	15.2	13.9
21 043	3400	2	Carter	1 064	27 106	1 459	25.5	99.7	0.1	0.1	0.1	0.4	6.0	19.1	10.7	12.2	15.3	14.9
21 045	...	9	Casey	1 154	14 908	2 068	12.9	99.3	0.3	0.1	0.2	0.5	6.2	18.5	8.4	11.7	15.3	14.1
21 047	1660	3	Christian	1 868	71 941	682	38.5	72.7	25.0	0.5	1.9	4.8	8.5	17.1	15.7	16.8	13.5	10.5
21 049	4280	2	Clark	659	32 457	1 299	49.3	93.7	5.9	0.1	0.2	0.5	6.4	17.6	8.7	13.1	17.2	14.6
21 051	...	9	Clay	1 220	22 780	1 620	18.7	97.9	1.7	0.1	0.2	0.3	7.2	21.5	10.1	13.8	15.6	13.0
21 053	...	9	Clinton	511	9 464	2 475	18.5	99.6	0.2	0.0	0.2	0.7	5.8	17.3	8.5	12.6	14.7	15.1
21 055	...	7	Crittenden	938	9 556	2 468	10.2	98.7	1.0	0.1	0.1	0.4	6.3	17.4	8.2	12.0	14.9	15.5

1. MSA = Metropolitan Statistical Area. PMSA = Primary MSA. NECMA = New England County Metropolitan Area. See Appendix A for explanation of these concepts. See Appendix B for list of metropolitan areas identified by type, with component counties.   2. County typology code from the Economic Research Service of USDA. See Appendix A for definition.   3. Dry land or land partially or temporarily covered by water.   4. Hispanic persons may be of any race.

Table B. States and Counties — **Population and Households**

	Population, 1999 (cont'd)				Population — change and components of change, 1980–1999							Households, 1990				
	Age (percent) (cont'd)				Total persons		Percent change		Components of change, 1990–1999						Percent	
STATE County	55 to 64 years	65 to 74 years	75 years and over	Percent female	1990	1980	1980–1990	1990–1999	Births	Deaths	Net migration	Number	Percent change, 1980–1990	Persons per house-hold	Female family house-holder[1]	One person
	16	17	18	19	20	21	22	23	24	25	26	27	28	29	30	31
KANSAS—Cont'd																
Osage	10.0	6.8	8.7	50.8	15 248	15 319	-0.5	12.8	1 838	1 717	1 910	5 806	3.7	2.57	6.6	23.1
Osborne	11.2	10.4	14.9	51.5	4 867	5 959	-18.3	-5.7	424	710	-129	2 057	-13.8	2.30	5.4	31.4
Ottawa	11.0	7.1	10.4	51.2	5 634	5 971	-5.6	4.5	575	753	451	2 266	-1.1	2.43	5.7	26.6
Pawnee	9.5	8.6	9.6	49.1	7 555	8 065	-6.3	-4.6	698	785	-232	2 923	-4.7	2.34	7.2	31.6
Phillips	10.1	9.9	12.9	51.2	6 590	7 406	-11.0	-9.6	617	896	-323	2 695	-6.5	2.38	4.9	28.9
Pottawatomie	8.1	5.8	7.1	49.9	16 128	14 782	9.1	17.4	2 384	1 460	1 912	5 938	9.9	2.66	6.0	22.6
Pratt	9.8	8.5	10.2	51.1	9 702	10 275	-5.6	-1.9	1 068	1 060	-160	3 937	-3.5	2.40	5.9	29.1
Rawlins	11.3	10.5	13.7	50.3	3 404	4 105	-17.1	-11.4	284	373	-293	1 361	-13.5	2.46	4.6	29.0
Reno	9.0	7.9	8.6	50.5	62 389	64 983	-4.0	2.1	7 436	5 998	74	24 239	-0.9	2.46	8.4	26.7
Republic	11.8	10.3	14.9	51.5	6 482	7 569	-14.4	-7.8	495	990	16	2 769	-11.1	2.27	3.6	31.4
Rice	10.1	8.2	10.7	51.8	10 610	11 900	-10.8	-3.6	1 159	1 228	-277	4 165	-8.0	2.43	6.5	27.9
Riley	4.0	3.8	3.7	45.5	67 139	63 505	5.7	-5.1	9 760	2 522	-14 840	21 280	10.4	2.58	6.4	23.6
Rooks	10.5	9.1	11.8	51.2	6 039	7 006	-13.8	-6.8	608	773	-232	2 444	-9.4	2.40	5.5	29.9
Rush	12.5	12.4	14.5	51.6	3 842	4 516	-14.9	-12.4	317	519	-250	1 642	-10.1	2.29	4.4	30.4
Russell	11.1	11.2	12.9	51.2	7 835	8 868	-11.6	-4.8	678	1 018	-11	3 371	-6.7	2.28	6.1	32.1
Saline	8.7	7.0	7.1	51.6	49 301	48 905	0.8	4.2	6 854	4 359	-316	19 826	6.5	2.44	9.3	27.3
Scott	9.3	3.8	5.4	49.5	5 289	5 782	-8.5	-6.6	637	520	-421	2 022	-2.5	2.57	4.9	24.5
Sedgwick	8.1	6.3	5.2	51.1	403 662	367 088	10.0	11.9	67 737	30 614	-1 549	156 571	13.7	2.54	10.2	26.7
Seward	6.9	5.0	4.6	49.3	18 743	17 071	9.8	7.3	4 063	1 199	-1 501	6 614	8.0	2.79	10.3	21.1
Shawnee	8.9	6.9	6.7	51.8	160 976	154 916	3.9	6.1	21 932	14 493	-2 795	63 768	8.4	2.46	10.5	27.6
Sheridan	11.4	9.4	10.5	49.4	3 043	3 544	-14.1	-12.1	248	301	-304	1 171	-7.0	2.57	3.1	25.2
Sherman	9.7	8.5	8.8	51.3	6 926	7 759	-10.7	-5.8	815	682	-526	2 733	-4.5	2.47	7.5	27.1
Smith	12.2	10.7	16.5	51.6	5 078	5 947	-14.6	-9.9	407	788	-103	2 165	-9.8	2.28	4.5	30.0
Stafford	10.3	8.5	11.4	51.1	5 365	5 694	-5.8	-6.9	497	765	-88	2 203	-4.5	2.36	5.4	29.9
Stanton	9.2	6.6	6.7	50.1	2 333	2 339	-0.3	-4.6	386	163	-328	831	4.7	2.77	5.9	21.9
Stevens	8.0	7.1	6.8	51.1	5 048	4 736	6.6	7.0	779	393	-17	1 885	11.3	2.65	5.4	24.6
Sumner	9.2	7.3	8.4	50.9	25 841	24 928	3.7	5.2	3 148	2 737	988	9 689	2.9	2.62	6.7	24.5
Thomas	8.3	6.9	7.5	50.8	8 258	8 451	-2.3	-3.5	1 089	741	-625	3 124	1.7	2.56	6.5	25.9
Trego	10.6	10.6	13.5	50.4	3 694	4 165	-11.3	-11.7	286	502	-203	1 464	-8.3	2.46	4.6	27.0
Wabaunsee	10.2	7.9	8.5	50.1	6 603	6 867	-3.8	-0.4	710	582	-149	2 482	-0.2	2.62	5.0	23.0
Wallace	10.3	8.3	9.1	49.4	1 821	2 045	-11.0	-1.1	231	169	-76	677	-8.5	2.65	3.7	26.3
Washington	11.4	9.7	14.4	50.7	7 073	8 543	-17.2	-8.5	681	1 018	-231	2 862	-12.5	2.73	3.9	29.9
Wichita	8.7	6.8	8.5	49.9	2 758	3 041	-9.3	-6.5	359	209	-324	996	-5.1	2.41	5.4	22.5
Wilson	10.4	9.1	11.0	51.7	10 289	12 128	-15.2	0.5	1 080	1 386	399	4 194	-12.1	2.41	6.2	28.7
Woodson	11.1	10.9	13.7	50.8	4 116	4 600	-10.5	-5.0	328	574	54	1 699	-7.3	2.33	5.7	30.8
Wyandotte	8.5	6.5	5.8	52.3	162 026	172 335	-6.0	-6.6	25 860	15 075	-21 493	61 514	-3.0	2.60	16.4	27.5
KENTUCKY	9.4	6.8	5.7	51.4	3 686 892	3 660 324	0.7	7.4	494 758	340 897	113 050	1 379 782	9.2	2.60	11.6	23.3
Adair	10.3	7.8	7.0	50.9	15 360	15 233	0.8	7.2	1 903	1 627	874	5 800	6.6	2.57	9.5	22.4
Allen	10.9	7.4	6.4	51.1	14 628	14 128	3.5	15.2	1 999	1 659	1 927	5 595	8.3	2.59	8.6	22.1
Anderson	9.1	5.6	5.2	51.0	14 571	12 567	15.9	29.1	2 236	1 218	3 247	5 438	23.2	2.66	9.0	20.0
Ballard	10.7	7.6	8.1	50.6	7 902	8 798	-10.2	7.8	936	1 030	736	3 191	-2.3	2.44	7.6	25.2
Barren	10.8	7.6	7.4	52.4	34 001	34 009	0.0	9.9	4 170	3 760	3 030	13 136	7.1	2.54	9.5	23.0
Bath	10.7	7.0	7.3	51.1	9 692	10 025	-3.3	10.8	1 245	1 106	951	3 659	6.5	2.61	10.1	22.1
Bell	9.4	7.3	6.0	51.8	31 506	34 330	-8.2	-7.9	4 015	3 344	-3 088	11 512	0.9	2.69	15.6	22.0
Boone	8.3	4.8	3.5	51.0	57 589	45 842	25.6	44.7	9 834	3 819	19 708	20 127	35.6	2.84	9.5	18.4
Bourbon	9.6	7.1	6.0	51.5	19 236	19 405	-0.9	0.7	2 330	1 834	-299	7 250	6.4	2.63	12.2	21.2
Boyd	11.4	8.6	6.9	51.3	51 096	55 513	-7.9	-4.4	5 660	5 492	-2 304	19 876	-0.4	2.50	10.9	24.0
Boyle	10.1	8.0	6.9	51.1	25 590	25 066	2.3	6.9	2 969	2 459	1 346	9 483	7.6	2.49	11.3	24.4
Bracken	11.1	6.7	6.7	51.4	7 766	7 738	0.4	9.2	1 016	833	562	2 872	6.1	2.68	9.7	21.9
Breathitt	9.2	5.4	5.2	50.4	15 703	17 004	-7.7	0.4	2 082	1 555	-420	5 555	6.6	2.63	13.3	19.6
Breckinridge	10.4	8.6	7.0	50.3	16 312	16 861	-3.3	8.7	1 860	1 703	1 297	6 159	4.7	2.63	8.8	22.8
Bullitt	7.9	4.5	2.8	49.9	47 567	43 346	9.7	28.1	7 257	2 945	9 128	15 965	23.3	2.97	9.2	13.5
Butler	9.7	6.9	6.4	50.4	11 245	11 064	1.6	6.9	1 348	1 213	673	4 180	8.9	2.64	8.6	21.4
Caldwell	11.5	8.7	8.7	52.5	13 232	13 473	-1.8	1.0	1 439	1 650	400	5 274	4.6	2.46	10.2	25.6
Calloway	9.5	7.2	7.2	51.6	30 735	30 031	2.3	8.3	3 032	3 055	2 671	11 607	7.8	2.34	7.8	27.1
Campbell	9.7	7.0	5.6	52.0	83 866	83 317	0.7	4.0	11 925	7 612	-729	31 169	8.9	2.66	11.7	25.3
Carlisle	12.2	8.7	9.0	51.7	5 238	5 487	-4.5	2.8	523	676	315	2 106	2.3	2.49	8.4	25.1
Carroll	10.1	7.3	5.9	51.4	9 292	9 270	0.2	5.2	1 255	1 052	306	3 505	3.8	2.61	12.0	24.4
Carter	9.6	6.6	5.6	50.9	24 340	25 060	-2.9	11.4	3 343	2 340	1 840	8 679	5.7	2.75	10.6	19.2
Casey	10.9	7.7	7.1	51.0	14 211	14 818	-4.1	4.9	1 814	1 515	451	5 436	5.4	2.59	9.7	22.1
Christian	7.2	5.5	5.2	47.5	68 941	66 878	3.1	4.4	13 262	5 082	-17 148	21 636	10.1	2.73	12.9	20.6
Clark	9.6	6.8	5.9	51.7	29 496	28 322	4.1	10.0	3 904	2 692	1 817	10 973	10.9	2.66	11.0	20.1
Clay	8.6	5.4	4.7	50.6	21 746	22 752	-4.4	4.8	3 208	1 937	-168	7 367	8.0	2.93	12.5	16.2
Clinton	10.5	8.1	7.3	51.9	9 135	9 321	-2.0	3.6	1 064	988	282	3 591	10.2	2.52	10.7	24.1
Crittenden	10.3	7.5	7.8	51.4	9 196	9 207	-0.1	3.9	901	1 096	590	3 646	5.2	2.48	8.2	25.6

1. No spouse present.

Table B. States and Counties — Vital Statistics, Health Resources, and Crime

STATE County	Births, average 1996–1998		Deaths, average 1996–1998				Physicians,[4] 1998		Hospitals,[4] 1998			Medicare enrollees 1999	Serious crimes known to police, 1998[6]	
			Number		Rate					Beds			Total	
	Total	Rate[1]	Total	Infant[2]	Total[1]	Infant[3]	Number	Rate[5]	Number	Number	Rate[5]		Number	Rate[7]
	32	33	34	35	36	37	38	39	40	41	42	43	44	45
KANSAS—Cont'd														
Osage............	202	11.9	179	1	10.5	6.6	6	35	0	0	0	2 909	NA	NA
Osborne.........	40	8.4	77	0	16.5	8.4	2	42	1	29	615	1 217	NA	NA
Ottawa..........	64	11.0	78	0	13.4	5.2	4	68	1	53	898	1 096	NA	NA
Pawnee..........	73	9.8	82	1	11.1	9.2	22	296	1	79	1 062	1 430	NA	NA
Phillips.........	59	9.6	91	0	14.8	0.0	9	148	1	62	1 020	1 408	NA	NA
Pottawatomie......	267	14.6	166	1	9.1	5.0	11	59	3	109	583	2 520	NA	NA
Pratt............	111	11.5	119	1	12.3	6.0	15	155	1	99	1 021	1 914	NA	NA
Rawlins.........	29	9.1	42	0	13.1	11.5	2	64	1	28	896	789	NA	NA
Reno............	832	13.2	654	8	10.4	9.2	112	177	1	160	253	11 516	NA	NA
Republic........	55	9.0	101	0	16.5	0.0	6	98	1	86	1 409	1 577	NA	NA
Rice............	121	12.0	126	1	12.4	11.0	7	68	1	44	425	2 186	NA	NA
Riley...........	936	14.6	270	2	4.2	2.5	120	189	2	155	244	5 075	NA	NA
Rooks...........	62	10.9	84	0	14.7	5.3	5	88	1	27	477	1 313	NA	NA
Rush............	31	8.9	56	0	16.2	0.0	2	59	1	60	794	990	NA	NA
Russell.........	75	9.9	100	0	13.1	0.0	4	53	1	76	2 227	1 969	NA	NA
Saline..........	740	14.3	508	8	9.8	11.3	118	229	1	187	362	8 305	NA	NA
Scott...........	64	12.7	62	0	12.3	5.2	4	80	1	27	538	497	NA	NA
Sedgwick........	7 218	16.4	3 519	63	8.0	8.7	952	212	5	1 770	395	57 277	NA	NA
Seward..........	467	23.3	132	2	6.6	4.3	30	150	1	77	385	2 115	NA	NA
Shawnee.........	2 365	14.3	1 623	21	9.8	9.0	482	292	2	642	388	27 122	NA	NA
Sheridan........	23	8.3	32	0	11.7	0.0	4	146	1	69	2 517	545	NA	NA
Sherman.........	91	13.8	75	0	11.4	3.7	7	108	1	49	753	1 265	NA	NA
Smith...........	39	8.3	80	0	17.1	8.6	4	87	1	54	1 177	1 287	NA	NA
Stafford........	58	11.3	84	1	16.6	23.1	2	40	1	25	500	1 094	NA	NA
Stanton.........	41	18.0	19	0	8.3	0.0	2	88	1	46	2 031	334	NA	NA
Stevens.........	87	16.2	47	0	8.8	3.8	2	37	1	17	317	792	NA	NA
Sumner..........	335	12.5	293	2	10.9	5.0	13	48	2	118	436	4 700	NA	NA
Thomas..........	116	14.1	84	1	10.2	8.7	8	100	1	40	498	1 245	NA	NA
Trego...........	30	9.0	51	0	15.3	11.0	5	152	1	73	2 224	807	NA	NA
Wabaunsee.......	71	10.7	69	0	10.3	0.0	3	45	0	0	0	1 157	NA	NA
Wallace.........	24	13.2	20	0	10.9	14.1	0	0	0	0	0	346	NA	NA
Washington......	74	11.2	97	0	14.7	0.0	2	31	2	75	1 156	1 772	NA	NA
Wichita.........	40	14.8	21	1	7.7	16.8	1	38	1	43	1 627	427	NA	NA
Wilson..........	118	11.5	155	2	15.0	14.1	7	69	2	80	783	2 156	NA	NA
Woodson.........	37	9.3	59	0	14.8	9.0	4	100	0	0	0	1 039	NA	NA
Wyandotte.......	2 721	17.8	1 625	25	10.6	9.1	353	232	3	1 102	723	22 512	NA	NA
KENTUCKY........	53 413	13.7	37 701	397	9.6	7.4	7 186	183	105	16 966	431	615 436	113 725	2 889
Adair...........	213	12.9	176	2	10.7	7.8	16	97	1	85	517	2 963	NA	NA
Allen...........	214	13.2	176	2	10.9	7.8	6	36	1	62	375	2 780	NA	NA
Anderson........	248	13.7	140	2	7.7	6.7	15	81	0	0	0	2 277	NA	NA
Ballard.........	103	12.3	110	0	13.1	3.2	2	24	0	0	0	1 913	NA	NA
Barren..........	463	12.6	407	2	11.1	4.3	48	130	1	194	525	6 440	NA	NA
Bath............	140	13.6	120	1	11.6	7.1	8	76	0	0	0	1 936	NA	NA
Bell............	408	13.7	360	5	12.1	11.4	48	165	2	247	848	6 106	NA	NA
Boone...........	1 175	15.4	456	6	6.0	5.1	93	117	1	155	195	8 133	2 889	3 766
Bourbon.........	243	12.6	202	2	10.5	9.6	23	119	1	68	351	2 928	NA	NA
Boyd............	580	11.6	608	6	12.2	9.8	149	301	2	539	1 088	9 964	NA	NA
Boyle...........	310	11.5	275	2	10.2	5.4	70	257	1	168	618	4 676	NA	NA
Bracken.........	108	13.0	87	1	10.4	9.2	2	24	0	0	0	1 349	NA	NA
Breathitt.......	199	12.8	174	2	11.1	8.4	18	115	1	59	376	2 762	NA	NA
Breckinridge....	216	12.5	173	2	10.0	10.8	10	57	1	45	258	3 164	NA	NA
Bullitt.........	791	13.6	345	3	6.0	3.4	12	20	0	0	0	4 971	NA	NA
Butler..........	152	12.9	133	1	11.3	8.8	3	25	0	0	0	1 859	NA	NA
Caldwell........	150	11.3	184	1	13.8	8.9	11	83	1	50	376	2 732	NA	NA
Calloway........	344	10.4	346	3	10.4	9.7	43	128	1	360	1 075	5 651	NA	NA
Campbell........	1 292	14.8	828	9	9.5	6.7	107	122	1	267	306	12 542	NA	NA
Carlisle........	56	10.5	68	0	12.7	6.0	1	19	0	0	0	1 132	NA	NA
Carroll.........	133	13.9	107	1	11.2	10.1	8	83	1	53	552	1 627	NA	NA
Carter..........	361	13.6	250	4	9.4	12.0	5	19	0	0	0	4 387	NA	NA
Casey...........	198	13.6	171	1	11.7	6.7	5	34	0	0	0	2 494	NA	NA
Christian.......	1 488	20.3	542	10	7.4	6.9	107	148	1	226	312	8 031	NA	NA
Clark...........	428	13.5	294	2	9.2	5.5	38	119	1	109	341	4 861	NA	NA
Clay............	306	13.5	225	3	9.9	9.8	9	39	1	62	272	3 592	NA	NA
Clinton.........	118	12.6	106	1	11.4	5.7	4	43	1	36	385	2 006	NA	NA
Crittenden......	100	10.6	116	1	12.3	13.3	4	42	1	46	480	1 730	NA	NA

1. Per 1,000 estimated resident population, average 1996–1998. 2. Deaths of infants under 1 year old. 3. Deaths of infants under 1 year old per 1,000 live births. 4. Data subject to copyright. 5. Per 100,000 resident population as of July 1 of the year shown. 6. Data for serious crimes have not been adjusted for underreporting; this may affect comparability between geographic areas and over time. 7. Per 100,000 population estimated by the FBI.

Table B. States and Counties — Crime, Education, Money Income, and Poverty

STATE County	Serious crimes known to police, 1998[1] (cont'd) Rate[2] Violent	Property	Education — School enrollment and attainment, 1990 Enrollment[3] Total	Percent private	High school graduate or more	Bachelor's degree or more	Local government expenditures, fiscal 1997[5] Total current expenditures (mil dol)	Current expenditures per student (dollars)	Money income 1989 Per capita[6] (dollars)	Households Median Dollars	Percent change, 1979–1989 (constant 1989 dollars)	Percent with $100,000 or more	Income and poverty, 1997 Median household income	Percent below poverty level All persons	Persons under 18	Persons 5–17 in families
	46	47	48	49	50	51	52	53	54	55	56	57	58	59	60	61
KANSAS—Cont'd																
Osage	NA	NA	3 705	3.2	76.9	9.3	18.1	5 407	10 823	24 867	-2.4	0.5	35 499	10.1	13.9	12.8
Osborne	NA	NA	971	2.8	76.1	11.0	3.1	5 823	9 913	18 365	-5.1	1.0	27 601	12.8	18.0	18.5
Ottawa	NA	NA	1 343	7.3	81.0	14.0	7.8	5 524	10 358	21 852	3.7	1.2	37 087	8.4	12.8	11.4
Pawnee	NA	NA	1 978	8.5	82.1	16.7	10.1	7 576	12 531	23 898	-1.5	1.7	33 528	12.4	18.1	17.2
Phillips	NA	NA	1 348	3.1	73.9	10.9	10.5	9 028	10 270	20 918	-5.2	0.9	32 418	12.1	16.8	15.2
Pottawatomie	NA	NA	4 455	8.7	81.8	15.6	24.0	6 352	10 984	25 305	1.3	1.5	38 587	8.4	12.5	11.5
Pratt	NA	NA	2 522	8.7	82.4	19.5	9.0	4 987	12 488	23 865	-7.8	1.9	34 857	11.5	15.1	15.1
Rawlins	NA	NA	802	1.9	80.4	14.4	4.1	6 901	10 468	21 332	2.1	1.3	29 655	11.9	17.1	16.3
Reno	NA	NA	15 511	9.1	77.4	14.9	57.3	5 189	12 074	24 665	-7.7	1.7	35 475	12.3	18.5	16.3
Republic	NA	NA	1 286	1.6	78.3	10.3	7.7	6 728	10 890	20 224	10.0	1.2	28 994	12.5	18.3	17.8
Rice	NA	NA	2 718	13.6	81.2	18.7	14.0	6 752	10 139	21 088	-18.7	0.5	32 195	13.3	17.2	17.4
Riley	NA	NA	28 488	3.4	91.7	34.3	41.0	5 620	10 067	21 700	4.8	1.5	33 744	14.1	13.4	16.3
Rooks	NA	NA	1 368	2.8	74.1	11.0	7.3	6 267	10 223	20 113	-13.0	0.9	29 792	13.2	18.1	17.7
Rush	NA	NA	795	1.5	72.6	11.5	4.7	6 421	10 516	19 356	-8.3	1.3	28 395	13.2	18.6	17.2
Russell	NA	NA	1 658	2.8	74.5	14.1	9.1	6 247	11 338	20 843	-8.5	2.3	28 214	14.1	19.7	18.5
Saline	NA	NA	11 801	15.8	82.4	17.7	48.5	5 504	13 153	25 728	-5.2	2.4	36 682	11.2	16.2	15.2
Scott	NA	NA	1 284	6.6	77.2	13.8	6.2	5 308	11 332	25 474	-1.7	1.2	38 781	7.9	10.1	10.1
Sedgwick	NA	NA	106 048	14.7	82.4	22.2	378.2	5 191	14 555	30 216	-1.1	3.1	40 875	11.3	17.0	14.7
Seward	NA	NA	5 073	6.0	72.2	11.6	24.5	4 815	11 341	26 055	-11.8	2.6	35 710	14.0	20.1	19.4
Shawnee	NA	NA	40 682	12.8	84.4	22.3	149.8	5 533	14 091	29 879	0.6	2.5	40 122	10.7	16.7	14.9
Sheridan	NA	NA	761	4.9	81.5	13.3	3.3	6 668	9 889	21 540	1.2	1.3	34 183	11.4	14.4	14.4
Sherman	NA	NA	1 681	4.1	75.0	12.5	7.2	5 705	10 356	21 138	-11.3	0.6	30 801	15.3	21.9	22.1
Smith	NA	NA	965	3.0	74.0	10.0	5.2	6 214	9 574	18 834	3.3	0.5	28 257	13.2	16.8	17.0
Stafford	NA	NA	1 312	4.6	78.7	16.5	7.3	6 061	10 496	19 778	-10.3	0.5	29 419	14.4	20.4	19.8
Stanton	NA	NA	622	3.1	76.9	16.9	3.6	6 417	11 025	24 545	3.5	2.6	39 024	9.2	11.8	13.9
Stevens	NA	NA	1 363	4.0	78.4	14.1	8.5	6 745	11 584	27 549	-3.2	2.6	40 593	10.3	15.0	15.5
Sumner	NA	NA	6 636	6.5	77.1	11.3	25.4	5 284	11 944	26 885	-3.7	1.3	38 987	9.5	12.8	11.9
Thomas	NA	NA	2 616	6.1	85.4	15.7	9.9	6 076	10 551	22 247	-12.9	1.9	34 654	11.9	14.9	15.1
Trego	NA	NA	832	3.5	72.9	12.1	4.1	6 515	10 464	19 921	-14.4	1.8	28 421	11.2	12.9	13.0
Wabaunsee	NA	NA	1 588	5.5	83.8	12.6	8.4	6 292	11 280	27 727	13.0	0.7	36 802	7.8	9.9	10.0
Wallace	NA	NA	464	4.1	77.8	12.5	2.9	6 875	9 366	20 417	-1.3	1.2	28 682	13.1	17.1	17.9
Washington	NA	NA	1 631	9.9	69.6	11.2	9.5	6 647	9 595	19 424	1.0	0.8	28 557	12.6	16.7	16.3
Wichita	NA	NA	719	2.9	71.7	12.5	3.3	6 162	10 196	23 395	-5.2	1.8	35 341	12.2	17.5	17.2
Wilson	NA	NA	2 338	4.1	74.6	11.4	12.7	5 805	9 734	18 776	-7.8	1.2	28 111	15.3	22.3	20.7
Woodson	NA	NA	964	4.5	70.6	8.4	3.8	5 770	10 424	19 637	4.8	0.8	26 400	15.4	22.8	21.5
Wyandotte	NA	NA	41 959	12.3	69.9	10.3	173.8	6 031	10 656	23 780	-8.2	0.8	30 056	18.3	27.6	24.8
KENTUCKY	284	2 605	918 315	12.0	64.6	13.6	3 382.0	5 155	11 153	22 534	-3.7	2.0	31 730	16.0	23.1	21.7
Adair	NA	NA	3 394	14.7	46.3	7.4	15.1	5 583	8 596	15 809	0.5	1.4	21 914	22.3	33.8	30.0
Allen	NA	NA	2 863	1.4	51.1	4.6	12.7	4 325	8 361	17 915	-1.7	0.8	28 798	13.9	20.0	18.6
Anderson	NA	NA	3 365	6.1	66.7	9.9	15.3	5 246	12 320	27 747	4.0	1.6	39 913	7.5	11.8	10.8
Ballard	NA	NA	1 754	1.7	64.2	8.7	7.4	5 290	10 262	19 371	-7.5	1.1	30 629	13.3	19.0	17.9
Barren	NA	NA	7 273	2.9	54.5	8.3	34.6	5 198	9 876	19 546	-6.5	1.1	29 580	15.8	22.8	20.9
Bath	NA	NA	2 038	1.3	46.3	6.2	9.8	5 281	8 034	15 940	-4.3	0.6	24 020	22.7	35.0	31.4
Bell	NA	NA	7 938	8.3	46.7	9.3	34.7	5 983	7 037	13 078	-20.9	1.0	19 896	29.5	39.3	37.9
Boone	241	3 525	14 796	17.5	76.4	15.3	61.7	4 868	13 576	34 485	0.4	2.7	48 999	6.3	9.5	8.7
Bourbon	NA	NA	4 392	3.8	64.0	11.8	20.6	5 863	10 858	22 445	6.7	2.1	33 314	13.9	20.9	19.6
Boyd	NA	NA	12 129	5.9	68.9	11.9	43.5	5 375	12 012	23 835	-12.7	2.1	32 239	16.5	25.9	22.4
Boyle	NA	NA	6 182	14.1	65.4	14.4	23.6	5 297	11 029	23 125	1.1	1.4	33 521	13.6	19.6	18.8
Bracken	NA	NA	1 723	3.4	56.0	6.5	7.3	4 672	9 297	19 684	-7.4	0.7	29 242	15.8	22.2	20.9
Breathitt	NA	NA	3 843	9.4	47.8	8.6	18.2	6 199	6 905	12 383	-21.1	0.5	18 404	32.9	44.9	41.2
Breckinridge	NA	NA	3 477	15.4	56.7	6.3	17.3	5 607	9 157	17 687	-2.6	1.4	27 050	17.6	26.5	23.2
Bullitt	NA	NA	12 462	8.5	64.7	6.3	51.9	5 150	10 907	29 455	-3.0	0.8	41 199	9.5	14.0	12.6
Butler	NA	NA	2 459	5.8	46.6	5.1	12.4	5 115	8 108	17 514	-2.6	0.6	25 578	19.1	27.8	25.7
Caldwell	NA	NA	2 921	2.5	61.9	8.2	10.7	4 955	9 658	17 997	-14.5	0.9	27 656	16.7	25.8	23.5
Calloway	NA	NA	10 207	2.4	69.1	19.4	27.1	5 950	10 434	19 408	-8.9	1.7	29 853	14.5	20.0	18.9
Campbell	NA	NA	21 324	21.2	71.0	14.9	66.9	5 721	12 603	29 228	3.2	2.1	39 201	10.0	14.6	14.3
Carlisle	NA	NA	1 130	2.8	62.3	6.6	4.1	4 804	9 735	19 404	-8.2	0.1	28 450	14.6	24.4	22.3
Carroll	NA	NA	2 311	8.7	59.6	10.7	9.6	5 420	10 202	20 179	-3.8	1.4	29 535	16.9	25.0	24.1
Carter	NA	NA	6 039	8.1	51.3	7.6	25.4	5 063	7 996	17 083	-5.1	0.6	23 986	23.8	34.6	31.3
Casey	NA	NA	2 906	7.4	43.1	6.3	14.1	5 698	7 719	14 993	7.5	0.5	22 182	22.0	32.6	29.2
Christian	NA	NA	16 280	7.1	72.2	10.4	48.9	5 410	9 708	21 032	4.0	1.0	27 968	17.3	24.7	23.6
Clark	NA	NA	6 882	9.8	65.1	13.0	27.6	5 124	11 655	25 323	-5.1	2.2	35 343	13.6	20.5	19.2
Clay	NA	NA	5 475	7.9	38.9	7.4	25.4	5 632	6 084	12 732	-3.8	0.7	19 231	33.7	43.8	42.9
Clinton	NA	NA	1 886	2.6	44.4	6.6	9.1	5 911	6 838	11 348	-6.5	1.1	17 104	29.7	42.5	39.4
Crittenden	NA	NA	1 923	10.8	59.6	5.1	8.2	5 240	9 807	18 566	-8.8	0.5	28 185	17.3	25.8	25.8

1. Data for serious crimes have not been adjusted for underreporting; this may affect comparability between geographic areas and over time. 2. Per 100,000 population estimated by the FBI. 3. All persons 3 years old and over enrolled in nursery school through college. 4. Persons 25 years old and over. 5. Elementary and secondary education expenditures, local government fiscal years ending between July 1, 1996 and June 30, 1997. 6. Based on population enumerated as of April 1, 1990.

STATE County	Personal income, 1998												
			Per capita[1]					Transfer payments					
									Government payments to individuals				
	Total (mil dol)	Percent change, 1997–1998	Dollars	Rank	Wages and salaries[2] (mil dol)	Proprietor's income (mil dol)	Dividends, interest, and rent (mil dol)	Total (mil dol)	Total (mil dol)	Social Security (mil dol)	Medical payments (mil dol)	Income maintenance (mil dol)	Unemployment insurance (mil dol)
	62	63	64	65	66	67	68	69	70	71	72	73	74
KANSAS—Cont'd													
Osage	326	4.1	18 986	2 062	80	19	60	59	56	26	19	3	1
Osborne	97	0.5	20 711	1 485	32	17	27	22	21	11	8	1	0
Ottawa	120	0.4	20 407	1 593	30	13	32	21	20	11	7	1	0
Pawnee	163	2.7	22 487	982	82	22	33	27	26	15	8	1	0
Phillips	148	5.3	24 529	555	62	27	39	26	25	13	10	1	0
Pottawatomie	374	3.6	20 082	1 685	190	25	83	52	49	23	18	3	1
Pratt	221	1.7	22 790	890	109	26	54	39	38	19	14	2	0
Rawlins	68	12.5	21 629	1 212	22	13	20	13	13	7	4	1	0
Reno	1 431	3.2	22 622	945	866	86	295	235	224	114	80	16	3
Republic	125	-1.0	20 455	1 575	51	15	33	26	25	14	8	1	0
Rice	208	1.5	19 933	1 733	82	30	47	42	40	21	13	3	1
Riley	1 325	3.9	20 728	1 475	644	68	230	124	113	47	31	10	3
Rooks	117	4.1	20 503	1 555	43	17	32	25	24	12	9	1	0
Rush	73	0.1	21 567	1 235	32	4	21	18	17	9	6	1	0
Russell	170	4.4	22 606	951	63	26	48	39	38	18	17	2	0
Saline	1 403	4.8	27 294	280	858	224	263	170	162	80	56	10	3
Scott	135	4.2	26 926	311	55	34	30	15	14	9	4	1	0
Sedgwick	12 011	6.0	26 821	317	9 292	883	2 205	1 369	1 292	596	490	112	20
Seward	460	1.8	22 899	872	343	65	68	51	48	22	18	5	1
Shawnee	4 345	5.0	25 508	436	3 292	233	870	597	568	251	185	44	10
Sheridan	83	18.8	30 613	150	22	34	18	11	10	6	3	1	0
Sherman	162	10.8	24 731	526	73	29	31	30	29	12	13	2	0
Smith	101	4.8	21 959	1 112	31	19	30	22	21	12	8	1	0
Stafford	117	4.2	23 208	816	37	28	28	26	25	11	12	1	0
Stanton	68	-9.0	30 330	157	23	26	14	7	6	3	2	0	0
Stevens	142	7.9	26 309	364	59	35	30	16	15	8	5	1	0
Sumner	636	4.2	23 393	767	191	48	88	93	88	42	32	5	1
Thomas	190	10.9	23 720	698	95	45	37	26	25	13	9	1	0
Trego	64	5.5	19 363	1 930	25	7	16	15	15	7	6	1	0
Wabaunsee	145	4.3	21 859	1 142	28	13	26	23	21	11	7	1	0
Wallace	40	17.2	21 887	1 129	12	11	10	7	7	3	3	1	0
Washington	130	-1.9	20 003	1 709	43	21	32	29	28	15	10	2	0
Wichita	82	-5.4	30 952	134	23	37	14	9	9	4	3	1	0
Wilson	192	-1.1	18 740	2 145	102	16	38	44	42	21	15	3	1
Woodson	67	-3.4	17 061	2 597	17	10	17	18	18	8	6	1	0
Wyandotte	2 964	2.1	19 434	1 911	3 104	97	389	619	592	214	246	70	15
KENTUCKY	87 274	4.9	22 183	X	55 214	6 034	15 335	15 064	14 353	5 729	5 566	1 705	243
Adair	259	0.1	15 758	2 835	97	24	41	80	77	24	35	10	4
Allen	276	2.5	16 672	2 683	144	18	53	58	55	24	21	6	1
Anderson	404	6.9	21 841	1 148	122	18	63	48	45	23	14	3	1
Ballard	212	11.0	24 933	496	127	17	28	37	36	15	16	3	1
Barren	795	5.5	21 515	1 249	540	70	126	136	130	55	51	14	3
Bath	180	6.5	17 021	2 608	48	15	25	44	42	15	16	8	1
Bell	454	1.5	15 560	2 870	251	25	74	171	166	52	68	31	1
Boone	2 063	9.4	25 860	408	2 163	108	270	190	175	84	61	10	4
Bourbon	499	6.2	25 806	411	187	83	92	64	61	27	23	7	1
Boyd	1 167	2.4	23 571	729	987	46	238	237	228	95	86	24	4
Boyle	617	6.6	22 777	896	472	39	133	99	94	43	34	9	1
Bracken	146	4.6	17 375	2 510	37	14	20	29	27	12	10	3	0
Breathitt	222	3.0	14 116	2 998	85	12	32	91	88	24	36	21	0
Breckinridge	292	2.5	16 739	2 667	73	23	61	68	65	26	25	8	1
Bullitt	1 205	8.6	20 307	1 626	299	53	142	144	133	64	44	6	2
Butler	189	3.3	15 829	2 820	91	13	26	49	47	16	22	11	1
Caldwell	255	2.1	19 124	2 014	99	22	53	58	55	25	21	5	1
Calloway	730	3.0	21 850	1 145	410	84	144	125	119	54	42	8	2
Campbell	2 054	4.8	23 529	739	790	85	349	298	282	128	105	22	5
Carlisle	112	4.6	20 984	1 398	21	11	20	22	21	10	8	2	0
Carroll	197	4.3	20 424	1 586	198	11	32	38	36	15	14	4	1
Carter	420	5.7	15 619	2 862	119	24	45	111	106	37	41	17	3
Casey	222	1.9	15 040	2 927	74	30	32	63	61	20	25	11	2
Christian	1 254	-0.8	17 314	2 526	1 859	77	244	192	185	72	74	24	3
Clark	733	4.6	22 961	859	376	50	131	109	103	45	39	11	2
Clay	321	3.6	14 107	3 000	124	16	37	119	115	28	47	32	1
Clinton	139	4.7	14 888	2 942	51	13	18	56	54	14	28	9	1
Crittenden	152	1.3	15 846	2 817	56	12	24	41	40	17	17	3	1

1. Based on the resident population estimated as of July 1 of the year shown.　2. Includes other labor income.

Table B. States and Counties — Earnings, Social Security, and Housing

STATE County	Earnings, 1998									Social Security beneficiaries, December 1998			Housing units, 1990	
	Total (mil dol)	Farm	Goods-related[1] Total	Manu-facturing	Service-related and other[2] Total	Retail trade	Finance, insurance, and real estate	Services	Government	Number	Rate[3]	Supplemental Security Income recipients, December 1998	Total	Percent change, 1980–1990
	75	76	77	78	79	80	81	82	83	84	85	86	87	88
KANSAS—Cont'd														
Osage	99	2.3	D	7.0	D	12.5	5.1	26.8	29.3	3 254	190	214	6 324	2.8
Osborne	49	16.5	D	10.3	D	10.8	6.5	16.8	18.2	1 317	279	53	2 496	-10.0
Ottawa	43	15.3	D	4.9	D	6.5	6.9	22.8	24.4	1 319	223	72	2 591	-2.8
Pawnee	104	12.8	D	1.5	D	5.9	4.3	12.6	46.8	1 616	217	111	3 412	-0.9
Phillips	89	15.7	D	D	D	6.8	5.7	12.3	19.7	1 565	257	79	3 264	-6.8
Pottawatomie	215	2.0	D	20.3	D	11.3	3.5	17.6	15.9	2 950	158	161	6 472	7.3
Pratt	135	6.4	12.4	3.1	60.9	10.7	4.2	25.1	20.3	2 122	219	90	4 620	3.8
Rawlins	35	24.6	D	1.4	D	4.7	5.5	17.1	24.8	863	276	42	1 744	-4.5
Reno	953	1.6	30.3	22.7	53.2	15.7	3.8	24.1	14.8	13 011	206	987	26 607	0.1
Republic	66	11.5	D	12.7	D	8.5	7.1	16.4	22.7	1 776	291	72	3 283	-13.6
Rice	111	14.4	D	10.6	D	6.9	3.8	14.4	21.0	2 453	237	115	4 868	-2.1
Riley	712	0.1	D	3.2	D	11.2	7.9	24.2	41.1	5 445	86	452	22 868	9.6
Rooks	60	11.3	D	5.1	D	9.2	4.7	9.1	26.1	1 485	262	61	2 979	-5.0
Rush	37	4.9	D	25.4	D	5.1	3.6	10.8	25.5	1 113	326	46	1 999	-4.8
Russell	89	7.5	30.5	11.1	44.4	10.3	3.5	19.2	17.7	2 112	279	140	4 079	-1.2
Saline	1 082	0.8	D	23.0	D	9.8	4.1	29.0	10.7	9 245	179	828	21 129	4.0
Scott	88	38.0	4.6	0.5	43.5	6.2	3.8	10.2	13.9	928	185	49	2 305	-1.7
Sedgwick	10 176	0.1	40.0	33.2	48.9	8.1	4.2	24.5	11.0	65 205	146	7 171	170 159	16.9
Seward	408	6.8	D	D	D	9.2	2.9	14.7	14.8	2 476	124	228	7 572	12.9
Shawnee	3 525	0.2	18.1	12.0	59.0	11.3	8.7	25.2	22.8	29 213	177	3 586	68 991	7.1
Sheridan	56	45.9	4.1	0.7	36.6	9.8	4.6	8.0	13.4	645	235	31	1 324	-8.3
Sherman	102	19.7	D	3.3	D	11.7	D	22.8	19.4	1 347	207	110	3 177	-3.5
Smith	50	27.9	12.4	8.0	43.1	7.6	5.3	18.0	16.6	1 422	310	58	2 615	-7.1
Stafford	65	32.9	10.2	2.8	35.8	5.8	5.0	12.6	21.1	1 247	249	61	2 666	-1.6
Stanton	49	56.8	D	0.6	D	2.7	D	4.9	14.8	368	162	16	956	-0.4
Stevens	94	31.9	D	D	D	5.9	D	6.5	19.2	919	171	41	2 116	7.0
Sumner	239	4.3	D	22.6	D	10.2	4.9	17.3	20.9	4 851	179	299	10 769	4.0
Thomas	140	21.0	D	1.7	D	12.5	3.9	18.7	18.6	1 424	177	71	3 534	1.1
Trego	31	1.6	D	2.8	D	12.0	5.6	19.3	29.3	924	281	44	1 851	-7.0
Wabaunsee	41	3.8	D	5.6	D	9.4	5.2	21.9	28.2	1 432	215	73	2 853	-1.3
Wallace	23	38.4	D	D	D	6.5	2.3	9.9	17.1	352	195	9	840	-5.8
Washington	64	26.1	D	3.0	D	7.6	5.2	11.2	26.6	1 929	297	100	3 355	-6.3
Wichita	60	61.4	D	D	D	3.4	D	5.1	10.6	484	183	20	1 190	-8.0
Wilson	118	-1.5	D	37.5	D	5.2	3.2	15.2	20.0	2 594	254	207	5 091	-5.2
Woodson	26	9.7	D	4.2	D	10.8	4.0	11.3	23.2	1 113	279	84	2 199	-4.1
Wyandotte	3 200	0.0	29.9	22.9	48.5	6.0	2.1	15.4	21.6	25 460	167	4 413	69 102	0.9
KENTUCKY	61 248	1.7	29.2	21.1	51.0	9.9	5.0	22.4	18.0	724 319	184	172 015	1 506 845	10.1
Adair	122	9.7	18.1	9.8	51.7	10.1	3.3	31.4	20.5	3 685	224	1 209	6 434	4.4
Allen	162	1.3	D	35.7	D	25.4	3.2	12.3	12.8	3 390	205	825	6 381	6.2
Anderson	139	0.6	D	43.1	D	9.6	4.0	12.6	16.2	2 837	153	298	5 804	20.8
Ballard	144	4.6	61.2	36.6	D	4.2	1.4	5.9	8.3	1 824	215	251	3 553	0.3
Barren	610	3.9	50.0	41.1	36.0	9.5	2.2	17.6	10.0	7 817	211	1 745	14 202	5.2
Bath	63	12.0	31.1	19.8	D	9.1	3.4	12.3	24.0	2 307	218	941	4 021	8.8
Bell	276	0.1	D	9.8	D	14.4	3.6	24.0	19.2	7 238	248	3 391	12 568	4.3
Boone	2 271	0.1	D	22.9	D	10.7	6.0	13.5	7.1	9 620	121	884	21 476	33.6
Bourbon	269	27.1	D	17.8	D	5.8	D	11.2	11.4	3 549	183	655	7 781	7.9
Boyd	1 033	0.0	D	23.9	D	9.5	3.4	29.8	11.5	10 861	219	2 253	21 365	-0.4
Boyle	512	1.4	D	28.8	D	9.7	2.8	25.9	11.4	5 328	196	1 048	10 191	7.1
Bracken	51	14.2	D	D	D	6.4	3.2	16.6	20.5	1 609	190	305	3 166	6.2
Breathitt	97	-0.4	D	2.8	D	16.0	4.1	25.7	33.6	3 557	227	2 496	6 127	10.5
Breckinridge	95	6.7	D	7.5	D	14.5	5.1	17.3	25.6	3 625	208	834	8 261	15.6
Bullitt	352	-0.7	D	26.9	D	12.7	3.6	13.0	18.5	7 581	128	848	16 629	21.7
Butler	104	0.2	D	39.8	D	7.0	2.4	13.0	19.0	2 427	204	606	4 698	9.9
Caldwell	121	4.0	D	19.4	D	16.2	5.2	16.7	20.4	3 172	238	523	5 794	8.2
Calloway	494	3.0	25.4	18.0	45.8	14.3	2.4	13.9	25.8	6 531	195	706	13 242	10.3
Campbell	875	-0.2	30.4	21.8	51.1	11.0	4.8	27.7	18.6	14 524	166	1 903	32 910	8.7
Carlisle	33	15.2	23.0	13.9	D	10.2	5.2	14.2	21.3	1 321	248	175	2 295	3.8
Carroll	209	1.3	61.9	55.6	D	7.6	0.9	8.0	9.1	2 018	210	462	3 870	1.3
Carter	143	1.5	D	17.3	D	17.9	4.3	17.2	25.8	5 101	190	1 842	9 290	5.9
Casey	104	11.1	D	26.1	D	10.1	2.2	15.6	17.4	3 159	214	1 319	6 046	4.0
Christian	1 935	0.6	D	11.9	D	4.2	1.4	8.0	68.1	9 596	132	2 098	23 429	10.5
Clark	426	3.2	D	32.0	D	11.5	2.6	15.6	11.4	5 809	182	1 097	11 635	11.7
Clay	140	0.7	D	7.2	D	13.8	2.4	21.6	42.6	4 413	194	3 679	7 930	7.1
Clinton	64	7.2	D	19.5	D	12.3	2.8	19.9	22.4	2 366	253	1 125	4 189	3.9
Crittenden	68	0.0	38.1	27.2	44.6	9.7	3.5	23.2	17.3	2 159	226	345	4 039	5.5

1. Covers mining, construction, and manufacturing. 2. Covers private sector earnings in agricultural services, forestry, and fisheries; transportation and public utilities; wholesale trade; retail trade; finance, insurance, and real estate; and services. 3. Per 1,000 resident population estimated as of July 1 of the year shown.

STATE County	Housing units, 1990 (cont'd)								Civilian labor force, 1999				Civilian employment, 1990[5]		
	Occupied units							Sub-stand-ard units[3] (percent)		Percent change, 1998–1999	Unemployment			Percent	
	Owner-occupied					Renter-occupied									
				Owner cost as a percent of income											
	Total	Percent	Median value[1]	With a mortgage	Without a mortgage	Median rent[2]	Rent as percent of income		Total		Total	Rate[4]	Total	Professional, managerial, and technical	Precision production, craft, and repair
	89	90	91	92	93	94	95	96	97	98	99	100	101	102	103
KANSAS—Cont'd															
Osage	5 806	79.2	38 300	18.6	12.8	280	22.8	2.1	10 182	4.6	404	4.0	6 730	20.5	15.5
Osborne	2 057	78.6	18 400	17.3	12.8	206	22.5	1.9	2 299	-0.2	41	1.8	2 272	16.3	8.7
Ottawa	2 266	78.7	27 500	15.4	12.3	253	20.0	2.0	3 172	3.0	75	2.4	2 536	21.6	13.2
Pawnee	2 923	71.3	35 300	17.9	12.1	282	21.5	1.2	3 742	12.2	70	1.9	3 414	25.7	10.0
Phillips	2 695	76.4	26 800	13.5	13.7	234	22.1	1.8	3 250	3.3	55	1.7	2 954	18.7	12.3
Pottawatomie	5 938	77.4	46 400	18.8	11.9	298	23.5	2.5	11 025	1.0	235	2.1	7 730	22.7	14.8
Pratt	3 937	73.9	37 500	16.5	12.0	313	21.1	1.2	4 962	-0.6	103	2.1	4 546	26.6	12.0
Rawlins	1 361	76.3	27 500	19.5	13.0	234	20.6	2.0	1 515	-2.0	37	2.4	1 555	17.3	8.4
Reno	24 239	69.9	40 100	16.3	12.3	306	22.7	2.1	33 424	1.8	991	3.0	28 858	22.8	12.9
Republic	2 769	78.4	18 900	20.2	11.8	212	19.3	1.2	3 168	2.9	53	1.7	2 991	19.5	10.4
Rice	4 165	75.2	27 200	15.3	12.0	250	20.1	1.4	4 793	3.0	159	3.3	4 602	20.6	12.7
Riley	21 280	44.1	63 500	20.3	12.2	379	30.0	3.9	30 993	-0.9	892	2.9	26 375	36.6	7.5
Rooks	2 444	77.6	25 800	20.1	13.2	233	21.3	1.8	3 152	-7.5	75	2.4	2 568	17.9	16.5
Rush	1 642	81.0	19 200	16.3	12.9	237	20.7	2.2	1 925	8.0	47	2.4	1 742	18.6	11.0
Russell	3 371	75.8	28 000	20.4	13.3	257	21.9	2.6	3 606	1.2	106	2.9	3 443	22.9	11.6
Saline	19 826	66.7	45 500	17.1	12.7	327	23.7	1.7	30 765	1.5	759	2.5	24 601	24.9	12.7
Scott	2 022	73.9	44 000	19.8	12.7	317	23.4	1.4	2 724	-4.3	41	1.5	2 505	20.5	10.3
Sedgwick	156 571	63.7	58 500	19.7	12.5	399	25.1	3.6	240 169	0.6	8 098	3.4	198 134	31.4	13.6
Seward	6 614	64.6	48 800	19.6	13.2	362	22.1	6.3	11 101	1.5	303	2.7	8 992	19.3	18.4
Shawnee	63 768	66.6	55 700	18.4	12.1	386	24.5	2.2	90 254	-0.5	2 803	3.1	80 143	32.4	8.6
Sheridan	1 171	79.6	27 600	14.4	13.5	212	18.8	3.0	1 521	-2.5	23	1.5	1 415	19.1	10.7
Sherman	2 733	69.7	37 900	14.9	12.2	276	24.0	2.5	4 267	7.0	64	1.5	3 292	21.4	9.4
Smith	2 165	79.6	20 700	17.2	12.3	195	21.5	1.6	2 504	12.0	33	1.3	2 345	16.4	8.8
Stafford	2 203	75.7	24 000	18.3	12.7	252	20.6	1.6	2 389	0.3	54	2.3	2 253	23.2	8.3
Stanton	831	64.6	44 500	18.8	12.8	286	19.1	4.3	1 095	2.3	21	1.9	1 065	20.2	8.7
Stevens	1 885	74.1	48 800	15.7	12.9	305	21.4	3.7	2 836	4.4	58	2.0	2 326	22.0	12.0
Sumner	9 689	76.6	39 300	17.2	12.8	299	21.4	2.6	14 393	10.5	462	3.2	11 408	21.0	19.1
Thomas	3 124	68.2	45 400	20.1	12.7	279	22.2	1.5	4 819	0.0	78	1.6	3 992	21.9	9.6
Trego	1 464	78.8	27 900	21.7	14.8	246	18.3	2.0	1 988	6.3	55	2.8	1 680	15.0	11.4
Wabaunsee	2 482	80.8	34 600	17.1	11.7	247	21.9	3.9	3 575	3.3	107	3.0	3 082	21.4	12.9
Wallace	677	74.0	28 400	19.0	14.1	257	23.8	2.2	896	11.6	14	1.6	845	16.6	8.6
Washington	2 862	78.3	18 500	15.6	12.4	193	20.3	3.2	3 475	0.8	86	2.5	3 216	20.4	7.8
Wichita	996	70.6	37 900	21.1	12.6	294	22.4	4.2	1 326	11.1	30	2.3	1 208	13.1	10.2
Wilson	4 194	77.7	23 500	21.3	14.1	268	27.9	2.3	5 649	-2.2	162	2.9	4 255	21.1	14.6
Woodson	1 699	78.0	18 800	16.5	14.2	257	24.6	4.1	1 530	3.9	76	5.0	1 557	17.1	11.8
Wyandotte	61 514	62.9	42 300	19.8	13.9	375	26.8	4.5	77 970	-0.8	4 207	5.4	70 343	20.3	11.6
KENTUCKY	1 379 782	69.6	50 500	18.0	12.3	319	24.9	4.7	1 969 791	2.4	88 032	4.5	1 563 960	24.7	12.9
Adair	5 800	79.9	35 100	20.0	12.8	234	25.9	6.9	7 581	-3.2	693	9.1	6 611	15.3	11.2
Allen	5 595	76.7	35 600	20.7	13.1	230	24.5	7.2	8 705	2.2	461	5.3	5 984	12.5	15.9
Anderson	5 438	82.1	51 500	16.8	12.2	328	22.2	3.8	10 123	4.9	296	2.9	7 429	21.8	14.3
Ballard	3 191	82.3	33 000	17.5	12.2	216	22.2	2.6	4 248	3.5	260	6.1	3 222	18.6	17.0
Barren	13 136	70.8	43 300	16.9	12.9	257	23.7	4.0	18 964	1.3	978	5.2	14 405	19.2	13.6
Bath	3 659	76.5	31 000	18.0	12.8	207	25.2	10.5	5 888	3.9	362	6.1	3 799	15.3	15.7
Bell	11 512	65.8	34 200	19.5	12.6	227	27.0	8.8	10 083	1.2	561	5.6	9 129	23.9	17.2
Boone	20 127	72.0	74 500	17.9	11.6	421	24.0	2.3	44 743	5.8	1 249	2.8	28 991	27.9	11.7
Bourbon	7 250	62.6	51 300	18.9	13.5	317	28.2	3.3	10 259	2.4	243	2.4	8 783	20.9	11.7
Boyd	19 876	72.7	45 400	15.8	12.0	297	24.2	1.7	22 910	1.9	1 534	6.7	20 071	25.7	14.3
Boyle	9 483	68.5	54 700	18.4	12.2	301	26.1	2.7	14 714	2.9	467	3.2	11 193	24.5	12.7
Bracken	2 872	75.4	39 400	17.8	13.4	229	21.5	8.8	4 056	7.1	159	3.9	3 083	16.3	14.2
Breathitt	5 555	71.8	28 700	21.6	12.9	205	26.5	20.0	4 273	1.5	360	8.4	4 405	22.3	14.1
Breckinridge	6 159	80.5	37 700	19.9	13.6	240	26.1	6.5	7 807	0.5	489	6.3	6 227	17.2	15.3
Bullitt	15 965	84.3	51 000	18.2	11.6	334	22.3	4.0	33 772	4.7	1 077	3.2	22 743	16.6	17.5
Butler	4 180	79.3	33 700	20.5	13.6	204	24.7	6.4	5 932	2.6	332	5.6	4 547	12.4	21.0
Caldwell	5 274	75.5	33 800	20.2	13.2	229	24.0	4.8	6 584	3.9	306	4.6	5 303	19.8	13.2
Calloway	11 607	72.4	51 800	17.5	13.4	272	26.6	2.5	17 963	1.7	762	4.2	13 706	26.6	9.8
Campbell	31 169	68.2	62 300	16.6	11.9	368	25.2	3.3	46 344	1.0	1 494	3.2	39 693	27.3	12.3
Carlisle	2 106	84.3	30 300	15.9	13.9	235	21.3	2.9	2 764	1.7	176	6.4	2 211	18.8	14.9
Carroll	3 505	65.6	41 700	15.3	11.9	261	24.1	7.3	5 146	1.4	214	4.2	3 857	21.0	16.0
Carter	8 679	80.0	37 100	18.7	12.4	272	28.4	8.9	12 031	4.5	1 542	12.8	8 648	18.3	15.1
Casey	5 436	80.0	30 900	17.2	13.2	207	23.4	13.4	6 826	-2.0	504	7.4	5 552	13.4	15.3
Christian	21 636	53.4	42 400	18.4	12.6	329	23.9	5.0	28 194	2.8	1 069	3.8	21 813	23.1	12.3
Clark	10 973	68.3	56 900	17.8	12.3	325	24.9	4.2	16 772	3.3	536	3.2	13 222	23.7	14.8
Clay	7 367	71.6	27 800	19.7	12.3	201	28.3	15.7	7 456	4.1	510	6.8	5 796	21.7	16.4
Clinton	3 591	75.9	27 400	20.9	13.6	198	29.0	11.2	5 640	25.5	218	3.9	3 418	15.0	12.8
Crittenden	3 646	79.2	30 900	15.4	11.9	232	26.5	4.8	4 023	-1.2	226	5.6	3 514	17.2	21.3

1. Specified owner-occupied units. 2. Specified renter-occupied units. 3. Overcrowded or lacking complete plumbing facilities. 4. Percent of civilian labor force. 5. Persons 16 years and older.

Table B. States and Counties — Nonfarm Employment and Agriculture

| | Private nonfarm establishments, employment and payroll, 1998 | | | | | | | | Agriculture, 1997 | | | |
| | Employment | | | | | | Annual payroll | | Farms | | | Farm operators |
STATE County	Number of establishments	Total	Health Care and Social Assistance	Manufacturing	Retail trade	Finance and Insurance	Professional Scientific and Technical Services	Total (mil dol)	Average per employee (dollars)	Number	Percent with— Less than 50 acres	500 acres and over	Whose principal occupation is farming (percent)
	104	105	106	107	108	109	110	111	112	113	114	115	116
KANSAS—Cont'd													
Osage	336	3 657	1 538	D	497	233	56	50	13 680	890	18.4	22.2	45.4
Osborne	175	1 267	253	205	278	75	34	20	15 509	465	6.0	55.5	72.3
Ottawa	133	931	292	24	129	106	21	16	17 378	498	12.9	45.0	58.0
Pawnee	196	2 092	946	81	293	118	40	42	20 286	425	6.8	51.3	68.7
Phillips	233	1 625	276	D	259	107	62	33	20 085	501	10.6	54.1	67.1
Pottawatomie	493	5 385	1 254	613	1 033	193	110	114	21 258	787	15.1	32.8	48.4
Pratt	376	3 014	615	127	699	121	95	61	20 171	434	6.5	52.3	62.7
Rawlins	110	569	161	34	120	54	15	10	17 297	431	3.9	70.8	77.5
Reno	1 744	24 923	3 546	5 444	3 948	803	505	599	24 027	1 363	18.6	29.9	53.3
Republic	219	1 888	375	461	297	81	40	31	16 572	684	9.1	42.0	68.3
Rice	310	2 290	321	315	332	147	51	44	19 257	519	12.1	47.8	61.5
Riley	1 402	17 523	2 863	659	3 303	978	714	325	18 556	468	20.9	31.2	54.5
Rooks	213	1 326	117	331	238	72	23	26	19 843	435	9.4	53.6	60.2
Rush	101	875	176	196	72	47	30	18	20 952	486	4.7	47.3	66.7
Russell	294	2 166	219	276	382	86	49	38	17 692	494	7.1	45.3	62.8
Saline	1 706	26 327	3 209	6 211	4 500	719	925	630	23 937	720	15.3	33.1	51.4
Scott	215	1 389	281	D	307	91	54	27	19 258	335	10.1	63.0	67.8
Sedgwick	11 776	232 884	29 516	60 894	26 285	8 282	10 124	7 016	30 127	1 395	30.9	21.9	47.0
Seward	702	9 117	1 115	D	1 533	236	208	217	23 825	251	10.4	59.4	64.9
Shawnee	4 609	81 210	15 499	7 842	10 790	5 384	3 420	2 173	26 758	823	30.6	14.2	40.8
Sheridan	103	627	149	18	117	49	12	12	18 515	442	5.2	63.1	70.4
Sherman	269	2 150	430	D	649	127	63	36	16 881	478	4.8	63.0	68.0
Smith	169	1 092	259	171	222	63	22	16	14 850	557	11.7	54.9	67.0
Stafford	143	949	264	69	120	79	16	16	17 026	475	7.2	52.4	65.5
Stanton	78	437	D	10	60	D	16	9	20 378	253	4.3	68.0	75.5
Stevens	171	1 193	128	D	178	60	54	26	21 490	304	6.2	62.5	68.1
Sumner	551	4 912	853	1 258	753	286	275	109	22 211	1 064	15.1	39.1	55.5
Thomas	354	2 603	425	D	554	112	58	45	17 296	553	6.1	61.5	63.7
Trego	127	737	D	D	167	29	24	12	15 753	399	4.8	63.7	69.2
Wabaunsee	128	663	D	60	149	49	D	11	17 151	597	12.7	36.2	47.7
Wallace	66	330	51	0	59	19	D	5	15 430	277	6.5	57.4	66.8
Washington	236	1 461	425	68	206	85	40	20	13 686	780	14.6	41.0	67.1
Wichita	98	493	D	40	106	37	9	9	17 414	310	7.1	67.4	74.2
Wilson	266	3 043	582	1 338	286	97	37	65	21 200	541	12.6	33.6	51.4
Woodson	108	555	81	D	87	42	15	9	16 787	371	14.6	38.8	59.3
Wyandotte	3 115	63 450	12 661	14 574	5 532	1 618	1 140	1 952	30 765	189	57.7	3.7	27.5
KENTUCKY	89 593	1 443 015	194 305	290 665	221 580	61 079	48 537	36 889	25 564	82 273	33.9	5.9	41.1
Adair	280	3 034	889	342	456	107	42	56	18 576	1 350	34.6	2.4	44.2
Allen	212	4 378	298	1 878	435	111	46	82	18 643	1 097	30.5	4.3	39.9
Anderson	274	3 338	234	1 409	486	102	63	82	24 465	691	32.9	2.0	26.9
Ballard	156	1 870	124	792	269	61	79	61	32 527	482	29.7	12.4	39.0
Barren	867	14 857	2 034	5 409	2 272	355	369	347	23 365	2 000	36.4	4.0	45.0
Bath	174	1 533	181	545	227	69	D	27	17 446	799	30.0	6.4	50.7
Bell	654	8 202	1 355	884	2 044	268	194	161	19 627	54	44.4	0.0	18.5
Boone	2 240	52 131	2 678	9 426	8 628	2 020	1 042	1 366	26 203	691	49.1	3.5	34.7
Bourbon	404	5 138	515	1 371	778	178	112	131	25 588	910	33.8	10.3	52.7
Boyd	1 570	25 638	4 538	4 213	4 388	764	1 024	785	30 610	207	35.7	2.9	22.7
Boyle	760	15 119	2 012	5 306	2 047	343	411	348	23 021	673	40.1	4.9	40.3
Bracken	125	1 125	D	D	154	D	14	18	16 429	656	26.4	3.0	44.4
Breathitt	233	2 451	800	29	548	131	38	42	17 220	193	33.2	9.3	29.0
Breckinridge	299	2 404	374	373	523	130	56	39	16 407	1 379	28.1	7.0	40.8
Bullitt	896	10 066	547	3 154	1 954	238	225	213	21 152	564	49.8	2.5	38.1
Butler	211	3 335	258	1 869	277	84	38	58	17 285	700	20.0	9.7	34.6
Caldwell	292	3 074	497	703	724	128	52	60	19 602	608	19.2	12.5	35.2
Calloway	817	11 928	1 931	2 878	2 130	266	204	250	20 962	749	39.3	9.9	40.7
Campbell	1 611	23 449	3 164	3 593	4 030	648	552	592	25 237	503	36.4	0.6	30.8
Carlisle	80	677	73	192	141	53	12	11	16 300	323	26.6	9.9	41.8
Carroll	231	5 000	184	2 539	657	49	D	154	30 846	324	25.9	6.5	43.2
Carter	446	4 215	538	632	1 098	185	94	61	14 564	872	31.0	2.5	33.9
Casey	203	2 463	218	977	320	76	D	40	16 144	1 332	32.0	4.5	43.5
Christian	1 347	21 380	4 801	4 653	2 926	724	404	469	21 915	1 158	25.0	12.3	47.9
Clark	751	11 522	994	3 929	2 155	225	285	266	23 117	847	41.3	7.9	45.5
Clay	295	2 899	701	376	621	112	72	52	17 949	402	33.3	6.0	40.5
Clinton	192	1 963	357	743	317	66	24	28	14 335	639	38.0	2.8	41.9
Crittenden	171	1 755	425	465	265	71	63	37	20 972	599	18.2	9.2	37.2

Table B. States and Counties — Agriculture, Land, and Water

STATE County	Acreage (1,000)	Percent change, 1992–1997	Average size of farm	Total irrigated (1,000)	Total cropland (1,000)	Average per farm ($1,000)	Average per acre (dollars)	Value of machinery and equipment Average per farm ($1,000)	Total (mil dol)	Average per farm (dollars)	Crops	Live-stock and poultry products	$10,000 or more	$100,000 or more	Percent of land owned by Fed. Gov. 1997	Water consumption 1995 (mil gal/day)
	117	118	119	120	121	122	123	124	125	126	127	128	129	130	131	132
KANSAS—Cont'd																
Osage	360	3.1	404	1	221	248	615	47	41	45 749	58.9	41.1	53.1	10.9	1.8	2.1
Osborne	505	-7.6	1 087	8	306	387	372	81	41	88 096	61.4	38.6	79.1	28.0	0.5	4.6
Ottawa	400	5.3	803	4	238	383	514	69	62	124 251	44.4	55.6	70.1	23.9	0.0	2.8
Pawnee	480	6.9	1 129	70	388	637	533	104	118	276 605	36.1	63.9	69.2	33.2	0.1	68.1
Phillips	555	-4.7	1 107	9	322	456	422	71	45	89 340	51.9	48.1	74.7	26.9	1.0	32.2
Pottawatomie	443	-1.8	563	13	199	390	686	50	52	65 834	33.4	66.6	57.2	13.0	1.6	39.7
Pratt	437	1.2	1 008	73	365	540	541	128	148	339 931	32.1	67.9	67.3	35.5	0.0	77.0
Rawlins	647	0.9	1 500	15	407	568	383	99	38	88 351	68.8	31.2	85.4	27.1	0.0	16.3
Reno	662	-5.6	486	28	500	361	728	58	134	98 303	44.0	56.0	59.6	19.4	0.7	58.2
Republic	428	-3.4	626	43	321	400	669	83	93	135 807	48.8	51.2	73.5	28.4	0.0	28.8
Rice	458	5.7	882	22	346	463	566	99	97	186 606	46.8	53.2	70.7	30.6	0.1	20.4
Riley	238	4.3	508	3	122	299	673	60	30	64 527	45.9	54.1	59.0	18.6	21.3	6.1
Rooks	570	-1.5	1 309	2	330	443	338	73	41	94 489	47.8	52.2	69.9	21.4	0.8	17.0
Rush	412	-3.4	848	6	329	370	421	73	30	60 746	72.5	27.5	70.6	19.5	0.0	10.1
Russell	429	-7.5	869	D	261	327	359	68	27	55 379	59.8	40.2	61.7	15.0	1.8	1.2
Saline	414	2.7	575	2	284	428	730	57	45	62 933	67.7	32.3	61.5	18.6	7.5	10.1
Scott	476	-1.6	1 422	46	394	694	510	147	451	1 347 057	9.5	90.5	84.2	51.6	0.0	63.6
Sedgwick	540	5.8	387	28	413	493	1 329	57	82	58 636	70.0	30.0	55.0	16.6	0.6	89.3
Seward	328	0.0	1 306	80	237	834	596	193	257	1 022 381	13.4	86.6	60.6	37.1	0.0	159.6
Shawnee	224	-1.3	272	12	148	280	1 084	39	29	35 362	73.7	26.3	42.0	9.7	0.6	42.9
Sheridan	507	-5.2	1 148	64	364	537	510	102	80	180 547	55.9	44.1	85.7	40.0	0.0	78.1
Sherman	653	5.3	1 365	98	527	684	493	116	83	173 565	64.5	35.5	79.1	35.1	0.0	89.8
Smith	492	-8.4	883	6	344	490	575	104	52	93 311	55.9	44.1	77.2	26.2	0.0	4.8
Stafford	435	-0.3	915	71	351	503	545	130	100	210 542	46.3	53.7	70.5	33.1	3.0	75.6
Stanton	400	-2.9	1 582	109	344	947	624	193	119	469 197	38.6	61.4	75.1	48.6	0.0	163.6
Stevens	512	13.5	1 684	162	408	908	525	250	154	507 326	44.4	55.6	71.7	43.8	0.2	189.1
Sumner	667	-3.0	627	5	555	412	603	74	89	83 744	80.1	19.9	68.8	25.9	0.0	6.9
Thomas	679	-3.4	1 229	88	584	705	595	116	118	212 719	53.4	46.6	82.5	34.5	0.0	91.0
Trego	462	-4.5	1 159	4	302	571	450	87	41	102 777	33.5	66.5	78.4	17.3	1.5	4.6
Wabaunsee	478	13.1	801	6	155	379	497	45	41	69 070	30.4	69.6	58.6	15.4	0.0	3.6
Wallace	480	1.7	1 733	42	266	614	376	106	36	130 115	60.7	39.3	66.1	30.3	0.0	62.2
Washington	536	2.9	688	7	348	444	683	80	85	108 655	42.6	57.4	71.9	26.4	0.0	5.6
Wichita	450	1.3	1 450	65	363	764	525	131	274	883 396	13.5	86.5	80.0	47.1	0.0	75.5
Wilson	301	-3.7	557	1	176	280	534	68	35	65 173	65.9	34.1	58.6	17.4	0.0	2.8
Woodson	254	-4.3	686	D	122	336	460	45	27	72 527	45.8	54.2	62.3	16.2	0.9	1.0
Wyandotte	22	-2.8	118	0	17	263	2 200	29	5	24 647	68.2	31.9	20.1	4.8	0.0	479.2
KENTUCKY	13 334	-2.4	162	58	8 549	230	1 450	33	3 064	37 247	51.5	48.5	44.0	6.8	4.6	4 420.2
Adair	160	-9.9	119	0	98	121	1 037	24	30	21 956	37.3	62.7	40.7	4.9	5.1	2.4
Allen	159	1.4	145	1	96	153	1 167	24	35	32 019	22.7	77.3	39.5	3.2	1.7	2.1
Anderson	84	-6.7	121	0	53	246	2 172	30	11	16 494	54.2	45.8	37.5	1.9	1.6	3.3
Ballard	119	5.9	246	0	96	322	1 380	58	35	71 998	62.8	37.2	49.6	14.7	0.0	23.5
Barren	250	0.3	125	1	185	180	1 455	31	60	29 894	42.6	57.4	47.6	6.6	2.4	7.7
Bath	129	-3.2	161	0	82	150	1 039	31	23	28 475	66.5	33.5	56.7	4.8	9.2	4.5
Bell	4	-26.3	68	0	2	104	1 524	14	0	2 352	24.4	75.6	1.9	0.0	3.7	7.6
Boone	80	-1.4	116	0	48	356	3 043	33	16	22 946	75.2	24.8	37.0	4.3	0.0	8.3
Bourbon	197	-5.1	216	1	141	522	2 385	42	90	98 757	31.8	68.2	69.9	17.8	0.0	3.0
Boyd	26	-6.8	126	0	11	182	1 480	24	2	10 969	20.3	79.7	13.5	2.4	0.0	80.0
Boyle	95	-12.1	141	0	66	228	1 609	31	27	40 178	38.9	61.1	46.4	8.2	0.0	4.8
Bracken	92	-7.4	140	1	54	160	1 117	29	18	26 888	80.0	20.0	57.5	5.2	0.0	1.6
Breathitt	47	8.5	242	0	6	217	827	17	1	7 351	83.9	16.1	23.3	0.0	0.0	1.1
Breckinridge	268	0.3	194	0	147	195	1 043	34	32	23 112	62.0	38.0	45.5	4.5	1.5	1.8
Bullitt	57	-7.3	100	0	32	306	2 937	36	8	13 445	50.6	49.4	25.5	2.1	18.6	3.9
Butler	151	7.4	216	0	79	192	922	29	22	30 766	39.9	60.1	29.1	5.9	0.0	1.5
Caldwell	148	14.7	243	D	99	204	812	34	23	37 221	70.2	29.7	33.7	7.4	0.0	1.3
Calloway	146	6.5	195	1	117	305	1 583	50	49	65 571	69.1	30.9	47.1	14.4	0.0	5.1
Campbell	45	4.9	90	0	25	274	2 890	27	5	10 817	59.1	40.9	21.7	2.0	0.0	31.8
Carlisle	90	14.3	279	0	74	285	1 006	46	25	77 243	65.7	34.3	46.7	14.6	0.0	2.6
Carroll	60	-1.7	185	1	29	209	1 313	32	9	26 829	77.8	22.2	54.6	4.9	0.0	43.5
Carter	109	-3.8	125	0	42	95	822	21	9	10 748	67.8	32.2	26.9	0.7	3.3	3.1
Casey	191	-0.7	143	0	95	114	884	22	29	21 625	51.2	48.8	43.9	4.1	0.0	1.9
Christian	310	3.6	267	2	230	370	1 393	60	83	71 293	76.5	23.5	52.3	14.9	2.9	10.4
Clark	147	1.3	173	1	102	318	1 951	29	35	41 879	45.2	54.8	51.0	9.1	0.0	108.5
Clay	57	-15.9	142	0	16	138	955	26	5	13 176	84.3	15.7	33.1	1.5	25.2	2.8
Clinton	78	4.1	122	0	44	163	1 383	23	11	17 179	43.1	56.9	39.9	2.2	5.3	1.3
Crittenden	142	13.2	236	0	85	180	775	27	10	16 502	50.3	49.7	28.7	3.7	0.0	1.0

Table B. States and Counties — Residential Construction, Wholesale and Retail Trade, and Real Estate

STATE County	Value of Residential Construction Authorized by Building Permits, 1999		Wholesale Trade, 1997				Retail Trade[1], 1997				Real Estate and Rental and Leasing, 1997			
	New Construction ($1,000)	Number of Housing Units	Number of Establishments	Number of Employees	Sales (mil dol)	Annual Payroll (mil dol)	Number of Establishments	Number of Employees	Sales (mil dol)	Annual Payroll (mil dol)	Number of Establishments	Number of Employees	Receipts (mil dol)	Annual Payroll (mil dol)
	133	134	135	136	137	138	139	140	141	142	143	144	145	146
KANSAS—Cont'd														
Osage	5 351	52	9	90	45.7	1.6	65	444	67.7	5.7	8	13	1.0	0.2
Osborne	340	5	13	156	65.9	2.8	45	244	34.2	2.8	1	D	D	D
Ottawa	0	0	12	92	72.1	2.6	24	132	16.8	1.7	NA	NA	NA	NA
Pawnee	300	3	11	92	43.1	2.3	42	298	40.8	4.2	3	7	0.2	0.0
Phillips	469	4	16	138	58.8	2.9	39	281	34.7	3.0	1	D	D	D
Pottawatomie	11 691	101	22	266	113.9	5.0	94	854	119.6	12.1	18	35	2.5	0.5
Pratt	2 155	30	30	357	258.0	8.7	62	632	88.0	9.5	10	D	D	D
Rawlins	0	0	12	77	47.0	2.0	23	114	13.8	1.2	1	D	D	D
Reno	20 404	177	94	1 239	474.6	36.3	327	3 961	667.0	65.7	55	185	54.9	2.4
Republic	0	0	24	153	85.8	2.3	51	255	34.5	3.6	3	4	0.3	0.0
Rice	1 953	24	19	116	47.7	3.1	50	337	40.1	4.1	5	D	D	D
Riley	18 254	169	42	493	140.7	12.1	305	3 331	442.9	43.6	73	245	18.4	2.8
Rooks	463	4	17	114	53.8	2.6	43	258	37.3	3.0	2	D	D	D
Rush	135	1	16	160	58.8	4.2	18	93	13.5	1.2	NA	NA	NA	NA
Russell	107	1	17	138	108.7	3.2	53	310	42.0	4.2	2	D	D	D
Saline	17 057	132	103	1 261	841.2	36.0	313	4 340	679.3	63.8	70	279	34.4	4.3
Scott	534	4	22	149	67.4	3.7	40	297	48.9	3.9	5	D	D	D
Sedgwick	238 575	2 433	798	9 903	5 875.1	336.3	1 804	25 223	4 265.4	423.1	541	2 663	340.6	54.2
Seward	2 406	20	48	299	133.3	9.2	135	1 394	249.1	21.5	31	112	12.1	2.3
Shawnee	102 770	865	204	2 298	947.1	65.9	768	10 625	1 619.6	166.7	199	1 216	88.8	22.4
Sheridan	NA	NA	9	109	56.6	3.1	22	110	15.9	1.4	NA	NA	NA	NA
Sherman	724	7	21	203	126.6	5.7	62	453	88.7	7.4	6	10	1.0	0.1
Smith	95	1	15	133	61.4	2.4	39	230	25.7	2.5	2	D	D	D
Stafford	0	0	15	157	57.1	3.4	21	108	12.0	1.1	1	D	D	D
Stanton	0	0	16	132	65.5	3.7	12	61	13.1	1.2	NA	NA	NA	NA
Stevens	500	2	19	181	113.9	4.9	23	138	26.4	2.1	2	D	D	D
Sumner	6 661	86	33	212	143.2	6.1	93	733	114.5	9.4	16	42	2.2	0.4
Thomas	3 755	54	28	255	207.8	6.5	70	606	81.5	8.0	9	35	2.3	0.4
Trego	0	0	11	52	38.6	1.1	29	177	21.4	2.0	2	D	D	D
Wabaunsee	2 602	32	5	21	6.7	0.2	30	139	18.4	1.9	2	D	D	D
Wallace	0	0	6	D	D	D	12	68	7.7	0.7	NA	NA	NA	NA
Washington	203	2	21	226	83.8	4.7	42	211	19.6	1.8	2	D	D	D
Wichita	176	4	8	43	31.7	1.2	22	104	19.1	1.7	2	D	D	D
Wilson	168	3	11	D	D	D	38	253	26.8	2.6	6	13	0.3	0.1
Woodson	371	7	9	D	D	D	25	101	11.7	1.2	3	6	0.1	0.0
Wyandotte	19 275	195	311	6 891	4 013.4	224.7	436	5 172	932.9	91.8	126	758	84.9	15.9
KENTUCKY	1 909 051	21 581	5 051	69 309	37 242.9	2 071.2	17 369	212 189	33 332.7	3 128.1	3 227	16 284	1 961.6	314.3
Adair	0	0	16	131	29.4	3.6	65	525	83.0	6.3	10	31	1.5	0.2
Allen	NA	NA	11	102	15.3	1.8	70	469	78.6	5.9	5	20	1.3	0.2
Anderson	15 233	189	10	D	D	D	54	528	92.7	8.0	7	D	D	D
Ballard	NA	NA	5	50	28.7	1.1	37	264	49.0	3.6	3	12	0.5	0.0
Barren	8 190	152	35	328	97.6	8.1	208	2 171	355.5	31.2	26	55	6.6	0.7
Bath	125	2	1	D	D	D	42	238	38.5	2.9	6	11	0.3	0.1
Bell	3 597	67	26	328	88.9	7.6	163	1 955	299.2	36.2	12	34	2.8	0.8
Boone	166 287	1 841	122	1 683	1 005.0	59.6	435	8 561	1 666.2	132.5	92	676	101.9	13.5
Bourbon	15 850	214	18	D	D	D	75	781	127.9	10.1	10	54	2.8	0.7
Boyd	1 895	21	94	1 435	515.3	38.7	345	4 313	641.6	60.8	63	215	25.8	4.4
Boyle	14 501	173	33	285	197.0	4.8	149	2 152	301.8	29.0	20	74	7.8	1.3
Bracken	NA	NA	4	47	18.2	1.0	27	127	19.7	1.5	3	14	0.5	0.1
Breathitt	0	0	5	75	40.1	1.7	52	715	102.8	8.7	5	15	1.6	0.3
Breckinridge	1 180	19	10	D	D	D	69	525	95.1	7.4	8	36	1.9	0.5
Bullitt	71 938	738	31	288	92.8	7.1	151	1 547	243.3	22.5	33	89	10.7	1.3
Butler	60	1	8	31	13.9	0.5	41	270	35.7	3.1	8	21	1.0	0.2
Caldwell	1 879	29	11	61	27.2	1.3	64	752	126.3	11.8	3	D	D	D
Calloway	7 507	249	53	D	D	D	192	2 020	336.5	28.4	25	94	7.6	1.1
Campbell	42 313	404	78	649	230.1	26.0	266	3 874	644.1	57.6	68	507	58.9	15.8
Carlisle	NA	NA	8	28	22.0	0.6	19	134	20.3	3.0	4	D	D	D
Carroll	319	7	13	234	63.4	3.6	59	549	121.8	8.7	3	D	D	D
Carter	432	13	12	D	D	D	130	1 071	179.2	14.8	14	D	D	D
Casey	400	5	17	87	18.2	1.4	53	310	44.2	4.2	3	11	0.4	0.1
Christian	31 186	610	79	1 281	682.5	39.9	301	2 836	464.9	43.7	74	266	26.6	4.0
Clark	43 628	469	34	D	D	D	147	1 922	348.2	30.3	24	60	6.0	0.5
Clay	0	0	14	70	13.4	1.1	78	812	110.2	9.4	11	35	1.2	0.2
Clinton	220	9	8	55	12.8	1.0	55	374	47.2	4.5	4	18	1.8	0.4
Crittenden	NA	NA	7	D	D	D	29	261	28.9	3.2	4	D	D	D

1. Establishments with payroll.

Table B. States and Counties — Professional, Manufacturing, and Accommodation and Foodservices

STATE County	Professional, Scientific, and Technical Services[1], 1997				Manufacturing, 1997				Accommodation and Foodservices, 1997			
	Number of Establishments	Number of Employees	Receipts (mil dol)	Annual Payroll (mil dol)	Number of Establishments	Number of Employees	Receipts (mil dol)	Annual Payroll (mil dol)	Number of Establishments	Number of Employees	Sales (mil dol)	Annual Payroll (mil dol)
	147	148	149	150	151	152	153	154	155	156	157	158
KANSAS—Cont'd												
Osage	13	52	2.4	0.9	NA	NA	NA	NA	32	189	5.2	1.1
Osborne	5	22	1.7	0.5	NA	NA	NA	NA	11	83	1.4	0.5
Ottawa	4	D	D	D	NA	NA	NA	NA	14	50	1.4	0.3
Pawnee	11	30	2.1	0.8	NA	NA	NA	NA	18	195	8.6	1.3
Phillips	14	51	3.4	1.5	NA	NA	NA	NA	18	150	3.1	0.8
Pottawatomie	27	83	4.9	1.4	22	720	134.2	25.8	32	320	7.3	1.9
Pratt	25	91	5.1	1.9	NA	NA	NA	NA	34	478	10.3	3.0
Rawlins	5	15	0.7	0.2	NA	NA	NA	NA	7	D	D	D
Reno	89	453	26.9	11.5	97	5 141	849.7	161.3	141	2 382	67.5	17.6
Republic	8	29	1.5	0.5	8	D	D	D	12	172	3.1	0.8
Rice	15	33	1.6	0.4	NA	NA	NA	NA	28	317	6.2	1.7
Riley	91	660	54.8	21.0	28	533	75.8	14.4	156	2 998	74.6	21.0
Rooks	7	18	1.3	0.5	NA	NA	NA	NA	19	79	1.6	0.4
Rush	7	15	0.9	0.4	NA	NA	NA	NA	8	D	D	D
Russell	14	57	2.5	0.8	NA	NA	NA	NA	21	288	6.2	1.6
Saline	84	702	52.1	20.4	87	6 434	1 212.2	193.2	136	2 464	68.9	21.0
Scott	14	36	1.8	0.5	NA	NA	NA	NA	12	148	3.3	0.8
Sedgwick	957	6 367	537.9	217.7	595	61 675	10 638.7	2 569.7	969	17 828	585.6	166.7
Seward	31	209	12.3	4.7	10	D	D	D	56	820	24.2	6.2
Shawnee	405	3 227	233.6	94.7	140	7 722	1 805.6	265.4	374	6 745	199.2	54.3
Sheridan	5	15	0.8	0.2	NA	NA	NA	NA	4	D	D	D
Sherman	18	57	2.6	0.7	NA	NA	NA	NA	20	246	6.6	1.7
Smith	9	22	0.7	0.2	NA	NA	NA	NA	14	81	2.3	0.6
Stafford	8	18	0.9	0.2	NA	NA	NA	NA	14	D	D	D
Stanton	5	13	0.6	0.2	NA	NA	NA	NA	6	D	D	D
Stevens	14	41	2.3	0.8	NA	NA	NA	NA	13	94	3.0	0.6
Sumner	27	70	3.4	1.1	44	1 262	194.6	45.1	36	444	10.7	3.2
Thomas	20	55	3.6	0.8	NA	NA	NA	NA	34	487	13.5	3.9
Trego	6	12	0.6	0.2	NA	NA	NA	NA	13	D	D	D
Wabaunsee	4	8	0.3	0.1	NA	NA	NA	NA	8	21	1.4	0.2
Wallace	1	D	D	D	NA	NA	NA	NA	2	D	D	D
Washington	10	28	1.4	0.3	NA	NA	NA	NA	17	159	2.8	0.7
Wichita	3	9	0.3	0.1	NA	NA	NA	NA	1	D	D	D
Wilson	12	29	1.8	0.3	29	1 256	261.5	35.0	13	D	D	D
Woodson	4	11	0.3	0.1	NA	NA	NA	NA	10	55	1.3	0.4
Wyandotte	157	1 127	88.8	33.4	262	15 083	7 678.2	638.9	230	3 191	109.3	30.3
KENTUCKY	6 189	41 991	3 820.3	1 260.1	4 218	288 405	86 636.1	9 198.1	6 546	129 442	4 056.1	1 140.6
Adair	16	28	1.9	0.6	20	533	30.8	8.3	19	221	7.3	2.0
Allen	8	38	1.5	0.5	12	1 858	285.1	41.6	20	232	6.3	1.7
Anderson	16	44	3.0	1.1	20	D	D	D	19	283	6.5	2.2
Ballard	7	54	2.0	1.1	12	D	D	D	6	D	D	D
Barren	44	204	13.5	4.5	55	5 672	796.0	154.5	85	1 338	44.6	11.9
Bath	12	25	1.1	0.3	NA	NA	NA	NA	11	105	2.7	0.7
Bell	36	157	9.4	4.1	22	858	125.8	18.6	50	766	26.0	6.5
Boone	125	857	117.1	35.9	134	9 050	1 857.4	305.7	171	4 381	156.0	43.2
Bourbon	23	58	2.6	0.8	19	D	D	D	27	308	9.9	2.6
Boyd	97	624	53.0	26.6	42	4 395	2 930.8	203.4	109	2 172	68.7	18.1
Boyle	46	208	16.9	5.9	33	4 604	778.3	130.5	54	1 088	32.5	8.8
Bracken	7	9	0.6	0.2	NA	NA	NA	NA	11	D	D	D
Breathitt	13	34	3.9	0.8	NA	NA	NA	NA	19	329	10.0	2.7
Breckinridge	11	41	1.4	0.4	NA	NA	NA	NA	22	188	4.7	1.5
Bullitt	45	143	8.5	2.6	49	2 959	344.8	85.6	56	1 169	36.0	10.4
Butler	6	21	0.7	0.2	15	1 886	355.1	37.6	12	134	3.0	0.9
Caldwell	16	38	2.0	0.5	19	659	121.6	18.7	24	283	7.2	2.0
Calloway	37	169	10.9	3.0	28	2 983	817.4	69.1	63	995	26.5	7.2
Campbell	101	387	30.0	9.8	83	3 043	726.1	105.0	169	D	D	D
Carlisle	4	12	0.4	0.1	NA	NA	NA	NA	7	D	D	D
Carroll	8	37	1.8	1.2	18	2 378	1 408.7	94.8	27	430	12.7	3.3
Carter	24	82	3.7	1.1	18	612	40.0	8.9	33	445	14.2	4.0
Casey	11	331	8.1	6.3	27	946	80.3	16.0	16	D	D	D
Christian	79	320	25.3	7.6	56	4 469	780.8	115.4	101	2 208	55.5	18.2
Clark	46	271	16.8	8.5	46	3 635	661.1	87.0	58	1 105	31.1	8.5
Clay	21	64	3.4	0.9	NA	NA	NA	NA	20	281	9.6	2.4
Clinton	12	21	1.3	0.2	15	671	45.7	9.9	16	155	6.5	1.8
Crittenden	9	29	1.3	0.5	NA	NA	NA	NA	12	D	D	D

1. Firms subject to federal tax.

Table B. States and Counties — Health and Other Services and Federal Funds

STATE County	Health Care and Social Assistance[1], 1997				Other Services[1], 1997				Federal funds and grants, fiscal 1999[2] Expenditures (mil dol)			
									Total	Direct payments for individuals[3]		
	Number of Establishments	Number of Employees	Receipts (mil dol)	Annual Payroll (mil dol)	Number of Establishments	Number of Employees	Receipts (mil dol)	Annual Payroll (mil dol)	Total	Social Security and government retirement	Medicare	Food stamps and Supplemental Security Income
	159	160	161	162	163	164	165	166	167	168	169	170
KANSAS—Cont'd												
Osage	22	317	9.0	4.2	21	38	3.6	0.6	73.4	38.7	11.7	1.4
Osborne	11	169	4.9	2.5	9	22	1.0	0.2	37.5	12.7	6.1	0.2
Ottawa	8	112	3.1	1.7	9	34	4.6	0.8	31.5	12.7	4.9	0.4
Pawnee	16	142	8.2	3.0	12	39	2.8	1.2	48.5	16.7	6.7	0.6
Phillips	15	50	2.6	0.7	15	42	2.5	0.6	39.1	15.2	7.3	0.2
Pottawatomie	27	322	10.2	5.2	27	73	4.9	1.1	61.5	31.8	13.1	1.2
Pratt	29	244	11.7	4.7	32	83	5.9	1.0	62.3	22.6	11.7	0.6
Rawlins	3	9	0.4	0.1	6	9	0.5	0.1	31.7	8.0	3.3	0.2
Reno	86	1 387	98.3	48.0	118	586	32.0	9.7	268.4	135.6	54.1	6.8
Republic	10	55	3.6	1.2	18	37	2.7	0.4	45.6	16.8	6.1	0.3
Rice	13	89	5.6	2.3	15	57	3.4	0.9	59.9	25.3	8.9	0.7
Riley	100	949	55.4	22.0	94	463	20.0	6.4	209.0	83.8	18.8	3.0
Rooks	7	41	1.4	0.6	12	33	2.0	0.6	37.7	14.6	8.0	0.4
Rush	4	15	1.1	0.7	5	11	0.6	0.2	31.7	10.7	5.5	0.3
Russell	14	170	6.8	2.7	18	46	4.5	0.7	49.0	21.2	10.0	0.7
Saline	125	1 149	91.8	36.6	110	697	49.0	15.8	252.5	106.9	37.7	5.2
Scott	7	44	3.4	1.6	19	37	3.0	0.5	32.0	5.9	3.6	0.3
Sedgwick	776	15 442	1 149.0	469.4	787	5 172	322.6	100.3	2 446.9	768.0	293.1	54.0
Seward	46	314	22.2	8.9	53	167	15.3	3.4	122.8	25.5	9.4	2.1
Shawnee	322	5 720	309.5	159.9	296	1 914	127.2	41.7	1 462.9	422.8	109.4	22.3
Sheridan	4	10	0.6	0.3	5	9	1.0	0.1	30.8	5.9	2.5	0.1
Sherman	12	144	5.9	2.3	23	151	5.8	1.7	54.8	14.9	7.2	0.7
Smith	11	160	4.2	2.0	11	29	1.6	0.3	36.3	13.6	5.3	0.3
Stafford	7	150	4.0	2.5	10	18	2.1	0.3	39.3	12.0	5.6	0.4
Stanton	4	31	0.5	0.2	3	D	D	D	25.8	3.9	1.3	0.1
Stevens	9	25	1.3	0.5	15	29	2.7	0.4	37.9	9.1	4.1	0.2
Sumner	44	444	15.2	6.6	33	101	7.0	1.6	128.6	59.8	21.8	2.0
Thomas	14	141	8.3	3.3	23	72	5.9	1.1	59.1	15.3	6.9	0.5
Trego	6	55	1.2	0.4	10	22	1.8	0.3	24.8	8.2	4.6	0.2
Wabaunsee	4	110	3.1	1.6	7	11	0.8	0.2	78.8	44.6	4.7	0.3
Wallace	1	D	D	D	4	7	0.6	0.1	22.6	4.0	2.2	0.1
Washington	14	116	3.3	1.3	16	29	1.8	0.4	56.8	17.8	7.1	0.4
Wichita	2	D	D	D	7	7	1.2	0.2	60.5	5.0	1.6	0.2
Wilson	19	229	8.3	3.7	17	37	2.8	0.6	53.0	24.0	9.8	1.2
Woodson	5	93	2.7	0.9	6	33	3.6	0.8	22.9	10.7	4.3	0.4
Wyandotte	223	4 049	301.9	108.6	231	1 379	78.5	25.1	897.2	293.1	151.8	31.5
KENTUCKY	6 805	94 720	5 936.2	2 620.3	5 383	31 164	1 870.3	551.4	22 198.1	7 584.3	2 904.6	1 088.3
Adair	23	353	14.7	7.6	13	31	2.3	0.6	93.9	27.5	16.8	7.1
Allen	13	55	2.7	1.1	9	27	2.0	0.3	67.2	27.9	13.5	4.3
Anderson	19	192	9.2	3.7	20	91	4.2	1.1	49.0	28.1	8.7	1.4
Ballard	5	154	3.7	1.7	9	43	2.4	0.7	45.6	21.6	10.7	1.6
Barren	75	1 002	53.7	26.1	40	198	12.3	3.0	141.5	64.5	25.2	9.2
Bath	10	102	2.6	1.2	13	20	1.3	0.2	47.6	19.1	5.8	5.9
Bell	61	557	28.5	11.7	39	184	9.3	2.9	506.7	70.7	31.2	21.7
Boone	142	1 452	94.8	38.1	132	1 244	68.7	19.5	247.9	111.4	34.0	6.4
Bourbon	32	274	21.4	6.9	23	94	4.0	1.1	84.5	35.8	14.3	3.8
Boyd	164	1 480	124.4	69.4	97	644	32.7	10.2	287.7	128.6	54.9	14.4
Boyle	76	724	49.1	24.4	41	195	7.9	2.4	108.4	52.1	19.7	6.2
Bracken	7	36	1.3	0.5	4	10	0.6	0.1	33.8	14.7	6.6	2.5
Breathitt	19	290	26.0	8.5	18	54	5.0	1.3	101.0	31.2	11.7	15.6
Breckinridge	18	144	6.7	2.0	20	80	4.5	1.1	81.0	37.9	13.6	4.1
Bullitt	47	537	21.8	10.3	69	285	18.2	4.6	199.3	72.5	22.9	5.8
Butler	10	78	2.9	1.4	12	62	7.6	0.9	49.6	19.4	10.5	3.3
Caldwell	18	93	8.1	1.9	17	55	3.7	0.7	63.5	31.0	11.5	3.0
Calloway	81	936	50.4	26.5	56	235	12.3	3.2	130.8	65.0	27.3	4.5
Campbell	117	1 487	84.5	41.8	116	640	41.1	12.2	308.9	159.2	65.5	14.0
Carlisle	4	70	2.6	1.0	5	11	0.6	0.1	27.2	12.3	5.9	0.9
Carroll	12	140	5.1	2.4	10	39	2.4	0.6	40.7	17.8	7.7	2.7
Carter	23	231	8.2	3.3	28	85	5.3	1.2	136.6	49.6	19.7	12.3
Casey	12	109	6.3	2.4	9	21	1.4	0.4	65.2	23.7	11.2	7.1
Christian	96	1 231	64.9	29.6	84	320	18.6	5.0	1 175.5	110.3	37.5	14.1
Clark	58	470	25.2	9.8	49	212	11.1	3.1	119.8	65.5	18.8	7.9
Clay	19	209	8.4	3.2	14	49	3.2	1.0	105.0	37.5	16.3	14.2
Clinton	13	200	9.0	4.2	4	9	0.7	0.1	59.2	17.6	14.1	4.2
Crittenden	9	153	5.2	3.0	13	30	2.2	0.4	44.9	20.5	10.1	2.3

1. Firms subject to federal tax.   2. October 1, 1998 to September 30, 1999.   3. State totals may include programs not allocated by county.

Table B. States and Counties — Federal Funds and Local Government Finances

	Federal funds and grants, fiscal 1999[1] (cont'd)							Local government finances, 1997				
	Expenditures (mil dol) (cont'd)							General revenue				
	Procurement contract awards			Grants[2]						Taxes		
STATE County	Salaries and wages	Defense	Other	Medicaid and other health-related	Nutrition and family welfare	Education	Other	Total (mil dol)	Intergovern-mental (mil dol)	Total (mil dol)	Per capita[3] (dollars) Total	Property
	171	172	173	174	175	176	177	178	179	180	181	182
KANSAS—Cont'd												
Osage	3.8	0.2	0.8	3.6	1.2	0.4	5.7	32.5	17.8	8.9	519	496
Osborne	1.4	0.0	0.9	2.5	0.3	0.2	0.3	9.6	3.2	3.5	774	729
Ottawa	1.1	0.0	0.3	2.0	0.4	0.1	0.4	17.4	9.3	5.2	895	786
Pawnee	2.1	0.0	0.4	1.6	1.0	0.2	0.3	18.9	10.3	5.5	904	879
Phillips	2.1	0.0	0.5	2.9	0.4	0.1	1.2	19.7	7.6	6.9	949	845
Pottawatomie	2.9	0.1	0.7	3.6	1.2	0.3	1.3	57.4	17.4	25.8	1 414	1 339
Pratt	1.8	0.0	0.5	1.4	0.6	0.2	1.5	26.6	9.8	10.6	1 091	1 015
Rawlins	0.8	0.0	0.2	1.6	0.2	0.1	0.7	9.4	3.8	4.8	1 510	928
Reno	13.1	0.0	2.7	19.0	7.8	1.9	3.3	144.5	54.7	57.5	915	757
Republic	1.7	0.0	0.4	1.6	0.4	0.2	4.1	16.7	7.0	6.9	1 125	1 046
Rice	2.3	0.0	0.5	2.0	1.2	0.5	0.5	26.4	12.5	9.9	991	918
Riley	19.3	7.2	9.5	11.7	4.8	5.8	31.2	92.3	37.6	35.8	566	428
Rooks	1.3	0.0	0.3	1.6	0.4	0.2	1.0	20.8	6.8	6.7	1 168	1 144
Rush	1.3	0.0	0.6	1.1	0.3	0.1	0.9	12.7	4.1	5.1	1 494	1 482
Russell	2.0	0.0	0.5	2.0	0.6	0.2	0.6	27.1	8.3	8.4	1 103	1 042
Saline	18.3	0.5	6.2	14.1	6.8	1.8	42.5	110.8	41.7	40.6	787	553
Scott	0.9	0.0	0.2	1.1	0.3	0.1	0.2	12.8	5.5	5.9	1 192	1 065
Sedgwick	336.5	630.8	59.4	144.0	58.1	16.0	49.2	961.5	388.0	342.5	781	546
Seward	4.5	54.7	0.8	5.0	2.4	0.9	0.9	87.9	22.2	25.9	1 287	944
Shawnee	159.6	8.3	25.4	108.5	148.7	70.6	221.8	423.2	144.6	175.0	1 061	836
Sheridan	0.5	0.1	0.1	0.9	0.1	0.1	0.2	9.5	2.9	3.7	1 345	1 328
Sherman	2.8	0.0	0.3	1.8	0.7	0.2	1.3	20.3	6.0	6.5	990	857
Smith	1.8	0.0	0.4	1.4	0.3	0.2	0.2	11.1	5.0	4.4	942	912
Stafford	1.7	0.0	0.3	0.9	0.4	0.2	0.3	20.9	6.8	8.4	1 643	1 548
Stanton	0.3	0.0	0.1	0.2	0.2	0.1	0.8	12.6	1.0	8.5	3 660	3 603
Stevens	1.0	0.0	0.2	1.1	0.3	0.1	0.0	25.4	2.4	19.1	3 527	3 447
Sumner	4.4	0.5	1.1	6.6	2.4	1.7	1.1	62.1	24.4	18.3	679	614
Thomas	2.4	0.0	0.5	1.8	0.6	0.4	1.1	28.6	11.5	8.8	1 073	987
Trego	0.8	0.0	0.2	1.4	0.2	0.1	0.4	13.2	3.7	3.7	1 120	1 101
Wabaunsee	1.4	0.0	0.3	0.9	0.4	0.1	22.3	13.6	7.7	4.4	654	610
Wallace	0.5	0.0	0.3	0.5	0.2	0.1	0.2	5.7	2.5	2.4	1 351	1 332
Washington	2.6	0.0	0.6	2.7	0.5	0.2	11.2	26.6	9.7	9.5	1 440	1 373
Wichita	0.5	32.4	0.9	0.7	0.3	0.1	0.4	8.8	2.7	3.4	1 243	1 176
Wilson	2.1	0.0	0.5	6.6	1.3	0.4	1.4	28.1	12.5	7.4	715	677
Woodson	1.1	0.2	0.3	2.0	0.3	0.1	0.0	7.5	3.3	3.2	807	785
Wyandotte	137.5	5.2	37.5	147.3	44.2	10.8	17.7	494.3	168.7	168.0	1 101	788
KENTUCKY	2 615.3	1 364.7	910.2	2 227.7	719.3	416.9	1 031.2	X	X	X	X	X
Adair	2.2	0.0	12.1	17.5	1.9	0.9	3.9	22.8	12.7	4.5	273	197
Allen	1.8	0.0	0.7	14.7	1.3	0.9	0.2	23.5	12.8	6.1	374	209
Anderson	1.7	0.1	0.4	4.7	1.0	0.6	1.9	24.1	12.5	7.6	422	308
Ballard	1.6	0.0	0.4	3.5	0.8	0.4	0.6	13.8	8.1	2.5	296	217
Barren	6.6	0.1	1.6	23.4	3.0	1.8	2.3	55.6	27.2	16.8	456	258
Bath	1.5	0.0	0.3	10.4	1.5	0.8	1.4	14.0	9.7	2.2	208	153
Bell	7.5	5.5	317.6	36.0	8.4	2.9	3.7	46.6	29.9	11.2	376	211
Boone	39.0	34.8	4.3	7.5	3.6	1.6	3.4	135.2	37.3	65.0	854	462
Bourbon	2.1	0.1	0.6	8.7	2.4	1.0	13.8	29.9	15.2	10.1	520	262
Boyd	31.1	2.2	7.3	25.8	6.7	2.6	6.6	83.0	34.3	25.5	512	314
Boyle	4.2	0.6	1.0	15.1	2.2	1.2	3.5	42.3	18.4	15.5	571	304
Bracken	1.3	0.0	0.4	5.7	0.7	0.5	0.8	10.9	7.0	2.4	287	217
Breathitt	3.6	0.0	0.4	30.0	6.0	1.6	0.2	22.9	16.3	3.7	240	126
Breckinridge	3.1	0.0	0.6	11.9	2.9	1.1	0.3	23.6	15.0	4.4	257	193
Bullitt	2.9	78.5	0.8	9.4	4.0	2.0	-0.4	64.1	41.0	17.7	305	236
Butler	1.7	0.0	0.4	9.9	1.2	0.7	0.1	20.1	12.1	5.0	423	150
Caldwell	2.4	0.0	0.5	7.4	1.2	0.8	1.4	30.5	9.5	4.4	330	132
Calloway	4.8	0.0	0.7	8.9	5.4	2.5	1.7	43.1	21.3	11.7	354	247
Campbell	13.8	2.7	5.3	22.6	7.8	3.5	10.8	118.2	46.8	52.6	602	351
Carlisle	1.0	0.0	0.2	2.4	0.5	0.3	0.2	6.1	4.1	1.2	218	157
Carroll	1.6	1.3	0.4	6.1	1.8	0.7	0.3	70.2	7.8	5.7	594	330
Carter	3.8	15.5	0.8	23.7	5.9	2.3	1.8	34.8	24.8	5.5	206	136
Casey	1.6	0.0	0.4	16.0	1.9	0.9	1.0	21.4	12.3	2.9	199	154
Christian	792.2	148.3	6.6	28.9	9.6	3.7	7.0	84.5	41.3	22.3	305	129
Clark	5.6	2.0	0.9	13.8	2.8	1.6	-0.4	59.1	21.4	18.0	569	254
Clay	20.2	9.4	-41.7	39.6	5.8	2.8	0.8	31.2	24.7	4.2	187	98
Clinton	1.4	0.0	0.3	15.8	1.6	1.7	1.9	12.1	9.6	1.6	175	126
Crittenden	1.7	0.3	0.4	5.0	0.8	0.5	1.0	11.6	7.2	2.6	275	159

1. October 1, 1998 to September 30, 1999.   2. State totals may include programs not allocated by county.   3. Based on the resident population estimated as of July 1 of the year shown.

STATE County	Total (mil dol)	Per capita[1] (dollars)	Education	Health and hospitals	Police protection	Public welfare	Highways	Total (mil dol)	Per capita[1] (dollars)	Federal civilian	Federal military	State and local	Demo-cratic	Republi-can	All other
	183	184	185	186	187	188	189	190	191	192	193	194	195	196	197
KANSAS—Cont'd															
Osage	31.0	1 812	62.0	1.7	3.9	0.0	9.1	17.7	1 035	94	84	1 146	38.3	57.0	4.7
Osborne	7.4	1 635	44.1	4.2	2.3	0.0	16.7	1.6	354	31	23	407	23.8	70.5	5.6
Ottawa	15.8	2 711	53.9	2.7	4.2	0.0	10.1	7.2	1 244	25	29	462	22.6	70.8	6.6
Pawnee	19.5	2 697	55.2	2.7	4.0	0.0	12.0	2.0	275	58	36	1 829	32.9	62.9	4.1
Phillips	19.3	3 187	55.9	4.0	3.0	3.8	8.1	8.7	1 433	39	30	784	21.9	73.7	4.4
Pottawatomie	55.4	3 044	53.5	11.2	2.7	0.0	8.3	73.9	4 062	60	91	1 359	26.3	64.5	9.2
Pratt	27.2	2 800	60.4	4.1	4.3	0.0	7.8	14.4	1 487	44	47	1 120	29.8	65.3	4.9
Rawlins	8.2	2 566	51.8	2.9	4.0	0.0	18.8	0.9	283	20	15	368	17.6	77.5	4.9
Reno	148.9	2 366	54.6	2.0	4.4	0.1	6.9	89.9	1 429	255	309	4 945	35.5	59.7	4.8
Republic	16.4	2 676	49.7	3.4	3.2	0.0	10.8	11.9	1 940	40	30	653	20.2	75.0	4.8
Rice	26.0	2 607	57.3	6.4	4.1	0.0	11.4	9.2	920	53	51	989	31.5	64.2	4.3
Riley	105.0	1 662	40.8	1.5	11.2	0.9	4.3	98.1	1 553	593	322	10 837	33.9	58.5	7.6
Rooks	21.9	3 824	35.1	15.3	3.3	5.9	10.6	5.9	1 028	29	28	720	21.5	72.6	5.8
Rush	12.6	3 676	40.4	20.7	2.8	0.0	12.2	1.3	366	29	17	398	27.2	66.6	6.1
Russell	30.0	3 928	32.4	21.7	1.4	0.0	9.8	5.1	662	39	37	681	25.4	69.9	4.7
Saline	112.3	2 176	44.7	1.1	4.4	0.0	6.9	138.0	2 673	325	252	3 656	34.8	57.7	7.6
Scott	12.9	2 587	51.1	3.8	4.2	0.1	6.8	8.7	1 743	19	25	508	18.2	78.6	3.2
Sedgwick	985.2	2 246	40.2	2.8	5.5	1.5	8.9	1 466.8	3 344	4 795	4 808	23 149	38.3	57.4	4.4
Seward	90.8	4 507	42.1	33.5	2.3	0.0	4.8	41.0	2 036	98	98	2 062	22.1	75.9	2.0
Shawnee	418.9	2 540	48.6	4.4	6.2	0.0	5.6	498.3	3 021	2 979	1 066	19 323	46.8	48.3	4.9
Sheridan	9.5	3 467	36.4	26.7	2.2	0.0	16.0	1.9	695	16	13	337	18.9	76.0	5.1
Sherman	19.9	3 015	37.3	26.3	3.6	0.2	7.9	2.3	342	58	32	713	25.4	70.6	4.0
Smith	10.4	2 230	52.4	3.9	2.7	0.0	11.2	2.8	594	41	22	320	24.5	70.2	5.3
Stafford	17.6	3 454	45.2	23.0	1.4	0.0	9.0	10.4	2 046	36	24	656	25.8	70.3	4.0
Stanton	11.5	4 932	38.5	21.2	5.4	3.8	8.0	2.3	998	0	11	305	20.9	76.3	2.8
Stevens	26.6	4 928	59.3	9.3	3.2	1.7	8.4	1.3	232	24	26	733	16.3	81.2	2.5
Sumner	59.6	2 209	44.4	15.2	3.5	3.5	9.4	40.0	1 483	94	132	1 890	34.7	60.4	5.0
Thomas	30.8	3 767	69.6	1.3	2.7	0.0	6.1	12.5	1 532	53	39	1 086	21.3	74.7	4.0
Trego	12.4	3 728	35.8	16.2	3.0	14.9	6.7	3.5	1 057	19	16	448	28.1	66.4	5.5
Wabaunsee	13.9	2 077	65.2	2.0	2.9	0.0	10.6	2.8	418	32	33	498	30.0	63.8	6.2
Wallace	5.6	3 084	58.8	3.0	2.4	0.0	10.1	3.0	1 658	10	0	207	12.0	85.6	2.4
Washington	26.9	4 075	36.2	12.4	2.4	0.0	11.3	1.8	272	56	32	816	21.0	74.9	4.1
Wichita	8.0	2 950	42.0	24.4	4.2	0.0	10.1	1.2	433	21	13	271	19.0	78.8	2.2
Wilson	27.3	2 648	50.1	23.8	3.3	0.1	6.3	7.5	730	45	50	903	29.0	67.1	3.9
Woodson	7.1	1 790	54.2	2.0	3.2	0.0	15.2	1.4	345	20	19	266	32.7	61.1	6.3
Wyandotte	480.2	3 146	43.2	2.2	7.2	0.0	2.9	1 698.0	11 125	2 519	747	14 916	67.1	29.1	3.8
KENTUCKY	X	X	X	X	X	X	X	X	X	36 894	47 221	245 003	41.4	56.5	2.1
Adair	21.6	1 309	63.3	13.1	2.2	0.0	5.4	21.6	1 309	47	57	744	24.3	74.5	1.2
Allen	21.2	1 306	59.2	8.5	4.9	0.2	8.0	35.0	2 157	40	57	694	30.3	68.7	1.0
Anderson	25.0	1 384	67.6	3.9	4.1	0.1	2.5	28.2	1 563	34	64	733	36.4	61.6	2.0
Ballard	13.7	1 644	50.8	1.1	1.9	0.0	6.7	119.5	14 315	34	29	387	49.9	48.4	1.7
Barren	56.2	1 528	62.3	0.8	3.2	0.0	5.8	101.2	2 753	126	128	1 918	35.6	63.1	1.2
Bath	13.1	1 265	74.6	1.6	2.2	0.0	6.0	8.7	836	33	37	531	46.7	51.5	1.9
Bell	49.7	1 669	68.2	1.4	3.4	0.0	3.4	18.8	632	151	101	1 665	45.1	52.6	2.3
Boone	145.5	1 910	40.8	1.0	4.8	0.5	3.9	328.8	4 317	842	277	3 566	28.9	68.8	2.3
Bourbon	30.4	1 571	65.4	4.1	3.8	0.0	4.1	24.3	1 254	46	67	953	42.9	54.6	2.4
Boyd	89.3	1 790	46.1	3.3	4.9	0.0	3.1	275.8	5 531	564	173	2 927	49.7	48.2	2.1
Boyle	40.3	1 487	55.5	5.5	4.5	0.1	5.3	67.2	2 484	85	94	1 760	38.4	59.3	2.3
Bracken	15.1	1 816	75.5	2.2	1.9	0.0	5.9	10.3	1 247	29	29	367	29.4	68.4	2.2
Breathitt	23.8	1 521	73.1	7.2	2.2	0.0	2.4	8.0	512	64	54	1 013	57.2	41.1	1.7
Breckinridge	23.7	1 370	72.1	0.1	2.5	0.0	5.9	36.1	2 087	76	61	757	34.8	63.9	1.3
Bullitt	72.6	1 252	73.4	3.0	4.9	0.0	2.9	30.5	525	56	206	1 939	36.1	62.0	1.9
Butler	24.1	2 051	58.9	2.6	1.7	0.0	6.9	36.6	3 117	34	41	679	25.9	72.9	1.1
Caldwell	27.9	2 091	37.9	35.7	2.7	0.0	4.4	39.5	2 960	54	46	805	40.6	57.7	1.8
Calloway	42.7	1 290	62.5	0.2	4.3	0.4	3.9	39.5	1 195	84	116	4 674	41.2	56.4	2.4
Campbell	115.7	1 324	55.5	0.4	8.6	0.4	3.7	130.8	1 496	233	303	4 807	35.6	61.5	2.9
Carlisle	6.4	1 193	64.5	3.6	1.6	0.0	16.8	1.4	252	22	18	213	44.3	54.2	1.5
Carroll	71.0	7 407	12.7	0.3	0.8	0.0	1.5	1 078.4	112 512	34	33	650	45.8	52.0	2.3
Carter	34.3	1 291	75.7	5.9	2.1	0.0	4.1	25.6	961	72	93	1 210	46.7	51.5	1.8
Casey	21.7	1 496	67.8	17.8	1.2	0.0	0.6	11.0	758	34	51	595	20.5	78.3	1.2
Christian	82.5	1 126	56.8	3.0	4.9	0.0	4.2	121.8	1 664	4 033	23 969	3 377	38.1	60.7	1.2
Clark	57.1	1 801	46.7	7.1	3.8	0.0	3.0	131.9	4 163	118	111	1 367	39.4	58.5	2.1
Clay	34.1	1 512	76.4	1.1	1.4	0.0	7.3	15.7	695	398	79	1 363	25.6	73.3	1.0
Clinton	12.3	1 325	82.5	0.0	1.6	0.0	6.4	8.1	871	27	32	494	24.0	74.9	1.1
Crittenden	12.1	1 276	64.6	0.5	2.5	0.0	9.8	14.1	1 485	35	33	393	38.8	59.4	1.8

1. Based on the resident population estimated as of July 1 of the year shown.

STATE/County code	MSA/PMSA/NECMA code[1]	County Type[2]	STATE County	Land area,[3] (sq km) 1990	Population and population characteristics, 1999													
								Race (percent)					Age (percent)					
					Total persons	Rank	Per square kilometer	White	Black	Am. Indian, Eskimo, Aleut	Asian and Pacific Islander	Percent Hispanic[4]	Under 5 years	5 to 17 years	18 to 24 years	25 to 34 years	35 to 44 years	45 to 54 years
					1	2	3	4	5	6	7	8	9	10	11	12	13	14	15
			KENTUCKY—Cont'd															
21 057	...	9	Cumberland	792	6 876	2 688	8.7	95.1	4.7	0.2	0.1	0.5	6.0	16.1	8.0	12.0	13.8	14.0
21 059	5990	3	Daviess	1 198	91 179	553	76.1	95.1	4.4	0.1	0.4	0.5	7.0	18.3	9.1	13.2	15.5	13.6
21 061	...	9	Edmonson	784	11 595	2 301	14.8	98.3	1.5	0.1	0.1	0.4	6.0	18.4	9.4	11.2	14.7	15.7
21 063	...	8	Elliott	606	6 533	2 729	10.8	99.9	0.0	0.0	0.0	0.4	6.9	20.7	9.6	12.6	15.5	13.8
21 065	...	6	Estill	658	15 506	2 034	23.6	99.8	0.1	0.0	0.0	0.5	6.0	18.8	9.9	12.4	14.9	14.3
21 067	4280	2	Fayette	737	243 785	224	330.8	83.5	14.0	0.2	2.3	1.7	6.5	14.7	13.8	16.8	17.2	12.5
21 069	...	7	Fleming	909	13 605	2 166	15.0	98.0	1.9	0.0	0.1	0.7	6.2	17.7	9.4	12.6	15.1	13.8
21 071	...	7	Floyd	1 021	43 266	1 016	42.4	98.8	0.9	0.1	0.3	0.5	6.8	20.4	9.7	13.0	16.6	13.3
21 073	...	4	Franklin	545	46 588	956	85.5	90.6	8.5	0.1	0.8	0.6	6.0	16.4	10.2	13.5	17.8	14.6
21 075	...	7	Fulton	541	7 451	2 642	13.8	80.2	19.5	0.1	0.2	0.4	5.9	18.0	8.6	11.3	14.3	13.2
21 077	1640	1	Gallatin	256	7 437	2 644	29.1	97.8	1.9	0.1	0.2	0.2	7.5	19.4	9.3	12.9	16.6	14.8
21 079	...	6	Garrard	599	14 333	2 110	23.9	95.7	4.1	0.1	0.1	0.4	5.9	17.0	8.4	13.2	15.6	15.2
21 081	1640	1	Grant	673	20 805	1 725	30.9	99.5	0.3	0.1	0.2	0.4	7.1	20.4	9.4	13.2	15.7	15.4
21 083	...	7	Graves	1 439	36 254	1 185	25.2	94.9	4.8	0.1	0.2	0.4	6.0	17.0	8.1	12.1	15.6	14.8
21 085	...	7	Grayson	1 305	23 828	1 583	18.3	99.2	0.4	0.2	0.3	0.6	6.1	18.5	8.7	12.6	15.2	14.7
21 087	...	9	Green	748	10 595	2 370	14.2	96.3	3.5	0.1	0.2	0.8	5.3	16.5	7.7	12.1	15.1	14.8
21 089	3400	2	Greenup	897	36 732	1 171	40.9	99.0	0.5	0.1	0.4	0.3	5.3	17.8	8.1	11.4	16.5	15.7
21 091	...	8	Hancock	489	8 977	2 506	18.4	98.2	1.3	0.2	0.4	0.6	6.9	20.7	8.5	13.1	17.5	14.9
21 093	...	4	Hardin	1 627	91 567	551	56.3	85.5	11.1	0.4	3.0	4.0	7.9	18.9	14.5	15.5	14.9	11.4
21 095	...	8	Harlan	1 210	34 273	1 247	28.3	96.1	3.6	0.1	0.2	0.5	6.7	20.3	9.2	12.5	16.4	12.9
21 097	...	6	Harrison	802	17 666	1 890	22.0	96.5	3.2	0.1	0.2	0.4	6.3	19.0	8.4	12.6	15.5	14.2
21 099	...	9	Hart	1 077	16 864	1 935	15.7	92.1	7.6	0.1	0.1	0.7	6.2	18.4	8.7	12.5	15.1	14.4
21 101	2440	2	Henderson	1 140	44 410	995	39.0	92.0	7.4	0.1	0.4	0.6	6.5	18.3	8.6	13.9	16.4	13.9
21 103	...	8	Henry	749	15 023	2 062	20.1	95.2	4.6	0.1	0.1	0.3	6.6	17.6	8.8	13.0	16.1	15.9
21 105	...	9	Hickman	633	5 146	2 827	8.1	90.4	9.5	0.0	0.1	0.4	6.1	16.0	7.2	12.0	14.8	14.7
21 107	...	7	Hopkins	1 426	46 155	964	32.4	92.5	7.0	0.1	0.4	0.6	6.4	18.0	8.3	12.7	16.4	14.1
21 109	...	8	Jackson	897	13 040	2 213	14.5	99.8	0.0	0.1	0.0	0.4	7.0	20.6	9.6	13.1	15.6	13.2
21 111	4520	2	Jefferson	997	672 900	73	674.9	81.0	17.8	0.1	1.0	1.0	6.4	16.4	9.2	14.2	16.7	13.3
21 113	4280	2	Jessamine	448	37 300	1 154	83.3	95.7	3.5	0.2	0.6	0.9	7.1	18.6	11.2	15.0	17.5	13.4
21 115	...	7	Johnson	677	23 999	1 578	35.4	99.3	0.1	0.1	0.4	0.2	6.0	19.6	9.4	12.9	17.0	14.3
21 117	1640	0	Kenton	421	147 221	355	349.7	96.1	3.1	0.1	0.7	0.8	7.9	18.4	9.7	15.2	16.4	12.6
21 119	...	9	Knott	912	17 931	1 873	19.7	99.1	0.7	0.1	0.2	0.3	6.5	21.1	11.2	13.6	16.3	13.0
21 121	...	7	Knox	1 004	31 976	1 316	31.8	98.6	1.1	0.2	0.1	0.5	7.0	20.1	10.8	12.5	15.6	14.1
21 123	...	7	Larue	682	13 150	2 200	19.3	95.2	4.4	0.3	0.1	0.8	5.9	17.7	7.6	12.6	15.1	15.1
21 125	...	7	Laurel	1 128	52 015	877	46.1	98.9	0.6	0.3	0.3	0.5	6.5	19.5	9.6	13.7	16.4	13.9
21 127	...	8	Lawrence	1 085	15 800	2 015	14.6	99.4	0.2	0.2	0.3	0.3	6.4	20.3	9.1	12.5	15.7	14.2
21 129	...	9	Lee	544	7 994	2 598	14.7	97.4	2.5	0.1	0.0	1.2	6.4	18.4	9.3	13.1	15.8	13.5
21 131	...	9	Leslie	1 046	13 558	2 171	13.0	99.7	0.1	0.1	0.1	0.6	7.4	20.9	10.0	14.2	15.8	12.8
21 133	...	7	Letcher	878	26 069	1 491	29.7	99.0	0.8	0.1	0.2	0.4	6.1	20.9	9.1	13.3	16.2	13.6
21 135	...	8	Lewis	1 255	13 471	2 177	10.7	99.6	0.2	0.2	0.0	0.3	6.2	20.1	9.4	12.8	15.4	14.1
21 137	...	7	Lincoln	872	22 540	1 632	25.8	96.4	3.3	0.2	0.1	0.4	6.6	18.6	9.3	12.9	15.2	14.4
21 139	...	9	Livingston	819	9 481	2 474	11.6	99.6	0.2	0.1	0.1	0.5	5.4	15.8	8.3	12.7	16.1	15.7
21 141	...	7	Logan	1 439	26 276	1 487	18.3	90.5	9.1	0.2	0.2	0.6	6.2	18.6	8.2	12.7	15.3	15.0
21 143	...	9	Lyon	559	8 060	2 592	14.4	92.3	7.0	0.4	0.3	0.6	3.8	11.4	8.6	16.2	16.4	15.4
21 145	...	5	McCracken	650	64 407	740	99.1	89.0	10.5	0.1	0.4	0.8	5.8	17.0	7.7	12.8	16.4	14.0
21 147	...	9	McCreary	1 108	16 754	1 948	15.1	99.0	0.6	0.3	0.0	0.4	7.3	21.5	10.5	12.3	15.8	13.7
21 149	...	8	McLean	659	9 897	2 437	15.0	99.4	0.5	0.1	0.1	0.2	5.8	17.7	8.7	11.6	16.1	14.1
21 151	4280	2	Madison	1 141	67 690	715	59.3	93.8	5.3	0.1	0.8	0.5	5.8	15.6	19.5	13.1	14.9	12.7
21 153	...	9	Magoffin	801	14 036	2 134	17.5	99.6	0.0	0.2	0.1	0.3	7.0	22.6	10.6	14.1	15.5	13.0
21 155	...	7	Marion	898	17 120	1 922	19.1	90.4	9.3	0.1	0.2	0.4	6.2	19.7	9.7	13.7	15.8	12.7
21 157	...	7	Marshall	790	30 250	1 369	38.3	99.6	0.1	0.2	0.2	0.7	5.6	15.8	7.2	11.8	15.0	15.6
21 159	...	9	Martin	598	11 901	2 282	19.9	99.6	0.0	0.2	0.1	0.5	7.4	22.1	10.0	13.9	16.5	12.4
21 161	...	6	Mason	625	16 825	1 941	26.9	91.7	8.1	0.0	0.2	0.7	6.4	17.9	8.8	12.6	15.3	13.3
21 163	...	6	Meade	799	29 195	1 403	36.5	88.3	9.8	0.4	1.5	3.7	9.9	21.9	9.5	19.1	14.5	11.1
21 165	...	9	Menifee	528	5 865	2 780	11.1	98.3	1.5	0.1	0.1	0.8	6.4	19.6	10.4	12.6	15.3	14.2
21 167	...	6	Mercer	650	20 809	1 724	32.0	94.8	4.5	0.1	0.6	0.7	5.9	17.1	8.4	12.4	15.9	15.2
21 169	...	9	Metcalfe	753	9 596	2 465	12.7	97.2	2.5	0.2	0.2	0.5	6.0	17.3	8.9	12.4	14.4	14.8
21 171	...	7	Monroe	857	11 157	2 335	13.0	96.6	3.2	0.1	0.1	0.8	5.9	17.1	8.4	12.4	14.5	15.3
21 173	...	6	Montgomery	514	21 636	1 675	42.1	95.2	4.5	0.1	0.1	0.6	6.1	18.7	9.1	12.4	17.1	14.0
21 175	...	9	Morgan	988	13 660	2 161	13.8	97.5	2.4	0.1	0.1	0.6	6.0	18.2	9.1	15.0	17.2	13.5
21 177	...	7	Muhlenberg	1 230	31 968	1 317	26.0	95.4	4.3	0.1	0.1	0.4	5.8	18.3	9.3	11.9	15.7	14.4
21 179	...	6	Nelson	1 095	36 971	1 160	33.8	93.0	6.6	0.1	0.4	0.7	7.2	20.5	9.4	14.4	16.6	13.3
21 181	...	8	Nicholas	509	7 126	2 668	14.0	98.0	1.4	0.1	0.5	0.5	5.6	18.2	8.6	12.0	15.6	15.0
21 183	...	6	Ohio	1 538	22 128	1 651	14.4	98.7	0.9	0.2	0.2	0.6	6.5	19.1	8.0	12.0	15.3	14.8
21 185	4520	2	Oldham	490	45 821	972	93.5	93.5	3.5	0.2	0.6	1.0	6.3	20.5	7.7	13.6	21.7	16.2
21 187	...	8	Owen	912	10 418	2 387	11.4	98.0	1.7	0.1	0.1	0.2	6.2	19.3	7.9	12.6	15.4	14.3

1. MSA = Metropolitan Statistical Area. PMSA = Primary MSA. NECMA = New England County Metropolitan Area. See Appendix A for explanation of these concepts. See Appendix B for list of metropolitan areas identified by type, with component counties. 2. County typology code from the Economic Research Service of USDA. See Appendix A for definition. 3. Dry land or land partially or temporarily covered by water. 4. Hispanic persons may be of any race.

Table B. States and Counties — **Population and Households**

STATE County	55 to 64 years (16)	65 to 74 years (17)	75 years and over (18)	Percent female (19)	Total persons 1990 (20)	Total persons 1980 (21)	Percent change 1980–1990 (22)	Percent change 1990–1999 (23)	Births (24)	Deaths (25)	Net migration (26)	Number (27)	Percent change, 1980–1990 (28)	Persons per household (29)	Female family householder[1] (30)	One person (31)
KENTUCKY—Cont'd																
Cumberland	12.0	9.1	8.9	52.6	6 784	7 289	-6.9	1.4	792	870	196	2 714	1.6	2.47	12.7	24.0
Daviess	9.9	7.4	6.1	52.2	87 189	85 949	1.4	4.6	11 608	7 762	418	33 036	9.4	2.58	11.5	24.8
Edmonson	11.1	7.7	5.9	50.6	10 357	9 962	4.0	12.0	1 087	987	1 160	3 843	14.5	2.64	9.3	18.6
Elliott	9.2	6.1	5.7	50.2	6 455	6 908	-6.6	1.2	708	612	-4	2 324	4.5	2.78	12.0	19.3
Estill	9.6	7.0	7.2	51.9	14 614	14 495	0.8	6.1	1 758	1 520	708	5 357	9.4	2.71	12.9	20.5
Fayette	8.0	5.8	4.6	52.2	225 366	204 165	10.4	8.2	31 466	17 019	4 616	89 529	18.7	2.38	12.2	29.1
Fleming	10.6	7.4	7.0	50.7	12 292	12 323	-0.3	10.7	1 500	1 362	1 205	4 626	7.3	2.62	9.0	22.6
Floyd	9.0	6.1	5.0	51.0	43 586	48 764	-10.6	-0.7	5 737	4 348	-1 599	15 664	-1.9	2.76	12.1	19.5
Franklin	9.6	6.6	5.3	51.6	44 143	41 830	5.5	5.5	5 459	3 891	989	17 385	10.9	2.44	12.0	27.0
Fulton	10.7	8.5	9.4	54.0	8 271	8 971	-7.8	-9.9	967	1 090	-679	3 378	-0.2	2.42	14.5	29.4
Gallatin	9.2	5.4	4.8	50.0	5 393	4 842	11.4	37.9	907	533	1 674	1 941	17.7	2.75	9.6	20.7
Garrard	11.4	6.8	6.4	51.3	11 579	10 853	6.7	23.8	1 423	1 216	2 561	4 435	12.6	2.59	9.8	20.0
Grant	8.8	5.5	4.5	50.4	15 737	13 308	18.3	32.2	2 755	1 475	3 809	5 585	26.3	2.78	9.5	19.5
Graves	10.3	8.0	8.0	51.8	33 550	34 049	-1.5	8.1	4 306	3 941	2 440	13 377	4.7	2.47	8.8	24.8
Grayson	11.0	7.3	6.0	51.0	21 050	20 854	0.9	13.2	2 700	2 115	2 276	7 991	10.6	2.61	8.9	21.5
Green	11.4	8.8	8.4	51.2	10 371	11 043	-6.1	2.2	1 088	1 131	306	4 089	2.7	2.49	8.0	22.4
Greenup	10.7	8.6	6.0	51.6	36 796	39 132	-6.1	-0.2	3 777	3 286	-443	13 414	3.8	2.71	9.1	18.1
Hancock	8.8	5.4	4.2	49.7	7 864	7 742	1.6	14.2	998	634	760	2 795	9.5	2.79	7.9	17.6
Hardin	7.2	5.6	4.2	48.2	89 240	88 911	0.4	4.2	14 329	5 379	-10 537	29 358	19.3	2.78	10.2	18.6
Harlan	9.1	7.3	5.6	51.6	36 574	41 889	-12.7	-6.3	4 540	3 508	-3 277	13 269	-4.2	2.74	13.3	21.9
Harrison	10.0	6.9	7.1	51.4	16 248	15 166	7.1	8.7	1 893	1 844	1 407	6 086	11.4	2.62	10.4	22.5
Hart	10.7	7.8	6.1	51.7	14 890	15 402	-3.3	13.3	1 954	1 688	1 758	5 740	5.6	2.58	9.9	22.8
Henderson	9.4	7.0	5.9	51.9	43 044	40 849	5.4	3.2	5 232	3 926	190	16 558	12.7	2.56	11.4	23.5
Henry	10.2	6.4	5.4	50.6	12 823	12 740	0.7	17.2	1 782	1 390	1 834	4 896	7.3	2.61	9.8	21.8
Hickman	10.9	8.2	10.1	52.8	5 566	6 065	-8.2	-7.5	528	707	-211	2 188	-1.8	2.47	9.7	23.8
Hopkins	9.6	7.6	7.1	51.9	46 126	46 174	-0.1	0.1	5 625	4 882	-577	17 760	7.3	2.56	11.1	23.0
Jackson	9.5	6.1	5.4	50.5	11 955	11 996	-0.3	9.1	1 545	1 112	702	4 381	8.7	2.71	10.6	20.2
Jefferson	9.9	7.7	6.2	52.8	665 123	684 638	-2.9	1.2	90 822	63 437	-17 754	264 138	5.4	2.48	14.5	27.5
Jessamine	7.8	5.4	4.1	50.9	30 508	26 065	17.0	22.3	4 918	2 248	4 203	10 601	26.0	2.77	10.1	16.6
Johnson	9.1	6.5	5.3	51.0	23 248	24 432	-4.8	3.2	2 844	2 244	230	8 469	3.3	2.71	10.9	20.5
Kenton	8.8	6.0	5.0	51.8	142 005	137 058	3.6	3.7	21 041	11 438	-3 904	52 690	9.6	2.66	12.2	25.2
Knott	8.0	5.7	4.6	50.6	17 906	17 940	-0.2	0.1	2 030	1 397	-555	6 086	11.4	2.86	12.6	18.2
Knox	8.8	5.9	5.3	51.6	29 676	30 239	-1.9	7.8	4 331	2 867	937	10 718	7.8	2.72	14.8	20.9
Larue	10.6	8.0	7.4	51.1	11 679	11 922	-2.0	12.6	1 445	1 261	1 322	4 503	5.5	2.56	9.0	22.4
Laurel	9.4	6.1	5.0	50.8	43 438	38 982	11.4	19.7	6 346	3 632	5 966	15 585	21.6	2.75	11.2	17.7
Lawrence	9.9	6.4	5.5	50.5	13 998	14 121	-0.9	12.9	1 717	1 479	1 610	5 007	7.4	2.77	10.4	20.2
Lee	10.0	6.6	6.9	50.2	7 422	7 754	-4.3	7.7	874	825	542	2 760	4.9	2.65	12.1	21.7
Leslie	8.7	5.4	4.8	50.5	13 642	14 882	-8.3	-0.6	1 601	1 051	-613	4 711	3.1	2.88	12.7	16.0
Letcher	9.1	6.5	5.1	51.3	27 000	30 687	-12.0	-3.4	3 095	2 684	-1 279	9 731	-2.8	2.76	11.8	19.7
Lewis	9.7	6.6	5.8	50.2	13 029	14 545	-10.4	3.4	1 743	1 285	24	4 713	0.9	2.74	9.7	19.7
Lincoln	10.2	6.9	5.8	50.5	20 096	19 053	5.2	12.2	2 675	2 031	1 852	7 431	14.0	2.67	9.7	20.2
Livingston	11.3	8.1	6.7	50.8	9 062	9 219	-1.7	4.6	947	1 050	558	3 593	5.1	2.49	7.5	22.7
Logan	10.3	7.2	6.6	51.7	24 416	24 138	1.2	4.6	3 295	2 699	1 336	9 302	8.8	2.60	9.9	23.0
Lyon	11.4	8.7	8.0	43.5	6 624	6 490	2.1	21.7	575	736	1 623	2 355	6.5	2.31	7.3	27.2
McCracken	10.4	8.4	7.5	52.9	62 879	61 310	2.6	2.4	7 622	6 670	802	25 625	9.2	2.41	11.7	27.0
McCreary	8.9	5.6	4.4	50.8	15 603	15 634	-0.2	7.4	2 368	1 639	462	5 479	12.9	2.80	14.4	20.1
McLean	10.4	7.3	6.9	50.5	9 628	10 090	-4.6	2.8	1 071	1 120	357	3 672	0.0	2.59	8.2	21.6
Madison	8.2	5.5	4.7	52.1	57 508	53 352	7.8	17.7	7 798	4 296	6 812	20 012	19.1	2.56	10.6	21.8
Magoffin	8.2	5.1	4.2	50.4	13 077	13 515	-3.2	7.3	1 853	1 169	314	4 440	7.0	2.90	10.5	16.8
Marion	9.3	6.5	6.3	50.2	16 499	17 910	-7.9	3.8	2 175	1 539	42	5 688	1.6	2.77	12.7	21.3
Marshall	12.0	9.2	7.8	51.1	27 205	25 637	6.1	11.2	2 872	2 945	3 205	10 789	14.4	2.48	6.9	21.5
Martin	7.9	5.8	4.1	50.8	12 526	13 925	-10.0	-5.0	1 795	974	-1 441	4 300	2.8	2.91	12.2	16.6
Mason	10.7	8.2	6.8	51.8	16 666	17 760	-6.2	1.0	2 053	1 991	157	6 537	2.8	2.52	11.5	25.3
Meade	6.7	4.3	3.1	50.2	24 170	22 854	5.8	20.8	3 053	1 415	2 760	8 080	12.8	2.98	7.9	14.4
Menifee	9.5	6.8	5.2	50.2	5 092	5 117	-0.5	15.2	632	488	642	1 842	10.3	2.68	9.6	19.8
Mercer	10.7	7.7	6.8	52.0	19 148	19 011	0.7	8.7	2 575	1 989	1 137	7 413	8.9	2.56	9.9	22.1
Metcalfe	11.1	8.1	7.1	52.0	8 963	9 484	-5.5	-2.1	1 165	1 005	500	3 433	5.1	2.57	8.9	22.0
Monroe	10.5	7.7	8.1	52.0	11 401	12 353	-7.7	-2.1	1 477	1 401	-289	4 505	2.0	2.50	10.1	23.9
Montgomery	9.9	6.7	5.9	51.6	19 561	20 046	-2.4	10.6	2 645	1 918	1 387	7 312	6.2	2.64	10.8	20.9
Morgan	9.4	6.1	5.6	45.6	11 648	12 103	-3.8	17.3	1 405	1 054	1 719	4 089	2.3	2.74	9.4	19.6
Muhlenberg	9.9	7.7	7.0	51.6	31 318	32 238	-2.9	2.1	3 468	3 395	673	11 683	5.1	2.62	9.9	21.5
Nelson	8.5	5.5	4.6	51.0	29 710	27 584	7.7	24.4	4 708	2 345	4 937	10 417	20.4	2.80	11.8	19.7
Nicholas	10.5	7.7	6.8	51.1	6 725	7 157	-6.0	6.0	817	737	338	2 621	0.9	2.54	9.4	23.9
Ohio	10.1	7.2	6.9	51.5	21 105	21 765	-3.0	4.8	2 464	2 419	1 048	7 816	3.0	2.66	8.3	20.8
Oldham	7.1	3.9	2.9	48.3	33 263	27 795	19.7	37.8	4 496	1 912	10 010	10 673	33.0	2.93	8.5	13.8
Owen	10.9	6.8	6.6	50.0	9 035	8 924	1.2	15.3	1 014	960	1 357	3 412	6.9	2.61	8.2	22.8

1. No spouse present.

Table B. States and Counties — **Vital Statistics, Health Resources, and Crime**

STATE County	Births, average 1996–1998 Total	Rate[1]	Deaths, average 1996–1998 Number Total	Number Infant[2]	Rate Total[1]	Rate Infant[3]	Physicians,[4] 1998 Number	Rate[5]	Hospitals,[4] 1998 Number	Beds Number	Beds Rate[5]	Medicare enrollees 1999	Serious crimes known to police, 1998[6] Total Number	Rate[7]
	32	33	34	35	36	37	38	39	40	41	42	43	44	45
KENTUCKY—Cont'd														
Cumberland	74	10.8	100	0	14.6	4.5	3	44	1	31	454	1 542	NA	NA
Daviess	1 268	13.9	857	11	9.4	8.9	163	179	2	526	577	14 918	NA	NA
Edmonson	115	10.3	109	1	9.8	5.8	3	26	0	0	0	1 602	NA	NA
Elliott	70	10.7	64	0	9.8	0.0	3	45	0	0	0	825	NA	NA
Estill	180	11.6	169	0	10.9	1.9	6	38	1	26	167	3 345	NA	NA
Fayette	3 410	14.2	1 916	26	8.0	7.7	1 303	539	5	1 906	788	29 568	13 616	5 636
Fleming	167	12.6	146	1	11.0	4.0	9	67	1	45	335	2 278	NA	NA
Floyd	576	13.3	466	5	10.8	9.3	60	138	3	295	681	7 908	NA	NA
Franklin	593	12.8	436	4	9.4	6.8	79	170	1	154	332	8 655	NA	NA
Fulton	105	13.7	115	2	15.0	22.3	16	212	1	65	862	1 873	NA	NA
Gallatin	105	15.4	69	1	10.1	6.4	3	42	0	0	0	902	NA	NA
Garrard	160	11.8	130	2	9.5	10.4	6	43	1	131	941	2 190	NA	NA
Grant	329	16.6	178	3	9.0	8.1	7	34	1	30	147	2 926	NA	NA
Graves	503	14.1	438	4	12.3	7.3	38	106	1	101	282	7 301	NA	NA
Grayson	299	12.8	243	2	10.4	5.6	15	63	1	71	299	4 217	NA	NA
Green	111	10.5	122	1	11.5	6.0	5	47	1	58	545	2 074	NA	NA
Greenup	400	10.8	372	3	10.1	6.7	32	87	0	0	0	6 311	NA	NA
Hancock	119	13.4	68	1	7.7	8.4	1	11	0	0	0	1 080	NA	NA
Hardin	1 522	16.8	600	12	6.6	7.9	179	196	1	296	324	10 874	NA	NA
Harlan	447	12.7	372	3	10.6	7.5	44	126	1	132	378	7 170	NA	NA
Harrison	214	12.4	198	2	11.4	7.8	12	68	1	81	461	2 853	NA	NA
Hart	218	13.2	184	2	11.1	10.7	7	42	1	36	215	2 793	NA	NA
Henderson	574	12.9	415	3	9.3	5.2	65	146	1	233	524	6 949	NA	NA
Henry	198	13.5	157	2	10.7	8.4	9	61	0	0	0	2 436	NA	NA
Hickman	55	10.5	71	0	13.5	0.0	3	57	0	0	0	869	NA	NA
Hopkins	604	13.0	535	7	11.5	11.6	97	209	1	429	925	8 391	NA	NA
Jackson	163	12.7	136	0	10.6	0.0	3	23	0	0	0	2 152	NA	NA
Jefferson	9 720	14.5	6 965	78	10.4	8.0	2 269	338	10	3 761	560	110 333	31 770	5 296
Jessamine	551	15.3	266	4	7.4	7.3	56	153	0	0	0	4 084	NA	NA
Johnson	298	12.4	257	2	10.7	6.7	40	167	1	78	325	4 329	NA	NA
Kenton	2 254	15.4	1 207	14	8.3	6.1	309	211	2	521	355	19 311	NA	NA
Knott	207	11.5	152	2	8.4	11.3	10	56	0	0	0	2 579	NA	NA
Knox	452	14.3	322	3	10.2	7.4	13	41	1	62	194	4 449	NA	NA
Larue	153	11.8	141	2	10.9	10.9	4	31	0	0	0	2 221	NA	NA
Laurel	744	14.8	413	5	8.2	6.7	46	91	1	80	158	7 149	NA	NA
Lawrence	165	10.7	167	1	10.8	4.0	13	83	1	106	677	2 611	NA	NA
Lee	89	11.2	95	1	11.9	7.5	3	37	0	0	0	1 475	NA	NA
Leslie	158	11.7	119	2	8.8	10.6	6	44	1	36	265	2 339	NA	NA
Letcher	299	11.3	298	4	11.3	12.3	30	115	2	149	569	4 882	NA	NA
Lewis	180	13.2	137	2	10.1	9.3	5	37	0	0	0	2 237	NA	NA
Lincoln	293	13.3	229	1	10.4	4.5	7	31	1	73	326	3 989	NA	NA
Livingston	93	9.9	113	0	12.2	0.0	6	64	1	26	276	1 895	NA	NA
Logan	354	13.6	284	2	10.9	6.6	15	57	1	106	405	4 446	NA	NA
Lyon	61	7.7	91	1	11.4	10.9	4	50	0	0	0	1 489	NA	NA
McCracken	831	12.8	734	6	11.3	7.2	189	293	2	769	1 193	11 979	NA	NA
McCreary	241	14.5	188	3	11.3	11.1	7	42	0	0	0	2 686	NA	NA
McLean	118	12.1	117	1	12.0	11.3	4	41	1	26	264	1 812	NA	NA
Madison	884	13.5	493	7	7.5	7.9	94	141	2	227	341	8 463	NA	NA
Magoffin	186	13.4	134	1	9.7	3.6	2	14	0	0	0	2 016	NA	NA
Marion	232	13.7	171	1	10.1	4.3	14	82	1	82	482	3 058	NA	NA
Marshall	283	9.5	329	3	11.0	9.4	20	66	1	41	135	5 910	NA	NA
Martin	179	14.6	118	2	9.6	11.2	4	33	0	0	0	2 041	NA	NA
Mason	220	13.0	204	3	12.1	15.2	25	147	1	117	687	2 910	NA	NA
Meade	294	10.5	164	4	5.9	13.6	11	38	0	0	0	2 201	NA	NA
Menifee	74	13.1	54	0	9.6	0.0	1	17	0	0	0	1 018	NA	NA
Mercer	268	13.1	209	1	10.2	5.0	14	68	1	59	285	3 565	NA	NA
Metcalfe	132	13.9	111	0	11.7	2.5	3	31	0	0	0	1 927	NA	NA
Monroe	157	13.9	152	1	13.5	4.2	6	54	1	49	437	2 453	NA	NA
Montgomery	286	13.8	213	2	10.2	8.2	18	86	1	97	463	3 490	NA	NA
Morgan	146	10.8	125	1	9.3	4.6	7	52	1	24	177	2 094	NA	NA
Muhlenberg	388	12.1	369	2	11.5	4.3	23	71	1	112	348	5 949	NA	NA
Nelson	540	15.4	289	2	8.2	3.7	29	81	1	47	131	5 156	NA	NA
Nicholas	94	13.5	79	0	11.3	3.5	5	71	1	73	1 043	1 289	NA	NA
Ohio	274	12.5	269	1	12.3	4.9	13	59	1	52	236	3 848	NA	NA
Oldham	510	11.8	227	2	5.2	4.6	52	117	1	123	277	3 364	NA	NA
Owen	114	11.3	101	1	10.0	11.7	5	49	1	50	487	1 282	NA	NA

1. Per 1,000 estimated resident population, average 1996–1998.   2. Deaths of infants under 1 year old.   3. Deaths of infants under 1 year old per 1,000 live births.   4. Data subject to copyright.   5. Per 100,000 resident population as of July 1 of the year shown.   6. Data for serious crimes have not been adjusted for underreporting; this may affect comparability between geographic areas and over time.   7. Per 100,000 population estimated by the FBI.

Table B. States and Counties — Crime, Education, Money Income, and Poverty

STATE County	Rate[2] Violent (46)	Property (47)	Enrollment[3] Total (48)	Percent private (49)	High school graduate or more (50)	Bachelor's degree or more (51)	Total current expenditures (mil dol) (52)	Current expenditures per student (dollars) (53)	Per capita[6] (dollars) (54)	Median Dollars (55)	Percent change, 1979–1989 (constant 1989 dollars) (56)	Percent with $100,000 or more (57)	Median household income (58)	All persons (59)	Persons under 18 (60)	Persons 5–17 in families (61)
KENTUCKY—Cont'd																
Cumberland	NA	NA	1 278	1.4	39.5	6.1	6.4	5 240	6 858	12 989	-8.4	0.1	18 217	26.9	40.4	37.8
Daviess	NA	NA	21 955	22.3	72.3	14.1	77.6	5 533	11 456	24 399	-8.5	1.9	34 335	13.2	18.8	17.5
Edmonson	NA	NA	2 509	1.3	48.6	5.4	10.1	5 316	7 181	15 134	-10.4	0.2	24 568	19.2	28.2	26.4
Elliott	NA	NA	1 597	0.5	44.0	5.6	8.8	6 767	6 823	13 890	-14.7	0.5	20 660	27.2	39.4	34.5
Estill	NA	NA	3 238	4.0	46.5	5.4	15.1	5 502	7 474	16 056	-10.6	0.5	23 937	22.7	33.7	30.3
Fayette	734	4 902	65 015	13.0	80.2	30.6	191.5	5 833	14 962	28 056	5.2	4.2	39 295	11.5	16.9	16.0
Fleming	NA	NA	2 823	1.1	53.8	8.7	12.8	5 329	8 950	18 014	-1.7	1.8	25 240	20.1	28.8	27.0
Floyd	NA	NA	10 744	4.5	50.8	7.4	42.4	5 270	7 922	15 661	-24.5	0.9	22 748	27.7	37.2	35.2
Franklin	NA	NA	10 592	9.8	76.0	21.3	34.3	5 021	13 383	27 484	0.7	1.9	37 284	11.0	17.1	16.0
Fulton	NA	NA	1 766	3.7	54.4	10.3	9.2	6 175	9 820	16 087	-11.8	1.7	23 741	24.5	38.0	35.1
Gallatin	NA	NA	1 240	10.4	59.8	5.0	5.8	4 624	9 717	21 454	-6.5	1.5	29 996	15.9	23.6	24.1
Garrard	NA	NA	2 395	6.9	54.3	6.3	10.9	4 884	10 011	21 057	9.1	1.4	30 355	14.8	22.9	20.4
Grant	NA	NA	3 940	4.7	61.6	7.2	18.7	4 587	10 356	24 502	-5.3	1.5	32 879	13.1	19.7	18.4
Graves	NA	NA	7 217	7.0	62.0	8.8	27.9	4 785	10 784	20 647	-9.7	1.3	29 677	14.1	21.1	19.5
Grayson	NA	NA	4 759	4.9	48.3	6.1	19.4	4 707	8 767	17 306	-3.9	1.0	25 009	19.9	28.6	27.1
Green	NA	NA	2 037	3.2	49.0	6.8	8.4	4 772	9 177	18 432	5.2	1.1	24 470	19.0	29.7	26.0
Greenup	NA	NA	8 921	5.0	64.7	11.1	34.0	5 449	11 165	24 527	-15.8	1.7	31 235	16.3	24.2	21.5
Hancock	NA	NA	1 987	6.9	69.3	6.9	8.3	5 257	10 891	26 080	-0.4	1.6	38 734	12.3	16.1	16.7
Hardin	NA	NA	22 617	7.9	75.3	12.9	79.0	5 156	10 624	24 431	6.1	1.6	35 603	12.2	16.9	15.8
Harlan	NA	NA	9 181	6.0	49.5	6.4	37.6	5 392	7 502	14 774	-21.1	0.7	21 442	29.9	39.1	37.1
Harrison	NA	NA	3 711	4.8	62.4	8.6	16.7	5 238	10 271	21 787	3.8	1.4	31 971	13.9	19.6	18.1
Hart	NA	NA	3 143	3.1	45.3	5.2	13.0	5 652	8 142	15 671	-3.3	0.8	23 194	23.5	34.5	31.8
Henderson	NA	NA	10 454	11.6	68.5	11.1	37.4	5 311	12 042	25 556	-7.5	1.8	35 263	13.1	18.9	17.3
Henry	NA	NA	2 646	3.7	60.9	8.2	13.5	5 111	10 344	22 528	6.2	1.1	31 846	15.3	22.4	21.3
Hickman	NA	NA	1 067	2.7	56.8	7.6	4.9	5 608	9 777	20 347	-7.2	0.3	28 542	16.5	24.3	25.4
Hopkins	NA	NA	10 894	7.3	62.5	9.6	42.8	6 119	10 751	22 155	-13.4	1.4	29 936	16.6	24.8	22.3
Jackson	NA	NA	2 812	3.9	38.3	4.9	13.5	5 461	7 097	11 885	-4.5	0.8	18 503	30.8	42.5	40.8
Jefferson	913	4 383	165 252	23.3	74.1	19.3	585.4	6 343	14 067	27 092	-3.0	3.3	38 733	12.2	19.4	17.1
Jessamine	NA	NA	8 578	25.0	69.0	19.1	28.7	6 234	11 733	27 059	9.0	2.5	36 726	12.4	17.8	16.5
Johnson	NA	NA	5 849	4.0	54.7	9.3	25.7	5 496	8 492	15 782	-21.2	1.1	24 052	25.3	34.9	32.0
Kenton	NA	NA	36 185	24.5	74.4	17.0	107.5	4 926	13 587	30 516	5.9	3.0	41 581	10.1	14.5	13.5
Knott	NA	NA	5 066	13.6	45.1	8.2	20.5	6 093	6 753	13 329	-24.5	0.6	22 470	29.4	35.9	35.7
Knox	NA	NA	7 439	11.8	46.6	8.0	30.3	5 484	7 776	12 697	-14.4	1.8	19 780	31.3	43.1	40.2
Larue	NA	NA	2 370	6.8	59.0	8.1	11.4	5 038	10 129	22 405	14.9	0.9	30 479	15.8	22.3	21.1
Laurel	NA	NA	10 549	7.8	52.7	8.2	44.6	4 997	8 879	18 584	-7.3	1.5	27 146	20.7	30.2	26.6
Lawrence	NA	NA	3 475	2.0	46.4	6.2	14.6	5 308	7 809	15 273	-3.2	1.7	22 608	27.5	36.5	35.2
Lee	NA	NA	1 729	4.7	43.4	5.8	7.4	5 064	6 869	12 461	-11.7	1.2	18 326	34.6	47.0	46.5
Leslie	NA	NA	3 464	4.7	40.4	6.6	14.7	5 777	7 190	13 692	-13.3	0.3	20 757	30.6	38.3	38.8
Letcher	NA	NA	6 971	5.5	45.6	6.7	27.0	5 429	7 340	15 112	-17.5	0.7	22 893	26.1	33.6	31.2
Lewis	NA	NA	3 235	2.3	45.4	6.7	12.8	4 985	7 477	15 775	-5.5	0.7	22 270	25.5	36.1	33.4
Lincoln	NA	NA	4 279	2.0	50.4	6.2	21.2	5 412	8 388	17 169	-2.2	0.7	25 282	20.5	29.5	28.4
Livingston	NA	NA	1 808	5.1	63.1	5.4	7.5	4 972	10 123	20 892	-5.6	1.2	30 822	14.6	22.8	20.8
Logan	NA	NA	5 306	5.5	57.7	8.1	22.8	5 095	9 907	21 279	3.9	1.2	30 547	14.1	20.7	18.5
Lyon	NA	NA	1 385	5.6	61.0	9.1	4.4	4 595	10 081	20 239	-14.1	0.8	29 466	14.7	21.2	19.4
McCracken	NA	NA	14 569	8.3	73.1	14.3	52.7	5 207	12 460	22 606	-11.1	2.1	33 538	14.4	22.5	20.2
McCreary	NA	NA	3 874	3.3	40.2	4.6	22.0	6 373	5 153	10 598	-16.1	0.0	16 433	35.3	46.6	46.2
McLean	NA	NA	2 179	4.6	58.6	6.6	8.1	4 861	9 599	20 474	-9.3	0.4	28 841	15.3	21.8	20.8
Madison	NA	NA	19 863	9.6	64.8	19.1	47.9	4 832	10 029	21 388	3.1	1.6	31 963	16.2	21.2	20.3
Magoffin	NA	NA	3 448	1.7	38.2	4.6	16.4	5 722	6 289	12 160	-20.2	0.5	19 292	33.6	41.9	41.7
Marion	NA	NA	3 791	17.7	58.9	6.4	15.8	5 319	9 121	18 181	-6.4	0.9	27 284	18.2	23.1	21.7
Marshall	NA	NA	5 709	7.0	67.6	9.6	23.7	4 457	11 374	22 413	-12.3	1.2	33 061	11.5	17.2	16.5
Martin	NA	NA	3 430	2.4	44.4	6.0	16.0	5 524	8 190	15 142	-34.0	0.9	22 497	30.8	39.7	38.3
Mason	NA	NA	3 942	9.0	60.7	10.2	15.1	5 431	9 888	20 582	-4.8	0.9	29 347	16.2	26.5	24.8
Meade	NA	NA	6 407	5.7	74.3	11.0	19.3	4 415	9 234	23 676	0.2	0.7	34 885	11.5	14.4	17.5
Menifee	NA	NA	1 152	1.2	46.0	4.9	6.0	5 725	6 911	14 650	-4.5	0.1	21 481	27.0	37.8	37.4
Mercer	NA	NA	4 037	5.0	62.8	8.9	17.3	5 029	10 821	22 774	-2.0	1.5	32 522	13.9	20.2	19.1
Metcalfe	NA	NA	1 732	2.2	45.2	5.0	8.6	5 219	7 542	14 815	-2.2	0.4	22 178	23.6	33.3	33.1
Monroe	NA	NA	2 314	2.3	47.1	6.9	11.8	5 604	8 347	15 214	1.4	0.9	23 348	22.5	32.6	31.3
Montgomery	NA	NA	4 544	3.4	56.1	9.2	20.1	5 276	9 636	20 025	-0.6	1.3	28 579	17.3	24.5	22.9
Morgan	NA	NA	2 704	3.3	44.1	6.7	13.5	5 647	6 871	13 229	-2.1	1.1	20 627	32.3	41.0	40.8
Muhlenberg	NA	NA	7 180	2.9	54.9	6.2	29.8	5 503	9 779	18 679	-23.3	1.5	26 698	17.3	25.4	23.3
Nelson	NA	NA	7 371	14.2	67.4	9.3	29.6	4 830	10 165	24 220	1.1	1.7	35 234	12.1	16.7	15.3
Nicholas	NA	NA	1 534	1.8	55.4	6.0	6.3	5 144	9 116	18 070	-3.5	0.6	25 311	20.5	28.1	28.9
Ohio	NA	NA	4 948	4.1	53.1	6.2	18.9	4 579	8 056	18 196	-21.4	0.6	26 333	18.9	26.5	24.6
Oldham	NA	NA	9 684	11.2	80.2	22.9	37.1	4 845	15 510	38 416	7.9	6.4	54 599	5.1	6.5	6.2
Owen	NA	NA	2 003	5.0	55.2	7.4	9.1	4 845	9 559	21 067	18.4	0.8	29 976	17.9	26.4	25.2

1. Data for serious crimes have not been adjusted for underreporting; this may affect comparability between geographic areas and over time.   2. Per 100,000 population estimated by the FBI.   3. All persons 3 years old and over enrolled in nursery school through college.   4. Persons 25 years old and over.   5. Elementary and secondary education expenditures, local government fiscal years ending between July 1, 1996 and June 30, 1997.   6. Based on population enumerated as of April 1, 1990.

STATE County	Personal income, 1998 Total (mil dol)	Percent change, 1997–1998	Per capita[1] Dollars	Per capita[1] Rank	Wages and salaries[2] (mil dol)	Proprietor's income (mil dol)	Dividends, interest, and rent (mil dol)	Transfer payments Total (mil dol)	Government payments to individuals Total (mil dol)	Social Security (mil dol)	Medical payments (mil dol)	Income maintenance (mil dol)	Unemployment insurance (mil dol)
	62	63	64	65	66	67	68	69	70	71	72	73	74
KENTUCKY—Cont'd													
Cumberland	98	4.3	14 296	2 984	36	7	14	40	39	11	20	6	1
Daviess	2 013	2.9	22 126	1 059	1 208	117	399	340	324	148	121	30	7
Edmonson	165	4.0	14 552	2 967	36	9	24	41	38	16	14	5	1
Elliott	77	1.7	11 734	3 089	16	6	11	27	26	8	10	6	1
Estill	238	3.4	15 253	2 906	64	10	30	70	67	20	29	12	1
Fayette	7 235	6.6	29 933	168	5 635	708	1 430	705	661	288	239	58	8
Fleming	216	5.7	16 016	2 790	80	25	37	50	47	18	19	7	1
Floyd	699	3.4	16 145	2 774	351	45	98	233	225	75	89	37	2
Franklin	1 238	5.7	26 628	332	1 066	53	230	189	180	79	61	18	3
Fulton	152	-0.9	20 198	1 652	86	13	30	41	39	15	15	6	1
Gallatin	121	6.7	16 853	2 644	62	8	11	21	20	8	8	2	0
Garrard	243	5.7	17 480	2 490	62	22	44	47	45	20	17	5	1
Grant	381	7.2	18 777	2 127	115	26	46	65	61	26	23	6	2
Graves	721	4.3	20 042	1 700	339	84	128	152	145	67	57	12	2
Grayson	389	5.7	16 377	2 729	186	31	49	97	92	35	39	12	2
Green	166	1.6	15 710	2 845	43	16	33	51	49	17	22	6	3
Greenup	709	3.3	19 165	1 993	292	31	87	165	158	52	53	14	4
Hancock	195	2.9	21 728	1 180	231	9	24	24	23	11	8	2	1
Hardin	1 868	4.3	20 619	1 519	1 600	109	337	272	257	92	101	26	5
Harlan	497	1.0	14 265	2 987	245	17	75	196	190	70	65	34	2
Harrison	344	5.6	19 622	1 854	156	14	57	59	56	26	20	6	1
Hart	268	6.9	16 044	2 787	94	33	37	65	62	22	26	10	1
Henderson	1 053	6.0	23 680	707	654	66	168	169	161	70	65	14	4
Henry	294	6.1	19 875	1 753	85	25	42	52	49	20	20	6	1
Hickman	109	9.8	21 066	1 370	31	22	17	22	21	9	9	2	0
Hopkins	923	3.0	19 907	1 744	545	63	176	195	186	82	67	19	2
Jackson	179	4.5	13 879	3 018	67	11	20	59	57	16	24	14	1
Jefferson	19 794	4.8	29 473	182	15 704	1 124	4 306	2 677	2 554	1 095	1 008	224	37
Jessamine	806	6.9	22 048	1 087	345	97	120	94	87	39	29	9	1
Johnson	383	2.3	15 964	2 798	171	24	50	120	116	38	47	19	1
Kenton	4 006	7.8	27 303	279	1 805	213	646	466	439	192	162	38	8
Knott	264	2.7	14 704	2 958	121	14	31	89	86	25	35	19	1
Knox	441	4.6	13 839	3 021	191	27	58	150	144	42	55	35	1
Larue	264	3.0	20 183	1 658	58	17	39	50	48	19	20	5	1
Laurel	912	4.8	17 928	2 369	537	68	128	190	181	68	67	28	3
Lawrence	221	4.2	14 160	2 994	80	13	25	73	71	23	27	13	1
Lee	110	3.0	13 673	3 032	39	9	14	43	42	12	18	8	0
Leslie	213	6.4	15 684	2 854	142	8	18	77	75	22	33	14	0
Letcher	387	2.8	14 769	2 953	170	18	48	139	134	47	51	24	1
Lewis	182	2.4	13 495	3 045	51	20	24	57	54	17	22	10	2
Lincoln	378	7.3	16 886	2 634	103	34	42	89	84	30	35	13	1
Livingston	204	3.9	21 628	1 213	69	13	30	41	39	18	15	3	1
Logan	492	1.9	18 766	2 130	285	41	81	99	94	38	41	9	2
Lyon	125	0.9	15 623	2 861	48	7	28	32	31	16	11	2	0
McCracken	1 640	3.3	25 457	442	1 188	96	338	272	260	116	94	23	4
McCreary	210	2.1	12 647	3 079	72	14	22	91	88	22	39	20	1
McLean	188	7.1	19 124	2 015	49	29	29	39	38	16	15	3	1
Madison	1 347	5.7	20 266	1 633	747	65	191	213	200	73	72	25	2
Magoffin	178	3.7	12 849	3 067	63	12	21	72	69	17	32	16	1
Marion	320	5.4	18 809	2 121	132	34	54	69	65	24	27	9	3
Marshall	631	3.2	20 924	1 414	383	49	122	124	118	59	44	6	2
Martin	190	2.4	15 695	2 849	99	13	29	68	66	23	23	15	1
Mason	342	5.9	20 222	1 644	257	30	62	63	60	26	23	7	1
Meade	489	4.5	17 029	2 605	105	21	66	63	58	24	19	6	1
Menifee	82	5.4	14 284	2 985	23	8	8	25	24	9	9	5	0
Mercer	435	5.4	21 046	1 376	215	29	71	70	67	32	24	6	1
Metcalfe	156	2.9	16 255	2 752	59	21	19	41	39	13	17	6	1
Monroe	211	3.2	18 967	2 068	90	21	27	59	57	17	28	8	1
Montgomery	417	5.3	19 828	1 769	232	33	66	83	79	30	32	11	1
Morgan	171	4.7	12 574	3 081	78	15	20	54	52	16	21	11	1
Muhlenberg	559	5.3	17 438	2 499	276	53	105	135	129	58	46	13	2
Nelson	768	7.9	21 388	1 270	362	48	117	114	107	47	41	11	4
Nicholas	115	3.3	16 404	2 721	39	9	13	28	27	10	12	3	0
Ohio	375	5.4	17 051	2 600	148	35	59	96	92	38	37	10	2
Oldham	1 324	9.6	29 802	173	337	81	199	87	79	38	29	4	1
Owen	181	5.8	17 508	2 481	50	12	23	33	31	12	12	4	1

1. Based on the resident population estimated as of July 1 of the year shown. 2. Includes other labor income.

STATE County	Earnings, 1998									Social Security beneficiaries, December 1998		Housing units, 1990	
		Percent by selected industries											
			Goods-related[1]		Service-related and other[2]								
	Total (mil dol)	Farm	Total	Manu-facturing	Total	Retail trade	Finance, insur-ance, and real estate	Services	Govern-ment	Number	Rate[3]	Supple-mental Security Income recipients, December 1998	Total	Percent change, 1980–1990
	75	76	77	78	79	80	81	82	83	84	85	86	87	88

KENTUCKY—Cont'd

Cumberland	43	6.0	18.5	14.8	D	11.5	5.7	29.5	24.5	1 762	258	741	3 051	-3.1
Daviess	1 325	0.5	31.5	20.4	51.9	11.6	5.1	22.2	16.0	17 479	192	2 717	35 041	10.7
Edmonson	45	4.4	D	0.8	D	8.2	3.8	22.6	47.2	2 353	207	522	5 009	18.7
Elliott	22	8.7	D	D	D	8.8	D	18.4	39.4	1 263	191	557	2 639	5.6
Estill	74	-0.2	D	15.8	D	12.8	3.9	15.4	27.7	2 985	191	1 273	5 863	11.7
Fayette	6 343	1.6	21.4	13.3	57.5	9.9	6.1	28.9	19.5	33 308	138	5 489	97 742	19.6
Fleming	106	10.8	D	15.3	D	12.6	3.3	12.9	26.4	2 783	207	756	5 163	11.6
Floyd	395	0.1	24.7	3.7	D	9.3	D	27.5	19.3	10 255	237	3 532	17 169	-1.1
Franklin	1 119	0.5	D	12.0	D	6.5	4.4	14.2	55.4	9 714	209	2 944	18 543	9.3
Fulton	99	4.3	D	31.9	D	10.8	3.6	13.5	18.4	1 971	261	594	3 684	1.5
Gallatin	70	2.8	D	48.6	D	6.3	1.6	8.3	13.1	1 013	141	235	2 290	28.7
Garrard	84	9.2	30.7	11.6	34.6	7.2	5.0	14.6	25.4	2 743	197	537	4 929	13.8
Grant	142	0.9	D	14.7	D	19.5	4.3	18.6	20.7	3 433	169	639	6 543	22.2
Graves	424	8.5	36.3	28.5	41.5	9.2	3.4	17.4	13.7	8 324	232	1 429	14 528	6.6
Grayson	218	3.7	39.8	30.6	D	9.9	3.0	11.5	18.5	4 964	209	1 276	10 446	9.4
Green	59	12.7	D	14.7	D	9.1	4.2	18.8	29.6	2 652	249	700	4 523	5.7
Greenup	323	1.6	D	31.6	D	7.8	2.6	13.7	14.3	6 445	175	1 434	14 657	5.8
Hancock	239	0.7	84.3	75.6	D	1.8	0.8	D	5.0	1 347	151	220	3 080	9.6
Hardin	1 709	0.0	20.6	16.5	30.4	8.1	2.3	13.6	49.0	12 572	137	2 411	32 375	19.1
Harlan	262	0.0	D	3.2	D	9.6	3.6	22.4	23.5	9 323	267	3 113	14 735	-0.5
Harrison	170	3.4	47.7	41.3	33.6	9.6	2.5	15.5	15.3	3 440	196	642	6 488	8.4
Hart	127	12.7	D	30.9	D	9.7	3.8	13.2	17.4	3 436	205	1 080	6 501	1.1
Henderson	720	2.4	47.6	39.2	39.1	7.8	3.1	18.7	11.0	8 241	185	1 295	17 932	15.5
Henry	110	14.1	D	21.6	D	9.3	4.1	17.7	19.0	2 681	182	539	5 447	6.7
Hickman	53	31.2	D	15.5	D	5.4	3.0	13.5	14.2	1 239	236	197	2 374	-1.3
Hopkins	608	0.3	32.0	18.8	51.8	9.7	3.6	28.1	15.9	9 727	210	1 792	19 325	9.3
Jackson	78	1.6	D	30.3	D	7.3	1.9	12.2	24.6	2 638	204	1 520	4 895	12.1
Jefferson	16 828	0.0	25.2	19.4	64.0	9.5	8.0	28.1	10.8	123 206	183	18 874	282 578	6.3
Jessamine	442	11.3	D	21.2	D	11.3	2.4	14.9	12.4	5 001	137	824	11 209	23.8
Johnson	195	-0.2	16.4	5.8	D	17.0	D	22.2	24.0	5 172	215	1 852	9 381	6.4
Kenton	2 018	0.0	19.3	10.4	63.7	12.3	7.1	33.7	17.0	21 884	149	3 207	56 086	9.5
Knott	134	0.1	45.6	0.6	33.4	6.2	1.8	13.1	21.1	3 543	197	1 814	6 718	14.5
Knox	219	0.4	21.2	15.0	53.1	15.1	3.6	20.6	25.3	6 351	199	3 658	11 731	8.4
Larue	75	6.3	27.6	17.1	43.3	8.8	4.8	19.2	22.8	2 669	204	486	4 824	3.8
Laurel	605	0.4	D	18.6	D	17.8	2.9	20.2	14.6	9 492	187	3 104	16 923	19.6
Lawrence	93	-0.7	D	6.3	D	13.3	3.1	24.0	21.1	3 157	202	1 327	5 684	8.8
Lee	48	0.8	20.2	10.4	D	15.0	3.8	22.1	27.3	1 778	222	913	3 025	8.1
Leslie	150	0.1	D	D	D	3.9	1.3	13.0	13.5	3 109	229	1 424	5 038	3.7
Letcher	188	0.1	D	2.4	D	10.4	2.3	26.7	20.6	6 187	236	2 285	10 808	1.4
Lewis	70	10.9	32.3	25.1	D	9.0	4.3	14.4	23.5	2 548	188	972	5 328	5.3
Lincoln	137	10.8	30.3	22.2	D	9.9	4.9	13.5	23.0	4 486	201	1 529	7 985	11.0
Livingston	82	2.2	D	4.3	D	10.7	1.6	19.8	17.3	2 217	235	293	4 177	8.7
Logan	326	2.2	D	50.5	D	7.0	2.4	13.4	10.6	5 228	200	1 103	10 303	8.8
Lyon	56	1.0	23.1	8.9	D	13.9	3.4	14.9	39.1	1 818	226	176	3 460	36.3
McCracken	1 284	0.2	D	17.0	D	12.0	3.8	30.2	12.6	13 707	213	2 170	27 581	11.2
McCreary	86	-0.8	D	25.1	D	11.7	3.1	15.0	32.8	3 367	202	2 061	6 039	16.7
McLean	78	26.7	D	6.2	D	9.2	2.7	D	17.5	2 060	209	286	4 042	4.9
Madison	812	1.0	D	27.9	D	11.7	2.5	20.2	26.2	9 744	147	2 512	21 456	19.4
Magoffin	76	0.9	28.7	10.9	D	8.2	D	D	25.4	2 620	189	1 562	4 800	7.0
Marion	167	8.1	39.5	32.0	D	8.7	2.7	21.9	14.9	3 446	202	1 119	6 115	3.3
Marshall	432	0.4	55.0	44.3	33.6	8.5	2.9	13.4	11.0	6 936	229	616	12 528	17.7
Martin	112	0.1	D	3.5	D	8.0	4.7	8.8	17.0	2 905	240	1 348	4 697	5.6
Mason	287	3.8	39.5	36.3	45.2	10.9	2.8	17.6	11.6	3 413	201	696	7 089	4.9
Meade	127	1.3	D	26.4	D	13.4	2.7	14.1	20.0	3 201	111	467	8 907	16.6
Menifee	31	4.5	D	15.3	D	7.1	2.0	19.6	34.6	1 284	224	538	2 421	29.6
Mercer	244	2.6	D	47.1	D	8.1	2.5	12.7	10.8	4 140	200	675	8 212	8.7
Metcalfe	80	15.0	D	38.1	D	6.6	3.2	7.9	16.8	2 152	225	707	3 793	6.4
Monroe	111	8.9	D	39.0	D	8.9	2.5	9.7	21.6	2 780	248	1 128	4 882	-5.1
Montgomery	265	2.3	D	32.3	D	12.3	3.1	18.3	12.4	4 144	198	1 138	7 759	7.2
Morgan	93	2.3	D	11.6	D	12.4	3.7	19.0	34.7	2 486	183	1 055	4 562	5.4
Muhlenberg	329	5.5	27.7	13.2	40.2	8.7	2.4	16.5	26.6	7 167	223	1 370	12 754	10.1
Nelson	411	0.4	49.1	35.4	39.7	10.4	3.3	16.8	10.9	6 004	167	1 039	11 078	20.1
Nicholas	49	9.6	40.4	37.0	D	6.2	2.3	17.1	19.5	1 461	209	397	2 930	5.7
Ohio	183	10.3	35.3	26.8	D	9.0	2.3	13.1	20.5	4 790	218	930	8 680	7.5
Oldham	417	1.3	25.1	12.7	51.2	9.4	5.6	27.7	22.5	4 256	96	349	11 202	28.8
Owen	62	9.3	D	D	D	6.7	3.7	20.0	22.1	1 711	167	357	4 723	18.9

1. Covers mining, construction, and manufacturing.   2. Covers private sector earnings in agricultural services, forestry, and fisheries; transportation and public utilities; wholesale trade; retail trade; finance, insurance, and real estate; and services.   3. Per 1,000 resident population estimated as of July 1 of the year shown.

STATE County	Total [89]	Percent [90]	Median value[1] [91]	With a mortgage [92]	Without a mortgage [93]	Median rent[2] [94]	Rent as percent of income [95]	Substandard units[3] (percent) [96]	Total [97]	Percent change, 1998–1999 [98]	Total [99]	Rate[4] [100]	Total [101]	Professional, managerial, and technical [102]	Precision production, craft, and repair [103]
KENTUCKY—Cont'd															
Cumberland	2 714	75.0	27 700	22.2	12.9	181	24.2	8.7	2 910	5.7	192	6.6	2 658	14.3	10.5
Daviess	33 036	68.8	48 000	16.3	11.8	286	24.9	2.7	50 659	2.9	2 572	5.1	39 290	23.9	13.5
Edmonson	3 843	85.6	33 000	22.7	13.0	227	32.7	7.2	5 010	2.5	286	5.7	3 711	16.3	17.1
Elliott	2 324	78.8	32 300	21.7	11.9	191	29.7	15.4	2 833	-2.9	393	13.9	1 809	16.9	21.7
Estill	5 357	74.5	30 400	20.3	13.0	253	26.2	12.4	5 821	-1.8	275	4.7	4 866	15.4	16.3
Fayette	89 529	53.0	73 900	18.4	11.7	394	24.9	2.5	146 093	3.2	2 846	1.9	117 906	37.2	7.8
Fleming	4 626	76.2	36 500	17.0	12.1	209	26.1	10.1	6 165	4.5	273	4.4	5 343	16.0	14.4
Floyd	15 664	74.6	37 800	22.7	12.7	266	27.5	6.1	14 134	1.0	1 073	7.6	12 765	23.0	18.7
Franklin	17 385	64.0	60 200	17.1	11.6	351	23.4	2.5	25 321	2.3	618	2.4	22 646	32.9	9.6
Fulton	3 378	66.5	33 900	20.3	13.6	253	29.0	4.2	3 444	-8.6	355	10.3	2 890	20.9	10.6
Gallatin	1 941	75.6	45 300	17.3	12.0	266	23.2	6.7	3 649	6.8	130	3.6	2 437	14.2	11.5
Garrard	4 435	74.5	45 800	20.5	12.8	248	24.2	6.2	7 450	4.3	201	2.7	5 024	15.4	15.6
Grant	5 585	77.0	49 600	18.7	13.0	297	24.0	6.0	10 117	3.2	399	3.9	6 931	18.2	14.0
Graves	13 377	77.9	38 500	17.6	12.2	262	24.2	2.2	17 448	2.1	993	5.7	13 367	18.2	13.7
Grayson	7 991	79.6	35 700	20.4	12.3	245	24.6	6.6	12 467	3.7	768	6.2	8 176	14.0	15.4
Green	4 089	78.9	31 700	17.3	12.2	203	23.9	5.0	4 316	-9.8	590	13.7	4 742	14.9	11.4
Greenup	13 414	81.6	44 100	16.7	12.3	319	23.4	3.9	16 732	1.8	1 068	6.4	14 194	23.7	15.5
Hancock	2 795	80.5	43 600	15.2	11.7	271	20.3	4.4	4 243	4.5	427	10.1	3 051	16.9	17.4
Hardin	29 358	63.5	58 300	20.3	11.8	353	23.7	3.9	36 971	1.3	2 084	5.6	30 858	26.0	11.3
Harlan	13 269	70.8	29 400	18.6	12.2	225	27.6	8.9	9 195	-1.9	1 023	11.1	9 932	20.9	23.3
Harrison	6 086	67.7	48 500	18.1	12.2	274	24.6	5.2	7 568	0.0	318	4.2	6 985	19.1	13.6
Hart	5 740	75.6	31 600	19.8	13.4	224	25.2	8.3	8 054	0.8	412	5.1	5 922	14.2	13.6
Henderson	16 558	66.9	51 000	16.3	12.7	319	24.1	3.1	24 284	0.1	1 035	4.3	19 857	22.4	14.5
Henry	4 896	76.2	41 100	16.9	12.6	268	25.0	7.0	7 597	12.4	267	3.5	5 851	18.3	10.6
Hickman	2 188	79.2	32 000	16.1	12.7	213	20.2	4.1	2 558	3.9	154	6.0	2 213	16.4	14.2
Hopkins	17 760	75.2	39 600	16.8	11.9	269	25.5	2.8	19 834	-1.0	1 134	5.7	18 634	22.8	15.8
Jackson	4 381	77.2	26 900	20.8	13.1	170	26.4	15.0	6 872	0.2	331	4.8	3 666	13.4	20.2
Jefferson	264 138	64.5	57 000	17.0	12.2	346	24.7	2.4	382 623	2.5	14 299	3.7	316 117	29.5	10.7
Jessamine	10 601	68.4	63 800	21.3	11.8	351	26.3	3.9	21 051	3.7	318	1.5	15 287	25.7	11.8
Johnson	8 469	73.8	40 100	22.2	12.8	276	26.8	7.0	9 429	-1.9	676	7.2	7 565	22.5	14.3
Kenton	52 690	65.8	65 200	17.3	12.1	370	23.3	2.7	80 619	1.5	2 544	3.2	69 688	28.9	11.5
Knott	6 086	78.4	27 700	20.4	13.1	199	28.7	10.7	5 954	1.2	496	8.3	4 673	22.4	21.6
Knox	10 718	68.8	35 300	21.2	12.8	245	33.5	10.2	11 379	3.7	628	5.5	8 752	20.6	17.0
Larue	4 503	79.7	39 500	19.8	12.7	225	24.0	3.3	6 280	1.1	301	4.8	4 848	16.6	17.4
Laurel	15 585	76.4	46 900	21.2	12.5	280	25.8	5.9	23 021	3.7	1 075	4.7	16 438	20.3	13.5
Lawrence	5 007	75.1	40 500	19.3	12.4	255	32.0	10.9	5 621	7.2	603	10.7	3 835	20.5	20.1
Lee	2 760	75.1	28 400	19.2	13.7	177	27.5	15.2	2 515	-2.4	145	5.8	2 104	16.5	18.7
Leslie	4 711	77.6	24 400	18.2	12.1	192	26.4	13.9	4 480	-0.4	255	5.7	3 650	17.1	28.2
Letcher	9 731	78.6	27 300	21.2	12.6	226	26.9	8.9	8 024	6.7	732	9.1	7 531	20.7	27.9
Lewis	4 713	78.8	31 400	18.9	12.7	207	24.9	14.0	4 794	-5.4	664	13.9	4 724	14.9	15.7
Lincoln	7 431	76.3	37 700	18.9	12.6	233	27.6	9.8	11 182	4.0	442	4.0	8 017	16.5	13.1
Livingston	3 593	84.8	36 500	20.1	13.8	310	21.2	4.1	4 927	1.9	261	5.3	3 891	15.3	17.8
Logan	9 302	73.4	41 200	16.8	13.4	271	24.4	4.3	13 263	1.5	453	3.4	10 955	15.5	16.4
Lyon	2 355	79.8	46 300	17.5	11.9	255	24.6	3.8	3 366	1.1	164	4.9	2 286	22.8	13.7
McCracken	25 625	68.2	48 500	15.8	12.2	291	24.7	1.8	33 835	0.4	1 270	3.8	27 571	26.1	12.5
McCreary	5 479	74.7	26 300	24.5	11.7	217	32.2	13.5	6 421	3.4	429	6.7	3 918	16.5	16.4
McLean	3 672	80.1	36 200	15.9	12.4	222	22.0	3.8	4 771	2.3	319	6.7	3 898	17.7	12.4
Madison	20 012	62.1	55 500	18.7	12.3	307	25.2	3.5	36 639	4.4	959	2.6	27 242	27.8	10.3
Magoffin	4 440	78.0	35 500	24.1	12.8	197	35.1	10.9	5 239	2.7	696	13.3	3 351	18.5	14.6
Marion	5 688	76.9	39 500	21.3	12.6	229	26.2	6.9	10 932	9.0	604	5.5	6 808	13.4	13.5
Marshall	10 789	82.8	47 600	19.0	11.9	280	25.4	1.2	14 794	2.4	830	5.6	10 878	20.3	16.1
Martin	4 300	78.7	37 500	16.9	12.9	256	29.8	7.2	3 107	4.2	388	12.5	3 272	17.4	28.2
Mason	6 537	64.9	43 800	17.5	12.3	244	22.6	6.1	8 901	6.0	262	2.9	7 286	20.1	13.3
Meade	8 080	61.3	49 700	19.3	12.0	362	22.2	5.7	10 818	1.8	481	4.4	7 862	19.9	16.3
Menifee	1 842	81.8	32 600	26.7	12.1	214	26.7	8.3	2 921	2.8	196	6.7	1 814	15.4	17.3
Mercer	7 413	72.8	46 600	18.6	11.9	290	25.9	3.9	10 963	-0.2	345	3.1	8 870	18.3	13.1
Metcalfe	3 433	77.4	31 300	17.5	12.8	203	28.2	9.8	5 054	3.3	355	7.0	3 837	10.8	12.0
Monroe	4 505	74.9	31 500	18.2	14.5	190	22.1	8.3	5 597	8.3	682	12.2	4 948	14.7	12.0
Montgomery	7 312	70.2	43 600	19.2	12.1	285	26.6	4.4	12 652	2.8	650	5.1	8 409	17.0	15.0
Morgan	4 089	76.5	36 600	25.5	14.3	223	27.6	9.8	5 083	0.3	391	7.7	3 503	20.9	15.1
Muhlenberg	11 683	80.8	37 300	18.0	12.1	246	24.7	4.5	12 614	2.2	1 063	8.4	11 432	17.5	17.7
Nelson	10 417	78.0	45 800	17.7	12.0	292	24.2	5.3	18 928	2.2	1 129	6.0	13 289	16.8	15.7
Nicholas	2 621	71.9	38 300	17.7	11.8	217	24.6	9.6	3 190	-0.5	128	4.0	3 022	14.7	10.9
Ohio	7 816	79.1	34 300	17.3	12.5	265	23.8	5.7	10 188	0.3	846	8.3	7 521	18.2	16.7
Oldham	10 673	83.1	86 500	19.7	11.7	367	24.3	2.1	24 837	4.9	485	2.0	15 824	32.9	11.0
Owen	3 412	75.6	38 200	19.6	12.4	226	25.4	10.3	4 348	-0.4	132	3.0	3 984	17.9	12.5

1. Specified owner-occupied units.   2. Specified renter-occupied units.   3. Overcrowded or lacking complete plumbing facilities.   4. Percent of civilian labor force.   5. Persons 16 years and older.

				Private nonfarm establishments, employment and payroll, 1998						Agriculture, 1997			
													Farm operators
		Employment						Annual payroll		Farms			
											Percent with—		
STATE County	Number of establishments	Total	Health Care and Social Assistance	Manufacturing	Retail trade	Finance and Insurance	Professional Scientific and Technical Services	Total (mil dol)	Average per employee (dollars)	Number	Less than 50 acres	500 acres and over	Whose principal occupation is farming (percent)
	104	105	106	107	108	109	110	111	112	113	114	115	116
KENTUCKY—Cont'd													
Cumberland	117	1 042	275	184	226	59	10	18	16 872	524	28.6	9.7	45.4
Daviess	2 395	39 917	5 800	8 175	6 565	1 298	1 030	971	24 317	1 042	43.2	11.8	43.2
Edmonson	99	651	171	D	132	65	D	11	16 195	706	35.0	3.4	36.1
Elliott	57	413	106	D	71	D	D	6	15 298	439	28.0	3.0	39.0
Estill	219	2 072	275	430	412	102	41	31	14 908	432	27.8	4.4	32.4
Fayette	7 673	141 945	24 035	16 608	21 789	5 778	8 533	3 805	26 803	745	42.7	8.6	52.8
Fleming	263	2 485	539	585	564	124	78	46	18 478	1 132	27.7	6.4	51.0
Floyd	877	9 880	1 999	345	1 553	286	385	249	25 184	59	44.1	3.4	27.1
Franklin	1 145	15 986	1 728	3 306	3 486	795	916	357	22 316	675	35.0	2.5	38.2
Fulton	206	2 897	309	1 063	523	114	24	55	18 931	162	22.8	32.1	66.7
Gallatin	93	776	145	19	159	30	14	15	18 731	253	28.9	4.3	41.5
Garrard	236	2 049	379	467	265	42	54	37	17 902	880	32.6	5.0	51.5
Grant	428	3 839	409	515	1 080	193	58	77	20 009	936	30.7	2.6	35.3
Graves	682	10 097	1 610	3 259	1 555	346	263	233	23 067	1 371	35.8	8.2	37.7
Grayson	459	7 174	822	2 932	878	171	91	133	18 575	1 412	27.8	3.9	35.8
Green	177	1 323	429	287	232	77	D	23	17 709	1 059	31.2	2.6	46.6
Greenup	504	5 377	531	638	878	237	D	142	26 426	733	33.8	3.4	31.1
Hancock	128	2 677	91	1 829	174	58	18	102	38 019	449	30.5	3.8	30.7
Hardin	1 943	30 894	6 375	6 727	5 660	904	1 170	670	21 692	1 637	41.7	4.9	39.2
Harlan	561	5 778	1 085	307	1 208	189	186	146	25 197	27	48.1	0.0	14.8
Harrison	301	4 308	733	1 749	646	120	D	103	23 851	1 079	27.7	5.6	46.1
Hart	265	2 459	348	593	614	122	87	42	17 017	1 352	26.8	2.7	48.1
Henderson	1 085	18 934	2 194	7 811	2 158	448	303	472	24 936	526	37.3	18.3	45.1
Henry	239	2 354	164	763	474	115	40	51	21 593	955	28.8	5.2	46.5
Hickman	95	1 101	178	327	125	52	17	22	19 639	294	28.2	21.1	44.9
Hopkins	1 104	15 133	3 182	2 587	2 586	503	394	369	24 362	538	26.2	11.2	38.7
Jackson	140	1 826	245	778	192	52	D	32	17 548	689	38.8	2.2	36.7
Jefferson	19 803	396 681	49 450	57 047	50 280	27 785	17 454	11 656	29 384	475	61.5	1.7	38.3
Jessamine	827	11 372	361	2 482	2 145	158	218	244	21 483	754	47.9	4.5	41.1
Johnson	501	4 656	574	310	1 530	244	173	87	18 667	182	36.3	1.1	25.8
Kenton	3 240	57 159	7 260	7 694	6 394	1 287	2 281	1 673	29 269	442	45.9	0.9	31.2
Knott	229	2 408	298	7	331	40	58	64	26 692	21	23.8	9.5	19.0
Knox	452	5 722	889	1 087	1 541	123	187	113	19 721	322	33.2	4.0	31.1
Larue	231	1 805	262	648	268	110	44	31	17 062	806	35.2	5.1	42.8
Laurel	1 018	15 356	1 045	2 712	2 723	439	286	332	21 616	1 083	48.3	1.6	34.8
Lawrence	217	2 218	459	D	469	69	36	52	23 317	297	25.6	4.0	35.0
Lee	117	1 967	831	D	180	60	D	23	11 714	161	32.3	5.0	28.6
Leslie	145	1 529	475	D	211	D	36	34	22 381	17	41.2	5.9	11.8
Letcher	437	4 865	827	118	768	160	162	120	24 647	31	29.0	0.0	35.5
Lewis	138	1 728	176	1 003	192	98	D	29	16 900	774	26.1	7.1	44.6
Lincoln	291	2 762	460	751	487	71	88	49	17 678	1 258	40.5	5.3	44.2
Livingston	153	1 748	327	98	180	43	12	43	24 660	405	15.1	14.1	33.3
Logan	525	8 634	732	4 817	989	182	113	205	23 774	1 203	26.2	10.4	46.4
Lyon	190	1 398	233	D	434	41	22	17	11 907	249	22.1	7.6	34.9
McCracken	2 148	35 552	5 693	4 147	6 690	886	1 043	869	24 447	457	48.1	5.3	34.8
McCreary	176	2 218	260	1 012	439	90	25	32	14 650	108	38.9	0.9	14.8
McLean	180	1 224	178	173	244	87	19	22	18 371	422	32.2	17.5	53.6
Madison	1 369	20 775	2 339	5 715	3 966	430	335	453	21 812	1 444	40.4	6.0	43.4
Magoffin	207	1 893	336	D	303	59	82	36	18 839	373	42.1	2.1	31.1
Marion	334	4 838	815	1 746	630	142	114	92	18 970	983	27.4	5.3	41.2
Marshall	635	8 404	730	2 752	1 104	303	227	260	30 880	673	37.6	4.0	24.7
Martin	178	2 197	190	D	312	D	49	70	31 640	9	11.1	0.0	0.0
Mason	465	8 609	943	3 380	1 389	244	93	191	22 158	751	28.6	6.4	52.2
Meade	323	2 717	164	D	695	148	54	67	24 808	841	41.3	5.4	33.7
Menifee	75	637	198	240	83	D	D	10	15 008	346	34.1	2.6	37.0
Mercer	417	6 363	449	2 939	878	101	89	162	25 452	976	38.2	3.2	39.9
Metcalfe	126	2 646	57	1 977	264	77	10	54	20 533	950	28.2	3.5	45.2
Monroe	224	3 558	488	2 037	414	87	16	61	17 223	973	31.1	7.0	39.9
Montgomery	509	7 634	787	2 672	1 330	223	125	149	19 537	734	36.4	6.0	44.0
Morgan	173	1 916	385	375	379	84	30	40	20 888	698	30.1	5.9	34.8
Muhlenberg	601	6 907	1 093	1 424	1 369	247	132	144	20 802	559	25.9	8.9	39.5
Nelson	878	12 060	972	3 428	1 799	277	211	270	22 395	1 249	37.2	5.0	36.4
Nicholas	90	1 248	214	D	110	D	5	20	16 068	567	26.6	8.8	50.6
Ohio	357	4 818	509	1 857	633	131	111	94	19 603	943	28.5	5.5	35.9
Oldham	950	8 623	978	1 098	1 562	293	345	200	23 174	392	42.1	9.7	40.8
Owen	119	1 193	250	D	199	63	30	27	22 476	803	20.3	7.8	44.5

	Agriculture, 1997 (cont'd)														
STATE County	Land in farms				Value of land and buildings			Value of products sold				Percent of farms with sales of —			
	Acreage (1,000)	Percent change, 1992–1997	Acres			Average per farm ($1,000)	Average per acre (dollars)	Value of machinery and equipment Average per farm ($1,000)	Total (mil dol)	Average per farm (dollars)	Percent from —		$10,000 or more	$100,000 or more	Percent of land owned by Fed. Gov. 1997	Water consumption 1995 (mil gal/day)
			Average size of farm	Total irrigated (1,000)	Total cropland (1,000)						Crops	Live-stock and poultry products				
	117	118	119	120	121	122	123	124	125	126	127	128	129	130	131	132

STATE County	117	118	119	120	121	122	123	124	125	126	127	128	129	130	131	132
KENTUCKY—Cont'd																
Cumberland	108	-0.5	207	D	40	132	670	21	8	14 525	62.1	37.9	40.3	1.1	1.3	0.8
Daviess	251	0.4	241	3	207	388	1 650	57	71	68 406	82.1	17.9	48.8	15.1	0.0	220.2
Edmonson	90	-2.6	127	0	53	134	1 305	23	11	15 175	40.9	59.1	30.7	2.7	23.7	1.2
Elliott	58	-3.9	131	D	21	102	816	19	4	9 205	81.5	18.5	31.9	0.2	4.6	0.4
Estill	62	-10.0	144	0	28	199	1 071	25	5	10 464	72.0	28.1	28.9	0.9	2.7	2.0
Fayette	136	-7.5	182	1	91	674	4 130	53	139	186 969	16.2	83.8	61.1	22.6	0.4	43.1
Fleming	189	-2.6	167	0	125	173	1 048	32	37	32 724	47.2	52.8	56.0	6.5	0.0	1.6
Floyd	7	-33.5	124	D	2	135	1 089	17	1	8 613	84.1	16.1	11.9	3.4	4.5	3.8
Franklin	83	-3.9	122	1	51	223	2 279	30	16	23 513	71.1	28.9	49.5	4.0	0.0	8.5
Fulton	94	-3.4	578	3	83	743	1 295	103	23	143 579	94.2	5.8	61.7	34.6	1.4	1.7
Gallatin	36	-11.2	144	0	21	197	1 364	31	7	26 662	78.3	21.7	45.1	7.1	0.0	0.8
Garrard	125	-9.6	142	0	86	199	1 357	29	30	33 923	49.7	50.3	57.8	7.2	0.0	1.7
Grant	115	-9.2	123	1	71	189	1 738	27	16	16 618	76.2	23.8	42.6	2.4	0.0	2.1
Graves	237	12.9	173	1	186	242	1 446	43	115	83 662	37.6	62.4	41.1	14.7	0.0	14.7
Grayson	209	1.4	148	0	130	155	1 066	26	33	23 260	36.7	63.3	38.7	4.0	2.2	3.4
Green	129	-4.4	122	0	85	127	1 096	28	24	22 529	53.9	46.1	49.0	3.8	0.0	1.6
Greenup	98	-2.0	134	0	37	140	1 209	22	8	11 327	64.4	35.6	27.6	1.2	0.0	16.4
Hancock	65	-7.1	145	0	37	177	1 300	30	12	26 923	69.7	30.3	41.0	4.5	0.0	250.9
Hardin	223	-1.3	136	0	158	235	1 689	31	39	23 792	58.8	41.2	37.4	5.1	14.8	13.4
Harlan	2	-53.5	86	D	1	142	1 650	17	0	6 817	35.9	64.1	18.5	0.0	1.0	4.8
Harrison	169	-4.8	157	3	113	226	1 427	30	29	26 862	72.1	27.9	54.1	5.7	0.0	3.4
Hart	186	-6.8	138	0	113	149	1 104	28	35	25 953	56.3	43.7	53.3	5.3	2.8	3.6
Henderson	196	-0.9	373	2	163	561	1 593	78	50	95 326	78.4	21.6	50.6	19.0	0.5	117.7
Henry	149	-6.8	156	3	101	243	1 714	37	37	38 571	69.9	30.1	62.0	8.1	0.0	3.0
Hickman	115	15.8	390	2	101	512	1 382	102	44	149 518	58.4	41.6	46.3	26.9	0.0	0.8
Hopkins	141	-2.6	263	0	105	279	1 077	44	27	50 950	62.9	37.1	34.2	10.4	0.0	18.1
Jackson	74	-9.0	107	0	34	106	966	21	9	13 536	62.3	37.7	30.6	1.0	26.2	1.2
Jefferson	34	-24.4	72	0	20	331	4 388	33	12	25 885	78.6	21.4	26.9	6.7	0.0	927.8
Jessamine	89	-10.6	117	1	61	329	2 663	31	66	88 133	22.0	78.0	50.9	9.5	0.0	3.9
Johnson	20	-11.4	112	0	5	139	1 191	20	1	6 918	81.1	18.9	20.3	0.0	4.1	2.0
Kenton	38	-14.1	85	0	23	271	2 394	25	5	11 524	61.7	38.3	23.1	0.0	0.0	8.5
Knott	4	23.7	177		1	159	902	21	0	3 037	18.8	81.2	14.3	0.0	1.3	0.9
Knox	46	1.0	144	0	19	166	946	25	3	9 855	64.8	35.2	17.4	0.0	0.0	1.0
Larue	117	-3.7	145	0	84	217	1 664	38	25	30 727	51.4	48.6	45.2	6.3	0.1	1.3
Laurel	96	-4.4	88	0	55	170	2 140	21	14	13 298	61.7	38.3	30.8	1.7	20.8	9.7
Lawrence	49	-0.1	165	0	12	119	899	24	2	6 763	75.3	24.6	18.9	0.0	6.5	15.9
Lee	24	14.1	149	0	9	93	666	18	2	11 052	67.1	32.9	27.3	0.6	5.7	0.7
Leslie	3	33.5	157		D	85	541	8	0	6 694	89.5	10.5	11.8	0.0	22.1	2.9
Letcher	3	-10.5	87	D	0	70	804	16	0	1 907	11.9	88.1	3.2	0.0	18.5	2.4
Lewis	143	-10.5	185	D	47	154	777	23	14	18 429	73.9	26.1	45.3	2.2	0.0	1.4
Lincoln	170	-2.1	135	0	110	163	1 186	24	39	30 662	44.0	56.0	45.7	7.0	0.0	2.3
Livingston	117	-1.4	290	D	74	210	768	31	10	24 539	39.7	60.3	31.9	4.7	0.5	23.8
Logan	273	-2.0	227	1	206	319	1 354	48	64	52 896	75.3	24.7	50.5	12.2	0.0	5.0
Lyon	48	-3.3	194	D	33	246	1 186	45	6	24 554	66.3	33.7	30.5	5.2	2.1	2.1
McCracken	67	5.6	146	0	55	195	1 406	33	16	36 035	69.7	30.3	32.6	7.9	2.0	1 005.5
McCreary	11	-22.1	101		5	96	1 078	22	1	4 767	25.4	74.6	13.0	0.0	61.3	1.1
McLean	134	-0.5	318	0	113	538	1 710	82	54	127 419	49.4	50.6	63.7	27.5	0.0	0.8
Madison	222	-10.3	153	0	140	270	1 811	26	44	30 670	48.2	51.8	52.8	5.3	5.1	11.8
Magoffin	41	-9.5	109	0	10	89	972	14	3	7 191	89.7	10.3	22.5	0.0	0.0	0.9
Marion	166	-5.6	169	1	101	188	1 147	40	34	34 171	43.4	56.6	57.0	9.2	0.0	2.9
Marshall	89	17.5	133	0	62	225	1 651	37	18	26 369	44.1	55.9	25.7	4.8	0.0	22.2
Martin	2	-55.4	248	D	D	288	1 164	31	0	5 550	14.0	86.0	0.0	0.0	0.0	5.8
Mason	131	-8.7	175	0	92	229	1 366	32	31	41 266	61.7	38.3	67.9	10.5	0.0	44.8
Meade	121	0.5	143	0	80	241	1 788	37	18	20 901	51.0	49.0	34.6	4.5	7.2	25.4
Menifee	38	-11.3	110	D	16	99	915	21	4	10 988	74.0	26.0	30.9	1.2	33.5	0.2
Mercer	126	-5.0	129	1	92	224	1 874	33	31	31 354	48.9	51.1	47.1	5.7	0.0	20.0
Metcalfe	134	-2.4	141	0	71	182	1 219	28	25	26 308	43.2	56.8	48.5	4.7	0.0	1.1
Monroe	167	0.7	172	0	91	169	1 013	28	26	26 312	36.4	63.6	43.4	6.5	0.0	1.9
Montgomery	112	-1.2	152	0	79	193	1 415	27	23	30 899	63.3	36.7	58.6	7.1	0.0	2.5
Morgan	111	6.0	159	0	41	94	629	20	10	13 995	76.5	23.5	36.1	1.1	7.0	1.4
Muhlenberg	115	-2.7	205	0	72	189	1 082	35	32	57 994	29.2	70.8	36.7	6.8	0.0	487.7
Nelson	176	-7.6	141	1	118	275	1 875	37	39	30 942	37.0	63.0	42.7	6.8	0.1	8.1
Nicholas	106	-5.1	187	1	67	181	1 023	32	16	28 261	69.3	30.7	55.7	4.4	0.0	2.5
Ohio	162	1.4	172	0	94	201	1 115	31	37	39 216	36.0	64.0	31.6	5.6	0.0	7.6
Oldham	71	-16.0	180	0	46	488	2 947	40	16	41 034	46.3	53.7	42.1	9.2	0.0	5.1
Owen	150	-15.0	187	2	85	230	1 189	41	22	27 817	74.0	26.0	54.5	5.7	0.0	2.3

Table B. States and Counties — **Residential Construction, Wholesale and Retail Trade, and Real Estate**

STATE County	Value of Residential Construction Authorized by Building Permits, 1999		Wholesale Trade, 1997				Retail Trade[1], 1997				Real Estate and Rental and Leasing, 1997			
	New Construction ($1,000)	Number of Housing Units	Number of Establish-ments	Number of Employees	Sales (mil dol)	Annual Payroll (mil dol)	Number of Establish-ments	Number of Employees	Sales (mil dol)	Annual Payroll (mil dol)	Number of Establish-ments	Number of Employees	Receipts (mil dol)	Annual Payroll (mil dol)
	133	134	135	136	137	138	139	140	141	142	143	144	145	146
KENTUCKY—Cont'd														
Cumberland	150	2	2	D	D	D	34	231	35.1	3.1	6	17	2.2	0.7
Daviess	34 047	679	141	1 678	872.9	43.7	470	6 011	853.8	84.5	75	476	33.9	7.7
Edmonson	NA	NA	2	D	D	D	22	140	18.9	1.5	2	D	D	D
Elliott	NA	NA	NA	NA	NA	NA	20	87	11.5	0.9	1	D	D	D
Estill	840	6	11	D	D	D	61	375	58.9	4.5	7	31	1.8	0.4
Fayette	211 830	2 205	492	6 529	4 181.5	203.8	1 251	20 363	3 133.1	308.7	368	2 018	289.5	40.7
Fleming	420	4	20	126	58.2	2.1	68	526	108.2	9.5	4	8	1.0	0.1
Floyd	185	3	55	771	312.6	19.7	185	1 568	259.4	22.9	30	156	17.1	2.7
Franklin	37 599	465	33	D	D	D	202	3 096	443.4	39.2	34	130	12.5	1.9
Fulton	397	4	12	D	D	D	61	498	70.5	7.0	5	9	0.8	0.1
Gallatin	32	1	6	D	D	D	19	179	21.6	2.0	5	D	D	D
Garrard	1 171	16	5	D	D	D	44	238	33.8	3.0	6	D	D	D
Grant	15 998	221	18	D	D	D	100	1 098	181.3	16.5	11	D	D	D
Graves	1 228	30	37	571	201.8	14.3	141	1 580	286.2	24.4	24	93	7.2	1.5
Grayson	150	3	17	D	D	D	103	942	131.4	12.0	13	70	3.2	1.0
Green	0	0	7	31	6.7	0.3	41	230	33.4	3.1	5	11	1.0	0.1
Greenup	1 173	14	18	D	D	D	111	788	119.7	11.2	15	33	3.2	0.4
Hancock	1 831	21	1	D	D	D	22	168	29.3	2.3	5	D	D	D
Hardin	50 448	620	68	596	134.7	13.1	422	5 431	897.0	82.9	83	241	23.6	3.6
Harlan	0	0	31	242	108.9	6.3	132	1 261	168.8	17.1	24	D	D	D
Harrison	4 724	74	11	D	D	D	64	695	106.6	9.0	9	46	2.8	0.5
Hart	2 592	48	10	D	D	D	90	589	76.7	7.3	7	D	D	D
Henderson	21 259	315	71	798	728.4	23.9	208	2 252	422.2	36.8	43	181	16.0	3.4
Henry	12 203	138	18	247	114.4	5.7	53	470	90.5	7.0	10	14	1.2	0.2
Hickman	NA	NA	6	97	40.4	2.3	19	93	13.5	1.4	5	31	0.5	0.2
Hopkins	5 008	51	57	435	190.0	10.5	246	2 805	409.0	39.9	37	114	8.6	1.3
Jackson	0	0	2	D	D	D	30	179	31.2	2.3	2	D	D	D
Jefferson	423 340	4 350	1 509	24 651	15 932.9	852.5	2 950	47 517	7 200.8	761.6	811	5 810	766.7	126.8
Jessamine	40 717	474	46	1 010	513.7	27.9	132	2 078	394.0	32.7	27	81	6.0	1.0
Johnson	994	6	24	187	60.1	5.4	127	1 606	229.2	20.7	10	32	1.6	0.3
Kenton	89 044	947	198	3 123	1 370.3	109.3	452	5 904	829.4	86.6	131	823	90.0	16.8
Knott	NA	NA	6	59	3.6	0.7	48	242	35.4	3.4	6	14	1.5	0.2
Knox	38	1	14	140	52.4	3.4	123	1 556	254.4	20.6	13	48	3.4	0.6
Larue	4 678	187	7	19	3.4	0.2	41	294	42.5	4.3	6	10	0.4	0.1
Laurel	1 610	48	67	1 239	520.2	28.3	230	2 827	499.8	40.6	31	108	10.2	2.2
Lawrence	0	0	9	D	D	D	51	440	63.7	5.5	4	16	0.7	0.2
Lee	NA	NA	6	50	16.3	2.0	27	179	25.8	2.8	5	D	D	D
Leslie	NA	NA	2	D	D	D	42	215	30.2	2.8	4	35	1.9	0.6
Letcher	0	0	14	374	111.3	5.1	92	837	110.2	10.8	3	16	1.0	0.2
Lewis	0	0	5	13	5.6	0.2	34	241	22.6	2.0	3	8	0.2	0.0
Lincoln	0	0	13	68	12.1	0.8	64	471	70.9	6.6	6	15	1.2	0.1
Livingston	NA	NA	4	39	4.4	0.4	33	188	22.7	2.7	3	13	1.1	0.2
Logan	4 026	50	27	203	79.8	3.5	106	975	147.8	13.8	13	34	6.1	0.3
Lyon	1 201	13	4	27	42.7	0.7	68	461	52.4	5.2	8	39	4.0	0.8
McCracken	28 978	275	136	2 700	1 557.0	72.3	515	6 266	1 012.0	91.1	79	418	62.7	11.3
McCreary	0	0	4	18	1.0	0.2	50	318	52.4	4.2	7	51	6.6	1.2
McLean	825	8	11	134	52.5	2.4	30	209	40.8	3.4	5	8	0.3	0.1
Madison	34 201	617	49	720	285.7	24.8	288	3 824	565.0	51.4	55	184	17.1	2.0
Magoffin	NA	NA	6	36	45.2	0.9	47	314	46.9	3.5	4	D	D	D
Marion	1 425	37	14	143	40.3	1.9	79	642	84.8	7.1	6	12	1.7	0.3
Marshall	16 240	153	38	292	124.2	7.6	128	1 054	179.2	16.4	16	110	11.7	2.3
Martin	NA	NA	8	48	73.9	2.1	51	344	58.0	5.3	4	D	D	D
Mason	2 656	37	31	394	93.7	7.4	109	1 467	246.3	20.2	12	28	3.7	0.6
Meade	1 690	26	12	51	59.0	1.5	85	570	122.8	9.4	14	35	2.6	0.3
Menifee	NA	NA	NA	NA	NA	NA	16	81	11.8	0.8	2	D	D	D
Mercer	9 574	106	18	67	23.7	1.2	84	637	125.6	10.1	11	100	2.6	0.5
Metcalfe	NA	NA	3	44	11.8	1.2	40	272	39.8	3.5	3	6	0.6	0.1
Monroe	NA	NA	12	D	D	D	64	405	63.7	5.3	6	7	1.2	0.1
Montgomery	8 952	158	31	243	126.7	5.2	117	1 479	225.2	18.1	25	75	6.0	1.0
Morgan	NA	NA	4	D	D	D	52	388	65.7	5.6	3	D	D	D
Muhlenberg	981	19	16	D	D	D	130	1 405	198.7	20.0	17	89	4.5	0.8
Nelson	39 135	486	41	448	133.3	12.8	178	1 445	218.8	19.5	27	80	7.9	1.1
Nicholas	103	1	1	D	D	D	14	114	18.5	1.6	5	11	0.5	0.0
Ohio	1 208	33	8	198	45.4	3.0	75	614	89.8	8.2	5	9	1.3	0.2
Oldham	96 473	611	58	451	272.6	15.0	113	1 209	192.1	19.1	23	108	12.2	1.5
Owen	349	11	6	17	3.0	0.2	23	220	50.4	2.9	4	14	0.5	0.1

1. Establishments with payroll.

STATE County	Professional, Scientific, and Technical Services[1], 1997				Manufacturing, 1997				Accommodation and Foodservices, 1997			
	Number of Establishments	Number of Employees	Receipts (mil dol)	Annual Payroll (mil dol)	Number of Establishments	Number of Employees	Receipts (mil dol)	Annual Payroll (mil dol)	Number of Establishments	Number of Employees	Sales (mil dol)	Annual Payroll (mil dol)
	147	148	149	150	151	152	153	154	155	156	157	158
KENTUCKY—Cont'd												
Cumberland	5	8	0.8	0.1	NA	NA	NA	NA	12	123	4.3	1.2
Daviess	145	857	56.4	23.3	114	8 011	2 938.2	276.8	150	3 331	100.6	26.6
Edmonson	4	D	D	D	NA	NA	NA	NA	11	179	6.1	1.9
Elliott	1	D	D	D	NA	NA	NA	NA	4	D	D	D
Estill	5	11	0.3	0.1	NA	NA	NA	NA	17	D	D	D
Fayette	765	8 482	1 043.1	292.0	283	17 403	4 313.9	654.0	610	15 216	508.1	146.9
Fleming	7	71	1.7	0.5	19	650	54.8	14.6	9	143	3.6	1.0
Floyd	56	300	21.7	8.5	NA	NA	NA	NA	43	608	19.3	5.4
Franklin	104	669	61.1	25.0	40	3 435	592.4	97.8	89	1 518	47.2	13.2
Fulton	9	15	0.9	0.2	14	1 087	194.1	23.4	15	D	D	D
Gallatin	3	6	0.4	0.1	NA	NA	NA	NA	9	103	4.7	0.7
Garrard	8	21	1.3	0.3	NA	NA	NA	NA	13	112	2.7	0.7
Grant	18	51	2.5	1.0	16	D	D	D	37	D	D	D
Graves	38	142	7.9	2.9	50	3 053	537.6	101.4	49	592	15.7	4.2
Grayson	19	57	2.7	0.9	31	2 462	382.5	47.8	36	370	12.9	3.0
Green	5	19	0.9	0.3	NA	NA	NA	NA	11	115	3.2	0.8
Greenup	29	130	6.5	2.0	13	600	108.6	23.4	33	789	20.3	5.6
Hancock	8	17	0.8	0.1	13	1 862	1 049.0	80.9	8	D	D	D
Hardin	109	509	34.2	13.0	68	7 162	1 633.9	216.8	141	2 975	85.7	24.3
Harlan	34	184	11.2	4.8	NA	NA	NA	NA	32	457	15.0	3.9
Harrison	13	36	1.7	0.6	19	1 730	353.3	54.9	18	D	D	D
Hart	13	38	2.4	0.6	10	D	D	D	17	189	5.5	1.5
Henderson	73	284	18.8	5.7	78	6 862	1 722.9	208.0	81	1 403	41.3	11.8
Henry	12	31	1.3	0.6	8	555	213.9	17.1	7	99	3.1	0.8
Hickman	4	14	0.9	0.4	NA	NA	NA	NA	3	D	D	D
Hopkins	69	334	23.3	7.7	55	2 606	572.8	89.7	74	982	30.4	8.3
Jackson	4	7	0.3	0.1	13	1 940	173.3	28.4	8	D	D	D
Jefferson	1 811	15 317	1 479.9	503.7	873	56 948	30 261.6	2 201.4	1 394	34 303	1 081.9	314.8
Jessamine	48	173	10.6	3.3	67	2 379	675.4	67.9	44	799	23.6	6.2
Johnson	34	189	14.2	3.6	NA	NA	NA	NA	28	470	15.3	4.3
Kenton	263	2 441	162.3	71.1	161	6 810	1 482.8	233.4	294	6 542	236.9	65.5
Knott	14	47	2.8	1.2	NA	NA	NA	NA	10	D	D	D
Knox	28	196	14.9	6.1	17	877	160.6	20.6	33	561	15.9	4.3
Larue	16	30	2.1	0.8	12	641	25.3	10.1	10	D	D	D
Laurel	60	246	18.6	4.7	44	2 595	319.1	57.4	64	1 698	50.9	14.4
Lawrence	10	34	2.5	0.8	NA	NA	NA	NA	18	280	8.3	2.2
Lee	5	8	0.3	0.1	NA	NA	NA	NA	8	D	D	D
Leslie	10	47	4.4	0.7	NA	NA	NA	NA	6	D	D	D
Letcher	27	169	9.5	3.2	NA	NA	NA	NA	19	314	9.5	2.7
Lewis	6	27	0.9	0.3	15	804	89.9	15.7	14	D	D	D
Lincoln	19	65	4.8	1.7	18	737	54.7	18.9	15	176	4.7	1.3
Livingston	9	31	1.3	0.4	NA	NA	NA	NA	11	249	8.7	3.1
Logan	23	83	5.1	1.8	41	4 650	781.7	126.0	29	479	11.6	2.6
Lyon	10	24	0.9	0.3	NA	NA	NA	NA	21	216	7.2	1.8
McCracken	133	947	67.3	21.8	58	4 081	978.9	155.2	184	4 116	125.1	35.3
McCreary	7	23	0.7	0.2	16	D	D	D	10	117	3.0	0.9
McLean	8	18	0.9	0.2	NA	NA	NA	NA	10	58	1.6	0.4
Madison	77	273	14.7	4.6	68	5 460	1 576.1	160.3	126	2 664	75.5	21.2
Magoffin	12	72	5.6	1.8	NA	NA	NA	NA	11	161	4.8	1.4
Marion	19	78	5.1	1.7	22	1 554	175.1	34.4	28	296	8.3	2.5
Marshall	37	224	12.8	6.4	35	2 881	1 715.5	141.0	72	774	24.0	6.3
Martin	13	31	2.5	0.6	NA	NA	NA	NA	15	235	7.6	2.1
Mason	20	72	4.2	1.4	19	3 167	545.5	85.6	42	526	20.2	4.9
Meade	10	36	1.6	0.5	NA	NA	NA	NA	24	284	9.4	2.7
Menifee	2	D	D	D	NA	NA	NA	NA	4	D	D	D
Mercer	24	52	3.7	1.0	16	3 053	888.7	94.9	36	403	14.0	3.7
Metcalfe	6	9	0.4	0.1	13	1 829	231.4	37.0	9	83	2.0	0.4
Monroe	7	14	0.8	0.1	32	1 966	160.9	35.8	21	D	D	D
Montgomery	23	101	5.9	1.6	32	2 124	281.4	45.4	38	785	20.5	5.5
Morgan	9	23	0.9	0.2	NA	NA	NA	NA	9	D	D	D
Muhlenberg	38	148	6.0	2.1	36	1 399	130.1	26.8	41	502	13.2	3.8
Nelson	46	181	11.5	3.2	56	3 616	960.2	99.0	55	863	27.2	7.5
Nicholas	4	6	0.3	0.1	5	D	D	D	4	59	0.8	0.2
Ohio	23	75	4.5	1.4	27	2 010	177.1	37.4	24	363	10.3	2.4
Oldham	78	261	23.2	9.3	41	1 004	252.5	37.5	51	957	29.2	8.4
Owen	5	25	2.4	1.4	NA	NA	NA	NA	6	75	1.8	0.5

1. Firms subject to federal tax.

Table B. States and Counties — Health and Other Services and Federal Funds

STATE County	Health Care and Social Assistance[1], 1997				Other Services[1], 1997				Federal funds and grants, fiscal 1999[2] Expenditures (mil dol)			
										Direct payments for individuals[3]		
	Number of Establishments	Number of Employees	Receipts (mil dol)	Annual Payroll (mil dol)	Number of Establishments	Number of Employees	Receipts (mil dol)	Annual Payroll (mil dol)	Total	Social Security and government retirement	Medicare	Food stamps and Supplemental Security Income
	159	160	161	162	163	164	165	166	167	168	169	170
KENTUCKY—Cont'd												
Cumberland	10	165	8.3	3.7	4	7	0.8	0.1	42.2	13.4	9.1	4.2
Daviess	202	2 568	184.0	76.4	144	829	50.4	14.5	360.4	173.4	67.7	18.6
Edmonson	8	137	5.3	2.2	3	13	1.3	0.2	50.8	17.6	7.4	2.8
Elliott	5	76	2.5	0.8	4	18	0.6	0.1	25.7	8.5	2.7	3.6
Estill	11	126	6.5	2.2	13	26	3.0	0.8	81.9	37.0	15.6	7.4
Fayette	612	10 905	793.3	352.1	456	3 266	177.5	56.7	1 247.1	397.6	129.1	37.1
Fleming	14	195	8.4	3.9	26	43	2.8	0.5	59.4	22.2	9.0	4.4
Floyd	85	702	40.1	16.3	43	155	12.0	3.2	244.3	103.2	41.3	26.3
Franklin	88	1 258	87.8	36.3	69	408	22.4	9.1	954.2	155.6	41.2	12.3
Fulton	19	322	18.7	7.7	9	32	2.2	0.5	55.4	21.2	9.6	3.2
Gallatin	4	D	D	D	4	6	0.5	0.1	24.5	10.1	4.4	2.0
Garrard	10	61	2.6	1.2	7	22	1.4	0.4	46.5	24.2	8.3	2.3
Grant	22	316	12.5	6.7	19	65	2.6	0.7	69.2	34.8	12.3	3.7
Graves	50	898	53.3	21.8	33	293	10.3	3.5	176.4	79.2	36.7	8.0
Grayson	23	204	10.6	5.2	27	93	4.5	1.3	106.8	46.4	20.0	6.5
Green	16	267	11.0	4.9	9	17	1.3	0.2	47.4	19.7	11.3	5.0
Greenup	48	444	21.5	8.3	32	104	6.6	1.6	155.5	88.6	30.9	9.1
Hancock	6	74	2.8	0.9	9	13	0.8	0.2	26.4	13.4	4.3	1.2
Hardin	189	2 319	154.9	71.4	136	825	43.5	14.2	862.6	245.0	45.7	16.4
Harlan	26	429	22.7	13.7	32	132	8.3	1.9	295.0	93.7	28.9	108.2
Harrison	31	295	13.2	6.0	22	69	4.4	1.0	69.7	31.5	11.2	3.5
Hart	17	266	10.4	4.7	16	38	2.9	0.5	68.9	28.3	12.1	5.6
Henderson	92	687	48.5	19.4	68	503	32.0	10.4	170.9	82.0	38.0	8.4
Henry	14	150	6.2	3.3	16	44	3.5	0.8	53.3	22.7	12.0	3.7
Hickman	6	120	3.7	1.5	4	14	1.1	0.3	27.8	9.0	4.9	0.9
Hopkins	55	1 047	38.3	18.6	71	449	28.0	8.6	246.3	108.5	35.2	12.2
Jackson	5	160	6.5	2.9	7	22	1.4	0.3	67.1	21.8	10.1	8.6
Jefferson	1 622	27 669	1 872.1	835.3	1 317	9 422	586.0	187.4	3 831.2	1 411.7	586.7	50.2
Jessamine	37	286	10.8	3.8	51	227	13.6	4.1	109.1	52.9	14.6	5.3
Johnson	52	525	47.1	13.8	32	116	5.5	1.5	126.6	53.1	19.8	12.5
Kenton	219	2 729	173.5	89.7	221	1 586	103.2	31.0	608.9	248.0	99.0	24.2
Knott	8	142	7.5	3.1	9	30	2.3	0.5	87.8	30.9	11.6	12.9
Knox	33	269	14.1	6.1	20	86	5.7	1.3	153.7	47.4	20.5	21.1
Larue	11	86	3.4	1.5	11	34	2.4	0.6	54.6	27.2	11.2	2.9
Laurel	46	292	22.1	8.5	53	273	19.1	4.3	214.9	81.7	26.9	23.7
Lawrence	24	441	27.4	9.7	19	76	4.4	1.1	78.7	31.1	11.4	9.0
Lee	4	26	1.4	0.9	5	16	0.8	0.2	46.2	15.9	6.6	5.9
Leslie	9	154	6.6	2.8	5	15	1.5	0.5	78.7	28.8	11.6	9.9
Letcher	21	329	17.2	6.3	23	79	5.5	1.1	149.4	61.9	22.5	16.0
Lewis	7	161	7.0	3.4	4	7	0.6	0.1	59.7	22.7	9.6	6.1
Lincoln	13	217	9.3	4.1	16	31	3.0	0.7	97.1	39.7	16.2	7.9
Livingston	8	62	3.8	1.5	6	14	0.9	0.1	59.4	22.5	10.1	1.8
Logan	40	479	28.4	10.3	33	127	9.9	2.3	117.7	47.1	25.9	5.7
Lyon	9	207	7.3	3.3	6	14	1.0	0.2	33.1	18.7	6.6	1.1
McCracken	191	2 250	186.3	91.5	117	737	49.6	12.3	641.9	146.2	60.3	14.1
McCreary	12	271	11.3	5.2	6	14	1.1	0.3	235.4	31.5	14.5	14.2
McLean	13	143	5.4	2.3	12	38	3.7	0.8	52.3	20.4	9.1	2.0
Madison	116	1 034	52.1	23.6	63	316	13.3	3.9	255.3	104.4	35.8	15.9
Magoffin	11	237	9.2	3.4	6	24	3.7	0.4	70.5	21.5	10.1	10.5
Marion	27	519	31.3	12.0	14	56	3.9	0.9	74.1	29.0	12.4	6.3
Marshall	36	428	21.6	9.1	31	175	15.2	4.3	121.1	71.0	26.0	4.1
Martin	12	140	5.1	2.0	11	101	5.2	2.8	67.2	28.4	7.9	9.9
Mason	39	770	53.8	18.1	30	167	6.5	2.0	84.1	29.8	13.6	3.7
Meade	22	135	5.5	2.0	12	47	2.8	0.6	69.4	41.3	10.3	3.4
Menifee	3	D	D	D	3	D	D	D	40.8	11.1	3.6	4.0
Mercer	21	231	9.8	4.2	20	57	3.0	0.8	72.8	39.2	12.0	4.1
Metcalfe	6	59	3.0	1.1	6	9	0.6	0.1	42.1	16.7	8.1	2.4
Monroe	16	189	8.8	2.8	15	56	3.0	0.6	69.8	21.8	14.7	5.4
Montgomery	47	446	21.0	9.1	33	174	9.4	3.0	94.5	38.9	14.4	7.2
Morgan	11	122	5.6	2.0	15	38	2.3	0.4	62.3	20.5	8.4	7.4
Muhlenberg	37	532	25.4	11.7	35	136	9.3	2.1	226.7	77.2	28.2	8.6
Nelson	43	521	22.4	9.2	39	166	6.5	1.8	108.5	53.0	21.5	6.1
Nicholas	6	27	1.4	0.8	7	15	0.5	0.2	30.5	13.4	5.7	2.1
Ohio	31	619	28.7	11.5	22	107	15.2	2.3	92.9	45.4	17.5	7.8
Oldham	57	256	14.6	5.8	52	248	14.4	4.9	67.3	35.7	14.2	1.3
Owen	11	285	11.4	5.0	11	34	1.5	0.5	29.5	13.2	6.4	2.3

1. Firms subject to federal tax.   2. October 1, 1998 to September 30, 1999.   3. State totals may include programs not allocated by county.

	Federal funds and grants, fiscal 1999[1] (cont'd)							Local government finances, 1997				
	Expenditures (mil dol) (cont'd)							General revenue				
	Procurement contract awards			Grants[2]							Taxes	
STATE County											Per capita[3] (dollars)	
	Salaries and wages	Defense	Other	Medicaid and other health-related	Nutrition and family welfare	Education	Other	Total (mil dol)	Intergovernmental (mil dol)	Total (mil dol)	Total	Property
	171	172	173	174	175	176	177	178	179	180	181	182
KENTUCKY—Cont'd												
Cumberland	0.9	0.0	0.2	10.2	1.2	0.5	1.5	9.9	6.1	2.8	413	284
Daviess	15.7	4.2	7.1	27.2	15.4	3.9	12.7	189.8	66.1	43.6	479	299
Edmonson	7.5	0.1	0.8	7.2	1.2	0.7	4.7	11.6	8.6	2.0	182	134
Elliott	0.5	0.0	0.1	7.2	1.4	0.7	0.2	11.3	8.4	1.3	198	146
Estill	1.7	0.0	0.3	16.0	2.6	1.3	-1.3	21.0	15.0	3.4	218	128
Fayette	189.0	124.6	70.9	112.9	23.8	17.2	103.9	487.9	102.9	218.7	912	394
Fleming	2.3	0.0	0.6	11.0	3.6	1.8	2.8	26.9	11.9	3.6	269	182
Floyd	7.4	2.7	6.7	38.3	6.5	3.5	6.3	60.6	39.4	11.6	268	197
Franklin	25.1	1.1	2.4	117.5	222.2	128.6	241.4	67.9	27.9	28.9	624	298
Fulton	2.1	1.9	0.5	8.4	1.6	1.1	0.2	16.9	9.3	3.4	447	257
Gallatin	1.2	0.3	0.2	2.8	0.7	0.3	1.5	18.6	4.8	2.2	329	240
Garrard	1.6	0.0	0.4	6.5	1.2	0.6	0.3	22.6	9.6	3.8	278	183
Grant	2.7	0.3	0.8	6.8	2.4	1.0	3.6	26.8	17.3	5.7	289	201
Graves	8.4	0.4	2.1	17.5	3.2	1.5	7.7	43.0	23.2	13.0	364	182
Grayson	3.1	0.4	0.8	18.0	3.8	1.3	2.9	31.5	18.4	7.4	320	156
Green	1.1	0.0	0.3	6.8	1.0	0.5	1.1	19.3	8.4	2.4	228	157
Greenup	3.2	1.2	0.9	15.2	3.4	1.7	0.4	56.8	28.4	15.7	424	379
Hancock	1.1	0.0	0.3	3.8	0.6	0.5	0.1	17.2	6.4	6.2	696	220
Hardin	506.2	0.5	3.5	23.0	8.0	3.9	1.5	211.7	66.1	31.8	354	207
Harlan	5.8	7.3	4.1	32.4	7.2	4.6	2.0	63.0	37.7	9.2	261	197
Harrison	2.9	0.3	0.5	9.1	1.7	0.8	6.6	24.8	14.1	7.0	404	177
Hart	1.7	0.0	0.4	13.1	1.9	1.1	2.0	17.6	11.3	4.0	240	151
Henderson	6.0	0.5	4.5	13.4	3.7	2.0	1.9	84.5	33.7	19.7	441	253
Henry	2.7	0.0	0.6	8.0	1.6	0.7	0.1	19.6	11.3	5.7	388	275
Hickman	0.9	0.0	0.2	3.2	0.6	0.3	1.6	7.1	5.1	1.4	275	179
Hopkins	19.6	130.6	-92.5	20.3	4.4	2.5	0.5	74.7	39.8	19.1	413	268
Jackson	1.5	0.0	0.4	18.4	2.7	1.4	1.5	16.6	13.7	2.2	169	112
Jefferson	366.5	726.9	83.0	263.3	83.1	47.5	133.3	1 438.0	409.4	609.2	908	432
Jessamine	3.7	0.6	7.0	8.6	2.3	1.5	9.9	53.8	23.4	21.0	582	350
Johnson	3.3	0.1	0.7	22.8	9.4	2.0	2.2	44.0	27.3	10.1	418	267
Kenton	133.2	1.4	12.4	37.9	14.6	4.8	28.7	330.3	104.3	106.0	725	412
Knott	2.5	0.0	0.7	21.8	3.9	1.9	0.7	26.4	18.6	5.0	280	238
Knox	7.7	0.0	0.7	39.1	11.7	3.7	0.7	43.2	29.9	6.3	201	143
Larue	2.0	0.0	0.5	6.8	1.3	0.7	0.1	15.8	10.9	3.3	257	203
Laurel	16.0	9.8	3.1	29.8	6.8	3.0	12.9	63.2	39.2	16.6	332	163
Lawrence	2.2	1.0	0.9	16.4	2.6	1.6	1.9	21.2	15.2	3.4	222	160
Lee	1.0	0.0	0.3	11.0	1.6	0.7	2.5	14.4	8.3	1.6	202	133
Leslie	1.9	0.0	0.9	18.3	3.0	1.2	2.8	20.4	16.0	3.7	271	220
Letcher	3.9	0.0	1.1	27.5	7.5	3.0	4.9	35.8	25.8	6.9	259	203
Lewis	1.0	0.0	0.3	14.0	2.1	1.0	2.0	16.8	13.0	2.3	167	124
Lincoln	2.8	0.0	0.7	21.0	3.9	1.5	1.1	27.3	20.4	4.4	199	146
Livingston	3.4	2.8	11.0	4.4	0.8	0.4	0.1	9.4	6.2	2.4	257	202
Logan	3.3	0.7	0.9	19.1	2.4	1.1	0.3	32.6	19.6	8.7	334	183
Lyon	1.5	0.0	0.2	2.6	0.4	0.3	0.5	7.4	3.7	2.3	283	206
McCracken	38.9	19.7	314.6	25.4	7.9	2.8	3.8	105.1	42.6	40.6	626	294
McCreary	3.9	5.1	140.2	17.5	4.1	2.1	1.7	24.8	20.3	2.1	124	90
McLean	1.7	0.0	0.4	3.8	0.9	0.6	8.1	15.2	8.1	2.7	275	172
Madison	26.6	6.9	1.9	30.5	8.7	5.0	6.5	100.2	48.9	30.4	465	203
Magoffin	1.2	0.1	0.3	21.2	3.5	1.5	0.1	21.5	16.8	2.8	201	143
Marion	3.1	0.0	0.6	13.2	5.0	1.2	1.0	25.4	15.1	6.5	382	203
Marshall	4.6	0.2	1.1	7.5	2.1	1.1	1.2	39.5	17.9	15.2	510	266
Martin	1.0	0.0	1.2	13.0	2.7	1.3	1.8	20.9	15.2	3.7	299	236
Mason	3.2	0.0	0.6	11.2	1.8	0.8	17.5	48.9	12.6	11.8	696	362
Meade	2.1	0.0	0.5	4.7	1.8	1.0	1.4	27.8	18.7	5.7	204	138
Menifee	8.5	0.0	0.7	5.9	0.9	0.4	5.3	7.9	5.3	1.5	262	183
Mercer	2.5	0.0	0.6	8.5	1.5	0.8	1.8	29.6	15.0	10.0	488	245
Metcalfe	1.4	0.0	0.4	9.7	1.2	0.7	0.7	11.9	8.4	2.8	298	146
Monroe	2.2	0.0	0.4	17.4	1.6	0.7	3.8	15.1	10.8	3.0	264	137
Montgomery	3.4	0.0	0.6	12.2	2.4	1.5	12.1	41.8	20.9	9.4	453	244
Morgan	1.6	0.0	0.6	15.4	4.2	1.2	1.9	18.4	13.9	2.4	180	106
Muhlenberg	29.4	0.4	59.1	15.2	3.3	1.5	1.6	39.7	23.9	7.7	241	189
Nelson	5.0	1.1	1.1	12.5	3.2	1.4	1.3	50.2	22.3	12.6	360	263
Nicholas	1.3	0.0	0.2	5.5	0.8	0.4	0.2	9.6	5.9	2.7	381	235
Ohio	3.9	0.0	1.0	10.4	2.7	1.5	0.0	37.7	18.2	6.3	288	181
Oldham	3.8	0.1	1.1	4.0	2.0	2.7	0.9	50.3	25.2	20.5	473	381
Owen	1.1	0.0	0.3	5.1	1.0	0.6	-1.4	12.1	8.5	2.8	275	217

1. October 1, 1998 to September 30, 1999.   2. State totals may include programs not allocated by county.   3. Based on the resident population estimated as of July 1 of the year shown.

STATE County	Local government finances, 1997 (cont'd)									Government employment, 1998			Presidential election, 2000		
	Direct general expenditure							Debt outstanding					Percent of vote cast —		
			Percent of total for —												
	Total (mil dol)	Per capita[1] (dollars)	Education	Health and hospitals	Police protection	Public welfare	Highways	Total (mil dol)	Per capita[1] (dollars)	Federal civilian	Federal military	State and local	Democratic	Republican	All other
	183	184	185	186	187	188	189	190	191	192	193	194	195	196	197
KENTUCKY—Cont'd															
Cumberland	9.7	1 408	62.8	12.0	2.6	0.0	8.6	5.6	813	17	24	349	24.5	73.9	1.7
Daviess	186.5	2 050	40.6	6.7	3.6	0.0	2.8	883.5	9 707	292	346	6 901	39.0	58.9	2.1
Edmonson	11.7	1 055	80.4	3.4	0.5	0.0	6.1	12.3	1 109	224	39	430	34.2	65.1	0.7
Elliott	11.9	1 812	72.3	0.8	0.1	0.0	5.9	6.2	947	0	23	289	64.0	34.7	1.2
Estill	24.9	1 609	75.2	5.1	1.7	0.0	3.2	16.5	1 066	25	54	688	33.8	64.4	1.8
Fayette	402.2	1 677	48.5	0.0	7.9	1.3	4.8	425.7	1 775	4 309	887	27 315	44.8	51.7	3.5
Fleming	26.0	1 967	46.8	41.6	1.6	0.0	2.7	10.3	783	49	47	837	35.0	63.4	1.6
Floyd	64.3	1 485	71.1	4.8	1.1	0.1	3.4	84.2	1 943	135	150	2 437	65.5	32.9	1.5
Franklin	62.0	1 341	51.7	2.3	5.4	0.0	3.9	48.0	1 039	467	182	15 525	50.1	47.1	2.7
Fulton	16.8	2 206	52.2	0.0	3.9	0.0	5.0	35.6	4 660	35	42	590	52.1	46.4	1.5
Gallatin	18.1	2 667	30.7	0.2	1.4	0.0	1.4	162.1	23 946	32	25	288	42.7	54.7	2.6
Garrard	23.9	1 749	51.1	31.9	1.3	0.0	3.7	11.6	846	32	48	791	29.4	69.4	1.2
Grant	27.1	1 366	70.2	0.9	2.2	0.0	7.1	22.9	1 157	58	71	905	36.2	62.0	1.8
Graves	44.9	1 263	62.9	0.2	3.0	0.1	7.9	159.7	4 488	168	124	1 598	42.8	55.2	2.0
Grayson	31.4	1 350	63.8	0.2	2.6	0.0	6.9	50.0	2 149	59	82	1 477	30.4	68.3	1.3
Green	17.7	1 674	44.0	41.8	1.4	0.0	5.7	7.7	726	28	37	643	22.8	76.0	1.2
Greenup	63.8	1 719	58.5	2.4	2.4	0.0	2.9	33.9	914	71	128	1 426	48.9	49.3	1.8
Hancock	15.5	1 757	51.8	2.1	1.9	0.2	1.8	695.4	78 610	23	31	415	41.8	56.3	1.9
Hardin	212.1	2 357	38.9	43.1	2.3	0.0	2.3	193.4	2 148	5 069	9 804	5 582	36.2	61.8	2.1
Harlan	62.0	1 754	58.1	23.7	2.1	0.0	4.0	14.9	420	114	121	2 150	50.9	47.3	1.8
Harrison	26.1	1 505	70.0	0.3	3.5	0.2	5.7	22.5	1 296	59	61	782	40.2	57.4	2.4
Hart	17.2	1 042	73.0	3.8	2.1	0.0	5.5	22.4	1 356	42	58	671	36.6	61.9	1.5
Henderson	81.2	1 819	45.7	0.3	4.5	0.5	1.8	539.6	12 094	134	154	2 321	50.2	48.0	1.8
Henry	20.4	1 384	69.6	4.2	3.1	0.2	4.1	12.4	842	60	51	603	38.7	59.3	2.0
Hickman	7.4	1 440	64.6	0.0	2.0	0.0	9.7	0.5	96	25	18	233	44.3	54.2	1.6
Hopkins	80.0	1 729	52.7	3.6	4.6	1.1	5.8	73.2	1 581	372	161	2 771	40.8	57.6	1.6
Jackson	15.7	1 228	81.8	0.0	0.6	0.0	5.4	13.7	1 067	37	45	711	14.4	84.0	1.5
Jefferson	1 533.9	2 287	35.1	2.3	5.9	1.7	2.3	3 266.0	4 870	7 136	2 538	39 565	49.6	48.0	2.5
Jessamine	56.8	1 577	59.6	1.7	4.1	0.0	3.4	71.9	1 995	71	127	1 893	30.8	66.9	2.4
Johnson	41.1	1 705	65.4	8.4	1.3	0.1	2.9	31.8	1 321	80	83	1 439	39.7	58.5	1.8
Kenton	366.4	2 506	28.2	2.5	5.2	0.0	4.0	674.1	4 610	3 752	509	5 900	34.0	62.9	3.1
Knott	27.1	1 501	75.2	1.8	1.8	0.0	5.0	5.2	291	53	62	866	67.3	31.4	1.2
Knox	38.8	1 232	73.7	9.7	2.1	0.0	1.0	8.3	262	168	113	1 744	37.2	61.1	1.6
Larue	15.2	1 179	69.7	0.1	1.6	0.0	5.9	9.7	753	45	45	551	33.3	65.3	1.3
Laurel	63.8	1 273	70.2	2.4	2.2	0.0	5.9	52.7	1 052	316	176	2 287	26.8	71.9	1.3
Lawrence	21.9	1 416	73.6	0.1	1.1	0.0	6.0	11.4	740	45	54	716	42.5	55.9	1.5
Lee	12.8	1 611	55.1	10.3	2.2	0.0	6.9	21.0	2 634	25	28	462	30.2	68.5	1.3
Leslie	18.4	1 359	76.8	0.2	1.0	2.3	6.1	6.2	457	38	47	708	27.3	71.2	1.5
Letcher	33.5	1 260	77.4	0.2	0.8	0.0	3.5	11.3	423	76	91	1 345	52.3	45.5	2.2
Lewis	23.5	1 733	56.4	1.2	1.6	0.1	3.7	114.4	8 435	20	47	558	28.3	70.4	1.3
Lincoln	30.3	1 374	79.0	2.0	1.7	0.1	3.7	16.1	731	54	78	899	35.3	63.1	1.6
Livingston	9.3	992	77.0	0.5	1.9	0.0	4.1	4.3	466	79	33	373	47.8	50.1	2.1
Logan	34.3	1 312	66.5	0.5	5.4	0.0	4.8	22.1	844	72	91	1 188	41.6	57.3	1.1
Lyon	8.9	1 105	48.2	2.0	3.3	0.4	7.2	6.3	786	34	28	700	49.1	49.4	1.5
McCracken	108.9	1 682	48.2	0.0	4.8	0.1	5.2	122.2	1 887	713	239	3 778	42.8	55.2	2.0
McCreary	26.9	1 624	78.2	0.9	0.3	0.0	5.4	13.3	803	124	58	796	29.5	69.2	1.3
McLean	13.9	1 437	54.7	20.0	1.7	0.0	1.7	26.7	2 748	39	34	475	43.4	55.2	1.4
Madison	98.0	1 499	59.0	8.4	2.8	0.0	3.2	113.8	1 742	617	245	5 693	39.3	57.8	2.9
Magoffin	20.3	1 469	77.0	4.4	0.7	0.0	4.7	6.2	446	22	48	752	47.7	51.1	1.2
Marion	24.4	1 435	62.6	1.0	3.7	0.0	7.7	28.7	1 688	53	59	781	45.0	52.8	2.3
Marshall	39.6	1 328	59.0	4.2	2.1	0.0	6.3	40.9	1 370	90	105	1 549	45.1	53.0	1.9
Martin	20.8	1 697	73.5	0.0	0.9	0.0	4.9	13.3	1 088	18	42	653	38.5	59.9	1.7
Mason	49.9	2 953	30.9	2.6	2.9	0.0	4.7	345.7	20 450	59	59	1 012	37.1	60.8	2.1
Meade	28.7	1 020	76.4	1.5	1.1	0.0	4.7	23.7	844	38	100	765	39.6	58.6	1.7
Menifee	7.6	1 345	77.6	0.1	0.8	0.0	9.8	5.7	1 015	61	20	327	46.2	52.0	1.8
Mercer	30.5	1 492	53.8	7.8	3.3	2.5	6.2	41.1	2 008	50	72	836	35.8	62.1	2.1
Metcalfe	10.7	1 133	75.4	0.8	3.2	0.0	6.8	7.4	780	32	33	558	34.2	64.3	1.4
Monroe	15.2	1 358	73.5	2.1	3.0	0.0	6.0	3.0	271	39	39	840	20.8	78.6	0.6
Montgomery	42.1	2 027	47.0	10.6	2.5	0.0	5.1	106.5	5 128	73	73	983	45.0	53.2	1.8
Morgan	17.5	1 302	72.1	2.7	2.4	0.0	9.4	13.7	1 016	36	47	1 122	44.2	54.1	1.7
Muhlenberg	39.2	1 226	69.9	3.7	2.1	0.0	4.0	56.6	1 770	587	111	1 575	52.7	46.2	1.2
Nelson	62.0	1 762	52.3	0.6	2.2	0.1	13.4	104.3	2 968	87	124	1 364	40.6	57.2	2.2
Nicholas	9.0	1 280	65.6	1.1	3.2	0.7	8.8	6.1	867	17	24	339	37.2	60.3	2.5
Ohio	36.6	1 668	49.1	0.3	2.0	0.1	4.2	163.4	7 444	92	76	1 415	37.2	60.9	1.9
Oldham	51.8	1 198	72.5	0.8	4.5	0.0	3.9	30.9	714	70	154	2 872	30.8	67.0	2.2
Owen	11.6	1 151	71.5	0.6	2.9	0.3	9.0	5.1	501	25	36	440	34.3	63.4	2.3

1. Based on the resident population estimated as of July 1 of the year shown.

STATE/ County code	MSA/ PMSA/ NECMA code[1]	County Type[2]	STATE County	Land area,[3] (sq km) 1990	Population and population characteristics, 1999													
								Race (percent)					Age (percent)					
					Total persons	Rank	Per square kilometer	White	Black	Am. Indian, Eskimo, Aleut	Asian and Pacific Islander	Percent Hispanic[4]	Under 5 years	5 to 17 years	18 to 24 years	25 to 34 years	35 to 44 years	45 to 54 years
				1	2	3	4	5	6	7	8	9	10	11	12	13	14	15
			KENTUCKY—Cont'd															
21 189	...	9	Owsley	513	5 375	2 815	10.5	99.6	0.3	0.1	0.0	0.4	6.3	19.1	9.6	11.9	15.2	14.0
21 191	1640	1	Pendleton	725	13 959	2 140	19.3	99.4	0.3	0.2	0.1	0.4	7.8	20.0	9.6	13.9	14.8	13.4
21 193	...	7	Perry	886	30 805	1 354	34.8	97.7	1.9	0.1	0.3	0.3	6.3	20.4	10.3	13.3	16.9	13.4
21 195	...	7	Pike	2 040	71 526	687	35.1	99.2	0.4	0.1	0.3	0.4	6.0	19.8	9.5	13.5	16.8	13.6
21 197	...	6	Powell	467	13 264	2 193	28.4	99.0	0.8	0.1	0.1	0.6	7.4	21.2	9.9	13.6	16.4	14.7
21 199	...	7	Pulaski	1 714	57 110	816	33.3	98.3	1.3	0.2	0.3	0.6	5.9	16.9	8.8	12.5	15.5	14.7
21 201	...	9	Robertson	259	2 265	3 038	8.7	99.6	0.4	0.0	0.0	0.3	5.8	17.4	9.6	12.0	14.5	15.1
21 203	...	6	Rockcastle	822	15 974	2 008	19.4	99.7	0.1	0.1	0.1	0.6	6.6	18.5	10.2	12.7	14.9	14.3
21 205	...	7	Rowan	727	22 168	1 649	30.5	97.5	1.6	0.2	0.7	0.6	5.6	14.2	25.9	11.7	12.9	11.9
21 207	...	9	Russell	657	16 182	1 994	24.6	99.2	0.7	0.1	0.0	0.4	5.7	16.3	8.9	12.5	14.8	14.7
21 209	4280	2	Scott	739	32 249	1 305	43.6	92.6	6.7	0.1	0.6	0.6	6.7	19.2	11.2	13.9	17.3	14.0
21 211	...	6	Shelby	995	30 552	1 361	30.7	89.3	10.1	0.1	0.5	0.5	6.4	17.6	8.8	13.1	17.7	15.6
21 213	...	6	Simpson	612	16 587	1 963	27.1	87.8	11.7	0.2	0.3	0.5	6.9	18.4	9.2	13.0	16.3	14.2
21 215	...	8	Spencer	482	10 441	2 385	21.7	97.9	1.8	0.0	0.3	0.1	6.5	19.3	8.8	14.1	16.7	14.5
21 217	...	7	Taylor	699	22 942	1 614	32.8	94.3	5.4	0.1	0.2	0.3	6.0	16.9	9.4	13.0	15.2	14.4
21 219	...	8	Todd	975	11 289	2 328	11.6	88.4	11.4	0.1	0.1	0.7	6.7	18.6	9.2	13.1	14.2	14.0
21 221	...	8	Trigg	1 148	12 593	2 243	11.0	87.1	12.4	0.2	0.3	0.6	5.4	16.0	7.8	10.6	14.4	15.6
21 223	...	8	Trimble	386	7 926	2 609	20.5	99.6	0.0	0.3	0.0	0.8	6.9	18.3	8.6	12.7	16.8	15.5
21 225	...	6	Union	894	16 499	1 971	18.5	84.5	15.0	0.2	0.3	0.9	5.7	21.5	13.7	11.3	15.1	11.8
21 227	...	5	Warren	1 412	87 683	574	62.1	90.0	8.7	0.2	1.2	0.9	6.0	16.6	15.4	13.2	15.8	13.5
21 229	...	7	Washington	779	11 047	2 343	14.2	90.4	9.3	0.1	0.1	0.9	6.8	18.6	9.3	12.9	14.6	13.4
21 231	...	7	Wayne	1 190	19 190	1 809	16.1	97.7	2.0	0.2	0.1	0.5	6.3	19.1	9.4	12.1	15.4	14.0
21 233	...	6	Webster	867	13 460	2 178	15.5	93.7	5.9	0.1	0.3	0.3	6.1	18.7	8.4	12.2	15.1	13.6
21 235	...	7	Whitley	1 140	36 130	1 188	31.7	98.9	0.7	0.2	0.2	0.4	6.6	18.9	11.5	12.0	15.1	14.1
21 237	...	9	Wolfe	577	7 507	2 638	13.0	99.7	0.2	0.1	0.1	0.1	6.4	21.1	8.7	13.8	15.9	14.0
21 239	4280	2	Woodford	494	22 773	1 621	46.1	92.8	6.8	0.1	0.2	0.8	6.9	17.7	8.6	13.6	18.6	15.5
22 000	...	X	LOUISIANA	112 836	4 372 035	X	38.7	65.9	32.4	0.4	1.3	2.7	7.2	20.0	11.0	13.1	15.4	13.0
22 001	3880	2	Acadia	1 697	57 947	811	34.1	79.4	20.4	0.1	0.2	0.9	7.8	22.2	9.6	12.3	14.0	13.1
22 003	...	6	Allen	1 980	24 218	1 570	12.2	72.6	25.8	1.3	0.3	6.2	6.2	18.2	9.2	15.2	17.0	13.7
22 005	0760	2	Ascension	755	74 049	667	98.1	74.1	25.3	0.2	0.4	2.0	7.8	22.6	10.7	14.1	16.4	13.4
22 007	...	6	Assumption	877	23 242	1 605	26.5	63.9	35.5	0.2	0.4	1.6	7.3	22.4	10.7	12.7	14.5	13.1
22 009	...	6	Avoyelles	2 156	40 710	1 066	18.9	69.1	30.5	0.3	0.2	2.1	6.8	20.3	9.8	12.3	14.4	13.0
22 011	...	6	Beauregard	3 005	32 265	1 304	10.7	82.5	16.4	0.4	0.7	1.7	7.0	20.1	9.9	12.7	15.6	13.7
22 013	...	6	Bienville	2 100	15 739	2 020	7.5	52.6	47.1	0.2	0.1	0.6	6.8	19.6	9.4	10.6	13.0	13.3
22 015	7680	2	Bossier	2 172	93 374	539	43.0	76.1	22.1	0.4	1.5	2.7	7.5	19.5	9.8	13.8	15.5	13.7
22 017	7680	2	Caddo	2 285	241 502	227	105.7	56.2	42.9	0.2	0.6	1.3	7.0	19.6	9.7	12.1	15.2	13.1
22 019	3960	3	Calcasieu	2 774	180 607	295	65.1	74.0	25.3	0.2	0.5	1.4	7.0	20.1	10.2	12.8	15.4	13.4
22 021	...	8	Caldwell	1 371	10 469	2 383	7.6	79.6	20.1	0.1	0.1	2.1	6.7	20.5	9.1	11.3	14.1	14.4
22 023	...	8	Cameron	3 401	8 969	2 508	2.6	93.0	6.4	0.2	0.4	2.0	7.6	20.6	9.1	13.9	14.1	13.3
22 025	...	7	Catahoula	1 823	10 905	2 354	6.0	71.4	28.4	0.1	0.1	0.8	7.0	21.3	9.1	11.4	14.0	13.1
22 027	...	6	Claiborne	1 954	16 826	1 940	8.6	50.1	49.7	0.1	0.1	0.2	6.0	17.5	10.3	12.6	14.3	12.5
22 029	...	7	Concordia	1 804	20 572	1 736	11.4	60.4	39.2	0.1	0.2	0.8	6.7	21.6	9.2	11.2	13.8	13.4
22 031	...	6	De Soto	2 272	25 146	1 525	11.1	52.4	47.2	0.3	0.0	1.8	7.2	20.7	9.8	11.5	14.5	12.9
22 033	0760	2	East Baton Rouge	1 180	393 294	146	333.3	60.3	37.7	0.2	1.8	1.9	7.0	18.7	14.0	13.6	16.3	12.6
22 035	...	7	East Carroll	1 092	8 719	2 533	8.0	32.8	66.9	0.1	0.2	1.4	8.6	25.1	10.5	10.4	11.8	11.5
22 037	...	6	East Feliciana	1 174	21 119	1 709	18.0	48.8	50.9	0.1	0.2	1.1	7.1	20.3	10.7	14.6	16.1	13.1
22 039	...	7	Evangeline	1 721	34 329	1 246	19.9	70.9	28.9	0.1	0.1	1.0	7.8	21.8	9.7	11.6	13.2	13.0
22 041	...	7	Franklin	1 615	21 993	1 658	13.6	65.6	34.2	0.1	0.2	0.6	6.9	22.0	9.7	10.5	13.2	12.8
22 043	...	8	Grant	1 671	19 211	1 808	11.5	83.0	16.3	0.4	0.2	1.2	7.3	21.1	9.5	12.3	14.5	14.1
22 045	...	4	Iberia	1 490	73 425	672	49.3	65.8	32.4	0.2	1.6	2.5	8.1	22.2	10.4	13.0	14.4	12.6
22 047	...	6	Iberville	1 602	31 357	1 338	19.6	49.7	49.9	0.2	0.2	2.3	7.3	19.8	11.3	14.3	15.6	12.6
22 049	...	6	Jackson	1 476	15 449	2 039	10.5	67.2	32.4	0.1	0.2	0.4	5.9	20.5	9.3	10.4	13.9	14.5
22 051	5560	0	Jefferson	792	447 790	126	565.4	77.6	19.0	0.4	3.0	7.5	6.6	18.3	9.9	13.8	16.6	13.9
22 053	...	6	Jefferson Davis	1 690	31 423	1 335	18.6	78.4	21.2	0.2	0.2	0.8	7.2	21.7	8.9	12.0	13.8	13.3
22 055	3880	2	Lafayette	699	187 403	285	268.1	73.8	24.8	0.2	1.2	2.0	7.7	19.4	12.1	14.8	16.1	12.1
22 057	3350	3	Lafourche	2 810	89 463	561	31.8	82.9	13.9	2.1	1.1	1.9	7.4	20.4	12.0	13.4	14.7	13.3
22 059	...	7	La Salle	1 616	13 705	2 156	8.5	88.5	10.6	0.6	0.4	0.4	6.0	19.9	8.6	11.2	15.0	14.0
22 061	...	4	Lincoln	1 221	41 129	1 059	33.7	56.6	42.2	0.1	1.1	1.1	5.9	16.5	25.0	10.9	12.1	10.8
22 063	0760	2	Livingston	1 678	91 182	552	54.3	93.1	6.3	0.2	0.3	1.2	7.3	22.1	9.8	13.4	17.1	13.7
22 065	...	7	Madison	1 617	12 987	2 217	8.0	37.1	62.7	0.1	0.1	1.4	7.5	24.4	10.2	11.4	14.1	11.8
22 067	...	6	Morehouse	2 057	31 242	1 344	15.2	55.5	44.2	0.1	0.2	0.6	6.9	21.9	9.8	11.0	13.6	11.6
22 069	...	6	Natchitoches	3 254	37 198	1 155	11.4	57.7	41.3	0.5	0.5	1.6	7.0	21.4	14.6	10.7	13.5	11.9
22 071	5560	0	Orleans	468	460 913	120	984.9	33.1	64.2	0.2	2.5	4.2	7.1	19.0	12.0	13.4	15.5	12.2
22 073	5200	3	Ouachita	1 582	146 672	356	92.7	65.3	33.6	0.2	0.7	1.1	7.3	20.5	12.6	12.2	14.5	12.6
22 075	5560	1	Plaquemines	2 188	26 094	1 490	11.9	70.2	25.4	1.8	2.6	3.0	7.6	21.4	10.7	14.1	14.7	12.9

1. MSA = Metropolitan Statistical Area. PMSA = Primary MSA. NECMA = New England County Metropolitan Area. See Appendix A for explanation of these concepts. See Appendix B for list of metropolitan areas identified by type, with component counties. 2. County typology code from the Economic Research Service of USDA. See Appendix A for definition. 3. Dry land or land partially or temporarily covered by water. 4. Hispanic persons may be of any race.

STATE County	55 to 64 years	65 to 74 years	75 years and over	Percent female	Total persons 1990	Total persons 1980	Percent change 1980–1990	Percent change 1990–1999	Births	Deaths	Net migration	Households 1990 Number	Percent change, 1980–1990	Persons per house-hold	Female family house-holder[1]	One person
	16	17	18	19	20	21	22	23	24	25	26	27	28	29	30	31
KENTUCKY—Cont'd																
Owsley	10.0	6.8	7.1	49.2	5 036	5 709	-11.8	6.7	620	611	339	1 848	-2.2	2.67	11.0	19.6
Pendleton	9.9	5.7	5.0	51.0	12 062	10 989	9.5	15.7	1 726	1 175	1 387	4 332	16.0	2.76	8.7	20.7
Perry	8.6	5.9	4.9	50.9	30 283	33 763	-10.3	1.7	4 456	2 715	-1 153	10 598	0.2	2.83	12.4	19.0
Pike	9.3	6.7	4.8	51.0	72 584	81 123	-10.5	-1.5	8 840	6 456	-3 299	26 148	-0.9	2.75	11.0	18.6
Powell	8.7	4.3	3.8	50.6	11 686	11 101	5.3	13.5	1 722	993	886	4 057	15.3	2.86	12.1	17.8
Pulaski	10.8	8.2	6.6	51.4	49 489	45 803	8.0	15.4	5 973	4 897	6 681	18 866	17.0	2.57	9.8	21.7
Robertson	10.7	7.6	7.4	50.5	2 124	2 270	-6.4	6.6	246	243	144	820	1.5	2.57	6.3	27.7
Rockcastle	9.9	6.6	6.2	50.4	14 803	13 973	5.9	7.9	1 717	1 514	1 006	5 464	15.5	2.68	10.7	20.7
Rowan	8.1	5.2	4.5	51.6	20 353	19 049	6.8	8.9	2 333	1 507	1 047	6 755	13.5	2.49	10.9	24.2
Russell	11.2	8.8	7.1	51.7	14 716	13 708	7.4	10.0	1 813	1 612	1 326	5 896	19.5	2.48	10.1	23.8
Scott	8.8	4.8	4.2	51.1	23 867	21 813	9.4	35.1	3 671	1 968	6 666	8 501	17.0	2.69	10.9	19.9
Shelby	9.8	5.7	5.3	51.9	24 824	23 328	6.4	23.1	3 552	2 488	4 681	9 048	15.1	2.65	10.7	20.1
Simpson	9.3	6.7	6.0	51.4	15 145	14 673	3.2	9.5	2 071	1 607	1 028	5 767	10.4	2.59	11.9	22.7
Spencer	10.3	5.3	4.6	49.5	6 801	5 929	14.7	53.5	1 110	648	3 145	2 451	21.0	2.75	7.5	18.5
Taylor	10.6	7.8	6.8	51.7	21 146	21 178	-0.2	8.5	2 702	2 128	1 303	8 216	8.7	2.52	9.6	22.4
Todd	10.4	7.4	6.3	51.4	10 940	11 874	-7.9	3.2	1 495	1 246	128	4 104	-0.7	2.64	10.5	22.3
Trigg	12.7	10.1	7.5	51.1	10 361	9 384	10.4	21.5	1 215	1 297	2 330	4 104	22.1	2.49	8.5	22.8
Trimble	9.8	6.0	5.4	50.7	6 090	6 253	-2.6	30.1	855	591	1 586	2 246	5.7	2.68	6.9	18.3
Union	8.5	6.6	5.8	48.8	16 557	17 821	-7.1	-0.4	1 853	1 432	-434	5 580	3.4	2.65	11.2	23.1
Warren	8.3	5.9	5.1	52.1	77 720	71 828	8.2	12.8	10 649	6 399	5 964	28 819	16.1	2.52	10.8	24.6
Washington	9.6	7.7	7.1	51.9	10 441	10 764	-3.0	5.8	1 214	1 044	469	3 709	6.5	2.76	10.2	19.9
Wayne	10.5	7.1	5.9	50.8	17 468	17 022	2.6	9.9	2 290	1 739	1 217	6 517	12.0	2.66	10.3	19.8
Webster	10.5	7.5	7.9	51.7	13 955	14 832	-5.9	-3.5	1 644	1 640	-453	5 372	-0.8	2.56	10.1	23.5
Whitley	9.1	6.8	5.9	52.0	33 326	33 396	-0.2	8.4	4 520	3 409	1 837	12 153	7.2	2.65	13.8	21.8
Wolfe	10.0	5.5	4.5	50.1	6 503	6 698	-2.9	15.4	992	729	762	2 451	7.4	2.63	12.4	22.9
Woodford	8.4	5.9	4.8	52.0	19 955	17 778	12.2	14.1	2 660	1 544	1 753	7 223	21.5	2.71	9.2	18.1
LOUISIANA	8.8	6.3	5.1	51.9	4 221 826	4 206 116	0.3	3.6	629 286	362 228	-113 794	1 499 269	6.2	2.74	15.6	23.7
Acadia	9.3	6.3	5.5	52.4	55 882	56 427	-1.0	3.7	8 822	5 247	-1 347	19 285	6.4	2.86	14.5	20.9
Allen	9.2	5.9	5.4	44.6	21 226	21 408	-0.9	14.1	3 109	2 233	2 166	7 080	-2.6	2.79	13.5	21.3
Ascension	7.5	4.3	3.3	51.0	58 214	50 068	16.3	27.2	10 370	4 116	9 649	19 337	24.8	2.99	13.1	16.8
Assumption	8.3	5.9	5.0	51.5	22 753	22 084	3.0	2.1	3 114	1 816	-740	7 397	14.2	3.05	13.2	18.3
Avoyelles	9.6	7.0	6.7	50.9	39 159	41 393	-5.4	4.0	5 389	4 245	517	13 480	-0.5	2.77	14.4	22.5
Beauregard	9.4	6.3	5.4	49.8	30 083	29 692	1.3	7.3	4 618	2 591	98	10 362	9.0	2.79	9.9	20.5
Bienville	10.4	7.7	9.2	52.3	16 232	16 387	-2.5	-3.0	2 062	1 917	-302	5 852	0.1	2.65	15.5	26.2
Bossier	8.9	6.6	4.7	52.1	86 088	80 721	6.6	8.5	12 835	6 101	-372	30 718	15.1	2.73	12.8	21.2
Caddo	9.4	7.2	6.5	53.5	248 253	252 437	-1.7	-2.7	35 410	23 964	-18 033	93 248	2.8	2.61	18.3	27.1
Calcasieu	9.7	6.6	4.9	51.6	168 134	167 223	0.5	7.4	25 632	14 184	1 466	60 328	7.0	2.74	13.2	22.2
Caldwell	10.1	6.5	7.3	51.2	9 806	10 761	-8.9	6.8	1 246	1 184	650	3 575	-7.9	2.68	13.2	22.6
Cameron	10.4	6.1	4.9	50.0	9 260	9 336	-0.8	-3.1	1 020	614	-670	3 153	4.4	2.92	7.9	17.0
Catahoula	10.4	7.1	6.6	51.6	11 065	12 287	-9.9	-1.4	1 387	1 129	-393	3 927	-3.9	2.77	12.8	22.8
Claiborne	10.1	7.9	8.9	48.4	17 405	17 095	1.8	-3.3	1 940	1 950	-508	6 065	-0.7	2.64	15.0	27.2
Concordia	10.7	7.6	5.7	52.8	20 828	22 981	-9.4	-1.2	2 891	2 057	-1 040	7 341	-3.1	2.80	18.5	21.8
De Soto	9.5	7.2	6.8	52.6	25 668	25 727	-1.5	-2.0	3 539	2 745	-609	9 129	1.9	2.75	18.0	23.7
East Baton Rouge	7.7	5.9	4.2	52.2	380 105	366 191	3.8	3.5	58 590	26 905	-17 796	138 620	11.5	2.65	15.3	24.9
East Carroll	9.3	6.6	6.2	53.3	9 709	11 772	-17.5	-10.2	1 642	1 108	-1 512	3 129	-13.4	3.00	27.5	24.3
East Feliciana	8.0	5.4	4.8	47.0	19 211	19 015	1.0	9.9	2 707	1 905	1 163	5 589	10.1	3.04	18.8	19.6
Evangeline	9.9	6.8	6.1	52.0	33 274	33 343	-0.2	3.2	5 358	3 437	-750	11 795	4.9	2.78	13.4	23.3
Franklin	10.0	7.3	7.7	52.8	22 387	24 141	-7.3	-1.8	3 062	2 521	-878	7 776	-3.7	2.81	15.8	22.6
Grant	9.5	5.9	5.8	51.6	17 526	16 703	4.9	9.6	2 392	1 816	1 135	6 261	8.5	2.76	12.2	21.2
Iberia	8.6	5.9	4.7	51.8	68 297	63 752	7.1	7.5	11 425	5 543	-565	22 847	14.7	2.96	15.5	19.3
Iberville	8.2	6.0	4.7	51.1	31 049	32 159	-3.5	1.0	4 609	2 682	-1 540	9 875	2.5	2.97	19.4	20.7
Jackson	10.2	7.6	7.7	52.2	15 859	17 321	-9.3	-2.6	1 888	1 741	-12	5 817	-4.7	2.65	13.1	25.2
Jefferson	8.9	7.0	4.9	52.1	448 306	454 592	-1.4	0.1	62 172	34 727	-27 441	166 398	6.9	2.68	13.5	24.9
Jefferson Davis	10.1	7.0	6.0	51.9	30 722	32 168	-4.5	2.3	4 713	2 977	-957	10 669	2.7	2.84	12.3	20.9
Lafayette	8.2	5.3	4.2	51.8	164 762	150 017	9.8	13.7	26 566	10 691	7 255	60 411	20.0	2.66	12.7	24.6
Lafourche	8.6	6.1	4.4	51.2	85 860	82 483	4.1	4.2	12 105	6 007	-2 232	28 835	13.6	2.93	11.8	17.3
La Salle	10.7	7.3	7.4	52.5	13 662	17 004	-19.7	0.3	1 739	1 597	-54	5 086	-16.2	2.64	9.7	23.6
Lincoln	7.5	5.8	5.6	51.6	41 745	39 763	5.0	-1.5	4 967	3 164	-2 362	13 669	11.3	2.57	13.7	26.1
Livingston	8.1	5.0	3.5	50.5	70 523	58 806	19.9	29.3	11 137	4 992	14 543	23 814	29.0	2.94	9.7	16.5
Madison	8.6	5.9	6.0	51.5	12 463	15 682	-20.5	4.2	2 209	1 470	-198	4 252	-18.1	2.87	24.1	25.4
Morehouse	10.2	7.9	7.0	53.1	31 938	34 803	-8.2	-2.2	4 598	3 516	-1 703	10 961	-5.6	2.85	18.1	22.3
Natchitoches	8.7	6.3	5.8	52.6	37 254	39 863	-8.0	-0.2	5 242	3 507	-1 600	12 644	-4.6	2.71	18.1	25.3
Orleans	8.6	6.5	5.6	53.7	496 938	557 927	-10.9	-7.2	77 500	50 388	-62 993	188 235	-8.8	2.55	24.1	32.2
Ouachita	8.8	6.1	5.4	53.0	142 191	139 241	2.1	3.2	20 944	12 200	-3 935	50 518	6.8	2.72	17.0	24.1
Plaquemines	9.0	5.8	3.8	49.4	25 575	26 049	-1.8	2.0	3 891	1 794	-1 622	8 213	6.0	3.04	12.4	17.1

1. No spouse present.

STATE County	Births, average 1996–1998		Deaths, average 1996–1998				Physicians,[4] 1998		Hospitals,[4] 1998			Medicare enrollees 1999	Serious crimes known to police, 1998[6]	
			Number		Rate					Beds			Total	
	Total	Rate[1]	Total	Infant[2]	Total[1]	Infant[3]	Number	Rate[5]	Number	Number	Rate[5]		Number	Rate[7]
	32	33	34	35	36	37	38	39	40	41	42	43	44	45
KENTUCKY—Cont'd														
Owsley	65	12.0	70	0	13.0	0.0	1	19	0	0	0	1 071	NA	NA
Pendleton	179	13.0	133	2	9.7	11.2	3	22	0	0	0	1 753	NA	NA
Perry	441	14.1	283	4	9.1	9.8	66	213	1	295	950	5 688	NA	NA
Pike	874	12.0	717	6	9.9	7.2	110	153	2	354	491	13 010	NA	NA
Powell	193	15.2	119	1	9.3	6.9	4	31	0	0	0	1 252	NA	NA
Pulaski	681	12.2	558	5	10.0	6.8	85	151	1	248	441	11 065	NA	NA
Robertson	26	11.8	30	0	13.5	12.8	1	45	0	0	0	373	NA	NA
Rockcastle	182	11.6	171	1	10.8	7.3	7	44	1	28	176	2 442	NA	NA
Rowan	241	11.0	161	2	7.3	6.9	47	212	1	169	761	2 823	NA	NA
Russell	187	11.5	187	1	11.5	7.1	13	80	1	47	290	3 344	NA	NA
Scott	428	14.5	226	3	7.7	7.0	34	111	1	79	257	3 418	NA	NA
Shelby	421	14.6	266	3	9.2	7.9	25	85	1	78	264	3 772	NA	NA
Simpson	219	13.5	170	2	10.5	9.2	9	55	1	58	354	2 423	NA	NA
Spencer	136	14.8	75	1	8.2	7.3	2	21	0	0	0	1 220	NA	NA
Taylor	278	12.1	239	2	10.4	7.2	26	113	1	98	427	4 461	NA	NA
Todd	163	14.6	139	1	12.4	4.1	4	36	0	0	0	1 838	NA	NA
Trigg	142	11.7	140	1	11.5	4.7	4	32	1	42	339	2 509	NA	NA
Trimble	106	14.4	63	0	8.5	0.0	3	39	0	0	0	1 057	NA	NA
Union	194	11.7	157	1	9.5	5.2	8	48	1	42	253	2 489	NA	NA
Warren	1 205	13.9	716	10	8.3	8.0	183	210	2	623	713	12 144	NA	NA
Washington	132	12.2	124	1	11.5	5.0	4	37	0	0	0	1 879	NA	NA
Wayne	257	13.6	188	3	10.0	11.7	14	73	1	30	157	3 345	NA	NA
Webster	179	13.2	172	0	12.7	1.9	3	22	0	0	0	2 527	NA	NA
Whitley	461	12.9	392	5	11.0	10.1	67	186	1	286	796	8 045	NA	NA
Wolfe	103	14.0	87	0	11.9	0.0	2	27	0	0	0	1 318	NA	NA
Woodford	283	12.7	169	1	7.6	4.7	43	188	1	66	289	2 731	NA	NA
LOUISIANA	66 039	15.2	39 976	609	9.2	9.2	9 110	209	133	18 314	419	597 485	266 435	6 098
Acadia	940	16.3	577	9	10.0	9.9	71	123	2	217	376	8 676	1 836	3 170
Allen	333	13.9	232	1	9.7	3.0	15	63	2	87	364	3 328	847	3 529
Ascension	1 174	16.8	474	11	6.8	9.4	28	39	3	189	264	6 778	2 697	3 839
Assumption	312	13.7	189	4	8.3	13.9	8	35	1	38	165	3 014	402	1 751
Avoyelles	565	13.9	467	5	11.5	8.3	22	54	2	103	252	6 947	NA	NA
Beauregard	470	14.8	298	3	9.3	7.1	27	84	2	193	604	4 647	712	2 230
Bienville	202	12.8	210	3	13.3	13.2	3	19	0	0	0	3 122	NA	NA
Bossier	1 397	15.1	693	13	7.5	9.3	142	152	2	214	229	10 827	4 797	5 152
Caddo	3 667	15.0	2 593	44	10.6	12.0	899	371	7	1 611	664	38 368	20 435	8 363
Calcasieu	2 795	15.6	1 603	24	8.9	8.7	300	166	6	862	478	25 334	12 791	7 276
Caldwell	132	12.9	139	1	13.5	7.6	6	58	2	89	859	1 787	128	1 232
Cameron	102	11.5	68	0	7.7	3.3	1	11	1	27	298	850	347	3 836
Catahoula	146	13.2	124	2	11.2	13.7	5	45	0	0	0	1 968	NA	NA
Claiborne	194	11.4	202	2	11.9	12.0	16	95	1	40	236	2 961	268	1 581
Concordia	310	14.9	237	2	11.4	7.5	15	72	1	46	222	3 448	658	3 160
De Soto	360	14.5	303	3	12.2	8.3	7	28	1	35	140	4 232	860	3 414
East Baton Rouge	6 105	15.4	3 041	69	7.7	11.4	1 057	268	5	1 557	394	44 853	39 320	10 279
East Carroll	157	17.4	110	0	12.2	2.1	6	67	1	29	326	1 458	NA	NA
East Feliciana	289	13.9	213	3	10.2	10.4	26	125	0	0	0	2 780	936	4 477
Evangeline	585	17.1	350	6	10.3	10.3	35	103	2	311	912	5 955	551	1 792
Franklin	321	14.5	279	2	12.6	7.3	8	36	1	46	208	3 652	NA	NA
Grant	257	13.7	188	3	10.1	11.7	5	26	0	0	0	2 820	622	3 327
Iberia	1 241	17.2	611	13	8.4	10.2	76	104	2	156	213	9 897	2 235	3 129
Iberville	462	14.8	303	5	9.7	10.8	24	77	1	151	484	4 352	NA	NA
Jackson	209	13.4	190	1	12.2	3.2	54	347	1	66	424	2 899	222	1 422
Jefferson	6 434	14.2	3 951	51	8.7	8.0	1 612	357	7	1 772	393	61 739	31 171	6 904
Jefferson Davis	502	15.8	335	5	10.6	9.3	25	79	2	70	221	4 870	1 533	4 821
Lafayette	2 889	15.7	1 239	29	6.7	10.0	451	242	5	1 024	549	20 695	11 196	6 109
Lafourche	1 253	14.2	654	8	7.4	6.4	113	127	3	251	281	11 453	3 003	3 497
La Salle	193	14.0	173	0	12.5	1.7	13	95	2	114	834	2 482	134	1 199
Lincoln	543	13.0	340	5	8.1	8.6	12	29	1	107	257	5 270	1 937	4 696
Livingston	1 301	15.2	567	8	6.6	6.4	11	12	0	0	0	8 801	2 342	2 729
Madison	229	17.6	142	2	10.9	8.7	5	39	1	50	390	1 821	NA	NA
Morehouse	484	15.8	384	8	12.1	17.2	30	95	1	119	378	5 637	1 123	3 525
Natchitoches	589	15.8	391	6	10.5	9.6	35	95	1	196	529	5 536	2 238	5 979
Orleans	7 636	16.2	5 269	71	11.2	9.3	2 089	449	14	3 229	694	67 155	41 096	8 722
Ouachita	2 203	15.0	1 340	19	9.1	8.6	332	226	5	1 012	689	19 459	12 707	8 676
Plaquemines	395	15.2	190	3	7.3	7.6	14	53	0	0	0	3 052	644	2 481

1. Per 1,000 estimated resident population, average 1996–1998.   2. Deaths of infants under 1 year old.   3. Deaths of infants under 1 year old per 1,000 live births.   4. Data subject to copyright.   5. Per 100,000 resident population as of July 1 of the year shown.   6. Data for serious crimes have not been adjusted for underreporting; this may affect comparability between geographic areas and over time.   7. Per 100,000 population estimated by the FBI.

Table B. States and Counties — Crime, Education, Money Income, and Poverty

STATE County	Serious crimes known to police, 1998 (cont'd) Rate[2] Violent	Property	Education — School enrollment and attainment, 1990 Enrollment[3] Total	Percent private	Attainment[4] (percent) High school graduate or more	Bachelor's degree or more	Local government expenditures, fiscal 1997[5] Total current expenditures (mil dol)	Current expenditures per student (dollars)	Money income 1989 Per capita[6] (dollars)	Households Median Dollars	Percent change, 1979–1989 (constant 1989 dollars)	Percent with $100,000 or more	Income and poverty, 1997 Median household income	Percent below poverty level All persons	Persons under 18	Persons 5–17 in families
	46	47	48	49	50	51	52	53	54	55	56	57	58	59	60	61
KENTUCKY—Cont'd																
Owsley	NA	NA	1 170	1.0	35.5	9.8	6.3	6 871	5 791	8 595	-23.1	0.4	14 392	40.9	50.0	54.0
Pendleton	NA	NA	2 810	3.1	60.1	6.8	13.3	4 796	9 525	22 500	0.6	0.8	32 811	14.4	19.7	20.1
Perry	NA	NA	7 631	2.7	47.6	6.7	35.4	5 648	7 914	16 202	-19.7	1.0	23 768	27.4	36.7	34.2
Pike	NA	NA	18 222	5.6	50.2	7.7	79.3	6 358	8 674	17 468	-22.9	1.4	26 026	22.6	29.6	27.4
Powell	NA	NA	2 769	1.7	50.1	5.3	15.0	5 688	7 474	16 828	-9.8	0.6	24 233	22.6	31.1	29.9
Pulaski	NA	NA	11 064	4.3	56.2	9.2	47.6	5 065	9 209	18 198	3.4	1.5	25 448	18.8	27.6	25.3
Robertson	NA	NA	439	3.0	50.8	7.7	2.0	5 526	8 630	19 756	7.4	0.2	26 181	20.3	29.8	30.2
Rockcastle	NA	NA	3 335	2.2	44.9	5.9	16.5	5 567	7 630	14 967	0.8	0.4	22 915	23.1	32.1	31.5
Rowan	NA	NA	8 195	2.6	57.9	17.3	16.5	5 217	7 639	15 922	-10.1	1.0	25 553	23.0	28.1	28.1
Russell	NA	NA	2 956	4.4	50.2	6.2	15.3	5 347	8 967	16 788	15.8	1.4	22 997	22.1	33.3	31.2
Scott	NA	NA	6 629	19.8	69.1	15.2	30.0	5 884	12 314	27 563	7.9	2.5	42 465	11.6	16.2	15.8
Shelby	NA	NA	5 791	9.5	69.9	12.9	22.6	4 795	13 064	28 500	6.3	2.6	40 134	10.1	14.3	14.0
Simpson	NA	NA	3 369	5.6	58.9	8.8	15.1	5 249	10 635	21 793	-3.7	1.0	33 233	11.8	17.2	17.1
Spencer	NA	NA	1 635	6.1	57.5	9.9	9.3	5 340	10 502	22 680	-4.6	1.7	33 958	11.7	16.6	16.6
Taylor	NA	NA	4 965	15.7	57.4	10.1	19.9	5 037	9 848	21 083	-4.2	1.3	28 552	16.6	23.9	22.6
Todd	NA	NA	2 322	5.2	50.6	7.1	9.2	4 695	9 227	20 309	9.9	1.2	29 247	16.2	25.0	23.6
Trigg	NA	NA	2 056	1.3	58.9	11.4	9.1	4 824	10 124	19 860	-5.8	1.3	29 190	14.1	22.3	21.0
Trimble	NA	NA	1 360	6.0	61.6	7.3	6.8	5 039	10 128	22 372	-0.5	0.7	30 948	14.8	22.2	21.0
Union	NA	NA	4 295	14.3	68.1	8.9	15.5	5 746	11 080	23 798	-14.4	2.8	31 197	14.5	18.0	19.4
Warren	NA	NA	22 735	4.4	70.9	19.2	72.2	5 210	11 819	24 175	2.5	2.0	34 891	14.4	20.8	19.1
Washington	NA	NA	2 541	16.8	57.8	7.5	9.1	5 063	9 559	20 606	0.0	1.2	29 266	15.6	20.2	20.5
Wayne	NA	NA	3 901	1.6	44.6	5.5	19.9	5 557	6 550	12 560	-10.3	0.4	20 242	27.5	39.0	37.0
Webster	NA	NA	3 243	3.0	60.7	6.0	13.7	5 169	10 263	21 189	-2.1	0.9	30 325	14.6	21.1	18.9
Whitley	NA	NA	8 931	17.8	53.0	11.3	40.3	5 637	8 028	14 979	-9.0	1.2	21 553	27.9	38.2	36.7
Wolfe	NA	NA	1 711	7.8	42.8	7.7	8.6	6 270	5 998	11 000	-16.3	0.2	16 323	36.6	46.4	50.6
Woodford	NA	NA	4 975	15.5	73.5	19.5	17.7	4 614	14 151	32 858	13.1	2.9	45 269	8.1	12.1	11.5
LOUISIANA	780	5 318	1 185 759	17.4	68.3	16.1	3 748.0	4 724	10 635	21 949	-14.0	2.4	30 466	18.4	26.0	24.5
Acadia	361	2 809	15 299	17.7	54.6	8.4	44.1	3 873	7 952	16 022	-29.2	1.6	24 975	20.4	27.3	26.1
Allen	662	2 867	5 507	4.6	57.1	6.7	18.7	3 996	7 394	15 838	-22.6	0.6	24 755	22.8	26.8	26.2
Ascension	300	3 539	16 832	13.1	68.5	9.3	71.6	4 814	10 482	27 435	-14.7	1.5	39 248	12.1	16.6	15.9
Assumption	288	1 463	6 013	9.1	50.4	6.7	23.6	4 465	8 077	20 021	-19.7	1.5	29 993	18.3	25.5	24.1
Avoyelles	NA	NA	9 956	14.0	50.5	7.4	31.8	4 008	6 874	13 451	-19.5	1.0	21 449	25.4	32.8	31.3
Beauregard	175	2 055	7 533	4.1	70.6	13.0	29.6	4 570	10 096	22 442	-9.7	1.6	31 486	15.8	22.1	21.8
Bienville	NA	NA	3 780	5.1	62.6	9.3	15.4	4 723	8 194	16 043	-7.7	0.7	22 995	24.5	35.4	34.7
Bossier	805	4 347	23 528	8.5	78.9	15.5	86.2	4 521	11 317	26 058	-5.9	1.5	35 521	12.8	19.2	18.4
Caddo	981	7 382	68 907	10.8	73.4	18.2	233.3	4 706	11 604	22 395	-13.1	2.9	29 667	20.4	29.5	27.0
Calcasieu	718	6 558	47 034	12.1	70.3	14.7	161.7	4 519	11 233	24 375	-22.3	2.3	34 175	14.1	20.3	18.3
Caldwell	212	1 020	2 284	3.4	57.1	9.3	9.5	4 500	8 308	16 069	-6.0	1.6	23 563	19.9	27.8	28.2
Cameron	741	3 095	2 332	3.6	61.1	7.9	12.1	5 510	10 289	25 164	-18.6	1.8	36 665	11.2	14.3	16.2
Catahoula	NA	NA	2 818	3.1	53.9	8.7	10.6	4 554	7 862	14 956	-9.2	1.5	21 091	25.2	34.0	34.6
Claiborne	142	1 439	3 978	6.8	60.9	10.1	13.3	4 081	8 076	16 073	-12.2	0.7	23 676	25.8	34.5	33.3
Concordia	480	2 680	5 757	12.4	56.9	9.1	20.6	4 652	8 391	17 265	-15.4	1.3	23 271	24.5	34.5	32.8
De Soto	711	2 703	6 387	5.2	64.0	9.5	28.0	5 086	8 330	16 315	-15.1	1.0	24 767	22.5	31.8	30.4
East Baton Rouge	852	9 427	120 056	19.5	80.5	27.5	291.8	4 745	13 126	27 224	-10.0	3.8	35 644	16.0	23.2	21.1
East Carroll	NA	NA	2 841	10.8	49.1	10.3	9.4	4 570	6 059	9 791	-24.9	1.3	14 910	42.7	52.9	52.2
East Feliciana	2 014	2 463	4 919	16.9	58.2	8.9	13.0	4 212	7 746	20 139	-14.2	1.4	26 864	20.6	26.0	26.0
Evangeline	166	1 626	8 897	13.4	48.2	8.3	30.2	3 890	7 041	13 797	-18.1	0.9	22 310	25.6	33.5	33.0
Franklin	NA	NA	6 011	3.5	53.7	10.3	19.5	4 211	7 607	15 159	-5.6	1.6	20 339	27.3	37.8	36.0
Grant	546	2 781	4 399	5.6	62.8	9.6	16.1	4 274	8 330	17 711	-6.4	1.3	26 425	18.4	26.2	25.3
Iberia	332	2 797	18 628	12.6	59.3	9.0	71.2	4 357	9 466	20 838	-27.8	2.0	29 951	18.5	25.1	24.5
Iberville	NA	NA	8 383	20.7	59.0	8.9	30.9	5 526	9 449	20 371	-13.3	2.0	27 838	21.8	28.7	27.6
Jackson	282	1 140	4 109	4.4	63.9	9.2	14.0	4 764	9 960	18 804	1.7	1.3	26 631	17.6	27.6	23.9
Jefferson	765	6 139	119 881	35.9	76.0	18.8	281.2	5 033	12 845	27 916	-15.7	3.0	37 312	13.1	20.6	18.9
Jefferson Davis	814	4 007	8 274	7.1	59.9	8.0	28.6	4 429	8 486	18 467	-26.7	1.2	26 645	18.9	25.0	24.7
Lafayette	664	5 445	49 203	14.9	73.3	22.5	134.7	4 307	11 983	24 339	-21.9	3.4	35 554	13.8	18.4	18.4
Lafourche	408	3 089	24 080	12.7	56.2	10.0	78.2	4 575	9 250	21 416	-28.6	1.3	32 795	14.7	19.7	19.6
La Salle	447	752	3 277	2.7	61.0	7.9	12.0	4 122	9 015	18 597	-9.0	1.2	27 398	15.6	21.9	21.4
Lincoln	545	4 151	18 451	5.3	74.5	26.2	30.5	4 272	9 342	19 254	-9.4	2.4	28 038	21.5	27.3	27.1
Livingston	481	2 248	19 330	8.5	66.7	8.7	73.1	3 952	9 946	25 470	-12.1	1.0	35 875	11.9	17.0	15.8
Madison	NA	NA	3 789	7.5	53.3	9.2	12.5	3 541	6 723	12 792	-8.7	1.4	18 956	32.6	41.9	40.8
Morehouse	832	2 693	8 645	12.3	57.8	10.5	24.6	3 975	8 547	17 309	7.1	1.6	22 387	24.8	34.3	32.3
Natchitoches	793	5 186	12 336	7.2	65.0	16.4	35.4	4 589	8 112	15 778	-13.4	1.6	23 874	24.9	33.5	32.7
Orleans	1 467	7 255	146 515	28.9	68.1	22.4	387.7	4 557	11 372	18 477	-6.7	3.6	25 200	27.9	40.1	36.2
Ouachita	1 204	7 472	42 399	9.1	71.6	18.9	126.8	4 289	10 593	21 129	-9.2	2.3	28 651	19.8	29.1	27.2
Plaquemines	497	1 984	7 064	17.7	58.0	7.5	27.8	4 756	9 500	24 076	-18.5	1.1	31 908	15.6	21.0	21.2

1. Data for serious crimes have not been adjusted for underreporting; this may affect comparability between geographic areas and over time.   2. Per 100,000 population estimated by the FBI.   3. All persons 3 years old and over enrolled in nursery school through college.   4. Persons 25 years old and over.   5. Elementary and secondary education expenditures, local government fiscal years ending between July 1, 1996 and June 30, 1997.   6. Based on population enumerated as of April 1, 1990.

Table B. States and Counties — **Personal Income**

STATE County	Total (mil dol)	Percent change, 1997–1998	Per capita Dollars	Per capita Rank	Wages and salaries[2] (mil dol)	Proprietor's income (mil dol)	Dividends, interest, and rent (mil dol)	Transfer payments Total (mil dol)	Government payments to individuals Total (mil dol)	Social Security (mil dol)	Medical payments (mil dol)	Income mainte-nance (mil dol)	Unemploy-ment insurance (mil dol)
	62	63	64	65	66	67	68	69	70	71	72	73	74
KENTUCKY—Cont'd													
Owsley	69	3.2	12 754	3 071	15	5	7	36	35	7	17	9	0
Pendleton	246	4.4	17 921	2 371	69	19	37	41	38	17	14	5	0
Perry	530	3.9	17 115	2 584	347	30	74	172	166	52	67	30	2
Pike	1 291	3.2	17 931	2 368	754	83	192	356	343	130	124	49	4
Powell	184	4.2	14 262	2 988	70	16	17	48	46	17	17	8	1
Pulaski	1 029	5.3	18 270	2 276	596	79	156	254	243	92	103	30	4
Robertson	35	3.0	15 649	2 859	7	4	4	9	9	3	4	1	0
Rockcastle	239	4.2	14 998	2 928	79	12	27	68	65	20	30	11	1
Rowan	337	4.9	15 215	2 912	218	22	51	75	71	25	26	10	1
Russell	259	0.1	16 004	2 795	110	33	37	87	84	27	33	11	8
Scott	785	7.2	25 503	440	1 058	89	99	78	73	31	27	8	1
Shelby	769	7.7	25 960	403	392	51	124	88	82	39	31	6	1
Simpson	309	2.1	18 741	2 144	221	19	60	54	51	22	21	5	1
Spencer	166	8.1	17 130	2 578	34	11	22	28	26	11	11	3	0
Taylor	391	-3.0	17 017	2 609	217	30	67	108	104	39	40	11	9
Todd	212	1.5	18 844	2 112	81	33	33	41	39	16	17	4	1
Trigg	207	0.5	16 715	2 675	89	7	42	49	46	23	17	4	1
Trimble	122	3.7	15 877	2 813	26	9	15	25	24	10	10	2	1
Union	298	-0.8	18 031	2 338	182	30	57	61	58	26	24	4	1
Warren	2 014	2.8	23 066	845	1 426	115	337	300	284	110	119	28	4
Washington	222	7.8	20 423	1 587	82	28	32	41	39	16	16	5	1
Wayne	287	5.8	15 065	2 926	117	35	41	89	86	26	37	17	2
Webster	249	1.5	18 422	2 233	141	14	49	53	51	25	17	5	1
Whitley	556	3.6	15 507	2 877	319	33	87	191	184	54	75	29	2
Wolfe	98	3.9	13 259	3 057	31	9	10	42	40	11	18	10	0
Woodford	692	8.0	30 458	154	330	146	106	58	53	28	16	4	1
LOUISIANA	96 878	4.7	22 206	X	60 057	7 669	16 014	16 965	16 216	5 490	7 615	2 130	146
Acadia	1 003	3.8	17 352	2 517	372	66	166	246	236	74	118	33	2
Allen	383	5.8	15 833	2 819	202	31	47	94	90	31	43	11	1
Ascension	1 672	8.7	23 326	786	1 190	141	185	206	193	70	93	21	2
Assumption	434	4.1	18 852	2 108	167	23	66	89	85	29	40	12	1
Avoyelles	656	2.3	16 091	2 783	239	48	99	190	183	52	93	31	1
Beauregard	574	3.1	17 935	2 367	259	42	82	111	106	39	47	12	1
Bienville	270	3.0	17 102	2 587	100	16	45	80	77	24	38	11	1
Bossier	2 098	7.3	22 726	913	1 242	129	300	301	286	101	131	27	3
Caddo	5 730	3.3	23 630	714	3 869	462	1 128	991	949	349	410	124	9
Calcasieu	3 988	3.7	22 139	1 054	2 759	260	655	664	633	249	283	57	7
Caldwell	168	0.0	16 196	2 763	62	14	27	54	52	13	30	6	0
Cameron	195	14.7	21 615	1 215	155	13	30	26	25	10	11	2	0
Catahoula	170	1.2	15 396	2 890	56	20	24	52	51	16	24	8	1
Claiborne	285	2.9	16 727	2 671	109	27	59	76	73	25	34	11	1
Concordia	335	-1.8	16 130	2 776	125	27	54	91	88	30	39	15	1
De Soto	500	4.5	20 012	1 707	192	58	71	104	100	36	42	17	1
East Baton Rouge	10 075	5.4	25 592	430	7 784	499	1 880	1 276	1 208	433	530	144	11
East Carroll	132	-2.4	14 872	2 947	55	10	18	52	50	10	27	12	0
East Feliciana	391	6.2	18 646	2 171	131	38	53	88	84	21	49	9	1
Evangeline	553	1.3	16 191	2 764	199	40	85	180	174	48	90	31	1
Franklin	334	-1.9	15 112	2 921	123	25	49	112	108	28	59	17	1
Grant	305	3.6	16 109	2 780	74	16	41	76	72	23	35	10	1
Iberia	1 501	5.8	20 574	1 536	950	82	260	256	244	92	107	34	3
Iberville	633	5.5	20 118	1 675	627	32	97	130	125	38	63	19	1
Jackson	288	1.9	18 574	2 189	122	22	54	79	77	27	37	9	0
Jefferson	11 805	4.3	26 251	370	6 763	970	2 095	1 608	1 531	619	679	146	13
Jefferson Davis	510	4.6	16 155	2 772	179	38	95	127	122	44	53	19	1
Lafayette	4 822	6.2	25 903	406	3 930	368	833	545	513	190	228	49	5
Lafourche	1 889	7.8	21 226	1 319	913	105	321	309	293	117	129	34	2
La Salle	232	2.7	16 950	2 624	98	18	37	68	66	22	30	10	0
Lincoln	802	4.5	19 492	1 894	518	55	133	157	150	41	66	15	1
Livingston	1 783	9.8	20 194	1 654	355	127	165	247	232	90	108	22	3
Madison	187	-0.8	14 480	2 971	86	8	24	60	58	14	28	13	1
Morehouse	528	0.1	16 772	2 662	243	24	81	161	155	48	76	24	2
Natchitoches	653	2.4	17 642	2 454	327	79	105	145	139	42	61	25	1
Orleans	11 819	3.2	25 439	446	9 915	1 810	2 083	2 257	2 178	606	1 041	402	15
Ouachita	3 117	3.5	21 230	1 316	1 967	316	532	548	522	176	234	71	5
Plaquemines	596	6.3	22 767	899	790	59	88	128	124	30	72	19	1

1. Based on the resident population estimated as of July 1 of the year shown.   2. Includes other labor income.

Table B. States and Counties — Earnings, Social Security, and Housing

STATE County	Earnings, 1998									Social Security beneficiaries, December 1998			Housing units, 1990	
	Total (mil dol)	Farm	Goods-related[1]		Service-related and other[2]				Government	Number	Rate[3]	Supplemental Security Income recipients, December 1998	Total	Percent change, 1980–1990
			Total	Manufacturing	Total	Retail trade	Finance, insurance, and real estate	Services						
	75	76	77	78	79	80	81	82	83	84	85	86	87	88
KENTUCKY—Cont'd														
Owsley	20	6.4	D	D	D	9.1	D	22.6	43.1	1 193	221	1 047	2 137	4.8
Pendleton	88	4.4	D	15.0	D	7.0	3.5	D	21.3	2 225	162	396	4 782	14.1
Perry	376	0.0	D	4.9	D	12.3	3.2	28.2	19.3	7 055	227	3 037	11 565	2.6
Pike	836	0.0	34.2	2.7	51.8	11.9	3.5	23.9	14.0	16 622	230	4 897	28 760	2.0
Powell	86	1.2	D	29.6	D	10.8	2.7	12.2	24.9	2 488	192	909	4 458	16.6
Pulaski	674	1.9	D	19.6	D	12.6	4.2	23.6	16.4	12 658	225	3 836	22 328	14.3
Robertson	11	18.9	D	D	D	7.2	D	14.4	29.7	425	192	115	955	5.6
Rockcastle	91	2.3	D	17.4	D	9.6	D	28.8	24.2	3 128	196	1 231	5 958	18.3
Rowan	239	0.8	D	10.9	D	11.6	2.8	26.7	35.8	3 410	154	1 082	7 375	10.9
Russell	143	5.7	28.7	20.8	43.7	14.9	3.2	14.4	21.9	4 121	254	1 456	7 375	16.2
Scott	1 147	5.4	D	68.5	D	3.5	0.8	8.2	4.3	4 026	131	788	9 173	17.9
Shelby	443	4.0	48.0	42.5	37.9	8.1	3.3	18.5	10.1	4 742	160	678	9 617	11.5
Simpson	241	0.4	D	55.9	D	11.6	2.3	10.0	10.7	2 909	177	482	6 172	8.0
Spencer	44	10.8	20.9	5.8	40.6	9.8	4.4	17.7	27.7	1 507	156	242	2 640	21.1
Taylor	247	1.4	D	28.0	D	12.7	4.8	17.7	18.2	5 237	228	1 372	8 798	7.1
Todd	114	20.1	D	33.8	D	5.7	2.1	8.7	12.5	2 229	199	460	4 415	-3.5
Trigg	95	1.3	D	37.2	D	7.9	3.2	11.8	25.2	2 949	238	405	5 284	20.7
Trimble	35	9.4	D	5.4	D	6.1	4.4	13.4	25.1	1 318	173	219	2 510	3.4
Union	212	2.0	D	13.7	D	8.1	2.3	17.9	10.5	3 017	182	347	6 091	7.4
Warren	1 542	0.5	33.1	25.0	50.8	13.0	5.6	22.7	15.7	13 835	158	2 761	31 065	16.4
Washington	110	12.5	D	32.5	D	6.5	3.2	11.6	12.7	2 292	210	532	4 009	6.7
Wayne	153	15.8	D	29.0	D	10.1	3.1	13.8	18.7	4 197	220	1 982	7 791	8.7
Webster	155	2.0	51.3	14.6	33.7	6.6	3.1	8.4	13.0	3 011	223	446	5 914	2.1
Whitley	351	-0.3	20.4	13.8	63.4	11.1	4.7	28.5	16.5	7 561	210	3 035	13 399	8.2
Wolfe	40	4.5	D	20.8	D	13.0	1.6	15.8	32.5	1 690	229	1 246	2 779	8.1
Woodford	476	25.5	D	33.3	D	4.3	2.5	11.7	5.7	3 319	145	333	7 689	20.0
LOUISIANA	67 725	0.6	26.4	13.6	54.3	9.0	5.4	26.3	18.7	701 704	161	174 456	1 716 241	10.8
Acadia	438	4.2	25.8	11.9	51.2	10.5	3.7	22.9	18.8	10 677	185	3 142	21 441	11.3
Allen	234	2.3	D	8.8	D	7.0	D	39.6	32.6	4 219	177	973	8 275	5.5
Ascension	1 331	0.3	57.6	32.3	33.2	7.8	2.4	12.1	8.9	8 676	121	1 681	21 165	27.3
Assumption	190	4.1	53.8	47.9	26.4	6.3	2.6	12.0	15.7	3 863	168	1 113	8 644	14.4
Avoyelles	287	0.0	D	8.8	D	10.8	4.5	33.0	25.4	8 100	198	3 090	15 428	4.8
Beauregard	301	0.5	41.4	31.8	41.4	10.4	6.8	14.8	16.7	5 155	161	1 040	12 666	10.8
Bienville	115	2.3	39.8	30.2	38.8	8.3	2.4	14.4	19.1	3 354	212	943	7 085	1.9
Bossier	1 371	-0.2	16.2	6.4	45.2	10.8	3.0	25.5	38.7	12 921	138	2 137	34 994	21.2
Caddo	4 331	0.0	25.1	15.5	55.5	8.5	4.7	28.2	19.4	42 834	177	10 072	107 615	10.3
Calcasieu	3 019	0.1	39.5	24.3	47.1	7.9	3.2	24.7	13.2	29 737	165	4 977	66 426	9.2
Caldwell	76	-1.5	19.2	12.8	58.0	12.5	3.6	29.0	24.3	1 873	181	485	4 533	-2.0
Cameron	168	0.9	26.7	11.9	56.6	3.3	0.5	6.1	15.8	1 324	146	139	5 031	12.1
Catahoula	75	12.2	D	7.6	D	10.8	4.9	15.2	25.0	2 342	212	733	5 138	5.3
Claiborne	136	8.7	28.0	17.2	D	9.6	2.6	10.1	31.6	3 375	199	863	7 513	6.7
Concordia	145	2.3	D	12.4	D	13.2	4.9	20.8	28.9	3 934	190	1 207	9 043	1.4
De Soto	250	3.6	50.8	24.1	29.2	6.7	2.9	10.7	16.4	4 882	196	1 363	10 919	9.5
East Baton Rouge	8 283	0.0	23.0	10.2	57.1	9.0	8.3	28.0	19.9	51 902	131	10 662	156 767	17.3
East Carroll	65	15.1	13.9	9.9	38.3	5.5	2.5	11.5	32.8	1 676	188	884	3 563	-13.3
East Feliciana	170	1.5	19.1	14.2	28.2	4.6	3.2	14.3	51.2	2 998	144	924	6 476	10.5
Evangeline	240	6.2	24.6	19.9	49.5	9.6	3.4	28.4	19.8	7 177	210	3 242	13 311	8.1
Franklin	148	9.0	D	8.9	D	16.4	4.9	19.4	25.7	4 171	188	1 489	8 719	-1.9
Grant	90	-1.6	D	29.4	D	6.6	2.4	12.5	32.6	3 335	176	787	7 494	10.5
Iberia	1 032	1.1	42.4	20.0	43.7	8.4	3.3	18.5	12.8	11 989	164	3 015	25 472	19.7
Iberville	659	1.0	D	49.0	D	3.9	1.4	9.8	15.0	5 102	164	1 559	11 352	3.4
Jackson	144	5.3	D	D	D	7.0	2.8	12.3	19.0	3 390	218	671	7 041	2.3
Jefferson	7 732	0.0	19.7	9.6	69.2	12.0	7.4	31.4	11.1	71 182	158	13 047	185 072	11.4
Jefferson Davis	217	7.4	19.1	10.6	52.3	14.4	4.4	19.3	21.2	5 867	186	1 264	11 963	8.4
Lafayette	4 298	0.1	33.4	7.4	56.3	9.8	4.0	27.7	10.3	24 098	129	523	67 431	26.9
Lafourche	1 017	0.6	23.8	14.6	54.9	8.2	2.8	18.1	20.6	14 710	165	4 901	31 332	15.9
La Salle	116	0.2	38.9	21.0	37.3	11.2	2.9	14.1	23.5	2 963	217	2 658	5 969	-9.7
Lincoln	572	1.7	29.6	16.2	40.8	8.8	5.7	17.8	27.9	5 528	133	1 251	15 286	14.5
Livingston	481	0.4	32.0	14.7	46.2	12.7	4.7	17.0	21.5	11 122	126	1 719	26 848	26.7
Madison	94	6.8	9.0	6.6	53.3	9.9	2.7	30.7	31.0	2 165	169	884	4 823	-19.9
Morehouse	267	3.0	D	23.7	D	10.9	3.1	20.9	16.4	6 238	198	2 116	12 314	-4.0
Natchitoches	406	2.8	D	22.0	D	9.8	3.5	17.1	28.1	6 108	165	2 139	15 210	2.1
Orleans	11 725	0.0	14.8	5.3	64.2	6.5	7.4	37.8	21.0	78 582	169	28 662	225 573	-0.4
Ouachita	2 284	0.3	22.4	16.7	61.2	10.5	8.2	25.6	16.1	21 956	149	5 209	56 300	9.4
Plaquemines	849	0.3	46.4	19.3	37.7	4.0	1.3	11.1	15.6	3 663	139	891	9 432	-1.2

1. Covers mining, construction, and manufacturing. 2. Covers private sector earnings in agricultural services, forestry, and fisheries; transportation and public utilities; wholesale trade; retail trade; finance, insurance, and real estate; and services. 3. Per 1,000 resident population estimated as of July 1 of the year shown.

Table B. States and Counties — Housing, Labor Force, and Employment

STATE County	Total	Percent	Median value[1]	With a mortgage	Without a mortgage	Median rent[2]	Rent as percent of income	Substandard units[3] (percent)	Total	Percent change, 1998–1999	Total	Rate[4]	Total	Professional, managerial, and technical	Precision production, craft, and repair
	89	90	91	92	93	94	95	96	97	98	99	100	101	102	103
KENTUCKY—Cont'd															
Owsley	1 848	74.7	24 400	27.9	14.9	140	31.5	18.0	1 741	0.8	93	5.3	1 176	24.9	13.3
Pendleton	4 332	75.1	43 700	21.3	13.2	274	24.5	6.9	6 665	0.3	257	3.9	5 190	15.2	14.5
Perry	10 598	75.0	34 800	20.0	12.5	231	24.8	10.6	11 886	0.2	922	7.8	9 198	20.4	16.6
Pike	26 148	76.9	41 300	21.6	12.2	301	26.8	4.6	27 634	1.1	2 094	7.6	22 398	21.1	21.3
Powell	4 057	76.8	37 400	22.2	12.4	260	27.0	10.9	6 533	-1.7	374	5.7	4 127	14.6	21.3
Pulaski	18 866	75.7	44 600	19.1	11.9	263	24.6	4.7	25 977	0.1	1 244	4.8	20 185	20.0	13.1
Robertson	820	72.7	33 700	17.8	11.6	161	21.1	12.3	1 058	7.7	51	4.8	834	15.3	9.8
Rockcastle	5 464	78.2	31 100	22.1	13.4	197	24.9	11.6	6 282	3.6	337	5.4	5 180	14.2	14.7
Rowan	6 755	66.7	44 400	18.7	13.4	250	26.4	6.2	9 476	2.9	357	3.8	8 102	28.2	8.4
Russell	5 896	80.6	38 900	19.0	13.0	228	24.2	5.0	5 930	-5.3	701	11.8	6 336	15.3	13.0
Scott	8 501	66.2	68 500	18.3	12.0	338	24.6	4.1	17 654	6.6	354	2.0	11 881	23.3	12.4
Shelby	9 048	71.1	58 600	19.7	11.9	301	23.7	4.3	18 029	7.7	429	2.4	12 565	23.6	10.9
Simpson	5 767	70.4	46 300	21.2	12.2	314	23.2	3.5	8 365	6.8	269	3.2	7 056	15.3	13.5
Spencer	2 451	74.4	49 300	20.5	12.1	282	23.9	3.9	5 145	8.3	177	3.4	3 116	17.8	13.6
Taylor	8 216	72.3	41 500	16.5	12.4	273	25.6	4.3	9 789	-14.4	1 526	15.6	9 954	16.1	12.8
Todd	4 104	75.8	34 100	20.3	12.9	247	25.3	6.2	5 379	1.2	161	3.0	4 702	12.4	11.6
Trigg	4 104	79.4	44 300	18.2	13.3	244	25.4	3.8	5 959	3.9	181	3.0	4 420	19.8	12.3
Trimble	2 246	81.5	43 800	19.9	11.9	268	23.9	6.5	3 173	4.2	89	2.8	2 611	15.7	18.7
Union	5 580	76.5	38 700	17.3	12.5	280	22.0	2.4	6 146	7.5	385	6.3	6 310	18.1	18.8
Warren	28 819	65.0	57 600	18.6	12.2	337	27.1	2.6	50 096	1.8	1 669	3.3	37 117	26.6	10.8
Washington	3 709	78.9	40 700	17.2	11.6	216	23.4	9.4	5 784	-4.7	224	3.9	4 504	15.1	12.9
Wayne	6 517	76.0	30 200	21.8	12.9	216	28.3	12.7	8 030	0.2	534	6.7	6 184	15.1	13.6
Webster	5 372	78.0	29 000	16.2	13.5	253	22.3	5.2	5 538	-1.0	387	7.0	5 340	15.6	20.2
Whitley	12 153	70.8	36 600	21.2	12.4	270	31.8	9.6	14 557	4.4	848	5.8	11 121	23.0	13.8
Wolfe	2 451	74.4	28 200	30.3	14.6	162	31.4	15.6	3 236	-3.2	166	5.1	1 868	19.5	13.8
Woodford	7 223	71.1	73 800	18.2	12.7	369	23.1	2.9	13 834	4.7	220	1.6	10 506	27.3	10.3
LOUISIANA	1 499 269	65.9	58 500	20.6	13.3	352	27.9	6.5	2 051 621	-0.6	103 966	5.1	1 641 614	28.1	12.5
Acadia	19 285	71.3	40 600	21.8	13.9	246	30.5	8.5	24 090	-1.7	1 873	7.8	18 641	19.8	17.5
Allen	7 080	77.7	35 400	22.4	13.5	232	31.7	6.5	9 992	8.6	654	6.5	6 302	19.3	14.7
Ascension	19 337	78.3	61 000	17.0	12.3	325	25.0	5.7	35 218	3.9	1 639	4.7	23 556	21.7	20.4
Assumption	7 397	82.5	45 200	20.5	13.0	276	31.3	10.3	9 184	-10.5	696	7.6	7 905	16.7	19.3
Avoyelles	13 480	74.8	34 900	23.9	14.1	215	29.4	7.4	16 129	-1.8	1 002	6.2	11 863	21.2	14.8
Beauregard	10 362	76.9	45 100	17.2	12.6	324	24.8	5.1	12 831	3.2	849	6.6	10 485	27.9	15.6
Bienville	5 852	78.6	33 600	20.1	15.1	235	25.4	10.0	5 556	-3.0	388	7.0	5 092	18.8	13.4
Bossier	30 718	66.7	61 000	20.5	12.5	378	25.6	5.6	46 949	0.1	2 146	4.6	35 082	28.1	12.0
Caddo	93 248	64.4	55 500	20.7	13.4	348	28.2	5.5	119 046	-2.0	5 440	4.6	98 879	29.4	10.6
Calcasieu	60 328	70.4	54 700	17.6	12.8	338	26.3	4.5	92 266	0.1	4 481	4.9	67 327	26.2	17.1
Caldwell	3 575	80.2	34 900	22.8	13.2	238	28.7	5.8	4 359	3.4	385	8.8	3 328	19.4	13.3
Cameron	3 153	85.1	44 500	19.2	12.8	275	18.7	8.2	4 033	-5.8	192	4.8	3 688	20.6	18.0
Catahoula	3 927	81.5	31 600	22.7	15.3	211	30.5	8.8	5 069	1.4	511	10.1	3 619	19.3	12.5
Claiborne	6 065	75.4	35 800	22.5	14.2	224	26.9	7.9	5 850	-4.4	464	7.9	5 390	22.4	14.0
Concordia	7 341	74.7	39 600	20.0	14.6	262	31.7	8.3	8 445	-3.3	1 128	13.4	6 931	22.0	14.0
De Soto	9 129	76.3	39 400	20.4	14.8	246	30.6	9.5	11 558	5.0	720	6.2	8 533	19.0	15.4
East Baton Rouge	138 620	60.0	69 200	18.3	12.4	375	26.7	4.7	215 588	1.5	7 804	3.6	172 715	35.7	10.1
East Carroll	3 129	61.5	30 700	31.2	16.9	183	35.1	10.7	3 143	-2.6	426	13.6	2 471	22.0	8.4
East Feliciana	5 589	79.9	46 700	23.5	12.5	272	26.5	10.5	7 803	2.5	386	4.9	6 234	21.7	12.7
Evangeline	11 795	69.5	32 700	23.6	14.7	224	32.2	9.3	12 316	-0.9	716	5.8	9 717	22.9	15.1
Franklin	7 776	75.6	34 100	22.1	13.8	235	29.0	7.8	10 024	0.6	830	8.3	7 359	20.8	13.5
Grant	6 261	80.7	39 400	21.4	13.8	285	28.5	6.1	7 156	8.8	498	7.0	6 117	21.7	14.1
Iberia	22 847	71.0	49 700	19.2	13.3	291	26.4	8.8	33 344	-4.6	2 706	8.1	25 256	19.8	17.6
Iberville	9 875	74.8	50 800	19.1	14.8	280	30.8	9.0	13 412	4.9	887	6.6	10 807	20.4	14.9
Jackson	5 817	77.7	37 900	19.5	13.5	228	27.4	6.2	5 913	-3.5	322	5.4	5 280	20.8	16.3
Jefferson	166 398	62.9	71 500	20.8	12.4	419	26.0	4.7	233 945	-0.9	8 812	3.8	207 479	30.4	11.1
Jefferson Davis	10 669	74.7	40 700	20.5	14.5	268	27.0	5.7	11 766	-4.0	826	7.0	10 361	21.1	16.8
Lafayette	60 411	61.3	62 700	18.5	13.1	329	24.3	5.4	98 738	-2.0	4 311	4.4	72 243	32.6	11.0
Lafourche	28 835	75.7	52 300	19.4	12.3	285	24.7	7.6	42 889	-3.5	1 657	3.9	32 168	22.0	19.0
La Salle	5 086	82.1	34 300	21.1	14.2	272	22.6	5.0	5 465	-0.4	423	7.7	4 953	21.9	15.6
Lincoln	13 669	62.1	56 200	20.1	12.9	326	33.6	4.4	19 779	4.4	483	2.4	15 759	32.6	8.0
Livingston	23 814	82.2	56 900	18.8	12.9	353	25.9	6.2	43 907	4.8	2 252	5.1	28 780	22.0	21.5
Madison	4 252	64.3	30 100	24.6	16.7	224	32.0	10.6	5 592	0.0	464	8.3	3 791	18.6	10.6
Morehouse	10 961	73.8	36 100	20.6	14.0	278	31.2	8.1	12 278	-3.2	1 315	10.7	10 348	21.1	13.2
Natchitoches	12 644	67.0	46 600	23.6	15.0	300	35.1	6.7	18 104	2.9	959	5.3	12 617	25.4	12.9
Orleans	188 235	43.7	69 600	23.2	14.2	379	31.2	8.5	198 011	-2.3	10 003	5.1	186 036	34.1	7.0
Ouachita	50 518	64.8	52 800	21.0	13.2	334	28.0	6.3	71 523	0.6	2 790	3.9	58 100	29.7	11.0
Plaquemines	8 213	75.9	62 200	20.5	13.2	396	23.6	9.0	10 782	1.3	557	5.2	9 219	22.5	16.7

1. Specified owner-occupied units. 2. Specified renter-occupied units. 3. Overcrowded or lacking complete plumbing facilities. 4. Percent of civilian labor force. 5. Persons 16 years and older.

STATE County	Number of establishments	Total	Health Care and Social Assistance	Manufacturing	Retail trade	Finance and Insurance	Professional Scientific and Technical Services	Total (mil dol)	Average per employee (dollars)	Number	Less than 50 acres	500 acres and over	Whose principal occupation is farming (percent)
	104	105	106	107	108	109	110	111	112	113	114	115	116
KENTUCKY—Cont'd													
Owsley	42	269	139	D	86	D	D	4	14 323	246	38.2	3.7	41.1
Pendleton	201	1 689	182	590	313	81	29	35	20 864	816	24.9	4.3	37.1
Perry	750	9 581	2 021	759	1 880	259	241	234	24 420	29	41.4	20.7	34.5
Pike	1 540	18 713	3 002	705	4 265	729	623	468	24 992	37	10.8	8.1	27.0
Powell	173	2 536	193	1 306	439	57	12	38	15 009	231	35.1	3.9	32.0
Pulaski	1 421	19 911	3 137	4 772	3 701	774	922	404	20 272	1 958	39.1	2.2	42.4
Robertson	31	164	D	D	D	D	D	2	11 396	272	18.8	5.5	48.5
Rockcastle	209	2 622	580	672	379	51	48	43	16 452	771	39.4	3.9	40.2
Rowan	451	6 090	1 463	1 047	1 303	159	72	106	17 433	413	44.3	2.2	32.7
Russell	343	3 860	384	1 045	833	117	51	66	17 121	943	46.7	2.3	38.8
Scott	651	18 734	922	9 911	1 777	203	213	723	38 613	851	35.5	8.2	49.9
Shelby	707	10 802	929	4 433	1 600	308	179	273	25 297	1 399	38.7	4.6	43.0
Simpson	384	7 437	455	3 293	870	142	65	183	24 548	582	35.2	8.2	47.6
Spencer	160	804	153	42	176	D	28	14	17 419	592	36.0	3.9	39.7
Taylor	666	8 250	1 011	2 639	1 572	241	92	152	18 425	971	39.8	2.6	40.3
Todd	218	2 401	175	1 289	250	85	D	44	18 390	679	21.2	15.3	49.9
Trigg	247	2 477	242	1 078	312	80	49	53	21 388	411	28.2	13.4	40.4
Trimble	74	456	111	D	74	45	D	11	24 967	526	35.7	2.3	37.3
Union	311	5 929	1 160	864	819	120	52	181	30 607	352	23.3	31.2	59.7
Warren	2 495	40 955	6 254	7 623	7 258	1 523	1 006	994	24 273	1 819	41.9	5.5	38.3
Washington	212	2 435	242	784	367	66	33	46	18 994	1 050	26.2	3.4	42.4
Wayne	299	4 048	403	1 699	677	137	49	70	17 194	803	36.6	6.7	44.8
Webster	260	3 141	221	857	449	146	D	82	26 136	455	25.3	14.9	46.4
Whitley	811	13 185	2 484	2 219	1 819	459	247	253	19 222	368	31.5	2.2	25.3
Wolfe	80	724	216	157	167	D	8	9	12 977	382	31.7	6.8	34.0
Woodford	496	8 136	538	3 701	1 182	198	243	217	26 656	678	36.9	8.8	51.2
LOUISIANA	100 667	1 577 220	234 869	171 549	226 586	68 110	74 826	40 802	25 870	23 823	34.1	17.3	47.4
Acadia	979	12 220	1 524	2 385	2 229	439	268	238	19 517	638	34.5	29.0	57.5
Allen	367	3 318	547	568	774	179	D	61	18 296	343	36.2	17.5	39.1
Ascension	1 462	23 839	2 101	5 507	3 989	594	463	722	30 288	279	53.8	8.6	37.6
Assumption	260	2 377	348	441	602	139	D	44	18 577	102	36.3	44.1	64.7
Avoyelles	729	8 195	2 038	575	1 508	375	134	131	16 044	827	31.9	17.9	48.7
Beauregard	607	6 813	1 084	1 271	1 364	543	241	170	24 901	676	32.8	10.7	38.5
Bienville	265	2 864	412	997	408	115	D	63	21 832	221	25.3	7.2	35.7
Bossier	1 883	29 730	3 319	2 771	4 994	815	620	605	20 334	372	35.2	18.8	39.5
Caddo	6 345	106 029	20 172	13 221	14 137	3 738	4 149	2 724	25 694	473	33.8	17.3	36.8
Calcasieu	4 285	71 390	10 410	11 154	10 766	2 033	2 878	1 825	25 560	749	35.6	17.5	34.6
Caldwell	208	1 832	602	64	280	117	D	34	18 785	217	28.6	14.7	45.2
Cameron	182	2 050	199	140	215	32	114	58	28 116	384	23.4	22.9	40.9
Catahoula	198	1 910	228	391	550	77	D	28	14 881	381	22.0	31.0	52.8
Claiborne	286	2 922	428	523	514	87	56	55	18 889	261	23.0	10.3	44.1
Concordia	354	3 521	715	70	770	179	85	65	18 430	292	17.5	50.7	72.6
De Soto	375	4 358	432	1 215	746	193	87	108	24 792	516	26.0	15.7	36.0
East Baton Rouge	11 459	204 953	28 516	12 327	27 502	12 053	14 092	5 579	27 222	441	44.4	7.5	31.5
East Carroll	148	946	161	D	251	51	80	18	18 752	244	15.6	50.8	79.1
East Feliciana	253	3 500	1 807	260	377	129	67	75	21 305	386	29.5	14.2	36.5
Evangeline	555	6 114	2 022	1 029	1 060	394	153	119	19 421	588	35.9	17.7	46.4
Franklin	429	4 296	1 065	371	1 019	198	420	65	15 118	732	24.7	21.7	59.3
Grant	200	1 639	173	486	205	D	D	32	19 361	186	32.8	13.4	36.6
Iberia	1 636	28 258	2 981	4 050	3 642	775	1 044	735	26 005	298	47.0	22.1	51.3
Iberville	558	10 643	897	4 263	1 090	248	171	405	38 025	161	21.1	35.4	55.9
Jackson	261	2 958	528	D	473	137	54	79	26 679	183	43.7	1.6	40.4
Jefferson	12 796	211 331	27 720	17 089	32 443	9 630	11 031	5 488	25 970	62	54.8	0.0	21.0
Jefferson Davis	602	6 105	889	705	1 440	332	143	109	17 776	576	26.2	34.9	55.4
Lafayette	6 575	99 052	13 449	5 790	14 221	3 106	6 933	2 644	26 693	577	62.4	7.3	40.4
Lafourche	1 798	24 658	3 148	2 788	3 995	974	1 483	602	24 422	398	33.7	17.6	42.7
La Salle	305	3 029	627	514	498	162	57	59	19 454	160	41.9	5.0	25.6
Lincoln	907	13 884	2 273	1 819	2 178	703	312	293	21 095	287	27.9	3.8	38.7
Livingston	1 220	10 819	1 042	1 339	2 273	320	341	208	19 200	345	58.3	2.3	38.0
Madison	225	2 299	779	85	464	62	76	35	15 077	279	11.5	53.4	72.4
Morehouse	543	6 455	1 574	1 257	1 081	209	93	155	24 014	402	18.2	40.3	61.2
Natchitoches	755	9 121	1 106	2 294	1 624	314	280	179	19 619	530	23.2	17.5	45.3
Orleans	10 762	211 827	32 922	10 018	20 096	12 179	13 008	6 071	28 661	10	100.0	0.0	50.0
Ouachita	4 067	61 306	10 387	8 075	9 299	5 234	3 335	1 482	24 168	377	37.9	11.9	42.4
Plaquemines	755	13 428	412	2 374	632	133	630	430	32 008	127	64.6	9.4	45.7

STATE County	Acreage (1,000) [117]	Percent change, 1992–1997 [118]	Average size of farm [119]	Total irrigated (1,000) [120]	Total cropland (1,000) [121]	Average per farm ($1,000) [122]	Average per acre (dollars) [123]	Value of machinery and equipment Average per farm ($1,000) [124]	Total (mil dol) [125]	Average per farm (dollars) [126]	Crops [127]	Livestock and poultry products [128]	$10,000 or more [129]	$100,000 or more [130]	Percent of land owned by Fed. Gov. 1997 [131]	Water consumption 1995 (mil gal/day) [132]
KENTUCKY—Cont'd																
Owsley	32	-11.8	129	0	9	109	1 133	26	3	11 845	92.5	7.5	32.5	0.4	13.0	0.4
Pendleton	117	-8.1	143	1	67	182	1 338	32	15	18 129	72.8	27.2	36.0	3.2	0.0	1.5
Perry	7	69.6	234	D	3	238	1 016	37	0	15 752	51.4	48.6	37.9	3.4	1.8	6.1
Pike	6	-2.5	158	D	1	143	907	19	0	4 756	31.2	68.8	24.3	0.0	2.9	8.2
Powell	28	-13.7	123	0	12	130	982	24	3	11 071	70.6	29.4	30.7	1.7	12.2	0.4
Pulaski	215	-1.4	110	0	138	166	1 478	27	36	18 362	45.1	54.9	39.7	3.7	11.9	390.3
Robertson	48	-9.7	176	0	26	139	711	27	7	24 550	75.8	24.2	52.6	4.0	0.0	0.2
Rockcastle	94	0.7	121	D	45	130	1 138	23	10	13 512	58.6	41.4	35.7	1.7	7.2	1.5
Rowan	42	-15.1	103	0	21	129	1 179	20	4	10 727	75.6	24.4	27.4	0.7	32.7	3.5
Russell	95	4.2	101	0	64	152	1 606	20	28	29 634	32.9	67.1	43.3	6.2	9.4	3.0
Scott	146	-5.3	171	3	100	392	2 287	38	65	76 948	40.5	59.5	56.3	12.3	0.0	3.4
Shelby	199	-13.6	142	2	140	353	2 538	39	56	40 146	59.2	40.8	55.7	9.3	0.0	4.7
Simpson	115	-2.6	198	0	98	348	1 720	47	32	55 166	77.1	22.9	51.5	13.6	0.0	2.0
Spencer	81	-13.8	137	1	56	260	1 825	33	20	33 779	60.2	39.8	53.5	7.4	8.2	1.2
Taylor	112	-12.9	116	0	73	149	1 384	29	24	25 188	47.7	52.3	46.1	5.1	6.7	6.1
Todd	190	15.1	280	0	144	378	1 409	53	70	102 631	59.5	40.5	58.3	21.5	0.0	1.9
Trigg	117	4.4	285	0	81	369	1 293	74	27	64 563	67.4	32.6	49.1	10.7	8.0	2.2
Trimble	64	-9.7	122	1	34	171	1 358	24	11	20 555	83.5	16.5	50.0	2.7	0.0	0.7
Union	212	7.4	601	2	185	881	1 482	110	59	166 542	81.9	18.1	65.6	33.0	2.5	7.3
Warren	255	0.7	140	0	171	242	1 808	34	65	35 867	37.8	62.2	37.9	5.9	0.0	16.5
Washington	157	-4.6	150	1	107	185	1 242	25	33	31 033	52.1	47.9	53.6	5.2	0.0	2.0
Wayne	131	-3.4	164	0	60	142	860	28	50	62 260	18.5	81.5	39.4	6.2	4.6	2.4
Webster	136	-2.6	300	D	110	324	1 122	61	32	69 416	72.7	27.3	47.5	15.6	0.0	151.6
Whitley	44	-3.3	118	0	24	151	1 209	25	3	8 535	35.5	64.5	18.8	1.1	14.8	2.0
Wolfe	57	-7.0	148	D	14	131	734	21	4	10 146	84.5	15.5	28.5	0.0	11.1	0.6
Woodford	123	-0.9	181	2	79	548	2 649	49	115	170 208	18.6	81.4	63.1	19.5	0.0	16.6
LOUISIANA	7 877	0.5	331	943	5 331	381	1 206	59	2 031	85 265	69.5	30.5	40.2	17.6	4.2	9 847.8
Acadia	273	1.8	428	101	240	461	1 115	71	67	104 377	96.0	4.0	55.2	28.8	0.0	110.0
Allen	116	-2.0	337	20	58	417	1 225	43	11	33 452	84.5	15.5	27.7	10.2	0.0	24.1
Ascension	55	-12.3	198	0	32	418	2 047	49	15	54 757	90.1	9.9	22.6	7.2	0.0	226.8
Assumption	64	-5.8	628	D	53	868	1 362	205	32	314 372	93.4	6.6	66.7	54.9	0.0	29.0
Avoyelles	259	1.3	314	12	211	406	1 387	56	61	73 864	93.2	6.8	48.4	17.3	3.6	17.5
Beauregard	165	20.6	244	3	62	247	1 072	30	11	16 194	37.1	62.9	23.4	3.6	0.0	29.5
Bienville	47	-8.3	212	0	16	202	937	34	6	26 584	9.5	90.5	24.9	5.0	0.0	1.8
Bossier	111	0.4	300	0	56	398	1 436	43	9	23 949	42.9	57.1	32.3	7.0	8.7	12.2
Caddo	173	1.7	365	3	94	358	998	43	27	58 014	69.3	30.7	33.6	11.0	0.0	86.5
Calcasieu	312	-5.0	416	30	140	500	1 301	33	20	27 307	68.6	31.4	28.8	8.3	0.0	312.0
Caldwell	70	6.7	324	6	49	282	967	50	11	52 103	88.3	11.7	33.2	12.9	0.0	3.1
Cameron	245	-5.1	638	17	75	478	727	50	11	28 796	64.3	35.7	24.5	7.3	14.4	27.5
Catahoula	229	-8.9	600	8	171	409	763	85	43	112 731	90.8	9.2	56.4	26.0	0.3	17.3
Claiborne	58	-8.7	224	0	22	211	1 170	41	36	139 713	2.5	97.5	35.6	15.3	4.6	2.8
Concordia	253	11.1	867	12	221	706	862	118	61	208 371	88.2	11.8	71.6	44.5	3.7	31.5
De Soto	157	5.9	304	0	50	275	965	35	19	37 655	7.3	92.7	28.5	7.8	0.0	14.1
East Baton Rouge	66	-16.4	150	0	32	329	1 912	41	8	18 745	37.9	62.1	24.3	4.1	0.0	151.7
East Carroll	210	8.4	862	53	186	797	946	175	62	254 765	98.3	1.7	83.2	55.7	0.2	38.0
East Feliciana	115	-15.9	298	0	40	418	1 548	32	8	19 534	16.2	83.9	30.6	4.1	0.0	3.3
Evangeline	181	2.3	308	57	147	305	1 103	35	44	75 660	85.1	14.9	41.8	18.5	0.0	188.1
Franklin	269	1.8	367	74	220	328	951	62	88	120 255	77.1	22.9	57.9	25.7	0.5	28.0
Grant	49	10.5	261	0	28	318	1 161	35	6	32 456	85.9	14.1	26.3	5.4	35.2	4.4
Iberia	103	-6.7	344	1	90	578	1 698	119	50	167 106	98.1	1.9	47.0	28.2	0.0	30.7
Iberville	96	19.0	599	0	71	968	1 661	172	37	230 951	94.1	5.9	55.9	30.4	3.8	1 217.7
Jackson	16	-6.9	86	0	6	154	1 794	27	25	139 084	1.1	98.9	27.9	15.3	0.0	21.2
Jefferson	5	20.9	78	0	2	142	1 823	19	2	37 945	16.4	83.5	17.7	6.5	2.3	1 139.9
Jefferson Davis	304	4.0	527	100	252	449	1 009	71	52	90 902	93.1	6.9	54.0	30.0	0.0	151.5
Lafayette	88	-0.1	152	11	74	351	2 954	40	24	41 606	88.7	11.3	23.9	6.2	0.0	33.1
Lafourche	135	1.5	339	0	69	481	1 328	68	32	80 922	83.1	16.9	44.0	13.8	0.0	29.6
La Salle	27	0.9	170	D	11	189	1 122	24	1	7 161	40.3	59.6	13.1	0.6	1.7	2.1
Lincoln	41	-29.7	144	0	20	212	1 279	35	35	122 914	4.2	95.8	39.0	14.6	0.0	8.2
Livingston	40	12.4	117	1	19	333	2 695	23	9	24 911	19.2	80.8	17.4	4.3	0.0	16.0
Madison	266	7.9	955	21	237	777	828	160	63	227 439	99.2	0.8	78.5	53.0	9.5	18.6
Morehouse	258	6.7	642	119	224	626	1 050	139	78	195 044	97.1	2.9	67.7	44.0	0.1	72.8
Natchitoches	189	3.2	356	3	109	369	1 033	38	50	94 467	35.1	64.9	42.3	15.8	16.2	24.2
Orleans	0	0.0	4	0	0	85	20 710	11	0	2 058	D	D	0.0	0.0	8.8	635.5
Ouachita	89	19.0	236	11	60	277	1 239	68	26	68 248	64.5	35.5	35.0	13.3	2.1	111.9
Plaquemines	37	-20.1	289	0	5	341	1 219	38	5	36 640	71.9	28.1	41.7	11.0	3.6	115.7

STATE County	Value of Residential Construction Authorized by Building Permits, 1999		Wholesale Trade, 1997				Retail Trade[1], 1997				Real Estate and Rental and Leasing, 1997			
	New Construction ($1,000)	Number of Housing Units	Number of Establish-ments	Number of Employees	Sales (mil dol)	Annual Payroll (mil dol)	Number of Establish-ments	Number of Employees	Sales (mil dol)	Annual Payroll (mil dol)	Number of Establish-ments	Number of Employees	Receipts (mil dol)	Annual Payroll (mil dol)
	133	134	135	136	137	138	139	140	141	142	143	144	145	146
KENTUCKY—Cont'd														
Owsley	NA	NA	NA	NA	NA	NA	16	99	25.9	1.0	2	D	D	D
Pendleton	185	3	10	D	D	D	40	287	35.5	2.9	6	D	D	D
Perry	1 006	13	50	467	233.7	14.4	183	1 917	294.6	25.7	17	78	17.7	1.5
Pike	2 646	38	78	711	318.4	21.3	347	4 618	664.7	61.2	42	140	21.7	3.3
Powell	NA	NA	8	115	23.2	2.2	39	297	38.1	3.0	6	20	0.8	0.2
Pulaski	7 828	101	76	1 068	318.4	21.1	336	3 508	543.3	48.7	57	203	16.3	3.3
Robertson	NA	NA	NA	NA	NA	NA	7	25	2.4	0.2	1	D	D	D
Rockcastle	NA	NA	9	62	11.4	0.9	54	365	44.3	4.3	4	33	1.5	0.2
Rowan	646	18	28	230	61.2	4.2	131	1 319	180.7	15.6	18	52	3.3	0.7
Russell	0	0	10	356	83.2	7.2	88	797	104.9	14.0	9	36	7.4	0.3
Scott	24 341	192	25	816	319.5	26.3	115	1 396	230.7	17.5	17	76	8.2	1.1
Shelby	53 456	513	46	375	140.4	11.2	111	1 338	253.0	19.6	32	108	10.7	1.5
Simpson	10 163	131	18	411	130.6	4.6	77	914	205.7	13.9	12	28	2.2	0.4
Spencer	34 356	353	7	D	D	D	23	147	16.9	2.5	2	D	D	D
Taylor	980	15	33	175	37.1	3.1	152	1 555	252.8	22.5	19	55	4.8	0.9
Todd	0	0	16	227	54.1	2.8	48	274	45.7	3.3	5	D	D	D
Trigg	1 650	9	10	66	18.3	1.8	52	324	51.8	4.1	8	36	3.4	0.5
Trimble	NA	NA	1	D	D	D	14	96	11.1	1.1	3	6	0.3	0.0
Union	834	15	21	226	66.8	4.4	77	623	91.4	7.7	5	18	0.6	0.1
Warren	87 002	997	155	2 029	1 367.4	57.4	525	7 144	1 108.8	102.5	100	407	38.9	6.0
Washington	621	5	10	D	D	D	41	301	44.6	3.9	5	11	0.9	0.1
Wayne	0	0	10	113	15.2	1.3	65	663	99.0	13.0	4	16	1.9	0.3
Webster	632	8	3	D	D	D	59	431	73.3	6.5	6	D	D	D
Whitley	5 501	96	28	D	D	D	164	1 609	275.6	23.5	29	99	8.1	1.4
Wolfe	NA	NA	3	15	3.9	0.1	27	161	25.7	1.7	1	D	D	D
Woodford	38 741	288	20	D	D	D	75	724	124.9	9.7	16	47	29.2	0.9
LOUISIANA	1 766 666	17 836	6 390	76 350	46 972.3	2 375.2	17 863	224 412	35 807.9	3 307.9	4 151	28 571	3 342.1	642.2
Acadia	17 421	240	61	598	280.7	12.9	199	2 093	278.0	27.9	34	96	8.1	1.6
Allen	2 464	51	16	113	37.7	2.0	93	672	99.1	7.8	13	37	1.9	0.4
Ascension	89 981	1 095	94	950	314.1	26.8	304	3 777	578.0	48.9	54	288	52.4	7.4
Assumption	9 914	97	15	114	32.5	2.7	59	599	75.1	7.5	8	D	D	D
Avoyelles	16 782	173	26	236	83.3	3.3	169	1 606	212.0	18.2	22	67	3.4	0.5
Beauregard	220	3	21	130	43.4	2.2	115	1 293	222.4	18.9	22	69	4.1	0.7
Bienville	0	0	10	76	188.8	2.2	65	414	57.3	5.0	10	51	5.6	1.3
Bossier	59 948	491	121	D	D	D	363	4 838	834.1	72.9	73	327	28.5	5.3
Caddo	78 809	596	451	5 864	2 586.1	176.2	1 053	13 945	2 338.2	221.5	247	1 185	120.6	22.9
Calcasieu	104 796	1 462	244	3 136	1 732.7	90.8	775	10 400	1 606.2	147.1	210	1 164	106.0	20.6
Caldwell	1 500	20	12	D	D	D	34	274	48.4	3.7	5	6	0.6	0.1
Cameron	3 766	41	19	115	416.8	4.7	34	240	29.1	2.4	4	11	1.5	0.2
Catahoula	500	15	15	193	111.8	3.0	52	407	62.2	4.9	3	D	D	D
Claiborne	0	0	20	173	121.7	4.2	63	486	63.7	6.3	7	17	1.0	0.2
Concordia	1 649	19	17	224	113.6	4.7	94	853	126.0	10.8	3	25	2.0	0.5
De Soto	0	0	17	D	D	D	83	748	116.3	9.6	48	129	9.6	1.7
East Baton Rouge	142 899	2 068	764	9 966	4 006.6	345.9	1 822	27 428	4 468.8	423.7	502	3 760	330.1	73.5
East Carroll	259	2	9	147	97.5	4.4	36	245	41.3	3.5	5	13	1.3	0.2
East Feliciana	109	1	11	D	D	D	45	373	45.0	4.3	13	38	2.2	0.7
Evangeline	7 493	120	17	122	30.4	2.3	129	1 012	144.5	13.4	21	73	4.0	0.7
Franklin	2 555	30	29	D	D	D	90	1 119	168.1	13.7	11	30	3.3	0.4
Grant	45	1	4	D	D	D	31	168	49.3	3.3	4	D	D	D
Iberia	20 619	179	118	1 447	359.2	44.4	282	3 354	613.9	54.1	82	1 274	218.2	47.5
Iberville	11 384	97	27	251	89.7	5.7	100	1 036	159.1	14.3	21	128	13.0	2.3
Jackson	0	0	8	36	28.0	1.1	53	521	59.8	5.6	10	28	2.1	0.4
Jefferson	118 809	920	1 168	15 313	10 041.1	500.0	2 038	32 403	5 787.0	535.8	533	5 485	627.9	121.6
Jefferson Davis	8 085	79	36	359	270.7	9.7	131	1 406	232.9	18.7	23	181	9.8	4.2
Lafayette	108 358	939	484	6 260	2 620.5	223.5	990	14 462	2 465.4	231.6	347	2 953	394.1	85.7
Lafourche	42 652	334	88	722	328.5	18.8	323	3 869	570.0	50.4	81	426	56.1	9.4
La Salle	0	0	8	43	8.8	0.8	64	515	68.4	6.0	4	12	0.4	0.1
Lincoln	8 869	102	34	376	105.8	9.1	163	2 233	328.0	28.8	41	150	10.0	1.4
Livingston	120 721	976	55	502	140.1	12.8	213	2 403	368.9	32.4	39	214	14.2	2.2
Madison	934	9	14	D	D	D	53	512	83.8	6.5	14	50	1.9	0.8
Morehouse	638	10	15	143	45.8	4.0	126	1 263	216.2	16.3	14	27	4.3	0.4
Natchitoches	12 860	158	33	247	91.0	4.6	141	1 612	230.4	19.7	34	82	6.5	0.7
Orleans	122 234	1 151	484	6 086	2 450.5	210.2	1 871	20 405	2 771.3	315.6	481	3 538	407.4	72.3
Ouachita	62 011	670	248	2 912	1 257.2	82.4	753	9 649	1 483.5	134.0	176	805	79.7	12.7
Plaquemines	12 167	151	87	1 168	837.8	36.4	76	674	85.8	8.4	44	286	45.0	8.4

1. Establishments with payroll.

STATE County	Professional, Scientific, and Technical Services[1], 1997				Manufacturing, 1997				Accommodation and Foodservices, 1997			
	Number of Establishments	Number of Employees	Receipts (mil dol)	Annual Payroll (mil dol)	Number of Establishments	Number of Employees	Receipts (mil dol)	Annual Payroll (mil dol)	Number of Establishments	Number of Employees	Sales (mil dol)	Annual Payroll (mil dol)
	147	148	149	150	151	152	153	154	155	156	157	158
KENTUCKY—Cont'd												
Owsley	3	D	D	D	NA	NA	NA	NA	2	D	D	D
Pendleton	8	12	0.7	0.2	12	D	D	D	12	D	D	D
Perry	54	211	14.1	5.9	9	614	91.4	16.5	51	1 008	34.6	8.7
Pike	102	627	49.3	19.6	26	587	74.3	10.7	84	1 425	44.9	10.9
Powell	6	10	0.5	0.1	16	1 185	175.3	19.2	15	D	D	D
Pulaski	79	686	29.2	11.1	84	4 564	672.1	107.1	82	1 548	45.4	13.2
Robertson	1	D	D	D	NA	NA	NA	NA	3	12	0.1	0.0
Rockcastle	11	36	1.7	0.4	11	D	D	D	17	270	8.6	2.3
Rowan	18	70	2.9	1.1	13	647	111.6	10.5	43	899	24.0	6.8
Russell	16	40	2.7	0.6	24	2 098	348.9	40.5	29	324	9.8	2.7
Scott	44	182	52.5	4.7	45	D	D	D	51	1 209	43.2	12.2
Shelby	49	129	9.3	3.3	42	4 095	942.2	126.2	43	685	21.4	5.8
Simpson	16	63	3.5	1.0	34	3 390	549.4	107.2	37	697	23.7	6.3
Spencer	7	21	1.2	0.3	NA	NA	NA	NA	7	D	D	D
Taylor	40	62	5.7	1.7	38	4 088	599.8	96.6	45	685	18.8	5.0
Todd	10	34	1.3	0.5	19	1 299	147.3	25.7	10	75	2.0	0.5
Trigg	8	37	2.4	0.9	19	1 083	158.0	26.5	18	224	6.1	1.8
Trimble	3	5	0.6	0.1	NA	NA	NA	NA	7	30	0.6	0.2
Union	13	41	2.1	0.6	18	1 214	167.0	29.3	23	D	D	D
Warren	146	946	58.1	20.2	104	D	D	D	192	4 375	136.0	40.0
Washington	11	25	2.0	0.4	13	1 049	179.6	25.1	13	131	4.1	1.0
Wayne	20	44	2.9	0.7	33	1 877	190.0	33.4	20	D	D	D
Webster	10	28	1.3	0.3	19	798	82.5	16.4	15	138	3.1	0.9
Whitley	39	130	9.2	2.9	33	1 927	201.1	43.5	68	1 128	35.1	9.4
Wolfe	4	7	0.6	0.1	NA	NA	NA	NA	6	D	D	D
Woodford	37	124	9.9	2.9	22	D	D	D	41	529	14.9	4.3
LOUISIANA	9 077	63 642	5 754.6	2 159.0	3 545	165 777	80 424.0	6 054.5	7 151	147 016	5 259.9	1 408.9
Acadia	54	233	18.1	5.7	47	2 247	283.9	38.5	58	D	D	D
Allen	17	35	2.2	0.6	11	658	97.5	16.7	26	288	10.9	2.3
Ascension	80	820	34.7	15.5	86	5 577	7 012.9	300.0	103	1 729	58.8	15.9
Assumption	15	45	2.2	0.7	NA	NA	NA	NA	13	116	3.3	0.9
Avoyelles	46	132	9.6	2.5	20	622	92.8	11.4	37	1 931	131.2	34.6
Beauregard	28	68	4.0	1.1	26	1 413	627.1	63.0	32	449	15.7	3.2
Bienville	11	15	1.5	0.4	14	1 052	226.3	33.0	16	D	D	D
Bossier	95	440	29.0	10.4	76	2 578	376.5	65.4	173	5 610	300.8	69.8
Caddo	557	3 317	277.3	102.7	216	11 997	4 515.6	445.7	408	7 743	236.9	66.0
Calcasieu	348	2 432	183.4	69.2	134	11 274	10 153.5	542.4	294	8 019	306.4	75.4
Caldwell	12	38	3.3	0.6	NA	NA	NA	NA	8	D	D	D
Cameron	11	118	6.7	3.0	NA	NA	NA	NA	11	54	2.0	0.4
Catahoula	11	24	1.3	0.4	NA	NA	NA	NA	11	100	2.7	0.7
Claiborne	16	36	2.6	0.5	10	507	109.5	11.5	18	D	D	D
Concordia	21	59	3.7	0.9	NA	NA	NA	NA	27	D	D	D
De Soto	20	75	3.4	0.9	16	1 166	493.3	43.9	15	D	D	D
East Baton Rouge	1 376	12 183	1 200.8	452.8	354	12 159	9 831.6	570.1	754	16 452	504.7	138.3
East Carroll	11	20	1.9	0.9	NA	NA	NA	NA	6	D	D	D
East Feliciana	15	29	1.9	0.9	NA	NA	NA	NA	17	150	3.4	0.9
Evangeline	34	100	5.4	1.8	18	944	191.0	36.0	34	D	D	D
Franklin	24	494	7.5	4.8	13	506	36.1	6.9	18	D	D	D
Grant	5	D	D	D	NA	NA	NA	NA	3	D	D	D
Iberia	113	562	34.6	13.4	100	4 962	911.0	141.8	83	1 302	33.9	9.0
Iberville	36	158	11.7	4.4	39	4 360	4 176.1	270.0	31	478	13.0	3.5
Jackson	14	45	2.4	0.6	5	D	D	D	18	D	D	D
Jefferson	1 359	9 307	861.4	333.4	444	16 356	2 893.2	508.6	948	18 676	681.2	185.7
Jefferson Davis	35	119	10.4	2.6	21	598	110.2	13.9	44	684	20.4	5.4
Lafayette	786	5 714	535.5	207.1	215	5 419	868.5	150.1	382	9 058	270.1	78.8
Lafourche	139	1 486	123.5	41.5	66	2 464	424.2	72.9	129	1 554	48.6	10.9
La Salle	20	56	2.7	0.9	8	D	D	D	13	150	4.6	1.2
Lincoln	55	222	16.6	4.9	35	1 788	346.0	53.0	66	1 206	34.5	8.4
Livingston	76	255	17.1	5.1	54	1 342	227.4	39.6	84	1 282	37.1	9.5
Madison	15	65	2.2	0.7	NA	NA	NA	NA	15	D	D	D
Morehouse	18	65	4.5	1.9	14	D	D	D	28	D	D	D
Natchitoches	47	280	21.6	6.1	18	1 664	537.9	42.5	65	1 370	40.9	11.2
Orleans	1 420	12 469	1 401.8	551.5	261	10 453	2 305.0	362.2	1 105	32 081	1 371.8	377.5
Ouachita	358	2 042	145.3	50.7	152	8 235	1 983.4	287.6	265	5 360	170.1	42.6
Plaquemines	38	489	28.1	13.1	44	2 231	2 779.2	102.1	51	1 600	55.5	20.4

1. Firms subject to federal tax.

Table B. States and Counties — Health and Other Services and Federal Funds

STATE County	Health Care and Social Assistance[1], 1997				Other Services[1], 1997				Federal funds and grants, fiscal 1999[2] Expenditures (mil dol)			
									Total	Direct payments for individuals[3]		
	Number of Establishments	Number of Employees	Receipts (mil dol)	Annual Payroll (mil dol)	Number of Establishments	Number of Employees	Receipts (mil dol)	Annual Payroll (mil dol)	Total	Social Security and government retirement	Medicare	Food stamps and Supplemental Security Income
	159	160	161	162	163	164	165	166	167	168	169	170
KENTUCKY—Cont'd												
Owsley	4	31	1.3	0.6	2	D	D	D	38.4	9.7	5.1	6.7
Pendleton	14	D	D	D	18	39	5.0	0.6	46.5	20.8	8.0	2.9
Perry	55	636	43.9	21.3	41	166	9.5	2.2	182.0	77.6	25.0	22.8
Pike	131	1 233	70.2	28.3	83	408	24.0	6.5	422.7	177.8	55.4	31.9
Powell	14	169	5.9	2.4	10	34	1.3	0.4	43.1	16.7	4.8	4.9
Pulaski	129	2 367	158.7	61.0	67	316	17.8	5.1	260.0	120.0	37.4	23.3
Robertson	4	D	D	D	1	D	D	D	8.9	3.6	1.9	0.6
Rockcastle	12	141	6.4	3.2	11	42	2.4	0.5	96.2	25.6	10.8	7.0
Rowan	29	540	28.3	15.3	19	91	4.6	1.0	82.2	30.9	11.3	6.8
Russell	18	233	9.9	3.9	15	56	3.0	0.9	86.3	33.6	13.8	7.7
Scott	42	634	34.9	14.3	45	276	12.2	4.5	87.8	41.2	15.1	4.2
Shelby	39	500	20.8	9.6	46	316	33.4	7.2	91.3	43.7	15.9	3.5
Simpson	27	232	11.2	4.3	28	180	11.5	3.1	61.6	25.7	13.7	2.8
Spencer	10	116	5.8	2.4	8	37	2.1	0.4	27.6	13.7	5.2	1.5
Taylor	59	421	22.6	10.3	41	134	7.7	1.6	99.3	47.1	20.6	6.1
Todd	11	147	5.3	2.1	12	41	2.2	0.7	53.1	20.1	10.3	2.4
Trigg	18	146	5.6	2.3	12	33	3.0	0.6	65.0	33.1	11.0	2.3
Trimble	4	86	2.9	1.3	6	17	0.7	0.3	24.5	12.9	5.4	1.1
Union	19	796	35.6	17.3	13	52	4.3	1.0	-89.6	31.3	13.1	2.5
Warren	232	3 877	262.9	105.0	133	1 020	43.6	14.1	349.4	141.4	62.5	17.9
Washington	17	137	6.1	2.1	7	51	2.5	0.9	41.5	17.2	8.5	2.6
Wayne	27	310	13.0	6.6	21	50	3.8	0.8	93.9	30.9	16.4	9.4
Webster	11	191	6.2	2.9	18	71	5.4	1.3	87.1	30.2	11.2	2.6
Whitley	65	770	44.2	20.3	51	225	12.8	3.4	232.1	96.4	38.6	21.5
Wolfe	4	194	6.3	2.7	3	14	1.1	0.2	44.5	13.1	4.6	6.1
Woodford	28	124	9.0	3.0	34	142	7.5	2.0	59.0	35.4	8.6	2.2
LOUISIANA	8 580	129 773	7 967.6	3 341.5	5 998	39 764	2 595.2	767.2	24 384.3	7 180.1	4 064.5	1 187.9
Acadia	74	930	39.7	16.2	65	296	20.8	5.4	271.5	89.4	48.9	19.7
Allen	30	435	29.0	9.1	14	46	3.7	0.6	144.9	38.0	22.9	6.9
Ascension	92	1 542	68.9	30.3	92	571	37.7	12.0	205.7	84.2	51.4	12.6
Assumption	13	307	8.8	4.1	17	117	6.0	1.3	90.7	32.3	23.7	7.2
Avoyelles	55	954	39.7	16.3	44	121	7.7	1.9	216.9	66.2	42.4	15.8
Beauregard	42	349	21.5	9.1	39	117	7.0	1.6	132.6	67.6	25.4	4.3
Bienville	10	191	7.1	2.7	16	197	10.3	3.3	88.8	33.0	21.1	4.8
Bossier	112	1 773	93.6	37.7	154	830	48.5	13.8	681.8	212.7	54.9	50.2
Caddo	549	8 870	622.6	278.6	379	2 579	169.1	49.7	1 166.0	467.8	231.4	37.3
Calcasieu	405	4 756	319.7	131.7	262	1 914	122.2	35.7	700.6	307.5	155.7	32.2
Caldwell	22	532	25.4	10.0	9	26	2.3	0.5	58.3	19.4	15.6	2.8
Cameron	4	23	1.5	0.8	8	30	2.7	0.6	33.8	9.7	6.1	2.9
Catahoula	10	92	4.3	2.3	9	30	1.2	0.2	84.5	19.3	12.3	4.2
Claiborne	13	112	5.9	2.2	10	28	2.2	0.4	79.5	29.2	16.8	5.9
Concordia	32	372	20.2	8.4	20	74	4.0	1.3	123.6	36.2	20.1	7.6
De Soto	15	199	8.6	3.8	22	80	5.1	1.3	119.5	44.4	23.9	9.7
East Baton Rouge	983	14 707	973.8	426.5	724	5 646	355.3	111.1	2 415.6	619.0	311.4	86.3
East Carroll	8	138	2.3	1.3	11	28	1.3	0.4	73.3	12.2	12.5	6.2
East Feliciana	14	300	9.9	4.8	15	136	8.9	3.3	84.9	28.3	22.2	5.5
Evangeline	81	1 528	71.9	27.1	17	48	2.8	0.5	205.4	57.4	36.5	19.2
Franklin	40	767	26.9	11.7	28	114	5.6	1.3	134.8	33.0	27.9	8.4
Grant	13	111	4.4	1.6	7	30	2.2	0.6	87.7	36.0	18.5	5.0
Iberia	149	1 810	115.1	42.6	129	827	65.4	18.9	267.9	109.0	53.0	21.1
Iberville	50	989	54.2	21.8	25	194	11.2	4.5	158.7	47.7	39.7	10.0
Jackson	14	396	11.4	5.7	14	70	3.3	0.8	82.0	32.1	23.0	3.9
Jefferson	1 170	17 797	1 165.4	469.1	865	6 614	431.3	135.6	1 815.7	702.8	429.1	79.8
Jefferson Davis	51	471	20.9	6.9	35	118	5.6	1.6	144.9	54.2	26.1	7.0
Lafayette	616	7 560	589.9	228.8	359	2 443	160.6	49.2	622.9	239.1	116.0	31.2
Lafourche	144	1 330	85.6	41.3	95	1 011	79.9	23.4	510.8	128.6	72.3	18.7
La Salle	19	136	6.2	2.9	13	34	2.3	0.6	68.2	27.9	17.2	2.5
Lincoln	61	1 299	85.0	25.4	41	223	15.6	3.7	155.4	54.8	31.2	10.6
Livingston	71	1 458	41.3	18.7	62	346	19.9	6.0	237.9	108.0	60.2	11.9
Madison	26	458	17.1	8.3	12	30	1.8	0.4	93.0	17.3	16.1	6.0
Morehouse	66	688	33.6	15.2	35	105	6.5	1.5	203.5	56.7	39.8	13.1
Natchitoches	51	516	24.7	10.0	45	180	10.0	2.3	200.6	57.5	30.9	13.4
Orleans	1 022	19 447	1 245.4	530.6	605	4 684	257.7	77.8	4 811.7	863.5	596.8	237.7
Ouachita	355	5 465	339.6	153.9	224	1 332	74.1	22.2	572.4	221.6	133.9	36.6
Plaquemines	23	258	13.7	6.3	46	400	41.8	15.4	204.0	36.7	20.9	6.1

1. Firms subject to federal tax. 2. October 1, 1998 to September 30, 1999. 3. State totals may include programs not allocated by county.

Table B. States and Counties — Federal Funds and Local Government Finances

	Federal funds and grants, fiscal 1999[1] (cont'd)							Local government finances, 1997				
	Expenditures (mil dol) (cont'd)							General revenue				
	Procurement contract awards			Grants[2]							Taxes	
											Per capita[3] (dollars)	
STATE County	Salaries and wages	Defense	Other	Medicaid and other health-related	Nutrition and family welfare	Education	Other	Total (mil dol)	Intergovern-mental (mil dol)	Total (mil dol)	Total	Property
	171	172	173	174	175	176	177	178	179	180	181	182
KENTUCKY—Cont'd												
Owsley	0.9	0.0	0.3	11.7	1.8	0.7	1.4	7.8	6.6	0.7	133	109
Pendleton	1.5	0.0	0.4	5.1	1.3	0.7	5.2	18.2	12.4	3.1	226	169
Perry	7.9	0.0	6.3	30.0	5.4	3.4	2.6	58.6	35.7	11.4	366	242
Pike	14.2	2.4	9.0	41.3	8.1	4.9	76.3	111.6	66.8	27.8	383	210
Powell	1.6	0.0	0.3	9.8	2.1	1.0	1.4	18.8	14.2	2.6	209	88
Pulaski	9.8	0.0	2.9	42.3	5.8	3.2	13.1	77.7	43.8	21.7	389	216
Robertson	0.2	0.0	0.1	1.5	0.3	0.2	0.0	2.9	2.0	0.5	253	222
Rockcastle	1.6	0.0	0.4	16.7	2.4	1.2	29.3	19.0	14.8	2.5	160	115
Rowan	4.2	0.1	0.7	14.5	2.0	3.8	2.4	27.6	16.7	8.1	367	150
Russell	2.6	0.6	0.4	16.6	5.6	1.1	3.3	28.3	13.6	4.8	296	198
Scott	3.0	0.0	0.8	9.1	1.7	1.2	9.1	88.6	19.6	23.2	786	315
Shelby	4.3	0.0	5.8	10.0	3.8	1.0	0.8	40.4	16.4	16.9	586	392
Simpson	1.7	0.0	0.5	7.5	1.4	0.8	1.8	29.5	12.2	7.5	465	269
Spencer	1.3	0.4	0.3	2.9	0.9	0.4	0.1	11.6	8.2	2.5	273	213
Taylor	4.5	0.9	0.7	12.2	2.1	1.0	0.9	57.3	30.5	7.2	316	205
Todd	1.7	0.1	0.4	9.2	1.2	0.5	0.4	15.6	10.4	2.8	249	145
Trigg	6.1	0.0	1.2	5.9	1.0	0.6	0.3	17.7	7.9	4.1	338	235
Trimble	0.8	0.0	0.2	2.4	1.1	0.4	-0.2	29.0	5.6	2.8	381	315
Union	2.6	0.0	-156.5	4.9	1.3	0.9	1.6	22.4	13.8	5.4	327	223
Warren	38.2	0.9	9.2	31.3	14.3	6.2	10.9	146.5	55.9	54.7	632	301
Washington	1.8	0.0	0.4	6.4	1.2	0.6	1.5	12.9	8.1	3.4	316	173
Wayne	2.0	0.0	0.4	27.0	3.2	1.7	2.3	24.5	18.6	3.8	204	143
Webster	2.0	0.0	27.6	6.0	1.4	0.6	0.0	35.3	21.3	7.0	515	409
Whitley	7.4	4.8	4.5	32.4	6.0	2.8	15.0	55.1	35.5	9.4	264	146
Wolfe	1.5	0.0	0.6	14.0	1.8	0.9	0.4	11.7	9.9	1.2	164	81
Woodford	2.1	0.0	1.0	4.8	1.3	0.7	0.5	36.1	12.8	16.6	744	352
LOUISIANA	2 164.9	1 449.9	1 216.7	2 615.2	907.2	513.5	1 191.9	X	X	X	X	X
Acadia	6.1	0.8	13.8	52.8	8.7	4.2	1.3	78.2	45.4	24.6	427	171
Allen	38.6	0.5	2.9	17.6	4.1	1.5	3.4	38.4	19.7	10.3	430	221
Ascension	6.9	0.7	4.6	20.4	6.8	3.1	12.9	169.6	57.8	75.8	1 083	402
Assumption	2.5	0.0	0.4	15.7	3.6	1.9	3.1	37.7	20.4	11.7	514	238
Avoyelles	5.4	2.0	3.8	49.5	7.4	3.1	5.4	60.1	41.7	14.5	354	90
Beauregard	6.3	0.1	0.9	15.5	2.6	1.7	5.1	75.6	23.2	24.8	779	401
Bienville	2.5	0.7	0.5	16.2	2.1	1.2	5.5	29.8	15.2	12.8	808	469
Bossier	245.0	42.9	2.1	25.4	9.1	3.8	20.0	235.4	79.6	75.8	817	245
Caddo	113.8	13.2	32.2	145.6	33.0	18.4	47.2	559.8	219.3	259.7	1 067	524
Calcasieu	32.9	13.7	16.0	63.1	18.0	9.1	35.2	480.0	111.0	238.5	1 334	449
Caldwell	1.4	0.0	0.3	8.9	1.4	0.9	1.5	14.2	9.1	4.3	416	184
Cameron	1.5	1.8	0.7	1.8	0.9	0.5	3.5	33.9	10.8	16.9	1 876	1 840
Catahoula	2.4	7.0	0.7	13.5	3.4	1.0	2.3	17.7	11.1	4.7	421	189
Claiborne	2.4	0.0	0.8	17.7	2.1	1.1	2.0	38.4	12.6	7.2	425	229
Concordia	3.4	5.5	0.4	21.7	4.0	3.0	4.8	28.1	18.1	7.9	383	120
De Soto	3.3	0.0	0.7	23.2	4.2	1.8	4.0	59.3	28.3	17.8	710	366
East Baton Rouge	137.5	43.7	31.3	170.4	372.2	186.3	408.1	794.9	243.5	391.9	994	318
East Carroll	1.1	0.0	0.4	15.9	4.4	1.4	3.6	21.1	9.4	8.2	907	591
East Feliciana	3.4	0.0	0.6	16.3	2.9	1.2	3.4	20.2	12.4	6.1	293	112
Evangeline	3.1	0.1	0.8	56.4	7.6	2.7	5.7	46.0	29.6	12.5	365	150
Franklin	3.5	0.0	0.6	29.1	4.5	2.0	2.3	26.3	17.7	6.9	314	79
Grant	4.3	0.2	1.9	13.3	2.9	1.2	1.8	22.7	17.3	3.7	197	109
Iberia	7.7	1.2	2.2	42.0	7.6	5.9	14.2	154.5	66.6	44.8	621	189
Iberville	10.8	4.7	1.1	28.2	7.2	2.2	4.8	84.5	22.6	51.7	1 662	522
Jackson	3.5	0.4	0.5	11.2	3.4	0.9	1.9	22.1	12.5	8.5	545	216
Jefferson	91.9	42.7	166.4	105.0	34.7	19.0	98.0	1 257.1	226.1	539.0	1 194	300
Jefferson Davis	3.8	0.0	2.7	18.5	4.9	2.3	4.2	60.1	30.0	19.0	600	277
Lafayette	52.1	8.3	30.3	63.7	17.0	10.8	33.2	266.9	99.7	121.6	660	150
Lafourche	8.3	61.5	156.9	29.4	10.7	6.1	12.2	217.2	74.7	51.0	579	220
La Salle	2.1	0.0	0.5	9.3	1.1	0.7	5.8	37.9	14.5	7.7	558	314
Lincoln	6.1	0.1	1.3	21.8	5.3	5.6	7.6	58.3	25.5	22.8	544	209
Livingston	6.7	0.0	1.6	20.2	5.8	3.0	17.7	107.2	66.4	30.0	351	120
Madison	2.1	1.0	0.7	18.9	4.8	1.6	3.9	21.1	13.4	5.4	416	159
Morehouse	3.8	0.1	1.0	37.5	6.8	2.7	10.5	70.8	22.5	19.3	608	250
Natchitoches	9.0	1.9	1.5	43.6	6.9	4.6	7.9	92.9	40.3	24.1	646	301
Orleans	705.5	902.4	536.6	500.5	105.2	53.0	175.3	1 235.2	447.5	510.8	1 089	441
Ouachita	26.4	5.6	7.1	76.8	16.2	11.0	14.7	289.6	116.9	136.3	927	353
Plaquemines	29.3	53.4	38.0	9.6	2.6	1.5	4.4	91.4	27.9	38.3	1 481	793

1. October 1, 1998 to September 30, 1999.   2. State totals may include programs not allocated by county.   3. Based on the resident population estimated as of July 1 of the year shown.

STATE County	Local government finances, 1997 (cont'd) Direct general expenditure — Total (mil dol)	Per capita[1] (dollars)	Percent of total for — Education	Health and hospitals	Police protection	Public welfare	Highways	Debt outstanding Total (mil dol)	Per capita[1] (dollars)	Government employment, 1998 Federal civilian	Federal military	State and local	Presidential election, 2000 Percent of vote cast — Democratic	Republican	All other
	183	184	185	186	187	188	189	190	191	192	193	194	195	196	197
KENTUCKY—Cont'd															
Owsley	7.7	1 438	78.9	0.0	0.7	0.0	8.0	4.1	764	15	19	326	18.6	80.3	1.2
Pendleton	23.1	1 665	73.0	1.9	2.9	0.0	5.0	12.8	925	30	47	571	34.8	63.4	1.9
Perry	67.8	2 179	50.3	0.1	2.5	0.1	3.2	199.9	6 427	157	108	2 451	50.1	48.2	1.7
Pike	114.4	1 576	67.5	4.1	1.7	0.6	5.0	76.2	1 051	293	250	3 259	54.6	44.1	1.3
Powell	18.9	1 499	75.4	0.0	2.1	0.0	3.9	9.9	788	42	45	756	46.0	51.8	2.2
Pulaski	78.2	1 406	58.0	10.4	2.8	0.1	5.5	66.8	1 201	191	196	3 598	25.1	73.6	1.3
Robertson	3.0	1 394	62.7	2.5	3.4	0.0	17.7	1.2	557	0	0	136	34.2	63.1	2.7
Rockcastle	19.7	1 250	83.2	0.2	1.7	0.0	4.5	13.3	845	34	55	720	22.4	76.1	1.5
Rowan	26.5	1 203	59.6	1.2	3.7	0.1	7.9	16.6	752	94	82	2 819	48.5	49.1	2.4
Russell	27.7	1 698	49.7	28.3	1.9	0.0	3.4	23.0	1 407	60	56	1 020	24.2	74.5	1.4
Scott	110.8	3 763	40.8	0.7	3.8	0.9	1.8	641.1	21 773	59	106	1 585	39.7	57.7	2.6
Shelby	39.5	1 369	56.1	0.3	2.5	0.1	3.8	44.2	1 532	83	103	1 361	34.8	63.3	1.8
Simpson	28.2	1 746	50.4	20.6	4.2	0.1	4.1	24.3	1 500	38	57	879	44.4	54.4	1.2
Spencer	13.0	1 416	71.7	0.1	1.2	0.0	4.5	4.8	522	27	33	398	32.6	66.0	1.4
Taylor	54.9	2 397	36.1	48.8	1.9	0.0	2.6	77.4	3 377	84	80	1 437	30.8	68.0	1.2
Todd	14.9	1 332	59.8	3.9	3.3	0.0	5.4	13.2	1 180	39	39	494	35.7	63.2	1.1
Trigg	16.8	1 389	51.1	26.4	2.1	0.0	5.0	4.6	383	155	43	627	39.5	58.6	1.9
Trimble	32.5	4 457	19.8	0.0	0.1	0.0	1.7	304.0	41 673	17	26	268	38.3	59.6	2.0
Union	22.3	1 351	62.7	1.2	4.8	0.1	6.3	9.8	593	52	57	669	47.4	51.2	1.3
Warren	144.4	1 669	49.3	6.9	4.5	0.3	4.0	318.7	3 684	774	310	6 718	36.9	61.4	1.7
Washington	12.2	1 139	76.6	1.5	1.8	0.0	2.4	2.7	247	36	38	455	31.8	66.3	1.9
Wayne	22.7	1 214	82.8	0.2	1.8	0.1	1.6	11.8	632	37	66	942	35.7	62.9	1.4
Webster	33.0	2 442	39.9	1.3	2.1	0.1	0.8	38.6	2 855	43	47	688	47.1	51.2	1.7
Whitley	53.2	1 494	73.1	7.2	2.1	0.0	2.9	25.1	707	100	125	1 982	34.8	63.7	1.5
Wolfe	9.8	1 335	82.9	0.0	0.5	0.1	7.7	2.1	283	31	26	442	46.8	52.2	0.9
Woodford	36.5	1 633	54.7	12.3	5.7	0.1	5.5	17.3	772	44	79	974	39.4	58.1	2.5
LOUISIANA	X	X	X	X	X	X	X	X	X	35 309	41 812	324 870	44.9	52.6	2.6
Acadia	80.1	1 389	58.2	0.4	6.4	0.0	3.5	31.0	537	110	319	3 176	NA	NA	NA
Allen	34.7	1 452	59.0	13.7	5.5	0.0	6.7	13.9	582	718	132	1 495	NA	NA	NA
Ascension	157.8	2 255	48.3	21.2	6.0	0.4	6.4	130.7	1 868	114	396	3 343	NA	NA	NA
Assumption	32.6	1 425	74.3	0.1	5.6	2.8	2.4	6.2	271	32	127	1 169	NA	NA	NA
Avoyelles	57.5	1 411	57.0	0.6	13.3	0.0	8.5	10.0	246	94	226	2 994	NA	NA	NA
Beauregard	76.8	2 415	43.1	30.1	4.9	0.2	9.0	33.0	1 036	113	177	1 634	NA	NA	NA
Bienville	26.6	1 678	61.5	0.8	6.3	0.2	2.5	9.6	606	53	87	780	NA	NA	NA
Bossier	213.7	2 304	46.0	24.3	5.6	2.3	4.0	108.5	1 169	1 952	5 903	6 269	NA	NA	NA
Caddo	532.5	2 188	46.4	1.5	7.6	0.0	3.5	397.8	1 634	2 707	1 342	18 969	NA	NA	NA
Calcasieu	455.7	2 548	39.3	7.7	8.3	0.4	7.4	617.0	3 450	621	1 005	12 267	NA	NA	NA
Caldwell	13.0	1 260	74.5	0.5	1.3	0.0	6.3	3.3	316	36	57	749	NA	NA	NA
Cameron	29.9	3 320	42.0	9.5	9.8	0.0	14.6	1.6	174	32	50	930	NA	NA	NA
Catahoula	19.8	1 787	56.0	0.6	3.0	0.0	7.6	4.8	435	58	61	692	NA	NA	NA
Claiborne	40.4	2 391	34.0	33.7	3.0	2.0	5.3	11.6	684	49	94	1 596	NA	NA	NA
Concordia	30.9	1 490	69.9	0.9	4.0	0.5	10.0	6.8	327	82	115	1 505	NA	NA	NA
De Soto	60.3	2 405	49.3	0.2	3.7	1.3	5.7	166.9	6 653	55	138	1 423	NA	NA	NA
East Baton Rouge	812.7	2 061	37.3	1.2	8.1	0.2	6.2	852.7	2 163	2 349	2 265	48 026	NA	NA	NA
East Carroll	19.4	2 157	50.3	10.7	9.2	3.3	4.3	0.6	64	27	49	874	NA	NA	NA
East Feliciana	19.2	924	71.4	0.3	5.0	0.4	5.4	14.8	711	43	116	3 100	NA	NA	NA
Evangeline	45.6	1 336	68.0	0.9	4.7	0.0	6.6	14.5	426	67	188	2 252	NA	NA	NA
Franklin	25.4	1 149	79.4	0.2	1.4	0.0	10.1	3.7	169	59	122	1 400	NA	NA	NA
Grant	20.7	1 114	82.0	0.3	1.9	0.0	4.8	4.3	232	95	113	1 041	NA	NA	NA
Iberia	148.5	2 060	50.0	22.0	4.1	0.4	3.4	73.0	1 013	132	407	4 315	NA	NA	NA
Iberville	72.2	2 319	45.8	0.1	11.4	3.3	6.4	105.5	3 391	227	172	3 069	NA	NA	NA
Jackson	21.2	1 366	68.7	0.8	3.9	0.0	7.9	3.7	239	32	86	990	NA	NA	NA
Jefferson	1 101.0	2 440	27.3	31.9	7.3	1.2	4.2	1 295.7	2 871	1 583	2 578	22 865	NA	NA	NA
Jefferson Davis	61.7	1 949	48.6	5.3	4.7	3.9	7.7	19.0	599	78	175	1 726	NA	NA	NA
Lafayette	250.2	1 359	60.6	0.3	4.7	0.0	4.7	527.0	2 863	992	1 043	11 024	NA	NA	NA
Lafourche	195.0	2 215	42.3	36.1	3.8	0.2	2.4	82.4	936	147	514	6 977	NA	NA	NA
La Salle	33.6	2 440	37.9	41.2	3.4	0.0	3.7	9.5	693	34	75	1 048	NA	NA	NA
Lincoln	57.8	1 378	57.2	1.2	6.4	0.0	7.4	30.7	731	114	242	5 845	NA	NA	NA
Livingston	108.5	1 269	78.0	0.2	2.5	0.3	3.7	40.5	474	119	487	3 714	NA	NA	NA
Madison	19.9	1 529	69.1	1.4	2.8	0.0	5.8	3.8	291	51	71	995	NA	NA	NA
Morehouse	68.8	2 167	37.9	30.0	7.4	0.0	2.3	78.9	2 488	76	174	1 617	NA	NA	NA
Natchitoches	91.2	2 445	44.6	24.0	7.1	0.7	2.3	64.9	1 740	191	212	3 990	NA	NA	NA
Orleans	1 121.7	2 391	36.0	2.4	6.2	0.3	1.7	1 648.7	3 515	13 082	6 081	44 814	NA	NA	NA
Ouachita	299.4	2 036	48.8	0.7	7.9	0.3	7.7	168.6	1 147	493	819	11 821	NA	NA	NA
Plaquemines	97.4	3 767	34.0	5.2	9.7	0.0	2.5	115.7	4 475	623	893	2 414	NA	NA	NA

1. Based on the resident population estimated as of July 1 of the year shown.

Table B. States and Counties — Land Area and Population

STATE/ County code	MSA/ PMSA/ NECMA code[1]	County Type[2]	STATE County	Land area[3] (sq km) 1990	Total persons	Rank	Per square kilometer	White	Black	Am. Indian, Eskimo, Aleut	Asian and Pacific Islander	Percent Hispanic[4]	Under 5 years	5 to 17 years	18 to 24 years	25 to 34 years	35 to 44 years	45 to 54 years
					1	2	3	4	5	6	7	8	9	10	11	12	13	14	15
			LOUISIANA—Cont'd															
22 077	...	6	Pointe Coupee	1 444	23 440	1 593	16.2	55.3	44.5	0.1	0.1	0.9	6.8	21.4	9.6	12.1	14.7	13.2
22 079	0220	3	Rapides	3 426	126 775	412	37.0	68.1	30.5	0.4	0.9	1.5	7.0	20.1	9.9	12.8	14.7	13.2
22 081	...	8	Red River	1 006	9 489	2 473	9.4	57.8	41.9	0.2	0.1	0.6	7.7	21.8	9.6	11.5	12.8	12.8
22 083	...	6	Richland	1 447	21 082	1 712	14.6	60.7	39.2	0.1	0.1	1.1	7.0	22.4	9.4	11.5	13.2	12.3
22 085	...	7	Sabine	2 241	23 812	1 585	10.6	77.6	19.2	3.1	0.2	6.0	7.0	19.9	8.7	10.8	13.0	13.9
22 087	5560	0	St. Bernard	1 205	65 406	731	54.3	92.9	5.2	0.6	1.3	8.2	6.6	18.2	9.6	12.7	15.6	12.8
22 089	5560	0	St. Charles	735	48 640	928	66.2	72.3	26.9	0.3	0.6	3.3	8.3	21.1	9.1	15.2	16.7	13.0
22 091	...	8	St. Helena	1 058	9 607	2 461	9.1	44.6	55.2	0.1	0.0	0.5	7.8	21.7	10.6	11.7	14.2	13.0
22 093	5560	1	St. James	638	21 197	1 699	33.2	46.7	53.1	0.0	0.1	0.6	7.7	21.5	11.2	13.0	14.7	13.0
22 095	5560	1	St. John the Baptist	567	42 494	1 032	74.9	59.8	39.4	0.2	0.5	3.0	8.7	23.0	9.3	15.0	16.6	12.2
22 097	3880	2	St. Landry	2 405	84 243	600	35.0	56.0	43.7	0.1	0.3	1.0	7.6	22.1	9.8	11.6	13.7	13.3
22 099	3880	2	St. Martin	1 916	47 645	943	24.9	62.7	36.1	0.2	1.0	1.5	8.1	22.2	10.7	13.3	14.6	13.1
22 101	...	4	St. Mary	1 588	56 795	819	35.8	62.2	34.2	1.3	2.2	2.5	8.0	22.0	10.2	13.3	14.4	13.4
22 103	5560	0	St. Tammany	2 213	192 945	280	87.2	86.5	12.4	0.4	0.7	2.9	7.3	20.8	7.8	12.7	18.7	14.5
22 105	...	4	Tangipahoa	2 047	98 285	526	48.0	68.0	31.4	0.2	0.4	1.4	7.2	21.7	12.2	12.1	15.2	12.7
22 107	...	9	Tensas	1 561	6 539	2 728	4.2	43.5	56.2	0.2	0.1	0.7	7.4	23.7	8.5	10.9	13.9	11.1
22 109	3350	3	Terrebonne	3 251	105 128	494	32.3	75.7	18.5	4.9	1.0	1.9	7.9	22.0	10.3	13.5	15.2	13.2
22 111	...	6	Union	2 273	22 165	1 650	9.8	69.4	30.4	0.1	0.2	0.9	6.6	19.8	9.1	11.0	14.4	14.2
22 113	...	6	Vermilion	3 040	52 258	873	17.2	82.5	15.5	0.2	1.8	1.5	7.4	21.4	9.1	12.5	13.9	12.8
22 115	...	5	Vernon	3 441	51 567	886	15.0	73.9	22.0	0.8	3.3	7.1	9.2	16.6	23.7	17.4	12.0	8.2
22 117	...	6	Washington	1 734	43 162	1 019	24.9	66.0	33.7	0.1	0.2	0.6	6.2	20.6	9.0	11.8	14.8	13.4
22 119	7680	2	Webster	1 543	42 797	1 027	27.7	65.1	34.5	0.2	0.2	0.7	6.4	19.1	8.9	11.2	14.0	14.1
22 121	0760	2	West Baton Rouge	495	20 421	1 742	41.3	60.2	39.4	0.2	0.2	1.3	7.4	20.4	10.8	13.9	15.6	13.8
22 123	...	9	West Carroll	931	12 175	2 268	13.1	81.0	18.7	0.3	0.1	1.1	6.6	20.7	8.5	10.6	13.7	14.4
22 125	...	8	West Feliciana	1 052	13 833	2 149	13.1	41.7	57.8	0.4	0.1	1.5	5.0	14.6	9.3	21.8	23.1	12.5
22 127	...	7	Winn	2 462	17 498	1 900	7.1	64.5	34.9	0.4	0.2	1.0	6.2	18.6	11.2	13.0	14.6	13.0
23 000	...	X	**MAINE**	79 939	1 253 040	X	15.7	98.3	0.5	0.5	0.8	0.7	5.4	17.8	8.8	13.3	17.4	14.4
23 001	4243	3	Androscoggin	1 218	101 337	513	83.2	98.4	0.6	0.2	0.7	1.1	5.7	18.1	9.9	13.6	16.1	14.0
23 003	...	5	Aroostook	17 280	75 836	654	4.4	97.3	1.2	0.8	0.6	0.8	5.2	17.9	9.0	13.3	16.3	13.7
23 005	6403	3	Cumberland	2 164	256 437	211	118.5	97.8	0.8	0.3	1.2	0.8	5.4	16.3	9.6	14.6	18.2	14.2
23 007	...	6	Franklin	4 398	28 797	1 419	6.5	99.2	0.1	0.3	0.4	0.5	5.2	18.9	9.8	12.0	16.6	14.8
23 009	...	6	Hancock	4 116	49 670	914	12.1	99.0	0.2	0.3	0.4	0.7	5.3	16.8	8.1	12.5	17.8	14.8
23 011	...	4	Kennebec	2 247	115 224	458	51.3	98.8	0.3	0.3	0.6	0.6	5.1	18.1	9.2	12.5	17.5	14.7
23 013	...	7	Knox	947	38 193	1 131	40.3	99.2	0.2	0.3	0.3	0.5	5.2	17.3	6.6	11.8	18.4	14.6
23 015	...	9	Lincoln	1 180	31 947	1 318	27.1	99.4	0.1	0.3	0.2	0.5	4.9	17.7	5.9	10.8	17.6	15.0
23 017	...	6	Oxford	5 383	54 288	846	10.1	99.2	0.2	0.2	0.4	0.5	5.5	18.7	6.7	12.5	16.4	14.7
23 019	0733	3	Penobscot	8 796	144 432	365	16.4	97.9	0.4	0.8	0.9	0.6	5.0	17.5	11.1	13.2	17.0	14.4
23 021	...	6	Piscataquis	10 273	18 077	1 867	1.8	99.1	0.1	0.4	0.4	0.4	4.6	19.4	6.3	10.8	16.7	15.2
23 023	...	6	Sagadahoc	658	36 267	1 184	55.1	97.5	1.2	0.2	1.1	1.3	6.2	18.0	8.2	15.1	18.3	14.9
23 025	...	7	Somerset	10 171	52 630	866	5.2	99.2	0.2	0.3	0.3	0.5	5.3	20.1	7.8	12.5	16.9	15.0
23 027	...	6	Waldo	1 890	36 965	1 161	19.6	99.2	0.2	0.3	0.3	0.6	5.5	19.6	7.4	11.9	18.3	14.7
23 029	...	7	Washington	6 653	35 352	1 212	5.3	95.7	0.2	3.7	0.3	0.5	4.9	18.7	8.0	11.4	15.8	14.7
23 031	...	4	York	2 567	177 588	301	69.2	98.5	0.4	0.2	0.9	0.8	5.7	18.3	7.7	14.0	18.1	14.2
24 000	...	X	**MARYLAND**	25 316	5 171 634	X	204.3	67.5	28.1	0.3	4.0	3.9	6.7	18.6	8.5	14.7	18.1	13.5
24 001	1900	3	Allegany	1 102	71 162	692	64.6	96.4	2.8	0.1	0.7	0.7	5.0	17.8	9.8	9.8	14.5	13.4
24 003	0720	0	Anne Arundel	1 077	480 483	115	446.1	81.3	15.7	0.4	2.6	2.5	6.6	18.9	8.8	14.4	18.5	14.6
24 005	0720	0	Baltimore	1 550	723 914	66	467.0	80.0	16.5	0.2	3.2	1.9	6.0	16.4	7.9	13.8	17.4	13.2
24 009	8840	1	Calvert	557	73 748	668	132.4	77.7	21.2	0.3	0.8	1.6	6.9	22.3	6.9	13.5	19.6	14.1
24 011	...	6	Caroline	829	29 768	1 385	35.8	76.8	22.5	0.2	0.4	1.3	6.9	20.6	7.3	12.7	16.2	13.3
24 013	0720	1	Carroll	1 163	152 468	336	131.1	95.7	3.1	0.2	0.9	1.3	6.7	20.7	7.6	13.1	19.1	14.5
24 015	9160	2	Cecil	902	84 238	601	93.4	93.1	5.9	0.3	0.7	1.5	6.8	21.7	8.2	12.9	17.9	13.7
24 017	8840	1	Charles	1 194	120 946	439	101.3	73.2	24.1	0.8	1.9	2.6	7.5	22.8	8.5	14.8	18.3	13.8
24 019	...	7	Dorchester	1 444	29 709	1 383	20.6	63.2	36.0	0.1	0.6	0.8	6.1	18.1	6.9	12.2	15.5	13.2
24 021	8840	1	Frederick	1 717	190 869	282	111.2	90.8	7.4	0.2	1.5	1.9	6.9	20.5	8.9	14.1	19.3	13.4
24 023	...	8	Garrett	1 679	29 389	1 397	17.5	99.1	0.6	0.1	0.2	0.7	5.8	22.0	7.4	11.7	15.3	13.6
24 025	0720	0	Harford	1 141	217 908	250	191.0	86.2	11.5	0.3	2.0	2.4	7.1	20.7	7.3	14.2	18.6	14.2
24 027	0720	0	Howard	653	243 112	226	372.3	77.8	15.8	0.3	6.2	3.1	7.0	19.6	7.0	15.9	21.2	15.2
24 029	...	6	Kent	724	19 089	1 816	26.4	73.0	26.3	0.3	0.5	3.2	5.4	16.1	10.8	10.9	14.0	13.6
24 031	8840	0	Montgomery	1 281	852 174	46	665.2	72.8	15.7	0.3	11.1	10.8	6.7	17.6	7.2	15.5	19.3	14.0
24 033	8840	0	Prince George's	1 260	781 781	56	620.5	36.7	58.2	0.3	4.8	5.2	7.0	18.5	10.7	16.4	18.8	13.6
24 035	0720	1	Queen Anne's	964	40 688	1 069	42.2	83.6	15.7	0.1	0.6	0.9	6.3	19.1	6.3	12.9	17.6	14.7
24 037	...	4	St. Mary's	936	88 758	568	94.8	79.5	18.3	0.4	1.8	2.5	8.1	21.9	9.7	15.6	16.7	12.4
24 039	...	7	Somerset	848	24 236	1 568	28.6	51.7	47.5	0.2	0.5	1.4	4.7	15.7	14.6	15.2	15.1	11.2
24 041	...	6	Talbot	697	33 550	1 270	48.1	74.9	24.5	0.1	0.5	0.8	5.5	16.1	6.0	11.3	15.6	13.7

1. MSA = Metropolitan Statistical Area. PMSA = Primary MSA. NECMA = New England County Metropolitan Area. See Appendix A for explanation of these concepts. See Appendix B for list of metropolitan areas identified by type, with component counties.   2. County typology code from the Economic Research Service of USDA. See Appendix A for definition.   3. Dry land or land partially or temporarily covered by water.   4. Hispanic persons may be of any race.

Table B. States and Counties — **Population and Households**

	Population, 1999 (cont'd) Age (percent) (cont'd)				Population — change and components of change, 1980–1999							Households, 1990				
STATE County	55 to 64 years	65 to 74 years	75 years and over	Percent female	Total persons 1990	Total persons 1980	Percent change 1980–1990	Percent change 1990–1999	Births	Deaths	Net migration	Number	Percent change, 1980–1990	Persons per household	Female family householder[1]	One person
	16	17	18	19	20	21	22	23	24	25	26	27	28	29	30	31
LOUISIANA—Cont'd																
Pointe Coupee	9.3	6.8	6.1	51.9	22 540	24 045	-6.3	4.0	3 252	2 144	-155	7 736	0.4	2.88	15.2	21.5
Rapides	9.2	7.0	6.0	52.5	131 556	135 282	-2.8	-3.6	17 927	11 841	-11 228	45 941	2.6	2.73	15.3	23.0
Red River	9.4	7.4	7.1	52.8	9 526	10 433	-10.0	-0.4	1 373	1 084	-329	3 321	-5.5	2.77	16.6	23.6
Richland	9.8	7.0	7.3	53.1	20 629	22 187	-7.0	2.2	3 230	2 299	-410	7 079	-2.0	2.84	16.8	22.2
Sabine	11.2	8.4	7.3	51.2	22 646	25 280	-10.4	5.1	2 891	2 535	895	8 361	-6.2	2.64	12.0	24.1
St. Bernard	10.4	8.7	5.4	52.2	66 631	64 097	4.0	-1.8	8 515	6 089	-3 500	23 156	12.5	2.85	13.1	18.3
St. Charles	8.6	4.7	3.3	51.3	42 437	37 259	13.9	14.6	6 856	2 655	2 148	14 333	24.8	2.94	12.6	17.6
St. Helena	9.1	6.0	5.9	52.3	9 874	9 827	0.5	-2.7	1 028	855	-408	3 328	8.3	2.94	16.1	22.9
St. James	8.3	5.7	4.9	52.4	20 879	21 495	-2.9	1.5	3 244	1 573	-1 300	6 432	6.4	3.22	18.2	15.6
St. John the Baptist	6.6	4.8	3.8	51.3	39 996	31 924	25.3	6.2	6 593	2 458	-1 516	12 710	36.6	3.13	15.1	16.2
St. Landry	9.6	6.7	5.7	52.4	80 312	84 128	-4.5	4.9	12 599	7 776	-665	27 477	2.4	2.88	16.5	21.8
St. Martin	8.1	5.7	4.3	51.6	44 097	40 214	9.7	8.0	6 909	3 202	-39	14 634	20.2	2.98	14.7	18.4
St. Mary	8.3	5.7	4.6	51.1	58 086	64 253	-9.6	-2.2	8 810	4 604	-5 380	19 456	-2.9	2.95	15.4	20.5
St. Tammany	8.5	5.9	3.9	50.8	144 500	110 869	30.3	33.5	22 557	10 781	36 750	50 346	41.0	2.84	10.4	18.5
Tangipahoa	8.7	5.4	4.8	52.1	85 709	80 698	6.2	14.7	14 797	8 551	6 552	29 663	14.3	2.79	16.4	23.1
Tensas	9.3	8.0	7.2	53.9	7 103	8 525	-16.7	-7.9	893	964	-479	2 515	-14.4	2.77	20.6	25.2
Terrebonne	8.3	5.6	4.0	51.3	96 982	94 393	2.7	8.4	15 708	6 984	-345	31 837	8.7	3.02	12.8	17.4
Union	10.6	7.3	7.0	52.1	20 796	21 167	-1.8	6.6	2 765	2 538	1 226	7 528	4.1	2.71	12.9	21.4
Vermilion	9.5	6.9	6.5	51.4	50 055	48 458	3.3	4.4	6 795	4 508	47	17 762	9.8	2.79	12.4	21.8
Vernon	5.1	4.2	3.5	43.7	61 961	53 475	15.9	-16.8	10 663	3 044	-21 782	19 111	23.6	2.87	8.1	17.4
Washington	10.1	7.8	6.2	51.6	43 185	44 207	-2.3	0.1	6 008	4 795	-1 099	15 475	0.5	2.70	16.5	23.9
Webster	10.8	8.0	7.5	52.7	41 989	43 631	-3.8	1.9	5 207	4 758	501	15 849	1.0	2.60	15.0	25.2
West Baton Rouge	8.4	5.7	3.9	51.7	19 419	19 086	1.7	5.2	3 143	1 500	-588	6 606	13.9	2.91	17.3	19.1
West Carroll	10.2	7.8	7.5	52.1	12 093	12 922	-6.4	0.7	1 440	1 343	29	4 394	-2.3	2.72	10.2	23.8
West Feliciana	6.7	3.7	3.2	33.7	12 915	12 186	6.0	7.1	1 145	732	519	2 741	18.5	2.87	17.9	22.4
Winn	9.6	7.2	6.6	48.3	16 498	17 253	-5.7	6.1	2 098	1 834	284	5 787	-4.5	2.69	13.8	24.6
MAINE	8.9	7.4	6.6	51.2	1 227 928	1 125 043	9.1	2.0	137 791	107 664	-3 452	465 312	17.7	2.56	9.5	23.3
Androscoggin	8.7	7.2	6.7	51.5	105 259	99 509	5.8	-3.7	11 994	9 310	-6 329	40 017	13.6	2.55	10.9	24.4
Aroostook	8.9	8.3	7.3	49.8	86 936	91 344	-4.8	-12.8	8 695	7 425	-13 063	31 366	6.9	2.62	8.6	21.7
Cumberland	8.4	6.9	6.3	51.9	243 135	215 789	12.7	5.5	29 475	20 519	4 737	94 512	20.1	2.49	9.8	25.2
Franklin	8.8	7.1	6.7	51.4	29 008	27 447	5.7	-0.7	2 994	2 363	-753	10 778	14.4	2.60	9.0	22.3
Hancock	9.6	7.6	7.5	50.7	46 948	41 781	12.4	5.8	4 806	4 916	2 867	18 342	18.8	2.48	8.2	24.0
Kennebec	8.8	7.4	6.6	51.6	115 904	109 889	5.5	-0.6	12 377	10 296	-2 468	43 889	13.8	2.55	9.9	24.2
Knox	9.4	8.7	8.1	51.1	36 310	32 941	10.2	5.2	3 852	3 798	1 949	14 344	17.9	2.45	9.2	26.0
Lincoln	9.8	9.6	8.6	51.0	30 357	25 691	18.2	5.2	3 101	2 974	1 549	11 968	26.1	2.52	7.5	23.6
Oxford	9.6	8.4	7.4	51.0	52 602	49 043	7.3	3.2	5 591	5 234	1 475	20 064	15.0	2.58	9.8	22.4
Penobscot	9.0	6.9	5.9	51.1	146 601	137 015	7.0	-1.5	15 137	11 806	-5 153	54 063	17.6	2.57	9.9	22.6
Piscataquis	9.7	9.1	8.3	51.0	18 653	17 634	5.8	-3.1	1 734	1 969	-273	7 194	14.4	2.56	8.3	23.3
Sagadahoc	7.4	6.3	5.6	50.5	33 535	28 795	16.5	8.1	4 080	2 511	1 090	12 581	25.4	2.63	9.3	21.6
Somerset	9.2	6.9	6.2	50.7	49 767	45 049	10.5	5.8	5 688	4 580	1 885	18 513	20.6	2.65	10.0	21.2
Waldo	9.3	7.2	6.1	50.6	33 018	28 414	16.2	12.0	3 856	2 860	3 039	12 415	26.3	2.63	9.3	21.7
Washington	10.1	8.4	7.9	50.7	35 308	34 963	1.0	0.1	3 773	3 856	191	13 418	9.8	2.55	10.0	23.6
York	8.5	7.3	6.1	51.2	164 587	139 739	17.8	7.9	20 638	13 247	5 805	61 848	24.6	2.63	8.9	21.4
MARYLAND	8.2	6.2	5.3	51.4	4 780 753	4 216 933	13.4	8.2	687 293	375 178	76 811	1 748 991	19.7	2.67	13.3	22.6
Allegany	10.9	9.0	9.8	52.4	74 946	80 548	-7.0	-5.0	7 692	9 180	-2 757	29 634	-0.1	2.43	11.0	27.7
Anne Arundel	8.3	5.7	4.3	49.7	427 239	370 775	15.2	12.5	60 509	28 003	17 522	149 114	23.2	2.76	10.0	18.2
Baltimore	9.5	8.4	7.4	52.2	692 134	655 615	5.6	4.6	86 779	62 502	9 637	268 280	13.0	2.53	11.1	23.4
Calvert	7.4	5.2	4.1	50.0	51 372	34 638	48.3	43.6	8 249	3 429	17 560	16 986	58.3	3.01	9.4	14.2
Caroline	9.3	6.8	6.8	51.1	27 035	23 143	16.8	9.9	3 656	2 806	1 910	9 983	21.5	2.66	11.6	21.7
Carroll	7.7	5.2	5.4	50.4	123 372	96 356	28.0	23.6	17 363	9 061	21 087	42 248	37.9	2.85	7.7	16.0
Cecil	8.4	5.7	4.6	49.8	71 347	60 430	18.1	18.1	10 042	5 536	8 463	24 725	27.7	2.81	10.2	17.9
Charles	6.6	4.4	3.3	50.2	101 154	72 751	39.0	19.6	15 277	5 758	9 788	32 950	54.1	3.03	11.9	14.2
Dorchester	10.7	8.8	8.5	52.5	30 236	30 623	-1.3	-1.7	3 488	3 577	-341	12 117	7.0	2.46	14.7	25.8
Frederick	7.4	4.8	4.5	50.4	150 208	114 792	30.9	27.1	24 058	10 177	26 866	52 570	40.2	2.78	8.7	18.0
Garrett	9.2	7.3	7.6	50.8	28 138	26 490	6.2	4.4	3 523	2 598	399	10 110	15.4	2.74	8.8	20.4
Harford	7.9	5.7	4.2	50.5	182 132	145 930	24.8	19.6	27 283	11 555	18 915	63 193	35.8	2.83	9.2	16.9
Howard	6.7	4.0	3.3	50.3	187 328	118 572	58.0	29.8	30 915	8 942	33 781	68 337	70.9	2.71	8.4	19.2
Kent	10.4	9.8	8.9	51.7	17 842	16 695	6.9	7.0	1 934	2 098	1 457	6 702	9.3	2.49	10.7	24.8
Montgomery	8.1	6.1	5.5	51.9	762 875	579 053	30.7	11.7	112 962	45 388	22 630	282 228	36.2	2.65	9.4	22.3
Prince George's	7.1	4.7	3.2	51.8	722 705	665 071	9.5	8.2	117 497	43 451	-16 620	258 011	14.8	2.76	16.3	21.6
Queen Anne's	10.2	7.1	5.7	50.4	33 953	25 508	33.1	19.8	4 153	2 795	5 410	12 489	41.1	2.69	8.5	17.8
St. Mary's	6.7	4.9	4.0	49.4	75 974	59 895	26.8	16.8	11 758	4 667	4 686	25 500	35.7	2.87	9.1	18.1
Somerset	9.2	7.2	7.1	46.1	23 440	19 188	22.2	3.4	2 398	2 714	1 184	7 977	18.2	2.48	14.8	25.7
Talbot	11.1	10.4	10.4	52.3	30 549	25 604	19.3	9.8	3 381	3 522	3 233	12 677	27.6	2.38	9.9	25.3

1. No spouse present.

Table B. States and Counties — Vital Statistics, Health Resources, and Crime

STATE County	Births, average 1996–1998 Total	Rate[1]	Deaths, average 1996–1998 Number Total	Number Infant[2]	Rate Total[1]	Rate Infant[3]	Physicians,[4] 1998 Number	Rate[5]	Hospitals,[4] 1998 Number	Beds Number	Rate[5]	Medicare enrollees 1999	Serious crimes known to police, 1998 Total Number	Rate[7]
	32	33	34	35	36	37	38	39	40	41	42	43	44	45
LOUISIANA—Cont'd														
Pointe Coupee	339	14.5	239	3	10.2	7.9	14	59	1	32	136	3 327	574	2 419
Rapides	1 869	14.8	1 278	21	10.1	11.2	306	241	3	746	588	19 949	8 134	6 747
Red River	133	13.8	117	1	12.2	5.0	5	52	1	74	771	1 542	186	1 911
Richland	343	16.4	260	3	12.4	8.7	18	86	2	101	480	3 785	NA	NA
Sabine	305	12.8	266	3	11.2	10.9	8	34	2	104	437	4 179	488	2 208
St. Bernard	865	13.1	680	4	10.3	4.2	50	76	2	226	342	10 829	423	636
St. Charles	721	15.2	310	4	6.5	5.5	32	66	1	104	215	4 872	2 160	4 510
St. Helena	98	10.1	93	1	9.7	13.7	4	42	1	25	261	1 002	NA	NA
St. James	320	15.2	178	3	8.5	10.4	10	47	1	41	194	2 815	951	5 603
St. John the Baptist	691	16.4	280	7	6.7	10.1	26	62	1	102	241	4 091	1 643	3 895
St. Landry	1 378	16.5	853	13	10.2	9.2	83	99	3	274	327	14 294	2 948	3 575
St. Martin	739	15.8	364	7	7.8	9.9	15	32	1	12	25	5 676	746	1 912
St. Mary	903	15.8	488	6	8.6	6.3	56	98	2	147	257	7 478	2 841	5 738
St. Tammany	2 544	13.8	1 291	16	7.0	6.3	447	237	4	610	323	21 547	7 240	3 907
Tangipahoa	1 609	16.8	946	13	9.9	8.3	91	94	4	385	397	13 585	6 831	7 143
Tensas	89	13.3	97	1	14.5	7.5	2	30	0	0	0	1 193	NA	NA
Terrebonne	1 666	16.2	772	17	7.5	10.2	136	130	2	396	379	13 508	6 954	6 713
Union	310	14.2	272	5	12.5	17.2	12	55	2	60	273	3 765	626	2 862
Vermilion	731	14.2	506	6	9.8	7.8	41	79	2	150	288	8 157	1 086	2 482
Vernon	955	18.3	344	9	6.6	9.4	52	101	1	66	128	4 697	1 539	3 091
Washington	669	15.5	542	8	12.5	11.5	42	98	3	235	546	7 821	2 037	4 709
Webster	571	13.4	525	5	12.3	8.2	29	68	3	266	623	8 062	940	2 198
West Baton Rouge	335	16.3	174	3	8.5	10.0	5	24	0	0	0	2 486	1 441	7 762
West Carroll	146	12.0	152	1	12.4	4.6	7	57	1	50	409	2 270	221	2 158
West Feliciana	112	8.4	84	1	6.3	8.9	11	82	1	24	178	1 022	246	1 846
Winn	224	12.6	201	3	11.3	11.9	10	56	1	73	412	2 482	288	1 615
MAINE	13 725	11.1	11 956	73	9.6	5.3	2 950	237	40	4 371	351	213 210	37 826	3 041
Androscoggin	1 173	11.6	1 008	6	9.9	5.4	238	235	2	440	434	17 884	4 082	4 033
Aroostook	754	9.8	820	5	10.7	6.2	129	170	5	459	603	15 355	1 657	2 146
Cumberland	3 030	12.0	2 276	14	9.0	4.5	1 007	397	6	1 049	414	40 254	9 431	3 746
Franklin	296	10.2	260	1	9.0	2.2	51	176	1	70	242	4 919	1 032	3 551
Hancock	486	9.8	544	3	11.0	5.5	115	230	3	139	278	9 098	1 290	2 595
Kennebec	1 203	10.4	1 151	6	10.0	5.3	312	271	3	451	391	20 004	3 209	2 765
Knox	501	13.2	404	2	10.7	4.0	115	304	1	157	415	7 444	765	2 034
Lincoln	310	9.8	338	1	10.7	4.3	78	245	2	82	258	6 599	496	1 567
Oxford	557	10.4	593	2	11.1	4.2	65	121	2	99	184	10 082	1 489	2 764
Penobscot	1 541	10.8	1 300	10	9.1	6.3	350	246	4	633	445	23 525	4 814	3 366
Piscataquis	161	8.8	216	2	11.8	14.5	20	109	2	96	525	3 782	468	2 551
Sagadahoc	401	11.3	284	1	8.0	1.7	56	157	1	53	148	4 675	854	2 391
Somerset	591	11.3	488	4	9.3	6.2	56	107	2	100	191	8 664	1 703	3 256
Waldo	377	10.5	307	2	8.5	4.4	59	162	1	49	134	5 795	470	1 303
Washington	363	10.1	441	3	12.3	7.3	43	121	2	95	268	7 120	818	2 358
York	1 980	11.4	1 525	12	8.8	6.1	256	146	3	399	228	27 890	5 119	2 945
MARYLAND	71 240	14.0	41 936	613	8.2	8.6	17 802	347	48	13 611	265	634 527	275 527	5 366
Allegany	778	10.8	1 008	3	13.9	4.3	172	241	2	462	648	15 306	2 576	3 535
Anne Arundel	6 442	13.7	3 221	42	6.8	6.5	950	200	3	996	209	53 407	20 997	4 432
Baltimore	8 965	12.4	6 917	71	9.6	7.9	2 941	407	4	1 514	210	114 589	40 085	5 518
Calvert	944	13.6	428	5	6.2	5.3	84	117	1	157	218	7 062	1 630	2 330
Caroline	362	12.4	307	4	10.5	12.0	12	41	0	0	0	4 517	1 158	3 890
Carroll	2 032	13.8	1 072	13	7.3	6.6	173	116	1	158	106	19 242	3 570	2 410
Cecil	1 102	13.6	645	9	8.0	8.2	86	104	1	166	201	9 782	3 004	3 727
Charles	1 597	13.8	656	10	5.7	6.3	120	102	1	131	111	9 701	5 253	4 528
Dorchester	332	11.2	383	3	12.9	9.0	52	176	1	114	386	5 675	1 041	3 455
Frederick	2 550	13.9	1 170	14	6.4	5.5	287	154	1	248	133	18 914	4 728	2 560
Garrett	345	11.7	280	3	9.5	8.7	29	99	1	76	260	4 473	601	2 020
Harford	2 938	13.9	1 392	20	6.6	6.7	313	146	2	494	230	22 826	5 545	2 588
Howard	3 330	14.5	1 076	14	4.7	4.2	1 088	460	1	223	94	15 068	7 723	3 349
Kent	198	10.5	220	2	11.6	8.4	51	269	1	64	338	4 485	476	2 477
Montgomery	11 990	14.4	5 050	78	6.1	6.5	6 108	726	5	1 493	178	94 403	31 092	3 472
Prince George's	11 971	15.5	5 043	151	6.5	12.6	1 274	164	5	1 281	165	66 001	54 090	6 963
Queen Anne's	452	11.6	331	5	8.5	11.8	30	76	0	0	0	4 682	1 103	2 799
St. Mary's	1 231	14.5	560	11	6.6	8.9	74	84	1	107	122	8 018	2 438	2 823
Somerset	239	9.8	275	3	11.3	11.2	23	95	1	39	161	3 901	829	3 360
Talbot	329	10.1	376	2	11.5	7.1	155	469	1	191	578	7 101	1 205	3 616

1. Per 1,000 estimated resident population, average 1996–1998.   2. Deaths of infants under 1 year old.   3. Deaths of infants under 1 year old per 1,000 live births.   4. Data subject to copyright.   5. Per 100,000 resident population as of July 1 of the year shown.   6. Data for serious crimes have not been adjusted for underreporting; this may affect comparability between geographic areas and over time.   7. Per 100,000 population estimated by the FBI.

Table B. States and Counties — Crime, Education, Money Income, and Poverty

STATE County	Violent	Property	Total	Percent private	High school graduate or more	Bachelor's degree or more	Total current expenditures (mil dol)	Current expenditures per student (dollars)	Per capita[6] (dollars)	Dollars	Percent change, 1979–1989 (constant 1989 dollars)	Percent with $100,000 or more	Median household income	All persons	Persons under 18	Persons 5–17 in families
	46	47	48	49	50	51	52	53	54	55	56	57	58	59	60	61
LOUISIANA—Cont'd																
Pointe Coupee	809	1 610	6 133	24.7	58.6	9.7	16.2	4 289	8 709	18 772	-10.6	1.3	27 541	20.1	27.1	26.7
Rapides	835	5 912	34 655	13.5	69.0	14.6	117.1	4 608	10 014	20 811	-7.3	2.1	27 231	20.0	29.1	26.8
Red River	360	1 551	2 410	10.4	57.4	8.7	9.9	4 169	7 213	14 831	-13.1	0.7	21 928	26.0	35.6	35.1
Richland	NA	NA	5 454	7.2	52.0	10.7	19.0	4 469	7 791	15 298	-4.4	0.6	20 515	27.5	37.8	36.3
Sabine	339	1 869	5 306	3.9	61.9	8.3	20.9	4 369	8 539	16 790	-11.7	1.2	25 824	19.0	26.3	26.8
St. Bernard	68	568	16 387	29.9	67.2	7.3	43.6	4 636	10 512	25 482	-19.5	1.2	32 478	13.2	19.7	18.8
St. Charles	791	3 719	11 898	18.2	74.0	14.8	65.3	6 348	11 901	31 777	-10.0	2.0	41 905	12.2	17.4	16.7
St. Helena	NA	NA	2 632	14.1	57.6	7.7	7.2	4 386	7 199	15 475	-4.3	0.4	22 255	24.6	37.1	33.0
St. James	1 555	4 048	5 860	16.8	61.1	8.1	24.3	5 382	8 959	23 105	-25.1	0.9	30 830	16.8	22.7	22.1
St. John the Baptist	263	3 632	11 725	32.2	71.5	11.4	33.7	4 668	10 454	29 035	-14.1	1.5	35 588	15.9	22.2	22.3
St. Landry	424	3 151	22 588	14.0	55.3	9.7	71.1	3 835	7 671	14 670	-22.5	1.5	22 364	25.3	33.5	32.2
St. Martin	218	1 694	11 958	9.9	53.7	6.7	39.8	4 194	7 990	19 116	-24.4	1.1	27 427	18.2	25.3	25.1
St. Mary	685	5 053	15 776	11.2	58.1	8.3	55.7	4 723	8 777	20 980	-32.1	1.3	29 528	19.8	26.6	26.6
St. Tammany	384	3 523	40 765	20.1	76.9	23.1	161.9	4 891	13 605	30 656	-7.6	4.8	43 653	9.9	14.3	13.6
Tangipahoa	699	6 444	24 866	10.5	60.7	12.9	74.8	3 852	8 150	16 849	-14.8	1.3	24 164	23.1	30.8	29.4
Tensas	NA	NA	1 942	18.4	58.1	11.7	7.1	4 252	7 896	11 931	-13.5	2.0	17 824	33.8	44.4	44.6
Terrebonne	917	5 796	27 274	12.0	59.6	9.4	91.1	4 106	9 505	21 765	-32.3	1.8	31 744	16.8	22.3	22.2
Union	759	2 103	4 870	4.7	64.3	11.0	14.7	3 656	8 903	18 083	-3.1	1.4	26 478	17.7	25.2	25.1
Vermilion	441	2 041	13 698	11.3	58.3	8.8	42.8	4 225	8 752	18 202	-24.1	1.4	27 680	17.4	23.1	22.9
Vernon	613	2 478	14 381	4.8	76.9	10.3	51.2	4 665	8 414	19 147	0.9	0.8	28 836	16.5	20.5	23.5
Washington	779	3 930	11 179	8.2	61.5	8.6	40.2	4 201	8 292	16 246	-12.6	1.3	22 584	24.7	34.8	32.4
Webster	461	1 737	10 156	6.5	63.9	10.0	35.3	4 202	9 191	18 716	-9.9	1.1	26 388	19.1	29.0	27.6
West Baton Rouge	689	7 073	5 078	21.4	66.0	9.9	18.2	4 299	10 255	24 852	-13.2	1.6	33 251	15.6	22.8	21.8
West Carroll	430	1 728	2 873	1.6	52.0	8.7	10.9	3 826	7 611	14 924	12.0	1.0	19 942	24.4	35.6	33.0
West Feliciana	203	1 643	2 637	11.9	57.2	7.8	13.3	5 617	6 796	19 402	-3.6	1.0	30 796	22.1	19.5	20.8
Winn	320	1 295	3 826	3.3	58.0	9.0	15.9	4 747	8 728	16 967	0.2	1.4	24 807	22.5	29.1	29.0
MAINE	126	2 915	304 868	12.3	78.8	18.8	1 352.0	6 327	12 957	27 854	20.3	2.4	33 140	10.7	14.9	13.4
Androscoggin	152	3 881	25 878	18.0	71.8	12.6	102.4	6 238	12 397	26 979	19.0	2.0	34 242	10.7	14.5	13.7
Aroostook	85	2 061	21 813	3.8	70.9	12.5	85.5	6 330	10 449	22 230	7.3	1.2	29 124	15.0	19.6	17.6
Cumberland	182	3 564	58 915	16.5	85.0	27.6	255.8	6 588	15 816	32 286	25.4	4.5	41 393	8.1	11.3	9.9
Franklin	48	3 503	8 106	5.0	79.7	17.7	33.9	6 265	10 830	24 432	8.0	0.9	30 712	12.7	17.6	15.9
Hancock	107	2 488	10 783	13.9	83.3	21.4	54.6	6 508	12 347	25 247	24.0	1.9	33 397	10.1	14.5	12.9
Kennebec	89	2 676	29 755	16.6	78.9	18.1	126.3	6 416	12 885	28 616	16.2	2.1	35 559	10.6	14.7	12.4
Knox	82	1 952	7 660	9.9	80.8	19.8	32.7	6 804	12 949	25 405	25.1	2.1	33 478	10.8	15.5	14.1
Lincoln	47	1 520	6 759	13.0	81.4	22.2	46.2	7 214	13 479	28 373	31.9	2.7	35 696	9.6	15.3	13.3
Oxford	56	2 708	12 130	8.4	76.9	12.7	68.2	6 293	11 373	24 535	12.4	1.6	30 688	12.3	17.4	15.9
Penobscot	104	3 262	41 743	9.7	79.1	17.7	143.8	6 066	12 231	26 631	12.0	2.3	33 574	12.1	16.4	14.5
Piscataquis	283	2 268	4 843	6.0	75.4	12.3	21.8	6 398	9 919	22 132	7.7	0.7	28 599	13.6	19.1	17.7
Sagadahoc	45	2 346	8 010	10.8	81.1	21.6	45.2	6 502	13 668	31 948	28.3	2.1	39 991	7.8	11.0	10.7
Somerset	285	2 971	12 262	6.7	71.9	10.5	73.6	6 057	10 471	22 829	15.1	1.2	28 300	14.9	20.6	18.8
Waldo	36	1 267	8 219	9.8	77.4	16.8	33.2	6 298	11 047	23 148	18.9	1.9	29 812	14.3	19.5	18.2
Washington	135	2 223	8 682	5.2	73.2	12.7	38.5	7 050	9 607	19 993	14.2	0.7	25 673	17.7	24.5	21.7
York	121	2 824	39 310	13.9	79.5	19.0	195.5	6 106	14 131	32 432	25.8	2.6	39 288	8.0	11.3	9.7
MARYLAND	797	4 569	1 212 333	19.0	78.4	26.5	5 529.0	6 755	17 730	39 386	15.9	6.9	45 289	9.5	14.9	13.5
Allegany	391	3 144	18 318	9.4	71.0	11.8	70.9	6 335	11 393	21 546	-7.4	1.7	28 794	15.9	24.2	22.7
Anne Arundel	544	3 888	108 751	16.7	81.1	24.6	456.3	6 309	18 509	45 147	18.8	7.6	56 147	5.3	9.7	8.8
Baltimore	844	4 674	164 527	22.6	78.4	25.0	703.0	6 755	18 658	38 837	7.1	6.4	44 715	7.6	12.8	11.2
Calvert	354	1 976	13 544	10.9	79.3	17.6	86.7	6 128	17 521	47 608	28.5	7.1	57 017	6.6	10.4	9.5
Caroline	679	3 211	5 886	7.6	66.8	10.8	33.8	6 053	11 926	27 758	14.6	1.8	32 902	12.8	20.4	19.4
Carroll	186	2 224	31 080	16.1	78.5	19.6	156.4	5 964	16 320	42 378	18.4	4.8	55 906	4.9	7.2	6.5
Cecil	574	3 153	17 521	12.8	72.2	12.1	88.8	5 961	14 314	36 019	17.3	3.2	44 650	9.0	14.2	13.2
Charles	542	3 986	27 744	16.4	81.0	16.2	131.3	6 207	16 555	46 415	14.3	5.6	54 110	7.4	12.2	10.9
Dorchester	627	2 828	6 171	7.2	64.7	10.9	33.7	6 418	12 437	24 922	8.0	2.0	29 361	15.5	25.3	24.1
Frederick	364	2 196	38 746	16.1	80.4	22.0	199.2	5 901	16 571	41 382	19.7	4.8	53 415	5.8	8.6	8.0
Garrett	108	1 912	6 779	5.4	68.4	9.5	33.8	6 541	10 124	22 733	3.8	1.2	30 197	15.8	24.2	22.6
Harford	251	2 337	47 534	15.4	81.6	21.5	226.5	6 007	16 612	41 680	15.2	4.9	52 231	6.4	9.6	8.9
Howard	191	3 158	52 053	18.8	91.1	46.9	280.7	7 223	22 704	54 348	17.4	11.9	68 024	4.4	6.6	6.3
Kent	203	2 274	4 193	28.3	71.4	16.9	20.0	6 888	15 488	30 104	28.5	4.8	36 391	10.7	17.1	16.4
Montgomery	243	3 499	193 806	24.7	90.6	49.9	1 007.4	8 223	25 591	54 089	11.3	16.2	62 130	5.6	8.8	8.2
Prince George's	1 012	5 951	202 502	17.5	83.2	25.5	839.9	6 709	17 391	43 127	14.9	5.5	47 882	9.3	15.1	12.8
Queen Anne's	272	2 527	7 643	12.4	76.8	19.9	39.9	6 273	17 489	39 190	35.0	5.9	48 226	7.5	11.3	11.6
St. Mary's	324	2 499	19 689	15.3	77.1	16.8	89.4	6 245	14 454	37 158	18.3	3.2	49 495	8.8	13.2	13.1
Somerset	531	2 829	5 775	9.9	61.2	9.6	22.2	6 942	10 232	23 379	16.5	1.2	26 867	21.8	29.1	26.8
Talbot	414	3 202	5 838	17.0	76.5	23.0	26.9	6 053	18 755	31 885	15.0	7.3	39 663	9.7	16.7	15.9

1. Data for serious crimes have not been adjusted for underreporting; this may affect comparability between geographic areas and over time.   2. Per 100,000 population estimated by the FBI.   3. All persons 3 years old and over enrolled in nursery school through college.   4. Persons 25 years old and over.   5. Elementary and secondary education expenditures, local government fiscal years ending between July 1, 1996 and June 30, 1997.   6. Based on population enumerated as of April 1, 1990.

STATE County	Total (mil dol)	Percent change, 1997–1998	Per capita[1] Dollars	Per capita[1] Rank	Wages and salaries[2] (mil dol)	Proprietor's income (mil dol)	Dividends, interest, and rent (mil dol)	Total (mil dol)	Total (mil dol)	Social Security (mil dol)	Medical payments (mil dol)	Income maintenance (mil dol)	Unemployment insurance (mil dol)
	62	63	64	65	66	67	68	69	70	71	72	73	74
LOUISIANA—Cont'd													
Pointe Coupee	437	5.0	18 559	2 191	153	16	73	97	93	27	40	23	1
Rapides	2 790	5.2	22 062	1 083	1 583	243	484	654	632	163	368	62	4
Red River	170	1.9	17 646	2 452	58	20	21	45	43	13	20	8	1
Richland	335	0.5	15 940	2 801	143	17	49	117	113	28	60	21	1
Sabine	404	2.7	16 979	2 616	144	63	71	102	98	38	41	13	1
St. Bernard	1 376	4.4	20 900	1 423	471	62	194	280	268	107	129	19	2
St. Charles	1 176	7.2	24 426	572	1 024	35	153	136	128	52	56	13	1
St. Helena	175	6.1	18 244	2 283	42	17	15	46	44	15	18	10	0
St. James	422	5.6	20 050	1 696	323	10	65	78	75	27	35	10	1
St. John the Baptist	864	5.5	20 480	1 567	415	32	94	126	119	44	55	14	2
St. Landry	1 447	3.2	17 275	2 539	531	108	228	391	377	114	184	63	4
St. Martin	790	6.1	16 640	2 690	269	37	104	161	152	54	69	22	2
St. Mary	1 133	6.3	19 805	1 779	1 057	52	204	214	204	76	88	32	2
St. Tammany	4 897	7.9	25 945	404	1 469	287	790	551	518	219	231	39	4
Tangipahoa	1 720	5.7	17 739	2 424	793	108	226	451	435	107	244	59	4
Tensas	116	2.6	17 622	2 462	45	11	18	38	37	9	17	10	0
Terrebonne	2 152	7.0	20 550	1 541	1 552	87	318	363	345	135	154	44	3
Union	406	-0.3	18 442	2 230	131	43	52	96	92	33	45	10	1
Vermilion	965	5.2	18 540	2 197	447	70	180	201	192	71	88	24	2
Vernon	968	2.1	18 837	2 113	713	35	120	138	130	38	60	17	2
Washington	772	2.8	17 894	2 379	314	46	111	239	232	69	122	31	1
Webster	802	4.2	18 765	2 131	329	49	124	206	199	72	95	20	2
West Baton Rouge	484	6.1	23 467	753	342	71	55	75	72	24	33	11	1
West Carroll	185	0.8	15 235	2 910	66	9	27	65	63	18	32	11	1
West Feliciana	205	8.3	14 981	2 929	256	10	33	33	30	9	14	5	0
Winn	272	1.9	15 360	2 897	139	20	36	76	73	22	37	10	1
MAINE	29 316	5.1	23 499	X	17 426	2 219	5 630	4 965	4 750	1 906	1 964	481	93
Androscoggin	2 296	3.5	22 671	931	1 319	121	341	446	429	163	191	46	9
Aroostook	1 422	4.5	18 557	2 192	784	119	211	363	350	125	150	41	9
Cumberland	7 623	6.5	29 960	165	5 676	488	1 617	940	897	374	375	83	9
Franklin	575	3.6	19 940	1 732	328	61	106	120	115	45	46	11	5
Hancock	1 221	5.1	24 502	559	618	148	330	192	183	83	71	15	5
Kennebec	2 705	3.6	23 502	745	1 764	176	460	474	454	178	181	49	10
Knox	930	5.3	24 475	563	447	110	262	151	145	67	56	13	2
Lincoln	804	3.7	25 321	459	264	74	265	127	121	60	43	10	2
Oxford	1 037	4.6	19 257	1 972	498	73	188	236	227	93	96	21	6
Penobscot	3 140	5.2	21 743	1 175	2 049	237	482	580	556	208	227	61	10
Piscataquis	323	3.5	17 742	2 423	151	34	59	80	77	30	30	7	1
Sagadahoc	828	4.5	23 236	808	574	48	155	108	102	45	39	9	2
Somerset	920	5.3	17 548	2 475	558	96	121	216	207	71	91	26	7
Waldo	697	6.3	19 070	2 035	234	76	128	139	132	51	53	16	4
Washington	645	4.2	18 129	2 313	316	59	104	184	178	58	81	22	5
York	4 149	5.5	23 708	700	1 846	300	801	608	578	256	235	49	7
MARYLAND	156 759	5.7	30 557	X	92 669	8 741	28 407	16 348	15 392	6 051	6 497	1 468	337
Allegany	1 474	2.7	20 429	1 583	890	70	272	401	388	137	170	27	12
Anne Arundel	14 633	5.4	30 827	139	8 839	725	2 599	1 254	1 167	519	452	76	32
Baltimore	23 284	4.2	32 269	107	13 316	994	5 054	2 704	2 569	1 231	1 014	146	62
Calvert	1 942	6.7	27 063	297	544	97	292	167	153	65	62	12	4
Caroline	542	5.9	18 375	2 245	257	28	94	102	97	44	40	9	0
Carroll	4 100	7.0	27 389	270	1 312	185	686	412	384	180	147	18	17
Cecil	2 030	9.5	24 646	539	756	114	291	238	222	96	90	17	4
Charles	3 155	6.9	26 725	326	1 130	116	464	268	246	88	108	23	5
Dorchester	614	4.5	20 766	1 465	311	42	130	134	129	54	53	13	5
Frederick	5 602	12.6	30 021	163	2 455	249	862	430	395	188	138	24	9
Garrett	536	2.3	18 293	2 265	243	99	93	117	112	43	45	11	4
Harford	5 710	6.0	26 613	333	2 360	216	884	541	501	224	188	34	13
Howard	8 533	6.9	36 294	57	4 769	482	1 400	421	377	181	132	21	8
Kent	496	5.1	26 128	384	194	41	177	89	86	44	32	5	2
Montgomery	35 575	6.3	42 393	21	20 441	2 551	7 790	1 986	1 829	833	721	111	20
Prince George's	21 750	5.4	27 996	238	12 739	725	3 033	1 837	1 692	555	750	178	32
Queen Anne's	1 067	3.8	26 878	314	267	71	201	104	96	48	34	6	1
St. Mary's	2 397	11.8	27 354	275	1 563	97	360	204	188	67	84	18	4
Somerset	388	5.5	16 006	2 794	186	23	65	94	90	34	37	9	3
Talbot	1 086	7.2	32 754	92	545	69	366	139	133	70	49	7	2

1. Based on the resident population estimated as of July 1 of the year shown. 2. Includes other labor income.

Table B. States and Counties — Earnings, Social Security, and Housing

STATE County	Earnings, 1998									Social Security beneficiaries, December 1998			Housing units, 1990	
			Goods-related[1]		Service-related and other[2]							Supplemental Security Income recipients, December 1998		
	Total (mil dol)	Farm	Total	Manu-facturing	Total	Retail trade	Finance, insurance, and real estate	Services	Govern-ment	Number	Rate[3]		Total	Percent change, 1980–1990
	75	76	77	78	79	80	81	82	83	84	85	86	87	88
LOUISIANA—Cont'd														
Pointe Coupee	169	0.5	24.7	14.3	D	12.3	3.6	14.6	22.9	3 796	161	1 208	9 695	10.8
Rapides	1 826	0.2	18.5	10.9	56.5	10.1	4.6	30.3	24.9	22 571	178	6 495	51 239	6.2
Red River	78	1.1	39.7	20.9	39.0	7.8	4.0	17.4	20.2	1 880	196	582	3 839	-5.1
Richland	160	1.5	23.1	15.0	54.8	9.7	4.0	26.8	20.6	4 010	191	1 378	8 031	1.8
Sabine	207	9.1	39.3	34.9	35.4	10.4	3.9	12.8	16.2	5 088	214	1 073	12 789	5.7
St. Bernard	532	0.1	32.0	21.3	51.9	11.1	2.7	24.3	16.0	12 708	192	1 781	25 147	16.5
St. Charles	1 059	0.0	60.4	36.7	30.7	3.1	1.1	7.1	9.0	6 075	126	981	16 016	29.1
St. Helena	59	18.9	22.6	16.0	D	4.4	2.8	13.0	29.3	2 299	240	579	3 840	7.2
St. James	333	2.3	D	56.3	D	3.9	2.5	7.2	14.1	3 363	159	620	6 934	7.5
St. John the Baptist	448	0.3	45.8	32.4	41.2	8.1	2.8	17.6	12.6	5 445	129	1 308	14 255	35.5
St. Landry	639	0.3	25.8	17.8	50.1	12.0	4.7	23.2	23.9	16 884	201	6 609	31 137	5.6
St. Martin	307	3.3	39.5	24.2	36.4	10.3	4.4	14.9	20.8	7 751	163	2 094	17 592	28.4
St. Mary	1 109	0.6	44.9	17.3	43.5	5.8	2.0	15.0	10.9	9 482	166	2 344	21 884	1.6
St. Tammany	1 756	0.1	15.6	5.9	61.5	14.6	7.1	28.8	23.0	25 620	136	3 434	57 993	40.4
Tangipahoa	901	2.5	14.0	8.9	48.6	16.8	3.7	18.5	34.8	14 915	154	5 647	33 640	15.0
Tensas	57	20.1	D	D	D	4.6	D	16.7	23.0	1 313	198	557	3 334	-14.3
Terrebonne	1 639	0.2	37.8	11.9	50.3	10.0	2.9	21.5	11.8	17 125	164	3 996	35 416	14.9
Union	174	11.5	D	34.6	D	7.4	2.2	13.3	15.9	4 373	199	856	9 304	7.9
Vermilion	517	4.4	36.2	9.8	42.4	10.0	3.4	12.9	17.0	9 845	189	1 782	20 361	13.9
Vernon	747	0.0	5.5	3.3	20.2	4.8	2.1	8.7	74.2	5 649	110	1 103	21 622	19.2
Washington	360	2.8	27.6	21.8	43.2	10.4	3.0	20.8	26.4	9 242	215	3 076	17 617	5.1
Webster	378	0.2	42.6	28.1	41.0	11.5	3.4	19.1	16.2	9 089	213	1 763	18 365	3.1
West Baton Rouge	413	2.5	D	30.9	D	4.4	2.2	10.1	10.1	3 068	148	693	7 298	13.4
West Carroll	75	7.4	21.6	14.1	D	8.5	2.4	15.4	29.1	2 637	216	722	4 831	-4.8
West Feliciana	266	0.3	D	D	D	2.2	1.8	6.5	31.4	1 227	91	373	3 392	17.0
Winn	159	-0.3	41.7	38.0	41.4	8.2	2.3	21.7	17.2	3 052	172	723	7 006	-1.1
MAINE	19 646	0.5	24.2	17.7	57.0	11.6	6.6	27.0	18.3	243 099	195	28 883	587 045	17.2
Androscoggin	1 440	0.4	D	19.3	62.6	11.5	5.5	33.9	12.1	20 664	204	2 995	43 815	14.2
Aroostook	904	2.9	D	21.0	50.2	10.9	3.0	24.4	21.3	17 561	231	2 971	38 421	7.0
Cumberland	6 165	0.0	D	11.2	D	12.3	12.5	30.5	14.5	44 664	176	4 588	109 890	19.7
Franklin	388	0.1	D	37.8	D	11.2	4.2	D	14.9	5 919	205	706	17 280	24.2
Hancock	766	1.3	D	20.2	D	12.5	3.6	29.7	15.1	10 264	206	718	30 396	21.3
Kennebec	1 940	0.6	D	9.2	D	9.5	3.2	26.9	31.1	23 829	207	3 342	51 648	13.6
Knox	557	0.0	D	12.0	D	12.3	8.0	29.1	14.6	8 321	220	830	19 009	16.4
Lincoln	338	0.6	19.6	10.1	64.9	16.5	4.4	29.3	14.9	7 410	233	502	17 538	17.1
Oxford	570	0.5	37.0	30.0	47.2	11.0	3.7	25.3	15.3	11 833	220	1 228	29 689	24.8
Penobscot	2 286	0.3	D	16.0	D	11.8	4.2	27.5	20.1	26 620	187	3 988	61 359	14.9
Piscataquis	185	0.7	D	D	D	10.5	D	16.1	18.6	3 948	216	433	13 194	23.0
Sagadahoc	622	0.1	D	D	D	5.6	1.7	14.7	14.1	5 540	155	343	14 633	21.7
Somerset	654	1.0	D	35.3	D	7.7	1.7	18.3	13.2	9 469	181	1 593	24 927	19.3
Waldo	310	0.8	28.5	18.3	D	11.9	D	D	15.3	6 801	187	908	16 181	20.2
Washington	375	4.6	D	19.2	D	10.3	D	19.1	22.7	8 156	230	1 152	19 124	5.4
York	2 147	0.2	27.9	20.8	46.9	13.4	3.2	22.6	25.0	32 087	183	2 499	79 941	19.7
MARYLAND	101 410	0.3	15.2	8.5	60.7	9.0	8.1	31.9	23.7	697 798	136	86 273	1 891 917	20.4
Allegany	960	0.0	25.9	19.3	D	11.6	4.2	26.4	22.0	16 090	226	1 865	32 513	1.9
Anne Arundel	9 564	0.1	14.9	9.0	49.0	9.1	4.7	22.5	36.1	58 427	123	4 383	157 194	21.8
Baltimore	14 310	0.3	D	13.3	D	10.4	8.9	30.8	17.6	130 311	181	9 521	281 553	15.4
Calvert	641	0.0	17.9	3.4	D	11.1	4.2	D	17.6	7 872	110	665	18 974	48.4
Caroline	284	1.1	D	17.5	D	11.8	2.7	D	15.5	5 405	183	682	10 745	21.9
Carroll	1 497	1.2	30.5	15.6	52.3	11.3	5.4	22.3	15.9	20 032	134	1 035	43 553	35.6
Cecil	871	2.8	27.8	20.8	46.0	11.5	3.0	18.9	23.4	11 448	139	998	27 656	20.4
Charles	1 245	0.0	D	4.0	D	16.1	5.8	20.4	30.5	11 293	96	1 260	34 487	51.8
Dorchester	353	3.2	D	30.7	43.6	8.3	3.4	18.7	16.7	6 524	221	827	14 269	11.9
Frederick	2 704	1.1	22.7	11.0	57.0	10.0	9.9	26.8	19.2	22 109	118	1 340	54 872	38.3
Garrett	342	2.9	27.3	10.7	55.7	13.4	5.6	23.5	14.1	5 492	188	666	14 119	15.4
Harford	2 577	1.0	D	6.9	D	11.0	3.9	20.2	39.0	26 358	123	1 810	66 446	34.4
Howard	5 251	0.3	D	6.5	D	9.2	8.4	36.7	10.5	19 719	83	1 396	72 583	70.8
Kent	235	7.8	22.3	13.7	57.5	10.0	4.8	30.4	12.4	5 030	266	311	8 181	11.4
Montgomery	22 992	0.1	10.6	5.4	67.1	7.5	9.0	40.9	22.2	91 071	108	9 501	295 723	36.8
Prince George's	13 464	0.1	13.4	4.3	53.9	11.5	4.7	25.3	32.6	71 707	92	9 389	270 090	14.2
Queen Anne's	338	1.1	25.9	12.5	54.4	16.7	5.4	19.5	18.7	5 528	139	353	13 944	39.0
St. Mary's	1 661	0.0	D	1.2	D	6.1	2.2	28.4	49.7	8 696	99	646	27 863	30.9
Somerset	209	1.3	8.7	4.1	D	9.2	2.4	D	43.4	4 446	183	1 060	9 393	20.3
Talbot	614	0.5	D	13.5	D	12.7	6.2	36.9	13.6	7 689	233	503	14 697	30.9

1. Covers mining, construction, and manufacturing.   2. Covers private sector earnings in agricultural services, forestry, and fisheries; transportation and public utilities; wholesale trade; retail trade; finance, insurance, and real estate; and services.   3. Per 1,000 resident population estimated as of July 1 of the year shown.

Table B. States and Counties — Housing, Labor Force, and Employment

STATE County	Housing units, 1990 (cont'd)								Civilian labor force, 1999				Civilian employment, 1990[5]		
		Occupied units									Unemployment			Percent	
			Owner-occupied			Renter-occupied									
				Owner cost as a percent of income											
	Total	Percent	Median value[1]	With a mort-gage	Without a mort-gage	Median rent[2]	Rent as per-cent of income	Sub-stand-ard units[3] (percent)	Total	Percent change, 1998–1999	Total	Rate[4]	Total	Professional, managerial, and technical	Precision production, craft, and repair
	89	90	91	92	93	94	95	96	97	98	99	100	101	102	103

LOUISIANA—Cont'd															
Pointe Coupee	7 736	74.1	48 300	21.6	13.2	237	33.0	8.8	9 750	-1.2	624	6.4	7 650	19.3	16.7
Rapides	45 941	66.5	52 600	19.6	13.4	338	27.6	5.2	61 657	3.2	2 785	4.5	48 788	29.2	10.5
Red River	3 321	75.6	35 500	21.7	15.1	231	31.6	10.5	3 352	-4.0	282	8.4	3 124	19.1	16.5
Richland	7 079	73.7	36 800	21.6	14.7	236	30.9	5.9	8 377	1.5	693	8.3	7 019	20.2	13.2
Sabine	8 361	80.1	37 800	22.7	13.6	249	31.2	9.5	8 930	-4.6	571	6.4	7 517	20.7	15.0
St. Bernard	23 156	75.8	63 300	19.9	12.3	406	28.7	5.3	31 202	-1.5	1 400	4.5	27 859	21.1	16.4
St. Charles	14 333	78.9	68 000	20.4	12.5	400	23.8	5.6	22 923	0.8	1 076	4.7	17 802	28.7	16.2
St. Helena	3 328	84.3	40 000	28.1	15.0	238	35.1	15.1	4 002	-1.8	205	5.1	3 162	15.9	16.2
St. James	6 432	82.4	57 100	17.3	12.8	234	31.8	10.4	9 245	2.5	949	10.3	7 598	18.4	18.5
St. John the Baptist	12 710	79.7	62 200	20.8	13.4	368	25.8	6.9	19 425	0.1	1 269	6.5	15 928	25.9	15.7
St. Landry	27 477	71.8	40 500	22.6	14.0	234	32.9	9.0	32 564	-3.1	2 457	7.5	25 000	24.0	14.6
St. Martin	14 634	79.9	44 400	21.7	13.8	266	28.8	11.5	21 720	-3.1	1 338	6.2	16 380	17.3	16.5
St. Mary	19 456	68.6	49 200	20.2	13.3	291	24.2	10.7	24 715	-9.0	2 793	11.3	20 980	21.9	14.1
St. Tammany	50 346	75.8	74 900	21.1	12.3	420	24.3	4.0	89 893	1.2	2 816	3.1	61 735	34.8	11.6
Tangipahoa	29 663	72.7	52 200	22.7	14.4	297	32.3	7.4	44 662	1.6	2 999	6.7	29 751	24.0	14.4
Tensas	2 515	71.7	34 000	26.5	15.4	179	35.1	8.4	3 131	-3.4	223	7.1	2 212	19.5	7.7
Terrebonne	31 837	73.2	52 900	20.4	12.9	347	27.1	8.8	49 127	-3.5	2 175	4.4	35 356	22.5	16.3
Union	7 528	82.3	39 600	20.8	13.7	258	27.9	6.8	12 689	3.6	534	4.2	7 459	21.4	16.4
Vermilion	17 762	75.7	43 800	21.6	13.4	263	30.2	8.3	22 530	-5.0	1 623	7.2	17 433	20.7	17.3
Vernon	19 111	50.4	47 800	21.9	13.5	351	24.5	6.0	17 413	-3.0	1 041	6.0	14 599	25.3	13.0
Washington	15 475	76.4	37 900	23.1	14.5	243	31.7	6.1	16 747	-0.8	1 010	6.0	14 061	19.8	14.3
Webster	15 849	74.1	40 600	21.2	13.8	276	28.6	5.0	19 318	-1.9	1 278	6.6	15 078	21.8	15.0
West Baton Rouge	6 606	75.9	58 400	17.3	12.8	319	25.7	6.8	10 356	2.3	437	4.2	8 039	23.0	14.0
West Carroll	4 394	77.7	30 400	23.0	13.2	238	32.5	6.9	5 491	-1.2	797	14.5	4 036	18.1	11.9
West Feliciana	2 741	68.2	61 300	20.7	14.2	248	22.6	9.9	3 784	-0.6	174	4.6	3 055	23.4	12.1
Winn	5 787	76.2	34 000	22.8	14.1	237	29.8	6.3	6 575	-3.4	423	6.4	5 562	18.6	14.1
MAINE	465 312	70.5	87 400	21.4	13.4	419	26.8	3.1	671 973	3.2	27 549	4.1	571 842	27.8	13.4
Androscoggin	40 017	62.2	86 800	21.4	13.9	374	25.9	2.4	59 994	4.2	2 417	4.0	50 588	23.4	14.5
Aroostook	31 366	69.5	45 900	18.5	14.0	332	27.6	2.8	37 990	3.3	2 140	5.6	34 343	22.9	12.1
Cumberland	94 512	64.3	118 300	22.7	13.2	522	27.2	1.7	142 167	2.1	3 309	2.3	123 322	33.9	10.2
Franklin	10 778	75.6	66 200	19.3	13.3	342	26.5	5.5	15 132	5.9	1 047	6.9	13 314	23.2	14.6
Hancock	18 342	75.7	85 200	20.9	13.6	403	25.9	4.9	28 741	5.1	1 509	5.3	21 000	27.7	16.0
Kennebec	43 889	70.9	79 300	19.4	12.6	382	25.9	2.6	59 899	1.0	2 723	4.5	56 080	30.3	12.7
Knox	14 344	73.6	92 500	22.6	14.0	399	28.1	3.0	19 997	-0.6	599	3.0	16 200	26.9	14.2
Lincoln	11 968	83.2	103 000	22.1	13.5	438	26.0	4.4	17 624	5.1	518	2.9	13 697	28.3	19.3
Oxford	20 064	76.1	69 900	19.7	12.6	333	25.9	4.6	26 534	0.9	1 766	6.7	22 593	21.7	16.1
Penobscot	54 063	69.7	69 100	19.3	13.1	397	26.9	3.2	77 866	4.2	3 311	4.3	67 389	28.1	12.8
Piscataquis	7 194	78.6	46 800	17.6	14.0	324	27.9	5.8	8 317	1.0	587	7.1	7 644	19.7	14.2
Sagadahoc	12 581	70.8	95 900	23.3	12.9	498	25.8	3.0	16 384	6.8	495	3.0	15 810	29.1	16.7
Somerset	18 513	77.3	56 400	19.2	13.1	344	26.7	4.6	25 958	1.2	1 916	7.4	21 652	20.8	14.7
Waldo	12 415	80.8	71 500	21.1	14.2	354	29.2	6.5	21 781	9.6	952	4.4	14 172	25.4	15.1
Washington	13 418	78.8	53 100	20.5	14.6	319	28.6	6.8	16 765	3.1	1 473	8.8	13 271	24.4	13.1
York	61 848	71.6	115 200	23.2	13.3	498	26.4	2.1	96 826	4.0	2 788	2.9	80 767	27.6	15.3
MARYLAND	1 748 991	65.0	116 500	21.1	12.4	548	25.4	3.3	2 765 644	0.3	97 909	3.5	2 481 342	37.0	10.3
Allegany	29 634	69.9	46 700	16.8	12.9	283	26.1	1.4	32 343	-2.7	2 306	7.1	29 731	26.5	11.5
Anne Arundel	149 114	72.9	127 900	21.3	12.4	616	25.0	2.0	255 436	1.4	7 199	2.8	224 381	36.4	11.7
Baltimore	268 280	66.3	99 900	19.7	12.1	529	23.6	1.6	394 041	0.0	14 753	3.7	366 276	36.4	10.9
Calvert	16 986	85.0	136 100	21.7	11.8	664	24.0	3.4	37 395	2.8	981	2.6	26 820	30.5	16.9
Caroline	9 983	73.5	75 000	21.2	13.4	348	25.6	4.2	16 063	-0.6	522	3.2	13 229	20.2	16.0
Carroll	42 248	78.5	126 700	21.7	11.8	484	23.8	1.3	81 474	2.0	2 054	2.5	65 924	31.8	15.5
Cecil	24 725	75.0	97 000	20.7	12.6	471	22.9	3.1	41 172	0.3	1 894	4.6	35 227	24.1	16.5
Charles	32 950	75.7	122 300	21.9	12.4	690	26.1	4.0	61 079	2.0	1 550	2.5	52 605	32.3	14.9
Dorchester	12 117	67.6	68 600	19.5	13.3	330	23.6	5.1	15 548	-2.3	1 133	7.3	14 379	20.3	15.2
Frederick	52 570	70.8	129 500	21.8	12.2	558	24.2	2.1	99 736	1.5	2 201	2.2	80 833	33.4	14.2
Garrett	10 110	79.1	60 200	20.9	12.4	310	24.9	4.3	13 476	-4.4	1 142	8.5	11 748	19.7	18.3
Harford	63 193	73.9	114 700	20.9	11.7	481	23.4	2.2	113 078	0.4	3 661	3.2	93 500	34.8	12.9
Howard	68 337	72.2	166 500	22.5	11.7	680	24.7	1.4	140 256	3.4	2 555	1.8	109 907	52.6	6.6
Kent	6 702	71.6	87 700	20.7	12.9	406	25.5	4.3	10 094	-2.2	382	3.8	8 822	23.9	13.6
Montgomery	282 228	67.9	200 800	22.1	11.5	740	26.5	3.4	474 003	1.5	8 734	1.8	431 572	53.0	6.3
Prince George's	258 011	58.9	122 600	21.7	11.8	642	25.6	5.5	442 972	0.3	15 484	3.5	412 742	35.9	9.0
Queen Anne's	12 489	81.0	118 000	21.9	12.9	471	24.4	3.0	20 912	1.3	603	2.9	17 506	30.6	13.9
St. Mary's	25 500	69.7	109 100	21.9	12.3	539	24.5	4.8	50 128	0.4	1 552	3.1	35 958	33.3	17.0
Somerset	7 977	72.2	55 600	21.3	13.4	302	26.5	6.4	11 513	-2.3	865	7.5	8 962	19.5	11.3
Talbot	12 677	68.1	118 100	20.6	12.3	429	25.1	3.4	18 937	-0.4	535	2.8	15 786	26.9	12.5

1. Specified owner-occupied units.   2. Specified renter-occupied units.   3. Overcrowded or lacking complete plumbing facilities.   4. Percent of civilian labor force.   5. Persons 16 years and older.

	Private nonfarm establishments, employment and payroll, 1998									Agriculture, 1997			
	Employment						Annual payroll		Farms			Farm operators
											Percent with—		
STATE County	Number of establishments	Total	Health Care and Social Assistance	Manufacturing	Retail trade	Finance and Insurance	Professional Scientific and Technical Services	Total (mil dol)	Average per employee (dollars)	Number	Less than 50 acres	500 acres and over	Whose principal occupation is farming (percent)
	104	105	106	107	108	109	110	111	112	113	114	115	116
LOUISIANA—Cont'd													
Pointe Coupee	334	3 821	471	636	929	144	87	78	20 386	402	30.6	25.9	51.0
Rapides	3 080	45 683	12 419	3 272	7 490	1 741	1 657	1 015	22 214	817	39.4	11.9	46.5
Red River	160	1 852	449	222	345	86	87	35	18 891	218	23.9	20.2	46.3
Richland	418	4 547	1 381	640	699	171	87	85	18 717	483	19.0	35.0	65.2
Sabine	481	4 760	553	1 171	868	307	107	88	18 478	373	30.6	5.4	45.3
St. Bernard	1 165	13 354	2 421	1 784	2 744	357	302	313	23 434	27	59.3	7.4	40.7
St. Charles	827	18 895	959	7 182	1 510	225	372	691	36 591	71	32.4	11.3	45.1
St. Helena	97	860	266	157	113	56	D	14	16 027	333	30.6	4.5	46.8
St. James	311	6 222	466	2 813	671	226	51	227	36 497	65	38.5	46.2	81.5
St. John the Baptist	636	10 782	959	2 180	1 543	290	220	296	27 469	27	40.7	22.2	44.4
St. Landry	1 540	16 440	3 874	1 802	3 566	834	553	331	20 111	966	44.5	15.7	45.7
St. Martin	665	9 060	870	3 023	1 459	304	439	177	19 513	243	42.0	20.2	51.9
St. Mary	1 485	25 701	1 546	5 981	2 959	529	998	707	27 507	103	20.4	49.5	68.0
St. Tammany	4 433	48 247	9 618	2 642	10 068	1 661	2 320	1 026	21 273	451	44.7	2.9	40.4
Tangipahoa	1 901	23 496	4 903	2 899	5 244	831	694	451	19 212	923	41.4	3.5	50.1
Tensas	107	716	145	D	113	61	24	14	19 493	202	7.9	54.5	77.2
Terrebonne	2 680	43 874	4 986	5 033	6 818	1 137	1 273	1 245	28 379	137	38.0	21.2	39.4
Union	331	4 749	716	1 799	542	165	D	91	19 192	436	30.3	3.2	48.9
Vermilion	964	9 819	1 297	893	1 981	435	245	203	20 656	995	34.0	20.7	59.4
Vernon	639	7 107	1 721	123	1 342	306	581	140	19 752	387	40.1	3.1	41.6
Washington	734	8 584	2 044	1 513	1 666	354	273	181	21 109	814	37.7	3.1	45.1
Webster	845	10 902	2 165	2 303	1 854	446	280	224	20 559	341	35.5	5.0	39.9
West Baton Rouge	413	8 346	330	1 894	943	181	52	254	30 480	95	49.5	22.1	37.9
West Carroll	191	1 775	394	185	458	65	D	34	19 412	539	21.5	19.5	53.1
West Feliciana	162	2 784	242	D	277	65	D	111	39 902	148	21.6	27.7	30.4
Winn	355	4 287	637	1 269	675	91	D	92	21 407	147	37.4	3.4	43.5
MAINE	38 334	456 715	79 828	80 640	74 220	21 374	16 708	11 559	25 309	5 810	29.6	9.3	49.4
Androscoggin	2 763	39 769	7 030	7 880	6 297	2 131	2 064	937	23 549	288	27.4	9.7	52.1
Aroostook	2 273	23 069	5 183	4 389	4 214	738	366	478	20 739	889	12.8	21.0	59.6
Cumberland	9 934	140 731	22 580	15 313	20 437	11 448	6 974	4 000	28 426	455	47.3	3.5	47.3
Franklin	842	10 469	1 646	3 288	1 485	284	113	230	21 934	223	22.0	5.8	46.2
Hancock	2 078	16 184	2 606	2 580	2 928	556	1 292	421	26 033	310	41.9	4.2	38.1
Kennebec	3 213	41 236	9 533	5 323	7 613	1 304	1 217	994	24 107	455	27.7	7.7	52.1
Knox	1 483	13 650	2 276	1 765	2 316	382	321	321	23 480	194	35.6	1.5	46.4
Lincoln	1 248	7 823	1 341	812	1 661	249	251	175	22 322	210	37.6	4.3	49.0
Oxford	1 372	15 002	2 214	4 158	2 098	327	216	341	22 740	358	32.1	7.5	47.8
Penobscot	4 061	53 154	10 778	7 124	9 817	1 670	1 600	1 283	24 137	525	31.0	11.4	47.2
Piscataquis	464	4 943	944	1 923	843	84	92	110	22 335	141	22.0	13.5	48.2
Sagadahoc	756	13 318	903	D	1 188	231	517	417	31 323	118	34.7	5.9	46.6
Somerset	1 195	15 110	2 352	4 223	2 328	315	249	412	27 265	431	18.3	11.8	56.6
Waldo	826	7 434	1 126	D	1 278	113	157	157	21 169	315	23.8	9.5	54.9
Washington	916	8 023	1 847	1 485	1 720	240	86	173	21 518	399	37.8	7.5	36.3
York	4 910	46 800	7 469	11 374	7 997	1 302	1 193	1 110	23 715	499	40.3	2.8	44.5
MARYLAND	126 577	1 938 727	258 901	163 123	273 016	104 336	172 671	59 818	30 854	12 084	43.3	8.2	51.6
Allegany	1 843	24 471	4 617	4 209	4 585	959	662	561	22 912	239	21.8	8.4	43.1
Anne Arundel	11 894	165 599	16 560	14 192	27 882	6 536	12 658	4 983	30 089	412	60.0	3.4	48.1
Baltimore	19 353	299 572	46 740	30 168	49 459	21 155	19 521	8 815	29 427	781	60.2	2.9	44.9
Calvert	1 440	13 644	2 157	527	2 492	324	673	363	26 626	349	52.7	3.7	45.8
Caroline	579	5 887	348	1 567	962	176	D	128	21 809	525	38.5	11.2	61.9
Carroll	3 845	40 396	5 904	4 291	7 576	1 422	1 354	908	22 472	1 041	48.9	5.8	47.6
Cecil	1 601	18 482	3 375	2 478	3 565	496	562	500	27 040	464	43.5	9.1	51.3
Charles	2 411	28 147	3 318	1 124	7 970	868	1 212	618	21 957	410	43.4	5.4	48.0
Dorchester	728	9 451	1 508	3 270	1 381	269	163	219	23 132	297	26.6	27.9	63.3
Frederick	4 852	64 779	6 369	8 444	10 418	6 470	3 830	1 759	27 157	1 304	35.9	5.6	51.2
Garrett	869	8 323	1 226	1 052	1 439	374	172	163	19 546	649	19.7	4.6	47.3
Harford	4 702	53 346	5 832	5 962	10 524	1 942	2 941	1 310	24 553	651	48.2	5.7	48.1
Howard	6 962	125 515	10 360	6 411	12 381	5 182	21 394	4 771	38 012	318	58.2	6.3	39.9
Kent	658	6 382	1 089	1 016	939	239	252	138	21 652	314	21.0	20.4	61.5
Montgomery	24 600	378 501	42 290	15 448	46 908	20 255	56 555	13 861	36 620	526	56.5	6.5	42.0
Prince George's	13 956	243 126	22 222	12 116	37 864	9 091	24 701	7 404	30 455	473	59.2	3.0	41.9
Queen Anne's	1 125	8 666	517	844	1 818	263	351	176	20 324	419	28.2	27.4	64.0
St. Mary's	1 646	20 782	2 100	633	3 916	470	4 986	556	26 763	621	43.3	3.7	52.7
Somerset	403	2 921	678	364	473	D	77	56	19 150	288	43.4	8.7	57.3
Talbot	1 425	16 275	2 637	2 907	2 549	587	652	390	23 969	240	25.4	24.2	57.9

Table B. States and Counties — Agriculture, Land, and Water

STATE County	Agriculture, 1997 (cont'd)															
	Land in farms				Value of land and buildings		Value of machinery and equipment Average per farm ($1,000)	Value of products sold		Percent from —		Percent of farms with sales of —		Percent of land owned by Fed. Gov. 1997	Water consumption 1995 (mil gal/day)
	Acreage (1,000)	Percent change, 1992–1997	Acres			Average per farm ($1,000)	Average per acre (dollars)		Total (mil dol)	Average per farm (dollars)	Crops	Live-stock and poultry products	$10,000 or more	$100,000 or more		
			Average size of farm	Total irrigated (1,000)	Total cropland (1,000)											
	117	118	119	120	121	122	123	124	125	126	127	128	129	130	131	132
LOUISIANA—Cont'd																
Pointe Coupee	201	4.2	500	3	160	582	1 131	89	54	133 487	90.3	9.7	49.5	23.1	3.7	290.1
Rapides	194	-7.8	238	7	122	333	1 464	56	55	67 534	88.5	11.5	39.8	16.4	11.6	497.7
Red River	113	15.5	519	D	51	420	931	51	11	50 114	68.3	31.7	36.2	11.0	0.0	1.6
Richland	237	-4.2	490	62	197	494	1 019	96	57	118 996	94.3	5.7	61.9	35.6	0.4	24.5
Sabine	57	-2.3	152	0	24	200	1 172	39	53	143 254	0.6	99.4	39.9	20.1	1.6	3.6
St. Bernard	3	-43.3	126	0	2	301	2 384	14	0	15 747	D	D	29.6	3.7	5.5	305.7
St. Charles	21	-7.2	301	D	9	484	1 610	44	5	71 337	87.5	12.5	39.4	7.0	2.8	1 953.5
St. Helena	66	31.5	197	0	24	251	1 251	38	30	90 762	1.6	98.4	32.7	12.0	0.0	6.3
St. James	45	5.5	698	D	40	1 050	1 506	249	27	410 626	99.8	0.2	72.3	52.3	0.0	246.7
St. John the Baptist	10	-43.9	353	D	6	777	2 200	104	4	131 351	98.4	1.7	48.1	22.2	0.0	731.5
St. Landry	265	-6.4	274	29	224	301	1 121	60	64	66 097	86.6	13.4	34.2	14.0	0.0	47.8
St. Martin	78	9.9	321	6	66	470	1 583	96	31	126 123	90.7	9.3	44.4	23.0	2.7	44.7
St. Mary	83	1.4	807		65	1 219	1 545	247	39	382 811	99.2	0.8	63.1	48.5	0.0	219.4
St. Tammany	42	4.7	93	1	17	305	3 530	49	12	27 504	66.6	33.4	26.8	6.7	3.9	23.9
Tangipahoa	120	-5.5	130	1	73	250	2 219	31	59	64 225	16.5	83.5	41.4	21.0	0.0	17.8
Tensas	241	-2.1	1 193	12	197	924	817	184	71	349 998	99.6	0.4	79.2	55.0	3.8	11.7
Terrebonne	53	20.2	386	0	31	676	1 650	75	14	103 506	85.6	14.4	41.6	14.6	0.0	33.1
Union	63	1.9	145	0	27	204	1 385	38	86	198 135	0.5	99.5	41.5	26.8	6.5	5.0
Vermilion	329	3.6	330	106	256	373	1 203	68	70	70 464	90.8	9.2	46.1	18.9	0.0	262.3
Vernon	44	-16.1	113	0	19	147	1 354	24	8	21 372	4.2	95.8	18.1	3.1	21.7	9.2
Washington	100	-13.8	123	1	60	233	1 922	41	45	55 427	26.1	73.9	33.4	16.6	0.2	31.6
Webster	50	-14.8	147	0	23	219	1 429	32	6	16 546	9.1	90.9	23.5	2.6	8.3	7.5
West Baton Rouge	29	-26.1	304	D	22	440	1 449	78	29	309 621	D	D	40.0	20.0	0.0	9.8
West Carroll	167	31.4	310	46	134	235	904	57	43	80 407	94.4	5.6	47.5	20.6	0.7	25.2
West Feliciana	76	-12.5	515	0	24	677	1 371	36	3	23 015	51.9	48.1	29.1	2.0	0.0	47.5
Winn	18	-22.3	122	D	8	111	953	25	3	20 925	6.2	93.8	21.8	2.0	21.9	3.0
MAINE	1 212	-3.7	209	22	540	251	1 190	49	439	75 503	48.4	51.6	41.2	13.2	1.0	221.0
Androscoggin	56	-9.8	194	1	23	304	1 715	71	62	216 587	12.7	87.3	47.9	19.4	0.0	14.0
Aroostook	325	-2.7	365	11	188	278	716	91	110	123 306	95.5	4.5	56.5	28.1	0.2	25.0
Cumberland	50	-7.7	110	1	26	322	2 600	35	17	38 061	64.5	35.5	38.9	10.5	0.6	36.9
Franklin	40	2.8	180	0	15	194	1 236	30	6	24 976	D	D	34.1	7.6	1.9	5.4
Hancock	43	-14.8	137	0	11	266	1 728	24	30	98 219	D	D	33.2	5.5	3.8	6.8
Kennebec	88	-7.2	194	0	45	258	1 509	52	45	99 299	13.7	86.3	41.3	14.5	0.1	29.8
Knox	25	-10.1	130	0	10	217	1 916	40	6	28 883	60.4	39.6	43.3	9.3	1.7	5.3
Lincoln	26	8.0	123	0	11	206	1 705	33	6	30 140	35.9	64.1	33.8	6.7	0.0	3.4
Oxford	64	1.5	179	1	21	293	1 417	45	20	54 607	53.2	46.8	33.8	8.4	3.8	10.5
Penobscot	117	-1.2	222	2	49	226	1 058	43	30	57 101	37.2	62.8	40.6	13.5	0.4	21.5
Piscataquis	34	-5.1	242	0	10	214	862	42	6	39 440	30.8	69.2	37.6	9.2	0.5	3.1
Sagadahoc	18	-6.0	151	0	7	288	1 893	35	3	25 993	46.0	54.0	28.8	5.9	0.1	4.6
Somerset	101	-5.4	235	0	36	219	921	57	25	57 371	19.8	80.2	45.9	13.5	0.3	8.3
Waldo	69	-4.8	218	0	28	222	952	34	15	46 884	17.2	82.8	42.2	12.7	0.2	3.8
Washington	98	3.5	246	4	36	215	885	35	43	107 956	61.1	38.9	35.6	5.3	1.7	5.0
York	58	-5.9	117	1	24	223	2 053	31	16	31 068	66.2	33.8	32.1	8.2	1.2	37.7
MARYLAND	2 155	-3.1	178	69	1 613	564	3 176	60	1 312	108 580	35.0	65.0	50.2	21.5	2.1	1 452.2
Allegany	42	10.3	175	0	20	263	1 625	31	3	13 899	34.6	65.4	24.3	2.5	2.8	45.1
Anne Arundel	35	-19.4	84	1	23	532	5 151	44	13	30 635	79.5	20.5	38.1	6.3	5.2	50.9
Baltimore	76	-8.7	97	1	54	457	4 742	49	51	65 530	68.3	31.7	37.6	11.3	0.4	282.9
Calvert	33	-9.6	96	0	18	375	3 584	32	8	22 075	89.1	10.9	39.8	4.6	0.2	7.4
Caroline	111	-12.3	212	16	95	500	2 297	95	95	181 181	30.2	69.8	69.1	38.7	0.0	17.0
Carroll	160	1.4	154	1	125	568	3 790	58	71	68 465	36.2	63.8	41.6	14.3	0.0	15.4
Cecil	86	7.1	185	1	63	683	3 628	56	59	127 267	38.8	61.2	43.5	15.1	0.6	9.0
Charles	56	-5.2	136	1	33	437	2 755	32	11	26 381	86.6	13.4	38.8	7.3	1.2	13.2
Dorchester	123	-0.9	414	15	99	862	2 018	102	82	277 411	41.9	58.1	79.5	51.2	2.3	18.6
Frederick	216	-3.2	166	1	171	626	3 769	60	102	77 960	17.2	82.8	47.1	18.8	1.9	39.0
Garrett	108	-3.0	166	0	54	249	1 578	46	21	32 353	11.5	88.5	38.4	10.2	0.2	9.1
Harford	94	-3.0	145	1	72	613	3 975	53	39	59 612	42.0	58.0	40.1	12.9	11.6	18.0
Howard	40	-11.5	125	1	31	691	5 490	51	20	61 667	61.6	38.4	34.3	11.0	0.1	3.6
Kent	118	-10.3	374	5	98	1 051	2 947	103	61	194 131	55.8	44.2	71.3	30.3	0.9	6.2
Montgomery	77	-5.8	147	1	61	659	4 396	55	29	54 303	69.4	30.6	34.6	11.8	3.3	728.5
Prince George's	48	-11.9	101	0	28	491	4 988	34	19	39 553	89.4	10.6	34.0	5.9	7.1	53.2
Queen Anne's	168	1.8	401	8	146	1 206	2 946	115	69	164 047	63.4	36.6	69.9	38.4	0.0	13.3
St. Mary's	72	-6.6	116	1	43	275	2 603	38	21	33 906	83.3	16.7	52.5	6.1	1.4	9.8
Somerset	55	-2.1	190	1	40	411	2 254	65	97	335 182	13.5	86.5	79.9	55.2	1.0	6.1
Talbot	110	0.5	457	2	93	1 414	3 157	118	49	202 208	50.0	50.0	73.3	40.8	0.0	7.0

STATE County	New Construction ($1,000)	Number of Housing Units	Number of Establish-ments	Number of Employees	Sales (mil dol)	Annual Payroll (mil dol)	Number of Establish-ments	Number of Employees	Sales (mil dol)	Annual Payroll (mil dol)	Number of Establish-ments	Number of Employees	Receipts (mil dol)	Annual Payroll (mil dol)
	Value of Residential Construction Authorized by Building Permits, 1999		Wholesale Trade, 1997				Retail Trade[1], 1997				Real Estate and Rental and Leasing, 1997			
	133	134	135	136	137	138	139	140	141	142	143	144	145	146
LOUISIANA—Cont'd														
Pointe Coupee	9 884	78	13	D	D	D	84	807	159.0	11.6	8	17	0.6	0.2
Rapides	49 451	509	173	1 789	581.1	45.6	586	7 397	1 188.3	108.5	92	660	57.8	12.4
Red River	100	1	6	53	13.8	0.9	39	265	53.6	3.7	4	13	0.7	0.2
Richland	5 124	76	28	259	160.4	5.6	85	844	188.0	12.8	14	40	2.9	0.7
Sabine	50	1	13	D	D	D	93	840	120.2	11.2	8	19	1.5	0.2
St. Bernard	9 264	154	62	D	D	D	214	2 887	362.7	33.6	37	148	13.2	3.0
St. Charles	24 802	227	84	1 485	2 627.1	50.7	119	1 316	210.8	17.5	29	109	14.5	2.1
St. Helena	726	12	1	D	D	D	17	101	11.1	1.1	1	D	D	D
St. James	2 933	26	15	282	277.7	10.5	55	609	72.4	7.4	10	20	2.2	0.3
St. John the Baptist	23 929	241	30	D	D	D	119	1 643	231.5	19.9	30	365	45.0	9.8
St. Landry	24 000	239	85	948	415.1	21.5	327	3 522	515.8	43.9	48	146	12.7	1.9
St. Martin	17 509	179	36	332	116.5	8.2	121	1 260	192.4	17.2	27	224	24.1	4.7
St. Mary	9 951	127	124	1 384	705.3	46.9	256	2 829	396.1	38.3	80	522	178.5	16.7
St. Tammany	244 364	2 063	252	2 070	6 604.0	75.3	749	9 479	1 511.5	135.3	156	739	86.4	14.5
Tangipahoa	57 846	648	106	1 482	725.4	38.0	415	5 442	894.8	74.6	72	309	29.5	5.4
Tensas	1 445	14	8	103	50.5	3.3	22	114	27.5	1.5	3	11	0.7	0.2
Terrebonne	34 761	407	212	2 467	790.5	69.5	482	6 237	1 064.1	93.3	137	1 651	247.6	54.0
Union	205	4	11	75	9.0	1.3	73	578	92.3	7.8	9	22	1.8	0.3
Vermilion	19 350	182	66	738	361.9	19.6	198	1 836	277.5	23.7	27	129	10.9	1.4
Vernon	380	5	30	221	53.6	4.8	143	1 392	216.1	19.3	29	78	6.4	0.8
Washington	14 890	150	28	178	57.0	3.7	184	1 627	241.2	20.0	13	44	2.4	0.5
Webster	3 238	24	36	D	D	D	197	1 844	293.5	24.5	25	116	9.2	1.4
West Baton Rouge	10 892	103	38	575	444.2	19.1	63	843	124.3	11.9	11	68	7.4	1.1
West Carroll	0	0	9	19	8.9	0.4	37	426	54.0	4.6	8	20	1.0	0.2
West Feliciana	10 123	66	7	30	11.7	0.8	35	275	40.7	3.5	2	D	D	D
Winn	0	0	17	159	56.7	4.9	65	692	81.1	7.9	8	20	1.4	0.3
MAINE	623 269	5 695	1 726	19 932	7 305.6	616.2	7 074	72 897	12 737.1	1 164.2	1 343	5 929	601.7	114.2
Androscoggin	32 092	329	126	1 244	277.8	35.7	533	6 362	1 247.1	96.4	109	418	46.9	7.2
Aroostook	7 762	106	101	766	211.1	19.8	471	4 285	591.9	57.9	71	197	13.1	2.2
Cumberland	192 356	1 496	574	8 884	3 673.3	296.8	1 570	20 735	3 825.9	346.5	407	2 731	293.4	63.5
Franklin	11 094	108	16	91	26.8	2.7	179	1 537	245.5	22.4	37	130	6.8	1.4
Hancock	45 338	340	73	354	138.6	8.4	388	2 895	490.0	49.3	63	127	13.9	2.2
Kennebec	32 068	388	133	2 135	821.9	67.6	589	7 166	1 289.7	120.5	109	439	37.7	7.6
Knox	29 748	257	79	550	171.7	13.8	278	2 309	394.0	35.8	42	92	11.1	1.3
Lincoln	19 003	179	52	259	66.5	5.5	236	1 545	299.7	25.2	28	58	11.6	1.2
Oxford	19 245	237	36	366	122.2	9.8	280	2 104	320.4	30.6	48	127	16.0	2.4
Penobscot	29 455	353	196	2 786	938.0	85.6	796	9 433	1 654.6	148.0	146	620	66.9	9.5
Piscataquis	3 390	45	11	D	D	D	100	871	120.6	12.3	17	37	2.6	0.5
Sagadahoc	16 466	151	21	111	78.7	1.9	124	1 044	183.5	17.1	27	93	8.1	1.6
Somerset	4 017	67	30	473	120.9	18.9	260	2 234	356.5	35.1	32	124	5.8	1.8
Waldo	14 424	144	29	165	149.2	4.2	165	1 226	192.5	18.2	15	41	3.0	0.4
Washington	9 070	117	50	D	D	D	204	1 712	260.2	23.5	13	38	2.5	0.4
York	148 993	1 292	199	1 479	438.6	41.1	901	7 439	1 265.1	125.1	179	657	62.1	11.1
MARYLAND	3 102 361	29 757	6 283	92 458	54 906.6	3 656.3	19 798	274 260	46 428.2	4 914.0	5 065	39 502	4 764.7	971.3
Allegany	9 009	86	71	D	D	D	385	4 719	663.5	63.5	56	198	23.7	3.4
Anne Arundel	340 737	3 633	653	9 148	8 829.7	366.4	1 863	27 922	4 757.6	487.0	415	3 531	407.1	82.4
Baltimore	336 301	3 752	1 003	12 047	6 707.2	491.6	3 138	49 690	8 243.4	902.7	743	7 047	947.9	182.5
Calvert	114 409	983	29	202	61.7	4.8	190	2 566	404.0	42.7	60	151	19.3	2.7
Caroline	20 147	199	26	325	163.2	9.1	104	901	191.3	13.7	17	36	2.1	0.4
Carroll	149 453	1 256	146	966	292.9	27.8	604	7 366	1 160.6	116.5	121	395	56.1	6.8
Cecil	75 508	750	53	D	D	D	284	3 526	613.4	58.2	60	177	20.3	3.0
Charles	138 706	1 211	75	1 088	234.9	27.6	490	7 750	1 243.6	128.0	84	290	31.2	5.7
Dorchester	10 366	94	51	402	121.6	10.7	132	1 476	285.9	27.7	30	97	5.8	1.3
Frederick	256 306	2 667	212	2 783	847.7	94.0	741	10 644	1 839.3	186.8	185	862	88.0	18.2
Garrett	30 783	239	40	303	121.7	5.7	157	1 367	222.9	20.6	20	113	8.5	1.5
Harford	221 088	2 046	198	1 502	1 024.7	47.1	741	10 518	1 755.4	174.6	170	780	74.1	13.8
Howard	247 286	2 295	631	13 185	9 392.3	528.3	766	11 823	2 010.8	216.2	254	1 899	335.2	64.7
Kent	15 071	106	25	162	49.8	3.5	125	908	132.3	13.9	31	65	9.3	0.8
Montgomery	526 927	4 253	971	14 752	8 795.9	778.9	3 000	46 311	8 914.4	957.8	1 123	11 375	1 321.4	305.1
Prince George's	240 621	2 615	759	13 904	9 053.7	542.9	2 425	38 214	6 390.5	675.8	599	5 013	638.5	110.7
Queen Anne's	54 007	433	71	526	209.0	14.3	217	1 833	321.5	28.7	31	62	8.4	1.0
St. Mary's	74 768	707	27	D	D	D	278	3 615	553.2	55.4	55	241	27.0	3.6
Somerset	5 604	66	19	D	D	D	73	485	68.0	6.1	10	30	1.6	0.3
Talbot	40 887	290	69	527	243.4	15.5	262	2 621	457.5	47.0	71	179	20.8	3.4

1. Establishments with payroll.

STATE County	Professional, Scientific, and Technical Services[1], 1997				Manufacturing, 1997				Accommodation and Foodservices, 1997			
	Number of Establishments	Number of Employees	Receipts (mil dol)	Annual Payroll (mil dol)	Number of Establishments	Number of Employees	Receipts (mil dol)	Annual Payroll (mil dol)	Number of Establishments	Number of Employees	Sales (mil dol)	Annual Payroll (mil dol)
	147	148	149	150	151	152	153	154	155	156	157	158
LOUISIANA—Cont'd												
Pointe Coupee	23	79	5.4	1.7	11	539	146.1	12.9	26	D	D	D
Rapides	247	1 956	124.2	42.2	73	3 179	1 165.9	103.0	224	3 985	119.8	31.7
Red River	6	17	1.0	0.2	NA	NA	NA	NA	6	D	D	D
Richland	24	85	5.9	1.9	14	600	132.1	16.6	27	296	8.7	2.1
Sabine	24	74	3.6	1.3	19	1 121	253.1	28.8	24	217	7.6	2.2
St. Bernard	69	224	17.9	4.9	54	1 769	2 603.6	83.1	107	1 431	43.0	11.6
St. Charles	63	430	30.1	15.1	37	5 068	8 501.5	302.2	47	701	19.0	5.2
St. Helena	7	D	D	D	NA	NA	NA	NA	5	D	D	D
St. James	14	39	2.7	1.0	26	2 858	3 842.3	149.5	14	203	6.6	1.8
St. John the Baptist	42	194	11.6	3.4	29	2 304	3 057.5	104.2	36	783	21.8	5.7
St. Landry	113	490	35.1	12.3	57	1 919	904.7	50.8	76	1 034	32.2	8.6
St. Martin	42	170	12.3	4.4	44	3 501	1 259.8	69.7	52	D	D	D
St. Mary	94	1 044	139.2	32.8	67	5 098	944.4	163.6	91	1 385	41.3	10.3
St. Tammany	401	1 789	125.4	45.5	127	2 699	373.7	61.3	345	5 415	170.7	44.8
Tangipahoa	133	530	36.2	12.0	74	2 933	420.4	59.5	159	2 898	79.7	21.9
Tensas	9	15	1.6	0.3	NA	NA	NA	NA	8	25	1.6	0.2
Terrebonne	190	1 111	93.2	36.8	119	3 990	539.5	129.3	173	3 133	105.9	31.1
Union	12	29	1.7	0.4	NA	NA	NA	NA	19	D	D	D
Vermilion	64	225	12.1	5.1	27	1 348	203.9	28.6	64	775	22.6	5.5
Vernon	31	599	21.0	12.9	NA	NA	NA	NA	58	782	23.0	5.9
Washington	43	148	11.7	2.8	28	1 536	466.3	54.7	49	626	18.3	4.4
Webster	43	151	8.7	3.3	45	2 336	504.6	67.2	56	637	18.1	4.2
West Baton Rouge	16	79	10.7	2.4	39	2 452	1 376.7	84.0	31	591	18.1	4.5
West Carroll	6	D	D	D	NA	NA	NA	NA	7	D	D	D
West Feliciana	12	25	1.5	0.4	6	D	D	D	18	176	7.1	1.8
Winn	13	22	1.2	0.3	24	1 252	300.0	37.8	20	209	6.2	1.5
MAINE	2 552	13 747	1 215.6	474.8	1 812	82 288	14 097.6	2 591.1	3 714	39 624	1 509.3	428.8
Androscoggin	151	1 672	191.6	54.3	183	8 233	1 218.6	226.6	180	2 438	77.4	23.3
Aroostook	89	342	18.1	7.2	89	3 906	895.0	125.4	162	1 807	50.0	14.8
Cumberland	973	6 408	614.6	253.8	382	14 304	2 232.7	477.2	792	11 749	429.9	121.3
Franklin	36	95	5.0	2.0	53	3 457	867.8	110.3	94	1 328	33.6	11.0
Hancock	111	309	24.2	8.7	94	2 397	551.0	103.8	315	1 741	105.0	28.4
Kennebec	230	926	71.1	26.3	129	5 488	753.4	165.8	257	3 282	109.1	32.0
Knox	74	275	15.0	6.2	92	1 602	267.7	44.3	131	1 306	58.0	17.5
Lincoln	74	D	D	D	68	D	D	D	158	870	49.1	14.4
Oxford	56	149	8.9	3.6	84	4 038	758.5	118.7	140	1 203	44.2	12.2
Penobscot	271	1 388	102.7	45.9	155	8 897	1 658.6	285.9	344	4 778	151.3	45.8
Piscataquis	13	D	D	D	26	1 905	114.7	36.1	50	351	10.8	2.8
Sagadahoc	62	535	42.7	19.4	29	D	D	D	64	743	25.6	7.7
Somerset	58	221	16.6	6.1	76	4 441	1 239.9	143.7	105	778	26.0	6.8
Waldo	40	100	7.4	2.8	53	1 180	117.8	24.8	86	546	23.2	6.2
Washington	34	82	3.7	1.1	41	1 676	364.8	52.6	113	707	22.0	6.3
York	280	973	77.7	30.7	258	11 649	2 093.5	360.2	723	5 997	294.1	78.1
MARYLAND	14 115	146 814	15 940.2	6 483.8	3 996	163 992	36 505.9	5 840.5	9 049	161 273	5 972.5	1 644.7
Allegany	94	515	25.5	13.9	67	4 169	785.9	139.2	165	2 434	75.5	19.8
Anne Arundel	1 321	9 033	1 025.4	366.7	339	14 878	2 703.8	618.4	852	17 645	637.3	175.6
Baltimore	2 132	17 132	1 708.2	682.1	575	31 065	6 883.3	1 235.1	1 359	24 414	842.4	233.5
Calvert	105	516	38.9	17.2	NA	NA	NA	NA	94	1 859	56.9	15.5
Caroline	21	70	2.7	1.0	31	1 533	167.6	36.6	27	255	7.9	1.9
Carroll	289	1 073	67.4	27.5	144	4 330	716.9	131.1	214	3 906	110.3	31.4
Cecil	109	363	27.3	9.7	55	2 766	678.3	100.9	131	2 011	75.2	20.1
Charles	145	993	91.9	33.0	58	1 100	170.3	38.5	186	3 895	125.3	33.5
Dorchester	42	126	7.3	3.1	48	3 580	867.2	86.9	60	765	21.3	6.0
Frederick	449	3 821	296.2	130.2	162	7 795	1 509.1	268.5	304	6 028	193.2	54.5
Garrett	36	151	7.6	3.2	49	1 135	103.5	22.8	73	961	26.7	8.0
Harford	408	2 608	237.5	90.5	152	5 301	1 274.6	178.8	293	5 777	185.9	51.6
Howard	1 050	15 883	1 950.3	772.1	245	6 927	1 177.3	257.2	366	7 078	242.5	68.5
Kent	39	284	13.1	4.3	27	1 031	189.4	25.4	66	585	20.1	5.7
Montgomery	4 314	49 186	5 997.5	2 419.3	527	15 190	3 111.9	680.5	1 407	25 248	1 062.1	298.0
Prince George's	1 364	23 023	2 186.8	967.6	372	11 179	2 008.1	408.5	1 027	20 122	718.4	193.8
Queen Anne's	71	291	20.7	8.5	34	877	106.7	21.8	80	1 482	54.9	15.7
St. Mary's	166	4 226	364.8	177.5	NA	NA	NA	NA	111	2 017	62.6	17.5
Somerset	18	81	4.0	1.8	NA	NA	NA	NA	28	335	10.5	3.0
Talbot	112	604	58.9	27.6	54	3 035	836.1	69.1	96	1 639	69.8	20.0

1. Firms subject to federal tax.

Table B. States and Counties — Health and Other Services and Federal Funds

STATE County	Health Care and Social Assistance[1], 1997				Other Services[1], 1997				Federal funds and grants, fiscal 1999[2] Expenditures (mil dol)			
									Total	Direct payments for individuals[3]		
	Number of Establishments	Number of Employees	Receipts (mil dol)	Annual Payroll (mil dol)	Number of Establishments	Number of Employees	Receipts (mil dol)	Annual Payroll (mil dol)	Total	Social Security and government retirement	Medicare	Food stamps and Supplemental Security Income
	159	160	161	162	163	164	165	166	167	168	169	170
LOUISIANA—Cont'd												
Pointe Coupee	20	235	9.0	4.0	20	66	4.9	1.1	100.2	32.9	17.3	5.8
Rapides	335	5 666	306.0	129.1	170	984	55.3	16.7	689.1	261.2	126.6	35.6
Red River	13	294	17.3	6.4	7	32	2.5	0.9	57.0	16.2	10.5	2.8
Richland	52	908	32.1	13.7	20	103	5.4	1.7	136.8	34.4	26.1	6.5
Sabine	21	393	22.5	8.6	25	89	6.8	1.6	120.1	50.6	22.6	5.7
St. Bernard	111	2 263	135.1	53.5	93	459	31.3	9.6	286.4	132.1	83.2	12.7
St. Charles	58	771	39.0	14.3	32	314	40.7	7.6	158.0	60.1	32.5	6.4
St. Helena	7	39	2.4	0.7	2	D	D	D	38.2	9.6	9.0	3.5
St. James	23	289	14.6	6.5	8	91	3.6	1.2	113.9	31.8	22.2	5.3
St. John the Baptist	59	990	57.4	26.7	42	211	9.9	3.0	156.6	53.7	30.0	10.3
St. Landry	163	2 333	130.3	51.2	98	441	26.6	8.0	444.2	139.2	86.2	39.1
St. Martin	34	584	19.4	10.2	30	91	7.0	1.8	170.6	59.5	32.5	12.3
St. Mary	73	809	41.9	19.2	96	479	46.4	10.3	236.1	86.8	46.2	17.6
St. Tammany	444	5 248	345.0	141.4	239	1 263	81.4	21.6	566.1	296.4	129.3	23.8
Tangipahoa	158	1 778	95.5	42.6	121	704	49.7	12.3	424.1	144.6	103.4	35.4
Tensas	8	149	4.8	2.6	3	D	D	D	61.0	10.6	9.0	3.3
Terrebonne	175	2 234	145.0	69.3	172	1 457	132.1	35.6	365.0	160.4	80.9	27.6
Union	20	352	12.6	5.1	14	54	3.1	0.7	100.9	41.5	25.5	3.9
Vermilion	73	805	36.6	12.5	61	384	24.5	9.2	215.8	84.2	46.0	11.2
Vernon	34	531	51.6	14.3	48	196	12.0	3.1	612.0	96.7	32.0	9.9
Washington	72	1 369	62.2	29.3	33	201	9.0	2.5	248.8	85.9	74.3	18.7
Webster	59	1 449	82.0	34.8	41	183	8.8	2.6	211.3	95.4	50.0	11.1
West Baton Rouge	20	439	11.9	6.1	21	151	11.2	3.2	113.9	28.6	19.4	5.5
West Carroll	7	254	7.7	3.7	17	54	2.8	0.7	73.1	21.6	15.8	3.4
West Feliciana	12	137	4.6	2.1	4	24	2.4	0.7	37.9	10.5	7.0	1.8
Winn	24	388	26.3	10.0	14	47	3.2	0.8	79.1	27.8	19.5	4.7
MAINE	2 727	28 944	1 608.4	766.3	1 923	8 820	612.3	169.6	7 281.5	2 642.4	851.6	206.1
Androscoggin	221	2 542	149.6	68.4	191	714	46.2	12.9	443.3	203.1	79.5	21.7
Aroostook	140	1 681	78.7	34.0	108	448	32.3	5.6	463.3	176.4	60.0	17.9
Cumberland	764	9 092	602.3	303.5	503	3 458	226.7	71.3	1 277.1	495.3	168.5	32.8
Franklin	51	709	28.8	12.0	37	120	9.8	2.0	120.3	56.9	20.2	4.6
Hancock	79	888	42.5	20.5	75	256	22.8	8.4	268.1	110.1	35.9	5.4
Kennebec	316	2 870	143.3	68.7	170	655	43.2	10.7	898.5	260.9	71.0	22.8
Knox	95	747	41.2	18.0	78	324	22.4	6.5	175.2	85.2	29.9	5.6
Lincoln	49	361	20.5	10.2	50	160	11.7	2.9	145.8	79.7	24.7	3.6
Oxford	84	834	38.1	18.2	71	220	15.6	4.0	231.7	117.3	43.3	9.4
Penobscot	310	3 432	209.8	98.2	208	980	82.3	20.4	735.0	289.4	96.2	28.4
Piscataquis	36	310	12.7	5.7	13	47	2.9	0.7	87.5	45.1	13.9	3.7
Sagadahoc	68	589	25.4	11.7	48	176	11.1	2.6	652.8	73.4	15.4	3.3
Somerset	75	1 024	35.6	15.8	68	200	13.2	3.2	217.0	99.2	33.3	12.1
Waldo	49	448	21.3	7.9	43	115	10.1	2.0	186.5	68.2	19.8	7.2
Washington	53	721	23.9	10.4	41	132	10.1	1.9	225.3	82.2	28.6	8.3
York	337	2 696	134.8	63.0	219	815	51.8	14.4	873.2	387.5	111.2	19.4
MARYLAND	10 841	116 241	8 060.7	3 538.0	7 871	55 241	3 561.3	1 129.2	41 990.2	10 396.8	3 838.7	644.1
Allegany	170	1 348	98.4	47.9	135	790	39.2	11.7	475.1	190.6	104.1	13.0
Anne Arundel	864	8 875	598.3	264.2	771	5 428	360.2	103.3	3 390.4	1 072.3	302.4	31.3
Baltimore	2 003	25 262	1 700.4	764.7	1 244	8 780	510.4	177.5	3 715.9	1 467.3	684.0	65.8
Calvert	108	971	59.8	29.7	69	397	20.7	6.5	220.7	143.8	35.0	5.2
Caroline	22	154	6.5	2.4	31	143	11.6	3.4	123.9	55.2	24.2	4.2
Carroll	265	2 346	130.7	56.9	271	1 596	86.9	26.7	475.5	267.2	100.1	8.0
Cecil	97	1 047	59.1	27.8	107	495	31.4	9.3	335.1	148.6	54.4	7.4
Charles	209	1 836	101.8	46.6	174	1 111	77.1	22.3	587.2	246.7	54.7	10.1
Dorchester	57	715	35.9	14.7	48	176	9.0	2.4	182.6	65.3	34.5	5.4
Frederick	315	3 258	203.2	96.0	280	1 384	102.0	28.8	741.6	311.5	82.7	9.1
Garrett	42	436	21.6	9.7	45	313	17.2	5.1	125.6	54.8	23.5	4.1
Harford	354	3 253	197.9	84.0	322	1 824	96.7	31.8	1 314.2	392.7	119.3	13.5
Howard	486	7 205	525.2	216.7	328	2 830	228.5	66.1	780.0	300.7	71.3	9.2
Kent	37	319	17.0	6.4	35	128	7.7	2.1	113.5	55.2	22.2	1.9
Montgomery	2 438	19 961	1 704.3	701.7	1 398	9 308	650.5	221.9	9 210.8	1 753.0	482.0	62.7
Prince George's	1 396	13 111	939.8	408.1	1 025	9 635	647.1	207.1	6 874.6	1 557.2	401.1	74.6
Queen Anne's	42	430	16.7	7.3	58	221	15.2	4.3	128.3	70.3	21.6	2.0
St. Mary's	108	1 289	66.1	30.8	97	526	28.6	8.7	2 143.6	182.5	45.6	8.4
Somerset	19	251	13.0	5.9	16	67	6.8	0.8	121.3	44.0	19.3	4.3
Talbot	97	1 195	76.2	37.2	88	482	26.6	8.5	199.8	91.7	33.4	2.9

1. Firms subject to federal tax.   2. October 1, 1998 to September 30, 1999.   3. State totals may include programs not allocated by county.

STATE County	Salaries and wages	Defense	Other	Medicaid and other health-related	Nutrition and family welfare	Education	Other	Total (mil dol)	Intergovern-mental (mil dol)	Total (mil dol)	Per capita Total	Per capita Property
	171	172	173	174	175	176	177	178	179	180	181	182
LOUISIANA—Cont'd												
Pointe Coupee	3.1	0.2	0.6	23.9	4.3	1.7	1.6	45.2	15.2	13.5	573	331
Rapides	92.6	10.7	26.3	77.0	18.6	8.2	16.1	251.4	107.2	113.8	900	376
Red River	1.6	0.7	0.3	11.8	1.8	0.7	3.0	16.2	10.5	4.8	494	229
Richland	4.9	0.0	0.7	26.6	3.9	1.8	5.2	54.3	24.2	8.7	415	216
Sabine	2.5	0.1	0.7	22.8	3.4	1.7	6.7	35.1	21.4	11.0	465	216
St. Bernard	6.4	20.5	1.8	15.3	5.1	2.9	1.5	83.4	36.4	36.5	551	187
St. Charles	7.7	16.4	12.0	11.9	4.2	1.9	3.8	173.9	32.7	96.4	2 020	1 225
St. Helena	0.7	0.0	0.2	10.7	2.0	0.9	1.2	17.9	8.4	3.1	318	164
St. James	3.2	0.9	29.9	10.8	4.1	1.5	3.4	71.9	19.0	29.6	1 409	861
St. John the Baptist	4.6	0.0	33.7	10.4	5.7	2.6	3.5	68.1	25.7	32.9	783	357
St. Landry	9.9	0.3	2.2	114.8	17.2	8.3	8.5	157.5	75.6	34.6	415	157
St. Martin	4.2	6.0	1.5	35.7	5.0	3.7	6.6	68.9	38.7	18.9	403	216
St. Mary	8.8	14.4	1.5	28.4	9.4	4.9	16.5	153.2	50.1	53.7	943	327
St. Tammany	29.5	9.1	7.5	29.4	15.2	5.8	12.6	416.9	119.6	143.6	778	331
Tangipahoa	14.9	0.4	3.6	81.2	14.7	8.9	6.5	248.2	84.9	54.5	572	142
Tensas	0.8	0.0	0.2	11.4	2.4	0.9	2.7	11.2	7.2	3.1	457	213
Terrebonne	15.3	3.1	6.8	38.0	9.2	7.1	11.4	290.7	90.4	77.6	752	267
Union	4.2	0.0	1.4	17.6	2.3	1.2	1.6	29.9	17.1	8.4	385	156
Vermilion	7.1	0.3	1.4	27.2	6.4	3.3	2.8	130.0	40.1	33.5	649	325
Vernon	325.9	111.1	3.3	19.5	5.3	2.5	3.0	72.8	49.8	19.4	375	120
Washington	6.3	2.0	1.1	42.5	6.2	3.4	5.3	78.9	38.5	23.9	555	204
Webster	5.8	0.1	1.2	31.8	6.5	2.7	3.5	66.7	33.6	25.0	586	193
West Baton Rouge	2.9	29.1	12.6	10.3	2.1	1.0	1.7	58.0	15.9	26.2	1 278	584
West Carroll	2.0	0.0	0.4	15.5	1.9	0.8	0.8	16.4	11.2	4.3	356	134
West Feliciana	0.9	8.1	0.3	5.9	1.7	0.7	0.3	55.9	10.0	9.7	729	227
Winn	3.2	0.0	0.8	13.3	2.4	1.2	4.7	23.5	14.5	7.1	397	132
MAINE	795.1	681.4	121.2	882.7	243.0	131.1	407.5	X	X	X	X	X
Androscoggin	19.9	1.6	4.6	73.1	14.6	6.7	11.2	207.6	72.2	111.1	1 099	1 053
Aroostook	31.5	18.5	10.3	92.5	14.9	5.0	24.5	183.2	73.3	72.3	938	897
Cumberland	249.1	75.9	33.8	132.1	25.3	11.2	34.9	611.2	131.2	364.6	1 450	1 414
Franklin	4.5	0.1	1.3	16.0	5.8	1.6	5.7	72.9	18.2	40.9	1 410	1 391
Hancock	28.9	1.6	10.8	51.8	6.3	1.8	12.3	107.2	25.4	70.1	1 412	1 352
Kennebec	75.7	0.3	11.5	127.7	97.9	50.3	161.7	223.1	80.4	122.5	1 057	1 024
Knox	7.0	0.1	1.8	33.3	4.5	2.0	5.2	75.8	11.3	57.5	1 530	1 473
Lincoln	5.7	0.2	2.3	17.4	3.5	0.9	7.6	80.6	17.9	57.5	1 820	1 754
Oxford	8.4	0.2	2.2	34.5	8.9	2.2	5.3	129.2	39.1	79.8	1 483	1 435
Penobscot	82.1	7.4	19.9	104.5	18.8	11.7	60.2	315.8	121.4	137.6	960	908
Piscataquis	2.7	0.0	0.6	13.9	2.5	0.8	3.4	51.9	15.4	18.9	1 031	993
Sagadahoc	27.0	504.0	0.9	11.2	4.0	0.9	12.3	72.6	22.1	44.5	1 247	1 229
Somerset	8.9	0.1	2.1	43.1	7.5	2.7	6.6	119.7	42.8	65.3	1 251	1 212
Waldo	5.8	40.8	1.5	26.0	5.1	1.8	7.5	69.3	22.8	41.3	1 147	1 089
Washington	17.7	4.1	6.5	45.8	8.0	4.5	10.6	73.8	29.5	38.2	1 061	1 009
York	220.3	26.5	11.1	59.9	15.4	5.0	13.4	349.5	103.1	213.3	1 229	1 172
MARYLAND	8 345.5	5 438.4	5 145.2	3 117.7	846.7	397.8	1 381.7	X	X	X	X	X
Allegany	32.8	0.8	13.7	58.0	10.8	4.8	40.8	167.3	79.9	51.3	710	456
Anne Arundel	797.5	593.5	229.9	129.5	135.2	10.3	62.7	1 002.6	225.8	574.2	1 222	680
Baltimore	804.1	241.3	108.7	170.1	33.6	16.1	102.2	1 526.6	394.0	870.0	1 207	661
Calvert	7.7	1.5	3.9	17.6	3.4	1.0	0.9	163.0	49.0	88.1	1 269	880
Caroline	4.4	0.0	1.3	21.4	2.8	0.8	3.8	55.0	26.7	20.9	707	449
Carroll	16.9	24.2	11.8	30.3	4.1	2.0	4.6	288.7	95.2	152.6	1 038	611
Cecil	59.8	20.2	7.2	19.7	5.8	1.7	5.3	154.3	60.7	71.6	886	577
Charles	159.1	49.8	5.5	31.4	10.5	2.6	11.9	255.0	88.5	112.5	978	604
Dorchester	7.7	11.4	5.4	25.9	4.7	1.9	13.1	65.9	29.7	25.2	842	590
Frederick	165.7	36.0	50.1	47.3	8.4	2.8	17.0	391.4	123.8	193.2	1 055	668
Garrett	4.6	3.3	1.0	17.8	5.0	1.4	8.0	68.7	33.5	26.9	911	646
Harford	405.0	289.3	10.4	39.5	10.2	3.5	17.2	400.7	134.3	206.7	972	600
Howard	45.0	146.7	113.6	20.5	5.4	2.3	53.1	525.1	103.9	328.3	1 435	800
Kent	3.9	0.1	3.5	10.0	1.6	0.4	7.3	36.5	12.8	19.6	1 029	707
Montgomery	2 748.4	1 126.1	2 317.9	419.5	57.1	27.6	168.0	2 584.5	596.7	1 501.9	1 817	987
Prince George's	1 723.4	752.8	1 785.4	235.5	66.0	32.4	196.4	1 927.6	657.4	842.0	1 093	605
Queen Anne's	4.3	3.8	2.8	9.6	2.2	0.6	3.2	88.3	28.7	44.9	1 149	671
St. Mary's	567.1	1 277.8	3.6	31.6	5.6	2.2	15.9	163.0	60.2	70.4	822	433
Somerset	3.7	5.2	1.7	23.8	2.9	3.7	8.0	41.8	24.9	11.7	478	310
Talbot	14.0	20.0	5.1	16.8	2.1	1.2	4.4	64.3	11.8	39.0	1 180	627

1. October 1, 1998 to September 30, 1999.   2. State totals may include programs not allocated by county.   3. Based on the resident population estimated as of July 1 of the year shown.

	Local government finances, 1997 (cont'd)							Debt outstanding		Government employment, 1998			Presidential election, 2000		
	Direct general expenditure												Percent of vote cast —		
			Percent of total for —												
STATE County	Total (mil dol)	Per capita[1] (dollars)	Education	Health and hospitals	Police protection	Public welfare	Highways	Total (mil dol)	Per capita[1] (dollars)	Federal civilian	Federal military	State and local	Democratic	Republican	All other
	183	184	185	186	187	188	189	190	191	192	193	194	195	196	197
LOUISIANA—Cont'd															
Pointe Coupee	45.4	1 923	41.9	20.0	9.1	0.2	4.4	72.5	3 066	67	130	1 359	NA	NA	NA
Rapides	250.5	1 981	51.6	0.1	7.9	0.0	4.4	201.5	1 593	2 180	704	11 222	NA	NA	NA
Red River	17.1	1 763	62.5	0.3	6.3	0.2	2.6	0.5	55	37	53	610	NA	NA	NA
Richland	49.4	2 370	41.2	37.6	5.4	0.3	6.2	5.3	252	112	116	1 233	NA	NA	NA
Sabine	32.9	1 383	66.2	0.2	5.5	0.2	8.2	14.0	589	47	132	1 243	NA	NA	NA
St. Bernard	92.5	1 396	48.8	3.2	4.5	0.6	5.1	123.9	1 870	122	365	3 020	NA	NA	NA
St. Charles	160.9	3 374	47.7	12.2	8.4	0.4	2.8	268.6	5 630	179	267	2 760	NA	NA	NA
St. Helena	18.0	1 840	42.3	35.5	3.8	1.8	6.1	3.1	316	11	57	755	NA	NA	NA
St. James	68.4	3 257	43.8	10.8	6.1	2.0	3.8	178.3	8 495	61	117	1 597	NA	NA	NA
St. John the Baptist	67.5	1 606	52.0	0.7	10.3	0.1	4.8	97.4	2 318	98	234	1 788	NA	NA	NA
St. Landry	161.7	1 938	45.4	24.0	4.7	0.2	3.5	60.6	726	199	463	5 300	NA	NA	NA
St. Martin	69.8	1 493	60.2	7.3	9.3	0.4	3.4	46.2	988	61	263	2 207	NA	NA	NA
St. Mary	139.1	2 442	43.4	23.8	5.9	0.4	2.5	75.8	1 331	142	397	3 661	NA	NA	NA
St. Tammany	418.6	2 268	43.8	29.5	6.0	0.2	4.7	293.1	1 588	589	1 048	10 756	NA	NA	NA
Tangipahoa	259.7	2 726	32.0	45.9	5.4	0.2	3.1	137.2	1 441	268	538	10 032	NA	NA	NA
Tensas	10.6	1 568	74.8	2.1	5.3	0.6	1.4	2.7	401	22	37	562	NA	NA	NA
Terrebonne	270.6	2 623	35.3	37.5	4.4	0.7	4.8	128.6	1 246	268	602	5 920	NA	NA	NA
Union	26.8	1 232	56.8	8.1	8.2	0.0	6.9	5.0	230	86	122	993	NA	NA	NA
Vermilion	119.7	2 315	38.5	29.1	6.5	0.8	6.4	37.8	731	147	288	3 094	NA	NA	NA
Vernon	80.6	1 555	65.3	0.4	4.6	2.8	8.7	30.1	582	2 758	7 940	2 744	NA	NA	NA
Washington	75.5	1 753	55.4	13.4	6.3	0.5	4.4	10.7	249	104	238	3 375	NA	NA	NA
Webster	71.8	1 686	50.8	0.1	5.3	1.3	5.6	28.9	679	113	236	1 947	NA	NA	NA
West Baton Rouge	57.6	2 815	38.9	0.5	6.7	0.4	5.7	166.4	8 127	71	115	1 401	NA	NA	NA
West Carroll	17.1	1 401	67.1	0.3	5.2	1.5	6.5	1.2	98	40	67	753	NA	NA	NA
West Feliciana	56.0	4 220	25.5	6.9	1.9	0.1	2.8	471.7	35 535	16	74	2 701	NA	NA	NA
Winn	25.9	1 459	67.2	2.0	7.0	0.1	5.1	4.4	249	71	98	929	NA	NA	NA
MAINE	X	X	X	X	X	X	X	X	X	13 021	10 838	79 403	49.0	44.0	7.0
Androscoggin	206.5	2 044	54.0	0.1	3.8	0.4	5.8	144.9	1 434	366	519	4 628	NA	NA	NA
Aroostook	181.3	2 352	52.7	13.0	2.0	0.6	6.7	66.6	864	759	458	4 889	NA	NA	NA
Cumberland	569.7	2 266	44.4	0.4	4.8	3.3	5.1	420.3	1 671	3 079	4 245	16 706	NA	NA	NA
Franklin	72.5	2 500	51.8	1.2	3.4	0.2	7.1	89.3	3 078	91	147	1 794	NA	NA	NA
Hancock	110.4	2 224	52.8	0.4	2.2	0.2	6.6	50.3	1 014	408	717	2 720	NA	NA	NA
Kennebec	218.0	1 881	62.0	0.3	3.6	0.5	6.8	164.3	1 418	1 608	590	13 903	NA	NA	NA
Knox	72.9	1 941	60.2	0.3	3.4	0.3	6.7	30.7	819	119	274	2 300	NA	NA	NA
Lincoln	73.8	2 335	63.3	1.1	2.5	0.6	7.8	17.6	557	101	184	1 585	NA	NA	NA
Oxford	135.4	2 518	72.9	0.5	2.0	0.3	6.7	79.3	1 475	167	273	2 732	NA	NA	NA
Penobscot	299.3	2 089	51.8	3.9	3.8	1.9	5.9	139.2	971	1 414	741	11 893	NA	NA	NA
Piscataquis	52.9	2 889	45.8	29.3	2.1	0.3	5.6	19.7	1 077	61	93	1 066	NA	NA	NA
Sagadahoc	74.6	2 093	69.7	0.5	3.7	0.1	4.4	35.7	1 001	371	466	1 530	NA	NA	NA
Somerset	116.6	2 233	71.6	0.6	3.4	0.4	4.9	74.3	1 422	158	266	2 617	NA	NA	NA
Waldo	64.3	1 786	65.8	0.8	2.9	0.4	7.0	25.3	702	109	185	1 488	NA	NA	NA
Washington	70.3	1 954	58.1	0.4	2.6	0.3	7.5	41.5	1 154	306	318	2 299	NA	NA	NA
York	344.3	1 984	60.8	0.6	5.2	1.4	5.4	201.4	1 161	3 904	1 362	7 253	NA	NA	NA
MARYLAND	X	X	X	X	X	X	X	X	X	153 567	51 984	303 307	57.0	40.0	3.0
Allegany	178.3	2 467	52.9	0.9	3.1	3.4	6.2	99.2	1 372	577	270	5 425	41.3	55.6	3.1
Anne Arundel	1 031.4	2 194	51.7	1.5	6.1	0.7	4.3	1 399.8	2 978	33 940	15 423	24 606	44.7	51.9	3.4
Baltimore	1 505.5	2 089	52.6	2.2	5.7	0.5	3.4	1 367.8	1 898	15 582	2 742	36 633	52.8	43.7	3.4
Calvert	154.5	2 226	60.3	1.7	3.2	0.9	4.5	158.4	2 282	129	314	2 603	43.6	53.7	2.7
Caroline	53.6	1 816	60.4	2.7	4.0	0.1	4.9	23.6	801	80	112	1 224	37.9	59.2	2.9
Carroll	269.6	1 835	67.3	1.1	0.9	0.9	2.3	213.5	1 453	326	573	6 261	31.5	65.2	3.3
Cecil	160.1	1 983	65.5	1.0	3.9	0.5	5.3	96.9	1 199	1 696	312	2 943	42.7	53.7	3.7
Charles	254.9	2 215	65.0	0.8	5.8	0.4	2.1	158.6	1 378	2 503	876	4 743	49.1	48.8	2.1
Dorchester	71.2	2 381	52.4	1.0	4.5	0.4	7.4	28.2	942	132	123	1 495	45.9	51.3	2.7
Frederick	382.9	2 090	58.2	3.2	3.8	2.2	4.1	313.5	1 711	2 509	1 968	8 169	39.1	57.7	3.3
Garrett	66.7	2 259	57.8	0.5	1.5	0.0	21.8	25.4	861	78	111	1 377	27.0	70.5	2.5
Harford	421.3	1 982	60.7	0.7	4.5	2.1	6.1	184.7	869	8 015	3 830	8 695	39.0	57.8	3.2
Howard	548.9	2 399	61.2	1.3	4.4	0.6	3.3	735.2	3 213	665	895	12 922	51.9	44.2	3.9
Kent	36.5	1 913	52.9	1.1	4.4	0.3	7.4	14.2	745	72	72	820	44.9	51.4	3.7
Montgomery	2 544.2	3 077	46.9	3.7	4.1	1.1	4.1	3 287.2	3 976	41 289	7 242	37 104	62.5	33.5	3.9
Prince George's	1 861.8	2 416	46.0	2.2	5.9	0.2	3.3	2 153.3	2 794	24 279	9 383	52 322	79.1	18.7	2.2
Queen Anne's	89.9	2 299	65.7	1.2	2.1	0.1	4.1	42.9	1 098	89	150	1 694	37.3	59.5	3.2
St. Mary's	165.7	1 934	60.7	0.8	4.0	5.1	2.4	86.4	1 008	6 594	3 366	3 820	49.8	47.5	2.8
Somerset	43.7	1 785	53.9	1.0	2.9	0.1	4.6	12.3	501	67	120	2 702	40.4	57.1	2.5
Talbot	59.8	1 808	55.1	1.9	5.4	0.2	5.3	15.1	456	566	126	1 305	38.4	58.3	3.3

1. Based on the resident population estimated as of July 1 of the year shown.

Table B. States and Counties — Land Area and Population

STATE/County code	MSA/PMSA/NECMA code[1]	County Type[2]	STATE County	Land area,[3] (sq km) 1990	Population and population characteristics, 1999													
								Race (percent)					Age (percent)					
					Total persons	Rank	Per square kilometer	White	Black	Am. Indian, Eskimo, Aleut	Asian and Pacific Islander	Percent Hispanic[4]	Under 5 years	5 to 17 years	18 to 24 years	25 to 34 years	35 to 44 years	45 to 54 years
				1	2	3	4	5	6	7	8	9	10	11	12	13	14	15
			MARYLAND—Cont'd															
24 043	3180	3	Washington	1 187	127 791	410	107.7	91.5	7.2	0.3	1.0	1.2	5.8	17.8	8.7	13.8	16.5	13.3
24 045	...	5	Wicomico	977	79 560	635	81.4	69.2	29.3	0.2	1.3	1.2	6.4	19.3	10.0	12.9	16.7	12.7
24 047	...	7	Worcester	1 226	43 672	1 005	35.6	70.8	28.3	0.2	0.7	1.1	5.8	16.8	6.4	12.2	15.5	12.7
24 510	0720	0	Baltimore city	209	632 681	82	3 027.2	30.9	67.4	0.4	1.3	1.3	7.3	18.5	9.4	15.2	16.3	11.5
25 000	...	X	**MASSACHUSETTS**	20 300	6 175 169	X	304.2	89.4	6.6	0.2	3.8	6.3	6.4	17.4	8.3	15.2	17.1	13.4
25 001	0743	3	Barnstable	1 025	212 519	256	207.3	96.3	2.1	0.7	0.9	1.7	5.4	15.8	4.9	12.0	16.3	12.4
25 003	6323	3	Berkshire	2 412	132 218	395	54.8	96.3	2.4	0.2	1.1	1.5	5.3	17.8	7.6	12.4	16.2	13.5
25 005	1123	2	Bristol	1 440	520 258	102	361.3	95.8	2.4	0.2	1.5	3.8	6.2	19.1	7.4	14.0	16.7	13.6
25 007	...	9	Dukes	269	14 048	2 131	52.2	93.4	3.7	2.3	0.6	1.5	6.0	17.4	3.9	13.8	22.3	12.6
25 009	1123	0	Essex	1 290	704 407	69	546.1	92.4	4.8	0.2	2.6	10.0	6.8	18.1	7.0	14.5	17.4	13.6
25 011	...	4	Franklin	1 819	70 806	696	38.9	97.6	1.0	0.3	1.1	1.7	6.2	19.2	5.8	13.7	19.7	12.9
25 013	8003	2	Hampden	1 602	438 279	131	273.6	88.1	10.3	0.2	1.4	13.2	7.0	19.5	7.8	13.8	15.8	12.5
25 015	8003	2	Hampshire	1 370	150 892	345	110.1	93.0	2.2	0.2	4.6	3.6	5.0	15.5	17.7	13.7	17.6	11.8
25 017	1123	0	Middlesex	2 133	1 426 606	18	668.8	90.2	3.7	0.2	5.9	4.6	5.9	15.8	8.5	16.5	17.5	13.9
25 019	...	7	Nantucket	124	8 206	2 576	66.2	96.3	3.1	0.1	0.5	1.3	6.3	15.5	4.9	17.9	21.3	13.4
25 021	1123	0	Norfolk	1 035	643 580	77	621.8	92.5	2.6	0.1	4.8	1.9	5.6	15.9	7.2	15.0	17.6	14.7
25 023	1123	1	Plymouth	1 711	473 026	117	276.5	93.1	5.3	0.2	1.4	3.1	6.7	20.4	6.8	13.9	18.4	14.5
25 025	1123	0	Suffolk	152	641 695	79	4 221.7	63.2	28.7	0.4	7.6	14.1	7.1	15.9	12.8	18.7	15.5	11.1
25 027	1123	2	Worcester	3 919	738 629	62	188.5	94.1	3.0	0.2	2.7	6.4	6.9	18.8	7.8	15.2	17.1	13.0
26 000	...	X	**MICHIGAN**	147 136	9 863 775	X	67.0	83.4	14.3	0.6	1.7	2.8	6.6	19.3	9.4	13.8	16.5	13.3
26 001	...	9	Alcona	1 747	11 147	2 336	6.4	98.7	0.4	0.5	0.4	0.7	4.6	16.3	5.7	9.0	12.8	14.8
26 003	...	7	Alger	2 377	10 083	2 417	4.2	91.3	5.0	3.3	0.5	0.7	5.0	18.4	8.3	12.3	16.8	13.4
26 005	3000	2	Allegan	2 143	103 406	501	48.3	97.2	1.5	0.6	0.7	4.2	7.5	22.2	7.8	13.7	16.9	13.1
26 007	...	7	Alpena	1 487	30 615	1 359	20.6	99.2	0.2	0.3	0.4	0.6	5.7	20.0	6.8	12.0	15.3	14.4
26 009	...	9	Antrim	1 235	21 953	1 660	17.8	98.4	0.3	1.1	0.2	0.7	6.2	19.4	6.5	11.6	15.1	13.8
26 011	...	8	Arenac	950	16 547	1 967	17.4	98.2	0.5	0.9	0.4	1.5	5.9	20.2	6.9	11.5	14.8	13.3
26 013	...	9	Baraga	2 342	8 672	2 538	3.7	85.7	3.4	10.6	0.2	0.6	5.6	18.9	8.8	12.2	16.9	13.6
26 015	...	6	Barry	1 440	54 648	845	38.0	98.9	0.3	0.4	0.4	1.4	6.5	20.6	7.2	12.4	17.2	14.9
26 017	6960	2	Bay	1 151	109 514	484	95.1	97.5	1.2	0.7	0.6	4.1	6.3	19.4	8.3	12.6	16.4	13.9
26 019	...	9	Benzie	832	15 257	2 050	18.3	97.3	0.4	1.9	0.4	1.4	6.0	17.6	6.6	11.5	15.6	14.6
26 021	0870	3	Berrien	1 479	159 709	324	108.0	81.6	16.6	0.4	1.3	2.1	6.4	20.1	8.2	12.5	15.6	13.5
26 023	...	6	Branch	1 314	43 825	1 004	33.4	96.3	2.6	0.6	0.6	1.6	6.7	20.1	7.6	13.2	16.2	13.8
26 025	3720	2	Calhoun	1 836	141 380	376	77.0	86.7	11.6	0.5	1.2	2.5	6.5	19.7	8.6	12.5	16.4	13.7
26 027	...	6	Cass	1 275	50 129	903	39.3	90.1	8.5	0.9	0.5	1.7	6.1	20.0	7.7	11.8	16.3	14.2
26 029	...	7	Charlevoix	1 080	25 034	1 529	23.2	97.8	0.1	1.8	0.3	0.7	6.6	19.6	6.9	12.4	16.4	13.7
26 031	...	7	Cheboygan	1 853	24 153	1 572	13.0	97.2	0.2	2.2	0.4	0.5	5.9	19.4	6.4	10.5	15.0	13.7
26 033	...	7	Chippewa	4 043	37 904	1 136	9.4	82.1	6.6	10.7	0.6	1.1	5.2	17.5	12.1	15.3	16.7	11.7
26 035	...	7	Clare	1 468	29 955	1 374	20.4	98.7	0.3	0.7	0.4	0.7	6.6	19.4	7.1	11.2	13.8	13.3
26 037	4040	2	Clinton	1 480	64 054	744	43.3	98.5	0.4	0.5	0.5	2.9	6.6	21.4	8.1	12.9	17.7	15.2
26 039	...	9	Crawford	1 446	14 265	2 115	9.9	96.6	1.7	1.2	0.5	0.9	6.4	19.2	7.1	12.7	14.8	13.7
26 041	...	7	Delta	3 031	38 848	1 114	12.8	97.4	0.1	2.0	0.4	0.5	5.7	20.4	7.1	11.4	16.0	13.5
26 043	...	7	Dickinson	1 985	26 944	1 467	13.6	98.7	0.2	0.5	0.6	0.6	6.0	19.6	6.2	12.0	16.3	12.6
26 045	4040	2	Eaton	1 493	101 612	511	68.1	94.7	3.9	0.5	0.9	3.1	6.2	20.6	8.4	12.8	18.4	14.8
26 047	...	7	Emmet	1 212	28 995	1 412	23.9	96.2	0.6	2.7	0.5	0.6	6.6	19.4	6.9	12.9	18.1	12.9
26 049	2640	2	Genesee	1 657	437 349	132	263.9	77.1	21.2	0.7	1.0	2.6	6.7	20.6	8.9	13.6	16.2	14.0
26 051	...	6	Gladwin	1 313	25 697	1 506	19.6	99.0	0.2	0.5	0.3	0.8	6.2	19.3	6.9	10.5	13.4	13.5
26 053	...	7	Gogebic	2 854	17 043	1 926	6.0	96.5	1.7	1.6	0.2	0.5	4.9	16.9	7.6	10.0	14.0	12.4
26 055	...	7	Grand Traverse	1 205	75 352	658	62.5	98.1	0.4	0.8	0.7	1.0	6.7	19.8	7.8	13.6	18.8	12.5
26 057	...	6	Gratiot	1 477	40 027	1 089	27.1	98.3	1.0	0.4	0.4	4.9	6.2	20.4	10.4	12.0	15.4	13.2
26 059	...	6	Hillsdale	1 551	47 042	946	30.3	99.0	0.3	0.4	0.4	1.3	6.8	20.8	9.5	11.9	15.4	13.6
26 061	...	7	Houghton	2 620	35 448	1 208	13.5	96.3	0.9	0.4	2.4	0.7	5.6	17.5	17.2	10.6	13.7	11.9
26 063	...	7	Huron	2 167	35 283	1 215	16.3	99.4	0.1	0.3	0.3	1.4	6.1	20.2	6.9	11.2	14.7	12.3
26 065	4040	2	Ingham	1 448	285 123	191	196.9	84.5	10.9	0.7	3.9	6.2	6.7	17.6	17.1	14.9	16.2	11.2
26 067	...	6	Ionia	1 485	67 126	719	45.2	90.2	9.0	0.4	0.3	2.9	6.4	19.9	14.1	15.3	16.3	11.9
26 069	...	7	Iosco	1 422	25 928	1 498	18.2	96.1	1.9	0.8	1.2	1.4	7.2	17.9	7.5	12.9	13.0	10.8
26 071	...	9	Iron	3 021	12 817	2 224	4.2	97.8	1.1	0.7	0.3	0.7	4.7	17.0	4.9	9.4	14.4	12.2
26 073	...	4	Isabella	1 487	59 122	801	39.8	95.5	1.3	1.9	1.2	1.7	5.9	17.3	25.8	11.8	13.6	10.1
26 075	3520	3	Jackson	1 830	157 271	328	85.9	90.5	8.4	0.4	0.7	2.0	6.4	18.9	8.3	14.0	17.2	13.4
26 077	3720	2	Kalamazoo	1 455	229 867	240	158.0	87.6	9.8	0.5	2.1	2.3	6.5	17.6	13.6	13.8	16.5	12.8
26 079	...	9	Kalkaska	1 453	15 808	2 013	10.9	98.7	0.2	0.8	0.3	0.9	7.0	22.2	7.0	12.8	15.7	12.9
26 081	3000	2	Kent	2 218	550 388	94	248.1	88.6	9.1	0.6	1.6	3.9	7.9	20.3	9.7	15.4	16.5	11.9
26 083	...	9	Keweenaw	1 402	2 142	3 056	1.5	99.2	0.1	0.2	0.5	0.6	4.9	17.2	4.3	9.2	17.2	14.8
26 085	...	9	Lake	1 470	10 627	2 367	7.2	84.2	14.6	0.9	0.2	1.0	6.1	17.9	5.8	9.9	12.9	14.1
26 087	2160	1	Lapeer	1 695	89 391	563	52.7	98.2	0.8	0.4	0.6	2.6	6.4	22.4	8.5	12.9	18.1	14.9

1. MSA = Metropolitan Statistical Area. PMSA = Primary MSA. NECMA = New England County Metropolitan Area. See Appendix A for explanation of these concepts. See Appendix B for list of metropolitan areas identified by type, with component counties.   2. County typology code from the Economic Research Service of USDA. See Appendix A for definition.   3. Dry land or land partially or temporarily covered by water.   4. Hispanic persons may be of any race.

Table B. States and Counties — Population and Households

STATE County	55 to 64 years (16)	65 to 74 years (17)	75 years and over (18)	Percent female (19)	Total persons 1990 (20)	Total persons 1980 (21)	Percent change 1980–1990 (22)	Percent change 1990–1999 (23)	Births (24)	Deaths (25)	Net migration (26)	Number (27)	Percent change, 1980–1990 (28)	Persons per household (29)	Female family householder[1] (30)	One person (31)
MARYLAND—Cont'd																
Washington	9.4	7.3	7.3	49.2	121 393	113 086	7.3	5.3	14 788	10 924	2 687	44 762	12.0	2.53	9.7	23.6
Wicomico	8.9	6.7	6.2	52.0	74 339	64 540	15.2	7.0	10 418	7 314	2 326	27 772	21.4	2.56	13.2	23.5
Worcester	11.2	10.7	8.7	52.0	35 028	30 889	13.4	24.7	4 492	4 449	8 765	14 142	21.3	2.44	11.5	24.7
Baltimore city	8.8	6.9	6.2	53.3	736 014	786 741	-6.4	-14.0	104 678	84 732	-121 777	276 484	-1.8	2.59	24.6	30.5
MASSACHUSETTS	8.3	7.0	7.0	51.8	6 016 425	5 737 093	4.9	2.6	778 803	506 880	-96 660	2 247 110	10.5	2.58	12.1	25.8
Barnstable	9.9	11.7	11.5	52.3	186 605	147 925	26.1	13.9	20 283	22 468	28 705	77 586	32.5	2.35	9.8	27.2
Berkshire	9.2	8.8	9.2	51.8	139 352	145 110	-4.0	-5.1	14 248	14 047	-6 917	54 315	3.7	2.45	10.8	27.5
Bristol	8.5	7.4	7.1	51.9	506 325	474 641	6.7	2.8	65 050	44 477	-4 914	187 668	12.4	2.64	12.5	23.8
Dukes	8.6	7.9	7.4	51.0	11 639	8 942	30.2	20.7	1 455	1 090	2 069	5 003	29.2	2.31	8.7	31.5
Essex	8.4	7.1	7.1	52.1	670 080	633 688	5.7	5.1	92 246	58 109	2 350	251 285	10.0	2.61	12.4	25.2
Franklin	7.6	7.4	7.5	50.9	70 086	64 317	9.0	1.0	7 584	6 090	-550	27 640	14.1	2.49	10.5	26.1
Hampden	8.3	7.8	7.4	52.3	456 310	443 018	3.0	-4.0	58 446	42 498	-32 645	169 906	7.5	2.60	15.4	25.6
Hampshire	6.9	6.2	5.7	52.5	146 568	138 813	5.6	3.0	13 434	10 554	1 956	50 052	13.1	2.54	9.9	24.8
Middlesex	8.5	6.6	6.7	51.8	1 398 468	1 367 034	2.3	2.0	181 530	106 085	-43 814	519 527	9.1	2.59	10.5	25.2
Nantucket	9.2	5.3	6.2	48.9	6 012	5 087	18.2	36.5	936	652	1 919	2 597	20.5	2.29	7.4	31.4
Norfolk	9.2	7.2	7.4	52.3	616 087	606 587	1.6	4.5	78 286	51 587	2 590	227 798	9.6	2.63	10.0	24.5
Plymouth	7.6	6.0	5.8	51.0	435 276	405 437	7.4	8.7	60 553	33 921	12 442	149 519	12.8	2.84	11.9	20.1
Suffolk	7.4	5.7	5.9	51.8	663 906	650 142	2.1	-3.3	90 236	54 840	-55 880	264 061	4.8	2.38	16.6	34.8
Worcester	7.9	6.6	6.7	51.0	709 711	646 352	9.8	4.1	94 516	60 462	-3 951	260 153	15.5	2.62	11.2	23.9
MICHIGAN	8.5	6.5	5.9	51.3	9 295 287	9 262 044	0.4	6.1	1 287 572	763 166	-99 730	3 419 331	7.0	2.66	12.9	23.7
Alcona	14.3	12.1	10.5	50.0	10 145	9 740	4.2	9.9	873	1 503	1 634	4 261	14.7	2.35	7.5	24.6
Alger	9.5	8.3	7.9	46.2	8 972	9 225	-2.7	12.4	837	981	1 285	3 337	1.8	2.52	8.5	24.3
Allegan	8.0	5.4	5.3	50.5	90 509	81 555	11.0	14.2	13 003	6 987	7 093	31 709	16.4	2.81	8.6	19.3
Alpena	10.5	7.7	7.8	51.4	30 605	32 315	-5.3	0.0	3 164	3 057	23	11 838	6.2	2.56	9.1	24.6
Antrim	11.3	8.6	7.7	50.9	18 185	16 194	12.3	20.7	2 286	2 046	3 560	6 980	22.0	2.58	8.5	21.5
Arenac	11.2	8.8	7.5	50.6	14 906	14 706	1.4	11.0	1 728	1 712	1 676	5 642	10.6	2.61	9.4	22.7
Baraga	7.9	7.7	8.4	46.4	7 954	8 484	-6.2	9.0	909	1 052	893	3 065	4.6	2.51	10.2	28.0
Barry	9.0	6.4	6.0	49.8	50 057	45 781	9.3	9.2	6 518	3 750	1 972	17 763	15.1	2.78	7.7	17.7
Bay	8.8	7.5	6.9	51.5	111 723	119 881	-6.8	-2.0	13 422	9 387	-5 923	42 188	2.0	2.62	11.0	24.1
Benzie	11.0	9.3	7.9	50.5	12 200	11 205	8.9	25.1	1 534	1 346	2 882	4 772	19.1	2.52	7.3	22.6
Berrien	9.1	7.5	7.0	52.1	161 378	171 276	-5.8	-1.0	21 271	14 324	-8 143	61 025	1.2	2.60	13.3	24.4
Branch	9.2	6.7	6.4	51.0	41 502	40 188	3.3	5.6	5 034	3 669	1 091	14 921	6.5	2.67	9.9	22.3
Calhoun	9.5	6.7	6.4	51.5	135 982	141 579	-4.0	4.0	18 010	12 961	706	51 812	1.3	2.54	13.1	25.3
Cass	9.6	7.6	6.7	50.8	49 477	49 499	0.0	1.3	4 960	4 140	11	18 239	5.8	2.70	10.4	20.3
Charlevoix	9.6	7.5	7.1	50.8	21 468	19 907	7.8	16.6	2 935	1 992	2 290	8 243	16.8	2.59	8.7	23.0
Cheboygan	10.9	9.5	8.6	51.4	21 398	20 649	3.6	12.9	2 546	2 458	2 725	8 201	12.7	2.58	9.6	22.1
Chippewa	8.9	6.3	6.2	44.3	34 604	29 029	19.2	9.5	3 885	2 651	2 147	11 541	16.2	2.56	10.0	25.4
Clare	11.9	9.1	7.5	51.3	24 952	23 822	4.7	20.1	3 407	3 176	4 823	9 698	11.7	2.54	10.5	22.5
Clinton	8.1	5.2	4.8	50.1	57 893	55 893	3.6	10.6	7 583	3 680	2 438	20 212	13.8	2.85	7.8	17.2
Crawford	10.8	8.0	7.1	49.2	12 260	9 465	29.5	16.4	1 543	1 200	1 694	4 441	34.0	2.62	9.6	21.0
Delta	9.6	8.1	8.1	51.1	37 780	38 947	-3.0	2.8	3 918	3 562	842	14 531	7.1	2.57	8.9	25.7
Dickinson	9.5	8.4	9.4	50.6	26 831	25 341	5.9	0.4	2 943	2 922	192	10 633	11.5	2.49	8.3	26.2
Eaton	7.9	5.5	5.4	51.4	92 879	88 337	5.1	9.4	11 159	6 415	3 589	34 027	12.9	2.69	9.4	21.2
Emmet	8.7	7.0	7.3	51.1	25 040	22 992	8.9	15.8	3 389	2 335	2 982	9 516	17.4	2.58	9.0	24.2
Genesee	8.6	6.1	5.3	52.2	430 459	450 449	-4.4	1.6	62 938	34 490	-20 398	161 296	4.3	2.64	16.7	23.9
Gladwin	12.2	10.2	7.9	50.5	21 896	19 957	9.7	17.4	2 577	2 543	3 819	8 357	16.7	2.59	8.6	21.7
Gogebic	10.6	11.0	12.7	50.3	18 052	19 686	-8.3	-5.6	1 540	2 431	-30	7 449	-1.7	2.33	9.2	31.8
Grand Traverse	7.9	6.3	6.5	51.2	64 273	54 899	17.1	17.2	8 310	5 219	8 190	23 965	25.0	2.62	9.2	22.5
Gratiot	8.4	6.5	7.3	51.1	38 982	40 448	-3.6	2.7	4 886	3 784	77	13 659	2.6	2.68	9.5	21.5
Hillsdale	9.0	6.4	6.7	50.8	43 431	42 071	3.2	8.3	5 374	3 733	2 095	15 637	8.7	2.70	8.7	21.1
Houghton	8.1	6.8	8.6	46.8	35 446	37 872	-6.4	0.0	3 742	3 861	227	13 172	1.5	2.44	8.4	31.5
Huron	10.0	9.4	9.2	50.8	34 951	36 459	-4.1	0.9	3 841	3 856	479	13 268	3.9	2.60	8.1	24.2
Ingham	6.4	5.0	4.8	52.0	281 912	275 520	2.3	1.1	38 176	17 027	-28 348	102 648	7.8	2.55	12.3	26.3
Ionia	6.9	4.5	4.6	43.4	57 024	51 815	10.1	17.7	7 603	3 971	6 571	18 447	13.7	2.81	9.7	20.6
Iosco	10.2	10.7	9.8	51.1	30 209	28 349	6.6	-14.2	3 231	3 149	-4 618	11 588	14.0	2.52	7.7	23.7
Iron	11.8	12.3	13.3	50.6	13 175	13 635	-3.4	-2.7	1 091	2 032	641	5 655	4.1	2.27	7.5	31.0
Isabella	6.5	4.8	4.2	51.9	54 624	54 110	0.9	8.2	6 056	3 197	1 781	17 591	9.6	2.74	9.4	20.6
Jackson	8.9	6.7	6.2	49.3	149 756	151 495	-1.1	5.0	19 762	12 930	1 155	53 660	5.3	2.62	11.5	23.2
Kalamazoo	7.7	5.8	5.7	51.9	223 411	212 378	5.2	2.9	29 751	15 956	-6 765	83 702	11.0	2.54	10.9	24.7
Kalkaska	9.6	6.9	5.9	49.5	13 497	10 952	23.2	17.1	1 875	1 185	1 655	4 934	30.0	2.71	8.8	20.3
Kent	7.5	5.4	5.4	51.5	500 631	444 506	12.6	9.9	83 888	35 535	-3 325	181 740	16.8	2.69	11.5	23.0
Keweenaw	12.7	8.7	11.0	49.5	1 701	1 963	-13.3	25.9	155	280	567	777	-6.7	2.19	6.3	34.5
Lake	14.0	9.4	8.0	50.9	8 583	7 711	11.3	23.8	1 030	1 352	2 373	3 536	15.9	2.39	9.8	27.9
Lapeer	7.6	5.0	4.4	49.6	74 768	70 038	6.8	19.6	10 274	4 976	9 484	24 659	16.3	2.97	8.9	15.7

1. No spouse present.

Table B. States and Counties — Vital Statistics, Health Resources, and Crime

STATE County	Births, average 1996–1998 Total	Rate[1]	Deaths, average 1996–1998 Number Total	Infant[2]	Rate Total[1]	Infant[3]	Physicians,[4] 1998 Number	Rate[5]	Hospitals,[4] 1998 Number	Beds Number	Rate[6]	Medicare enrollees 1999	Serious crimes known to police, 1998[6] Total Number	Rate[7]
	32	33	34	35	36	37	38	39	40	41	42	43	44	45
MARYLAND—Cont'd														
Washington	1 569	12.3	1 218	8	9.5	5.1	236	185	1	320	251	19 944	3 319	2 569
Wicomico	1 072	13.5	770	8	9.7	7.5	233	294	1	400	504	11 681	4 263	5 332
Worcester	489	11.6	524	5	12.5	10.9	58	136	1	32	75	9 632	2 856	6 727
Baltimore city	9 983	15.1	9 011	128	13.7	12.9	3 253	504	12	4 945	766	103 995	274 257	5 344
MASSACHUSETTS	80 684	13.2	55 084	413	9.0	5.1	21 233	345	90	20 369	331	954 180	211 203	3 436
Barnstable	2 054	10.0	2 571	9	12.5	4.2	581	279	2	385	185	55 123	7 294	3 539
Berkshire	1 350	10.1	1 553	7	11.6	5.4	374	281	4	595	447	26 555	3 051	2 578
Bristol	6 581	12.8	4 867	32	9.4	4.9	670	129	5	1 232	238	87 194	17 937	3 463
Dukes	158	11.7	131	1	9.6	6.3	49	353	1	80	576	2 405	NA	NA
Essex	9 568	13.8	6 368	57	9.2	6.0	1 446	207	9	2 044	292	110 320	20 625	3 077
Franklin	730	10.3	660	5	9.3	7.3	105	149	1	128	181	11 452	2 586	3 809
Hampden	5 874	13.3	4 600	40	10.4	6.9	938	213	7	1 746	397	75 696	23 754	5 466
Hampshire	1 343	9.0	1 124	4	7.5	2.7	497	333	2	227	152	20 019	2 812	2 106
Middlesex	19 235	13.5	11 417	78	8.0	4.1	6 022	423	21	4 066	286	204 598	31 376	2 299
Nantucket	110	14.5	74	1	9.8	9.1	18	229	1	39	497	1 060	604	8 006
Norfolk	8 320	13.0	5 669	29	8.8	3.5	3 141	489	6	1 317	205	97 747	11 317	1 955
Plymouth	6 402	13.9	3 833	32	8.3	5.0	667	143	4	741	158	62 971	12 176	2 802
Suffolk	9 254	14.4	5 555	60	8.7	6.5	4 826	752	15	5 521	860	87 737	39 393	6 094
Worcester	9 705	13.4	6 665	56	9.2	5.8	1 899	259	12	2 248	307	111 133	22 728	3 156
MICHIGAN	133 589	13.7	84 028	1 089	8.6	8.1	21 525	219	167	31 719	323	1 389 107	459 720	4 683
Alcona	91	8.3	175	0	16.0	0.0	6	54	0	0	0	3 046	230	2 086
Alger	91	9.2	102	1	10.2	14.7	9	91	1	40	405	1 976	133	1 330
Allegan	1 409	14.0	803	11	8.0	7.8	56	55	2	106	104	11 400	2 295	2 386
Alpena	329	10.8	335	3	11.0	9.1	53	174	1	169	556	6 500	645	2 096
Antrim	235	11.2	238	2	11.3	8.5	22	102	0	0	0	4 144	NA	NA
Arenac	173	10.6	187	2	11.4	9.6	11	67	1	81	494	3 627	417	2 530
Baraga	97	11.5	121	1	14.3	10.3	6	71	1	61	725	1 677	89	1 049
Barry	691	12.7	425	6	7.8	8.2	48	88	1	91	167	6 505	911	1 914
Bay	1 344	12.2	1 036	10	9.4	7.7	144	131	1	341	310	17 914	3 815	3 440
Benzie	169	11.8	152	0	10.6	2.0	26	177	1	48	327	2 960	258	1 859
Berrien	2 200	13.7	1 543	20	9.6	9.2	242	151	4	733	457	28 086	7 496	4 661
Branch	532	12.3	411	4	9.5	7.5	47	108	1	130	298	6 569	1 300	3 282
Calhoun	1 839	13.2	1 435	13	10.3	6.9	222	157	4	527	374	22 299	7 932	5 803
Cass	601	12.1	455	4	9.1	7.2	54	109	1	57	115	6 759	1 612	3 212
Charlevoix	330	13.7	229	3	9.5	8.1	47	192	1	40	164	4 379	NA	NA
Cheboygan	277	11.8	290	2	12.4	8.4	28	118	1	129	543	4 711	510	2 418
Chippewa	427	11.3	299	2	7.9	5.5	32	84	1	137	361	5 616	712	1 893
Clare	351	12.1	354	2	12.2	4.7	23	78	1	64	216	6 745	890	3 054
Clinton	795	12.7	417	2	6.6	2.9	57	90	1	48	76	6 048	873	1 544
Crawford	154	11.1	137	1	9.9	8.7	22	155	1	130	919	2 250	355	2 546
Delta	411	10.6	392	1	10.1	3.2	54	139	1	66	169	7 585	NA	NA
Dickinson	299	11.0	330	2	12.2	6.7	70	259	2	126	465	5 384	615	2 263
Eaton	1 210	12.0	730	6	7.3	4.7	98	97	2	81	80	9 769	3 172	3 246
Emmet	363	12.8	246	1	8.7	1.8	137	478	1	249	868	5 025	NA	NA
Genesee	6 384	14.6	3 760	78	8.6	12.2	828	190	5	1 779	408	61 100	30 625	7 142
Gladwin	267	10.7	290	3	11.6	11.2	16	63	1	42	166	5 440	558	2 358
Gogebic	165	9.5	263	3	15.1	18.1	23	135	1	53	310	4 730	453	2 586
Grand Traverse	901	12.3	602	5	8.2	5.9	304	410	1	328	442	12 542	1 961	2 669
Gratiot	496	12.4	435	5	10.9	10.1	60	150	1	100	249	6 437	1 002	2 493
Hillsdale	569	12.3	418	4	9.1	7.0	38	82	1	68	146	6 847	1 110	2 649
Houghton	378	10.5	423	3	11.8	7.1	48	134	2	122	342	6 264	574	1 596
Huron	390	11.1	430	3	12.2	7.7	39	110	3	207	586	7 819	660	1 863
Ingham	3 907	13.6	1 862	29	6.5	7.3	906	318	4	1 503	527	35 951	14 906	5 257
Ionia	807	13.2	421	5	6.9	5.8	36	58	1	77	125	6 984	1 228	2 078
Iosco	270	10.9	343	1	13.8	3.7	24	96	1	69	275	6 743	900	3 566
Iron	106	8.1	221	0	17.0	0.0	12	93	2	71	551	3 733	232	1 768
Isabella	632	11.0	363	3	6.3	5.3	61	105	1	118	203	6 162	1 848	3 271
Jackson	2 062	13.3	1 428	20	9.2	9.7	195	125	2	507	325	23 609	5 955	3 872
Kalamazoo	3 146	13.7	1 787	29	7.8	9.1	733	319	2	817	356	30 734	NA	NA
Kalkaska	190	12.3	132	2	8.5	8.8	4	26	1	81	520	2 174	483	3 112
Kent	9 045	16.7	3 952	70	7.3	7.8	1 350	248	4	1 405	258	67 897	26 369	4 867
Keweenaw	22	10.6	30	0	14.9	0.0	3	144	0	0	0	503	36	1 725
Lake	119	11.7	142	1	14.0	8.4	2	19	0	0	0	2 468	615	6 031
Lapeer	1 095	12.6	568	10	6.5	9.1	74	84	1	182	206	8 695	1 437	1 806

1. Per 1,000 estimated resident population, average 1996–1998. 2. Deaths of infants under 1 year old. 3. Deaths of infants under 1 year old per 1,000 live births. 4. Data subject to copyright. 5. Per 100,000 resident population as of July 1 of the year shown. 6. Data for serious crimes have not been adjusted for underreporting; this may affect comparability between geographic areas and over time. 7. Per 100,000 population estimated by the FBI.

Table B. States and Counties — Crime, Education, Money Income, and Poverty

STATE County	Serious crimes known to police, 1998[1] (cont'd) Rate[2] Violent	Property	Education — School enrollment and attainment, 1990 — Enrollment[3] Total	Percent private	Attainment[4] (percent) High school graduate or more	Bachelor's degree or more	Local government expenditures, fiscal 1997[5] Total current expenditures (mil dol)	Current expenditures per student (dollars)	Money income 1989 Per capita[6] (dollars)	Households Median Dollars	Percent change, 1979–1989 (constant 1989 dollars)	Percent with $100,000 or more	Income and poverty, 1997 Median household income	Percent below poverty level All persons	Persons under 18	Persons 5–17 in families
	46	47	48	49	50	51	52	53	54	55	56	57	58	59	60	61
MARYLAND—Cont'd																
Washington	379	2 190	25 860	10.8	69.3	11.4	118.8	5 971	12 970	29 632	6.4	2.0	37 327	10.1	15.7	14.2
Wicomico	659	4 673	19 738	11.6	72.1	18.5	82.6	5 940	13 425	28 512	7.5	3.0	34 827	13.5	21.6	20.0
Worcester	803	5 924	7 077	10.5	70.8	14.8	45.6	6 744	14 341	27 586	16.3	3.3	32 815	11.9	21.8	20.2
Baltimore city	794	4 550	181 558	21.5	60.7	15.5	728.9	6 702	11 994	24 045	12.0	2.4	27 713	23.7	34.4	32.4
MASSACHUSETTS	621	2 815	1 530 134	28.1	80.0	27.2	6 847.0	7 331	17 224	36 952	25.4	6.7	43 015	10.7	17.0	16.1
Barnstable	623	2 916	37 509	13.9	88.4	28.1	215.2	6 832	16 402	31 766	21.9	4.1	40 791	8.9	15.5	14.9
Berkshire	303	2 275	34 224	21.7	77.9	20.9	153.2	7 133	14 857	30 470	14.5	3.5	37 284	11.3	18.2	17.2
Bristol	615	2 848	123 204	17.9	65.0	15.9	547.1	6 568	13 853	31 520	21.5	3.0	38 866	11.9	18.8	17.1
Dukes	NA	NA	2 488	15.2	90.4	32.1	22.9	9 530	18 280	31 994	40.7	7.6	40 852	6.7	10.1	10.5
Essex	452	2 625	161 455	23.8	80.2	25.9	768.8	6 917	17 586	37 913	25.1	7.2	44 187	10.6	17.0	16.4
Franklin	1 274	2 535	17 354	12.9	82.4	24.2	84.6	6 987	13 944	30 350	18.7	2.3	38 330	10.5	16.5	17.0
Hampden	1 508	3 958	116 349	22.6	73.6	17.6	540.3	7 294	14 029	31 100	14.8	3.2	36 746	16.6	26.9	25.7
Hampshire	275	1 831	53 875	22.4	83.0	31.9	141.7	6 721	14 414	34 154	22.2	4.4	42 287	9.4	11.3	11.5
Middlesex	283	2 016	355 828	33.4	84.3	35.4	1 535.8	7 748	20 343	43 847	28.0	10.2	53 268	7.3	10.9	10.2
Nantucket	597	7 409	1 094	19.7	89.4	32.9	9.9	8 516	20 591	40 331	26.6	6.8	48 151	4.2	7.7	7.7
Norfolk	155	1 800	151 086	33.2	88.0	34.4	651.8	7 079	21 091	46 215	25.9	11.1	54 528	5.0	7.0	7.0
Plymouth	474	2 328	112 932	17.9	83.8	22.2	534.3	6 522	16 523	40 905	30.2	6.6	49 165	8.6	13.2	12.3
Suffolk	1 259	4 835	185 123	45.3	75.4	27.7	693.7	9 065	15 414	29 399	37.1	4.6	36 260	20.7	35.4	34.9
Worcester	654	2 502	177 613	23.5	77.4	22.2	815.8	6 712	15 500	35 774	24.2	4.5	40 489	11.1	16.8	15.8
MICHIGAN	621	4 062	2 581 042	13.1	76.8	17.4	11 686.0	6 932	14 154	31 020	-3.7	3.8	38 883	11.5	18.0	16.8
Alcona	82	2 004	2 013	3.0	68.6	9.0	6.5	6 122	9 466	18 013	0.2	0.7	25 466	13.7	26.5	23.6
Alger	190	1 140	2 058	5.4	73.0	11.5	9.9	5 760	9 669	21 569	-9.5	0.5	31 877	11.8	16.2	16.4
Allegan	279	2 107	23 805	13.1	74.4	12.0	105.9	5 864	12 498	30 596	2.0	2.3	43 128	8.2	12.1	11.6
Alpena	192	1 904	8 200	7.4	73.6	11.4	34.7	5 941	10 930	22 598	-11.1	1.4	31 836	12.9	20.6	18.8
Antrim	NA	NA	4 087	4.7	76.4	13.7	25.8	6 205	10 856	22 636	-3.7	1.4	34 015	9.4	16.0	15.4
Arenac	352	2 178	3 838	2.0	65.4	7.1	16.5	5 127	9 730	19 489	-11.8	1.1	27 758	16.6	27.6	25.4
Baraga	177	872	1 936	9.8	70.5	8.3	8.7	5 740	9 021	19 424	-3.5	0.6	29 412	13.3	19.0	19.1
Barry	225	1 689	13 088	8.0	78.3	10.8	47.8	5 852	12 417	30 516	-2.5	1.5	43 955	8.7	13.4	13.1
Bay	318	3 122	30 302	14.9	74.0	11.0	118.8	6 701	12 597	27 940	-12.5	2.1	36 836	12.3	19.7	18.3
Benzie	108	1 751	2 608	6.4	76.6	15.1	13.4	5 444	10 415	21 577	-4.0	1.0	31 666	9.4	16.0	15.5
Berrien	608	4 053	42 700	17.9	74.7	16.7	198.3	6 676	12 636	27 245	-0.1	2.4	35 846	14.1	23.0	21.3
Branch	290	2 992	10 467	6.8	73.8	10.3	53.1	6 721	11 033	25 332	-6.4	1.6	33 824	12.2	18.7	18.1
Calhoun	909	4 894	36 371	12.9	76.8	13.8	165.7	6 826	12 729	27 476	-6.9	1.9	37 295	13.5	21.7	21.0
Cass	297	2 915	12 605	8.1	72.3	9.2	44.7	5 754	12 167	28 002	1.3	1.8	36 600	12.2	19.3	18.4
Charlevoix	NA	NA	5 172	4.0	79.7	16.0	35.3	7 938	11 632	24 738	5.2	1.6	36 885	9.0	13.3	14.0
Cheboygan	218	2 200	5 056	6.5	73.5	10.0	28.4	7 227	9 568	21 006	-3.7	0.8	29 623	12.5	21.2	19.7
Chippewa	96	1 797	9 582	4.3	73.6	10.8	38.2	6 437	9 468	21 449	2.4	1.3	30 477	14.7	20.8	19.9
Clare	168	2 886	5 967	5.2	66.9	6.8	36.2	6 376	9 152	17 163	-9.8	0.9	25 237	17.0	28.6	27.0
Clinton	88	1 456	16 612	13.2	83.7	14.6	59.4	6 038	14 153	36 180	0.1	2.5	50 538	5.9	9.3	8.3
Crawford	230	2 316	2 966	4.2	73.2	12.6	12.2	5 208	9 610	21 497	8.4	0.8	29 587	14.6	25.8	24.0
Delta	NA	NA	10 107	5.1	76.9	11.3	49.7	6 504	10 810	22 791	-9.8	1.1	33 301	12.2	18.0	17.3
Dickinson	63	2 200	6 531	7.7	78.5	13.0	33.4	6 257	12 338	24 809	3.6	1.8	35 854	9.2	13.5	13.0
Eaton	265	2 981	26 580	11.7	85.5	18.5	103.5	6 197	14 896	35 734	-2.1	2.7	46 527	7.1	11.4	10.5
Emmet	NA	NA	5 905	10.0	81.5	19.2	31.1	6 022	12 606	26 015	2.8	3.2	36 641	8.8	14.0	13.7
Genesee	1 032	6 110	122 685	10.5	76.8	12.8	568.8	6 777	13 583	31 030	-11.8	2.5	40 153	14.2	23.5	21.5
Gladwin	249	2 109	5 140	8.1	64.8	6.5	22.1	5 490	9 482	18 587	-9.5	0.8	27 911	15.4	24.5	25.8
Gogebic	183	2 403	4 170	8.1	76.3	11.4	18.6	6 381	9 481	17 343	-5.7	0.8	26 003	15.7	24.8	23.2
Grand Traverse	222	2 447	17 423	9.7	84.9	22.1	96.1	7 048	13 289	29 034	3.8	3.1	39 841	7.6	11.6	11.4
Gratiot	157	2 336	11 017	14.3	77.1	10.9	55.5	6 584	10 673	24 530	-7.3	1.2	33 952	12.0	18.2	16.5
Hillsdale	255	2 394	11 461	16.1	75.2	11.3	49.0	6 226	11 198	26 019	0.8	1.1	35 694	11.1	16.5	16.4
Houghton	95	1 501	12 529	4.5	73.9	18.0	36.3	5 903	9 012	17 650	-8.1	1.1	28 170	15.0	19.8	19.4
Huron	119	1 744	8 370	11.4	68.0	8.9	40.3	6 369	10 089	21 852	-5.9	1.2	33 362	12.0	17.6	17.0
Ingham	601	4 656	105 704	7.8	83.9	29.2	376.1	7 633	13 740	30 162	-0.5	3.5	40 626	13.4	19.3	18.7
Ionia	234	1 844	15 466	11.9	77.2	8.9	72.8	5 886	10 896	29 430	0.7	1.4	38 443	11.1	14.0	14.2
Iosco	182	3 384	7 128	5.7	76.3	10.4	38.2	5 901	9 556	20 091	2.2	0.5	27 140	13.6	21.9	23.1
Iron	190	1 578	2 689	2.4	73.0	10.0	13.3	5 770	9 077	16 307	-14.1	0.4	25 527	13.6	19.8	19.4
Isabella	212	3 059	23 877	5.4	79.7	21.5	43.4	6 319	9 961	22 659	-9.9	1.8	33 561	13.9	17.3	17.4
Jackson	427	3 445	38 772	14.2	77.7	12.9	174.8	6 757	12 556	29 156	-6.1	2.3	38 253	11.6	17.3	16.3
Kalamazoo	NA	NA	70 282	11.2	83.4	27.1	233.9	6 770	14 548	31 060	-0.5	4.0	41 517	10.8	16.2	15.4
Kalkaska	296	2 816	3 516	4.8	69.6	7.1	12.3	5 912	9 502	22 078	-3.9	0.6	30 783	12.9	18.7	20.1
Kent	618	4 249	138 741	23.5	80.3	20.7	637.6	6 660	14 378	32 358	4.1	3.6	44 512	8.7	13.4	12.6
Keweenaw	0	1 725	334	5.1	64.3	11.1	0.1	6 455	8 620	13 821	-9.1	0.8	24 887	11.3	16.5	17.5
Lake	677	5 354	1 973	5.3	61.3	6.6	6.1	7 455	8 195	14 562	-4.9	0.5	22 291	20.3	34.5	34.1
Lapeer	132	1 674	21 293	8.3	77.6	9.3	86.7	5 743	13 313	35 874	0.0	2.6	47 774	6.9	9.8	9.3

1. Data for serious crimes have not been adjusted for underreporting; this may affect comparability between geographic areas and over time.   2. Per 100,000 population estimated by the FBI.   3. All persons 3 years old and over enrolled in nursery school through college.   4. Persons 25 years old and over.   5. Elementary and secondary education expenditures, local government fiscal years ending between July 1, 1996 and June 30, 1997.   6. Based on population enumerated as of April 1, 1990.

Personal income, 1998

STATE County	Total (mil dol)	Percent change, 1997–1998	Per capita[1] Dollars	Rank	Wages and salaries[2] (mil dol)	Proprietor's income (mil dol)	Dividends, interest, and rent (mil dol)	Transfer payments Total (mil dol)	Government payments to individuals Total (mil dol)	Social Security (mil dol)	Medical payments (mil dol)	Income maintenance (mil dol)	Unemployment insurance (mil dol)
	62	63	64	65	66	67	68	69	70	71	72	73	74
MARYLAND—Cont'd													
Washington	2 968	5.3	23 282	798	1 921	102	526	453	429	193	162	31	11
Wicomico	1 822	4.5	22 929	866	1 227	107	323	295	281	115	118	26	6
Worcester	1 074	4.9	25 109	479	520	107	304	194	186	95	63	11	9
Baltimore city	15 980	3.4	24 750	522	15 885	1 430	2 142	3 765	3 644	948	1 807	635	73
MASSACHUSETTS	205 814	6.5	33 496	X	137 604	16 401	37 374	26 555	25 474	9 060	12 470	2 205	750
Barnstable	6 799	6.9	32 612	99	2 653	607	1 964	1 127	1 090	531	430	50	38
Berkshire	3 684	4.4	27 731	250	2 077	278	821	694	670	263	319	50	17
Bristol	13 497	6.4	26 108	389	7 060	746	1 885	2 405	2 314	777	1 150	226	88
Dukes	465	7.3	33 599	75	208	64	155	52	50	24	19	2	3
Essex	22 930	7.0	32 740	93	11 420	1 444	4 178	3 005	2 882	1 057	1 369	262	94
Franklin	1 811	4.8	25 642	422	812	147	326	341	329	107	173	24	10
Hampden	11 617	4.5	26 441	349	6 949	626	1 933	2 523	2 445	709	1 328	276	59
Hampshire	3 792	4.9	25 225	466	1 856	298	733	447	421	186	149	27	15
Middlesex	56 695	6.9	39 857	33	40 525	4 318	11 064	5 116	4 866	2 002	2 180	340	138
Nantucket	349	9.3	44 267	14	191	61	92	25	24	12	10	1	1
Norfolk	25 333	6.8	39 453	35	13 591	1 766	4 976	2 315	2 202	981	945	116	61
Plymouth	13 680	7.0	29 292	188	6 004	1 138	2 088	1 767	1 685	614	807	133	58
Suffolk	24 270	6.0	37 844	44	32 211	3 671	4 051	3 753	3 640	717	2 252	452	82
Worcester	20 890	7.0	28 587	212	12 049	1 236	3 107	2 986	2 857	1 080	1 339	246	86
MICHIGAN	264 016	4.7	26 885	X	177 528	14 568	47 631	35 056	33 245	14 719	12 929	3 409	981
Alcona	206	3.9	18 593	2 186	47	15	65	61	59	32	19	4	2
Alger	170	2.8	16 996	2 615	85	14	31	41	40	19	14	3	1
Allegan	2 476	4.1	24 356	581	1 334	115	427	275	256	134	86	18	9
Alpena	674	3.6	22 125	1 060	412	42	131	139	133	64	48	11	6
Antrim	474	4.9	22 073	1 077	148	42	149	88	84	46	29	4	2
Arenac	303	2.7	18 452	2 227	116	22	63	78	75	33	30	7	2
Baraga	152	3.3	17 678	2 443	91	8	27	36	35	16	13	3	2
Barry	1 343	4.7	24 650	537	370	68	345	159	148	82	46	11	5
Bay	2 690	2.5	24 458	567	1 470	103	500	436	416	191	154	37	13
Benzie	307	3.2	20 812	1 455	90	21	93	63	61	30	22	3	2
Berrien	3 874	2.6	24 235	601	2 347	248	761	636	607	276	222	73	16
Branch	844	1.6	19 306	1 951	431	36	156	147	139	69	51	11	4
Calhoun	3 285	2.2	23 333	785	2 454	175	528	543	517	225	193	55	14
Cass	1 049	3.7	20 982	1 400	335	41	180	170	161	81	53	16	4
Charlevoix	579	1.8	23 627	715	335	51	129	89	84	43	30	5	3
Cheboygan	498	3.7	20 928	1 411	203	28	133	113	108	53	36	7	3
Chippewa	645	4.1	17 008	2 613	403	37	114	126	119	51	43	11	6
Clare	488	3.0	16 549	2 704	196	29	101	146	141	65	52	14	4
Clinton	1 541	3.0	24 310	589	436	62	309	154	143	81	44	8	5
Crawford	236	2.8	16 723	2 672	118	20	54	53	50	25	17	4	2
Delta	852	4.9	21 878	1 132	500	49	159	170	162	71	58	12	7
Dickinson	627	3.5	23 187	821	450	25	138	110	105	52	37	6	4
Eaton	2 422	2.3	23 978	645	1 091	87	451	268	250	139	77	16	8
Emmet	751	4.3	26 222	373	463	78	190	101	96	47	33	6	6
Genesee	10 433	1.7	23 947	653	7 155	343	1 847	1 749	1 668	671	660	217	73
Gladwin	448	4.0	17 683	2 441	130	23	77	123	118	57	45	10	3
Gogebic	334	2.2	19 381	1 921	150	21	72	94	90	42	34	7	3
Grand Traverse	1 970	6.3	26 535	340	1 427	173	449	244	230	116	85	13	8
Gratiot	785	-1.1	19 545	1 872	416	34	152	148	141	63	56	12	4
Hillsdale	948	3.4	20 361	1 615	507	60	161	152	143	71	53	12	4
Houghton	667	2.9	18 732	2 148	368	31	136	148	141	61	55	11	4
Huron	853	4.3	24 179	610	423	70	208	157	151	76	58	10	4
Ingham	6 945	1.8	24 296	592	6 396	403	1 220	873	820	333	324	98	26
Ionia	1 123	3.0	16 832	2 652	518	42	158	157	146	72	51	13	5
Iosco	490	2.4	19 048	2 040	226	33	117	138	133	67	48	9	4
Iron	247	2.1	19 141	2 003	102	13	54	75	72	34	29	4	2
Isabella	1 150	4.7	19 696	1 821	729	60	206	187	176	67	75	15	4
Jackson	3 525	3.1	22 576	961	2 031	214	665	551	523	247	190	50	14
Kalamazoo	6 283	3.4	27 364	272	4 505	344	1 253	744	701	330	255	69	15
Kalkaska	266	0.6	17 122	2 581	153	18	36	57	55	25	20	4	3
Kent	15 701	6.0	28 820	202	12 626	1 116	2 795	1 594	1 493	698	526	148	49
Keweenaw	38	2.0	17 968	2 351	12	2	9	10	10	5	3	1	0
Lake	162	3.4	15 518	2 876	40	13	35	58	56	25	20	7	1
Lapeer	2 005	5.1	22 727	912	637	83	294	225	208	102	77	13	10

1. Based on the resident population estimated as of July 1 of the year shown. 2. Includes other labor income.

Table B. States and Counties — Earnings, Social Security, and Housing

STATE County	Earnings, 1998									Social Security beneficiaries, December 1998			Housing units, 1990	
					Percent by selected industries									
			Goods-related[1]		Service-related and other[2]							Supplemental Security Income recipients, December 1998		
	Total (mil dol)	Farm	Total	Manufacturing	Total	Retail trade	Finance, insurance, and real estate	Services	Government	Number	Rate[3]		Total	Percent change, 1980–1990
	75	76	77	78	79	80	81	82	83	84	85	86	87	88
MARYLAND—Cont'd														
Washington	2 022	0.4	D	19.5	D	10.9	3.4	29.5	15.7	22 057	173	1 997	47 448	11.9
Wicomico	1 334	2.2	D	19.2	D	10.1	4.9	28.0	15.2	13 441	169	1 642	30 108	22.0
Worcester	626	3.3	D	8.9	D	22.5	8.1	27.3	15.9	11 019	258	698	41 800	40.0
Baltimore city	17 315	0.0	11.6	8.4	68.2	5.2	14.0	36.8	20.3	116 020	180	33 388	303 706	0.3
MASSACHUSETTS	154 006	0.1	20.9	16.0	66.6	8.3	10.6	35.6	12.3	1 045 541	170	166 532	2 472 711	12.0
Barnstable	3 261	0.2	D	5.2	D	17.7	6.8	33.4	17.8	59 558	286	3 727	135 192	35.3
Berkshire	2 355	0.1	26.9	20.6	60.7	12.0	4.5	34.7	12.3	29 991	225	3 634	64 324	8.6
Bristol	7 805	0.3	32.2	26.4	53.8	12.4	3.6	23.6	13.8	97 637	189	18 384	201 235	13.9
Dukes	272	0.2	15.6	1.3	68.3	21.5	7.6	27.9	15.9	2 601	187	173	11 604	31.6
Essex	12 864	0.1	32.0	26.8	55.7	9.9	5.1	29.2	12.2	121 035	173	20 173	271 977	11.3
Franklin	959	1.1	29.4	23.3	54.0	10.8	5.3	27.0	15.5	12 921	183	1 841	30 394	13.3
Hampden	7 575	0.1	24.6	19.5	57.1	9.5	8.6	28.6	18.2	85 190	194	19 557	180 025	7.7
Hampshire	2 154	0.8	16.9	10.8	54.7	10.4	3.1	32.5	27.6	22 233	149	2 012	53 068	13.8
Middlesex	44 844	0.1	24.4	19.4	67.1	7.1	5.3	42.1	8.5	219 611	154	25 513	543 796	10.3
Nantucket	252	0.0	16.3	1.2	71.5	23.7	10.3	26.2	12.2	1 175	150	71	7 021	46.8
Norfolk	15 357	0.0	18.9	13.0	72.1	10.8	13.2	32.3	9.0	105 794	165	8 384	236 816	11.3
Plymouth	7 141	0.5	17.0	9.9	64.8	13.7	5.5	27.0	17.7	71 424	153	9 019	168 555	11.4
Suffolk	35 882	0.0	D	5.4	D	4.1	23.8	41.0	13.1	91 081	142	35 110	289 276	4.5
Worcester	13 284	0.1	29.2	24.4	54.6	9.5	6.7	26.6	16.1	125 275	171	18 447	279 428	16.5
MICHIGAN	192 096	0.2	36.9	31.2	49.7	8.1	5.7	24.2	13.2	1 613 854	164	212 560	3 847 926	7.2
Alcona	62	-0.6	37.8	28.8	42.0	13.8	2.9	20.8	20.7	3 743	337	253	10 414	11.1
Alger	100	0.2	48.4	43.2	31.5	7.8	4.7	13.3	19.9	2 238	226	215	5 775	14.0
Allegan	1 449	1.9	62.4	56.1	25.1	6.9	2.1	9.6	10.6	15 234	150	1 132	36 395	14.2
Alpena	454	-0.6	D	27.2	D	10.1	3.2	15.9	24.8	7 325	241	857	14 431	3.2
Antrim	190	3.0	D	28.2	D	9.4	3.7	21.0	19.6	5 241	244	341	13 145	21.9
Arenac	138	4.4	D	18.0	D	9.6	3.0	31.4	19.4	3 893	237	454	8 891	15.5
Baraga	99	0.0	D	29.8	D	6.5	2.8	23.6	25.8	1 862	221	232	4 684	9.7
Barry	438	0.6	D	31.7	D	8.1	6.1	19.6	16.3	9 129	167	555	20 887	9.1
Bay	1 573	0.4	34.5	29.2	49.5	10.5	5.0	24.2	15.6	21 197	193	2 300	44 234	1.9
Benzie	111	1.5	D	13.7	D	14.1	4.9	25.7	21.0	3 463	236	256	8 557	14.0
Berrien	2 595	0.7	42.3	37.0	45.5	8.5	3.5	22.9	11.5	30 943	193	4 882	69 532	1.1
Branch	466	0.5	D	30.6	D	8.7	3.0	14.2	28.4	7 928	182	672	18 449	2.5
Calhoun	2 629	0.1	41.7	37.1	40.1	9.3	4.8	17.8	18.2	25 710	182	3 940	55 619	2.6
Cass	376	-0.2	44.2	37.9	36.3	7.3	4.1	15.8	19.7	9 228	186	842	22 644	4.9
Charlevoix	385	0.0	48.5	37.6	36.3	8.2	3.5	17.3	15.2	4 847	198	308	13 119	18.0
Cheboygan	230	0.2	25.2	12.0	56.2	19.1	3.2	27.6	18.4	6 189	261	464	14 090	12.8
Chippewa	440	-0.2	15.6	10.6	46.2	9.9	2.6	26.6	38.4	6 420	169	699	18 023	9.8
Clare	224	0.9	26.3	17.5	51.2	17.7	2.7	19.6	21.7	7 720	261	1 024	19 135	3.2
Clinton	498	1.8	35.0	23.8	42.9	10.8	2.5	19.7	20.3	8 834	139	467	20 959	13.5
Crawford	137	0.0	28.1	23.0	46.9	10.0	2.4	27.5	25.0	2 938	208	263	8 727	16.5
Delta	550	0.2	D	30.9	D	13.5	3.2	19.4	15.8	8 430	216	798	17 928	6.1
Dickinson	475	0.0	38.7	25.4	39.2	9.0	2.1	16.3	22.1	6 207	229	419	12 902	14.7
Eaton	1 178	0.4	22.0	12.6	58.3	9.7	12.5	23.9	19.3	14 990	148	781	35 517	12.7
Emmet	541	0.0	D	12.5	D	13.5	5.5	36.6	11.4	5 403	188	580	14 731	17.8
Genesee	7 498	0.0	D	36.7	D	8.9	3.8	23.7	13.0	72 977	167	12 645	170 808	4.8
Gladwin	152	0.3	D	24.1	D	13.2	3.1	19.0	20.7	6 457	255	607	14 885	10.2
Gogebic	171	0.1	19.0	14.7	52.6	11.5	3.8	31.2	28.5	5 062	296	469	10 997	8.8
Grand Traverse	1 600	0.0	26.7	14.5	60.4	13.1	6.7	31.8	12.9	12 979	175	1 187	28 740	21.7
Gratiot	450	0.7	30.5	26.6	51.9	8.2	3.4	28.4	16.9	7 339	183	989	14 699	2.9
Hillsdale	567	2.2	53.7	49.8	29.8	6.6	2.2	13.8	14.3	8 175	175	854	18 547	8.5
Houghton	399	0.1	D	8.4	D	9.6	5.1	22.0	39.4	7 338	205	766	17 296	5.0
Huron	493	7.0	D	32.7	D	9.0	2.9	18.4	13.7	8 967	254	718	19 755	10.7
Ingham	6 799	0.1	24.6	19.6	46.8	8.0	6.8	24.8	28.6	36 743	129	6 706	108 542	9.1
Ionia	561	0.6	D	27.5	D	9.4	4.0	14.3	30.6	8 335	135	836	19 674	11.7
Iosco	259	0.4	D	17.1	48.0	12.9	3.9	22.8	23.7	7 842	312	555	19 517	8.4
Iron	115	0.1	21.7	12.7	42.4	12.9	3.9	19.0	36.0	4 119	320	295	9 039	16.8
Isabella	790	0.4	22.5	11.4	50.1	11.3	3.0	28.5	27.0	7 777	134	1 207	19 950	9.8
Jackson	2 245	0.0	33.2	26.8	50.2	9.1	3.7	22.1	16.6	27 080	173	3 457	57 979	4.0
Kalamazoo	4 849	0.6	38.7	33.1	47.2	7.4	7.7	24.1	13.5	35 619	155	4 315	88 955	11.5
Kalkaska	170	0.5	45.3	16.9	41.0	8.1	1.9	12.2	13.2	3 052	196	346	9 151	20.5
Kent	13 742	0.2	36.9	30.2	54.6	9.5	6.4	23.3	8.2	76 515	140	10 911	192 698	16.6
Keweenaw	15	0.0	16.4	13.5	D	10.1	1.2	34.8	35.3	578	278	47	2 257	5.0
Lake	53	0.0	24.6	17.6	D	14.4	3.3	20.2	29.1	3 036	290	514	12 114	15.2
Lapeer	720	0.4	39.6	29.1	37.0	12.1	3.2	14.6	23.0	11 239	127	683	26 445	14.8

1. Covers mining, construction, and manufacturing. 2. Covers private sector earnings in agricultural services, forestry, and fisheries; transportation and public utilities; wholesale trade; retail trade; finance, insurance, and real estate; and services. 3. Per 1,000 resident population estimated as of July 1 of the year shown.

STATE County	Occupied units								Civilian labor force, 1999		Unemployment		Civilian employment, 1990[5]		
			Owner-occupied			Renter-occupied								Percent	
				Owner cost as a percent of income											
	Total	Percent	Median value[1]	With a mortgage	Without a mortgage	Median rent[2]	Rent as percent of income	Substandard units[3] (percent)	Total	Percent change, 1998–1999	Total	Rate[4]	Total	Professional, managerial, and technical	Precision production, craft, and repair
	89	90	91	92	93	94	95	96	97	98	99	100	101	102	103
MARYLAND—Cont'd															
Washington	44 762	63.8	83 000	18.7	12.4	358	21.7	2.2	68 018	-2.4	2 318	3.4	56 191	23.0	14.4
Wicomico	27 772	66.7	71 100	19.7	13.4	439	25.3	2.4	47 775	-0.3	2 207	4.6	37 233	26.5	13.1
Worcester	14 142	69.3	83 500	20.3	13.1	398	24.6	4.2	25 068	-1.0	2 210	8.8	17 322	22.8	13.6
Baltimore city	276 484	48.6	54 700	19.4	13.7	413	27.3	4.9	295 128	-2.9	21 069	7.1	314 688	27.6	9.3
MASSACHUSETTS	2 247 110	59.3	162 800	22.3	13.8	580	26.8	2.7	3 277 898	0.1	104 780	3.2	3 027 950	36.2	10.0
Barnstable	77 586	72.4	162 800	25.1	14.4	646	30.6	1.4	106 621	1.6	4 544	4.3	82 526	31.0	12.4
Berkshire	54 315	65.2	114 900	21.0	13.3	437	26.2	1.0	64 717	-1.0	2 428	3.8	65 136	32.0	12.7
Bristol	187 668	59.1	141 700	22.0	13.9	424	25.4	2.2	262 432	-0.6	12 018	4.6	241 998	26.8	12.9
Dukes	5 003	71.3	195 800	26.4	15.0	647	31.2	1.9	9 293	2.4	353	3.8	5 868	30.2	18.1
Essex	251 285	61.2	176 200	23.2	14.2	597	27.6	2.7	367 454	1.3	12 894	3.5	331 079	35.9	10.8
Franklin	27 640	65.6	114 100	22.4	13.9	478	27.0	2.2	37 747	-0.3	1 117	3.0	35 245	33.1	13.1
Hampden	169 906	60.2	123 200	21.0	13.4	484	27.4	3.1	210 931	-0.2	8 396	4.0	210 581	28.6	11.5
Hampshire	50 052	62.3	134 700	21.0	13.4	526	26.8	2.5	80 805	0.6	1 999	2.5	76 948	35.8	9.1
Middlesex	519 527	59.6	192 800	21.8	13.5	671	25.5	2.3	819 405	0.6	20 348	2.5	757 556	43.4	8.5
Nantucket	2 597	62.7	299 400	27.8	17.8	926	32.2	3.5	6 456	5.3	110	1.7	3 569	30.8	19.8
Norfolk	227 798	67.7	182 900	21.9	13.4	674	25.3	1.4	358 944	-0.9	8 497	2.4	328 006	41.0	8.5
Plymouth	149 519	73.0	156 400	23.4	14.8	620	28.2	2.1	245 604	1.6	8 045	3.3	215 264	31.5	11.7
Suffolk	264 061	32.5	162 100	22.9	14.4	625	28.5	6.7	339 576	-0.9	11 608	3.4	331 135	35.8	6.9
Worcester	260 153	61.4	140 000	22.2	13.6	522	25.5	2.2	367 914	-0.7	12 424	3.4	343 039	33.4	11.2
MICHIGAN	3 419 331	71.0	60 600	18.0	13.5	423	27.2	2.9	5 136 130	2.1	193 841	3.8	4 166 196	28.3	12.0
Alcona	4 261	86.4	48 200	22.8	14.1	326	30.5	3.0	5 112	-1.0	402	7.9	3 256	20.8	14.0
Alger	3 337	80.0	39 200	17.4	14.0	296	26.5	3.9	4 480	2.5	263	5.9	3 261	19.1	12.0
Allegan	31 709	80.7	59 300	18.5	12.9	377	24.6	3.0	57 613	3.0	1 681	2.9	41 879	19.5	15.8
Alpena	11 838	78.1	41 600	18.0	14.1	307	28.7	1.7	16 474	0.9	1 065	6.5	12 439	23.9	12.3
Antrim	6 980	80.9	53 000	22.1	14.9	342	25.6	3.4	10 523	2.2	674	6.4	7 332	20.2	16.3
Arenac	5 642	81.4	41 800	20.2	14.9	319	31.0	3.0	7 118	1.9	517	7.3	5 372	18.5	14.1
Baraga	3 065	73.9	37 900	18.0	13.4	235	25.0	4.0	4 456	2.8	307	6.9	2 761	22.9	13.9
Barry	17 763	84.0	54 700	19.3	12.8	366	25.7	3.0	33 774	5.1	998	3.0	22 709	20.1	16.2
Bay	42 188	76.9	44 100	16.8	13.5	344	28.5	1.9	56 500	1.8	2 718	4.8	48 026	24.0	13.8
Benzie	4 772	81.9	50 200	22.7	14.1	337	27.5	3.5	7 828	1.3	445	5.7	5 000	22.8	15.4
Berrien	61 025	69.6	52 800	16.9	13.2	368	26.9	2.9	84 718	2.6	3 403	4.0	73 154	27.7	13.5
Branch	14 921	76.1	40 800	17.0	13.6	346	27.0	2.9	22 342	2.7	807	3.6	17 807	20.0	12.3
Calhoun	51 812	71.0	42 700	16.2	13.6	374	27.2	2.1	70 339	2.5	2 961	4.2	58 597	25.8	11.4
Cass	18 239	78.9	48 600	17.7	13.9	364	24.8	2.8	27 163	3.8	916	3.4	22 870	19.9	15.8
Charlevoix	8 243	77.1	53 600	21.1	15.6	353	25.7	2.5	14 540	3.1	752	5.2	9 635	21.6	17.0
Cheboygan	8 201	79.5	47 400	21.0	14.5	315	26.9	3.3	12 904	0.4	1 352	10.5	8 164	19.3	13.7
Chippewa	11 541	73.4	37 500	18.4	13.9	323	24.8	3.7	18 092	1.8	1 310	7.2	12 299	23.0	9.3
Clare	9 698	78.4	36 800	21.2	14.6	320	30.3	3.9	10 867	4.0	855	7.9	7 986	19.6	14.7
Clinton	20 212	83.0	68 000	17.6	13.1	393	23.1	1.8	34 644	1.4	780	2.3	28 979	25.3	14.1
Crawford	4 441	80.3	44 500	21.2	14.1	350	28.3	3.6	5 815	1.9	379	6.5	4 758	22.3	12.0
Delta	14 531	76.2	43 200	19.4	14.2	297	26.8	2.4	19 444	1.6	1 254	6.4	14 886	21.8	14.3
Dickinson	10 633	79.4	42 900	18.7	15.5	347	22.7	1.2	14 402	0.8	766	5.3	11 301	24.8	12.3
Eaton	34 027	72.9	68 200	18.0	12.7	436	23.1	1.8	56 759	2.0	1 339	2.4	47 712	28.3	12.0
Emmet	9 516	74.2	64 700	21.1	14.1	379	25.1	2.5	18 221	3.7	1 289	7.1	11 822	27.3	14.1
Genesee	161 296	70.4	50 500	16.0	13.3	401	31.3	3.0	198 398	-1.4	10 968	5.5	179 087	24.6	13.6
Gladwin	8 357	81.6	42 700	19.4	14.1	307	29.6	4.8	9 606	4.5	678	7.1	6 892	17.6	18.0
Gogebic	7 449	78.2	23 300	16.7	14.8	257	28.7	3.0	8 143	0.3	562	6.9	6 494	21.8	11.6
Grand Traverse	23 965	74.8	66 700	21.0	13.5	446	25.5	2.2	46 028	0.3	1 678	3.6	31 333	29.8	11.9
Gratiot	13 659	76.2	38 800	16.5	13.2	333	26.1	2.4	19 800	2.6	894	4.5	16 362	21.0	11.9
Hillsdale	15 637	77.2	41 400	17.4	13.5	321	24.9	2.9	24 879	6.0	814	3.3	18 810	20.8	14.4
Houghton	13 172	69.5	28 300	18.8	14.5	281	29.0	4.0	17 829	2.1	824	4.6	12 990	30.7	9.4
Huron	13 268	79.4	44 500	20.9	14.8	297	25.7	2.1	18 430	2.1	898	4.9	13 660	18.9	13.0
Ingham	102 648	58.4	61 800	18.7	13.3	422	27.1	3.1	155 558	1.6	4 254	2.7	140 135	34.1	7.8
Ionia	18 447	77.3	47 700	16.5	12.9	341	25.1	3.5	28 116	2.5	1 223	4.3	23 420	19.2	13.1
Iosco	11 588	68.4	47 400	21.4	14.6	340	24.6	2.1	11 642	-1.5	958	8.2	9 728	23.6	11.9
Iron	5 655	80.1	30 100	20.1	16.2	269	29.5	2.8	5 695	1.3	386	6.8	4 552	21.8	12.1
Isabella	17 591	65.0	53 200	19.5	13.2	393	33.5	2.6	33 165	5.4	1 039	3.1	24 050	27.8	8.2
Jackson	53 660	73.7	47 900	16.1	12.7	376	25.0	2.1	78 070	2.0	2 658	3.4	64 317	24.7	12.5
Kalamazoo	83 702	64.4	62 800	17.2	13.1	417	27.4	2.3	130 243	3.2	3 795	2.9	110 927	33.0	9.1
Kalkaska	4 934	80.5	44 500	21.2	14.7	354	25.6	5.5	7 819	-0.7	482	6.2	5 184	17.2	17.2
Kent	181 740	69.7	68 200	18.7	13.0	431	24.9	2.2	331 012	3.1	10 276	3.1	247 711	27.3	11.4
Keweenaw	777	86.5	19 200	20.7	17.1	231	25.0	1.5	867	2.1	76	8.8	499	27.3	8.4
Lake	3 536	80.8	29 800	23.6	16.1	303	33.0	4.5	3 514	6.0	285	8.1	2 291	17.8	14.0
Lapeer	24 659	81.0	62 300	18.9	12.9	407	27.3	2.9	44 496	2.7	1 799	4.0	32 919	21.3	16.9

1. Specified owner-occupied units. 2. Specified renter-occupied units. 3. Overcrowded or lacking complete plumbing facilities. 4. Percent of civilian labor force. 5. Persons 16 years and older.

Table B. States and Counties — Nonfarm Employment and Agriculture

	Private nonfarm establishments, employment and payroll, 1998									Agriculture, 1997			
	Employment						Annual payroll		Farms			Farm operators
											Percent with—		
STATE County	Number of establishments	Total	Health Care and Social Assistance	Manufacturing	Retail trade	Finance and Insurance	Professional Scientific and Technical Services	Total (mil dol)	Average per employee (dollars)	Number	Less than 50 acres	500 acres and over	Whose principal occupation is farming (percent)
	104	105	106	107	108	109	110	111	112	113	114	115	116
MARYLAND—Cont'd													
Washington	3 222	51 788	7 764	9 502	7 568	5 115	1 095	1 312	25 338	768	34.1	4.7	54.9
Wicomico	2 451	35 020	5 944	5 802	6 042	1 387	1 081	851	24 306	580	56.2	9.1	60.5
Worcester	2 136	17 198	1 208	1 971	3 130	497	368	381	22 180	415	50.8	16.4	68.0
Baltimore city	13 855	298 655	64 138	28 825	21 175	19 895	17 320	9 518	31 871	NA	NA	NA	NA
MASSACHUSETTS	167 929	2 924 913	452 465	409 938	340 548	214 807	201 084	105 871	36 196	5 574	56.0	2.7	52.5
Barnstable	7 938	66 257	12 080	2 900	13 734	3 052	3 403	1 779	26 843	221	89.6	0.0	49.8
Berkshire	4 114	54 752	9 279	8 450	8 548	2 374	2 003	1 524	27 842	387	39.5	7.0	50.1
Bristol	12 399	195 504	30 751	49 415	33 092	4 853	4 629	5 147	26 326	555	58.7	1.3	55.9
Dukes	957	4 794	753	109	1 013	235	D	149	31 168	64	76.6	1.6	50.0
Essex	17 706	268 252	42 791	58 246	36 410	11 107	10 976	8 549	31 871	396	64.6	1.0	51.0
Franklin	1 625	21 865	3 552	5 630	2 948	777	372	553	25 291	543	35.0	4.4	50.6
Hampden	10 314	180 610	32 849	31 974	24 445	18 334	6 337	5 131	28 407	418	51.9	2.2	50.0
Hampshire	3 316	44 100	7 266	5 545	6 988	1 020	1 412	1 062	24 073	539	53.2	3.0	51.6
Middlesex	41 848	787 896	89 914	114 813	80 019	28 124	85 252	32 400	41 122	531	67.4	1.3	53.3
Nantucket	742	3 905	273	61	D	D	183	134	34 295	14	85.7	7.1	92.9
Norfolk	18 905	326 590	44 049	35 257	40 235	36 275	17 914	11 856	36 301	185	73.0	0.5	50.3
Plymouth	11 009	142 940	24 632	16 265	26 366	5 732	6 773	4 092	28 627	732	66.5	3.0	60.0
Suffolk	19 870	539 259	101 712	20 775	30 136	86 944	53 073	24 654	45 718	5	100.0	0.0	60.0
Worcester	17 171	287 961	52 564	60 498	35 770	15 816	8 577	8 832	30 671	984	45.3	2.4	49.4
MICHIGAN	235 403	3 919 567	486 987	828 751	537 895	164 990	192 200	128 649	32 822	46 027	31.9	10.7	47.9
Alcona	229	1 309	179	316	291	D	64	28	21 595	207	17.9	8.2	45.9
Alger	327	2 536	248	839	292	101	31	57	22 448	60	18.3	13.3	48.3
Allegan	2 069	36 293	2 669	17 888	4 016	483	447	1 080	29 755	1 337	40.6	8.3	48.4
Alpena	887	10 306	1 645	2 452	1 648	374	167	268	26 049	412	24.0	8.3	41.7
Antrim	632	5 378	534	1 391	D	116	567	105	19 614	261	26.4	8.4	46.0
Arenac	460	5 159	1 270	756	875	112	70	105	20 433	325	17.8	12.9	51.4
Baraga	232	2 136	356	752	314	71	4	48	22 512	54	16.7	25.9	51.9
Barry	1 005	11 151	1 067	3 471	1 718	635	234	267	23 966	881	27.1	8.3	38.5
Bay	2 635	35 189	5 519	7 857	6 704	1 334	943	955	27 138	730	28.2	14.2	56.0
Benzie	443	2 961	295	605	494	125	77	57	19 155	140	30.7	7.1	50.7
Berrien	4 082	60 344	7 130	16 521	8 212	1 879	1 489	1 630	27 011	1 182	49.1	5.8	54.2
Branch	924	11 887	1 534	3 819	2 057	393	271	272	22 854	980	26.2	11.9	45.6
Calhoun	3 058	60 436	8 581	16 804	7 865	3 222	976	1 732	28 650	1 085	24.4	11.0	45.4
Cass	821	8 765	677	3 853	D	234	199	218	24 822	700	29.0	14.3	52.0
Charlevoix	1 019	9 922	703	3 400	1 211	230	225	261	26 289	188	24.5	8.0	39.4
Cheboygan	922	6 181	1 058	699	1 422	197	221	140	22 572	210	21.0	11.9	39.0
Chippewa	943	9 773	1 451	624	1 825	280	217	182	18 604	319	11.3	20.4	43.6
Clare	631	5 805	843	1 013	1 341	194	109	121	20 829	350	24.0	9.4	50.3
Clinton	1 165	12 621	1 261	2 662	2 389	243	465	339	26 894	1 123	29.4	9.8	43.6
Crawford	307	2 994	787	481	543	107	91	63	20 904	27	48.1	3.7	48.1
Delta	1 179	13 086	1 516	2 940	2 499	563	689	319	24 401	253	14.6	15.8	49.0
Dickinson	952	12 997	2 239	2 529	2 173	360	230	347	26 728	116	26.7	11.2	42.2
Eaton	1 968	25 677	2 373	4 277	6 074	1 064	728	569	22 174	1 062	33.9	9.4	43.8
Emmet	1 318	13 122	2 691	1 633	2 399	363	362	334	25 459	207	23.2	8.2	42.0
Genesee	9 220	149 767	22 125	31 739	25 494	5 134	5 119	4 461	29 784	796	49.5	6.4	44.5
Gladwin	475	4 253	581	1 179	932	129	77	96	22 578	424	21.5	5.4	46.7
Gogebic	490	5 176	777	679	880	167	99	83	16 073	48	25.0	0.0	31.2
Grand Traverse	3 374	40 556	6 305	5 909	7 502	1 754	2 357	1 062	26 181	413	39.7	5.8	47.9
Gratiot	884	12 566	2 795	2 902	1 915	391	111	287	22 804	873	26.0	18.1	54.9
Hillsdale	905	14 553	1 211	6 721	1 542	317	172	341	23 403	1 236	29.6	9.9	40.0
Houghton	946	9 577	2 008	811	2 111	346	313	177	18 473	128	21.1	4.7	33.6
Huron	1 047	11 013	1 273	4 270	1 767	355	186	279	25 312	1 184	20.5	21.4	66.8
Ingham	7 170	127 773	16 844	21 013	18 923	9 531	5 937	3 913	30 623	827	42.1	10.5	45.2
Ionia	1 008	12 447	1 162	4 427	2 294	451	254	302	24 232	1 004	28.1	11.8	46.5
Iosco	682	5 633	614	736	1 323	284	119	119	21 180	238	30.7	8.4	47.9
Iron	435	3 261	654	359	550	149	101	60	18 469	86	17.4	14.0	43.0
Isabella	1 315	18 049	2 691	1 984	3 110	472	489	365	20 243	911	23.4	12.8	51.7
Jackson	3 442	53 517	7 148	12 218	8 471	1 450	1 389	1 470	27 475	987	34.7	8.0	38.0
Kalamazoo	5 960	109 688	14 780	20 886	15 299	4 715	4 474	3 396	30 959	696	44.0	12.8	48.3
Kalkaska	383	4 122	371	1 283	634	74	53	109	26 383	139	30.9	4.3	35.3
Kent	15 198	324 049	34 454	80 117	38 084	13 479	12 985	10 106	31 188	1 136	42.3	7.0	42.9
Keweenaw	61	310	D	42	D	D	D	5	17 261	5	60.0	0.0	40.0
Lake	180	1 125	205	128	241	D	12	18	16 306	126	24.6	6.3	29.4
Lapeer	1 709	19 962	2 369	6 109	3 865	493	486	457	22 916	1 020	37.8	7.9	47.8

STATE County	Agriculture, 1997 (cont'd)															
	Land in farms				Value of land and buildings		Value of machinery and equipment Average per farm ($1,000)	Value of products sold				Percent of farms with sales of —		Percent of land owned by Fed. Gov. 1997	Water consumption 1995 (mil gal/day)
		Acres								Percent from —					
	Acreage (1,000)	Percent change, 1992–1997	Average size of farm	Total irrigated (1,000)	Total cropland (1,000)	Average per farm ($1,000)	Average per acre (dollars)		Total (mil dol)	Average per farm (dollars)	Crops	Live-stock and poultry products	$10,000 or more	$100,000 or more		
	117	118	119	120	121	122	123	124	125	126	127	128	129	130	131	132
MARYLAND—Cont'd																
Washington	126	1.8	164	1	95	454	2 819	68	61	78 912	21.1	78.9	50.5	27.9	4.8	60.0
Wicomico	91	-0.4	156	6	71	406	2 686	61	186	321 197	16.0	84.0	81.0	53.3	0.0	19.8
Worcester	112	3.6	269	4	83	505	2 191	70	148	355 548	16.6	83.4	83.6	63.4	2.5	14.5
Baltimore city	NA	NA	NA	NA	NA	NA	NA	NA	NA	NA	NA	NA	NA	NA	0.2	4.8
MASSACHUSETTS	518	-1.5	93	25	224	455	5 207	40	454	81 522	78.6	21.4	46.4	15.4	1.8	1 145.7
Barnstable	5	-5.1	21	2	2	329	15 774	32	18	82 466	94.5	5.5	57.9	14.5	15.5	39.5
Berkshire	63	3.0	162	0	31	547	3 150	35	21	53 553	40.0	60.0	35.9	11.9	0.0	24.0
Bristol	37	9.3	67	2	18	456	7 625	31	34	61 444	73.6	26.4	47.0	13.5	0.1	114.6
Dukes	5	-18.4	77	0	1	661	8 640	22	1	19 524	78.9	21.1	28.1	9.4	0.8	2.8
Essex	26	2.2	65	1	12	527	8 602	54	25	63 361	79.2	20.8	45.2	13.9	1.4	115.0
Franklin	75	1.5	138	2	32	315	2 279	39	41	74 962	61.6	38.4	42.7	15.8	0.0	9.1
Hampden	37	1.1	90	1	16	358	4 617	29	29	69 633	85.8	14.2	37.6	13.4	2.0	232.0
Hampshire	52	-1.7	97	1	27	302	3 859	36	36	65 888	70.8	29.2	44.5	12.6	0.9	26.0
Middlesex	31	-4.0	58	2	15	503	9 762	41	58	108 421	86.5	13.5	45.4	14.1	2.0	108.3
Nantucket	1	0.0	75	0	D	680	9 077	66	3	210 821	100.0	0.0	71.4	21.4	0.3	1.6
Norfolk	10	-1.0	53	0	4	574	9 917	35	8	44 680	88.8	11.2	46.5	11.4	0.4	56.7
Plymouth	73	2.0	100	12	21	695	6 654	61	123	167 605	96.7	3.3	66.5	29.9	0.5	105.4
Suffolk	0	0.0	1	0	D	339	242 143	19	0	52 620	100.0	0.0	100.0	20.0	0.8	4.4
Worcester	103	-10.0	105	1	44	378	4 236	39	58	58 891	54.9	45.1	41.1	11.8	1.7	306.3
MICHIGAN	9 873	-2.1	215	393	7 892	358	1 671	66	3 568	77 516	61.7	38.3	49.1	15.8	8.8	12 059.3
Alcona	43	0.9	210	D	30	216	965	51	6	27 016	39.1	60.9	37.2	6.3	25.4	2.3
Alger	16	0.2	267	0	9	229	858	41	2	33 806	28.8	71.2	43.3	15.0	26.8	3.9
Allegan	237	-3.7	177	13	198	353	1 979	75	187	139 684	39.5	60.5	53.2	22.6	0.0	50.6
Alpena	78	1.4	189	1	56	228	1 172	46	11	27 078	39.4	60.6	33.3	7.3	0.0	409.3
Antrim	55	6.1	211	3	33	253	1 231	45	17	65 922	72.9	27.1	44.8	14.2	0.0	8.4
Arenac	86	5.2	265	1	69	326	1 286	87	23	71 133	71.1	28.9	48.0	18.8	0.0	52.9
Baraga	15	7.1	278	D	9	231	833	43	1	21 001	36.7	63.3	37.0	5.6	7.6	2.1
Barry	165	-0.1	187	2	126	319	1 813	45	48	54 258	30.2	69.8	31.6	9.3	0.0	8.6
Bay	176	-2.8	241	5	162	388	1 606	89	61	84 141	93.1	6.9	63.7	23.7	0.0	627.3
Benzie	23	12.8	161	0	12	297	2 026	41	7	47 400	71.2	28.8	40.7	16.4	4.9	3.5
Berrien	174	4.2	147	11	146	283	1 913	63	81	68 846	88.5	11.5	52.9	16.2	0.0	2 195.8
Branch	234	2.7	239	31	185	305	1 352	63	77	78 826	57.7	42.3	48.3	16.0	0.0	21.0
Calhoun	243	-0.8	224	9	188	301	1 333	53	61	56 208	57.3	42.7	50.4	11.5	0.5	60.7
Cass	177	-4.9	253	15	141	400	1 590	76	67	96 416	47.0	53.0	54.0	20.1	0.0	17.5
Charlevoix	31	-24.2	165	0	18	241	1 511	33	4	22 080	39.3	60.7	29.8	5.3	0.1	117.4
Cheboygan	51	23.4	241	0	28	249	1 052	43	6	27 847	20.7	79.3	28.6	8.6	0.0	4.1
Chippewa	99	6.4	310	0	68	265	881	40	7	23 043	39.3	60.7	36.1	6.0	27.2	10.4
Clare	63	-1.8	180	D	41	239	1 317	31	13	36 999	13.4	86.6	38.6	8.3	0.4	4.2
Clinton	244	-4.7	217	3	210	358	1 583	70	92	81 492	44.8	55.2	55.1	15.5	0.0	11.8
Crawford	3	156.8	95	D	1	158	1 662	25	0	4 326	34.2	65.8	14.8	0.0	10.7	2.7
Delta	70	-3.8	278	1	41	205	759	47	8	32 260	45.5	54.5	39.9	7.9	32.0	75.9
Dickinson	28	1.1	244	0	14	230	943	50	4	33 975	46.5	53.5	42.2	10.3	0.0	11.2
Eaton	232	-0.9	218	1	190	334	1 524	55	55	51 740	71.8	28.2	44.7	12.6	0.0	17.7
Emmet	40	0.3	194	0	25	352	1 820	44	5	26 321	35.9	64.1	40.1	6.3	0.0	6.1
Genesee	118	-13.9	148	1	99	301	2 106	52	28	35 169	73.2	26.8	36.2	7.8	0.0	54.5
Gladwin	68	9.7	160	0	49	173	1 204	31	10	22 539	41.9	58.1	36.8	4.7	0.0	3.3
Gogebic	4	-30.1	87	D	2	99	1 129	28	0	4 830	77.6	22.4	10.4	0.0	44.0	4.3
Grand Traverse	62	-7.8	150	2	42	330	2 051	42	17	41 537	79.9	20.1	47.7	11.1	0.0	17.6
Gratiot	277	0.0	317	2	245	454	1 401	90	102	117 342	63.9	36.1	59.8	25.0	0.0	9.2
Hillsdale	257	11.0	208	4	210	271	1 276	47	72	58 033	58.3	41.7	42.2	12.3	0.0	62.0
Houghton	23	-20.3	181	0	12	165	818	34	2	17 238	30.6	69.4	28.9	3.1	23.5	6.4
Huron	424	-3.4	358	2	384	606	1 681	116	211	178 559	47.5	52.5	72.4	33.9	0.0	53.3
Ingham	190	-1.9	230	2	159	390	1 680	71	53	64 564	60.8	39.2	47.6	15.1	0.0	163.3
Ionia	237	-7.2	236	2	197	334	1 439	65	87	86 846	40.2	59.8	51.9	17.1	0.0	12.8
Iosco	43	-9.2	179	1	29	206	1 235	42	7	28 442	23.8	76.2	35.3	7.1	35.7	5.5
Iron	24	-20.6	277	0	12	190	685	39	2	18 525	65.1	34.9	30.2	3.5	22.3	4.8
Isabella	217	8.3	238	1	176	290	1 217	55	57	62 377	47.3	52.7	51.9	15.9	0.0	10.4
Jackson	181	-14.1	184	3	138	272	1 600	51	44	44 895	53.7	46.3	41.7	9.1	0.0	37.3
Kalamazoo	147	-4.6	211	18	120	439	2 038	74	105	151 572	64.2	35.8	54.2	22.3	1.8	111.7
Kalkaska	21	33.6	154	4	13	171	1 111	40	5	36 405	78.0	22.0	28.1	6.5	4.7	4.5
Kent	186	-2.4	164	6	150	453	2 686	74	121	106 550	76.0	24.0	48.2	18.8	0.0	184.3
Keweenaw	D	D	D	0	0	80	1 249	18	0	994	0.0	100.0	0.0	0.0	36.5	0.3
Lake	23	27.6	182	0	14	190	992	44	2	16 454	48.3	51.7	25.4	3.2	30.5	1.2
Lapeer	178	-8.1	175	2	144	433	2 425	66	54	53 191	59.5	40.5	41.9	11.5	0.0	13.5

STATE County	Value of Residential Construction Authorized by Building Permits, 1999		Wholesale Trade, 1997				Retail Trade[1], 1997				Real Estate and Rental and Leasing, 1997			
	New Construction ($1,000)	Number of Housing Units	Number of Establishments	Number of Employees	Sales (mil dol)	Annual Payroll (mil dol)	Number of Establishments	Number of Employees	Sales (mil dol)	Annual Payroll (mil dol)	Number of Establishments	Number of Employees	Receipts (mil dol)	Annual Payroll (mil dol)
	133	134	135	136	137	138	139	140	141	142	143	144	145	146
MARYLAND—Cont'd														
Washington	62 974	642	156	2 184	922.7	62.9	598	7 450	1 220.5	117.3	105	479	43.4	7.3
Wicomico	38 073	523	130	1 410	502.1	41.7	464	6 111	994.1	100.0	91	580	52.9	11.1
Worcester	79 935	720	76	1 181	476.0	39.1	505	3 285	546.0	59.1	137	1 095	53.9	16.5
Baltimore city	13 396	191	792	14 152	6 171.2	499.2	2 256	23 159	3 438.4	414.7	597	4 807	568.2	124.9
MASSACHUSETTS	2 666 006	18 967	9 993	146 827	112 792.4	6 484.8	26 209	335 736	58 578.0	5 894.8	5 834	41 233	5 925.4	1 214.1
Barnstable	366 137	2 224	259	1 361	462.8	45.5	1 592	13 675	2 518.8	256.5	286	917	138.1	21.4
Berkshire	47 179	327	136	D	D	D	832	8 513	1 280.7	137.7	122	410	43.9	7.5
Bristol	210 513	1 792	709	12 089	11 586.3	471.3	2 365	32 400	5 158.7	511.1	375	1 564	193.6	31.8
Dukes	51 947	309	22	D	D	D	222	931	207.6	24.3	45	112	19.3	2.9
Essex	226 320	1 618	1 071	14 836	9 270.7	671.4	2 703	34 590	6 156.2	585.5	563	2 555	319.4	58.2
Franklin	21 770	195	87	782	349.0	29.3	295	2 880	410.8	46.2	45	101	13.6	1.6
Hampden	110 576	846	573	7 696	4 481.2	285.4	1 862	24 675	3 919.9	384.7	373	1 852	238.0	40.2
Hampshire	58 075	432	109	D	D	D	604	6 976	964.6	107.5	128	500	61.1	8.7
Middlesex	475 250	3 316	2 914	49 166	33 893.5	2 386.3	5 701	78 812	14 462.1	1 491.7	1 412	9 998	1 669.0	305.0
Nantucket	74 909	232	13	D	D	D	178	799	195.7	23.0	37	124	27.3	6.5
Norfolk	247 395	1 753	1 451	23 872	21 949.4	1 128.8	2 599	38 832	7 332.9	715.5	687	5 682	981.6	196.0
Plymouth	227 846	1 695	700	9 214	5 772.6	361.1	1 917	27 147	4 895.9	472.3	337	1 399	243.6	31.3
Suffolk	171 951	1 209	923	11 910	10 935.6	523.8	2 543	30 091	4 842.5	532.2	887	13 000	1 585.4	432.5
Worcester	376 137	3 019	1 026	12 865	12 038.3	493.9	2 796	35 415	6 231.7	606.7	537	3 019	391.6	70.5
MICHIGAN	6 204 660	54 257	13 936	189 057	158 757.3	7 629.6	39 564	529 441	93 706.1	8 922.3	8 302	50 941	6 492.7	1 126.2
Alcona	17 505	181	1	D	D	D	40	290	49.7	3.9	2	D	D	D
Alger	5 865	98	7	7	D	D	55	294	37.1	3.3	9	24	11.0	0.8
Allegan	87 900	802	100	1 003	369.4	29.9	365	3 757	642.0	59.5	64	258	23.5	3.7
Alpena	13 597	101	45	396	143.3	10.3	162	1 719	288.5	25.0	23	127	9.1	2.0
Antrim	38 322	308	24	96	32.5	3.0	96	628	106.5	11.6	24	74	6.6	1.1
Arenac	2 938	28	27	227	74.6	5.3	79	758	127.8	10.6	19	31	4.1	0.4
Baraga	3 075	46	6	67	27.0	1.8	43	337	48.8	4.2	3	D	D	D
Barry	44 218	359	50	317	87.0	8.4	180	1 697	262.3	24.0	28	80	6.2	1.1
Bay	47 631	451	123	1 393	600.0	41.7	541	6 661	1 101.7	104.8	89	364	35.4	6.8
Benzie	33 320	294	9	48	4.6	0.7	78	532	104.8	10.0	16	27	3.3	0.8
Berrien	85 886	658	193	1 887	938.3	60.0	674	8 078	1 302.5	125.6	164	627	186.3	10.5
Branch	18 851	162	49	639	411.8	19.0	174	2 002	321.3	30.4	28	84	14.4	1.6
Calhoun	49 386	539	145	1 646	1 392.4	60.8	567	7 779	1 239.0	114.7	88	425	44.2	6.7
Cass	28 504	329	54	351	252.5	11.1	143	985	159.0	14.6	28	67	7.1	0.8
Charlevoix	56 185	390	14	113	33.9	3.4	172	1 288	202.8	19.3	29	96	9.1	1.3
Cheboygan	22 543	222	21	85	48.9	3.0	195	1 475	254.0	24.0	24	49	6.5	1.1
Chippewa	16 562	247	21	140	24.9	3.2	187	1 839	289.6	25.5	26	107	8.4	1.6
Clare	10 017	147	15	90	47.2	2.8	140	1 319	217.8	21.4	16	32	3.6	0.4
Clinton	66 217	449	56	685	522.2	23.2	207	2 378	426.2	40.1	38	152	17.8	3.3
Crawford	9 046	129	11	D	D	D	65	629	116.0	9.3	11	33	2.6	0.4
Delta	19 714	195	59	452	95.5	10.9	232	2 552	380.0	35.7	24	77	7.5	1.0
Dickinson	9 320	103	54	505	119.1	14.1	177	2 222	316.6	31.4	23	71	4.8	0.7
Eaton	66 787	606	86	774	673.9	25.1	342	5 587	898.7	82.4	77	342	40.7	6.4
Emmet	56 850	501	32	228	75.4	6.7	298	2 509	404.7	41.9	41	120	12.0	2.0
Genesee	284 384	2 806	422	5 884	1 899.4	217.2	1 809	25 369	4 521.3	409.3	350	1 613	193.6	28.7
Gladwin	30 954	341	15	40	11.2	1.1	90	895	152.8	14.2	22	36	4.2	0.6
Gogebic	5 052	57	16	115	35.4	2.6	102	920	135.0	11.4	17	160	3.1	0.9
Grand Traverse	94 061	1 006	167	1 580	729.9	51.9	634	7 300	1 232.7	117.5	113	441	52.7	9.7
Gratiot	11 701	120	37	493	196.0	14.1	200	1 891	295.8	26.9	20	55	5.5	0.7
Hillsdale	33 573	315	48	416	215.6	12.7	163	1 556	255.8	23.2	29	81	5.8	0.9
Houghton	9 820	107	27	179	33.7	5.3	181	2 052	262.3	25.4	24	80	5.9	0.7
Huron	20 139	219	51	536	194.5	14.0	211	1 800	262.6	23.3	22	41	3.6	0.7
Ingham	96 355	985	365	5 830	3 313.4	213.5	1 207	18 762	2 992.6	301.9	295	2 999	223.2	54.1
Ionia	42 812	464	42	325	143.5	11.1	184	2 189	331.2	32.1	17	109	6.2	1.9
Iosco	16 119	148	11	79	7.9	1.4	160	1 475	224.3	21.7	25	60	5.0	0.6
Iron	5 466	57	17	86	18.4	2.1	77	632	92.9	9.2	15	70	1.6	0.3
Isabella	34 316	530	69	817	327.9	23.7	220	3 187	458.6	44.0	46	581	21.3	7.0
Jackson	95 935	1 007	196	2 339	1 047.2	83.7	564	8 108	1 289.4	126.9	96	465	41.9	7.3
Kalamazoo	152 336	1 069	337	6 278	1 870.1	233.2	978	15 421	2 388.2	230.2	237	2 032	180.7	40.8
Kalkaska	10 276	133	27	225	76.2	8.2	70	660	144.3	11.6	15	56	5.3	1.1
Kent	395 875	3 480	1 314	28 386	15 882.2	1 043.6	2 194	38 200	6 491.8	658.0	567	4 030	493.9	88.5
Keweenaw	1 947	25	3	7	0.7	0.2	10	19	2.7	0.3	3	2	0.2	0.0
Lake	3 133	118	7	27	4.0	0.5	36	244	36.8	3.7	6	11	1.6	0.2
Lapeer	79 537	587	68	373	136.0	13.2	278	3 706	705.7	58.2	52	170	14.9	2.6

1. Establishments with payroll.

Table B. States and Counties — Professional, Manufacturing, and Accommodation and Foodservices

STATE County	Professional, Scientific, and Technical Services[1], 1997				Manufacturing, 1997				Accommodation and Foodservices, 1997			
	Number of Establishments	Number of Employees	Receipts (mil dol)	Annual Payroll (mil dol)	Number of Establishments	Number of Employees	Receipts (mil dol)	Annual Payroll (mil dol)	Number of Establishments	Number of Employees	Sales (mil dol)	Annual Payroll (mil dol)
	147	148	149	150	151	152	153	154	155	156	157	158
MARYLAND—Cont'd												
Washington	163	854	63.5	22.7	147	9 173	1 924.5	294.2	230	4 135	127.6	36.4
Wicomico	169	967	76.5	29.2	95	5 690	1 041.6	158.1	159	2 964	86.8	25.0
Worcester	103	319	23.1	8.7	38	1 754	275.4	30.9	393	5 697	309.7	77.8
Baltimore city	1 395	14 695	1 645.0	666.3	688	30 216	9 822.2	1 006.2	1 328	20 021	849.9	232.0
MASSACHUSETTS	18 086	177 345	22 744.1	9 261.4	9 554	417 135	77 876.6	16 379.0	14 800	227 476	9 269.9	2 575.6
Barnstable	571	1 919	173.7	63.9	226	2 561	349.4	82.4	1 144	11 852	624.3	177.3
Berkshire	247	1 420	129.3	50.6	207	9 176	1 423.0	344.7	485	7 060	247.3	75.6
Bristol	793	4 101	324.7	112.5	915	49 363	7 651.4	1 654.2	1 112	16 980	557.3	152.7
Dukes	44	109	10.3	4.3	NA	NA	NA	NA	139	888	87.9	25.3
Essex	1 735	9 589	1 058.1	377.4	1 200	57 660	13 728.1	2 362.4	1 573	22 544	872.0	238.5
Franklin	110	359	28.8	9.0	119	5 700	756.0	182.2	150	1 715	49.8	14.3
Hampden	738	5 108	398.3	173.7	802	33 350	5 953.5	1 204.0	931	13 492	430.3	119.7
Hampshire	265	1 411	93.8	34.2	180	5 760	1 048.3	192.3	332	4 816	147.8	42.8
Middlesex	5 744	73 319	9 250.9	4 134.1	2 437	118 002	22 587.1	5 216.5	3 045	48 816	2 055.4	558.2
Nantucket	44	133	14.3	6.0	NA	NA	NA	NA	106	899	69.1	20.1
Norfolk	2 286	16 489	1 983.8	768.5	863	36 648	6 528.4	1 515.2	1 299	21 115	802.5	222.0
Plymouth	937	5 219	530.4	228.1	613	16 063	2 210.8	534.4	887	14 410	482.0	135.0
Suffolk	3 140	50 260	7 923.2	2 969.3	624	21 366	4 317.9	745.4	2 075	41 647	2 129.0	598.5
Worcester	1 432	7 909	824.4	329.8	1 336	61 344	11 303.4	2 340.9	1 522	21 242	715.1	195.6
MICHIGAN	18 614	162 971	16 231.7	6 882.9	16 045	833 429	214 900.7	34 418.9	18 958	320 014	10 158.7	2 835.8
Alcona	10	94	3.4	1.7	NA	NA	NA	NA	38	194	5.5	1.3
Alger	8	13	1.1	0.3	13	873	195.8	29.7	57	392	12.6	3.1
Allegan	82	330	17.3	7.1	203	15 984	3 108.9	585.9	174	2 136	65.6	18.1
Alpena	33	127	8.6	3.5	58	2 445	480.1	90.8	74	1 130	27.2	7.4
Antrim	31	589	11.2	5.9	56	1 323	164.9	38.7	71	930	49.3	15.6
Arenac	20	54	4.4	1.5	37	732	91.8	18.9	51	499	14.7	3.8
Baraga	3	5	0.1	0.0	26	715	115.2	21.6	21	211	4.6	1.3
Barry	45	170	12.9	4.8	71	3 145	525.2	102.1	84	1 095	28.0	7.9
Bay	138	834	62.8	28.6	152	7 459	1 928.6	347.0	241	3 922	106.5	29.6
Benzie	19	49	2.6	0.9	23	657	70.1	12.3	60	819	28.7	8.0
Berrien	255	1 338	124.6	48.9	397	16 996	2 394.2	539.1	383	5 328	163.5	44.0
Branch	35	212	15.3	6.2	90	3 572	516.5	102.4	78	1 026	30.0	7.4
Calhoun	168	836	68.8	29.1	222	16 973	4 514.8	613.8	307	5 010	147.5	42.5
Cass	52	193	11.8	4.3	87	3 384	570.8	95.9	76	708	20.0	5.2
Charlevoix	57	191	14.1	5.4	69	3 624	724.1	116.9	84	1 384	45.0	16.4
Cheboygan	40	145	10.3	3.4	37	711	76.6	17.9	128	715	33.6	8.6
Chippewa	44	198	10.2	4.5	31	818	63.2	15.0	147	1 475	49.0	12.3
Clare	31	109	7.4	3.2	28	924	120.9	23.9	80	895	25.2	6.7
Clinton	84	410	39.2	13.6	62	2 586	450.3	100.3	83	1 213	32.4	9.2
Crawford	16	52	2.9	1.1	17	503	104.3	15.8	47	409	14.7	3.9
Delta	47	730	23.3	12.8	59	2 834	702.4	124.3	132	1 529	40.0	10.5
Dickinson	51	224	19.4	6.4	50	2 478	655.3	100.6	92	1 124	26.7	7.7
Eaton	133	580	38.1	17.3	94	D	D	D	156	3 008	88.4	25.4
Emmet	86	312	24.7	9.7	57	1 377	168.2	39.1	143	1 970	88.5	24.7
Genesee	660	4 149	274.3	125.2	355	34 414	11 240.3	1 744.6	794	13 618	403.9	111.2
Gladwin	22	64	5.3	1.2	46	1 406	206.8	42.1	42	475	11.7	3.4
Gogebic	25	103	4.9	2.2	27	709	62.5	14.8	70	1 175	40.0	10.5
Grand Traverse	284	1 990	133.7	58.1	190	5 867	875.9	177.1	233	3 895	134.2	37.3
Gratiot	38	94	5.7	1.9	51	2 282	265.7	77.0	67	1 009	29.8	7.6
Hillsdale	38	123	6.5	2.8	104	6 510	1 134.5	176.1	75	815	23.6	6.3
Houghton	48	266	15.4	7.1	43	698	72.1	16.3	118	1 272	30.3	8.3
Huron	38	150	7.1	3.2	67	4 216	612.8	126.9	103	719	23.2	6.1
Ingham	680	5 171	520.7	222.7	272	D	D	D	597	13 137	368.9	104.8
Ionia	56	205	12.3	4.5	80	4 308	852.8	138.0	85	893	26.0	6.5
Iosco	33	101	5.3	2.3	34	1 299	164.7	31.5	88	795	25.8	6.6
Iron	30	105	6.6	2.7	NA	NA	NA	NA	49	577	11.5	3.9
Isabella	86	457	39.4	16.2	58	2 221	402.5	61.2	103	2 498	68.5	19.5
Jackson	200	1 354	90.8	45.5	351	12 248	2 271.8	422.0	267	4 467	137.0	37.7
Kalamazoo	481	3 366	306.0	134.4	399	22 007	4 108.6	820.9	452	9 317	260.6	78.2
Kalkaska	13	42	3.5	1.3	19	1 187	178.2	34.5	29	296	9.0	2.4
Kent	1 303	11 722	1 113.1	457.4	1 205	80 020	14 765.5	3 189.9	954	20 741	617.5	181.6
Keweenaw	NA	NA	NA	NA	NA	NA	NA	NA	21	D	D	D
Lake	6	15	0.7	0.2	NA	NA	NA	NA	36	201	7.9	1.9
Lapeer	98	430	28.6	10.1	139	6 118	837.2	155.6	119	2 045	52.1	14.1

1. Firms subject to federal tax.

STATE County	Health Care and Social Assistance[1], 1997				Other Services[1], 1997				Federal funds and grants, fiscal 1999[2] Expenditures (mil dol)	Direct payments for individuals[3]		
	Number of Establishments	Number of Employees	Receipts (mil dol)	Annual Payroll (mil dol)	Number of Establishments	Number of Employees	Receipts (mil dol)	Annual Payroll (mil dol)	Total	Social Security and government retirement	Medicare	Food stamps and Supplemental Security Income
	159	160	161	162	163	164	165	166	167	168	169	170
MARYLAND—Cont'd												
Washington	225	3 006	208.0	95.5	207	1 524	81.7	25.4	510.8	259.1	95.0	13.2
Wicomico	200	2 520	159.9	86.6	146	986	60.1	18.1	326.8	141.6	56.2	10.9
Worcester	67	597	27.2	11.1	85	364	19.7	6.0	287.3	133.1	39.8	3.1
Baltimore city	1 220	16 856	1 093.8	486.1	891	6 733	426.4	131.5	7 444.8	1 367.9	932.7	273.8
MASSACHUSETTS	11 887	182 902	11 361.4	5 310.5	10 806	61 557	4 359.8	1 338.6	37 803.0	11 062.8	6 283.9	876.1
Barnstable	482	5 989	336.5	163.8	439	1 819	124.6	36.0	1 419.8	662.8	300.2	18.9
Berkshire	268	4 334	254.6	113.7	231	1 074	62.7	18.7	869.0	295.0	164.9	17.6
Bristol	844	12 815	711.6	350.6	878	4 340	295.9	79.6	2 560.5	925.5	524.6	84.6
Dukes	33	D	D	D	36	D	D	D	54.3	27.6	13.8	1.1
Essex	1 317	19 159	1 104.7	558.8	1 181	6 614	441.3	149.5	3 821.7	1 260.2	696.7	109.6
Franklin	107	1 502	72.7	35.1	116	471	29.1	7.9	276.7	129.0	60.8	9.2
Hampden	806	13 261	794.1	367.4	742	4 092	278.1	85.2	2 338.0	857.1	427.0	117.8
Hampshire	225	2 407	143.5	65.9	195	818	56.7	16.1	595.6	233.3	98.8	8.8
Middlesex	2 991	42 136	2 707.8	1 227.3	2 661	16 875	1 307.7	428.7	9 077.0	2 353.9	1 392.0	118.1
Nantucket	20	D	D	D	20	D	D	D	29.4	13.3	6.9	0.2
Norfolk	1 672	25 589	1 542.9	714.3	1 266	7 302	501.0	159.0	2 791.6	934.4	678.0	27.6
Plymouth	811	13 663	737.4	372.8	702	3 550	243.6	70.3	1 709.8	767.8	393.5	43.5
Suffolk	1 067	20 943	1 517.1	737.0	1 157	8 142	558.9	160.9	7 600.3	1 320.9	807.1	217.3
Worcester	1 244	20 902	1 425.3	599.7	1 182	6 312	444.3	122.9	3 066.2	1 260.1	719.7	101.8
MICHIGAN	18 943	186 954	11 811.5	5 696.8	14 705	93 792	6 159.1	1 893.8	43 871.6	17 110.4	7 716.1	1 546.7
Alcona	7	153	5.4	2.6	8	19	1.7	0.2	72.0	38.5	13.1	1.4
Alger	12	147	4.8	1.9	13	31	1.9	0.4	49.2	24.5	9.7	1.4
Allegan	98	1 251	64.8	32.7	125	560	33.5	9.6	256.6	130.1	50.2	6.8
Alpena	72	661	33.8	15.2	61	393	18.3	6.8	169.1	76.8	30.7	5.7
Antrim	31	277	10.2	5.2	32	94	6.4	1.7	93.1	47.9	17.6	1.8
Arenac	39	938	21.1	9.2	28	107	6.8	1.7	86.0	42.6	17.3	2.7
Baraga	16	104	3.9	2.0	7	20	1.4	0.2	119.8	19.4	7.3	1.2
Barry	61	498	26.9	11.5	86	415	26.0	7.9	141.5	78.5	26.1	3.8
Bay	210	2 225	132.9	65.2	198	1 004	55.9	16.2	446.7	213.0	92.3	16.9
Benzie	22	146	7.0	3.2	19	48	2.7	0.7	61.5	35.8	10.4	1.3
Berrien	281	2 395	154.1	71.3	262	1 452	77.6	25.1	712.0	326.2	131.0	34.2
Branch	72	570	34.3	13.7	59	199	13.9	3.3	152.7	76.5	30.3	2.8
Calhoun	300	3 100	176.3	79.3	207	1 433	91.5	26.9	740.3	295.2	113.8	27.9
Cass	46	233	11.0	4.7	60	216	11.8	3.3	165.5	79.1	28.6	6.2
Charlevoix	48	216	12.2	4.5	59	208	15.3	4.0	90.4	51.3	16.3	2.1
Cheboygan	53	295	15.9	6.9	53	237	10.2	3.1	111.5	56.0	20.6	3.1
Chippewa	40	366	19.1	9.7	56	193	10.8	2.8	186.2	72.8	23.7	4.0
Clare	40	456	19.3	7.3	35	77	5.1	1.1	151.1	78.8	31.0	6.5
Clinton	65	666	30.8	13.3	71	268	17.6	5.2	168.5	72.7	26.2	3.2
Crawford	21	141	10.0	4.3	13	59	3.5	1.2	57.0	28.5	10.4	1.8
Delta	61	443	20.4	9.1	79	450	27.9	6.8	180.7	93.5	33.6	4.7
Dickinson	85	755	37.3	16.9	69	301	20.2	5.0	139.2	67.4	20.0	2.2
Eaton	158	1 269	59.5	26.2	103	592	32.4	9.3	595.7	123.9	45.8	3.8
Emmet	85	1 233	114.2	52.0	52	192	12.9	3.3	112.0	59.0	19.5	2.8
Genesee	1 037	9 466	610.5	310.7	627	4 165	255.2	74.4	1 820.0	757.9	386.7	101.9
Gladwin	22	191	7.3	3.3	23	81	5.0	1.3	116.3	64.7	26.0	3.8
Gogebic	26	364	14.3	9.2	31	113	6.8	1.7	110.2	54.5	21.1	2.3
Grand Traverse	272	2 175	157.5	72.2	187	1 045	70.5	22.1	295.5	151.0	48.5	5.9
Gratiot	76	885	44.7	21.8	63	234	17.2	4.4	174.3	73.0	31.4	6.5
Hillsdale	66	411	22.7	10.6	57	219	12.8	3.4	160.8	79.2	27.5	5.6
Houghton	60	650	26.5	12.7	54	175	12.9	3.1	168.9	73.6	29.1	4.4
Huron	88	566	27.3	12.9	53	190	12.1	2.8	179.9	84.1	33.6	3.6
Ingham	659	5 597	407.3	198.4	438	3 073	162.9	53.7	2 524.3	623.1	189.6	50.9
Ionia	78	747	34.4	14.9	75	354	21.5	6.2	173.8	81.3	32.7	5.4
Iosco	35	226	11.1	5.5	45	159	7.8	2.2	151.8	89.5	30.0	3.3
Iron	21	295	15.3	7.6	17	57	3.0	0.7	78.6	41.9	15.6	1.4
Isabella	101	1 005	50.8	23.8	80	414	22.7	5.6	159.2	72.4	25.4	7.2
Jackson	299	2 649	180.0	85.7	238	1 294	77.2	22.2	575.6	281.5	112.2	24.6
Kalamazoo	467	5 746	407.2	205.0	412	2 814	176.6	55.9	857.8	368.6	135.1	30.4
Kalkaska	14	73	4.3	2.1	26	174	10.8	3.6	51.3	26.0	10.2	2.1
Kent	1 075	12 469	832.0	420.3	975	7 146	503.4	149.3	1 841.8	806.2	288.0	72.1
Keweenaw	2	D	D	D	2	D	D	D	11.8	6.3	2.6	0.2
Lake	11	182	7.4	4.1	6	D	D	D	61.2	28.8	11.3	3.1
Lapeer	116	915	51.3	26.9	95	454	30.0	7.9	215.8	108.2	42.1	5.0

1. Firms subject to federal tax. 2. October 1, 1998 to September 30, 1999. 3. State totals may include programs not allocated by county.

STATE County	Federal funds and grants, fiscal 1999[1] (cont'd)							Local government finances, 1997				
	Expenditures (mil dol) (cont'd)							General revenue				
	Procurement contract awards			Grants[2]							Taxes	
											Per capita[3] (dollars)	
	Salaries and wages	Defense	Other	Medicaid and other health-related	Nutrition and family welfare	Education	Other	Total (mil dol)	Intergovern-mental (mil dol)	Total (mil dol)	Total	Property
	171	172	173	174	175	176	177	178	179	180	181	182
MARYLAND—Cont'd												
Washington	28.1	7.8	11.5	52.2	11.5	3.2	21.3	237.6	87.8	104.0	811	520
Wicomico	17.9	11.7	9.6	41.2	12.6	3.2	13.5	160.1	60.8	70.8	892	544
Worcester	8.7	55.2	2.3	21.2	3.4	1.2	15.4	126.3	16.9	82.7	1 964	1 405
Baltimore city	716.0	759.9	439.4	1 627.4	441.7	193.2	522.6	2 137.2	1 192.6	698.2	1 062	719
MASSACHUSETTS	2 918.9	4 449.9	1 303.4	4 773.8	1 158.6	554.2	2 351.5	X	X	X	X	X
Barnstable	118.9	79.4	22.4	68.6	16.5	8.2	105.2	522.1	107.6	331.0	1 614	1 548
Berkshire	38.3	86.6	141.0	73.6	20.7	7.4	15.8	303.3	146.3	129.8	967	934
Bristol	83.5	351.7	25.6	383.6	83.5	27.3	43.2	1 091.3	577.8	400.1	776	763
Dukes	3.1	0.0	1.8	4.1	0.9	0.3	1.2	63.2	11.9	40.2	2 960	2 844
Essex	203.1	925.1	61.1	330.7	90.6	45.2	55.4	1 592.7	618.7	719.9	1 041	1 022
Franklin	12.2	2.0	4.7	30.0	14.3	3.8	5.2	168.4	82.1	69.9	980	965
Hampden	294.0	30.5	78.6	275.7	112.6	37.7	51.9	1 178.9	658.3	373.1	846	834
Hampshire	64.1	43.7	12.2	49.8	9.4	6.8	48.8	277.1	118.9	115.6	770	754
Middlesex	668.4	2 216.1	446.2	1 033.4	116.7	212.7	407.5	3 181.5	949.3	1 844.5	1 301	1 262
Nantucket	3.4	0.0	0.6	1.6	0.2	0.1	3.0	42.7	7.6	25.8	3 439	3 163
Norfolk	69.0	484.4	116.4	330.0	34.5	19.3	31.7	1 404.2	333.0	797.8	1 248	1 220
Plymouth	149.4	28.7	35.7	177.9	48.1	21.1	25.1	947.6	427.4	426.0	922	897
Suffolk	1 026.5	152.6	273.0	1 562.8	515.0	79.8	1 391.6	2 940.7	1 773.0	871.5	1 356	1 273
Worcester	184.8	48.9	83.8	417.7	89.9	40.5	73.7	1 569.7	789.0	602.0	830	811
MICHIGAN	2 932.4	1 167.8	897.0	4 394.0	2 095.9	899.0	2 375.1	X	X	X	X	X
Alcona	2.1	0.0	0.6	11.4	1.3	0.6	2.5	19.4	7.3	7.1	644	643
Alger	3.4	0.0	0.6	6.6	1.1	0.9	0.4	23.0	13.6	5.0	501	484
Allegan	8.9	3.2	2.3	25.7	8.9	3.3	5.5	211.8	124.8	49.3	490	479
Alpena	5.6	10.7	1.6	13.4	16.3	2.1	3.8	154.5	55.4	18.3	598	582
Antrim	3.0	0.9	7.2	8.5	1.9	0.9	2.0	59.1	27.0	20.4	974	949
Arenac	2.4	0.8	0.6	10.1	2.8	1.8	1.4	32.4	20.0	7.0	427	418
Baraga	1.5	0.1	3.5	6.2	1.8	1.0	77.7	32.3	13.2	3.7	436	429
Barry	5.3	1.2	1.5	11.9	4.3	1.5	2.2	94.4	57.1	19.1	357	350
Bay	14.2	0.6	4.2	41.0	16.4	7.1	24.1	334.9	155.4	85.0	769	752
Benzie	2.6	0.0	0.8	7.5	1.2	0.6	1.1	35.6	14.0	13.6	954	932
Berrien	22.7	2.0	8.9	98.6	26.9	11.6	35.3	404.7	221.7	101.0	629	610
Branch	4.9	0.0	1.3	14.4	5.9	2.4	2.4	149.2	65.5	20.1	462	444
Calhoun	122.0	25.2	11.9	75.0	26.9	10.8	16.2	416.5	226.4	100.4	708	605
Cass	4.7	0.0	3.3	17.8	5.2	2.9	7.4	94.6	53.4	21.2	425	417
Charlevoix	4.9	2.3	0.9	7.2	2.3	0.9	1.2	81.5	32.8	31.7	1 342	1 321
Cheboygan	5.7	1.0	1.0	11.2	2.9	1.2	7.9	63.1	30.5	17.9	759	748
Chippewa	18.6	7.4	4.9	30.1	11.1	2.7	5.2	88.8	47.3	17.2	455	447
Clare	3.1	0.1	0.9	14.1	6.8	2.1	3.0	75.5	45.5	17.1	588	577
Clinton	23.7	0.0	2.2	7.2	4.0	1.6	17.0	118.2	68.5	26.2	415	400
Crawford	8.0	0.7	0.8	3.4	2.0	0.7	0.5	27.4	13.4	9.4	679	665
Delta	10.0	1.0	2.1	17.9	7.4	3.8	3.3	101.0	58.7	20.4	526	523
Dickinson	26.2	1.2	4.6	7.6	3.6	0.8	4.0	106.5	35.8	20.3	749	721
Eaton	21.2	0.0	2.0	16.6	271.5	2.7	98.7	200.1	114.9	49.2	491	475
Emmet	5.2	0.0	3.6	11.1	2.5	1.2	3.8	97.4	38.4	30.1	1 063	1 037
Genesee	77.8	0.5	32.3	203.0	99.2	35.9	81.8	1 466.8	790.4	256.3	589	571
Gladwin	2.7	0.0	0.7	10.0	4.0	1.7	0.0	46.2	26.1	11.7	470	457
Gogebic	7.3	0.1	1.8	12.0	3.2	1.3	5.8	62.3	31.4	9.9	568	562
Grand Traverse	29.7	0.2	11.0	28.3	9.3	1.9	5.1	232.8	109.4	64.3	879	849
Gratiot	6.0	0.3	1.5	20.6	9.1	2.6	7.3	98.1	66.1	16.8	419	411
Hillsdale	5.9	0.3	1.9	17.5	5.6	2.2	3.7	104.1	55.0	17.8	385	373
Houghton	9.8	2.4	3.9	19.9	6.7	2.5	12.6	106.5	56.1	14.3	399	389
Huron	5.4	0.1	1.5	17.9	4.0	1.9	7.0	101.2	48.4	25.7	730	715
Ingham	109.1	22.4	28.5	280.0	394.8	272.7	495.4	880.5	450.2	237.6	836	734
Ionia	6.0	0.6	4.5	17.8	6.0	2.6	7.4	130.3	85.2	24.1	394	386
Iosco	5.1	2.0	2.1	6.8	3.8	1.5	5.4	79.6	44.8	18.4	732	719
Iron	2.8	0.2	0.7	8.2	1.4	0.7	4.9	45.4	26.7	8.2	629	620
Isabella	7.3	0.1	1.6	19.8	5.5	3.9	1.9	118.3	67.0	18.8	327	306
Jackson	25.5	9.9	6.5	54.6	23.8	6.6	16.0	370.0	218.4	75.9	489	432
Kalamazoo	92.2	9.1	24.3	91.3	27.9	15.1	35.5	582.0	292.0	158.5	692	669
Kalkaska	1.6	0.1	0.4	6.0	1.9	0.8	1.8	32.9	11.8	11.1	721	703
Kent	166.0	59.9	64.4	169.3	49.0	24.4	107.3	1 474.4	767.5	416.1	771	654
Keweenaw	0.4	0.0	0.1	0.7	0.3	0.2	1.0	4.8	1.9	0.8	397	383
Lake	2.4	0.0	0.4	7.8	2.4	0.8	3.6	14.8	7.1	6.4	633	598
Lapeer	8.5	0.1	2.3	23.1	6.8	2.8	9.4	169.5	100.2	34.1	392	357

1. October 1, 1998 to September 30, 1999. 2. State totals may include programs not allocated by county. 3. Based on the resident population estimated as of July 1 of the year shown.

Table B. States and Counties — Local Government Finances, Government Employment, and Elections

STATE County	Local government finances, 1997 (cont'd)									Government employment, 1998			Presidential election, 2000		
	Direct general expenditure							Debt outstanding					Percent of vote cast —		
						Percent of total for —									
	Total (mil dol)	Per capita¹ (dollars)	Education	Health and hospitals	Police protection	Public welfare	Highways	Total (mil dol)	Per capita¹ (dollars)	Federal civilian	Federal military	State and local	Democratic	Republican	All other
	183	184	185	186	187	188	189	190	191	192	193	194	195	196	197
MARYLAND—Cont'd															
Washington	234.3	1 828	58.6	0.8	3.9	0.3	4.8	230.5	1 799	950	771	6 942	38.4	58.9	2.7
Wicomico	166.0	2 093	59.0	1.1	5.4	1.8	4.8	88.1	1 110	346	304	5 517	45.5	51.4	3.1
Worcester	129.5	3 075	39.3	1.3	7.6	0.3	6.3	112.1	2 662	222	191	2 624	45.2	51.8	3.0
Baltimore city	2 110.8	3 212	33.7	3.9	9.7	0.0	6.6	1 794.7	2 731	12 861	2 710	71 361	82.5	14.1	3.4
MASSACHUSETTS	X	X	X	X	X	X	X	X	X	54 691	24 278	360 422	59.8	32.5	7.7
Barnstable	579.2	2 823	47.9	0.9	5.6	0.5	6.2	414.6	2 021	1 859	1 317	10 894	NA	NA	NA
Berkshire	324.7	2 418	55.8	0.6	3.7	0.1	6.8	145.7	1 085	456	433	7 239	NA	NA	NA
Bristol	1 073.8	2 083	53.4	0.8	6.3	0.7	3.5	586.5	1 138	1 209	1 898	24 124	NA	NA	NA
Dukes	71.9	5 298	46.0	1.4	5.0	0.0	4.4	61.9	4 561	41	45	1 121	NA	NA	NA
Essex	1 648.9	2 385	50.5	2.4	5.0	0.6	3.3	1 251.5	1 810	4 444	2 344	32 806	NA	NA	NA
Franklin	176.1	2 468	59.8	0.4	2.9	0.2	7.4	76.1	1 067	181	228	4 552	NA	NA	NA
Hampden	1 169.2	2 651	52.3	1.6	5.6	1.2	3.1	1 756.6	3 983	5 338	1 526	26 706	NA	NA	NA
Hampshire	285.1	1 899	55.0	0.7	4.2	2.2	5.6	131.1	873	1 278	498	14 465	NA	NA	NA
Middlesex	3 110.1	2 194	52.9	0.7	5.8	0.2	4.3	1 247.5	880	13 344	6 634	64 488	NA	NA	NA
Nantucket	42.3	5 631	25.8	1.6	5.0	5.2	4.3	21.8	2 903	53	56	582	NA	NA	NA
Norfolk	1 381.6	2 161	48.9	7.7	6.3	0.1	4.6	535.6	838	1 344	2 110	28 917	NA	NA	NA
Plymouth	1 001.0	2 166	55.6	1.5	5.4	0.2	4.5	344.0	744	4 597	1 573	22 728	NA	NA	NA
Suffolk	1 994.5	3 102	34.1	4.9	11.0	5.3	3.5	4 668.6	7 262	17 484	3 178	74 102	NA	NA	NA
Worcester	1 588.0	2 189	58.2	0.7	5.0	0.1	4.6	895.5	1 234	3 063	2 438	47 698	NA	NA	NA
MICHIGAN	X	X	X	X	X	X	X	X	X	56 255	21 763	577 804	51.3	46.1	2.6
Alcona	17.8	1 625	37.9	1.8	5.8	1.0	26.4	4.3	392	40	22	380	45.0	52.6	2.5
Alger	22.8	2 289	45.4	1.3	1.8	0.6	21.6	17.8	1 785	84	20	519	47.4	49.1	3.5
Allegan	222.7	2 214	54.5	7.9	3.0	4.3	8.8	113.2	1 126	186	202	4 304	34.5	62.8	2.7
Alpena	153.2	5 001	31.5	45.5	1.6	0.4	4.5	72.9	2 378	99	61	3 031	49.9	47.9	2.2
Antrim	62.7	2 989	45.9	9.5	2.6	10.0	6.8	54.5	2 599	55	43	1 240	37.6	58.9	3.5
Arenac	33.3	2 027	52.0	1.9	3.2	1.0	12.1	13.4	815	50	33	764	50.7	47.1	2.2
Baraga	29.0	3 432	32.5	28.7	2.3	1.0	14.1	12.8	1 516	28	17	792	41.3	54.1	4.6
Barry	110.2	2 059	60.0	3.6	2.4	0.9	7.7	74.6	1 393	101	108	1 867	37.2	59.9	2.9
Bay	335.8	3 041	56.0	7.2	3.6	4.3	6.0	203.2	1 840	278	238	6 152	54.7	42.9	2.4
Benzie	34.8	2 438	41.7	0.7	2.5	0.9	12.1	11.3	791	40	43	666	43.9	51.7	4.4
Berrien	397.8	2 475	57.8	7.5	4.1	0.9	4.9	189.4	1 178	442	335	8 313	43.2	54.7	2.1
Branch	146.3	3 354	41.0	30.9	1.7	4.0	5.3	54.9	1 259	105	87	3 508	42.4	55.4	2.2
Calhoun	451.4	3 183	48.8	5.4	4.3	2.2	6.4	250.0	1 763	3 342	325	7 641	49.6	47.7	2.7
Cass	95.7	1 916	69.2	0.7	2.5	5.2	2.5	40.6	812	90	99	2 157	44.4	53.2	2.4
Charlevoix	88.3	3 738	49.0	8.9	2.0	4.8	8.0	25.3	1 072	64	112	1 624	39.7	56.2	4.1
Cheboygan	66.2	2 814	52.4	0.9	3.1	1.1	10.1	41.2	1 749	69	124	1 082	43.5	54.0	2.5
Chippewa	92.8	2 447	44.7	14.5	2.5	0.9	10.5	41.2	1 086	345	207	4 214	44.4	52.4	3.2
Clare	79.8	2 751	65.8	0.6	2.4	0.9	8.9	17.0	587	59	59	1 439	49.9	47.1	3.0
Clinton	133.4	2 114	63.5	0.4	3.2	0.5	9.2	164.9	2 614	295	427	1 805	41.6	56.1	2.3
Crawford	32.9	2 369	56.6	0.6	4.6	1.3	11.6	16.1	1 156	136	28	796	43.8	52.6	3.6
Delta	102.3	2 636	63.9	9.9	3.3	0.7	3.4	47.2	1 216	226	79	2 122	46.0	51.2	2.7
Dickinson	107.5	3 974	34.3	38.6	2.8	0.5	6.0	93.7	3 462	627	55	2 069	43.1	54.0	2.9
Eaton	244.4	2 439	65.3	2.4	3.1	1.8	5.6	162.5	1 623	229	206	5 588	47.1	50.3	2.6
Emmet	103.7	3 659	39.0	10.8	2.6	4.4	10.7	91.8	3 239	104	58	1 598	37.1	58.5	4.5
Genesee	1 443.2	3 315	47.5	22.9	4.3	1.2	3.6	652.5	1 499	1 409	870	22 930	62.8	34.9	2.3
Gladwin	51.9	2 085	51.9	1.6	2.4	0.6	13.2	29.7	1 193	55	50	983	47.9	49.4	2.7
Gogebic	62.9	3 609	43.3	11.7	3.2	8.0	9.8	14.1	808	165	34	1 370	48.8	47.1	4.1
Grand Traverse	260.6	3 562	55.0	6.4	3.1	7.2	4.1	281.3	3 845	465	271	4 696	37.6	58.5	3.9
Gratiot	99.4	2 483	63.5	4.5	2.5	0.6	7.3	54.6	1 365	112	80	2 074	43.1	54.8	2.2
Hillsdale	101.4	2 192	51.4	0.5	2.6	15.7	10.2	143.7	3 108	109	93	2 488	37.2	60.0	2.8
Houghton	114.7	3 203	42.8	18.9	1.4	8.4	7.9	80.5	2 247	146	106	4 347	40.0	55.5	4.5
Huron	101.9	2 889	42.3	9.1	2.5	5.4	14.8	54.0	1 532	101	75	2 084	42.9	55.4	1.8
Ingham	924.3	3 253	55.0	1.6	4.6	3.3	3.1	799.2	2 813	2 337	694	45 594	57.4	39.2	3.4
Ionia	147.2	2 408	64.3	5.0	2.3	0.5	6.6	141.1	2 309	117	123	4 224	39.6	58.1	2.4
Iosco	81.3	3 234	52.8	2.0	1.7	4.3	7.6	68.8	2 739	112	69	1 741	49.2	48.0	2.8
Iron	42.2	3 230	35.0	7.4	1.8	13.4	13.7	11.7	893	57	26	1 408	48.7	47.9	3.3
Isabella	128.4	2 228	43.1	19.9	2.2	0.9	8.1	66.3	1 151	143	122	6 434	48.5	47.7	3.7
Jackson	396.5	2 552	58.8	7.3	3.4	3.4	5.1	218.2	1 404	439	312	9 123	45.5	51.8	2.8
Kalamazoo	613.7	2 678	51.4	5.8	6.7	1.2	5.5	697.7	3 044	1 619	464	16 906	48.5	47.9	3.6
Kalkaska	35.1	2 274	35.4	25.4	4.9	2.8	8.4	22.3	1 440	29	31	722	40.5	56.1	3.4
Kent	1 561.1	2 894	56.7	6.9	4.2	0.8	4.6	1 688.3	3 130	3 050	1 112	23 355	38.1	59.4	2.5
Keweenaw	4.7	3 469	2.2	0.4	3.5	2.0	43.2	0.7	349	72	0	94	40.2	55.1	4.7
Lake	16.4	1 615	39.6	2.9	4.1	3.4	2.7	3.0	291	65	21	409	55.1	41.8	3.2
Lapeer	165.5	1 904	55.6	5.8	3.8	1.2	10.0	131.4	1 512	157	176	4 484	42.3	54.7	3.0

1. Based on the resident population estimated as of July 1 of the year shown.

Table B. States and Counties — Land Area and Population

STATE/ County code	MSA/ PMSA/ NECMA code[1]	County Type[2]	STATE County	Land area,[3] (sq km) 1990	Total persons	Rank	Per square kilometer	White	Black	Am. Indian, Eskimo, Aleut	Asian and Pacific Islander	Percent Hispanic[4]	Under 5 years	5 to 17 years	18 to 24 years	25 to 34 years	35 to 44 years	45 to 54 years
					1	2	3	4	5	6	7	8	9	10	11	12	13	14	15
			MICHIGAN—Cont'd															
26 089	...	9	Leelanau	903	19 370	1 795	21.5	96.8	0.2	2.6	0.4	1.5	6.4	18.4	5.7	11.4	18.5	13.1
26 091	0440	1	Lenawee	1 944	99 780	519	51.3	96.6	2.2	0.4	0.8	7.9	6.6	21.0	9.3	12.6	16.9	13.3
26 093	0440	1	Livingston	1 472	151 496	339	102.9	98.2	0.5	0.6	0.8	1.1	6.6	21.2	7.7	12.9	19.9	16.1
26 095	...	9	Luce	2 339	6 754	2 704	2.9	87.1	7.6	5.0	0.3	1.6	5.2	18.5	8.1	11.5	17.3	13.6
26 097	...	7	Mackinac	2 646	11 103	2 340	4.2	84.2	0.3	15.3	0.2	0.4	5.8	19.1	6.1	11.5	15.1	13.7
26 099	2160	0	Macomb	1 244	792 082	55	636.7	96.1	1.6	0.4	1.9	1.5	5.9	17.1	8.8	14.0	16.3	14.2
26 101	...	7	Manistee	1 409	23 665	1 588	16.8	96.8	2.0	0.9	0.3	2.2	5.3	17.7	6.7	11.8	16.2	14.2
26 103	...	5	Marquette	4 717	62 758	767	13.3	95.6	2.0	1.3	1.1	1.0	6.2	18.9	12.3	13.8	17.0	11.5
26 105	...	7	Mason	1 283	27 966	1 438	21.8	97.9	0.4	0.8	0.5	2.1	6.2	19.6	7.2	11.2	15.8	13.5
26 107	...	7	Mecosta	1 439	40 704	1 067	28.3	96.0	2.6	0.7	0.7	1.3	5.9	17.4	20.6	10.6	13.2	11.6
26 109	...	7	Menominee	2 703	24 449	1 555	9.0	98.2	0.0	1.5	0.3	0.3	5.6	20.2	6.6	11.8	16.1	12.8
26 111	6960	2	Midland	1 350	81 994	620	60.7	96.9	1.1	0.4	1.6	1.8	6.5	19.8	8.9	13.1	17.1	14.4
26 113	...	9	Missaukee	1 468	14 151	2 123	9.6	98.9	0.0	0.6	0.4	0.8	6.9	22.5	6.6	12.1	14.4	13.3
26 115	2160	1	Monroe	1 427	144 913	363	101.6	97.0	2.0	0.4	0.6	2.1	6.7	21.2	8.5	13.0	17.0	14.0
26 117	...	6	Montcalm	1 834	61 406	780	33.5	96.6	2.2	0.8	0.5	2.3	6.9	21.3	8.4	13.8	16.1	13.2
26 119	...	9	Montmorency	1 418	10 014	2 423	7.1	99.3	0.0	0.5	0.2	0.9	5.1	17.9	5.4	9.1	13.3	12.2
26 121	3000	2	Muskegon	1 319	168 037	313	127.4	83.6	15.0	0.9	0.5	3.0	7.2	20.5	8.3	13.5	16.2	12.7
26 123	...	6	Newaygo	2 182	46 356	961	21.2	97.5	1.4	0.7	0.5	3.4	7.5	21.9	6.9	12.4	15.5	13.7
26 125	2160	0	Oakland	2 260	1 179 978	30	522.1	88.2	7.9	0.4	3.5	2.4	6.3	17.8	7.9	14.7	18.4	14.7
26 127	...	8	Oceana	1 400	24 900	1 535	17.8	98.1	0.3	1.2	0.4	8.0	7.3	22.0	6.8	11.8	15.0	13.9
26 129	...	7	Ogemaw	1 462	21 201	1 698	14.5	98.8	0.2	0.8	0.2	0.8	6.1	19.9	6.4	10.8	13.7	13.4
26 131	...	9	Ontonagon	3 397	7 668	2 626	2.3	98.3	0.2	1.2	0.2	0.6	5.2	17.5	5.4	9.8	15.0	15.3
26 133	...	9	Osceola	1 466	22 220	1 647	15.2	98.7	0.4	0.6	0.3	0.9	6.7	22.4	7.2	11.2	15.0	13.5
26 135	...	9	Oscoda	1 463	8 899	2 516	6.1	99.3	0.0	0.5	0.1	0.9	6.1	17.3	5.8	10.7	12.2	13.7
26 137	...	7	Otsego	1 333	22 719	1 622	17.0	98.4	0.3	0.6	0.7	0.5	6.7	21.2	7.0	12.4	16.2	13.0
26 139	3000	2	Ottawa	1 465	230 261	239	157.2	97.1	0.6	0.4	1.9	5.4	7.7	21.2	10.7	13.7	16.6	12.6
26 141	...	7	Presque Isle	1 710	14 596	2 093	8.5	99.2	0.2	0.3	0.3	0.3	5.2	18.7	5.8	9.6	13.6	12.5
26 143	...	7	Roscommon	1 350	23 562	1 590	17.5	99.0	0.3	0.5	0.2	0.7	4.9	15.8	5.3	9.5	12.2	12.8
26 145	6960	2	Saginaw	2 095	209 245	259	99.9	79.5	19.0	0.5	0.9	8.0	6.8	20.6	8.8	12.6	16.0	13.7
26 147	2160	0	St. Clair	1 876	161 755	320	86.2	96.6	2.3	0.5	0.5	2.3	6.7	20.6	8.5	12.9	16.6	13.8
26 149	...	6	St. Joseph	1 305	61 448	778	47.1	95.9	3.1	0.4	0.7	1.2	7.0	21.3	7.8	12.6	16.2	13.0
26 151	...	8	Sanilac	2 496	43 451	1 013	17.4	99.0	0.2	0.5	0.3	3.0	6.6	21.4	7.1	12.0	15.0	13.0
26 153	...	7	Schoolcraft	3 051	8 788	2 524	2.9	92.2	1.8	5.8	0.2	0.5	5.0	19.3	6.3	11.6	15.4	13.7
26 155	...	4	Shiawassee	1 396	72 346	678	51.8	98.8	0.2	0.6	0.5	2.0	6.4	21.4	8.4	12.5	16.8	14.3
26 157	...	6	Tuscola	2 105	58 195	810	27.6	98.0	0.8	0.6	0.5	2.7	6.3	21.7	7.9	12.2	16.7	14.4
26 159	3720	2	Van Buren	1 583	75 917	653	48.0	91.0	7.5	1.0	0.5	4.2	7.0	21.9	7.4	12.4	16.8	13.4
26 161	0440	0	Washtenaw	1 839	306 073	183	166.4	81.5	12.1	0.4	6.0	2.6	6.1	15.4	17.1	16.7	17.7	12.2
26 163	2160	0	Wayne	1 591	2 106 495	9	1 324.0	55.4	42.7	0.4	1.5	3.0	7.0	19.7	9.1	14.5	15.9	12.7
26 165	...	7	Wexford	1 465	29 560	1 391	20.2	98.5	0.3	0.7	0.5	0.8	7.0	21.1	7.4	12.6	15.9	12.7
27 000	...	X	MINNESOTA	206 207	4 775 508	X	23.2	92.9	3.1	1.2	2.7	1.9	6.7	19.9	9.5	13.2	17.0	13.1
27 001	...	9	Aitkin	4 712	14 293	2 113	3.0	97.7	0.2	1.7	0.4	0.5	4.7	18.6	4.6	8.2	14.0	15.0
27 003	5120	0	Anoka	1 098	298 990	185	272.3	96.4	0.8	0.9	2.0	1.5	7.3	21.7	9.1	14.1	18.3	14.1
27 005	...	6	Becker	3 394	29 757	1 379	8.8	92.1	0.1	7.2	0.6	0.7	6.2	22.4	6.7	10.3	15.6	13.3
27 007	...	7	Beltrami	6 489	39 210	1 104	6.0	80.9	0.4	17.9	0.8	0.7	7.1	23.0	12.6	11.3	15.4	11.4
27 009	6980	3	Benton	1 057	34 832	1 232	33.0	98.5	0.3	0.5	0.7	0.8	7.7	22.3	11.5	14.1	15.5	11.3
27 011	...	9	Big Stone	1 287	5 571	2 801	4.3	99.1	0.1	0.4	0.4	0.5	5.9	19.2	4.9	8.4	13.5	13.3
27 013	...	5	Blue Earth	1 949	53 874	854	27.6	96.8	0.7	0.3	2.3	1.4	5.5	17.0	21.5	11.0	13.8	10.6
27 015	...	7	Brown	1 582	26 903	1 469	17.0	99.2	0.1	0.1	0.6	0.9	6.1	20.1	9.1	10.6	14.3	12.4
27 017	...	6	Carlton	2 228	31 492	1 329	14.1	94.0	0.6	5.0	0.4	0.6	5.8	21.3	7.6	11.3	16.0	13.4
27 019	5120	1	Carver	925	67 023	721	72.5	97.9	0.4	0.3	1.5	0.9	8.3	21.7	8.2	15.1	18.3	13.2
27 021	...	9	Cass	5 226	27 042	1 465	5.2	87.6	0.3	11.7	0.4	0.7	5.9	21.2	5.5	9.3	14.7	14.2
27 023	...	7	Chippewa	1 510	13 028	2 215	8.6	99.1	0.1	0.2	0.6	1.2	5.8	21.0	5.8	9.7	15.2	12.9
27 025	5120	1	Chisago	1 082	42 302	1 033	39.1	98.7	0.3	0.4	0.5	0.7	7.1	23.7	7.3	12.0	17.6	14.0
27 027	2520	3	Clay	2 707	51 717	885	19.1	97.0	0.5	1.2	1.2	3.7	6.2	18.7	17.9	10.5	14.6	11.5
27 029	...	9	Clearwater	2 576	8 146	2 581	3.2	91.5	0.1	8.2	0.2	0.3	6.0	23.1	6.4	9.2	14.7	14.3
27 031	...	9	Cook	3 757	4 772	2 856	1.3	91.2	0.3	7.7	0.9	0.5	5.7	17.5	5.0	10.4	19.2	14.7
27 033	...	7	Cottonwood	1 658	11 908	2 281	7.2	98.7	0.1	0.1	1.1	0.8	5.5	20.0	5.6	8.8	14.0	13.3
27 035	...	7	Crow Wing	2 581	52 608	867	20.4	98.3	0.4	0.8	0.5	0.7	6.1	20.3	7.4	10.1	15.4	13.4
27 037	5120	0	Dakota	1 476	349 131	164	236.5	94.9	1.9	0.4	2.8	2.4	8.0	21.2	8.7	15.7	19.2	13.6
27 039	...	6	Dodge	1 138	17 396	1 908	15.3	99.0	0.1	0.3	0.6	1.8	7.5	23.8	7.7	12.3	15.9	13.6
27 041	...	7	Douglas	1 643	31 274	1 343	19.0	99.0	0.1	0.3	0.6	0.5	6.0	20.5	8.1	10.0	14.8	13.0
27 043	...	7	Faribault	1 848	16 247	1 990	8.8	99.1	0.1	0.2	0.6	3.0	5.3	20.4	5.4	9.0	13.9	13.0
27 045	...	8	Fillmore	2 231	20 688	1 729	9.3	99.3	0.1	0.2	0.4	0.6	6.1	21.2	6.7	9.5	14.3	12.5
27 047	...	7	Freeborn	1 833	31 503	1 328	17.2	99.1	0.1	0.2	0.6	5.2	5.8	19.0	6.7	10.0	14.9	13.9
27 049	...	6	Goodhue	1 965	43 367	1 015	22.1	98.3	0.3	0.7	0.7	0.7	6.4	21.3	7.0	11.5	16.4	13.2

1. MSA = Metropolitan Statistical Area. PMSA = Primary MSA. NECMA = New England County Metropolitan Area. See Appendix A for explanation of these concepts. See Appendix B for list of metropolitan areas identified by type, with component counties. 2. County typology code from the Economic Research Service of USDA. See Appendix A for definition. 3. Dry land or land partially or temporarily covered by water. 4. Hispanic persons may be of any race.

Table B. States and Counties — **Population and Households**

STATE County	55 to 64 years (16)	65 to 74 years (17)	75 years and over (18)	Percent female (19)	1990 (20)	1980 (21)	1980–1990 (22)	1990–1999 (23)	Births (24)	Deaths (25)	Net migration (26)	Number (27)	Percent change, 1980–1990 (28)	Persons per house-hold (29)	Female family house-holder[1] (30)	One person (31)
MICHIGAN—Cont'd																
Leelanau	10.1	8.7	7.7	50.0	16 527	14 007	18.0	17.2	1 951	1 541	2 764	6 274	24.9	2.62	7.2	20.1
Lenawee	8.3	6.3	5.8	49.9	91 476	89 948	1.7	9.1	11 303	7 483	4 697	31 635	5.3	2.77	9.9	20.2
Livingston	7.4	4.5	3.6	49.4	115 645	100 289	15.3	31.0	16 269	7 211	26 774	38 887	24.1	2.94	6.9	15.1
Luce	10.0	7.2	7.4	45.2	5 763	6 659	-13.5	17.2	655	650	981	2 154	-1.7	2.57	8.5	25.1
Mackinac	12.0	8.6	8.0	50.3	10 674	10 178	4.9	4.0	1 185	1 170	448	4 240	15.2	2.49	8.3	25.2
Macomb	9.4	8.0	6.3	51.5	717 400	694 600	3.3	10.4	91 758	58 628	-1 146	264 991	15.3	2.68	10.1	22.2
Manistee	10.9	8.5	8.8	50.0	21 265	23 019	-7.6	11.3	2 172	2 617	2 914	8 580	1.1	2.45	8.3	26.2
Marquette	7.2	6.4	6.7	49.2	70 887	74 101	-4.3	-11.5	7 445	5 285	-10 709	25 435	3.8	2.61	8.6	23.5
Mason	9.9	8.3	8.4	50.8	25 537	26 365	-3.1	9.5	2 922	2 709	2 303	9 984	3.0	2.51	9.1	24.6
Mecosta	8.4	6.6	5.8	49.0	37 308	36 961	0.9	9.1	4 076	2 834	2 236	12 260	10.1	2.66	8.7	20.8
Menominee	9.6	8.2	9.2	50.3	24 920	26 201	-4.9	-1.9	2 467	2 502	-347	9 766	5.2	2.52	8.5	26.5
Midland	8.4	6.3	5.5	50.7	75 651	73 578	2.8	8.4	10 093	4 823	1 316	27 791	13.4	2.67	7.9	20.4
Missaukee	9.7	7.7	6.8	50.3	12 147	10 009	21.4	16.5	1 559	1 138	1 620	4 389	28.1	2.74	6.9	19.3
Monroe	8.5	5.8	5.3	50.6	133 600	134 659	-0.8	8.5	16 307	9 983	5 320	46 508	7.9	2.84	10.3	18.9
Montcalm	8.6	6.1	5.7	48.6	53 059	47 555	11.6	15.7	7 619	4 614	5 459	18 563	12.2	2.75	9.9	20.1
Montmorency	14.1	12.4	10.5	50.7	8 936	7 492	19.3	12.1	850	1 333	1 596	3 600	27.9	2.45	7.9	23.6
Muskegon	8.7	6.8	6.1	50.9	158 983	157 589	0.9	5.7	22 635	13 874	852	57 798	6.0	2.66	13.9	23.1
Newaygo	9.7	6.4	5.8	50.4	38 206	34 917	9.4	21.3	5 904	3 619	5 961	13 776	13.5	2.74	9.0	19.4
Oakland	8.6	6.1	5.4	51.4	1 083 592	1 011 793	7.1	8.9	150 852	77 373	23 152	410 488	15.6	2.61	9.6	23.6
Oceana	9.4	7.4	6.5	50.6	22 455	22 002	2.1	10.9	3 225	2 086	1 387	8 071	8.8	2.75	8.7	19.8
Ogemaw	12.1	9.8	7.9	50.4	18 681	16 436	13.7	13.5	2 313	2 347	2 613	7 190	21.0	2.56	8.9	22.1
Ontonagon	11.4	9.7	10.8	49.0	8 854	9 861	-10.2	-13.4	742	1 094	-819	3 641	3.3	2.39	6.9	27.9
Osceola	10.1	7.5	6.4	50.2	20 146	18 928	6.4	10.3	2 671	1 961	1 450	7 347	12.0	2.71	9.2	21.6
Oscoda	13.8	11.3	9.1	50.5	7 842	6 858	14.3	13.5	926	992	1 146	3 160	25.5	2.45	6.8	24.3
Otsego	9.6	7.5	6.4	50.7	17 957	14 993	19.8	26.5	2 565	1 668	3 893	6 522	32.5	2.72	7.9	20.1
Ottawa	7.1	5.3	5.0	50.6	187 768	157 174	19.5	22.6	30 451	11 821	24 269	62 664	24.2	2.90	6.9	16.7
Presque Isle	11.8	12.1	10.7	50.5	13 743	14 267	-3.7	6.2	1 248	1 618	1 298	5 376	7.3	2.53	7.3	24.3
Roscommon	15.1	14.1	10.2	50.8	19 776	16 374	20.8	19.1	2 050	2 918	4 712	8 516	30.6	2.30	7.2	25.9
Saginaw	8.3	6.7	6.4	52.1	211 946	228 059	-7.1	-1.3	29 386	17 622	-13 996	78 256	2.8	2.67	15.3	23.2
St. Clair	8.7	6.3	5.8	51.1	145 607	138 802	4.9	11.1	19 350	12 494	9 622	52 882	11.8	2.73	10.9	21.3
St. Joseph	8.9	6.5	6.7	51.0	58 913	56 083	5.0	4.3	7 896	5 389	199	21 579	9.0	2.70	10.1	21.6
Sanilac	9.6	7.8	7.5	50.7	39 928	40 789	-2.1	8.8	5 041	4 256	2 858	14 658	5.0	2.70	8.4	22.0
Schoolcraft	10.9	8.9	8.9	50.4	8 302	8 575	-3.2	5.9	911	1 009	610	3 294	8.2	2.50	8.4	24.8
Shiawassee	8.2	6.3	5.7	51.1	69 770	71 140	-1.9	3.7	8 872	5 211	-891	24 864	6.4	2.78	10.1	19.4
Tuscola	8.3	6.4	6.1	50.4	55 498	56 961	-2.6	4.9	6 750	4 539	647	19 469	6.4	2.79	9.2	19.1
Van Buren	8.8	6.1	6.2	50.9	70 060	66 814	4.9	8.4	10 078	6 046	2 061	25 402	9.9	2.73	11.3	20.9
Washtenaw	6.4	4.4	4.0	50.8	282 937	264 740	6.9	8.2	36 930	14 682	1 715	104 528	12.5	2.50	9.3	26.3
Wayne	8.6	6.9	5.8	52.7	2 111 687	2 337 843	-9.7	-0.2	321 598	194 722	-228 987	780 535	-5.3	2.67	20.8	26.7
Wexford	9.4	7.2	6.8	51.1	26 360	25 102	5.0	12.1	3 590	2 491	2 180	9 923	10.5	2.63	10.5	22.9
MINNESOTA	8.3	6.1	6.2	50.7	4 375 665	4 075 970	7.4	9.1	603 264	338 093	142 020	1 647 853	14.0	2.58	8.6	25.1
Aitkin	12.9	12.0	10.0	50.3	12 425	13 404	-7.3	15.0	1 285	1 717	2 334	5 126	2.4	2.39	5.2	26.8
Anoka	6.7	5.3	3.4	50.0	243 641	195 998	24.3	22.7	39 265	10 371	27 284	82 437	35.8	2.93	9.7	15.6
Becker	10.0	7.3	8.1	50.2	27 881	29 336	-5.0	6.7	3 494	2 931	1 414	10 477	3.6	2.62	8.3	24.6
Beltrami	7.9	5.5	5.9	50.3	34 384	30 982	11.0	14.0	5 236	2 842	2 545	11 870	18.4	2.74	11.6	22.9
Benton	7.2	4.6	5.8	50.5	30 185	25 187	19.8	15.4	4 635	2 506	2 610	10 935	32.1	2.71	8.2	23.9
Big Stone	11.5	9.6	13.8	52.1	6 285	7 716	-18.5	-11.4	550	933	-307	2 463	-14.3	2.43	4.6	29.0
Blue Earth	7.3	6.3	6.9	50.4	54 044	52 314	3.3	-0.3	5 755	3 777	-1 996	19 277	7.0	2.59	7.4	24.3
Brown	9.6	8.1	9.7	51.7	26 984	28 645	-5.8	-0.3	2 951	2 502	-458	10 321	3.3	2.54	5.9	28.0
Carlton	9.8	7.6	7.2	49.3	29 259	29 936	-2.3	7.6	3 167	2 767	1 912	10 842	7.3	2.62	8.3	24.6
Carver	7.3	3.9	4.0	49.6	47 915	37 046	29.3	39.9	9 037	2 732	12 869	16 601	38.2	2.84	6.8	17.9
Cass	12.3	8.9	8.1	49.9	21 791	21 050	3.5	24.1	2 614	2 670	5 328	8 302	11.5	2.56	7.7	23.6
Chippewa	10.0	8.6	11.1	51.5	13 228	14 941	-11.5	-1.5	1 427	1 497	-80	5 245	-6.1	2.48	5.4	27.8
Chisago	8.0	5.0	5.3	49.2	30 521	25 717	18.7	38.6	4 933	2 464	9 361	10 551	26.4	2.84	6.9	18.7
Clay	8.2	5.9	6.4	51.6	50 422	49 327	2.2	2.6	6 089	3 440	-1 227	17 490	8.0	2.64	8.9	23.4
Clearwater	9.5	6.9	9.9	49.3	8 309	8 761	-5.2	-2.0	913	963	-84	3 064	2.8	2.65	8.0	25.1
Cook	10.6	9.1	7.8	49.9	3 868	4 092	-5.5	23.4	461	332	795	1 632	3.1	2.33	5.3	29.2
Cottonwood	10.6	9.4	12.8	51.1	12 694	14 854	-14.5	-6.2	1 309	1 481	-574	5 060	-7.6	2.45	5.3	27.8
Crow Wing	10.6	8.5	8.1	51.3	44 249	41 722	6.1	18.9	5 691	4 525	7 346	17 204	13.4	2.52	8.1	25.3
Dakota	6.5	3.9	3.1	50.5	275 210	194 279	41.6	26.9	47 697	12 731	37 292	98 293	53.4	2.78	8.9	18.8
Dodge	7.9	5.7	6.2	50.2	15 731	14 773	6.5	10.6	2 231	1 208	711	5 538	10.9	2.81	5.6	19.9
Douglas	9.6	8.5	9.6	50.5	28 674	27 839	3.0	9.1	3 196	2 931	2 427	10 988	10.0	2.56	6.3	24.5
Faribault	11.1	9.7	12.2	51.8	16 937	19 714	-14.1	-4.1	1 570	1 969	-225	6 772	-8.2	2.45	6.2	28.7
Fillmore	10.2	8.7	10.9	50.3	20 777	21 930	-5.3	-0.4	2 317	2 438	100	7 822	-0.1	2.59	5.4	25.2
Freeborn	10.2	9.4	10.0	51.0	33 060	36 329	-9.0	-4.7	3 309	3 347	-1 415	13 029	-1.5	2.49	6.7	25.9
Goodhue	9.0	6.7	8.6	50.5	40 690	38 749	5.0	6.6	4 816	4 188	2 220	15 198	11.5	2.60	6.5	24.9

1. No spouse present.

Table B. States and Counties — Vital Statistics, Health Resources, and Crime

STATE County	Births, average 1996–1998		Deaths, average 1996–1998				Physicians,[4] 1998		Hospitals,[4] 1998			Medicare enrollees 1999	Serious crimes known to police, 1998[6]	
			Number		Rate					Beds			Total	
	Total	Rate[1]	Total	Infant[2]	Total[1]	Infant[3]	Number	Rate[5]	Number	Number	Rate[5]		Number	Rate[7]
	32	33	34	35	36	37	38	39	40	41	42	43	44	45

STATE County	32	33	34	35	36	37	38	39	40	41	42	43	44	45
MICHIGAN—Cont'd														
Leelanau	200	10.7	166	1	8.8	3.3	33	172	1	90	470	3 051	284	1 559
Lenawee	1 186	12.1	833	5	8.5	4.5	98	100	4	317	322	14 895	2 353	2 537
Livingston	1 889	13.3	868	11	6.1	5.8	164	112	1	93	64	11 840	2 743	1 924
Luce	63	9.6	70	1	10.7	10.6	10	151	1	69	1 039	1 327	NA	NA
Mackinac	115	10.4	132	1	11.9	8.7	14	126	1	75	676	2 281	722	6 468
Macomb	9 860	12.6	6 684	60	8.5	6.1	976	124	7	1 466	186	117 132	29 334	3 751
Manistee	232	10.0	282	2	12.2	7.2	38	163	1	173	742	5 009	531	2 281
Marquette	626	10.2	601	5	9.8	7.5	172	279	2	376	611	10 017	1 765	2 844
Mason	293	10.5	296	3	10.7	10.2	44	157	1	85	304	5 190	1 114	3 982
Mecosta	461	11.7	322	5	8.2	10.1	46	115	1	74	185	5 914	882	2 241
Menominee	284	11.6	278	1	11.3	4.7	10	41	1	78	319	4 736	582	2 371
Midland	1 017	12.5	560	7	6.9	6.9	193	236	1	307	375	10 798	1 647	2 018
Missaukee	160	11.7	129	1	9.4	6.2	5	36	0	0	0	2 227	365	2 656
Monroe	1 842	13.0	1 167	11	8.2	6.2	123	86	1	173	121	18 341	4 475	3 131
Montcalm	822	13.8	523	6	8.8	7.3	73	121	4	300	495	9 383	1 495	2 697
Montmorency	102	10.2	152	0	15.2	0.0	3	30	0	0	0	3 144	169	1 686
Muskegon	2 369	14.3	1 541	18	9.3	7.7	265	159	3	618	371	27 012	NA	NA
Newaygo	635	14.1	419	4	9.3	5.8	37	81	1	73	159	6 423	1 373	3 056
Oakland	15 940	13.6	8 662	96	7.4	6.0	5 371	457	12	3 458	294	148 289	44 168	4 018
Oceana	346	14.1	228	3	9.3	8.7	18	72	1	35	141	4 626	461	2 331
Ogemaw	236	11.3	252	2	12.1	8.5	35	165	1	92	434	4 345	658	3 126
Ontonagon	63	7.8	117	0	14.4	0.0	6	76	1	87	1 104	1 912	124	1 954
Osceola	276	12.5	219	2	9.9	7.2	11	50	1	110	498	4 280	300	1 356
Oscoda	95	10.8	109	0	12.4	3.5	4	45	0	0	0	1 699	162	1 824
Otsego	279	12.8	181	3	8.3	9.6	38	172	1	111	502	3 714	468	2 137
Ottawa	3 422	15.5	1 395	23	6.3	6.8	308	137	3	336	150	26 719	5 979	2 749
Presque Isle	141	9.8	178	1	12.4	4.7	9	62	0	0	0	3 712	111	832
Roscommon	204	8.8	338	2	14.6	9.8	21	89	0	0	0	7 210	874	3 755
Saginaw	2 855	13.5	1 917	25	9.1	8.8	437	208	3	848	404	32 905	10 105	5 274
St. Clair	2 066	13.1	1 398	12	8.9	5.8	212	133	4	473	296	22 687	4 470	3 122
St. Joseph	857	14.0	599	5	9.8	6.2	58	95	2	117	191	9 181	2 405	4 017
Sanilac	548	12.8	477	2	11.2	3.0	29	67	3	144	335	7 613	795	1 928
Schoolcraft	90	10.4	125	2	14.3	22.1	9	102	1	47	534	1 947	NA	NA
Shiawassee	928	12.8	579	6	8.0	6.8	78	107	1	155	214	10 338	1 568	2 197
Tuscola	684	11.8	521	7	9.0	10.7	35	60	2	109	187	8 828	996	2 018
Van Buren	1 044	13.8	656	11	8.7	10.5	60	79	2	224	296	11 197	2 996	3 941
Washtenaw	3 928	13.1	1 652	21	5.5	5.4	2 240	739	5	1 637	540	29 531	12 972	4 368
Wayne	31 687	14.9	20 402	348	9.6	11.0	3 922	185	27	8 232	389	296 587	169 318	7 971
Wexford	374	12.9	288	3	9.9	7.1	50	171	1	154	528	5 164	1 135	3 877
MINNESOTA	64 467	13.8	37 097	381	7.9	5.9	10 190	216	142	17 140	363	648 272	191 197	4 047
Aitkin	140	10.1	182	1	13.1	7.1	8	57	1	84	594	3 666	639	4 570
Anoka	4 219	14.7	1 212	25	4.2	5.9	282	97	2	470	161	21 507	13 031	4 508
Becker	376	12.8	327	1	11.2	2.7	40	136	1	160	545	5 172	511	1 733
Beltrami	566	14.7	312	7	8.1	12.4	57	147	1	98	253	5 371	1 833	4 696
Benton	498	14.8	289	4	8.6	7.4	33	97	0	0	0	3 143	983	2 895
Big Stone	58	10.1	97	0	16.9	5.8	7	124	2	137	2 423	1 517	116	2 022
Blue Earth	625	11.6	429	4	8.0	5.9	107	199	1	153	285	8 606	2 096	3 847
Brown	278	10.2	274	1	10.1	3.6	26	96	3	126	466	5 345	431	1 570
Carlton	355	11.6	299	1	9.8	3.8	30	97	2	253	821	5 486	853	2 757
Carver	1 043	16.5	311	4	4.9	4.2	86	133	1	106	164	5 197	1 213	1 904
Cass	278	10.8	293	2	11.3	8.4	28	106	0	0	0	5 281	1 522	5 863
Chippewa	145	11.1	163	1	12.5	9.2	7	54	1	35	268	2 562	146	1 112
Chisago	584	14.8	270	3	6.8	4.6	32	78	2	115	282	5 030	1 219	3 065
Clay	635	12.3	376	5	7.3	7.3	16	31	0	0	0	7 072	1 463	2 800
Clearwater	89	10.7	111	0	13.4	0.0	6	72	1	18	217	1 551	169	2 044
Cook	49	10.4	34	0	7.1	6.8	15	313	1	63	1 315	922	134	2 804
Cottonwood	137	11.3	171	1	14.0	9.7	10	83	2	43	357	2 840	158	1 278
Crow Wing	609	11.9	481	3	9.4	4.9	94	182	2	322	623	10 568	2 214	4 297
Dakota	5 195	15.5	1 497	24	4.5	4.7	365	107	3	304	89	23 018	11 200	3 320
Dodge	242	14.2	133	1	7.8	4.1	10	58	0	0	0	2 258	334	1 948
Douglas	356	11.6	332	2	10.8	4.7	51	164	1	110	354	6 372	1 033	3 334
Faribault	157	9.6	211	1	12.9	8.5	13	80	1	43	265	3 902	289	1 744
Fillmore	245	11.8	261	3	12.6	10.9	17	82	2	129	620	4 498	180	863
Freeborn	332	10.5	361	2	11.4	5.0	34	108	1	115	364	6 556	833	2 617
Goodhue	506	11.8	436	3	10.2	6.6	60	139	3	124	287	6 986	1 582	3 674

1. Per 1,000 estimated resident population, average 1996–1998.   2. Deaths of infants under 1 year old.   3. Deaths of infants under 1 year old per 1,000 live births.   4. Data subject to copyright.   5. Per 100,000 resident population as of July 1 of the year shown.   6. Data for serious crimes have not been adjusted for underreporting; this may affect comparability between geographic areas and over time.   7. Per 100,000 population estimated by the FBI.

Table B. States and Counties — Crime, Education, Money Income, and Poverty

STATE County	Serious crimes known to police, 1998[1] (cont'd) Rate[2] Violent	Serious crimes known to police Property	Education — Enrollment[3] Total	Enrollment Percent private	Attainment[4] High school graduate or more	Attainment Bachelor's degree or more	Local government expenditures, fiscal 1997[5] Total current expenditures (mil dol)	Current expenditures per student (dollars)	Money income 1989 Per capita[6] (dollars)	Households Median Dollars	Percent change, 1979–1989 (constant 1989 dollars)	Percent with $100,000 or more	Income and poverty, 1997 Median household income	Percent below poverty level All persons	Persons under 18	Persons 5–17 in families
	46	47	48	49	50	51	52	53	54	55	56	57	58	59	60	61
MICHIGAN—Cont'd																
Leelanau	110	1 449	3 922	14.7	85.1	24.1	16.1	6 197	13 307	28 589	7.0	2.5	41 624	8.3	13.0	14.0
Lenawee	259	2 278	26 130	16.3	76.3	12.9	124.2	6 479	12 654	31 012	-0.2	1.9	40 778	9.4	13.7	13.5
Livingston	142	1 782	33 332	11.4	85.6	19.6	147.4	6 087	17 327	45 439	10.5	6.3	61 915	3.8	5.2	5.1
Luce	NA	NA	1 418	2.0	69.6	9.6	7.2	5 706	9 264	20 370	-8.3	0.7	28 252	16.4	22.7	22.9
Mackinac	340	6 128	2 360	3.1	71.4	10.4	12.1	6 486	9 751	19 397	-7.1	0.9	28 367	11.8	19.2	19.2
Macomb	422	3 329	186 105	12.9	76.9	13.5	856.2	7 132	16 187	38 931	-4.1	3.9	49 601	5.9	9.4	8.7
Manistee	275	2 006	4 785	8.9	73.3	10.5	24.3	6 500	10 118	19 977	-16.9	0.9	28 889	14.5	23.3	22.2
Marquette	197	2 647	21 668	4.4	81.8	20.3	73.2	6 759	11 025	25 137	-9.2	1.5	35 478	11.3	14.5	14.6
Mason	286	3 696	6 294	5.3	76.1	11.8	37.5	7 032	10 848	21 701	-10.1	1.5	31 189	13.2	21.3	20.5
Mecosta	163	2 078	15 778	4.9	77.7	17.9	43.9	6 575	9 271	20 784	-5.2	1.0	31 055	15.4	23.3	21.9
Menominee	167	2 204	6 022	8.4	74.3	9.3	25.6	5 794	10 336	21 586	-9.3	1.0	32 472	11.1	16.0	15.4
Midland	154	1 864	22 189	16.3	83.2	27.4	99.7	6 961	15 615	33 948	-5.9	5.5	48 093	9.0	13.0	13.0
Missaukee	175	2 481	3 020	12.2	69.4	8.0	12.2	4 892	9 139	20 932	1.4	0.8	30 571	13.9	21.0	20.9
Monroe	237	2 894	36 833	12.8	74.1	10.5	162.2	6 534	13 893	35 462	-0.9	2.8	48 607	7.6	11.2	10.4
Montcalm	325	2 372	14 100	6.4	73.4	8.2	85.6	6 132	10 081	23 880	-3.7	1.0	25 297	13.3	18.4	19.3
Montmorency	140	1 546	1 857	3.4	67.6	8.7	7.1	5 714	9 307	17 819	3.7	0.9	25 297	15.1	26.9	27.0
Muskegon	NA	NA	42 908	10.2	74.2	11.1	220.7	6 579	11 345	25 617	-5.5	1.6	34 951	14.4	21.9	20.8
Newaygo	260	2 796	10 046	7.7	71.1	10.5	62.7	5 996	10 307	23 468	-0.6	1.0	33 631	12.6	19.2	19.0
Oakland	416	3 602	286 218	16.0	84.6	30.2	1 453.2	7 884	21 125	43 407	2.3	10.1	59 677	6.0	9.6	8.5
Oceana	308	2 023	6 093	5.9	73.3	10.4	25.1	5 969	9 582	22 383	-5.7	1.0	31 324	16.8	25.2	25.9
Ogemaw	337	2 789	4 458	6.1	63.0	7.2	15.3	5 192	8 991	17 665	0.3	0.9	25 383	17.4	26.8	27.0
Ontonagon	236	1 718	1 866	1.7	74.6	9.2	12.6	8 800	10 939	21 147	-4.1	1.2	27 811	13.6	22.4	22.0
Osceola	172	1 184	5 400	5.8	72.1	8.7	30.8	5 148	9 258	20 880	-3.9	0.9	29 712	15.5	23.1	23.3
Oscoda	68	1 756	1 528	9.3	66.6	7.9	7.3	5 189	8 719	17 772	-5.1	0.7	25 044	17.1	27.8	29.6
Otsego	160	1 977	4 340	12.6	79.5	13.7	26.1	5 663	11 366	26 356	2.5	1.8	37 938	8.6	13.0	12.8
Ottawa	232	2 517	55 248	21.5	79.8	18.7	237.2	6 398	14 347	36 507	7.7	3.7	51 677	4.9	6.3	6.6
Presque Isle	60	772	3 187	16.4	65.7	8.7	11.8	5 145	9 654	20 941	0.0	0.3	28 886	12.1	18.8	18.6
Roscommon	357	3 398	3 969	5.9	69.4	7.9	30.3	7 062	9 709	17 047	-6.4	0.7	24 172	16.6	31.1	30.1
Saginaw	831	4 443	60 862	11.2	74.8	13.0	244.1	6 586	12 355	27 980	-15.4	2.0	36 318	15.3	24.6	22.8
St. Clair	307	2 815	38 403	8.2	74.8	10.7	175.0	6 330	13 257	30 692	-0.9	2.9	42 617	8.9	13.3	12.8
St. Joseph	387	3 630	15 261	10.7	73.8	10.9	71.6	5 888	12 039	27 510	2.0	2.1	36 779	11.1	16.6	16.5
Sanilac	213	1 715	10 303	5.0	72.1	8.4	51.3	5 737	10 330	23 107	-5.5	1.0	32 199	12.2	18.7	18.0
Schoolcraft	NA	NA	2 059	8.6	71.6	8.9	7.6	5 714	9 740	20 112	-3.6	0.6	28 681	15.6	25.0	23.5
Shiawassee	200	1 997	18 869	8.9	78.7	10.3	91.3	6 184	12 244	30 283	-8.4	1.5	38 430	10.1	14.3	14.4
Tuscola	174	1 844	14 722	9.5	73.0	8.1	80.9	6 450	11 543	27 374	-10.9	1.2	36 568	11.0	16.0	15.9
Van Buren	420	3 521	18 843	6.9	71.8	12.1	112.2	6 313	11 233	25 491	-1.2	1.7	33 852	14.9	22.2	22.4
Washtenaw	451	3 917	103 484	8.8	87.2	41.9	318.2	7 549	17 115	36 307	4.7	6.6	51 286	8.7	12.0	11.9
Wayne	1 379	6 592	569 252	15.7	70.0	13.7	2 541.4	7 102	13 016	27 997	-10.3	3.1	35 357	18.0	28.5	25.9
Wexford	355	3 522	6 764	6.7	74.6	12.6	37.8	6 436	10 952	22 915	2.1	1.4	31 841	13.5	21.0	20.6
MINNESOTA	310	3 737	1 175 027	14.4	82.4	21.8	5 087.0	6 005	14 389	30 909	3.8	3.6	41 591	8.9	13.1	11.8
Aitkin	236	4 334	2 629	2.3	70.5	9.5	14.0	5 835	9 281	17 564	-1.7	0.9	26 746	14.9	25.9	22.3
Anoka	194	4 314	67 791	10.0	86.7	15.5	366.6	5 945	14 554	40 076	2.2	2.7	53 308	5.3	8.1	7.3
Becker	34	1 699	7 079	5.5	72.9	12.0	29.6	5 743	9 889	20 920	-1.5	1.3	30 323	14.6	21.5	19.2
Beltrami	159	4 537	11 596	3.6	75.9	20.4	57.8	6 963	8 938	20 925	2.0	0.8	29 851	18.9	26.8	24.3
Benton	153	2 742	8 347	14.1	77.3	14.8	26.3	5 031	11 018	26 619	2.4	1.0	38 241	8.5	12.4	11.2
Big Stone	157	1 865	1 333	3.9	72.3	10.1	8.2	5 732	9 575	19 408	-6.0	0.9	27 919	13.7	21.9	20.0
Blue Earth	114	3 733	21 082	7.4	82.7	22.7	62.2	5 830	11 125	25 366	-3.0	1.6	37 135	10.5	12.9	12.0
Brown	22	1 548	6 678	30.6	71.7	12.3	26.0	5 628	11 244	25 032	-3.0	1.6	36 938	7.4	10.0	9.2
Carlton	165	2 592	7 616	6.2	75.1	12.2	39.1	5 954	10 878	24 900	-9.5	0.9	36 871	10.3	14.6	13.2
Carver	74	1 830	12 839	23.6	84.6	21.4	67.1	6 635	16 116	39 188	14.2	5.3	58 797	3.7	4.9	4.7
Cass	512	5 351	5 018	4.1	72.5	11.4	29.8	6 274	8 991	18 732	2.3	0.9	27 704	15.3	24.5	21.6
Chippewa	61	1 051	3 137	2.1	73.7	10.9	19.1	6 978	11 067	22 227	-0.8	1.5	34 301	9.7	13.8	12.3
Chisago	156	2 909	8 041	6.3	80.1	11.9	40.9	5 307	12 526	31 281	0.9	2.1	46 563	6.1	8.7	7.9
Clay	205	2 595	18 459	16.2	80.5	21.5	54.6	5 862	10 836	25 891	-6.8	1.5	37 711	12.5	16.6	15.0
Clearwater	193	1 851	2 076	2.0	64.9	9.8	11.2	6 000	8 359	17 752	4.9	0.7	26 177	19.1	28.0	25.6
Cook	126	2 678	798	8.8	84.9	20.7	4.3	5 826	12 067	22 908	-6.6	1.3	33 460	7.7	11.8	12.1
Cottonwood	32	1 246	2 874	7.4	71.7	12.3	15.5	6 702	10 335	21 661	-8.5	0.9	31 272	11.0	16.7	15.6
Crow Wing	194	4 103	11 049	5.1	75.7	13.5	58.7	5 814	10 911	22 250	4.7	1.1	32 616	11.8	18.0	16.3
Dakota	139	3 181	75 104	14.0	90.7	27.6	395.7	5 798	17 237	42 218	6.8	5.4	57 802	4.6	6.6	6.0
Dodge	140	1 808	4 164	3.8	78.7	11.7	20.6	5 161	11 932	29 071	3.2	1.7	42 511	6.9	8.9	8.4
Douglas	136	3 198	7 540	8.8	76.1	12.7	31.6	5 566	10 264	22 067	0.7	1.2	34 444	9.4	13.0	11.9
Faribault	127	1 617	4 121	7.3	74.4	12.0	21.2	7 367	11 276	22 421	-7.2	1.4	31 670	10.5	15.6	14.0
Fillmore	62	801	4 831	6.5	70.2	10.5	21.0	5 887	10 146	22 155	0.7	1.4	31 850	10.6	14.5	13.9
Freeborn	141	2 476	7 760	4.2	75.5	11.5	29.7	5 627	11 452	24 764	-10.3	1.2	33 893	10.3	16.2	14.6
Goodhue	181	3 493	10 269	7.3	78.0	14.1	53.1	5 665	12 892	29 237	2.4	2.3	43 192	6.8	9.2	8.5

1. Data for serious crimes have not been adjusted for underreporting; this may affect comparability between geographic areas and over time. 2. Per 100,000 population estimated by the FBI. 3. All persons 3 years old and over enrolled in nursery school through college. 4. Persons 25 years old and over. 5. Elementary and secondary education expenditures, local government fiscal years ending between July 1, 1996 and June 30, 1997. 6. Based on population enumerated as of April 1, 1990.

STATE County	Personal income, 1998 Total (mil dol)	Percent change, 1997–1998	Per capita[1] Dollars	Per capita[1] Rank	Wages and salaries[2] (mil dol)	Proprietor's income (mil dol)	Dividends, interest, and rent (mil dol)	Transfer payments Total (mil dol)	Government payments to individuals Total (mil dol)	Social Security (mil dol)	Medical payments (mil dol)	Income maintenance (mil dol)	Unemployment insurance (mil dol)
	62	63	64	65	66	67	68	69	70	71	72	73	74
MICHIGAN—Cont'd													
Leelanau	506	5.9	26 448	348	145	36	142	68	64	39	19	3	2
Lenawee	2 307	6.6	23 400	766	1 162	91	370	324	306	153	111	23	9
Livingston	4 487	7.4	30 666	145	1 492	178	702	310	283	161	90	13	9
Luce	123	-1.2	18 135	2 311	71	10	23	32	31	12	14	3	1
Mackinac	262	3.6	23 735	692	125	21	61	53	51	24	17	3	5
Macomb	22 255	3.6	28 283	225	15 058	722	4 286	2 663	2 518	1 283	979	119	77
Manistee	439	2.9	18 697	2 158	199	23	108	110	105	51	40	7	3
Marquette	1 308	3.7	20 894	1 426	824	49	246	240	228	98	84	16	8
Mason	573	4.3	20 551	1 539	325	28	121	116	111	52	36	9	4
Mecosta	690	4.3	17 181	2 568	340	43	139	134	127	61	40	12	3
Menominee	512	4.5	20 980	1 401	258	30	97	94	89	45	30	6	4
Midland	2 438	4.0	29 897	169	1 642	115	535	244	229	120	80	17	6
Missaukee	237	7.7	17 058	2 599	71	24	42	48	46	23	15	4	2
Monroe	3 683	7.0	25 687	417	1 595	199	568	449	422	212	151	31	10
Montcalm	1 005	2.5	16 583	2 696	586	66	143	200	189	89	69	18	6
Montmorency	169	4.2	16 868	2 639	50	13	46	60	58	31	20	4	2
Muskegon	3 507	4.5	21 016	1 385	2 165	137	598	631	601	279	210	75	17
Newaygo	817	5.5	17 856	2 391	313	55	144	160	151	72	50	15	7
Oakland	49 796	8.7	42 378	22	36 273	3 144	9 917	3 599	3 382	1 663	1 336	202	89
Oceana	469	4.4	18 934	2 083	183	30	89	97	93	44	32	10	5
Ogemaw	336	2.7	15 938	2 802	149	30	66	105	101	47	38	9	3
Ontonagon	149	1.8	18 985	2 063	72	12	28	42	41	19	15	3	2
Osceola	401	4.8	18 133	2 312	246	28	66	89	85	40	30	9	4
Oscoda	130	1.8	14 655	2 960	44	17	21	40	39	19	14	3	1
Otsego	494	6.5	22 229	1 033	334	50	95	75	71	38	24	4	3
Ottawa	6 044	4.3	26 812	319	3 955	343	1 118	522	481	273	148	24	16
Presque Isle	246	1.0	16 951	2 622	90	17	57	70	67	36	21	5	3
Roscommon	436	3.0	18 656	2 167	141	43	104	146	141	74	51	9	3
Saginaw	4 915	2.4	23 402	765	3 710	236	894	839	800	345	291	112	25
St. Clair	3 823	4.3	23 976	648	1 672	169	667	529	500	236	182	40	17
St. Joseph	1 319	0.9	21 566	1 237	807	59	229	208	197	98	71	17	6
Sanilac	908	4.5	21 084	1 362	365	59	173	174	166	77	68	12	6
Schoolcraft	171	2.4	19 473	1 902	77	14	33	44	42	18	16	3	2
Shiawassee	1 454	0.9	20 056	1 693	536	57	210	244	231	104	91	17	9
Tuscola	1 130	1.8	19 487	1 896	424	48	166	209	198	90	80	15	7
Van Buren	1 461	3.4	19 313	1 950	669	81	208	269	255	113	98	29	8
Washtenaw	10 522	6.7	34 751	67	8 003	455	1 953	756	700	319	269	56	13
Wayne	53 051	3.2	25 065	481	40 455	3 288	7 877	9 264	8 873	3 124	3 892	1 376	209
Wexford	586	3.7	20 114	1 676	426	39	109	113	107	50	38	10	5
MINNESOTA	138 307	7.1	29 263	X	92 973	8 550	28 760	15 428	14 487	6 095	5 883	1 242	349
Aitkin	270	5.2	19 023	2 047	87	23	70	76	73	34	26	5	2
Anoka	7 704	8.6	26 354	358	3 736	322	1 061	622	564	254	208	43	20
Becker	590	7.2	20 012	1 706	276	67	124	117	111	45	43	12	4
Beltrami	759	6.0	19 630	1 850	441	54	150	152	144	44	59	23	3
Benton	742	9.4	21 751	1 172	377	47	135	87	80	34	31	7	3
Big Stone	117	3.3	20 627	1 518	42	11	35	27	26	12	11	2	0
Blue Earth	1 386	7.9	25 790	414	925	124	333	168	158	71	56	12	3
Brown	635	2.8	23 466	754	379	49	165	99	94	47	35	5	3
Carlton	656	4.5	20 948	1 407	401	31	121	121	114	51	44	9	4
Carver	2 060	10.0	31 775	118	997	107	347	127	114	55	44	5	4
Cass	503	7.0	19 126	2 013	198	55	128	121	116	49	44	11	3
Chippewa	313	6.8	23 998	642	159	36	74	48	46	21	17	3	2
Chisago	1 038	14.6	25 357	452	335	54	174	112	104	47	41	6	4
Clay	1 050	4.9	20 387	1 608	466	54	216	170	160	64	61	14	2
Clearwater	142	5.3	17 262	2 541	62	13	27	38	36	12	16	4	1
Cook	120	5.2	25 272	462	60	16	32	18	17	9	6	1	1
Cottonwood	272	3.4	22 596	952	114	41	73	53	50	25	20	4	1
Crow Wing	1 168	7.2	22 581	960	684	82	265	218	208	94	75	16	5
Dakota	10 849	8.5	31 717	122	5 219	318	1 928	690	622	295	214	38	22
Dodge	397	5.8	23 148	827	133	36	71	50	46	20	20	3	1
Douglas	710	6.7	22 860	879	393	56	176	119	112	53	42	7	2
Faribault	353	1.9	21 697	1 194	147	39	96	72	69	32	29	4	1
Fillmore	438	6.4	21 107	1 352	164	51	102	83	79	35	35	5	1
Freeborn	690	3.8	21 873	1 134	359	45	156	130	124	63	46	8	1
Goodhue	1 155	7.2	26 774	321	647	84	266	141	132	66	51	6	3

1. Based on the resident population estimated as of July 1 of the year shown.   2. Includes other labor income.

Table B. States and Counties — Earnings, Social Security, and Housing

STATE County	Earnings, 1998									Social Security beneficiaries, December 1998			Housing units, 1990	
			Percent by selected industries									Supplemental Security Income recipients, December 1998		
			Goods-related[1]		Service-related and other[2]									
	Total (mil dol)	Farm	Total	Manufacturing	Total	Retail trade	Finance, insurance, and real estate	Services	Government	Number	Rate[3]		Total	Percent change, 1980–1990
	75	76	77	78	79	80	81	82	83	84	85	86	87	88

MICHIGAN—Cont'd														
Leelanau	181	3.4	D	5.5	D	11.9	5.4	36.5	14.6	4 270	223	134	11 171	23.1
Lenawee	1 253	1.5	D	38.9	D	10.3	4.0	17.1	16.8	17 215	175	1 704	35 104	4.0
Livingston	1 670	0.0	38.8	26.7	49.8	10.2	8.2	20.8	11.5	16 770	115	593	41 863	19.8
Luce	81	1.6	D	22.6	D	9.1	2.2	8.1	44.6	1 413	213	219	3 594	0.6
Mackinac	146	-0.2	D	5.4	D	16.5	2.1	35.7	23.3	2 944	265	220	9 254	21.4
Macomb	15 779	0.1	51.9	45.3	37.5	7.7	3.1	18.8	10.5	133 210	169	7 477	274 843	16.2
Manistee	222	0.4	37.8	28.4	38.8	10.1	2.4	17.3	23.0	5 854	251	480	13 330	8.9
Marquette	873	0.0	D	3.6	D	8.9	4.1	D	25.8	11 335	184	1 034	31 049	1.7
Mason	353	1.1	D	35.4	D	9.5	2.5	18.9	17.9	6 119	219	596	14 119	6.7
Mecosta	382	1.3	D	18.2	D	10.4	2.2	16.5	37.8	7 128	178	789	17 274	11.3
Menominee	288	1.1	40.5	36.5	42.3	8.3	2.5	17.2	16.2	5 435	222	426	12 509	8.3
Midland	1 757	-0.2	D	51.2	D	4.9	2.5	21.9	8.1	13 147	161	1 065	29 343	11.3
Missaukee	96	11.8	33.2	23.5	36.1	10.0	2.9	11.3	19.0	2 859	206	240	7 112	16.3
Monroe	1 794	1.1	45.1	38.5	40.7	9.3	2.0	14.5	13.1	23 055	161	1 864	48 312	6.5
Montcalm	651	2.3	D	36.6	D	10.5	2.4	17.3	17.2	10 586	175	1 262	22 817	9.2
Montmorency	63	-0.2	D	23.6	D	10.2	2.9	18.6	20.7	3 596	359	257	8 791	11.5
Muskegon	2 302	0.4	D	33.7	D	9.8	2.7	21.3	15.7	31 869	191	5 162	61 962	6.4
Newaygo	367	2.9	29.9	23.5	42.7	9.2	4.4	20.1	24.5	8 641	189	962	20 105	9.8
Oakland	39 418	0.0	30.0	24.5	63.8	7.6	9.2	33.5	6.2	166 080	141	13 919	432 684	15.9
Oceana	213	7.6	31.0	21.6	41.0	9.7	2.6	19.4	20.4	5 286	213	679	12 857	12.8
Ogemaw	179	1.7	23.1	15.8	53.1	16.9	3.6	17.1	22.0	5 549	262	579	13 977	7.7
Ontonagon	84	0.1	D	30.5	D	9.7	2.7	11.9	27.8	2 301	292	237	5 332	5.8
Osceola	274	0.3	59.7	48.4	25.8	6.2	1.3	12.0	14.2	4 879	221	655	11 444	15.3
Oscoda	61	0.4	40.5	34.7	36.9	13.1	2.7	15.7	22.2	2 271	256	197	8 112	11.0
Otsego	384	0.1	36.7	18.4	50.7	14.4	3.5	21.9	12.7	4 329	196	318	10 669	17.5
Ottawa	4 298	1.4	51.1	43.4	36.6	6.8	4.6	15.8	10.9	29 633	132	1 602	66 624	23.5
Presque Isle	107	2.5	D	8.4	D	14.2	3.3	D	21.6	4 154	288	340	8 917	6.6
Roscommon	184	0.0	D	7.3	D	21.4	3.8	20.0	26.2	8 283	353	623	19 881	10.9
Saginaw	3 946	0.1	42.8	37.7	46.1	9.0	4.0	23.1	11.0	38 338	182	6 946	81 931	3.0
St. Clair	1 841	0.1	32.9	25.1	52.4	10.2	4.4	21.7	14.9	26 109	163	2 517	57 494	10.8
St. Joseph	866	0.7	D	52.3	D	6.7	D	10.6	14.4	11 043	180	1 005	24 242	7.8
Sanilac	423	4.1	43.2	35.5	36.3	9.3	3.0	16.9	16.4	9 111	212	674	19 465	5.3
Schoolcraft	91	0.1	28.1	18.6	42.2	11.6	6.1	16.7	29.8	2 199	250	225	5 487	10.3
Shiawassee	593	-0.6	29.6	22.5	50.8	11.8	5.5	22.7	20.2	11 718	161	1 272	25 833	5.6
Tuscola	472	2.5	30.1	22.9	39.2	9.3	4.3	14.7	28.2	10 283	177	998	21 231	5.9
Van Buren	750	2.7	D	27.5	D	9.6	D	13.5	22.4	13 199	174	1 835	31 530	9.5
Washtenaw	8 458	0.0	31.0	27.0	42.4	8.1	3.4	22.8	26.6	32 347	107	3 420	111 256	13.3
Wayne	43 743	0.0	36.8	33.3	50.1	6.7	5.8	23.1	13.2	344 974	163	78 073	832 710	-4.8
Wexford	465	0.2	D	33.9	D	10.0	2.5	23.7	14.8	5 974	205	741	12 862	11.1
MINNESOTA	101 523	1.0	D	20.5	D	8.9	8.9	26.5	13.3	723 599	153	63 674	1 848 445	14.6
Aitkin	110	-1.3	D	13.7	D	14.2	3.5	23.0	22.6	4 314	305	260	12 934	16.3
Anoka	4 058	0.0	42.5	33.3	44.8	10.4	2.6	20.6	12.7	28 408	97	1 512	85 519	36.0
Becker	342	4.5	D	14.5	D	11.0	D	25.1	20.2	6 023	205	530	15 563	0.9
Beltrami	495	0.2	16.1	6.1	56.2	11.9	3.3	29.2	27.5	6 045	156	1 029	14 670	12.0
Benton	424	2.6	D	27.4	D	12.2	2.1	15.5	10.0	4 429	130	299	11 521	30.7
Big Stone	53	8.6	D	2.6	D	10.8	5.5	17.5	28.8	1 624	287	115	3 192	-8.6
Blue Earth	1 049	2.7	22.1	13.9	56.9	10.9	4.7	25.4	18.4	8 683	161	895	20 358	5.0
Brown	428	2.9	D	33.3	D	8.4	D	19.9	11.5	5 815	215	239	10 814	3.3
Carlton	431	-0.4	39.7	26.9	38.7	7.7	3.0	18.0	22.0	6 097	198	434	12 342	4.8
Carver	1 104	1.1	D	39.6	D	6.2	4.1	20.4	12.6	6 419	99	191	17 449	38.6
Cass	253	-0.2	12.6	3.2	60.4	13.7	4.7	33.8	27.2	6 471	245	569	18 863	7.3
Chippewa	195	8.3	D	21.7	D	9.2	3.7	13.9	15.0	2 834	217	146	5 755	-6.0
Chisago	389	1.2	34.1	19.9	48.2	10.1	3.5	27.7	16.5	5 566	136	288	11 946	24.9
Clay	520	1.6	D	8.3	D	12.1	3.5	24.2	26.4	7 743	150	723	18 546	4.1
Clearwater	75	-0.8	30.2	17.2	39.3	8.6	2.8	15.5	31.3	1 735	209	241	4 008	4.8
Cook	77	0.0	16.7	5.5	D	13.5	2.3	36.2	26.0	1 023	213	48	4 312	24.8
Cottonwood	155	15.4	D	18.7	D	8.0	4.5	17.3	16.5	3 141	261	225	5 495	-5.3
Crow Wing	767	-0.4	D	16.7	D	13.4	5.9	24.2	20.3	11 505	223	881	29 916	16.5
Dakota	5 537	0.2	29.0	21.2	58.6	10.5	7.5	22.4	12.2	32 584	95	1 673	102 707	53.6
Dodge	169	10.2	D	26.7	D	6.9	3.5	12.2	17.5	2 614	152	145	5 771	4.3
Douglas	449	0.6	32.2	20.7	49.2	13.2	4.0	19.4	17.9	7 012	226	430	14 590	10.7
Faribault	186	6.4	32.9	24.4	44.6	7.5	5.0	16.1	16.1	4 096	252	209	7 416	-6.7
Fillmore	215	12.3	D	17.9	D	9.8	4.9	16.6	16.5	4 716	227	227	8 356	-1.1
Freeborn	405	3.2	D	27.6	D	11.9	4.1	22.5	12.8	7 660	243	410	13 783	-0.2
Goodhue	731	4.3	30.2	25.8	53.1	7.3	3.6	24.3	12.4	7 805	181	359	15 936	10.9

1. Covers mining, construction, and manufacturing. 2. Covers private sector earnings in agricultural services, forestry, and fisheries; transportation and public utilities; wholesale trade; retail trade; finance, insurance, and real estate; and services. 3. Per 1,000 resident population estimated as of July 1 of the year shown.

Table B. States and Counties — Housing, Labor Force, and Employment

STATE County	Housing units, 1990 (cont'd) Occupied units — Owner-occupied — Total	Percent	Median value[1]	Owner cost as a percent of income — With a mortgage	Without a mortgage	Renter-occupied — Median rent[2]	Rent as percent of income	Sub-standard units[3] (percent)	Civilian labor force, 1999 — Total	Percent change, 1998-1999	Unemployment — Total	Rate[4]	Civilian employment, 1990[5] — Total	Percent — Professional, managerial, and technical	Precision production, craft, and repair
	89	90	91	92	93	94	95	96	97	98	99	100	101	102	103
MICHIGAN—Cont'd															
Leelanau	6 274	81.5	73 100	21.6	13.7	414	24.2	2.7	11 320	0.9	375	3.3	7 701	29.1	14.2
Lenawee	31 635	75.9	54 000	17.2	12.8	382	25.4	2.8	48 807	3.3	1 744	3.6	40 681	22.2	13.5
Livingston	38 887	84.5	97 300	20.0	13.5	521	24.3	1.9	81 383	5.3	1 784	2.2	58 567	30.8	14.9
Luce	2 154	79.1	30 800	18.6	12.1	306	29.5	3.4	2 668	-2.4	220	8.2	2 073	22.9	9.5
Mackinac	4 240	76.0	43 900	19.4	13.6	297	25.9	3.2	7 572	2.2	731	9.7	3 893	21.0	14.3
Macomb	264 991	77.2	76 800	18.4	13.4	493	24.5	2.0	443 435	2.1	14 387	3.2	355 676	28.2	14.2
Manistee	8 580	78.2	40 400	18.8	14.0	287	29.3	2.1	11 103	6.2	671	6.0	7 967	20.8	13.9
Marquette	25 435	64.2	44 800	17.6	13.6	333	25.2	2.3	32 993	2.9	1 889	5.7	28 858	27.5	13.3
Mason	9 984	75.9	43 300	18.8	13.7	304	27.9	1.8	14 494	1.4	896	6.2	10 244	22.4	14.2
Mecosta	12 260	69.9	49 100	19.1	13.5	339	35.1	3.3	18 490	4.2	758	4.1	15 094	25.6	10.2
Menominee	9 766	78.9	37 900	19.5	15.2	293	24.8	3.0	13 110	0.2	637	4.9	10 758	19.2	13.1
Midland	27 791	76.9	63 300	17.0	11.7	407	25.5	1.9	43 702	2.8	1 284	2.9	34 488	37.2	12.3
Missaukee	4 389	83.0	40 500	19.7	13.6	340	30.9	3.7	6 965	9.0	409	5.9	4 637	18.4	12.1
Monroe	46 508	77.8	67 200	16.1	13.3	423	26.3	2.1	74 181	2.4	2 361	3.2	60 862	21.8	15.8
Montcalm	18 563	79.4	42 600	18.0	14.1	340	25.2	3.1	25 858	-0.3	1 520	5.9	20 595	17.5	17.1
Montmorency	3 600	81.5	41 700	23.0	14.8	329	33.2	4.2	3 575	-0.3	418	11.7	2 664	19.8	15.2
Muskegon	57 798	74.4	46 300	16.9	13.2	362	29.7	3.1	85 594	2.7	4 004	4.7	65 424	23.6	13.6
Newaygo	13 776	82.2	44 300	19.9	13.9	348	28.4	4.4	21 410	3.8	1 478	6.9	15 139	20.9	15.5
Oakland	410 488	72.7	95 400	19.4	13.2	557	24.4	2.1	681 730	2.4	17 171	2.5	557 134	39.0	10.0
Oceana	8 071	80.3	43 300	19.0	14.2	333	28.5	3.9	14 402	0.5	1 066	7.4	8 889	18.2	15.5
Ogemaw	7 190	81.4	39 500	22.7	15.0	327	31.4	4.1	8 860	2.4	626	7.1	6 029	18.8	14.1
Ontonagon	3 641	81.0	28 100	15.5	13.2	248	24.6	3.4	3 069	-0.8	275	9.0	3 464	18.9	18.5
Osceola	7 347	79.9	37 500	20.0	14.5	300	27.3	3.6	11 068	0.1	618	5.6	7 527	19.7	13.4
Oscoda	3 160	81.9	37 400	21.4	14.9	317	35.1	4.2	3 636	5.6	295	8.1	2 490	19.2	12.3
Otsego	6 522	79.1	56 000	21.1	13.7	365	25.5	2.5	13 784	4.1	639	4.6	8 042	23.3	13.5
Ottawa	62 664	80.7	74 600	18.4	12.6	454	23.3	2.2	140 441	3.8	3 797	2.7	96 179	26.7	12.6
Presque Isle	5 376	83.7	44 000	20.7	13.7	276	28.1	3.5	6 303	1.6	686	10.9	4 915	19.6	14.4
Roscommon	8 516	81.9	44 500	21.9	14.3	326	35.1	2.7	8 196	0.3	629	7.7	6 108	23.5	12.4
Saginaw	78 256	70.7	48 100	16.5	13.5	389	30.4	3.0	102 935	1.4	4 579	4.4	87 273	24.4	12.4
St. Clair	52 882	75.7	59 400	17.9	14.1	409	28.4	2.3	80 920	2.7	3 553	4.4	64 179	22.9	16.3
St. Joseph	21 579	74.8	44 800	16.9	12.6	345	25.4	3.0	33 179	1.4	1 068	3.2	26 307	20.1	13.9
Sanilac	14 658	79.4	42 400	18.8	15.0	337	26.1	2.6	21 367	2.5	1 358	6.4	15 998	18.9	14.1
Schoolcraft	3 294	77.0	32 300	18.3	13.3	273	29.5	2.2	4 373	1.7	413	9.4	2 862	21.8	10.2
Shiawassee	24 864	77.7	47 200	16.4	13.0	363	25.5	2.0	37 365	2.5	1 653	4.4	31 533	20.9	15.0
Tuscola	19 469	81.2	46 000	17.7	13.1	358	28.7	2.7	29 057	2.1	1 560	5.4	22 632	18.5	14.8
Van Buren	25 402	76.7	48 000	19.3	13.9	343	27.7	3.7	37 554	2.6	1 629	4.3	29 997	22.8	13.4
Washtenaw	104 528	55.3	96 000	19.9	13.1	536	27.8	3.1	177 932	3.5	3 219	1.8	151 680	42.9	7.7
Wayne	780 535	63.9	48 500	17.4	13.9	406	29.8	4.1	970 409	1.0	40 632	4.2	843 731	26.1	11.2
Wexford	9 923	74.7	41 200	17.2	13.2	356	28.1	3.1	15 458	6.3	1 030	6.7	10 540	24.4	12.2
MINNESOTA	1 647 853	71.8	74 000	20.4	12.4	422	26.7	2.4	2 698 511	0.6	75 453	2.8	2 192 417	30.3	10.1
Aitkin	5 126	83.9	48 600	23.0	14.1	243	28.2	4.5	6 013	0.8	449	7.5	4 445	21.0	12.6
Anoka	82 437	81.2	83 500	21.1	11.5	498	27.0	1.9	177 766	1.7	3 968	2.2	132 961	26.2	13.8
Becker	10 477	77.8	49 000	19.6	13.2	269	28.2	3.9	14 040	3.5	772	5.5	11 354	21.7	12.4
Beltrami	11 870	73.1	49 200	21.1	13.1	320	30.9	6.1	19 596	-0.7	1 010	5.2	13 931	29.7	8.9
Benton	10 935	67.0	60 800	19.3	12.9	395	26.0	2.7	20 357	3.6	636	3.1	14 938	21.8	12.2
Big Stone	2 463	80.9	27 000	17.1	12.7	227	27.6	1.5	2 656	-4.9	102	3.8	2 657	18.8	11.4
Blue Earth	19 277	64.0	59 500	18.3	12.3	374	29.0	2.3	33 658	2.2	778	2.3	27 709	24.9	10.3
Brown	10 321	77.3	48 900	16.3	12.0	283	24.6	2.0	14 553	-2.4	529	3.6	12 798	20.9	12.3
Carlton	10 842	81.1	45 200	16.4	12.2	291	26.9	3.4	16 164	4.3	674	4.2	11 846	24.7	12.8
Carver	16 601	79.0	95 700	22.4	12.5	442	25.2	1.8	39 185	2.2	848	2.2	26 057	27.9	12.4
Cass	8 302	82.9	50 500	21.4	13.8	294	27.5	4.9	12 290	3.6	734	6.0	7 683	22.1	12.5
Chippewa	5 245	75.4	34 200	17.5	12.5	267	24.9	1.4	6 732	-3.1	337	5.0	5 930	22.1	11.6
Chisago	10 551	85.0	72 600	22.3	12.6	375	28.9	1.8	21 105	3.5	692	3.3	13 992	23.1	14.7
Clay	17 490	68.3	58 600	18.1	12.2	335	31.7	3.0	29 774	-1.2	734	2.5	24 274	27.2	8.2
Clearwater	3 064	81.6	29 600	20.1	14.8	240	28.5	7.4	4 163	5.3	468	11.2	2 909	22.1	11.6
Cook	1 632	76.6	55 600	20.6	12.6	316	21.8	8.4	2 925	-0.2	111	3.8	1 782	27.1	10.7
Cottonwood	5 060	77.6	29 600	15.5	11.8	245	24.1	1.2	5 554	-1.4	247	4.4	5 527	20.7	8.7
Crow Wing	17 204	76.7	54 200	19.2	12.7	329	28.7	2.6	27 526	1.4	1 224	4.4	18 184	26.5	11.9
Dakota	98 293	73.9	95 900	21.9	11.9	542	25.3	1.8	212 219	1.9	3 945	1.9	153 515	34.2	9.6
Dodge	5 538	80.9	53 000	19.6	12.9	281	24.4	2.1	9 111	2.1	290	3.2	7 748	23.5	10.1
Douglas	10 988	74.2	56 400	20.7	12.7	297	28.2	2.3	16 410	-2.6	562	3.4	12 805	23.6	11.5
Faribault	6 772	78.8	32 200	14.6	12.6	265	23.1	1.3	7 862	-2.1	304	3.9	7 275	20.7	12.7
Fillmore	7 822	78.1	38 000	17.2	12.8	249	22.6	3.5	9 883	-0.5	326	3.3	9 479	18.6	10.8
Freeborn	13 029	76.7	42 800	17.1	12.3	286	24.9	1.7	16 751	1.8	442	2.6	14 897	21.8	10.4
Goodhue	15 198	76.5	63 300	18.0	12.6	321	24.5	1.5	23 184	-1.2	679	2.9	19 554	23.8	12.2

1. Specified owner-occupied units.   2. Specified renter-occupied units.   3. Overcrowded or lacking complete plumbing facilities.   4. Percent of civilian labor force.   5. Persons 16 years and older.

	Private nonfarm establishments, employment and payroll, 1998								Agriculture, 1997			
	Employment						Annual payroll		Farms			Farm operators
										Percent with—		
STATE County	Number of establishments	Total	Health Care and Social Assistance	Manufacturing	Retail trade	Finance and Insurance	Professional Scientific and Technical Services	Total (mil dol)	Average per employee (dollars)	Number	Less than 50 acres	500 acres and over	Whose principal occupation is farming (percent)
	104	105	106	107	108	109	110	111	112	113	114	115	116
MICHIGAN—Cont'd													
Leelanau	672	4 026	342	166	675	93	120	89	22 217	369	26.3	4.9	61.0
Lenawee	2 145	29 979	3 589	9 579	4 915	929	468	781	26 053	1 317	30.1	14.7	45.0
Livingston	3 629	42 785	3 702	10 516	7 099	2 103	1 591	1 217	28 443	637	51.8	6.9	43.6
Luce	197	1 533	295	185	299	65	D	33	21 563	31	29.0	22.6	29.0
Mackinac	533	2 714	280	116	D	122	53	69	25 337	72	15.3	15.3	45.8
Macomb	18 676	320 622	27 920	92 816	48 771	6 904	13 561	11 489	35 833	523	49.5	5.5	52.2
Manistee	643	5 737	1 086	1 434	957	190	80	132	23 060	284	23.2	6.7	47.9
Marquette	1 718	20 557	4 912	669	3 592	931	594	521	25 351	108	33.3	11.1	30.6
Mason	803	8 969	1 103	2 650	1 585	214	225	220	24 584	413	30.0	8.7	46.0
Mecosta	920	9 753	1 347	1 989	1 995	282	177	190	19 439	597	17.9	8.0	43.7
Menominee	539	6 956	618	2 822	790	236	130	159	22 843	348	14.1	19.3	50.9
Midland	1 951	36 652	5 643	6 574	5 044	D	964	1 418	38 685	418	33.7	9.6	40.4
Missaukee	325	2 148	D	577	474	70	29	44	20 324	335	17.9	18.2	57.0
Monroe	2 476	36 779	3 471	9 535	5 767	1 328	630	1 181	32 116	1 058	44.0	11.2	44.4
Montcalm	1 062	14 910	1 409	6 339	2 721	394	191	355	23 816	954	25.3	12.8	48.2
Montmorency	251	1 700	164	436	277	54	D	38	22 188	103	15.5	13.6	42.7
Muskegon	3 630	56 611	8 326	16 139	8 930	1 761	1 177	1 535	27 116	410	44.6	7.1	44.9
Newaygo	748	8 164	D	1 839	1 361	276	277	212	25 911	670	22.8	8.7	47.3
Oakland	41 626	746 998	78 155	90 903	85 093	48 635	75 544	29 478	39 462	544	66.9	2.2	34.7
Oceana	574	3 986	351	1 176	787	130	85	85	21 399	573	28.1	11.0	51.5
Ogemaw	611	5 355	989	936	1 400	126	102	103	19 193	261	15.3	13.8	50.2
Ontonagon	232	1 735	324	375	357	86	15	41	23 465	92	5.4	20.7	56.5
Osceola	433	6 946	648	3 818	D	108	110	168	24 141	496	16.5	8.5	45.4
Oscoda	221	1 696	190	514	340	D	29	29	16 979	80	21.2	5.0	53.8
Otsego	890	10 356	1 232	1 918	1 755	251	330	242	23 376	139	17.3	13.7	36.0
Ottawa	5 614	98 821	8 566	39 758	12 162	2 206	2 779	2 834	28 677	1 292	48.4	5.4	50.9
Presque Isle	438	3 263	323	272	864	121	64	69	21 186	296	12.2	12.8	48.3
Roscommon	702	4 840	542	352	1 490	235	71	86	17 854	36	44.4	2.8	38.9
Saginaw	5 035	86 367	13 855	20 261	14 944	2 916	2 953	2 716	31 446	1 163	30.0	13.8	55.0
St. Clair	3 577	47 265	6 832	12 457	8 224	1 297	1 020	1 255	26 548	940	35.0	6.7	45.3
St. Joseph	1 301	20 742	1 931	10 277	2 520	520	290	587	28 302	791	28.2	15.8	52.2
Sanilac	995	11 284	1 383	4 783	1 756	365	200	242	21 476	1 448	21.5	16.2	62.0
Schoolcraft	273	1 978	334	241	479	121	D	49	24 678	45	22.2	22.2	44.4
Shiawassee	1 309	15 644	2 401	3 733	3 091	458	365	352	22 482	915	30.1	12.9	45.1
Tuscola	1 101	12 441	2 614	2 801	2 143	428	151	290	23 307	1 140	25.4	16.8	53.6
Van Buren	1 451	16 113	2 038	4 770	2 631	331	499	415	25 745	1 059	37.5	6.1	50.0
Washtenaw	8 071	150 034	28 426	29 632	18 599	3 475	11 488	5 452	36 341	1 030	39.9	8.8	46.4
Wayne	36 089	755 495	103 494	129 792	87 598	33 703	31 744	27 507	36 410	303	65.3	5.9	45.2
Wexford	828	13 028	1 717	4 507	2 104	271	309	317	24 353	251	21.9	5.6	41.0
MINNESOTA	134 981	2 271 671	304 550	378 392	295 669	129 833	110 695	70 095	30 856	73 367	18.0	20.8	60.0
Aitkin	401	2 887	586	437	535	90	D	54	18 653	587	13.3	14.8	40.2
Anoka	6 278	92 836	10 346	23 701	13 960	1 510	2 880	2 913	31 379	473	49.0	4.4	35.9
Becker	953	14 405	1 285	1 412	1 922	195	189	275	19 068	1 084	11.4	16.4	53.5
Beltrami	989	11 744	2 365	1 227	2 500	280	238	248	21 129	656	8.5	21.0	47.0
Benton	672	10 806	891	2 744	1 860	100	217	264	24 407	834	21.9	7.8	53.8
Big Stone	204	1 604	452	71	346	68	D	26	16 107	420	13.1	45.7	71.7
Blue Earth	1 660	27 029	4 819	5 752	5 752	847	715	577	21 335	1 037	19.1	29.4	67.0
Brown	746	12 389	1 799	3 726	1 778	367	377	272	21 916	1 054	13.1	20.2	75.0
Carlton	673	7 964	1 128	2 145	1 404	310	144	229	28 800	527	12.9	5.9	40.4
Carver	1 646	25 950	2 459	9 880	2 546	445	1 346	770	29 669	779	28.5	5.6	60.5
Cass	770	4 873	564	182	1 035	161	137	83	17 131	598	13.9	17.6	49.0
Chippewa	393	4 485	596	1 277	898	182	77	91	20 252	618	14.7	33.7	74.6
Chisago	1 002	8 935	1 529	2 259	1 501	271	352	201	22 446	762	30.8	5.8	37.1
Clay	1 132	14 804	1 881	1 177	2 800	357	329	274	18 508	887	14.0	39.8	69.6
Clearwater	202	1 957	508	301	262	73	115	37	18 772	570	6.3	19.6	50.4
Cook	259	1 842	161	110	306	D	27	34	18 292	11	9.1	9.1	18.2
Cottonwood	389	3 879	880	982	742	161	74	69	17 915	784	11.5	37.0	73.3
Crow Wing	1 817	19 398	3 377	2 825	3 964	499	1 061	449	23 165	593	20.9	10.6	42.7
Dakota	8 099	140 687	11 420	17 402	23 073	5 777	5 512	4 590	32 626	890	36.3	14.4	49.7
Dodge	401	3 436	153	1 041	532	126	69	90	26 164	674	24.6	22.0	60.7
Douglas	1 198	13 232	1 984	2 748	2 637	296	336	285	21 554	1 042	14.8	11.0	57.1
Faribault	514	4 749	758	1 458	622	219	128	97	20 332	878	13.4	35.0	76.5
Fillmore	663	5 430	936	1 238	977	256	124	98	18 041	1 546	19.2	16.2	62.5
Freeborn	933	11 966	2 073	3 206	2 129	351	229	257	21 458	1 151	25.0	24.0	63.6
Goodhue	1 245	19 286	2 597	5 087	2 430	589	395	452	23 457	1 489	25.5	14.4	57.0

Table B. States and Counties — Agriculture, Land, and Water

STATE County	Agriculture, 1997 (cont'd)															
	Land in farms					Value of land and buildings		Value of machinery and equipment Average per farm ($1,000)	Value of products sold				Percent of farms with sales of —		Percent of land owned by Fed. Gov. 1997	Water consumption 1995 (mil gal/day)
			Acres								Percent from —					
	Acreage (1,000)	Percent change, 1992–1997	Average size of farm	Total irrigated (1,000)	Total cropland (1,000)	Average per farm ($1,000)	Average per acre (dollars)		Total (mil dol)	Average per farm (dollars)	Crops	Live-stock and poultry products	$10,000 or more	$100,000 or more		
	117	118	119	120	121	122	123	124	125	126	127	128	129	130	131	†32
MICHIGAN—Cont'd																
Leelanau	62	-4.4	168	2	38	500	3 087	70	29	77 845	82.9	17.1	64.2	20.6	19.0	7.2
Lenawee	336	0.1	255	3	302	444	1 720	72	103	78 093	76.2	23.8	54.7	19.6	0.0	24.4
Livingston	98	-17.4	154	2	75	399	2 360	71	28	44 671	65.1	34.9	42.4	11.0	0.0	24.8
Luce	D	D	D	D	7	336	902	53	2	75 029	81.5	18.5	45.2	19.4	0.0	1.2
Mackinac	22	-2.2	299	D	14	196	657	34	3	35 373	13.5	86.5	36.1	4.2	22.3	14.7
Macomb	69	-1.7	132	2	59	430	3 446	61	45	85 534	92.3	7.7	54.1	16.4	0.9	80.0
Manistee	48	-1.0	167	3	28	239	1 368	47	9	32 030	89.2	10.8	33.8	7.7	24.3	37.2
Marquette	27	15.8	247	0	12	261	1 060	37	3	27 278	38.2	61.8	25.9	6.5	1.7	257.0
Mason	77	5.6	187	3	56	245	1 127	50	24	57 194	67.8	32.2	47.9	13.8	21.4	27.5
Mecosta	112	-7.5	188	7	82	217	1 270	50	25	41 651	40.4	59.6	37.9	8.9	0.7	15.9
Menominee	110	-0.3	315	0	63	226	728	60	18	52 592	13.3	86.7	46.0	16.7	0.0	7.6
Midland	80	-10.5	191	1	62	346	1 642	64	17	41 278	76.1	23.9	42.3	10.8	0.0	88.5
Missaukee	90	2.3	269	2	66	289	1 046	80	35	103 575	13.5	86.5	50.1	24.2	0.0	4.6
Monroe	210	-3.4	198	5	196	447	2 293	77	94	88 977	89.8	10.2	57.8	17.7	0.0	1 763.5
Montcalm	238	6.1	249	45	186	316	1 262	76	88	92 096	71.9	28.1	46.8	15.9	0.4	26.8
Montmorency	21	-4.4	204	D	14	200	993	46	3	31 755	36.7	63.3	39.8	8.7	0.0	2.8
Muskegon	73	-1.2	178	8	53	283	1 631	69	44	108 379	54.0	46.0	42.7	17.1	5.5	321.7
Newaygo	122	6.3	183	4	90	236	1 341	57	49	72 449	41.5	58.5	47.9	15.7	19.8	17.2
Oakland	45	-5.5	83	1	33	486	5 645	49	32	59 654	91.6	8.4	33.3	8.8	0.0	110.8
Oceana	128	-0.8	223	3	86	295	1 327	68	50	86 896	74.7	25.3	55.5	18.0	15.1	8.2
Ogemaw	73	-2.3	281	0	51	294	1 111	74	22	84 841	13.6	86.4	52.5	19.5	6.1	3.6
Ontonagon	33	-1.5	353		17	169	479	37	2	23 963	24.9	75.1	30.4	5.4	30.2	30.6
Osceola	108	-0.7	218	1	72	242	1 120	59	19	38 879	17.7	82.3	37.1	11.1	0.0	6.9
Oscoda	14	-0.7	174	0	8	195	1 121	25	2	23 494	19.1	80.9	43.8	3.8	41.5	1.5
Otsego	34	-4.3	248	1	19	343	1 300	62	4	27 407	65.7	34.3	30.2	7.2	0.0	4.2
Ottawa	171	-3.1	132	15	141	396	3 066	78	300	232 187	53.4	46.6	58.0	26.2	0.0	639.7
Presque Isle	82	3.1	279	3	54	204	878	37	13	44 206	59.7	40.3	41.2	11.8	0.3	6.3
Roscommon	4	3.5	115	0	3	149	1 299	23	1	14 255	73.1	26.9	41.7	0.0	0.0	3.6
Saginaw	298	-6.3	256	3	268	459	1 711	80	84	72 256	89.0	11.0	63.5	18.1	1.6	30.9
St. Clair	163	-10.5	173	1	141	416	2 517	56	36	38 378	76.7	23.3	43.7	8.2	0.0	1 562.5
St. Joseph	217	-7.5	275	91	185	504	1 762	96	81	102 533	77.1	22.9	59.2	20.0	0.0	58.1
Sanilac	430	-3.2	297	4	381	401	1 379	92	133	91 514	56.6	43.4	60.6	23.3	0.0	16.8
Schoolcraft	16	12.4	350	D	9	294	842	37	1	27 326	47.6	52.4	44.4	6.7	27.9	12.0
Shiawassee	214	-9.6	234	1	184	366	1 547	85	45	49 399	72.2	27.8	55.1	13.8	0.0	12.1
Tuscola	333	2.8	292	9	292	512	1 800	104	106	92 739	80.7	19.3	56.8	23.1	0.0	12.7
Van Buren	177	-14.3	167	20	136	322	1 789	67	101	95 034	86.6	13.4	51.9	17.0	0.0	102.1
Washtenaw	180	-4.6	175	5	153	507	2 892	56	57	54 874	61.1	38.9	47.7	12.9	0.1	54.6
Wayne	39	77.7	129	1	30	447	3 790	66	27	89 635	96.2	3.8	46.2	14.5	0.0	2 165.4
Wexford	43	39.7	173	0	29	200	1 171	36	9	34 621	63.8	36.2	32.3	7.2	30.9	8.7
MINNESOTA	25 995	1.3	354	380	21 492	408	1 164	85	8 290	112 997	50.7	49.3	64.4	28.1	6.2	3 391.5
Aitkin	164	-2.7	279	5	81	161	518	35	14	24 563	36.2	63.8	30.7	4.8	1.2	5.0
Anoka	57	-7.6	121	2	40	315	2 697	58	24	50 305	70.5	29.5	37.8	9.3	0.0	142.2
Becker	389	2.8	359	2	269	233	652	57	100	92 131	33.4	66.6	49.9	17.3	4.4	5.1
Beltrami	225	0.0	343	3	121	154	509	36	17	26 267	30.4	69.6	40.7	5.0	4.5	7.8
Benton	176	-4.2	211	11	131	212	986	71	90	107 446	21.8	78.2	59.7	21.3	0.0	18.3
Big Stone	254	-3.1	605	1	227	506	815	100	55	130 039	70.1	29.9	78.1	36.9	3.1	1.4
Blue Earth	403	5.3	389	1	370	738	1 941	113	221	213 568	44.8	55.2	79.3	43.1	0.0	32.1
Brown	350	1.0	332	3	321	588	1 778	103	182	172 526	42.8	57.2	89.2	41.5	0.0	3.7
Carlton	107	-5.2	203	0	56	142	590	38	8	16 035	19.6	80.4	25.6	2.7	0.0	22.4
Carver	153	-7.7	197	1	126	418	2 075	101	62	79 661	36.8	63.2	65.5	26.4	0.0	7.8
Cass	192	-4.1	321	3	95	178	574	31	21	34 514	12.2	87.8	42.5	6.0	17.3	4.0
Chippewa	318	-2.6	515	2	298	677	1 304	129	101	163 804	82.6	17.4	79.8	43.9	0.0	9.5
Chisago	122	-12.6	159	1	84	262	1 618	46	30	39 696	62.2	37.8	37.1	9.6	0.7	3.8
Clay	581	2.5	655	4	529	666	1 035	127	138	155 202	81.7	18.3	69.4	38.2	1.3	7.9
Clearwater	212	0.6	372	7	115	161	459	36	20	35 826	45.3	54.7	47.5	5.6	0.0	13.4
Cook	D	D	D	D	1	213	1 051	35	0	9 210	77.2	22.8	18.2	0.0	62.4	126.1
Cottonwood	368	-1.8	470	1	333	653	1 387	121	160	204 420	49.8	50.2	85.1	51.1	0.5	3.2
Crow Wing	135	3.3	228	1	69	186	846	34	14	23 978	27.1	72.9	36.6	5.4	0.1	9.0
Dakota	221	0.1	249	41	196	570	2 268	96	103	115 707	62.5	37.5	61.7	26.1	0.5	224.2
Dodge	247	2.4	366	D	224	579	1 599	104	105	155 481	55.8	44.2	70.2	36.1	0.0	2.0
Douglas	268	3.0	257	2	201	202	799	55	59	56 508	36.2	63.8	55.5	17.9	2.1	5.5
Faribault	413	-0.4	471	0	389	783	1 681	133	171	194 818	66.3	33.7	90.2	53.9	0.0	2.8
Fillmore	435	-1.9	281	0	327	297	1 048	77	148	95 900	41.3	58.7	68.1	26.8	0.0	14.7
Freeborn	380	3.4	330	1	351	523	1 603	95	163	141 674	61.6	38.4	73.5	38.8	0.2	6.6
Goodhue	385	1.2	258	2	315	384	1 537	76	161	107 886	40.3	59.7	69.0	31.1	0.3	599.8

Table B. States and Counties — Residential Construction, Wholesale and Retail Trade, and Real Estate

STATE County	Value of Residential Construction Authorized by Building Permits, 1999		Wholesale Trade, 1997				Retail Trade[1], 1997				Real Estate and Rental and Leasing, 1997			
	New Construction ($1,000)	Number of Housing Units	Number of Establishments	Number of Employees	Sales (mil dol)	Annual Payroll (mil dol)	Number of Establishments	Number of Employees	Sales (mil dol)	Annual Payroll (mil dol)	Number of Establishments	Number of Employees	Receipts (mil dol)	Annual Payroll (mil dol)
	133	134	135	136	137	138	139	140	141	142	143	144	145	146
MICHIGAN—Cont'd														
Leelanau	45 253	386	18	90	20.0	1.7	143	661	92.0	10.5	23	59	4.6	1.0
Lenawee	75 862	639	92	685	429.5	22.6	375	4 859	826.3	75.8	80	270	31.5	4.1
Livingston	191 192	2 105	246	1 859	1 064.1	73.2	476	6 435	1 308.4	121.7	117	439	55.5	7.7
Luce	2 360	58	10	61	10.8	1.2	36	333	64.7	4.6	5	28	4.0	0.3
Mackinac	13 255	149	12	92	29.6	1.6	133	448	83.7	8.2	16	22	2.0	0.6
Macomb	694 080	5 648	1 040	12 592	6 608.7	521.7	2 901	47 125	9 010.8	859.9	625	3 058	456.3	64.0
Manistee	10 512	92	26	D	D	D	116	947	189.8	16.3	15	44	3.9	0.7
Marquette	19 877	250	68	545	159.1	15.4	331	3 822	522.7	51.1	66	286	21.8	4.2
Mason	15 939	173	25	118	41.0	3.2	159	1 470	223.0	21.0	19	62	7.4	0.8
Mecosta	21 223	307	31	187	43.0	4.9	175	1 925	301.1	25.6	46	115	10.2	1.7
Menominee	8 842	142	24	337	192.4	10.5	85	967	162.0	12.5	9	30	3.8	0.6
Midland	31 410	300	73	758	311.0	29.0	353	4 449	722.1	72.2	60	223	27.2	3.5
Missaukee	8 902	88	11	57	17.6	1.3	57	506	103.1	7.8	9	18	1.5	0.2
Monroe	101 241	896	96	1 213	731.5	46.2	448	5 489	1 035.0	91.1	74	278	30.0	4.4
Montcalm	22 162	281	48	287	158.7	7.1	217	2 613	403.7	36.5	20	64	7.2	1.0
Montmorency	8 261	105	3	D	D	D	48	312	49.9	4.1	10	47	1.6	0.3
Muskegon	92 132	919	162	1 852	891.4	57.6	591	8 672	1 365.4	132.3	112	469	55.5	7.2
Newaygo	17 563	252	27	323	56.0	9.4	156	1 394	244.2	22.8	21	54	4.5	0.7
Oakland	1 046 060	7 078	3 526	45 311	68 519.0	2 332.1	5 530	83 826	16 585.0	1 623.9	1 772	14 568	1 987.1	390.9
Oceana	12 276	123	11	72	14.6	2.3	110	786	124.3	10.7	13	24	2.3	0.4
Ogemaw	7 714	144	18	207	69.9	6.0	148	1 351	230.8	20.1	23	58	4.1	0.7
Ontonagon	750	15	2	D	D	D	51	388	60.4	5.2	3	2	0.1	0.0
Osceola	19 555	219	11	129	51.2	3.0	88	694	105.5	9.8	4	19	2.4	0.3
Oscoda	6 496	72	3	D	D	D	44	318	44.7	4.2	9	16	1.3	0.3
Otsego	22 014	223	38	387	207.8	11.3	163	1 903	334.8	29.9	31	184	12.1	1.9
Ottawa	259 244	2 027	326	3 471	2 213.3	110.2	828	12 375	1 920.7	193.1	168	774	93.6	15.9
Presque Isle	11 534	125	15	181	41.7	3.6	93	768	122.5	11.0	9	21	1.6	0.3
Roscommon	21 546	272	22	72	10.5	1.3	149	1 553	267.0	25.5	26	51	3.5	0.6
Saginaw	74 449	609	269	3 643	1 614.3	120.1	1 101	14 917	2 477.0	228.2	155	820	80.1	14.0
St. Clair	107 631	974	131	1 415	596.4	50.6	629	7 801	1 315.1	124.8	102	444	53.9	7.6
St. Joseph	24 378	226	59	680	252.1	27.8	230	2 627	399.3	37.4	52	199	19.7	3.0
Sanilac	15 586	231	37	238	99.5	5.2	183	1 707	287.6	25.7	29	105	9.3	2.2
Schoolcraft	3 810	73	12	D	D	D	56	410	78.6	6.2	8	17	0.9	0.2
Shiawassee	27 435	271	67	476	182.6	11.5	234	3 080	571.4	46.6	37	148	63.8	3.8
Tuscola	15 967	239	54	408	202.4	9.8	212	2 048	412.6	33.1	22	68	6.2	0.8
Van Buren	36 634	464	61	405	160.5	11.7	267	2 694	503.8	44.2	48	169	11.8	2.1
Washtenaw	375 850	2 617	435	4 778	3 338.4	182.3	1 204	18 464	3 371.9	329.6	315	2 147	184.5	47.9
Wayne	476 769	4 187	2 357	40 193	37 963.4	1 614.4	6 690	85 476	15 852.1	1 483.7	1 256	9 014	1 478.6	225.7
Wexford	16 595	174	29	334	83.5	9.0	174	2 127	359.1	33.1	28	156	12.7	2.2
MINNESOTA	4 052 938	33 344	9 348	131 787	99 444.5	5 024.0	20 883	282 282	48 077.7	4 525.7	5 051	30 172	3 886.4	687.2
Aitkin	20 204	213	16	D	D	D	60	490	77.7	6.5	9	26	1.3	0.2
Anoka	330 755	2 740	351	4 520	1 824.1	161.2	826	13 478	2 232.6	206.0	235	1 166	117.9	18.0
Becker	19 657	185	42	263	78.6	7.4	182	1 609	258.6	22.7	29	107	7.8	1.7
Beltrami	7 482	120	44	414	101.2	10.0	200	2 453	365.8	34.5	24	89	18.4	1.1
Benton	19 316	194	45	1 083	535.4	28.4	102	1 356	186.8	20.6	15	65	6.8	1.2
Big Stone	1 325	11	15	D	D	D	42	254	26.9	2.6	4	D	D	D
Blue Earth	25 575	244	108	1 520	558.0	39.0	325	5 166	744.4	70.4	62	344	29.2	6.2
Brown	7 796	64	41	438	417.7	9.8	152	1 850	234.7	22.2	23	84	9.2	1.4
Carlton	13 834	173	25	417	193.2	11.5	129	1 364	226.6	19.5	12	62	5.7	0.7
Carver	155 283	1 004	122	2 205	570.1	59.8	177	2 389	413.8	40.0	61	320	32.3	8.1
Cass	53 598	523	18	D	D	D	163	959	164.8	15.9	17	45	4.9	0.9
Chippewa	3 066	31	27	240	191.4	6.9	75	844	125.9	10.8	13	51	1.6	0.3
Chisago	77 691	695	33	D	D	D	148	1 421	221.9	20.0	39	171	7.4	1.5
Clay	27 714	299	67	765	410.6	17.8	193	2 828	458.0	37.8	38	127	10.1	1.4
Clearwater	400	4	10	75	17.7	1.4	40	260	34.5	3.0	3	8	0.3	0.1
Cook	7 121	82	2	D	D	D	48	271	44.0	4.5	19	30	3.9	0.5
Cottonwood	1 784	18	28	206	169.6	4.5	72	665	103.2	8.7	7	21	1.1	0.4
Crow Wing	71 851	705	79	713	178.7	16.4	376	3 749	708.3	61.9	76	220	28.3	3.5
Dakota	441 102	3 377	686	9 650	5 578.3	359.6	1 140	22 202	4 010.9	374.2	331	1 597	237.1	34.3
Dodge	22 510	213	22	321	156.1	10.1	68	448	70.5	6.5	6	23	16.6	0.5
Douglas	34 799	360	56	488	174.6	13.1	233	2 472	368.7	33.3	48	126	13.1	1.9
Faribault	1 935	17	40	D	D	D	84	634	80.5	7.7	6	7	0.9	0.1
Fillmore	9 638	97	35	319	240.8	8.4	135	810	149.2	12.7	9	11	1.7	0.1
Freeborn	13 012	144	68	646	522.1	19.1	183	1 965	310.8	29.5	21	61	6.6	0.6
Goodhue	29 448	240	63	1 051	680.4	31.3	244	2 390	337.0	32.7	43	107	10.9	1.6

1. Establishments with payroll.

Table B. States and Counties — **Professional, Manufacturing, and Accommodation and Foodservices**

STATE County	Professional, Scientific, and Technical Services[1], 1997				Manufacturing, 1997				Accommodation and Foodservices, 1997			
	Number of Establishments	Number of Employees	Receipts (mil dol)	Annual Payroll (mil dol)	Number of Establishments	Number of Employees	Receipts (mil dol)	Annual Payroll (mil dol)	Number of Establishments	Number of Employees	Sales (mil dol)	Annual Payroll (mil dol)
	147	148	149	150	151	152	153	154	155	156	157	158
MICHIGAN—Cont'd												
Leelanau	36	220	11.5	4.4	NA	NA	NA	NA	78	884	32.5	10.1
Lenawee	106	371	23.5	9.4	163	8 940	1 736.1	359.3	182	2 485	73.5	19.6
Livingston	288	1 629	103.7	50.5	264	10 560	2 782.8	374.1	193	3 494	116.1	29.9
Luce	7	16	0.7	0.2	NA	NA	NA	NA	33	275	7.3	2.0
Mackinac	21	109	10.2	4.9	NA	NA	NA	NA	129	723	50.4	13.3
Macomb	1 305	11 709	1 069.4	509.2	2 116	93 551	23 988.0	4 321.9	1 342	24 413	796.5	216.4
Manistee	28	77	4.7	2.0	31	1 300	244.6	48.4	73	671	18.5	5.2
Marquette	120	590	35.2	16.7	39	730	81.0	16.0	175	2 642	64.7	20.1
Mason	53	190	12.6	4.9	40	2 682	435.8	84.2	80	1 010	29.5	8.4
Mecosta	41	141	9.6	3.8	41	1 837	363.2	50.7	87	1 587	41.2	11.4
Menominee	26	92	5.0	2.5	56	2 901	425.2	78.0	51	D	D	D
Midland	142	697	71.5	23.4	71	5 613	1 690.8	285.4	132	2 688	78.1	22.9
Missaukee	9	32	2.4	0.8	23	548	73.0	17.5	25	179	4.6	1.2
Monroe	120	501	36.3	14.1	138	9 278	2 560.1	425.6	219	3 339	98.0	26.2
Montcalm	35	134	5.7	1.4	77	5 456	923.8	172.0	89	1 027	27.7	7.5
Montmorency	12	25	1.6	0.7	NA	NA	NA	NA	38	275	7.1	1.7
Muskegon	229	1 087	91.2	40.4	335	16 398	2 903.3	562.1	321	5 256	153.8	42.2
Newaygo	37	258	11.6	4.7	46	1 727	484.7	51.7	62	686	19.9	5.4
Oakland	5 522	60 999	6 922.0	2 990.6	2 366	90 481	27 172.7	3 747.5	2 453	48 174	1 668.0	478.6
Oceana	21	96	5.6	1.7	51	1 385	214.5	31.2	66	410	16.9	5.2
Ogemaw	24	78	7.4	2.1	29	872	85.9	23.3	69	654	20.8	5.7
Ontonagon	9	15	0.8	0.4	NA	NA	NA	NA	40	303	6.5	1.8
Osceola	20	58	3.9	1.8	36	3 582	661.3	99.2	43	334	10.6	2.6
Oscoda	6	27	0.8	0.3	NA	NA	NA	NA	24	210	5.6	1.7
Otsego	51	317	19.4	8.0	39	1 870	255.5	53.8	69	1 686	56.9	18.3
Ottawa	344	2 565	192.0	91.9	591	38 244	7 688.1	1 310.8	328	6 073	173.2	50.4
Presque Isle	14	59	2.2	1.3	NA	NA	NA	NA	57	295	9.1	2.5
Roscommon	28	61	3.8	1.5	NA	NA	NA	NA	79	994	26.5	7.5
Saginaw	320	2 908	195.1	86.5	239	20 681	5 172.2	1 148.6	408	9 236	270.5	78.9
St. Clair	176	851	56.8	25.2	294	14 162	2 667.6	431.5	290	4 520	138.3	38.4
St. Joseph	49	244	12.6	6.1	163	10 651	2 402.7	371.4	128	1 436	45.5	11.4
Sanilac	42	164	9.7	2.3	88	5 244	726.3	123.6	75	736	21.3	6.1
Schoolcraft	9	24	0.9	0.4	NA	NA	NA	NA	43	221	7.5	1.9
Shiawassee	70	334	26.5	11.9	86	4 139	453.8	99.6	110	1 467	41.1	11.0
Tuscola	43	127	9.0	3.0	65	2 818	486.4	96.9	84	1 101	29.0	8.2
Van Buren	77	439	37.2	13.7	127	4 879	1 007.8	152.1	146	1 677	51.6	15.1
Washtenaw	993	7 818	954.4	380.0	412	29 254	7 350.2	1 395.5	627	13 266	430.2	119.5
Wayne	2 512	29 950	3 133.0	1 233.0	2 390	133 703	54 375.0	6 514.3	3 313	58 336	2 023.7	542.5
Wexford	42	257	18.2	8.4	57	4 331	719.1	126.7	88	1 487	39.7	11.6
MINNESOTA	12 391	96 677	10 447.9	4 091.3	8 091	382 530	76 244.9	13 126.1	9 982	179 487	5 934.2	1 688.8
Aitkin	15	87	3.1	1.6	NA	NA	NA	NA	59	469	16.5	4.4
Anoka	533	2 440	167.8	68.0	614	24 754	3 860.7	908.7	351	7 744	215.4	62.3
Becker	45	157	9.9	4.2	42	1 320	193.0	35.7	104	973	33.3	8.4
Beltrami	47	208	13.3	6.0	43	1 112	175.9	32.0	100	1 339	40.9	11.4
Benton	25	179	12.9	5.4	53	2 797	300.2	71.4	53	962	26.8	7.5
Big Stone	8	28	1.5	0.8	NA	NA	NA	NA	21	155	3.3	0.8
Blue Earth	90	596	48.6	16.6	78	4 144	1 160.8	126.7	137	2 657	72.6	19.5
Brown	44	367	23.1	9.7	41	4 292	1 580.8	113.0	62	1 044	23.5	6.5
Carlton	33	133	7.2	3.1	30	2 131	425.0	89.8	74	808	23.4	6.4
Carver	140	1 096	75.2	31.5	143	10 470	1 920.0	391.7	109	1 566	43.6	12.8
Cass	34	100	6.6	2.5	NA	NA	NA	NA	121	669	26.8	6.0
Chippewa	13	61	3.4	1.5	24	1 498	116.3	34.5	30	329	7.6	2.0
Chisago	63	297	13.0	6.3	101	2 462	282.1	70.3	67	772	18.5	5.2
Clay	56	307	24.9	9.6	38	1 225	229.4	35.7	107	1 615	40.7	11.4
Clearwater	10	D	D	D	NA	NA	NA	NA	20	D	D	D
Cook	13	D	D	D	NA	NA	NA	NA	71	748	36.1	9.8
Cottonwood	18	66	3.4	1.7	16	930	486.9	20.5	24	258	6.0	1.6
Crow Wing	94	784	67.1	25.1	95	2 957	458.3	91.2	211	2 480	121.3	33.2
Dakota	854	4 016	399.0	151.1	439	17 957	5 922.4	636.3	488	11 244	344.9	100.8
Dodge	18	50	2.7	1.0	29	1 322	398.6	37.5	24	D	D	D
Douglas	54	270	15.7	7.8	72	2 806	448.4	76.0	106	1 258	42.2	11.1
Faribault	22	85	3.3	1.3	28	1 578	260.6	36.5	31	D	D	D
Fillmore	28	87	3.5	1.2	42	1 122	224.8	27.9	60	D	D	D
Freeborn	33	202	14.6	5.9	66	3 062	564.5	86.7	79	978	26.5	7.0
Goodhue	66	286	27.2	9.5	81	5 522	972.8	166.6	104	1 623	39.4	12.0

1. Firms subject to federal tax.

Table B. States and Counties — Health and Other Services and Federal Funds

STATE County	Health Care and Social Assistance[1], 1997				Other Services[1], 1997				Federal funds and grants, fiscal 1999[2]			
									Expenditures (mil dol)			
									Total	Direct payments for individuals[3]		
	Number of Establishments	Number of Employees	Receipts (mil dol)	Annual Payroll (mil dol)	Number of Establishments	Number of Employees	Receipts (mil dol)	Annual Payroll (mil dol)		Social Security and government retirement	Medicare	Food stamps and Supplemental Security Income
	159	160	161	162	163	164	165	166	167	168	169	170
MICHIGAN—Cont'd												
Leelanau	34	147	8.8	3.7	26	145	11.3	2.7	60.2	36.3	11.2	1.0
Lenawee	183	1 335	71.3	33.2	134	605	38.8	12.0	346.6	174.0	71.0	10.4
Livingston	246	2 017	98.3	49.0	209	1 109	82.4	25.5	288.2	153.2	58.7	4.3
Luce	11	D	D	D	7	37	2.6	0.5	34.3	15.0	7.1	1.3
Mackinac	17	76	3.5	1.5	14	57	2.9	0.8	52.3	27.2	10.2	0.9
Macomb	1 492	14 800	995.8	477.1	1 366	8 618	573.3	184.6	3 479.3	1 425.3	708.8	50.7
Manistee	59	448	18.3	8.4	32	101	6.0	1.5	108.1	59.0	22.7	2.9
Marquette	137	1 582	98.4	56.2	99	485	29.1	7.9	270.6	139.7	48.3	5.7
Mason	74	509	27.3	12.9	36	166	9.6	2.9	114.9	61.9	21.7	3.7
Mecosta	68	612	27.1	13.5	61	276	14.2	4.1	136.2	69.2	21.8	5.3
Menominee	32	351	11.6	5.6	32	106	7.7	1.8	101.1	53.3	17.0	2.1
Midland	202	1 822	112.6	56.3	124	698	46.4	12.0	244.7	129.8	43.6	7.7
Missaukee	21	154	5.6	2.5	13	27	2.7	0.4	48.0	25.1	8.9	1.6
Monroe	171	1 480	90.2	41.9	141	892	60.7	22.4	426.5	229.3	100.1	12.7
Montcalm	73	596	31.7	13.9	76	350	22.4	6.5	217.2	108.1	43.1	7.4
Montmorency	13	179	6.2	3.1	11	30	2.4	0.5	61.6	36.6	13.8	1.8
Muskegon	272	2 682	157.8	82.2	234	1 299	67.2	21.8	744.5	316.4	116.6	35.5
Newaygo	43	542	26.3	12.3	53	187	12.4	2.7	149.0	77.9	27.3	6.0
Oakland	3 713	35 580	2 427.4	1 186.9	2 108	16 274	1 133.6	363.1	3 931.6	1 907.5	906.7	96.6
Oceana	31	192	7.4	3.9	41	107	6.0	1.4	103.9	52.3	18.3	3.9
Ogemaw	52	499	21.9	9.8	37	169	9.2	2.6	96.5	51.4	20.4	4.2
Ontonagon	10	120	3.9	2.0	8	32	2.8	0.4	59.6	23.0	8.8	0.9
Osceola	24	178	9.9	3.9	29	80	4.5	1.1	100.1	49.5	17.5	3.7
Oscoda	11	D	D	D	11	31	2.4	0.4	36.5	20.2	8.1	1.6
Otsego	66	499	28.1	12.1	55	250	20.9	4.9	95.2	44.8	13.2	2.1
Ottawa	332	4 128	213.1	105.4	346	2 032	141.6	40.5	655.1	319.5	89.6	9.5
Presque Isle	25	247	12.7	4.2	27	74	5.8	1.1	72.6	42.0	13.5	1.7
Roscommon	40	473	21.2	9.2	48	125	7.8	2.1	143.7	84.8	34.5	4.5
Saginaw	410	3 465	248.1	121.5	336	2 127	126.7	39.1	937.2	398.6	165.8	51.4
St. Clair	271	2 176	148.7	72.5	242	1 229	87.2	24.0	510.0	232.1	112.1	15.9
St. Joseph	98	805	36.6	15.3	97	578	40.2	13.8	214.6	108.2	42.0	7.0
Sanilac	82	527	25.2	10.5	59	189	15.2	2.8	183.8	84.6	39.0	4.7
Schoolcraft	8	136	5.7	3.5	19	55	3.6	0.8	54.8	23.3	9.6	1.3
Shiawassee	114	972	54.2	28.1	84	443	25.8	8.1	246.1	126.9	54.8	8.1
Tuscola	81	923	32.6	15.5	72	352	19.4	5.8	213.2	104.5	42.2	6.7
Van Buren	94	688	34.6	16.0	95	330	18.4	5.4	294.8	131.0	53.8	11.4
Washtenaw	703	6 534	525.1	228.3	392	2 628	158.7	53.6	1 446.0	377.0	162.4	24.5
Wayne	3 115	35 576	2 186.2	1 040.1	2 621	20 451	1 407.6	440.8	10 602.9	3 656.9	2 206.8	634.3
Wexford	67	477	33.2	15.5	51	304	17.4	5.0	138.9	61.7	21.0	3.5
MINNESOTA	8 033	106 839	5 864.5	2 946.0	7 614	55 723	3 394.6	1 103.6	21 665.8	7 557.0	2 699.6	465.3
Aitkin	12	264	7.3	3.6	11	30	3.0	0.6	83.9	40.9	12.9	1.8
Anoka	384	5 016	282.6	143.4	399	2 502	170.0	49.4	1 148.2	255.9	75.2	10.0
Becker	30	424	21.0	8.4	63	668	21.5	8.5	150.7	57.3	18.3	3.9
Beltrami	65	995	47.5	25.5	62	574	23.3	6.6	183.6	62.8	22.7	7.8
Benton	29	491	18.8	9.2	38	174	13.7	2.9	103.8	62.0	11.1	4.1
Big Stone	8	48	2.7	0.8	14	34	2.4	0.4	37.8	14.1	5.6	0.6
Blue Earth	118	2 027	103.3	53.6	101	662	36.1	10.6	215.9	92.9	27.1	5.1
Brown	35	414	18.1	9.9	47	190	12.4	3.3	112.1	53.9	17.5	1.6
Carlton	39	292	16.0	7.3	43	110	8.0	2.1	144.0	65.5	20.9	2.5
Carver	79	922	51.3	29.7	76	675	46.5	18.7	139.9	59.4	20.5	1.2
Cass	20	193	7.9	3.6	21	62	4.2	1.0	146.9	62.5	21.2	3.7
Chippewa	21	171	8.6	4.0	20	86	7.6	1.6	61.9	25.1	7.6	0.8
Chisago	49	1 150	47.6	27.8	50	192	11.8	2.6	105.4	61.3	20.4	2.1
Clay	56	496	24.9	11.6	76	299	17.9	4.9	187.6	83.0	26.5	6.8
Clearwater	12	71	3.6	2.0	8	21	2.2	0.2	44.2	15.9	6.7	1.4
Cook	2	D	D	D	4	8	0.7	0.2	26.4	10.7	2.7	0.2
Cottonwood	28	310	9.6	4.6	29	76	5.9	1.2	68.9	27.5	9.8	1.1
Crow Wing	99	1 353	63.0	35.8	84	352	21.1	5.2	228.6	124.0	39.5	6.3
Dakota	501	7 009	344.1	156.2	488	4 515	279.0	101.7	709.2	342.0	84.6	12.0
Dodge	16	66	3.3	1.5	34	173	14.3	4.7	61.9	23.1	10.0	0.9
Douglas	61	573	34.2	16.9	65	241	15.1	3.6	131.5	66.7	20.6	2.2
Faribault	33	150	7.0	2.8	27	55	5.3	0.9	90.0	38.1	13.6	1.2
Fillmore	27	263	10.5	4.7	32	74	7.0	1.2	100.1	43.0	18.1	1.3
Freeborn	47	447	33.3	14.2	50	225	9.8	2.4	157.0	73.6	24.4	2.9
Goodhue	65	764	39.2	14.2	74	383	29.0	6.3	153.1	76.8	25.6	1.8

1. Firms subject to federal tax.   2. October 1, 1998 to September 30, 1999.   3. State totals may include programs not allocated by county.

Table B. States and Counties — Federal Funds and Local Government Finances

STATE County	Federal funds and grants, fiscal 1999[1] (cont'd)							Local government finances, 1997				
	Expenditures (mil dol) (cont'd)							General revenue				
	Procurement contract awards			Grants[2]							Taxes	
											Per capita[3] (dollars)	
	Salaries and wages	Defense	Other	Medicaid and other health-related	Nutrition and family welfare	Education	Other	Total (mil dol)	Intergovern-mental (mil dol)	Total (mil dol)	Total	Property
	171	172	173	174	175	176	177	178	179	180	181	182
MICHIGAN—Cont'd												
Leelanau	5.1	0.2	0.9	2.5	1.0	0.9	0.4	36.1	14.2	16.1	859	835
Lenawee	11.6	0.4	2.9	34.5	11.5	4.7	6.3	228.8	140.4	50.6	517	470
Livingston	13.7	3.4	3.7	16.5	6.6	2.9	20.5	309.9	156.2	73.7	520	495
Luce	0.9	0.0	0.2	7.1	1.1	0.5	0.8	41.8	13.8	2.8	429	423
Mackinac	3.9	0.0	1.1	4.8	1.4	0.8	1.3	41.3	13.8	12.8	1 153	1 118
Macomb	333.8	627.7	31.1	129.9	43.4	26.6	78.2	1 901.7	986.7	553.4	706	681
Manistee	5.2	0.3	2.2	7.1	2.9	3.9	0.8	86.2	39.9	14.6	631	616
Marquette	15.6	3.4	3.7	22.2	8.5	3.1	13.8	182.2	95.4	38.5	622	600
Mason	5.0	1.5	1.6	9.4	5.8	1.2	1.5	86.5	42.6	26.6	955	875
Mecosta	5.4	0.0	1.3	12.9	3.3	3.2	3.3	98.4	43.5	21.9	558	513
Menominee	4.0	1.6	2.4	9.2	2.7	1.2	3.3	52.7	32.8	11.5	470	463
Midland	9.6	2.1	3.1	18.8	7.7	3.6	3.3	227.3	101.3	77.1	950	935
Missaukee	1.7	0.1	0.5	4.4	1.6	1.0	0.4	27.5	17.4	5.9	428	406
Monroe	13.0	1.9	3.6	29.6	16.4	5.3	3.6	374.5	167.1	117.0	822	797
Montcalm	7.9	0.0	2.0	25.1	6.4	3.0	4.0	148.1	97.1	31.2	524	511
Montmorency	0.9	0.0	0.2	5.2	1.4	0.6	0.8	19.1	8.4	5.5	554	545
Muskegon	21.9	89.7	13.0	77.6	32.0	12.2	23.0	506.9	268.0	87.9	530	466
Newaygo	4.7	1.2	1.4	13.7	6.8	3.4	2.8	126.0	77.4	22.4	498	492
Oakland	285.6	54.4	109.8	225.0	75.0	37.7	175.3	3 356.3	1 516.9	1 217.3	1 044	994
Oceana	3.2	0.6	8.2	9.4	4.1	1.5	0.6	66.2	35.5	13.5	549	546
Ogemaw	2.9	0.0	0.6	9.1	3.0	1.4	1.1	39.3	21.8	9.1	437	412
Ontonagon	2.5	6.1	1.6	6.5	1.2	0.6	6.4	23.9	13.8	6.2	768	754
Osceola	3.1	0.6	0.9	13.5	3.2	1.4	3.0	53.2	35.1	11.0	499	490
Oscoda	1.8	0.0	0.3	2.1	1.1	0.5	0.5	16.9	11.3	4.5	511	500
Otsego	10.9	0.0	2.3	7.9	1.9	0.6	10.5	53.7	23.7	19.3	884	866
Ottawa	27.6	41.4	89.2	27.0	8.5	7.3	19.7	532.8	264.8	147.3	668	649
Presque Isle	2.3	0.5	0.6	8.1	1.3	0.7	0.6	28.2	14.9	10.4	720	713
Roscommon	2.0	0.0	0.5	8.6	3.4	1.1	3.4	68.0	29.1	23.5	1 015	994
Saginaw	71.6	10.9	17.7	104.5	50.3	16.0	28.5	547.4	319.8	107.1	507	421
St. Clair	25.6	11.6	6.4	48.6	21.3	7.5	20.9	411.8	201.6	117.9	747	694
St. Joseph	7.1	0.1	5.4	20.7	6.4	3.3	3.6	172.1	92.8	31.6	515	506
Sanilac	5.9	2.4	1.6	17.5	5.1	2.3	3.2	107.9	62.6	20.5	479	467
Schoolcraft	2.6	0.6	6.5	7.6	1.3	0.9	0.7	33.5	13.5	4.6	531	525
Shiawassee	7.9	0.0	1.9	22.0	8.6	3.4	3.9	164.4	106.5	25.7	356	344
Tuscola	7.6	0.5	1.9	22.2	7.8	3.3	3.1	152.4	102.0	24.0	413	399
Van Buren	8.3	0.4	10.4	48.7	16.4	4.7	3.1	232.7	128.1	50.6	669	654
Washtenaw	167.7	87.5	54.6	318.5	24.1	15.4	172.1	834.2	343.8	302.6	1 010	978
Wayne	914.0	33.6	238.9	1 476.2	567.2	179.1	512.3	7 365.7	4 120.9	1 847.0	868	666
Wexford	7.2	17.4	1.2	13.4	3.6	1.7	7.3	87.3	45.0	20.1	691	671
MINNESOTA	1 778.3	1 198.0	609.3	2 218.2	837.9	354.4	1 088.0	X	X	X	X	X
Aitkin	2.3	0.1	0.6	13.6	1.8	0.7	7.8	35.3	17.9	11.9	855	846
Anoka	12.2	1.9	6.2	35.6	18.1	8.8	18.7	769.2	368.8	225.2	785	758
Becker	9.6	0.0	6.3	22.8	9.2	2.5	4.8	68.6	39.0	16.2	555	545
Beltrami	14.9	0.0	5.4	36.9	11.7	4.7	10.8	107.5	69.2	20.7	534	526
Benton	3.5	0.1	0.4	10.2	2.3	1.0	3.3	63.4	37.4	17.6	523	515
Big Stone	1.9	0.0	0.4	3.8	0.7	0.3	0.1	38.2	19.1	4.6	810	802
Blue Earth	21.1	0.5	4.9	22.4	6.3	2.8	6.7	152.6	72.9	47.1	872	852
Brown	4.2	1.2	1.2	7.5	1.6	0.8	0.9	73.4	32.9	18.2	669	661
Carlton	13.0	0.1	1.4	21.6	5.0	2.3	8.8	93.6	54.2	22.4	731	721
Carver	12.5	0.1	24.1	6.3	6.4	1.1	0.5	229.6	65.8	75.6	1 197	1 150
Cass	10.0	0.2	1.1	30.5	7.5	2.2	6.1	75.7	37.1	27.4	1 065	1 060
Chippewa	2.9	0.0	0.5	4.9	2.5	0.7	1.0	43.7	22.9	10.5	807	798
Chisago	5.6	0.1	1.5	7.5	2.3	1.1	0.1	99.4	50.0	25.8	653	621
Clay	6.8	0.0	1.6	18.5	6.3	2.5	7.7	143.8	77.1	28.1	542	539
Clearwater	1.5	0.0	0.4	12.1	1.9	0.9	1.7	26.5	16.0	7.7	936	933
Cook	3.7	0.0	1.0	2.9	0.5	0.2	4.5	25.5	6.3	7.1	1 488	1 266
Cottonwood	2.9	0.0	0.7	4.5	1.0	0.7	2.1	42.1	19.1	10.3	843	840
Crow Wing	8.9	1.5	2.3	29.8	6.2	2.1	5.4	147.4	57.3	45.2	884	861
Dakota	104.2	68.2	22.0	25.7	12.6	6.6	9.5	900.5	380.4	306.5	916	885
Dodge	2.0	0.0	0.5	4.5	1.3	0.6	5.3	51.7	28.1	12.4	727	715
Douglas	6.3	0.3	1.3	17.0	2.7	1.1	3.6	108.7	38.3	23.9	779	766
Faribault	2.9	0.0	0.8	7.2	0.7	0.7	1.9	52.3	20.9	12.9	784	780
Fillmore	4.1	0.0	1.1	11.3	3.2	1.1	0.1	56.3	36.4	10.7	517	509
Freeborn	5.0	0.0	14.0	12.8	3.2	1.3	2.2	78.4	43.4	19.4	614	558
Goodhue	6.5	0.1	2.2	11.2	3.7	1.3	5.5	136.4	49.7	52.4	1 227	1 221

1. October 1, 1998 to September 30, 1999. 2. State totals may include programs not allocated by county. 3. Based on the resident population estimated as of July 1 of the year shown.

STATE County	Local government finances, 1997 (cont'd) Direct general expenditure							Debt outstanding		Government employment, 1998			Presidential election, 2000 Percent of vote cast —		
	Total (mil dol)	Per capita[1] (dollars)	Education	Health and hospitals	Police protection	Public welfare	Highways	Total (mil dol)	Per capita[1] (dollars)	Federal civilian	Federal military	State and local	Democratic	Republican	All other
	183	184	185	186	187	188	189	190	191	192	193	194	195	196	197
MICHIGAN—Cont'd															
Leelanau	39.6	2 112	53.3	3.2	3.0	1.3	9.9	32.7	1 744	145	38	658	38.6	57.0	4.4
Lenawee	227.3	2 320	57.9	6.9	2.7	4.0	7.1	76.3	779	231	196	5 495	45.8	51.6	2.6
Livingston	306.3	2 158	54.9	5.2	3.5	0.3	5.4	495.8	3 493	243	291	4 844	38.1	59.1	2.7
Luce	42.2	6 410	17.4	64.4	0.6	0.6	5.7	5.3	804	20	13	1 090	37.7	58.4	3.9
Mackinac	45.0	4 045	37.3	17.9	2.2	0.6	9.7	27.7	2 490	60	64	933	42.4	54.8	2.8
Macomb	1 924.5	2 456	55.3	5.2	6.0	2.1	5.0	1 051.4	1 342	6 797	1 889	27 433	50.0	47.5	2.5
Manistee	83.7	3 611	32.4	31.6	1.9	6.8	7.7	11.5	498	97	51	1 485	49.3	47.3	3.4
Marquette	193.6	3 133	43.1	9.8	2.6	3.2	8.9	184.9	2 992	307	136	6 313	53.1	43.1	3.8
Mason	83.7	3 006	58.9	6.9	1.8	6.1	7.1	17.8	638	99	71	1 730	42.9	54.3	2.9
Mecosta	118.2	3 017	60.3	18.6	2.5	0.4	2.1	60.7	1 551	92	81	4 241	42.7	54.7	2.6
Menominee	51.6	2 109	53.1	7.2	3.8	0.7	10.7	35.9	1 468	75	49	1 470	44.1	53.0	3.0
Midland	220.2	2 710	49.0	7.5	3.8	1.2	6.6	301.4	3 710	169	164	3 578	41.0	56.3	2.7
Missaukee	29.6	2 161	43.8	8.8	1.0	0.7	15.7	22.4	1 639	30	28	562	31.7	65.8	2.5
Monroe	365.9	2 571	52.8	6.3	3.0	1.0	6.0	590.5	4 150	255	286	5 927	51.1	46.8	2.1
Montcalm	162.2	2 719	73.1	2.5	2.1	0.9	6.5	112.9	1 892	143	120	3 104	42.0	55.4	2.5
Montmorency	18.3	1 835	41.2	1.3	3.7	2.4	11.5	12.6	1 265	15	20	434	42.7	54.9	2.4
Muskegon	563.6	3 398	55.5	6.6	2.8	4.2	4.4	345.9	2 085	392	333	8 870	54.7	43.3	2.0
Newaygo	140.5	3 118	63.0	8.9	1.5	1.2	5.3	81.7	1 812	90	91	2 457	39.3	58.3	2.5
Oakland	3 498.2	2 999	52.5	4.8	5.5	0.1	5.6	2 263.7	1 941	5 276	2 352	50 431	49.3	48.1	2.6
Oceana	77.0	3 129	51.0	4.9	2.1	8.3	18.1	34.2	1 390	68	49	1 313	42.7	54.9	2.4
Ogemaw	38.4	1 832	42.2	10.6	3.3	1.9	13.7	12.6	602	57	42	1 256	49.7	47.8	2.6
Ontonagon	25.8	3 180	56.7	0.7	1.5	1.7	20.8	10.5	1 291	53	16	660	36.5	59.6	4.0
Osceola	59.1	2 683	69.5	1.8	1.7	0.6	6.9	30.5	1 384	64	44	1 157	40.3	57.2	2.5
Oscoda	14.3	1 621	52.4	1.7	3.6	0.4	19.8	2.8	315	41	18	379	42.0	55.3	2.7
Otsego	54.8	2 513	60.6	0.7	2.2	0.9	11.5	47.3	2 171	199	45	1 068	38.4	58.1	3.5
Ottawa	583.9	2 649	53.0	9.9	3.0	0.9	6.5	752.4	3 414	487	516	12 058	26.8	71.2	2.1
Presque Isle	28.3	1 969	45.1	1.1	2.7	1.0	14.4	14.2	988	53	29	715	45.8	51.7	2.5
Roscommon	67.0	2 892	64.5	2.2	2.2	1.4	7.2	31.6	1 366	38	47	1 408	49.8	47.9	2.4
Saginaw	546.0	2 584	47.6	11.0	4.5	1.0	4.5	351.4	1 663	1 340	441	9 600	54.2	43.9	1.9
St. Clair	419.2	2 658	49.7	8.3	3.8	1.0	6.7	241.3	1 530	457	386	6 377	48.2	49.0	2.8
St. Joseph	173.1	2 827	51.1	19.7	2.5	0.7	7.0	64.8	1 058	124	122	3 602	38.9	58.6	2.5
Sanilac	114.2	2 672	49.2	9.4	2.7	5.4	9.7	71.8	1 679	120	85	2 317	38.5	59.1	2.4
Schoolcraft	33.4	3 823	24.7	30.3	1.9	7.3	11.2	7.5	861	57	18	746	48.5	49.7	1.8
Shiawassee	169.2	2 343	56.7	5.1	3.4	5.1	8.8	90.4	1 252	144	144	3 498	48.2	49.1	2.7
Tuscola	149.2	2 569	60.3	8.2	2.4	3.7	9.5	55.0	947	149	117	3 512	44.0	53.6	2.4
Van Buren	241.6	3 192	54.7	18.4	2.3	1.0	5.8	135.3	1 787	163	150	4 811	46.8	50.2	3.0
Washtenaw	878.0	2 932	52.3	5.4	5.0	0.9	3.6	713.7	2 383	2 727	672	61 774	59.8	36.2	4.0
Wayne	7 119.6	3 347	39.4	6.7	6.9	1.5	5.0	5 738.0	2 698	17 380	4 769	109 636	69.0	29.0	1.9
Wexford	86.4	2 965	53.5	12.5	3.0	1.0	7.0	61.6	2 114	145	59	1 725	41.0	55.6	3.4
MINNESOTA	X	X	X	X	X	X	X	X	X	33 229	20 084	328 799	47.9	45.5	6.6
Aitkin	36.0	2 597	44.5	2.6	3.5	10.3	14.9	16.3	1 176	47	57	743	46.4	45.5	8.2
Anoka	796.9	2 780	58.9	0.6	3.7	6.5	4.7	867.9	3 028	238	1 187	13 185	46.7	47.6	5.7
Becker	86.8	2 967	53.0	0.2	2.3	10.0	13.0	52.2	1 787	198	119	1 829	36.6	56.9	6.5
Beltrami	117.3	3 029	61.4	0.1	2.6	11.6	5.5	72.1	1 863	302	158	3 691	42.4	48.5	9.1
Benton	63.9	1 897	46.4	0.9	3.3	8.8	13.3	71.8	2 131	54	139	1 264	40.3	51.4	8.3
Big Stone	32.4	5 687	29.5	19.3	2.2	4.4	13.0	287.9	50 604	38	23	574	48.0	46.0	6.0
Blue Earth	158.4	2 931	45.7	0.4	3.9	6.0	15.3	108.5	2 009	369	224	5 001	45.0	47.2	7.8
Brown	80.2	2 946	42.1	9.8	4.4	7.2	8.2	81.3	2 987	74	110	1 538	36.2	57.4	6.3
Carlton	98.4	3 205	47.2	1.7	3.1	9.0	9.0	157.8	5 141	83	125	2 796	57.2	37.0	5.9
Carver	249.7	3 950	32.4	18.8	1.2	4.2	8.9	293.7	4 648	198	262	3 810	35.6	59.4	5.1
Cass	75.9	2 948	45.5	2.4	3.5	9.3	14.0	40.0	1 554	244	107	1 778	40.7	52.5	6.8
Chippewa	52.6	4 038	49.6	0.3	3.0	12.2	13.1	36.8	2 824	46	53	961	46.5	46.9	6.7
Chisago	109.3	2 772	54.7	8.2	2.8	6.7	8.3	103.0	2 612	109	166	1 894	43.6	49.7	6.6
Clay	147.6	2 848	42.5	1.8	4.5	9.8	9.7	157.2	3 034	115	209	4 446	43.4	50.1	6.5
Clearwater	28.0	3 413	54.5	0.1	3.3	7.9	14.1	14.1	1 723	30	34	814	38.3	55.9	5.8
Cook	29.3	6 189	25.3	33.9	3.5	3.9	11.8	24.7	5 211	114	19	447	41.5	45.9	12.6
Cottonwood	44.3	3 617	39.2	13.1	2.7	8.0	14.3	19.8	1 611	57	49	875	40.5	54.5	5.0
Crow Wing	152.8	2 990	46.0	12.4	4.3	7.6	8.0	79.6	1 557	153	209	4 172	40.0	53.5	6.5
Dakota	945.1	2 825	53.8	0.6	4.3	5.7	7.6	1 419.1	4 241	1 551	1 391	15 071	46.9	47.9	5.2
Dodge	60.6	3 563	51.3	0.4	2.4	17.0	10.6	39.0	2 295	40	70	1 058	41.9	52.3	5.8
Douglas	103.5	3 367	33.7	28.4	2.8	6.0	9.3	52.0	1 692	120	126	2 555	36.9	57.0	6.1
Faribault	48.0	2 923	40.7	15.8	3.2	0.0	13.2	38.5	2 344	58	66	1 018	43.0	51.5	5.5
Fillmore	59.0	2 854	40.4	2.5	3.7	4.5	27.0	27.1	1 312	78	84	1 235	49.1	45.4	5.4
Freeborn	78.4	2 483	42.5	1.3	4.1	11.9	13.7	32.5	1 030	90	128	1 460	52.8	42.4	4.8
Goodhue	147.0	3 442	46.7	2.6	4.0	5.0	8.8	208.1	4 872	122	175	2 689	44.8	48.8	6.4

1. Based on the resident population estimated as of July 1 of the year shown.

STATE/ County code	MSA/ PMSA/ NECMA code[1]	County Type[2]	STATE County	Land area,[3] (sq km) 1990	Total persons	Rank	Per square kilometer	White	Black	Am. Indian, Eskimo, Aleut	Asian and Pacific Islander	Percent Hispanic[4]	Under 5 years	5 to 17 years	18 to 24 years	25 to 34 years	35 to 44 years	45 to 54 years
					1	2	3	4	5	6	7	8	9	10	11	12	13	14	15
			MINNESOTA—Cont'd															
27 051	...	9	Grant	1 415	6 077	2 765	4.3	99.3	0.1	0.3	0.3	0.2	5.5	19.9	4.6	9.0	13.7	13.4
27 053	5120	0	Hennepin	1 442	1 064 419	31	738.2	85.2	8.7	1.5	4.5	2.1	6.6	16.8	10.1	15.8	18.4	13.1
27 055	3870	3	Houston	1 446	19 489	1 790	13.5	99.0	0.2	0.3	0.5	0.4	6.8	21.3	6.7	11.3	16.4	12.4
27 057	...	9	Hubbard	2 389	17 031	1 927	7.1	97.9	0.0	1.9	0.2	0.4	5.7	20.9	5.4	9.3	15.2	14.9
27 059	5120	1	Isanti	1 137	30 887	1 351	27.2	98.3	0.4	0.6	0.7	0.7	6.8	24.2	7.3	11.7	17.5	14.7
27 061	...	6	Itasca	6 903	44 154	999	6.4	95.9	0.2	3.5	0.3	0.6	5.4	21.9	6.4	9.3	16.7	13.8
27 063	...	7	Jackson	1 818	11 378	2 313	6.3	97.6	0.0	0.1	2.3	1.5	5.9	20.7	6.3	10.1	14.6	12.3
27 065	...	6	Kanabec	1 360	14 427	2 105	10.6	98.6	0.3	0.5	0.6	0.8	6.6	23.3	6.8	10.9	15.5	13.8
27 067	...	7	Kandiyohi	2 062	40 826	1 063	19.8	98.6	0.4	0.5	0.5	5.7	6.9	21.6	9.2	11.2	15.5	12.5
27 069	...	9	Kittson	2 841	5 175	2 826	1.8	99.5	0.0	0.2	0.3	1.2	5.9	19.2	5.3	9.3	15.2	12.9
27 071	...	7	Koochiching	8 035	14 895	2 070	1.9	96.3	0.3	2.9	0.5	1.6	5.3	19.4	7.9	10.5	15.7	14.2
27 073	...	9	Lac qui Parle	1 981	7 813	2 619	3.9	99.2	0.2	0.2	0.5	0.4	5.6	20.1	4.2	9.2	13.8	12.9
27 075	...	6	Lake	5 437	10 765	2 359	2.0	99.1	0.1	0.6	0.3	0.6	4.8	17.8	5.1	9.1	15.1	14.4
27 077	...	9	Lake of the Woods	3 358	4 621	2 862	1.4	98.9	0.0	0.5	0.5	1.2	7.2	19.8	6.1	11.3	15.6	14.7
27 079	...	6	Le Sueur	1 162	25 464	1 515	21.9	99.2	0.1	0.2	0.4	0.9	6.5	22.3	7.2	10.9	15.6	13.5
27 081	...	9	Lincoln	1 391	6 424	2 740	4.6	99.6	0.0	0.2	0.2	0.5	4.4	21.2	5.0	7.7	13.1	13.5
27 083	...	7	Lyon	1 850	24 256	1 565	13.1	98.5	0.4	0.3	0.7	1.5	6.1	21.1	11.6	10.8	14.5	11.9
27 085	...	6	McLeod	1 274	34 552	1 237	27.1	98.9	0.2	0.2	0.7	1.5	7.0	21.6	8.0	11.7	16.0	13.0
27 087	...	9	Mahnomen	1 440	5 091	2 832	3.5	74.2	0.0	25.6	0.1	0.9	5.5	26.1	5.7	9.5	13.1	13.7
27 089	...	8	Marshall	4 590	10 094	2 414	2.2	99.3	0.0	0.5	0.2	1.6	5.4	22.9	5.5	9.3	14.7	13.7
27 091	...	7	Martin	1 837	21 792	1 667	11.9	99.2	0.1	0.2	0.6	0.9	5.9	20.1	5.6	10.1	15.3	13.2
27 093	...	6	Meeker	1 576	21 763	1 669	13.8	98.9	0.2	0.2	0.7	1.9	6.5	22.5	6.4	10.2	15.4	13.2
27 095	...	6	Mille Lacs	1 488	21 350	1 690	14.3	95.8	0.2	3.6	0.3	0.8	6.4	22.1	6.8	10.2	14.8	13.4
27 097	...	6	Morrison	2 913	30 522	1 362	10.5	99.3	0.2	0.3	0.2	0.6	6.7	24.1	7.2	10.5	14.6	12.2
27 099	...	4	Mower	1 843	37 152	1 157	20.2	98.3	0.3	0.1	1.3	1.1	5.6	19.4	6.9	9.9	14.2	12.7
27 101	...	9	Murray	1 825	9 519	2 470	5.2	99.7	0.0	0.0	0.3	0.4	5.4	20.9	5.6	8.5	14.5	12.7
27 103	...	7	Nicollet	1 172	29 272	1 402	25.0	98.3	0.4	0.2	1.1	1.2	6.4	20.0	15.4	11.5	16.9	12.2
27 105	...	7	Nobles	1 853	19 113	1 813	10.3	96.1	0.3	0.4	3.2	2.0	5.8	19.9	7.7	10.3	14.1	12.9
27 107	...	8	Norman	2 270	7 517	2 636	3.3	98.6	0.1	1.0	0.3	1.4	5.2	21.4	4.9	9.1	13.7	13.3
27 109	6820	3	Olmsted	1 691	119 077	443	70.4	93.7	1.1	0.3	4.9	1.5	7.4	19.6	8.7	14.8	17.1	14.0
27 111	...	6	Otter Tail	5 128	55 583	833	10.8	98.8	0.1	0.5	0.6	0.7	5.9	20.2	6.5	9.6	15.0	13.5
27 113	...	7	Pennington	1 597	13 557	2 172	8.5	98.5	0.1	0.8	0.6	1.3	5.9	20.9	9.9	10.2	15.6	13.2
27 115	...	6	Pine	3 655	24 616	1 545	6.7	96.0	1.5	1.9	0.6	2.1	5.8	22.2	6.7	11.2	14.8	13.8
27 117	...	7	Pipestone	1 207	9 993	2 425	8.3	97.2	0.1	1.5	1.3	0.7	6.4	21.5	6.7	9.9	13.5	11.7
27 119	2985	3	Polk	5 104	30 787	1 355	6.0	97.7	0.4	1.4	0.5	5.6	6.4	21.5	8.4	10.2	15.0	12.7
27 121	...	6	Pope	1 736	10 886	2 355	6.3	99.5	0.1	0.2	0.2	0.1	5.9	21.3	5.0	8.9	14.3	13.0
27 123	5120	0	Ramsey	404	486 254	111	1 203.6	84.3	6.9	1.0	7.7	4.5	7.2	17.8	11.0	14.4	16.5	12.1
27 125	...	9	Red Lake	1 120	4 202	2 896	3.8	99.5	0.1	0.3	0.1	1.6	6.1	23.4	5.7	10.2	14.7	13.0
27 127	...	7	Redwood	2 279	16 421	1 977	7.2	97.7	0.0	1.8	0.3	0.8	6.3	21.4	5.8	9.8	14.0	13.2
27 129	...	7	Renville	2 546	16 808	1 942	6.6	99.1	0.1	0.4	0.5	2.0	6.1	21.2	5.7	9.9	13.9	12.3
27 131	...	4	Rice	1 289	54 988	839	42.7	97.1	0.7	0.3	1.8	1.8	6.1	19.8	15.4	11.6	15.5	12.8
27 133	...	6	Rock	1 250	9 619	2 459	7.7	99.2	0.2	0.4	0.3	0.5	5.7	21.8	5.8	9.4	14.6	12.5
27 135	...	9	Roseau	4 306	16 085	1 998	3.7	97.7	0.0	1.1	1.1	0.3	8.3	23.0	8.2	13.1	14.9	12.7
27 137	2240	3	St. Louis	16 124	193 433	278	12.0	96.3	0.8	2.0	0.9	0.8	5.3	18.9	9.1	10.4	17.0	13.2
27 139	5120	1	Scott	924	82 994	614	89.8	97.1	0.7	0.7	1.5	1.2	8.3	22.6	8.4	15.3	18.5	13.9
27 141	5120	1	Sherburne	1 131	63 356	756	56.0	98.1	0.6	0.5	0.8	1.0	7.6	24.2	10.9	13.5	18.3	13.0
27 143	...	8	Sibley	1 525	14 774	2 081	9.7	99.4	0.0	0.1	0.4	1.5	6.5	21.6	6.5	10.3	14.4	13.4
27 145	6980	3	Stearns	3 482	130 081	399	37.4	98.1	0.5	0.3	1.1	0.7	6.5	21.1	16.2	11.7	14.5	11.0
27 147	...	7	Steele	1 113	32 061	1 311	28.8	98.7	0.2	0.2	0.9	3.0	6.9	21.6	7.9	11.9	16.2	13.1
27 149	...	7	Stevens	1 456	9 973	2 430	6.8	97.0	0.8	0.5	1.7	0.8	5.1	18.0	20.0	8.2	12.9	10.1
27 151	...	7	Swift	1 926	11 344	2 316	5.9	95.1	3.1	1.2	0.6	2.6	4.8	19.6	6.7	11.8	15.5	12.8
27 153	...	6	Todd	2 440	24 240	1 566	9.9	99.3	0.1	0.3	0.4	0.4	5.9	24.4	6.7	9.5	14.8	13.4
27 155	...	9	Traverse	1 487	4 168	2 900	2.8	96.5	0.0	3.0	0.6	0.2	5.4	19.7	3.9	8.5	12.2	12.4
27 157	...	6	Wabasha	1 360	21 140	1 707	15.5	98.9	0.1	0.2	0.7	0.7	6.6	21.7	7.1	10.9	16.1	13.7
27 159	...	7	Wadena	1 387	13 238	2 196	9.5	98.8	0.1	0.6	0.4	0.6	6.1	21.3	6.9	9.3	13.4	13.7
27 161	...	7	Waseca	1 096	18 560	1 843	16.9	98.0	0.8	0.5	0.7	1.5	6.4	21.9	7.8	11.5	17.0	12.0
27 163	5120	0	Washington	1 015	202 606	269	199.6	96.2	1.4	0.5	1.9	2.1	7.1	22.6	7.6	13.2	20.3	15.5
27 165	...	7	Watonwan	1 125	11 548	2 305	10.3	98.9	0.1	0.3	0.7	8.0	6.4	20.8	6.5	10.3	13.5	12.7
27 167	...	6	Wilkin	1 946	7 287	2 655	3.7	98.8	0.1	0.6	0.6	1.0	6.5	21.3	7.1	11.0	14.8	12.4
27 169	...	4	Winona	1 622	47 785	940	29.5	97.5	0.6	0.2	1.7	1.2	5.7	18.5	17.6	10.5	14.9	11.6
27 171	5120	1	Wright	1 712	87 864	571	51.3	98.8	0.2	0.4	0.7	0.7	7.8	24.5	8.3	13.0	17.2	13.4
27 173	...	7	Yellow Medicine	1 963	11 310	2 325	5.8	98.6	0.0	1.1	0.3	1.2	5.8	20.8	6.2	9.5	13.3	13.4

1. MSA = Metropolitan Statistical Area. PMSA = Primary MSA. NECMA = New England County Metropolitan Area. See Appendix A for explanation of these concepts. See Appendix B for list of metropolitan areas identified by type, with component counties.   2. County typology code from the Economic Research Service of USDA. See Appendix A for definition.   3. Dry land or land partially or temporarily covered by water.   4. Hispanic persons may be of any race.

STATE County	55 to 64 years	65 to 74 years	75 years and over	Percent female	Total persons 1990	Total persons 1980	Percent change 1980-1990	Percent change 1990-1999	Births	Deaths	Net migration	Number	Percent change, 1980-1990	Persons per household	Female family householder[1]	One person
	16	17	18	19	20	21	22	23	24	25	26	27	28	29	30	31
MINNESOTA—Cont'd																
Grant	11.7	9.3	12.9	51.2	6 246	7 171	-12.9	-2.7	593	863	128	2 454	-7.5	2.47	5.3	27.3
Hennepin	8.0	5.6	5.5	51.5	1 032 431	941 411	9.7	3.1	147 410	75 058	-37 305	419 060	14.6	2.41	10.0	29.0
Houston	9.7	7.2	8.3	50.2	18 497	18 382	0.6	5.4	2 257	1 714	506	6 844	8.0	2.65	7.2	23.4
Hubbard	11.4	8.7	8.4	50.4	14 939	14 098	6.0	14.0	1 601	1 636	2 169	5 781	15.0	2.55	6.0	23.5
Isanti	7.5	4.6	5.6	49.9	25 921	23 600	9.8	19.2	3 366	1 923	3 586	8 810	17.4	2.86	7.1	19.0
Itasca	10.0	8.8	7.8	50.3	40 844	43 069	-5.1	8.1	4 240	4 013	3 266	15 461	3.3	2.60	7.9	23.1
Jackson	10.8	8.8	10.5	50.4	11 677	13 690	-14.7	-2.6	1 148	1 220	-193	4 560	-8.6	2.51	5.3	25.7
Kanabec	9.4	7.0	6.7	49.9	12 802	12 161	5.3	12.7	1 453	1 136	1 346	4 753	11.8	2.67	7.4	24.0
Kandiyohi	8.5	6.9	7.6	50.5	38 761	36 763	5.4	5.3	5 156	3 323	353	14 298	11.1	2.64	6.8	23.9
Kittson	10.3	9.6	12.2	50.4	5 767	6 672	-13.6	-10.3	538	791	-321	2 274	-8.5	2.46	5.3	28.7
Koochiching	10.2	8.7	8.0	49.4	16 299	17 571	-7.2	-8.6	1 553	1 543	-1 394	6 025	-1.7	2.58	8.5	24.8
Lac qui Parle	11.3	10.1	12.9	50.3	8 924	10 592	-15.7	-12.4	807	1 105	-780	3 505	-9.8	2.48	3.6	27.7
Lake	13.5	10.8	9.5	50.2	10 415	13 043	-20.1	3.4	950	1 133	571	4 242	-7.3	2.42	6.2	25.4
Lake of the Woods	9.9	8.1	7.4	49.8	4 076	3 764	8.3	13.4	456	392	492	1 576	13.5	2.55	5.9	23.4
Le Sueur	9.1	7.1	7.7	50.0	23 239	23 434	-0.8	9.6	3 011	1 918	1 207	8 468	5.4	2.71	6.2	23.1
Lincoln	11.2	10.2	13.6	50.7	6 890	8 207	-16.0	-6.8	679	999	-126	2 704	-7.7	2.47	4.3	28.0
Lyon	8.2	7.3	8.4	50.8	24 789	25 207	-1.7	-2.2	3 262	2 088	-1 657	9 073	4.5	2.56	6.3	26.1
McLeod	8.5	6.5	7.6	50.2	32 030	29 657	8.0	7.9	4 342	2 732	1 022	11 815	13.9	2.67	6.2	23.4
Mahnomen	10.1	7.8	8.6	49.7	5 044	5 535	-8.9	0.9	727	558	-94	1 805	1.3	2.75	8.2	24.3
Marshall	10.3	8.9	9.3	49.3	10 993	13 027	-15.6	-8.2	1 134	1 164	-837	4 194	-6.0	2.59	4.9	26.3
Martin	9.8	9.0	11.0	51.0	22 914	24 687	-7.2	-4.9	2 345	2 329	-1 067	9 129	-2.1	2.46	6.4	27.8
Meeker	9.9	7.7	8.3	50.4	20 846	20 594	1.2	4.4	2 453	2 091	631	7 651	6.6	2.67	5.4	24.0
Mille Lacs	9.7	7.6	9.0	50.6	18 670	18 430	1.3	14.4	2 383	2 073	2 433	6 911	7.5	2.65	7.3	23.9
Morrison	9.6	7.5	7.7	49.8	29 604	29 311	1.0	3.1	3 735	2 677	-67	10 399	9.4	2.79	7.1	23.2
Mower	11.4	9.7	10.3	51.3	37 385	40 390	-7.4	-0.6	4 178	4 016	-254	15 028	0.4	2.44	7.2	27.8
Murray	12.1	10.0	10.2	50.4	9 660	11 507	-16.1	-1.5	989	939	-148	3 758	-6.9	2.53	4.1	26.2
Nicollet	8.1	4.4	5.1	50.4	28 076	26 929	4.3	4.3	3 233	1 656	-281	9 478	10.5	2.69	7.1	22.1
Nobles	10.4	8.6	10.2	50.7	20 098	21 840	-8.0	-4.9	2 682	1 904	-1 716	7 683	-1.7	2.55	5.9	25.1
Norman	11.5	8.6	12.2	50.2	7 975	9 379	-15.0	-5.7	838	1 102	-161	3 118	-9.1	2.48	4.5	29.3
Olmsted	7.6	5.2	5.4	51.4	106 470	92 006	15.7	11.8	16 359	6 319	2 858	40 058	22.6	2.59	7.5	24.6
Otter Tail	11.2	8.4	9.8	50.2	50 714	51 937	-2.4	9.6	5 360	5 549	5 191	19 510	5.2	2.53	5.8	25.8
Pennington	9.0	6.4	8.8	50.1	13 306	15 258	-12.8	1.9	1 569	1 353	80	5 173	-4.9	2.50	8.1	28.1
Pine	10.6	7.5	7.4	47.8	21 264	19 871	7.0	15.8	2 472	2 097	3 018	7 577	10.6	2.64	7.2	24.2
Pipestone	10.3	9.0	10.8	51.9	10 491	11 690	-10.3	-4.7	1 185	1 173	-472	4 078	-6.4	2.51	5.6	28.7
Polk	9.4	7.3	9.0	50.4	32 589	34 844	-6.5	-5.5	3 868	3 796	-1 841	11 984	-1.4	2.61	7.9	26.0
Pope	10.8	9.6	11.3	50.5	10 745	11 657	-7.8	1.3	1 036	1 336	489	4 135	-2.5	2.54	4.9	26.3
Ramsey	7.9	6.5	6.6	52.2	485 760	459 784	5.7	0.1	71 633	37 247	-32 884	190 500	11.7	2.47	11.3	29.3
Red Lake	9.8	7.9	9.1	49.1	4 525	5 471	-17.3	-7.1	443	510	-246	1 730	-4.8	2.58	5.1	30.5
Redwood	10.1	8.7	10.7	50.8	17 254	19 341	-10.8	-4.8	1 914	2 025	-671	6 554	-4.2	2.57	5.2	27.0
Renville	11.0	9.0	10.8	50.2	17 673	20 401	-13.4	-4.9	1 890	1 979	-723	6 790	-7.2	2.55	4.7	26.6
Rice	7.7	5.2	6.0	50.1	49 183	46 087	6.7	11.8	5 963	3 790	3 795	16 347	14.5	2.66	7.8	24.1
Rock	10.2	9.6	10.6	51.2	9 806	10 703	-8.4	-1.9	1 078	978	-251	3 754	-2.6	2.57	5.1	25.6
Roseau	7.9	5.4	6.4	48.6	15 026	12 574	19.5	7.0	2 394	1 281	-23	5 415	25.0	2.73	6.2	22.0
St. Louis	9.8	8.0	8.3	51.1	198 232	222 229	-10.8	-2.4	19 553	20 407	-3 378	78 901	-3.2	2.43	9.2	28.8
Scott	6.5	3.3	3.1	49.1	57 846	43 784	32.1	43.5	11 658	3 033	16 496	19 367	43.4	2.95	7.2	15.5
Sherburne	6.1	3.2	3.0	48.8	41 945	29 908	40.2	51.0	7 601	2 707	16 504	13 643	52.1	2.98	6.8	15.2
Sibley	10.9	7.5	8.9	49.9	14 366	15 448	-7.0	2.8	1 701	1 401	151	5 323	-0.3	2.66	4.6	23.8
Stearns	7.6	5.9	5.6	49.8	119 324	108 161	10.3	9.0	15 203	6 561	2 447	39 776	23.9	2.81	7.3	21.5
Steele	8.8	6.6	7.1	50.8	30 729	30 328	1.3	4.3	3 889	2 361	-98	11 342	7.0	2.65	6.3	23.1
Stevens	9.2	7.5	8.9	51.5	10 634	11 322	-6.1	-6.2	880	878	-634	3 823	-1.5	2.57	5.4	25.5
Swift	9.8	8.7	10.2	45.6	10 724	12 900	-17.0	5.8	1 168	1 305	781	4 268	-9.1	2.46	5.3	29.5
Todd	10.1	7.3	8.0	49.8	23 363	24 991	-6.5	3.8	2 652	2 263	575	8 589	0.9	2.69	5.4	24.7
Traverse	12.5	10.7	14.7	51.7	4 463	5 542	-19.5	-6.6	463	558	-182	1 778	-12.8	2.44	5.1	28.2
Wabasha	9.1	7.1	7.6	50.0	19 744	19 335	2.1	7.1	2 322	1 847	990	7 286	8.0	2.67	5.7	23.0
Wadena	10.0	8.7	10.6	51.0	13 154	14 192	-7.3	0.6	1 505	1 594	232	4 978	3.2	2.56	7.3	27.3
Waseca	8.7	7.1	7.7	49.4	18 079	18 448	-2.0	2.7	2 196	1 599	-54	6 649	2.8	2.64	6.9	24.6
Washington	7.1	3.7	2.9	49.8	145 860	113 571	28.4	38.9	23 505	7 157	38 381	49 246	40.3	2.91	8.5	16.1
Watonwan	10.4	8.7	10.6	50.8	11 682	12 361	-5.5	-1.1	1 641	1 199	-538	4 530	-2.3	2.54	5.5	27.9
Wilkin	10.8	7.1	9.0	50.3	7 516	8 454	-11.1	-3.0	847	740	-312	2 805	-4.4	2.63	6.0	25.3
Winona	8.0	5.9	7.3	50.9	47 828	46 256	3.4	0.1	5 262	3 935	-1 270	16 930	8.5	2.61	7.1	25.5
Wright	7.0	4.3	4.5	49.3	68 710	58 681	17.1	27.9	11 370	4 435	12 339	23 013	24.9	2.95	6.9	17.5
Yellow Medicine	10.9	8.7	11.4	50.2	11 684	13 653	-14.4	-3.2	1 217	1 322	-221	4 607	-7.7	2.48	4.4	28.6

1. No spouse present.

Table B. States and Counties — **Vital Statistics, Health Resources, and Crime**

STATE County	Births, average 1996–1998 Total	Rate[1]	Deaths, average 1996–1998 Number Total	Number Infant[2]	Rate Total[1]	Rate Infant[3]	Physicians,[4] 1998 Number	Rate[5]	Hospitals,[4] 1998 Number	Beds Number	Beds Rate[5]	Medicare enrollees 1999	Serious crimes known to police, 1998[6] Total Number	Rate[7]
	32	33	34	35	36	37	38	39	40	41	42	43	44	45
MINNESOTA—Cont'd														
Grant	62	10.0	86	0	14.0	0.0	5	81	1	20	324	1 559	138	2 229
Hennepin	15 484	14.6	8 125	109	7.7	7.0	3 729	352	8	3 411	322	137 044	64 288	6 051
Houston	204	10.7	180	0	9.4	1.6	19	99	1	89	462	3 351	238	1 228
Hubbard	176	10.5	186	0	11.2	1.9	18	106	1	45	266	3 470	696	4 119
Isanti	384	13.0	230	3	7.8	7.8	40	133	1	86	286	3 316	775	2 600
Itasca	429	9.9	430	4	9.9	10.1	52	119	3	244	556	8 345	1 193	2 716
Jackson	119	10.3	125	0	10.7	0.0	9	78	1	41	356	2 160	158	1 339
Kanabec	156	11.2	129	1	9.3	6.4	5	35	1	49	346	2 187	536	3 786
Kandiyohi	533	13.0	366	3	8.9	6.2	99	241	1	122	297	6 708	1 259	3 039
Kittson	59	11.1	82	0	15.3	5.6	5	94	2	205	3 852	1 215	86	1 592
Koochiching	156	10.0	163	1	10.4	6.4	13	84	1	44	283	2 969	601	3 801
Lac qui Parle	81	10.0	118	0	14.5	0.0	5	62	2	106	1 321	1 884	127	1 555
Lake	102	9.6	128	0	12.0	0.0	17	161	1	80	757	2 209	148	1 370
Lake of the Woods	33	7.3	43	0	9.4	0.0	5	110	1	73	1 600	828	88	1 923
Le Sueur	314	12.6	208	1	8.3	2.1	15	59	2	131	517	4 348	401	1 598
Lincoln	70	10.7	105	0	15.9	0.0	7	108	3	231	3 576	1 570	6	91
Lyon	340	13.9	234	2	9.6	4.9	28	115	2	145	596	4 318	525	2 124
McLeod	460	13.6	279	2	8.3	4.3	36	106	2	215	632	5 229	912	2 685
Mahnomen	82	15.9	58	1	11.4	12.2	4	79	1	66	1 300	993	360	7 016
Marshall	116	11.0	117	1	11.1	5.8	2	19	1	18	175	2 077	130	1 225
Martin	230	10.4	267	1	12.1	5.8	20	91	1	108	491	4 694	627	2 796
Meeker	279	12.9	226	2	10.4	7.2	12	55	1	38	175	3 695	611	2 816
Mille Lacs	273	13.2	238	1	11.5	4.9	23	109	2	149	708	4 530	935	4 486
Morrison	405	13.3	313	2	10.3	4.1	26	85	1	55	180	5 369	720	2 341
Mower	433	11.7	414	2	11.2	4.6	55	148	1	94	254	8 353	1 219	3 256
Murray	97	10.2	92	0	9.6	0.0	5	53	1	32	336	1 976	80	833
Nicollet	326	11.0	182	2	6.1	5.1	41	139	1	121	409	2 673	755	2 493
Nobles	293	14.8	192	2	9.7	5.7	22	114	2	146	756	3 955	359	1 805
Norman	80	10.4	105	0	13.7	0.0	4	53	1	77	1 022	1 647	62	797
Olmsted	1 732	15.1	740	7	6.5	4.2	1 438	1 232	3	1 343	1 151	13 725	3 311	2 865
Otter Tail	580	10.7	627	2	11.5	4.0	68	124	2	267	486	10 997	1 257	2 299
Pennington	177	13.0	145	1	10.7	5.7	15	111	1	150	1 106	2 335	527	3 858
Pine	262	11.1	226	2	9.6	7.6	11	46	2	233	974	4 360	1 181	4 968
Pipestone	120	11.8	122	0	12.0	2.8	8	79	1	87	862	2 232	167	1 643
Polk	385	12.1	392	3	12.3	8.7	19	61	2	252	814	5 784	720	2 225
Pope	108	9.9	157	0	14.4	3.1	6	55	2	53	487	2 429	195	1 774
Ramsey	7 412	15.3	4 083	59	8.4	8.0	1 421	293	6	1 514	312	76 070	29 106	5 960
Red Lake	45	10.3	51	0	11.9	7.5	1	23	0	0	0	854	71	1 621
Redwood	192	11.6	219	1	13.2	5.2	9	55	1	35	212	3 541	437	2 602
Renville	196	11.5	217	1	12.7	3.4	7	41	1	30	177	3 500	306	1 778
Rice	676	12.6	416	2	7.8	3.5	67	124	2	114	211	6 842	1 878	3 475
Rock	115	11.7	109	1	11.1	11.6	5	51	1	38	390	2 026	130	1 304
Roseau	252	15.6	141	1	8.7	5.3	9	56	1	101	627	2 207	438	2 665
St. Louis	2 024	10.4	2 182	11	11.2	5.6	464	240	8	1 368	707	36 169	7 155	3 639
Scott	1 410	18.5	352	3	4.6	2.4	42	53	1	67	85	5 215	2 015	2 627
Sherburne	932	16.1	318	3	5.5	3.6	23	38	0	0	0	4 560	1 586	2 718
Sibley	190	13.0	146	1	10.0	3.5	4	27	1	17	117	2 617	56	381
Stearns	1 623	12.7	723	8	5.7	4.9	279	218	5	655	511	17 886	3 679	2 861
Steele	408	13.0	257	3	8.2	6.5	39	123	1	65	205	4 855	1 093	3 438
Stevens	97	9.6	95	1	9.4	6.9	8	79	1	38	375	1 831	192	1 878
Swift	131	12.0	139	0	12.8	0.0	6	56	2	138	1 277	2 436	220	2 015
Todd	275	11.5	222	1	9.3	3.6	11	46	2	262	1 091	4 132	570	2 359
Traverse	47	11.0	63	0	14.7	7.1	5	118	1	35	824	1 079	56	1 298
Wabasha	227	11.0	199	2	9.6	8.8	30	143	2	112	535	3 737	471	2 251
Wadena	159	12.1	165	1	12.6	6.3	9	68	1	48	365	3 043	441	3 376
Waseca	253	13.9	169	2	9.3	6.6	14	77	1	26	143	3 016	526	2 871
Washington	2 684	14.0	851	10	4.4	3.6	310	158	2	92	47	11 654	5 652	2 926
Watonwan	173	15.0	132	1	11.4	3.9	9	78	2	37	323	2 386	274	2 314
Wilkin	98	13.3	74	1	10.1	10.2	2	27	1	171	2 339	1 263	245	3 298
Winona	569	11.8	423	4	8.8	7.0	47	98	1	203	422	6 944	1 599	3 286
Wright	1 299	15.6	514	6	6.2	4.6	45	53	2	147	173	8 771	2 281	2 720
Yellow Medicine	126	10.9	144	1	12.5	8.0	4	35	2	193	1 691	2 622	82	703

1. Per 1,000 estimated resident population, average 1996–1998.   2. Deaths of infants under 1 year old.   3. Deaths of infants under 1 year old per 1,000 live births.   4. Data subject to copyright.   5. Per 100,000 resident population as of July 1 of the year shown.   6. Data for serious crimes have not been adjusted for underreporting; this may affect comparability between geographic areas and over time.   7. Per 100,000 population estimated by the FBI.

Table B. States and Counties — Crime, Education, Money Income, and Poverty

STATE County	Serious crimes known to police, 1998[1] (cont'd) Rate[2] Violent	Property	Education — School enrollment and attainment, 1990 — Enrollment[3] Total	Percent private	Attainment[4] (percent) High school graduate or more	Bachelor's degree or more	Local government expenditures, fiscal 1997[5] Total current expenditures (mil dol)	Current expenditures per student (dollars)	Money income 1989 Per capita[6] (dollars)	Households Median Dollars	Percent change, 1979–1989 (constant 1989 dollars)	Percent with $100,000 or more	Income and poverty, 1997 Median household income	Percent below poverty level All persons	Persons under 18	Persons 5–17 in families
	46	47	48	49	50	51	52	53	54	55	56	57	58	59	60	61
MINNESOTA—Cont'd																
Grant	65	2 164	1 380	0.8	71.9	11.4	9.0	5 732	9 622	19 773	-2.0	0.9	30 909	12.0	17.5	16.2
Hennepin	653	5 398	258 020	16.8	88.2	31.6	1 137.4	7 497	18 496	35 659	6.0	6.3	48 054	9.4	15.5	13.4
Houston	52	1 176	4 620	14.4	75.9	14.4	20.0	5 456	11 587	25 846	2.8	1.8	38 078	8.0	11.1	10.6
Hubbard	160	3 959	3 615	4.4	76.4	14.7	16.9	5 664	9 527	20 151	3.2	0.9	28 457	13.9	20.6	19.0
Isanti	107	2 493	7 273	5.7	78.2	11.5	31.1	5 449	11 909	31 308	6.4	1.9	43 409	7.3	10.5	9.5
Itasca	134	2 582	11 081	6.5	77.5	12.5	54.0	6 388	10 541	22 442	-17.1	0.9	32 769	12.3	17.9	16.3
Jackson	25	1 314	2 831	5.9	74.2	10.0	11.2	5 549	11 287	23 157	-3.0	1.5	33 304	9.5	13.2	12.7
Kanabec	332	3 454	3 317	2.4	69.9	8.9	14.7	5 113	9 887	22 495	0.4	0.8	31 555	12.5	18.2	17.2
Kandiyohi	237	2 802	10 609	7.0	76.3	15.7	42.5	6 369	11 574	25 368	1.7	2.1	36 767	11.2	16.2	14.5
Kittson	167	1 425	1 291	3.2	71.0	12.5	8.0	6 654	11 050	23 518	6.4	1.1	31 221	12.2	18.8	17.1
Koochiching	171	3 630	4 100	10.4	73.0	10.4	16.1	6 099	11 732	23 411	-12.8	1.0	34 633	11.7	18.1	16.9
Lac qui Parle	24	1 531	2 012	2.8	72.2	10.9	13.4	6 214	10 368	21 646	1.9	0.9	32 011	9.3	11.8	11.5
Lake	120	1 250	2 299	5.5	80.2	12.2	12.8	5 629	11 415	23 478	-31.3	0.6	35 598	8.1	12.7	11.7
Lake of the Woods	109	1 814	933	2.3	75.2	11.0	4.8	5 619	10 623	24 383	23.8	0.3	32 302	9.1	13.8	14.1
Le Sueur	64	1 534	6 142	12.1	76.3	13.1	27.2	5 390	11 792	27 706	1.8	2.2	40 833	7.2	10.0	8.9
Lincoln	91	0	1 635	3.7	67.7	8.4	6.9	6 385	9 616	19 211	10.7	1.4	27 341	12.0	16.4	15.3
Lyon	133	1 991	7 542	9.1	75.9	16.8	39.9	7 910	11 121	24 689	-0.7	2.2	37 367	9.2	12.3	11.2
McLeod	171	2 514	8 036	16.6	75.5	11.7	35.9	5 672	12 689	29 549	4.4	2.0	43 010	6.3	8.7	8.1
Mahnomen	1 559	5 457	1 403	5.7	64.7	10.5	10.9	7 010	7 737	16 924	-3.7	0.4	24 664	20.5	30.4	27.1
Marshall	19	1 206	2 895	3.1	68.5	10.2	16.9	6 609	9 675	21 707	0.3	0.4	30 975	11.6	16.6	14.7
Martin	103	2 693	5 669	12.0	75.2	13.0	27.5	6 668	11 387	24 414	-4.8	1.9	34 839	10.4	14.9	13.5
Meeker	217	2 599	5 209	6.7	73.4	10.0	33.7	5 327	10 843	24 516	4.2	1.9	36 119	8.6	11.9	11.1
Mille Lacs	254	4 232	4 782	5.7	70.1	9.4	34.0	5 441	10 167	22 689	2.7	1.5	31 218	12.6	19.1	17.2
Morrison	55	2 286	7 841	9.6	67.7	9.0	40.4	6 379	9 666	22 102	9.2	1.3	31 100	13.3	18.6	16.7
Mower	203	3 053	9 073	10.5	75.8	12.9	37.8	6 197	11 599	23 763	-12.6	1.4	34 330	10.1	15.4	13.7
Murray	21	812	2 350	11.5	69.7	8.5	9.3	5 819	10 871	22 673	2.2	1.6	31 594	9.8	13.4	12.7
Nicollet	106	2 387	9 314	32.6	81.5	22.4	16.9	6 943	12 358	30 491	6.6	2.1	42 786	7.4	9.1	9.1
Nobles	90	1 715	4 981	7.8	70.4	11.1	23.5	6 174	10 860	22 942	-5.8	1.3	32 516	10.9	16.3	14.6
Norman	26	771	1 853	0.6	69.7	9.7	9.9	6 543	9 948	21 238	2.1	0.8	29 518	13.9	20.2	17.9
Olmsted	266	2 599	28 118	15.4	88.0	29.5	141.6	6 824	16 214	35 789	6.4	5.1	49 000	7.0	10.1	9.0
Otter Tail	155	2 144	11 799	8.6	71.6	13.0	78.0	8 233	10 467	21 909	4.0	1.1	31 721	11.4	16.8	14.9
Pennington	205	3 653	3 593	5.5	72.3	13.7	15.2	6 021	10 426	21 571	-12.0	1.1	31 848	11.2	15.8	15.1
Pine	177	4 791	5 461	4.7	69.2	9.5	27.5	5 941	9 538	21 191	3.2	1.1	30 820	13.3	19.6	17.5
Pipestone	49	1 594	2 575	13.7	70.4	9.9	12.8	5 965	10 050	20 737	5.9	1.5	31 021	10.9	14.9	14.6
Polk	155	2 070	8 740	8.5	73.0	12.9	38.1	5 817	10 199	22 559	-5.2	1.2	32 126	14.3	20.1	17.8
Pope	64	1 710	2 571	2.8	72.1	10.2	11.3	5 787	9 465	20 131	1.1	0.8	31 165	10.8	15.4	14.7
Ramsey	550	5 410	130 778	25.5	85.0	28.8	573.1	6 820	15 645	32 043	0.9	3.9	42 284	11.5	19.2	16.9
Red Lake	0	1 621	1 149	9.5	64.3	9.3	7.8	8 071	8 963	19 926	2.0	0.6	29 033	12.1	15.4	15.2
Redwood	185	2 417	3 948	10.4	71.3	11.1	18.5	5 680	10 489	22 827	0.4	1.4	34 606	9.1	12.4	12.0
Renville	76	1 702	4 323	10.7	71.7	10.2	16.3	5 507	10 795	23 278	-6.1	1.6	34 940	10.9	15.9	14.9
Rice	178	3 297	16 008	39.1	78.7	19.3	50.4	6 208	11 936	29 596	4.2	2.5	42 685	7.9	10.1	9.2
Rock	211	1 093	2 504	10.3	69.8	10.8	10.1	5 430	11 383	24 483	2.7	2.1	34 775	7.9	10.4	10.3
Roseau	37	2 628	3 518	3.4	71.8	10.2	18.7	5 519	10 280	25 910	16.0	0.9	36 832	7.7	9.9	10.0
St. Louis	275	3 364	53 991	8.5	80.3	17.3	207.5	6 336	11 833	24 093	-16.7	1.4	36 254	11.7	16.8	14.1
Scott	145	2 482	15 572	17.1	84.8	17.2	74.7	6 275	15 341	40 798	8.4	4.4	59 412	3.9	5.5	5.3
Sherburne	125	2 593	12 613	10.7	84.2	16.7	64.8	5 486	13 147	35 585	9.2	2.6	51 450	5.6	7.1	6.8
Sibley	20	361	3 574	11.2	68.2	8.9	14.6	5 956	10 899	24 957	1.1	1.6	33 692	9.1	13.1	12.9
Stearns	152	2 709	40 146	17.1	78.3	17.5	145.6	5 767	11 620	27 512	2.5	2.6	38 806	8.5	11.6	10.6
Steele	151	3 287	7 913	13.9	79.4	16.0	33.8	5 251	12 993	30 571	8.1	2.4	43 657	7.3	10.6	9.6
Stevens	78	1 800	3 873	5.1	77.0	17.0	10.9	6 080	9 814	21 921	4.2	0.8	36 408	9.8	11.5	11.5
Swift	192	1 823	2 493	7.3	68.2	11.2	10.5	5 501	9 222	18 740	-6.0	0.5	30 259	12.3	15.7	14.4
Todd	112	2 247	6 336	7.6	68.4	7.8	34.7	7 053	8 535	18 836	0.8	0.6	27 846	15.0	20.9	18.5
Traverse	23	1 275	968	2.7	71.2	9.8	4.7	6 094	9 882	20 746	2.0	1.0	29 980	13.8	20.9	19.2
Wabasha	100	2 151	4 948	9.5	76.4	12.4	21.5	5 156	11 862	26 998	6.7	2.0	38 159	7.5	10.8	10.2
Wadena	214	3 162	3 293	5.4	70.6	11.6	19.7	5 927	8 640	17 333	-7.2	0.7	27 036	16.2	20.9	20.9
Waseca	158	2 713	4 970	8.7	77.5	13.6	24.2	5 685	11 514	26 992	-0.9	1.2	38 187	8.5	11.5	10.9
Washington	121	2 805	42 488	13.6	90.0	26.2	182.2	5 423	17 435	44 122	8.5	6.4	61 994	4.0	5.2	4.9
Watonwan	160	2 154	2 782	10.5	72.2	10.1	12.9	5 693	10 658	22 496	-9.0	1.3	31 722	10.3	15.9	15.2
Wilkin	54	3 244	1 858	9.0	73.8	11.6	8.8	5 608	10 108	23 081	-10.9	1.1	35 206	11.4	16.6	14.7
Winona	41	3 245	16 128	19.2	77.7	19.7	40.9	6 085	11 323	25 937	2.2	1.8	36 450	10.1	13.6	12.1
Wright	79	2 641	18 754	9.8	80.1	12.1	101.2	5 777	12 687	33 456	7.0	2.6	47 713	5.9	7.8	7.5
Yellow Medicine	51	652	2 905	6.2	72.6	9.9	14.2	6 304	10 513	21 537	-0.1	1.4	32 582	9.7	11.5	12.0

1. Data for serious crimes have not been adjusted for underreporting; this may affect comparability between geographic areas and over time.   2. Per 100,000 population estimated by the FBI.   3. All persons 3 years old and over enrolled in nursery school through college.   4. Persons 25 years old and over.   5. Elementary and secondary education expenditures, local government fiscal years ending between July 1, 1996 and June 30, 1997.   6. Based on population enumerated as of April 1, 1990.

Table B. States and Counties — **Personal Income**

STATE County	Personal income, 1998 Total (mil dol)	Percent change, 1997–1998	Per capita[1] Dollars	Per capita[1] Rank	Wages and salaries[2] (mil dol)	Proprietor's income (mil dol)	Dividends, interest, and rent (mil dol)	Transfer payments Total (mil dol)	Government payments to individuals Total (mil dol)	Social Security (mil dol)	Medical payments (mil dol)	Income maintenance (mil dol)	Unemployment insurance (mil dol)
	62	63	64	65	66	67	68	69	70	71	72	73	74
MINNESOTA—Cont'd													
Grant	132	3.3	21 529	1 247	51	21	35	28	27	12	11	2	1
Hennepin	42 491	6.7	40 126	30	38 741	2 776	9 599	3 764	3 554	1 347	1 582	365	69
Houston	464	7.1	24 100	622	123	46	95	65	61	29	25	3	1
Hubbard	335	6.6	19 791	1 782	139	30	78	74	71	32	27	6	2
Isanti	671	7.8	22 329	1 010	247	52	106	85	79	35	31	6	3
Itasca	883	4.4	20 100	1 680	459	66	192	182	173	78	66	14	6
Jackson	251	4.5	21 864	1 136	113	35	62	42	40	19	15	3	1
Kanabec	261	5.3	18 414	2 235	109	19	53	47	44	19	16	4	2
Kandiyohi	1 021	7.9	24 976	494	590	72	266	143	135	57	52	10	3
Kittson	116	11.5	21 808	1 156	43	11	30	24	23	10	10	1	0
Koochiching	329	3.3	21 823	1 151	196	17	66	65	62	28	23	5	2
Lac qui Parle	176	4.8	22 062	1 082	60	35	44	36	34	16	14	2	1
Lake	230	4.4	21 558	1 239	124	15	59	49	46	20	17	2	1
Lake of the Woods	90	5.6	19 763	1 789	39	5	22	17	16	7	7	1	0
Le Sueur	596	7.3	23 502	741	234	44	131	80	75	35	30	4	2
Lincoln	127	12.8	19 597	1 858	41	23	31	29	27	12	12	2	1
Lyon	622	6.9	25 488	441	407	56	140	86	81	36	33	2	2
McLeod	895	5.3	26 216	374	624	58	195	103	96	47	37	5	3
Mahnomen	83	3.0	16 434	2 716	51	3	19	24	23	8	10	3	1
Marshall	200	3.0	19 497	1 892	67	11	53	42	40	17	17	3	1
Martin	519	1.4	23 569	730	256	46	143	91	87	43	34	5	2
Meeker	458	5.3	21 064	1 371	171	30	109	72	68	32	26	5	2
Mille Lacs	411	6.9	19 490	1 895	215	37	76	93	89	37	39	7	2
Morrison	584	9.2	19 134	2 010	279	56	121	112	106	44	42	10	4
Mower	912	5.4	24 567	550	443	75	209	165	158	78	62	10	2
Murray	201	9.7	21 073	1 368	66	39	51	37	35	18	13	2	1
Nicollet	690	4.3	23 404	764	391	36	138	70	64	33	21	5	1
Nobles	449	4.5	23 319	789	245	62	107	75	72	34	27	6	2
Norman	160	13.9	21 159	1 343	56	20	44	35	34	14	16	2	1
Olmsted	3 611	9.0	30 880	137	2 980	205	703	334	310	141	125	24	5
Otter Tail	1 167	6.4	21 295	1 296	532	127	292	222	211	98	82	15	5
Pennington	308	7.1	22 765	901	215	18	66	50	48	19	19	4	1
Pine	443	6.2	18 403	2 237	191	28	82	95	90	40	34	8	3
Pipestone	216	4.4	21 499	1 251	96	39	52	41	39	17	16	3	1
Polk	685	9.7	22 024	1 098	322	50	139	128	122	49	52	11	2
Pope	227	6.6	20 792	1 457	92	18	57	47	45	20	18	3	1
Ramsey	15 962	5.7	32 863	86	13 333	708	3 515	1 900	1 804	636	814	210	31
Red Lake	78	11.2	18 303	2 263	29	12	15	18	17	6	7	2	1
Redwood	385	3.1	23 347	782	183	44	105	63	59	29	23	4	1
Renville	370	4.1	21 857	1 143	165	41	98	65	61	30	24	4	2
Rice	1 215	5.3	22 421	996	705	55	257	147	136	65	52	9	4
Rock	217	1.2	22 271	1 023	83	27	58	37	35	18	12	2	1
Roseau	349	5.8	21 690	1 196	256	12	82	45	42	18	18	3	1
St. Louis	4 958	6.1	25 630	423	2 979	394	1 021	855	816	337	318	69	21
Scott	2 298	10.7	29 049	193	1 036	130	325	143	127	58	47	7	6
Sherburne	1 342	11.3	22 248	1 026	532	71	194	115	103	49	35	8	5
Sibley	287	8.0	19 591	1 860	89	24	70	51	48	23	20	3	1
Stearns	2 928	10.3	22 747	907	2 246	227	588	362	336	141	122	25	10
Steele	868	8.5	27 371	271	620	53	173	96	89	45	34	5	2
Stevens	231	2.5	22 992	855	130	26	59	37	35	15	14	2	0
Swift	236	6.5	20 500	1 557	110	23	55	46	44	19	19	3	1
Todd	399	6.5	16 584	2 695	166	32	83	90	85	33	34	9	2
Traverse	94	2.6	22 240	1 028	35	10	33	21	20	9	9	2	0
Wabasha	505	9.8	24 176	612	196	50	112	71	67	32	27	4	1
Wadena	248	7.2	18 947	2 077	148	19	50	62	60	22	27	6	1
Waseca	416	4.4	22 433	991	242	31	94	57	54	27	18	4	1
Washington	5 979	9.9	30 399	156	2 151	180	1 075	364	325	168	104	18	10
Watonwan	254	2.3	22 093	1 069	122	35	59	45	43	20	17	3	1
Wilkin	149	2.8	20 172	1 662	62	9	36	27	25	11	11	2	0
Winona	1 128	7.5	23 495	747	700	76	260	150	140	65	54	9	2
Wright	2 053	6.8	24 143	616	743	132	304	201	184	85	70	11	8
Yellow Medicine	227	4.4	19 913	1 739	102	33	49	48	45	21	19	3	1

1. Based on the resident population estimated as of July 1 of the year shown. 2. Includes other labor income.

Table B. States and Counties — Earnings, Social Security, and Housing

STATE County	Earnings, 1998 Total (mil dol)	Farm	Goods-related[1] Total	Manufacturing	Service-related and other[2] Total	Retail trade	Finance, insurance, and real estate	Services	Government	Social Security beneficiaries, December 1998 Number	Rate[3]	Supplemental Security Income recipients, December 1998	Housing units, 1990 Total	Percent change, 1980–1990
	75	76	77	78	79	80	81	82	83	84	85	86	87	88
MINNESOTA—Cont'd														
Grant	71	13.8	D	10.7	D	6.8	4.8	23.7	15.7	1 677	271	86	3 178	-0.4
Hennepin	41 517	0.0	20.7	16.4	69.8	8.4	13.6	29.8	9.5	145 950	138	18 235	443 583	16.9
Houston	168	6.3	D	13.8	D	7.0	4.1	23.1	17.3	3 706	192	184	7 257	8.8
Hubbard	170	0.7	D	23.9	D	11.6	4.6	24.3	17.7	4 189	247	299	10 042	10.3
Isanti	299	-0.7	29.1	18.8	51.4	10.7	3.6	28.7	20.3	4 198	139	250	9 693	15.8
Itasca	525	-0.4	D	18.2	D	10.1	3.5	D	20.7	9 515	217	756	22 494	6.0
Jackson	149	15.6	23.9	18.6	D	6.1	4.0	15.0	15.8	2 458	213	113	5 121	-7.3
Kanabec	128	-1.9	D	19.3	D	19.7	5.0	15.6	21.5	2 554	180	197	6 098	11.2
Kandiyohi	662	2.3	D	15.8	D	9.7	3.9	22.0	22.6	7 358	179	634	16 669	10.4
Kittson	54	13.5	D	4.4	54.8	8.4	4.3	20.9	23.3	1 317	247	69	2 865	-5.1
Koochiching	213	-0.4	D	34.4	D	9.6	2.2	21.9	18.2	3 347	215	237	7 825	8.1
Lac qui Parle	95	23.9	D	12.8	D	8.2	4.0	13.9	20.8	2 140	267	109	3 955	-7.4
Lake	138	0.1	D	14.3	D	10.3	2.5	D	21.1	2 309	219	90	6 776	10.9
Lake of the Woods	44	-4.0	D	26.0	D	10.2	2.1	26.9	23.6	974	213	51	3 050	12.6
Le Sueur	278	3.8	47.1	35.2	35.7	7.8	3.5	16.0	13.4	4 412	174	239	9 785	2.9
Lincoln	64	19.8	14.8	3.4	49.4	6.8	2.9	23.1	15.9	1 755	272	110	3 050	-7.5
Lyon	464	5.6	D	29.3	D	8.0	5.8	14.1	18.6	4 557	187	322	9 675	5.2
McLeod	682	2.2	D	52.5	D	6.4	2.6	9.1	12.3	5 813	171	133	12 391	13.5
Mahnomen	53	-7.2	D	D	D	8.4	8.6	47.0	19.8	1 116	220	116	2 505	3.9
Marshall	79	5.0	20.9	10.9	48.4	8.6	5.4	15.5	25.8	2 377	230	313	5 049	-3.9
Martin	302	7.4	28.9	22.8	50.0	9.0	4.3	19.7	13.6	5 282	240	228	9 847	0.6
Meeker	201	1.3	D	25.2	D	9.4	D	14.7	18.2	4 235	195	228	9 139	7.0
Mille Lacs	252	2.1	D	18.1	D	9.1	4.8	33.3	17.0	4 674	222	340	9 065	9.3
Morrison	335	3.1	25.1	16.6	49.8	10.3	3.8	22.1	22.0	6 224	204	530	12 434	7.0
Mower	518	4.7	D	31.9	D	9.4	3.1	21.6	15.3	9 187	248	605	15 831	1.0
Murray	106	25.0	D	6.5	D	6.5	4.5	15.1	15.4	2 403	252	102	4 611	-1.5
Nicollet	427	2.5	D	39.7	D	5.7	3.8	17.4	18.8	3 877	131	199	9 963	11.2
Nobles	308	7.2	D	22.8	D	10.9	3.8	14.6	17.3	4 458	231	320	8 094	-1.4
Norman	76	14.5	D	D	D	9.9	5.6	20.3	20.7	1 869	248	108	3 648	-9.2
Olmsted	3 185	0.7	D	22.3	62.6	7.1	3.6	45.6	9.0	16 213	139	1 360	41 603	21.1
Otter Tail	659	4.4	25.8	15.1	51.7	11.7	4.1	20.9	18.1	12 926	235	749	29 295	8.7
Pennington	233	-0.4	D	23.6	D	9.1	2.9	20.0	17.7	2 512	185	219	5 682	-5.0
Pine	219	1.0	D	5.9	D	12.6	3.0	31.7	27.7	5 232	219	429	12 738	23.7
Pipestone	135	8.1	D	17.4	D	11.2	D	17.1	18.2	2 331	231	156	4 387	-5.4
Polk	371	8.9	20.8	15.2	47.6	8.9	3.4	21.1	22.7	6 405	207	496	14 275	-3.3
Pope	110	6.9	D	15.2	51.4	10.5	3.8	16.8	20.7	2 746	252	123	5 836	3.1
Ramsey	14 041	0.0	29.7	24.9	53.6	6.8	8.8	27.2	16.7	71 264	147	11 389	201 016	13.6
Red Lake	41	13.9	D	8.1	D	10.8	3.4	15.8	20.6	928	217	57	1 899	-7.0
Redwood	227	8.9	D	19.9	D	8.5	3.9	20.6	15.8	3 813	231	198	7 144	-3.3
Renville	205	16.1	25.6	19.3	42.4	6.3	5.5	14.8	15.9	3 850	228	179	7 442	-5.9
Rice	759	0.4	35.1	26.9	46.7	8.5	2.8	25.4	17.8	7 766	144	529	17 520	11.8
Rock	110	15.6	D	7.4	D	10.0	11.1	19.0	21.2	2 356	242	93	3 963	-3.2
Roseau	268	-0.7	63.3	61.5	26.2	5.6	2.3	13.3	11.1	2 464	153	159	6 236	23.9
St. Louis	3 373	0.0	22.6	9.4	57.7	10.1	3.6	28.4	19.8	40 029	207	239	95 403	0.1
Scott	1 167	0.2	40.0	23.4	48.1	8.3	3.3	25.0	11.7	6 809	86	340	20 302	43.1
Sherburne	603	1.0	D	18.5	D	11.7	3.8	15.5	19.1	5 854	97	110	14 964	44.7
Sibley	113	8.8	25.7	13.6	44.4	7.7	4.0	16.6	21.1	3 073	211	4 116	5 625	-0.1
Stearns	2 473	2.1	24.0	17.6	57.5	17.0	4.6	23.3	16.4	18 378	143	1 497	43 806	21.8
Steele	672	2.4	D	39.6	D	7.6	D	13.7	9.0	5 373	169	236	11 840	5.2
Stevens	156	9.2	D	13.6	D	8.0	4.4	19.1	24.9	1 950	192	126	4 108	-2.7
Swift	134	6.3	D	24.2	D	7.8	3.5	18.8	19.2	2 584	239	170	4 795	-7.5
Todd	197	2.8	D	30.5	D	8.7	3.8	16.2	19.8	4 823	201	453	11 234	5.1
Traverse	45	9.4	D	13.6	D	8.1	6.4	12.4	24.9	1 210	285	46	2 220	-7.8
Wabasha	246	8.4	36.0	29.0	41.3	8.6	3.2	14.9	14.3	4 091	195	189	8 205	7.9
Wadena	168	-0.5	24.0	17.6	54.0	10.2	3.3	24.3	22.5	3 200	243	370	5 801	6.7
Waseca	273	4.4	D	41.5	D	5.3	3.2	14.1	17.5	3 438	189	177	7 011	1.8
Washington	2 331	0.5	35.9	29.1	49.5	12.0	9.2	19.1	14.0	18 547	94	657	51 648	38.9
Watonwan	157	12.6	D	27.2	D	6.1	3.8	16.0	13.9	2 593	226	126	4 886	-1.3
Wilkin	72	9.1	D	3.7	D	7.0	5.5	26.0	18.2	1 407	192	62	3 140	-4.4
Winona	776	4.2	D	32.3	D	8.1	2.4	19.2	15.5	7 980	166	570	17 630	6.8
Wright	876	1.1	D	18.1	D	11.7	4.5	19.1	16.4	10 393	122	513	26 353	20.9
Yellow Medicine	134	13.1	D	13.3	D	6.7	3.5	22.9	23.0	2 761	242	156	4 983	-7.5

1. Covers mining, construction, and manufacturing. 2. Covers private sector earnings in agricultural services, forestry, and fisheries; transportation and public utilities; wholesale trade; retail trade; finance, insurance, and real estate; and services. 3. Per 1,000 resident population estimated as of July 1 of the year shown.

STATE County	Total	Percent	Median value[1]	With a mortgage	Without a mortgage	Median rent[2]	Rent as percent of income	Sub-standard units[3] (percent)	Total	Percent change, 1998–1999	Total	Rate[4]	Total	Professional, managerial, and technical	Precision production, craft, and repair
	89	90	91	92	93	94	95	96	97	98	99	100	101	102	103
MINNESOTA—Cont'd															
Grant	2 454	79.5	29 100	18.1	13.7	227	26.6	2.0	2 778	-0.9	151	5.4	2 628	21.1	11.3
Hennepin	419 060	63.4	91 000	21.0	12.1	487	27.0	2.3	653 448	0.4	14 168	2.2	571 425	37.1	7.6
Houston	6 844	79.6	52 400	18.2	12.2	300	24.7	2.1	10 960	-0.5	389	3.5	9 042	23.7	11.4
Hubbard	5 781	83.1	48 700	19.5	12.5	275	27.7	3.0	8 286	-0.4	405	4.9	5 869	25.0	11.1
Isanti	8 810	83.1	64 400	21.1	12.5	357	28.0	3.3	15 740	1.9	558	3.5	11 987	22.2	16.6
Itasca	15 461	83.1	44 300	17.8	12.5	297	27.9	3.6	19 783	0.4	1 424	7.2	15 202	24.2	13.1
Jackson	4 560	76.2	32 100	17.3	11.9	239	23.4	2.4	6 158	-3.5	195	3.2	5 176	17.7	8.7
Kanabec	4 753	82.6	49 200	21.0	13.1	313	28.4	4.2	6 750	-5.4	448	6.6	5 530	17.3	14.5
Kandiyohi	14 298	72.9	56 800	20.0	12.7	315	28.0	2.5	21 477	-0.6	743	3.5	17 913	26.0	10.2
Kittson	2 274	81.8	28 000	14.5	13.2	253	24.6	2.1	2 263	-1.0	132	5.8	2 420	19.8	12.8
Koochiching	6 025	77.9	41 800	15.6	11.9	312	25.4	4.9	6 286	-3.9	430	6.8	7 159	21.6	17.8
Lac qui Parle	3 505	78.9	26 000	16.2	12.1	235	25.7	2.1	3 663	-4.4	126	3.4	3 723	20.0	10.7
Lake	4 242	82.9	39 400	15.0	11.5	271	25.4	3.7	5 457	-1.1	207	3.8	4 303	21.4	16.2
Lake of the Woods	1 576	84.5	40 900	15.5	12.1	244	25.9	4.8	2 432	-0.6	117	4.8	1 900	22.4	10.7
Le Sueur	8 468	82.0	57 800	19.2	13.0	315	23.5	2.4	14 707	4.3	491	3.3	10 939	21.3	15.1
Lincoln	2 704	79.9	22 900	19.1	13.4	209	23.2	1.6	3 031	-2.8	113	3.7	2 919	17.4	9.1
Lyon	9 073	68.4	48 200	16.5	12.4	300	23.9	1.9	14 983	-0.7	396	2.6	11 940	24.5	10.0
McLeod	11 815	77.0	62 100	20.0	12.5	330	23.5	1.9	20 169	-5.5	664	3.3	15 972	20.7	14.3
Mahnomen	1 805	79.4	33 900	20.1	14.8	246	24.7	5.2	2 179	0.2	163	7.5	1 668	26.0	12.2
Marshall	4 194	82.1	34 600	17.1	12.7	217	24.3	3.2	4 447	-3.0	434	9.8	4 351	18.5	11.3
Martin	9 129	74.9	40 500	18.8	12.8	265	22.8	1.2	10 814	-3.3	377	3.5	10 375	22.4	10.8
Meeker	7 651	79.6	49 100	18.1	12.8	301	26.6	2.9	9 319	-0.4	502	5.4	9 299	20.9	13.8
Mille Lacs	6 911	79.7	50 800	19.9	13.9	308	27.9	4.3	9 359	3.3	581	6.2	7 960	19.1	13.5
Morrison	10 399	81.8	47 100	20.8	13.6	274	26.6	4.5	14 859	-2.8	905	6.1	12 135	19.2	13.0
Mower	15 028	77.3	42 600	16.6	12.1	278	26.0	1.6	18 884	0.9	403	2.1	16 391	22.1	10.9
Murray	3 758	79.4	30 400	14.8	13.0	242	22.8	1.5	4 247	-6.5	177	4.2	4 149	18.2	10.7
Nicollet	9 478	72.9	65 200	17.5	12.1	363	25.2	1.9	18 735	1.2	350	1.9	14 620	29.7	10.3
Nobles	7 683	75.4	39 600	15.8	12.4	299	22.8	2.4	9 352	-1.1	301	3.2	9 219	20.7	13.0
Norman	3 118	80.1	30 200	15.6	13.1	231	21.9	1.8	3 263	-3.5	165	5.1	3 183	21.2	12.1
Olmsted	40 058	72.4	72 300	18.6	11.8	410	23.4	2.1	72 567	3.6	1 457	2.0	57 318	40.1	7.6
Otter Tail	19 510	78.1	46 600	18.6	12.9	290	26.3	2.3	26 650	-1.4	1 156	4.3	22 038	23.5	10.6
Pennington	5 173	74.0	41 400	17.0	13.5	242	25.7	2.0	7 975	-0.5	461	5.8	5 691	23.9	11.2
Pine	7 577	82.5	44 900	19.5	13.3	287	27.6	5.4	11 349	-1.8	704	6.2	8 030	20.0	12.3
Pipestone	4 078	76.7	31 700	15.7	12.6	237	24.7	2.1	4 831	-9.6	140	2.9	4 491	19.5	10.8
Polk	11 984	74.7	47 200	19.8	12.6	293	27.6	2.1	16 345	-0.9	619	3.8	13 789	22.8	10.0
Pope	4 135	78.7	39 200	18.5	13.2	243	24.9	2.1	5 383	-3.5	167	3.1	4 480	20.3	9.2
Ramsey	190 500	62.2	83 600	20.9	12.7	450	27.4	3.2	281 343	0.1	6 447	2.3	252 277	36.1	7.8
Red Lake	1 730	78.8	28 200	16.3	12.4	199	24.6	3.1	1 837	-2.4	172	9.4	1 755	19.0	10.5
Redwood	6 554	77.1	32 800	17.0	12.5	250	23.1	1.9	8 749	-3.9	251	2.9	7 573	20.5	10.0
Renville	6 790	79.2	31 600	15.8	12.5	261	22.6	2.6	8 049	-1.7	379	4.7	7 445	20.4	10.0
Rice	16 347	75.5	67 800	19.7	12.6	370	26.7	2.1	27 913	-1.7	819	2.9	25 025	27.3	11.3
Rock	3 754	75.3	36 600	15.8	12.1	248	22.2	1.8	4 516	-5.6	132	2.9	4 488	17.9	9.2
Roseau	5 415	82.6	49 400	16.9	12.5	326	23.7	4.1	8 763	-2.7	356	4.1	7 199	15.7	11.2
St. Louis	78 901	74.2	42 200	15.2	12.5	291	28.6	2.2	101 829	-0.6	4 116	4.0	83 314	28.5	12.6
Scott	19 367	81.9	90 900	22.9	12.7	475	25.1	2.2	46 885	3.6	1 092	2.3	30 750	26.8	13.6
Sherburne	13 643	80.5	74 800	20.9	11.8	442	29.3	2.8	32 924	4.0	893	2.7	20 410	24.4	15.1
Sibley	5 323	81.5	44 400	18.4	12.7	253	21.6	2.3	6 503	-0.4	262	4.0	6 741	15.6	13.2
Stearns	39 776	71.4	61 400	19.2	12.6	388	26.8	2.4	76 076	2.8	2 262	3.0	58 886	24.7	10.3
Steele	11 342	77.1	61 200	17.0	12.3	321	21.5	1.8	19 500	0.1	488	2.5	15 553	24.0	12.1
Stevens	3 823	67.2	37 700	15.8	12.9	286	24.8	3.3	5 554	0.2	158	2.8	4 703	25.5	8.5
Swift	4 268	77.5	27 500	15.9	12.6	206	23.8	1.8	5 478	-3.5	214	3.9	4 464	20.2	10.0
Todd	8 589	80.8	35 000	18.1	14.1	235	25.8	3.3	9 180	-0.5	479	5.2	9 445	17.1	11.7
Traverse	1 778	79.0	23 400	15.4	12.3	237	20.4	1.1	1 666	-7.3	96	5.8	1 770	19.8	9.8
Wabasha	7 286	81.7	51 900	17.0	13.2	301	23.3	2.6	12 680	0.7	304	2.4	9 236	22.7	11.9
Wadena	4 978	76.4	36 200	18.6	13.5	235	27.3	3.3	7 025	0.9	380	5.4	5 250	23.1	10.5
Waseca	6 649	77.3	53 500	18.1	12.6	310	24.0	1.4	9 365	-3.3	303	3.2	8 627	22.0	13.0
Washington	49 246	83.9	94 200	21.5	12.2	489	26.2	1.5	114 677	2.3	2 126	1.9	76 652	34.4	10.6
Watonwan	4 530	74.8	35 500	16.1	11.7	252	21.5	1.8	5 676	2.1	218	3.8	5 343	17.7	12.9
Wilkin	2 805	77.6	38 400	17.1	12.2	260	26.3	2.5	3 805	-3.3	88	2.3	3 247	21.4	12.1
Winona	16 930	72.1	54 400	17.7	13.2	323	26.1	2.6	27 542	-2.7	734	2.7	23 826	25.1	11.0
Wright	23 013	82.0	75 000	21.1	12.6	380	25.8	2.7	47 362	2.1	1 381	2.9	34 050	22.1	15.4
Yellow Medicine	4 607	77.9	31 100	16.7	13.1	242	24.1	1.8	5 217	-3.1	226	4.3	4 904	22.0	12.5

1. Specified owner-occupied units. 2. Specified renter-occupied units. 3. Overcrowded or lacking complete plumbing facilities. 4. Percent of civilian labor force. 5. Persons 16 years and older.

Table B. States and Counties — Nonfarm Employment and Agriculture

	Private nonfarm establishments, employment and payroll, 1998								Agriculture, 1997			
	Employment						Annual payroll		Farms			Farm operators
										Percent with—		
STATE County	Number of establishments	Total	Health Care and Social Assistance	Manufacturing	Retail trade	Finance and Insurance	Professional Scientific and Technical Services	Total (mil dol)	Average per employee (dollars)	Number	Less than 50 acres	500 acres and over	Whose principal occupation is farming (percent)
	104	105	106	107	108	109	110	111	112	113	114	115	116

MINNESOTA—Cont'd													
Grant	231	1 723	408	166	306	98	45	29	16 746	468	13.5	36.1	67.7
Hennepin	38 350	820 439	88 768	104 912	81 897	71 276	63 365	30 195	36 803	574	56.3	5.1	41.6
Houston	418	4 212	1 073	638	507	161	92	79	18 806	954	11.4	17.7	61.5
Hubbard	564	4 672	802	974	1 000	141	61	94	20 138	431	10.4	14.2	37.8
Isanti	697	7 097	1 798	1 446	1 230	215	147	155	21 823	746	34.7	8.4	35.8
Itasca	1 224	13 334	1 917	2 597	2 459	340	441	322	24 142	415	14.9	11.1	36.6
Jackson	326	3 788	D	864	407	121	135	73	19 185	963	13.7	28.6	71.0
Kanabec	286	3 508	700	815	675	107	77	71	20 246	626	17.7	8.8	43.9
Kandiyohi	1 255	18 294	4 418	3 119	3 269	599	469	403	22 044	1 131	22.3	20.3	57.9
Kittson	171	1 146	343	D	222	72	33	20	17 390	558	5.4	52.9	61.6
Koochiching	459	4 949	620	D	828	409	75	118	23 944	213	4.2	25.8	38.5
Lac qui Parle	261	2 371	476	341	403	109	D	45	19 023	790	10.1	37.5	74.9
Lake	280	3 002	520	539	381	92	113	71	23 559	37	29.7	2.7	27.0
Lake of the Woods	157	1 181	D	219	236	D	D	23	19 066	196	11.2	34.2	41.8
Le Sueur	672	8 280	703	2 668	970	209	558	199	24 031	877	24.9	12.4	55.0
Lincoln	186	1 393	563	D	285	53	17	22	15 574	724	13.0	25.4	66.6
Lyon	775	13 476	1 580	2 014	1 951	763	162	333	24 689	931	15.5	33.1	71.1
McLeod	912	18 060	1 832	9 457	2 159	411	214	490	27 133	1 008	22.9	12.5	64.7
Mahnomen	124	799	D	D	201	D	D	15	18 412	341	8.5	36.4	72.4
Marshall	344	2 120	392	271	306	140	19	42	19 928	1 144	6.6	41.1	60.0
Martin	698	8 425	1 364	2 160	1 572	334	225	184	21 861	987	16.6	32.3	69.8
Meeker	587	5 763	809	1 664	787	165	121	129	22 331	1 016	21.8	15.8	61.7
Mille Lacs	605	8 583	1 396	1 076	1 025	195	63	168	19 568	711	21.9	7.3	48.5
Morrison	781	8 435	1 472	1 998	1 509	276	100	167	19 834	1 808	12.3	8.3	55.9
Mower	918	12 340	2 326	2 916	2 003	361	D	320	25 955	1 123	20.8	23.1	65.2
Murray	288	2 101	394	285	338	137	90	38	18 171	836	13.8	35.8	78.5
Nicollet	619	11 487	1 594	4 274	840	226	255	277	24 119	723	16.3	22.0	69.4
Nobles	667	8 341	1 312	2 326	1 372	289	133	166	19 884	1 021	14.1	24.2	74.4
Norman	215	1 572	458	D	359	93	59	28	17 651	670	10.6	44.5	68.2
Olmsted	2 892	68 663	D	10 989	9 330	1 489	2 350	2 183	31 799	1 317	28.3	10.9	51.3
Otter Tail	1 588	17 462	3 134	3 715	3 156	527	303	331	18 934	2 647	11.6	16.7	58.3
Pennington	363	6 425	853	1 784	969	129	83	134	20 788	528	7.0	32.4	57.0
Pine	602	4 820	862	436	1 033	209	69	82	17 098	950	12.4	11.6	45.7
Pipestone	330	3 705	635	653	562	78	D	64	17 211	690	18.7	23.3	71.9
Polk	819	8 589	1 749	1 319	1 372	307	230	167	19 455	1 366	8.6	45.0	66.8
Pope	334	3 384	781	535	389	114	178	68	19 999	825	12.8	22.3	62.1
Ramsey	13 410	300 709	40 208	38 130	32 937	21 418	14 151	10 157	33 777	59	74.6	1.7	45.8
Red Lake	116	1 176	205	417	145	58	5	26	22 064	376	7.4	33.8	52.1
Redwood	604	5 447	896	1 172	950	210	120	111	20 364	1 168	11.8	34.5	80.4
Renville	604	6 074	722	1 322	760	214	122	123	20 300	1 114	12.4	35.8	76.6
Rice	1 338	20 014	3 019	5 094	2 918	473	351	504	25 175	1 191	24.9	9.8	47.4
Rock	266	2 865	495	91	529	557	47	55	19 310	704	19.7	25.1	69.5
Roseau	391	7 960	702	4 811	784	163	D	183	23 031	1 051	9.2	31.6	47.7
St. Louis	5 556	76 907	16 447	5 144	12 772	2 959	2 586	1 899	24 692	713	19.5	8.4	31.7
Scott	2 029	27 811	2 315	4 550	2 497	474	588	833	29 940	805	46.5	6.0	40.4
Sherburne	1 179	12 880	1 785	3 083	2 319	320	247	328	25 457	512	36.5	9.4	42.2
Sibley	355	3 304	371	1 293	444	162	63	71	21 596	958	20.6	18.1	68.4
Stearns	3 843	65 890	9 172	13 066	11 143	2 171	1 766	1 674	25 410	2 982	16.8	6.5	66.5
Steele	898	20 163	D	8 503	2 423	2 362	183	556	27 572	774	23.5	15.9	61.9
Stevens	354	3 575	848	246	630	134	157	75	20 954	497	16.5	44.1	71.8
Swift	333	3 522	506	857	464	124	D	67	19 022	739	10.8	37.9	70.1
Todd	546	4 666	611	1 628	768	190	94	97	20 887	1 741	13.7	8.0	54.9
Traverse	132	1 022	198	86	258	D	D	15	15 046	385	7.3	56.9	79.0
Wabasha	589	6 847	1 133	2 136	969	163	109	151	21 997	963	16.0	12.0	63.0
Wadena	299	4 417	1 733	795	622	98	54	79	17 963	625	13.3	13.4	52.0
Waseca	481	6 982	1 099	2 934	745	273	123	166	23 843	709	19.2	22.7	63.9
Washington	4 197	52 281	4 824	9 827	10 018	1 933	1 667	1 600	30 603	653	49.0	6.3	43.6
Watonwan	335	3 566	528	1 095	412	146	70	68	19 072	576	12.5	31.1	75.0
Wilkin	173	1 936	522	D	264	68	D	35	17 985	441	8.8	54.9	80.7
Winona	1 267	24 355	2 522	7 432	2 633	509	825	550	22 585	1 044	14.7	14.6	66.3
Wright	2 078	22 644	3 874	4 568	3 932	606	776	544	24 003	1 422	31.6	7.5	49.9
Yellow Medicine	358	3 837	747	630	514	123	D	76	19 821	876	11.9	38.5	72.6

Table B. States and Counties — Agriculture, Land, and Water

STATE County	Land in farms Acreage (1,000)	Percent change, 1992–1997	Acres Average size of farm	Total irrigated (1,000)	Total cropland (1,000)	Value of land and buildings Average per farm ($1,000)	Average per acre (dollars)	Value of machinery and equipment Average per farm ($1,000)	Value of products sold Total (mil dol)	Average per farm (dollars)	Percent from Crops	Live-stock and poultry products	Percent of farms with sales of $10,000 or more	$100,000 or more	Percent of land owned by Fed. Gov. 1997	Water consumption 1995 (mil gal/day)
	117	118	119	120	121	122	123	124	125	126	127	128	129	130	131	132
MINNESOTA—Cont'd																
Grant	278	3.5	595	3	251	584	1 000	124	61	129 757	81.7	18.3	68.4	36.3	2.3	1.7
Hennepin	69	-12.5	120	2	54	433	3 323	56	44	76 217	77.3	22.7	42.9	15.0	0.5	253.2
Houston	298	9.6	313	0	187	305	1 093	61	78	81 404	38.1	61.9	67.1	24.5	2.5	2.9
Hubbard	131	16.5	303	24	71	222	692	47	23	54 198	77.8	22.2	30.2	5.6	0.0	6.8
Isanti	139	5.6	187	1	99	273	1 584	38	25	33 408	65.8	34.2	35.3	8.8	0.0	3.0
Itasca	104	-4.0	250	0	55	168	591	35	5	11 958	34.0	66.0	30.1	1.0	16.5	174.6
Jackson	384	-4.3	398	0	355	642	1 651	96	150	156 169	59.1	40.9	85.8	42.4	0.8	1.7
Kanabec	139	-4.9	222	D	68	168	773	36	17	26 570	26.4	73.6	36.9	7.3	0.0	1.6
Kandiyohi	379	4.9	335	9	327	465	1 412	83	224	197 763	32.5	67.5	62.6	30.1	2.0	9.4
Kittson	501	3.8	899	D	431	536	585	127	56	99 626	90.7	9.3	58.4	30.6	0.0	0.7
Koochiching	77	11.1	360	D	42	135	435	29	4	16 519	29.9	70.1	33.3	2.3	0.6	42.9
Lac qui Parle	398	-1.8	503	3	362	519	1 059	104	113	143 139	62.4	37.6	82.7	38.4	2.3	3.5
Lake	4	-20.6	107	0	2	106	986	14	0	3 356	46.0	54.0	10.8	0.0	51.5	133.0
Lake of the Woods	118	13.1	600	D	78	297	452	61	8	39 886	81.5	18.5	48.0	11.7	4.0	1.2
Le Sueur	215	4.7	245	D	184	440	1 770	88	85	96 378	48.9	51.1	59.6	25.8	0.0	3.7
Lincoln	270	5.7	372	0	234	292	794	68	69	95 244	44.7	55.3	66.4	25.0	0.0	1.3
Lyon	403	2.0	433	0	366	503	1 180	86	147	158 058	49.7	50.3	77.6	45.4	0.0	5.8
McLeod	250	-0.3	248	0	223	362	1 566	91	83	82 130	55.4	44.6	73.0	24.8	0.2	7.4
Mahnomen	190	1.6	557	0	153	365	635	80	25	72 309	73.6	26.4	66.9	21.4	8.0	0.7
Marshall	774	3.9	677	1	691	381	563	110	91	79 624	89.7	10.3	56.6	23.0	3.9	1.0
Martin	421	1.8	426	1	398	839	1 933	130	254	257 064	43.2	56.8	89.5	53.3	0.0	45.1
Meeker	293	-2.6	289	3	249	335	1 217	93	139	137 190	34.2	65.8	66.8	25.4	1.2	4.3
Mille Lacs	135	-5.2	189	0	84	183	918	47	26	36 879	25.5	74.5	45.6	11.0	0.1	2.7
Morrison	430	1.8	238	14	250	175	731	67	157	86 708	16.2	83.8	59.5	21.3	0.2	9.6
Mower	404	2.9	360	2	375	567	1 596	103	163	144 955	62.0	38.0	77.8	39.3	0.0	7.3
Murray	384	2.1	459	D	355	546	1 159	108	126	151 214	54.6	45.4	87.0	48.9	0.0	2.1
Nicollet	249	3.0	345	0	233	595	1 746	123	172	238 322	35.2	64.8	86.9	46.1	0.0	6.3
Nobles	390	-6.4	382		366	561	1 462	107	159	155 287	48.5	51.5	89.1	41.7	0.0	5.0
Norman	483	5.5	721	1	435	521	780	106	75	112 303	91.2	8.8	67.2	34.6	0.0	0.8
Olmsted	304	-0.8	231	0	245	328	1 425	75	106	80 729	48.4	51.6	57.3	22.6	0.0	41.3
Otter Tail	840	2.4	317	48	595	226	723	70	201	76 098	40.1	59.9	56.6	19.4	1.3	77.5
Pennington	313	11.7	592	0	264	281	489	70	24	45 255	81.2	18.8	50.0	15.2	0.0	2.8
Pine	247	-6.2	260	3	129	213	769	37	38	39 848	26.0	74.0	42.6	9.2	0.8	2.7
Pipestone	244	-3.7	353	3	213	368	1 075	86	118	171 658	29.6	70.4	83.0	34.1	0.1	2.7
Polk	1 052	0.8	770	7	937	597	794	149	194	141 764	91.8	8.2	66.6	36.6	1.0	18.4
Pope	325	4.8	394	29	268	323	800	85	80	97 217	60.7	39.3	66.4	27.3	2.7	11.9
Ramsey	D	D	D	0	3	242	3 119	43	6	105 681	98.6	1.4	57.6	16.9	2.1	142.9
Red Lake	205	12.0	545	D	172	307	650	62	21	56 128	67.8	32.2	57.2	16.2	0.1	0.6
Redwood	508	3.3	435	D	473	689	1 593	120	210	179 558	55.8	44.2	89.1	52.6	0.0	2.8
Renville	601	0.2	540	2	567	913	1 703	165	301	269 849	56.1	43.9	87.7	51.3	0.0	3.0
Rice	251	10.1	211	1	209	404	1 976	72	127	106 977	36.2	63.8	56.1	19.9	0.0	6.9
Rock	281	4.0	399	D	260	543	1 400	100	135	191 537	40.7	59.3	83.8	43.5	0.0	3.3
Roseau	577	7.7	549	0	467	246	427	64	53	50 759	64.5	35.5	46.4	14.1	0.1	2.1
St. Louis	155	1.6	218	1	87	135	633	26	10	13 575	51.0	49.0	21.3	2.5	20.2	203.6
Scott	118	-10.7	146	0	100	416	2 969	62	46	57 329	46.8	53.2	46.1	16.6	1.4	9.7
Sherburne	105	-11.0	205	26	77	370	1 896	73	43	83 516	64.1	35.9	38.3	14.3	11.2	86.6
Sibley	310	-0.7	323	1	283	507	1 563	115	144	150 349	47.7	52.3	80.2	37.9	0.0	3.0
Stearns	646	0.3	217	30	492	227	1 099	72	302	101 356	18.1	81.9	69.1	31.2	0.6	27.7
Steele	227	-2.2	293	1	210	457	1 563	93	96	124 590	58.2	41.8	71.8	34.1	0.0	3.5
Stevens	299	4.7	602	13	284	648	1 098	137	107	214 580	55.8	44.2	78.3	47.7	2.2	3.8
Swift	388	-0.5	525	20	352	506	941	118	119	161 311	64.0	36.0	79.0	39.4	1.4	8.4
Todd	387	-1.9	223	8	248	155	687	49	113	64 641	22.7	77.3	53.1	15.5	0.1	7.3
Traverse	315	1.6	818	D	300	726	882	146	68	177 181	88.4	11.6	87.8	52.5	0.6	0.6
Wabasha	253	3.0	263	1	184	306	1 207	79	94	97 107	33.3	66.7	74.0	32.4	0.9	3.8
Wadena	175	2.2	280	14	100	162	636	47	53	84 717	22.9	77.1	45.8	10.9	0.0	7.6
Waseca	235	-0.7	332	D	213	586	1 777	101	118	166 811	51.2	48.8	81.0	38.2	0.0	2.9
Washington	90	-11.0	138	4	69	484	3 652	62	57	87 685	87.3	12.7	41.3	14.1	0.3	320.9
Watonwan	256	2.4	444	0	237	707	1 711	116	120	208 562	54.3	45.7	88.4	51.4	0.0	3.1
Wilkin	458	8.7	1 038	3	435	964	942	174	101	227 982	94.4	5.6	81.6	50.3	0.4	1.2
Winona	290	-0.4	277	0	191	307	1 084	86	122	116 920	21.3	78.7	70.3	30.3	0.7	12.0
Wright	252	-7.8	177	2	201	364	2 145	60	93	65 287	47.1	52.9	54.3	17.1	0.4	348.2
Yellow Medicine	415	1.8	474	1	380	504	1 102	117	125	142 838	66.0	34.0	81.1	45.3	0.2	1.5

STATE County	Value of Residential Construction Authorized by Building Permits, 1999		Wholesale Trade, 1997				Retail Trade[1], 1997				Real Estate and Rental and Leasing, 1997			
	New Construction ($1,000)	Number of Housing Units	Number of Establish-ments	Number of Employees	Sales (mil dol)	Annual Payroll (mil dol)	Number of Establish-ments	Number of Employees	Sales (mil dol)	Annual Payroll (mil dol)	Number of Establish-ments	Number of Employees	Receipts (mil dol)	Annual Payroll (mil dol)
	133	134	135	136	137	138	139	140	141	142	143	144	145	146
MINNESOTA—Cont'd														
Grant	1 131	15	18	168	209.1	3.8	44	287	53.4	4.1	7	D	D	D
Hennepin	723 704	5 252	3 723	61 454	59 929.0	2 700.6	4 644	78 226	14 615.8	1 409.6	1 796	14 720	2 205.9	409.7
Houston	12 024	94	31	536	70.0	10.1	70	500	76.3	6.0	5	11	1.8	0.1
Hubbard	4 976	66	22	111	29.0	2.2	107	846	125.2	11.4	9	42	3.3	0.8
Isanti	29 942	294	19	D	D	D	103	1 195	193.6	15.7	18	54	3.7	0.5
Itasca	30 554	314	43	395	467.5	9.7	256	2 376	361.0	34.0	31	83	7.1	1.1
Jackson	1 602	18	23	254	131.3	6.9	55	478	57.6	5.6	3	7	0.5	0.1
Kanabec	6 192	81	9	D	D	D	75	665	114.0	9.5	7	D	D	D
Kandiyohi	21 500	195	73	1 071	548.8	31.5	267	3 022	447.6	44.2	52	189	31.4	3.0
Kittson	1 029	12	20	171	89.3	3.3	36	220	38.0	2.7	6	10	0.4	0.0
Koochiching	2 782	34	10	D	D	D	104	787	124.6	11.9	12	35	3.9	0.7
Lac qui Parle	1 228	12	21	207	124.6	5.2	56	355	50.1	3.8	7	12	0.6	0.1
Lake	7 694	78	9	D	D	D	53	407	121.4	9.3	2	D	D	D
Lake of the Woods	0	0	8	43	15.8	0.8	29	202	26.2	2.5	6	14	1.3	0.2
Le Sueur	12 394	154	30	415	154.0	11.6	117	955	150.1	13.1	19	35	2.8	0.4
Lincoln	287	4	15	99	40.2	1.9	34	228	35.9	4.2	5	9	0.5	0.0
Lyon	7 667	79	54	889	915.8	31.7	155	2 013	290.5	27.6	26	87	5.4	0.8
McLeod	37 476	258	43	413	239.0	13.6	188	2 079	286.6	27.7	28	72	8.7	1.0
Mahnomen	0	0	8	48	29.7	1.2	28	147	28.8	2.7	3	7	0.3	0.1
Marshall	290	3	32	D	D	D	45	293	72.0	5.6	2	D	D	D
Martin	3 910	31	53	377	419.4	12.6	131	1 552	250.4	21.3	18	47	4.2	0.7
Meeker	15 876	168	26	203	100.8	5.3	103	787	128.2	11.9	19	36	3.9	0.3
Mille Lacs	13 801	140	27	219	87.1	5.1	118	997	133.1	12.2	12	23	1.7	0.2
Morrison	20 569	303	31	282	161.5	5.3	141	1 468	247.8	20.1	13	42	4.3	0.5
Mower	13 457	117	44	279	443.3	9.8	191	1 957	269.0	26.0	21	112	4.2	1.0
Murray	2 726	36	15	124	78.6	3.0	53	335	54.0	4.3	3	D	D	D
Nicollet	30 165	349	41	492	207.3	21.1	80	756	121.7	10.3	19	72	3.8	0.7
Nobles	2 918	24	43	D	D	D	155	1 376	206.6	19.0	12	51	2.6	0.5
Norman	883	8	15	141	57.6	3.3	43	357	80.5	5.7	4	D	D	D
Olmsted	164 406	1 385	125	1 176	605.4	37.5	583	9 254	1 431.6	136.5	124	654	72.9	9.7
Otter Tail	15 672	183	73	602	233.4	10.2	317	2 922	474.8	43.3	47	113	10.4	1.4
Pennington	1 586	15	19	939	302.9	21.0	85	1 000	149.5	15.3	13	37	3.2	0.6
Pine	8 572	109	14	101	25.4	2.0	116	875	153.2	12.3	26	111	5.3	1.0
Pipestone	425	4	31	457	256.1	9.1	67	557	94.3	6.6	6	D	D	D
Polk	12 049	118	57	415	206.2	10.0	152	1 377	211.7	19.7	15	66	3.3	0.9
Pope	2 967	33	22	290	192.2	8.0	54	379	58.7	5.1	4	11	0.6	0.1
Ramsey	115 231	889	927	15 680	9 328.6	633.3	1 878	32 511	5 485.7	564.7	625	4 875	560.0	111.9
Red Lake	382	6	10	70	35.0	1.8	30	150	32.5	2.6	NA	NA	NA	NA
Redwood	2 653	22	51	478	400.0	16.1	87	927	126.9	11.7	26	40	2.3	0.2
Renville	3 679	33	31	478	364.7	13.3	104	681	111.7	9.8	9	29	1.4	0.3
Rice	41 549	313	63	1 009	543.5	32.2	242	2 788	416.8	40.5	37	130	11.7	1.5
Rock	1 283	13	22	126	108.5	3.2	50	517	85.6	7.2	8	16	0.9	0.1
Roseau	2 096	26	20	145	69.7	4.0	89	769	119.7	10.3	12	40	1.9	0.3
St. Louis	74 695	756	280	D	D	D	1 087	12 385	1 892.0	186.2	175	918	85.3	14.8
Scott	284 421	2 175	153	1 613	1 917.8	64.5	229	2 318	419.3	37.0	67	204	23.2	2.8
Sherburne	133 984	1 154	51	351	78.5	7.1	154	2 120	502.9	34.4	38	133	13.5	1.5
Sibley	6 930	67	13	110	146.7	3.6	62	497	63.1	5.3	8	14	1.0	0.2
Stearns	102 671	1 023	193	3 688	1 068.9	117.1	661	9 866	1 664.3	149.4	135	668	57.4	10.3
Steele	18 618	187	55	415	225.7	13.1	174	2 042	272.4	27.5	17	125	7.3	1.4
Stevens	1 570	14	22	379	151.6	11.0	64	569	119.4	8.5	12	17	1.6	0.2
Swift	3 363	31	21	266	180.6	6.5	65	486	68.5	6.7	7	39	1.2	0.3
Todd	12 931	208	32	217	49.3	4.1	112	780	124.1	10.1	13	28	1.8	0.2
Traverse	844	7	8	72	96.4	2.9	31	213	31.6	2.7	4	D	D	D
Wabasha	13 939	116	25	199	49.0	4.3	107	882	124.7	13.1	12	28	3.3	0.6
Wadena	4 438	48	17	D	D	D	66	589	104.8	9.0	7	18	1.7	0.2
Waseca	5 737	55	26	156	62.6	3.3	70	742	106.3	10.0	6	13	0.8	0.1
Washington	413 434	2 794	205	1 471	2 029.3	69.8	601	9 304	1 674.4	142.6	160	702	84.5	12.0
Watonwan	1 108	14	24	219	211.8	6.7	59	427	55.3	5.0	3	5	1.1	0.1
Wilkin	4 689	46	20	260	149.7	6.8	36	272	38.1	3.8	3	5	0.5	0.1
Winona	21 544	109	80	682	418.3	17.8	224	2 506	384.8	36.5	41	129	19.7	1.9
Wright	170 081	1 401	85	669	221.2	18.2	283	3 870	682.9	59.7	70	248	26.1	3.3
Yellow Medicine	1 719	28	24	124	91.7	2.7	66	514	79.7	6.5	6	18	1.0	0.1

1. Establishments with payroll.

STATE County	Professional, Scientific, and Technical Services[1], 1997				Manufacturing, 1997				Accommodation and Foodservices, 1997			
	Number of Establishments	Number of Employees	Receipts (mil dol)	Annual Payroll (mil dol)	Number of Establishments	Number of Employees	Receipts (mil dol)	Annual Payroll (mil dol)	Number of Establishments	Number of Employees	Sales (mil dol)	Annual Payroll (mil dol)
	147	148	149	150	151	152	153	154	155	156	157	158
MINNESOTA—Cont'd												
Grant	9	19	1.2	0.7	NA	NA	NA	NA	11	D	D	D
Hennepin	5 655	58 051	7 181.2	2 758.4	2 404	106 772	17 291.6	4 090.1	2 196	54 567	2 078.4	616.4
Houston	20	53	4.7	0.7	NA	NA	NA	NA	33	260	6.9	1.3
Hubbard	24	73	3.4	1.0	32	940	166.1	19.6	70	429	16.9	3.8
Isanti	41	149	10.7	4.1	59	1 330	153.5	35.6	43	570	14.5	4.1
Itasca	61	472	20.9	8.8	58	2 432	534.3	92.0	116	1 365	41.9	10.9
Jackson	12	122	15.9	3.4	18	D	D	D	16	D	D	D
Kanabec	13	46	2.7	0.8	17	803	96.7	19.4	23	D	D	D
Kandiyohi	74	381	27.4	9.7	66	3 265	605.5	84.0	88	1 551	41.5	11.0
Kittson	5	23	1.6	0.9	NA	NA	NA	NA	11	D	D	D
Koochiching	18	65	3.2	1.2	11	D	D	D	52	599	18.1	5.1
Lac qui Parle	10	D	D	D	NA	NA	NA	NA	17	D	D	D
Lake	10	27	1.4	0.3	12	507	84.4	18.6	49	481	15.6	3.9
Lake of the Woods	4	D	D	D	NA	NA	NA	NA	35	304	11.3	2.6
Le Sueur	31	575	40.4	24.6	51	2 751	728.9	79.5	47	D	D	D
Lincoln	5	D	D	D	NA	NA	NA	NA	15	83	2.3	0.4
Lyon	32	134	9.2	3.6	28	1 833	456.0	40.5	52	879	22.0	6.4
McLeod	49	195	9.1	3.5	67	9 080	1 670.5	291.0	67	1 040	26.9	7.1
Mahnomen	4	D	D	D	NA	NA	NA	NA	14	D	D	D
Marshall	9	28	1.5	0.6	NA	NA	NA	NA	27	D	D	D
Martin	31	207	13.6	5.7	44	2 111	294.1	61.6	52	775	18.1	5.2
Meeker	26	99	6.2	2.2	58	1 740	356.8	41.1	36	D	D	D
Mille Lacs	26	54	2.2	0.8	38	1 029	158.0	24.4	65	D	D	D
Morrison	21	67	4.0	1.3	44	1 883	256.3	47.3	91	804	22.4	5.6
Mower	38	191	13.3	5.1	37	D	D	D	87	1 211	31.5	8.5
Murray	14	89	5.2	2.0	NA	NA	NA	NA	22	D	D	D
Nicollet	34	207	12.4	4.7	34	3 748	868.2	79.9	44	826	22.9	6.1
Nobles	25	87	4.9	1.5	24	2 690	823.8	62.9	44	737	17.6	5.5
Norman	6	55	5.0	2.4	NA	NA	NA	NA	26	D	D	D
Olmsted	206	2 145	164.4	84.1	77	10 477	3 085.4	482.1	274	5 924	204.3	58.5
Otter Tail	65	199	12.0	4.0	91	3 732	661.7	82.1	138	1 354	37.9	9.7
Pennington	20	68	4.8	1.8	16	2 047	594.7	50.9	32	839	22.0	7.0
Pine	21	56	3.3	1.1	NA	NA	NA	NA	68	911	27.7	7.9
Pipestone	13	23	1.1	0.2	15	652	96.9	16.6	28	D	D	D
Polk	29	154	9.7	4.5	40	1 350	300.3	36.3	80	1 127	25.0	6.7
Pope	14	142	7.6	4.3	29	529	84.6	13.3	36	D	D	D
Ramsey	1 569	12 225	1 240.6	530.7	765	41 550	9 294.6	1 581.6	1 011	20 952	654.9	196.6
Red Lake	3	D	D	D	NA	NA	NA	NA	9	D	D	D
Redwood	23	94	4.7	1.8	21	1 250	165.9	34.9	41	397	10.5	2.9
Renville	26	104	8.7	3.5	34	884	155.7	21.5	33	1 068	39.9	12.5
Rice	81	254	23.0	7.6	86	4 838	954.9	161.3	110	1 825	55.0	15.5
Rock	12	21	1.6	0.3	NA	NA	NA	NA	20	D	D	D
Roseau	17	54	2.6	0.9	18	D	D	D	44	718	14.6	5.2
St. Louis	318	2 186	147.8	66.6	228	5 446	879.4	155.8	591	8 610	289.8	73.3
Scott	157	395	40.2	15.5	148	5 039	989.5	180.8	122	2 049	57.0	16.1
Sherburne	59	167	11.7	5.0	96	3 278	463.2	103.2	74	1 095	33.4	9.7
Sibley	17	42	3.2	1.1	25	1 054	352.1	28.7	18	180	4.2	0.8
Stearns	224	1 325	100.8	41.9	219	12 609	2 216.6	369.1	309	5 558	150.4	40.0
Steele	55	162	10.5	3.6	67	6 292	1 006.9	191.7	65	1 004	26.4	7.0
Stevens	17	131	9.0	4.0	NA	NA	NA	NA	24	D	D	D
Swift	16	58	3.0	1.3	13	829	56.5	19.3	28	219	6.6	1.5
Todd	16	76	3.4	1.4	47	1 519	278.2	46.4	49	D	D	D
Traverse	1	D	D	D	NA	NA	NA	NA	10	D	D	D
Wabasha	29	71	5.1	1.6	39	1 934	368.5	51.3	51	D	D	D
Wadena	14	52	2.4	0.7	21	784	74.4	19.8	22	D	D	D
Waseca	29	103	4.9	1.6	29	3 298	467.1	108.6	32	D	D	D
Washington	443	1 180	135.0	44.3	210	9 456	2 795.0	436.0	296	5 543	165.2	51.0
Watonwan	12	68	3.4	1.0	21	1 102	139.3	22.7	20	D	D	D
Wilkin	9	149	3.4	2.7	NA	NA	NA	NA	19	D	D	D
Winona	71	569	33.2	10.9	116	7 115	1 071.9	196.1	115	1 725	45.7	11.9
Wright	129	693	44.3	17.5	179	4 315	583.6	127.4	130	2 159	54.3	15.1
Yellow Medicine	13	47	4.3	1.1	NA	NA	NA	NA	21	D	D	D

1. Firms subject to federal tax.

Table B. States and Counties — **Health and Other Services and Federal Funds**

STATE County	Health Care and Social Assistance[1], 1997				Other Services[1], 1997				Federal funds and grants, fiscal 1999[2] Expenditures (mil dol)			
										Direct payments for individuals[3]		
	Number of Establishments	Number of Employees	Receipts (mil dol)	Annual Payroll (mil dol)	Number of Establishments	Number of Employees	Receipts (mil dol)	Annual Payroll (mil dol)	Total	Social Security and government retirement	Medicare	Food stamps and Supplemental Security Income
	159	160	161	162	163	164	165	166	167	168	169	170
MINNESOTA—Cont'd												
Grant	13	221	5.3	2.9	11	33	2.3	0.4	44.0	15.0	6.0	0.4
Hennepin	2 292	32 525	2 031.0	1 019.3	1 929	23 352	1 348.6	514.2	5 584.8	1 686.0	700.5	149.6
Houston	17	174	7.5	3.3	33	77	6.5	1.3	68.9	35.9	11.2	1.0
Hubbard	26	238	14.5	5.0	19	48	3.5	0.7	77.8	39.5	13.9	1.8
Isanti	43	519	28.4	13.5	45	166	10.7	2.4	76.3	39.1	13.9	1.8
Itasca	75	855	39.9	18.9	61	216	14.4	3.4	191.9	97.7	30.4	5.2
Jackson	15	462	8.9	5.2	31	87	7.3	1.3	58.9	20.7	7.6	0.7
Kanabec	13	192	8.0	4.8	15	48	2.6	0.6	52.3	24.6	7.1	1.4
Kandiyohi	77	1 519	69.9	41.4	70	266	17.5	4.4	177.0	72.6	22.9	5.0
Kittson	10	157	4.7	1.7	7	18	1.5	0.3	45.2	12.3	5.2	0.3
Koochiching	21	230	9.5	5.0	17	67	4.1	0.8	68.6	35.3	10.2	1.7
Lac qui Parle	15	98	3.5	1.5	19	67	5.5	0.8	49.0	17.9	6.9	0.6
Lake	13	87	2.0	0.6	18	93	5.7	1.5	51.7	31.3	7.9	1.1
Lake of the Woods	5	10	0.6	0.1	7	12	1.1	0.2	20.2	9.5	3.1	0.4
Le Sueur	40	344	12.4	5.4	36	107	8.0	1.6	92.1	44.4	14.7	1.4
Lincoln	8	66	2.7	1.1	9	14	1.0	0.2	40.8	14.1	6.5	0.4
Lyon	50	707	27.0	14.0	56	168	11.9	2.2	106.5	43.3	15.0	1.9
McLeod	68	586	33.4	15.0	64	278	21.8	4.9	111.9	53.7	18.6	1.4
Mahnomen	7	29	1.2	0.4	5	D	D	D	31.0	10.2	3.2	0.9
Marshall	10	81	1.9	0.9	24	74	7.3	0.9	84.6	20.9	9.2	0.6
Martin	47	448	27.8	10.2	37	113	7.8	1.7	113.4	48.3	17.6	1.4
Meeker	23	215	10.2	5.7	19	56	3.1	0.9	80.4	37.3	12.9	1.2
Mille Lacs	28	285	11.7	6.1	38	121	10.1	2.3	101.8	49.1	19.6	2.3
Morrison	40	490	24.1	12.2	48	172	14.5	2.9	141.0	57.8	19.7	2.6
Mower	71	637	26.3	11.7	75	377	19.9	4.7	185.6	89.0	33.4	3.7
Murray	12	176	5.6	3.3	13	27	2.2	0.4	53.2	18.9	7.3	0.5
Nicollet	31	225	12.2	5.7	48	202	10.5	2.8	68.6	30.1	9.8	1.4
Nobles	28	455	21.2	9.5	43	149	8.7	2.1	93.4	38.5	13.3	2.3
Norman	10	42	1.9	0.8	10	37	1.9	0.3	57.8	16.8	6.6	0.7
Olmsted	168	2 241	102.8	50.7	180	1 363	69.8	20.4	443.8	157.6	59.5	9.6
Otter Tail	73	896	41.7	22.6	81	320	18.4	4.2	242.6	116.8	40.6	4.1
Pennington	15	183	12.9	3.8	29	92	5.4	1.5	70.2	24.6	8.5	1.0
Pine	34	587	25.8	10.7	22	51	3.2	0.7	119.0	50.3	15.3	2.6
Pipestone	16	88	4.1	1.8	20	72	4.9	1.0	52.6	21.2	8.0	0.8
Polk	49	475	16.0	7.0	55	237	12.7	3.1	190.1	60.4	24.8	3.7
Pope	15	77	3.6	1.3	24	50	3.7	0.7	55.5	25.4	9.7	0.9
Ramsey	1 030	15 342	939.0	502.5	826	6 378	401.6	124.5	3 385.4	947.9	378.4	92.8
Red Lake	2	D	D	D	2	D	D	D	35.0	7.9	3.7	0.3
Redwood	41	587	14.3	6.9	32	64	5.2	1.1	93.9	34.9	11.5	1.1
Renville	26	518	14.4	7.6	32	65	6.5	1.1	93.4	34.4	12.0	1.3
Rice	84	1 398	64.4	35.5	81	331	23.6	6.3	161.5	78.0	23.7	3.4
Rock	10	106	3.6	1.8	22	89	7.1	1.6	47.9	20.7	7.1	0.5
Roseau	19	134	5.5	1.6	17	66	4.2	1.1	64.9	21.6	9.3	0.7
St. Louis	376	5 334	240.6	125.7	327	1 807	124.4	35.9	1 003.9	440.3	150.2	29.8
Scott	99	1 131	53.9	25.5	120	607	51.1	12.6	122.4	65.3	18.2	1.8
Sherburne	77	665	30.5	15.1	59	302	14.8	4.5	108.0	58.1	14.3	1.8
Sibley	15	57	3.2	1.0	27	62	4.4	0.8	61.9	24.2	10.9	0.7
Stearns	238	3 178	239.5	121.3	243	1 493	89.0	24.7	441.9	180.0	58.4	7.5
Steele	46	667	33.2	17.2	55	223	18.0	4.1	107.5	51.0	17.5	1.7
Stevens	15	54	3.7	1.3	25	116	6.0	1.3	61.1	17.5	7.9	0.6
Swift	14	189	6.6	3.3	21	68	6.4	1.3	63.3	22.8	9.6	0.9
Todd	24	150	10.0	4.6	30	68	6.5	1.2	102.4	42.3	15.1	2.7
Traverse	7	55	2.7	1.2	8	14	1.4	0.3	33.3	10.4	4.4	0.5
Wabasha	27	316	15.6	6.0	34	90	6.1	1.3	92.8	39.7	14.6	1.0
Wadena	17	156	9.5	4.5	18	48	3.5	0.7	66.7	30.2	11.7	2.1
Waseca	42	585	18.7	8.5	37	98	6.7	1.2	86.3	30.3	10.0	1.3
Washington	265	3 251	177.8	89.2	219	1 700	99.3	29.4	260.9	149.9	44.7	4.4
Watonwan	20	216	8.9	3.6	17	49	4.5	0.7	59.4	24.6	7.9	0.9
Wilkin	6	52	1.3	0.5	6	8	1.0	0.2	40.3	13.6	4.3	0.6
Winona	71	705	38.2	17.1	67	296	16.9	4.3	156.8	77.4	26.2	3.5
Wright	126	1 244	56.2	26.7	124	482	29.2	7.4	187.1	101.5	34.2	3.4
Yellow Medicine	22	191	6.9	3.4	31	175	10.6	3.0	71.9	24.6	9.7	0.7

1. Firms subject to federal tax.   2. October 1, 1998 to September 30, 1999.   3. State totals may include programs not allocated by county.

STATE County	Federal funds and grants, fiscal 1999[1] (cont'd)							Local government finances, 1997				
	Expenditures (mil dol) (cont'd)							General revenue				
	Procurement contract awards			Grants[2]							Taxes	
											Per capita[3] (dollars)	
	Salaries and wages	Defense	Other	Medicaid and other health-related	Nutrition and family welfare	Education	Other	Total (mil dol)	Intergovernmental (mil dol)	Total (mil dol)	Total	Property
	171	172	173	174	175	176	177	178	179	180	181	182
MINNESOTA—Cont'd												
Grant	1.4	0.0	0.4	4.2	1.8	0.3	1.8	21.5	11.6	6.1	989	977
Hennepin	692.5	854.7	244.8	712.7	124.2	52.6	237.7	3 868.0	1 284.4	1 435.9	1 363	1 263
Houston	3.3	0.3	0.7	7.5	1.2	0.6	0.1	44.8	27.4	9.4	491	480
Hubbard	2.2	0.0	0.6	12.1	2.4	0.9	2.2	44.6	21.0	12.4	742	730
Isanti	3.6	0.2	1.2	8.5	2.3	0.9	0.3	70.7	41.6	18.2	614	595
Itasca	8.4	1.8	1.6	26.0	8.3	2.9	8.6	170.3	62.0	43.2	991	986
Jackson	2.0	0.0	0.5	4.2	1.0	0.5	0.1	40.8	17.9	10.9	935	931
Kanabec	2.4	0.0	0.5	6.4	3.4	0.7	4.2	40.3	20.5	6.9	489	481
Kandiyohi	10.2	0.0	17.9	18.7	5.5	1.9	1.2	154.2	60.6	26.9	654	636
Kittson	2.7	0.0	0.4	4.2	0.6	0.2	0.2	22.0	10.2	7.8	1 455	1 443
Koochiching	6.1	0.1	1.0	9.4	2.5	0.8	0.6	45.7	24.7	11.2	714	701
Lac qui Parle	1.9	0.1	0.4	3.0	0.6	0.3	1.7	33.7	16.9	7.1	881	877
Lake	1.4	1.2	0.5	4.9	1.1	0.4	1.9	40.0	21.6	9.7	901	891
Lake of the Woods	1.2	0.0	0.2	3.4	0.4	0.2	0.2	17.0	8.2	3.4	738	729
Le Sueur	3.1	0.0	0.8	9.4	1.6	0.8	3.2	59.4	33.3	15.2	610	601
Lincoln	1.4	0.0	0.3	4.2	0.3	0.4	0.0	17.1	10.2	4.6	694	693
Lyon	6.6	3.2	1.2	9.1	4.1	1.5	1.8	93.8	38.7	20.6	840	827
McLeod	4.5	0.0	2.0	6.8	1.5	0.9	11.0	133.0	45.4	21.3	633	618
Mahnomen	0.8	0.0	0.9	6.0	1.4	1.0	0.1	26.6	20.0	4.8	944	942
Marshall	3.4	0.2	0.9	6.8	1.2	0.5	1.5	40.7	24.2	9.5	898	895
Martin	3.6	0.2	0.8	6.0	3.3	0.9	6.0	59.2	27.6	16.3	734	723
Meeker	4.2	0.0	0.8	7.2	2.0	0.8	0.0	72.0	38.0	15.8	735	727
Mille Lacs	3.2	0.0	1.0	13.9	3.8	1.4	4.0	61.9	37.4	16.3	788	777
Morrison	18.8	1.7	1.3	19.2	5.4	1.9	2.2	81.0	50.2	16.5	542	531
Mower	7.8	2.9	1.6	18.0	3.5	1.4	0.1	111.3	55.1	21.8	588	578
Murray	2.1	0.0	0.6	3.8	0.4	0.4	0.1	29.6	16.6	7.1	742	739
Nicollet	2.7	0.0	0.5	5.3	1.4	0.6	1.4	59.0	23.9	15.0	499	483
Nobles	4.8	0.0	0.9	10.2	2.5	0.9	2.7	74.3	31.4	13.6	689	674
Norman	2.0	0.0	0.5	4.5	0.8	0.4	0.4	31.1	15.6	7.0	909	897
Olmsted	50.7	4.8	9.3	109.4	7.6	4.2	13.7	326.5	131.8	102.9	898	812
Otter Tail	11.1	0.0	5.7	31.7	5.6	2.3	2.6	169.5	70.0	33.5	619	606
Pennington	4.4	0.0	0.8	12.5	1.8	2.0	0.7	43.7	23.5	9.9	730	708
Pine	17.9	0.0	1.6	15.1	3.0	1.1	7.7	60.1	34.9	15.2	645	636
Pipestone	2.8	0.0	0.5	6.4	1.1	0.5	0.6	26.8	15.5	7.4	734	725
Polk	6.5	0.6	1.7	21.3	9.8	1.8	11.3	109.7	64.9	23.8	742	715
Pope	1.8	0.1	0.5	4.9	1.1	0.6	0.0	33.3	17.0	7.2	663	655
Ramsey	301.1	230.7	84.0	290.3	361.5	134.9	464.9	2 041.7	784.1	603.4	1 246	1 154
Red Lake	1.1	0.0	8.8	2.6	1.7	0.2	0.5	15.3	9.3	2.6	602	594
Redwood	3.4	0.0	1.2	9.1	1.3	0.8	3.6	62.7	31.9	14.9	892	873
Renville	3.6	0.1	0.9	8.6	1.3	1.0	0.2	49.5	22.9	13.0	764	761
Rice	7.6	3.5	1.9	21.0	3.1	3.0	3.0	156.4	61.4	31.8	593	576
Rock	1.7	0.0	0.4	2.6	0.7	0.4	2.0	33.6	13.7	6.3	637	631
Roseau	3.1	0.0	0.6	7.9	2.5	0.6	0.2	61.3	27.5	9.6	591	587
St. Louis	116.3	3.8	31.8	133.9	34.1	12.3	31.0	710.7	335.6	160.2	822	749
Scott	13.3	0.0	4.3	5.9	2.9	1.7	0.6	178.4	71.7	67.6	889	834
Sherburne	9.8	0.4	1.5	7.5	2.6	1.3	6.0	145.0	58.0	51.3	887	867
Sibley	2.3	0.0	0.6	4.2	0.9	0.5	2.1	40.1	21.5	10.2	701	692
Stearns	66.1	0.0	24.9	41.1	10.8	5.1	17.6	382.6	184.1	100.0	784	738
Steele	4.1	1.4	5.2	7.2	1.6	0.9	2.1	84.2	44.2	20.1	638	620
Stevens	4.0	0.1	0.5	5.3	0.8	0.5	5.0	26.3	16.0	6.4	632	628
Swift	2.9	0.0	2.2	6.4	1.2	0.5	0.2	39.1	18.7	7.6	700	691
Todd	4.1	0.0	0.9	18.9	3.3	1.5	4.9	81.6	44.5	14.5	606	600
Traverse	1.1	0.0	0.3	1.9	0.5	0.2	0.5	17.2	7.8	4.0	928	873
Wabasha	3.3	0.0	14.0	7.2	1.3	0.8	0.5	60.5	28.4	14.0	674	664
Wadena	2.7	0.1	0.6	13.6	2.0	0.8	0.3	46.5	27.3	7.6	583	577
Waseca	14.9	4.6	0.9	5.3	1.4	0.8	1.0	53.6	27.6	14.2	781	762
Washington	15.6	3.2	4.4	15.8	6.9	3.8	5.8	448.3	179.8	156.2	816	777
Watonwan	2.5	0.0	5.9	1.9	0.5	0.6	0.4	30.4	16.8	8.7	739	735
Wilkin	1.4	0.0	0.4	3.4	0.7	0.4	0.3	25.9	14.1	6.2	836	828
Winona	7.3	3.6	1.9	15.4	3.3	1.9	1.9	102.8	57.2	27.2	563	528
Wright	10.3	0.1	2.6	15.5	5.5	2.2	0.8	219.3	100.5	68.3	821	797
Yellow Medicine	2.5	0.0	1.7	6.3	1.1	0.5	3.4	50.3	19.6	9.8	847	843

1. October 1, 1998 to September 30, 1999.   2. State totals may include programs not allocated by county.   3. Based on the resident population estimated as of July 1 of the year shown.

Table B. States and Counties — Local Government Finances, Government Employment, and Elections

STATE County	Local government finances, 1997 (cont'd)									Government employment, 1998			Presidential election, 2000		
	Direct general expenditure							Debt outstanding					Percent of vote cast —		
			Percent of total for —												
	Total (mil dol)	Per capita[1] (dollars)	Education	Health and hospitals	Police protection	Public welfare	Highways	Total (mil dol)	Per capita[1] (dollars)	Federal civilian	Federal military	State and local	Democratic	Republican	All other
	183	184	185	186	187	188	189	190	191	192	193	194	195	196	197
MINNESOTA—Cont'd															
Grant	22.4	3 649	49.5	3.5	3.1	7.5	16.8	10.5	1 702	25	25	371	41.6	49.8	8.6
Hennepin	3 978.8	3 778	35.1	12.1	4.9	4.7	4.8	5 234.9	4 971	13 748	4 904	80 682	53.6	39.3	7.1
Houston	45.9	2 388	50.8	0.4	3.0	6.4	16.4	14.8	770	73	79	947	44.3	49.9	5.8
Hubbard	44.4	2 649	43.4	0.2	2.5	19.6	14.2	26.5	1 581	40	69	1 009	37.8	55.2	7.0
Isanti	66.7	2 256	51.0	1.9	3.9	10.9	11.5	83.8	2 834	71	122	1 729	41.8	51.4	6.8
Itasca	173.8	3 990	35.3	17.6	2.4	11.1	12.0	178.2	4 092	195	178	3 041	48.7	44.0	7.3
Jackson	41.0	3 503	30.9	13.5	2.4	15.9	15.1	10.9	928	30	47	929	43.5	51.0	5.5
Kanabec	41.9	2 995	41.3	21.0	3.3	8.7	12.2	19.0	1 350	47	57	840	41.6	51.1	7.3
Kandiyohi	163.2	3 973	29.4	33.1	3.6	7.7	8.1	140.2	3 411	186	167	4 194	42.6	52.0	5.4
Kittson	21.4	3 999	41.6	5.2	3.1	6.7	20.6	16.7	3 109	52	22	333	42.0	51.3	6.7
Koochiching	52.9	3 374	45.7	1.4	4.3	13.0	10.1	56.2	3 586	131	63	982	42.2	51.2	6.6
Lac qui Parle	33.1	4 089	44.3	16.4	2.6	5.0	14.3	7.8	969	34	33	692	50.4	43.6	6.0
Lake	42.0	3 923	33.9	1.2	4.3	8.4	18.2	65.8	6 143	33	43	893	54.5	37.6	7.9
Lake of the Woods	13.9	3 051	39.7	0.6	5.7	6.2	21.1	360.1	79 325	21	22	292	38.8	55.6	5.6
Le Sueur	63.7	2 558	47.8	3.9	3.2	8.2	10.3	58.4	2 349	61	103	1 283	43.5	49.8	6.7
Lincoln	17.3	2 644	44.7	0.5	3.4	4.6	21.4	7.6	1 158	27	26	335	48.4	46.1	5.5
Lyon	99.6	4 061	44.7	18.2	3.1	4.3	8.7	65.2	2 659	131	99	2 710	41.2	53.0	5.8
McLeod	132.2	3 924	31.4	29.5	3.2	7.6	7.7	116.9	3 469	81	138	2 702	41.4	50.4	8.1
Mahnomen	27.3	5 363	44.6	0.3	4.2	23.7	8.0	8.2	1 610	18	21	339	36.7	56.0	7.3
Marshall	40.7	3 870	47.3	1.3	1.9	5.6	24.7	13.7	1 302	64	42	616	40.2	54.8	5.0
Martin	62.9	2 827	50.0	0.2	4.0	6.8	13.9	42.4	1 907	69	89	1 333	36.4	57.0	6.5
Meeker	79.0	3 670	52.5	10.4	2.8	8.8	8.1	57.7	2 683	69	88	1 192	41.2	51.7	7.0
Mille Lacs	61.8	2 990	63.6	1.0	3.0	9.1	6.9	48.5	2 348	62	85	1 301	42.7	50.9	6.4
Morrison	87.8	2 877	57.9	2.3	2.6	8.6	9.6	57.4	1 881	355	124	1 717	35.9	55.8	8.2
Mower	107.5	2 895	40.6	1.4	3.5	12.4	13.3	877.2	23 623	150	150	2 278	57.9	37.2	4.9
Murray	31.4	3 297	35.8	9.9	2.7	3.0	18.8	11.0	1 157	39	39	562	44.0	50.6	5.3
Nicollet	60.7	2 022	30.7	14.6	4.4	6.0	16.1	42.1	1 400	47	120	2 342	45.9	47.1	6.9
Nobles	74.7	3 787	35.0	22.4	3.1	7.8	11.5	29.1	1 476	93	78	1 684	42.4	53.7	3.9
Norman	30.6	3 971	39.9	14.6	1.8	5.6	18.8	9.4	1 213	39	31	537	43.3	49.7	7.1
Olmsted	335.5	2 927	51.7	1.4	4.4	7.7	6.8	254.0	2 216	913	477	6 401	43.5	51.6	4.9
Otter Tail	182.2	3 361	47.3	7.7	2.7	6.2	12.2	100.3	1 850	225	223	3 446	34.5	59.5	6.0
Pennington	43.3	3 195	40.0	0.1	4.4	11.7	13.7	34.5	2 547	79	55	1 261	38.9	53.5	7.6
Pine	66.5	2 819	53.9	5.8	3.9	8.8	10.1	46.2	1 959	323	97	1 445	47.0	44.8	8.2
Pipestone	29.9	2 964	48.3	0.5	2.9	7.2	11.6	11.6	1 151	49	41	855	40.3	55.0	4.7
Polk	122.6	3 821	40.1	0.2	3.8	12.0	12.3	72.1	2 247	118	125	2 703	40.8	53.8	5.4
Pope	32.4	2 968	38.9	14.1	3.2	4.2	17.3	23.1	2 115	34	44	722	46.3	46.9	6.8
Ramsey	2 130.7	4 399	31.3	1.8	3.8	7.8	4.9	2 838.1	5 860	5 140	2 141	49 996	56.7	35.9	7.4
Red Lake	19.2	4 409	58.1	0.4	3.8	5.4	11.2	12.8	2 946	21	17	277	39.7	52.2	8.1
Redwood	58.2	3 496	37.9	11.1	2.7	7.0	14.2	40.3	2 422	63	67	1 299	34.6	59.2	6.2
Renville	58.4	3 421	30.4	7.1	3.1	12.1	14.5	33.6	1 971	61	69	1 198	43.5	49.7	6.8
Rice	173.9	3 245	45.7	17.0	3.6	6.2	7.3	138.2	2 578	135	219	3 571	50.5	41.8	7.7
Rock	32.9	3 322	35.7	23.3	3.0	4.3	11.5	41.1	4 158	35	39	838	41.5	55.3	3.1
Roseau	62.5	3 835	35.6	19.7	2.5	3.5	11.7	61.5	3 771	62	65	846	29.7	65.5	4.8
St. Louis	710.1	3 642	32.6	7.3	4.9	9.5	11.8	540.8	2 774	2 118	903	16 878	59.8	33.0	7.3
Scott	207.6	2 728	45.9	0.9	4.3	4.9	11.6	217.2	2 855	253	320	3 335	40.0	54.7	5.3
Sherburne	148.9	2 572	52.8	0.7	3.0	5.6	6.4	316.9	5 476	169	245	2 846	39.3	54.5	6.2
Sibley	40.5	2 778	41.2	2.3	3.7	13.8	17.8	25.2	1 732	39	59	811	36.6	55.7	7.6
Stearns	380.7	2 985	44.7	4.2	3.6	6.9	9.9	587.2	4 604	1 496	525	9 582	39.7	51.9	8.4
Steele	85.5	2 711	46.0	0.9	4.0	9.9	12.9	87.3	2 768	78	129	1 648	42.9	51.2	5.9
Stevens	26.2	2 587	45.7	1.8	4.4	9.4	17.1	13.2	1 300	78	41	1 296	42.3	49.2	8.5
Swift	40.5	3 737	29.9	14.2	3.4	13.3	13.6	20.8	1 920	52	44	898	49.6	43.7	6.7
Todd	84.3	3 517	58.0	6.0	2.6	9.1	11.6	38.5	1 608	77	97	1 275	37.3	54.4	8.4
Traverse	19.8	4 630	27.7	18.2	3.2	8.1	15.1	7.1	1 658	22	17	429	42.0	51.0	7.0
Wabasha	59.0	2 842	42.6	7.5	3.1	13.7	9.0	32.5	1 565	62	85	1 141	42.9	49.8	7.3
Wadena	47.5	3 665	48.0	1.7	3.0	19.8	9.9	39.2	3 023	48	53	1 433	35.3	58.5	6.2
Waseca	59.4	3 267	57.6	0.6	3.4	11.1	9.3	39.2	2 156	263	74	1 234	41.7	52.0	6.3
Washington	471.0	2 459	47.6	1.4	5.8	4.5	7.8	595.8	3 111	250	796	8 255	46.4	48.1	5.5
Watonwan	31.4	2 676	47.2	1.2	5.2	10.6	14.7	10.2	866	48	46	720	44.0	49.9	6.1
Wilkin	29.5	4 006	43.4	2.0	3.7	7.3	23.3	32.7	4 434	28	30	387	31.6	61.5	6.9
Winona	104.3	2 162	47.3	2.0	5.0	9.0	11.3	65.5	1 356	146	196	3 587	46.3	45.0	8.7
Wright	237.9	2 861	53.3	6.2	3.1	7.2	7.9	283.5	3 410	178	345	4 242	38.7	55.0	6.3
Yellow Medicine	52.0	4 492	31.2	26.3	2.5	9.7	12.1	18.7	1 619	47	46	1 175	45.8	47.1	7.1

1. Based on the resident population estimated as of July 1 of the year shown.

Table B. States and Counties — Land Area and Population

STATE/County code	MSA/PMSA/NECMA code[1]	County Type[2]	STATE County	Land area,[3] (sq km) 1990	Total persons	Rank	Per square kilometer	White	Black	Am. Indian, Eskimo, Aleut	Asian and Pacific Islander	Percent Hispanic[4]	Under 5 years	5 to 17 years	18 to 24 years	25 to 34 years	35 to 44 years	45 to 54 years
					1	2	3	4	5	6	7	8	9	10	11	12	13	14	15
28 000	...	X	MISSISSIPPI	121 506	2 768 619	X	22.8	62.4	36.5	0.4	0.7	0.9	7.3	19.9	10.9	13.7	15.1	12.4
28 001	...	7	Adams	1 192	33 657	1 266	28.2	48.6	51.1	0.1	0.2	0.5	7.0	19.4	8.2	12.4	15.1	12.7
28 003	...	7	Alcorn	1 036	33 080	1 282	31.9	87.3	12.4	0.1	0.2	0.6	6.0	18.0	8.7	12.5	15.5	14.2
28 005	...	9	Amite	1 890	13 906	2 142	7.4	52.1	47.7	0.1	0.1	0.3	6.9	20.5	9.2	12.3	13.8	12.9
28 007	...	6	Attala	1 904	18 338	1 852	9.6	57.5	42.1	0.2	0.2	0.3	6.6	19.1	9.3	11.4	13.6	12.7
28 009	...	8	Benton	1 054	8 091	2 587	7.7	58.4	41.3	0.1	0.1	0.6	6.9	20.9	9.7	12.9	12.5	11.8
28 011	...	5	Bolivar	2 270	39 826	1 091	17.5	34.6	64.9	0.1	0.4	1.0	8.4	23.2	14.7	11.5	14.1	10.5
28 013	...	9	Calhoun	1 519	14 891	2 071	9.8	70.9	29.0	0.1	0.0	0.7	6.5	18.4	9.8	11.9	14.1	13.1
28 015	...	9	Carroll	1 626	9 967	2 432	6.1	57.7	42.0	0.1	0.2	0.5	6.8	19.7	8.8	11.9	14.4	14.5
28 017	...	7	Chickasaw	1 299	18 121	1 863	13.9	58.6	41.1	0.1	0.1	0.5	7.9	20.1	10.0	13.2	14.1	12.3
28 019	...	9	Choctaw	1 086	9 366	2 481	8.6	67.6	32.1	0.1	0.1	0.5	6.7	21.8	8.4	12.3	14.1	13.1
28 021	...	8	Claiborne	1 261	11 596	2 300	9.2	17.3	82.3	0.2	0.2	0.7	6.8	20.4	21.7	11.2	12.5	10.0
28 023	...	7	Clarke	1 791	18 445	1 848	10.3	63.0	36.9	0.1	0.1	0.5	6.8	20.1	9.4	12.1	14.9	12.4
28 025	...	7	Clay	1 058	21 657	1 674	20.5	55.6	44.1	0.1	0.2	0.5	7.4	21.5	10.9	12.8	14.8	11.3
28 027	...	7	Coahoma	1 435	31 094	1 346	21.7	33.1	66.3	0.1	0.5	0.9	8.5	23.8	10.4	12.2	13.3	11.2
28 029	...	6	Copiah	2 012	28 892	1 414	14.4	46.9	52.9	0.1	0.1	0.5	7.3	20.6	12.1	12.5	14.0	11.9
28 031	...	7	Covington	1 072	17 889	1 877	16.7	62.3	37.5	0.1	0.2	0.4	7.7	21.4	10.1	12.6	14.1	13.3
28 033	4920	1	De Soto	1 239	102 131	509	82.4	85.3	14.2	0.2	0.3	0.6	7.6	19.5	9.3	14.4	16.8	15.0
28 035	3285	5	Forrest	1 209	74 927	660	62.0	65.7	33.3	0.1	0.9	1.1	7.1	17.6	17.0	14.1	13.8	11.0
28 037	...	9	Franklin	1 462	8 160	2 580	5.6	60.8	39.1	0.0	0.1	0.3	7.3	20.7	8.3	12.6	14.2	11.5
28 039	...	6	George	1 239	20 185	1 753	16.3	89.0	10.4	0.4	0.2	0.6	7.4	21.6	9.8	13.2	14.7	13.6
28 041	...	8	Greene	1 847	12 630	2 237	6.8	71.8	27.9	0.1	0.1	1.0	6.1	19.2	10.4	18.2	16.6	12.2
28 043	...	7	Grenada	1 093	22 450	1 640	20.5	55.7	43.9	0.2	0.2	0.5	7.3	19.8	9.6	13.0	15.3	12.4
28 045	0920	2	Hancock	1 235	41 518	1 051	33.6	89.1	9.7	0.5	0.7	2.5	7.1	18.7	8.0	12.5	14.5	13.2
28 047	0920	2	Harrison	1 505	178 567	299	118.6	75.0	21.0	0.3	3.7	2.6	8.0	18.5	10.6	15.5	14.9	11.8
28 049	3560	2	Hinds	2 251	245 737	220	109.2	45.7	53.5	0.1	0.7	0.6	7.3	18.6	12.0	15.1	16.2	11.8
28 051	...	6	Holmes	1 958	21 562	1 680	11.0	22.7	77.0	0.1	0.2	0.3	8.4	24.2	12.2	11.8	12.6	10.3
28 053	...	7	Humphreys	1 083	11 214	2 332	10.4	30.0	69.4	0.1	0.5	0.5	8.8	24.6	10.7	12.6	12.9	11.0
28 055	...	9	Issaquena	1 070	1 635	3 087	1.5	40.9	58.7	0.1	0.3	0.1	8.7	21.8	10.0	12.8	12.4	14.7
28 057	...	9	Itawamba	1 379	21 085	1 711	15.3	91.8	7.8	0.1	0.3	0.8	6.1	17.5	11.2	12.2	14.5	14.3
28 059	0920	2	Jackson	1 882	133 120	393	70.7	76.2	22.2	0.2	1.4	1.5	7.3	20.3	9.6	13.8	16.1	14.0
28 061	...	9	Jasper	1 751	18 110	1 864	10.3	46.4	53.4	0.0	0.1	0.4	6.7	22.0	9.8	12.6	14.5	12.5
28 063	...	9	Jefferson	1 345	8 385	2 560	6.2	13.2	86.6	0.0	0.2	0.5	7.9	24.2	10.4	12.8	13.5	11.9
28 065	...	9	Jefferson Davis	1 058	13 770	2 151	13.0	42.5	57.1	0.2	0.2	0.3	7.1	22.1	10.4	11.9	14.4	12.6
28 067	...	5	Jones	1 797	63 054	760	35.1	72.5	26.9	0.4	0.2	0.5	6.6	19.1	9.4	12.8	15.1	12.6
28 069	...	9	Kemper	1 984	10 487	2 380	5.3	40.3	57.6	2.0	0.1	0.3	6.6	20.4	12.4	11.5	13.3	11.5
28 071	...	7	Lafayette	1 635	34 914	1 230	21.4	69.5	27.7	0.1	2.7	0.9	5.5	14.8	25.3	13.8	13.8	10.7
28 073	3285	7	Lamar	1 288	38 127	1 133	29.6	86.0	13.2	0.2	0.6	0.9	7.9	20.8	10.2	15.5	16.3	12.4
28 075	...	5	Lauderdale	1 822	75 978	652	41.7	62.0	37.2	0.1	0.7	0.9	7.3	19.0	10.5	13.6	15.0	12.2
28 077	...	9	Lawrence	1 115	13 066	2 208	11.7	64.3	35.4	0.1	0.2	0.3	6.8	21.1	8.9	12.6	14.0	12.8
28 079	...	6	Leake	1 509	19 602	1 783	13.0	57.5	37.9	4.6	0.1	0.3	6.8	20.2	9.3	12.1	14.0	12.4
28 081	...	5	Lee	1 165	75 211	659	64.6	76.2	23.4	0.1	0.3	0.8	7.7	19.0	9.4	14.9	16.1	13.0
28 083	...	7	Leflore	1 533	36 816	1 167	24.0	36.2	63.2	0.1	0.5	0.4	7.8	21.8	12.3	13.2	14.1	10.9
28 085	...	7	Lincoln	1 517	32 105	1 310	21.2	67.3	32.4	0.1	0.2	0.3	6.2	20.3	9.2	12.4	15.4	12.5
28 087	...	5	Lowndes	1 301	60 527	788	46.5	59.5	39.6	0.1	0.7	1.2	8.2	19.6	11.8	15.1	15.5	11.5
28 089	3560	2	Madison	1 863	74 562	665	40.0	52.5	46.9	0.1	0.5	0.7	8.4	19.5	10.6	17.4	16.2	11.0
28 091	...	7	Marion	1 405	26 538	1 478	18.9	67.0	32.7	0.1	0.2	0.7	6.9	21.9	9.0	12.7	14.4	11.7
28 093	...	6	Marshall	1 830	32 323	1 302	17.7	46.8	52.8	0.2	0.2	0.5	7.6	20.9	11.5	13.5	14.5	12.5
28 095	...	7	Monroe	1 979	38 230	1 128	19.3	67.1	32.7	0.1	0.1	0.6	7.2	20.0	9.7	12.7	14.9	13.0
28 097	...	7	Montgomery	1 054	12 394	2 258	11.8	53.6	46.1	0.1	0.2	0.4	6.6	20.1	9.6	11.4	13.5	12.9
28 099	...	7	Neshoba	1 476	27 639	1 446	18.7	65.7	20.2	13.8	0.2	0.6	7.2	21.7	9.5	12.5	14.5	11.9
28 101	...	7	Newton	1 497	21 741	1 670	14.5	65.0	31.0	3.9	0.1	0.6	6.6	19.5	11.5	11.9	14.2	12.0
28 103	...	9	Noxubee	1 800	12 497	2 248	6.9	29.7	69.9	0.3	0.1	0.2	8.7	22.8	10.4	13.5	12.8	10.8
28 105	...	7	Oktibbeha	1 186	39 765	1 092	33.5	59.4	36.9	0.1	3.6	1.2	6.3	15.4	26.7	13.6	12.6	10.1
28 107	...	7	Panola	1 772	33 913	1 258	19.1	48.8	50.9	0.1	0.2	0.6	8.0	22.4	10.6	13.1	14.1	11.6
28 109	...	6	Pearl River	2 102	47 969	938	22.8	83.5	15.8	0.4	0.3	1.2	7.2	20.1	9.6	12.4	15.2	13.9
28 111	...	9	Perry	1 676	12 039	2 273	7.2	74.6	24.6	0.7	0.1	0.6	7.5	22.0	9.8	13.2	14.5	12.7
28 113	...	7	Pike	1 059	37 910	1 135	35.8	51.5	48.2	0.1	0.2	0.6	6.8	21.5	9.6	12.2	15.0	12.0
28 115	...	7	Pontotoc	1 288	25 685	1 507	19.9	83.2	16.4	0.2	0.2	0.5	7.0	19.2	9.7	13.8	15.3	12.9
28 117	...	7	Prentiss	1 075	24 497	1 551	22.8	86.5	13.3	0.1	0.1	0.6	6.5	17.3	12.0	12.0	14.0	13.1
28 119	...	9	Quitman	1 049	9 780	2 446	9.3	38.3	61.3	0.2	0.3	0.6	8.4	23.4	10.7	11.9	13.6	10.8
28 121	3560	2	Rankin	2 006	112 348	470	56.0	80.5	18.8	0.1	0.5	0.9	6.5	18.9	9.0	14.8	18.0	13.7
28 123	...	6	Scott	1 578	24 911	1 533	15.8	59.3	40.3	0.3	0.1	0.7	7.9	20.3	9.8	12.8	14.2	11.9
28 125	...	9	Sharkey	1 108	6 543	2 725	5.9	31.1	68.4	0.1	0.4	0.5	8.7	25.5	11.4	11.9	14.3	10.1
28 127	...	6	Simpson	1 525	25 375	1 518	16.6	65.0	34.7	0.2	0.2	0.4	7.2	20.7	9.0	13.3	15.2	12.7
28 129	...	8	Smith	1 647	15 431	2 042	9.4	75.8	24.0	0.2	0.1	0.8	7.0	19.9	9.4	12.6	14.5	13.2
28 131	...	6	Stone	1 154	13 488	2 176	11.7	75.6	24.0	0.2	0.2	0.7	7.6	19.9	12.4	12.8	15.0	12.6

1. MSA = Metropolitan Statistical Area. PMSA = Primary MSA. NECMA = New England County Metropolitan Area. See Appendix A for explanation of these concepts. See Appendix B for list of metropolitan areas identified by type, with component counties. 2. County typology code from the Economic Research Service of USDA. See Appendix A for definition. 3. Dry land or land partially or temporarily covered by water. 4. Hispanic persons may be of any race.

STATE County	Population, 1999 (cont'd) Age (percent) (cont'd)				Population — change and components of change, 1980–1999							Households, 1990				
					Total persons		Percent change		Components of change, 1990–1999						Percent	
	55 to 64 years	65 to 74 years	75 years and over	Percent female	1990	1980	1980– 1990	1990– 1999	Births	Deaths	Net migration	Number	Percent change, 1980– 1990	Persons per house- hold	Female family house- holder[1]	One person
	16	17	18	19	20	21	22	23	24	25	26	27	28	29	30	31
MISSISSIPPI	8.7	6.6	5.5	52.1	2 575 475	2 520 770	2.2	7.5	389 349	246 225	51 526	911 374	10.2	2.75	15.9	23.4
Adams	10.0	8.7	6.6	54.2	35 356	38 071	-7.1	-4.8	4 947	4 064	-2 516	13 262	3.6	2.64	19.8	25.1
Alcorn	9.8	7.8	7.3	52.0	31 722	33 036	-4.0	4.3	3 930	3 518	1 049	12 449	4.3	2.52	10.5	25.0
Amite	9.8	8.1	6.4	51.8	13 328	13 369	-0.3	4.3	1 505	1 214	351	4 830	10.7	2.76	14.4	24.3
Attala	10.3	8.6	8.3	53.0	18 481	19 865	-7.0	-0.8	2 391	2 198	-265	6 945	1.2	2.63	13.7	26.3
Benton	9.8	8.6	6.9	51.5	8 046	8 153	-1.3	0.6	1 102	784	-235	2 842	10.3	2.82	13.9	21.7
Bolivar	6.7	5.7	5.3	54.0	41 875	45 965	-8.9	-4.9	6 670	4 216	-4 430	13 292	-2.1	3.02	26.3	24.0
Calhoun	9.7	8.0	8.4	52.2	14 908	15 664	-4.8	0.1	1 951	1 708	-208	5 662	4.5	2.60	12.7	24.9
Carroll	9.4	7.8	6.7	52.0	9 237	9 776	-5.5	7.9	921	736	584	3 352	4.7	2.75	14.6	22.3
Chickasaw	8.7	7.0	6.7	52.3	18 085	17 851	1.3	0.2	2 906	1 806	-1 019	6 480	10.4	2.77	15.3	22.7
Choctaw	9.5	7.0	7.2	52.7	9 071	8 996	0.8	3.3	1 057	927	192	3 217	7.3	2.76	13.6	23.1
Claiborne	6.7	5.8	4.9	53.5	11 370	12 279	-7.4	2.0	1 695	1 045	-384	3 342	-6.5	2.82	25.1	27.6
Clarke	9.3	7.6	7.4	52.6	17 313	16 945	2.2	6.5	2 253	1 796	747	6 334	9.9	2.71	15.5	23.2
Clay	8.3	6.8	6.2	52.8	21 120	21 082	0.2	2.5	3 310	2 174	-531	7 251	7.0	2.83	19.4	23.0
Coahoma	8.4	6.2	6.0	54.5	31 665	36 918	-14.2	-1.8	5 671	3 607	-2 548	10 530	-9.9	2.93	25.1	26.4
Copiah	8.3	6.9	6.4	52.4	27 592	26 503	4.1	4.7	3 892	2 802	287	9 304	9.2	2.83	18.6	23.1
Covington	8.7	6.5	5.6	51.8	16 527	15 927	3.8	8.2	2 777	1 735	373	5 786	11.9	2.84	14.4	22.1
De Soto	8.3	5.7	3.4	50.9	67 910	53 930	25.9	50.4	11 929	4 848	27 086	23 273	42.5	2.91	11.1	14.8
Forrest	7.8	6.2	5.3	53.4	68 314	66 018	3.5	9.7	10 161	6 860	3 455	25 150	9.5	2.54	16.8	27.6
Franklin	10.5	7.6	7.3	52.2	8 377	8 208	2.1	-2.6	1 042	993	-236	3 086	5.8	2.69	14.2	24.7
George	8.8	5.8	5.1	50.8	16 673	15 297	9.0	21.1	3 012	1 432	1 966	5 779	19.7	2.86	10.4	18.9
Greene	7.5	5.4	4.4	42.9	10 220	9 827	4.0	23.6	1 350	997	2 060	3 327	8.5	2.90	12.9	19.6
Grenada	8.8	7.4	6.4	53.5	21 555	21 115	2.1	4.2	3 134	2 427	248	7 701	8.3	2.75	17.0	23.6
Hancock	11.0	9.5	5.4	50.4	31 760	24 496	29.7	30.7	4 402	3 161	8 556	11 817	44.4	2.64	11.3	23.3
Harrison	8.8	7.1	4.8	51.0	165 365	157 665	4.9	8.0	26 522	14 850	-1 206	59 557	14.1	2.65	13.9	24.2
Hinds	8.0	6.1	5.0	53.2	254 441	250 998	1.4	-3.4	38 340	21 823	-24 636	91 023	6.0	2.70	19.2	25.6
Holmes	7.7	6.5	6.4	53.7	21 604	22 970	-5.9	-0.2	3 710	2 469	-1 214	7 139	1.5	2.97	28.3	25.5
Humphreys	7.6	5.7	6.1	53.6	12 134	13 931	-12.9	-7.6	1 905	1 157	-1 628	3 926	-8.0	3.07	24.2	23.7
Issaquena	8.7	5.7	5.1	51.4	1 909	2 513	-24.0	-14.4	233	154	-337	633	-17.1	3.02	14.8	23.2
Itawamba	10.4	7.3	6.6	50.9	20 017	20 518	-2.4	5.3	2 540	2 115	715	7 497	6.3	2.59	8.1	21.9
Jackson	8.9	6.1	3.9	50.5	115 243	118 015	-2.3	15.5	16 800	8 728	9 680	40 454	7.6	2.82	13.5	19.3
Jasper	8.7	6.7	6.5	52.0	17 114	17 265	-0.9	5.8	2 583	1 725	188	5 956	6.5	2.86	16.0	21.6
Jefferson	7.6	6.4	5.5	53.0	8 653	9 181	-5.8	-3.1	1 342	869	-720	2 814	1.4	3.07	27.9	23.1
Jefferson Davis	8.6	7.0	5.8	52.6	14 051	13 846	1.5	-2.0	1 971	1 479	-720	4 787	9.8	2.91	18.2	22.0
Jones	10.1	7.5	6.7	52.4	62 031	61 912	0.2	1.6	8 240	6 473	-581	22 506	4.4	2.69	13.7	22.9
Kemper	8.7	7.6	7.9	51.6	10 356	10 148	2.0	1.3	1 235	997	-75	3 626	11.7	2.77	17.1	25.7
Lafayette	7.0	5.1	4.8	51.2	31 826	31 030	2.6	9.7	3 665	2 366	1 882	11 090	15.2	2.47	11.2	26.8
Lamar	8.1	5.0	4.0	51.4	30 424	23 821	27.7	25.3	4 666	2 176	5 219	10 883	38.6	2.78	11.6	19.1
Lauderdale	8.8	7.2	6.4	53.0	75 555	77 285	-2.2	0.6	11 050	7 435	-3 644	28 232	4.9	2.59	17.1	26.4
Lawrence	9.5	7.6	6.6	52.3	12 458	12 518	-0.5	4.9	1 745	1 245	149	4 506	8.4	2.74	13.6	23.4
Leake	10.1	7.3	7.7	52.2	18 436	18 790	-1.9	6.3	2 893	2 226	562	6 788	6.4	2.69	13.3	24.3
Lee	8.7	6.0	5.2	52.3	65 579	57 061	14.9	14.7	11 046	6 134	4 923	24 450	22.4	2.65	13.1	23.4
Leflore	7.8	6.3	5.8	52.3	37 341	41 525	-10.1	-1.4	6 408	4 109	-2 748	12 749	-2.0	2.82	23.6	27.1
Lincoln	9.7	7.4	6.8	52.5	30 278	30 174	0.3	6.0	4 281	3 135	783	11 089	9.5	2.69	14.1	23.8
Lowndes	7.8	5.7	4.8	52.7	59 308	57 304	3.5	2.1	9 810	4 778	-4 258	21 402	14.7	2.71	16.7	23.5
Madison	7.2	5.1	4.6	52.7	53 794	41 613	29.3	38.6	10 607	4 444	14 780	19 276	51.6	2.74	16.7	25.1
Marion	9.5	7.8	6.2	51.7	25 544	25 708	-0.6	3.9	3 562	2 745	270	9 110	6.4	2.75	13.7	23.0
Marshall	8.5	6.7	5.0	52.4	30 361	29 296	3.6	6.5	5 008	2 916	-33	10 077	18.3	2.93	17.9	20.8
Monroe	9.2	6.9	6.3	52.9	36 582	36 404	0.5	4.5	5 023	3 643	405	13 348	8.9	2.72	15.1	22.9
Montgomery	9.9	8.0	7.9	53.5	12 387	13 366	-7.3	0.1	1 765	1 457	-262	4 532	-0.2	2.70	17.1	25.0
Neshoba	9.6	6.7	6.4	52.0	24 800	23 789	4.2	11.4	3 836	2 773	1 857	8 848	10.0	2.77	13.7	21.9
Newton	9.7	7.3	7.2	52.1	20 291	19 967	1.6	7.1	3 091	2 304	709	7 358	6.1	2.68	13.5	23.0
Noxubee	8.2	6.3	6.4	52.8	12 604	13 212	-4.6	-0.8	2 097	1 341	-810	4 140	3.0	3.04	22.6	24.2
Oktibbeha	6.2	4.7	4.5	50.4	38 375	36 018	6.5	3.6	4 919	2 534	-901	12 916	17.6	2.58	14.3	25.7
Panola	8.8	6.1	5.4	52.6	29 996	28 164	6.5	13.1	5 028	3 155	2 124	10 130	14.1	2.91	18.0	22.6
Pearl River	10.1	6.9	4.8	51.7	38 714	33 795	14.6	23.9	5 599	3 781	7 474	13 760	25.0	2.77	12.2	20.3
Perry	8.4	6.5	5.4	51.6	10 865	9 864	10.1	10.8	1 720	956	439	3 802	20.3	2.84	13.1	21.2
Pike	9.2	7.4	6.4	53.3	36 882	36 173	2.0	2.8	5 425	4 148	-126	13 408	8.6	2.70	18.4	25.7
Pontotoc	9.7	6.6	5.8	51.5	22 237	20 918	6.3	15.5	3 210	2 147	2 434	8 346	13.1	2.65	10.6	22.3
Prentiss	9.5	8.4	7.2	52.1	23 278	24 025	-3.1	5.2	3 059	2 107	351	8 647	4.2	2.63	11.6	22.4
Quitman	8.1	6.8	6.4	53.1	10 490	12 636	-17.0	-6.8	1 798	1 096	-1 378	3 521	-10.4	2.95	19.7	25.1
Rankin	8.6	6.0	4.3	50.9	87 161	69 427	25.5	28.9	12 902	6 503	18 838	29 858	37.3	2.82	11.2	17.7
Scott	9.2	7.1	6.7	52.2	24 137	24 556	-1.7	3.2	4 107	2 431	-851	8 511	6.2	2.82	15.9	22.0
Sharkey	7.1	5.6	5.3	53.8	7 066	7 964	-11.3	-7.4	1 227	781	-966	2 084	-7.9	3.36	23.3	20.3
Simpson	9.2	6.6	6.2	51.2	23 953	23 441	2.2	5.9	3 461	2 485	517	8 357	8.9	2.78	13.4	22.6
Smith	10.0	6.8	6.5	50.9	14 798	15 077	-1.9	4.3	1 933	1 485	227	5 276	5.2	2.78	9.4	21.2
Stone	8.7	6.4	4.6	50.9	10 750	9 716	10.6	25.5	1 714	1 207	2 257	3 685	23.0	2.76	12.4	22.0

1. No spouse present.

Table B. States and Counties — **Vital Statistics, Health Resources, and Crime**

STATE County	Births, average 1996–1998 Total	Births, average 1996–1998 Rate[1]	Deaths, average 1996–1998 Number Total	Deaths, average 1996–1998 Number Infant[2]	Deaths, average 1996–1998 Rate Total[1]	Deaths, average 1996–1998 Rate Infant[3]	Physicians,[4] 1998 Number	Physicians,[4] 1998 Rate[5]	Hospitals,[4] 1998 Number	Hospitals,[4] 1998 Beds Number	Hospitals,[4] 1998 Beds Rate[5]	Medicare enrollees 1999	Serious crimes known to police, 1998[6] Total Number	Serious crimes known to police, 1998[6] Total Rate[7]
	32	33	34	35	36	37	38	39	40	41	42	43	44	45
MISSISSIPPI	41 820	15.3	27 344	443	10.0	10.6	4 204	153	104	12 563	456	413 900	120 647	4 384
Adams	508	14.7	439	7	12.7	14.4	68	199	2	238	695	6 213	2 362	6 788
Alcorn	440	13.5	394	3	12.0	6.1	35	107	1	150	458	6 542	NA	NA
Amite	157	11.5	132	1	9.7	4.2	5	36	0	0	0	2 277	NA	NA
Attala	250	13.6	266	3	14.4	13.3	13	71	1	72	391	3 921	192	1 036
Benton	114	14.1	100	2	12.3	17.5	0	0	0	0	0	1 496	NA	NA
Bolivar	698	17.2	440	9	10.8	13.4	25	62	1	119	295	6 126	NA	NA
Calhoun	204	13.7	183	1	12.3	3.3	5	34	2	77	519	2 954	123	1 095
Carroll	98	9.8	90	0	9.0	0.0	6	60	0	0	0	1 510	NA	NA
Chickasaw	312	17.1	196	2	10.8	6.4	12	67	2	160	888	3 634	75	493
Choctaw	118	12.7	95	1	10.2	8.5	5	53	1	88	938	1 369	NA	NA
Claiborne	181	15.5	113	2	9.7	12.9	5	43	1	27	232	1 469	114	1 137
Clarke	233	12.9	177	1	9.8	2.9	5	27	1	42	230	3 200	150	1 063
Clay	350	16.2	228	3	10.5	9.5	17	79	1	60	277	3 299	NA	NA
Coahoma	611	19.5	377	9	12.0	15.3	46	148	1	195	627	4 942	NA	NA
Copiah	405	14.1	291	5	10.1	12.4	13	45	1	49	169	5 232	NA	NA
Covington	302	17.1	213	2	12.1	6.6	7	39	1	82	461	3 094	327	1 854
De Soto	1 482	16.0	654	14	7.1	9.7	59	61	1	130	134	10 503	NA	NA
Forrest	1 099	14.9	723	7	9.8	6.1	254	342	2	672	904	11 344	4 088	7 126
Franklin	119	14.4	113	0	13.6	2.8	3	36	1	53	637	1 417	NA	NA
George	332	17.4	165	2	8.6	6.0	11	56	1	53	270	2 958	NA	NA
Greene	149	12.6	103	1	8.8	6.7	2	17	0	0	0	1 415	NA	NA
Grenada	326	14.6	277	3	12.4	8.2	31	138	1	118	526	4 029	1 071	4 730
Hancock	459	11.7	381	4	9.7	8.7	63	156	1	66	164	6 021	1 023	2 586
Harrison	2 783	15.8	1 697	25	9.6	9.1	450	253	4	722	406	25 765	12 021	6 793
Hinds	4 019	16.2	2 446	48	9.8	11.9	880	356	5	2 038	825	32 957	21 966	9 727
Holmes	394	18.3	251	7	11.7	16.9	10	46	2	113	525	3 842	NA	NA
Humphreys	195	17.1	121	2	10.6	10.3	9	79	1	28	247	1 785	NA	NA
Issaquena	20	12.3	16	0	9.8	16.7	0	0	0	0	0	154	NA	NA
Itawamba	251	12.0	250	2	11.9	9.3	8	38	0	0	0	3 130	NA	NA
Jackson	1 789	13.9	1 016	17	7.9	9.7	249	190	2	446	341	15 174	NA	NA
Jasper	298	16.9	183	2	10.4	7.8	2	11	1	114	645	3 140	NA	NA
Jefferson	132	15.6	98	3	11.6	22.7	3	36	1	30	356	1 379	NA	NA
Jefferson Davis	205	14.7	161	2	11.6	8.1	7	51	1	101	729	2 071	NA	NA
Jones	906	14.3	672	13	10.6	14.0	82	129	2	301	474	11 570	2 556	4 252
Kemper	134	12.8	105	1	10.1	10.0	2	19	1	24	227	1 755	NA	NA
Lafayette	409	11.9	288	4	8.4	10.6	74	214	1	150	434	3 763	NA	NA
Lamar	569	15.9	256	3	7.2	5.9	8	22	1	23	62	3 700	NA	NA
Lauderdale	1 165	15.2	829	16	10.8	13.4	223	293	3	619	813	12 821	2 779	3 594
Lawrence	177	13.7	139	2	10.8	9.4	6	46	1	53	406	2 888	NA	NA
Leake	321	16.6	250	2	12.9	6.2	11	57	1	76	392	3 789	NA	NA
Lee	1 158	15.7	689	15	9.3	12.7	196	263	1	607	813	11 417	4 088	5 594
Leflore	669	18.0	417	7	11.2	10.5	54	146	1	187	506	5 734	1 830	5 208
Lincoln	466	14.7	366	6	11.6	12.2	35	110	1	95	299	5 284	NA	NA
Lowndes	1 020	16.7	543	14	8.9	14.1	99	162	2	404	660	8 145	NA	NA
Madison	1 192	16.9	506	12	7.2	9.8	224	307	1	127	174	7 720	2 037	3 359
Marion	380	14.5	308	3	11.7	7.9	13	49	1	90	341	4 823	NA	NA
Marshall	513	15.9	320	4	9.9	7.8	8	25	1	40	124	4 935	NA	NA
Monroe	498	13.1	386	6	10.2	12.7	44	115	2	122	319	5 956	NA	NA
Montgomery	191	15.4	165	5	13.2	27.9	6	48	2	68	547	2 524	NA	NA
Neshoba	441	16.1	307	4	11.2	9.8	21	76	2	224	810	3 872	NA	NA
Newton	336	15.6	253	7	11.8	19.8	16	74	1	39	181	4 545	NA	NA
Noxubee	219	17.7	124	6	10.1	27.4	7	57	1	109	881	2 067	NA	NA
Oktibbeha	536	13.6	293	4	7.5	7.5	34	87	1	96	244	4 647	NA	NA
Panola	541	16.4	366	10	11.1	18.5	21	63	1	70	210	5 368	772	2 501
Pearl River	615	13.5	434	4	9.5	6.5	26	55	2	145	309	7 217	NA	NA
Perry	194	16.4	100	1	8.5	5.2	4	34	1	82	695	1 587	9	76
Pike	578	15.2	461	4	12.1	7.5	61	161	2	166	438	6 970	NA	NA
Pontotoc	353	14.2	241	3	9.7	8.5	9	35	1	61	240	3 858	NA	NA
Prentiss	336	13.9	223	4	9.2	10.9	19	78	1	78	321	4 871	NA	NA
Quitman	177	17.9	120	1	12.1	7.5	4	40	1	96	968	1 865	NA	NA
Rankin	1 520	14.2	745	12	7.0	7.7	217	198	3	233	213	12 364	NA	NA
Scott	432	17.2	274	4	10.9	8.5	12	48	2	104	416	4 461	NA	NA
Sharkey	123	18.4	77	0	11.5	2.7	2	30	1	29	436	993	NA	NA
Simpson	371	14.7	289	5	11.4	12.6	15	59	2	113	446	4 221	409	1 610
Smith	213	14.1	163	2	10.7	10.9	5	33	1	22	144	2 312	NA	NA
Stone	184	14.3	142	3	11.0	14.5	8	61	1	34	258	2 193	NA	NA

1. Per 1,000 estimated resident population, average 1996–1998. 2. Deaths of infants under 1 year old. 3. Deaths of infants under 1 year old per 1,000 live births. 4. Data subject to copyright. 5. Per 100,000 resident population as of July 1 of the year shown. 6. Data for serious crimes have not been adjusted for underreporting; this may affect comparability between geographic areas and over time. 7. Per 100,000 population estimated by the FBI.

Table B. States and Counties — Crime, Education, Money Income, and Poverty

STATE County	Serious crimes known to police, 1998[1] (cont'd) Rate[2]		Education School enrollment and attainment, 1990				Local government expenditures, fiscal 1997[5]		Money income 1989				Income and poverty, 1997		
			Enrollment[3]		Attainment[4] (percent)					Households Median				Percent below poverty level		
	Violent	Property	Total	Percent private	High school graduate or more	Bachelor's degree or more	Total current expenditures (mil dol)	Current expenditures per student (dollars)	Per capita[6] (dollars)	Dollars	Percent change, 1979–1989 (constant 1989 dollars)	Percent with $100,000 or more	Median household income	All persons	Persons under 18	Persons 5–17 in families
	46	47	48	49	50	51	52	53	54	55	56	57	58	59	60	61
MISSISSIPPI	411	3 973	727 486	11.1	64.3	14.7	2 036.0	4 039	9 648	20 136	-0.7	1.7	28 527	18.1	24.5	22.6
Adams	943	5 845	9 515	17.8	67.3	14.8	24.0	4 314	9 469	17 214	-9.5	1.9	23 444	22.6	30.8	27.9
Alcorn	NA	NA	7 289	4.4	56.3	9.6	24.5	4 314	9 301	18 538	-8.2	0.5	28 057	15.2	21.7	20.1
Amite	NA	NA	3 338	18.9	57.1	8.7	8.2	4 411	8 268	15 669	-2.1	1.2	24 072	18.4	24.8	22.8
Attala	59	977	4 529	10.7	51.4	10.0	14.3	3 840	7 685	15 380	-1.4	1.0	21 854	21.5	30.9	26.7
Benton	NA	NA	2 053	4.3	46.4	7.8	5.2	3 927	6 982	15 794	-16.2	0.2	23 458	19.5	26.3	24.5
Bolivar	NA	NA	14 519	7.6	54.9	15.2	37.0	3 963	6 889	14 020	-8.4	1.3	21 110	29.4	34.9	32.5
Calhoun	196	899	3 296	8.0	52.8	8.2	11.0	3 806	8 806	18 182	8.2	0.6	24 965	16.8	24.8	21.9
Carroll	NA	NA	2 399	22.5	54.0	10.3	5.6	4 781	8 241	16 639	2.9	1.4	24 421	18.0	25.9	23.1
Chickasaw	151	342	4 446	7.4	52.9	9.5	14.8	3 951	8 725	18 259	-5.3	1.4	24 926	16.6	23.0	20.8
Choctaw	NA	NA	2 462	11.1	57.6	10.8	8.0	4 144	8 076	17 313	9.0	0.9	23 367	21.5	29.2	28.2
Claiborne	469	668	5 013	7.0	58.7	16.1	9.3	4 400	5 932	12 876	-21.6	0.1	20 137	28.6	31.4	29.4
Clarke	99	964	4 352	3.3	61.6	8.2	12.8	3 719	8 987	19 055	-3.3	0.8	26 236	14.8	20.9	18.7
Clay	NA	NA	6 109	15.2	60.4	12.9	16.4	3 884	9 224	18 337	-11.8	1.9	25 464	21.2	28.3	25.3
Coahoma	NA	NA	10 082	9.7	54.0	14.7	29.1	4 241	7 197	13 780	-7.9	1.3	19 895	30.0	36.4	32.9
Copiah	NA	NA	7 933	10.8	61.1	9.4	19.6	3 817	7 815	16 583	-1.7	1.1	23 107	20.7	27.4	25.5
Covington	533	1 321	4 453	4.5	55.5	8.6	14.3	3 869	7 847	17 589	7.3	0.8	23 798	19.4	25.8	24.1
De Soto	NA	NA	17 526	15.6	71.2	9.5	57.2	3 439	12 509	31 756	2.8	1.9	43 386	7.6	11.1	10.3
Forrest	406	6 720	23 219	7.4	72.1	19.8	53.1	4 422	9 765	17 986	-7.2	1.9	27 652	18.3	24.9	21.9
Franklin	NA	NA	2 196	8.8	58.1	7.4	8.0	4 356	7 426	14 341	-9.0	0.7	22 749	19.7	25.8	25.8
George	NA	NA	4 468	6.6	58.8	8.3	12.8	3 291	8 000	18 397	-19.0	0.4	28 656	15.5	20.9	19.2
Greene	NA	NA	2 704	3.9	62.4	6.0	7.9	3 959	6 882	17 958	3.9	0.3	24 753	22.3	25.4	24.2
Grenada	397	4 333	5 617	10.7	56.5	10.8	16.4	3 658	9 125	19 955	-2.3	1.3	26 468	18.1	25.4	22.7
Hancock	215	2 371	7 738	18.3	68.0	14.3	23.9	3 939	10 180	20 720	-5.9	1.9	29 168	15.3	22.5	21.7
Harrison	409	6 384	42 908	12.9	74.7	16.3	132.2	4 413	10 434	22 157	-1.4	1.6	30 706	14.9	21.4	19.9
Hinds	1 029	8 698	78 082	19.3	75.2	26.4	190.2	4 343	12 222	24 676	-1.7	3.4	32 033	18.5	25.8	22.3
Holmes	NA	NA	6 968	9.3	48.0	9.7	18.0	3 756	5 969	9 809	-16.7	1.3	15 307	36.0	41.1	39.2
Humphreys	NA	NA	3 716	18.9	46.4	10.4	9.3	3 605	7 201	12 696	-4.3	1.6	18 014	32.0	40.2	37.5
Issaquena	NA	NA	549	18.4	43.7	5.6	0.0	0	6 412	13 005	-15.4	0.5	19 249	33.2	41.8	43.4
Itawamba	NA	NA	4 855	2.8	49.0	6.7	14.1	3 871	9 476	20 770	1.5	0.4	30 194	11.6	17.3	14.7
Jackson	NA	NA	32 942	8.1	74.4	14.4	104.4	4 163	11 246	26 444	-7.1	1.7	34 411	13.6	19.0	16.9
Jasper	NA	NA	4 644	9.3	60.0	9.8	13.2	4 053	7 524	16 130	-5.6	0.6	23 612	19.8	25.0	23.4
Jefferson	NA	NA	2 746	6.5	53.0	10.3	8.3	4 513	5 349	10 267	-16.7	0.2	16 349	28.3	32.3	31.6
Jefferson Davis	NA	NA	3 895	7.3	57.4	8.9	11.0	4 206	7 303	15 442	-12.4	0.6	21 064	24.3	33.8	29.6
Jones	324	3 928	16 426	6.4	64.3	12.2	47.9	4 116	9 663	19 239	-7.6	1.7	26 639	16.5	22.1	20.9
Kemper	NA	NA	2 863	11.1	56.3	7.9	7.4	4 853	8 033	14 315	-4.6	1.1	21 607	20.2	25.8	24.1
Lafayette	NA	NA	14 147	6.1	70.2	29.2	21.6	4 343	9 196	18 186	-5.9	1.7	27 958	14.3	17.7	16.3
Lamar	NA	NA	8 907	8.6	73.3	20.9	25.7	3 495	10 619	23 263	-1.2	2.2	32 363	14.9	19.3	19.6
Lauderdale	344	3 250	19 601	7.8	69.7	13.3	57.4	4 092	10 649	20 414	-0.6	2.2	28 225	17.5	24.8	22.7
Lawrence	NA	NA	3 502	4.9	61.9	9.2	10.2	3 967	8 294	17 519	-15.5	0.8	24 574	17.5	23.6	21.4
Leake	NA	NA	4 649	14.5	54.3	9.2	12.7	3 902	7 279	15 975	4.5	0.4	23 054	19.5	26.8	24.1
Lee	408	5 186	16 256	6.1	67.8	15.0	60.1	4 163	11 702	24 647	7.7	2.5	33 160	12.0	17.4	15.6
Leflore	330	4 878	11 746	9.7	55.3	15.7	31.4	4 288	9 003	15 219	-4.9	2.0	21 027	29.1	35.0	32.6
Lincoln	NA	NA	7 818	9.2	63.0	11.6	24.5	4 112	9 134	18 193	-10.1	1.3	25 922	17.7	23.8	21.6
Lowndes	NA	NA	16 936	12.9	69.0	18.6	45.9	4 089	11 108	22 985	8.1	1.8	30 068	17.7	24.6	23.3
Madison	272	3 087	15 338	23.8	71.5	29.3	41.5	3 526	12 020	25 887	27.1	3.4	37 445	14.3	19.0	19.2
Marion	NA	NA	7 036	7.2	58.8	8.4	19.5	4 028	8 490	16 084	-10.8	1.0	22 516	22.3	31.1	27.3
Marshall	NA	NA	7 902	20.0	51.7	9.4	20.1	3 760	7 599	18 492	0.2	0.5	26 328	19.1	25.4	23.9
Monroe	NA	NA	9 135	5.1	55.6	8.4	26.0	3 893	8 979	20 047	2.1	1.0	27 782	14.9	20.7	19.0
Montgomery	NA	NA	3 328	7.4	56.6	9.5	10.1	4 526	7 660	15 396	-3.5	0.5	21 719	22.4	30.2	27.7
Neshoba	NA	NA	7 071	11.7	60.9	10.1	15.9	3 804	8 249	18 237	0.0	0.9	27 149	16.9	22.6	21.2
Newton	NA	NA	5 685	10.1	60.1	9.7	16.4	4 359	8 923	19 302	9.0	1.2	25 659	16.4	23.0	20.6
Noxubee	NA	NA	3 546	17.3	49.6	7.9	9.4	3 833	6 654	14 205	-2.2	1.0	20 005	28.3	35.5	34.2
Oktibbeha	NA	NA	17 325	7.2	73.0	31.7	27.5	4 756	9 166	18 507	0.8	1.4	27 224	20.0	24.2	23.3
Panola	227	2 274	8 085	6.8	54.3	8.7	25.2	3 719	7 537	17 686	9.3	0.8	23 572	21.6	27.8	26.0
Pearl River	NA	NA	10 674	7.7	68.4	11.4	30.7	3 692	9 418	20 133	-0.6	1.8	27 091	17.5	24.9	22.0
Perry	0	76	2 980	3.9	61.8	7.1	10.5	4 331	7 418	16 230	-12.1	0.9	24 328	19.2	24.6	23.8
Pike	NA	NA	10 425	6.8	60.6	12.8	29.1	4 025	8 119	15 149	-14.1	1.4	21 689	23.2	29.6	27.5
Pontotoc	NA	NA	5 157	2.9	57.4	8.1	18.1	3 660	9 143	20 223	6.5	0.5	28 991	12.7	17.1	16.8
Prentiss	NA	NA	6 024	2.4	52.9	8.4	20.3	4 134	8 947	17 736	-5.1	1.7	25 784	15.6	19.8	19.7
Quitman	NA	NA	2 974	13.0	45.5	9.0	7.0	4 072	6 450	13 730	0.4	0.6	18 118	31.5	38.1	36.8
Rankin	NA	NA	23 316	14.7	73.8	19.0	64.0	3 478	12 749	31 668	3.0	2.6	41 627	9.7	14.0	12.0
Scott	NA	NA	6 136	5.0	53.1	9.4	21.8	3 799	8 187	17 040	-5.4	1.4	23 642	19.1	25.5	24.0
Sharkey	NA	NA	2 329	11.1	51.3	12.4	8.0	5 114	6 032	13 304	-3.8	0.8	17 245	35.9	43.7	41.8
Simpson	138	1 472	6 122	10.4	58.0	8.7	16.5	3 690	8 284	19 053	-3.0	0.7	25 392	19.5	25.6	24.4
Smith	NA	NA	3 516	4.8	57.0	7.6	11.3	3 688	8 799	19 111	9.8	0.9	26 406	17.2	22.8	22.2
Stone	NA	NA	3 243	3.2	68.1	12.4	10.4	3 963	8 816	19 045	-13.3	1.4	25 433	20.7	25.7	27.5

1. Data for serious crimes have not been adjusted for underreporting; this may affect comparability between geographic areas and over time.   2. Per 100,000 population estimated by the FBI.   3. All persons 3 years old and over enrolled in nursery school through college.   4. Persons 25 years old and over.   5. Elementary and secondary education expenditures, local government fiscal years ending between July 1, 1996 and June 30, 1997.   6. Based on population enumerated as of April 1, 1990.

Table B. States and Counties — **Personal Income**

| | Personal income, 1998 | | | | | | | | | | | | |
STATE County	Total (mil dol)	Percent change, 1997–1998	Per capita[1] Dollars	Per capita[1] Rank	Wages and salaries[2] (mil dol)	Proprietor's income (mil dol)	Dividends, interest, and rent (mil dol)	Transfer payments Total (mil dol)	Government payments to individuals Total (mil dol)	Social Security (mil dol)	Medical payments (mil dol)	Income mainte- nance (mil dol)	Unemploy- ment insurance (mil dol)
	62	63	64	65	66	67	68	69	70	71	72	73	74
MISSISSIPPI	54 410	5.5	19 776	X	32 603	4 124	8 415	10 307	9 809	3 724	3 967	1 404	117
Adams	664	3.7	19 461	1 905	393	65	131	156	150	60	56	24	2
Alcorn	635	4.1	19 372	1 927	384	46	93	142	136	60	53	16	2
Amite	203	6.5	14 622	2 965	62	22	33	51	49	19	18	9	0
Attala	317	3.7	17 289	2 535	139	27	56	88	84	33	33	13	1
Benton	120	3.5	14 881	2 944	40	6	14	32	30	11	13	5	0
Bolivar	663	0.8	16 499	2 708	362	23	99	175	168	48	65	44	3
Calhoun	270	3.6	18 159	2 305	99	30	46	67	64	26	26	9	1
Carroll	170	3.6	17 029	2 604	30	11	25	36	34	15	11	6	0
Chickasaw	318	2.3	17 643	2 453	172	29	53	77	74	31	30	10	1
Choctaw	132	4.1	14 063	3 001	47	12	17	34	32	12	12	6	0
Claiborne	167	3.5	14 501	2 968	181	8	24	46	43	13	19	9	1
Clarke	292	2.9	16 013	2 792	110	23	43	70	67	29	26	8	1
Clay	383	5.2	17 735	2 429	251	26	66	83	79	31	28	14	1
Coahoma	523	-1.0	16 727	2 670	289	19	90	155	149	42	66	32	2
Copiah	448	5.2	15 555	2 872	173	38	63	116	111	41	45	18	1
Covington	299	5.1	16 885	2 635	106	47	40	71	67	26	26	11	1
De Soto	2 390	14.1	24 616	543	852	149	243	227	209	105	70	17	3
Forrest	1 439	3.7	19 313	1 949	1 036	109	297	286	273	96	113	32	2
Franklin	119	4.7	14 300	2 983	52	7	17	35	33	13	12	5	1
George	325	12.9	16 572	2 699	89	16	39	66	63	24	28	7	1
Greene	164	5.7	12 833	3 068	49	14	17	41	39	14	16	5	1
Grenada	428	5.4	19 103	2 022	313	29	76	101	97	34	45	12	1
Hancock	786	7.9	19 519	1 882	492	39	159	144	137	60	56	12	1
Harrison	4 047	6.8	22 838	882	2 970	269	689	656	625	226	276	65	6
Hinds	6 017	3.1	24 333	586	5 122	493	1 177	863	818	320	310	115	9
Holmes	290	2.3	13 472	3 048	119	20	38	113	109	24	49	29	1
Humphreys	195	3.3	17 204	2 560	86	30	29	54	52	14	23	13	1
Issaquena	21	-6.1	12 859	3 066	8	-2	3	6	5	2	2	2	0
Itawamba	411	6.9	19 484	1 900	145	23	58	74	70	33	25	6	1
Jackson	2 769	11.7	21 170	1 338	2 026	85	388	403	379	170	145	36	5
Jasper	277	4.5	15 687	2 852	117	34	34	70	67	26	26	11	1
Jefferson	96	4.7	11 390	3 092	31	5	9	45	43	11	15	10	1
Jefferson Davis	206	5.0	14 944	2 934	62	18	28	55	53	20	20	9	1
Jones	1 310	5.6	20 598	1 530	766	128	191	291	279	104	133	27	2
Kemper	174	3.5	16 460	2 712	49	14	26	43	41	14	15	7	1
Lafayette	662	5.6	19 034	2 042	418	49	115	109	103	38	47	9	0
Lamar	695	6.4	18 761	2 134	296	68	67	98	92	42	34	10	1
Lauderdale	1 633	2.8	21 456	1 258	1 141	84	263	306	293	110	119	39	4
Lawrence	225	4.8	17 337	2 523	104	26	30	62	60	26	23	7	1
Leake	374	7.8	19 259	1 971	149	66	46	88	84	30	37	12	1
Lee	1 753	4.8	23 486	749	1 594	94	285	243	229	105	88	24	3
Leflore	667	1.4	17 915	2 373	417	45	116	176	169	46	73	34	2
Lincoln	584	6.1	18 326	2 256	308	73	84	130	124	52	49	15	2
Lowndes	1 236	3.5	20 249	1 637	902	83	197	191	180	69	66	31	2
Madison	1 829	8.3	25 096	480	727	110	321	198	184	74	72	29	1
Marion	427	5.3	16 180	2 767	187	35	71	116	111	43	46	16	1
Marshall	575	5.8	17 878	2 385	183	45	52	118	113	41	43	20	1
Monroe	635	3.5	16 667	2 686	322	43	101	144	137	60	51	16	3
Montgomery	205	3.6	16 566	2 700	71	20	31	57	55	20	24	9	0
Neshoba	555	6.3	20 198	1 651	361	71	62	111	106	39	47	13	1
Newton	409	6.8	18 944	2 078	178	57	58	98	95	35	41	11	1
Noxubee	196	2.8	15 809	2 825	83	19	31	52	50	16	18	14	1
Oktibbeha	703	5.4	17 728	2 433	449	39	132	117	110	38	40	18	1
Panola	512	3.1	15 368	2 895	276	39	71	130	123	45	48	24	3
Pearl River	764	6.0	16 304	2 741	214	64	116	181	172	73	67	19	1
Perry	163	3.8	13 774	3 027	81	13	20	45	43	17	16	7	1
Pike	671	4.7	17 737	2 425	392	62	101	168	161	56	65	25	2
Pontotoc	439	7.2	17 333	2 524	242	30	53	80	76	33	31	8	1
Prentiss	376	2.7	15 445	2 884	212	18	52	91	87	36	34	10	2
Quitman	138	-2.0	13 980	3 006	45	7	17	49	48	13	20	12	1
Rankin	2 701	9.4	24 646	538	1 425	183	330	317	297	126	130	21	2
Scott	488	8.0	19 503	1 889	260	111	56	102	98	33	44	14	1
Sharkey	84	-0.4	12 734	3 072	41	3	13	31	30	8	13	8	1
Simpson	468	4.3	18 489	2 215	154	74	55	118	113	36	58	12	2
Smith	301	9.2	19 709	1 809	110	80	28	61	58	26	21	8	0
Stone	209	4.8	15 811	2 824	94	17	23	57	55	19	23	6	0

1. Based on the resident population estimated as of July 1 of the year shown.   2. Includes other labor income.

STATE County	Earnings, 1998 Total (mil dol)	Farm	Goods-related[1] Total	Manu-facturing	Service-related and other[2] Total	Retail trade	Finance, insur-ance, and real estate	Services	Govern-ment	Social Security bene-ficiaries, December 1998 Number	Rate[3]	Supple-mental Security Income recipients, December 1998	Housing units, 1990 Total	Percent change, 1980–1990
	75	76	77	78	79	80	81	82	83	84	85	86	87	88
MISSISSIPPI	36 726	2.3	27.9	20.7	48.7	9.7	4.5	22.8	21.1	501 039	182	135 036	1 010 423	10.8
Adams	458	0.1	37.7	18.6	47.6	11.6	3.5	23.6	14.6	7 517	220	2 043	14 715	8.4
Alcorn	430	0.2	D	41.8	D	13.4	3.1	13.4	16.0	8 079	247	1 988	13 704	7.0
Amite	84	14.0	D	35.9	D	6.7	D	12.5	15.6	2 721	198	794	5 695	7.9
Attala	166	0.9	36.2	21.8	D	14.3	4.9	15.3	17.0	4 703	256	1 277	7 674	0.7
Benton	46	0.9	39.3	34.0	D	D	1.3	15.6	17.0	1 677	206	585	3 379	10.5
Bolivar	385	2.7	23.7	20.2	49.1	9.5	3.1	15.8	24.4	7 158	178	4 075	14 514	-0.3
Calhoun	129	12.2	37.3	35.6	34.3	9.4	2.5	9.3	16.2	3 784	255	983	6 260	3.7
Carroll	41	3.3	D	17.7	D	9.2	D	19.6	21.1	2 168	217	538	3 948	10.2
Chickasaw	202	4.7	53.1	51.0	30.6	7.8	1.8	11.8	11.5	4 381	243	1 218	6 997	10.3
Choctaw	59	4.5	D	29.5	D	6.5	1.9	16.2	24.5	1 768	188	526	3 539	3.6
Claiborne	188	1.4	D	9.2	D	3.9	1.0	6.4	23.3	1 950	167	932	4 099	-6.8
Clarke	134	2.7	48.9	43.4	33.7	5.7	2.4	14.2	14.7	3 968	218	869	7 065	9.3
Clay	278	0.3	D	52.2	D	6.8	2.0	16.4	10.0	4 179	193	1 208	7 737	5.9
Coahoma	308	1.9	D	14.2	D	10.2	5.1	34.3	19.0	6 043	194	2 985	11 495	-11.1
Copiah	211	5.9	36.6	30.1	D	8.3	2.0	14.9	24.7	5 724	198	1 872	10 260	7.2
Covington	153	9.2	D	24.4	D	7.2	2.0	10.9	17.0	3 756	211	1 192	6 535	13.3
De Soto	1 001	-0.3	D	28.1	D	12.8	4.1	20.8	9.9	12 441	128	1 508	24 472	42.7
Forrest	1 145	0.6	18.5	11.8	49.2	10.2	5.6	22.9	31.7	12 310	166	2 885	27 740	10.9
Franklin	59	1.2	D	25.5	D	5.9	D	11.7	26.4	1 795	216	432	3 555	4.3
George	106	2.7	D	14.7	D	14.3	3.5	D	29.4	3 221	164	560	6 663	16.4
Greene	64	8.8	23.9	17.0	D	8.5	1.9	9.2	42.5	2 080	177	487	3 864	13.0
Grenada	343	0.4	46.2	41.4	37.3	11.2	3.1	15.3	16.1	4 614	206	1 364	8 712	13.4
Hancock	531	-0.2	D	11.6	D	6.6	2.8	33.6	33.0	7 380	183	1 022	16 561	32.1
Harrison	3 239	0.0	12.5	6.5	52.5	9.5	4.0	28.5	35.1	30 042	169	6 146	67 813	17.0
Hinds	5 615	0.3	12.8	7.3	63.6	9.2	9.7	29.1	23.3	39 780	161	10 376	99 860	9.0
Holmes	138	4.9	D	28.8	D	10.1	2.6	21.8	22.5	3 890	181	2 516	7 972	2.3
Humphreys	115	28.0	23.7	21.6	33.1	7.0	2.7	14.2	15.2	2 266	200	1 223	4 231	-10.7
Issaquena	6	0.0	D	4.6	D	D	D	14.5	38.4	279	171	102	698	-23.0
Itawamba	168	4.7	D	30.1	D	6.8	1.5	11.1	18.2	4 428	210	640	8 116	6.2
Jackson	2 111	0.0	D	40.0	D	6.6	2.1	16.0	19.7	20 418	156	2 495	45 542	6.8
Jasper	151	9.7	45.2	30.7	D	7.1	2.0	13.5	15.3	3 796	215	1 239	6 700	8.3
Jefferson	36	5.8	D	D	41.4	5.0	1.2	13.6	42.6	1 871	222	962	3 167	1.1
Jefferson Davis	80	9.5	D	16.3	D	11.4	2.3	14.5	22.7	2 988	216	860	5 336	8.8
Jones	894	5.7	40.4	25.3	35.0	8.7	2.3	14.5	18.9	13 410	211	3 303	25 044	4.7
Kemper	63	12.6	32.1	28.0	32.0	7.1	3.4	12.9	23.3	2 232	211	707	4 151	16.7
Lafayette	467	0.2	18.2	12.5	45.0	12.1	3.2	24.8	36.6	4 991	144	975	12 478	14.3
Lamar	364	2.7	17.6	9.5	70.0	21.7	3.3	34.3	9.8	5 263	143	862	11 849	37.8
Lauderdale	1 225	0.2	D	14.1	D	11.2	4.0	27.8	22.4	14 382	189	3 771	31 232	7.5
Lawrence	130	9.9	D	45.6	D	5.6	1.6	8.9	15.3	3 506	269	776	5 160	11.6
Leake	216	22.7	34.9	28.9	D	9.2	2.8	13.1	10.0	4 363	225	1 230	7 614	7.4
Lee	1 688	0.2	38.2	34.6	52.9	9.6	4.4	27.0	8.8	13 603	182	2 717	25 971	21.5
Leflore	462	1.7	25.6	21.9	48.8	9.9	3.7	18.7	24.0	6 635	180	3 191	13 799	0.4
Lincoln	381	3.3	26.8	17.4	59.2	19.7	3.1	19.4	10.7	6 828	215	1 483	12 133	10.0
Lowndes	984	1.5	32.2	24.0	44.4	9.9	2.7	19.1	21.9	9 137	149	2 645	23 117	16.3
Madison	837	0.4	19.4	11.3	67.3	15.6	11.8	23.8	12.9	9 410	129	2 296	20 761	48.4
Marion	222	6.6	30.6	13.2	44.7	13.3	3.6	15.6	18.1	5 952	226	1 520	10 132	7.0
Marshall	228	-0.6	D	27.4	D	9.1	4.2	23.0	15.7	5 934	184	2 079	10 984	16.4
Monroe	364	0.4	48.0	39.7	37.9	9.5	2.2	16.9	13.7	8 154	213	1 566	14 285	7.8
Montgomery	91	2.6	D	19.5	D	12.2	3.6	22.1	21.5	2 859	230	894	4 987	0.0
Neshoba	432	8.0	D	19.4	D	7.4	2.6	D	11.8	5 491	199	1 359	9 770	9.9
Newton	235	17.0	D	27.9	D	7.9	2.3	14.3	21.4	4 983	232	1 195	8 095	4.3
Noxubee	102	9.3	D	38.1	D	7.7	2.5	10.0	18.9	2 547	206	1 373	4 645	6.1
Oktibbeha	488	0.5	17.7	15.3	29.2	9.9	3.7	12.7	52.7	5 079	129	1 835	13 861	17.6
Panola	315	-0.2	36.2	28.4	44.7	12.2	2.4	16.9	19.2	6 641	199	2 371	11 482	11.5
Pearl River	278	-0.6	D	11.3	D	18.3	3.6	21.7	22.6	9 396	201	1 600	15 793	24.0
Perry	94	4.6	D	51.3	D	6.4	2.2	6.6	17.4	2 471	209	571	4 292	22.1
Pike	454	3.1	D	23.9	D	13.1	3.1	17.0	22.4	7 713	203	2 465	14 995	12.2
Pontotoc	272	1.4	D	57.3	D	6.6	2.0	11.3	10.0	4 538	179	887	9 001	10.5
Prentiss	229	-0.2	D	42.4	D	8.6	2.8	13.0	18.7	5 139	212	1 165	9 155	2.3
Quitman	52	1.3	D	15.1	57.8	11.5	11.8	23.9	21.8	2 099	212	1 227	3 880	-9.6
Rankin	1 608	1.5	26.2	15.6	56.0	8.4	6.6	19.0	16.3	15 386	140	2 087	31 872	32.8
Scott	371	22.7	D	33.9	29.6	7.2	2.6	11.0	10.3	4 846	194	1 553	9 488	6.3
Sharkey	44	8.6	D	D	D	9.6	3.3	22.3	27.7	1 140	171	600	2 290	-8.8
Simpson	228	19.9	D	10.8	D	10.9	2.6	20.4	19.2	5 027	198	1 339	9 374	7.4
Smith	190	34.9	D	32.5	D	3.3	0.9	7.7	9.0	3 738	244	728	5 850	2.4
Stone	111	0.4	D	24.2	D	8.9	3.0	22.5	27.2	2 594	197	514	4 148	19.6

1. Covers mining, construction, and manufacturing. 2. Covers private sector earnings in agricultural services, forestry, and fisheries; transportation and public utilities; wholesale trade; retail trade; finance, insurance, and real estate; and services. 3. Per 1,000 resident population estimated as of July 1 of the year shown.

Table B. States and Counties — Housing, Labor Force, and Employment

STATE County	Housing units, 1990 (cont'd)								Civilian labor force, 1999				Civilian employment, 1990[5]		
	Occupied units							Sub-standard units[3] (percent)			Unemployment			Percent	
	Owner-occupied					Renter-occupied									
				Owner cost as a percent of income											
	Total	Percent	Median value[1]	With a mortgage	Without a mortgage	Median rent[2]	Rent as percent of income		Total	Percent change, 1998–1999	Total	Rate[4]	Total	Professional, managerial, and technical	Precision production, craft, and repair
	89	90	91	92	93	94	95	96	97	98	99	100	101	102	103
MISSISSIPPI	911 374	71.5	45 600	20.8	13.5	309	27.1	7.2	1 269 955	0.1	64 666	5.1	1 028 773	24.6	12.9
Adams	13 262	71.5	43 900	21.7	14.9	282	29.0	4.7	14 271	-3.3	1 251	8.8	12 895	27.0	11.5
Alcorn	12 449	75.7	38 800	19.3	13.1	240	26.7	3.1	14 893	1.7	776	5.2	13 226	20.7	14.7
Amite	4 830	86.0	36 800	22.9	14.3	198	20.9	9.3	5 716	3.5	280	4.9	4 426	19.3	11.9
Attala	6 945	78.2	36 500	21.8	13.9	231	25.9	10.4	7 708	0.6	647	8.4	6 753	17.8	13.0
Benton	2 842	86.0	35 100	25.2	13.3	225	21.1	10.6	3 295	1.7	201	6.1	2 804	14.2	13.4
Bolivar	13 292	59.4	39 200	21.0	15.5	258	31.5	13.0	16 434	-2.0	1 217	7.4	14 284	23.9	9.3
Calhoun	5 662	80.8	33 900	19.3	13.0	234	22.7	6.3	6 103	-3.8	257	4.2	6 275	14.7	14.4
Carroll	3 352	80.5	34 400	23.5	15.6	224	23.4	10.0	4 345	0.2	227	5.2	3 543	18.8	15.5
Chickasaw	6 480	78.5	37 800	20.2	12.4	230	24.7	7.3	7 593	-3.3	478	6.3	7 816	15.8	16.8
Choctaw	3 217	85.6	36 000	22.5	12.8	235	23.6	7.4	2 912	-1.4	230	7.9	3 285	18.4	17.4
Claiborne	3 342	74.2	39 000	22.6	17.8	240	28.6	13.7	3 272	-6.1	345	10.5	3 078	28.3	9.5
Clarke	6 334	83.6	36 000	21.1	13.4	249	19.8	5.4	8 739	2.8	635	7.3	7 209	19.3	16.4
Clay	7 251	74.4	41 500	20.4	12.6	262	26.7	9.9	8 720	-2.2	648	7.4	8 297	19.8	11.9
Coahoma	10 530	56.7	36 700	21.3	15.5	247	30.0	13.0	11 626	-0.5	1 042	9.0	9 878	26.6	9.5
Copiah	9 304	79.7	35 600	22.7	14.8	243	28.8	9.2	10 927	-1.6	957	8.8	10 080	18.8	13.0
Covington	5 786	85.4	37 300	23.5	13.7	227	25.1	9.1	8 093	-2.6	457	5.6	6 238	21.1	16.1
De Soto	23 273	81.3	62 400	21.3	12.2	430	27.3	4.8	52 367	3.2	1 344	2.6	33 128	21.2	15.8
Forrest	25 150	60.9	45 200	21.4	12.8	299	28.2	5.1	33 170	-2.0	1 111	3.3	28 133	28.0	11.6
Franklin	3 086	85.0	35 900	22.8	13.4	201	27.7	8.8	3 289	-0.3	275	8.4	2 670	20.2	18.8
George	5 779	86.2	37 500	20.3	13.3	264	26.9	7.0	8 594	4.9	602	7.0	6 033	18.5	21.7
Greene	3 327	86.4	33 800	21.9	13.8	228	26.2	10.0	5 301	-1.2	371	7.0	3 353	17.5	22.3
Grenada	7 701	70.1	44 300	18.7	13.4	295	24.9	6.6	10 047	0.2	533	5.3	8 495	20.6	14.5
Hancock	11 817	79.0	52 800	21.1	13.0	331	27.1	5.5	17 889	4.7	721	4.0	11 201	27.4	16.1
Harrison	59 557	61.4	55 100	20.9	12.4	345	25.5	4.6	85 394	2.4	2 931	3.4	63 470	29.5	11.9
Hinds	91 023	61.6	57 500	21.4	13.7	390	25.6	6.5	128 359	-1.0	5 184	4.0	114 761	31.7	9.0
Holmes	7 139	70.7	30 200	29.6	16.1	206	35.1	14.3	7 096	-0.2	1 196	16.9	5 611	19.4	12.9
Humphreys	3 926	58.7	36 600	24.8	16.2	235	31.2	14.1	4 747	-0.6	466	9.8	4 378	18.3	10.9
Issaquena	633	67.5	36 600	17.5	16.1	213	27.4	15.2	623	-6.7	94	15.1	674	14.5	8.0
Itawamba	7 497	85.3	35 500	19.8	12.4	249	20.8	3.6	11 104	-0.8	481	4.3	9 409	15.1	13.9
Jackson	40 454	73.5	50 900	18.9	13.0	348	25.4	4.8	68 915	3.3	2 625	3.8	48 343	28.2	17.9
Jasper	5 956	88.3	36 000	22.4	13.7	193	27.0	10.4	7 894	0.4	393	5.0	6 033	20.7	14.5
Jefferson	2 814	77.7	34 500	27.9	14.6	204	35.1	17.3	2 687	9.6	472	17.6	2 312	21.5	13.5
Jefferson Davis	4 787	84.6	36 700	22.7	13.7	238	33.5	10.6	4 990	4.2	787	15.8	4 659	18.0	15.7
Jones	22 506	76.4	41 500	20.3	13.4	269	25.6	5.3	30 906	0.2	1 038	3.4	24 247	22.4	14.0
Kemper	3 626	80.4	36 600	22.9	13.1	201	25.0	13.0	4 523	4.4	547	12.1	3 647	17.6	11.1
Lafayette	11 090	61.7	51 100	21.0	12.4	356	33.9	4.4	17 354	1.5	316	1.8	13 606	34.8	9.2
Lamar	10 883	75.3	55 400	19.1	12.5	333	26.2	3.0	17 159	0.5	508	3.0	13 119	32.0	13.8
Lauderdale	28 232	66.4	47 300	19.1	12.8	297	25.4	5.7	34 691	-1.0	1 945	5.6	30 435	26.0	12.4
Lawrence	4 506	86.4	40 200	23.4	15.2	244	24.5	5.6	5 273	-0.6	387	7.3	4 488	17.2	16.6
Leake	6 788	84.8	34 700	22.3	13.2	211	26.4	9.2	9 828	0.7	573	5.8	6 875	16.4	16.2
Lee	24 450	69.0	54 000	18.8	12.9	319	23.7	3.3	39 571	0.8	1 517	3.8	31 178	23.6	11.2
Leflore	12 749	52.3	42 700	21.7	13.0	245	30.0	12.0	15 180	0.1	1 277	8.4	13 082	25.4	8.8
Lincoln	11 089	78.6	43 800	21.8	14.7	259	29.8	5.6	13 869	1.9	664	4.8	11 433	22.0	12.6
Lowndes	21 402	63.6	49 500	18.9	13.2	322	24.5	6.1	26 272	-4.6	1 538	5.9	25 260	26.3	13.8
Madison	19 276	64.1	66 300	21.9	15.4	437	24.9	8.2	36 843	1.8	1 139	3.1	23 857	37.0	7.9
Marion	9 110	79.5	38 800	25.2	12.6	250	24.4	8.3	10 634	0.0	684	6.4	8 678	19.7	16.2
Marshall	10 077	79.5	41 900	22.5	13.8	241	25.4	11.8	14 044	-0.6	833	5.9	11 389	16.1	18.2
Monroe	13 348	78.0	39 200	19.0	14.4	258	25.9	5.3	15 042	-1.5	1 097	7.3	15 923	15.8	13.8
Montgomery	4 532	74.2	35 400	22.7	16.2	224	27.4	8.3	5 446	1.0	326	6.0	4 742	20.9	13.1
Neshoba	8 848	80.1	38 000	19.8	13.3	216	22.9	8.3	16 154	-0.9	744	4.6	10 060	18.2	13.8
Newton	7 358	81.5	37 600	20.6	12.1	204	23.8	6.7	8 268	-2.5	553	6.7	8 283	18.0	16.0
Noxubee	4 140	78.2	31 700	21.8	14.1	175	25.4	18.8	4 389	-1.3	511	11.6	4 166	12.7	13.8
Oktibbeha	12 916	59.0	51 200	18.4	13.4	330	33.7	7.2	20 818	1.1	460	2.2	16 243	35.5	8.9
Panola	10 130	76.1	39 300	20.6	13.9	249	24.5	12.4	12 343	-2.7	1 000	8.1	11 167	18.0	12.1
Pearl River	13 760	79.1	45 100	20.8	13.0	290	28.0	5.2	19 869	0.0	807	4.1	14 723	27.0	16.6
Perry	3 802	82.5	34 300	21.3	12.9	227	28.2	9.8	4 412	6.3	301	6.8	3 801	18.5	16.3
Pike	13 408	74.8	41 000	23.5	14.5	243	28.5	6.7	16 781	2.2	848	5.1	13 020	21.3	11.8
Pontotoc	8 346	80.5	41 200	19.3	13.1	255	24.1	3.9	13 239	2.3	448	3.4	10 443	15.8	16.3
Prentiss	8 647	78.9	36 700	21.0	13.4	225	25.7	3.0	12 173	-0.5	768	6.3	10 190	19.0	14.9
Quitman	3 521	68.4	27 900	21.8	15.4	228	29.3	14.6	3 218	-1.0	285	8.9	3 306	19.3	10.4
Rankin	29 858	79.4	64 400	19.4	13.2	423	24.7	4.5	59 912	1.4	1 291	2.2	42 184	30.1	12.9
Scott	8 511	80.7	34 900	21.5	13.7	270	26.5	9.7	12 462	5.1	412	3.3	9 810	17.5	17.0
Sharkey	2 084	61.2	40 800	22.0	14.5	223	28.4	17.2	2 480	-2.0	450	18.1	2 347	18.7	10.2
Simpson	8 357	81.0	38 900	22.3	12.6	246	27.4	9.4	9 808	-7.0	619	6.3	9 376	18.6	16.9
Smith	5 276	85.7	36 900	21.8	12.9	227	26.9	7.2	5 735	-4.4	220	3.8	5 955	15.1	15.1
Stone	3 685	79.8	39 100	20.7	13.1	263	32.0	5.6	5 073	-3.5	258	5.1	4 189	24.3	14.8

1. Specified owner-occupied units.   2. Specified renter-occupied units.   3. Overcrowded or lacking complete plumbing facilities.   4. Percent of civilian labor force.   5. Persons 16 years and older.

Table B. States and Counties — Nonfarm Employment and Agriculture

| | Private nonfarm establishments, employment and payroll, 1998 | | | | | | | | | Agriculture, 1997 | | | |
STATE County	Number of establish-ments	Total	Health Care and Social Assistance	Manufac-turing	Retail trade	Finance and Insurance	Professional Scientific and Technical Services	Total (mil dol)	Average per employee (dollars)	Number	Less than 50 acres	500 acres and over	Whose principal occupation is farming (percent)
	104	105	106	107	108	109	110	111	112	113	114	115	116
MISSISSIPPI	59 771	937 023	126 613	230 175	138 422	34 047	24 890	21 067	22 483	31 318	22.3	14.5	40.7
Adams	1 076	11 727	1 934	1 708	2 324	415	243	233	19 892	132	26.5	21.2	37.1
Alcorn	862	12 959	1 555	4 694	2 317	293	173	302	23 282	449	28.5	8.0	26.7
Amite	188	1 640	45	723	242	35	26	35	21 122	471	15.1	9.6	38.2
Attala	396	5 605	565	1 032	1 285	218	69	104	18 611	385	12.7	14.3	34.3
Benton	79	1 113	108	477	187	D	D	22	19 695	213	15.5	17.4	33.8
Bolivar	771	9 633	1 608	2 467	1 722	497	172	190	19 735	394	11.7	57.4	79.7
Calhoun	334	3 355	209	1 740	467	90	48	64	19 151	427	11.5	18.5	44.3
Carroll	115	778	15	D	186	11	3	13	16 532	423	12.8	19.6	36.9
Chickasaw	437	6 902	532	4 361	720	105	60	129	18 746	447	17.4	15.0	36.5
Choctaw	157	1 502	211	584	188	D	8	30	20 001	217	11.1	7.4	33.6
Claiborne	145	2 278	194	513	237	51	19	83	36 518	170	13.5	25.3	40.6
Clarke	313	4 053	386	2 082	285	95	52	81	19 969	269	29.0	8.9	33.5
Clay	433	7 804	578	3 669	742	167	121	197	25 276	367	16.6	14.4	37.9
Coahoma	679	9 180	1 698	1 410	1 488	405	227	191	20 841	181	10.5	59.1	82.9
Copiah	463	5 946	582	2 719	795	149	60	103	17 369	510	18.2	11.6	38.6
Covington	308	4 298	348	2 046	422	103	41	75	17 377	475	22.3	7.4	40.8
De Soto	1 749	28 534	1 864	6 932	4 931	619	900	652	22 848	467	41.8	12.4	32.5
Forrest	2 099	32 546	6 706	5 229	5 474	1 345	950	734	22 543	291	36.8	5.2	39.2
Franklin	150	1 360	277	209	194	47	28	28	20 812	158	17.7	12.0	36.1
George	292	2 761	506	354	700	121	100	48	17 492	419	47.0	3.1	26.7
Greene	133	854	94	D	196	D	12	12	14 568	334	23.4	7.2	29.3
Grenada	622	10 015	1 253	4 081	1 445	286	136	234	23 350	211	13.3	19.9	41.2
Hancock	718	8 672	740	541	1 524	247	633	208	23 993	239	33.1	5.0	32.2
Harrison	4 382	71 987	12 788	4 178	10 334	2 512	1 937	1 611	22 375	275	60.0	0.7	25.8
Hinds	6 768	135 733	24 034	10 682	17 014	9 070	6 069	3 526	25 979	723	23.5	13.8	32.5
Holmes	289	3 899	402	2 139	612	111	D	63	16 249	352	11.1	25.0	42.0
Humphreys	190	2 708	233	1 263	320	97	34	46	16 945	240	15.8	45.4	77.1
Issaquena	15	89	0	0	4	D	0	1	13 079	82	7.3	54.9	72.0
Itawamba	334	4 662	305	1 625	518	70	28	99	21 185	387	19.4	9.8	36.4
Jackson	2 311	43 018	4 558	16 765	5 966	895	1 864	1 196	27 812	321	53.9	4.0	33.6
Jasper	287	3 948	258	1 749	461	105	137	74	18 849	367	15.5	7.6	42.5
Jefferson	79	745	185	D	103	D	10	14	18 250	158	12.7	23.4	48.7
Jefferson Davis	194	2 471	337	999	355	53	18	35	14 005	389	16.7	7.5	41.6
Jones	1 442	21 443	2 517	7 054	3 053	557	442	477	22 222	773	37.9	2.6	44.1
Kemper	127	2 254	84	1 609	181	49	4	35	15 344	382	17.5	13.6	37.7
Lafayette	897	12 302	2 729	2 049	2 025	266	789	225	18 258	372	12.6	11.3	29.8
Lamar	760	8 420	719	754	2 813	230	250	149	17 680	401	31.4	6.5	38.4
Lauderdale	2 109	33 674	7 083	5 946	5 569	1 211	623	781	23 203	356	25.6	9.6	27.8
Lawrence	234	2 675	292	D	318	52	D	66	24 775	308	16.9	7.5	41.6
Leake	347	5 605	750	2 900	713	172	42	90	16 000	583	22.5	6.2	42.4
Lee	2 284	46 890	6 151	17 845	6 445	1 618	1 234	1 175	25 056	488	27.7	11.9	34.2
Leflore	885	13 262	2 285	3 749	1 903	405	351	275	20 726	246	8.9	56.5	74.8
Lincoln	787	10 022	1 445	1 252	1 678	268	181	217	21 616	499	18.6	6.4	36.9
Lowndes	1 673	25 209	2 433	6 907	3 966	665	452	554	21 991	378	22.8	21.4	38.1
Madison	1 795	24 706	1 723	2 451	5 753	1 599	941	568	22 975	465	22.2	20.4	33.5
Marion	563	6 289	790	1 139	1 151	218	122	119	18 843	485	23.1	9.3	41.6
Marshall	431	6 733	927	1 343	880	203	34	119	17 678	469	21.7	16.6	34.5
Monroe	762	10 338	1 238	4 707	1 417	284	128	242	23 446	504	19.2	18.7	39.9
Montgomery	249	3 057	674	1 053	489	127	33	49	16 145	286	15.7	18.5	36.7
Neshoba	561	10 168	1 089	4 427	1 336	254	86	224	22 012	543	21.0	5.9	45.3
Newton	376	5 144	476	2 452	752	126	261	98	19 066	454	16.7	23.3	41.9
Noxubee	240	2 563	206	1 177	345	114	15	47	18 146	329	21.0	14.0	30.4
Oktibbeha	793	9 543	1 224	2 191	2 147	358	364	169	17 729				
Panola	651	9 490	671	3 044	1 485	321	207	186	19 636	573	14.7	20.1	35.3
Pearl River	778	7 603	1 001	1 059	2 238	297	224	132	17 345	609	36.8	6.6	33.7
Perry	152	2 044	258	954	252	61	14	56	27 403	246	32.5	4.9	37.0
Pike	993	12 879	1 752	4 097	2 347	343	207	251	19 480	437	23.3	4.1	46.7
Pontotoc	466	8 652	349	6 056	734	149	103	178	20 550	552	25.0	9.8	29.9
Prentiss	548	8 095	987	4 037	826	185	129	146	18 004	412	20.9	8.3	32.3
Quitman	146	1 154	251	242	232	65	19	21	17 879	179	10.6	50.8	68.2
Rankin	2 408	38 772	6 440	5 744	4 660	2 099	922	940	24 256	558	26.9	10.6	36.2
Scott	517	9 538	617	5 418	1 048	220	72	171	17 878	674	29.1	5.0	49.0
Sharkey	143	1 009	238	D	191	D	D	17	17 037	110	9.1	65.5	80.9
Simpson	439	4 686	1 359	454	996	192	143	76	16 219	550	25.5	5.3	44.2
Smith	205	3 458	292	2 077	282	70	40	81	23 534	635	26.8	4.9	52.0
Stone	273	2 759	488	668	442	100	91	55	19 881	212	33.5	5.7	30.2

Table B. States and Counties — Agriculture, Land, and Water

STATE County	Land in farms — Acreage (1,000)	Land in farms — Percent change, 1992–1997	Acres — Average size of farm	Acres — Total irrigated (1,000)	Acres — Total cropland (1,000)	Value of land and buildings — Average per farm ($1,000)	Value of land and buildings — Average per acre (dollars)	Value of machinery and equipment Average per farm ($1,000)	Value of products sold — Total (mil dol)	Value of products sold — Average per farm (dollars)	Percent from — Crops	Percent from — Livestock and poultry products	Percent of farms with sales of — $10,000 or more	Percent of farms with sales of — $100,000 or more	Percent of land owned by Fed. Gov. 1997	Water consumption 1995 (mil gal/day)
	117	118	119	120	121	122	123	124	125	126	127	128	129	130	131	132
MISSISSIPPI	10 125	-0.6	323	1 076	5 947	337	1 052	52	3 127	99 859	41.3	58.7	33.4	14.4	5.8	3 088.0
Adams	65	-19.3	489	0	29	295	702	39	6	43 844	79.4	20.6	26.5	6.1	9.1	51.2
Alcorn	81	2.0	180	D	43	189	1 205	29	8	16 875	67.1	32.9	19.2	3.3	0.0	3.2
Amite	118	4.5	251	D	43	379	1 699	36	28	59 599	1.8	98.2	27.2	8.9	7.4	2.3
Attala	129	19.2	334	0	43	266	819	35	13	34 164	61.5	38.5	21.6	5.7	0.5	3.9
Benton	81	-10.5	382	D	43	272	797	57	8	38 409	86.8	13.2	30.5	7.0	20.8	0.7
Bolivar	455	6.5	1 154	230	416	1 040	957	256	157	397 286	92.3	7.7	84.3	59.6	1.9	472.4
Calhoun	142	11.7	332	D	83	276	801	70	25	57 856	88.0	12.0	38.9	12.9	4.4	45.9
Carroll	143	-6.0	338	3	64	246	814	51	15	36 565	70.1	29.9	29.6	6.9	0.0	6.4
Chickasaw	138	-7.4	309	D	81	226	750	34	30	67 496	26.3	73.7	32.2	10.1	9.0	2.4
Choctaw	58	34.6	267	D	16	220	722	29	9	39 420	9.9	90.1	22.6	3.7	3.1	2.4
Claiborne	81	-8.7	478	D	29	343	800	41	6	36 493	42.5	57.5	29.4	5.3	1.1	34.4
Clarke	52	-24.6	193	0	19	160	930	22	5	17 796	6.2	93.8	21.9	1.9	0.0	2.9
Clay	132	4.5	359	D	61	250	689	28	11	30 857	38.6	61.4	31.3	7.9	0.7	6.6
Coahoma	273	-7.5	1 507	111	252	1 451	966	276	96	531 588	95.7	4.3	82.9	64.1	0.0	146.4
Copiah	121	-5.0	237	0	45	222	915	29	45	88 751	5.3	94.7	27.5	8.4	1.7	4.8
Covington	86	7.1	180	0	33	242	1 276	28	43	91 479	8.8	91.2	32.0	12.8	0.0	6.9
De Soto	149	6.7	320	7	103	539	1 913	39	27	57 680	87.5	12.5	22.9	8.4	5.6	16.7
Forrest	46	24.4	158	1	16	257	1 851	30	12	41 072	23.2	76.8	21.0	7.6	20.5	41.8
Franklin	42	-9.6	269	0	13	270	935	37	4	23 154	19.9	80.1	17.7	3.8	26.2	1.1
George	42	-2.9	100	1	19	167	1 528	29	9	21 730	67.8	32.2	22.7	6.0	2.8	1.9
Greene	59	20.2	176	0	17	153	1 063	24	12	35 419	7.8	92.2	25.4	5.7	7.2	1.4
Grenada	91	-9.0	431	3	45	313	757	45	10	45 985	73.6	26.4	26.5	8.5	17.8	20.8
Hancock	36	20.8	152	0	17	268	1 725	26	2	8 951	23.0	77.0	19.2	1.3	4.4	6.3
Harrison	18	5.1	65	0	8	223	3 316	32	3	9 354	59.1	40.9	15.6	2.9	16.7	153.4
Hinds	196	-15.0	272	0	89	334	1 226	51	52	71 239	21.7	78.3	23.5	4.6	0.6	48.3
Holmes	190	-14.9	539	36	119	452	915	78	37	105 359	93.9	6.1	33.8	17.0	4.1	47.6
Humphreys	198	10.1	826	43	145	816	1 063	168	124	516 587	40.0	60.0	78.3	62.5	3.0	158.0
Issaquena	113	-1.1	1 375	12	96	1 275	956	253	30	365 415	90.8	9.2	85.4	53.7	0.0	34.4
Itawamba	82	5.9	211	D	37	221	868	29	14	37 416	19.9	80.1	24.8	7.5	2.9	2.1
Jackson	33	30.4	102	0	15	251	2 499	22	5	14 927	54.9	45.1	17.4	1.6	9.8	68.2
Jasper	75	-16.1	204	D	25	240	1 152	35	28	77 577	0.6	99.4	29.4	12.0	3.1	3.1
Jefferson	64	-3.8	402	D	25	348	727	36	8	48 932	53.8	46.2	29.7	7.0	3.0	1.5
Jefferson Davis	79	-2.9	202	0	34	172	988	35	15	39 426	7.3	92.7	26.0	6.4	0.0	2.0
Jones	91	-6.1	118	0	39	230	1 628	36	99	128 511	1.5	98.5	38.7	21.0	7.4	16.6
Kemper	97	4.0	253		33	242	803	23	8	21 911	3.6	96.4	23.0	3.9	0.4	1.6
Lafayette	102	3.2	275	D	44	260	901	28	6	16 465	69.9	30.1	17.7	2.7	19.8	5.2
Lamar	74	39.9	185	0	25	368	1 669	28	34	84 052	6.0	94.0	32.4	9.2	0.0	8.7
Lauderdale	75	-7.7	210	0	22	165	825	23	5	13 295	44.6	55.4	18.0	1.1	1.6	14.7
Lawrence	55	-12.5	179	0	24	216	1 120	36	24	77 334	5.7	94.3	23.4	8.4	0.0	33.7
Leake	104	8.4	178	D	40	201	1 141	37	97	167 008	1.7	98.3	37.7	24.9	0.5	3.8
Lee	135	-3.6	277	D	93	283	1 074	44	21	42 669	60.0	40.0	31.1	9.6	1.0	12.5
Leflore	267	2.0	1 087	93	230	1 271	1 168	271	115	467 318	73.3	26.7	80.9	56.5	1.0	192.9
Lincoln	99	-0.1	198	0	44	240	1 180	32	31	63 091	4.6	95.4	30.5	9.4	2.1	13.3
Lowndes	145	15.2	384	1	71	347	970	41	45	119 865	21.2	78.8	31.0	10.8	2.6	14.9
Madison	182	-8.5	392	D	90	513	1 128	41	24	52 013	77.1	22.9	30.5	12.0	0.8	12.1
Marion	97	8.2	201	0	36	334	1 261	23	29	58 920	1.7	98.3	30.5	10.5	0.0	4.2
Marshall	181	-0.4	387	D	88	437	1 083	43	14	30 068	68.2	31.8	29.9	5.8	11.0	3.2
Monroe	162	-7.2	322	1	100	292	940	49	17	33 508	61.0	39.0	28.4	10.1	2.9	18.5
Montgomery	92	15.4	323	0	38	240	756	38	10	34 928	67.0	33.0	29.0	9.8	0.0	1.9
Neshoba	141	2.6	231	0	51	227	1 081	36	87	143 502	1.0	99.0	37.2	18.6	0.0	3.8
Newton	100	4.5	185	D	44	199	1 152	35	89	162 993	1.2	98.8	38.3	19.5	1.8	3.7
Noxubee	194	-4.2	426	2	100	363	794	54	44	95 942	33.8	66.2	46.7	20.5	3.0	4.1
Oktibbeha	85	5.3	259	0	42	280	1 118	28	9	26 713	17.4	82.6	21.9	4.9	5.7	8.3
Panola	238	9.4	416	10	151	386	956	51	31	54 140	88.1	11.9	33.7	9.4	1.4	14.8
Pearl River	103	10.9	169	0	44	240	1 381	23	9	14 513	26.7	73.3	25.0	3.8	2.5	5.8
Perry	32	-0.3	130	0	11	193	1 285	28	9	37 264	6.4	93.6	20.3	6.9	43.2	20.1
Pike	71	-11.9	161	0	35	253	1 629	22	50	113 449	1.4	98.6	30.0	12.1	0.0	7.2
Pontotoc	115	-7.5	208	0	65	194	886	33	9	15 616	61.9	38.1	19.4	3.1	0.4	2.8
Prentiss	88	2.4	214	D	51	189	921	31	8	18 391	70.0	30.0	21.8	4.4	1.2	2.1
Quitman	170	-8.8	947	29	156	747	786	139	46	257 976	98.0	2.0	74.3	48.0	1.6	111.8
Rankin	117	-1.4	210	0	50	298	1 467	32	51	91 945	8.0	92.0	35.1	13.3	0.0	12.7
Scott	107	-2.3	159	0	46	217	1 345	39	175	258 952	0.7	99.3	46.9	30.3	20.6	10.1
Sharkey	166	-9.0	1 505	22	153	1 266	845	265	59	537 224	81.9	18.1	88.2	72.7	23.3	64.1
Simpson	94	-3.4	170	D	39	227	1 335	33	103	187 502	1.2	98.8	40.2	21.8	0.0	4.0
Smith	95	-0.2	149	0	36	234	1 518	32	129	203 532	0.9	99.1	47.6	30.6	21.4	6.0
Stone	42	25.9	196	0	13	418	2 038	27	4	19 587	43.2	56.9	19.8	3.3	13.8	2.3

STATE County	New Construction ($1,000)	Number of Housing Units	Number of Establishments	Number of Employees	Sales (mil dol)	Annual Payroll (mil dol)	Number of Establishments	Number of Employees	Sales (mil dol)	Annual Payroll (mil dol)	Number of Establishments	Number of Employees	Receipts (mil dol)	Annual Payroll (mil dol)
	133	134	135	136	137	138	139	140	141	142	143	144	145	146
MISSISSIPPI	989 518	12 871	3 173	36 520	18 445.2	1 012.1	12 791	138 372	20 774.5	1 935.3	2 125	8 354	794.2	132.1
Adams	731	13	57	369	80.4	9.2	225	2 356	328.9	33.3	46	128	9.3	2.1
Alcorn	4 996	55	49	692	264.3	16.9	200	2 152	315.1	29.4	28	128	7.2	1.9
Amite	173	3	7	D	D	D	44	228	34.6	3.1	2	D	D	D
Attala	570	9	18	210	46.2	3.9	93	1 022	146.7	13.9	9	23	0.5	0.1
Benton	16	1	1	D	D	D	24	178	23.6	1.8	1	D	D	D
Bolivar	2 227	31	41	685	355.4	18.8	187	1 775	296.3	24.1	33	77	6.2	0.9
Calhoun	103	1	12	130	27.3	2.7	86	525	63.2	6.6	4	8	0.2	0.0
Carroll	NA	NA	9	32	17.3	0.9	24	161	15.5	1.9	NA	NA	NA	NA
Chickasaw	170	5	29	244	66.6	3.3	94	741	102.0	9.1	14	39	6.6	1.0
Choctaw	130	2	5	D	D	D	29	183	26.5	2.3	1	D	D	D
Claiborne	0	0	1	D	D	D	34	229	46.8	4.3	2	D	D	D
Clarke	922	11	14	142	33.1	2.3	63	325	38.3	3.7	7	13	0.7	0.1
Clay	2 631	31	18	217	561.8	14.1	94	771	109.5	9.4	12	26	2.9	0.4
Coahoma	1 069	11	37	529	203.2	14.3	160	1 613	250.4	22.2	39	100	11.1	1.4
Copiah	220	2	20	187	66.4	3.6	107	815	100.1	9.4	5	30	0.7	0.2
Covington	1 131	23	15	150	426.1	2.6	63	479	92.4	7.2	7	16	1.0	0.2
De Soto	190 435	2 428	78	D	D	D	278	4 248	663.2	58.5	69	205	31.8	4.1
Forrest	14 012	136	113	1 602	1 282.5	37.6	427	5 509	852.4	77.9	97	410	34.3	5.5
Franklin	0	0	5	D	D	D	37	198	25.4	2.2	4	14	1.4	0.3
George	0	0	12	D	D	D	70	706	92.4	8.0	5	10	0.5	0.1
Greene	60	1	5	92	18.6	1.9	36	203	28.2	2.1	2	D	D	D
Grenada	3 890	47	34	252	123.2	5.6	139	1 506	249.5	20.9	25	99	8.3	1.3
Hancock	9 315	94	30	251	68.8	7.6	128	1 583	214.2	19.9	34	124	9.1	1.7
Harrison	145 379	1 370	195	2 082	650.9	51.9	883	10 553	1 613.9	153.3	208	841	75.3	12.7
Hinds	109 282	1 663	454	6 671	2 600.7	206.0	1 092	17 356	2 760.8	280.3	295	1 560	152.6	24.6
Holmes	1 538	22	10	73	22.5	0.6	95	673	95.0	8.6	10	24	2.1	0.3
Humphreys	305	4	14	D	D	D	44	334	70.4	5.0	7	16	1.1	0.2
Issaquena	0	0	2	D	D	D	2	D	D	D	NA	NA	NA	NA
Itawamba	1 073	20	13	188	43.2	3.9	65	555	85.1	6.8	7	11	0.4	0.1
Jackson	84 787	1 526	70	576	272.6	16.7	512	6 119	948.6	82.3	100	367	29.4	5.6
Jasper	591	18	9	61	11.1	1.5	63	480	76.1	7.2	6	31	4.0	0.7
Jefferson	135	7	4	D	D	D	22	D	D	D	1	D	D	D
Jefferson Davis	0	0	4	17	2.0	0.2	51	357	45.5	4.6	4	8	0.7	0.1
Jones	2 969	51	102	764	211.8	20.8	303	3 059	467.1	43.3	49	275	19.1	6.0
Kemper	0	0	4	D	D	D	37	176	27.7	2.5	1	D	D	D
Lafayette	12 467	111	22	89	46.8	2.0	174	2 099	254.2	26.4	36	150	11.0	1.7
Lamar	998	24	29	D	D	D	170	2 250	283.4	28.0	22	67	7.2	1.3
Lauderdale	5 255	62	106	1 869	973.6	50.4	496	5 305	793.7	76.2	74	259	23.7	3.7
Lawrence	0	0	9	43	8.5	0.6	62	350	40.1	4.0	4	D	D	D
Leake	446	5	17	105	17.7	1.5	99	769	125.2	10.9	4	D	D	D
Lee	11 708	119	201	2 121	831.0	56.7	541	6 341	975.8	92.3	73	353	32.9	6.0
Leflore	4 390	56	56	803	905.1	23.4	222	2 033	277.8	26.4	40	95	9.7	1.3
Lincoln	1 584	17	37	762	415.6	17.9	164	1 809	315.2	24.7	20	75	7.2	1.5
Lowndes	18 201	319	93	1 098	333.5	30.0	367	3 856	601.2	54.3	58	332	27.5	5.2
Madison	118 480	1 227	118	1 565	1 180.0	45.4	377	4 987	679.8	69.6	72	235	28.6	4.5
Marion	844	11	29	D	D	D	130	1 154	167.4	15.0	14	41	4.2	0.6
Marshall	3 255	68	14	99	46.1	2.1	115	892	102.0	10.8	14	38	2.1	0.5
Monroe	1 365	22	33	200	104.5	5.4	169	1 525	228.1	21.3	18	50	3.1	0.5
Montgomery	3 036	107	10	57	20.7	1.0	68	507	63.1	5.5	2	D	D	D
Neshoba	825	10	32	297	85.3	5.9	117	1 384	226.0	18.4	9	150	17.5	3.0
Newton	415	8	8	D	D	D	91	829	116.0	10.6	9	18	1.1	0.4
Noxubee	29	1	9	57	21.2	0.9	62	378	50.9	4.3	4	4	0.3	0.1
Oktibbeha	20 022	408	11	63	25.3	1.5	172	2 029	241.4	23.5	37	109	12.7	2.0
Panola	1 842	44	37	465	248.0	14.6	186	1 525	239.7	20.8	14	32	2.3	0.4
Pearl River	38 560	541	34	276	58.0	3.8	178	2 086	336.3	30.2	26	83	9.5	1.1
Perry	310	5	3	D	D	D	36	253	29.4	2.7	4	7	0.7	0.1
Pike	913	14	64	527	164.0	11.9	252	2 339	343.0	33.2	34	130	9.6	1.6
Pontotoc	2 758	43	24	204	73.1	4.6	103	808	120.2	9.7	10	37	2.1	0.7
Prentiss	2 181	28	29	223	85.3	4.7	129	891	138.4	11.5	16	28	1.9	0.2
Quitman	0	0	4	D	D	D	35	249	44.4	3.9	4	4	0.8	0.1
Rankin	92 453	1 055	200	3 150	1 609.8	112.2	350	5 001	808.9	72.9	92	429	74.2	9.6
Scott	1 885	22	34	208	103.6	3.6	144	1 216	156.2	14.6	8	28	1.3	0.3
Sharkey	150	5	10	91	18.3	1.8	33	204	25.4	2.8	6	11	1.0	0.1
Simpson	3 674	42	13	76	31.3	1.6	103	1 039	147.9	13.3	13	33	1.9	0.3
Smith	187	3	7	D	D	D	49	279	35.5	3.4	5	16	2.3	0.3
Stone	1 755	22	17	76	17.0	1.3	59	425	63.6	6.7	7	26	1.8	0.3

1. Establishments with payroll.

STATE County	Professional, Scientific, and Technical Services[1], 1997				Manufacturing, 1997				Accommodation and Foodservices, 1997			
	Number of Establishments	Number of Employees	Receipts (mil dol)	Annual Payroll (mil dol)	Number of Establishments	Number of Employees	Receipts (mil dol)	Annual Payroll (mil dol)	Number of Establishments	Number of Employees	Sales (mil dol)	Annual Payroll (mil dol)
	147	148	149	150	151	152	153	154	155	156	157	158
MISSISSIPPI	3 627	21 671	1 761.6	662.1	3 008	227 800	39 658.3	5 599.4	4 050	84 834	3 064.8	814.5
Adams	66	234	14.9	3.9	38	2 299	550.0	76.0	88	1 189	37.7	10.3
Alcorn	43	191	10.7	3.6	58	4 918	955.6	150.8	66	913	26.9	6.8
Amite	11	22	4.2	0.3	10	691	97.3	17.2	4	D	D	D
Attala	17	39	8.5	2.2	22	1 267	119.9	21.8	28	373	10.8	2.3
Benton	3	D	D	D	NA	NA	NA	NA	1	D	D	D
Bolivar	42	139	10.2	3.6	22	2 724	417.8	67.0	49	626	17.9	4.3
Calhoun	15	47	4.0	1.1	34	1 874	296.2	35.4	16	D	D	D
Carroll	4	7	0.5	0.1	NA	NA	NA	NA	2	D	D	D
Chickasaw	16	62	2.2	0.7	80	4 896	420.8	93.4	27	D	D	D
Choctaw	3	D	D	D	10	598	105.0	13.9	5	D	D	D
Claiborne	7	15	1.1	0.2	10	629	88.6	13.9	6	46	1.5	0.4
Clarke	15	41	2.4	0.8	18	2 084	304.1	51.4	12	94	3.4	0.9
Clay	18	103	5.8	2.3	25	3 640	926.0	113.6	32	408	11.5	3.1
Coahoma	44	246	19.3	7.9	28	1 353	236.6	35.6	37	540	17.2	4.3
Copiah	15	50	3.5	0.8	32	2 735	407.7	52.6	30	425	12.6	3.0
Covington	12	37	2.5	0.7	17	1 950	194.2	32.2	15	D	D	D
De Soto	83	445	24.4	8.7	131	7 232	1 369.6	213.4	114	2 639	72.7	18.6
Forrest	166	799	61.1	19.8	84	5 170	1 037.1	116.3	163	D	D	D
Franklin	7	39	2.2	0.8	NA	NA	NA	NA	4	D	D	D
George	19	73	4.4	1.9	NA	NA	NA	NA	25	D	D	D
Greene	5	9	0.3	0.1	NA	NA	NA	NA	9	78	1.8	0.5
Grenada	29	127	8.8	4.1	24	4 194	571.8	109.5	46	806	24.4	5.9
Hancock	55	614	54.2	23.5	NA	NA	NA	NA	72	784	24.7	6.2
Harrison	335	2 049	152.0	55.6	139	4 498	1 079.7	133.6	377	9 573	323.4	87.8
Hinds	652	5 400	544.0	216.5	208	11 540	2 484.4	314.8	449	10 351	322.4	92.6
Holmes	7	27	3.2	0.5	14	1 674	214.5	31.4	18	113	3.1	0.8
Humphreys	7	21	1.4	0.4	4	D	D	D	9	D	D	D
Issaquena	NA	NA	NA	NA	NA	NA	NA	NA	NA	NA	NA	NA
Itawamba	10	31	1.3	0.5	40	1 366	371.6	30.1	29	341	6.9	1.5
Jackson	161	1 603	134.3	61.4	98	16 340	4 447.7	534.5	191	3 469	97.4	25.5
Jasper	16	150	6.8	3.3	15	1 720	151.3	30.0	12	D	D	D
Jefferson	4	12	1.3	0.1	NA	NA	NA	NA	5	131	2.3	0.5
Jefferson Davis	7	13	0.5	0.1	9	769	56.0	8.9	16	D	D	D
Jones	83	478	48.2	12.1	68	6 820	991.3	162.7	84	1 309	37.3	10.0
Kemper	2	D	D	D	NA	NA	NA	NA	4	30	0.6	0.2
Lafayette	70	422	27.6	14.1	29	2 017	304.5	43.2	109	1 665	43.2	11.5
Lamar	36	195	14.1	6.4	22	770	116.8	16.4	48	D	D	D
Lauderdale	117	483	33.9	10.6	83	6 076	916.6	164.2	147	2 855	87.4	23.9
Lawrence	4	10	0.6	0.1	9	D	D	D	15	126	2.9	0.7
Leake	16	36	1.5	0.3	18	2 481	242.0	29.8	20	D	D	D
Lee	140	865	64.0	26.6	191	17 717	2 708.4	472.9	158	3 037	84.7	23.2
Leflore	63	324	23.6	7.8	40	3 572	510.9	76.6	51	841	28.0	7.3
Lincoln	41	298	17.0	7.0	28	1 383	301.4	35.1	42	715	21.2	5.2
Lowndes	90	459	31.4	12.3	71	7 611	1 313.9	223.2	105	2 071	59.5	14.9
Madison	131	1 042	103.7	32.2	57	2 414	396.6	57.2	113	2 402	78.8	20.8
Marion	21	112	5.7	2.9	26	1 000	103.9	15.7	32	434	10.5	2.8
Marshall	20	32	4.3	0.6	29	1 777	201.3	41.2	19	322	7.7	1.9
Monroe	35	114	5.5	1.5	71	4 889	1 121.2	124.8	46	503	13.4	3.1
Montgomery	10	54	3.2	0.7	21	1 165	116.6	21.8	20	196	5.4	1.3
Neshoba	18	69	4.7	1.7	32	2 572	347.8	57.1	37	725	17.1	3.8
Newton	16	232	5.9	3.1	20	2 256	165.7	49.5	26	D	D	D
Noxubee	8	27	0.6	0.1	20	1 201	210.8	22.8	8	105	3.0	1.0
Oktibbeha	61	286	12.6	4.1	35	2 132	372.3	49.8	85	1 546	40.2	10.2
Panola	30	201	11.0	5.4	44	2 943	575.0	68.5	46	829	23.0	5.6
Pearl River	49	174	13.6	5.2	47	905	190.3	20.3	66	877	23.2	5.7
Perry	5	14	0.8	0.2	7	D	D	D	6	68	1.5	0.4
Pike	52	163	10.7	3.2	36	3 924	580.3	64.7	61	923	26.0	6.5
Pontotoc	19	75	4.3	1.1	92	5 549	720.2	116.5	25	340	8.0	1.9
Prentiss	21	87	7.5	2.0	46	4 507	702.2	86.1	34	425	10.9	2.8
Quitman	6	21	0.7	0.2	NA	NA	NA	NA	5	D	D	D
Rankin	129	740	73.8	24.4	127	5 763	1 088.2	150.3	127	2 286	78.1	20.7
Scott	19	66	2.9	1.1	28	5 487	607.4	95.8	36	448	13.0	3.4
Sharkey	7	22	1.4	0.6	NA	NA	NA	NA	3	D	D	D
Simpson	22	86	6.0	2.1	15	1 182	360.4	22.2	21	D	D	D
Smith	13	41	4.0	0.5	17	1 801	392.8	41.2	8	53	1.6	0.4
Stone	13	65	5.2	1.8	15	682	124.6	15.3	18	D	D	D

1. Firms subject to federal tax.

Table B. States and Counties — **Health and Other Services and Federal Funds**

STATE County	Health Care and Social Assistance[1], 1997				Other Services[1], 1997				Federal funds and grants, fiscal 1999[2] Expenditures (mil dol)			
										Direct payments for individuals[3]		
	Number of Establishments	Number of Employees	Receipts (mil dol)	Annual Payroll (mil dol)	Number of Establishments	Number of Employees	Receipts (mil dol)	Annual Payroll (mil dol)	Total	Social Security and government retirement	Medicare	Food stamps and Supplemental Security Income
	159	160	161	162	163	164	165	166	167	168	169	170
MISSISSIPPI	4 139	55 529	3 632.3	1 547.0	3 491	17 449	1 057.1	299.6	16 487.9	5 118.3	2 159.7	771.9
Adams	82	1 136	74.8	29.7	55	260	13.0	4.0	175.0	72.7	26.4	12.7
Alcorn	73	540	32.5	11.9	55	163	9.2	2.5	148.7	70.2	30.8	9.0
Amite	5	20	1.5	0.7	5	42	1.3	0.4	58.3	24.8	12.0	4.3
Attala	21	309	15.3	6.6	29	132	12.2	2.3	100.0	41.8	20.3	6.6
Benton	6	112	3.8	1.9	3	3	0.2	0.0	38.5	14.9	7.5	2.3
Bolivar	48	735	38.7	15.2	49	167	12.9	2.7	239.3	59.0	31.3	24.4
Calhoun	19	153	8.2	2.6	12	55	2.5	0.6	74.5	29.6	15.5	4.4
Carroll	6	23	0.9	0.4	8	17	1.8	0.2	43.7	15.5	7.4	2.5
Chickasaw	27	396	20.7	8.0	22	64	3.2	0.8	88.5	37.4	17.8	5.8
Choctaw	8	37	2.7	0.8	7	18	1.6	0.3	36.5	14.4	6.0	2.6
Claiborne	12	149	5.8	2.9	7	14	0.6	0.1	48.7	16.6	9.4	6.0
Clarke	17	185	7.8	3.0	16	53	2.9	0.7	72.2	34.9	15.2	4.1
Clay	34	271	12.4	4.8	29	150	10.7	3.1	94.7	37.6	14.3	5.6
Coahoma	63	1 435	96.3	31.8	45	169	7.8	2.3	188.6	48.4	31.5	19.2
Copiah	26	431	16.0	6.5	27	109	8.1	1.7	150.7	58.0	27.5	10.5
Covington	13	130	5.7	2.3	16	66	6.0	1.3	84.9	35.2	15.7	7.1
De Soto	87	859	62.2	26.0	112	533	35.9	9.8	246.6	144.3	43.3	7.6
Forrest	122	2 562	159.7	91.3	101	753	45.2	12.9	376.7	149.6	60.2	19.2
Franklin	7	92	3.6	1.8	6	27	1.3	0.4	48.6	16.7	7.1	2.7
George	12	166	8.9	3.1	27	79	4.0	0.9	73.7	38.1	17.4	5.1
Greene	6	103	3.7	1.3	8	32	1.9	0.7	37.4	16.5	8.9	2.5
Grenada	59	652	39.1	14.4	29	133	10.6	2.3	113.6	43.8	26.6	7.2
Hancock	48	322	19.4	7.8	45	187	8.8	2.9	473.8	87.1	33.1	7.7
Harrison	372	5 503	407.7	157.6	284	1 663	89.6	28.6	1 578.1	457.7	150.6	38.3
Hinds	528	7 452	562.2	250.5	391	3 003	176.0	55.8	1 913.9	468.2	177.8	73.3
Holmes	20	267	14.0	6.0	15	43	2.0	0.4	151.2	35.6	26.8	15.5
Humphreys	14	159	6.7	3.0	15	36	2.9	0.5	76.4	16.0	13.9	6.7
Issaquena	NA	NA	NA	NA	NA	NA	NA	NA	14.2	1.7	1.2	0.7
Itawamba	19	309	9.6	4.2	19	60	2.7	0.6	72.9	33.1	15.9	1.7
Jackson	237	1 763	124.0	53.4	162	744	41.0	11.7	1 439.5	265.1	84.7	19.1
Jasper	14	64	2.5	1.0	16	82	5.5	1.4	77.8	33.3	14.9	6.4
Jefferson	3	15	0.8	0.1	4	9	0.4	0.1	58.8	14.4	7.6	5.1
Jefferson Davis	12	62	3.1	1.2	7	19	1.3	0.3	61.2	22.7	11.7	5.2
Jones	76	1 147	65.7	32.0	101	543	33.3	8.9	275.8	134.2	57.5	15.8
Kemper	4	140	3.7	1.9	6	11	0.7	0.2	48.7	17.8	7.8	3.4
Lafayette	72	713	58.8	25.9	40	238	10.1	3.3	126.8	46.8	14.6	1.5
Lamar	61	745	67.0	29.7	27	107	8.4	2.0	89.3	46.2	18.0	4.4
Lauderdale	149	2 063	164.4	82.5	136	690	36.6	10.7	435.1	167.3	67.4	22.6
Lawrence	11	120	4.3	1.4	7	27	2.5	0.5	69.2	33.8	14.8	4.4
Leake	25	775	37.9	18.5	18	44	3.8	0.8	98.9	40.7	23.2	5.9
Lee	161	2 064	168.4	92.8	127	859	52.7	21.9	281.5	134.0	49.3	13.2
Leflore	67	954	61.6	26.2	57	325	17.6	5.4	212.3	56.8	37.1	18.9
Lincoln	55	739	42.8	16.4	34	191	11.7	2.7	124.6	59.5	23.2	7.9
Lowndes	132	1 159	79.5	29.4	102	540	33.1	9.5	345.7	110.1	33.6	15.4
Madison	87	758	46.4	21.7	74	482	45.1	11.4	428.3	99.7	35.0	15.6
Marion	32	419	22.4	8.8	37	142	8.8	2.1	131.0	53.5	25.7	9.3
Marshall	19	332	17.2	5.9	16	86	3.8	1.1	152.8	53.1	22.8	13.1
Monroe	46	586	27.8	12.0	60	182	13.3	2.8	171.2	69.1	32.1	7.6
Montgomery	17	210	9.1	4.1	17	59	3.6	0.6	76.9	25.7	15.3	4.5
Neshoba	22	535	31.8	15.0	38	133	9.9	2.4	120.8	43.9	23.7	7.1
Newton	27	432	21.9	8.3	22	46	3.2	0.8	113.5	51.0	27.0	5.8
Noxubee	12	53	2.5	1.2	9	22	1.6	0.3	65.9	18.6	8.2	7.9
Oktibbeha	63	625	32.7	12.6	58	252	11.4	3.4	203.0	56.3	16.5	10.4
Panola	50	646	33.1	13.2	25	84	4.4	1.0	152.0	56.6	24.7	13.7
Pearl River	59	451	23.7	9.1	43	206	10.1	2.9	200.8	95.9	40.7	10.3
Perry	6	41	2.0	0.6	10	38	2.3	0.7	42.3	19.3	7.8	2.7
Pike	72	680	40.7	18.4	48	245	12.8	3.7	184.4	79.1	38.2	13.6
Pontotoc	28	285	10.6	4.1	32	104	5.2	1.3	85.1	40.7	17.9	3.2
Prentiss	37	331	14.7	6.3	37	148	10.1	2.8	101.2	48.8	20.1	5.0
Quitman	7	219	11.3	4.1	12	36	2.1	0.3	67.7	16.7	10.9	6.9
Rankin	154	3 534	269.9	104.4	143	744	55.9	13.4	291.4	159.7	52.1	10.2
Scott	25	290	15.0	6.2	32	173	10.1	2.9	124.1	48.5	26.3	6.5
Sharkey	11	138	6.3	2.5	10	19	1.0	0.2	42.8	9.5	6.5	3.9
Simpson	35	855	31.4	12.9	23	65	4.5	0.9	112.9	48.7	22.9	4.9
Smith	8	171	4.7	2.3	8	10	1.1	0.2	62.3	26.3	10.8	5.7
Stone	18	390	31.8	9.3	12	34	2.3	0.7	70.2	32.9	12.9	3.6

1. Firms subject to federal tax.   2. October 1, 1998 to September 30, 1999.   3. State totals may include programs not allocated by county.

Table B. States and Counties — Federal Funds and Local Government Finances

STATE County	Federal funds and grants, fiscal 1999[1] (cont'd) Expenditures (mil dol) (cont'd) — Procurement contract awards — Salaries and wages	Defense	Other	Grants[2] — Medicaid and other health-related	Nutrition and family welfare	Education	Other	Local government finances, 1997 General revenue — Total (mil dol)	Intergovern-mental (mil dol)	Taxes Total (mil dol)	Per capita[3] (dollars) Total	Property
	171	172	173	174	175	176	177	178	179	180	181	182
MISSISSIPPI	1 698.5	1 528.1	411.2	1 578.7	599.5	327.0	882.1	X	X	X	X	X
Adams	6.1	6.4	3.0	23.7	9.6	2.6	2.6	97.3	30.6	19.6	566	512
Alcorn	4.7	0.0	2.0	18.4	2.0	1.8	5.2	104.5	37.1	12.3	376	342
Amite	2.6	0.0	0.8	9.6	1.5	1.1	0.4	15.0	9.2	3.5	253	233
Attala	3.0	0.1	1.1	16.6	2.3	1.7	3.2	43.0	15.6	7.7	417	394
Benton	1.1	0.0	0.5	7.6	1.8	0.5	0.7	9.9	6.3	2.7	335	334
Bolivar	4.9	0.1	1.1	46.6	14.1	4.5	17.0	88.6	43.7	16.8	415	398
Calhoun	2.7	0.3	0.8	12.4	1.5	0.6	0.7	22.6	12.5	4.8	318	292
Carroll	1.1	0.8	0.3	6.9	1.0	0.6	3.8	11.5	5.9	3.2	318	314
Chickasaw	2.9	0.0	0.7	15.9	2.0	1.0	0.5	24.9	15.5	6.1	335	322
Choctaw	2.0	0.0	0.6	6.7	1.1	0.6	1.2	19.6	8.4	2.6	275	256
Claiborne	1.1	0.0	0.9	9.7	1.9	1.0	0.6	51.3	16.6	2.6	222	214
Clarke	1.9	0.0	0.4	12.2	1.8	1.1	0.2	26.5	13.2	7.2	400	362
Clay	4.6	0.0	6.6	13.6	3.0	2.7	1.3	29.9	18.1	8.4	391	340
Coahoma	4.8	0.4	0.8	36.0	10.3	4.8	3.3	64.7	39.3	13.7	437	423
Copiah	4.0	1.0	19.1	21.0	3.6	2.8	0.6	48.6	25.8	11.5	399	376
Covington	3.0	0.0	0.5	13.7	2.2	1.4	5.2	34.0	14.3	6.6	374	356
De Soto	7.4	1.1	2.2	17.2	3.6	1.5	8.1	110.6	53.7	42.4	461	427
Forrest	43.0	11.2	7.6	25.9	10.1	5.5	26.4	283.2	61.6	42.0	569	514
Franklin	2.1	0.0	0.6	5.4	1.1	0.6	11.5	14.5	9.8	3.1	374	370
George	2.4	0.0	0.6	5.3	2.1	0.9	0.3	20.6	13.5	5.3	282	255
Greene	0.9	0.0	0.4	5.6	1.2	0.6	0.6	12.9	8.6	3.2	269	248
Grenada	10.4	1.0	1.5	13.6	2.3	1.3	1.5	62.1	19.7	10.5	468	433
Hancock	120.2	47.8	158.6	5.5	2.7	1.6	7.3	80.6	23.2	19.2	488	453
Harrison	573.7	211.6	23.9	47.9	19.8	7.5	14.5	488.5	152.4	136.1	775	608
Hinds	225.8	18.8	38.5	181.6	241.6	109.6	332.9	527.0	243.2	185.2	748	702
Holmes	3.1	7.4	0.7	33.5	5.9	3.2	4.5	41.8	27.4	8.0	371	346
Humphreys	1.5	1.9	0.6	14.1	2.8	1.9	3.5	19.9	10.5	4.7	418	381
Issaquena	0.3	1.1	0.1	1.3	0.6	0.2	0.8	1.9	0.6	1.0	583	564
Itawamba	2.5	0.7	0.5	10.0	1.2	0.6	3.2	51.8	29.4	10.0	473	471
Jackson	101.8	858.1	7.8	15.5	11.4	5.5	36.5	379.4	89.6	90.9	707	648
Jasper	3.0	0.0	0.5	15.0	2.4	1.4	0.5	28.4	13.1	6.3	357	332
Jefferson	1.3	0.1	0.2	12.5	1.8	4.0	5.2	15.5	8.3	3.3	388	373
Jefferson Davis	1.3	0.0	0.3	11.9	6.1	1.2	0.0	16.9	10.7	4.0	288	282
Jones	11.5	0.1	2.4	31.5	5.7	4.2	5.5	169.4	66.4	27.7	437	401
Kemper	1.8	0.0	0.4	10.1	1.3	0.9	2.3	24.5	14.0	4.9	472	462
Lafayette	15.2	6.2	1.3	13.1	2.2	1.4	18.6	45.6	26.3	12.2	356	334
Lamar	2.6	0.0	0.6	8.4	2.2	1.4	2.4	48.7	24.2	13.2	368	357
Lauderdale	94.9	11.9	4.1	42.0	7.6	4.6	5.8	144.2	78.3	40.1	523	482
Lawrence	3.5	0.0	0.6	8.8	1.5	0.9	0.0	23.4	10.2	7.0	541	531
Leake	3.9	0.0	0.6	17.8	2.1	1.5	1.2	22.5	13.7	5.1	262	261
Lee	28.6	0.3	6.2	25.0	7.8	3.2	5.5	137.9	67.7	43.6	590	569
Leflore	9.7	4.3	0.9	34.3	7.1	7.2	5.1	106.9	34.7	18.1	488	468
Lincoln	5.5	0.0	1.0	15.1	3.1	1.9	5.2	44.5	23.6	12.1	383	364
Lowndes	73.8	57.3	4.1	27.9	5.5	3.9	6.4	103.5	57.6	30.8	504	464
Madison	9.5	128.9	53.1	26.7	6.1	5.5	17.4	124.4	55.6	32.8	462	434
Marion	3.3	6.9	0.7	18.4	8.7	1.9	0.5	48.8	24.1	8.2	308	289
Marshall	4.5	0.5	1.1	25.7	21.5	3.6	1.3	61.3	27.2	9.9	307	281
Monroe	5.5	0.2	1.9	20.4	3.4	2.2	20.9	61.0	28.8	12.0	314	307
Montgomery	3.9	0.2	0.5	14.1	7.1	1.1	2.7	24.8	10.1	4.4	356	325
Neshoba	5.2	0.1	0.5	25.1	4.7	3.9	5.6	28.3	17.4	6.8	252	222
Newton	4.6	0.0	0.7	15.9	1.9	0.9	1.8	43.9	23.9	6.9	322	296
Noxubee	1.9	0.4	1.4	16.7	2.8	1.2	1.0	23.8	10.7	4.3	352	321
Oktibbeha	16.2	2.3	6.9	18.8	3.9	7.4	51.6	77.9	28.0	15.6	399	363
Panola	5.7	0.6	2.3	24.0	4.5	2.5	6.2	51.5	27.8	12.7	387	358
Pearl River	5.3	21.3	1.2	12.8	3.6	2.1	0.8	72.7	43.5	17.2	378	362
Perry	1.4	0.0	0.4	6.1	1.4	1.3	0.1	63.6	11.3	4.7	397	374
Pike	7.4	0.1	1.9	25.5	5.0	3.2	3.8	113.3	39.1	15.8	415	398
Pontotoc	3.0	0.1	0.8	12.4	1.5	0.8	0.9	30.2	18.1	7.0	283	272
Prentiss	2.7	0.0	0.5	15.5	1.6	1.2	0.9	55.6	34.5	8.2	339	336
Quitman	1.4	0.0	0.3	14.9	2.3	1.0	1.9	19.7	8.7	4.1	422	370
Rankin	29.0	0.0	3.1	17.2	4.0	3.0	10.7	174.1	68.9	50.9	476	441
Scott	8.0	0.0	0.8	16.6	3.3	1.6	11.0	38.1	22.9	9.5	376	324
Sharkey	1.5	0.0	0.5	6.8	1.5	0.9	0.7	12.3	7.8	3.4	511	496
Simpson	2.9	0.0	0.7	13.2	2.3	1.7	15.0	38.9	18.8	8.4	332	304
Smith	2.7	0.0	0.5	10.7	1.4	0.9	3.0	19.9	12.0	4.7	310	283
Stone	3.7	0.0	0.9	3.5	1.2	0.6	6.5	73.0	38.3	15.7	1 220	1 209

1. October 1, 1998 to September 30, 1999. 2. State totals may include programs not allocated by county. 3. Based on the resident population estimated as of July 1 of the year shown.

STATE County	Total (mil dol)	Per capita[1] (dollars)	Education	Health and hospitals	Police protection	Public welfare	Highways	Total (mil dol)	Per capita[1] (dollars)	Federal civilian	Federal military	State and local	Democratic	Republican	All other
	183	184	185	186	187	188	189	190	191	192	193	194	195	196	197
MISSISSIPPI	X	X	X	X	X	X	X	X	X	26 375	35 509	197 560	40.7	57.6	1.7
Adams	88.5	2 563	30.0	36.1	5.1	0.2	4.6	74.8	2 165	134	247	2 181	NA	NA	NA
Alcorn	105.8	3 232	23.9	45.4	2.0	0.3	4.9	41.6	1 270	96	224	2 201	NA	NA	NA
Amite	14.1	1 027	60.1	0.8	7.7	0.0	12.4	3.4	249	64	94	403	NA	NA	NA
Attala	42.1	2 289	36.2	26.3	3.5	1.1	9.1	5.5	299	65	126	985	NA	NA	NA
Benton	9.1	1 136	61.7	0.3	4.2	0.4	10.5	1.0	120	21	56	293	NA	NA	NA
Bolivar	86.6	2 135	44.4	27.7	4.3	0.7	5.5	24.7	610	102	276	3 535	NA	NA	NA
Calhoun	21.4	1 421	54.2	13.9	4.6	0.1	8.1	7.9	524	43	101	773	NA	NA	NA
Carroll	10.1	1 000	61.8	0.7	3.5	0.7	15.2	2.3	227	27	68	298	NA	NA	NA
Chickasaw	26.3	1 440	61.3	0.6	7.5	0.0	11.7	8.4	457	51	123	831	NA	NA	NA
Choctaw	16.2	1 739	50.8	15.6	3.9	9.3	10.3	4.7	510	65	64	515	NA	NA	NA
Claiborne	48.8	4 160	19.3	9.0	1.8	0.1	2.8	325.8	27 776	30	80	1 537	NA	NA	NA
Clarke	23.2	1 288	59.6	1.0	5.7	0.7	11.0	11.7	649	39	125	736	NA	NA	NA
Clay	32.9	1 526	55.1	2.5	3.8	0.8	1.2	15.7	726	85	148	877	NA	NA	NA
Coahoma	65.8	2 101	61.1	0.3	6.1	0.3	5.1	44.2	1 412	88	213	2 122	NA	NA	NA
Copiah	49.8	1 722	71.6	1.1	5.5	0.0	7.9	16.2	562	71	198	2 010	NA	NA	NA
Covington	31.5	1 800	49.5	23.4	5.5	0.3	5.2	3.0	169	68	122	878	NA	NA	NA
De Soto	116.7	1 268	58.6	1.6	6.5	0.0	9.2	111.4	1 211	135	663	3 348	NA	NA	NA
Forrest	299.0	4 054	18.6	59.9	2.7	0.2	2.4	105.7	1 433	705	715	10 739	NA	NA	NA
Franklin	12.7	1 541	68.1	1.7	3.4	0.6	10.5	1.8	223	62	57	509	NA	NA	NA
George	20.3	1 072	65.1	1.0	6.1	0.0	15.5	7.6	405	46	134	1 096	NA	NA	NA
Greene	12.8	1 080	64.0	1.4	3.8	0.5	10.1	6.2	527	16	80	1 077	NA	NA	NA
Grenada	62.5	2 782	29.3	42.9	3.7	0.0	9.7	23.4	1 043	236	153	1 621	NA	NA	NA
Hancock	75.8	1 931	34.6	25.3	4.6	0.2	5.9	53.0	1 349	1 549	465	1 941	NA	NA	NA
Harrison	516.0	2 938	32.4	25.9	5.0	1.0	4.3	359.7	2 048	6 510	12 164	11 008	NA	NA	NA
Hinds	532.3	2 151	51.0	1.1	7.3	1.0	5.6	399.6	1 615	4 630	1 904	31 991	NA	NA	NA
Holmes	42.1	1 967	77.2	1.4	3.2	0.5	5.4	10.2	474	64	147	1 108	NA	NA	NA
Humphreys	21.8	1 931	50.3	12.1	4.1	0.6	9.9	5.8	514	32	78	621	NA	NA	NA
Issaquena	3.7	2 282	0.0	1.7	9.0	0.0	14.3	5.7	3 486	0	11	97	NA	NA	NA
Itawamba	51.7	2 456	83.1	0.2	1.7	0.1	4.7	22.4	1 065	52	144	917	NA	NA	NA
Jackson	418.2	3 253	29.6	36.3	3.0	0.2	4.8	685.6	5 333	886	2 976	9 055	NA	NA	NA
Jasper	27.2	1 546	52.1	20.1	3.1	0.1	8.3	13.3	756	62	121	860	NA	NA	NA
Jefferson	19.3	2 280	45.7	10.7	3.4	0.0	12.3	13.4	1 576	23	63	630	NA	NA	NA
Jefferson Davis	16.4	1 175	69.7	0.7	4.0	0.4	8.0	0.9	66	30	95	729	NA	NA	NA
Jones	174.1	2 745	45.3	30.5	2.5	0.3	3.8	158.5	2 500	244	434	6 066	NA	NA	NA
Kemper	23.6	2 270	78.5	0.0	2.2	0.1	10.4	1.1	103	36	72	524	NA	NA	NA
Lafayette	44.9	1 307	55.9	0.6	6.5	0.0	7.2	37.1	1 078	288	266	5 332	NA	NA	NA
Lamar	50.3	1 405	56.9	4.2	3.5	0.3	8.7	55.5	1 550	48	252	1 354	NA	NA	NA
Lauderdale	129.6	1 689	60.0	3.0	5.3	0.0	5.0	105.6	1 376	899	2 012	5 825	NA	NA	NA
Lawrence	22.8	1 762	50.3	22.8	2.6	1.5	8.1	12.0	925	56	89	719	NA	NA	NA
Leake	22.5	1 159	62.6	0.7	4.6	0.2	8.5	5.5	284	87	133	681	NA	NA	NA
Lee	126.0	1 703	51.5	0.7	6.2	0.2	11.8	111.0	1 501	489	556	4 547	NA	NA	NA
Leflore	104.6	2 814	31.1	41.8	4.5	0.9	4.2	34.2	921	184	258	3 616	NA	NA	NA
Lincoln	44.2	1 394	60.7	0.8	4.9	0.7	8.1	35.4	1 117	102	217	1 457	NA	NA	NA
Lowndes	111.6	1 823	44.9	0.9	4.6	0.5	8.5	168.5	2 753	904	1 815	3 351	NA	NA	NA
Madison	116.5	1 644	40.9	10.9	6.2	0.2	8.1	122.9	1 734	190	498	3 244	NA	NA	NA
Marion	44.4	1 679	49.8	26.4	4.3	0.0	5.2	8.6	325	61	181	1 407	NA	NA	NA
Marshall	59.5	1 835	35.1	11.7	3.3	0.4	4.8	5.4	167	114	221	1 163	NA	NA	NA
Monroe	61.6	1 615	44.8	19.4	5.2	0.4	8.6	16.1	421	154	262	1 585	NA	NA	NA
Montgomery	25.1	2 022	42.1	31.6	2.2	0.5	5.2	4.0	323	37	85	769	NA	NA	NA
Neshoba	27.0	994	63.6	1.8	5.9	0.0	7.8	13.1	481	507	189	1 274	NA	NA	NA
Newton	43.5	2 035	70.4	8.4	3.0	0.1	7.4	14.2	663	84	147	1 749	NA	NA	NA
Noxubee	22.2	1 794	47.1	21.9	3.9	0.6	11.9	7.1	571	47	85	672	NA	NA	NA
Oktibbeha	81.8	2 088	42.5	29.5	3.9	0.1	3.9	34.7	887	364	279	7 861	NA	NA	NA
Panola	51.7	1 573	51.9	14.7	9.0	0.2	7.0	19.0	578	122	229	2 016	NA	NA	NA
Pearl River	70.9	1 555	73.8	0.8	4.9	0.0	4.8	23.2	509	99	321	2 467	NA	NA	NA
Perry	62.2	5 278	19.2	5.4	1.6	0.0	1.8	577.6	48 993	25	81	715	NA	NA	NA
Pike	111.7	2 941	35.8	37.8	2.5	0.1	3.5	69.2	1 821	139	260	3 332	NA	NA	NA
Pontotoc	33.1	1 339	62.9	0.2	4.2	0.3	8.6	14.4	581	60	174	918	NA	NA	NA
Prentiss	64.5	2 666	66.5	1.1	2.6	0.2	3.4	36.5	1 509	56	166	1 476	NA	NA	NA
Quitman	21.0	2 142	39.0	30.6	4.8	0.0	5.7	5.4	546	32	68	417	NA	NA	NA
Rankin	203.8	1 905	45.2	23.5	4.4	0.4	6.7	120.4	1 125	539	751	8 497	NA	NA	NA
Scott	39.9	1 590	58.9	2.0	6.7	0.1	8.5	27.4	1 091	214	171	1 100	NA	NA	NA
Sharkey	12.3	1 865	70.5	1.4	5.0	0.3	7.0	0.8	120	36	45	436	NA	NA	NA
Simpson	41.1	1 631	45.2	22.6	4.2	1.3	7.4	12.2	483	51	173	1 645	NA	NA	NA
Smith	18.8	1 241	69.1	1.5	5.3	1.0	9.8	3.2	213	62	105	571	NA	NA	NA
Stone	71.4	5 545	86.3	5.7	1.2	0.1	2.6	8.7	674	82	90	1 037	NA	NA	NA

1. Based on the resident population estimated as of July 1 of the year shown.

Table B. States and Counties — **Land Area and Population**

STATE/ County code	MSA/ PMSA/ NECMA code[1]	County Type[2]	STATE County	Land area,[3] (sq km) 1990	Total persons	Rank	Per square kilometer	White	Black	Am. Indian, Eskimo, Aleut	Asian and Pacific Islander	Percent Hispanic[4]	Under 5 years	5 to 17 years	18 to 24 years	25 to 34 years	35 to 44 years	45 to 54 years
					1	2	3	4	5	6	7	8	9	10	11	12	13	14	15
			MISSISSIPPI—Cont'd															
28 133	...	7	Sunflower	1 797	33 257	1 277	18.5	32.5	66.9	0.2	0.4	0.9	7.0	20.9	12.1	15.4	16.1	11.0
28 135	...	9	Tallahatchie	1 668	14 587	2 095	8.7	38.7	60.7	0.1	0.5	0.6	8.4	22.9	10.9	12.2	13.1	11.5
28 137	...	6	Tate	1 048	24 417	1 557	23.3	62.6	37.0	0.2	0.2	0.8	7.3	20.3	12.3	13.1	14.8	12.6
28 139	...	7	Tippah	1 186	21 069	1 713	17.8	81.6	18.2	0.1	0.1	0.5	6.8	18.9	10.1	12.8	14.1	13.0
28 141	...	6	Tishomingo	1 099	18 742	1 836	17.1	95.6	4.1	0.2	0.1	0.5	6.1	16.2	8.8	12.0	14.6	14.0
28 143	...	8	Tunica	1 178	7 935	2 607	6.7	22.9	76.6	0.1	0.3	1.1	9.5	25.8	11.6	12.2	12.6	10.4
28 145	...	7	Union	1 076	24 121	1 573	22.4	83.6	16.2	0.1	0.2	0.6	6.5	18.8	9.5	12.7	15.3	13.1
28 147	...	9	Walthall	1 046	14 211	2 120	13.6	54.9	44.7	0.1	0.3	0.4	7.2	22.4	9.6	12.2	13.5	12.2
28 149	...	4	Warren	1 519	49 148	919	32.4	57.8	41.4	0.1	0.7	0.7	7.0	21.1	8.9	13.4	16.4	13.0
28 151	...	5	Washington	1 875	64 265	742	34.3	39.3	60.0	0.1	0.6	0.7	8.3	23.4	10.4	13.1	14.6	11.2
28 153	...	7	Wayne	2 099	20 637	1 730	9.8	61.3	38.3	0.1	0.2	0.5	7.6	22.2	9.9	13.9	14.8	12.6
28 155	...	9	Webster	1 095	10 633	2 366	9.7	76.3	23.6	0.0	0.1	0.7	6.3	19.4	9.4	11.8	13.8	12.7
28 157	...	9	Wilkinson	1 753	9 042	2 504	5.2	30.5	69.4	0.1	0.0	0.5	7.5	20.5	9.6	13.0	14.3	12.1
28 159	...	7	Winston	1 572	19 253	1 805	12.2	55.3	43.7	0.9	0.1	0.4	6.7	20.7	9.0	11.3	15.0	12.0
28 161	...	7	Yalobusha	1 210	12 627	2 238	10.4	59.7	40.1	0.1	0.1	0.6	6.9	19.5	8.9	12.1	14.5	12.5
28 163	...	6	Yazoo	2 382	25 208	1 523	10.6	44.7	55.0	0.1	0.2	0.5	8.0	22.5	9.3	12.7	13.3	11.7
29 000	...	X	**MISSOURI**	178 446	5 468 338	X	30.6	87.2	11.3	0.4	1.1	1.7	6.6	19.0	9.5	13.2	16.3	12.9
29 001	...	7	Adair	1 470	24 200	1 571	16.5	97.5	1.1	0.2	1.2	1.1	5.2	14.9	26.2	10.8	13.4	10.2
29 003	7000	3	Andrew	1 127	15 585	2 029	13.8	99.3	0.2	0.3	0.2	1.0	6.1	20.5	7.7	11.5	16.9	13.3
29 005	...	9	Atchison	1 411	7 021	2 677	5.0	98.2	1.3	0.3	0.2	1.7	4.8	17.4	11.4	9.8	14.7	11.9
29 007	...	6	Audrain	1 796	23 449	1 592	13.1	91.7	7.6	0.1	0.6	0.5	6.1	19.9	6.8	10.6	15.6	12.6
29 009	...	7	Barry	2 018	33 189	1 279	16.4	98.5	0.1	0.9	0.5	0.8	6.1	19.4	7.7	11.1	14.2	14.3
29 011	...	6	Barton	1 539	12 133	2 270	7.9	98.6	0.1	0.9	0.4	0.8	6.5	20.6	7.0	12.1	14.9	12.1
29 013	...	6	Bates	2 198	16 061	2 001	7.3	98.5	0.9	0.5	0.1	0.8	6.2	20.0	6.9	10.6	14.7	13.1
29 015	...	9	Benton	1 827	17 345	1 909	9.5	99.2	0.1	0.5	0.2	0.8	4.6	16.6	6.0	8.6	13.3	15.3
29 017	...	9	Bollinger	1 608	11 829	2 289	7.4	99.2	0.2	0.3	0.4	1.0	6.6	20.0	8.3	11.2	15.4	13.6
29 019	1740	3	Boone	1 775	130 179	398	73.3	86.8	9.0	0.3	3.8	1.5	6.7	16.2	20.3	15.5	16.3	10.3
29 021	7000	3	Buchanan	1 061	81 635	622	76.9	95.4	3.8	0.3	0.5	2.9	6.7	19.1	9.4	12.6	15.3	12.0
29 023	...	7	Butler	1 807	40 379	1 075	22.3	93.0	6.2	0.3	0.5	0.8	6.0	19.5	8.1	11.3	15.2	13.1
29 025	...	6	Caldwell	1 112	8 926	2 513	8.0	99.6	0.2	0.2	0.0	1.0	6.6	20.0	7.1	10.5	14.7	13.6
29 027	...	6	Callaway	2 173	37 904	1 136	17.4	93.0	6.1	0.3	0.6	0.7	6.7	19.2	10.8	13.5	17.3	12.7
29 029	...	7	Camden	1 697	34 596	1 236	20.4	99.0	0.3	0.4	0.3	1.0	5.1	15.9	6.0	9.8	14.8	15.1
29 031	...	5	Cape Girardeau	1 499	67 200	717	44.8	93.0	5.8	0.2	1.0	0.7	6.2	17.6	13.9	12.4	16.0	12.1
29 033	...	6	Carroll	1 799	10 108	2 412	5.6	97.2	2.5	0.1	0.2	0.5	5.9	20.2	6.8	9.9	14.4	13.0
29 035	...	9	Carter	1 315	6 292	2 752	4.8	99.0	0.0	0.8	0.1	0.9	6.6	20.7	7.9	10.3	14.6	14.1
29 037	3760	1	Cass	1 811	83 099	612	45.9	97.4	1.3	0.6	0.6	1.9	7.2	21.1	8.1	13.2	16.9	14.1
29 039	...	7	Cedar	1 233	13 395	2 183	10.9	99.1	0.1	0.6	0.2	0.8	5.6	18.0	6.5	9.1	13.3	13.6
29 041	...	9	Chariton	1 958	8 557	2 548	4.4	95.2	4.6	0.2	0.1	0.2	6.1	19.5	6.3	10.2	13.9	12.8
29 043	7920	2	Christian	1 459	51 353	891	35.2	98.9	0.2	0.5	0.3	0.9	6.8	21.2	8.2	13.4	18.0	13.4
29 045	...	9	Clark	1 314	7 367	2 648	5.6	99.7	0.1	0.1	0.1	0.4	6.0	20.7	7.6	10.6	15.6	13.7
29 047	3760	0	Clay	1 027	180 111	296	175.4	96.3	2.1	0.5	1.1	3.3	6.8	18.3	9.2	14.5	17.9	13.8
29 049	3760	1	Clinton	1 085	19 522	1 789	18.0	96.8	2.6	0.4	0.2	1.1	6.7	21.2	7.1	11.8	16.2	15.1
29 051	...	4	Cole	1 014	69 512	704	68.6	90.5	8.6	0.4	0.6	1.0	6.2	18.3	9.6	15.4	18.4	12.3
29 053	...	6	Cooper	1 463	16 153	1 996	11.0	89.3	9.9	0.4	0.4	0.8	5.7	18.4	15.1	10.8	14.2	11.4
29 055	...	6	Crawford	1 923	22 427	1 642	11.7	99.5	0.1	0.2	0.2	0.9	6.2	20.5	7.5	11.7	14.5	13.7
29 057	...	8	Dade	1 270	7 939	2 606	6.3	98.5	0.3	0.8	0.3	1.4	6.4	18.8	6.3	10.7	13.6	12.7
29 059	...	8	Dallas	1 403	15 570	2 030	11.1	98.9	0.2	0.6	0.2	0.8	6.6	20.8	7.2	11.2	14.8	13.8
29 061	...	9	Daviess	1 469	8 051	2 594	5.5	99.4	0.0	0.4	0.2	0.8	6.6	20.7	6.7	10.0	13.6	13.7
29 063	...	8	De Kalb	1 099	11 288	2 329	10.3	89.2	9.1	1.2	0.5	3.1	4.9	15.4	10.3	18.6	16.6	11.6
29 065	...	7	Dent	1 952	14 257	2 116	7.3	98.9	0.2	0.5	0.4	0.9	5.8	20.6	6.9	10.5	14.8	13.9
29 067	...	6	Douglas	2 110	12 421	2 254	5.9	99.0	0.0	0.7	0.2	1.1	6.3	19.6	6.8	10.1	14.4	14.5
29 069	...	7	Dunklin	1 413	32 526	1 296	23.0	89.9	9.6	0.2	0.3	0.7	6.2	20.5	8.1	10.7	14.5	13.9
29 071	7040	1	Franklin	2 388	93 128	544	39.0	98.3	1.2	0.2	0.4	0.8	7.2	20.9	9.1	13.0	16.0	13.4
29 073	...	6	Gasconade	1 345	14 975	2 066	11.1	99.6	0.1	0.2	0.2	0.4	6.3	18.4	7.0	11.6	14.2	12.2
29 075	...	8	Gentry	1 273	6 872	2 690	5.4	99.4	0.1	0.4	0.1	0.5	5.9	19.0	6.6	10.7	12.0	13.2
29 077	7920	2	Greene	1 748	227 002	244	129.9	96.2	2.2	0.6	1.1	1.2	5.9	16.7	13.8	12.8	16.3	12.4
29 079	...	7	Grundy	1 129	10 134	2 409	9.0	99.2	0.1	0.4	0.3	1.0	5.4	17.9	6.8	10.1	14.6	13.8
29 081	...	7	Harrison	1 878	8 413	2 557	4.5	99.2	0.1	0.3	0.4	0.6	5.3	17.6	6.3	10.5	12.9	13.8
29 083	...	6	Henry	1 819	21 288	1 692	11.7	97.9	1.4	0.4	0.4	1.0	6.0	18.4	7.3	10.7	14.9	13.5
29 085	...	9	Hickory	1 033	8 728	2 532	8.4	99.0	0.1	0.7	0.1	0.6	4.1	15.4	5.1	7.6	12.4	13.6
29 087	...	8	Holt	1 196	5 562	2 803	4.7	99.4	0.2	0.3	0.1	0.4	6.3	19.5	6.7	10.4	15.1	11.8
29 089	...	6	Howard	1 206	9 661	2 457	8.0	90.3	9.2	0.3	0.2	0.5	5.9	19.0	11.4	11.0	14.6	12.0
29 091	...	7	Howell	2 403	36 070	1 192	15.0	98.9	0.3	0.5	0.4	0.8	6.2	19.7	7.7	10.7	15.1	13.8
29 093	...	9	Iron	1 428	10 936	2 349	7.7	99.0	0.6	0.1	0.2	0.6	5.8	21.2	7.6	10.4	14.6	13.7
29 095	3760	0	Jackson	1 566	654 484	75	417.9	73.0	25.1	0.5	1.5	4.1	7.1	18.5	9.2	14.7	16.6	12.4

1. MSA = Metropolitan Statistical Area. PMSA = Primary MSA. NECMA = New England County Metropolitan Area. See Appendix A for explanation of these concepts. See Appendix B for list of metropolitan areas identified by type, with component counties. 2. County typology code from the Economic Research Service of USDA. See Appendix A for definition. 3. Dry land or land partially or temporarily covered by water. 4. Hispanic persons may be of any race.

Table B. States and Counties — **Population and Households**

STATE County	Population, 1999 (cont'd) Age (percent) (cont'd) 55 to 64 years	65 to 74 years	75 years and over	Percent female	Population — change and components of change, 1980–1999 Total persons 1990	Total persons 1980	Percent change 1980–1990	Percent change 1990–1999	Components of change, 1990–1999 Births	Deaths	Net migration	Households, 1990 Number	Percent change, 1980–1990	Persons per household	Percent Female family householder[1]	One person
	16	17	18	19	20	21	22	23	24	25	26	27	28	29	30	31
MISSISSIPPI—Cont'd																
Sunflower	7.1	5.3	5.1	46.4	35 129	34 844	0.8	-5.3	5 209	3 239	-3 815	9 650	-0.4	3.06	23.4	25.3
Tallahatchie	8.3	6.7	5.9	53.0	15 210	17 157	-11.3	-4.1	2 289	1 488	-1 387	5 034	-4.8	3.01	20.2	24.4
Tate	8.2	5.9	5.5	51.8	21 432	20 119	6.5	13.9	3 115	2 024	1 928	7 024	16.4	2.92	14.0	18.7
Tippah	9.5	7.2	7.5	52.0	19 523	18 739	4.2	7.9	2 696	2 282	1 219	7 158	11.7	2.68	10.5	21.9
Tishomingo	11.2	9.1	8.0	52.3	17 683	18 434	-4.1	6.0	2 123	2 217	1 227	7 059	4.9	2.48	9.0	23.5
Tunica	7.0	6.1	4.8	53.5	8 164	9 652	-15.4	-2.8	1 453	938	-734	2 526	-10.2	3.22	26.4	23.0
Union	10.0	7.1	7.1	51.7	22 085	21 741	1.6	9.2	3 190	2 205	1 126	8 367	7.6	2.62	9.7	23.0
Walthall	9.3	6.9	6.7	51.7	14 352	13 761	4.3	-1.0	2 128	1 541	-660	4 929	11.5	2.88	14.7	22.2
Warren	8.2	6.3	5.6	52.8	47 880	51 627	-7.3	2.6	7 553	4 918	-1 274	17 407	0.3	2.72	16.5	24.9
Washington	7.9	5.9	5.2	53.3	67 935	72 344	-6.1	-5.4	11 523	6 748	-8 374	22 593	-1.5	2.98	23.7	23.2
Wayne	8.7	5.6	4.8	52.2	19 517	19 135	2.0	5.7	3 124	1 773	-178	6 858	10.8	2.83	15.8	21.1
Webster	9.9	8.3	8.4	52.0	10 222	10 300	-0.8	4.0	1 294	1 228	378	3 826	6.5	2.63	13.3	25.5
Wilkinson	8.4	7.7	6.9	53.3	9 678	10 021	-3.4	-6.6	1 217	1 209	-637	3 347	4.9	2.85	24.3	23.4
Winston	10.1	7.6	7.5	52.8	19 433	19 474	-0.2	-0.9	2 369	2 102	-371	7 061	7.8	2.73	15.8	24.5
Yalobusha	9.9	8.5	7.2	53.2	12 033	13 183	-8.7	4.9	1 675	1 425	386	4 614	0.7	2.59	15.6	28.1
Yazoo	9.2	6.7	6.6	53.2	25 506	27 349	-6.7	-1.2	4 307	2 958	-1 579	8 813	-0.1	2.86	20.3	25.0
MISSOURI	8.9	7.1	6.5	51.5	5 116 901	4 916 766	4.1	6.9	697 038	492 127	139 371	1 961 206	9.4	2.54	10.6	26.0
Adair	6.8	5.8	6.7	52.9	24 577	24 870	-1.2	-1.5	2 537	2 107	-752	9 060	1.3	2.35	7.5	30.2
Andrew	9.0	7.1	7.8	50.9	14 632	13 980	4.7	6.5	1 631	1 399	771	5 429	10.1	2.64	6.8	20.6
Atchison	9.8	9.5	10.7	50.7	7 457	8 605	-13.3	-5.8	636	877	-166	2 961	-10.2	2.35	6.8	28.0
Audrain	9.9	9.5	9.0	51.6	23 599	26 458	-10.8	-4.0	2 884	2 758	-191	9 205	-5.9	2.50	8.5	25.5
Barry	11.2	8.4	7.7	50.8	27 547	24 408	12.9	20.5	4 161	3 330	4 894	10 858	16.7	2.51	7.0	23.5
Barton	10.0	7.8	8.9	51.2	11 312	11 292	0.2	7.3	1 576	1 393	678	4 524	2.7	2.46	7.1	27.7
Bates	11.1	8.1	9.4	51.4	15 025	15 873	-5.3	6.9	1 859	1 979	1 208	5 918	-2.9	2.49	7.3	25.4
Benton	14.9	11.6	9.2	50.7	13 859	12 183	13.8	25.2	1 304	2 049	4 243	5 764	18.9	2.37	6.2	24.7
Bollinger	10.6	7.6	6.9	50.3	10 619	10 301	3.1	11.4	1 225	1 202	1 208	3 946	6.2	2.65	7.2	20.6
Boone	5.9	4.5	4.2	51.4	112 379	100 376	12.0	15.8	15 980	6 725	8 922	41 937	18.8	2.42	9.5	27.5
Buchanan	9.3	7.6	8.0	52.3	83 083	87 888	-5.5	-1.7	10 796	9 068	-2 880	32 486	-1.3	2.48	11.4	27.7
Butler	10.6	8.6	7.6	52.1	38 765	37 693	2.8	4.2	4 827	4 833	1 760	15 334	8.1	2.48	11.3	24.8
Caldwell	10.0	8.0	9.4	51.9	8 380	8 660	-3.2	6.5	969	1 011	619	3 222	-2.4	2.54	6.7	24.8
Callaway	8.5	5.6	5.7	51.1	32 809	32 252	1.7	15.5	4 262	2 791	3 686	11 552	8.4	2.63	8.8	21.8
Camden	14.4	12.2	6.7	49.8	27 495	20 017	37.4	25.8	2 929	3 027	7 253	11 305	41.5	2.41	5.7	20.6
Cape Girardeau	8.2	6.9	6.8	51.7	61 633	58 837	4.8	9.0	7 656	5 797	3 876	23 390	11.6	2.49	8.9	25.4
Carroll	10.1	9.1	10.8	52.0	10 748	12 131	-11.4	-6.0	1 220	1 324	-495	4 332	-9.2	2.44	7.4	28.5
Carter	11.1	7.4	7.2	50.2	5 515	5 428	1.6	14.1	740	727	780	2 128	8.5	2.56	8.8	26.5
Cass	8.1	5.7	5.1	51.1	63 808	51 029	25.0	30.2	9 307	5 272	14 994	22 892	31.4	2.75	8.2	19.1
Cedar	12.5	10.3	11.1	52.2	12 093	11 894	1.7	10.8	1 334	1 830	1 824	5 003	4.4	2.37	6.8	27.4
Chariton	10.8	9.4	11.1	51.7	9 202	10 489	-12.3	-7.0	782	1 237	-168	3 661	-9.5	2.47	5.8	27.6
Christian	8.1	5.9	5.1	50.6	32 644	22 402	45.7	57.3	5 557	2 811	16 000	11 937	49.6	2.70	8.0	17.8
Clark	9.5	7.7	8.6	50.0	7 547	8 493	-11.1	-2.4	749	876	-36	2 859	-8.1	2.61	6.9	24.5
Clay	8.5	6.4	4.5	51.5	153 411	136 488	12.4	17.4	21 619	11 265	14 691	58 915	18.4	2.55	9.0	23.5
Clinton	9.2	5.8	7.0	51.1	16 595	15 916	4.3	17.6	2 087	1 884	2 763	6 112	10.0	2.66	7.2	21.7
Cole	7.8	6.0	6.0	48.6	63 579	56 663	12.2	9.3	8 292	4 950	2 783	22 976	16.2	2.53	8.8	27.4
Cooper	8.5	7.7	8.1	46.8	14 835	14 643	1.3	8.9	1 761	1 594	1 212	5 359	-0.4	2.53	7.8	25.0
Crawford	10.6	7.8	7.5	51.0	19 173	18 300	4.8	17.0	2 770	2 228	2 769	7 299	10.8	2.59	7.4	23.0
Dade	11.1	9.0	11.3	51.9	7 449	7 383	0.9	6.6	810	1 056	766	2 976	1.6	2.43	6.1	27.7
Dallas	11.0	7.4	7.3	50.6	12 646	12 096	4.5	23.1	1 830	1 494	2 632	4 899	9.9	2.55	7.2	23.6
Daviess	10.9	8.3	9.4	52.0	7 865	8 905	-11.7	2.4	1 054	1 013	168	3 040	-10.0	2.55	5.7	25.5
De Kalb	8.1	6.5	8.0	39.5	9 967	8 222	21.2	13.3	922	1 114	1 524	3 054	-0.7	2.55	5.8	25.0
Dent	10.5	8.5	8.5	51.5	13 702	14 517	-5.6	4.1	1 588	1 716	730	5 327	-1.3	2.53	8.2	23.8
Douglas	10.8	8.5	9.1	51.1	11 876	11 594	2.4	4.0	1 400	1 256	452	4 587	10.1	2.56	6.3	23.3
Dunklin	9.6	8.2	8.2	53.3	33 112	36 324	-8.8	-1.8	4 472	4 385	-563	13 128	-3.4	2.48	12.3	27.2
Franklin	8.6	6.2	5.5	50.4	80 603	71 233	13.2	15.5	11 671	7 321	8 373	28 856	20.2	2.76	8.4	20.0
Gasconade	10.6	9.6	10.1	51.3	14 006	13 181	6.3	6.9	1 615	1 802	1 195	5 543	10.2	2.48	6.2	25.8
Gentry	10.5	9.3	12.7	52.3	6 854	7 887	-13.1	0.3	758	1 058	346	2 756	-11.6	2.40	6.2	29.3
Greene	8.3	7.1	6.7	51.9	207 949	185 302	12.2	9.2	27 770	19 236	11 281	81 463	17.7	2.43	9.2	26.6
Grundy	10.5	9.4	11.5	53.1	10 536	11 959	-11.9	-3.8	1 168	1 620	80	4 346	-10.7	2.36	7.2	29.1
Harrison	11.7	9.3	12.6	51.5	8 469	9 890	-14.4	-0.7	845	1 298	435	3 574	-13.6	2.32	5.8	29.7
Henry	10.3	8.9	10.0	51.6	20 044	19 672	1.9	6.2	2 200	2 719	1 827	8 189	5.5	2.41	7.8	28.0
Hickory	17.1	14.4	10.3	50.6	7 335	6 367	15.2	19.0	719	1 338	2 034	3 183	21.0	2.27	5.2	24.4
Holt	10.2	8.6	11.5	50.8	6 034	6 882	-12.3	-7.8	512	767	-190	2 440	-11.9	2.42	5.2	28.8
Howard	9.6	7.3	9.1	51.1	9 631	10 008	-3.8	0.3	1 045	1 089	109	3 571	-2.5	2.49	8.5	26.9
Howell	10.3	8.3	8.2	51.5	31 447	28 807	9.2	14.7	4 337	3 907	4 297	12 283	14.2	2.51	8.4	24.4
Iron	10.5	7.3	8.9	52.6	10 726	11 084	-3.2	2.0	1 288	1 663	624	3 995	5.0	2.58	8.7	23.5
Jackson	8.6	6.9	6.1	52.4	633 234	629 266	0.6	3.4	91 466	58 013	-25 641	252 582	4.3	2.46	13.6	29.6

1. No spouse present.

Items 16—31

Table B. States and Counties — Vital Statistics, Health Resources, and Crime

STATE County	Births, average 1996–1998 Total	Rate[1]	Deaths, average 1996–1998 Number Total	Number Infant[2]	Rate Total[1]	Rate Infant[3]	Physicians,[4] 1998 Number	Rate[5]	Hospitals,[4] 1998 Number	Beds Number	Beds Rate[5]	Medicare enrollees 1999	Serious crimes known to police, 1998[6] Total Number	Rate[7]
	32	33	34	35	36	37	38	39	40	41	42	43	44	45
MISSISSIPPI—Cont'd														
Sunflower	523	15.0	348	7	10.0	13.4	20	58	2	155	448	4 078	NA	NA
Tallahatchie	216	14.5	154	3	10.3	13.9	4	27	1	77	517	2 396	NA	NA
Tate	355	15.1	225	5	9.6	13.1	10	42	1	52	217	3 458	NA	NA
Tippah	307	14.7	251	5	12.0	15.2	7	33	1	106	504	4 376	NA	NA
Tishomingo	227	12.2	255	2	13.8	7.3	10	54	1	88	472	4 454	NA	NA
Tunica	160	20.0	99	3	12.3	16.6	5	62	0	0	0	1 187	NA	NA
Union	353	15.0	240	3	10.2	7.5	23	97	1	153	642	4 187	NA	NA
Walthall	220	15.3	166	3	11.6	15.2	9	63	1	49	341	2 194	NA	NA
Warren	796	16.2	514	10	10.4	12.1	81	164	2	343	694	6 781	2 454	4 948
Washington	1 197	18.2	705	14	10.7	12.0	95	146	2	287	440	9 134	5 736	9 142
Wayne	342	16.9	206	5	10.2	13.7	14	69	1	77	378	2 747	NA	NA
Webster	140	13.4	132	0	12.6	0.0	8	76	1	76	721	1 986	NA	NA
Wilkinson	126	13.7	124	1	13.4	7.9	9	98	1	66	719	1 678	NA	NA
Winston	248	12.8	209	1	10.8	4.0	10	52	1	185	954	3 425	NA	NA
Yalobusha	180	14.6	161	1	13.1	3.7	5	40	1	85	687	2 959	NA	NA
Yazoo	457	18.0	315	4	12.4	8.0	20	78	1	34	133	4 215	NA	NA
MISSOURI	74 409	13.8	54 434	567	10.1	7.6	11 722	216	134	21 768	400	854 472	262 506	4 826
Adair	281	11.5	224	2	9.2	7.1	87	358	2	194	799	3 391	NA	NA
Andrew	178	11.5	156	0	10.1	1.9	16	103	1	205	1 317	2 034	NA	NA
Atchison	62	8.7	90	0	12.7	0.0	5	71	1	44	629	1 426	49	682
Audrain	320	13.6	304	2	12.9	7.3	43	182	1	165	700	4 656	525	2 212
Barry	470	14.3	373	4	11.4	9.2	16	48	2	71	214	6 649	295	896
Barton	179	14.9	150	2	12.5	9.3	9	75	1	44	364	2 157	221	1 837
Bates	191	12.1	214	2	13.6	8.7	4	25	1	33	209	3 221	NA	NA
Benton	160	9.6	237	1	14.2	8.3	7	41	0	0	0	4 434	345	2 073
Bollinger	122	10.7	122	1	10.7	10.9	1	9	0	0	0	1 963	NA	NA
Boone	1 736	13.6	752	9	5.9	5.2	813	630	3	931	721	13 703	5 965	4 617
Buchanan	1 117	13.7	978	8	11.9	6.9	158	193	1	277	339	15 118	5 157	6 263
Butler	523	12.9	538	6	13.3	10.8	91	224	2	376	927	8 170	NA	NA
Caldwell	107	12.3	111	0	12.8	3.1	2	23	0	0	0	1 758	40	457
Callaway	458	12.4	316	4	8.6	8.7	34	91	1	36	96	5 333	NA	NA
Camden	319	9.6	352	2	10.6	7.3	56	165	1	91	268	6 387	517	1 544
Cape Girardeau	785	11.9	648	6	9.8	7.6	191	288	2	510	769	10 120	2 824	4 249
Carroll	120	11.8	133	0	13.0	0.0	3	29	1	52	509	2 268	NA	NA
Carter	86	13.6	88	1	14.0	11.7	1	16	0	0	0	1 288	NA	NA
Cass	1 012	13.0	626	4	8.0	3.6	45	56	2	89	111	10 003	1 552	2 048
Cedar	150	11.5	192	1	14.7	4.4	11	83	1	34	257	3 303	154	1 174
Chariton	79	9.0	139	0	15.9	4.2	2	23	0	0	0	1 790	147	1 660
Christian	680	14.5	370	5	7.9	7.4	16	33	0	0	0	6 473	443	937
Clark	80	10.6	90	1	12.1	12.6	2	27	0	0	0	1 291	NA	NA
Clay	2 443	14.1	1 313	13	7.6	5.2	296	168	3	608	345	22 391	12 266	7 000
Clinton	240	12.9	210	2	11.3	8.3	6	31	1	38	199	2 978	NA	NA
Cole	891	13.0	593	6	8.6	6.4	171	247	3	290	418	9 285	2 394	3 455
Cooper	189	11.8	179	1	11.2	5.3	13	81	1	49	306	2 746	NA	NA
Crawford	308	14.0	256	1	11.6	4.3	8	36	0	0	0	3 839	500	2 256
Dade	85	10.8	118	0	14.9	0.0	5	63	0	0	0	1 807	174	2 176
Dallas	200	13.3	157	1	10.5	6.7	5	33	0	0	0	2 628	16	105
Daviess	119	15.2	107	0	13.7	0.0	2	26	0	0	0	1 552	98	1 250
De Kalb	102	9.2	118	1	10.6	9.8	2	18	0	0	0	1 420	156	1 396
Dent	171	12.2	196	0	13.9	0.0	12	85	1	46	326	3 064	NA	NA
Douglas	142	11.6	144	1	11.7	7.0	4	32	0	0	0	2 270	41	331
Dunklin	476	14.5	479	4	14.6	7.7	23	70	1	116	355	6 747	NA	NA
Franklin	1 284	14.1	840	6	9.2	4.9	91	99	2	194	211	13 784	3 008	3 283
Gasconade	172	11.6	195	1	13.2	3.9	18	121	1	41	275	3 227	NA	NA
Gentry	80	11.6	114	0	16.4	0.0	4	58	1	35	504	1 832	2	29
Greene	3 093	13.7	2 199	21	9.7	6.9	669	295	5	1 657	731	36 349	12 998	5 723
Grundy	130	12.7	165	0	16.1	2.6	7	69	1	48	472	2 359	271	2 628
Harrison	99	11.7	124	0	14.7	3.4	5	59	1	23	270	2 116	NA	NA
Henry	249	11.8	288	2	13.6	6.7	23	108	1	108	509	4 872	781	3 682
Hickory	74	8.6	148	1	17.3	18.0	1	12	0	0	0	2 304	NA	NA
Holt	49	8.8	73	1	13.0	13.5	3	54	0	0	0	1 234	NA	NA
Howard	100	10.2	111	1	11.4	10.0	6	62	0	0	0	1 781	NA	NA
Howell	483	13.6	417	3	11.7	6.9	38	106	2	140	391	7 570	953	2 661
Iron	136	12.4	189	1	17.3	4.9	12	110	1	50	460	2 323	NA	NA
Jackson	9 961	15.2	6 306	88	9.7	8.8	1 534	234	14	3 347	511	94 515	58 462	8 961

1. Per 1,000 estimated resident population, average 1996–1998.   2. Deaths of infants under 1 year old.   3. Deaths of infants under 1 year old per 1,000 live births.   4. Data subject to copyright.   5. Per 100,000 resident population as of July 1 of the year shown.   6. Data for serious crimes have not been adjusted for underreporting; this may affect comparability between geographic areas and over time.   7. Per 100,000 population estimated by the FBI.

Table B. States and Counties — Crime, Education, Money Income, and Poverty

STATE County	Serious crimes known to police, 1998[1] (cont'd) Rate[2] Violent	Property	Education — School enrollment and attainment, 1990 Enrollment[3] Total	Percent private	Attainment[4] (percent) High school graduate or more	Bachelor's degree or more	Local government expenditures, fiscal 1997[5] Total current expenditures (mil dol)	Current expenditures per student (dollars)	Money income — 1989 Per capita[6] (dollars)	Households Median Dollars	Percent change, 1979–1989 (constant 1989 dollars)	Percent with $100,000 or more	Income and poverty, 1997 Median household income	Percent below poverty level All persons	Persons under 18	Persons 5–17 in families
	46	47	48	49	50	51	52	53	54	55	56	57	58	59	60	61
MISSISSIPPI—Cont'd																
Sunflower	NA	NA	10 209	10.9	49.2	12.4	25.7	3 821	7 067	14 431	-10.5	1.4	19 878	34.3	37.7	33.6
Tallahatchie	NA	NA	4 221	10.7	48.2	7.9	12.6	4 041	6 180	13 593	2.7	0.8	18 628	27.6	34.5	32.2
Tate	NA	NA	5 963	8.2	61.0	11.7	18.1	3 815	9 212	22 207	9.4	1.5	30 911	14.9	19.7	18.9
Tippah	NA	NA	4 654	5.8	54.4	9.0	16.1	3 858	8 747	17 991	3.8	0.8	26 316	14.8	19.9	18.7
Tishomingo	NA	NA	3 671	3.4	55.0	6.6	12.5	3 880	8 735	17 500	-17.6	0.8	25 993	13.9	20.5	19.3
Tunica	NA	NA	2 637	12.7	45.9	8.5	9.6	4 833	6 449	10 965	-1.2	1.9	19 322	26.6	30.5	30.7
Union	NA	NA	5 131	4.6	57.3	10.1	17.7	3 860	9 735	21 128	9.6	1.1	29 875	12.6	18.1	16.4
Walthall	NA	NA	4 017	4.6	55.0	10.1	11.6	3 898	7 263	14 135	-17.7	0.7	20 201	27.2	33.2	33.4
Warren	813	4 135	13 893	11.5	67.7	19.1	40.5	4 239	10 861	22 804	-14.3	1.6	31 459	16.9	23.7	20.5
Washington	749	8 393	20 778	15.0	58.8	14.3	54.2	4 054	8 704	17 492	-1.6	2.1	24 001	26.0	32.9	29.4
Wayne	NA	NA	5 389	6.7	56.1	8.9	16.5	3 904	7 545	16 095	-6.8	0.6	24 508	20.7	25.4	25.2
Webster	NA	NA	2 533	5.0	58.6	10.8	8.1	3 906	8 354	17 094	-9.8	0.8	23 856	17.4	26.1	22.9
Wilkinson	NA	NA	2 428	21.7	48.3	8.9	7.7	4 240	6 670	11 910	-22.1	0.7	18 282	28.8	35.2	35.2
Winston	NA	NA	5 227	8.7	59.1	10.8	15.0	4 086	8 907	18 320	2.3	1.7	26 181	18.9	25.0	23.8
Yalobusha	NA	NA	2 860	7.0	55.7	9.9	9.1	3 925	8 049	15 885	-7.9	0.9	23 057	21.9	29.0	28.8
Yazoo	NA	NA	7 116	16.8	53.4	12.0	20.6	4 161	7 786	14 234	-13.6	1.9	20 670	27.5	35.5	32.6
MISSOURI	556	4 270	1 292 623	17.9	73.9	17.8	4 776.0	5 304	12 989	26 362	1.0	2.8	34 502	12.2	17.7	15.9
Adair	NA	NA	9 691	7.6	74.3	22.7	14.1	4 614	9 197	17 285	-15.1	1.4	28 246	15.4	18.2	17.5
Andrew	NA	NA	3 534	6.0	78.6	13.5	12.9	4 500	10 984	26 103	1.6	1.6	37 621	8.7	11.6	10.6
Atchison	111	571	1 900	22.9	76.8	14.2	6.4	5 467	10 042	20 126	-7.8	1.6	31 287	12.4	15.0	15.1
Audrain	101	2 111	5 146	10.1	68.0	10.9	17.6	4 642	11 310	23 424	-9.9	1.5	32 606	12.5	18.1	16.1
Barry	219	677	5 625	3.7	67.4	8.5	28.2	4 505	9 465	19 169	2.8	1.3	26 543	15.5	24.1	20.5
Barton	108	1 729	2 502	5.1	68.2	8.2	9.8	4 437	10 229	19 951	6.0	1.9	28 536	13.6	19.6	17.3
Bates	NA	NA	3 274	5.2	66.9	8.4	13.2	4 348	9 598	20 085	1.1	0.6	28 735	14.2	20.2	18.3
Benton	180	1 893	2 692	4.7	64.5	7.7	11.2	4 159	6 925	16 925	-2.1	0.6	23 451	17.3	27.8	24.4
Bollinger	NA	NA	2 263	4.7	52.7	6.9	8.5	4 086	8 757	19 430	16.7	1.0	26 068	16.4	23.0	21.5
Boone	356	4 261	42 951	9.7	84.8	36.5	99.4	4 929	12 707	25 647	-1.4	2.6	38 421	11.4	14.3	13.5
Buchanan	342	5 921	20 161	9.4	72.1	13.5	66.4	4 662	11 193	23 019	-4.0	1.7	31 544	14.4	19.8	18.4
Butler	NA	NA	8 922	6.1	56.8	8.6	29.2	4 204	9 000	16 285	-2.6	1.4	24 073	20.0	29.0	26.1
Caldwell	80	377	1 905	4.3	75.4	8.1	9.1	4 957	9 491	19 448	-0.8	1.1	28 742	13.5	17.9	17.0
Callaway	NA	NA	8 652	23.0	70.1	13.9	24.3	4 815	11 024	26 663	-6.7	1.0	35 105	10.6	14.7	13.4
Camden	161	1 383	5 096	7.5	73.6	12.4	23.4	4 659	12 403	22 564	14.5	2.9	30 225	12.1	21.6	18.8
Cape Girardeau	175	4 074	17 779	11.5	74.4	19.2	41.0	4 361	11 858	24 510	-1.4	2.1	36 264	11.6	16.1	14.4
Carroll	NA	NA	2 447	3.3	70.3	11.7	9.7	5 006	10 102	19 697	-2.0	1.4	27 937	14.6	20.8	18.9
Carter	NA	NA	1 303	2.0	56.0	8.8	7.0	4 870	7 470	15 357	-2.8	0.5	20 808	24.8	36.3	33.1
Cass	232	1 816	16 185	11.4	80.0	13.0	66.1	4 477	12 991	31 373	-1.5	1.9	43 100	7.2	10.1	9.5
Cedar	145	1 029	2 387	6.8	63.9	7.6	10.6	4 449	8 864	16 939	2.7	0.8	23 423	18.3	27.4	25.2
Chariton	361	1 299	1 965	10.6	71.3	10.4	7.4	4 941	10 589	20 829	0.4	1.2	28 790	12.6	16.9	16.4
Christian	27	910	8 153	8.9	76.6	12.5	35.8	4 102	10 862	25 995	9.7	1.2	36 236	9.1	13.8	11.7
Clark	NA	NA	1 730	5.5	67.4	7.9	6.9	4 581	8 849	19 674	-4.5	0.5	29 168	14.5	19.4	18.6
Clay	897	6 103	38 853	16.0	84.7	20.0	145.7	4 829	15 369	34 370	-2.5	2.7	46 602	5.5	8.3	7.5
Clinton	NA	NA	3 996	4.9	77.1	10.3	15.2	4 588	11 492	26 306	-3.2	1.5	37 405	9.4	12.2	12.0
Cole	188	3 267	15 956	21.5	77.3	22.3	49.6	4 580	13 918	30 362	0.2	2.4	42 486	8.2	10.8	9.7
Cooper	NA	NA	3 462	18.5	70.9	11.5	13.5	5 247	10 006	22 785	-0.6	1.0	31 567	11.6	15.0	14.3
Crawford	397	1 859	4 432	4.5	58.6	7.1	14.0	3 843	9 284	19 711	-0.3	1.0	27 143	15.8	23.3	19.8
Dade	325	1 851	1 505	6.8	71.8	9.0	6.7	4 522	9 490	18 724	-0.4	1.4	24 307	16.4	22.6	21.2
Dallas	0	105	2 537	7.7	63.0	6.5	10.0	4 684	8 530	16 673	3.7	1.5	27 477	16.2	22.9	21.8
Daviess	332	918	1 658	10.8	70.6	8.9	7.7	5 501	9 008	18 351	-3.5	0.7	30 996	16.7	17.0	17.3
De Kalb	197	1 199	2 041	6.9	73.1	8.3	7.1	4 863	9 047	22 771	14.0	1.4	30 990	16.5	17.0	17.3
Dent	NA	NA	3 035	4.9	53.9	7.9	11.8	4 575	9 033	16 594	-8.3	1.0	24 695	19.5	27.0	25.6
Douglas	105	226	2 585	8.0	59.8	7.5	8.2	4 290	8 899	16 187	5.7	1.0	21 955	21.5	30.8	27.7
Dunklin	NA	NA	7 748	3.6	51.2	8.0	29.2	4 607	9 028	15 388	-6.1	1.3	23 341	23.9	33.8	31.0
Franklin	265	3 018	19 681	15.2	67.5	9.3	72.4	4 331	11 606	28 622	2.8	1.3	39 611	8.4	11.8	10.6
Gasconade	NA	NA	2 938	8.1	61.1	8.0	13.0	4 106	10 774	22 328	5.5	1.2	31 080	10.7	15.3	14.1
Gentry	29	0	1 437	3.4	71.0	10.3	7.1	4 966	9 535	17 594	-1.9	1.0	26 553	13.0	16.5	16.3
Greene	408	5 315	57 451	15.9	78.9	20.7	156.7	4 416	12 468	24 285	0.8	2.7	33 087	12.2	18.5	15.7
Grundy	330	2 298	2 357	3.4	71.3	10.1	9.0	5 031	9 858	18 084	-6.8	1.9	28 036	14.8	20.9	19.3
Harrison	NA	NA	1 675	3.1	71.6	8.3	9.0	5 505	10 118	17 460	2.6	1.5	24 936	15.6	23.0	21.8
Henry	170	3 512	4 197	4.7	67.6	10.3	15.6	4 449	9 835	18 476	-9.1	0.8	20 755	19.4	32.1	28.7
Hickory	NA	NA	1 137	5.0	60.4	6.4	9.0	4 727	8 583	16 010	11.0	0.4	28 075	14.1	18.9	18.7
Holt	NA	NA	1 328	2.2	75.4	12.2	5.2	5 164	9 757	18 729	-3.8	1.2				
Howard	NA	NA	2 613	27.6	69.9	16.8	8.0	4 689	9 854	21 378	6.1	0.8	28 827	13.9	18.7	17.0
Howell	173	2 488	6 815	6.4	61.2	8.7	32.0	4 387	8 776	16 564	1.3	1.4	23 423	19.6	28.6	25.0
Iron	NA	NA	2 462	4.1	56.3	6.8	12.3	4 852	8 232	17 303	-12.2	0.5	23 782	20.8	30.2	26.2
Jackson	1 179	7 782	155 666	17.1	79.5	20.0	652.2	6 121	13 712	27 853	-1.6	2.6	37 732	12.2	18.4	16.1

1. Data for serious crimes have not been adjusted for underreporting; this may affect comparability between geographic areas and over time.   2. Per 100,000 population estimated by the FBI.   3. All persons 3 years old and over enrolled in nursery school through college.   4. Persons 25 years old and over.   5. Elementary and secondary education expenditures, local government fiscal years ending between July 1, 1996 and June 30, 1997.   6. Based on population enumerated as of April 1, 1990.

STATE County	Personal income, 1998 Total (mil dol)	Percent change, 1997–1998	Per capita[1] Dollars	Per capita[1] Rank	Wages and salaries[2] (mil dol)	Proprietor's income (mil dol)	Dividends, interest, and rent (mil dol)	Transfer payments Total (mil dol)	Government payments to individuals Total (mil dol)	Social Security (mil dol)	Medical payments (mil dol)	Income mainte-nance (mil dol)	Unemploy-ment insurance (mil dol)
	62	63	64	65	66	67	68	69	70	71	72	73	74
MISSISSIPPI—Cont'd													
Sunflower	466	1.0	13 884	3 016	304	35	68	127	120	35	51	28	2
Tallahatchie	196	-6.8	13 223	3 061	61	5	32	66	63	21	25	15	1
Tate	496	7.3	20 670	1 496	169	35	53	85	81	29	29	10	1
Tippah	362	5.1	17 202	2 561	200	23	53	90	86	33	37	11	1
Tishomingo	303	4.3	16 217	2 758	154	20	53	83	79	35	32	7	2
Tunica	152	-1.7	18 857	2 105	458	4	27	34	32	9	13	9	1
Union	457	6.3	19 166	1 991	228	32	68	86	82	38	31	9	1
Walthall	223	5.8	15 504	2 878	77	33	28	58	56	20	23	10	1
Warren	1 183	4.6	23 967	650	819	58	189	181	172	59	76	24	3
Washington	1 164	1.9	17 863	2 389	715	89	167	260	248	82	93	61	5
Wayne	346	6.1	17 032	2 602	161	48	48	73	69	26	25	14	1
Webster	175	3.4	16 502	2 707	76	11	32	49	47	21	18	5	0
Wilkinson	134	2.8	14 647	2 963	49	6	20	45	43	13	19	9	1
Winston	342	3.0	17 746	2 421	170	25	59	78	75	30	28	12	1
Yalobusha	211	3.1	17 026	2 607	87	16	32	60	58	21	25	9	0
Yazoo	455	5.6	17 847	2 393	216	41	77	116	111	38	46	23	1
MISSOURI	136 754	3.8	25 150	X	89 563	9 667	26 900	20 233	19 273	8 195	8 104	1 640	298
Adair	459	1.2	18 938	2 082	279	33	95	93	89	32	40	6	2
Andrew	330	2.9	21 202	1 329	56	23	75	46	44	21	17	3	1
Atchison	144	-2.3	20 472	1 570	48	26	34	29	28	13	10	2	0
Audrain	536	5.1	22 765	902	315	31	115	104	100	46	43	7	1
Barry	604	6.2	18 215	2 290	364	76	125	130	124	54	52	10	2
Barton	231	-1.6	19 138	2 009	130	16	46	46	44	20	18	4	1
Bates	285	-0.3	17 995	2 346	84	27	61	70	67	30	28	5	1
Benton	268	3.7	15 792	2 828	71	27	59	90	87	41	34	6	1
Bollinger	168	1.2	14 556	2 966	40	13	24	44	42	18	16	5	1
Boone	3 302	5.9	25 606	426	2 297	218	653	349	326	132	143	27	2
Buchanan	1 854	4.7	22 669	933	1 243	113	351	345	331	140	137	27	4
Butler	825	4.4	20 407	1 592	464	85	127	214	207	70	95	24	3
Caldwell	150	1.5	17 067	2 596	34	16	32	35	33	15	14	3	1
Callaway	759	5.3	20 250	1 636	389	51	124	121	115	52	48	8	2
Camden	733	5.5	21 585	1 230	349	66	193	145	139	74	48	7	2
Cape Girardeau	1 561	5.1	23 573	726	1 087	103	331	227	216	95	83	16	4
Carroll	196	-4.2	19 260	1 970	60	18	51	46	44	20	18	4	1
Carter	95	0.0	14 889	2 941	29	12	14	31	30	11	14	4	0
Cass	1 804	5.7	22 393	1 002	456	117	288	232	218	101	86	11	7
Cedar	222	4.1	16 833	2 651	71	22	52	67	64	29	27	5	1
Chariton	163	-2.9	18 874	2 097	48	24	39	40	38	17	17	3	1
Christian	979	9.8	19 990	1 714	268	98	162	137	129	60	50	9	2
Clark	118	-9.0	15 878	2 812	32	2	25	30	28	12	12	2	1
Clay	4 762	4.9	26 991	305	2 948	274	698	500	469	227	186	20	7
Clinton	416	4.4	21 860	1 140	100	30	65	60	56	25	24	3	1
Cole	1 827	4.9	26 399	354	1 584	96	358	214	202	92	82	12	3
Cooper	311	2.9	19 373	1 925	131	26	64	61	58	25	26	3	1
Crawford	399	4.4	17 888	2 380	140	29	65	93	89	39	37	8	2
Dade	143	1.5	18 208	2 292	43	13	28	34	33	15	13	2	1
Dallas	252	8.2	16 480	2 709	58	27	42	59	57	24	23	6	1
Daviess	144	-6.1	18 180	2 301	42	17	32	30	29	14	11	2	1
De Kalb	164	2.1	14 561	2 962	72	21	25	36	34	16	14	2	1
Dent	262	4.6	18 531	2 202	118	21	45	70	68	27	30	7	1
Douglas	182	2.0	14 630	2 964	58	17	34	52	50	21	20	6	1
Dunklin	593	-2.2	18 138	2 310	251	41	90	184	178	56	88	26	2
Franklin	2 103	5.3	22 900	871	955	98	356	286	269	131	105	18	5
Gasconade	309	5.4	20 853	1 437	141	18	69	61	58	29	24	3	1
Gentry	132	-10.2	19 113	2 019	48	18	29	35	34	14	16	2	0
Greene	5 678	3.6	25 059	482	4 157	595	1 186	813	773	329	306	61	8
Grundy	204	-1.2	19 980	1 718	88	16	44	47	45	19	18	4	1
Harrison	167	4.9	19 754	1 793	60	20	36	42	40	16	19	3	0
Henry	408	3.3	19 207	1 984	186	33	94	102	98	43	43	8	1
Hickory	124	1.6	14 446	2 973	24	11	28	51	50	24	19	4	1
Holt	113	-1.6	20 386	1 610	34	18	26	26	25	11	10	2	0
Howard	188	2.3	19 352	1 936	61	17	40	40	38	15	18	3	0
Howell	629	4.3	17 582	2 471	335	53	121	168	162	67	68	17	2
Iron	176	1.2	16 144	2 775	99	11	31	57	55	22	25	6	1
Jackson	17 281	3.2	26 380	356	15 154	1 595	3 016	2 414	2 298	940	991	208	39

1. Based on the resident population estimated as of July 1 of the year shown.   2. Includes other labor income.

Table B. States and Counties — Earnings, Social Security, and Housing

STATE County	Earnings, 1998 Total (mil dol)	Farm	Goods-related[1] Total	Manu-facturing	Service-related and other[2] Total	Retail trade	Finance, insur-ance, and real estate	Services	Govern-ment	Social Security beneficiaries, December 1998 Number	Rate[3]	Supplemental Security Income recipients, December 1998	Housing units, 1990 Total	Percent change, 1980–1990
	75	76	77	78	79	80	81	82	83	84	85	86	87	88
MISSISSIPPI—Cont'd														
Sunflower	339	8.4	21.3	19.2	36.5	8.7	2.1	11.2	33.8	5 241	152	2 283	10 167	-1.0
Tallahatchie	65	1.1	13.8	10.7	D	10.9	2.9	D	33.2	3 326	223	1 552	5 492	-5.5
Tate	204	2.8	D	27.9	D	14.6	3.7	18.0	21.0	4 022	168	1 022	7 474	16.9
Tippah	223	1.4	D	50.2	D	8.5	3.4	9.6	12.3	4 781	227	1 412	7 846	10.1
Tishomingo	174	0.2	52.2	44.5	D	9.3	2.9	13.8	11.8	4 808	258	951	8 455	7.4
Tunica	462	0.0	5.1	2.4	91.4	1.8	0.5	87.3	3.5	1 475	183	731	2 990	-2.0
Union	260	0.8	45.9	42.3	42.2	15.8	2.6	15.0	11.1	5 187	218	936	9 104	10.2
Walthall	110	17.3	D	23.2	D	6.9	2.5	16.1	17.4	2 882	201	963	5 643	14.4
Warren	878	0.0	D	20.1	D	8.9	2.2	30.8	27.4	7 969	161	2 103	19 512	1.2
Washington	804	2.8	D	20.2	56.5	9.2	2.6	27.0	17.9	11 392	175	5 217	24 567	1.6
Wayne	209	11.8	35.0	19.1	38.0	11.5	3.0	12.0	15.1	3 831	188	1 359	7 723	12.8
Webster	87	0.5	48.0	42.1	38.0	8.7	2.3	17.6	13.5	3 026	287	595	4 326	10.4
Wilkinson	56	0.5	D	D	D	9.2	4.1	25.1	26.9	1 996	218	956	4 242	12.5
Winston	195	1.9	D	38.6	D	9.4	2.5	18.0	11.2	4 093	211	1 055	7 613	5.9
Yalobusha	103	0.0	D	40.9	D	10.4	3.7	9.0	19.4	3 000	243	1 011	5 414	-3.8
Yazoo	257	4.4	D	27.9	39.9	7.9	7.2	15.4	23.1	5 342	209	1 955	9 549	0.2
MISSOURI	99 230	0.4	24.9	18.2	59.7	9.4	7.9	27.0	15.0	987 660	182	111 929	2 199 129	10.6
Adair	312	-0.3	20.2	16.1	55.2	13.0	3.9	31.5	24.9	4 170	172	549	10 097	2.7
Andrew	79	4.8	D	3.3	D	15.1	D	19.0	22.5	2 618	168	157	5 841	5.9
Atchison	74	13.7	D	2.2	D	10.6	5.3	25.3	16.0	1 563	223	101	3 298	-8.8
Audrain	346	0.8	D	39.8	D	9.3	3.5	11.6	21.2	5 421	230	360	10 039	-4.8
Barry	440	7.3	D	41.1	D	8.6	2.5	16.0	11.2	7 255	219	687	12 908	15.5
Barton	146	1.3	50.1	44.0	34.2	9.5	3.4	11.3	14.5	2 639	218	242	5 014	3.6
Bates	111	6.2	D	8.0	D	12.5	4.7	15.9	24.6	3 954	251	318	6 782	-3.2
Benton	98	1.4	D	9.5	D	18.0	6.2	18.4	26.7	5 123	301	391	10 280	23.5
Bollinger	53	1.1	D	12.8	D	10.8	D	18.3	23.0	2 531	220	341	4 542	6.7
Boone	2 515	0.1	14.3	8.5	48.7	9.6	9.1	22.2	36.9	15 455	120	1 789	44 695	19.4
Buchanan	1 356	0.4	D	23.5	D	9.8	5.4	25.7	15.1	16 664	204	2 091	35 652	-1.5
Butler	549	3.3	D	16.6	D	11.7	2.9	27.4	19.6	9 832	242	2 228	17 046	7.2
Caldwell	50	7.5	D	2.0	D	13.8	5.1	14.2	28.3	1 997	226	151	3 649	-5.3
Callaway	439	2.3	24.9	16.0	D	7.6	2.8	D	26.5	6 366	170	542	13 003	10.9
Camden	415	0.0	D	11.3	D	20.6	7.5	30.6	11.4	8 738	257	432	25 662	51.4
Cape Girardeau	1 190	0.1	25.7	18.1	60.5	11.6	4.5	28.9	13.9	11 526	174	1 231	25 315	11.3
Carroll	79	8.8	D	12.0	52.2	10.6	6.6	19.9	20.9	2 535	248	230	5 001	-8.8
Carter	41	-1.6	20.5	16.6	D	12.6	3.9	18.0	32.6	1 503	235	341	2 693	18.8
Cass	573	0.1	26.3	6.5	51.0	16.1	5.2	19.9	22.5	11 845	147	515	24 337	27.2
Cedar	94	2.1	D	16.4	D	14.9	4.3	17.4	25.9	3 830	290	356	6 035	7.2
Chariton	71	15.8	D	12.4	D	7.6	6.3	15.9	17.6	2 149	249	161	4 479	-6.9
Christian	366	-0.3	D	16.5	D	15.5	6.6	17.1	14.2	7 670	157	639	12 812	48.5
Clark	34	-14.1	D	D	D	13.9	5.3	16.9	39.9	1 544	207	123	3 398	-2.8
Clay	3 222	0.0	32.4	26.4	55.8	11.0	4.6	23.9	11.7	25 061	142	1 291	63 000	20.4
Clinton	130	-1.3	D	4.6	D	14.9	11.8	30.0	19.2	3 064	161	226	6 559	7.1
Cole	1 680	0.2	D	7.0	D	7.3	5.8	21.3	41.0	11 085	160	876	24 939	18.1
Cooper	157	2.0	27.0	19.9	47.1	10.8	3.8	15.7	23.9	3 149	196	209	6 002	2.3
Crawford	169	-1.9	D	29.2	D	17.4	3.6	19.6	13.8	4 960	224	509	9 030	4.2
Dade	56	4.2	D	10.0	D	8.0	3.5	14.2	25.3	2 059	261	177	3 543	1.9
Dallas	84	-0.5	D	11.8	D	19.2	6.4	17.8	22.5	3 421	224	389	5 484	8.2
Daviess	60	9.9	30.4	17.5	D	8.9	4.5	9.6	24.8	1 817	232	114	3 613	-5.5
De Kalb	93	6.5	D	2.4	D	10.5	3.4	11.2	45.7	2 087	188	85	3 358	-3.6
Dent	138	0.2	D	13.4	D	12.4	4.3	13.9	19.2	3 637	258	540	6 115	-3.2
Douglas	76	6.0	D	30.0	D	12.2	3.0	14.9	18.8	3 095	249	435	5 105	9.5
Dunklin	292	1.1	D	19.9	D	14.6	4.8	23.3	16.7	7 998	245	2 365	14 102	-4.8
Franklin	1 053	0.2	44.1	34.5	44.0	11.7	3.7	17.7	11.7	15 559	170	1 272	32 451	17.9
Gasconade	159	-0.6	D	38.7	D	11.2	3.0	13.7	15.2	3 600	242	187	7 158	8.1
Gentry	66	15.2	D	14.9	D	14.2	3.6	19.3	18.5	2 015	290	155	3 232	-9.6
Greene	4 752	0.0	21.2	15.7	66.4	13.3	6.3	29.2	12.4	40 478	179	4 819	87 910	17.3
Grundy	104	0.3	D	22.9	D	11.4	4.3	21.9	23.3	2 534	249	251	5 113	-8.1
Harrison	80	12.0	D	2.2	D	23.7	3.8	16.4	23.8	2 338	275	208	4 245	-12.5
Henry	219	1.4	D	20.0	D	13.9	4.9	18.4	19.6	5 512	260	608	9 317	5.2
Hickory	34	0.8	D	8.2	D	16.0	5.3	21.0	26.3	3 034	352	200	5 482	15.8
Holt	52	25.7	D	6.2	44.4	10.1	4.5	12.2	18.6	1 441	259	104	3 190	-14.0
Howard	78	2.8	D	22.3	D	8.4	4.0	23.3	17.2	1 939	199	225	4 025	-1.8
Howell	387	-0.2	28.4	23.2	55.8	14.6	3.7	24.9	16.0	9 412	263	1 362	13 326	12.3
Iron	110	0.2	D	20.0	D	7.1	2.4	18.4	14.0	2 831	260	480	4 700	7.1
Jackson	16 748	0.0	19.4	12.4	65.5	7.8	11.0	30.2	15.1	107 718	164	12 425	280 729	7.0

1. Covers mining, construction, and manufacturing.   2. Covers private sector earnings in agricultural services, forestry, and fisheries; transportation and public utilities; wholesale trade; retail trade; finance, insurance, and real estate; and services.   3. Per 1,000 resident population estimated as of July 1 of the year shown.

STATE County	Housing units, 1990 (cont'd)								Civilian labor force, 1999				Civilian employment, 1990[5]		
	Occupied units										Unemployment			Percent	
			Owner-occupied			Renter-occupied									
				Owner cost as a percent of income											
	Total	Percent	Median value[1]	With a mortgage	Without a mortgage	Median rent[2]	Rent as percent of income	Substandard units[3] (percent)	Total	Percent change, 1998–1999	Total	Rate[4]	Total	Professional, managerial, and technical	Precision production, craft, and repair
	89	90	91	92	93	94	95	96	97	98	99	100	101	102	103
MISSISSIPPI—Cont'd															
Sunflower	9 650	60.1	37 800	22.1	15.6	253	29.4	13.2	10 762	1.9	1 069	9.9	10 293	20.6	11.1
Tallahatchie	5 034	69.5	31 500	23.9	14.5	189	26.6	17.3	5 137	-2.2	503	9.8	4 896	15.0	12.9
Tate	7 024	75.6	49 500	20.4	13.7	293	26.3	10.7	10 082	-3.9	585	5.8	9 143	19.9	13.9
Tippah	7 158	79.4	35 200	20.6	12.4	241	22.7	6.1	10 168	-1.6	480	4.7	8 247	16.5	16.3
Tishomingo	7 059	79.4	38 700	20.6	12.5	212	21.8	2.7	9 186	-0.3	743	8.1	7 300	17.6	16.5
Tunica	2 526	53.8	35 400	26.5	14.3	222	35.1	21.2	5 591	10.5	360	6.4	2 360	16.4	9.1
Union	8 367	78.2	39 700	21.1	12.6	248	22.1	3.7	12 233	1.2	468	3.8	10 168	16.2	15.6
Walthall	4 929	84.3	39 100	30.3	15.9	223	27.3	12.7	6 154	4.3	341	5.5	4 653	16.9	14.3
Warren	17 407	68.9	50 600	18.7	13.4	332	28.5	5.8	25 940	-0.6	1 178	4.5	19 373	32.5	12.2
Washington	22 593	59.6	41 700	20.6	15.2	318	31.3	11.2	26 425	-6.7	2 513	9.5	24 131	24.3	10.4
Wayne	6 858	83.7	37 100	26.5	12.9	220	27.3	9.7	8 559	-2.1	535	6.3	7 091	18.7	17.1
Webster	3 826	78.5	36 000	21.2	12.4	205	24.7	6.7	4 327	-3.4	228	5.3	3 819	17.8	12.4
Wilkinson	3 347	81.4	35 700	25.7	19.0	207	24.2	10.2	2 983	-10.3	455	15.3	2 957	15.2	9.3
Winston	7 061	81.6	35 100	21.0	12.9	256	28.7	8.2	7 647	-1.2	486	6.4	7 523	18.4	14.2
Yalobusha	4 614	79.2	35 500	23.0	14.1	205	25.9	8.5	4 531	-8.8	374	8.3	4 549	16.8	13.7
Yazoo	8 813	66.3	38 400	21.1	14.8	234	30.1	10.9	9 357	-1.6	754	8.1	8 298	19.8	11.6
MISSOURI	1 961 206	68.8	59 800	18.4	12.3	368	25.2	3.0	2 847 386	-0.3	95 947	3.4	2 367 395	27.8	11.1
Adair	9 060	59.4	41 900	17.8	13.0	307	33.3	2.2	13 759	-2.0	250	1.8	11 011	29.9	8.7
Andrew	5 429	78.6	45 900	16.9	11.9	303	21.5	1.0	8 283	2.9	237	2.9	6 645	21.6	13.0
Atchison	2 961	65.9	28 800	18.9	12.2	243	21.0	1.1	3 078	-4.6	65	2.1	3 258	21.7	11.3
Audrain	9 205	74.2	36 000	16.1	12.4	276	24.6	3.1	13 105	1.0	343	2.6	10 332	22.3	12.7
Barry	10 858	77.2	42 300	20.5	12.2	280	22.8	4.6	15 305	1.9	549	3.6	11 640	13.9	15.3
Barton	4 524	73.8	31 800	17.8	12.8	253	20.8	2.5	7 301	3.1	183	2.5	5 057	16.9	11.0
Bates	5 918	74.6	31 400	19.4	13.3	266	26.4	3.3	7 505	1.8	315	4.2	5 939	19.5	15.5
Benton	5 764	81.4	38 300	22.2	12.7	262	30.5	4.8	6 022	-0.3	340	5.6	4 831	18.2	12.2
Bollinger	3 946	81.7	29 400	15.3	13.4	241	27.3	8.1	5 277	0.6	214	4.1	4 151	15.7	14.9
Boone	41 937	55.0	65 700	17.5	12.0	381	27.3	2.1	81 391	-2.2	1 005	1.2	58 017	38.3	7.8
Buchanan	32 486	68.0	40 800	15.2	11.9	304	24.0	2.0	41 809	0.9	1 522	3.6	35 952	23.4	11.5
Butler	15 334	68.1	36 300	18.7	12.8	255	27.5	3.3	19 564	-1.2	786	4.0	15 285	22.8	12.0
Caldwell	3 222	76.2	25 600	17.5	12.9	243	24.4	2.4	3 183	-2.1	148	4.6	3 354	16.9	12.3
Callaway	11 552	76.9	48 900	17.2	12.2	313	22.1	2.9	20 968	-1.1	528	2.5	15 556	23.4	11.8
Camden	11 305	80.7	71 700	22.3	11.6	346	24.5	2.9	17 079	2.3	791	4.6	11 544	26.0	13.2
Cape Girardeau	23 390	67.7	56 900	17.8	12.2	327	27.2	1.9	37 247	1.7	1 005	2.7	29 939	27.2	10.7
Carroll	4 332	73.4	26 900	16.7	12.4	231	24.2	2.4	4 834	-0.8	190	3.9	4 206	19.1	8.8
Carter	2 128	73.8	29 900	19.2	13.6	241	27.9	7.8	2 781	0.9	174	6.3	1 917	21.6	10.4
Cass	22 892	76.4	64 600	20.1	12.5	404	24.4	2.3	43 701	2.2	1 074	2.5	31 131	24.1	16.0
Cedar	5 003	79.6	34 200	19.7	11.8	231	25.7	3.2	5 033	-6.8	180	3.6	4 655	19.2	8.0
Chariton	3 661	77.9	26 100	17.6	13.1	222	20.4	3.7	4 125	7.4	166	4.0	4 012	15.6	11.2
Christian	11 937	79.6	58 500	19.9	12.0	340	23.0	2.7	26 920	3.9	679	2.5	15 889	20.2	14.7
Clark	2 859	75.9	26 300	16.4	12.8	225	25.9	5.7	3 650	1.8	174	4.8	3 252	13.5	13.1
Clay	58 915	67.5	68 500	18.0	11.7	429	23.1	2.0	103 945	0.5	2 503	2.4	81 396	28.5	11.1
Clinton	6 112	77.6	47 900	18.0	13.0	312	24.0	2.2	9 552	1.2	290	3.0	7 428	20.7	14.8
Cole	22 976	67.6	60 200	17.3	11.8	334	22.0	1.6	39 383	-1.2	765	1.9	30 764	33.2	9.4
Cooper	5 359	75.0	39 600	17.7	13.1	274	24.6	3.0	8 343	-1.5	243	2.9	6 419	21.5	13.9
Crawford	7 299	78.4	37 900	20.9	12.6	278	26.3	3.7	9 692	-4.3	494	5.1	7 583	16.9	16.8
Dade	2 976	77.3	30 900	18.3	12.6	218	22.1	3.9	3 272	-2.0	130	4.0	3 086	17.5	13.2
Dallas	4 899	78.8	33 000	23.2	13.1	233	26.7	4.7	6 443	-0.6	267	4.1	4 947	15.6	16.6
Daviess	3 040	75.3	24 600	16.2	13.6	238	22.9	4.6	3 533	-2.7	116	3.3	3 059	17.8	11.2
De Kalb	3 054	73.1	33 200	17.2	12.1	229	23.1	3.2	4 810	1.1	132	2.7	3 416	21.8	12.0
Dent	5 327	73.9	34 800	19.6	12.7	258	28.8	4.5	6 344	-6.2	398	6.3	4 952	20.8	11.2
Douglas	4 587	77.6	34 000	18.5	12.8	247	23.0	6.2	5 508	-1.8	297	5.4	4 756	13.1	14.4
Dunklin	13 128	66.8	30 000	18.3	13.2	229	28.4	3.7	14 099	-5.1	709	5.0	11 883	20.0	13.3
Franklin	28 856	78.0	58 300	18.5	11.9	348	23.3	4.0	46 046	-0.3	1 634	3.5	37 568	19.8	16.3
Gasconade	5 543	80.3	41 800	17.9	12.6	253	22.9	2.8	7 856	1.4	229	2.9	6 288	16.9	14.9
Gentry	2 756	74.5	23 000	17.3	13.8	219	22.3	2.7	3 545	-0.9	90	2.5	2 878	21.4	9.8
Greene	81 463	63.4	58 200	17.9	11.6	344	25.8	2.2	124 929	0.5	2 848	2.3	101 750	27.5	10.1
Grundy	4 346	72.5	24 200	16.1	13.6	231	25.3	2.4	4 934	2.3	154	3.1	4 420	20.2	10.6
Harrison	3 574	73.9	20 200	16.3	13.1	201	23.4	3.8	4 359	1.0	102	2.3	3 678	20.1	9.1
Henry	8 189	73.4	36 500	20.0	13.4	275	27.0	3.1	10 417	1.0	394	3.8	8 179	20.3	14.1
Hickory	3 183	84.2	37 500	22.4	11.8	225	27.2	2.9	2 901	7.5	150	5.2	2 351	18.2	11.3
Holt	2 440	73.6	22 600	16.9	12.8	203	22.5	3.4	2 643	0.5	91	3.4	2 449	19.8	10.7
Howard	3 571	75.0	31 400	15.8	13.0	263	23.7	2.5	4 719	0.3	160	3.4	4 319	21.8	10.8
Howell	12 283	73.8	36 800	18.9	13.0	243	26.6	6.0	17 562	-0.7	689	3.9	12 712	17.6	13.4
Iron	3 995	75.9	34 900	17.8	12.8	256	28.2	6.7	4 196	-2.7	300	7.1	3 716	20.2	14.5
Jackson	252 582	61.3	58 400	18.4	12.4	402	25.5	2.8	359 498	-0.2	12 620	3.5	309 069	29.2	9.9

1. Specified owner-occupied units. 2. Specified renter-occupied units. 3. Overcrowded or lacking complete plumbing facilities. 4. Percent of civilian labor force. 5. Persons 16 years and older.

Table B. States and Counties — **Nonfarm Employment and Agriculture**

STATE County	Number of establish-ments	Total	Health Care and Social Assistance	Manufac-turing	Retail trade	Finance and Insurance	Professional Scientific and Technical Services	Total (mil dol)	Average per employee (dollars)	Number	Less than 50 acres	500 acres and over	Whose principal occupation is farming (percent)
	104	105	106	107	108	109	110	111	112	113	114	115	116
MISSISSIPPI—Cont'd													
Sunflower	498	7 174	1 026	2 739	1 187	229	98	142	19 727	350	8.9	52.6	70.3
Tallahatchie	191	1 494	303	352	281	47	21	27	17 831	355	12.4	38.0	52.7
Tate	418	5 374	360	2 074	1 133	188	70	100	18 683	508	24.0	13.2	40.0
Tippah	411	6 810	535	3 321	797	176	82	145	21 257	501	18.4	7.8	33.9
Tishomingo	417	5 192	422	2 723	613	149	61	106	20 371	258	21.7	6.2	26.4
Tunica	175	17 350	201	380	299	72	D	418	24 108	95	1.1	74.7	88.4
Union	459	9 121	670	4 420	1 085	194	80	199	21 772	549	23.3	6.4	29.0
Walthall	231	2 756	403	1 032	386	79	24	47	16 897	538	21.4	6.7	47.2
Warren	1 179	20 077	2 164	4 852	2 968	455	818	452	22 513	159	17.0	32.7	49.7
Washington	1 507	22 631	3 070	5 404	3 717	483	424	449	19 854	283	8.8	60.4	76.7
Wayne	379	5 257	664	1 520	832	175	45	103	19 671	458	31.2	6.1	40.8
Webster	195	3 047	389	1 706	289	62	48	49	15 938	289	19.4	11.4	38.1
Wilkinson	170	1 944	376	465	231	57	15	34	17 408	196	19.9	26.5	40.8
Winston	407	5 457	481	2 042	747	135	158	124	22 705	458	19.9	7.2	34.3
Yalobusha	238	3 035	224	1 527	384	96	44	59	19 531	278	14.4	13.7	37.1
Yazoo	452	5 579	679	1 998	1 048	190	70	126	22 590	424	9.7	39.9	53.3
MISSOURI	143 912	2 310 122	320 300	382 003	304 009	123 925	108 911	64 669	27 994	98 860	20.1	15.5	45.3
Adair	632	8 993	2 282	1 473	1 528	233	123	178	19 809	861	14.4	18.2	43.3
Andrew	241	2 228	345	23	1 022	57	31	39	17 365	820	18.4	15.5	50.1
Atchison	223	1 591	583	33	347	82	18	26	16 336	471	11.9	46.5	72.0
Audrain	655	8 303	1 441	2 958	1 126	259	126	205	24 692	1 005	15.1	23.5	57.7
Barry	783	12 292	957	6 891	1 411	304	589	258	21 026	1 598	27.8	6.4	45.7
Barton	301	4 620	445	2 312	593	146	128	95	20 579	896	15.3	24.2	53.3
Bates	389	2 871	527	416	601	148	65	48	16 729	1 250	17.3	18.9	47.8
Benton	407	2 402	235	369	586	116	61	37	15 315	804	14.1	15.0	49.8
Bollinger	212	1 411	178	296	283	42	21	21	14 870	832	13.5	12.5	40.0
Boone	3 675	58 592	13 754	5 700	8 956	4 822	1 960	1 353	23 095	1 227	28.8	10.8	35.6
Buchanan	2 342	34 603	5 790	6 818	4 431	1 508	1 030	849	24 533	776	28.5	12.5	45.7
Butler	1 067	14 393	3 134	3 150	2 432	452	275	291	20 242	678	22.3	25.1	52.2
Caldwell	185	1 011	209	55	168	83	19	17	17 012	845	17.0	13.6	43.0
Callaway	695	9 767	2 138	1 865	1 178	270	96	252	25 841	1 338	19.7	10.3	37.5
Camden	1 516	11 896	1 304	1 471	2 713	446	398	238	19 970	584	14.0	15.6	36.6
Cape Girardeau	2 282	34 596	6 960	5 876	6 273	1 209	863	783	22 636	1 161	21.7	9.7	46.6
Carroll	249	1 950	374	391	289	111	23	30	15 271	952	15.7	25.8	55.9
Carter	137	818	122	272	144	D	12	12	14 329	202	15.3	15.3	33.2
Cass	1 631	13 180	1 977	1 201	2 807	455	300	266	20 189	1 519	31.4	8.7	41.2
Cedar	301	2 615	607	564	406	114	66	44	16 831	865	18.3	11.2	45.5
Chariton	203	1 372	141	354	244	110	22	23	17 046	1 071	14.5	23.4	54.2
Christian	1 103	9 918	963	2 711	1 562	329	197	182	18 395	1 209	34.7	5.0	41.4
Clark	152	888	81	95	272	64	13	14	15 670	634	9.5	24.3	55.0
Clay	4 504	78 899	8 916	14 354	12 196	1 704	4 579	2 391	30 310	634	34.7	9.8	35.0
Clinton	412	2 980	792	220	744	205	61	53	17 879	768	25.0	14.6	40.1
Cole	2 106	35 630	5 448	3 089	5 013	1 831	1 099	812	22 786	1 045	20.0	5.4	34.3
Cooper	415	4 064	684	853	696	133	69	69	16 874	879	15.1	20.7	51.3
Crawford	487	4 917	563	1 476	1 073	134	136	94	19 032	691	15.8	12.7	38.2
Dade	150	1 171	110	334	141	49	14	20	17 377	808	17.3	17.3	47.6
Dallas	263	2 869	983	556	477	119	44	35	12 036	1 130	23.3	8.2	44.8
Daviess	183	1 352	172	477	187	66	D	20	14 780	886	15.8	20.2	47.5
De Kalb	202	1 712	327	43	267	245	D	29	16 923	769	17.7	16.8	45.0
Dent	337	3 742	503	1 004	601	131	61	79	21 142	727	11.8	17.3	36.0
Douglas	201	1 719	231	425	347	57	21	26	15 205	1 206	16.7	12.1	47.3
Dunklin	773	7 863	2 129	1 219	1 652	425	128	141	17 915	473	16.5	43.3	70.2
Franklin	2 368	30 900	3 000	10 863	4 596	724	722	724	23 426	1 592	25.4	7.4	37.4
Gasconade	438	4 206	308	1 624	729	114	84	89	21 053	762	11.7	10.0	37.3
Gentry	206	1 770	536	378	291	58	24	30	16 732	667	13.5	22.0	43.8
Greene	7 533	129 375	21 480	18 849	19 012	5 483	4 964	3 051	23 582	1 997	40.7	5.0	36.8
Grundy	277	2 837	524	922	454	107	50	56	19 866	667	15.0	18.4	46.9
Harrison	260	2 271	521	77	662	107	32	34	14 773	901	13.2	25.7	48.3
Henry	658	6 676	1 331	1 900	1 090	254	121	137	20 530	938	17.9	19.0	46.7
Hickory	152	831	129	98	142	35	D	11	12 668	521	10.4	19.0	56.2
Holt	130	872	147	105	214	69	4	17	18 975	465	12.0	34.2	63.0
Howard	214	1 901	453	356	189	83	32	33	17 510	709	13.3	18.2	44.6
Howell	984	12 040	2 303	3 768	2 045	266	223	227	18 814	1 637	22.0	9.2	38.7
Iron	243	2 294	611	334	316	74	18	56	24 268	274	14.6	11.3	35.0
Jackson	18 077	349 080	46 967	38 053	38 510	27 688	23 054	11 423	32 723	765	45.0	7.2	36.7

STATE County	Acreage (1,000)	Percent change, 1992–1997	Average size of farm	Total irrigated (1,000)	Total cropland (1,000)	Average per farm ($1,000)	Average per acre (dollars)	Value of machinery and equipment Average per farm ($1,000)	Total (mil dol)	Average per farm (dollars)	Crops	Livestock and poultry products	$10,000 or more	$100,000 or more	Percent of land owned by Fed. Gov. 1997	Water consumption 1995 (mil gal/day)
	117	118	119	120	121	122	123	124	125	126	127	128	129	130	131	132
MISSISSIPPI—Cont'd																
Sunflower	348	-3.5	995	156	296	1 160	1 147	239	164	469 528	61.7	38.3	81.1	61.4	0.6	352.8
Tallahatchie	297	8.7	836	95	250	743	947	131	83	232 887	96.9	3.1	49.6	34.6	5.0	107.4
Tate	135	-4.5	265	1	77	288	1 136	36	24	48 042	47.4	52.6	36.0	10.2	5.7	5.7
Tippah	114	5.4	227	D	47	181	799	22	9	18 921	65.1	34.9	20.8	3.2	5.2	2.5
Tishomingo	45	9.4	174	D	17	187	887	27	3	10 766	32.1	67.8	15.1	1.2	7.7	4.4
Tunica	202	-12.4	2 130	60	185	1 971	938	346	64	676 490	89.9	10.1	87.4	66.3	1.2	140.4
Union	102	2.2	186	0	50	142	756	24	10	17 971	46.0	54.0	19.3	4.0	4.0	3.0
Walthall	110	2.2	205	D	50	250	1 310	27	51	94 370	2.4	97.6	34.2	16.5	0.0	2.2
Warren	98	-14.2	615	D	51	547	902	71	12	77 345	92.5	7.5	34.0	15.1	0.8	81.8
Washington	343	0.2	1 211	137	308	1 285	1 095	271	146	517 598	78.6	21.4	85.5	64.7	3.1	302.9
Wayne	76	3.8	165	0	28	215	1 349	46	63	136 739	2.1	97.9	38.9	22.5	17.3	2.2
Webster	79	3.5	272	D	35	201	731	44	13	43 294	56.7	43.3	28.0	8.7	0.6	1.4
Wilkinson	109	21.4	557	D	38	573	1 052	37	5	27 020	28.8	71.2	27.0	4.6	6.1	2.5
Winston	88	6.1	192	D	36	155	1 008	25	8	18 082	14.4	85.6	19.7	3.3	13.9	3.3
Yalobusha	86	9.7	308	D	41	196	707	49	9	34 150	80.0	20.0	26.3	5.8	19.8	2.7
Yazoo	312	-13.7	737	15	209	548	746	89	75	176 468	78.5	21.5	51.4	29.2	5.2	29.9
MISSOURI	28 826	1.0	292	882	19 229	309	1 069	41	5 368	54 297	43.0	57.0	44.4	10.8	4.3	7 029.0
Adair	268	0.4	311	D	171	211	650	32	22	25 324	47.7	52.3	47.2	4.8	0.0	4.0
Andrew	227	-0.1	276	0	178	321	1 174	47	40	49 318	70.0	30.0	55.2	14.1	0.0	3.0
Atchison	294	-3.2	625	6	256	708	1 119	117	63	132 798	89.1	10.9	81.3	44.8	0.7	19.0
Audrain	382	1.5	381	16	316	481	1 193	73	82	81 576	63.0	37.0	63.9	23.1	0.0	10.0
Barry	285	-2.3	178	0	163	217	1 309	29	152	95 115	2.7	97.3	42.4	13.4	11.3	7.3
Barton	335	7.8	374	9	252	309	776	52	64	71 699	52.3	47.7	55.4	16.9	0.0	4.7
Bates	445	3.4	356	1	297	341	942	44	66	52 644	49.1	50.9	51.4	11.4	0.0	2.8
Benton	232	-2.8	289	0	124	249	918	39	31	38 143	20.6	79.4	43.9	6.8	6.6	1.9
Bollinger	209	5.7	251	7	117	222	1 008	25	19	22 908	42.7	57.3	36.1	4.2	0.4	9.7
Boone	250	-8.1	204	4	172	331	1 599	37	40	32 684	42.0	58.0	34.8	5.9	0.8	18.2
Buchanan	182	0.3	234	0	145	303	1 217	56	32	41 487	79.4	20.6	46.9	11.9	0.0	57.6
Butler	255	0.0	376	108	218	441	1 191	80	60	88 338	91.5	8.5	51.0	22.9	11.0	155.8
Caldwell	227	-2.1	269	D	164	217	886	29	26	30 232	52.6	47.4	40.8	5.8	0.0	1.2
Callaway	330	-2.5	247	4	210	309	1 217	39	54	40 658	40.1	59.9	35.5	7.1	2.2	26.6
Camden	172	5.7	295	0	71	227	782	23	16	26 736	3.2	96.8	30.3	5.0	0.0	3.7
Cape Girardeau	261	3.1	225	9	197	325	1 361	49	46	39 814	50.0	50.0	44.3	9.5	0.0	12.2
Carroll	396	4.9	416	2	324	392	967	65	59	61 938	75.5	24.5	56.2	17.8	0.0	2.7
Carter	63	14.4	311	D	20	244	790	28	3	15 193	7.5	92.5	27.7	3.5	32.7	0.7
Cass	310	-4.8	204	5	229	320	1 517	36	56	36 603	61.2	38.8	37.1	6.1	0.1	6.4
Cedar	204	8.3	235	0	111	204	890	24	21	24 127	12.4	87.6	38.4	3.9	3.5	2.1
Chariton	414	2.6	387	1	332	368	996	59	85	79 565	56.0	44.0	59.3	19.0	1.3	1.7
Christian	203	-3.9	168	0	115	304	1 760	26	26	21 290	7.9	92.1	31.2	3.7	14.3	4.7
Clark	248	1.4	392	2	184	325	813	52	36	56 079	81.8	18.2	57.1	15.9	0.3	1.7
Clay	134	3.2	212	0	93	421	1 825	42	26	41 512	43.6	56.4	36.4	8.2	2.6	25.7
Clinton	216	4.1	282	0	156	356	1 254	39	35	45 007	51.8	48.2	46.1	11.8	1.8	2.1
Cole	179	-4.3	171	0	98	185	1 154	26	26	25 324	18.8	81.2	30.6	3.8	0.0	9.3
Cooper	302	0.9	343	0	224	332	941	56	53	60 099	45.3	54.7	57.6	16.0	0.4	2.9
Crawford	182	-9.8	264	0	82	230	902	20	9	12 630	17.1	82.9	30.5	1.6	10.4	2.5
Dade	249	-1.5	308	4	159	283	903	34	31	37 882	32.0	68.0	48.1	8.0	5.7	3.8
Dallas	222	-2.8	196	0	127	202	1 152	21	28	25 093	4.7	95.3	36.4	5.8	0.0	2.1
Daviess	302	8.2	341	0	209	263	717	39	57	64 538	42.2	57.8	48.3	11.9	0.0	1.8
De Kalb	215	2.0	280	D	162	252	882	35	29	38 063	51.4	48.6	45.3	10.9	0.0	1.2
Dent	222	1.4	305	0	96	249	746	22	10	13 578	7.7	92.3	35.2	1.7	15.3	1.7
Douglas	302	0.2	250	0	135	200	781	17	30	24 487	4.5	95.5	35.2	6.5	7.8	2.7
Dunklin	313	8.4	662	87	303	970	1 486	149	110	232 604	98.7	1.3	79.1	46.9	0.0	45.4
Franklin	290	-2.2	182	1	180	301	1 624	31	47	29 293	31.7	68.3	30.0	5.3	0.0	966.6
Gasconade	188	-4.6	247	0	96	264	1 045	29	15	19 929	26.6	73.4	33.1	4.6	0.0	2.6
Gentry	249	1.1	373	D	191	283	776	46	54	81 109	33.4	66.6	51.7	14.1	0.0	1.3
Greene	277	-2.8	139	0	183	310	2 206	23	33	16 732	16.0	84.0	28.8	3.1	0.3	175.9
Grundy	222	-1.8	333	1	170	227	727	41	29	43 256	72.9	27.1	44.7	11.2	0.0	3.2
Harrison	387	-2.9	430	0	255	275	635	37	44	49 272	56.2	43.8	47.8	11.0	0.0	2.9
Henry	315	-1.7	336	1	235	267	831	36	43	45 461	40.8	59.2	50.5	9.2	9.6	358.0
Hickory	172	-1.3	330	1	85	229	696	27	15	27 985	8.5	91.5	45.5	4.4	4.7	1.1
Holt	231	-0.8	497	9	204	455	1 040	80	53	114 557	83.8	16.2	77.4	33.1	1.9	2.5
Howard	242	1.4	342	3	159	354	1 046	37	31	44 328	64.2	35.8	50.4	11.3	0.8	1.6
Howell	387	4.0	236	0	162	238	975	20	50	30 637	3.3	96.7	35.5	4.9	8.3	5.4
Iron	63	-9.4	228	0	29	208	936	16	6	23 277	D	D	23.0	1.5	27.2	5.1
Jackson	151	12.4	197	1	114	377	2 122	37	28	36 060	80.7	19.3	32.3	7.3	0.3	546.7

Table B. States and Counties — Residential Construction, Wholesale and Retail Trade, and Real Estate

STATE County	Value of Residential Construction Authorized by Building Permits, 1999		Wholesale Trade, 1997				Retail Trade[1], 1997				Real Estate and Rental and Leasing, 1997			
	New Construction ($1,000)	Number of Housing Units	Number of Establishments	Number of Employees	Sales (mil dol)	Annual Payroll (mil dol)	Number of Establishments	Number of Employees	Sales (mil dol)	Annual Payroll (mil dol)	Number of Establishments	Number of Employees	Receipts (mil dol)	Annual Payroll (mil dol)
	133	134	135	136	137	138	139	140	141	142	143	144	145	146
MISSISSIPPI—Cont'd														
Sunflower	2 661	50	31	D	D	D	144	1 250	212.3	16.8	13	49	2.8	0.6
Tallahatchie	409	9	10	59	24.2	1.5	45	276	35.3	3.3	5	16	6.3	1.5
Tate	17 524	177	15	151	34.2	2.1	93	1 182	220.4	17.0	13	31	2.1	0.3
Tippah	1 540	22	20	181	59.9	2.8	105	831	106.7	10.2	11	38	6.1	0.7
Tishomingo	220	3	31	288	82.7	6.3	98	635	91.1	8.7	9	52	1.3	0.3
Tunica	16 155	340	11	109	110.6	2.9	40	304	61.8	4.8	10	20	1.6	0.2
Union	1 978	27	21	217	334.5	9.2	107	1 084	138.3	12.8	11	34	3.3	0.4
Walthall	125	1	14	181	53.3	1.9	54	378	56.2	5.3	2	D	D	D
Warren	3 833	39	46	359	151.6	10.6	281	3 316	454.7	43.7	46	127	14.2	2.0
Washington	11 441	104	78	795	393.8	24.5	324	3 441	507.2	48.2	78	305	25.5	4.0
Wayne	2 013	72	25	159	174.4	7.6	99	868	124.1	12.7	8	21	1.9	0.2
Webster	970	10	6	D	D	D	45	329	42.4	3.9	3	5	0.3	0.1
Wilkinson	0	0	12	88	27.3	1.5	31	228	31.1	2.7	3	8	0.7	0.1
Winston	1 089	12	13	242	98.0	8.6	90	741	103.9	10.2	7	123	5.6	1.9
Yalobusha	578	19	11	36	48.9	1.1	50	372	41.0	4.2	6	17	0.8	0.1
Yazoo	134	2	28	224	93.5	6.1	121	1 043	196.5	16.0	17	45	3.3	0.5
MISSOURI	2 742 784	26 881	9 522	125 929	91 411.9	4 639.8	24 181	297 556	51 269.9	4 945.0	5 500	31 301	3 991.1	698.1
Adair	5 087	59	30	376	87.6	6.8	143	1 595	225.2	21.7	26	198	11.1	2.5
Andrew	2 545	41	9	D	D	D	47	513	86.8	7.1	9	21	1.5	0.2
Atchison	1 002	25	13	D	D	D	45	376	59.5	4.8	5	12	0.8	0.1
Audrain	2 596	28	46	356	125.1	7.4	122	1 108	166.5	16.8	16	33	2.9	0.7
Barry	4 522	67	39	252	98.1	5.3	160	1 383	255.3	19.8	26	85	4.9	0.8
Barton	772	15	17	D	D	D	58	546	78.4	6.7	6	18	1.8	0.4
Bates	838	9	23	183	72.0	3.7	82	636	81.4	7.8	4	12	0.8	0.1
Benton	592	8	13	131	29.6	1.9	82	587	99.3	8.2	18	40	4.9	0.9
Bollinger	70	2	16	135	56.6	3.4	41	274	40.5	3.8	3	5	0.5	0.1
Boone	119 968	1 216	138	1 651	684.7	49.9	602	8 880	1 469.7	135.3	173	642	75.2	11.0
Buchanan	32 294	318	153	D	D	D	399	4 841	797.9	73.4	86	433	32.3	5.8
Butler	1 322	19	66	523	170.0	12.2	248	2 419	425.7	35.9	25	122	8.1	1.9
Caldwell	140	2	14	57	22.9	0.9	31	175	25.4	2.2	4	D	D	D
Callaway	9 633	177	35	238	130.0	5.0	119	1 109	208.2	16.3	19	56	4.2	0.8
Camden	7 487	132	58	244	88.4	5.0	328	2 639	437.0	42.1	80	272	26.8	4.6
Cape Girardeau	37 435	404	144	1 585	647.2	42.0	473	5 997	959.5	88.0	87	273	27.7	4.9
Carroll	203	2	24	105	78.8	2.1	52	286	36.3	3.2	7	15	0.7	0.1
Carter	257	4	5	20	4.7	0.4	29	149	17.9	1.3	7	17	1.3	0.2
Cass	90 886	889	58	D	D	D	218	2 833	492.9	44.4	60	176	17.5	3.3
Cedar	2 271	40	12	40	11.4	0.6	67	416	70.0	5.5	8	D	D	D
Chariton	598	7	20	190	121.4	4.2	49	260	47.9	3.6	9	D	D	D
Christian	49 515	626	58	403	134.3	8.6	176	1 298	247.7	20.7	42	109	7.9	1.2
Clark	0	0	17	155	69.1	3.5	38	327	44.2	3.8	5	D	D	D
Clay	96 229	865	334	4 707	5 773.2	165.4	721	11 919	2 476.5	211.4	179	1 179	169.4	27.9
Clinton	25 072	276	14	D	D	D	72	787	129.3	11.5	14	29	3.5	0.4
Cole	68 184	570	100	3 286	897.5	65.9	349	4 884	764.1	72.0	74	194	23.5	3.7
Cooper	3 820	31	26	125	63.2	2.8	71	640	96.5	8.6	10	36	1.7	0.3
Crawford	2 116	30	19	117	46.3	3.8	83	1 014	224.5	14.2	23	39	4.2	0.7
Dade	0	0	8	328	104.6	8.0	27	156	20.9	1.7	3	5	0.2	0.0
Dallas	NA	NA	17	75	23.8	1.2	59	423	80.9	6.8	13	22	0.9	0.2
Daviess	566	23	13	119	41.6	2.1	45	203	24.8	2.3	2	D	D	D
De Kalb	175	1	12	77	29.6	2.2	28	232	44.9	3.1	2	D	D	D
Dent	1 247	18	11	D	D	D	77	675	105.5	9.1	19	34	2.9	0.7
Douglas	1 221	12	8	56	27.1	0.8	40	324	46.6	4.3	3	9	0.8	0.1
Dunklin	2 985	45	53	384	134.3	9.0	186	1 690	256.6	25.2	27	98	6.4	1.2
Franklin	101 172	632	104	753	185.3	19.5	398	4 495	803.1	74.5	86	254	20.8	3.8
Gasconade	737	10	26	D	D	D	84	605	91.2	9.8	13	102	6.8	2.3
Gentry	582	7	12	D	D	D	48	304	40.9	4.1	3	10	0.5	0.0
Greene	202 258	1 805	576	8 856	5 101.7	263.9	1 302	17 819	3 271.8	294.0	336	1 736	151.7	32.3
Grundy	1 671	21	13	136	59.1	2.6	54	451	65.7	6.5	11	21	1.2	0.2
Harrison	1 111	9	19	225	74.6	4.6	56	605	92.7	8.7	9	23	1.2	0.2
Henry	4 243	70	48	534	218.6	14.2	136	1 126	177.1	15.0	18	37	2.7	0.4
Hickory	0	0	4	3	2.0	0.2	28	141	22.5	1.7	6	D	D	D
Holt	260	3	6	34	45.7	1.2	28	191	39.4	2.9	2	D	D	D
Howard	710	7	13	129	48.4	3.1	41	199	24.8	2.1	3	9	0.3	0.1
Howell	5 240	57	55	418	273.4	10.5	213	2 123	351.7	30.1	38	155	9.4	2.2
Iron	205	7	5	D	D	D	53	317	56.1	4.3	9	20	0.9	0.3
Jackson	527 107	5 311	1 197	19 252	11 305.8	712.5	2 670	39 198	7 239.1	704.8	746	4 888	793.7	127.3

1. Establishments with payroll.

Table B. States and Counties — Professional, Manufacturing, and Accommodation and Foodservices

STATE County	Professional, Scientific, and Technical Services[1], 1997				Manufacturing, 1997				Accommodation and Foodservices, 1997			
	Number of Establishments	Number of Employees	Receipts (mil dol)	Annual Payroll (mil dol)	Number of Establishments	Number of Employees	Receipts (mil dol)	Annual Payroll (mil dol)	Number of Establishments	Number of Employees	Sales (mil dol)	Annual Payroll (mil dol)
	147	148	149	150	151	152	153	154	155	156	157	158
MISSISSIPPI—Cont'd												
Sunflower	27	90	6.5	1.7	22	2 654	508.3	48.3	27	299	9.8	2.5
Tallahatchie	10	19	1.6	0.5	7	500	41.2	5.6	11	56	1.1	0.3
Tate	21	54	2.8	0.8	16	2 047	199.9	45.3	25	357	10.4	2.4
Tippah	12	42	2.3	0.9	42	3 247	344.1	71.2	21	D	D	D
Tishomingo	16	43	3.1	1.5	46	3 361	321.6	70.8	21	D	D	D
Tunica	6	19	2.5	0.5	NA	NA	NA	NA	26	11 575	826.9	226.1
Union	27	75	4.8	1.4	39	4 204	445.8	97.2	38	D	D	D
Walthall	7	19	0.9	0.2	24	940	68.9	15.8	17	149	4.3	1.2
Warren	76	577	34.2	17.4	43	4 698	1 181.8	131.7	97	3 294	160.8	38.0
Washington	83	361	36.2	10.5	65	5 067	1 030.3	121.8	95	1 486	47.5	12.3
Wayne	15	37	1.7	0.4	16	1 323	294.9	28.7	20	D	D	D
Webster	11	52	3.2	1.1	17	1 567	149.8	25.2	5	D	D	D
Wilkinson	6	13	0.7	0.1	NA	NA	NA	NA	9	79	2.2	0.6
Winston	20	176	5.9	3.2	26	1 850	318.3	53.5	22	326	8.9	2.4
Yalobusha	10	54	2.4	0.9	17	1 576	224.2	33.4	10	D	D	D
Yazoo	19	67	9.4	1.3	21	1 987	236.1	52.1	24	340	9.9	2.5
MISSOURI	10 601	93 792	9 953.3	3 643.6	7 497	371 448	93 115.5	11 647.0	11 150	203 849	6 780.8	1 933.3
Adair	34	112	6.8	2.2	10	1 619	412.4	39.8	59	1 364	29.0	8.7
Andrew	10	18	0.9	0.4	NA	NA	NA	NA	14	149	3.5	1.0
Atchison	6	13	0.7	0.2	NA	NA	NA	NA	21	D	D	D
Audrain	24	137	7.7	4.2	38	2 721	531.3	79.7	46	626	17.1	4.2
Barry	39	D	D	D	61	7 537	1 096.2	154.3	66	667	17.9	4.6
Barton	19	122	6.4	2.8	19	2 080	269.6	52.0	25	324	7.2	2.0
Bates	16	56	2.4	0.8	NA	NA	NA	NA	23	282	7.1	1.8
Benton	16	49	2.0	0.6	NA	NA	NA	NA	43	427	9.6	2.5
Bollinger	10	16	0.7	0.2	NA	NA	NA	NA	10	61	1.5	0.3
Boone	272	1 588	112.4	39.1	87	5 703	1 595.0	165.3	312	5 983	180.1	48.4
Buchanan	133	779	64.4	21.7	96	7 365	2 293.8	235.1	196	3 208	96.2	26.7
Butler	44	245	14.8	5.5	53	3 010	494.5	66.7	76	1 210	36.4	9.3
Caldwell	6	13	0.4	0.1	NA	NA	NA	NA	9	58	1.0	0.4
Callaway	22	85	5.5	1.9	37	1 896	320.6	59.6	48	739	22.6	5.9
Camden	73	275	19.9	6.4	53	1 269	132.0	32.6	200	2 412	103.9	31.4
Cape Girardeau	119	731	48.4	16.3	93	5 912	1 569.7	163.3	137	3 017	89.4	24.9
Carroll	11	21	1.0	0.2	NA	NA	NA	NA	13	D	D	D
Carter	5	D	D	D	NA	NA	NA	NA	18	63	2.0	0.5
Cass	80	209	16.5	5.3	71	1 057	116.6	24.6	104	1 647	50.4	12.8
Cedar	12	40	2.5	0.4	15	505	76.5	9.9	33	291	6.4	1.7
Chariton	11	18	1.0	0.2	NA	NA	NA	NA	11	39	1.1	0.2
Christian	44	156	8.1	2.9	101	D	D	D	62	841	20.3	5.9
Clark	5	D	D	D	NA	NA	NA	NA	4	31	0.8	0.3
Clay	337	3 362	401.0	154.3	214	14 743	9 891.7	569.6	320	12 228	527.2	145.2
Clinton	17	48	2.2	0.7	NA	NA	NA	NA	22	D	D	D
Cole	173	910	75.1	29.8	53	D	D	D	134	2 751	84.5	24.6
Cooper	17	64	3.6	1.0	16	865	138.6	19.2	32	391	10.2	2.8
Crawford	23	63	3.8	0.9	52	1 639	142.9	33.8	47	447	11.6	3.1
Dade	6	17	0.6	0.2	NA	NA	NA	NA	11	D	D	D
Dallas	11	25	1.1	0.3	11	530	40.2	8.7	27	298	6.7	1.9
Daviess	7	13	0.8	0.2	NA	NA	NA	NA	10	79	2.2	0.5
De Kalb	11	28	0.9	0.3	NA	NA	NA	NA	27	415	10.3	2.9
Dent	18	51	2.0	0.7	27	951	84.3	17.3	22	300	8.3	2.2
Douglas	8	10	0.7	0.2	NA	NA	NA	NA	8	148	3.6	1.0
Dunklin	39	113	6.9	1.5	26	1 281	259.7	28.5	51	563	14.6	3.7
Franklin	125	578	39.4	15.8	210	10 641	1 836.3	284.4	160	2 514	70.9	20.2
Gasconade	26	67	5.2	1.0	38	1 643	161.8	41.9	36	357	7.4	2.0
Gentry	6	15	0.8	0.3	NA	NA	NA	NA	12	62	1.3	0.3
Greene	574	4 028	363.7	121.3	371	19 475	3 788.6	513.1	595	11 812	350.3	100.0
Grundy	10	40	2.1	0.4	11	798	242.4	20.7	17	238	5.0	1.5
Harrison	8	25	0.8	0.2	NA	NA	NA	NA	17	320	8.8	2.2
Henry	28	85	4.9	1.2	32	1 780	390.1	33.0	53	568	16.2	4.1
Hickory	6	16	0.6	0.2	NA	NA	NA	NA	20	121	3.5	0.8
Holt	3	8	0.2	0.1	NA	NA	NA	NA	12	99	2.7	0.7
Howard	8	19	1.2	0.4	NA	NA	NA	NA	12	152	2.9	0.8
Howell	41	160	9.2	4.1	70	3 690	485.6	72.5	76	1 093	29.3	8.0
Iron	8	17	0.6	0.2	NA	NA	NA	NA	18	151	3.8	1.0
Jackson	1 728	19 506	2 015.2	843.0	907	38 785	8 984.7	1 301.5	1 393	28 200	1 005.3	292.5

1. Firms subject to federal tax.

STATE County	Health Care and Social Assistance[1], 1997				Other Services[1], 1997				Federal funds and grants, fiscal 1999[2] Expenditures (mil dol)			
										Direct payments for individuals[3]		
	Number of Establishments	Number of Employees	Receipts (mil dol)	Annual Payroll (mil dol)	Number of Establishments	Number of Employees	Receipts (mil dol)	Annual Payroll (mil dol)	Total	Social Security and government retirement	Medicare	Food stamps and Supplemental Security Income
	159	160	161	162	163	164	165	166	167	168	169	170
MISSISSIPPI—Cont'd												
Sunflower	35	457	25.5	9.4	41	172	10.4	3.0	152.7	39.8	27.1	13.6
Tallahatchie	8	122	7.2	2.5	13	34	1.5	0.3	95.1	21.4	14.0	8.3
Tate	27	335	18.8	6.6	31	111	7.4	1.8	91.9	38.7	16.4	5.2
Tippah	20	253	9.6	4.7	12	34	1.8	0.5	97.2	42.9	21.8	5.8
Tishomingo	19	303	14.4	5.1	23	64	4.5	1.1	115.6	47.6	19.9	3.9
Tunica	7	166	5.9	2.9	12	34	1.3	0.4	48.0	11.6	7.1	3.3
Union	35	280	17.6	6.5	25	94	6.1	1.4	91.0	44.6	18.4	3.8
Walthall	18	230	11.3	4.8	11	41	2.3	0.5	63.4	23.8	13.5	5.5
Warren	66	1 867	143.5	54.9	69	278	15.5	4.5	383.2	101.6	48.1	13.2
Washington	125	1 267	84.3	32.9	111	508	27.8	7.9	331.1	101.8	49.1	35.2
Wayne	27	268	14.6	5.6	18	57	3.3	0.8	71.5	30.5	12.6	7.7
Webster	12	176	7.9	3.2	8	19	1.8	0.3	59.6	21.5	9.7	2.8
Wilkinson	13	200	9.1	4.3	10	43	5.6	0.6	45.3	16.3	8.5	4.9
Winston	21	205	9.2	4.6	20	67	3.5	0.8	88.2	37.9	15.4	6.4
Yalobusha	14	62	4.2	1.1	5	17	1.1	0.2	76.2	32.4	16.5	4.6
Yazoo	24	326	17.6	6.8	35	106	6.7	1.6	183.9	44.5	26.4	12.0
MISSOURI	10 213	131 485	7 885.4	3 596.7	9 427	52 060	3 203.3	963.1	33 231.0	10 702.3	4 471.2	836.1
Adair	77	2 068	114.5	51.6	45	211	9.9	2.5	93.0	35.9	20.6	3.2
Andrew	14	131	5.1	2.5	18	69	4.4	1.2	51.6	21.9	9.0	1.2
Atchison	10	412	17.1	7.5	17	25	2.3	0.3	47.0	15.1	6.4	0.6
Audrain	60	452	26.1	11.8	49	241	15.7	4.2	117.3	53.4	27.5	3.2
Barry	36	277	9.9	4.2	46	139	8.8	2.1	137.4	74.3	27.3	4.7
Barton	17	199	7.5	2.9	24	90	4.6	1.0	51.4	22.9	10.6	1.7
Bates	23	272	12.1	4.4	33	62	4.1	0.8	76.8	35.4	15.5	2.1
Benton	16	190	7.6	3.1	28	45	3.5	0.7	93.6	54.9	19.8	2.7
Bollinger	6	79	2.4	1.0	14	59	3.5	0.8	49.6	20.9	8.4	1.9
Boone	328	4 024	321.4	129.7	230	1 269	67.1	20.6	537.9	177.6	73.4	15.7
Buchanan	174	2 235	138.5	62.8	161	786	46.6	13.2	380.5	181.3	78.7	16.6
Butler	92	2 502	160.4	53.5	64	243	13.6	4.1	255.2	96.6	38.6	12.6
Caldwell	4	D	D	D	11	18	1.4	0.2	40.6	19.6	8.2	1.1
Callaway	34	395	14.9	5.9	46	267	13.6	4.1	141.2	62.4	27.3	3.5
Camden	61	569	32.8	13.3	82	293	14.3	4.0	152.2	83.6	30.8	3.4
Cape Girardeau	201	2 170	162.1	73.5	129	584	36.4	10.6	254.3	119.1	39.2	10.6
Carroll	16	136	6.4	2.3	16	45	2.8	1.0	62.7	24.0	11.1	1.5
Carter	8	98	2.9	1.4	3	15	2.1	0.3	38.7	16.0	5.4	2.1
Cass	83	713	31.4	14.9	115	487	27.9	8.2	300.8	149.2	43.5	4.8
Cedar	14	211	8.0	3.6	13	28	1.6	0.3	69.9	36.9	14.4	2.4
Chariton	8	151	4.3	1.9	14	31	1.6	0.4	54.8	19.5	9.4	0.9
Christian	49	672	22.6	8.7	67	256	18.2	3.9	137.4	81.8	23.0	4.3
Clark	5	33	2.0	0.6	10	19	1.5	0.2	36.3	13.5	6.4	1.0
Clay	382	4 689	308.2	148.7	317	1 839	115.9	35.2	450.2	202.0	114.3	6.7
Clinton	24	177	7.8	3.2	33	101	5.1	1.2	69.9	35.7	15.0	1.5
Cole	160	1 936	127.1	70.5	115	609	30.8	9.4	1 103.5	187.3	49.0	6.5
Cooper	22	199	7.9	3.2	34	151	8.3	2.5	72.0	32.4	13.9	1.5
Crawford	26	412	10.8	4.5	27	71	7.5	1.1	94.5	45.1	17.2	4.0
Dade	4	12	0.7	0.1	10	28	2.1	0.4	39.2	19.1	7.4	0.9
Dallas	18	176	4.7	1.9	17	38	2.7	0.5	59.5	29.8	11.2	2.8
Daviess	8	51	1.6	0.5	10	10	0.8	0.1	43.7	17.2	6.9	0.8
De Kalb	13	214	7.6	2.9	9	30	2.3	0.6	35.2	15.6	5.7	0.9
Dent	21	213	7.9	3.3	20	61	3.3	0.7	81.6	34.4	14.6	1.5
Douglas	11	150	6.2	2.3	10	33	1.6	0.5	53.8	23.7	9.3	2.5
Dunklin	57	1 841	75.0	29.9	45	129	8.6	1.8	220.1	70.2	35.1	13.7
Franklin	159	1 507	74.1	30.9	140	561	34.3	11.0	291.1	167.5	61.3	11.0
Gasconade	23	309	9.9	4.5	19	66	4.6	1.2	62.7	36.4	14.4	1.4
Gentry	22	216	7.1	3.2	9	32	1.8	0.4	45.2	17.6	9.8	0.6
Greene	457	7 245	532.1	253.3	514	3 519	184.4	56.9	983.0	450.1	154.8	33.2
Grundy	17	159	4.9	2.0	23	94	4.1	1.0	57.8	25.5	11.2	1.5
Harrison	16	133	5.0	1.9	24	63	4.3	0.8	53.9	20.9	11.0	1.2
Henry	35	581	30.9	14.1	37	156	7.7	2.0	117.6	56.6	24.0	3.6
Hickory	5	D	D	D	9	17	1.2	0.2	49.5	27.5	11.0	1.4
Holt	5	114	4.2	1.7	11	17	1.3	0.2	37.4	13.6	6.4	0.5
Howard	16	298	8.4	3.7	10	24	1.4	0.2	50.8	18.8	10.8	1.3
Howell	63	631	29.1	10.9	61	218	16.0	3.3	189.1	83.5	29.8	8.7
Iron	19	151	5.3	1.7	15	57	2.9	0.9	57.4	26.6	11.2	4.3
Jackson	1 334	18 242	1 254.8	614.8	1 265	8 921	539.1	170.9	4 249.3	1 400.5	592.3	67.5

1. Firms subject to federal tax.   2. October 1, 1998 to September 30, 1999.   3. State totals may include programs not allocated by county.

	Federal funds and grants, fiscal 1999[1] (cont'd)							Local government finances, 1997				
	Expenditures (mil dol) (cont'd)							General revenue				
	Procurement contract awards			Grants[2]						Taxes		
STATE County											Per capita[3] (dollars)	
	Salaries and wages	Defense	Other	Medicaid and other health-related	Nutrition and family welfare	Education	Other	Total (mil dol)	Intergovern-mental (mil dol)	Total (mil dol)	Total	Property
	171	172	173	174	175	176	177	178	179	180	181	182
MISSISSIPPI—Cont'd												
Sunflower	4.0	0.0	0.8	27.3	8.6	3.4	2.5	72.1	39.3	13.4	383	354
Tallahatchie	2.6	4.6	0.5	18.9	3.3	1.7	2.9	23.2	13.2	4.4	291	266
Tate	3.7	0.0	1.1	13.6	2.7	1.3	2.1	52.9	30.4	10.9	463	436
Tippah	3.3	0.7	0.7	15.8	1.6	1.1	1.3	36.4	18.1	6.0	286	278
Tishomingo	3.4	23.3	2.6	11.7	1.3	0.5	0.5	23.8	15.2	4.9	263	228
Tunica	0.9	0.0	0.2	10.1	2.4	1.5	0.5	43.3	32.1	6.2	772	674
Union	3.2	0.0	3.0	11.9	1.5	1.0	0.6	32.5	19.7	8.0	339	304
Walthall	1.4	0.0	0.3	12.9	2.3	1.2	0.4	26.6	12.5	4.3	301	277
Warren	94.1	82.4	5.4	22.3	5.3	2.5	1.3	99.7	47.8	38.3	778	711
Washington	21.4	2.4	6.0	50.3	18.7	7.0	6.6	167.1	71.9	33.0	501	462
Wayne	1.9	0.0	0.7	13.0	2.9	1.3	0.2	49.0	17.8	4.9	241	229
Webster	1.9	0.0	0.3	7.6	1.2	0.5	10.8	15.8	8.8	3.3	320	313
Wilkinson	0.5	0.0	0.1	10.8	1.8	0.9	1.1	15.6	9.5	3.8	418	397
Winston	2.6	0.0	0.6	15.4	2.7	1.5	3.8	36.2	18.2	5.5	286	246
Yalobusha	3.8	0.5	0.6	11.2	1.4	0.9	1.7	25.6	11.5	4.0	321	294
Yazoo	17.9	2.5	1.8	25.6	6.3	2.6	23.1	44.5	27.6	11.8	466	441
MISSOURI	3 313.4	4 318.6	1 386.7	2 757.0	898.4	458.2	1 364.9	X	X	X	X	X
Adair	4.4	1.0	0.9	16.9	3.0	1.6	0.5	38.8	11.5	12.6	518	264
Andrew	3.1	0.0	0.5	3.8	1.0	0.4	6.1	19.9	10.0	6.4	416	330
Atchison	1.9	0.4	0.5	2.1	0.5	0.2	9.3	14.5	6.4	6.2	870	717
Audrain	4.1	0.0	1.0	8.6	2.1	1.1	3.0	37.2	15.1	14.1	597	368
Barry	6.2	0.5	1.9	16.2	2.6	1.4	1.1	48.4	24.9	16.3	498	374
Barton	2.1	0.1	0.5	4.1	0.8	0.3	0.4	16.1	7.5	6.3	526	349
Bates	2.9	0.0	0.8	7.9	1.6	0.7	0.5	20.3	11.0	6.6	415	325
Benton	4.3	0.5	0.6	6.9	1.3	0.7	0.4	23.7	9.5	6.7	407	291
Bollinger	1.6	0.0	0.4	12.5	1.1	0.5	0.1	13.5	7.6	4.6	401	318
Boone	92.6	4.8	17.9	55.6	9.5	11.8	60.0	223.9	79.2	93.9	731	424
Buchanan	23.8	0.3	3.8	40.1	10.5	4.1	9.8	149.4	58.1	65.2	797	411
Butler	21.1	0.0	5.0	48.3	5.8	3.1	4.8	61.2	27.8	22.8	564	294
Caldwell	1.9	0.0	0.5	2.9	0.6	0.4	0.3	14.8	7.8	3.8	433	360
Callaway	22.0	0.0	3.1	12.2	2.1	1.2	0.4	56.5	19.7	26.2	709	359
Camden	3.3	0.0	0.9	8.8	1.6	1.1	17.9	55.5	16.5	25.7	773	400
Cape Girardeau	22.4	0.9	6.8	24.3	3.8	2.6	14.8	94.7	31.5	44.6	676	327
Carroll	2.8	0.0	0.8	4.9	1.1	0.6	1.1	16.7	8.2	6.0	593	465
Carter	2.4	0.0	0.2	5.7	1.3	0.4	5.0	8.9	6.1	2.0	318	268
Cass	39.1	4.2	2.8	8.6	3.1	2.3	25.1	145.1	57.4	49.9	641	470
Cedar	2.5	0.9	0.5	9.0	1.0	0.5	0.7	24.6	10.5	5.6	430	299
Chariton	2.3	1.3	0.6	5.5	0.6	0.4	2.1	12.3	4.9	4.6	526	421
Christian	6.1	0.0	1.5	10.4	2.0	1.6	5.3	58.3	30.8	20.5	437	320
Clark	1.6	0.0	0.4	2.3	0.8	0.5	2.1	16.2	6.5	4.1	540	452
Clay	41.1	0.2	17.4	19.7	5.0	5.0	11.9	529.7	94.2	161.7	929	622
Clinton	3.0	0.0	0.9	6.5	1.0	0.6	1.2	26.2	12.9	8.9	476	351
Cole	16.6	5.4	4.2	99.6	300.0	126.5	293.7	105.1	36.9	52.0	755	462
Cooper	2.9	0.1	0.6	8.3	1.2	0.6	2.8	25.3	11.7	7.8	483	300
Crawford	1.9	0.1	1.7	10.0	1.9	1.2	11.0	22.9	12.2	7.8	352	244
Dade	1.6	0.0	0.4	5.1	0.7	0.8	0.2	13.3	6.0	3.3	415	308
Dallas	1.8	0.0	0.5	11.1	1.1	0.7	0.1	15.1	8.4	4.6	306	182
Daviess	2.2	0.6	1.0	3.3	0.8	0.5	3.1	16.9	10.3	4.4	563	452
De Kalb	1.6	0.0	0.4	1.5	0.5	0.6	2.6	11.2	6.2	3.5	311	249
Dent	3.5	9.2	0.5	14.5	1.8	0.9	0.2	20.4	10.2	6.1	433	291
Douglas	2.0	0.0	0.4	12.1	1.4	0.9	1.2	11.8	7.9	3.1	255	195
Dunklin	5.3	0.6	1.2	56.7	7.5	2.8	2.0	47.5	26.6	14.4	440	341
Franklin	12.4	0.1	3.1	20.5	4.9	2.9	3.2	131.8	51.3	58.2	639	415
Gasconade	2.1	0.0	0.5	5.2	0.8	0.5	0.2	29.2	13.1	9.5	645	439
Gentry	2.4	0.2	0.5	4.6	0.8	0.4	1.0	42.6	36.9	4.4	583	492
Greene	128.6	1.1	30.6	77.0	22.3	9.6	23.9	384.5	131.0	161.1	714	398
Grundy	2.8	0.2	0.5	5.8	2.2	0.8	0.6	23.9	11.6	5.6	547	371
Harrison	2.6	0.0	0.8	4.9	0.8	0.6	1.1	22.0	8.4	5.9	707	541
Henry	4.3	0.1	1.3	10.5	1.5	1.0	9.5	33.8	15.8	13.1	624	414
Hickory	1.8	0.8	0.5	4.1	0.9	0.3	0.7	12.6	8.1	3.5	407	342
Holt	1.7	0.0	0.4	3.8	0.4	0.2	0.5	9.5	4.0	4.2	753	497
Howard	1.8	0.3	1.0	7.6	0.8	0.5	1.7	15.6	6.7	5.4	550	392
Howell	5.5	7.5	1.2	26.9	7.1	1.9	15.2	57.4	33.1	15.8	444	295
Iron	1.3	0.0	0.4	11.1	1.5	0.7	0.3	19.1	9.9	7.6	690	548
Jackson	806.4	139.2	647.4	263.5	80.6	43.5	139.5	1 962.8	630.3	904.0	1 395	665

1. October 1, 1998 to September 30, 1999. 2. State totals may include programs not allocated by county. 3. Based on the resident population estimated as of July 1 of the year shown.

Table B. States and Counties — Local Government Finances, Government Employment, and Elections

STATE County	Total (mil dol)	Per capita[1] (dollars)	Education	Health and hospitals	Police protection	Public welfare	Highways	Total (mil dol)	Per capita[1] (dollars)	Federal civilian	Federal military	State and local	Democratic	Republican	All other
	183	184	185	186	187	188	189	190	191	192	193	194	195	196	197
MISSISSIPPI—Cont'd															
Sunflower	71.9	2 058	61.7	14.8	4.8	0.6	5.5	21.9	628	72	237	4 223	NA	NA	NA
Tallahatchie	22.7	1 510	57.8	15.2	6.7	0.5	2.8	3.0	200	56	102	840	NA	NA	NA
Tate	51.4	2 181	77.0	1.0	4.4	0.2	4.8	18.0	763	82	164	1 535	NA	NA	NA
Tippah	36.9	1 764	47.0	25.4	2.7	1.5	6.8	6.1	293	60	144	996	NA	NA	NA
Tishomingo	22.4	1 205	57.5	0.1	5.6	0.7	8.5	3.9	212	68	128	667	NA	NA	NA
Tunica	31.7	3 921	44.3	0.3	7.6	0.3	27.7	6.2	770	21	55	547	NA	NA	NA
Union	32.2	1 362	56.5	1.1	3.5	0.4	10.3	11.8	499	60	163	988	NA	NA	NA
Walthall	28.4	1 982	43.1	27.5	5.9	0.5	3.8	1.5	107	24	98	725	NA	NA	NA
Warren	93.3	1 895	45.9	1.9	6.7	0.8	6.5	59.7	1 213	2 348	368	2 602	NA	NA	NA
Washington	159.4	2 422	36.5	24.1	5.6	0.7	4.5	53.0	805	493	463	4 138	NA	NA	NA
Wayne	49.3	2 450	36.4	45.3	3.0	0.1	5.0	10.2	509	35	139	1 164	NA	NA	NA
Webster	14.0	1 346	63.6	0.1	5.8	0.0	12.4	8.8	842	41	72	408	NA	NA	NA
Wilkinson	15.2	1 652	60.2	2.3	3.7	0.0	16.2	6.0	650	11	63	560	NA	NA	NA
Winston	38.9	2 018	39.9	2.8	3.8	0.1	15.7	9.9	514	48	133	729	NA	NA	NA
Yalobusha	22.1	1 796	42.3	24.0	4.6	0.1	8.1	6.7	543	97	85	671	NA	NA	NA
Yazoo	43.9	1 729	48.8	0.3	6.5	0.1	15.2	27.6	1 086	355	175	1 422	NA	NA	NA
MISSOURI	X	X	X	X	X	X	X	X	X	58 899	37 557	351 621	47.0	50.0	3.0
Adair	38.7	1 591	42.0	26.0	4.0	0.0	5.6	21.8	895	88	112	2 689	NA	NA	NA
Andrew	20.3	1 327	65.9	2.7	1.4	0.1	13.5	5.3	349	44	70	651	NA	NA	NA
Atchison	14.1	1 978	52.5	4.6	3.1	0.0	21.9	2.5	350	38	32	425	NA	NA	NA
Audrain	38.7	1 641	51.9	0.7	6.3	6.6	10.9	30.7	1 301	86	106	2 494	NA	NA	NA
Barry	49.7	1 521	66.0	1.4	2.9	0.8	9.8	21.1	645	152	150	1 652	NA	NA	NA
Barton	16.4	1 370	64.2	1.8	4.1	0.0	10.0	8.0	671	43	55	797	NA	NA	NA
Bates	20.1	1 268	68.9	0.4	4.5	0.0	10.7	6.2	389	62	71	1 021	NA	NA	NA
Benton	22.5	1 364	54.4	0.8	2.9	25.0	6.9	6.1	372	107	77	776	NA	NA	NA
Bollinger	13.7	1 193	72.9	1.8	2.6	0.4	6.8	2.3	196	35	52	406	NA	NA	NA
Boone	227.7	1 775	52.0	1.3	5.0	2.0	8.3	248.9	1 940	1 971	616	26 701	NA	NA	NA
Buchanan	155.1	1 896	46.0	1.2	6.0	0.2	5.8	27.1	331	519	378	5 683	NA	NA	NA
Butler	66.7	1 650	64.8	0.0	3.5	0.0	4.2	28.5	705	517	184	2 754	NA	NA	NA
Caldwell	14.0	1 613	67.8	2.6	1.1	10.3	8.1	2.9	329	41	40	570	NA	NA	NA
Callaway	57.7	1 563	53.7	3.8	4.8	0.0	5.8	26.6	721	183	182	3 929	NA	NA	NA
Camden	57.7	1 735	49.5	2.1	3.5	8.4	12.7	26.4	793	67	153	1 605	NA	NA	NA
Cape Girardeau	94.8	1 436	49.0	0.5	6.2	0.0	6.7	98.6	1 493	398	310	5 240	NA	NA	NA
Carroll	17.4	1 710	59.9	4.1	4.0	0.0	12.3	6.0	591	55	46	625	NA	NA	NA
Carter	9.1	1 440	83.5	1.8	1.7	0.0	3.7	0.3	55	69	29	393	NA	NA	NA
Cass	146.6	1 882	62.0	8.5	4.5	0.1	5.2	98.9	1 269	246	838	3 160	NA	NA	NA
Cedar	23.7	1 820	48.8	26.3	6.8	0.0	8.7	1.9	146	57	60	788	NA	NA	NA
Chariton	12.7	1 441	62.0	3.2	3.3	0.0	15.1	2.1	236	53	39	460	NA	NA	NA
Christian	59.4	1 264	70.6	0.8	4.3	0.0	6.9	32.7	696	102	221	1 616	NA	NA	NA
Clark	16.4	2 180	52.7	3.4	1.4	18.1	13.4	4.2	564	37	34	559	NA	NA	NA
Clay	498.1	2 862	36.5	39.8	2.5	0.3	3.3	212.3	1 220	314	1 238	10 394	NA	NA	NA
Clinton	25.9	1 391	61.6	1.2	7.6	0.0	9.4	16.3	874	66	86	807	NA	NA	NA
Cole	104.5	1 519	50.7	1.2	6.0	0.0	13.7	41.1	598	516	313	19 494	NA	NA	NA
Cooper	25.5	1 587	62.0	1.1	4.1	5.2	9.1	5.6	348	53	80	1 395	NA	NA	NA
Crawford	21.4	971	70.8	4.7	4.8	0.0	5.4	6.6	298	36	100	837	NA	NA	NA
Dade	14.5	1 821	57.5	0.7	3.0	21.2	10.2	4.3	547	35	36	612	NA	NA	NA
Dallas	16.4	1 086	73.5	0.0	4.2	0.0	9.5	1.2	81	38	69	613	NA	NA	NA
Daviess	14.2	1 822	66.4	6.0	2.6	0.1	7.1	4.0	520	53	35	520	NA	NA	NA
De Kalb	10.6	953	70.6	1.6	3.5	0.0	6.3	7.0	630	33	50	1 505	NA	NA	NA
Dent	21.2	1 503	73.2	0.6	3.2	0.0	5.8	3.7	261	85	64	917	NA	NA	NA
Douglas	11.3	916	77.7	0.5	5.0	0.0	6.8	0.0	2	51	56	435	NA	NA	NA
Dunklin	47.7	1 453	67.3	0.3	5.9	0.0	5.8	13.6	416	106	148	1 595	NA	NA	NA
Franklin	135.0	1 484	60.4	2.0	5.9	0.1	10.5	97.8	1 075	232	415	3 778	NA	NA	NA
Gasconade	28.8	1 949	56.1	17.5	3.9	0.0	6.8	8.9	603	50	67	951	NA	NA	NA
Gentry	11.4	1 661	65.0	4.1	3.4	0.0	11.6	1.2	176	44	31	419	NA	NA	NA
Greene	373.7	1 657	51.0	1.6	4.8	1.1	8.7	405.8	1 799	2 190	1 063	14 105	NA	NA	NA
Grundy	24.5	2 390	64.3	1.6	3.2	12.1	7.5	7.9	774	55	46	921	NA	NA	NA
Harrison	20.8	2 481	47.2	22.8	2.3	0.0	10.8	4.3	511	52	38	724	NA	NA	NA
Henry	33.7	1 601	50.7	14.5	3.6	0.0	11.0	11.5	547	88	96	1 459	NA	NA	NA
Hickory	15.1	1 746	83.0	0.4	2.3	0.0	2.9	4.7	539	43	39	292	NA	NA	NA
Holt	9.0	1 601	60.7	0.8	2.7	0.0	14.4	2.5	447	40	25	322	NA	NA	NA
Howard	15.3	1 561	56.4	2.6	4.0	1.8	7.4	5.7	586	40	44	486	NA	NA	NA
Howell	53.8	1 511	67.2	9.0	3.9	0.0	8.3	4.9	139	112	163	2 173	NA	NA	NA
Iron	18.6	1 689	74.4	1.5	3.7	0.0	9.7	0.8	69	28	49	563	NA	NA	NA
Jackson	1 993.4	3 076	42.9	3.9	7.4	0.3	3.8	1 825.1	2 817	17 192	3 213	43 180	NA	NA	NA

1. Based on the resident population estimated as of July 1 of the year shown.

Table B. States and Counties — **Land Area and Population**

STATE/County code	MSA/PMSA/NECMA code[1]	County Type[2]	STATE County	Land area,[3] (sq km) 1990	Population and population characteristics, 1999			Race (percent)					Age (percent)					
					Total persons	Rank	Per square kilometer	White	Black	Am. Indian, Eskimo, Aleut	Asian and Pacific Islander	Percent Hispanic[4]	Under 5 years	5 to 17 years	18 to 24 years	25 to 34 years	35 to 44 years	45 to 54 years
				1	2	3	4	5	6	7	8	9	10	11	12	13	14	15
			MISSOURI—Cont'd															
29 097	3710	3	Jasper	1 657	100 267	516	60.5	96.1	1.6	1.6	0.7	1.3	6.3	19.1	9.7	12.5	15.9	12.5
29 099	7040	1	Jefferson	1 701	198 116	274	116.5	98.4	0.9	0.2	0.5	1.0	7.7	21.4	8.9	14.8	17.6	13.3
29 101	...	6	Johnson	2 151	48 053	934	22.3	90.8	6.7	0.4	2.0	2.4	7.3	17.5	21.9	13.6	13.4	10.6
29 103	...	9	Knox	1 310	4 312	2 883	3.3	99.4	0.3	0.2	0.1	0.2	5.7	18.1	6.8	10.1	13.8	14.1
29 105	...	6	Laclede	1 984	31 419	1 336	15.8	98.6	0.5	0.5	0.5	0.8	6.7	19.9	8.4	12.3	15.5	13.6
29 107	3760	1	Lafayette	1 630	32 810	1 289	20.1	98.5	3.4	0.3	0.3	1.0	6.5	19.8	8.3	11.6	15.5	13.7
29 109	...	6	Lawrence	1 588	33 494	1 272	21.1	98.7	0.1	0.9	0.3	1.0	6.6	20.3	7.9	11.5	14.9	14.0
29 111	...	7	Lewis	1 308	10 230	2 402	7.8	95.6	4.0	0.2	0.2	0.3	5.4	17.8	14.1	10.3	13.2	13.2
29 113	7040	1	Lincoln	1 633	37 733	1 143	23.1	96.8	2.6	0.3	0.3	1.1	7.8	21.8	7.7	13.8	16.2	13.5
29 115	...	7	Linn	1 607	13 867	2 146	8.6	98.7	1.0	0.2	0.2	1.0	5.9	19.3	6.4	10.6	14.4	12.2
29 117	...	7	Livingston	1 385	14 024	2 136	10.1	96.4	3.0	0.3	0.3	0.6	5.8	18.6	7.4	11.4	15.5	12.8
29 119	...	8	McDonald	1 397	20 158	1 754	14.4	96.6	0.0	3.0	0.4	1.0	7.2	20.4	8.5	12.0	14.6	14.5
29 121	...	7	Macon	2 082	15 450	2 038	7.4	96.6	2.9	0.3	0.2	0.5	5.4	19.5	7.3	10.5	15.5	13.0
29 123	...	9	Madison	1 287	11 650	2 298	9.1	99.1	0.1	0.3	0.4	0.8	6.1	19.5	7.7	11.3	14.2	13.0
29 125	...	9	Maries	1 367	8 423	2 555	6.2	99.3	0.3	0.2	0.2	0.8	6.4	19.4	7.8	10.7	13.8	15.0
29 127	...	5	Marion	1 135	27 719	1 442	24.4	93.6	5.5	0.3	0.6	0.6	6.6	20.6	8.0	11.9	15.9	11.5
29 129	...	9	Mercer	1 177	3 956	2 917	3.4	99.7	0.1	0.2	0.1	0.2	4.8	18.5	5.3	9.8	13.9	13.0
29 131	...	7	Miller	1 534	22 624	1 629	14.7	99.2	0.2	0.4	0.2	0.7	6.7	20.3	8.0	11.7	15.1	12.4
29 133	...	7	Mississippi	1 070	13 339	2 187	12.5	76.8	22.9	0.2	0.1	0.4	6.7	22.4	8.1	11.1	14.0	12.7
29 135	...	6	Moniteau	1 079	13 313	2 190	12.3	97.8	1.4	0.4	0.4	0.6	6.3	21.5	8.1	12.1	16.1	12.2
29 137	...	9	Monroe	1 673	9 137	2 497	5.5	94.9	4.6	0.2	0.2	0.7	6.5	20.8	6.8	11.1	14.5	13.3
29 139	...	8	Montgomery	1 395	12 110	2 272	8.7	96.6	3.0	0.1	0.3	0.6	6.5	20.0	7.0	11.2	14.3	13.9
29 141	...	9	Morgan	1 547	18 908	1 823	12.2	98.5	0.8	0.4	0.3	0.7	6.0	16.9	6.7	9.6	13.1	14.9
29 143	...	7	New Madrid	1 756	19 933	1 766	11.4	81.1	18.6	0.1	0.2	0.6	6.7	22.8	8.4	11.3	14.6	12.7
29 145	3710	3	Newton	1 623	49 714	911	30.6	96.7	0.5	1.9	0.8	1.1	6.7	19.8	8.3	11.7	16.0	14.4
29 147	...	6	Nodaway	2 271	20 531	1 739	9.0	97.9	0.9	0.2	1.0	0.8	5.2	16.9	23.2	10.4	12.3	10.1
29 149	...	9	Oregon	2 050	10 295	2 398	5.0	99.3	0.1	0.4	0.2	0.5	5.2	18.5	7.2	9.4	15.3	14.8
29 151	...	9	Osage	1 570	12 524	2 246	8.0	99.4	0.2	0.2	0.0	0.7	6.5	21.2	10.2	12.1	14.7	12.5
29 153	...	9	Ozark	1 934	9 970	2 431	5.2	99.2	0.1	0.5	0.2	0.9	4.5	18.3	5.9	9.3	14.2	14.7
29 155	...	7	Pemiscot	1 277	21 150	1 705	16.6	69.7	29.8	0.2	0.3	0.5	7.7	24.3	8.8	10.8	14.0	11.5
29 157	...	7	Perry	1 229	17 431	1 906	14.2	99.0	0.2	0.2	0.6	0.6	6.6	21.7	8.2	11.7	15.5	11.9
29 159	...	7	Pettis	1 774	37 110	1 158	20.9	95.1	4.1	0.3	0.5	1.1	6.6	19.4	8.3	12.5	15.1	12.7
29 161	...	7	Phelps	1 743	38 954	1 113	22.3	95.3	1.3	0.4	3.0	1.2	6.0	17.5	14.6	12.1	14.6	12.8
29 163	...	6	Pike	1 743	16 411	1 979	9.4	92.9	6.6	0.3	0.2	1.1	6.4	20.4	7.1	10.7	14.5	13.7
29 165	3760	0	Platte	1 089	71 688	685	65.8	94.9	2.6	0.5	2.0	2.9	6.7	18.8	8.7	14.4	19.5	15.1
29 167	...	6	Polk	1 650	25 740	1 504	15.6	98.5	0.5	0.6	0.5	1.1	6.0	18.5	13.1	10.9	13.9	12.3
29 169	...	7	Pulaski	1 417	38 230	1 128	27.0	80.4	14.6	0.6	4.4	6.5	8.6	21.2	14.0	17.5	15.6	8.8
29 171	...	9	Putnam	1 342	4 872	2 849	3.6	99.3	0.3	0.2	0.1	0.6	5.2	17.3	6.8	9.9	13.8	13.5
29 173	...	9	Ralls	1 220	9 169	2 495	7.5	97.5	2.1	0.2	0.2	0.3	5.6	21.0	6.8	11.0	17.1	14.0
29 175	...	6	Randolph	1 249	23 863	1 581	19.1	90.1	9.1	0.3	0.4	1.1	5.8	18.8	9.2	13.5	16.6	12.4
29 177	3760	1	Ray	1 475	23 759	1 586	16.1	97.6	1.7	0.5	0.2	0.8	6.8	21.4	7.3	12.0	16.2	15.0
29 179	...	9	Reynolds	2 101	6 627	2 716	3.2	99.5	0.2	0.2	0.2	0.6	5.7	20.1	6.9	10.5	14.5	14.9
29 181	...	9	Ripley	1 630	14 174	2 122	8.7	99.2	0.1	0.4	0.3	1.0	6.2	20.6	7.5	10.2	13.5	13.8
29 183	7040	0	St. Charles	1 454	280 448	197	192.9	95.9	2.9	0.2	1.0	1.6	8.1	21.0	8.3	15.5	18.9	12.9
29 185	...	9	St. Clair	1 753	9 276	2 487	5.3	99.1	0.3	0.5	0.2	0.6	5.3	17.8	6.3	9.2	13.3	13.2
29 186	...	6	Ste. Genevieve	1 301	17 462	1 904	13.4	99.3	0.3	0.2	0.2	0.4	6.5	20.7	7.6	12.2	15.7	12.8
29 187	...	6	St. Francois	1 164	55 790	830	47.9	96.8	2.6	0.2	0.4	0.7	5.9	19.3	9.1	13.2	15.7	12.8
29 189	7040	0	St. Louis	1 315	996 181	34	757.6	81.2	16.7	0.1	2.0	1.4	6.3	17.7	8.3	13.3	17.4	13.5
29 195	...	7	Saline	1 957	22 782	1 619	11.6	92.4	7.1	0.2	0.3	1.2	5.8	19.4	10.2	11.4	15.2	12.2
29 197	...	9	Schuyler	797	4 415	2 876	5.5	99.7	0.0	0.2	0.1	0.6	6.8	18.6	7.1	10.8	14.1	13.7
29 199	...	9	Scotland	1 136	4 921	2 846	4.3	99.7	0.1	0.2	0.0	0.3	6.9	18.7	6.9	10.5	13.4	13.5
29 201	...	5	Scott	1 091	40 564	1 073	37.2	88.8	10.7	0.2	0.2	0.7	7.0	21.4	8.7	12.0	16.2	12.9
29 203	...	9	Shannon	2 600	8 298	2 567	3.2	99.5	0.1	0.3	0.1	0.5	6.7	19.7	7.5	11.4	15.1	14.1
29 205	...	9	Shelby	1 297	6 660	2 713	5.1	98.4	1.3	0.2	0.1	0.5	6.4	20.2	6.1	10.8	13.8	13.1
29 207	...	7	Stoddard	2 142	29 633	1 388	13.8	97.8	1.8	0.2	0.2	0.6	5.6	19.0	8.3	10.9	15.2	14.2
29 209	...	8	Stone	1 200	27 506	1 449	22.9	98.8	0.1	0.7	0.3	0.9	4.9	16.6	6.7	9.4	14.1	15.4
29 211	...	9	Sullivan	1 686	6 864	2 692	4.1	99.5	0.3	0.2	0.0	0.8	5.1	17.9	7.8	9.6	14.5	14.5
29 213	...	6	Taney	1 638	35 490	1 205	21.7	98.8	0.1	0.6	0.5	1.1	5.4	16.3	9.2	10.2	14.4	14.2
29 215	...	9	Texas	3 053	22 470	1 639	7.4	99.1	0.2	0.4	0.4	0.7	6.0	20.1	7.0	10.4	14.8	13.5
29 217	...	7	Vernon	2 160	19 488	1 791	9.0	96.8	0.3	0.6	0.5	0.8	6.4	19.9	8.9	10.9	15.7	12.8
29 219	7040	1	Warren	1 118	25 435	1 516	22.8	96.3	3.3	0.2	0.3	1.2	7.6	20.1	7.6	12.9	15.8	13.7
29 221	...	6	Washington	1 968	23 354	1 598	11.9	96.8	2.8	0.2	0.2	0.6	6.8	22.2	9.2	13.0	15.8	13.2
29 223	...	9	Wayne	1 971	13 046	2 212	6.6	99.2	0.3	0.4	0.1	0.6	5.5	17.5	7.5	9.7	12.4	14.6
29 225	7920	2	Webster	1 537	29 977	1 373	19.5	98.4	0.8	0.6	0.3	0.9	6.9	21.4	8.7	12.2	15.9	14.0
29 227	...	9	Worth	690	2 295	3 032	3.3	99.5	0.2	0.0	0.3	0.5	5.6	19.1	5.5	9.3	12.1	14.2
29 229	...	6	Wright	1 767	19 934	1 765	11.3	98.9	0.4	0.6	0.1	0.6	6.7	21.5	7.5	11.2	14.2	13.4

1. MSA = Metropolitan Statistical Area. PMSA = Primary MSA. NECMA = New England County Metropolitan Area. See Appendix A for explanation of these concepts. See Appendix B for list of metropolitan areas identified by type, with component counties.   2. County typology code from the Economic Research Service of USDA. See Appendix A for definition.   3. Dry land or land partially or temporarily covered by water.   4. Hispanic persons may be of any race.

Table B. States and Counties — **Population and Households**

	Population, 1999 (cont'd)				Population — change and components of change, 1980–1999							Households, 1990				
	Age (percent) (cont'd)				Total persons		Percent change		Components of change, 1990–1999						Percent	
STATE County	55 to 64 years	65 to 74 years	75 years and over	Percent female	1990	1980	1980–1990	1990–1999	Births	Deaths	Net migration	Number	Percent change, 1980–1990	Persons per house-hold	Female family house-holder[1]	One person
	16	17	18	19	20	21	22	23	24	25	26	27	28	29	30	31
MISSOURI—Cont'd																
Jasper	9.1	7.6	7.3	52.1	90 465	86 958	4.0	10.8	13 517	9 926	6 554	36 134	7.7	2.44	9.8	27.4
Jefferson	7.4	5.1	3.8	50.2	171 380	146 183	17.2	15.6	24 635	12 239	14 718	59 199	25.5	2.87	9.2	16.7
Johnson	6.6	4.6	4.5	49.3	42 514	39 059	8.8	13.0	6 060	2 678	1 585	14 579	16.3	2.60	6.9	21.6
Knox	11.7	8.8	10.9	51.6	4 482	5 508	-18.6	-3.8	459	635	21	1 819	-12.5	2.40	6.3	28.1
Laclede	9.4	7.3	6.8	51.1	27 158	24 323	11.7	15.7	3 833	2 894	3 390	10 420	15.5	2.56	8.0	23.2
Lafayette	9.4	6.9	8.3	50.7	31 107	29 931	3.9	5.5	3 675	3 577	1 721	11 732	7.4	2.57	7.9	24.8
Lawrence	9.5	7.5	7.8	51.1	30 236	28 973	4.4	10.8	4 280	3 511	2 582	11 724	9.2	2.53	7.9	25.2
Lewis	9.3	7.5	9.3	52.0	10 233	10 901	-6.1	0.0	1 132	1 166	68	3 745	-5.3	2.49	7.0	26.4
Lincoln	8.4	5.6	5.2	49.9	28 892	22 193	30.2	30.6	4 367	2 392	6 883	10 316	35.1	2.77	7.3	20.7
Linn	10.8	9.2	11.2	52.7	13 885	15 495	-10.4	0.1	1 699	1 948	291	5 704	-9.6	2.37	6.5	30.6
Livingston	9.9	8.6	10.0	53.9	14 592	15 739	-7.3	-3.9	1 678	1 818	-389	5 645	-6.2	2.44	7.7	28.7
McDonald	10.5	6.3	5.9	50.1	16 938	14 917	13.5	19.0	2 648	1 788	2 409	6 386	15.6	2.61	7.9	22.5
Macon	10.0	8.7	10.2	52.1	15 345	16 313	-5.9	0.7	1 748	2 081	485	6 160	-3.5	2.44	6.6	27.0
Madison	10.6	8.6	9.1	51.5	11 127	10 725	3.7	4.7	1 272	1 471	760	4 344	5.8	2.52	8.9	24.0
Maries	11.1	8.1	7.8	50.4	7 976	7 551	5.6	5.6	863	855	468	3 028	9.7	2.60	6.8	23.5
Marion	9.0	7.5	9.0	52.6	27 682	28 638	-3.3	0.1	3 684	3 363	-191	10 728	0.3	2.50	9.4	28.4
Mercer	13.8	9.5	11.4	50.7	3 723	4 685	-20.5	6.3	360	485	376	1 577	-17.4	2.32	4.2	29.8
Miller	9.7	7.9	8.2	50.9	20 700	18 539	11.7	9.3	2 805	2 316	1 532	7 977	16.1	2.56	8.5	25.1
Mississippi	8.9	8.1	8.0	53.0	14 442	15 726	-8.2	-7.6	1 910	1 801	-1 179	5 411	-1.8	2.63	16.1	24.7
Moniteau	8.8	7.1	7.8	50.2	12 298	12 068	1.9	8.3	1 635	1 309	732	4 583	4.8	2.59	7.1	25.5
Monroe	9.4	7.8	9.8	50.6	9 104	9 716	-6.3	0.4	968	984	83	3 471	-4.1	2.56	6.3	26.9
Montgomery	10.1	7.5	9.4	51.3	11 355	11 537	-1.6	6.6	1 297	1 492	983	4 341	1.8	2.54	7.5	26.1
Morgan	13.8	10.2	8.9	50.7	15 574	13 807	12.8	21.4	1 992	2 211	3 565	6 269	18.1	2.44	6.0	23.6
New Madrid	9.1	7.7	6.7	52.1	20 928	22 945	-8.8	-4.8	2 759	2 423	-1 290	7 795	-2.1	2.65	13.7	24.3
Newton	9.7	6.9	6.3	50.9	44 445	40 555	9.6	11.9	6 117	4 339	3 653	16 886	13.5	2.59	7.5	22.1
Nodaway	7.4	6.4	8.0	51.4	21 709	21 996	-1.3	-5.4	2 023	1 882	-1 265	7 620	-0.9	2.48	6.5	27.1
Oregon	11.8	8.8	9.0	51.5	9 470	10 238	-7.5	8.7	1 089	1 278	1 046	3 851	-0.9	2.43	7.4	25.2
Osage	9.0	7.2	6.6	48.0	12 018	12 014	0.0	4.2	1 482	1 091	158	4 262	7.1	2.78	5.9	22.3
Ozark	13.8	10.6	8.6	50.2	8 598	7 961	8.0	16.0	928	1 046	1 511	3 486	15.2	2.44	6.0	22.9
Pemiscot	9.0	6.9	7.0	52.9	21 921	24 987	-12.3	-3.5	3 682	2 728	-1 678	8 210	-7.6	2.62	17.2	27.6
Perry	9.2	6.9	8.2	50.2	16 648	16 784	-0.8	4.7	2 088	1 714	464	6 111	5.7	2.67	7.0	23.5
Pettis	10.0	7.7	7.7	51.5	35 437	36 378	-2.6	4.7	4 758	3 981	987	14 056	1.6	2.50	9.0	25.9
Phelps	8.7	7.2	6.5	48.7	35 248	33 633	4.8	10.5	4 126	3 471	3 111	13 277	15.4	2.46	8.3	26.1
Pike	10.3	8.4	8.4	51.4	15 969	17 568	-9.1	2.8	1 904	1 784	374	6 083	-3.4	2.57	8.4	25.7
Platte	7.2	5.5	4.0	50.3	57 867	46 341	24.9	23.9	8 630	3 559	8 860	22 142	35.0	2.58	7.9	22.9
Polk	9.4	7.9	8.0	50.7	21 826	18 822	16.0	17.9	2 913	2 519	3 629	8 031	18.4	2.55	6.5	22.9
Pulaski	5.7	4.7	4.0	46.4	41 307	42 011	-1.7	-7.4	6 245	2 283	-9 752	12 397	17.8	2.84	9.0	18.0
Putnam	12.2	10.1	11.2	51.1	5 079	6 092	-16.6	-4.1	512	726	34	2 166	-9.8	2.31	6.1	30.3
Ralls	9.7	7.6	7.2	50.9	8 476	8 984	-5.7	8.2	887	841	678	3 226	1.4	2.60	6.1	21.5
Randolph	8.4	6.8	8.3	48.3	24 370	25 460	-4.3	-2.1	2 975	2 785	-639	8 943	-3.2	2.50	8.8	26.9
Ray	9.3	6.0	6.0	50.6	21 968	21 378	2.8	8.2	2 728	1 995	1 122	8 020	6.8	2.71	7.4	20.4
Reynolds	11.4	8.2	7.7	50.7	6 661	7 230	-7.9	-0.5	685	651	-32	2 542	-3.7	2.58	7.5	21.0
Ripley	11.7	8.5	8.1	52.3	12 303	12 458	-1.2	15.2	1 574	1 572	1 911	4 788	4.7	2.54	9.6	24.7
St. Charles	6.6	5.1	3.5	50.3	212 751	144 107	47.6	31.8	35 472	12 077	44 680	74 331	60.0	2.83	8.0	18.0
St. Clair	13.2	10.4	11.4	51.8	8 457	8 622	-1.9	9.7	905	1 238	1 164	3 499	2.7	2.36	6.3	28.2
Ste. Genevieve	9.8	7.6	7.2	50.1	16 037	15 180	5.6	8.9	1 788	1 336	1 030	5 707	15.5	2.77	6.6	20.2
St. Francois	9.7	7.7	6.7	49.2	48 904	42 600	14.8	14.1	6 123	5 700	6 589	17 670	16.3	2.59	10.1	23.1
St. Louis	9.2	7.8	6.5	52.4	993 508	974 180	2.0	0.3	127 165	85 327	-36 904	380 110	10.3	2.57	10.7	24.6
Saline	9.1	7.8	8.9	51.4	23 523	24 913	-5.6	-3.2	2 676	2 708	-641	8 903	-4.9	2.46	9.5	28.1
Schuyler	10.2	8.4	10.4	51.2	4 236	4 979	-14.9	4.2	491	606	307	1 729	-10.6	2.42	6.8	27.0
Scotland	10.5	8.4	11.0	51.3	4 822	5 415	-11.0	2.1	634	619	94	1 956	-4.9	2.40	6.3	30.0
Scott	8.2	7.1	6.4	52.4	39 376	39 647	-0.7	3.0	5 505	3 834	-355	14 761	5.7	2.63	12.3	23.6
Shannon	10.4	7.9	7.1	50.9	7 613	7 885	-3.4	9.0	931	758	537	2 917	3.1	2.58	7.0	22.8
Shelby	9.8	8.0	11.7	52.6	6 942	7 826	-11.3	-4.1	781	1 023	-20	2 809	-9.1	2.39	6.6	29.8
Stoddard	10.0	8.4	8.5	51.8	28 895	29 009	-0.4	2.6	3 021	3 570	1 382	11 383	6.4	2.48	9.2	24.6
Stone	14.5	11.1	7.4	50.9	19 078	15 587	22.4	44.2	2 649	2 291	8 136	7 885	29.1	2.40	5.8	21.5
Sullivan	11.5	8.6	10.6	51.4	6 326	7 434	-14.9	8.5	756	931	725	2 615	-11.4	2.33	6.2	28.8
Taney	13.0	9.5	7.9	51.1	25 561	20 467	24.9	38.8	3 840	3 297	9 474	10 321	28.4	2.36	6.8	24.2
Texas	10.8	8.8	8.5	51.5	21 476	21 070	1.9	4.6	2 488	2 421	1 017	8 441	7.4	2.52	7.9	24.7
Vernon	10.0	7.7	7.7	52.7	19 041	19 806	-3.9	2.3	2 448	2 206	285	7 301	-2.6	2.46	9.0	28.0
Warren	9.0	7.2	6.1	50.3	19 534	14 900	31.1	30.2	2 846	1 690	4 791	7 070	37.5	2.73	6.6	20.1
Washington	8.7	6.1	5.1	48.1	20 380	17 983	13.3	14.6	2 756	1 898	2 163	6 982	17.3	2.83	10.4	19.7
Wayne	12.6	10.4	9.8	51.0	11 543	11 277	2.4	13.0	1 383	1 584	1 756	4 607	7.7	2.47	8.9	23.2
Webster	8.6	6.2	6.0	49.4	23 753	20 414	16.4	26.2	3 796	2 214	4 744	8 391	21.1	2.74	7.5	19.9
Worth	12.3	8.5	13.5	52.3	2 440	3 008	-18.9	-5.9	244	379	-1	1 037	-14.8	2.28	5.2	32.4
Wright	10.5	7.4	7.6	51.3	16 758	16 188	3.5	19.0	2 210	1 958	2 965	6 510	7.9	2.54	8.0	25.8

1. No spouse present.

Table B. States and Counties — **Vital Statistics, Health Resources, and Crime**

STATE County	Births, average 1996–1998 Total	Births, average 1996–1998 Rate[1]	Deaths, average 1996–1998 Number Total	Deaths Number Infant[2]	Deaths Rate Total[1]	Deaths Rate Infant[3]	Physicians,[4] 1998 Number	Physicians,[4] 1998 Rate[5]	Hospitals,[4] 1998 Number	Hospitals Beds Number	Hospitals Beds Rate[5]	Medicare enrollees 1999	Serious crimes known to police, 1998[6] Total Number	Serious crimes Rate[7]
	32	33	34	35	36	37	38	39	40	41	42	43	44	45
MISSOURI—Cont'd														
Jasper	1 534	15.5	1 101	9	11.1	5.9	259	260	4	705	708	19 116	4 273	4 391
Jefferson	2 728	14.2	1 422	14	7.4	5.2	81	41	1	228	117	19 626	5 362	2 756
Johnson	634	13.5	312	3	6.6	4.2	41	86	1	70	147	4 902	NA	NA
Knox	54	12.5	64	1	14.6	12.3	1	23	0	0	0	992	NA	NA
Laclede	425	14.0	337	2	11.1	5.5	24	77	1	48	155	5 400	NA	NA
Lafayette	368	11.3	375	2	11.6	5.4	18	55	1	37	113	5 705	468	1 429
Lawrence	482	14.7	410	2	12.5	4.8	35	106	2	174	525	5 800	NA	NA
Lewis	142	13.9	131	0	12.8	2.4	3	29	0	0	0	1 905	138	1 349
Lincoln	494	14.0	276	4	7.8	8.1	15	41	1	36	98	4 536	NA	NA
Linn	180	13.0	204	1	14.7	7.4	9	65	1	34	246	3 283	NA	NA
Livingston	172	12.1	196	2	13.8	13.5	11	78	1	80	565	2 948	NA	NA
McDonald	347	17.7	202	4	10.3	10.6	1	5	0	0	0	2 852	68	342
Macon	200	13.1	221	2	14.5	8.3	9	59	1	38	249	3 279	NA	NA
Madison	139	12.1	162	2	14.1	12.0	12	105	1	147	1 280	2 474	NA	NA
Maries	100	12.0	95	1	11.4	10.0	3	35	0	0	0	1 293	NA	NA
Marion	399	14.3	375	5	13.5	13.4	51	184	1	105	378	5 396	1 022	3 648
Mercer	42	10.4	54	0	13.5	0.0	1	25	0	0	0	825	81	2 013
Miller	319	14.2	263	1	11.7	2.1	7	31	0	0	0	4 352	NA	NA
Mississippi	205	15.1	181	2	13.4	9.8	4	30	0	0	0	2 704	NA	NA
Moniteau	197	14.9	147	2	11.1	10.2	7	53	0	0	0	2 250	NA	NA
Monroe	104	11.6	121	0	13.4	3.2	5	55	0	0	0	1 810	14	154
Montgomery	135	11.3	158	1	13.3	9.9	8	66	0	0	0	2 354	143	1 199
Morgan	212	11.7	247	1	13.7	4.7	10	54	0	0	0	4 169	290	1 593
New Madrid	274	13.4	265	2	12.9	8.5	9	44	0	0	0	3 387	NA	NA
Newton	703	14.5	503	4	10.4	5.7	28	57	1	54	110	6 193	NA	NA
Nodaway	211	10.1	208	1	10.0	6.3	22	106	1	55	265	3 245	395	1 876
Oregon	120	11.9	134	1	13.3	8.3	2	20	0	0	0	2 229	35	349
Osage	170	13.6	128	1	10.3	5.9	5	40	0	0	0	1 856	NA	NA
Ozark	110	11.2	120	0	12.3	0.0	2	20	0	0	0	2 152	70	723
Pemiscot	385	17.8	292	5	13.5	12.1	15	70	1	209	971	3 787	159	734
Perry	228	13.1	182	2	10.4	7.3	11	63	1	55	316	2 898	113	642
Pettis	535	14.5	435	5	11.8	8.7	41	111	1	147	397	6 725	NA	NA
Phelps	446	11.7	385	3	10.1	7.5	72	187	1	227	588	6 501	NA	NA
Pike	202	12.5	191	2	11.8	8.3	19	116	1	25	153	3 034	NA	NA
Platte	932	13.6	397	5	5.8	5.4	108	154	1	55	78	6 812	4 182	6 048
Polk	331	13.0	289	2	11.4	6.0	25	98	1	74	290	4 926	633	2 470
Pulaski	615	16.1	245	5	6.4	8.1	47	122	0	0	0	4 274	334	912
Putnam	58	11.7	76	0	15.2	0.0	4	81	1	26	529	1 169	NA	NA
Ralls	91	10.3	89	1	10.2	7.3	2	23	0	0	0	1 166	NA	NA
Randolph	325	13.5	313	1	13.0	2.0	26	108	1	101	420	4 206	1 004	4 174
Ray	300	12.9	225	2	9.7	6.7	10	42	1	50	211	2 935	480	2 053
Reynolds	70	10.6	75	1	11.3	19.0	3	45	1	29	438	1 260	NA	NA
Ripley	169	12.2	175	1	12.6	7.9	7	50	1	26	185	2 921	163	1 166
St. Charles	3 993	15.1	1 489	24	5.7	6.0	248	91	4	659	242	26 841	7 975	2 997
St. Clair	97	10.7	146	0	16.1	0.0	7	77	2	72	793	2 097	NA	NA
Ste. Genevieve	185	10.8	157	1	9.1	7.2	14	80	1	34	194	2 734	248	1 431
St. Francois	664	12.1	644	7	11.8	10.1	65	117	2	210	378	10 392	NA	NA
St. Louis	12 933	12.9	9 537	99	9.5	7.7	4 037	404	12	3 981	399	158 038	39 713	3 962
Saline	279	12.2	285	3	12.5	11.9	21	92	1	56	247	4 544	618	2 681
Schuyler	53	12.1	67	1	15.2	12.5	2	45	0	0	0	1 056	80	1 817
Scotland	75	15.5	65	0	13.3	0.0	3	62	1	32	665	1 037	NA	NA
Scott	591	14.7	432	6	10.7	9.6	50	124	1	148	368	7 216	NA	NA
Shannon	98	12.1	72	1	8.9	13.6	2	24	0	0	0	1 380	26	317
Shelby	76	11.1	101	0	14.8	4.4	4	59	0	0	0	1 550	66	961
Stoddard	320	10.8	386	3	13.1	8.3	19	64	1	50	169	6 081	NA	NA
Stone	315	11.9	272	1	10.3	4.2	12	45	0	0	0	5 239	468	1 755
Sullivan	98	14.4	94	1	13.8	6.8	3	43	1	47	668	1 470	NA	NA
Taney	500	14.7	376	3	11.0	6.7	43	125	1	99	287	7 221	NA	NA
Texas	263	11.8	258	3	11.6	12.7	11	49	1	53	237	4 551	NA	NA
Vernon	274	14.2	246	4	12.7	13.4	28	144	1	97	499	3 776	965	5 002
Warren	303	12.8	197	2	8.3	6.6	6	24	0	0	0	3 371	695	2 922
Washington	307	13.5	224	2	9.9	5.4	7	30	1	42	183	3 100	538	2 355
Wayne	143	11.1	171	2	13.3	13.9	10	77	0	0	0	3 538	NA	NA
Webster	450	15.8	262	3	9.2	7.4	19	65	0	0	0	4 848	192	670
Worth	23	10.1	43	0	18.6	14.3	1	44	0	0	0	568	42	1 788
Wright	248	12.8	224	2	11.5	8.1	9	46	0	0	0	3 889	NA	NA

1. Per 1,000 estimated resident population, average 1996–1998.   2. Deaths of infants under 1 year old.   3. Deaths of infants under 1 year old per 1,000 live births.   4. Data subject to copyright.   5. Per 100,000 resident population as of July 1 of the year shown.   6. Data for serious crimes have not been adjusted for underreporting; this may affect comparability between geographic areas and over time.   7. Per 100,000 population estimated by the FBI.

Table B. States and Counties — Crime, Education, Money Income, and Poverty

STATE County	Serious crimes known to police, 1998[1] (cont'd) Rate[2] Violent	Property	Education — School enrollment and attainment, 1990 — Enrollment[3] Total	Percent private	Attainment[4] (percent) High school graduate or more	Bachelor's degree or more	Local government expenditures, fiscal 1997[5] Total current expenditures (mil dol)	Current expenditures per student (dollars)	Money income 1989 Per capita[6] (dollars)	Households Median Dollars	Percent change, 1979-1989 (constant 1989 dollars)	Percent with $100,000 or more	Income and poverty, 1997 Median household income	Percent below poverty level All persons	Persons under 18	Persons 5-17 in families
	46	47	48	49	50	51	52	53	54	55	56	57	58	59	60	61
MISSOURI—Cont'd																
Jasper	251	4 140	21 911	8.9	71.4	13.4	77.7	4 290	10 621	20 924	0.0	1.5	29 877	14.0	20.5	17.7
Jefferson	362	2 394	44 624	14.2	71.6	9.0	151.0	4 271	12 226	32 281	-1.7	1.4	43 172	7.8	11.0	9.9
Johnson	NA	NA	15 605	2.7	80.7	21.4	36.4	4 552	10 202	23 044	1.7	1.2	33 270	12.1	15.1	14.5
Knox	NA	NA	928	8.2	72.2	8.1	4.1	5 485	9 048	17 293	-8.0	0.7	23 041	18.2	26.7	24.8
Laclede	NA	NA	5 951	4.1	64.4	8.0	24.5	4 325	9 522	20 122	7.9	1.1	28 136	15.0	21.7	19.6
Lafayette	34	1 395	7 264	11.6	71.1	11.5	28.7	4 862	11 470	24 669	-5.9	1.2	33 304	10.8	14.9	14.4
Lawrence	NA	NA	6 607	7.1	68.9	9.7	26.2	4 438	9 672	20 643	6.8	0.8	27 968	14.7	20.2	18.9
Lewis	88	1 261	2 748	29.5	71.7	10.3	8.2	4 525	9 298	20 575	-10.4	0.7	29 314	14.6	18.5	17.5
Lincoln	NA	NA	7 019	14.2	66.8	8.0	25.6	3 913	11 123	28 054	7.6	0.9	38 449	10.1	14.1	13.0
Linn	NA	NA	2 835	3.1	70.8	10.6	15.2	5 033	9 391	17 367	-8.0	0.6	26 477	14.2	19.1	17.6
Livingston	NA	NA	3 318	8.9	71.7	12.5	12.8	5 083	11 316	21 647	-3.0	1.9	31 104	13.1	17.8	17.0
McDonald	106	236	3 582	5.8	61.1	6.6	11.9	3 573	8 409	17 312	-0.2	0.7	24 802	19.0	28.1	25.4
Macon	NA	NA	3 387	6.8	70.3	11.5	13.5	5 135	9 976	20 271	-4.1	0.9	28 263	11.9	16.9	15.3
Madison	NA	NA	2 449	1.4	54.4	6.7	10.6	4 946	8 560	17 100	6.1	0.7	24 462	17.7	25.1	23.4
Maries	NA	NA	1 755	8.7	61.2	8.3	6.8	4 281	9 426	19 041	-2.1	0.5	27 017	14.3	20.1	18.7
Marion	507	3 141	6 721	17.0	70.9	12.9	24.6	4 605	10 110	21 420	-8.2	1.3	31 109	13.8	18.6	17.2
Mercer	621	1 392	807	0.2	71.0	8.2	4.0	5 477	9 132	16 629	0.7	0.4	25 537	14.4	18.6	17.3
Miller	NA	NA	4 451	4.8	63.0	7.5	23.3	4 509	9 356	18 985	-4.5	0.8	26 659	15.3	21.3	20.5
Mississippi	NA	NA	3 646	3.9	49.2	7.2	12.4	4 453	8 945	16 159	-7.1	1.4	22 987	26.1	37.6	34.8
Moniteau	NA	NA	2 683	13.9	67.8	8.7	11.0	4 470	10 172	22 110	1.9	1.5	31 941	9.6	13.0	12.0
Monroe	11	143	2 170	12.9	69.8	8.1	9.4	4 943	9 444	19 804	-4.7	1.1	29 763	12.1	15.4	15.7
Montgomery	17	1 182	2 424	4.1	62.6	7.8	10.0	4 581	10 128	21 726	5.6	0.8	30 011	12.8	18.1	17.0
Morgan	93	1 500	2 764	10.0	64.3	7.2	9.5	4 340	9 867	19 158	10.1	1.3	25 603	15.8	25.0	23.8
New Madrid	NA	NA	5 199	4.5	52.0	6.7	18.6	4 810	9 034	17 491	3.9	1.6	24 772	22.3	30.7	28.2
Newton	NA	NA	10 467	7.5	72.8	12.1	30.2	3 819	11 136	22 263	6.0	1.8	31 236	12.9	18.2	16.9
Nodaway	43	1 833	8 413	4.8	80.7	17.5	18.8	5 737	9 268	20 347	-3.8	1.7	32 332	12.3	12.3	12.4
Oregon	140	209	1 979	4.9	59.3	7.8	9.3	4 767	7 622	13 705	3.0	0.4	19 847	23.8	34.6	31.4
Osage	NA	NA	2 888	19.8	65.0	7.1	8.5	4 923	10 032	24 983	4.9	0.5	36 171	7.9	9.8	9.5
Ozark	10	713	1 774	3.9	60.9	8.0	8.7	4 671	8 611	16 417	7.0	0.9	20 938	21.2	33.3	28.1
Pemiscot	198	536	5 570	2.2	49.5	6.8	22.2	5 021	7 709	13 911	-9.2	0.7	20 938	28.4	37.6	35.6
Perry	63	579	3 849	24.7	56.4	6.4	11.7	4 556	10 370	23 803	11.5	0.9	33 561	9.9	12.1	11.6
Pettis	NA	NA	8 450	9.6	72.2	12.5	27.9	4 501	11 010	22 101	-1.6	1.6	30 831	13.1	19.7	17.6
Phelps	NA	NA	11 050	8.9	70.1	18.3	31.0	4 568	10 531	20 885	0.8	1.5	29 529	15.5	22.1	20.2
Pike	NA	NA	3 622	11.2	67.5	10.6	14.1	4 686	9 887	21 178	-2.3	1.0	29 673	13.5	18.2	17.6
Platte	899	5 149	15 060	13.2	87.8	25.6	62.7	5 342	16 737	38 173	1.2	4.5	52 960	4.9	6.8	6.6
Polk	191	2 279	5 756	31.7	67.0	12.0	21.9	4 463	8 873	18 672	3.8	1.5	26 487	16.6	22.6	20.6
Pulaski	172	740	10 369	7.9	78.5	12.8	40.1	5 083	9 159	21 559	5.6	0.5	31 701	14.3	16.6	16.8
Putnam	NA	NA	980	3.0	64.5	8.7	4.6	5 050	9 025	15 549	-4.9	1.5	23 135	17.5	26.0	23.8
Ralls	NA	NA	1 951	10.1	70.2	7.8	4.0	4 240	10 554	22 070	-14.0	1.1	31 825	12.0	15.3	15.6
Randolph	420	3 754	6 038	7.0	68.4	10.8	19.7	5 032	10 855	21 425	-3.5	0.9	27 987	16.8	20.9	19.9
Ray	231	1 822	5 307	7.0	71.2	8.4	17.7	4 502	11 213	27 124	-3.2	1.3	36 927	9.7	13.1	13.0
Reynolds	NA	NA	1 465	0.5	53.1	6.5	7.7	5 648	8 667	17 008	-1.3	1.1	22 584	23.3	33.3	32.1
Ripley	129	1 037	2 704	4.9	48.5	6.1	11.5	4 556	7 295	13 740	2.4	0.4	19 671	26.0	36.6	34.2
St. Charles	201	2 796	59 400	25.2	83.3	21.2	227.0	5 054	15 366	40 307	7.3	3.1	54 759	4.7	6.4	5.9
St. Clair	NA	NA	1 596	5.8	60.8	7.9	7.6	4 872	9 097	17 265	9.7	0.3	23 256	19.2	27.8	26.0
Ste. Genevieve	300	1 131	3 608	25.1	62.8	7.4	9.9	4 479	10 775	26 712	-1.0	1.7	37 170	9.4	12.8	12.0
St. Francois	NA	NA	11 213	8.7	62.5	9.1	45.6	4 385	9 585	20 745	-6.1	1.0	28 589	16.3	23.0	20.2
St. Louis	275	3 687	259 509	31.5	82.3	29.2	998.2	6 478	18 625	38 127	2.8	7.0	47 825	7.2	11.2	9.2
Saline	204	2 477	6 057	21.9	67.3	11.9	20.4	5 096	10 624	21 685	-1.6	1.5	28 818	13.1	17.7	16.4
Schuyler	45	1 772	867	4.2	68.0	8.0	3.8	4 599	9 059	16 729	-6.2	1.4	23 895	16.5	22.2	22.9
Scotland	NA	NA	898	7.1	69.5	8.5	4.1	5 171	8 581	15 944	-4.5	0.4	24 060	18.0	24.5	25.4
Scott	NA	NA	9 513	8.4	62.4	9.5	31.5	3 970	9 907	20 764	-3.9	1.2	28 760	17.4	25.0	22.2
Shannon	146	171	1 660	8.1	54.0	6.0	4.5	5 021	7 720	14 910	-1.0	0.6	19 753	25.4	37.0	34.0
Shelby	0	961	1 443	3.6	74.2	8.0	6.8	5 208	9 545	18 316	-0.9	1.3	27 598	14.0	18.9	18.3
Stoddard	NA	NA	6 326	2.5	55.9	8.2	24.1	4 173	9 644	18 259	0.1	1.5	26 222	17.0	24.5	22.2
Stone	405	1 350	3 443	7.0	70.6	11.1	19.7	4 464	11 173	21 049	9.6	1.7	28 623	13.1	23.0	20.2
Sullivan	NA	NA	1 214	1.3	65.8	6.8	5.1	5 182	9 193	15 826	-2.2	0.5	23 817	17.0	24.2	21.9
Taney	NA	NA	5 591	23.5	70.8	14.3	26.1	4 607	11 198	20 260	2.0	1.8	27 001	13.1	22.2	18.7
Texas	NA	NA	4 861	6.6	60.9	7.0	21.7	4 626	8 507	16 757	1.9	1.3	22 773	20.7	28.8	27.0
Vernon	197	4 805	4 464	14.0	67.8	13.1	16.2	4 571	9 587	19 641	-2.3	1.0	26 489	16.4	22.1	21.2
Warren	227	2 695	4 498	22.6	68.0	9.1	14.4	4 087	11 640	28 944	7.2	1.7	38 839	8.5	11.6	12.1
Washington	149	2 206	5 094	6.7	50.8	5.7	18.3	4 471	7 650	17 117	-10.6	0.4	24 649	23.5	30.4	28.9
Wayne	NA	NA	2 391	5.2	48.9	5.9	10.2	4 584	8 434	13 815	-2.6	0.9	18 786	25.4	37.9	35.0
Webster	21	649	5 484	7.1	66.8	8.5	18.9	4 375	9 116	20 525	2.0	1.0	28 577	15.5	21.7	20.6
Worth	213	1 575	492	1.8	74.3	8.7	2.3	4 687	8 475	14 568	-7.0	0.3	23 440	19.1	25.5	24.5
Wright	NA	NA	3 839	4.7	59.7	7.4	19.9	4 903	7 692	15 770	-3.3	0.4	22 330	20.5	27.1	26.3

1. Data for serious crimes have not been adjusted for underreporting; this may affect comparability between geographic areas and over time.   2. Per 100,000 population estimated by the FBI.   3. All persons 3 years old and over enrolled in nursery school through college.   4. Persons 25 years old and over.   5. Elementary and secondary education expenditures, local government fiscal years ending between July 1, 1996 and June 30, 1997.   6. Based on population enumerated as of April 1, 1990.

Table B. States and Counties — **Personal Income**

STATE County	Total (mil dol) 62	Percent change, 1997–1998 63	Per capita[1] Dollars 64	Per capita[1] Rank 65	Wages and salaries[2] (mil dol) 66	Proprietor's income (mil dol) 67	Dividends, interest, and rent (mil dol) 68	Transfer payments Total (mil dol) 69	Gov't payments to individuals Total (mil dol) 70	Social Security (mil dol) 71	Medical payments (mil dol) 72	Income maintenance (mil dol) 73	Unemployment insurance (mil dol) 74
MISSOURI—Cont'd													
Jasper	2 206	3.9	22 140	1 053	1 670	187	409	406	389	159	174	33	5
Jefferson	4 074	6.2	20 843	1 443	1 109	154	502	522	487	227	190	32	10
Johnson	871	4.9	18 272	2 274	529	37	163	122	115	47	44	9	1
Knox	76	-6.6	17 431	2 501	25	5	21	20	20	8	9	2	0
Laclede	578	5.0	18 649	2 168	324	57	110	113	107	45	43	11	2
Lafayette	698	0.0	21 371	1 275	214	50	127	142	136	55	68	7	2
Lawrence	574	3.1	17 338	2 521	196	53	93	130	124	56	49	10	2
Lewis	171	-4.1	16 776	2 659	66	5	33	39	37	16	16	3	0
Lincoln	755	8.2	20 635	1 516	215	45	108	113	106	47	47	7	1
Linn	273	0.1	19 771	1 788	133	25	58	68	66	25	28	4	1
Livingston	323	-0.2	22 872	876	162	31	84	62	59	26	26	5	1
McDonald	323	2.8	16 156	2 771	134	35	44	67	64	26	26	9	1
Macon	283	-0.2	18 462	2 223	119	18	65	70	67	28	30	4	1
Madison	196	3.1	16 969	2 619	64	15	36	58	56	23	24	5	1
Maries	145	2.4	17 168	2 571	35	5	29	34	33	13	15	2	0
Marion	596	3.0	21 375	1 274	379	33	114	126	121	47	56	10	2
Mercer	33	-50.1	8 162	3 107	46	-23	12	16	16	7	6	1	0
Miller	386	3.4	17 186	2 564	172	36	65	88	84	34	37	7	2
Mississippi	233	-1.3	17 313	2 527	88	23	36	70	67	23	31	11	1
Moniteau	257	1.8	19 421	1 916	98	19	56	46	44	20	19	3	1
Monroe	170	-4.9	18 826	2 117	80	10	38	37	36	15	15	3	1
Montgomery	235	2.4	19 518	1 883	85	21	44	52	50	21	23	3	1
Morgan	331	5.3	17 949	2 360	93	45	77	84	81	38	32	6	1
New Madrid	333	-0.6	16 379	2 727	238	17	49	97	93	30	45	15	1
Newton	1 023	5.0	20 783	1 461	435	88	159	167	158	73	62	12	3
Nodaway	399	1.2	19 288	1 961	221	34	83	65	62	28	24	5	0
Oregon	142	3.8	13 975	3 007	54	9	24	51	49	18	20	6	1
Osage	273	3.6	21 907	1 127	81	20	48	39	37	17	15	2	1
Ozark	138	3.7	13 907	3 014	32	10	29	45	44	19	17	5	1
Pemiscot	348	-5.0	16 207	2 762	152	21	49	117	113	31	56	22	2
Perry	361	3.6	20 618	1 520	222	16	69	62	59	27	25	4	1
Pettis	809	5.2	21 823	1 152	511	59	151	150	144	60	60	11	2
Phelps	770	5.0	19 980	1 716	420	56	154	147	140	55	60	12	1
Pike	305	4.2	18 581	2 187	143	15	62	71	68	28	32	5	1
Platte	2 156	6.0	30 801	140	1 121	138	295	160	147	74	55	6	2
Polk	439	6.2	17 181	2 567	162	42	83	103	99	37	45	8	1
Pulaski	801	-0.4	20 369	1 613	587	35	108	104	99	32	42	11	2
Putnam	81	-1.0	16 613	2 692	21	5	21	24	23	9	10	2	0
Ralls	187	-1.3	21 026	1 381	71	14	37	34	32	13	12	2	1
Randolph	441	5.5	18 451	2 228	247	28	75	105	101	34	44	8	2
Ray	454	3.4	19 168	1 990	111	42	59	75	70	33	28	4	1
Reynolds	103	3.6	15 560	2 869	59	7	16	34	33	12	15	4	0
Ripley	190	3.7	13 545	3 041	53	17	31	72	70	25	31	10	1
St. Charles	7 230	7.9	26 570	336	2 931	227	954	615	567	288	217	25	10
St. Clair	148	1.8	16 283	2 745	45	10	34	45	43	20	17	4	0
Ste. Genevieve	351	4.1	20 204	1 648	161	17	71	60	57	28	23	3	1
St. Francois	898	-2.2	16 214	2 761	491	59	153	249	239	98	105	22	3
St. Louis	36 702	3.6	36 800	50	25 962	2 249	9 045	3 466	3 290	1 656	1 287	177	48
Saline	500	-0.8	22 044	1 090	249	45	94	128	124	39	72	7	1
Schuyler	63	-2.0	14 174	2 993	16	4	14	20	19	7	9	2	0
Scotland	86	-6.3	17 877	2 386	27	11	20	23	22	8	11	2	0
Scott	801	1.7	19 884	1 750	398	80	124	178	171	62	77	20	2
Shannon	114	3.4	13 782	3 026	38	15	15	36	34	12	14	5	1
Shelby	133	-8.3	19 654	1 837	55	13	33	30	29	13	13	2	0
Stoddard	536	-2.0	18 050	2 332	230	60	91	134	129	52	57	13	2
Stone	582	8.4	21 666	1 202	142	71	123	112	107	54	36	7	4
Sullivan	136	2.7	19 505	1 886	83	13	20	34	33	10	18	3	0
Taney	732	6.2	21 239	1 309	503	77	157	153	147	69	56	8	6
Texas	321	3.2	14 340	2 980	134	27	58	93	89	34	38	10	2
Vernon	355	-4.1	18 238	2 285	185	22	68	103	99	33	54	7	1
Warren	512	6.4	20 885	1 429	166	24	80	82	77	37	33	4	1
Washington	362	3.6	15 714	2 842	112	27	37	94	90	31	41	13	2
Wayne	183	3.5	14 002	3 004	48	15	27	76	74	28	32	9	1
Webster	473	5.5	16 227	2 756	152	42	61	95	89	38	38	8	1
Worth	38	-3.3	16 459	2 713	10	6	9	10	9	4	4	1	0
Wright	275	5.0	14 023	3 003	106	35	51	81	77	30	33	10	1

1. Based on the resident population estimated as of July 1 of the year shown.   2. Includes other labor income.

Table B. States and Counties — Earnings, Social Security, and Housing

STATE County	Earnings, 1998 Total (mil dol)	Farm	Goods-related[1] Total	Manu- facturing	Service-related and other[2] Total	Retail trade	Finance, insur- ance, and real estate	Services	Govern- ment	Social Security bene- ficiaries, December 1998 Number	Rate[3]	Supple- mental Security Income recipients, December 1998	Housing units, 1990 Total	Percent change, 1980–1990
	75	76	77	78	79	80	81	82	83	84	85	86	87	88
MISSOURI—Cont'd														
Jasper	1 857	0.5	28.6	23.6	61.1	11.0	3.3	24.2	9.9	20 007	201	2 773	39 554	9.2
Jefferson	1 263	-0.2	28.8	15.7	52.7	13.1	4.8	22.7	18.6	26 406	135	1 864	63 423	24.0
Johnson	565	-0.6	D	13.6	D	8.2	2.6	10.0	55.2	5 943	125	507	16 010	15.2
Knox	30	4.8	D	7.5	D	10.6	5.5	18.6	30.8	1 143	262	132	2 254	-10.3
Laclede	381	0.1	D	39.8	D	16.4	2.8	16.5	10.7	6 305	203	888	11 564	17.5
Lafayette	264	4.5	20.3	12.1	51.8	13.3	5.2	20.2	23.3	6 696	205	447	12 820	8.0
Lawrence	249	4.6	D	15.1	D	16.2	4.1	14.9	19.2	7 495	226	718	12 788	8.8
Lewis	72	-3.8	D	20.1	D	10.8	4.3	25.3	23.3	2 093	205	167	4 244	-3.1
Lincoln	260	3.3	32.1	16.4	44.3	12.5	4.3	14.4	20.3	5 601	153	436	12 284	27.2
Linn	159	3.3	D	31.5	D	10.2	3.1	15.3	15.7	3 382	245	305	6 566	-8.0
Livingston	193	2.3	25.6	17.1	54.4	12.3	6.5	21.6	17.8	3 370	238	331	6 294	-6.1
McDonald	169	9.9	47.7	40.4	29.9	8.9	2.6	8.0	12.5	3 625	182	536	7 327	14.4
Macon	137	-3.8	D	18.3	D	12.9	5.0	14.6	31.8	3 608	236	277	6 955	-3.6
Madison	79	-0.3	D	17.8	D	15.0	2.8	16.3	24.6	2 958	258	389	5 282	5.3
Maries	40	-9.4	D	18.4	D	13.0	6.5	20.5	20.7	1 789	211	146	3 715	8.7
Marion	412	0.7	D	24.5	D	10.3	3.1	25.6	13.7	6 020	217	861	12 026	1.9
Mercer	23	-1.3	D	6.1	D	9.1	5.0	14.7	30.5	1 010	252	70	2 225	-9.6
Miller	207	3.4	29.2	17.3	52.7	15.9	4.8	17.5	14.7	4 558	203	484	9 766	23.2
Mississippi	111	10.9	D	14.9	D	14.2	3.4	13.1	18.6	3 127	233	731	5 757	-4.6
Moniteau	117	4.4	D	25.1	D	9.7	3.9	12.2	24.7	2 547	192	143	5 043	8.8
Monroe	90	2.2	D	40.7	D	7.7	2.9	10.2	21.7	2 026	225	178	4 114	0.5
Montgomery	105	-3.0	35.1	24.0	51.3	10.4	5.5	16.8	16.6	2 696	223	220	5 241	1.4
Morgan	137	11.8	D	15.4	D	18.4	5.0	13.8	16.6	4 853	263	362	12 642	21.4
New Madrid	255	4.2	45.9	44.3	38.2	9.5	2.0	8.5	11.7	4 218	207	1 123	8 557	-5.2
Newton	523	3.7	D	31.5	D	11.6	2.6	17.2	10.8	9 379	191	697	18 384	14.6
Nodaway	254	1.6	33.6	26.3	38.4	9.4	4.1	16.2	26.4	3 620	174	297	8 349	-1.9
Oregon	63	-4.2	D	18.0	D	15.5	5.6	17.1	20.2	2 644	260	533	4 484	-0.3
Osage	101	1.8	D	30.9	D	11.6	3.8	14.1	17.4	2 241	180	119	5 414	7.2
Ozark	42	-2.4	D	10.7	D	12.1	6.8	24.7	28.1	2 653	268	370	4 451	18.8
Pemiscot	173	1.7	D	14.6	D	10.7	3.3	17.5	30.9	4 676	217	1 853	8 806	-10.3
Perry	237	-1.1	D	42.1	D	9.0	3.4	13.2	11.2	3 443	198	296	6 867	6.4
Pettis	570	2.8	41.0	33.4	41.3	10.8	4.3	15.5	15.0	7 682	207	863	15 443	1.2
Phelps	476	-0.8	13.6	8.0	45.8	13.0	3.3	21.4	41.4	7 414	192	967	14 715	13.9
Pike	158	1.0	D	20.5	D	10.7	3.8	15.7	27.5	3 580	219	343	7 128	-3.5
Platte	1 259	0.8	14.7	9.0	76.2	6.9	6.0	23.5	8.3	8 053	115	319	24 362	35.8
Polk	204	0.4	D	9.3	D	13.4	4.5	28.9	21.7	5 046	198	645	8 979	15.9
Pulaski	622	0.4	D	2.2	D	6.5	1.7	8.7	74.4	4 721	123	716	13 838	16.6
Putnam	26	-3.4	D	D	D	11.2	7.9	10.7	40.8	1 329	271	165	2 590	-10.3
Ralls	85	6.0	43.3	37.6	D	6.5	3.7	11.3	14.1	1 708	194	122	3 766	10.4
Randolph	276	1.0	D	14.0	D	11.8	5.5	18.3	20.0	4 439	185	611	10 131	0.0
Ray	153	1.9	D	14.5	D	10.3	7.7	17.9	22.2	3 973	168	212	8 611	4.6
Reynolds	67	-1.0	D	21.6	D	4.8	1.5	D	18.0	1 664	251	312	3 537	2.6
Ripley	71	3.2	D	18.1	D	15.8	3.6	18.4	27.7	3 558	253	783	5 597	4.9
St. Charles	3 158	0.2	34.4	21.9	53.2	13.1	4.1	24.7	12.2	31 591	116	1 397	79 113	58.1
St. Clair	55	-3.3	D	2.4	D	15.3	4.8	24.5	33.1	2 654	292	253	4 645	11.6
Ste. Genevieve	178	0.4	D	33.6	D	8.6	4.0	11.8	15.0	3 312	189	179	6 766	14.1
St. Francois	550	0.2	26.0	18.7	51.0	13.2	4.0	24.9	22.8	12 256	221	1 837	20 321	16.7
St. Louis	28 211	0.0	27.2	20.9	65.4	8.4	9.6	31.3	7.4	175 113	175	11 186	401 839	12.2
Saline	294	5.4	D	25.7	D	8.5	3.4	18.0	21.5	4 958	218	542	10 033	-2.6
Schuyler	20	-8.6	D	6.5	D	18.5	4.8	13.7	37.3	1 008	227	136	1 986	-5.7
Scotland	38	2.9	D	11.1	D	13.6	4.2	13.1	36.2	1 165	242	129	2 302	-2.3
Scott	477	1.0	20.6	14.2	63.4	11.5	4.7	27.5	15.0	8 310	206	1 649	15 881	4.4
Shannon	53	-1.3	D	32.9	D	9.4	3.0	16.1	25.5	1 886	229	350	3 312	2.2
Shelby	68	3.2	37.1	26.3	38.5	6.5	4.4	11.4	21.2	1 676	246	139	3 277	-9.5
Stoddard	290	7.9	D	20.7	D	12.8	3.8	16.8	14.1	7 135	241	1 149	12 288	2.5
Stone	213	0.7	D	4.2	D	12.5	6.2	38.5	13.0	6 622	247	402	11 294	27.7
Sullivan	96	18.2	D	41.5	D	5.6	2.7	9.3	12.8	1 536	218	253	3 093	-11.7
Taney	581	0.1	D	3.3	D	21.2	9.3	41.2	8.4	8 571	248	539	13 273	29.2
Texas	161	0.1	27.0	19.9	48.7	13.2	4.7	14.0	24.2	4 893	219	788	9 525	9.4
Vernon	207	-2.5	D	25.1	D	11.8	5.7	19.8	24.3	4 412	227	677	8 181	-1.9
Warren	190	0.5	43.7	33.0	42.5	11.2	5.5	14.1	13.3	4 270	174	212	8 841	35.2
Washington	139	-1.4	D	8.7	D	12.2	3.7	21.1	36.2	4 165	181	903	8 075	13.6
Wayne	62	-0.4	D	16.1	D	15.2	4.9	17.8	30.0	3 890	298	734	6 406	13.1
Webster	194	0.9	35.9	24.6	45.0	13.1	4.8	15.1	18.2	5 206	179	639	9 067	17.7
Worth	16	9.3	D	D	D	7.9	5.3	12.3	30.5	655	285	48	1 269	-13.0
Wright	141	6.0	D	18.1	D	18.5	3.8	13.6	21.6	4 551	232	823	7 214	7.6

1. Covers mining, construction, and manufacturing.   2. Covers private sector earnings in agricultural services, forestry, and fisheries; transportation and public utilities; wholesale trade; retail trade; finance, insurance, and real estate; and services.   3. Per 1,000 resident population estimated as of July 1 of the year shown.

Table B. States and Counties — Housing, Labor Force, and Employment

STATE County	Housing units, 1990 (cont'd) Occupied units Total	Percent	Owner-occupied Median value[1]	Owner cost as a percent of income With a mortgage	Without a mortgage	Renter-occupied Median rent[2]	Rent as percent of income	Sub-standard units[3] (percent)	Civilian labor force, 1999 Total	Percent change, 1998–1999	Unemployment Total	Rate[4]	Civilian employment, 1990[5] Total	Percent Professional, managerial, and technical	Precision production, craft, and repair
	89	90	91	92	93	94	95	96	97	98	99	100	101	102	103
MISSOURI—Cont'd															
Jasper	36 134	69.3	38 300	16.9	12.0	301	24.8	2.4	54 527	-1.9	1 588	2.9	41 148	22.7	12.3
Jefferson	59 199	81.2	65 300	18.4	12.1	418	25.4	2.9	100 923	0.2	3 290	3.3	82 349	20.5	17.5
Johnson	14 579	58.6	55 300	18.3	11.6	341	27.7	3.2	22 642	-3.2	498	2.2	17 708	25.7	10.9
Knox	1 819	75.0	20 500	20.7	13.8	230	24.8	1.9	1 997	0.8	52	2.6	1 915	16.8	8.7
Laclede	10 420	73.5	42 100	20.7	12.9	271	23.2	3.6	15 755	-2.3	687	4.4	11 591	17.9	15.0
Lafayette	11 732	74.1	45 300	18.9	11.8	307	24.3	2.7	16 352	-0.5	576	3.5	13 851	20.1	13.6
Lawrence	11 724	74.4	37 900	17.9	12.1	267	23.7	3.2	15 744	1.1	548	3.5	13 157	19.3	12.1
Lewis	3 745	74.0	28 000	16.7	12.8	222	24.0	2.5	5 592	-2.1	175	3.1	4 491	20.7	11.1
Lincoln	10 316	80.0	55 200	17.9	12.9	341	26.8	3.4	17 761	2.2	586	3.3	13 072	18.4	17.5
Linn	5 704	77.6	22 400	15.9	14.0	234	23.7	2.7	6 368	-1.1	374	5.9	5 708	20.3	10.9
Livingston	5 645	70.9	35 800	16.7	12.6	269	26.1	2.5	7 115	-5.0	183	2.6	6 163	22.6	10.9
McDonald	6 386	75.6	31 800	19.2	13.2	239	23.8	5.7	8 299	-4.8	319	3.8	6 932	13.5	15.7
Macon	6 160	76.5	32 700	16.7	12.6	244	22.5	2.3	7 510	0.1	304	4.0	6 370	20.1	14.5
Madison	4 344	76.7	33 100	20.3	12.4	261	26.4	4.0	4 346	-4.4	251	5.8	4 154	16.6	15.6
Maries	3 028	82.2	35 000	22.1	13.4	224	25.3	4.1	4 447	0.1	137	3.1	3 418	18.4	11.7
Marion	10 728	69.1	36 000	14.3	12.1	256	22.8	2.7	15 737	0.3	569	3.6	11 999	23.5	11.1
Mercer	1 577	75.0	18 900	16.7	13.7	195	24.2	3.0	1 598	0.3	48	3.0	1 364	17.1	13.6
Miller	7 977	76.2	43 700	22.2	14.2	277	26.0	4.2	11 533	-1.3	554	4.8	8 871	16.8	17.6
Mississippi	5 411	64.9	32 300	19.9	14.2	230	29.0	4.1	5 978	-1.4	313	5.2	5 429	17.1	11.4
Moniteau	4 583	78.8	38 700	17.6	12.2	264	23.7	2.7	7 243	-1.7	191	2.6	5 678	16.4	14.1
Monroe	3 471	77.5	31 800	18.4	13.5	240	22.4	4.0	4 549	-4.4	194	4.3	3 812	19.0	11.7
Montgomery	4 341	78.9	33 000	17.1	12.2	272	24.1	4.1	5 836	-0.7	249	4.3	4 803	18.1	14.3
Morgan	6 269	80.7	45 300	21.1	12.2	273	28.3	3.4	8 356	-1.4	345	4.1	6 435	16.0	17.3
New Madrid	7 795	64.0	32 800	18.4	13.6	266	27.1	5.5	8 774	-1.1	456	5.2	7 596	18.2	12.3
Newton	16 886	76.9	42 900	18.2	12.1	292	23.5	3.0	27 393	-1.1	988	3.6	20 419	22.0	14.5
Nodaway	7 620	65.4	37 100	17.8	12.5	277	29.4	2.2	12 824	0.1	159	1.2	10 298	22.9	10.0
Oregon	3 851	79.0	26 000	21.8	14.9	210	26.2	4.2	4 410	1.4	182	4.1	3 377	18.4	11.4
Osage	4 262	82.9	43 700	19.7	11.6	235	22.3	2.8	7 331	-0.8	329	4.5	5 882	15.4	14.5
Ozark	3 486	82.0	36 500	21.7	12.1	241	23.9	6.7	4 071	-2.7	187	4.6	3 277	19.0	11.2
Pemiscot	8 210	56.9	28 800	19.2	14.6	234	29.2	6.4	8 274	-2.9	571	6.9	7 412	18.1	12.9
Perry	6 111	81.1	43 500	16.2	12.4	276	21.1	4.3	10 793	-1.9	237	2.2	7 660	15.1	15.4
Pettis	14 056	74.5	40 100	18.7	13.1	319	26.0	2.7	21 641	-0.4	847	3.9	15 835	22.2	12.5
Phelps	13 277	65.6	47 200	17.9	11.8	294	26.6	2.9	19 744	-1.1	517	2.6	14 793	30.7	11.1
Pike	6 083	74.7	32 600	15.9	12.6	259	25.5	4.8	8 216	4.9	315	3.8	6 869	19.5	13.5
Platte	22 142	65.1	81 200	18.6	11.7	443	21.8	1.7	42 889	1.0	848	2.0	31 998	33.5	11.1
Polk	8 031	73.5	39 600	20.1	12.1	261	25.6	3.9	12 285	1.7	388	3.2	9 207	21.6	10.8
Pulaski	12 397	55.6	51 400	23.2	12.2	353	24.0	4.2	12 069	0.1	756	6.3	11 288	23.6	9.8
Putnam	2 166	77.0	21 300	20.7	13.0	205	24.0	3.1	1 989	5.5	65	3.3	1 966	16.8	10.2
Ralls	3 226	80.3	37 900	18.3	13.2	270	26.9	3.1	5 293	0.4	201	3.8	3 886	16.6	15.2
Randolph	8 943	73.0	33 200	17.8	13.3	276	25.3	2.4	10 935	3.5	435	4.0	9 868	21.9	12.6
Ray	8 020	79.0	46 400	18.0	12.5	331	25.0	2.7	11 381	1.1	458	4.0	9 328	18.6	14.7
Reynolds	2 542	76.5	29 300	22.4	13.5	224	24.6	6.9	3 196	-2.8	144	4.5	2 402	16.6	15.7
Ripley	4 788	75.7	29 200	20.7	13.2	241	31.6	6.0	5 340	0.1	237	4.4	3 800	19.2	11.2
St. Charles	74 331	76.4	83 600	20.0	11.5	485	23.0	2.0	152 712	2.2	3 307	2.2	112 393	32.5	13.0
St. Clair	3 499	75.2	28 400	22.2	13.2	217	24.0	4.2	3 735	-2.9	161	4.3	3 188	19.6	14.8
Ste. Genevieve	5 707	82.7	53 800	18.7	12.1	295	24.9	4.2	8 717	-2.5	297	3.4	7 189	16.9	16.4
St. Francois	17 670	74.0	40 200	17.9	12.3	307	27.1	3.8	24 674	-2.6	1 429	5.8	17 811	21.8	13.7
St. Louis	380 110	73.9	83 500	18.1	11.8	482	24.1	1.6	544 849	-1.1	15 088	2.8	507 521	38.0	8.5
Saline	8 903	70.6	37 600	19.0	12.7	308	23.4	2.6	11 845	-1.2	313	2.6	10 528	19.0	12.4
Schuyler	1 729	75.4	20 400	18.7	14.8	203	24.6	3.3	2 382	-0.5	81	3.4	1 770	17.1	10.8
Scotland	1 956	73.6	24 300	18.5	14.1	190	24.6	3.9	2 199	4.4	64	2.9	2 035	18.5	13.2
Scott	14 761	69.1	41 700	17.8	12.9	295	27.4	2.8	20 290	1.0	834	4.1	16 912	20.6	12.5
Shannon	2 917	78.7	25 900	21.0	12.5	194	26.5	8.6	4 009	0.1	207	5.2	3 007	12.7	13.7
Shelby	2 809	75.7	22 900	18.4	12.9	202	23.6	3.1	3 401	-3.1	195	5.7	2 843	17.2	10.1
Stoddard	11 383	71.9	34 100	17.5	13.3	253	24.7	2.5	13 001	-1.3	634	4.9	11 779	17.3	14.9
Stone	7 885	81.6	58 800	21.2	11.5	305	23.5	3.4	13 671	-1.0	1 088	8.0	7 582	21.2	15.3
Sullivan	2 615	75.6	16 100	18.4	15.0	209	22.6	4.3	3 992	-1.4	79	2.0	2 616	16.7	15.0
Taney	10 321	74.7	55 400	20.2	12.5	307	24.6	2.9	30 053	0.8	1 858	6.2	10 947	25.9	12.4
Texas	8 441	75.3	33 700	21.8	12.8	220	25.0	4.8	8 861	-3.3	781	8.8	8 401	14.9	14.2
Vernon	7 301	72.5	32 100	18.4	13.7	272	24.2	3.2	8 984	-0.8	258	2.9	8 000	23.6	10.0
Warren	7 070	80.8	63 600	20.0	12.2	341	24.9	3.1	12 147	2.6	425	3.5	8 964	18.6	15.1
Washington	6 982	78.5	34 200	19.4	13.4	292	30.4	9.5	9 534	-3.2	693	7.3	6 824	16.5	13.7
Wayne	4 607	76.5	29 000	20.4	12.9	246	26.7	6.1	3 406	-1.5	266	7.8	3 891	15.9	14.5
Webster	8 391	77.8	41 200	20.8	12.5	268	24.3	5.5	13 971	2.3	405	2.9	10 061	15.6	16.3
Worth	1 037	75.9	14 999	18.3	13.3	183	22.4	2.0	841	-4.2	32	3.8	938	16.5	12.3
Wright	6 510	73.7	31 100	20.0	13.9	219	27.0	3.9	7 239	4.8	375	5.2	6 543	13.9	11.8

1. Specified owner-occupied units.   2. Specified renter-occupied units.   3. Overcrowded or lacking complete plumbing facilities.   4. Percent of civilian labor force.   5. Persons 16 years and older.

Table B. States and Counties — Nonfarm Employment and Agriculture

STATE County	Number of establishments	Employment Total	Health Care and Social Assistance	Manufacturing	Retail trade	Finance and Insurance	Professional Scientific and Technical Services	Annual payroll Total (mil dol)	Average per employee (dollars)	Farms Number	Percent with— Less than 50 acres	500 acres and over	Farm operators Whose principal occupation is farming (percent)
	104	105	106	107	108	109	110	111	112	113	114	115	116
MISSOURI—Cont'd													
Jasper	3 024	53 535	6 805	12 250	7 791	1 200	949	1 210	22 604	1 355	30.0	8.5	39.3
Jefferson	3 398	34 432	5 008	5 852	6 335	810	763	761	22 089	659	31.1	5.8	33.8
Johnson	832	9 110	1 324	1 987	1 690	362	178	174	19 153	1 626	21.9	12.1	42.0
Knox	114	597	80	D	107	50	18	10	15 923	602	10.6	29.7	61.1
Laclede	801	11 162	1 048	4 740	1 927	305	120	227	20 374	1 300	18.1	12.5	41.1
Lafayette	823	6 920	887	1 133	1 624	297	120	116	16 697	1 215	25.3	16.8	52.0
Lawrence	627	7 043	1 157	1 761	1 169	160	89	144	20 503	1 733	28.7	8.3	42.5
Lewis	232	2 127	329	D	260	98	9	38	17 638	719	15.2	20.6	49.5
Lincoln	730	6 654	876	1 130	1 203	223	345	138	20 772	989	25.8	14.6	45.1
Linn	354	4 397	629	1 998	547	148	73	89	20 159	933	14.1	22.5	47.5
Livingston	463	5 172	946	894	1 038	197	141	102	19 720	738	15.4	20.5	47.3
McDonald	336	4 856	202	3 123	450	91	51	89	18 340	1 078	23.1	7.6	39.7
Macon	360	3 824	449	1 144	782	161	81	62	16 238	1 155	13.7	17.3	42.3
Madison	272	2 588	476	528	464	82	105	38	14 788	386	10.9	15.5	36.3
Maries	132	1 054	131	264	207	70	D	21	19 603	817	12.9	16.5	42.8
Marion	824	11 412	1 735	3 391	1 777	334	267	251	21 993	695	15.7	18.7	49.1
Mercer	87	483	79	D	82	42	5	9	19 296	539	12.1	24.9	45.8
Miller	621	6 099	331	1 432	1 048	154	207	126	20 626	1 067	12.7	9.5	41.3
Mississippi	289	2 832	320	590	594	97	21	48	16 977	267	10.5	57.3	77.5
Moniteau	332	3 141	338	1 071	506	123	47	57	18 278	1 024	17.5	9.7	40.5
Monroe	215	2 204	258	D	249	77	31	47	21 496	886	12.4	21.0	45.5
Montgomery	354	2 788	316	800	442	143	34	50	17 817	765	17.1	20.3	41.3
Morgan	505	3 161	151	858	884	109	102	53	16 622	869	19.4	10.8	47.4
New Madrid	375	6 006	623	2 603	1 021	146	D	147	24 394	429	7.7	55.5	76.0
Newton	1 027	16 669	3 718	4 428	1 676	426	168	358	21 466	1 622	31.3	6.0	39.3
Nodaway	529	6 323	953	1 680	1 010	205	113	129	20 370	1 257	14.3	26.1	57.9
Oregon	214	1 680	248	420	397	63	30	25	15 029	798	17.3	14.8	45.0
Osage	266	2 618	194	944	390	89	26	53	20 128	1 147	13.3	11.5	41.7
Ozark	169	932	99	154	264	70	18	14	15 524	781	12.5	14.7	47.5
Pemiscot	380	4 685	1 109	927	667	142	39	83	17 663	306	12.7	58.2	78.1
Perry	466	7 346	704	3 178	860	187	91	166	22 546	857	20.0	10.6	43.4
Pettis	1 034	16 743	2 174	5 695	2 209	423	270	363	21 678	1 249	20.7	16.1	50.2
Phelps	1 047	11 605	2 856	1 356	2 256	319	428	210	18 132	758	21.0	12.9	34.7
Pike	409	3 556	625	780	631	141	D	79	22 150	944	17.1	18.8	46.0
Platte	1 762	33 722	2 182	2 160	2 677	3 442	999	851	25 244	714	31.4	13.6	43.1
Polk	568	6 483	1 589	841	948	184	119	115	17 707	1 575	23.5	9.7	44.8
Pulaski	676	5 598	1 064	697	1 196	281	175	95	16 913	539	16.7	15.8	35.6
Putnam	107	598	122	67	137	59	26	9	14 890	615	12.7	24.7	50.6
Ralls	175	2 067	240	930	203	41	20	46	22 078	550	13.8	26.2	48.5
Randolph	556	7 284	1 230	1 336	1 273	477	103	156	21 476	801	16.0	14.2	42.8
Ray	409	3 440	653	567	643	105	109	64	18 693	1 075	23.7	12.3	40.6
Reynolds	168	1 766	247	589	129	41	10	43	24 175	302	10.9	19.9	34.1
Ripley	234	1 886	433	556	374	67	29	30	16 095	472	13.8	18.2	46.8
St. Charles	6 001	85 552	9 126	15 067	14 564	1 892	4 093	2 190	25 599	680	29.4	16.0	48.8
St. Clair	190	1 473	636	80	301	83	D	20	13 834	778	16.1	22.1	53.1
Ste. Genevieve	368	4 869	607	1 821	467	134	79	113	23 186	631	17.7	11.6	37.1
St. Francois	1 283	16 284	3 784	3 644	2 806	440	370	312	19 158	649	25.6	6.3	34.4
St. Louis	30 262	582 360	66 113	82 380	74 037	33 707	38 204	18 952	32 543	291	45.7	9.6	40.5
Saline	576	7 399	1 273	2 417	1 019	189	72	148	19 949	936	14.4	28.8	57.7
Schuyler	91	382	34	11	146	37	D	5	13 398	493	13.8	18.1	52.5
Scotland	138	771	128	168	172	63	15	12	15 131	600	12.3	22.2	52.3
Scott	1 143	14 049	2 125	3 453	1 949	481	292	285	20 310	541	21.8	26.1	53.0
Shannon	153	1 309	187	671	146	51	6	19	14 225	470	16.8	15.7	36.0
Shelby	198	1 691	95	614	224	83	56	36	21 378	644	12.3	27.3	59.9
Stoddard	740	7 572	1 040	2 240	1 306	251	94	144	18 958	941	22.6	27.1	59.1
Stone	648	4 173	256	314	783	168	59	93	22 295	684	23.4	9.4	39.9
Sullivan	122	2 516	343	D	172	D	D	48	19 239	791	9.2	25.7	49.9
Taney	1 730	16 859	1 327	785	3 072	380	515	362	21 449	459	17.0	17.4	40.3
Texas	483	4 704	684	1 436	877	184	65	87	18 589	1 478	16.6	13.3	47.2
Vernon	501	5 925	1 129	1 478	987	321	103	118	19 862	1 265	21.1	17.2	46.8
Warren	536	5 864	578	2 026	954	130	54	127	21 672	555	26.8	13.3	41.8
Washington	335	2 755	556	617	523	88	27	52	19 003	499	14.6	11.6	33.7
Wayne	241	1 826	307	523	462	85	26	26	14 004	380	10.3	12.4	36.6
Webster	593	4 902	491	1 336	894	238	113	93	18 928	1 691	31.3	6.9	40.0
Worth	69	298	31	88	D	14	D	4	12 993	356	12.4	26.1	50.0
Wright	393	3 652	375	891	837	156	62	66	17 960	1 331	19.8	12.1	51.3

Table B. States and Counties — **Agriculture, Land, and Water**

STATE County	Agriculture, 1997 (cont'd)														Percent of land owned by Fed. Gov. 1997	Water consumption 1995 (mil gal/day)
	Land in farms				Value of land and buildings		Value of machinery and equipment Average per farm ($1,000)	Value of products sold				Percent of farms with sales of —			
		Acres								Percent from —					
	Acreage (1,000)	Percent change, 1992–1997	Average size of farm	Total irrigated (1,000)	Total cropland (1,000)	Average per farm ($1,000)	Average per acre (dollars)		Total (mil dol)	Average per farm (dollars)	Crops	Live-stock and poultry products	$10,000 or more	$100,000 or more		
	117	118	119	120	121	122	123	124	125	126	127	128	129	130	131	132
MISSOURI—Cont'd																
Jasper	271	-3.5	200	6	180	230	1 196	29	76	56 399	36.7	63.3	35.9	7.8	0.0	25.9
Jefferson	109	-8.8	166	0	57	290	2 021	21	9	13 606	41.6	58.4	19.9	2.1	0.0	835.2
Johnson	400	7.7	246	1	279	275	1 112	40	54	33 082	38.4	61.6	39.8	6.3	0.7	5.5
Knox	281	4.7	466	0	207	382	796	64	37	60 814	59.5	40.5	58.5	16.3	0.0	0.8
Laclede	317	4.0	244	0	166	218	920	24	32	24 734	6.1	93.9	37.5	7.2	5.5	5.0
Lafayette	349	-1.9	287	2	286	389	1 421	56	108	88 799	53.4	46.6	57.0	19.3	0.2	4.4
Lawrence	338	1.5	195	1	223	248	1 277	32	122	70 304	7.8	92.2	40.2	9.1	0.0	5.3
Lewis	269	7.9	374	D	190	328	879	58	41	56 521	70.6	29.4	52.7	15.3	0.0	1.7
Lincoln	262	3.7	265	2	188	438	1 654	53	52	52 947	53.5	46.5	44.7	11.8	0.1	3.1
Linn	346	2.4	371	1	251	233	684	33	49	52 086	33.9	66.1	54.0	11.6	0.0	2.3
Livingston	273	0.7	370	1	213	325	876	52	37	50 378	78.7	21.3	48.8	11.7	0.0	2.5
McDonald	232	16.4	215	0	97	251	1 256	27	155	143 799	1.0	99.0	36.4	13.1	0.0	5.3
Macon	381	-0.4	329	0	249	216	676	38	35	30 230	55.0	45.0	45.2	7.1	1.0	2.8
Madison	110	-1.7	285	D	48	187	707	26	7	17 007	7.7	92.3	30.1	2.6	14.7	1.4
Maries	229	-1.8	280	0	105	231	735	36	19	23 557	8.4	91.6	41.1	5.0	0.0	3.3
Marion	221	0.6	318	4	164	339	1 025	53	40	57 489	62.2	37.8	53.5	15.7	0.0	7.6
Mercer	230	9.3	426	D	159	351	882	36	123	227 791	D	D	45.6	5.8	0.0	1.8
Miller	255	5.2	239	1	118	213	874	28	76	71 191	3.2	96.8	41.1	10.5	0.0	3.2
Mississippi	264	-0.5	987	70	255	1 596	1 591	200	80	299 051	99.1	0.9	91.8	60.7	0.0	19.2
Moniteau	223	2.7	218	0	147	195	931	37	53	51 629	17.7	82.3	46.6	8.0	0.0	2.8
Monroe	328	7.3	370	3	240	342	901	56	56	62 679	52.9	47.1	53.4	15.8	5.5	3.2
Montgomery	248	10.1	324	1	171	397	1 174	61	37	47 849	62.2	37.8	51.5	13.9	0.0	2.2
Morgan	202	0.2	233	0	112	221	1 001	32	91	104 835	6.1	93.9	48.4	15.1	0.0	2.4
New Madrid	386	4.5	899	150	375	1 304	1 462	203	109	255 031	97.0	3.0	89.7	58.7	0.0	848.7
Newton	256	-0.2	158	0	168	232	1 352	24	123	76 067	4.8	95.2	34.7	9.7	0.1	7.2
Nodaway	492	-3.2	391	0	396	327	845	50	84	66 707	63.5	36.5	65.9	19.6	0.0	3.9
Oregon	248	-1.6	311	0	100	253	816	30	20	25 470	5.9	94.1	40.0	4.9	20.9	4.0
Osage	305	-3.8	266	1	140	238	919	31	51	44 834	10.2	89.8	41.8	10.6	0.8	34.8
Ozark	253	1.1	324	0	85	247	724	27	21	26 932	2.9	97.1	41.5	7.4	11.2	5.2
Pemiscot	296	1.3	966	49	291	1 424	1 383	199	86	280 575	99.3	0.7	87.9	62.7	0.0	28.2
Perry	201	-3.6	235	0	131	253	1 083	45	32	37 589	48.9	51.1	46.7	9.2	0.0	2.7
Pettis	366	2.0	293	1	263	285	996	60	104	83 278	28.1	71.9	53.8	15.0	0.0	5.6
Phelps	196	-2.4	259	0	84	220	867	21	9	12 208	13.7	86.3	28.9	1.8	14.7	3.9
Pike	317	-1.9	336	1	218	397	1 184	51	55	57 810	63.5	36.5	53.2	15.1	0.8	9.8
Platte	180	-4.5	253	1	139	435	1 874	50	36	50 106	84.2	15.8	50.1	13.0	0.5	364.9
Polk	348	0.5	221	1	209	248	1 221	26	50	31 439	9.6	90.4	39.6	7.0	1.9	4.3
Pulaski	140	0.5	259	0	65	183	731	28	12	22 174	6.7	93.3	32.8	2.4	13.6	7.5
Putnam	261	2.9	425	D	154	242	599	37	27	43 740	27.8	72.2	58.2	11.2	0.0	2.2
Ralls	232	1.2	421	1	172	469	1 061	70	39	70 450	66.7	33.3	53.1	17.8	3.0	1.8
Randolph	230	4.0	287	1	143	236	887	35	27	33 364	40.7	59.3	36.3	7.0	1.1	877.3
Ray	274	-1.0	255	3	202	297	1 275	45	39	36 335	63.6	36.4	41.4	7.5	0.2	3.9
Reynolds	113	25.8	375	0	34	229	599	19	3	10 282	8.6	91.4	29.8	1.0	20.0	3.7
Ripley	152	-0.7	322	8	70	214	795	28	11	22 731	50.5	49.5	35.2	5.7	23.8	19.2
St. Charles	187	-8.3	275	2	148	728	2 664	62	42	62 436	79.9	20.1	51.9	15.1	0.0	446.4
St. Clair	263	2.3	338	0	162	240	724	32	25	31 638	36.2	63.8	46.8	8.1	7.1	1.5
Ste. Genevieve	168	-0.5	266	0	86	292	1 102	28	18	28 376	38.9	61.1	39.6	6.0	3.2	1.8
St. Francois	113	-3.6	174	1	61	263	1 254	33	13	20 492	46.3	53.7	29.6	2.3	0.3	306.5
St. Louis	45	-16.6	155	1	31	418	2 789	31	21	73 314	84.3	15.7	39.5	16.8	(1)0.0	176.4
Saline	430	3.8	459	2	347	543	1 214	74	103	109 651	66.6	33.4	69.9	27.1	1.5	5.1
Schuyler	160	-3.3	324	D	111	212	624	33	14	29 097	43.0	57.0	51.5	6.9	0.0	0.7
Scotland	225	3.5	374	D	165	288	769	60	34	56 797	60.6	39.4	57.7	17.3	0.0	0.9
Scott	241	9.9	445	66	223	578	1 337	101	77	141 644	77.7	22.3	60.8	29.0	0.0	19.5
Shannon	133	11.1	284	0	51	158	588	23	6	11 702	5.8	94.2	34.3	0.4	18.3	1.0
Shelby	272	-0.3	423	2	210	400	912	65	59	90 893	50.8	49.2	66.1	23.4	0.0	2.5
Stoddard	449	2.4	477	204	415	769	1 566	114	154	163 274	76.3	23.7	55.5	30.3	2.2	153.3
Stone	136	-1.5	199	0	62	219	1 273	20	16	23 228	4.8	95.2	33.0	5.1	8.4	3.8
Sullivan	326	-1.3	412	D	212	299	664	35	185	234 391	4.9	95.1	53.1	7.6	0.0	3.1
Taney	158	-1.6	345	0	40	389	1 148	38	10	21 650	5.3	94.7	35.1	1.7	19.5	9.5
Texas	430	-6.5	291	0	206	205	758	24	37	24 727	6.0	94.0	39.5	6.0	6.6	5.4
Vernon	389	-3.3	307	4	274	260	883	32	88	69 353	31.5	68.5	43.4	9.2	0.0	4.9
Warren	133	5.2	239	1	85	351	1 766	36	22	40 525	55.0	45.0	40.2	11.4	0.0	3.6
Washington	127	13.3	254	0	53	219	804	20	25	49 464	1.8	98.2	26.7	2.0	16.8	8.9
Wayne	98	5.0	257	0	38	182	780	29	4	11 066	27.5	72.5	22.4	1.3	26.8	1.8
Webster	297	2.4	176	0	166	210	1 192	23	46	27 408	5.0	95.0	36.0	6.3	0.0	4.2
Worth	150	12.1	422	D	105	253	552	29	13	36 642	53.1	46.9	53.9	9.3	0.0	0.5
Wright	312	-1.5	235	1	163	200	881	24	42	31 550	3.8	96.2	41.0	10.4	1.6	3.8

1. St. Louis City included with St. Louis County.

Table B. States and Counties — **Residential Construction, Wholesale and Retail Trade, and Real Estate**

STATE County	Value of Residential Construction Authorized by Building Permits, 1999		Wholesale Trade, 1997				Retail Trade[1], 1997				Real Estate and Rental and Leasing, 1997			
	New Construction ($1,000)	Number of Housing Units	Number of Establishments	Number of Employees	Sales (mil dol)	Annual Payroll (mil dol)	Number of Establishments	Number of Employees	Sales (mil dol)	Annual Payroll (mil dol)	Number of Establishments	Number of Employees	Receipts (mil dol)	Annual Payroll (mil dol)
	133	134	135	136	137	138	139	140	141	142	143	144	145	146
MISSOURI—Cont'd														
Jasper	40 668	505	198	2 164	897.0	54.3	597	7 658	1 153.1	108.8	115	455	39.7	7.5
Jefferson	138 799	1 304	158	1 115	352.6	35.7	549	6 265	1 110.0	99.9	134	460	42.5	8.4
Johnson	10 250	200	37	373	93.8	8.0	154	1 551	243.8	22.1	29	79	6.8	1.1
Knox	260	3	7	D	D	D	31	115	20.4	1.3	1	D	D	D
Laclede	4 985	59	44	337	126.4	7.3	191	1 964	318.9	28.1	35	89	7.0	1.3
Lafayette	12 547	110	48	362	220.3	9.1	185	1 516	201.4	19.3	16	49	7.8	0.5
Lawrence	10 538	195	26	108	205.6	2.2	120	1 202	270.8	21.4	17	36	4.6	0.3
Lewis	171	2	13	D	D	D	49	261	47.2	4.0	16	15	1.2	0.1
Lincoln	8 814	109	47	254	144.2	6.5	110	1 249	234.1	18.9	26	60	7.8	0.9
Linn	902	10	23	123	34.0	2.8	71	531	80.4	7.0	8	19	0.6	0.1
Livingston	3 182	28	36	591	196.3	12.6	83	987	150.4	14.8	12	32	5.2	0.6
McDonald	1 279	18	16	D	D	D	79	478	82.6	6.4	11	22	1.6	0.3
Macon	1 017	10	23	227	82.9	3.7	73	642	85.6	7.7	8	21	1.2	0.1
Madison	2 150	28	11	64	19.0	0.6	53	475	62.9	7.0	4	13	0.9	0.1
Maries	NA	NA	8	142	87.0	0.7	30	199	31.5	2.3	3	7	0.5	0.2
Marion	9 421	105	37	437	138.6	8.4	178	1 889	298.6	25.4	26	85	4.8	1.0
Mercer	0	0	4	33	11.8	0.6	16	78	17.5	1.1	NA	NA	NA	NA
Miller	4 387	83	22	182	62.8	2.9	130	1 004	208.1	17.8	33	73	8.0	1.4
Mississippi	826	21	22	236	313.2	6.2	67	588	94.7	7.6	6	10	0.7	0.1
Moniteau	469	4	19	D	D	D	59	447	108.9	7.2	10	19	0.8	0.1
Monroe	4 120	55	13	40	17.0	0.9	42	267	47.1	3.8	3	4	0.6	0.1
Montgomery	1 067	10	21	180	93.7	4.0	67	438	74.4	6.3	5	12	0.6	0.1
Morgan	NA	NA	23	129	31.1	2.0	112	921	146.0	12.8	20	D	D	D
New Madrid	1 752	21	31	482	310.5	11.2	95	741	145.0	10.4	11	53	1.6	0.4
Newton	6 501	101	52	411	195.1	10.0	193	1 644	291.2	24.8	36	130	10.6	1.8
Nodaway	4 648	41	29	266	240.0	5.0	100	1 029	128.1	12.5	20	51	3.3	0.4
Oregon	70	1	14	113	29.0	2.0	46	378	57.1	4.9	5	13	0.7	0.1
Osage	NA	NA	15	34	24.4	0.9	52	387	91.9	7.1	4	D	D	D
Ozark	75	2	8	D	D	D	37	249	39.6	3.2	4	16	0.7	0.1
Pemiscot	1 345	23	25	239	213.8	5.7	91	667	129.8	10.4	9	D	D	D
Perry	5 569	70	17	122	39.1	3.9	83	880	170.2	14.7	14	36	1.7	0.4
Pettis	2 468	26	67	765	211.6	18.3	204	2 230	355.7	33.5	40	142	12.0	2.4
Phelps	10 046	130	44	428	99.0	9.6	209	2 352	375.8	33.7	27	88	6.3	1.2
Pike	1 118	21	28	D	D	D	95	636	86.1	9.0	7	19	0.8	0.1
Platte	66 546	526	119	1 943	3 334.6	92.4	204	2 471	581.5	40.4	74	731	99.4	13.0
Polk	6 765	103	26	788	120.2	7.0	110	919	167.2	14.6	16	52	3.2	0.5
Pulaski	5 201	86	15	D	D	D	143	1 041	178.8	15.6	29	88	7.6	1.2
Putnam	198	3	10	D	D	D	18	116	17.7	1.4	5	D	D	D
Ralls	57	1	12	86	61.3	2.6	31	172	23.2	2.3	3	D	D	D
Randolph	3 148	23	26	188	76.9	4.7	110	1 384	211.7	19.1	16	98	13.9	1.4
Ray	12 602	127	19	D	D	D	72	608	109.9	8.9	13	34	1.9	0.3
Reynolds	NA	NA	7	59	8.3	0.7	27	123	19.1	1.5	2	D	D	D
Ripley	305	3	7	32	11.0	0.5	54	371	68.4	5.1	3	D	D	D
St. Charles	411 091	3 903	345	2 729	1 831.7	91.9	934	13 688	2 343.7	220.7	189	1 095	304.6	24.6
St. Clair	NA	NA	8	38	34.4	0.5	48	314	42.5	3.5	3	4	0.3	0.0
Ste. Genevieve	3 968	47	24	137	36.0	3.2	64	469	82.5	6.7	5	D	D	D
St. Francois	17 330	252	51	556	145.1	14.4	260	2 792	440.1	39.9	39	121	9.1	1.6
St. Louis	366 734	2 882	2 639	38 765	39 755.5	1 890.0	4 287	72 497	12 385.5	1 347.8	1 319	10 396	1 405.8	275.6
Saline	2 283	22	41	459	226.2	12.0	122	1 025	140.9	12.9	16	71	2.7	0.5
Schuyler	509	5	3	D	D	D	22	138	22.6	1.6	1	D	D	D
Scotland	67	1	9	56	25.3	0.7	33	170	24.2	2.1	3	D	D	D
Scott	6 253	77	80	1 142	629.5	30.8	243	2 248	355.1	34.3	33	81	5.7	1.0
Shannon	0	6	10	61	22.3	1.5	29	128	19.1	1.5	10	11	0.9	0.2
Shelby	203	2	20	98	32.3	1.9	45	233	28.0	2.8	4	D	D	D
Stoddard	4 667	53	52	355	177.2	8.1	152	1 292	245.1	18.7	24	41	3.9	0.6
Stone	3 786	53	17	51	28.0	1.2	131	828	134.0	13.1	32	61	6.4	0.9
Sullivan	610	6	2	D	D	D	31	191	34.4	2.7	4	5	0.2	0.0
Taney	34 801	516	40	302	73.0	6.9	391	2 976	442.6	47.3	78	831	66.0	18.1
Texas	715	11	26	184	66.7	3.0	105	916	136.7	11.9	11	50	3.5	0.9
Vernon	1 406	16	29	164	56.3	3.3	89	1 003	143.7	14.5	13	37	4.2	0.8
Warren	42 139	360	26	145	53.7	4.3	114	1 027	188.8	15.3	17	45	7.1	0.8
Washington	100	1	15	65	11.3	1.0	67	633	101.7	11.6	8	31	1.0	0.3
Wayne	NA	NA	5	18	3.6	0.2	53	457	57.5	5.2	4	7	0.4	0.1
Webster	5 732	89	23	120	25.8	2.2	114	876	146.3	11.9	19	46	2.5	0.6
Worth	0	0	7	D	D	D	14	58	6.1	0.6	3	D	D	D
Wright	1 657	25	20	147	94.8	2.4	94	795	130.4	10.7	14	39	2.3	0.4

1. Establishments with payroll.

Table B. States and Counties — Professional, Manufacturing, and Accommodation and Foodservices

STATE County	Professional, Scientific, and Technical Services[1], 1997				Manufacturing, 1997				Accommodation and Foodservices, 1997			
	Number of Establishments	Number of Employees	Receipts (mil dol)	Annual Payroll (mil dol)	Number of Establishments	Number of Employees	Receipts (mil dol)	Annual Payroll (mil dol)	Number of Establishments	Number of Employees	Sales (mil dol)	Annual Payroll (mil dol)
	147	148	149	150	151	152	153	154	155	156	157	158
MISSOURI—Cont'd												
Jasper	145	948	53.9	23.0	198	11 904	2 154.6	289.8	222	4 100	109.5	31.7
Jefferson	152	570	40.9	16.0	182	5 304	1 199.3	168.2	214	3 981	113.8	31.8
Johnson	42	108	15.2	2.5	31	1 856	183.2	46.7	83	1 144	31.5	8.2
Knox	6	15	0.7	0.2	NA	NA	NA	NA	4	24	0.7	0.2
Laclede	31	101	6.0	2.2	57	5 177	809.7	130.4	62	827	27.9	6.9
Lafayette	36	117	11.5	2.4	42	1 166	130.4	22.9	70	D	D	D
Lawrence	26	63	3.6	1.3	54	1 614	259.0	34.8	54	690	17.6	4.8
Lewis	6	D	D	D	NA	NA	NA	NA	18	66	2.1	0.4
Lincoln	27	296	4.2	1.4	43	1 078	176.8	29.0	48	700	19.4	5.1
Linn	11	52	2.2	1.0	24	1 739	137.8	45.0	26	241	6.6	1.7
Livingston	22	123	8.2	2.6	28	903	117.1	23.6	28	405	11.7	3.1
McDonald	11	29	3.2	0.7	34	3 052	469.8	52.5	34	218	7.2	2.0
Macon	16	76	3.6	1.4	15	D	D	D	26	355	9.8	3.0
Madison	8	77	2.8	0.8	16	553	28.7	8.3	23	278	5.7	1.6
Maries	5	D	D	D	NA	NA	NA	NA	9	D	D	D
Marion	44	226	15.0	5.5	46	3 179	1 707.1	87.5	69	1 053	28.9	8.2
Mercer	2	D	D	D	NA	NA	NA	NA	8	49	0.8	0.3
Miller	36	180	16.7	3.7	29	1 500	128.5	31.8	63	1 090	40.0	12.5
Mississippi	9	21	1.3	0.2	14	571	66.4	10.7	16	D	D	D
Moniteau	14	35	1.9	0.5	22	1 095	173.8	19.5	21	210	5.5	1.4
Monroe	7	14	0.8	0.1	7	1 047	74.8	27.9	22	160	3.4	0.9
Montgomery	9	16	0.7	0.1	32	811	82.1	16.6	17	240	4.7	1.2
Morgan	20	80	3.6	1.3	29	649	115.0	12.0	51	330	11.4	3.2
New Madrid	17	39	2.5	1.3	17	2 504	529.8	83.4	28	298	7.9	2.2
Newton	37	144	6.8	2.3	63	4 315	692.9	109.8	87	1 664	50.0	14.3
Nodaway	22	92	5.6	1.6	23	1 677	647.2	48.2	41	764	18.4	4.7
Oregon	9	17	0.7	0.2	NA	NA	NA	NA	18	139	4.2	1.1
Osage	7	11	0.6	0.2	24	914	169.8	20.3	21	D	D	D
Ozark	5	17	0.6	0.2	NA	NA	NA	NA	14	63	2.3	0.5
Pemiscot	13	28	1.9	0.5	12	893	131.1	19.8	36	404	10.6	3.0
Perry	14	75	4.1	1.8	31	2 855	609.3	61.9	39	469	12.5	3.5
Pettis	50	215	13.2	4.9	69	5 324	958.9	130.2	76	1 313	36.2	10.8
Phelps	64	282	18.0	7.0	55	1 132	218.2	29.6	103	1 346	45.1	12.1
Pike	16	87	6.0	2.2	27	771	277.4	25.7	25	304	8.7	2.3
Platte	138	830	105.3	34.1	47	1 599	344.7	52.4	157	3 218	139.2	38.3
Polk	27	93	4.2	1.6	34	859	81.1	13.9	40	462	12.0	3.3
Pulaski	27	144	9.8	3.0	18	682	36.4	9.4	77	914	29.5	10.7
Putnam	3	20	0.8	0.3	NA	NA	NA	NA	5	D	D	D
Ralls	3	17	1.3	0.4	10	913	253.9	21.6	17	239	6.1	2.1
Randolph	17	83	5.9	1.3	37	1 381	182.6	30.5	45	656	16.1	4.2
Ray	31	104	14.4	2.4	21	654	63.9	16.5	26	244	7.1	1.8
Reynolds	6	D	D	D	33	634	52.7	10.9	14	70	3.0	1.0
Ripley	5	14	0.6	0.2	42	629	42.8	10.0	16	156	4.1	1.0
St. Charles	446	2 971	208.6	71.0	279	12 160	4 432.9	431.9	418	8 656	245.2	71.3
St. Clair	6	13	0.8	0.2	NA	NA	NA	NA	14	D	D	D
Ste. Genevieve	17	73	3.9	1.2	32	1 752	208.2	47.8	32	399	9.5	2.6
St. Francois	73	330	16.5	5.7	66	3 797	394.6	80.3	100	1 602	45.1	13.1
St. Louis	3 296	35 334	4 078.7	1 437.2	1 272	78 218	25 347.9	3 359.8	2 030	46 507	1 579.7	465.7
Saline	23	56	3.1	0.8	24	2 530	647.5	55.4	50	603	15.3	4.0
Schuyler	1	D	D	D	NA	NA	NA	NA	8	51	0.8	0.2
Scotland	5	D	D	D	NA	NA	NA	NA	10	66	2.3	0.5
Scott	59	209	16.2	5.6	77	3 008	532.6	66.1	78	1 102	35.1	9.8
Shannon	3	D	D	D	22	710	40.9	8.1	16	44	2.1	0.5
Shelby	10	41	3.8	1.0	5	D	D	D	11	94	1.5	0.4
Stoddard	26	103	5.5	2.1	40	2 372	264.0	42.4	47	504	14.6	4.1
Stone	23	60	3.6	0.8	NA	NA	NA	NA	86	530	19.2	5.8
Sullivan	4	13	1.1	0.8	5	D	D	D	7	D	D	D
Taney	80	295	18.9	6.5	59	798	87.8	15.8	328	4 947	245.4	68.6
Texas	16	39	2.4	0.8	53	1 399	169.6	26.2	32	212	4.7	1.3
Vernon	25	89	4.9	1.6	21	1 561	425.8	44.0	41	520	13.8	3.6
Warren	19	49	2.8	0.8	37	2 042	242.7	50.1	34	503	14.3	4.1
Washington	13	30	1.0	0.4	NA	NA	NA	NA	17	D	D	D
Wayne	9	22	1.6	0.3	28	510	44.0	8.3	20	144	3.5	0.9
Webster	24	75	3.3	1.2	44	D	D	D	38	420	11.7	3.1
Worth	2	D	D	D	NA	NA	NA	NA	6	13	0.4	0.1
Wright	13	31	1.2	0.3	18	730	102.0	14.2	40	303	8.3	2.0

1. Firms subject to federal tax.

Table B. States and Counties — Health and Other Services and Federal Funds

STATE County	Health Care and Social Assistance[1], 1997				Other Services[1], 1997				Federal funds and grants, fiscal 1999[2] Expenditures (mil dol)			
										Direct payments for individuals[3]		
	Number of Establishments	Number of Employees	Receipts (mil dol)	Annual Payroll (mil dol)	Number of Establishments	Number of Employees	Receipts (mil dol)	Annual Payroll (mil dol)	Total	Social Security and government retirement	Medicare	Food stamps and Supplemental Security Income
	159	160	161	162	163	164	165	166	167	168	169	170
MISSOURI—Cont'd												
Jasper	235	2 360	144.4	65.4	227	1 189	69.2	18.9	580.4	222.0	88.4	19.6
Jefferson	216	2 633	108.7	48.1	291	1 426	83.0	24.4	470.7	267.9	102.4	15.3
Johnson	59	650	26.9	11.0	55	212	10.9	2.8	303.8	77.6	21.6	4.3
Knox	7	53	1.6	0.8	11	51	11.7	0.7	30.2	9.7	6.4	0.7
Laclede	41	492	26.2	10.3	48	133	8.4	2.0	129.9	69.9	20.9	6.4
Lafayette	45	489	18.8	8.6	48	146	7.6	2.0	145.8	67.7	30.6	3.4
Lawrence	36	211	12.7	4.3	44	106	6.4	1.6	126.5	66.1	24.5	4.6
Lewis	8	120	3.3	1.8	19	52	3.7	0.8	49.4	20.0	8.8	1.0
Lincoln	39	376	12.6	4.6	53	155	9.6	2.5	108.0	54.9	23.0	3.0
Linn	24	476	13.8	5.9	31	86	6.0	1.1	80.0	36.3	18.3	1.8
Livingston	34	537	19.3	7.4	32	97	6.5	1.6	82.9	31.5	14.8	1.9
McDonald	15	148	6.1	2.8	18	64	1.6	0.6	82.0	33.2	12.6	4.1
Macon	20	226	7.2	3.0	29	73	4.5	1.0	81.6	35.2	18.1	1.8
Madison	16	150	4.5	1.5	11	24	2.3	0.4	63.9	28.4	11.4	2.8
Maries	9	145	5.1	1.9	10	28	1.8	0.4	29.7	14.8	7.4	0.8
Marion	61	798	39.7	19.7	43	216	15.0	3.8	133.2	61.1	27.3	5.5
Mercer	6	85	2.6	1.3	5	9	0.9	0.2	25.3	8.5	4.0	0.4
Miller	26	261	9.4	5.0	43	141	8.0	2.2	96.2	52.5	22.3	3.2
Mississippi	13	255	7.5	3.1	20	56	3.2	0.8	93.3	28.1	12.2	5.3
Moniteau	19	158	7.3	2.6	18	63	2.7	0.8	49.5	24.4	11.8	1.0
Monroe	14	78	2.8	1.2	12	25	1.7	0.4	51.0	19.9	10.0	1.0
Montgomery	19	268	8.9	4.1	25	245	8.4	3.2	60.8	26.6	12.1	1.5
Morgan	13	61	2.7	1.4	33	87	4.9	0.9	88.4	50.2	18.6	2.8
New Madrid	14	479	14.5	6.5	21	86	6.0	1.0	140.7	34.7	15.6	7.2
Newton	63	1 108	60.4	21.3	72	222	10.3	2.5	149.2	72.7	28.6	4.2
Nodaway	29	391	13.5	5.6	43	136	8.3	1.9	85.7	33.2	14.1	1.7
Oregon	8	203	7.2	3.2	14	28	2.1	0.5	54.5	25.2	8.9	2.4
Osage	10	229	6.6	2.4	15	33	2.7	0.4	41.3	19.5	10.6	0.7
Ozark	4	93	3.1	1.4	11	19	1.1	0.2	49.3	24.8	8.0	2.0
Pemiscot	26	361	11.3	4.5	21	102	5.8	1.4	157.6	37.4	21.0	11.5
Perry	29	255	8.8	3.2	31	106	10.2	2.1	65.2	31.4	13.6	0.8
Pettis	89	998	43.5	19.4	77	821	36.8	13.8	169.3	82.8	32.5	5.7
Phelps	88	1 529	56.6	27.3	66	306	16.7	4.4	206.6	92.7	28.9	5.5
Pike	24	273	9.1	4.0	23	68	6.9	1.3	91.1	34.4	16.0	2.2
Platte	101	1 309	60.2	28.5	106	604	59.2	11.3	205.3	44.7	29.7	50.4
Polk	32	626	15.1	6.8	41	111	7.1	1.2	109.1	55.3	21.8	4.0
Pulaski	26	300	9.1	3.4	54	204	11.1	2.9	676.8	94.4	18.2	5.6
Putnam	9	31	1.3	0.4	8	17	1.0	0.2	29.3	11.8	6.5	0.9
Ralls	8	260	8.2	3.7	9	34	1.8	0.4	36.5	12.7	6.5	0.8
Randolph	44	864	45.9	18.2	48	189	10.3	2.6	112.1	50.6	25.9	3.9
Ray	21	164	5.7	2.9	42	113	6.3	1.7	75.3	36.5	17.0	2.0
Reynolds	10	194	5.7	2.5	3	7	0.6	0.1	34.8	14.5	6.6	2.2
Ripley	15	251	9.3	3.9	13	23	1.7	0.4	77.3	32.9	12.5	5.0
St. Charles	417	5 042	344.0	161.4	425	2 506	145.7	48.2	697.8	375.0	119.6	13.2
St. Clair	8	213	5.9	2.8	5	11	1.8	0.2	58.2	23.5	9.6	1.7
Ste. Genevieve	26	189	7.0	2.9	21	75	4.5	1.2	62.6	32.2	12.0	1.5
St. Francois	123	1 649	68.7	33.9	83	271	15.1	3.9	247.7	121.9	51.6	11.9
St. Louis	2 719	29 766	2 077.0	972.8	1 877	12 884	819.2	270.5	3 898.3	2 019.7	854.1	91.7
Saline	44	499	18.7	7.7	43	141	9.0	2.3	116.2	48.4	23.4	3.2
Schuyler	6	22	1.0	0.5	6	11	0.8	0.1	25.6	11.0	5.3	0.5
Scotland	3	21	0.5	0.2	15	32	2.4	0.4	29.2	10.1	5.8	0.7
Scott	87	1 452	56.1	23.1	57	262	19.8	5.0	190.7	82.4	31.0	10.2
Shannon	4	9	0.5	0.3	7	13	1.1	0.2	38.3	15.6	5.8	2.4
Shelby	7	44	2.4	1.6	15	52	2.4	0.7	39.2	16.5	8.1	0.9
Stoddard	47	977	33.1	15.6	40	169	10.3	3.2	176.4	65.1	26.8	6.7
Stone	19	195	10.8	3.5	37	117	7.1	2.0	109.7	67.2	20.1	3.1
Sullivan	9	177	6.1	2.7	11	24	1.9	0.5	40.7	13.6	8.6	1.2
Taney	64	537	31.1	11.8	66	267	14.0	4.4	152.2	89.4	31.0	4.0
Texas	17	295	8.3	3.7	32	77	5.9	0.9	107.9	57.2	16.5	7.5
Vernon	48	639	24.7	9.7	27	77	4.3	1.1	89.9	41.2	16.5	4.0
Warren	27	210	7.2	2.6	29	81	5.4	2.1	76.7	41.6	17.5	2.0
Washington	18	83	4.8	2.0	17	37	2.0	0.5	83.7	36.0	14.5	6.9
Wayne	10	244	7.5	2.6	9	26	2.1	0.5	84.1	40.3	14.8	4.5
Webster	22	150	4.4	2.0	36	112	6.8	1.6	104.1	54.9	19.4	3.2
Worth	6	27	1.0	0.3	4	10	0.7	0.1	15.2	5.8	2.1	0.3
Wright	23	351	13.7	6.1	29	72	5.4	1.1	90.6	40.9	17.1	3.5

1. Firms subject to federal tax.　2. October 1, 1998 to September 30, 1999.　3. State totals may include programs not allocated by county.

STATE County	Salaries and wages	Defense	Other	Medicaid and other health-related	Nutrition and family welfare	Education	Other	Total (mil dol)	Intergovern- mental (mil dol)	Total (mil dol)	Total	Property
	171	172	173	174	175	176	177	178	179	180	181	182
MISSOURI—Cont'd												
Jasper	18.7	18.6	129.0	48.9	12.0	4.5	9.2	183.4	61.0	68.6	694	359
Jefferson	17.7	2.3	5.0	28.5	10.5	5.2	12.3	257.6	113.4	103.1	534	374
Johnson	146.9	25.0	1.4	8.0	2.8	3.8	1.3	66.3	32.2	21.3	449	289
Knox	1.9	0.0	0.5	2.7	0.4	0.2	0.1	10.8	7.0	2.8	635	466
Laclede	4.4	0.0	0.9	20.0	2.8	1.2	2.1	41.4	19.1	14.7	482	268
Lafayette	6.6	1.6	2.1	7.4	4.0	1.7	10.5	48.4	21.7	16.8	515	314
Lawrence	6.6	0.0	1.0	14.3	2.6	1.7	2.2	59.6	23.6	19.2	584	302
Lewis	2.7	0.3	0.8	5.1	0.9	0.5	0.9	17.0	7.5	4.3	427	330
Lincoln	4.9	0.4	1.0	10.2	1.5	0.6	1.1	75.7	22.4	16.9	479	321
Linn	3.1	0.3	1.5	8.0	1.3	0.7	0.8	28.2	15.6	8.2	590	361
Livingston	5.3	0.0	1.0	9.6	1.2	0.7	6.7	25.7	10.7	8.9	617	340
McDonald	4.7	0.2	0.6	13.1	1.9	0.9	10.4	21.1	12.6	5.4	272	192
Macon	4.5	0.0	2.3	7.6	1.1	0.6	2.6	38.1	11.6	8.7	571	369
Madison	1.4	0.0	0.4	8.2	1.4	0.6	7.3	24.2	9.2	4.1	350	281
Maries	0.7	0.0	0.2	4.4	0.5	0.3	0.1	10.3	5.6	3.5	417	334
Marion	2.8	1.3	0.5	18.4	4.7	1.4	3.0	51.0	20.2	18.0	646	394
Mercer	0.9	0.0	0.2	2.6	0.3	0.1	3.4	7.9	3.5	2.7	676	587
Miller	2.9	0.0	0.8	10.2	1.8	1.0	0.4	36.3	17.4	14.5	643	514
Mississippi	2.1	0.0	0.5	24.7	4.1	2.1	2.4	32.8	13.3	9.5	708	400
Moniteau	2.3	0.0	0.5	5.0	0.7	0.5	0.2	17.7	8.0	6.3	476	381
Monroe	3.0	0.7	0.5	5.9	0.6	0.5	1.1	21.3	12.4	5.6	621	449
Montgomery	2.6	0.0	0.7	6.5	0.9	0.7	2.6	16.1	7.2	5.7	485	297
Morgan	2.3	0.0	0.6	7.5	1.3	0.7	3.4	17.3	7.8	7.2	397	295
New Madrid	3.4	0.0	0.8	34.1	10.6	1.8	1.0	32.5	15.0	13.0	635	489
Newton	8.8	0.1	3.9	15.5	3.2	3.9	5.6	64.6	31.5	20.4	422	286
Nodaway	5.6	0.1	1.2	7.0	2.5	2.4	3.9	34.0	15.2	13.0	621	419
Oregon	1.7	0.0	0.5	13.1	1.5	0.6	0.3	12.1	7.8	3.2	321	231
Osage	1.8	0.0	0.8	5.1	0.3	0.4	0.2	13.1	6.8	4.5	358	298
Ozark	1.4	0.2	0.4	10.6	1.1	0.7	0.1	12.0	7.4	3.6	369	276
Pemiscot	3.6	0.7	0.7	49.2	7.5	3.0	0.6	37.1	22.2	9.7	449	301
Perry	2.8	2.8	2.5	7.1	1.3	0.5	-1.5	33.9	9.9	8.8	503	346
Pettis	7.6	1.2	1.8	20.7	3.8	1.7	0.7	108.3	27.0	24.0	651	377
Phelps	32.7	2.7	3.0	20.3	3.0	2.3	12.7	123.2	41.1	18.9	490	257
Pike	3.7	10.6	0.9	9.0	1.6	1.3	3.7	31.4	11.2	9.1	563	402
Platte	45.9	2.4	4.0	9.4	2.4	2.0	6.8	104.0	38.2	48.4	705	542
Polk	3.9	0.0	1.0	15.1	1.8	1.9	1.9	63.7	20.5	9.2	363	251
Pulaski	424.9	88.9	1.0	14.2	6.4	11.9	8.1	55.9	37.7	11.9	311	223
Putnam	1.3	0.0	0.3	3.5	0.4	0.3	0.3	8.9	4.5	2.7	546	436
Ralls	4.1	0.1	1.0	2.5	0.5	0.3	2.0	8.6	4.3	3.2	359	228
Randolph	4.0	0.3	0.9	12.3	2.3	1.1	4.3	47.1	19.8	17.1	714	432
Ray	3.1	0.0	0.7	4.4	1.9	0.8	1.5	48.7	18.7	12.0	518	365
Reynolds	1.3	0.6	0.4	7.3	1.0	0.6	0.2	9.9	4.9	4.1	607	570
Ripley	2.3	0.0	0.4	18.4	2.7	1.0	0.5	18.9	10.9	5.7	409	371
St. Charles	30.0	14.0	86.8	25.1	9.3	5.0	8.4	481.6	153.7	246.6	933	623
St. Clair	1.6	0.0	0.4	5.7	3.9	0.5	7.9	22.6	10.4	3.2	351	294
Ste. Genevieve	1.7	6.0	0.4	4.4	1.0	0.5	0.4	30.8	7.8	9.1	530	362
St. Francois	7.1	0.5	1.9	30.1	8.7	3.1	8.4	83.2	44.8	25.0	458	284
St. Louis	335.7	106.5	60.5	175.9	47.7	28.9	151.8	2 001.6	563.8	1 188.8	1 185	772
Saline	4.7	0.0	1.2	13.9	2.0	1.1	2.9	42.0	20.6	13.3	582	369
Schuyler	2.0	0.0	0.4	2.8	0.5	0.2	0.2	7.7	3.5	2.1	476	397
Scotland	1.2	0.0	0.3	2.3	0.5	0.3	0.0	14.2	5.8	2.9	590	452
Scott	5.8	3.8	1.3	34.5	6.2	2.3	1.7	66.6	32.2	21.8	541	356
Shannon	2.1	0.0	0.2	7.8	3.6	0.4	0.2	6.8	4.4	1.6	200	143
Shelby	2.3	0.0	0.6	3.4	0.6	0.4	0.1	13.2	6.9	3.8	551	431
Stoddard	8.2	0.0	1.9	29.5	3.6	2.0	2.3	41.7	20.4	14.5	490	383
Stone	2.0	0.1	0.6	7.2	1.8	1.2	6.2	29.2	14.6	11.7	443	348
Sullivan	2.5	0.0	0.5	7.7	0.7	0.2	0.1	12.7	4.7	3.9	585	489
Taney	5.1	4.3	1.0	9.3	1.4	0.7	4.2	72.2	17.5	43.0	1 265	506
Texas	4.1	0.2	0.8	15.8	2.6	1.9	0.6	90.6	35.2	33.3	1 482	463
Vernon	4.9	0.0	0.9	9.5	1.9	1.0	0.2	46.6	15.4	11.0	576	346
Warren	3.2	0.4	0.7	4.5	1.1	0.8	1.2	25.9	9.6	12.9	547	345
Washington	2.7	0.0	0.7	16.8	3.6	1.5	0.4	36.0	17.6	7.4	326	216
Wayne	3.0	2.5	0.9	14.0	2.0	0.9	0.7	15.4	8.8	4.9	384	229
Webster	4.1	0.1	1.1	16.3	1.8	1.4	0.8	32.2	17.3	8.1	285	207
Worth	1.1	0.4	0.3	1.5	0.2	0.2	0.1	5.0	2.2	1.1	478	311
Wright	2.9	0.0	0.8	20.7	1.9	1.2	0.3	30.7	17.6	7.0	361	255

1. October 1, 1998 to September 30, 1999.   2. State totals may include programs not allocated by county.   3. Based on the resident population estimated as of July 1 of the year shown.

Table B. States and Counties — Local Government Finances, Government Employment, and Elections

STATE County	Local government finances, 1997 (cont'd)									Government employment, 1998			Presidential election, 2000		
	Direct general expenditure							Debt outstanding					Percent of vote cast —		
			Percent of total for —												
	Total (mil dol)	Per capita¹ (dollars)	Education	Health and hospitals	Police protection	Public welfare	Highways	Total (mil dol)	Per capita¹ (dollars)	Federal civilian	Federal military	State and local	Democratic	Republican	All other
	183	184	185	186	187	188	189	190	191	192	193	194	195	196	197
MISSOURI—Cont'd															
Jasper	191.9	1 942	48.0	9.4	4.8	0.5	8.7	54.5	551	347	451	5 842	NA	NA	NA
Jefferson	258.9	1 340	69.2	2.0	4.5	0.0	5.9	95.3	493	419	884	7 046	NA	NA	NA
Johnson	65.6	1 386	64.7	8.2	5.2	0.2	7.0	28.3	598	863	3 189	4 755	NA	NA	NA
Knox	10.3	2 362	41.9	2.6	0.1	32.1	14.8	1.4	312	40	20	387	NA	NA	NA
Laclede	39.8	1 308	66.4	1.0	2.5	0.4	15.7	8.2	271	83	140	1 300	NA	NA	NA
Lafayette	50.5	1 554	63.4	0.1	4.2	0.0	10.3	30.5	937	110	154	2 114	NA	NA	NA
Lawrence	59.3	1 805	50.6	17.3	6.1	4.7	7.7	8.7	265	82	150	1 651	NA	NA	NA
Lewis	17.4	1 715	52.0	1.5	2.7	17.1	7.0	4.6	452	63	46	594	NA	NA	NA
Lincoln	75.7	2 152	39.9	43.3	3.2	0.0	5.0	22.8	647	116	165	1 574	NA	NA	NA
Linn	30.0	2 149	60.3	2.6	2.7	0.7	12.9	10.7	769	66	62	846	NA	NA	NA
Livingston	26.0	1 812	54.9	3.6	3.0	5.7	9.3	5.0	348	104	64	1 070	NA	NA	NA
McDonald	21.0	1 063	66.5	0.7	3.8	2.7	7.6	3.6	184	64	90	680	NA	NA	NA
Macon	38.6	2 527	39.6	23.7	1.3	16.1	8.0	8.3	544	80	69	1 595	NA	NA	NA
Madison	25.6	2 210	42.9	36.0	2.3	0.7	3.4	2.5	218	29	52	746	NA	NA	NA
Maries	10.4	1 250	70.7	4.6	2.0	0.0	8.6	0.4	47	13	38	348	NA	NA	NA
Marion	51.5	1 850	52.8	3.1	4.9	7.8	5.7	84.9	3 050	85	125	1 869	NA	NA	NA
Mercer	8.4	2 102	63.7	3.3	2.4	0.0	14.0	1.7	420	22	18	254	NA	NA	NA
Miller	40.4	1 786	73.1	1.9	2.3	4.2	4.2	21.7	961	54	101	1 005	NA	NA	NA
Mississippi	27.7	2 056	48.0	4.4	4.7	0.6	9.4	14.1	1 046	45	61	716	NA	NA	NA
Moniteau	18.1	1 368	67.8	5.0	5.6	0.0	7.7	6.7	507	43	60	1 056	NA	NA	NA
Monroe	20.7	2 296	48.0	2.1	3.4	24.0	5.9	30.2	3 344	79	41	734	NA	NA	NA
Montgomery	16.4	1 381	65.2	3.1	4.5	0.0	11.1	1.4	120	54	55	621	NA	NA	NA
Morgan	17.4	961	59.8	0.9	3.9	8.2	8.9	1.2	65	49	83	876	NA	NA	NA
New Madrid	33.6	1 637	66.2	2.6	4.8	0.2	7.9	14.5	706	63	92	1 031	NA	NA	NA
Newton	59.3	1 227	71.3	3.3	4.8	0.0	5.0	5.6	116	139	222	1 930	NA	NA	NA
Nodaway	34.4	1 646	60.8	1.7	4.8	0.0	12.7	21.8	1 041	98	94	2 556	NA	NA	NA
Oregon	12.4	1 241	81.5	0.5	0.4	0.0	6.7	0.6	63	31	46	478	NA	NA	NA
Osage	13.9	1 112	72.8	1.1	2.4	0.0	12.8	4.3	346	40	56	623	NA	NA	NA
Ozark	12.3	1 279	75.2	2.9	2.4	0.0	7.2	6.4	664	27	45	483	NA	NA	NA
Pemiscot	36.5	1 694	68.4	0.4	6.3	0.3	5.4	8.8	408	87	97	1 951	NA	NA	NA
Perry	37.1	2 122	34.7	32.2	3.5	0.0	6.1	10.1	577	58	79	941	NA	NA	NA
Pettis	110.2	2 996	39.0	41.1	2.8	0.0	4.0	42.0	1 141	141	168	2 723	NA	NA	NA
Phelps	120.4	3 130	30.5	48.4	2.1	1.9	3.3	48.8	1 268	549	293	5 216	NA	NA	NA
Pike	33.6	2 084	48.0	23.9	5.1	0.0	8.1	7.3	450	85	74	1 593	NA	NA	NA
Platte	116.6	1 698	68.0	3.4	4.1	0.1	6.1	87.6	1 276	333	319	2 623	NA	NA	NA
Polk	61.6	2 420	38.2	45.6	2.7	0.0	7.0	19.9	781	80	115	1 537	NA	NA	NA
Pulaski	52.3	1 369	82.1	6.1	2.7	0.2	2.8	7.0	183	1 959	7 801	1 683	NA	NA	NA
Putnam	9.3	1 876	54.8	1.7	3.2	12.9	15.0	3.7	753	26	22	433	NA	NA	NA
Ralls	8.7	981	55.6	3.7	5.1	0.1	15.9	7.4	836	53	40	381	NA	NA	NA
Randolph	54.9	2 299	61.4	1.2	3.4	0.0	5.7	28.1	1 175	83	109	1 944	NA	NA	NA
Ray	46.6	2 005	42.3	21.1	1.7	9.4	11.2	24.7	1 062	63	107	1 208	NA	NA	NA
Reynolds	11.5	1 718	74.5	3.9	2.6	0.0	7.2	0.5	68	23	30	465	NA	NA	NA
Ripley	18.6	1 342	68.5	7.9	2.0	0.0	15.4	10.6	763	56	64	636	NA	NA	NA
St. Charles	532.6	2 015	53.3	1.2	5.5	0.1	8.6	480.9	1 820	562	1 232	10 087	NA	NA	NA
St. Clair	22.9	2 523	38.7	25.3	2.0	0.0	10.1	4.6	504	34	41	674	NA	NA	NA
Ste. Genevieve	33.3	1 933	31.5	33.7	4.7	7.5	5.6	7.5	437	36	79	869	NA	NA	NA
St. Francois	89.2	1 634	71.8	2.1	3.4	0.3	5.9	27.3	501	130	251	4 374	NA	NA	NA
St. Louis	2 003.9	1 997	55.4	1.5	7.0	0.0	5.2	1 349.7	1 345	5 952	4 562	48 433	NA	NA	NA
Saline	39.3	1 718	56.1	2.3	3.2	0.6	9.9	19.0	832	103	103	2 261	NA	NA	NA
Schuyler	7.6	1 746	53.3	5.1	2.2	18.3	11.3	1.5	333	32	20	293	NA	NA	NA
Scotland	12.5	2 593	36.1	18.2	2.5	25.6	9.0	1.1	222	29	22	548	NA	NA	NA
Scott	61.4	1 523	58.3	2.5	6.5	0.0	5.6	257.4	6 384	117	182	2 132	NA	NA	NA
Shannon	7.3	896	67.9	0.0	1.3	0.0	10.8	0.8	93	68	37	428	NA	NA	NA
Shelby	12.8	1 884	57.5	4.9	2.5	13.0	12.5	2.4	350	46	31	593	NA	NA	NA
Stoddard	42.3	1 431	65.3	2.8	4.1	0.0	10.6	8.6	290	165	134	1 278	NA	NA	NA
Stone	31.0	1 171	82.7	0.0	1.9	0.3	2.1	18.9	715	39	121	933	NA	NA	NA
Sullivan	12.9	1 942	44.3	27.2	3.8	0.0	14.1	2.9	441	49	32	455	NA	NA	NA
Taney	80.1	2 357	37.5	1.4	4.0	0.0	8.6	127.5	3 755	105	156	1 481	NA	NA	NA
Texas	122.5	5 457	19.5	9.9	0.6	0.0	66.5	35.0	1 558	91	101	1 284	NA	NA	NA
Vernon	47.8	2 495	40.3	30.4	3.2	5.0	6.1	15.7	819	92	88	1 762	NA	NA	NA
Warren	25.8	1 090	61.0	3.3	9.8	0.0	8.3	10.8	458	54	111	865	NA	NA	NA
Washington	38.4	1 691	52.7	22.0	3.6	0.0	5.1	10.4	458	68	104	1 547	NA	NA	NA
Wayne	14.9	1 158	73.3	1.9	3.1	0.9	4.7	2.2	171	88	59	594	NA	NA	NA
Webster	30.8	1 084	66.5	0.0	3.1	11.1	8.9	3.2	113	80	131	1 140	NA	NA	NA
Worth	5.0	2 132	51.1	1.7	2.2	23.4	10.3	0.5	196	21	10	198	NA	NA	NA
Wright	29.9	1 538	73.3	0.8	3.2	7.2	4.7	1.6	80	56	88	960	NA	NA	NA

1. Based on the resident population estimated as of July 1 of the year shown.

Table B. States and Counties — **Land Area and Population**

STATE/County code	MSA/PMSA/NECMA code[1]	County Type[2]	STATE County	Land area[3] (sq km) 1990	Total persons	Rank	Per square kilometer	White	Black	Am. Indian, Eskimo, Aleut	Asian and Pacific Islander	Percent Hispanic[4]	Under 5 years	5 to 17 years	18 to 24 years	25 to 34 years	35 to 44 years	45 to 54 years
				1	2	3	4	5	6	7	8	9	10	11	12	13	14	15
			MISSOURI—Cont'd															
29 510	7040	0	St. Louis city	160	333 960	169	2 087.3	45.4	53.1	0.2	1.3	1.8	7.5	19.2	10.2	15.1	14.8	10.4
30 000	...	X	**MONTANA**	376 991	882 779	X	2.3	92.5	0.4	6.5	0.6	1.8	6.0	19.3	10.1	10.7	15.6	15.0
30 001	...	7	Beaverhead	14 355	8 790	2 523	0.6	97.7	0.1	1.8	0.4	1.6	5.8	19.2	12.7	10.2	14.5	15.3
30 003	...	6	Big Horn	12 937	12 573	2 245	1.0	40.2	0.2	59.2	0.5	2.7	9.4	27.4	10.1	10.9	14.3	12.3
30 005	...	9	Blaine	10 946	7 074	2 672	0.6	56.7	0.1	43.1	0.1	0.8	7.9	24.9	8.6	10.4	13.8	12.4
30 007	...	9	Broadwater	3 086	4 167	2 901	1.4	98.0	0.0	1.8	0.2	1.2	5.5	20.8	6.2	9.1	14.0	16.8
30 009	...	8	Carbon	5 304	9 543	2 469	1.8	98.9	0.1	0.8	0.2	1.4	4.8	20.3	5.5	8.3	16.5	15.3
30 011	...	9	Carter	8 650	1 454	3 095	0.2	99.2	0.0	0.6	0.1	0.8	5.6	17.6	6.7	9.4	13.4	17.8
30 013	3040	3	Cascade	6 988	78 282	641	11.2	92.6	1.6	4.7	1.2	2.1	6.6	18.4	10.2	12.0	14.1	15.0
30 015	...	8	Chouteau	10 291	5 066	2 833	0.5	95.4	0.1	4.3	0.3	0.6	5.5	19.3	6.5	8.8	14.5	13.5
30 017	...	7	Custer	9 799	11 837	2 288	1.2	97.5	0.2	2.0	0.3	1.6	5.1	19.9	9.1	9.5	14.3	14.1
30 019	...	9	Daniels	3 694	1 963	3 063	0.5	98.8	0.0	0.3	0.9	0.8	3.8	18.8	4.7	7.3	14.3	14.7
30 021	...	7	Dawson	6 147	8 670	2 539	1.4	98.7	0.0	1.0	0.3	0.8	5.3	19.2	8.4	9.2	14.1	14.6
30 023	...	7	Deer Lodge	1 909	9 721	2 453	5.1	96.2	0.4	3.1	0.3	2.0	4.5	17.0	9.7	9.0	14.0	14.7
30 025	...	9	Fallon	4 197	2 885	2 998	0.7	98.1	0.8	0.4	0.7	1.4	6.2	20.4	5.4	9.8	13.2	14.7
30 027	...	7	Fergus	11 239	12 180	2 266	1.1	98.7	0.1	1.1	0.1	0.7	5.2	18.8	6.9	9.0	13.7	15.1
30 029	...	5	Flathead	13 205	72 773	676	5.5	97.6	0.1	1.8	0.5	1.3	5.7	19.9	7.6	10.1	17.5	16.1
30 031	...	5	Gallatin	6 493	63 881	746	9.8	97.4	0.2	1.4	0.9	1.4	5.8	16.4	19.8	12.5	16.1	13.3
30 033	...	9	Garfield	12 091	1 420	3 099	0.1	98.6	0.6	0.4	0.4	0.8	5.6	22.3	6.6	9.4	14.0	14.9
30 035	...	7	Glacier	7 756	12 603	2 242	1.6	39.8	0.1	60.0	0.1	0.7	9.3	27.5	9.1	12.0	12.9	11.9
30 037	...	8	Golden Valley	3 044	1 049	3 111	0.3	97.9	0.0	1.6	0.5	1.1	6.1	20.5	6.7	9.0	13.6	14.4
30 039	...	9	Granite	4 474	2 662	3 015	0.6	98.6	0.0	1.0	0.4	0.4	5.5	18.8	7.0	8.8	14.7	18.0
30 041	...	7	Hill	7 502	17 050	1 925	2.3	81.3	0.1	18.0	0.6	1.1	6.9	21.9	10.3	11.1	14.7	12.7
30 043	...	9	Jefferson	4 291	10 367	2 391	2.4	97.8	0.1	1.9	0.2	1.3	5.6	21.5	6.4	9.7	19.4	18.6
30 045	...	8	Judith Basin	4 843	2 284	3 035	0.5	99.3	0.0	0.4	0.3	0.5	4.9	18.0	6.1	9.8	13.9	17.1
30 047	...	7	Lake	3 869	25 885	1 500	6.7	75.7	0.1	24.1	0.4	2.1	6.8	22.1	8.4	9.1	14.3	14.4
30 049	...	5	Lewis and Clark	8 964	54 075	850	6.0	96.5	0.2	2.7	0.6	1.4	5.9	19.0	9.6	10.7	17.5	15.9
30 051	...	9	Liberty	3 703	2 253	3 041	0.6	96.2	2.0	0.6	1.2	3.2	6.5	18.7	4.7	10.0	12.2	12.3
30 053	...	7	Lincoln	9 357	18 819	1 831	2.0	97.7	0.1	1.8	0.4	1.3	5.7	20.4	7.2	9.2	15.3	16.8
30 055	...	9	McCone	6 844	1 924	3 065	0.3	96.8	0.6	1.7	0.9	2.2	4.8	20.1	7.0	8.8	14.1	13.3
30 057	...	9	Madison	9 289	6 927	2 684	0.7	99.0	0.0	0.8	0.2	1.7	4.9	18.4	7.2	9.4	15.7	16.1
30 059	...	8	Meagher	6 195	1 777	3 077	0.3	98.2	0.1	1.4	0.3	1.9	5.5	18.5	6.4	9.7	14.1	14.4
30 061	...	9	Mineral	3 159	3 867	2 925	1.2	96.2	0.2	2.7	0.8	1.6	5.4	20.4	6.6	9.3	14.7	16.9
30 063	5140	5	Missoula	6 729	89 344	565	13.3	95.8	0.3	2.7	1.2	1.5	5.9	17.4	14.9	12.0	16.6	14.4
30 065	...	8	Musselshell	4 836	4 552	2 867	0.9	98.8	0.0	0.9	0.2	1.1	3.9	19.6	6.6	7.8	15.9	15.3
30 067	...	7	Park	6 879	15 982	2 006	2.3	98.0	0.5	1.0	0.5	2.0	5.8	17.7	6.4	10.6	18.9	15.2
30 069	...	9	Petroleum	4 284	506	3 136	0.1	99.4	0.0	0.6	0.0	0.0	6.3	18.8	7.1	10.3	14.0	16.8
30 071	...	9	Phillips	13 312	4 692	2 860	0.4	90.5	0.1	9.1	0.3	0.8	5.9	22.1	7.1	10.4	12.8	14.4
30 073	...	7	Pondera	4 208	6 244	2 754	1.5	87.1	0.1	12.5	0.4	0.5	6.8	21.7	6.9	10.0	13.3	13.6
30 075	...	9	Powder River	8 540	1 777	3 077	0.2	97.5	0.0	2.3	0.2	1.3	5.5	17.8	6.7	8.3	13.2	13.8
30 077	...	7	Powell	6 024	6 945	2 683	1.2	93.8	0.4	5.4	0.5	1.6	4.8	15.3	8.5	13.8	17.9	16.8
30 079	...	9	Prairie	4 498	1 360	3 100	0.3	98.5	0.0	1.2	0.4	1.5	3.9	18.5	5.3	6.7	14.6	15.6
30 081	...	7	Ravalli	6 201	35 811	1 197	5.8	98.1	0.2	1.4	0.3	1.8	5.3	19.7	7.0	8.0	15.8	17.7
30 083	...	7	Richland	5 398	10 053	2 419	1.9	97.7	0.3	1.6	0.4	3.2	6.5	21.8	7.7	10.6	14.6	14.2
30 085	...	7	Roosevelt	6 101	10 912	2 351	1.8	47.3	0.1	52.2	0.3	0.9	9.3	25.3	8.8	11.8	13.8	11.6
30 087	...	7	Rosebud	12 982	9 869	2 439	0.8	69.4	0.4	29.8	0.5	2.2	7.7	27.3	8.7	11.3	16.8	13.1
30 089	...	9	Sanders	7 154	10 233	2 400	1.4	93.0	0.2	6.3	0.6	1.5	5.4	20.6	6.6	8.3	15.5	16.0
30 091	...	9	Sheridan	4 343	4 100	2 908	0.9	98.4	0.0	1.2	0.3	1.0	4.8	18.1	5.0	8.5	13.4	14.1
30 093	...	5	Silver Bow	1 860	33 954	1 256	18.3	97.6	0.1	1.8	0.5	2.9	5.4	17.1	10.7	10.0	14.0	15.4
30 095	...	8	Stillwater	4 648	8 328	2 565	1.8	98.7	0.0	1.0	0.2	1.8	6.1	20.1	7.0	9.5	16.3	16.2
30 097	...	9	Sweet Grass	4 805	3 584	2 944	0.7	99.1	0.1	0.7	0.2	0.2	5.4	19.4	6.2	8.0	15.6	16.2
30 099	...	8	Teton	5 886	6 432	2 738	1.1	97.9	0.0	1.9	0.2	0.8	5.4	21.5	6.9	8.6	14.0	16.6
30 101	...	7	Toole	4 949	4 638	2 861	0.9	96.7	0.2	2.8	0.4	1.0	6.4	21.8	6.9	10.9	15.2	16.3
30 103	...	8	Treasure	2 535	859	3 119	0.3	98.4	0.0	1.4	0.2	4.0	5.4	20.5	7.2	8.1	13.5	15.8
30 105	...	7	Valley	12 745	8 132	2 583	0.6	89.2	0.1	10.5	0.3	0.9	5.2	19.5	6.5	9.1	14.1	14.7
30 107	...	9	Wheatland	3 686	2 276	3 036	0.6	98.5	0.0	1.1	0.4	1.2	5.5	19.5	6.6	8.5	13.1	14.5
30 109	...	9	Wibaux	2 303	1 117	3 107	0.5	99.6	0.0	0.2	0.2	0.4	4.7	20.9	6.4	8.9	13.8	14.7
30 111	0880	3	Yellowstone	6 825	127 258	411	18.6	95.5	0.5	3.3	0.6	3.3	6.0	18.6	10.3	11.4	15.5	15.0
31 000	...	X	**NEBRASKA**	199 113	1 666 028	X	8.4	93.6	4.1	0.9	1.4	4.6	6.9	19.7	10.2	12.4	15.7	12.9
31 001	...	5	Adams	1 459	29 289	1 400	20.1	98.1	0.8	0.5	0.7	2.0	6.4	17.8	11.1	11.7	15.1	13.0
31 003	...	9	Antelope	2 220	7 243	2 659	3.3	99.4	0.0	0.3	0.2	0.2	7.3	22.0	5.1	9.8	13.6	12.4
31 005	...	9	Arthur	1 853	412	3 138	0.2	99.3	0.2	0.5	0.0	0.2	6.3	18.0	4.4	10.0	11.4	16.3
31 007	...	9	Banner	1 933	831	3 122	0.4	99.0	0.6	0.4	0.0	4.8	6.5	21.7	6.0	8.9	16.4	15.5

1. MSA = Metropolitan Statistical Area. PMSA = Primary MSA. NECMA = New England County Metropolitan Area. See Appendix A for explanation of these concepts. See Appendix B for list of metropolitan areas identified by type, with component counties.   2. County typology code from the Economic Research Service of USDA. See Appendix A for definition.   3. Dry land or land partially or temporarily covered by water.   4. Hispanic persons may be of any race.

Table B. States and Counties — Population and Households

STATE County	55 to 64 years	65 to 74 years	75 years and over	Percent female	1990	1980	1980–1990	1990–1999	Births	Deaths	Net migration	Number	Percent change, 1980–1990	Persons per house-hold	Female family house-holder[1]	One person
	16	17	18	19	20	21	22	23	24	25	26	27	28	29	30	31
MISSOURI—Cont'd																
St. Louis city	8.6	6.8	7.4	54.2	396 685	452 801	-12.4	-15.8	62 588	46 645	-77 601	164 931	-7.4	2.34	20.5	39.2
MONTANA	10.0	6.8	6.5	50.3	799 065	786 690	1.6	10.5	103 358	69 332	50 625	306 163	7.9	2.53	8.6	26.3
Beaverhead	9.7	5.9	6.8	48.9	8 424	8 186	2.9	4.3	1 029	763	120	3 211	7.5	2.51	7.7	27.6
Big Horn	7.4	4.2	4.0	50.7	11 337	11 096	2.2	10.9	2 262	887	-111	3 448	4.7	3.25	15.5	18.4
Blaine	9.6	6.1	6.4	49.8	6 728	6 999	-3.9	5.1	1 072	588	-117	2 379	5.4	2.76	12.7	26.4
Broadwater	11.5	8.7	7.4	49.0	3 318	3 267	1.6	25.6	434	338	767	1 280	12.3	2.56	7.0	24.6
Carbon	12.3	8.2	8.7	51.0	8 080	8 099	-0.2	18.1	824	832	1 495	3 269	5.6	2.44	7.0	27.4
Carter	12.7	8.1	8.7	47.9	1 503	1 799	-16.5	-3.3	153	167	-32	589	-9.5	2.52	4.4	28.7
Cascade	10.1	7.0	6.6	50.9	77 691	80 696	-3.7	0.8	11 393	6 596	-5 411	30 133	2.5	2.51	9.3	26.2
Chouteau	12.2	10.3	9.2	48.9	5 452	6 092	-10.5	-7.1	492	564	-304	2 064	-4.8	2.57	5.9	24.7
Custer	11.2	8.3	8.5	51.1	11 697	13 109	-10.8	1.2	1 405	1 375	152	4 631	-5.5	2.44	9.1	29.3
Daniels	13.3	11.4	11.7	50.9	2 266	2 835	-20.1	-13.4	153	291	-153	919	-12.1	2.42	5.1	29.2
Dawson	11.5	8.5	9.0	50.4	9 505	11 805	-19.5	-8.8	839	828	-824	3 691	-11.7	2.54	6.5	26.6
Deer Lodge	12.3	10.0	8.8	50.6	10 356	12 518	-17.3	-6.1	949	1 234	-321	4 060	-8.2	2.32	9.3	32.5
Fallon	13.0	8.5	8.9	50.6	3 103	3 763	-17.5	-7.0	285	293	-198	1 166	-11.5	2.64	4.9	23.8
Fergus	12.1	8.8	10.4	50.9	12 083	13 076	-7.6	0.8	1 303	1 649	480	4 603	-2.4	2.49	6.2	27.6
Flathead	10.3	6.8	6.0	50.1	59 218	51 966	14.0	22.9	7 965	5 109	10 920	22 834	21.5	2.56	8.0	24.1
Gallatin	7.5	4.7	3.9	48.6	50 484	42 865	17.7	26.5	6 617	2 652	9 534	19 015	27.4	2.50	6.8	24.2
Garfield	11.7	7.6	8.0	48.9	1 589	1 656	-4.0	-10.6	170	140	-195	577	-2.0	2.73	4.3	24.1
Glacier	7.7	5.1	4.5	51.0	12 121	10 628	14.0	4.0	2 210	1 015	-684	3 816	11.1	3.03	15.7	21.7
Golden Valley	14.8	7.4	7.5	49.4	912	1 026	-11.1	15.0	131	74	82	330	-9.3	2.45	3.6	27.9
Granite	11.5	8.2	7.6	47.9	2 548	2 700	-5.6	4.5	292	288	124	1 051	5.3	2.40	5.8	29.7
Hill	9.5	6.5	6.3	50.5	17 654	17 985	-1.8	-3.4	2 547	1 369	-1 758	6 426	1.9	2.64	9.9	26.2
Jefferson	9.1	5.3	4.5	48.7	7 939	7 029	12.9	30.6	869	619	2 192	2 867	21.4	2.68	6.5	21.4
Judith Basin	12.3	9.6	8.3	48.9	2 282	2 646	-13.8	0.1	254	179	-67	908	-4.9	2.44	3.6	26.5
Lake	11.0	7.1	6.8	49.8	21 041	19 056	10.4	23.0	2 844	2 087	4 158	7 814	17.9	2.62	11.0	24.1
Lewis and Clark	9.5	6.2	5.7	50.9	47 495	43 039	10.4	13.9	6 108	3 735	4 308	18 649	16.1	2.47	9.8	28.0
Liberty	10.5	12.1	12.9	52.1	2 295	2 329	-1.5	-1.8	244	193	-64	788	-5.6	2.58	5.8	28.2
Lincoln	10.4	8.6	6.4	49.6	17 481	17 752	-1.5	7.7	1 953	1 541	1 001	6 668	10.0	2.60	7.2	23.3
McCone	12.5	10.6	8.9	50.0	2 276	2 702	-15.8	-15.5	205	189	-359	844	-5.8	2.65	3.3	22.6
Madison	12.7	7.4	8.3	48.1	5 989	5 448	9.9	15.7	632	647	973	2 387	13.9	2.43	5.1	28.2
Meagher	12.5	10.5	8.4	48.1	1 819	2 154	-15.6	-2.3	236	199	-69	709	-8.0	2.39	4.4	29.2
Mineral	12.0	8.6	6.1	49.3	3 315	3 675	-9.8	16.7	342	287	510	1 282	-3.5	2.55	7.6	25.5
Missoula	8.1	5.5	5.3	50.7	78 687	76 016	3.5	13.5	9 976	5 282	6 208	30 782	9.9	2.47	9.5	27.3
Musselshell	12.9	8.8	9.2	49.7	4 106	4 428	-7.3	10.9	410	528	582	1 661	-2.2	2.41	5.2	30.8
Park	11.1	7.2	7.1	51.1	14 515	12 869	12.5	10.1	1 816	1 345	1 038	5 619	14.1	2.46	7.2	28.0
Petroleum	12.1	9.1	5.5	46.2	519	655	-20.8	-2.5	46	37	-17	209	-9.9	2.48	4.3	23.0
Phillips	10.8	7.8	8.7	50.7	5 163	5 367	-3.8	-9.1	587	481	-571	1 931	0.8	2.59	7.6	26.8
Pondera	11.0	7.9	9.1	50.3	6 433	6 731	-4.4	-2.9	756	649	-289	2 246	-3.8	2.63	6.6	25.4
Powder River	12.8	11.9	10.0	49.3	2 090	2 520	-17.1	-15.0	208	190	-321	805	-9.4	2.55	4.7	25.8
Powell	9.8	6.5	6.7	40.7	6 620	6 958	-4.9	4.9	618	644	380	2 234	-3.6	2.44	6.5	28.6
Prairie	12.9	10.7	11.8	47.9	1 383	1 836	-24.7	-1.7	114	147	21	568	-14.8	2.40	3.2	26.9
Ravalli	12.0	7.5	6.9	50.2	25 010	22 493	11.2	43.2	3 154	2 647	10 377	9 698	21.1	2.53	6.5	23.9
Richland	9.9	7.5	7.2	50.6	10 716	12 243	-12.5	-6.2	1 171	961	-839	3 956	-7.8	2.68	6.8	24.3
Roosevelt	8.5	5.4	5.6	51.5	10 999	10 467	5.1	-0.8	2 004	938	-1 142	3 694	9.0	2.94	15.3	22.8
Rosebud	7.4	4.3	3.5	48.7	10 505	9 899	6.1	-6.1	1 647	740	-1 569	3 479	9.1	2.98	10.6	21.4
Sanders	11.9	8.0	7.7	49.0	8 669	8 675	0.0	18.0	978	922	1 553	3 397	6.8	2.53	5.5	27.1
Sheridan	12.4	11.2	12.7	50.8	4 732	5 414	-12.6	-13.4	336	545	-413	1 899	-5.8	2.44	5.6	27.4
Silver Bow	11.3	7.8	8.2	50.7	33 941	38 092	-10.9	0.0	3 937	3 876	26	13 899	-4.8	2.39	9.5	31.9
Stillwater	11.4	6.6	6.8	49.6	6 536	5 598	16.8	27.4	772	614	1 645	2 523	21.8	2.56	5.8	24.1
Sweet Grass	12.6	7.1	9.3	50.3	3 154	3 216	-1.9	13.6	311	356	485	1 281	3.6	2.42	4.1	29.7
Teton	11.2	7.3	8.3	49.8	6 271	6 491	-3.4	2.6	710	679	143	2 329	0.6	2.54	4.7	26.6
Toole	11.3	5.8	5.4	50.5	5 046	5 559	-9.2	-8.1	549	488	-444	1 922	-6.2	2.46	6.7	29.4
Treasure	11.1	8.7	9.7	49.9	874	981	-10.9	-1.7	73	68	-17	339	-5.0	2.58	5.3	23.6
Valley	12.0	9.3	9.5	49.9	8 239	10 250	-19.6	-1.3	957	864	-178	3 268	-11.0	2.49	7.4	27.9
Wheatland	12.2	9.6	10.5	49.2	2 246	2 359	-4.8	1.3	271	243	6	849	-3.9	2.33	4.8	32.9
Wibaux	11.4	8.4	11.0	49.9	1 191	1 476	-19.3	-6.2	124	154	-38	454	-11.0	2.54	6.4	28.4
Yellowstone	10.1	6.9	6.2	51.4	113 419	108 035	5.0	12.2	15 621	9 206	7 850	44 689	12.0	2.49	9.7	26.5
NEBRASKA	8.5	6.8	6.9	51.1	1 578 417	1 569 825	0.5	5.6	217 510	139 754	11 445	602 363	5.4	2.54	8.3	26.5
Adams	8.9	7.5	8.5	51.2	29 625	30 656	-3.4	-1.1	3 849	3 014	-1 095	11 593	-1.3	2.41	7.6	28.8
Antelope	9.6	9.4	10.9	50.9	7 965	8 675	-8.2	-9.1	888	850	-730	3 045	-4.9	2.59	5.1	26.8
Arthur	10.7	12.1	10.9	49.5	462	513	-9.9	-10.8	41	43	-44	187	-5.6	2.47	5.3	24.1
Banner	9.3	9.1	6.6	48.1	852	918	-7.2	-2.5	69	53	-35	305	-3.2	2.79	4.3	13.8

1. No spouse present.

Table B. States and Counties — Vital Statistics, Health Resources, and Crime

STATE County	Births, average 1996–1998 Total	Rate[1]	Deaths, average 1996–1998 Number Total	Infant[2]	Rate Total[1]	Infant[3]	Physicians,[4] 1998 Number	Rate[5]	Hospitals,[4] 1998 Number	Beds Number	Rate[5]	Medicare enrollees 1999	Serious crimes known to police, 1998[6] Total Number	Rate[7]
	32	33	34	35	36	37	38	39	40	41	42	43	44	45
MISSOURI—Cont'd														
St. Louis city	5 745	16.6	4 666	76	13.5	13.2	1 457	429	12	3 411	1 005	58 283	51 459	14 952
MONTANA	10 833	12.3	7 819	77	8.9	7.1	1 775	202	54	4 084	464	135 415	35 822	4 071
Beaverhead	96	10.7	90	1	10.0	6.9	18	203	1	31	350	1 339	NA	NA
Big Horn	246	19.6	102	3	8.1	13.6	14	111	1	54	428	1 167	NA	NA
Blaine	115	16.1	64	1	9.0	8.7	5	70	0	0	0	942	66	931
Broadwater	42	10.3	40	0	9.8	7.9	7	169	1	42	1 016	759	NA	NA
Carbon	84	9.0	88	1	9.4	11.9	11	116	1	46	487	1 713	156	1 812
Carter	15	10.1	15	0	10.1	21.7	1	65	1	10	651	263	NA	NA
Cascade	1 107	13.9	739	9	9.3	8.1	201	254	2	402	509	12 698	98	1 870
Chouteau	48	9.1	55	0	10.4	0.0	2	39	2	82	1 581	1 048	98	1 870
Custer	134	11.0	152	1	12.5	5.0	29	241	1	141	1 172	2 259	554	4 568
Daniels	15	7.3	29	0	14.0	22.2	3	150	1	54	2 699	487	NA	NA
Dawson	86	9.6	93	1	10.4	7.8	10	113	1	104	1 175	1 688	340	3 754
Deer Lodge	98	9.7	129	0	12.9	3.4	17	170	2	134	1 340	2 164	304	3 038
Fallon	28	9.6	34	0	11.4	0.0	2	68	1	52	1 768	543	34	1 119
Fergus	119	9.5	164	1	13.2	11.2	15	122	1	132	1 076	2 521	303	2 422
Flathead	890	12.4	582	7	8.1	7.5	169	235	2	249	347	11 425	NA	NA
Gallatin	753	12.3	306	3	5.0	4.4	141	225	1	86	138	6 246	2 377	4 079
Garfield	20	14.1	17	0	12.2	0.0	0	0	0	0	0	251	NA	NA
Glacier	227	18.0	118	2	9.4	10.3	15	120	1	59	470	1 356	NA	NA
Golden Valley	14	13.3	8	0	7.8	0.0	0	0	0	0	0	217	NA	NA
Granite	35	13.4	36	0	13.5	0.0	3	112	1	31	1 162	429	114	4 326
Hill	268	15.3	150	2	8.6	6.2	22	127	1	140	806	2 444	1 079	6 145
Jefferson	87	8.9	74	0	7.5	3.8	18	178	0	0	0	1 256	NA	NA
Judith Basin	25	11.0	20	0	8.7	13.2	0	0	0	0	0	426	NA	NA
Lake	324	12.8	234	2	9.3	6.2	41	160	2	121	472	4 038	NA	NA
Lewis and Clark	661	12.4	417	3	7.8	4.5	131	244	1	79	147	7 559	NA	NA
Liberty	22	9.3	25	0	10.9	15.4	2	86	1	67	2 884	625	35	1 462
Lincoln	190	10.1	187	2	10.0	10.5	20	107	1	26	139	3 456	NA	NA
McCone	19	9.4	18	0	8.8	0.0	1	51	0	0	0	373	2	98
Madison	64	9.4	69	1	10.1	20.7	9	131	2	23	335	1 189	69	999
Meagher	26	14.3	21	0	11.7	0.0	4	223	1	37	2 059	383	40	2 214
Mineral	35	9.4	32	0	8.7	9.5	4	107	1	30	800	766	NA	NA
Missoula	1 035	11.7	617	6	7.0	5.8	273	307	2	336	378	10 947	3 342	4 335
Musselshell	47	10.1	60	1	12.9	28.6	2	43	1	48	1 042	891	208	4 512
Park	177	11.1	146	1	9.2	3.8	20	126	1	35	221	2 598	NA	NA
Petroleum	6	11.1	4	0	7.8	0.0	0	0	0	0	0	83	NA	NA
Phillips	50	10.1	52	0	10.6	0.0	2	41	1	21	436	894	117	2 383
Pondera	78	12.3	68	1	10.7	8.5	7	109	1	94	1 468	1 205	NA	NA
Powder River	17	9.0	21	0	11.3	0.0	0	0	0	0	0	306	19	994
Powell	61	8.8	66	0	9.5	5.4	4	57	1	35	500	1 119	NA	NA
Prairie	12	8.7	18	0	13.7	0.0	0	0	1	21	1 575	311	NA	NA
Ravalli	365	10.6	317	1	9.2	3.6	44	125	1	48	137	6 128	NA	NA
Richland	114	11.2	105	1	10.3	5.8	13	129	1	49	485	1 715	NA	NA
Roosevelt	197	17.9	88	2	8.0	11.8	12	109	3	116	1 056	1 472	49	440
Rosebud	162	15.8	81	2	7.9	14.4	4	40	1	75	746	995	213	2 084
Sanders	102	10.0	111	1	10.9	9.8	13	128	1	44	432	1 989	NA	NA
Sheridan	35	8.1	69	0	15.9	0.0	4	94	1	103	2 413	1 062	93	2 140
Silver Bow	400	11.6	436	2	12.6	5.8	76	220	1	115	333	6 459	NA	NA
Stillwater	80	10.3	66	0	8.5	0.0	5	62	1	23	285	1 278	24	306
Sweet Grass	38	11.3	40	1	11.7	17.4	3	88	0	0	0	637	49	1 439
Teton	76	12.0	79	0	12.5	4.4	3	47	0	0	0	1 104	NA	NA
Toole	56	11.7	55	0	11.5	0.0	6	127	1	83	1 756	578	111	2 301
Treasure	7	8.6	5	0	6.3	0.0	0	0	0	0	0	173	6	714
Valley	98	11.8	102	0	12.3	0.0	10	122	1	42	513	1 648	212	2 553
Wheatland	28	11.9	28	1	11.6	23.5	2	84	1	44	1 854	490	NA	NA
Wibaux	13	11.1	20	0	17.5	0.0	0	0	0	0	0	215	NA	NA
Yellowstone	1 684	13.4	1 055	14	8.4	8.1	357	283	2	520	412	19 040	5 679	4 733
NEBRASKA	23 380	14.1	15 321	183	9.3	7.8	3 142	189	89	7 870	473	252 231	73 259	4 405
Adams	396	13.4	340	4	11.5	10.9	66	224	1	190	645	5 208	1 467	4 914
Antelope	89	12.2	86	0	11.8	0.0	9	125	1	49	682	1 436	79	1 069
Arthur	5	12.5	5	0	12.6	0.0	0	0	0	0	0	98	2	465
Banner	8	9.2	5	0	6.1	0.0	0	0	0	0	0	90	NA	NA

1. Per 1,000 estimated resident population, average 1996–1998.   2. Deaths of infants under 1 year old.   3. Deaths of infants under 1 year old per 1,000 live births.   4. Data subject to copyright.   5. Per 100,000 resident population as of July 1 of the year shown.   6. Data for serious crimes have not been adjusted for underreporting; this may affect comparability between geographic areas and over time.   7. Per 100,000 population estimated by the FBI.

Table B. States and Counties — Crime, Education, Money Income, and Poverty

STATE County	Serious crimes known to police, 1998 [1] (cont'd) Rate [2]		Education — School enrollment and attainment, 1990				Local government expenditures, fiscal 1997 [5]		Money income — 1989				Income and poverty, 1997			
			Enrollment [3]		Attainment [4] (percent)					Households			Percent below poverty level			
										Median						
	Violent	Property	Total	Percent private	High school graduate or more	Bachelor's degree or more	Total current expenditures (mil dol)	Current expenditures per student (dollars)	Per capita [6] (dollars)	Dollars	Percent change, 1979–1989 (constant 1989 dollars)	Percent with $100,000 or more	Median household income	All persons	Persons under 18	Persons 5–17 in families
	46	47	48	49	50	51	52	53	54	55	56	57	58	59	60	61
MISSOURI—Cont'd																
St. Louis city	2 571	12 381	96 794	30.2	62.8	15.3	326.0	7 305	10 798	19 458	0.9	1.3	26 364	25.7	38.4	34.6
MONTANA	139	3 932	215 759	8.5	81.0	19.8	902.0	5 481	11 213	22 988	-11.1	1.7	29 672	15.5	21.3	19.1
Beaverhead	NA	NA	2 701	3.6	83.9	20.6	9.5	5 521	10 376	20 925	-2.5	0.8	29 796	16.7	21.0	19.8
Big Horn	NA	NA	3 571	11.2	69.2	12.8	19.1	7 256	7 148	19 101	-18.1	0.7	24 317	29.6	34.8	32.6
Blaine	56	875	1 995	3.1	70.4	14.4	11.7	7 203	8 290	18 512	-15.0	1.0	23 670	26.8	32.9	30.7
Broadwater	NA	NA	752	1.1	73.9	13.5	3.7	4 499	10 125	20 257	-11.2	1.3	29 034	16.2	22.9	20.5
Carbon	12	1 800	1 959	2.9	78.1	19.2	10.1	5 999	10 727	19 042	-7.1	1.5	29 010	12.9	16.2	15.4
Carter	NA	NA	296	7.4	76.0	10.8	1.6	7 165	10 670	16 458	-12.6	3.4	23 505	19.3	23.6	24.9
Cascade	NA	NA	18 971	12.3	82.9	18.4	71.9	4 908	12 011	23 700	-11.9	2.3	31 489	14.4	20.1	17.6
Chouteau	114	1 756	1 247	3.1	83.4	16.8	7.6	6 790	11 290	22 362	-11.8	2.5	30 365	13.2	16.5	16.6
Custer	503	4 065	3 087	5.8	77.1	16.0	10.6	4 813	10 310	21 348	-8.0	0.8	29 451	17.0	24.4	21.3
Daniels	NA	NA	517	1.4	74.4	11.5	3.4	8 052	9 963	21 433	-5.3	1.1	30 409	13.6	19.2	17.0
Dawson	132	3 622	2 531	5.1	74.5	13.2	10.1	5 699	10 629	23 414	-18.9	0.9	31 964	12.3	15.9	15.3
Deer Lodge	130	2 908	2 291	2.9	74.5	11.5	8.3	4 702	9 444	20 281	-23.9	0.5	26 692	19.4	26.7	24.7
Fallon	197	922	714	2.5	75.3	10.6	5.6	7 303	10 308	23 162	-14.6	1.4	33 260	11.0	12.4	11.9
Fergus	88	2 334	2 705	6.4	77.4	14.5	15.1	6 255	10 995	21 398	4.3	2.4	28 446	14.4	18.9	16.9
Flathead	NA	NA	14 832	9.0	82.1	17.2	64.9	4 679	11 718	24 145	-10.5	1.6	32 387	14.2	20.4	17.1
Gallatin	132	3 947	18 710	6.8	90.4	33.8	46.9	4 999	12 252	23 345	-9.1	2.2	35 710	11.6	13.9	13.1
Garfield	NA	NA	387	2.8	72.6	8.8	1.7	6 444	9 843	17 201	-13.8	3.4	24 808	14.4	18.0	19.3
Glacier	NA	NA	3 909	3.3	72.0	14.5	22.2	6 875	7 458	18 598	-17.2	0.2	22 491	33.6	40.2	36.7
Golden Valley	NA	NA	176	9.1	72.4	14.7	1.7	7 765	8 505	18 062	-4.4	0.6	20 453	21.2	25.5	26.0
Granite	228	4 093	529	2.6	75.9	16.9	3.3	5 691	10 049	18 278	-14.3	2.5	26 063	18.1	24.5	24.5
Hill	165	5 980	5 539	7.5	78.4	18.1	22.5	6 132	11 121	25 467	-8.2	1.8	30 736	19.2	25.3	22.9
Jefferson	NA	NA	2 287	11.4	81.3	20.8	9.5	4 694	13 233	31 400	11.7	3.5	41 820	10.4	14.5	12.1
Judith Basin	NA	NA	496	5.6	80.4	19.8	3.4	7 096	12 060	22 578	3.7	3.2	26 198	17.6	24.1	21.8
Lake	NA	NA	5 495	4.5	77.3	15.7	25.5	5 143	9 274	19 755	-3.9	1.3	27 169	21.4	28.9	26.4
Lewis and Clark	NA	NA	12 205	15.4	87.4	27.8	53.1	5 202	12 342	26 409	-7.1	1.3	36 409	12.6	17.6	15.3
Liberty	42	1 420	554	16.6	77.2	16.9	3.7	7 074	10 544	24 969	3.9	2.4	27 412	14.4	16.1	18.0
Lincoln	NA	NA	4 496	7.3	73.3	12.5	18.9	4 960	9 813	20 898	-20.3	1.1	27 934	18.7	27.9	23.7
McCone	0	98	589	2.5	79.5	14.3	2.4	6 873	9 347	20 487	2.0	0.9	28 974	14.4	17.2	18.2
Madison	29	970	1 405	5.8	85.0	19.7	7.3	6 185	10 718	22 066	8.5	0.6	28 831	13.0	17.0	16.4
Meagher	498	1 716	372	8.3	73.9	14.4	1.9	5 920	9 201	18 936	-13.2	0.4	22 471	19.7	25.9	25.4
Mineral	NA	NA	846	3.5	74.0	13.1	5.9	6 355	9 440	20 938	-22.2	0.5	26 068	20.3	29.4	26.6
Missoula	237	4 098	25 497	6.4	85.4	27.7	75.4	5 223	11 944	23 388	-14.2	2.1	33 248	15.3	20.0	17.8
Musselshell	260	4 252	974	8.0	70.9	11.4	5.0	5 770	8 941	16 661	-13.0	1.1	22 923	19.4	26.2	23.2
Park	NA	NA	3 063	18.3	81.7	19.3	13.7	5 510	11 378	22 658	-7.5	1.7	29 845	13.8	19.1	19.0
Petroleum	NA	NA	94	0.0	81.9	17.5	0.9	7 719	9 876	19 219	5.7	1.9	24 234	19.5	24.9	28.9
Phillips	41	2 342	1 245	9.0	74.1	13.1	8.1	7 635	10 793	22 245	11.3	2.1	26 699	19.3	24.7	22.6
Pondera	NA	NA	1 634	5.4	73.7	15.0	10.8	6 788	9 811	23 533	-12.9	1.3	28 198	20.1	26.5	23.4
Powder River	157	837	473	3.2	75.2	15.3	3.0	6 804	12 722	22 354	-11.5	3.7	29 283	15.3	18.5	20.2
Powell	NA	NA	1 500	4.0	76.5	16.6	7.1	6 131	9 978	21 621	-12.2	0.9	29 595	19.7	24.4	22.7
Prairie	NA	NA	299	2.0	71.1	13.2	1.6	6 754	8 497	16 694	5.4	0.9	24 999	12.7	17.2	16.0
Ravalli	NA	NA	6 025	9.8	79.1	18.2	29.2	4 530	10 130	21 113	-5.0	1.2	28 589	15.6	23.3	20.6
Richland	NA	NA	2 767	5.7	75.4	13.4	13.2	5 874	10 091	23 264	-21.2	1.3	31 885	14.5	18.7	17.3
Roosevelt	63	377	3 079	2.9	70.1	11.3	21.3	7 250	7 751	19 445	-21.7	0.7	23 953	31.1	39.8	37.1
Rosebud	176	1 908	3 303	10.1	78.3	13.4	18.2	7 459	10 415	27 192	-3.1	0.6	34 889	19.9	24.8	22.6
Sanders	NA	NA	2 083	5.6	75.2	14.8	11.4	5 679	9 459	18 616	-12.0	1.2	24 183	19.8	27.4	24.9
Sheridan	46	2 094	1 012	2.7	74.5	11.7	6.3	7 180	10 001	20 728	-17.3	0.6	29 761	12.5	15.6	15.6
Silver Bow	NA	NA	8 527	12.0	78.3	17.9	30.8	5 271	11 364	21 216	-13.2	1.6	30 795	16.1	23.2	20.2
Stillwater	0	306	1 520	2.1	78.2	16.9	9.2	5 770	10 975	23 582	6.3	1.3	33 897	10.6	14.2	13.2
Sweet Grass	88	1 351	674	2.2	78.9	20.0	3.4	5 965	10 838	20 867	9.0	1.8	29 456	12.3	16.6	15.4
Teton	NA	NA	1 488	9.6	78.6	17.8	7.8	5 722	10 772	22 072	-6.0	1.6	27 944	15.9	20.4	19.6
Toole	498	1 803	1 208	8.7	77.4	14.0	6.6	6 101	11 375	25 108	5.9	1.2	30 673	15.9	19.7	18.2
Treasure	0	714	217	1.8	85.1	13.2	1.4	8 218	10 244	18 152	-10.7	4.1	24 321	15.8	22.8	21.4
Valley	72	2 481	1 889	5.0	78.6	13.2	11.3	7 039	10 529	21 781	-10.7	0.9	29 581	18.0	25.3	22.0
Wheatland	NA	NA	519	8.3	72.2	10.6	3.2	6 839	8 656	16 946	-19.4	0.7	21 293	19.8	27.9	28.0
Wibaux	NA	NA	277	2.5	68.3	10.9	1.4	6 342	9 338	19 375	3.5	0.2	25 010	18.1	23.8	21.3
Yellowstone	187	4 546	30 202	11.0	83.7	21.5	113.7	5 092	12 416	25 942	-11.3	2.2	35 680	12.1	16.8	14.5
NEBRASKA	451	3 954	433 409	14.9	81.8	18.9	1 707.0	5 848	12 452	26 016	-2.5	2.2	35 337	9.6	12.6	10.2
Adams	144	4 770	7 591	20.2	81.2	15.6	31.3	6 626	12 650	24 399	-4.9	2.3	35 771	9.7	12.5	10.2
Antelope	68	1 001	2 014	11.7	77.5	9.9	11.3	8 862	9 221	18 447	3.8	1.2	30 271	13.0	15.1	13.2
Arthur	233	232	98	0.0	83.7	13.8	0.9	8 650	9 094	19 038	-5.9	0.0	19 468	13.5	15.4	14.3
Banner	NA	NA	213	2.3	87.7	12.0	1.6	6 870	9 120	22 176	11.3	0.6	29 688	6.9	7.1	8.2

1. Data for serious crimes have not been adjusted for underreporting; this may affect comparability between geographic areas and over time.   2. Per 100,000 population estimated by the FBI.   3. All persons 3 years old and over enrolled in nursery school through college.   4. Persons 25 years old and over.   5. Elementary and secondary education expenditures, local government fiscal years ending between July 1, 1996 and June 30, 1997.   6. Based on population enumerated as of April 1, 1990.

Table B. States and Counties — **Personal Income**

	Personal income, 1998												
			Per capita[1]					Transfer payments					
									Government payments to individuals				
STATE County	Total (mil dol)	Percent change, 1997–1998	Dollars	Rank	Wages and salaries[2] (mil dol)	Proprietor's income (mil dol)	Dividends, interest, and rent (mil dol)	Total (mil dol)	Total (mil dol)	Social Security (mil dol)	Medical payments (mil dol)	Income mainte-nance (mil dol)	Unemploy-ment insurance (mil dol)
	62	63	64	65	66	67	68	69	70	71	72	73	74
MISSOURI—Cont'd													
St. Louis city	8 925	2.7	26 332	361	11 249	623	1 938	1 902	1 842	542	850	306	32
MONTANA	18 671	5.6	21 229	X	10 253	1 756	4 415	3 063	2 903	1 275	980	242	65
Beaverhead	177	4.2	20 072	1 687	91	13	47	34	32	13	12	2	1
Big Horn	167	6.5	13 239	3 059	124	12	28	38	36	10	14	7	1
Blaine	109	10.7	15 358	2 898	40	16	27	26	24	8	9	4	1
Broadwater	77	4.2	18 684	2 160	32	9	18	16	15	7	5	1	0
Carbon	186	4.0	19 745	1 798	52	16	68	33	31	15	11	2	1
Carter	20	5.6	13 139	3 062	6	0	9	5	4	2	2	0	0
Cascade	1 863	4.3	23 721	697	1 075	133	430	299	285	120	100	23	5
Chouteau	108	2.9	20 905	1 422	31	13	39	21	20	10	7	1	0
Custer	247	2.9	20 487	1 561	124	16	66	48	46	20	16	4	1
Daniels	52	5.7	26 120	385	20	10	16	9	8	5	3	0	0
Dawson	182	7.5	20 612	1 523	101	13	42	35	33	15	10	2	0
Deer Lodge	174	3.5	17 490	2 489	77	9	40	48	46	21	16	4	1
Fallon	61	2.7	20 647	1 506	34	8	12	11	11	5	4	1	0
Fergus	241	3.6	19 630	1 847	100	28	70	50	48	22	18	3	1
Flathead	1 605	9.3	22 327	1 012	891	166	399	241	228	108	72	14	7
Gallatin	1 428	6.5	22 820	888	824	183	352	142	131	61	34	8	2
Garfield	22	11.1	15 761	2 833	7	3	8	4	4	2	1	0	0
Glacier	193	6.0	15 374	2 894	110	20	32	49	47	12	17	11	2
Golden Valley	17	6.3	16 095	2 782	4	1	6	4	3	2	1	0	0
Granite	49	5.2	18 556	2 193	18	6	15	10	10	5	3	1	0
Hill	361	6.7	20 789	1 458	188	42	80	69	66	20	22	6	2
Jefferson	223	6.8	22 088	1 072	67	19	39	28	26	12	8	1	1
Judith Basin	41	4.6	17 882	2 383	10	5	15	8	7	4	2	1	0
Lake	424	2.9	16 574	2 698	195	29	105	95	90	38	32	10	2
Lewis and Clark	1 265	4.4	23 600	723	838	105	286	175	165	76	51	12	3
Liberty	46	9.1	19 827	1 771	18	8	15	8	8	4	3	0	0
Lincoln	305	4.7	16 297	2 743	142	39	62	78	74	35	24	7	3
McCone	36	12.9	18 457	2 225	14	6	9	7	6	3	2	1	0
Madison	119	4.4	17 337	2 522	42	11	39	22	21	11	7	1	0
Meagher	36	4.0	19 870	1 755	12	6	10	8	7	3	3	0	0
Mineral	56	6.7	14 863	2 948	23	7	12	17	16	7	5	1	1
Missoula	2 066	5.9	23 234	809	1 314	207	439	273	257	105	86	23	5
Musselshell	66	1.8	14 351	2 978	22	5	19	19	19	8	7	1	0
Park	[3]295	[3]3.5	[3]18 708	[3]2 155	[3]123	[3]36	[3]83	[3]54	[3]51	[3]20	[3]16	[3]3	[3]2
Petroleum	7	13.4	14 151	2 996	2	1	2	2	2	1	0	0	0
Phillips	82	8.6	17 011	2 610	35	11	21	18	17	8	6	2	0
Pondera	126	4.4	19 866	1 756	49	14	39	26	25	11	9	2	0
Powder River	29	3.2	16 314	2 740	11	2	10	6	5	3	2	0	0
Powell	120	2.8	17 201	2 562	62	12	27	24	23	10	7	2	0
Prairie	25	15.2	18 533	2 201	7	5	7	6	6	3	2	1	0
Ravalli	623	6.6	17 737	2 426	219	82	173	122	115	56	38	8	4
Richland	196	6.6	19 298	1 954	105	17	47	36	34	16	13	2	1
Roosevelt	173	9.0	15 767	2 830	86	18	34	47	45	14	19	9	1
Rosebud	181	2.0	18 066	2 328	142	5	30	29	27	10	9	4	1
Sanders	156	5.4	15 284	2 903	63	10	38	42	40	19	13	3	1
Sheridan	93	10.0	21 947	1 113	31	15	31	18	18	10	6	1	0
Silver Bow	763	3.0	22 093	1 070	447	55	156	153	147	66	53	13	2
Stillwater	159	8.1	19 736	1 801	82	12	43	26	25	12	9	1	0
Sweet Grass	65	2.6	19 032	2 043	22	5	25	11	10	6	3	1	0
Teton	119	2.5	18 799	2 123	42	16	37	23	22	11	7	1	0
Toole	107	1.7	22 589	956	54	16	27	18	17	8	6	1	0
Treasure	14	10.7	15 707	2 846	5	0	5	3	3	2	1	0	0
Valley	177	6.9	21 439	1 259	74	23	47	35	34	14	13	3	0
Wheatland	38	-2.7	16 217	2 759	13	3	12	11	10	4	4	1	0
Wibaux	18	14.7	15 887	2 810	5	3	5	4	4	2	2	0	0
Yellowstone	3 083	5.7	24 425	573	1 927	230	663	423	400	182	134	28	8
NEBRASKA	43 053	5.0	25 924	X	26 595	4 568	8 912	5 495	5 213	2 372	2 036	350	46
Adams	714	4.3	24 280	594	407	56	180	108	103	51	39	6	1
Antelope	167	2.9	22 886	873	51	44	41	29	27	13	11	2	0
Arthur	3	54.4	7 000	3 108	2	-4	2	1	1	1	0	0	0
Banner	13	-6.0	15 122	2 920	5	2	3	2	2	1	0	0	0

1. Based on the resident population estimated as of July 1 of the year shown.   2. Includes other labor income.   3. Yellowstone Park included with Park County.

Table B. States and Counties — Earnings, Social Security, and Housing

STATE County	Earnings, 1998									Social Security beneficiaries, December 1998		Supplemental Security Income recipients, December 1998	Housing units, 1990	
			Goods-related[1]		Service-related and other[2]									
	Total (mil dol)	Farm	Total	Manu-facturing	Total	Retail trade	Finance, insur-ance, and real estate	Services	Govern-ment	Number	Rate[3]		Total	Percent change, 1980–1990
	75	76	77	78	79	80	81	82	83	84	85	86	87	88
MISSOURI—Cont'd														
St. Louis city	11 872	0.0	D	17.1	D	5.7	9.8	29.8	16.9	67 752	200	18 972	194 919	-3.6
MONTANA	12 009	2.0	17.9	7.9	58.3	11.8	5.9	26.6	21.8	153 476	174	13 853	361 155	10.0
Beaverhead	105	6.9	D	2.3	D	10.4	8.5	20.6	27.3	1 518	171	123	4 128	10.3
Big Horn	136	5.6	27.0	0.8	34.7	5.9	2.8	20.8	32.7	1 485	118	325	4 304	11.3
Blaine	56	19.2	D	1.3	D	8.5	4.0	12.8	39.6	1 112	156	173	2 930	13.4
Broadwater	42	11.3	D	23.2	D	6.2	2.9	11.8	15.3	910	220	62	1 593	9.9
Carbon	68	2.5	15.1	4.2	60.7	15.2	7.4	28.4	21.7	1 960	208	98	4 828	10.7
Carter	6	-27.2	D	10.1	D	9.5	6.8	D	42.7	296	193	11	816	2.6
Cascade	1 208	0.6	10.0	3.4	60.1	12.6	7.6	28.3	29.3	14 326	181	1 452	33 063	2.7
Chouteau	45	27.8	5.1	1.9	38.5	8.8	5.5	11.5	28.6	1 150	222	51	2 668	-0.8
Custer	140	-1.0	D	2.7	D	14.7	5.9	26.3	30.8	2 492	207	241	5 405	-1.2
Daniels	30	21.7	D	1.6	D	6.4	3.3	13.2	17.7	547	273	25	1 220	-6.4
Dawson	114	5.9	D	1.3	D	10.2	3.4	18.9	21.0	1 756	198	67	4 487	-3.2
Deer Lodge	86	0.2	D	3.9	D	11.3	3.1	33.5	35.3	2 404	240	218	4 830	-7.1
Fallon	42	3.6	31.0	1.9	D	7.6	2.4	14.9	17.7	631	215	34	1 525	0.4
Fergus	128	5.8	15.5	4.7	54.6	12.1	4.8	26.3	24.1	2 761	225	220	5 732	6.3
Flathead	1 057	0.3	30.4	21.1	55.3	12.6	6.3	25.8	13.9	12 916	180	982	26 979	20.0
Gallatin	1 006	1.3	20.4	9.0	56.7	14.3	5.9	25.3	21.6	7 127	114	379	21 350	24.3
Garfield	11	23.6	9.0	4.8	D	8.2	D	D	29.9	271	195	14	924	6.5
Glacier	130	8.0	D	0.8	D	10.0	3.0	26.8	34.9	1 630	130	405	4 797	19.9
Golden Valley	5	20.8	D	D	D	D	0.0	D	38.8	225	216	13	432	-8.5
Granite	25	4.6	D	19.6	D	11.4	D	D	29.2	587	220	33	1 924	17.7
Hill	229	9.2	5.5	1.0	66.1	10.5	3.9	27.8	19.2	2 437	140	345	7 345	2.1
Jefferson	86	0.0	41.8	7.0	D	6.0	2.4	16.1	27.7	1 464	145	119	3 302	15.2
Judith Basin	15	27.1	D	1.9	D	6.5	6.5	7.2	34.8	475	207	17	1 346	-1.0
Lake	225	-0.7	22.0	13.1	61.6	13.1	4.5	36.5	17.2	4 899	191	494	10 972	21.4
Lewis and Clark	943	0.2	11.0	3.9	54.2	10.0	8.0	27.5	34.7	8 998	168	786	21 412	15.3
Liberty	25	29.3	19.1	3.5	D	6.1	2.1	11.0	22.9	422	182	6	1 007	-12.7
Lincoln	181	0.1	31.1	24.3	39.1	10.1	3.6	15.7	29.7	4 193	224	407	8 002	14.0
McCone	20	26.4	D	0.0	D	5.9	D	10.5	19.7	390	199	38	1 161	3.6
Madison	53	-2.1	D	5.1	D	13.7	6.5	19.9	25.2	1 407	205	29	3 902	42.4
Meagher	19	18.0	D	5.4	D	8.8	D	25.2	22.0	453	252	17	1 259	4.8
Mineral	31	0.4	21.3	16.6	D	19.3	D	17.6	33.1	818	218	67	1 635	-0.7
Missoula	1 521	-0.2	16.5	8.9	64.5	12.5	6.5	29.9	19.3	12 324	138	1 527	33 466	9.6
Musselshell	27	6.1	19.6	5.1	D	11.6	4.1	20.3	25.2	1 036	225	71	2 183	7.1
Park	[4]159	[4]3.1	[4]20.0	[4]8.9	[4]62.5	[4]14.0	[4]4.4	[4]32.2	[4]14.3	2 540	160	207	6 926	16.1
Petroleum	3	37.7	D	0.0	D	D	2.6	D	35.9	96	192	3	293	-4.2
Phillips	46	12.4	14.0	2.9	48.5	10.0	4.4	16.3	25.1	1 005	208	116	2 765	10.0
Pondera	63	18.0	D	3.1	D	10.0	4.8	16.9	20.6	1 316	206	118	2 618	-3.1
Powder River	13	-1.7	D	D	D	14.5	3.7	13.8	39.9	365	200	14	1 096	-2.4
Powell	73	3.3	D	17.9	D	7.3	2.4	12.7	44.0	1 158	165	88	2 835	0.2
Prairie	12	36.9	D	D	D	6.0	D	5.9	29.5	341	256	11	749	-7.3
Ravalli	300	0.1	D	12.9	D	12.1	7.5	22.7	19.9	7 083	201	429	11 099	21.5
Richland	122	7.6	D	9.8	D	11.3	3.3	21.0	16.4	1 974	195	131	4 825	2.9
Roosevelt	104	10.1	D	D	D	10.0	4.1	26.6	32.6	1 805	164	281	4 265	12.0
Rosebud	147	0.9	25.9	2.3	55.8	4.8	2.2	20.1	17.3	1 281	127	176	4 251	12.3
Sanders	73	-3.7	D	12.7	D	9.9	3.6	24.6	28.1	2 347	230	210	4 335	12.8
Sheridan	47	22.7	D	2.3	D	9.7	3.8	19.5	24.1	1 166	273	50	2 417	0.0
Silver Bow	502	0.1	20.5	5.3	62.0	11.7	3.9	28.8	17.3	7 355	213	832	15 474	-3.7
Stillwater	94	1.3	D	10.5	D	7.1	1.7	10.6	12.4	1 452	180	84	3 291	22.8
Sweet Grass	28	-4.4	22.7	6.7	D	22.1	3.9	16.9	26.6	725	213	26	1 639	10.8
Teton	59	19.3	D	1.5	D	7.0	4.6	10.6	21.3	1 321	209	72	2 725	-0.8
Toole	70	10.0	D	1.4	D	7.9	3.5	12.8	25.1	939	199	67	2 354	-3.2
Treasure	6	20.0	D	0.0	D	5.9	D	5.5	32.5	192	221	5	448	-3.0
Valley	97	12.9	8.6	2.2	55.0	10.4	4.5	21.6	23.6	1 826	223	159	5 304	-5.5
Wheatland	16	9.8	D	7.3	D	14.1	4.9	19.8	31.9	491	207	29	1 129	-1.0
Wibaux	9	28.5	D	D	D	6.2	2.2	15.6	26.8	255	222	19	563	-17.2
Yellowstone	2 157	0.4	16.2	6.7	68.9	12.4	6.6	31.0	14.5	21 012	167	1 837	48 781	14.1
NEBRASKA	31 163	4.8	19.9	13.7	58.4	8.6	7.3	25.2	17.0	281 839	170	21 154	660 621	5.7
Adams	463	5.0	26.5	19.7	52.0	10.0	3.2	25.7	16.5	5 822	198	390	12 491	-1.3
Antelope	96	35.9	D	3.5	D	7.8	2.8	14.8	14.3	1 721	240	77	3 478	-5.7
Arthur	-2	0.0	-5.9	0.0	D	D	0.0	D	0.0	109	255	12	242	3.9
Banner	7	48.9	D	1.7	D	D	D	3.0	24.8	138	157	3	366	-10.7

1. Covers mining, construction, and manufacturing. 2. Covers private sector earnings in agricultural services, forestry, and fisheries; transportation and public utilities; wholesale trade; retail trade; finance, insurance, and real estate; and services. 3. Per 1,000 resident population estimated as of July 1 of the year shown. 4. Yellowstone Park included with Park County.

Table B. States and Counties — Housing, Labor Force, and Employment

	Housing units, 1990 (cont'd)								Civilian labor force, 1999				Civilian employment, 1990[5]		
	Occupied units										Unemployment			Percent	
	Owner-occupied			Owner cost as a percent of income		Renter-occupied										
STATE County	Total	Percent	Median value[1]	With a mort-gage	Without a mort-gage	Median rent[2]	Rent as per-cent of income	Sub-stand-ard units[3] (percent)	Total	Percent change, 1998–1999	Total	Rate[4]	Total	Professional, managerial, and technical	Precision production, craft, and repair
	89	90	91	92	93	94	95	96	97	98	99	100	101	102	103
MISSOURI—Cont'd															
St. Louis city	164 931	45.1	50 700	19.1	13.6	342	27.9	5.8	153 394	-2.2	10 005	6.5	161 434	27.3	7.7
MONTANA	306 163	67.3	56 600	20.2	12.5	311	25.0	3.2	474 006	1.3	24 645	5.2	350 723	26.9	10.4
Beaverhead........................	3 211	61.5	55 500	15.7	13.9	262	20.4	3.9	5 324	2.4	243	4.6	3 770	24.8	10.3
Big Horn............................	3 448	62.6	41 600	19.0	13.8	247	23.8	13.3	5 424	3.0	524	9.7	3 595	25.8	7.4
Blaine................................	2 379	62.2	40 800	19.6	13.0	235	23.7	5.6	3 115	5.6	248	8.0	2 706	20.2	9.4
Broadwater.........................	1 280	74.9	46 800	21.0	11.4	287	20.2	2.3	2 217	2.8	125	5.6	1 446	19.7	8.5
Carbon..............................	3 269	73.1	45 700	21.5	14.2	287	19.3	2.2	5 016	4.9	263	5.2	3 431	23.5	9.5
Carter...............................	589	77.4	22 500	35.0	12.9	242	22.2	4.6	1 089	7.9	27	2.5	827	9.3	3.7
Cascade............................	30 133	63.7	60 100	20.5	11.9	318	25.7	2.5	38 017	-1.4	2 027	5.3	31 669	27.9	10.2
Chouteau...........................	2 064	69.3	41 900	17.8	12.6	272	25.3	1.2	3 005	5.5	92	3.1	2 372	19.7	8.7
Custer...............................	4 631	66.9	37 400	17.8	13.0	270	24.3	3.1	6 103	-2.4	269	4.4	5 351	25.5	7.6
Daniels..............................	919	79.4	30 800	22.2	14.8	226	16.5	1.6	1 322	-0.7	41	3.1	1 035	18.8	10.5
Dawson.............................	3 691	72.7	37 100	16.2	13.0	271	22.3	1.6	5 528	10.8	210	3.8	4 416	22.1	11.9
Deer Lodge........................	4 060	72.9	34 000	16.4	12.5	199	21.5	2.1	4 005	1.3	313	7.8	3 501	24.5	10.9
Fallon...............................	1 166	77.0	36 700	18.5	11.5	249	17.5	1.3	1 766	1.0	96	5.4	1 419	17.8	12.5
Fergus..............................	4 603	71.5	40 800	18.8	12.1	269	25.1	2.7	6 296	-1.8	340	5.4	5 160	20.2	10.6
Flathead............................	22 834	70.6	64 200	21.4	12.3	332	25.7	3.4	38 003	-1.2	2 685	7.1	25 607	24.2	11.8
Gallatin.............................	19 015	58.5	70 200	21.3	11.8	342	27.9	2.9	41 852	2.5	1 200	2.9	25 153	30.7	10.2
Garfield.............................	577	70.9	32 000	16.8	15.2	280	23.5	5.2	1 054	8.8	33	3.1	809	12.4	5.4
Glacier..............................	3 816	60.9	43 800	17.6	12.8	257	23.4	10.7	5 272	-7.4	788	14.9	4 137	27.3	10.7
Golden Valley.....................	330	79.1	30 800	17.9	13.1	243	19.3	4.4	580	9.6	33	5.7	431	14.2	5.3
Granite..............................	1 051	75.4	37 700	24.0	13.2	252	19.7	6.6	1 279	4.8	94	7.3	1 001	18.0	10.4
Hill...................................	6 426	63.1	53 200	17.5	13.0	292	22.9	3.8	9 706	4.5	535	5.5	7 551	25.8	11.1
Jefferson...........................	2 867	80.7	63 700	16.6	12.8	299	18.4	3.7	4 851	-3.6	229	4.7	3 680	33.3	11.1
Judith Basin.......................	908	72.9	30 600	14.2	11.1	253	20.0	2.6	1 345	16.3	53	3.9	1 065	18.8	5.1
Lake.................................	7 814	70.2	61 300	20.5	12.8	263	24.7	5.5	12 442	9.6	781	6.3	8 268	23.9	13.7
Lewis and Clark	18 649	68.5	61 800	20.3	12.3	329	25.1	2.0	26 985	-4.8	1 260	4.7	23 036	38.5	7.9
Liberty..............................	788	71.7	41 300	16.0	12.6	267	21.8	4.5	1 346	16.2	54	4.0	862	21.2	13.8
Lincoln..............................	6 668	73.3	48 900	17.2	12.2	280	21.6	4.8	7 330	-2.1	886	12.1	6 500	24.4	11.8
McCone.............................	844	78.2	32 300	18.5	14.1	297	16.8	1.6	1 303	3.8	48	3.7	1 050	13.8	9.1
Madison............................	2 387	68.8	56 800	22.0	13.2	319	22.5	5.3	4 108	8.4	181	4.4	2 802	18.8	12.0
Meagher............................	709	67.4	36 500	18.1	11.9	275	20.2	4.4	1 150	14.3	66	5.7	851	14.8	8.9
Mineral.............................	1 282	72.9	43 700	18.9	12.3	258	22.8	7.2	1 635	-5.3	162	9.9	1 393	20.7	9.7
Missoula............................	30 782	60.1	66 200	20.3	12.2	334	28.0	3.3	52 281	-0.4	1 947	3.7	37 122	30.8	9.1
Musselshell........................	1 661	78.1	29 600	17.3	12.3	264	23.7	5.2	1 880	-5.9	151	8.0	1 597	16.8	11.0
Park.................................	5 619	66.3	48 100	21.5	12.3	299	24.4	3.1	10 796	1.4	579	5.4	6 389	22.3	16.0
Petroleum..........................	209	76.1	15 500	27.5	15.2	291	18.6	7.1	349	7.7	23	6.6	277	21.7	6.9
Phillips..............................	1 931	69.8	41 500	19.0	13.1	273	21.0	4.0	2 538	0.9	193	7.6	2 304	17.2	11.1
Pondera............................	2 246	69.5	42 100	18.4	12.0	271	22.7	5.5	3 558	5.4	165	4.6	2 700	21.7	11.3
Powder River......................	805	73.4	43 800	18.8	12.3	305	16.9	5.3	1 335	2.1	49	3.7	1 063	18.3	9.3
Powell..............................	2 234	71.8	41 900	17.7	12.4	253	20.1	1.2	2 522	-0.6	127	5.0	2 411	29.4	9.6
Prairie..............................	568	78.9	19 100	13.9	13.4	239	14.3	3.2	700	2.3	28	4.0	607	17.6	7.7
Ravalli..............................	9 698	75.1	61 500	21.5	12.1	313	25.7	4.3	17 557	2.5	1 069	6.1	9 928	24.7	11.8
Richland............................	3 956	70.7	44 200	16.8	12.6	280	18.4	1.5	5 815	1.8	398	6.8	4 537	19.8	14.6
Roosevelt..........................	3 694	63.9	40 400	18.4	14.0	280	25.5	5.3	4 701	13.4	432	9.2	3 866	22.8	11.2
Rosebud............................	3 479	68.8	51 800	13.7	12.9	285	17.6	8.5	4 759	9.6	351	7.4	4 345	19.4	16.1
Sanders............................	3 397	75.1	42 000	20.4	13.9	243	18.5	5.5	4 330	5.5	394	9.1	3 061	26.4	9.3
Sheridan............................	1 899	77.0	39 500	21.8	12.5	276	23.1	1.7	2 242	3.3	123	5.5	1 858	20.6	12.8
Silver Bow.........................	13 899	70.8	44 300	17.4	13.4	265	25.6	2.2	16 967	-6.1	982	5.8	13 935	29.6	10.6
Stillwater...........................	2 523	73.6	56 200	16.1	13.0	303	20.6	2.8	4 666	10.6	197	4.2	2 982	17.9	17.8
Sweet Grass.......................	1 281	72.1	48 000	17.4	12.3	252	24.8	1.8	1 857	3.4	61	3.3	1 368	18.4	9.7
Teton...............................	2 329	73.4	44 900	20.2	12.0	271	22.6	2.9	3 563	8.3	126	3.5	2 731	20.7	10.8
Toole...............................	1 922	71.9	39 100	16.8	12.1	243	20.6	2.3	2 920	1.0	113	3.9	2 387	23.9	8.4
Treasure...........................	339	64.6	35 200	13.9	11.2	188	26.5	2.9	568	19.1	21	3.7	421	18.3	7.8
Valley...............................	3 268	71.4	36 800	16.2	12.8	272	24.7	2.9	4 661	3.8	205	4.4	3 685	20.1	11.3
Wheatland.........................	849	75.3	27 600	20.5	13.3	226	21.6	2.2	1 344	-2.4	75	5.6	978	14.5	8.7
Wibaux.............................	454	72.5	28 900	21.4	14.1	214	16.5	1.9	631	4.8	21	3.3	478	20.7	9.0
Yellowstone........................	44 689	65.7	62 800	21.4	12.0	343	25.5	1.6	73 001	3.7	2 911	4.0	54 760	28.6	9.9
NEBRASKA......................	602 363	66.5	50 400	19.4	12.6	348	23.7	1.9	911 100	-0.6	26 055	2.9	772 813	26.2	10.3
Adams..............................	11 593	64.5	44 800	17.4	12.5	301	23.9	1.3	15 734	0.1	350	2.2	14 314	25.0	11.5
Antelope...........................	3 045	74.0	26 100	17.9	14.4	216	19.6	3.5	3 045	2.0	111	3.6	3 258	17.2	8.9
Arthur...............................	187	60.4	23 200	10.0	11.6	197	11.5	1.1	211	2.4	4	1.9	218	11.5	2.8
Banner..............................	305	63.0	32 500	16.3	13.5	242	35.1	1.3	440	2.1	11	2.5	395	17.2	9.1

1. Specified owner-occupied units.   2. Specified renter-occupied units.   3. Overcrowded or lacking complete plumbing facilities.   4. Percent of civilian labor force.   5. Persons 16 years and older.

Table B. States and Counties — Nonfarm Employment and Agriculture

	Private nonfarm establishments, employment and payroll, 1998									Agriculture, 1997			
		Employment						Annual payroll		Farms			Farm operators
											Percent with—		
STATE County	Number of establishments	Total	Health Care and Social Assistance	Manufacturing	Retail trade	Finance and Insurance	Professional Scientific and Technical Services	Total (mil dol)	Average per employee (dollars)	Number	Less than 50 acres	500 acres and over	Whose principal occupation is farming (percent)
	104	105	106	107	108	109	110	111	112	113	114	115	116
MISSOURI—Cont'd													
St. Louis city	9 850	273 593	40 422	35 156	16 109	20 902	15 783	9 533	34 843	NA	NA	NA	NA
MONTANA	30 957	277 144	45 242	20 686	48 285	12 780	12 362	5 961	21 508	24 279	18.4	53.0	64.7
Beaverhead	351	2 161	376	73	439	104	68	39	17 832	360	19.2	57.2	61.9
Big Horn	221	2 225	539	D	416	71	57	55	24 570	530	13.4	60.0	67.4
Blaine	167	1 035	304	D	224	61	21	22	21 008	541	6.3	68.8	74.9
Broadwater	112	713	90	218	83	30	D	14	19 596	219	13.2	51.1	68.9
Carbon	313	1 866	304	96	256	59	68	29	15 501	623	15.4	35.6	62.0
Carter	28	133	D	D	20	D	D	2	14 496	305	3.3	88.5	81.6
Cascade	2 522	26 152	5 017	944	5 091	1 613	1 129	534	20 407	903	20.3	44.3	57.5
Chouteau	157	782	243	40	148	66	13	12	15 107	750	2.8	84.0	83.1
Custer	398	3 839	1 009	D	813	134	109	73	19 036	405	18.8	53.3	63.2
Daniels	82	572	102	D	130	42	13	11	19 773	363	3.3	80.4	72.2
Dawson	317	2 333	546	D	482	98	D	38	16 165	502	8.2	72.5	70.9
Deer Lodge	238	2 401	960	110	219	64	42	47	19 507	83	24.1	44.6	53.0
Fallon	116	750	D	D	124	38	10	15	20 431	309	7.1	73.1	69.9
Fergus	422	2 855	660	219	464	159	91	52	18 105	816	11.0	67.2	70.0
Flathead	3 051	24 981	3 121	4 001	4 320	1 116	823	564	22 573	898	49.0	12.6	43.1
Gallatin	3 104	25 362	2 374	2 166	4 772	756	1 236	509	20 078	835	31.3	30.4	54.6
Garfield	24	142	D	D	38	D	D	2	12 683	244	3.3	90.2	91.4
Glacier	279	1 968	396	D	412	76	47	44	22 183	425	9.4	68.5	64.5
Golden Valley	15	47	D	D	3	0	0	1	10 702	118	7.6	72.9	76.3
Granite	84	469	62	D	73	D	D	8	17 139	117	8.5	67.5	77.8
Hill	524	4 692	1 208	59	894	146	153	83	17 616	692	4.2	73.4	71.7
Jefferson	196	1 349	116	112	167	35	D	36	26 585	266	28.2	36.5	48.1
Judith Basin	55	144	12	D	17	D	9	2	13 333	329	8.5	72.9	80.5
Lake	674	5 179	979	900	1 062	231	159	96	18 447	1 011	40.2	14.5	52.0
Lewis and Clark	1 911	20 267	3 963	694	3 195	1 637	1 329	440	21 715	502	43.6	25.5	42.0
Liberty	70	447	125	D	78	24	D	9	20 045	280	1.1	88.6	87.1
Lincoln	577	3 797	577	718	640	127	85	76	19 952	252	35.3	6.7	40.5
McCone	46	334	D	D	43	23	D	6	19 374	430	2.8	83.7	77.7
Madison	266	1 078	113	106	174	67	69	23	21 159	460	16.7	47.0	68.7
Meagher	61	271	105	0	40	D	D	4	13 963	142	9.9	65.5	76.1
Mineral	108	700	150	121	205	10	4	11	15 071	71	36.6	14.1	56.3
Missoula	3 541	37 491	6 051	2 949	6 877	1 481	1 877	834	22 239	482	53.1	13.9	35.5
Musselshell	142	649	139	D	134	27	20	10	14 707	232	9.1	63.8	64.2
Park	692	4 165	602	619	553	138	162	76	18 281	420	20.0	50.0	61.0
Petroleum	9	18	D	D	D	0	0	0	6 722	88	2.3	81.8	73.9
Phillips	149	958	212	25	212	51	D	15	16 170	489	8.2	71.0	75.5
Pondera	206	1 411	321	81	269	71	D	25	17 595	474	8.9	69.0	78.9
Powder River	71	207	D	D	63	D	7	2	11 324	297	4.7	81.5	82.2
Powell	143	1 014	189	D	134	37	19	20	19 536	230	13.9	57.4	59.6
Prairie	34	186	D	D	30	20	D	2	12 962	158	5.7	75.3	82.9
Ravalli	1 099	7 809	1 057	973	1 210	341	266	151	19 370	1 080	56.8	6.8	48.2
Richland	396	3 134	511	400	510	132	113	61	19 325	571	10.3	62.7	72.0
Roosevelt	236	1 761	392	96	402	88	44	27	15 502	609	4.9	71.8	68.3
Rosebud	194	2 662	159	D	390	52	D	81	30 260	362	7.5	68.8	73.2
Sanders	345	1 732	424	222	246	68	D	30	17 147	412	18.9	25.5	52.9
Sheridan	164	1 000	283	D	200	65	32	14	13 683	581	2.6	77.5	75.9
Silver Bow	1 155	12 162	2 006	456	2 084	352	936	284	23 338	116	17.2	32.8	44.0
Stillwater	203	2 025	196	297	341	57	D	65	32 289	473	18.6	53.1	63.4
Sweet Grass	114	601	12	53	169	20	30	11	17 646	301	12.3	57.1	70.1
Teton	190	1 083	204	51	227	79	D	20	18 073	557	10.2	58.2	72.9
Toole	208	1 314	226	46	152	72	36	26	19 687	382	2.6	80.9	74.6
Treasure	25	89	D	D	21	D	3	1	15 258	110	5.5	64.5	72.7
Valley	259	1 880	491	52	323	115	67	33	17 537	655	4.3	69.2	72.5
Wheatland	63	335	D	D	84	21	10	4	12 081	144	3.5	80.6	77.8
Wibaux	25	154	D	0	D	6	6	2	12 890	178	5.6	69.1	66.9
Yellowstone	4 783	53 847	7 789	3 122	8 601	2 591	2 891	1 297	24 081	1 097	32.5	32.0	53.5
NEBRASKA	48 655	720 252	95 015	109 645	104 866	47 979	30 406	18 178	25 239	51 454	14.2	42.2	69.5
Adams	962	13 812	2 628	3 698	2 096	320	243	292	21 152	623	15.2	44.6	74.5
Antelope	243	1 404	275	111	332	93	24	24	17 093	803	12.0	41.2	75.7
Arthur	12	D	0	0	D	D	D	D	D	83	4.8	88.0	85.5
Banner	7	20	0	0	0	D	0	0	18 400	220	3.6	77.3	69.5

Table B. States and Counties — Agriculture, Land, and Water

STATE County	Agriculture, 1997 (cont'd)														
	Land in farms					Value of land and buildings		Value of machinery and equipment Average per farm ($1,000)	Value of products sold				Percent of farms with sales of —		Percent of land owned by Fed. Gov. 1997	Water consumption 1995 (mil gal/day)
	Acreage (1,000)	Percent change, 1992–1997	Acres			Average per farm ($1,000)	Average per acre (dollars)		Total (mil dol)	Average per farm (dollars)	Percent from —		$10,000 or more	$100,000 or more		
			Average size of farm	Total irrigated (1,000)	Total cropland (1,000)						Crops	Live-stock and poultry products				
	117	118	119	120	121	122	123	124	125	126	127	128	129	130	131	132
MISSOURI—Cont'd																
St. Louis city	NA	NA	NA	NA	NA	NA	NA	NA	NA	NA	NA	NA	NA	NA	[1]NA	147.8
MONTANA	58 608	-1.7	2 414	1 994	17 629	699	294	78	1 871	77 051	48.3	51.7	61.6	22.1	28.8	8 847.2
Beaverhead	1 152	-14.2	3 200	225	203	1 359	401	101	55	153 815	18.4	81.6	66.9	30.3	58.8	570.7
Big Horn	2 770	-7.7	5 227	53	408	1 217	229	85	61	115 332	45.0	55.0	70.4	27.5	2.0	315.4
Blaine	2 258	-3.5	4 173	63	660	731	190	94	48	88 609	53.3	46.7	70.1	26.6	17.1	274.2
Broadwater	453	0.6	2 067	53	131	839	378	97	20	92 131	66.8	33.2	71.7	28.3	32.0	241.0
Carbon	736	22.9	1 181	82	172	564	459	61	44	70 257	35.5	64.5	64.2	17.8	42.9	448.8
Carter	1 589	-1.8	5 211	5	245	592	107	77	27	88 494	13.9	86.1	81.0	31.8	27.9	4.1
Cascade	1 441	1.2	1 596	33	508	620	373	61	67	73 899	48.0	52.0	55.6	16.1	12.5	153.2
Chouteau	2 212	-2.9	2 949	12	1 346	1 015	351	150	93	123 608	83.9	16.1	81.9	44.7	6.2	36.5
Custer	1 898	-9.0	4 685	28	170	919	187	70	33	80 459	21.8	78.2	66.2	24.0	16.3	74.9
Daniels	765	0.5	2 106	2	529	535	251	110	26	70 645	79.4	20.6	68.0	23.7	0.2	5.0
Dawson	1 417	6.2	2 823	18	466	452	166	88	35	69 220	59.3	40.7	69.1	24.5	4.2	72.4
Deer Lodge	102	-24.7	1 225	18	22	683	558	52	4	50 807	20.3	79.7	53.0	16.9	38.4	48.0
Fallon	953	0.9	3 084	1	232	630	200	75	20	66 042	27.3	72.7	67.3	21.7	11.7	6.6
Fergus	2 249	0.7	2 756	16	676	666	259	82	72	88 041	44.7	55.3	72.2	27.9	18.1	74.7
Flathead	216	-21.9	241	27	106	450	1 649	37	27	29 693	67.0	33.0	31.6	7.3	70.6	64.9
Gallatin	760	8.7	910	91	253	832	976	66	59	70 545	52.5	47.5	53.3	19.9	38.0	489.2
Garfield	2 163	8.2	8 866	5	302	952	111	95	32	131 271	30.5	69.5	82.0	40.6	23.8	12.4
Glacier	1 623	-6.3	3 818	24	497	842	224	77	45	106 867	62.6	37.4	68.5	28.5	20.2	86.9
Golden Valley	638	0.2	5 407	10	117	1 249	236	109	13	109 674	35.0	65.0	72.9	32.2	4.3	85.4
Granite	268	-23.3	2 294	36	45	951	449	74	10	82 412	15.0	85.0	72.6	33.3	63.6	103.5
Hill	1 643	0.0	2 374	5	1 080	709	294	126	67	96 907	82.6	17.4	71.5	36.7	1.8	18.4
Jefferson	364	-0.8	1 369	26	76	549	433	30	9	32 198	22.9	77.1	36.8	10.2	52.1	148.1
Judith Basin	835	-3.8	2 537	6	289	713	300	124	38	114 269	38.5	61.5	80.5	33.7	26.2	65.0
Lake	597	-5.4	590	100	150	443	816	40	38	37 134	42.8	57.2	49.3	7.5	16.0	308.5
Lewis and Clark	822	-6.9	1 638	40	97	709	447	42	19	37 842	35.4	64.6	34.5	8.2	47.4	183.4
Liberty	915	-3.8	3 269	8	631	981	298	169	38	137 423	76.1	23.9	84.3	41.1	2.1	22.4
Lincoln	46	-7.7	183	5	17	461	1 997	23	4	14 582	38.8	61.2	21.4	2.4	73.8	36.6
McCone	1 313	1.8	3 053	7	555	491	151	109	29	66 740	62.2	37.8	76.5	21.9	14.5	14.8
Madison	1 080	-15.1	2 347	108	154	1 109	501	65	35	77 079	27.9	72.1	59.6	21.3	46.2	540.4
Meagher	940	3.1	6 620	46	114	1 987	303	97	23	161 251	18.2	81.8	68.3	38.7	31.6	349.6
Mineral	16	-14.1	230	1	6	401	1 744	27	1	16 662	25.1	74.9	31.0	4.2	82.0	8.1
Missoula	262	5.8	544	22	47	494	993	34	8	16 643	27.4	72.6	28.2	3.1	42.1	113.6
Musselshell	953	-7.7	4 106	12	134	851	207	55	17	75 176	32.3	67.7	53.4	18.1	9.7	81.7
Park	749	-3.7	1 784	49	132	1 178	640	76	20	48 708	30.2	69.8	55.2	14.0	45.0	333.0
Petroleum	541	-19.2	6 152	11	64	1 110	188	77	9	106 484	23.8	76.2	78.4	33.0	36.3	56.7
Phillips	1 978	0.4	4 045	42	634	683	175	89	41	83 569	39.8	60.2	73.8	26.6	41.0	210.0
Pondera	878	-1.7	1 853	63	564	678	374	122	58	121 694	75.2	24.8	80.6	39.2	10.3	212.1
Powder River	1 559	-4.3	5 250	9	166	712	142	74	27	91 895	11.5	88.5	79.5	27.9	28.4	15.1
Powell	649	-3.9	2 824	63	75	1 290	451	51	18	77 423	12.7	87.3	61.7	23.0	48.7	211.2
Prairie	613	-10.3	3 879	11	123	600	158	108	20	128 428	30.9	69.1	80.4	36.7	40.1	74.4
Ravalli	184	-24.1	170	77	83	394	2 451	30	24	22 175	25.3	74.7	31.3	5.3	72.9	167.0
Richland	1 215	1.5	2 127	48	507	561	273	111	54	94 702	65.0	35.0	73.9	29.9	3.9	316.7
Roosevelt	1 430	1.1	2 348	10	784	479	216	112	39	63 731	77.4	22.6	68.0	22.0	0.4	44.5
Rosebud	2 681	3.7	7 406	31	207	919	127	78	38	104 049	23.1	76.9	71.5	29.0	10.3	165.3
Sanders	410	7.6	995	18	62	464	453	31	12	27 995	36.7	63.3	42.0	5.8	51.7	76.1
Sheridan	1 001	4.1	1 723	6	677	422	272	95	36	61 874	80.6	19.4	74.2	20.5	2.5	5.2
Silver Bow	100	0.2	864	8	15	446	587	30	3	27 910	7.0	93.0	37.1	7.8	51.3	39.3
Stillwater	897	0.9	1 896	26	250	682	384	53	29	61 313	28.1	71.9	63.4	15.6	17.5	113.6
Sweet Grass	839	0.2	2 789	45	101	1 199	423	73	21	70 914	9.4	90.6	66.4	21.3	24.9	323.6
Teton	1 117	-5.3	2 005	118	581	686	360	103	72	129 196	63.9	36.1	72.0	36.3	18.3	518.8
Toole	1 091	2.6	2 856	6	680	730	278	119	39	102 560	79.2	20.8	71.5	36.6	2.6	8.5
Treasure	606	1.1	5 505	17	47	905	175	124	18	159 700	35.5	64.5	72.7	28.2	2.0	117.2
Valley	1 787	5.8	2 728	50	740	535	199	95	48	72 954	54.0	46.0	70.2	19.4	35.3	153.4
Wheatland	834	-2.0	5 790	19	182	1 224	217	104	23	158 571	28.2	71.8	78.5	34.7	7.3	184.6
Wibaux	475	-3.2	2 671	0	139	449	170	72	11	59 337	40.0	60.0	69.7	21.9	4.7	2.5
Yellowstone	1 526	4.9	1 391	80	381	524	372	57	96	87 551	31.4	68.6	51.3	16.7	5.2	440.4
NEBRASKA	45 525	2.6	885	6 939	22 093	567	645	85	9 832	191 074	38.6	61.4	77.6	35.4	1.3	10 543.2
Adams	344	2.8	553	185	288	702	1 283	143	159	255 834	49.3	50.7	81.5	48.5	0.2	188.7
Antelope	492	0.6	613	184	378	500	842	90	156	194 496	49.2	50.8	80.9	44.8	0.0	130.0
Arthur	465	1.2	5 606	16	59	1 168	208	61	13	162 497	14.8	85.2	91.6	44.6	0.0	18.0
Banner	446	9.4	2 029	22	210	612	310	93	49	221 591	29.4	70.6	75.9	25.0	0.0	26.4

1. St. Louis City included with St. Louis County.

Table B. States and Counties — Residential Construction, Wholesale and Retail Trade, and Real Estate

STATE County	Value of Residential Construction Authorized by Building Permits, 1999		Wholesale Trade, 1997				Retail Trade[1], 1997				Real Estate and Rental and Leasing, 1997			
	New Construction ($1,000)	Number of Housing Units	Number of Establishments	Number of Employees	Sales (mil dol)	Annual Payroll (mil dol)	Number of Establishments	Number of Employees	Sales (mil dol)	Annual Payroll (mil dol)	Number of Establishments	Number of Employees	Receipts (mil dol)	Annual Payroll (mil dol)
	133	134	135	136	137	138	139	140	141	142	143	144	145	146
MISSOURI—Cont'd														
St. Louis city	37 522	487	902	16 599	10 582.9	646.4	1 241	14 511	2 361.7	282.4	401	3 520	402.9	76.7
MONTANA	226 260	2 566	1 577	14 381	7 709.5	372.3	5 042	48 337	7 779.1	746.5	1 186	4 265	353.4	58.1
Beaverhead	258	2	11	95	16.3	1.6	60	474	69.5	7.2	13	36	2.1	0.6
Big Horn	219	3	10	D	D	D	50	415	56.5	5.7	7	D	D	D
Blaine	179	3	13	81	58.2	1.2	36	204	30.5	2.7	3	4	0.4	0.0
Broadwater	345	6	8	61	37.1	1.8	17	103	12.7	1.1	3	5	0.1	0.0
Carbon	360	6	13	55	9.9	1.0	45	267	32.8	3.2	14	28	1.4	0.2
Carter	0	0	1	D	D	D	4	18	2.6	0.2	NA	NA	NA	NA
Cascade	11 819	101	141	1 231	1 114.8	32.6	427	5 049	803.0	81.8	100	395	30.4	4.6
Chouteau	387	3	14	89	108.7	2.1	34	169	33.5	2.4	6	D	D	D
Custer	691	8	20	147	94.3	2.6	72	770	113.5	10.7	13	19	1.1	0.1
Daniels	100	1	7	29	23.7	0.7	17	125	30.9	2.7	NA	NA	NA	NA
Dawson	0	0	22	117	39.7	2.6	61	522	69.6	6.9	9	30	9.4	0.9
Deer Lodge	928	9	2	D	D	D	42	259	49.5	3.8	7	21	1.0	0.2
Fallon	0	0	7	52	15.1	0.5	20	120	22.5	1.6	2	D	D	D
Fergus	350	6	27	199	187.8	4.4	80	581	89.6	7.2	11	54	2.5	0.4
Flathead	28 914	255	102	784	347.1	19.7	475	4 285	696.4	70.0	132	467	34.0	5.9
Gallatin	54 938	753	129	1 126	476.1	31.9	472	4 594	710.3	73.6	142	516	50.6	6.9
Garfield	0	0	1	D	D	D	5	35	4.4	0.4	NA	NA	NA	NA
Glacier	70	1	15	77	72.2	1.5	54	426	71.1	6.8	9	100	4.2	2.4
Golden Valley	0	0	2	D	D	D	2	D	D	D	NA	NA	NA	NA
Granite	0	0	3	12	3.6	0.3	11	73	13.2	0.9	1	D	D	D
Hill	1 606	17	28	218	145.2	4.9	90	907	140.7	13.0	22	69	4.6	0.7
Jefferson	70	2	10	18	6.9	0.5	25	148	17.8	1.9	10	D	D	D
Judith Basin	0	0	6	D	D	D	8	26	4.4	0.2	1	D	D	D
Lake	2 320	21	23	129	34.1	2.2	125	1 056	157.5	15.8	24	35	2.4	0.4
Lewis and Clark	4 453	51	76	772	217.0	18.2	304	3 196	529.4	49.7	80	377	27.1	5.1
Liberty	0	0	5	40	43.9	0.9	14	72	11.1	0.9	2	D	D	D
Lincoln	150	2	10	30	4.9	0.7	94	602	91.5	8.7	18	47	2.5	0.4
McCone	0	0	5	55	25.1	1.3	8	58	8.0	0.7	NA	NA	NA	NA
Madison	0	0	6	17	5.7	0.4	40	165	24.6	2.3	10	14	0.5	0.2
Meagher	0	0	1	D	D	D	12	43	8.2	0.6	NA	NA	NA	NA
Mineral	645	5	NA	NA	NA	NA	19	164	20.3	2.5	3	D	D	D
Missoula	37 232	422	183	1 991	775.9	50.0	540	6 800	1 069.0	105.7	138	593	46.2	8.2
Musselshell	165	2	7	28	7.8	0.6	22	134	15.6	1.6	4	11	1.6	0.1
Park	1 659	32	23	138	33.9	3.3	111	588	102.7	8.5	28	39	6.2	0.5
Petroleum	0	0	1	D	D	D	2	D	D	D	NA	NA	NA	NA
Phillips	0	0	5	37	15.7	0.8	29	209	31.1	2.8	2	D	D	D
Pondera	108	2	21	132	55.3	2.4	32	260	51.8	4.2	7	15	1.0	0.2
Powder River	0	0	NA	NA	NA	NA	14	78	9.0	0.9	1	D	D	D
Powell	0	0	6	D	D	D	24	131	15.8	1.9	5	5	0.6	0.1
Prairie	0	0	3	D	D	D	5	37	5.2	0.4	NA	NA	NA	NA
Ravalli	6 771	108	44	283	166.4	8.7	154	1 197	179.8	16.8	53	178	10.7	2.3
Richland	578	5	26	228	188.7	4.2	66	506	83.6	7.5	12	34	2.5	0.3
Roosevelt	64	1	10	42	57.5	1.1	53	367	53.0	5.2	7	16	1.0	0.1
Rosebud	0	0	NA	NA	NA	NA	39	392	42.4	4.6	6	66	2.3	1.2
Sanders	62	1	12	51	65.0	1.2	51	239	33.2	3.2	11	10	0.9	0.1
Sheridan	516	4	13	67	44.1	1.1	41	176	26.2	2.3	2	D	D	D
Silver Bow	6 801	79	55	534	192.0	10.7	220	2 147	333.1	32.0	39	134	11.3	2.0
Stillwater	2 065	16	6	14	6.1	0.3	37	339	47.7	4.0	4	1	0.7	0.1
Sweet Grass	2 624	34	2	D	D	D	26	177	36.4	2.9	6	11	0.5	0.1
Teton	663	7	10	66	31.2	1.6	33	247	50.1	3.6	7	13	0.5	0.1
Toole	185	7	18	99	71.5	2.8	30	181	24.2	2.5	8	32	1.4	0.2
Treasure	0	0	3	22	8.8	0.6	5	25	2.2	0.2	NA	NA	NA	NA
Valley	0	0	15	126	71.2	2.5	52	342	53.1	4.8	7	28	1.2	0.3
Wheatland	0	0	3	17	3.8	0.3	14	89	10.6	0.8	2	D	D	D
Wibaux	0	0	1	D	D	D	2	D	D	D	NA	NA	NA	NA
Yellowstone	57 961	591	389	4 915	2 648.9	143.4	717	8 736	1 575.6	144.9	195	770	85.9	12.3
NEBRASKA	827 968	8 696	3 157	41 002	38 015.4	1 170.2	8 295	102 684	16 529.3	1 554.6	1 587	8 240	891.1	160.8
Adams	6 546	81	60	D	D	D	180	2 204	289.5	30.4	39	97	10.9	1.3
Antelope	1 962	21	21	162	88.4	3.1	51	314	52.1	3.7	2	D	D	D
Arthur	NA	NA	NA	NA	NA	NA	3	5	0.3	0.0	NA	NA	NA	NA
Banner	NA	NA	1	D	D	D	NA	NA	NA	NA	NA	NA	NA	NA

1. Establishments with payroll.

STATE County	Professional, Scientific, and Technical Services[1], 1997				Manufacturing, 1997				Accommodation and Foodservices, 1997			
	Number of Establishments	Number of Employees	Receipts (mil dol)	Annual Payroll (mil dol)	Number of Establishments	Number of Employees	Receipts (mil dol)	Annual Payroll (mil dol)	Number of Establishments	Number of Employees	Sales (mil dol)	Annual Payroll (mil dol)
	147	148	149	150	151	152	153	154	155	156	157	158
MISSOURI—Cont'd												
St. Louis city	963	13 915	1 819.8	663.7	802	33 836	8 605.5	1 243.6	954	18 843	686.6	195.8
MONTANA	2 082	10 735	769.4	297.7	1 160	19 611	4 866.3	560.1	3 278	38 533	1 198.9	325.4
Beaverhead.........	22	51	2.9	0.9	NA	NA	NA	NA	47	337	11.1	2.4
Big Horn.........	13	50	2.3	1.0	NA	NA	NA	NA	35	241	8.1	2.0
Blaine.........	8	12	0.6	0.3	NA	NA	NA	NA	18	101	2.5	0.7
Broadwater.........	4	7	0.6	0.2	NA	NA	NA	NA	17	128	3.3	0.8
Carbon.........	14	51	2.1	0.7	NA	NA	NA	NA	52	417	14.3	4.4
Carter.........	1	D	D	D	NA	NA	NA	NA	5	17	0.4	0.1
Cascade.........	176	994	69.3	28.6	80	925	228.5	23.9	267	3 592	109.7	29.4
Chouteau.........	4	10	0.5	0.1	NA	NA	NA	NA	22	71	1.7	0.4
Custer.........	26	117	5.7	2.4	NA	NA	NA	NA	43	629	17.2	4.9
Daniels.........	3	9	0.4	0.1	NA	NA	NA	NA	10	D	D	D
Dawson.........	12	50	1.5	0.5	NA	NA	NA	NA	29	415	9.4	2.6
Deer Lodge.........	10	25	2.7	0.4	NA	NA	NA	NA	39	420	12.2	3.3
Fallon.........	5	11	0.3	0.1	NA	NA	NA	NA	12	88	2.9	0.5
Fergus.........	27	77	4.2	1.0	NA	NA	NA	NA	49	652	16.5	4.2
Flathead.........	187	659	44.8	16.0	124	3 887	790.5	121.5	319	3 940	132.1	35.9
Gallatin.........	259	1 031	87.6	33.3	148	1 992	273.8	48.3	285	4 694	154.0	44.1
Garfield.........	1	D	D	D	NA	NA	NA	NA	5	D	D	D
Glacier.........	16	46	2.8	1.2	NA	NA	NA	NA	52	403	18.5	4.4
Golden Valley.........	NA	NA	NA	NA	NA	NA	NA	NA	4	13	0.5	0.1
Granite.........	4	2	0.5	0.1	NA	NA	NA	NA	15	85	1.8	0.4
Hill.........	32	156	9.0	3.6	NA	NA	NA	NA	53	679	18.6	4.9
Jefferson.........	11	21	1.5	0.5	NA	NA	NA	NA	27	205	5.1	1.2
Judith Basin.........	1	D	D	D	NA	NA	NA	NA	13	D	D	D
Lake.........	37	127	7.1	2.7	30	840	115.3	19.5	86	594	20.5	5.3
Lewis and Clark.........	159	1 174	104.9	39.3	46	D	D	D	182	2 343	67.7	18.1
Liberty.........	5	14	0.8	0.2	NA	NA	NA	NA	4	16	0.5	0.1
Lincoln.........	23	56	3.1	1.0	33	657	125.4	21.3	68	439	16.7	3.8
McCone.........	1	D	D	D	NA	NA	NA	NA	5	D	D	D
Madison.........	8	16	1.0	0.4	NA	NA	NA	NA	44	117	7.7	1.9
Meagher.........	3	3	0.3	0.1	NA	NA	NA	NA	16	57	2.6	0.6
Mineral.........	3	4	0.4	0.0	NA	NA	NA	NA	24	178	4.8	1.5
Missoula.........	276	1 617	109.7	45.2	136	2 690	562.3	89.4	329	4 782	145.6	40.4
Musselshell.........	11	20	1.1	0.3	NA	NA	NA	NA	20	D	D	D
Park.........	46	138	7.4	2.6	36	535	63.3	13.3	111	1 043	34.0	9.7
Petroleum.........	NA	NA	NA	NA	NA	NA	NA	NA	3	D	D	D
Phillips.........	5	14	0.8	0.3	NA	NA	NA	NA	23	140	4.0	0.9
Pondera.........	10	45	1.8	0.8	NA	NA	NA	NA	18	D	D	D
Powder River.........	2	D	D	D	NA	NA	NA	NA	7	D	D	D
Powell.........	4	5	0.3	0.1	NA	NA	NA	NA	25	D	D	D
Prairie.........	2	D	D	D	NA	NA	NA	NA	5	D	D	D
Ravalli.........	52	223	11.9	6.4	66	870	95.2	21.3	92	793	21.1	6.0
Richland.........	25	95	6.1	2.3	NA	NA	NA	NA	40	401	10.3	2.7
Roosevelt.........	11	36	1.8	0.8	NA	NA	NA	NA	29	210	5.9	1.5
Rosebud.........	7	14	0.7	0.2	NA	NA	NA	NA	29	301	7.5	1.8
Sanders.........	11	38	1.1	0.5	NA	NA	NA	NA	27	189	4.9	1.2
Sheridan.........	8	30	1.3	0.4	NA	NA	NA	NA	26	D	D	D
Silver Bow.........	88	861	60.2	25.7	NA	NA	NA	NA	130	1 354	47.8	12.3
Stillwater.........	11	20	1.7	0.4	NA	NA	NA	NA	24	D	D	D
Sweet Grass.........	4	25	1.2	0.5	NA	NA	NA	NA	15	170	6.2	1.7
Teton.........	4	8	0.3	0.1	NA	NA	NA	NA	26	122	3.3	0.8
Toole.........	10	32	1.7	0.5	NA	NA	NA	NA	27	135	4.8	1.0
Treasure.........	2	D	D	D	NA	NA	NA	NA	4	D	D	D
Valley.........	9	44	2.9	1.0	NA	NA	NA	NA	33	261	7.6	•1.8
Wheatland.........	2	D	D	D	NA	NA	NA	NA	14	77	1.8	0.4
Wibaux.........	3	6	0.2	0.1	NA	NA	NA	NA	9	D	D	D
Yellowstone.........	404	2 664	199.7	74.9	182	3 223	1 797.9	110.1	365	6 691	205.3	58.7
NEBRASKA.........	3 076	25 720	2 273.4	838.0	1 960	106 690	27 859.2	3 040.5	4 070	61 048	1 726.6	488.2
Adams.........	41	188	12.2	5.2	63	3 526	593.0	88.9	82	1 230	29.1	8.4
Antelope.........	11	19	0.9	0.3	NA	NA	NA	NA	17	146	2.8	0.7
Arthur.........	NA	NA	NA	NA	NA	NA	NA	NA	NA	NA	NA	NA
Banner.........	NA	NA	NA	NA	NA	NA	NA	NA	NA	NA	NA	NA

1. Firms subject to federal tax.

STATE County	Health Care and Social Assistance[1], 1997				Other Services[1], 1997				Federal funds and grants, fiscal 1999[2]			
									Expenditures (mil dol)			
										Direct payments for individuals[3]		
	Number of Establishments	Number of Employees	Receipts (mil dol)	Annual Payroll (mil dol)	Number of Establishments	Number of Employees	Receipts (mil dol)	Annual Payroll (mil dol)	Total	Social Security and government retirement	Medicare	Food stamps and Supplemental Security Income
	159	160	161	162	163	164	165	166	167	168	169	170
MISSOURI—Cont'd												
St. Louis city	581	9 806	612.5	263.9	673	4 693	334.1	101.2	7 490.4	762.1	467.8	159.1
MONTANA	2 034	15 673	928.6	412.6	1 612	6 986	449.1	117.0	6 225.0	1 817.6	530.6	112.7
Beaverhead	29	194	9.8	3.6	18	45	3.3	0.6	52.9	17.9	7.1	0.8
Big Horn	7	113	2.5	1.7	6	23	1.2	0.3	94.6	15.1	5.8	3.2
Blaine	5	25	1.2	0.4	8	17	1.3	0.3	64.0	11.8	3.3	1.1
Broadwater	6	20	0.6	0.2	9	8	1.2	0.1	21.8	9.9	2.7	0.4
Carbon	10	120	4.2	2.0	10	21	0.9	0.2	38.4	19.5	7.0	0.7
Carter	1	D	D	D	1	D	D	D	14.2	2.5	0.7	0.1
Cascade	205	1 729	104.2	40.5	153	690	43.3	11.4	1 076.0	199.3	55.3	10.6
Chouteau	6	44	1.1	0.5	6	8	0.7	0.1	67.9	11.9	3.8	0.2
Custer	38	273	13.7	7.7	17	80	5.6	1.4	74.2	28.3	7.8	1.8
Daniels	3	16	0.7	0.2	5	6	0.7	0.1	24.0	5.8	1.9	0.1
Dawson	20	92	4.1	1.4	22	81	5.1	1.3	47.9	20.5	6.3	0.4
Deer Lodge	30	153	9.2	3.1	9	23	1.8	0.4	51.4	26.6	9.4	1.1
Fallon	NA	NA	NA	NA	9	20	1.9	0.3	16.1	5.8	1.9	0.2
Fergus	36	239	11.1	3.9	21	64	4.3	0.7	73.9	28.0	10.9	1.0
Flathead	195	1 213	77.8	32.0	163	710	50.7	12.0	306.8	158.1	36.8	6.9
Gallatin	165	1 134	63.6	27.0	139	642	36.4	9.2	224.2	85.7	19.3	3.1
Garfield	NA	NA	NA	NA	1	D	D	D	13.4	2.4	0.9	0.1
Glacier	16	40	2.2	0.6	18	90	5.5	1.3	98.5	17.5	6.5	4.1
Golden Valley	1	D	D	D	NA	NA	NA	NA	7.3	2.3	0.7	0.1
Granite	2	D	D	D	NA	NA	NA	NA	18.1	5.7	1.7	0.2
Hill	25	107	6.3	3.0	52	167	8.8	2.2	132.8	34.1	11.2	3.2
Jefferson	18	129	5.2	2.8	7	21	1.2	0.3	39.9	18.7	4.1	0.7
Judith Basin	1	D	D	D	1	D	D	D	16.2	4.8	1.4	0.1
Lake	39	400	13.8	7.3	32	53	3.9	0.8	131.5	50.7	15.2	4.6
Lewis and Clark	159	1 257	70.4	27.3	88	412	24.0	6.5	756.9	125.4	29.2	13.7
Liberty	2	D	D	D	5	5	0.6	0.1	29.3	7.2	1.8	0.0
Lincoln	33	214	9.7	3.3	30	70	5.4	1.1	108.8	49.5	10.9	3.4
McCone	3	D	D	D	1	D	D	D	31.4	3.5	1.7	0.2
Madison	3	9	0.6	0.1	10	39	2.5	0.5	38.7	14.4	4.2	0.1
Meagher	4	18	0.5	0.1	1	D	D	D	11.9	4.5	1.3	0.1
Mineral	7	15	0.7	0.2	5	8	0.4	0.1	21.4	10.9	2.5	0.7
Missoula	285	2 305	151.7	70.7	184	956	61.9	17.0	385.9	151.5	43.3	11.4
Musselshell	3	9	0.4	0.1	4	9	0.8	0.2	27.9	10.7	3.6	0.5
Park	31	342	13.8	6.1	35	147	9.1	2.2	74.2	35.1	10.6	1.4
Petroleum	NA	NA	NA	NA	NA	NA	NA	NA	3.2	0.9	0.3	0.0
Phillips	6	19	0.7	0.4	11	31	2.6	0.4	38.7	10.0	4.0	0.6
Pondera	12	46	2.2	0.5	10	25	2.0	0.4	81.5	13.6	5.8	0.9
Powder River	1	D	D	D	5	6	0.5	0.1	15.4	3.1	0.9	0.1
Powell	9	96	1.9	1.0	6	9	0.5	0.1	26.8	14.2	4.0	0.8
Prairie	NA	NA	NA	NA	2	D	D	D	10.0	3.2	1.2	0.0
Ravalli	56	395	17.6	7.2	51	186	11.1	2.9	151.0	86.0	20.6	3.2
Richland	21	86	5.8	1.5	23	61	4.6	1.1	87.5	18.4	7.9	1.0
Roosevelt	10	214	6.9	4.4	11	19	1.2	0.2	160.2	17.4	7.2	3.1
Rosebud	11	40	2.0	0.5	6	22	2.0	0.4	61.0	13.5	3.9	1.9
Sanders	19	110	6.8	3.0	10	26	1.6	0.3	51.2	27.1	7.1	1.4
Sheridan	5	37	1.7	0.9	6	19	1.5	0.3	44.8	11.6	3.9	0.3
Silver Bow	114	1 055	53.4	24.7	71	282	16.6	4.3	205.2	81.7	31.3	6.5
Stillwater	7	128	4.0	1.9	11	26	2.3	0.4	33.4	15.7	4.6	0.5
Sweet Grass	2	D	D	D	3	5	0.5	0.1	16.5	7.1	2.0	0.2
Teton	9	76	7.0	1.6	5	4	0.5	0.2	46.4	13.7	4.9	0.5
Toole	13	47	3.8	1.6	3	6	0.5	0.1	42.0	8.1	4.4	0.5
Treasure	NA	NA	NA	NA	NA	NA	NA	NA	4.4	1.9	0.7	0.0
Valley	15	63	4.2	1.9	15	38	3.2	0.5	68.6	21.4	6.2	1.2
Wheatland	2	D	D	D	1	D	D	D	16.5	5.9	2.8	0.2
Wibaux	NA	NA	NA	NA	1	D	D	D	9.0	2.2	0.6	0.1
Yellowstone	334	2 942	228.1	114.5	291	1 788	114.1	34.1	560.6	244.2	75.1	13.4
NEBRASKA	3 057	34 763	2 027.7	970.3	3 288	16 940	1 039.2	297.1	8 793.3	3 201.7	982.8	154.2
Adams	71	598	49.0	23.2	50	229	16.4	4.3	136.6	62.4	18.8	2.7
Antelope	9	127	3.9	2.2	18	36	2.3	0.4	57.8	14.7	5.9	0.5
Arthur	NA	NA	NA	NA	1	D	D	D	1.9	1.0	0.2	0.0
Banner	NA	NA	NA	NA	NA	NA	NA	NA	7.1	0.9	0.3	0.0

1. Firms subject to federal tax.   2. October 1, 1998 to September 30, 1999.   3. State totals may include programs not allocated by county.

Table B. States and Counties — Federal Funds and Local Government Finances

STATE County	Federal funds and grants, fiscal 1999[1] (cont'd) Expenditures (mil dol) (cont'd)							Local government finances, 1997 General revenue				
	Procurement contract awards			Grants[2]							Taxes	
												Per capita[3] (dollars)	
	Salaries and wages	Defense	Other	Medicaid and other health-related	Nutrition and family welfare	Education	Other	Total (mil dol)	Intergovern-mental (mil dol)	Total (mil dol)	Total	Property
	171	172	173	174	175	176	177	178	179	180	181	182
MISSOURI—Cont'd												
St. Louis city	730.8	3 837.9	274.9	731.0	133.4	41.1	224.9	1 446.8	474.8	554.4	1 622	667
MONTANA	666.8	99.2	420.8	402.4	165.3	145.9	685.8	X	X	X	X	X
Beaverhead	7.6	0.0	1.7	3.4	0.8	0.5	10.0	33.4	6.9	9.8	1 091	1 075
Big Horn	16.8	0.0	3.3	5.8	1.6	8.2	24.5	28.8	15.5	9.0	713	699
Blaine	7.8	0.0	3.3	5.9	1.8	5.4	6.6	20.0	12.0	4.9	697	681
Broadwater	1.4	0.1	0.2	1.3	0.3	0.1	1.5	7.3	2.9	3.2	784	763
Carbon	2.8	0.0	0.5	2.9	0.6	0.3	0.4	18.0	8.8	6.2	657	627
Carter	0.8	0.0	0.3	0.5	0.1	0.1	2.9	3.3	1.1	1.7	1 162	1 147
Cascade	181.3	61.8	11.4	48.0	9.2	4.4	21.1	135.2	61.8	42.8	541	514
Chouteau	1.4	0.0	1.1	0.8	0.3	0.2	2.9	21.8	4.7	7.9	1 515	1 473
Custer	12.0	0.0	1.0	7.3	1.5	0.7	8.7	28.0	11.4	6.9	572	551
Daniels	1.0	0.0	2.5	0.3	0.1	0.1	0.4	8.4	2.7	2.6	1 244	1 225
Dawson	2.6	0.1	0.5	3.0	1.4	0.8	0.2	23.9	10.4	7.2	795	778
Deer Lodge	3.3	0.0	0.4	5.6	2.3	0.6	1.2	15.8	7.7	4.9	491	467
Fallon	0.4	0.0	0.2	0.5	0.1	0.2	0.5	14.7	9.4	3.1	1 012	990
Fergus	6.2	0.2	1.6	5.6	1.4	0.7	2.6	23.3	10.7	8.5	677	659
Flathead	31.4	1.2	9.9	31.7	6.6	3.2	14.8	135.0	51.0	52.9	737	677
Gallatin	25.7	1.0	13.5	17.1	3.2	2.7	41.1	105.6	35.5	37.6	616	555
Garfield	0.7	0.0	0.2	0.3	0.0	0.1	0.2	3.4	1.4	1.4	965	947
Glacier	14.2	0.3	4.8	11.1	4.1	9.7	9.2	36.5	20.0	7.6	599	586
Golden Valley	0.3	0.0	0.1	0.0	0.0	0.0	0.0	3.1	1.2	1.4	1 370	1 341
Granite	1.4	0.0	0.1	0.8	0.3	0.1	7.6	8.3	2.4	3.1	1 161	1 141
Hill	6.0	0.2	2.0	14.4	4.3	9.0	9.0	39.2	21.0	11.9	678	660
Jefferson	8.0	1.5	0.6	3.3	0.5	0.3	1.2	17.6	6.7	7.2	727	712
Judith Basin	1.3	0.0	0.2	0.8	0.1	0.1	0.1	5.9	2.2	2.9	1 254	1 234
Lake	5.6	3.9	5.2	12.1	3.7	8.2	17.3	42.8	20.6	13.0	513	503
Lewis and Clark	59.4	17.6	132.8	44.9	61.9	34.1	225.0	105.2	41.1	37.5	703	665
Liberty	1.2	0.0	0.2	0.3	0.1	0.1	0.2	10.1	2.9	3.1	1 304	1 288
Lincoln	17.0	5.2	3.2	6.1	3.0	1.2	8.7	32.1	17.6	8.3	442	429
McCone	0.7	0.0	0.1	0.8	0.2	0.1	8.9	4.6	1.6	2.4	1 174	1 156
Madison	2.6	0.0	0.6	1.3	0.2	0.2	13.6	19.4	4.6	7.7	1 117	953
Meagher	1.0	0.0	0.9	1.1	0.1	0.1	1.4	4.1	1.4	2.3	1 247	1 224
Mineral	1.9	0.1	0.5	0.8	0.4	0.3	3.2	12.1	6.7	3.8	1 008	990
Missoula	62.1	1.5	19.5	38.7	10.4	9.3	27.7	158.2	57.6	74.9	843	814
Musselshell	0.8	0.0	0.2	1.6	0.3	0.2	6.0	9.4	5.5	2.5	552	537
Park	3.8	0.0	0.7	5.4	1.2	1.1	11.0	27.2	10.2	9.0	566	542
Petroleum	0.2	0.0	0.0	0.0	0.0	0.0	0.3	2.3	1.3	0.5	967	936
Phillips	2.3	0.0	0.4	4.2	0.4	0.4	2.6	15.3	6.9	4.4	907	882
Pondera	2.1	0.6	26.0	3.2	0.5	2.4	5.8	15.8	9.0	4.7	723	699
Powder River	0.8	0.0	0.5	0.3	0.1	0.2	4.0	10.8	3.3	2.7	1 425	1 365
Powell	3.0	0.0	0.5	1.9	0.6	0.7	0.5	11.6	5.7	3.9	549	524
Prairie	0.4	0.0	0.1	0.5	0.0	0.1	0.0	6.5	1.9	1.5	1 159	1 138
Ravalli	17.9	0.1	5.2	9.1	2.8	1.5	2.5	46.7	23.5	16.7	482	465
Richland	3.4	0.1	36.4	3.5	1.0	0.5	1.7	24.4	12.2	6.7	655	639
Roosevelt	8.9	0.3	66.4	7.1	2.9	12.4	18.0	38.8	20.3	7.5	675	663
Rosebud	6.3	0.0	1.8	6.6	2.1	4.0	12.9	54.1	12.1	11.7	1 143	1 130
Sanders	4.5	0.0	0.6	4.3	1.0	1.1	3.5	20.6	9.1	8.2	801	782
Sheridan	3.0	0.1	0.4	2.1	0.3	0.3	8.6	11.6	5.9	3.6	838	822
Silver Bow	13.6	1.0	31.1	20.5	6.1	2.0	6.8	64.5	25.1	23.8	691	607
Stillwater	1.6	0.0	1.1	0.8	0.3	0.3	2.0	15.5	6.4	6.6	849	825
Sweet Grass	1.3	0.0	0.3	0.5	0.1	0.1	4.2	7.4	2.0	2.3	673	655
Teton	2.2	0.0	0.5	2.4	0.4	0.2	0.4	18.7	5.8	5.6	889	830
Toole	3.2	0.1	1.3	1.6	0.4	0.2	1.2	23.8	6.8	5.9	1 217	1 182
Treasure	0.3	0.0	0.1	0.0	0.1	0.0	0.1	2.2	0.7	1.1	1 347	1 327
Valley	6.8	1.6	1.7	4.0	0.6	1.0	3.2	21.6	9.5	8.0	963	946
Wheatland	1.5	0.0	0.2	0.8	0.1	0.1	2.1	5.2	2.0	2.7	1 145	1 123
Wibaux	0.2	0.0	0.1	0.8	0.1	0.0	0.5	3.6	1.7	1.5	1 350	1 333
Yellowstone	92.8	0.4	22.8	44.6	15.2	6.9	15.4	248.1	82.9	83.5	664	613
NEBRASKA	992.2	226.8	243.6	748.8	283.9	171.0	447.6	X	X	X	X	X
Adams	6.1	2.8	1.1	15.3	4.5	1.3	1.1	89.3	24.9	40.4	1 357	1 194
Antelope	1.7	0.0	1.0	3.6	0.6	0.4	10.7	17.3	6.6	8.6	1 175	1 067
Arthur	0.1	0.0	0.0	0.0	0.0	0.0	0.0	1.7	0.2	1.2	2 836	2 785
Banner	0.1	0.0	0.0	0.0	0.0	0.1	0.0	3.0	0.7	1.6	1 866	1 740

1. October 1, 1998 to September 30, 1999. 2. State totals may include programs not allocated by county. 3. Based on the resident population estimated as of July 1 of the year shown.

STATE County	Local government finances, 1997 (cont'd) Direct general expenditure Total (mil dol)	Per capita[1] (dollars)	Percent of total for — Education	Health and hospitals	Police protection	Public welfare	Highways	Debt outstanding Total (mil dol)	Per capita[1] (dollars)	Government employment, 1998 Federal civilian	Federal military	State and local	Presidential election, 2000 Percent of vote cast — Democratic	Republican	All other
	183	184	185	186	187	188	189	190	191	192	193	194	195	196	197
MISSOURI—Cont'd															
St. Louis city	1 294.2	3 786	37.2	2.4	8.6	0.0	1.1	947.1	2 770	17 456	2 452	26 827	NA	NA	NA
MONTANA	X	X	X	X	X	X	X	X	X	12 647	8 474	61 856	33.4	58.4	8.2
Beaverhead	27.1	3 008	41.3	34.2	3.2	0.5	3.8	7.6	841	193	50	741	18.8	73.2	8.0
Big Horn	31.1	2 464	69.5	1.2	3.0	1.5	6.7	2.3	179	448	71	749	55.1	38.8	6.0
Blaine	20.2	2 849	65.4	1.2	3.8	1.7	9.0	4.0	570	193	40	482	44.4	50.2	5.4
Broadwater	7.5	1 844	54.1	3.0	7.1	1.8	3.9	2.5	624	37	23	174	21.8	70.2	8.1
Carbon	19.0	2 019	57.8	1.6	4.6	1.6	6.5	7.6	811	67	53	464	28.9	60.7	10.4
Carter	3.6	2 406	53.6	6.7	3.0	2.4	12.6	0.5	319	19	0	122	8.2	88.3	3.5
Cascade	145.9	1 843	53.3	1.9	4.1	0.8	3.0	71.9	908	1 474	3 896	3 791	39.0	53.9	7.2
Chouteau	22.5	4 290	40.4	32.3	2.3	1.3	6.0	10.5	2 009	35	29	470	23.5	69.7	6.8
Custer	26.9	2 218	61.2	3.2	5.6	1.3	5.4	3.9	325	331	68	837	29.5	62.0	8.5
Daniels	9.1	4 401	46.8	25.2	2.5	1.1	3.5	4.4	2 140	27	11	164	26.6	65.8	7.6
Dawson	24.1	2 667	62.1	2.5	3.6	1.9	6.1	7.2	795	44	50	836	31.1	62.0	6.9
Deer Lodge	16.7	1 671	55.7	3.2	7.9	0.8	3.7	11.8	1 181	82	56	896	57.4	32.1	10.5
Fallon	13.7	4 505	49.8	8.4	3.5	2.4	8.2	0.5	162	18	17	268	18.2	75.4	6.5
Fergus	24.0	1 924	74.7	1.5	3.8	1.5	4.3	3.8	303	151	69	906	21.7	69.9	8.4
Flathead	130.6	1 821	62.7	2.9	5.4	0.7	3.9	46.7	651	839	405	3 290	24.1	65.1	10.9
Gallatin	108.3	1 772	49.5	1.0	3.4	4.6	4.0	82.9	1 357	543	365	7 352	30.8	57.9	11.3
Garfield	3.8	2 614	51.5	4.8	4.9	2.5	8.1	0.0	18	23	0	111	8.1	86.9	4.9
Glacier	41.0	3 233	65.5	12.8	2.3	1.8	3.6	3.9	309	424	70	804	51.0	39.4	9.6
Golden Valley	3.3	3 140	72.9	0.5	2.5	1.2	5.0	2.0	1 855	0	0	79	16.4	75.4	8.2
Granite	8.4	3 206	42.1	4.0	5.0	17.9	7.3	1.0	367	42	15	239	18.2	73.0	8.7
Hill	39.6	2 256	67.1	1.1	4.7	0.8	4.7	14.5	824	127	104	1 393	41.2	50.6	8.2
Jefferson	19.1	1 937	58.4	1.6	4.1	1.2	4.2	12.9	1 306	61	57	773	28.9	63.2	7.9
Judith Basin	5.6	2 410	66.0	1.7	2.2	1.2	8.8	0.0	17	37	13	168	19.7	74.9	5.5
Lake	44.7	1 765	67.2	5.9	4.3	0.6	4.4	7.3	290	137	144	1 129	33.5	55.6	10.8
Lewis and Clark	103.8	1 950	53.9	3.0	5.2	3.3	5.0	66.3	1 245	1 354	306	7 154	35.9	54.3	9.7
Liberty	9.9	4 155	44.5	32.0	2.8	1.5	5.5	1.4	568	24	13	221	22.4	69.4	8.2
Lincoln	35.4	1 886	64.7	1.9	6.0	0.2	8.8	4.7	252	551	105	903	20.4	69.7	9.9
McCone	5.1	2 522	56.5	3.9	3.8	2.4	6.0	0.0	3	20	11	149	20.5	71.7	7.8
Madison	19.6	2 845	42.3	13.8	3.7	12.6	6.0	1.5	210	76	39	415	23.0	71.3	5.7
Meagher	4.5	2 483	50.4	2.9	6.0	1.0	17.2	0.4	217	28	10	131	18.6	73.6	7.8
Mineral	12.5	3 352	55.3	0.6	3.9	0.3	2.8	5.6	1 505	65	21	250	22.6	63.7	13.7
Missoula	163.4	1 839	56.4	4.7	5.4	0.4	3.6	111.4	1 254	1 281	515	7 687	36.7	45.8	17.5
Musselshell	9.1	1 983	64.1	1.3	4.4	1.6	4.4	1.0	215	[3]82	[3]89	[3]665	22.8	70.6	6.6
Park	28.6	1 800	58.8	2.6	4.8	0.1	3.6	8.0	502	0	0	234	28.7	60.3	11.1
Petroleum	3.0	5 882	32.7	0.3	0.9	3.5	4.3	1.1	2 195	0	0	60	11.5	81.4	7.1
Phillips	16.8	3 432	61.1	1.2	4.1	1.5	8.3	6.6	1 345	53	27	367	18.7	76.1	5.2
Pondera	16.7	2 591	72.7	2.0	4.0	0.9	5.7	4.6	716	43	36	437	26.0	63.9	10.2
Powder River	8.1	4 247	43.7	1.2	2.8	18.8	6.2	0.3	178	17	10	216	11.2	83.9	4.9
Powell	12.5	1 762	62.3	1.5	6.0	0.2	8.9	0.9	129	74	39	968	22.0	67.8	10.2
Prairie	6.4	4 790	29.2	38.3	2.4	1.9	3.2	1.8	1 379	12	0	170	21.3	70.3	8.4
Ravalli	49.8	1 441	68.0	0.9	4.6	2.1	4.1	15.1	437	464	198	1 251	25.6	64.5	9.9
Richland	23.9	2 348	65.0	1.1	5.1	1.0	7.9	12.3	1 210	73	57	611	24.8	69.6	5.6
Roosevelt	40.0	3 594	61.6	18.0	3.3	1.1	3.5	5.3	479	227	62	795	52.0	40.5	7.5
Rosebud	54.6	5 353	39.7	0.7	2.8	0.7	2.5	426.0	41 732	187	56	584	39.0	51.1	9.8
Sanders	21.6	2 104	61.8	0.8	4.2	0.9	7.5	7.7	750	145	57	528	24.3	65.5	10.2
Sheridan	12.0	2 765	63.2	0.7	5.1	2.5	8.4	1.5	337	73	24	293	34.7	58.2	7.1
Silver Bow	77.3	2 245	41.7	2.4	5.2	1.3	3.9	73.4	2 130	322	209	2 119	52.6	36.9	10.5
Stillwater	16.2	2 062	66.5	1.6	4.0	0.8	7.7	2.8	353	34	45	381	23.4	69.9	6.7
Sweet Grass	7.8	2 295	49.9	3.2	4.9	16.1	6.3	0.9	264	83	19	277	16.4	78.0	5.6
Teton	19.9	3 136	50.3	19.9	2.5	0.7	5.3	8.6	1 360	61	36	425	25.1	68.1	6.7
Toole	21.5	4 453	36.3	36.7	4.0	1.4	6.6	4.9	1 014	70	27	563	25.7	66.9	7.3
Treasure	2.5	2 920	63.2	1.3	3.7	0.9	7.7	0.5	580	0	0	80	22.1	71.7	6.3
Valley	23.4	2 815	56.4	1.0	3.5	3.3	5.2	6.8	818	134	46	582	31.2	61.3	7.4
Wheatland	5.6	2 387	67.8	1.9	5.4	0.7	7.1	0.4	150	41	13	153	24.0	70.0	6.0
Wibaux	4.1	3 727	39.6	3.3	7.6	2.6	13.4	0.2	201	0	0	92	22.7	69.4	7.9
Yellowstone	245.0	1 948	51.1	3.9	7.0	1.0	3.1	122.8	976	1 713	728	6 857	35.1	58.5	6.4
NEBRASKA	X	X	X	X	X	X	X	X	X	15 840	15 873	129 070	33.3	62.2	4.5
Adams	82.2	2 764	71.3	0.5	4.9	0.2	8.0	92.5	3 108	112	130	2 492	29.6	65.6	4.7
Antelope	18.7	2 537	65.0	0.2	0.7	0.0	14.5	2.0	278	39	32	519	20.1	76.1	3.8
Arthur	1.7	3 869	54.4	0.2	1.3	0.0	6.9	0.0	12	0	0	41	9.6	86.4	4.0
Banner	2.9	3 385	69.5	0.0	1.1	0.0	13.6	0.0	0	0	0	65	14.1	84.4	1.5

1. Based on the resident population estimated as of July 1 of the year shown. 3. Yellowstone Park included with Park County.

Table B. States and Counties — Land Area and Population

STATE/ County code	MSA/ PMSA/ NECMA code[1]	County Type[2]	STATE County	Land area,[3] (sq km) 1990	Total persons	Rank	Per square kilometer	White	Black	Am. Indian, Eskimo, Aleut	Asian and Pacific Islander	Percent Hispanic[4]	Under 5 years	5 to 17 years	18 to 24 years	25 to 34 years	35 to 44 years	45 to 54 years
				1	2	3	4	5	6	7	8	9	10	11	12	13	14	15
			NEBRASKA—Cont'd															
31 009	...	9	Blaine	1 841	575	3 133	0.3	99.7	0.2	0.2	0.0	0.0	5.6	22.6	6.1	9.9	13.0	17.7
31 011	...	9	Boone	1 779	6 355	2 747	3.6	99.4	0.2	0.3	0.2	0.9	7.3	20.6	5.4	10.5	12.6	12.7
31 013	...	7	Box Butte	2 785	12 674	2 235	4.6	96.3	0.4	2.6	0.7	10.4	7.5	24.6	6.4	12.1	16.5	11.5
31 015	...	9	Boyd	1 399	2 520	3 021	1.8	99.0	0.0	1.0	0.0	0.5	5.8	20.5	3.4	8.5	13.5	13.2
31 017	...	9	Brown	3 163	3 499	2 951	1.1	99.3	0.0	0.3	0.3	1.3	5.9	20.0	5.3	9.1	14.3	14.2
31 019	...	5	Buffalo	2 507	40 249	1 081	16.1	98.2	0.5	0.5	0.8	5.4	6.7	18.8	19.0	11.5	14.4	10.8
31 021	...	8	Burt	1 276	7 907	2 610	6.2	98.4	0.1	1.2	0.3	1.8	5.9	20.2	5.6	9.0	14.2	13.3
31 023	...	6	Butler	1 512	8 607	2 543	5.7	99.2	0.1	0.2	0.4	0.6	6.1	21.4	6.4	9.8	14.2	13.5
31 025	5920	2	Cass	1 449	24 841	1 537	17.1	98.4	0.3	0.6	0.7	1.9	7.2	21.1	8.2	11.9	16.1	14.7
31 027	...	9	Cedar	1 917	9 612	2 460	5.0	99.4	0.2	0.2	0.2	0.5	7.3	22.2	6.6	9.7	12.8	11.9
31 029	...	9	Chase	2 317	4 253	2 891	1.8	99.6	0.0	0.3	0.1	4.0	6.7	21.1	5.0	9.9	14.5	13.4
31 031	...	7	Cherry	15 438	6 326	2 748	0.4	96.3	0.1	3.2	0.3	0.8	7.1	20.0	5.7	10.5	14.5	15.1
31 033	...	7	Cheyenne	3 099	9 428	2 479	3.0	98.5	0.3	1.0	0.2	6.5	6.8	20.2	7.0	10.8	14.4	12.5
31 035	...	9	Clay	1 484	7 094	2 670	4.8	99.4	0.1	0.3	0.3	1.2	5.8	20.8	5.9	10.3	14.3	14.6
31 037	...	7	Colfax	1 070	10 691	2 362	10.0	99.4	0.1	0.4	0.2	4.3	6.5	18.2	7.1	10.6	11.7	11.5
31 039	...	7	Cuming	1 482	9 981	2 427	6.7	99.4	0.1	0.1	0.4	0.3	6.5	20.6	6.5	9.7	13.1	13.3
31 041	...	7	Custer	6 671	11 825	2 290	1.8	99.1	0.1	0.6	0.2	1.5	6.1	20.6	5.2	8.9	14.2	13.8
31 043	7720	3	Dakota	684	19 140	1 812	28.0	93.9	0.6	2.0	3.5	11.5	8.4	22.1	9.7	13.3	15.1	13.1
31 045	...	7	Dawes	3 616	8 831	2 519	2.4	93.6	0.7	4.4	1.3	2.8	5.8	18.5	20.1	8.9	12.8	11.2
31 047	...	7	Dawson	2 624	23 277	1 604	8.9	99.0	0.2	0.4	0.4	6.5	6.7	21.4	7.1	10.5	15.8	14.0
31 049	...	9	Deuel	1 139	1 988	3 062	1.7	98.8	0.3	0.5	0.5	8.5	6.2	19.7	5.4	10.7	11.9	12.3
31 051	...	8	Dixon	1 234	6 360	2 746	5.2	99.6	0.1	0.2	0.1	0.1	6.9	20.9	6.9	9.4	14.8	12.9
31 053	...	4	Dodge	1 384	35 201	1 221	25.4	98.6	0.4	0.4	0.6	1.4	6.1	18.9	9.1	10.5	14.4	13.8
31 055	5920	2	Douglas	857	446 277	128	520.7	85.8	11.9	0.7	1.6	5.5	7.2	19.2	10.7	14.1	16.6	13.0
31 057	...	9	Dundy	2 383	2 179	3 050	0.9	99.6	0.0	0.2	0.2	1.2	4.8	19.6	6.2	9.6	14.7	12.1
31 059	...	9	Fillmore	1 493	6 912	2 687	4.6	99.0	0.4	0.5	0.1	1.1	6.0	20.6	5.7	9.8	14.2	13.4
31 061	...	9	Franklin	1 492	3 677	2 935	2.5	99.3	0.2	0.3	0.2	0.4	6.0	17.1	5.0	9.3	12.8	14.8
31 063	...	9	Frontier	2 524	3 157	2 979	1.3	99.2	0.2	0.1	0.4	1.3	6.2	21.4	6.3	10.0	14.5	16.3
31 065	...	9	Furnas	1 860	5 411	2 811	2.9	99.3	0.1	0.3	0.2	1.3	4.8	19.1	5.2	8.9	14.0	13.0
31 067	...	6	Gage	2 215	22 710	1 623	10.3	98.7	0.2	0.5	0.6	1.0	6.0	17.8	7.7	11.1	14.7	13.7
31 069	...	9	Garden	4 415	2 073	3 059	0.5	100.0	0.0	0.0	0.0	1.0	5.6	15.8	5.2	9.2	12.5	14.6
31 071	...	9	Garfield	1 476	2 015	3 061	1.4	99.5	0.0	0.1	0.4	0.2	5.6	18.9	4.7	8.0	12.4	15.9
31 073	...	9	Gosper	1 187	2 256	3 040	1.9	97.7	0.8	0.4	1.1	3.1	4.8	17.9	4.5	9.1	13.3	15.9
31 075	...	9	Grant	2 011	714	3 130	0.4	96.9	0.8	0.8	1.4	2.2	8.0	19.7	4.8	11.8	15.0	15.1
31 077	...	9	Greeley	1 476	2 812	3 004	1.9	99.7	0.0	0.1	0.2	0.1	6.0	23.3	5.1	8.6	13.2	12.3
31 079	...	5	Hall	1 415	51 764	884	36.6	97.3	0.4	0.4	1.9	8.4	7.2	20.9	8.9	12.2	15.7	12.6
31 081	...	7	Hamilton	1 408	9 566	2 467	6.8	99.0	0.3	0.1	0.5	1.5	6.7	21.4	6.0	10.7	15.8	14.0
31 083	...	9	Harlan	1 432	3 671	2 936	2.6	99.9	0.1	0.1	0.0	0.3	5.5	18.5	4.3	8.8	15.4	13.6
31 085	...	9	Hayes	1 847	1 066	3 108	0.6	99.4	0.0	0.2	0.4	1.1	5.8	21.5	5.4	9.9	14.5	16.4
31 087	...	9	Hitchcock	1 839	3 366	2 963	1.8	99.5	0.1	0.3	0.1	1.2	5.8	21.7	5.3	9.1	14.2	12.6
31 089	...	7	Holt	6 249	11 884	2 285	1.9	99.4	0.1	0.3	0.3	0.5	7.3	21.3	6.2	10.5	13.9	12.2
31 091	...	9	Hooker	1 868	689	3 131	0.4	100.0	0.0	0.0	0.0	3.8	5.2	18.4	6.1	7.0	13.5	14.7
31 093	...	9	Howard	1 475	6 540	2 726	4.4	99.5	0.0	0.3	0.2	1.5	6.4	21.4	6.3	9.3	14.1	14.2
31 095	...	7	Jefferson	1 484	8 288	2 569	5.6	99.5	0.1	0.3	0.1	1.9	6.0	18.2	6.2	9.5	14.2	13.1
31 097	...	8	Johnson	974	4 548	2 868	4.7	95.8	0.0	0.0	4.2	2.1	5.8	18.8	5.2	10.4	12.4	14.3
31 099	...	7	Kearney	1 337	6 861	2 693	5.1	99.7	0.0	0.1	0.2	3.4	6.9	19.8	7.4	11.4	15.6	13.8
31 101	...	7	Keith	2 749	8 877	2 517	3.2	98.9	0.1	0.7	0.3	7.4	6.4	20.7	5.8	10.4	14.3	14.1
31 103	...	9	Keya Paha	2 003	952	3 112	0.5	99.9	0.0	0.1	0.0	0.2	4.6	21.2	4.2	10.3	13.2	14.6
31 105	...	6	Kimball	2 465	4 027	2 914	1.6	99.5	0.0	0.2	0.2	6.7	6.4	19.2	4.8	10.4	13.5	14.5
31 107	...	9	Knox	2 870	9 048	2 502	3.2	93.7	0.0	5.9	0.3	0.2	5.8	19.5	4.8	8.6	13.5	12.6
31 109	4360	3	Lancaster	2 173	237 657	233	109.4	94.3	2.4	0.7	2.5	3.6	6.5	17.0	15.7	13.9	16.6	12.1
31 111	...	5	Lincoln	6 641	33 866	1 259	5.1	98.5	0.4	0.5	0.6	9.6	6.7	21.8	7.8	10.5	15.9	13.4
31 113	...	9	Logan	1 478	895	3 116	0.6	99.4	0.4	0.0	0.1	0.9	7.5	24.9	4.5	9.8	15.0	11.7
31 115	...	9	Loup	1 476	654	3 132	0.4	99.7	0.0	0.0	0.3	0.3	6.0	20.3	5.4	10.7	12.2	16.4
31 117	...	9	McPherson	2 225	547	3 134	0.2	99.6	0.4	0.0	0.0	0.3	6.0	20.7	3.7	10.4	11.2	13.9
31 119	...	5	Madison	1 483	34 184	1 251	23.1	97.8	0.7	0.9	0.6	3.4	7.5	20.2	9.9	13.1	15.1	11.7
31 121	...	7	Merrick	1 255	8 052	2 593	6.4	99.2	0.1	0.2	0.5	1.9	6.6	20.6	6.6	10.2	14.3	14.8
31 123	...	9	Morrill	3 688	5 294	2 820	1.4	98.7	0.1	0.8	0.4	14.6	7.2	21.1	5.8	9.9	14.6	14.1
31 125	...	9	Nance	1 143	4 057	2 912	3.5	99.4	0.0	0.2	0.3	1.9	7.1	21.1	5.4	10.5	13.4	12.8
31 127	...	7	Nemaha	1 060	7 618	2 630	7.2	98.8	0.8	0.4	0.2	0.5	5.9	18.2	11.1	9.9	14.9	13.2
31 129	...	9	Nuckolls	1 490	5 121	2 830	3.4	99.8	0.0	0.0	0.0	0.7	5.2	19.2	4.5	8.7	13.1	12.9
31 131	...	6	Otoe	1 595	14 803	2 080	9.3	99.2	0.2	0.2	0.4	1.6	6.2	19.6	6.7	10.0	14.3	14.3
31 133	...	9	Pawnee	1 118	3 087	2 981	2.8	99.7	0.1	0.0	0.2	1.1	5.6	16.7	5.5	7.6	13.2	12.6
31 135	...	9	Perkins	2 287	3 205	2 977	1.4	98.9	0.0	0.7	0.5	3.1	6.5	22.7	4.9	8.6	15.6	13.7
31 137	...	7	Phelps	1 399	9 831	2 442	7.0	99.4	0.1	0.2	0.3	1.9	6.5	20.0	6.8	10.6	15.3	13.7
31 139	...	9	Pierce	1 487	7 945	2 605	5.3	99.3	0.1	0.4	0.2	0.5	7.3	21.6	6.7	10.9	13.4	13.7

1. MSA = Metropolitan Statistical Area. PMSA = Primary MSA. NECMA = New England County Metropolitan Area. See Appendix A for explanation of these concepts. See Appendix B for list of metropolitan areas identified by type, with component counties. 2. County typology code from the Economic Research Service of USDA. See Appendix A for definition. 3. Dry land or land partially or temporarily covered by water. 4. Hispanic persons may be of any race.

	Population, 1999 (cont'd)				Population — change and components of change, 1980-1999							Households, 1990				
	Age (percent) (cont'd)				Total persons		Percent change		Components of change, 1990-1999						Percent	
STATE County	55 to 64 years	65 to 74 years	75 years and over	Percent female	1990	1980	1980-1990	1990-1999	Births	Deaths	Net migration	Number	Percent change, 1980-1990	Persons per household	Female family householder[1]	One person
	16	17	18	19	20	21	22	23	24	25	26	27	28	29	30	31
NEBRASKA—Cont'd																
Blaine	11.8	5.9	7.3	51.0	675	867	-22.1	-14.8	91	48	-140	268	-12.7	2.52	2.6	28.0
Boone	10.6	9.6	10.7	49.9	6 667	7 391	-9.8	-4.7	758	693	-355	2 560	-4.5	2.56	3.9	27.7
Box Butte	7.4	6.4	7.5	50.7	13 130	13 696	-4.1	-3.5	1 619	1 147	-890	4 898	-2.8	2.64	7.6	26.4
Boyd	11.2	10.1	13.8	50.4	2 835	3 331	-14.9	-11.1	296	372	-232	1 148	-9.4	2.41	4.2	30.7
Brown	10.3	9.7	11.3	51.3	3 657	4 377	-16.4	-4.3	407	455	-98	1 499	-11.7	2.40	5.9	29.4
Buffalo	7.2	5.5	6.2	50.9	37 447	34 797	7.6	7.5	5 015	2 772	656	13 736	11.8	2.53	7.2	26.0
Burt	11.1	8.8	11.9	51.2	7 868	8 813	-10.7	0.5	740	1 048	385	3 139	-6.9	2.44	5.5	29.1
Butler	10.1	8.3	10.3	50.1	8 601	9 330	-7.8	0.1	1 007	1 014	48	3 253	-3.7	2.59	4.9	27.4
Cass	9.0	6.1	5.8	49.9	21 318	20 297	5.0	16.5	2 918	1 850	2 341	7 797	9.0	2.70	6.5	21.0
Cedar	10.1	8.7	10.7	50.2	10 131	11 375	-10.9	-5.1	1 255	1 102	-639	3 652	-4.4	2.71	3.9	26.4
Chase	9.8	9.6	10.0	50.6	4 381	4 758	-7.9	-2.9	461	503	-67	1 704	-1.0	2.52	5.5	26.8
Cherry	10.0	7.9	9.2	50.3	6 307	6 758	-6.7	0.3	772	605	-128	2 438	-2.6	2.56	5.3	25.8
Cheyenne	10.2	9.0	9.0	51.6	9 494	10 057	-5.6	-0.7	1 121	953	-195	3 851	-2.1	2.44	7.5	28.7
Clay	9.7	8.8	10.0	51.0	7 123	8 106	-12.1	-0.4	801	775	-32	2 741	-9.0	2.54	4.5	24.8
Colfax	8.4	11.0	14.8	50.5	9 139	9 890	-7.6	17.0	1 277	997	1 385	3 562	-3.3	2.52	5.3	28.9
Cuming	10.7	9.0	10.5	50.3	10 117	11 664	-13.3	-1.3	1 225	1 142	-187	3 851	-5.0	2.56	3.5	27.0
Custer	10.7	9.1	11.4	51.4	12 270	13 877	-11.6	-3.6	1 389	1 593	-205	4 953	-6.0	2.43	5.2	28.9
Dakota	7.4	5.7	5.3	50.1	16 742	16 573	1.0	14.3	3 122	1 507	840	6 035	5.6	2.73	10.5	22.9
Dawes	7.7	6.9	8.0	50.5	9 021	9 609	-6.1	-2.1	971	880	-264	3 327	-4.9	2.43	8.5	29.8
Dawson	9.7	7.3	7.6	51.0	19 940	22 304	-10.6	16.7	3 603	2 152	1 731	7 829	-4.3	2.51	6.3	25.6
Deuel	9.9	11.5	12.4	50.8	2 237	2 462	-9.1	-11.1	179	284	-134	915	-5.0	2.41	4.8	29.3
Dixon	10.3	7.6	10.3	50.3	6 143	7 137	-13.9	3.5	695	681	226	2 338	-8.3	2.58	5.8	26.3
Dodge	9.8	8.3	9.1	52.0	34 500	35 847	-3.8	2.0	3 980	3 582	409	13 445	1.2	2.48	6.8	26.8
Douglas	8.0	6.0	5.1	51.7	416 444	397 038	4.9	7.2	65 271	32 498	-1 923	161 113	10.3	2.53	12.2	28.1
Dundy	10.6	10.6	11.8	51.4	2 582	2 861	-9.8	-15.6	238	317	-313	1 085	-5.5	2.32	5.0	31.5
Fillmore	10.1	8.8	11.4	51.5	7 103	7 920	-10.3	-2.7	752	911	-5	2 829	-6.0	2.41	4.2	29.3
Franklin	11.3	10.2	13.5	51.7	3 938	4 377	-10.0	-6.6	381	627	7	1 655	-5.0	2.32	3.7	30.3
Frontier	10.7	6.6	8.0	49.8	3 101	3 647	-15.0	1.8	296	298	67	1 206	-10.3	2.53	3.6	27.1
Furnas	10.7	9.4	14.9	51.5	5 553	6 486	-14.4	-2.6	571	900	212	2 334	-10.7	2.28	4.4	33.8
Gage	10.5	8.4	10.0	51.8	22 794	24 456	-6.8	-0.4	2 367	2 820	453	9 019	-2.4	2.40	6.7	28.2
Garden	11.6	11.8	13.7	51.8	2 460	2 802	-12.2	-15.7	178	376	-185	1 040	-8.0	2.30	4.9	30.3
Garfield	9.5	11.0	14.1	51.5	2 141	2 363	-9.4	-5.9	203	323	9	864	-5.5	2.40	4.7	28.7
Gosper	12.1	11.6	10.7	48.8	1 928	2 140	-9.9	17.0	215	254	372	764	-1.3	2.45	3.7	21.2
Grant	12.7	7.8	5.0	50.0	769	877	-12.3	-7.2	94	56	-93	303	-5.9	2.54	6.6	24.1
Greeley	9.6	9.5	12.3	51.0	3 006	3 462	-13.2	-6.5	326	350	-164	1 133	-6.6	2.59	6.4	30.1
Hall	8.4	7.1	7.0	51.2	48 925	47 690	2.6	5.8	7 684	4 563	-148	18 678	7.0	2.56	8.5	26.0
Hamilton	9.7	7.5	8.2	51.0	8 862	9 301	-4.7	7.9	1 106	866	487	3 235	-1.1	2.67	4.3	21.7
Harlan	11.4	11.0	11.3	51.5	3 810	4 292	-11.2	-3.6	369	488	-3	1 585	-6.1	2.37	3.7	29.2
Hayes	12.0	8.3	6.1	48.4	1 222	1 356	-9.9	-12.8	102	97	-156	480	0.0	2.55	3.3	22.7
Hitchcock	9.7	9.8	11.8	50.2	3 750	4 079	-8.1	-10.2	311	379	-299	1 467	-4.5	2.48	4.3	28.6
Holt	9.6	9.2	9.7	50.4	12 599	13 552	-7.0	-5.7	1 416	1 221	-869	4 744	-1.0	2.62	5.1	27.3
Hooker	9.4	10.7	14.9	50.9	793	990	-19.9	-13.1	58	148	-6	332	-12.2	2.29	4.5	33.7
Howard	10.9	8.5	8.9	50.9	6 057	6 773	-10.6	8.0	701	647	439	2 309	-2.3	2.59	4.8	25.2
Jefferson	10.9	10.1	11.9	51.2	8 759	9 817	-10.8	-5.4	793	1 152	-77	3 634	-7.7	2.37	5.1	28.8
Johnson	10.9	9.6	12.5	51.5	4 673	5 285	-11.6	-2.7	456	607	43	1 940	-4.9	2.36	5.2	30.8
Kearney	9.9	6.8	8.3	50.1	6 629	7 053	-6.0	3.5	777	708	178	2 523	-0.8	2.54	4.8	24.1
Keith	10.9	9.3	8.2	51.3	8 584	9 364	-8.3	3.4	912	891	292	3 430	-1.7	2.47	6.7	27.3
Keya Paha	11.1	10.9	9.8	48.1	1 029	1 301	-20.9	-7.5	130	99	-106	419	-12.5	2.46	2.1	24.8
Kimball	10.4	10.8	9.9	51.2	4 108	4 882	-15.9	-2.0	369	465	27	1 650	-8.3	2.45	6.8	26.7
Knox	11.3	10.9	13.0	51.1	9 564	11 457	-16.5	-5.4	1 037	1 340	-167	3 817	-8.6	2.44	5.1	29.7
Lancaster	7.3	5.6	5.2	51.0	213 641	192 884	10.8	11.2	29 673	14 365	9 330	82 759	15.3	2.44	8.7	27.5
Lincoln	9.0	7.5	7.4	51.1	32 508	36 455	-10.8	4.2	4 186	3 090	384	12 676	-4.3	2.53	8.0	27.0
Logan	11.6	7.5	6.7	50.2	878	983	-10.7	1.9	73	71	19	320	-8.3	2.74	4.4	21.9
Loup	10.6	9.0	9.5	51.8	683	859	-20.5	-4.2	50	60	-16	276	-13.5	2.47	4.0	27.2
McPherson	11.0	11.5	11.7	48.4	546	593	-7.9	0.2	42	31	-8	212	-4.1	2.58	2.8	23.6
Madison	8.1	6.7	7.7	50.8	32 655	31 382	4.1	4.7	5 164	3 204	-347	12 283	6.0	2.57	7.0	26.7
Merrick	9.8	7.7	9.4	50.3	8 062	8 945	-10.0	0.1	1 021	911	-89	3 061	-2.2	2.57	4.3	25.3
Morrill	10.1	7.5	9.7	50.1	5 423	6 085	-10.9	-2.4	597	676	-29	2 083	-6.6	2.55	3.8	25.7
Nance	10.9	8.7	10.1	50.4	4 275	4 740	-9.8	-5.1	459	514	-159	1 585	-7.4	2.58	4.3	27.3
Nemaha	9.2	7.9	9.9	50.2	7 980	8 367	-4.6	-4.5	730	880	-189	3 079	-3.8	2.41	5.7	28.9
Nuckolls	11.3	11.3	13.8	51.9	5 786	6 726	-14.0	-11.5	455	746	-356	2 359	-8.9	2.40	4.3	29.0
Otoe	10.3	8.4	10.1	51.7	14 252	15 183	-6.1	3.9	1 587	1 807	818	5 657	-2.5	2.46	6.5	28.0
Pawnee	11.3	13.1	14.4	51.7	3 317	3 937	-15.7	-6.9	257	508	38	1 408	-10.8	2.31	3.9	31.0
Perkins	9.0	9.0	9.9	49.8	3 367	3 637	-7.4	-4.8	285	384	-54	1 283	-5.7	2.58	4.8	25.8
Phelps	9.5	7.5	9.9	51.7	9 715	9 769	-0.6	1.2	1 178	1 105	69	3 769	1.9	2.51	5.3	26.2
Pierce	9.7	8.0	8.8	50.7	7 827	8 481	-7.7	1.5	912	862	95	2 929	-3.8	2.62	4.5	25.2

1. No spouse present.

Table B. States and Counties — Vital Statistics, Health Resources, and Crime

STATE County	Births, average 1996–1998		Deaths, average 1996–1998				Physicians,[4] 1998		Hospitals,[4] 1998			Medicare enrollees 1999	Serious crimes known to police, 1998[6]	
			Number		Rate					Beds			Total	
	Total	Rate[1]	Total	Infant[2]	Total[1]	Infant[3]	Number	Rate[5]	Number	Number	Rate[5]		Number	Rate[7]
	32	33	34	35	36	37	38	39	40	41	42	43	44	45

NEBRASKA—Cont'd

STATE County	32	33	34	35	36	37	38	39	40	41	42	43	44	45
Blaine	7	11.3	7	0	11.3	0.0	0	0	0	0	0	89	0	0
Boone	80	12.5	76	1	11.8	8.3	7	110	1	34	533	1 370	110	1 718
Box Butte	170	13.2	122	1	9.5	7.8	8	62	1	36	281	1 956	351	2 707
Boyd	31	11.7	36	1	13.7	21.5	5	195	1	29	1 131	694	27	1 020
Brown	39	11.0	48	0	13.3	8.5	5	141	1	23	647	824	60	1 656
Buffalo	569	14.1	292	3	7.2	4.7	119	293	1	183	451	5 373	1 777	4 404
Burt	78	9.8	116	0	14.5	0.0	5	63	1	23	288	1 825	100	1 480
Butler	108	12.5	99	0	11.4	3.1	3	35	1	34	392	1 701	161	1 868
Cass	319	13.3	204	3	8.5	9.4	16	65	0	0	0	3 251	483	2 005
Cedar	117	11.9	122	1	12.4	11.4	2	21	0	0	0	1 915	56	568
Chase	48	11.3	57	1	13.5	14.0	2	47	1	26	612	934	35	821
Cherry	79	12.4	61	1	9.5	8.4	3	47	1	36	569	1 233	213	3 314
Cheyenne	124	13.0	110	0	11.5	0.0	12	127	1	106	1 119	1 903	289	3 017
Clay	79	11.1	85	1	11.9	8.4	2	28	0	0	0	1 487	92	1 282
Colfax	152	14.3	109	2	10.3	15.4	6	56	1	49	457	3 686	203	1 918
Cuming	136	13.5	114	0	11.3	0.0	5	50	1	49	490	1 984	81	809
Custer	130	10.7	175	1	14.5	10.3	8	67	3	146	1 214	2 618	189	1 558
Dakota	365	19.6	173	2	9.3	6.4	5	27	0	0	0	2 390	641	3 410
Dawes	99	11.0	94	1	10.5	6.7	8	89	2	51	568	1 511	210	2 315
Dawson	414	17.8	249	5	10.7	12.9	18	78	3	118	509	3 642	860	3 704
Deuel	17	8.5	28	0	13.9	0.0	2	99	0	0	0	532	26	1 280
Dixon	79	12.6	71	0	11.2	4.2	1	16	0	0	0	1 227	89	1 382
Dodge	429	12.2	394	4	11.2	10.1	33	93	1	262	742	6 740	1 234	3 501
Douglas	7 087	16.1	3 560	60	8.1	8.5	1 597	360	8	2 604	587	58 505	28 288	6 389
Dundy	20	8.7	35	0	15.2	0.0	2	87	1	14	608	501	27	1 164
Fillmore	70	10.1	90	0	13.0	0.0	5	72	1	33	476	1 450	73	1 056
Franklin	33	8.7	63	0	16.6	0.0	3	80	1	20	536	928	50	1 304
Frontier	31	10.0	31	0	10.0	0.0	0	0	0	0	0	526	NA	NA
Furnas	58	10.6	94	1	17.2	17.2	4	74	1	65	1 208	1 504	109	2 002
Gage	250	11.0	305	1	13.4	4.0	26	115	1	143	631	5 039	1 015	4 421
Garden	14	6.6	41	0	18.6	0.0	3	140	1	56	2 619	630	51	2 285
Garfield	22	10.7	34	0	16.4	15.2	2	98	0	0	0	560	7	335
Gosper	22	9.5	28	0	12.4	15.4	0	0	0	0	0	501	28	1 220
Grant	10	13.3	7	0	8.8	33.3	1	131	0	0	0	145	6	813
Greeley	37	12.6	31	0	10.8	0.0	0	0	0	0	0	645	3	102
Hall	843	16.3	504	9	9.7	11.1	88	170	1	197	380	8 080	4 031	7 773
Hamilton	110	11.7	94	1	10.0	9.1	11	116	1	82	866	1 496	NA	NA
Harlan	35	9.4	55	0	14.6	9.4	2	53	1	25	667	836	65	1 716
Hayes	6	5.9	10	0	9.6	0.0	0	0	0	0	0	119	1	92
Hitchcock	33	9.7	48	0	14.1	0.0	0	0	0	0	0	778	26	758
Holt	133	11.0	125	1	10.3	10.1	8	66	2	47	390	2 403	142	1 158
Hooker	6	8.9	14	0	20.2	0.0	1	142	0	0	0	223	3	417
Howard	76	11.8	71	0	11.0	4.4	2	31	1	37	573	1 203	109	1 675
Jefferson	75	9.0	120	0	14.3	4.4	5	60	1	73	871	2 024	232	2 754
Johnson	47	10.2	61	0	13.3	7.1	2	44	1	30	657	1 083	NA	NA
Kearney	77	11.5	76	1	11.3	8.6	6	88	1	80	1 167	1 174	168	2 506
Keith	95	11.1	91	1	10.6	10.5	5	58	1	41	473	1 655	304	3 513
Keya Paha	11	11.1	10	0	10.4	0.0	0	0	0	0	0	189	2	203
Kimball	37	9.3	45	0	11.2	0.0	1	24	1	30	735	926	124	3 066
Knox	113	12.1	139	0	14.9	2.9	6	65	1	77	836	2 345	68	723
Lancaster	3 302	14.1	1 608	24	6.9	7.2	508	216	3	702	298	29 038	15 350	6 555
Lincoln	443	13.2	347	5	10.3	12.0	54	161	1	105	313	5 759	698	2 075
Logan	8	9.0	8	0	9.0	41.7	0	0	0	0	0	163	1	111
Loup	9	12.7	6	0	8.8	0.0	0	0	0	0	0	97	0	0
McPherson	6	10.0	3	0	5.9	0.0	0	0	0	0	0	125	1	179
Madison	538	15.5	353	4	10.2	6.8	67	194	3	199	575	5 857	1 275	3 644
Merrick	102	12.6	105	1	13.0	6.5	1	12	1	79	981	1 485	170	2 071
Morrill	62	11.5	74	1	13.7	10.7	4	73	1	20	367	1 039	115	2 113
Nance	47	11.3	58	1	13.8	14.1	2	49	1	20	488	817	46	1 084
Nemaha	75	9.7	106	1	13.6	13.3	5	65	1	39	507	1 446	112	1 428
Nuckolls	45	8.5	79	1	14.8	14.7	5	96	1	49	938	1 372	11	204
Otoe	173	11.8	198	1	13.6	7.7	8	54	2	67	453	2 891	323	2 207
Pawnee	24	7.5	54	0	16.9	0.0	3	96	1	17	543	888	49	1 539
Perkins	26	8.1	40	0	12.3	0.0	4	126	1	76	2 397	628	40	1 212
Phelps	124	12.4	118	1	11.8	5.4	9	91	1	55	555	1 812	294	2 956
Pierce	92	11.6	92	1	11.6	10.9	4	51	2	59	746	1 412	67	844

1. Per 1,000 estimated resident population, average 1996–1998.   2. Deaths of infants under 1 year old.   3. Deaths of infants under 1 year old per 1,000 live births.   4. Data subject to copyright.   5. Per 100,000 resident population as of July 1 of the year shown.   6. Data for serious crimes have not been adjusted for underreporting; this may affect comparability between geographic areas and over time.   7. Per 100,000 population estimated by the FBI.

Table B. States and Counties — Crime, Education, Money Income, and Poverty

STATE County	Serious crimes known to police, 1998[1] (cont'd) Rate[2] Violent	Property	Education School enrollment and attainment, 1990 Enrollment[3] Total	Percent private	Attainment[4] (percent) High school graduate or more	Bachelor's degree or more	Local government expenditures, fiscal 1997[5] Total current expenditures (mil dol)	Current expenditures per student (dollars)	Money income 1989 Per capita[6] (dollars)	Households Median Dollars	Percent change, 1979–1989 (constant 1989 dollars)	Percent with $100,000 or more	Income and poverty, 1997 Percent below poverty level Median household income	All persons	Persons under 18	Persons 5–17 in families
	46	47	48	49	50	51	52	53	54	55	56	57	58	59	60	61
NEBRASKA—Cont'd																
Blaine	0	0	167	4.8	85.3	15.8	1.4	8 029	9 681	19 716	12.4	1.5	22 144	14.6	18.2	17.7
Boone	16	1 702	1 612	15.1	76.1	9.4	7.9	5 863	10 062	21 653	18.5	2.0	31 324	12.0	14.8	12.5
Box Butte	208	2 499	3 465	6.8	84.0	13.0	15.2	5 289	11 880	26 493	-13.7	1.3	39 126	11.3	14.3	11.5
Boyd	38	982	619	1.6	72.1	9.9	4.0	6 307	8 979	16 329	4.2	0.9	23 212	13.2	14.9	14.0
Brown	0	1 656	790	3.8	79.8	11.3	5.1	7 322	9 209	17 067	-6.6	0.9	25 684	15.1	20.4	17.0
Buffalo	307	4 097	13 295	4.6	83.3	23.7	42.2	5 889	11 190	23 999	-5.8	2.0	36 296	10.3	12.3	10.0
Burt	59	1 421	1 748	5.0	77.6	13.5	9.0	5 298	10 030	21 061	-0.1	0.9	31 585	10.4	12.6	10.9
Butler	23	1 845	2 058	25.4	72.5	8.0	7.5	5 445	11 662	23 267	2.0	1.1	34 451	8.5	10.4	8.2
Cass	37	1 968	5 762	10.4	82.1	13.6	19.9	5 485	11 792	28 490	0.1	1.5	42 623	7.7	10.3	8.2
Cedar	30	538	2 613	26.5	75.2	10.3	10.5	5 623	8 978	21 014	8.5	1.0	33 078	9.1	11.0	9.5
Chase	47	774	1 080	3.3	79.0	15.1	6.7	6 113	10 011	21 488	4.4	1.1	32 125	11.8	14.7	12.5
Cherry	218	3 096	1 295	3.6	75.2	13.1	6.2	5 351	10 758	18 962	-18.4	3.0	27 326	15.9	19.7	17.7
Cheyenne	115	2 902	2 313	8.3	80.3	15.1	14.5	6 961	11 517	23 400	-7.4	1.5	33 886	11.6	16.5	12.8
Clay	56	1 226	1 752	6.1	76.9	11.7	10.7	6 505	10 511	22 949	-1.0	1.5	34 467	10.6	14.6	11.3
Colfax	123	1 795	2 051	10.2	70.4	8.5	10.5	4 842	10 180	22 140	1.7	1.2	31 357	8.0	10.5	8.6
Cuming	60	749	2 409	31.9	71.5	11.8	9.2	5 428	10 171	21 623	-10.9	1.1	33 874	8.9	11.5	9.4
Custer	49	1 509	2 740	5.0	80.5	10.8	14.3	6 077	11 116	21 440	3.7	2.0	29 595	13.9	18.7	14.6
Dakota	96	3 314	4 330	14.1	74.9	11.7	15.5	4 513	10 635	25 397	-10.2	0.7	35 037	10.3	14.1	11.5
Dawes	55	2 260	3 366	3.4	80.0	23.1	7.8	5 594	9 357	17 784	-17.7	1.2	26 992	17.7	20.7	17.5
Dawson	207	3 497	4 993	2.9	78.8	12.3	25.6	5 012	10 849	22 420	-18.4	1.6	32 285	10.6	15.1	11.1
Deuel	0	1 280	513	1.9	79.2	12.9	4.4	8 205	10 434	21 272	-7.9	1.2	31 843	7.6	9.3	9.0
Dixon	47	1 335	1 388	4.4	76.1	11.0	10.7	8 604	9 074	20 047	0.0	0.5	32 331	8.9	10.4	9.4
Dodge	167	3 334	8 608	18.7	78.3	13.5	37.1	5 815	11 638	24 817	-8.2	1.3	36 298	8.5	11.3	8.9
Douglas	1 119	5 270	116 102	22.0	84.5	24.9	420.4	5 546	14 644	29 857	0.5	3.8	42 260	10.0	14.1	10.7
Dundy	43	1 121	569	2.1	71.3	13.0	2.7	7 383	10 894	21 271	8.5	1.0	30 745	11.1	15.4	12.2
Fillmore	58	998	1 611	7.5	81.4	11.9	9.7	7 119	11 961	23 219	-0.2	1.4	35 954	9.2	12.8	10.4
Franklin	52	1 252	731	2.3	71.1	11.8	4.1	6 820	10 968	20 553	6.3	0.7	27 938	11.9	16.5	14.1
Frontier	NA	NA	819	3.1	81.0	10.5	5.1	6 929	9 611	20 364	-5.3	0.4	30 504	12.9	16.9	14.5
Furnas	37	1 965	1 225	4.5	75.3	12.0	8.6	6 521	9 432	17 949	-1.7	0.6	27 410	12.0	15.5	12.2
Gage	109	4 312	5 041	9.8	73.7	11.3	21.6	6 403	11 099	22 876	-1.9	1.1	32 052	9.8	12.0	10.1
Garden	134	2 151	508	4.3	76.4	13.9	3.7	8 217	10 135	18 614	-12.9	0.3	26 114	9.1	11.5	11.6
Garfield	96	239	447	4.3	73.8	12.9	2.4	5 734	9 043	17 308	-4.6	0.2	26 029	13.8	17.0	15.0
Gosper	0	1 220	425	3.1	79.1	13.9	1.6	6 101	11 738	25 669	16.6	1.1	33 076	5.7	8.1	6.9
Grant	0	813	166	1.2	89.5	14.6	1.8	7 266	10 273	19 063	-8.0	2.9	26 679	8.7	12.9	11.2
Greeley	0	102	825	18.2	78.9	11.5	4.7	7 119	8 595	18 248	16.8	0.4	25 604	12.1	14.8	12.0
Hall	382	7 391	12 047	9.5	79.3	14.6	47.5	5 070	11 526	25 546	-8.7	1.6	35 764	10.2	13.9	10.9
Hamilton	NA	NA	2 206	8.6	79.9	13.0	9.6	5 451	11 103	25 026	-5.3	2.1	38 914	6.9	8.6	7.3
Harlan	53	1 663	769	4.2	80.9	12.9	2.2	5 314	9 721	18 478	-5.2	0.8	27 747	11.1	15.0	12.8
Hayes	0	92	274	2.2	80.6	10.7	1.6	9 349	13 871	20 531	10.8	4.0	29 356	10.0	12.2	11.8
Hitchcock	0	758	918	6.1	80.4	12.1	7.2	12 784	10 689	19 735	-5.1	1.2	26 894	12.8	15.9	14.4
Holt	16	1 142	2 880	16.3	76.1	12.8	12.8	5 597	10 164	20 059	3.5	2.1	29 517	12.9	16.0	13.6
Hooker	0	417	173	4.0	79.5	13.5	1.5	6 673	9 381	18 682	1.9	0.0	24 862	15.3	23.2	17.0
Howard	92	1 583	1 436	6.4	75.2	8.6	8.5	5 256	9 551	21 688	-4.4	0.6	30 893	10.1	13.0	11.0
Jefferson	12	2 742	1 888	7.0	75.1	12.7	12.1	5 976	11 126	21 740	2.1	1.3	31 028	10.4	13.3	11.1
Johnson	NA	NA	1 009	4.7	73.6	8.5	6.3	6 387	11 229	19 925	3.2	1.3	29 246	11.5	14.8	12.4
Kearney	119	2 387	1 504	7.9	80.3	17.9	8.3	5 952	11 751	27 207	5.6	0.8	38 847	7.9	9.7	8.6
Keith	150	3 363	2 029	7.4	81.5	13.1	11.1	7 077	10 771	22 909	-13.7	0.8	32 269	10.3	13.3	10.9
Keya Paha	0	203	216	0.0	76.8	8.1	1.1	5 885	7 907	17 202	-7.4	0.0	20 756	19.1	25.8	21.5
Kimball	124	2 942	953	4.9	73.8	12.7	4.3	5 883	11 105	23 232	-7.9	0.2	31 373	7.3	9.4	9.1
Knox	96	627	2 139	11.2	71.1	8.8	12.9	6 079	9 881	17 877	-1.4	1.7	26 711	15.6	20.1	16.7
Lancaster	506	6 049	67 322	12.9	88.1	27.6	204.3	5 823	13 803	28 900	-1.0	2.5	39 478	9.0	11.5	8.9
Lincoln	208	1 867	8 459	9.6	81.4	14.2	32.5	5 317	12 091	25 915	-15.9	1.3	35 907	11.8	15.7	12.4
Logan	0	111	264	4.2	82.9	13.4	1.6	7 473	9 186	21 250	19.3	1.0	30 037	12.2	15.6	14.5
Loup	0	0	178	6.7	78.3	9.8	1.1	8 007	8 817	17 933	-13.5	0.7	18 136	16.2	23.1	19.0
McPherson	0	179	126	4.0	78.0	9.0	0.7	6 571	10 601	17 500	-18.8	2.3	20 856	15.2	17.9	19.0
Madison	137	3 507	8 863	20.0	78.3	13.2	33.1	4 920	11 054	24 461	-8.8	1.4	36 880	9.0	12.0	9.8
Merrick	61	2 010	1 918	8.5	77.0	11.7	9.2	5 755	10 194	22 518	-11.9	1.8	32 345	9.4	12.1	10.4
Morrill	37	2 076	1 290	3.4	74.1	12.7	6.8	5 818	10 102	19 398	5.2	1.1	27 932	14.6	19.6	16.5
Nance	141	943	1 002	5.2	71.0	10.7	4.7	5 397	8 936	20 742	11.5	0.6	29 499	10.9	15.0	13.0
Nemaha	102	1 326	2 486	2.9	77.2	18.5	10.5	7 913	11 343	22 383	-0.6	1.8	34 185	10.9	13.6	10.8
Nuckolls	0	204	1 277	13.5	74.2	10.1	6.3	6 693	9 862	20 250	-7.4	1.0	28 679	11.4	13.7	11.6
Otoe	55	2 152	3 285	8.9	77.4	13.1	14.6	5 383	10 990	23 189	-4.3	1.0	35 448	8.9	10.7	9.1
Pawnee	63	1 476	658	5.9	75.0	11.1	4.3	6 412	9 316	18 286	9.8	0.1	26 157	13.6	17.9	15.4
Perkins	61	1 151	857	3.9	79.0	16.7	4.8	7 338	9 933	23 132	1.2	0.5	32 473	10.1	11.6	11.0
Phelps	101	2 855	2 266	6.5	85.0	15.5	14.9	7 508	12 837	26 693	4.1	2.8	37 595	8.9	11.9	9.8
Pierce	50	794	1 954	21.9	73.8	9.1	8.1	5 192	10 430	22 293	2.5	1.4	34 408	9.4	10.9	9.6

1. Data for serious crimes have not been adjusted for underreporting; this may affect comparability between geographic areas and over time.   2. Per 100,000 population estimated by the FBI.   3. All persons 3 years old and over enrolled in nursery school through college.   4. Persons 25 years old and over.   5. Elementary and secondary education expenditures, local government fiscal years ending between July 1, 1996 and June 30, 1997.   6. Based on population enumerated as of April 1, 1990.

STATE County	Personal income, 1998												
	Total (mil dol)	Percent change, 1997–1998	Per capita[1] Dollars	Per capita[1] Rank	Wages and salaries[2] (mil dol)	Proprietor's income (mil dol)	Dividends, interest, and rent (mil dol)	Transfer payments Total (mil dol)	Government payments to individuals Total (mil dol)	Social Security (mil dol)	Medical payments (mil dol)	Income maintenance (mil dol)	Unemployment insurance (mil dol)
	62	63	64	65	66	67	68	69	70	71	72	73	74
NEBRASKA—Cont'd													
Blaine	5	10.6	9 358	3 104	5	-3	3	2	1	1	0	0	0
Boone	130	-2.3	20 399	1 595	45	22	37	24	23	11	9	2	0
Box Butte	295	4.1	23 134	830	197	32	56	41	39	16	13	2	1
Boyd	44	-0.2	17 195	2 563	14	7	14	12	12	5	5	1	0
Brown	66	-0.5	18 763	2 132	26	5	22	14	14	7	5	1	0
Buffalo	910	6.4	22 564	966	590	80	178	117	110	50	40	7	1
Burt	170	2.5	21 396	1 266	49	33	39	36	34	17	15	2	0
Butler	183	2.5	21 035	1 379	52	29	48	31	29	15	10	2	0
Cass	610	9.1	24 911	498	120	42	94	72	68	32	26	4	1
Cedar	204	-1.2	21 173	1 337	64	46	50	32	30	16	11	2	0
Chase	111	5.3	26 008	395	38	31	28	17	17	9	6	1	0
Cherry	114	3.5	18 046	2 334	46	6	42	21	20	10	7	1	0
Cheyenne	225	4.0	23 696	704	128	25	47	37	35	18	13	2	0
Clay	165	4.6	23 075	843	77	32	39	27	26	13	10	1	0
Colfax	205	0.9	19 274	1 965	115	29	51	38	36	15	17	2	0
Cuming	274	-1.0	27 462	267	96	93	58	36	34	19	13	2	0
Custer	261	0.7	21 863	1 138	89	54	70	49	47	23	18	3	0
Dakota	384	4.0	20 441	1 577	344	30	61	54	51	23	21	4	0
Dawes	153	7.3	17 293	2 533	75	7	37	33	31	13	10	2	0
Dawson	505	3.2	21 798	1 162	292	73	107	75	71	35	28	4	1
Deuel	47	4.7	23 239	807	14	7	17	9	9	5	3	0	0
Dixon	134	-1.2	21 237	1 311	43	33	24	21	20	10	8	1	0
Dodge	835	4.1	23 662	710	407	70	192	138	132	67	50	6	1
Douglas	14 485	5.3	32 671	94	11 256	1 486	2 863	1 479	1 403	561	599	118	13
Dundy	67	4.6	29 441	183	19	17	22	11	10	5	4	1	0
Fillmore	185	2.8	26 716	328	57	50	54	25	23	13	8	1	0
Franklin	76	6.9	20 425	1 585	18	14	23	17	16	8	6	1	0
Frontier	62	6.4	19 859	1 758	20	13	14	10	10	5	3	1	0
Furnas	115	2.9	21 135	1 349	42	13	35	26	25	12	10	2	0
Gage	550	6.9	24 120	618	232	63	116	131	127	45	72	5	0
Garden	46	2.2	21 802	1 160	17	3	16	10	10	5	4	0	0
Garfield	43	2.6	20 871	1 433	14	7	14	9	8	4	3	0	0
Gosper	46	3.6	19 988	1 715	11	6	14	9	8	5	2	0	0
Grant	9	16.3	11 624	3 090	5	-3	5	2	2	1	1	0	0
Greeley	51	-0.3	17 829	2 398	16	7	18	11	11	5	4	1	0
Hall	1 225	4.3	23 671	709	843	99	257	173	164	74	63	11	2
Hamilton	216	4.2	22 886	874	71	44	51	29	27	15	9	1	0
Harlan	76	5.7	20 656	1 502	22	16	19	16	16	8	5	1	0
Hayes	22	2.8	20 486	1 564	6	5	4	3	3	1	1	0	0
Hitchcock	59	4.3	17 284	2 538	17	5	17	14	13	7	4	1	0
Holt	253	-0.4	21 018	1 384	91	60	63	46	44	20	18	3	0
Hooker	10	5.1	14 155	2 995	6	-4	6	4	4	2	1	0	0
Howard	118	1.6	18 187	2 299	28	20	28	21	20	10	8	1	0
Jefferson	184	6.4	22 029	1 095	74	26	49	35	34	17	12	2	0
Johnson	88	3.7	19 238	1 976	28	11	25	18	18	9	6	1	0
Kearney	173	1.3	25 244	463	54	41	40	27	26	11	12	1	0
Keith	178	4.5	20 511	1 550	79	24	45	33	31	17	10	2	0
Keya Paha	10	-2.7	10 760	3 096	3	0	4	3	3	2	1	0	0
Kimball	84	4.4	20 664	1 498	37	8	24	16	16	9	5	1	0
Knox	178	-1.6	19 374	1 924	59	22	48	43	41	18	18	4	0
Lancaster	6 474	7.0	27 487	266	4 488	440	1 315	673	633	285	236	40	5
Lincoln	762	5.1	22 756	905	472	55	149	128	122	44	41	8	2
Logan	15	2.0	16 765	2 663	4	3	4	3	3	2	1	0	0
Loup	2	-5.7	3 674	3 110	2	-5	3	2	2	1	1	0	0
McPherson	3	-2.6	5 926	3 109	1	-4	3	2	2	1	0	0	0
Madison	824	2.3	23 827	674	548	95	167	116	110	52	43	7	2
Merrick	166	1.6	20 538	1 543	50	33	37	28	27	14	10	2	0
Morrill	93	-1.0	17 228	2 551	30	14	22	20	19	9	7	2	0
Nance	81	0.8	19 664	1 831	19	20	17	17	17	8	7	1	0
Nemaha	200	10.5	26 008	394	127	21	43	31	30	14	12	2	0
Nuckolls	108	6.9	20 783	1 460	35	17	30	25	25	13	10	1	0
Otoe	318	3.9	21 605	1 222	143	29	84	57	54	28	21	3	0
Pawnee	69	7.1	21 968	1 110	15	14	18	15	14	7	5	1	0
Perkins	78	10.4	24 466	564	25	27	17	13	12	7	4	1	0
Phelps	269	4.3	27 140	291	127	63	59	40	38	19	16	2	0
Pierce	162	0.9	20 392	1 605	45	31	37	25	24	12	9	1	0

1. Based on the resident population estimated as of July 1 of the year shown.   2. Includes other labor income.

Table B. States and Counties — Earnings, Social Security, and Housing

STATE County	Total (mil dol)	Farm	Goods-related[1] Total	Manu-facturing	Service-related and other[2] Total	Retail trade	Finance, insurance, and real estate	Services	Govern-ment	Social Security beneficiaries, December 1998 Number	Rate[3]	Supplemental Security Income recipients, December 1998	Housing units, 1990 Total	Percent change, 1980–1990
	75	76	77	78	79	80	81	82	83	84	85	86	87	88
NEBRASKA—Cont'd														
Blaine	1	-252.0	D	D	D	30.7	D	35.1	179.7	92	159	7	381	3.5
Boone	66	25.6	D	3.0	D	9.4	3.9	12.5	23.9	1 487	233	67	2 878	-6.1
Box Butte	230	9.7	10.5	6.6	67.7	5.6	2.5	9.8	12.1	1 972	154	152	5 534	-0.3
Boyd	21	-1.0	D	D	D	8.7	5.4	16.7	28.9	744	290	41	1 538	5.6
Brown	31	-2.2	D	D	D	10.5	6.4	16.9	33.9	940	265	44	1 950	-2.3
Buffalo	669	3.8	24.8	19.0	55.5	14.0	3.4	25.8	15.9	5 878	145	338	14 538	8.2
Burt	82	29.0	10.8	5.9	41.1	6.4	4.3	14.7	19.1	2 077	260	107	3 740	-1.7
Butler	82	27.5	D	16.9	D	5.9	2.1	14.7	18.3	1 938	223	78	3 801	-0.2
Cass	162	10.6	D	8.9	D	9.4	5.0	16.2	18.8	3 688	151	134	8 951	7.6
Cedar	110	29.1	D	8.5	D	5.6	D	14.1	17.9	2 159	224	74	4 149	1.3
Chase	69	36.9	5.1	1.9	40.2	8.7	4.4	9.7	17.8	1 021	240	49	2 011	-4.2
Cherry	53	-1.7	D	1.4	D	18.4	6.5	22.9	26.5	1 336	211	108	3 023	2.0
Cheyenne	152	5.5	16.1	12.4	D	29.5	3.2	D	13.6	2 079	219	136	4 345	-2.9
Clay	109	25.1	D	9.7	D	3.5	D	8.5	24.9	1 554	217	67	3 173	-5.4
Colfax	144	17.1	D	D	D	5.2	2.8	12.5	10.9	1 959	183	71	3 971	-1.8
Cuming	189	39.6	D	11.8	D	6.5	3.1	11.8	9.2	2 338	234	67	4 132	-4.4
Custer	143	26.1	13.2	9.5	43.9	8.2	5.1	17.1	16.8	3 008	250	154	5 728	-7.3
Dakota	373	2.1	D	D	D	6.3	7.6	10.8	7.4	2 773	148	245	6 486	5.8
Dawes	82	-8.6	D	1.0	D	17.6	3.8	24.4	40.9	1 652	184	116	3 909	-1.4
Dawson	365	14.3	D	33.9	D	7.3	2.5	10.8	14.5	4 119	178	255	9 021	-3.7
Deuel	21	14.9	D	D	D	11.2	7.0	13.9	25.2	580	286	26	1 075	-3.8
Dixon	76	33.8	D	D	D	2.8	2.6	7.8	14.0	1 317	209	63	2 613	-8.3
Dodge	477	6.0	D	22.1	D	12.6	4.0	19.3	16.8	7 766	220	328	14 601	2.5
Douglas	12 741	0.1	D	11.3	D	8.1	10.6	32.7	11.6	63 412	143	7 296	172 335	10.7
Dundy	36	43.4	D	D	D	3.6	D	10.9	16.9	594	258	26	1 326	-7.8
Fillmore	106	35.7	9.5	3.1	37.5	5.3	3.5	8.7	17.2	1 586	229	67	3 102	-5.3
Franklin	32	33.0	D	1.3	D	7.0	6.0	12.8	22.9	1 048	281	56	1 950	-5.1
Frontier	34	28.2	D	D	D	5.1	5.6	11.8	26.0	617	200	22	1 565	-12.6
Furnas	55	16.9	D	2.2	D	7.8	4.6	22.7	24.0	1 544	287	100	2 905	-5.7
Gage	294	11.5	D	21.0	D	10.2	3.1	19.1	22.2	5 550	245	428	9 735	-1.8
Garden	20	11.5	D	D	D	15.7	7.1	8.5	36.1	603	282	21	1 343	-4.1
Garfield	21	16.5	D	8.8	D	10.3	3.0	14.2	17.8	585	287	27	1 021	-5.0
Gosper	16	32.3	6.5	0.8	D	6.3	8.5	8.4	25.3	642	276	17	1 212	-3.0
Grant	2	-201.1	D	D	D	33.5	D	51.0	119.3	179	235	6	425	-1.2
Greeley	23	17.8	10.5	4.3	D	6.5	4.9	16.0	26.9	710	249	31	1 284	-9.8
Hall	942	2.0	D	23.9	D	11.7	5.0	20.9	15.2	8 865	171	734	19 528	4.0
Hamilton	115	28.6	D	11.5	D	6.1	3.5	17.1	14.7	1 833	194	55	3 589	-0.4
Harlan	38	30.5	D	D	D	8.5	3.6	12.2	19.0	988	264	41	2 409	13.2
Hayes	11	50.1	D	D	D	3.2	3.4	D	19.5	195	182	7	583	-13.1
Hitchcock	23	14.2	D	D	D	8.6	3.3	6.0	36.4	867	252	48	1 873	7.6
Holt	151	16.1	5.7	2.5	64.4	8.6	3.6	18.5	13.9	2 715	225	205	5 472	1.1
Hooker	2	-198.8	D	0.8	D	25.3	12.3	99.3	91.6	251	358	6	433	-3.6
Howard	47	32.6	D	D	D	11.4	3.9	11.2	23.7	1 361	211	58	2 598	-2.4
Jefferson	100	18.2	D	19.4	D	10.0	3.0	14.4	14.5	2 192	262	124	4 082	-4.4
Johnson	39	11.0	D	D	D	10.8	5.0	16.1	28.3	1 212	266	44	2 153	-2.2
Kearney	95	37.3	10.5	4.6	D	4.4	3.1	14.4	14.4	1 299	190	85	2 756	-2.5
Keith	103	11.5	D	8.5	D	15.9	5.8	21.7	16.2	2 051	237	102	4 938	3.2
Keya Paha	3	-3.6	D	4.2	D	11.1	0.0	D	43.6	236	243	13	584	3.2
Kimball	45	2.8	D	D	D	14.3	3.7	21.1	21.1	1 047	256	48	1 967	-3.2
Knox	81	12.6	D	D	D	10.3	3.7	19.4	29.4	2 539	275	187	4 799	-0.1
Lancaster	4 928	0.4	20.2	14.3	58.1	8.1	8.4	27.1	21.4	31 980	136	3 067	86 734	13.6
Lincoln	527	1.2	D	2.0	D	12.3	3.8	23.1	17.4	5 518	165	567	14 210	-3.7
Logan	7	35.3	D	D	D	8.5	D	8.1	24.4	176	200	12	387	-3.7
Loup	-3	0.0	D	0.0	D	D	D	D	0.0	163	245	9	399	8.7
McPherson	-2	0.0	D	0.0	D	0.0	0.0	0.0	0.0	123	218	10	257	-2.7
Madison	643	3.4	D	22.7	D	10.1	3.1	20.7	15.3	6 282	182	488	13 069	6.0
Merrick	83	30.8	D	3.7	D	6.1	4.9	12.1	18.3	1 776	221	102	3 533	-2.0
Morrill	45	23.4	D	1.7	D	6.8	D	12.0	28.2	1 139	209	80	2 530	-2.4
Nance	39	37.1	D	0.9	D	5.0	4.9	13.9	23.0	1 015	248	78	1 807	-8.6
Nemaha	148	8.3	14.4	9.8	23.8	4.3	2.2	11.4	53.5	1 691	220	112	3 432	-1.9
Nuckolls	52	13.7	D	0.9	D	10.5	5.1	28.4	19.5	1 547	296	63	2 699	-6.9
Otoe	172	6.2	D	23.6	D	11.1	4.1	17.7	19.9	3 299	223	151	6 137	-2.9
Pawnee	29	31.8	D	10.1	D	6.8	3.3	15.2	22.7	976	312	60	1 674	-6.9
Perkins	52	39.3	D	2.0	D	4.0	2.2	10.9	17.3	742	234	22	1 537	-1.4
Phelps	190	28.8	21.7	17.1	37.8	5.7	3.4	15.2	11.8	2 075	209	98	4 084	0.0
Pierce	76	23.1	12.6	1.6	D	8.1	3.7	17.9	17.0	1 587	201	64	3 177	-1.9

1. Covers mining, construction, and manufacturing. 2. Covers private sector earnings in agricultural services, forestry, and fisheries; transportation and public utilities; wholesale trade; retail trade; finance, insurance, and real estate; and services. 3. Per 1,000 resident population estimated as of July 1 of the year shown.

STATE County	Housing units, 1990 (cont'd)								Civilian labor force, 1999				Civilian employment, 1990[5]		
	Occupied units										Unemployment			Percent	
			Owner-occupied			Renter-occupied									
				Owner cost as a percent of income											
	Total	Percent	Median value[1]	With a mortgage	Without a mortgage	Median rent[2]	Rent as percent of income	Substandard units[3] (percent)	Total	Percent change, 1998–1999	Total	Rate[4]	Total	Professional, managerial, and technical	Precision production, craft, and repair
	89	90	91	92	93	94	95	96	97	98	99	100	101	102	103
NEBRASKA—Cont'd															
Blaine	268	64.6	22 300	16.7	14.7	150	10.0	2.3	370	2.8	9	2.4	358	16.8	6.7
Boone	2 560	73.1	30 500	16.6	13.0	226	17.2	0.9	2 943	3.2	81	2.8	2 897	16.4	11.2
Box Butte	4 898	67.9	44 000	16.3	12.6	283	21.9	2.9	6 503	-0.9	317	4.9	5 869	16.6	14.0
Boyd	1 148	79.3	16 800	16.4	14.6	224	16.8	2.0	1 113	1.8	41	3.7	1 108	17.9	6.9
Brown	1 499	73.6	29 400	21.8	13.7	263	23.0	1.5	1 781	2.2	73	4.1	1 586	19.0	10.2
Buffalo	13 736	61.8	49 500	19.2	13.3	320	25.0	1.8	24 425	1.0	787	3.2	19 558	23.5	10.4
Burt	3 139	71.1	29 600	15.8	13.0	247	22.9	1.1	3 473	-2.4	157	4.5	3 301	18.7	12.5
Butler	3 253	75.2	30 200	19.2	12.3	279	20.2	2.6	4 191	-0.4	123	2.9	3 813	18.1	11.1
Cass	7 797	76.7	48 200	21.5	12.6	345	21.8	1.6	12 734	0.5	320	2.5	9 877	21.4	13.4
Cedar	3 652	76.9	31 100	17.5	12.9	222	17.0	1.8	4 645	-2.1	128	2.8	4 485	15.3	10.7
Chase	1 704	74.9	38 000	20.6	13.6	270	19.2	1.5	1 952	3.0	41	2.1	1 880	18.1	10.1
Cherry	2 438	63.5	35 500	18.9	13.3	266	23.4	3.9	3 425	4.6	77	2.2	2 955	16.6	7.6
Cheyenne	3 851	70.4	35 700	15.8	12.0	277	21.1	2.2	5 194	1.0	136	2.6	4 616	20.8	10.9
Clay	2 741	75.8	28 100	15.5	12.6	254	20.0	1.0	3 487	1.2	85	2.4	3 137	20.1	9.8
Colfax	3 562	75.9	34 300	15.8	13.2	258	18.8	2.3	4 808	-4.1	119	2.5	4 193	15.8	15.7
Cuming	3 851	71.7	38 500	17.1	12.4	266	18.7	1.2	5 325	3.0	114	2.1	4 755	15.9	8.7
Custer	4 953	71.0	27 900	15.1	12.0	234	21.3	1.9	5 456	0.5	124	2.3	5 579	17.9	9.3
Dakota	6 035	68.3	43 700	17.9	12.9	348	23.1	4.0	10 179	-2.0	298	2.9	8 147	18.9	16.8
Dawes	3 327	63.1	33 400	15.1	13.7	291	30.3	2.3	4 617	-0.8	190	4.1	3 913	26.9	8.8
Dawson	7 829	69.7	40 800	18.2	12.3	291	21.7	1.7	13 125	1.0	397	3.0	9 672	18.5	11.3
Deuel	915	74.0	28 800	15.7	13.0	246	21.1	2.2	861	-3.4	33	3.8	986	16.7	12.0
Dixon	2 338	74.2	27 100	15.7	13.0	237	18.4	1.8	2 418	-1.9	70	2.9	2 798	16.9	12.5
Dodge	13 445	67.6	42 800	17.8	12.8	311	22.6	1.3	19 111	-1.7	565	3.0	16 481	20.5	13.2
Douglas	161 113	62.7	59 900	20.4	12.7	393	24.8	2.0	254 368	-0.7	7 198	2.8	211 964	32.5	8.9
Dundy	1 085	69.5	23 600	20.2	12.6	229	17.9	0.8	1 081	0.2	22	2.0	1 202	20.5	6.0
Fillmore	2 829	74.6	30 900	19.3	12.5	272	19.4	0.9	3 147	2.8	77	2.4	3 187	18.6	11.2
Franklin	1 655	78.9	19 300	17.7	12.7	231	17.2	1.1	1 604	-0.3	43	2.7	1 617	19.2	9.4
Frontier	1 206	71.8	25 100	14.8	13.2	231	19.3	1.2	1 498	-1.2	43	2.9	1 489	17.0	5.3
Furnas	2 334	75.9	19 900	18.4	13.0	208	20.6	1.7	2 498	-1.0	70	2.8	2 352	19.0	9.1
Gage	9 019	70.7	36 600	17.1	12.0	280	21.5	1.4	12 273	-2.1	368	3.0	10 837	19.7	12.3
Garden	1 040	68.7	30 700	18.0	12.7	230	18.8	1.1	1 079	3.1	27	2.5	1 148	19.3	5.5
Garfield	864	71.6	24 000	19.6	12.5	212	19.3	2.2	964	-5.6	21	2.2	1 003	16.1	10.7
Gosper	764	77.2	40 300	17.5	11.4	280	17.0	2.2	1 359	2.6	23	1.7	977	18.0	9.5
Grant	303	63.4	25 900	19.2	12.9	245	22.2	0.6	386	6.0	9	2.3	372	17.2	7.5
Greeley	1 133	78.5	19 200	18.3	12.8	209	16.5	2.4	1 392	-7.9	53	3.8	1 370	18.8	9.3
Hall	18 678	63.6	48 200	17.7	12.6	319	22.6	2.0	31 023	-0.3	1 038	3.3	24 542	22.7	12.0
Hamilton	3 235	69.4	41 400	17.9	12.4	296	19.4	2.3	5 374	-0.5	117	2.2	4 267	20.6	11.6
Harlan	1 585	77.7	28 400	20.3	13.6	262	22.6	0.6	1 761	1.7	52	3.0	1 768	17.3	9.6
Hayes	480	70.4	19 600	13.2	13.4	235	17.5	1.1	469	-5.6	18	3.8	495	15.2	3.6
Hitchcock	1 467	75.5	22 700	18.1	12.2	250	15.9	1.5	1 614	3.0	38	2.4	1 588	17.8	8.4
Holt	4 744	69.9	35 200	19.7	13.5	261	20.4	2.8	6 675	4.8	197	3.0	5 754	19.0	8.7
Hooker	332	76.8	26 300	18.5	13.0	223	16.1	1.7	435	12.1	11	2.5	358	20.1	7.8
Howard	2 309	74.4	31 600	15.9	12.9	236	17.3	2.2	3 472	-0.9	117	3.4	2 729	15.8	10.7
Jefferson	3 634	76.2	19 400	15.5	12.3	257	18.7	2.1	3 951	-0.6	122	3.1	4 140	19.5	12.4
Johnson	1 940	76.4	25 900	16.3	12.4	247	21.4	2.7	2 169	16.1	89	4.1	2 201	18.4	17.6
Kearney	2 523	72.2	42 500	17.5	12.6	307	20.0	1.1	3 665	2.6	84	2.3	3 107	23.8	9.3
Keith	3 430	69.7	41 500	21.7	12.7	285	21.9	1.3	4 583	2.7	134	2.9	4 311	19.1	10.2
Keya Paha	419	70.9	17 500	12.5	13.3	183	15.2	1.2	472	7.5	13	2.8	493	8.9	5.7
Kimball	1 650	74.5	35 300	18.1	11.6	289	19.1	2.5	1 947	-1.3	37	1.9	1 881	18.3	14.8
Knox	3 817	73.4	24 900	18.5	14.1	202	20.2	2.1	4 730	0.9	169	3.6	4 104	16.6	8.2
Lancaster	82 759	60.5	62 200	18.9	11.9	378	25.6	1.4	142 384	-0.4	3 397	2.4	117 484	32.7	9.5
Lincoln	12 676	67.9	42 900	16.4	11.8	288	23.9	1.7	17 159	-6.9	572	3.3	14 962	21.0	13.5
Logan	320	66.6	29 200	28.8	12.3	282	16.4	3.5	433	-8.5	10	2.3	392	19.6	7.1
Loup	276	72.8	14 999	27.5	11.9	182	12.6	3.3	388	2.9	9	2.3	329	13.4	5.5
McPherson	212	63.7	30 600	10.0	11.5	179	28.8	7.0	304	-5.9	3	1.0	272	9.2	5.5
Madison	12 283	65.4	48 000	19.6	12.8	307	22.7	2.1	19 691	-4.2	851	4.3	16 235	21.0	13.0
Merrick	3 061	73.0	33 200	17.8	12.4	266	17.9	1.3	4 551	-2.6	108	2.4	3 853	17.1	11.2
Morrill	2 083	68.4	28 400	16.7	13.5	272	22.7	2.2	2 762	2.1	109	3.9	2 390	16.4	9.4
Nance	1 585	76.3	24 300	16.0	12.8	235	18.9	1.2	1 696	-0.8	56	3.3	1 914	16.8	8.8
Nemaha	3 079	69.3	33 500	16.8	13.1	255	21.1	1.6	3 831	-6.6	175	4.6	3 679	26.1	9.6
Nuckolls	2 359	78.7	22 000	16.0	12.8	219	22.0	2.2	2 266	0.5	50	2.2	2 431	16.8	10.8
Otoe	5 657	71.5	38 800	15.3	12.7	296	21.6	2.2	7 583	-1.9	237	3.1	6 735	20.5	12.1
Pawnee	1 408	80.8	14 999	17.9	13.3	190	23.9	3.1	1 603	6.2	48	3.0	1 491	17.4	11.2
Perkins	1 283	77.5	36 600	16.9	12.8	301	16.8	1.3	1 481	0.4	40	2.7	1 438	17.9	9.1
Phelps	3 769	71.9	39 700	16.3	11.4	284	19.6	1.2	4 958	-1.8	108	2.2	4 881	19.8	11.6
Pierce	2 929	76.6	34 200	17.0	14.4	244	17.7	2.0	3 933	-3.0	122	3.1	3 440	17.7	13.0

1. Specified owner-occupied units.   2. Specified renter-occupied units.   3. Overcrowded or lacking complete plumbing facilities.   4. Percent of civilian labor force.   5. Persons 16 years and older.

Table B. States and Counties — Nonfarm Employment and Agriculture

STATE County	Number of establishments	Total	Health Care and Social Assistance	Manufacturing	Retail trade	Finance and Insurance	Professional Scientific and Technical Services	Total (mil dol)	Average per employee (dollars)	Number	Less than 50 acres	500 acres and over	Whose principal occupation is farming (percent)
	104	105	106	107	108	109	110	111	112	113	114	115	116
NEBRASKA—Cont'd													
Blaine	13	D	0	D	D	D	D	D	D	118	10.2	72.0	88.1
Boone	201	1 530	348	62	303	76	22	27	17 576	767	9.8	38.1	75.6
Box Butte	374	3 539	513	490	708	197	90	62	17 583	508	6.5	61.0	73.4
Boyd	77	424	140	D	66	35	16	6	14 042	361	9.7	54.3	70.9
Brown	148	791	161	D	198	67	D	12	14 794	349	14.3	56.7	63.9
Buffalo	1 269	19 485	3 165	4 271	3 995	642	413	422	21 670	1 081	16.1	39.0	67.9
Burt	221	1 199	220	73	226	D	63	22	18 055	580	14.7	35.5	70.9
Butler	183	1 674	320	511	200	75	34	32	19 389	804	13.4	32.6	68.7
Cass	495	3 593	398	292	704	179	66	76	21 131	694	22.6	28.2	62.7
Cedar	287	1 779	173	325	304	104	38	33	18 336	971	12.5	33.5	72.5
Chase	135	1 014	155	D	298	80	14	18	17 800	374	7.2	68.4	70.3
Cherry	246	1 496	258	D	422	81	D	25	16 444	672	9.2	75.7	79.8
Cheyenne	328	3 778	429	442	1 035	165	55	82	21 628	645	4.7	62.8	73.6
Clay	203	1 237	179	67	205	D	D	23	18 520	538	14.9	46.5	75.8
Colfax	277	3 732	365	D	384	113	D	78	20 791	604	20.4	28.3	69.2
Cuming	362	3 123	416	756	478	165	59	59	19 027	995	19.8	23.7	74.4
Custer	374	2 533	638	D	580	137	68	44	17 188	1 307	13.4	57.3	71.3
Dakota	456	12 422	334	5 129	893	941	127	327	26 297	289	13.8	27.7	57.8
Dawes	293	2 282	319	D	706	83	65	32	13 911	471	10.0	59.2	66.7
Dawson	704	9 253	905	3 886	1 447	290	165	193	20 839	858	16.2	45.1	73.8
Deuel	82	451	16	0	199	39	D	7	16 534	251	5.6	62.9	66.1
Dixon	128	639	223	D	106	58	3	9	14 504	583	14.9	27.8	67.2
Dodge	1 068	13 651	1 921	3 478	2 380	451	341	289	21 156	798	19.7	29.1	68.4
Douglas	13 789	293 617	34 664	29 425	35 074	24 410	14 736	8 828	30 066	368	37.0	19.3	51.4
Dundy	73	469	173	D	77	17	21	8	17 437	323	6.8	68.7	77.1
Fillmore	238	1 640	324	90	231	116	15	33	20 279	584	9.8	50.5	82.0
Franklin	104	539	192	D	99	47	37	8	15 434	430	10.5	48.8	74.0
Frontier	88	504	77	D	74	D	D	9	17 048	362	8.3	68.8	79.6
Furnas	177	1 335	360	51	287	72	55	26	19 103	432	10.6	55.3	74.8
Gage	687	7 411	1 386	1 750	1 336	226	110	137	18 425	1 144	16.3	34.4	65.1
Garden	61	388	D	0	88	35	8	6	14 930	308	7.1	61.0	72.1
Garfield	86	519	D	60	137	D	22	7	14 017	206	11.2	51.0	68.0
Gosper	54	176	D	D	12	36	D	3	15 523	252	6.7	58.3	83.3
Grant	24	99	0	0	27	D	D	2	21 202	88	14.8	76.1	77.3
Greeley	85	428	53	D	123	D	D	7	15 696	387	8.8	49.1	74.7
Hall	1 845	26 442	3 231	6 143	4 874	1 272	488	598	22 627	702	20.8	32.3	65.2
Hamilton	275	2 526	265	737	283	113	D	55	21 819	661	11.3	43.9	75.0
Harlan	96	556	150	D	108	40	D	8	14 059	371	11.9	52.3	70.1
Hayes	21	63	D	D	D	D	D	1	15 841	257	5.8	63.8	74.7
Hitchcock	62	281	D	0	89	D	D	5	19 480	339	8.6	65.2	77.0
Holt	424	2 867	561	157	603	157	65	47	16 233	1 291	12.3	54.0	68.3
Hooker	35	179	D	D	45	D	0	3	17 916	88	4.5	76.1	73.9
Howard	156	854	180	15	245	66	21	14	15 930	646	12.4	34.2	71.8
Jefferson	251	2 678	312	663	461	86	41	49	18 136	626	11.2	37.2	67.4
Johnson	134	778	198	D	189	63	D	11	14 451	491	9.8	29.7	62.9
Kearney	192	1 623	548	103	157	81	14	28	17 097	492	10.4	52.4	80.3
Keith	375	2 989	443	412	621	163	88	50	16 859	375	10.1	51.7	69.1
Keya Paha	22	D	0	D	12	0	D	D	D	225	3.1	79.6	85.8
Kimball	161	1 390	88	330	205	59	26	23	16 786	326	4.9	71.8	64.1
Knox	285	1 481	337	D	408	111	D	20	13 274	1 053	12.2	40.2	73.5
Lancaster	6 696	117 339	16 922	15 368	15 904	9 423	8 069	2 928	24 955	1 457	32.3	19.1	46.0
Lincoln	969	9 691	1 625	359	2 181	476	286	181	18 638	1 019	15.8	52.4	61.1
Logan	15	D	0	D	15	D	0	D	D	124	8.9	58.1	86.3
Loup	8	D	0	0	D	D	0	D	D	143	7.0	60.1	79.7
McPherson	7	D	0	0	D	0	0	D	D	112	7.1	80.4	81.2
Madison	1 319	19 313	2 760	5 262	3 231	490	356	414	21 425	782	19.8	30.7	65.5
Merrick	237	1 948	319	332	351	68	36	37	19 076	553	13.6	37.4	70.0
Morrill	117	806	131	D	177	40	D	14	17 390	474	12.0	53.2	71.7
Nance	115	490	138	D	106	49	14	7	14 822	419	13.6	41.5	76.6
Nemaha	198	1 687	306	D	313	81	38	31	18 231	483	9.7	36.9	67.9
Nuckolls	189	1 270	395	D	278	78	40	19	14 733	496	9.9	51.0	69.8
Otoe	445	4 583	754	1 368	741	198	73	88	19 303	821	19.2	29.2	67.6
Pawnee	81	456	115	D	42	39	26	7	15 175	444	8.3	33.6	61.3
Perkins	110	771	194	15	116	39	D	14	18 567	490	4.3	59.4	73.3
Phelps	343	3 888	767	955	526	189	91	85	21 915	552	11.8	50.5	82.8
Pierce	212	1 440	305	52	348	89	23	25	17 354	717	14.6	31.9	67.1

Table B. States and Counties — Agriculture, Land, and Water

STATE County	Acreage (1,000)	Percent change, 1992–1997	Average size of farm	Total irrigated (1,000)	Total cropland (1,000)	Average per farm ($1,000)	Average per acre (dollars)	Value of machinery and equipment Average per farm ($1,000)	Total (mil dol)	Average per farm (dollars)	Crops	Live-stock and poultry products	$10,000 or more	$100,000 or more	Percent of land owned by Fed. Gov. 1997	Water consumption 1995 (mil gal/day)
	117	118	119	120	121	122	123	124	125	126	127	128	129	130	131	132
NEBRASKA—Cont'd																
Blaine	452	-1.9	3 831	9	44	757	196	58	16	138 027	11.0	89.0	78.0	34.7	2.3	29.5
Boone	448	2.3	584	129	317	511	952	85	164	213 762	33.7	66.3	85.5	38.9	0.0	87.6
Box Butte	697	7.2	1 371	136	389	528	347	107	151	296 892	40.8	59.2	76.4	36.8	0.0	171.1
Boyd	297	0.2	822	5	113	272	307	62	31	85 106	33.5	66.5	80.9	21.9	0.0	4.4
Brown	701	7.8	2 008	52	133	726	364	68	87	250 341	18.1	81.9	75.4	32.1	0.2	19.4
Buffalo	621	5.7	575	208	380	535	941	83	159	146 671	51.7	48.3	76.1	36.3	0.0	207.5
Burt	292	8.3	504	38	264	646	1 371	88	113	194 000	53.7	46.3	79.0	44.1	0.0	46.3
Butler	354	5.2	440	95	307	476	1 178	82	102	127 451	65.8	34.2	75.9	34.5	0.0	100.6
Cass	301	1.5	433	D	255	663	1 576	74	67	96 772	83.8	16.2	70.5	30.7	0.0	16.2
Cedar	445	3.8	459	63	359	444	925	84	154	158 153	31.9	68.1	81.2	40.6	0.1	52.9
Chase	557	6.8	1 488	168	317	1 048	756	121	104	278 593	68.6	31.4	84.0	54.3	0.1	180.1
Cherry	3 882	-0.2	5 777	44	395	1 153	200	84	100	149 226	7.7	92.3	80.1	36.2	5.3	98.9
Cheyenne	779	1.0	1 208	48	559	541	434	92	111	172 597	34.1	65.9	79.8	23.3	0.0	66.2
Clay	365	2.1	678	182	288	831	1 229	111	171	317 096	43.8	56.2	83.8	54.3	11.1	198.3
Colfax	230	0.6	381	52	203	479	1 417	86	179	295 749	25.1	74.9	82.3	38.7	0.0	60.2
Cuming	360	3.9	361	32	313	549	1 571	73	507	509 501	11.8	88.2	86.3	43.8	0.0	43.8
Custer	1 552	8.9	1 188	199	486	547	444	67	289	220 766	26.4	73.6	78.3	33.7	0.0	241.2
Dakota	142	2.9	492	12	120	504	1 015	75	29	100 188	80.9	19.1	64.7	26.0	0.5	20.7
Dawes	822	-2.4	1 745	16	198	460	266	50	28	59 863	27.0	73.0	66.0	13.8	8.1	43.2
Dawson	650	-1.4	757	219	354	625	859	84	399	465 589	22.4	77.6	82.3	45.1	0.0	332.6
Deuel	282	6.2	1 122	16	231	538	497	88	21	83 956	73.9	26.1	79.7	24.3	0.0	43.1
Dixon	243	-0.2	416	16	194	352	868	59	117	200 988	24.0	76.0	74.1	29.3	0.0	42.6
Dodge	323	8.1	405	93	295	664	1 654	96	141	176 815	51.0	49.0	82.2	40.1	0.0	100.7
Douglas	113	17.5	306	16	92	676	2 261	93	44	119 956	56.4	43.6	57.3	23.9	0.3	363.9
Dundy	591	11.7	1 830	85	217	849	480	110	87	268 209	46.3	53.7	83.0	47.1	0.0	102.7
Fillmore	357	5.0	611	195	326	842	1 383	114	142	242 554	62.0	38.0	90.2	56.5	0.7	163.2
Franklin	351	8.6	816	87	192	632	812	90	56	129 496	66.9	33.1	80.5	39.5	0.5	99.6
Frontier	531	1.0	1 467	55	226	686	480	86	76	208 946	36.2	63.8	82.0	42.0	1.9	76.2
Furnas	450	4.5	1 042	54	279	514	539	89	77	177 901	50.1	49.9	83.8	39.8	0.2	73.6
Gage	519	2.0	454	48	410	394	899	71	115	100 326	55.1	44.9	75.1	29.1	0.0	42.2
Garden	1 078	0.7	3 499	38	197	890	252	76	58	186 855	24.4	75.6	78.2	33.1	4.0	58.0
Garfield	308	-8.9	1 495	13	67	446	326	51	29	140 121	14.4	85.6	76.7	26.2	0.1	103.3
Gosper	234	1.8	929	68	127	560	577	99	52	204 972	51.1	48.9	85.7	45.6	0.4	164.9
Grant	477	-12.7	5 419	1	41	1 087	201	67	11	127 084	5.6	94.4	77.3	40.9	0.0	3.7
Greeley	291	-4.3	752	58	124	483	646	77	46	119 946	40.4	59.6	80.6	35.9	0.5	44.5
Hall	342	8.0	488	175	258	733	1 449	106	146	208 512	47.1	52.9	74.9	38.7	3.4	169.6
Hamilton	344	7.0	520	238	310	869	1 626	127	149	225 844	64.4	35.6	88.2	58.1	0.6	224.9
Harlan	325	6.4	877	76	219	554	721	103	83	223 006	41.9	58.1	77.1	40.2	2.4	122.0
Hayes	426	6.1	1 659	35	173	926	591	77	68	265 256	26.9	73.1	82.1	38.5	0.0	61.5
Hitchcock	406	0.6	1 198	29	239	654	465	118	34	99 410	66.8	33.2	83.2	33.3	1.4	49.5
Holt	1 464	5.5	1 134	209	618	554	547	98	246	190 607	35.1	64.9	77.8	30.2	0.0	168.0
Hooker	371	-0.9	4 221	3	20	667	158	29	9	97 062	1.6	98.4	80.7	30.7	0.0	6.1
Howard	330	1.5	511	111	210	405	828	73	116	179 093	32.7	67.3	79.9	31.9	1.6	42.3
Jefferson	315	-3.6	503	55	238	457	916	72	77	122 997	54.5	45.5	75.7	30.4	0.0	41.2
Johnson	197	5.3	401	10	146	306	826	48	30	60 289	59.4	40.6	66.8	20.2	0.0	8.4
Kearney	320	3.2	650	189	267	852	1 366	148	197	399 506	43.2	56.8	85.2	57.7	0.8	167.7
Keith	607	-9.3	1 618	78	254	684	422	97	103	274 101	32.0	68.0	75.7	35.7	0.0	122.7
Keya Paha	500	12.0	2 221	11	104	596	275	58	27	120 633	16.1	83.9	86.2	27.1	0.0	9.1
Kimball	565	11.9	1 734	25	339	468	286	74	23	70 197	60.8	39.2	66.9	19.9	0.0	38.6
Knox	596	-2.8	566	38	327	294	497	70	165	156 379	17.1	82.9	78.5	27.0	0.2	51.3
Lancaster	421	1.5	289	13	344	400	1 410	51	82	56 545	72.4	27.6	51.6	17.4	1.4	21.0
Lincoln	1 420	-2.0	1 394	196	434	737	494	72	192	188 732	36.6	63.4	74.0	33.1	0.0	1 086.3
Logan	323	-3.9	2 605	15	58	646	250	74	19	154 087	33.9	66.1	83.9	43.5	0.0	19.9
Loup	339	2.8	2 372	11	39	639	254	56	15	104 425	17.2	82.8	82.5	25.9	0.0	35.9
McPherson	443	-4.7	3 958	7	36	705	178	41	14	124 563	7.2	92.8	80.4	31.2	0.0	8.9
Madison	329	2.3	421	79	275	467	1 082	92	116	148 042	44.9	55.1	72.6	30.6	0.0	68.7
Merrick	274	-5.9	495	163	220	603	1 255	94	163	295 044	36.0	64.0	82.6	43.4	0.0	125.2
Morrill	861	18.9	1 816	117	232	658	363	72	148	311 459	24.6	75.4	79.1	36.9	0.0	116.0
Nance	244	3.1	583	60	165	440	787	84	67	158 869	46.5	53.5	85.7	38.9	0.0	39.3
Nemaha	239	5.8	495	4	202	586	1 148	67	56	116 127	64.2	35.8	79.5	30.2	0.0	636.9
Nuckolls	327	-1.7	660	50	228	426	766	78	54	109 156	70.5	29.5	83.7	36.5	0.0	54.0
Otoe	354	8.7	432	4	276	400	973	70	71	86 677	67.7	32.3	72.1	26.4	0.0	308.3
Pawnee	230	2.5	517	D	145	328	685	43	28	63 133	50.9	49.1	63.3	18.0	0.0	2.4
Perkins	553	3.7	1 128	120	446	606	521	97	65	132 353	83.1	16.9	76.3	34.9	0.0	141.1
Phelps	379	0.7	686	224	302	876	1 376	165	336	609 402	25.5	74.5	89.7	63.2	1.2	337.6
Pierce	309	4.0	431	92	258	416	945	82	108	150 820	42.2	57.8	79.6	36.7	0.0	78.4

Table B. States and Counties — **Residential Construction, Wholesale and Retail Trade, and Real Estate**

STATE County	Value of Residential Construction Authorized by Building Permits, 1999		Wholesale Trade, 1997				Retail Trade[1], 1997				Real Estate and Rental and Leasing, 1997			
	New Construction ($1,000)	Number of Housing Units	Number of Establishments	Number of Employees	Sales (mil dol)	Annual Payroll (mil dol)	Number of Establishments	Number of Employees	Sales (mil dol)	Annual Payroll (mil dol)	Number of Establishments	Number of Employees	Receipts (mil dol)	Annual Payroll (mil dol)
	133	134	135	136	137	138	139	140	141	142	143	144	145	146
NEBRASKA—Cont'd														
Blaine	NA	NA	3	D	D	D	4	7	0.9	0.1	NA	NA	NA	NA
Boone	1 168	10	21	200	164.8	4.2	49	334	60.5	5.2	4	8	0.6	0.1
Box Butte	230	2	24	250	84.0	6.1	72	698	107.3	9.7	16	31	1.4	0.3
Boyd	0	0	6	D	D	D	15	62	7.9	0.6	2	D	D	D
Brown	277	4	9	D	D	D	30	191	28.8	2.5	1	D	D	D
Buffalo	29 036	271	68	915	589.2	22.5	239	3 234	455.3	48.7	43	155	14.8	1.8
Burt	2 362	33	18	129	52.2	3.8	51	241	49.2	3.7	4	10	0.4	0.1
Butler	961	9	13	D	D	D	25	210	23.3	2.4	2	D	D	D
Cass	17 892	200	28	D	D	D	77	740	113.5	8.8	15	41	4.0	0.6
Cedar	779	8	24	154	79.8	3.2	51	308	62.9	4.3	6	15	0.7	0.2
Chase	1 189	13	19	222	118.5	5.4	35	240	44.8	3.7	1	D	D	D
Cherry	1 048	15	13	51	37.2	1.2	49	399	60.7	5.8	3	D	D	D
Cheyenne	4 031	47	18	D	D	D	61	964	649.8	22.2	7	34	0.9	0.2
Clay	2 015	20	19	185	100.2	4.1	40	202	43.9	2.9	4	8	0.2	0.15
Colfax	868	10	23	207	81.4	4.5	51	383	76.3	5.9	5	8	0.3	0.1
Cuming	1 546	13	24	D	D	D	60	466	97.8	6.7	7	17	1.8	0.2
Custer	302	3	19	142	74.3	2.7	83	534	81.2	6.7	8	16	1.6	0.1
Dakota	6 116	100	30	D	D	D	80	878	105.0	11.5	16	D	D	D
Dawes	463	8	16	D	D	D	61	663	81.4	6.7	12	26	1.2	0.1
Dawson	1 656	21	46	504	306.3	11.4	149	1 401	185.4	18.9	19	70	4.2	0.6
Deuel	402	3	5	D	D	D	15	136	24.6	1.6	1	D	D	D
Dixon	791	10	9	80	47.1	1.7	16	97	23.5	1.4	1	D	D	D
Dodge	11 673	150	71	748	587.7	21.1	185	2 313	479.8	37.8	37	172	13.5	2.4
Douglas	232 509	2 751	1 039	17 083	11 542.8	574.0	1 931	34 920	5 634.5	591.7	574	4 411	553.6	106.0
Dundy	115	1	5	D	D	D	17	84	15.7	1.4	3	5	0.3	0.0
Fillmore	460	3	21	170	83.0	4.5	38	229	30.5	2.5	4	9	0.2	0.1
Franklin	733	4	7	43	20.9	0.9	23	97	13.0	1.2	NA	NA	NA	NA
Frontier	467	6	7	D	D	D	17	78	6.3	0.6	NA	NA	NA	NA
Furnas	285	4	11	D	D	D	41	285	55.2	4.0	1	D	D	D
Gage	4 031	57	46	277	148.3	6.6	153	1 310	190.1	15.8	20	98	3.8	0.9
Garden	60	1	4	D	D	D	15	80	9.6	0.9	NA	NA	NA	NA
Garfield	0	0	3	D	D	D	26	135	33.0	1.8	2	D	D	D
Gosper	862	7	4	D	D	D	5	17	2.0	0.1	NA	NA	NA	NA
Grant	NA	NA	2	D	D	D	6	41	2.9	0.4	NA	NA	NA	NA
Greeley	275	2	7	D	D	D	19	111	32.8	1.9	1	D	D	D
Hall	15 624	154	116	1 534	690.4	41.5	347	4 646	722.1	69.2	61	178	22.4	3.3
Hamilton	3 305	33	26	376	208.8	8.1	35	302	39.9	4.2	10	21	0.9	0.3
Harlan	440	8	7	D	D	D	20	103	17.0	1.3	NA	NA	NA	NA
Hayes	78	1	2	D	D	D	1	D	D	D	1	D	D	D
Hitchcock	94	1	7	D	D	D	14	93	18.2	1.3	1	D	D	D
Holt	1 398	11	40	341	166.2	4.7	95	610	99.6	7.5	6	17	1.3	0.1
Hooker	0	0	1	D	D	D	8	43	4.1	0.5	NA	NA	NA	NA
Howard	2 212	25	7	54	30.7	1.7	38	210	25.1	2.8	2	D	D	D
Jefferson	0	0	22	246	144.3	5.7	51	448	60.6	6.1	7	34	0.8	0.2
Johnson	1 124	17	7	71	29.0	1.1	34	196	29.1	2.6	4	8	0.3	0.0
Kearney	640	8	11	131	135.3	3.8	28	166	24.2	2.1	3	5	0.2	0.0
Keith	3 672	34	24	213	190.6	4.8	75	669	97.8	9.6	8	11	0.9	0.2
Keya Paha	NA	NA	3	D	D	D	6	12	2.1	0.2	1	D	D	D
Kimball	80	1	10	D	D	D	30	183	21.1	2.1	2	D	D	D
Knox	442	5	17	D	D	D	73	373	61.3	4.5	4	12	0.3	0.1
Lancaster	180 207	1 686	304	D	D	D	996	15 734	2 270.4	232.0	267	1 480	150.3	25.4
Lincoln	14 744	139	56	461	259.7	11.9	198	2 107	314.5	28.9	31	100	7.7	1.3
Logan	NA	NA	NA	NA	NA	NA	2	D	D	D	NA	NA	NA	NA
Loup	0	0	NA	NA	NA	NA	3	D	D	D	NA	NA	NA	NA
McPherson	NA	NA	2	D	D	D	2	D	D	D	NA	NA	NA	NA
Madison	12 985	141	81	D	D	D	226	3 048	479.6	41.6	46	147	12.8	2.0
Merrick	3 128	41	20	137	109.4	3.7	39	250	31.5	3.2	4	5	0.2	0.1
Morrill	177	2	11	119	30.7	2.7	23	162	23.9	2.0	4	5	0.5	0.0
Nance	941	8	10	D	D	D	21	111	14.8	1.2	5	4	0.2	0.0
Nemaha	1 732	26	12	D	D	D	45	323	51.5	3.7	4	6	0.5	0.1
Nuckolls	160	2	13	109	44.9	1.7	40	284	43.2	3.7	2	D	D	D
Otoe	10 909	117	21	159	131.3	3.6	98	694	110.6	9.5	11	15	1.7	0.3
Pawnee	135	3	6	D	D	D	12	53	7.1	0.6	2	D	D	D
Perkins	498	6	20	125	136.7	2.8	18	92	12.4	1.2	2	D	D	D
Phelps	1 763	17	25	D	D	D	70	533	81.8	7.4	6	17	0.9	0.2
Pierce	1 972	21	18	97	40.0	1.9	51	312	45.1	3.6	2	D	D	D

1. Establishments with payroll.

STATE County	Professional, Scientific, and Technical Services[1], 1997				Manufacturing, 1997				Accommodation and Foodservices, 1997			
	Number of Establishments	Number of Employees	Receipts (mil dol)	Annual Payroll (mil dol)	Number of Establishments	Number of Employees	Receipts (mil dol)	Annual Payroll (mil dol)	Number of Establishments	Number of Employees	Sales (mil dol)	Annual Payroll (mil dol)
	147	148	149	150	151	152	153	154	155	156	157	158
NEBRASKA—Cont'd												
Blaine	1	D	D	D	NA	NA	NA	NA	1	D	D	D
Boone	2	D	D	D	NA	NA	NA	NA	14	60	1.8	0.4
Box Butte	21	63	3.7	1.3	NA	NA	NA	NA	35	441	10.3	3.1
Boyd	3	7	0.5	0.1	NA	NA	NA	NA	6	17	0.5	0.1
Brown	4	10	0.5	0.2	NA	NA	NA	NA	16	95	2.3	0.6
Buffalo	65	343	21.1	8.0	47	4 392	817.1	122.1	118	2 322	65.8	18.7
Burt	8	26	1.7	0.4	NA	NA	NA	NA	17	141	3.1	0.7
Butler	7	24	1.1	0.6	NA	NA	NA	NA	18	D	D	D
Cass	24	D	D	D	NA	NA	NA	NA	45	340	10.3	2.6
Cedar	9	17	1.0	0.3	NA	NA	NA	NA	21	D	D	D
Chase	3	7	0.3	0.1	NA	NA	NA	NA	12	75	1.8	0.5
Cherry	12	33	2.1	0.4	NA	NA	NA	NA	27	179	5.9	1.5
Cheyenne	15	50	2.3	0.8	NA	NA	NA	NA	37	456	12.5	3.4
Clay	10	22	0.9	0.2	NA	NA	NA	NA	21	D	D	D
Colfax	5	17	1.1	0.3	4	D	D	D	31	D	D	D
Cuming	16	57	2.7	0.8	30	803	522.2	18.0	33	265	6.2	1.5
Custer	15	42	2.5	0.5	NA	NA	NA	NA	32	206	5.0	1.0
Dakota	26	97	5.5	1.8	23	D	D	D	41	656	21.2	6.1
Dawes	14	46	2.5	1.0	NA	NA	NA	NA	37	398	9.4	2.5
Dawson	34	109	6.0	2.1	26	3 899	1 300.0	88.8	63	759	19.4	4.8
Deuel	2	D	D	D	NA	NA	NA	NA	10	50	1.1	0.4
Dixon	4	4	0.2	0.0	NA	NA	NA	NA	9	39	1.4	0.2
Dodge	48	285	13.2	5.8	67	3 437	1 009.7	87.5	99	1 490	41.3	10.2
Douglas	1 244	12 434	1 125.5	466.4	555	27 335	7 140.4	897.4	1 033	19 822	618.8	184.4
Dundy	8	8	0.6	0.1	NA	NA	NA	NA	8	D	D	D
Fillmore	5	13	0.9	0.3	NA	NA	NA	NA	23	121	3.7	0.7
Franklin	6	23	1.2	0.3	NA	NA	NA	NA	10	44	1.3	0.2
Frontier	2	D	D	D	NA	NA	NA	NA	4	D	D	D
Furnas	8	46	2.6	1.5	NA	NA	NA	NA	17	D	D	D
Gage	25	80	4.2	1.3	34	1 700	305.5	43.9	50	583	15.6	4.1
Garden	3	3	0.2	0.0	NA	NA	NA	NA	10	42	1.1	0.2
Garfield	2	D	D	D	NA	NA	NA	NA	8	61	0.9	0.2
Gosper	5	12	0.9	0.2	NA	NA	NA	NA	5	16	0.6	0.1
Grant	NA	NA	NA	NA	NA	NA	NA	NA	3	D	D	D
Greeley	1	D	D	D	NA	NA	NA	NA	6	25	0.9	0.1
Hall	99	427	32.4	11.9	81	5 791	1 823.3	156.3	155	2 833	71.5	21.0
Hamilton	14	37	2.6	0.7	21	691	332.7	19.9	12	129	2.9	0.9
Harlan	4	7	0.9	0.1	NA	NA	NA	NA	15	D	D	D
Hayes	NA	NA	NA	NA	NA	NA	NA	NA	1	D	D	D
Hitchcock	1	D	D	D	NA	NA	NA	NA	4	D	D	D
Holt	14	56	2.7	0.8	NA	NA	NA	NA	30	313	7.3	1.6
Hooker	NA	NA	NA	NA	NA	NA	NA	NA	4	19	0.5	0.1
Howard	7	13	0.5	0.1	NA	NA	NA	NA	17	107	1.9	0.5
Jefferson	13	27	1.3	0.4	11	649	67.5	11.8	19	D	D	D
Johnson	3	9	0.4	0.1	NA	NA	NA	NA	10	73	1.4	0.4
Kearney	8	17	1.0	0.2	NA	NA	NA	NA	15	D	D	D
Keith	15	70	4.3	1.5	NA	NA	NA	NA	57	584	20.0	4.7
Keya Paha	1	D	D	D	NA	NA	NA	NA	2	D	D	D
Kimball	12	28	1.3	0.3	NA	NA	NA	NA	18	205	6.3	1.7
Knox	14	19	1.2	0.2	NA	NA	NA	NA	30	122	3.4	0.6
Lancaster	483	7 161	688.0	211.6	267	15 322	3 855.1	502.3	545	11 230	318.5	91.8
Lincoln	53	269	17.0	6.2	NA	NA	NA	NA	96	1 645	44.8	13.1
Logan	NA	NA	NA	NA	NA	NA	NA	NA	2	D	D	D
Loup	NA	NA	NA	NA	NA	NA	NA	NA	1	D	D	D
McPherson	1	D	D	D	NA	NA	NA	NA	1	D	D	D
Madison	66	262	16.1	7.1	52	4 908	1 402.4	154.3	101	1 541	40.2	11.3
Merrick	6	16	0.6	0.3	NA	NA	NA	NA	17	168	3.4	0.9
Morrill	NA	NA	NA	NA	NA	NA	NA	NA	16	109	2.3	0.7
Nance	3	10	0.3	0.1	NA	NA	NA	NA	4	12	0.4	0.1
Nemaha	8	14	0.6	0.2	NA	NA	NA	NA	21	221	4.8	1.4
Nuckolls	8	29	0.8	0.3	NA	NA	NA	NA	14	D	D	D
Otoe	20	57	4.3	1.3	17	1 354	212.3	35.0	47	658	17.4	4.7
Pawnee	3	D	D	D	NA	NA	NA	NA	8	36	0.9	0.2
Perkins	5	12	0.6	0.2	NA	NA	NA	NA	9	D	D	D
Phelps	21	79	6.6	1.8	8	D	D	D	20	221	5.7	1.5
Pierce	8	29	1.2	0.4	NA	NA	NA	NA	14	58	1.7	0.3

1. Firms subject to federal tax.

STATE County	Health Care and Social Assistance[1], 1997				Other Services[1], 1997				Federal funds and grants, fiscal 1999[2] Expenditures (mil dol)			
										Direct payments for individuals[3]		
	Number of Establishments	Number of Employees	Receipts (mil dol)	Annual Payroll (mil dol)	Number of Establishments	Number of Employees	Receipts (mil dol)	Annual Payroll (mil dol)	Total	Social Security and government retirement	Medicare	Food stamps and Supplemental Security Income
	159	160	161	162	163	164	165	166	167	168	169	170
NEBRASKA—Cont'd												
Blaine	NA	NA	NA	NA	NA	NA	NA	NA	2.9	0.9	0.3	0.0
Boone	9	90	2.6	1.2	13	22	2.1	0.4	41.0	13.0	4.9	0.4
Box Butte	20	180	8.1	3.1	25	117	6.1	1.5	53.4	25.4	5.8	1.2
Boyd	5	82	2.2	0.8	4	6	0.3	0.0	17.2	6.5	3.4	0.2
Brown	6	82	2.6	1.2	10	28	1.4	0.2	21.8	8.5	2.6	0.2
Buffalo	92	827	67.8	36.4	82	463	29.9	8.6	144.8	63.5	19.7	2.7
Burt	10	154	4.4	2.5	16	37	2.8	0.5	47.5	18.9	8.1	0.8
Butler	9	140	5.1	2.8	13	39	2.2	0.5	48.6	17.8	5.3	0.5
Cass	22	279	9.0	4.7	24	101	7.0	1.7	97.3	50.0	13.4	1.5
Cedar	13	165	5.4	2.7	17	58	3.6	0.9	50.2	17.9	6.1	0.4
Chase	7	77	2.4	1.1	8	23	2.2	0.4	35.0	9.7	3.6	0.3
Cherry	10	51	3.1	1.2	10	23	2.4	0.3	26.4	12.9	3.8	0.5
Cheyenne	17	146	6.3	3.1	21	71	4.4	1.1	60.7	23.0	7.8	1.0
Clay	7	130	3.1	1.9	12	23	1.6	0.2	58.8	16.8	4.7	0.4
Colfax	16	198	7.1	3.5	28	77	4.5	1.1	55.5	20.8	10.9	0.5
Cuming	12	126	4.6	1.9	30	104	9.3	1.6	48.4	19.4	7.2	0.4
Custer	17	245	10.4	4.8	24	58	3.7	0.7	68.9	27.5	9.4	0.7
Dakota	20	235	12.5	5.5	32	275	29.7	8.5	91.5	28.4	10.6	1.7
Dawes	19	131	6.5	3.0	22	41	2.5	0.5	44.4	18.7	4.8	1.1
Dawson	32	395	18.4	8.6	52	181	16.5	3.1	96.7	40.2	13.1	2.2
Deuel	3	10	0.7	0.1	5	22	0.7	0.2	21.5	6.1	1.9	0.1
Dixon	8	133	3.5	1.5	15	33	2.4	0.5	32.7	12.1	4.6	0.3
Dodge	77	852	42.7	19.4	96	360	19.3	5.1	149.4	78.6	27.1	2.8
Douglas	966	11 736	835.2	393.7	899	6 682	398.4	127.0	2 093.4	839.2	293.8	61.7
Dundy	3	9	0.6	0.1	3	6	0.5	0.1	21.4	5.5	2.8	0.1
Fillmore	12	152	5.1	2.7	20	53	2.6	0.6	45.5	15.6	4.9	0.4
Franklin	5	113	2.7	1.6	6	11	0.8	0.1	26.1	9.8	3.4	0.3
Frontier	2	D	D	D	9	28	1.5	0.4	21.6	5.7	2.0	0.1
Furnas	6	102	4.0	2.2	15	39	2.5	0.4	48.7	16.6	5.8	0.4
Gage	28	287	12.8	5.4	58	181	9.8	2.2	115.3	54.3	14.3	2.2
Garden	2	D	D	D	1	D	D	D	26.7	6.9	2.5	0.1
Garfield	2	D	D	D	3	5	0.4	0.1	10.7	5.4	2.0	0.1
Gosper	2	D	D	D	1	D	D	D	18.2	5.8	1.4	0.1
Grant	NA	NA	NA	NA	2	D	D	D	5.1	1.6	0.4	0.0
Greeley	3	D	D	D	7	16	1.4	0.3	21.0	6.5	2.0	0.2
Hall	109	1 263	75.6	38.6	118	858	50.2	15.6	237.2	101.8	30.0	5.3
Hamilton	14	84	4.0	1.6	19	53	4.3	0.9	54.2	17.6	5.0	0.4
Harlan	3	7	0.5	0.2	8	25	2.3	0.3	28.9	9.8	3.3	0.1
Hayes	NA	NA	NA	NA	1	D	D	D	11.0	1.3	0.8	0.1
Hitchcock	NA	NA	NA	NA	4	11	0.5	0.1	26.6	8.9	2.5	0.2
Holt	20	179	7.7	3.4	30	83	6.7	1.2	67.3	23.6	10.1	1.1
Hooker	2	D	D	D	3	5	0.2	0.0	4.2	2.1	0.7	0.0
Howard	6	74	2.5	1.3	9	21	1.6	0.3	33.0	13.0	5.0	0.3
Jefferson	9	136	4.8	2.5	16	35	1.9	0.4	54.3	21.4	6.3	0.7
Johnson	7	83	3.7	1.5	8	17	1.4	0.3	27.4	10.8	3.4	0.2
Kearney	10	30	1.6	0.4	14	43	3.2	0.6	45.5	13.5	5.2	0.5
Keith	15	130	6.1	2.5	28	112	6.7	1.5	46.6	19.2	5.2	0.7
Keya Paha	NA	NA	NA	NA	1	D	D	D	4.6	1.8	0.6	0.0
Kimball	6	23	1.4	0.4	10	34	2.1	0.3	37.6	11.0	2.6	0.2
Knox	12	97	4.1	1.8	15	29	2.4	0.4	60.4	21.5	8.8	1.1
Lancaster	548	6 380	376.7	184.1	418	2 512	134.2	42.0	1 250.5	407.7	101.9	21.5
Lincoln	80	813	49.0	18.5	70	335	19.7	5.6	166.1	78.1	20.8	4.0
Logan	NA	NA	NA	NA	1	D	D	D	7.4	1.9	0.6	0.0
Loup	1	D	D	D	2	D	D	D	3.0	1.0	0.6	0.0
McPherson	NA	NA	NA	NA	1	D	D	D	3.6	1.4	0.3	0.0
Madison	91	932	53.2	26.0	90	410	23.6	6.5	133.9	64.2	18.5	3.0
Merrick	12	164	4.6	2.5	19	41	2.8	0.6	42.6	16.5	6.4	0.5
Morrill	3	D	D	D	6	27	1.0	0.3	27.1	11.5	3.6	0.5
Nance	6	109	3.5	1.8	9	21	1.2	0.3	24.7	8.3	3.4	0.3
Nemaha	12	62	3.6	1.6	17	44	3.4	0.7	38.2	16.2	5.6	0.6
Nuckolls	9	65	3.5	1.5	12	32	2.6	0.5	35.8	14.3	4.8	0.7
Otoe	31	362	14.8	6.8	28	85	5.9	1.4	66.9	32.3	10.0	1.0
Pawnee	4	63	2.3	1.0	10	30	1.9	0.3	23.5	9.1	3.3	0.3
Perkins	4	24	1.0	0.3	10	24	3.3	0.6	37.0	7.6	2.7	0.1
Phelps	12	118	7.9	4.3	23	94	7.3	1.4	55.9	21.8	6.7	0.4
Pierce	8	104	3.2	1.2	14	38	6.1	0.6	40.0	14.3	5.1	0.4

1. Firms subject to federal tax.   2. October 1, 1998 to September 30, 1999.   3. State totals may include programs not allocated by county.

STATE County	Federal funds and grants, fiscal 1999[1] (cont'd)							Local government finances, 1997				
	Expenditures (mil dol) (cont'd)							General revenue				
	Procurement contract awards		Grants[2]							Taxes		
											Per capita[3] (dollars)	
	Salaries and wages	Defense	Other	Medicaid and other health-related	Nutrition and family welfare	Education	Other	Total (mil dol)	Intergovern-mental (mil dol)	Total (mil dol)	Total	Property
	171	172	173	174	175	176	177	178	179	180	181	182
NEBRASKA—Cont'd												
Blaine	0.3	0.0	0.1	0.3	0.1	0.0	0.3	2.0	0.4	1.4	2 180	2 055
Boone	1.5	0.0	0.4	2.4	0.5	0.3	0.5	21.1	4.0	8.7	1 360	1 233
Box Butte	3.0	0.0	0.9	3.3	1.0	0.6	0.1	35.2	11.5	12.2	941	776
Boyd	0.9	0.0	0.2	1.2	0.3	0.3	2.3	8.8	4.0	3.2	1 202	1 079
Brown	0.8	0.0	0.2	2.1	0.3	0.2	1.6	11.5	2.5	4.4	1 227	1 149
Buffalo	8.0	0.0	6.7	9.3	4.7	1.0	7.9	84.7	23.5	41.6	1 034	843
Burt	1.7	0.0	0.4	3.9	1.1	0.3	0.3	22.6	5.4	10.7	1 355	1 159
Butler	2.4	0.1	0.6	3.3	0.4	0.3	1.3	25.2	4.6	12.7	1 475	1 408
Cass	3.6	0.1	1.5	5.1	2.1	0.6	8.5	42.7	12.1	21.3	888	842
Cedar	3.5	0.1	0.5	3.3	0.7	0.5	2.9	21.5	8.1	8.9	904	801
Chase	0.9	0.0	0.2	1.2	0.4	0.1	1.0	16.9	3.2	8.0	1 887	1 740
Cherry	2.0	0.0	0.7	2.7	0.6	0.4	0.5	19.8	3.5	8.1	1 272	1 147
Cheyenne	2.8	0.0	0.8	4.2	0.6	0.3	2.2	32.0	7.7	16.3	1 706	1 366
Clay	8.4	0.0	2.2	1.5	0.5	0.8	4.2	20.6	5.7	12.2	1 699	1 595
Colfax	2.9	0.0	5.1	3.6	0.5	0.2	1.0	19.8	7.0	8.7	826	739
Cuming	2.3	0.0	0.4	2.1	2.0	0.4	0.3	21.8	5.5	11.1	1 112	1 021
Custer	2.8	0.0	0.6	6.6	1.1	0.6	1.8	31.1	9.5	17.1	1 414	1 311
Dakota	3.5	26.8	1.4	10.2	1.7	0.7	0.4	29.8	13.4	12.0	641	598
Dawes	5.6	0.0	1.4	3.0	2.1	0.5	1.2	17.5	6.6	7.9	870	671
Dawson	4.7	1.2	0.9	9.0	2.0	0.5	0.7	83.0	19.7	30.2	1 304	1 097
Deuel	0.5	0.0	0.1	1.5	0.2	0.1	2.1	8.8	1.5	4.6	2 269	2 024
Dixon	1.5	0.2	1.2	2.1	0.4	0.2	0.4	15.4	5.3	6.7	1 039	950
Dodge	6.8	0.3	1.9	10.8	3.2	1.1	1.8	112.1	25.6	35.0	997	852
Douglas	302.6	22.3	82.4	263.3	65.4	28.3	96.6	1 131.3	333.7	571.6	1 296	947
Dundy	0.7	0.0	0.2	1.2	0.1	0.1	0.3	10.1	1.2	3.9	1 669	1 514
Fillmore	1.7	0.0	0.5	2.7	0.5	0.1	0.4	20.6	4.4	10.3	1 496	1 445
Franklin	1.2	0.0	0.3	1.2	0.2	0.2	0.0	11.3	1.9	5.4	1 426	1 292
Frontier	0.9	0.0	0.3	1.2	0.2	0.1	0.5	8.9	2.7	5.0	1 558	1 465
Furnas	1.7	0.0	0.4	4.8	0.4	0.2	2.5	18.9	5.2	9.5	1 752	1 652
Gage	5.3	0.0	1.3	11.7	2.1	2.1	1.7	51.3	20.3	19.1	837	794
Garden	0.7	0.0	8.4	1.2	0.2	0.1	0.1	12.5	1.8	6.7	3 006	2 865
Garfield	0.5	0.0	0.1	0.9	0.1	0.1	0.1	5.3	2.1	1.9	914	828
Gosper	0.4	0.0	0.1	0.0	0.1	0.0	0.0	6.2	1.2	4.5	1 979	1 201
Grant	0.3	0.0	0.1	0.0	0.0	0.0	2.6	2.9	0.4	2.1	2 837	2 682
Greeley	0.9	0.0	0.3	0.9	0.3	0.1	2.2	10.5	3.9	4.3	1 454	1 376
Hall	29.0	-0.5	7.9	21.9	5.5	2.3	8.9	118.2	34.3	53.6	1 038	823
Hamilton	1.6	0.0	0.4	3.6	0.6	0.3	4.3	23.8	8.7	11.7	1 239	1 212
Harlan	1.4	0.0	0.2	1.2	0.2	0.3	0.0	9.0	2.6	2.9	764	690
Hayes	0.2	0.0	0.0	0.3	0.0	0.0	0.0	3.0	0.7	2.0	1 833	1 782
Hitchcock	0.8	0.0	0.2	1.5	0.2	0.2	2.1	9.1	4.0	3.5	1 034	944
Holt	2.5	0.0	0.5	6.6	1.3	0.5	3.0	26.0	8.6	13.7	1 122	958
Hooker	0.3	0.0	0.0	0.0	0.0	0.0	0.6	3.3	0.4	1.8	2 459	2 240
Howard	1.4	0.0	0.3	2.1	0.5	0.3	1.1	17.5	5.9	7.1	1 094	983
Jefferson	1.8	0.0	0.4	4.8	2.5	0.7	2.4	20.8	6.5	10.9	1 304	1 157
Johnson	1.7	0.0	0.3	1.8	0.3	0.3	1.5	15.8	5.2	6.1	1 342	1 225
Kearney	1.3	0.3	0.3	1.5	0.2	0.2	0.2	22.0	2.8	10.9	1 626	1 465
Keith	1.8	0.4	0.4	2.4	0.6	0.2	3.9	22.5	6.4	12.8	1 490	1 045
Keya Paha	0.2	0.0	0.1	0.6	0.1	0.1	0.0	2.1	0.5	1.4	1 440	1 387
Kimball	0.7	0.1	0.3	1.2	0.3	0.1	11.1	13.0	1.7	5.1	1 271	1 111
Knox	2.5	0.0	2.0	9.8	1.5	2.2	0.9	24.2	10.6	10.2	1 083	965
Lancaster	140.9	19.2	33.7	123.6	127.3	59.0	174.1	605.8	149.9	273.2	1 171	924
Lincoln	12.0	4.2	2.2	14.7	3.2	1.6	4.2	97.2	27.5	48.5	1 446	1 202
Logan	0.1	0.0	0.0	0.6	0.1	0.1	2.5	2.6	0.7	1.4	1 532	1 427
Loup	0.1	0.0	0.0	0.0	0.0	0.0	0.5	1.8	0.6	1.1	1 632	1 552
McPherson	0.1	0.0	0.0	0.6	0.0	0.1	0.5	1.2	0.3	0.8	1 457	1 417
Madison	12.1	0.0	2.7	14.1	2.7	0.9	1.6	96.5	32.7	40.2	1 154	942
Merrick	1.7	0.1	0.4	3.0	0.6	0.4	0.5	27.3	6.5	11.4	1 398	1 240
Morrill	1.0	0.0	0.3	1.8	0.6	0.3	0.1	20.7	5.5	8.7	1 596	1 460
Nance	0.7	0.0	0.2	3.3	0.3	0.1	0.4	8.3	3.2	3.8	901	813
Nemaha	1.8	0.4	0.4	3.3	0.5	0.5	0.0	21.9	7.0	7.9	1 017	882
Nuckolls	1.4	0.0	0.4	3.0	0.4	0.2	0.5	12.6	5.1	5.4	1 003	897
Otoe	2.9	0.0	1.5	5.1	1.2	0.4	0.7	35.4	9.3	20.3	1 394	1 042
Pawnee	1.0	0.0	0.3	2.1	0.2	0.1	0.0	11.6	3.8	4.1	1 285	1 199
Perkins	0.8	0.0	0.2	0.0	0.1	0.2	0.0	17.9	1.8	5.8	1 750	1 708
Phelps	1.8	0.0	0.4	3.3	0.5	0.4	0.0	24.2	6.0	14.1	1 421	1 241
Pierce	1.4	0.0	0.3	1.8	0.4	0.3	2.1	22.1	5.6	9.8	1 238	977

1. October 1, 1998 to September 30, 1999.   2. State totals may include programs not allocated by county.   3. Based on the resident population estimated as of July 1 of the year shown.

STATE County	Total (mil dol)	Per capita[1] (dollars)	Educa-tion	Health and hospitals	Police protec-tion	Public welfare	High-ways	Total (mil dol)	Per capita[1] (dollars)	Federal civilian	Federal military	State and local	Demo-cratic	Republi-can	All other
	183	184	185	186	187	188	189	190	191	192	193	194	195	196	197
NEBRASKA—Cont'd															
Blaine	2.0	3 172	71.0	0.0	1.6	0.0	9.7	0.0	0	25	0	67	12.3	85.7	2.0
Boone	23.8	3 723	47.9	26.3	1.2	0.0	8.0	7.2	1 121	38	28	565	20.1	76.7	3.2
Box Butte	33.6	2 602	49.7	17.6	4.9	0.1	7.9	6.7	520	60	57	955	31.7	63.0	5.2
Boyd	8.1	3 080	60.3	0.4	1.3	0.0	7.1	7.1	2 698	17	11	277	21.3	75.0	3.7
Brown	12.0	3 336	44.1	16.6	3.1	0.0	10.2	11.0	3 050	21	16	400	14.8	81.7	3.5
Buffalo	94.3	2 345	52.6	0.2	4.1	0.1	8.7	51.2	1 274	156	178	3 253	23.9	72.5	3.7
Burt	21.8	2 763	45.4	9.6	2.9	6.2	12.4	5.9	746	38	35	615	36.1	60.6	3.3
Butler	27.3	3 175	33.2	15.2	3.4	0.0	11.1	18.1	2 104	53	38	543	26.9	68.9	4.2
Cass	45.4	1 891	60.8	3.4	3.2	0.1	8.4	39.7	1 656	77	108	1 036	35.6	59.8	4.7
Cedar	19.7	2 009	57.2	0.1	2.6	6.4	10.9	8.6	873	97	43	654	24.9	70.0	5.1
Chase	17.0	4 003	41.1	25.5	0.8	0.0	6.4	4.4	1 036	25	19	546	16.3	80.3	3.4
Cherry	20.4	3 183	32.1	28.5	2.7	0.2	14.7	2.4	379	51	28	484	15.7	81.6	2.8
Cheyenne	30.9	3 234	49.9	0.5	2.8	0.0	6.3	30.5	3 193	50	42	737	20.2	76.6	3.2
Clay	19.5	2 725	60.0	1.0	2.4	0.1	8.0	5.9	826	160	32	684	24.1	72.3	3.6
Colfax	20.0	1 895	56.9	0.1	2.8	0.1	13.0	3.0	280	76	47	581	26.0	70.5	3.4
Cuming	20.3	2 040	50.6	0.2	2.7	6.8	14.4	9.0	907	55	44	650	20.3	76.7	3.0
Custer	31.1	2 573	50.8	7.9	2.5	0.0	17.6	13.1	1 081	52	53	891	18.0	78.4	3.6
Dakota	28.7	1 531	57.5	0.6	7.1	0.0	5.9	9.4	500	84	83	835	44.5	51.5	4.1
Dawes	18.5	2 052	44.4	6.2	3.6	6.3	6.9	10.8	1 195	141	40	978	22.7	70.4	6.9
Dawson	79.8	3 452	44.0	18.0	4.4	0.0	9.3	36.2	1 563	104	102	1 808	23.2	73.4	3.4
Deuel	8.5	4 200	53.9	0.1	3.1	8.2	8.4	0.9	420	14	0	195	20.6	75.8	3.6
Dixon	19.6	3 055	57.6	8.8	2.7	0.0	10.3	1.7	271	39	28	402	29.4	65.7	4.9
Dodge	116.3	3 312	33.4	35.7	2.1	2.8	5.7	8.7	246	129	157	2 560	34.7	61.3	4.0
Douglas	1 031.1	2 338	48.1	3.0	5.5	0.6	5.6	1 499.9	3 401	5 726	2 542	30 119	40.0	55.2	4.8
Dundy	9.1	3 923	33.1	30.7	1.8	0.0	9.7	1.2	509	16	10	232	17.7	79.2	3.1
Fillmore	21.9	3 171	47.9	17.9	1.4	5.4	8.7	3.0	441	38	31	756	28.3	67.5	4.2
Franklin	10.4	2 720	41.4	21.3	2.4	0.0	13.7	1.4	354	31	16	293	25.2	71.7	3.1
Frontier	9.2	2 891	63.5	0.3	4.5	0.0	14.3	0.4	116	17	14	357	17.5	79.1	3.4
Furnas	17.3	3 185	54.4	0.3	2.5	0.0	7.8	24.4	4 495	40	24	598	22.0	76.1	2.0
Gage	52.8	2 306	53.4	1.5	3.9	0.0	9.7	36.6	1 601	108	100	2 234	37.0	58.3	4.8
Garden	12.3	5 519	32.3	18.4	1.5	7.6	5.8	0.5	230	22	0	300	16.7	79.0	4.3
Garfield	5.2	2 501	52.5	0.1	3.1	0.1	8.1	0.5	247	10	0	157	21.0	74.6	4.5
Gosper	5.8	2 542	29.8	0.1	3.3	0.0	13.5	1.0	447	15	10	167	22.5	74.7	2.9
Grant	3.1	4 201	64.6	0.2	2.3	0.1	13.4	1.2	1 566	0	0	90	12.7	84.2	3.1
Greeley	10.3	3 505	48.3	0.1	0.6	7.5	8.9	5.9	1 995	15	13	279	31.8	64.0	4.2
Hall	117.4	2 271	51.2	0.7	4.4	0.2	7.1	104.3	2 019	607	230	3 625	32.1	63.6	4.3
Hamilton	18.8	1 991	58.6	0.6	2.6	0.0	9.0	2.8	297	36	42	573	23.7	72.4	3.9
Harlan	9.4	2 500	27.8	24.2	2.0	0.0	11.3	1.9	509	38	17	267	23.7	73.3	3.0
Hayes	3.0	2 730	62.5	0.0	2.0	0.0	19.8	0.3	269	13	0	81	11.6	85.1	3.3
Hitchcock	10.4	3 041	71.7	0.1	1.9	0.0	7.6	8.5	2 491	16	15	361	21.1	76.1	2.8
Holt	26.0	2 131	55.4	0.4	2.5	0.1	13.1	9.4	772	58	53	831	17.1	79.7	3.2
Hooker	3.2	4 439	49.1	25.3	1.3	0.1	7.0	0.1	127	0	0	93	18.1	77.5	4.4
Howard	16.6	2 564	54.8	0.2	1.9	0.0	8.2	5.3	816	32	28	440	33.8	62.3	4.0
Jefferson	21.4	2 551	68.7	0.2	3.4	0.1	7.9	7.6	901	39	37	507	35.4	61.1	3.5
Johnson	15.5	3 387	47.0	14.2	1.3	0.0	13.7	4.1	887	38	20	424	37.6	57.3	5.1
Kearney	19.7	2 947	45.5	11.7	2.5	0.3	5.5	6.7	1 009	31	30	512	21.8	74.7	3.5
Keith	22.8	2 646	56.8	2.3	2.2	0.5	8.5	5.6	646	34	38	564	20.2	76.7	3.1
Keya Paha	2.1	2 123	56.0	0.2	1.0	0.0	23.5	0.0	4	0	0	69	15.2	82.3	2.5
Kimball	12.9	3 193	35.7	17.6	3.3	13.1	7.9	0.5	129	18	18	372	20.8	75.8	3.4
Knox	22.3	2 375	61.0	0.2	2.5	0.1	14.9	8.1	867	55	41	1 014	26.1	70.0	3.9
Lancaster	589.1	2 525	45.1	13.3	3.6	2.8	5.0	639.3	2 740	2 577	1 093	26 604	41.7	51.8	6.5
Lincoln	86.8	2 588	55.3	5.6	1.3	0.2	5.8	18.8	560	239	148	2 402	34.4	61.0	4.6
Logan	2.3	2 610	75.0	0.2	3.1	0.0	8.9	0.0	0	0	0	80	14.6	81.6	3.9
Loup	1.6	2 432	69.9	0.0	3.3	0.0	12.2	0.0	0	0	0	55	22.2	75.1	2.6
McPherson	1.2	2 121	71.4	0.0	1.7	0.0	11.0	0.1	167	0	0	36	21.6	75.0	3.5
Madison	106.3	3 049	55.0	1.2	3.4	1.8	6.8	58.9	1 691	241	153	3 193	15.9	81.1	3.0
Merrick	26.1	3 193	43.3	22.7	1.3	0.0	9.4	13.5	1 653	36	36	571	25.4	71.3	3.4
Morrill	18.3	3 371	39.6	11.8	2.0	8.1	7.3	6.6	1 213	24	24	488	21.5	74.7	3.8
Nance	10.4	2 467	67.2	0.5	2.5	0.0	10.9	2.6	617	19	18	391	29.8	66.4	3.8
Nemaha	21.2	2 709	54.1	16.0	0.8	0.1	10.2	7.2	925	40	34	1 546	31.6	64.6	3.8
Nuckolls	12.5	2 321	54.5	0.1	3.4	0.4	13.4	1.1	211	35	23	389	26.4	69.6	4.0
Otoe	32.3	2 218	50.2	1.9	4.8	0.1	12.1	22.6	1 548	63	65	1 034	33.1	62.7	4.1
Pawnee	10.9	3 442	43.5	20.9	1.2	0.0	8.6	1.4	446	25	14	254	34.4	61.7	3.9
Perkins	16.4	4 974	30.9	57.1	2.0	0.0	1.8	2.0	610	20	14	384	16.7	80.6	2.7
Phelps	24.8	2 506	66.0	0.0	2.4	0.1	9.5	7.3	732	42	44	793	20.2	77.3	2.6
Pierce	20.5	2 595	45.4	17.7	1.8	0.0	10.9	11.2	1 416	35	35	469	17.8	79.0	3.2

1. Based on the resident population estimated as of July 1 of the year shown.

STATE/ County code	MSA/ PMSA/ NECMA code[1]	County Type[2]	STATE County	Land area,[3] (sq km) 1990	Population and population characteristics, 1999			Race (percent)					Age (percent)					
					Total persons	Rank	Per square kilometer	White	Black	Am. Indian, Eskimo, Aleut	Asian and Pacific Islander	Percent Hispanic[4]	Under 5 years	5 to 17 years	18 to 24 years	25 to 34 years	35 to 44 years	45 to 54 years
				1	2	3	4	5	6	7	8	9	10	11	12	13	14	15
			NEBRASKA—Cont'd															
31 141	...	7	Platte	1 756	30 378	1 365	17.3	99.1	0.2	0.2	0.5	1.8	8.0	23.3	8.4	12.3	15.9	13.4
31 143	...	9	Polk	1 137	5 518	2 806	4.9	99.3	0.1	0.3	0.3	1.1	5.6	20.9	5.2	9.0	14.9	13.2
31 145	...	7	Red Willow	1 856	11 304	2 326	6.1	99.3	0.1	0.3	0.3	3.5	6.3	19.4	8.6	10.5	13.9	12.7
31 147	...	7	Richardson	1 434	9 330	2 483	6.5	97.7	0.1	2.0	0.2	0.9	6.4	18.1	6.3	9.7	13.5	14.1
31 149	...	9	Rock	2 612	1 690	3 084	0.6	99.9	0.0	0.1	0.0	0.7	5.7	21.1	4.6	9.5	14.8	12.2
31 151	...	6	Saline	1 490	13 111	2 204	8.8	98.2	0.1	0.2	1.4	1.2	5.8	19.0	11.4	10.0	13.9	12.6
31 153	5920	2	Sarpy	623	122 495	430	196.6	90.8	5.5	0.5	3.2	6.6	8.3	22.5	10.1	14.9	17.9	12.8
31 155	...	6	Saunders	1 953	19 260	1 803	9.9	99.3	0.1	0.3	0.3	1.2	6.7	21.1	6.7	11.0	15.2	14.0
31 157	...	5	Scotts Bluff	1 915	36 078	1 190	18.8	96.8	0.4	2.0	0.9	25.1	6.8	21.6	8.0	10.9	14.9	12.1
31 159	...	6	Seward	1 489	16 435	1 975	11.0	99.1	0.2	0.3	0.4	1.1	6.1	19.3	13.9	9.7	14.5	12.8
31 161	...	9	Sheridan	6 323	6 423	2 741	1.0	90.5	0.2	8.9	0.5	1.9	5.7	21.8	5.9	8.9	14.2	12.4
31 163	...	9	Sherman	1 466	3 470	2 956	2.4	99.4	0.0	0.1	0.5	0.5	5.7	21.4	6.4	7.9	13.2	13.7
31 165	...	9	Sioux	5 353	1 424	3 098	0.3	98.4	0.0	1.5	0.1	5.6	5.3	19.7	4.9	9.5	14.0	18.1
31 167	...	9	Stanton	1 113	6 100	2 764	5.5	98.6	0.4	0.7	0.2	0.8	8.2	23.7	7.1	12.0	14.8	13.9
31 169	...	9	Thayer	1 488	6 170	2 761	4.1	99.5	0.1	0.3	0.1	1.8	5.1	18.9	5.6	8.7	13.1	13.4
31 171	...	9	Thomas	1 846	809	3 123	0.4	99.4	0.0	0.6	0.0	2.5	5.2	25.5	6.1	9.1	17.4	15.9
31 173	...	8	Thurston	1 020	7 054	2 674	6.9	52.2	0.2	47.5	0.2	1.3	10.4	25.5	8.5	10.5	11.6	11.5
31 175	...	9	Valley	1 471	4 527	2 869	3.1	99.3	0.2	0.3	0.2	0.7	5.3	19.0	5.7	8.3	13.9	13.2
31 177	5920	2	Washington	1 011	18 837	1 829	18.6	98.7	0.6	0.3	0.3	1.2	5.7	20.9	8.9	10.3	17.0	15.0
31 179	...	7	Wayne	1 149	9 201	2 492	8.0	98.6	0.5	0.3	0.6	0.5	5.9	17.0	21.7	10.0	11.6	11.2
31 181	...	9	Webster	1 489	3 933	2 921	2.6	99.2	0.1	0.2	0.6	0.5	5.5	18.6	4.5	9.3	12.4	14.1
31 183	...	9	Wheeler	1 490	924	3 113	0.6	97.9	0.6	0.1	1.3	1.6	8.5	23.1	4.9	11.6	12.1	14.6
31 185	...	7	York	1 491	14 392	2 106	9.7	98.3	0.8	0.4	0.5	1.5	6.9	19.5	8.7	10.7	15.0	13.2
32 000	...	X	NEVADA	284 397	1 809 253	X	6.4	85.6	7.7	1.8	4.9	16.8	7.9	19.3	8.6	13.7	16.4	13.4
32 001	...	6	Churchill	12 767	23 405	1 596	1.8	88.6	1.2	6.1	4.1	9.4	8.4	22.7	7.7	12.0	15.4	12.5
32 003	4120	2	Clark	20 489	1 217 155	27	59.4	83.1	10.5	1.0	5.3	18.0	7.9	19.2	8.8	13.9	16.2	13.4
32 005	...	7	Douglas	1 839	37 602	1 147	20.4	95.2	0.4	2.3	2.0	9.9	7.3	19.3	5.2	11.2	18.8	13.4
32 007	...	5	Elko	44 500	45 465	978	1.0	90.4	0.7	7.6	1.3	20.7	10.1	25.9	8.3	14.3	16.7	12.6
32 009	...	9	Esmeralda	9 295	1 121	3 106	0.1	91.5	1.0	6.5	1.0	13.8	5.7	18.5	7.0	11.2	16.8	14.1
32 011	...	9	Eureka	10 816	1 854	3 071	0.2	95.3	0.8	2.9	1.0	14.3	9.1	19.7	6.6	12.9	15.6	15.7
32 013	...	7	Humboldt	24 989	17 876	1 878	0.7	91.7	1.0	6.5	0.9	28.2	9.4	24.8	8.4	14.2	16.9	11.8
32 015	...	7	Lander	14 229	6 709	2 708	0.5	93.9	0.1	5.7	0.4	20.5	10.1	27.5	7.7	13.5	16.3	12.3
32 017	...	8	Lincoln	27 544	4 226	2 893	0.2	94.8	2.7	1.8	0.6	7.1	7.5	27.5	4.9	8.7	11.7	11.8
32 019	...	6	Lyon	5 164	31 459	1 332	6.1	94.2	0.5	4.0	1.3	12.3	8.1	21.5	5.5	10.6	14.8	13.7
32 021	...	7	Mineral	9 730	5 176	2 825	0.5	78.1	6.9	13.4	1.6	12.7	7.7	21.3	6.0	10.0	13.2	11.6
32 023	4120	2	Nye	47 001	29 709	1 383	0.6	93.6	1.7	3.5	1.3	10.6	6.6	17.3	5.1	10.2	13.2	13.5
32 027	...	9	Pershing	15 564	4 803	2 855	0.3	93.1	0.4	5.6	0.9	24.1	10.5	23.6	7.3	12.5	13.4	12.6
32 029	...	8	Storey	682	2 988	2 990	4.4	95.4	0.4	2.5	1.7	6.8	6.5	18.8	5.0	10.4	20.7	18.5
32 031	6720	2	Washoe	16 427	319 816	176	19.5	89.1	2.6	2.3	5.9	14.4	7.8	18.0	9.3	14.2	17.7	13.5
32 033	...	7	White Pine	22 990	9 843	2 441	0.4	91.9	3.8	3.6	0.6	14.7	7.3	20.7	7.3	12.9	16.5	13.8
32 510	...	4	Carson City city	372	50 046	907	134.5	92.4	2.0	3.4	2.2	12.3	6.9	17.1	7.4	12.3	16.9	13.5
33 000	...	X	NEW HAMPSHIRE	23 231	1 201 134	X	51.7	97.8	0.8	0.2	1.2	1.6	6.2	19.2	8.2	14.8	18.6	13.4
33 001	...	6	Belknap	1 039	53 680	858	51.7	98.8	0.2	0.3	0.7	0.9	5.5	20.1	5.9	12.9	17.7	13.1
33 003	...	6	Carroll	2 419	40 184	1 084	16.6	99.2	0.2	0.2	0.4	0.6	5.3	18.4	4.9	12.4	18.4	13.2
33 005	...	4	Cheshire	1 832	72 401	677	39.5	98.8	0.3	0.2	0.6	0.7	5.6	18.9	10.5	12.4	17.4	13.4
33 007	...	7	Coos	4 664	32 725	1 291	7.0	99.1	0.1	0.2	0.5	0.7	5.1	19.5	6.0	11.8	16.1	13.3
33 009	...	5	Grafton	4 438	78 570	638	17.7	97.7	0.6	0.3	1.5	1.3	5.3	17.8	13.0	12.6	17.3	12.6
33 011	1123	2	Hillsborough	2 270	367 233	155	161.8	97.1	1.1	0.2	1.7	2.7	6.6	19.4	7.7	15.9	18.8	13.5
33 013	...	4	Merrimack	2 420	129 931	401	53.7	98.5	0.5	0.2	0.8	1.1	6.0	19.6	7.3	14.9	19.0	13.2
33 015	1123	2	Rockingham	1 801	275 488	200	153.0	97.4	1.0	0.2	1.4	1.5	6.5	19.5	6.7	15.9	20.1	13.9
33 017	1123	2	Strafford	955	110 667	477	115.9	97.8	0.6	0.3	1.3	1.3	6.1	17.9	13.0	15.1	16.4	12.4
33 019	...	7	Sullivan	1 392	40 255	1 080	28.9	98.9	0.2	0.4	0.5	0.7	5.7	19.8	6.2	12.2	17.9	13.4
34 000	...	X	NEW JERSEY	19 215	8 143 412	X	423.8	79.3	14.7	0.3	5.8	12.6	6.7	17.9	8.3	13.6	17.5	13.5
34 001	0560	2	Atlantic	1 453	239 626	230	164.9	75.6	20.3	0.4	3.7	10.1	7.1	17.5	8.8	14.5	16.6	12.3
34 003	0875	0	Bergen	607	857 052	45	1 411.9	83.3	5.6	0.2	11.0	8.5	5.7	15.7	7.2	12.6	17.6	15.0
34 005	6160	0	Burlington	2 084	424 510	138	203.7	79.7	16.5	0.3	3.6	4.6	6.6	19.1	8.3	13.5	17.5	13.4
34 007	6160	0	Camden	576	503 093	105	873.4	76.3	19.3	0.3	4.0	10.2	7.6	20.6	8.0	13.8	17.0	12.5
34 009	0560	2	Cape May	661	98 009	527	148.3	91.7	6.8	0.3	1.2	2.9	6.4	17.2	6.9	11.6	15.2	12.2
34 011	8760	3	Cumberland	1 267	140 112	379	110.6	77.5	19.7	1.3	1.5	18.3	7.2	20.4	8.4	12.9	16.4	12.5
34 013	5640	0	Essex	327	747 355	58	2 285.5	52.1	43.3	0.3	4.3	16.5	6.9	18.6	9.2	14.3	17.2	12.7
34 015	6160	0	Gloucester	841	250 492	214	297.9	87.1	10.4	0.2	2.2	2.6	7.0	21.0	8.4	13.2	18.0	12.8
34 017	3640	0	Hudson	121	552 819	93	4 568.0	74.2	15.5	0.4	9.9	41.3	6.8	16.9	9.4	16.4	16.7	12.4
34 019	5015	1	Hunterdon	1 114	124 553	419	111.8	95.4	2.2	0.1	2.3	2.4	6.4	18.5	6.8	12.5	21.1	16.6

1. MSA = Metropolitan Statistical Area. PMSA = Primary MSA. NECMA = New England County Metropolitan Area. See Appendix A for explanation of these concepts. See Appendix B for list of metropolitan areas identified by type, with component counties. 2. County typology code from the Economic Research Service of USDA. See Appendix A for definition. 3. Dry land or land partially or temporarily covered by water. 4. Hispanic persons may be of any race.

Table B. States and Counties — Population and Households

STATE County	55 to 64 years	65 to 74 years	75 years and over	Percent female	Total persons 1990	Total persons 1980	Percent change 1980–1990	Percent change 1990–1999	Births	Deaths	Net migration	Number	Percent change, 1980–1990	Persons per household	Female family householder[1]	One person
	16	17	18	19	20	21	22	23	24	25	26	27	28	29	30	31
NEBRASKA—Cont'd																
Platte	8.9	5.0	4.9	50.5	29 820	28 852	3.4	1.9	4 291	2 188	-1 365	10 954	8.6	2.69	6.1	24.7
Polk	10.5	8.8	12.0	50.8	5 655	6 320	-10.3	-2.4	617	754	10	2 223	-4.3	2.48	4.7	27.1
Red Willow	9.9	9.3	9.4	52.4	11 705	12 615	-7.2	-3.4	1 395	1 162	-574	4 723	-1.5	2.44	7.1	28.5
Richardson	10.2	9.7	11.9	51.7	9 937	11 315	-12.2	-6.1	985	1 492	-61	4 120	-8.0	2.35	6.0	31.1
Rock	9.9	10.0	12.1	50.8	2 019	2 383	-15.3	-16.3	174	221	-272	798	-9.6	2.52	5.8	26.9
Saline	9.3	7.5	10.5	51.0	12 715	13 131	-3.2	3.1	1 355	1 591	683	4 829	-1.9	2.45	4.9	28.8
Sarpy	5.8	4.7	2.9	50.2	102 583	86 015	19.3	19.4	18 016	4 198	3 551	33 960	29.1	2.97	8.4	15.1
Saunders	10.2	7.0	8.1	49.7	18 285	18 716	-2.3	5.3	2 271	1 635	407	6 809	3.1	2.65	5.6	23.6
Scotts Bluff	8.8	8.7	8.2	51.9	36 025	38 344	-6.0	0.1	4 882	3 731	-999	14 056	1.8	2.52	9.0	27.1
Seward	8.6	7.1	8.0	49.6	15 450	15 789	-2.1	6.4	1 594	1 469	918	5 432	3.3	2.63	5.0	22.5
Sheridan	10.6	9.9	10.6	51.1	6 750	7 544	-10.5	-4.8	720	831	-196	2 618	-6.9	2.52	6.6	27.8
Sherman	10.7	10.0	10.9	49.5	3 718	4 226	-12.0	-6.7	361	481	-115	1 431	-6.5	2.55	3.9	28.0
Sioux	12.1	8.1	8.1	49.6	1 549	1 845	-16.0	-8.1	123	89	-158	612	-7.7	2.53	5.6	22.7
Stanton	8.8	5.3	6.2	50.3	6 244	6 549	-4.7	-2.3	745	440	-436	2 167	0.7	2.85	5.9	19.5
Thayer	10.3	11.0	13.9	51.3	6 635	7 582	-12.5	-7.0	592	919	-109	2 669	-8.7	2.40	4.1	28.3
Thomas	11.1	5.4	4.2	51.8	851	973	-12.5	-4.9	82	60	-54	316	-11.7	2.69	5.7	21.2
Thurston	9.0	6.6	6.4	50.4	6 936	7 186	-3.5	1.7	1 383	734	-519	2 288	-2.5	2.98	16.3	23.3
Valley	10.4	10.7	13.6	51.8	5 169	5 633	-8.2	-12.4	490	656	-457	2 141	-1.3	2.37	4.1	31.2
Washington	9.1	6.3	6.8	50.7	16 607	15 508	7.1	13.4	1 804	1 443	1 911	6 017	14.5	2.68	5.5	21.3
Wayne	8.3	6.4	8.0	51.4	9 364	9 858	-5.0	-1.7	1 031	666	-506	3 232	-3.0	2.53	4.9	25.6
Webster	12.6	9.9	13.1	51.6	4 279	4 858	-11.9	-8.1	406	719	-19	1 755	-8.4	2.35	4.0	29.8
Wheeler	11.0	7.1	7.0	49.7	948	1 060	-10.6	-2.5	120	67	-72	350	-4.9	2.71	4.6	23.7
York	9.1	7.9	9.0	51.4	14 428	14 798	-2.5	-0.2	1 742	1 478	-252	5 467	0.7	2.53	5.1	26.1
NEVADA	9.3	6.9	4.6	49.1	1 201 675	800 508	50.1	50.6	227 622	110 437	488 789	466 297	53.2	2.53	10.2	25.7
Churchill	9.5	6.2	5.7	49.5	17 938	13 917	28.9	30.5	3 275	1 775	3 764	6 666	31.4	2.62	7.9	23.0
Clark	9.4	6.8	4.4	49.4	741 368	463 087	60.1	64.2	152 563	71 482	392 510	287 025	65.1	2.54	11.2	25.5
Douglas	9.5	9.6	5.6	49.1	27 637	19 421	42.3	36.1	3 289	2 161	8 923	10 571	43.1	2.59	7.4	18.2
Elko	6.3	3.0	2.7	46.8	33 463	17 269	93.8	35.9	6 911	1 740	6 805	11 777	85.5	2.79	7.7	22.4
Esmeralda	10.2	9.1	7.4	43.9	1 344	777	73.0	-16.6	116	98	-236	588	89.1	2.28	4.8	34.0
Eureka	9.5	6.5	4.3	44.8	1 547	1 198	29.1	19.8	183	108	223	617	38.3	2.49	3.2	30.6
Humboldt	7.5	4.1	2.9	46.2	12 844	9 449	35.9	39.2	2 646	830	3 207	4 538	37.6	2.76	7.4	23.2
Lander	6.2	3.4	2.9	47.9	6 266	4 076	53.7	7.1	1 271	327	-522	2 212	55.1	2.82	6.2	21.6
Lincoln	9.7	9.2	8.9	47.4	3 775	3 732	1.2	11.9	422	412	460	1 325	4.3	2.63	8.1	29.3
Lyon	11.1	8.9	5.9	48.3	20 001	13 594	47.1	57.3	3 002	2 399	10 822	7 680	52.4	2.58	7.2	22.1
Mineral	10.4	11.5	8.2	49.3	6 475	6 217	4.1	-20.1	786	614	-1 480	2 529	11.4	2.50	9.1	26.7
Nye	10.9	15.3	8.0	46.7	17 781	9 048	96.5	67.1	2 405	2 076	11 690	6 664	94.1	2.50	5.1	25.0
Pershing	8.9	5.8	5.4	48.6	4 336	3 408	27.2	10.8	694	297	78	1 614	28.5	2.65	5.8	25.2
Storey	11.2	4.5	4.3	48.6	2 526	1 503	68.1	18.3	143	129	462	1 006	69.6	2.44	6.8	25.0
Washoe	8.9	6.1	4.6	49.1	254 667	193 623	31.5	25.6	42 608	20 661	43 796	102 294	32.5	2.43	9.4	27.6
White Pine	9.3	6.6	5.6	43.0	9 264	8 167	13.4	6.3	1 194	802	172	3 296	9.8	2.59	7.0	26.6
Carson City city	9.9	9.0	7.1	48.4	40 443	32 022	26.3	23.7	6 114	4 526	8 115	15 895	31.6	2.39	9.6	27.2
NEW HAMPSHIRE	7.7	6.4	5.7	50.8	1 109 252	920 610	20.5	8.3	142 027	83 680	36 602	411 186	27.1	2.62	8.5	22.0
Belknap	8.4	9.0	7.3	50.7	49 216	42 884	14.8	9.1	5 677	4 780	3 816	18 839	21.0	2.58	8.5	22.8
Carroll	9.6	9.6	8.1	50.9	35 410	27 931	26.8	13.5	3 916	3 704	4 657	14 253	28.7	2.45	7.6	24.3
Cheshire	8.1	7.0	6.6	51.4	70 121	62 116	12.9	3.3	7 650	5 765	603	25 856	18.4	2.57	8.7	22.8
Coos	9.9	9.5	8.8	51.4	34 828	35 147	-0.9	-6.0	3 388	3 782	-1 577	13 799	6.7	2.48	8.2	25.6
Grafton	7.9	6.9	6.5	50.6	74 929	65 806	13.9	4.9	8 064	6 045	1 874	27 542	18.6	2.51	8.2	24.4
Hillsborough	7.4	5.7	5.0	50.9	335 838	276 608	21.4	9.3	48 202	23 562	7 746	124 567	30.0	2.64	8.9	22.1
Merrimack	7.8	5.9	6.2	50.6	120 240	98 302	22.3	8.1	14 669	9 825	5 162	44 595	28.6	2.59	8.6	22.5
Rockingham	7.1	5.6	4.7	50.3	245 845	190 345	29.2	12.1	33 194	15 393	12 259	89 118	35.1	2.72	7.7	19.3
Strafford	7.6	6.2	5.3	51.4	104 233	85 408	22.0	6.2	12 860	7 193	1 026	37 744	29.7	2.59	9.1	21.9
Sullivan	8.9	8.6	7.2	50.7	38 592	36 063	7.0	4.3	4 407	3 631	1 036	14 873	11.8	2.56	8.6	22.9
NEW JERSEY	8.9	7.1	6.5	51.5	7 747 750	7 365 011	5.0	5.1	1 079 022	667 367	-665	2 794 711	9.7	2.70	12.1	23.1
Atlantic	8.9	7.1	7.2	51.7	224 327	194 119	15.6	6.8	34 698	22 511	3 895	85 123	18.5	2.56	13.7	26.6
Bergen	10.4	8.1	7.6	52.0	825 380	845 385	-2.4	3.8	99 344	70 151	6 154	308 880	2.8	2.64	9.4	23.2
Burlington	8.6	7.3	5.7	50.6	395 066	362 542	9.0	7.5	50 262	28 790	5 959	136 554	18.9	2.79	10.3	19.6
Camden	8.3	6.7	5.8	51.8	502 824	471 650	6.6	0.1	71 186	42 011	-27 341	178 758	10.0	2.76	14.7	23.1
Cape May	10.1	10.2	10.3	51.8	95 089	82 266	15.6	3.1	11 556	11 787	3 287	37 856	17.0	2.44	10.3	27.5
Cumberland	8.5	7.1	6.6	50.7	138 053	132 866	3.9	1.5	19 381	13 054	-8 429	47 118	6.4	2.79	15.8	21.6
Essex	8.8	6.4	5.9	52.6	777 964	851 304	-8.6	-3.9	119 961	73 818	-74 800	278 752	-7.2	2.72	19.2	27.1
Gloucester	8.1	6.4	5.0	51.1	230 082	199 917	15.1	8.9	30 485	17 698	8 273	78 845	21.1	2.87	10.7	18.9
Hudson	9.2	6.5	5.7	51.7	553 099	556 972	-0.7	0.1	84 200	47 535	-35 537	208 739	0.4	2.62	16.5	28.7
Hunterdon	8.0	5.0	5.0	49.9	107 852	87 361	23.4	15.5	13 551	6 534	9 901	37 906	32.9	2.76	6.3	17.9

1. No spouse present.

STATE County	Births, average 1996-1998 Total	Rate[1]	Deaths, average 1996-1998 Number Total	Infant[2]	Rate Total[1]	Infant[3]	Physicians,[4] 1998 Number	Rate[5]	Hospitals,[4] 1998 Number	Beds Number	Rate[5]	Medicare enrollees 1999	Serious crimes known to police, 1998[6] Total Number	Rate[7]
	32	33	34	35	36	37	38	39	40	41	42	43	44	45
NEBRASKA—Cont'd														
Platte	454	14.8	250	4	8.2	9.5	26	85	1	81	264	3 073	927	3 027
Polk	64	11.4	82	0	14.6	0.0	2	36	1	21	373	1 120	92	1 629
Red Willow	147	12.9	122	1	10.8	6.8	13	116	1	44	391	2 409	341	2 984
Richardson	92	9.7	158	1	16.7	14.6	6	64	2	69	732	2 287	145	1 512
Rock	18	10.2	22	0	12.6	18.5	2	115	1	54	3 098	416	34	1 953
Saline	145	11.2	173	1	13.3	9.2	7	54	2	130	1 003	2 534	301	2 302
Sarpy	1 971	16.6	518	12	4.4	6.3	131	108	1	185	153	7 019	3 277	2 754
Saunders	232	12.1	190	1	9.9	4.3	6	31	1	30	156	3 127	236	1 228
Scotts Bluff	497	13.7	419	3	11.5	6.0	83	230	1	218	604	7 216	1 628	4 471
Seward	162	10.0	166	1	10.2	4.1	8	49	1	49	301	2 502	356	2 179
Sheridan	61	9.3	84	0	12.8	0.0	5	77	1	40	620	1 418	274	4 124
Sherman	35	10.1	56	0	15.9	9.4	3	87	0	0	0	801	53	1 475
Sioux	11	7.4	9	0	5.8	0.0	1	67	0	0	0	131	5	329
Stanton	88	14.2	46	0	7.4	0.0	0	0	0	0	0	615	56	900
Thayer	62	9.9	98	0	15.5	5.3	3	48	1	20	319	1 601	96	1 525
Thomas	7	9.1	7	0	8.3	0.0	0	0	0	0	0	142	11	1 372
Thurston	149	20.6	77	2	10.6	11.2	3	42	1	47	655	1 005	7	97
Valley	48	10.2	64	0	13.5	6.9	5	109	1	96	2 086	1 155	NA	NA
Washington	212	11.5	161	2	8.7	7.9	14	75	1	46	247	2 362	404	2 179
Wayne	102	10.9	66	1	7.1	6.5	5	53	1	31	330	1 398	143	1 532
Webster	39	9.8	74	0	18.3	0.0	2	50	1	16	398	1 044	89	2 202
Wheeler	13	13.8	10	0	10.7	0.0	0	0	0	0	0	152	11	1 152
York	173	11.9	163	1	11.2	5.8	13	90	2	108	744	2 650	458	3 124
NEVADA	27 245	16.3	13 676	179	8.2	6.6	3 104	178	23	3 716	213	228 631	92 250	5 281
Churchill	370	16.4	201	3	8.9	8.1	27	116	1	40	172	3 069	752	3 173
Clark	18 785	17.0	9 043	119	8.2	6.3	2 021	174	8	2 249	194	150 920	68 095	5 909
Douglas	341	9.4	273	3	7.6	7.8	59	159	0	0	0	5 502	876	2 330
Elko	786	17.5	200	3	4.5	4.2	39	85	1	50	108	2 828	1 897	4 011
Esmeralda	10	9.0	12	0	10.1	32.3	4	352	0	0	0	139	20	1 647
Eureka	22	12.1	14	0	7.6	0.0	1	50	0	0	0	227	56	2 893
Humboldt	320	18.4	94	3	5.4	9.4	15	83	1	30	165	1 433	568	3 121
Lander	140	19.9	40	1	5.8	4.8	3	43	1	6	86	447	84	1 134
Lincoln	50	12.2	41	1	10.0	13.2	3	71	1	19	450	747	61	1 320
Lyon	367	12.8	290	4	10.1	10.0	14	47	1	44	146	5 477	719	2 395
Mineral	68	12.0	68	1	12.1	19.7	3	55	1	35	641	1 071	161	2 699
Nye	304	11.3	278	3	10.3	8.8	13	45	1	45	156	6 342	1 049	3 706
Pershing	79	14.7	32	0	6.0	4.2	1	18	1	34	626	517	156	2 783
Storey	10	3.4	18	0	6.1	0.0	0	0	0	0	0	157	75	2 401
Washoe	4 754	15.5	2 450	33	8.0	6.9	801	255	4	1 009	322	38 743	15 576	4 890
White Pine	129	12.7	86	2	8.5	12.9	7	69	1	39	387	1 382	284	2 669
Carson City city	710	14.6	535	4	11.0	5.6	93	189	1	116	235	9 488	1 821	3 614
NEW HAMPSHIRE	14 421	12.3	9 449	66	8.1	4.6	2 700	228	26	3 179	268	166 751	28 675	2 420
Belknap	567	10.9	537	2	10.4	2.9	119	227	1	115	219	10 313	NA	NA
Carroll	397	10.2	442	3	11.4	8.4	85	216	2	128	325	8 355	NA	NA
Cheshire	750	10.5	649	3	9.1	4.4	137	191	1	177	246	11 105	NA	NA
Coos	311	9.4	418	2	12.6	5.3	56	170	3	172	523	7 273	NA	NA
Grafton	822	10.5	690	3	8.8	4.1	552	705	5	613	783	12 247	NA	NA
Hillsborough	4 935	13.8	2 673	22	7.5	4.5	702	193	5	938	258	45 536	NA	NA
Merrimack	1 473	11.7	1 110	7	8.8	4.8	333	261	3	347	272	18 940	NA	NA
Rockingham	3 412	12.8	1 739	13	6.5	3.9	446	164	3	405	149	31 658	NA	NA
Strafford	1 305	12.1	794	8	7.4	5.9	179	165	2	213	196	14 256	NA	NA
Sullivan	447	11.2	396	2	9.9	5.2	91	227	1	71	177	6 890	NA	NA
NEW JERSEY	114 045	14.1	72 318	746	9.0	6.5	22 333	275	94	30 258	373	1 194 539	296 527	3 654
Atlantic	3 509	14.8	2 451	29	10.4	8.4	457	192	4	1 043	438	37 333	16 774	7 036
Bergen	10 785	12.6	7 544	45	8.8	4.2	3 885	453	6	3 153	367	140 168	19 324	2 252
Burlington	5 173	12.4	3 291	29	7.9	5.6	1 069	254	3	922	219	56 371	11 182	2 655
Camden	7 175	14.2	4 586	61	9.1	8.5	1 619	320	8	2 067	409	72 152	24 710	4 860
Cape May	1 101	11.3	1 299	6	13.3	5.8	195	199	1	239	244	21 847	5 787	5 853
Cumberland	1 942	13.8	1 441	23	10.2	11.8	219	156	3	631	450	22 159	7 216	5 082
Essex	12 310	16.3	7 411	133	9.8	10.8	2 745	366	13	4 875	650	102 848	48 803	6 449
Gloucester	3 196	13.0	2 000	16	8.1	5.0	333	134	1	339	137	30 868	9 346	3 769
Hudson	8 781	15.8	4 889	77	8.8	8.8	903	162	9	2 435	437	72 790	25 641	4 614
Hunterdon	1 460	12.1	730	6	6.1	4.1	276	225	1	197	161	13 318	1 710	1 407

1. Per 1,000 estimated resident population, average 1996–1998.   2. Deaths of infants under 1 year old.   3. Deaths of infants under 1 year old per 1,000 live births.   4. Data subject to copyright.   5. Per 100,000 resident population as of July 1 of the year shown.   6. Data for serious crimes have not been adjusted for underreporting; this may affect comparability between geographic areas and over time.   7. Per 100,000 population estimated by the FBI.

Table B. States and Counties — Crime, Education, Money Income, and Poverty

STATE County	Violent	Property	Total	Percent private	High school graduate or more	Bachelor's degree or more	Total current expenditures (mil dol)	Current expenditures per student (dollars)	Per capita (dollars)	Dollars	Percent change, 1979–1989 (constant 1989 dollars)	Percent with $100,000 or more	Median household income	All persons	Persons under 18	Persons 5–17 in families
	46	47	48	49	50	51	52	53	54	55	56	57	58	59	60	61
NEBRASKA—Cont'd																
Platte	111	2 916	8 187	25.4	79.5	12.8	31.7	6 402	11 566	26 123	-9.9	1.8	39 189	7.5	9.3	8.0
Polk	53	1 576	1 364	7.5	81.0	12.4	7.4	6 178	11 377	25 959	12.6	1.1	37 296	6.9	8.2	7.3
Red Willow	210	2 774	3 025	7.0	82.2	14.9	13.5	6 078	11 146	22 336	-12.8	1.0	31 965	13.0	17.5	14.2
Richardson	73	1 439	2 137	13.9	73.3	11.7	9.6	5 482	9 943	19 521	0.2	0.2	28 765	13.0	16.3	13.3
Rock	115	1 838	489	0.0	79.4	10.1	2.3	6 368	9 396	18 974	-9.1	1.2	27 051	14.5	19.5	17.4
Saline	69	2 233	3 419	24.1	76.0	12.6	14.1	5 260	10 732	24 455	-4.1	0.6	35 541	7.9	9.1	7.8
Sarpy	88	2 666	33 538	16.1	91.0	25.4	104.7	5 573	13 284	35 575	3.8	1.9	49 644	4.1	4.9	4.4
Saunders	36	1 192	4 535	13.4	79.1	12.0	16.9	5 584	11 115	26 058	-0.3	1.3	37 441	7.5	8.9	7.8
Scotts Bluff	176	4 295	9 589	4.7	74.3	13.9	35.5	4 993	10 644	21 369	-11.9	1.6	30 152	15.6	21.5	16.8
Seward	49	2 130	4 701	31.4	80.5	14.8	18.2	6 297	11 154	27 200	2.4	1.0	40 984	7.2	8.1	7.1
Sheridan	361	3 763	1 656	2.8	74.4	15.5	7.2	5 273	10 891	19 237	-14.4	2.7	27 075	16.1	21.3	17.0
Sherman	56	1 419	908	1.9	72.2	11.4	4.3	6 814	8 176	17 025	-4.3	0.4	25 454	11.5	13.2	11.9
Sioux	0	329	356	2.2	77.1	17.8	1.4	8 593	11 001	18 810	-20.8	1.8	26 965	9.2	9.8	11.8
Stanton	64	836	1 720	11.2	79.4	7.6	2.9	5 363	9 861	24 375	-7.9	0.9	35 443	10.0	10.8	10.9
Thayer	95	1 430	1 482	10.7	72.7	10.2	8.7	7 322	10 172	20 298	-10.3	1.4	31 115	11.2	14.6	11.9
Thomas	249	1 123	226	1.3	78.8	11.4	1.1	7 951	7 865	17 273	-23.2	0.0	24 909	12.7	15.3	13.6
Thurston	42	55	1 949	6.5	70.6	8.8	10.0	6 050	7 940	18 588	-10.5	1.4	25 623	23.0	27.5	24.5
Valley	NA	NA	1 143	9.0	75.7	11.6	4.9	5 864	9 589	19 201	1.4	0.0	28 202	12.4	16.4	13.3
Washington	70	2 109	4 727	15.1	82.7	15.4	16.4	4 759	13 132	29 805	-1.0	2.7	45 194	5.1	6.0	4.8
Wayne	96	1 436	3 495	4.5	80.4	19.8	9.2	5 197	9 128	20 956	-9.5	1.0	33 981	9.6	9.6	9.1
Webster	0	2 202	891	2.5	74.0	10.3	4.8	6 060	9 339	18 349	-5.3	0.9	27 807	11.7	14.9	12.5
Wheeler	0	1 152	230	6.1	79.0	12.1	1.4	8 506	10 329	22 604	21.2	1.1	31 594	9.7	12.2	12.6
York	157	2 967	3 644	18.7	81.8	13.0	13.5	6 067	11 434	25 722	-2.6	1.9	38 051	8.2	11.1	8.8
NEVADA	644	4 637	280 411	8.7	78.8	15.3	1 434.0	5 084	15 214	31 011	1.6	3.8	39 280	10.7	15.4	13.7
Churchill	363	2 810	4 499	4.5	79.5	13.1	26.3	5 548	12 611	29 007	22.5	2.5	38 009	10.7	13.7	12.9
Clark	779	5 130	168 500	9.5	77.3	13.8	878.2	4 903	15 109	30 746	1.3	3.7	39 586	11.1	16.4	14.2
Douglas	122	2 208	6 731	8.0	87.3	20.0	42.9	5 878	17 620	35 209	-0.6	5.7	46 026	7.3	10.8	10.4
Elko	402	3 609	9 073	5.1	78.5	13.3	58.2	5 533	14 050	33 715	24.0	3.1	49 822	7.3	8.4	8.7
Esmeralda	247	1 400	274	10.9	71.5	11.1	1.4	11 602	12 776	25 577	-12.1	1.2	33 366	15.2	17.8	21.0
Eureka	620	2 273	307	2.3	75.2	13.6	6.0	18 078	14 474	31 047	40.5	3.7	45 572	8.2	8.9	10.4
Humboldt	170	2 951	3 403	4.4	75.5	12.2	22.0	5 448	13 544	33 269	36.0	2.1	47 512	8.0	9.4	9.9
Lander	216	918	1 574	2.0	73.2	10.8	9.4	5 167	13 167	33 988	12.6	2.9	49 667	8.8	9.6	10.3
Lincoln	173	1 147	1 066	2.7	77.6	13.1	9.0	8 154	9 074	20 872	-12.6	0.7	32 993	14.8	17.7	18.7
Lyon	263	2 132	4 659	5.2	75.2	9.4	32.9	5 613	11 704	25 065	-7.3	1.5	33 684	11.4	15.8	15.1
Mineral	268	2 431	1 516	6.9	73.1	9.1	6.6	5 759	11 785	26 278	6.8	0.2	33 738	16.3	23.1	22.1
Nye	336	3 370	3 369	3.5	75.1	9.5	27.8	5 588	15 454	30 211	8.9	2.6	36 580	12.7	20.7	18.4
Pershing	392	2 391	1 083	1.3	73.1	7.2	6.6	6 549	11 488	27 519	15.8	1.4	40 197	10.9	12.5	14.2
Storey	288	2 113	553	6.1	84.4	17.6	4.2	8 469	15 623	32 457	11.2	2.3	55 008	4.2	5.4	4.8
Washoe	448	4 442	61 679	8.9	82.5	20.7	246.2	4 956	16 365	31 891	-2.7	4.5	42 070	9.8	13.8	12.7
White Pine	179	2 490	2 600	6.7	73.1	11.4	11.9	6 433	12 317	27 427	2.0	2.3	39 026	13.4	15.3	15.4
Carson City city	419	3 195	9 525	7.0	82.7	16.3	42.3	5 269	15 131	31 570	0.9	2.8	40 712	10.6	15.4	14.0
NEW HAMPSHIRE	107	2 313	276 765	20.7	82.2	24.4	1 174.0	5 920	15 959	36 329	27.4	4.5	42 023	7.5	10.0	8.2
Belknap	NA	NA	11 408	13.6	80.4	20.5	60.3	6 065	14 439	31 474	23.3	3.2	38 787	8.7	13.1	10.4
Carroll	NA	NA	7 423	12.2	83.5	23.4	47.8	6 597	14 041	28 145	23.8	2.8	35 001	10.2	15.8	13.1
Cheshire	NA	NA	18 976	16.8	80.8	23.9	80.3	6 124	13 887	31 648	17.7	2.9	39 730	8.2	10.5	8.9
Coos	NA	NA	7 660	7.6	70.0	11.0	32.7	5 655	11 963	25 897	12.8	1.5	31 735	12.1	17.2	14.2
Grafton	NA	NA	21 591	26.0	81.4	26.4	103.5	6 957	13 611	30 065	23.5	3.6	38 469	9.4	12.3	10.2
Hillsborough	NA	NA	82 585	25.7	82.2	26.4	326.2	5 487	17 404	40 404	29.0	5.6	46 650	6.9	9.2	7.5
Merrimack	NA	NA	29 435	21.8	83.2	25.4	122.9	5 939	16 057	35 801	27.8	4.2	43 679	7.3	9.6	7.9
Rockingham	NA	NA	59 612	21.5	86.2	25.9	267.7	6 458	17 694	41 881	31.6	6.0	54 161	5.1	6.5	5.4
Strafford	NA	NA	29 658	14.1	79.8	21.7	87.7	5 615	13 999	32 812	21.5	2.7	39 969	9.7	13.2	11.0
Sullivan	NA	NA	8 417	9.3	75.0	16.5	32.6	6 086	12 935	29 053	13.3	1.7	37 006	9.8	14.1	12.2
NEW JERSEY	440	3 214	1 867 402	22.2	76.7	24.9	11 772.0	9 588	18 714	40 927	23.3	8.8	47 903	9.3	14.8	14.2
Atlantic	607	6 429	50 006	16.9	72.9	16.4	341.1	8 679	16 016	33 716	27.7	4.6	38 124	10.8	18.1	17.2
Bergen	147	2 105	186 843	28.0	81.6	31.7	1 174.9	10 419	24 080	49 249	22.2	14.6	59 557	5.3	8.1	7.6
Burlington	242	2 413	97 234	18.1	81.9	23.6	593.8	8 887	17 707	42 373	19.3	6.6	52 543	5.8	9.0	9.0
Camden	697	4 163	125 512	19.6	75.5	21.0	798.1	9 078	15 773	36 190	19.6	5.6	41 441	12.8	20.0	19.2
Cape May	357	5 496	19 171	15.6	74.0	17.2	144.2	9 451	15 536	30 435	29.3	4.2	36 211	11.0	18.2	18.1
Cumberland	730	4 352	33 115	13.3	63.4	10.8	224.9	8 978	12 560	29 985	16.3	2.6	34 935	15.8	24.7	23.9
Essex	1 303	5 146	197 601	22.4	70.1	24.0	1 251.4	10 612	17 574	34 518	27.2	9.1	39 823	17.3	27.0	25.3
Gloucester	234	3 535	61 760	15.9	77.5	18.1	356.9	8 290	15 207	39 387	18.5	3.9	49 279	7.4	11.0	10.5
Hudson	821	3 793	128 644	29.0	64.1	19.7	725.5	9 578	14 480	30 917	28.2	4.2	34 848	17.1	28.6	27.1
Hunterdon	77	1 330	26 315	16.9	85.9	34.6	192.4	9 860	23 236	54 628	35.2	15.2	72 398	3.1	3.9	4.2

1. Data for serious crimes have not been adjusted for underreporting; this may affect comparability between geographic areas and over time.   2. Per 100,000 population estimated by the FBI.   3. All persons 3 years old and over enrolled in nursery school through college.   4. Persons 25 years old and over.   5. Elementary and secondary education expenditures, local government fiscal years ending between July 1, 1996 and June 30, 1997.   6. Based on population enumerated as of April 1, 1990.

Table B. States and Counties — **Personal Income**

STATE County	Personal income, 1998 Total (mil dol)	Per capita¹ Percent change, 1997–1998	Per capita¹ Dollars	Per capita¹ Rank	Wages and salaries² (mil dol)	Proprietor's income (mil dol)	Dividends, interest, and rent (mil dol)	Transfer payments Total (mil dol)	Government payments to individuals Total (mil dol)	Social Security (mil dol)	Medical payments (mil dol)	Income maintenance (mil dol)	Unemployment insurance (mil dol)
	62	63	64	65	66	67	68	69	70	71	72	73	74
NEBRASKA—Cont'd													
Platte	743	1.8	24 222	602	483	85	158	84	79	45	24	4	1
Polk	133	2.2	23 654	712	33	35	31	21	20	11	7	1	0
Red Willow	251	4.0	22 284	1 018	118	33	67	48	46	21	17	3	0
Richardson	208	3.8	22 087	1 073	66	44	49	45	43	20	17	3	0
Rock	36	1.0	20 754	1 469	12	6	10	7	7	3	3	0	0
Saline	286	5.3	22 075	1 076	167	37	67	44	42	23	15	2	0
Sarpy	2 787	6.3	23 158	826	1 523	91	400	207	188	89	59	9	2
Saunders	410	4.6	21 321	1 290	108	62	76	61	58	29	23	3	1
Scotts Bluff	793	4.5	22 031	1 094	426	105	157	149	143	68	52	13	1
Seward	379	4.8	23 111	833	161	60	79	48	45	25	15	2	0
Sheridan	113	2.3	17 572	2 473	41	5	34	26	25	12	9	2	0
Sherman	59	3.1	16 976	2 617	16	8	17	14	13	7	5	1	0
Sioux	16	0.4	10 697	3 097	5	-3	6	3	3	2	1	0	0
Stanton	123	-2.2	19 788	1 784	56	24	17	14	13	7	4	1	0
Thayer	155	6.2	24 809	513	57	30	42	29	28	14	11	1	0
Thomas	11	-1.4	14 182	2 992	6	-3	5	3	3	1	1	0	0
Thurston	121	3.3	16 807	2 656	66	18	19	30	29	8	14	5	0
Valley	97	1.5	20 848	1 438	37	12	26	20	20	10	8	1	0
Washington	503	5.7	26 933	310	216	27	89	51	47	25	18	2	0
Wayne	194	4.3	20 837	1 447	91	32	36	28	27	13	9	2	0
Webster	82	3.2	20 392	1 604	24	15	21	18	17	9	7	1	0
Wheeler	21	-14.8	22 571	963	9	5	6	3	3	1	1	0	0
York	372	5.4	25 541	433	227	55	77	50	47	26	17	2	0
NEVADA	50 919	7.7	29 200	X	33 169	4 058	11 170	5 280	5 004	2 243	1 724	361	180
Churchill	510	6.4	22 041	1 091	314	39	100	69	66	27	24	6	3
Clark	33 542	8.6	28 884	199	22 543	2 736	6 731	3 574	3 391	1 501	1 198	249	116
Douglas	1 409	7.0	38 263	43	627	128	517	112	106	62	27	4	3
Elko	1 085	2.4	23 574	725	637	58	166	77	70	26	21	7	5
Esmeralda	20	4.7	17 235	2 548	11	0	3	3	3	2	1	0	0
Eureka	41	-0.8	20 718	1 479	270	3	7	5	4	2	1	1	0
Humboldt	402	0.6	22 239	1 029	298	34	64	35	32	13	10	3	2
Lander	152	-3.6	21 862	1 139	106	12	22	14	13	5	4	2	1
Lincoln	85	6.4	20 375	1 612	56	3	16	15	14	6	5	1	0
Lyon	649	8.4	21 547	1 242	240	27	142	105	100	52	29	6	5
Mineral	130	1.0	24 443	569	76	6	22	24	23	8	9	3	1
Nye	657	13.1	22 913	867	351	33	138	118	114	64	34	6	3
Pershing	114	1.8	23 585	724	86	2	19	14	13	5	5	2	0
Storey	78	5.4	26 462	345	33	3	15	7	7	4	1	0	0
Washoe	10 342	6.6	33 040	85	6 384	848	2 778	900	850	376	287	56	33
White Pine	202	0.1	20 068	1 688	134	11	37	32	30	13	10	3	1
Carson City city	1 500	5.4	30 508	152	1 004	116	394	176	168	78	59	10	7
NEW HAMPSHIRE	34 958	7.4	29 480	X	20 581	2 627	6 492	3 807	3 589	1 668	1 436	217	34
Belknap	1 473	6.9	27 824	244	749	121	357	206	196	99	73	12	1
Carroll	1 089	6.1	27 664	254	459	133	332	171	163	80	65	9	1
Cheshire	1 832	6.7	25 442	445	1 014	134	394	245	232	114	91	14	1
Coos	768	7.8	23 370	779	411	76	133	168	162	70	73	10	1
Grafton	2 255	6.8	28 826	201	1 608	227	559	286	271	121	117	15	2
Hillsborough	11 351	8.0	31 315	129	7 526	770	1 853	1 087	1 020	463	414	69	7
Merrimack	3 765	6.1	29 438	185	2 311	224	739	431	408	191	163	24	3
Rockingham	8 775	8.3	32 423	103	4 558	725	1 462	714	664	323	247	32	13
Strafford	2 684	6.6	24 515	556	1 505	144	453	344	324	137	131	23	3
Sullivan	965	4.6	24 199	606	439	73	209	156	148	70	61	10	1
NEW JERSEY	278 349	6.1	34 383	X	168 135	22 411	51 091	31 393	29 876	12 459	12 566	2 308	1 100
Atlantic	7 553	6.4	31 738	120	5 177	1 429	1 143	1 016	971	367	427	71	62
Bergen	40 244	8.1	47 101	9	22 237	5 140	8 958	3 078	2 917	1 536	1 065	100	77
Burlington	12 452	5.2	29 556	180	7 327	637	2 133	1 377	1 299	599	509	63	37
Camden	13 797	4.2	27 360	273	7 828	892	2 255	2 035	1 941	721	854	211	59
Cape May	2 773	3.3	28 297	224	1 107	200	640	530	512	222	211	22	37
Cumberland	3 195	5.1	22 756	906	1 993	232	489	643	617	219	271	63	41
Essex	24 771	3.6	33 102	84	17 574	2 095	4 504	3 722	3 582	1 051	1 701	565	122
Gloucester	6 447	5.7	25 995	398	2 978	326	865	816	770	339	307	42	32
Hudson	14 915	4.1	26 970	306	11 111	1 229	1 771	2 421	2 317	670	1 102	313	128
Hunterdon	5 198	7.7	42 471	19	2 210	342	932	300	277	146	99	8	7

1. Based on the resident population estimated as of July 1 of the year shown.   2. Includes other labor income.

Table B. States and Counties — Earnings, Social Security, and Housing

STATE County	Earnings, 1998									Social Security beneficiaries, December 1998		Supplemental Security Income recipients, December 1998	Housing units, 1990	
			Percent by selected industries											
			Goods-related[1]		Service-related and other[2]									
	Total (mil dol)	Farm	Total	Manu-facturing	Total	Retail trade	Finance, insur-ance, and real estate	Services	Govern-ment	Number	Rate[3]		Total	Percent change, 1980-1990
	75	76	77	78	79	80	81	82	83	84	85	86	87	88

NEBRASKA—Cont'd

Platte	568	7.3	D	34.8	D	7.8	3.8	14.8	14.8	5 301	172	252	11 716	7.1
Polk	68	44.1	D	2.0	D	5.4	2.9	11.8	16.1	1 306	232	39	2 742	6.5
Red Willow	151	10.8	D	8.8	D	13.4	4.9	19.1	18.3	2 549	226	175	5 279	-0.6
Richardson	110	22.0	D	7.2	D	8.9	3.7	18.7	14.9	2 535	269	166	4 704	-4.4
Rock	18	23.5	D	2.6	D	4.5	2.8	11.6	27.5	426	244	22	1 001	-3.8
Saline	204	11.6	D	41.8	D	7.4	2.6	12.4	14.9	2 785	215	108	5 299	-1.7
Sarpy	1 613	0.4	D	4.7	D	6.4	2.4	15.3	42.3	10 440	86	353	35 994	30.0
Saunders	170	22.8	D	7.3	D	8.7	4.2	15.1	19.3	3 478	181	148	7 594	0.1
Scotts Bluff	531	7.4	D	11.6	D	11.3	5.1	24.7	16.3	8 187	227	824	15 514	1.3
Seward	221	17.1	21.7	16.5	47.0	6.4	3.4	20.1	14.2	2 871	176	93	5 908	3.8
Sheridan	46	-9.1	D	1.0	D	16.5	7.6	18.7	37.3	1 571	243	93	3 211	1.1
Sherman	23	19.6	D	2.7	D	9.2	4.7	15.5	29.7	937	273	49	1 874	3.3
Sioux	2	-99.1	D	0.0	D	19.2	D	34.1	91.9	234	157	5	869	5.8
Stanton	80	21.1	D	D	D	1.6	1.7	7.1	9.4	920	148	27	2 355	2.9
Thayer	87	26.3	20.8	17.5	35.1	6.2	4.9	10.2	17.8	1 783	284	84	3 017	-5.2
Thomas	3	-101.4	D	D	D	26.7	D	28.7	63.4	198	248	10	404	-5.2
Thurston	83	11.8	D	10.0	D	4.3	3.6	32.0	25.1	1 163	162	203	2 548	-0.9
Valley	50	15.2	D	2.0	46.6	9.2	5.3	14.4	32.1	1 290	280	76	2 469	-2.9
Washington	243	6.6	D	15.1	D	8.6	2.6	21.6	27.3	2 846	153	86	6 378	12.1
Wayne	123	19.7	22.5	15.6	31.6	6.4	5.3	12.8	26.2	1 597	170	81	3 517	-1.5
Webster	40	30.0	D	0.8	D	8.6	4.4	12.1	19.2	1 165	290	64	2 048	-7.1
Wheeler	14	70.3	D	D	D	2.1	D	3.0	11.9	199	215	8	561	3.5
York	282	11.5	D	17.1	D	9.5	3.1	16.2	12.1	2 977	205	110	5 861	1.2
NEVADA	37 227	0.2	18.2	4.7	67.0	9.4	8.5	38.4	14.6	260 634	149	23 366	518 858	52.6
Churchill	353	2.5	15.2	6.2	43.6	9.4	2.9	25.2	38.7	3 497	150	288	7 290	26.3
Clark	25 278	0.0	16.2	3.2	70.6	9.7	9.6	41.2	13.1	172 560	148	16 858	317 188	66.4
Douglas	755	0.0	D	9.9	D	6.5	10.2	49.4	9.9	6 959	188	159	14 121	50.2
Elko	694	0.9	20.7	1.1	D	8.7	D	35.0	20.3	3 286	71	307	13 461	75.6
Esmeralda	12	3.0	D	1.9	D	3.2	0.0	D	26.2	213	188	25	966	162.5
Eureka	273	1.0	93.4	0.1	D	0.6	D	1.0	3.5	231	116	19	817	35.0
Humboldt	331	3.0	46.5	2.0	35.1	9.8	1.8	11.9	15.4	1 623	89	187	5 044	31.8
Lander	117	2.0	D	D	D	6.6	0.6	8.3	19.1	595	85	72	2 586	55.4
Lincoln	59	1.5	D	D	D	6.9	1.3	D	38.5	826	196	46	1 800	6.8
Lyon	267	3.2	34.5	21.0	43.3	8.9	3.3	19.1	19.0	6 308	210	357	8 722	50.0
Mineral	81	-0.6	23.5	0.5	D	5.7	1.6	42.3	26.1	1 197	219	111	2 994	-0.8
Nye	384	2.7	23.7	1.1	56.4	6.1	1.8	43.9	17.2	7 633	265	296	8 073	88.1
Pershing	89	3.1	52.9	1.4	D	7.2	D	3.5	27.4	634	117	57	1 908	34.9
Storey	37	0.0	D	D	D	10.7	D	14.2	18.7	481	158	19	1 085	49.4
Washoe	7 232	0.0	18.2	8.3	67.5	9.4	7.3	35.7	14.3	43 543	139	3 656	112 193	30.4
White Pine	145	0.5	32.0	0.8	D	8.6	3.5	13.9	35.4	1 569	156	121	3 982	8.7
Carson City city	1 119	0.0	D	13.2	D	9.5	5.2	21.1	37.2	9 471	192	561	16 628	24.4
NEW HAMPSHIRE	23 208	0.2	29.0	22.3	59.3	11.6	7.3	28.0	11.5	192 107	162	11 290	503 904	30.4
Belknap	870	0.0	31.1	20.8	56.6	16.9	3.2	27.0	12.3	11 382	217	620	30 306	26.3
Carroll	592	0.2	21.7	9.0	66.1	21.4	4.0	33.6	12.0	9 415	239	392	32 146	40.7
Cheshire	1 148	0.6	D	22.4	D	14.1	10.7	22.6	11.9	12 803	178	724	30 350	19.6
Coos	487	0.5	D	24.8	D	12.2	2.3	24.5	13.6	8 398	255	540	18 712	16.9
Grafton	1 835	0.1	24.8	20.0	63.9	10.8	3.6	41.9	11.1	13 915	178	706	42 206	30.9
Hillsborough	8 296	0.0	31.6	26.4	59.2	9.9	9.7	28.0	9.2	52 374	144	3 570	135 622	34.0
Merrimack	2 535	0.4	22.8	15.4	57.7	9.9	8.3	28.2	19.1	22 047	173	1 427	50 870	28.3
Rockingham	5 283	0.1	26.9	19.1	64.5	13.5	6.0	27.3	8.5	36 991	136	1 442	101 773	33.7
Strafford	1 649	0.1	32.8	27.3	48.1	10.2	5.5	20.2	19.0	16 679	154	1 201	42 387	30.6
Sullivan	511	0.8	D	32.5	D	11.6	3.4	19.2	15.3	8 086	202	626	19 532	18.5
NEW JERSEY	190 546	0.1	19.7	15.2	66.2	7.5	9.5	31.3	14.1	1 317 284	162	145 159	3 075 310	10.9
Atlantic	6 606	0.4	D	3.2	D	6.8	3.2	60.3	14.3	41 337	174	4 869	106 877	19.6
Bergen	27 378	0.0	19.3	16.1	73.4	7.3	8.0	34.7	7.3	149 914	175	8 156	324 817	5.9
Burlington	7 965	0.4	18.3	12.7	63.3	9.5	7.6	30.1	18.0	64 087	152	4 116	143 236	18.2
Camden	8 720	0.1	18.5	12.8	63.9	9.2	6.6	33.2	17.5	79 777	158	11 879	190 145	9.5
Cape May	1 307	0.2	D	2.5	D	17.8	6.6	D	27.0	24 668	252	1 575	85 537	18.6
Cumberland	2 225	2.1	29.0	22.7	46.0	8.3	4.7	20.7	22.8	25 252	180	4 452	50 294	6.2
Essex	19 669	0.0	13.0	9.9	68.3	5.2	14.7	31.1	18.7	114 378	152	25 526	298 710	-5.8
Gloucester	3 305	0.9	28.6	19.9	53.0	11.6	3.2	21.9	17.5	37 545	151	2 804	82 459	19.3
Hudson	12 340	0.0	13.2	10.5	69.2	7.2	18.2	22.5	17.7	78 508	141	21 300	229 682	3.8
Hunterdon	2 552	0.2	32.1	24.9	55.0	8.9	7.5	28.4	12.7	14 835	121	676	39 987	33.2

1. Covers mining, construction, and manufacturing. 2. Covers private sector earnings in agricultural services, forestry, and fisheries; transportation and public utilities; wholesale trade; retail trade; finance, insurance, and real estate; and services. 3. Per 1,000 resident population estimated as of July 1 of the year shown.

STATE County	Total [89]	Percent [90]	Median value[1] [91]	With a mortgage [92]	Without a mortgage [93]	Median rent[2] [94]	Rent as percent of income [95]	Substandard units[3] (percent) [96]	Total [97]	Percent change, 1998–1999 [98]	Total [99]	Rate[4] [100]	Total [101]	Professional, managerial, and technical [102]	Precision production, craft, and repair [103]
NEBRASKA—Cont'd															
Platte	10 954	73.4	51 900	18.5	12.2	315	20.6	2.0	16 951	-3.9	595	3.5	14 757	22.5	12.8
Polk	2 223	76.3	30 700	14.4	11.8	247	17.1	1.1	2 343	0.5	48	2.0	2 598	17.6	10.2
Red Willow	4 723	69.7	39 000	18.3	12.5	281	21.8	1.0	5 966	1.6	166	2.8	5 582	21.9	11.4
Richardson	4 120	71.7	24 800	15.9	12.8	218	20.8	1.9	4 314	-2.0	251	5.8	4 169	19.5	11.7
Rock	798	70.1	26 600	16.0	13.5	232	22.1	2.4	874	-2.9	37	4.2	974	13.7	6.6
Saline	4 829	73.3	37 500	15.9	12.4	296	18.5	1.2	7 030	1.3	140	2.0	6 020	20.9	12.5
Sarpy	33 960	63.0	66 900	21.8	12.1	473	23.5	2.2	60 396	0.6	1 289	2.1	45 877	30.9	8.6
Saunders	6 809	79.7	43 600	20.2	13.0	299	21.0	1.8	10 029	-4.0	288	2.9	8 723	18.7	13.0
Scotts Bluff	14 056	64.3	40 400	19.8	13.3	306	25.8	3.3	18 064	0.0	783	4.3	16 361	23.8	10.8
Seward	5 432	70.4	48 900	17.5	12.2	327	21.6	1.5	8 843	-4.1	242	2.7	7 841	21.2	11.5
Sheridan	2 618	69.3	28 800	16.3	14.1	269	25.5	3.3	2 867	0.1	87	3.0	2 942	20.2	8.7
Sherman	1 431	75.6	16 400	19.9	14.3	231	19.7	1.8	1 462	-0.7	44	3.0	1 613	15.5	9.1
Sioux	612	64.2	27 000	24.2	12.4	307	16.7	5.3	778	-0.4	15	1.9	755	19.1	4.6
Stanton	2 167	76.1	41 700	21.0	12.2	274	20.3	1.6	3 269	-3.4	102	3.1	2 903	17.3	11.9
Thayer	2 669	78.1	24 200	17.0	12.8	254	18.5	1.1	3 271	2.0	71	2.2	3 019	18.7	9.2
Thomas	316	71.2	24 800	21.1	13.1	286	23.3	4.4	462	1.5	27	5.8	374	13.9	8.6
Thurston	2 288	60.7	30 700	16.7	12.2	197	17.7	9.2	2 817	-4.9	315	11.2	2 349	22.3	10.2
Valley	2 141	71.8	23 800	16.2	13.2	228	23.2	1.4	2 469	-0.4	64	2.6	2 576	18.6	8.6
Washington	6 017	74.9	58 200	18.4	12.8	327	23.9	2.9	10 765	-0.3	231	2.1	8 567	25.8	12.3
Wayne	3 232	64.8	44 100	17.4	12.7	262	24.3	1.3	6 264	7.4	223	3.6	4 514	21.8	8.2
Webster	1 755	78.4	22 600	17.6	13.3	200	21.2	1.5	1 795	0.7	41	2.3	1 728	18.3	11.2
Wheeler	350	66.0	18 800	11.4	13.1	227	16.8	4.5	407	20.8	14	3.4	427	16.6	4.2
York	5 467	68.6	45 200	19.1	12.0	309	21.6	1.0	9 092	-0.5	136	1.5	6 813	20.2	11.4
NEVADA	466 297	54.8	95 700	22.4	11.9	509	26.8	6.4	941 600	2.4	41 863	4.4	607 437	24.8	11.4
Churchill	6 666	63.1	84 500	21.4	12.0	459	24.4	4.6	9 325	-3.7	801	8.6	7 273	24.5	16.5
Clark	287 025	51.9	93 300	22.4	11.6	516	27.3	6.8	649 848	4.4	28 675	4.4	370 583	23.7	10.9
Douglas	10 571	68.9	121 000	22.6	11.8	621	26.3	4.3	17 439	-0.9	852	4.9	13 859	27.4	12.3
Elko	11 777	64.5	81 600	18.3	11.9	435	21.9	8.8	20 033	-5.4	1 059	5.3	16 587	22.5	19.4
Esmeralda	588	60.4	41 400	18.6	12.7	351	16.8	11.1	607	10.4	67	11.0	673	18.0	19.5
Eureka	617	68.2	54 600	15.0	13.6	424	14.3	5.5	903	-1.1	38	4.2	808	18.1	21.0
Humboldt	4 538	67.3	74 000	18.9	11.6	449	18.4	8.7	7 934	-7.3	509	6.4	6 400	23.6	15.4
Lander	2 212	70.3	58 300	15.6	14.7	374	18.8	7.3	2 570	-12.3	238	9.3	2 918	18.6	22.3
Lincoln	1 325	73.5	50 900	16.1	11.7	264	21.7	7.4	1 045	-8.9	63	6.0	1 371	23.0	9.7
Lyon	7 680	72.4	74 900	22.2	12.4	391	25.0	5.1	12 586	2.0	1 066	8.5	8 583	21.2	16.2
Mineral	2 529	66.5	56 900	16.4	14.6	432	20.8	7.8	2 039	-15.4	166	8.1	2 861	22.8	14.7
Nye	6 664	70.2	70 800	17.9	11.8	380	17.7	7.3	15 041	5.9	742	4.9	8 256	20.6	22.4
Pershing	1 614	60.7	66 500	21.2	12.7	389	21.1	7.7	2 240	-10.8	83	3.7	1 947	19.5	15.5
Storey	1 006	73.0	99 500	23.2	11.9	441	27.8	3.5	1 553	-1.8	59	3.8	1 384	30.1	11.4
Washoe	102 294	54.1	111 200	23.4	12.2	509	26.6	5.7	173 249	-1.2	6 423	3.7	140 734	27.7	9.5
White Pine	3 296	72.6	53 000	14.1	14.3	387	21.2	5.0	3 221	-9.2	121	3.8	3 840	25.1	17.2
Carson City city	15 895	60.3	99 300	20.9	10.6	480	27.4	3.0	21 970	-3.1	902	4.1	19 360	30.6	12.4
NEW HAMPSHIRE	411 186	68.2	129 400	24.4	14.7	549	26.4	2.1	665 927	2.1	18 068	2.7	574 237	32.6	12.5
Belknap	18 839	71.5	114 000	24.0	14.5	510	27.4	2.2	30 029	2.7	713	2.4	24 333	27.8	14.9
Carroll	14 253	75.3	119 000	25.7	14.7	521	27.9	2.7	21 352	2.0	539	2.5	16 948	26.7	14.5
Cheshire	25 856	70.4	110 600	23.9	15.4	516	28.0	2.7	38 476	0.1	1 036	2.7	36 083	28.8	13.5
Coos	13 799	70.3	71 600	20.5	14.6	340	27.1	2.3	16 694	0.6	692	4.1	15 472	20.8	14.5
Grafton	27 542	67.2	105 700	23.4	15.2	479	27.1	3.3	43 887	1.1	826	1.9	37 497	31.5	11.0
Hillsborough	124 567	63.7	137 500	24.2	14.6	588	26.0	1.8	205 978	2.4	5 540	2.7	179 821	34.9	11.3
Merrimack	44 595	69.7	117 800	24.4	14.9	534	26.2	2.0	75 348	3.2	1 567	2.1	61 201	33.6	12.4
Rockingham	89 118	72.2	149 800	25.3	14.3	614	25.4	1.8	154 999	3.0	5 192	3.3	131 222	35.7	12.6
Strafford	37 744	64.8	116 400	24.8	14.6	522	27.3	1.9	57 714	0.1	1 380	2.4	53 105	29.5	13.9
Sullivan	14 873	70.7	90 900	23.8	15.9	440	27.1	2.8	21 448	1.8	582	2.7	18 555	24.7	15.1
NEW JERSEY	2 794 711	64.9	162 300	23.4	15.1	592	26.3	4.1	4 206 799	1.2	193 300	4.6	3 868 698	34.0	10.0
Atlantic	85 123	64.5	105 900	22.4	15.6	574	27.4	4.0	127 031	-0.2	9 201	7.2	113 910	25.6	10.0
Bergen	308 880	67.9	227 700	23.2	15.3	689	25.6	2.6	447 320	1.5	16 381	3.7	436 439	39.4	8.9
Burlington	136 554	75.4	122 500	22.4	13.7	597	25.8	2.1	225 031	1.9	7 528	3.3	197 588	34.1	10.3
Camden	178 758	69.8	99 300	22.2	15.0	507	27.3	3.8	260 236	1.6	12 023	4.6	238 771	33.1	10.7
Cape May	37 856	72.0	112 800	23.7	15.6	565	28.1	2.2	45 605	-0.6	4 610	10.1	40 777	29.1	11.6
Cumberland	47 118	68.5	73 900	20.8	14.4	480	27.9	4.7	64 320	-1.0	5 502	8.6	60 937	22.8	12.6
Essex	278 752	45.3	196 100	22.9	15.0	528	26.8	8.1	369 446	0.9	21 031	5.7	364 513	31.6	8.3
Gloucester	78 845	78.3	99 300	22.2	14.5	521	26.4	2.0	131 329	2.0	5 893	4.5	112 523	30.7	13.7
Hudson	208 739	32.5	157 000	24.0	15.6	525	25.0	9.9	283 560	0.7	20 534	7.2	268 816	27.2	8.8
Hunterdon	37 906	80.5	209 900	25.4	14.4	721	26.2	0.9	68 895	1.5	1 453	2.1	58 463	42.3	10.6

1. Specified owner-occupied units.   2. Specified renter-occupied units.   3. Overcrowded or lacking complete plumbing facilities.   4. Percent of civilian labor force.   5. Persons 16 years and older.

Table B. States and Counties — Nonfarm Employment and Agriculture

| | Private nonfarm establishments, employment and payroll, 1998 | | | | | | | | Agriculture, 1997 | | | |
| | | Employment | | | | | Annual payroll | | Farms | | | Farm operators |
STATE County	Number of establish-ments	Total	Health Care and Social Assistance	Manufac-turing	Retail trade	Finance and Insurance	Professional Scientific and Technical Services	Total (mil dol)	Average per employee (dollars)	Number	Less than 50 acres	500 acres and over	Whose principal occu-pation is farming (percent)
	104	105	106	107	108	109	110	111	112	113	114	115	116
NEBRASKA—Cont'd													
Platte	992	15 781	1 050	6 290	1 991	515	485	361	22 883	1 024	18.8	30.1	69.7
Polk	139	944	273	D	134	71	24	17	17 479	601	16.6	34.1	76.0
Red Willow	430	4 274	628	505	1 136	174	140	72	16 796	438	17.6	53.4	69.2
Richardson	305	2 176	469	321	385	118	60	36	16 518	717	12.1	29.4	55.9
Rock	61	412	D	D	58	18	D	6	13 667	316	8.2	64.6	75.0
Saline	311	5 227	494	2 361	602	144	51	113	21 654	727	14.7	31.9	66.6
Sarpy	2 010	26 503	2 229	2 070	5 058	1 609	1 507	653	24 654	367	30.8	19.9	57.8
Saunders	452	3 139	405	497	591	167	103	57	18 265	1 176	18.8	25.9	66.8
Scotts Bluff	1 227	12 633	2 235	1 377	2 476	484	462	269	21 256	789	14.6	26.5	68.1
Seward	408	5 562	556	1 128	515	197	61	109	19 603	833	22.2	30.1	60.5
Sheridan	198	1 179	253	12	344	111	39	16	13 585	656	10.8	60.4	71.6
Sherman	80	435	84	19	93	28	7	6	13 223	483	9.1	41.8	71.0
Sioux	16	42	0	0	16	D	D	0	9 762	343	8.2	65.0	74.9
Stanton	87	517	12	D	70	34	7	7	14 273	609	13.8	27.4	63.5
Thayer	218	1 783	391	447	293	108	24	36	20 189	569	8.6	45.2	76.8
Thomas	38	220	0	D	D	D	D	3	14 550	87	8.0	75.9	69.0
Thurston	135	1 457	412	324	215	40	18	30	20 478	379	13.2	33.8	62.8
Valley	175	1 181	311	46	243	75	59	20	16 633	445	11.9	48.3	76.4
Washington	454	5 322	622	927	692	167	142	124	23 262	692	25.6	20.8	58.5
Wayne	256	3 686	362	1 640	394	400	38	66	17 875	612	17.0	30.7	69.4
Webster	104	644	168	16	119	39	5	10	15 388	433	12.0	46.2	63.7
Wheeler	16	96	0	D	18	14	D	1	8 760	186	10.8	61.3	70.4
York	518	6 357	896	1 052	914	286	131	133	20 910	712	14.5	40.9	78.5
NEVADA	44 613	800 861	60 524	39 029	95 507	27 360	33 347	21 847	27 280	2 829	39.6	26.1	55.1
Churchill	511	4 687	695	266	1 003	121	156	104	22 083	511	50.1	9.8	56.2
Clark	26 691	549 060	38 764	17 892	63 916	19 612	23 235	14 998	27 315	209	70.3	3.8	40.2
Douglas	1 289	18 349	484	1 996	1 215	382	647	454	24 724	156	53.2	14.1	48.1
Elko	1 012	17 108	1 027	179	2 199	387	371	449	26 243	402	25.1	49.5	59.5
Esmeralda	15	166	0	D	D	0	D	5	29 452	20	10.0	35.0	85.0
Eureka	39	2 767	D	D	D	D	D	133	48 086	84	4.8	45.2	66.7
Humboldt	409	6 615	345	320	1 044	83	97	199	30 029	218	20.2	49.1	65.6
Lander	98	1 451	94	D	286	19	7	42	28 802	76	21.1	46.1	72.4
Lincoln	80	511	D	0	180	35	D	8	14 722	121	30.6	19.8	49.6
Lyon	546	6 001	399	1 598	743	82	425	138	22 947	305	42.6	22.0	59.7
Mineral	89	1 551	313	D	129	D	7	36	23 015	37	54.1	21.6	37.8
Nye	543	5 444	352	206	765	131	84	135	24 706	144	42.4	23.6	56.2
Pershing	95	1 470	107	35	167	D	9	50	33 929	120	15.8	35.0	62.5
Storey	82	321	D	0	90	D	25	5	15 623	8	62.5	0.0	50.0
Washoe	10 674	161 330	15 048	12 262	19 630	5 470	7 123	4 458	27 634	285	56.1	17.5	36.8
White Pine	215	2 287	286	D	412	61	28	66	28 835	115	24.3	35.7	61.7
Carson City city	2 209	21 677	2 537	4 097	3 666	925	1 117	563	25 973	18	33.3	27.8	55.6
NEW HAMPSHIRE	36 842	518 526	68 223	101 513	85 811	24 936	22 048	14 864	28 666	2 937	41.2	5.2	42.9
Belknap	1 865	20 889	3 061	4 584	4 528	544	555	521	24 936	184	41.8	3.8	37.0
Carroll	1 833	17 639	2 275	1 700	3 262	334	2 277	333	18 894	177	36.7	4.5	37.9
Cheshire	1 952	27 490	3 833	6 130	5 007	1 813	572	715	25 992	293	40.6	5.8	36.5
Coos	975	11 540	2 054	2 876	2 084	336	146	266	23 050	185	24.3	10.3	45.9
Grafton	2 875	46 559	7 639	7 366	6 293	864	1 110	1 150	24 691	406	27.8	8.4	44.3
Hillsborough	10 779	176 318	21 437	38 701	25 800	7 925	8 382	5 501	31 198	391	51.2	1.8	47.6
Merrimack	3 991	51 764	9 496	9 774	7 473	2 996	2 262	1 460	28 201	413	41.4	6.5	45.8
Rockingham	9 078	114 513	11 798	16 882	23 288	5 003	4 815	3 553	31 027	407	55.0	1.5	46.4
Strafford	2 403	39 309	5 180	8 591	5 931	4 737	1 652	1 065	27 098	235	45.5	3.0	42.1
Sullivan	1 091	12 505	1 450	4 909	2 145	384	277	301	24 048	246	35.8	8.1	36.6
NEW JERSEY	230 860	3 368 365	405 935	405 275	417 791	200 646	234 816	125 787	37 344	9 101	66.5	3.8	43.1
Atlantic	6 310	121 092	12 525	4 900	14 519	2 621	3 797	3 273	27 030	424	69.8	1.9	46.7
Bergen	32 941	446 352	45 357	57 476	52 286	21 107	26 628	17 865	40 025	121	92.6	0.8	52.1
Burlington	10 086	158 802	19 806	20 054	23 412	10 662	10 273	5 117	32 225	857	64.8	3.7	50.4
Camden	12 595	178 439	29 852	20 976	26 435	8 243	12 779	5 451	30 549	211	79.6	1.4	40.3
Cape May	4 045	24 929	3 827	742	5 286	884	993	643	25 777	149	70.5	2.0	38.3
Cumberland	3 058	44 863	6 604	11 995	7 188	1 606	1 320	1 250	27 873	573	61.8	4.7	53.1
Essex	19 880	332 831	52 830	36 200	26 885	33 139	23 557	12 440	37 376	21	90.5	0.0	47.6
Gloucester	5 510	73 288	7 919	10 477	13 979	1 889	3 024	2 130	29 059	652	66.3	3.2	48.5
Hudson	13 254	210 152	19 391	23 771	21 551	21 835	9 194	7 802	37 126	NA	NA	NA	NA
Hunterdon	3 776	40 135	4 627	5 689	6 505	1 382	3 711	1 604	39 959	1 313	65.0	3.0	37.8

Table B. States and Counties — Agriculture, Land, and Water

STATE County	Land in farms — Acreage (1,000)	Percent change, 1992–1997	Acres — Average size of farm	Acres — Total irrigated (1,000)	Acres — Total cropland (1,000)	Value of land and buildings — Average per farm ($1,000)	Value of land and buildings — Average per acre (dollars)	Value of machinery and equipment Average per farm ($1,000)	Value of products sold — Total (mil dol)	Value of products sold — Average per farm (dollars)	Percent from — Crops	Percent from — Livestock and poultry products	Percent of farms with sales of — $10,000 or more	Percent of farms with sales of — $100,000 or more	Percent of land owned by Fed. Gov. 1997	Water consumption 1995 (mil gal/day)
	117	118	119	120	121	122	123	124	125	126	127	128	129	130	131	132
NEBRASKA—Cont'd																
Platte	420	2.4	410	148	356	658	1 582	104	225	219 502	36.1	63.9	84.0	43.1	0.0	117.0
Polk	259	3.4	430	132	220	584	1 415	106	166	275 579	38.1	61.9	86.5	46.3	0.0	116.2
Red Willow	436	-0.6	996	54	262	578	562	95	92	211 040	41.0	59.0	74.2	36.1	0.3	62.2
Richardson	319	5.5	444	2	242	367	904	52	69	96 572	60.7	39.3	75.7	26.6	0.0	2.6
Rock	631	-4.1	1 997	41	169	581	281	66	56	176 043	26.7	73.3	74.1	33.9	0.0	25.7
Saline	318	1.8	437	75	265	396	975	76	77	105 298	67.9	32.1	77.9	31.6	0.0	66.3
Sarpy	102	-3.2	277	8	90	623	2 357	69	57	155 882	38.5	61.5	67.6	25.1	4.3	64.8
Saunders	436	-0.3	371	76	382	581	1 556	89	144	122 166	57.3	42.7	76.0	28.0	0.5	123.1
Scotts Bluff	443	6.0	561	173	227	373	619	78	232	293 785	24.6	75.4	77.4	32.3	1.1	371.3
Seward	321	1.8	385	108	279	606	1 521	89	147	176 233	46.8	53.2	71.3	34.1	0.3	99.4
Sheridan	1 487	0.3	2 267	56	335	555	232	60	66	100 779	29.1	70.9	70.6	26.2	0.0	81.5
Sherman	324	8.7	671	59	178	367	510	77	43	89 291	54.5	45.5	77.0	29.8	0.7	115.1
Sioux	1 115	10.8	3 250	41	97	744	249	56	71	205 982	13.0	87.0	81.6	35.3	7.0	30.0
Stanton	226	4.3	372	23	183	341	928	68	104	170 418	26.8	73.2	71.6	29.6	0.0	22.3
Thayer	368	5.9	648	116	288	674	979	109	107	188 864	59.0	41.0	83.1	42.4	0.0	111.5
Thomas	369	2.4	4 236	2	14	678	160	41	8	96 126	9.5	90.5	77.0	27.6	17.3	7.6
Thurston	189	-2.6	499	6	170	476	1 023	82	60	157 132	50.6	49.4	74.7	38.8	0.2	7.6
Valley	333	-1.9	747	72	154	468	691	77	90	202 807	29.7	70.3	83.8	35.3	0.9	45.7
Washington	219	-3.9	317	15	196	635	2 083	89	93	133 736	48.7	51.3	69.8	29.3	1.7	445.0
Wayne	257	3.3	420	18	233	431	1 013	79	92	151 118	41.4	58.6	75.5	37.3	0.0	21.0
Webster	314	1.9	725	37	183	442	569	51	114	262 592	23.2	76.8	73.0	27.9	0.0	116.6
Wheeler	293	10.9	1 574	49	122	582	343	133	127	681 953	10.6	89.4	79.6	41.9	0.0	30.4
York	353	2.0	496	228	320	888	1 788	142	178	250 437	56.5	43.5	88.1	56.7	0.1	232.1
NEVADA	6 409	-30.8	2 266	765	847	876	388	70	357	126 039	42.5	57.5	51.8	18.0	84.6	2 259.3
Churchill	129	-51.8	253	47	54	463	2 203	54	38	74 478	29.7	70.3	48.3	11.2	78.8	140.0
Clark	71	-13.7	338	6	9	814	1 610	47	19	90 557	33.4	66.6	28.7	7.2	88.3	412.7
Douglas	90	13.0	579	38	26	1 200	1 993	47	9	56 382	24.4	75.6	48.1	15.4	51.2	130.8
Elko	2 855	-9.4	7 103	205	237	933	132	57	49	122 458	8.6	91.4	60.4	22.1	71.9	358.6
Esmeralda	27	-98.6	1 373	16	12	1 264	921	164	4	200 822	83.8	16.2	90.0	45.0	97.6	35.9
Eureka	215	-8.9	2 559	49	41	881	344	118	13	156 344	52.8	47.2	75.0	42.9	79.3	99.0
Humboldt	733	-0.6	3 364	157	172	887	267	141	57	262 912	67.8	32.2	67.9	35.8	81.1	279.9
Lander	486	-1.6	6 395	26	32	1 477	231	109	13	168 342	42.1	57.9	72.4	40.8	84.8	95.3
Lincoln	49	-0.2	404	16	17	368	953	48	7	60 469	54.4	45.6	41.3	10.7	98.4	54.4
Lyon	174	-7.7	572	74	79	909	1 738	86	54	175 922	54.9	45.1	59.0	22.0	66.7	194.2
Mineral	D	D	D	10	11	3 171	D	88	2	48 681	40.5	59.5	45.9	13.5	86.4	23.0
Nye	86	-38.9	594	17	28	558	956	69	28	193 003	26.6	73.4	39.6	10.4	97.6	72.6
Pershing	119	-80.9	995	40	50	794	711	114	33	272 326	44.5	55.5	66.7	25.0	74.3	86.0
Storey	D	D	D	0	0	332	D	33	0	11 626	D	D	50.0	0.0	8.1	3.2
Washoe	772	8.6	2 709	35	42	1 326	498	32	23	79 012	67.4	32.6	34.4	7.0	68.9	153.2
White Pine	247	6.7	2 152	29	34	892	437	68	8	71 617	21.9	78.1	58.3	18.3	94.5	105.1
Carson City city	7	44.5	401	1	1	438	1 091	40	0	11 021	D	D	22.2	0.0	52.2	15.2
NEW HAMPSHIRE	415	7.5	141	3	133	324	2 250	38	149	50 891	49.3	50.7	33.0	9.4	12.8	445.5
Belknap	21	-1.8	112	0	5	228	2 020	29	4	19 924	65.2	34.8	29.3	3.3	0.5	6.7
Carroll	24	-3.4	136	0	6	278	2 096	27	4	20 089	63.7	36.3	26.6	4.5	24.1	8.1
Cheshire	42	22.5	142	0	12	367	2 234	45	28	93 972	11.5	88.5	29.0	10.6	0.5	9.2
Coos	43	-6.7	232	0	14	213	840	41	8	42 111	20.3	79.7	37.3	9.2	20.1	46.3
Grafton	76	-0.2	187	0	27	290	1 533	38	17	42 808	17.4	82.6	36.0	14.0	31.1	19.4
Hillsborough	38	-6.1	96	1	15	397	3 473	31	16	41 586	72.1	27.9	32.5	8.7	1.3	59.1
Merrimack	63	34.9	154	1	17	315	2 362	42	29	70 796	70.8	29.2	32.0	11.1	1.8	244.9
Rockingham	35	4.3	87	1	14	322	4 301	43	17	41 204	74.0	26.0	34.4	9.1	0.9	24.5
Strafford	26	4.3	111	0	9	357	2 932	37	9	38 865	64.0	36.0	38.3	6.0	0.1	21.7
Sullivan	47	24.4	192	0	13	382	1 999	39	18	73 739	58.7	41.3	31.7	10.2	0.1	5.6
NEW JERSEY	833	-1.8	91	93	595	594	6 642	48	697	76 627	85.0	15.0	39.0	12.8	2.8	2 137.5
Atlantic	31	3.5	73	12	19	363	5 251	69	63	149 690	99.0	1.0	46.2	19.8	5.3	46.2
Bergen	3	-12.2	22	0	1	554	21 468	31	9	74 444	96.0	4.0	57.0	15.7	0.0	121.9
Burlington	104	6.9	121	11	70	615	5 250	88	102	102 141	86.6	13.4	47.7	14.6	4.1	233.8
Camden	9	12.6	43	3	7	359	8 288	27	17	82 811	98.5	1.5	38.9	12.3	0.0	72.6
Cape May	10	-19.4	65	1	6	296	4 669	39	7	45 685	95.9	4.1	34.9	8.1	2.1	25.6
Cumberland	66	-3.9	116	19	51	421	3 738	77	94	164 315	96.0	4.0	53.8	27.9	0.0	87.4
Essex	D	D	D	0	0	500	29 020	64	1	58 235	99.3	0.7	71.4	19.0	0.1	31.8
Gloucester	58	-5.9	90	13	46	457	5 103	50	67	102 717	91.5	8.5	46.3	18.9	0.0	73.2
Hudson	NA	NA	NA	NA	NA	NA	NA	NA	NA	NA	NA	NA	NA	NA	1.5	0.2
Hunterdon	105	-0.7	80	1	78	582	7 346	35	36	27 461	78.1	21.9	28.1	5.0	0.0	73.2

Table B. States and Counties — Residential Construction, Wholesale and Retail Trade, and Real Estate

STATE County	Value of Residential Construction Authorized by Building Permits, 1999		Wholesale Trade, 1997				Retail Trade[1], 1997				Real Estate and Rental and Leasing, 1997			
	New Construction ($1,000)	Number of Housing Units	Number of Establish-ments	Number of Employees	Sales (mil dol)	Annual Payroll (mil dol)	Number of Establish-ments	Number of Employees	Sales (mil dol)	Annual Payroll (mil dol)	Number of Establish-ments	Number of Employees	Receipts (mil dol)	Annual Payroll (mil dol)
	133	134	135	136	137	138	139	140	141	142	143	144	145	146
NEBRASKA—Cont'd														
Platte	7 846	61	55	680	324.8	14.8	176	1 984	293.7	27.9	23	90	7.1	1.0
Polk	459	6	11	141	117.1	4.0	24	126	23.8	1.7	1	D	D	D
Red Willow	1 006	13	20	D	D	D	109	1 124	176.3	15.7	14	51	3.3	0.5
Richardson	778	9	25	119	74.0	2.6	66	387	59.4	4.6	7	11	1.0	0.1
Rock	0	0	7	D	D	D	10	57	6.4	0.6	NA	NA	NA	NA
Saline	3 626	31	15	109	72.7	2.8	62	584	95.6	8.9	6	24	1.1	0.4
Sarpy	160 373	1 636	84	D	D	D	291	4 663	695.6	63.7	72	D	D	D
Saunders	9 167	99	21	150	72.1	2.7	79	602	92.8	7.5	8	14	1.2	0.2
Scotts Bluff	8 924	91	79	826	225.8	19.0	239	2 624	391.9	38.8	40	136	9.2	1.9
Seward	9 675	72	25	235	94.2	5.9	63	564	80.7	6.8	10	45	1.6	0.3
Sheridan	682	8	17	245	117.2	3.6	58	397	56.9	4.4	4	D	D	D
Sherman	0	0	4	D	D	D	18	84	17.8	1.2	1	D	D	D
Sioux	NA	NA	2	5	D	D	5	17	2.2	0.2	NA	NA	NA	NA
Stanton	1 048	11	5	D	D	D	13	59	8.2	0.8	4	11	0.3	0.1
Thayer	305	4	16	112	96.0	2.1	45	285	44.2	3.5	3	D	D	D
Thomas	NA	NA	1	D	D	D	6	27	4.2	0.3	1	D	D	D
Thurston	1 637	12	9	54	31.4	1.2	29	239	42.4	3.1	1	D	D	D
Valley	272	3	13	151	101.4	3.1	38	226	27.3	2.9	3	8	0.4	0.1
Washington	26 820	203	22	D	D	D	72	675	233.9	14.3	14	D	D	D
Wayne	1 194	12	11	D	D	D	46	386	47.0	4.5	7	D	D	D
Webster	245	4	13	103	48.4	2.0	22	143	21.3	2.0	NA	NA	NA	NA
Wheeler	0	0	1	D	D	D	4	16	1.7	0.1	NA	NA	NA	NA
York	2 342	26	38	363	207.4	10.2	98	1 027	160.2	13.9	12	24	1.9	0.3
NEVADA	2 976 683	32 643	2 253	27 251	12 806.9	918.5	6 222	89 452	18 220.8	1 798.2	2 460	16 890	2 276.5	381.5
Churchill	15 320	153	17	123	29.3	2.3	87	1 023	177.6	16.9	21	80	4.1	0.8
Clark	2 369 607	26 856	1 298	15 824	6 366.0	526.9	3 803	58 477	12 321.5	1 201.7	1 521	12 437	1 672.5	291.4
Douglas	77 616	485	46	205	67.6	6.8	141	1 143	203.3	23.5	95	506	61.1	8.8
Elko	11 687	119	61	636	268.9	24.2	171	2 226	426.8	39.1	34	237	22.3	4.2
Esmeralda	NA	NA	1	D	D	D	2	D	D	D	NA	NA	NA	NA
Eureka	NA	NA	3	4	3.4	0.1	7	D	D	D	1	D	D	D
Humboldt	1 700	15	29	161	64.2	4.4	79	967	193.7	15.7	11	23	2.1	0.2
Lander	161	2	7	46	19.8	1.0	20	311	36.6	4.0	3	12	2.3	0.1
Lincoln	916	13	1	D	D	D	15	141	12.5	1.5	5	14	0.6	0.1
Lyon	17 473	200	26	145	46.0	4.5	81	723	140.6	13.9	22	63	6.9	0.8
Mineral	20	2	2	D	D	D	23	172	32.1	2.7	2	D	D	D
Nye	0	0	19	D	D	D	107	777	140.4	13.0	20	62	4.3	0.7
Pershing	308	3	2	D	D	D	21	177	36.4	2.4	2	D	D	D
Storey	2 976	32	2	D	D	D	24	82	7.5	1.4	1	D	D	D
Washoe	442 266	4 424	639	9 339	5 663.6	324.9	1 328	19 418	3 751.1	389.5	614	3 058	444.5	66.1
White Pine	1 750	12	12	64	17.6	1.6	51	376	55.5	6.1	6	27	3.2	0.6
Carson City city	34 883	327	88	557	222.4	18.7	262	3 383	678.4	66.1	102	343	51.2	7.4
NEW HAMPSHIRE	781 944	6 326	2 033	22 631	11 371.1	875.0	6 645	84 170	15 890.1	1 428.2	1 399	6 639	719.4	151.1
Belknap	50 713	344	74	628	181.7	25.9	414	4 073	713.8	69.2	75	241	26.6	4.9
Carroll	46 675	365	61	371	80.8	10.6	428	3 267	551.1	55.4	73	314	33.6	6.5
Cheshire	31 552	313	92	1 187	403.5	37.6	402	5 097	1 155.4	92.0	68	312	26.2	5.9
Coos	7 691	86	27	308	81.0	6.6	229	1 959	423.8	32.8	23	111	6.2	1.1
Grafton	40 749	309	112	944	333.4	31.6	589	6 164	1 031.6	110.2	122	432	38.8	7.9
Hillsborough	215 224	1 798	721	8 588	4 792.9	366.4	1 692	25 208	4 927.0	455.6	436	2 269	233.8	53.1
Merrimack	75 058	629	189	2 328	799.5	78.0	628	7 629	1 500.7	127.7	139	882	116.2	20.2
Rockingham	246 277	1 857	605	6 504	4 328.9	271.2	1 617	22 905	4 218.8	356.8	331	1 702	192.0	45.2
Strafford	54 283	486	109	1 508	281.0	39.9	436	5 807	1 020.0	92.8	91	279	34.8	4.9
Sullivan	13 722	139	43	265	88.4	7.4	210	2 061	347.8	35.8	41	97	11.2	1.4
NEW JERSEY	3 162 436	31 976	17 812	266 944	227 366.7	11 886.1	34 837	420 724	79 914.9	7 926.0	8 292	47 558	8 881.9	1 376.5
Atlantic	102 067	1 401	234	2 312	831.5	81.0	1 258	14 308	2 513.2	253.8	236	1 424	203.3	27.0
Bergen	232 706	1 661	3 876	55 657	62 435.3	2 713.6	4 284	52 065	10 766.1	1 052.8	1 360	8 772	1 821.6	278.9
Burlington	234 717	2 755	769	13 262	16 206.9	547.1	1 570	22 857	4 410.8	426.6	322	2 872	788.8	85.9
Camden	72 900	867	922	10 789	6 139.0	400.0	2 052	26 577	4 612.4	481.0	376	3 159	432.5	92.7
Cape May	114 837	1 226	74	907	201.0	21.6	784	4 990	961.1	102.7	208	589	126.5	18.9
Cumberland	30 999	371	189	2 230	989.4	69.4	578	7 157	1 226.5	130.1	115	486	52.0	9.4
Essex	111 822	1 343	1 478	23 082	17 599.5	1 025.5	2 819	27 068	4 518.1	512.9	915	6 280	1 084.7	165.4
Gloucester	120 166	1 527	381	6 268	6 023.1	218.8	989	14 030	2 441.7	231.3	152	663	81.8	14.2
Hudson	133 605	1 921	1 065	21 629	11 271.5	864.6	2 327	22 670	3 842.9	384.9	542	3 070	628.1	96.1
Hunterdon	100 672	708	208	1 595	1 201.5	74.9	600	6 415	1 454.5	143.7	98	270	57.2	6.2

1. Establishments with payroll.

STATE County	Professional, Scientific, and Technical Services[1], 1997				Manufacturing, 1997				Accommodation and Foodservices, 1997			
	Number of Establishments	Number of Employees	Receipts (mil dol)	Annual Payroll (mil dol)	Number of Establishments	Number of Employees	Receipts (mil dol)	Annual Payroll (mil dol)	Number of Establishments	Number of Employees	Sales (mil dol)	Annual Payroll (mil dol)
	147	148	149	150	151	152	153	154	155	156	157	158
NEBRASKA—Cont'd												
Platte	54	307	23.1	8.4	74	6 120	1 217.2	164.1	75	1 130	29.7	8.3
Polk	9	18	1.1	0.2	NA	NA	NA	NA	12	56	1.5	0.3
Red Willow	29	119	6.1	2.3	NA	NA	NA	NA	39	536	12.7	3.5
Richardson	16	41	2.0	0.6	NA	NA	NA	NA	26	214	4.7	1.3
Rock	2	D	D	D	NA	NA	NA	NA	9	33	0.7	0.2
Saline	16	36	1.7	0.6	19	2 512	659.9	64.7	39	442	10.0	2.7
Sarpy	141	1 410	146.1	55.8	55	D	D	D	155	2 462	72.2	20.5
Saunders	21	95	5.6	2.8	NA	NA	NA	NA	39	D	D	D
Scotts Bluff	68	379	19.3	9.1	54	1 732	357.5	46.2	100	1 207	33.1	9.2
Seward	21	48	3.7	0.7	18	1 039	111.7	30.1	37	589	12.6	3.2
Sheridan	8	20	1.0	0.3	NA	NA	NA	NA	24	D	D	D
Sherman	4	D	D	D	NA	NA	NA	NA	9	D	D	D
Sioux	1	D	D	D	NA	NA	NA	NA	2	D	D	D
Stanton	3	D	D	D	NA	NA	NA	NA	6	D	D	D
Thayer	9	21	1.0	0.2	NA	NA	NA	NA	14	124	2.4	0.5
Thomas	NA	NA	NA	NA	NA	NA	NA	NA	4	43	1.0	0.3
Thurston	4	13	0.9	0.1	NA	NA	NA	NA	8	95	3.0	1.3
Valley	12	46	1.6	0.8	NA	NA	NA	NA	20	D	D	D
Washington	21	D	D	D	21	861	372.1	25.1	45	489	11.8	3.0
Wayne	13	28	1.6	0.4	15	1 473	221.3	28.6	26	411	7.6	2.0
Webster	3	D	D	D	NA	NA	NA	NA	9	40	1.3	0.3
Wheeler	NA	NA	NA	NA	NA	NA	NA	NA	5	D	D	D
York	22	117	6.4	2.4	33	1 207	214.6	32.8	43	804	22.1	6.3
NEVADA	4 171	28 963	2 974.4	1 171.1	1 615	37 849	6 361.8	1 178.0	3 632	241 672	15 322.7	4 665.3
Churchill	28	120	6.2	2.8	NA	NA	NA	NA	53	706	26.0	8.0
Clark	2 405	20 281	2 105.8	832.7	814	D	D	D	2 164	185 322	12 412.3	3 771.0
Douglas	149	526	47.0	20.9	65	1 897	241.8	66.3	92	8 414	523.9	151.1
Elko	68	353	27.4	10.9	NA	NA	NA	NA	134	6 268	301.0	78.6
Esmeralda	1	D	D	D	NA	NA	NA	NA	5	12	0.5	0.1
Eureka	NA	NA	NA	NA	NA	NA	NA	NA	6	55	2.0	0.4
Humboldt	18	80	4.9	2.3	NA	NA	NA	NA	53	1 125	46.4	15.2
Lander	1	D	D	D	NA	NA	NA	NA	19	160	5.8	1.3
Lincoln	2	D	D	D	NA	NA	NA	NA	18	100	2.5	0.7
Lyon	31	240	18.4	6.8	50	1 561	280.4	47.9	43	465	15.8	4.4
Mineral	3	8	0.1	0.1	NA	NA	NA	NA	12	258	9.7	3.2
Nye	17	73	13.6	2.4	NA	NA	NA	NA	54	1 035	40.5	12.8
Pershing	4	5	0.3	0.1	NA	NA	NA	NA	21	289	7.6	2.2
Storey	5	16	1.3	0.5	NA	NA	NA	NA	10	49	2.4	0.7
Washoe	1 193	6 422	659.7	259.7	418	11 522	1 931.3	361.9	778	34 517	1 815.8	583.1
White Pine	13	23	3.0	1.7	NA	NA	NA	NA	37	493	17.4	4.8
Carson City city	233	806	86.2	30.2	186	4 157	514.5	120.8	133	2 404	93.1	27.7
NEW HAMPSHIRE	3 341	18 268	1 626.6	713.1	2 328	98 934	19 813.1	3 361.4	3 029	43 942	1 543.5	449.8
Belknap	110	479	36.6	16.4	133	4 658	497.4	133.4	213	2 237	89.1	26.1
Carroll	108	1 906	43.0	23.2	93	1 634	180.7	45.9	269	3 810	143.2	42.4
Cheshire	144	553	41.1	16.7	168	6 212	787.3	196.4	133	2 178	68.9	21.2
Coos	43	142	10.0	4.8	50	3 051	494.3	94.0	121	1 572	56.2	18.2
Grafton	227	1 024	87.9	39.0	148	6 886	881.5	205.6	325	4 761	156.3	47.3
Hillsborough	1 210	7 164	741.2	330.5	737	36 656	6 260.7	1 397.9	702	12 020	412.7	120.6
Merrimack	392	1 938	196.2	85.9	224	9 674	1 314.4	304.9	261	3 807	126.1	36.2
Rockingham	873	3 862	386.0	161.0	500	16 582	6 596.5	573.3	727	9 947	384.2	109.3
Strafford	167	949	68.7	29.0	159	9 080	2 106.2	281.5	209	2 830	84.3	22.1
Sullivan	67	251	15.9	6.6	116	4 501	694.2	128.6	69	780	22.6	6.3
NEW JERSEY	25 849	220 238	25 943.8	10 441.0	11 812	409 788	97 060.8	15 430.2	16 974	251 872	13 407.4	3 608.2
Atlantic	513	3 885	380.8	157.4	160	4 927	600.3	143.0	766	55 638	5 015.2	1 328.3
Bergen	4 134	24 327	3 087.0	1 149.8	1 806	59 877	10 419.7	2 223.7	1 910	24 315	1 116.9	304.0
Burlington	1 048	10 752	1 204.1	466.6	464	18 766	3 945.9	740.7	711	11 085	391.4	109.3
Camden	1 464	11 673	1 073.7	485.3	677	21 055	3 617.6	729.5	881	11 826	440.4	120.2
Cape May	211	795	69.1	26.7	82	813	110.4	19.1	961	4 642	368.1	95.0
Cumberland	200	1 061	88.9	34.1	210	12 985	1 896.1	398.3	218	2 554	78.8	21.1
Essex	2 232	23 080	3 055.9	1 213.8	1 206	35 578	8 416.4	1 359.9	1 320	16 915	853.8	234.2
Gloucester	404	2 099	213.9	71.8	290	11 013	6 882.8	416.5	386	6 419	201.6	53.6
Hudson	977	7 208	931.6	342.8	979	26 470	4 220.8	787.8	1 127	10 056	466.5	119.6
Hunterdon	493	3 163	709.5	183.4	175	5 064	1 104.4	194.8	237	2 439	102.5	28.9

1. Firms subject to federal tax.

Table B. States and Counties — **Health and Other Services and Federal Funds**

STATE County	Health Care and Social Assistance[1], 1997				Other Services[1], 1997				Federal funds and grants, fiscal 1999[2]			
									Expenditures (mil dol)			
										Direct payments for individuals[3]		
	Number of Establishments	Number of Employees	Receipts (mil dol)	Annual Payroll (mil dol)	Number of Establishments	Number of Employees	Receipts (mil dol)	Annual Payroll (mil dol)	Total	Social Security and government retirement	Medicare	Food stamps and Supplemental Security Income
	159	160	161	162	163	164	165	166	167	168	169	170
NEBRASKA—Cont'd												
Platte	49	561	30.8	14.2	79	309	18.6	5.4	132.4	52.6	11.7	2.0
Polk	7	21	0.9	0.3	10	25	1.7	0.3	32.8	12.1	4.6	0.1
Red Willow	28	185	9.5	3.8	24	93	4.9	1.2	60.8	27.8	8.6	1.0
Richardson	20	248	8.8	3.9	17	57	3.2	0.7	57.0	25.4	9.2	0.9
Rock	3	D	D	D	7	19	1.1	0.3	10.0	3.8	1.1	0.1
Saline	25	237	9.3	4.2	20	67	3.8	0.9	65.9	28.0	7.9	0.5
Sarpy	121	1 820	71.1	37.9	142	753	44.7	14.1	710.7	170.1	20.7	2.7
Saunders	21	234	6.6	3.3	26	57	5.0	0.9	88.1	36.8	12.8	0.9
Scotts Bluff	91	886	58.3	30.2	91	460	25.6	7.4	177.3	83.8	23.0	6.1
Seward	22	262	10.4	5.9	37	117	9.0	2.1	62.0	29.3	7.1	0.6
Sheridan	7	34	2.9	1.0	16	23	1.8	0.3	35.6	15.9	4.8	0.6
Sherman	4	D	D	D	7	9	0.8	0.1	24.2	7.9	2.7	0.2
Sioux	NA	NA	NA	NA	2	D	D	D	5.6	1.6	0.3	0.0
Stanton	4	D	D	D	6	11	1.3	0.2	19.8	6.6	2.0	0.2
Thayer	6	82	3.1	1.7	17	31	3.0	0.4	41.5	16.8	4.8	0.4
Thomas	NA	NA	NA	NA	2	D	D	D	4.1	1.5	0.7	0.1
Thurston	4	D	D	D	7	19	1.5	0.3	72.1	11.2	5.8	1.5
Valley	9	75	3.2	1.5	12	35	3.3	0.5	30.5	11.8	4.2	0.4
Washington	14	108	6.4	2.6	27	74	3.8	1.0	64.2	28.9	9.4	0.6
Wayne	11	228	7.6	3.8	20	65	3.0	0.9	35.1	14.1	4.1	0.5
Webster	8	132	3.3	1.7	4	17	1.6	0.2	28.6	10.8	4.1	0.3
Wheeler	NA	NA	NA	NA	NA	NA	NA	NA	6.4	1.5	0.6	0.0
York	27	154	8.2	3.6	49	205	11.9	3.4	68.5	30.1	9.1	1.2
NEVADA	3 226	39 476	3 406.5	1 358.9	2 175	16 185	1 061.7	328.0	7 941.9	3 351.1	1 022.6	162.1
Churchill	24	234	8.4	4.4	30	102	6.5	1.9	193.2	53.5	14.6	1.7
Clark	2 053	29 105	2 567.0	988.7	1 324	11 045	707.8	221.1	4 842.7	2 248.5	707.7	120.6
Douglas	67	358	28.2	11.3	44	177	11.5	3.2	119.8	75.9	19.1	1.5
Elko	52	459	34.6	13.7	57	422	38.4	9.6	108.2	38.4	9.1	1.8
Esmeralda	NA	NA	NA	NA	1	D	D	D	12.5	9.7	0.4	0.1
Eureka	NA	NA	NA	NA	2	D	D	D	9.4	2.3	0.9	0.1
Humboldt	19	122	8.7	2.7	28	115	6.1	1.7	42.3	19.1	5.7	1.1
Lander	2	D	D	D	4	D	D	D	18.6	6.5	2.4	0.3
Lincoln	2	D	D	D	2	D	D	D	19.4	10.6	3.0	1.1
Lyon	16	100	3.9	1.7	25	256	15.3	5.4	114.8	73.4	18.9	2.5
Mineral	6	135	5.3	2.5	6	15	1.6	0.3	71.4	18.7	4.4	1.1
Nye	19	118	6.8	3.1	22	88	9.6	1.4	131.1	85.1	19.8	2.0
Pershing	3	16	0.3	0.1	1	D	D	D	14.8	6.4	2.1	0.2
Storey	1	D	D	D	NA	NA	NA	NA	4.8	2.3	0.6	0.1
Washoe	779	7 430	649.9	288.0	518	3 269	217.6	68.7	1 204.5	547.5	171.0	24.3
White Pine	11	109	5.6	2.8	7	30	2.1	0.6	40.0	17.8	4.4	1.2
Carson City city	172	1 274	86.7	39.8	104	634	42.2	13.5	530.8	132.7	38.4	2.4
NEW HAMPSHIRE	2 373	28 889	1 734.1	836.3	2 159	11 379	794.5	236.6	5 301.4	2 249.7	688.7	81.4
Belknap	116	1 145	69.8	32.6	108	437	27.6	7.6	251.3	129.5	42.5	4.7
Carroll	82	920	41.2	17.3	67	204	13.6	3.3	175.5	106.7	30.3	3.5
Cheshire	106	1 454	71.2	34.8	126	690	50.7	13.6	265.7	137.2	43.5	5.0
Coos	43	340	16.6	7.7	52	210	18.7	3.8	175.3	84.4	34.8	3.4
Grafton	148	1 312	107.0	64.7	153	753	45.4	13.5	406.4	157.4	51.2	4.0
Hillsborough	742	9 268	587.4	284.8	640	4 143	286.7	93.3	1 608.1	623.2	189.6	26.6
Merrimack	260	3 170	208.9	109.2	265	1 218	96.4	25.4	693.6	237.3	78.4	9.6
Rockingham	580	8 259	465.7	205.7	537	2 853	186.5	58.2	942.1	468.8	132.4	10.7
Strafford	230	2 534	136.7	67.4	144	701	50.9	14.5	450.7	217.9	57.5	9.0
Sullivan	66	487	29.7	12.0	67	170	18.0	3.3	162.3	84.5	28.5	4.9
NEW JERSEY	18 905	172 723	13 702.4	5 900.2	15 077	78 644	5 434.8	1 665.1	40 397.6	14 796.4	7 083.7	982.3
Atlantic	540	5 024	376.4	175.3	429	2 485	130.7	42.1	1 249.3	455.4	233.7	34.3
Bergen	2 738	24 529	2 115.1	914.8	2 088	11 009	807.5	256.1	3 661.8	1 724.7	760.0	45.4
Burlington	747	8 697	624.8	287.6	656	3 844	265.5	87.6	2 664.1	851.2	290.3	26.9
Camden	1 144	11 362	836.3	391.6	846	5 239	332.6	100.1	2 331.0	942.6	463.7	93.6
Cape May	208	1 289	94.5	43.3	168	803	42.6	14.7	552.9	269.5	136.9	9.3
Cumberland	238	2 191	161.8	74.8	243	1 156	65.2	20.6	670.5	253.6	142.5	29.7
Essex	1 966	17 414	1 352.7	619.9	1 371	8 525	595.8	191.2	4 518.1	1 212.1	746.8	212.3
Gloucester	385	4 443	272.5	134.0	424	2 172	141.1	40.0	862.2	410.5	188.6	18.2
Hudson	1 003	6 962	521.4	213.4	915	4 477	264.3	77.8	2 726.6	726.7	477.3	146.2
Hunterdon	224	1 932	132.7	62.1	200	956	65.3	20.3	289.9	164.6	65.6	2.0

1. Firms subject to federal tax.   2. October 1, 1998 to September 30, 1999.   3. State totals may include programs not allocated by county.

Table B. States and Counties — Federal Funds and Local Government Finances

STATE County	Federal funds and grants, fiscal 1999[1] (cont'd)							Local government finances, 1997				
	Expenditures (mil dol) (cont'd)							General revenue				
	Procurement contract awards		Grants[2]								Taxes	
											Per capita[3] (dollars)	
	Salaries and wages	Defense	Other	Medicaid and other health-related	Nutrition and family welfare	Education	Other	Total (mil dol)	Intergovern-mental (mil dol)	Total (mil dol)	Total	Property
	171	172	173	174	175	176	177	178	179	180	181	182
NEBRASKA—Cont'd												
Platte	6.6	0.2	25.8	6.6	1.6	1.0	1.2	86.2	17.0	31.3	1 026	900
Polk	1.0	0.0	0.3	1.2	0.2	0.2	0.0	16.8	3.1	8.9	1 589	1 456
Red Willow	3.6	0.0	0.8	3.0	1.0	0.5	1.5	29.2	12.0	10.7	940	854
Richardson	2.2	0.1	0.6	5.1	1.7	0.3	1.0	17.5	6.7	8.5	889	814
Rock	0.3	0.0	0.1	0.6	0.2	0.1	0.0	7.3	1.1	3.5	1 999	1 898
Saline	3.2	0.0	6.1	3.9	0.6	0.7	1.0	39.0	10.2	14.0	1 075	921
Sarpy	313.0	144.3	7.8	10.2	4.3	22.2	5.2	204.2	77.1	89.1	752	619
Saunders	5.3	1.1	3.2	3.3	0.9	0.6	6.8	39.6	10.9	18.1	944	875
Scotts Bluff	9.3	0.0	3.7	21.9	8.2	2.7	7.7	106.5	36.9	39.3	1 084	920
Seward	2.7	0.0	0.8	2.4	0.8	1.5	1.0	36.9	9.5	20.3	1 249	1 169
Sheridan	1.1	0.0	0.7	2.1	0.8	0.4	1.6	21.9	6.1	6.9	1 044	839
Sherman	0.8	0.0	0.2	2.4	2.9	0.2	0.0	8.9	3.1	4.4	1 222	1 158
Sioux	0.4	0.0	0.1	0.3	0.0	0.1	0.9	2.9	1.0	1.7	1 151	1 098
Stanton	1.0	0.0	0.1	1.2	0.2	0.2	0.4	8.0	3.5	3.1	503	472
Thayer	1.6	0.0	0.6	3.0	0.5	0.2	0.0	20.1	4.1	9.3	1 477	1 416
Thomas	1.5	0.0	0.1	0.0	0.0	0.1	0.0	2.3	0.6	1.2	1 513	1 429
Thurston	6.0	1.6	9.0	16.8	3.9	7.4	1.5	21.7	11.1	4.1	565	531
Valley	1.4	0.0	0.3	5.1	0.4	0.4	0.1	21.5	3.4	6.8	1 428	1 244
Washington	2.4	1.7	0.6	4.2	0.6	0.4	6.3	39.2	12.7	20.7	1 121	979
Wayne	2.0	0.0	0.3	2.1	0.4	0.5	0.3	18.9	6.0	8.1	868	725
Webster	1.2	0.0	0.3	2.4	0.3	0.2	0.1	12.4	4.3	4.7	1 174	1 094
Wheeler	0.3	0.0	0.1	0.0	0.1	0.1	0.0	2.4	0.6	1.6	1 730	1 709
York	2.8	0.0	0.6	3.0	0.8	0.3	0.3	44.4	9.2	18.7	1 282	1 182
NEVADA	902.6	273.7	527.9	373.8	217.2	102.3	555.8	X	X	X	X	X
Churchill	53.4	51.6	3.2	10.2	1.7	1.0	0.9	65.3	33.1	11.6	511	416
Clark	606.0	149.5	464.5	216.6	91.9	33.6	154.3	3 420.1	1 268.5	1 030.0	931	516
Douglas	4.5	2.1	3.4	1.3	1.4	1.8	8.4	105.6	44.2	38.5	1 067	812
Elko	15.5	0.1	3.2	9.6	3.1	1.3	23.4	141.1	77.1	25.3	557	446
Esmeralda	0.4	0.0	0.1	0.2	0.6	0.1	0.2	4.6	2.6	1.5	1 275	1 235
Eureka	0.2	0.0	0.0	0.2	0.6	0.1	4.6	18.3	6.4	9.7	5 236	5 079
Humboldt	6.0	0.0	0.9	3.9	1.3	0.7	1.8	73.0	35.4	15.7	896	733
Lander	3.5	0.0	1.1	1.4	0.8	0.3	2.2	30.0	13.0	6.8	952	904
Lincoln	1.4	0.0	0.4	0.5	0.9	0.2	0.0	16.8	12.0	2.9	650	601
Lyon	3.4	0.2	4.3	5.1	2.0	1.0	3.1	67.2	41.8	16.9	585	467
Mineral	4.0	37.5	0.2	3.6	0.8	0.3	0.6	27.1	9.7	4.2	736	623
Nye	8.3	0.0	1.8	2.5	1.3	0.9	9.0	87.9	42.6	21.4	786	677
Pershing	0.5	0.0	0.2	1.1	0.9	0.1	2.3	24.5	9.7	6.0	1 115	961
Storey	0.2	0.0	0.0	0.0	0.6	0.1	0.8	12.4	6.2	5.1	1 693	1 323
Washoe	163.4	22.8	37.1	80.9	23.8	10.7	111.3	874.3	369.6	293.3	959	668
White Pine	6.5	0.0	2.3	3.4	1.3	0.8	1.5	32.8	16.2	7.3	718	644
Carson City city	25.5	9.9	5.2	33.2	70.5	39.0	172.7	168.6	56.2	26.7	551	399
NEW HAMPSHIRE	453.3	359.7	122.0	507.7	145.1	85.6	381.6	X	X	X	X	X
Belknap	11.7	5.9	2.6	29.0	4.9	1.9	17.0	138.3	17.8	99.5	1 908	1 899
Carroll	7.6	0.0	1.9	14.7	3.1	1.8	4.9	108.7	13.0	79.7	2 049	2 022
Cheshire	10.0	2.5	2.7	33.9	8.4	2.6	11.2	175.7	33.5	120.9	1 691	1 678
Coos	7.6	0.0	1.7	24.1	7.2	1.4	8.8	96.4	28.1	59.2	1 784	1 751
Grafton	29.1	24.6	15.8	80.1	6.3	2.9	26.3	204.9	30.1	149.8	1 918	1 895
Hillsborough	213.1	248.8	61.2	129.3	25.3	13.1	53.6	716.7	93.3	518.3	1 448	1 425
Merrimack	44.8	6.8	7.7	75.9	59.0	35.5	115.1	264.4	40.9	190.6	1 513	1 501
Rockingham	103.8	67.1	20.6	56.6	14.5	7.0	50.9	539.2	64.6	419.0	1 569	1 554
Strafford	19.9	3.0	6.0	41.5	11.3	6.8	67.2	213.5	41.2	148.5	1 374	1 354
Sullivan	5.6	1.0	1.7	22.6	5.2	1.9	2.2	82.0	20.5	51.3	1 289	1 265
NEW JERSEY	3 598.8	2 838.0	1 368.1	3 446.4	1 181.4	616.3	2 017.5	X	X	X	X	X
Atlantic	171.2	5.8	123.7	117.0	28.8	8.5	37.7	880.9	301.3	477.6	2 019	1 991
Bergen	173.2	401.7	186.2	161.6	19.6	12.7	137.6	2 628.6	520.4	1 691.6	1 987	1 966
Burlington	418.7	840.0	48.1	91.9	24.0	22.1	36.7	1 072.7	406.6	529.6	1 267	1 247
Camden	168.1	174.7	54.0	233.2	80.0	23.8	56.6	1 870.8	767.6	677.5	1 343	1 326
Cape May	43.0	4.0	12.3	26.0	6.3	4.3	36.5	428.4	95.2	252.1	2 569	2 516
Cumberland	40.6	19.0	8.9	99.2	28.2	7.9	17.3	463.2	280.5	121.7	864	853
Essex	427.7	114.2	104.9	665.8	201.7	58.7	609.2	2 458.7	908.0	1 243.5	1 656	1 591
Gloucester	28.3	30.1	71.3	57.2	14.9	5.2	27.6	669.6	282.4	293.1	1 191	1 173
Hudson	426.7	10.8	147.2	488.7	105.0	31.3	82.0	1 636.7	711.2	666.5	1 209	1 191
Hunterdon	18.8	2.6	7.7	18.7	1.5	1.0	5.6	345.8	68.3	230.2	1 909	1 886

1. October 1, 1998 to September 30, 1999.   2. State totals may include programs not allocated by county.   3. Based on the resident population estimated as of July 1 of the year shown.

STATE County	Total (mil dol)	Per capita[1] (dollars)	Education	Health and hospitals	Police protection	Public welfare	Highways	Total (mil dol)	Per capita[1] (dollars)	Federal civilian	Federal military	State and local	Democratic	Republican	All other
	183	184	185	186	187	188	189	190	191	192	193	194	195	196	197
NEBRASKA—Cont'd															
Platte	57.3	1 877	60.4	0.2	4.3	0.4	8.6	1 463.2	47 954	125	136	2 397	20.3	76.7	3.0
Polk	17.2	3 058	47.3	19.6	1.9	0.1	10.8	5.1	906	24	25	474	23.3	73.7	3.0
Red Willow	23.8	2 095	62.8	0.4	2.8	0.0	5.4	15.9	1 397	68	50	1 016	23.6	73.2	3.1
Richardson	17.3	1 806	61.8	0.2	6.7	0.1	13.6	2.8	296	49	42	597	33.3	63.2	3.5
Rock	7.0	4 033	35.1	33.2	2.4	0.1	7.4	1.1	661	0	0	231	15.8	81.1	3.1
Saline	40.7	3 125	40.7	17.4	3.5	1.3	6.7	6.9	528	70	57	1 162	45.1	50.2	4.7
Sarpy	224.4	1 892	52.3	0.4	4.3	0.1	7.8	165.1	1 393	2 468	8 428	4 187	32.3	64.0	3.7
Saunders	39.4	2 059	47.7	15.1	2.3	0.7	11.2	15.1	788	104	85	1 189	32.0	63.8	4.2
Scotts Bluff	107.5	2 962	48.4	0.4	4.1	0.3	6.3	16.5	455	172	159	2 683	28.4	67.9	3.6
Seward	34.2	2 099	57.2	0.2	3.4	0.0	9.5	12.6	774	59	72	943	32.1	63.5	4.4
Sheridan	20.5	3 100	37.8	28.9	2.4	6.6	7.6	4.3	642	30	28	766	15.2	81.7	3.1
Sherman	9.0	2 500	55.6	0.1	2.0	0.1	17.0	7.7	2 164	21	15	287	33.1	62.9	4.0
Sioux	2.9	1 932	51.8	0.0	1.8	0.1	17.2	0.0	9	17	0	85	13.0	83.6	3.3
Stanton	8.3	1 335	40.0	0.1	4.5	0.2	19.7	25.8	4 169	21	27	331	20.1	76.2	3.7
Thayer	20.7	3 299	44.5	20.4	2.0	0.0	7.4	2.5	403	37	28	638	27.3	69.7	3.0
Thomas	2.1	2 680	60.8	0.0	1.4	0.0	9.6	0.0	16	14	0	84	13.9	83.3	2.8
Thurston	19.6	2 731	55.6	20.1	1.7	0.0	5.3	7.6	1 056	145	32	591	44.4	50.0	5.7
Valley	17.6	3 679	30.5	37.5	1.3	0.1	7.1	2.3	485	33	20	653	25.8	71.1	3.1
Washington	44.0	2 380	56.2	0.4	4.3	0.1	10.0	23.7	1 283	52	82	1 476	29.6	66.8	3.7
Wayne	19.5	2 092	51.1	0.1	2.3	0.1	10.5	4.0	435	39	41	1 048	25.4	70.4	4.2
Webster	13.1	3 258	40.0	12.9	2.3	0.4	15.9	5.3	1 327	29	18	299	30.0	66.9	3.0
Wheeler	2.5	2 639	58.4	0.0	1.6	0.8	22.0	0.1	110	0	0	72	18.8	77.5	3.8
York	35.7	2 447	40.0	0.6	3.6	0.0	10.3	26.0	1 777	60	64	1 024	21.8	74.6	3.7
NEVADA	X	X	X	X	X	X	X	X	X	14 155	11 329	96 433	46.0	49.5	4.5
Churchill	62.4	2 744	47.1	1.4	7.4	1.5	4.1	29.8	1 310	740	1 154	1 271	24.7	70.2	5.1
Clark	3 710.3	3 355	31.8	8.3	7.2	1.3	7.3	5 998.0	5 423	8 426	8 944	54 990	51.3	44.7	4.0
Douglas	96.4	2 672	45.8	2.8	7.6	1.2	3.1	63.3	1 755	97	78	1 764	32.0	61.3	6.7
Elko	142.2	3 131	48.6	12.5	5.9	0.6	6.9	37.0	814	367	97	3 280	17.9	77.8	4.3
Esmeralda	4.5	3 835	34.7	1.8	16.1	0.6	12.1	0.0	10	0	0	106	23.6	67.8	8.6
Eureka	22.3	11 985	35.8	2.9	4.7	1.2	12.3	2.5	1 346	0	0	248	17.8	75.0	7.2
Humboldt	64.6	3 695	38.1	17.2	4.4	1.1	6.0	128.7	7 363	140	38	1 143	22.1	71.3	6.5
Lander	32.8	4 611	29.9	28.3	4.6	1.1	4.1	12.1	1 701	82	15	473	18.6	76.4	5.0
Lincoln	15.8	3 555	60.9	0.7	6.1	1.4	7.0	6.3	1 425	33	0	586	23.6	70.1	6.3
Lyon	67.6	2 347	57.1	5.1	7.5	1.3	5.9	40.5	1 404	57	63	1 351	33.0	60.6	6.4
Mineral	27.2	4 756	30.2	39.6	5.8	1.2	1.9	7.2	1 248	96	16	428	39.9	53.5	6.5
Nye	84.6	3 113	36.0	22.1	8.0	0.8	6.4	32.1	1 182	181	72	1 391	37.1	56.7	6.2
Pershing	23.4	4 350	32.1	33.4	4.4	1.1	4.3	11.6	2 155	13	11	673	26.4	67.8	5.8
Storey	9.4	3 137	47.1	1.0	14.8	0.0	2.0	6.6	2 191	0	0	197	36.7	55.9	7.4
Washoe	877.3	2 869	32.5	2.5	7.8	2.5	5.9	985.2	3 222	3 178	692	18 633	42.6	52.0	5.4
White Pine	30.8	3 016	44.1	15.4	8.6	0.6	6.4	15.5	1 515	186	21	1 038	30.2	63.1	6.8
Carson City city	151.7	3 135	30.0	36.4	5.4	0.7	3.3	105.5	2 181	542	107	8 861	37.8	57.0	5.2
NEW HAMPSHIRE	X	X	X	X	X	X	X	X	X	8 083	4 374	68 780	46.8	48.1	5.1
Belknap	132.8	2 547	47.8	0.5	4.8	11.1	5.0	48.9	937	229	185	3 157	40.0	55.2	4.8
Carroll	104.4	2 684	50.3	1.2	4.1	7.6	6.6	57.2	1 470	129	138	2 249	41.3	52.8	6.0
Cheshire	167.5	2 341	51.3	0.7	3.6	8.4	6.2	46.6	652	200	252	4 449	52.0	41.3	6.6
Coos	84.3	2 538	41.0	1.2	2.8	15.2	5.7	34.7	1 046	151	115	2 308	47.3	46.7	6.0
Grafton	197.9	2 533	53.7	0.9	3.9	7.4	6.0	83.6	1 070	680	282	5 756	47.3	46.7	6.0
Hillsborough	703.2	1 965	51.9	0.8	5.4	5.6	5.5	405.3	1 133	3 963	1 315	14 420	46.8	48.7	4.5
Merrimack	283.2	2 248	55.2	0.4	4.5	8.2	5.2	161.6	1 283	868	450	13 371	48.1	47.2	4.8
Rockingham	578.5	2 166	58.4	1.1	5.5	5.2	4.1	247.4	926	1 421	1 102	10 915	45.9	49.1	5.0
Strafford	197.5	1 827	50.2	0.4	5.0	8.4	3.7	113.2	1 047	332	395	9 394	51.4	42.7	5.8
Sullivan	81.6	2 050	43.3	1.0	3.8	17.5	6.6	41.3	1 038	110	140	2 761	44.1	49.8	6.1
NEW JERSEY	X	X	X	X	X	X	X	X	X	65 637	30 205	491 838	56.1	40.3	3.6
Atlantic	1 007.3	4 258	42.2	1.0	7.7	4.3	3.6	690.7	2 919	2 508	704	17 301	NA	NA	NA
Bergen	2 623.4	3 082	50.9	5.3	6.7	2.9	3.1	971.5	1 141	3 156	2 070	37 858	NA	NA	NA
Burlington	1 126.3	2 695	57.5	2.7	4.2	3.2	7.8	637.0	1 524	5 949	6 338	21 003	NA	NA	NA
Camden	1 800.1	3 568	47.3	2.8	5.3	7.1	5.7	1 923.9	3 813	3 377	1 219	30 211	NA	NA	NA
Cape May	441.4	4 498	35.3	2.0	6.9	4.1	5.0	467.7	4 766	362	1 423	7 990	NA	NA	NA
Cumberland	441.6	3 134	55.9	3.2	4.0	7.7	4.3	153.1	1 086	759	339	11 204	NA	NA	NA
Essex	2 458.0	3 274	34.7	4.7	7.7	11.5	2.3	1 101.7	1 467	9 402	1 823	63 285	NA	NA	NA
Gloucester	678.8	2 759	62.6	1.1	4.8	1.9	3.7	586.6	2 384	542	597	14 956	NA	NA	NA
Hudson	1 555.6	2 821	28.9	5.2	7.7	7.3	2.3	1 414.7	2 565	8 293	1 483	35 769	NA	NA	NA
Hunterdon	377.4	3 130	59.7	1.5	3.9	1.2	6.6	232.4	1 928	377	295	6 653	NA	NA	NA

1. Based on the resident population estimated as of July 1 of the year shown.

Table B. States and Counties — Land Area and Population

STATE/ County code	MSA/ PMSA/ NECMA code[1]	County Type[2]	STATE County	Land area,[3] (sq km) 1990	Population and population characteristics, 1999				Race (percent)					Age (percent)					
					Total persons	Rank	Per square kilometer	White	Black	Am. Indian, Eskimo, Aleut	Asian and Pacific Islander	Percent Hispanic[4]	Under 5 years	5 to 17 years	18 to 24 years	25 to 34 years	35 to 44 years	45 to 54 years
				1	2	3	4	5	6	7	8	9	10	11	12	13	14	15
			NEW JERSEY—Cont'd															
34 021	8480	2	Mercer	585	333 861	170	570.7	73.4	21.3	0.2	5.1	8.3	6.5	17.4	10.1	13.4	17.6	13.2
34 023	5015	0	Middlesex	805	717 949	67	891.9	79.7	9.2	0.3	10.8	12.2	6.6	16.3	10.0	15.1	17.4	13.1
34 025	5190	0	Monmouth	1 222	611 444	84	500.4	85.2	9.9	0.2	4.7	5.8	6.7	19.0	7.2	12.5	18.8	14.4
34 027	5640	0	Morris	1 215	463 545	119	381.5	89.7	3.4	0.1	6.8	6.6	6.1	17.5	7.7	12.6	19.0	16.4
34 029	5190	0	Ocean	1 648	497 533	109	301.9	94.8	3.4	0.2	1.6	4.9	6.3	17.9	6.4	10.9	15.5	11.6
34 031	0875	0	Passaic	479	485 064	112	1 012.7	76.1	19.2	0.5	4.1	29.6	7.5	18.8	9.5	14.1	16.9	12.7
34 033	6160	1	Salem	875	64 534	739	73.8	81.3	17.2	0.4	1.0	3.2	6.2	20.4	7.2	11.3	16.8	13.5
34 035	5015	0	Somerset	789	288 090	189	365.1	85.2	7.1	0.1	7.6	6.0	6.7	16.4	7.0	15.1	19.2	15.0
34 037	5640	1	Sussex	1 350	144 700	364	107.2	97.1	1.1	0.2	1.6	3.4	7.7	21.3	6.8	13.3	20.9	14.6
34 039	5640	0	Union	268	498 759	108	1 861.0	74.4	20.8	0.3	4.5	18.6	6.4	16.7	8.1	13.7	17.0	13.6
34 041	5640	1	Warren	927	100 312	515	108.2	96.7	1.7	0.2	1.4	2.9	7.1	19.1	7.1	13.0	18.2	14.0
35 000	...	X	NEW MEXICO	314 334	1 739 844	X	5.5	86.3	2.6	9.5	1.5	40.7	7.6	20.9	10.1	12.1	16.0	13.2
35 001	0200	2	Bernalillo	3 020	523 472	101	173.3	89.7	3.9	3.9	2.5	39.7	7.0	18.2	10.7	13.2	17.1	13.8
35 003	...	9	Catron	17 944	2 862	2 999	0.2	98.8	0.3	0.8	0.1	30.4	5.3	19.0	5.7	7.7	15.7	15.8
35 005	...	5	Chaves	15 725	62 394	771	4.0	95.3	3.0	0.8	0.9	39.3	7.5	22.4	10.1	10.3	14.0	12.3
35 006	...	6	Cibola	11 757	26 894	1 471	2.3	60.0	0.9	38.6	0.9	34.9	7.4	23.4	8.9	12.5	14.5	11.9
35 007	...	7	Colfax	9 730	13 666	2 160	1.4	97.8	0.8	0.9	0.4	50.5	6.6	20.9	7.2	9.4	15.1	13.9
35 009	...	5	Curry	3 642	43 570	1 008	12.0	86.9	8.9	0.8	3.3	27.1	8.0	21.9	11.7	13.1	13.9	12.1
35 011	...	9	De Baca	6 022	2 359	3 028	0.4	98.0	0.1	1.9	0.0	35.4	5.5	19.0	5.5	8.8	12.7	15.0
35 013	4100	3	Dona Ana	9 861	170 361	309	17.3	95.9	1.9	0.8	1.3	58.6	8.4	21.3	14.5	11.8	14.2	11.7
35 015	...	5	Eddy	10 832	53 122	862	4.9	95.8	2.7	0.6	0.8	38.0	7.1	22.4	8.3	10.2	14.7	12.9
35 017	...	7	Grant	10 272	31 335	1 340	3.1	98.0	0.7	0.9	0.4	53.0	6.9	21.6	9.9	8.7	14.4	13.3
35 019	...	9	Guadalupe	7 849	4 023	2 915	0.5	97.6	0.7	0.7	1.0	85.5	7.5	21.7	8.0	11.2	13.1	13.4
35 021	...	9	Harding	5 505	854	3 120	0.2	99.1	0.2	0.6	0.1	49.4	5.4	19.7	6.0	6.2	14.4	11.7
35 023	...	7	Hidalgo	8 925	6 027	2 768	0.7	97.7	0.2	0.9	1.1	52.4	7.7	24.7	8.8	10.6	14.1	12.9
35 025	...	5	Lea	11 379	55 067	838	4.8	93.1	5.4	0.8	0.6	31.6	7.7	23.9	9.3	11.1	14.2	12.5
35 027	...	7	Lincoln	12 513	16 778	1 945	1.3	97.7	0.7	1.2	0.4	30.1	5.8	18.1	6.6	9.6	15.8	15.3
35 028	7490	3	Los Alamos	283	18 281	1 855	64.6	95.2	0.7	0.7	3.5	11.8	4.8	18.5	4.9	9.0	17.6	21.9
35 029	...	6	Luna	7 680	24 360	1 559	3.2	96.8	2.1	0.6	0.5	50.5	7.3	22.1	7.6	8.5	12.2	13.0
35 031	...	5	McKinley	14 113	66 923	724	4.7	25.6	0.6	73.0	0.7	13.4	9.7	27.5	10.3	14.3	14.5	10.6
35 033	...	8	Mora	5 002	4 945	2 840	1.0	98.8	0.1	0.5	0.6	86.1	7.0	21.4	8.4	9.9	14.7	12.9
35 035	...	4	Otero	17 164	54 185	849	3.2	85.1	5.8	6.2	2.9	26.3	8.1	20.7	10.7	12.9	14.1	12.2
35 037	...	7	Quay	7 447	9 872	2 438	1.3	94.4	3.3	1.7	0.6	40.2	5.9	19.7	6.9	8.9	14.5	15.3
35 039	...	6	Rio Arriba	15 172	38 180	1 132	2.5	83.5	0.5	15.7	0.3	73.6	8.9	22.6	9.6	11.9	16.0	12.6
35 041	...	7	Roosevelt	6 342	17 416	1 907	2.7	95.8	1.8	1.3	1.2	30.0	6.9	20.9	15.4	10.3	12.8	12.6
35 043	0200	2	Sandoval	9 608	90 253	558	9.4	74.9	2.3	21.4	1.4	29.4	8.8	22.4	7.9	14.0	17.3	11.8
35 045	...	5	San Juan	14 282	109 899	482	7.7	60.1	0.7	38.8	0.6	13.9	8.2	26.5	8.7	12.7	15.4	12.0
35 047	...	6	San Miguel	12 218	28 488	1 426	2.3	96.4	1.1	1.2	1.3	80.7	8.2	21.5	12.1	11.3	15.3	12.8
35 049	7490	3	Santa Fe	4 945	124 228	421	25.1	94.9	1.0	3.2	0.9	51.6	6.8	18.1	9.0	11.5	19.9	15.4
35 051	...	6	Sierra	10 828	11 008	2 345	1.0	98.2	0.7	1.0	0.2	26.4	5.2	14.3	5.7	6.9	10.1	13.9
35 053	...	7	Socorro	17 216	16 500	1 970	1.0	86.2	1.0	10.7	2.1	49.6	7.4	22.1	11.6	11.6	14.8	13.1
35 055	...	7	Taos	5 707	27 116	1 458	4.8	91.5	0.5	7.2	0.7	66.8	7.3	20.3	8.0	10.3	18.1	14.7
35 057	...	8	Torrance	8 664	16 408	1 980	1.9	96.7	1.0	2.0	0.4	41.7	7.0	23.6	7.4	11.6	18.0	14.4
35 059	...	9	Union	9 920	3 903	2 924	0.4	99.5	0.0	0.4	0.1	36.0	6.8	20.0	6.2	9.1	13.2	14.6
35 061	0200	2	Valencia	2 765	65 095	732	23.5	94.2	1.6	3.3	0.9	53.0	8.1	22.3	8.5	12.1	16.8	13.8
36 000	...	X	NEW YORK	122 310	18 196 601	X	148.8	76.2	17.7	0.4	5.6	14.6	6.7	17.7	8.9	14.4	16.6	13.4
36 001	0160	2	Albany	1 357	292 006	187	215.2	87.5	9.6	0.2	2.6	2.4	5.9	16.1	11.3	13.9	17.0	12.4
36 003	...	7	Allegany	2 668	50 553	898	18.9	98.2	0.7	0.2	0.9	0.9	6.3	20.1	13.8	10.5	14.3	12.5
36 005	5600	0	Bronx	109	1 194 099	28	10 955.0	52.9	42.3	0.6	4.2	48.6	8.9	20.5	9.8	15.1	15.1	11.6
36 007	0960	2	Broome	1 831	195 246	276	106.6	94.8	2.4	0.2	2.6	1.6	6.2	16.8	10.2	13.3	15.2	13.0
36 009	...	4	Cattaraugus	3 393	84 477	596	24.9	95.8	1.0	2.5	0.6	0.9	6.8	21.4	8.8	11.7	15.6	12.7
36 011	8160	2	Cayuga	1 796	81 703	621	45.5	94.5	4.4	0.4	0.7	2.1	6.7	19.9	8.0	14.2	16.5	12.4
36 013	3610	3	Chautauqua	2 751	137 431	382	50.0	96.6	2.4	0.5	0.6	4.0	6.3	19.5	9.2	12.1	15.1	12.7
36 015	2335	3	Chemung	1 057	91 738	550	86.8	92.1	6.4	0.3	1.2	2.0	6.4	19.2	8.4	12.8	15.9	13.0
36 017	...	6	Chenango	2 317	50 704	897	21.9	98.3	0.9	0.3	0.5	1.3	6.9	21.1	6.6	12.6	16.1	13.9
36 019	...	5	Clinton	2 692	79 722	633	29.6	93.4	5.1	0.3	1.2	3.3	6.9	18.4	11.8	16.0	15.7	12.0
36 021	...	6	Columbia	1 647	63 002	763	38.3	94.6	4.5	0.2	0.7	2.2	6.4	18.4	6.5	12.0	17.1	14.4
36 023	...	4	Cortland	1 294	48 006	937	37.1	98.1	0.8	0.3	0.7	1.3	6.5	19.0	14.4	12.4	15.2	12.4
36 025	...	6	Delaware	3 746	46 362	960	12.4	97.8	1.3	0.3	0.6	1.6	6.0	18.9	8.8	10.4	14.9	13.4
36 027	2281	2	Dutchess	2 076	268 237	204	129.2	87.1	9.2	0.2	3.5	4.9	6.6	17.7	9.1	14.6	17.7	14.1
36 029	1280	0	Erie	2 706	925 957	38	342.2	84.7	13.0	0.7	1.6	3.1	6.2	17.3	8.7	13.5	15.7	12.9
36 031	...	6	Essex	4 654	37 507	1 149	8.1	95.8	3.3	0.3	0.6	2.7	6.2	17.9	7.0	13.7	16.7	13.7
36 033	...	7	Franklin	4 226	48 511	930	11.5	88.0	5.9	5.7	0.4	4.3	6.0	19.2	9.1	16.1	16.7	12.7
36 035	...	4	Fulton	1 285	52 851	864	41.1	97.1	2.0	0.2	0.7	1.4	6.1	20.6	7.2	12.3	16.3	13.3

1. MSA = Metropolitan Statistical Area. PMSA = Primary MSA. NECMA = New England County Metropolitan Area. See Appendix A for explanation of these concepts. See Appendix B for list of metropolitan areas identified by type, with component counties. 2. County typology code from the Economic Research Service of USDA. See Appendix A for definition. 3. Dry land or land partially or temporarily covered by water. 4. Hispanic persons may be of any race.

Table B. States and Counties — **Population and Households**

STATE County	55 to 64 years	65 to 74 years	75 years and over	Percent female	Total persons 1990	Total persons 1980	1980–1990 Percent change	1990–1999 Percent change	Births	Deaths	Net migration	Number	Percent change, 1980–1990	Persons per household	Female family householder[1]	One person
	16	17	18	19	20	21	22	23	24	25	26	27	28	29	30	31
NEW JERSEY—Cont'd																
Mercer	8.7	6.9	6.1	51.5	325 759	307 863	5.8	2.5	42 859	27 660	-5 889	116 941	10.5	2.65	13.2	24.2
Middlesex	8.6	7.4	5.5	50.8	671 712	595 893	12.7	6.9	93 233	49 698	4 972	238 833	21.4	2.71	10.0	21.3
Monmouth	8.8	6.3	6.3	51.4	553 192	503 173	9.9	10.5	75 745	47 379	30 680	197 570	16.1	2.74	9.8	22.0
Morris	9.0	6.0	5.8	51.1	421 330	407 630	3.4	10.0	56 507	28 564	15 645	148 751	12.8	2.78	8.0	19.0
Ocean	8.5	10.8	12.0	52.3	433 203	346 038	25.2	14.8	56 673	57 523	65 840	168 147	31.1	2.54	8.6	24.9
Passaic	8.4	6.1	5.9	51.7	470 872	447 585	1.3	3.0	73 951	39 380	-19 141	155 269	1.2	2.85	14.7	21.7
Salem	8.9	8.2	7.5	51.5	65 294	64 676	1.0	-1.2	7 718	6 341	-1 844	23 794	6.6	2.68	12.7	22.4
Somerset	9.3	6.1	5.2	50.8	240 222	203 129	18.3	19.9	38 032	16 692	27 194	88 346	31.1	2.67	8.2	20.6
Sussex	6.5	4.3	4.6	50.0	130 936	116 119	12.8	10.5	18 273	8 598	4 528	44 456	19.4	2.91	7.6	16.2
Union	9.8	7.7	7.0	52.0	493 819	504 094	-2.0	1.0	69 068	43 741	-18 483	180 076	1.2	2.71	12.7	23.0
Warren	8.5	6.5	6.5	51.3	91 675	84 429	8.5	9.4	12 339	7 902	4 471	33 997	15.6	2.66	9.1	22.2
NEW MEXICO	8.6	6.4	5.1	50.8	1 515 069	1 303 302	16.2	14.8	254 934	111 862	80 606	542 709	22.9	2.74	11.9	23.0
Bernalillo	8.5	6.5	5.1	51.3	480 577	420 261	14.4	8.9	75 483	34 351	834	185 582	22.9	2.55	11.9	26.1
Catron	11.9	10.1	9.0	47.0	2 563	2 720	-5.8	11.7	247	198	262	1 010	5.2	2.54	5.8	27.1
Chaves	9.5	7.0	6.9	50.4	57 849	51 103	13.2	7.9	8 774	5 267	1 161	20 589	13.2	2.74	11.7	23.3
Cibola	8.2	8.0	5.3	51.0	23 794	30 346	-21.6	13.0	4 153	1 645	706	7 292	0.0	3.17	16.0	17.8
Colfax	10.6	8.3	8.0	49.8	12 925	13 667	-5.4	5.7	1 604	1 251	420	4 959	1.2	2.53	10.9	25.3
Curry	8.2	5.5	5.7	51.3	42 207	42 019	0.4	3.2	8 748	3 080	-5 572	15 113	4.8	2.72	11.1	21.2
De Baca	13.4	8.9	11.3	50.7	2 252	2 454	-8.2	4.8	215	286	185	913	-7.7	2.41	7.9	28.5
Dona Ana	8.1	5.8	4.2	50.4	135 510	96 340	40.7	25.7	28 576	8 241	14 603	45 043	0.0	2.92	12.0	19.6
Eddy	10.1	7.0	7.3	50.8	48 605	47 855	1.6	9.3	7 514	4 777	1 929	17 472	4.8	2.74	9.9	21.8
Grant	9.8	8.6	6.8	50.6	27 676	26 204	5.6	13.2	4 114	2 765	2 415	9 773	13.8	2.77	11.3	21.2
Guadalupe	9.9	7.5	7.7	50.1	4 156	4 496	-7.6	-3.2	534	355	-303	1 520	1.5	2.72	16.2	23.2
Harding	11.5	13.0	12.2	49.1	987	1 090	-9.4	-13.5	75	106	-98	396	-3.9	2.49	7.1	29.5
Hidalgo	9.4	6.0	5.7	49.4	5 958	6 049	-1.5	1.2	898	466	-357	2 004	5.2	2.92	10.5	20.5
Lea	9.4	6.5	5.4	50.4	55 765	55 993	-0.4	-1.3	9 003	4 341	-5 325	19 306	1.9	2.86	10.5	20.3
Lincoln	11.6	9.8	7.1	50.2	12 219	10 997	11.1	37.3	1 697	1 205	4 093	4 789	16.6	2.48	9.6	24.9
Los Alamos	11.3	8.2	3.8	49.3	18 115	17 599	2.9	0.9	1 818	871	-712	7 213	14.8	2.50	5.0	22.9
Luna	11.9	9.7	7.8	51.7	18 110	15 585	16.2	34.5	3 616	2 150	4 865	6 797	22.3	2.63	11.8	25.4
McKinley	6.2	3.9	2.9	51.7	60 686	56 536	7.3	10.3	14 755	3 736	-4 684	16 588	10.0	3.61	20.1	17.0
Mora	11.1	7.8	6.8	49.4	4 264	4 205	1.4	16.0	518	347	520	1 519	9.3	2.79	12.4	22.8
Otero	8.6	7.4	5.2	50.0	51 928	44 665	16.3	4.3	8 581	3 534	-4 383	18 155	24.3	2.77	9.8	20.1
Quay	10.7	8.9	9.2	51.4	10 823	10 577	2.3	-8.8	1 298	1 138	-1 088	4 238	7.7	2.53	10.1	25.6
Rio Arriba	8.3	5.6	4.3	50.2	34 365	29 282	17.4	11.1	6 008	2 557	469	11 461	26.3	2.97	14.3	19.9
Roosevelt	8.7	6.2	6.3	51.0	16 702	15 695	6.4	4.3	2 905	1 175	-1 040	5 991	6.1	2.58	10.5	25.5
Sandoval	7.3	6.3	4.3	50.8	63 319	34 400	84.1	42.5	11 468	4 049	19 543	20 867	99.4	3.02	11.5	16.8
San Juan	7.5	5.2	3.8	50.9	91 605	81 433	12.5	20.0	17 255	5 459	6 617	28 740	14.9	3.16	13.0	17.7
San Miguel	7.9	5.8	5.1	50.2	25 743	22 751	13.2	10.7	3 868	2 167	1 116	8 701	18.1	2.81	16.2	22.8
Santa Fe	8.6	6.1	4.7	51.1	98 928	75 519	31.0	25.6	14 107	6 594	18 085	37 840	43.9	2.54	11.5	26.9
Sierra	14.8	14.4	14.9	50.8	9 912	8 454	17.2	11.1	1 129	1 971	1 987	4 428	18.2	2.16	7.6	33.0
Socorro	8.2	6.1	5.0	49.0	14 764	12 566	17.5	11.8	2 453	1 201	532	5 217	29.6	2.75	10.6	24.0
Taos	9.1	6.6	5.4	50.9	23 118	19 456	18.8	17.3	3 310	1 740	2 490	8 752	35.3	2.64	13.2	25.6
Torrance	9.1	4.9	3.9	47.2	10 285	7 491	37.3	59.5	1 684	846	5 250	3 670	38.8	2.80	9.0	21.0
Union	11.4	8.7	10.1	51.2	4 124	4 725	-12.7	-5.4	516	497	-228	1 615	-6.3	2.52	9.0	27.2
Valencia	8.9	5.6	4.0	49.7	45 235	30 769	47.0	43.9	8 010	3 496	16 314	15 170	-20.6	2.89	11.1	17.3
NEW YORK	9.0	7.0	6.3	51.8	17 990 778	17 558 165	2.5	1.1	2 539 280	1 519 562	-781 122	6 639 322	4.7	2.63	13.8	27.2
Albany	8.6	7.3	7.5	52.3	292 812	285 909	2.4	-0.3	33 357	26 462	-15 233	115 824	8.7	2.40	11.5	30.3
Allegany	8.6	6.7	7.2	50.0	50 470	51 742	-2.5	0.2	5 662	4 272	-1 161	17 011	3.1	2.68	8.6	23.2
Bronx	8.2	5.5	5.4	53.7	1 203 789	1 168 972	3.0	-0.8	227 788	111 876	-123 951	424 112	-1.2	2.74	28.0	28.1
Broome	8.9	8.4	8.0	51.5	212 160	213 648	-0.7	-8.0	23 610	19 163	-20 823	81 843	6.6	2.50	10.0	26.9
Cattaraugus	9.0	7.2	6.8	51.1	84 234	85 697	-1.7	0.3	10 346	7 776	-2 095	30 456	4.0	2.65	10.6	24.8
Cayuga	8.2	7.2	6.8	49.2	82 313	79 894	3.0	-0.7	9 749	7 244	-2 890	29 075	8.1	2.68	10.8	23.6
Chautauqua	9.1	7.8	8.2	51.0	141 895	146 925	-3.4	-3.1	16 334	13 917	-6 532	53 696	1.7	2.54	10.3	26.1
Chemung	9.0	8.0	7.3	50.8	95 195	97 656	-2.5	-3.6	10 843	8 904	-5 095	35 275	2.2	2.56	11.5	25.5
Chenango	8.4	7.3	7.2	50.6	51 768	49 344	4.9	-2.1	6 220	4 761	-2 399	19 141	13.5	2.66	8.7	23.3
Clinton	7.5	6.0	5.7	48.6	85 969	80 750	6.5	-7.3	9 633	5 614	-11 075	29 123	17.0	2.68	8.9	22.1
Columbia	9.1	7.9	8.2	50.3	62 982	59 487	5.9	0.0	6 662	6 245	-197	23 696	11.1	2.57	9.9	24.0
Cortland	7.5	6.3	6.4	51.9	48 963	48 820	0.3	-2.0	5 930	3 877	-2 880	17 247	5.7	2.65	9.7	23.6
Delaware	9.3	9.3	9.0	50.5	47 352	46 824	0.9	-2.1	4 874	4 823	-890	17 646	7.1	2.56	8.8	25.3
Dutchess	8.2	6.2	5.9	49.4	259 462	245 055	5.9	3.4	32 912	19 658	-3 660	89 567	11.1	2.69	9.3	22.2
Erie	9.7	8.7	7.3	52.0	968 584	1 015 472	-4.6	-4.4	118 502	94 175	-64 267	376 994	3.2	2.50	13.3	27.9
Essex	9.1	7.9	7.8	48.0	37 152	36 176	2.7	1.0	4 065	3 664	81	13 721	6.5	2.54	8.8	25.7
Franklin	8.2	6.2	5.8	46.2	46 540	44 929	3.6	4.2	5 124	4 117	1 108	16 284	7.6	2.61	10.3	25.8
Fulton	9.0	7.5	7.6	50.8	54 191	55 153	-1.7	-2.5	6 386	5 363	-2 173	20 995	3.6	2.54	10.7	25.8

1. No spouse present.

Table B. States and Counties — Vital Statistics, Health Resources, and Crime

STATE County	Births, average 1996–1998 Total	Births Rate[1]	Deaths, average 1996–1998 Number Total	Deaths Number Infant[2]	Deaths Rate Total[1]	Deaths Rate Infant[3]	Physicians,[4] 1998 Number	Physicians Rate[5]	Hospitals,[4] 1998 Number	Hospitals Beds Number	Hospitals Beds Rate[5]	Medicare enrollees 1999	Serious crimes known to police, 1998[6] Total Number	Crimes Rate[7]
	32	33	34	35	36	37	38	39	40	41	42	43	44	45
NEW JERSEY—Cont'd														
Mercer	4 455	13.5	3 000	34	9.1	7.6	1 093	330	5	1 674	505	51 102	13 130	3 951
Middlesex	9 992	14.1	5 563	53	7.8	5.3	1 882	263	6	1 907	266	96 143	21 909	3 070
Monmouth	8 206	13.7	5 114	39	8.6	4.8	1 723	286	5	1 857	308	86 022	16 071	2 675
Morris	6 351	14.0	3 219	26	7.1	4.0	1 476	321	4	1 909	415	57 136	8 074	1 764
Ocean	6 266	13.0	6 547	34	13.6	5.5	737	150	5	1 433	293	116 856	13 608	2 809
Passaic	7 802	16.1	4 170	46	8.6	5.9	923	190	6	1 947	401	65 020	17 401	3 567
Salem	784	12.0	699	6	10.7	7.7	85	131	2	243	374	10 512	1 882	2 828
Somerset	4 259	15.4	1 886	18	6.8	4.2	1 120	396	1	374	132	31 666	6 258	2 243
Sussex	1 858	13.1	968	9	6.8	4.7	191	134	2	271	189	15 056	1 692	1 182
Union	7 379	14.8	4 643	47	9.3	6.4	1 266	253	7	2 422	484	79 780	22 450	4 472
Warren	1 262	12.9	867	8	8.8	6.3	136	138	2	320	325	15 204	1 823	1 840
NEW MEXICO	27 139	15.7	12 680	177	7.4	6.5	3 684	212	36	4 015	231	229 124	116 711	6 719
Bernalillo	8 077	15.3	3 915	49	7.4	6.1	1 956	372	8	1 619	308	69 080	52 118	9 862
Catron	24	8.7	23	0	8.3	0.0	3	105	0	0	0	647	22	784
Chaves	940	15.1	558	9	8.9	9.2	88	141	2	277	443	10 041	998	3 834
Cibola	(8)NA	(8)NA	(8)NA	(8)NA	(8)NA	(8)NA	3	11	1	43	164	2 329	998	3 834
Colfax	157	11.5	136	1	9.9	4.2	29	213	1	46	338	2 540	NA	NA
Curry	892	19.1	351	9	7.5	10.1	54	119	1	106	234	5 848	2 326	4 957
De Baca	25	10.6	34	0	14.4	13.3	2	84	1	25	1 046	583	NA	NA
Dona Ana	3 013	18.1	965	21	5.8	6.9	239	141	1	221	131	19 601	9 671	5 789
Eddy	802	15.0	526	6	9.9	7.1	59	110	2	174	325	8 686	3 760	7 032
Grant	463	14.8	320	4	10.2	7.9	50	158	1	68	215	5 421	NA	NA
Guadalupe	55	13.4	41	0	9.9	6.1	1	25	1	20	494	790	NA	NA
Harding	5	5.5	12	0	13.2	0.0	0	0	0	0	0	251	NA	NA
Hidalgo	92	14.6	46	1	7.4	10.9	2	32	0	0	0	842	29	455
Lea	948	16.9	465	6	8.3	6.0	48	86	2	278	496	7 692	2 558	5 842
Lincoln	187	11.7	144	0	9.1	0.0	31	189	1	38	232	3 318	NA	NA
Los Alamos	187	10.2	87	1	4.8	3.6	47	256	1	53	289	2 112	283	1 542
Luna	410	17.3	245	3	10.4	8.1	24	100	1	119	494	4 598	1 379	5 741
McKinley	1 407	20.9	407	9	6.0	6.4	142	210	1	70	104	5 786	3 248	5 467
Mora	50	10.4	40	1	8.3	13.3	2	41	0	0	0	908	0	0
Otero	878	15.9	391	6	7.1	6.5	58	106	1	67	123	7 266	NA	NA
Quay	122	12.0	122	0	12.0	0.0	6	60	1	37	369	2 098	NA	NA
Rio Arriba	626	16.7	297	3	7.9	4.8	33	87	1	80	212	5 277	NA	NA
Roosevelt	291	15.8	123	1	6.7	2.3	16	88	1	151	830	2 562	852	4 581
Sandoval	1 247	14.6	493	9	5.8	7.2	76	86	0	0	0	10 004	1 966	2 295
San Juan	1 850	17.8	647	11	6.2	6.1	158	149	1	126	119	11 422	4 544	4 372
San Miguel	409	14.2	245	6	8.5	14.7	38	131	1	56	193	4 271	NA	NA
Santa Fe	1 583	13.1	753	10	6.2	6.1	406	329	1	208	169	14 644	NA	NA
Sierra	114	10.4	221	1	20.2	5.8	15	136	1	47	426	3 521	NA	NA
Socorro	255	15.7	132	1	8.1	5.2	11	67	1	32	196	2 006	906	5 553
Taos	354	13.4	193	1	7.3	2.8	47	175	1	29	108	4 012	1 021	4 141
Torrance	217	14.8	94	2	6.4	7.7	4	26	0	0	0	1 742	65	502
Union	49	12.1	50	0	12.4	6.8	3	75	1	25	627	877	NA	NA
Valencia	(8)1 411	(8)16.0	(8)603	(8)8	(8)6.8	(8)5.7	33	51	0	0	0	8 165	NA	NA
NEW YORK	259 803	14.3	159 889	1 729	8.8	6.7	58 578	322	235	73 682	405	2 694 015	652 202	3 589
Albany	3 341	11.4	2 859	25	9.7	7.4	1 322	452	3	1 322	452	45 195	13 084	4 436
Allegany	562	11.0	474	2	9.3	3.6	46	90	2	177	347	7 888	886	1 789
Bronx	22 877	19.2	10 963	181	9.2	7.9	2 146	179	12	5 509	461	145 145	NA	NA
Broome	2 235	11.3	2 129	19	10.7	8.7	503	256	3	802	408	38 140	6 376	3 202
Cattaraugus	1 072	12.6	874	8	10.2	7.5	113	133	3	353	415	14 541	2 066	2 418
Cayuga	948	11.6	785	6	9.6	6.3	106	130	1	266	327	12 701	1 988	2 410
Chautauqua	1 627	11.7	1 467	13	10.5	7.8	193	140	4	687	497	25 821	4 280	3 050
Chemung	1 056	11.4	952	5	10.3	4.4	232	252	2	495	538	16 581	3 058	3 278
Chenango	609	11.8	518	3	10.1	4.4	63	123	1	132	259	8 823	1 086	2 070
Clinton	804	10.1	631	6	7.9	7.5	140	175	1	409	511	10 703	1 274	1 599
Columbia	647	10.2	696	6	11.0	8.8	103	163	1	194	307	11 084	1 493	2 325
Cortland	581	12.1	436	3	9.0	5.2	61	127	1	260	541	6 955	1 865	3 810
Delaware	470	10.1	542	4	11.7	7.8	45	98	2	214	464	9 158	800	1 715
Dutchess	3 367	12.8	2 180	16	8.3	4.7	610	230	3	686	259	39 721	6 592	2 539
Erie	11 771	12.5	10 095	99	10.7	8.4	2 974	318	12	4 100	439	168 739	39 291	4 151
Essex	389	10.3	422	2	11.2	5.2	38	101	3	95	253	7 269	681	1 771
Franklin	489	10.0	442	3	9.1	6.1	85	175	2	245	504	7 714	NA	NA
Fulton	650	12.2	572	5	10.7	7.2	70	132	1	208	393	9 255	1 419	2 657

1. Per 1,000 estimated resident population, average 1996–1998.   2. Deaths of infants under 1 year old.   3. Deaths of infants under 1 year old per 1,000 live births.   4. Data subject to copyright.   5. Per 100,000 resident population as of July 1 of the year shown.   6. Data for serious crimes have not been adjusted for underreporting; this may affect comparability between geographic areas and over time.   7. Per 100,000 population estimated by the FBI.   8. Cibola County included with Valencia County.

Table B. States and Counties — Crime, Education, Money Income, and Poverty

STATE County	Serious crimes known to police, 1998[1] (cont'd) Rate[2] Violent	Property	Education School enrollment and attainment, 1990 Enrollment[3] Total	Percent private	Attainment[4] (percent) High school graduate or more	Bachelor's degree or more	Local government expenditures, fiscal 1997[5] Total current expenditures (mil dol)	Current expenditures per student (dollars)	Money income 1989 Per capita[6] (dollars)	Households Median Dollars	Percent change, 1979–1989 (constant 1989 dollars)	Percent with $100,000 or more	Income and poverty, 1997 Median household income	Percent below poverty level All persons	Persons under 18	Persons 5–17 in families
	46	47	48	49	50	51	52	53	54	55	56	57	58	59	60	61
NEW JERSEY—Cont'd																
Mercer	468	3 483	86 125	29.5	77.1	29.5	512.8	10 006	18 936	41 227	25.1	9.0	49 251	9.4	14.8	14.3
Middlesex	267	2 803	167 895	18.2	79.4	26.5	914.5	9 336	18 714	45 623	19.3	8.2	52 646	6.8	10.7	10.2
Monmouth	208	2 467	135 897	23.9	82.8	28.4	865.8	9 175	20 565	45 912	30.1	11.2	57 985	6.6	9.9	9.5
Morris	119	1 645	104 706	25.3	87.0	36.7	689.7	10 446	25 177	56 273	26.1	17.4	67 919	3.4	4.8	4.8
Ocean	214	2 595	93 686	19.1	74.9	15.3	588.2	8 573	15 598	33 110	21.8	3.5	42 053	7.8	13.3	12.5
Passaic	460	3 107	109 773	22.1	68.8	18.7	660.1	9 503	16 048	37 596	25.3	6.7	39 783	12.5	20.2	19.7
Salem	328	2 500	16 232	12.1	72.6	11.8	108.4	9 025	13 961	33 155	9.8	2.2	42 378	10.5	16.1	16.2
Somerset	143	2 100	56 216	22.6	86.3	38.3	372.7	9 690	25 111	55 519	26.3	16.1	74 586	4.1	6.6	6.3
Sussex	84	1 098	34 646	17.3	85.1	24.9	241.9	9 276	18 566	48 823	33.2	7.5	59 626	4.1	5.6	6.0
Union	495	3 977	115 297	23.3	75.2	25.0	707.2	9 757	19 660	41 791	15.3	10.1	50 254	9.3	15.4	14.9
Warren	108	1 732	20 728	16.0	77.6	19.6	151.9	9 108	16 716	39 929	25.6	4.9	50 002	6.7	10.1	10.3
NEW MEXICO	961	5 758	435 989	8.2	75.1	20.4	1 557.0	4 682	11 246	24 087	-1.9	2.5	30 836	19.3	27.5	25.7
Bernalillo	1 247	8 615	133 386	11.2	82.1	26.7	406.6	4 564	13 594	27 382	0.6	3.4	36 853	14.6	21.5	19.7
Catron	0	784	613	3.1	73.3	18.7	3.6	7 175	8 537	18 460	7.3	0.0	22 661	24.9	35.8	35.6
Chaves	NA	NA	15 920	7.6	67.3	14.3	59.0	4 513	10 550	21 764	4.9	2.5	27 531	23.1	32.4	30.7
Cibola	626	3 208	7 281	8.2	66.7	8.8	18.3	4 635	6 803	16 848	NA	0.9	23 722	24.8	29.1	30.1
Colfax	NA	NA	3 388	5.2	71.1	14.7	14.5	5 064	10 076	20 800	0.2	1.1	27 382	20.1	30.8	29.2
Curry	695	4 262	12 521	5.0	75.8	13.7	45.0	4 238	9 843	21 303	-2.8	1.4	21 721	20.5	29.0	27.9
De Baca	NA	NA	444	0.9	63.0	11.4	2.9	5 903	8 896	15 686	-3.5	1.1	26 379	22.0	31.8	31.5
Dona Ana	526	5 263	46 488	4.4	70.4	21.9	166.3	4 544	9 374	21 859	5.1	1.4	26 379	26.6	37.7	34.4
Eddy	578	6 454	13 489	4.8	67.3	10.9	52.7	4 454	10 490	23 418	-5.1	2.3	31 228	18.6	25.3	23.6
Grant	NA	NA	8 301	3.3	70.5	16.4	30.3	4 915	9 381	21 350	-19.9	1.7	28 882	20.3	27.3	26.4
Guadalupe	NA	NA	1 047	3.0	57.8	6.1	6.9	6 712	6 529	13 350	-9.5	0.8	18 820	29.7	37.0	38.7
Harding	NA	NA	246	1.6	65.9	15.7	1.7	9 544	9 731	19 020	3.3	1.0	27 213	13.8	15.2	18.2
Hidalgo	110	345	1 549	2.4	71.6	11.7	8.9	5 801	10 092	23 504	4.3	0.9	28 400	22.6	29.1	28.1
Lea	838	5 004	16 457	5.8	63.8	11.5	56.2	4 153	10 025	23 352	-24.2	1.6	31 337	20.7	27.1	25.8
Lincoln	NA	NA	2 658	4.6	77.1	16.1	20.1	5 625	10 701	19 489	-13.4	1.5	25 831	19.3	31.0	28.7
Los Alamos	387	1 155	5 020	10.2	94.7	53.4	23.6	6 523	22 900	54 801	17.2	10.2	74 253	2.7	3.4	3.5
Luna	633	5 108	4 560	1.7	58.8	11.1	21.3	3 792	8 116	15 684	-5.0	0.8	19 349	29.8	44.9	39.8
McKinley	619	4 848	19 705	7.4	58.5	11.1	79.4	4 954	6 628	17 468	-14.0	1.1	21 681	34.7	45.4	38.6
Mora	0	0	1 161	0.9	59.7	14.2	6.5	5 908	7 021	12 993	2.0	0.7	18 160	29.9	39.2	39.7
Otero	NA	NA	14 677	7.5	81.6	15.0	42.3	4 177	10 053	22 624	0.6	1.0	29 412	17.7	25.8	25.5
Quay	NA	NA	2 497	1.0	70.3	9.9	12.0	5 128	9 461	18 711	-9.9	1.1	23 105	26.5	37.7	36.1
Rio Arriba	NA	NA	9 651	9.1	65.9	10.3	37.4	5 414	7 859	18 373	4.8	0.5	25 036	22.5	29.7	29.7
Roosevelt	285	4 296	6 019	4.2	66.1	18.1	18.1	4 922	9 254	18 699	10.5	1.7	24 368	26.5	36.1	34.6
Sandoval	285	2 010	17 097	8.3	79.3	19.1	56.7	4 915	10 849	28 950	18.8	1.8	40 139	12.9	17.7	17.6
San Juan	1 084	3 288	29 208	4.9	69.2	12.3	112.5	4 461	8 911	22 300	-20.3	1.4	30 160	20.7	25.9	24.0
San Miguel	NA	NA	8 384	6.7	68.4	16.2	30.7	4 891	8 149	17 885	17.8	1.2	22 772	29.3	37.7	37.7
Santa Fe	NA	NA	25 743	17.6	82.6	32.3	67.3	4 382	15 327	29 403	10.7	4.7	37 882	11.9	17.2	16.7
Sierra	NA	NA	1 586	5.2	83.7	8.5	8.6	4 546	10 124	15 612	17.0	1.4	20 724	23.4	40.9	37.2
Socorro	1 250	4 303	4 873	7.3	67.2	17.1	13.5	5 080	9 154	19 165	4.8	1.5	24 025	31.4	43.1	41.4
Taos	1 314	2 827	5 954	8.4	71.8	18.5	30.8	5 463	8 950	19 619	8.1	1.2	26 334	24.6	33.3	31.3
Torrance	116	386	2 793	3.2	72.0	10.9	27.9	4 658	10 603	18 227	-2.6	1.8	26 320	20.7	29.2	29.1
Union	NA	NA	830	5.5	63.6	12.0	6.4	6 432	10 603	18 227	-2.6	1.8	26 320	20.7	29.2	29.1
Valencia	NA	NA	12 443	7.2	73.3	12.1	54.5	4 246	10 244	24 312	NA	1.5	30 092	18.3	26.1	24.1
NEW YORK	638	2 951	4 656 218	24.0	74.8	23.1	24 237.0	8 525	16 501	32 965	18.2	6.8	36 369	15.6	24.7	23.8
Albany	443	3 993	77 425	25.1	80.9	28.3	338.1	8 348	16 363	33 358	17.0	4.6	40 490	10.9	17.4	16.7
Allegany	139	1 650	16 500	19.2	76.9	15.6	73.5	8 015	9 907	24 164	5.9	1.3	31 291	18.1	27.0	25.9
Bronx	NA	NA	342 170	22.0	58.5	12.2	(7)	(7)	10 535	21 944	19.6	2.3	24 031	30.2	41.9	42.8
Broome	187	3 015	55 770	11.2	78.9	20.7	261.6	7 709	13 626	28 743	5.5	2.5	35 340	13.8	22.5	21.3
Cattaraugus	183	2 235	23 035	18.5	74.5	12.8	137.3	7 666	10 595	23 421	-1.2	1.6	31 348	15.7	22.9	22.8
Cayuga	211	2 199	20 367	11.5	73.3	13.0	91.9	7 148	11 671	27 568	5.4	1.5	35 508	12.9	19.3	19.0
Chautauqua	272	2 778	37 059	7.9	74.4	14.2	199.9	7 712	11 287	24 183	-3.2	1.4	31 051	16.7	25.4	24.9
Chemung	276	3 002	23 886	17.8	77.2	15.4	114.6	8 024	12 069	26 135	2.5	2.0	33 988	13.8	21.0	21.0
Chenango	255	1 815	12 733	6.2	75.5	13.1	80.8	7 759	11 830	26 032	8.9	1.6	31 757	15.5	24.7	24.5
Clinton	292	1 307	24 367	10.2	74.2	16.5	116.3	8 488	11 444	26 903	13.2	1.9	34 918	15.2	21.2	21.5
Columbia	385	1 940	14 263	13.7	73.6	18.5	87.9	8 772	14 044	29 785	18.6	3.6	36 697	11.9	19.5	19.4
Cortland	255	3 555	15 358	6.3	76.8	18.2	62.9	7 904	11 228	26 791	12.2	1.7	33 758	14.5	21.3	20.8
Delaware	219	1 496	11 803	6.0	74.0	13.2	68.3	8 410	11 180	24 132	6.1	1.4	30 362	14.6	23.1	23.3
Dutchess	261	2 278	67 685	24.7	79.8	24.8	363.2	8 369	17 420	42 250	24.4	6.1	47 828	8.4	12.9	12.5
Erie	479	3 672	247 150	18.8	76.4	20.0	1 210.8	8 390	13 560	28 005	-2.4	2.9	36 711	13.9	21.5	20.5
Essex	265	1 506	8 326	14.6	74.2	15.8	46.1	8 955	11 354	25 002	8.8	1.5	32 051	14.4	21.8	22.3
Franklin	NA	NA	11 907	12.4	69.5	11.7	78.8	8 470	9 771	21 791	6.0	0.8	29 235	18.7	26.1	25.4
Fulton	247	2 410	13 102	6.8	70.5	11.4	77.0	7 520	11 330	23 862	2.4	1.2	30 502	15.2	25.0	24.5

1. Data for serious crimes have not been adjusted for underreporting; this may affect comparability between geographic areas and over time.   2. Per 100,000 population estimated by the FBI.   3. All persons 3 years old and over enrolled in nursery school through college.   4. Persons 25 years old and over.   5. Elementary and secondary education expenditures, local government fiscal years ending between July 1, 1996 and June 30, 1997.   6. Based on population enumerated as of April 1, 1990.   7. Bronx, Kings, Queens, and Richmond Counties included with New York County.

Table B. States and Counties — **Personal Income**

STATE County	Personal income, 1998 Total (mil dol)	Percent change, 1997–1998	Per capita[1] Dollars	Per capita[1] Rank	Wages and salaries[2] (mil dol)	Proprietor's income (mil dol)	Dividends, interest, and rent (mil dol)	Transfer payments Total (mil dol)	Government payments to individuals Total (mil dol)	Social Security (mil dol)	Medical payments (mil dol)	Income mainte-nance (mil dol)	Unemploy-ment insurance (mil dol)
	62	63	64	65	66	67	68	69	70	71	72	73	74
NEW JERSEY—Cont'd													
Mercer	12 447	6.1	37 551	46	8 941	846	2 375	1 386	1 324	520	586	112	36
Middlesex	23 723	5.8	33 289	82	19 034	1 249	3 791	2 427	2 292	1 049	904	117	89
Monmouth	21 496	6.9	35 636	61	9 827	1 202	4 268	2 091	1 979	886	808	102	78
Morris	21 994	6.9	47 915	7	14 745	1 783	4 257	1 300	1 214	616	460	37	34
Ocean	13 142	4.5	26 815	318	4 206	722	3 142	2 510	2 418	1 219	969	76	57
Passaic	12 921	5.9	26 748	324	7 298	749	2 249	1 927	1 836	666	824	196	82
Salem	1 704	4.0	26 234	372	932	98	264	282	270	111	120	19	9
Somerset	13 999	7.4	49 594	6	9 634	1 685	2 312	774	721	370	263	25	21
Sussex	4 177	5.6	29 180	192	1 210	236	632	371	344	162	135	15	13
Union	18 629	7.9	37 340	47	11 428	1 169	3 644	2 031	1 937	831	812	138	68
Warren	2 773	5.7	28 093	233	1 338	149	467	356	337	156	141	15	10
NEW MEXICO	36 688	5.0	21 164	X	22 545	2 775	7 161	5 593	5 290	2 084	1 882	722	91
Bernalillo	13 870	4.2	26 434	350	10 331	810	2 822	1 641	1 549	652	535	179	27
Catron	43	4.4	15 167	2 914	17	3	13	11	11	6	2	1	0
Chaves	1 188	10.3	18 979	2 064	561	205	232	226	215	94	75	31	3
Cibola	358	7.0	13 521	3 043	162	18	38	92	87	28	32	13	2
Colfax	258	5.5	18 960	2 073	131	20	63	56	54	23	19	6	1
Curry	906	0.5	20 201	1 649	521	100	158	156	149	49	56	22	2
De Baca	39	2.9	16 324	2 738	15	5	9	10	10	5	3	1	0
Dona Ana	2 805	6.4	16 599	2 693	1 512	266	532	495	465	163	173	77	8
Eddy	1 045	3.4	19 546	1 871	597	101	187	202	193	87	73	21	1
Grant	551	0.8	17 409	2 504	307	32	114	128	123	54	45	14	1
Guadalupe	57	-1.0	14 120	2 997	32	3	10	18	17	6	7	4	0
Harding	15	-7.7	16 645	2 689	5	2	3	3	3	2	1	0	0
Hidalgo	109	1.3	17 623	2 461	66	11	13	23	22	7	7	3	0
Lea	1 059	4.3	18 756	2 137	625	99	157	197	187	80	73	24	2
Lincoln	318	5.5	19 375	1 922	133	35	101	65	62	32	20	5	1
Los Alamos	701	5.1	38 350	41	899	25	197	34	31	18	9	1	0
Luna	333	2.9	13 902	3 015	142	34	65	95	91	41	29	11	4
McKinley	908	5.8	13 482	3 047	551	47	107	229	217	41	83	57	3
Mora	61	5.7	12 667	3 078	20	1	10	22	22	7	7	5	1
Otero	995	2.1	18 310	2 260	647	57	191	164	155	65	52	18	2
Quay	175	1.1	17 497	2 484	79	20	38	46	44	18	16	7	0
Rio Arriba	543	5.3	14 340	2 982	224	26	88	142	136	45	51	26	3
Roosevelt	316	6.9	17 717	2 435	129	60	50	69	66	22	23	10	0
Sandoval	1 788	4.4	20 313	1 625	784	77	277	229	213	94	72	21	4
San Juan	1 928	5.4	18 161	2 304	1 308	164	283	308	289	108	103	41	7
San Miguel	439	4.6	15 291	2 902	197	26	67	131	126	32	53	25	2
Santa Fe	3 444	7.3	28 040	236	1 737	312	938	320	298	140	97	27	5
Sierra	213	5.0	19 406	1 917	67	21	59	71	69	31	25	7	0
Socorro	251	6.6	15 368	2 896	130	18	43	59	56	17	20	13	1
Taos	479	5.9	17 905	2 377	224	62	106	99	94	34	34	15	3
Torrance	252	7.8	15 726	2 839	68	17	26	46	44	16	15	8	1
Union	94	2.9	23 568	731	32	31	16	17	16	7	6	2	0
Valencia	1 148	7.4	17 999	2 344	291	67	147	187	176	62	64	25	3
NEW YORK	583 061	5.2	32 108	X	376 822	55 750	105 431	93 972	90 265	26 760	46 035	11 781	1 610
Albany	8 959	4.9	30 576	151	8 707	592	1 818	1 413	1 354	470	522	131	16
Allegany	882	3.3	17 444	2 496	413	68	152	210	200	78	79	27	5
Bronx	23 637	3.4	19 841	1 764	7 798	947	2 675	7 611	7 367	1 297	4 369	1 380	152
Broome	4 818	4.1	24 514	558	3 189	361	954	903	862	384	337	90	12
Cattaraugus	1 601	3.2	18 845	2 111	908	104	264	359	341	137	134	40	9
Cayuga	1 700	3.3	20 687	1 492	746	104	282	314	298	126	119	30	7
Chautauqua	2 820	4.5	20 387	1 609	1 633	173	496	642	613	255	247	73	11
Chemung	2 077	4.1	22 524	974	1 278	93	368	423	404	167	165	43	6
Chenango	1 003	4.0	19 668	1 830	479	75	181	205	195	84	75	21	5
Clinton	1 649	6.1	20 664	1 497	1 017	115	256	308	291	108	122	36	7
Columbia	1 604	5.6	25 425	447	587	128	351	282	269	113	114	25	4
Cortland	944	3.7	19 570	1 865	527	78	160	184	174	70	71	21	5
Delaware	903	5.1	19 470	1 904	490	82	208	211	202	92	80	17	3
Dutchess	7 913	9.0	29 812	172	4 059	412	1 440	1 035	981	419	412	80	13
Erie	24 447	4.1	26 183	379	15 780	1 393	4 438	4 556	4 365	1 716	1 785	551	71
Essex	777	4.6	20 697	1 491	418	59	155	167	160	65	66	15	5
Franklin	874	4.8	17 956	2 356	468	70	135	205	195	74	82	24	5
Fulton	1 163	4.4	21 906	1 128	488	92	218	258	247	96	110	25	5

1. Based on the resident population estimated as of July 1 of the year shown.   2. Includes other labor income.

Table B. States and Counties — Earnings, Social Security, and Housing

STATE County	Earnings, 1998									Social Security beneficiaries, December 1998		Supplemental Security Income recipients, December 1998	Housing units, 1990	
	Total (mil dol)	Farm	Goods-related[1]		Service-related and other[2]				Government					
			Total	Manufacturing	Total	Retail trade	Finance, insurance, and real estate	Services		Number	Rate[3]		Total	Percent change, 1980–1990
	75	76	77	78	79	80	81	82	83	84	85	86	87	88
NEW JERSEY—Cont'd														
Mercer	9 786	0.0	16.4	13.1	57.8	5.6	9.3	34.2	25.7	55 021	166	7 941	123 666	10.8
Middlesex	20 282	0.1	D	20.4	D	6.8	10.2	29.0	11.6	107 258	150	9 268	250 174	23.0
Monmouth	11 029	0.2	D	5.8	D	9.5	8.3	37.6	18.5	93 145	154	6 813	218 408	17.6
Morris	16 528	0.1	23.8	19.1	67.6	6.9	12.0	29.9	8.5	61 231	133	3 282	155 745	12.9
Ocean	4 928	0.1	15.3	5.8	63.2	14.9	5.3	32.8	21.3	129 118	264	4 600	219 863	26.7
Passaic	8 046	0.0	29.9	23.2	54.9	9.5	6.3	25.9	15.2	72 323	149	13 313	162 512	1.8
Salem	1 030	1.3	31.6	25.8	D	7.0	2.7	D	15.5	12 434	192	1 161	25 349	4.9
Somerset	11 320	0.0	19.3	15.6	74.4	5.7	11.5	27.4	6.2	36 699	130	1 769	92 653	32.8
Sussex	1 447	0.0	18.3	9.1	61.1	10.2	8.6	31.8	20.6	17 346	121	1 355	51 574	17.6
Union	12 597	0.0	29.1	24.6	60.6	6.5	6.5	29.1	10.3	85 702	171	8 626	187 033	2.3
Warren	1 487	0.0	37.9	30.3	47.2	9.5	2.8	21.5	15.0	16 686	169	1 096	36 589	16.2
NEW MEXICO	25 320	2.4	17.0	7.3	53.4	10.6	5.2	27.2	27.2	266 307	153	45 631	632 058	24.5
Bernalillo	11 141	0.1	14.6	7.8	62.9	10.3	6.4	34.3	22.4	78 785	150	11 065	201 235	24.1
Catron	20	-5.1	D	4.3	D	6.7		12.4	55.3	766	269	78	1 552	11.2
Chaves	766	16.6	22.7	12.8	40.3	9.7	3.5	17.4	20.4	11 830	189	1 976	23 386	12.3
Cibola	181	0.7	D	7.8	D	11.4	1.9	D	32.5	3 555	135	609	9 692	NA
Colfax	151	2.0	D	5.4	D	13.6	5.2	28.9	42.7	2 934	216	376	8 265	19.9
Curry	621	8.9	D	1.9	D	9.9	3.0	13.6	31.6	6 528	144	1 363	16 906	4.3
De Baca	20	18.6	10.7	1.9	D	12.5	2.7	10.3	31.6	629	263	87	1 329	-1.6
Dona Ana	1 777	7.3	D	4.8	D	10.4	4.0	21.4	37.8	22 461	133	4 582	49 148	NA
Eddy	697	3.5	33.8	6.2	45.8	9.5	3.2	18.4	16.9	10 318	193	1 417	20 134	10.9
Grant	339	-0.6	39.4	6.3	33.6	9.8	3.6	13.2	27.6	6 423	203	714	11 349	17.8
Guadalupe	35	-5.1	D	D	D	21.4	D	17.5	30.8	927	229	261	2 149	0.3
Harding	7	19.9	D	D	D	5.7	D	D	35.2	264	294	19	614	11.0
Hidalgo	77	11.7	D	D	D	9.9	1.4	8.1	20.9	978	157	180	2 413	3.7
Lea	724	4.6	33.3	2.0	48.3	9.7	3.0	19.9	13.9	9 424	168	1 391	23 333	10.7
Lincoln	168	-0.6	D	3.7	D	19.0	6.9	27.1	22.6	3 841	234	300	12 622	29.6
Los Alamos	924	0.0	2.0	0.3	D	2.1	2.2	23.7	69.3	2 177	119	52	7 565	14.9
Luna	176	10.2	D	8.4	D	14.1	2.1	17.4	29.5	5 368	223	750	7 766	23.5
McKinley	598	0.0	D	3.7	D	16.3	3.1	18.4	37.6	6 894	102	3 617	20 933	15.5
Mora	21	-10.6	8.7	2.3	D	5.4	D	27.1	46.4	1 112	229	342	2 486	18.1
Otero	703	0.4	D	2.4	D	7.4	2.9	18.9	54.3	8 776	161	1 060	23 177	29.0
Quay	100	5.7	10.5	2.0	D	12.1	4.5	20.0	29.9	2 404	240	414	5 576	13.5
Rio Arriba	251	0.0	11.2	4.9	55.7	11.6	3.3	33.1	33.1	6 812	180	1 867	14 357	29.3
Roosevelt	188	29.5	8.0	3.2	36.7	11.0	1.7	13.4	25.8	2 981	164	574	6 902	6.0
Sandoval	861	0.2	D	D	D	9.4	3.0	15.7	13.2	11 648	132	3 263	23 667	92.6
San Juan	1 473	3.9	29.3	3.2	49.1	11.3	2.9	19.3	17.6	14 060	133	1 861	34 248	15.2
San Miguel	222	0.1	D	2.2	D	11.7	3.5	22.2	49.9	4 827	166	1 355	11 066	11.7
Santa Fe	2 049	0.2	11.6	3.8	61.7	13.5	9.4	33.0	26.5	16 679	135	1 867	41 464	46.4
Sierra	88	6.7	D	1.0	D	13.2	7.3	22.9	30.8	4 007	363	463	6 457	19.8
Socorro	148	6.1	D	2.8	D	9.1	2.1	26.3	45.3	2 442	150	645	6 289	35.7
Taos	286	0.3	D	2.5	60.9	17.1	5.6	32.7	19.8	4 804	179	1 054	12 020	28.7
Torrance	86	6.6	10.3	3.8	D	12.9	2.6	17.2	37.7	2 257	146	364	4 878	47.4
Union	63	46.4	D	1.1	D	6.3	4.9	11.2	16.7	979	246	101	2 299	1.2
Valencia	358	2.7	D	8.0	D	13.0	3.7	15.3	31.3	8 385	130	1 411	16 781	-24.9
NEW YORK	432 572	0.1	15.3	11.6	70.1	6.4	20.7	31.0	14.5	2 963 912	163	608 373	7 226 891	5.2
Albany	9 299	0.0	D	6.4	D	7.6	9.2	28.5	32.0	52 129	178	6 397	124 255	7.4
Allegany	481	1.0	D	24.7	41.5	9.5	1.8	24.3	26.7	9 391	184	1 539	21 951	5.9
Bronx	8 745	0.0	D	4.8	D	7.1	7.9	47.2	14.1	159 574	133	80 145	440 955	-2.3
Broome	3 549	0.1	D	24.6	D	8.8	4.4	27.6	18.4	43 567	222	5 150	87 969	7.3
Cattaraugus	1 012	0.7	28.6	25.0	47.1	9.7	2.9	20.8	23.6	16 540	194	2 679	36 839	5.7
Cayuga	850	2.8	24.1	18.9	48.5	8.7	2.7	24.1	24.6	14 522	179	1 979	33 280	7.5
Chautauqua	1 806	1.1	34.1	29.7	45.6	10.1	2.6	22.8	19.2	29 745	215	4 156	62 682	2.9
Chemung	1 371	0.2	32.6	26.4	48.6	9.9	3.7	24.1	18.5	19 413	211	2 870	37 290	1.6
Chenango	554	1.4	34.6	30.3	42.2	8.8	7.6	17.5	21.8	10 271	201	1 505	22 164	17.5
Clinton	1 133	1.2	D	18.1	D	10.8	2.6	20.1	28.7	13 461	168	2 523	32 190	14.6
Columbia	715	2.8	D	15.1	D	9.5	5.3	28.8	21.3	12 818	203	1 750	29 139	12.3
Cortland	604	1.0	D	26.6	D	11.3	3.2	25.8	20.6	8 345	174	1 323	18 681	5.6
Delaware	572	1.4	38.6	33.7	35.4	10.2	3.7	14.7	24.5	11 047	240	1 276	27 361	20.3
Dutchess	4 471	0.1	33.3	28.0	47.8	7.9	4.5	28.4	18.8	45 524	172	5 009	97 632	12.4
Erie	17 173	0.1	24.8	20.1	56.0	8.9	7.7	27.8	18.1	190 778	204	25 810	402 131	3.4
Essex	477	0.2	22.5	12.2	47.1	12.5	2.4	24.6	30.2	7 855	209	994	21 493	12.4
Franklin	539	1.8	D	6.2	D	9.6	3.1	28.0	41.3	9 569	197	1 705	21 962	8.0
Fulton	580	0.3	D	24.1	D	10.4	3.2	20.7	24.4	11 458	217	1 744	26 260	3.0

1. Covers mining, construction, and manufacturing.
2. Covers private sector earnings in agricultural services, forestry, and fisheries; transportation and public utilities; wholesale trade; retail trade; finance, insurance, and real estate; and services.
3. Per 1,000 resident population estimated as of July 1 of the year shown.

Table B. States and Counties — Housing, Labor Force, and Employment

STATE County	Occupied units Total	Owner-occupied Percent	Median value[1]	Owner cost as a percent of income With a mortgage	Owner cost as a percent of income Without a mortgage	Renter-occupied Median rent[2]	Rent as percent of income	Sub-standard units[3] (percent)	Civilian labor force, 1999 Total	Percent change, 1998–1999	Unemployment Total	Rate[4]	Civilian employment, 1990[5] Total	Percent Professional, managerial, and technical	Precision production, craft, and repair
	89	90	91	92	93	94	95	96	97	98	99	100	101	102	103
NEW JERSEY—Cont'd															
Mercer	116 941	66.5	137 900	22.2	14.4	570	25.7	3.1	167 185	0.2	6 692	4.0	166 432	38.8	8.0
Middlesex	238 833	67.4	164 700	23.4	15.1	667	25.2	3.5	405 593	1.2	15 217	3.8	360 509	35.1	9.8
Monmouth	197 570	72.6	180 400	24.5	15.6	634	28.0	2.0	309 030	1.1	12 283	4.0	275 140	38.0	9.9
Morris	148 751	74.0	217 300	23.3	14.0	724	24.8	1.9	261 242	2.1	7 331	2.8	234 721	41.6	9.1
Ocean	168 147	82.9	126 000	26.1	16.7	681	31.7	1.8	212 531	1.6	9 754	4.6	181 415	29.0	13.5
Passaic	155 269	55.8	185 500	24.4	15.2	583	27.0	7.1	235 527	1.4	14 650	6.2	225 555	27.2	11.5
Salem	23 794	72.3	82 700	20.3	13.6	452	26.9	2.5	32 121	-0.7	1 504	4.7	29 766	25.7	14.2
Somerset	88 346	75.3	196 300	23.7	14.3	719	25.5	1.8	167 718	2.2	4 136	2.5	136 761	45.1	8.1
Sussex	44 456	82.3	156 300	25.8	15.4	697	28.9	1.5	75 796	1.4	2 636	3.5	67 578	34.8	12.6
Union	180 076	62.5	180 500	23.2	15.1	596	25.7	4.7	266 211	1.3	12 800	4.8	252 215	32.5	9.6
Warren	33 997	69.5	143 900	25.1	15.2	552	27.1	1.7	51 073	1.3	2 141	4.2	45 869	28.3	14.0
NEW MEXICO	542 709	67.4	70 100	21.6	12.5	372	26.5	8.8	809 713	-2.6	45 520	5.6	629 272	31.6	12.0
Bernalillo	185 582	60.7	85 300	22.3	12.3	402	27.4	5.4	283 661	-2.4	10 931	3.9	227 463	36.3	10.0
Catron	1 010	76.3	39 700	35.1	12.8	249	19.7	11.2	1 110	-4.1	109	9.8	901	24.9	9.1
Chaves	20 589	69.9	44 600	19.4	12.7	335	27.9	7.3	24 778	-7.0	2 072	8.4	22 913	24.8	11.5
Cibola	7 292	73.8	37 500	18.3	13.0	245	21.3	16.7	10 790	-6.0	875	8.1	7 473	24.3	13.3
Colfax	4 959	70.6	46 700	20.7	13.4	266	26.5	4.5	6 542	1.4	361	5.5	5 143	24.2	10.1
Curry	15 113	61.6	51 300	20.9	12.8	349	25.5	5.5	18 762	-3.5	782	4.2	15 267	24.9	13.3
De Baca	913	74.5	33 000	23.9	13.3	245	28.9	5.0	954	-3.4	42	4.4	855	18.7	9.5
Dona Ana	45 029	64.6	67 300	20.7	12.3	347	28.2	9.7	68 148	0.0	5 153	7.6	53 059	32.1	10.5
Eddy	17 472	72.9	44 800	17.3	11.7	304	23.4	6.8	23 285	-4.5	1 896	8.1	18 649	23.9	17.8
Grant	9 773	70.3	50 900	19.4	11.9	302	23.6	7.8	12 380	-4.6	1 072	8.7	10 034	22.5	16.5
Guadalupe	1 520	70.9	33 100	28.9	15.5	229	33.3	7.6	1 813	-5.0	150	8.3	1 487	19.4	10.1
Harding	396	77.8	16 000	13.1	14.2	229	17.7	4.3	404	-6.9	14	3.5	400	17.8	11.5
Hidalgo	2 004	61.2	36 700	20.2	13.3	191	15.6	7.2	2 490	-5.8	240	9.6	2 421	15.7	18.9
Lea	19 306	71.5	39 600	17.6	12.1	312	24.5	7.7	23 513	-6.2	2 191	9.3	21 346	22.1	20.0
Lincoln	4 789	72.4	67 400	25.8	14.7	348	26.8	5.4	7 299	-3.4	299	4.1	5 182	24.5	10.7
Los Alamos	7 213	74.4	126 100	17.3	10.5	467	18.1	2.6	10 128	-2.5	159	1.6	9 942	64.5	6.5
Luna	6 797	71.1	47 200	23.6	12.1	252	27.8	10.4	11 154	-3.7	2 680	24.0	5 419	22.2	12.3
McKinley	16 588	71.1	42 800	19.6	12.8	294	19.6	41.2	24 485	-3.7	1 761	7.2	19 765	27.1	17.2
Mora	1 519	81.2	30 200	13.8	14.7	235	29.5	15.2	1 652	-3.9	286	17.3	1 129	19.8	12.1
Otero	18 155	62.3	58 000	21.3	11.7	355	24.7	5.7	20 199	-0.7	933	4.6	17 904	28.0	15.0
Quay	4 238	72.2	37 600	20.2	13.4	279	27.1	3.1	4 361	-3.8	170	3.9	4 359	20.1	8.9
Rio Arriba	11 461	80.4	58 800	21.0	13.8	285	27.0	13.3	19 179	0.5	1 413	7.4	12 695	25.9	13.9
Roosevelt	5 991	64.4	41 000	20.0	12.5	268	28.0	5.4	7 193	-4.7	251	3.5	6 864	25.2	9.6
Sandoval	20 867	82.8	69 600	23.5	12.5	468	26.1	10.6	42 112	-0.4	1 740	4.1	26 501	30.7	12.7
San Juan	28 740	72.0	58 400	19.7	12.5	345	24.3	19.6	48 643	-3.7	3 716	7.6	32 280	26.8	16.6
San Miguel	8 701	72.0	47 500	24.8	14.3	270	26.5	11.9	11 761	-3.8	824	7.0	9 152	32.6	9.4
Santa Fe	37 840	67.7	103 300	22.6	12.0	489	27.7	6.4	62 882	-2.0	1 809	2.9	49 452	38.3	9.8
Sierra	4 428	73.3	49 500	23.3	12.3	226	26.9	4.4	3 966	-9.0	128	3.2	3 017	22.1	13.6
Socorro	5 217	68.7	52 500	21.1	13.1	305	28.4	9.8	6 274	-2.3	333	5.3	5 867	30.5	12.3
Taos	8 752	74.8	71 700	23.5	14.1	369	32.5	9.8	12 733	-4.9	1 487	11.7	9 128	25.5	15.3
Torrance	3 670	82.0	46 500	24.5	14.5	318	27.0	9.2	6 310	-1.1	309	4.9	3 931	20.8	14.6
Union	1 615	72.4	36 200	22.5	13.6	284	27.9	5.2	1 912	-1.5	46	2.4	1 671	16.3	11.8
Valencia	15 170	83.4	72 100	22.8	13.0	344	27.9	7.4	28 842	0.0	1 290	4.5	17 603	25.1	14.3
NEW YORK	6 639 322	52.2	131 600	21.5	14.4	486	26.3	6.8	8 883 034	0.1	459 191	5.2	8 370 718	33.5	9.4
Albany	115 824	57.0	110 900	19.9	12.8	481	24.9	1.7	156 577	-0.2	4 562	2.9	149 954	37.5	7.3
Allegany	17 011	73.1	37 600	16.5	13.3	318	27.2	2.7	23 262	1.2	1 796	7.7	21 003	27.3	12.8
Bronx	424 112	17.9	173 900	22.7	14.5	443	27.0	17.3	463 730	-1.1	37 569	8.1	441 957	24.1	8.8
Broome	81 843	65.4	79 000	19.7	12.9	388	26.6	1.5	97 941	-0.3	4 077	4.2	98 783	34.9	10.1
Cattaraugus	30 456	73.2	42 100	17.7	13.3	314	25.9	2.8	41 222	0.4	2 980	7.2	35 967	23.6	12.1
Cayuga	29 075	70.9	59 800	20.1	14.5	391	28.0	2.4	37 630	-0.6	1 985	5.3	35 840	23.8	13.0
Chautauqua	53 696	68.6	47 800	18.0	13.5	326	28.6	1.6	66 007	-2.3	3 433	5.2	62 263	24.1	12.0
Chemung	35 275	68.3	53 600	17.5	14.6	361	27.3	1.6	44 863	0.1	2 175	4.9	41 063	28.5	11.8
Chenango	19 141	74.4	55 900	19.3	13.5	344	24.6	2.6	23 847	-0.4	1 426	6.0	23 540	25.1	13.2
Clinton	29 123	63.9	65 000	18.7	13.0	385	25.8	2.6	39 595	1.4	2 621	6.6	35 380	26.5	9.9
Columbia	23 696	69.5	103 100	20.3	13.9	437	27.2	2.3	33 860	3.1	1 056	3.1	29 520	28.8	12.4
Cortland	17 247	64.4	66 200	19.3	14.0	396	27.6	1.5	22 740	-5.6	1 584	7.0	22 941	28.9	10.8
Delaware	17 646	71.7	67 000	20.8	14.0	361	28.3	2.1	20 845	-0.5	1 101	5.3	20 169	24.4	14.7
Dutchess	89 567	69.1	149 200	22.3	14.1	600	25.8	2.0	119 951	1.3	4 184	3.5	127 925	39.1	10.6
Erie	376 994	63.7	74 000	19.1	13.9	384	28.5	1.7	460 650	-0.9	24 169	5.2	442 126	30.5	10.4
Essex	13 721	72.1	62 200	20.0	13.6	368	26.2	3.0	18 256	0.1	1 568	8.6	15 289	26.8	12.5
Franklin	16 284	68.9	48 900	18.4	14.2	324	27.6	3.7	22 093	5.9	1 743	7.9	18 281	25.3	10.4
Fulton	20 995	71.4	56 000	19.9	14.3	348	28.1	2.4	26 895	0.2	1 639	6.1	23 909	23.8	12.7

1. Specified owner-occupied units. 2. Specified renter-occupied units. 3. Overcrowded or lacking complete plumbing facilities. 4. Percent of civilian labor force. 5. Persons 16 years and older.

Table B. States and Counties — Nonfarm Employment and Agriculture

STATE County	Number of establishments	Employment Total	Health Care and Social Assistance	Manufacturing	Retail trade	Finance and Insurance	Professional Scientific and Technical Services	Annual payroll Total (mil dol)	Average per employee (dollars)	Farms Number	Percent with— Less than 50 acres	500 acres and over	Farm operators Whose principal occupation is farming (percent)
	104	105	106	107	108	109	110	111	112	113	114	115	116
NEW JERSEY—Cont'd													
Mercer	9 317	156 991	21 501	10 394	17 763	9 238	13 287	5 693	36 265	285	64.9	4.6	42.5
Middlesex	20 219	363 121	31 805	49 448	39 466	21 836	34 779	14 795	40 744	275	73.5	5.5	44.7
Monmouth	18 278	200 524	30 383	12 736	33 869	8 855	14 785	6 716	33 491	874	80.0	3.5	45.5
Morris	17 162	280 256	24 807	30 630	28 624	17 736	29 679	13 408	47 844	383	73.6	1.8	40.2
Ocean	10 666	105 202	22 629	7 170	25 272	3 517	5 129	2 687	25 545	235	83.4	0.0	36.4
Passaic	11 956	164 987	20 718	33 876	23 637	9 010	9 794	5 402	32 744	55	80.0	0.0	36.4
Salem	1 351	17 946	2 606	4 100	2 656	603	D	634	35 307	660	50.8	**6.5**	44.8
Somerset	9 454	165 200	14 634	15 750	14 854	15 316	17 633	7 973	48 263	437	66.4	4.8	35.5
Sussex	3 470	27 181	4 786	2 174	4 812	1 859	1 239	730	26 845	827	62.2	3.4	33.6
Union	14 789	225 532	25 137	39 486	23 267	8 554	11 690	9 169	40 656	19	94.7	0.0	57.9
Warren	2 721	30 163	4 191	7 231	5 525	754	1 111	989	32 789	730	54.4	4.7	41.8
NEW MEXICO	42 608	540 186	76 641	40 561	89 883	21 847	35 771	13 134	24 313	14 094	37.0	35.5	51.1
Bernalillo	15 585	249 348	33 927	19 520	34 689	11 767	24 932	6 631	26 593	468	76.9	7.3	32.3
Catron	59	238	D	D	D	D	D	3	12 966	217	9.7	59.9	65.0
Chaves	1 525	16 056	2 299	2 795	2 954	602	464	323	20 092	562	29.9	44.1	61.4
Cibola	363	4 654	681	512	796	118	97	96	20 610	166	24.7	59.0	57.8
Colfax	500	3 963	469	281	657	158	103	69	17 343	322	14.3	51.9	64.6
Curry	1 072	10 635	2 143	313	2 455	D	302	194	18 204	655	13.4	51.0	56.6
De Baca	62	339	98	D	69	D	D	5	16 035	191	24.1	52.9	65.4
Dona Ana	3 183	34 739	5 874	2 398	6 604	1 413	2 538	674	19 389	1 290	75.7	7.8	40.4
Eddy	1 283	15 947	2 314	1 138	2 726	586	297	385	24 115	467	34.3	34.5	53.5
Grant	694	7 972	1 092	318	1 198	235	D	201	25 203	286	19.6	52.4	53.8
Guadalupe	113	1 077	128	0	365	D	D	15	14 257	236	15.7	64.8	58.9
Harding	20	54	D	D	D	D	D	1	21 926	172	3.5	78.5	70.3
Hidalgo	108	1 451	117	D	248	D	D	35	23 881	146	10.3	65.1	58.2
Lea	1 487	16 044	1 797	762	2 456	484	380	367	22 866	528	19.1	47.0	51.7
Lincoln	708	4 406	481	56	1 077	242	182	76	17 344	337	21.4	57.0	63.5
Los Alamos	446	5 830	967	D	521	307	787	173	29 738	4	100.0	0.0	69.3
Luna	414	3 408	432	473	962	136	73	57	16 621	192	17.7	48.4	69.3
McKinley	1 037	13 792	2 838	642	3 816	339	245	289	20 937	224	21.4	47.8	39.3
Mora	61	412	204	D	66	D	D	7	15 925	398	19.1	34.9	46.0
Otero	1 035	11 229	1 848	499	2 297	446	D	203	18 061	417	48.9	21.3	48.0
Quay	295	2 097	307	146	583	134	D	32	15 338	583	9.4	60.4	65.7
Rio Arriba	637	6 248	1 482	230	1 175	157	98	119	19 082	940	56.6	16.5	43.5
Roosevelt	342	2 923	351	224	766	125	D	47	16 186	738	15.2	49.1	57.0
Sandoval	1 172	18 750	962	5 519	2 828	273	D	579	30 873	353	48.4	22.4	43.6
San Juan	2 416	31 938	3 965	1 182	5 906	876	886	868	27 180	666	64.3	7.5	44.7
San Miguel	536	5 063	1 887	131	1 097	180	111	100	19 817	643	18.5	46.3	45.9
Santa Fe	4 517	44 430	6 026	1 320	8 583	1 825	2 273	1 060	23 852	336	53.9	23.2	37.8
Sierra	313	1 931	272	D	388	76	D	29	14 803	180	24.4	49.4	65.6
Socorro	271	2 410	396	143	389	91	91	41	16 983	395	41.5	32.4	56.5
Taos	1 109	8 242	1 107	215	1 549	214	240	138	16 733	422	53.1	11.1	38.9
Torrance	235	1 842	109	65	467	D	D	30	16 192	473	15.2	51.2	54.1
Union	119	732	115	D	120	93	D	12	15 970	448	7.8	70.8	67.6
Valencia	833	8 267	1 920	1 025	2 017	299	222	150	18 163	639	80.8	4.2	38.8
NEW YORK	481 962	6 993 814	1 134 481	752 511	800 566	587 464	485 199	274 635	39 268	31 757	24.3	10.7	58.0
Albany	8 815	162 226	26 057	9 333	22 054	16 178	11 331	4 843	29 852	396	35.6	3.8	45.7
Allegany	842	12 131	2 032	3 024	1 545	193	207	247	20 352	724	14.0	8.6	47.5
Bronx	14 233	194 171	76 716	12 250	20 919	2 983	3 639	5 779	29 763	NA	NA	NA	NA
Broome	4 280	81 593	12 341	19 740	11 460	3 402	3 160	2 224	27 261	511	26.6	4.9	47.2
Cattaraugus	1 772	24 039	3 230	5 165	4 127	704	405	549	22 837	946	17.0	7.2	52.6
Cayuga	1 561	19 050	3 299	4 502	3 255	693	572	437	22 944	846	17.3	15.7	59.3
Chautauqua	3 107	46 937	8 123	13 743	6 862	853	1 060	1 090	23 231	1 557	33.2	5.3	56.0
Chemung	1 933	36 456	6 495	9 262	6 052	908	919	895	24 550	313	23.3	8.0	39.0
Chenango	1 027	12 572	1 863	3 640	1 842	1 045	319	305	24 278	801	18.6	10.2	60.5
Clinton	1 888	23 507	3 786	4 388	4 764	515	498	539	22 917	488	15.6	16.0	55.3
Columbia	1 640	14 983	3 589	2 357	2 291	591	684	367	20 252	464	31.0	13.4	62.5
Cortland	1 036	17 235	3 591	4 592	2 535	389	643	349	24 142	452	15.3	14.4	54.2
Delaware	1 115	12 610	2 092	4 433	1 809	437	248	304	28 045	717	15.9	12.3	59.7
Dutchess	6 593	82 574	15 020	11 961	13 504	3 315	3 926	2 316	27 439	539	33.0	9.8	54.7
Erie	22 528	399 282	65 946	62 229	53 170	23 208	19 562	10 956	27 439	973	37.2	5.4	53.2
Essex	1 168	9 786	1 681	1 438	1 656	221	350	220	22 519	197	22.8	14.2	42.1
Franklin	1 043	9 336	2 550	1 118	1 688	319	198	193	20 691	476	9.9	14.3	68.5
Fulton	1 080	13 418	2 125	3 750	1 949	335	213	309	23 018	176	18.8	5.1	62.5

Items 104–116

Table B. States and Counties — **Agriculture, Land, and Water**

STATE County	Agriculture, 1997 (cont'd)															
	Land in farms					Value of land and buildings		Value of machinery and equipment	Value of products sold				Percent of farms with sales of —		Percent of land owned by Fed. Gov. 1997	Water consumption 1995 (mil gal/day)
		Acres									Percent from —					
	Acreage (1,000)	Percent change, 1992–1997	Average size of farm	Total irrigated (1,000)	Total cropland (1,000)	Average per farm ($1,000)	Average per acre (dollars)	Average per farm ($1,000)	Total (mil dol)	Average per farm (dollars)	Crops	Live-stock and poultry products	$10,000 or more	$100,000 or more		
	117	118	119	120	121	122	123	124	125	126	127	128	129	130	131	132
NEW JERSEY—Cont'd																
Mercer	28	-21.1	100	1	23	1 359	13 871	44	13	46 510	92.5	7.5	38.2	10.5	0.0	506.1
Middlesex	28	12.4	102	2	22	756	8 225	50	34	124 927	96.7	3.3	50.2	16.7	0.0	49.2
Monmouth	59	0.7	68	6	46	676	9 710	54	68	77 772	92.2	7.8	41.3	12.2	3.9	79.4
Morris	22	-6.9	58	1	14	710	13 552	38	30	78 215	96.0	4.0	31.6	10.4	4.6	101.6
Ocean	11	13.8	48	1	6	349	6 791	19	8	34 767	68.1	31.9	32.3	8.9	6.8	59.7
Passaic	2	11.6	41	0	0	576	14 201	24	4	70 232	93.9	6.1	40.0	10.9	0.0	300.2
Salem	92	-6.1	139	18	75	537	3 887	66	68	102 892	64.2	35.8	45.8	15.9	2.4	33.1
Somerset	46	5.1	106	1	31	796	8 454	49	14	32 096	71.0	29.0	34.3	8.0	0.9	127.0
Sussex	73	-3.9	88	1	41	477	5 493	25	19	23 201	58.7	41.3	25.6	6.4	6.9	20.1
Union	D	D	D	0	0	1 085	80 852	49	10	525 587	99.8	0.2	78.9	31.6	0.0	26.7
Warren	83	-5.8	114	2	58	737	6 502	41	46	63 021	42.8	57.2	32.7	12.7	3.8	68.8
NEW MEXICO	45 787	-2.3	3 249	805	2 179	625	195	44	1 618	114 780	28.6	71.4	38.9	12.2	34.0	3 505.3
Bernalillo	465	12.0	993	11	18	403	436	23	31	66 298	17.9	82.1	15.8	4.1	16.0	189.9
Catron	1 795	15.6	8 274	2	12	928	112	26	14	66 793	0.5	99.5	48.4	10.1	62.7	17.3
Chaves	2 944	-5.4	5 239	66	D	1 075	194	71	220	391 684	15.4	84.6	62.6	29.9	31.8	289.6
Cibola	1 699	-18.3	10 237	2	21	1 231	123	26	6	34 290	3.7	96.3	33.7	5.4	28.5	8.8
Colfax	2 227	6.8	6 917	27	46	1 348	187	40	40	124 955	3.5	96.5	57.1	18.6	3.2	47.5
Curry	948	2.5	1 447	93	444	588	434	90	195	298 378	24.4	75.6	57.4	29.2	0.4	229.9
De Baca	1 442	7.3	7 548	8	18	873	120	55	25	131 798	18.1	81.9	55.5	23.0	2.4	52.6
Dona Ana	581	10.5	451	82	91	541	1 305	65	235	182 546	54.5	45.5	32.7	13.3	76.1	441.4
Eddy	1 276	12.0	2 731	46	65	578	203	60	85	181 127	29.7	70.3	52.2	18.4	60.3	237.8
Grant	1 174	-2.9	4 103	3	13	558	133	33	7	25 590	3.0	97.0	38.1	7.3	48.7	60.8
Guadalupe	1 419	-7.4	6 013	2	7	722	121	25	12	52 645	2.1	97.9	38.1	10.2	3.3	19.3
Harding	1 255	-2.7	7 296	D	20	D	D	26	14	79 845	0.2	99.8	58.7	14.5	5.1	4.1
Hidalgo	1 105	31.1	7 567	10	23	1 125	153	49	18	125 417	69.2	30.8	64.4	21.9	42.4	40.6
Lea	2 002	-6.8	3 792	41	104	563	161	52	60	114 379	25.6	74.4	47.7	15.3	15.1	157.5
Lincoln	1 975	4.9	5 861	3	9	858	139	36	14	41 620	0.8	99.2	48.4	12.5	35.1	34.7
Los Alamos	D	D	D	D	D	D	D	9	D	D			0.0	0.0	48.4	5.3
Luna	603	-24.3	3 143	31	D	738	243	103	49	255 557	78.3	21.7	65.1	35.4	40.0	131.5
McKinley	3 157	-2.1	14 094	4	D	1 396	99	34	9	41 651	0.8	99.2	21.9	3.6	17.9	18.2
Mora	975	7.7	2 449	13	41	634	261	27	11	27 787	3.9	96.1	21.4	5.3	8.8	33.3
Otero	1 081	-7.3	2 592	6	D	605	241	21	10	23 247	35.7	64.3	26.6	5.3	69.5	46.6
Quay	1 856	4.9	3 183	41	245	514	167	58	41	69 691	32.9	67.1	61.4	16.1	0.1	134.3
Rio Arriba	1 463	-5.8	1 557	24	65	370	250	25	10	11 101	19.7	80.3	22.2	1.2	52.4	85.1
Roosevelt	1 419	-13.8	1 923	68	349	521	275	65	128	173 839	30.3	69.7	55.0	21.3	5.3	143.7
Sandoval	780	1.3	2 209	11	32	374	178	26	10	28 291	21.4	78.6	23.2	3.1	40.5	67.5
San Juan	D	D	D	69	84	314	92	31	D	D			22.7	2.4	25.3	345.0
San Miguel	2 557	-0.9	3 976	12	50	762	189	24	21	32 121	5.3	94.7	21.5	5.1	12.7	30.9
Santa Fe	652	25.9	1 940	11	23	685	312	29	13	37 223	52.6	47.4	20.2	4.8	27.4	45.7
Sierra	1 287	4.3	7 149	6	D	1 467	215	33	16	87 589	27.7	72.3	53.9	13.9	61.9	42.3
Socorro	1 651	-11.6	4 180	15	20	652	165	39	25	63 872	18.6	81.4	45.3	10.9	52.5	147.1
Taos	310	-4.2	735	14	27	390	554	21	4	8 882	35.1	64.9	14.2	1.2	53.6	98.3
Torrance	1 477	-17.8	3 123	20	65	498	175	45	31	65 215	38.2	61.8	35.9	9.9	8.0	42.3
Union	2 227	-5.8	4 972	47	90	682	141	58	130	291 281	10.3	89.7	71.4	28.3	2.4	76.5
Valencia	384	9.9	600	17	17	295	494	24	27	41 625	23.6	76.4	21.9	4.1	7.3	179.9
NEW YORK	7 254	-2.7	228	69	4 722	287	1 284	60	2 835	89 256	35.3	64.7	54.0	21.6	0.7	10 277.6
Albany	57	-2.1	143	0	36	236	1 878	40	16	39 823	42.7	57.3	43.9	7.6	0.0	566.1
Allegany	158	-2.6	218	1	90	163	801	33	35	48 138	11.8	88.2	39.5	12.0	0.0	9.5
Bronx	NA	NA	NA	NA	NA	NA	NA	NA	NA	NA	NA	NA	NA	NA	0.0	7.5
Broome	86	-12.4	168	0	47	155	1 025	39	24	46 997	19.4	80.6	32.3	11.5	0.1	132.6
Cattaraugus	192	-5.9	203	0	105	192	986	46	53	56 526	19.5	80.5	46.6	15.1	0.0	15.8
Cayuga	252	-0.9	298	1	193	318	1 092	76	115	136 452	32.6	67.4	63.8	28.3	0.0	17.2
Chautauqua	245	-5.8	157	1	145	172	1 145	46	89	56 951	32.9	67.1	52.0	15.5	0.0	1 204.1
Chemung	59	0.5	189	0	36	186	983	41	13	41 209	31.1	68.9	33.9	12.1	0.0	18.2
Chenango	183	-2.5	229	0	104	195	857	53	53	66 359	7.3	92.7	54.2	22.0	0.0	9.2
Clinton	149	-5.9	305	0	77	275	946	72	69	142 066	23.0	77.0	54.7	28.9	0.4	15.6
Columbia	115	2.6	248	3	79	627	2 586	86	73	156 627	26.0	74.0	62.3	23.5	0.0	8.7
Cortland	121	-13.1	267	0	67	270	977	64	37	82 848	8.2	91.8	53.5	26.1	0.0	11.3
Delaware	184	-4.3	256	0	95	246	1 044	46	43	60 666	11.1	88.9	53.1	21.8	0.0	490.2
Dutchess	107	-3.0	198	1	63	791	4 619	53	34	63 013	48.5	51.5	53.6	15.2	0.4	39.2
Erie	143	-1.9	147	2	103	249	1 698	58	78	79 990	39.9	60.1	47.1	18.4	0.0	1 094.9
Essex	48	-12.4	245	0	25	316	1 338	51	9	40 639	31.6	68.4	42.1	9.6	0.0	10.9
Franklin	163	18.1	342	D	78	217	640	65	44	93 037	12.6	87.4	66.4	32.8	0.0	10.3
Fulton	34	-2.0	195	0	22	232	1 215	62	10	54 686	13.2	86.8	51.1	22.2	0.0	7.6

Table B. States and Counties — Residential Construction, Wholesale and Retail Trade, and Real Estate

STATE County	Value of Residential Construction Authorized by Building Permits, 1999		Wholesale Trade, 1997				Retail Trade[1], 1997				Real Estate and Rental and Leasing, 1997			
	New Construction ($1,000)	Number of Housing Units	Number of Establishments	Number of Employees	Sales (mil dol)	Annual Payroll (mil dol)	Number of Establishments	Number of Employees	Sales (mil dol)	Annual Payroll (mil dol)	Number of Establishments	Number of Employees	Receipts (mil dol)	Annual Payroll (mil dol)
	133	134	135	136	137	138	139	140	141	142	143	144	145	146
NEW JERSEY—Cont'd														
Mercer	113 932	1 159	472	8 480	4 403.0	291.5	1 442	18 217	3 183.1	326.1	289	1 685	256.7	43.1
Middlesex	249 996	3 102	1 866	36 168	24 256.4	1 554.4	2 785	39 421	7 364.0	720.8	616	4 098	743.5	129.7
Monmouth	355 806	2 974	1 197	9 577	6 298.1	410.3	2 870	34 839	6 400.5	627.7	599	2 795	444.5	74.8
Morris	240 710	1 853	1 397	20 533	20 939.4	1 027.2	2 241	30 767	6 499.9	635.5	536	2 920	620.8	109.8
Ocean	393 570	4 192	429	2 903	937.2	95.4	1 923	23 431	4 728.3	431.5	386	1 345	190.3	30.2
Passaic	54 051	533	1 006	13 154	9 085.0	601.8	1 843	25 468	4 659.9	469.0	415	1 710	251.4	45.8
Salem	16 479	147	45	517	440.3	19.3	226	2 682	401.3	41.5	52	183	20.5	3.6
Somerset	259 343	2 146	672	12 018	18 285.3	643.4	1 178	15 351	3 305.8	306.7	271	1 555	249.8	45.8
Sussex	94 247	687	181	D	D	D	502	4 689	953.6	92.7	82	256	36.5	5.6
Union	38 691	513	1 222	22 744	15 712.5	1 085.7	2 100	22 616	4 809.2	464.9	648	3 184	756.1	88.6
Warren	91 118	890	129	D	D	D	466	5 106	862.2	90.1	74	242	35.2	4.7
NEW MEXICO	1 079 858	9 716	2 182	21 344	7 397.6	601.1	7 421	86 300	14 984.5	1 455.5	1 887	8 844	893.9	165.2
Bernalillo	440 154	4 441	1 037	12 824	4 594.3	388.2	2 307	34 361	6 497.7	623.6	751	4 519	504.2	85.0
Catron	NA	NA	NA	NA	NA	NA	12	37	3.1	0.3	3	22	1.6	0.4
Chaves	3 186	36	74	599	231.3	13.8	269	2 702	411.0	40.5	74	198	18.6	3.1
Cibola	NA	NA	17	82	21.8	1.4	77	809	149.3	11.3	13	80	4.0	1.2
Colfax	NA	NA	13	D	D	D	95	606	104.6	9.1	16	49	3.0	0.5
Curry	3 833	37	44	342	120.5	7.3	235	2 455	342.6	34.6	53	177	9.8	1.8
De Baca	NA	NA	1	D	D	D	13	59	8.7	0.8	2	D	D	D
Dona Ana	97 389	920	122	978	283.6	25.0	511	6 266	1 059.1	98.1	175	530	44.8	7.4
Eddy	6 167	58	69	384	274.7	10.3	232	2 312	372.7	38.9	58	217	15.6	3.8
Grant	NA	NA	32	198	56.6	4.1	125	1 165	190.4	17.9	31	89	6.7	1.2
Guadalupe	NA	NA	5	7	9.8	0.2	27	333	32.0	3.5	2	D	D	D
Harding	NA	NA	NA	NA	NA	NA	3	13	8.1	0.5	NA	NA	NA	NA
Hidalgo	NA	NA	3	D	D	D	36	238	49.3	3.7	1	D	D	D
Lea	249	1	121	964	308.7	27.2	248	2 375	405.3	42.6	58	360	43.0	10.5
Lincoln	25 133	149	16	35	7.7	0.6	148	1 079	149.1	15.1	53	129	11.4	1.7
Los Alamos	19 545	138	9	75	41.4	4.1	59	555	74.1	8.0	16	D	D	D
Luna	3 455	40	22	233	49.3	3.1	95	950	177.5	12.3	13	38	2.7	0.5
McKinley	6 270	63	74	761	191.9	13.5	269	3 670	585.5	59.6	36	156	11.7	2.1
Mora	NA	NA	NA	NA	NA	NA	12	57	7.3	0.7	2	D	D	D
Otero	12 311	100	22	121	29.7	2.5	215	2 281	326.5	32.3	47	170	11.8	2.1
Quay	NA	NA	10	33	4.5	0.4	71	594	99.6	8.5	12	44	1.7	0.4
Rio Arriba	1 649	13	19	84	40.2	1.6	104	1 149	189.0	18.2	15	33	2.4	0.4
Roosevelt	1 485	22	17	103	33.7	2.0	71	626	121.2	10.6	11	18	1.0	0.1
Sandoval	40 276	449	48	456	248.3	11.2	155	1 902	274.0	31.0	42	193	18.0	3.1
San Juan	23 973	176	158	1 278	381.9	35.7	494	5 896	990.8	96.7	87	495	35.1	15.3
San Miguel	NA	NA	16	62	19.4	1.3	114	1 087	168.4	15.1	14	53	2.8	0.5
Santa Fe	61 993	781	167	1 260	340.2	39.3	846	7 868	1 422.9	149.4	200	D	D	D
Sierra	NA	NA	7	21	7.5	0.8	60	379	62.6	5.2	15	47	1.8	0.4
Socorro	2 342	45	6	102	12.3	1.4	57	385	70.6	6.3	10	26	1.5	0.2
Taos	5 569	66	16	59	11.8	1.0	259	1 554	206.8	23.7	39	145	7.3	1.4
Torrance	NA	NA	10	57	10.4	1.2	44	441	73.2	5.6	6	6	0.5	0.1
Union	NA	NA	2	D	D	D	27	103	15.3	1.3	2	D	D	D
Valencia	42 775	421	25	104	38.1	1.7	131	1 993	336.2	30.4	30	96	8.5	1.2
NEW YORK	4 414 787	42 619	37 499	414 249	319 697.6	17 185.8	75 241	805 208	139 303.9	14 329.8	27 214	145 326	27 770.1	4 447.8
Albany	111 327	992	581	8 866	4 335.8	322.3	1 483	21 444	3 567.2	348.1	343	2 535	383.6	57.6
Allegany	7 039	110	26	235	54.8	3.9	181	1 646	210.6	20.4	18	57	3.4	0.6
Bronx	73 822	1 153	755	10 728	5 373.6	389.9	3 110	21 641	3 434.9	352.5	2 171	7 435	1 212.8	182.5
Broome	26 198	252	261	D	D	D	829	11 881	1 763.3	164.2	128	613	82.3	10.1
Cattaraugus	14 202	206	86	979	409.1	28.0	380	4 190	570.7	56.1	52	182	16.1	2.8
Cayuga	12 600	155	78	746	201.3	20.7	265	3 250	516.8	50.5	42	187	18.7	3.1
Chautauqua	23 657	227	159	2 171	748.6	57.6	591	7 096	1 011.1	96.6	86	395	41.9	7.0
Chemung	22 788	296	107	1 667	447.2	49.2	412	5 963	875.9	82.9	66	345	47.9	7.4
Chenango	3 625	64	30	332	64.3	6.7	204	1 793	293.8	27.3	32	66	7.4	1.1
Clinton	23 461	241	115	1 515	407.0	29.6	445	4 967	756.6	70.8	65	219	18.2	2.5
Columbia	27 796	198	81	686	250.6	20.2	260	2 647	424.1	42.0	49	128	11.6	2.4
Cortland	6 695	84	35	401	195.7	11.8	200	2 658	423.9	38.5	24	90	11.1	1.3
Delaware	11 709	145	40	278	150.8	7.4	243	1 810	307.8	29.2	38	118	13.1	1.6
Dutchess	176 919	1 238	274	D	D	D	1 097	13 506	2 259.5	225.7	256	1 502	165.9	28.5
Erie	243 887	2 221	1 680	25 712	14 962.5	884.6	3 628	55 286	8 036.3	797.2	738	5 325	719.1	126.1
Essex	19 850	170	22	178	49.7	5.2	251	1 611	283.8	25.9	34	89	10.1	2.2
Franklin	6 493	106	37	310	126.7	6.8	215	1 834	283.9	26.0	25	71	6.6	1.3
Fulton	10 393	116	78	763	336.1	22.7	195	2 019	331.8	30.1	26	72	7.8	1.1

1. Establishments with payroll.

STATE County	Professional, Scientific, and Technical Services[1], 1997				Manufacturing, 1997				Accommodation and Foodservices, 1997			
	Number of Establish-ments	Number of Employees	Receipts (mil dol)	Annual Payroll (mil dol)	Number of Establish-ments	Number of Employees	Receipts (mil dol)	Annual Payroll (mil dol)	Number of Establish-ments	Number of Employees	Sales (mil dol)	Annual Payroll (mil dol)
	147	148	149	150	151	152	153	154	155	156	157	158
NEW JERSEY—Cont'd												
Mercer	1 223	10 930	1 407.3	586.2	352	13 537	2 413.6	579.7	703	9 870	394.0	109.9
Middlesex	2 682	33 101	3 953.4	1 790.4	977	49 983	13 688.0	1 950.6	1 318	17 941	761.8	201.0
Monmouth	2 195	13 292	1 460.2	617.6	587	12 820	2 318.3	402.7	1 377	18 131	689.8	194.5
Morris	2 452	26 674	3 528.4	1 443.6	749	24 461	7 531.5	979.6	1 080	14 790	665.8	184.0
Ocean	831	4 325	347.8	151.1	309	7 174	939.8	201.1	946	10 569	420.2	108.7
Passaic	1 083	7 338	817.1	256.0	1 059	34 589	6 464.2	1 237.6	764	8 212	338.9	91.0
Salem	86	301	22.3	9.1	48	4 188	1 156.2	207.5	109	1 246	45.1	12.5
Somerset	1 501	23 781	2 218.9	898.2	376	16 289	5 148.4	856.7	618	8 092	356.6	102.2
Sussex	329	1 059	109.1	40.6	146	2 854	320.8	87.2	254	3 006	106.2	31.4
Union	1 554	10 502	1 178.1	480.0	996	40 157	13 883.3	1 619.7	1 064	11 982	513.2	138.3
Warren	237	892	86.8	36.4	164	7 188	1 982.3	294.4	224	2 144	80.6	20.8
NEW MEXICO	3 702	31 535	3 243.4	1 307.3	1 593	39 664	17 906.1	1 135.8	3 825	67 134	2 144.9	599.1
Bernalillo	1 881	23 092	2 578.3	1 040.4	703	D	D	D	1 202	26 744	878.1	248.1
Catron	2	D	D	D	NA	NA	NA	NA	11	45	1.7	0.4
Chaves	87	458	37.5	13.6	51	D	D	D	115	1 970	54.8	14.7
Cibola	18	62	3.1	1.1	NA	NA	NA	NA	46	642	21.4	5.3
Colfax	31	77	5.0	2.0	NA	NA	NA	NA	79	1 205	34.6	12.7
Curry	66	249	13.5	5.3	NA	NA	NA	NA	83	1 631	45.9	13.1
De Baca	2	D	D	D	NA	NA	NA	NA	8	44	1.2	0.3
Dona Ana	222	1 334	107.3	45.7	111	2 290	395.5	46.9	253	4 278	121.7	32.6
Eddy	53	231	20.3	9.0	41	1 057	641.4	43.9	102	1 761	52.5	14.3
Grant	37	173	8.7	3.3	NA	NA	NA	NA	72	823	25.1	6.2
Guadalupe	2	D	D	D	NA	NA	NA	NA	33	317	10.1	2.4
Harding	2	D	D	D	NA	NA	NA	NA	3	10	0.1	0.0
Hidalgo	2	D	D	D	2	D	D	D	24	301	7.9	2.6
Lea	67	338	19.9	8.4	45	524	379.7	14.8	109	1 510	42.0	11.3
Lincoln	53	154	10.4	3.8	NA	NA	NA	NA	99	866	30.1	7.6
Los Alamos	67	728	76.2	32.1	NA	NA	NA	NA	42	696	20.5	6.3
Luna	20	68	2.7	1.1	16	776	49.5	10.7	51	595	16.0	4.4
McKinley	38	219	10.6	3.7	NA	NA	NA	NA	133	2 061	69.3	17.5
Mora	3	D	D	D	NA	NA	NA	NA	4	12	0.2	0.1
Otero	53	240	12.3	5.3	26	593	93.8	10.5	99	1 324	37.0	9.9
Quay	12	48	1.8	0.8	NA	NA	NA	NA	46	526	16.2	3.9
Rio Arriba	35	87	5.9	1.6	NA	NA	NA	NA	89	1 059	33.9	9.5
Roosevelt	12	37	2.2	0.6	NA	NA	NA	NA	30	581	12.4	3.3
Sandoval	97	396	28.0	10.7	57	D	D	D	92	1 501	46.0	12.1
San Juan	166	919	50.9	19.9	71	1 147	257.8	30.3	173	3 478	100.0	27.3
San Miguel	30	87	4.0	1.3	NA	NA	NA	NA	69	796	24.0	5.8
Santa Fe	464	1 964	205.9	85.1	162	1 436	124.8	31.7	361	7 498	304.8	89.1
Sierra	18	41	1.9	0.6	NA	NA	NA	NA	47	437	13.0	3.2
Socorro	20	102	7.6	2.8	NA	NA	NA	NA	51	658	18.7	5.2
Taos	71	181	11.8	4.0	NA	NA	NA	NA	167	2 232	63.7	19.1
Torrance	10	24	1.6	0.4	NA	NA	NA	NA	32	361	8.9	2.5
Union	7	17	1.0	0.3	NA	NA	NA	NA	20	226	4.8	1.2
Valencia	54	180	12.7	3.8	40	967	110.3	22.3	80	946	28.3	7.0
NEW YORK	45 619	416 892	57 475.0	21 773.1	23 908	785 891	146 720.2	26 515.8	38 045	473 327	21 671.1	6 101.1
Albany	860	8 250	848.7	330.0	272	9 065	2 182.4	335.9	841	12 586	449.2	125.0
Allegany	49	148	11.4	3.7	57	2 919	542.8	102.4	87	961	29.1	7.8
Bronx	391	1 980	158.6	50.7	527	12 941	1 252.3	319.6	1 067	8 264	371.6	95.7
Broome	316	2 334	183.7	68.6	242	20 429	3 147.6	787.8	476	6 940	204.2	58.1
Cattaraugus	79	357	31.5	7.8	95	5 341	930.5	162.9	227	3 309	79.5	23.4
Cayuga	90	532	36.1	15.0	100	3 859	618.6	110.4	172	1 688	52.5	14.2
Chautauqua	168	815	48.5	19.2	222	13 084	2 973.6	409.1	368	4 323	124.9	35.4
Chemung	104	827	56.5	18.3	94	9 098	1 357.3	278.1	213	2 965	86.2	24.4
Chenango	65	267	19.9	6.7	86	3 829	790.4	120.3	97	848	24.0	6.0
Clinton	92	328	20.9	8.1	82	4 188	777.9	131.8	189	2 243	64.7	20.0
Columbia	132	538	43.8	16.1	86	2 531	331.1	62.2	142	1 130	41.9	11.1
Cortland	62	457	36.4	13.8	70	4 521	736.1	123.5	125	1 845	53.0	13.7
Delaware	75	224	10.1	3.6	60	4 386	783.7	147.9	124	740	31.1	7.3
Dutchess	591	3 149	284.3	113.6	210	11 848	3 032.9	521.3	558	6 243	252.1	64.4
Erie	1 790	15 551	1 413.9	527.1	1 251	63 234	14 054.5	2 422.1	2 143	31 916	935.4	271.6
Essex	59	145	11.9	3.5	40	1 474	285.2	50.4	219	1 942	86.9	28.1
Franklin	53	170	10.8	4.0	26	1 165	144.4	24.9	127	899	30.6	7.9
Fulton	59	183	12.4	4.0	116	3 548	443.6	86.6	112	957	28.2	7.3

1. Firms subject to federal tax.

Table B. States and Counties — **Health and Other Services and Federal Funds**

STATE County	Health Care and Social Assistance[1], 1997				Other Services[1], 1997				Federal funds and grants, fiscal 1999[2] Expenditures (mil dol)			
										Direct payments for individuals[3]		
	Number of Establishments	Number of Employees	Receipts (mil dol)	Annual Payroll (mil dol)	Number of Establishments	Number of Employees	Receipts (mil dol)	Annual Payroll (mil dol)	Total	Social Security and government retirement	Medicare	Food stamps and Supplemental Security Income
	159	160	161	162	163	164	165	166	167	168	169	170
NEW JERSEY—Cont'd												
Mercer	792	6 837	576.4	260.0	538	2 985	210.3	62.1	2 960.9	716.2	342.3	51.8
Middlesex	1 429	13 628	1 231.2	469.8	1 261	6 628	511.4	145.4	2 711.4	1 133.0	556.4	54.9
Monmouth	1 695	13 866	1 057.5	462.7	1 177	5 961	382.6	119.5	3 080.6	1 153.1	504.4	39.1
Morris	1 330	11 147	930.5	387.8	1 031	5 308	403.3	119.0	1 576.0	726.2	290.9	16.9
Ocean	984	12 337	855.6	362.5	767	3 074	185.1	50.9	2 579.2	1 428.7	635.7	30.9
Passaic	1 033	8 552	840.7	306.5	823	3 926	287.8	89.5	1 939.9	727.9	387.8	81.5
Salem	108	744	56.1	22.9	102	285	20.0	4.5	264.9	125.9	67.1	7.1
Somerset	706	7 075	613.1	252.4	498	2 331	175.9	54.8	837.8	440.1	148.9	9.5
Sussex	244	2 849	151.9	67.9	250	886	61.8	16.6	373.3	199.1	82.9	6.3
Union	1 194	10 405	800.1	348.7	1 100	5 844	432.1	137.8	2 024.4	942.0	469.4	59.7
Warren	197	1 440	101.0	42.3	190	750	53.8	14.5	364.9	186.5	92.7	6.7
NEW MEXICO	2 923	32 824	2 057.3	864.3	2 318	13 448	759.1	227.2	13 580.2	3 326.9	900.7	338.5
Bernalillo	1 152	16 080	1 115.2	463.3	896	6 596	374.4	121.2	4 929.3	1 142.3	294.7	87.7
Catron	NA	NA	NA	NA	2	D	D	D	19.1	9.6	1.5	0.4
Chaves	121	826	48.5	22.8	79	335	19.5	5.0	263.1	126.8	35.6	14.8
Cibola	20	203	10.3	4.2	28	72	3.7	0.9	94.4	33.9	0.0	5.1
Colfax	18	154	8.0	3.3	22	54	2.8	0.8	76.2	32.6	10.3	2.5
Curry	96	738	41.0	16.5	76	334	17.7	4.7	337.3	94.7	24.1	4.6
De Baca	3	D	D	D	3	7	0.4	0.1	12.1	6.3	2.1	0.4
Dona Ana	272	3 149	177.9	75.3	169	1 025	43.9	13.2	925.7	283.1	72.1	43.7
Eddy	84	1 101	70.4	26.4	84	353	25.1	5.5	344.0	106.9	38.5	10.2
Grant	46	298	18.7	8.4	46	149	6.9	1.7	140.3	70.4	19.5	5.7
Guadalupe	4	37	0.9	0.6	5	22	1.4	0.3	27.9	7.8	3.5	1.4
Harding	1	D	D	D	1	D	D	D	5.4	2.6	0.7	0.1
Hidalgo	5	D	D	D	4	5	0.6	0.1	28.2	12.2	3.6	1.3
Lea	86	1 121	70.6	23.1	100	722	43.4	12.7	200.9	90.7	40.2	12.8
Lincoln	35	214	9.3	5.6	23	96	5.4	1.3	76.7	44.6	10.0	2.2
Los Alamos	48	352	20.1	10.0	16	68	4.3	1.5	1 476.1	24.7	7.5	0.3
Luna	34	155	8.3	3.1	18	78	4.3	1.0	112.1	53.8	15.5	6.5
McKinley	41	391	15.1	5.9	69	332	16.1	4.5	405.5	81.6	23.6	28.6
Mora	3	72	1.4	0.9	1	D	D	D	30.7	9.7	2.7	1.9
Otero	61	491	27.0	11.6	59	284	13.8	4.2	492.7	149.0	23.7	8.2
Quay	19	123	4.7	2.1	19	79	4.4	0.9	62.7	24.4	8.4	3.1
Rio Arriba	46	545	30.4	13.0	27	68	4.4	0.9	201.6	61.7	19.6	10.8
Roosevelt	12	44	2.9	1.4	27	82	5.2	1.1	91.5	29.9	12.9	4.5
Sandoval	57	610	37.7	15.5	55	302	13.7	4.0	261.2	134.5	35.2	10.7
San Juan	169	1 379	85.8	39.6	176	1 076	66.4	18.7	417.4	147.9	45.9	20.2
San Miguel	55	523	21.5	9.8	29	88	4.5	1.1	171.1	46.1	17.6	9.8
Santa Fe	298	2 831	164.1	74.0	170	854	54.5	15.8	894.3	221.5	52.8	11.1
Sierra	9	54	1.6	0.7	16	62	2.3	0.7	97.6	45.7	14.3	3.6
Socorro	12	81	5.5	2.2	12	24	2.1	0.4	86.7	26.1	7.0	5.2
Taos	53	397	23.0	8.4	31	86	5.5	1.2	131.5	48.4	13.4	7.0
Torrance	7	29	1.7	0.8	10	21	1.1	0.2	62.5	24.5	5.2	3.5
Union	4	57	3.3	1.0	5	16	1.0	0.2	36.8	9.4	3.5	0.7
Valencia	52	628	28.4	12.4	40	151	9.3	3.1	230.4	121.7	35.4	10.0
NEW YORK	36 054	358 075	26 008.3	10 970.9	30 104	146 365	10 014.6	2 858.7	101 808.6	31 322.5	16 712.2	4 168.5
Albany	601	7 195	516.5	239.9	513	3 599	270.1	79.1	4 981.3	813.3	204.5	40.8
Allegany	66	1 028	34.0	14.3	49	181	10.5	2.2	201.6	91.7	34.0	9.9
Bronx	1 050	15 530	1 014.2	448.1	1 254	4 612	319.1	93.3	(4)	(4)	(4)	(4)
Broome	343	3 912	286.7	131.3	296	1 407	93.2	24.7	953.6	438.3	161.7	33.9
Cattaraugus	112	1 266	87.1	25.9	94	400	27.0	6.1	394.4	166.8	60.4	14.7
Cayuga	136	969	60.5	25.6	85	411	31.5	7.1	317.9	147.7	58.0	11.2
Chautauqua	243	2 304	109.8	49.9	178	721	45.2	11.3	631.6	290.7	106.5	26.6
Chemung	162	1 675	123.1	60.7	108	553	36.1	9.8	424.8	197.8	69.3	17.2
Chenango	62	417	22.8	9.8	59	164	12.2	2.7	202.0	101.4	30.5	8.5
Clinton	146	1 302	79.3	33.9	115	466	29.7	8.3	321.5	142.5	46.5	14.7
Columbia	106	1 196	63.4	26.8	94	308	27.3	6.1	272.6	128.5	46.3	7.9
Cortland	82	967	44.5	20.5	71	484	45.9	15.9	172.7	80.9	27.8	7.7
Delaware	54	243	15.8	5.1	60	162	12.1	2.5	308.0	104.1	38.1	6.5
Dutchess	583	4 980	347.7	145.8	448	1 802	125.0	33.3	993.5	484.9	176.9	25.2
Erie	1 916	25 392	1 397.0	624.4	1 603	9 094	585.9	169.4	4 836.7	2 033.3	784.9	176.6
Essex	39	288	14.5	7.2	43	148	9.7	2.0	194.8	88.3	30.5	5.4
Franklin	71	354	30.1	11.0	49	129	7.0	1.6	216.5	86.9	31.8	8.9
Fulton	70	430	26.6	9.7	59	343	19.6	6.6	205.7	104.4	37.9	9.1

1. Firms subject to federal tax. 2. October 1, 1998 to September 30, 1999. 3. State totals may include programs not allocated by county. 4. Bronx, Kings, Queens, and Richmond Counties included with New York County.

Table B. States and Counties — **Federal Funds and Local Government Finances**

STATE County	Expenditures (mil dol) (cont'd)							Local government finances, 1997 — General revenue				
	Procurement contract awards			Grants[2]						Taxes		
	Salaries and wages	Defense	Other	Medicaid and other health- related	Nutrition and family welfare	Education	Other	Total (mil dol)	Intergovern- mental (mil dol)	Total (mil dol)	Per capita[3] (dollars)	
											Total	Property
	171	172	173	174	175	176	177	178	179	180	181	182
NEW JERSEY—Cont'd												
Mercer	152.6	104.1	164.7	340.6	361.0	199.2	489.5	1 212.4	434.8	560.9	1 701	1 678
Middlesex	206.3	70.5	208.7	223.6	37.4	17.5	153.5	1 989.8	532.9	1 136.3	1 605	1 576
Monmouth	508.8	546.1	42.1	189.5	34.2	17.8	20.5	1 901.5	504.4	1 053.5	1 767	1 727
Morris	230.5	172.1	22.9	63.6	8.1	5.5	30.5	1 449.5	291.0	922.2	2 030	2 012
Ocean	194.0	106.3	18.0	93.2	29.1	11.0	19.6	1 213.5	365.3	699.3	1 455	1 438
Passaic	97.6	169.4	38.6	263.1	69.6	19.0	46.3	1 224.9	436.1	624.7	1 291	1 275
Salem	12.2	3.3	3.0	27.7	6.7	2.5	4.0	239.0	105.9	83.4	1 263	1 234
Somerset	98.7	10.4	41.7	39.1	8.5	2.3	34.7	779.7	132.4	527.7	1 906	1 882
Sussex	19.7	12.3	13.6	23.9	3.5	3.0	7.2	411.4	137.9	229.5	1 615	1 602
Union	146.6	25.3	45.5	199.1	44.7	15.1	52.6	1 626.8	571.6	831.7	1 670	1 647
Warren	15.4	15.2	5.0	23.7	7.5	1.9	6.4	313.5	99.9	162.5	1 653	1 638
NEW MEXICO	1 646.4	615.0	3 316.0	991.5	450.6	344.3	963.6	X	X	X	X	X
Bernalillo	768.2	357.6	1 645.3	258.2	77.1	32.6	207.3	1 290.2	662.0	345.2	656	395
Catron	3.4	0.0	2.1	1.5	0.3	0.1	0.0	7.1	5.6	1.0	368	348
Chaves	18.3	0.2	8.1	36.4	9.9	4.6	1.9	167.8	72.4	25.7	409	160
Cibola	14.4	-0.6	3.6	2.0	9.4	4.5	18.8	43.5	32.6	6.7	259	111
Colfax	2.9	1.6	0.5	7.2	2.4	0.7	14.4	39.7	24.6	9.1	667	349
Curry	125.8	14.4	1.5	23.5	9.9	3.1	1.9	87.7	59.6	16.7	358	152
De Baca	0.6	0.0	0.1	1.5	0.5	0.1	0.0	6.1	4.6	0.8	325	220
Dona Ana	154.2	136.7	34.4	68.5	27.1	16.8	64.9	371.2	203.5	61.6	365	198
Eddy	25.1	6.5	104.7	26.5	10.8	2.9	5.3	116.9	63.9	30.1	566	272
Grant	10.3	0.0	1.8	16.7	4.8	2.1	6.5	84.6	41.2	12.0	382	203
Guadalupe	1.2	0.1	0.2	9.4	1.1	0.4	1.8	13.3	10.3	2.2	532	312
Harding	0.5	0.0	0.1	0.4	0.1	0.1	0.0	4.2	3.3	0.5	555	377
Hidalgo	2.8	0.0	0.3	3.3	1.5	0.4	0.5	20.0	11.0	3.1	483	350
Lea	5.7	0.0	1.4	23.9	8.9	4.9	0.5	139.3	79.3	37.9	673	342
Lincoln	4.7	0.0	1.7	4.8	1.9	1.0	4.7	49.0	25.3	14.2	884	557
Los Alamos	10.7	3.4	1 409.1	10.2	0.2	0.5	9.3	62.1	41.4	11.6	635	259
Luna	9.1	0.4	1.1	11.4	4.1	1.9	4.7	43.7	30.1	7.1	296	160
McKinley	92.1	1.8	16.0	77.5	23.7	45.1	13.0	135.2	96.0	24.3	359	193
Mora	1.8	0.0	0.3	10.0	2.3	0.8	1.1	13.2	10.0	1.7	355	207
Otero	190.6	71.7	3.8	19.7	7.1	5.6	8.3	85.5	57.5	17.0	305	159
Quay	3.1	0.4	0.6	7.2	2.2	0.7	-0.5	23.5	16.3	4.9	482	217
Rio Arriba	13.4	3.5	5.9	54.0	11.4	7.3	11.6	72.6	52.0	13.6	360	191
Roosevelt	2.8	0.0	1.0	12.1	3.5	2.3	0.0	29.4	20.8	4.5	241	117
Sandoval	12.6	0.5	7.5	31.7	11.3	10.5	4.6	121.4	71.9	31.0	361	194
San Juan	72.5	0.0	11.2	50.5	15.4	29.5	8.7	281.4	146.4	67.4	651	394
San Miguel	7.3	0.1	1.2	48.1	10.9	5.5	19.8	70.7	47.2	13.4	465	298
Santa Fe	57.8	1.9	36.6	88.1	153.2	62.3	193.9	232.7	112.8	75.0	616	244
Sierra	4.8	0.4	2.7	8.3	1.4	0.4	14.3	19.7	13.4	3.5	314	231
Socorro	8.3	1.3	7.1	14.9	3.7	1.8	9.8	26.8	19.0	4.0	245	135
Taos	11.3	0.1	3.4	29.8	6.9	2.6	7.5	58.3	39.3	12.9	484	229
Torrance	2.4	12.9	0.7	7.7	2.2	0.6	1.3	40.1	30.7	6.8	465	365
Union	2.2	0.0	0.4	3.3	0.6	0.2	12.3	12.7	8.8	1.9	454	225
Valencia	5.8	0.0	1.3	23.1	11.6	3.3	16.2	80.8	60.4	13.8	219	143
NEW YORK	7 521.2	3 217.6	3 555.2	16 378.8	5 313.2	1 870.1	5 307.8	X	X	X	X	X
Albany	315.4	16.7	84.1	359.6	1 437.5	482.1	1 055.9	1 003.4	251.1	540.9	1 838	1 228
Allegany	7.1	4.8	2.0	26.1	10.9	2.8	7.4	162.2	87.4	57.5	1 113	873
Bronx	(4)	(4)	(4)	(4)	(4)	(4)	(4)	(4)	(4)	(4)	(4)	(4)
Broome	43.6	77.6	12.1	97.4	24.9	10.0	41.6	679.9	250.3	314.4	1 582	1 170
Cattaraugus	15.3	1.9	35.1	46.8	16.3	7.7	21.9	303.8	144.5	112.9	1 324	932
Cayuga	10.4	1.9	5.6	45.1	12.0	5.7	11.4	239.4	101.6	93.9	1 141	819
Chautauqua	23.1	18.9	12.3	79.3	27.8	10.0	28.3	483.0	200.9	189.6	1 354	1 078
Chemung	25.5	2.1	5.7	59.5	17.4	4.3	13.9	284.8	128.5	107.2	1 151	822
Chenango	6.5	1.9	2.1	29.1	7.4	3.0	8.4	176.0	79.5	74.1	1 416	1 234
Clinton	26.7	2.0	8.2	45.2	10.8	4.3	12.7	255.3	118.4	93.7	1 162	837
Columbia	9.7	1.8	7.3	48.2	7.0	2.4	6.7	202.3	67.1	102.9	1 606	1 259
Cortland	6.5	0.7	5.9	21.9	8.9	2.5	8.2	158.4	69.7	63.7	1 303	859
Delaware	9.9	9.8	5.8	30.4	6.8	58.8	17.7	197.1	76.0	76.5	1 644	1 475
Dutchess	62.4	4.7	15.1	152.0	20.7	9.0	21.2	866.8	254.0	462.0	1 745	1 391
Erie	436.6	146.9	97.7	632.9	196.8	58.9	170.2	3 231.0	1 155.0	1 413.2	1 496	1 047
Essex	21.8	2.5	3.2	27.7	6.2	1.3	6.4	144.6	41.3	75.0	1 955	1 617
Franklin	8.8	0.5	7.8	42.8	8.6	3.0	9.5	167.8	77.3	58.8	1 202	998
Fulton	5.6	1.7	1.4	31.1	6.8	3.0	2.3	201.8	87.2	71.3	1 339	1 096

1. October 1, 1998 to September 30, 1999.   2. State totals may include programs not allocated by county.   3. Based on the resident population estimated as of July 1 of the year shown.   4. Bronx, Kings, Queens, and Richmond Counties included with New York County.

STATE County	Local government finances, 1997 (cont'd)									Government employment, 1998			Presidential election, 2000		
	Direct general expenditure							Debt outstanding					Percent of vote cast —		
			Percent of total for —												
	Total (mil dol)	Per capita[1] (dollars)	Education	Health and hospitals	Police protection	Public welfare	Highways	Total (mil dol)	Per capita[1] (dollars)	Federal civilian	Federal military	State and local	Democratic	Republican	All other
	183	184	185	186	187	188	189	190	191	192	193	194	195	196	197
NEW JERSEY—Cont'd															
Mercer	1 200.7	3 641	49.0	2.4	5.9	5.8	3.0	1 028.7	3 119	3 140	842	48 380	NA	NA	NA
Middlesex	2 003.7	2 830	52.9	3.5	6.5	3.7	2.3	1 370.5	1 935	3 395	1 855	47 869	NA	NA	NA
Monmouth	1 898.0	3 183	52.8	1.8	6.0	4.0	2.8	1 326.5	2 225	8 967	4 410	29 477	NA	NA	NA
Morris	1 469.8	3 236	53.3	2.2	5.6	2.9	4.1	921.9	2 030	5 148	1 184	22 676	NA	NA	NA
Ocean	1 228.4	2 555	53.9	1.5	5.7	2.5	4.2	1 088.4	2 264	2 987	1 823	20 082	NA	NA	NA
Passaic	1 181.5	2 441	39.2	0.8	7.3	10.7	3.3	769.7	1 590	1 890	1 171	23 763	NA	NA	NA
Salem	239.5	3 627	49.7	2.1	3.8	6.8	3.9	338.5	5 126	185	156	3 936	NA	NA	NA
Somerset	778.0	2 811	56.2	3.5	4.5	2.0	4.5	507.6	1 834	2 598	682	12 406	NA	NA	NA
Sussex	398.8	2 807	64.0	2.8	4.6	2.7	4.2	239.2	1 684	370	345	6 553	NA	NA	NA
Union	1 640.0	3 292	47.5	3.3	6.5	3.8	4.2	813.2	1 632	1 958	1 209	25 312	NA	NA	NA
Warren	327.9	3 336	54.8	2.8	3.4	4.6	5.9	168.6	1 716	274	237	5 154	NA	NA	NA
NEW MEXICO	X	X	X	X	X	X	X	X	X	29 867	18 427	138 207	48.0	48.0	4.0
Bernalillo	1 330.4	2 529	41.1	2.5	7.4	0.4	5.4	1 311.5	2 493	13 476	6 330	43 440	NA	NA	NA
Catron	8.1	2 886	47.4	1.1	5.8	0.0	16.1	0.5	166	117	10	217	NA	NA	NA
Chaves	159.1	2 525	41.8	28.5	4.0	2.5	3.8	116.1	1 843	377	230	4 495	NA	NA	NA
Cibola	41.7	1 608	51.4	0.4	3.3	0.7	3.7	12.9	497	396	93	1 551	NA	NA	NA
Colfax	38.4	2 801	46.2	6.4	5.5	0.8	9.1	18.5	1 349	53	48	1 370	NA	NA	NA
Curry	91.6	1 959	66.2	1.4	5.9	0.8	5.3	29.4	629	995	3 549	2 341	NA	NA	NA
De Baca	6.2	2 675	50.9	1.6	6.8	0.9	9.6	3.5	1 506	15	0	231	NA	NA	NA
Dona Ana	387.8	2 302	48.7	22.3	3.4	1.1	3.6	251.1	1 490	3 608	670	14 177	NA	NA	NA
Eddy	118.9	2 233	50.9	7.6	6.8	1.4	5.6	35.5	666	479	189	2 869	NA	NA	NA
Grant	81.0	2 583	38.6	33.5	4.8	0.0	3.1	36.2	1 156	237	111	2 943	NA	NA	NA
Guadalupe	13.3	3 251	55.0	0.3	6.0	0.0	9.4	1.9	467	24	14	362	NA	NA	NA
Harding	4.1	4 551	51.2	0.1	2.7	0.0	17.4	1.1	1 177	16	0	87	NA	NA	NA
Hidalgo	20.1	3 161	50.1	1.3	3.9	1.6	5.6	56.1	8 835	57	22	465	NA	NA	NA
Lea	132.1	2 342	56.5	4.6	9.9	1.0	6.8	23.5	416	117	198	3 284	NA	NA	NA
Lincoln	46.7	2 920	45.2	0.6	7.2	0.0	6.6	32.6	2 037	123	58	1 025	NA	NA	NA
Los Alamos	61.0	3 337	42.1	1.0	6.5	0.9	8.3	109.9	6 014	209	70	9 635	NA	NA	NA
Luna	42.8	1 788	51.9	1.6	7.9	6.2	8.5	4.7	196	179	85	1 379	NA	NA	NA
McKinley	155.3	2 297	59.2	0.6	4.9	0.8	3.6	51.0	754	2 382	238	3 966	NA	NA	NA
Mora	13.0	2 715	56.0	0.1	2.5	0.0	16.6	1.7	365	37	17	291	NA	NA	NA
Otero	86.1	1 544	52.2	0.7	7.6	0.7	6.7	31.7	568	2 114	4 535	2 754	NA	NA	NA
Quay	24.2	2 398	54.7	1.7	7.8	0.6	6.0	6.0	597	75	35	987	NA	NA	NA
Rio Arriba	72.5	1 919	56.6	0.7	3.7	1.5	5.1	16.6	439	423	133	2 612	NA	NA	NA
Roosevelt	28.6	1 543	65.3	0.0	6.7	0.6	3.9	8.8	477	62	64	1 804	NA	NA	NA
Sandoval	132.0	1 538	55.0	0.6	9.5	2.0	7.6	152.1	1 772	370	310	3 113	NA	NA	NA
San Juan	308.1	2 976	56.5	0.3	3.9	0.9	4.0	1 075.2	10 387	1 644	376	5 799	NA	NA	NA
San Miguel	73.4	2 537	61.6	0.8	4.8	0.2	4.2	23.9	828	157	102	3 849	NA	NA	NA
Santa Fe	256.5	2 106	40.2	1.2	6.2	3.9	8.7	349.9	2 873	1 245	441	13 751	NA	NA	NA
Sierra	22.7	2 066	40.3	1.7	5.2	1.4	10.4	10.2	925	116	39	744	NA	NA	NA
Socorro	27.7	1 704	54.1	0.0	3.0	0.1	11.7	5.8	359	222	58	1 976	NA	NA	NA
Taos	63.0	2 374	60.8	0.6	3.6	0.9	7.7	37.4	1 409	270	95	1 584	NA	NA	NA
Torrance	41.5	2 824	77.1	1.2	3.3	1.6	4.1	14.9	1 016	82	54	966	NA	NA	NA
Union	12.1	2 932	54.0	1.0	5.5	2.0	11.7	0.6	147	55	14	336	NA	NA	NA
Valencia	89.6	1 424	73.4	0.1	4.4	1.2	2.9	44.7	711	135	228	3 804	NA	NA	NA
NEW YORK	X	X	X	X	X	X	X	X	X	138 893	57 885	1 242 103	60.2	35.2	4.6
Albany	1 001.7	3 404	39.5	2.8	4.7	15.2	3.9	1 036.5	3 522	6 479	991	62 955	60.3	33.5	6.1
Allegany	178.0	3 448	54.4	2.8	1.2	12.0	9.0	89.8	1 740	145	103	3 594	33.9	61.2	4.9
Bronx	(3)	(3)	(3)	(3)	(3)	(3)	(3)	(3)	(3)	8 456	2 491	15 809	86.3	11.8	1.9
Broome	677.0	3 406	46.0	2.3	2.9	14.0	4.7	285.2	1 435	843	414	17 000	52.1	42.4	5.4
Cattaraugus	311.5	3 654	50.0	3.6	2.0	12.8	8.8	123.2	1 445	232	180	7 185	40.6	54.5	4.9
Cayuga	257.6	3 130	48.1	3.2	2.3	10.7	7.2	156.8	1 905	186	166	5 397	50.1	44.1	5.8
Chautauqua	511.1	3 650	49.3	1.7	2.8	13.4	7.8	276.8	1 977	414	283	9 312	46.0	49.5	4.5
Chemung	297.6	3 197	43.8	2.8	2.8	17.0	5.2	123.1	1 322	444	198	6 922	46.2	49.8	4.0
Chenango	175.7	3 356	50.4	2.5	0.9	8.5	8.5	59.7	1 140	124	103	3 732	45.0	49.5	5.5
Clinton	255.6	3 169	51.5	3.8	1.6	11.6	6.7	101.4	1 257	524	163	7 389	50.9	43.4	5.7
Columbia	218.4	3 409	54.2	4.0	1.7	11.6	7.5	98.6	1 538	191	129	4 000	47.0	45.8	7.1
Cortland	157.4	3 223	45.1	3.9	2.5	11.0	7.8	72.5	1 485	99	98	3 404	46.8	47.6	5.7
Delaware	207.3	4 453	42.3	8.6	1.4	11.6	11.5	72.7	1 562	157	93	4 136	41.9	52.8	5.3
Dutchess	889.0	3 359	48.6	5.3	4.1	9.0	4.7	485.9	1 836	1 443	539	20 265	46.9	47.1	6.0
Erie	3 346.2	3 543	41.2	6.8	4.2	14.6	3.9	1 675.1	1 774	9 100	2 295	63 083	56.6	37.7	5.7
Essex	148.4	3 868	36.3	4.2	1.1	12.5	9.9	54.6	1 424	389	76	3 800	44.2	49.2	6.6
Franklin	175.6	3 588	50.8	3.0	1.5	11.6	5.4	82.9	1 694	151	98	6 011	50.8	43.8	5.4
Fulton	225.9	4 239	48.5	1.1	2.2	13.9	4.5	215.9	4 051	112	109	4 089	43.0	52.8	4.3

1. Based on the resident population estimated as of July 1 of the year shown.   3. Bronx, Kings, Queens, and Richmond Counties included with New York County.

STATE/ County code	MSA/ PMSA/ NECMA code[1]	County Type[2]	STATE County	Land area,[3] (sq km) 1990	Population and population characteristics, 1999												
								Race (percent)					Age (percent)				
					Total persons	Rank	Per square kilometer	White	Black	Am. Indian, Eskimo, Aleut	Asian and Pacific Islander	Percent Hispanic[4]	Under 5 years	5 to 17 years	18 to 24 years	25 to 34 years	35 to 44 years	45 to 54 years
				1	2	3	4	5	6	7	8	9	10	11	12	13	14	15
			NEW YORK—Cont'd															
36 037	6840	1	Genesee	1 280	60 469	790	47.2	95.9	2.1	1.3	0.6	1.0	6.8	20.1	7.8	13.4	15.9	13.5
36 039	...	6	Greene	1 678	48 348	932	28.8	92.3	6.6	0.4	0.7	4.8	6.0	17.5	8.5	13.8	16.5	13.6
36 041	...	8	Hamilton	4 457	5 190	2 824	1.2	99.2	0.3	0.3	0.2	0.6	4.1	16.5	5.7	10.2	14.7	16.1
36 043	8680	2	Herkimer	3 657	63 354	757	17.3	99.0	0.4	0.2	0.4	0.8	6.3	19.9	7.5	11.7	15.7	13.6
36 045	...	5	Jefferson	3 295	109 920	481	33.4	90.8	7.3	0.5	1.4	4.2	7.8	20.0	12.6	16.1	15.2	10.7
36 047	5600	0	Kings	183	2 268 297	7	12 395.1	51.6	41.1	0.4	6.9	23.8	7.6	19.6	8.9	14.9	16.1	11.9
36 049	...	6	Lewis	3 304	27 289	1 453	8.3	98.6	0.6	0.3	0.6	0.6	7.5	23.2	6.8	13.2	15.0	12.4
36 051	6840	1	Livingston	1 637	65 851	728	40.2	95.3	3.5	0.4	0.8	2.4	6.1	18.5	12.8	14.0	16.3	12.7
36 053	8160	2	Madison	1 699	71 127	694	41.9	97.5	1.2	0.5	0.8	1.1	6.4	19.3	13.1	12.4	15.6	13.4
36 055	6840	0	Monroe	1 708	712 419	68	417.1	83.5	13.4	0.3	2.7	4.8	7.1	18.1	9.3	14.4	16.9	13.2
36 057	0160	2	Montgomery	1 048	50 369	899	48.1	97.9	1.2	0.2	0.7	7.0	6.6	19.1	6.7	11.8	15.4	12.1
36 059	5380	0	Nassau	743	1 305 057	25	1 756.5	85.2	9.8	0.2	4.8	7.7	5.7	16.5	7.9	12.7	16.7	14.6
36 061	5600	0	New York	73	1 551 844	15	21 258.1	62.2	26.8	0.5	10.5	30.7	5.5	12.7	8.6	17.7	18.9	14.3
36 063	1280	0	Niagara	1 354	216 164	252	159.6	92.1	6.3	1.0	0.6	1.3	6.4	18.7	7.7	13.1	15.7	13.0
36 065	8680	2	Oneida	3 141	229 714	241	73.1	91.8	6.6	0.8	1.4	3.3	6.3	18.1	9.3	13.5	15.3	12.6
36 067	8160	2	Onondaga	2 021	456 215	124	225.7	87.9	9.1	0.8	2.2	2.0	6.8	18.1	9.9	14.1	16.1	12.5
36 069	6840	1	Ontario	1 669	99 791	518	59.8	96.7	2.2	0.3	0.8	1.8	6.6	19.0	8.4	13.0	17.7	13.7
36 071	5660	2	Orange	2 114	334 199	168	158.1	89.7	8.2	0.3	1.8	9.1	7.9	20.7	8.6	14.3	17.8	13.2
36 073	6840	1	Orleans	1 014	45 022	984	44.4	89.8	9.1	0.5	0.6	4.0	6.6	20.2	8.6	15.1	16.7	12.9
36 075	8160	2	Oswego	2 469	123 875	422	50.2	98.4	0.6	0.4	0.6	1.3	7.2	21.4	10.4	13.6	16.0	12.8
36 077	...	6	Otsego	2 598	60 619	786	23.3	97.5	1.5	0.2	0.8	1.6	5.8	18.0	13.4	10.8	15.2	13.1
36 079	5600	1	Putnam	600	94 844	533	158.1	97.2	1.2	0.2	1.4	3.5	7.0	18.7	7.2	13.9	19.7	16.2
36 081	5600	0	Queens	283	2 000 642	11	7 069.4	59.5	23.0	0.4	17.0	22.6	6.4	15.8	8.4	15.7	16.4	13.3
36 083	0160	2	Rensselaer	1 694	151 445	341	89.4	93.9	3.8	0.2	2.0	1.6	6.5	17.9	10.7	13.8	16.4	12.6
36 085	5600	0	Richmond	152	413 280	139	2 718.9	83.8	9.0	0.2	7.0	10.2	7.1	18.4	8.4	14.3	17.5	14.3
36 087	5600	0	Rockland	451	284 022	192	629.8	82.3	11.1	0.3	6.3	8.4	6.6	19.4	7.8	12.1	16.7	16.0
36 089	...	5	St. Lawrence	6 956	112 853	466	16.2	95.0	3.0	0.9	1.1	2.3	6.0	19.3	13.8	12.8	15.1	12.3
36 091	0160	2	Saratoga	2 103	199 733	271	95.0	97.1	1.5	0.2	1.3	1.4	6.7	19.1	8.3	14.3	18.2	14.3
36 093	0160	2	Schenectady	534	143 871	367	269.4	92.9	4.9	0.2	2.0	2.2	6.4	16.9	8.0	13.2	16.4	12.9
36 095	0160	2	Schoharie	1 611	32 050	1 312	19.9	97.7	1.5	0.3	0.5	2.2	5.8	19.2	10.8	11.5	16.1	13.4
36 097	...	8	Schuyler	851	19 229	1 807	22.6	98.1	1.2	0.3	0.4	1.2	6.3	20.6	6.9	11.9	16.5	14.1
36 099	...	6	Seneca	842	31 925	1 319	37.9	97.2	1.6	0.3	1.0	1.3	6.8	19.7	6.6	12.7	16.6	13.4
36 101	...	4	Steuben	3 607	97 699	528	27.1	97.5	1.3	0.3	0.9	0.7	6.7	20.8	6.7	12.0	15.9	13.7
36 103	5380	0	Suffolk	2 360	1 383 847	21	586.4	89.9	7.2	0.3	2.7	8.6	6.5	18.5	8.5	13.8	17.0	15.0
36 105	...	6	Sullivan	2 512	69 331	706	27.6	89.1	9.4	0.2	1.3	8.9	6.8	18.8	7.5	13.6	17.0	13.5
36 107	0960	2	Tioga	1 343	52 216	874	38.9	98.0	0.9	0.2	0.9	1.0	7.0	21.1	6.4	13.5	16.2	14.5
36 109	...	5	Tompkins	1 233	97 656	529	79.2	88.2	3.8	0.4	7.6	2.9	5.3	14.8	24.3	14.1	15.4	10.5
36 111	...	4	Ulster	2 918	167 293	315	57.3	92.0	5.8	0.3	1.8	5.6	6.4	17.1	8.4	14.3	17.7	13.7
36 113	2975	3	Warren	2 253	61 441	779	27.3	98.4	0.6	0.2	0.8	1.1	6.3	19.0	8.1	12.8	16.9	13.5
36 115	2975	3	Washington	2 164	60 141	792	27.8	96.1	3.3	0.2	0.3	2.6	6.6	19.6	8.0	14.0	16.2	13.4
36 117	6840	1	Wayne	1 565	95 521	531	61.0	95.2	3.8	0.3	0.7	2.4	7.3	21.0	7.1	13.8	17.0	13.9
36 119	5600	0	Westchester	1 121	905 572	40	807.8	78.9	15.2	0.2	5.6	12.2	6.3	16.1	7.8	13.8	17.0	14.7
36 121	...	6	Wyoming	1 536	44 189	997	28.8	93.1	6.2	0.3	0.5	3.3	6.3	16.1	7.9	15.7	17.3	13.1
36 123	...	6	Yates	876	24 556	1 548	28.0	98.3	0.9	0.2	0.5	1.4	6.8	20.2	7.5	11.8	16.1	13.3
37 000	...	X	NORTH CAROLINA	126 180	7 650 789	X	60.6	75.3	22.0	1.3	1.4	2.3	7.0	18.4	9.3	14.5	16.2	13.2
37 001	3120	3	Alamance	1 115	121 100	436	108.6	79.2	19.7	0.3	0.8	1.5	6.4	16.5	9.1	13.1	15.7	13.9
37 003	3290	2	Alexander	674	31 984	1 315	47.5	93.1	6.3	0.2	0.3	1.5	6.4	19.3	7.8	13.8	16.3	14.9
37 005	...	9	Alleghany	608	9 850	2 440	16.2	97.7	2.1	0.1	0.1	1.5	5.0	16.7	5.8	11.3	14.2	14.3
37 007	...	6	Anson	1 377	24 238	1 567	17.6	50.4	49.1	0.4	0.2	0.5	6.1	20.3	8.2	13.4	16.4	12.1
37 009	...	9	Ashe	1 104	24 284	1 564	22.0	98.9	0.7	0.1	0.3	0.7	5.0	17.3	6.5	11.7	15.4	15.1
37 011	...	9	Avery	640	15 844	2 012	24.8	98.6	1.0	0.2	0.3	1.3	5.9	17.8	8.7	11.8	15.6	13.8
37 013	...	6	Beaufort	2 144	45 150	982	21.1	68.1	31.6	0.1	0.2	0.9	6.3	20.2	6.6	11.7	15.7	13.5
37 015	...	9	Bertie	1 811	20 392	1 744	11.3	38.3	61.2	0.3	0.1	0.3	6.6	22.4	6.8	12.5	13.8	12.2
37 017	...	6	Bladen	2 266	30 919	1 349	13.6	58.2	39.8	1.8	0.2	1.0	6.1	20.9	7.2	11.8	15.9	13.9
37 019	9200	3	Brunswick	2 214	71 214	691	32.2	80.8	18.4	0.6	0.3	1.6	6.3	17.5	6.3	11.8	14.5	14.0
37 021	0480	3	Buncombe	1 700	196 274	275	115.5	90.4	8.5	0.3	0.8	1.5	6.4	17.2	7.4	12.8	16.4	13.7
37 023	3290	2	Burke	1 312	83 101	611	63.3	90.4	7.5	0.2	1.8	1.0	6.5	18.4	8.3	12.9	15.7	14.7
37 025	1520	0	Cabarrus	944	124 844	418	132.3	85.7	13.3	0.4	0.7	1.1	7.1	18.7	7.8	13.8	16.6	14.3
37 027	3290	2	Caldwell	1 222	76 429	650	62.5	93.8	5.7	0.2	0.3	1.0	6.6	17.9	7.9	13.4	16.0	14.9
37 029	...	8	Camden	623	6 866	2 691	11.0	73.9	25.4	0.4	0.3	0.8	6.3	18.4	6.7	13.2	15.6	15.1
37 031	...	6	Carteret	1 376	60 031	793	43.6	89.9	8.6	0.6	1.0	1.8	6.3	16.8	7.0	13.7	15.5	13.4
37 033	...	8	Caswell	1 103	22 436	1 641	20.3	57.1	42.6	0.1	0.2	1.3	5.6	17.7	8.4	13.4	16.7	14.9
37 035	3290	2	Catawba	1 036	134 307	390	129.6	89.3	9.2	0.2	1.2	1.7	6.7	18.4	8.0	13.9	16.6	14.2
37 037	6640	2	Chatham	1 769	46 503	957	26.3	75.9	23.4	0.4	0.4	3.0	6.8	16.4	6.7	13.8	17.8	13.2
37 039	...	7	Cherokee	1 179	23 173	1 607	19.7	95.3	2.1	2.2	0.4	1.5	5.5	18.4	6.4	10.7	14.6	13.9

1. MSA = Metropolitan Statistical Area. PMSA = Primary MSA. NECMA = New England County Metropolitan Area. See Appendix A for explanation of these concepts. See Appendix B for list of metropolitan areas identified by type, with component counties. 2. County typology code from the Economic Research Service of USDA. See Appendix A for definition. 3. Dry land or land partially or temporarily covered by water. 4. Hispanic persons may be of any race.

Table B. States and Counties — Population and Households

STATE County	55 to 64 years	65 to 74 years	75 years and over	Percent female	1990	1980	1980–1990	1990–1999	Births	Deaths	Net migration	Number	Percent change, 1980–1990	Persons per house-hold	Female family house-holder[1]	One person
	16	17	18	19	20	21	22	23	24	25	26	27	28	29	30	31
NEW YORK—Cont'd																
Genesee	8.6	7.1	6.9	50.9	60 060	59 400	1.1	0.7	7 627	5 194	-1 874	21 614	7.5	2.72	9.5	21.6
Greene	9.3	7.3	7.6	47.9	44 739	40 861	9.5	8.1	5 037	4 436	3 149	16 596	11.2	2.54	9.7	25.6
Hamilton	11.9	11.9	8.8	49.8	5 279	5 034	4.9	-1.7	432	557	52	2 153	12.0	2.41	7.9	25.5
Herkimer	8.8	8.6	7.9	51.2	65 809	66 714	-1.4	-3.7	7 219	6 396	-3 058	24 936	5.3	2.59	9.5	25.0
Jefferson	6.8	5.4	5.4	47.4	110 943	88 151	25.9	-0.9	17 714	8 237	-12 948	37 851	22.9	2.74	9.7	21.1
Kings	8.5	6.6	5.8	53.3	2 300 664	2 231 028	3.1	-1.4	393 246	195 092	-226 335	828 199	0.0	2.74	21.5	28.6
Lewis	8.5	6.7	6.6	49.8	26 796	25 035	7.0	1.8	3 523	2 085	-915	9 253	14.9	2.86	8.0	20.4
Livingston	7.9	5.9	5.7	51.1	62 372	57 006	9.4	5.6	6 849	4 552	1 407	21 197	16.1	2.68	8.9	21.9
Madison	7.7	6.3	5.7	50.4	69 166	65 150	6.2	2.8	8 372	5 053	-1 174	23 567	13.3	2.72	9.2	21.4
Monroe	8.0	6.7	6.4	51.7	713 968	702 238	1.7	-0.2	97 981	56 079	-41 922	271 944	7.8	2.54	12.5	26.2
Montgomery	9.2	9.5	9.6	51.9	51 981	53 439	-2.7	-3.1	5 930	5 925	-1 457	20 185	1.7	2.52	10.9	26.9
Nassau	10.8	8.7	6.3	51.5	1 287 873	1 321 582	-2.6	1.3	165 360	103 986	-37 837	431 515	1.9	2.94	10.2	17.1
New York	9.6	6.4	6.2	52.8	1 487 536	1 428 285	4.1	4.3	191 915	127 903	5 466	716 422	1.7	1.99	12.8	48.6
Niagara	9.4	8.6	7.3	51.6	220 756	227 354	-2.9	-2.1	26 764	20 791	-9 857	84 809	5.7	2.56	11.6	26.1
Oneida	8.5	8.5	7.9	49.9	250 836	253 466	-1.0	-8.4	28 848	23 451	-27 212	92 562	5.2	2.55	11.2	27.0
Onondaga	8.5	7.3	6.6	51.9	468 973	463 920	1.1	-2.7	61 966	37 667	-36 093	177 898	7.4	2.55	11.9	26.4
Ontario	8.3	6.8	6.4	50.7	95 101	88 909	7.0	4.9	11 888	8 225	1 344	34 929	15.3	2.64	9.2	22.1
Orange	7.3	5.3	4.9	49.6	307 571	259 603	18.5	8.7	47 174	22 417	1 125	101 506	20.5	2.89	10.2	19.7
Orleans	7.8	6.3	5.8	49.0	41 846	38 496	8.7	7.6	5 376	3 640	1 580	14 428	11.2	2.74	10.3	21.6
Oswego	7.6	5.8	5.1	50.4	121 785	113 901	6.9	1.7	15 722	9 166	-4 177	42 434	14.0	2.76	10.0	21.6
Otsego	8.5	7.4	7.8	51.7	60 390	59 075	2.4	0.4	5 978	5 455	-112	21 725	7.4	2.56	8.3	24.9
Putnam	7.5	4.9	4.9	49.8	83 941	77 193	8.7	13.0	11 893	4 976	4 224	28 094	15.3	2.95	7.2	15.7
Queens	9.7	7.6	6.8	52.4	1 951 598	1 891 325	3.2	2.5	297 481	164 567	-77 429	720 149	1.2	2.67	14.3	27.2
Rensselaer	8.4	7.0	6.7	50.6	154 429	151 966	1.6	-1.9	18 759	13 297	-8 090	57 612	9.2	2.58	11.2	25.5
Richmond	8.3	6.4	5.4	51.2	378 977	352 029	7.7	9.1	56 324	31 587	10 563	130 519	13.9	2.85	12.4	20.9
Rockland	9.5	6.2	5.7	51.6	265 475	259 530	2.3	7.0	39 264	18 529	-1 484	84 874	8.9	3.03	9.8	17.8
St. Lawrence	8.2	6.5	6.0	48.4	111 974	114 347	-2.1	0.8	12 369	9 433	-1 819	37 964	6.0	2.67	9.6	23.5
Saratoga	7.7	6.3	5.2	50.3	181 276	153 759	17.9	10.2	24 052	12 131	6 676	66 425	27.9	2.67	8.4	21.4
Schenectady	9.2	8.5	8.5	51.9	149 285	149 946	-0.4	-3.6	18 351	14 553	-8 850	59 181	5.4	2.45	11.1	28.1
Schoharie	8.8	7.4	7.1	50.7	31 840	29 710	7.2	0.7	3 356	2 849	-217	11 257	16.3	2.64	9.0	22.4
Schuyler	8.5	7.7	7.4	49.8	18 662	17 686	5.5	3.0	2 157	1 639	106	6 818	12.9	2.67	9.1	21.6
Seneca	9.1	7.9	7.1	50.8	33 683	33 733	-0.1	-5.2	3 842	3 067	-2 591	12 285	7.7	2.64	9.4	22.0
Steuben	9.3	7.8	7.1	50.5	99 088	99 217	-0.1	-1.4	11 969	9 312	-3 707	37 299	6.1	2.60	9.7	24.6
Suffolk	8.8	6.3	5.5	51.0	1 321 339	1 284 231	2.9	4.7	188 557	99 516	-22 993	424 719	10.1	3.04	10.4	16.0
Sullivan	9.0	7.3	6.5	48.2	69 277	65 155	6.3	0.1	8 795	6 943	-1 489	24 576	6.8	2.60	9.5	25.3
Tioga	8.8	6.6	5.9	50.4	52 337	49 812	5.1	-0.2	6 152	3 771	-2 399	18 838	14.0	2.76	8.7	19.5
Tompkins	6.0	4.7	4.8	50.2	94 097	87 085	8.1	3.8	9 205	5 271	-135	33 338	12.8	2.46	8.0	27.2
Ulster	8.6	7.0	6.8	49.8	165 380	158 158	4.5	1.2	19 826	14 630	-2 806	60 807	8.9	2.58	10.2	24.3
Warren	8.8	7.3	7.3	51.4	59 209	54 854	7.9	3.8	7 037	5 414	788	22 559	16.2	2.58	10.0	24.3
Washington	8.6	7.2	6.6	48.5	59 330	54 795	8.3	1.4	6 803	5 230	-583	20 256	13.2	2.75	10.0	21.2
Wayne	8.1	6.1	5.8	50.1	89 123	84 581	5.4	7.2	12 300	6 810	1 205	31 977	12.4	2.75	9.5	20.1
Westchester	9.8	7.3	7.2	52.3	874 866	866 599	1.0	3.5	120 148	72 227	-16 606	320 030	4.1	2.64	11.6	24.8
Wyoming	7.4	6.2	6.0	45.7	42 507	39 895	6.5	4.0	4 665	3 323	459	13 897	8.8	2.79	8.5	20.5
Yates	9.2	7.3	7.8	51.1	22 810	21 459	6.3	7.7	3 057	2 269	1 035	8 419	9.2	2.63	8.3	22.7
NORTH CAROLINA	9.0	6.9	5.6	51.5	6 632 448	5 880 095	12.8	15.4	967 386	586 354	612 390	2 517 026	23.2	2.54	12.3	23.7
Alamance	10.3	8.3	6.8	52.5	108 213	99 319	9.0	7.1	14 417	10 746	9 529	42 652	18.6	2.47	12.0	24.5
Alexander	9.4	6.5	5.6	50.4	27 544	24 999	10.2	16.1	3 550	2 230	3 186	10 331	21.1	2.64	9.2	19.6
Alleghany	11.5	10.5	10.6	51.9	9 590	9 587	0.0	2.7	885	1 154	566	3 894	8.3	2.41	7.8	25.4
Anson	8.8	7.7	7.0	50.8	23 474	25 649	-8.5	3.3	3 230	2 643	263	8 531	1.7	2.71	17.3	23.9
Ashe	11.2	8.8	9.1	51.4	22 209	22 325	-0.5	9.3	2 252	2 481	2 399	8 848	10.2	2.48	9.2	21.9
Avery	9.9	8.7	7.3	51.4	14 867	14 409	3.2	6.6	1 739	1 567	874	5 520	14.4	2.52	8.7	22.3
Beaufort	10.3	8.3	7.4	52.7	42 283	40 355	4.8	6.8	5 339	4 876	2 522	16 157	13.4	2.58	13.5	24.2
Bertie	9.9	8.7	7.1	53.6	20 388	21 024	-3.0	0.0	2 661	2 333	-241	7 412	7.5	2.74	19.1	24.2
Bladen	9.6	8.1	6.6	52.8	28 663	30 491	-6.0	7.0	3 956	3 282	1 671	10 760	6.4	2.62	16.4	24.0
Brunswick	12.3	11.4	5.9	50.9	50 985	35 777	42.5	39.7	6 847	5 272	18 682	20 069	61.7	2.52	10.1	21.1
Buncombe	9.9	8.4	7.9	52.3	174 357	160 934	8.6	12.6	21 687	18 599	19 353	70 802	17.5	2.40	10.9	26.6
Burke	9.9	7.4	6.2	50.5	75 740	72 504	4.5	9.7	9 855	6 762	4 506	29 184	15.2	2.51	10.8	22.6
Cabarrus	9.7	6.5	5.6	51.4	98 935	85 895	15.2	26.2	14 273	8 802	20 443	37 515	22.6	2.59	10.6	21.4
Caldwell	9.9	7.3	6.0	51.0	70 709	67 746	4.4	8.1	9 105	6 111	2 959	27 172	16.5	2.57	10.8	20.8
Camden	11.0	7.9	5.8	49.9	5 904	5 829	1.3	16.3	535	548	983	2 180	12.9	2.69	10.3	20.0
Carteret	10.9	9.8	6.7	50.7	52 407	41 092	27.9	14.5	6 023	5 122	6 352	21 238	40.4	2.43	9.5	23.9
Caswell	9.1	7.7	6.4	49.3	20 662	20 705	0.0	8.6	2 340	2 026	1 525	7 468	14.6	2.69	13.7	21.3
Catawba	9.6	7.1	5.6	51.4	118 412	105 208	12.6	13.4	16 406	10 242	9 957	45 700	22.5	2.55	10.6	22.5
Chatham	9.7	8.7	7.1	51.3	38 979	33 415	16.0	19.3	5 288	3 684	5 991	15 293	26.8	2.51	10.5	22.5
Cherokee	11.1	10.5	8.9	51.6	20 170	18 933	6.5	14.9	2 298	2 300	3 047	7 966	16.3	2.50	9.6	22.1

1. No spouse present.

Table B. States and Counties — **Vital Statistics, Health Resources, and Crime**

STATE County	Births, average 1996–1998 Total	Rate[1]	Deaths, average 1996–1998 Number Total	Number Infant[2]	Rate Total[1]	Rate Infant[3]	Physicians,[4] 1998 Number	Rate[5]	Hospitals,[4] 1998 Number	Beds Number	Beds Rate[5]	Medicare enrollees 1999	Serious crimes known to police, 1998[6] Total Number	Rate[7]
	32	33	34	35	36	37	38	39	40	41	42	43	44	45
NEW YORK—Cont'd														
Genesee	734	12.1	576	8	9.5	11.3	77	127	2	166	274	9 791	1 419	2 291
Greene	499	10.5	506	1	10.7	2.7	32	67	1	195	408	8 567	1 128	2 352
Hamilton	42	8.1	61	0	11.6	0.0	4	77	0	0	0	1 248	101	1 933
Herkimer	688	10.6	709	4	10.9	6.3	68	106	2	320	500	11 886	1 411	2 143
Jefferson	1 749	15.6	914	10	8.1	5.5	195	176	3	391	352	15 149	2 327	2 053
Kings	40 217	17.7	19 509	331	8.6	8.2	4 547	200	19	9 324	411	291 465	NA	NA
Lewis	348	12.6	219	3	8.0	8.6	4	15	1	189	687	4 012	469	1 660
Livingston	693	10.5	510	5	7.8	7.2	56	85	1	72	109	8 725	1 801	2 703
Madison	845	11.9	547	4	7.7	5.1	98	138	2	334	470	10 055	1 265	1 762
Monroe	9 670	13.5	6 157	74	8.6	7.7	2 587	361	7	2 481	346	107 977	34 055	4 735
Montgomery	591	11.5	625	3	12.2	4.5	81	160	2	381	751	11 480	1 147	2 225
Nassau	17 361	13.3	11 096	92	8.5	5.3	6 767	520	15	5 925	455	219 926	21 912	1 677
New York	19 636	12.7	12 546	121	8.1	6.2	13 136	847	18	11 672	753	209 874	323 150	4 392
Niagara	2 673	12.2	2 299	20	10.5	7.6	283	130	5	974	447	39 463	4 982	2 466
Oneida	2 675	11.5	2 516	21	10.8	7.7	514	223	4	959	416	45 090	7 237	3 097
Onondaga	6 072	13.2	4 127	43	8.9	7.0	1 649	360	4	1 674	365	71 885	18 120	3 918
Ontario	1 165	11.7	911	8	9.2	6.9	222	223	3	667	669	14 939	2 396	2 392
Orange	4 895	15.0	2 466	31	7.6	6.4	579	176	6	1 054	320	41 060	8 101	2 545
Orleans	541	12.1	397	4	8.9	6.8	33	74	1	101	227	6 159	904	2 017
Oswego	1 476	11.9	999	10	8.0	6.8	98	79	2	271	219	17 331	2 874	2 289
Otsego	568	9.3	602	3	9.9	5.9	221	364	2	438	721	10 631	1 124	1 824
Putnam	1 237	13.4	570	6	6.2	5.1	147	157	1	188	201	10 200	1 285	1 388
Queens	32 070	16.1	16 890	200	8.5	6.2	4 733	237	13	4 681	234	282 485	NA	NA
Rensselaer	1 831	11.9	1 398	14	9.1	7.5	235	154	3	616	403	23 641	2 748	1 776
Richmond	5 789	14.4	3 472	31	8.6	5.4	1 304	320	5	1 387	341	57 651	NA	NA
Rockland	4 408	15.8	2 003	23	7.2	5.2	1 013	360	2	745	265	38 885	6 724	2 398
St. Lawrence	1 210	10.6	1 018	9	8.9	7.2	149	131	5	372	327	18 018	2 965	2 591
Saratoga	2 561	13.1	1 358	10	6.9	4.0	283	143	1	227	115	25 919	3 011	1 528
Schenectady	1 780	12.2	1 606	11	11.0	6.0	430	295	2	619	425	29 040	5 620	3 809
Schoharie	337	10.3	311	3	9.5	7.9	21	65	1	70	216	5 224	470	1 444
Schuyler	210	11.0	185	1	9.7	3.2	12	63	1	173	905	2 944	178	927
Seneca	374	11.6	311	2	9.7	4.5	27	85	0	0	0	5 468	792	2 456
Steuben	1 170	11.9	1 010	10	10.3	8.3	121	124	3	651	665	17 142	2 725	2 770
Suffolk	19 911	14.6	10 870	105	8.0	5.3	3 649	266	13	4 236	309	193 418	17 471	1 279
Sullivan	843	12.1	742	6	10.7	7.1	107	155	2	295	427	12 642	2 479	3 516
Tioga	624	11.9	430	2	8.2	3.7	38	72	0	0	0	7 337	751	1 415
Tompkins	847	8.8	583	4	6.1	4.7	203	211	1	204	212	10 344	2 823	2 962
Ulster	1 915	11.5	1 590	11	9.6	5.7	329	198	3	413	248	26 867	4 161	2 487
Warren	671	11.0	604	2	9.9	3.0	191	312	1	440	718	11 017	2 076	3 347
Washington	634	10.5	556	4	9.2	6.3	46	76	1	113	187	9 520	1 275	2 096
Wayne	1 254	13.3	764	10	8.1	7.7	80	84	2	336	354	14 801	2 191	2 336
Westchester	12 696	14.2	7 665	63	8.6	4.9	5 302	590	14	3 695	412	138 356	24 923	2 775
Wyoming	459	10.4	357	3	8.1	6.5	29	66	1	262	595	6 100	1 090	2 439
Yates	337	13.9	263	2	10.9	5.0	28	116	1	217	897	4 467	415	1 716
NORTH CAROLINA	107 724	14.5	66 769	993	9.0	9.2	15 823	210	121	21 735	288	1 111 273	401 615	5 322
Alamance	1 655	14.0	1 210	16	10.2	9.5	171	143	1	220	184	21 429	5 711	4 765
Alexander	416	13.5	259	3	8.4	8.0	13	42	1	44	141	4 391	697	2 237
Alleghany	101	10.3	126	1	12.9	6.6	19	193	1	46	467	2 426	104	1 049
Anson	338	13.9	277	5	11.4	14.8	11	45	1	125	513	4 250	993	4 321
Ashe	253	10.6	278	3	11.6	10.5	26	108	1	115	479	4 907	364	1 495
Avery	165	10.6	185	1	11.8	8.1	39	248	2	115	731	3 269	321	2 018
Beaufort	560	12.6	534	8	12.1	14.3	74	166	2	146	328	8 430	1 814	4 036
Bertie	267	13.0	270	3	13.2	10.0	11	54	1	16	78	4 213	580	2 792
Bladen	449	14.7	361	4	11.8	8.9	14	46	1	62	202	5 361	1 372	4 411
Brunswick	748	11.4	650	4	9.9	5.3	52	76	2	100	146	13 352	2 649	3 953
Buncombe	2 366	12.3	2 123	18	11.0	7.5	689	354	2	714	366	35 895	7 884	4 078
Burke	1 112	13.6	798	10	9.7	9.0	140	169	2	228	276	13 083	2 787	3 368
Cabarrus	1 688	14.5	1 035	7	8.9	4.3	209	174	1	331	276	19 243	4 227	3 586
Caldwell	1 001	13.3	687	9	9.1	8.7	74	97	1	81	106	11 563	2 487	3 250
Camden	41	6.2	66	2	9.9	40.3	6	87	0	0	0	1 031	96	1 414
Carteret	613	10.3	598	4	10.1	7.1	91	152	1	117	195	10 126	2 254	3 713
Caswell	244	11.1	236	4	10.7	17.8	4	18	0	0	0	3 214	495	2 246
Catawba	1 775	13.6	1 191	11	9.1	6.2	270	204	2	459	346	20 180	7 009	5 308
Chatham	615	13.8	436	8	9.8	13.0	48	106	2	50	110	6 612	1 531	3 358
Cherokee	260	11.7	280	3	12.6	11.5	39	171	2	222	975	5 479	451	1 992

1. Per 1,000 estimated resident population, average 1996–1998.   2. Deaths of infants under 1 year old.   3. Deaths of infants under 1 year old per 1,000 live births.   4. Data subject to copyright.   5. Per 100,000 resident population as of July 1 of the year shown.   6. Data for serious crimes have not been adjusted for underreporting; this may affect comparability between geographic areas and over time.   7. Per 100,000 population estimated by the FBI.

STATE County	Serious crimes known to police, 1998[1] (cont'd) Rate[2] Violent	Property	Education — School enrollment and attainment, 1990 Enrollment[3] Total	Percent private	Attainment[4] (percent) High school graduate or more	Bachelor's degree or more	Local government expenditures, fiscal 1997[5] Total current expenditures (mil dol)	Current expenditures per student (dollars)	Money income 1989 Per capita[6] (dollars)	Households Median Dollars	Percent change, 1979–1989 (constant 1989 dollars)	Percent with $100,000 or more	Income and poverty, 1997 Percent below poverty level Median household income	All persons	Persons under 18	Persons 5–17 in families
	46	47	48	49	50	51	52	53	54	55	56	57	58	59	60	61
NEW YORK—Cont'd																
Genesee	157	2 134	15 324	12.1	77.4	14.0	88.7	7 784	12 705	30 955	4.9	1.6	37 859	9.8	15.3	15.1
Greene	678	1 674	10 571	12.3	72.8	13.4	62.1	8 278	12 722	27 469	19.8	2.4	34 408	13.6	21.4	21.0
Hamilton	19	1 914	1 121	7.1	77.3	15.1	10.5	14 952	11 682	23 195	12.7	1.6	31 015	11.0	19.6	19.6
Herkimer	211	1 932	16 331	7.8	72.6	12.9	94.7	7 536	10 543	23 075	-1.9	1.0	30 321	13.9	21.6	21.5
Jefferson	153	1 900	25 873	10.3	76.4	13.6	148.1	7 504	11 160	25 929	14.2	1.7	31 515	15.9	23.2	23.0
Kings	NA	NA	643 175	25.4	63.7	16.6	(7)	(7)	12 388	25 684	28.6	3.7	26 108	26.5	39.7	37.9
Lewis	556	1 104	6 648	5.9	73.6	10.5	40.0	7 540	10 455	25 599	5.5	1.4	32 416	14.4	20.7	21.8
Livingston	233	2 470	18 902	11.2	77.5	18.1	83.0	7 817	12 585	30 981	8.8	2.4	39 354	11.1	16.1	15.3
Madison	75	1 687	20 667	21.9	79.2	18.2	97.7	7 515	12 334	29 547	9.6	2.5	38 293	11.2	16.3	16.1
Monroe	332	4 403	188 654	25.9	80.1	26.3	1 013.8	8 294	16 162	35 337	4.4	4.8	41 954	12.5	19.9	19.3
Montgomery	206	2 019	11 785	11.0	70.1	10.8	67.2	8 281	11 640	24 068	2.4	1.4	30 482	14.8	24.5	24.1
Nassau	150	1 527	317 875	28.8	84.2	30.0	2 174.0	11 402	23 352	54 283	24.1	17.0	61 026	5.8	9.6	8.6
New York	1 167	3 225	332 012	38.6	75.3	42.2	(7) 885.4	(7) 7 414	27 862	32 262	38.4	12.9	38 224	20.7	38.4	40.2
Niagara	174	2 292	54 566	15.4	75.8	13.6	302.9	8 193	12 710	28 408	-5.0	1.6	36 218	12.1	19.0	18.5
Oneida	270	2 827	63 045	15.4	75.1	16.7	310.9	8 000	12 227	26 710	4.4	2.1	34 668	15.1	23.4	22.4
Onondaga	403	3 515	128 198	26.6	80.7	24.4	627.4	7 899	14 703	31 783	7.9	3.6	38 447	12.7	19.4	18.6
Ontario	113	2 279	24 035	18.9	81.0	19.5	144.8	7 952	14 601	33 133	9.6	3.1	41 266	9.2	14.9	14.5
Orange	316	2 229	84 728	19.6	77.2	19.5	492.4	8 289	15 198	39 198	29.8	5.2	46 446	11.4	16.7	16.4
Orleans	259	1 758	10 575	7.7	71.5	10.7	61.2	7 053	11 776	28 359	-1.9	1.5	34 942	12.6	18.4	19.0
Oswego	94	2 195	34 681	6.9	74.7	12.9	205.9	7 888	11 792	29 083	7.4	1.7	35 809	14.1	21.1	20.8
Otsego	206	1 618	18 563	14.3	77.7	19.9	80.2	7 836	11 657	25 099	14.5	2.2	32 474	13.9	19.7	20.3
Putnam	76	1 312	20 679	22.3	86.5	27.8	152.9	10 573	20 536	53 634	32.8	12.6	62 646	4.4	5.9	6.3
Queens	NA	NA	468 837	27.7	71.1	20.6	(7)	(7)	15 348	34 186	19.8	4.9	35 820	17.0	29.3	26.2
Rensselaer	132	1 644	41 951	29.9	77.7	19.5	195.0	8 252	14 031	31 958	19.4	2.8	39 550	11.7	18.6	18.5
Richmond	NA	NA	99 464	31.6	78.6	20.7	(7)	(7)	17 507	43 861	23.4	8.3	51 141	9.7	15.5	15.2
Rockland	247	2 151	75 625	34.2	83.3	33.0	457.1	11 729	20 195	52 731	22.7	15.1	58 362	9.7	17.4	15.8
St. Lawrence	165	2 426	34 891	19.9	73.1	15.1	156.0	8 105	10 346	23 799	3.9	1.3	31 169	18.5	25.4	24.7
Saratoga	106	1 422	46 244	19.2	83.0	25.2	278.0	8 104	15 644	36 635	19.3	4.1	46 290	7.3	11.0	10.7
Schenectady	382	3 427	35 063	22.5	80.7	23.0	178.2	8 171	15 378	31 569	11.3	3.6	41 079	11.0	19.0	18.7
Schoharie	101	1 343	8 954	4.9	73.7	14.4	49.0	8 490	11 333	26 077	13.2	1.5	33 209	13.6	19.8	21.1
Schuyler	26	901	4 350	9.0	74.2	13.6	20.5	8 731	10 825	25 712	6.0	1.1	32 241	12.9	20.1	21.1
Seneca	205	2 251	7 738	15.4	76.2	14.2	41.5	7 524	12 408	28 604	4.1	1.4	35 650	11.9	19.1	19.7
Steuben	181	2 589	24 272	9.2	75.0	14.4	155.7	7 933	11 933	25 312	0.8	1.8	33 732	15.5	23.4	23.1
Suffolk	83	1 196	347 688	17.7	82.2	23.0	2 524.9	11 018	18 481	49 128	31.1	10.8	53 560	7.6	11.9	10.8
Sullivan	379	3 137	16 233	10.0	71.2	14.4	111.1	9 552	12 567	27 582	26.7	2.6	33 123	16.2	25.6	25.5
Tioga	62	1 353	13 564	9.9	80.6	18.0	71.2	7 178	13 064	31 497	8.5	2.4	38 503	11.1	17.3	17.4
Tompkins	106	2 856	40 342	51.6	87.2	41.7	115.3	8 492	13 171	27 742	14.9	4.6	38 162	13.7	16.8	18.0
Ulster	323	2 164	40 410	13.7	76.6	21.6	254.2	9 050	14 921	34 033	29.4	3.6	37 096	12.3	20.0	19.1
Warren	231	3 116	14 438	14.4	78.3	19.4	90.2	7 988	14 378	30 434	24.2	3.2	37 703	11.7	18.9	18.2
Washington	395	1 701	14 495	8.9	74.0	11.6	84.8	7 734	12 221	28 660	15.9	1.4	33 905	12.9	19.3	19.4
Wayne	139	2 197	21 576	10.2	74.3	14.0	148.9	7 789	13 313	32 469	9.3	2.2	40 181	10.6	15.7	15.1
Westchester	319	2 456	213 279	32.3	81.0	35.3	1 518.3	11 744	25 584	48 405	27.1	17.8	55 040	9.3	15.2	14.6
Wyoming	237	2 202	10 427	8.1	70.3	9.7	46.3	7 526	10 552	27 515	2.5	1.3	35 915	11.6	15.4	15.8
Yates	91	1 625	5 457	20.1	73.7	15.0	23.8	7 521	11 065	24 874	9.0	1.5	31 926	15.3	24.7	26.1
NORTH CAROLINA	579	4 743	1 624 913	11.1	70.0	17.4	5 965.0	4 929	12 885	26 647	9.8	2.6	35 320	12.6	18.6	17.0
Alamance	499	4 266	23 920	18.2	67.9	14.6	86.6	4 571	13 290	27 231	3.7	2.2	35 281	8.8	13.8	12.1
Alexander	132	2 105	6 005	4.9	59.0	7.9	23.0	4 510	11 624	26 539	5.5	1.3	35 302	10.1	15.6	14.1
Alleghany	131	918	1 881	1.6	52.6	9.0	9.3	6 331	10 237	18 476	3.0	2.5	27 730	14.2	20.2	20.3
Anson	509	3 812	5 574	5.3	60.8	7.3	22.7	5 012	9 402	21 836	6.0	0.8	26 968	15.5	22.5	20.5
Ashe	115	1 380	4 420	3.5	55.6	8.1	17.7	5 148	9 545	18 951	9.0	1.3	28 407	15.3	23.5	21.4
Avery	88	1 930	3 648	19.8	62.2	12.4	14.4	5 762	9 729	20 403	9.3	1.5	28 614	17.4	25.6	22.4
Beaufort	369	3 667	10 145	7.3	65.9	10.8	39.9	5 198	10 722	21 738	8.2	1.9	28 614	17.4	25.6	22.4
Bertie	544	2 248	4 839	5.8	54.9	8.0	21.0	5 370	8 392	17 795	8.1	0.9	22 816	22.9	31.5	29.1
Bladen	852	3 559	7 310	4.1	56.4	7.7	29.9	5 115	9 497	19 015	4.8	0.9	26 984	18.8	27.5	22.7
Brunswick	358	3 595	10 890	4.3	69.2	10.7	50.5	5 310	11 688	23 480	8.7	1.8	30 689	14.0	22.7	20.9
Buncombe	475	3 603	38 449	13.3	74.5	19.1	152.1	5 213	13 211	25 847	9.9	2.4	35 159	12.3	19.1	16.9
Burke	366	3 002	16 414	7.1	60.1	10.6	63.1	4 616	11 604	25 879	7.8	1.4	32 113	11.8	18.6	16.4
Cabarrus	271	3 315	21 672	9.7	67.4	12.3	93.8	4 568	13 552	30 133	13.2	2.6	41 781	8.0	12.7	10.9
Caldwell	299	2 951	14 987	6.0	56.8	8.9	58.2	4 838	11 522	25 691	5.3	1.5	32 838	11.2	17.3	16.0
Camden	133	1 281	1 396	9.0	66.2	10.1	7.0	5 879	10 465	26 699	6.2	0.4	35 423	12.2	18.8	16.6
Carteret	224	3 489	11 371	9.9	75.5	16.2	43.6	5 139	13 227	25 811	9.9	2.4	34 348	11.8	18.7	17.6
Caswell	277	1 969	4 613	6.0	55.0	6.6	17.9	4 976	9 817	22 736	7.0	1.1	31 152	14.3	20.3	18.0
Catawba	354	4 954	27 090	10.5	66.7	14.2	104.0	4 806	13 764	29 228	7.4	2.6	38 456	9.3	15.5	12.8
Chatham	331	3 027	8 101	6.5	70.0	19.5	34.4	5 114	13 321	28 539	10.7	2.2	41 632	13.1	13.1	11.6
Cherokee	128	1 864	4 239	4.4	59.9	8.0	18.2	5 062	9 258	19 625	20.5	0.7	25 489	17.0	24.6	23.1

1. Data for serious crimes have not been adjusted for underreporting; this may affect comparability between geographic areas and over time. 2. Per 100,000 population estimated by the FBI. 3. All persons 3 years old and over enrolled in nursery school through college. 4. Persons 25 years old and over. 5. Elementary and secondary education expenditures, local government fiscal years ending between July 1, 1996 and June 30, 1997. 6. Based on population enumerated as of April 1, 1990. 7. Bronx, Kings, Queens, and Richmond Counties included with New York County.

Table B. States and Counties — Personal Income

STATE County	Total (mil dol) [62]	Percent change, 1997–1998 [63]	Per capita[1] Dollars [64]	Per capita[1] Rank [65]	Wages and salaries[2] (mil dol) [66]	Proprietor's income (mil dol) [67]	Dividends, interest, and rent (mil dol) [68]	Transfer payments Total (mil dol) [69]	Gov. payments to individuals Total (mil dol) [70]	Social Security (mil dol) [71]	Medical payments (mil dol) [72]	Income maintenance (mil dol) [73]	Unemployment insurance (mil dol) [74]
NEW YORK—Cont'd													
Genesee	1 336	2.4	22 007	1 104	643	85	230	235	223	100	85	18	6
Greene	1 046	8.8	21 726	1 184	370	52	199	207	197	86	77	19	4
Hamilton	114	3.9	22 051	1 086	37	12	33	26	25	12	9	2	1
Herkimer	1 271	3.1	19 854	1 761	466	76	219	289	276	116	116	25	6
Jefferson	2 313	4.5	20 832	1 449	1 617	124	351	395	375	142	144	52	12
Kings	54 561	3.5	24 076	627	14 615	2 915	6 959	14 297	13 834	2 459	8 240	2 520	297
Lewis	464	5.5	16 922	2 626	186	47	81	101	96	40	38	10	4
Livingston	1 367	2.8	20 827	1 452	535	66	226	219	206	91	77	22	5
Madison	1 555	4.0	21 926	1 119	590	117	271	245	231	98	94	20	5
Monroe	21 404	3.9	29 938	166	15 659	1 290	4 191	3 273	3 127	1 152	1 343	450	45
Montgomery	1 118	4.5	22 013	1 102	498	63	209	272	262	110	115	22	5
Nassau	55 120	4.3	42 368	23	24 688	4 177	13 729	5 910	5 644	2 428	2 557	301	64
New York	111 648	7.5	72 194	1	161 616	28 312	20 145	10 296	9 980	1 964	5 650	1 497	188
Niagara	5 093	3.1	23 387	768	2 680	212	819	1 008	963	413	383	98	22
Oneida	5 302	4.8	22 981	857	3 252	295	1 031	1 142	1 095	422	476	123	15
Onondaga	12 055	4.7	26 325	362	8 930	783	2 176	2 002	1 909	742	809	225	25
Ontario	2 504	3.0	25 160	474	1 346	134	431	366	345	152	133	30	7
Orange	8 242	6.0	24 992	491	3 883	427	1 375	1 238	1 172	419	549	125	17
Orleans	822	1.5	18 314	2 259	335	45	133	157	148	66	54	17	4
Oswego	2 487	2.8	20 088	1 683	1 155	133	330	452	426	180	164	50	10
Otsego	1 258	4.5	20 762	1 467	642	107	257	246	233	98	95	20	4
Putnam	3 123	5.8	33 453	77	775	160	547	292	273	115	119	15	4
Queens	56 656	5.9	28 425	218	18 386	1 977	8 899	12 515	12 107	2 695	7 145	1 720	225
Rensselaer	3 754	4.8	24 662	533	1 610	154	666	653	622	237	276	60	10
Richmond	12 690	4.4	31 187	132	3 019	585	1 848	2 636	2 553	609	1 507	319	44
Rockland	10 299	7.5	36 654	51	4 180	917	1 915	1 155	1 098	411	528	88	16
St. Lawrence	2 053	6.4	18 141	2 308	1 186	148	325	479	456	170	192	59	12
Saratoga	5 217	6.2	26 424	351	1 980	296	890	623	583	265	223	42	11
Schenectady	4 197	5.0	28 922	197	2 464	222	935	696	666	274	295	58	9
Schoharie	639	7.7	19 922	1 737	249	40	103	123	117	49	48	11	2
Schuyler	340	4.4	17 715	2 436	116	24	56	79	75	32	30	7	2
Seneca	699	2.2	21 875	1 133	308	41	123	133	126	56	51	10	2
Steuben	2 220	5.4	22 657	937	1 448	137	363	430	410	166	153	49	9
Suffolk	44 745	5.2	32 648	97	22 145	2 243	8 486	5 526	5 246	2 085	2 372	420	79
Sullivan	1 660	4.4	23 925	658	667	185	339	375	361	128	180	35	6
Tioga	1 101	3.5	21 006	1 390	481	62	174	177	167	78	58	18	3
Tompkins	2 148	4.4	22 089	1 071	1 534	158	463	280	261	108	95	30	3
Ulster	3 973	6.3	23 817	678	1 719	235	812	728	694	281	306	68	9
Warren	1 559	4.1	25 445	444	994	154	356	254	241	110	91	21	6
Washington	1 126	5.0	18 712	2 154	501	85	196	237	225	94	91	24	4
Wayne	2 170	2.6	22 821	887	876	120	314	351	331	146	127	24	5
Westchester	42 581	5.1	47 267	8	18 921	3 283	9 452	4 321	4 138	1 504	1 963	399	48
Wyoming	802	5.9	18 157	2 306	386	66	129	147	138	61	52	12	5
Yates	461	3.8	19 004	2 057	152	39	94	97	92	43	34	9	2
NORTH CAROLINA	190 009	5.7	25 181	X	125 325	13 213	34 719	26 131	24 823	10 497	10 089	2 496	435
Alamance	2 972	5.0	24 836	508	1 785	155	590	445	424	209	164	27	9
Alexander	666	7.1	21 298	1 295	272	56	100	95	89	40	37	7	1
Alleghany	232	6.9	23 687	706	98	36	47	45	43	19	18	4	1
Anson	500	2.6	20 496	1 558	232	47	77	112	108	38	51	12	2
Ashe	485	4.6	20 161	1 665	189	75	92	106	102	40	43	12	2
Avery	351	5.0	22 328	1 011	153	63	67	71	69	26	33	6	1
Beaufort	905	2.1	20 340	1 618	505	52	189	193	185	75	75	23	5
Bertie	377	3.6	18 497	2 213	168	45	54	101	97	32	45	16	1
Bladen	614	-4.1	19 908	1 743	328	37	84	147	142	47	64	22	3
Brunswick	1 351	5.4	19 731	1 802	603	105	282	296	284	133	110	24	6
Buncombe	5 056	5.1	25 998	397	3 213	285	1 201	775	741	335	291	60	10
Burke	1 700	3.8	20 644	1 508	1 065	110	299	298	283	125	120	21	5
Cabarrus	3 186	7.5	26 480	341	1 640	196	539	405	384	175	166	24	5
Caldwell	1 675	6.6	22 060	1 084	898	118	236	264	250	113	104	24	5
Camden	134	4.3	19 679	1 828	35	4	30	24	23	9	9	2	0
Carteret	1 402	5.1	23 442	758	502	92	377	225	215	99	82	15	0
Caswell	411	3.7	18 463	2 222	101	16	60	81	77	30	33	10	1
Catawba	3 596	6.4	27 157	288	2 926	216	713	433	410	208	153	28	7
Chatham	1 253	4.5	27 489	265	437	91	360	158	150	74	60	9	2
Cherokee	397	7.0	17 469	2 492	215	29	76	116	112	47	45	11	4

1. Based on the resident population estimated as of July 1 of the year shown. 2. Includes other labor income.

Table B. States and Counties — Earnings, Social Security, and Housing

STATE County	Earnings, 1998									Social Security beneficiaries, December 1998		Housing units, 1990		
	Total (mil dol)	Percent by selected industries								Number	Rate[3]	Supplemental Security Income recipients, December 1998	Total	Percent change, 1980–1990
		Farm	Goods-related[1]		Service-related and other[2]									
			Total	Manufacturing	Total	Retail trade	Finance, insurance, and real estate	Services	Government					
	75	76	77	78	79	80	81	82	83	84	85	86	87	88
NEW YORK—Cont'd														
Genesee	728	4.0	27.3	21.6	44.0	9.4	2.5	20.3	24.6	11 308	186	1 093	22 596	6.3
Greene	422	0.3	D	10.0	D	10.6	3.9	21.1	35.4	9 995	209	1 125	25 000	17.1
Hamilton	49	0.0	18.4	5.8	42.6	13.9	3.2	21.0	39.0	1 411	272	128	8 234	16.6
Herkimer	542	1.7	D	26.4	D	11.3	3.1	18.9	25.1	13 999	219	1 772	30 799	8.0
Jefferson	1 741	0.9	D	9.6	D	8.9	2.9	16.9	49.1	17 464	157	2 837	50 519	20.2
Kings	17 530	0.0	D	7.7	D	7.7	14.5	38.8	10.4	295 992	131	140 810	873 671	-0.9
Lewis	233	4.0	D	27.6	D	8.5	1.8	11.4	29.6	4 984	181	659	13 182	13.6
Livingston	601	1.3	20.3	14.1	38.2	12.6	2.7	15.5	40.2	10 307	156	1 087	23 084	13.7
Madison	707	1.9	19.9	14.0	57.4	11.3	4.8	29.9	20.7	11 486	162	1 311	26 641	11.4
Monroe	16 948	0.1	D	34.4	D	7.5	5.4	27.8	10.8	124 296	174	17 279	285 524	8.0
Montgomery	562	1.3	D	25.7	D	9.8	4.1	27.7	16.7	13 170	259	1 546	21 851	3.1
Nassau	28 865	0.0	12.1	7.3	74.2	10.8	12.4	36.6	13.7	237 903	183	16 318	446 292	2.8
New York	189 929	0.0	8.0	6.7	80.6	3.4	36.7	31.2	11.4	208 460	134	77 162	785 127	4.0
Niagara	2 892	0.4	D	35.5	D	9.8	2.8	18.9	17.8	45 737	210	4 976	90 385	6.1
Oneida	3 547	0.5	19.6	15.5	55.3	9.8	8.1	28.4	24.6	50 853	220	7 543	101 251	5.7
Onondaga	9 713	0.1	25.4	20.3	59.8	8.3	8.6	26.7	14.6	82 002	179	10 765	190 878	7.8
Ontario	1 480	0.8	30.6	21.6	48.3	12.9	3.6	21.3	20.2	17 341	174	1 680	38 947	14.3
Orange	4 310	0.4	15.2	10.2	56.2	11.3	5.4	24.6	28.1	47 815	145	6 378	110 814	18.8
Orleans	380	4.1	20.7	14.9	34.5	8.4	2.4	16.6	40.7	7 621	171	930	16 345	8.7
Oswego	1 289	0.6	D	21.8	D	9.4	2.1	16.8	28.4	21 055	170	2 847	48 548	13.2
Otsego	749	0.9	D	10.8	D	11.4	6.9	35.6	19.7	11 911	196	1 509	26 385	10.5
Putnam	935	0.1	D	12.0	D	8.3	9.0	30.6	19.8	11 874	127	779	31 898	14.5
Queens	20 363	0.0	19.4	9.4	71.7	7.9	6.4	31.4	8.9	295 428	148	71 922	752 690	1.7
Rensselaer	1 764	0.2	19.8	11.4	58.4	9.5	5.5	33.7	21.6	26 842	176	3 119	62 591	9.1
Richmond	3 604	0.0	11.4	3.1	78.6	9.9	6.1	44.2	10.0	66 278	163	10 758	139 726	17.4
Rockland	5 096	0.0	D	13.3	D	8.5	6.4	30.3	16.7	42 617	151	4 951	88 264	10.1
St. Lawrence	1 334	1.3	27.2	21.0	41.2	9.9	2.4	21.0	30.3	20 896	184	3 915	47 521	8.8
Saratoga	2 276	0.2	D	16.0	D	12.0	7.8	26.0	21.2	29 774	151	2 592	75 105	24.4
Schenectady	2 686	0.0	29.2	23.3	56.8	9.0	4.3	35.3	14.0	30 564	210	3 682	62 769	5.4
Schoharie	288	1.2	D	9.6	D	14.7	5.7	15.7	35.9	5 976	184	757	14 431	14.1
Schuyler	140	0.3	25.4	19.4	48.0	12.3	2.1	25.0	26.2	3 890	203	501	8 472	12.1
Seneca	348	1.3	D	27.4	D	10.6	2.7	16.7	24.9	6 716	210	744	14 314	7.2
Steuben	1 584	0.8	D	43.5	D	7.5	4.7	17.3	17.8	19 729	201	2 926	43 019	6.2
Suffolk	24 388	0.2	20.0	13.6	60.2	8.9	7.8	29.5	19.7	222 507	162	21 863	481 317	11.5
Sullivan	852	0.2	7.7	2.7	66.0	8.8	8.0	30.5	26.0	15 190	220	2 738	41 814	-8.8
Tioga	543	1.0	D	51.7	D	7.2	2.0	11.9	16.0	9 206	175	1 003	20 254	12.6
Tompkins	1 692	0.5	14.5	11.4	72.0	7.4	3.6	53.7	12.9	11 895	124	1 570	35 338	14.0
Ulster	1 954	0.5	18.5	13.4	55.6	11.1	5.6	28.5	25.4	31 791	191	4 326	71 716	3.5
Warren	1 148	0.0	D	16.6	D	12.3	7.9	33.3	13.1	12 721	208	1 507	31 737	18.3
Washington	586	2.8	33.6	27.1	31.5	7.8	1.8	15.3	32.1	11 177	185	1 438	24 216	10.5
Wayne	996	2.1	39.1	33.5	35.5	9.0	2.1	16.2	23.3	17 241	182	2 153	35 188	9.6
Westchester	22 204	0.0	20.2	14.6	65.6	7.1	11.7	32.4	14.1	148 128	165	14 408	336 727	6.3
Wyoming	452	8.2	24.4	19.7	33.5	8.9	3.6	11.7	33.9	7 200	163	655	15 848	5.1
Yates	191	3.0	D	15.8	D	11.5	3.5	26.2	20.4	5 116	211	582	11 629	8.1
NORTH CAROLINA	138 538	1.6	29.3	22.5	51.4	9.2	7.0	22.6	17.7	1 299 374	172	194 304	2 818 193	23.9
Alamance	1 940	0.4	D	30.9	D	10.8	4.9	27.3	9.4	24 243	203	2 406	45 312	18.7
Alexander	328	5.4	56.0	50.5	27.1	7.5	1.7	12.7	11.5	5 149	165	527	11 197	19.3
Alleghany	135	17.4	D	28.1	D	7.2	3.3	15.9	11.8	2 625	267	403	5 344	14.4
Anson	278	10.2	37.6	31.8	29.1	6.6	1.5	10.7	23.1	5 074	208	1 030	9 255	2.0
Ashe	264	14.2	D	30.1	D	9.2	3.0	14.6	11.9	5 680	236	1 030	11 119	16.7
Avery	216	14.3	D	13.9	D	10.6	4.2	28.5	12.7	3 443	219	534	8 923	26.1
Beaufort	556	0.1	38.6	33.3	45.5	8.9	2.7	19.6	16.0	10 045	226	1 942	19 598	14.1
Bertie	213	18.2	37.5	35.2	27.5	4.6	1.8	11.7	16.8	4 922	241	1 590	8 331	5.4
Bladen	365	6.1	46.7	43.6	27.9	6.6	1.4	11.1	19.3	6 683	218	1 914	12 685	11.0
Brunswick	708	0.3	D	17.5	D	10.5	8.5	17.1	17.2	16 114	236	1 924	37 114	72.2
Buncombe	3 498	0.7	25.3	18.5	58.0	11.3	4.8	30.5	15.9	40 719	209	4 528	77 951	17.9
Burke	1 175	2.2	D	42.8	D	7.6	1.8	16.8	21.1	15 377	186	1 817	31 575	14.7
Cabarrus	1 836	0.4	38.4	29.1	44.9	10.5	5.2	19.5	16.3	20 264	169	1 961	39 713	22.3
Caldwell	1 016	3.1	51.6	46.1	34.2	8.2	1.9	15.2	11.0	13 905	183	1 441	29 454	15.2
Camden	39	-0.6	20.9	3.6	D	11.7	D	26.4	25.0	1 267	184	141	2 466	14.8
Carteret	594	0.3	D	7.6	D	17.8	6.7	21.4	23.5	12 409	207	1 170	34 576	45.6
Caswell	117	4.8	D	21.8	D	5.6	1.8	15.5	40.1	4 184	188	843	8 254	7.8
Catawba	3 142	0.4	D	43.1	D	10.1	2.8	16.2	8.9	24 193	183	1 919	49 192	20.8
Chatham	528	5.9	48.3	38.4	D	7.7	2.4	16.7	11.6	8 701	192	748	16 642	29.0
Cherokee	244	1.8	D	27.8	D	12.5	3.5	23.4	17.0	6 286	276	1 020	10 319	20.9

1. Covers mining, construction, and manufacturing. 2. Covers private sector earnings in agricultural services, forestry, and fisheries; transportation and public utilities; wholesale trade; retail trade; finance, insurance, and real estate; and services. 3. Per 1,000 resident population estimated as of July 1 of the year shown.

Table B. States and Counties — Housing, Labor Force, and Employment

STATE County	Housing units, 1990 (cont'd) Occupied units Owner-occupied Total	Percent	Median value[1]	Owner cost as a percent of income With a mortgage	Without a mortgage	Renter-occupied Median rent[2]	Rent as percent of income	Sub-standard units[3] (percent)	Civilian labor force, 1999 Total	Percent change, 1998–1999	Unemployment Total	Rate[4]	Civilian employment, 1990[5] Total	Percent Professional, managerial, and technical	Precision production, craft, and repair
	89	90	91	92	93	94	95	96	97	98	99	100	101	102	103
NEW YORK—Cont'd															
Genesee	21 614	72.8	65 800	20.5	13.6	402	24.5	1.8	31 898	-2.0	1 681	5.3	28 880	24.6	13.4
Greene	16 596	72.9	91 700	22.2	14.5	421	27.1	2.0	21 800	-0.4	1 185	5.4	18 756	25.3	13.7
Hamilton	2 153	77.5	71 800	20.1	13.2	351	23.5	3.4	2 573	0.4	273	10.6	2 230	26.5	17.4
Herkimer	24 936	71.4	54 400	17.2	14.4	316	26.7	2.1	31 248	-0.6	1 653	5.3	27 558	23.3	13.3
Jefferson	37 851	59.3	59 400	20.0	14.1	400	26.3	2.6	44 020	0.8	4 077	9.3	40 821	26.3	12.5
Kings	828 199	25.9	196 100	21.8	14.4	477	26.8	14.0	965 131	-0.2	75 706	7.8	929 335	28.8	8.3
Lewis	9 253	76.3	49 800	17.3	13.2	358	28.4	3.2	12 016	-0.7	1 098	9.1	11 035	21.1	12.6
Livingston	21 197	73.3	72 800	20.7	14.0	412	25.7	1.6	34 566	-0.9	1 740	5.0	29 942	27.2	13.4
Madison	23 567	74.3	69 300	20.5	14.5	398	26.9	2.2	35 453	0.0	1 681	4.7	32 626	27.6	13.2
Monroe	271 944	65.1	90 700	21.1	13.7	478	28.4	1.6	382 767	0.1	15 052	3.9	353 883	36.0	10.3
Montgomery	20 185	66.3	61 600	19.6	14.4	341	24.7	2.4	23 566	-0.4	1 513	6.4	22 264	22.8	12.2
Nassau	431 515	80.4	209 500	23.1	16.0	749	27.7	2.8	692 015	0.4	20 824	3.0	661 486	37.6	8.7
New York	716 422	17.9	487 300	19.7	12.8	513	24.0	10.8	826 381	0.1	47 013	5.7	770 084	50.6	3.4
Niagara	84 809	68.1	62 700	19.2	14.2	362	27.6	1.5	108 396	-1.4	6 749	6.2	100 560	24.8	13.3
Oneida	92 562	65.2	72 300	18.7	13.7	373	27.0	2.0	112 311	1.2	4 576	4.1	106 191	29.3	11.0
Onondaga	177 898	63.5	81 000	20.6	13.8	440	26.9	1.8	232 833	0.0	8 195	3.5	228 180	34.5	9.4
Ontario	34 929	73.3	78 300	21.1	13.2	437	25.8	1.7	53 537	-0.2	2 268	4.2	47 221	30.3	12.4
Orange	101 506	67.5	141 700	23.3	15.5	595	29.0	3.5	158 139	1.8	5 552	3.5	141 415	31.1	12.1
Orleans	14 428	74.4	56 900	20.4	13.7	388	26.1	2.6	20 827	-0.6	1 132	5.4	17 869	20.8	14.5
Oswego	42 434	73.0	65 100	17.7	13.4	392	28.0	2.7	56 895	0.4	3 677	6.5	51 881	24.0	15.6
Otsego	21 725	73.0	67 800	20.6	14.3	380	29.3	2.1	31 974	2.9	1 681	5.3	27 007	29.8	10.5
Putnam	28 094	81.9	195 000	24.0	14.7	765	27.7	1.5	54 489	2.7	1 598	2.9	45 002	35.8	12.2
Queens	720 149	42.4	191 000	21.8	14.0	560	25.3	11.7	992 652	0.4	58 941	5.9	938 996	29.3	9.1
Rensselaer	57 612	63.9	93 200	20.3	13.1	421	24.0	2.1	79 776	-0.7	3 177	4.0	76 367	30.9	10.8
Richmond	130 519	63.7	186 300	21.6	13.7	578	26.0	3.9	196 266	0.3	11 384	5.8	177 265	32.6	9.6
Rockland	84 874	72.1	217 100	22.9	15.0	708	28.0	4.7	147 459	1.7	5 134	3.5	136 170	40.4	9.1
St. Lawrence	37 964	68.8	44 100	16.5	13.1	331	28.2	2.5	51 206	0.2	4 334	8.5	44 157	26.9	11.2
Saratoga	66 425	72.3	107 500	20.6	12.9	501	25.3	1.6	103 726	0.8	3 432	3.3	90 694	35.1	10.3
Schenectady	59 181	65.7	94 000	20.6	13.6	452	27.1	1.3	72 532	-1.2	2 588	3.6	70 726	34.1	10.0
Schoharie	11 257	74.1	73 600	20.3	14.4	392	26.2	3.4	15 268	0.7	810	5.3	13 998	25.7	12.8
Schuyler	6 818	77.3	48 500	19.6	13.5	344	26.4	3.7	9 020	4.1	530	5.9	8 177	24.0	12.8
Seneca	12 285	74.3	57 500	19.5	13.9	396	26.4	2.2	15 789	4.1	876	5.5	15 205	27.1	14.5
Steuben	37 299	73.1	46 200	17.4	13.0	341	26.1	2.5	47 560	-0.3	2 755	5.8	43 056	26.9	13.2
Suffolk	424 719	80.1	165 900	23.9	16.7	802	30.4	2.5	718 678	1.2	26 406	3.7	665 182	32.5	12.0
Sullivan	24 576	68.7	93 400	22.6	15.4	459	29.6	4.4	30 959	0.4	1 856	6.0	29 816	27.2	12.3
Tioga	18 838	78.8	72 800	19.9	12.9	382	27.4	1.9	26 347	-0.2	1 010	3.8	24 636	33.2	14.1
Tompkins	33 338	55.3	94 700	21.3	12.9	489	33.6	2.8	50 625	1.4	1 447	2.9	46 056	44.4	8.0
Ulster	60 807	69.2	114 300	21.5	14.0	529	27.4	2.5	82 020	1.0	2 963	3.6	80 213	34.7	11.8
Warren	22 559	69.3	91 200	20.7	13.7	452	26.6	1.6	31 122	-1.9	1 594	5.1	27 380	30.3	11.9
Washington	20 256	73.8	70 200	20.3	13.7	407	28.3	2.6	28 436	0.1	1 351	4.8	25 490	21.5	13.1
Wayne	31 977	76.7	70 700	20.4	14.3	410	27.0	1.8	49 650	-0.2	2 534	5.1	42 674	25.4	15.2
Westchester	320 030	59.7	283 500	23.0	15.5	600	25.8	4.4	447 294	-0.3	15 421	3.4	445 942	42.0	8.2
Wyoming	13 897	75.1	52 500	19.5	13.9	354	25.3	1.6	20 598	0.1	1 501	7.3	18 167	20.7	14.7
Yates	8 419	76.5	55 500	20.8	14.1	333	27.4	3.0	13 439	1.3	559	4.2	10 215	24.5	14.3
NORTH CAROLINA	2 517 026	68.0	65 800	20.5	12.9	382	24.4	3.9	3 874 423	2.1	122 153	3.2	3 238 414	25.7	13.3
Alamance	42 652	71.8	65 300	19.3	12.6	381	23.9	2.8	65 722	1.6	1 568	2.4	57 514	22.9	15.0
Alexander	10 331	82.3	58 100	18.6	11.7	312	22.4	4.5	16 723	2.3	363	2.2	15 084	14.9	16.8
Alleghany	3 894	80.0	48 300	21.9	12.3	275	25.5	3.5	5 487	5.0	179	3.3	4 510	17.7	13.1
Anson	8 531	75.5	41 600	18.6	14.4	296	23.3	8.1	10 755	-2.4	714	6.6	10 801	14.2	14.1
Ashe	8 848	82.7	57 600	21.8	12.4	265	24.2	4.9	10 986	3.5	727	6.6	10 341	14.9	16.8
Avery	5 520	81.0	55 100	18.7	12.8	293	22.4	4.0	7 647	2.7	256	3.3	6 629	21.4	14.7
Beaufort	16 157	74.1	52 600	19.9	13.6	289	28.3	6.1	19 792	0.1	1 473	7.4	19 187	21.0	15.2
Bertie	7 412	74.2	39 100	20.2	14.0	229	24.0	13.1	8 775	1.6	472	5.4	8 269	15.0	15.3
Bladen	10 760	77.5	41 000	21.8	15.0	245	24.2	6.1	19 472	0.5	971	5.0	12 109	17.7	15.2
Brunswick	20 069	81.5	70 600	22.0	12.7	378	26.6	3.7	31 973	6.4	1 370	4.3	22 310	20.4	16.6
Buncombe	70 802	70.3	64 400	20.3	13.0	372	24.9	2.4	100 893	0.0	2 235	2.2	85 640	28.0	13.1
Burke	29 184	74.8	52 800	18.3	12.1	326	20.1	3.4	42 055	0.6	1 040	2.5	39 339	21.5	16.8
Cabarrus	37 515	73.7	65 500	18.4	12.6	370	22.3	3.0	65 611	4.6	1 304	2.0	51 808	23.7	15.2
Caldwell	27 172	74.8	51 600	18.5	12.3	320	21.9	3.7	39 569	0.4	717	1.8	37 802	17.0	16.8
Camden	2 180	80.9	59 400	23.2	12.6	242	22.2	8.2	3 129	2.0	79	2.5	2 655	21.2	20.9
Carteret	21 238	74.2	73 100	22.7	12.3	385	25.3	2.1	29 031	1.9	1 130	3.9	23 837	26.8	14.3
Caswell	7 468	78.5	47 300	18.4	13.3	250	23.5	6.0	12 552	4.4	274	2.2	9 633	13.8	15.9
Catawba	45 700	72.8	62 400	18.5	11.8	371	20.9	2.5	72 796	1.3	1 421	2.0	66 768	19.7	14.0
Chatham	15 293	77.1	63 600	20.6	12.3	399	24.8	4.1	26 289	0.1	446	1.7	20 878	24.6	14.8
Cherokee	7 966	81.0	52 900	20.8	13.0	266	26.7	3.9	11 093	15.4	781	7.0	8 317	18.2	17.7

1. Specified owner-occupied units. 2. Specified renter-occupied units. 3. Overcrowded or lacking complete plumbing facilities. 4. Percent of civilian labor force. 5. Persons 16 years and older.

Table B. States and Counties — Nonfarm Employment and Agriculture

| | Private nonfarm establishments, employment and payroll, 1998 | | | | | | | | | Agriculture, 1997 | | | |
| | Employment | | | | | | Annual payroll | | Farms | | | Farm operators |
STATE County	Number of establishments	Total	Health Care and Social Assistance	Manufacturing	Retail trade	Finance and Insurance	Professional Scientific and Technical Services	Total (mil dol)	Average per employee (dollars)	Number	Percent with— Less than 50 acres	500 acres and over	Whose principal occupation is farming (percent)
	104	105	106	107	108	109	110	111	112	113	114	115	116
NEW YORK—Cont'd													
Genesee	1 333	16 714	2 573	3 802	2 394	359	427	395	23 662	516	28.7	15.5	58.1
Greene	1 100	8 915	687	802	1 691	329	317	176	19 718	244	24.2	10.7	46.7
Hamilton	203	663	54	22	D	D	D	14	20 661	13	61.5	0.0	30.8
Herkimer	1 178	13 640	2 146	4 714	2 037	388	191	305	22 327	583	15.6	11.8	67.6
Jefferson	2 304	26 366	5 082	3 676	5 525	865	632	621	23 541	916	12.9	17.4	62.2
Kings	36 980	409 177	125 539	48 002	46 980	14 940	10 851	11 605	28 362	8	100.0	0.0	25.0
Lewis	553	4 768	806	1 576	755	109	94	109	22 957	623	9.5	12.8	72.4
Livingston	1 233	11 735	1 409	2 320	2 562	315	395	246	20 956	625	21.8	17.9	54.9
Madison	1 351	18 837	2 509	2 848	2 748	539	633	400	21 256	692	16.8	14.2	67.6
Monroe	16 463	361 798	50 968	79 541	42 202	13 773	17 741	11 818	32 665	480	46.7	12.3	52.5
Montgomery	1 142	15 964	3 704	4 891	2 294	657	285	355	22 233	542	18.1	11.8	67.5
Nassau	46 238	532 641	88 205	37 789	82 709	44 381	36 380	18 035	33 859	55	83.6	0.0	49.1
New York	105 128	1 951 646	197 778	74 913	102 196	339 880	257 285	122 513	62 774	2	100.0	0.0	100.0
Niagara	4 590	67 088	9 698	18 388	11 035	1 257	1 731	1 748	26 061	687	39.9	7.7	49.5
Oneida	4 977	86 713	15 447	15 422	13 035	10 153	2 696	2 002	23 093	928	18.8	11.2	63.8
Onondaga	11 571	226 050	29 347	32 913	29 768	13 640	11 634	6 605	29 221	602	33.1	12.6	58.6
Ontario	2 518	36 166	5 735	7 280	7 536	879	1 166	953	26 358	692	28.6	16.2	56.5
Orange	7 867	87 960	13 071	9 664	17 312	4 100	2 935	2 316	26 333	624	38.5	5.0	69.7
Orleans	703	6 803	1 388	1 807	1 334	251	75	140	20 615	456	29.6	15.4	58.3
Oswego	2 017	23 772	3 818	5 090	4 338	704	538	652	27 441	605	25.1	4.8	52.1
Otsego	1 335	17 455	4 169	1 602	3 088	1 260	658	393	22 537	865	13.9	11.8	63.6
Putnam	2 475	17 231	3 300	1 542	2 858	976	850	524	30 393	48	54.2	0.0	33.3
Queens	35 408	444 825	82 691	48 371	48 356	11 767	10 325	13 841	31 116	2	100.0	0.0	0.0
Rensselaer	2 695	41 552	8 176	4 572	5 972	1 547	2 580	1 055	25 390	459	26.8	9.8	50.5
Richmond	7 073	79 611	24 726	2 251	13 428	2 784	3 305	2 186	27 454	7	100.0	0.0	42.9
Rockland	8 297	92 559	18 200	10 394	12 681	4 095	4 614	2 995	32 356	21	81.0	0.0	42.9
St. Lawrence	2 150	28 654	5 573	5 034	4 974	811	619	683	23 823	1 363	10.3	14.9	59.9
Saratoga	3 955	50 296	5 593	7 050	9 822	4 285	2 141	1 326	26 370	472	36.9	6.6	49.8
Schenectady	2 995	47 683	10 649	5 095	7 362	1 649	4 246	1 473	30 883	151	33.1	1.3	39.1
Schoharie	573	5 747	782	1 069	1 306	256	213	119	20 639	518	21.2	9.5	60.0
Schuyler	344	3 065	766	699	499	79	97	69	22 500	318	19.5	6.3	50.9
Seneca	658	7 359	919	1 959	1 691	159	185	185	25 169	413	24.0	16.0	62.5
Steuben	1 787	29 921	4 914	7 389	4 279	925	1 043	980	32 741	1 295	14.1	13.7	53.9
Suffolk	41 675	487 168	70 584	68 195	69 499	24 090	30 992	16 063	32 972	606	71.6	2.3	67.0
Sullivan	1 943	17 387	3 484	624	2 860	680	483	416	23 930	311	24.8	8.4	62.4
Tioga	786	11 017	823	5 624	1 181	213	463	366	33 264	497	18.7	9.7	60.8
Tompkins	2 122	39 804	3 400	4 037	4 435	888	1 837	963	24 190	447	30.0	11.4	51.7
Ulster	4 253	46 526	7 741	6 779	8 369	3 942	2 319	1 061	22 794	409	38.4	5.1	57.2
Warren	2 263	31 566	4 676	4 190	5 330	1 441	1 375	808	25 604	58	37.9	5.2	41.4
Washington	1 047	9 778	1 375	3 733	1 747	214	171	236	24 177	738	18.0	14.8	64.8
Wayne	1 643	22 136	2 667	7 833	3 328	460	645	535	24 174	840	31.2	8.8	59.3
Westchester	30 096	368 745	66 424	18 732	45 045	20 689	21 787	15 104	40 962	91	60.4	3.3	47.3
Wyoming	763	8 586	1 337	2 566	1 577	348	245	185	21 599	702	19.8	13.4	63.7
Yates	494	5 090	1 012	786	799	87	139	97	19 116	657	19.8	4.3	64.5
NORTH CAROLINA	198 690	3 223 178	375 399	771 282	430 667	133 120	126 888	86 781	26 924	49 406	39.6	8.2	49.3
Alamance	3 275	57 559	6 236	20 494	7 710	1 270	1 132	1 360	23 621	731	34.3	4.5	45.6
Alexander	604	9 028	487	5 554	1 018	131	143	190	21 061	565	41.9	2.8	48.5
Alleghany	271	3 186	533	1 367	335	55	41	58	18 255	545	38.3	7.2	42.0
Anson	456	5 908	344	2 631	734	96	81	137	23 193	442	26.0	8.4	50.0
Ashe	522	5 873	831	2 064	840	119	55	117	19 913	1 043	48.7	3.0	40.7
Avery	574	5 791	1 087	818	805	70	109	110	18 948	429	59.0	0.7	42.2
Beaufort	1 146	15 433	1 930	5 284	2 332	367	610	341	22 123	385	27.3	23.4	66.8
Bertie	379	5 446	740	2 816	424	83	50	99	18 229	371	25.9	19.9	70.6
Bladen	541	10 596	1 129	6 482	874	132	145	208	19 649	553	34.7	13.4	54.6
Brunswick	1 666	16 360	1 445	2 545	2 425	388	377	405	24 727	213	44.6	7.0	53.1
Buncombe	6 273	92 346	16 297	18 887	13 755	2 202	2 876	2 261	24 489	1 009	59.3	2.3	39.6
Burke	1 543	30 774	3 136	16 520	3 402	391	507	724	23 541	354	55.6	1.7	35.6
Cabarrus	2 906	45 564	5 440	13 084	7 429	830	1 263	1 219	26 752	481	34.1	4.4	38.3
Caldwell	1 545	28 910	2 229	14 694	3 388	427	310	648	22 430	331	42.9	3.6	34.7
Camden	114	870	D	D	115	D	D	20	23 164	76	27.6	39.5	69.7
Carteret	1 879	17 308	2 514	1 633	3 745	437	452	307	17 766	101	47.5	7.9	58.4
Caswell	232	1 580	384	270	286	D	D	26	16 685	564	24.6	13.8	51.2
Catawba	4 319	89 436	6 759	40 535	10 290	1 484	1 297	2 229	24 923	596	40.6	3.7	39.8
Chatham	961	13 343	1 373	6 915	1 387	174	231	291	21 822	956	39.0	2.5	44.0
Cherokee	589	7 352	1 154	2 643	1 258	202	237	147	19 977	243	50.6	3.7	41.6

STATE County	Acreage (1,000)	Percent change, 1992–1997	Average size of farm	Total irrigated (1,000)	Total cropland (1,000)	Average per farm ($1,000)	Average per acre (dollars)	Value of machinery and equipment Average per farm ($1,000)	Total (mil dol)	Average per farm (dollars)	Crops	Live-stock and poultry products	$10,000 or more	$100,000 or more	Percent of land owned by Fed. Gov. 1997	Water consumption 1995 (mil gal/day)
	117	118	119	120	121	122	123	124	125	126	127	128	129	130	131	132
NEW YORK—Cont'd																
Genesee	171	-0.7	331	5	143	342	1 085	103	110	212 430	43.9	56.1	58.5	26.2	1.6	11.2
Greene	49	6.0	200	0	25	282	1 352	46	9	35 988	36.4	63.6	40.6	9.8	0.0	9.5
Hamilton	1	0.0	61	0	D	126	2 083	34	0	6 065	89.9	10.1	15.4	0.0	0.0	1.0
Herkimer	142	-13.0	243	0	90	207	876	59	46	78 600	7.9	92.1	61.9	27.8	0.0	16.3
Jefferson	291	-3.3	318	0	194	219	711	66	77	84 144	9.2	90.8	57.2	25.3	10.9	30.1
Kings	0	0.0	1	0	0	102	102 188	16	0	46 719	100.0	0.0	62.5	12.5	5.4	25.0
Lewis	180	6.0	288	0	102	187	646	68	62	99 015	5.1	94.9	73.5	41.9	2.3	7.4
Livingston	197	-3.7	316	1	154	334	1 091	95	73	116 698	36.9	63.1	49.0	21.9	0.0	12.7
Madison	186	-5.1	269	0	121	238	953	64	66	94 928	13.4	86.6	64.3	31.1	0.1	11.4
Monroe	103	-6.3	215	3	90	402	1 998	61	48	99 904	79.8	20.2	53.5	22.7	0.0	344.2
Montgomery	135	-2.9	249	0	105	215	832	64	49	89 894	16.0	84.0	62.0	28.0	0.0	15.3
Nassau	1	-30.5	25	0	1	994	39 340	47	3	56 716	91.7	8.3	60.0	14.5	0.3	216.0
New York	D	D	D	D	D	D	D	D	D	D	D		100.0	100.0	1.0	81.8
Niagara	127	-5.7	185	2	112	226	1 222	69	58	84 026	66.1	33.9	49.1	15.1	0.4	434.2
Oneida	216	-11.1	233	0	139	239	1 032	54	74	79 802	21.5	78.5	60.6	27.3	0.6	39.0
Onondaga	147	1.5	244	1	112	297	1 243	74	71	117 859	29.4	70.6	55.3	22.8	0.3	169.5
Ontario	186	2.2	269	1	154	388	1 441	83	78	112 692	48.4	51.6	58.1	21.4	0.0	17.9
Orange	95	-8.0	152	5	66	576	3 819	76	70	111 934	63.6	36.4	69.9	29.6	3.3	1 368.8
Orleans	143	7.0	314	2	122	326	1 076	91	62	136 246	85.5	14.5	53.1	25.4	2.1	4.4
Oswego	103	-8.4	169	1	59	186	1 174	52	31	51 991	56.6	43.4	44.6	13.9	0.0	1 171.4
Otsego	207	-5.1	239	0	116	232	923	51	52	59 667	8.6	91.4	50.6	21.5	0.0	9.7
Putnam	3	-14.2	72	0	2	478	6 682	35	3	60 997	96.9	3.1	47.9	12.5	0.1	131.2
Queens	D	D	D	D	D	D	D	D	D	D	D		50.0	0.0	4.0	44.5
Rensselaer	99	6.4	216	1	59	407	1 813	51	29	62 528	33.5	66.5	45.3	15.5	0.0	37.7
Richmond	0	0.0	4	0	D	625	150 764	43	0	67 486	D	D	71.4	28.6	3.3	2.8
Rockland	1	-44.0	27	0	0	1 392	52 106	56	2	112 448	D	D	47.6	28.6	0.0	46.7
St. Lawrence	396	-0.1	291	0	220	192	666	48	89	65 354	7.5	92.5	54.4	19.4	0.0	21.0
Saratoga	73	4.2	155	0	46	368	2 429	52	30	63 252	29.6	70.4	44.3	11.7	1.2	20.4
Schenectady	18	-4.4	120	0	11	272	2 369	35	6	40 447	71.8	28.2	27.2	7.3	0.9	31.1
Schoharie	111	-6.1	214	1	70	231	1 089	40	27	52 071	21.7	78.3	48.5	18.0	0.0	130.6
Schuyler	65	0.4	205	0	37	203	1 056	42	14	44 133	24.8	75.2	40.9	11.0	4.9	4.1
Seneca	117	2.1	284	0	97	314	1 326	60	41	99 440	49.4	50.6	66.6	28.1	8.0	4.8
Steuben	349	-3.9	269	3	217	200	762	50	79	60 745	30.2	69.8	48.7	16.7	0.1	65.1
Suffolk	36	2.5	59	16	30	642	10 648	72	168	276 993	92.8	7.2	71.9	35.5	1.0	174.1
Sullivan	58	3.7	187	0	35	380	1 861	62	23	75 126	9.1	90.9	49.8	16.7	0.1	150.8
Tioga	109	-4.9	220	1	63	182	854	43	28	55 405	11.7	88.3	46.5	17.1	0.0	8.9
Tompkins	95	3.8	214	0	64	348	1 419	69	48	106 372	16.2	83.8	50.1	19.2	0.0	260.2
Ulster	69	-1.4	169	5	38	536	3 136	53	42	103 368	87.5	12.5	47.9	15.9	0.1	481.9
Warren	9	53.1	158	0	2	299	1 887	45	2	37 581	61.1	38.9	36.2	12.1	0.0	13.8
Washington	195	-5.4	264	1	123	320	1 234	62	78	105 073	13.1	86.9	60.4	27.8	0.0	10.5
Wayne	167	-4.5	199	2	125	311	1 595	74	108	128 055	66.0	34.0	58.8	26.7	0.0	483.3
Westchester	8	25.5	83	0	3	690	8 342	60	11	116 135	69.6	30.4	59.3	20.9	0.0	365.6
Wyoming	195	-7.2	278	2	136	292	1 099	93	135	191 815	10.0	90.0	59.0	34.6	0.0	10.6
Yates	105	2.7	159	1	77	246	1 477	54	40	61 277	48.1	51.9	64.7	19.0	0.0	112.4
NORTH CAROLINA	9 122	2.1	185	156	5 608	376	2 081	49	7 677	155 376	33.8	66.2	46.2	20.5	7.4	7 730.2
Alamance	108	6.7	147	2	59	340	2 402	42	35	47 337	37.7	62.3	38.0	12.7	0.0	27.6
Alexander	60	12.9	106	0	35	218	2 322	26	47	82 817	9.9	90.1	43.9	20.0	0.0	5.0
Alleghany	86	17.8	158	0	42	357	2 035	34	25	46 496	43.8	56.2	40.6	9.5	5.2	2.9
Anson	82	15.5	185	0	35	341	1 791	41	99	222 973	5.2	94.8	47.3	30.3	2.3	13.4
Ashe	105	0.9	101	0	47	238	2 213	28	22	21 246	74.9	25.1	33.7	2.7	0.1	3.6
Avery	27	35.2	63	1	14	201	3 568	29	17	39 411	98.1	1.9	46.9	9.1	18.7	8.7
Beaufort	155	7.2	404	2	136	577	1 430	103	82	212 196	68.2	31.8	69.6	38.2	0.5	16.6
Bertie	154	-9.2	416	9	97	468	1 216	100	111	298 986	59.8	40.2	79.8	44.7	1.3	8.1
Bladen	128	0.2	232	3	75	346	1 586	56	239	431 696	15.2	84.8	58.6	31.3	0.0	8.7
Brunswick	37	-8.1	173	1	24	454	2 449	35	30	142 283	41.9	58.1	46.9	18.8	1.3	11.9
Buncombe	87	-7.0	87	1	36	323	3 603	23	34	34 106	73.0	27.0	20.3	3.4	10.2	37.8
Burke	29	-8.2	83	1	14	255	3 337	36	28	79 779	34.1	65.9	30.8	11.9	14.8	29.0
Cabarrus	63	0.2	131	0	40	464	3 520	22	21	43 368	24.8	75.2	28.5	6.0	0.0	30.8
Caldwell	37	19.5	112	0	18	236	2 216	31	24	71 638	58.1	41.9	27.8	11.5	16.3	13.4
Camden	52	20.2	680	D	48	1 053	1 549	173	20	259 827	93.7	6.3	67.1	42.1	4.3	0.9
Carteret	60	-6.5	593	0	46	980	1 646	62	19	187 703	96.0	4.0	55.4	27.7	16.7	8.4
Caswell	138	10.3	244	3	54	371	1 542	40	28	50 327	77.1	22.9	54.3	13.1	0.0	3.6
Catawba	72	14.7	121	1	48	336	2 809	32	24	40 933	27.1	72.9	25.5	7.0	0.0	806.0
Chatham	113	4.6	118	1	54	293	2 248	30	121	126 261	3.8	96.2	41.8	20.0	3.2	396.5
Cherokee	25	2.2	101	0	10	241	2 687	27	13	51 899	11.3	88.7	18.5	4.1	44.7	7.6

Table B. States and Counties — Residential Construction, Wholesale and Retail Trade, and Real Estate

STATE County	Value of Residential Construction Authorized by Building Permits, 1999		Wholesale Trade, 1997				Retail Trade[1], 1997				Real Estate and Rental and Leasing, 1997			
	New Construction ($1,000)	Number of Housing Units	Number of Establishments	Number of Employees	Sales (mil dol)	Annual Payroll (mil dol)	Number of Establishments	Number of Employees	Sales (mil dol)	Annual Payroll (mil dol)	Number of Establishments	Number of Employees	Receipts (mil dol)	Annual Payroll (mil dol)
	133	134	135	136	137	138	139	140	141	142	143	144	145	146
NEW YORK—Cont'd														
Genesee	15 989	177	99	1 140	385.6	31.5	231	2 649	366.4	35.6	42	136	15.3	2.5
Greene	13 701	128	39	516	222.6	14.8	230	1 673	278.3	27.1	33	122	12.2	1.8
Hamilton	3 668	42	2	D	D	D	35	140	23.7	2.6	3	D	D	D
Herkimer	11 809	132	33	D	D	D	254	2 183	313.4	29.7	45	96	9.8	1.1
Jefferson	14 547	144	93	958	280.7	26.0	514	5 679	1 016.3	90.8	94	407	56.9	7.5
Kings	183 065	2 894	2 953	25 838	11 371.6	742.8	6 994	45 941	7 983.6	821.8	3 230	10 872	1 924.2	256.5
Lewis	7 974	176	25	186	68.8	3.7	99	743	134.0	11.1	10	D	D	D
Livingston	22 271	202	68	633	212.6	18.7	245	2 676	411.3	38.4	34	132	13.0	2.3
Madison	14 477	131	63	473	159.8	13.4	260	2 935	463.3	43.2	48	134	10.4	2.1
Monroe	305 228	2 602	1 113	15 298	9 311.1	634.8	2 546	43 294	6 513.2	634.1	614	5 984	684.3	127.4
Montgomery	4 870	58	54	561	148.6	14.7	222	2 381	378.4	34.0	21	100	7.5	1.9
Nassau	199 433	1 151	4 124	36 401	23 793.6	1 597.9	6 751	81 902	16 483.6	1 615.9	2 157	9 913	1 894.6	287.4
New York	201 871	3 791	11 629	119 913	151 792.8	6 473.4	11 222	102 965	19 502.4	2 447.2	8 510	59 793	14 318.2	2 331.7
Niagara	51 120	443	237	2 573	656.6	64.4	886	11 500	1 607.6	159.9	111	509	50.8	8.1
Oneida	31 934	303	245	D	D	D	971	12 664	1 846.1	180.5	163	652	79.1	11.5
Onondaga	110 317	952	992	13 949	11 159.8	526.1	1 974	30 203	4 372.3	443.4	403	4 020	364.9	88.9
Ontario	93 080	827	152	1 092	471.6	36.4	520	7 791	1 118.6	106.3	62	226	22.5	4.3
Orange	195 920	1 842	448	D	D	D	1 438	17 131	3 047.7	290.4	278	1 075	156.1	22.6
Orleans	7 971	80	26	205	36.3	3.9	139	1 371	191.5	18.1	17	52	3.9	0.7
Oswego	20 906	267	73	443	140.0	11.0	396	4 609	747.1	69.5	60	264	34.2	6.3
Otsego	17 182	556	50	427	99.4	9.8	298	3 064	539.3	47.4	36	135	11.7	2.0
Putnam	67 878	395	126	729	278.2	27.0	320	2 707	497.6	49.9	107	251	37.8	6.8
Queens	134 657	2 169	2 787	27 165	12 942.0	952.6	5 933	48 425	8 756.0	890.1	2 385	11 853	1 919.0	297.2
Rensselaer	57 760	476	131	1 066	780.5	33.5	440	5 814	854.3	86.0	75	300	43.7	7.0
Richmond	214 708	2 414	358	1 763	627.1	55.5	1 197	13 522	2 235.3	219.4	234	842	152.1	18.8
Rockland	116 659	870	662	5 606	5 826.0	221.0	1 114	11 601	2 229.9	228.2	338	1 260	231.7	44.8
St. Lawrence	17 203	255	74	665	316.4	18.3	483	5 161	791.8	73.6	70	203	18.8	3.5
Saratoga	133 355	1 012	195	2 324	1 539.6	74.8	721	9 063	1 509.8	139.0	137	666	95.1	13.5
Schenectady	31 193	284	121	1 733	618.3	60.0	582	7 606	1 174.0	119.1	76	461	45.2	10.7
Schoharie	6 204	76	12	89	24.4	1.9	134	1 364	190.1	18.4	17	54	5.2	0.8
Schuyler	3 504	47	14	D	D	D	72	713	119.5	11.7	11	D	D	D
Seneca	6 033	70	28	311	53.9	6.0	174	1 560	250.3	22.6	17	D	D	D
Steuben	26 975	380	46	366	89.9	8.1	403	4 526	663.4	63.8	59	261	22.1	4.1
Suffolk	630 184	5 167	3 400	42 107	21 953.6	1 616.1	6 393	68 059	13 509.7	1 352.7	1 281	5 853	1 009.5	166.2
Sullivan	22 524	257	82	688	235.8	16.7	344	2 842	485.9	49.0	82	231	26.1	3.9
Tioga	13 111	120	31	D	D	D	145	1 205	218.1	20.0	13	55	4.1	0.6
Tompkins	31 152	399	71	432	239.6	13.8	373	4 367	616.3	65.7	81	450	42.1	8.2
Ulster	62 040	550	183	2 163	522.0	59.5	771	8 107	1 278.3	132.1	135	418	54.6	7.9
Warren	36 028	316	93	D	D	D	466	5 236	850.6	83.9	63	265	39.2	5.2
Washington	21 500	233	44	D	D	D	209	1 693	265.2	25.9	24	76	6.1	0.9
Wayne	35 346	394	78	745	327.1	26.0	296	3 569	576.4	54.2	46	148	15.2	2.3
Westchester	381 734	1 666	1 947	31 486	23 918.0	1 313.0	4 191	46 984	9 189.0	958.6	1 760	7 321	1 533.8	235.8
Wyoming	8 712	106	32	202	107.4	4.7	159	1 609	247.0	23.8	16	89	3.6	1.0
Yates	6 532	91	21	D	D	D	107	739	105.4	10.6	23	105	6.1	1.4
NORTH CAROLINA	8 616 858	84 754	12 284	157 774	98 080.1	5 574.1	35 563	416 287	72 356.8	6 697.4	7 346	39 349	5 026.0	900.6
Alamance	99 613	888	172	1 756	550.7	53.7	643	7 630	1 245.1	117.8	97	397	69.3	7.3
Alexander	21 510	169	24	91	23.1	1.9	100	900	142.5	11.6	8	21	1.2	0.2
Alleghany	17 276	146	3	D	D	D	53	317	59.0	4.7	7	13	0.8	0.1
Anson	4 718	39	17	208	86.2	6.5	96	771	105.4	9.8	11	26	1.8	0.4
Ashe	27 815	276	24	69	44.2	1.3	103	830	163.0	13.2	19	37	4.1	0.7
Avery	39 215	180	19	98	35.1	2.6	108	822	130.9	11.9	38	187	11.0	2.7
Beaufort	39 082	297	77	683	245.4	16.6	234	2 398	386.0	33.1	30	118	8.4	1.3
Bertie	1 347	24	21	268	158.6	4.8	69	458	70.8	6.5	7	14	1.1	0.2
Bladen	7 102	66	29	298	144.7	7.5	111	895	129.4	11.9	12	56	9.8	1.1
Brunswick	145 439	1 533	57	367	77.0	8.6	276	2 490	441.9	38.1	86	949	64.7	15.0
Buncombe	160 846	1 245	340	D	D	D	1 136	13 179	2 193.4	210.4	221	1 037	131.9	21.8
Burke	32 180	321	78	583	248.4	16.0	315	3 079	557.8	46.2	43	103	10.3	1.6
Cabarrus	196 706	2 877	157	1 480	953.9	45.4	468	6 467	1 131.8	103.6	98	497	60.0	11.1
Caldwell	47 723	444	77	842	791.3	31.6	330	3 329	515.1	45.8	39	116	11.3	1.9
Camden	7 829	77	5	D	D	D	24	128	14.9	1.6	1	D	D	D
Carteret	80 728	681	61	623	141.3	13.5	406	3 510	598.7	53.4	112	478	46.8	7.1
Caswell	9 749	78	5	75	4.5	1.1	49	267	44.0	3.9	3	4	0.5	0.0
Catawba	140 728	1 225	308	5 844	2 543.2	177.7	779	10 011	1 719.8	161.1	146	643	80.5	13.2
Chatham	89 737	512	58	523	262.9	12.8	177	1 451	226.1	21.3	20	61	3.6	0.6
Cherokee	19 320	253	24	186	51.1	3.1	139	1 266	217.0	18.3	17	89	11.2	2.0

1. Establishments with payroll.

STATE County	Professional, Scientific, and Technical Services[1], 1997				Manufacturing, 1997				Accommodation and Foodservices, 1997			
	Number of Establishments	Number of Employees	Receipts (mil dol)	Annual Payroll (mil dol)	Number of Establishments	Number of Employees	Receipts (mil dol)	Annual Payroll (mil dol)	Number of Establishments	Number of Employees	Sales (mil dol)	Annual Payroll (mil dol)
	147	148	149	150	151	152	153	154	155	156	157	158
NEW YORK—Cont'd												
Genesee	67	715	25.7	10.4	107	3 979	778.1	127.0	131	1 770	51.7	14.5
Greene	58	283	25.1	6.1	37	740	118.4	22.4	207	1 508	62.6	16.4
Hamilton	3	6	0.7	0.1	NA	NA	NA	NA	59	140	10.4	2.8
Herkimer	58	192	8.7	2.9	71	4 971	662.4	135.8	153	1 225	40.6	10.6
Jefferson	98	591	36.8	16.0	84	3 896	812.6	132.0	295	2 835	102.5	28.1
Kings	1 906	7 731	790.0	250.4	2 672	48 589	5 725.5	1 139.9	2 221	15 748	734.5	188.1
Lewis	20	58	3.1	1.0	24	1 560	505.3	53.1	67	314	10.9	2.4
Livingston	77	344	20.4	8.0	48	2 196	500.5	59.5	138	1 399	39.3	10.3
Madison	89	495	41.7	12.0	69	2 526	506.7	69.3	171	1 948	59.9	17.5
Monroe	1 623	15 316	1 643.0	622.2	1 007	82 459	21 774.7	3 521.8	1 439	22 914	760.6	219.4
Montgomery	55	237	21.1	7.0	84	4 790	637.7	123.6	115	910	36.9	8.5
Nassau	5 784	34 253	3 832.4	1 425.5	1 653	42 717	7 117.3	1 550.8	2 881	35 707	1 544.2	431.3
New York	15 163	230 278	38 237.5	14 755.2	5 165	93 784	14 028.9	2 551.8	7 219	127 621	8 318.2	2 423.4
Niagara	253	1 269	128.7	36.2	310	18 164	4 403.5	836.5	592	6 876	207.6	58.3
Oneida	344	2 312	177.2	62.8	280	15 079	2 485.3	447.1	528	5 931	180.1	50.8
Onondaga	1 057	10 334	935.4	370.6	510	33 289	6 614.4	1 296.3	1 062	16 009	509.8	151.5
Ontario	171	946	108.6	34.5	161	7 196	999.1	226.4	262	3 516	110.7	31.5
Orange	605	2 643	269.0	96.7	346	D	D	D	687	6 763	256.5	67.0
Orleans	27	66	5.5	1.1	48	2 269	496.0	71.2	66	598	15.2	4.1
Oswego	108	436	31.0	12.8	108	5 082	2 210.7	204.9	262	3 128	87.0	25.4
Otsego	84	299	27.5	8.1	68	1 481	225.0	38.0	165	1 675	62.8	16.7
Putnam	248	853	73.2	28.6	74	1 595	258.9	60.3	144	1 207	45.7	12.0
Queens	1 756	7 829	678.8	231.1	2 043	50 505	6 412.8	1 433.2	2 666	25 321	1 336.5	357.1
Rensselaer	226	1 546	125.6	53.3	110	5 023	767.2	169.1	269	3 092	92.0	25.8
Richmond	574	2 143	210.4	68.0	162	2 156	316.2	59.6	553	5 427	239.6	55.3
Rockland	923	4 197	526.9	177.3	309	10 739	3 649.8	413.3	558	5 553	246.6	64.4
St. Lawrence	109	445	26.2	10.5	85	5 311	1 602.2	201.4	259	2 497	74.9	20.3
Saratoga	369	2 011	132.0	47.3	139	6 400	1 513.9	263.2	380	5 431	197.3	58.4
Schenectady	227	3 994	484.7	196.4	119	5 134	1 687.8	212.2	313	3 126	106.6	29.8
Schoharie	31	116	5.5	2.1	28	1 024	180.8	24.0	51	547	14.4	4.1
Schuyler	21	38	3.2	0.6	17	574	88.8	18.3	49	281	11.4	3.1
Seneca	33	97	9.2	3.1	31	2 037	457.2	71.2	72	646	23.3	7.0
Steuben	113	550	35.4	13.2	74	8 070	1 338.5	264.2	211	2 332	74.7	21.4
Suffolk	3 680	21 383	2 149.9	773.5	2 535	70 317	12 009.2	2 433.5	2 795	29 208	1 266.9	336.3
Sullivan	140	407	33.4	9.1	54	D	D	D	246	3 607	148.1	43.4
Tioga	53	417	60.8	14.2	48	5 055	1 569.6	239.8	84	749	24.2	6.7
Tompkins	188	1 411	135.8	49.5	94	3 613	667.1	123.6	312	3 477	113.2	31.7
Ulster	321	2 013	183.7	69.3	215	6 449	785.0	183.7	468	5 662	215.7	63.1
Warren	151	1 114	127.8	40.2	84	4 014	820.7	144.0	407	4 078	179.5	51.6
Washington	59	125	8.5	2.5	99	3 852	642.0	122.7	100	584	19.8	4.8
Wayne	98	386	23.0	8.5	145	8 041	1 435.2	221.8	140	1 473	46.2	12.4
Westchester	3 550	20 530	2 818.2	1 016.6	869	18 797	3 012.0	626.3	1 833	19 829	1 018.1	285.1
Wyoming	37	143	8.0	3.0	55	3 011	371.9	79.1	73	544	16.4	4.1
Yates	27	85	6.1	2.3	27	522	225.2	15.6	55	322	13.0	3.1
NORTH CAROLINA	14 351	101 610	9 760.9	3 693.5	11 306	773 548	161 900.5	21 297.9	14 579	262 848	8 625.0	2 393.2
Alamance	173	878	66.5	29.8	282	21 490	3 324.8	588.2	246	5 028	145.1	39.9
Alexander	31	106	5.4	2.0	99	5 512	635.0	129.2	38	575	15.5	4.5
Alleghany	15	27	1.3	0.4	22	1 422	245.3	27.2	25	246	6.2	1.8
Anson	19	73	4.0	1.4	37	3 426	364.8	74.3	30	406	12.1	3.3
Ashe	17	46	2.8	0.8	37	2 093	242.1	42.2	43	464	12.5	3.8
Avery	20	59	8.2	1.5	11	802	85.4	14.6	47	468	22.1	5.6
Beaufort	60	569	24.3	9.7	65	5 772	927.8	139.8	68	924	29.1	7.2
Bertie	5	40	2.3	0.8	16	D	D	D	15	162	4.4	1.1
Bladen	25	147	10.1	3.0	36	6 559	1 040.9	127.4	50	544	17.9	4.7
Brunswick	89	281	20.8	6.4	57	2 340	1 013.3	86.9	155	1 843	67.4	16.7
Buncombe	466	2 386	174.1	77.3	332	D	D	D	506	9 130	334.3	98.9
Burke	91	447	25.9	10.3	171	17 279	2 126.9	416.7	118	2 451	63.1	16.7
Cabarrus	158	808	59.2	24.6	166	13 099	7 991.8	409.7	155	3 317	123.7	31.7
Caldwell	55	259	17.6	7.2	167	15 254	1 633.1	344.4	102	1 332	40.9	10.8
Camden	4	18	0.8	0.4	NA	NA	NA	NA	3	D	D	D
Carteret	93	319	30.8	9.0	69	1 576	173.1	29.4	202	3 010	106.0	28.7
Caswell	13	29	2.8	0.8	NA	NA	NA	NA	14	88	2.7	0.7
Catawba	238	1 109	86.6	30.8	575	40 469	5 512.8	1 035.2	315	6 274	179.7	52.0
Chatham	63	170	12.3	4.8	76	7 109	1 014.3	158.2	51	D	D	D
Cherokee	34	178	8.0	4.0	27	2 776	315.0	56.3	47	525	15.4	4.0

1. Firms subject to federal tax.

Table B. States and Counties — Health and Other Services and Federal Funds

STATE County	Health Care and Social Assistance[1], 1997				Other Services[1], 1997				Federal funds and grants, fiscal 1999[2] Expenditures (mil dol)			
										Direct payments for individuals[3]		
	Number of Establishments	Number of Employees	Receipts (mil dol)	Annual Payroll (mil dol)	Number of Establishments	Number of Employees	Receipts (mil dol)	Annual Payroll (mil dol)	Total	Social Security and government retirement	Medicare	Food stamps and Supplemental Security Income
	159	160	161	162	163	164	165	166	167	168	169	170
NEW YORK—Cont'd												
Genesee	90	912	44.9	18.3	90	559	31.0	8.5	247.7	119.4	44.6	5.7
Greene	63	444	25.2	9.9	61	191	16.7	3.8	189.7	101.5	35.6	6.4
Hamilton	1	D	D	D	9	17	1.6	0.3	29.1	14.9	5.1	0.4
Herkimer	63	454	24.5	9.9	86	512	61.8	15.2	264.4	132.7	53.1	9.0
Jefferson	157	1 324	89.2	47.9	129	482	33.6	9.0	874.4	194.7	57.2	17.5
Kings	3 102	28 475	2 029.6	781.4	2 747	10 809	715.0	212.2	(4)	(4)	(4)	(4)
Lewis	26	D	D	D	30	50	5.5	0.9	99.8	47.1	14.4	3.4
Livingston	79	449	26.6	10.3	75	300	16.3	4.1	202.2	104.5	38.4	6.6
Madison	87	669	46.2	19.8	81	206	17.2	3.7	225.1	122.0	37.4	7.2
Monroe	1 299	14 414	951.7	402.5	1 048	6 001	401.6	118.8	3 233.0	1 279.4	554.8	122.3
Montgomery	103	992	56.7	24.9	86	323	18.2	4.4	246.2	126.4	54.1	7.8
Nassau	4 486	45 327	3 665.3	1 504.1	3 201	17 088	1 105.6	342.1	6 254.5	2 749.0	1 381.4	89.5
New York	5 360	39 451	3 780.3	1 523.5	4 188	26 361	1 825.5	505.9	(4)44 212.6	(4)10 269.7	(4)8 097.6	(4)2 799.4
Niagara	359	3 906	182.8	78.7	305	1 279	78.8	20.4	1 015.0	476.2	181.6	31.8
Oneida	421	4 299	287.8	133.6	328	1 733	112.9	29.0	1 307.3	567.6	191.9	46.9
Onondaga	894	9 567	722.2	341.2	762	5 753	413.2	119.8	2 261.2	879.0	313.0	74.4
Ontario	142	1 391	86.3	33.6	133	495	31.5	8.5	401.4	193.8	65.2	10.1
Orange	651	5 619	366.9	158.9	548	2 588	189.5	50.7	1 545.1	531.7	219.1	41.4
Orleans	62	417	25.5	9.9	50	108	8.6	2.0	156.6	72.9	27.4	5.4
Oswego	119	1 103	58.1	25.8	133	426	32.8	7.6	420.8	212.6	70.0	17.4
Otsego	75	536	35.2	15.5	84	298	22.6	5.9	253.9	121.4	44.6	7.3
Putnam	189	1 999	132.1	58.2	168	670	50.3	12.6	235.7	131.7	57.8	3.5
Queens	2 966	32 874	2 271.0	935.6	2 834	12 307	766.9	235.7	(4)	(4)	(4)	(4)
Rensselaer	244	2 820	150.8	67.9	187	755	51.1	13.2	810.7	299.0	110.8	20.8
Richmond	732	8 746	651.7	299.6	600	2 398	153.3	41.5	(4)	(4)	(4)	(4)
Rockland	761	6 753	508.3	227.1	527	1 985	147.2	38.2	1 026.7	461.5	228.2	27.8
St. Lawrence	158	1 295	76.0	31.2	113	475	25.6	6.4	484.2	208.6	71.0	23.4
Saratoga	286	2 050	132.7	51.6	203	1 027	63.3	17.9	600.6	331.8	97.6	13.3
Schenectady	311	4 202	274.7	126.0	196	1 239	84.3	22.9	1 019.2	346.9	125.7	22.8
Schoharie	33	297	14.5	5.2	43	103	7.3	1.6	123.0	60.8	21.2	3.6
Schuyler	18	181	8.0	3.6	15	38	2.9	0.5	74.5	35.7	10.8	3.0
Seneca	38	372	19.7	7.5	31	96	7.1	1.3	129.6	70.9	21.6	3.6
Steuben	139	1 282	75.5	33.7	106	371	24.2	5.9	454.4	213.9	70.8	18.2
Suffolk	3 042	33 419	2 448.6	1 030.0	2 986	12 507	944.8	266.3	6 150.5	2 444.7	1 121.7	115.1
Sullivan	130	1 001	58.9	22.9	112	563	29.0	7.5	369.5	147.2	72.6	13.6
Tioga	46	322	14.1	6.0	50	166	10.7	2.8	463.4	86.1	25.8	6.5
Tompkins	157	1 307	85.1	35.3	108	555	32.4	8.8	444.9	126.1	37.5	9.6
Ulster	343	3 292	191.7	75.6	243	938	55.6	15.1	654.5	317.9	118.0	23.6
Warren	146	1 371	104.1	52.7	107	511	39.9	12.1	253.1	129.2	42.8	7.0
Washington	45	614	25.9	11.6	62	157	11.4	2.6	214.7	113.1	38.4	7.5
Wayne	99	761	40.6	17.2	106	317	24.3	5.9	339.1	169.8	61.8	11.0
Westchester	2 629	23 146	1 909.4	815.9	1 883	8 331	617.8	180.7	4 059.9	1 674.7	904.0	92.8
Wyoming	40	513	22.7	11.5	47	180	10.3	2.7	141.1	71.6	25.3	3.9
Yates	21	D	D	D	25	113	8.2	1.8	96.4	54.0	16.7	3.3
NORTH CAROLINA	12 582	173 770	10 708.8	4 859.6	11 483	64 802	4 060.6	1 204.0	37 227.6	14 120.7	4 770.2	1 155.5
Alamance	212	3 555	289.1	106.9	202	1 339	80.3	23.2	438.7	244.3	88.8	11.6
Alexander	31	317	14.0	7.1	41	176	10.9	2.7	86.7	47.6	18.4	3.1
Alleghany	12	200	5.7	2.5	11	20	1.6	0.2	52.7	25.6	9.5	1.7
Anson	23	261	10.8	5.5	28	106	6.8	1.8	126.3	46.0	22.5	6.1
Ashe	27	244	11.7	5.6	25	70	5.1	1.1	109.2	49.6	18.8	4.2
Avery	26	342	12.6	6.6	25	77	5.2	1.4	75.3	35.9	15.7	3.1
Beaufort	63	893	45.4	20.6	91	387	24.1	7.2	217.5	100.3	31.5	11.1
Bertie	20	355	13.7	5.0	20	76	5.0	1.0	120.7	41.9	18.1	8.7
Bladen	54	719	27.4	12.4	23	81	4.0	1.1	157.8	59.8	23.7	10.5
Brunswick	94	1 170	67.3	26.0	68	239	16.7	3.8	318.0	181.5	51.5	12.0
Buncombe	459	6 057	428.7	214.9	347	1 834	104.9	33.0	963.0	457.9	150.2	29.2
Burke	122	1 068	69.6	35.7	81	468	27.4	8.9	291.1	146.0	54.2	10.0
Cabarrus	163	2 348	148.2	73.7	216	965	57.8	17.5	409.2	228.1	93.5	10.8
Caldwell	94	1 492	62.5	28.6	98	433	26.8	7.2	238.2	130.8	49.5	7.5
Camden	2	D	D	D	5	25	2.2	0.8	32.1	17.4	4.8	0.7
Carteret	95	1 123	51.2	24.0	103	409	20.0	5.1	294.8	170.9	39.5	6.8
Caswell	20	303	8.7	3.8	10	18	0.9	0.2	81.2	33.7	13.4	5.0
Catawba	251	4 733	345.0	149.4	239	1 385	82.6	26.1	445.6	238.6	75.5	13.5
Chatham	43	525	25.3	9.4	56	209	12.9	4.3	157.0	75.7	30.2	3.5
Cherokee	43	285	16.7	6.6	19	63	5.3	1.2	119.7	61.4	19.4	4.9

1. Firms subject to federal tax. 2. October 1, 1998 to September 30, 1999. 3. State totals may include programs not allocated by county. 4. Bronx, Kings, Queens, and Richmond Counties included with New York County.

Table B. States and Counties — **Federal Funds and Local Government Finances**

	Federal funds and grants, fiscal 1999[1] (cont'd)							Local government finances, 1997				
	Expenditures (mil dol) (cont'd)							General revenue				
	Procurement contract awards			Grants[2]							Taxes	
											Per capita[3] (dollars)	
STATE County	Salaries and wages	Defense	Other	Medicaid and other health-related	Nutrition and family welfare	Education	Other	Total (mil dol)	Intergovern-mental (mil dol)	Total (mil dol)	Total	Property
	171	172	173	174	175	176	177	178	179	180	181	182
NEW YORK—Cont'd												
Genesee	23.5	0.8	11.1	24.4	5.1	3.4	3.2	260.1	85.4	82.5	1 335	966
Greene	6.5	0.6	2.5	20.8	5.6	2.3	6.0	154.2	56.6	83.4	1 743	1 418
Hamilton	1.2	0.0	0.3	1.2	0.4	0.6	4.8	29.9	4.1	22.5	4 318	3 966
Herkimer	7.8	4.0	1.9	34.0	7.5	3.7	6.1	204.9	93.8	79.9	1 217	958
Jefferson	422.1	52.1	5.8	58.4	16.9	15.8	21.5	362.1	171.4	125.0	1 105	827
Kings	(4)	(4)	(4)	(4)	(4)	(4)	(4)	(4)	(4)	(4)	(4)	(4)
Lewis	3.5	0.8	2.3	16.9	3.9	1.1	4.4	106.8	42.3	30.7	1 089	925
Livingston	8.7	1.2	3.2	21.9	5.5	2.5	2.9	189.8	79.6	74.2	1 116	897
Madison	8.8	0.4	2.4	29.2	7.1	2.9	2.6	204.7	92.8	85.0	1 187	1 028
Monroe	178.3	90.8	61.4	429.6	131.3	87.9	148.6	2 629.4	938.4	1 206.5	1 681	1 220
Montgomery	6.6	3.5	3.5	27.2	6.5	2.3	2.5	176.4	71.2	61.6	1 197	936
Nassau	385.7	694.0	124.2	490.8	73.9	38.7	55.3	5 981.3	1 189.9	4 027.2	3 089	2 527
New York	(4)3 219.1	(4)457.5	(4)2 079.5	(4)10 453.0	(4)2 534.7	(4)663.9	(4)2 164.4	(4)45 887.1	(4)16 661.7	(4)19 368.2	(4)2 638	(4)1 006
Niagara	77.4	26.2	11.2	106.5	37.9	11.1	32.4	807.0	303.7	323.9	1 471	1 125
Oneida	120.5	73.9	14.0	170.5	34.0	12.3	42.8	827.8	337.3	325.9	1 398	1 017
Onondaga	227.4	252.1	55.6	229.6	66.1	23.0	91.0	1 571.2	614.0	706.1	1 530	1 145
Ontario	46.0	2.2	9.4	34.2	8.4	3.8	17.8	342.9	125.9	157.9	1 579	1 177
Orange	382.1	118.6	24.9	141.0	37.3	16.3	16.4	1 503.0	395.0	553.4	1 691	1 355
Orleans	4.9	0.0	6.9	16.6	6.7	2.3	7.7	129.0	61.3	48.3	1 079	830
Oswego	14.9	1.7	6.6	56.4	17.9	6.3	12.4	452.0	179.9	213.6	1 705	1 584
Otsego	9.5	0.5	5.6	39.2	7.3	3.0	10.7	172.2	73.4	71.8	1 168	967
Putnam	11.5	0.6	3.3	16.0	2.5	3.3	5.0	294.9	58.2	204.2	2 211	1 960
Queens	(4)	(4)	(4)	(4)	(4)	(4)	(4)	(4)	(4)	(4)	(4)	(4)
Rensselaer	30.5	4.7	6.2	253.1	19.5	6.5	43.8	531.7	218.2	208.5	1 351	1 061
Richmond	(4)	(4)	(4)	(4)	(4)	(4)	(4)	(4)	(4)	(4)	(4)	(4)
Rockland	37.8	5.5	15.1	146.3	31.0	9.7	48.7	1 184.5	247.5	761.3	2 720	2 185
St. Lawrence	25.9	1.2	6.4	84.6	21.8	7.8	22.4	368.5	167.6	124.5	1 090	837
Saratoga	68.5	1.8	7.0	43.0	12.0	4.5	15.3	534.7	177.4	285.2	1 451	1 107
Schenectady	49.2	315.3	14.2	73.2	17.4	5.3	38.1	471.9	164.1	229.7	1 561	1 221
Schoharie	4.8	0.0	1.3	19.2	4.0	1.5	4.5	101.5	48.6	43.1	1 325	1 099
Schuyler	3.0	0.1	1.0	11.4	2.6	1.2	4.8	51.4	24.0	19.4	1 014	821
Seneca	8.4	0.2	1.2	16.0	2.2	1.4	0.8	99.3	48.3	39.2	1 193	906
Steuben	39.9	6.1	10.7	50.8	12.6	5.9	18.5	368.7	173.9	128.4	1 296	952
Suffolk	647.0	255.3	574.7	630.1	140.8	52.4	126.9	5 486.0	1 485.4	3 377.9	2 479	1 995
Sullivan	12.5	0.0	9.4	85.0	9.1	3.7	9.6	312.2	96.2	156.8	2 229	1 928
Tioga	8.1	306.0	5.4	13.7	6.5	2.0	2.1	150.1	74.6	54.4	1 028	841
Tompkins	19.0	7.9	6.5	63.1	11.0	6.7	140.1	293.8	104.5	136.1	1 408	1 028
Ulster	28.0	7.7	7.4	108.7	19.1	5.9	9.0	596.9	179.9	335.1	2 007	1 643
Warren	15.8	2.2	3.7	32.1	6.5	2.2	5.1	219.5	69.3	117.9	1 905	1 398
Washington	8.0	2.0	2.0	27.5	8.8	2.7	1.6	197.6	85.3	74.6	1 229	1 036
Wayne	11.6	4.9	4.6	47.5	10.1	3.7	7.2	315.9	136.5	126.2	1 325	1 087
Westchester	291.3	218.9	120.4	458.1	114.9	39.8	76.1	4 215.4	872.0	2 548.0	2 843	2 351
Wyoming	5.7	0.0	9.6	13.2	2.8	2.5	1.5	133.8	45.8	43.0	965	731
Yates	4.9	0.0	1.0	9.6	2.1	1.1	1.1	66.2	23.6	35.1	1 455	1 249
NORTH CAROLINA	5 275.1	1 045.5	1 004.3	3 991.8	1 306.4	599.1	1 710.7	X	X	X	X	X
Alamance	13.4	3.1	3.7	44.8	8.8	4.0	5.9	226.3	114.5	61.3	520	387
Alexander	2.7	0.3	0.8	8.6	2.4	1.1	0.3	41.1	23.9	11.1	364	232
Alleghany	2.2	0.0	1.4	9.8	0.9	0.6	0.5	17.7	9.4	5.4	553	406
Anson	2.9	16.9	0.9	21.4	4.2	1.7	0.7	85.5	31.6	11.4	470	358
Ashe	4.1	0.0	0.8	24.5	2.2	1.1	1.7	31.4	17.8	10.3	428	290
Avery	2.3	0.1	0.6	12.0	1.9	1.0	1.9	29.2	14.9	11.5	734	551
Beaufort	6.3	0.5	2.4	32.6	5.7	3.5	2.3	116.0	51.3	24.1	545	396
Bertie	4.1	1.8	0.6	31.0	4.9	2.4	0.4	39.1	28.0	7.7	377	280
Bladen	5.7	0.1	7.6	32.3	6.2	3.1	1.6	85.9	38.1	16.8	548	419
Brunswick	14.3	14.8	1.8	26.8	5.7	2.1	4.7	149.7	56.0	63.1	957	762
Buncombe	118.9	12.3	48.4	79.9	17.3	10.3	24.8	427.7	186.5	144.1	748	554
Burke	6.9	10.4	1.8	31.8	6.2	7.3	13.9	144.5	78.8	35.8	438	377
Cabarrus	15.2	0.2	3.6	31.5	8.6	4.8	7.0	227.4	103.6	76.3	658	513
Caldwell	7.0	1.1	2.4	23.6	6.8	3.1	2.7	130.4	77.2	30.9	408	295
Camden	1.5	0.0	0.2	2.8	0.7	0.2	1.1	12.0	8.2	3.2	485	357
Carteret	20.8	13.4	8.6	16.4	7.6	2.3	2.8	146.5	53.3	41.4	693	485
Caswell	2.3	0.0	0.8	19.7	3.0	1.1	0.9	32.4	20.6	8.3	381	257
Catawba	30.1	0.6	11.2	27.0	8.5	4.8	29.4	358.8	139.7	83.4	640	473
Chatham	6.1	12.3	1.4	15.2	2.9	1.3	7.3	74.4	33.8	27.4	611	469
Cherokee	6.3	0.3	0.9	18.0	3.5	1.3	2.4	40.7	24.0	10.3	460	282

1. October 1, 1998 to September 30, 1999.   2. State totals may include programs not allocated by county.   3. Based on the resident population estimated as of July 1 of the year shown.   4. Bronx, Kings, Queens, and Richmond Counties included with New York County.

Table B. States and Counties — Local Government Finances, Government Employment, and Elections

STATE County	Total (mil dol) [183]	Per capita[1] (dollars) [184]	Education [185]	Health and hospitals [186]	Police protection [187]	Public welfare [188]	Highways [189]	Total (mil dol) [190]	Per capita[1] (dollars) [191]	Federal civilian [192]	Federal military [193]	State and local [194]	Democratic [195]	Republican [196]	All other [197]
NEW YORK—Cont'd															
Genesee	254.4	4 116	46.5	2.6	2.1	11.1	5.0	100.0	1 617	577	124	4 686	39.1	55.5	5.4
Greene	146.3	3 057	50.1	3.1	1.7	10.4	8.9	39.0	815	112	97	3 711	40.2	53.7	6.1
Hamilton	30.1	5 766	39.2	5.2	1.4	3.4	17.1	6.4	1 237	15	11	617	30.3	64.9	4.9
Herkimer	221.6	3 373	57.9	3.4	1.8	8.4	8.4	92.4	1 406	136	136	4 528	44.1	51.1	4.8
Jefferson	370.0	3 271	47.6	3.9	2.2	11.0	7.5	297.2	2 627	2 834	10 891	7 868	46.1	50.0	3.9
Kings	(3)	(3)	(3)	(3)	(3)	(3)	(3)	(3)	(3)	8 778	5 023	23 909	80.6	15.7	3.7
Lewis	108.3	3 840	39.8	23.0	0.8	8.1	8.2	44.6	1 581	65	56	2 061	39.7	55.9	4.5
Livingston	190.4	2 863	47.5	3.6	2.2	20.9	7.9	84.2	1 266	165	134	6 668	38.5	56.0	5.5
Madison	222.9	3 111	58.9	3.0	1.7	6.2	8.1	127.2	1 776	162	144	4 016	42.4	52.5	5.2
Monroe	2 740.4	3 818	44.1	4.2	3.9	15.5	3.2	1 861.9	2 594	3 105	1 540	42 922	50.9	44.5	4.6
Montgomery	192.7	3 745	45.3	2.1	2.5	12.0	5.2	110.5	2 148	119	103	2 935	49.3	46.9	3.8
Nassau	6 346.0	4 868	40.8	6.3	8.6	7.1	3.3	4 870.5	3 736	7 094	2 990	71 876	57.9	38.5	3.6
New York	(3)42 603.8	(3)5 802	(3)22.2	(3)9.5	(3)6.8	(3)17.5	(3)2.5	(3)52 567.4	(3)7 159	32 214	3 362	421 912	79.8	14.2	6.0
Niagara	814.2	3 697	48.1	2.5	3.4	11.4	4.4	661.7	3 004	1 166	458	11 366	51.2	43.9	4.9
Oneida	834.9	3 580	42.9	2.1	2.8	11.9	4.8	421.4	1 807	2 198	601	20 369	45.8	49.6	4.6
Onondaga	1 676.2	3 632	43.9	2.4	3.6	14.1	4.7	1 078.8	2 338	4 332	1 269	35 494	54.0	41.1	4.9
Ontario	343.9	3 440	52.8	3.4	2.6	8.5	6.0	288.2	2 883	1 225	203	6 729	43.0	52.0	5.0
Orange	1 533.0	4 686	38.2	1.9	2.9	10.3	3.1	658.7	2 013	5 516	6 449	19 429	46.0	49.7	4.4
Orleans	127.3	2 846	52.0	3.7	2.5	14.6	6.4	53.0	1 185	92	90	4 299	37.8	58.1	4.1
Oswego	448.8	3 581	49.2	2.4	2.9	11.5	6.9	231.3	1 846	243	268	8 830	47.2	48.0	4.9
Otsego	177.4	2 885	50.5	3.4	1.5	13.9	10.2	88.4	1 438	171	124	4 344	45.2	48.2	6.6
Putnam	293.1	3 173	56.0	3.1	4.2	4.5	6.5	127.3	1 378	208	189	3 575	43.5	51.4	5.1
Queens	(3)	(3)	(3)	(3)	(3)	(3)	(3)	(3)	(3)	12 923	4 132	20 298	75.0	22.0	3.0
Rensselaer	572.3	3 708	53.0	2.3	2.4	11.9	3.7	318.2	2 061	395	337	9 691	50.9	43.2	5.9
Richmond	(3)	(3)	(3)	(3)	(3)	(3)	(3)	(3)	(3)	1 264	1 144	5 455	51.9	45.0	3.1
Rockland	1 152.2	4 117	45.2	7.9	4.8	8.3	3.9	557.8	1 993	668	570	18 319	56.7	39.5	3.8
St. Lawrence	369.2	3 234	43.9	9.7	1.8	10.9	7.4	187.3	1 641	501	253	10 135	53.8	41.4	4.9
Saratoga	519.4	2 642	57.8	2.5	2.3	9.4	5.7	256.2	1 303	388	1 667	10 867	45.6	49.0	5.3
Schenectady	491.9	3 341	44.2	1.8	3.6	19.0	4.4	226.4	1 538	727	368	9 221	53.1	41.8	5.2
Schoharie	107.1	3 298	58.1	3.0	1.0	8.5	9.9	53.4	1 645	93	66	2 574	39.8	55.1	5.2
Schuyler	49.7	2 592	44.7	6.9	1.5	10.5	10.7	20.7	1 080	56	39	1 034	40.5	53.7	5.8
Seneca	97.3	2 965	55.6	3.4	2.5	9.3	6.0	60.6	1 847	223	70	2 197	47.7	47.0	5.3
Steuben	381.9	3 855	58.2	3.3	1.4	10.7	8.5	165.2	1 668	955	199	6 865	36.0	59.7	4.3
Suffolk	5 546.5	4 070	52.2	2.6	6.8	6.7	2.9	3 577.2	2 625	12 696	3 023	83 523	53.4	42.0	4.6
Sullivan	320.4	4 554	41.1	5.5	2.1	13.4	9.0	217.9	3 097	222	140	5 681	50.3	44.5	5.2
Tioga	145.1	2 739	54.5	4.2	2.2	9.7	6.2	45.2	853	173	113	2 443	40.8	54.5	4.7
Tompkins	289.6	2 996	47.8	4.5	2.9	9.3	5.6	195.3	2 021	315	216	5 814	54.4	33.3	12.2
Ulster	600.5	3 597	48.4	3.0	2.6	15.1	5.8	270.1	1 618	464	351	12 625	48.8	42.8	8.5
Warren	220.3	3 560	46.0	4.7	3.0	9.7	7.6	126.6	2 045	268	132	4 070	42.6	52.4	5.0
Washington	197.5	3 255	55.0	2.4	1.7	12.9	7.5	115.5	1 904	136	123	4 918	40.9	53.5	5.6
Wayne	314.7	3 302	54.0	5.5	1.9	12.0	5.4	159.2	1 671	199	193	6 675	39.1	56.6	4.3
Westchester	4 269.8	4 764	38.4	10.1	4.6	10.7	2.7	2 024.3	2 259	6 022	1 820	54 302	58.6	37.5	3.9
Wyoming	136.4	3 060	37.5	23.7	2.4	8.9	10.5	39.6	887	113	89	4 138	33.7	61.3	5.0
Yates	60.1	2 492	43.6	2.9	3.1	9.1	13.2	22.4	927	76	49	1 031	39.4	55.4	5.2
NORTH CAROLINA	X	X	X	X	X	X	X	X	X	61 370	120 100	533 782	43.1	56.0	0.9
Alamance	228.8	1 940	47.0	10.3	5.2	5.4	2.0	169.1	1 434	271	371	5 789	NA	NA	NA
Alexander	37.9	1 236	64.0	5.8	4.1	8.1	0.8	3.4	111	54	97	1 245	NA	NA	NA
Alleghany	17.0	1 741	58.3	4.1	3.4	6.3	0.4	7.0	720	49	31	489	NA	NA	NA
Anson	85.4	3 510	38.0	20.6	2.4	4.6	0.8	25.9	1 064	63	76	2 305	NA	NA	NA
Ashe	30.1	1 257	63.7	2.4	3.3	10.9	1.5	4.7	198	76	75	1 045	NA	NA	NA
Avery	28.5	1 822	55.8	3.3	3.9	5.7	1.9	2.3	147	51	49	943	NA	NA	NA
Beaufort	119.3	2 698	44.0	23.0	3.2	6.2	0.6	57.6	1 302	132	138	2 909	NA	NA	NA
Bertie	35.8	1 752	62.8	4.5	3.9	11.5	1.6	2.1	103	101	64	1 125	NA	NA	NA
Bladen	89.7	2 932	43.4	22.4	3.2	7.2	1.1	81.3	2 658	119	95	2 270	NA	NA	NA
Brunswick	142.6	2 163	45.0	11.2	5.1	5.7	1.8	50.9	772	344	260	3 401	NA	NA	NA
Buncombe	434.7	2 255	44.2	9.6	5.4	5.6	2.4	326.5	1 694	2 654	665	12 449	NA	NA	NA
Burke	140.1	1 714	58.0	3.3	6.0	6.6	1.6	69.8	854	151	257	7 881	NA	NA	NA
Cabarrus	224.2	1 933	46.4	5.2	6.0	7.0	2.1	223.2	1 924	248	373	8 866	NA	NA	NA
Caldwell	134.2	1 775	57.0	5.8	4.5	9.2	1.8	26.8	355	131	236	3 866	NA	NA	NA
Camden	11.7	1 744	66.7	0.4	2.5	9.5	0.0	1.5	219	12	21	337	NA	NA	NA
Carteret	163.1	2 731	37.7	29.8	5.1	4.9	1.2	60.1	1 006	252	414	3 948	NA	NA	NA
Caswell	32.3	1 491	58.5	8.6	3.6	9.0	0.1	7.8	357	51	69	1 587	NA	NA	NA
Catawba	351.0	2 693	37.2	26.3	3.6	6.8	3.7	162.0	1 242	548	413	7 973	NA	NA	NA
Chatham	85.1	1 897	58.9	7.1	4.3	6.7	1.0	49.9	1 112	131	141	1 905	NA	NA	NA
Cherokee	44.4	1 991	65.5	4.7	3.1	6.6	1.1	15.5	694	148	71	1 191	NA	NA	NA

1. Based on the resident population estimated as of July 1 of the year shown.   3. Bronx, Kings, Queens, and Richmond Counties included with New York County.

Table B. States and Counties — Land Area and Population

| STATE/County code | MSA/PMSA/NECMA code[1] | County Type[2] | STATE County | Land area,[3] (sq km) 1990 | Population and population characteristics, 1999 | | | Race (percent) | | | | | Age (percent) | | | | | |
| | | | | | Total persons | Rank | Per square kilometer | White | Black | Am. Indian, Eskimo, Aleut | Asian and Pacific Islander | Percent Hispanic[4] | Under 5 years | 5 to 17 years | 18 to 24 years | 25 to 34 years | 35 to 44 years | 45 to 54 years |
				1	2	3	4	5	6	7	8	9	10	11	12	13	14	15
			NORTH CAROLINA—Cont'd															
37 041	...	7	Chowan	447	14 309	2 112	32.0	61.2	38.3	0.2	0.4	1.2	6.6	20.1	6.0	11.5	14.9	12.8
37 043	...	9	Clay	556	8 745	2 528	15.7	98.2	1.1	0.6	0.2	1.2	4.8	18.9	5.5	10.0	14.8	13.3
37 045	...	4	Cleveland	1 203	94 024	537	78.2	77.7	21.4	0.1	0.8	0.9	6.7	18.7	8.3	12.8	15.8	14.3
37 047	...	6	Columbus	2 426	52 946	863	21.8	65.3	31.3	3.2	0.2	0.9	6.5	21.2	7.0	12.5	15.5	13.9
37 049	...	5	Craven	1 801	89 391	563	49.6	71.8	26.2	0.5	1.6	4.3	8.5	19.1	10.8	14.8	14.0	10.6
37 051	2560	2	Cumberland	1 692	283 650	193	167.6	63.3	31.3	1.8	3.6	9.3	9.3	20.5	13.5	17.0	14.4	10.5
37 053	5720	1	Currituck	678	18 305	1 854	27.0	87.6	11.1	0.6	0.7	1.9	7.5	19.8	6.2	14.5	16.0	14.0
37 055	...	7	Dare	989	29 640	1 387	30.0	95.5	3.7	0.2	0.6	1.8	7.0	16.3	6.1	15.8	17.5	12.6
37 057	3120	2	Davidson	1 430	142 852	369	99.9	88.9	10.0	0.4	0.6	1.0	6.7	18.4	7.7	13.9	16.4	14.7
37 059	3120	2	Davie	687	32 693	1 292	47.6	90.1	9.2	0.4	0.3	1.0	5.8	18.7	6.8	12.4	16.8	14.7
37 061	...	6	Duplin	2 118	43 379	1 014	20.5	66.0	33.4	0.3	0.2	5.0	6.8	20.6	7.6	13.0	15.5	13.4
37 063	6640	2	Durham	753	204 097	266	271.0	59.4	37.4	0.3	2.9	2.2	7.2	17.0	11.1	17.2	17.9	11.9
37 065	6895	3	Edgecombe	1 308	54 659	844	41.8	43.0	56.6	0.2	0.2	0.8	7.2	21.9	7.8	13.9	16.5	12.9
37 067	3120	2	Forsyth	1 061	288 810	188	272.2	73.5	25.2	0.2	1.1	1.7	6.7	16.6	9.0	14.9	16.6	13.5
37 069	6640	6	Franklin	1 273	45 612	977	35.8	62.8	36.6	0.2	0.3	1.5	6.7	19.2	8.2	14.6	16.6	13.9
37 071	1520	0	Gaston	923	185 169	288	200.6	85.5	13.3	0.3	0.9	1.1	7.2	19.2	8.2	13.6	16.1	13.4
37 073	...	8	Gates	882	10 180	2 408	11.5	54.1	45.5	0.1	0.2	0.5	6.9	19.5	6.9	13.8	14.5	13.4
37 075	...	9	Graham	756	7 609	2 631	10.1	92.3	0.5	6.9	0.2	0.9	5.8	17.9	7.5	10.9	14.6	14.3
37 077	...	6	Granville	1 376	44 546	992	32.4	59.4	39.8	0.3	0.5	1.8	6.5	18.3	7.8	15.0	16.6	14.6
37 079	...	8	Greene	688	18 537	1 845	26.9	56.4	43.4	0.1	0.1	2.2	6.2	20.1	7.4	15.2	16.7	13.3
37 081	3120	2	Guilford	1 684	391 380	147	232.4	71.0	26.6	0.5	1.8	1.7	6.5	16.9	10.4	14.6	16.7	13.5
37 083	...	4	Halifax	1 879	55 832	829	29.7	46.0	50.1	3.4	0.4	0.8	6.7	21.1	7.3	13.0	15.2	12.6
37 085	...	6	Harnett	1 541	84 501	595	54.8	75.2	23.0	1.0	0.8	3.5	8.2	19.5	11.0	14.2	14.9	12.7
37 087	...	6	Haywood	1 435	52 002	878	36.2	97.9	1.5	0.4	0.2	1.1	5.6	15.8	6.4	11.0	14.6	15.1
37 089	...	6	Henderson	968	82 264	617	85.0	95.4	3.5	0.3	0.7	2.7	5.8	16.4	5.8	11.1	14.6	13.1
37 091	...	6	Hertford	916	21 937	1 661	23.9	40.7	57.7	1.1	0.5	0.7	6.6	20.9	7.8	11.9	14.8	13.3
37 093	...	6	Hoke	1 013	31 324	1 341	30.9	40.9	43.0	15.4	0.7	1.7	8.5	24.1	9.4	15.1	15.2	11.9
37 095	...	9	Hyde	1 587	5 828	2 783	3.7	63.3	36.3	0.3	0.1	1.8	5.7	18.8	8.3	13.7	16.3	12.9
37 097	...	4	Iredell	1 488	117 519	448	79.0	82.8	16.3	0.2	0.7	1.6	6.8	18.5	7.7	13.6	16.0	14.6
37 099	...	7	Jackson	1 271	30 260	1 368	23.8	86.4	1.7	11.3	0.6	1.2	5.2	16.4	15.8	11.1	14.5	13.8
37 101	6640	2	Johnston	2 051	110 850	475	54.0	80.9	18.5	0.3	0.4	3.3	7.3	19.4	7.8	14.4	16.9	14.6
37 103	...	8	Jones	1 226	9 320	2 484	7.6	60.0	39.6	0.1	0.3	1.2	7.2	19.8	6.4	12.7	14.3	13.1
37 105	...	6	Lee	666	49 452	916	74.3	75.6	23.1	0.5	0.9	3.7	7.3	19.8	7.3	13.4	16.1	13.2
37 107	...	4	Lenoir	1 036	58 842	804	56.8	59.5	39.9	0.1	0.5	1.5	6.3	20.4	7.2	12.6	15.7	13.8
37 109	1520	1	Lincoln	774	58 895	803	76.1	90.8	8.3	0.3	0.6	2.6	7.1	18.8	7.7	13.6	16.2	14.3
37 111	...	6	McDowell	1 144	40 565	1 072	35.5	94.1	4.7	0.2	1.0	0.7	6.2	18.3	7.5	13.3	16.0	14.2
37 113	...	7	Macon	1 338	28 906	1 413	21.6	97.6	1.6	0.4	0.5	1.4	5.3	15.6	5.6	10.1	14.3	14.4
37 115	0480	3	Madison	1 164	18 906	1 824	16.2	98.6	0.9	0.1	0.4	1.1	5.7	17.6	9.6	11.1	15.3	14.1
37 117	...	6	Martin	1 198	26 133	1 489	21.8	54.5	45.1	0.1	0.3	0.6	6.6	20.4	7.2	12.0	15.5	13.5
37 119	1520	0	Mecklenburg	1 366	648 400	76	474.7	70.2	26.5	0.4	2.8	2.7	7.6	18.0	9.1	17.3	17.9	13.0
37 121	...	9	Mitchell	574	14 763	2 084	25.7	99.1	0.4	0.1	0.3	0.8	5.7	16.9	6.1	11.5	14.8	14.3
37 123	...	7	Montgomery	1 272	24 323	1 560	19.1	72.8	25.6	0.4	1.2	4.8	6.9	20.0	8.3	13.3	15.4	12.5
37 125	...	6	Moore	1 810	72 885	674	40.3	80.3	18.6	0.6	0.4	1.7	6.0	17.3	6.2	11.6	13.4	11.8
37 127	6895	3	Nash	1 399	92 369	547	66.0	67.3	31.9	0.4	0.5	1.5	6.5	19.1	7.7	13.8	16.7	13.0
37 129	9200	3	New Hanover	515	150 895	344	293.0	78.1	20.6	0.4	0.9	1.6	6.2	17.6	9.9	13.7	16.9	13.3
37 131	...	9	Northampton	1 389	21 234	1 694	15.3	39.8	59.9	0.2	0.1	0.9	5.9	19.2	6.8	12.0	14.5	13.3
37 133	3605	3	Onslow	1 986	142 480	371	71.7	76.4	19.3	0.7	3.6	9.8	9.9	17.4	21.8	19.5	12.4	7.4
37 135	6640	2	Orange	1 035	111 533	472	107.8	79.2	16.4	0.4	4.1	2.9	6.1	14.9	18.1	16.7	16.7	11.2
37 137	...	9	Pamlico	873	12 314	2 263	14.1	73.2	26.2	0.3	0.3	1.2	5.8	17.9	5.5	11.0	14.2	13.6
37 139	...	7	Pasquotank	588	35 629	1 202	60.6	60.1	38.7	0.2	1.0	1.8	7.5	19.8	10.4	14.4	14.5	11.5
37 141	...	8	Pender	2 255	40 293	1 078	17.9	67.6	31.7	0.4	0.3	2.0	6.6	18.6	7.2	13.1	16.0	14.4
37 143	...	9	Perquimans	640	11 294	2 327	17.6	66.3	33.2	0.2	0.3	0.5	6.2	18.5	5.9	11.7	13.2	13.5
37 145	...	6	Person	1 016	33 856	1 260	33.3	68.6	30.7	0.7	0.1	1.6	6.9	18.7	7.1	13.9	16.1	14.0
37 147	3150	3	Pitt	1 688	127 960	409	75.8	64.3	34.3	0.2	1.2	1.8	7.2	18.8	14.3	14.9	15.8	11.4
37 149	...	8	Polk	616	16 893	1 933	27.4	91.9	7.6	0.1	0.3	1.8	5.3	15.2	5.6	10.1	13.8	13.3
37 151	3120	2	Randolph	2 040	123 410	426	60.5	92.7	6.2	0.5	0.6	1.5	7.1	18.2	7.6	14.0	16.3	14.3
37 153	...	7	Richmond	1 228	45 718	975	37.2	68.5	29.5	1.3	0.8	1.2	6.7	21.1	8.2	12.1	14.9	13.2
37 155	...	4	Robeson	2 458	116 597	453	47.4	34.3	24.3	41.0	0.4	1.1	7.9	23.4	9.0	14.0	15.2	11.9
37 157	...	4	Rockingham	1 467	90 287	557	61.5	78.7	20.7	0.2	0.4	1.5	6.6	18.2	7.4	13.1	16.1	14.1
37 159	1520	1	Rowan	1 325	126 585	414	95.5	82.4	16.6	0.3	0.7	1.3	6.9	18.3	8.0	13.6	15.5	13.5
37 161	...	6	Rutherford	1 461	61 507	777	42.1	87.8	11.7	0.2	0.3	1.3	6.6	19.0	7.6	12.1	14.9	13.7
37 163	...	6	Sampson	2 449	52 812	865	21.6	63.9	33.6	2.2	0.3	3.1	6.4	21.0	7.4	12.6	15.3	13.7
37 165	...	7	Scotland	827	35 882	1 196	43.4	55.4	36.4	7.8	0.4	1.8	7.1	23.2	8.9	12.2	16.6	13.0
37 167	...	6	Stanly	1 023	56 547	823	55.3	87.0	11.8	0.3	0.8	1.3	7.3	18.6	7.9	12.7	15.4	13.5
37 169	3120	2	Stokes	1 170	43 894	1 003	37.5	93.4	6.0	0.2	0.4	1.6	6.4	19.2	7.5	13.7	16.6	14.9
37 171	...	6	Surry	1 390	67 940	714	48.9	94.8	4.8	0.1	0.3	2.1	6.2	17.8	7.5	12.4	15.4	14.6

1. MSA = Metropolitan Statistical Area. PMSA = Primary MSA. NECMA = New England County Metropolitan Area. See Appendix A for explanation of these concepts. See Appendix B for list of metropolitan areas identified by type, with component counties.   2. County typology code from the Economic Research Service of USDA. See Appendix A for definition.   3. Dry land or land partially or temporarily covered by water.   4. Hispanic persons may be of any race.

Table B. States and Counties — **Population and Households**

STATE County	55 to 64 years	65 to 74 years	75 years and over	Percent female	1990	1980	1980–1990	1990–1999	Births	Deaths	Net migration	Number	Percent change, 1980–1990	Persons per house-hold	Female family house-holder[1]	One person
	16	17	18	19	20	21	22	23	24	25	26	27	28	29	30	31
NORTH CAROLINA—Cont'd																
Chowan	10.5	9.2	8.4	53.4	13 506	12 558	7.5	5.9	1 906	1 634	574	5 113	17.5	2.59	15.0	24.2
Clay	11.0	12.1	9.6	51.0	7 155	6 619	8.1	22.2	647	839	1 824	2 928	17.6	2.44	6.9	23.9
Cleveland	9.8	7.4	6.3	52.0	84 958	83 435	1.5	10.7	12 097	8 462	5 637	32 037	12.6	2.59	13.0	21.9
Columbus	9.8	7.7	6.0	52.3	49 587	51 037	-2.8	6.8	6 931	5 271	1 850	18 459	6.9	2.65	14.9	23.6
Craven	8.2	8.5	5.6	50.4	81 812	71 043	14.9	9.3	14 499	6 593	-2 398	29 542	25.7	2.64	11.9	20.7
Cumberland	6.5	5.1	3.2	49.5	274 713	247 160	11.1	3.3	52 761	16 136	-41 408	91 500	22.1	2.77	14.1	19.4
Currituck	10.3	6.7	5.0	49.6	13 736	11 089	23.9	33.3	1 696	1 377	4 209	5 038	29.3	2.68	8.1	19.5
Dare	10.3	8.8	5.5	50.3	22 746	13 377	70.0	30.3	2 797	1 773	5 843	9 349	74.5	2.41	7.3	24.2
Davidson	9.7	6.9	5.6	50.9	126 688	113 162	11.9	12.8	16 619	10 742	10 572	48 944	22.3	2.56	10.5	21.0
Davie	10.0	8.0	6.7	50.9	27 859	24 599	13.3	17.4	3 324	2 555	4 134	10 785	26.3	2.55	8.8	20.8
Duplin	9.7	7.3	6.1	51.6	39 995	40 952	-2.3	8.5	6 307	4 664	1 841	14 925	6.7	2.64	14.1	23.8
Durham	7.2	5.6	5.1	52.8	181 844	152 235	19.5	12.2	28 709	14 985	9 034	72 297	30.0	2.40	14.3	28.9
Edgecombe	8.8	6.1	5.0	54.3	56 692	55 988	1.3	-3.6	8 284	5 691	-4 396	20 319	10.4	2.75	21.1	23.1
Forsyth	9.3	7.0	6.3	53.0	265 855	243 704	9.1	8.6	37 807	23 356	9 352	107 419	19.2	2.40	13.1	27.8
Franklin	9.1	6.2	5.5	51.5	36 414	30 055	21.2	25.3	5 070	3 572	7 730	13 503	35.3	2.61	13.8	23.1
Gaston	9.6	6.8	5.8	52.0	174 769	162 568	7.7	6.0	24 295	15 950	2 580	65 347	15.9	2.64	12.9	20.8
Gates	10.0	8.2	6.8	50.6	9 305	8 875	4.8	9.4	1 048	1 065	911	3 352	16.0	2.75	12.1	21.0
Graham	10.6	9.0	8.2	49.8	7 196	7 217	-0.3	5.7	837	815	412	2 772	11.7	2.59	8.9	20.3
Granville	9.4	6.4	5.4	50.0	38 341	34 043	12.6	16.2	5 187	3 704	4 758	13 134	25.7	2.68	14.1	22.0
Greene	9.5	6.6	5.3	49.0	15 384	16 117	-4.5	20.5	1 961	1 385	2 605	5 395	6.6	2.72	16.2	22.0
Guilford	9.2	6.5	5.7	52.7	347 431	317 154	9.5	12.6	48 473	30 166	26 668	137 706	20.7	2.44	12.8	26.6
Halifax	9.6	7.9	6.7	52.4	55 516	55 076	0.8	0.6	7 749	6 151	-1 105	20 335	11.2	2.66	19.8	24.6
Harnett	9.0	5.7	4.8	51.3	67 833	59 570	13.9	24.6	12 112	6 199	10 321	25 150	24.8	2.60	12.5	23.0
Haywood	11.6	10.5	9.3	52.3	46 948	46 495	1.0	10.8	5 067	5 290	5 422	19 211	13.0	2.40	9.2	23.9
Henderson	11.2	11.8	10.4	51.8	69 747	58 580	18.3	17.9	7 965	8 948	13 771	28 709	28.2	2.38	8.2	23.8
Hertford	9.6	8.2	7.1	54.0	22 317	23 368	-4.5	-1.7	2 823	2 487	-658	8 150	8.7	2.65	18.1	25.3
Hoke	8.2	4.4	3.3	50.4	22 856	20 383	12.1	37.0	4 451	1 831	5 806	7 405	22.9	2.92	21.7	19.2
Hyde	9.5	7.5	7.7	46.8	5 411	5 873	-7.9	7.7	570	614	465	2 094	3.2	2.57	15.3	24.6
Iredell	10.1	6.8	5.9	51.5	93 205	82 538	12.6	26.1	13 595	8 779	19 516	35 573	22.1	2.59	11.3	21.5
Jackson	9.4	7.1	6.8	51.5	26 835	25 811	4.0	12.8	2 925	2 375	2 948	9 683	13.9	2.46	10.1	23.2
Johnston	9.4	5.8	4.5	51.1	81 306	70 599	15.2	36.3	13 916	7 859	23 356	31 566	25.5	2.55	11.5	23.6
Jones	9.7	9.7	6.9	53.2	9 361	9 705	-3.0	-0.4	1 062	972	-120	3 492	9.0	2.70	13.8	22.2
Lee	9.9	7.7	5.4	51.6	41 370	36 718	12.7	19.5	6 549	4 022	5 623	15 689	21.5	2.59	13.6	22.2
Lenoir	9.8	8.1	6.2	53.4	57 274	59 819	-4.3	2.7	8 048	6 193	-120	21 938	6.1	2.54	17.3	26.0
Lincoln	9.2	7.4	5.6	50.9	50 319	42 372	18.8	17.0	7 063	4 306	5 994	18 764	27.9	2.65	9.7	19.1
McDowell	10.1	7.6	6.8	50.2	35 681	35 135	1.6	13.7	4 378	3 452	4 028	13 680	11.9	2.56	10.0	21.9
Macon	12.8	11.3	10.6	51.9	23 504	20 178	16.5	23.0	2 497	3 028	6 013	9 834	27.7	2.34	7.9	24.3
Madison	10.5	8.0	8.1	50.4	16 953	16 827	0.7	11.5	1 916	1 848	1 932	6 488	11.0	2.48	8.0	23.3
Martin	9.8	8.3	6.6	53.2	25 078	25 948	-3.4	4.2	3 190	2 624	564	9 317	8.1	2.66	16.3	23.8
Mecklenburg	7.9	5.1	4.1	51.9	511 211	404 270	26.5	26.8	85 340	37 016	89 192	200 219	36.2	2.50	12.5	26.0
Mitchell	11.7	9.3	9.7	51.9	14 433	14 428	0.0	2.3	1 503	1 749	638	5 779	9.8	2.47	8.3	21.9
Montgomery	8.7	8.3	6.5	49.4	23 359	22 469	3.9	4.1	3 472	2 093	-336	8 290	6.8	2.69	13.5	22.2
Moore	11.3	13.3	9.2	52.1	59 000	50 505	16.8	23.5	7 596	6 758	13 234	23 827	28.2	2.43	10.4	23.8
Nash	8.8	8.1	6.2	52.3	76 677	67 153	14.2	20.5	11 287	7 306	12 165	29 041	23.7	2.60	13.7	23.8
New Hanover	9.1	7.6	5.7	52.5	120 284	103 471	16.2	25.4	16 992	11 081	25 052	48 139	27.7	2.43	13.3	25.8
Northampton	10.7	10.0	7.6	51.8	21 004	22 195	-6.3	1.1	2 516	2 539	314	7 591	7.0	2.64	18.9	23.9
Onslow	4.7	4.2	2.7	42.7	149 838	112 784	32.9	-4.9	30 591	6 169	-47 584	40 658	34.2	2.84	9.5	15.4
Orange	6.6	5.2	4.5	52.4	93 662	77 055	21.8	19.1	10 676	5 492	13 074	36 104	33.5	2.34	9.4	28.0
Pamlico	12.2	10.8	8.8	52.5	11 368	10 398	9.3	8.3	1 110	1 281	1 154	4 523	23.0	2.49	12.1	23.3
Pasquotank	8.4	7.2	6.3	51.5	31 298	28 462	10.0	13.8	4 181	3 222	3 292	11 384	17.1	2.63	14.8	23.9
Pender	10.6	8.1	5.3	50.6	28 855	22 262	29.6	39.6	4 069	3 012	10 403	11 112	47.9	2.56	12.3	21.5
Perquimans	11.6	10.6	8.7	52.1	10 447	9 486	10.1	8.1	1 083	1 218	999	3 988	21.5	2.58	11.7	21.6
Person	9.7	7.2	6.4	52.1	30 180	29 164	3.5	12.2	3 960	3 027	2 823	11 423	15.9	2.61	13.5	22.8
Pitt	7.7	5.6	4.4	52.5	108 480	90 146	20.3	18.0	16 176	8 841	8 506	40 491	34.1	2.53	14.5	25.7
Polk	11.9	12.4	12.6	52.8	14 458	12 984	11.0	16.8	1 506	2 072	3 100	6 110	21.6	2.32	8.4	26.2
Randolph	9.4	7.3	5.9	51.1	106 546	91 300	16.7	15.8	14 841	8 866	11 165	41 096	24.8	2.57	9.6	20.9
Richmond	9.7	8.0	6.2	52.1	44 511	45 161	-1.4	2.7	6 301	4 740	-216	16 793	6.2	2.59	15.2	24.9
Robeson	7.9	6.0	4.6	52.5	105 170	101 610	3.5	10.9	18 026	9 792	3 499	36 154	15.2	2.85	20.3	21.8
Rockingham	9.9	7.8	6.8	52.3	86 064	83 426	3.2	4.9	10 648	8 692	2 523	33 446	12.9	2.55	12.5	23.8
Rowan	10.1	7.4	6.6	51.2	110 605	99 186	11.5	14.4	14 129	11 645	13 733	42 512	18.3	2.52	10.9	24.1
Rutherford	10.2	8.2	7.7	51.8	56 956	53 787	5.8	8.0	7 490	6 130	3 404	22 198	15.5	2.53	11.1	23.7
Sampson	9.7	7.6	6.2	52.0	47 297	49 687	-4.8	11.7	6 845	5 116	3 919	17 526	5.3	2.67	14.4	22.7
Scotland	7.9	6.3	4.8	53.3	33 763	32 273	4.6	6.3	5 266	3 150	116	11 837	14.4	2.76	19.8	22.1
Stanly	10.1	7.8	6.7	51.7	51 765	48 517	6.7	9.2	6 584	5 147	3 482	19 747	13.6	2.57	10.0	22.3
Stokes	8.8	6.7	6.1	50.9	37 224	33 086	12.5	17.9	4 620	3 186	5 366	14 123	25.5	2.61	9.0	20.0
Surry	10.4	8.2	7.5	52.0	61 704	59 449	3.8	10.1	8 091	6 307	4 655	24 252	13.9	2.51	9.7	22.6

1. No spouse present.

STATE County	Births, average 1996–1998 Total	Births, average 1996–1998 Rate[1]	Deaths Number Total	Deaths Number Infant[2]	Deaths Rate Total[1]	Deaths Rate Infant[3]	Physicians,[4] 1998 Number	Physicians,[4] 1998 Rate[5]	Hospitals,[4] 1998 Number	Hospitals,[4] 1998 Beds Number	Hospitals,[4] 1998 Beds Rate[5]	Medicare enrollees 1999	Serious crimes Total Number	Serious crimes Total Rate[7]
	32	33	34	35	36	37	38	39	40	41	42	43	44	45
NORTH CAROLINA—Cont'd														
Chowan	216	15.2	172	3	12.1	13.9	26	183	1	111	782	2 914	516	3 585
Clay	64	7.7	104	1	12.5	15.6	8	93	0	0	0	2 109	116	1 377
Cleveland	1 296	14.1	940	12	10.2	9.0	112	121	3	421	454	16 042	4 813	5 275
Columbus	775	14.8	591	8	11.3	9.9	44	84	1	136	258	9 890	3 238	6 070
Craven	1 568	17.9	782	10	8.9	6.6	193	219	1	276	313	14 626	4 265	4 833
Cumberland	5 602	19.7	1 820	61	6.4	10.9	534	188	2	515	181	28 345	17 688	6 127
Currituck	180	10.4	149	3	8.6	16.7	8	45	0	0	0	2 399	660	3 794
Dare	305	11.0	206	2	7.4	6.6	19	66	0	0	0	4 229	1 781	6 287
Davidson	1 809	13.0	1 223	14	8.8	7.7	91	64	2	195	138	18 926	4 536	3 207
Davie	376	12.0	315	2	10.1	6.2	40	125	1	46	143	5 154	1 019	3 214
Duplin	740	17.2	501	7	11.7	9.9	23	53	1	80	186	7 116	1 732	3 949
Durham	3 196	16.0	1 723	32	8.6	10.0	1 735	857	2	1 187	586	25 014	18 791	9 261
Edgecombe	830	14.9	621	8	11.2	9.6	47	85	1	127	230	9 665	3 749	6 635
Forsyth	4 205	14.7	2 604	50	9.1	11.8	1 161	404	3	1 648	573	44 787	20 931	7 206
Franklin	568	13.0	403	3	9.2	5.3	24	54	1	67	150	5 619	1 419	3 207
Gaston	2 566	14.0	1 805	20	9.9	7.8	252	137	1	404	219	28 298	11 529	6 187
Gates	109	10.9	117	1	11.7	9.2	1	10	0	0	0	1 792	138	1 357
Graham	89	11.6	91	0	11.9	0.0	5	65	0	0	0	1 639	60	771
Granville	565	13.4	426	4	10.1	7.1	41	96	1	66	154	6 600	2 013	4 700
Greene	255	14.1	163	3	9.0	10.4	4	22	0	0	0	2 252	568	3 100
Guilford	5 388	14.1	3 337	53	8.7	9.9	857	221	3	1 155	298	55 746	28 388	7 314
Halifax	748	13.2	666	10	11.8	13.4	58	103	2	262	464	11 560	3 298	5 723
Harnett	1 380	17.1	712	12	8.8	8.7	60	73	2	134	163	9 611	4 323	5 426
Haywood	530	10.4	604	6	11.9	11.3	88	171	1	141	274	11 394	1 243	2 392
Henderson	935	11.8	1 026	10	12.9	10.7	200	247	2	281	348	20 651	2 334	2 894
Hertford	276	12.4	274	4	12.3	14.5	28	126	1	124	556	4 272	1 083	4 761
Hoke	574	19.4	212	5	7.2	9.3	7	23	0	0	0	2 465	1 396	4 673
Hyde	54	9.8	64	1	11.5	18.4	2	36	0	0	0	1 008	135	2 467
Iredell	1 565	14.3	1 019	13	9.3	8.5	195	172	3	442	390	16 950	5 037	4 552
Jackson	321	10.8	284	2	9.5	7.3	78	258	1	186	616	4 903	799	2 653
Johnston	1 721	16.8	933	15	9.1	8.5	65	61	1	127	119	13 859	5 090	4 915
Jones	102	10.8	113	1	12.0	9.8	5	53	0	0	0	1 789	132	1 447
Lee	756	15.7	448	8	9.3	11.0	86	174	1	137	278	8 411	3 433	6 974
Lenoir	853	14.4	682	11	11.5	13.3	97	164	1	252	427	11 344	3 802	6 274
Lincoln	792	13.9	496	5	8.7	6.7	57	98	1	75	129	8 534	2 283	3 927
McDowell	396	10.1	326	4	8.3	10.9	31	77	1	65	162	7 020	1 005	2 531
Macon	291	10.5	358	2	12.9	6.9	47	166	2	105	371	7 074	520	1 853
Madison	225	12.1	203	2	10.9	10.4	8	43	0	0	0	3 489	NA	NA
Martin	428	16.2	356	5	13.5	11.7	19	73	1	49	187	4 733	1 192	4 456
Mecklenburg	9 835	16.0	4 171	69	6.8	7.0	1 685	267	6	1 895	300	67 832	55 244	8 933
Mitchell	150	10.2	195	1	13.2	4.4	16	108	1	40	270	3 310	NA	NA
Montgomery	401	16.7	243	4	10.1	9.1	14	58	1	86	357	4 209	1 157	4 688
Moore	873	12.5	810	10	11.6	11.4	233	326	1	359	503	17 220	2 385	3 344
Nash	1 181	13.2	810	16	9.1	13.5	147	162	2	285	313	12 673	4 701	5 188
New Hanover	1 871	12.7	1 259	13	8.6	7.0	465	310	2	611	408	23 593	10 962	7 342
Northampton	250	11.8	277	5	13.1	18.6	4	19	0	0	0	4 565	501	3 748
Onslow	3 234	22.6	711	24	5.0	7.3	182	128	1	133	93	11 422	5 447	3 748
Orange	1 158	10.7	633	14	5.8	12.1	1 244	1 130	1	648	588	11 200	6 151	5 578
Pamlico	120	9.8	152	0	12.4	2.8	10	81	0	0	0	2 371	273	2 207
Pasquotank	443	12.7	344	9	9.8	20.3	73	206	1	130	366	5 541	1 420	4 083
Pender	430	11.3	347	2	9.2	5.4	18	46	1	66	167	6 115	1 207	3 124
Perquimans	108	9.7	139	2	12.5	18.6	4	35	0	0	0	2 429	292	2 580
Person	423	12.8	342	6	10.3	13.4	19	56	1	93	276	5 418	993	2 939
Pitt	1 833	14.8	996	25	8.0	13.8	559	441	1	571	451	15 761	10 161	8 259
Polk	163	9.8	237	3	14.3	18.4	42	249	1	26	154	4 464	406	2 418
Randolph	1 707	14.3	997	12	8.4	7.0	99	82	1	105	87	17 925	5 008	4 122
Richmond	672	14.6	513	7	11.1	10.4	35	76	2	193	418	8 357	2 694	5 745
Robeson	2 024	17.7	1 102	27	9.6	13.2	96	83	1	280	242	17 186	5 551	4 796
Rockingham	1 145	12.8	980	11	10.9	9.6	95	106	2	372	413	15 983	3 988	4 410
Rowan	1 582	12.8	1 341	12	10.9	7.8	188	150	1	238	190	18 139	4 359	3 472
Rutherford	786	13.1	698	6	11.6	7.2	74	122	1	114	187	11 215	2 054	3 399
Sampson	822	15.9	595	6	11.5	7.3	47	90	1	146	278	8 507	2 552	4 886
Scotland	571	16.0	361	7	10.1	12.3	49	137	1	174	486	5 145	2 255	6 313
Stanly	711	12.8	601	9	10.9	12.2	56	100	1	119	212	9 748	2 387	4 270
Stokes	517	12.1	364	3	8.6	5.8	15	35	1	93	215	5 328	1 011	2 329
Surry	915	13.8	729	7	11.0	7.3	73	109	2	253	377	13 219	2 397	3 547

1. Per 1,000 estimated resident population, average 1996–1998.   2. Deaths of infants under 1 year old.   3. Deaths of infants under 1 year old per 1,000 live births.   4. Data subject to copyright.   5. Per 100,000 resident population as of July 1 of the year shown.   6. Data for serious crimes have not been adjusted for underreporting; this may affect comparability between geographic areas and over time.   7. Per 100,000 population estimated by the FBI.

Table B. States and Counties — Crime, Education, Money Income, and Poverty

STATE County	Serious crimes known to police, 1998[1] (cont'd) Rate[2] Violent	Property	Education — School enrollment and attainment, 1990 — Enrollment[3] Total	Percent private	Attainment[4] (percent) High school graduate or more	Bachelor's degree or more	Local government expenditures, fiscal 1997[5] Total current expenditures (mil dol)	Current expenditures per student (dollars)	Money income 1989 Per capita[6] (dollars)	Households Median Dollars	Percent change, 1979-1989 (constant 1989 dollars)	Percent with $100,000 or more	Income and poverty, 1997 Median household income	Percent below poverty level All persons	Persons under 18	Persons 5-17 in families
	46	47	48	49	50	51	52	53	54	55	56	57	58	59	60	61
NORTH CAROLINA—Cont'd																
Chowan	424	3 161	3 168	4.6	63.3	12.2	13.8	5 396	10 606	20 397	6.0	1.9	27 900	18.7	27.3	25.4
Clay	119	1 258	1 615	3.0	62.9	12.6	6.8	5 359	9 456	18 532	7.9	0.9	26 800	15.2	23.0	21.6
Cleveland	587	4 688	19 330	8.5	63.5	11.1	84.0	5 059	11 875	26 476	4.2	1.8	33 552	13.2	20.5	17.2
Columbus	598	5 472	12 617	5.0	59.4	9.1	51.9	4 968	9 134	18 468	1.1	1.2	25 504	20.5	27.8	25.1
Craven	590	4 243	20 091	9.5	75.9	15.1	70.9	4 736	11 619	25 619	17.0	1.7	33 214	13.8	20.0	19.4
Cumberland	574	5 553	73 885	9.7	80.3	16.6	229.5	4 497	11 100	25 462	13.1	1.6	33 836	15.5	21.2	19.7
Currituck	385	3 409	3 078	5.4	67.7	8.2	17.2	5 610	12 630	27 905	30.2	1.2	36 287	10.8	16.4	16.3
Dare	247	6 040	4 547	12.2	81.0	21.4	25.0	5 740	15 107	29 322	29.1	3.8	35 258	8.1	12.5	12.5
Davidson	262	2 945	27 585	6.9	64.2	10.0	108.7	4 611	12 597	27 913	9.3	2.0	36 099	10.1	15.3	13.5
Davie	218	2 996	6 323	6.7	69.6	14.7	24.7	4 931	14 648	29 659	12.4	3.8	39 871	7.8	11.8	10.4
Duplin	461	3 488	9 603	4.5	56.4	6.6	38.5	4 578	9 406	19 695	5.6	0.8	27 384	18.4	24.9	21.6
Durham	981	8 280	51 606	26.7	78.9	33.4	165.2	5 686	15 030	30 526	18.3	3.3	40 007	12.4	19.4	17.4
Edgecombe	807	5 828	14 587	6.4	58.5	8.1	40.8	5 035	9 530	21 390	-2.3	0.8	27 464	21.9	30.6	26.5
Forsyth	773	6 433	64 607	21.1	77.6	24.1	228.1	5 449	16 151	30 449	9.4	4.5	39 536	10.8	16.2	14.6
Franklin	312	2 895	8 429	16.2	62.4	9.2	33.5	4 731	10 959	25 049	27.1	1.3	33 713	13.5	20.7	18.1
Gaston	765	5 422	40 639	10.4	60.9	10.8	137.9	4 640	12 447	28 126	5.6	1.8	36 590	12.0	18.0	16.0
Gates	167	1 190	2 202	5.0	60.9	7.4	11.2	5 687	11 561	23 408	7.0	1.9	30 087	15.4	22.9	21.9
Graham	26	745	1 624	1.7	56.9	10.0	7.8	6 156	8 877	16 754	-11.1	1.3	24 355	18.3	26.1	26.1
Granville	472	4 228	8 398	5.6	62.0	9.6	35.5	4 771	10 993	26 488	16.4	1.2	34 779	12.3	17.4	16.2
Greene	218	2 882	3 799	8.7	59.2	8.9	15.7	5 378	9 567	22 703	11.7	0.9	29 993	16.1	23.2	20.2
Guilford	789	6 525	88 607	13.4	76.1	24.8	319.0	5 431	15 373	30 148	9.2	4.3	39 721	11.2	17.3	15.0
Halifax	512	5 211	13 501	6.9	53.9	8.6	58.1	5 285	8 980	18 932	8.0	1.1	24 741	23.6	31.5	28.3
Harnett	614	4 812	16 468	15.9	64.0	9.5	62.7	4 319	10 053	21 743	7.1	1.3	31 941	14.7	20.7	19.2
Haywood	239	2 153	9 656	5.0	68.0	12.8	38.8	5 138	11 731	22 462	3.3	1.5	31 013	13.7	22.3	19.5
Henderson	222	2 672	13 784	9.7	76.2	19.5	53.7	4 764	13 702	26 967	13.5	2.1	35 260	11.4	18.6	17.0
Hertford	470	4 291	6 125	13.7	58.1	10.7	21.2	4 763	9 016	18 180	-9.3	0.9	23 724	23.1	31.3	29.1
Hoke	382	4 291	6 430	5.0	55.7	8.4	27.5	4 705	8 688	22 770	6.1	0.7	27 525	18.1	24.7	22.5
Hyde	164	2 303	1 188	11.4	60.0	7.7	6.4	7 834	9 434	17 665	8.3	2.3	23 568	24.8	32.6	32.5
Iredell	643	3 909	20 320	6.8	66.5	11.8	84.8	4 665	13 000	28 627	13.0	2.1	38 086	9.2	13.2	12.2
Jackson	156	2 497	8 915	4.3	68.7	19.7	18.8	5 152	10 326	21 520	12.8	1.5	29 776	16.1	21.7	20.2
Johnston	464	4 451	18 463	6.6	64.6	11.1	80.8	4 614	11 839	25 169	21.9	1.6	36 406	12.3	18.2	15.9
Jones	164	1 283	2 135	7.6	62.4	8.1	9.7	6 004	8 832	19 392	3.5	0.5	27 219	18.0	26.6	25.2
Lee	439	6 535	9 869	6.7	72.4	14.3	39.9	4 636	12 042	26 419	6.6	1.5	34 864	12.9	19.0	17.7
Lenoir	718	5 556	14 394	6.0	62.9	11.5	51.8	4 990	10 647	21 207	-1.7	1.5	27 982	18.6	26.6	23.8
Lincoln	353	3 574	11 002	6.7	62.0	10.5	44.5	4 587	12 440	28 662	7.8	1.9	35 811	10.6	14.5	15.4
McDowell	169	2 362	7 920	3.9	58.5	8.1	30.1	4 857	10 516	22 562	0.1	1.1	30 957	11.6	16.4	14.8
Macon	82	1 771	4 334	5.1	66.7	13.2	19.7	5 045	11 017	20 450	9.5	1.1	28 696	13.2	20.2	19.3
Madison	NA	NA	4 027	23.1	56.4	11.3	13.8	5 420	9 149	18 956	18.8	0.7	27 466	16.7	23.0	22.1
Martin	527	3 929	6 221	4.2	58.3	9.5	26.8	5 316	9 486	19 995	1.2	0.8	26 053	20.1	27.8	25.9
Mecklenburg	1 422	7 511	129 647	16.5	81.6	28.3	485.6	5 192	16 910	33 830	13.2	5.1	45 350	9.7	14.7	13.2
Mitchell	NA	NA	2 835	5.3	55.3	9.2	12.3	5 179	10 219	20 554	2.0	1.1	29 238	13.4	19.2	18.3
Montgomery	413	4 275	5 579	5.7	55.3	7.8	21.4	4 992	10 695	22 682	5.5	1.7	28 832	16.0	23.3	21.5
Moore	335	3 009	12 901	8.1	74.3	19.9	51.5	4 959	14 934	28 053	15.6	3.9	36 688	10.9	18.2	17.0
Nash	530	4 658	18 427	11.6	65.1	13.7	87.2	4 864	12 684	25 834	13.1	2.7	34 079	13.7	20.3	17.9
New Hanover	761	6 581	31 336	10.0	78.1	21.2	104.0	4 813	13 863	27 320	6.3	2.9	38 480	13.0	19.8	17.7
Northampton	334	2 204	5 042	6.8	52.8	8.8	20.0	4 997	8 244	18 029	4.0	0.9	24 218	23.1	32.8	29.2
Onslow	309	3 439	33 122	8.6	83.0	13.4	86.7	4 153	10 713	23 386	13.1	1.0	30 682	14.6	18.0	18.6
Orange	368	5 210	35 128	9.3	83.6	46.1	84.4	5 939	15 776	29 968	19.7	6.0	39 410	10.5	12.5	12.6
Pamlico	218	1 989	2 635	2.7	65.9	11.6	11.4	5 388	10 665	21 060	6.8	1.2	28 629	16.8	25.9	24.4
Pasquotank	403	3 680	8 699	6.1	67.4	14.4	31.4	5 074	10 718	21 816	5.9	2.3	29 305	19.0	25.3	24.8
Pender	251	2 873	6 367	5.2	64.6	11.6	27.9	4 671	11 460	23 270	16.9	1.7	30 705	15.0	22.0	21.1
Perquimans	292	2 288	2 194	7.5	61.2	8.8	11.3	5 683	9 821	20 022	9.5	1.5	26 489	19.5	29.4	28.3
Person	358	2 581	6 770	6.1	63.2	7.6	28.3	5 077	11 158	25 625	12.0	1.0	33 501	11.6	16.5	16.4
Pitt	927	7 332	35 790	6.7	71.0	21.9	93.4	4 760	11 642	23 324	7.8	2.3	31 987	17.7	23.2	22.1
Polk	179	2 239	2 558	11.6	69.6	20.1	12.7	5 774	14 213	26 801	19.1	3.5	34 909	8.7	14.7	13.2
Randolph	178	3 944	22 444	8.8	62.0	9.1	87.7	4 412	12 102	27 130	4.3	1.7	35 453	8.8	13.3	12.4
Richmond	612	5 133	10 872	6.7	60.4	7.9	39.8	4 801	9 841	21 953	-2.4	1.0	27 349	18.2	26.3	23.4
Robeson	544	4 252	29 676	3.7	57.0	11.0	110.0	4 629	8 878	19 716	2.3	1.5	25 518	22.8	28.8	26.2
Rockingham	477	3 933	18 946	5.4	59.2	8.8	70.6	4 884	11 546	25 402	3.8	1.2	32 305	12.1	17.3	16.3
Rowan	366	3 106	25 239	12.9	66.0	11.7	93.0	4 807	12 018	26 354	2.9	1.5	35 112	11.8	17.6	16.1
Rutherford	285	3 114	12 624	6.3	59.4	9.8	49.3	4 869	11 287	23 828	6.8	1.3	30 981	13.7	20.2	18.6
Sampson	461	4 425	11 810	5.1	61.3	8.1	48.2	4 841	9 480	19 709	2.3	1.3	28 919	17.5	23.8	22.0
Scotland	529	5 784	9 478	11.6	60.7	13.6	37.6	5 077	9 768	22 561	-3.2	1.2	29 323	18.8	25.6	23.0
Stanly	322	3 948	11 585	10.1	62.1	9.4	45.1	4 708	11 265	25 374	4.3	1.3	34 437	10.8	15.5	14.9
Stokes	247	2 082	8 407	6.3	62.8	7.3	34.3	4 957	12 181	27 945	9.1	1.5	35 618	10.3	15.3	13.6
Surry	392	3 155	13 340	4.5	57.3	9.4	55.2	5 018	11 342	23 444	5.2	1.7	30 848	11.8	17.5	16.2

1. Data for serious crimes have not been adjusted for underreporting; this may affect comparability between geographic areas and over time. 2. Per 100,000 population estimated by the FBI. 3. All persons 3 years old and over enrolled in nursery school through college. 4. Persons 25 years old and over. 5. Elementary and secondary education expenditures, local government fiscal years ending between July 1, 1996 and June 30, 1997. 6. Based on population enumerated as of April 1, 1990.

Table B. States and Counties — Personal Income

STATE County	Total (mil dol)	Percent change, 1997–1998	Per capita¹ Dollars	Per capita¹ Rank	Wages and salaries² (mil dol)	Proprietor's income (mil dol)	Dividends, interest, and rent (mil dol)	Transfer payments Total (mil dol)	Gov't payments to individuals Total (mil dol)	Social Security (mil dol)	Medical payments (mil dol)	Income maintenance (mil dol)	Unemployment insurance (mil dol)
	62	63	64	65	66	67	68	69	70	71	72	73	74
NORTH CAROLINA—Cont'd													
Chowan	302	4.0	21 238	1 310	138	30	66	67	65	25	28	9	0
Clay	162	5.9	18 861	2 104	39	16	37	40	38	18	15	3	0
Cleveland	1 966	5.1	21 126	1 350	1 129	84	333	364	347	153	135	35	13
Columbus	1 057	-0.8	20 046	1 698	498	115	157	276	267	84	128	39	5
Craven	2 090	4.8	23 527	740	1 574	98	453	321	307	126	124	34	4
Cumberland	6 851	3.5	24 104	621	5 209	315	997	830	788	253	287	118	13
Currituck	394	8.0	22 162	1 047	85	20	63	54	51	22	19	5	1
Dare	665	7.7	23 096	835	365	89	164	90	85	42	33	4	3
Davidson	3 251	5.3	23 034	847	1 448	180	620	451	426	206	163	33	8
Davie	894	6.6	27 937	240	282	56	198	110	104	50	42	7	2
Duplin	887	-13.2	20 574	1 535	432	127	133	184	176	61	76	24	5
Durham	5 764	3.8	28 492	215	7 496	329	1 161	666	631	250	261	66	8
Edgecombe	1 064	-0.2	19 349	1 937	713	70	177	255	246	80	112	39	6
Forsyth	9 006	6.9	31 304	130	6 476	630	1 900	1 001	951	439	372	82	14
Franklin	933	4.4	20 932	1 410	276	67	129	150	142	50	67	18	2
Gaston	4 267	4.0	23 210	815	2 461	282	662	674	642	284	266	59	11
Gates	180	2.6	17 775	2 413	42	14	31	40	38	16	17	4	0
Graham	128	3.0	16 877	2 638	55	15	21	38	36	13	16	4	1
Granville	920	5.3	21 007	1 389	584	42	154	145	137	59	57	15	2
Greene	331	-8.7	18 001	2 343	106	32	46	65	62	22	28	9	1
Guilford	11 330	5.2	29 229	190	9 672	652	2 305	1 310	1 242	562	486	107	22
Halifax	1 034	3.5	18 357	2 250	509	76	163	291	281	97	116	54	5
Harnett	1 577	4.9	19 129	2 011	607	116	256	265	250	88	111	31	5
Haywood	1 107	3.2	21 494	1 253	467	91	238	238	229	109	84	19	7
Henderson	2 121	5.6	26 115	387	984	176	631	382	367	192	137	21	4
Hertford	388	2.6	17 626	2 459	214	11	65	111	107	38	46	17	1
Hoke	412	2.4	13 582	3 037	196	24	54	91	86	29	36	14	1
Hyde	106	-2.0	18 157	2 307	47	11	21	26	25	8	12	4	1
Iredell	2 768	7.1	24 382	578	1 633	184	480	381	361	166	153	25	5
Jackson	623	8.9	20 777	1 462	327	49	124	115	110	44	42	10	2
Johnston	2 482	7.9	23 288	794	921	215	325	350	331	126	148	38	4
Jones	179	-7.4	19 160	1 997	49	19	26	43	41	15	19	5	1
Lee	1 208	5.2	24 563	551	824	73	221	182	173	76	71	15	3
Lenoir	1 253	0.1	21 287	1 297	866	70	224	280	269	95	125	34	5
Lincoln	1 243	4.3	21 422	1 260	527	72	146	180	170	79	68	13	4
McDowell	782	6.3	19 522	1 878	511	52	107	145	138	66	51	12	3
Macon	599	6.3	21 191	1 333	252	53	156	132	127	63	47	9	2
Madison	349	5.5	18 599	2 184	99	25	54	78	75	27	31	11	1
Martin	488	1.3	18 657	2 166	308	32	82	116	112	38	48	16	3
Mecklenburg	22 233	9.7	35 245	63	20 354	1 918	3 830	1 659	1 548	693	606	148	26
Mitchell	288	4.2	19 449	1 909	150	19	49	67	65	27	26	6	2
Montgomery	477	5.5	19 789	1 783	289	45	74	95	91	34	42	10	1
Moore	2 033	5.7	28 493	214	836	180	705	329	317	167	114	19	3
Nash	2 142	4.3	23 572	727	1 306	164	334	300	284	111	111	36	6
New Hanover	3 948	6.2	26 346	359	2 549	323	977	564	538	234	213	50	10
Northampton	394	3.4	18 452	2 226	139	52	58	109	105	38	45	17	1
Onslow	3 170	3.4	22 109	1 064	2 398	143	428	317	299	99	123	39	4
Orange	3 106	4.2	28 256	227	1 958	208	669	267	247	112	102	17	2
Pamlico	262	5.5	21 256	1 306	68	13	61	53	51	22	20	5	1
Pasquotank	697	4.3	19 581	1 863	419	37	133	140	133	47	59	16	2
Pender	730	2.8	18 535	2 200	202	61	128	147	140	58	58	14	3
Perquimans	197	3.2	17 609	2 465	43	18	38	51	49	21	19	6	1
Person	705	2.8	20 990	1 394	374	26	105	125	120	49	52	11	3
Pitt	2 884	3.7	22 772	897	1 854	149	502	420	398	140	172	58	6
Polk	479	4.8	28 614	210	100	37	190	81	78	45	27	4	1
Randolph	2 746	5.9	22 622	946	1 362	229	371	383	362	176	141	22	8
Richmond	867	3.4	18 845	2 110	432	76	123	225	217	72	94	24	4
Robeson	1 987	2.1	17 179	2 569	1 097	102	254	502	482	140	231	81	10
Rockingham	1 879	2.8	20 866	1 435	950	99	316	370	354	152	149	32	10
Rowan	2 701	4.6	21 594	1 225	1 515	121	504	438	416	191	156	32	5
Rutherford	1 229	4.5	20 183	1 659	708	77	190	241	230	104	89	22	6
Sampson	1 041	-7.5	19 880	1 751	460	124	139	218	209	78	93	26	4
Scotland	679	3.2	19 026	2 045	524	16	97	152	146	50	65	22	3
Stanly	1 211	6.2	21 689	1 197	600	86	212	205	195	93	79	14	3
Stokes	896	5.2	20 714	1 484	202	50	125	126	118	54	47	10	2
Surry	1 475	4.1	21 939	1 117	952	140	243	268	256	112	109	20	6

1. Based on the resident population estimated as of July 1 of the year shown. 2. Includes other labor income.

Table B. States and Counties — Earnings, Social Security, and Housing

STATE County	Earnings, 1998									Social Security beneficiaries, December 1998		Supplemental Security Income recipients, December 1998	Housing units, 1990	
			Goods-related[1]		Service-related and other[2]									
	Total (mil dol)	Farm	Total	Manufacturing	Total	Retail trade	Finance, insurance, and real estate	Services	Government	Number	Rate[3]		Total	Percent change, 1980–1990
	75	76	77	78	79	80	81	82	83	84	85	86	87	88
NORTH CAROLINA—Cont'd														
Chowan	168	12.2	D	22.2	D	9.2	3.4	21.7	15.6	3 421	241	571	5 910	12.3
Clay	55	2.6	D	6.3	D	13.0	6.1	24.2	21.3	2 353	274	294	4 158	23.4
Cleveland	1 213	1.2	D	40.1	D	8.5	2.8	20.2	12.9	18 824	203	2 575	34 232	12.6
Columbus	613	9.9	D	30.0	D	9.8	D	19.3	16.8	12 108	230	3 825	20 513	7.6
Craven	1 673	0.0	D	10.5	D	6.7	2.5	15.1	53.9	16 336	185	2 540	32 293	26.4
Cumberland	5 523	0.2	D	9.2	D	8.2	3.2	12.5	57.6	34 238	120	7 429	98 360	20.9
Currituck	105	-0.2	21.6	2.5	D	19.9	7.1	15.6	28.7	2 909	162	265	7 367	36.3
Dare	454	0.0	D	4.7	D	23.0	11.8	20.1	18.1	4 923	170	264	21 567	96.0
Davidson	1 628	0.4	D	40.8	D	9.5	3.2	16.5	11.5	24 562	174	2 333	53 266	20.3
Davie	338	0.3	D	36.5	D	8.4	D	19.2	13.1	6 028	188	542	11 496	21.3
Duplin	559	18.2	D	31.2	D	7.3	D	10.7	15.6	9 057	211	2 182	16 395	5.2
Durham	7 825	0.1	D	39.7	D	5.1	4.1	32.3	9.9	29 063	144	4 349	77 710	33.2
Edgecombe	783	5.6	D	20.9	D	6.9	D	15.4	20.0	11 295	205	3 198	21 827	7.6
Forsyth	7 106	0.1	D	24.0	D	9.5	9.9	30.0	8.2	49 400	172	5 565	115 715	20.7
Franklin	343	9.4	D	22.4	D	10.1	D	17.8	19.0	6 927	155	1 682	14 957	34.1
Gaston	2 743	0.4	D	40.5	D	9.3	3.4	19.7	10.6	33 584	182	3 891	69 133	16.8
Gates	56	17.6	D	10.1	35.4	5.9	2.3	13.9	32.9	2 133	212	364	3 696	14.6
Graham	70	3.5	D	D	D	8.4	1.9	10.5	21.1	1 918	251	392	4 132	15.5
Granville	626	0.9	D	35.3	D	5.9	1.8	8.2	38.1	7 997	186	1 527	14 164	22.5
Greene	138	18.2	23.9	16.6	27.6	5.7	1.2	12.4	30.3	3 142	172	745	5 944	6.4
Guilford	10 324	0.3	30.6	24.4	58.8	9.3	7.9	23.7	10.4	63 051	163	7 014	146 812	21.9
Halifax	585	5.2	28.5	24.0	40.4	11.3	3.3	14.8	25.9	13 803	245	4 618	22 480	10.8
Harnett	722	3.3	D	23.9	D	10.8	3.0	19.8	19.3	12 054	146	2 234	27 896	25.8
Haywood	558	2.3	D	24.8	D	14.6	3.2	20.7	19.1	13 174	256	1 475	23 975	17.7
Henderson	1 160	6.2	D	28.6	D	10.7	3.6	21.1	12.7	22 156	274	1 585	34 131	25.5
Hertford	225	0.8	27.1	21.9	50.7	11.8	2.2	27.6	21.5	5 298	238	1 519	8 870	7.4
Hoke	220	5.5	46.3	38.3	21.2	4.6	1.4	10.7	27.1	4 143	136	911	7 999	23.5
Hyde	58	6.6	13.2	7.7	42.2	10.6	4.7	11.2	38.0	1 196	213	284	2 905	2.4
Iredell	1 817	2.3	40.5	32.6	45.9	11.7	2.5	21.5	11.3	19 672	174	1 937	39 191	21.1
Jackson	376	2.9	15.8	8.4	51.6	10.6	3.3	32.4	29.7	5 724	189	798	14 052	17.5
Johnston	1 136	6.0	D	25.4	D	12.4	3.6	16.3	15.5	17 206	161	3 609	34 172	22.2
Jones	68	18.9	14.6	7.1	44.1	6.9	1.5	21.7	22.4	2 215	234	417	3 829	4.8
Lee	897	1.5	51.3	45.5	37.3	10.3	2.4	15.1	9.9	9 480	192	1 292	16 954	21.1
Lenoir	935	2.2	34.5	27.6	40.6	9.0	3.2	19.6	22.7	12 804	217	2 948	23 739	5.2
Lincoln	599	2.4	D	39.4	D	9.1	4.2	13.2	15.4	9 534	164	975	20 189	24.9
McDowell	564	3.4	D	53.3	D	7.4	1.4	11.5	12.5	8 344	208	1 101	15 091	8.2
Macon	305	1.5	D	12.0	D	15.6	5.8	28.7	14.8	8 031	283	786	17 174	28.6
Madison	124	6.1	30.8	23.5	D	6.9	2.2	22.7	21.3	3 994	213	926	7 667	7.0
Martin	340	5.1	48.6	43.4	28.6	7.5	1.6	10.4	17.8	5 380	205	1 437	10 104	8.4
Mecklenburg	22 271	0.4	18.0	11.3	73.0	8.2	16.7	25.5	8.6	76 688	122	8 785	216 416	38.6
Mitchell	169	3.3	40.3	24.2	D	7.8	3.2	20.0	17.4	3 687	249	669	6 983	15.3
Montgomery	334	5.9	56.2	48.7	D	6.6	2.1	9.3	14.9	4 450	185	882	10 421	9.5
Moore	1 016	5.8	20.9	13.8	61.6	9.7	4.3	40.1	11.6	19 137	268	1 460	27 358	30.0
Nash	1 470	4.1	D	29.6	D	12.2	6.7	18.2	12.4	14 801	163	3 168	31 024	20.6
New Hanover	2 872	0.2	25.1	15.9	57.1	13.1	7.0	26.0	17.6	27 007	180	3 748	57 076	31.8
Northampton	192	24.3	D	17.2	D	5.0	D	12.2	23.4	5 511	260	1 490	8 974	2.9
Onslow	2 541	0.7	D	2.5	D	6.5	1.7	8.1	73.3	13 802	97	2 383	47 526	34.1
Orange	2 167	0.6	9.3	5.3	41.5	8.6	8.4	19.9	48.6	12 471	113	1 192	38 683	34.7
Pamlico	81	3.7	18.0	8.0	52.2	12.4	2.2	23.0	26.2	3 000	243	373	6 050	20.7
Pasquotank	456	1.0	11.0	5.7	44.0	12.1	4.5	17.3	44.0	6 404	181	1 155	12 298	17.1
Pender	264	7.8	D	13.1	D	9.3	D	16.4	25.4	7 547	191	1 126	15 437	50.0
Perquimans	61	12.7	D	D	D	9.4	D	16.7	29.7	2 850	253	442	4 972	19.2
Person	399	-0.7	48.9	42.1	37.2	9.6	2.3	13.7	14.7	6 436	191	1 032	12 548	17.4
Pitt	2 003	0.8	D	18.0	D	10.6	4.1	19.5	31.1	18 708	148	4 898	43 070	30.6
Polk	137	2.5	30.3	22.0	D	9.5	4.3	30.4	17.3	5 139	305	269	7 273	22.7
Randolph	1 591	5.4	49.2	40.0	34.9	7.9	2.2	15.9	10.4	21 350	176	1 840	43 634	23.8
Richmond	508	6.5	31.4	25.9	44.2	10.7	2.7	18.6	17.9	9 748	211	1 969	18 218	6.9
Robeson	1 199	1.4	37.5	30.7	41.0	11.0	2.2	19.9	20.2	20 731	179	7 430	39 045	17.2
Rockingham	1 049	0.8	49.1	41.1	37.1	9.4	2.7	17.2	13.0	18 662	207	2 823	35 657	10.5
Rowan	1 636	1.3	41.7	34.2	39.7	10.4	2.3	17.6	17.3	23 018	183	2 095	46 264	18.5
Rutherford	785	0.0	D	44.9	D	9.0	2.6	15.8	12.7	12 972	213	1 682	25 220	15.7
Sampson	584	17.2	28.2	22.9	35.3	8.5	2.2	13.0	19.2	11 034	210	2 192	19 183	5.2
Scotland	540	0.1	54.0	50.8	34.4	7.2	1.7	19.0	11.5	6 544	183	1 677	12 759	14.8
Stanly	687	3.1	47.2	38.8	36.2	10.2	2.4	17.2	13.5	11 309	202	998	21 808	13.7
Stokes	252	4.3	33.4	17.9	41.0	9.7	2.6	19.6	21.2	7 119	164	819	15 160	19.3
Surry	1 092	5.0	D	33.5	D	9.9	2.3	12.6	12.4	14 642	218	1 971	26 022	11.8

1. Covers mining, construction, and manufacturing. 2. Covers private sector earnings in agricultural services, forestry, and fisheries; transportation and public utilities; wholesale trade; retail trade; finance, insurance, and real estate; and services. 3. Per 1,000 resident population estimated as of July 1 of the year shown.

Table B. States and Counties — Housing, Labor Force, and Employment

STATE County	Housing units, 1990 (cont'd) Occupied units Owner-occupied Total	Percent	Median value[1]	Owner cost as a percent of income With a mortgage	Without a mortgage	Renter-occupied Median rent[2]	Rent as percent of income	Substandard units[3] (percent)	Civilian labor force, 1999 Total	Percent change, 1998–1999	Unemployment Total	Rate[4]	Civilian employment, 1990[5] Total	Percent Professional, managerial, and technical	Precision production, craft, and repair
	89	90	91	92	93	94	95	96	97	98	99	100	101	102	103
NORTH CAROLINA—Cont'd															
Chowan	5 113	70.6	60 700	22.0	13.7	279	24.4	5.5	6 436	3.6	193	3.0	5 736	19.6	13.1
Clay	2 928	84.4	56 500	21.3	12.2	262	29.2	4.0	4 000	16.0	123	3.1	2 944	17.7	17.1
Cleveland	32 037	72.8	53 400	18.6	12.4	327	23.8	3.7	44 716	0.4	2 202	4.9	42 546	19.8	15.8
Columbus	18 459	75.8	45 800	21.2	15.0	275	30.4	6.8	23 058	-1.6	1 955	8.5	20 348	19.7	15.0
Craven	29 542	63.3	65 900	21.8	12.7	374	24.2	4.3	36 127	2.6	1 501	4.2	31 305	24.5	14.5
Cumberland	91 500	57.7	63 500	23.1	13.9	406	26.1	4.3	115 622	2.8	4 409	3.8	96 204	26.5	11.8
Currituck	5 038	80.3	79 200	22.6	14.4	423	22.7	4.0	8 886	5.8	204	2.3	6 357	19.8	22.3
Dare	9 349	71.1	108 100	24.3	12.5	516	27.6	2.2	17 512	4.2	837	4.8	12 199	26.3	16.4
Davidson	48 944	73.6	60 800	18.0	12.2	351	22.9	2.9	78 788	1.8	1 786	2.3	68 344	18.9	17.2
Davie	10 785	82.1	68 000	17.8	12.3	362	22.9	2.8	17 469	3.6	438	2.5	14 623	21.5	15.8
Duplin	14 925	75.9	42 600	18.9	14.0	267	24.6	6.2	21 701	0.2	1 346	6.2	18 301	16.2	15.1
Durham	72 297	53.0	85 500	21.8	13.2	444	24.6	2.6	115 980	0.4	2 306	2.0	96 658	40.7	8.8
Edgecombe	20 319	61.8	47 100	20.1	14.8	304	25.8	8.2	24 558	-1.5	1 971	8.0	26 297	17.4	12.7
Forsyth	107 419	63.5	75 700	18.9	12.4	384	24.0	1.9	152 549	1.1	3 440	2.3	136 304	32.7	10.6
Franklin	13 503	75.5	55 500	21.4	14.9	312	24.5	9.2	23 304	1.7	583	2.5	17 501	19.1	14.9
Gaston	65 347	69.3	57 700	18.6	13.0	360	22.0	3.8	99 579	2.2	3 482	3.5	89 280	20.0	15.8
Gates	3 352	81.1	49 700	19.5	13.3	237	17.4	11.7	4 559	3.0	124	2.7	3 898	14.2	16.0
Graham	2 772	81.7	47 400	18.4	12.2	226	27.1	4.5	3 858	-6.4	307	8.0	2 823	20.8	18.3
Granville	13 134	73.4	59 100	20.0	13.5	323	22.9	8.8	22 850	2.0	681	3.0	18 113	22.2	14.0
Greene	5 395	70.3	48 600	21.2	12.6	288	22.7	8.6	8 940	4.6	416	4.7	6 993	17.6	14.2
Guilford	137 706	61.3	79 400	20.8	12.8	428	24.4	2.4	217 758	2.1	5 160	2.4	188 433	29.2	10.4
Halifax	20 335	65.3	44 800	19.5	14.7	287	26.8	10.6	22 056	-0.8	1 573	7.1	21 954	18.1	13.8
Harnett	25 150	68.4	50 800	21.4	14.5	326	26.0	5.0	36 320	0.9	1 185	3.3	29 629	19.8	16.5
Haywood	19 211	77.1	59 600	20.4	12.8	305	24.4	3.0	23 313	-7.2	935	4.0	20 763	22.4	15.3
Henderson	28 709	76.7	78 400	20.1	11.5	372	24.1	2.3	36 132	3.0	863	2.4	30 618	24.0	14.7
Hertford	8 150	68.6	44 900	21.8	14.0	275	25.3	9.4	9 949	0.3	397	4.0	9 519	19.4	14.0
Hoke	7 405	75.3	44 800	20.5	14.1	322	25.7	8.8	11 539	7.5	799	6.9	9 117	16.7	16.2
Hyde	2 094	77.0	43 700	24.6	13.9	263	25.6	11.2	3 029	1.5	191	6.3	2 160	17.0	11.8
Iredell	35 573	75.1	63 300	18.5	12.5	360	22.3	3.5	60 120	4.0	1 420	2.4	48 907	20.1	15.1
Jackson	9 683	75.6	63 000	19.2	12.1	300	25.1	2.7	15 874	2.4	604	3.8	12 346	27.3	13.3
Johnston	31 566	69.9	59 400	21.8	14.4	322	25.1	4.0	58 758	3.2	1 128	1.9	41 608	22.1	18.1
Jones	3 492	78.1	43 700	22.0	14.7	287	28.5	6.5	4 465	8.3	238	5.3	4 109	15.3	14.4
Lee	15 689	72.6	61 100	21.1	13.2	350	25.6	3.3	25 813	1.1	838	3.2	19 590	24.2	17.1
Lenoir	21 938	63.1	52 400	20.6	14.7	287	26.4	5.2	29 555	1.5	1 848	6.3	26 237	23.8	13.9
Lincoln	18 764	78.9	60 500	19.2	12.0	338	23.3	3.7	31 763	2.6	885	2.8	26 148	19.4	17.8
McDowell	13 680	77.1	45 100	16.7	12.0	296	21.4	3.5	20 127	3.1	797	4.0	17 266	17.8	16.8
Macon	9 834	82.8	62 500	21.8	12.7	318	23.9	2.8	13 445	-0.5	494	3.7	10 077	20.4	18.9
Madison	6 488	77.8	47 800	20.1	12.2	234	24.4	6.6	8 917	0.3	243	2.7	7 586	20.0	15.9
Martin	9 317	68.8	46 600	20.5	13.4	268	23.5	8.1	11 278	-1.0	917	8.1	11 079	18.0	15.2
Mecklenburg	200 219	59.7	86 900	20.4	12.4	467	24.1	3.0	362 035	4.1	7 276	2.0	281 201	33.0	9.2
Mitchell	5 779	82.5	48 700	21.5	12.7	282	21.6	4.0	7 008	-1.8	452	6.4	6 253	17.1	17.7
Montgomery	8 290	77.1	43 900	19.7	12.9	287	22.6	7.6	11 567	1.7	481	4.2	11 205	14.8	16.0
Moore	23 827	77.6	80 300	20.9	12.1	356	24.7	3.7	29 213	3.0	1 005	3.4	26 342	24.2	13.6
Nash	29 041	64.4	63 200	18.7	13.5	345	22.9	6.3	42 518	1.2	2 191	5.2	38 532	24.3	13.1
New Hanover	48 139	62.7	72 000	20.7	13.0	417	27.4	2.1	79 034	4.4	2 404	3.0	60 179	29.9	12.3
Northampton	7 591	76.6	38 100	21.5	14.7	231	23.9	8.9	8 073	0.0	529	6.6	8 069	16.3	13.0
Onslow	40 658	53.7	62 200	23.4	13.2	398	25.3	4.8	46 631	3.5	1 651	3.5	38 674	24.0	13.8
Orange	36 104	55.3	101 500	22.0	12.5	472	28.9	2.2	63 520	0.4	702	1.1	50 671	44.4	9.0
Pamlico	4 523	81.1	54 300	21.2	13.1	328	30.6	3.4	5 451	3.1	203	3.7	4 718	20.3	16.2
Pasquotank	11 384	65.2	59 300	23.0	14.2	359	29.2	4.6	14 690	2.3	524	3.6	12 673	24.6	16.7
Pender	11 112	82.6	60 200	20.4	13.4	350	24.8	6.1	16 146	1.7	776	4.8	12 868	21.7	16.6
Perquimans	3 988	76.8	53 200	22.4	12.8	306	26.4	4.7	4 627	-0.2	133	2.9	4 220	17.9	13.5
Person	11 423	72.5	55 700	19.5	13.2	309	23.8	7.0	17 317	0.3	707	4.1	15 576	19.4	16.8
Pitt	40 491	58.1	65 300	20.3	13.5	350	28.2	5.4	64 785	2.2	2 897	4.5	53 492	30.0	10.5
Polk	6 110	79.9	68 200	19.9	12.2	332	21.9	2.8	7 663	3.0	242	3.2	6 511	23.7	15.2
Randolph	41 096	77.0	60 200	18.6	12.3	341	23.0	3.1	70 278	2.2	1 845	2.6	59 463	17.7	17.5
Richmond	16 793	72.3	40 000	19.9	14.6	301	22.9	4.6	18 499	0.1	1 187	6.4	20 375	16.9	14.6
Robeson	36 154	70.1	44 200	21.0	14.6	273	27.1	8.0	54 258	3.4	4 225	7.8	44 412	18.4	16.5
Rockingham	33 446	74.3	48 800	17.8	12.8	307	22.1	4.7	44 178	-2.0	2 110	4.8	42 607	17.5	15.4
Rowan	42 512	73.6	54 600	18.2	12.4	347	22.8	2.8	65 432	3.3	1 908	2.9	54 730	20.3	15.4
Rutherford	22 198	73.0	46 300	18.1	13.1	310	22.7	3.3	29 567	1.7	2 007	6.8	27 581	17.8	15.3
Sampson	17 526	72.9	46 500	19.9	13.8	283	26.6	6.2	23 246	1.6	1 064	4.6	21 789	16.9	16.2
Scotland	11 837	69.4	48 000	20.0	14.0	312	28.8	6.0	16 709	-2.7	1 066	6.4	14 777	21.6	11.0
Stanly	19 747	76.6	52 800	19.6	12.6	329	21.3	3.3	26 402	3.0	933	3.5	26 260	18.5	17.3
Stokes	14 123	81.0	59 100	17.0	12.4	319	20.8	4.9	22 930	2.2	514	2.2	19 065	17.2	17.9
Surry	24 252	76.6	48 600	17.5	12.7	292	23.0	3.3	34 460	0.1	1 226	3.6	31 213	18.0	17.1

1. Specified owner-occupied units. 2. Specified renter-occupied units. 3. Overcrowded or lacking complete plumbing facilities. 4. Percent of civilian labor force. 5. Persons 16 years and older.

	Private nonfarm establishments, employment and payroll, 1998								Agriculture, 1997			
		Employment					Annual payroll		Farms			Farm operators
										Percent with—		
STATE County	Number of establishments	Total	Health Care and Social Assistance	Manufacturing	Retail trade	Finance and Insurance	Professional Scientific and Technical Services	Total (mil dol)	Average per employee (dollars)	Number	Less than 50 acres	500 acres and over	Whose principal occupation is farming (percent)
	104	105	106	107	108	109	110	111	112	113	114	115	116

STATE County	104	105	106	107	108	109	110	111	112	113	114	115	116
NORTH CAROLINA—Cont'd												
Chowan	340	4 603	981	1 432	686	123	78	89	19 247	151	26.5	27.2	71.5
Clay	201	1 326	276	180	278	47	D	25	18 700	166	41.0	4.8	45.2
Cleveland	2 128	35 351	3 939	15 287	4 852	773	445	853	24 129	864	33.9	3.1	34.1
Columbus	1 200	14 980	2 286	5 008	2 496	510	171	312	20 813	884	35.9	11.2	49.4
Craven	2 138	26 162	4 702	4 349	4 375	776	1 172	613	23 427	277	34.3	18.4	61.0
Cumberland	5 312	86 766	13 542	13 194	15 400	2 993	2 874	1 902	21 926	433	37.9	12.9	43.0
Currituck	404	2 482	219	100	737	D	D	47	19 129	86	40.7	29.1	62.8
Dare	1 626	11 401	517	294	2 783	298	552	234	20 492	9	55.6	33.3	66.7
Davidson	2 673	43 974	3 705	20 868	5 303	916	531	1 043	23 712	929	40.7	3.3	40.5
Davie	672	9 052	751	2 902	933	126	144	195	21 533	557	35.7	3.8	43.4
Duplin	1 012	12 457	1 452	4 623	1 808	244	196	233	18 730	1 224	40.1	10.0	61.7
Durham	5 770	156 006	18 991	32 314	13 483	4 051	12 596	5 545	35 545	159	40.3	8.2	46.5
Edgecombe	963	17 695	1 965	6 070	1 569	330	289	449	25 372	315	29.2	33.0	66.7
Forsyth	8 320	170 994	22 765	25 747	20 962	13 748	6 609	5 122	29 955	621	56.2	2.3	45.7
Franklin	730	7 891	1 259	2 257	1 074	179	182	182	23 050	524	23.1	13.9	50.6
Gaston	4 178	74 878	7 111	31 382	10 009	1 414	1 455	1 854	24 764	333	41.7	1.8	40.5
Gates	134	967	100	185	255	D	D	17	17 402	147	21.1	26.5	68.0
Graham	176	1 707	133	D	245	D	D	34	20 114	110	60.9	0.9	35.5
Granville	795	13 930	2 420	6 554	1 344	145	131	337	24 185	637	22.8	11.5	51.8
Greene	206	1 989	642	370	298	D	D	35	17 808	313	26.2	20.8	70.3
Guilford	13 360	256 664	24 052	50 663	31 730	18 636	10 601	7 427	28 936	920	43.9	4.6	47.6
Halifax	1 133	14 313	2 443	3 190	3 017	415	232	311	21 723	339	26.0	28.0	66.4
Harnett	1 466	20 815	1 939	6 281	2 592	351	331	421	20 235	626	40.9	9.6	53.7
Haywood	1 372	13 833	2 213	2 599	2 813	330	340	320	23 159	776	56.6	2.2	38.8
Henderson	2 102	29 114	3 907	8 271	4 256	675	597	726	24 940	488	56.8	2.9	52.9
Hertford	574	7 084	1 207	1 635	1 267	155	185	136	19 176	169	16.0	26.0	72.8
Hoke	284	5 217	626	3 122	486	94	D	115	21 962	162	37.0	20.4	55.6
Hyde	180	970	33	159	166	D	D	17	17 243	100	17.0	53.0	74.0
Iredell	3 119	46 931	5 650	16 479	6 478	796	974	1 189	25 339	1 189	39.4	5.1	46.1
Jackson	890	8 036	2 056	866	1 451	197	254	158	19 608	217	56.7	2.8	40.6
Johnston	2 489	28 497	2 770	7 069	4 615	671	738	641	22 486	1 216	40.1	8.0	54.9
Jones	165	1 298	330	247	165	18	D	26	20 343	154	24.7	26.6	70.1
Lee	1 391	24 645	1 922	11 455	3 212	338	329	597	24 236	311	43.1	4.5	44.7
Lenoir	1 531	27 563	5 680	7 212	3 748	650	515	641	23 268	447	30.9	20.4	67.8
Lincoln	1 275	18 081	1 624	7 744	2 445	326	278	428	23 677	497	39.0	3.8	36.6
McDowell	763	14 898	1 095	8 477	1 679	197	180	312	20 912	223	43.9	3.1	40.4
Macon	1 026	8 352	1 381	1 458	1 820	257	176	174	20 840	309	50.8	0.0	35.6
Madison	305	2 991	389	967	343	D	D	60	20 126	907	49.4	1.5	45.5
Martin	550	6 637	897	1 906	1 244	164	107	122	18 440	389	25.7	19.0	71.0
Mecklenburg	23 466	456 674	38 034	41 523	48 186	37 033	30 425	15 866	34 743	295	47.8	2.4	45.1
Mitchell	358	4 306	605	1 662	537	85	60	90	20 986	306	58.8	2.0	30.1
Montgomery	536	8 976	362	5 255	848	202	55	194	21 598	256	35.2	6.2	44.9
Moore	2 010	28 696	7 035	5 749	4 174	567	731	645	22 464	683	41.6	6.0	48.0
Nash	2 274	40 076	4 735	10 669	6 013	1 783	958	1 000	24 963	472	32.8	16.1	61.7
New Hanover	5 983	72 044	10 427	8 288	12 821	2 463	4 192	1 795	24 919	62	67.7	4.8	27.4
Northampton	319	2 912	453	839	501	D	51	59	20 417	342	24.6	31.3	68.7
Onslow	2 599	28 155	4 385	1 930	6 330	928	801	487	17 300	369	40.7	8.4	56.9
Orange	2 783	33 867	8 312	1 183	5 795	2 879	2 131	855	25 240	485	32.6	6.0	50.1
Pamlico	235	1 676	171	71	381	D	30	33	19 764	67	25.4	38.8	67.2
Pasquotank	931	9 847	1 999	828	2 605	325	270	196	19 935	174	25.9	29.9	70.7
Pender	726	5 473	955	1 153	870	90	106	100	18 236	283	31.4	13.4	58.3
Perquimans	180	1 215	170	119	237	24	26	19	15 547	202	21.8	25.7	71.3
Person	760	11 189	837	5 219	1 526	193	170	255	22 793	401	27.9	15.2	56.9
Pitt	3 051	50 143	9 453	8 980	8 409	1 808	1 507	1 175	23 425	474	26.8	23.0	67.1
Polk	443	3 651	1 020	900	434	89	77	70	19 199	188	38.3	4.3	36.2
Randolph	2 754	46 166	3 139	23 826	4 795	808	551	1 094	23 700	1 366	39.5	2.7	46.1
Richmond	978	13 514	1 868	4 888	2 250	288	225	283	20 966	251	29.5	9.2	51.4
Robeson	1 990	32 002	4 659	11 615	4 993	849	554	684	21 375	1 004	35.8	14.8	53.8
Rockingham	1 789	30 153	3 784	13 631	4 005	536	351	698	23 163	780	32.2	6.8	49.4
Rowan	2 460	43 574	5 884	14 256	4 965	846	631	1 106	25 392	779	35.4	4.7	40.3
Rutherford	1 303	21 816	2 115	10 453	2 833	337	202	471	21 582	505	32.5	3.4	34.9
Sampson	1 072	12 642	1 960	4 007	2 137	324	168	279	22 067	1 186	36.6	9.9	58.9
Scotland	732	16 710	1 643	8 147	1 992	219	104	390	23 343	123	28.5	24.4	51.2
Stanly	1 390	19 078	2 186	8 046	2 935	348	217	428	22 439	558	34.8	5.7	38.9
Stokes	561	5 303	879	1 311	747	96	111	115	21 691	926	38.0	3.0	48.3
Surry	1 803	36 277	2 805	15 033	4 573	685	433	779	21 476	1 194	42.3	2.8	47.0

STATE County	Land in farms		Acres			Value of land and buildings		Value of machinery and equipment Average per farm ($1,000)	Value of products sold		Percent from —		Percent of farms with sales of —		Percent of land owned by Fed. Gov. 1997	Water consumption 1995 (mil gal/day)
	Acreage (1,000)	Percent change, 1992–1997	Average size of farm	Total irrigated (1,000)	Total cropland (1,000)	Average per farm ($1,000)	Average per acre (dollars)		Total (mil dol)	Average per farm (dollars)	Crops	Livestock and poultry products	$10,000 or more	$100,000 or more		
	117	118	119	120	121	122	123	124	125	126	127	128	129	130	131	132
NORTH CAROLINA—Cont'd																
Chowan	51	-4.9	340	3	38	519	1 611	119	34	225 181	76.7	23.3	70.9	43.0	0.0	3.3
Clay	18	14.3	110	0	9	309	3 377	29	5	28 181	14.4	85.6	27.7	5.4	55.7	4.7
Cleveland	104	10.7	120	0	62	328	2 667	25	34	38 990	27.0	73.0	24.4	6.8	0.0	39.3
Columbus	170	4.3	192	1	116	275	1 508	53	140	158 273	48.0	52.0	58.9	23.4	0.0	7.4
Craven	84	-4.7	303	1	62	356	1 302	84	67	241 636	52.9	47.1	63.5	36.1	15.1	14.2
Cumberland	103	4.2	238	2	57	461	2 205	66	68	156 313	32.8	67.2	45.7	18.9	10.4	35.7
Currituck	40	-5.8	460	0	34	836	1 816	103	15	174 005	93.1	6.9	58.1	36.0	3.4	2.2
Dare	5	-29.1	551	0	4	555	1 007	76	1	92 923	D	D	66.7	33.3	25.1	4.6
Davidson	99	7.6	107	1	56	392	3 690	30	24	25 452	44.9	55.1	28.5	6.5	0.3	22.0
Davie	71	2.3	127	0	42	372	2 814	36	16	28 099	38.1	61.9	29.6	7.9	0.0	5.6
Duplin	238	-4.3	195	6	157	457	2 321	68	746	609 844	9.5	90.5	72.7	51.5	0.0	29.1
Durham	22	11.2	140	1	11	555	4 228	46	7	45 576	85.6	14.4	43.4	17.6	2.2	31.4
Edgecombe	172	-4.7	545	5	116	723	1 408	113	149	472 312	43.5	56.5	71.1	49.8	0.0	12.3
Forsyth	51	6.4	82	1	30	269	3 561	29	16	26 187	83.8	16.2	29.5	6.3	0.0	61.5
Franklin	137	16.1	261	5	72	480	1 947	49	61	116 015	66.0	34.0	49.4	20.2	0.0	9.1
Gaston	35	-0.4	105	0	20	324	3 207	26	10	29 872	33.4	66.6	21.6	4.2	0.0	399.1
Gates	62	-4.6	422	0	49	630	1 469	145	45	305 737	38.3	61.7	71.4	40.8	5.2	2.4
Graham	7	-20.1	65	D	3	119	2 335	18	1	9 946	21.7	78.3	18.2	0.9	67.2	42.3
Granville	162	3.7	254	5	59	385	1 650	40	37	58 102	85.9	14.1	55.6	17.3	2.1	7.4
Greene	103	-7.9	330	2	80	680	2 110	137	181	578 160	29.1	70.9	84.7	56.9	0.0	5.0
Guilford	112	-1.9	122	3	60	356	3 063	34	49	53 121	68.2	31.8	38.7	12.5	0.2	95.3
Halifax	185	-9.1	547	3	128	679	1 314	110	97	286 794	54.7	45.3	64.3	43.1	0.0	13.2
Harnett	116	-9.4	185	3	73	426	2 512	58	94	150 292	47.1	52.9	50.0	27.2	2.2	96.9
Haywood	65	-6.8	84	0	28	262	3 057	24	15	18 874	37.3	62.7	26.4	3.9	43.3	84.7
Henderson	45	-14.4	91	2	28	394	4 808	41	47	95 785	85.9	14.1	44.5	11.9	8.3	14.4
Hertford	76	1.9	452	4	53	594	1 283	116	61	358 317	44.4	55.6	86.4	44.4	0.0	5.0
Hoke	67	17.4	413	0	42	594	1 500	92	66	407 919	27.5	72.5	54.3	27.8	35.5	4.5
Hyde	95	1.4	953	D	83	1 150	1 171	153	33	329 965	91.1	8.9	83.0	54.0	8.9	0.5
Iredell	157	5.9	132	1	98	376	2 553	38	100	83 780	9.6	90.4	36.6	14.1	0.0	23.6
Jackson	19	45.2	87	0	6	296	3 856	27	6	28 735	89.3	10.7	33.6	5.1	34.6	4.5
Johnston	211	-8.3	174	3	138	419	2 490	52	179	147 557	53.9	46.1	54.7	22.5	0.0	13.5
Jones	72	4.0	466	0	50	647	1 362	98	108	698 891	24.2	75.8	73.4	48.7	13.4	5.1
Lee	45	22.2	145	1	22	370	2 942	36	26	83 853	59.2	40.8	41.8	16.1	0.0	8.6
Lenoir	150	5.4	335	1	110	703	2 020	107	200	446 473	36.5	63.5	77.2	51.2	0.0	11.5
Lincoln	63	8.9	127	0	39	287	2 273	25	19	38 660	16.3	83.7	25.6	7.0	0.0	10.6
McDowell	21	-1.5	93	1	9	208	2 463	22	13	60 418	61.7	38.3	25.6	8.1	28.2	10.5
Macon	23	3.6	74	0	11	261	4 286	18	3	11 157	46.4	53.6	21.0	1.6	56.4	17.0
Madison	80	-13.9	88	0	27	196	2 385	16	10	11 158	77.6	22.4	27.6	0.7	23.0	4.2
Martin	115	-12.7	296	1	81	356	1 286	78	63	161 846	85.6	14.4	80.7	39.3	0.0	5.9
Mecklenburg	29	3.6	98	0	16	604	5 456	67	43	145 769	79.4	20.6	28.8	7.1	0.0	2 749.0
Mitchell	25	9.4	82	0	11	147	1 984	26	4	12 394	80.0	20.0	28.8	0.7	18.8	6.6
Montgomery	42	13.0	163	1	15	305	1 510	34	46	180 312	7.8	92.2	37.5	25.0	11.8	6.8
Moore	101	15.7	147	5	37	306	2 116	44	113	165 771	18.2	81.8	45.1	29.3	0.6	26.6
Nash	175	-2.1	371	14	110	794	2 076	123	168	355 426	50.8	49.2	67.6	39.2	0.0	24.0
New Hanover	5	81.2	88	0	4	300	3 422	54	4	69 753	D	D	43.5	9.7	1.1	66.6
Northampton	160	3.5	469	2	104	597	1 260	108	92	269 673	45.1	54.9	78.4	45.3	0.0	4.8
Onslow	63	-0.9	172	0	42	291	1 729	48	102	275 201	21.6	78.4	55.6	31.4	15.4	14.8
Orange	73	8.2	150	1	41	446	3 226	46	26	53 268	46.6	53.4	39.6	12.4	0.0	16.0
Pamlico	50	14.2	750	1	43	980	1 307	217	23	341 358	90.5	9.5	64.2	49.3	0.0	3.0
Pasquotank	86	4.0	496	D	79	731	1 545	114	33	190 271	96.7	3.3	76.4	38.5	2.6	5.3
Pender	69	5.9	243	1	42	434	2 043	55	110	387 196	20.7	79.3	60.8	33.9	0.0	4.1
Perquimans	77	11.9	382	0	70	603	1 660	106	38	188 338	58.4	41.6	77.2	44.1	0.6	2.1
Person	120	3.9	300	3	56	504	1 694	50	29	72 423	85.9	14.1	58.4	22.7	0.0	678.3
Pitt	193	-0.3	408	2	144	767	1 865	112	196	413 795	49.8	50.2	76.8	49.6	0.8	26.0
Polk	31	33.5	163	D	10	373	2 268	34	3	17 631	50.6	49.4	22.3	5.3	0.0	2.7
Randolph	148	2.3	109	1	78	282	2 530	38	147	107 855	10.3	89.7	39.3	22.3	1.8	23.7
Richmond	54	4.8	217	1	26	336	1 360	37	66	263 348	16.6	83.4	53.4	39.0	1.3	11.9
Robeson	285	-2.3	284	2	214	377	1 378	60	221	220 562	45.8	54.2	60.1	27.2	0.0	37.8
Rockingham	134	2.2	172	4	55	260	1 611	34	37	47 657	81.1	18.9	49.2	12.3	0.0	68.8
Rowan	108	2.4	138	1	71	322	2 341	42	32	40 858	41.2	58.8	31.2	6.8	0.0	71.9
Rutherford	61	11.2	121	0	30	220	1 850	22	5	10 768	23.7	76.3	19.8	1.8	0.0	32.9
Sampson	271	1.8	228	9	183	464	1 971	72	733	617 925	13.7	86.3	70.0	42.1	0.0	20.6
Scotland	54	-0.9	435	1	36	459	1 201	80	55	447 609	23.0	77.0	60.2	41.5	2.1	8.9
Stanly	95	6.4	170	0	67	289	1 808	46	68	121 307	20.4	79.6	38.9	15.9	0.1	13.3
Stokes	110	4.8	119	1	50	205	2 030	29	34	36 486	68.9	31.1	50.4	7.9	0.0	898.3
Surry	130	7.3	109	2	70	221	2 154	34	98	82 382	32.4	67.6	44.9	15.4	0.2	25.5

Table B. States and Counties — Residential Construction, Wholesale and Retail Trade, and Real Estate

STATE County	Value of Residential Construction Authorized by Building Permits, 1999		Wholesale Trade, 1997				Retail Trade[1], 1997				Real Estate and Rental and Leasing, 1997			
	New Construction ($1,000)	Number of Housing Units	Number of Establishments	Number of Employees	Sales (mil dol)	Annual Payroll (mil dol)	Number of Establishments	Number of Employees	Sales (mil dol)	Annual Payroll (mil dol)	Number of Establishments	Number of Employees	Receipts (mil dol)	Annual Payroll (mil dol)
	133	134	135	136	137	138	139	140	141	142	143	144	145	146
NORTH CAROLINA—Cont'd														
Chowan	6 501	50	14	207	72.1	5.7	67	730	109.6	9.8	9	14	1.5	0.1
Clay	15 813	161	1	D	D	D	38	324	52.2	3.8	9	20	1.4	0.3
Cleveland	45 694	408	126	1 434	1 355.9	39.1	431	4 707	707.4	68.9	76	354	45.8	6.6
Columbus	8 992	101	62	463	241.3	10.6	296	2 565	387.7	37.4	28	97	8.7	1.4
Craven	54 756	556	76	746	307.6	23.2	443	4 560	772.6	71.3	74	325	28.1	5.2
Cumberland	88 852	1 023	205	2 454	845.3	66.5	1 061	14 929	2 563.3	239.3	272	1 182	137.5	23.4
Currituck	80 916	343	20	D	D	D	81	541	98.6	10.2	20	110	11.0	3.4
Dare	131 862	818	41	374	103.9	7.1	389	2 494	442.4	43.4	106	872	61.8	16.8
Davidson	97 633	925	193	1 972	791.9	67.8	494	5 131	892.0	88.7	100	371	29.4	7.2
Davie	39 324	321	33	406	109.2	8.3	107	902	166.2	14.4	10	15	2.6	0.4
Duplin	12 365	114	44	D	D	D	226	1 879	280.4	25.2	18	65	7.5	0.9
Durham	352 578	3 328	249	4 343	2 306.3	158.4	1 010	13 322	2 032.6	213.2	246	1 301	160.8	30.6
Edgecombe	6 009	65	47	602	454.3	19.9	196	1 631	214.2	21.5	43	354	45.6	7.8
Forsyth	241 082	2 605	478	6 706	3 625.1	219.9	1 489	20 888	3 731.2	344.9	350	1 819	276.6	38.7
Franklin	45 430	417	34	481	166.1	13.8	127	1 057	176.2	15.0	19	60	5.3	0.9
Gaston	134 220	1 316	269	2 047	958.5	67.6	767	9 662	1 587.9	146.5	119	423	37.0	6.8
Gates	7 424	27	6	51	16.7	1.1	29	248	41.8	3.1	3	10	0.5	0.1
Graham	4 580	66	2	D	D	D	36	278	44.6	3.5	5	5	0.7	0.1
Granville	44 430	466	32	222	219.0	8.2	151	1 334	217.1	19.9	24	60	4.2	0.6
Greene	1 612	150	13	122	34.8	2.7	38	302	47.7	4.2	4	8	0.5	0.1
Guilford	403 792	4 481	1 347	21 568	13 448.1	882.9	2 059	29 817	5 179.3	530.8	529	3 704	441.0	82.9
Halifax	11 363	95	36	424	101.7	11.1	306	3 255	462.0	43.7	29	210	17.6	3.7
Harnett	54 768	825	62	756	257.7	18.5	284	2 713	443.2	37.0	45	154	10.7	2.0
Haywood	60 334	457	49	349	127.3	9.4	266	2 847	569.8	46.5	48	119	11.3	1.8
Henderson	121 495	917	91	613	228.0	15.8	386	4 192	901.3	75.2	66	252	28.1	4.9
Hertford	4 757	58	27	264	126.0	5.7	134	1 313	176.9	17.7	14	51	2.7	1.0
Hoke	30 217	302	7	102	30.3	2.8	74	486	67.5	5.9	11	24	1.4	0.3
Hyde	710	10	9	61	21.8	1.3	36	164	26.8	2.5	5	D	D	D
Iredell	257 649	2 111	196	2 443	1 373.6	76.5	510	5 993	1 065.8	93.2	95	341	33.8	6.4
Jackson	69 902	434	16	66	18.2	1.6	178	1 472	220.6	20.1	44	112	9.8	2.2
Johnston	206 070	2 148	117	1 269	836.8	26.3	486	4 580	857.9	71.5	65	221	20.4	3.3
Jones	2 062	20	7	60	12.9	1.2	30	142	33.7	2.2	1	D	D	D
Lee	36 986	408	75	1 159	517.1	32.2	292	3 109	591.9	51.0	59	196	18.2	3.3
Lenoir	16 846	163	80	1 382	486.7	28.2	352	3 597	565.6	51.2	45	170	14.1	2.5
Lincoln	88 357	894	73	1 035	629.9	29.4	212	2 346	406.2	36.6	40	151	13.0	2.5
McDowell	15 131	143	30	293	59.0	6.1	167	1 557	273.4	22.0	22	50	5.0	0.8
Macon	73 392	410	30	101	16.5	1.7	241	1 750	308.1	27.5	38	80	10.6	1.5
Madison	13 290	126	9	D	D	D	51	327	49.0	4.0	8	16	0.6	0.1
Martin	4 855	42	32	220	76.1	5.3	117	1 263	195.1	17.1	10	33	1.7	0.4
Mecklenburg	1 221 583	14 014	2 638	38 333	35 019.8	1 574.3	2 971	44 557	8 517.2	815.7	994	9 430	1 449.2	292.7
Mitchell	6 717	66	11	D	D	D	81	486	97.3	7.3	15	38	3.2	0.6
Montgomery	22 360	131	22	110	58.6	3.0	100	825	137.0	11.7	10	150	5.2	3.1
Moore	116 034	909	92	579	297.6	16.5	360	4 003	616.7	60.5	70	240	19.8	4.7
Nash	50 402	725	125	2 204	1 038.8	67.9	524	5 885	1 035.5	93.0	80	404	50.2	7.3
New Hanover	232 303	2 307	324	3 528	1 216.9	95.4	1 026	12 352	2 461.1	210.9	252	1 140	117.7	22.4
Northampton	5 944	56	22	243	214.8	6.1	66	532	85.4	8.9	4	D	D	D
Onslow	69 941	970	69	D	D	D	564	6 542	1 090.1	96.7	129	497	53.0	7.5
Orange	185 510	1 540	78	428	312.3	12.0	387	5 549	837.2	95.0	126	414	60.0	9.3
Pamlico	11 570	87	12	144	19.0	2.4	49	364	53.8	5.0	9	16	2.4	0.2
Pasquotank	12 067	128	46	606	150.7	12.8	201	2 548	405.0	37.6	37	133	10.1	1.9
Pender	35 528	353	33	326	99.1	8.0	131	906	153.9	13.5	28	94	9.9	1.7
Perquimans	10 882	66	9	87	32.6	1.7	38	274	31.7	3.0	3	D	D	D
Person	28 969	189	30	273	81.1	6.4	160	1 556	250.2	22.7	13	76	4.3	0.9
Pitt	104 762	1 189	181	2 153	1 246.8	66.4	643	7 956	1 384.8	124.8	121	495	51.4	7.9
Polk	13 858	156	14	39	19.7	0.8	61	417	63.3	5.9	21	34	3.7	0.5
Randolph	68 810	873	174	1 637	582.0	44.5	457	4 821	845.0	77.1	58	211	22.3	3.2
Richmond	18 213	321	38	368	96.9	8.9	229	2 165	368.2	32.8	34	139	8.8	1.5
Robeson	29 769	315	82	843	349.6	22.0	450	4 844	1 011.7	79.8	46	260	14.0	4.5
Rockingham	35 058	374	59	394	177.6	10.0	421	3 974	619.8	55.4	59	224	17.6	2.8
Rowan	98 233	817	117	1 392	548.3	39.7	450	4 820	799.2	74.3	69	236	25.3	5.0
Rutherford	34 496	346	66	525	334.9	15.0	286	2 861	443.5	41.1	51	164	12.8	3.0
Sampson	13 468	146	52	587	231.1	17.6	246	2 125	373.8	31.1	25	85	5.3	1.2
Scotland	12 867	159	29	212	75.0	6.1	178	1 856	255.3	26.1	27	113	7.3	1.4
Stanly	25 933	278	61	474	228.3	15.8	265	2 722	472.3	44.5	32	123	12.2	1.9
Stokes	24 785	212	18	D	D	D	118	774	135.5	11.7	12	63	2.2	0.4
Surry	26 867	216	90	1 147	646.3	24.8	381	5 594	780.0	75.6	60	183	20.0	2.5

1. Establishments with payroll.

Table B. States and Counties — Professional, Manufacturing, and Accommodation and Foodservices

STATE County	Professional, Scientific, and Technical Services[1], 1997				Manufacturing, 1997				Accommodation and Foodservices, 1997			
	Number of Establishments	Number of Employees	Receipts (mil dol)	Annual Payroll (mil dol)	Number of Establishments	Number of Employees	Receipts (mil dol)	Annual Payroll (mil dol)	Number of Establishments	Number of Employees	Sales (mil dol)	Annual Payroll (mil dol)
	147	148	149	150	151	152	153	154	155	156	157	158
NORTH CAROLINA—Cont'd												
Chowan	13	65	4.7	1.9	18	1 061	114.2	23.8	27	364	10.1	2.5
Clay	12	25	2.1	0.7	NA	NA	NA	NA	13	D	D	D
Cleveland	110	425	26.4	9.9	173	14 655	2 497.0	399.9	131	2 422	60.5	17.6
Columbus	46	129	10.0	2.2	46	4 767	895.5	129.9	75	1 058	26.7	6.7
Craven	145	1 022	71.2	32.1	86	4 344	796.4	118.5	159	3 004	87.1	24.8
Cumberland	329	2 084	142.1	47.7	121	12 282	2 766.9	384.6	495	10 654	318.4	91.2
Currituck	19	36	2.7	0.8	NA	NA	NA	NA	45	339	13.7	4.0
Dare	76	345	20.7	7.7	NA	NA	NA	NA	274	2 854	140.0	37.6
Davidson	129	438	31.4	10.5	326	21 576	2 249.4	521.7	177	2 802	87.4	24.8
Davie	28	91	5.2	2.0	45	2 886	406.9	76.4	41	D	D	D
Duplin	47	121	7.2	2.4	48	4 688	675.9	95.2	65	976	28.6	7.6
Durham	614	7 922	1 119.6	369.6	181	31 489	11 223.8	1 027.2	468	9 414	378.5	105.7
Edgecombe	42	301	17.0	5.0	50	7 720	1 606.6	234.0	52	747	22.1	6.2
Forsyth	781	5 462	536.2	203.9	399	26 545	9 676.3	908.6	632	12 945	408.0	116.2
Franklin	35	131	8.9	3.4	55	2 259	444.6	67.3	37	D	D	D
Gaston	231	1 157	80.5	29.7	492	31 175	5 772.7	863.2	297	5 315	158.7	42.3
Gates	4	10	0.5	0.1	NA	NA	NA	NA	4	53	1.2	0.4
Graham	3	D	D	D	3	D	D	D	17	160	7.7	2.4
Granville	38	117	8.7	2.7	57	6 990	1 534.2	185.2	52	680	23.3	5.9
Greene	10	23	1.5	0.5	NA	NA	NA	NA	10	117	2.9	0.8
Guilford	1 155	8 157	762.2	273.6	862	47 158	10 546.4	1 431.2	924	19 991	637.5	185.4
Halifax	51	229	9.6	3.4	59	4 136	567.7	113.7	76	1 531	51.7	13.4
Harnett	90	292	23.9	8.5	82	5 959	633.7	149.2	88	1 289	37.1	10.0
Haywood	58	250	14.1	6.5	49	3 321	726.3	130.2	151	2 038	65.9	17.5
Henderson	120	429	28.8	11.6	132	8 361	1 745.8	260.1	167	3 146	97.2	28.6
Hertford	16	74	6.0	2.2	30	1 695	459.2	37.2	39	632	16.8	4.6
Hoke	13	30	1.9	0.5	11	3 151	414.8	72.8	19	189	5.4	1.3
Hyde	5	13	0.7	0.2	NA	NA	NA	NA	33	158	10.2	2.4
Iredell	176	872	88.0	26.3	263	16 978	3 172.6	476.5	195	3 470	117.5	31.9
Jackson	49	194	14.6	4.7	36	699	76.3	15.9	102	942	32.9	8.6
Johnston	133	506	33.9	13.2	114	6 588	1 622.3	192.1	151	2 548	90.9	23.7
Jones	4	7	0.4	0.1	NA	NA	NA	NA	6	41	1.3	0.3
Lee	63	271	17.5	6.5	108	12 130	2 167.9	319.4	83	1 390	40.5	11.4
Lenoir	65	424	28.5	13.9	82	7 120	1 596.1	201.4	95	1 678	51.5	14.6
Lincoln	69	236	14.0	5.9	112	8 047	990.9	196.4	73	962	26.8	7.1
McDowell	28	126	7.0	3.0	63	6 084	866.3	140.9	64	861	26.7	7.0
Macon	38	142	7.2	3.2	34	1 358	174.7	32.5	92	943	30.0	8.2
Madison	11	23	0.8	0.3	NA	NA	NA	NA	24	230	6.1	1.9
Martin	21	73	4.5	2.0	22	1 902	307.9	40.6	43	659	17.5	4.8
Mecklenburg	2 315	27 365	2 902.6	1 123.7	1 001	42 494	8 831.4	1 429.8	1 553	33 351	1 194.2	330.2
Mitchell	10	38	1.9	0.8	32	1 868	151.4	37.1	25	324	8.9	2.6
Montgomery	14	60	2.7	0.9	78	5 292	666.7	112.1	28	D	D	D
Moore	130	562	42.8	16.8	105	5 943	903.7	129.8	154	3 202	133.0	34.6
Nash	113	688	60.8	22.2	104	9 879	1 721.8	267.8	168	3 481	111.6	30.2
New Hanover	497	3 123	251.6	103.9	203	8 378	2 698.2	338.8	455	8 834	281.4	76.7
Northampton	18	42	2.4	0.6	13	749	233.0	20.5	12	D	D	D
Onslow	137	725	34.9	11.9	37	1 829	346.4	37.7	249	4 420	127.9	34.5
Orange	349	1 746	149.0	63.4	78	1 209	142.1	34.0	283	4 443	154.1	44.3
Pamlico	12	28	1.9	0.4	NA	NA	NA	NA	18	293	13.6	4.4
Pasquotank	52	231	15.8	5.1	31	884	148.6	18.5	74	1 183	31.7	9.3
Pender	36	65	4.7	1.3	39	1 123	135.8	24.3	48	499	15.2	4.5
Perquimans	8	28	1.6	0.5	NA	NA	NA	NA	11	D	D	D
Person	34	125	8.3	2.8	39	5 138	1 084.8	135.5	45	716	20.8	5.4
Pitt	219	1 303	88.0	35.3	119	9 305	2 741.9	280.8	237	5 342	153.5	41.8
Polk	28	65	4.4	1.4	25	904	150.9	19.9	36	431	10.9	3.3
Randolph	127	464	42.9	12.9	411	24 954	3 612.7	559.8	150	2 433	75.9	21.0
Richmond	47	186	11.1	3.8	58	4 814	719.7	114.5	69	1 140	28.6	7.1
Robeson	93	534	29.0	7.9	96	11 890	2 407.9	264.0	171	2 685	85.3	22.4
Rockingham	79	327	16.4	5.6	124	13 958	3 214.4	387.0	124	1 913	60.2	16.5
Rowan	120	451	45.0	15.0	201	14 324	3 677.9	413.8	158	2 891	82.4	22.4
Rutherford	52	177	12.7	3.3	97	11 480	1 514.2	278.6	93	1 280	37.4	10.2
Sampson	48	162	9.8	3.6	61	4 202	768.5	102.4	66	903	26.6	7.3
Scotland	27	86	6.7	2.9	59	8 534	1 533.3	234.0	52	1 134	28.9	7.0
Stanly	50	187	11.3	4.0	124	8 086	1 167.5	210.3	92	1 338	34.1	9.1
Stokes	29	72	4.3	1.3	33	1 218	167.7	37.0	39	D	D	D
Surry	101	371	23.5	7.4	149	14 915	1 697.3	300.1	149	1 899	56.6	15.4

1. Firms subject to federal tax.

Table B. States and Counties — Health and Other Services and Federal Funds

STATE County	Health Care and Social Assistance[1], 1997				Other Services[1], 1997				Federal funds and grants, fiscal 1999[2] Expenditures (mil dol)		Direct payments for individuals[3]	
	Number of Establishments	Number of Employees	Receipts (mil dol)	Annual Payroll (mil dol)	Number of Establishments	Number of Employees	Receipts (mil dol)	Annual Payroll (mil dol)	Total	Social Security and government retirement	Medicare	Food stamps and Supplemental Security Income
	159	160	161	162	163	164	165	166	167	168	169	170
NORTH CAROLINA—Cont'd												
Chowan	29	419	17.5	8.5	17	68	4.2	1.0	72.4	36.1	10.8	3.3
Clay	7	125	5.0	2.0	10	22	1.0	0.3	43.2	24.0	7.3	1.3
Cleveland	158	1 782	102.2	51.5	133	466	30.8	8.6	444.3	180.6	63.1	15.2
Columbus	89	1 544	62.7	32.4	77	310	18.8	4.7	284.3	110.0	56.1	19.5
Craven	158	1 872	128.5	55.6	124	679	35.1	10.6	924.5	244.3	56.1	15.3
Cumberland	407	6 135	366.5	159.9	402	2 631	145.7	45.1	3 103.1	681.4	109.4	52.0
Currituck	16	67	3.5	1.0	20	56	4.3	1.0	75.6	43.2	10.2	2.1
Dare	33	474	20.9	8.9	46	184	10.9	3.3	125.0	68.2	15.7	1.6
Davidson	136	1 834	87.1	41.6	147	603	38.3	10.6	401.6	213.9	82.7	14.1
Davie	33	521	21.9	8.7	27	102	4.9	1.5	109.1	60.9	21.3	2.3
Duplin	69	815	29.0	11.9	63	273	16.5	4.5	208.8	82.7	34.5	9.4
Durham	387	5 893	338.6	159.6	333	2 215	121.0	43.2	1 533.5	323.5	124.1	29.8
Edgecombe	55	1 370	75.8	32.7	75	340	16.9	4.8	269.1	75.2	56.4	18.5
Forsyth	538	7 866	624.0	257.2	511	3 492	188.9	65.2	1 159.9	551.6	194.7	37.6
Franklin	44	1 217	46.3	18.9	37	132	8.4	2.2	149.6	62.1	29.6	9.0
Gaston	268	3 601	222.2	106.3	293	1 736	108.7	31.1	622.7	334.9	133.4	28.1
Gates	4	D	D	D	8	44	2.8	0.6	47.7	23.0	7.6	1.6
Graham	3	106	4.1	1.8	11	25	1.7	0.4	37.8	18.1	6.2	1.8
Granville	53	782	26.6	11.7	39	138	9.2	2.6	219.1	71.6	28.5	8.7
Greene	15	271	10.0	4.7	10	37	3.3	0.9	66.6	23.4	11.4	4.0
Guilford	816	11 217	822.5	392.9	768	5 117	346.8	101.1	1 728.5	711.4	239.6	50.9
Halifax	73	1 286	57.4	27.3	93	442	23.0	6.7	327.6	125.9	49.8	26.7
Harnett	95	908	41.9	17.2	88	370	18.5	4.8	281.4	119.9	51.7	15.0
Haywood	97	1 131	55.1	24.3	85	391	16.8	5.4	256.4	135.8	40.9	8.4
Henderson	158	1 545	103.1	44.9	122	489	30.9	9.0	393.3	246.8	77.1	9.1
Hertford	52	569	21.7	9.4	48	225	12.4	3.0	118.3	45.9	16.8	8.2
Hoke	23	302	10.8	4.6	17	51	2.9	0.7	92.5	38.5	12.0	7.1
Hyde	4	18	1.0	0.2	3	15	0.8	0.2	38.3	11.1	4.8	1.7
Iredell	254	3 584	223.7	87.6	169	939	54.8	16.6	366.9	197.1	85.6	11.0
Jackson	55	560	41.8	19.2	48	189	10.6	2.5	113.3	57.5	18.1	4.3
Johnston	126	1 766	77.5	34.3	138	513	33.4	9.1	367.2	160.6	73.1	17.0
Jones	12	222	13.8	6.3	4	8	0.4	0.1	55.6	24.4	9.2	2.4
Lee	95	1 679	97.1	48.2	83	358	21.0	6.0	204.8	110.4	36.6	6.8
Lenoir	138	1 891	100.5	43.4	88	613	28.6	8.8	321.9	129.2	63.8	16.9
Lincoln	80	793	42.8	21.7	80	332	17.0	5.0	171.8	99.7	34.5	3.5
McDowell	47	615	27.5	13.0	35	148	8.1	2.3	144.3	79.4	23.7	5.7
Macon	52	509	27.1	12.5	61	218	12.7	3.5	147.4	82.9	25.6	3.8
Madison	19	253	12.2	5.6	14	39	3.4	0.9	129.1	34.8	14.2	4.6
Martin	35	435	17.9	8.0	28	99	4.4	1.3	128.7	53.6	21.0	6.9
Mecklenburg	1 223	17 239	1 346.8	597.4	1 297	10 102	675.5	215.0	2 011.7	867.3	287.0	67.8
Mitchell	22	216	10.5	4.5	19	82	6.2	1.5	77.8	34.5	12.5	2.5
Montgomery	31	333	11.9	5.6	33	91	3.9	1.1	102.7	46.1	18.6	5.2
Moore	136	2 037	147.2	78.6	98	393	27.4	7.7	358.3	232.8	61.1	7.8
Nash	150	3 089	204.2	82.6	136	907	57.7	16.0	334.6	177.1	44.5	17.4
New Hanover	402	5 653	372.8	157.1	331	1 889	116.3	35.2	674.4	324.0	98.5	26.6
Northampton	16	243	9.9	4.6	20	45	2.6	0.5	130.9	49.6	17.9	9.4
Onslow	188	2 489	127.1	57.5	195	914	45.5	13.4	1 538.9	283.2	42.5	16.4
Orange	217	2 446	122.8	60.3	144	738	40.4	13.0	547.0	150.8	55.4	7.0
Pamlico	15	183	7.4	3.1	15	54	3.9	1.0	62.8	35.3	7.8	2.1
Pasquotank	77	803	49.5	24.4	59	277	15.0	4.3	221.0	76.2	26.0	8.2
Pender	35	432	21.8	8.4	41	147	8.9	2.4	156.6	81.1	24.6	6.4
Perquimans	11	169	5.7	2.5	11	44	1.6	0.4	65.0	32.6	8.8	2.9
Person	42	344	16.4	7.7	53	147	10.2	2.2	125.8	58.3	23.2	5.6
Pitt	205	3 334	216.7	115.5	158	875	49.1	13.7	467.4	182.6	72.7	27.6
Polk	30	401	15.8	6.8	17	47	3.7	1.0	84.0	52.7	13.9	1.4
Randolph	144	1 747	87.5	39.0	188	1 064	70.9	15.7	326.4	181.6	68.8	9.4
Richmond	80	1 051	55.8	22.1	66	279	16.9	4.5	213.3	104.1	38.8	11.4
Robeson	154	2 076	95.9	47.2	120	437	27.6	7.2	554.0	194.1	86.1	40.8
Rockingham	141	1 697	84.6	36.4	126	480	26.9	8.0	355.9	178.8	74.7	14.4
Rowan	186	2 571	128.8	58.8	150	645	38.9	12.3	484.1	234.2	82.0	13.8
Rutherford	93	1 060	47.1	22.6	81	269	16.1	4.2	236.8	126.1	39.3	9.2
Sampson	66	758	34.7	17.2	70	332	22.7	6.2	235.9	95.2	39.6	11.6
Scotland	70	715	42.3	20.2	47	189	10.5	2.9	156.0	61.6	22.1	10.5
Stanly	98	1 115	44.2	21.9	81	410	34.5	11.9	194.7	110.4	39.6	5.8
Stokes	30	488	21.2	8.8	38	157	9.6	3.0	111.7	60.6	20.4	3.9
Surry	108	1 278	71.4	34.7	93	407	25.2	6.5	285.7	137.7	58.2	9.1

1. Firms subject to federal tax.   2. October 1, 1998 to September 30, 1999.   3. State totals may include programs not allocated by county.

	Federal funds and grants, fiscal 1999[1] (cont'd)							Local government finances, 1997				
	Expenditures (mil dol) (cont'd)							General revenue				
	Procurement contract awards			Grants[2]							Taxes	
											Per capita[3] (dollars)	
STATE County	Salaries and wages	Defense	Other	Medicaid and other health-related	Nutrition and family welfare	Education	Other	Total (mil dol)	Intergovern-mental (mil dol)	Total (mil dol)	Total	Property
	171	172	173	174	175	176	177	178	179	180	181	182
NORTH CAROLINA—Cont'd												
Chowan	2.1	0.0	0.7	9.2	4.4	0.8	0.4	27.5	16.2	7.7	544	394
Clay	1.3	0.0	0.4	7.4	0.7	0.4	0.2	12.8	8.1	3.8	462	313
Cleveland	10.0	29.4	64.9	50.1	12.5	4.9	6.4	239.4	98.2	46.0	500	378
Columbus	6.9	0.1	1.5	60.9	11.4	4.5	2.4	109.6	72.1	23.8	453	335
Craven	446.0	80.4	3.2	46.6	9.2	5.5	7.8	267.0	91.9	42.5	487	341
Cumberland	1 678.9	298.9	27.9	106.3	46.2	17.9	51.5	709.7	294.8	158.4	558	407
Currituck	2.1	0.0	8.7	4.5	1.2	0.7	0.8	40.7	15.9	19.9	1 164	856
Dare	11.9	5.7	1.7	3.4	1.2	0.5	13.6	84.3	22.9	44.6	1 599	1 127
Davidson	9.9	7.9	13.7	32.7	9.3	5.0	6.8	214.6	126.4	59.3	426	298
Davie	3.1	4.6	1.1	10.8	1.7	1.1	1.2	58.4	24.5	15.0	480	354
Duplin	6.7	7.0	1.2	38.8	7.4	3.4	5.0	93.6	57.6	21.2	491	364
Durham	228.3	31.1	302.6	337.0	29.2	16.8	91.5	634.3	189.7	202.0	1 012	827
Edgecombe	26.7	0.1	6.9	47.7	14.3	4.9	4.5	104.3	59.5	26.9	485	380
Forsyth	63.7	4.2	21.7	179.7	31.1	14.0	40.1	895.3	329.0	400.2	1 400	1 100
Franklin	4.3	0.5	1.2	30.5	4.7	2.1	1.0	71.2	37.0	22.1	507	379
Gaston	20.2	2.5	5.5	60.0	21.1	8.5	4.1	382.4	193.2	108.2	590	469
Gates	1.3	0.0	0.4	8.1	1.7	0.5	0.4	16.6	11.1	4.1	413	306
Graham	1.8	0.0	0.3	6.7	1.0	0.7	1.0	14.6	9.6	3.5	453	311
Granville	41.0	4.1	29.6	25.0	4.9	3.2	-0.4	90.9	42.4	19.3	457	325
Greene	2.1	0.0	0.4	10.0	7.1	1.1	0.4	28.4	18.1	6.6	364	253
Guilford	228.0	130.6	63.1	116.6	38.9	25.1	90.5	940.2	391.5	346.5	907	734
Halifax	6.6	0.2	4.1	69.6	17.6	6.1	7.7	133.8	78.7	30.5	538	411
Harnett	6.4	8.5	4.9	44.9	10.4	3.7	3.3	169.5	92.0	31.7	393	272
Haywood	7.2	15.1	1.6	28.3	5.6	1.9	9.4	158.3	55.7	32.4	633	474
Henderson	10.8	3.6	2.7	24.8	6.7	2.9	5.8	204.4	67.3	45.1	568	409
Hertford	3.6	0.0	0.6	24.0	5.1	2.5	6.3	50.9	33.3	11.9	530	387
Hoke	2.9	0.2	2.1	15.7	5.4	1.9	3.8	47.8	31.1	11.2	381	276
Hyde	1.5	5.0	0.2	6.4	1.1	0.5	0.3	13.8	7.6	4.3	803	618
Iredell	12.5	0.4	5.2	31.6	8.4	3.6	6.4	186.6	96.0	57.0	524	369
Jackson	3.2	0.0	0.6	17.1	2.5	4.1	2.5	52.1	29.3	17.7	597	400
Johnston	10.3	1.9	2.4	66.8	10.1	3.6	8.6	227.5	104.6	56.0	549	389
Jones	1.2	0.2	0.3	9.4	2.1	0.7	0.5	17.0	11.4	4.1	456	345
Lee	7.3	1.3	2.8	23.6	4.8	2.5	4.0	104.1	56.2	29.9	616	483
Lenoir	19.2	1.3	4.8	51.0	10.0	5.4	8.7	140.4	79.2	32.2	540	397
Lincoln	5.7	2.1	1.7	13.3	4.0	1.7	4.0	92.6	46.2	30.4	531	391
McDowell	3.9	0.0	0.9	19.7	4.0	1.5	4.8	61.5	37.6	17.0	436	292
Macon	8.3	1.8	2.7	15.3	4.4	1.1	1.2	47.1	20.2	18.9	686	498
Madison	2.6	0.0	5.7	23.0	2.4	2.0	37.4	27.5	17.6	7.3	396	293
Martin	3.8	0.0	0.6	23.3	7.8	1.7	0.9	88.9	35.1	15.9	605	464
Mecklenburg	278.9	37.4	85.0	153.6	56.8	29.7	101.5	2 651.2	669.9	668.8	1 090	824
Mitchell	2.3	0.0	0.4	16.4	4.1	3.1	0.7	30.0	19.9	6.9	466	319
Montgomery	2.5	7.6	0.6	15.0	3.0	1.2	1.4	49.3	28.9	12.5	513	401
Moore	8.3	0.1	2.3	27.5	5.2	3.5	1.7	144.4	79.6	43.3	617	450
Nash	3.6	4.1	1.7	48.9	15.0	5.0	5.5	280.2	116.1	47.0	523	398
New Hanover	48.9	22.7	16.4	57.2	16.8	6.3	32.7	543.3	166.8	117.5	796	559
Northampton	2.6	0.1	0.6	29.3	10.0	1.6	1.6	41.3	25.7	10.5	496	403
Onslow	970.1	133.7	5.7	32.2	11.1	5.3	27.3	222.6	130.6	48.8	341	218
Orange	19.8	0.9	23.8	209.6	12.1	18.2	41.3	213.3	85.1	95.0	875	727
Pamlico	1.9	0.2	0.4	7.3	1.5	0.6	0.2	28.3	17.6	7.0	574	441
Pasquotank	46.7	0.0	10.2	14.8	6.2	5.2	17.1	130.8	48.1	17.3	507	351
Pender	3.8	1.3	1.7	20.8	4.5	1.9	7.1	61.5	31.5	21.8	573	428
Perquimans	1.4	1.5	0.4	8.1	2.1	0.8	1.5	22.1	12.0	5.6	507	398
Person	3.2	0.1	0.7	23.5	4.6	2.3	1.2	75.3	35.5	21.7	653	504
Pitt	20.4	0.9	6.3	82.1	17.7	9.2	25.9	615.5	129.6	64.9	536	396
Polk	2.3	0.0	0.6	6.4	1.0	0.6	4.8	23.7	12.8	8.1	490	382
Randolph	10.5	1.1	5.3	27.3	7.0	4.0	8.1	188.0	105.1	54.2	454	330
Richmond	5.9	0.1	2.0	33.0	6.5	3.3	3.9	89.0	53.0	21.5	467	340
Robeson	28.0	0.1	6.9	115.6	28.4	11.2	19.1	224.3	138.8	47.1	412	287
Rockingham	8.9	2.4	5.1	50.0	9.7	4.4	2.5	168.9	89.0	48.2	535	413
Rowan	63.4	0.4	5.3	29.8	12.6	6.1	23.6	213.5	118.7	61.6	499	378
Rutherford	6.4	0.4	1.6	36.1	6.9	3.5	5.6	115.9	63.9	28.3	471	334
Sampson	6.9	0.1	3.6	44.4	9.2	3.7	3.7	101.5	65.3	23.9	462	344
Scotland	3.3	0.1	0.9	32.3	15.3	2.5	2.5	73.8	43.6	20.0	561	416
Stanly	9.1	0.1	1.7	16.2	3.6	2.3	2.0	106.4	61.8	26.7	481	359
Stokes	3.8	0.0	1.2	14.8	2.4	1.3	2.3	59.6	33.8	17.2	404	282
Surry	8.2	0.1	1.9	39.3	4.5	2.8	21.6	125.8	69.8	33.6	505	343

1. October 1, 1998 to September 30, 1999.   2. State totals may include programs not allocated by county.   3. Based on the resident population estimated as of July 1 of the year shown.

Table B. States and Counties — Local Government Finances, Government Employment, and Elections

STATE County	Direct general expenditure Total (mil dol) 183	Per capita[1] (dollars) 184	Percent of total for — Education 185	Health and hospitals 186	Police protection 187	Public welfare 188	High- ways 189	Debt outstanding Total (mil dol) 190	Per capita[1] (dollars) 191	Government employment, 1998 Federal civilian 192	Federal military 193	State and local 194	Presidential election, 2000 Percent of vote cast — Demo- cratic 195	Republi- can 196	All other 197
NORTH CAROLINA—Cont'd															
Chowan	30.2	2 132	48.7	3.7	4.5	10.5	1.5	15.1	1 066	38	44	843	NA	NA	NA
Clay	12.7	1 529	58.6	7.9	5.0	2.8	0.3	2.0	238	24	27	410	NA	NA	NA
Cleveland	238.4	2 594	41.0	32.3	3.6	6.6	1.0	177.9	1 935	203	288	5 074	NA	NA	NA
Columbus	109.9	2 093	60.4	5.3	3.6	7.7	1.5	57.5	1 096	147	164	3 351	NA	NA	NA
Craven	281.6	3 223	35.5	35.5	3.4	4.5	1.2	115.2	1 319	6 253	8 537	7 490	NA	NA	NA
Cumberland	746.1	2 627	37.7	26.6	5.8	5.7	1.4	475.3	1 673	10 355	45 494	19 320	NA	NA	NA
Currituck	41.0	2 396	55.8	1.4	3.7	4.1	0.1	25.5	1 492	47	56	952	NA	NA	NA
Dare	82.8	2 969	30.9	8.8	8.5	3.4	2.7	42.6	1 529	221	238	2 204	NA	NA	NA
Davidson	221.3	1 591	60.3	7.2	5.0	5.4	1.4	69.4	499	184	439	5 995	NA	NA	NA
Davie	62.4	2 001	51.3	23.8	3.0	4.2	0.6	16.6	532	56	100	1 340	NA	NA	NA
Duplin	87.1	2 017	55.1	2.6	3.9	8.4	3.3	36.3	841	154	134	3 054	NA	NA	NA
Durham	620.3	3 107	31.1	26.7	5.4	5.7	2.3	541.5	2 712	4 513	683	13 366	NA	NA	NA
Edgecombe	98.8	1 776	52.8	8.6	4.3	13.7	1.0	9.0	162	497	172	4 386	NA	NA	NA
Forsyth	738.9	2 585	38.2	3.7	5.8	4.8	2.7	558.8	1 955	1 173	901	15 335	NA	NA	NA
Franklin	74.2	1 704	52.2	5.9	4.0	9.4	0.7	39.2	900	75	139	2 086	NA	NA	NA
Gaston	404.7	2 207	42.2	8.5	5.4	6.7	4.3	256.6	1 400	387	573	8 473	NA	NA	NA
Gates	16.7	1 665	76.9	0.8	1.2	7.4	0.3	0.1	14	32	31	594	NA	NA	NA
Graham	13.6	1 773	61.2	3.7	3.1	6.6	1.2	4.8	628	76	24	468	NA	NA	NA
Granville	83.7	1 985	47.0	20.0	3.9	5.9	1.8	40.5	961	737	133	6 263	NA	NA	NA
Greene	28.4	1 576	57.6	3.5	4.8	10.1	0.6	10.9	605	59	57	1 331	NA	NA	NA
Guilford	932.9	2 443	41.3	8.4	6.7	6.5	3.0	575.4	1 507	4 322	1 268	26 134	NA	NA	NA
Halifax	143.0	2 521	53.2	10.2	3.9	8.6	1.6	45.6	804	132	175	4 974	NA	NA	NA
Harnett	154.9	1 921	47.3	21.1	4.1	6.3	2.5	61.3	760	119	264	4 326	NA	NA	NA
Haywood	163.8	3 202	31.9	42.3	3.1	4.3	1.4	75.8	1 481	137	160	3 344	NA	NA	NA
Henderson	191.8	2 417	35.4	38.5	3.8	4.9	0.8	30.7	386	224	251	4 430	NA	NA	NA
Hertford	50.7	2 267	58.3	6.1	3.8	10.3	1.7	5.7	255	73	69	1 702	NA	NA	NA
Hoke	46.2	1 572	62.4	2.6	4.1	8.8	0.8	15.5	527	46	95	2 016	NA	NA	NA
Hyde	13.0	2 423	54.4	8.6	3.1	9.3	0.2	4.0	736	44	18	756	NA	NA	NA
Iredell	181.2	1 664	59.6	3.6	5.3	5.9	1.2	77.2	709	257	353	6 216	NA	NA	NA
Jackson	48.7	1 644	57.1	6.1	3.4	8.2	0.9	19.6	663	69	95	3 689	NA	NA	NA
Johnston	235.9	2 315	47.7	20.4	3.9	4.8	1.3	76.1	747	197	331	5 503	NA	NA	NA
Jones	16.8	1 867	62.0	4.2	3.5	12.4	0.7	1.2	135	23	29	519	NA	NA	NA
Lee	107.3	2 214	58.2	2.8	5.6	5.5	1.7	74.1	1 529	161	153	2 697	NA	NA	NA
Lenoir	163.2	2 736	59.8	5.7	2.4	6.2	1.1	105.5	1 769	335	183	6 605	NA	NA	NA
Lincoln	88.4	1 546	58.3	4.5	4.7	6.9	0.4	102.9	1 798	105	180	2 893	NA	NA	NA
McDowell	58.4	1 495	63.3	3.6	4.4	8.8	1.4	6.5	167	98	124	2 385	NA	NA	NA
Macon	43.0	1 558	49.2	6.0	5.2	6.8	2.5	8.0	289	237	88	1 250	NA	NA	NA
Madison	27.1	1 466	56.9	5.2	3.6	12.4	1.7	2.3	125	71	58	888	NA	NA	NA
Martin	86.4	3 281	40.2	19.6	2.9	5.2	0.7	242.9	9 228	89	81	2 022	NA	NA	NA
Mecklenburg	2 495.5	4 069	26.2	35.3	4.6	5.1	2.1	2 850.3	4 647	4 870	2 067	45 215	NA	NA	NA
Mitchell	29.6	2 000	71.0	1.9	2.8	7.4	1.4	2.8	189	62	46	1 142	NA	NA	NA
Montgomery	49.6	2 042	61.8	4.4	5.0	6.3	1.6	20.3	835	82	75	1 584	NA	NA	NA
Moore	151.0	2 152	47.8	19.5	5.1	3.7	1.8	49.5	705	159	222	3 858	NA	NA	NA
Nash	287.3	3 194	39.0	35.7	3.9	4.1	2.0	41.6	463	88	283	5 544	NA	NA	NA
New Hanover	559.6	3 790	25.9	42.7	3.3	4.6	1.0	311.4	2 109	855	648	12 922	NA	NA	NA
Northampton	40.3	1 900	55.1	7.5	3.5	12.2	1.5	14.1	665	56	66	1 533	NA	NA	NA
Onslow	245.6	1 717	54.8	7.5	4.2	4.9	1.4	93.6	655	5 281	37 705	6 845	NA	NA	NA
Orange	207.1	1 909	49.3	2.1	6.5	4.8	1.3	147.3	1 358	345	423	26 173	NA	NA	NA
Pamlico	26.9	2 208	60.9	3.2	2.6	8.0	1.0	13.3	1 090	32	60	702	NA	NA	NA
Pasquotank	139.1	4 065	39.3	40.0	2.4	3.4	0.5	67.2	1 964	640	696	4 706	NA	NA	NA
Pender	62.1	1 635	54.6	5.0	3.7	7.6	0.5	28.8	758	80	123	2 196	NA	NA	NA
Perquimans	23.1	2 074	52.5	1.3	3.0	7.4	1.0	7.3	653	41	35	612	NA	NA	NA
Person	74.2	2 233	53.2	5.1	3.5	7.2	0.9	101.5	3 054	66	105	1 992	NA	NA	NA
Pitt	538.9	4 452	21.3	56.9	2.9	3.2	1.0	243.6	2 012	373	404	17 018	NA	NA	NA
Polk	23.5	1 422	56.5	2.7	7.8	6.8	1.9	11.3	686	41	52	752	NA	NA	NA
Randolph	200.1	1 674	61.5	7.6	3.9	4.7	1.3	107.0	895	191	377	5 461	NA	NA	NA
Richmond	85.9	1 862	57.5	3.1	4.2	8.0	1.4	38.6	836	126	144	3 028	NA	NA	NA
Robeson	227.7	1 993	56.0	8.5	4.5	10.0	1.3	82.6	722	550	360	7 843	NA	NA	NA
Rockingham	162.5	1 803	53.4	7.4	6.3	5.7	2.7	82.6	917	175	280	4 294	NA	NA	NA
Rowan	220.0	1 781	58.7	2.6	4.5	6.0	2.5	88.2	714	1 716	391	5 732	NA	NA	NA
Rutherford	115.5	1 920	53.0	10.0	4.6	6.4	1.6	56.8	944	129	189	3 336	NA	NA	NA
Sampson	102.1	1 971	58.7	9.0	4.3	7.3	1.4	36.4	703	136	163	3 761	NA	NA	NA
Scotland	75.2	2 112	53.2	6.7	4.4	8.8	1.0	16.0	449	55	111	1 953	NA	NA	NA
Stanly	104.5	1 881	57.4	3.4	4.1	5.9	2.2	32.7	588	155	175	2 885	NA	NA	NA
Stokes	59.4	1 390	62.1	7.2	3.7	7.3	0.4	21.4	501	82	135	1 620	NA	NA	NA
Surry	129.3	1 944	61.5	7.0	3.9	5.6	1.5	60.4	908	177	208	4 470	NA	NA	NA

1. Based on the resident population estimated as of July 1 of the year shown.

STATE/County code	MSA/PMSA/NECMA code[1]	County Type[2]	STATE County	Land area[3] (sq km) 1990	Population and population characteristics, 1999													
								Race (percent)						Age (percent)						
					Total persons	Rank	Per square kilometer	White	Black	Am. Indian, Eskimo, Aleut	Asian and Pacific Islander		Percent Hispanic[4]	Under 5 years	5 to 17 years	18 to 24 years	25 to 34 years	35 to 44 years	45 to 54 years
					1	2	3	4	5	6	7	8	9	10	11	12	13	14	15
			NORTH CAROLINA— Cont'd																
37 173	...	9	Swain	1 368	12 341	2 262	9.0	67.9	1.9	29.6	0.5		1.2	6.8	19.8	7.8	12.7	14.5	13.2
37 175	...	6	Transylvania	980	28 853	1 415	29.4	94.4	4.7	0.4	0.5		1.3	5.6	16.8	7.7	10.9	13.2	13.3
37 177	...	9	Tyrrell	1 010	3 940	2 920	3.9	57.5	42.1	0.1	0.3		0.6	6.1	20.6	7.2	13.3	14.9	12.7
37 179	1520	1	Union	1 651	115 144	460	69.7	82.8	16.2	0.4	0.5		1.7	7.9	21.0	8.3	14.1	16.8	14.4
37 181	...	6	Vance	657	42 496	1 031	64.7	54.2	45.4	0.2	0.3		1.4	7.2	20.6	8.5	13.3	16.2	12.7
37 183	6640	2	Wake	2 160	586 940	88	271.7	75.5	20.9	0.3	3.3		2.7	7.4	17.4	10.6	18.2	18.7	13.1
37 185	...	8	Warren	1 110	18 848	1 826	17.0	38.0	57.1	4.7	0.1		1.1	6.1	18.5	7.0	11.8	14.8	12.4
37 187	...	7	Washington	901	13 443	2 180	14.9	53.8	45.7	0.1	0.4		0.9	6.8	21.4	7.4	11.4	15.5	13.1
37 189	...	7	Watauga	810	41 419	1 052	51.1	96.9	2.2	0.2	0.7		1.5	4.9	13.8	25.0	11.3	13.7	12.0
37 191	2980	3	Wayne	1 431	111 711	471	78.1	65.4	33.0	0.3	1.4		2.6	7.4	19.4	8.6	15.9	15.9	12.8
37 193	...	7	Wilkes	1 961	63 640	752	32.5	94.5	5.1	0.2	0.3		1.3	6.0	18.5	7.4	13.3	16.2	14.7
37 195	...	4	Wilson	961	68 801	708	71.6	61.3	38.1	0.1	0.5		1.6	6.4	20.3	8.1	12.6	16.3	13.2
37 197	3120	2	Yadkin	869	35 245	1 216	40.6	95.3	4.4	0.1	0.1		2.9	6.3	17.4	7.1	13.0	15.7	14.9
37 199	...	8	Yancey	809	16 860	1 937	20.8	98.7	1.0	0.2	0.1		0.7	5.9	17.3	6.8	11.5	15.7	13.9
38 000	...	X	**NORTH DAKOTA**	178 695	633 666	X	3.5	93.7	0.6	4.8	0.8		1.1	6.2	19.1	10.8	12.3	15.4	13.0
38 001	...	9	Adams	2 559	2 644	3 016	1.0	99.4	0.3	0.4	0.0		0.1	5.1	18.2	5.2	9.0	15.9	14.2
38 003	...	7	Barnes	3 864	11 864	2 287	3.1	98.6	0.3	0.5	0.5		0.4	5.2	17.3	10.8	9.4	14.2	13.6
38 005	...	9	Benson	3 596	6 781	2 701	1.9	56.0	0.0	43.9	0.1		0.3	9.4	25.9	8.4	10.4	12.5	11.8
38 007	...	9	Billings	2 982	1 066	3 108	0.4	99.1	0.3	0.3	0.4		0.2	6.0	23.8	6.2	10.1	16.6	14.2
38 009	...	7	Bottineau	4 322	7 241	2 660	1.7	98.9	0.1	0.8	0.2		0.3	4.8	18.9	6.9	8.9	15.2	13.9
38 011	...	9	Bowman	3 010	3 269	2 972	1.1	99.7	0.0	0.1	0.2		0.2	5.1	19.9	5.2	9.3	15.0	14.1
38 013	...	9	Burke	2 858	2 189	3 048	0.8	99.1	0.0	0.5	0.3		0.6	3.6	18.1	4.2	7.6	14.0	13.8
38 015	1010	3	Burleigh	4 230	67 371	716	15.9	96.0	0.2	3.2	0.6		0.9	6.1	19.1	9.9	13.0	17.2	14.0
38 017	2520	3	Cass	4 573	118 405	445	25.9	97.1	0.3	1.2	1.4		1.1	6.2	17.0	15.2	14.4	17.1	12.7
38 019	...	9	Cavalier	3 857	4 821	2 853	1.2	99.0	0.0	0.9	0.1		0.1	5.3	17.8	5.4	8.5	13.8	14.9
38 021	...	9	Dickey	2 930	5 662	2 793	1.9	99.2	0.1	0.4	0.3		0.7	4.6	18.4	9.9	8.7	13.3	13.9
38 023	...	9	Divide	3 262	2 294	3 033	0.7	99.2	0.0	0.4	0.4		0.3	4.8	15.9	4.2	8.1	13.3	14.6
38 025	...	9	Dunn	5 206	3 457	2 959	0.7	87.9	0.3	11.3	0.5		1.0	6.6	21.4	5.8	9.8	15.0	13.5
38 027	...	9	Eddy	1 637	2 795	3 007	1.7	98.1	0.0	1.8	0.1		0.1	4.7	18.9	5.1	9.2	14.3	12.1
38 029	...	8	Emmons	3 911	4 302	2 885	1.1	99.8	0.0	0.1	0.1		0.2	4.7	17.4	5.3	8.1	11.8	15.0
38 031	...	9	Foster	1 645	3 787	2 930	2.3	99.2	0.0	0.7	0.1		0.4	5.7	19.1	5.5	9.8	13.0	14.0
38 033	...	9	Golden Valley	2 595	1 782	3 076	0.7	97.3	0.0	2.0	0.7		0.3	5.3	22.6	5.9	8.8	13.2	12.7
38 035	2985	3	Grand Forks	3 724	64 674	738	17.4	93.7	2.4	2.2	1.7		2.4	7.1	17.2	19.1	15.4	14.7	10.8
38 037	...	8	Grant	4 298	2 854	3 001	0.7	98.7	0.0	1.0	0.2		0.4	4.8	18.3	4.9	7.7	13.7	15.2
38 039	...	9	Griggs	1 835	2 778	3 008	1.5	99.4	0.0	0.3	0.3		0.1	4.8	18.3	4.9	7.7	15.6	12.8
38 041	...	9	Hettinger	2 933	2 839	3 002	1.0	99.1	0.0	0.6	0.3		0.1	5.0	17.8	4.7	8.1	13.3	14.4
38 043	...	8	Kidder	3 501	2 798	3 006	0.8	99.9	0.0	0.0	0.1		0.3	4.7	19.7	4.8	8.4	13.0	14.2
38 045	...	9	La Moure	2 971	4 700	2 859	1.6	99.7	0.0	0.2	0.1		0.2	4.9	19.6	4.8	8.7	13.1	13.7
38 047	...	9	Logan	2 571	2 268	3 037	0.9	99.2	0.3	0.2	0.4		0.4	4.8	17.4	4.1	9.3	11.7	15.4
38 049	...	9	McHenry	4 854	5 962	2 775	1.2	99.2	0.1	0.5	0.3		0.3	4.7	19.7	4.9	8.1	14.4	15.3
38 051	...	9	McIntosh	2 526	3 397	2 960	1.3	99.4	0.0	0.4	0.2		0.3	3.9	14.0	3.5	7.3	10.0	13.0
38 053	...	9	McKenzie	7 102	5 541	2 805	0.8	82.6	0.1	17.3	0.1		1.1	7.9	23.2	5.9	11.0	15.9	13.6
38 055	...	8	McLean	5 466	9 603	2 464	1.8	93.3	0.0	6.5	0.2		0.4	5.2	21.3	4.7	8.9	16.0	14.1
38 057	...	7	Mercer	2 708	9 210	2 490	3.4	96.0	0.3	3.0	0.7		0.8	7.4	22.5	4.8	13.8	17.2	13.5
38 059	1010	3	Morton	4 989	24 568	1 547	4.9	97.6	0.1	2.0	0.3		0.5	5.7	21.4	7.3	11.0	15.8	13.7
38 061	...	9	Mountrail	4 724	6 516	2 732	1.4	76.1	0.1	23.6	0.2		0.6	6.4	22.5	6.3	9.5	15.1	13.1
38 063	...	8	Nelson	2 543	3 656	2 938	1.4	99.7	0.0	0.2	0.1		0.1	4.0	16.3	3.7	8.0	12.7	14.7
38 065	...	8	Oliver	1 874	2 158	3 055	1.2	97.8	0.0	2.1	0.0		0.2	5.9	24.5	5.2	9.9	19.5	14.0
38 067	...	9	Pembina	2 898	8 351	2 562	2.9	97.1	0.1	2.0	0.2		1.5	5.4	19.8	5.8	10.1	15.7	13.8
38 069	...	7	Pierce	2 636	4 594	2 863	1.7	98.9	0.1	0.5	0.4		0.1	4.4	19.0	5.2	8.7	12.6	14.4
38 071	...	7	Ramsey	3 072	11 944	2 280	3.9	93.8	0.2	5.6	0.3		0.4	5.8	18.4	8.6	11.1	14.4	13.5
38 073	...	8	Ransom	2 235	5 731	2 790	2.6	99.3	0.1	0.3	0.2		0.7	5.0	19.2	5.2	10.0	15.0	13.8
38 075	...	9	Renville	2 266	2 799	3 005	1.2	98.0	0.4	0.9	0.6		0.2	4.6	20.8	5.5	9.8	14.5	15.1
38 077	...	6	Richland	3 722	17 924	1 874	4.8	96.6	0.2	2.6	0.7		0.4	5.8	18.9	13.6	11.2	13.9	12.3
38 079	...	9	Rolette	2 338	14 229	2 118	6.1	28.9	0.2	70.7	0.1		0.6	10.2	28.6	9.3	12.8	12.6	10.3
38 081	...	9	Sargent	2 224	4 288	2 888	1.9	99.4	0.1	0.3	0.2		0.4	5.1	19.5	5.9	9.7	16.1	16.6
38 083	...	9	Sheridan	2 517	1 665	3 085	0.7	99.4	0.0	0.5	0.1		0.1	4.9	16.5	3.7	8.2	13.8	15.4
38 085	...	9	Sioux	2 834	4 156	2 902	1.5	20.0	0.1	79.3	0.6		0.6	11.2	32.9	9.4	12.5	13.4	9.9
38 087	...	9	Slope	3 155	887	3 117	0.3	94.4	2.6	1.4	1.7		2.1	4.6	21.5	5.9	9.0	13.6	13.0
38 089	...	7	Stark	3 466	22 490	1 636	6.5	98.2	0.2	0.8	0.7		1.2	6.3	20.3	9.7	12.6	14.9	12.8
38 091	...	8	Steele	1 845	2 182	3 049	1.2	99.8	0.0	0.1	0.1		0.3	5.4	18.9	4.2	9.4	13.0	17.0
38 093	...	7	Stutsman	5 754	21 090	1 710	3.7	98.3	0.3	0.7	0.7		0.6	5.2	17.8	9.1	11.0	15.2	13.5
38 095	...	9	Towner	2 656	2 955	2 991	1.1	98.0	0.0	1.8	0.2		0.3	5.9	18.5	5.9	9.4	14.5	12.8
38 097	...	8	Traill	2 232	8 555	2 549	3.8	98.8	0.1	0.7	0.4		2.0	5.2	18.8	10.3	8.8	13.9	13.9
38 099	...	6	Walsh	3 320	13 356	2 186	4.0	98.1	0.3	0.9	0.7		4.9	5.9	19.4	6.6	10.9	14.7	13.7

1. MSA = Metropolitan Statistical Area. PMSA = Primary MSA. NECMA = New England County Metropolitan Area. See Appendix A for explanation of these concepts. See Appendix B for list of metropolitan areas identified by type, with component counties.   2. County typology code from the Economic Research Service of USDA. See Appendix A for definition.   3. Dry land or land partially or temporarily covered by water.   4. Hispanic persons may be of any race.

Table B. States and Counties — **Population and Households**

STATE County	55 to 64 years	65 to 74 years	75 years and over	Percent female	Total persons 1990	Total persons 1980	Percent change 1980–1990	Percent change 1990–1999	Births	Deaths	Net migration	Number	Percent change 1980–1990	Persons per household	Female family householder[1]	One person
	16	17	18	19	20	21	22	23	24	25	26	27	28	29	30	31
NORTH CAROLINA—Cont'd																
Swain	10.5	7.3	7.4	49.9	11 268	10 283	9.6	9.5	1 575	1 302	839	4 173	17.1	2.55	13.2	23.6
Transylvania	11.1	12.0	9.4	51.2	25 520	23 417	9.0	13.1	2 674	2 720	3 489	9 924	21.0	2.45	8.0	22.4
Tyrrell	9.4	8.1	7.8	49.1	3 856	3 975	-3.0	2.2	383	447	158	1 471	6.5	2.62	14.5	24.4
Union	8.3	5.2	4.0	50.9	84 210	70 436	19.6	36.7	15 046	6 510	22 401	29 307	27.9	2.82	10.5	17.1
Vance	9.2	6.7	5.5	52.9	38 892	36 748	5.8	9.3	6 057	4 194	1 854	14 166	15.7	2.69	18.2	22.9
Wake	7.0	4.3	3.4	51.1	426 311	301 429	41.4	37.7	72 285	26 090	114 728	165 743	55.6	2.46	10.0	25.7
Warren	11.3	9.8	8.1	50.8	17 265	16 232	6.4	9.2	1 896	1 944	1 675	6 305	19.9	2.68	17.9	22.6
Washington	9.3	8.2	6.9	52.9	13 997	14 801	-5.4	-4.0	1 868	1 352	-1 054	5 052	6.8	2.72	16.5	22.8
Watauga	7.9	6.2	5.4	51.2	36 952	31 666	16.7	12.1	3 342	2 303	3 533	13 693	27.4	2.37	7.1	25.1
Wayne	8.7	6.6	4.8	50.2	104 666	97 054	7.8	6.7	15 140	8 773	-1 483	36 889	14.2	2.65	14.4	22.4
Wilkes	9.7	7.6	6.6	50.9	59 393	58 657	1.3	7.2	7 349	5 306	2 372	23 021	12.2	2.55	9.9	21.1
Wilson	9.2	7.7	6.1	53.2	66 061	63 132	4.6	4.1	9 352	6 829	435	25 093	16.4	2.57	16.7	25.0
Yadkin	10.3	8.0	7.3	51.2	30 488	28 439	7.2	15.6	3 997	2 945	3 843	12 068	18.2	2.49	9.3	22.1
Yancey	10.9	9.3	8.7	51.5	15 419	14 934	3.2	9.3	1 706	1 499	1 273	6 124	16.1	2.49	8.3	22.1
NORTH DAKOTA	8.7	7.1	7.5	50.3	638 800	652 717	-2.1	-0.8	78 833	54 150	-32 082	240 878	5.8	2.55	7.3	26.5
Adams	10.6	9.7	12.1	50.5	3 174	3 584	-11.4	-16.7	250	394	-360	1 266	-5.0	2.44	4.0	29.9
Barnes	9.7	8.9	10.8	50.9	12 545	13 960	-10.1	-5.4	1 182	1 482	-339	4 975	-2.3	2.40	6.2	29.6
Benson	8.8	5.9	7.0	49.4	7 198	7 944	-9.4	-5.8	1 114	642	-857	2 415	-4.5	2.97	13.9	22.7
Billings	11.0	6.8	5.3	47.7	1 108	1 138	-2.6	-3.8	97	30	-102	387	5.4	2.86	1.8	19.1
Bottineau	10.3	9.2	11.9	49.7	8 011	9 239	-13.3	-9.6	616	904	-452	3 105	-5.0	2.46	5.4	28.3
Bowman	11.3	9.5	10.5	50.8	3 596	4 229	-15.0	-9.1	312	385	-239	1 420	-5.6	2.48	5.3	29.0
Burke	13.7	11.4	13.7	49.7	3 002	3 822	-21.5	-27.1	192	338	-647	1 252	-13.3	2.38	4.3	29.5
Burleigh	8.4	6.4	5.9	51.6	60 131	54 811	9.7	12.0	8 045	4 058	3 499	22 684	16.8	2.57	8.8	25.4
Cass	7.4	5.0	5.0	50.2	102 874	88 247	16.6	15.1	14 457	6 443	7 777	40 281	23.5	2.45	7.4	28.2
Cavalier	12.1	10.2	12.1	50.3	6 064	7 636	-20.6	-20.5	484	677	-1 038	2 375	-11.6	2.51	3.3	27.9
Dickey	10.5	9.0	11.7	50.5	6 107	7 207	-15.3	-7.3	614	768	-279	2 299	-6.3	2.46	4.8	28.3
Divide	11.2	12.5	15.4	50.3	2 899	3 494	-17.0	-20.9	168	420	-340	1 193	-8.9	2.34	5.0	29.2
Dunn	10.0	10.1	7.8	49.1	4 005	4 627	-13.4	-13.7	385	362	-558	1 194	-11.0	2.40	4.8	31.7
Eddy	12.7	10.0	13.1	50.6	2 951	3 554	-17.0	-5.3	265	410	2	1 849	-3.9	2.58	3.9	24.3
Emmons	12.7	12.3	12.7	49.2	4 830	5 877	-17.8	-10.9	501	554	-449	1 541	-5.1	2.52	4.7	26.9
Foster	11.6	8.8	12.3	51.4	3 983	4 611	-13.6	-4.9	412	512	-83	811	-4.6	2.50	4.2	30.9
Golden Valley	9.6	10.8	11.1	50.3	2 108	2 391	-11.8	-15.5	222	179	-363	811	-4.6	2.50	4.2	30.9
Grand Forks	6.2	4.7	4.8	49.3	70 683	66 100	6.9	-8.5	10 280	3 860	-14 026	25 340	14.6	2.56	8.0	25.6
Grant	11.5	11.1	12.8	49.1	3 549	4 274	-17.0	-19.6	272	347	-605	1 374	-8.3	2.55	3.6	26.4
Griggs	11.6	11.0	13.4	49.9	3 303	3 714	-11.1	-15.9	269	442	-344	1 294	-7.0	2.51	4.8	25.4
Hettinger	12.2	12.3	12.3	50.4	3 445	4 275	-19.4	-17.6	256	361	-492	1 341	-10.4	2.53	3.3	25.8
Kidder	12.6	11.3	11.4	48.8	3 332	3 833	-13.1	-16.0	261	336	-448	1 247	-7.8	2.64	3.4	22.0
La Moure	11.7	10.9	12.6	49.7	5 383	6 473	-16.8	-12.7	404	568	-504	2 075	-8.4	2.55	3.3	27.5
Logan	14.1	11.2	12.1	49.5	2 847	3 493	-18.5	-20.3	236	322	-473	1 096	-9.0	2.53	2.4	24.5
McHenry	11.4	10.1	11.5	49.1	6 528	7 858	-16.9	-8.7	527	689	-382	2 551	-9.9	2.54	5.3	26.4
McIntosh	13.8	15.0	19.5	52.0	4 021	4 800	-16.2	-15.5	296	693	-207	1 687	-9.0	2.30	3.1	28.4
McKenzie	8.3	8.0	6.2	49.2	6 383	7 132	-10.5	-13.2	770	542	-1 057	2 301	-3.4	2.75	7.3	25.2
McLean	9.8	10.0	9.8	49.4	10 457	12 383	-15.6	-8.2	866	1 105	-575	3 933	-8.0	2.61	5.1	25.4
Mercer	7.4	6.9	6.6	49.5	9 808	9 404	4.3	-6.1	965	634	-911	3 560	9.3	2.72	4.6	22.2
Morton	9.7	8.0	7.5	50.6	23 700	25 177	-5.9	3.7	2 754	1 962	168	8 677	1.7	2.68	7.5	23.6
Mountrail	9.2	8.6	9.3	50.3	7 021	7 679	-8.6	-7.2	929	883	-538	2 587	-3.3	2.64	9.9	26.6
Nelson	12.4	12.1	16.1	50.7	4 410	5 233	-15.7	-17.1	321	742	-317	1 831	-7.7	2.31	5.2	31.9
Oliver	9.4	6.3	5.5	47.2	2 381	2 495	-4.6	-9.4	141	109	-250	809	1.4	2.94	3.0	18.7
Pembina	10.4	8.7	10.3	50.4	9 238	10 399	-11.2	-9.6	905	1 048	-720	3 555	-5.3	2.54	5.7	27.6
Pierce	11.1	10.0	14.6	50.4	5 052	6 166	-18.1	-9.1	492	644	-286	1 974	-6.6	2.45	5.3	29.7
Ramsey	9.8	8.2	10.2	50.9	12 681	13 048	-2.8	-5.8	1 521	1 440	-808	4 977	7.8	2.44	9.0	29.4
Ransom	12.0	8.4	11.4	48.2	5 921	6 698	-11.6	-3.2	604	852	82	2 284	-5.0	2.47	4.6	27.8
Renville	10.4	8.2	11.1	49.8	3 160	3 608	-12.4	-11.4	223	326	-255	1 209	-6.1	2.56	6.1	24.8
Richland	9.1	6.8	8.3	48.2	18 148	19 207	-5.5	-1.2	2 011	1 632	-561	6 518	1.6	2.55	5.9	27.0
Rolette	7.0	4.7	4.4	50.7	12 772	12 177	4.9	11.4	2 742	1 071	-175	4 150	21.2	3.04	21.3	22.3
Sargent	10.5	8.7	8.0	48.5	4 549	5 512	-17.5	-5.7	468	418	-298	1 763	-9.9	2.55	4.0	26.5
Sheridan	13.4	12.5	11.7	47.7	2 148	2 819	-23.8	-22.5	138	174	-425	858	-14.8	2.47	2.8	23.5
Sioux	5.9	3.5	1.4	48.5	3 761	3 620	3.9	10.5	893	242	-247	1 022	11.1	3.68	23.5	16.8
Slope	13.2	12.2	7.0	48.0	907	1 157	-21.6	-2.2	85	27	-76	333	-14.2	2.72	4.2	24.0
Stark	8.6	7.6	7.3	50.9	22 832	23 697	-3.7	-1.5	2 704	1 730	-1 269	8 479	8.3	2.62	7.9	26.1
Steele	13.1	10.4	8.6	49.4	2 420	3 106	-22.1	-9.8	223	261	-189	991	-13.2	2.44	2.1	27.9
Stutsman	10.3	8.7	9.1	51.2	22 241	24 154	-7.9	-5.2	2 236	2 137	-1 186	8 661	0.1	2.44	7.1	29.3
Towner	10.3	9.9	12.7	50.3	3 627	4 052	-10.5	-18.5	294	428	-527	1 433	-4.2	2.47	5.7	30.6
Traill	9.8	7.7	10.5	50.6	8 752	9 624	-9.1	-2.3	874	1 097	41	3 327	-2.9	2.50	5.2	27.1
Walsh	10.1	9.0	9.7	50.1	13 840	15 371	-10.0	-3.5	1 377	1 709	-1 114	5 229	-0.3	2.56	6.4	27.4

1. No spouse present.

Table B. States and Counties — Vital Statistics, Health Resources, and Crime

STATE County	Births, average 1996–1998 Total	Rate[1]	Deaths, average 1996–1998 Number Total	Infant[2]	Rate Total[1]	Infant[3]	Physicians,[4] 1998 Number	Rate[5]	Hospitals,[4] 1998 Number	Beds Number	Rate[5]	Medicare enrollees 1999	Serious crimes known to police, 1998[6] Total Number	Rate[7]
	32	33	34	35	36	37	38	39	40	41	42	43	44	45
NORTH CAROLINA—Cont'd														
Swain	166	13.7	141	0	11.6	2.0	11	89	1	24	195	2 379	NA	NA
Transylvania	284	10.2	319	5	11.4	16.4	56	197	1	90	316	6 744	823	2 905
Tyrrell	40	10.6	50	1	13.3	33.3	0	0	0	0	0	727	71	1 857
Union	1 819	17.1	781	15	7.4	8.2	81	74	1	226	205	10 986	4 783	4 497
Vance	654	15.7	475	9	11.4	14.3	47	111	1	87	206	7 196	3 055	7 229
Wake	8 582	15.5	3 085	71	5.6	8.3	1 289	226	7	1 295	227	54 809	27 178	4 961
Warren	195	10.8	228	1	12.6	5.1	7	38	0	0	0	3 413	665	3 597
Washington	186	13.5	149	3	10.8	17.9	5	37	1	49	360	2 549	398	2 850
Watauga	355	8.7	273	3	6.7	9.4	87	212	2	205	500	4 955	1 476	3 566
Wayne	1 670	14.9	1 003	16	9.0	9.8	165	147	1	267	238	16 621	5 869	5 157
Wilkes	797	12.8	615	6	9.8	7.5	51	81	1	130	207	10 255	1 681	2 648
Wilson	1 083	15.9	739	11	10.9	10.2	96	141	1	277	406	11 387	4 869	7 068
Yadkin	471	13.6	329	3	9.5	5.7	15	43	1	50	143	5 961	882	2 725
Yancey	178	10.8	169	1	10.3	3.7	15	90	0	0	0	3 619	82	546
NORTH DAKOTA	8 211	12.8	5 941	55	9.3	6.7	1 327	208	46	4 304	674	103 066	17 105	2 681
Adams	23	8.5	42	0	15.1	0.0	12	442	1	45	1 658	582	24	878
Barnes	129	10.7	154	1	12.8	5.2	7	59	1	50	418	2 565	106	883
Benson	127	18.5	71	1	10.4	10.5	2	29	0	0	0	1 085	NA	NA
Billings	8	7.6	3	0	2.8	0.0	0	0	0	0	0	85	NA	NA
Bottineau	54	7.3	100	1	13.6	12.3	4	55	1	67	927	1 603	81	1 088
Bowman	35	10.6	48	0	14.5	9.5	4	121	1	36	1 085	763	12	366
Burke	14	6.1	34	0	14.5	0.0	0	0	0	0	0	648	1	50
Burleigh	849	12.8	452	8	6.8	9.4	254	380	2	513	767	9 466	2 340	3 528
Cass	1 628	14.1	741	10	6.4	6.3	431	369	3	667	571	13 421	3 714	3 253
Cavalier	41	8.1	69	0	13.5	0.0	3	60	1	28	559	1 147	50	976
Dickey	56	9.8	81	0	14.3	0.0	6	106	1	30	532	1 217	76	1 355
Divide	15	6.3	50	0	20.5	21.7	2	85	1	25	1 057	580	20	832
Dunn	33	9.0	46	0	12.7	0.0	0	0	0	0	0	581	0	0
Eddy	28	9.7	47	0	16.3	0.0	0	0	0	0	0	684	NA	NA
Emmons	46	10.5	55	0	12.5	0.0	2	46	1	25	580	1 126	48	1 103
Foster	39	10.2	64	0	16.8	0.0	5	132	1	70	1 841	861	17	453
Golden Valley	19	10.0	16	0	8.4	0.0	2	107	0	0	0	451	6	317
Grand Forks	1 034	15.0	416	5	6.0	4.5	185	277	2	413	618	7 033	3 398	4 938
Grant	25	8.2	39	1	12.9	40.0	2	67	1	50	1 684	710	10	421
Griggs	25	8.5	46	0	16.0	0.0	2	70	1	69	2 428	711	NA	NA
Hettinger	22	7.4	41	0	13.9	15.4	0	0	0	0	0	780	1	34
Kidder	24	8.1	39	0	13.2	0.0	0	0	0	0	0	659	28	961
La Moure	42	8.6	61	1	12.5	15.9	0	0	0	0	0	1 188	26	649
Logan	27	11.1	34	1	14.2	25.0	0	0	0	0	0	596	NA	NA
McHenry	62	10.1	73	0	11.9	5.3	2	33	0	0	0	1 522	59	961
McIntosh	28	7.8	71	0	20.1	0.0	2	58	2	94	2 731	1 211	19	535
McKenzie	70	12.2	57	1	9.9	14.3	10	176	1	26	458	844	48	836
McLean	87	8.9	122	0	12.5	0.0	6	62	2	84	866	2 170	141	1 453
Mercer	82	8.7	77	0	8.2	0.0	3	32	1	32	340	1 369	145	1 543
Morton	305	12.5	213	0	8.7	1.1	13	53	1	36	146	4 170	806	3 319
Mountrail	94	14.1	96	2	14.3	21.2	4	60	1	25	377	1 292	57	861
Nelson	29	7.5	71	1	18.7	23.3	3	81	1	14	377	1 151	NA	NA
Oliver	15	6.9	12	0	5.6	21.7	0	0	0	0	0	239	12	544
Pembina	83	9.7	112	2	13.0	20.0	1	12	1	90	1 061	1 794	121	1 411
Pierce	53	11.3	68	0	14.7	6.3	9	195	1	220	4 759	1 064	94	2 068
Ramsey	154	12.5	160	1	13.0	4.3	26	215	1	55	454	2 527	560	4 546
Ransom	63	10.8	96	0	16.6	0.0	6	104	1	70	1 212	1 245	NA	NA
Renville	25	8.7	33	0	11.6	0.0	2	71	0	0	0	568	24	845
Richland	214	11.8	163	2	8.9	7.8	12	66	0	0	0	2 807	404	2 227
Rolette	286	20.3	115	2	8.2	7.0	17	120	1	101	710	1 579	129	917
Sargent	49	11.1	46	0	10.3	6.8	0	0	0	0	0	838	71	1 877
Sheridan	12	6.8	17	0	9.6	27.8	0	0	0	0	0	462	16	901
Sioux	91	22.0	28	1	6.7	14.7	2	48	0	0	0	272	NA	NA
Slope	9	11.0	3	0	3.1	0.0	0	0	0	0	0	97	0	0
Stark	269	11.8	203	3	8.9	9.9	34	149	2	135	593	4 010	NA	NA
Steele	23	10.0	25	0	10.9	0.0	0	0	0	0	0	456	NA	NA
Stutsman	214	10.1	244	1	11.6	4.7	32	153	1	56	267	4 321	526	2 503
Towner	29	9.4	49	0	15.8	0.0	2	66	1	32	1 060	673	31	1 012
Traill	95	11.0	119	1	13.8	10.5	4	47	2	52	609	1 695	51	714
Walsh	145	10.7	187	1	13.7	4.6	17	126	2	49	362	2 678	334	2 455

1. Per 1,000 estimated resident population, average 1996–1998.   2. Deaths of infants under 1 year old.   3. Deaths of infants under 1 year old per 1,000 live births.   4. Data subject to copyright.   5. Per 100,000 resident population as of July 1 of the year shown.   6. Data for serious crimes have not been adjusted for underreporting; this may affect comparability between geographic areas and over time.   7. Per 100,000 population estimated by the FBI.

Table B. States and Counties — Crime, Education, Money Income, and Poverty

STATE County	Serious crimes known to police, 1998[1] (cont'd) Rate[2] Violent	Property	Education — Enrollment[3] Total	Percent private	Attainment[4] (percent) High school graduate or more	Bachelor's degree or more	Local government expenditures, fiscal 1997[5] Total current expenditures (mil dol)	Current expenditures per student (dollars)	Money income, 1989 Per capita[6] (dollars)	Households Median Dollars	Percent change, 1979–1989 (constant 1989 dollars)	Percent with $100,000 or more	Income and poverty, 1997 Median household income	Percent below poverty level All persons	Persons under 18	Persons 5–17 in families
	46	47	48	49	50	51	52	53	54	55	56	57	58	59	60	61
NORTH CAROLINA—Cont'd																
Swain	NA	NA	2 526	6.3	59.0	9.9	9.7	5 796	8 922	16 068	-2.8	0.9	21 858	20.9	29.8	28.0
Transylvania	325	2 580	5 724	19.7	72.1	17.9	19.9	5 010	12 737	25 179	-6.4	2.1	34 547	12.4	20.3	19.5
Tyrrell	157	1 700	887	8.5	58.0	7.6	5.7	7 079	7 884	16 363	-8.4	0.0	21 616	25.7	33.9	31.4
Union	382	4 115	21 170	14.8	69.0	13.2	86.8	4 529	13 135	30 957	11.1	3.2	41 145	8.9	13.7	12.9
Vance	831	6 398	9 756	7.8	57.1	9.5	36.9	4 803	10 457	21 555	7.8	2.2	26 499	19.3	27.4	25.6
Wake	501	4 460	114 706	16.1	85.4	35.3	411.2	4 796	17 195	36 222	15.9	5.2	51 391	7.8	11.3	10.2
Warren	298	3 299	3 857	6.4	53.7	7.1	17.0	5 224	8 502	16 937	-0.2	0.9	23 025	23.4	29.6	29.9
Washington	372	2 478	3 637	5.8	60.6	8.7	13.9	5 121	9 827	21 840	-2.2	1.2	27 726	20.5	29.3	27.1
Watauga	176	3 390	14 404	2.8	72.0	27.4	24.2	4 984	10 628	20 252	9.5	2.3	31 013	14.5	16.1	15.0
Wayne	641	4 516	27 469	11.4	71.2	12.7	87.8	4 556	10 843	23 560	8.7	1.2	31 410	16.6	22.1	20.6
Wilkes	306	2 342	12 767	3.9	54.1	8.8	49.5	4 927	10 816	22 261	-2.0	1.8	30 700	13.3	19.4	17.3
Wilson	945	6 123	17 118	13.3	62.2	14.4	60.1	4 946	11 641	24 021	5.9	2.1	30 191	18.7	26.0	24.2
Yadkin	213	2 512	6 340	4.4	58.9	7.1	26.2	4 837	11 843	25 062	9.7	1.5	33 929	10.1	14.6	14.1
Yancey	40	506	3 045	3.8	60.7	10.0	13.4	5 333	9 462	19 401	7.3	1.1	27 797	15.6	22.7	21.8
NORTH DAKOTA	89	2 592	177 543	7.5	76.7	18.1	577.0	4 808	11 051	23 213	-9.4	1.6	31 764	12.5	16.8	15.3
Adams	0	878	661	0.0	72.5	11.2	2.6	4 994	10 382	20 722	-11.3	2.1	27 346	13.2	18.1	16.4
Barnes	17	866	3 396	3.9	75.4	15.4	10.9	5 239	10 102	20 419	-13.0	0.9	29 588	13.9	18.6	17.1
Benson	NA	NA	2 010	1.8	65.4	9.2	6.5	6 072	6 983	16 917	-21.3	0.6	21 833	28.7	38.5	35.8
Billings	NA	NA	282	11.7	71.5	12.6	1.5	13 473	9 172	22 639	-33.3	0.5	29 541	12.1	14.0	17.1
Bottineau	13	1 075	1 984	2.9	74.9	14.3	7.8	5 827	10 557	22 294	1.0	1.8	30 156	12.6	17.2	15.2
Bowman	92	274	834	3.1	74.3	13.9	4.3	5 562	10 060	21 478	-7.2	0.3	31 058	10.7	13.7	13.5
Burke	0	50	653	2.3	66.9	8.7	2.8	6 324	9 176	19 160	-5.0	0.3	28 783	12.1	17.0	15.3
Burleigh	92	3 436	16 359	16.1	80.4	25.1	49.1	4 347	13 018	28 450	-11.1	2.5	39 664	9.2	12.3	10.4
Cass	114	3 139	31 588	7.3	87.1	26.5	89.2	4 763	13 240	26 806	-9.2	2.8	38 871	9.0	11.5	9.6
Cavalier	0	976	1 330	8.5	68.4	12.6	5.3	5 718	10 653	21 250	-13.0	1.7	31 223	12.9	18.3	16.8
Dickey	89	1 266	1 620	26.7	68.8	16.0	4.7	4 657	9 747	20 248	1.2	1.1	28 090	15.3	19.7	18.2
Divide	0	832	563	2.5	69.4	12.8	2.3	5 042	10 603	21 507	-8.7	0.5	29 291	12.6	18.3	17.4
Dunn	0	0	972	8.8	70.5	10.1	4.3	6 645	8 689	19 824	-6.7	0.9	25 257	16.7	21.2	21.2
Eddy	NA	NA	635	0.0	66.5	11.0	3.2	5 317	9 398	19 310	-9.5	0.5	26 181	13.0	19.8	16.8
Emmons	0	1 103	1 022	0.6	57.3	9.0	4.5	5 567	8 421	16 892	-8.2	0.3	23 504	15.7	21.5	20.6
Foster	27	426	947	6.0	69.4	12.1	4.6	4 580	9 393	20 760	-13.0	0.8	30 687	12.4	16.1	15.8
Golden Valley	0	317	568	2.5	74.6	15.7	2.8	5 938	9 290	20 281	-14.9	0.2	26 669	14.5	20.0	18.8
Grand Forks	109	4 829	24 841	5.0	85.6	25.8	51.4	4 260	11 414	25 162	-3.0	1.8	35 959	11.2	14.1	13.2
Grant	0	421	770	0.9	62.6	8.9	3.1	6 662	8 511	17 368	10.2	0.6	20 257	22.5	33.7	30.6
Griggs	NA	NA	729	2.3	67.9	12.1	2.1	5 150	8 816	19 417	-12.7	0.8	28 108	14.4	20.7	19.2
Hettinger	34	0	685	15.6	69.5	12.2	4.2	6 556	9 203	19 601	-0.7	1.0	28 249	13.6	18.9	18.3
Kidder	0	961	796	5.0	60.5	11.3	3.4	5 724	8 700	17 378	-0.8	0.4	23 779	17.2	23.7	22.5
La Moure	25	624	1 215	7.5	66.4	12.4	6.1	5 279	9 271	19 710	-3.7	1.0	28 985	12.0	15.5	15.7
Logan	NA	NA	552	2.9	51.9	9.3	2.9	5 676	10 304	19 490	11.6	1.9	23 910	16.2	22.4	21.5
McHenry	33	928	1 508	1.1	66.7	9.7	6.4	5 012	8 871	18 275	-5.0	0.6	24 851	16.9	24.0	20.8
McIntosh	0	535	1 067	0.5	48.8	9.5	3.4	5 405	9 133	17 798	4.8	0.3	23 018	17.0	27.8	24.5
McKenzie	35	801	1 684	3.9	72.7	14.2	9.2	7 638	9 832	24 662	-4.6	1.0	32 034	19.6	25.8	25.4
McLean	0	1 453	2 551	4.2	68.2	11.9	11.1	4 743	9 733	21 853	-14.1	0.6	32 129	12.7	15.9	14.0
Mercer	11	1 532	2 468	2.1	71.2	11.2	11.0	4 755	12 195	31 969	2.1	1.0	47 215	7.8	8.5	8.1
Morton	428	2 891	6 351	9.6	70.4	13.8	21.3	4 261	10 534	23 685	-14.0	1.1	32 755	13.0	18.3	15.7
Mountrail	30	831	1 866	2.7	73.0	12.9	8.3	4 990	9 265	19 399	-10.1	0.6	27 543	17.6	24.0	21.7
Nelson	NA	NA	902	2.7	69.4	10.6	4.5	5 471	9 590	19 360	-1.7	0.4	25 831	11.1	15.1	14.6
Oliver	0	544	635	8.2	68.2	10.8	1.8	4 686	9 749	23 000	-18.3	0.0	34 989	12.2	14.1	13.8
Pembina	23	1 388	2 186	1.6	73.1	13.1	10.8	5 356	11 308	23 256	-0.8	1.6	34 875	10.4	14.7	12.8
Pierce	44	2 024	1 059	7.5	65.9	13.4	3.9	4 569	8 993	20 216	-0.7	0.0	26 796	14.4	20.4	17.5
Ramsey	97	4 449	3 311	6.1	74.5	16.3	12.5	5 192	11 125	21 780	-14.7	1.3	30 355	14.8	22.0	19.0
Ransom	NA	NA	1 217	1.5	73.1	11.1	5.2	3 995	11 297	23 017	0.6	1.3	32 823	9.6	11.1	10.5
Renville	0	845	725	1.1	74.2	9.8	4.0	5 098	10 759	22 659	0.2	1.5	30 684	10.5	13.8	13.1
Richland	77	2 150	5 540	6.6	75.9	13.0	16.8	5 116	10 562	24 248	-7.2	1.9	36 591	11.4	14.6	13.2
Rolette	14	903	4 011	2.6	59.4	11.7	19.0	5 750	6 773	15 163	-19.1	0.4	21 831	30.7	36.2	34.3
Sargent	0	1 877	1 040	1.5	72.7	9.7	3.8	4 248	10 867	23 838	0.2	0.7	36 041	8.9	10.9	10.1
Sheridan	113	788	388	0.3	49.5	8.2	1.5	6 173	8 152	17 145	-11.7	0.0	23 067	22.4	32.8	29.7
Sioux	NA	NA	1 399	7.2	68.3	9.9	4.2	7 217	5 185	14 838	-22.8	0.5	19 120	37.4	40.8	41.7
Slope	0	0	231	17.3	71.5	10.4	0.3	5 489	8 234	18 355	-9.8	0.6	22 759	12.6	14.1	14.9
Stark	NA	NA	6 335	17.6	73.1	14.8	17.7	4 298	10 136	22 048	-21.0	0.8	32 028	13.7	17.0	15.5
Steele	NA	NA	527	1.3	71.9	13.7	2.2	5 859	11 586	23 307	-13.7	1.3	32 659	12.9	20.3	17.8
Stutsman	95	2 408	5 644	20.4	73.5	16.7	16.6	4 754	11 369	22 415	-11.2	1.7	32 213	12.7	17.3	15.3
Towner	65	947	733	0.5	71.9	12.7	3.4	5 426	9 481	18 608	-23.2	1.0	27 205	14.8	19.3	19.1
Traill	0	714	2 477	3.5	76.6	17.7	9.6	5 166	10 509	22 050	-14.6	1.1	35 162	10.9	14.1	13.0
Walsh	73	2 382	3 159	2.3	68.0	13.0	13.9	5 572	10 766	21 973	4.5	1.5	29 847	14.5	20.4	18.3

1. Data for serious crimes have not been adjusted for underreporting; this may affect comparability between geographic areas and over time.   2. Per 100,000 population estimated by the FBI.   3. All persons 3 years old and over enrolled in nursery school through college.   4. Persons 25 years old and over.   5. Elementary and secondary education expenditures, local government fiscal years ending between July 1, 1996 and June 30, 1997.   6. Based on population enumerated as of April 1, 1990.

STATE County	Personal income, 1998												
	Total (mil dol)	Percent change, 1997–1998	Per capita[1] Dollars	Per capita[1] Rank	Wages and salaries[2] (mil dol)	Proprietor's income (mil dol)	Dividends, interest, and rent (mil dol)	Transfer payments Total (mil dol)	Government payments to individuals Total (mil dol)	Social Security (mil dol)	Medical payments (mil dol)	Income maintenance (mil dol)	Unemployment insurance (mil dol)
	62	63	64	65	66	67	68	69	70	71	72	73	74
NORTH CAROLINA—Cont'd													
Swain	198	3.3	16 156	2 770	128	12	34	57	55	21	23	7	2
Transylvania	665	4.6	23 378	775	327	52	217	129	124	67	44	8	1
Tyrrell	62	-5.3	15 475	2 881	21	3	11	17	17	6	7	2	0
Union	2 455	7.4	22 277	1 019	1 316	152	329	278	258	122	99	20	4
Vance	799	3.7	19 008	2 055	462	42	132	183	175	64	75	28	3
Wake	19 266	9.8	33 780	72	13 083	1 394	3 195	1 299	1 199	534	470	100	18
Warren	298	3.3	15 874	2 814	101	29	41	81	78	27	34	13	1
Washington	248	-2.1	18 366	2 246	84	14	43	64	61	24	24	10	2
Watauga	859	6.4	20 996	1 393	483	102	185	119	112	47	40	10	2
Wayne	2 205	3.1	19 710	1 808	1 410	133	374	405	386	142	164	51	6
Wilkes	1 381	6.4	22 014	1 101	738	145	222	235	224	92	97	23	3
Wilson	1 626	5.9	23 823	675	1 162	89	258	289	277	106	118	34	6
Yadkin	763	5.1	21 860	1 141	266	62	113	121	115	54	47	9	2
Yancey	304	5.4	18 308	2 262	113	32	57	75	72	30	28	9	1
NORTH DAKOTA	14 600	9.1	22 892	X	8 708	1 489	3 101	2 293	2 183	923	829	141	29
Adams	50	7.8	18 543	2 196	24	2	13	13	13	6	6	1	0
Barnes	241	12.9	20 187	1 656	105	27	67	48	46	23	17	2	1
Benson	99	13.4	14 494	2 970	44	7	23	31	30	9	11	4	1
Billings	15	36.9	13 748	3 030	8	0	4	2	2	1	1	0	0
Bottineau	152	14.6	20 837	1 448	49	25	46	32	31	14	12	2	0
Bowman	75	13.7	22 700	923	29	13	23	15	14	7	6	1	0
Burke	51	22.9	22 301	1 016	17	4	17	12	11	6	4	1	0
Burleigh	1 680	5.8	25 117	477	1 155	114	321	226	214	90	84	11	3
Cass	3 172	8.2	27 139	292	2 377	274	610	320	299	129	101	15	3
Cavalier	118	13.9	23 550	732	39	17	39	21	21	10	8	1	0
Dickey	117	13.6	20 654	1 503	45	21	28	26	25	10	12	1	0
Divide	55	29.3	23 380	774	14	11	20	11	11	6	4	0	0
Dunn	51	22.6	14 221	2 990	21	0	17	13	13	5	6	1	0
Eddy	52	10.9	18 140	2 309	20	5	14	14	14	6	6	1	0
Emmons	80	26.5	18 396	2 239	26	14	21	19	18	9	7	1	0
Foster	88	19.0	23 201	818	41	15	22	17	16	8	6	1	0
Golden Valley	30	16.2	16 234	2 755	14	-2	11	8	7	4	2	0	0
Grand Forks	1 559	3.8	23 339	783	1 135	111	282	182	171	67	57	11	2
Grant	41	29.8	13 912	3 013	13	3	13	13	13	6	5	1	0
Griggs	66	26.8	23 128	831	23	16	18	13	13	6	5	1	0
Hettinger	61	17.3	20 997	1 392	16	15	17	14	14	6	6	1	0
Kidder	54	27.6	18 773	2 129	13	12	15	13	12	5	5	1	0
La Moure	101	22.7	21 138	1 347	28	23	28	21	20	10	8	1	0
Logan	46	27.0	19 600	1 855	11	9	14	11	11	5	5	1	0
McHenry	105	15.7	17 310	2 528	27	13	29	28	27	12	11	2	1
McIntosh	72	18.8	20 892	1 427	24	10	22	21	20	9	10	1	0
McKenzie	107	19.6	18 781	2 126	59	11	27	21	20	8	8	2	0
McLean	206	13.5	21 246	1 307	87	27	53	44	42	19	17	2	1
Mercer	211	2.7	22 476	984	171	9	36	29	28	12	11	1	1
Morton	505	11.9	20 533	1 547	235	30	90	96	92	35	40	5	2
Mountrail	138	19.9	20 907	1 421	50	26	31	31	30	11	12	2	0
Nelson	81	17.9	21 779	1 167	25	11	24	22	22	10	10	1	0
Oliver	40	17.5	17 962	2 355	30	0	8	6	6	3	2	0	0
Pembina	251	22.5	29 538	181	126	63	57	34	32	16	11	2	1
Pierce	95	15.1	20 551	1 540	41	11	24	22	21	9	9	1	0
Ramsey	273	8.8	22 525	973	134	27	66	53	51	22	20	3	1
Ransom	122	4.0	21 145	1 346	50	15	25	26	25	10	11	1	0
Renville	60	25.4	21 397	1 265	17	15	14	12	11	5	5	1	0
Richland	391	2.4	21 633	1 210	221	61	83	59	56	25	19	3	1
Rolette	207	3.7	14 654	2 961	120	8	24	67	64	13	26	16	1
Sargent	106	3.2	23 884	666	78	14	26	15	14	7	5	1	0
Sheridan	34	29.4	19 942	1 731	8	7	10	9	9	4	4	1	0
Sioux	43	5.6	10 341	3 099	37	-3	4	16	15	2	7	4	0
Slope	12	94.8	13 927	3 012	2	4	4	2	2	1	1	0	0
Stark	475	6.9	20 921	1 416	259	47	105	84	80	33	32	5	1
Steele	51	20.0	22 907	870	14	13	16	8	8	5	2	0	0
Stutsman	495	12.8	23 614	720	259	67	105	88	85	37	33	5	1
Towner	65	21.5	21 537	1 244	24	9	21	14	13	6	5	1	0
Traill	193	14.2	22 619	947	78	39	42	34	32	16	12	1	0
Walsh	290	20.0	21 356	1 280	118	63	68	52	50	24	19	3	1

1. Based on the resident population estimated as of July 1 of the year shown. 2. Includes other labor income.

Table B. States and Counties — Earnings, Social Security, and Housing

STATE County	Total (mil dol)	Farm	Goods-related[1] Total	Manu- facturing	Service-related and other[2] Total	Retail trade	Finance, insur- ance, and real estate	Services	Govern- ment	Number	Rate[3]	Supple- mental Security Income recipients, December 1998	Total	Percent change, 1980– 1990
	75	76	77	78	79	80	81	82	83	84	85	86	87	88
NORTH CAROLINA—Cont'd														
Swain	140	0.6	D	6.6	D	16.7	1.6	43.8	24.8	2 980	242	421	5 664	16.7
Transylvania	379	2.4	D	40.2	D	7.9	3.8	20.2	11.2	7 669	269	579	12 893	26.0
Tyrrell	24	-0.2	12.6	9.5	43.4	12.1	3.0	14.4	44.2	887	238	195	1 907	8.0
Union	1 468	3.9	D	30.5	D	9.1	D	12.3	11.6	14 580	133	1 249	30 760	27.8
Vance	503	1.3	D	27.7	D	17.5	3.1	19.4	18.4	8 789	208	2 301	15 743	14.0
Wake	14 477	0.2	16.4	8.2	65.9	9.3	9.2	31.1	17.5	60 958	107	7 794	177 146	56.3
Warren	130	14.0	24.7	19.1	32.3	6.9	1.7	17.6	29.0	3 895	213	1 125	8 714	24.3
Washington	99	5.3	16.1	8.4	42.3	11.4	2.6	16.8	36.3	3 013	221	698	5 644	3.9
Watauga	585	2.4	D	7.1	D	15.4	5.2	27.5	27.1	6 008	147	749	19 538	33.3
Wayne	1 543	2.7	D	15.0	D	9.4	4.4	18.6	32.9	19 495	174	4 655	39 483	12.7
Wilkes	883	7.4	D	26.6	D	20.2	6.1	11.7	14.5	12 334	196	2 033	24 960	12.9
Wilson	1 251	1.9	D	28.6	D	8.7	7.5	17.4	14.8	14 058	206	2 997	26 662	13.7
Yadkin	328	5.8	46.0	34.4	34.7	10.5	1.8	14.3	13.5	6 932	198	731	12 921	16.4
Yancey	145	9.4	D	30.4	D	10.9	2.2	14.7	17.2	4 233	255	776	7 994	16.2
NORTH DAKOTA	10 196	5.5	16.6	8.0	57.1	9.5	5.6	25.0	20.8	114 172	179	8 506	276 340	6.8
Adams	26	-6.8	D	1.9	D	14.7	3.7	45.3	16.6	702	259	32	1 504	-3.8
Barnes	132	5.2	D	9.0	D	9.8	6.3	23.8	20.7	2 825	236	160	5 801	-2.9
Benson	51	5.5	D	10.1	D	4.7	5.1	35.9	26.1	1 306	189	202	3 163	2.6
Billings	8	5.2	D	0.0	D	D	0.0	D	40.0	161	152	6	533	3.1
Bottineau	74	16.0	D	2.5	D	11.8	4.9	20.6	20.2	1 746	242	62	4 661	-0.4
Bowman	41	13.5	D	1.6	D	11.3	4.2	22.3	14.2	838	253	36	1 691	-1.8
Burke	21	10.2	D	D	D	7.9	5.8	D	32.3	715	316	29	1 691	-6.9
Burleigh	1 269	0.5	13.5	6.0	64.4	10.6	6.3	32.7	21.6	10 654	159	894	23 803	14.2
Cass	2 651	1.8	17.5	9.6	67.7	9.4	9.1	29.8	13.1	14 746	126	1 240	42 407	20.4
Cavalier	57	13.6	10.5	1.3	D	D	7.2	18.6	15.9	1 296	259	47	3 038	-2.7
Dickey	66	23.8	13.0	9.5	51.8	8.5	2.8	22.8	11.4	1 394	247	97	2 763	-2.6
Divide	26	27.7	D	D	D	7.6	4.7	23.3	18.0	714	302	22	1 667	-6.5
Dunn	21	-14.8	D	D	D	10.7	4.0	D	30.4	737	207	43	2 057	11.2
Eddy	25	5.8	D	D	D	8.7	5.5	22.1	19.7	759	267	41	1 470	-4.6
Emmons	40	20.8	7.3	1.1	D	8.2	D	18.5	16.7	1 255	291	58	2 200	-5.3
Foster	57	18.0	D	D	D	8.8	3.7	20.3	12.5	947	249	29	1 876	2.7
Golden Valley	13	-30.6	D	D	D	11.3	7.4	31.8	30.0	488	260	9	1 035	0.2
Grand Forks	1 246	3.6	D	4.2	D	10.3	3.5	22.4	35.6	7 635	114	562	27 085	10.3
Grant	16	-8.5	D	4.6	D	8.6	7.9	28.4	28.7	841	283	67	2 011	2.1
Griggs	38	29.4	9.8	8.1	47.8	6.9	3.8	13.8	13.1	805	283	35	1 660	-4.5
Hettinger	31	36.5	D	2.8	D	4.4	3.9	13.0	18.1	854	292	33	1 637	-1.9
Kidder	25	32.8	D	1.1	D	6.0	5.7	9.9	19.6	764	266	39	1 672	-3.9
La Moure	51	33.8	D	4.0	D	5.5	5.8	11.2	16.5	1 289	271	60	2 434	-3.7
Logan	20	26.2	D	D	D	7.1	6.4	15.5	19.6	703	299	42	1 335	-6.1
McHenry	41	17.6	D	D	D	6.6	3.5	12.1	26.2	1 629	268	104	3 320	-3.4
McIntosh	33	15.6	10.2	6.1	59.7	9.1	6.1	30.7	14.5	1 295	376	63	2 031	-7.6
McKenzie	69	7.6	D	1.3	D	4.2	3.7	32.0	19.5	974	171	86	3 178	7.9
McLean	114	14.3	D	1.1	D	5.3	3.6	13.1	18.5	2 350	242	150	5 515	-4.2
Mercer	179	-1.8	29.5	0.6	63.2	4.8	1.6	10.2	9.1	1 536	163	76	4 496	13.0
Morton	265	1.5	D	13.2	D	11.6	4.2	21.9	15.5	4 552	185	312	9 467	0.9
Mountrail	76	23.3	D	D	D	7.1	6.6	15.2	20.1	1 480	223	146	3 675	14.8
Nelson	36	15.7	D	D	D	8.1	8.0	21.8	18.8	1 189	320	45	2 261	-7.4
Oliver	30	-0.9	D	0.9	D	2.2	D	4.8	10.5	400	181	7	968	0.8
Pembina	189	26.2	D	22.3	D	6.1	D	9.4	12.0	1 959	231	92	4 294	-3.2
Pierce	52	5.1	D	7.3	D	9.9	6.1	30.0	12.5	1 233	267	65	2 355	-0.9
Ramsey	161	2.4	D	3.7	D	15.6	6.6	25.4	23.7	2 731	225	224	5 616	6.8
Ransom	66	17.6	14.4	10.1	52.1	8.4	4.0	18.0	15.9	1 320	229	52	2 569	-5.3
Renville	32	32.5	8.8	1.0	D	7.7	2.5	16.1	17.2	642	229	15	1 558	1.8
Richland	281	14.4	D	28.8	D	6.6	2.4	14.9	13.2	3 165	173	144	7 394	3.0
Rolette	127	-2.6	D	7.5	D	8.9	4.7	33.3	37.6	1 949	137	631	4 742	20.9
Sargent	92	12.4	D	D	D	3.4	2.1	3.7	6.9	910	204	41	2 057	-6.9
Sheridan	14	31.1	D	D	D	5.8	4.8	5.3	18.8	564	333	35	1 061	-10.1
Sioux	35	-13.3	D	D	D	3.7	D	60.8	37.8	357	85	193	1 175	10.6
Slope	6	61.5	D	D	D	D	0.0	D	11.1	157	182	8	481	-6.2
Stark	306	0.9	25.0	9.2	D	12.7	D	25.0	16.5	4 390	193	398	9 585	12.9
Steele	27	42.3	12.0	6.8	D	5.0	5.0	D	13.7	551	243	11	1 311	-9.4
Stutsman	326	5.0	D	15.6	D	10.2	4.8	21.9	18.0	4 581	219	475	9 770	1.1
Towner	33	10.7	D	16.4	D	8.6	5.2	22.2	14.5	762	252	31	1 770	4.6
Traill	117	30.0	D	D	43.8	6.7	4.3	13.8	15.0	1 853	217	52	3 770	-4.0
Walsh	181	28.3	D	5.0	43.8	6.6	3.9	15.3	18.8	2 974	220	113	6 093	-1.0

1. Covers mining, construction, and manufacturing.   2. Covers private sector earnings in agricultural services, forestry, and fisheries; transportation and public utilities; wholesale trade; retail trade; finance, insurance, and real estate; and services.   3. Per 1,000 resident population estimated as of July 1 of the year shown.

STATE County	Housing units, 1990 (cont'd)								Civilian labor force, 1999				Civilian employment, 1990[5]		
	Occupied units										Unemployment			Percent	
		Owner-occupied				Renter-occupied									
				Owner cost as a percent of income											
	Total	Percent	Median value[1]	With a mortgage	Without a mortgage	Median rent[2]	Rent as percent of income	Sub-standard units[3] (percent)	Total	Percent change, 1998–1999	Total	Rate[4]	Total	Professional, managerial, and technical	Precision production, craft, and repair
	89	90	91	92	93	94	95	96	97	98	99	100	101	102	103
NORTH CAROLINA—Cont'd															
Swain	4 173	76.3	49 100	14.9	12.7	235	24.1	5.0	5 548	-2.4	638	11.5	4 450	21.1	14.5
Transylvania	9 924	78.9	72 200	17.4	11.5	345	27.1	3.0	11 152	1.3	202	1.8	10 835	24.3	16.0
Tyrrell	1 471	76.4	37 400	23.1	14.3	270	24.4	8.3	1 744	0.6	150	8.6	1 532	14.4	12.1
Union	29 307	75.9	70 600	19.3	12.7	406	24.5	4.4	59 565	4.7	1 186	2.0	43 685	22.5	16.5
Vance	14 166	65.3	53 100	18.6	13.5	301	26.6	7.9	19 126	2.4	1 328	6.9	18 184	20.2	12.8
Wake	165 743	60.9	97 200	22.0	12.6	480	24.1	2.6	345 115	2.4	4 705	1.4	240 692	40.6	8.7
Warren	6 305	76.4	48 200	22.4	14.2	246	26.6	12.1	6 913	0.7	434	6.3	6 770	15.7	12.6
Washington	5 052	73.6	45 500	15.6	14.4	266	26.1	5.5	5 910	3.3	356	6.0	5 736	13.5	14.9
Watauga	13 693	64.2	73 200	20.3	12.6	374	35.1	3.6	22 522	3.1	319	1.4	18 198	31.3	10.7
Wayne	36 889	62.7	58 000	21.1	13.8	322	24.1	4.1	47 881	0.7	1 943	4.1	44 564	23.2	13.1
Wilkes	23 021	79.4	52 800	21.5	12.4	299	22.9	3.7	31 699	4.6	822	2.6	29 920	16.7	13.6
Wilson	25 093	59.3	59 600	20.7	13.9	321	26.4	4.4	35 458	3.6	2 693	7.6	31 193	23.0	12.1
Yadkin	12 068	81.2	52 900	17.8	12.6	294	22.0	4.2	18 200	2.1	465	2.6	15 301	19.5	16.7
Yancey	6 124	80.8	51 300	21.9	13.2	259	26.1	5.4	6 307	1.2	317	5.0	6 547	18.1	17.3
NORTH DAKOTA	240 878	65.6	50 800	20.3	13.0	313	23.9	2.5	336 822	-2.9	11 456	3.4	287 558	26.4	9.8
Adams	1 266	70.4	34 000	20.9	14.4	242	20.2	2.5	1 370	-3.2	39	2.8	1 504	22.5	6.3
Barnes	4 975	68.5	38 400	16.7	12.1	251	23.9	1.2	5 477	-9.3	175	3.2	5 346	22.0	10.0
Benson	2 415	68.2	18 900	17.1	14.2	243	24.8	11.1	2 870	9.3	222	7.7	2 372	15.9	8.2
Billings	387	77.5	50 800	21.7	11.8	294	13.5	6.8	520	-2.8	26	5.0	472	14.4	11.4
Bottineau	3 105	78.3	37 400	21.7	12.8	274	24.3	2.2	3 230	-5.9	157	4.9	3 173	25.3	11.0
Bowman	1 420	78.9	44 000	21.8	12.8	240	20.9	1.3	1 778	-1.7	42	2.4	1 786	21.1	10.9
Burke	1 252	81.8	19 900	16.6	13.1	233	21.6	2.0	996	-3.4	37	3.7	1 176	21.3	9.5
Burleigh	22 684	64.8	67 500	20.7	12.2	348	23.3	2.0	39 392	-2.3	1 056	2.7	30 963	34.8	8.1
Cass	40 281	54.8	67 900	20.8	12.5	350	24.8	1.8	71 387	-2.5	1 262	1.8	54 931	30.7	8.7
Cavalier	2 375	79.7	39 300	21.0	13.5	276	22.4	1.4	2 512	1.7	76	3.0	2 346	22.5	10.2
Dickey	2 299	70.1	32 900	17.2	12.4	243	23.1	2.1	2 845	-2.2	47	1.7	2 750	20.4	7.5
Divide	1 193	79.6	27 600	21.0	11.9	220	19.3	4.0	1 144	-2.1	30	2.6	1 115	20.2	6.3
Dunn	1 433	78.4	27 300	21.1	13.5	233	23.4	4.2	1 891	-8.2	87	4.6	1 773	14.7	9.2
Eddy	1 194	71.5	27 400	18.5	13.2	267	23.0	1.6	1 404	9.3	74	5.3	1 182	25.5	9.1
Emmons	1 849	82.2	31 500	22.6	14.3	193	25.4	3.3	2 020	-0.4	81	4.0	1 819	18.0	8.6
Foster	1 541	74.0	36 500	20.0	13.1	254	20.1	0.9	2 179	-2.9	56	2.6	1 759	20.0	9.8
Golden Valley	811	75.6	31 800	20.3	14.3	264	18.9	1.9	899	2.3	37	4.1	964	19.0	9.8
Grand Forks	25 340	48.7	62 700	20.6	12.2	367	25.1	2.3	35 364	-4.7	910	2.6	31 544	31.8	8.3
Grant	1 374	81.4	24 100	24.8	14.7	187	18.5	1.9	1 524	5.5	58	3.8	1 508	13.4	5.6
Griggs	1 294	75.9	29 500	20.9	13.2	230	20.5	0.9	1 557	-7.7	34	2.2	1 396	18.3	10.2
Hettinger	1 341	82.0	24 900	20.1	14.2	197	18.7	2.5	1 297	-6.4	49	3.8	1 429	18.6	8.4
Kidder	1 247	83.8	22 600	20.6	12.8	210	22.8	1.6	1 422	-0.8	68	4.8	1 386	12.4	7.9
La Moure	2 075	79.1	22 300	18.5	12.9	222	23.3	2.6	2 244	-2.1	61	2.7	2 167	14.9	8.9
Logan	1 096	86.6	20 900	21.0	14.4	222	21.3	2.6	1 130	3.0	21	1.9	1 193	16.8	5.9
McHenry	2 551	80.6	22 600	17.1	13.2	207	21.7	2.0	2 757	-5.7	142	5.2	2 454	18.5	10.0
McIntosh	1 687	81.9	20 300	18.1	13.3	211	22.5	1.7	1 706	-0.8	39	2.3	1 756	17.4	9.0
McKenzie	2 301	74.3	43 900	19.6	11.4	233	16.7	5.5	3 009	-6.9	133	4.4	2 666	17.4	12.7
McLean	3 993	79.0	40 100	16.5	13.3	250	25.7	2.6	4 485	-3.7	309	6.9	4 189	21.4	13.9
Mercer	3 560	80.4	52 200	16.4	13.7	278	18.2	1.7	4 589	-5.5	324	7.1	4 293	21.6	19.6
Morton	8 677	73.1	51 100	20.4	12.9	315	26.1	1.9	13 542	-1.7	526	3.9	11 274	22.6	12.3
Mountrail	2 587	75.4	31 400	18.2	14.0	240	22.4	5.5	3 042	1.1	219	7.2	2 747	22.9	13.0
Nelson	1 831	76.0	23 900	22.2	12.0	214	20.3	0.7	1 603	-6.0	71	4.4	1 635	21.2	11.4
Oliver	809	85.4	47 300	15.0	11.7	255	17.2	4.5	1 018	-11.4	55	5.4	1 073	13.1	14.6
Pembina	3 555	77.4	41 700	18.8	12.8	268	20.7	2.5	4 929	-3.7	307	6.2	4 006	17.0	11.4
Pierce	1 974	73.9	35 400	19.2	15.7	271	24.8	1.2	2 487	1.4	83	3.3	2 103	22.2	7.9
Ramsey	4 977	64.1	45 700	20.8	12.6	288	23.4	2.6	6 499	-1.4	213	3.3	5 717	27.6	10.1
Ransom	2 284	74.9	32 200	15.7	13.6	245	21.4	0.7	2 652	-3.4	67	2.5	2 470	21.3	8.5
Renville	1 209	78.5	35 000	22.0	12.4	273	22.6	2.6	1 332	-5.6	37	2.8	1 273	19.8	13.4
Richland	6 518	68.9	43 800	19.8	12.9	281	23.6	1.6	9 152	-5.7	267	2.9	7 800	21.4	10.7
Rolette	4 150	64.9	39 400	16.3	14.7	189	23.9	13.4	5 773	10.4	792	13.7	3 725	28.3	10.7
Sargent	1 763	79.4	25 000	13.5	12.1	223	18.2	1.9	2 406	-1.4	49	2.0	2 055	13.0	10.4
Sheridan	858	85.1	14 999	17.3	13.6	219	24.6	2.8	672	-6.7	48	7.1	719	19.5	10.4
Sioux	1 022	43.6	20 700	21.0	12.6	147	16.1	22.2	1 674	-0.8	122	7.3	1 015	27.8	5.3
Slope	333	82.0	14 999	23.8	11.8	233	28.3	1.2	410	1.2	24	5.9	428	7.7	8.4
Stark	8 479	68.7	42 800	20.9	14.1	266	24.0	2.7	12 511	-2.7	528	4.2	10 541	24.2	12.3
Steele	991	75.6	24 800	19.1	12.8	214	17.8	1.2	1 045	-9.1	13	1.2	979	20.9	15.8
Stutsman	8 661	65.7	45 400	19.0	12.7	285	24.4	1.4	11 704	-2.2	316	2.7	10 292	28.0	10.3
Towner	1 433	70.8	30 900	20.3	13.3	265	22.8	1.5	1 277	-13.2	35	2.7	1 439	19.0	10.8
Traill	3 327	71.0	40 200	19.8	13.1	270	24.0	2.2	3 717	-1.0	124	3.3	3 476	21.7	11.8
Walsh	5 229	75.0	41 900	20.8	13.2	281	22.7	2.5	6 333	2.6	265	4.2	6 066	25.2	9.6

1. Specified owner-occupied units. 2. Specified renter-occupied units. 3. Overcrowded or lacking complete plumbing facilities. 4. Percent of civilian labor force. 5. Persons 16 years and older.

Table B. States and Counties — Nonfarm Employment and Agriculture

| | | Private nonfarm establishments, employment and payroll, 1998 | | | | | | | | Agriculture, 1997 | | | |
| | | Employment | | | | | | Annual payroll | | Farms | | | Farm operators |
STATE County	Number of establishments	Total	Health Care and Social Assistance	Manufacturing	Retail trade	Finance and Insurance	Professional Scientific and Technical Services	Total (mil dol)	Average per employee (dollars)	Number	Percent with— Less than 50 acres	Percent with— 500 acres and over	Whose principal occupation is farming (percent)
	104	105	106	107	108	109	110	111	112	113	114	115	116
NORTH CAROLINA—Cont'd													
Swain	394	4 820	516	468	497	51	50	87	18 001	77	46.8	3.9	42.9
Transylvania	727	9 302	1 099	3 240	1 282	265	178	237	25 488	174	60.9	1.7	35.6
Tyrrell	74	329	D	D	D	D	D	6	17 772	83	25.3	28.9	67.5
Union	2 675	37 152	2 308	13 892	4 422	633	588	943	25 385	1 142	48.9	5.7	48.7
Vance	940	15 073	1 795	4 980	2 714	252	193	307	20 380	232	17.2	16.8	53.0
Wake	19 160	300 548	31 188	24 187	41 885	14 127	23 527	9 312	30 984	772	43.0	5.8	54.5
Warren	283	2 582	182	860	371	44	45	46	17 723	282	19.1	14.9	53.2
Washington	270	3 831	377	D	479	D	D	129	33 664	203	35.5	27.1	62.1
Watauga	1 513	15 839	2 776	1 178	3 251	264	454	281	17 729	674	57.7	2.1	38.0
Wayne	2 338	36 626	6 382	9 179	6 195	1 256	711	804	21 964	827	39.5	13.1	62.8
Wilkes	1 285	22 541	2 203	8 702	2 807	361	324	510	22 635	1 170	45.6	2.3	47.9
Wilson	1 811	31 620	3 341	9 000	4 323	1 654	1 582	815	25 763	385	33.8	22.6	67.8
Yadkin	641	8 690	916	3 440	915	106	401	181	20 839	884	42.2	3.8	46.8
Yancey	321	3 643	362	1 533	558	76	171	79	21 640	604	63.9	1.3	31.5
NORTH DAKOTA	20 288	249 476	45 894	23 209	41 402	12 526	7 596	5 534	22 182	30 504	6.4	63.9	74.3
Adams	104	748	304	D	161	36	17	15	20 266	367	4.4	72.8	69.5
Barnes	385	3 917	856	427	610	156	80	64	16 225	772	7.5	60.0	75.6
Benson	117	1 083	D	174	74	34	2	21	18 968	604	4.6	64.2	75.8
Billings	27	148	0	0	2	0	0	4	30 358	237	5.5	67.5	73.8
Bottineau	269	1 597	369	87	329	87	43	25	15 752	808	4.8	61.5	70.5
Bowman	165	953	219	30	220	49	36	15	16 044	358	6.1	65.1	69.6
Burke	92	389	0	0	71	34	6	7	17 653	479	2.3	71.2	72.4
Burleigh	2 252	32 964	7 352	1 250	5 292	1 712	1 227	765	23 193	867	12.8	50.4	54.9
Cass	4 059	71 056	10 383	6 828	10 440	4 847	2 623	1 793	25 228	919	10.8	61.8	81.8
Cavalier	183	1 282	309	D	241	95	14	22	17 466	682	2.9	74.6	84.2
Dickey	207	1 713	426	107	310	68	32	29	16 770	517	7.0	58.6	78.7
Divide	83	579	255	D	70	33	13	7	12 409	535	4.3	76.1	78.1
Dunn	90	659	D	D	123	38	D	12	18 390	618	8.1	72.3	74.1
Eddy	86	525	166	D	60	23	8	8	14 619	288	3.8	74.0	77.8
Emmons	146	1 106	216	19	180	76	16	22	20 115	744	3.2	65.1	71.0
Foster	151	1 548	322	D	247	36	13	29	18 811	282	5.7	65.6	83.0
Golden Valley	77	438	D	D	90	18	D	7	16 137	244	4.9	71.3	76.2
Grand Forks	1 767	27 734	5 639	1 870	5 553	1 058	1 035	599	21 603	768	8.1	55.1	71.7
Grant	86	483	185	20	69	40	7	7	14 923	596	6.5	71.1	77.7
Griggs	112	888	D	132	141	D	18	16	18 347	357	7.0	58.5	72.0
Hettinger	99	472	96	D	81	39	D	7	15 136	436	3.9	71.3	78.0
Kidder	64	392	124	D	74	35	14	6	14 587	513	3.7	71.5	72.1
La Moure	157	897	130	113	138	96	7	14	15 349	616	5.8	62.8	78.6
Logan	75	402	110	D	47	29	D	5	12 254	401	3.5	73.3	80.5
McHenry	146	657	102	D	104	56	6	11	17 411	905	5.2	61.7	70.2
McIntosh	121	907	370	D	146	71	5	13	14 499	505	4.8	60.4	70.3
McKenzie	160	1 127	156	46	178	83	28	20	17 936	668	6.0	67.2	74.4
McLean	250	2 040	400	D	306	153	18	53	26 032	969	5.1	63.1	72.9
Mercer	259	3 592	432	88	442	86	35	123	34 177	473	7.0	53.9	61.7
Morton	652	7 055	1 207	937	869	238	270	143	20 334	907	9.0	62.1	69.9
Mountrail	202	1 607	369	D	287	72	43	26	16 189	755	2.8	70.3	73.0
Nelson	150	928	313	D	122	67	9	15	15 880	471	3.8	62.6	74.3
Oliver	39	405	D	D	18	D	5	21	50 642	327	6.1	59.0	69.4
Pembina	329	3 439	405	1 272	632	118	23	81	23 456	615	7.3	57.9	82.6
Pierce	160	1 443	430	D	254	88	27	26	17 701	491	5.1	69.2	77.0
Ramsey	434	4 394	1 030	183	947	226	111	76	17 250	525	7.0	66.3	74.3
Ransom	208	1 494	371	231	283	65	30	26	17 206	485	10.3	52.6	72.6
Renville	90	577	D	7	114	30	D	9	16 208	390	1.8	74.1	80.5
Richland	566	6 582	648	2 330	849	150	124	142	21 551	874	10.2	55.6	80.5
Rolette	205	3 409	528	407	464	72	8	64	18 715	511	7.6	58.5	70.5
Sargent	133	1 999	D	D	178	42	13	70	35 012	449	8.0	60.8	77.3
Sheridan	45	187	D	D	31	16	8	4	18 802	380	3.2	71.3	76.3
Sioux	35	735	D	0	60	0	D	16	21 297	193	3.6	76.7	81.9
Slope	12	81	0	0	0	0	0	2	20 025	263	4.2	72.6	82.5
Stark	866	8 202	1 568	823	1 610	295	233	157	19 142	802	12.8	56.1	68.0
Steele	72	364	D	70	44	43	3	7	20 170	290	5.5	75.2	84.5
Stutsman	682	8 783	1 960	1 528	1 430	379	135	179	20 416	979	6.8	64.9	74.0
Towner	107	778	D	251	96	48	D	13	17 190	428	6.5	72.0	79.7
Traill	309	2 487	615	D	338	159	39	45	17 930	471	8.5	67.1	83.2
Walsh	445	3 746	769	406	684	163	71	70	18 677	755	5.7	57.9	78.3

STATE County	Acreage (1,000)	Percent change, 1992–1997	Average size of farm	Total irrigated (1,000)	Total cropland (1,000)	Average per farm ($1,000)	Average per acre (dollars)	Value of machinery and equipment Average per farm ($1,000)	Total (mil dol)	Average per farm (dollars)	Crops	Live-stock and poultry products	$10,000 or more	$100,000 or more	Percent of land owned by Fed. Gov. 1997	Water consumption 1995 (mil gal/day)
	117	118	119	120	121	122	123	124	125	126	127	128	129	130	131	132
NORTH CAROLINA—Cont'd																
Swain	7	10.4	86	0	2	192	2 228	24	2	30 158	31.8	68.2	20.8	7.8	69.3	22.7
Transylvania	13	5.6	73	0	6	318	4 382	31	10	59 279	33.3	66.7	31.6	6.3	30.8	29.5
Tyrrell	55	-19.4	661	0	51	850	1 287	150	36	429 966	54.6	45.4	73.5	41.0	15.5	0.5
Union	178	6.7	156	0	131	428	2 790	45	284	248 304	10.9	89.1	47.2	31.6	0.0	27.5
Vance	67	-2.1	287	3	27	396	1 558	86	20	84 341	97.4	2.6	58.2	24.6	3.9	22.0
Wake	113	-5.7	147	6	60	508	3 886	45	71	91 720	80.3	19.7	48.3	20.9	0.7	78.8
Warren	80	-7.9	284	2	35	309	1 237	50	38	133 356	35.8	64.2	51.1	24.5	0.0	2.9
Washington	107	4.2	528	2	92	658	1 302	132	68	332 784	62.2	37.8	66.0	40.9	6.2	5.6
Watauga	57	20.2	84	0	24	260	2 854	24	12	17 272	58.9	41.1	36.1	3.3	6.5	6.3
Wayne	229	27.5	277	2	147	542	2 025	83	337	407 604	21.4	78.6	71.0	41.8	0.8	32.0
Wilkes	127	10.8	109	0	59	258	2 178	31	215	183 665	4.1	95.9	44.3	28.4	1.4	18.5
Wilson	128	-9.8	333	2	91	613	2 021	114	120	312 840	70.1	29.9	68.6	42.6	0.0	16.8
Yadkin	102	-2.1	115	1	67	269	2 359	39	50	56 742	44.7	55.3	41.4	14.7	0.0	6.3
Yancey	40	5.4	66	0	14	142	2 316	17	5	8 853	80.0	20.0	20.4	0.8	18.9	2.3
NORTH DAKOTA	39 359	-0.2	1 290	180	27 025	513	401	112	2 869	94 064	76.5	23.5	75.1	28.4	3.9	1 122.4
Adams	630	5.8	1 716		375	399	228	101	28	75 871	53.9	46.1	76.0	28.6	0.0	0.8
Barnes	870	1.4	1 127	2	767	537	485	137	80	103 586	87.7	12.3	80.8	36.4	0.6	2.3
Benson	758	-2.5	1 255	2	610	412	320	116	50	82 735	78.5	21.5	78.8	28.1	1.3	2.7
Billings	794	-3.1	3 350	0	124	797	247	81	12	51 435	30.0	70.0	75.9	14.8	49.6	1.4
Bottineau	960	1.0	1 188	D	811	460	417	104	61	75 398	90.5	9.5	72.9	26.7	1.8	1.9
Bowman	715	5.5	1 998	1	335	422	223	78	26	73 205	49.1	50.9	72.6	19.8	4.0	2.9
Burke	615	10.1	1 285		455	390	325	106	29	60 100	86.6	13.4	71.8	18.8	4.2	0.8
Burleigh	896	2.1	1 033	3	480	322	331	54	36	41 567	52.3	47.7	58.2	10.6	1.7	12.2
Cass	1 068	-0.3	1 162	8	1 013	942	826	164	169	183 941	91.7	8.3	82.4	53.1	0.2	18.8
Cavalier	875	2.4	1 284	D	812	636	499	163	72	105 924	97.6	2.4	88.1	41.2	1.0	0.9
Dickey	580	-7.6	1 122	10	454	511	459	140	64	123 022	68.3	31.7	75.0	33.1	0.9	7.1
Divide	733	1.0	1 371	3	555	404	316	111	35	65 446	84.9	15.1	76.8	25.2	1.4	2.3
Dunn	1 336	-1.3	2 161	2	429	517	238	73	39	63 774	29.9	70.1	80.3	19.1	2.5	3.4
Eddy	344	-6.8	1 195	2	258	466	355	94	23	78 200	66.1	33.9	77.8	29.5	1.0	1.5
Emmons	824	-1.2	1 107	4	509	293	266	85	51	68 902	50.1	49.9	75.8	19.8	0.8	6.4
Foster	370	1.2	1 313	3	312	603	476	129	36	127 502	69.3	30.7	80.1	36.5	0.2	2.2
Golden Valley	579	14.6	2 372	1	221	565	224	96	18	74 860	56.5	43.5	73.8	24.6	15.4	3.0
Grand Forks	775	0.7	1 009	15	719	777	762	155	130	168 764	91.5	8.5	68.8	39.6	1.4	15.6
Grant	970	-4.9	1 627	2	448	400	252	74	35	58 553	37.6	62.4	74.7	16.1	0.9	7.9
Griggs	390	-1.5	1 092	4	318	422	375	109	28	78 767	83.7	16.3	70.6	27.2	0.4	1.6
Hettinger	707	2.8	1 622	D	578	520	328	115	44	101 926	81.1	18.9	77.8	33.7	0.1	0.6
Kidder	725	0.1	1 413	7	416	307	221	75	34	66 159	46.8	53.2	76.6	18.1	1.7	6.1
La Moure	671	0.3	1 089	7	570	457	427	133	73	118 228	74.1	25.9	80.2	35.7	0.7	5.1
Logan	531	-11.3	1 325	2	287	349	254	110	32	80 612	35.2	64.8	79.3	24.4	1.4	2.0
McHenry	1 067	1.7	1 179	8	683	382	333	66	57	62 476	63.4	36.6	70.9	17.3	2.9	18.6
McIntosh	508	-6.8	1 006		348	315	321	73	35	69 873	43.8	56.2	70.1	19.2	2.1	1.1
McKenzie	1 170	0.3	1 751	23	522	464	263	90	46	69 610	54.9	45.1	76.0	24.0	29.7	13.0
McLean	1 143	1.3	1 179	5	866	450	360	98	74	76 650	82.8	17.2	73.7	24.9	1.7	161.0
Mercer	551	3.6	1 165	2	284	322	280	67	23	48 708	53.5	46.5	67.7	11.8	0.5	277.9
Morton	1 229	-0.4	1 355	4	565	452	296	75	60	66 496	30.3	69.7	69.8	20.0	0.5	37.5
Mountrail	997	-0.4	1 321	D	650	404	318	105	49	65 130	78.0	22.0	74.0	21.2	0.7	1.5
Nelson	535	-3.2	1 136	D	441	506	476	108	37	77 838	84.6	15.4	68.6	26.8	0.8	1.1
Oliver	400	4.2	1 224	4	186	271	240	62	19	58 368	38.8	61.2	73.4	20.5	0.0	434.5
Pembina	633	5.4	1 030	D	587	1 006	1 008	203	128	207 327	96.7	3.3	78.5	45.4	0.3	2.1
Pierce	567	-3.2	1 155	0	444	427	363	102	36	73 489	75.4	24.6	77.8	24.8	1.3	1.7
Ramsey	658	2.8	1 254	0	597	504	391	188	45	85 590	93.9	6.1	72.6	29.3	1.6	0.6
Ransom	515	6.2	1 062	17	360	586	511	123	61	126 570	76.7	23.3	70.7	34.6	8.4	13.2
Renville	516	2.3	1 322	D	456	605	494	146	38	96 901	92.1	7.9	87.9	32.6	3.0	0.3
Richland	809	1.2	926	2	748	836	901	162	166	189 914	82.1	17.9	83.4	47.4	4.0	3.8
Rolette	493	-5.7	965		356	318	345	85	30	57 933	73.4	26.6	65.8	18.4	0.7	2.0
Sargent	477	-3.9	1 062	6	403	589	550	121	65	143 729	74.2	25.8	80.4	45.2	2.1	6.3
Sheridan	492	-5.6	1 295		340	456	372	91	27	72 075	63.8	36.2	76.8	24.5	0.8	0.5
Sioux	705	-5.5	3 652	D	D	813	216	80	15	75 273	22.8	77.2	80.8	22.8	1.2	0.9
Slope	757	-3.7	2 879	0	D	559	199	93	21	81 490	57.3	42.7	81.7	21.3	21.8	1.0
Stark	806	-4.3	1 005	1	536	320	349	64	46	57 088	47.6	52.4	68.3	17.3	0.1	1.7
Steele	413	-6.2	1 423	4	377	685	496	201	47	161 097	95.9	4.1	85.9	52.8	0.6	0.9
Stutsman	1 265	-0.4	1 292	7	985	471	380	115	93	94 528	72.6	27.4	73.1	32.4	2.2	6.3
Towner	570	-3.5	1 332	D	499	524	376	124	42	99 052	93.1	6.9	76.2	35.3	0.8	0.7
Traill	494	-1.3	1 050		480	847	815	193	85	179 445	97.3	2.7	87.9	58.2	0.1	1.4
Walsh	718	-2.6	950	1	642	734	783	151	122	162 111	96.0	4.0	72.5	35.1	0.2	2.2

Table B. States and Counties — **Residential Construction, Wholesale and Retail Trade, and Real Estate**

STATE County	Value of Residential Construction Authorized by Building Permits, 1999		Wholesale Trade, 1997				Retail Trade[1], 1997				Real Estate and Rental and Leasing, 1997			
	New Construction ($1,000)	Number of Housing Units	Number of Establishments	Number of Employees	Sales (mil dol)	Annual Payroll (mil dol)	Number of Establishments	Number of Employees	Sales (mil dol)	Annual Payroll (mil dol)	Number of Establishments	Number of Employees	Receipts (mil dol)	Annual Payroll (mil dol)
	133	134	135	136	137	138	139	140	141	142	143	144	145	146
NORTH CAROLINA—Cont'd														
Swain	8 661	98	9	109	27.3	2.7	118	472	62.1	6.3	7	12	0.5	0.1
Transylvania	55 356	286	16	68	20.9	1.8	110	1 127	158.2	14.9	32	73	7.9	1.4
Tyrrell	652	7		14	16.0	0.3	19	107	18.1	1.4	1	D	D	D
Union	252 326	2 569	241	2 214	813.4	75.6	383	4 245	753.0	69.2	67	222	25.9	4.4
Vance	13 239	129	33	489	274.0	13.2	251	2 763	454.0	42.1	46	146	17.2	2.6
Wake	1 431 413	13 527	1 249	18 833	13 259.1	826.0	2 719	38 755	7 391.9	664.3	792	4 777	862.5	130.1
Warren	12 518	94	9	22	5.6	0.6	55	369	44.1	5.3	6	D	D	D
Washington	2 606	31	15	91	36.4	2.5	65	446	71.0	6.4	7	32	2.0	0.5
Watauga	104 788	854	47	422	166.1	12.0	342	3 207	519.8	44.3	69	231	18.4	3.1
Wayne	39 715	555	151	2 217	891.1	59.4	523	6 169	1 033.0	88.1	81	263	21.0	4.5
Wilkes	34 697	279	66	818	431.1	22.8	259	2 906	458.6	41.3	38	127	16.7	2.3
Wilson	37 681	469	121	1 264	471.1	33.6	393	4 416	735.4	66.2	63	192	19.3	3.0
Yadkin	19 935	182	32	D	D	D	144	851	167.9	13.6	15	46	5.1	0.5
Yancey	5 626	96	5	15	1.5	0.2	66	541	112.6	8.8	13	28	2.1	0.3
NORTH DAKOTA	223 249	2 579	1 604	16 992	8 618.4	454.4	3 569	40 685	6 702.1	616.1	657	3 325	287.0	46.3
Adams	0	0	10	67	51.0	1.4	21	169	34.3	2.7	2	D	D	D
Barnes	848	12	35	281	150.2	6.3	76	602	81.1	7.4	3	2	0.3	0.0
Benson	150	1	10	36	31.8	1.3	18	76	14.7	0.7	4	D	D	D
Billings	203	2	1	D	D	D	6	10	1.4	0.2	NA	NA	NA	NA
Bottineau	0	0	13	71	84.2	2.4	54	325	57.3	4.7	9	D	D	D
Bowman	200	1	5	97	56.1	2.2	27	196	43.5	2.8	2	D	0.1	0.0
Burke	323	4	7	41	33.4	0.7	16	89	14.5	0.9	4	6	0.1	0.0
Burleigh	52 235	417	143	1 574	619.8	43.5	366	5 114	814.6	82.5	92	563	48.9	6.9
Cass	85 981	1 088	366	5 945	2 755.5	182.6	572	9 697	1 669.2	161.3	163	1 067	111.5	17.3
Cavalier	0	0	20	113	93.6	3.2	33	241	48.7	3.4	2	D	D	D
Dickey	499	4	22	153	93.2	3.5	41	297	46.9	4.3	3	4	0.2	0.0
Divide	0	0	8	45	59.8	1.2	15	70	9.0	1.0	4	7	0.4	0.0
Dunn	0	0	9	35	9.5	0.8	19	110	29.3	1.6	2	D	D	D
Eddy	0	0	7	42	23.1	0.9	11	59	9.9	0.7	2	D	D	D
Emmons	804	13	9	64	34.3	0.8	34	174	35.1	2.4	2	D	D	D
Foster	605	6	17	109	68.0	2.7	30	222	38.7	3.2	NA	NA	NA	NA
Golden Valley	278	7	4	58	32.8	1.3	17	88	17.7	1.2				
Grand Forks	16 715	192	130	1 511	552.4	41.3	351	5 596	934.7	81.4	70	524	33.9	7.0
Grant	0	0	10	51	19.4	0.9	15	77	14.0	1.1	2	D	D	D
Griggs	0	0	15	83	36.7	2.1	22	133	22.6	1.9	3	D	D	D
Hettinger	0	0	9	54	27.3	1.2	13	79	16.9	1.1	3	D	D	D
Kidder	210	4	5	23	9.8	0.4	11	62	13.9	0.6	1	D	D	D
La Moure	410	5	17	155	88.6	2.9	22	105	18.7	1.6	3	3	0.1	0.0
Logan	0	0	8	111	96.9	1.2	12	52	11.8	0.8	1	D	D	D
McHenry	342	4	19	92	64.7	2.3	23	109	14.3	1.1	7	13	0.5	0.0
McIntosh	0	0	8	43	22.2	0.9	27	146	29.0	2.1	2	D	D	D
McKenzie	1 485	18	11	62	18.3	1.6	27	179	23.8	2.2	2	D	D	D
McLean	1 365	24	22	124	114.3	3.2	46	343	47.0	3.9	4	13	0.4	0.1
Mercer	619	8	12	58	22.8	1.1	46	440	56.2	5.2	5	6	0.3	0.0
Morton	13 261	151	49	409	193.4	9.2	101	944	196.0	18.4	21	53	3.9	0.5
Mountrail	724	10	13	D	D	D	46	299	47.0	3.7	4	D	D	D
Nelson	270	3	20	188	92.1	3.4	22	114	15.5	1.2	5	11	0.2	0.0
Oliver	70	1	2	D	D	D	3	23	4.0	0.2	NA	NA	NA	NA
Pembina	1 016	8	28	211	113.7	4.4	77	620	103.0	8.4	4	9	0.2	0.0
Pierce	350	5	13	183	90.1	3.5	30	252	42.5	3.0	4	3	0.3	0.0
Ramsey	1 638	14	35	374	170.5	9.3	92	1 014	141.2	14.0	11	161	5.2	1.1
Ransom	3 409	71	9	154	130.2	4.6	39	275	39.4	3.3	4	8	0.4	0.0
Renville	100	5	15	56	57.8	1.4	14	105	27.7	1.9	1	D	D	D
Richland	3 175	36	54	479	208.3	8.7	91	797	137.9	11.9	18	73	5.7	0.7
Rolette	525	4	10	71	79.4	1.5	49	486	79.7	6.5	4	D	D	D
Sargent	3 773	76	11	80	48.5	1.6	28	161	25.5	2.0	3	7	0.2	0.0
Sheridan	0	0	5	25	7.5	0.4	8	33	6.1	0.5	3	7	0.1	0.0
Sioux	0	0	2	D	D	D	11	60	14.0	0.7	1	D	D	D
Slope	0	0	NA	NA	NA	NA	NA	NA	NA	NA	1	D	D	D
Stark	4 745	34	57	434	276.6	9.8	166	1 591	255.9	23.5	30	74	6.3	1.1
Steele	250	1	7	42	47.1	1.4	8	51	12.3	0.7	1	D	D	D
Stutsman	6 012	79	37	300	235.0	8.0	137	1 419	207.8	19.4	24	95	6.9	1.1
Towner	200	1	11	D	D	D	19	87	10.4	0.8	4	23	1.0	0.1
Traill	3 132	30	30	293	184.0	6.6	47	314	49.2	4.4	8	D	D	D
Walsh	1 165	12	42	383	151.7	8.2	91	706	116.1	10.2	10	18	0.5	0.2

1. Establishments with payroll.

Table B. States and Counties — **Professional, Manufacturing, and Accommodation and Foodservices**

STATE County	Professional, Scientific, and Technical Services[1], 1997				Manufacturing, 1997				Accommodation and Foodservices, 1997			
	Number of Establishments	Number of Employees	Receipts (mil dol)	Annual Payroll (mil dol)	Number of Establishments	Number of Employees	Receipts (mil dol)	Annual Payroll (mil dol)	Number of Establishments	Number of Employees	Sales (mil dol)	Annual Payroll (mil dol)
	147	148	149	150	151	152	153	154	155	156	157	158
NORTH CAROLINA—Cont'd												
Swain	6	46	2.1	1.1	NA	NA	NA	NA	79	796	38.1	10.4
Transylvania	50	150	11.6	3.9	28	3 071	715.1	119.3	72	798	34.0	10.7
Tyrrell	3	D	D	D	NA	NA	NA	NA	8	D	D	D
Union	141	744	65.2	19.9	228	13 113	2 543.5	356.9	151	2 618	73.0	18.6
Vance	34	208	10.2	4.1	53	5 085	1 218.0	119.2	66	1 532	38.6	10.7
Wake	2 366	18 158	2 000.3	798.8	639	23 789	10 420.0	784.7	1 229	24 776	896.6	251.0
Warren	15	36	2.1	0.7	13	813	95.5	15.3	13	D	D	D
Washington	8	20	0.8	0.3	15	D	D	D	22	334	9.6	2.5
Watauga	97	331	21.0	7.2	56	1 223	97.4	24.8	165	2 847	91.3	25.0
Wayne	129	596	43.4	16.0	101	9 495	1 417.5	231.1	158	2 953	84.4	23.1
Wilkes	73	336	19.9	6.5	108	8 082	1 081.2	168.1	97	1 436	42.9	10.8
Wilson	90	1 238	61.9	27.5	96	8 954	4 980.3	288.1	138	2 771	85.4	23.1
Yadkin	27	198	7.0	3.5	43	3 616	787.3	94.5	70	922	26.2	7.7
Yancey	21	115	4.3	1.8	21	1 645	373.4	39.3	26	268	7.4	2.2
NORTH DAKOTA	1 077	7 076	418.0	175.7	704	21 956	5 115.9	604.8	1 827	26 330	684.9	189.0
Adams	6	13	0.5	0.2	NA	NA	NA	NA	9	54	1.2	0.4
Barnes	15	58	4.3	1.5	NA	NA	NA	NA	36	318	8.1	2.1
Benson	3	2	0.3	0.1	NA	NA	NA	NA	12	D	D	D
Billings	NA	NA	NA	NA	NA	NA	NA	NA	8	92	6.7	1.9
Bottineau	12	33	2.4	0.9	NA	NA	NA	NA	30	151	4.8	1.3
Bowman	8	29	1.9	0.9	NA	NA	NA	NA	18	128	3.2	0.7
Burke	3	6	0.3	0.0	NA	NA	NA	NA	18	D	D	D
Burleigh	176	1 604	87.5	37.2	54	1 310	99.7	47.3	156	3 485	96.8	27.8
Cass	272	2 318	164.1	65.9	183	6 757	1 512.2	173.5	294	7 184	195.0	55.2
Cavalier	10	17	0.7	0.2	NA	NA	NA	NA	23	D	D	D
Dickey	8	22	0.9	0.4	NA	NA	NA	NA	20	177	3.2	0.8
Divide	4	13	0.5	0.2	NA	NA	NA	NA	8	52	1.4	0.2
Dunn	2	D	D	D	NA	NA	NA	NA	10	D	D	D
Eddy	1	D	D	D	NA	NA	NA	NA	13	55	1.9	0.4
Emmons	7	11	0.5	0.1	NA	NA	NA	NA	15	D	D	D
Foster	7	13	0.7	0.2	NA	NA	NA	NA	14	D	D	D
Golden Valley	5	10	0.9	0.3	NA	NA	NA	NA	7	57	1.3	0.3
Grand Forks	109	771	51.3	24.1	52	1 737	251.5	39.0	180	4 126	93.8	27.1
Grant	3	4	0.2	0.0	NA	NA	NA	NA	8	37	1.0	0.2
Griggs	3	D	D	D	NA	NA	NA	NA	12	71	1.7	0.5
Hettinger	3	8	0.2	0.1	NA	NA	NA	NA	9	34	0.9	0.2
Kidder	2	D	D	D	NA	NA	NA	NA	5	49	1.3	0.4
La Moure	3	7	0.2	0.0	NA	NA	NA	NA	16	D	D	D
Logan	2	D	D	D	NA	NA	NA	NA	8	33	0.9	0.2
McHenry	5	10	0.7	0.1	NA	NA	NA	NA	14	D	D	D
McIntosh	2	D	D	D	NA	NA	NA	NA	16	67	1.5	0.3
McKenzie	5	23	0.7	0.4	NA	NA	NA	NA	21	75	2.3	0.5
McLean	7	14	0.8	0.2	NA	NA	NA	NA	35	155	4.2	0.9
Mercer	10	33	1.7	0.5	NA	NA	NA	NA	32	276	6.3	1.9
Morton	30	286	8.6	3.6	27	883	573.4	27.2	49	580	15.7	4.1
Mountrail	4	22	0.5	0.3	NA	NA	NA	NA	30	158	4.1	1.0
Nelson	5	14	0.3	0.1	NA	NA	NA	NA	17	68	2.0	0.5
Oliver	2	D	D	D	NA	NA	NA	NA	5	D	D	D
Pembina	13	25	1.8	0.7	16	D	D	D	29	244	5.5	1.3
Pierce	8	27	1.1	0.3	NA	NA	NA	NA	17	104	3.2	0.9
Ramsey	19	51	3.3	1.1	NA	NA	NA	NA	43	551	15.2	4.2
Ransom	8	15	0.6	0.2	NA	NA	NA	NA	25	176	4.2	0.9
Renville	4	5	0.1	0.0	NA	NA	NA	NA	12	D	D	D
Richland	29	112	6.6	2.5	34	2 261	373.0	69.2	44	384	11.3	2.6
Rolette	4	8	0.4	0.1	NA	NA	NA	NA	21	109	3.6	0.7
Sargent	5	8	0.3	0.1	5	D	D	D	17	D	D	D
Sheridan	3	3	0.1	0.0	NA	NA	NA	NA	5	46	1.6	0.3
Sioux	NA	NA	NA	NA	NA	NA	NA	NA	3	23	0.9	0.2
Slope	NA	NA	NA	NA	NA	NA	NA	NA	2	D	D	D
Stark	46	214	12.0	6.0	30	718	75.8	17.6	64	1 059	26.6	7.2
Steele	2	D	D	D	NA	NA	NA	NA	8	21	0.8	0.1
Stutsman	26	119	6.4	3.4	28	1 446	250.3	41.0	61	850	22.1	6.3
Towner	5	12	0.7	0.3	NA	NA	NA	NA	9	40	1.5	0.3
Traill	12	31	1.8	0.8	NA	NA	NA	NA	36	363	6.9	1.8
Walsh	17	57	3.2	0.9	NA	NA	NA	NA	41	271	7.4	1.7

1. Firms subject to federal tax.

Table B. States and Counties — Health and Other Services and Federal Funds

STATE County	Health Care and Social Assistance[1], 1997				Other Services[1], 1997				Federal funds and grants, fiscal 1999[2] Expenditures (mil dol)			
										Direct payments for individuals[3]		
	Number of Establish-ments	Number of Employees	Receipts (mil dol)	Annual Payroll (mil dol)	Number of Establish-ments	Number of Employees	Receipts (mil dol)	Annual Payroll (mil dol)	Total	Social Security and government retirement	Medicare	Food stamps and Supplemental Security Income
	159	160	161	162	163	164	165	166	167	168	169	170
NORTH CAROLINA—Cont'd												
Swain	17	430	14.8	7.5	18	70	3.5	1.0	92.5	29.3	9.8	3.3
Transylvania	51	543	25.7	11.5	33	85	5.2	1.3	133.9	84.5	22.7	3.7
Tyrrell	2	D	D	D	5	10	1.2	0.2	36.9	7.9	2.8	1.1
Union	114	1 263	75.0	36.2	158	788	46.4	12.8	249.8	133.5	43.5	8.5
Vance	69	1 252	49.6	24.2	41	147	9.4	2.4	192.3	78.9	28.4	13.1
Wake	1 202	16 538	1 124.1	514.0	1 005	7 036	559.0	152.3	3 073.8	806.5	244.8	47.8
Warren	13	237	8.3	4.0	15	53	2.5	0.5	91.8	35.4	13.3	6.2
Washington	15	147	4.1	1.8	18	61	4.5	0.9	69.2	29.8	10.4	4.4
Watauga	98	1 386	70.3	35.3	61	288	13.4	3.9	124.6	58.7	19.8	4.3
Wayne	181	2 357	114.4	56.0	151	998	58.5	18.5	719.0	238.9	73.6	24.5
Wilkes	81	966	48.9	21.7	66	302	18.9	5.5	228.7	108.3	41.5	10.5
Wilson	133	1 903	100.6	48.5	108	776	39.2	12.7	304.9	127.7	54.2	16.8
Yadkin	33	471	19.7	9.0	40	248	11.2	3.8	126.7	61.8	23.2	3.5
Yancey	16	243	8.5	3.5	14	30	1.9	0.6	78.5	37.1	11.9	4.2
NORTH DAKOTA	1 013	13 181	904.1	386.4	1 281	6 294	364.3	101.3	4 535.2	1 185.6	424.6	58.1
Adams	7	104	5.2	3.0	8	14	1.2	0.2	19.7	6.3	2.6	0.1
Barnes	17	106	4.2	2.3	28	99	5.8	1.5	85.8	27.3	9.1	1.1
Benson	2	D	D	D	3	D	D	D	79.4	11.9	5.1	1.9
Billings	NA	NA	NA	NA	2	D	D	D	5.1	0.9	0.3	0.0
Bottineau	6	15	1.1	0.2	12	29	2.0	0.4	58.1	17.3	7.3	0.5
Bowman	7	82	4.0	1.3	15	25	2.9	0.4	26.0	7.6	3.4	0.2
Burke	NA	NA	NA	NA	5	5	0.4	0.0	26.6	6.7	3.2	0.2
Burleigh	137	1 456	121.5	55.6	135	811	44.5	13.6	573.2	123.4	37.5	6.1
Cass	244	5 939	474.2	191.5	261	2 059	115.5	36.1	495.6	174.7	46.8	8.4
Cavalier	8	26	2.6	1.0	12	31	1.7	0.4	63.8	11.7	4.7	0.2
Dickey	10	43	3.8	2.2	13	32	1.8	0.4	46.3	12.1	5.6	0.4
Divide	3	8	0.8	0.4	6	12	1.1	0.1	23.4	6.5	2.8	0.1
Dunn	1	D	D	D	3	5	0.2	0.0	22.4	5.4	2.7	0.2
Eddy	2	D	D	D	8	15	1.3	0.2	21.3	7.1	3.1	0.2
Emmons	5	8	0.5	0.2	7	11	0.7	0.2	31.0	10.0	4.4	0.3
Foster	9	94	3.0	1.2	14	55	2.9	0.8	47.5	9.0	3.5	0.2
Golden Valley	4	D	D	D	6	13	0.9	0.2	14.9	4.7	1.9	0.1
Grand Forks	84	1 492	65.4	44.1	113	731	36.6	11.3	424.3	86.4	29.6	4.5
Grant	4	17	0.6	0.2	6	9	0.7	0.1	24.6	6.1	4.1	0.3
Griggs	3	D	D	D	5	15	0.7	0.2	26.5	6.9	3.0	0.2
Hettinger	4	D	D	D	6	11	1.0	0.2	32.7	7.7	3.5	0.1
Kidder	2	D	D	D	2	D	D	D	23.2	6.0	3.2	0.2
La Moure	4	16	0.6	0.3	9	13	0.9	0.1	45.6	11.5	4.7	0.3
Logan	5	53	1.1	0.5	4	9	0.7	0.1	19.5	4.9	2.6	0.2
McHenry	6	17	0.6	0.2	7	12	1.4	0.1	50.7	16.0	6.7	0.6
McIntosh	4	30	1.5	0.9	8	14	1.0	0.2	28.8	10.0	6.0	0.2
McKenzie	3	D	D	D	9	28	1.4	0.4	32.0	9.0	3.3	0.8
McLean	10	136	3.6	1.9	19	48	3.0	0.7	77.5	23.7	9.5	0.7
Mercer	10	57	3.5	1.3	15	59	2.7	0.6	32.8	14.2	6.2	0.5
Morton	24	133	7.1	3.7	49	219	15.2	4.3	104.3	46.0	17.8	2.2
Mountrail	7	12	0.6	0.1	10	16	1.2	0.3	58.5	14.5	5.9	0.9
Nelson	8	118	2.0	0.9	11	12	1.2	0.2	43.4	11.9	5.5	0.2
Oliver	2	D	D	D	1	D	D	D	12.0	2.6	1.2	0.0
Pembina	10	53	2.6	1.3	16	43	2.5	0.4	73.4	19.3	7.7	0.5
Pierce	8	80	4.9	2.2	9	31	1.1	0.4	34.1	10.4	4.8	0.3
Ramsey	24	209	11.7	5.4	22	91	5.1	1.4	109.6	28.5	10.8	1.5
Ransom	15	60	2.3	0.8	13	24	2.1	0.4	41.7	13.0	5.4	0.5
Renville	3	2	0.3	0.0	6	41	3.6	0.7	23.6	6.9	2.8	0.1
Richland	21	181	10.2	4.2	27	89	5.3	1.2	89.5	30.7	10.1	1.1
Rolette	9	52	3.4	1.7	9	26	1.3	0.3	147.7	19.0	7.5	5.6
Sargent	4	D	D	D	7	12	0.4	0.1	34.0	8.4	3.5	0.2
Sheridan	NA	NA	NA	NA	4	13	0.3	0.0	20.2	4.2	2.3	0.2
Sioux	1	D	D	D	NA	NA	NA	NA	40.3	3.7	1.7	1.7
Slope	NA	NA	NA	NA	1	D	D	D	7.0	0.9	0.3	0.0
Stark	43	284	15.7	7.3	64	257	18.4	4.4	99.3	40.6	16.8	2.6
Steele	1	D	D	D	8	16	1.0	0.2	26.0	5.3	2.2	0.1
Stutsman	39	509	21.0	7.4	44	192	10.7	2.6	139.9	46.6	14.7	2.4
Towner	3	D	D	D	6	11	1.2	0.2	33.7	7.0	3.3	0.2
Traill	11	73	4.0	2.5	20	39	4.2	0.7	60.4	18.8	7.1	0.5
Walsh	19	99	4.2	2.1	38	123	6.7	1.5	92.0	28.4	11.8	1.0

1. Firms subject to federal tax.　2. October 1, 1998 to September 30, 1999.　3. State totals may include programs not allocated by county.

STATE County	Salaries and wages (171)	Defense (172)	Other (173)	Medicaid and other health-related (174)	Nutrition and family welfare (175)	Education (176)	Other (177)	Total (mil dol) (178)	Intergovern-mental (mil dol) (179)	Total (mil dol) (180)	Total (181)	Property (182)
NORTH CAROLINA—Cont'd												
Swain	12.2	0.2	5.0	15.0	3.6	1.0	12.1	18.2	12.8	3.7	307	173
Transylvania	6.6	0.2	2.4	8.7	2.0	1.1	1.2	45.6	21.4	18.8	674	507
Tyrrell	0.5	0.0	0.1	4.4	1.1	0.4	14.8	9.5	6.2	2.3	618	495
Union	10.0	7.4	2.7	20.4	10.6	3.5	1.5	191.0	90.3	59.4	559	425
Vance	4.8	0.1	9.0	36.3	10.8	3.5	1.4	106.3	68.6	21.3	512	367
Wake	258.6	31.0	78.0	252.8	462.6	198.6	638.2	1 333.0	472.2	477.3	865	639
Warren	2.0	0.0	0.5	23.7	4.8	1.3	2.4	35.6	20.4	9.7	533	414
Washington	2.2	0.0	1.2	11.3	3.7	1.2	0.6	33.3	17.8	6.2	451	340
Watauga	5.2	0.0	1.9	14.3	2.4	2.6	11.4	82.5	28.1	24.8	610	429
Wayne	191.9	51.0	3.4	72.3	21.9	8.6	8.9	200.0	123.1	47.0	420	291
Wilkes	9.1	0.2	2.1	43.6	5.9	3.6	2.2	120.4	69.1	28.6	458	305
Wilson	8.5	3.6	3.5	50.7	13.6	5.5	10.0	167.4	85.4	43.8	646	493
Yadkin	3.6	0.1	1.0	16.3	3.8	1.2	10.6	55.7	26.8	14.9	431	299
Yancey	2.3	0.0	0.7	17.5	2.1	0.9	0.7	26.1	15.1	6.9	421	283
NORTH DAKOTA	618.1	149.4	105.1	294.9	140.4	96.6	477.5	X	X	X	X	X
Adams	0.8	0.0	0.2	1.9	0.3	0.1	0.0	6.3	2.3	2.4	881	863
Barnes	4.8	2.1	1.1	5.0	1.4	0.8	5.1	23.9	10.1	8.7	724	708
Benson	5.0	2.4	2.5	8.1	4.0	3.6	17.1	14.1	7.7	4.0	590	579
Billings	1.1	0.1	0.0	0.0	0.0	0.1	0.7	5.3	3.1	0.9	770	736
Bottineau	3.0	0.0	0.6	2.7	0.9	0.2	1.2	17.3	6.4	6.5	873	853
Bowman	0.8	0.0	0.2	0.8	0.4	0.2	5.1	8.1	4.6	2.4	730	717
Burke	2.3	0.0	0.3	1.1	0.2	0.1	2.6	7.0	2.4	3.3	1 416	1 373
Burleigh	50.4	0.5	6.7	35.8	54.4	32.5	196.9	127.7	39.8	50.2	753	623
Cass	100.0	11.6	13.1	33.4	9.3	2.8	45.2	238.0	72.1	97.6	852	711
Cavalier	1.6	0.0	0.3	2.1	0.6	0.2	0.1	16.1	3.8	8.3	1 604	1 565
Dickey	1.6	0.1	0.4	2.9	0.7	0.2	5.3	10.4	3.9	4.6	820	814
Divide	1.1	0.0	0.2	2.1	0.2	0.1	0.0	7.2	2.2	3.4	1 408	1 378
Dunn	1.0	0.2	2.3	1.3	0.5	0.7	1.9	8.4	4.2	2.9	787	779
Eddy	1.0	0.2	0.2	1.3	0.4	0.1	0.4	10.7	2.5	4.4	1 521	1 501
Emmons	1.1	0.0	0.2	2.9	0.6	0.2	0.3	15.1	4.2	6.1	1 398	1 390
Foster	1.5	0.0	4.3	0.8	0.4	0.2	16.8	10.6	3.3	4.7	1 257	1 243
Golden Valley	0.5	0.0	0.1	0.8	0.2	0.1	0.6	6.6	2.3	2.6	1 342	1 315
Grand Forks	136.3	59.3	7.2	24.2	7.9	9.0	18.3	139.4	49.2	54.9	789	622
Grant	1.1	0.0	0.2	2.7	0.4	0.2	0.6	5.5	2.2	2.5	823	815
Griggs	1.1	0.0	0.2	0.8	0.4	0.1	0.4	10.2	2.4	5.9	2 065	2 045
Hettinger	1.1	0.0	0.2	3.5	0.4	0.1	0.2	7.3	2.8	3.2	1 095	1 091
Kidder	1.1	0.0	0.2	1.6	0.4	0.2	1.5	13.5	3.6	6.1	2 098	2 097
La Moure	1.8	0.4	0.4	2.7	0.6	0.3	4.1	24.3	13.4	7.7	1 564	1 545
Logan	0.6	0.0	0.2	1.9	0.2	0.1	0.1	5.0	2.2	2.0	841	835
McHenry	2.7	0.0	0.6	3.2	2.2	0.3	2.6	11.9	5.9	4.4	708	679
McIntosh	1.1	0.0	0.2	2.4	0.3	0.1	0.1	7.3	2.5	2.8	798	793
McKenzie	2.2	0.5	2.4	1.1	0.9	0.3	3.1	17.6	10.5	4.2	736	718
McLean	4.7	4.8	0.9	8.6	1.1	0.5	1.4	20.9	12.1	4.8	496	488
Mercer	1.9	0.8	0.4	3.2	0.6	0.2	0.0	31.8	12.2	8.4	895	881
Morton	5.2	0.1	2.8	8.6	3.8	0.6	6.4	49.9	21.3	17.1	701	689
Mountrail	4.4	0.0	0.5	5.4	2.6	1.2	10.5	18.7	9.6	5.4	808	791
Nelson	1.4	0.0	0.4	2.7	0.4	0.1	1.7	10.4	3.6	5.5	1 442	1 432
Oliver	0.2	0.0	0.0	1.1	0.1	0.1	3.4	12.8	2.5	1.0	473	429
Pembina	6.7	1.2	0.8	4.8	0.7	0.2	2.4	20.0	7.3	8.1	942	908
Pierce	1.3	0.0	0.3	3.2	0.6	0.2	1.1	8.7	3.4	4.1	887	821
Ramsey	9.6	10.1	2.6	6.7	1.8	0.5	10.7	27.1	10.5	10.0	810	726
Ransom	1.8	0.0	0.6	1.9	0.5	0.1	1.5	12.4	5.1	5.0	866	818
Renville	0.9	0.0	0.2	0.8	0.2	0.1	0.5	7.9	3.5	3.1	1 084	1 046
Richland	3.7	0.0	1.0	5.3	1.5	0.4	3.4	36.0	14.8	13.1	716	708
Rolette	22.7	6.9	26.1	19.3	9.6	4.6	14.9	27.7	19.8	4.4	313	291
Sargent	1.8	0.0	0.4	2.1	0.6	0.1	1.1	9.6	3.2	4.1	929	923
Sheridan	0.5	0.2	0.1	2.7	0.3	0.1	1.1	3.6	1.4	1.3	742	736
Sioux	6.9	0.0	2.5	4.1	4.9	4.3	4.1	6.8	5.2	1.2	293	292
Slope	0.1	0.0	0.0	0.3	0.0	0.0	0.2	3.8	1.0	0.6	704	647
Stark	6.7	0.0	0.8	8.6	3.5	1.0	6.5	41.7	18.0	14.0	618	527
Steele	0.8	0.2	0.1	0.3	0.2	0.1	1.5	5.1	1.6	2.8	1 247	1 228
Stutsman	9.3	0.3	2.2	17.9	3.7	0.5	7.7	41.5	16.2	14.2	763	677
Towner	1.0	0.0	0.2	1.1	0.4	0.1	2.8	7.3	2.5	3.2	1 051	1 041
Traill	2.1	0.0	1.0	2.4	1.2	0.5	3.3	22.4	7.4	8.3	963	939
Walsh	3.2	0.0	0.9	4.5	1.4	0.7	10.0	28.9	11.2	12.0	877	840

1. October 1, 1998 to September 30, 1999.　2. State totals may include programs not allocated by county.　3. Based on the resident population estimated as of July 1 of the year shown.

Table B. States and Counties — Local Government Finances, Government Employment, and Elections

	Local government finances, 1997 (cont'd)									Government employment, 1998			Presidential election, 2000		
	Direct general expenditure							Debt outstanding					Percent of vote cast —		
STATE County	Total (mil dol)	Per capita[1] (dollars)	Education	Health and hospitals	Police protection	Public welfare	Highways	Total (mil dol)	Per capita[1] (dollars)	Federal civilian	Federal military	State and local	Democratic	Republican	All other
	183	184	185	186	187	188	189	190	191	192	193	194	195	196	197
NORTH CAROLINA—Cont'd															
Swain	19.2	1 575	54.2	7.3	4.7	8.8	0.5	8.2	672	338	38	793	NA	NA	NA
Transylvania	45.1	1 619	47.7	5.2	6.7	10.5	1.1	9.2	331	169	88	1 216	NA	NA	NA
Tyrrell	10.3	2 725	58.6	1.5	4.1	7.2	0.5	2.1	562	15	12	382	NA	NA	NA
Union	169.7	1 596	55.0	3.9	6.4	7.2	1.0	189.1	1 778	202	342	5 377	NA	NA	NA
Vance	109.4	2 630	48.9	16.6	3.9	7.2	1.5	28.5	684	104	131	3 278	NA	NA	NA
Wake	1 231.5	2 233	46.8	5.4	4.7	3.9	2.5	7 733.2	14 020	4 203	2 429	61 473	NA	NA	NA
Warren	35.7	1 963	54.1	7.3	3.4	10.7	0.4	22.5	1 238	46	57	1 285	NA	NA	NA
Washington	33.1	2 409	44.7	17.7	3.6	9.3	1.3	11.6	845	52	42	1 212	NA	NA	NA
Watauga	73.0	1 793	35.7	5.5	5.3	6.9	2.8	35.0	860	113	133	4 900	NA	NA	NA
Wayne	192.4	1 718	58.5	4.8	4.1	6.9	3.0	104.1	929	1 455	4 592	8 236	NA	NA	NA
Wilkes	122.4	1 960	56.8	17.4	2.9	6.6	1.0	29.9	479	200	195	4 233	NA	NA	NA
Wilson	166.6	2 458	45.9	7.5	5.4	8.7	1.6	45.3	668	203	212	5 707	NA	NA	NA
Yadkin	54.1	1 565	54.1	17.9	4.2	7.4	1.3	6.9	198	76	109	1 516	NA	NA	NA
Yancey	26.3	1 602	55.2	15.2	2.3	7.2	0.6	3.8	233	75	52	789	NA	NA	NA
NORTH DAKOTA	X	X	X	X	X	X	X	X	X	8 985	13 097	49 267	33.1	60.7	6.3
Adams	6.3	2 302	43.4	0.4	3.1	4.2	20.6	1.7	635	19	22	162	25.2	72.6	2.2
Barnes	22.9	1 894	51.4	2.3	2.9	3.3	11.9	3.4	284	93	97	964	34.6	61.8	3.6
Benson	13.0	1 909	52.7	1.6	1.6	6.7	14.7	0.7	100	124	56	325	45.2	50.1	4.6
Billings	4.8	4 348	32.1	0.9	3.7	2.3	42.3	0.0	0	39	0	78	16.1	77.3	6.7
Bottineau	17.4	2 331	48.1	0.0	1.8	3.4	15.9	1.5	201	64	59	518	32.6	65.3	2.0
Bowman	8.3	2 512	56.4	0.4	2.9	3.3	18.5	0.0	10	21	27	226	23.1	75.5	1.5
Burke	7.0	3 002	43.1	0.4	1.9	2.5	13.4	0.2	65	58	18	174	29.0	68.5	2.5
Burleigh	119.6	1 794	45.0	0.7	5.9	3.6	9.0	100.5	1 508	919	544	7 359	29.5	67.4	3.1
Cass	237.8	2 075	42.3	1.2	3.9	2.4	4.5	326.6	2 851	2 053	989	8 277	38.0	59.4	2.6
Cavalier	17.1	3 316	32.3	0.0	2.4	4.0	15.2	6.2	1 203	39	41	298	26.9	65.8	7.3
Dickey	11.6	2 060	62.4	0.5	2.2	4.4	11.1	4.8	848	32	46	284	29.5	67.8	2.7
Divide	8.8	3 625	27.7	24.2	2.4	2.3	25.3	1.9	773	30	19	145	39.7	57.5	2.7
Dunn	7.8	2 149	58.8	0.0	2.8	1.5	21.4	0.1	23	30	29	231	28.3	67.1	4.5
Eddy	9.1	3 182	35.8	0.0	3.2	1.2	6.8	0.5	160	29	23	170	37.2	57.1	5.8
Emmons	15.3	3 491	31.6	0.9	0.7	1.8	9.6	4.7	1 080	31	35	233	20.8	73.3	5.9
Foster	9.3	2 472	52.4	0.5	1.8	3.7	10.2	2.7	705	29	31	228	27.9	69.1	3.0
Golden Valley	7.0	3 681	41.7	3.8	3.6	4.7	11.3	0.0	25	12	15	138	19.8	77.7	2.4
Grand Forks	138.0	1 982	41.5	3.1	4.1	1.5	5.3	117.6	1 689	1 282	3 955	8 070	39.2	58.8	2.0
Grant	5.8	1 919	56.3	1.2	0.9	6.7	20.3	1.9	614	32	24	160	16.8	76.9	6.3
Griggs	10.5	3 698	21.2	0.9	1.4	2.9	9.3	1.4	509	28	23	165	33.4	63.4	3.2
Hettinger	7.7	2 608	57.1	0.0	2.1	6.2	10.8	0.8	270	27	24	192	23.9	71.7	4.4
Kidder	12.0	4 096	30.6	3.2	1.0	2.1	9.0	2.1	720	30	23	162	22.7	67.1	10.2
La Moure	28.9	5 888	23.8	0.0	0.9	2.2	6.5	8.9	1 808	43	39	279	28.5	65.8	5.7
Logan	4.8	1 993	66.9	0.6	2.1	2.6	13.3	0.3	136	23	19	140	19.7	71.8	8.5
McHenry	11.8	1 908	57.7	0.0	2.2	4.5	17.0	1.9	308	72	49	368	33.4	63.3	3.3
McIntosh	7.1	2 002	51.5	0.0	2.3	2.1	18.0	0.7	188	25	28	190	21.9	73.6	4.6
McKenzie	18.1	3 140	53.9	1.4	2.2	2.4	15.0	0.2	43	71	46	377	28.2	70.5	1.4
McLean	20.4	2 093	57.4	0.5	4.6	1.7	7.9	1.4	167	129	79	680	32.3	63.8	3.8
Mercer	33.3	3 530	35.9	0.4	3.2	1.9	8.1	107.7	11 407	47	76	581	24.1	71.1	4.8
Morton	49.5	2 029	46.9	2.0	3.1	4.1	7.8	27.5	1 128	118	199	1 368	31.6	64.3	4.1
Mountrail	17.6	2 647	54.0	2.0	2.0	3.0	6.1	1.3	190	109	54	423	45.0	52.5	2.5
Nelson	10.0	2 623	46.9	0.4	2.2	3.9	17.2	3.7	962	36	30	219	38.4	57.6	4.1
Oliver	13.1	5 919	14.6	1.5	1.6	0.5	7.6	160.7	72 492	0	18	126	24.0	69.9	6.1
Pembina	19.3	2 245	58.3	0.6	3.0	2.5	7.6	3.8	442	124	98	532	29.8	66.2	4.0
Pierce	7.6	1 675	55.5	4.4	3.2	5.3	11.8	0.7	164	32	37	209	26.1	70.3	3.6
Ramsey	24.9	2 009	55.5	0.0	3.0	6.4	10.6	9.1	735	185	98	1 142	34.4	62.4	3.2
Ransom	10.5	1 806	54.8	1.7	3.7	4.8	12.0	5.4	922	39	47	436	40.7	56.1	3.2
Renville	9.3	3 248	46.9	0.7	2.1	1.9	21.5	1.1	369	23	23	178	34.2	63.3	2.5
Richland	38.1	2 093	52.0	1.7	2.8	2.8	13.2	11.2	615	81	148	1 328	32.0	64.3	3.7
Rolette	26.9	1 902	76.5	0.3	1.9	3.4	5.1	6.0	427	588	115	683	62.9	33.2	3.8
Sargent	9.0	2 028	46.8	2.3	2.8	3.6	14.0	4.4	984	49	36	213	44.9	51.6	3.5
Sheridan	3.2	1 776	50.6	0.7	2.8	6.3	17.2	0.3	173	16	14	109	17.6	77.3	5.1
Sioux	5.4	1 331	81.4	0.1	0.8	0.6	7.5	0.0	2	164	34	184	70.6	26.2	3.1
Slope	2.7	3 135	10.3	0.0	1.4	2.2	24.5	0.2	178	0	0	36	20.0	74.4	5.6
Stark	40.3	1 775	52.4	0.2	4.9	5.6	8.7	8.2	361	157	185	1 696	29.4	67.4	3.2
Steele	5.0	2 226	47.1	0.9	2.7	5.0	22.7	0.3	112	21	18	123	40.2	55.4	4.4
Stutsman	44.0	2 083	40.1	0.6	4.6	4.4	14.7	5.7	272	207	170	1 683	34.6	61.9	3.5
Towner	7.5	2 443	48.9	9.3	2.1	4.2	11.7	4.4	1 418	23	24	156	35.4	59.9	4.7
Traill	22.1	2 561	48.8	0.6	1.6	3.2	13.8	6.4	740	44	69	645	37.6	59.5	2.8
Walsh	28.6	2 090	51.7	0.3	2.3	1.4	12.5	3.9	288	72	110	1 343	34.3	61.1	4.6

1. Based on the resident population estimated as of July 1 of the year shown.

Table B. States and Counties — Land Area and Population

STATE/ County code	MSA/ PMSA/ NECMA code[1]	County Type[2]	STATE County	Land area,[3] (sq km) 1990	Population and population characteristics, 1999			Race (percent)					Age (percent)					
					Total persons	Rank	Per square kilometer	White	Black	Am. Indian, Eskimo, Aleut	Asian and Pacific Islander	Percent Hispanic[4]	Under 5 years	5 to 17 years	18 to 24 years	25 to 34 years	35 to 44 years	45 to 54 years
				1	2	3	4	5	6	7	8	9	10	11	12	13	14	15
			NORTH DAKOTA—Cont'd															
38 101	...	5	Ward	5 214	58 360	809	11.2	93.6	2.7	2.1	1.6	2.4	7.2	18.8	12.9	14.2	15.0	11.9
38 103	...	9	Wells	3 293	5 094	2 831	1.5	99.8	0.0	0.1	0.1	0.2	4.7	16.9	4.3	8.7	12.5	14.7
38 105	...	7	Williams	5 363	19 764	1 774	3.7	93.6	0.1	6.0	0.3	0.7	6.1	20.9	6.9	11.7	15.9	13.5
39 000	...	X	OHIO	106 067	11 256 654	X	106.1	87.0	11.6	0.2	1.2	1.6	6.6	18.7	9.5	13.6	16.2	13.3
39 001	...	6	Adams	1 512	28 698	1 422	19.0	99.2	0.3	0.3	0.2	0.6	6.5	21.9	8.6	12.1	14.9	13.8
39 003	4320	3	Allen	1 048	106 898	489	102.0	86.1	12.9	0.2	0.8	1.5	6.8	19.7	9.3	13.3	15.8	12.6
39 005	...	4	Ashland	1 099	51 973	879	47.3	98.0	1.1	0.1	0.8	0.6	6.4	20.1	10.0	12.0	15.3	13.6
39 007	1680	1	Ashtabula	1 820	103 344	502	56.8	95.6	3.6	0.2	0.5	2.0	6.7	20.1	7.9	12.2	15.9	13.3
39 009	...	4	Athens	1 313	61 599	775	46.9	93.5	3.3	0.3	3.0	0.9	5.0	15.5	27.2	12.2	13.6	10.6
39 011	4320	3	Auglaize	1 039	47 167	945	45.4	99.1	0.2	0.1	0.6	0.7	7.1	20.9	7.6	12.7	15.9	13.3
39 013	9000	3	Belmont	1 392	71 259	690	51.2	95.4	4.2	0.2	0.3	0.5	5.1	17.1	7.8	12.2	16.5	13.3
39 015	1640	1	Brown	1 274	41 576	1 049	32.6	98.4	1.4	0.1	0.1	0.2	6.8	21.5	8.3	13.3	15.7	13.7
39 017	3200	0	Butler	1 210	333 486	171	275.6	93.4	5.2	0.1	1.3	0.7	6.7	18.9	11.6	13.8	16.6	13.2
39 019	1320	2	Carroll	1 022	29 286	1 401	28.7	99.0	0.6	0.3	0.2	0.5	6.3	20.4	7.4	12.6	16.4	14.1
39 021	...	6	Champaign	1 110	38 572	1 120	34.7	96.1	3.3	0.2	0.5	0.8	6.2	19.5	8.6	12.3	16.2	16.3
39 023	2000	3	Clark	1 036	144 962	362	139.9	89.0	10.1	0.2	0.6	0.9	6.2	18.7	9.3	11.9	15.9	14.6
39 025	1640	0	Clermont	1 171	178 749	298	152.6	98.4	1.0	0.2	0.4	0.7	7.5	21.3	8.8	15.2	17.7	13.7
39 027	...	6	Clinton	1 064	40 701	1 068	38.3	96.8	2.4	0.2	0.6	0.5	6.6	20.3	10.0	13.1	16.1	13.2
39 029	9320	2	Columbiana	1 379	111 300	473	80.7	98.0	1.5	0.2	0.3	0.5	6.3	19.5	7.7	12.1	16.1	13.6
39 031	...	2	Coshocton	1 461	36 204	1 186	24.8	97.9	1.4	0.2	0.5	0.4	6.4	19.8	7.3	12.1	15.7	14.1
39 033	4800	3	Crawford	1 042	47 010	948	45.1	98.9	0.6	0.1	0.4	0.7	6.4	19.2	7.9	12.2	15.4	14.3
39 035	1680	0	Cuyahoga	1 187	1 371 717	24	1 155.6	70.6	27.4	0.2	1.8	2.8	6.5	17.3	8.6	13.8	15.7	12.8
39 037	...	6	Darke	1 554	54 063	851	34.8	99.1	0.4	0.2	0.3	0.9	6.4	20.2	8.0	12.3	15.2	13.9
39 039	...	4	Defiance	1 065	39 651	1 095	37.2	97.6	1.6	0.3	0.6	8.7	6.7	21.0	8.9	12.5	16.3	13.8
39 041	1840	1	Delaware	1 146	103 679	499	90.5	96.7	2.4	0.2	0.7	0.7	6.8	20.1	8.2	12.8	19.7	15.5
39 043	...	4	Erie	659	77 893	642	118.2	90.0	9.3	0.2	0.5	2.0	6.2	18.8	7.5	12.2	16.1	14.1
39 045	1840	1	Fairfield	1 310	126 723	413	96.7	98.1	1.2	0.2	0.5	0.6	6.2	20.1	9.0	12.6	17.8	15.1
39 047	...	6	Fayette	1 053	28 399	1 430	27.0	96.4	2.9	0.2	0.6	0.5	6.3	19.3	8.2	12.2	16.0	14.0
39 049	1840	0	Franklin	1 399	1 027 821	33	734.7	79.0	18.0	0.2	2.8	1.3	7.1	17.4	12.2	16.6	16.8	13.2
39 051	8400	2	Fulton	1 054	42 202	1 035	40.0	98.9	0.4	0.2	0.5	6.3	7.0	21.7	7.9	13.3	16.4	13.2
39 053	...	6	Gallia	1 214	33 248	1 278	27.4	95.7	3.3	0.3	0.6	0.7	6.3	19.8	8.9	13.0	15.4	14.5
39 055	1680	1	Geauga	1 047	89 598	560	85.6	97.8	1.5	0.1	0.6	0.5	6.7	19.6	7.0	10.9	17.6	15.7
39 057	2000	2	Greene	1 075	149 149	349	138.7	89.8	7.7	0.3	2.2	1.3	6.0	18.7	11.6	12.4	17.0	14.5
39 059	...	7	Guernsey	1 352	40 955	1 062	30.3	97.4	1.9	0.2	0.5	0.4	6.4	20.0	7.8	12.4	15.8	13.9
39 061	1640	0	Hamilton	1 055	840 443	49	796.6	75.0	23.4	0.1	1.5	0.8	7.1	18.5	9.6	14.3	15.5	12.3
39 063	...	4	Hancock	1 376	69 401	705	50.4	97.8	1.1	0.2	0.9	3.4	6.8	19.5	9.1	13.7	16.2	13.6
39 065	...	6	Hardin	1 218	31 652	1 326	26.0	98.4	0.9	0.2	0.5	0.6	6.1	19.0	13.7	12.0	14.3	13.4
39 067	...	6	Harrison	1 045	16 070	1 999	15.4	96.9	2.8	0.1	0.2	0.3	5.2	19.4	7.2	11.3	15.6	13.7
39 069	...	6	Henry	1 079	29 870	1 376	27.7	98.7	0.5	0.3	0.5	6.0	7.1	21.0	7.8	12.9	15.0	13.0
39 071	...	6	Highland	1 433	41 091	1 060	28.7	97.2	2.3	0.2	0.3	0.4	6.6	20.5	8.1	12.3	15.3	13.8
39 073	...	6	Hocking	1 095	29 170	1 405	26.6	98.5	1.1	0.2	0.2	0.5	6.3	19.4	8.4	12.5	15.6	15.3
39 075	...	7	Holmes	1 096	38 295	1 126	34.9	99.5	0.2	0.1	0.2	0.5	9.9	25.2	9.1	12.3	13.8	11.6
39 077	...	4	Huron	1 277	60 513	789	47.4	98.2	1.3	0.2	0.4	2.4	7.4	21.1	8.6	13.2	15.9	13.0
39 079	...	7	Jackson	1 089	32 660	1 294	30.0	98.7	0.8	0.2	0.2	0.4	6.4	20.7	8.3	12.6	15.9	13.3
39 081	8080	3	Jefferson	1 061	73 662	669	69.4	92.9	6.4	0.2	0.5	0.7	5.0	17.4	8.1	10.7	15.4	13.3
39 083	...	6	Knox	1 365	53 903	853	39.5	98.3	0.9	0.2	0.6	0.5	5.8	18.7	11.2	11.9	15.6	13.7
39 085	1680	0	Lake	591	227 145	243	384.3	97.0	1.9	0.1	1.0	0.9	6.1	17.6	7.9	13.9	16.9	14.4
39 087	3400	2	Lawrence	1 180	64 344	741	54.5	96.7	3.0	0.1	0.2	0.3	6.0	20.1	8.5	11.8	15.3	14.6
39 089	1840	0	Licking	1 778	136 485	386	76.8	97.3	2.0	0.2	0.5	0.6	6.5	19.0	9.2	13.1	16.4	14.9
39 091	...	6	Logan	1 187	46 816	949	39.4	96.7	2.3	0.1	0.8	0.5	6.7	20.5	8.4	12.7	15.6	13.2
39 093	1680	0	Lorain	1 276	282 100	196	221.1	89.8	9.1	0.3	0.8	7.2	6.7	20.0	9.2	13.3	16.7	13.3
39 095	8400	2	Lucas	882	446 482	127	506.2	81.5	16.7	0.3	1.5	4.4	7.2	19.0	10.1	13.9	15.9	12.2
39 097	1840	1	Madison	1 205	41 348	1 054	34.3	90.8	8.2	0.3	0.7	0.7	6.1	17.7	9.6	16.8	17.8	13.7
39 099	9320	2	Mahoning	1 076	252 597	213	234.8	82.3	17.0	0.2	0.6	2.9	5.9	18.0	8.1	11.8	15.4	12.6
39 101	...	4	Marion	1 046	66 870	725	63.9	92.4	6.7	0.3	0.6	1.1	6.4	18.3	8.3	14.8	17.3	13.4
39 103	1680	1	Medina	1 092	147 277	354	134.9	98.2	0.8	0.2	0.8	0.8	6.5	20.8	7.7	12.8	18.7	15.3
39 105	...	6	Meigs	1 112	24 012	1 577	21.6	98.8	0.9	0.2	0.1	0.3	6.0	20.4	7.9	11.7	15.9	14.5
39 107	...	7	Mercer	1 200	41 017	1 061	34.2	99.3	0.1	0.3	0.4	1.0	7.8	22.2	7.8	12.7	14.9	11.5
39 109	2000	2	Miami	1 054	98 721	522	93.7	96.7	2.2	0.2	0.9	0.5	6.3	19.5	8.0	12.5	16.6	15.2
39 111	...	6	Monroe	1 180	15 454	2 036	13.1	99.6	0.2	0.1	0.1	0.2	5.4	19.1	7.4	11.0	15.5	15.3
39 113	2000	2	Montgomery	1 196	565 866	91	473.1	78.5	19.8	0.2	1.4	1.0	6.6	17.5	9.5	14.1	15.9	13.3
39 115	...	8	Morgan	1 082	14 525	2 098	13.4	94.7	4.7	0.5	0.1	0.3	6.4	21.5	7.2	11.9	15.1	13.5
39 117	...	6	Morrow	1 050	32 146	1 308	30.6	99.3	0.3	0.2	0.2	0.5	6.6	21.6	8.1	12.6	16.6	15.2
39 119	...	4	Muskingum	1 721	84 812	593	49.3	94.5	4.9	0.3	0.3	0.4	6.5	19.6	9.4	12.7	15.4	13.4
39 121	...	8	Noble	1 033	14 810	2 079	14.3	90.6	9.0	0.2	0.1	0.8	5.8	18.3	9.8	15.9	17.3	12.6

1. MSA = Metropolitan Statistical Area. PMSA = Primary MSA. NECMA = New England County Metropolitan Area. See Appendix A for explanation of these concepts. See Appendix B for list of metropolitan areas identified by type, with component counties.   2. County typology code from the Economic Research Service of USDA. See Appendix A for definition.   3. Dry land or land partially or temporarily covered by water.   4. Hispanic persons may be of any race.

Table B. States and Counties — **Population and Households**

STATE County	Age (percent) (cont'd) 55 to 64 years	65 to 74 years	75 years and over	Percent female	Total persons 1990	1980	Percent change 1980–1990	1990–1999	Components of change, 1990–1999 Births	Deaths	Net migration	Households, 1990 Number	Percent change, 1980–1990	Persons per household	Female family householder[1]	One person
	16	17	18	19	20	21	22	23	24	25	26	27	28	29	30	31
NORTH DAKOTA—Cont'd																
Ward	7.6	6.1	6.3	50.4	57 921	58 392	-0.8	0.8	9 397	3 986	-6 200	21 485	8.0	2.59	8.0	24.9
Wells	12.4	10.8	15.1	51.8	5 864	6 979	-16.0	-13.1	418	813	-353	2 406	-5.6	2.39	5.0	29.1
Williams	8.9	8.3	7.9	50.9	21 129	22 237	-5.0	-6.5	2 365	1 962	-1 727	8 041	1.3	2.58	7.4	26.8
OHIO	8.8	7.0	6.3	51.7	10 847 115	10 797 603	0.5	3.8	1 454 713	957 171	-113 278	4 087 546	6.6	2.59	11.7	25.0
Adams	9.1	6.6	6.5	50.8	25 371	24 328	4.3	13.1	3 315	2 541	2 633	9 192	11.2	2.72	11.2	21.4
Allen	8.6	7.1	6.8	50.0	109 755	112 241	-2.2	-2.6	14 467	9 543	-7 451	39 408	0.6	2.66	11.7	23.6
Ashland	8.9	6.8	7.0	51.0	47 507	46 178	2.9	9.4	5 994	4 139	2 776	17 101	7.5	2.66	8.0	22.6
Ashtabula	9.4	7.5	7.1	51.5	99 880	104 215	-4.2	3.5	12 691	9 782	927	36 760	2.6	2.66	11.0	22.8
Athens	6.7	4.6	4.5	50.8	59 549	56 399	5.6	3.4	5 979	4 277	491	20 139	9.7	2.53	9.8	25.8
Auglaize	8.6	7.5	7.5	51.3	44 585	42 554	4.8	5.8	5 880	3 915	805	15 976	9.9	2.76	7.6	21.0
Belmont	10.3	9.0	8.8	51.0	71 074	82 569	-13.9	0.3	7 032	8 434	1 801	28 161	-6.9	2.49	10.8	26.1
Brown	9.0	5.8	5.9	50.6	34 966	31 920	9.5	18.9	5 081	3 320	4 944	12 379	15.9	2.79	9.6	19.1
Butler	8.5	5.6	5.0	51.5	291 479	258 787	12.6	14.4	40 928	21 539	18 275	104 535	18.6	2.68	10.4	20.8
Carroll	9.3	7.3	6.2	50.6	26 521	25 598	3.6	10.4	2 943	2 272	2 163	9 667	12.7	2.70	7.6	20.6
Champaign	8.4	6.3	6.2	50.5	36 019	33 649	7.0	7.1	4 517	3 356	1 504	13 253	12.4	2.67	8.3	21.2
Clark	9.0	7.4	7.1	51.9	147 538	150 236	-1.8	-1.7	18 377	14 436	-6 214	55 198	3.4	2.60	11.9	23.3
Clermont	7.6	4.6	3.8	50.8	150 094	128 483	16.9	19.1	23 688	10 586	15 901	52 726	26.1	2.82	10.0	18.2
Clinton	8.5	6.2	6.0	51.2	35 444	34 603	2.4	14.8	5 017	3 111	3 450	13 038	7.3	2.65	9.5	22.3
Columbiana	9.7	8.2	7.0	51.6	108 276	113 572	-4.7	2.8	12 689	10 691	1 421	40 775	1.9	2.63	10.3	22.9
Coshocton	9.6	7.7	7.3	51.5	35 427	36 024	-1.7	2.2	4 275	3 520	148	13 433	2.8	2.60	8.7	23.7
Crawford	9.3	7.7	7.6	51.6	47 870	50 075	-4.4	-1.8	5 736	4 717	-1 739	18 383	1.2	2.57	9.9	23.8
Cuyahoga	9.4	8.4	7.5	53.0	1 412 140	1 498 400	-5.8	-2.9	192 476	143 148	-101 608	563 243	0.0	2.46	14.9	30.2
Darke	8.7	7.4	7.8	51.4	53 617	55 096	-2.7	0.8	6 598	5 034	-935	19 459	3.2	2.71	7.9	21.0
Defiance	8.2	6.5	6.0	50.5	39 350	39 987	-1.6	0.8	4 840	2 973	-1 460	14 070	5.7	2.74	8.1	21.5
Delaware	8.3	4.6	4.1	50.3	66 929	53 840	24.3	54.9	9 856	4 515	25 787	23 116	31.2	2.78	7.2	17.0
Erie	9.4	8.6	7.0	51.4	76 781	79 655	-3.6	1.4	9 665	7 256	-1 072	28 932	4.3	2.61	10.4	24.1
Fairfield	8.6	5.5	5.2	50.2	103 468	93 678	10.5	22.5	14 070	8 166	17 563	36 813	15.9	2.74	8.8	19.0
Fayette	9.4	7.1	7.5	51.3	27 466	27 467	0.0	3.4	3 447	3 061	633	10 221	5.5	2.64	10.5	21.8
Franklin	7.6	5.4	4.7	51.9	961 437	869 126	10.6	6.9	149 925	70 377	-10 660	378 723	17.3	2.47	12.6	28.0
Fulton	8.0	6.1	6.4	50.9	38 498	37 751	2.0	9.6	5 285	3 092	1 617	13 504	7.7	2.82	7.2	19.5
Gallia	9.3	6.4	6.5	51.0	30 954	30 098	2.8	7.4	3 770	2 837	1 482	11 367	10.6	2.63	10.2	22.4
Geauga	8.5	7.9	6.2	50.5	81 087	74 474	8.9	10.5	11 213	5 418	3 090	26 906	17.6	2.98	7.1	14.9
Greene	8.7	6.4	4.7	51.1	136 731	129 769	5.4	9.1	15 741	9 481	-3 958	48 351	12.2	2.70	9.2	19.3
Guernsey	9.5	7.1	7.1	52.1	39 024	42 024	-7.1	4.9	5 065	4 208	1 198	14 894	-1.0	2.57	11.4	25.1
Hamilton	8.7	6.9	7.0	52.7	866 228	873 203	-0.8	-3.0	119 384	78 638	-64 802	338 881	5.2	2.50	14.0	29.9
Hancock	8.3	6.5	6.4	51.4	65 536	64 581	1.5	5.9	9 079	5 428	429	24 642	6.9	2.61	8.0	23.5
Hardin	8.5	6.4	6.8	50.8	31 111	32 719	-4.9	1.7	3 791	2 812	-348	11 250	1.1	2.60	8.6	24.7
Harrison	10.2	8.6	8.6	51.4	16 085	18 152	-11.4	0.1	1 732	1 916	218	6 111	-2.8	2.59	9.0	23.4
Henry	8.9	6.9	7.4	50.8	29 108	28 383	2.6	2.6	3 791	2 435	-513	10 401	6.9	2.75	7.2	21.3
Highland	9.6	6.8	5.7	51.2	35 728	33 477	6.7	15.0	4 929	3 581	4 089	13 230	11.0	2.67	10.0	22.4
Hocking	9.5	6.6	6.3	49.8	25 533	24 304	5.1	14.2	3 262	2 374	2 810	9 351	8.8	2.66	9.1	21.2
Holmes	7.6	5.0	5.6	50.6	32 849	29 416	11.7	16.6	7 572	2 281	268	9 315	14.1	3.42	6.1	15.8
Huron	8.6	6.3	5.9	51.1	56 238	54 608	3.0	7.6	8 512	4 603	540	20 239	8.3	2.75	9.2	21.2
Jackson	9.5	6.7	6.6	52.0	30 230	30 592	-1.2	8.0	3 931	3 157	1 770	11 260	5.2	2.65	12.0	22.6
Jefferson	10.7	10.1	8.7	52.6	80 298	91 564	-12.3	-8.3	7 910	9 040	-5 247	31 311	-4.3	2.51	11.7	25.5
Knox	9.3	7.0	6.9	51.5	47 473	46 304	2.5	13.5	5 884	4 679	5 356	17 230	8.4	2.57	8.7	22.8
Lake	9.2	7.9	6.1	51.5	215 500	212 801	1.3	5.4	26 390	16 831	-429	80 421	11.6	2.65	9.6	22.0
Lawrence	9.8	7.4	6.4	52.2	61 834	63 849	-3.2	4.1	7 402	6 165	1 487	22 899	3.9	2.67	12.2	21.6
Licking	9.1	6.1	5.7	51.4	128 300	120 981	6.0	6.4	17 230	11 100	8 388	47 254	11.9	2.65	9.5	21.3
Logan	9.4	7.0	6.4	51.2	42 310	39 155	8.1	10.6	6 035	4 220	2 823	15 952	11.9	2.62	8.7	23.0
Lorain	8.4	6.8	5.5	51.1	271 126	274 909	-1.4	-0.4	37 405	21 774	-3 844	96 064	5.8	2.76	11.7	20.8
Lucas	8.4	6.7	6.4	52.2	462 361	471 741	-2.0	-3.4	65 293	41 500	-38 465	177 500	3.1	2.56	13.9	27.3
Madison	7.6	5.7	4.9	45.5	37 078	33 004	12.3	11.5	4 803	2 843	2 426	11 990	12.5	2.74	9.2	19.8
Mahoning	10.1	9.9	8.0	52.7	264 806	289 487	-8.5	-4.6	31 232	29 162	-13 302	101 136	-1.4	2.57	13.9	25.5
Marion	8.5	6.8	6.2	48.2	64 274	67 974	-5.4	4.0	8 228	5 650	117	23 484	-1.3	2.62	10.7	22.8
Medina	7.8	5.7	4.8	50.7	122 354	113 150	8.1	20.4	16 794	8 425	16 802	41 792	16.2	2.90	7.7	16.3
Meigs	9.6	7.1	6.8	51.3	22 987	23 641	-2.8	4.5	2 560	2 441	985	8 662	3.0	2.62	10.1	22.7
Mercer	8.9	7.3	7.0	50.1	39 443	38 334	2.9	4.0	5 746	3 280	-768	13 398	10.1	2.91	6.7	20.4
Miami	9.0	6.8	6.1	51.3	93 184	90 381	3.1	5.9	11 753	7 843	1 929	34 559	8.1	2.67	8.7	21.0
Monroe	9.8	8.1	8.7	50.7	15 497	17 382	-10.8	-0.3	1 473	1 521	57	5 754	-3.5	2.66	8.1	21.7
Montgomery	8.9	7.6	6.4	52.2	573 809	571 697	0.4	-1.4	76 865	49 336	-47 129	226 192	6.8	2.49	13.2	27.0
Morgan	9.5	7.3	7.6	51.3	14 194	14 241	-0.3	2.3	1 694	1 508	195	5 170	5.3	2.70	9.4	21.9
Morrow	8.6	5.3	5.3	50.1	27 749	26 480	4.8	15.8	3 662	2 076	2 860	9 656	10.1	2.85	8.1	16.7
Muskingum	9.3	6.8	6.9	52.2	82 068	83 340	-1.5	3.3	10 883	8 178	292	30 753	4.5	2.61	11.5	23.8
Noble	8.8	5.3	6.2	44.1	11 336	11 310	0.2	30.6	1 323	1 044	3 188	4 137	4.8	2.70	7.6	22.7

1. No spouse present.

Table B. States and Counties — Vital Statistics, Health Resources, and Crime

STATE County	Births, average 1996–1998 Total	Rate¹	Deaths, average 1996–1998 Number Total	Number Infant²	Rate Total¹	Rate Infant³	Physicians,⁴ 1998 Number	Rate⁵	Hospitals,⁴ 1998 Number	Beds Number	Beds Rate⁵	Medicare enrollees 1999	Serious crimes known to police, 1998⁶ Total Number	Rate⁷
	32	33	34	35	36	37	38	39	40	41	42	43	44	45
NORTH DAKOTA—Cont'd														
Ward.........................	1 002	16.9	437	6	7.4	6.3	153	261	3	768	1 309	8 207	1 904	3 256
Wells........................	38	7.3	85	0	16.3	0.0	6	115	1	149	2 865	1 441	43	821
Williams....................	243	12.0	212	1	10.4	4.1	38	189	2	128	635	3 712	361	1 777
OHIO......................	152 173	13.6	105 479	1 193	9.4	7.8	24 240	216	188	39 924	356	1 692 072	485 066	4 328
Adams.......................	374	13.2	301	2	10.6	6.2	16	56	1	64	224	4 904	NA	NA
Allen.........................	1 495	13.9	1 050	13	9.7	8.5	212	198	3	581	542	16 993	5 166	5 587
Ashland.....................	659	12.7	476	3	9.2	4.5	46	88	1	65	124	7 520	NA	NA
Ashtabula..................	1 303	12.7	1 077	9	10.5	6.7	90	87	3	280	271	17 311	NA	NA
Athens.......................	611	10.0	482	5	7.9	7.6	92	150	2	150	244	7 397	NA	NA
Auglaize....................	596	12.7	435	4	9.3	7.3	31	66	1	122	259	8 092	NA	NA
Belmont.....................	742	10.7	920	6	13.2	8.1	77	111	3	391	565	14 188	666	1 144
Brown.......................	548	13.6	372	4	9.3	6.7	33	81	1	58	142	5 441	NA	NA
Butler.......................	4 477	13.7	2 484	35	7.6	7.7	375	113	5	792	240	40 559	15 082	4 608
Carroll......................	301	10.5	251	2	8.7	6.7	14	48	0	0	0	3 267	164	640
Champaign................	497	13.0	350	3	9.2	6.0	16	42	1	73	191	5 353	1 046	2 864
Clark.........................	1 902	13.0	1 607	15	11.0	7.7	207	142	2	464	319	24 229	NA	NA
Clermont...................	2 555	14.8	1 227	21	7.1	8.3	183	104	1	151	86	15 626	NA	NA
Clinton......................	577	14.6	351	2	8.9	4.0	61	153	1	81	203	5 976	795	2 018
Columbiana................	1 343	12.1	1 172	11	10.5	8.4	119	107	2	361	324	19 577	1 248	1 147
Coshocton..................	436	12.1	394	5	10.9	10.7	33	91	1	151	418	6 009	391	1 079
Crawford...................	608	12.9	516	3	10.9	4.9	50	106	3	242	513	8 262	815	2 284
Cuyahoga..................	19 447	14.0	15 133	189	10.9	9.7	5 457	395	23	7 398	536	238 811	NA	NA
Darke........................	693	12.8	525	5	9.7	6.7	31	57	1	92	170	8 483	422	1 017
Defiance....................	546	13.6	339	3	8.5	4.9	50	126	2	111	279	5 712	NA	NA
Delaware...................	1 247	14.2	533	7	6.1	5.3	198	215	2	110	119	8 390	1 924	2 250
Erie...........................	968	12.3	821	6	10.4	5.8	188	240	2	444	567	13 324	3 995	5 063
Fairfield....................	1 644	13.5	894	8	7.3	5.1	163	131	1	219	177	15 033	NA	NA
Fayette.....................	374	13.1	345	3	12.1	7.1	20	70	1	44	154	4 309	1 122	3 915
Franklin....................	16 120	15.8	7 914	144	7.8	8.9	2 940	288	11	3 872	379	121 170	78 804	8 022
Fulton.......................	558	13.5	348	3	8.4	6.0	28	67	1	86	205	6 390	882	2 130
Gallia........................	399	12.1	331	4	10.0	9.2	88	263	1	269	805	5 291	NA	NA
Geauga......................	1 191	13.6	612	7	7.0	5.9	305	344	1	122	137	9 141	NA	NA
Greene......................	1 674	11.4	1 083	5	7.4	2.8	233	159	1	210	143	14 701	5 311	3 794
Guernsey...................	526	12.9	461	3	11.3	5.1	52	127	1	141	344	7 196	1 425	3 487
Hamilton...................	12 171	14.3	8 384	118	9.8	9.7	3 074	363	12	4 114	485	134 956	NA	NA
Hancock....................	928	13.5	622	5	9.1	5.0	99	144	1	150	218	9 282	NA	NA
Hardin......................	406	12.8	314	2	9.9	5.7	21	66	1	51	161	4 738	NA	NA
Harrison....................	184	11.5	207	1	12.9	7.2	9	56	1	48	298	3 260	181	1 118
Henry.......................	384	12.9	266	2	8.9	5.2	13	43	1	44	147	4 555	396	1 455
Highland...................	557	14.0	407	2	10.2	3.6	30	74	2	95	235	6 420	522	1 584
Hocking....................	344	12.0	271	2	9.4	6.8	21	72	1	91	314	4 060	514	1 784
Holmes.....................	857	22.9	252	5	6.8	6.2	28	74	1	55	145	2 932	196	580
Huron.......................	893	14.9	501	5	8.4	5.6	66	109	3	212	352	9 716	1 113	1 850
Jackson....................	448	13.8	347	3	10.7	6.7	23	71	1	49	150	5 251	282	1 078
Jefferson..................	813	10.7	995	12	13.1	14.3	87	117	2	374	502	16 324	514	927
Knox.........................	637	12.1	529	6	10.1	8.9	54	101	2	117	219	8 372	NA	NA
Lake.........................	2 708	12.1	1 932	15	8.6	5.7	300	134	2	339	151	35 298	NA	NA
Lawrence...................	791	12.3	683	5	10.6	6.3	44	68	2	183	284	11 115	NA	NA
Licking.....................	1 879	13.9	1 270	15	9.4	8.0	136	99	1	185	135	18 470	4 070	3 176
Logan.......................	644	14.1	457	4	10.0	6.7	43	93	1	87	188	7 218	949	2 062
Lorain......................	3 814	13.5	2 393	35	8.5	9.2	393	139	5	970	344	38 920	NA	NA
Lucas........................	6 490	14.4	4 481	41	10.0	6.3	1 417	316	8	2 676	597	67 781	30 517	6 982
Madison....................	501	12.1	327	6	7.9	11.3	30	72	1	107	257	5 393	NA	NA
Mahoning..................	3 092	12.0	3 156	33	12.3	10.6	580	227	4	1 284	503	52 028	NA	NA
Marion......................	823	12.7	626	5	9.6	6.5	112	173	2	233	360	10 610	3 585	5 548
Medina.....................	1 897	13.4	978	9	6.9	4.9	183	127	3	198	137	16 842	NA	NA
Meigs.......................	276	11.5	287	1	12.0	4.8	11	46	1	69	287	3 804	NA	NA
Mercer......................	603	14.7	361	3	8.8	5.0	43	104	1	87	211	6 508	NA	NA
Miami.......................	1 250	12.8	869	6	8.9	4.8	142	145	2	287	292	14 873	1 741	2 241
Monroe.....................	151	9.8	175	1	11.4	8.8	6	39	0	0	0	2 722	NA	NA
Montgomery..............	7 789	13.9	5 485	66	9.8	8.5	1 570	281	8	2 957	530	92 510	30 386	5 669
Morgan.....................	174	12.0	169	1	11.6	3.8	4	28	0	0	0	2 272	86	587
Morrow.....................	389	12.6	225	2	7.3	6.0	6	19	1	66	210	3 440	160	570
Muskingum................	1 159	13.7	914	8	10.8	6.9	145	172	2	511	605	14 490	3 156	3 767
Noble.......................	126	10.3	111	1	9.1	5.3	6	49	0	0	0	1 673	120	973

1. Per 1,000 estimated resident population, average 1996–1998.   2. Deaths of infants under 1 year old.   3. Deaths of infants under 1 year old per 1,000 live births.   4. Data subject to copyright.   5. Per 100,000 resident population as of July 1 of the year shown.   6. Data for serious crimes have not been adjusted for underreporting; this may affect comparability between geographic areas and over time.   7. Per 100,000 population estimated by the FBI.

Table B. States and Counties — Crime, Education, Money Income, and Poverty

	Serious crimes known to police, 1998 [1] (cont'd) Rate [2]		Education						Money income				Income and poverty, 1997		
			School enrollment and attainment, 1990				Local government expenditures, fiscal 1997 [5]		1989				Percent below poverty level		
			Enrollment [3]		Attainment [4] (percent)					Households						
										Median						
STATE County	Violent	Property	Total	Percent private	High school graduate or more	Bachelor's degree or more	Total current expenditures (mil dol)	Current expenditures per student (dollars)	Per capita [6] (dollars)	Dollars	Percent change, 1979–1989 (constant 1989 dollars)	Percent with $100,000 or more	Median household income	All persons	Persons under 18	Persons 5–17 in families
	46	47	48	49	50	51	52	53	54	55	56	57	58	59	60	61
NORTH DAKOTA—Cont'd																
Ward	99	3 157	16 826	6.6	82.8	19.0	47.4	4 450	10 708	22 996	-11.6	1.4	33 095	11.8	15.7	14.5
Wells	19	802	1 200	2.8	63.2	11.3	5.9	5 473	9 957	18 568	-9.0	1.1	27 798	14.2	19.1	17.8
Williams	59	1 718	5 491	5.4	76.8	14.3	21.4	5 025	11 165	23 249	-26.1	1.5	33 249	13.1	17.5	15.7
OHIO	363	3 965	2 798 226	16.4	75.7	17.0	10 948.0	5 935	13 461	28 706	-3.5	2.9	36 029	11.0	16.0	14.3
Adams	NA	NA	6 283	3.0	58.4	5.2	26.7	4 873	8 407	16 318	-8.1	0.9	24 708	18.3	25.3	23.1
Allen	569	5 018	28 723	17.2	76.1	11.4	103.2	5 301	11 830	27 166	-6.8	1.9	35 411	11.4	15.8	14.4
Ashland	NA	NA	12 557	22.7	76.0	13.0	47.3	5 896	11 623	26 668	-4.6	1.8	36 428	8.1	11.5	10.8
Ashtabula	NA	NA	23 643	10.4	72.4	9.0	98.9	5 294	10 672	24 126	-16.0	1.2	32 318	13.4	19.9	17.8
Athens	NA	NA	26 587	2.2	74.6	23.4	56.6	5 942	9 170	19 169	-3.4	1.5	28 965	19.1	23.6	21.6
Auglaize	NA	NA	11 176	10.0	76.5	9.8	44.1	4 679	12 398	30 090	2.8	1.8	39 705	6.1	7.9	7.5
Belmont	34	1 110	16 446	9.8	72.3	9.0	54.7	5 395	10 329	20 987	-24.3	0.9	27 061	16.3	23.3	20.3
Brown	NA	NA	8 495	6.8	64.9	7.4	39.7	4 829	10 498	25 286	0.6	1.3	33 138	12.0	17.5	15.9
Butler	486	4 122	81 500	12.7	76.0	18.7	279.6	5 184	13 947	32 440	-1.2	3.3	43 534	8.1	11.1	9.8
Carroll	70	570	6 398	8.7	71.5	7.9	17.4	4 223	10 693	25 787	-6.4	0.9	34 161	10.8	16.3	14.3
Champaign	90	2 774	8 821	10.1	75.4	9.7	39.9	5 304	12 539	31 198	12.9	1.2	40 807	7.5	10.9	9.8
Clark	NA	NA	37 618	14.6	73.4	12.2	135.6	5 243	12 348	27 743	-1.7	1.7	36 145	12.5	19.4	17.5
Clermont	NA	NA	38 213	12.8	72.8	14.5	144.2	4 974	13 338	32 465	-3.6	2.5	44 605	6.7	9.8	8.7
Clinton	188	1 830	9 126	11.8	74.3	11.6	40.2	4 676	11 736	27 157	4.8	1.8	37 516	9.0	13.1	11.7
Columbiana	59	1 088	25 882	7.5	71.8	8.5	100.7	5 360	10 567	23 368	-16.6	1.2	32 222	13.3	19.1	17.4
Coshocton	25	1 054	7 948	8.4	71.3	8.1	34.6	5 249	10 685	23 617	-11.1	1.5	31 900	11.5	17.7	15.3
Crawford	28	2 256	11 499	11.6	73.8	9.3	43.3	5 066	11 401	24 981	-7.7	1.2	33 105	10.1	15.2	13.5
Cuyahoga	NA	NA	344 407	25.7	74.0	20.1	1 481.1	7 374	14 912	28 595	-5.3	4.0	36 754	13.6	21.4	18.5
Darke	63	954	12 837	6.7	73.5	8.8	46.7	4 902	11 693	27 640	1.6	1.5	37 160	7.4	9.7	9.3
Defiance	NA	NA	10 477	14.2	76.8	12.5	36.5	4 745	12 545	31 505	-3.7	1.5	41 686	7.1	9.9	9.3
Delaware	82	2 168	18 442	23.4	84.4	26.4	75.8	5 877	17 437	37 896	13.1	8.0	56 641	4.5	6.4	5.3
Erie	241	4 822	18 429	15.2	76.2	13.8	100.6	6 859	13 833	30 470	-5.0	2.7	39 321	9.3	14.2	12.6
Fairfield	NA	NA	25 629	11.1	78.8	15.5	109.9	5 143	13 609	31 284	1.6	3.1	42 060	6.9	10.3	9.0
Fayette	143	3 772	6 080	6.0	65.3	8.5	25.6	4 814	10 300	22 704	-3.1	1.0	32 477	12.0	16.8	16.1
Franklin	635	7 387	263 166	15.2	81.0	26.6	1 021.0	6 237	14 907	30 375	6.1	3.5	39 498	11.1	17.1	15.4
Fulton	99	2 031	10 059	9.2	78.3	10.3	53.1	5 636	12 467	31 890	2.0	1.6	41 290	5.6	7.5	7.1
Gallia	NA	NA	8 017	8.9	64.2	10.9	32.8	5 754	9 711	20 972	-13.2	1.3	28 349	18.4	27.0	24.3
Geauga	NA	NA	21 009	26.2	82.0	25.9	77.4	6 029	17 587	41 113	0.7	9.4	52 425	5.0	7.3	7.0
Greene	150	3 644	42 519	18.1	82.4	26.0	134.4	5 557	14 384	35 116	3.2	3.3	46 768	7.3	10.3	9.4
Guernsey	225	3 262	9 358	6.6	71.4	9.2	32.7	5 020	9 929	21 143	-11.5	0.9	28 306	15.4	23.1	20.7
Hamilton	NA	NA	225 274	24.8	75.6	23.7	826.7	6 428	15 354	29 498	0.9	4.7	38 763	11.4	16.6	14.6
Hancock	NA	NA	16 673	17.4	82.9	18.7	66.4	5 604	14 239	31 897	4.0	2.5	40 758	7.3	10.0	8.9
Hardin	NA	NA	9 170	26.6	74.0	11.6	32.9	5 182	10 957	24 589	-7.6	1.3	33 666	11.5	15.1	14.7
Harrison	37	1 081	3 959	4.9	69.8	7.0	14.5	4 683	9 146	19 943	-22.4	0.6	27 254	14.7	21.2	19.5
Henry	22	1 433	7 223	12.3	75.4	10.3	35.3	6 536	12 115	31 032	0.9	1.1	40 653	6.4	8.8	8.6
Highland	243	1 341	8 717	4.6	66.5	8.2	36.6	4 468	9 848	21 505	-1.6	1.5	29 740	12.5	17.0	16.4
Hocking	87	1 697	5 737	4.9	67.8	8.1	19.2	4 479	10 265	22 727	-4.9	1.1	30 865	12.9	18.9	17.5
Holmes	56	524	7 224	23.2	46.9	6.6	22.1	4 654	9 191	25 448	1.3	2.1	33 441	10.0	12.8	14.2
Huron	47	1 803	13 876	13.4	74.1	9.4	58.8	4 909	11 552	27 401	-7.0	1.5	36 500	8.8	12.8	11.7
Jackson	4	1 074	7 474	5.4	60.9	7.9	27.0	4 468	9 228	18 298	-12.5	0.9	27 774	16.4	22.8	21.1
Jefferson	128	799	19 180	19.1	71.9	8.8	67.0	5 434	11 001	22 142	-27.3	1.1	28 443	15.5	23.0	20.7
Knox	NA	NA	12 476	25.5	75.2	12.8	45.0	5 393	10 688	24 701	-0.4	1.2	34 027	10.1	14.7	13.2
Lake	NA	NA	53 639	20.1	81.1	17.5	231.4	6 524	15 465	35 605	-5.0	3.2	43 115	5.7	8.3	7.5
Lawrence	NA	NA	15 207	4.2	65.9	8.2	62.7	5 238	9 336	19 454	-22.5	0.9	26 075	20.1	29.2	26.1
Licking	151	3 025	31 787	16.0	76.4	13.0	127.9	5 349	12 864	29 606	-0.3	2.3	39 845	9.1	13.0	11.7
Logan	67	1 995	9 826	5.5	74.5	8.9	44.9	5 581	11 741	26 857	8.3	1.4	37 531	9.5	13.7	12.6
Lorain	NA	NA	73 473	16.7	75.3	12.3	270.3	5 858	12 733	31 098	-8.9	2.0	40 496	10.4	15.1	13.5
Lucas	702	6 280	124 450	20.1	76.2	17.0	431.9	6 165	13 778	28 245	-4.9	3.3	37 064	13.6	20.3	17.8
Madison	NA	NA	8 756	10.4	69.5	9.0	39.8	5 657	12 053	29 935	2.2	1.6	39 761	8.7	11.8	11.1
Mahoning	NA	NA	66 193	13.7	74.6	14.0	243.1	5 940	11 668	24 062	-17.9	1.9	31 236	14.4	21.1	18.6
Marion	223	5 325	15 485	9.7	73.8	9.9	65.3	5 294	11 547	26 330	-7.4	1.6	34 456	11.9	16.6	15.3
Medina	NA	NA	33 184	13.0	82.4	18.0	153.4	5 688	14 852	38 083	-0.4	3.7	49 194	4.9	6.4	6.0
Meigs	NA	NA	5 587	5.0	64.0	7.3	21.1	5 012	8 644	17 707	-17.1	0.7	25 223	20.4	28.3	27.3
Mercer	NA	NA	9 731	5.8	75.5	8.6	47.2	4 675	11 673	29 618	-3.5	1.6	38 887	6.5	8.5	8.1
Miami	89	2 152	23 538	11.7	76.6	14.1	100.4	5 533	13 896	31 425	5.0	2.7	41 678	7.0	10.4	9.6
Monroe	NA	NA	3 685	8.7	69.4	6.8	17.8	5 814	9 101	20 413	-23.2	0.4	27 923	16.9	24.1	22.2
Montgomery	455	5 214	149 601	20.1	77.8	20.0	547.8	6 368	14 495	30 111	1.9	3.0	37 174	11.1	16.7	15.0
Morgan	27	560	3 450	3.7	71.6	7.4	13.5	5 078	9 373	21 396	-6.7	0.6	29 443	15.3	21.9	19.8
Morrow	175	395	7 188	6.3	71.3	7.2	25.0	4 501	10 581	27 318	-0.2	1.1	36 005	10.1	13.5	13.7
Muskingum	227	3 540	20 345	13.4	71.1	10.1	88.4	5 288	10 844	23 967	-1.2	1.4	31 000	14.1	21.8	19.4
Noble	32	941	2 537	1.2	69.9	5.6	11.1	4 290	9 028	21 617	-10.7	0.5	29 206	15.8	17.7	18.2

1. Data for serious crimes have not been adjusted for underreporting; this may affect comparability between geographic areas and over time. 2. Per 100,000 population estimated by the FBI. 3. All persons 3 years old and over enrolled in nursery school through college. 4. Persons 25 years old and over. 5. Elementary and secondary education expenditures, local government fiscal years ending between July 1, 1996 and June 30, 1997. 6. Based on population enumerated as of April 1, 1990.

Table B. States and Counties — **Personal Income**

STATE County	Total (mil dol)	Percent change, 1997–1998	Per capita[1] Dollars	Per capita[1] Rank	Wages and salaries[2] (mil dol)	Proprietor's income (mil dol)	Dividends, interest, and rent (mil dol)	Transfer payments Total (mil dol)	Gov't payments to individuals Total (mil dol)	Social Security (mil dol)	Medical payments (mil dol)	Income maintenance (mil dol)	Unemployment insurance (mil dol)
	62	63	64	65	66	67	68	69	70	71	72	73	74
NORTH DAKOTA—Cont'd													
Ward	1 376	5.6	23 497	746	881	109	265	195	185	73	67	12	3
Wells	113	9.9	21 633	1 211	40	13	36	26	25	12	10	1	0
Williams	428	4.9	21 242	1 308	225	33	104	80	77	36	27	4	1
OHIO	292 999	4.5	26 073	X	190 959	17 401	55 822	42 197	39 915	16 628	15 616	3 509	664
Adams	449	5.8	15 735	2 837	173	42	77	124	118	37	51	19	3
Allen	2 391	3.4	22 295	1 017	1 758	115	490	402	380	174	134	34	6
Ashland	1 054	3.5	20 405	1 594	588	53	225	159	149	75	50	8	3
Ashtabula	2 191	6.8	21 221	1 321	1 021	102	342	450	429	161	186	8	8
Athens	1 076	4.0	17 459	2 493	603	50	207	200	188	57	72	31	3
Auglaize	1 130	4.1	24 012	640	652	70	245	155	145	68	57	7	2
Belmont	1 412	7.0	19 648	1 840	578	73	294	345	330	143	130	27	5
Brown	827	6.8	20 265	1 634	202	58	119	143	135	52	58	12	3
Butler	8 395	6.3	25 372	450	4 150	332	1 498	1 009	941	424	341	69	14
Carroll	600	8.3	20 640	1 513	180	64	95	96	90	43	32	7	2
Champaign	903	3.9	23 543	735	334	63	146	127	120	53	45	8	2
Clark	3 468	3.2	23 870	668	1 933	131	598	615	585	225	249	53	8
Clermont	4 364	7.9	24 828	510	1 553	187	572	503	467	217	162	32	10
Clinton	1 008	5.6	25 114	478	816	55	163	136	128	55	48	9	2
Columbiana	2 282	5.1	20 487	1 562	985	154	379	455	432	191	172	34	7
Coshocton	740	3.7	20 491	1 560	412	50	148	140	133	59	53	10	3
Crawford	1 020	2.8	21 614	1 216	518	53	208	187	178	82	63	14	4
Cuyahoga	42 581	3.8	30 846	138	32 390	3 734	8 842	6 401	6 120	2 369	2 580	645	84
Darke	1 245	1.0	23 026	849	546	102	233	180	169	84	59	10	3
Defiance	954	1.7	23 944	655	709	50	166	126	118	59	38	7	3
Delaware	3 301	10.5	33 614	74	977	160	727	227	208	97	68	11	3
Erie	2 106	3.2	26 922	312	1 285	149	423	300	284	132	104	17	6
Fairfield	3 145	7.4	25 376	449	959	125	531	363	337	153	123	22	5
Fayette	562	2.0	19 712	1 807	270	23	101	104	98	39	41	9	2
Franklin	30 060	5.7	29 425	186	25 559	2 009	5 115	3 236	3 028	1 123	1 191	326	43
Fulton	1 028	2.5	24 598	547	630	83	199	133	125	61	45	6	3
Gallia	614	4.8	18 478	2 219	344	29	111	167	161	45	83	19	3
Geauga	2 903	6.0	32 765	90	1 031	147	620	241	223	116	70	8	4
Greene	3 798	2.9	25 674	420	2 535	156	803	415	386	166	124	27	5
Guernsey	728	3.9	17 781	2 409	396	43	131	175	167	66	71	14	4
Hamilton	26 863	4.2	31 708	123	23 277	1 767	6 511	3 332	3 159	1 266	1 277	289	38
Hancock	1 871	5.1	27 112	295	1 337	99	393	206	192	101	59	11	3
Hardin	616	3.4	19 431	1 912	270	54	99	106	100	45	37	8	1
Harrison	286	4.2	17 736	2 427	101	17	56	71	68	29	26	6	1
Henry	696	1.0	23 308	792	358	51	125	101	95	45	37	4	2
Highland	749	4.6	18 516	2 204	310	63	118	148	140	58	56	12	3
Hocking	545	5.9	18 848	2 109	208	24	79	105	99	39	56	9	3
Holmes	648	5.3	17 120	2 582	390	105	111	82	74	29	32	6	2
Huron	1 335	2.8	22 177	1 043	851	80	230	208	196	82	68	12	7
Jackson	573	4.1	17 591	2 469	295	39	91	130	123	46	46	17	3
Jefferson	1 442	3.4	19 335	1 939	773	74	294	385	370	158	145	33	5
Knox	1 102	3.0	20 644	1 509	556	80	202	210	199	79	91	12	3
Lake	6 427	4.9	28 337	223	3 434	239	1 161	803	758	368	278	28	13
Lawrence	1 098	3.0	17 035	2 601	341	49	161	301	288	100	114	43	4
Licking	3 481	9.3	25 791	413	1 635	183	567	445	417	185	150	31	9
Logan	1 122	4.3	24 205	604	680	79	157	160	150	65	58	10	2
Lorain	6 964	4.9	24 719	529	3 693	263	1 163	936	993	408	347	77	21
Lucas	11 815	2.9	26 335	360	8 582	667	2 220	1 941	1 849	674	779	208	34
Madison	873	4.0	21 235	1 313	375	58	132	119	111	47	45	8	1
Mahoning	5 918	2.1	23 183	823	3 332	293	1 216	1 250	1 198	502	478	113	21
Marion	1 448	4.2	21 583	1 231	886	60	256	254	240	99	89	22	4
Medina	3 981	6.8	27 675	253	1 648	164	667	416	387	178	145	16	7
Meigs	382	5.5	15 951	2 800	161	36	53	101	96	34	37	14	3
Mercer	962	4.0	23 406	763	446	129	191	132	123	63	41	6	4
Miami	2 631	3.6	26 788	320	1 446	112	477	321	301	149	104	16	5
Monroe	265	4.9	17 251	2 543	181	13	47	62	58	25	22	6	2
Montgomery	15 510	3.1	27 203	286	11 748	611	3 159	2 164	2 050	853	806	189	29
Morgan	261	3.4	17 952	2 359	131	14	47	61	58	23	22	6	2
Morrow	544	4.4	17 286	2 537	148	41	76	89	82	39	28	7	2
Muskingum	1 790	5.2	21 155	1 344	1 060	94	311	334	316	136	116	34	7
Noble	200	4.5	13 564	3 038	93	13	36	44	41	17	16	4	1

1. Based on the resident population estimated as of July 1 of the year shown. 2. Includes other labor income.

Table B. States and Counties — Earnings, Social Security, and Housing

STATE County	Earnings, 1998 Total (mil dol)	Farm	Goods-related[1] Total	Manu- facturing	Service-related and other[2] Total	Retail trade	Finance, insur- ance, and real estate	Services	Govern- ment	Social Security bene- ficiaries, December 1998 Number	Rate[3]	Supple- mental Security Income recipients, December 1998	Housing units, 1990 Total	Percent change, 1980- 1990
	75	76	77	78	79	80	81	82	83	84	85	86	87	88
NORTH DAKOTA—Cont'd														
Ward	990	2.2	9.4	2.1	52.5	10.7	3.5	25.3	36.0	8 797	150	677	23 585	9.6
Wells	54	10.3	D	1.0	D	11.3	5.3	22.7	15.2	1 513	291	97	2 869	-0.6
Williams	258	2.7	22.4	2.5	58.8	11.3	4.2	27.5	16.2	4 181	207	297	10 180	13.7
OHIO	208 360	0.5	31.4	25.5	53.5	9.2	6.8	24.8	14.6	1 893 846	169	248 540	4 371 945	6.4
Adams	216	5.1	D	15.8	D	12.3	3.0	14.1	21.9	5 326	186	1 805	10 237	12.3
Allen	1 873	0.1	36.0	29.5	49.9	9.9	3.0	24.4	14.2	19 823	185	2 668	42 758	2.1
Ashland	641	0.6	44.2	38.4	39.5	8.7	2.2	23.0	15.6	8 622	165	468	18 139	6.2
Ashtabula	1 123	0.2	42.1	35.0	42.1	9.9	2.7	19.3	15.6	18 884	183	2 492	41 214	1.7
Athens	653	0.1	8.0	3.9	38.0	11.2	3.2	17.8	54.1	7 806	127	2 195	21 737	9.4
Auglaize	721	2.6	56.4	49.2	28.1	7.7	2.4	12.7	13.0	7 802	166	390	16 907	9.1
Belmont	651	-0.2	24.0	10.2	56.2	17.8	4.5	22.9	20.1	16 452	238	1 874	30 575	-4.0
Brown	260	4.3	29.1	21.7	41.2	9.6	2.6	20.5	25.3	6 680	164	894	13 720	15.8
Butler	4 482	0.1	33.8	25.4	51.1	10.4	7.1	19.6	15.2	47 564	144	5 339	110 353	19.3
Carroll	243	13.4	39.7	32.2	34.6	9.0	2.5	12.6	12.2	5 068	174	328	11 536	11.8
Champaign	397	5.0	48.0	42.4	31.9	8.5	3.4	13.7	15.2	6 311	165	527	14 030	12.2
Clark	2 064	0.7	D	35.1	D	10.3	3.5	21.5	14.1	26 760	184	3 783	58 377	3.5
Clermont	1 740	-0.2	D	21.8	D	14.2	4.8	20.6	14.1	24 562	140	2 179	55 315	23.6
Clinton	871	1.0	D	21.6	D	6.0	3.4	10.9	11.6	6 922	173	653	13 740	6.8
Columbiana	1 139	1.5	36.8	27.8	46.1	9.7	3.3	20.4	15.6	21 844	196	2 629	44 035	2.3
Coshocton	462	2.4	44.5	38.5	41.4	7.1	2.4	18.6	11.6	7 018	194	765	14 964	5.2
Crawford	571	1.7	D	43.9	D	8.0	4.2	16.3	12.8	9 358	198	1 011	19 514	-0.1
Cuyahoga	36 124	0.0	25.5	20.9	62.2	7.1	9.5	31.8	12.3	259 477	188	40 580	604 538	1.3
Darke	648	4.1	D	34.9	D	8.7	3.8	17.4	11.2	9 848	182	684	20 338	1.6
Defiance	759	0.8	59.2	54.4	31.0	8.4	2.9	13.2	9.0	6 620	166	617	14 737	3.4
Delaware	1 136	0.9	29.2	19.6	54.7	11.4	7.1	25.4	15.3	10 796	117	612	24 377	29.6
Erie	1 434	0.7	41.8	36.2	44.5	9.2	3.0	24.8	13.1	14 524	186	1 192	32 827	4.8
Fairfield	1 083	0.0	28.7	21.1	48.7	12.6	6.2	21.4	22.6	17 892	144	1 676	39 014	15.1
Fayette	294	1.4	D	31.4	D	19.8	3.4	13.8	17.7	4 948	174	755	10 816	4.2
Franklin	27 568	0.0	17.2	12.1	65.5	11.9	12.6	27.3	17.2	130 483	128	23 291	405 418	16.8
Fulton	712	3.4	56.2	48.5	D	6.8	2.4	12.1	11.4	6 749	161	374	14 095	5.7
Gallia	374	0.8	15.3	10.6	D	11.8	3.3	28.6	18.5	5 997	179	1 734	12 564	9.8
Geauga	1 179	0.1	43.6	33.3	45.7	8.0	3.7	22.1	10.6	12 246	138	443	27 922	15.0
Greene	2 691	0.4	11.5	7.9	35.5	8.7	2.7	19.1	52.5	20 334	139	1 782	50 238	11.5
Guernsey	439	-0.3	31.5	23.3	47.6	11.0	3.5	22.0	21.2	8 290	202	1 301	17 262	3.7
Hamilton	25 043	0.0	28.0	23.0	61.2	7.5	9.1	28.7	10.8	142 168	168	21 694	361 421	5.3
Hancock	1 436	0.9	D	36.9	D	10.1	3.4	18.4	8.3	11 233	163	714	26 107	6.1
Hardin	324	7.7	D	35.2	D	7.9	2.5	21.0	15.1	5 343	168	554	11 976	-0.2
Harrison	118	0.2	38.3	19.1	41.2	7.6	2.8	16.0	20.4	3 530	219	395	7 301	3.3
Henry	409	2.7	D	39.0	D	7.4	2.5	12.6	15.5	5 065	169	294	11 000	1.8
Highland	373	2.3	42.1	32.3	37.5	11.6	4.0	14.1	18.1	7 580	188	1 058	14 842	6.8
Hocking	232	-1.4	D	34.2	D	8.8	3.1	13.6	24.6	4 853	167	770	10 481	9.4
Holmes	495	4.0	D	39.6	D	9.6	2.4	13.5	9.2	3 566	94	266	10 007	13.9
Huron	931	2.6	50.6	40.9	36.6	7.7	2.1	13.4	10.2	9 503	158	924	21 382	5.9
Jackson	334	2.6	D	36.2	D	12.4	3.6	12.3	14.6	6 066	186	1 570	12 452	6.8
Jefferson	847	0.2	29.8	23.3	54.8	10.3	3.1	26.1	15.3	17 818	239	2 418	33 911	-4.9
Knox	636	3.2	41.2	30.0	40.6	8.2	2.7	23.2	15.0	9 458	177	884	18 508	7.2
Lake	3 673	1.7	D	35.8	D	9.8	4.1	19.5	12.3	38 860	174	1 710	83 194	10.7
Lawrence	390	0.0	D	18.6	D	13.4	2.9	18.0	29.0	12 571	195	3 846	24 788	5.2
Licking	1 818	2.1	32.5	24.3	50.9	12.9	7.5	20.4	14.5	21 980	161	2 314	50 032	11.2
Logan	759	3.0	48.5	42.1	38.8	7.3	2.8	17.0	9.7	7 681	166	684	19 473	5.0
Lorain	3 957	0.7	D	38.4	D	8.3	3.0	18.7	15.1	45 088	160	4 785	99 937	4.2
Lucas	9 248	0.3	30.1	23.2	55.5	9.0	5.1	28.9	14.1	76 327	170	14 802	191 388	3.5
Madison	433	1.8	D	27.4	D	8.4	2.6	15.8	27.3	5 588	134	484	12 621	11.1
Mahoning	3 624	0.3	21.1	13.4	62.7	12.8	5.7	29.8	15.9	57 422	225	7 901	107 915	-0.6
Marion	946	0.8	33.7	28.8	43.8	9.4	2.9	17.7	21.7	11 810	182	1 997	25 149	-0.6
Medina	1 811	0.6	33.7	25.1	53.2	10.8	7.2	23.2	12.4	19 381	135	868	43 330	14.0
Meigs	196	7.6	D	2.9	D	11.4	2.5	D	17.3	4 432	185	1 035	9 795	5.4
Mercer	575	14.0	D	28.3	D	8.2	4.3	11.3	13.8	7 317	178	341	14 969	5.2
Miami	1 558	0.7	D	40.0	D	10.3	3.7	20.4	11.1	16 759	171	1 229	35 985	6.8
Monroe	194	-0.8	D	56.4	D	4.9	2.0	D	14.1	3 154	205	485	6 567	1.2
Montgomery	12 358	0.1	33.3	28.5	52.5	7.4	5.0	28.1	14.1	98 524	176	13 821	240 820	5.8
Morgan	145	1.5	D	22.5	D	5.6	2.2	8.1	14.7	2 872	198	468	6 681	8.9
Morrow	190	5.5	34.3	24.9	37.1	9.1	2.7	16.8	23.1	4 657	148	432	10 312	8.6
Muskingum	1 154	0.1	32.8	25.0	53.1	12.2	3.2	24.8	14.1	16 367	194	2 686	33 029	3.5
Noble	106	-2.3	D	D	D	8.5	3.1	12.9	35.0	2 223	180	241	4 998	4.3

1. Covers mining, construction, and manufacturing. finance, insurance, and real estate; and services.
2. Covers private sector earnings in agricultural services, forestry, and fisheries; transportation and public utilities; wholesale trade; retail trade; finance, insurance, and real estate; and services.
3. Per 1,000 resident population estimated as of July 1 of the year shown.

STATE County	Housing units, 1990 (cont'd)								Civilian labor force, 1999				Civilian employment, 1990[5]		
	Occupied units										Unemployment			Percent	
		Owner-occupied				Renter-occupied									
				Owner cost as a percent of income											
	Total	Percent	Median value[1]	With a mortgage	Without a mortgage	Median rent[2]	Rent as percent of income	Substandard units[3] (percent)	Total	Percent change, 1998–1999	Total	Rate[4]	Total	Professional, managerial, and technical	Precision production, craft, and repair
	89	90	91	92	93	94	95	96	97	98	99	100	101	102	103
NORTH DAKOTA—Cont'd															
Ward	21 485	59.7	54 200	21.0	12.9	322	24.8	1.9	28 304	-4.1	967	3.4	23 571	26.2	9.4
Wells	2 406	74.7	29 100	17.5	14.3	229	24.4	2.0	2 505	-0.9	105	4.2	2 332	21.4	8.6
Williams	8 041	70.7	43 100	19.1	12.8	266	20.8	2.4	9 240	-9.2	571	6.2	9 410	23.4	12.7
OHIO	4 087 546	67.5	63 500	18.2	12.5	379	25.3	2.2	5 749 099	1.2	245 754	4.3	4 931 357	28.5	11.6
Adams	9 192	73.2	36 900	19.9	13.3	275	33.3	8.3	11 788	6.4	1 115	9.5	8 699	17.6	15.3
Allen	39 408	71.7	52 100	15.7	11.9	346	24.8	2.1	51 306	2.8	2 438	4.8	46 585	23.3	12.9
Ashland	17 101	74.0	53 600	16.6	12.0	337	23.7	2.8	26 310	4.1	1 082	4.1	22 062	22.5	12.7
Ashtabula	36 760	71.9	45 800	17.5	12.9	335	26.4	2.5	47 312	1.0	2 751	5.8	40 782	20.7	15.9
Athens	20 139	62.0	47 600	18.2	12.6	355	35.1	4.4	26 832	1.2	1 300	4.8	23 672	32.9	9.4
Auglaize	15 976	76.9	58 500	16.2	11.7	347	21.1	2.1	24 677	3.8	972	3.9	20 880	21.9	13.3
Belmont	28 161	73.8	42 100	17.8	12.3	285	26.9	2.4	31 599	0.1	1 788	5.7	26 979	23.6	14.3
Brown	12 379	76.0	49 200	18.0	13.3	303	23.9	6.0	19 760	2.2	1 075	5.4	15 042	18.0	17.1
Butler	104 535	69.2	73 000	18.9	12.3	415	25.8	2.0	185 181	3.8	5 958	3.2	137 316	30.0	11.4
Carroll	9 667	78.5	46 600	18.0	11.7	288	19.8	2.2	13 621	1.5	731	5.4	10 888	17.3	15.0
Champaign	13 253	73.9	55 400	15.7	12.5	348	20.9	2.5	18 643	-1.5	711	3.8	17 277	19.8	14.5
Clark	55 198	69.1	54 900	16.9	12.6	361	26.3	2.2	69 349	-0.5	3 033	4.4	65 055	25.8	12.5
Clermont	52 726	72.1	71 200	20.0	12.4	407	24.2	2.4	94 582	2.2	3 524	3.7	72 989	26.0	15.0
Clinton	13 038	67.7	52 200	16.9	12.6	350	24.9	2.8	25 677	2.0	851	3.3	16 268	21.8	13.3
Columbiana	40 775	75.0	42 600	18.0	12.5	306	26.4	2.0	52 513	0.6	3 069	5.8	44 381	20.3	14.8
Coshocton	13 433	75.7	44 500	15.7	11.8	292	24.9	2.8	17 673	-0.3	1 067	6.0	14 824	18.3	12.4
Crawford	18 383	71.1	43 100	15.7	12.2	303	24.0	2.3	22 227	1.7	1 229	5.5	20 781	20.5	15.1
Cuyahoga	563 243	62.0	72 100	19.5	13.0	397	26.7	1.9	681 196	1.0	31 312	4.6	629 512	32.1	9.6
Darke	19 459	76.4	52 300	15.7	11.9	327	22.4	2.2	29 445	1.8	1 456	4.9	24 783	18.9	14.0
Defiance	14 070	78.4	53 300	16.4	11.8	364	23.2	2.1	21 300	-1.2	896	4.2	18 586	20.3	14.8
Delaware	23 116	78.1	95 900	21.0	12.6	426	23.6	1.3	52 291	7.2	1 062	2.0	33 902	33.4	10.4
Erie	28 932	71.3	65 100	17.1	12.4	361	23.6	1.9	42 137	0.7	1 827	4.3	35 398	25.1	13.1
Fairfield	36 813	74.7	68 900	18.8	12.2	375	23.5	1.7	65 829	3.6	1 888	2.9	48 647	27.8	12.9
Fayette	10 221	64.9	43 800	17.4	12.6	316	25.5	3.0	15 540	5.3	590	3.8	11 906	17.0	11.5
Franklin	378 723	54.9	73 800	19.7	12.2	430	24.7	2.1	593 396	2.0	14 957	2.5	496 524	34.8	7.8
Fulton	13 504	78.5	59 700	17.0	12.3	387	22.3	2.0	23 262	3.7	944	4.1	18 618	20.5	15.1
Gallia	11 367	73.8	48 400	19.6	13.5	307	32.4	4.5	14 901	2.7	1 225	8.2	11 526	24.7	14.8
Geauga	26 906	85.7	107 700	20.4	12.5	453	23.1	3.1	47 542	2.7	1 533	3.2	39 815	34.4	13.6
Greene	48 351	69.4	78 200	18.5	11.7	434	25.4	2.1	72 123	4.8	2 406	3.3	62 830	37.3	10.2
Guernsey	14 894	73.0	38 600	18.0	12.6	279	26.9	3.0	19 046	-0.2	1 659	8.7	15 617	23.3	14.8
Hamilton	338 881	58.3	72 200	18.6	12.3	355	24.9	2.8	439 432	0.0	15 553	3.5	406 974	34.6	8.9
Hancock	24 642	74.2	63 300	16.5	11.7	366	22.6	1.6	41 593	1.9	1 175	2.8	31 675	27.5	12.6
Hardin	11 250	71.7	42 100	15.6	12.6	289	25.5	2.7	15 483	1.1	549	3.5	13 135	21.6	11.5
Harrison	6 111	75.7	33 300	19.2	12.3	277	28.7	3.8	6 791	2.0	446	6.6	5 727	18.3	15.2
Henry	10 401	78.4	55 200	16.1	12.8	336	19.8	1.7	15 789	4.1	885	5.6	13 445	20.1	15.5
Highland	13 230	72.9	42 200	19.9	13.3	306	26.1	5.2	19 312	0.8	939	4.9	14 491	18.4	14.5
Hocking	9 351	75.8	43 400	16.7	12.6	311	27.0	4.9	12 179	-0.7	867	7.1	10 328	18.4	16.5
Holmes	9 315	77.2	63 400	18.9	11.7	297	18.9	7.7	18 778	4.7	561	3.0	13 643	12.8	14.9
Huron	20 239	71.6	56 700	16.8	11.9	362	23.4	2.4	30 584	3.2	2 229	7.3	25 225	19.6	14.5
Jackson	11 260	73.4	39 400	20.4	13.6	283	30.3	5.6	14 621	3.4	1 026	7.0	10 408	21.9	13.3
Jefferson	31 311	73.5	42 900	15.8	12.6	289	26.6	2.1	29 882	-2.1	2 048	6.9	29 528	20.8	16.5
Knox	17 230	72.2	49 100	19.0	12.5	321	24.0	2.3	26 328	0.6	1 291	4.9	21 118	24.0	11.4
Lake	80 421	75.8	74 200	18.6	12.4	475	24.1	1.1	124 832	1.7	5 012	4.0	109 281	29.7	14.1
Lawrence	22 899	72.2	43 700	17.0	12.7	299	31.3	4.4	26 931	1.8	1 932	7.2	22 263	21.5	15.0
Licking	47 254	72.0	61 600	17.9	11.8	357	25.6	1.8	72 518	-0.3	2 659	3.7	59 694	26.2	13.1
Logan	15 952	73.3	53 000	16.1	12.6	339	23.1	2.3	28 582	8.3	811	2.8	18 919	18.5	14.8
Lorain	96 064	71.9	66 100	18.5	12.3	378	24.6	2.4	141 236	1.0	6 816	4.8	122 333	25.4	13.8
Lucas	177 500	65.0	57 300	17.4	13.6	390	26.3	1.9	231 023	1.1	12 074	5.2	204 890	29.0	10.7
Madison	11 990	70.2	62 300	19.3	12.5	377	22.2	2.5	20 850	1.8	525	2.5	16 522	20.1	13.2
Mahoning	101 136	71.7	47 900	18.6	13.4	342	27.9	1.7	117 434	-1.2	6 501	5.5	106 433	25.7	12.0
Marion	23 484	70.9	42 500	16.1	12.4	343	24.7	2.3	31 293	-1.9	1 203	3.8	27 324	22.4	14.5
Medina	41 792	79.3	83 700	20.2	12.2	441	24.3	1.7	78 020	3.2	2 902	3.7	60 441	28.0	14.4
Meigs	8 662	78.7	35 700	20.1	13.8	264	33.6	5.4	8 508	-0.9	971	11.4	7 677	20.6	19.3
Mercer	13 398	79.8	61 100	17.8	11.5	324	21.8	2.6	19 865	-1.5	1 580	8.0	18 263	18.2	12.9
Miami	34 559	72.7	65 000	16.4	12.1	382	23.5	1.6	51 005	0.6	1 962	3.8	44 993	26.3	13.3
Monroe	5 754	79.9	39 600	15.6	12.8	274	27.9	6.5	6 053	0.6	563	9.3	5 414	18.2	18.0
Montgomery	226 192	62.9	65 000	17.7	12.6	403	25.1	2.1	278 502	-0.9	10 657	3.8	265 950	33.1	10.0
Morgan	5 170	77.2	39 900	15.5	12.3	262	27.9	6.4	4 945	-1.2	677	13.7	5 036	17.9	15.3
Morrow	9 656	81.0	47 600	18.3	12.8	336	22.8	2.5	14 360	5.9	743	5.2	12 536	17.4	17.1
Muskingum	30 753	73.0	47 100	16.8	12.2	301	26.1	2.7	43 107	2.5	2 877	6.7	34 894	22.2	12.9
Noble	4 137	80.0	37 200	18.2	12.4	290	24.5	6.1	5 408	-0.3	457	8.5	4 291	14.3	17.1

1. Specified owner-occupied units.   2. Specified renter-occupied units.   3. Overcrowded or lacking complete plumbing facilities.   4. Percent of civilian labor force.   5. Persons 16 years and older.

	Private nonfarm establishments, employment and payroll, 1998								Agriculture, 1997			
		Employment						Annual payroll		Farms			Farm operators
STATE County	Number of establish-ments	Total	Health Care and Social Assistance	Manufac-turing	Retail trade	Finance and Insurance	Professional Scientific and Technical Services	Total (mil dol)	Average per employee (dollars)	Number	Percent with— Less than 50 acres	500 acres and over	Whose principal occu-pation is farming (percent)
	104	105	106	107	108	109	110	111	112	113	114	115	116
NORTH DAKOTA—Cont'd													
Ward	1 684	21 581	4 186	779	4 701	668	866	445	20 603	1 172	8.1	57.8	69.0
Wells	212	1 380	424	19	260	83	46	21	15 280	593	4.9	65.3	77.9
Williams	833	6 759	1 240	155	1 332	302	172	132	19 556	850	6.0	67.3	72.9
OHIO	270 343	4 806 046	628 383	994 788	632 285	246 164	207 796	140 265	29 185	68 591	30.7	10.0	45.2
Adams	412	4 459	884	1 011	1 002	147	104	83	18 690	1 315	30.5	4.9	41.8
Allen	2 833	49 878	9 329	9 886	7 806	1 312	1 030	1 297	26 004	918	27.7	12.0	46.7
Ashland	1 069	17 971	1 659	7 393	2 113	368	489	439	24 443	929	26.9	7.8	47.4
Ashtabula	2 269	29 842	4 713	10 226	4 721	625	419	687	23 012	993	28.9	4.4	46.5
Athens	1 174	12 428	2 387	1 292	2 705	495	367	233	18 711	481	18.5	4.4	37.2
Auglaize	1 048	18 808	1 752	8 482	2 161	418	257	497	26 415	1 001	27.3	10.8	49.1
Belmont	1 654	19 491	3 624	1 836	5 303	879	404	383	19 659	622	16.7	9.5	44.1
Brown	572	6 344	1 303	1 269	989	213	99	142	22 326	1 378	36.3	5.2	42.2
Butler	6 197	102 274	12 052	20 067	13 398	6 382	3 580	2 975	29 091	849	40.8	6.6	43.7
Carroll	475	5 274	515	1 919	701	98	83	116	21 925	683	21.5	4.2	42.9
Champaign	730	10 287	1 068	4 480	1 204	283	108	265	25 776	836	35.8	16.6	46.8
Clark	2 808	49 917	7 528	13 561	7 345	1 448	833	1 289	25 832	671	42.0	14.8	43.5
Clermont	3 221	45 663	4 390	7 485	9 823	2 276	1 800	1 333	29 196	744	50.0	5.1	32.8
Clinton	800	23 048	1 596	4 924	2 009	610	164	613	26 612	761	28.3	19.6	54.0
Columbiana	2 440	30 406	4 688	9 503	4 843	965	837	699	22 985	980	36.2	4.4	41.8
Coshocton	743	15 600	1 609	5 075	1 497	269	354	471	30 165	864	20.1	8.0	43.6
Crawford	1 016	15 362	1 776	6 809	1 772	401	227	385	25 093	712	25.3	17.6	51.8
Cuyahoga	38 566	749 942	109 728	118 495	78 608	52 376	46 000	24 475	32 636	118	78.8	0.0	53.4
Darke	1 247	16 416	1 834	5 275	2 372	594	217	395	24 080	1 726	33.8	10.0	44.7
Defiance	883	17 186	1 457	7 233	2 586	469	242	522	30 393	861	25.7	10.6	41.9
Delaware	2 274	36 427	2 444	6 361	3 825	6 635	1 477	1 080	29 644	627	41.8	14.2	49.3
Erie	2 093	31 994	3 870	9 710	4 858	721	525	923	28 862	380	36.1	15.0	48.7
Fairfield	2 472	29 605	4 279	6 008	5 536	722	762	648	21 895	1 024	37.5	9.2	47.9
Fayette	715	9 205	1 056	2 696	2 591	209	90	197	21 439	520	26.5	32.5	62.7
Franklin	27 644	589 962	67 498	50 517	79 587	59 826	34 326	18 312	31 039	407	40.8	11.5	44.5
Fulton	1 081	18 876	1 665	9 932	1 723	384	344	500	26 513	794	30.4	14.0	48.0
Gallia	647	9 380	2 297	1 035	1 603	326	333	233	24 871	776	24.7	3.4	35.4
Geauga	2 587	27 712	2 779	9 511	3 357	556	1 080	786	28 345	661	44.9	2.1	43.1
Greene	2 893	43 882	4 717	5 030	8 793	1 138	5 524	1 062	24 200	764	40.8	13.5	45.7
Guernsey	949	12 593	2 051	3 180	1 802	322	205	304	24 156	802	20.6	5.0	42.5
Hamilton	24 944	531 128	70 382	74 084	59 338	29 693	34 111	17 525	32 995	302	59.9	3.6	43.4
Hancock	1 777	38 904	3 459	12 394	4 637	856	635	1 074	27 605	979	25.4	18.1	46.6
Hardin	526	8 132	777	2 648	1 060	213	80	187	22 938	837	23.2	17.9	52.2
Harrison	341	3 121	583	790	370	D	D	68	21 630	423	15.6	11.6	44.2
Henry	626	8 936	1 171	3 783	1 030	270	92	245	27 387	872	22.7	16.6	50.0
Highland	734	10 431	1 459	3 860	1 738	357	128	218	20 945	1 239	28.2	10.0	42.3
Hocking	534	6 053	919	2 051	875	156	148	133	22 033	353	24.4	1.4	31.4
Holmes	923	11 878	1 300	4 674	1 540	284	234	261	21 999	1 404	24.6	2.5	60.4
Huron	1 257	23 599	2 028	11 135	2 555	500	327	612	25 943	782	24.9	16.0	46.8
Jackson	637	10 325	946	3 695	1 489	1 570	147	216	20 962	408	17.4	6.4	33.6
Jefferson	1 642	20 850	4 432	2 004	3 856	859	387	492	23 605	410	16.8	6.6	38.8
Knox	1 085	17 340	2 111	5 017	2 052	425	254	431	24 834	1 103	28.6	8.4	45.7
Lake	6 442	94 736	9 119	26 394	16 325	2 186	3 238	2 646	27 930	274	68.6	2.2	54.4
Lawrence	934	10 383	2 139	1 879	2 441	313	149	213	20 493	490	28.6	2.4	34.7
Licking	2 862	45 602	5 344	9 583	6 388	3 640	1 491	1 174	25 738	1 218	35.0	8.3	42.2
Logan	930	18 710	1 716	6 727	1 955	340	682	535	28 576	895	30.5	12.7	39.4
Lorain	5 708	91 049	11 419	26 410	13 044	2 545	2 051	2 533	27 824	778	43.7	6.8	44.1
Lucas	11 266	218 620	39 742	32 338	28 912	7 740	10 520	D	28 884	385	53.0	14.3	45.5
Madison	704	10 326	942	3 496	1 338	173	D	256	24 767	667	28.5	24.7	57.3
Mahoning	6 506	96 202	17 139	13 047	14 733	3 951	2 766	2 330	24 219	542	39.5	3.7	45.4
Marion	1 411	24 668	3 579	7 051	3 594	590	473	620	25 134	543	28.2	22.7	52.3
Medina	3 762	49 811	5 602	11 479	8 292	2 553	1 421	1 296	26 026	851	47.9	4.6	42.9
Meigs	368	3 334	569	D	657	135	78	96	28 912	491	17.7	4.7	39.5
Mercer	972	13 854	1 482	4 406	2 123	666	252	308	22 205	1 255	26.6	10.4	50.6
Miami	2 244	37 906	3 147	14 505	5 347	851	637	1 026	27 061	983	42.6	11.5	43.9
Monroe	283	3 876	183	D	377	112	137	D	35 243	589	12.4	4.9	43.5
Montgomery	13 428	282 914	40 635	54 307	34 652	11 153	13 938	8 538	30 177	760	50.7	6.4	39.9
Morgan	202	2 319	351	843	349	102	D	54	23 240	500	12.2	6.8	40.4
Morrow	401	4 502	781	1 612	643	84	72	99	21 894	759	31.2	9.4	43.1
Muskingum	2 034	33 631	5 386	10 069	5 060	863	495	763	22 696	1 018	22.7	7.1	43.6
Noble	208	2 242	383	705	368	81	21	52	23 308	519	15.0	4.6	32.8

Table B. States and Counties — Agriculture, Land, and Water

STATE County	Acreage (1,000) [117]	Percent change, 1992-1997 [118]	Average size of farm [119]	Total irrigated (1,000) [120]	Total cropland (1,000) [121]	Average per farm ($1,000) [122]	Average per acre (dollars) [123]	Value of machinery and equipment Average per farm ($1,000) [124]	Total (mil dol) [125]	Average per farm (dollars) [126]	Crops [127]	Livestock and poultry products [128]	$10,000 or more [129]	$100,000 or more [130]	Percent of land owned by Fed. Gov. 1997 [131]	Water consumption 1995 (mil gal/day) [132]
NORTH DAKOTA—Cont'd																
Ward	1 208	4.0	1 030	1	949	555	529	96	83	70 742	82.8	17.2	75.1	24.2	1.5	9.3
Wells	744	-0.9	1 255	D	617	509	422	146	62	103 856	83.8	16.2	74.7	35.6	1.8	0.9
Williams	1 205	1.9	1 418	14	829	426	312	97	53	62 379	80.5	19.5	72.1	19.2	2.2	11.0
OHIO	14 103	-1.0	206	34	11 341	415	2 039	58	4 684	68 293	60.4	39.6	52.3	15.7	1.4	10 523.3
Adams	195	-0.7	148	0	110	209	1 476	35	27	20 744	58.6	41.4	42.1	4.5	0.0	735.0
Allen	190	-2.1	207	D	173	446	2 112	72	59	64 678	76.6	23.4	68.4	19.4	0.2	39.9
Ashland	164	-4.1	176	0	128	383	2 135	64	49	52 672	38.4	61.6	53.7	15.2	0.2	6.4
Ashtabula	149	-4.3	150	0	103	242	1 637	50	35	35 153	43.7	56.3	39.1	8.2	0.0	211.0
Athens	83	2.3	172	0	39	230	1 241	30	6	12 906	33.9	66.1	24.5	3.7	5.0	7.0
Auglaize	213	4.0	213	D	195	464	2 109	75	86	85 472	55.3	44.7	71.4	24.7	0.0	14.5
Belmont	148	17.7	238	0	65	213	936	41	12	19 788	18.7	81.3	32.0	5.3	0.0	239.6
Brown	196	-3.1	142	0	144	269	1 827	42	38	27 412	81.8	18.2	48.4	5.9	0.0	3.8
Butler	135	-2.5	158	0	108	517	3 024	50	35	41 262	61.4	38.6	43.0	11.7	0.3	73.9
Carroll	113	-7.1	166	0	68	236	1 508	43	21	31 153	45.2	54.8	36.7	7.0	2.2	3.6
Champaign	222	2.6	265	D	196	561	2 110	75	71	85 265	76.0	24.0	58.4	22.6	0.0	5.1
Clark	172	-3.9	256	2	154	595	2 278	72	73	109 416	86.7	13.3	55.0	20.0	0.0	25.4
Clermont	88	-10.8	119	0	66	322	2 906	38	17	22 399	84.2	15.8	33.7	5.8	2.2	547.4
Clinton	223	-1.8	293	0	201	606	2 211	67	66	86 502	84.4	15.6	64.9	24.7	0.0	2.3
Columbiana	138	-4.0	141	1	99	267	2 113	48	47	47 880	36.1	63.9	40.4	13.2	0.0	14.2
Coshocton	170	5.0	197	D	104	293	1 391	57	37	42 968	39.6	60.4	40.9	10.4	1.7	238.4
Crawford	227	1.6	318	0	207	578	1 792	84	75	105 623	71.1	28.9	72.8	24.9	0.0	5.7
Cuyahoga	4	6.7	36	0	3	435	13 094	60	17	145 310	97.0	3.0	44.9	21.2	1.0	429.1
Darke	329	-1.9	191	0	302	460	2 439	67	247	143 147	30.1	69.9	68.1	25.6	0.0	7.6
Defiance	186	-5.4	216	0	166	382	1 757	57	45	52 553	74.2	25.8	59.8	14.3	0.0	6.3
Delaware	161	-4.9	256	0	145	721	3 019	53	54	85 814	85.8	14.2	54.1	17.5	2.0	16.8
Erie	90	1.0	237	0	81	483	2 168	82	35	93 321	83.1	16.9	63.7	22.6	3.3	22.1
Fairfield	197	-0.5	192	0	162	482	2 439	54	51	50 103	74.0	26.0	50.1	14.4	0.0	13.1
Fayette	243	2.8	466	0	224	914	1 913	100	72	138 805	89.5	10.5	72.7	37.3	0.9	3.5
Franklin	80	-17.9	196	0	69	588	3 041	64	41	101 143	92.3	7.7	52.6	17.0	1.2	162.3
Fulton	197	-4.2	249	0	185	554	2 268	72	88	110 639	64.5	35.5	74.7	28.5	0.0	5.8
Gallia	117	6.5	151	0	53	200	1 243	34	15	19 529	41.2	58.8	33.2	3.6	5.9	1 285.3
Geauga	59	-8.9	90	0	38	348	3 985	29	18	27 658	49.0	51.0	38.4	7.1	0.0	7.8
Greene	178	-3.1	233	1	155	549	2 474	68	59	76 695	82.8	17.2	54.1	19.5	2.9	18.2
Guernsey	138	7.5	172	0	70	167	989	27	11	13 408	22.4	77.6	23.2	2.5	0.0	7.0
Hamilton	29	0.5	97	1	21	384	4 819	35	17	57 289	83.2	16.8	35.1	14.2	0.3	310.9
Hancock	277	0.4	283	0	259	651	2 237	76	82	83 620	82.3	17.7	76.1	24.4	0.0	18.2
Hardin	247	-0.5	295	D	225	483	1 612	61	115	137 360	47.4	52.6	68.7	23.2	0.0	3.7
Harrison	110	-2.9	259	0	53	234	964	44	10	23 664	23.6	76.4	30.0	4.0	3.6	2.2
Henry	244	-0.3	280	1	230	596	2 114	78	75	86 114	89.5	10.5	79.5	25.9	0.0	9.4
Highland	242	5.0	196	0	190	354	1 807	48	46	37 271	73.8	26.2	47.1	9.3	1.7	4.3
Hocking	48	-0.1	136	0	23	220	1 422	32	3	9 724	68.5	31.5	18.4	2.0	8.2	4.6
Holmes	172	-3.0	122	0	113	349	2 744	44	88	62 546	8.9	91.1	65.0	17.5	0.0	5.3
Huron	232	5.7	296	3	203	454	1 711	91	78	99 154	82.3	17.7	64.1	20.1	0.0	10.9
Jackson	74	0.0	181	0	43	222	1 173	51	18	42 928	75.1	24.9	28.9	3.7	0.6	2.4
Jefferson	71	4.9	174	D	40	156	1 052	26	7	16 348	29.1	70.9	23.4	3.2	0.0	2 146.8
Knox	206	-2.2	187	0	159	364	1 915	50	62	56 111	45.5	54.5	49.6	14.1	0.7	7.4
Lake	19	12.1	70	4	13	388	6 196	60	74	268 510	99.3	0.7	47.4	17.2	0.0	803.9
Lawrence	59	-4.1	121	0	23	126	1 030	22	4	8 070	56.3	43.7	17.3	1.2	24.1	8.7
Licking	237	4.4	195	0	184	466	2 497	56	129	105 813	32.7	67.3	43.2	11.0	0.1	18.2
Logan	219	7.9	245	D	188	383	1 624	57	89	99 528	45.9	54.1	50.6	15.6	0.0	6.2
Lorain	131	-8.6	168	1	110	477	2 926	84	83	106 647	83.1	16.9	50.6	13.9	0.0	544.5
Lucas	80	7.5	207	1	75	628	2 768	85	61	158 117	75.1	24.9	60.8	26.0	1.6	753.7
Madison	262	0.5	393	0	238	810	2 033	94	80	120 355	83.9	16.1	69.1	34.0	0.0	4.1
Mahoning	73	0.6	135	1	56	322	2 650	48	32	59 035	56.1	43.9	44.8	12.0	0.1	7.9
Marion	221	1.7	406	0	207	701	1 654	111	64	118 347	81.3	18.7	68.5	26.2	0.5	9.1
Medina	104	0.0	122	0	81	433	3 950	50	34	40 047	52.7	47.3	39.4	8.8	0.0	16.8
Meigs	85	-2.6	173	1	39	201	1 138	28	13	26 439	69.8	30.2	28.7	4.9	0.0	8.5
Mercer	261	-3.0	208	D	237	582	2 812	81	288	229 213	19.1	80.9	80.6	39.5	0.0	6.9
Miami	192	-3.8	196	1	174	562	2 814	56	64	65 206	77.8	22.2	57.7	18.9	0.0	42.1
Monroe	110	-0.3	186	0	48	161	871	38	7	12 560	13.7	86.3	21.6	3.1	7.6	3.7
Montgomery	106	-1.0	139	0	93	410	2 956	56	36	47 603	81.8	18.2	47.8	11.2	0.6	178.9
Morgan	98	-13.8	197	0	42	186	1 100	25	8	16 804	19.8	80.2	27.2	2.8	1.1	3.8
Morrow	161	-2.3	212	0	132	380	1 804	46	42	54 855	66.7	33.3	46.8	11.7	0.2	2.6
Muskingum	180	-4.2	177	0	103	204	1 266	41	26	25 320	38.6	61.4	34.2	5.6	2.3	19.5
Noble	99	-4.8	191	D	51	156	772	25	4	7 366	16.9	83.1	16.6	1.0	0.2	1.4

Table B. States and Counties — Residential Construction, Wholesale and Retail Trade, and Real Estate

STATE County	Value of Residential Construction Authorized by Building Permits, 1999		Wholesale Trade, 1997				Retail Trade[1], 1997				Real Estate and Rental and Leasing, 1997			
	New Construction ($1,000)	Number of Housing Units	Number of Establishments	Number of Employees	Sales (mil dol)	Annual Payroll (mil dol)	Number of Establishments	Number of Employees	Sales (mil dol)	Annual Payroll (mil dol)	Number of Establishments	Number of Employees	Receipts (mil dol)	Annual Payroll (mil dol)
	133	134	135	136	137	138	139	140	141	142	143	144	145	146
NORTH DAKOTA—Cont'd														
Ward.................	15 289	220	95	1 203	701.6	32.9	339	4 819	753.7	74.3	60	234	27.1	3.6
Wells.................	200	2	18	148	91.2	3.7	42	238	41.4	3.4	7	12	0.7	0.1
Williams.................	672	6	89	693	331.0	17.4	138	1 417	207.5	19.7	27	109	12.9	3.0
OHIO.................	6 401 999	55 888	17 322	254 226	158 310.2	9 192.2	44 521	630 098	102 938.8	9 924.5	9 692	62 628	7 243.7	1 334.6
Adams.................	430	7	9	50	32.1	1.2	105	913	134.5	12.0	9	25	1.3	0.3
Allen.................	30 899	236	190	D	D	D	542	7 908	1 291.4	116.0	107	454	37.7	6.8
Ashland.................	24 516	223	47	282	121.3	7.3	183	2 242	311.1	33.0	34	124	10.0	2.0
Ashtabula.................	44 804	481	86	572	152.0	12.9	429	4 962	711.1	68.9	78	249	22.9	3.9
Athens.................	4 410	45	37	298	72.5	7.7	232	2 609	345.7	36.3	61	252	16.6	3.4
Auglaize.................	21 958	197	46	D	D	D	192	2 114	341.5	30.1	32	97	10.0	1.3
Belmont.................	3 276	54	58	D	D	D	383	5 359	737.6	68.3	48	226	11.5	2.8
Brown.................	11 682	101	15	239	73.7	5.6	114	922	141.7	12.4	18	56	3.2	0.5
Butler.................	315 218	3 408	454	D	D	D	922	13 529	2 188.6	208.5	235	1 324	149.7	25.7
Carroll.................	2 960	22	25	180	83.6	5.2	79	819	129.6	11.3	7	23	1.5	0.1
Champaign.................	17 119	164	31	427	160.8	11.4	124	1 254	204.1	18.3	27	83	6.2	0.8
Clark.................	43 122	449	124	1 704	1 035.2	49.6	528	7 439	1 102.9	107.9	82	317	32.4	5.0
Clermont.................	213 380	1 869	186	2 602	1 935.9	96.5	540	8 901	1 656.2	141.0	112	525	62.7	8.8
Clinton.................	28 187	230	39	360	192.2	11.1	154	2 101	434.7	33.4	23	200	56.1	5.7
Columbiana.................	8 733	104	111	866	278.0	24.5	468	4 934	823.4	68.7	65	303	22.5	4.7
Coshocton.................	1 661	10	31	203	70.5	4.7	146	1 538	209.8	20.1	13	73	7.1	2.3
Crawford.................	10 050	87	52	520	175.4	13.3	173	1 726	251.8	23.6	27	83	6.6	1.1
Cuyahoga.................	449 373	2 854	3 292	52 577	31 169.4	2 131.0	5 700	78 658	12 662.9	1 310.3	1 516	16 216	1 939.1	351.0
Darke.................	20 310	193	65	985	491.2	30.1	206	2 398	385.4	37.4	30	133	15.5	3.6
Defiance.................	14 469	154	46	568	306.7	16.4	195	2 580	424.8	39.7	24	123	11.0	2.2
Delaware.................	336 225	2 959	173	1 596	828.4	62.2	258	4 080	792.9	70.2	86	230	29.0	4.5
Erie.................	43 677	479	94	1 123	397.0	31.0	382	4 784	732.0	71.4	77	292	27.2	5.1
Fairfield.................	120 818	810	104	649	209.1	18.6	405	5 430	841.7	81.9	87	418	38.6	7.2
Fayette.................	12 406	158	44	329	749.2	10.8	246	2 154	329.8	30.6	14	48	7.0	0.9
Franklin.................	894 567	10 615	1 843	36 442	22 320.0	1 411.7	4 276	76 175	13 622.2	1 355.4	1 262	10 255	1 089.3	237.6
Fulton.................	12 799	111	68	603	365.4	16.9	179	1 715	294.2	26.3	32	171	15.6	2.5
Gallia.................	415	7	27	187	45.2	2.6	172	1 665	281.5	24.0	25	74	4.4	0.9
Geauga.................	122 433	594	194	1 425	691.5	53.9	317	3 311	565.0	55.6	68	194	30.0	3.8
Greene.................	111 593	1 062	110	1 316	1 540.4	47.0	564	8 922	1 321.9	125.0	104	386	52.6	6.9
Guernsey.................	8 358	107	42	390	97.3	10.8	167	1 722	294.0	24.9	30	160	11.3	1.8
Hamilton.................	307 505	2 629	2 047	37 207	32 788.6	1 413.1	3 774	59 154	9 310.4	938.2	1 076	7 783	1 197.0	207.2
Hancock.................	38 260	275	103	1 053	507.6	30.5	323	4 557	767.9	67.6	63	389	39.4	7.4
Hardin.................	8 415	141	19	D	D	D	111	1 089	160.7	14.5	13	47	2.9	0.4
Harrison.................	0	0	18	185	63.1	6.0	60	379	55.2	5.0	8	103	2.9	0.9
Henry.................	12 014	91	43	283	216.7	7.8	106	1 060	191.5	16.3	15	74	7.4	1.3
Highland.................	4 002	52	45	424	218.2	7.8	160	1 698	258.5	22.9	24	112	7.5	1.1
Hocking.................	868	9	14	D	D	D	92	880	145.1	14.3	16	45	3.5	0.4
Holmes.................	276	5	38	418	92.5	9.4	159	1 495	242.0	24.0	11	28	1.9	0.5
Huron.................	16 311	156	54	573	204.4	16.0	234	2 616	445.0	38.1	45	144	12.8	2.6
Jackson.................	11 421	128	27	304	72.5	7.2	162	1 542	234.8	21.5	13	42	2.9	0.5
Jefferson.................	2 649	38	69	D	D	D	335	3 969	531.4	52.9	50	198	15.9	3.2
Knox.................	39 264	418	58	362	168.3	9.0	183	2 076	313.4	28.8	39	147	9.8	1.5
Lake.................	149 107	901	425	4 392	1 590.9	148.8	975	15 509	2 831.2	260.7	180	801	87.0	13.9
Lawrence.................	2 526	30	37	D	D	D	206	2 503	360.7	31.7	24	D	D	D
Licking.................	138 418	1 066	144	1 600	623.1	45.1	502	6 392	1 105.2	104.2	100	493	37.4	8.4
Logan.................	25 550	237	45	1 671	844.2	47.2	187	1 919	309.0	26.9	29	79	6.9	1.2
Lorain.................	243 208	1 574	245	2 627	997.6	74.8	929	13 595	2 379.8	210.1	204	868	76.6	13.7
Lucas.................	183 329	1 535	751	10 580	6 302.2	377.3	1 860	29 585	4 842.2	473.7	403	2 530	289.8	55.5
Madison.................	20 291	198	38	904	355.4	26.2	122	1 423	276.8	22.5	19	75	5.5	0.8
Mahoning.................	95 344	802	407	5 559	2 132.4	177.3	1 187	16 420	2 547.9	235.5	173	1 028	102.8	19.4
Marion.................	18 245	210	61	559	219.3	17.5	237	3 549	548.9	53.8	55	202	17.5	3.9
Medina.................	242 667	1 514	295	2 724	1 155.8	93.5	524	7 764	1 346.0	123.4	99	378	46.0	7.0
Meigs.................	1 656	21	12	70	21.7	1.5	98	798	113.9	11.0	8	26	1.6	0.3
Mercer.................	20 856	182	57	952	384.7	24.1	192	2 151	330.0	32.3	29	116	16.4	3.0
Miami.................	50 585	321	110	1 832	3 072.8	56.2	371	5 018	845.4	72.4	82	332	33.2	5.5
Monroe.................	123	1	8	38	D	D	58	445	50.5	5.3	7	D	D	D
Montgomery.................	203 037	1 867	888	12 913	7 638.5	508.0	2 143	35 936	5 603.5	549.9	533	3 336	393.4	75.4
Morgan.................	0	0	10	D	D	D	35	345	45.4	3.8	4	D	D	D
Morrow.................	8 496	89	8	D	D	D	65	670	113.5	8.6	18	43	2.6	0.3
Muskingum.................	8 385	186	79	1 114	415.6	30.0	428	4 690	787.9	68.1	67	214	23.1	4.4
Noble.................	2 355	32	8	109	28.2	2.1	47	393	54.0	4.9	3	D	D	D

1. Establishments with payroll.

Table B. States and Counties — Professional, Manufacturing, and Accommodation and Foodservices

STATE County	Professional, Scientific, and Technical Services¹, 1997				Manufacturing, 1997				Accommodation and Foodservices, 1997			
	Number of Establish-ments	Number of Employees	Receipts (mil dol)	Annual Payroll (mil dol)	Number of Establish-ments	Number of Employees	Receipts (mil dol)	Annual Payroll (mil dol)	Number of Establish-ments	Number of Employees	Sales (mil dol)	Annual Payroll (mil dol)
	147	148	149	150	151	152	153	154	155	156	157	158
NORTH DAKOTA—Cont'd												
Ward	86	818	38.0	17.4	58	770	281.6	18.0	158	2 896	72.1	20.9
Wells	14	31	1.1	0.3	NA	NA	NA	NA	21	164	2.9	0.7
Williams	42	171	8.5	4.0	NA	NA	NA	NA	63	819	20.8	6.0
OHIO	21 182	182 805	18 294.7	6 948.0	17 974	984 201	241 902.9	35 950.5	22 631	401 206	12 411.0	3 444.2
Adams	23	82	4.9	1.1	31	D	D	D	37	508	13.9	3.7
Allen	171	951	59.8	21.9	132	9 529	6 631.7	407.8	231	4 260	127.5	33.1
Ashland	48	396	28.5	10.2	98	7 135	1 157.5	215.7	102	1 440	40.7	11.4
Ashtabula	105	340	23.8	7.8	175	9 984	1 794.3	302.6	235	2 759	83.8	21.7
Athens	61	333	18.7	8.1	43	1 351	222.1	32.5	141	2 364	57.4	16.2
Auglaize	46	207	18.1	4.7	93	8 236	1 737.6	288.7	102	1 533	37.9	10.4
Belmont	81	327	23.7	7.3	55	1 523	272.5	36.9	152	2 281	67.6	18.0
Brown	28	84	5.4	1.7	25	1 110	280.8	33.4	60	531	15.6	3.8
Butler	444	3 148	291.9	89.2	396	20 391	6 567.8	819.2	519	9 919	286.3	79.6
Carroll	20	52	3.8	1.1	40	1 782	302.3	56.7	45	459	10.5	2.7
Champaign	26	93	5.4	1.5	55	3 452	946.8	101.3	64	776	20.0	5.2
Clark	146	738	43.5	16.7	230	13 231	4 071.5	520.0	248	4 662	132.8	36.6
Clermont	258	1 541	183.0	58.8	167	7 892	1 544.3	305.5	224	4 370	133.9	37.7
Clinton	34	166	8.5	3.8	50	4 969	809.6	135.5	74	1 268	36.3	10.1
Columbiana	127	850	51.5	22.3	209	8 616	1 109.3	246.3	210	2 526	70.1	19.2
Coshocton	31	321	26.5	6.4	55	4 814	1 191.3	162.9	52	719	19.2	5.7
Crawford	41	159	9.2	3.1	90	6 575	1 194.7	211.6	94	1 160	30.5	7.8
Cuyahoga	3 936	40 008	4 384.1	1 769.9	2 712	116 680	23 382.3	4 640.6	3 031	55 025	1 846.3	493.4
Darke	50	166	11.7	4.7	92	5 811	1 147.4	172.4	91	1 143	32.4	8.5
Defiance	42	221	19.2	5.9	48	7 150	1 338.9	329.2	72	1 281	33.4	8.9
Delaware	211	1 435	304.2	79.3	117	5 131	1 285.7	187.6	160	2 623	79.3	23.9
Erie	107	470	38.4	17.2	117	9 176	2 251.5	409.2	248	4 622	167.9	46.6
Fairfield	159	587	45.5	17.0	154	6 251	833.7	188.2	185	3 478	106.8	30.4
Fayette	26	75	5.7	1.5	45	2 959	572.8	83.5	56	1 002	32.4	9.2
Franklin	2 934	30 270	3 163.8	1 195.7	1 061	48 265	11 837.7	1 754.6	2 330	49 486	1 669.9	483.2
Fulton	43	204	17.9	5.2	110	9 108	1 673.4	276.5	78	1 002	27.8	7.3
Gallia	31	314	12.4	7.0	18	948	117.6	26.9	59	970	30.9	7.9
Geauga	236	716	66.9	24.6	233	9 851	1 380.2	306.2	146	1 977	58.6	16.8
Greene	328	5 471	628.3	231.4	141	4 952	738.0	166.2	248	5 129	157.3	44.3
Guernsey	49	203	17.2	5.3	59	3 773	899.9	113.7	91	1 459	49.3	14.1
Hamilton	2 527	29 765	3 162.6	1 244.3	1 450	76 053	20 077.9	3 027.9	1 967	40 513	1 365.9	387.4
Hancock	104	508	35.5	14.2	97	11 964	2 792.4	422.5	172	3 184	87.5	25.8
Hardin	22	61	3.3	0.8	38	2 412	484.3	84.6	58	647	17.2	5.0
Harrison	19	72	2.0	0.6	24	678	105.8	14.2	37	225	5.7	1.4
Henry	26	87	4.7	1.4	54	3 947	1 721.1	148.6	60	D	D	D
Highland	38	107	5.2	1.4	41	3 851	653.8	94.4	58	743	22.9	5.8
Hocking	22	142	6.1	2.8	26	2 102	341.2	60.4	51	619	20.4	5.5
Holmes	32	180	10.1	3.7	164	4 621	710.1	100.2	58	845	26.0	7.5
Huron	61	488	24.6	10.0	110	11 114	2 152.7	326.0	110	1 696	43.6	12.5
Jackson	29	139	9.4	2.3	37	3 631	780.5	83.4	49	694	21.7	5.6
Jefferson	88	352	17.6	6.9	45	2 244	463.3	78.7	166	1 724	48.6	13.6
Knox	46	211	14.2	5.1	72	4 924	972.3	174.4	96	1 418	36.9	10.5
Lake	499	3 214	235.8	103.3	769	25 423	4 661.0	893.2	482	9 435	257.2	68.6
Lawrence	40	140	8.4	3.2	44	1 969	998.1	65.0	73	1 078	32.1	8.3
Licking	162	1 433	76.2	32.9	150	9 489	2 455.1	321.1	266	4 206	124.4	35.8
Logan	54	658	38.6	13.9	58	6 295	3 766.0	238.9	101	1 502	37.0	10.5
Lorain	329	1 766	119.0	53.4	437	27 252	11 225.5	1 054.4	489	7 639	215.9	56.2
Lucas	932	9 186	895.0	329.7	652	33 116	12 071.0	1 404.8	1 034	18 683	602.0	161.6
Madison	35	264	19.3	7.2	51	3 401	606.5	102.8	61	1 219	39.6	11.0
Mahoning	426	2 485	189.4	76.5	405	13 001	2 110.0	398.6	536	8 653	255.8	69.3
Marion	81	399	23.0	8.2	86	6 842	1 924.7	229.8	116	1 947	57.7	15.4
Medina	276	1 157	89.1	33.2	306	10 672	1 744.7	346.7	229	4 400	117.6	33.6
Meigs	21	63	2.9	0.9	NA	NA	NA	NA	26	313	10.1	2.3
Mercer	27	179	14.9	4.8	62	4 473	775.7	130.8	79	1 027	27.5	7.4
Miami	135	534	36.5	16.6	265	13 848	2 611.8	454.9	178	3 231	91.4	26.2
Monroe	16	54	2.6	0.7	21	D	D	D	18	D	D	D
Montgomery	1 206	12 424	1 232.1	442.6	927	56 299	15 734.7	2 337.3	1 129	23 022	717.5	202.7
Morgan	13	53	3.5	0.6	10	921	135.5	27.5	15	178	4.2	1.2
Morrow	13	46	1.8	0.6	27	1 778	366.2	57.5	39	370	10.2	2.5
Muskingum	79	397	31.4	11.0	113	10 096	1 214.6	248.8	189	3 177	91.6	25.2
Noble	6	22	1.1	0.4	12	D	D	D	18	204	6.1	1.7

1. Firms subject to federal tax.

Table B. States and Counties — Health and Other Services and Federal Funds

	Health Care and Social Assistance[1], 1997				Other Services[1], 1997				Federal funds and grants, fiscal 1999[2] Expenditures (mil dol)			
										Direct payments for individuals[3]		
STATE County	Number of Establishments	Number of Employees	Receipts (mil dol)	Annual Payroll (mil dol)	Number of Establishments	Number of Employees	Receipts (mil dol)	Annual Payroll (mil dol)	Total	Social Security and government retirement	Medicare	Food stamps and Supplemental Security Income
	159	160	161	162	163	164	165	166	167	168	169	170
NORTH DAKOTA—Cont'd												
Ward	105	1 081	92.6	29.7	110	592	28.7	8.7	469.4	115.7	34.0	5.1
Wells	6	29	1.8	0.6	13	23	2.0	0.4	46.4	14.5	5.6	0.3
Williams	49	251	14.3	5.2	52	234	16.4	3.9	99.1	43.2	15.1	2.0
OHIO	20 399	261 520	15 440.1	7 477.0	17 314	116 165	7 087.5	2 165.7	53 262.2	20 419.4	8 676.4	1 770.8
Adams	31	393	15.2	6.1	18	47	2.3	0.4	152.3	51.0	21.6	11.4
Allen	201	2 625	161.8	86.0	182	1 071	61.2	17.0	561.7	325.4	77.0	21.8
Ashland	83	851	37.4	18.6	75	350	19.7	5.8	147.7	84.9	27.7	3.0
Ashtabula	149	2 319	122.5	53.6	140	585	27.0	7.6	425.7	206.3	97.0	16.2
Athens	77	891	49.5	21.9	53	266	10.7	3.4	260.9	78.6	36.2	14.8
Auglaize	67	815	41.3	17.8	74	431	25.4	8.7	148.0	75.2	36.8	1.9
Belmont	121	1 643	66.0	29.6	93	418	21.5	6.3	353.3	177.6	73.4	13.5
Brown	28	646	22.5	10.8	37	106	7.4	1.5	137.3	61.3	25.7	5.2
Butler	464	5 629	329.1	164.6	422	2 924	192.6	59.6	972.4	487.9	182.9	36.5
Carroll	24	277	13.4	5.5	25	152	8.9	3.0	78.0	39.3	13.8	2.5
Champaign	37	328	16.7	6.4	59	236	13.9	3.6	132.9	64.8	22.2	3.7
Clark	240	2 758	159.6	78.1	202	1 384	72.8	21.4	669.9	330.4	120.9	26.0
Clermont	187	2 554	127.9	62.1	220	1 177	71.5	21.9	377.9	196.6	67.9	15.0
Clinton	52	634	35.3	16.7	55	266	12.0	4.6	153.6	72.7	28.0	3.8
Columbiana	182	2 229	106.7	49.7	164	737	37.8	12.9	465.2	229.2	97.4	18.9
Coshocton	52	679	30.1	13.1	46	178	9.5	2.5	134.2	66.6	24.8	4.1
Crawford	77	810	36.0	16.2	53	326	19.8	6.1	186.4	95.4	40.7	5.9
Cuyahoga	3 042	36 747	2 409.7	1 137.5	2 511	19 147	1 466.9	396.0	7 902.0	2 805.5	1 529.0	316.2
Darke	61	729	32.3	15.6	88	348	21.4	5.6	188.3	93.5	35.1	4.3
Defiance	59	736	47.0	18.9	59	275	16.5	4.5	137.7	66.6	24.2	4.1
Delaware	132	1 349	71.2	30.6	98	459	29.9	7.9	266.5	101.7	33.1	4.0
Erie	168	1 369	87.3	45.4	123	647	29.0	9.2	328.2	160.2	68.3	8.9
Fairfield	226	2 544	137.0	62.5	157	811	44.3	14.5	338.9	178.3	66.8	10.3
Fayette	41	547	22.6	10.5	37	159	6.8	1.8	108.6	47.2	18.6	5.1
Franklin	2 171	28 471	1 920.5	962.2	1 579	12 799	783.6	249.5	6 051.1	1 625.9	605.7	173.4
Fulton	62	717	37.4	15.7	63	258	16.1	4.3	144.0	72.0	30.4	1.5
Gallia	45	885	62.1	30.0	34	127	6.6	1.8	147.9	57.5	25.8	11.6
Geauga	158	1 490	73.1	33.8	140	695	44.3	13.5	170.0	106.1	38.2	1.8
Greene	212	2 290	138.0	67.2	217	1 318	69.4	24.8	1 755.5	262.8	57.5	12.0
Guernsey	81	946	44.5	21.9	65	293	12.8	3.8	184.3	80.9	34.1	9.8
Hamilton	1 956	27 934	1 781.5	898.4	1 591	11 379	724.4	232.3	5 353.7	1 620.8	732.7	154.9
Hancock	130	1 505	90.6	45.0	107	656	36.8	11.6	196.1	98.9	35.2	4.6
Hardin	28	383	14.0	5.5	32	111	6.0	1.7	100.6	33.7	22.9	2.4
Harrison	14	280	10.5	4.7	19	42	2.4	0.6	73.1	39.0	14.9	2.8
Henry	30	451	17.0	7.9	37	165	12.6	3.1	107.1	51.6	19.4	1.7
Highland	49	624	25.4	11.9	39	240	15.0	4.4	163.7	73.2	28.9	6.6
Hocking	38	442	19.8	8.4	37	130	6.0	1.5	98.0	46.5	19.4	5.6
Holmes	41	1 047	45.7	20.1	34	120	10.6	2.2	59.8	31.2	8.7	0.9
Huron	77	997	52.7	25.2	67	388	20.2	5.8	210.8	117.9	41.8	6.9
Jackson	28	415	17.8	6.9	44	168	10.3	2.1	145.5	59.8	21.3	8.8
Jefferson	135	1 788	87.0	39.1	121	820	38.7	12.4	430.6	205.5	93.4	16.3
Knox	98	1 237	56.2	23.2	60	511	17.2	5.5	187.2	93.3	37.9	4.6
Lake	429	4 882	258.6	119.2	464	2 577	166.6	52.4	724.5	419.1	171.1	11.9
Lawrence	54	1 013	36.8	16.6	63	217	11.9	3.4	304.1	135.1	52.0	25.2
Licking	185	3 415	147.2	75.7	176	1 191	62.0	24.2	562.6	250.8	78.9	15.7
Logan	73	605	32.5	14.1	55	394	29.3	6.6	173.6	83.3	34.9	4.7
Lorain	444	5 189	310.7	162.5	379	2 474	131.6	40.4	983.3	468.5	207.7	36.6
Lucas	944	13 899	900.9	461.4	798	5 289	332.8	100.2	1 965.7	789.7	429.2	113.4
Madison	54	457	25.9	9.4	31	159	9.9	2.5	148.5	62.2	25.6	3.0
Mahoning	629	7 696	434.1	203.3	415	2 852	162.8	49.9	1 341.3	592.6	278.5	59.8
Marion	116	1 754	99.9	50.3	95	389	20.5	6.0	261.3	123.6	50.1	12.4
Medina	265	3 147	151.0	71.5	239	1 347	75.0	22.7	349.7	209.6	78.9	5.8
Meigs	16	336	13.0	4.7	19	45	3.1	0.7	104.1	44.2	17.4	7.1
Mercer	63	816	36.1	16.7	71	298	22.3	5.6	84.5	21.7	26.6	0.9
Miami	151	1 606	99.0	45.2	154	824	44.1	13.5	350.5	179.6	63.3	7.6
Monroe	9	140	5.1	1.7	21	60	2.9	0.6	68.9	30.1	12.6	2.6
Montgomery	1 167	15 974	1 017.3	491.6	914	9 895	499.5	183.9	3 096.6	1 264.5	463.0	96.5
Morgan	10	129	5.4	2.6	13	33	2.1	0.6	59.6	26.1	10.1	3.2
Morrow	28	368	12.6	5.9	20	61	3.1	0.7	76.2	39.7	11.3	3.5
Muskingum	159	1 935	124.7	58.6	141	999	56.4	17.8	359.0	167.0	59.8	17.4
Noble	17	353	10.7	5.0	14	28	1.7	0.4	39.9	18.1	6.9	1.6

1. Firms subject to federal tax.　2. October 1, 1998 to September 30, 1999.　3. State totals may include programs not allocated by county.

Table B. States and Counties — Federal Funds and Local Government Finances

	Federal funds and grants, fiscal 1999[1] (cont'd)							Local government finances, 1997				
	Expenditures (mil dol) (cont'd)							General revenue				
	Procurement contract awards			Grants[2]							Taxes	
											Per capita[3] (dollars)	
STATE County	Salaries and wages	Defense	Other	Medicaid and other health-related	Nutrition and family welfare	Education	Other	Total (mil dol)	Intergovern-mental (mil dol)	Total (mil dol)	Total	Property
	171	172	173	174	175	176	177	178	179	180	181	182
NORTH DAKOTA—Cont'd												
Ward	188.0	47.3	11.5	16.8	8.7	8.3	5.3	98.9	45.5	33.7	573	490
Wells	1.5	0.0	0.4	2.9	0.5	0.2	2.4	10.9	4.3	4.4	841	810
Williams	4.8	0.1	3.9	8.7	3.0	1.0	1.9	40.2	16.9	16.4	805	743
OHIO	4 340.9	2 596.7	1 910.8	4 955.7	2 305.3	911.0	2 082.4	X	X	X	X	X
Adams	3.8	0.0	1.1	45.9	6.6	2.5	4.7	71.9	26.7	26.5	930	774
Allen	24.5	17.7	6.4	38.9	16.4	6.3	12.8	223.2	93.9	88.2	817	535
Ashland	5.7	0.1	2.7	8.6	3.7	2.1	3.9	99.4	40.0	41.5	799	567
Ashtabula	13.8	11.0	19.2	30.4	16.0	6.1	5.5	225.3	115.7	74.7	725	550
Athens	19.5	0.7	6.1	41.6	11.0	5.6	31.6	132.6	76.6	39.4	643	488
Auglaize	5.0	3.1	1.3	7.2	3.1	1.4	2.1	96.6	40.3	35.6	758	508
Belmont	10.1	0.3	4.0	30.4	12.8	4.2	20.6	131.6	65.4	42.8	616	427
Brown	4.4	0.0	1.4	18.3	6.3	2.0	2.0	105.9	54.9	21.4	531	423
Butler	31.5	29.6	20.4	92.0	29.5	11.0	35.2	673.7	251.8	283.0	866	645
Carroll	2.5	0.0	0.8	10.0	2.9	1.2	3.0	38.1	21.4	10.8	372	316
Champaign	4.2	7.0	1.1	12.4	3.2	1.5	1.5	86.3	34.8	29.1	762	500
Clark	38.6	7.3	5.0	68.3	20.7	9.2	21.3	307.5	139.9	118.4	810	551
Clermont	16.5	1.1	4.6	38.3	16.2	5.9	7.5	375.5	149.5	144.7	836	699
Clinton	8.1	0.1	1.7	15.7	3.8	2.7	2.6	122.5	42.5	30.8	782	564
Columbiana	25.5	3.4	3.8	39.1	18.3	6.1	16.4	212.6	113.6	67.8	608	471
Coshocton	5.3	2.3	1.1	12.0	6.1	1.7	6.5	77.3	27.7	35.9	992	768
Crawford	4.1	0.3	1.2	14.3	5.7	2.5	2.7	94.5	39.9	36.0	764	586
Cuyahoga	851.2	132.8	484.8	915.9	266.6	98.8	283.7	4 906.0	1 641.5	2 262.7	1 632	962
Darke	6.1	0.9	1.8	13.3	10.8	2.0	4.0	96.2	44.4	36.5	671	457
Defiance	5.0	0.1	4.4	9.1	5.0	1.6	4.2	115.4	53.5	38.5	965	709
Delaware	11.8	3.3	8.9	10.4	2.7	2.2	32.9	178.1	52.5	88.6	1 013	833
Erie	11.7	1.2	9.9	17.2	8.5	3.5	32.1	223.6	75.5	96.3	1 223	924
Fairfield	13.0	5.3	4.0	23.7	8.1	3.6	13.7	231.4	97.6	90.9	749	530
Fayette	2.6	0.0	1.0	14.6	4.6	1.5	0.3	61.1	23.4	17.4	608	433
Franklin	590.6	252.0	223.1	644.2	916.0	339.4	557.8	3 051.9	952.6	1 557.1	1 531	946
Fulton	6.6	1.4	1.5	5.6	2.3	1.4	8.6	89.7	30.1	44.9	1 085	724
Gallia	3.9	2.0	1.0	30.6	7.8	2.1	2.6	74.5	28.0	20.6	624	564
Geauga	6.9	0.3	2.1	6.3	2.2	2.3	1.7	181.1	57.3	97.1	1 105	956
Greene	770.4	548.4	12.7	39.1	10.3	7.7	6.2	319.0	115.1	130.0	930	697
Guernsey	5.7	0.2	1.5	24.1	6.1	2.3	15.5	80.6	34.9	31.0	761	546
Hamilton	543.0	819.1	468.5	545.4	131.7	51.3	122.6	2 694.5	846.9	1 282.5	1 506	974
Hancock	9.0	0.1	2.0	13.9	5.4	2.6	8.0	146.1	55.7	63.4	921	659
Hardin	5.8	2.6	1.5	7.8	3.7	2.9	1.9	55.6	29.0	19.6	617	367
Harrison	3.3	0.1	0.7	6.7	2.9	1.2	1.0	38.1	17.5	15.4	955	523
Henry	4.9	0.0	1.3	5.4	1.8	1.4	6.0	74.5	36.6	26.7	892	691
Highland	5.4	0.3	1.3	24.1	6.0	2.0	1.2	88.1	41.5	19.1	479	320
Hocking	2.7	0.0	0.9	11.3	3.9	1.3	5.0	65.6	26.0	15.9	553	376
Holmes	3.7	0.0	1.2	5.9	1.3	2.0	2.2	54.2	23.6	22.2	595	555
Huron	7.6	0.2	2.0	13.9	5.3	2.6	3.3	146.7	59.2	64.3	1 071	502
Jackson	3.7	0.0	1.3	33.9	7.3	2.2	5.5	54.8	33.4	11.9	367	305
Jefferson	13.9	2.5	7.5	42.2	14.0	5.0	22.5	140.4	66.4	52.4	689	591
Knox	5.7	0.0	1.7	19.2	5.4	3.1	7.5	96.7	45.2	37.0	704	522
Lake	26.0	6.7	11.4	28.4	11.9	7.3	23.6	621.7	166.6	336.2	1 503	1 097
Lawrence	6.8	1.1	1.6	54.2	16.8	6.0	3.2	112.5	76.3	22.9	355	249
Licking	25.0	96.2	3.6	39.0	14.6	5.7	18.5	302.5	133.6	126.1	904	639
Logan	10.7	1.0	3.1	14.8	4.2	1.8	1.4	100.0	41.5	40.2	875	716
Lorain	82.2	4.5	9.0	76.0	38.7	16.3	23.8	679.1	261.1	292.7	1 036	706
Lucas	119.6	28.8	25.7	238.0	79.4	28.7	69.0	1 329.5	486.9	587.8	1 302	767
Madison	4.5	0.0	1.1	14.3	2.8	1.5	21.0	90.0	42.3	33.8	815	627
Mahoning	85.5	4.8	18.6	142.8	51.5	17.7	71.1	554.5	258.4	215.5	837	593
Marion	8.8	2.0	2.0	23.5	13.8	3.1	5.5	147.0	64.6	50.7	778	547
Medina	16.3	4.4	5.0	14.3	5.3	4.2	2.1	318.4	122.1	135.7	956	813
Meigs	3.5	0.2	0.9	17.4	5.3	1.9	4.5	41.5	28.4	9.2	384	309
Mercer	5.3	0.0	1.4	6.1	3.4	1.4	2.2	102.0	43.9	31.7	774	553
Miami	11.8	33.5	5.5	21.7	7.0	3.1	3.0	222.6	79.7	92.9	951	655
Monroe	3.0	1.2	2.0	11.5	2.5	1.1	2.0	30.5	15.3	12.4	812	707
Montgomery	277.4	270.2	169.9	255.6	92.4	35.9	108.5	1 745.3	605.7	741.8	1 321	795
Morgan	3.7	0.4	0.8	8.0	2.5	1.1	2.8	26.5	16.4	7.5	515	405
Morrow	2.9	0.0	0.8	6.3	2.9	1.4	1.3	51.0	27.6	15.3	492	392
Muskingum	16.9	0.5	4.1	44.8	12.3	5.0	22.6	192.6	93.8	66.9	792	525
Noble	1.4	0.0	1.0	5.4	3.3	0.8	1.2	23.8	13.9	6.6	539	454

1. October 1, 1998 to September 30, 1999.   2. State totals may include programs not allocated by county.   3. Based on the resident population estimated as of July 1 of the year shown.

Table B. States and Counties — Local Government Finances, Government Employment, and Elections

STATE County	Local government finances, 1997 (cont'd) Direct general expenditure Total (mil dol)	Per capita[1] (dollars)	Education	Health and hospitals	Police protection	Public welfare	Highways	Debt outstanding Total (mil dol)	Per capita[1] (dollars)	Government employment, 1998 Federal civilian	Federal military	State and local	Presidential election, 2000 Percent of vote cast — Democratic	Republican	All other
	183	184	185	186	187	188	189	190	191	192	193	194	195	196	197
NORTH DAKOTA—Cont'd															
Ward	89.3	1 520	55.8	2.4	5.5	3.9	5.9	44.7	760	1 304	4 913	3 597	34.4	64.0	1.6
Wells	10.0	1 895	61.4	0.0	1.7	5.6	14.1	0.8	159	37	42	289	28.0	68.2	3.7
Williams	42.0	2 058	55.3	0.5	4.1	3.2	8.1	16.3	800	110	163	1 375	30.5	67.8	1.7
OHIO	X	X	X	X	X	X	X	X	X	83 126	36 706	683 434	46.4	50.0	3.6
Adams	96.4	3 386	62.7	12.9	2.2	4.3	5.0	45.3	1 591	77	74	1 516	NA	NA	NA
Allen	219.4	2 032	51.1	3.1	5.1	4.8	3.9	89.0	824	469	281	6 690	NA	NA	NA
Ashland	97.3	1 871	58.9	2.4	4.8	4.4	8.8	13.3	256	114	135	2 778	NA	NA	NA
Ashtabula	217.2	2 106	49.5	5.9	4.6	10.1	6.0	33.3	323	258	276	5 016	NA	NA	NA
Athens	127.8	2 085	57.2	3.0	3.7	12.0	6.9	37.4	611	240	174	10 015	NA	NA	NA
Auglaize	90.2	1 920	55.8	1.7	3.2	7.8	6.6	49.4	1 051	95	121	2 736	NA	NA	NA
Belmont	127.7	1 835	48.9	9.6	4.5	7.1	6.3	43.4	624	167	178	3 951	NA	NA	NA
Brown	95.1	2 362	54.1	21.3	1.9	4.0	4.7	24.8	616	89	105	1 927	NA	NA	NA
Butler	685.0	2 096	52.2	5.4	5.7	5.0	5.6	758.6	2 322	558	875	18 661	NA	NA	NA
Carroll	37.1	1 283	48.6	6.2	5.1	8.7	13.0	4.5	155	50	75	898	NA	NA	NA
Champaign	90.0	2 354	47.7	12.1	3.9	5.3	6.8	20.0	523	82	98	1 781	NA	NA	NA
Clark	304.7	2 084	49.2	8.9	5.5	10.3	4.2	106.5	728	629	379	7 133	NA	NA	NA
Clermont	369.9	2 136	50.0	2.7	4.3	4.5	3.8	608.4	3 514	311	453	6 462	NA	NA	NA
Clinton	115.9	2 947	41.4	31.3	3.5	2.0	4.6	44.8	1 139	146	103	2 880	NA	NA	NA
Columbiana	200.7	1 797	55.4	3.7	4.3	8.2	5.3	72.1	646	572	288	4 613	NA	NA	NA
Coshocton	74.8	2 069	49.4	2.5	4.1	8.7	7.0	9.2	255	105	93	1 554	NA	NA	NA
Crawford	98.7	2 095	46.3	4.7	5.3	6.7	8.0	28.8	613	88	122	2 034	NA	NA	NA
Cuyahoga	4 613.2	3 326	38.3	12.5	6.4	5.0	3.8	4 727.5	3 409	17 306	4 154	84 516	NA	NA	NA
Darke	91.7	1 688	54.5	1.3	5.7	9.2	8.9	10.5	193	125	140	2 129	NA	NA	NA
Defiance	95.6	2 395	42.5	8.2	5.1	6.5	16.4	4.9	122	109	103	1 927	NA	NA	NA
Delaware	196.0	2 243	57.0	4.1	4.3	2.4	5.2	175.0	2 002	230	238	4 327	NA	NA	NA
Erie	218.1	2 770	50.1	2.1	4.4	6.7	4.1	75.7	962	193	210	4 975	NA	NA	NA
Fairfield	227.9	1 877	54.0	4.6	4.7	3.1	7.5	99.3	817	258	321	6 552	NA	NA	NA
Fayette	62.2	2 173	44.1	22.8	4.1	4.7	7.0	22.7	794	57	73	1 479	NA	NA	NA
Franklin	2 999.8	2 949	38.5	8.1	7.2	5.0	4.9	2 872.2	2 823	13 392	3 285	100 541	NA	NA	NA
Fulton	90.5	2 189	60.8	1.0	4.2	2.7	12.3	46.8	1 133	109	108	2 455	NA	NA	NA
Gallia	72.3	2 185	50.1	21.9	3.5	2.9	8.3	11.9	360	79	86	1 924	NA	NA	NA
Geauga	182.2	2 073	51.4	6.0	4.6	2.6	8.4	73.9	841	137	229	3 466	NA	NA	NA
Greene	313.8	2 246	47.8	2.7	7.7	5.3	4.7	233.8	1 674	12 006	3 485	9 809	NA	NA	NA
Guernsey	72.7	1 782	48.9	1.6	4.7	10.1	8.3	37.5	918	119	106	2 458	NA	NA	NA
Hamilton	2 677.2	3 144	34.2	8.5	6.3	5.6	4.8	1 063.9	1 249	9 948	2 336	54 245	NA	NA	NA
Hancock	153.0	2 223	46.9	7.7	5.7	7.0	7.4	79.9	1 161	178	179	2 988	NA	NA	NA
Hardin	54.5	1 719	65.4	2.3	5.4	3.3	8.7	6.2	195	86	82	1 603	NA	NA	NA
Harrison	36.2	2 242	42.3	1.3	7.2	11.9	14.0	3.4	208	62	41	874	NA	NA	NA
Henry	73.5	2 460	57.5	0.6	3.2	9.5	10.9	23.0	768	78	77	1 841	NA	NA	NA
Highland	84.5	2 122	45.7	21.6	3.1	3.5	4.5	17.9	450	107	104	1 972	NA	NA	NA
Hocking	63.0	2 192	32.9	32.8	2.8	5.9	7.3	17.1	593	54	75	1 583	NA	NA	NA
Holmes	49.0	1 312	50.1	0.5	4.9	11.7	13.6	18.4	492	78	98	1 393	NA	NA	NA
Huron	126.4	2 105	54.6	1.7	6.6	5.1	7.2	35.3	589	140	156	2 580	NA	NA	NA
Jackson	53.2	1 643	54.6	2.9	3.7	7.6	8.0	28.1	868	71	84	1 405	NA	NA	NA
Jefferson	137.2	1 805	51.7	1.1	4.9	12.6	6.1	34.5	453	264	193	3 715	NA	NA	NA
Knox	92.9	1 769	52.7	2.2	4.4	6.5	7.7	61.6	1 174	112	137	2 656	NA	NA	NA
Lake	570.3	2 549	50.2	7.7	5.6	2.0	5.1	248.1	1 109	510	596	11 081	NA	NA	NA
Lawrence	115.5	1 791	60.4	3.2	2.2	7.4	4.5	29.6	459	151	166	3 544	NA	NA	NA
Licking	286.8	2 057	51.4	7.1	2.8	6.6	4.9	64.2	460	530	367	6 573	NA	NA	NA
Logan	97.0	2 111	55.9	1.3	5.8	5.2	6.7	46.8	1 019	143	123	2 126	NA	NA	NA
Lorain	651.2	2 305	52.1	5.8	5.5	4.2	4.1	243.7	863	1 178	738	13 065	NA	NA	NA
Lucas	1 375.4	3 047	35.1	7.9	5.8	5.1	3.5	906.1	2 008	2 140	1 230	29 864	NA	NA	NA
Madison	78.9	1 901	56.6	3.0	4.0	9.0	7.7	9.1	220	93	107	2 962	NA	NA	NA
Mahoning	532.3	2 067	48.8	6.1	5.4	5.3	4.6	269.2	1 046	1 576	678	15 600	NA	NA	NA
Marion	140.4	2 156	50.2	4.5	5.6	9.0	4.8	129.2	1 984	172	168	5 870	NA	NA	NA
Medina	307.5	2 166	53.4	4.5	5.2	2.4	4.4	124.3	875	304	372	5 791	NA	NA	NA
Meigs	43.2	1 800	53.6	0.9	3.2	12.9	13.3	6.8	285	77	62	1 137	NA	NA	NA
Mercer	102.9	2 511	54.0	12.0	3.3	5.0	6.8	41.5	1 014	98	106	2 536	NA	NA	NA
Miami	218.1	2 232	50.7	3.7	5.6	3.2	5.9	75.6	773	227	255	4 399	NA	NA	NA
Monroe	31.4	2 047	59.8	1.5	3.9	4.5	13.2	13.8	897	63	40	887	NA	NA	NA
Montgomery	1 649.0	2 938	41.0	4.2	6.5	6.4	4.7	990.2	1 764	6 437	4 411	29 629	NA	NA	NA
Morgan	26.1	1 786	54.5	1.0	3.8	10.5	9.1	1.9	127	45	37	654	NA	NA	NA
Morrow	47.1	1 515	56.9	5.1	3.2	5.4	11.8	13.7	439	56	81	1 395	NA	NA	NA
Muskingum	178.6	2 113	53.7	3.6	5.7	6.9	5.2	84.1	995	311	219	4 595	NA	NA	NA
Noble	21.2	1 723	55.1	2.8	2.6	7.2	14.5	6.2	501	28	32	1 058	NA	NA	NA

1. Based on the resident population estimated as of July 1 of the year shown.

STATE/ County code	MSA/ PMSA/ NECMA code[1]	County Type[2]	STATE County	Land area,[3] (sq km) 1990	Total persons	Rank	Per square kilometer	White	Black	Am. Indian, Eskimo, Aleut	Asian and Pacific Islander	Percent Hispanic[4]	Under 5 years	5 to 17 years	18 to 24 years	25 to 34 years	35 to 44 years	45 to 54 years
				1	2	3	4	5	6	7	8	9	10	11	12	13	14	15
			OHIO—Cont'd															
39 123	...	6	Ottawa	661	41 281	1 056	62.5	98.7	0.8	0.1	0.3	4.7	5.4	18.1	7.1	12.0	16.1	14.0
39 125	...	6	Paulding	1 078	20 073	1 759	18.6	98.1	1.4	0.3	0.2	4.0	7.0	22.0	8.2	12.7	15.7	13.7
39 127	...	6	Perry	1 062	34 261	1 248	32.3	99.5	0.2	0.1	0.1	0.3	6.8	21.7	8.5	13.1	15.8	13.1
39 129	1840	1	Pickaway	1 301	53 431	860	41.1	92.7	6.7	0.3	0.3	0.9	5.9	17.3	9.7	15.7	17.8	14.8
39 131	...	7	Pike	1 144	27 988	1 437	24.5	97.8	1.6	0.3	0.3	0.4	6.6	21.7	8.6	12.7	15.2	13.5
39 133	0080	2	Portage	1 275	151 579	338	118.9	95.6	3.1	0.2	1.1	0.7	6.0	18.1	14.5	13.4	16.0	13.0
39 135	...	6	Preble	1 100	43 472	1 011	39.5	99.1	0.5	0.2	0.2	0.4	6.3	20.3	7.9	12.7	16.5	14.4
39 137	...	6	Putnam	1 253	35 206	1 220	28.1	99.6	0.1	0.2	0.1	5.5	7.9	22.9	8.2	13.4	14.5	11.8
39 139	4800	3	Richland	1 287	129 607	403	100.7	89.5	9.6	0.2	0.7	1.0	6.1	18.6	8.9	12.9	15.8	14.2
39 141	...	4	Ross	1 783	75 731	655	42.5	91.7	7.5	0.3	0.6	0.7	5.7	18.5	8.5	15.0	17.1	14.3
39 143	...	4	Sandusky	1 060	61 810	773	58.3	96.5	3.0	0.2	0.4	7.4	6.7	20.6	8.2	13.1	15.8	12.6
39 145	...	4	Scioto	1 586	80 353	628	50.7	96.3	2.9	0.5	0.3	0.4	6.1	20.3	8.4	12.4	15.0	13.6
39 147	...	5	Seneca	1 426	59 768	795	41.9	96.9	2.4	0.2	0.6	3.7	6.5	21.1	9.4	12.4	15.5	12.1
39 149	...	6	Shelby	1 060	47 949	939	45.2	97.0	1.6	0.1	1.3	0.5	7.3	21.8	8.3	13.6	15.8	13.0
39 151	1320	2	Stark	1 492	373 174	152	250.1	91.3	7.8	0.3	0.6	1.0	6.1	18.2	8.5	12.6	16.4	13.7
39 153	0080	2	Summit	1 069	537 856	98	503.1	84.9	13.5	0.2	1.4	0.8	6.4	17.7	9.1	13.6	16.8	13.1
39 155	9320	2	Trumbull	1 595	225 339	247	141.3	91.4	7.8	0.2	0.6	0.9	6.0	18.0	8.2	12.1	16.2	14.1
39 157	...	4	Tuscarawas	1 470	88 773	567	60.4	98.6	0.9	0.2	0.3	0.4	6.3	19.2	7.4	12.7	16.1	13.7
39 159	...	6	Union	1 131	40 776	1 064	36.1	95.3	3.9	0.2	0.6	0.7	6.7	19.8	8.5	15.5	17.8	14.1
39 161	...	6	Van Wert	1 062	30 092	1 371	28.3	98.7	0.8	0.1	0.4	2.1	6.6	20.4	7.6	12.9	15.8	12.8
39 163	...	9	Vinton	1 073	12 362	2 260	11.5	99.8	0.0	0.1	0.0	0.4	6.4	21.2	8.6	12.4	15.7	14.0
39 165	1640	1	Warren	1 036	153 292	334	148.0	96.8	2.2	0.2	0.8	0.6	7.0	19.0	7.9	15.3	18.3	14.6
39 167	6020	3	Washington	1 645	63 029	762	38.3	97.9	1.5	0.2	0.5	0.5	5.8	18.9	8.8	12.3	16.1	14.3
39 169	...	4	Wayne	1 438	111 045	474	77.2	97.4	1.7	0.1	0.7	0.6	7.1	20.4	9.2	13.0	16.2	13.3
39 171	...	7	Williams	1 092	37 755	1 142	34.6	99.2	0.1	0.1	0.5	2.9	6.8	20.6	7.7	13.4	15.6	13.4
39 173	8400	2	Wood	1 599	120 292	440	75.2	97.4	1.1	0.2	1.3	3.4	5.9	18.1	16.7	12.8	15.9	12.0
39 175	...	7	Wyandot	1 051	22 921	1 616	21.8	99.4	0.1	0.1	0.4	0.9	6.5	20.1	7.7	12.6	15.0	13.4
40 000	...	X	**OKLAHOMA**	177 878	3 358 044	X	18.9	83.0	7.8	7.8	1.3	4.1	6.9	19.3	10.2	12.4	15.1	13.1
40 001	...	6	Adair	1 491	20 544	1 738	13.8	57.1	0.1	42.8	0.1	1.8	7.3	22.5	10.4	12.1	13.5	12.9
40 003	...	8	Alfalfa	2 245	5 887	2 779	2.6	93.5	3.7	2.7	0.1	2.5	5.1	16.1	7.6	12.0	12.8	14.2
40 005	...	7	Atoka	2 534	13 379	2 184	5.3	81.7	6.2	11.9	0.2	1.3	5.9	19.5	8.8	12.1	14.6	13.3
40 007	...	9	Beaver	4 699	6 016	2 769	1.3	98.5	0.2	1.3	0.0	7.5	6.2	21.7	6.1	11.0	14.6	13.5
40 009	...	7	Beckham	2 336	19 799	1 771	8.5	94.6	2.9	2.1	0.4	6.6	7.3	21.2	8.2	12.1	14.3	12.0
40 011	...	6	Blaine	2 405	10 284	2 399	4.3	86.6	4.8	8.3	0.3	3.7	7.1	20.3	7.6	10.7	13.1	12.9
40 013	...	6	Bryan	2 354	34 941	1 228	14.8	84.3	1.4	13.7	0.5	2.2	6.4	18.5	12.2	10.5	13.6	13.1
40 015	...	6	Caddo	3 311	30 664	1 356	9.3	73.6	3.4	22.7	0.3	5.9	7.1	20.4	9.3	12.0	13.8	12.8
40 017	5880	2	Canadian	2 331	86 498	582	37.1	91.3	2.6	4.0	2.1	3.8	7.4	22.0	7.9	13.1	17.9	13.9
40 019	...	5	Carter	2 134	44 533	993	20.9	82.5	9.0	8.0	0.5	2.7	6.7	20.1	7.7	11.2	14.7	12.7
40 021	...	6	Cherokee	1 945	39 506	1 099	20.3	66.0	1.2	32.5	0.2	2.0	6.8	19.6	12.5	12.0	13.7	12.7
40 023	...	7	Choctaw	2 005	15 025	2 061	7.5	72.0	13.5	14.3	0.2	1.4	6.8	20.7	8.2	9.9	13.2	12.7
40 025	...	9	Cimarron	4 753	2 922	2 995	0.6	98.6	0.1	0.9	0.4	18.3	6.9	21.0	7.0	9.5	13.6	13.0
40 027	5880	2	Cleveland	1 389	203 449	267	146.5	89.2	3.2	4.9	2.7	4.2	6.9	19.1	14.7	14.4	16.8	12.8
40 029	...	9	Coal	1 342	6 126	2 763	4.6	83.2	0.9	15.9	0.0	0.9	6.0	20.5	8.4	10.7	13.7	12.7
40 031	4200	3	Comanche	2 770	106 621	490	38.5	73.9	17.8	4.6	3.7	9.2	8.4	20.5	13.0	14.6	14.2	11.1
40 033	...	6	Cotton	1 649	6 609	2 720	4.0	89.1	2.4	8.4	0.1	4.8	6.2	19.7	8.1	11.2	12.8	13.9
40 035	...	6	Craig	1 971	14 468	2 100	7.3	77.4	3.7	18.5	0.4	1.2	5.6	17.2	7.9	11.3	14.6	15.4
40 037	8560	2	Creek	2 475	68 169	711	27.5	88.3	3.4	8.0	0.3	1.6	6.8	20.0	8.5	10.8	15.2	14.3
40 039	...	7	Custer	2 555	25 577	1 511	10.0	88.9	3.7	6.5	0.9	8.6	7.1	19.5	15.8	11.9	12.9	11.3
40 041	...	6	Delaware	1 919	34 977	1 224	18.2	75.3	0.1	24.4	0.2	1.2	5.8	17.7	7.9	9.7	12.5	14.5
40 043	...	9	Dewey	2 591	4 859	2 852	1.9	94.1	0.2	5.6	0.2	1.9	5.9	20.4	6.3	10.9	12.9	13.9
40 045	...	9	Ellis	3 184	4 194	2 897	1.3	97.8	0.3	1.7	0.3	4.7	5.3	21.0	5.1	8.8	15.3	13.4
40 047	2340	3	Garfield	2 742	56 954	817	20.8	92.8	3.8	2.1	1.3	2.9	6.7	19.2	8.7	12.3	14.3	12.9
40 049	...	6	Garvin	2 096	26 720	1 475	12.7	90.0	2.9	6.8	0.3	1.9	5.8	19.5	8.0	10.7	13.3	13.0
40 051	...	6	Grady	2 852	46 084	967	16.2	90.6	4.0	5.1	0.4	2.7	6.9	21.3	9.1	11.8	15.2	14.1
40 053	...	8	Grant	2 592	5 237	2 823	2.0	98.4	0.1	1.3	0.3	1.6	6.8	18.7	5.8	10.3	13.3	12.2
40 055	...	7	Greer	1 656	6 387	2 743	3.9	89.0	7.7	2.8	0.5	7.6	5.1	15.5	9.1	12.7	13.6	12.6
40 057	...	7	Harmon	1 393	3 336	2 968	2.4	88.8	9.6	1.0	0.6	25.8	7.2	21.6	8.0	9.2	11.6	10.4
40 059	...	9	Harper	2 691	3 580	2 945	1.3	98.9	0.1	0.8	0.2	2.7	5.4	19.7	5.1	9.7	13.4	13.0
40 061	...	6	Haskell	1 495	11 421	2 310	7.6	84.9	1.0	14.0	0.1	1.1	5.9	19.5	7.9	9.9	13.4	13.7
40 063	...	7	Hughes	2 090	14 064	2 129	6.7	78.3	5.6	15.9	0.2	2.1	5.0	17.9	8.1	10.7	14.0	13.6
40 065	...	5	Jackson	2 079	28 392	1 431	13.7	86.7	9.6	1.9	1.8	17.6	9.2	21.4	11.7	13.5	14.1	11.1
40 067	...	9	Jefferson	1 965	6 518	2 731	3.3	93.7	0.9	4.9	0.4	6.7	5.7	19.1	7.8	9.7	13.9	12.0
40 069	...	7	Johnston	1 669	10 310	2 396	6.2	82.3	2.3	15.2	0.2	1.7	6.1	20.5	10.0	10.3	13.9	13.3
40 071	...	5	Kay	2 380	46 448	958	19.5	90.2	1.9	7.2	0.6	2.6	6.9	19.1	8.2	11.0	13.6	12.6
40 073	...	6	Kingfisher	2 339	13 496	2 175	5.8	94.7	2.5	2.6	0.2	4.7	6.9	21.3	6.9	12.1	13.7	12.8

1. MSA = Metropolitan Statistical Area. PMSA = Primary MSA. NECMA = New England County Metropolitan Area. See Appendix A for explanation of these concepts. See Appendix B for list of metropolitan areas identified by type, with component counties. 2. County typology code from the Economic Research Service of USDA. See Appendix A for definition. 3. Dry land or land partially or temporarily covered by water. 4. Hispanic persons may be of any race.

Table B. States and Counties — **Population and Households**

STATE County	Population, 1999 (cont'd) — Age (percent) (cont'd)				Population — change and components of change, 1980–1999 — Total persons		Percent change		Components of change, 1990–1999			Households, 1990			Percent	
	55 to 64 years	65 to 74 years	75 years and over	Percent female	1990	1980	1980–1990	1990–1999	Births	Deaths	Net migration	Number	Percent change, 1980–1990	Persons per household	Female family householder[1]	One person
	16	17	18	19	20	21	22	23	24	25	26	27	28	29	30	31
OHIO—Cont'd																
Ottawa	10.2	9.4	7.8	50.9	40 029	40 076	-0.1	3.1	4 179	3 738	931	15 170	6.8	2.60	7.7	21.9
Paulding	8.2	6.5	6.0	50.7	20 488	21 302	-3.8	-2.0	2 284	1 554	-1 067	7 252	3.5	2.81	7.5	19.8
Perry	8.8	6.1	6.0	50.9	31 557	31 032	1.7	8.6	4 614	2 911	1 106	11 264	7.0	2.77	10.2	20.8
Pickaway	8.3	5.7	4.8	45.0	48 248	43 662	10.5	10.7	5 806	3 760	3 286	15 602	10.2	2.72	9.3	18.8
Pike	9.2	6.1	6.4	51.0	24 249	22 802	6.3	15.4	3 439	2 578	2 948	8 805	14.3	2.70	12.4	21.5
Portage	8.2	6.1	4.9	51.1	142 585	135 856	5.0	6.3	17 183	9 326	1 510	49 229	11.3	2.72	9.5	20.3
Preble	9.1	6.9	5.9	50.5	40 113	38 223	4.9	8.4	4 731	3 210	1 956	14 347	9.3	2.77	8.1	18.1
Putnam	8.1	6.4	6.8	50.2	33 819	32 991	2.5	4.1	4 940	2 567	-883	11 082	9.6	3.02	6.7	18.2
Richland	9.4	7.5	6.6	50.3	126 137	131 205	-3.9	2.8	16 215	11 101	-4 214	47 573	2.5	2.57	10.4	24.1
Ross	8.9	6.3	5.7	47.5	69 330	65 004	6.7	9.2	8 537	6 291	4 371	24 325	10.4	2.62	11.2	22.6
Sandusky	8.9	7.2	7.0	50.9	61 963	63 267	-2.1	-0.2	8 071	5 392	-2 640	22 464	4.2	2.71	9.9	21.7
Scioto	9.8	7.0	7.4	51.8	80 327	84 545	-5.0	0.0	9 857	8 770	-812	29 786	0.9	2.58	12.9	25.2
Seneca	8.8	7.2	7.2	51.2	59 733	61 901	-3.5	0.1	7 414	5 026	-2 204	21 277	2.2	2.71	9.4	22.9
Shelby	8.2	6.2	6.0	50.1	44 915	43 089	4.2	6.8	6 599	3 269	-154	15 626	10.2	2.83	8.0	19.7
Stark	9.3	8.0	7.2	52.1	367 585	378 823	-3.0	1.5	46 449	34 384	-5 287	139 573	4.1	2.58	10.9	23.9
Summit	9.3	7.5	6.5	52.1	514 990	524 472	-1.8	4.4	69 030	46 885	-2 675	199 998	5.3	2.54	12.3	25.7
Trumbull	9.8	8.8	6.9	51.7	227 795	241 863	-5.8	-1.1	27 191	21 354	-7 565	86 056	2.3	2.62	11.6	23.5
Tuscarawas	9.6	7.6	7.5	52.0	84 090	84 614	-0.6	5.6	11 087	8 265	2 150	31 971	4.9	2.60	8.6	23.4
Union	8.3	4.6	4.7	53.2	31 969	29 536	8.2	27.5	4 685	2 498	6 651	11 037	10.2	2.73	8.2	19.6
Van Wert	9.2	7.0	7.7	51.1	30 464	30 458	0.0	-1.2	3 651	2 711	-1 213	11 266	3.0	2.67	7.4	21.6
Vinton	9.4	6.1	6.2	50.5	11 098	11 584	-4.2	11.4	1 664	1 170	803	4 069	3.7	2.70	9.2	20.9
Warren	8.4	5.2	4.4	49.6	113 973	99 276	14.8	34.5	17 461	7 897	29 744	39 150	23.8	2.80	8.7	16.3
Washington	9.5	7.2	7.2	51.6	62 254	64 266	-3.1	1.2	7 493	5 777	-767	23 636	5.7	2.57	9.2	23.4
Wayne	8.4	6.3	6.1	51.0	101 461	97 408	4.2	9.4	14 847	8 049	3 158	35 619	10.5	2.76	8.4	21.0
Williams	8.4	7.0	7.2	50.9	36 956	36 369	1.6	2.2	4 578	3 084	-596	13 807	7.1	2.65	7.7	22.4
Wood	7.5	5.6	5.4	51.8	113 269	107 372	5.5	6.2	12 869	7 756	2 206	39 677	11.8	2.64	7.9	22.8
Wyandot	9.7	6.9	8.2	51.8	22 254	22 651	-1.8	3.0	2 731	2 262	285	8 168	4.2	2.67	8.7	22.2
OKLAHOMA	9.5	7.1	6.3	51.2	3 145 576	3 025 487	4.0	6.8	437 373	298 499	71 324	1 206 135	7.8	2.53	10.4	25.6
Adair	9.4	6.1	5.8	50.7	18 421	18 575	-0.8	11.5	3 389	2 007	820	6 386	4.5	2.85	12.3	21.1
Alfalfa	11.4	9.4	11.5	46.8	6 416	7 077	-9.3	-8.2	483	820	-177	2 469	-13.9	2.33	5.2	28.5
Atoka	10.9	7.7	7.1	47.4	12 778	12 748	0.2	4.7	1 474	1 336	512	4 495	-4.7	2.60	10.0	23.8
Beaver	10.8	8.1	8.0	49.8	6 023	6 806	-11.5	0.1	597	525	-64	2 327	-8.0	2.56	5.0	22.7
Beckham	9.7	6.7	8.4	50.9	18 812	19 243	-2.2	5.2	2 374	2 426	236	7 351	-1.7	2.51	9.4	27.2
Blaine	10.1	8.4	9.7	51.6	11 470	13 443	-14.7	-10.3	1 407	1 567	-996	4 418	-13.0	2.53	7.5	27.3
Bryan	10.3	7.7	7.7	51.6	32 089	30 535	5.1	8.9	4 137	3 530	2 325	12 524	7.8	2.49	10.5	26.1
Caddo	10.1	6.8	7.8	49.9	29 550	30 905	-4.4	3.8	3 920	3 527	805	10 879	-1.7	2.66	11.8	24.0
Canadian	7.7	5.4	4.8	49.9	74 409	56 452	31.8	16.2	9 400	4 781	7 723	25 597	37.3	2.81	8.8	18.1
Carter	10.5	8.1	8.4	51.9	42 919	43 610	-1.6	3.8	5 684	4 974	1 044	16 601	1.9	2.52	11.1	25.3
Cherokee	9.9	6.8	6.0	51.3	34 049	30 684	11.0	16.0	5 018	3 248	3 752	12 657	19.5	2.59	11.7	23.2
Choctaw	11.2	8.6	8.5	52.5	15 302	17 203	-11.1	-1.8	1 917	1 772	-361	5 952	-6.5	2.53	13.1	27.2
Cimarron	9.9	10.1	9.1	49.4	3 301	3 648	-9.5	-11.5	383	356	-403	1 300	-5.7	2.51	5.8	26.3
Cleveland	7.0	4.8	3.4	49.8	174 253	133 173	30.8	16.8	21 265	9 193	17 129	63 991	39.8	2.60	9.2	23.2
Coal	11.5	7.5	9.1	51.7	5 780	6 041	-4.3	6.0	760	750	357	2 279	1.3	2.51	10.3	28.5
Comanche	7.9	5.9	4.3	49.9	111 486	112 456	-0.9	-4.4	19 771	7 642	-22 248	37 569	6.9	2.72	12.1	20.4
Cotton	10.7	8.1	9.3	52.4	6 651	7 338	-9.4	-0.6	781	854	55	2 609	-7.8	2.51	9.2	25.3
Craig	11.4	8.4	8.2	51.3	14 104	15 014	-6.1	2.6	1 596	1 683	499	5 272	-3.9	2.45	8.6	27.5
Creek	9.6	7.9	6.9	51.3	60 915	59 016	3.2	11.9	8 240	5 740	4 978	22 470	7.5	2.68	9.4	20.7
Custer	8.0	6.4	7.2	50.8	26 897	25 995	3.5	-4.9	3 335	2 489	-2 111	9 918	4.6	2.55	8.9	25.4
Delaware	13.6	10.5	7.8	51.1	28 070	23 946	17.2	24.6	3 678	3 802	7 066	11 003	24.9	2.51	8.0	22.4
Dewey	10.3	8.5	10.9	51.4	5 551	5 922	-6.3	-12.5	472	877	-263	2 221	-3.6	2.46	5.9	27.6
Ellis	10.2	9.8	11.1	50.7	4 497	5 596	-19.6	-6.7	392	524	-154	1 826	-17.8	2.43	6.4	27.1
Garfield	10.0	7.9	7.9	51.9	56 735	62 820	-9.7	0.4	7 340	5 869	-1 499	22 460	-5.8	2.45	9.1	26.9
Garvin	11.2	8.7	9.8	52.0	26 605	27 856	-4.5	0.4	3 125	3 482	577	10 417	-0.9	2.47	9.6	26.0
Grady	9.3	6.1	6.3	51.4	41 747	39 490	5.7	10.4	5 327	3 993	3 085	15 544	8.7	2.64	9.5	21.6
Grant	12.0	9.4	11.5	52.2	5 689	6 518	-12.7	-7.9	511	717	-232	2 327	-12.4	2.40	5.5	27.8
Greer	11.1	8.8	11.5	46.5	6 559	7 028	-6.7	-2.6	578	980	238	2 551	-11.1	2.24	8.4	33.5
Harmon	10.2	9.3	12.4	52.0	3 793	4 519	-16.1	-12.0	431	544	-338	1 486	-15.5	2.45	8.1	31.0
Harper	12.2	9.4	12.0	50.6	4 063	4 715	-13.8	-11.9	347	545	-268	1 645	-13.6	2.42	5.4	27.5
Haskell	11.6	9.5	8.5	51.0	10 940	11 010	-0.6	4.4	1 345	1 416	593	4 319	3.1	2.51	8.5	25.4
Hughes	11.8	8.8	9.9	49.6	13 014	14 338	-9.2	8.1	1 467	1 894	1 512	5 224	-6.5	2.43	11.5	27.2
Jackson	7.7	5.6	5.8	50.8	28 764	30 356	-5.2	-1.3	5 147	2 472	-4 078	10 455	-0.2	2.65	10.3	22.4
Jefferson	11.0	9.2	11.6	52.0	7 010	8 294	-15.5	-7.0	655	1 007	-111	2 843	-10.4	2.40	8.1	29.7
Johnston	10.7	7.4	7.9	51.0	10 032	10 356	-3.1	2.8	1 168	1 244	391	3 783	-1.3	2.55	11.3	25.2
Kay	10.1	8.6	8.8	51.5	48 056	49 852	-3.6	-3.3	6 563	5 445	-2 595	19 083	-1.8	2.46	7.8	27.2
Kingfisher	9.7	8.0	8.7	51.1	13 212	14 187	-6.9	2.1	1 579	1 317	71	4 932	-4.4	2.64	7.0	23.8

1. No spouse present.

Table B. States and Counties — Vital Statistics, Health Resources, and Crime

STATE County	Births, average 1996–1998		Deaths, average 1996–1998				Physicians,[4] 1998		Hospitals,[4] 1998			Medicare enrollees 1999	Serious crimes known to police, 1998[6]	
			Number		Rate					Beds			Total	
	Total	Rate[1]	Total	Infant[2]	Total[1]	Infant[3]	Number	Rate[5]	Number	Number	Rate[5]		Number	Rate[7]
	32	33	34	35	36	37	38	39	40	41	42	43	44	45

OHIO—Cont'd

STATE County	Total	Rate	Total	Infant	Total	Infant	Number	Rate	Number	Number	Rate	Medicare	Number	Rate
Ottawa	426	10.4	403	4	9.9	8.6	47	115	1	41	100	7 839	NA	NA
Paulding	261	13.0	172	2	8.6	6.4	4	20	1	51	254	2 844	NA	NA
Perry	506	14.8	335	4	9.8	7.2	9	26	0	0	0	5 301	656	2 152
Pickaway	619	11.6	438	5	8.2	8.6	30	56	2	131	244	6 274	697	1 307
Pike	358	13.1	306	5	11.2	13.9	24	86	1	40	144	4 233	NA	NA
Portage	1 806	12.0	1 061	11	7.1	5.9	146	97	1	285	188	18 107	NA	NA
Preble	514	12.0	360	2	8.4	4.5	18	42	0	0	0	6 121	882	2 067
Putnam	484	13.8	289	3	8.2	6.2	11	31	0	0	0	5 016	NA	NA
Richland	1 685	13.2	1 248	15	9.8	8.7	175	137	3	411	323	21 022	5 657	4 419
Ross	920	12.3	696	6	9.3	6.2	107	142	1	212	281	10 758	2 953	3 919
Sandusky	845	13.5	582	4	9.3	4.7	51	82	1	130	209	8 818	NA	NA
Scioto	1 064	13.2	960	11	11.9	10.3	97	121	2	281	350	14 841	3 693	4 564
Seneca	759	12.6	538	6	8.9	7.5	51	85	2	134	223	10 978	1 166	1 939
Shelby	697	14.8	372	4	7.9	5.7	44	93	1	106	223	6 213	NA	NA
Stark	4 798	12.8	3 771	29	10.1	6.0	778	209	5	1 710	458	66 417	11 847	4 043
Summit	7 280	13.6	5 154	49	9.6	6.7	1 389	258	6	1 936	360	83 638	NA	NA
Trumbull	2 791	12.4	2 386	24	10.6	8.7	380	169	2	660	293	38 330	NA	NA
Tuscarawas	1 168	13.2	916	8	10.4	6.8	93	105	2	273	308	14 987	1 793	2 029
Union	536	13.9	286	5	7.4	9.9	32	81	1	56	142	3 800	NA	NA
Van Wert	374	12.3	309	2	10.2	5.3	17	56	1	99	328	4 453	808	2 663
Vinton	172	14.2	135	2	11.2	9.7	1	8	0	0	0	1 761	NA	NA
Warren	2 060	14.7	945	11	6.7	5.2	177	121	0	0	0	15 370	NA	NA
Washington	756	11.9	655	4	10.3	5.7	86	136	2	250	394	10 690	1 378	2 214
Wayne	1 595	14.6	928	14	8.5	8.8	129	117	2	128	116	15 471	NA	NA
Williams	486	12.8	344	4	9.1	8.2	29	76	1	78	205	5 997	528	1 569
Wood	1 342	11.3	852	10	7.2	7.5	202	169	1	98	82	14 258	3 782	3 324
Wyandot	277	12.2	242	2	10.7	6.0	9	39	1	31	136	3 904	381	2 002
OKLAHOMA	47 974	14.4	33 664	392	10.1	8.2	5 679	170	110	11 495	343	503 506	167 479	5 004
Adair	369	18.3	211	3	10.5	7.2	10	49	1	34	167	3 149	464	2 286
Alfalfa	54	8.9	83	0	13.7	6.2	1	17	0	0	0	1 367	54	884
Atoka	163	12.3	151	1	11.4	8.2	6	45	1	45	340	2 153	256	1 902
Beaver	47	7.9	67	1	11.3	28.6	3	50	1	24	396	1 007	124	2 055
Beckham	270	13.9	263	2	13.6	7.4	30	153	2	128	654	3 256	838	4 476
Blaine	142	13.4	176	1	16.6	7.0	8	76	2	97	923	2 049	308	2 882
Bryan	463	13.5	425	3	12.4	7.2	29	84	1	103	297	6 536	1 232	3 572
Caddo	396	12.9	376	4	12.2	10.9	13	42	2	87	281	5 368	935	2 996
Canadian	1 026	12.2	553	11	6.6	10.4	44	51	1	54	63	8 153	3 162	3 701
Carter	638	14.4	545	3	12.3	5.2	71	160	2	206	463	8 713	2 690	6 042
Cherokee	580	15.1	384	2	10.0	4.0	46	118	1	61	156	5 404	1 146	2 966
Choctaw	206	13.6	205	1	13.6	6.5	10	66	1	66	438	3 334	474	3 079
Cimarron	37	12.4	36	0	12.1	0.0	1	34	1	20	676	613	36	1 344
Cleveland	2 367	12.0	1 117	13	5.7	5.6	314	156	1	236	117	16 084	10 623	5 340
Coal	87	14.3	77	0	12.7	3.8	4	67	1	20	333	1 203	162	2 650
Comanche	2 075	18.2	845	19	7.4	9.3	200	176	2	339	299	12 333	6 074	5 282
Cotton	89	13.2	92	1	13.6	15.0	3	45	0	0	0	1 253	166	2 459
Craig	173	11.9	189	1	13.1	3.9	22	152	1	28	194	3 202	384	2 635
Creek	902	13.6	646	6	9.8	7.0	38	57	3	220	328	8 699	1 933	2 897
Custer	360	14.0	286	3	11.2	9.3	27	106	2	96	377	3 847	918	3 528
Delaware	436	12.9	428	3	12.7	6.9	23	67	1	62	182	5 779	824	2 410
Dewey	39	7.8	91	1	18.4	25.9	4	81	1	18	365	1 096	148	2 911
Ellis	45	10.6	55	0	12.9	0.0	6	140	1	59	1 375	956	33	774
Garfield	798	14.0	675	7	11.9	8.8	121	213	2	298	524	10 223	3 687	6 444
Garvin	334	12.4	405	2	15.0	7.0	19	70	2	75	277	5 933	889	3 261
Grady	597	13.1	468	5	10.3	8.4	45	98	1	156	340	6 186	2 121	4 630
Grant	45	8.3	79	0	14.7	0.0	2	37	0	0	0	1 183	46	844
Greer	59	9.1	103	0	16.0	0.0	7	110	1	40	628	1 419	133	2 067
Harmon	45	12.7	51	1	14.4	14.9	3	86	1	24	690	732	113	3 225
Harper	34	9.2	53	0	14.5	0.0	2	56	1	25	695	873	79	2 163
Haskell	146	12.9	153	2	13.5	11.4	6	53	1	41	361	2 469	257	2 237
Hughes	172	12.3	205	1	14.7	3.9	8	57	2	72	511	3 071	401	3 034
Jackson	529	18.2	274	1	9.4	2.5	51	177	1	103	358	3 744	1 314	4 535
Jefferson	62	9.3	120	1	18.0	16.1	4	61	1	41	623	1 626	92	1 367
Johnston	134	13.1	146	0	14.2	2.5	5	48	1	36	348	1 855	128	1 574
Kay	686	14.6	607	5	12.9	7.3	63	135	2	168	360	9 280	2 771	5 863
Kingfisher	178	13.2	146	0	10.8	1.9	9	67	1	28	207	2 380	297	2 184

1. Per 1,000 estimated resident population, average 1996–1998.   2. Deaths of infants under 1 year old.   3. Deaths of infants under 1 year old per 1,000 live births.   4. Data subject to copyright.   5. Per 100,000 resident population as of July 1 of the year shown.   6. Data for serious crimes have not been adjusted for underreporting; this may affect comparability between geographic areas and over time.   7. Per 100,000 population estimated by the FBI.

Table B. States and Counties — Crime, Education, Money Income, and Poverty

STATE County	Serious crimes known to police, 1998 (cont'd) Rate[2]		Education — School enrollment and attainment, 1990				Local government expenditures, fiscal 1997[5]		Money income — 1989				Income and poverty, 1997			
			Enrollment[3]		Attainment[4] (percent)				Per capita[6] (dollars)	Households			Percent below poverty level			
										Median						
	Violent	Property	Total	Percent private	High school graduate or more	Bachelor's degree or more	Total current expenditures (mil dol)	Current expenditures per student (dollars)		Dollars	Percent change, 1979–1989 (constant 1989 dollars)	Percent with $100,000 or more	Median household income	All persons	Persons under 18	Persons 5–17 in families
	46	47	48	49	50	51	52	53	54	55	56	57	58	59	60	61
OHIO—Cont'd																
Ottawa	NA	NA	9 302	11.3	75.9	13.5	43.8	6 516	14 144	31 360	0.8	2.2	39 823	6.9	10.2	9.4
Paulding	NA	NA	5 226	6.7	72.2	6.9	20.9	4 902	11 254	28 345	-10.4	0.9	37 556	7.7	10.3	10.2
Perry	115	2 037	7 878	8.8	68.6	5.8	33.3	4 964	9 247	21 517	-9.0	0.8	29 116	15.4	20.6	20.3
Pickaway	118	1 189	10 829	9.7	69.7	9.0	46.3	4 872	11 490	28 403	-0.2	1.1	37 886	11.3	15.3	14.5
Pike	NA	NA	5 966	4.7	60.8	8.0	32.1	5 486	8 958	19 486	-1.5	0.7	27 989	18.2	27.0	23.9
Portage	NA	NA	47 037	9.0	79.3	17.6	140.2	5 662	12 509	30 253	-3.9	2.8	40 060	8.7	11.8	10.8
Preble	141	1 926	9 843	4.8	72.5	7.0	41.3	5 064	11 466	27 582	-4.2	1.2	37 214	8.0	11.0	11.0
Putnam	NA	NA	9 150	12.3	77.5	8.8	37.4	4 842	11 943	32 492	1.9	1.1	42 741	5.5	6.6	6.5
Richland	290	4 129	29 632	12.6	73.5	11.6	136.7	6 104	12 514	27 329	-5.0	1.8	34 413	11.5	16.5	15.2
Ross	118	3 801	16 760	6.9	67.6	9.2	70.4	5 701	10 758	24 286	-9.2	1.7	33 580	14.6	19.5	18.4
Sandusky	NA	NA	15 840	13.6	76.6	10.7	67.2	5 775	12 230	29 060	-5.7	1.9	36 864	9.5	13.4	12.1
Scioto	256	4 308	20 304	4.6	63.8	8.5	82.9	5 590	9 253	17 595	-15.7	1.4	25 807	21.0	28.1	27.1
Seneca	78	1 861	16 634	20.5	75.3	10.1	54.2	5 353	11 226	26 988	-8.1	1.3	34 234	9.6	12.8	12.0
Shelby	NA	NA	11 431	8.9	72.9	11.2	44.1	4 885	13 150	30 929	5.5	2.4	40 543	7.6	10.5	9.8
Stark	512	3 531	88 455	16.0	76.0	14.3	357.0	5 426	13 003	27 852	-10.8	2.3	38 323	10.5	15.8	13.9
Summit	NA	NA	130 885	13.9	78.3	19.7	508.3	5 990	14 409	28 996	-5.9	3.5	38 774	10.9	16.8	14.5
Trumbull	NA	NA	54 893	13.3	75.2	11.4	215.6	5 742	12 899	28 186	-13.9	2.0	36 410	11.2	17.4	15.1
Tuscarawas	144	1 885	18 700	9.5	71.9	9.0	80.3	5 076	11 141	24 773	-8.0	1.4	32 877	10.2	15.2	13.5
Union	NA	NA	7 918	12.0	76.2	12.0	29.9	5 280	13 644	33 244	13.6	2.8	43 392	6.7	8.8	8.8
Van Wert	158	2 505	7 423	12.7	79.2	9.3	27.9	6 189	11 913	28 642	-4.7	1.6	37 296	6.4	8.4	8.1
Vinton	NA	NA	2 670	3.1	58.7	4.8	11.5	4 631	8 826	19 066	-4.1	1.2	26 697	18.7	25.6	25.2
Warren	NA	NA	28 785	14.6	75.5	18.0	120.1	5 131	14 615	36 728	5.5	3.9	50 152	5.6	7.4	7.1
Washington	167	2 047	15 478	15.3	77.5	13.2	58.3	5 260	11 438	24 456	-9.9	1.6	33 426	12.3	17.4	15.9
Wayne	NA	NA	26 038	17.3	73.6	13.9	114.4	5 918	12 237	29 190	-3.3	2.4	37 947	8.8	12.6	11.9
Williams	48	1 521	9 085	7.3	76.1	8.9	37.8	5 140	12 473	28 451	-3.4	2.0	37 571	6.8	9.2	8.9
Wood	112	3 212	40 718	8.3	83.8	21.9	119.0	6 389	13 853	31 197	-1.3	4.3	42 790	7.1	8.4	7.7
Wyandot	84	1 918	5 411	10.0	76.5	8.7	18.5	4 562	11 279	27 454	0.7	1.3	35 245	7.0	8.8	8.8
OKLAHOMA	539	4 465	838 811	10.0	74.6	17.8	2 990.0	4 817	11 893	23 577	-4.6	2.3	30 002	16.3	23.7	21.6
Adair	217	2 069	4 936	6.4	56.1	9.6	26.5	5 400	7 378	16 886	10.5	0.5	23 123	23.7	33.3	29.8
Alfalfa	65	819	1 416	6.9	77.3	17.3	5.3	5 558	9 999	18 407	-21.8	1.9	25 826	16.4	20.4	20.7
Atoka	52	1 850	3 085	4.2	59.8	10.2	12.3	5 298	8 308	13 898	-7.1	0.7	21 062	27.5	35.4	33.3
Beaver	66	1 989	1 470	2.6	75.3	15.4	8.3	6 487	11 910	27 372	-1.1	0.8	34 960	10.0	13.2	12.6
Beckham	160	4 316	4 911	4.0	66.5	12.3	18.2	4 664	10 400	19 154	-12.5	2.2	26 701	20.3	27.0	26.2
Blaine	271	2 611	2 716	4.1	71.2	12.4	12.3	5 374	9 787	20 395	-10.9	1.5	27 252	20.3	29.0	27.2
Bryan	319	3 253	8 532	3.1	67.3	16.9	31.2	4 683	9 082	16 610	-2.3	0.9	24 270	21.2	29.3	27.6
Caddo	279	2 717	7 355	1.6	66.2	11.6	35.7	5 367	8 735	17 857	-12.4	1.4	25 045	23.8	32.2	30.1
Canadian	321	3 380	21 552	8.3	82.3	16.7	75.0	4 294	13 077	33 855	-2.7	2.1	44 610	8.9	12.2	11.1
Carter	705	5 337	10 656	6.7	70.3	13.4	45.4	4 932	11 266	21 800	-4.7	2.1	28 017	19.2	27.2	25.4
Cherokee	158	2 808	10 522	5.9	69.9	21.1	35.5	5 111	9 446	17 513	-0.5	1.4	24 399	23.6	33.0	31.1
Choctaw	578	2 501	3 646	4.3	57.9	7.1	16.2	5 262	7 548	12 451	-17.1	0.4	19 213	29.6	40.0	38.6
Cimarron	523	821	839	4.2	71.0	15.1	4.6	6 640	9 929	19 173	-10.5	2.0	27 257	14.4	20.0	20.7
Cleveland	423	4 917	59 525	8.0	83.9	25.9	151.8	4 211	13 182	29 975	-1.8	2.5	41 085	10.9	15.2	13.3
Coal	507	2 143	1 370	3.0	60.4	9.1	6.2	5 039	7 695	14 177	-3.9	0.5	20 617	25.1	35.5	34.5
Comanche	506	4 776	30 373	6.9	81.1	18.4	110.3	4 771	10 602	24 378	5.5	1.5	31 132	17.6	25.6	24.0
Cotton	178	2 281	1 644	7.1	62.8	8.9	6.1	4 802	9 147	18 978	1.6	0.5	27 095	18.0	24.3	24.4
Craig	261	2 374	3 143	4.9	66.8	10.0	14.1	4 675	9 886	18 986	-7.1	1.2	25 754	16.2	22.3	21.0
Creek	250	2 647	15 474	7.7	68.9	10.6	59.6	4 528	10 608	23 795	-7.4	1.2	31 800	14.2	21.1	18.6
Custer	204	3 324	8 929	2.3	75.1	20.4	26.4	5 017	10 461	22 592	-5.5	1.3	30 093	17.3	22.8	22.0
Delaware	249	2 161	5 999	4.6	66.2	10.8	30.7	4 937	9 572	18 681	10.1	2.0	25 455	19.3	31.0	27.3
Dewey	138	2 773	1 287	3.8	68.2	12.1	7.7	6 515	9 726	18 968	-15.1	1.3	26 943	15.1	19.8	19.3
Ellis	70	704	1 043	1.4	73.8	14.0	5.4	6 665	10 082	20 017	-10.6	1.0	26 892	14.5	20.3	19.6
Garfield	654	5 790	13 899	14.1	76.5	17.3	50.6	4 760	11 564	23 243	-16.4	2.1	31 256	14.9	22.4	20.2
Garvin	396	2 865	5 996	4.7	63.4	10.1	26.0	4 608	9 548	18 659	-9.9	1.4	25 109	18.9	28.0	24.3
Grady	609	4 021	11 023	4.9	69.0	13.2	37.9	4 407	10 420	21 885	-5.6	1.4	31 241	16.8	23.4	21.8
Grant	37	807	1 239	5.6	77.9	15.6	6.4	5 611	11 255	21 659	-7.9	2.3	28 870	14.3	19.7	19.8
Greer	249	1 818	1 204	6.0	64.7	10.0	5.7	5 616	9 089	17 010	4.5	1.4	23 992	27.1	37.1	34.7
Harmon	314	2 911	877	1.4	58.0	10.5	4.2	5 495	7 817	13 880	-10.8	0.6	20 799	31.5	43.8	44.3
Harper	137	2 026	895	2.1	76.1	13.6	4.6	5 800	11 752	22 813	-17.9	2.0	32 818	9.5	12.8	12.6
Haskell	339	1 898	2 638	2.1	56.4	7.7	10.8	4 977	8 320	15 592	-4.0	1.3	22 419	23.2	32.8	30.6
Hughes	461	2 573	2 946	3.5	58.7	7.7	14.2	5 336	8 849	15 168	1.2	0.7	21 394	25.5	34.1	31.6
Jackson	338	4 197	7 871	2.7	74.1	16.5	28.8	4 503	10 224	21 715	8.8	1.5	30 330	16.8	23.2	23.5
Jefferson	193	1 174	1 485	2.1	58.7	6.6	7.2	5 045	8 430	15 553	-8.9	0.7	22 347	22.4	31.5	29.4
Johnston	164	1 071	2 915	2.2	61.0	9.3	11.2	5 306	7 821	15 264	12.6	1.0	21 713	24.2	33.0	31.7
Kay	415	5 448	11 494	7.9	76.8	18.5	41.6	4 538	12 394	24 295	-6.4	2.0	31 732	14.6	22.1	19.8
Kingfisher	88	2 096	3 355	7.8	76.2	13.4	16.0	5 090	11 141	25 367	-10.5	1.3	34 556	11.6	15.8	15.0

1. Data for serious crimes have not been adjusted for underreporting; this may affect comparability between geographic areas and over time.   2. Per 100,000 population estimated by the FBI.   3. All persons 3 years old and over enrolled in nursery school through college.   4. Persons 25 years old and over.   5. Elementary and secondary education expenditures, local government fiscal years ending between July 1, 1996 and June 30, 1997.   6. Based on population enumerated as of April 1, 1990.

STATE County	Personal income, 1998												
			Per capita[1]					Transfer payments					
									Government payments to individuals				
	Total (mil dol)	Percent change, 1997–1998	Dollars	Rank	Wages and salaries[2] (mil dol)	Proprietor's income (mil dol)	Dividends, interest, and rent (mil dol)	Total (mil dol)	Total (mil dol)	Social Security (mil dol)	Medical payments (mil dol)	Income mainte- nance (mil dol)	Unemploy- ment insurance (mil dol)
	62	63	64	65	66	67	68	69	70	71	72	73	74
OHIO—Cont'd													
Ottawa	1 076	4.2	26 242	371	473	56	221	175	166	77	67	6	4
Paulding	396	-0.6	19 703	1 812	146	20	62	62	58	30	19	4	1
Perry	541	4.4	15 821	2 823	193	28	72	129	122	48	49	13	3
Pickaway	1 054	4.3	19 777	1 787	567	49	161	149	138	61	48	13	3
Pike	495	4.5	17 836	2 395	377	28	89	124	118	40	49	17	4
Portage	3 522	5.1	23 350	781	1 739	179	587	457	426	187	156	27	8
Preble	935	5.2	21 681	1 199	324	62	138	139	130	62	48	7	2
Putnam	840	2.4	23 820	677	330	62	168	105	97	48	34	5	2
Richland	2 833	3.2	21 846	1 146	1 937	146	496	486	460	208	165	37	10
Ross	1 475	4.6	19 557	1 868	908	74	231	252	237	94	86	28	6
Sandusky	1 404	3.6	22 615	948	858	71	243	222	210	98	77	12	6
Scioto	1 468	2.9	18 178	2 302	680	84	225	418	402	125	171	60	9
Seneca	1 262	2.3	21 036	1 378	675	67	230	243	231	96	101	13	5
Shelby	1 199	5.0	25 209	469	1 025	60	202	144	134	66	46	9	3
Stark	9 287	5.3	24 898	500	5 611	486	1 804	1 473	1 397	635	525	104	21
Summit	15 008	4.7	27 940	239	9 572	631	2 886	2 159	2 049	867	806	183	32
Trumbull	5 492	2.2	24 264	598	3 516	284	993	971	925	412	363	71	18
Tuscarawas	1 846	5.1	20 845	1 441	993	147	340	316	298	144	101	21	7
Union	925	6.4	23 191	820	1 143	51	133	97	89	41	32	6	1
Van Wert	663	3.2	22 025	1 096	357	43	127	97	90	51	26	4	1
Vinton	194	4.9	15 916	2 805	62	9	34	47	45	15	18	7	1
Warren	3 957	9.9	27 097	296	1 663	166	551	397	367	164	137	18	6
Washington	1 367	3.5	21 586	1 229	767	96	244	245	232	102	88	19	5
Wayne	2 542	5.5	23 079	842	1 509	224	495	350	328	150	127	21	4
Williams	925	3.4	24 428	571	589	54	178	129	121	57	45	6	2
Wood	3 064	3.9	25 624	424	1 841	150	605	346	321	143	112	16	5
Wyandot	498	3.3	21 817	1 155	277	39	91	79	75	36	28	4	2
OKLAHOMA	73 350	5.0	21 964	X	43 371	7 725	13 005	11 445	10 867	4 769	3 911	1 041	112
Adair	320	6.1	15 678	2 855	115	40	38	75	72	24	29	11	0
Alfalfa	108	-0.4	17 904	2 378	34	24	27	24	23	13	8	1	0
Atoka	191	5.3	14 343	2 979	74	30	30	50	48	18	18	7	0
Beaver	117	4.7	19 431	1 913	40	18	28	19	18	9	6	1	0
Beckham	323	3.1	16 184	2 766	154	31	79	71	67	30	25	7	1
Blaine	205	4.4	19 706	1 810	78	29	52	44	42	19	16	5	0
Bryan	620	5.8	17 848	2 392	278	45	93	144	138	56	51	15	0
Caddo	501	4.6	16 215	2 760	215	52	110	112	107	44	38	15	1
Canadian	1 872	6.2	21 917	1 122	672	104	276	215	201	84	63	11	2
Carter	947	3.7	21 344	1 284	558	139	183	183	175	79	65	18	2
Cherokee	643	6.0	16 480	2 710	276	70	98	147	140	49	50	16	1
Choctaw	230	2.8	15 237	2 907	86	17	36	74	72	26	27	12	1
Cimarron	63	7.3	21 098	1 354	23	13	17	11	10	6	3	1	0
Cleveland	4 261	6.4	21 203	1 328	1 511	207	587	440	405	186	122	30	5
Coal	81	0.1	13 386	3 052	28	4	14	26	25	9	10	3	0
Comanche	2 299	4.0	21 257	1 305	1 631	116	343	323	306	111	93	42	2
Cotton	119	2.1	17 924	2 370	25	15	22	25	24	11	9	2	0
Craig	260	4.6	18 008	2 340	166	13	48	68	65	25	31	5	0
Creek	1 165	4.2	17 358	2 513	486	77	187	218	207	98	71	17	2
Custer	489	3.1	19 140	2 006	264	45	120	89	85	36	30	8	1
Delaware	609	5.3	17 753	2 419	161	62	117	132	126	59	43	12	1
Dewey	95	4.5	19 306	1 952	33	15	26	20	19	9	8	1	0
Ellis	82	4.7	19 335	1 940	24	13	25	17	16	8	6	1	0
Garfield	1 294	3.4	22 720	917	720	111	265	254	245	100	113	15	2
Garvin	525	3.0	19 590	1 861	214	47	107	163	159	53	87	10	1
Grady	782	4.3	17 078	2 593	325	65	136	138	130	61	41	15	2
Grant	119	0.7	22 204	1 037	38	22	34	23	22	11	8	1	0
Greer	125	3.6	19 704	1 811	45	14	21	30	29	12	12	3	0
Harmon	62	3.7	17 736	2 428	20	11	11	17	17	6	7	2	0
Harper	85	-4.1	23 708	701	25	17	26	15	14	8	5	1	0
Haskell	182	2.7	16 009	2 793	64	15	35	52	50	20	18	6	1
Hughes	204	-1.5	14 499	2 969	59	21	41	63	61	25	24	7	1
Jackson	562	4.9	19 700	1 817	385	39	102	95	90	33	35	11	1
Jefferson	116	-2.8	17 630	2 457	43	13	23	32	31	13	12	3	0
Johnston	145	3.8	14 046	3 002	69	11	22	43	41	16	14	6	0
Kay	1 037	2.3	22 273	1 022	620	105	232	175	167	91	51	11	2
Kingfisher	293	2.7	21 715	1 187	158	32	68	46	43	22	16	3	0

1. Based on the resident population estimated as of July 1 of the year shown.   2. Includes other labor income.

Table B. States and Counties — Earnings, Social Security, and Housing

STATE County	Earnings, 1998									Social Security beneficiaries, December 1998			Housing units, 1990	
						Percent by selected industries								
			Goods-related[1]		Service-related and other[2]									
	Total (mil dol)	Farm	Total	Manufacturing	Total	Retail trade	Finance, insurance, and real estate	Services	Government	Number	Rate[3]	Supplemental Security Income recipients, December 1998	Total	Percent change, 1980–1990
	75	76	77	78	79	80	81	82	83	84	85	86	87	88
OHIO—Cont'd														
Ottawa	529	0.9	31.9	24.6	51.6	11.2	3.5	16.5	15.6	8 607	210	291	23 340	1.2
Paulding	165	1.8	D	34.8	D	8.5	2.3	11.2	22.1	3 440	171	318	7 951	4.2
Perry	221	1.6	40.9	26.1	35.7	7.6	2.6	14.9	21.8	5 981	174	912	12 260	6.9
Pickaway	615	1.0	D	39.4	D	7.9	2.6	9.9	26.7	7 391	138	893	16 385	8.3
Pike	405	-0.4	D	57.6	D	7.5	1.2	11.3	13.5	5 326	192	1 520	9 722	11.6
Portage	1 918	0.5	36.8	29.8	36.6	8.8	2.5	15.2	26.1	20 935	138	1 811	52 299	10.0
Preble	386	3.1	D	37.1	D	9.1	2.8	14.4	16.4	7 263	168	438	15 174	8.7
Putnam	392	4.1	D	40.6	D	8.4	D	10.9	14.0	5 510	156	274	11 600	5.5
Richland	2 083	0.6	D	34.5	D	9.8	3.7	19.7	14.7	23 661	186	2 679	50 350	2.4
Ross	983	0.4	D	28.8	D	10.9	2.3	17.3	26.9	11 716	155	2 700	26 173	10.2
Sandusky	929	1.3	49.4	43.7	D	8.5	2.8	18.2	12.7	11 085	178	825	23 753	2.4
Scioto	764	0.0	20.8	14.0	54.1	12.9	3.6	27.8	25.1	16 140	201	5 656	32 408	2.3
Seneca	742	0.1	D	38.3	D	8.8	3.1	18.7	14.3	11 104	185	997	22 473	1.0
Shelby	1 086	1.5	65.1	59.3	24.9	4.2	1.4	11.5	8.4	7 468	157	575	16 509	7.9
Stark	6 097	0.3	39.6	32.2	48.7	10.6	4.6	22.9	11.4	70 461	189	6 860	146 910	2.6
Summit	10 203	0.0	31.6	25.9	55.8	9.7	5.4	25.7	12.7	94 992	177	11 353	211 477	5.5
Trumbull	3 800	0.0	54.1	50.3	35.6	8.9	3.0	15.9	10.3	45 254	201	4 717	90 533	2.6
Tuscarawas	1 141	2.1	39.6	31.2	44.7	11.9	3.4	18.2	13.6	16 579	187	1 483	33 982	5.4
Union	1 194	0.8	D	68.6	D	3.5	D	7.7	8.1	4 806	122	344	11 599	9.2
Van Wert	400	1.3	D	46.4	D	8.0	6.1	15.5	11.0	5 825	193	329	11 998	3.2
Vinton	71	-0.8	D	D	D	7.9	5.6	12.9	30.1	1 996	164	505	4 856	10.3
Warren	1 829	0.0	34.9	27.3	50.9	13.6	7.1	19.6	14.1	18 289	125	1 220	40 636	22.1
Washington	863	0.6	38.4	28.4	47.7	9.7	3.7	23.3	13.3	12 113	191	1 709	25 752	7.5
Wayne	1 733	3.8	46.6	38.2	35.6	8.7	4.1	14.0	14.0	16 951	154	1 402	37 036	7.9
Williams	643	0.8	D	51.3	D	6.4	3.1	15.0	10.6	6 576	173	381	14 745	5.7
Wood	1 991	1.3	38.8	32.3	39.3	7.7	3.2	15.6	20.7	15 989	134	981	41 760	10.7
Wyandot	316	2.3	53.7	42.2	31.8	7.0	2.6	9.8	12.2	4 172	183	269	8 596	3.6
OKLAHOMA	51 096	1.3	25.9	16.0	52.3	9.4	5.3	24.0	20.5	584 643	175	73 365	1 406 499	13.7
Adair	155	16.6	D	32.4	D	7.4	1.9	11.9	21.2	3 713	182	973	7 124	7.5
Alfalfa	58	31.8	7.3	2.4	D	7.8	3.8	10.7	23.8	1 512	250	69	3 357	3.2
Atoka	104	1.1	D	15.9	D	13.1	2.4	10.9	35.0	2 697	204	627	5 110	10.5
Beaver	58	16.7	25.5	5.0	D	4.8	2.7	7.3	23.9	1 130	187	48	2 923	5.5
Beckham	185	1.5	23.8	4.3	59.4	16.5	4.5	28.6	15.3	3 966	203	581	9 117	11.0
Blaine	107	16.1	26.9	19.7	32.9	7.7	3.8	13.9	24.2	2 499	238	225	5 729	-2.4
Bryan	323	-0.4	D	11.8	D	11.3	3.5	34.2	21.9	7 508	216	1 369	14 875	11.6
Caddo	268	10.4	D	2.9	D	7.6	3.9	20.2	26.2	5 980	193	908	13 191	6.2
Canadian	776	1.0	41.5	30.8	35.3	9.7	3.1	15.3	22.2	10 071	118	519	28 560	38.1
Carter	697	-0.6	41.6	19.2	47.1	11.9	3.3	21.5	11.8	9 610	216	1 518	19 201	7.6
Cherokee	346	11.8	D	1.0	D	11.2	2.9	26.5	36.1	6 626	169	1 072	15 935	24.9
Choctaw	104	1.8	D	1.9	56.4	14.1	3.0	22.3	27.7	3 776	250	1 118	6 844	-5.2
Cimarron	36	38.1	D	1.6	D	9.3	3.3	7.5	25.9	721	244	37	1 690	6.2
Cleveland	1 718	-0.2	16.6	8.1	48.0	13.2	4.8	23.3	35.6	22 274	111	1 960	71 038	43.4
Coal	32	-8.7	D	D	D	10.6	D	25.1	31.4	1 338	223	283	2 725	8.2
Comanche	1 747	0.4	D	10.0	D	7.3	2.8	13.2	57.6	14 701	130	2 125	43 589	9.1
Cotton	40	25.0	D	2.5	D	7.9	3.8	15.3	27.7	1 420	212	142	3 152	-0.3
Craig	179	-1.2	D	18.0	D	9.4	3.5	16.2	33.1	3 189	221	511	6 041	-0.5
Creek	563	-0.8	41.4	29.7	44.1	8.4	3.6	17.8	15.3	11 834	176	1 005	25 143	11.0
Custer	309	3.2	22.0	13.5	48.5	11.8	4.3	19.9	26.2	4 390	172	541	11 636	11.5
Delaware	222	14.7	21.3	12.6	46.1	12.8	4.9	24.6	18.0	7 616	223	866	16 808	57.8
Dewey	47	13.6	D	5.5	D	6.8	4.5	13.3	29.6	1 192	242	93	2 733	1.9
Ellis	37	23.3	D	2.1	D	11.5	D	13.0	35.6	1 043	243	40	2 449	-0.6
Garfield	831	2.5	19.6	8.2	54.0	10.0	4.0	23.6	23.9	11 538	203	1 180	26 502	3.6
Garvin	261	-1.0	33.3	12.5	41.8	11.4	3.8	12.3	25.8	6 712	248	942	11 932	4.9
Grady	390	3.3	35.0	25.9	42.2	9.6	3.3	18.6	19.6	7 735	168	954	17 788	12.9
Grant	60	28.5	11.4	1.7	D	3.5	4.8	D	17.4	1 299	243	77	2 955	-0.9
Greer	59	16.8	4.8	3.2	D	5.5	2.8	12.3	43.4	1 615	254	232	3 126	-5.4
Harmon	31	23.9	D	6.9	D	8.3	5.2	7.9	30.4	857	246	159	1 793	-8.2
Harper	43	27.8	15.6	1.6	D	6.7	4.3	12.2	26.8	982	273	43	2 077	-2.9
Haskell	79	5.1	18.3	4.0	48.2	12.8	2.3	21.8	28.3	2 787	245	508	5 138	8.2
Hughes	80	10.2	10.0	1.5	46.3	12.9	3.2	18.7	33.4	3 464	246	539	6 021	-4.5
Jackson	424	5.2	D	6.6	D	8.2	3.0	12.1	56.8	4 349	151	716	12 125	3.3
Jefferson	56	8.2	D	19.3	42.2	13.9	4.5	13.4	23.6	1 817	276	237	3 522	-4.4
Johnston	79	3.6	D	D	D	6.9	0.9	12.8	29.0	2 303	223	387	4 478	3.3
Kay	725	1.3	D	27.1	D	10.2	2.7	D	11.8	10 462	224	794	22 456	5.6
Kingfisher	190	8.3	25.1	7.5	54.4	8.2	3.5	14.8	12.2	2 709	200	164	5 791	2.2

1. Covers mining, construction, and manufacturing; finance, insurance, and real estate; and services. 2. Covers private sector earnings in agricultural services, forestry, and fisheries; transportation and public utilities; wholesale trade; retail trade; finance, insurance, and real estate; and services. 3. Per 1,000 resident population estimated as of July 1 of the year shown.

Table B. States and Counties — Housing, Labor Force, and Employment

	Housing units, 1990 (cont'd)								Civilian labor force, 1999				Civilian employment, 1990[5]		
STATE County	Occupied units										Unemployment		Percent		
		Owner-occupied				Renter-occupied									
				Owner cost as a percent of income											
	Total	Percent	Median value[1]	With a mortgage	Without a mortgage	Median rent[2]	Rent as percent of income	Substandard units[3] (percent)	Total	Percent change, 1998–1999	Total	Rate[4]	Total	Professional, managerial, and technical	Precision production, craft, and repair
	89	90	91	92	93	94	95	96	97	98	99	100	101	102	103

OHIO—Cont'd

Ottawa	15 170	78.3	68 600	16.8	12.5	379	22.8	1.9	20 581	0.2	1 335	6.5	18 274	24.7	15.3
Paulding	7 252	83.2	42 500	15.1	12.3	295	20.2	3.0	9 948	-0.7	449	4.5	8 936	16.0	13.7
Perry	11 264	78.1	36 900	17.9	12.7	290	25.7	4.5	14 669	3.0	1 182	8.1	12 179	17.7	15.3
Pickaway	15 602	71.7	62 200	17.4	11.9	357	23.4	2.8	24 973	2.5	803	3.2	19 787	20.9	15.0
Pike	8 805	69.4	42 300	17.5	12.9	297	30.9	7.6	11 630	-0.7	990	8.5	8 019	22.5	15.6
Portage	49 229	70.1	69 200	19.1	12.1	407	27.7	2.1	82 993	0.9	3 302	4.0	68 974	25.7	13.5
Preble	14 347	77.1	52 700	18.2	12.6	329	21.6	2.1	21 120	-3.1	865	4.1	17 968	18.5	16.4
Putnam	11 082	84.3	58 000	15.6	11.9	326	18.5	1.9	20 651	1.8	764	3.7	15 648	19.2	16.5
Richland	47 573	70.8	52 200	16.5	12.3	343	24.0	1.9	62 120	1.9	3 991	6.4	56 207	22.6	14.6
Ross	24 325	70.5	49 200	17.7	12.7	317	25.5	4.3	34 657	-1.4	1 767	5.1	26 080	23.1	12.8
Sandusky	22 464	74.5	57 200	16.2	12.3	365	23.1	1.9	32 518	1.3	1 716	5.3	27 857	19.7	17.0
Scioto	29 786	69.7	37 100	17.8	13.1	281	30.1	4.1	32 897	0.1	2 806	8.5	25 320	26.4	12.3
Seneca	21 277	74.0	47 700	16.3	11.8	322	22.9	2.1	28 667	-1.2	1 518	5.3	26 213	20.4	14.4
Shelby	15 626	74.3	59 900	16.6	11.8	369	22.6	2.6	27 922	-1.6	1 145	4.1	21 474	22.6	14.0
Stark	139 573	70.1	57 700	16.9	12.1	356	24.5	1.5	188 553	0.5	8 419	4.5	164 452	27.0	11.2
Summit	199 998	68.7	61 900	18.8	12.7	394	26.5	1.4	281 068	1.7	11 897	4.2	236 637	30.9	11.2
Trumbull	86 056	73.1	53 300	16.6	12.3	346	24.4	1.7	111 506	-0.7	5 918	5.3	98 808	22.8	13.4
Tuscarawas	31 971	75.0	49 900	17.9	12.0	311	24.7	1.7	44 270	0.4	2 280	5.2	35 842	19.9	13.0
Union	11 037	74.4	67 400	18.4	12.8	395	23.6	1.9	17 836	0.2	509	2.9	15 129	23.0	13.3
Van Wert	11 266	80.6	46 000	15.8	11.6	325	21.1	1.4	16 580	2.1	599	3.6	14 390	19.1	12.4
Vinton	4 069	80.4	34 900	19.2	13.2	267	26.7	9.7	3 734	-1.8	437	11.7	3 820	15.2	14.8
Warren	39 150	74.7	77 600	19.1	11.8	434	23.7	2.2	77 431	4.6	2 327	3.0	55 033	29.2	12.3
Washington	23 636	74.5	51 900	16.8	11.9	300	24.2	2.4	32 493	0.0	1 915	5.9	27 251	27.0	12.7
Wayne	35 619	71.2	65 700	18.9	11.6	367	23.4	2.8	57 460	1.3	2 030	3.5	47 862	22.5	12.6
Williams	13 807	77.0	48 200	16.2	11.8	327	22.5	1.7	20 930	-0.6	952	4.5	18 115	17.1	16.7
Wood	39 677	69.9	72 200	17.7	12.2	395	25.3	1.9	67 085	2.4	2 336	3.5	55 716	30.6	10.9
Wyandot	8 168	75.7	46 600	16.7	11.8	293	20.6	1.7	12 513	1.4	568	4.5	10 371	19.3	14.9
OKLAHOMA	1 206 135	68.1	48 100	20.0	12.8	340	25.4	3.7	1 647 638	1.3	56 693	3.4	1 369 138	27.9	12.0
Adair	6 386	73.0	30 200	18.7	13.0	226	26.2	7.8	8 815	-5.4	490	5.6	7 030	17.6	13.5
Alfalfa	2 469	81.1	23 900	18.4	13.1	239	16.7	1.3	2 500	-0.6	43	1.7	2 649	18.5	7.9
Atoka	4 495	75.0	30 300	21.2	13.9	230	29.7	4.8	4 866	0.3	170	3.5	4 332	19.1	8.7
Beaver	2 327	77.7	47 800	18.7	11.6	288	18.5	3.6	2 564	-11.8	93	3.6	2 857	21.8	14.4
Beckham	7 351	69.8	31 200	19.3	13.8	272	22.8	3.5	9 725	0.7	456	4.7	7 571	25.1	12.9
Blaine	4 418	76.1	34 000	20.3	13.4	272	22.2	3.8	4 535	-3.5	160	3.5	4 732	18.1	13.1
Bryan	12 524	69.7	36 000	19.9	12.7	278	29.3	3.8	16 874	3.9	354	2.1	12 530	24.8	11.3
Caddo	10 879	72.6	31 400	20.6	14.1	259	25.5	4.2	13 034	3.4	510	3.9	10 629	21.1	11.8
Canadian	25 597	76.5	58 100	20.3	12.4	415	24.0	3.0	46 467	3.5	898	1.9	36 215	28.2	11.9
Carter	16 601	72.4	38 100	19.8	13.0	311	24.7	3.2	20 308	-1.1	1 008	5.0	17 541	24.8	12.5
Cherokee	12 657	68.2	43 300	20.5	13.5	291	32.1	5.5	18 404	5.5	600	3.3	13 245	27.9	10.7
Choctaw	5 952	72.3	30 900	22.0	14.4	197	26.4	4.9	5 416	-2.3	338	6.2	5 086	17.7	12.1
Cimarron	1 300	74.5	29 000	15.0	12.8	226	20.9	2.9	1 747	-2.1	38	2.2	1 566	14.0	5.7
Cleveland	63 991	63.1	61 800	20.5	12.2	383	26.5	2.9	112 651	4.2	2 338	2.1	87 247	33.5	10.9
Coal	2 279	73.7	25 100	23.1	14.1	226	27.0	5.9	2 526	-0.5	159	6.3	2 114	20.8	14.0
Comanche	37 569	60.2	54 000	21.3	12.3	377	25.7	4.8	41 120	-0.2	1 491	3.6	37 640	31.0	8.9
Cotton	2 609	77.0	32 800	18.4	12.5	279	24.6	3.9	2 103	-9.3	94	4.5	2 465	19.2	14.5
Craig	5 272	75.5	33 000	20.2	12.2	288	27.0	3.5	6 590	-3.4	173	2.6	5 830	19.6	12.8
Creek	22 470	77.6	44 500	20.8	12.7	320	25.8	3.7	33 362	0.6	1 188	3.6	26 546	21.6	16.0
Custer	9 918	63.5	46 900	17.4	12.6	307	26.0	3.7	11 736	-5.3	388	3.3	12 369	25.7	12.1
Delaware	11 003	79.1	44 500	22.5	12.7	302	27.2	5.0	17 189	2.9	625	3.6	10 664	21.9	14.2
Dewey	2 221	80.9	27 900	15.6	13.0	229	22.2	2.3	1 974	-6.0	77	3.9	2 180	17.8	12.6
Ellis	1 826	80.3	29 800	17.5	12.6	291	16.3	3.0	1 620	-1.9	71	4.4	2 034	20.4	12.9
Garfield	22 460	69.1	38 000	19.9	12.3	339	24.0	2.0	27 386	-1.6	827	3.0	24 402	24.7	12.5
Garvin	10 417	74.4	32 800	20.9	13.4	300	25.6	3.4	11 189	-2.2	647	5.8	10 349	19.6	15.9
Grady	15 544	75.8	42 000	20.2	12.7	309	26.1	2.8	19 237	-5.9	834	4.3	17 571	21.8	13.9
Grant	2 327	80.2	26 100	16.9	12.4	280	19.7	1.7	2 174	-9.4	57	2.6	2 384	21.4	11.4
Greer	2 551	75.6	21 800	21.6	13.6	238	28.2	3.9	2 483	-4.0	75	3.0	2 224	20.5	9.1
Harmon	1 486	75.2	22 800	23.9	14.9	176	22.4	5.8	1 247	-8.2	42	3.4	1 266	18.5	10.6
Harper	1 645	79.0	29 100	16.0	12.7	274	17.5	1.9	1 716	-0.9	53	3.1	1 890	21.1	13.3
Haskell	4 319	78.0	31 300	18.4	13.1	247	27.2	6.4	4 929	1.3	334	6.8	3 652	17.7	14.8
Hughes	5 224	77.1	21 000	21.9	14.4	245	29.9	4.5	5 323	-2.5	395	7.4	4 496	18.3	14.3
Jackson	10 455	60.8	43 800	20.5	12.7	357	23.9	4.9	12 839	1.1	417	3.2	9 572	28.5	9.1
Jefferson	2 843	73.4	22 800	21.0	14.3	209	24.1	3.7	3 180	-0.9	111	3.5	2 612	17.1	14.7
Johnston	3 783	73.1	28 600	21.5	14.1	247	30.8	5.0	4 918	5.1	195	4.0	3 526	20.3	11.9
Kay	19 083	72.9	42 600	17.5	12.2	327	24.4	2.4	21 835	-3.1	1 433	6.6	21 246	28.1	13.6
Kingfisher	4 932	79.2	47 900	21.2	13.1	319	21.5	4.5	6 701	-4.5	174	2.6	5 967	22.5	14.0

1. Specified owner-occupied units.   2. Specified renter-occupied units.   3. Overcrowded or lacking complete plumbing facilities.   4. Percent of civilian labor force.   5. Persons 16 years and older.

Table B. States and Counties — Nonfarm Employment and Agriculture

STATE County	Number of establishments	Total	Health Care and Social Assistance	Manufacturing	Retail trade	Finance and Insurance	Professional Scientific and Technical Services	Total (mil dol)	Average per employee (dollars)	Number	Less than 50 acres	500 acres and over	Whose principal occupation is farming (percent)
	104	105	106	107	108	109	110	111	112	113	114	115	116
OHIO—Cont'd													
Ottawa	1 146	11 942	1 100	2 927	1 609	309	D	315	26 375	474	31.4	12.4	38.6
Paulding	338	4 205	539	1 666	567	114	76	94	22 292	542	21.2	26.6	49.8
Perry	489	5 007	839	1 730	714	172	123	110	21 900	606	25.1	5.0	38.1
Pickaway	839	12 124	1 669	4 589	1 720	326	245	332	27 370	703	31.4	21.5	56.5
Pike	455	9 775	1 105	5 098	1 542	181	46	273	27 958	435	19.8	6.2	38.6
Portage	3 043	41 767	3 127	13 001	5 713	1 214	863	1 080	25 849	719	45.9	4.0	42.6
Preble	723	9 179	689	3 263	1 439	221	165	218	23 757	977	35.9	10.4	44.7
Putnam	732	10 210	915	4 377	1 249	297	126	243	23 803	1 352	23.1	10.3	40.3
Richland	3 061	53 050	6 526	15 214	8 451	1 217	1 062	1 323	24 936	908	28.6	7.0	48.3
Ross	1 364	22 006	4 118	5 150	3 674	427	478	605	27 476	885	25.2	13.1	42.1
Sandusky	1 444	24 249	2 539	10 395	2 965	536	442	606	24 989	795	30.3	14.1	46.9
Scioto	1 496	18 044	5 003	2 023	3 709	670	444	352	19 527	630	28.4	5.6	35.1
Seneca	1 381	20 758	2 443	6 674	2 528	507	280	485	23 341	1 210	24.0	13.7	45.3
Shelby	1 030	23 816	1 751	12 635	1 977	317	385	769	32 289	991	27.7	10.3	43.6
Stark	9 362	161 496	23 933	41 001	23 494	5 567	4 011	4 206	26 044	1 086	45.5	4.7	43.8
Summit	14 385	246 220	33 071	41 679	32 687	8 929	10 954	7 687	31 220	251	64.5	1.2	41.0
Trumbull	4 776	87 887	10 052	33 041	13 016	2 262	1 893	2 591	29 479	788	33.0	4.2	45.1
Tuscarawas	2 379	32 534	3 887	10 069	5 160	734	628	741	22 784	920	28.2	5.3	46.8
Union	788	19 557	1 128	9 027	1 359	197	1 220	862	44 096	811	31.8	14.5	46.1
Van Wert	643	11 157	1 362	4 738	1 346	713	147	274	24 519	707	21.9	23.9	57.1
Vinton	150	1 715	249	D	192	D	D	40	23 077	202	19.3	4.5	30.2
Warren	2 806	52 958	3 822	13 326	6 751	2 607	2 603	1 479	27 920	741	49.7	6.7	39.3
Washington	1 565	22 160	2 865	5 376	3 044	743	486	562	25 364	900	19.6	4.0	38.8
Wayne	2 570	43 616	4 007	16 258	5 252	1 456	801	1 175	26 946	1 601	35.5	5.8	58.7
Williams	921	17 476	1 637	9 007	1 592	495	321	442	25 314	908	25.7	10.9	39.4
Wood	2 656	46 724	3 449	13 538	5 952	839	1 999	1 346	28 809	1 015	27.1	19.8	51.0
Wyandot	568	9 276	785	4 934	812	233	87	210	22 586	608	24.2	22.0	52.1
OKLAHOMA	84 881	1 167 709	171 498	168 140	165 852	57 364	49 645	28 667	24 550	74 214	20.5	21.6	44.5
Adair	209	3 027	414	1 548	488	99	D	58	19 143	1 090	26.0	8.4	43.7
Alfalfa	145	860	204	D	133	64	D	13	15 312	709	8.9	43.4	62.1
Atoka	227	2 072	492	332	479	70	D	33	15 788	1 087	16.7	15.5	42.2
Beaver	169	919	76	61	115	D	28	19	20 753	738	3.9	56.9	56.1
Beckham	625	5 558	1 192	120	1 121	233	135	94	16 840	825	14.4	34.8	46.5
Blaine	304	2 665	854	588	330	128	45	48	17 875	841	8.2	39.4	52.6
Bryan	613	9 253	1 511	1 080	1 404	409	191	174	18 773	1 516	20.0	14.2	39.9
Caddo	536	4 409	783	314	944	241	112	87	19 835	1 496	11.8	29.4	53.5
Canadian	1 586	17 871	1 480	2 824	2 947	487	406	368	20 577	1 165	25.2	26.0	50.0
Carter	1 363	16 627	2 813	2 710	2 658	555	313	364	21 905	1 165	22.1	15.0	33.6
Cherokee	671	6 403	1 734	153	1 698	251	176	106	16 596	1 154	27.5	7.5	39.0
Choctaw	274	2 946	718	220	558	102	47	43	14 624	991	17.7	18.9	44.2
Cimarron	96	500	D	0	109	D	13	8	15 466	481	3.1	66.3	66.5
Cleveland	4 097	44 316	6 826	3 802	8 386	1 431	2 074	916	20 660	1 017	42.4	7.4	35.0
Coal	63	859	247	D	138	D	D	14	16 062	586	13.0	26.8	48.0
Comanche	2 149	27 604	5 158	D	5 182	1 383	1 229	568	20 578	512	18.2	25.2	44.3
Cotton	95	539	146	D	120	D	14	6	11 408	512	8.8	36.5	54.7
Craig	381	5 200	1 565	906	601	159	82	106	20 448	1 120	18.3	17.3	42.2
Creek	1 240	15 256	2 199	4 275	1 857	522	332	334	21 907	1 475	32.7	10.4	30.6
Custer	822	7 922	1 416	1 171	1 531	368	304	146	18 378	788	10.3	41.9	58.8
Delaware	645	5 443	1 306	688	1 138	280	149	92	16 937	1 303	24.2	8.6	45.0
Dewey	124	766	87	D	198	72	D	16	20 796	713	6.2	43.3	54.1
Ellis	120	717	250	D	157	D	D	13	18 431	622	5.1	50.0	52.1
Garfield	1 669	20 739	3 850	1 396	3 495	686	1 563	433	20 858	1 069	13.5	35.3	55.1
Garvin	635	6 366	1 232	1 410	1 088	202	99	124	19 510	1 380	19.9	18.3	45.4
Grady	935	10 740	1 588	2 872	1 441	371	247	218	20 311	1 625	20.6	19.5	46.6
Grant	142	784	D	D	D	72	18	19	23 953	688	4.5	50.9	63.8
Greer	121	871	229	D	139	57	12	15	16 746	478	7.3	38.3	53.6
Harmon	82	513	90	D	177	D	15	8	15 969	338	5.6	48.5	55.0
Harper	117	534	126	D	91	D	28	9	16 809	443	5.6	56.7	55.8
Haskell	210	2 073	691	93	420	D	37	33	15 845	872	17.3	15.7	46.6
Hughes	235	2 043	446	70	403	D	D	31	15 237	897	11.5	17.9	44.0
Jackson	570	7 660	1 512	1 118	1 459	312	564	144	18 781	723	16.0	34.3	50.1
Jefferson	142	1 140	301	280	150	74	28	17	14 815	499	11.4	36.9	54.3
Johnston	154	2 061	441	773	194	D	12	44	21 563	624	20.0	21.3	38.0
Kay	1 286	18 153	1 714	4 397	2 660	531	1 111	429	23 624	929	18.5	32.2	55.8
Kingfisher	424	4 591	557	376	610	288	88	101	21 983	998	12.0	34.7	55.1

STATE County	Land in farms Acreage (1,000) [117]	Percent change, 1992–1997 [118]	Acres Average size of farm [119]	Total irrigated (1,000) [120]	Total cropland (1,000) [121]	Value of land and buildings Average per farm ($1,000) [122]	Average per acre (dollars) [123]	Value of machinery and equipment Average per farm ($1,000) [124]	Value of products sold Total (mil dol) [125]	Average per farm (dollars) [126]	Percent from — Crops [127]	Live-stock and poultry products [128]	Percent of farms with sales of — $10,000 or more [129]	$100,000 or more [130]	Percent of land owned by Fed. Gov. 1997 [131]	Water consumption 1995 (mil gal/day) [132]
OHIO—Cont'd																
Ottawa	106	-1.1	223	1	97	470	2 212	72	29	60 427	93.1	6.9	62.7	14.8	1.9	50.9
Paulding	210	-4.1	387		196	615	1 639	84	54	99 897	82.8	17.2	69.0	27.5	0.0	3.2
Perry	97	0.6	159	0	63	217	1 409	33	15	25 331	62.0	37.9	35.5	5.9	7.2	3.5
Pickaway	267	3.2	380	1	241	784	2 046	79	79	112 857	83.1	16.9	62.2	25.7	0.3	37.4
Pike	78	-11.0	180	0	44	230	1 208	44	8	17 281	52.1	47.9	26.4	3.9	1.3	4.2
Portage	87	-8.9	122	1	62	372	3 138	40	24	33 071	55.7	44.3	36.3	7.6	6.9	17.1
Preble	197	-3.4	202	0	172	424	2 195	55	68	69 531	64.5	35.5	56.0	19.3	0.0	4.5
Putnam	292	1.9	216	0	275	452	2 107	71	103	76 097	68.0	32.0	77.4	19.3	0.0	4.8
Richland	156	-3.4	171	0	120	329	2 045	54	47	51 922	49.0	51.0	50.4	16.0	0.0	16.3
Ross	252	-0.5	284	D	184	432	1 551	48	46	51 758	80.4	19.6	43.4	12.1	0.6	41.9
Sandusky	199	-1.3	251	0	186	439	1 824	73	66	83 018	85.7	14.3	70.1	22.6	0.0	19.8
Scioto	103	7.3	163	0	59	218	1 318	34	14	22 123	61.9	38.1	29.2	4.6	3.1	11.7
Seneca	293	-1.1	242	D	261	430	1 720	67	84	69 166	73.2	26.8	71.8	19.0	0.0	5.1
Shelby	202	-0.5	204	0	181	491	2 328	61	72	72 451	57.4	42.6	69.5	22.8	0.0	13.4
Stark	137	-0.2	126	1	107	347	3 091	44	73	67 217	39.0	61.0	46.3	13.6	0.2	44.5
Summit	17	-9.3	69	0	11	341	5 553	31	9	35 586	84.7	15.3	41.0	9.2	5.6	82.7
Trumbull	112	-7.0	143	0	82	283	1 815	53	25	32 319	53.7	46.3	42.1	8.0	2.9	231.2
Tuscarawas	141	-4.5	154	0	90	308	1 939	45	56	61 119	20.5	79.5	40.9	14.6	0.7	40.1
Union	205	-8.2	252	0	185	531	2 271	72	70	85 851	61.7	38.3	55.6	18.7	0.0	5.8
Van Wert	237	-2.0	336	D	225	719	2 093	103	73	102 619	86.7	13.3	80.9	31.0	0.0	4.8
Vinton	37	-11.6	184	D	20	185	942	22	2	8 437	40.2	59.8	19.3	1.0	0.6	1.2
Warren	118	-8.2	160	0	94	554	3 858	51	34	45 589	84.0	16.0	38.2	9.9	2.0	21.5
Washington	147	4.6	163	0	72	214	1 406	38	20	22 698	36.8	63.2	29.4	4.8	7.9	690.5
Wayne	241	-2.5	150	1	195	402	2 807	63	156	97 287	22.1	77.9	65.0	24.9	0.0	19.2
Williams	203	8.7	224	D	175	342	1 560	50	51	56 590	69.0	31.0	51.1	13.3	0.0	5.2
Wood	304	0.7	299	0	288	633	2 151	89	96	95 027	90.8	9.2	75.2	26.9	0.0	11.8
Wyandot	209	-3.2	344	0	191	566	1 638	93	64	104 753	71.9	28.1	70.2	28.3	0.0	7.1
OKLAHOMA	33 219	3.3	448	506	14 844	272	610	37	4 146	55 870	21.9	78.1	40.0	8.5	2.6	1 781.3
Adair	225	8.9	207	1	100	206	913	31	74	68 183	1.6	98.4	33.4	10.8	0.0	9.6
Alfalfa	502	2.9	708	3	376	485	713	71	90	126 777	35.3	64.7	76.0	24.5	4.5	3.3
Atoka	421	11.9	387	1	128	173	430	25	20	18 808	7.7	92.3	33.5	2.2	1.3	55.5
Beaver	1 048	6.2	1 420	22	397	476	325	71	89	120 056	16.0	84.0	58.0	14.9	0.0	33.6
Beckham	499	1.1	605	2	222	281	475	39	25	30 007	33.2	66.8	44.7	6.4	0.0	7.9
Blaine	547	6.4	650	3	304	363	549	62	77	91 994	22.7	77.3	64.1	11.8	0.4	5.2
Bryan	420	1.7	277	6	192	186	684	26	33	21 469	27.6	72.4	31.9	3.4	1.7	16.0
Caddo	727	0.0	486	45	403	331	670	52	91	60 919	47.9	52.1	55.9	14.7	0.2	47.6
Canadian	467	-6.6	401	4	280	397	978	59	67	57 156	29.1	70.9	51.8	13.9	1.9	9.9
Carter	382	2.5	328	1	118	220	709	23	22	18 850	9.5	90.5	24.8	3.3	0.0	4.2
Cherokee	238	8.5	206	1	91	186	951	28	66	56 916	58.9	41.1	28.4	5.5	3.2	23.0
Choctaw	338	12.3	341	0	132	172	507	19	24	24 429	12.9	87.1	34.9	3.6	3.5	12.7
Cimarron	1 077	4.1	2 239	69	454	705	320	102	181	375 359	16.8	83.2	65.7	29.5	9.9	216.9
Cleveland	162	3.4	160	1	84	251	1 577	24	12	11 969	32.3	67.7	22.0	1.9	1.7	25.4
Coal	273	3.0	466	0	90	229	457	25	18	30 477	4.2	95.8	45.1	3.9	0.0	6.7
Comanche	435	7.0	422	1	194	309	720	39	32	31 380	35.0	65.0	42.1	7.2	23.4	21.1
Cotton	350	-2.2	684	0	194	286	485	38	36	71 092	29.5	70.5	61.9	13.9	0.9	2.4
Craig	418	-6.4	374	1	166	236	659	36	62	55 057	10.1	89.9	42.0	6.9	0.0	3.1
Creek	351	4.6	238	0	122	168	724	19	15	9 893	14.6	85.4	19.4	1.1	2.7	7.1
Custer	625	-1.5	793	3	312	465	602	80	65	82 151	31.5	68.5	66.0	19.3	1.2	13.3
Delaware	265	9.3	203	0	129	219	1 114	28	94	72 441	3.1	96.9	38.5	13.6	0.0	5.9
Dewey	619	6.2	869	2	227	352	385	52	34	48 051	31.5	68.5	58.1	9.8	0.9	4.2
Ellis	670	-4.3	1 077	13	194	296	285	43	35	56 762	24.5	75.5	55.3	10.1	0.0	45.0
Garfield	615	-7.1	575	0	459	384	693	59	83	77 621	46.5	53.5	66.5	19.0	0.3	6.1
Garvin	449	6.8	325	2	196	201	672	35	34	24 815	25.4	74.6	36.3	4.8	0.0	5.5
Grady	609	7.6	375	7	278	253	656	38	89	54 936	15.5	84.5	42.4	8.7	0.0	17.5
Grant	585	-2.6	850	D	431	559	664	90	61	88 888	64.1	35.9	78.1	23.1	0.0	2.9
Greer	314	-7.3	658	9	173	238	395	44	17	36 108	52.7	47.3	50.6	10.5	0.2	4.7
Harmon	304	6.4	900	21	161	371	402	56	22	64 315	56.1	43.9	61.8	18.0	0.0	16.4
Harper	580	-4.5	1 308	7	201	369	291	50	100	225 782	8.7	91.3	65.2	19.4	0.9	15.6
Haskell	268	-0.1	307	1	116	226	670	32	33	38 193	3.3	96.7	38.4	8.0	2.3	4.1
Hughes	355	2.4	396	4	116	190	473	30	41	45 177	10.2	89.8	34.0	5.4	0.0	16.9
Jackson	477	1.4	659	50	333	379	609	68	69	95 000	61.2	38.8	55.0	20.1	0.5	46.1
Jefferson	441	9.0	884	0	135	385	421	33	51	101 823	8.9	91.1	53.1	14.6	0.5	7.1
Johnston	334	3.1	535	1	92	300	557	30	28	44 165	6.9	93.1	37.3	5.1	3.2	5.6
Kay	469	-1.8	505	0	331	351	695	59	56	60 803	65.8	34.2	58.8	18.1	4.0	25.2
Kingfisher	555	6.3	556	5	367	431	768	68	99	99 669	21.5	78.5	66.7	20.1	0.0	8.8

Table B. States and Counties — Residential Construction, Wholesale and Retail Trade, and Real Estate

STATE County	Value of Residential Construction Authorized by Building Permits, 1999		Wholesale Trade, 1997				Retail Trade[1], 1997				Real Estate and Rental and Leasing, 1997			
	New Construction ($1,000)	Number of Housing Units	Number of Establishments	Number of Employees	Sales (mil dol)	Annual Payroll (mil dol)	Number of Establishments	Number of Employees	Sales (mil dol)	Annual Payroll (mil dol)	Number of Establishments	Number of Employees	Receipts (mil dol)	Annual Payroll (mil dol)
	133	134	135	136	137	138	139	140	141	142	143	144	145	146
OHIO—Cont'd														
Ottawa	20 541	253	42	184	85.8	5.1	171	1 648	353.3	29.3	60	364	21.4	4.1
Paulding	6 722	74	19	155	69.8	4.0	62	638	102.4	8.9	6	32	1.8	0.3
Perry	3 887	40	15	D	D	D	83	648	105.2	8.9	14	44	2.7	1.7
Pickaway	23 197	199	38	326	141.8	9.1	147	1 630	284.0	23.8	34	82	7.8	1.0
Pike	1 074	11	16	103	26.1	2.8	98	1 105	153.5	12.9	8	52	3.8	0.4
Portage	135 082	808	183	2 648	1 180.5	96.5	465	5 828	1 117.9	92.8	104	409	39.4	6.3
Preble	23 038	227	32	586	249.6	20.2	112	1 334	218.3	18.7	17	83	5.0	1.0
Putnam	8 309	74	51	330	162.0	7.7	115	1 344	181.2	17.2	14	103	4.4	1.1
Richland	48 957	504	157	1 902	633.2	53.8	590	8 848	1 297.7	127.7	98	407	43.3	6.3
Ross	7 381	77	63	531	147.5	12.8	279	3 882	581.9	52.7	51	167	22.4	3.9
Sandusky	16 010	165	64	880	213.7	24.2	241	2 945	470.3	43.2	32	129	9.8	2.0
Scioto	306	5	68	550	219.3	12.3	321	3 629	543.0	53.4	40	185	17.5	2.6
Seneca	11 833	200	63	756	359.2	20.7	231	2 447	407.9	38.9	39	101	7.9	1.1
Shelby	31 058	271	51	666	276.3	18.6	167	2 126	309.4	28.4	32	186	16.9	4.1
Stark	207 933	1 463	517	8 242	4 151.7	275.8	1 618	23 170	3 671.2	357.2	274	1 273	126.1	22.9
Summit	379 918	2 836	1 070	13 375	8 443.7	501.6	2 172	32 463	5 515.7	546.7	476	2 994	373.8	68.4
Trumbull	54 248	559	231	2 867	1 212.0	80.4	913	12 617	1 943.2	192.9	175	1 139	123.5	21.8
Tuscarawas	17 547	156	109	1 096	300.2	26.4	439	5 240	758.8	75.6	73	285	29.8	5.1
Union	70 789	497	38	280	165.6	11.5	103	1 291	279.1	22.0	28	105	16.1	2.7
Van Wert	8 322	92	40	D	D	D	110	1 279	207.6	17.9	14	34	10.0	0.9
Vinton	0	0	4	D	D	D	28	201	27.1	2.3	4	D	D	D
Warren	352 893	3 500	181	2 324	6 034.5	91.2	455	6 709	1 111.7	106.3	95	414	48.4	8.0
Washington	5 439	56	74	826	166.6	19.3	279	3 063	501.0	45.8	48	146	17.7	2.7
Wayne	81 340	461	144	1 489	654.1	41.5	393	5 250	801.4	79.5	80	345	26.7	6.1
Williams	13 812	126	49	557	344.7	17.4	153	1 573	227.7	21.4	25	80	6.5	1.1
Wood	78 401	651	169	2 731	1 496.8	82.5	436	5 864	947.2	83.4	97	597	77.3	14.3
Wyandot	8 948	85	28	296	129.6	7.4	94	842	109.4	11.2	11	44	2.3	0.5
OKLAHOMA	1 430 600	14 186	5 191	59 641	32 132.3	1 756.1	14 352	161 613	27 065.6	2 406.9	3 344	15 354	1 576.0	284.5
Adair	282	4	4	31	5.6	0.4	54	482	67.0	5.1	5	11	0.6	0.1
Alfalfa	0	0	19	129	52.0	2.1	25	136	18.4	1.5	4	5	0.3	0.1
Atoka	140	1	19	124	48.8	2.2	49	530	71.9	6.2	4	6	0.4	0.1
Beaver	0	0	10	30	10.3	0.7	25	116	14.4	1.1	2	D	D	D
Beckham	2 892	35	31	163	58.0	3.5	130	1 036	204.1	13.6	24	151	15.1	3.4
Blaine	290	2	17	D	D	D	69	357	42.6	3.7	6	6	0.2	0.0
Bryan	1 947	29	44	597	287.4	12.3	127	1 243	206.8	17.6	27	83	4.4	0.9
Caddo	8 206	143	26	284	111.4	5.8	142	998	128.7	11.7	10	D	D	D
Canadian	33 206	358	87	670	819.0	17.5	212	2 957	620.1	46.6	69	309	29.7	5.6
Carter	7 107	93	78	835	244.7	23.7	275	2 594	413.3	35.5	50	166	13.5	2.4
Cherokee	1 888	22	21	201	44.5	2.7	144	1 843	235.0	20.2	26	62	6.7	1.3
Choctaw	1 210	22	14	D	D	D	71	551	75.4	5.9	5	D	D	D
Cimarron	0	0	7	36	13.7	0.6	19	116	24.4	1.5	2	D	D	D
Cleveland	129 297	1 276	159	1 462	528.6	37.2	616	7 679	1 318.6	115.2	205	764	68.7	11.6
Coal	80	1	2	D	D	D	18	150	17.1	1.4	NA	NA	NA	NA
Comanche	15 447	138	84	766	200.6	16.4	436	5 216	691.8	67.8	133	523	48.7	8.1
Cotton	305	4	7	40	10.7	0.6	20	114	21.7	1.3	3	3	0.2	0.0
Craig	300	2	24	208	74.9	3.7	67	571	99.2	8.6	10	34	3.7	0.5
Creek	9 264	105	77	914	255.9	25.4	186	1 854	284.4	23.7	28	87	6.2	1.1
Custer	2 247	29	45	367	211.8	9.9	172	1 472	235.0	18.9	38	111	11.3	2.1
Delaware	11 127	111	15	82	27.1	1.1	132	1 067	148.9	13.8	24	67	4.9	0.9
Dewey	0	0	7	34	14.9	0.8	32	174	20.8	1.8	5	19	2.0	0.6
Ellis	50	1	7	34	14.9	0.8	28	143	20.1	1.7	2	D	D	D
Garfield	13 126	85	122	1 967	570.1	48.9	302	3 423	501.7	47.8	70	287	24.6	4.8
Garvin	2 610	155	26	287	67.8	5.3	127	1 097	172.0	13.4	18	48	6.4	1.3
Grady	10 336	91	63	576	173.4	14.7	162	1 512	241.3	19.7	32	93	8.8	1.7
Grant	0	0	18	D	D	D	18	92	12.8	0.9	1	D	D	D
Greer	0	0	5	49	13.4	0.4	26	129	15.4	1.5	3	6	0.5	0.0
Harmon	NA	NA	3	D	D	D	25	154	20.2	1.9	3	6	0.5	0.1
Harper	0	0	9	42	13.4	0.9	17	90	10.8	0.9	3	4	0.1	0.0
Haskell	689	9	7	90	41.5	1.2	42	395	57.9	5.2	7	12	0.6	0.1
Hughes	582	10	14	222	35.7	2.8	64	431	58.6	4.8	9	6	0.2	0.0
Jackson	2 727	28	34	161	66.7	3.9	125	1 420	241.2	19.8	23	57	4.4	0.7
Jefferson	92	1	5	D	D	D	30	164	25.5	1.8	6	17	0.9	0.2
Johnston	308	5	7	54	14.4	1.1	37	167	22.1	1.9	5	D	D	D
Kay	9 813	81	61	444	210.2	12.0	263	2 718	397.6	36.5	53	134	11.5	1.7
Kingfisher	1 871	14	33	234	159.3	7.3	60	576	90.0	7.3	10	22	1.2	0.2

1. Establishments with payroll.

Table B. States and Counties — Professional, Manufacturing, and Accommodation and Foodservices

STATE County	Professional, Scientific, and Technical Services[1], 1997				Manufacturing, 1997				Accommodation and Foodservices, 1997			
	Number of Establishments	Number of Employees	Receipts (mil dol)	Annual Payroll (mil dol)	Number of Establishments	Number of Employees	Receipts (mil dol)	Annual Payroll (mil dol)	Number of Establishments	Number of Employees	Sales (mil dol)	Annual Payroll (mil dol)
	147	148	149	150	151	152	153	154	155	156	157	158
OHIO—Cont'd												
Ottawa	51	156	11.7	4.1	56	2 886	634.2	100.8	168	1 346	62.6	15.7
Paulding	13	62	3.9	1.5	39	1 628	256.5	46.4	32	332	10.1	2.6
Perry	20	107	5.1	2.2	35	1 763	238.9	50.8	38	294	8.3	2.0
Pickaway	51	168	10.4	4.0	44	4 726	1 134.4	188.6	72	1 069	31.7	9.2
Pike	13	44	2.3	0.5	28	4 953	1 202.3	190.2	51	643	21.2	5.6
Portage	194	635	55.4	18.9	298	12 984	2 154.2	417.8	267	4 761	124.6	35.1
Preble	42	158	7.7	2.3	61	3 274	698.0	109.2	67	689	22.1	6.0
Putnam	25	89	5.2	1.5	42	4 005	1 237.1	129.9	54	D	D	D
Richland	168	933	73.3	23.5	220	15 212	2 444.7	567.1	272	4 613	140.1	38.6
Ross	66	263	22.8	7.1	48	D	D	D	119	2 225	61.3	16.8
Sandusky	80	383	23.8	8.9	124	10 156	2 533.6	307.1	110	1 699	50.0	12.9
Scioto	68	368	19.3	7.4	63	1 942	290.8	55.0	151	2 199	65.4	17.9
Seneca	63	234	13.2	4.1	101	6 882	1 124.6	231.2	128	1 325	33.9	9.7
Shelby	55	363	22.9	13.4	136	13 278	5 129.2	470.5	95	1 554	48.6	12.4
Stark	640	3 610	312.3	109.0	629	39 352	8 222.5	1 324.1	761	14 302	389.8	107.6
Summit	1 305	9 742	996.9	382.8	1 091	42 312	6 846.7	1 506.1	1 156	20 197	612.2	173.1
Trumbull	278	2 058	129.6	58.2	282	34 101	11 235.6	1 622.1	449	7 323	203.5	55.7
Tuscarawas	113	1 212	46.0	27.1	226	9 823	2 054.6	304.1	212	3 365	90.6	25.7
Union	45	1 079	231.5	69.4	40	8 462	7 467.2	370.7	57	766	23.1	6.8
Van Wert	30	102	7.5	2.5	50	4 553	942.1	140.8	58	878	21.9	5.6
Vinton	6	21	1.1	0.3	17	624	91.2	15.4	15	D	D	D
Warren	215	1 557	180.8	56.4	198	12 145	2 186.4	407.3	243	4 694	154.7	44.6
Washington	77	385	29.8	10.9	104	5 242	1 900.9	187.8	122	2 023	65.4	18.6
Wayne	126	671	43.9	14.7	252	16 172	3 105.0	521.5	178	3 206	79.0	23.9
Williams	30	136	9.2	2.4	131	9 132	1 831.5	267.1	84	1 197	30.3	9.1
Wood	177	1 674	187.3	50.2	192	13 357	2 602.3	512.7	270	4 905	134.4	37.0
Wyandot	25	81	4.3	1.1	53	4 188	573.1	112.1	57	656	16.3	4.5
OKLAHOMA	7 009	40 633	3 543.0	1 323.7	4 087	164 060	37 453.2	4 963.2	6 534	105 934	3 151.3	856.8
Adair	13	39	1.6	0.5	14	1 626	312.6	33.9	15	D	D	D
Alfalfa	8	18	1.0	0.2	NA	NA	NA	NA	6	D	D	D
Atoka	13	32	1.5	0.4	NA	NA	NA	NA	15	D	D	D
Beaver	10	28	1.8	0.3	NA	NA	NA	NA	8	D	D	D
Beckham	30	127	6.7	1.6	NA	NA	NA	NA	56	721	19.7	5.1
Blaine	18	55	2.5	0.8	15	622	98.0	17.1	24	236	5.0	1.5
Bryan	35	128	6.0	2.3	31	949	122.5	19.3	50	733	23.5	5.8
Caddo	26	92	3.7	1.3	NA	NA	NA	NA	48	277	8.0	2.0
Canadian	139	336	24.0	7.3	64	3 003	1 024.4	82.3	122	1 704	49.4	12.7
Carter	86	288	16.9	5.8	45	2 801	1 012.6	105.4	97	1 466	44.3	12.5
Cherokee	39	146	6.7	2.1	NA	NA	NA	NA	78	930	26.6	7.0
Choctaw	14	29	2.0	0.4	NA	NA	NA	NA	25	D	D	D
Cimarron	5	11	0.4	0.1	NA	NA	NA	NA	11	91	1.8	0.4
Cleveland	395	1 656	138.9	47.5	151	4 287	902.3	116.4	330	6 474	188.1	51.6
Coal	2	D	D	D	NA	NA	NA	NA	3	D	D	D
Comanche	127	1 062	63.0	30.5	51	3 325	900.8	119.8	203	3 660	96.9	28.9
Cotton	7	14	0.5	0.2	NA	NA	NA	NA	7	D	D	D
Craig	13	41	3.6	0.7	18	978	128.1	21.7	39	409	14.1	3.9
Creek	78	246	19.0	6.3	96	4 032	703.3	116.4	86	991	31.2	7.8
Custer	53	259	14.2	4.6	23	D	D	D	65	1 110	27.7	7.8
Delaware	38	115	7.1	2.8	30	673	45.2	12.1	67	808	24.1	6.7
Dewey	6	13	0.8	0.3	NA	NA	NA	NA	5	D	D	D
Ellis	9	19	0.7	0.3	NA	NA	NA	NA	7	D	D	D
Garfield	92	432	33.6	12.1	66	2 389	506.2	62.7	123	1 896	51.9	14.7
Garvin	35	94	4.8	1.4	26	1 153	615.4	29.4	44	458	13.3	3.5
Grady	69	202	16.6	4.9	64	2 792	747.0	70.0	63	983	24.5	6.5
Grant	6	14	0.9	0.2	NA	NA	NA	NA	7	30	0.8	0.2
Greer	6	7	0.3	0.1	NA	NA	NA	NA	8	55	1.4	0.4
Harmon	3	7	0.3	0.1	NA	NA	NA	NA	3	D	D	D
Harper	7	19	0.7	0.2	NA	NA	NA	NA	8	34	0.7	0.2
Haskell	11	29	1.3	0.4	NA	NA	NA	NA	16	D	D	D
Hughes	11	33	1.6	0.5	NA	NA	NA	NA	21	D	D	D
Jackson	29	404	15.3	6.5	12	896	205.1	16.3	56	841	24.2	6.3
Jefferson	8	16	0.5	0.1	NA	NA	NA	NA	13	D	D	D
Johnston	6	10	0.6	0.2	10	678	98.4	17.1	12	142	2.8	0.9
Kay	73	829	36.4	14.9	74	4 019	2 001.2	126.5	102	1 446	40.3	10.8
Kingfisher	18	77	3.1	1.3	NA	NA	NA	NA	27	D	D	D

1. Firms subject to federal tax.

STATE County	Health Care and Social Assistance[1], 1997				Other Services[1], 1997				Federal funds and grants, fiscal 1999[2]			
									Expenditures (mil dol)			
										Direct payments for individuals[3]		
	Number of Establishments	Number of Employees	Receipts (mil dol)	Annual Payroll (mil dol)	Number of Establishments	Number of Employees	Receipts (mil dol)	Annual Payroll (mil dol)	Total	Social Security and government retirement	Medicare	Food stamps and Supplemental Security Income
	159	160	161	162	163	164	165	166	167	168	169	170
OHIO—Cont'd												
Ottawa	48	538	26.8	13.5	67	344	18.7	5.4	166.5	94.9	36.8	2.3
Paulding	23	193	6.8	2.9	16	96	4.2	1.3	61.8	22.9	12.3	1.1
Perry	24	400	13.4	6.7	22	64	4.0	0.8	131.6	64.7	25.0	6.3
Pickaway	52	953	37.2	19.2	50	175	10.9	2.9	157.5	75.4	26.6	4.9
Pike	30	522	18.9	8.4	20	61	4.0	1.0	311.2	46.9	17.1	8.3
Portage	174	1 715	100.7	46.4	182	984	49.4	16.3	420.8	210.3	84.7	10.9
Preble	39	585	23.1	9.0	57	262	13.5	4.0	136.4	72.7	26.6	2.5
Putnam	34	516	17.9	8.0	36	137	8.6	2.5	86.2	33.2	19.7	2.0
Richland	256	2 797	156.8	72.6	199	1 512	81.1	31.0	491.1	243.3	91.7	18.5
Ross	107	1 218	60.6	28.6	92	554	26.4	8.4	337.2	134.4	43.2	17.0
Sandusky	116	966	50.8	22.5	96	620	30.8	10.6	201.7	102.6	44.3	6.4
Scioto	151	2 448	105.9	52.2	82	347	17.8	4.4	428.3	168.6	75.1	35.8
Seneca	108	927	50.5	22.4	80	382	17.4	5.2	233.7	123.3	47.3	6.4
Shelby	62	643	36.7	17.1	52	249	19.0	4.8	140.1	67.8	27.8	4.1
Stark	732	9 505	603.8	291.3	685	4 541	265.0	82.0	1 486.6	768.9	299.1	50.3
Summit	1 130	14 026	863.9	438.0	977	6 761	368.7	117.2	2 365.8	962.6	488.6	91.7
Trumbull	476	5 373	297.3	135.8	310	1 805	98.9	26.8	908.1	473.7	216.7	35.5
Tuscarawas	159	2 663	103.8	48.7	161	917	66.3	18.5	312.0	172.0	57.8	9.8
Union	47	435	26.2	12.5	51	226	11.6	4.0	93.9	43.2	17.9	1.3
Van Wert	51	529	30.2	13.2	38	233	10.2	3.0	92.3	43.5	17.7	2.9
Vinton	6	179	4.2	2.3	4	13	1.8	0.2	46.1	19.5	7.4	2.8
Warren	156	2 400	94.2	43.0	161	1 201	72.7	28.1	347.1	193.9	58.3	7.8
Washington	101	1 419	81.8	36.0	113	509	31.8	8.3	262.3	123.9	48.9	11.5
Wayne	135	1 906	93.7	44.8	141	665	50.2	10.9	321.7	174.2	60.2	9.4
Williams	48	762	46.3	17.6	51	291	22.7	4.7	132.5	67.0	27.7	2.3
Wood	143	1 915	83.5	37.8	169	1 187	70.3	21.3	347.0	156.6	66.5	6.0
Wyandot	24	269	11.4	5.1	43	177	12.1	3.5	86.5	42.1	16.2	1.2
OKLAHOMA	6 991	91 803	5 061.4	2 244.0	4 572	26 308	1 599.4	458.5	19 188.7	6 950.0	2 596.9	528.8
Adair	21	373	11.1	5.3	9	23	1.2	0.2	113.5	34.1	18.2	5.4
Alfalfa	8	55	1.7	0.8	10	18	1.1	0.2	47.5	15.4	6.7	0.4
Atoka	19	257	6.9	3.1	16	42	2.8	0.5	67.8	24.5	12.6	3.7
Beaver	6	26	1.3	0.5	9	33	1.8	0.3	38.4	11.0	3.5	0.3
Beckham	62	589	23.3	10.6	29	121	15.8	2.0	83.6	36.0	17.1	4.0
Blaine	16	237	7.9	3.4	14	36	1.7	0.4	71.7	23.3	11.8	1.5
Bryan	54	1 038	61.3	23.5	30	176	9.4	3.0	204.3	77.9	34.5	7.1
Caddo	44	420	12.1	5.6	29	79	4.9	1.0	180.6	68.9	27.2	6.7
Canadian	93	1 101	39.9	16.5	84	384	21.8	6.4	280.1	137.3	36.4	5.5
Carter	128	1 418	76.0	35.2	70	325	17.2	4.5	202.5	99.9	45.0	9.0
Cherokee	54	535	22.3	8.0	30	115	6.7	1.7	227.0	71.6	29.3	8.2
Choctaw	22	289	10.7	5.3	15	66	2.7	0.7	120.8	36.2	18.8	6.1
Cimarron	3	D	D	D	10	30	1.3	0.2	29.3	7.3	2.3	0.3
Cleveland	361	3 856	203.4	91.1	198	1 123	60.7	16.7	683.3	317.5	75.5	66.4
Coal	6	31	1.4	0.6	2	D	D	D	34.7	13.8	6.5	1.3
Comanche	208	2 349	141.5	52.8	146	778	36.3	10.9	1 153.6	293.0	52.6	18.3
Cotton	8	122	3.4	1.7	8	26	1.8	0.4	42.3	16.4	7.1	0.9
Craig	21	102	5.2	1.8	18	44	3.7	1.0	75.0	36.3	14.7	0.9
Creek	86	1 358	49.0	22.6	70	301	22.8	6.6	212.0	117.6	41.9	7.7
Custer	64	632	26.6	10.9	38	201	11.8	3.0	100.2	30.1	23.9	2.3
Delaware	46	555	21.6	8.6	25	94	4.5	1.2	140.4	70.9	29.6	5.8
Dewey	5	24	0.9	0.3	4	16	1.0	0.2	32.4	11.9	6.6	0.7
Ellis	8	96	3.0	1.5	8	22	1.0	0.2	29.9	10.0	5.6	0.3
Garfield	145	1 487	90.8	40.6	104	476	26.0	7.0	369.1	134.6	50.1	8.6
Garvin	42	842	28.5	14.9	24	117	7.7	1.7	173.3	68.5	37.8	5.0
Grady	67	997	45.4	22.2	49	213	13.9	3.8	164.2	83.4	27.7	7.2
Grant	3	D	D	D	9	12	1.4	0.2	50.1	13.4	6.8	0.4
Greer	12	188	7.8	4.1	4	13	0.7	0.2	44.2	16.4	10.3	1.3
Harmon	3	D	D	D	4	15	0.7	0.1	27.4	7.4	5.8	1.1
Harper	8	74	2.0	0.8	10	17	1.5	0.3	24.6	9.2	4.2	0.2
Haskell	20	256	9.6	4.5	13	49	2.5	0.7	70.7	30.5	13.6	2.9
Hughes	18	271	9.0	4.4	5	19	1.4	0.2	84.9	36.4	16.6	3.1
Jackson	48	489	19.0	7.8	26	131	9.3	2.3	291.5	71.2	24.3	4.9
Jefferson	13	273	7.5	4.3	9	23	1.5	0.3	45.3	18.4	8.8	1.2
Johnston	15	232	7.0	3.7	7	14	0.9	0.2	59.2	21.6	9.4	2.2
Kay	110	864	44.9	19.0	80	304	18.5	4.8	276.6	112.4	37.1	5.8
Kingfisher	14	224	7.7	3.1	26	95	6.1	1.4	65.5	27.6	11.4	1.2

1. Firms subject to federal tax.   2. October 1, 1998 to September 30, 1999.   3. State totals may include programs not allocated by county.

STATE County	Federal funds and grants, fiscal 1999[1] (cont'd)							Local government finances, 1997				
	Expenditures (mil dol) (cont'd)							General revenue				
	Procurement contract awards		Grants[2]				Total (mil dol)	Intergovern-mental (mil dol)	Taxes			
									Total (mil dol)	Per capita[3] (dollars)		
	Salaries and wages	Defense	Other	Medicaid and other health-related	Nutrition and family welfare	Education	Other				Total	Property
	171	172	173	174	175	176	177	178	179	180	181	182
OHIO—Cont'd												
Ottawa	11.3	0.7	2.1	4.6	2.4	1.4	5.8	108.8	32.4	52.6	1 294	1 082
Paulding	2.5	0.0	0.7	4.8	1.7	0.9	3.1	47.4	19.9	11.7	582	450
Perry	3.4	0.2	1.0	17.6	5.2	2.2	2.3	60.0	39.7	12.2	357	289
Pickaway	4.8	0.0	1.6	20.2	5.8	2.1	2.3	124.5	54.7	37.0	696	516
Pike	3.5	0.0	175.0	25.9	8.0	2.4	21.8	66.4	46.4	12.6	458	392
Portage	16.4	8.2	4.4	29.1	13.8	9.7	15.8	395.7	115.2	138.7	920	643
Preble	4.9	0.1	1.2	8.5	3.9	2.2	3.7	120.1	36.8	32.7	762	466
Putnam	4.1	0.0	3.1	6.4	1.9	1.7	0.8	78.0	38.3	23.2	660	437
Richland	42.8	5.9	6.6	43.0	14.5	6.9	8.3	303.0	140.9	120.7	945	634
Ross	58.2	0.0	6.1	43.6	10.7	4.1	6.5	139.6	69.3	51.0	678	423
Sandusky	6.2	0.0	2.6	13.3	9.1	2.5	3.8	141.4	55.9	56.8	911	598
Scioto	10.0	0.0	2.8	86.3	21.7	11.2	4.9	170.5	104.3	35.7	442	321
Seneca	7.4	0.0	1.8	14.8	5.4	2.9	7.2	114.0	52.9	43.5	724	463
Shelby	4.6	0.1	1.3	9.8	4.3	1.6	9.8	112.8	38.7	47.8	1 009	622
Stark	74.8	17.2	28.8	117.3	45.5	20.5	38.9	799.1	335.4	328.9	880	612
Summit	148.8	232.2	43.9	197.3	73.7	30.8	54.9	1 507.5	496.2	727.6	1 369	853
Trumbull	27.0	5.4	6.9	62.2	31.4	12.5	21.4	485.5	209.1	193.4	855	593
Tuscarawas	11.3	1.1	3.1	26.3	10.4	5.4	10.1	189.0	77.9	77.1	874	577
Union	3.8	0.4	1.0	7.6	2.2	1.1	4.7	103.6	21.2	36.3	938	807
Van Wert	3.5	0.0	1.5	5.6	2.0	0.9	2.1	59.9	26.2	22.6	747	540
Vinton	1.4	0.0	0.7	9.1	2.4	0.9	1.2	24.8	16.5	5.2	431	373
Warren	14.9	8.2	4.2	25.6	8.8	3.0	17.2	293.9	89.4	143.4	1 024	782
Washington	11.3	0.6	3.1	27.0	8.9	4.9	15.7	123.0	51.0	54.5	857	591
Wayne	13.9	1.7	3.1	24.5	9.7	5.4	9.6	318.8	110.1	98.7	901	653
Williams	4.6	0.4	1.3	6.1	2.2	1.4	7.7	85.9	34.3	35.0	923	603
Wood	13.7	1.7	4.7	18.0	5.5	7.4	35.2	281.3	91.2	138.1	1 159	738
Wyandot	3.1	0.0	2.1	6.9	1.3	0.8	1.4	62.2	19.3	16.3	718	536
OKLAHOMA	2 760.6	1 197.7	471.8	1 324.9	648.3	355.6	901.9	X	X	X	X	X
Adair	2.3	11.3	0.5	28.3	4.8	5.4	2.6	34.2	24.8	4.9	245	213
Alfalfa	2.3	0.0	0.7	1.6	0.3	0.2	6.0	9.0	4.6	2.9	484	356
Atoka	3.0	0.0	0.6	12.1	2.4	1.3	4.7	19.6	11.3	4.5	334	230
Beaver	1.4	0.0	0.4	0.6	0.4	0.1	7.5	19.9	8.8	7.7	1 289	1 113
Beckham	2.6	0.0	0.6	9.3	2.1	1.5	1.1	36.2	15.6	15.5	837	519
Blaine	3.3	0.1	0.7	4.3	4.9	1.2	8.7	25.4	13.0	4.4	417	308
Bryan	6.5	8.5	4.1	30.6	12.9	5.8	5.5	47.8	28.4	11.9	347	174
Caddo	17.1	0.0	2.3	18.0	7.7	4.2	6.1	59.7	36.2	12.9	417	268
Canadian	54.9	0.8	9.5	7.0	6.1	3.8	5.3	130.1	57.5	41.5	491	335
Carter	7.2	0.0	1.5	21.5	5.7	3.5	5.5	78.3	38.0	27.3	618	331
Cherokee	20.3	0.1	6.5	31.1	22.2	7.8	19.0	80.6	34.9	10.1	262	109
Choctaw	2.9	0.2	1.2	23.8	5.4	1.8	11.2	24.5	16.2	4.4	291	118
Cimarron	0.8	0.0	0.2	0.8	0.2	0.3	0.1	13.3	5.8	2.3	759	582
Cleveland	46.4	41.4	10.2	23.0	11.8	12.2	58.3	376.5	129.3	97.9	497	300
Coal	1.3	0.0	0.3	7.1	1.1	1.2	0.5	12.7	6.0	4.6	754	651
Comanche	562.0	130.8	11.6	27.7	16.8	7.9	12.6	265.5	104.9	49.1	431	208
Cotton	1.6	0.0	0.3	3.8	0.8	0.4	1.7	9.4	6.2	1.8	275	166
Craig	2.9	0.0	0.7	10.6	1.4	1.5	4.1	25.4	11.0	8.3	577	268
Creek	7.1	0.1	1.7	19.2	7.0	3.0	3.8	100.0	55.7	27.4	414	261
Custer	8.0	0.0	1.3	6.1	2.8	2.0	6.2	61.2	20.6	19.0	739	456
Delaware	3.4	0.2	0.7	17.4	4.7	3.0	3.5	41.1	23.7	13.3	392	248
Dewey	1.7	0.0	0.4	1.7	0.3	0.3	0.1	17.8	8.5	3.1	622	439
Ellis	1.0	0.0	0.3	0.8	0.3	0.3	4.6	11.8	6.3	4.1	964	791
Garfield	58.8	66.5	2.5	12.6	4.8	3.1	5.9	99.4	42.6	35.9	633	324
Garvin	4.7	26.5	1.0	16.9	2.9	1.9	2.3	55.9	25.4	12.1	447	265
Grady	5.4	0.1	1.2	16.9	5.6	2.9	2.9	87.6	33.3	16.9	371	232
Grant	1.8	0.0	1.0	1.1	0.3	0.1	2.4	12.3	6.4	4.5	842	767
Greer	1.3	0.0	0.3	5.5	0.7	0.4	0.3	15.6	6.6	2.4	369	268
Harmon	0.9	0.0	0.2	3.1	0.7	0.4	0.2	6.4	4.1	1.2	356	243
Harper	1.1	0.0	0.2	0.6	0.2	0.1	0.5	9.6	4.9	2.7	757	601
Haskell	2.8	0.1	0.5	11.1	5.1	1.1	0.4	18.6	12.0	3.0	266	115
Hughes	4.4	0.0	0.6	14.5	2.0	1.7	1.7	44.8	15.8	5.3	401	247
Jackson	108.4	30.0	1.1	13.2	5.1	2.1	10.2	88.6	33.2	13.1	458	239
Jefferson	1.7	0.1	0.4	6.7	0.5	0.5	2.2	16.7	8.5	3.9	592	491
Johnston	2.5	3.8	0.6	10.1	3.0	1.5	1.1	17.2	12.1	3.3	325	258
Kay	9.4	63.4	2.6	10.8	4.9	2.8	5.9	81.1	33.2	29.2	624	408
Kingfisher	3.1	2.4	2.3	1.5	1.1	0.8	1.9	26.9	12.8	9.7	717	467

1. October 1, 1998 to September 30, 1999.   2. State totals may include programs not allocated by county.   3. Based on the resident population estimated as of July 1 of the year shown.

Table B. States and Counties — Local Government Finances, Government Employment, and Elections

STATE County	Direct general expenditure							Debt outstanding		Government employment, 1998			Presidential election, 2000 Percent of vote cast —		
	Total (mil dol)	Per capita¹ (dollars)	Educa-tion	Health and hospitals	Police protec-tion	Public welfare	High-ways	Total (mil dol)	Per capita¹ (dollars)	Federal civilian	Federal military	State and local	Demo-cratic	Republi-can	All other
	183	184	185	186	187	188	189	190	191	192	193	194	195	196	197
OHIO—Cont'd															
Ottawa	107.5	2 644	47.3	8.7	4.8	5.9	7.0	39.5	971	166	142	2 039	NA	NA	NA
Paulding	43.7	2 166	50.6	22.8	3.5	3.0	8.7	10.5	520	55	52	1 146	NA	NA	NA
Perry	56.2	1 647	62.3	3.3	2.3	7.6	6.8	10.5	307	74	88	1 678	NA	NA	NA
Pickaway	120.3	2 261	41.0	30.7	2.6	3.5	4.9	23.5	442	91	138	4 171	NA	NA	NA
Pike	63.6	2 306	63.2	3.1	2.5	7.0	6.2	3.7	133	66	72	1 665	NA	NA	NA
Portage	394.3	2 615	40.7	29.3	3.5	4.0	5.0	138.4	918	306	410	14 195	NA	NA	NA
Preble	111.3	2 597	40.4	36.5	3.0	2.0	5.7	16.6	388	101	111	1 928	NA	NA	NA
Putnam	74.5	2 124	54.6	4.4	4.0	8.9	9.6	20.1	572	81	91	1 984	NA	NA	NA
Richland	297.1	2 326	49.2	7.6	5.0	4.7	5.9	60.8	476	702	330	7 788	NA	NA	NA
Ross	137.9	1 834	55.7	3.8	5.4	5.6	7.8	38.6	513	1 385	196	4 841	NA	NA	NA
Sandusky	132.3	2 124	55.5	1.3	6.3	10.0	6.8	46.9	753	125	160	3 254	NA	NA	NA
Scioto	162.1	2 008	61.2	1.5	2.5	11.2	4.5	55.0	682	194	207	5 374	NA	NA	NA
Seneca	111.6	1 860	52.9	5.5	6.2	5.1	7.0	37.2	619	142	156	3 084	NA	NA	NA
Shelby	96.5	2 035	50.5	2.7	4.8	1.4	8.3	25.6	540	101	122	2 528	NA	NA	NA
Stark	779.9	2 087	51.0	6.6	5.7	5.5	4.7	297.2	795	1 216	965	17 725	NA	NA	NA
Summit	1 433.3	2 696	39.5	8.7	6.0	4.9	5.9	968.9	1 822	2 749	1 415	30 212	NA	NA	NA
Trumbull	486.4	2 151	47.8	5.5	7.6	6.0	4.4	162.7	720	504	583	10 561	NA	NA	NA
Tuscarawas	181.5	2 057	51.5	4.2	4.3	3.8	5.9	73.8	836	219	229	4 635	NA	NA	NA
Union	92.7	2 400	39.9	34.7	3.3	1.4	2.1	59.7	1 545	73	102	2 617	NA	NA	NA
Van Wert	58.9	1 944	53.1	1.0	5.8	9.7	7.8	10.5	346	72	78	1 337	NA	NA	NA
Vinton	24.4	2 023	53.5	4.3	3.0	8.6	6.2	0.7	57	23	31	789	NA	NA	NA
Warren	290.3	2 072	54.2	3.5	6.4	3.0	6.3	228.2	1 629	274	376	6 521	NA	NA	NA
Washington	120.7	1 897	51.7	8.2	5.1	5.6	10.5	23.5	370	260	163	3 132	NA	NA	NA
Wayne	287.4	2 623	44.5	25.2	3.3	4.3	4.8	117.9	1 076	263	284	6 872	NA	NA	NA
Williams	79.1	2 090	50.7	5.4	3.8	7.7	8.6	13.3	352	95	98	2 120	NA	NA	NA
Wood	269.8	2 264	47.2	7.7	5.1	5.1	5.6	97.7	820	236	330	13 172	NA	NA	NA
Wyandot	58.2	2 561	36.3	33.6	3.6	5.8	6.7	8.6	378	66	59	1 242	NA	NA	NA
OKLAHOMA	X	X	X	X	X	X	X	X	X	44 493	41 819	227 140	38.4	60.3	1.3
Adair	33.4	1 659	79.9	1.6	2.5	0.0	4.8	5.5	273	45	101	1 099	39.5	58.6	1.9
Alfalfa	9.6	1 581	55.6	0.6	3.5	0.1	16.4	1.9	317	46	30	465	23.3	75.2	1.5
Atoka	20.4	1 528	60.0	11.8	3.1	0.1	8.2	5.9	440	74	66	1 132	44.1	54.9	1.0
Beaver	16.8	2 814	48.5	12.0	2.6	0.0	27.3	1.8	299	32	30	527	13.8	85.2	1.0
Beckham	33.8	1 821	57.9	1.7	5.9	0.0	17.7	7.6	409	55	97	934	36.9	62.3	0.9
Blaine	26.4	2 492	47.3	22.0	1.5	1.8	9.1	4.2	392	79	52	915	34.2	64.3	1.4
Bryan	48.8	1 427	66.6	1.4	4.2	0.1	7.6	26.0	762	120	173	2 541	47.3	51.8	0.9
Caddo	57.2	1 848	71.8	5.6	1.7	0.0	4.8	12.5	405	415	154	1 904	46.4	52.5	1.1
Canadian	136.5	1 612	61.9	9.5	3.4	0.0	4.7	56.1	662	621	855	4 054	26.7	72.3	1.0
Carter	88.7	2 011	57.7	2.1	5.5	0.4	9.1	25.9	587	127	222	2 707	40.5	58.7	0.8
Cherokee	77.5	2 024	46.3	38.9	1.8	0.0	3.9	12.5	325	479	195	3 958	50.2	47.8	2.0
Choctaw	24.6	1 614	66.2	5.1	3.4	0.6	8.0	8.2	535	65	75	965	52.7	46.3	1.0
Cimarron	13.7	4 452	32.4	34.4	2.4	0.0	17.1	0.9	308	19	19	351	15.3	82.9	1.8
Cleveland	369.2	1 872	46.5	24.5	5.4	0.1	3.9	204.1	1 035	766	1 114	18 652	36.5	62.2	1.3
Coal	11.0	1 823	69.1	5.9	1.1	0.0	12.1	3.4	562	25	30	351	48.6	50.6	0.8
Comanche	259.6	2 278	44.8	33.8	3.9	0.0	2.7	87.0	763	3 810	14 303	7 818	40.8	58.3	0.9
Cotton	10.2	1 519	59.3	0.7	1.3	0.1	13.5	2.8	422	33	33	397	43.0	55.9	1.0
Craig	25.2	1 743	61.1	13.0	3.7	0.0	8.4	9.0	625	60	72	1 896	46.8	51.3	1.8
Creek	91.4	1 383	70.8	2.4	4.9	0.1	6.5	67.2	1 016	118	334	2 762	41.1	57.2	1.7
Custer	57.6	2 234	49.1	18.3	4.0	0.3	8.2	23.9	926	161	127	2 774	32.0	67.0	1.0
Delaware	42.5	1 256	72.5	2.0	4.4	0.0	6.1	13.3	393	67	170	1 258	41.3	57.1	1.7
Dewey	16.3	3 229	47.3	23.6	0.8	0.0	14.7	3.5	693	40	25	518	27.0	72.4	0.6
Ellis	9.8	2 332	56.0	1.6	2.7	0.0	21.7	0.4	94	25	21	435	23.2	75.2	1.6
Garfield	99.7	1 758	54.5	0.6	4.7	0.0	6.7	128.6	2 268	381	1 430	3 675	30.2	68.7	1.1
Garvin	55.4	2 051	47.6	22.9	3.3	0.1	7.2	23.2	860	93	135	2 350	42.6	56.2	1.2
Grady	87.5	1 927	43.8	33.3	3.4	0.0	6.3	24.9	549	101	229	2 611	37.1	61.7	1.2
Grant	13.9	2 579	56.1	0.9	3.6	0.6	25.1	2.8	518	37	27	363	28.3	70.4	1.3
Greer	16.2	2 533	36.5	27.8	4.0	0.0	8.7	0.3	49	27	32	890	39.0	59.8	1.2
Harmon	6.8	1 960	62.9	2.8	5.4	0.0	14.1	0.1	40	23	17	335	42.1	57.4	0.5
Harper	8.7	2 416	58.8	1.8	3.3	0.1	18.1	0.0	0	27	18	406	22.2	77.0	0.8
Haskell	17.6	1 549	61.7	11.4	3.8	0.3	9.5	1.6	141	66	57	753	54.2	44.1	1.7
Hughes	42.0	3 207	37.2	14.3	1.4	0.0	4.9	43.9	3 351	45	70	937	50.9	47.9	1.2
Jackson	87.1	3 033	36.8	29.2	3.5	9.1	4.9	60.5	2 108	1 633	2 194	2 294	30.8	68.5	0.6
Jefferson	15.4	2 307	46.7	1.2	2.1	0.0	11.5	46.1	6 917	41	33	461	48.0	50.9	1.1
Johnston	17.5	1 701	65.7	1.1	2.8	0.0	17.2	3.1	300	50	51	807	46.0	52.7	1.2
Kay	86.4	1 844	53.8	1.2	6.2	0.0	6.0	70.6	1 507	191	232	2 782	33.7	64.8	1.5
Kingfisher	24.8	1 838	65.5	0.3	3.8	0.0	9.9	6.4	471	59	67	774	21.5	77.5	1.0

1. Based on the resident population estimated as of July 1 of the year shown.

Table B. States and Counties — Land Area and Population

STATE/ County code	MSA/ PMSA/ NECMA code[1]	County Type[2]	STATE County	Land area,[3] (sq km) 1990	Population and population characteristics, 1999												
								Race (percent)					Age (percent)				
					Total persons	Rank	Per square kilometer	White	Black	Am. Indian, Eskimo, Aleut	Asian and Pacific Islander	Percent Hispanic[4]	Under 5 years	5 to 17 years	18 to 24 years	25 to 34 years	35 to 44 years	45 to 54 years
				1	2	3	4	5	6	7	8	9	10	11	12	13	14	15
			OKLAHOMA—Cont'd															
40 075	...	6	Kiowa	2 628	10 498	2 378	4.0	87.3	5.7	6.6	0.4	8.1	6.8	20.6	7.3	10.6	12.5	11.9
40 077	...	7	Latimer	1 871	10 204	2 405	5.5	83.0	1.7	15.0	0.3	1.5	6.5	20.3	11.5	10.5	12.9	12.5
40 079	...	6	Le Flore	4 108	46 770	953	11.4	85.8	2.6	11.3	0.3	1.5	6.7	20.5	9.3	11.2	14.4	14.2
40 081	5880	2	Lincoln	2 483	31 811	1 322	12.8	90.7	2.9	6.0	0.3	1.6	6.6	21.2	7.7	10.9	14.5	14.4
40 083	5880	2	Logan	1 929	30 437	1 364	15.8	82.6	13.7	3.2	0.5	3.1	6.6	20.7	11.3	10.9	15.3	13.3
40 085	...	9	Love	1 335	8 581	2 546	6.4	89.6	3.3	6.9	0.2	6.0	6.2	20.2	8.3	10.2	14.8	14.2
40 087	5880	2	McClain	1 475	26 706	1 476	18.1	92.2	1.1	6.4	0.2	3.8	6.1	20.8	8.4	11.3	15.0	15.4
40 089	...	7	McCurtain	4 798	34 795	1 233	7.3	74.8	11.0	13.9	0.4	1.9	7.3	21.8	9.4	10.8	14.0	13.6
40 091	...	7	McIntosh	1 606	19 269	1 802	12.0	77.0	5.6	17.2	0.2	1.3	5.1	17.3	7.0	8.6	11.9	14.4
40 093	...	6	Major	2 478	7 659	2 628	3.1	98.0	0.1	1.7	0.2	2.6	6.4	20.4	6.5	10.5	13.5	14.0
40 095	...	6	Marshall	961	12 377	2 259	12.9	87.9	2.1	9.8	0.2	3.6	5.6	20.4	6.5	10.0	12.5	13.9
40 097	...	6	Mayes	1 700	38 270	1 127	22.5	82.4	0.2	17.1	0.3	1.4	6.5	19.3	8.1	10.0	12.5	13.9
40 099	...	7	Murray	1 083	12 477	2 250	11.5	87.4	1.9	10.6	0.2	2.2	5.7	19.5	7.5	10.0	14.7	13.2
40 101	...	4	Muskogee	2 108	70 091	702	33.3	71.9	14.9	12.7	0.5	1.9	6.5	20.3	9.1	11.6	14.7	12.6
40 103	...	7	Noble	1 896	11 334	2 320	6.0	89.6	2.0	8.1	0.3	1.7	6.7	20.1	7.9	11.7	14.1	14.2
40 105	...	6	Nowata	1 463	10 079	2 418	6.9	80.4	4.0	15.5	0.1	1.1	6.0	18.4	7.6	10.1	13.4	14.2
40 107	...	6	Okfuskee	1 618	11 242	2 330	6.9	68.3	12.4	19.1	0.2	1.8	6.0	19.5	8.5	11.1	13.6	14.3
40 109	5880	2	Oklahoma	1 837	636 539	80	346.5	77.9	15.5	4.0	2.6	6.4	7.4	18.5	10.5	13.7	15.6	12.6
40 111	...	6	Okmulgee	1 805	38 788	1 116	21.5	75.0	13.0	11.7	0.3	1.8	6.8	19.9	9.4	10.3	14.2	13.9
40 113	8560	2	Osage	5 830	42 970	1 024	7.4	74.3	11.4	14.0	0.3	2.4	6.6	20.6	7.8	11.6	16.4	14.8
40 115	...	6	Ottawa	1 221	30 881	1 352	25.3	81.5	0.4	17.6	0.5	1.8	6.0	17.6	9.7	10.0	13.4	13.6
40 117	...	6	Pawnee	1 475	16 548	1 966	11.2	89.0	0.9	9.9	0.2	1.1	6.6	20.0	7.5	10.6	15.0	14.6
40 119	...	4	Payne	1 778	65 418	730	36.8	89.1	3.7	4.2	3.0	2.4	5.7	15.5	25.0	13.5	12.6	10.2
40 121	...	7	Pittsburg	3 383	43 472	1 011	12.9	83.0	4.8	11.9	0.4	1.8	5.5	18.2	8.1	11.5	14.6	13.8
40 123	...	6	Pontotoc	1 864	34 686	1 235	18.6	83.5	2.8	13.3	0.4	1.8	6.1	18.6	12.3	10.9	13.9	12.6
40 125	5880	2	Pottawatomie	2 041	62 654	768	30.7	85.7	2.5	11.1	0.8	2.4	6.4	20.2	11.3	11.1	14.3	13.4
40 127	...	7	Pushmataha	3 619	11 542	2 306	3.2	84.1	1.2	14.6	0.1	1.9	6.0	19.0	7.8	9.4	13.2	14.5
40 129	...	9	Roger Mills	2 958	3 593	2 943	1.2	95.7	0.2	4.0	0.1	2.3	6.4	21.0	6.9	10.4	14.3	13.1
40 131	8560	6	Rogers	1 748	70 567	698	40.4	86.4	1.0	12.3	0.4	1.7	6.6	20.0	8.2	10.9	16.1	15.5
40 133	...	6	Seminole	1 638	24 546	1 549	15.0	75.5	8.2	16.0	0.2	1.9	6.1	20.0	8.7	10.3	13.4	13.3
40 135	2720	3	Sequoyah	1 745	37 886	1 138	21.7	77.4	2.5	19.9	0.3	1.3	6.8	20.7	9.6	11.2	14.2	14.4
40 137	...	4	Stephens	2 272	43 076	1 021	19.0	93.1	2.5	3.9	0.5	3.3	6.1	19.6	7.1	10.7	14.6	12.4
40 139	...	7	Texas	5 277	18 329	1 853	3.5	97.5	0.5	1.5	0.4	15.2	7.2	22.0	9.9	11.5	15.1	13.4
40 141	...	6	Tillman	2 259	9 419	2 480	4.2	85.6	10.3	3.8	0.4	20.5	7.0	21.8	8.6	9.7	12.2	12.5
40 143	8560	2	Tulsa	1 477	548 296	95	371.2	83.1	10.5	4.8	1.5	3.7	7.4	18.4	10.2	13.8	16.5	12.8
40 145	8560	2	Wagoner	1 458	56 115	827	38.5	86.3	4.5	8.7	0.5	2.1	6.9	22.5	8.6	11.6	17.2	15.4
40 147	...	4	Washington	1 080	47 674	942	44.1	88.6	2.8	7.5	1.1	2.5	6.3	18.4	7.3	10.4	15.2	13.9
40 149	...	7	Washita	2 599	11 692	2 296	4.5	97.3	0.2	2.2	0.3	5.4	6.5	20.7	6.9	10.6	13.2	12.8
40 151	...	7	Woods	3 332	8 171	2 579	2.5	96.1	0.8	2.5	0.6	4.6	6.7	21.1	8.2	12.8	14.8	13.1
40 153	...	7	Woodward	3 218	18 588	1 841	5.8	96.1	0.6	1.6	0.4	2.5	5.4	15.9	12.8	9.3	11.7	12.3
41 000	...	X	OREGON	248 647	3 316 154	X	13.3	93.4	1.9	1.4	3.3	6.4	6.6	18.3	9.4	12.8	15.9	14.7
41 001	...	7	Baker	7 947	16 259	1 986	2.0	98.4	0.2	1.0	0.5	3.0	6.0	18.9	6.2	10.2	13.2	15.7
41 003	1890	4	Benton	1 752	77 192	646	44.1	91.4	1.1	0.8	6.7	3.9	5.8	16.0	19.6	13.4	14.9	12.6
41 005	6440	0	Clackamas	4 839	338 251	166	69.9	96.4	0.5	0.7	2.4	4.1	6.3	19.2	8.1	11.8	17.2	17.1
41 007	...	6	Clatsop	2 143	35 323	1 213	16.5	96.5	0.5	1.1	1.9	3.3	6.4	18.7	8.2	11.6	15.1	14.8
41 009	6440	1	Columbia	1 701	45 368	979	26.7	97.4	0.2	1.4	1.1	3.1	6.8	21.0	7.6	11.2	16.1	16.6
41 011	...	5	Coos	4 145	61 670	774	14.9	96.0	0.3	2.3	1.3	3.7	5.7	17.8	7.0	10.5	13.7	15.5
41 013	...	7	Crook	7 717	17 686	1 887	2.3	97.7	0.1	1.7	0.5	4.5	6.7	19.6	8.0	10.8	14.2	14.6
41 015	...	7	Curry	4 215	21 170	1 703	5.0	96.7	0.2	2.3	0.8	2.9	4.9	13.7	4.9	8.4	12.5	14.0
41 017	...	5	Deschutes	7 817	110 810	476	14.2	98.1	0.2	0.9	0.9	3.5	6.3	18.8	7.6	12.0	17.1	15.6
41 019	...	4	Douglas	13 045	101 805	510	7.8	97.3	0.2	1.6	1.0	3.8	6.2	18.8	7.5	10.5	13.8	14.9
41 021	...	9	Gilliam	3 119	2 074	3 058	0.7	98.6	0.0	0.6	0.8	3.2	5.6	20.1	5.0	11.1	13.3	13.9
41 023	...	9	Grant	11 730	7 855	2 617	0.7	98.5	0.1	1.1	0.3	3.0	6.1	19.1	6.4	10.8	14.8	16.0
41 025	...	7	Harney	26 249	7 295	2 653	0.3	95.7	0.1	3.5	0.7	5.1	6.5	19.5	6.2	11.2	14.0	16.6
41 027	...	6	Hood River	1 353	19 917	1 767	14.7	95.8	0.6	1.2	2.5	24.0	7.7	19.9	8.1	13.9	15.0	13.7
41 029	4890	3	Jackson	7 214	175 822	302	24.4	97.0	0.3	1.3	1.3	6.5	6.2	18.1	8.3	10.8	15.2	15.1
41 031	...	7	Jefferson	4 613	16 861	1 936	3.7	81.8	0.3	17.3	0.6	15.1	9.1	20.1	8.4	12.5	12.8	12.5
41 033	...	4	Josephine	4 247	74 919	661	17.6	97.2	0.3	1.4	1.1	4.7	5.8	17.7	6.6	9.6	14.1	15.9
41 035	...	5	Klamath	15 397	63 435	754	4.1	93.9	1.0	4.1	1.1	8.3	6.6	19.1	9.4	11.1	14.4	14.5
41 037	...	7	Lake	21 073	7 173	2 666	0.3	96.3	0.1	2.7	0.9	6.1	6.7	19.5	5.6	10.5	13.8	15.5
41 039	2400	2	Lane	11 795	314 901	179	26.7	95.4	0.9	1.1	2.6	4.0	6.1	17.5	11.6	12.3	15.9	14.4
41 041	...	7	Lincoln	2 537	44 985	985	17.7	96.0	0.2	2.4	1.3	2.6	5.5	16.8	6.0	10.1	15.2	14.8
41 043	...	4	Linn	5 935	105 337	492	17.7	97.2	0.3	1.2	1.3	4.0	6.7	19.2	8.9	11.7	14.4	15.4
41 045	...	7	Malheur	25 609	28 445	1 429	1.1	93.9	0.5	1.4	4.2	28.5	8.2	22.5	8.5	10.9	12.6	13.2
41 047	7080	2	Marion	3 069	272 760	202	88.9	94.8	1.2	1.6	2.5	12.7	7.3	19.6	9.7	13.2	15.1	14.1

1. MSA = Metropolitan Statistical Area. PMSA = Primary MSA. NECMA = New England County Metropolitan Area. See Appendix A for explanation of these concepts. See Appendix B for list of metropolitan areas identified by type, with component counties. 2. County typology code from the Economic Research Service of USDA. See Appendix A for definition. 3. Dry land or land partially or temporarily covered by water. 4. Hispanic persons may be of any race.

STATE County	Age (percent) (cont'd) 55 to 64 years	65 to 74 years	75 years and over	Percent female	Total persons 1990	Total persons 1980	Percent change 1980–1990	Percent change 1990–1999	Births	Deaths	Net migration	Households 1990 Number	Percent change, 1980–1990	Persons per household	Female family householder[1]	One person
	16	17	18	19	20	21	22	23	24	25	26	27	28	29	30	31
OKLAHOMA—Cont'd																
Kiowa	11.1	8.1	11.1	52.0	11 347	12 711	-10.7	-7.5	1 222	1 635	-399	4 551	-9.7	2.43	11.0	28.8
Latimer	10.3	8.1	7.4	49.7	10 333	9 840	5.0	-1.2	1 209	1 235	-72	3 693	8.7	2.64	10.0	22.8
Le Flore	9.8	7.1	6.9	50.5	43 270	40 698	6.3	8.1	5 989	4 818	2 466	15 938	10.0	2.65	10.3	22.4
Lincoln	10.5	7.4	6.9	50.6	29 216	26 601	9.8	8.9	3 386	2 875	2 131	10 839	12.3	2.67	7.8	21.4
Logan	9.3	6.0	6.6	50.8	29 011	26 881	7.9	4.9	3 253	2 640	911	10 180	8.1	2.65	10.0	22.6
Love	10.6	7.9	7.7	50.5	7 788	7 469	9.2	10.2	943	817	692	2 992	5.6	2.57	8.4	23.3
McClain	10.1	6.8	6.0	49.8	22 795	20 291	12.3	17.2	2 865	2 007	3 115	8 332	17.9	2.71	7.2	18.5
McCurtain	10.0	6.9	6.4	51.8	33 433	36 151	-7.5	4.1	5 072	3 606	-10	12 234	-1.1	2.69	13.4	23.0
McIntosh	14.4	11.9	9.3	51.7	16 779	15 562	7.8	14.8	1 871	2 391	3 062	6 786	14.3	2.43	9.4	24.3
Major	10.6	8.4	9.8	51.2	8 055	8 772	-8.2	-4.9	736	886	-222	3 121	-4.6	2.54	6.0	23.6
Marshall	12.4	10.7	9.5	51.2	10 829	10 550	2.6	14.3	1 360	1 493	1 718	4 350	4.6	2.41	8.2	25.2
Mayes	11.0	9.4	7.4	50.8	33 366	32 261	3.4	14.7	4 689	3 651	3 948	12 672	9.0	2.61	8.4	21.7
Murray	11.4	8.8	9.2	51.0	12 042	12 147	-0.9	3.6	1 321	1 635	782	4 651	2.5	2.49	9.2	26.3
Muskogee	10.1	7.9	7.2	52.0	68 078	67 033	1.6	3.0	9 454	7 601	-169	25 174	1.8	2.59	12.5	25.5
Noble	10.2	6.8	8.3	51.1	11 045	11 573	-4.6	2.6	1 295	1 194	219	4 225	-2.8	2.55	7.7	26.0
Nowata	12.1	8.8	9.4	51.0	9 992	11 486	-13.0	0.9	1 205	1 193	104	3 994	-7.7	2.45	8.6	26.4
Okfuskee	10.9	7.9	8.3	49.1	11 551	11 125	3.8	-2.7	1 350	1 434	-192	4 164	0.9	2.58	10.8	25.8
Oklahoma	9.3	6.9	5.5	51.9	599 611	568 933	5.4	6.2	94 864	54 408	-4 047	237 879	7.8	2.46	12.6	28.6
Okmulgee	10.5	7.6	7.5	51.4	36 490	39 169	-6.8	6.3	4 639	4 404	2 185	14 044	-1.9	2.52	12.4	26.5
Osage	10.1	6.6	5.5	50.0	41 645	39 327	5.9	3.2	3 996	3 262	800	15 383	7.0	2.63	9.2	23.3
Ottawa	11.7	10.0	8.0	52.6	30 561	32 870	-7.0	1.0	3 977	3 910	374	12 124	-1.0	2.42	9.7	27.3
Pawnee	10.4	8.1	7.3	50.1	15 575	15 310	1.7	6.2	1 892	1 616	747	6 006	4.5	2.57	7.2	23.1
Payne	6.9	5.3	5.3	49.3	61 507	62 435	-1.5	6.4	7 322	4 218	972	23 834	7.8	2.34	7.6	29.1
Pittsburg	11.3	8.9	8.1	49.4	40 950	40 524	0.1	6.2	4 751	4 941	2 849	15 911	5.8	2.44	10.2	26.4
Pontotoc	10.1	7.6	8.0	52.3	34 119	32 598	4.7	1.7	4 297	3 838	208	13 310	8.5	2.46	10.3	27.1
Pottawatomie	9.9	6.7	6.8	51.9	58 760	55 239	6.4	6.6	7 686	6 272	2 610	21 796	8.6	2.60	10.2	24.0
Pushmataha	12.3	8.9	8.9	50.7	10 997	11 773	-6.6	5.0	1 185	1 463	854	4 370	0.3	2.48	8.4	26.5
Roger Mills	9.7	9.3	8.9	50.2	4 147	4 799	-13.6	-13.4	350	418	-472	1 586	-10.3	2.59	6.3	23.8
Rogers	9.5	7.5	5.6	50.7	55 170	46 436	18.8	27.9	7 627	4 356	12 225	19 866	26.9	2.75	7.7	17.8
Seminole	10.9	8.6	8.8	51.9	25 412	27 465	-7.5	-3.4	3 233	3 206	-831	9 665	-4.9	2.57	11.9	25.7
Sequoyah	10.0	6.9	6.2	50.8	33 828	30 749	10.0	12.0	4 799	3 544	2 851	12 335	17.8	2.71	11.3	20.8
Stephens	11.5	9.2	8.7	52.0	42 299	43 419	-2.6	1.8	4 822	4 800	856	16 764	1.5	2.49	8.2	24.5
Texas	9.8	6.0	5.1	50.0	16 419	17 727	-7.4	11.6	2 341	1 270	846	5 933	-1.9	2.57	7.4	23.4
Tillman	9.6	8.7	9.8	51.3	10 384	12 398	-16.2	-9.3	1 276	1 315	-891	3 933	-16.0	2.57	10.2	26.4
Tulsa	9.1	6.6	5.2	51.7	503 341	470 593	7.0	8.9	79 273	42 533	9 538	202 537	11.5	2.43	11.0	28.8
Wagoner	8.8	5.2	3.9	50.4	47 883	41 801	14.5	17.2	6 078	3 054	5 332	16 946	23.1	2.81	8.6	17.2
Washington	10.8	9.8	7.9	52.0	48 066	48 113	0.0	-0.8	5 278	4 860	-622	19 242	2.6	2.46	7.9	24.8
Washita	10.9	9.8	9.5	51.2	11 441	13 798	-17.1	2.2	1 237	1 421	469	4 421	-14.0	2.53	6.4	24.1
Woods	10.5	9.8	12.2	52.1	9 103	10 923	-16.7	-10.2	855	1 217	-539	3 803	-14.1	2.26	6.2	32.4
Woodward	9.7	6.8	6.7	49.7	18 976	21 172	-10.4	-2.0	2 319	1 714	-938	7 087	-6.5	2.57	8.1	24.4
OREGON	9.1	6.6	6.5	50.6	2 842 337	2 633 156	7.9	16.7	399 411	255 204	337 146	1 103 313	11.3	2.52	9.2	25.3
Baker	11.7	8.4	9.7	49.8	15 317	16 134	-5.1	6.2	1 679	1 808	1 120	6 118	-0.8	2.45	7.2	26.0
Benton	7.2	5.4	5.1	49.4	70 811	68 211	3.8	9.0	7 695	3 896	1 633	26 126	9.0	2.47	7.1	25.2
Clackamas	8.9	5.8	5.6	50.6	278 850	241 911	15.3	21.3	37 320	21 778	44 563	103 530	22.2	2.67	8.2	20.5
Clatsop	10.1	7.5	7.6	50.1	33 301	32 489	2.5	6.1	3 879	3 514	1 732	13 374	4.5	2.43	8.3	28.0
Columbia	9.3	5.9	5.5	49.5	37 557	35 646	5.4	20.8	4 651	3 157	6 367	13 910	9.2	2.68	7.6	21.3
Coos	11.4	9.6	8.9	50.4	60 273	64 047	-5.9	-2.8	6 314	6 958	2 228	24 134	1.1	2.45	9.1	24.6
Crook	10.7	8.1	7.2	49.3	14 111	13 091	7.8	25.3	2 001	1 532	3 161	5 455	11.5	2.56	6.4	22.7
Curry	13.8	15.8	12.0	50.3	19 327	16 992	13.7	9.5	1 741	2 529	2 711	8 311	22.9	2.30	5.9	24.4
Deschutes	10.2	7.0	5.5	49.9	74 976	62 142	20.7	47.8	11 098	6 712	31 393	29 217	27.2	2.54	7.6	21.0
Douglas	10.9	9.1	8.3	50.3	94 649	93 748	1.0	7.6	10 851	9 946	6 627	35 872	7.5	2.60	8.8	21.5
Gilliam	12.9	8.8	9.2	50.0	1 717	2 057	-16.5	20.8	144	164	385	696	-10.5	2.47	5.0	25.3
Grant	11.2	7.6	8.0	49.3	7 853	8 210	-4.3	0.0	935	721	-198	3 092	2.9	2.51	5.9	24.6
Harney	10.7	7.5	7.7	49.5	7 060	8 314	-15.1	3.3	756	646	136	2 760	-6.2	2.54	7.2	24.6
Hood River	8.7	6.5	6.4	48.5	16 903	15 835	6.7	17.8	2 781	1 430	1 731	6 425	7.8	2.59	7.5	24.2
Jackson	10.1	8.3	8.0	51.0	146 387	132 456	10.5	20.1	18 979	14 902	25 882	57 238	16.8	2.50	9.1	24.0
Jefferson	8.9	8.8	7.0	49.6	13 676	11 599	17.9	23.3	2 717	1 210	1 744	4 744	20.6	2.84	9.8	18.8
Josephine	11.7	9.8	8.9	51.1	62 649	58 855	6.4	19.6	7 350	8 107	13 202	25 081	14.6	2.46	9.3	23.7
Klamath	10.4	7.6	6.8	49.4	57 702	59 117	-2.4	9.9	7 828	5 556	3 609	22 341	3.0	2.54	8.4	24.2
Lake	11.0	9.2	8.2	49.6	7 186	7 532	-4.6	-0.2	829	721	-97	2 765	-0.9	2.57	6.3	22.5
Lane	8.7	6.8	6.6	51.1	282 912	275 226	2.8	11.3	33 949	23 564	22 445	110 799	7.0	2.49	9.4	25.5
Lincoln	12.5	10.7	8.4	51.6	38 889	35 264	10.3	15.7	4 252	4 630	6 566	16 455	12.6	2.34	7.7	26.5
Linn	9.7	7.1	6.9	50.5	91 227	89 495	1.9	15.5	12 596	8 586	10 322	34 716	5.9	2.60	9.0	22.2
Malheur	9.9	7.2	7.1	50.5	26 038	26 896	-3.2	9.2	4 599	2 530	429	9 457	1.9	2.71	8.8	24.1
Marion	8.8	5.7	6.5	50.3	228 483	204 692	11.6	19.4	38 696	21 300	27 573	83 494	12.5	2.60	10.3	24.6

1. No spouse present.

Table B. States and Counties — Vital Statistics, Health Resources, and Crime

STATE County	Births, average 1996–1998 Total	Rate[1]	Deaths, average 1996–1998 Number Total	Number Infant[2]	Rate Total[1]	Rate Infant[3]	Physicians,[4] 1998 Number	Rate[5]	Hospitals,[4] 1998 Number	Beds Number	Beds Rate[5]	Medicare enrollees 1999	Serious crimes known to police, 1998[6] Total Number	Total Rate[7]
	32	33	34	35	36	37	38	39	40	41	42	43	44	45

OKLAHOMA—Cont'd

STATE County	32	33	34	35	36	37	38	39	40	41	42	43	44	45
Kiowa	130	12.1	178	1	16.6	7.7	5	47	1	50	471	2 368	312	2 856
Latimer	124	12.1	127	1	12.4	10.8	14	136	1	33	320	1 452	282	2 717
Le Flore	690	14.9	526	4	11.3	5.3	24	52	1	84	180	8 248	1 049	2 236
Lincoln	384	12.3	339	4	10.9	9.6	11	35	2	44	140	4 764	753	2 401
Logan	355	11.6	296	3	9.7	9.4	13	42	1	32	103	3 786	894	2 895
Love	106	12.4	95	1	11.1	6.3	1	12	1	40	469	1 492	243	2 801
McClain	322	12.5	227	3	8.8	8.3	13	50	1	32	122	3 760	912	3 501
McCurtain	556	16.0	398	6	11.5	11.4	16	46	1	89	256	5 847	1 356	3 903
McIntosh	218	11.6	284	3	15.1	12.2	6	31	1	33	173	4 680	825	4 349
Major	79	10.2	96	0	12.4	0.0	3	38	1	24	307	1 473	221	2 818
Marshall	165	13.6	155	2	12.8	12.1	7	57	1	25	203	2 787	282	2 320
Mayes	531	14.3	405	4	10.9	7.5	22	58	1	43	114	5 956	901	2 496
Murray	156	12.6	178	2	14.4	10.7	12	97	1	48	389	2 381	474	3 798
Muskogee	1 038	14.8	859	10	12.3	9.6	121	173	1	225	321	12 537	3 873	5 533
Noble	146	12.9	135	1	11.9	4.6	7	61	1	42	368	1 888	225	1 983
Nowata	124	12.5	122	2	12.3	13.4	5	50	1	32	321	2 035	343	3 433
Okfuskee	146	12.8	146	1	12.8	6.9	4	35	1	20	175	2 259	419	3 685
Oklahoma	10 565	16.7	6 222	105	9.8	9.9	1 952	308	13	3 325	525	89 648	51 614	8 115
Okmulgee	521	13.6	475	3	12.4	6.4	27	69	2	118	304	6 798	1 453	3 770
Osage	408	9.6	369	2	8.7	4.9	65	152	3	411	959	3 622	1 201	2 800
Ottawa	438	14.2	434	4	14.1	9.1	24	78	1	119	385	7 183	1 292	4 187
Pawnee	208	12.8	179	1	11.0	6.4	9	55	2	43	262	2 751	388	2 373
Payne	794	12.3	479	6	7.4	7.6	95	146	2	177	272	7 963	2 548	3 929
Pittsburg	488	11.3	538	3	12.5	5.5	50	117	1	171	400	7 922	1 425	3 269
Pontotoc	476	13.7	427	4	12.2	7.7	57	165	1	144	416	6 352	1 306	3 718
Pottawatomie	854	13.8	708	8	11.4	9.8	66	106	2	160	257	9 734	3 001	4 882
Pushmataha	131	11.3	172	0	14.8	2.5	7	60	1	46	397	2 444	288	2 481
Roger Mills	31	8.6	37	1	10.2	32.3	4	112	1	15	419	709	75	2 063
Rogers	838	12.7	501	7	7.6	8.8	64	94	1	86	126	7 412	1 818	2 744
Seminole	355	14.3	349	5	14.0	13.1	13	52	1	39	157	4 958	968	3 883
Sequoyah	537	14.5	397	5	10.7	9.3	17	45	1	41	109	6 219	989	2 718
Stephens	523	12.1	555	4	12.8	7.0	34	78	1	100	230	8 308	1 531	3 480
Texas	295	16.3	152	2	8.4	5.7	13	70	1	49	263	2 230	846	4 637
Tillman	121	12.7	140	1	14.6	8.2	5	53	1	58	610	1 920	223	2 289
Tulsa	8 682	16.2	4 823	66	9.0	7.6	1 498	276	6	1 898	349	81 941	33 484	6 192
Wagoner	659	12.2	354	5	6.5	8.1	30	54	1	100	181	4 417	1 063	1 944
Washington	531	11.2	539	3	11.4	5.0	82	173	1	233	490	9 657	1 808	3 780
Washita	133	11.4	155	0	13.3	0.0	2	17	1	38	322	2 321	214	1 815
Woods	92	11.0	128	1	15.3	14.4	4	48	1	50	598	1 892	188	2 258
Woodward	238	12.8	179	1	9.6	4.2	19	102	1	68	367	2 801	865	4 593
OREGON	44 247	13.7	29 022	248	9.0	5.6	7 552	230	62	7 352	224	483 898	185 323	5 647
Baker	176	10.7	205	0	12.6	1.9	22	134	1	129	784	3 447	917	5 519
Benton	829	10.7	444	4	5.7	4.4	188	242	1	124	159	7 996	2 757	3 559
Clackamas	4 102	12.4	2 500	26	7.6	6.3	697	208	3	339	101	38 834	16 105	4 806
Clatsop	402	11.4	375	1	10.6	2.5	50	141	2	69	195	6 124	1 783	4 956
Columbia	519	11.9	351	2	8.1	4.5	15	34	0	0	0	5 913	1 178	2 661
Coos	647	10.4	813	3	13.0	5.2	126	203	3	178	286	13 239	2 738	4 375
Crook	224	13.2	172	1	10.2	3.0	13	75	1	35	203	3 039	608	3 543
Curry	176	8.3	302	1	14.3	5.7	35	165	1	24	113	6 282	525	2 437
Deschutes	1 327	13.0	821	7	8.1	5.5	232	220	2	223	211	16 209	4 995	4 909
Douglas	1 125	11.1	1 148	9	11.3	8.0	189	186	3	284	279	20 045	2 930	2 844
Gilliam	18	9.3	17	0	8.6	0.0	0	0	0	0	0	416	52	2 628
Grant	93	11.6	84	1	10.5	7.1	5	62	1	75	929	1 473	89	1 099
Harney	83	11.7	78	0	11.0	4.0	5	69	1	52	722	1 276	189	2 655
Hood River	297	15.4	160	1	8.3	3.4	42	215	1	54	276	2 737	732	3 687
Jackson	2 093	12.3	1 756	12	10.3	5.6	429	248	3	471	272	31 590	9 434	5 498
Jefferson	313	19.0	151	2	9.2	7.5	17	102	1	109	656	2 875	582	3 599
Josephine	787	10.8	945	4	12.9	5.5	116	156	2	146	196	16 934	3 616	4 864
Klamath	832	13.3	636	7	10.1	8.8	107	169	1	256	405	10 491	2 242	3 516
Lake	73	10.1	76	1	10.6	13.7	8	112	1	67	937	1 512	148	1 996
Lane	3 669	11.8	2 772	22	8.9	6.0	650	207	4	620	197	47 785	20 623	6 545
Lincoln	437	9.7	532	3	11.8	6.9	86	190	2	75	165	9 737	2 563	5 555
Linn	1 441	13.9	999	8	9.7	5.5	124	119	2	120	115	16 976	5 996	5 728
Malheur	499	17.6	287	4	10.1	8.7	49	172	1	74	259	4 746	1 177	4 080
Marion	4 459	16.8	2 401	29	9.1	6.4	488	182	3	466	174	40 408	17 489	6 518

1. Per 1,000 estimated resident population, average 1996–1998.   2. Deaths of infants under 1 year old.   3. Deaths of infants under 1 year old per 1,000 live births.   4. Data subject to copyright.   5. Per 100,000 resident population as of July 1 of the year shown.   6. Data for serious crimes have not been adjusted for underreporting; this may affect comparability between geographic areas and over time.   7. Per 100,000 population estimated by the FBI.

Table B. States and Counties — Crime, Education, Money Income, and Poverty

STATE County	Serious crimes known to police, 1998[1] (cont'd) Rate[2] Violent	Rate[2] Property	Education School enrollment and attainment, 1990 Enrollment[3] Total	Enrollment[3] Percent private	Attainment[4] (percent) High school graduate or more	Attainment[4] (percent) Bachelor's degree or more	Local government expenditures, fiscal 1997[5] Total current expenditures (mil dol)	Current expenditures per student (dollars)	Money income 1989 Per capita[6] (dollars)	Households Median Dollars	Households Median Percent change, 1979–1989 (constant 1989 dollars)	Percent with $100,000 or more	Income and poverty, 1997 Percent below poverty level Median household income	All persons	Persons under 18	Persons 5–17 in families
	46	47	48	49	50	51	52	53	54	55	56	57	58	59	60	61
OKLAHOMA—Cont'd																
Kiowa	284	2 572	2 622	3.1	65.0	11.1	11.6	5 561	9 213	16 322	0.5	1.1	22 095	23.2	30.4	31.0
Latimer	713	2 004	2 990	3.1	63.1	11.0	14.6	7 529	9 427	17 477	9.8	0.7	23 720	24.1	35.5	30.8
Le Flore	350	1 886	10 631	3.2	61.2	9.6	46.5	4 841	8 752	18 832	4.2	1.2	26 057	21.7	30.7	28.1
Lincoln	328	2 073	7 301	4.2	68.8	10.1	26.0	4 506	9 952	21 515	-1.5	1.1	31 148	15.2	23.1	20.1
Logan	301	2 594	8 398	6.5	72.0	14.8	21.6	4 718	10 946	24 050	1.7	1.9	35 771	13.8	19.3	17.5
Love	646	2 155	1 889	3.2	66.5	9.3	8.0	4 767	9 960	20 320	-7.3	1.9	27 775	16.7	25.1	23.8
McClain	591	2 910	6 015	5.1	72.2	13.3	24.7	4 559	11 114	25 437	-4.7	2.2	34 208	13.9	20.0	18.4
McCurtain	699	3 204	8 607	1.8	59.2	9.6	39.7	5 209	8 291	16 413	-4.4	1.0	23 132	26.5	36.0	33.7
McIntosh	511	3 838	3 616	2.2	61.5	10.7	17.1	5 060	9 403	17 738	7.3	0.8	22 904	22.3	36.0	32.2
Major	306	2 512	1 960	5.4	70.9	13.1	6.7	4 880	10 745	23 568	-7.6	2.1	31 859	13.9	18.7	18.8
Marshall	313	2 007	2 162	4.0	60.7	9.7	10.0	4 720	9 889	16 292	-2.5	2.0	23 597	18.9	29.6	27.2
Mayes	150	2 346	7 937	5.8	67.9	10.8	32.0	4 547	10 049	21 209	0.2	1.7	29 381	17.2	25.7	23.3
Murray	441	3 357	2 839	5.0	64.0	13.5	11.0	4 633	9 439	18 321	-13.7	0.9	25 266	19.5	27.2	26.7
Muskogee	736	4 797	17 050	7.5	68.3	14.1	73.8	5 285	9 756	20 407	-1.6	1.2	27 432	20.0	27.8	25.3
Noble	256	1 727	2 648	2.5	72.8	12.7	12.8	5 411	10 969	23 227	-0.7	1.7	31 827	14.0	18.8	18.7
Nowata	360	3 073	2 385	3.6	67.4	7.4	9.9	4 933	9 339	18 274	-18.0	0.6	26 073	17.2	23.9	23.6
Okfuskee	334	3 351	2 784	4.8	60.7	8.2	12.5	5 161	8 471	15 738	2.9	1.8	21 202	27.6	37.1	34.8
Oklahoma	749	7 366	157 291	14.4	79.1	22.6	491.9	4 572	13 794	26 129	-5.3	3.1	34 513	15.8	24.4	21.6
Okmulgee	524	3 246	9 541	5.2	66.3	8.8	34.8	4 715	8 799	17 368	-5.6	0.9	24 039	22.5	31.5	29.2
Osage	562	2 238	10 652	7.7	73.0	13.1	25.9	5 397	11 123	24 617	-6.8	1.1	32 421	15.2	22.8	20.2
Ottawa	246	3 941	7 848	3.0	67.8	10.4	32.6	5 302	9 057	17 716	-11.7	1.1	25 013	19.7	29.5	26.7
Pawnee	257	2 116	3 696	6.3	73.0	10.4	11.8	4 370	10 416	21 199	-9.7	1.4	29 496	16.7	23.9	22.9
Payne	413	3 516	26 211	3.1	82.2	30.1	52.4	5 084	10 907	19 591	-2.1	1.8	30 444	16.6	20.8	19.8
Pittsburg	388	2 881	9 422	3.7	64.3	10.3	41.7	4 941	9 832	18 906	-0.9	1.2	26 665	19.8	29.0	26.1
Pontotoc	604	3 114	9 151	2.3	69.3	18.0	34.2	4 851	10 005	17 945	-11.2	1.7	25 859	20.8	30.4	28.0
Pottawatomie	407	4 475	15 912	16.6	70.3	12.2	58.3	4 711	10 391	21 914	-2.4	1.2	30 409	19.5	29.0	25.6
Pushmataha	525	1 956	2 352	2.6	57.8	7.8	12.9	5 204	7 426	13 613	-7.5	0.3	19 362	29.2	42.1	39.2
Roger Mills	138	1 925	1 007	1.8	72.1	9.5	3.7	8 676	9 886	20 106	-6.8	2.3	27 240	16.9	23.0	23.2
Rogers	186	2 558	14 798	9.8	78.1	13.0	51.9	4 200	12 235	29 389	-5.4	1.9	41 466	9.1	14.1	12.5
Seminole	401	3 482	6 423	3.9	62.1	9.6	26.1	5 098	9 044	17 007	-11.2	1.2	22 426	26.7	39.0	34.7
Sequoyah	349	2 369	8 466	3.3	59.6	8.8	39.1	4 829	9 074	18 441	-1.2	0.9	26 044	21.0	29.7	27.4
Stephens	225	3 255	10 064	4.0	70.8	14.7	40.0	4 786	10 839	22 647	-9.7	1.3	30 175	16.5	23.6	21.5
Texas	373	4 264	4 577	4.4	75.5	15.1	18.2	5 173	11 096	23 587	-15.1	1.5	36 041	11.3	15.9	15.0
Tillman	195	2 094	2 624	2.9	61.7	11.4	10.6	5 181	8 597	17 799	-2.4	1.1	22 989	23.6	32.6	31.9
Tulsa	903	5 289	133 622	20.3	81.7	23.7	465.9	4 644	14 742	27 228	-6.9	4.0	35 280	13.3	20.0	18.3
Wagoner	139	1 805	13 136	11.3	74.7	12.0	25.0	4 343	11 839	28 544	-2.5	1.5	37 904	12.8	18.3	16.7
Washington	481	3 299	11 909	10.6	79.6	25.8	38.6	4 380	15 086	28 857	-9.7	3.9	37 346	12.3	19.1	17.1
Washita	254	1 561	2 590	3.6	66.6	11.0	12.6	5 588	9 642	18 385	-27.0	2.1	25 393	19.9	27.7	26.8
Woods	252	2 006	2 707	2.7	76.1	23.5	9.5	6 422	12 261	19 762	-13.0	2.8	28 010	15.5	22.0	20.4
Woodward	276	4 317	4 718	6.5	73.4	13.0	18.8	4 949	11 000	23 796	-21.9	2.1	32 899	14.6	19.6	19.1
OREGON	420	5 227	724 233	11.7	81.5	20.6	3 184.0	5 920	13 418	27 250	-3.1	2.8	37 284	11.6	16.3	13.9
Baker	211	5 308	3 275	6.0	75.0	13.3	20.3	6 586	10 802	22 150	-0.8	1.7	29 203	16.8	24.4	20.8
Benton	169	3 390	29 624	5.8	89.3	41.3	59.2	5 693	12 994	27 295	0.6	3.3	43 632	9.1	10.0	9.1
Clackamas	209	4 597	71 771	12.4	85.7	23.6	309.4	5 746	16 360	35 419	-0.2	5.2	49 455	6.4	8.6	6.9
Clatsop	200	4 756	8 040	7.9	81.8	16.7	32.7	5 998	12 568	25 135	-1.7	1.7	33 502	13.3	18.3	17.2
Columbia	45	2 616	9 429	8.8	78.0	11.0	52.4	5 808	12 798	29 507	-5.2	1.9	42 924	8.6	11.1	10.1
Coos	165	4 210	14 061	5.9	75.5	12.3	70.0	6 545	11 088	22 146	-17.9	1.6	29 933	16.7	23.6	20.7
Crook	70	3 473	3 108	6.7	71.8	10.1	16.7	5 441	11 017	24 275	-6.6	1.4	33 188	12.8	18.6	16.5
Curry	74	2 363	3 227	4.2	78.1	12.8	21.1	6 244	12 475	22 579	-8.0	2.4	28 463	13.9	22.9	20.5
Deschutes	210	4 699	18 147	8.5	83.2	18.9	101.1	5 617	13 401	27 317	-1.7	3.2	37 046	10.6	15.9	13.4
Douglas	89	2 755	22 054	7.0	74.5	11.7	107.8	6 108	10 809	23 693	-15.3	1.2	32 005	14.6	20.5	17.7
Gilliam	51	2 577	423	7.3	85.4	18.7	4.3	11 173	12 137	24 020	-6.5	2.4	34 685	9.4	11.5	11.7
Grant	62	1 037	1 772	2.8	77.2	12.5	11.7	7 319	11 310	24 640	-3.3	1.2	32 939	14.5	19.7	17.6
Harney	169	2 486	1 620	2.6	78.0	14.1	10.8	7 503	10 990	22 334	-21.3	1.4	29 809	14.8	21.9	18.9
Hood River	96	3 591	3 894	9.6	71.3	18.0	24.0	6 606	11 421	25 242	-6.6	1.7	34 380	13.0	18.8	17.1
Jackson	294	5 204	34 122	9.6	80.1	17.6	166.2	5 866	12 492	25 069	-3.3	2.1	32 807	13.8	20.3	16.5
Jefferson	155	3 444	3 368	5.7	73.9	12.2	24.8	6 980	9 863	23 532	-9.2	2.0	31 915	16.6	23.0	21.6
Josephine	211	4 653	13 135	11.9	75.2	12.0	66.2	5 651	10 809	20 936	-4.5	1.6	26 988	18.7	28.5	24.0
Klamath	320	3 196	14 456	5.9	76.2	12.4	72.5	6 319	11 138	23 054	-10.7	1.6	30 781	15.9	22.8	19.9
Lake	54	1 942	1 649	4.9	75.0	14.5	10.3	6 546	11 231	24 659	-5.0	2.3	30 427	14.7	20.1	18.5
Lane	384	6 161	80 983	8.3	83.0	22.2	292.6	5 973	12 570	25 268	-7.3	2.4	34 672	13.3	18.0	15.2
Lincoln	299	5 256	8 225	7.7	80.5	16.7	42.9	5 934	12 058	22 883	-6.9	1.5	30 394	14.7	23.0	20.3
Linn	239	5 489	22 122	9.2	76.2	11.0	103.2	5 652	11 443	25 209	-6.2	1.4	36 107	12.3	17.2	14.8
Malheur	83	3 997	7 341	6.6	69.9	13.1	37.6	6 432	9 949	20 242	-7.1	2.0	28 204	19.6	26.0	23.4
Marion	229	6 289	57 717	14.3	78.7	17.5	277.6	5 680	12 228	26 876	-0.4	2.2	36 853	13.2	19.0	15.7

1. Data for serious crimes have not been adjusted for underreporting; this may affect comparability between geographic areas and over time.   2. Per 100,000 population estimated by the FBI.   3. All persons 3 years old and over enrolled in nursery school through college.   4. Persons 25 years old and over.   5. Elementary and secondary education expenditures, local government fiscal years ending between July 1, 1996 and June 30, 1997.   6. Based on population enumerated as of April 1, 1990.

Table B. States and Counties — **Personal Income**

STATE County	Personal income, 1998 Total (mil dol)	Percent change, 1997–1998	Per capita[1] Dollars	Per capita[1] Rank	Wages and salaries[2] (mil dol)	Proprietor's income (mil dol)	Dividends, interest, and rent (mil dol)	Transfer payments Total (mil dol)	Government payments to individuals Total (mil dol)	Social Security (mil dol)	Medical payments (mil dol)	Income mainte-nance (mil dol)	Unemploy-ment insurance (mil dol)
	62	63	64	65	66	67	68	69	70	71	72	73	74
OKLAHOMA—Cont'd													
Kiowa	190	7.5	17 789	2 407	65	29	40	51	49	20	19	6	0
Latimer	182	0.8	17 693	2 439	100	8	32	49	47	18	16	5	1
Le Flore	789	3.6	16 919	2 628	263	106	115	190	182	67	68	24	1
Lincoln	563	4.9	17 976	2 349	156	34	92	99	93	44	31	9	1
Logan	617	7.1	20 509	1 553	147	52	87	97	91	41	32	7	1
Love	135	1.8	15 774	2 829	44	6	22	31	30	14	11	3	0
McClain	493	5.0	18 809	2 120	143	37	69	77	72	34	34	5	1
McCurtain	599	5.9	17 210	2 556	297	114	75	141	135	48	55	21	1
McIntosh	292	2.2	15 386	2 891	85	20	60	92	89	39	32	9	1
Major	147	-0.4	18 874	2 098	62	22	36	26	25	14	8	2	0
Marshall	205	4.1	16 697	2 680	91	13	40	57	55	25	21	5	0
Mayes	685	4.8	18 205	2 293	312	47	113	140	134	64	46	12	1
Murray	206	4.0	16 720	2 674	87	18	37	53	51	22	18	4	1
Muskogee	1 299	4.9	18 538	2 198	831	94	223	292	280	108	105	30	4
Noble	222	3.5	19 503	1 890	129	14	50	40	38	18	16	2	0
Nowata	162	3.6	16 188	2 765	46	11	30	40	39	19	13	3	0
Okfuskee	168	2.4	14 767	2 954	62	14	25	52	50	19	21	6	0
Oklahoma	15 841	4.6	25 031	487	13 440	1 538	2 945	2 037	1 928	828	709	201	23
Okmulgee	603	4.6	15 599	2 864	248	33	97	170	163	64	59	18	2
Osage	756	3.9	17 618	2 463	220	27	130	122	115	64	30	10	1
Ottawa	573	2.3	18 537	2 199	217	72	100	146	140	63	52	12	1
Pawnee	298	3.4	18 181	2 300	74	23	52	59	56	28	19	4	1
Payne	1 267	3.4	19 405	1 918	789	74	246	189	178	76	60	14	1
Pittsburg	739	2.2	17 184	2 566	380	59	155	173	165	71	59	18	2
Pontotoc	653	3.5	18 868	2 100	349	52	128	148	142	59	53	15	1
Pottawatomie	1 135	4.2	18 224	2 289	500	94	203	211	200	86	68	22	2
Pushmataha	155	1.2	13 512	3 044	59	10	26	57	55	20	22	8	1
Roger Mills	66	2.1	18 457	2 224	21	9	24	13	12	6	4	1	0
Rogers	1 405	6.4	20 657	1 501	604	106	211	187	175	87	56	10	2
Seminole	385	2.2	15 555	2 874	164	26	70	119	114	43	47	14	2
Sequoyah	637	4.2	16 964	2 620	179	70	81	145	139	55	53	18	2
Stephens	845	3.8	19 422	1 915	376	123	179	175	167	85	53	13	2
Texas	496	6.8	26 751	323	249	132	70	49	46	24	15	3	0
Tillman	155	5.4	16 259	2 749	62	20	28	40	39	17	15	5	0
Tulsa	16 297	7.1	29 990	164	11 690	2 673	2 789	1 740	1 645	768	593	133	17
Wagoner	985	4.7	17 836	2 396	163	63	123	141	131	66	40	11	2
Washington	1 248	4.4	26 271	367	605	90	358	184	176	98	56	10	1
Washita	181	1.5	15 261	2 904	57	18	44	46	44	20	17	4	0
Woods	188	6.1	22 640	940	71	32	52	37	35	17	11	2	0
Woodward	357	0.3	19 151	2 000	216	41	69	59	56	28	19	4	1
OREGON	85 043	4.9	25 912	X	53 304	6 799	19 260	11 140	10 566	4 814	3 608	903	447
Baker	313	0.5	19 049	2 039	142	17	91	71	68	32	23	6	3
Benton	2 125	3.7	27 307	278	1 346	106	571	187	173	87	44	14	4
Clackamas	10 281	5.2	30 709	144	4 481	671	2 288	865	807	425	238	45	32
Clatsop	801	3.3	22 662	935	432	68	198	134	128	63	42	10	5
Columbia	1 024	6.1	23 004	853	320	61	184	137	129	64	42	9	6
Coos	1 326	3.4	21 332	1 288	607	102	340	305	295	133	100	28	15
Crook	344	4.4	19 905	1 746	183	23	89	67	64	30	22	5	3
Curry	463	4.4	21 993	1 106	152	34	167	116	112	62	34	7	4
Deschutes	2 620	7.1	24 784	517	1 298	328	719	355	336	169	103	23	19
Douglas	2 092	4.1	20 543	1 542	1 110	139	503	436	418	199	133	34	21
Gilliam	29	-9.4	14 353	2 977	25	-8	13	7	6	4	1	0	0
Grant	160	-0.5	19 963	1 725	78	9	43	33	32	14	11	3	3
Harney	148	5.0	20 534	1 546	78	12	33	29	28	13	9	2	2
Hood River	417	2.3	21 262	1 302	244	36	112	57	54	27	16	4	5
Jackson	4 022	5.4	23 214	813	1 988	425	1 090	660	629	310	198	51	27
Jefferson	307	7.6	18 328	2 255	183	15	66	60	57	24	22	6	2
Josephine	1 473	4.9	19 862	1 757	551	146	427	374	361	164	127	38	11
Klamath	1 251	2.1	19 800	1 781	668	96	275	259	248	102	85	25	11
Lake	143	-1.3	19 996	1 713	69	10	38	31	30	15	9	3	2
Lane	7 568	5.4	24 151	615	4 217	638	1 829	1 139	1 084	480	373	102	38
Lincoln	992	4.7	21 913	1 124	439	82	301	206	198	98	65	15	8
Linn	2 216	3.6	21 218	1 324	1 332	163	429	389	371	167	126	35	20
Malheur	558	4.8	19 542	1 873	336	59	138	106	101	43	37	11	4
Marion	6 250	5.1	23 240	806	3 776	563	1 372	957	910	389	343	83	32

1. Based on the resident population estimated as of July 1 of the year shown.   2. Includes other labor income.

Table B. States and Counties — Earnings, Social Security, and Housing

STATE County	Earnings, 1998									Social Security beneficiaries, December 1998		Supplemental Security Income recipients, December 1998	Housing units, 1990	
			Goods-related[1]		Service-related and other[2]									
	Total (mil dol)	Farm	Total	Manu-facturing	Total	Retail trade	Finance, insurance, and real estate	Services	Govern-ment	Number	Rate[3]		Total	Percent change, 1980–1990
	75	76	77	78	79	80	81	82	83	84	85	86	87	88
OKLAHOMA—Cont'd														
Kiowa	94	18.6	D	D	D	8.4	4.0	17.2	27.0	2 716	256	417	5 645	-3.3
Latimer	108	-2.0	36.2	7.9	26.2	5.4	1.7	12.6	39.6	2 553	247	300	4 303	8.0
Le Flore	369	10.4	D	16.6	D	10.3	4.2	14.5	25.7	9 292	200	2 081	18 029	15.1
Lincoln	189	-2.9	20.9	9.2	61.6	11.0	11.6	18.3	20.4	5 918	189	602	12 302	15.7
Logan	199	2.0	19.9	5.2	50.6	10.6	4.6	24.9	27.6	5 100	165	387	12 277	16.2
Love	50	-7.3	D	29.4	D	13.8	2.6	16.8	23.2	1 765	207	186	3 583	11.8
McClain	180	1.4	31.2	11.3	44.1	16.1	4.6	14.2	23.3	4 330	165	319	9 300	20.6
McCurtain	411	11.4	D	33.6	D	7.8	2.1	16.0	17.4	6 910	199	1 791	13 828	0.7
McIntosh	106	-2.8	13.8	8.0	64.1	19.0	4.8	29.7	24.8	5 185	272	677	10 708	28.6
Major	84	10.6	D	7.0	D	8.3	3.7	13.8	15.6	1 788	228	87	3 855	8.1
Marshall	104	-3.3	D	32.2	D	12.0	3.6	15.4	19.6	3 216	261	405	7 389	43.2
Mayes	359	0.7	D	38.2	D	9.5	2.7	13.6	20.5	7 905	210	815	15 470	11.4
Murray	105	1.1	D	7.5	D	13.2	3.1	17.6	34.6	2 843	230	338	5 742	11.5
Muskogee	925	-0.3	29.3	20.3	44.4	10.0	3.0	18.7	26.6	13 915	199	2 327	28 882	5.1
Noble	144	3.6	D	D	D	7.9	3.2	11.3	17.0	2 193	192	200	4 894	0.5
Nowata	56	0.3	D	17.9	D	7.3	5.1	22.5	25.1	2 412	242	201	4 534	-6.6
Okfuskee	76	0.7	28.6	6.9	38.6	8.8	3.4	20.8	32.1	2 604	228	543	4 894	2.5
Oklahoma	14 977	0.0	20.2	11.1	56.7	9.4	6.6	27.5	23.0	98 381	155	13 304	279 340	15.5
Okmulgee	281	-1.3	30.2	23.1	45.6	11.6	4.1	22.1	25.5	8 102	208	1 337	16 431	5.2
Osage	247	-1.6	48.8	14.7	28.6	6.0	2.7	15.1	24.2	7 743	181	461	18 196	11.6
Ottawa	289	8.4	D	18.2	D	11.2	3.2	22.7	19.4	7 922	256	973	14 064	0.8
Pawnee	98	-3.4	D	4.5	D	11.8	4.8	28.2	29.5	3 470	211	314	7 407	15.1
Payne	864	-0.3	D	10.7	D	9.9	3.4	20.2	43.5	9 072	139	993	27 381	12.9
Pittsburg	439	-0.9	20.6	13.6	43.3	11.2	3.4	18.7	37.0	9 615	225	1 489	19 433	8.2
Pontotoc	400	-0.6	20.4	13.5	59.3	11.2	6.1	33.0	21.0	7 410	214	1 177	15 094	13.5
Pottawatomie	595	0.4	30.8	23.1	53.0	16.4	3.3	26.6	15.8	11 493	185	1 499	24 528	11.5
Pushmataha	69	-7.5	13.5	7.3	56.7	13.9	3.3	31.3	37.3	2 900	250	653	5 190	3.8
Roger Mills	30	10.8	14.9	1.9	D	7.6	3.8	13.3	38.7	817	228	70	2 048	2.1
Rogers	711	-0.5	42.8	33.6	41.9	7.6	3.3	15.3	15.8	10 154	149	645	21 455	26.5
Seminole	189	-1.5	33.9	19.7	D	11.5	3.0	20.1	24.3	5 737	232	960	11 404	1.3
Sequoyah	249	-0.4	14.9	9.1	60.2	14.4	4.3	32.3	25.3	7 570	202	1 551	14 314	20.4
Stephens	500	0.2	39.5	24.6	47.4	11.6	4.6	25.0	12.9	10 141	234	829	19 675	9.5
Texas	380	31.0	D	D	D	6.4	2.0	9.7	11.8	2 660	143	180	7 328	3.5
Tillman	82	19.1	D	18.7	34.1	5.8	3.2	11.4	24.9	2 213	233	306	4 704	-10.5
Tulsa	14 363	0.1	30.5	20.8	61.6	8.2	6.3	27.3	7.8	84 202	155	9 352	227 834	16.6
Wagoner	226	0.6	30.3	16.8	50.0	10.9	3.5	28.0	19.1	7 999	145	619	19 262	22.7
Washington	695	0.4	D	10.6	D	9.7	4.1	D	10.0	10 857	228	706	21 707	7.2
Washita	75	10.1	D	6.3	D	7.3	3.3	18.3	28.7	2 698	229	213	6 101	2.7
Woods	103	19.2	9.6	4.7	42.2	12.0	6.8	12.5	28.9	2 026	242	106	4 782	-2.8
Woodward	257	4.3	27.2	4.2	46.6	11.7	6.8	13.0	21.9	3 374	182	254	8 512	4.2
OREGON	60 103	1.2	26.1	18.6	57.0	10.4	7.1	25.2	15.7	547 705	167	49 046	1 193 567	10.2
Baker	159	-3.2	D	12.8	52.8	12.6	4.2	23.5	30.3	3 981	242	318	7 525	3.0
Benton	1 452	1.9	D	32.6	D	6.6	2.9	22.3	24.2	9 519	122	592	27 024	7.3
Clackamas	5 152	1.9	25.5	15.9	60.5	12.3	8.2	22.9	12.1	46 167	138	2 383	109 003	20.8
Clatsop	499	0.3	30.5	23.1	48.7	15.1	2.9	23.1	20.5	7 121	201	578	17 367	4.5
Columbia	381	2.8	34.4	25.6	44.3	10.5	3.6	13.0	18.6	7 118	160	398	14 576	6.9
Coos	709	1.9	D	14.4	D	13.0	3.9	21.3	26.8	15 399	248	1 510	26 668	3.8
Crook	206	-0.4	D	27.4	D	7.7	2.8	13.6	21.6	3 509	204	214	6 066	7.7
Curry	185	-1.0	D	15.8	D	18.5	4.7	20.8	22.3	7 144	338	339	9 885	32.0
Deschutes	1 626	-0.2	24.8	11.7	60.4	13.2	9.7	28.0	15.0	19 116	181	1 091	35 928	27.8
Douglas	1 249	0.1	32.6	27.0	45.5	9.9	3.4	20.9	21.8	23 327	229	1 689	38 298	7.4
Gilliam	18	-38.6	5.4	2.1	D	11.9	2.4	9.6	34.9	449	222	28	932	-11.2
Grant	87	-1.6	21.3	15.6	36.1	8.8	3.5	12.7	44.2	1 670	207	148	3 774	-1.0
Harney	90	1.6	26.1	20.0	37.2	11.2	1.7	16.5	35.1	1 491	207	140	3 305	-2.1
Hood River	280	7.3	20.2	12.6	55.9	11.8	2.2	23.4	16.7	3 102	159	197	7 569	5.8
Jackson	2 413	0.4	23.1	15.3	60.4	16.4	5.7	26.8	16.1	36 028	208	2 555	60 376	15.5
Jefferson	198	3.1	35.5	32.4	38.5	8.3	2.0	17.8	22.9	3 137	189	260	6 311	21.4
Josephine	697	0.4	23.7	15.0	57.0	16.1	5.5	26.0	18.9	19 483	262	1 520	26 912	15.4
Klamath	764	1.2	D	18.1	D	10.7	4.7	23.9	22.3	12 161	192	1 165	25 954	2.3
Lake	78	-0.8	D	D	D	10.5	2.6	12.6	43.3	1 749	245	136	3 434	3.2
Lane	4 855	0.6	27.2	19.2	54.6	12.0	5.6	26.3	17.7	54 223	173	4 804	116 676	5.0
Lincoln	521	-0.2	D	10.3	D	17.6	4.7	27.1	24.9	11 223	247	689	22 389	6.9
Linn	1 495	3.3	42.3	34.4	40.9	9.2	4.0	16.0	13.5	19 497	187	1 739	36 482	3.8
Malheur	394	10.2	D	11.3	48.7	11.7	3.0	19.4	25.3	5 400	189	632	10 649	0.1
Marion	4 339	3.7	D	11.5	D	10.3	5.8	24.1	28.3	45 108	168	4 429	86 869	9.1

1. Covers mining, construction, and manufacturing.   2. Covers private sector earnings in agricultural services, forestry, and fisheries; transportation and public utilities; wholesale trade; retail trade; finance, insurance, and real estate; and services.   3. Per 1,000 resident population estimated as of July 1 of the year shown.

Table B. States and Counties — Housing, Labor Force, and Employment

	Housing units, 1990 (cont'd)								Civilian labor force, 1999				Civilian employment, 1990[5]		
	Occupied units										Unemployment			Percent	
			Owner-occupied			Renter-occupied										
				Owner cost as a percent of income											
STATE County	Total	Percent	Median value[1]	With a mortgage	Without a mortgage	Median rent[2]	Rent as percent of income	Substandard units[3] (percent)	Total	Percent change, 1998–1999	Total	Rate[4]	Total	Professional, managerial, and technical	Precision production, craft, and repair
	89	90	91	92	93	94	95	96	97	98	99	100	101	102	103
OKLAHOMA—Cont'd															
Kiowa	4 551	74.2	27 000	20.7	13.4	229	24.5	4.1	4 694	1.4	160	3.4	4 339	19.9	8.1
Latimer	3 693	74.9	33 900	20.6	13.9	261	24.2	7.7	4 655	0.8	371	8.0	3 474	24.5	14.3
Le Flore	15 938	75.3	34 900	20.3	14.1	277	27.6	4.5	19 995	0.9	1 076	5.4	16 317	20.7	15.4
Lincoln	10 839	80.5	35 100	19.3	13.3	296	26.4	4.1	14 305	-1.9	583	4.1	11 673	20.9	16.0
Logan	10 180	77.4	46 200	18.5	14.0	306	25.1	3.4	14 896	3.2	359	2.4	12 430	24.4	13.5
Love	2 992	78.7	35 900	22.3	12.5	270	26.4	4.3	3 764	-2.5	128	3.4	3 275	19.0	13.1
McClain	8 332	80.2	46 500	20.4	13.6	348	26.1	2.7	13 216	3.8	311	2.4	10 240	24.3	15.1
McCurtain	12 234	73.1	29 200	17.9	13.5	238	26.9	8.6	15 725	4.8	990	6.3	12 085	18.7	13.5
McIntosh	6 786	77.8	38 700	20.2	13.1	256	29.0	4.9	8 038	3.1	498	6.2	5 844	23.4	12.9
Major	3 121	80.8	37 700	20.4	12.0	281	19.8	1.7	3 856	-5.7	119	3.1	3 430	19.2	13.4
Marshall	4 350	78.5	37 000	20.3	12.6	284	28.3	4.0	5 315	2.3	215	4.0	3 999	22.8	9.4
Mayes	12 672	76.8	42 400	19.6	12.2	299	26.4	4.9	16 215	8.9	640	3.9	13 207	20.1	17.6
Murray	4 651	72.5	33 700	17.7	12.7	246	22.1	4.2	5 392	-2.1	341	6.3	4 739	21.8	13.0
Muskogee	25 174	69.9	40 900	19.3	13.5	295	28.1	4.1	32 197	2.4	1 374	4.3	26 378	24.2	12.2
Noble	4 225	75.0	33 500	17.3	12.7	285	22.7	3.5	5 711	-1.2	139	2.4	4 854	21.3	13.7
Nowata	3 994	78.1	27 900	20.4	13.1	267	23.7	3.8	3 783	5.2	182	4.8	4 033	21.0	13.2
Okfuskee	4 164	76.5	25 700	21.7	13.3	219	26.3	6.8	3 686	-12.6	213	5.8	3 795	17.7	13.1
Oklahoma	237 879	61.3	53 300	19.9	12.3	368	25.4	4.1	333 534	2.5	9 110	2.7	280 519	31.3	10.1
Okmulgee	14 044	72.6	30 900	20.3	12.7	273	29.8	4.1	14 239	-2.4	1 041	7.3	13 449	22.5	14.6
Osage	15 383	78.6	43 300	19.8	12.9	266	26.4	3.9	20 388	0.1	730	3.6	17 380	24.0	16.9
Ottawa	12 124	73.9	30 200	17.9	12.3	250	26.2	2.9	13 256	2.1	641	4.8	11 958	22.5	11.5
Pawnee	6 006	79.0	39 200	21.0	13.6	308	26.6	3.9	6 315	0.2	329	5.2	6 642	22.6	14.4
Payne	23 834	54.5	50 700	20.4	12.1	343	32.9	2.2	37 202	5.0	469	1.3	28 234	33.6	9.3
Pittsburg	15 911	75.4	34 700	20.8	13.1	286	24.8	2.7	17 953	2.8	1 117	6.2	14 934	25.1	13.8
Pontotoc	13 310	69.0	39 900	20.1	13.6	283	26.1	2.8	17 226	3.0	561	3.3	14 237	26.6	12.4
Pottawatomie	21 796	73.9	42 400	19.6	13.1	325	27.7	3.1	28 967	2.2	1 063	3.7	24 045	25.3	13.9
Pushmataha	4 370	76.6	27 700	22.7	11.9	205	28.1	8.4	4 891	-4.7	253	5.2	3 775	22.3	10.5
Roger Mills	1 586	79.1	25 900	25.8	15.2	197	19.6	3.6	1 942	-4.8	66	3.4	1 811	16.3	10.8
Rogers	19 866	79.4	63 700	20.6	12.5	358	24.8	4.0	35 794	2.9	1 103	3.1	25 548	24.4	17.8
Seminole	9 665	73.0	27 300	20.9	14.1	246	27.0	4.6	9 833	-4.3	699	7.1	9 082	23.5	14.4
Sequoyah	12 335	73.8	37 800	19.4	14.1	288	27.5	5.5	17 331	0.9	872	5.0	13 610	18.1	14.5
Stephens	16 764	74.7	39 000	18.5	13.0	294	26.3	3.1	17 447	-4.3	1 106	6.3	16 581	27.0	15.1
Texas	6 214	71.6	44 500	17.2	12.4	287	21.1	3.4	14 165	3.3	297	2.1	7 779	19.4	12.9
Tillman	3 933	75.0	22 700	21.1	13.6	258	21.0	4.7	3 530	-6.7	134	3.8	3 854	22.7	9.7
Tulsa	202 537	60.7	60 700	20.1	12.7	366	24.4	2.9	300 538	0.9	9 731	3.2	244 911	32.9	11.0
Wagoner	16 946	79.0	58 300	19.2	12.1	347	24.7	3.5	28 769	0.9	776	2.7	22 060	23.4	16.5
Washington	19 242	74.5	51 900	16.4	11.6	358	24.4	1.8	19 535	6.0	768	3.9	21 213	36.4	11.5
Washita	4 421	76.5	28 400	17.1	12.9	287	20.4	3.8	4 878	-2.8	182	3.7	4 705	19.6	15.0
Woods	3 803	73.0	32 700	16.5	12.8	254	22.7	2.0	4 382	-1.6	82	1.9	4 099	25.3	10.0
Woodward	7 087	72.5	40 300	19.1	11.7	295	21.0	3.1	8 802	-11.2	509	5.8	8 371	21.1	14.5
OREGON	1 103 313	63.1	67 100	20.4	13.4	408	25.5	3.9	1 760 442	0.1	100 361	5.7	1 319 960	28.8	10.7
Baker	6 118	68.8	42 100	20.6	14.6	289	22.4	3.6	7 350	-3.1	617	8.4	6 154	19.9	9.3
Benton	26 126	55.1	72 900	20.1	12.2	387	29.4	3.7	40 782	-2.9	1 195	2.9	32 984	41.2	6.8
Clackamas	103 530	71.7	85 100	20.4	12.9	472	24.0	2.9	194 234	-0.7	7 806	4.0	141 004	31.0	11.2
Clatsop	13 374	63.2	62 500	19.6	14.1	352	24.4	3.7	17 170	-2.0	967	5.6	14 788	23.4	12.5
Columbia	13 910	74.1	62 800	17.7	12.4	350	22.2	4.0	22 718	-0.3	1 397	6.1	16 369	21.6	16.4
Coos	24 134	66.5	49 800	20.0	14.0	331	25.6	4.1	26 790	-2.6	2 338	8.7	23 384	23.6	11.1
Crook	5 455	71.4	50 300	15.8	12.4	335	21.2	3.8	7 585	0.4	684	9.0	5 968	16.5	9.8
Curry	8 311	72.5	83 400	22.1	13.1	387	22.7	4.3	8 359	0.3	610	7.3	7 352	19.7	13.5
Deschutes	29 217	71.0	74 500	21.0	13.4	438	25.9	3.6	57 614	4.6	3 697	6.4	35 860	26.9	12.2
Douglas	35 872	68.9	56 000	21.2	13.3	350	23.8	4.5	45 245	-1.0	4 222	9.3	37 639	21.4	10.7
Gilliam	696	66.7	31 600	15.8	13.9	363	23.8	1.3	1 200	-1.3	66	5.5	785	22.9	6.4
Grant	3 092	70.8	46 900	17.2	12.8	310	18.9	4.2	4 051	-3.5	494	12.2	3 302	24.7	9.2
Harney	2 760	70.3	37 800	18.0	13.2	290	19.7	4.0	4 104	3.3	312	7.6	3 051	20.1	11.6
Hood River	6 425	62.1	77 200	20.2	12.4	393	24.4	9.4	10 990	-1.5	954	8.7	7 720	25.0	9.0
Jackson	57 238	66.2	74 900	22.0	13.3	413	27.6	4.4	89 158	1.2	5 910	6.6	62 704	25.1	10.7
Jefferson	4 744	64.9	53 700	19.1	13.1	346	21.4	9.3	8 570	2.4	556	6.5	5 598	18.8	9.7
Josephine	25 081	70.4	74 700	22.7	13.7	391	28.8	5.4	29 116	1.5	2 435	8.4	23 039	22.9	12.2
Klamath	22 341	65.2	52 700	19.3	13.0	329	24.6	4.8	28 753	-0.6	2 496	8.7	23 638	21.7	11.3
Lake	2 765	67.8	41 900	16.9	14.1	299	20.4	5.0	3 371	-1.9	343	10.2	3 182	22.4	10.3
Lane	110 799	60.8	65 800	20.2	13.3	418	28.5	3.7	163 186	0.5	9 291	5.7	129 698	28.3	10.4
Lincoln	16 455	66.0	69 400	22.2	12.8	376	25.7	3.7	21 097	-1.4	1 743	8.3	16 352	26.1	9.6
Linn	34 716	65.6	51 300	18.8	13.6	376	24.5	3.3	52 731	-0.9	4 198	8.0	39 402	20.4	13.7
Malheur	9 457	64.1	46 300	20.8	14.4	289	25.9	7.6	14 821	1.6	1 314	8.9	10 794	20.0	8.4
Marion	83 494	62.9	59 900	20.8	13.0	401	25.4	4.6	137 801	-0.6	8 674	6.3	101 478	28.2	10.4

1. Specified owner-occupied units.   2. Specified renter-occupied units.   3. Overcrowded or lacking complete plumbing facilities.   4. Percent of civilian labor force.   5. Persons 16 years and older.

	Private nonfarm establishments, employment and payroll, 1998								Agriculture, 1997			
STATE County	Number of establishments	Employment						Annual payroll		Farms			Farm operators
		Total	Health Care and Social Assistance	Manufacturing	Retail trade	Finance and Insurance	Professional Scientific and Technical Services	Total (mil dol)	Average per employee (dollars)	Number	Percent with—		Whose principal occupation is farming (percent)
											Less than 50 acres	500 acres and over	
	104	105	106	107	108	109	110	111	112	113	114	115	116
OKLAHOMA—Cont'd													
Kiowa	238	2 090	674	D	325	138	51	34	16 468	702	9.5	46.4	57.8
Latimer	168	1 713	537	D	216	60	25	30	17 792	643	20.2	14.5	41.4
Le Flore	757	8 017	1 890	1 080	1 801	369	347	149	18 542	1 744	29.0	9.9	40.8
Lincoln	540	5 195	737	654	1 036	594	113	94	18 063	1 916	19.0	9.9	35.4
Logan	525	4 234	927	312	807	141	93	69	16 222	983	20.7	20.8	42.2
Love	143	1 464	137	461	277	D	21	27	18 402	629	16.2	18.6	40.9
McClain	538	4 433	581	613	989	217	120	87	19 618	1 046	30.1	13.5	39.1
McCurtain	610	8 315	1 189	2 749	1 178	258	446	174	20 872	1 573	28.0	8.0	42.7
McIntosh	396	3 223	942	386	714	128	103	47	14 541	906	20.2	10.9	44.8
Major	226	1 789	270	199	362	72	25	38	21 070	877	11.1	35.5	51.8
Marshall	287	3 395	462	1 380	411	88	45	64	18 897	414	18.6	17.9	39.9
Mayes	721	9 325	805	3 475	1 303	238	194	214	22 958	1 406	29.9	8.6	39.7
Murray	263	2 369	429	171	533	108	57	42	17 583	454	18.5	19.6	41.6
Muskogee	1 623	23 917	4 819	4 891	3 769	660	449	534	22 346	1 468	28.3	8.7	40.8
Noble	245	3 606	489	D	532	121	26	86	23 910	739	11.1	31.9	48.8
Nowata	177	1 418	259	328	186	101	D	24	16 970	764	18.5	17.9	43.1
Okfuskee	157	1 959	682	273	240	69	D	37	18 877	784	14.5	17.5	40.4
Oklahoma	21 276	337 110	48 434	40 653	42 019	18 641	17 047	8 707	25 829	996	46.0	7.0	33.4
Okmulgee	659	6 608	1 611	1 041	1 505	267	143	131	19 794	1 107	23.6	11.5	40.7
Osage	536	4 388	768	897	773	172	112	83	19 002	1 196	20.7	29.3	42.6
Ottawa	731	6 995	1 345	1 778	1 110	306	145	131	18 722	972	31.4	9.1	39.8
Pawnee	305	2 561	542	254	504	126	69	48	18 867	671	18.0	23.0	42.0
Payne	1 568	19 196	2 797	2 665	3 307	685	835	366	19 092	1 281	26.9	14.0	34.1
Pittsburg	877	9 611	2 200	913	1 936	453	241	178	18 543	1 586	21.7	14.6	39.6
Pontotoc	878	11 208	2 545	2 070	1 926	662	309	207	18 506	1 133	22.9	13.9	39.3
Pottawatomie	1 330	18 461	2 490	3 997	3 058	566	339	350	18 940	1 448	22.5	10.4	39.3
Pushmataha	212	1 677	525	251	327	66	42	26	15 417	776	19.2	14.4	43.8
Roger Mills	83	502	129	0	113	D	13	8	16 540	680	3.5	52.1	59.4
Rogers	1 253	15 937	1 968	4 865	2 028	447	308	383	24 059	1 408	38.2	9.3	34.9
Seminole	528	6 127	1 133	1 565	904	175	112	103	16 790	1 018	20.2	11.3	35.9
Sequoyah	609	5 936	1 312	474	1 430	267	130	91	15 340	1 125	30.0	7.7	36.5
Stephens	1 074	12 375	1 600	2 057	2 193	737	225	270	21 824	1 165	20.5	17.4	44.7
Texas	548	6 927	639	2 480	1 001	196	125	138	19 936	785	6.5	58.2	55.5
Tillman	194	1 635	316	D	224	70	35	30	18 521	638	7.5	42.0	57.5
Tulsa	18 112	314 790	35 837	40 656	36 593	18 785	16 221	9 316	29 595	954	50.3	6.6	30.1
Wagoner	733	6 841	817	1 885	995	158	161	132	19 358	973	32.2	10.1	36.3
Washington	1 179	16 607	2 351	1 407	2 602	D	856	550	33 129	768	32.8	10.8	40.8
Washita	258	1 721	389	159	308	103	62	27	15 433	994	9.7	38.7	60.8
Woods	284	2 198	423	D	541	153	63	34	15 683	705	7.2	51.9	60.6
Woodward	684	6 211	1 043	519	1 060	409	137	129	20 806	800	12.1	39.0	50.6
OREGON	99 183	1 310 750	150 105	211 636	182 706	59 843	62 828	37 723	28 780	34 030	56.3	12.9	46.0
Baker	568	3 781	630	586	790	151	165	72	19 105	704	27.0	35.9	62.6
Benton	1 968	29 170	3 684	9 055	3 321	545	1 574	922	31 611	726	65.4	7.4	41.5
Clackamas	9 332	106 042	10 538	17 969	16 266	4 552	4 160	3 054	28 801	3 745	78.9	1.0	35.9
Clatsop	1 351	11 729	1 416	1 016	2 208	228	241	226	19 233	229	49.8	3.1	40.2
Columbia	838	9 042	773	2 927	1 284	216	243	263	29 139	686	63.4	2.3	34.3
Coos	1 750	16 728	2 930	1 657	3 079	505	501	372	22 246	675	42.1	9.6	54.7
Crook	406	4 774	399	1 463	503	81	83	114	23 854	521	46.1	26.9	44.7
Curry	692	4 700	592	755	1 080	169	130	93	19 786	168	33.9	26.8	60.1
Deschutes	4 137	39 781	4 227	4 896	7 800	1 301	1 525	939	23 603	1 235	74.7	3.5	35.5
Douglas	2 698	30 760	4 418	7 089	4 433	670	794	725	23 558	1 908	49.5	4.5	45.0
Gilliam	57	556	D	D	67	D	7	13	24 000	166	2.4	81.3	75.9
Grant	294	1 604	247	D	308	70	63	34	20 911	407	23.8	49.6	58.2
Harney	211	1 463	207	D	334	51	D	31	21 521	504	17.9	52.6	64.1
Hood River	744	7 241	958	901	1 321	98	230	140	19 333	537	67.2	0.7	56.8
Jackson	5 157	58 195	8 568	7 412	9 705	1 823	1 767	1 389	23 870	1 623	66.7	4.7	41.0
Jefferson	290	4 255	325	1 807	618	90	55	98	23 106	399	30.8	26.3	57.9
Josephine	1 817	16 368	2 570	2 984	3 271	596	420	350	21 381	616	74.0	1.1	46.8
Klamath	1 629	17 014	2 555	2 820	3 209	575	807	420	24 694	1 066	35.2	22.6	57.6
Lake	196	1 311	292	297	219	34	28	26	19 516	418	17.0	39.7	61.5
Lane	9 726	114 500	14 943	19 059	18 276	4 386	5 794	2 882	25 171	2 104	65.3	4.2	37.2
Lincoln	1 679	13 336	1 520	973	2 825	412	334	261	19 607	306	54.9	3.9	42.2
Linn	2 514	34 977	3 252	9 828	4 651	915	1 018	919	26 274	2 009	57.4	9.2	45.1
Malheur	768	8 597	1 094	1 295	2 039	241	226	176	20 437	1 207	28.7	22.5	66.5
Marion	7 328	91 691	13 100	11 643	14 610	6 080	3 274	2 266	24 709	2 546	65.0	5.8	47.5

STATE County	Acreage (1,000) 117	Percent change, 1992-1997 118	Average size of farm 119	Total irrigated (1,000) 120	Total cropland (1,000) 121	Average per farm ($1,000) 122	Average per acre (dollars) 123	Value of machinery and equipment Average per farm ($1,000) 124	Total (mil dol) 125	Average per farm (dollars) 126	Crops 127	Live-stock and poultry products 128	$10,000 or more 129	$100,000 or more 130	Percent of land owned by Fed. Gov. 1997 131	Water con-sumption 1995 (mil gal/day) 132
OKLAHOMA—Cont'd																
Kiowa	595	6.7	848	1	362	380	448	60	52	73 826	36.8	63.2	65.8	17.0	0.4	11.5
Latimer	202	4.2	314	2	63	205	579	32	11	16 659	5.7	94.3	26.1	2.5	0.6	2.2
Le Flore	407	6.9	234	4	189	211	902	27	119	68 066	6.5	93.5	34.1	12.8	23.4	14.2
Lincoln	431	8.4	225	0	181	189	838	23	24	12 271	12.8	87.2	23.2	2.2	0.0	8.4
Logan	381	10.6	387	1	183	315	837	32	39	40 084	27.3	72.7	39.6	6.2	0.0	6.3
Love	266	4.0	423	4	87	231	533	30	16	24 723	22.1	77.9	38.5	5.6	4.1	2.6
McClain	268	5.5	256	2	121	242	947	36	31	30 083	21.5	78.5	34.3	5.4	0.0	4.9
McCurtain	328	4.0	208	1	135	180	745	30	137	87 146	3.0	97.0	35.7	14.7	7.7	11.3
McIntosh	254	7.0	280	0	105	199	644	24	16	17 535	16.5	83.5	31.1	2.5	3.8	4.8
Major	491	-0.6	560	5	244	337	583	47	55	62 489	27.0	73.0	55.3	13.5	0.0	11.0
Marshall	164	0.4	395	1	42	218	558	30	6	14 677	19.5	80.5	26.6	2.4	11.7	2.5
Mayes	284	2.0	202	0	147	225	1 080	27	33	23 771	13.5	86.5	33.5	5.9	2.9	84.5
Murray	203	-11.9	448	D	49	289	615	31	20	45 064	3.0	97.0	36.6	6.6	3.5	14.4
Muskogee	333	-4.2	227	7	183	179	768	27	32	21 565	39.6	60.4	29.1	3.9	2.7	83.5
Noble	413	5.6	559	0	222	313	573	44	40	53 690	45.3	54.7	55.1	14.9	0.0	3.2
Nowata	309	9.3	405	D	99	240	596	23	29	37 325	6.6	93.4	36.6	4.1	2.2	1.7
Okfuskee	282	9.4	360	0	101	214	587	23	18	22 384	11.9	88.1	32.1	4.0	0.0	2.2
Oklahoma	160	2.2	161	1	78	272	1 688	24	15	15 003	56.7	43.3	23.6	2.5	1.3	77.4
Okmulgee	302	7.5	273	0	123	200	732	28	19	17 000	22.3	77.7	27.1	2.9	0.7	8.2
Osage	1 207	8.2	1 010	0	158	430	436	30	103	86 022	5.5	94.5	42.6	9.4	2.1	19.4
Ottawa	215	3.8	221	0	130	204	977	30	53	54 294	53.4	46.6	32.6	7.1	0.0	5.0
Pawnee	263	-6.6	393	0	93	194	521	28	18	26 640	19.9	80.1	37.7	6.3	1.1	25.3
Payne	339	3.1	265	0	142	212	777	22	22	17 467	17.4	82.6	28.3	2.8	0.0	6.1
Pittsburg	491	2.2	310	2	148	188	631	20	25	15 530	13.0	87.0	30.5	2.0	7.5	10.4
Pontotoc	335	-5.0	296	2	130	181	593	22	23	20 604	8.0	92.0	28.3	2.3	0.0	6.7
Pottawatomie	336	12.5	232	1	155	175	809	23	33	22 790	13.7	86.3	24.5	2.8	0.0	11.4
Pushmataha	256	6.8	330	0	71	178	570	27	8	9 928	4.7	95.3	24.7	1.3	1.6	2.7
Roger Mills	691	4.6	1 016	5	162	375	381	40	28	40 458	16.6	83.4	59.3	11.8	4.2	6.9
Rogers	313	0.9	222	1	125	236	1 004	23	27	19 268	21.9	78.1	23.9	3.1	2.2	79.0
Seminole	278	10.6	273	1	109	155	557	21	14	14 172	16.2	83.8	22.7	2.1	0.0	17.3
Sequoyah	293	36.4	261	2	95	190	762	30	39	34 760	12.1	87.9	24.2	2.8	1.5	14.1
Stephens	427	1.4	366	3	171	192	542	29	24	20 848	13.0	87.0	31.7	4.5	0.5	7.1
Texas	1 087	3.4	1 384	138	632	718	511	130	668	850 985	7.8	92.2	61.7	23.9	0.4	375.0
Tillman	466	-3.2	730	14	322	385	551	58	41	64 457	59.2	40.8	60.0	17.1	0.6	7.0
Tulsa	143	6.7	150	3	72	264	1 790	22	20	20 676	65.8	34.2	22.1	3.6	0.1	17.2
Wagoner	241	10.9	247	1	139	266	1 100	29	29	29 657	64.5	35.5	30.1	5.2	6.3	20.3
Washington	238	10.0	309	0	74	202	752	20	16	21 382	26.2	73.8	27.9	4.3	4.0	4.1
Washita	586	1.4	589	3	399	334	558	66	69	69 161	36.3	63.7	66.2	17.4	0.0	7.1
Woods	805	8.2	1 141	3	290	668	587	59	81	115 461	27.3	72.7	69.1	20.7	0.0	6.4
Woodward	722	5.1	902	6	214	329	358	37	50	62 121	17.7	82.3	50.9	11.9	1.0	16.3
OREGON	17 449	-0.9	513	1 949	5 286	479	960	55	2 969	87 252	71.2	28.8	38.2	13.4	50.3	7 906.0
Baker	1 008	23.0	1 431	143	161	727	504	62	54	76 528	25.3	74.7	56.4	17.6	50.9	462.8
Benton	131	9.9	180	20	92	413	2 527	55	70	96 697	87.3	12.7	31.5	11.3	17.6	80.9
Clackamas	180	20.6	48	24	107	367	7 447	37	276	73 765	78.4	21.6	31.4	8.4	46.1	228.5
Clatsop	23	-8.9	99	0	13	372	3 112	27	5	23 253	13.4	86.6	24.9	6.1	0.6	126.7
Columbia	66	-8.9	96	1	23	335	4 004	26	25	36 225	81.4	18.6	15.0	1.5	2.5	99.6
Coos	163	-6.8	242	11	43	345	1 450	30	31	45 225	46.7	53.3	42.7	12.4	21.5	36.6
Crook	916	2.4	1 759	72	77	608	359	67	31	60 338	42.5	57.5	42.4	14.8	49.6	226.2
Curry	85	14.6	505	3	17	754	2 017	41	13	77 743	67.1	32.9	42.9	12.5	59.8	19.8
Deschutes	124	-10.5	101	40	44	368	2 715	37	21	17 405	45.9	54.1	22.3	2.9	74.7	180.8
Douglas	402	0.0	211	17	118	324	1 814	27	35	18 521	27.8	72.2	27.0	3.4	48.0	189.7
Gilliam	743	-3.0	4 474	4	298	1 180	265	172	25	147 746	81.0	19.0	75.3	40.4	7.0	31.1
Grant	1 081	-6.3	2 655	48	87	938	339	50	17	41 998	14.5	85.5	50.4	12.3	60.6	223.5
Harney	1 359	-6.7	2 696	152	215	795	294	59	39	77 150	19.3	80.7	59.7	20.8	71.9	549.1
Hood River	28	5.0	53	19	21	436	6 681	60	63	117 888	98.6	1.4	57.5	31.7	62.3	117.5
Jackson	246	-6.1	152	53	70	353	1 784	32	51	31 396	74.5	25.5	22.1	3.4	47.7	363.6
Jefferson	783	47.5	1 964	52	100	766	384	105	43	108 150	81.2	18.8	57.9	25.1	27.5	163.7
Josephine	35	11.5	56	12	17	219	4 177	27	16	26 305	54.0	46.0	20.1	3.1	56.8	59.6
Klamath	714	-0.9	669	243	235	507	872	72	101	94 392	51.0	49.0	54.0	18.8	54.4	694.8
Lake	737	-11.6	1 762	200	187	775	529	72	43	102 294	47.3	52.7	64.6	25.4	67.1	686.0
Lane	224	-7.6	106	23	120	336	3 428	34	87	41 430	62.2	37.8	24.3	6.7	53.5	350.1
Lincoln	32	-6.1	104	1	10	278	3 285	24	4	13 488	61.8	38.2	19.9	2.0	29.4	41.8
Linn	393	3.5	196	30	305	456	2 552	62	174	86 717	78.5	21.5	33.7	14.2	37.3	184.0
Malheur	1 257	-4.6	1 042	239	279	655	587	104	208	172 509	58.7	41.3	67.2	28.5	74.2	610.2
Marion	306	1.4	120	92	251	500	4 248	88	438	172 179	83.6	16.4	45.3	19.9	29.4	265.7

Table B. States and Counties — **Residential Construction, Wholesale and Retail Trade, and Real Estate**

STATE County	New Construction ($1,000)	Number of Housing Units	Number of Establishments	Number of Employees	Sales (mil dol)	Annual Payroll (mil dol)	Number of Establishments	Number of Employees	Sales (mil dol)	Annual Payroll (mil dol)	Number of Establishments	Number of Employees	Receipts (mil dol)	Annual Payroll (mil dol)
	Value of Residential Construction Authorized by Building Permits, 1999		Wholesale Trade, 1997				Retail Trade[1], 1997				Real Estate and Rental and Leasing, 1997			
	133	134	135	136	137	138	139	140	141	142	143	144	145	146
OKLAHOMA—Cont'd														
Kiowa	136	2	18	123	44.7	2.4	56	353	37.5	3.3	8	13	1.6	0.3
Latimer	256	8	6	D	D	D	31	237	26.1	2.9	4	29	2.5	0.8
Le Flore	3 438	48	27	120	42.4	2.3	162	1 578	247.2	20.0	25	55	3.6	0.5
Lincoln	2 179	26	21	D	D	D	154	1 011	136.3	12.6	11	13	0.7	0.1
Logan	1 756	17	18	D	D	D	96	816	133.3	10.5	21	37	3.4	0.5
Love	80	2	6	79	28.7	1.9	35	290	51.7	3.5	1	D	D	D
McClain	14 612	169	19	D	D	D	96	940	192.0	14.6	13	27	2.2	0.5
McCurtain	801	18	30	239	69.8	4.8	138	1 119	167.2	15.1	11	46	2.1	0.5
McIntosh	2 213	64	10	17	6.7	0.3	94	650	140.1	9.2	11	22	1.4	0.2
Major	320	2	17	151	69.4	2.3	48	323	59.6	4.1	3	7	0.6	0.1
Marshall	392	1	12	124	48.7	3.5	56	416	56.6	5.3	11	26	1.0	0.2
Mayes	3 573	41	36	216	71.5	5.2	135	1 313	191.8	16.5	15	69	3.4	0.5
Murray	939	11	10	73	25.5	1.1	49	492	93.1	7.3	3	17	1.2	0.2
Muskogee	7 622	82	91	1 185	313.2	30.4	349	3 613	561.7	52.8	56	218	16.7	3.3
Noble	760	8	9	50	17.2	0.9	57	478	72.3	6.4	10	22	2.1	0.2
Nowata	303	4	9	107	28.4	1.6	33	180	27.3	2.1	7	22	1.6	0.6
Okfuskee	0	0	2	D	D	D	33	235	37.5	2.7	3	6	0.5	0.1
Oklahoma	525 983	4 727	1 517	21 108	15 144.3	638.9	3 098	41 034	7 479.8	681.3	913	5 379	612.2	107.7
Okmulgee	2 167	25	30	150	42.7	3.2	142	1 324	207.3	17.8	14	36	2.0	0.4
Osage	6 141	64	23	147	29.5	3.2	112	748	95.8	8.8	13	35	1.9	0.4
Ottawa	1 217	18	30	D	D	D	138	1 136	180.8	15.2	23	67	5.9	0.7
Pawnee	121	2	9	D	D	D	55	484	69.9	6.2	10	17	0.8	0.2
Payne	18 514	224	62	664	211.2	13.1	299	3 336	466.1	43.4	70	278	16.2	3.3
Pittsburg	6 872	70	51	333	114.2	8.2	185	2 059	326.3	26.7	39	150	8.3	1.9
Pontotoc	2 264	18	53	492	257.6	10.4	180	1 859	266.9	23.5	27	73	7.2	1.2
Pottawatomie	10 451	107	44	D	D	D	276	2 847	397.8	37.0	55	200	18.5	2.5
Pushmataha	199	3	10	130	11.1	1.4	56	294	42.0	3.3	5	3	0.4	0.0
Roger Mills	0	0	3	6	4.6	0.1	22	110	14.8	1.4	1	D	D	D
Rogers	61 822	567	65	518	357.8	16.7	192	1 994	353.2	28.6	38	243	15.8	3.2
Seminole	789	7	28	169	53.8	4.6	104	813	116.1	10.6	17	73	4.2	0.7
Sequoyah	7 726	137	15	110	47.6	1.4	159	1 387	218.9	17.0	16	44	2.1	0.5
Stephens	5 367	45	53	441	90.6	10.0	221	2 074	314.1	27.7	29	115	11.3	2.5
Texas	7 045	102	40	D	D	D	99	936	130.2	11.6	21	57	3.9	0.6
Tillman	215	2	13	155	33.4	3.0	43	346	31.4	2.6	2	D	D	D
Tulsa	417 090	4 082	1 438	18 675	9 427.0	658.2	2 440	35 520	6 410.4	590.8	802	4 358	506.2	92.5
Wagoner	43 174	537	34	209	98.3	4.3	109	971	149.2	12.0	33	113	10.1	2.0
Washington	5 208	75	34	284	52.0	7.1	216	2 613	425.8	38.7	42	161	10.2	2.5
Washita	0	0	16	118	33.2	2.0	51	310	46.2	3.8	12	46	2.0	0.5
Woods	140	4	21	170	48.0	3.2	58	533	65.4	6.8	8	10	0.6	0.2
Woodward	1 277	12	50	342	68.9	6.7	128	1 074	179.2	15.3	22	107	10.6	2.6
OREGON	2 652 791	23 249	5 943	74 790	53 679.1	2 578.7	14 467	178 349	33 396.8	3 308.8	4 556	23 058	2 704.0	470.9
Baker	5 343	34	19	90	13.2	2.0	93	805	121.3	11.7	23	55	5.0	0.6
Benton	45 900	401	63	681	112.6	15.9	294	3 175	473.9	53.2	111	379	38.9	5.5
Clackamas	394 668	2 761	685	8 723	6 383.3	314.7	1 092	16 098	3 448.3	312.3	422	2 231	240.5	44.9
Clatsop	23 275	157	39	383	88.4	7.0	274	2 173	332.4	36.8	57	181	14.3	2.1
Columbia	44 725	335	26	161	61.5	4.4	137	1 360	199.8	22.1	28	83	7.6	1.2
Coos	3 721	42	60	496	233.2	14.6	289	3 040	505.2	52.1	64	208	18.5	3.4
Crook	16 075	140	16	72	21.5	1.5	57	494	89.3	8.4	14	24	3.6	0.4
Curry	18 240	120	20	62	14.2	1.1	121	1 041	148.4	16.8	31	76	8.3	1.4
Deschutes	323 379	2 055	191	1 303	571.0	39.7	687	7 130	1 297.1	128.7	198	1 028	140.5	16.9
Douglas	47 803	478	84	1 152	404.1	27.0	457	4 416	669.0	71.2	126	391	34.9	5.1
Gilliam	67	1	3	D	D	D	13	72	8.7	1.1	NA	NA	NA	NA
Grant	NA	NA	4	28	5.9	0.8	45	316	42.4	4.4	7	7	0.6	0.1
Harney	6 630	74	6	31	9.7	0.7	41	299	51.5	5.4	7	15	1.1	0.2
Hood River	15 485	111	27	181	92.2	9.9	129	1 286	170.3	19.8	23	72	7.2	0.8
Jackson	189 945	1 757	284	2 678	1 022.7	69.8	835	9 564	2 075.3	172.2	248	1 003	95.9	15.2
Jefferson	13 888	269	18	221	78.0	5.3	57	647	109.9	11.4	17	34	2.8	0.4
Josephine	46 717	440	59	441	175.6	9.2	326	3 322	590.3	57.9	71	313	20.6	3.6
Klamath	30 059	204	66	954	293.1	22.1	290	3 116	544.8	55.5	67	200	20.7	2.8
Lake	2 755	28	7	D	D	D	48	266	39.4	4.3	9	D	D	D
Lane	195 895	1 830	535	6 144	2 498.6	179.6	1 462	18 145	3 322.6	328.3	463	2 042	226.5	35.0
Lincoln	27 496	233	39	296	72.5	7.0	372	2 794	415.2	43.8	77	183	22.7	2.6
Linn	56 136	616	131	1 534	766.0	44.5	391	4 662	800.9	78.7	97	361	31.5	5.2
Malheur	7 990	54	50	951	171.0	18.0	163	1 903	302.9	30.7	26	68	6.0	1.0
Marion	199 934	1 776	326	3 247	1 184.0	91.9	1 081	14 637	2 672.5	266.3	380	1 748	194.5	36.3

1. Establishments with payroll.

STATE County	Professional, Scientific, and Technical Services[1], 1997				Manufacturing, 1997				Accommodation and Foodservices, 1997			
	Number of Establishments	Number of Employees	Receipts (mil dol)	Annual Payroll (mil dol)	Number of Establishments	Number of Employees	Receipts (mil dol)	Annual Payroll (mil dol)	Number of Establishments	Number of Employees	Sales (mil dol)	Annual Payroll (mil dol)
	147	148	149	150	151	152	153	154	155	156	157	158
OKLAHOMA—Cont'd												
Kiowa	14	41	1.6	0.4	NA	NA	NA	NA	15	D	D	D
Latimer	5	14	0.5	0.1	NA	NA	NA	NA	14	107	2.8	0.8
Le Flore	48	314	13.4	6.8	32	1 104	137.0	24.4	55	616	18.2	4.7
Lincoln	35	123	5.5	1.5	21	737	132.0	14.1	46	570	12.4	3.3
Logan	30	101	7.4	2.6	NA	NA	NA	NA	43	D	D	D
Love	7	21	0.7	0.2	NA	NA	NA	NA	17	157	5.3	1.3
McClain	34	81	3.8	1.3	19	D	D	D	38	D	D	D
McCurtain	29	388	10.7	6.0	25	2 758	794.7	79.6	51	537	14.9	3.7
McIntosh	19	84	4.5	1.7	NA	NA	NA	NA	46	439	12.6	3.4
Major	9	20	1.5	0.3	NA	NA	NA	NA	16	D	D	D
Marshall	15	43	2.1	0.6	20	1 196	130.5	24.3	27	222	7.3	1.8
Mayes	30	97	5.8	2.7	68	3 357	731.5	102.4	72	755	19.7	5.0
Murray	18	64	4.5	1.1	NA	NA	NA	NA	24	266	8.4	2.3
Muskogee	72	363	25.4	8.1	87	4 780	990.3	155.3	135	2 097	58.8	15.2
Noble	12	22	1.7	0.6	13	D	D	D	20	316	7.2	2.0
Nowata	11	20	1.2	0.3	NA	NA	NA	NA	12	139	3.1	0.9
Okfuskee	7	17	1.1	0.3	NA	NA	NA	NA	12	96	2.9	0.7
Oklahoma	2 262	14 060	1 266.2	502.1	851	39 462	9 922.1	1 281.5	1 493	29 780	918.6	255.9
Okmulgee	30	114	5.8	2.2	35	1 120	295.4	38.5	59	664	20.7	5.5
Osage	34	116	4.1	1.1	21	939	137.1	31.2	42	389	9.5	2.5
Ottawa	35	104	5.5	1.9	67	1 819	276.4	41.4	59	676	18.1	5.1
Pawnee	22	74	22.7	2.0	NA	NA	NA	NA	28	199	5.7	1.4
Payne	116	694	59.3	20.6	60	2 584	846.8	76.5	149	2 867	66.5	18.3
Pittsburg	61	203	14.1	4.0	27	875	217.1	20.7	75	1 275	37.3	10.2
Pontotoc	61	293	20.1	7.3	47	1 743	209.7	36.6	59	1 151	29.3	8.2
Pottawatomie	72	288	22.2	6.5	72	3 673	654.9	119.7	135	2 726	76.3	21.1
Pushmataha	14	36	2.6	0.6	NA	NA	NA	NA	17	96	3.3	0.8
Roger Mills	4	D	D	D	NA	NA	NA	NA	9	57	1.3	0.3
Rogers	67	237	16.8	6.3	122	4 562	822.9	147.4	89	1 324	38.0	10.0
Seminole	26	77	4.0	1.2	30	1 689	252.3	33.4	33	413	11.7	2.9
Sequoyah	31	93	7.5	2.4	NA	NA	NA	NA	74	900	24.0	6.3
Stephens	56	216	15.3	4.6	58	1 941	470.4	49.8	85	1 159	30.9	8.3
Texas	25	112	6.5	2.7	13	D	D	D	55	617	16.7	4.4
Tillman	13	38	1.4	0.7	NA	NA	NA	NA	14	D	D	D
Tulsa	1 953	13 985	1 437.7	533.5	1 136	39 402	7 858.1	1 310.7	1 316	23 663	771.3	207.7
Wagoner	45	104	11.5	2.5	66	1 924	432.7	50.8	60	786	23.1	5.1
Washington	76	827	76.2	24.4	48	1 327	183.8	50.0	92	1 595	51.6	14.0
Washita	16	51	2.7	0.8	NA	NA	NA	NA	9	37	0.9	0.1
Woods	21	45	2.9	0.5	NA	NA	NA	NA	23	317	6.3	1.8
Woodward	36	116	6.8	2.1	30	591	260.5	21.5	46	613	18.3	4.6
OREGON	8 117	52 514	4 734.6	1 925.0	5 768	213 111	47 666.0	7 095.3	8 363	124 425	4 385.7	1 236.6
Baker	27	105	7.4	2.4	NA	NA	NA	NA	62	540	19.0	4.7
Benton	210	1 367	116.7	50.1	106	8 547	1 391.9	494.5	205	2 807	85.9	24.0
Clackamas	745	3 526	348.4	129.8	589	18 655	3 667.4	632.2	571	10 002	331.1	94.6
Clatsop	60	212	12.6	4.0	49	858	142.4	21.2	200	2 250	89.4	25.5
Columbia	36	208	10.2	3.6	57	3 079	1 008.5	128.4	75	782	24.3	7.2
Coos	96	377	26.8	9.2	104	1 937	391.2	57.6	186	2 004	61.4	17.0
Crook	18	62	3.7	1.3	21	1 506	225.3	39.4	34	383	12.7	3.4
Curry	38	94	6.1	2.0	32	727	116.2	26.2	112	785	30.5	8.1
Deschutes	295	1 206	105.1	37.4	202	4 884	698.6	129.5	305	4 722	194.2	55.6
Douglas	140	550	30.9	13.2	157	7 141	1 494.7	226.4	274	3 635	138.1	37.9
Gilliam	4	D	D	D	NA	NA	NA	NA	8	67	1.7	0.4
Grant	16	49	2.4	1.1	NA	NA	NA	NA	32	179	5.8	1.4
Harney	7	25	1.7	0.5	NA	NA	NA	NA	25	170	5.2	1.5
Hood River	53	180	12.4	5.2	58	1 128	157.5	27.2	76	1 107	36.2	10.8
Jackson	341	1 917	99.5	35.4	301	7 428	1 424.0	201.7	474	6 253	205.3	60.3
Jefferson	12	35	3.0	0.7	21	1 793	351.3	52.2	31	371	11.9	3.2
Josephine	106	280	17.0	5.2	117	2 812	439.6	76.8	168	1 928	66.9	18.0
Klamath	88	775	35.2	13.7	72	3 013	562.6	86.1	156	1 899	73.1	17.2
Lake	7	20	1.2	0.4	NA	NA	NA	NA	26	196	6.1	1.5
Lane	797	4 682	374.3	138.8	624	19 262	3 881.8	589.8	809	12 022	387.8	110.5
Lincoln	74	297	21.2	7.0	59	1 060	255.2	34.4	274	3 644	134.7	37.8
Linn	142	861	48.9	21.5	184	9 794	1 918.8	347.8	183	2 400	73.1	20.3
Malheur	38	171	10.4	3.5	28	D	D	D	73	947	33.3	9.1
Marion	519	2 708	210.3	82.7	402	12 651	2 232.8	354.4	529	8 872	281.6	78.1

1. Firms subject to federal tax.

Table B. States and Counties — Health and Other Services and Federal Funds

STATE County	Health Care and Social Assistance[1], 1997				Other Services[1], 1997				Federal funds and grants, fiscal 1999[2] Expenditures (mil dol)			
										Direct payments for individuals[3]		
	Number of Establishments	Number of Employees	Receipts (mil dol)	Annual Payroll (mil dol)	Number of Establishments	Number of Employees	Receipts (mil dol)	Annual Payroll (mil dol)	Total	Social Security and government retirement	Medicare	Food stamps and Supplemental Security Income
	159	160	161	162	163	164	165	166	167	168	169	170
OKLAHOMA—Cont'd												
Kiowa	19	200	6.2	2.6	12	39	2.2	0.5	82.6	28.4	13.9	2.4
Latimer	24	426	12.5	7.6	9	26	1.3	0.3	49.0	19.1	10.5	2.3
Le Flore	63	1 000	32.2	16.2	39	117	9.9	1.9	254.0	103.8	46.8	12.2
Lincoln	36	510	14.3	6.0	15	56	2.4	0.9	118.7	66.4	20.7	4.3
Logan	40	1 045	22.9	11.2	28	99	5.5	1.7	122.4	51.3	21.2	3.7
Love	9	152	4.7	2.3	3	D	D	D	38.2	18.1	8.1	1.0
McClain	32	365	11.8	5.1	25	83	5.6	1.4	97.5	49.0	18.6	2.2
McCurtain	47	669	19.1	9.0	32	140	8.1	1.5	200.1	66.9	38.6	12.0
McIntosh	39	908	29.1	14.3	19	46	3.0	0.7	113.7	60.0	22.5	3.6
Major	6	28	1.5	0.5	3	D	D	D	37.9	16.0	6.6	0.5
Marshall	18	265	10.3	5.1	14	33	3.1	0.6	63.6	34.5	14.7	2.4
Mayes	48	462	15.9	6.4	39	117	7.3	1.7	147.3	73.9	28.3	6.2
Murray	22	341	11.2	5.2	13	33	2.3	0.4	64.8	31.2	12.6	2.0
Muskogee	175	2 633	111.4	49.5	76	399	24.2	7.3	407.0	172.1	65.7	14.7
Noble	17	327	9.5	4.6	9	12	1.3	0.3	55.2	22.0	9.4	1.2
Nowata	13	212	4.7	2.7	11	29	2.0	0.5	47.5	23.6	8.9	1.2
Okfuskee	17	435	10.5	4.5	3	11	0.5	0.1	89.3	28.9	12.7	2.9
Oklahoma	1 916	25 018	1 706.7	750.5	1 209	9 534	541.1	166.5	5 233.2	1 450.5	484.6	62.3
Okmulgee	63	921	33.0	15.5	37	108	7.3	1.5	212.5	83.8	39.1	9.9
Osage	41	471	14.9	7.1	21	44	2.5	0.5	136.3	54.8	20.6	4.4
Ottawa	57	695	22.7	11.7	34	118	7.1	1.9	198.1	85.7	40.0	6.6
Pawnee	23	262	8.9	4.2	16	35	2.8	0.6	73.1	34.2	14.5	2.3
Payne	113	1 283	60.8	28.2	92	441	19.6	5.6	290.0	102.5	42.0	6.9
Pittsburg	71	1 391	62.8	31.6	38	190	10.8	2.9	272.8	114.7	40.8	9.5
Pontotoc	82	1 037	48.4	22.0	57	325	18.3	5.7	196.8	79.2	34.1	7.6
Pottawatomie	105	1 694	74.2	32.8	65	272	15.7	4.1	281.4	151.9	41.3	11.9
Pushmataha	19	339	12.0	5.1	11	29	1.8	0.3	76.2	29.2	14.9	3.2
Roger Mills	3	D	D	D	3	D	D	D	23.0	7.0	4.3	0.4
Rogers	83	1 388	69.8	26.3	63	307	21.0	6.9	202.6	102.4	33.6	4.4
Seminole	33	792	22.9	10.8	21	43	3.9	0.7	151.7	60.5	27.4	6.9
Sequoyah	52	812	30.5	12.6	34	107	5.8	1.4	178.7	75.2	31.7	9.3
Stephens	83	979	44.1	19.4	56	214	12.4	2.8	212.8	111.5	39.3	6.2
Texas	34	192	13.4	4.2	32	103	6.5	1.3	96.0	27.0	12.9	1.3
Tillman	10	182	3.5	1.8	9	25	1.3	0.3	71.5	21.9	11.3	2.5
Tulsa	1 489	20 172	1 369.8	608.8	1 006	6 871	473.8	138.7	2 158.7	1 013.4	411.7	75.4
Wagoner	48	877	34.1	16.3	42	103	6.4	1.4	126.6	61.5	26.3	5.2
Washington	108	947	63.5	31.7	68	369	20.5	6.8	190.8	118.5	39.3	5.3
Washita	10	68	2.9	1.2	16	49	3.4	0.9	70.8	26.6	12.7	1.5
Woods	21	200	6.6	2.6	16	56	2.6	0.6	55.4	21.7	9.2	0.5
Woodward	41	357	16.1	6.4	34	134	10.0	2.3	72.7	34.5	14.1	2.1
OREGON	7 328	68 285	4 431.4	1 899.6	4 794	28 185	1 897.5	561.9	15 592.2	6 295.4	1 970.5	420.5
Baker	31	124	7.8	2.3	33	148	6.7	1.4	103.7	43.5	11.3	2.6
Benton	148	1 994	140.5	52.6	88	461	26.3	7.9	308.9	117.3	29.2	4.9
Clackamas	638	5 206	377.7	161.5	417	2 263	158.1	44.8	985.6	469.8	159.0	83.2
Clatsop	79	685	39.6	15.1	44	175	11.9	3.5	171.1	80.1	26.3	4.6
Columbia	59	340	20.0	8.6	33	119	6.3	1.8	137.4	76.6	26.1	3.5
Coos	156	1 328	85.3	30.9	79	298	23.2	5.9	345.7	171.1	49.2	13.6
Crook	36	202	9.3	3.1	14	49	3.2	0.9	81.1	39.2	12.6	2.0
Curry	45	237	11.9	3.8	28	65	4.3	0.8	128.9	80.5	23.1	3.0
Deschutes	253	2 073	147.7	57.1	159	904	56.1	18.4	378.3	224.5	55.4	10.0
Douglas	233	1 999	126.3	60.1	132	669	38.5	11.0	504.3	267.4	70.7	15.3
Gilliam	3	27	0.7	0.3	1	D	D	D	19.8	4.8	1.3	0.1
Grant	13	72	3.1	1.1	8	16	1.9	0.3	46.6	19.6	5.3	1.1
Harney	16	111	4.2	2.0	13	48	2.1	0.6	43.0	16.4	4.1	0.9
Hood River	55	367	18.2	7.0	24	160	6.5	1.6	71.7	33.7	9.6	1.7
Jackson	384	3 810	244.3	110.5	222	1 192	80.6	21.6	763.4	408.8	106.3	23.0
Jefferson	15	76	4.6	2.0	17	69	3.1	0.8	77.4	35.8	8.9	2.3
Josephine	164	1 555	81.9	30.7	94	369	23.7	5.6	378.0	214.4	55.2	16.7
Klamath	158	881	58.3	25.3	83	343	25.1	6.5	304.4	145.4	42.3	11.1
Lake	9	42	2.6	1.1	10	9	1.5	0.2	54.1	19.9	5.2	1.2
Lane	751	7 176	492.8	217.7	473	3 210	194.0	57.1	1 306.4	616.9	184.5	47.1
Lincoln	99	677	37.9	15.2	53	251	16.1	4.2	228.0	126.9	37.5	6.4
Linn	154	1 466	89.1	44.8	123	611	37.6	11.6	408.6	209.2	63.2	15.1
Malheur	70	381	23.5	8.3	52	188	13.6	3.4	121.2	52.7	16.0	5.2
Marion	629	5 965	354.9	156.3	373	2 003	116.9	37.4	1 543.9	575.1	155.9	39.6

1. Firms subject to federal tax.　2. October 1, 1998 to September 30, 1999.　3. State totals may include programs not allocated by county.

	Federal funds and grants, fiscal 1999[1] (cont'd)							Local government finances, 1997				
	Expenditures (mil dol) (cont'd)							General revenue				
	Procurement contract awards			Grants[2]						Taxes		
											Per capita[3] (dollars)	
STATE County	Salaries and wages	Defense	Other	Medicaid and other health-related	Nutrition and family welfare	Education	Other	Total (mil dol)	Intergovern-mental (mil dol)	Total (mil dol)	Total	Property
	171	172	173	174	175	176	177	178	179	180	181	182
OKLAHOMA—Cont'd												
Kiowa	2.9	0.1	0.5	8.6	1.8	1.0	5.5	19.7	12.0	4.4	410	241
Latimer	1.2	0.0	0.4	5.4	1.7	2.3	1.9	31.1	16.9	11.2	1 089	986
Le Flore	9.1	0.0	3.7	35.5	6.4	5.2	24.3	73.2	42.8	15.3	329	198
Lincoln	4.9	0.0	1.0	10.9	3.1	1.3	3.6	43.0	24.0	10.6	342	188
Logan	3.9	0.4	11.6	8.4	3.1	4.5	5.7	45.5	20.3	9.0	295	189
Love	0.9	0.0	0.2	4.8	0.7	0.4	2.0	10.6	7.2	2.3	266	166
McClain	3.3	0.0	0.8	7.3	1.6	1.4	8.6	55.7	23.8	18.2	705	493
McCurtain	6.3	0.1	1.4	40.2	6.8	12.7	7.2	56.9	37.9	12.4	360	244
McIntosh	2.2	0.3	0.5	15.5	2.6	2.3	2.8	27.0	16.0	7.3	389	181
Major	1.7	0.0	0.5	1.4	0.6	1.2	0.6	14.8	7.8	3.4	431	305
Marshall	1.3	0.0	0.3	6.3	1.2	1.1	0.5	21.1	10.2	5.5	461	292
Mayes	3.7	0.0	0.9	14.7	3.1	3.8	10.3	45.5	25.8	14.1	382	186
Murray	3.5	0.0	0.4	8.4	1.5	0.8	3.0	22.2	12.6	4.9	400	230
Muskogee	58.3	0.4	7.1	51.3	11.2	7.3	11.5	194.4	56.5	50.8	732	411
Noble	2.4	0.1	0.9	2.8	1.7	1.3	4.5	21.4	9.2	8.6	766	682
Nowata	1.6	1.6	0.6	4.9	0.9	0.8	0.9	14.3	9.2	2.9	293	180
Okfuskee	1.9	0.1	19.1	16.8	2.8	1.2	1.2	18.4	12.0	4.4	392	299
Oklahoma	1 282.4	705.2	225.3	252.6	282.4	103.8	332.9	1 385.1	405.6	562.2	892	382
Okmulgee	6.3	0.6	1.0	26.7	12.9	5.0	18.3	64.1	33.9	12.7	334	147
Osage	28.0	0.0	2.3	9.1	5.0	3.8	4.2	44.0	27.0	9.1	214	127
Ottawa	6.5	16.7	6.2	14.7	6.5	3.8	5.1	54.6	28.4	17.4	570	412
Pawnee	4.6	0.0	1.0	5.0	6.1	1.0	2.4	22.6	12.0	5.1	312	178
Payne	19.8	8.5	13.6	12.7	4.1	22.7	44.8	155.2	47.9	34.2	533	298
Pittsburg	42.9	14.3	3.5	26.5	5.2	5.7	5.3	101.0	40.9	20.8	482	169
Pontotoc	13.4	0.0	5.8	25.1	8.0	7.2	8.6	102.3	32.3	19.7	566	234
Pottawatomie	9.8	0.7	2.6	29.4	16.3	5.2	5.5	122.5	56.9	28.4	460	234
Pushmataha	1.7	0.2	0.3	13.0	1.9	1.3	8.6	19.3	14.6	2.9	250	129
Roger Mills	1.7	0.0	0.4	1.8	0.4	0.2	1.0	5.9	3.3	1.7	477	394
Rogers	21.1	0.3	2.1	12.1	6.1	3.0	14.8	79.8	40.2	29.8	453	292
Seminole	6.0	0.2	1.1	20.5	6.3	4.0	15.5	49.0	23.8	9.8	391	256
Sequoyah	7.6	1.3	1.2	28.4	5.0	5.1	11.5	52.0	36.7	8.6	232	126
Stephens	5.6	0.1	6.6	14.8	4.7	2.4	16.2	62.9	37.1	17.0	390	222
Texas	3.2	0.0	2.0	2.8	1.3	1.4	7.6	35.3	17.0	11.1	616	371
Tillman	2.0	1.0	0.4	7.4	3.3	0.8	1.0	18.3	11.9	3.7	382	260
Tulsa	207.7	53.4	69.1	119.3	52.1	33.4	71.0	1 254.5	357.4	493.4	921	470
Wagoner	3.6	0.0	0.7	13.0	3.9	2.3	3.3	40.3	23.1	10.7	197	101
Washington	1.8	0.2	1.3	8.2	4.5	3.1	3.2	83.0	31.4	32.9	695	412
Washita	2.3	5.6	0.5	3.0	1.0	1.2	0.6	25.9	13.3	7.0	600	486
Woods	2.1	0.0	2.1	1.4	0.6	1.3	2.1	17.9	8.8	7.3	884	678
Woodward	5.1	0.0	2.0	3.1	1.3	1.2	1.5	36.9	18.2	11.8	633	321
OREGON	1 505.9	303.8	461.7	1 628.8	574.8	308.9	1 005.8	X	X	X	X	X
Baker	12.2	0.0	3.0	15.4	1.6	0.8	10.9	36.7	19.9	9.7	588	515
Benton	33.5	2.5	10.5	25.6	5.0	6.1	62.4	158.2	62.1	64.3	841	723
Clackamas	90.3	8.8	27.9	70.5	29.7	10.4	28.9	760.2	290.8	280.6	848	770
Clatsop	19.4	4.5	9.6	16.0	3.2	2.7	2.7	115.1	48.7	43.8	1 233	1 029
Columbia	4.6	4.4	1.3	12.0	4.8	1.8	1.8	117.7	46.1	39.5	902	770
Coos	25.6	7.9	10.4	30.9	10.0	4.6	18.4	230.4	81.8	46.6	745	656
Crook	13.2	0.0	3.6	5.9	1.4	1.0	1.1	43.8	24.4	10.2	601	551
Curry	6.0	0.8	2.1	6.5	1.8	1.0	3.9	63.1	32.6	14.7	690	600
Deschutes	33.8	0.9	8.2	23.0	7.3	3.8	8.7	259.4	94.0	107.5	1 061	873
Douglas	62.9	0.0	14.3	44.3	13.4	6.5	4.5	251.4	139.7	62.5	614	539
Gilliam	0.3	0.0	0.1	0.3	0.3	0.1	4.0	11.5	4.2	2.8	1 426	1 400
Grant	11.0	0.0	2.6	2.8	0.8	0.4	2.9	53.5	37.5	6.7	842	582
Harney	8.5	0.0	1.6	2.8	0.8	0.3	5.5	29.7	14.4	4.6	661	593
Hood River	6.0	3.1	2.8	6.8	4.4	0.9	2.5	51.1	21.2	11.9	608	557
Jackson	78.2	1.1	21.2	66.7	20.2	8.1	20.4	386.3	176.3	123.7	724	630
Jefferson	6.6	0.4	0.6	9.1	3.3	3.1	3.7	51.6	21.5	11.2	676	598
Josephine	14.8	1.8	4.5	37.4	9.4	4.5	14.1	159.4	89.6	37.5	510	450
Klamath	43.1	1.4	9.5	26.3	8.7	5.3	4.8	262.4	83.1	41.9	666	580
Lake	10.6	0.0	9.8	2.5	0.8	0.4	2.7	25.4	11.1	6.2	848	765
Lane	96.4	5.6	28.7	175.1	45.0	33.1	49.5	846.7	365.1	256.5	824	689
Lincoln	13.4	4.5	6.8	18.6	5.4	2.3	5.7	175.7	44.2	64.2	1 408	1 174
Linn	20.9	1.5	6.6	47.3	15.1	5.7	18.0	257.9	128.6	78.5	759	679
Malheur	8.8	0.1	1.7	15.0	4.7	2.6	4.1	85.9	49.5	16.4	575	497
Marion	80.2	0.7	20.7	160.9	158.5	100.4	235.7	666.4	314.9	198.5	749	673

1. October 1, 1998 to September 30, 1999.   2. State totals may include programs not allocated by county.   3. Based on the resident population estimated as of July 1 of the year shown.

STATE County	Local government finances, 1997 (cont'd)							Debt outstanding		Government employment, 1998			Presidential election, 2000		
	Direct general expenditure												Percent of vote cast —		
			Percent of total for —												
	Total (mil dol)	Per capita¹ (dollars)	Education	Health and hospitals	Police protec-tion	Public welfare	High-ways	Total (mil dol)	Per capita¹ (dollars)	Federal civilian	Federal military	State and local	Demo-cratic	Republi-can	All other
	183	184	185	186	187	188	189	190	191	192	193	194	195	196	197
OKLAHOMA—Cont'd															
Kiowa	20.9	1 926	61.5	1.0	4.0	0.0	16.0	22.5	2 079	60	53	894	41.2	57.9	0.9
Latimer	30.3	2 948	82.1	0.1	0.9	0.0	9.7	2.9	280	23	51	1 603	50.8	47.4	1.8
Le Flore	71.4	1 536	65.3	8.9	3.8	0.2	7.9	10.6	228	219	232	3 090	43.6	54.8	1.6
Lincoln	41.9	1 349	63.6	9.4	4.2	0.0	6.9	19.6	632	82	156	1 234	35.4	63.1	1.5
Logan	47.9	1 565	53.2	20.6	3.6	0.0	6.6	26.4	864	70	154	1 856	35.0	63.6	1.3
Love	10.8	1 255	75.3	0.8	2.8	0.0	10.0	2.2	255	24	42	387	45.4	53.6	1.0
McClain	52.5	2 035	64.0	14.7	3.8	0.0	5.6	22.7	878	65	130	1 351	34.9	64.0	1.0
McCurtain	57.2	1 660	72.6	2.2	3.7	0.7	5.0	14.9	433	151	173	2 273	35.8	63.0	1.2
McIntosh	26.2	1 394	65.6	1.3	4.8	0.2	12.5	10.9	580	37	95	879	54.1	44.3	1.7
Major	14.9	1 915	46.6	15.5	3.2	0.0	24.1	3.5	450	41	39	427	18.9	79.7	1.3
Marshall	23.0	1 911	54.9	18.9	4.6	0.0	6.2	6.7	557	25	61	703	45.1	53.9	1.0
Mayes	45.4	1 223	71.5	1.2	4.8	0.0	6.2	13.8	373	73	187	2 102	47.3	50.9	1.8
Murray	21.1	1 703	53.5	1.7	4.9	0.0	19.4	10.2	827	90	61	1 184	46.0	53.0	1.0
Muskogee	192.7	2 777	42.8	28.7	3.1	0.0	4.5	186.3	2 686	1 395	348	5 330	50.7	47.9	1.4
Noble	21.2	1 883	63.1	1.7	4.3	0.2	11.4	10.8	961	51	57	825	30.1	68.8	1.1
Nowata	13.7	1 381	74.3	0.0	2.2	0.0	10.3	6.8	691	35	50	460	44.2	53.8	2.0
Okfuskee	18.8	1 668	65.7	5.6	3.7	0.0	11.3	4.2	376	37	57	797	47.9	50.4	1.7
Oklahoma	1 319.5	2 093	41.9	6.2	8.8	0.3	4.4	1 664.9	2 641	23 748	10 743	47 667	36.6	62.3	1.1
Okmulgee	62.5	1 638	57.2	12.6	3.8	0.0	1.4	20.5	536	136	193	2 184	54.5	44.0	1.5
Osage	44.6	1 050	58.2	7.2	4.1	0.1	10.8	10.7	253	203	236	1 769	47.4	51.2	1.5
Ottawa	54.8	1 791	71.6	0.7	4.3	0.0	4.4	9.1	299	133	155	1 983	49.5	49.3	1.2
Pawnee	22.9	1 412	51.5	15.2	2.4	0.0	13.6	13.0	800	183	82	714	41.1	57.1	1.8
Payne	153.1	2 381	41.2	30.6	4.7	0.1	4.3	113.6	1 767	275	344	13 915	37.4	61.2	1.5
Pittsburg	102.2	2 366	42.7	34.1	2.7	0.1	4.5	50.4	1 166	1 190	219	3 235	46.6	52.1	1.3
Pontotoc	98.1	2 819	37.8	41.7	2.3	0.0	3.8	36.0	1 033	248	172	2 528	42.0	56.9	1.2
Pottawatomie	119.0	1 925	54.8	18.6	3.3	0.1	5.8	51.3	829	184	310	2 832	39.3	59.3	1.4
Pushmataha	17.7	1 536	73.9	1.6	3.0	0.0	11.6	1.4	124	38	58	945	45.3	53.6	1.1
Roger Mills	5.8	1 621	65.8	2.5	1.5	0.0	13.3	1.8	504	39	18	398	26.1	73.1	0.7
Rogers	78.1	1 189	69.6	0.8	3.6	0.0	8.9	43.1	657	456	339	2 921	37.3	61.2	1.5
Seminole	49.1	1 961	53.8	19.9	2.7	0.0	4.3	17.8	711	122	123	1 511	48.1	51.0	0.9
Sequoyah	52.8	1 432	73.7	0.4	3.7	0.0	6.0	27.0	732	143	203	1 972	44.3	54.0	1.8
Stephens	70.6	1 618	62.5	0.4	4.3	0.3	7.4	35.8	820	103	216	2 006	37.0	62.1	0.9
Texas	35.5	1 962	54.8	1.1	3.8	0.0	12.4	15.2	843	71	93	1 607	17.8	81.5	0.7
Tillman	18.6	1 930	56.4	4.0	4.4	0.1	14.0	8.1	843	49	47	658	41.8	57.3	0.9
Tulsa	1 268.3	2 367	41.2	2.4	6.3	0.0	2.5	2 209.9	4 124	4 233	2 728	28 040	37.3	61.3	1.3
Wagoner	40.1	739	62.9	2.4	4.8	0.0	11.0	33.7	622	80	275	1 293	38.3	60.3	1.4
Washington	74.2	1 566	59.1	0.5	5.8	0.0	5.5	34.8	734	115	236	2 067	32.0	66.5	1.5
Washita	25.8	2 208	62.8	5.8	2.8	0.0	14.5	5.1	439	53	59	734	35.0	63.8	1.2
Woods	16.6	2 014	67.9	1.6	3.4	0.2	6.6	1.6	193	43	42	1 130	30.5	68.6	0.9
Woodward	36.0	1 929	61.5	5.9	4.7	0.5	8.7	18.4	986	114	92	1 785	27.5	71.4	1.2
OREGON	X	X	X	X	X	X	X	X	X	29 971	12 704	213 424	47.0	46.5	6.5
Baker	36.6	2 229	58.2	2.9	5.7	1.6	7.6	8.1	495	312	56	965	26.6	68.0	5.4
Benton	139.9	1 828	45.9	8.3	9.3	1.7	5.9	27.2	355	658	339	10 280	50.9	41.4	7.7
Clackamas	804.6	2 430	46.3	2.9	4.5	1.5	5.1	543.7	1 642	2 004	1 338	13 070	47.1	47.8	5.1
Clatsop	112.7	3 172	47.1	5.9	5.5	0.0	4.9	60.4	1 699	185	470	2 432	50.4	42.2	7.5
Columbia	112.3	2 566	51.6	3.6	3.5	0.9	8.3	102.7	2 347	82	151	1 869	48.7	44.2	7.1
Coos	230.1	3 680	42.8	29.1	3.9	0.5	3.5	45.5	727	389	420	4 879	39.5	53.2	7.3
Crook	54.4	3 209	42.6	3.6	3.1	0.7	7.1	31.8	1 873	349	59	806	29.9	64.8	5.3
Curry	62.1	2 919	38.9	10.8	3.9	0.2	14.6	12.1	569	126	103	1 068	35.5	56.9	7.6
Deschutes	252.5	2 491	52.1	5.2	7.8	0.5	5.4	195.3	1 927	815	360	5 581	38.1	55.5	6.4
Douglas	256.0	2 515	51.7	8.9	4.8	0.0	7.9	37.0	364	1 552	404	5 515	30.1	64.2	5.8
Gilliam	10.4	5 340	43.9	8.3	4.7	0.0	12.1	1.4	719	0	0	216	32.9	62.3	4.8
Grant	52.5	6 563	29.2	12.0	1.2	2.7	41.2	2.2	279	355	27	762	15.3	80.0	4.7
Harney	27.8	3 948	41.9	28.9	2.3	0.2	12.5	0.7	99	227	24	698	20.5	75.0	4.5
Hood River	47.5	2 422	54.5	1.3	2.9	0.0	9.2	38.1	1 944	161	66	1 230	47.6	43.5	8.8
Jackson	398.8	2 333	49.9	8.6	6.6	0.0	5.7	125.9	736	1 752	596	8 586	39.1	54.3	6.6
Jefferson	56.9	3 433	53.9	23.3	2.3	0.3	3.6	43.9	2 649	161	56	1 181	38.9	55.6	5.5
Josephine	170.1	2 316	60.3	5.5	6.0	1.4	0.7	54.0	735	334	253	3 425	32.3	60.4	7.3
Klamath	242.1	3 842	34.6	38.4	2.6	0.2	5.0	290.0	4 603	920	221	3 696	27.1	67.7	5.2
Lake	25.8	3 522	43.0	22.0	4.1	0.0	11.4	4.7	644	297	24	636	19.0	75.9	5.1
Lane	874.9	2 810	47.8	3.5	4.9	1.1	7.3	757.5	2 433	2 042	1 099	22 585	51.6	40.5	7.9
Lincoln	175.2	3 842	34.5	26.3	4.0	2.5	6.0	109.1	2 392	242	216	3 221	51.4	40.0	8.6
Linn	280.1	2 708	54.0	2.5	4.2	1.5	8.4	102.2	988	341	356	5 876	37.6	57.1	5.3
Malheur	89.4	3 136	62.8	4.1	3.2	0.0	4.9	57.0	2 001	192	97	2 942	22.5	73.3	4.3
Marion	685.0	2 584	53.8	5.5	4.8	0.0	5.7	401.2	1 513	1 473	929	30 018	43.6	50.7	5.7

1. Based on the resident population estimated as of July 1 of the year shown.

Table B. States and Counties — **Land Area and Population**

STATE/County code	MSA/PMSA/NECMA code[1]	County Type[2]	STATE County	Land area,[3] (sq km) 1990	Total persons	Rank	Per square kilometer	White	Black	Am. Indian, Eskimo, Aleut	Asian and Pacific Islander	Percent Hispanic[4]	Under 5 years	5 to 17 years	18 to 24 years	25 to 34 years	35 to 44 years	45 to 54 years
				1	2	3	4	5	6	7	8	9	10	11	12	13	14	15
			OREGON—Cont'd															
41 049	...	9	Morrow	5 265	10 513	2 375	2.0	98.1	0.1	1.3	0.6	16.5	7.6	22.2	7.7	11.8	14.1	14.2
41 051	6440	0	Multnomah	1 127	633 224	81	561.9	85.1	7.2	1.2	6.5	5.4	6.7	16.3	10.4	15.4	17.2	13.9
41 053	7080	2	Polk	1 919	62 396	770	32.5	96.2	0.5	1.6	1.8	8.8	6.3	19.0	10.8	10.4	14.3	13.4
41 055	...	9	Sherman	2 132	1 786	3 075	0.8	97.1	0.3	1.7	0.8	3.0	6.7	19.1	4.0	10.9	14.5	12.5
41 057	...	6	Tillamook	2 855	24 420	1 556	8.6	97.5	0.2	1.2	1.1	2.9	5.6	17.1	5.8	9.7	13.5	14.5
41 059	...	4	Umatilla	8 328	66 803	726	8.0	94.5	0.8	3.5	1.3	13.8	7.3	20.6	9.6	12.7	14.2	13.9
41 061	...	7	Union	5 275	24 807	1 539	4.7	97.0	0.5	1.1	1.4	2.6	6.2	20.2	10.5	10.4	14.6	14.5
41 063	...	9	Wallowa	8 147	7 258	2 658	0.9	99.0	0.1	0.5	0.5	3.0	5.9	19.2	5.5	9.9	14.3	15.2
41 065	...	7	Wasco	6 167	23 346	1 599	3.8	94.0	0.4	4.0	1.5	7.8	6.5	19.9	6.7	10.5	14.6	14.9
41 067	6440	0	Washington	1 875	409 305	141	218.3	92.6	0.8	0.6	6.0	7.3	7.4	19.0	9.1	15.1	17.3	14.7
41 069	...	9	Wheeler	4 442	1 559	3 091	0.4	99.0	0.1	0.8	0.1	1.9	4.6	15.8	5.5	7.1	12.8	17.8
41 071	6440	1	Yamhill	1 853	83 424	608	45.0	96.6	0.6	1.3	1.6	9.9	7.2	21.1	10.1	12.3	14.9	13.9
42 000	...	X	PENNSYLVANIA	116 083	11 994 016	X	103.3	88.4	9.8	0.2	1.7	2.7	5.9	17.8	8.5	13.1	16.2	13.5
42 001	...	6	Adams	1 347	87 697	573	65.1	97.7	1.5	0.1	0.7	2.2	6.2	19.0	9.1	13.1	16.4	13.7
42 003	6280	0	Allegheny	1 891	1 256 806	26	664.6	85.3	13.1	0.1	1.5	1.0	5.5	15.8	8.1	13.3	16.1	13.2
42 005	...	6	Armstrong	1 694	73 001	673	43.1	98.8	1.0	0.1	0.2	0.3	5.2	18.8	6.8	12.1	15.9	13.5
42 007	6280	0	Beaver	1 127	182 687	290	162.1	92.9	6.7	0.1	0.3	0.9	5.4	17.7	6.9	12.0	15.4	13.7
42 009	...	6	Bedford	2 628	49 699	912	18.9	99.2	0.4	0.1	0.3	0.4	5.5	19.4	7.1	11.8	15.0	15.0
42 011	6680	2	Berks	2 225	358 211	160	161.0	94.7	3.7	0.1	1.4	7.3	6.1	17.7	8.4	13.1	16.2	13.5
42 013	0280	3	Blair	1 362	129 937	400	95.4	98.4	1.0	0.1	0.4	0.5	5.5	18.9	7.7	11.7	16.0	13.6
42 015	...	6	Bradford	2 980	62 146	772	20.9	98.9	0.3	0.2	0.6	0.5	6.3	20.6	6.6	12.0	15.9	14.5
42 017	6160	0	Bucks	1 574	594 047	87	377.4	94.2	3.3	0.1	2.4	2.4	6.4	18.9	7.3	14.0	18.1	14.4
42 019	6280	1	Butler	2 042	172 522	305	84.5	98.7	0.6	0.1	0.6	0.6	5.9	19.0	8.8	13.0	17.2	13.9
42 021	3680	3	Cambria	1 782	153 766	333	86.3	96.6	3.0	0.1	0.4	1.0	4.9	18.2	8.1	11.0	15.7	12.8
42 023	...	7	Cameron	1 029	5 571	2 801	5.4	99.4	0.1	0.3	0.1	0.1	6.2	18.6	6.2	10.8	15.3	13.2
42 025	0240	2	Carbon	991	58 759	806	59.3	99.1	0.3	0.1	0.5	1.4	5.4	17.6	6.8	12.2	15.4	13.6
42 027	8050	3	Centre	2 869	132 190	396	46.1	92.7	2.6	0.2	4.5	1.6	5.1	13.5	25.0	14.3	14.0	11.2
42 029	6160	0	Chester	1 958	430 001	135	219.6	90.8	7.4	0.2	1.6	3.1	6.5	18.4	8.1	13.8	18.4	14.9
42 031	...	7	Clarion	1 560	41 651	1 048	26.7	98.5	0.6	0.2	0.8	0.4	5.0	18.2	14.8	11.1	14.2	13.5
42 033	...	6	Clearfield	2 972	80 732	626	27.2	99.0	0.5	0.1	0.4	0.4	5.6	19.1	7.5	12.6	15.6	13.8
42 035	...	6	Clinton	2 307	36 774	1 169	15.9	99.0	0.5	0.2	0.4	0.3	5.1	18.2	11.2	10.8	14.8	13.5
42 037	7560	2	Columbia	1 258	63 674	751	50.6	98.9	0.5	0.1	0.5	0.8	5.1	16.6	14.1	11.3	15.0	13.1
42 039	...	4	Crawford	2 623	89 109	566	34.0	97.8	1.6	0.2	0.5	0.5	5.8	20.0	9.1	11.4	15.9	13.7
42 041	3240	2	Cumberland	1 425	210 663	257	147.8	95.6	2.3	0.2	1.9	1.1	5.1	16.4	10.8	12.7	17.0	14.1
42 043	3240	2	Dauphin	1 361	245 576	221	180.4	80.5	17.5	0.2	1.8	3.6	6.3	17.9	7.5	14.2	17.5	13.4
42 045	6160	0	Delaware	477	541 502	97	1 135.2	84.1	13.0	0.1	2.7	1.6	6.2	17.2	9.3	13.8	15.6	12.8
42 047	...	7	Elk	2 146	34 344	1 245	16.0	99.3	0.1	0.1	0.4	0.3	5.9	19.4	6.7	12.2	14.9	13.6
42 049	2360	2	Erie	2 077	276 993	199	133.4	92.7	6.4	0.2	0.8	1.8	6.3	19.7	10.1	12.7	15.9	12.7
42 051	6280	1	Fayette	2 046	143 775	368	70.3	95.4	4.2	0.1	0.2	0.5	5.3	19.1	7.0	11.4	15.9	13.4
42 053	...	9	Forest	1 109	4 938	2 843	4.5	97.7	1.9	0.3	0.1	1.1	4.2	20.2	6.1	8.5	13.6	14.6
42 055	...	4	Franklin	1 999	128 812	405	64.4	96.3	2.8	0.2	0.8	1.3	5.7	18.5	8.0	12.4	16.2	14.4
42 057	...	8	Fulton	1 133	14 616	2 092	12.9	98.6	1.0	0.2	0.2	0.4	6.2	20.3	7.3	12.2	15.2	15.0
42 059	...	6	Greene	1 492	42 072	1 040	28.2	96.4	2.9	0.2	0.5	1.0	5.3	19.7	8.8	12.9	17.5	12.6
42 061	...	6	Huntingdon	2 267	44 753	989	19.7	94.0	5.6	0.1	0.3	0.7	5.5	17.7	10.0	12.6	16.7	13.8
42 063	...	6	Indiana	2 148	87 831	572	40.9	97.4	1.5	0.1	0.9	0.6	5.2	18.4	15.0	11.4	15.2	12.6
42 065	...	7	Jefferson	1 698	46 086	966	27.1	99.5	0.2	0.1	0.2	0.3	5.7	19.8	6.9	12.0	15.3	13.5
42 067	...	8	Juniata	1 014	22 204	1 648	21.9	99.3	0.2	0.1	0.3	0.4	5.9	20.0	7.4	12.6	16.0	14.4
42 069	7560	2	Lackawanna	1 188	206 520	262	173.8	98.1	0.8	0.1	0.9	0.7	5.3	16.7	8.4	11.5	15.2	13.2
42 071	4000	2	Lancaster	2 458	460 035	121	187.2	95.0	3.1	0.1	1.7	5.3	7.0	19.6	8.7	13.5	16.1	13.0
42 073	...	4	Lawrence	934	94 508	535	101.2	95.9	3.6	0.1	0.4	0.5	5.4	18.1	7.5	11.0	15.3	13.3
42 075	3240	2	Lebanon	937	117 856	447	125.8	97.9	0.8	0.1	1.2	3.4	5.8	18.4	7.7	12.6	16.1	13.8
42 077	0240	2	Lehigh	898	299 855	184	333.9	94.9	3.0	0.2	1.9	7.3	6.0	16.8	7.8	13.6	16.6	13.4
42 079	7560	2	Luzerne	2 308	312 000	180	135.2	97.8	1.5	0.1	0.7	0.9	5.1	16.3	7.8	11.6	15.4	13.5
42 081	9140	3	Lycoming	3 198	116 709	452	36.5	96.4	2.8	0.2	0.6	0.8	6.0	18.9	8.2	12.5	16.2	13.4
42 083	...	7	McKean	2 542	45 987	970	18.1	97.4	1.8	0.3	0.5	1.7	5.7	19.2	7.6	12.2	15.9	13.8
42 085	7610	3	Mercer	1 740	121 458	434	69.8	93.5	5.9	0.1	0.5	0.6	5.3	18.0	8.8	11.3	15.2	13.6
42 087	...	6	Mifflin	1 064	46 793	950	44.0	99.2	0.4	0.1	0.3	0.4	6.1	18.6	7.5	11.8	15.2	14.9
42 089	...	6	Monroe	1 573	128 541	406	81.7	96.6	2.2	0.2	1.1	3.2	6.7	18.8	8.3	13.8	17.9	13.5
42 091	6160	0	Montgomery	1 251	724 087	65	578.8	89.7	6.6	0.1	3.6	1.8	5.9	16.5	7.2	13.7	16.9	14.2
42 093	...	6	Montour	339	17 571	1 896	51.8	98.2	0.6	0.1	1.2	0.9	6.4	18.4	7.1	13.8	15.8	13.9
42 095	0240	2	Northampton	968	259 736	207	268.3	95.6	2.7	0.1	1.6	6.8	6.0	17.6	9.3	13.0	16.7	13.5
42 097	...	4	Northumberland	1 191	93 163	542	78.2	99.1	0.5	0.1	0.3	0.9	5.3	17.5	7.3	12.0	15.4	13.9
42 099	3240	2	Perry	1 434	44 280	996	30.9	99.3	0.3	0.1	0.3	0.7	6.3	20.5	7.3	13.4	18.4	14.1
42 101	6160	0	Philadelphia	350	1 417 601	19	4 050.3	52.2	43.6	0.3	3.9	7.5	6.8	18.7	9.7	14.6	15.0	12.1
42 103	5660	1	Pike	1 417	41 357	1 053	29.2	97.9	1.2	0.2	0.7	3.5	7.1	18.4	5.2	13.8	16.8	13.2

1. MSA = Metropolitan Statistical Area. PMSA = Primary MSA. NECMA = New England County Metropolitan Area. See Appendix A for explanation of these concepts. See Appendix B for list of metropolitan areas identified by type, with component counties. 2. County typology code from the Economic Research Service of USDA. See Appendix A for definition. 3. Dry land or land partially or temporarily covered by water. 4. Hispanic persons may be of any race.

Table B. States and Counties — **Population and Households**

STATE County	Population, 1999 (cont'd) Age (percent) (cont'd)				Population — change and components of change, 1980–1999 Total persons		Percent change		Components of change, 1990–1999			Households, 1990			Percent	
	55 to 64 years	65 to 74 years	75 years and over	Percent female	1990	1980	1980–1990	1990–1999	Births	Deaths	Net migration	Number	Percent change, 1980–1990	Persons per house-hold	Female family house-holder[1]	One person
	16	17	18	19	20	21	22	23	24	25	26	27	28	29	30	31
OREGON—Cont'd																
Morrow	10.2	6.1	6.0	49.0	7 625	7 519	1.4	37.9	1 265	647	2 278	2 803	6.1	2.71	7.5	21.5
Multnomah	8.5	5.5	6.1	51.1	583 887	562 647	3.8	8.4	85 161	53 754	20 039	242 140	3.9	2.36	10.9	31.9
Polk	8.9	8.4	8.5	51.5	49 541	45 203	9.6	25.9	6 180	4 399	11 363	18 167	10.7	2.64	9.1	21.9
Sherman	13.4	10.9	8.0	48.8	1 918	2 172	-11.7	-6.9	168	186	-93	784	-4.4	2.44	5.6	26.1
Tillamook	13.5	11.2	9.2	50.6	21 570	21 164	1.9	13.2	2 309	2 477	3 080	8 846	5.3	2.39	7.1	25.7
Umatilla	9.0	6.4	6.3	49.2	59 249	58 861	0.7	12.7	9 455	5 461	3 783	22 020	4.5	2.60	9.5	24.3
Union	9.2	6.6	7.8	50.5	23 598	23 921	-1.4	5.1	2 819	2 144	623	9 035	3.8	2.55	7.6	24.0
Wallowa	11.7	8.9	9.4	49.9	6 911	7 273	-5.0	5.0	650	730	450	2 796	-0.6	2.45	6.2	25.9
Wasco	10.0	8.1	8.9	51.2	21 683	21 732	-0.2	7.7	2 690	2 423	1 487	8 607	4.8	2.48	9.5	25.9
Washington	7.5	4.9	5.1	50.9	311 554	245 860	26.7	31.4	55 476	21 476	64 704	118 997	30.9	2.59	8.7	23.3
Wheeler	14.4	12.1	10.1	49.1	1 396	1 513	-7.7	11.7	123	171	220	584	-0.3	2.37	4.1	24.5
Yamhill	8.5	5.9	6.1	49.6	65 551	55 332	18.5	27.3	9 475	5 439	13 968	22 424	16.8	2.77	9.0	19.6
PENNSYLVANIA	9.1	8.1	7.7	51.9	11 882 842	11 864 720	0.2	0.9	1 438 566	1 163 384	-136 205	4 495 966	6.5	2.57	11.3	25.6
Adams	8.4	7.0	7.1	51.0	78 274	68 292	14.6	12.0	9 446	7 004	7 193	28 067	22.6	2.68	8.1	19.9
Allegheny	9.8	9.3	8.7	53.2	1 336 449	1 450 195	-7.8	-6.0	149 034	141 506	-82 146	541 261	0.1	2.41	12.5	29.7
Armstrong	9.6	9.0	9.0	51.7	73 478	77 768	-5.5	-0.6	7 759	8 045	72	28 309	0.9	2.56	8.6	24.1
Beaver	10.4	10.1	8.3	52.3	186 093	204 441	-9.0	-1.8	20 136	18 760	-3 958	71 939	0.3	2.54	11.2	24.4
Bedford	9.7	8.6	7.9	51.1	47 919	46 784	2.4	3.7	5 066	4 242	1 124	18 038	10.7	2.64	7.7	21.6
Berks	9.3	7.6	8.0	51.5	336 523	312 509	7.7	6.4	42 701	32 481	11 533	127 649	11.4	2.56	9.1	23.5
Blair	9.6	8.5	8.6	52.8	130 542	136 660	-4.4	-0.5	14 257	14 253	-120	50 332	2.5	2.54	11.4	25.9
Bradford	8.7	7.6	7.8	51.2	60 967	62 919	-3.1	1.9	7 132	5 761	6	22 492	4.9	2.67	8.7	22.3
Bucks	8.3	6.8	5.7	50.9	541 174	479 180	12.9	9.8	68 899	40 973	24 016	190 507	21.6	2.80	8.4	19.2
Butler	8.5	6.9	6.7	51.1	152 013	147 912	2.8	13.5	19 475	13 964	15 503	55 325	12.1	2.65	8.3	22.4
Cambria	9.9	10.2	9.3	51.7	163 062	183 263	-11.0	-5.7	15 681	17 454	-6 861	62 004	-2.2	2.53	10.4	26.9
Cameron	9.8	10.5	9.6	50.7	5 913	6 674	-11.4	-5.8	675	583	-403	2 395	-6.1	2.45	9.7	29.4
Carbon	10.4	9.7	8.9	51.5	56 803	53 285	6.9	3.4	5 538	6 493	3 091	21 989	11.9	2.55	9.2	24.1
Centre	6.6	5.3	5.0	48.6	124 812	112 760	10.7	5.9	12 533	6 981	2 114	42 683	18.2	2.55	6.2	23.6
Chester	8.1	6.4	5.4	51.0	376 389	316 660	18.9	14.2	50 901	26 408	30 004	133 257	27.2	2.73	8.3	20.2
Clarion	8.7	7.1	7.4	51.6	41 699	43 362	-3.8	0.1	4 396	3 838	-462	14 990	5.8	2.59	8.0	24.0
Clearfield	9.2	8.5	8.1	50.6	78 097	83 578	-6.6	3.4	8 678	8 039	2 307	29 808	2.3	2.58	9.3	24.4
Clinton	9.7	8.6	8.1	51.9	37 182	38 971	-4.6	-1.1	4 041	3 793	-510	13 844	2.3	2.54	9.6	24.8
Columbia	8.8	8.1	7.8	52.5	63 202	61 967	2.0	0.7	6 193	6 050	545	23 478	8.3	2.53	8.6	24.1
Crawford	8.7	7.6	7.8	51.0	86 166	88 869	-3.0	3.4	10 367	8 341	1 214	32 185	4.0	2.60	9.3	24.6
Cumberland	8.7	7.8	7.4	51.3	195 257	179 625	8.7	7.9	21 484	16 680	11 094	73 452	17.0	2.51	7.6	24.2
Dauphin	8.9	7.3	7.1	52.2	237 813	232 317	2.4	3.3	32 048	22 440	-1 203	95 264	8.1	2.45	11.7	28.4
Delaware	9.1	8.4	7.7	52.4	547 658	555 029	-1.3	-1.1	68 492	52 385	-22 293	201 374	4.7	2.63	11.9	25.1
Elk	9.8	9.1	8.4	50.8	34 878	38 338	-9.0	-1.5	3 913	3 487	-835	13 131	1.8	2.63	8.4	24.2
Erie	8.3	7.6	6.7	51.3	275 575	279 780	-1.5	0.5	35 734	24 406	-9 120	101 564	4.9	2.61	11.5	25.4
Fayette	9.9	9.3	8.7	52.3	145 351	159 417	-8.8	-1.1	16 370	16 807	-493	56 110	-0.8	2.56	12.3	25.0
Forest	10.3	11.7	10.7	46.7	4 802	5 072	-5.3	2.8	422	688	433	1 908	-0.2	2.40	7.1	26.3
Franklin	9.0	8.0	7.8	51.4	121 082	113 629	6.6	6.4	14 151	10 848	4 770	45 675	14.3	2.59	7.8	21.8
Fulton	9.3	7.5	7.0	50.5	13 837	12 842	7.7	5.6	1 549	1 039	318	5 139	15.0	2.68	8.0	20.7
Greene	8.3	7.2	7.6	53.0	39 550	40 476	-2.3	6.4	4 190	4 207	2 657	14 624	3.3	2.62	10.6	24.3
Huntingdon	9.1	7.2	7.5	48.1	44 164	42 253	4.5	1.3	4 636	3 739	-135	15 527	7.4	2.58	8.5	24.3
Indiana	8.0	7.2	7.0	51.6	89 994	92 281	-2.5	-2.4	8 779	7 819	-2 848	31 710	5.7	2.65	8.2	23.2
Jefferson	9.5	8.4	8.9	51.4	46 083	48 303	-4.6	0.0	4 981	4 930	122	17 608	2.0	2.57	9.0	24.7
Juniata	9.2	6.9	7.5	50.6	20 625	19 188	7.5	7.7	2 600	1 994	1 044	7 598	13.5	2.66	6.6	20.4
Lackawanna	9.9	9.7	10.1	53.1	219 097	227 908	-3.9	-5.7	22 176	26 271	-7 603	84 528	3.0	2.50	11.9	28.4
Lancaster	8.0	6.9	7.2	51.4	422 822	362 346	16.7	8.8	62 474	35 497	11 859	150 956	21.9	2.71	7.9	20.9
Lawrence	10.1	10.0	9.2	52.5	96 246	107 150	-10.2	-1.8	10 301	10 343	-1 282	36 350	-3.1	2.57	10.8	24.2
Lebanon	9.1	8.2	8.3	51.3	113 744	108 582	4.8	3.6	13 484	10 545	1 512	42 688	12.5	2.58	8.7	22.9
Lehigh	9.0	8.5	8.4	52.0	291 130	272 349	6.9	3.0	35 390	27 117	1 381	112 887	11.4	2.51	9.4	25.0
Luzerne	10.2	9.8	10.2	52.6	328 149	343 079	-4.4	-4.9	31 589	40 197	-6 075	128 483	2.4	2.47	11.9	28.6
Lycoming	9.1	7.8	8.0	51.6	118 710	118 416	0.2	-1.7	13 984	11 231	-4 403	44 949	6.8	2.56	9.9	24.1
McKean	9.6	7.3	8.0	50.1	47 131	50 635	-6.9	-2.4	5 149	5 081	-1 042	17 837	-2.5	2.52	9.9	26.4
Mercer	9.8	9.1	8.9	51.3	121 003	128 299	-5.7	0.4	12 844	12 427	500	45 591	2.1	2.54	10.3	24.6
Mifflin	9.4	8.2	8.3	52.0	46 197	46 908	-1.5	1.3	5 700	4 644	-316	17 697	5.3	2.58	8.7	24.5
Monroe	8.7	6.8	5.6	50.5	95 681	69 409	37.7	34.3	13 438	8 878	28 380	34 206	35.9	2.69	7.5	19.2
Montgomery	9.2	8.2	8.2	52.1	678 193	643 371	5.4	6.8	86 279	59 891	19 214	254 995	14.2	2.58	8.3	24.6
Montour	8.8	7.2	8.6	52.7	17 735	16 675	6.4	-0.9	2 173	2 097	-191	6 543	17.9	2.52	7.7	26.3
Northampton	8.9	8.0	7.2	51.3	247 110	225 418	9.6	5.1	27 812	21 704	7 451	90 955	13.6	2.62	9.1	24.1
Northumberland	9.7	9.1	9.7	51.7	96 771	100 381	-3.6	-3.7	9 480	11 445	-1 237	38 736	2.4	2.46	9.5	27.4
Perry	8.3	6.4	5.4	50.0	41 172	35 718	15.3	7.5	5 119	3 223	1 336	14 949	21.1	2.73	7.7	18.4
Philadelphia	8.4	7.4	7.2	53.7	1 585 577	1 688 210	-6.1	-10.6	233 282	174 269	-223 638	603 075	-2.7	2.56	20.3	31.6
Pike	10.4	8.6	6.4	50.2	28 032	18 271	53.1	47.5	3 509	2 501	12 314	10 536	47.9	2.62	6.1	20.0

1. No spouse present.

Table B. States and Counties — Vital Statistics, Health Resources, and Crime

STATE County	Births, average 1996–1998 Total	Rate[1]	Deaths, average 1996–1998 Number Total	Infant[2]	Rate Total[1]	Infant[3]	Physicians,[4] 1998 Number	Rate[5]	Hospitals,[4] 1998 Number	Beds Number	Rate[5]	Medicare enrollees 1999	Serious crimes known to police, 1998[6] Total Number	Rate[7]
	32	33	34	35	36	37	38	39	40	41	42	43	44	45
OREGON—Cont'd														
Morrow	148	15.5	74	0	7.7	2.2	3	30	1	44	441	1 261	442	4 535
Multnomah	9 147	14.6	5 778	45	9.2	5.0	2 396	380	8	2 130	338	88 920	53 172	8 418
Polk	696	11.6	491	3	8.2	3.8	73	119	1	51	83	8 566	2 828	4 647
Sherman	19	10.7	21	0	11.8	0.0	0	0	0	0	0	411	45	2 468
Tillamook	236	9.7	280	1	11.6	2.8	44	181	1	45	185	5 323	743	3 011
Umatilla	1 018	15.7	584	8	9.0	7.5	94	144	2	98	150	9 712	3 064	4 676
Union	292	11.7	241	2	9.7	5.7	51	205	1	69	278	4 073	743	3 178
Wallowa	66	8.8	82	1	11.1	15.2	5	68	1	32	434	1 510	119	1 586
Wasco	299	13.0	266	2	11.6	6.7	37	160	1	49	212	4 325	1 168	4 963
Washington	6 589	16.8	2 502	30	6.4	4.5	1 037	259	4	742	186	38 374	17 121	4 323
Wheeler	12	7.3	19	0	11.7	0.0	0	0	0	0	0	378	26	1 603
Yamhill	1 103	13.8	658	8	8.2	7.0	119	145	2	102	124	10 850	3 184	3 922
PENNSYLVANIA	146 154	12.2	127 968	1 101	10.7	7.5	32 665	272	214	46 466	387	2 088 116	392 788	3 273
Adams	994	11.6	808	2	9.5	2.0	87	101	1	102	118	12 543	1 167	1 411
Allegheny	14 663	11.4	15 215	109	11.9	7.4	5 496	433	22	7 470	589	244 854	39 716	3 246
Armstrong	792	10.8	855	4	11.6	5.0	70	96	1	187	256	15 850	764	1 264
Beaver	1 995	10.7	2 062	14	11.1	7.0	238	129	2	558	303	36 009	2 295	1 517
Bedford	567	11.5	490	2	9.9	4.1	39	79	1	78	158	9 064	752	1 605
Berks	4 433	12.5	3 663	37	10.3	8.3	676	190	3	874	246	60 126	11 878	2 749
Blair	1 438	11.0	1 558	10	11.9	7.2	283	217	4	593	454	24 773	3 594	3 447
Bradford	722	11.6	649	4	10.4	5.5	170	272	3	404	647	11 092	1 059	1 703
Bucks	7 273	12.5	4 741	43	8.1	6.0	1 490	253	7	1 254	213	77 746	15 179	2 625
Butler	2 094	12.4	1 594	11	9.4	5.2	218	128	1	286	167	26 668	2 767	1 697
Cambria	1 556	9.9	1 879	13	11.9	8.1	344	220	4	872	559	33 850	2 410	1 718
Cameron	59	10.3	67	1	11.8	11.4	5	89	0	0	0	1 305	125	2 189
Carbon	569	9.7	715	4	12.2	7.6	44	75	2	270	459	12 113	1 097	1 867
Centre	1 262	9.5	782	5	5.9	4.2	235	177	2	232	175	15 106	2 261	1 703
Chester	5 410	13.0	3 025	32	7.3	6.0	1 178	279	5	745	177	49 477	8 509	2 072
Clarion	440	10.5	419	3	10.0	6.1	58	139	1	88	210	6 895	454	1 372
Clearfield	869	10.7	878	4	10.9	4.6	139	172	2	286	354	14 828	1 657	2 430
Clinton	440	11.9	415	3	11.2	6.1	46	124	2	315	851	6 739	707	2 478
Columbia	626	9.8	665	4	10.4	5.9	108	168	2	391	610	11 792	1 251	2 409
Crawford	1 087	12.2	935	10	10.5	9.5	129	144	2	248	277	15 928	1 893	2 148
Cumberland	2 232	10.7	1 880	14	9.0	6.4	508	243	3	552	265	34 113	4 842	2 349
Dauphin	3 203	13.0	2 446	22	9.9	7.0	1 001	408	4	1 435	584	38 447	8 677	3 664
Delaware	6 971	12.8	5 713	42	10.5	6.1	2 347	433	9	2 112	389	91 421	16 791	3 118
Elk	396	11.4	376	3	10.8	7.6	45	130	2	304	880	6 588	938	2 691
Erie	3 568	12.9	2 702	29	9.7	8.2	631	228	6	1 167	422	44 902	8 634	3 095
Fayette	1 666	11.5	1 842	11	12.7	6.8	149	103	3	440	304	31 329	2 812	2 550
Forest	39	7.9	81	1	16.3	25.4	1	20	0	0	0	1 327	207	4 223
Franklin	1 627	12.8	1 225	11	9.6	6.6	155	121	2	297	232	20 828	3 034	2 386
Fulton	172	11.9	129	1	8.9	5.8	3	21	1	96	662	2 239	225	1 559
Greene	429	10.5	453	4	11.1	10.1	32	79	1	107	263	7 202	576	1 638
Huntingdon	483	10.8	408	2	9.1	4.1	52	117	1	104	233	7 432	846	1 876
Indiana	886	9.9	873	10	9.8	10.9	117	132	1	150	169	14 804	1 779	2 050
Jefferson	508	10.9	534	3	11.5	6.6	63	136	2	127	275	9 179	770	1 794
Juniata	291	13.2	228	2	10.4	5.7	5	23	0	0	0	3 468	134	658
Lackawanna	2 209	10.5	2 821	12	13.4	5.4	520	249	5	1 143	548	45 259	NA	NA
Lancaster	6 512	14.4	4 017	47	8.9	7.2	787	172	5	1 118	245	68 534	10 155	2 274
Lawrence	1 076	11.3	1 136	10	11.9	9.6	120	126	3	526	554	21 494	2 441	2 610
Lebanon	1 424	12.2	1 203	10	10.3	6.8	248	211	2	216	184	20 799	2 946	2 517
Lehigh	3 674	12.3	3 019	31	10.1	8.5	1 045	349	4	1 077	360	51 836	11 073	3 725
Luzerne	3 111	9.8	4 418	20	13.9	6.4	719	229	6	1 337	426	69 133	6 497	2 341
Lycoming	1 338	11.3	1 205	12	10.2	9.2	250	213	4	612	522	21 386	3 206	2 952
McKean	515	11.0	583	4	12.4	7.1	53	114	2	269	578	8 679	704	1 525
Mercer	1 358	11.1	1 418	7	11.6	5.2	237	194	4	638	523	24 230	2 590	2 173
Mifflin	578	12.3	502	6	10.7	9.8	67	143	1	232	494	8 336	841	1 943
Monroe	1 422	11.6	1 011	9	8.3	6.6	174	139	1	228	182	18 857	3 961	3 924
Montgomery	9 231	12.9	6 814	51	9.5	5.6	3 898	542	9	2 062	287	123 967	20 946	2 945
Montour	208	11.7	240	2	13.5	11.2	285	1 607	1	460	2 594	3 461	304	1 694
Northampton	2 823	11.0	2 414	21	9.4	7.4	409	158	3	880	340	46 507	4 880	2 324
Northumberland	943	9.9	1 251	4	13.2	3.9	76	81	2	193	205	20 035	1 939	2 348
Perry	534	12.1	376	3	8.5	5.6	26	59	0	0	0	6 012	547	1 241
Philadelphia	22 326	15.3	18 196	278	12.5	12.4	5 199	362	31	8 778	611	241 843	106 088	7 319
Pike	411	10.6	346	3	8.9	6.5	22	55	0	0	0	5 967	819	2 177

1. Per 1,000 estimated resident population, average 1996–1998.   2. Deaths of infants under 1 year old.   3. Deaths of infants under 1 year old per 1,000 live births.   4. Data subject to copyright.   5. Per 100,000 resident population as of July 1 of the year shown.   6. Data for serious crimes have not been adjusted for underreporting; this may affect comparability between geographic areas and over time.   7. Per 100,000 population estimated by the FBI.

Table B. States and Counties — Crime, Education, Money Income, and Poverty

	Serious crimes known to police, 1998[1] (cont'd) Rate[2]		Education — School enrollment and attainment, 1990				Local government expenditures, fiscal 1997[5]		Money income — 1989				Income and poverty, 1997 — Percent below poverty level			
			Enrollment[3]		Attainment[4] (percent)					Households						
										Median						
STATE County	Violent	Property	Total	Percent private	High school graduate or more	Bachelor's degree or more	Total current expenditures (mil dol)	Current expenditures per student (dollars)	Per capita[6] (dollars)	Dollars	Percent change, 1979-1989 (constant 1989 dollars)	Percent with $100,000 or more	Median household income	All persons	Persons under 18	Persons 5-17 in families
	46	47	48	49	50	51	52	53	54	55	56	57	58	59	60	61
OREGON—Cont'd																
Morrow	554	3 981	1 909	5.4	73.9	11.8	14.3	6 872	10 412	23 969	-19.7	1.1	33 181	7.0	8.3	8.9
Multnomah	1 147	7 271	140 543	16.9	82.9	23.7	648.6	6 900	14 462	26 928	-0.1	3.0	38 225	12.2	17.6	15.1
Polk	164	4 483	14 360	8.9	80.0	21.2	38.6	6 051	12 405	26 292	-6.1	2.4	38 415	10.5	14.3	12.9
Sherman	0	2 468	436	0.5	83.1	18.9	4.6	11 662	13 242	25 030	6.5	3.4	31 298	12.0	15.8	15.2
Tillamook	170	2 841	4 478	9.0	76.3	13.1	23.1	5 861	11 550	21 965	-8.1	1.7	30 713	13.6	20.7	18.9
Umatilla	124	4 552	14 893	5.7	75.1	13.3	79.0	6 266	11 178	22 791	-13.6	1.6	31 454	15.6	21.0	18.3
Union	111	3 067	6 995	7.0	80.2	17.0	28.7	6 141	10 698	22 484	-10.3	1.4	32 912	13.9	17.3	15.4
Wallowa	13	1 573	1 541	4.6	81.2	15.7	10.4	7 293	10 811	21 300	-6.8	1.0	30 361	13.1	16.8	16.0
Wasco	217	4 746	5 345	9.3	77.4	14.5	28.8	7 415	12 542	24 908	-12.7	2.1	34 540	12.9	18.3	16.5
Washington	221	4 102	81 871	15.6	88.2	29.8	361.7	5 532	16 351	35 554	-1.7	4.4	49 753	6.7	9.3	8.0
Wheeler	432	1 171	287	2.1	69.4	10.7	2.8	9 989	9 299	15 224	-10.4	1.0	23 385	12.5	18.2	18.7
Yamhill	244	3 678	18 012	20.4	79.1	17.1	85.1	5 615	12 990	28 303	0.1	2.7	40 252	10.5	13.8	12.5
PENNSYLVANIA	421	2 852	2 829 553	23.6	74.7	17.9	12 821.0	7 106	14 068	29 069	2.8	3.6	37 267	10.9	16.6	14.8
Adams	106	1 305	17 801	22.6	70.0	13.2	124.5	8 864	13 018	30 304	8.4	2.1	40 958	6.4	9.9	8.9
Allegheny	422	2 824	311 846	24.9	79.0	22.6	1 500.6	8 722	15 115	28 136	-6.4	4.1	38 893	10.9	17.1	14.9
Armstrong	89	1 175	15 880	7.2	71.1	8.1	86.2	7 312	10 565	22 554	-13.0	0.9	31 017	12.2	18.7	16.2
Beaver	201	1 316	42 110	15.1	74.9	11.9	195.3	6 704	11 683	24 276	-27.7	1.5	33 583	11.4	16.5	15.1
Bedford	113	1 492	10 101	6.6	68.5	7.8	52.1	6 076	9 954	21 622	-2.0	1.1	30 173	11.8	17.8	16.3
Berks	394	3 053	75 295	18.3	70.0	15.1	421.1	6 859	14 604	32 048	9.1	3.1	40 587	8.8	14.1	12.3
Blair	203	2 546	29 518	13.6	75.0	10.5	124.2	5 943	11 233	23 271	-6.0	1.3	30 881	13.7	19.3	17.5
Bradford	151	1 552	14 009	8.2	75.7	12.9	78.5	6 496	10 810	23 970	-0.8	1.7	32 185	13.2	19.1	17.4
Bucks	159	2 466	136 047	27.1	82.9	24.8	729.3	8 447	18 292	43 347	17.5	7.6	54 664	4.7	6.7	5.8
Butler	91	1 606	39 210	10.7	78.6	15.6	159.1	5 839	12 747	29 358	-5.1	2.1	39 390	8.4	12.1	11.2
Cambria	259	1 459	38 054	19.2	71.2	10.8	160.9	7 639	10 460	21 462	-18.8	1.2	28 786	12.7	18.4	16.2
Cameron	158	2 031	1 158	3.2	73.1	9.8	6.2	5 212	10 190	20 839	-11.6	1.8	31 084	10.8	16.4	16.4
Carbon	191	1 676	11 659	15.0	69.4	8.4	57.7	6 867	11 729	25 501	-1.0	1.5	33 551	9.3	14.8	13.7
Centre	105	1 598	50 857	5.9	83.6	32.3	111.7	7 868	11 854	26 060	4.6	2.9	38 108	9.9	11.8	11.2
Chester	221	1 851	97 407	27.5	84.9	34.7	495.4	8 199	20 601	45 642	22.6	10.8	59 569	5.0	7.2	6.6
Clarion	57	1 315	12 677	5.2	73.1	11.7	60.5	7 659	9 698	21 602	-17.7	1.1	30 562	14.5	18.7	17.7
Clearfield	305	2 125	17 185	9.4	70.2	8.6	94.8	5 936	10 430	21 773	-12.8	1.3	30 176	13.4	19.3	17.5
Clinton	74	2 404	9 725	6.6	72.5	11.7	40.3	7 455	10 287	22 128	-11.1	1.4	30 139	13.7	20.8	19.3
Columbia	135	2 274	16 898	6.8	73.1	12.5	71.1	6 420	10 959	24 211	2.1	1.3	33 201	10.5	15.5	13.8
Crawford	142	2 006	21 135	16.6	74.1	11.8	75.7	6 124	10 833	23 083	-9.3	1.7	31 749	13.5	19.6	17.8
Cumberland	136	2 213	49 188	20.1	81.0	22.9	253.3	7 056	15 796	34 493	6.8	3.7	45 284	5.0	7.6	6.7
Dauphin	389	3 275	52 439	15.7	77.6	18.6	257.5	6 860	14 890	30 985	7.9	2.9	41 140	9.5	16.0	14.3
Delaware	543	2 575	137 289	40.5	81.4	24.8	558.5	8 017	17 210	37 337	11.7	6.5	44 913	8.5	13.0	11.6
Elk	189	2 502	7 546	24.8	74.9	9.5	28.9	6 075	10 775	24 866	-10.9	0.8	37 483	7.8	10.7	10.4
Erie	312	2 783	74 816	25.9	77.5	16.2	290.2	6 720	12 317	26 581	-5.4	2.3	35 341	12.7	18.7	16.7
Fayette	236	2 314	31 668	11.1	67.8	9.3	130.2	6 019	9 791	19 195	-19.8	1.0	25 878	19.1	29.8	25.7
Forest	163	4 060	983	16.8	70.5	7.9	5.8	7 269	9 349	19 170	-9.6	0.3	25 702	15.4	29.6	27.0
Franklin	359	2 027	26 020	12.6	69.4	12.4	106.5	5 935	13 060	28 806	1.6	2.3	37 843	8.0	12.6	11.7
Fulton	90	1 469	2 958	3.9	64.0	7.4	16.3	6 258	10 267	23 736	4.3	1.0	33 127	10.4	15.9	15.5
Greene	145	1 493	9 684	11.8	68.0	11.3	49.0	7 191	10 005	19 903	-20.7	1.1	27 444	18.6	25.6	23.8
Huntingdon	182	1 694	10 103	16.8	71.2	9.4	40.6	6 031	10 471	23 067	6.3	1.3	31 879	12.6	17.8	16.9
Indiana	608	1 442	28 253	6.6	74.0	14.4	97.8	7 180	10 260	22 966	-14.1	1.6	31 510	15.4	21.5	19.2
Jefferson	133	1 661	10 364	5.7	72.6	8.9	46.8	6 693	10 580	22 063	-12.0	1.3	30 457	12.8	19.0	17.5
Juniata	79	579	4 162	7.7	65.2	7.3	17.1	4 387	10 759	25 359	9.0	0.9	33 092	8.7	13.6	12.7
Lackawanna	NA	NA	49 554	31.0	73.3	14.8	210.7	7 567	12 358	24 816	3.8	2.3	32 536	10.9	16.3	14.4
Lancaster	174	2 100	97 202	22.1	70.5	16.7	451.7	6 691	14 235	33 255	10.6	3.4	43 119	7.6	11.8	11.0
Lawrence	259	2 351	21 996	14.1	73.0	11.8	91.8	5 926	10 830	22 317	-19.7	1.4	30 367	13.9	21.7	19.6
Lebanon	216	2 301	24 342	17.3	70.0	11.8	110.5	6 171	13 209	29 469	-0.5	2.2	38 657	7.9	12.4	11.3
Lehigh	341	3 384	64 915	22.7	74.6	19.6	309.9	7 152	15 458	32 455	3.1	3.6	41 477	8.6	14.2	12.5
Luzerne	191	2 150	71 492	24.2	72.0	13.1	294.3	7 162	12 002	23 600	0.7	1.8	32 463	10.8	16.4	14.5
Lycoming	232	2 720	27 909	12.3	74.5	12.3	133.0	6 535	11 714	25 552	1.5	1.8	32 767	11.9	18.2	16.4
McKean	108	1 417	10 551	10.3	75.4	12.2	64.0	7 990	10 817	23 106	-6.7	1.4	32 005	13.7	19.4	18.2
Mercer	175	1 998	28 594	20.5	75.1	13.6	145.5	7 437	11 336	24 599	-14.5	1.6	32 005	13.2	20.4	18.4
Mifflin	171	1 772	9 266	11.9	68.2	8.7	48.4	7 628	10 609	22 778	-2.6	1.1	30 416	12.8	20.5	19.3
Monroe	315	3 609	23 230	12.3	78.0	17.6	147.0	6 024	13 630	32 465	21.1	2.8	40 120	8.5	13.4	11.5
Montgomery	219	2 726	160 332	36.5	83.8	32.1	843.1	8 993	21 990	43 720	15.9	10.9	55 580	4.8	7.1	6.3
Montour	234	1 460	3 826	16.7	75.2	18.7	17.7	6 419	13 769	27 260	1.3	3.5	36 113	10.3	15.5	15.4
Northampton	177	2 147	61 028	28.1	73.1	16.7	284.1	7 027	14 562	32 890	6.2	3.3	43 437	7.1	10.7	10.0
Northumberland	340	2 008	19 007	16.2	68.5	8.6	81.4	5 601	10 819	22 124	2.1	1.1	30 951	11.5	17.1	15.5
Perry	79	1 162	8 994	8.8	72.3	8.9	42.7	5 513	11 941	29 539	8.3	1.2	39 305	7.7	12.0	11.3
Philadelphia	1 465	5 854	395 033	36.2	64.3	15.2	1 511.2	7 123	12 091	24 603	11.5	2.2	28 897	21.7	32.8	28.9
Pike	189	1 988	5 636	10.3	79.2	14.7	27.9	6 403	13 785	30 314	22.8	2.9	39 790	7.7	12.7	11.6

1. Data for serious crimes have not been adjusted for underreporting; this may affect comparability between geographic areas and over time.   2. Per 100,000 population estimated by the FBI.   3. All persons 3 years old and over enrolled in nursery school through college.   4. Persons 25 years old and over.   5. Elementary and secondary education expenditures, local government fiscal years ending between July 1, 1996 and June 30, 1997.   6. Based on population enumerated as of April 1, 1990.

Table B. States and Counties — **Personal Income**

STATE County	Total (mil dol)	Percent change, 1997–1998	Per capita[1] Dollars	Per capita[1] Rank	Wages and salaries[2] (mil dol)	Proprietor's income (mil dol)	Dividends, interest, and rent (mil dol)	Transfer payments Total (mil dol)	Government payments to individuals Total (mil dol)	Social Security (mil dol)	Medical payments (mil dol)	Income maintenance (mil dol)	Unemployment insurance (mil dol)
	62	63	64	65	66	67	68	69	70	71	72	73	74
OREGON—Cont'd													
Morrow	183	14.4	18 353	2 251	115	16	35	26	24	13	6	1	2
Multnomah	19 334	4.2	30 662	146	17 380	1 768	4 197	2 224	2 114	822	826	215	88
Polk	1 371	6.5	22 334	1 009	433	95	323	184	174	91	51	12	6
Sherman	29	1.3	16 247	2 754	19	-3	11	8	7	4	2	1	0
Tillamook	501	4.9	20 613	1 522	205	58	143	106	102	55	31	6	3
Umatilla	1 379	7.0	21 018	1 383	792	100	269	236	224	91	82	23	10
Union	504	2.8	20 272	1 632	270	36	117	97	93	38	32	8	4
Wallowa	144	-3.0	19 636	1 845	59	14	44	30	29	14	8	2	3
Wasco	528	6.0	22 876	875	273	38	129	90	86	42	26	7	4
Washington	12 270	5.9	30 621	149	8 848	749	2 282	913	843	420	262	50	42
Wheeler	24	-0.9	15 555	2 873	7	0	10	6	6	4	2	0	0
Yamhill	1 852	5.8	22 586	957	849	132	381	241	227	109	78	16	8
PENNSYLVANIA	329 687	4.7	27 469	X	199 348	27 370	62 016	53 391	51 057	20 698	21 757	4 399	1 484
Adams	2 000	4.8	23 083	840	828	133	397	266	249	129	86	14	9
Allegheny	40 150	3.4	31 665	125	27 913	3 984	8 132	6 429	6 183	2 460	2 786	460	150
Armstrong	1 593	7.0	21 728	1 182	560	134	291	342	328	141	132	26	12
Beaver	4 251	4.2	23 066	844	1 877	243	628	874	838	376	335	57	25
Bedford	922	5.4	18 657	2 165	434	96	158	191	182	83	64	15	8
Berks	9 787	4.6	27 511	264	5 897	806	1 806	1 408	1 339	613	540	89	44
Blair	2 900	4.9	22 216	1 036	1 763	280	483	610	585	197	234	53	17
Bradford	1 232	4.0	19 746	1 796	685	109	228	232	220	104	76	23	4
Bucks	19 189	5.6	32 643	98	8 701	1 094	3 534	1 938	1 824	861	734	86	58
Butler	4 112	5.8	24 078	626	2 159	295	703	627	594	269	235	37	20
Cambria	3 276	3.3	21 058	1 373	1 668	244	580	911	881	316	418	58	21
Cameron	133	2.7	23 672	708	76	8	26	28	27	13	10	2	1
Carbon	1 295	4.8	22 059	1 085	406	94	247	274	263	116	101	13	12
Centre	3 072	4.3	23 272	801	2 078	321	584	358	332	148	103	22	10
Chester	17 582	6.3	41 675	25	9 407	1 430	3 478	1 376	1 294	567	566	57	32
Clarion	853	5.2	20 435	1 582	411	129	145	178	170	71	69	14	5
Clearfield	1 646	4.2	20 390	1 606	878	170	291	362	346	146	131	28	18
Clinton	732	4.0	19 810	1 778	355	51	126	161	154	66	58	13	7
Columbia	1 353	6.3	21 165	1 340	748	106	260	255	242	109	93	16	12
Crawford	1 837	4.6	20 576	1 534	965	196	310	378	361	153	143	33	10
Cumberland	6 124	4.5	29 218	191	4 797	364	1 283	668	628	309	223	24	17
Dauphin	7 211	6.4	29 380	187	6 401	365	1 232	934	886	369	345	76	27
Delaware	17 519	4.0	32 288	106	8 754	1 511	3 727	2 313	2 208	963	927	144	58
Elk	844	2.9	24 385	577	535	59	164	148	141	69	52	8	6
Erie	6 570	3.6	23 622	717	4 129	492	1 264	1 099	1 045	451	389	109	36
Fayette	2 887	4.1	19 996	1 712	984	220	501	803	775	284	315	101	22
Forest	89	4.4	17 947	2 361	36	10	18	27	26	13	10	2	1
Franklin	2 986	4.6	23 282	797	1 562	223	603	486	461	193	212	25	10
Fulton	288	6.1	19 830	1 767	158	40	47	46	43	20	16	5	2
Greene	734	4.0	17 385	2 509	424	42	113	191	183	71	72	23	6
Huntingdon	783	4.4	17 491	2 487	365	66	129	160	152	67	53	13	9
Indiana	1 839	5.0	20 809	1 456	938	261	334	365	348	144	123	32	15
Jefferson	969	3.9	20 979	1 402	436	126	180	210	201	83	77	16	9
Juniata	423	5.0	19 140	2 005	149	43	83	77	72	32	26	5	5
Lackawanna	5 120	3.1	24 572	549	2 908	434	1 030	1 120	1 079	421	477	66	33
Lancaster	12 012	5.5	26 303	365	7 152	1 227	2 353	1 405	1 316	698	442	86	35
Lawrence	2 014	4.3	21 223	1 320	963	177	352	481	463	199	188	39	12
Lebanon	2 859	4.8	24 303	590	1 266	188	515	428	405	205	142	24	15
Lehigh	8 861	5.0	29 657	177	6 319	821	1 707	1 228	1 170	543	467	75	41
Luzerne	7 560	3.1	24 029	638	4 353	524	1 465	1 690	1 629	651	681	98	58
Lycoming	2 558	4.4	21 791	1 164	1 562	212	496	469	446	204	157	38	20
McKean	1 021	3.0	22 045	1 088	528	118	188	203	194	89	72	19	7
Mercer	2 585	4.4	21 231	1 314	1 414	200	483	557	533	243	211	44	11
Mifflin	881	3.9	18 761	2 135	476	87	137	192	183	82	70	17	7
Monroe	2 809	7.6	22 396	1 001	1 355	184	499	414	389	201	131	23	15
Montgomery	30 532	5.1	42 431	20	21 475	3 020	6 995	2 780	2 640	1 286	1 081	97	72
Montour	552	6.9	31 402	128	503	22	67	127	123	31	84	4	5
Northampton	6 847	5.3	26 479	343	2 887	405	1 299	1 024	973	464	386	54	28
Northumberland	1 981	4.9	21 089	1 357	890	136	333	438	420	184	162	27	16
Perry	937	4.8	21 163	1 342	191	70	139	130	121	51	41	8	5
Philadelphia	35 542	4.9	24 769	519	29 574	2 588	5 222	8 930	8 650	2 250	4 344	1 558	196
Pike	856	7.9	21 332	1 287	199	58	180	132	124	77	32	7	2

1. Based on the resident population estimated as of July 1 of the year shown.   2. Includes other labor income.

Table B. States and Counties — Earnings, Social Security, and Housing

STATE County	Earnings, 1998									Social Security beneficiaries, December 1998		Supplemental Security Income recipients, December 1998	Housing units, 1990	
	Total (mil dol)	Farm	Goods-related[1]		Service-related and other[2]					Number	Rate[3]		Total	Percent change, 1980–1990
			Total	Manufacturing	Total	Retail trade	Finance, insurance, and real estate	Services	Government					
	75	76	77	78	79	80	81	82	83	84	85	86	87	88
OREGON—Cont'd														
Morrow	131	17.3	30.2	26.7	32.7	4.4	1.6	8.4	19.8	1 479	148	98	3 412	6.2
Multnomah	19 149	0.1	19.2	12.8	66.3	8.8	10.4	29.3	14.4	91 585	145	14 140	255 751	3.9
Polk	528	7.2	30.0	20.8	45.8	7.7	2.7	26.7	17.1	10 512	171	678	18 978	8.1
Sherman	16	-37.9	D	D	D	29.1	1.4	18.6	64.4	395	221	30	900	-8.4
Tillamook	263	7.0	25.4	17.5	45.0	12.0	3.4	20.7	22.6	6 326	260	327	13 324	4.6
Umatilla	892	3.9	D	15.0	D	12.5	2.8	19.3	22.6	10 906	167	1 111	24 333	3.5
Union	306	0.6	D	19.0	D	12.3	3.0	18.6	25.1	4 502	181	424	9 974	2.9
Wallowa	73	-7.6	24.9	17.2	50.6	16.1	6.0	16.5	32.1	1 734	235	112	3 755	3.3
Wasco	311	5.6	D	16.7	D	14.0	3.2	23.5	23.5	4 905	213	400	10 476	5.9
Washington	9 596	0.7	38.8	31.1	54.3	9.2	5.8	23.2	6.2	45 244	113	3 260	124 716	28.5
Wheeler	7	-17.6	D	D	D	17.5	4.7	11.3	63.8	440	281	18	782	0.9
Yamhill	982	8.1	33.6	24.5	43.0	10.2	4.7	20.2	15.3	12 547	153	755	23 194	14.6
PENNSYLVANIA	226 718	0.3	26.9	20.6	59.5	8.7	8.0	29.9	13.3	2 329 732	194	275 662	4 938 140	7.4
Adams	962	2.1	35.7	26.4	45.4	10.0	2.7	22.2	16.8	15 059	174	824	30 141	23.0
Allegheny	31 897	0.0	22.2	16.2	67.0	7.8	9.4	35.2	10.9	268 633	212	29 249	580 738	1.7
Armstrong	694	2.2	30.7	15.3	50.9	12.4	2.7	22.0	16.3	16 564	226	2 147	31 757	2.3
Beaver	2 120	0.0	D	22.9	D	9.3	3.3	25.1	13.9	41 590	226	3 776	76 336	1.7
Bedford	530	1.4	D	27.6	D	15.3	2.4	14.9	14.8	10 280	208	1 107	21 738	9.7
Berks	6 703	0.8	35.5	29.4	53.0	9.2	6.4	25.8	10.7	67 215	189	5 281	134 482	12.1
Blair	2 042	0.5	D	17.5	D	13.1	3.2	26.4	14.9	24 079	184	4 185	54 349	4.4
Bradford	794	1.7	D	33.7	D	9.3	2.8	25.4	13.2	12 711	204	1 764	27 058	7.4
Bucks	9 795	0.2	30.0	20.8	59.8	11.6	6.4	28.6	10.0	89 615	152	4 791	199 934	20.9
Butler	2 454	0.1	38.0	29.4	47.5	9.3	3.2	19.1	14.3	30 135	176	2 946	59 061	11.4
Cambria	1 912	0.2	21.2	13.2	60.1	10.6	6.3	31.4	18.5	37 403	240	4 314	67 374	0.4
Cameron	84	0.0	D	59.9	D	6.5	D	8.1	15.7	1 474	262	147	4 399	-0.7
Carbon	501	0.2	D	25.3	D	11.0	5.7	24.5	18.4	13 504	229	912	27 380	18.1
Centre	2 399	0.5	18.7	13.8	41.8	7.7	3.6	21.7	38.9	16 653	125	1 520	46 195	16.8
Chester	10 837	0.9	26.5	21.0	65.1	8.0	13.1	30.3	7.5	58 497	139	3 056	139 597	26.7
Clarion	540	0.7	30.1	19.7	46.4	12.6	2.6	16.2	22.8	8 293	198	1 046	18 022	4.8
Clearfield	1 049	0.2	27.7	17.9	56.3	17.5	3.1	22.4	15.8	17 414	216	2 014	34 300	3.3
Clinton	406	0.8	38.3	34.1	38.2	11.8	2.9	15.3	22.6	7 750	209	917	16 478	2.7
Columbia	854	0.1	D	30.5	D	10.4	2.7	19.6	18.0	13 000	203	1 255	25 598	7.2
Crawford	1 160	0.8	43.3	37.2	42.1	9.5	2.3	22.9	13.8	17 979	201	2 474	40 462	2.7
Cumberland	5 161	0.3	15.8	11.1	66.4	10.2	11.4	24.8	17.5	34 783	167	1 603	77 108	17.4
Dauphin	6 766	0.1	21.7	16.5	52.9	6.4	7.3	25.0	25.4	42 466	173	4 846	102 684	7.3
Delaware	10 265	0.0	24.1	18.5	66.1	9.9	9.7	34.8	9.8	100 967	186	7 428	211 024	4.7
Elk	595	0.1	63.4	58.9	28.6	5.7	1.8	14.7	8.1	7 540	218	525	17 249	5.5
Erie	4 621	0.4	38.3	32.5	48.0	9.6	5.4	23.8	13.3	50 878	184	7 024	108 585	4.7
Fayette	1 204	0.0	22.9	15.1	59.6	14.6	2.9	27.1	17.4	34 331	237	7 845	61 406	0.6
Forest	46	0.0	D	14.9	D	9.6	1.0	30.2	30.9	1 506	301	151	8 445	-2.2
Franklin	1 785	1.6	D	29.4	D	10.8	3.3	19.8	19.5	23 813	186	1 886	48 629	14.1
Fulton	198	0.9	D	50.2	D	6.9	D	10.5	12.5	2 579	178	335	6 184	16.7
Greene	467	-0.6	45.2	4.7	34.5	7.7	2.0	14.2	20.9	8 399	206	1 742	15 982	6.1
Huntingdon	431	3.2	D	20.9	D	9.5	4.3	19.9	25.6	8 318	187	1 065	19 286	14.1
Indiana	1 199	0.9	33.4	12.1	44.0	9.8	4.9	16.9	21.7	17 071	193	2 454	34 770	7.1
Jefferson	562	0.7	43.6	32.6	43.7	9.1	2.4	19.5	12.0	9 977	216	1 264	21 242	2.8
Juniata	192	3.8	43.9	34.5	41.0	10.5	3.8	12.4	11.2	3 976	180	404	8 505	9.2
Lackawanna	3 342	0.0	27.6	22.6	59.2	10.3	7.2	30.0	13.2	50 442	242	5 192	91 707	2.4
Lancaster	8 379	1.1	40.2	30.4	50.0	10.1	5.8	21.7	8.7	76 166	167	6 168	156 462	20.9
Lawrence	1 140	0.2	30.6	21.4	54.0	11.3	6.7	24.2	15.2	22 684	239	2 785	38 844	-1.9
Lebanon	1 453	0.9	D	24.9	D	12.2	3.1	22.5	19.0	23 346	199	1 555	44 634	11.3
Lehigh	7 141	0.1	D	26.8	D	8.0	6.6	29.7	8.5	59 444	199	5 517	118 335	11.6
Luzerne	4 877	0.1	25.5	19.4	59.0	9.8	6.4	25.5	15.5	78 297	250	7 456	138 724	1.9
Lycoming	1 773	0.5	31.7	26.0	53.5	10.4	5.0	25.2	14.3	23 785	203	2 999	49 580	4.3
McKean	645	0.3	45.3	36.5	37.6	8.5	2.1	18.4	16.8	10 194	219	1 442	21 454	-0.5
Mercer	1 614	0.6	35.5	29.9	51.8	11.3	3.9	26.3	12.1	27 235	223	3 059	48 689	2.2
Mifflin	563	2.1	42.2	36.5	44.7	10.5	2.9	19.4	11.0	9 784	208	1 298	19 641	5.8
Monroe	1 539	0.0	D	14.5	D	11.9	4.6	25.8	26.2	22 753	181	1 357	54 823	47.3
Montgomery	24 496	0.0	30.2	23.8	63.3	6.8	13.7	30.4	6.4	127 140	177	5 792	265 856	14.3
Montour	525	1.4	D	6.3	D	3.2	2.3	68.0	9.8	3 667	207	398	6 885	15.2
Northampton	3 292	0.1	30.3	22.8	55.2	9.9	6.1	27.4	14.4	50 902	197	3 807	95 345	13.1
Northumberland	1 026	0.7	39.0	32.8	45.6	13.2	2.9	16.8	14.7	22 730	242	2 260	41 900	2.5
Perry	261	5.2	D	10.1	D	13.7	3.2	17.3	23.3	6 257	141	520	17 063	15.4
Philadelphia	32 162	0.0	D	9.7	D	5.8	10.4	42.4	18.2	269 556	188	80 686	674 899	-1.6
Pike	257	0.1	D	6.3	D	14.2	7.3	29.8	25.1	8 464	211	338	30 852	74.0

1. Covers mining, construction, and manufacturing.   2. Covers private sector earnings in agricultural services, forestry, and fisheries; transportation and public utilities; wholesale trade; retail trade; finance, insurance, and real estate; and services.   3. Per 1,000 resident population estimated as of July 1 of the year shown.

Table B. States and Counties — Housing, Labor Force, and Employment

	Housing units, 1990 (cont'd)								Civilian labor force, 1999				Civilian employment, 1990[5]		
	Occupied units										Unemployment			Percent	
		Owner-occupied				Renter-occupied									
				Owner cost as a percent of income											
STATE County	Total	Percent	Median value[1]	With a mort-gage	Without a mort-gage	Median rent[2]	Rent as per-cent of income	Sub-stand-ard units[3] (percent)	Total	Percent change, 1998–1999	Total	Rate[4]	Total	Professional, managerial, and technical	Precision production, craft, and repair
	89	90	91	92	93	94	95	96	97	98	99	100	101	102	103
OREGON—Cont'd															
Morrow	2 803	68.0	43 500	17.8	12.4	332	23.7	6.7	4 170	-2.1	445	10.7	3 238	16.1	11.8
Multnomah	242 140	55.3	61 800	20.3	14.1	407	25.6	3.6	367 424	-0.7	19 043	5.2	292 646	30.9	10.1
Polk	18 167	66.4	63 600	20.1	13.2	360	27.6	3.3	30 286	0.3	1 611	5.3	21 315	31.6	9.3
Sherman	784	66.1	30 600	21.8	12.9	295	21.6	1.1	1 050	-1.6	55	5.2	774	18.9	8.1
Tillamook	8 846	71.3	61 300	20.6	12.6	341	25.6	2.2	11 281	1.4	588	5.2	8 344	22.3	11.8
Umatilla	22 020	62.0	47 800	19.2	13.7	313	23.0	5.8	36 321	4.0	2 358	6.5	25 612	20.8	10.8
Union	9 035	64.4	43 900	18.4	13.8	309	24.9	4.0	12 264	-1.9	733	6.0	9 920	26.2	10.6
Wallowa	2 796	69.2	47 400	18.0	13.8	287	18.7	2.4	3 528	-1.4	318	9.0	2 892	23.9	10.1
Wasco	8 607	65.1	50 000	17.0	13.0	324	23.7	3.8	12 111	0.5	911	7.5	8 811	24.7	11.4
Washington	118 997	60.8	85 500	20.5	12.8	489	24.1	3.0	242 604	0.2	9 897	4.1	164 686	36.4	10.2
Wheeler	584	70.7	30 400	18.6	13.4	247	22.1	3.6	598	-3.4	58	9.7	499	16.2	12.2
Yamhill	22 424	67.6	62 300	20.6	13.1	389	25.0	4.5	41 976	0.3	2 009	4.8	28 978	25.4	13.1
PENNSYLVANIA	4 495 966	70.6	69 700	20.2	13.3	404	26.1	2.3	5 968 988	0.6	262 336	4.4	5 434 532	28.9	11.6
Adams	28 067	73.3	79 600	21.6	11.9	386	21.8	2.4	41 672	0.0	1 527	3.7	40 056	20.4	14.3
Allegheny	541 261	66.2	57 100	19.7	13.7	389	26.6	1.3	646 609	0.1	25 018	3.9	604 923	34.8	9.1
Armstrong	28 309	76.4	44 300	18.7	12.8	290	26.7	2.0	31 419	0.0	1 978	6.3	28 624	18.1	16.2
Beaver	71 939	73.3	50 500	19.8	13.7	321	26.8	1.6	85 533	0.2	4 104	4.8	75 901	24.8	12.5
Bedford	18 038	79.1	46 800	20.1	12.6	280	24.7	3.2	25 640	2.8	1 547	6.0	20 013	16.7	14.5
Berks	127 649	73.9	81 800	19.7	12.5	413	24.7	2.2	182 574	0.1	7 441	4.1	166 292	25.2	13.1
Blair	50 332	72.6	41 100	17.0	13.2	299	26.8	1.6	63 477	1.7	2 880	4.5	55 022	23.0	13.2
Bradford	22 492	75.3	50 900	18.6	13.5	317	25.5	2.8	27 524	0.1	1 146	4.2	26 226	23.0	13.2
Bucks	190 507	75.7	140 000	23.1	13.5	604	26.1	1.5	326 011	2.1	11 205	3.4	283 836	33.7	12.2
Butler	55 325	76.6	62 900	18.1	12.0	352	24.7	1.5	87 336	1.9	3 680	4.2	68 777	25.9	13.6
Cambria	62 004	73.3	39 900	18.8	13.3	276	25.0	1.9	65 691	-0.5	3 802	5.8	60 374	24.7	12.7
Cameron	2 395	73.2	39 800	17.1	13.4	266	22.0	2.1	2 763	3.4	226	8.2	2 318	18.7	15.2
Carbon	21 989	77.9	62 900	20.3	13.0	335	26.0	1.3	27 195	0.3	1 819	6.7	24 290	19.2	15.6
Centre	42 683	59.8	74 700	20.3	11.8	448	31.3	4.4	65 375	-1.1	1 757	2.7	57 809	35.9	8.1
Chester	133 257	74.5	155 900	22.2	13.0	581	24.6	1.4	233 240	2.5	6 118	2.6	198 581	38.7	9.4
Clarion	14 990	72.5	46 200	18.1	12.4	298	28.4	2.2	18 990	0.2	938	4.9	16 296	22.0	13.4
Clearfield	29 808	78.5	40 000	19.7	13.6	295	26.3	2.7	37 582	-0.7	2 876	7.7	30 777	21.1	15.0
Clinton	13 844	72.8	46 300	18.5	13.9	295	26.4	2.0	17 563	2.4	1 005	5.7	15 342	22.4	12.1
Columbia	23 478	73.5	54 800	17.8	13.2	337	24.4	2.1	32 701	-0.4	1 713	5.2	28 882	21.2	13.0
Crawford	32 185	73.4	43 200	17.8	13.0	305	26.9	3.1	41 727	1.1	2 274	5.4	35 834	23.4	13.5
Cumberland	73 452	71.8	85 000	19.2	11.7	457	23.1	1.4	120 239	-0.3	3 329	2.8	101 690	31.6	9.2
Dauphin	95 264	63.7	71 300	18.6	12.2	428	23.9	2.1	138 821	-0.3	5 215	3.8	120 247	31.1	9.8
Delaware	201 374	72.6	113 200	21.4	14.1	526	26.5	2.0	279 470	1.1	10 346	3.7	266 074	35.5	11.1
Elk	13 131	79.7	49 900	16.6	12.9	290	25.8	1.4	17 780	-1.9	1 077	6.1	14 961	18.2	13.9
Erie	101 564	68.6	54 000	17.5	12.7	329	25.5	1.9	140 809	1.3	7 032	5.0	122 635	26.8	12.4
Fayette	56 110	72.3	39 700	20.0	12.9	281	30.0	2.7	57 019	0.6	3 915	6.9	49 221	22.5	14.4
Forest	1 908	81.0	35 700	17.5	12.9	290	22.7	3.9	1 787	3.4	137	7.7	1 802	20.6	11.9
Franklin	45 675	72.7	70 500	18.2	11.8	344	21.3	2.3	64 568	-1.5	2 973	4.6	59 552	23.9	13.8
Fulton	5 139	78.8	50 700	17.7	12.7	295	22.6	4.1	6 557	-2.6	276	4.2	6 127	17.1	16.3
Greene	14 624	72.5	38 400	18.0	13.0	270	27.9	3.8	16 073	-1.4	1 178	7.3	13 506	23.8	18.1
Huntingdon	15 527	76.3	43 100	18.7	13.4	279	24.5	3.0	18 711	-0.3	1 585	8.5	17 482	20.5	13.6
Indiana	31 710	73.5	50 500	20.9	13.0	334	29.7	3.6	36 147	-1.9	2 472	6.8	35 222	24.8	14.8
Jefferson	17 608	77.2	42 500	20.0	12.5	285	27.0	1.9	21 545	-1.0	1 493	6.9	18 320	19.9	14.7
Juniata	7 598	77.5	51 700	18.6	11.7	280	18.8	3.5	10 321	3.1	612	5.9	9 530	16.7	15.3
Lackawanna	84 528	67.0	68 900	19.0	14.0	323	24.8	1.5	103 390	-1.2	5 382	5.2	97 407	25.9	11.9
Lancaster	150 956	69.4	89 400	20.7	11.9	441	23.8	2.9	243 503	0.8	6 602	2.7	215 292	24.0	13.6
Lawrence	36 350	76.1	41 500	18.2	13.6	298	28.6	2.2	40 185	0.0	2 293	5.7	37 804	24.4	12.3
Lebanon	42 868	71.0	71 000	19.8	12.1	355	22.2	1.7	65 013	-1.1	2 009	3.1	56 716	21.9	14.1
Lehigh	112 887	69.3	97 800	21.4	13.0	461	26.0	2.0	156 124	0.9	6 134	3.9	144 250	29.8	11.5
Luzerne	128 483	69.4	56 000	18.1	14.0	319	25.2	1.4	153 707	-1.4	9 060	5.9	143 046	24.5	12.2
Lycoming	44 949	69.7	54 900	18.9	12.9	334	25.3	2.2	56 481	-0.9	2 843	5.0	52 566	22.6	12.3
McKean	17 837	74.0	37 400	15.9	12.8	292	25.4	1.1	21 059	-0.9	1 125	5.3	19 317	23.2	13.2
Mercer	45 591	75.0	41 900	17.1	13.0	321	26.4	2.3	57 899	2.1	2 898	5.0	50 027	23.3	11.8
Mifflin	17 697	72.8	44 800	19.3	12.7	286	23.4	3.2	21 809	0.1	1 467	6.7	19 831	17.5	14.0
Monroe	34 206	75.7	116 500	23.4	13.1	517	26.8	1.8	51 512	-0.9	3 202	6.2	45 021	24.7	14.3
Montgomery	254 995	72.3	143 400	21.6	13.1	593	24.8	1.3	400 399	2.2	11 934	3.0	358 563	39.4	9.6
Montour	6 543	71.6	62 200	16.8	11.9	329	22.2	2.6	8 657	1.6	221	2.6	8 248	31.2	9.7
Northampton	90 955	73.6	105 400	21.7	12.4	452	25.9	1.7	130 070	0.9	5 191	4.0	117 962	27.4	12.4
Northumberland	38 736	73.3	39 500	17.8	13.0	284	24.6	1.6	43 521	1.2	2 188	5.0	41 584	19.4	12.7
Perry	14 949	79.5	64 400	20.5	12.2	342	21.6	3.6	24 199	0.0	913	3.8	20 076	19.3	15.1
Philadelphia	603 075	61.9	49 400	19.3	14.8	452	29.8	5.1	640 912	0.1	38 314	6.0	651 621	28.6	9.0
Pike	10 536	83.3	117 700	26.0	14.1	548	26.6	2.0	18 538	5.7	659	3.6	12 528	24.4	16.8

1. Specified owner-occupied units.   2. Specified renter-occupied units.   3. Overcrowded or lacking complete plumbing facilities.   4. Percent of civilian labor force.   5. Persons 16 years and older.

Table B. States and Counties — Nonfarm Employment and Agriculture

	Private nonfarm establishments, employment and payroll, 1998									Agriculture, 1997			
		Employment						Annual payroll		Farms			Farm operators
											Percent with—		
STATE County	Number of establish-ments	Total	Health Care and Social Assistance	Manufac-turing	Retail trade	Finance and Insurance	Professional Scientific and Technical Services	Total (mil dol)	Average per employee (dollars)	Number	Less than 50 acres	500 acres and over	Whose principal occu-pation is farming (percent)
	104	105	106	107	108	109	110	111	112	113	114	115	116
OREGON—Cont'd													
Morrow	158	1 899	124	742	255	71	10	49	25 604	420	24.8	52.6	59.3
Multnomah	23 396	399 456	45 058	49 017	40 656	24 732	26 646	12 740	31 894	577	82.1	1.6	35.2
Polk	1 149	12 653	1 452	2 462	1 579	234	310	273	21 566	1 147	60.0	6.8	43.6
Sherman	43	291	D	0	89	D	0	4	12 275	168	9.5	76.8	73.8
Tillamook	718	6 181	750	1 120	975	127	125	128	20 655	313	37.4	2.6	63.9
Umatilla	1 586	18 721	2 603	4 004	3 591	515	355	409	21 833	1 488	48.6	27.8	51.7
Union	728	6 971	1 140	1 322	1 337	167	194	150	21 485	832	39.7	25.1	43.9
Wallowa	322	1 500	253	207	307	70	44	30	19 847	459	29.0	38.6	55.6
Wasco	692	7 383	1 227	755	1 540	207	169	162	22 010	470	32.3	36.2	55.7
Washington	12 227	204 003	15 420	38 854	26 990	9 270	10 929	7 414	36 342	1 681	72.5	3.3	39.3
Wheeler	43	124	D	D	19	13	0	2	13 694	157	7.6	54.8	65.0
Yamhill	1 958	23 800	2 765	6 219	3 161	625	543	573	24 072	1 813	67.1	4.9	36.8
PENNSYLVANIA	292 659	4 906 190	740 333	818 215	645 472	272 427	266 917	145 569	29 670	45 457	29.2	5.4	56.4
Adams	1 788	26 680	3 410	7 986	3 047	635	405	600	22 478	984	36.8	7.7	55.5
Allegheny	34 987	672 404	104 998	55 654	78 790	47 456	50 145	21 562	32 068	334	52.1	1.2	34.7
Armstrong	1 494	15 767	2 493	3 019	3 348	531	473	343	21 783	654	18.8	6.4	45.4
Beaver	3 485	50 231	8 575	10 579	8 117	1 420	1 996	1 286	25 606	499	35.1	1.6	40.7
Bedford	1 068	12 861	1 341	3 372	2 309	358	181	272	21 113	943	17.4	8.4	57.9
Berks	8 024	143 449	15 694	41 596	19 416	5 674	6 212	4 139	28 852	1 586	39.0	5.0	63.0
Blair	3 231	49 527	8 526	9 268	8 207	1 819	2 098	1 151	23 235	422	20.6	10.2	68.5
Bradford	1 306	18 449	3 900	6 002	3 136	571	375	457	24 790	1 279	15.1	11.1	64.4
Bucks	17 329	232 062	27 703	41 176	36 971	8 501	13 325	6 939	29 900	739	58.9	5.4	47.5
Butler	4 230	59 153	7 737	14 605	9 682	1 997	1 629	1 574	26 614	972	30.7	2.8	46.9
Cambria	3 531	49 851	9 361	7 938	7 860	3 419	2 267	1 095	21 968	525	26.1	7.6	47.4
Cameron	146	2 026	180	1 254	271	D	D	48	23 733	26	30.8	3.8	38.5
Carbon	1 112	14 085	1 778	3 508	1 968	438	233	269	19 085	167	40.1	3.6	44.3
Centre	3 116	44 202	5 086	8 711	7 807	1 772	2 649	1 023	23 149	788	26.8	6.1	57.0
Chester	11 701	177 037	23 457	19 387	22 024	8 773	19 320	6 756	38 164	1 424	45.6	4.8	64.0
Clarion	1 073	12 766	1 726	2 767	2 250	828	218	296	23 205	457	15.8	9.4	43.3
Clearfield	1 937	27 208	4 808	4 995	4 545	819	528	579	21 282	339	25.1	4.4	44.2
Clinton	761	9 737	1 131	3 329	1 962	236	149	203	20 814	266	24.1	6.0	60.2
Columbia	1 526	23 698	3 144	8 239	3 346	588	692	549	23 173	702	24.5	4.8	52.1
Crawford	2 114	27 645	4 212	8 760	4 042	565	579	657	23 755	1 069	19.5	6.9	55.2
Cumberland	5 358	111 899	14 528	13 615	14 471	10 964	4 712	3 057	27 318	970	31.6	4.9	60.8
Dauphin	6 535	138 356	21 082	14 657	15 293	9 623	6 217	4 009	28 976	625	34.2	4.2	50.2
Delaware	13 349	211 561	33 620	19 353	28 318	10 991	14 734	7 532	35 600	63	68.3	3.2	42.9
Elk	995	15 687	2 002	8 485	1 516	267	175	416	26 549	145	25.5	1.4	34.5
Erie	6 859	116 678	17 158	33 358	16 055	4 714	2 845	3 036	26 022	1 123	31.7	4.2	55.8
Fayette	2 772	32 766	6 769	3 715	6 753	842	791	640	19 546	747	28.8	4.7	41.4
Forest	147	1 020	249	D	D	D	D	19	19 023	34	17.6	5.9	44.1
Franklin	2 752	42 695	5 424	13 029	6 419	1 259	1 075	1 001	23 446	1 304	27.7	6.1	65.1
Fulton	292	5 135	460	D	403	129	29	123	23 869	449	12.0	6.7	44.8
Greene	668	8 270	1 199	664	1 234	247	134	245	29 662	666	17.4	7.8	38.3
Huntingdon	836	9 584	1 519	2 372	1 461	423	271	198	20 656	586	15.7	7.5	53.2
Indiana	2 007	23 999	3 477	3 083	4 574	1 141	1 001	537	22 383	767	22.0	6.4	54.0
Jefferson	1 215	13 635	2 114	4 781	1 861	339	290	308	22 581	436	19.3	4.8	45.2
Juniata	492	5 808	617	2 619	707	209	48	119	20 432	611	27.7	2.6	63.2
Lackawanna	5 393	90 808	16 202	16 087	13 420	4 426	2 725	2 073	22 834	238	30.3	2.5	54.2
Lancaster	11 242	201 341	23 726	52 897	30 359	6 663	6 416	5 387	26 753	4 556	39.6	1.3	74.2
Lawrence	2 118	28 297	4 880	5 441	4 181	1 252	656	660	23 328	621	26.4	3.5	54.9
Lebanon	2 538	40 426	9 288	9 632	6 287	962	832	939	23 227	885	36.4	2.5	63.6
Lehigh	8 187	158 672	25 064	22 066	18 227	8 289	7 249	5 107	32 184	425	42.6	10.6	62.6
Luzerne	7 636	122 507	20 701	23 026	18 011	5 607	3 810	2 922	23 853	451	35.3	3.5	48.1
Lycoming	2 883	47 148	7 935	12 625	7 407	2 000	1 252	1 070	22 705	841	19.9	4.8	52.3
McKean	1 151	15 364	2 376	5 314	2 026	391	239	345	22 449	209	17.7	7.2	38.3
Mercer	2 954	44 553	8 393	11 285	7 596	1 089	758	1 016	22 795	1 030	20.4	4.7	51.7
Mifflin	937	14 430	2 224	5 668	2 330	339	157	344	23 816	619	25.5	1.8	69.6
Monroe	3 180	37 352	3 958	5 216	7 575	888	1 396	815	21 828	176	34.7	5.1	42.0
Montgomery	25 388	476 769	58 634	64 046	54 779	43 917	34 361	17 351	36 392	462	55.4	2.2	48.3
Montour	383	10 567	4 900	1 511	741	729	203	355	33 634	259	23.2	5.8	56.0
Northampton	5 619	76 870	8 743	17 985	10 026	4 759	2 262	2 034	26 463	396	44.4	11.1	56.1
Northumberland	1 861	25 010	3 076	7 668	4 130	738	411	549	21 969	596	30.4	7.6	56.2
Perry	718	5 632	633	818	1 252	210	137	97	17 287	618	21.8	6.1	52.1
Philadelphia	26 181	586 689	122 210	45 209	51 050	47 061	55 156	20 194	34 420	9	66.7	0.0	77.8
Pike	688	5 328	394	308	1 162	113	151	101	18 960	40	45.0	7.5	45.0

Table B. States and Counties — **Agriculture, Land, and Water**

STATE County	Land in farms — Acreage (1,000) [117]	Land in farms — Percent change, 1992–1997 [118]	Acres — Average size of farm [119]	Acres — Total irrigated (1,000) [120]	Acres — Total cropland (1,000) [121]	Value of land and buildings — Average per farm ($1,000) [122]	Value of land and buildings — Average per acre (dollars) [123]	Value of machinery and equipment Average per farm ($1,000) [124]	Value of products sold — Total (mil dol) [125]	Value of products sold — Average per farm (dollars) [126]	Percent from — Crops [127]	Percent from — Livestock and poultry products [128]	Percent of farms with sales of — $10,000 or more [129]	Percent of farms with sales of — $100,000 or more [130]	Percent of land owned by Fed. Gov. 1997 [131]	Water consumption 1995 (mil gal/day) [132]

OREGON—Cont'd

STATE County	117	118	119	120	121	122	123	124	125	126	127	128	129	130	131	132
Morrow	1 118	0.0	2 662	95	486	909	338	164	142	336 979	77.0	23.0	60.2	31.7	16.1	347.5
Multnomah	34	11.2	60	8	19	374	7 030	36	41	71 621	96.2	3.8	31.9	10.2	25.8	197.8
Polk	171	2.0	149	14	128	498	3 214	48	91	79 420	77.3	22.7	32.0	11.5	9.3	68.3
Sherman	425	-12.9	2 530	2	278	852	326	168	24	142 484	82.8	17.2	71.4	44.6	10.0	21.9
Tillamook	36	-11.1	114	6	20	387	4 082	66	63	199 693	0.6	99.4	54.0	43.8	19.2	85.3
Umatilla	1 345	-8.3	904	129	707	611	759	89	249	167 474	76.2	23.8	47.6	22.2	20.8	378.1
Union	532	12.5	639	62	176	471	823	55	48	57 369	70.7	29.3	42.9	10.8	47.5	202.8
Wallowa	621	-10.5	1 353	49	109	625	537	49	27	59 774	35.5	64.5	56.0	15.5	57.2	168.1
Wasco	1 135	-1.5	2 415	27	214	825	353	87	57	121 249	82.8	17.2	53.6	27.2	15.2	130.2
Washington	131	-6.5	78	26	100	458	6 045	46	186	110 675	90.6	9.4	37.2	12.7	2.6	106.9
Wheeler	680	-6.6	4 331	9	35	1 246	298	50	7	42 053	9.5	90.5	54.1	10.2	24.4	51.3
Yamhill	186	3.5	103	21	128	457	4 459	45	163	89 817	79.2	20.8	32.5	11.1	14.6	155.6
PENNSYLVANIA	7 168	-0.3	158	36	5 032	372	2 390	53	3 998	87 942	32.1	67.9	54.1	21.1	2.5	9 684.9
Adams	179	3.9	182	3	138	495	2 911	68	150	152 480	40.1	59.9	53.8	21.3	1.7	26.9
Allegheny	27	-18.4	81	0	18	256	3 403	35	9	27 058	76.3	23.7	34.1	8.4	0.1	904.2
Armstrong	120	-0.3	183	0	80	279	1 642	47	41	62 344	69.8	30.2	37.0	7.8	0.9	144.6
Beaver	54	-7.3	108	0	34	246	2 553	36	12	24 886	40.5	59.5	33.3	5.8	0.0	695.9
Bedford	199	0.0	211	0	125	321	1 568	52	58	61 575	16.9	83.1	48.6	22.1	0.0	12.0
Berks	222	-0.2	140	1	188	547	3 673	71	248	156 235	47.7	52.3	65.0	29.4	1.0	85.1
Blair	84	10.3	199	0	60	379	2 008	57	51	120 855	13.9	86.1	65.2	38.2	0.1	35.7
Bradford	307	-1.4	240	0	192	288	1 219	51	97	75 816	9.6	90.4	59.4	26.9	0.0	13.7
Bucks	84	8.5	113	1	71	710	5 713	54	70	94 339	79.1	20.9	49.7	16.6	0.2	94.9
Butler	119	-8.1	122	0	83	333	2 674	47	28	28 448	46.5	53.5	39.5	7.8	0.0	30.9
Cambria	88	14.0	167	0	59	233	1 322	48	22	41 921	53.8	46.2	39.2	10.5	0.1	22.6
Cameron	4	0.0	159	0	2	175	1 105	27	0	8 759	D	D	19.2	0.0	0.0	0.8
Carbon	20	4.0	119	0	14	388	3 194	48	8	45 745	83.7	16.3	46.1	7.8	1.1	37.4
Centre	136	-2.9	173	0	93	522	2 761	51	51	64 109	26.3	73.7	58.8	23.2	0.0	33.6
Chester	175	-0.9	123	1	139	670	5 658	67	343	240 778	77.5	22.5	62.7	32.2	0.1	274.1
Clarion	94	-1.0	206	0	63	233	1 139	52	17	36 164	25.3	74.7	39.6	10.9	0.0	4.5
Clearfield	53	-4.3	155	0	35	222	1 429	40	9	25 500	38.1	61.9	37.5	8.0	0.0	319.7
Clinton	41	5.9	155	1	30	315	1 940	60	21	77 991	32.4	67.6	54.1	25.9	0.0	35.7
Columbia	110	8.2	157	1	83	301	1 995	55	38	54 471	58.8	41.2	45.6	11.1	0.0	9.3
Crawford	207	-1.8	194	1	135	188	1 088	51	58	54 656	17.2	82.8	51.8	16.5	0.8	16.9
Cumberland	143	0.8	148	1	122	460	3 098	57	85	87 133	24.1	75.9	61.8	24.9	0.3	54.6
Dauphin	87	-3.9	138	1	70	445	3 264	58	54	85 747	22.7	77.3	55.4	19.2	1.7	123.0
Delaware	5	-3.2	77	0	3	693	9 013	46	7	111 874	90.5	9.5	42.9	19.0	0.7	828.2
Elk	17	6.8	118	0	11	242	2 192	51	2	14 223	30.1	69.9	26.2	4.1	24.5	17.5
Erie	168	-0.2	149	1	114	290	1 892	63	69	61 366	63.4	36.6	51.0	14.4	0.0	97.2
Fayette	109	2.5	145	0	70	223	1 620	50	20	26 781	42.5	57.5	33.5	5.9	0.4	43.0
Forest	5	7.2	158	D	3	206	1 305	51	1	29 743	18.5	81.5	41.2	11.8	50.1	0.5
Franklin	238	1.6	182	3	191	484	2 595	74	195	149 527	10.9	89.1	66.9	40.6	4.1	20.8
Fulton	94	5.9	210	0	51	294	1 266	66	21	47 183	16.4	83.6	41.2	15.4	0.0	2.0
Greene	131	3.9	197	0	67	174	991	34	7	10 654	24.5	75.5	18.2	2.0	0.0	43.9
Huntingdon	125	-4.0	213	0	76	362	1 722	54	41	70 184	12.5	87.5	50.0	19.5	4.4	9.3
Indiana	139	-3.1	181	1	90	262	1 484	50	46	60 065	56.0	44.0	48.4	12.1	1.3	239.6
Jefferson	80	1.2	183	0	52	184	1 073	40	16	36 285	43.6	56.4	34.6	10.6	0.0	6.8
Juniata	87	2.0	142	0	58	295	1 981	50	64	104 441	10.1	89.9	64.3	27.2	0.0	4.2
Lackawanna	30	-20.2	124	0	20	328	2 702	49	11	46 736	50.1	49.9	47.9	13.4	0.0	51.5
Lancaster	392	1.0	86	5	331	472	5 578	52	767	168 293	13.3	86.7	82.1	43.5	0.0	165.7
Lawrence	87	1.4	140	0	63	225	1 595	54	25	40 895	25.5	74.5	46.1	10.6	0.0	154.1
Lebanon	111	5.4	125	1	96	500	4 093	69	171	193 376	10.8	89.2	72.7	43.3	0.5	24.0
Lehigh	92	10.4	216	0	81	750	3 705	66	57	133 456	69.4	30.6	57.9	18.8	0.0	49.1
Luzerne	57	14.6	127	0	37	308	2 564	48	18	40 613	66.9	33.1	42.6	10.6	0.1	104.9
Lycoming	136	1.9	161	2	87	283	1 873	50	43	51 357	36.9	63.1	50.7	15.2	0.3	16.3
McKean	39	-2.4	187	0	18	185	1 056	24	4	20 483	24.7	75.3	33.5	6.7	25.5	15.2
Mercer	167	3.5	162	0	113	248	1 595	45	46	44 753	39.0	61.0	48.8	11.5	0.3	85.4
Mifflin	79	-2.0	128	0	53	261	2 068	58	52	83 751	9.3	90.7	66.4	26.8	0.0	15.5
Monroe	26	24.5	149	0	14	410	2 987	56	5	30 120	56.3	43.7	41.5	8.0	2.2	15.4
Montgomery	42	-5.6	90	0	34	500	4 667	51	29	63 625	56.9	43.1	52.2	15.8	1.1	141.6
Montour	40	-2.5	154	0	30	344	2 084	57	26	101 890	68.2	31.8	52.5	15.8	0.0	21.2
Northampton	78	-3.3	198	0	69	642	3 288	69	29	72 204	68.0	32.0	56.6	21.0	0.5	471.6
Northumberland	115	5.4	193	1	91	376	2 068	50	59	99 613	36.8	63.2	58.9	19.8	0.0	30.6
Perry	115	10.5	186	0	79	347	1 902	48	59	94 898	15.6	84.4	53.2	22.7	0.0	3.9
Philadelphia	0	0.0	32	0	D	709	22 395	78	1	85 864	D	D	77.8	22.2	1.5	574.5
Pike	6	-7.0	139	0	D	523	3 761	39	1	34 625	83.6	16.4	42.5	5.0	5.3	4.1

Table B. States and Counties — Residential Construction, Wholesale and Retail Trade, and Real Estate

STATE County	New Construction ($1,000)	Number of Housing Units	Number of Establishments	Number of Employees	Sales (mil dol)	Annual Payroll (mil dol)	Number of Establishments	Number of Employees	Sales (mil dol)	Annual Payroll (mil dol)	Number of Establishments	Number of Employees	Receipts (mil dol)	Annual Payroll (mil dol)
	Value of Residential Construction Authorized by Building Permits, 1999		Wholesale Trade, 1997				Retail Trade[1], 1997				Real Estate and Rental and Leasing, 1997			
	133	134	135	136	137	138	139	140	141	142	143	144	145	146
OREGON—Cont'd														
Morrow	NA	NA	12	73	103.1	2.1	30	217	38.8	3.2	4	D	D	D
Multnomah	315 125	3 641	1 850	28 384	25 188.5	1 017.7	3 025	39 841	7 334.5	791.4	1 118	8 335	1 053.2	208.9
Polk	31 797	242	41	425	87.3	8.7	143	1 592	232.4	24.3	54	145	14.5	1.9
Sherman	300	2	2	D	D	D	13	91	12.9	1.3	NA	NA	NA	NA
Tillamook	28 543	227	22	114	18.8	2.0	123	1 044	144.1	15.0	28	104	6.7	1.3
Umatilla	25 977	257	75	954	331.6	22.8	290	3 188	567.2	53.7	61	164	14.5	2.2
Union	5 335	47	34	301	96.2	7.4	129	1 355	227.7	23.5	22	61	6.2	0.7
Wallowa	NA	NA	4	11	5.1	0.2	52	336	61.8	6.2	13	29	2.6	0.4
Wasco	4 540	33	36	550	115.7	11.3	134	1 468	256.9	26.1	28	81	7.0	1.3
Washington	430 253	3 879	1 035	13 622	13 153.8	603.2	1 499	25 124	5 453.5	512.3	579	3 098	418.9	64.6
Wheeler	134	1	1	D	D	D	6	19	8.5	0.5	1	D	D	D
Yamhill	71 894	727	73	485	259.1	14.8	269	3 313	627.2	58.4	82	306	36.1	4.6
PENNSYLVANIA	4 634 786	42 662	17 138	237 567	159 354.2	8 588.2	50 208	650 144	109 948.5	10 561.9	8 684	57 519	7 668.6	1 360.5
Adams	78 109	712	88	1 211	909.7	33.2	330	3 072	472.7	45.6	45	139	12.6	1.8
Allegheny	346 441	3 215	2 490	33 034	28 256.0	1 269.4	5 353	78 841	12 929.7	1 218.0	1 274	9 616	1 645.6	239.8
Armstrong	11 279	133	48	285	65.1	5.9	310	3 255	487.1	43.3	31	116	12.1	2.7
Beaver	43 564	432	148	1 515	570.5	46.5	668	8 513	1 180.5	113.7	80	374	35.1	7.2
Bedford	17 382	202	44	451	207.7	11.7	216	2 298	438.9	35.6	18	41	4.1	0.5
Berks	187 957	1 789	439	7 051	3 121.7	253.0	1 468	19 302	3 330.7	326.2	215	1 324	191.3	28.1
Blair	24 823	261	160	2 836	1 641.3	82.3	639	8 310	1 331.2	117.7	90	419	34.8	6.9
Bradford	10 633	158	55	512	175.1	10.7	296	3 315	521.2	46.4	31	92	10.0	1.5
Bucks	368 717	2 904	1 433	16 257	8 415.9	684.2	2 549	36 195	7 217.4	701.3	506	3 166	420.4	82.5
Butler	128 335	1 053	272	4 732	4 540.8	140.5	709	9 317	1 480.2	137.0	112	492	76.0	10.6
Cambria	18 218	214	144	2 115	580.7	57.5	693	8 555	1 244.8	111.5	77	347	32.4	5.1
Cameron	656	5	2	D	D	D	27	287	31.0	3.8	NA	NA	NA	NA
Carbon	22 085	191	34	240	91.4	7.0	219	2 102	316.7	30.9	27	81	5.5	1.3
Centre	90 262	837	100	D	D	D	617	7 861	1 153.9	108.7	111	704	83.1	14.0
Chester	442 428	3 308	1 013	10 955	15 420.9	459.6	1 517	22 625	5 879.6	490.8	328	2 052	319.1	55.0
Clarion	8 417	113	47	470	568.5	13.8	226	2 100	330.5	32.3	17	74	5.9	1.7
Clearfield	16 754	190	80	713	280.5	17.7	397	4 935	768.4	68.8	42	294	23.9	6.0
Clinton	13 386	155	28	D	D	D	176	1 877	296.2	24.6	19	74	7.9	1.1
Columbia	16 187	184	50	D	D	D	317	3 462	533.9	45.1	46	178	18.6	3.3
Crawford	17 216	212	81	652	175.5	14.6	360	3 970	628.8	58.6	49	165	15.3	1.9
Cumberland	131 687	1 244	260	3 589	2 439.6	122.7	955	15 697	2 759.5	268.2	177	1 390	195.7	35.7
Dauphin	102 528	1 172	341	9 844	8 700.1	320.2	1 125	15 204	2 532.8	246.1	196	1 369	198.2	29.3
Delaware	149 659	1 108	807	9 947	9 506.8	438.9	2 080	28 710	5 003.6	516.4	411	4 236	574.0	100.6
Elk	11 793	134	40	335	89.7	8.7	163	1 668	219.9	20.4	15	49	6.1	0.9
Erie	84 051	775	334	4 069	1 277.8	131.9	1 225	16 323	2 562.1	239.0	180	834	75.5	13.8
Fayette	20 811	340	123	1 566	406.8	29.3	599	7 056	1 110.2	96.3	77	296	28.4	4.7
Forest	3 314	41	4	D	D	D	35	162	28.6	2.3	5	6	0.4	0.2
Franklin	65 544	680	102	1 862	610.3	49.0	566	6 249	1 035.7	94.4	77	296	29.3	4.6
Fulton	3 190	45	7	32	6.6	0.5	55	402	70.7	5.3	5	37	2.8	0.7
Greene	7 029	76	34	364	78.9	6.9	136	1 240	259.2	18.4	15	40	4.1	0.4
Huntingdon	12 837	177	24	D	D	D	169	1 495	252.8	22.5	17	36	3.2	0.5
Indiana	17 105	189	80	870	418.8	19.6	391	4 986	723.6	64.3	58	223	15.7	2.8
Jefferson	9 442	139	62	515	121.4	12.0	209	1 828	299.2	24.6	26	87	5.1	1.0
Juniata	6 437	79	24	D	D	D	71	649	123.6	9.0	12	15	1.3	0.2
Lackawanna	43 774	420	286	3 636	1 126.0	95.7	1 039	13 167	1 966.3	189.8	145	747	72.7	12.8
Lancaster	262 112	2 273	663	11 020	10 936.6	341.6	2 012	29 237	4 671.7	480.8	281	1 906	247.2	41.9
Lawrence	26 084	244	90	1 070	430.2	29.0	370	4 286	627.1	61.4	58	264	27.6	5.2
Lebanon	57 729	591	118	D	D	D	490	6 480	1 209.1	106.8	59	270	29.2	4.0
Lehigh	190 098	1 690	560	7 469	4 668.7	255.6	1 376	18 976	3 509.2	333.2	264	1 659	207.1	33.1
Luzerne	66 857	622	388	5 697	2 149.6	152.3	1 406	18 945	2 856.4	269.2	208	1 240	113.0	26.5
Lycoming	30 066	297	137	2 195	481.9	51.4	605	7 600	1 149.3	108.4	78	299	32.2	4.7
McKean	5 458	67	44	426	229.2	12.7	200	1 969	280.5	26.8	21	58	4.5	0.5
Mercer	32 674	351	124	1 692	656.3	41.9	618	7 852	1 285.0	112.8	84	281	29.6	5.0
Mifflin	9 801	119	53	552	111.7	12.4	195	2 427	368.4	34.8	27	88	8.7	1.3
Monroe	192 030	1 374	93	1 012	345.3	28.5	658	7 621	1 160.6	111.7	111	808	60.9	12.4
Montgomery	356 642	3 675	2 004	29 378	22 878.2	1 395.6	3 689	54 728	9 607.4	1 025.8	876	6 649	1 019.2	199.7
Montour	9 150	80	15	209	65.8	5.2	76	797	131.3	10.0	10	24	2.7	0.3
Northampton	134 222	1 233	312	4 465	2 066.2	167.7	832	10 051	1 831.8	168.1	115	648	79.3	16.6
Northumberland	16 116	178	72	1 016	582.6	26.5	367	3 689	658.7	58.9	58	231	15.5	3.5
Perry	16 089	179	17	D	D	D	141	1 280	205.3	17.5	7	D	D	D
Philadelphia	27 003	367	1 403	22 298	12 004.0	848.4	4 782	51 398	8 118.2	887.1	964	9 550	1 158.1	253.5
Pike	53 928	433	23	D	D	D	107	1 203	182.6	16.9	27	274	40.9	3.0

1. Establishments with payroll.

Table B. States and Counties — Professional, Manufacturing, and Accommodation and Foodservices

STATE County	Professional, Scientific, and Technical Services[1], 1997				Manufacturing, 1997				Accommodation and Foodservices, 1997			
	Number of Establishments	Number of Employees	Receipts (mil dol)	Annual Payroll (mil dol)	Number of Establishments	Number of Employees	Receipts (mil dol)	Annual Payroll (mil dol)	Number of Establishments	Number of Employees	Sales (mil dol)	Annual Payroll (mil dol)
	147	148	149	150	151	152	153	154	155	156	157	158
OREGON—Cont'd												
Morrow	3	D	D	D	10	741	183.4	20.9	18	123	4.2	0.9
Multnomah	2 682	23 427	2 336.0	967.7	1 309	47 763	8 715.4	1 600.4	1 937	33 949	1 315.1	373.6
Polk	63	200	14.2	5.6	63	2 358	357.4	63.4	77	997	30.7	7.8
Sherman	NA	NA	NA	NA	NA	NA	NA	NA	9	D	D	D
Tillamook	32	96	5.8	2.4	31	1 227	317.8	32.5	128	1 086	35.5	10.1
Umatilla	67	235	16.7	5.4	75	4 623	790.6	107.2	159	1 950	66.4	17.2
Union	35	163	10.4	3.8	28	1 250	273.9	37.2	77	773	23.6	6.3
Wallowa	14	31	1.8	0.6	NA	NA	NA	NA	47	198	5.8	1.4
Wasco	38	154	9.7	4.0	26	751	374.7	28.1	73	925	34.3	11.8
Washington	1 203	8 082	800.5	354.2	828	38 997	14 360.2	1 413.2	798	14 299	495.8	140.6
Wheeler	NA	NA	NA	NA	NA	NA	NA	NA	6	D	D	D
Yamhill	111	408	32.6	12.4	159	6 092	1 268.3	194.9	146	1 997	58.3	17.0
PENNSYLVANIA	23 184	235 025	26 240.3	10 448.3	17 128	826 521	172 193.2	27 641.3	24 465	365 158	12 227.2	3 364.1
Adams	81	341	22.2	7.6	127	8 209	1 401.3	214.1	190	2 789	89.3	25.5
Allegheny	3 432	44 926	5 155.6	1 988.1	1 500	55 620	10 576.1	2 130.8	2 912	52 581	1 711.4	477.5
Armstrong	77	421	28.6	8.5	92	3 617	409.2	94.9	135	1 133	32.8	8.2
Beaver	208	1 760	108.0	45.3	221	10 311	3 161.9	383.1	307	3 796	108.3	28.1
Bedford	34	123	6.6	2.2	61	3 231	472.8	76.6	108	1 674	49.5	14.4
Berks	546	5 520	476.6	215.2	587	41 614	7 729.4	1 510.7	706	10 091	330.4	90.9
Blair	181	1 838	151.6	53.5	157	8 966	1 592.4	251.7	254	4 003	108.8	29.6
Bradford	67	318	17.9	5.2	73	6 405	1 273.7	191.5	117	1 185	35.3	9.7
Bucks	1 729	11 075	1 155.1	489.6	1 236	41 592	7 593.0	1 518.9	1 047	15 741	569.3	147.8
Butler	262	1 519	132.2	51.3	276	14 891	2 990.0	533.0	317	5 439	156.6	42.8
Cambria	184	1 619	98.6	42.3	153	7 403	1 349.5	186.3	314	4 143	111.4	30.6
Cameron	7	27	1.4	0.4	20	1 259	151.4	34.6	14	106	2.6	0.7
Carbon	63	182	11.2	3.9	63	3 646	311.9	76.2	97	1 200	41.8	11.3
Centre	211	2 332	167.5	85.9	159	8 546	1 409.3	255.4	287	5 241	154.8	41.2
Chester	1 567	18 172	2 446.6	972.8	629	20 791	4 332.2	771.1	642	10 790	365.4	102.7
Clarion	42	180	17.7	6.8	49	2 711	441.7	76.4	108	1 331	38.7	9.9
Clearfield	91	428	26.1	8.2	107	4 864	791.0	120.2	153	1 840	56.1	14.5
Clinton	30	139	8.3	2.5	54	3 212	677.1	89.2	79	932	28.6	6.9
Columbia	67	629	29.4	14.1	100	D	D	D	154	2 218	59.3	15.9
Crawford	97	442	31.2	11.0	301	8 714	1 263.4	289.4	180	2 357	67.3	19.0
Cumberland	404	3 989	326.3	155.4	221	13 804	3 307.3	444.8	415	7 623	235.2	65.6
Dauphin	560	5 277	559.2	198.0	222	14 871	3 590.9	522.4	611	10 456	394.4	107.3
Delaware	1 417	13 750	1 876.1	669.2	522	19 341	7 315.2	867.0	1 025	13 991	514.1	134.1
Elk	41	130	7.2	2.2	130	8 338	1 393.3	288.0	82	617	18.5	4.4
Erie	379	2 330	177.7	62.4	570	32 813	5 779.3	1 142.3	614	9 599	265.2	73.3
Fayette	115	700	49.4	14.7	128	3 842	656.7	106.0	278	4 886	157.3	47.7
Forest	3	D	D	D	NA	NA	NA	NA	20	142	4.9	1.2
Franklin	158	948	61.7	25.2	191	12 763	2 212.0	379.5	217	3 274	105.8	28.1
Fulton	12	31	1.6	0.4	22	D	D	D	24	278	10.0	2.7
Greene	27	99	5.9	1.9	27	630	81.5	15.1	56	620	19.4	4.7
Huntingdon	36	233	10.2	4.4	44	2 300	493.0	59.5	84	778	22.9	6.3
Indiana	89	601	62.6	20.2	88	3 175	344.1	98.9	167	2 707	64.8	17.5
Jefferson	56	253	14.4	5.5	88	4 634	680.9	132.0	89	928	23.9	6.4
Juniata	18	34	2.2	0.5	57	2 443	290.6	61.1	33	312	8.5	2.0
Lackawanna	358	2 585	230.1	88.2	306	16 052	2 562.7	463.0	520	7 421	219.3	59.4
Lancaster	639	5 130	439.8	165.6	918	52 908	10 585.4	1 752.0	877	15 724	506.4	145.6
Lawrence	103	553	37.7	14.8	169	5 092	1 076.6	156.4	196	2 488	67.3	17.2
Lebanon	113	608	42.2	17.9	199	9 376	1 710.3	254.3	209	2 687	76.0	22.3
Lehigh	651	4 837	410.7	164.1	504	23 277	7 690.1	877.2	648	11 892	412.7	114.7
Luzerne	466	3 666	251.7	98.7	408	24 362	4 501.1	700.8	694	9 780	292.7	79.8
Lycoming	137	1 014	68.8	27.1	208	12 982	2 460.4	370.2	283	3 571	106.1	28.5
McKean	57	226	11.4	3.3	67	5 346	875.7	158.7	118	1 057	30.0	7.8
Mercer	130	679	49.4	22.0	198	10 457	2 440.8	326.8	270	3 953	113.3	32.6
Mifflin	24	117	7.0	2.2	72	5 373	922.7	163.1	83	989	26.0	7.0
Monroe	235	1 110	77.4	31.5	113	4 744	812.9	171.1	345	6 179	241.8	67.7
Montgomery	2 934	29 664	3 693.5	1 488.4	1 398	67 234	20 666.6	2 649.5	1 504	23 896	915.4	254.0
Montour	17	D	D	D	22	1 530	820.4	65.8	39	586	15.8	4.5
Northampton	422	2 211	255.1	80.9	353	18 244	2 638.4	546.1	513	5 497	195.0	50.0
Northumberland	79	351	25.4	6.9	115	7 812	1 526.7	217.3	180	1 641	43.7	11.7
Perry	29	92	6.6	1.5	32	845	82.7	19.1	61	467	14.8	3.4
Philadelphia	2 444	49 894	6 317.4	2 690.5	1 342	47 928	11 098.1	1 582.4	2 989	38 521	1 691.6	461.1
Pike	53	137	11.9	3.7	NA	NA	NA	NA	91	1 221	49.0	15.2

1. Firms subject to federal tax.

Table B. States and Counties — Health and Other Services and Federal Funds

STATE County	Health Care and Social Assistance[1], 1997 Number of Establishments	Number of Employees	Receipts (mil dol)	Annual Payroll (mil dol)	Other Services[1], 1997 Number of Establishments	Number of Employees	Receipts (mil dol)	Annual Payroll (mil dol)	Federal funds and grants, fiscal 1999[2] Expenditures (mil dol) Total	Direct payments for individuals[3] Social Security and government retirement	Medicare	Food stamps and Supplemental Security Income
	159	160	161	162	163	164	165	166	167	168	169	170
OREGON—Cont'd												
Morrow	4	20	0.6	0.3	8	29	1.6	0.5	55.7	17.1	5.8	0.7
Multnomah	1 649	17 599	1 221.2	535.8	1 268	9 706	688.9	211.7	3 783.4	1 253.0	460.1	52.3
Polk	92	510	24.7	10.2	58	229	14.3	3.6	280.2	75.5	28.9	4.6
Sherman	1	D	D	D	2	D	D	D	31.2	5.1	1.8	0.3
Tillamook	32	252	12.1	5.2	26	102	7.7	1.8	125.4	68.5	21.0	2.5
Umatilla	141	1 047	56.9	21.7	87	303	21.1	5.9	369.7	127.8	39.0	9.6
Union	71	517	26.4	10.0	34	112	7.9	2.0	112.4	53.0	17.7	3.6
Wallowa	14	85	4.3	1.6	18	41	3.3	0.7	49.0	18.4	5.4	0.7
Wasco	58	387	27.9	11.3	32	95	7.0	1.6	134.1	54.9	15.1	2.8
Washington	915	9 348	572.9	246.9	593	3 512	257.1	78.3	833.8	418.1	167.3	21.9
Wheeler	2	D	D	D	3	D	D	D	7.2	4.6	1.5	0.1
Yamhill	151	1 716	102.3	39.4	92	429	30.6	8.3	273.5	134.0	48.6	7.1
PENNSYLVANIA	24 888	262 603	17 633.5	7 994.9	19 754	107 502	7 085.7	2 049.0	69 448.0	25 904.5	12 835.2	1 984.3
Adams	109	807	44.7	22.0	106	496	33.0	9.6	306.8	167.1	50.8	4.4
Allegheny	3 230	39 435	2 895.2	1 276.4	2 570	15 947	1 084.0	308.5	9 270.3	3 018.7	1 775.0	216.5
Armstrong	125	1 089	50.7	21.4	97	307	20.0	4.4	386.5	188.3	91.8	13.1
Beaver	310	2 700	186.7	87.5	255	1 360	67.6	20.3	834.5	429.9	214.2	27.9
Bedford	88	465	27.8	11.1	73	195	12.4	2.8	215.3	105.7	44.1	6.3
Berks	601	6 387	412.6	200.5	559	3 102	183.2	56.4	1 343.0	694.7	283.1	38.5
Blair	284	2 816	200.5	83.6	251	1 319	72.7	18.9	673.8	309.7	132.0	26.9
Bradford	81	1 044	40.3	21.6	68	225	14.1	3.4	286.8	127.0	44.5	10.6
Bucks	1 329	13 239	859.9	379.8	1 132	6 494	450.6	145.0	1 943.0	1 028.0	460.1	32.2
Butler	311	2 751	160.1	71.3	296	1 456	95.1	28.2	772.3	332.9	162.2	18.0
Cambria	351	2 749	180.8	92.5	220	1 097	69.8	19.0	992.0	405.2	202.0	28.3
Cameron	10	40	2.0	1.0	9	12	1.2	0.2	37.0	15.0	6.4	0.8
Carbon	101	616	37.2	14.4	59	183	13.4	3.0	268.3	148.9	70.6	5.7
Centre	212	2 520	169.1	72.4	159	958	52.2	14.5	678.4	183.9	68.4	8.8
Chester	893	10 268	660.5	321.3	672	4 641	414.5	117.1	1 500.0	657.5	270.9	19.9
Clarion	71	685	38.0	18.2	58	252	20.5	4.5	187.8	83.1	46.8	7.8
Clearfield	159	1 397	81.0	30.1	103	509	34.9	8.6	365.8	178.6	85.3	13.4
Clinton	49	254	15.5	5.7	42	136	9.8	2.1	171.0	77.5	33.3	6.1
Columbia	113	1 185	57.7	24.3	89	320	18.8	4.2	257.6	131.7	58.2	6.4
Crawford	167	1 530	85.4	40.1	126	527	38.1	10.1	382.6	186.8	81.5	17.0
Cumberland	425	5 511	392.2	192.7	389	2 333	136.9	44.6	1 187.1	528.8	145.7	8.6
Dauphin	545	5 434	343.1	155.6	417	2 535	171.0	52.1	3 331.4	686.1	203.9	36.7
Delaware	1 280	14 634	995.3	454.5	985	5 017	332.8	104.5	2 495.7	1 177.9	626.3	56.5
Elk	66	329	21.1	10.0	49	192	11.8	2.9	140.9	77.2	34.8	2.6
Erie	560	5 498	423.4	190.6	476	2 174	135.0	39.6	1 194.3	531.2	227.4	52.3
Fayette	269	3 290	153.4	65.3	209	867	47.7	11.7	913.4	380.9	221.8	54.4
Forest	6	105	7.1	3.5	6	27	0.9	0.3	32.4	16.5	7.7	0.6
Franklin	181	1 666	109.9	50.1	219	938	52.9	14.4	614.8	313.8	83.8	11.1
Fulton	15	98	4.1	1.3	21	53	4.2	0.7	57.9	29.3	10.0	1.9
Greene	61	450	24.9	10.9	46	190	12.3	3.5	200.0	90.4	49.4	11.6
Huntingdon	65	325	19.5	8.0	55	130	8.6	1.8	190.5	89.7	36.5	6.6
Indiana	200	1 402	77.0	30.2	126	573	42.3	9.2	415.7	180.4	89.3	16.0
Jefferson	112	663	43.9	14.9	81	290	20.5	4.4	217.8	109.2	50.6	7.7
Juniata	22	208	9.5	3.7	22	72	5.6	1.1	75.8	40.1	16.5	2.0
Lackawanna	536	5 276	351.1	158.7	349	2 096	109.4	33.1	1 235.6	546.6	284.8	31.2
Lancaster	710	8 212	523.8	252.0	808	4 429	276.4	81.6	1 510.9	810.5	278.2	38.7
Lawrence	183	1 709	100.0	45.6	139	648	32.5	8.6	524.0	250.2	125.5	19.9
Lebanon	194	1 655	107.1	49.7	192	785	52.1	13.6	539.9	267.2	85.3	9.3
Lehigh	845	8 416	625.6	307.6	583	4 350	295.2	91.8	1 207.7	503.1	284.3	45.2
Luzerne	736	8 132	501.2	218.3	499	2 288	136.0	34.6	1 830.4	859.4	413.1	45.3
Lycoming	218	2 050	134.4	58.6	176	887	57.5	15.2	525.9	245.7	99.0	19.9
McKean	89	598	37.3	15.0	69	222	12.2	3.1	230.0	102.0	44.0	9.6
Mercer	303	2 686	162.7	72.5	203	876	44.3	12.9	586.7	299.7	140.9	22.2
Mifflin	79	550	40.2	19.3	53	198	14.2	3.0	206.6	92.7	45.7	8.4
Monroe	226	1 759	108.5	48.9	191	733	54.3	12.8	546.2	247.3	96.8	10.7
Montgomery	2 171	27 990	2 082.6	949.7	1 524	9 822	622.2	209.1	3 241.4	1 554.1	698.7	38.3
Montour	26	573	31.5	10.6	20	55	3.9	0.8	79.1	38.1	18.7	2.1
Northampton	515	4 607	284.1	115.7	409	2 186	139.2	42.8	1 159.9	584.3	278.4	14.9
Northumberland	147	1 673	68.6	28.3	121	553	34.3	8.5	439.6	232.3	104.5	12.4
Perry	45	326	13.5	5.4	42	93	5.8	1.1	159.6	82.2	30.0	3.4
Philadelphia	2 574	27 295	1 931.1	899.0	1 913	10 971	737.4	199.6	12 566.5	2 966.4	2 242.3	677.7
Pike	46	307	16.4	5.6	29	91	6.9	1.4	119.0	75.5	24.6	2.4

1. Firms subject to federal tax. 2. October 1, 1998 to September 30, 1999. 3. State totals may include programs not allocated by county.

STATE County	Federal funds and grants, fiscal 1999[1] (cont'd)							Local government finances, 1997				
	Expenditures (mil dol) (cont'd)							General revenue				
	Procurement contract awards			Grants[2]						Taxes		
											Per capita[3] (dollars)	
	Salaries and wages	Defense	Other	Medicaid and other health-related	Nutrition and family welfare	Education	Other	Total (mil dol)	Intergovern-mental (mil dol)	Total (mil dol)	Total	Property
	171	172	173	174	175	176	177	178	179	180	181	182
OREGON—Cont'd												
Morrow	2.4	1.7	1.6	1.3	0.7	0.4	9.2	39.8	11.7	13.5	1 402	1 266
Multnomah	649.7	157.9	212.4	608.6	92.3	44.0	186.3	2 776.0	1 020.6	1 000.1	1 601	1 091
Polk	6.6	0.6	1.3	30.8	56.4	7.2	55.2	77.2	43.4	21.5	358	330
Sherman	3.4	2.6	0.2	0.9	0.0	0.1	5.0	8.7	4.7	2.3	1 260	1 225
Tillamook	6.6	0.1	2.3	8.0	2.0	1.6	9.5	75.2	38.2	21.9	899	816
Umatilla	33.9	50.9	10.2	29.4	11.8	4.0	20.3	167.4	92.6	42.3	654	589
Union	9.2	0.0	1.7	9.6	3.7	1.5	4.2	57.1	31.2	14.6	582	522
Wallowa	4.4	0.0	2.2	4.9	0.6	0.4	7.8	28.0	14.2	7.9	1 064	1 012
Wasco	14.6	10.6	1.3	8.6	2.6	1.2	14.3	79.2	39.4	21.4	921	839
Washington	43.2	25.8	15.4	81.3	16.6	10.8	23.8	935.0	299.4	377.5	965	838
Wheeler	0.4	0.0	0.1	0.3	0.0	0.1	-0.2	5.9	3.3	1.7	1 039	898
Yamhill	31.3	3.3	4.8	22.5	9.7	3.4	1.1	179.1	84.5	55.3	689	605
PENNSYLVANIA	5 423.6	3 841.1	2 092.6	6 684.7	2 312.7	977.6	3 165.7	X	X	X	X	X
Adams	21.3	4.1	8.0	34.0	5.1	1.7	4.9	175.1	77.6	69.1	805	565
Allegheny	798.7	1 172.6	478.6	946.7	189.2	46.3	356.2	4 249.4	1 711.3	1 679.0	1 311	973
Armstrong	12.5	0.5	3.5	38.2	8.6	2.4	24.9	141.8	69.6	54.8	745	618
Beaver	20.7	2.2	12.2	71.3	25.1	6.2	10.2	466.9	204.0	148.2	798	644
Bedford	7.3	1.8	7.3	27.1	4.5	1.7	6.1	86.7	45.4	28.8	584	460
Berks	64.0	38.5	21.7	98.4	27.1	9.5	45.0	888.2	318.7	394.0	1 113	880
Blair	45.4	0.5	13.1	73.2	20.3	5.8	38.1	243.5	120.0	78.2	598	430
Bradford	11.5	0.7	22.0	33.9	7.9	2.6	21.7	158.2	80.2	40.5	650	483
Bucks	77.7	117.6	31.6	87.7	26.4	7.3	56.6	1 386.5	370.1	708.6	1 216	1 025
Butler	59.7	5.8	86.7	59.8	13.2	3.4	21.1	331.8	133.8	131.7	778	600
Cambria	74.7	114.9	10.3	77.5	18.9	5.9	39.7	375.6	173.7	96.1	610	473
Cameron	1.0	0.0	0.3	4.0	2.3	0.2	4.7	13.2	5.8	4.7	819	691
Carbon	6.8	1.7	1.7	17.9	4.5	1.2	8.4	119.8	47.8	49.8	846	651
Centre	28.9	66.1	7.4	61.3	9.7	6.7	206.4	229.7	80.9	92.8	698	468
Chester	162.7	48.5	155.9	73.9	19.5	7.0	62.8	920.8	250.5	491.5	1 180	961
Clarion	6.1	0.5	2.1	18.6	4.4	2.6	9.6	91.8	53.8	24.9	596	456
Clearfield	15.3	0.7	5.0	38.2	8.8	3.9	12.8	155.2	84.8	53.0	657	516
Clinton	8.2	12.9	1.9	16.1	4.8	1.8	1.4	89.0	36.8	29.5	800	621
Columbia	8.9	10.5	2.2	21.8	5.6	1.6	5.2	115.1	51.3	45.5	709	492
Crawford	12.8	0.0	6.3	36.6	13.1	3.8	15.3	166.8	78.8	54.8	614	491
Cumberland	356.8	51.3	8.5	35.7	6.4	2.3	31.2	429.4	127.2	209.5	1 008	686
Dauphin	172.4	90.9	50.0	295.0	806.9	300.3	629.5	717.3	261.3	267.3	1 087	776
Delaware	129.4	151.1	30.9	175.9	47.3	14.9	49.3	1 290.2	354.4	614.0	1 131	1 023
Elk	5.6	0.1	1.5	8.8	2.8	0.7	5.7	64.2	24.5	26.2	750	527
Erie	80.0	25.6	15.9	114.3	44.0	10.2	65.5	628.4	305.3	212.1	759	598
Fayette	25.7	2.1	6.4	146.6	27.6	7.8	27.6	223.0	136.0	60.7	418	316
Forest	2.2	0.0	1.1	3.1	0.6	0.1	0.5	11.4	4.3	5.9	1 205	899
Franklin	79.2	49.6	4.1	37.6	8.4	2.6	16.0	198.8	81.0	80.1	628	466
Fulton	1.6	1.4	0.8	8.5	1.5	0.4	1.3	26.8	14.7	9.3	647	525
Greene	8.1	0.5	-15.1	36.8	5.9	2.6	6.2	83.2	35.2	35.5	840	717
Huntingdon	6.5	0.8	2.1	23.9	5.3	1.4	13.1	67.4	36.5	22.7	502	392
Indiana	15.5	2.7	3.6	55.8	9.7	3.9	23.1	157.5	84.9	52.6	590	452
Jefferson	7.7	0.0	1.7	21.9	5.7	1.6	8.4	77.4	40.0	26.4	568	427
Juniata	3.7	0.0	0.8	8.0	2.1	0.4	0.4	24.2	12.5	7.8	356	227
Lackawanna	59.0	119.1	17.3	105.8	25.4	5.6	25.0	452.9	170.2	182.8	868	612
Lancaster	90.4	43.5	45.4	102.9	30.9	11.5	37.8	904.6	306.8	395.6	871	677
Lawrence	25.4	0.7	17.7	47.1	15.0	4.0	6.4	179.8	94.2	59.8	627	478
Lebanon	96.1	10.2	6.0	26.4	5.8	1.6	20.9	231.1	93.0	94.3	804	608
Lehigh	72.8	85.6	23.6	85.1	21.0	7.1	66.7	818.9	272.3	322.8	1 084	851
Luzerne	152.7	19.9	54.0	149.9	35.0	10.7	55.6	626.7	245.8	254.8	802	592
Lycoming	36.2	13.6	8.5	46.3	15.2	3.9	24.8	254.6	105.3	97.0	819	555
McKean	27.3	0.0	4.5	22.7	6.1	1.9	8.5	116.0	59.0	33.0	705	545
Mercer	17.1	0.7	3.7	48.8	16.9	4.0	19.0	237.6	127.1	74.1	607	449
Mifflin	6.5	0.3	2.0	26.1	4.7	1.6	15.8	80.8	39.7	26.1	554	409
Monroe	96.0	45.3	11.2	17.0	6.9	3.0	8.1	267.8	69.1	167.2	1 365	1 215
Montgomery	240.2	287.8	136.4	133.1	26.3	7.4	102.8	1 819.3	435.4	980.0	1 375	1 133
Montour	2.1	0.0	0.7	6.5	1.6	0.3	8.0	40.2	11.4	14.0	778	507
Northampton	74.9	7.4	20.8	77.1	21.7	5.2	54.1	652.1	222.4	284.9	1 107	869
Northumberland	12.5	0.1	4.4	52.5	7.6	2.5	3.4	188.7	94.3	51.3	539	328
Perry	5.0	0.6	1.9	12.0	2.6	0.7	17.7	72.2	33.2	30.4	689	447
Philadelphia	1 676.1	729.3	501.7	2 329.4	521.6	125.2	542.8	6 608.1	3 309.2	2 309.6	1 591	575
Pike	9.8	0.1	1.2	3.1	1.1	0.7	0.4	59.7	13.8	37.7	964	918

1. October 1, 1998 to September 30, 1999.   2. State totals may include programs not allocated by county.   3. Based on the resident population estimated as of July 1 of the year shown.

STATE County	Total (mil dol) 183	Per capita[1] (dollars) 184	Education 185	Health and hospitals 186	Police protection 187	Public welfare 188	High-ways 189	Total (mil dol) 190	Per capita[1] (dollars) 191	Federal civilian 192	Federal military 193	State and local 194	Demo-cratic 195	Republi-can 196	All other 197
OREGON—Cont'd															
Morrow	45.8	4 760	45.8	16.7	2.9	0.0	6.7	29.7	3 080	69	45	726	33.2	61.6	5.2
Multnomah	2 594.4	4 154	34.1	6.1	5.3	0.0	5.0	2 960.6	4 740	11 731	2 596	49 962	63.5	28.2	8.3
Polk	86.4	1 437	52.0	10.5	6.1	0.0	5.5	47.7	792	120	209	3 017	41.9	52.7	5.4
Sherman	8.8	4 861	55.9	1.1	5.5	0.0	10.4	1.0	532	84	0	176	30.7	63.9	5.4
Tillamook	75.4	3 091	40.7	3.7	2.8	0.4	15.8	47.4	1 946	133	116	1 558	46.6	46.7	6.8
Umatilla	175.5	2 710	58.9	5.0	5.2	1.1	4.3	90.8	1 403	765	230	4 580	33.9	61.3	4.8
Union	54.7	2 182	55.7	0.6	5.0	0.0	7.9	14.8	590	221	84	2 322	29.6	64.9	5.5
Wallowa	25.1	3 380	45.0	27.3	3.5	0.0	6.6	7.4	996	137	25	600	19.5	76.4	4.2
Wasco	76.8	3 302	42.0	6.9	3.9	6.0	8.7	79.7	3 426	338	78	1 555	43.3	50.2	6.5
Washington	949.0	2 425	46.3	2.6	6.1	0.0	6.7	752.9	1 924	808	1 360	13 832	48.7	46.3	5.0
Wheeler	5.2	3 215	57.5	3.8	2.5	0.0	12.9	0.4	228	0	0	174	24.0	69.4	6.5
Yamhill	179.5	2 238	50.8	4.7	3.4	0.6	6.0	167.1	2 084	581	279	3 385	40.1	54.0	5.9
PENNSYLVANIA	X	X	X	X	X	X	X	X	X	111 517	45 066	601 726	50.6	46.4	3.0
Adams	213.8	2 493	71.4	0.2	1.4	3.2	3.3	174.2	2 031	456	292	3 955	NA	NA	NA
Allegheny	4 129.5	3 225	42.9	7.1	4.4	3.0	3.4	6 637.9	5 183	15 280	4 960	59 794	NA	NA	NA
Armstrong	133.8	1 818	66.3	0.2	1.2	6.4	5.5	87.2	1 185	247	247	2 951	NA	NA	NA
Beaver	472.0	2 542	48.5	4.0	3.0	5.8	3.9	1 106.6	5 960	404	622	8 112	NA	NA	NA
Bedford	94.6	1 920	68.8	3.8	0.6	0.4	4.8	76.7	1 556	139	167	2 157	NA	NA	NA
Berks	906.5	2 560	55.6	3.1	2.9	6.8	2.9	1 461.7	4 129	1 186	1 223	17 757	NA	NA	NA
Blair	242.1	1 849	59.3	0.3	2.9	5.5	3.7	328.0	2 505	967	442	7 320	NA	NA	NA
Bradford	156.0	2 504	55.0	4.2	1.3	7.3	4.7	445.6	7 154	202	212	2 952	NA	NA	NA
Bucks	1 463.3	2 512	58.9	3.0	4.0	2.7	4.7	1 563.1	2 683	1 508	1 985	19 196	NA	NA	NA
Butler	341.1	2 016	60.0	3.5	1.5	3.7	3.9	575.4	3 401	1 454	577	7 342	NA	NA	NA
Cambria	377.0	2 395	46.9	3.7	1.6	9.3	3.1	813.4	5 167	1 119	653	8 413	NA	NA	NA
Cameron	13.3	2 324	50.0	0.4	1.2	3.5	7.5	9.6	1 683	17	19	386	NA	NA	NA
Carbon	116.2	1 976	52.3	0.3	2.2	8.0	3.4	123.7	2 103	133	200	2 615	NA	NA	NA
Centre	225.8	1 698	54.9	3.5	2.9	3.9	3.7	243.4	1 830	476	543	30 627	NA	NA	NA
Chester	991.7	2 381	57.1	5.8	3.0	3.2	3.2	1 377.1	3 306	1 966	1 424	16 901	NA	NA	NA
Clarion	105.2	2 517	73.6	0.7	0.8	0.2	4.1	101.8	2 434	115	141	3 343	NA	NA	NA
Clearfield	147.1	1 824	70.9	1.1	1.3	1.3	5.0	146.0	1 810	265	274	4 449	NA	NA	NA
Clinton	84.1	2 281	53.2	0.5	1.3	2.3	4.0	88.5	2 400	141	125	2 486	NA	NA	NA
Columbia	120.1	1 869	66.3	0.0	2.4	0.4	4.4	76.1	1 185	163	217	4 166	NA	NA	NA
Crawford	171.9	1 925	51.4	5.2	1.7	5.5	5.2	139.6	1 563	278	303	4 208	NA	NA	NA
Cumberland	449.5	2 163	64.1	2.8	2.6	3.3	3.3	443.8	2 135	7 029	1 511	10 666	NA	NA	NA
Dauphin	762.3	3 101	46.8	5.0	3.1	7.4	3.2	1 236.1	5 029	2 892	890	38 288	NA	NA	NA
Delaware	1 385.4	2 551	46.6	3.9	4.5	5.5	2.4	2 533.1	4 665	2 270	1 878	21 132	NA	NA	NA
Elk	63.5	1 819	52.7	5.6	2.3	2.6	6.5	69.6	1 994	106	117	1 315	NA	NA	NA
Erie	657.1	2 352	51.9	5.6	3.9	5.4	3.4	883.8	3 163	1 596	982	14 038	NA	NA	NA
Fayette	217.8	1 501	63.7	6.1	1.4	1.3	4.4	157.1	1 083	501	500	4 992	NA	NA	NA
Forest	10.5	2 141	57.5	0.2	1.0	1.5	8.6	4.4	888	63	17	351	NA	NA	NA
Franklin	194.0	1 523	57.6	4.4	2.2	5.9	4.3	186.0	1 460	2 733	440	5 343	NA	NA	NA
Fulton	24.4	1 690	70.1	0.1	0.5	0.6	7.3	28.0	1 939	36	49	706	NA	NA	NA
Greene	89.4	2 119	66.0	0.4	0.6	0.3	5.7	151.5	3 590	132	137	2 544	NA	NA	NA
Huntingdon	69.4	1 537	64.7	0.6	1.4	1.6	5.4	78.1	1 729	132	150	2 871	NA	NA	NA
Indiana	159.9	1 793	65.8	0.1	1.1	5.1	4.3	220.0	2 467	278	315	6 730	NA	NA	NA
Jefferson	85.3	1 831	68.5	0.1	2.1	0.0	5.2	45.6	980	128	156	1 924	NA	NA	NA
Juniata	22.6	1 031	67.4	2.4	0.8	2.0	8.4	3.1	143	79	75	582	NA	NA	NA
Lackawanna	490.1	2 329	47.8	0.2	3.3	3.9	3.6	688.0	3 269	1 154	712	9 912	NA	NA	NA
Lancaster	1 006.5	2 217	55.1	2.5	3.2	4.2	3.5	1 478.9	3 257	1 631	1 541	16 671	NA	NA	NA
Lawrence	176.2	1 846	55.7	5.5	2.3	5.0	3.8	156.4	1 638	482	321	4 087	NA	NA	NA
Lebanon	238.6	2 036	58.0	3.5	2.7	7.4	3.6	313.5	2 675	2 274	444	4 679	NA	NA	NA
Lehigh	847.0	2 845	44.3	2.6	2.5	10.2	3.1	1 952.1	6 557	1 375	1 043	14 010	NA	NA	NA
Luzerne	657.1	2 069	59.9	0.3	3.0	5.7	3.7	886.8	2 792	3 431	1 099	14 715	NA	NA	NA
Lycoming	245.0	2 070	56.5	0.1	2.3	3.2	4.7	326.2	2 755	662	402	5 478	NA	NA	NA
McKean	131.3	2 805	61.0	0.2	1.3	5.9	3.9	133.1	2 843	586	157	2 295	NA	NA	NA
Mercer	253.9	2 080	63.9	4.1	2.4	1.8	4.2	227.7	1 866	299	412	5 342	NA	NA	NA
Mifflin	78.3	1 659	64.9	1.0	2.3	0.3	3.9	67.6	1 433	110	159	1 608	NA	NA	NA
Monroe	292.3	2 386	68.9	0.1	2.1	3.5	3.6	406.6	3 318	3 250	444	6 431	NA	NA	NA
Montgomery	1 837.6	2 579	54.2	3.8	4.4	2.0	2.9	2 865.2	4 021	4 655	3 759	28 122	NA	NA	NA
Montour	41.9	2 333	48.3	0.5	2.3	0.8	4.0	201.9	11 234	39	60	1 347	NA	NA	NA
Northampton	704.9	2 740	52.8	2.5	3.1	6.3	2.5	1 078.2	4 191	1 353	874	10 968	NA	NA	NA
Northumberland	190.3	2 001	51.3	5.1	2.2	7.8	4.5	192.1	2 020	217	317	4 333	NA	NA	NA
Perry	65.7	1 488	67.3	0.2	1.0	0.1	6.8	58.9	1 333	97	150	1 689	NA	NA	NA
Philadelphia	5 669.8	3 906	29.4	8.6	7.2	5.3	1.8	7 942.6	5 472	36 094	5 542	80 275	NA	NA	NA
Pike	62.0	1 587	57.9	0.2	2.0	1.3	4.4	62.2	1 590	124	136	1 688	NA	NA	NA

1. Based on the resident population estimated as of July 1 of the year shown.

Table B. States and Counties — Land Area and Population

STATE/ County code	MSA/ PMSA/ NECMA code[1]	County Type[2]	STATE County	Land area,[3] (sq km) 1990	Total persons	Rank	Per square kilometer	White	Black	Am. Indian, Eskimo, Aleut	Asian and Pacific Islander	Percent Hispanic[4]	Under 5 years	5 to 17 years	18 to 24 years	25 to 34 years	35 to 44 years	45 to 54 years
				1	2	3	4	5	6	7	8	9	10	11	12	13	14	15
			PENNSYLVANIA—Cont'd															
42 105	...	7	Potter	2 800	17 115	1 923	6.1	99.1	0.4	0.2	0.3	0.7	6.1	21.3	6.1	11.1	15.3	13.9
42 107	...	4	Schuylkill	2 017	148 788	350	73.8	97.6	1.8	0.1	0.5	1.0	4.9	16.9	7.2	12.1	15.7	13.2
42 109	...	7	Snyder	858	37 875	1 139	44.1	98.2	0.5	0.1	0.4	0.6	6.3	18.8	11.1	12.5	15.5	13.6
42 111	3680	3	Somerset	2 784	80 028	631	28.7	99.4	0.2	0.1	0.3	0.4	5.4	18.8	6.9	12.4	16.2	13.2
42 113	...	8	Sullivan	1 165	6 038	2 767	5.2	98.2	1.1	0.5	0.2	0.5	4.8	18.4	8.0	10.6	13.4	12.5
42 115	...	8	Susquehanna	2 132	42 190	1 036	19.8	99.1	0.3	0.2	0.4	0.6	6.3	20.5	6.3	12.4	15.7	14.6
42 117	...	6	Tioga	2 936	41 657	1 047	14.2	98.7	0.7	0.3	0.4	0.5	5.7	19.6	9.5	11.1	14.7	14.7
42 119	...	6	Union	820	40 546	1 074	49.4	92.1	6.6	0.3	1.0	4.2	5.3	15.9	13.7	12.9	17.8	13.8
42 121	...	4	Venango	1 749	57 562	814	32.9	98.5	1.0	0.1	0.3	0.5	5.7	20.0	6.2	11.9	16.3	13.8
42 123	...	6	Warren	2 288	43 505	1 010	19.0	99.3	0.1	0.2	0.4	0.4	5.8	19.1	6.2	11.8	16.0	14.8
42 125	6280	0	Washington	2 220	204 888	264	92.3	95.5	3.9	0.1	0.4	0.9	5.0	17.5	7.5	11.5	16.5	14.2
42 127	...	6	Wayne	1 889	46 080	968	24.4	98.1	1.4	0.1	0.4	1.7	5.7	18.6	6.9	12.1	15.8	13.4
42 129	6280	0	Westmoreland	2 648	370 658	154	140.0	97.0	2.3	0.1	0.6	0.6	5.1	17.0	7.1	11.7	16.5	14.3
42 131	7560	2	Wyoming	1 029	29 298	1 399	28.5	98.7	0.7	0.1	0.5	0.7	6.2	20.8	9.4	11.9	16.8	13.8
42 133	9280	2	York	2 343	376 586	150	160.7	94.9	4.0	0.2	1.0	2.2	6.2	18.2	7.7	13.8	17.6	14.5
44 000	...	X	**RHODE ISLAND**	2 707	990 819	X	366.0	92.1	5.1	0.5	2.3	6.9	6.3	18.1	8.5	14.5	16.5	12.6
44 001	6483	2	Bristol	64	49 102	922	767.2	98.5	0.4	0.2	0.9	2.4	5.7	16.9	8.2	12.5	16.1	13.6
44 003	6483	2	Kent	440	162 120	319	368.5	97.9	0.8	0.2	1.1	1.8	5.6	18.1	5.8	14.1	17.7	14.0
44 005	...	4	Newport	269	83 024	613	308.6	93.7	4.3	0.5	1.6	2.9	6.0	18.2	7.3	14.3	18.1	13.4
44 007	6483	2	Providence	1 070	574 108	90	536.5	88.8	7.6	0.5	3.1	10.5	6.6	18.0	9.0	15.0	15.7	12.0
44 009	6483	2	Washington	862	122 465	432	142.1	96.0	1.2	1.1	1.7	1.6	6.1	18.6	10.3	13.9	18.0	13.1
45 000	...	X	**SOUTH CAROLINA**	77 988	3 885 736	X	49.8	69.1	29.8	0.2	0.9	1.4	6.5	18.1	10.1	14.4	16.2	13.5
45 001	...	6	Abbeville	1 316	24 681	1 543	18.8	67.4	32.2	0.1	0.3	0.6	6.1	17.8	10.3	11.8	15.3	13.7
45 003	0600	2	Aiken	2 779	135 401	389	48.7	74.5	24.6	0.2	0.7	1.2	6.6	18.8	8.5	14.1	16.1	13.4
45 005	...	7	Allendale	1 057	11 325	2 322	10.7	31.6	68.1	0.1	0.1	1.5	6.4	19.9	12.2	14.6	15.7	11.6
45 007	3160	2	Anderson	1 860	162 793	318	87.5	82.4	17.1	0.1	0.3	0.7	5.9	17.6	8.4	13.1	16.1	15.2
45 009	...	7	Bamberg	1 019	16 289	1 984	16.0	38.2	61.5	0.1	0.2	0.7	6.0	20.3	13.6	11.5	14.3	12.1
45 011	...	6	Barnwell	1 421	21 784	1 668	15.3	56.4	43.3	0.2	0.1	1.0	7.1	21.3	8.6	13.3	15.9	12.8
45 013	...	5	Beaufort	1 520	112 973	465	74.3	70.3	28.0	0.3	1.4	3.7	7.6	15.6	12.8	15.5	13.5	10.1
45 015	1440	2	Berkeley	2 848	142 300	374	50.0	72.1	24.7	0.3	2.9	3.3	8.8	21.5	10.2	17.2	16.5	11.9
45 017	...	8	Calhoun	985	14 236	2 117	14.5	47.9	51.9	0.1	0.1	0.5	6.3	18.8	8.4	12.9	16.7	14.7
45 019	1440	2	Charleston	2 376	319 921	175	134.6	62.6	35.9	0.2	1.3	1.9	7.3	16.4	11.0	16.5	15.8	12.4
45 021	3160	2	Cherokee	1 017	50 074	905	49.2	78.1	21.1	0.2	0.6	1.0	6.3	18.6	9.2	12.9	16.1	14.5
45 023	...	6	Chester	1 504	34 927	1 229	23.2	59.1	40.5	0.2	0.1	0.4	6.6	19.4	9.1	13.0	15.7	14.2
45 025	...	6	Chesterfield	2 069	41 531	1 050	20.1	65.7	34.0	0.2	0.1	0.5	6.3	19.4	8.9	12.8	16.1	14.3
45 027	...	6	Clarendon	1 573	30 901	1 350	19.6	42.6	57.2	0.1	0.1	0.7	6.2	19.7	9.0	12.9	16.0	13.8
45 029	...	6	Colleton	2 736	37 659	1 145	13.8	53.8	45.6	0.5	0.1	0.8	6.6	20.6	8.3	12.4	15.9	14.1
45 031	...	4	Darlington	1 456	66 488	727	45.7	59.2	40.5	0.1	0.2	0.5	6.1	20.1	8.8	12.7	16.9	14.1
45 033	...	6	Dillon	1 049	29 718	1 381	28.3	54.3	43.9	1.5	0.3	0.4	7.1	22.4	8.9	12.7	15.2	13.1
45 035	1440	2	Dorchester	1 489	90 582	556	60.8	74.2	23.7	0.7	1.4	2.1	7.9	19.8	9.6	16.7	17.5	12.9
45 037	0600	2	Edgefield	1 300	19 989	1 762	15.4	52.1	47.6	0.0	0.2	0.6	6.6	19.3	8.9	14.5	16.7	13.3
45 039	...	6	Fairfield	1 778	22 573	1 630	12.7	41.3	58.4	0.1	0.2	0.6	6.1	19.9	9.4	12.9	15.7	12.9
45 041	2655	2	Florence	2 070	125 229	417	60.5	60.1	39.4	0.1	0.4	0.7	6.4	20.0	9.4	13.3	16.9	14.0
45 043	...	6	Georgetown	2 110	54 934	841	26.0	56.8	42.9	0.1	0.2	0.6	6.3	20.0	7.8	12.1	15.2	12.4
45 045	3160	2	Greenville	2 052	358 936	157	174.9	80.5	18.4	0.2	0.9	1.6	6.4	16.9	9.5	14.7	16.7	14.5
45 047	...	5	Greenwood	1 180	63 717	748	54.0	68.5	30.9	0.1	0.6	0.7	6.1	17.4	10.0	13.0	15.5	13.9
45 049	...	7	Hampton	1 450	19 108	1 814	13.2	45.5	54.3	0.0	0.1	0.5	7.1	21.8	8.5	12.0	15.4	13.2
45 051	5330	3	Horry	2 936	178 550	300	60.8	81.1	17.5	0.2	1.1	1.4	5.9	16.2	8.7	14.5	15.4	13.2
45 053	...	8	Jasper	1 695	17 232	1 916	10.2	41.5	58.1	0.1	0.3	0.7	7.3	21.2	8.9	13.5	14.8	13.3
45 055	...	6	Kershaw	1 881	49 291	918	26.2	70.7	28.8	0.2	0.4	1.0	5.9	19.3	7.7	13.2	16.9	14.4
45 057	...	6	Lancaster	1 422	59 577	800	41.9	74.0	25.7	0.1	0.2	0.6	6.5	18.6	8.8	13.1	16.2	14.7
45 059	...	6	Laurens	1 847	63 360	755	34.3	70.6	29.1	0.1	0.3	0.6	6.2	17.9	9.9	12.6	15.8	14.7
45 061	...	6	Lee	1 063	20 315	1 746	19.1	36.9	62.7	0.2	0.2	0.7	5.9	20.0	9.8	15.0	16.2	12.2
45 063	1760	2	Lexington	1 815	208 972	260	115.1	87.8	11.1	0.2	0.9	1.4	6.6	18.5	8.5	14.9	18.2	14.9
45 065	...	8	McCormick	931	9 606	2 462	10.3	41.0	58.8	0.1	0.1	0.4	4.1	16.8	10.8	14.7	15.5	12.6
45 067	...	6	Marion	1 267	34 475	1 239	27.2	44.5	54.7	0.2	0.5	0.5	6.3	22.2	8.1	12.3	16.0	13.4
45 069	...	7	Marlboro	1 242	29 492	1 392	23.7	47.8	49.6	2.5	0.1	0.4	6.2	20.0	10.0	13.7	15.8	13.2
45 071	...	6	Newberry	1 634	34 385	1 243	21.0	64.1	35.3	0.2	0.4	0.7	5.9	17.7	9.6	12.6	15.4	14.1
45 073	...	6	Oconee	1 619	65 081	733	40.2	90.4	9.0	0.1	0.4	1.6	5.6	17.1	7.8	12.6	15.2	14.8
45 075	...	4	Orangeburg	2 865	87 519	575	30.5	40.8	58.4	0.3	0.5	0.5	6.1	19.4	12.1	12.5	15.2	13.2
45 077	3160	2	Pickens	1 287	108 126	486	84.0	91.1	7.6	0.2	1.1	1.0	5.6	15.7	16.4	12.8	15.0	13.4
45 079	1760	2	Richland	1 959	307 279	181	156.9	55.7	42.2	0.3	1.9	2.5	6.1	16.5	13.6	17.0	17.0	12.1
45 081	...	6	Saluda	1 169	16 983	1 929	14.5	65.9	33.9	0.1	0.1	0.7	5.6	18.7	8.3	12.5	15.4	14.6
45 083	3160	2	Spartanburg	2 100	249 636	215	118.9	77.6	21.2	0.2	1.1	1.1	6.1	17.1	9.6	13.6	16.6	14.7

1. MSA = Metropolitan Statistical Area. PMSA = Primary MSA. NECMA = New England County Metropolitan Area. See Appendix A for explanation of these concepts. See Appendix B for list of metropolitan areas identified by type, with component counties.   2. County typology code from the Economic Research Service of USDA. See Appendix A for definition.   3. Dry land or land partially or temporarily covered by water.   4. Hispanic persons may be of any race.

Table B. States and Counties — **Population and Households**

STATE County	\[55 to 64 years\] (16)	\[65 to 74 years\] (17)	\[75 years and over\] (18)	\[Percent female\] (19)	Total persons 1990 (20)	Total persons 1980 (21)	Percent change 1980–1990 (22)	Percent change 1990–1999 (23)	Births (24)	Deaths (25)	Net migration (26)	Households Number (27)	Percent change 1980–1990 (28)	Persons per household (29)	Female family householder[1] (30)	One person (31)
PENNSYLVANIA—Cont'd																
Potter	9.6	8.3	8.4	51.2	16 717	17 726	-5.7	2.4	2 006	1 697	154	6 246	1.7	2.63	8.1	23.1
Schuylkill	10.4	9.8	9.7	50.5	152 585	160 630	-5.0	-2.5	14 725	19 073	1 224	60 773	1.4	2.47	10.0	28.0
Snyder	8.3	7.0	6.7	51.1	36 680	33 584	9.2	3.3	4 200	2 890	-6	12 764	19.5	2.70	6.6	20.2
Somerset	9.3	9.1	8.6	50.3	78 218	81 243	-3.7	2.3	8 062	7 800	1 833	29 574	3.6	2.60	8.6	23.2
Sullivan	10.3	9.8	12.1	49.9	6 104	6 349	-3.9	-1.1	506	917	373	2 280	5.1	2.49	8.0	26.7
Susquehanna	8.7	7.7	7.8	50.5	40 380	37 876	6.6	4.5	4 420	3 904	1 429	14 898	14.5	2.69	8.3	21.5
Tioga	9.0	7.9	7.8	51.0	41 126	40 973	0.4	1.3	4 072	3 760	362	14 974	8.7	2.61	8.1	22.1
Union	7.6	6.2	7.0	44.9	36 176	32 870	10.1	12.1	3 617	3 027	3 920	11 689	16.8	2.64	7.0	22.2
Venango	9.8	8.3	8.1	51.5	59 381	64 444	-7.9	-3.1	6 294	5 902	-2 013	22 408	-1.3	2.58	9.6	23.9
Warren	9.6	8.2	8.5	51.2	45 050	47 449	-5.1	-3.4	4 939	4 514	-1 808	17 244	3.1	2.54	8.2	24.5
Washington	9.9	9.4	8.4	52.0	204 584	217 074	-5.8	0.1	21 201	22 154	2 091	78 533	1.9	2.54	10.3	24.5
Wayne	9.2	9.1	9.2	49.7	39 944	35 237	13.4	15.4	5 011	4 691	6 013	14 638	18.2	2.65	8.3	22.1
Westmoreland	10.1	9.7	8.5	52.1	370 321	392 184	-5.6	0.1	37 720	38 910	3 007	144 080	3.5	2.53	9.5	24.2
Wyoming	7.5	6.8	6.6	50.4	28 076	26 433	6.2	4.4	3 328	2 322	295	10 002	12.8	2.72	9.1	22.0
York	8.6	6.8	6.6	50.9	339 574	312 963	8.5	10.9	42 025	28 024	20 988	128 666	14.6	2.60	8.4	21.3
RHODE ISLAND	7.9	7.6	8.0	51.9	1 003 464	947 154	5.9	-1.3	125 103	89 187	-46 911	377 977	11.6	2.55	11.7	26.2
Bristol	8.8	9.4	8.8	51.5	48 859	46 942	4.1	0.5	5 187	4 295	-523	17 559	13.8	2.64	8.9	21.7
Kent	8.5	8.3	7.9	52.0	161 143	154 163	4.5	0.6	18 656	14 526	-2 640	62 058	14.6	2.57	9.7	25.5
Newport	7.6	7.5	7.6	51.7	87 194	81 383	7.1	-4.8	9 875	6 606	-8 583	32 687	15.7	2.53	10.2	25.4
Providence	7.8	7.5	8.3	52.2	596 270	571 349	4.4	-3.7	78 208	55 607	-42 763	226 362	7.9	2.53	13.2	27.7
Washington	7.2	6.5	6.3	50.9	109 998	93 317	17.9	11.3	13 177	8 153	7 598	39 311	26.5	2.64	9.0	21.6
SOUTH CAROLINA	9.0	6.9	5.3	51.7	3 486 310	3 120 729	11.7	11.5	498 067	301 259	161 777	1 258 044	22.1	2.68	14.0	22.4
Abbeville	10.1	7.4	7.5	52.6	23 862	22 627	5.5	3.4	2 967	2 237	191	8 780	14.0	2.64	14.2	23.6
Aiken	9.7	7.4	5.4	51.6	120 991	105 630	14.5	11.9	17 817	10 925	7 896	44 883	23.1	2.66	12.5	22.5
Allendale	7.5	6.5	5.7	48.3	11 727	10 700	9.6	-3.4	1 656	1 167	-863	3 791	9.9	2.81	25.7	26.0
Anderson	10.3	7.3	6.1	52.1	145 177	133 235	9.0	12.1	19 184	13 735	12 517	55 481	18.2	2.59	11.7	22.7
Bamberg	8.5	7.7	6.1	53.2	16 902	18 118	-6.7	-3.6	2 189	1 599	-1 160	5 587	-0.7	2.84	20.8	24.3
Barnwell	8.9	6.6	5.5	52.1	20 293	19 868	2.1	7.3	3 209	2 060	383	7 100	9.7	2.82	17.9	22.3
Beaufort	8.8	10.2	6.0	49.7	86 425	65 364	32.2	30.7	15 201	6 914	14 261	30 712	52.7	2.59	11.7	20.5
Berkeley	6.4	4.7	2.8	49.3	128 658	94 745	35.9	10.6	20 450	7 090	-2 158	42 386	46.5	3.01	10.9	15.7
Calhoun	9.3	6.8	6.2	52.7	12 753	12 206	4.5	11.6	1 636	1 143	1 022	4 487	14.7	2.82	15.7	22.4
Charleston	8.2	7.2	5.2	52.1	295 159	276 556	6.7	8.4	44 213	22 489	-29 043	107 069	18.2	2.61	15.1	24.7
Cherokee	9.7	6.8	5.9	52.1	44 506	40 983	8.6	12.5	6 511	4 227	3 378	16 456	20.2	2.67	14.2	22.8
Chester	9.6	6.7	5.8	52.7	32 170	30 148	6.7	8.6	4 512	3 031	1 364	11 448	14.8	2.80	17.5	22.5
Chesterfield	9.8	6.8	5.6	52.2	38 575	38 161	1.1	7.7	5 315	3 836	901	14 047	9.3	2.72	15.9	22.7
Clarendon	9.1	7.6	5.6	50.8	28 450	27 464	3.6	8.6	3 776	3 044	1 799	9 544	14.0	2.96	19.9	20.6
Colleton	9.7	6.9	5.5	52.2	34 377	31 776	8.2	9.5	5 097	3 347	1 620	12 040	16.5	2.83	16.1	21.5
Darlington	9.2	6.7	5.4	53.0	61 851	62 717	-1.4	7.5	8 874	6 288	2 245	21 999	9.7	2.76	17.8	22.1
Dillon	8.6	6.7	5.4	53.6	29 114	31 083	-6.3	2.1	4 599	3 035	-868	9 887	5.9	2.91	21.1	22.9
Dorchester	6.8	5.2	3.7	50.5	83 060	59 045	40.7	9.1	12 191	5 429	3 720	28 213	53.6	2.87	11.5	17.0
Edgefield	9.0	6.3	5.3	50.4	18 360	17 528	4.7	8.9	2 559	1 709	821	6 424	16.0	2.82	14.4	21.9
Fairfield	9.1	7.5	6.4	51.9	22 295	20 700	7.7	1.2	3 147	2 701	-83	7 467	17.5	2.93	18.7	21.9
Florence	8.9	6.5	4.9	53.0	114 344	110 163	3.8	9.5	16 534	11 189	5 873	40 217	12.6	2.78	17.3	21.8
Georgetown	9.2	10.4	6.5	52.5	46 302	42 461	9.0	18.6	6 953	4 409	6 224	16 275	22.1	2.83	15.0	20.6
Greenville	9.4	6.4	5.4	52.0	320 127	287 895	11.2	12.1	45 122	26 587	21 113	122 878	21.0	2.54	12.1	24.7
Greenwood	9.9	7.5	6.7	53.1	59 567	55 859	6.6	7.0	8 478	5 872	1 727	22 730	11.9	2.55	14.0	25.3
Hampton	8.5	7.4	6.0	53.3	18 186	18 159	0.2	5.1	2 897	1 709	-207	6 322	6.3	2.87	17.7	22.7
Horry	10.8	9.7	5.5	51.5	144 053	101 419	42.0	23.9	19 315	13 557	27 697	55 764	60.3	2.52	11.2	22.3
Jasper	8.8	6.5	5.7	51.4	15 487	14 504	6.8	11.3	2 680	1 365	493	5 298	16.1	2.87	19.4	21.7
Kershaw	10.1	7.2	5.4	51.8	43 599	39 015	11.7	13.1	6 217	3 890	3 472	15 810	20.4	2.73	12.8	20.4
Lancaster	9.6	6.9	5.6	52.2	54 516	53 361	2.2	9.3	7 366	4 940	2 739	19 778	11.0	2.74	13.9	20.1
Laurens	10.2	6.6	6.1	52.1	58 132	52 214	11.3	9.0	7 689	6 076	3 739	20 660	21.5	2.68	14.2	22.3
Lee	8.2	6.9	5.8	50.0	18 437	18 929	-2.6	10.2	2 479	1 618	1 069	6 054	8.1	3.02	22.5	21.1
Lexington	8.5	5.8	4.1	51.4	167 526	140 353	19.4	24.7	26 366	12 262	27 689	61 633	29.4	2.70	10.7	18.9
McCormick	8.4	9.1	8.1	46.7	8 868	7 797	13.7	8.3	900	906	788	2 731	13.8	2.75	17.2	22.7
Marion	8.9	7.2	5.5	54.7	33 899	34 179	-0.8	1.7	4 835	3 462	-673	11 766	9.4	2.86	22.4	22.6
Marlboro	8.8	6.8	5.5	51.6	29 716	31 634	-6.1	-0.8	4 136	3 047	-1 206	10 163	3.5	2.82	21.1	24.0
Newberry	9.5	7.8	7.4	52.2	33 172	31 242	6.2	3.7	4 223	3 315	397	12 314	13.0	2.63	15.0	24.9
Oconee	11.0	8.9	6.9	51.1	57 494	48 611	18.3	13.2	7 061	5 173	5 840	22 358	28.7	2.55	10.0	22.0
Orangeburg	8.8	7.2	5.6	53.4	84 804	82 276	3.1	3.2	11 958	8 305	-728	28 909	12.7	2.81	19.3	22.7
Pickens	8.8	6.5	5.8	50.4	93 896	79 292	18.4	15.2	11 711	7 261	10 039	33 422	28.6	2.58	8.8	21.5
Richland	7.7	5.6	4.3	51.7	286 321	269 600	6.2	7.3	40 113	21 535	619	101 590	18.9	2.56	15.2	26.5
Saluda	10.1	7.6	7.0	51.2	16 441	16 136	1.4	3.3	2 242	1 791	154	5 824	10.5	2.76	12.8	21.1
Spartanburg	9.6	6.8	5.8	51.8	226 793	203 023	11.7	10.1	30 472	21 711	14 635	84 503	20.8	2.61	13.1	22.5

1. No spouse present.

Items 16—31

Table B. States and Counties — **Vital Statistics, Health Resources, and Crime**

STATE County	Births, average 1996–1998 Total	Births, average 1996–1998 Rate[1]	Deaths, average 1996–1998 Number Total	Deaths, average 1996–1998 Number Infant[2]	Deaths, average 1996–1998 Rate Total[1]	Deaths, average 1996–1998 Rate Infant[3]	Physicians,[4] 1998 Number	Physicians,[4] 1998 Rate[5]	Hospitals,[4] 1998 Number	Hospitals,[4] 1998 Beds Number	Hospitals,[4] 1998 Beds Rate[5]	Medicare enrollees 1999	Serious crimes known to police, 1998[6] Total Number	Serious crimes known to police, 1998[6] Total Rate[7]
	32	33	34	35	36	37	38	39	40	41	42	43	44	45
PENNSYLVANIA—Cont'd														
Potter	216	12.6	195	1	11.3	3.1	27	157	1	120	698	3 344	241	1 865
Schuylkill	1 447	9.7	2 068	12	13.8	8.1	178	120	4	605	408	32 620	2 338	1 782
Snyder	427	11.2	307	3	8.1	7.0	44	115	0	0	0	6 023	663	1 802
Somerset	842	10.5	905	5	11.3	5.5	95	118	3	230	287	15 577	759	990
Sullivan	51	8.4	107	0	17.5	0.0	3	49	0	0	0	1 499	126	2 068
Susquehanna	461	11.0	454	2	10.8	5.1	38	90	2	139	330	7 276	493	1 329
Tioga	403	9.7	440	2	10.6	5.8	54	130	1	103	248	7 519	535	1 322
Union	374	9.0	353	4	8.5	11.6	100	245	1	135	330	5 829	415	1 083
Venango	636	10.9	654	4	11.2	6.3	90	156	2	308	532	11 150	1 517	2 617
Warren	496	11.2	496	3	11.2	6.7	79	180	1	105	239	8 035	820	1 891
Washington	2 225	10.8	2 387	13	11.6	6.0	290	141	3	713	347	40 969	4 141	2 184
Wayne	517	11.5	554	2	12.3	3.9	67	148	1	95	210	10 837	1 039	2 359
Westmoreland	3 808	10.2	4 333	22	11.6	5.9	637	171	6	1 169	314	71 849	6 305	1 700
Wyoming	326	11.1	272	1	9.3	4.1	28	96	1	63	216	4 424	476	1 753
York	4 471	12.1	3 167	24	8.5	5.3	638	171	3	768	206	54 564	11 381	3 146
RHODE ISLAND	12 569	12.7	9 657	80	9.8	6.4	2 924	296	10	2 814	285	170 331	34 756	3 518
Bristol	522	10.6	472	2	9.6	3.2	187	381	0	0	0	8 822	1 089	2 222
Kent	1 879	11.6	1 634	10	10.1	5.1	383	237	1	359	222	28 806	4 839	2 989
Newport	979	11.8	724	5	8.7	4.8	202	244	1	200	241	13 470	3 203	3 874
Providence	7 822	13.6	5 892	59	10.2	7.5	1 863	325	6	2 030	354	102 381	22 601	3 933
Washington	1 367	11.5	935	5	7.8	3.9	289	240	2	225	186	16 760	2 820	2 354
SOUTH CAROLINA	52 403	13.8	34 190	482	9.0	9.2	6 967	182	64	11 249	293	555 082	221 607	5 777
Abbeville	342	14.0	237	1	9.7	3.9	19	77	0	0	0	3 818	1 140	4 578
Aiken	1 848	13.9	1 221	15	9.2	8.3	172	128	2	273	204	20 035	6 220	4 577
Allendale	170	14.6	119	1	10.3	3.9	9	79	1	78	681	1 581	412	3 490
Anderson	2 107	13.3	1 582	21	10.0	10.0	234	146	1	445	277	26 351	7 591	4 702
Bamberg	213	12.9	183	2	11.1	7.8	12	73	1	84	509	2 502	571	3 369
Barnwell	327	15.1	230	3	10.6	8.2	12	55	1	35	161	3 419	851	3 821
Beaufort	1 612	15.1	806	10	7.6	6.0	344	316	3	234	215	18 044	7 068	6 500
Berkeley	1 980	14.8	838	14	6.3	7.2	32	23	0	0	0	11 099	6 189	4 520
Calhoun	172	12.5	137	1	9.9	7.7	6	43	0	0	0	1 766	434	3 196
Charleston	4 201	13.5	2 460	46	7.9	11.0	1 488	470	7	1 760	556	42 505	23 588	8 118
Cherokee	701	14.4	484	9	9.9	12.4	45	92	1	125	254	7 198	2 696	5 465
Chester	468	13.8	332	5	9.8	11.4	18	52	1	163	474	5 420	1 998	5 809
Chesterfield	561	13.8	433	6	10.6	10.1	28	68	1	66	161	6 222	1 879	4 600
Clarendon	393	12.8	329	5	10.7	11.9	23	75	1	56	182	4 900	1 500	4 792
Colleton	528	14.2	370	5	10.0	10.1	34	91	1	116	310	5 764	2 193	5 807
Darlington	906	13.8	703	10	10.7	11.0	60	90	2	150	226	9 488	4 055	6 042
Dillon	474	16.0	330	4	11.1	9.2	22	74	1	90	303	4 510	2 067	6 823
Dorchester	1 145	13.3	677	12	7.9	10.2	59	67	1	111	126	10 540	3 848	4 231
Edgefield	267	13.5	190	4	9.6	13.7	5	25	0	0	0	2 542	731	3 628
Fairfield	322	14.4	281	3	12.6	10.3	11	49	1	41	183	3 517	1 168	5 118
Florence	1 787	14.4	1 245	18	10.0	10.1	278	223	4	765	612	18 410	8 201	6 463
Georgetown	719	13.7	506	8	9.6	11.1	108	201	1	141	262	11 462	3 319	6 216
Greenville	5 000	14.3	3 042	34	8.7	6.7	818	231	4	1 314	371	52 429	20 365	5 727
Greenwood	915	14.4	676	13	10.7	14.2	158	248	1	355	558	10 887	4 484	6 941
Hampton	293	15.4	191	2	10.0	6.8	8	42	1	36	188	3 658	769	4 089
Horry	2 145	12.7	1 634	20	9.7	9.5	290	166	3	480	275	28 923	18 222	10 557
Jasper	292	17.3	161	2	9.5	8.0	12	71	0	0	0	2 213	1 291	7 464
Kershaw	651	13.6	445	6	9.3	9.2	59	121	1	198	407	8 251	1 798	3 721
Lancaster	776	13.4	559	6	9.7	7.7	53	90	1	166	282	8 486	3 466	5 869
Laurens	829	13.3	691	8	11.1	9.2	50	79	1	80	126	9 906	3 365	5 328
Lee	238	11.7	198	5	9.8	19.6	3	15	0	0	0	2 749	732	3 554
Lexington	2 953	14.7	1 480	20	7.4	6.8	210	102	1	287	140	23 687	9 324	4 561
McCormick	88	9.3	105	1	11.0	11.3	7	73	0	0	0	1 806	313	3 221
Marion	481	13.8	388	8	11.1	16.6	31	90	2	190	549	5 753	1 706	4 793
Marlboro	426	14.3	350	4	11.8	8.6	20	68	1	108	365	4 704	2 246	7 450
Newberry	463	13.5	352	3	10.2	7.2	31	90	1	64	186	6 311	828	2 370
Oconee	775	12.2	579	6	9.1	7.3	82	128	1	195	304	11 940	1 876	2 898
Orangeburg	1 218	13.9	914	15	10.4	12.3	123	140	1	292	332	14 403	6 685	7 591
Pickens	1 302	12.4	841	12	8.0	9.0	122	114	2	132	123	15 184	3 254	3 049
Richland	4 194	13.8	2 404	38	7.9	9.1	1 129	368	4	1 267	413	37 254	23 186	7 491
Saluda	242	14.3	192	4	11.3	15.1	7	41	0	0	0	2 432	580	3 385
Spartanburg	3 281	13.4	2 420	22	9.9	6.6	409	165	3	681	275	38 460	16 284	6 541

1. Per 1,000 estimated resident population, average 1996–1998.   2. Deaths of infants under 1 year old.   3. Deaths of infants under 1 year old per 1,000 live births.   4. Data subject to copyright.   5. Per 100,000 resident population as of July 1 of the year shown.   6. Data for serious crimes have not been adjusted for underreporting; this may affect comparability between geographic areas and over time.   7. Per 100,000 population estimated by the FBI.

Table B. States and Counties — Crime, Education, Money Income, and Poverty

STATE County	Serious crimes known to police, 1998[1] (cont'd) Rate[2] Violent	Property	Education — School enrollment and attainment, 1990 — Enrollment[3] Total	Percent private	Attainment[4] (percent) High school graduate or more	Bachelor's degree or more	Local government expenditures, fiscal 1997[5] Total current expenditures (mil dol)	Current expenditures per student (dollars)	Money income 1989 Per capita[6] (dollars)	Households Median Dollars	Percent change, 1979–1989 (constant 1989 dollars)	Percent with $100,000 or more	Income and poverty, 1997 Median household income	Percent below poverty level All persons	Persons under 18	Persons 5–17 in families
	46	47	48	49	50	51	52	53	54	55	56	57	58	59	60	61
PENNSYLVANIA—Cont'd																
Potter	147	1 718	3 821	5.8	73.8	9.8	19.6	5 727	9 905	21 377	-1.8	1.2	30 554	14.5	22.3	20.6
Schuylkill	240	1 542	30 220	16.4	68.4	8.1	138.5	6 675	11 193	23 028	3.0	1.2	31 675	10.4	15.3	13.7
Snyder	294	1 508	8 384	27.6	64.4	10.6	33.3	5 905	10 859	25 864	-0.7	2.0	32 807	9.9	14.3	14.7
Somerset	90	900	16 854	8.3	68.9	8.9	77.9	5 932	10 422	21 674	-12.1	1.5	28 665	13.7	19.5	18.1
Sullivan	82	1 986	1 205	6.2	70.2	8.6	7.5	7 748	9 839	20 107	-4.2	1.0	28 046	12.8	16.7	19.3
Susquehanna	205	1 124	9 366	7.0	76.0	11.1	54.3	6 056	10 907	24 736	4.1	1.3	32 383	12.5	18.9	17.1
Tioga	138	1 184	10 837	5.9	72.9	12.6	42.8	5 910	10 290	22 571	-2.3	1.4	31 160	13.3	19.2	18.1
Union	91	992	10 400	40.9	73.1	17.5	54.9	12 231	11 679	27 622	3.9	2.8	36 528	11.2	14.8	14.2
Venango	155	2 462	13 511	10.5	74.2	10.8	68.4	6 097	10 696	22 593	-19.7	1.3	29 474	13.9	20.0	18.7
Warren	95	1 796	9 866	9.0	76.6	10.7	41.1	5 671	12 350	26 351	-4.5	2.1	33 863	10.6	16.0	14.8
Washington	180	2 004	46 605	13.3	73.2	13.6	226.4	7 359	12 744	25 469	-14.0	2.4	34 998	11.7	17.0	15.4
Wayne	261	2 098	8 747	9.9	74.2	13.1	59.8	6 448	11 257	24 912	12.7	1.9	31 509	12.0	18.8	17.3
Westmoreland	214	1 486	83 126	16.1	77.7	15.4	369.5	6 385	12 612	25 736	-13.7	2.1	34 073	10.2	14.8	13.0
Wyoming	111	1 642	7 273	17.5	77.6	13.2	32.9	6 543	11 628	27 207	6.1	1.8	35 110	11.1	15.8	15.5
York	254	2 892	72 386	15.9	72.8	13.9	320.9	5 870	14 544	32 605	5.8	2.7	43 488	6.8	10.7	9.5
RHODE ISLAND	312	3 206	254 635	24.7	72.0	21.3	1 152.0	7 612	14 981	32 181	19.3	4.1	36 699	11.2	17.3	15.8
Bristol	131	2 091	12 290	34.2	73.9	27.4	53.5	7 727	17 897	37 539	20.7	8.0	47 141	6.9	9.9	9.3
Kent	282	2 707	37 497	19.5	76.8	20.5	190.9	8 164	16 390	36 070	16.6	4.7	44 089	6.9	10.4	9.4
Newport	364	3 510	21 798	25.2	82.8	30.1	94.9	8 012	16 819	35 829	26.9	5.2	43 684	7.9	11.7	11.2
Providence	370	3 563	149 473	27.8	67.0	18.3	604.3	7 095	13 871	29 580	19.0	3.2	34 311	14.2	22.5	20.6
Washington	85	2 269	33 577	12.5	82.8	29.1	151.1	7 557	16 182	36 948	21.8	5.2	47 467	6.5	8.6	8.3
SOUTH CAROLINA	903	4 874	913 010	11.6	68.3	16.6	3 297.0	5 050	11 897	26 256	6.5	2.3	33 325	14.9	23.0	21.5
Abbeville	988	3 590	6 030	10.7	58.9	10.8	19.4	5 077	10 214	23 170	0.7	0.6	31 037	14.1	21.9	20.2
Aiken	598	3 979	31 894	11.4	70.7	17.2	108.6	4 418	13 127	29 994	11.8	2.9	38 084	13.7	21.6	19.3
Allendale	1 076	2 414	3 245	5.6	52.3	9.5	12.8	5 776	7 458	15 013	-7.1	1.2	20 942	35.1	44.4	42.7
Anderson	668	4 034	33 898	12.0	64.0	12.9	125.8	4 853	12 027	25 748	-0.5	1.7	34 662	10.8	16.7	15.1
Bamberg	855	2 514	5 435	10.7	59.2	11.2	16.6	5 466	8 438	17 496	-0.4	1.8	23 858	26.4	36.3	35.5
Barnwell	647	3 174	5 341	4.3	59.9	11.9	25.4	5 187	10 611	23 501	10.9	1.9	29 085	21.5	30.5	29.8
Beaufort	928	5 572	19 811	14.8	83.4	26.5	84.0	5 719	15 213	30 450	17.3	5.7	38 867	13.0	22.0	22.0
Berkeley	721	3 799	36 362	10.3	75.4	11.6	120.4	4 612	10 942	29 106	7.2	1.0	36 249	14.1	20.6	20.1
Calhoun	847	2 349	3 068	13.9	61.9	11.7	12.3	6 013	9 983	23 750	13.1	1.2	29 479	19.2	29.0	28.1
Charleston	1 003	7 115	76 617	16.2	75.5	22.4	215.6	4 962	13 068	26 875	8.2	3.0	35 150	16.8	26.7	26.4
Cherokee	1 020	4 445	10 400	6.8	57.2	9.3	43.4	5 124	10 406	24 655	-0.6	1.1	31 489	14.1	22.2	20.5
Chester	1 087	4 722	7 895	4.0	56.9	9.1	32.6	4 957	9 806	23 054	-1.2	1.2	29 110	17.2	26.1	24.1
Chesterfield	925	3 675	9 907	5.1	53.9	7.7	40.1	5 102	9 455	21 069	2.4	1.1	28 422	18.8	28.6	25.6
Clarendon	981	3 811	7 371	7.1	54.9	10.2	29.1	4 738	8 181	17 645	-5.2	1.4	23 906	26.8	38.2	34.5
Colleton	1 136	4 671	8 973	8.9	61.7	9.6	36.0	5 107	9 193	20 617	5.4	1.4	25 682	22.6	33.9	31.2
Darlington	881	5 161	15 789	7.6	62.3	12.4	60.5	5 525	10 510	22 642	4.0	1.9	28 644	20.2	31.4	27.8
Dillon	1 842	4 981	7 947	2.9	52.5	8.5	30.5	4 776	8 077	18 365	0.4	1.0	23 572	25.7	36.6	33.7
Dorchester	559	3 672	21 910	13.7	76.7	17.3	83.8	4 716	11 884	30 764	6.9	1.7	36 590	13.1	19.4	18.7
Edgefield	690	2 938	4 803	9.4	62.6	12.2	21.9	5 360	10 651	23 021	13.5	1.3	29 031	18.8	26.2	26.4
Fairfield	1 617	3 501	5 789	7.4	58.1	9.6	26.3	7 229	9 011	21 484	2.0	1.0	27 752	19.5	28.8	26.3
Florence	980	5 483	32 153	8.9	64.3	14.8	110.1	4 793	11 007	24 264	4.0	2.4	30 557	19.4	28.7	25.8
Georgetown	1 084	5 132	13 007	5.6	63.9	15.6	61.1	5 797	11 084	23 981	-0.1	2.9	30 915	18.6	29.9	27.8
Greenville	905	4 822	79 865	22.0	71.6	21.0	265.8	4 756	13 918	29 088	8.5	3.2	38 807	10.5	16.2	14.7
Greenwood	1 683	5 258	15 478	8.0	64.1	16.0	57.7	5 064	11 429	23 584	-3.7	1.7	32 937	13.8	20.5	19.6
Hampton	994	3 095	5 215	4.3	58.9	8.8	24.6	5 809	8 578	18 615	2.3	0.9	25 108	23.9	34.8	33.1
Horry	1 156	9 401	33 637	7.7	74.3	16.0	139.4	5 339	12 385	24 959	10.4	2.4	31 312	14.4	25.1	23.4
Jasper	919	6 545	4 340	18.7	54.5	4.8	14.5	4 718	7 984	18 071	-0.2	0.7	25 154	25.5	31.4	35.7
Kershaw	604	3 117	10 842	9.1	67.8	12.5	46.8	4 970	11 937	28 282	11.9	1.8	34 077	12.4	20.4	18.1
Lancaster	838	5 031	12 893	5.0	60.0	9.6	50.4	4 641	11 041	25 320	-4.1	1.6	32 656	14.8	23.1	21.9
Laurens	1 347	3 981	14 061	13.4	57.4	11.3	43.0	4 640	10 739	24 905	-1.1	1.2	30 159	14.3	22.4	20.4
Lee	772	2 782	5 292	9.4	53.5	7.5	16.4	4 995	7 569	18 174	-4.2	0.3	23 160	28.3	38.2	35.1
Lexington	617	3 944	43 506	8.7	77.3	21.0	222.5	5 280	14 259	32 914	7.6	2.9	42 697	9.4	15.4	13.5
McCormick	895	2 326	2 005	17.1	52.5	7.1	7.6	5 650	7 929	19 226	-2.4	1.3	27 056	19.6	28.7	27.5
Marion	846	3 947	9 695	3.9	55.3	9.1	34.4	4 869	8 185	17 825	-6.3	0.8	23 302	24.1	32.7	30.8
Marlboro	1 546	5 904	7 533	3.5	50.9	7.9	27.2	4 889	7 948	18 068	-8.2	0.8	23 539	23.2	31.6	29.5
Newberry	587	1 783	8 270	13.1	62.1	12.5	32.1	5 537	10 487	23 405	-2.9	1.5	30 637	14.4	22.3	21.0
Oconee	463	2 435	13 156	6.5	63.4	13.3	55.4	5 574	12 352	25 723	12.6	1.9	34 286	11.1	16.1	16.9
Orangeburg	1 488	6 103	26 054	11.6	62.4	13.7	91.3	5 600	9 004	20 216	4.7	1.5	26 554	23.3	32.0	29.0
Pickens	312	2 737	30 836	7.7	65.4	16.9	67.3	4 368	11 427	26 336	0.8	1.6	35 825	11.1	15.3	14.6
Richland	1 033	6 458	83 610	13.6	79.4	28.0	248.3	5 855	13 243	28 848	9.7	3.2	35 903	14.8	22.1	20.4
Saluda	654	2 731	3 983	6.1	59.8	8.0	11.1	4 971	9 814	22 176	9.3	0.8	29 005	16.8	25.4	24.4
Spartanburg	1 085	5 456	53 949	12.6	63.0	14.3	220.7	5 560	12 218	26 941	6.5	2.1	35 713	11.6	17.9	16.6

1. Data for serious crimes have not been adjusted for underreporting; this may affect comparability between geographic areas and over time.   2. Per 100,000 population estimated by the FBI.   3. All persons 3 years old and over enrolled in nursery school through college.   4. Persons 25 years old and over.   5. Elementary and secondary education expenditures, local government fiscal years ending between July 1, 1996 and June 30, 1997.   6. Based on population enumerated as of April 1, 1990.

Table B. States and Counties — Personal Income

STATE County	Total (mil dol)	Percent change, 1997–1998	Per capita[1] Dollars	Rank	Wages and salaries[2] (mil dol)	Proprietor's income (mil dol)	Dividends, interest, and rent (mil dol)	Transfer payments Total (mil dol)	Government payments to individuals Total (mil dol)	Social Security (mil dol)	Medical payments (mil dol)	Income mainte- nance (mil dol)	Unemploy- ment insurance (mil dol)
	62	63	64	65	66	67	68	69	70	71	72	73	74
PENNSYLVANIA—Cont'd													
Potter............	371	5.4	21 644	1 207	182	62	55	72	69	32	25	7	3
Schuylkill............	3 268	3.4	21 777	1 169	1 455	248	594	715	686	304	247	40	30
Snyder............	958	3.6	25 237	465	419	95	169	288	281	57	206	7	6
Somerset............	1 611	3.5	20 091	1 682	690	226	269	375	360	142	153	26	13
Sullivan............	123	4.9	20 179	1 660	43	15	28	30	29	16	10	1	1
Susquehanna............	859	4.1	20 409	1 591	209	117	156	155	147	73	48	13	4
Tioga............	781	4.7	18 799	2 122	354	86	138	160	152	73	53	14	5
Union............	866	4.7	21 516	1 248	551	77	167	184	176	55	105	7	4
Venango............	1 421	3.1	24 583	548	648	97	222	470	459	115	305	23	7
Warren............	993	2.6	22 685	927	512	81	173	219	211	85	103	12	5
Washington............	5 378	6.4	26 190	376	2 339	371	876	1 046	1 006	417	443	67	27
Wayne............	940	5.7	20 701	1 488	347	101	211	198	190	98	66	12	7
Westmoreland............	9 235	4.3	24 799	515	4 188	697	1 592	1 768	1 695	739	712	101	58
Wyoming............	609	4.3	20 838	1 445	340	67	95	103	97	42	36	8	6
York............	9 565	4.8	25 596	428	5 577	816	1 729	1 133	1 060	568	327	79	36
RHODE ISLAND............	27 914	5.3	28 262	X	16 137	1 754	5 465	4 692	4 509	1 643	2 022	424	149
Bristol............	1 615	6.4	32 832	88	408	82	407	196	187	91	66	9	6
Kent............	4 672	5.5	28 946	196	2 385	201	861	723	693	288	278	44	37
Newport............	2 565	3.9	31 054	133	1 518	130	643	323	308	124	127	24	10
Providence............	15 463	4.9	26 953	308	10 390	1 120	2 798	3 024	2 918	968	1 388	322	83
Washington............	3 599	7.5	29 792	174	1 436	221	755	426	404	174	162	24	12
SOUTH CAROLINA.........	85 898	5.8	22 372	X	55 137	5 263	14 860	13 266	12 594	5 318	4 948	1 356	184
Abbeville............	469	4.5	19 019	2 050	247	22	80	88	84	40	26	8	2
Aiken............	3 166	4.8	23 627	716	2 223	172	600	464	440	204	163	44	4
Allendale............	186	5.4	16 293	2 744	133	5	23	50	48	14	21	10	1
Anderson............	3 557	5.4	22 130	1 056	1 813	243	580	548	520	269	174	39	6
Bamberg............	282	4.4	17 130	2 577	119	12	37	74	71	23	29	12	1
Barnwell............	504	18.4	23 086	837	407	16	54	97	93	29	44	14	2
Beaufort............	3 387	6.1	30 765	142	1 880	231	1 108	371	353	189	116	27	3
Berkeley............	2 237	6.1	16 258	2 750	1 004	88	309	307	283	123	91	39	4
Calhoun............	276	5.6	19 625	1 852	140	12	42	43	41	18	13	7	1
Charleston............	7 611	6.6	24 040	636	5 894	700	1 561	1 010	956	365	393	120	12
Cherokee............	930	7.9	18 894	2 091	610	36	129	167	159	76	59	14	2
Chester............	602	5.3	17 521	2 479	356	24	82	127	121	52	47	13	3
Chesterfield............	738	3.3	17 965	2 354	429	46	96	157	150	59	60	22	3
Clarendon............	493	3.1	16 016	2 791	185	27	82	133	128	43	53	23	2
Colleton............	644	4.3	17 243	2 547	280	50	94	160	154	54	68	23	2
Darlington............	1 304	4.7	19 652	1 839	788	61	191	278	267	94	118	39	5
Dillon............	499	1.9	16 788	2 658	255	24	60	139	133	38	64	25	2
Dorchester............	1 825	8.8	20 735	1 474	718	70	261	313	297	97	152	26	3
Edgefield............	376	10.7	18 809	2 119	155	15	49	70	67	26	26	10	1
Fairfield............	442	5.7	19 730	1 803	282	19	59	97	93	31	45	11	2
Florence............	2 757	4.8	22 114	1 063	1 946	150	393	532	510	153	247	69	7
Georgetown............	1 139	5.8	21 207	1 327	563	85	288	231	221	94	90	23	5
Greenville............	9 604	5.8	27 131	294	7 814	680	1 762	1 097	1 034	519	367	84	10
Greenwood............	1 435	3.2	22 562	967	1 019	93	242	225	213	106	69	20	4
Hampton............	362	6.1	18 900	2 089	183	19	57	86	83	28	36	13	1
Horry............	4 030	7.2	23 088	836	2 363	403	870	630	599	309	196	51	12
Jasper............	311	6.1	18 225	2 288	100	26	35	60	57	17	26	10	1
Kershaw............	996	5.7	20 484	1 565	544	53	180	170	162	77	58	15	2
Lancaster............	1 151	4.9	19 557	1 867	557	65	159	201	191	86	75	18	4
Laurens............	1 311	3.8	20 762	1 468	607	47	189	357	346	100	215	19	2
Lee............	272	1.8	13 390	3 050	100	15	39	75	72	24	29	15	2
Lexington............	5 162	7.3	25 174	471	2 416	285	801	528	491	243	165	38	7
McCormick............	149	3.7	15 591	2 866	61	9	29	37	35	17	12	4	1
Marion............	584	3.4	16 892	2 633	320	19	77	158	152	45	73	22	3
Marlboro............	442	1.0	14 921	2 936	231	17	56	127	122	41	53	20	2
Newberry............	677	3.6	19 671	1 829	345	38	112	129	123	58	45	12	2
Oconee............	1 456	5.6	22 702	920	836	58	314	233	221	117	76	15	3
Orangeburg............	1 647	4.7	18 777	2 128	952	84	257	368	352	126	131	61	7
Pickens............	2 190	6.8	20 460	1 573	1 046	125	328	296	277	145	95	17	3
Richland............	8 094	6.5	26 547	339	7 233	490	1 348	1 074	1 022	345	454	98	8
Saluda............	337	4.8	19 783	1 786	111	27	47	63	60	26	23	8	1
Spartanburg............	5 506	5.0	22 274	1 021	4 089	287	805	806	763	369	261	67	13

1. Based on the resident population estimated as of July 1 of the year shown.   2. Includes other labor income.

Table B. States and Counties — Earnings, Social Security, and Housing

STATE County	Earnings, 1998 Total (mil dol)	Farm	Goods-related¹ Total	Manu-facturing	Service-related and other² Total	Retail trade	Finance, insurance, and real estate	Services	Govern-ment	Social Security beneficiaries, Dec 1998 Number	Rate³	Supplemental Security Income recipients, Dec 1998	Housing units, 1990 Total	Percent change, 1980–1990
	75	76	77	78	79	80	81	82	83	84	85	86	87	88
PENNSYLVANIA—Cont'd														
Potter	244	2.7	20.6	15.2	62.8	7.4	1.5	19.1	13.9	3 883	226	505	11 334	4.4
Schuylkill	1 702	0.6	39.0	30.6	45.0	10.0	3.1	20.3	15.5	36 666	247	2 854	66 457	2.5
Snyder	514	3.1	D	32.1	D	13.0	2.7	14.3	18.5	6 895	180	559	13 629	16.7
Somerset	916	2.1	34.5	19.4	46.7	11.4	3.2	20.1	16.6	17 545	219	1 997	35 713	6.9
Sullivan	59	1.4	D	D	D	10.9	3.7	26.5	20.9	1 875	307	97	5 458	12.4
Susquehanna	326	4.8	29.4	13.3	46.1	11.9	3.6	19.1	19.6	8 812	209	841	20 308	18.1
Tioga	440	3.6	30.3	25.6	42.9	10.7	2.7	17.4	23.3	8 869	213	1 174	18 202	7.1
Union	627	2.1	D	18.9	D	7.1	2.2	29.7	27.8	6 384	156	443	12 886	15.1
Venango	745	0.1	35.3	30.3	45.6	10.1	3.2	21.1	19.3	13 315	230	1 973	26 961	1.2
Warren	592	0.4	38.6	32.1	44.7	17.2	3.2	16.2	16.4	9 639	220	813	22 236	1.6
Washington	2 710	0.1	33.3	20.6	53.2	11.2	3.2	26.1	13.6	46 395	226	5 101	84 113	3.7
Wayne	448	1.7	22.3	8.5	55.9	12.4	5.8	26.6	20.1	11 391	252	793	28 480	45.3
Westmoreland	4 885	0.1	32.3	24.2	54.9	11.3	3.8	24.5	12.7	82 645	222	7 471	153 554	3.7
Wyoming	407	1.9	D	D	D	7.6	2.3	13.4	10.0	5 159	177	467	11 857	11.2
York	6 393	0.2	43.7	36.1	45.7	10.1	4.0	20.5	10.5	62 940	169	5 139	134 761	14.6
RHODE ISLAND	17 890	0.2	22.6	17.6	59.3	8.8	8.0	31.2	17.9	190 022	192	26 158	414 572	11.2
Bristol	489	0.2	30.6	22.4	52.5	9.3	4.0	29.7	16.7	10 106	206	414	18 567	13.4
Kent	2 586	0.1	D	19.3	D	12.6	9.9	28.8	13.8	32 446	201	2 707	65 450	14.8
Newport	1 648	0.6	D	8.8	D	8.9	2.7	29.0	41.4	14 724	178	1 361	37 475	13.9
Providence	11 510	0.0	22.8	18.0	62.3	7.5	9.1	33.1	14.8	113 587	198	20 372	243 224	7.9
Washington	1 657	0.7	25.8	19.7	50.6	11.9	3.8	24.1	22.9	19 135	159	1 221	49 856	21.9
SOUTH CAROLINA	60 400	0.5	30.1	22.9	49.8	10.6	6.2	22.1	19.5	661 592	172	109 792	1 424 155	23.4
Abbeville	269	1.0	58.1	53.1	26.0	4.8	1.8	11.7	15.0	5 026	204	604	9 846	15.2
Aiken	2 395	0.7	55.0	44.7	32.6	7.0	4.3	16.5	11.6	24 187	180	3 570	49 266	23.8
Allendale	138	1.5	37.3	35.0	30.5	9.1	1.4	11.2	30.7	1 955	171	785	4 242	6.8
Anderson	2 055	0.7	41.4	33.5	41.8	12.3	4.5	17.0	16.0	32 414	202	3 182	60 745	18.3
Bamberg	131	1.1	D	26.2	D	10.7	3.4	17.2	27.2	3 116	189	867	6 408	0.4
Barnwell	423	0.6	26.1	22.4	D	4.9	1.3	D	10.5	3 868	178	1 139	7 854	7.9
Beaufort	2 111	0.2	11.7	2.5	55.3	12.2	12.3	23.8	32.8	21 124	194	1 895	45 981	68.4
Berkeley	1 092	0.9	D	31.9	D	8.0	2.1	13.2	21.7	16 771	123	2 797	45 697	43.8
Calhoun	152	2.6	59.2	54.0	D	3.9	D	8.5	15.4	2 512	179	557	5 225	20.8
Charleston	6 593	0.2	D	5.8	D	11.1	7.1	29.8	28.9	46 538	147	8 808	123 550	23.7
Cherokee	645	0.3	D	45.7	D	9.8	1.8	11.8	10.3	9 349	190	1 110	17 610	17.8
Chester	380	0.5	47.5	42.2	33.0	7.9	1.5	8.5	19.0	6 599	192	867	12 293	14.5
Chesterfield	475	3.0	57.4	52.7	27.1	7.5	2.5	10.9	12.5	6 191	201	1 913	12 101	9.2
Clarendon	212	2.2	27.0	19.2	43.6	13.1	4.0	18.0	27.2	7 581	203	1 939	14 926	22.9
Colleton	329	1.0	30.5	22.5	49.9	11.4	4.3	19.3	18.6	12 003	181	2 786	23 601	9.8
Darlington	849	0.7	50.4	39.7	38.3	8.0	2.2	16.8	10.6	12 728	186	3 101	24 888	9.8
Dillon	279	1.2	36.9	35.1	45.8	14.8	2.6	20.9	16.1	5 561	187	2 139	10 590	4.3
Dorchester	788	0.5	34.9	26.3	46.1	11.7	3.1	18.6	18.5	12 853	146	2 381	30 632	51.5
Edgefield	169	2.0	40.8	36.2	28.6	7.6	1.7	11.9	28.6	3 509	175	783	7 290	17.4
Fairfield	301	1.4	D	38.5	D	3.8	1.2	9.4	15.2	4 229	189	942	8 730	17.1
Florence	2 096	0.3	D	20.0	D	10.3	8.5	24.9	18.6	20 311	163	6 072	43 209	10.3
Georgetown	649	0.8	D	21.9	D	13.9	8.4	21.3	19.1	11 358	211	1 662	21 134	28.7
Greenville	8 495	0.1	32.1	24.1	57.8	10.7	6.9	25.0	10.1	60 254	170	7 230	131 645	21.7
Greenwood	1 113	0.6	45.8	39.3	35.9	10.7	3.8	15.8	17.6	12 685	199	1 603	24 735	13.9
Hampton	203	0.5	30.7	26.9	42.8	10.8	2.8	18.6	26.0	4 019	209	1 129	7 058	6.3
Horry	2 766	0.1	17.1	8.6	70.4	20.4	10.2	32.5	12.4	37 571	215	4 288	89 960	63.6
Jasper	126	1.5	22.5	7.2	D	10.3	1.6	26.7	25.0	2 490	147	676	6 070	14.7
Kershaw	597	2.0	46.4	36.1	35.1	8.7	4.5	13.3	16.4	9 677	199	1 440	17 479	14.7
Lancaster	622	1.9	45.7	39.1	39.3	12.9	5.1	16.8	13.1	10 515	179	1 310	20 929	8.9
Laurens	655	1.0	D	34.4	D	16.0	2.6	15.4	18.7	12 543	198	1 942	23 201	18.2
Lee	115	6.0	D	24.9	D	10.3	3.2	17.7	23.4	3 452	169	1 120	6 537	6.5
Lexington	2 700	1.1	29.5	19.8	55.6	11.4	5.2	20.7	13.8	28 741	140	2 924	67 556	28.3
McCormick	70	3.6	D	22.0	D	4.7	D	14.2	43.6	2 175	228	602	3 347	12.4
Marion	339	-0.3	D	41.7	D	9.5	3.6	14.3	21.7	6 401	185	1 877	12 777	7.0
Marlboro	249	1.4	D	39.8	D	7.5	1.4	14.8	22.3	5 789	196	382	10 955	2.5
Newberry	383	3.1	46.8	40.7	33.3	7.7	2.1	14.9	16.8	7 218	209	1 054	14 455	17.6
Oconee	895	0.9	45.9	38.0	D	7.1	2.2	D	13.1	14 128	221	1 202	25 983	28.5
Orangeburg	1 036	1.1	35.2	30.0	41.4	11.6	3.5	18.4	22.3	16 968	193	4 827	32 340	11.1
Pickens	1 171	0.2	D	24.5	D	11.7	6.2	19.0	23.4	17 285	161	1 372	35 865	26.0
Richland	7 723	0.1	11.3	6.6	56.2	8.6	11.5	26.0	32.5	42 571	139	7 598	109 564	19.2
Saluda	138	10.3	43.0	37.7	29.0	6.8	4.7	9.5	17.6	3 383	199	612	6 792	13.6
Spartanburg	4 377	0.2	43.6	36.6	44.1	11.0	3.3	17.8	12.2	44 443	180	6 000	89 927	19.3

1. Covers mining, construction, and manufacturing.   2. Covers private sector earnings in agricultural services, forestry, and fisheries; transportation and public utilities; wholesale trade; retail trade; finance, insurance, and real estate; and services.   3. Per 1,000 resident population estimated as of July 1 of the year shown.

STATE County	Housing units, 1990 (cont'd)								Civilian labor force, 1999				Civilian employment, 1990[5]		
	Occupied units										Unemployment			Percent	
			Owner-occupied			Renter-occupied									
				Owner cost as a percent of income											
	Total	Percent	Median value[1]	With mort-gage	Without a mort-gage	Median rent[2]	Rent as per-cent of income	Sub-stand-ard units[3] (percent)	Total	Percent change, 1998–1999	Total	Rate[4]	Total	Professional, managerial, and technical	Precision production, craft, and repair
	89	90	91	92	93	94	95	96	97	98	99	100	101	102	103
PENNSYLVANIA—Cont'd															
Potter	6 246	75.4	40 900	18.3	13.6	299	26.4	2.9	8 896	2.2	479	5.4	6 778	20.7	13.2
Schuylkill	60 773	78.1	38 200	17.3	13.7	284	24.3	1.6	67 766	1.5	4 601	6.8	64 562	19.1	15.4
Snyder	12 764	77.2	56 700	20.0	11.9	324	22.6	4.2	19 023	2.6	788	4.1	17 103	16.9	12.8
Somerset	29 574	77.4	43 400	20.0	13.4	283	24.6	2.4	36 852	0.7	2 130	5.8	31 594	20.9	14.3
Sullivan	2 280	78.6	47 000	20.8	14.6	259	24.2	3.3	2 564	-2.2	157	6.1	2 376	19.4	15.5
Susquehanna	14 898	79.2	64 200	20.1	13.8	342	25.7	2.3	18 203	1.1	919	5.0	17 444	21.9	15.6
Tioga	14 974	75.5	43 900	18.2	12.6	286	26.6	2.4	19 248	-1.5	905	4.7	17 188	23.3	13.1
Union	11 689	74.6	66 800	19.2	12.6	351	23.6	1.8	18 637	0.6	559	3.0	15 630	26.2	10.7
Venango	22 408	74.5	38 600	17.0	12.5	305	26.1	1.7	26 071	0.1	1 526	5.9	23 858	24.4	12.5
Warren	17 244	77.2	43 900	17.3	12.4	304	23.5	2.0	20 221	-2.5	806	4.0	20 229	21.5	13.4
Washington	78 533	75.6	53 600	17.9	12.6	320	27.0	1.9	95 623	0.6	4 598	4.8	83 675	25.6	13.9
Wayne	14 638	79.2	89 800	22.3	13.9	386	26.0	1.6	19 315	3.1	1 180	6.1	17 487	21.6	16.2
Westmoreland	144 080	76.3	56 800	19.2	12.6	321	25.2	1.4	181 296	0.0	8 795	4.9	158 570	28.9	12.6
Wyoming	10 002	76.9	67 600	18.9	13.1	360	24.0	2.6	14 816	-2.1	841	5.7	12 729	25.3	14.6
York	128 666	74.4	79 700	19.2	11.9	409	23.4	1.7	193 015	0.9	6 921	3.6	176 908	24.0	14.2
RHODE ISLAND	377 977	59.5	133 500	22.7	13.9	489	27.5	2.6	503 778	1.1	20 890	4.1	487 913	30.1	12.0
Bristol	17 559	71.3	162 100	23.5	14.1	511	27.3	1.7	25 425	1.0	792	3.1	24 539	33.9	10.9
Kent	62 058	72.0	122 500	22.8	14.0	526	27.1	1.6	86 623	0.9	3 396	3.9	82 956	30.2	12.7
Newport	32 687	59.4	160 900	23.3	14.2	627	27.7	1.7	40 000	2.5	1 486	3.7	40 271	36.8	10.4
Providence	226 362	53.5	127 400	23.5	14.0	465	27.5	3.3	287 273	0.4	13 141	4.6	284 662	27.9	12.1
Washington	39 311	68.9	152 700	22.7	12.9	580	27.6	1.7	64 459	4.2	2 076	3.2	55 485	34.5	11.7
SOUTH CAROLINA	1 258 044	69.8	61 100	19.8	13.0	376	24.4	5.0	1 961 962	0.2	87 782	4.5	1 603 425	25.4	13.8
Abbeville	8 780	80.1	43 600	16.5	12.8	242	23.5	5.0	12 333	-4.1	732	5.9	10 713	18.8	14.8
Aiken	44 883	74.6	61 700	17.3	13.0	375	23.2	4.3	63 801	0.5	3 120	4.9	55 268	28.4	16.6
Allendale	3 791	68.2	39 100	21.3	14.8	232	30.0	9.7	4 994	-3.8	379	7.6	3 952	19.2	12.9
Anderson	55 481	75.2	53 700	18.8	12.5	326	23.6	3.3	84 549	-0.7	2 655	3.1	70 331	22.8	15.7
Bamberg	5 587	72.5	43 100	21.1	14.6	225	26.9	9.6	7 882	4.5	672	8.5	6 469	18.5	12.5
Barnwell	7 100	73.2	44 900	18.0	14.2	279	22.6	7.7	11 505	0.7	884	7.7	8 609	24.2	14.0
Beaufort	30 712	64.9	112 100	23.2	12.8	500	24.6	3.9	51 818	2.9	1 192	2.3	33 743	29.6	11.9
Berkeley	42 386	69.7	68 500	21.6	13.2	424	23.2	5.3	63 513	-2.3	2 392	3.8	52 228	23.2	18.7
Calhoun	4 487	81.9	45 000	18.4	13.2	224	22.4	11.6	6 788	-0.7	506	7.5	5 573	18.9	15.8
Charleston	107 069	57.6	73 800	21.7	13.5	437	26.5	4.2	162 222	5.9	5 346	3.3	132 506	31.0	13.5
Cherokee	16 456	75.2	46 900	17.4	12.9	290	23.3	4.9	25 685	0.1	1 148	4.5	21 125	16.8	17.3
Chester	11 448	76.4	40 700	17.7	13.4	282	22.9	7.9	15 897	1.0	1 450	9.1	14 313	16.3	15.2
Chesterfield	14 047	75.4	42 200	16.9	12.9	266	22.7	6.9	20 222	0.0	1 487	7.4	17 334	15.5	14.8
Clarendon	9 544	77.4	45 900	21.5	15.1	237	27.0	12.3	12 617	-1.9	987	7.8	11 109	18.8	14.4
Colleton	12 040	79.4	47 400	22.1	14.6	289	26.4	8.3	15 147	-3.3	854	5.6	14 161	18.2	15.5
Darlington	21 999	74.6	49 000	19.1	13.8	294	27.5	7.2	31 120	-1.8	2 333	7.5	27 574	20.3	13.7
Dillon	9 887	67.0	40 800	17.2	13.6	255	26.3	11.7	14 506	-1.8	1 417	9.8	11 789	18.2	11.8
Dorchester	28 213	71.0	73 600	22.0	13.0	428	24.0	4.5	43 896	-7.1	1 516	3.5	36 188	27.8	16.0
Edgefield	6 424	76.3	52 100	20.8	14.4	268	24.9	6.9	9 511	2.4	524	5.5	8 324	20.7	14.2
Fairfield	7 467	78.1	47 500	18.2	13.3	262	23.9	11.1	10 821	-2.3	1 019	9.4	9 570	16.9	12.7
Florence	40 217	70.5	54 900	18.6	13.7	342	25.0	6.6	63 202	-1.2	3 465	5.5	51 984	24.7	13.4
Georgetown	16 275	79.4	63 800	22.1	13.8	351	24.4	7.7	25 150	-3.9	2 166	8.6	19 699	21.2	14.6
Greenville	122 878	66.2	66 300	18.6	12.6	383	23.0	2.6	192 867	-0.5	4 757	2.5	161 895	29.9	11.8
Greenwood	22 730	69.1	50 100	18.3	12.6	308	24.1	4.6	33 455	-3.8	2 294	6.9	27 811	24.0	14.7
Hampton	6 322	74.4	43 700	21.5	14.1	240	24.1	8.0	8 777	1.9	511	5.8	7 133	17.8	14.0
Horry	55 764	68.5	75 600	23.0	12.8	425	25.5	4.2	104 862	1.8	4 065	3.9	66 730	24.8	13.6
Jasper	5 298	78.0	44 400	21.8	14.3	265	24.8	7.2	8 317	1.0	292	3.5	6 145	15.4	14.4
Kershaw	15 810	81.4	60 200	17.3	13.0	321	23.4	5.0	23 236	-2.1	1 201	5.2	20 663	21.8	15.6
Lancaster	19 778	74.8	49 400	17.6	12.7	316	23.8	5.4	29 175	0.3	1 240	4.3	25 854	17.8	17.2
Laurens	20 660	75.9	44 700	16.4	12.6	296	23.1	5.1	27 742	-8.0	1 078	3.9	26 860	18.7	14.9
Lee	6 054	78.7	42 000	21.0	13.9	235	21.0	13.7	7 944	-2.9	681	8.6	7 245	14.5	12.6
Lexington	61 633	76.1	74 900	19.8	12.2	425	23.2	3.1	119 679	1.3	2 444	2.0	89 550	30.4	13.4
McCormick	2 731	77.3	39 200	18.4	12.6	217	23.2	8.6	4 155	-1.9	501	12.1	3 236	17.3	14.9
Marion	11 766	71.3	42 600	20.6	14.3	273	27.9	9.4	16 878	5.6	2 188	13.0	14 096	17.2	11.7
Marlboro	10 163	68.9	37 100	19.8	13.8	271	26.6	11.2	12 078	2.9	1 479	12.2	11 847	15.7	13.6
Newberry	12 314	76.1	49 200	17.4	13.0	276	23.5	5.6	17 968	-2.3	876	4.9	15 100	20.1	13.1
Oconee	22 358	76.9	56 900	17.5	11.9	305	21.5	3.2	29 039	1.7	1 181	4.1	27 173	20.7	17.6
Orangeburg	28 909	73.2	50 500	19.6	13.6	269	25.6	8.8	42 085	-0.2	4 866	11.6	35 112	20.2	13.7
Pickens	33 422	73.2	59 800	17.4	11.9	344	24.7	2.7	56 567	0.5	1 914	3.4	45 581	26.0	15.3
Richland	101 590	59.2	71 200	20.7	12.6	429	25.5	4.0	161 637	0.3	4 453	2.8	137 105	36.2	8.4
Saluda	5 824	81.6	46 600	20.5	12.4	229	21.3	8.5	8 960	-1.4	473	5.3	7 362	16.2	16.5
Spartanburg	84 503	69.8	54 200	17.7	12.7	353	23.2	4.0	133 406	-0.4	5 763	4.3	111 272	23.3	14.2

1. Specified owner-occupied units.   2. Specified renter-occupied units.   3. Overcrowded or lacking complete plumbing facilities.   4. Percent of civilian labor force.   5. Persons 16 years and older.

Table B. States and Counties — Nonfarm Employment and Agriculture

	Private nonfarm establishments, employment and payroll, 1998								Agriculture, 1997			
		Employment						Annual payroll		Farms		Farm operators
											Percent with—	
STATE County	Number of establishments	Total	Health Care and Social Assistance	Manufacturing	Retail trade	Finance and Insurance	Professional Scientific and Technical Services	Total (mil dol)	Average per employee (dollars)	Number	Less than 50 acres	500 acres and over	Whose principal occupation is farming (percent)
	104	105	106	107	108	109	110	111	112	113	114	115	116
PENNSYLVANIA—Cont'd													
Potter	449	5 468	864	1 199	549	120	76	145	26 558	292	14.4	13.7	55.5
Schuylkill	3 175	43 076	6 278	14 572	7 075	1 553	723	1 002	23 259	605	32.9	6.8	50.1
Snyder	808	12 746	724	4 190	2 649	343	156	255	20 018	671	27.6	3.3	62.0
Somerset	1 932	20 551	3 028	4 897	3 175	765	500	442	21 518	958	15.9	8.2	62.2
Sullivan	179	1 368	373	326	177	D	39	25	18 262	123	10.6	8.1	52.0
Susquehanna	787	6 338	1 059	1 147	1 156	390	173	119	18 831	703	13.2	10.1	62.9
Tioga	859	10 443	1 553	3 126	1 904	371	213	205	19 653	823	13.7	11.2	58.2
Union	827	14 600	2 625	3 606	1 467	328	192	320	21 910	498	28.9	2.6	63.7
Venango	1 270	16 826	2 965	4 356	2 856	528	264	401	23 829	351	21.9	1.4	40.7
Warren	1 011	15 654	2 358	4 609	2 608	463	220	406	25 961	390	21.0	3.1	49.0
Washington	4 802	68 993	9 061	11 558	9 046	1 580	2 289	1 930	27 979	1 307	23.1	3.1	45.7
Wayne	1 430	12 669	2 061	1 035	2 386	543	374	251	19 804	564	14.7	6.0	58.2
Westmoreland	9 003	123 335	17 336	23 694	19 975	4 018	3 630	3 172	25 722	1 035	27.6	4.6	48.3
Wyoming	633	8 887	979	3 098	1 236	219	145	242	27 211	307	16.6	7.5	58.3
York	8 160	149 419	16 254	45 149	20 317	4 127	3 892	4 167	27 886	1 698	43.9	6.8	50.7
RHODE ISLAND	28 245	402 485	68 633	74 181	46 781	24 277	15 973	11 116	27 618	735	59.6	2.0	50.3
Bristol	1 114	12 166	1 583	2 744	1 322	271	201	261	21 465	37	62.2	0.0	62.2
Kent	4 930	69 634	9 378	11 980	12 161	6 503	2 156	1 837	26 381	74	64.9	2.7	43.2
Newport	2 725	26 597	4 756	2 460	3 727	988	2 168	697	26 211	139	56.1	2.2	62.6
Providence	16 064	261 016	47 276	50 472	23 311	15 630	9 381	7 466	28 605	255	63.1	0.4	46.3
Washington	3 412	33 072	5 640	6 525	6 260	885	2 067	854	25 825	230	55.7	3.9	47.8
SOUTH CAROLINA	94 985	1 526 106	161 581	343 295	213 800	58 771	58 476	38 559	25 266	20 189	34.4	10.6	39.4
Abbeville	329	6 408	547	3 926	548	128	45	156	24 268	471	25.7	6.2	32.5
Aiken	2 593	49 345	4 166	19 620	6 417	1 013	3 468	1 664	33 725	729	37.6	7.4	37.6
Allendale	165	2 264	232	1 286	271	D	D	49	21 508	131	21.4	31.3	39.7
Anderson	3 640	55 329	6 440	19 373	8 734	1 321	893	1 335	24 135	1 271	38.9	4.4	33.9
Bamberg	297	3 499	689	1 177	528	106	D	71	20 155	254	21.3	25.6	46.1
Barnwell	403	6 868	443	3 807	979	105	217	157	22 924	325	28.3	15.4	36.3
Beaufort	3 983	41 244	4 223	1 238	7 986	1 225	2 411	979	23 743	99	56.6	18.2	42.4
Berkeley	1 672	22 156	1 653	6 658	3 522	411	513	541	24 407	292	47.9	7.2	36.6
Calhoun	192	2 516	302	1 268	209	D	32	56	22 362	293	21.5	21.2	40.3
Charleston	10 218	162 111	26 739	10 552	22 925	5 426	9 394	3 995	24 647	266	53.4	8.6	43.2
Cherokee	1 054	20 287	1 028	9 139	2 302	285	157	479	23 617	412	32.3	4.9	26.7
Chester	589	10 448	746	5 232	1 126	181	104	259	24 809	340	21.8	11.2	42.6
Chesterfield	729	13 120	1 014	6 376	1 662	211	85	298	22 747	537	23.1	10.2	38.0
Clarendon	533	5 968	984	1 494	1 164	176	109	108	18 023	304	30.3	27.0	56.2
Colleton	829	8 483	863	1 790	1 906	317	257	168	19 845	416	34.3	15.1	40.1
Darlington	1 272	21 432	1 784	6 434	2 629	404	290	585	27 284	346	32.4	23.7	51.7
Dillon	543	8 761	1 270	3 667	1 563	154	91	165	18 870	199	21.6	26.6	58.3
Dorchester	1 654	20 722	1 961	3 990	3 512	549	617	461	22 238	314	41.7	9.6	40.1
Edgefield	364	4 400	414	2 095	412	59	44	90	20 390	271	29.5	13.3	36.9
Fairfield	342	6 812	559	2 657	818	92	63	219	32 126	172	27.9	16.3	29.7
Florence	3 281	54 875	9 886	10 924	8 990	4 349	1 382	1 310	23 866	615	33.3	15.4	52.7
Georgetown	1 725	19 239	1 965	4 926	3 280	430	452	424	22 065	206	41.7	15.0	38.3
Greenville	11 405	244 949	16 956	44 896	25 605	9 557	12 496	7 254	29 615	761	50.3	2.5	33.6
Greenwood	1 560	29 025	3 448	11 497	3 931	701	561	721	24 836	377	37.9	8.2	32.1
Hampton	428	4 613	281	1 367	1 041	118	89	101	21 843	207	25.1	24.2	40.6
Horry	6 991	80 708	6 230	6 582	15 240	2 828	2 147	1 615	20 007	896	31.1	9.8	54.9
Jasper	381	3 253	338	171	507	157	56	53	16 245	123	35.8	13.8	33.3
Kershaw	1 123	14 785	1 408	4 629	2 078	394	356	348	23 525	324	35.2	9.6	38.0
Lancaster	1 158	16 978	1 969	4 907	2 831	750	161	406	23 937	500	32.6	5.6	35.2
Laurens	921	17 250	1 636	6 580	1 930	505	263	373	21 619	686	30.2	9.2	33.5
Lee	266	2 350	346	498	466	62	41	44	18 769	222	18.5	30.6	48.6
Lexington	4 878	63 898	5 693	9 880	10 948	2 123	1 945	1 521	23 806	799	44.1	3.8	40.9
McCormick	129	1 206	79	337	174	D	27	23	18 805	92	28.3	12.0	28.3
Marion	670	10 345	1 085	5 199	1 608	378	112	209	20 194	200	25.0	23.0	53.5
Marlboro	426	6 323	774	2 980	941	156	48	143	22 580	180	22.8	33.9	54.4
Newberry	720	11 652	1 162	5 067	1 462	463	134	238	20 400	499	24.2	8.2	38.7
Oconee	1 432	20 842	1 864	7 109	2 705	343	414	515	24 727	611	40.4	3.1	33.1
Orangeburg	1 901	28 575	3 156	9 661	4 695	863	482	640	22 401	965	25.9	14.9	41.6
Pickens	2 149	30 441	3 352	11 281	4 422	617	557	641	21 063	532	53.2	1.9	32.0
Richland	8 961	169 495	24 344	14 560	22 085	16 682	12 348	4 460	26 312	350	42.6	6.6	42.0
Saluda	266	4 354	435	2 614	388	58	121	84	19 302	556	26.3	8.8	45.1
Spartanburg	6 170	115 285	9 577	34 172	14 013	2 403	2 912	3 110	26 979	1 067	48.0	2.7	32.5

Items 104—116

Table B. States and Counties — Agriculture, Land, and Water

STATE County	Agriculture, 1997 (cont'd)															
	Land in farms					Value of land and buildings		Value of machinery and equipment Average per farm ($1,000)	Value of products sold		Percent from —		Percent of farms with sales of —		Percent of land owned by Fed. Gov. 1997	Water consumption 1995 (mil gal/day)
			Acres													
	Acreage (1,000)	Percent change, 1992–1997	Average size of farm	Total irrigated (1,000)	Total cropland (1,000)	Average per farm ($1,000)	Average per acre (dollars)		Total (mil dol)	Average per farm (dollars)	Crops	Live-stock and poultry products	$10,000 or more	$100,000 or more		
	117	118	119	120	121	122	123	124	125	126	127	128	129	130	131	132
PENNSYLVANIA—Cont'd																
Potter	83	-7.3	286	0	44	247	938	43	20	67 738	24.7	75.3	44.9	19.9	0.0	4.1
Schuylkill	90	1.5	149	1	70	359	2 561	63	67	110 609	31.0	69.0	53.7	19.8	0.0	55.5
Snyder	93	6.6	138	1	68	269	2 250	41	75	111 575	12.5	87.5	67.2	25.5	0.0	299.3
Somerset	206	-6.2	215	1	128	274	1 226	59	60	62 541	12.7	87.3	56.7	18.4	0.2	40.1
Sullivan	27	-11.9	222	0	17	296	1 471	57	7	57 424	5.8	94.2	50.4	20.3	0.0	3.4
Susquehanna	169	-4.8	240	0	95	329	1 437	48	43	61 190	7.3	92.7	55.3	23.3	0.0	5.5
Tioga	202	-4.6	246	0	124	260	1 057	46	47	57 493	12.7	87.3	54.3	19.7	1.3	6.2
Union	63	0.4	127	0	54	363	2 660	51	49	99 208	16.8	83.2	68.5	32.1	1.5	7.5
Venango	46	-12.9	132	0	28	162	1 195	29	7	18 560	27.0	73.0	31.1	4.8	0.0	12.9
Warren	64	-3.7	165	D	32	164	1 002	36	15	37 516	14.3	85.7	36.2	11.0	25.6	72.2
Washington	186	-8.3	142	1	115	266	1 802	39	27	20 357	38.5	61.5	30.3	4.1	0.0	451.6
Wayne	110	-10.2	194	0	60	331	1 746	47	25	44 580	11.1	88.9	49.1	17.6	0.0	5.4
Westmoreland	148	-4.0	143	0	101	363	2 481	47	36	35 226	45.0	55.0	41.0	8.7	0.7	120.0
Wyoming	61	-3.2	199	0	37	282	1 395	49	30	97 856	13.3	86.7	48.9	15.6	0.0	17.6
York	261	3.6	154	1	217	472	3 187	57	129	75 748	39.9	60.1	50.0	17.3	0.2	2 350.0
RHODE ISLAND	55	10.5	75	3	26	442	5 885	39	48	65 578	81.8	18.2	46.7	13.2	0.5	136.2
Bristol	2	71.0	46	0	1	594	12 845	27	3	75 400	92.9	7.1	48.6	8.1	0.0	5.4
Kent	6	7.3	87	0	2	381	4 383	28	3	36 283	85.3	14.7	43.2	8.1	0.1	7.4
Newport	10	4.1	75	0	7	580	7 742	46	15	104 402	81.0	19.0	57.6	21.6	1.6	10.1
Providence	15	22.8	58	0	6	334	5 781	29	10	37 928	64.7	35.2	42.0	9.8	0.0	96.8
Washington	22	9.8	95	2	10	475	4 972	51	19	80 617	89.1	10.9	46.1	14.3	0.4	16.6
SOUTH CAROLINA	4 593	2.7	228	86	2 463	325	1 482	45	1 588	78 665	49.8	50.2	31.0	11.3	5.2	6 202.9
Abbeville	81	-9.7	172	0	36	213	1 531	22	8	17 599	17.4	82.6	21.0	1.7	7.6	4.4
Aiken	134	-2.1	184	2	62	254	1 315	39	59	80 595	24.5	75.5	27.4	10.4	9.6	303.1
Allendale	92	13.4	701	5	55	778	1 095	63	14	105 526	92.3	7.7	37.4	14.5	1.6	11.0
Anderson	166	3.0	131	1	90	308	2 761	28	35	27 174	41.7	58.3	18.9	3.1	1.4	81.7
Bamberg	101	16.0	397	4	53	352	936	49	21	81 554	67.1	32.9	44.1	20.1	0.0	2.6
Barnwell	97	29.4	299	6	48	323	1 045	32	15	44 970	78.1	21.9	33.2	8.9	33.1	3.6
Beaufort	39	-13.0	395	2	11	674	1 772	40	8	84 377	90.6	9.4	33.3	9.1	3.1	29.8
Berkeley	51	0.8	176	1	18	277	1 856	35	22	75 765	92.5	7.5	31.2	3.8	26.4	490.7
Calhoun	102	12.4	349	7	62	369	1 150	72	26	89 837	83.8	16.2	40.3	18.1	0.0	125.4
Charleston	44	37.8	166	2	17	437	2 658	46	27	100 974	85.3	14.7	39.1	15.4	14.8	147.7
Cherokee	65	-1.9	157	D	31	206	1 512	20	13	32 023	23.0	77.0	16.5	2.4	0.9	8.8
Chester	81	-14.2	237	0	33	319	1 179	34	12	34 338	11.4	88.6	23.8	6.5	3.4	3.8
Chesterfield	124	13.0	231	1	55	245	1 062	36	72	133 811	12.3	87.7	27.7	12.3	8.9	9.6
Clarendon	142	4.6	468	2	112	395	912	94	77	252 123	56.7	43.3	55.6	38.2	1.0	3.9
Colleton	155	22.9	372	1	50	396	1 122	41	15	36 516	75.7	24.3	30.5	7.5	0.0	8.3
Darlington	158	0.7	457	1	115	397	909	102	61	177 045	77.2	22.8	47.1	27.5	0.0	37.7
Dillon	91	-16.4	458	D	69	487	1 054	143	66	331 251	52.0	48.0	70.9	38.7	0.0	5.4
Dorchester	65	5.4	208	D	38	208	1 246	41	22	68 490	48.7	51.3	33.4	10.2	0.0	6.7
Edgefield	71	3.5	264	3	28	304	1 219	36	15	56 235	65.6	34.4	31.4	10.7	9.6	3.3
Fairfield	47	-16.8	271	0	15	286	1 116	28	14	78 512	2.3	97.7	19.8	5.2	2.4	860.8
Florence	169	-13.5	274	2	114	337	1 230	67	69	112 367	89.4	10.6	53.2	21.5	0.0	50.0
Georgetown	53	43.7	258	1	15	562	2 238	48	15	72 277	87.4	12.6	32.0	11.7	0.0	45.9
Greenville	70	5.0	92	2	38	299	3 413	30	18	23 012	75.4	24.6	16.0	2.8	0.0	176.9
Greenwood	68	-2.8	181	D	28	253	1 381	23	12	32 603	D	D	19.9	1.9	3.8	12.8
Hampton	117	21.0	567	1	58	572	1 065	73	16	76 204	91.7	8.3	41.1	16.9	0.1	4.1
Horry	184	-6.3	205	1	117	384	1 943	72	83	92 397	86.8	13.2	55.6	24.0	0.5	94.1
Jasper	68	-6.6	554	1	16	549	896	58	5	38 320	93.9	6.2	23.6	5.7	3.7	2.0
Kershaw	73	37.0	224	0	24	343	1 454	40	60	184 408	4.3	95.7	32.1	13.6	0.0	19.4
Lancaster	75	29.6	150	0	31	229	1 638	25	41	81 359	4.7	95.3	22.6	7.6	0.0	18.6
Laurens	127	-1.0	185	1	62	369	1 992	34	19	27 063	40.5	59.5	24.2	2.6	4.5	6.6
Lee	120	-12.0	539	0	89	507	914	87	45	204 427	61.6	38.4	54.5	32.9	0.0	3.4
Lexington	93	12.5	117	6	49	238	2 280	38	108	135 706	20.9	79.1	34.2	15.4	0.0	188.8
McCormick	20	6.9	221	0	7	360	1 632	32	7	75 688	D	D	15.2	2.2	20.7	2.9
Marion	80	2.8	401	1	53	534	1 259	97	33	163 593	94.8	5.2	53.5	26.5	0.0	11.6
Marlboro	117	11.0	647	1	84	603	979	132	36	202 605	79.1	20.9	48.3	34.4	0.0	10.2
Newberry	95	0.6	190	0	49	259	1 496	36	43	85 639	7.5	92.5	24.4	9.8	13.7	6.3
Oconee	66	-5.0	109	1	31	331	2 721	32	44	72 517	8.7	91.3	22.7	9.7	20.1	2 533.6
Orangeburg	272	3.7	282	15	164	319	1 169	56	88	91 088	55.7	44.3	38.8	14.2	0.2	24.9
Pickens	47	6.5	88	0	25	264	3 191	24	6	11 105	61.3	38.7	14.3	1.9	0.0	17.9
Richland	57	-14.3	162	1	28	341	2 549	28	11	30 943	43.4	56.6	26.0	6.6	14.2	495.0
Saluda	111	0.3	200	2	54	274	1 432	43	56	100 606	10.4	89.6	33.1	12.1	1.5	4.0
Spartanburg	107	0.0	100	1	64	256	2 767	30	23	21 663	57.6	42.4	18.0	2.3	0.0	65.6

STATE County	Value of Residential Construction Authorized by Building Permits, 1999		Wholesale Trade, 1997				Retail Trade[1], 1997				Real Estate and Rental and Leasing, 1997			
	New Construction ($1,000)	Number of Housing Units	Number of Establishments	Number of Employees	Sales (mil dol)	Annual Payroll (mil dol)	Number of Establishments	Number of Employees	Sales (mil dol)	Annual Payroll (mil dol)	Number of Establishments	Number of Employees	Receipts (mil dol)	Annual Payroll (mil dol)
	133	134	135	136	137	138	139	140	141	142	143	144	145	146
PENNSYLVANIA—Cont'd														
Potter	5 653	94	13	58	17.4	1.0	77	611	88.3	8.3	5	45	1.6	0.3
Schuylkill	35 774	388	134	1 798	632.2	42.0	659	7 129	1 062.5	106.3	76	255	21.9	5.4
Snyder	9 972	107	29	444	160.4	11.8	190	2 558	365.6	33.5	16	59	6.4	0.9
Somerset	20 016	229	87	840	274.5	21.8	367	3 361	543.1	46.2	38	136	16.0	2.3
Sullivan	2 874	41	5	D	D	D	29	186	24.7	2.3	5	15	2.9	0.1
Susquehanna	12 221	160	34	D	D	D	161	1 221	217.8	17.3	10	26	5.6	0.5
Tioga	11 306	148	28	293	93.3	6.8	170	1 924	287.9	26.3	18	43	3.2	0.5
Union	14 866	162	33	313	89.9	10.0	140	1 492	225.3	19.6	29	149	19.7	2.8
Venango	7 990	101	53	530	128.3	12.1	247	2 792	417.4	37.8	37	119	14.9	1.6
Warren	5 160	73	36	285	67.1	8.4	185	2 742	718.6	52.9	18	91	4.8	1.2
Washington	86 634	750	305	3 803	1 481.0	132.5	778	9 187	1 531.6	152.6	129	551	72.1	9.9
Wayne	24 119	260	35	262	67.5	5.9	246	2 444	397.0	38.4	37	150	10.6	1.8
Westmoreland	144 636	1 156	473	6 482	3 967.1	221.0	1 557	19 333	3 230.2	280.5	237	1 015	114.5	20.2
Wyoming	8 962	105	23	D	D	D	126	1 241	214.3	17.4	11	32	1.8	0.4
York	226 495	2 228	450	9 498	3 428.1	275.9	1 447	20 356	3 250.6	315.4	236	1 138	128.3	21.5
RHODE ISLAND	336 166	3 414	1 590	18 762	7 602.7	635.2	4 169	45 747	7 505.8	752.1	922	4 649	573.4	105.4
Bristol	14 076	215	55	324	108.4	9.4	168	1 311	211.6	20.6	43	77	13.2	1.7
Kent	46 482	457	312	3 491	1 778.6	128.9	804	11 839	1 985.5	187.9	164	1 228	179.9	31.2
Newport	36 247	291	102	561	242.3	18.6	485	3 844	626.2	66.1	97	351	47.3	9.9
Providence	128 410	1 531	1 003	13 417	5 094.4	450.9	2 163	22 850	3 663.7	374.6	510	2 765	291.3	57.1
Washington	110 951	920	118	969	378.9	27.2	549	5 903	1 018.3	103.0	108	228	41.7	5.6
SOUTH CAROLINA	3 614 665	36 161	5 035	58 910	34 179.8	1 866.8	18 481	209 256	33 634.3	3 107.2	3 541	18 760	2 012.6	377.1
Abbeville	9 501	108	10	36	12.1	0.9	65	469	58.6	5.2	5	16	0.6	0.2
Aiken	76 193	719	97	D	D	D	533	6 455	936.6	87.1	101	277	28.2	4.8
Allendale	127	3	11	44	17.9	0.9	46	311	53.6	3.8	7	15	0.7	0.2
Anderson	120 491	1 323	186	1 704	873.0	46.4	743	8 860	1 349.1	124.7	113	418	50.3	6.6
Bamberg	2 406	37	10	D	D	D	78	524	68.4	6.4	6	24	1.0	0.2
Barnwell	3 296	34	8	D	D	D	107	1 020	116.2	11.6	12	27	2.9	0.3
Beaufort	438 193	2 952	118	548	169.4	15.2	751	7 444	1 340.9	129.2	273	1 886	231.0	44.3
Berkeley	73 298	682	75	926	577.6	25.7	292	3 347	537.5	47.1	67	547	66.2	10.2
Calhoun	5 514	89	10	114	24.1	2.9	37	267	31.1	2.9	2	D	D	D
Charleston	549 611	4 464	472	5 296	3 727.1	175.5	1 850	22 298	3 483.7	347.7	466	2 618	269.0	48.9
Cherokee	4 816	67	42	D	D	D	232	2 137	366.7	30.3	35	107	12.3	1.5
Chester	7 491	58	27	905	331.5	24.2	129	1 142	186.1	14.4	12	38	5.6	0.9
Chesterfield	12 309	316	33	330	91.8	8.6	182	1 632	240.9	21.4	19	45	2.1	0.6
Clarendon	10 338	128	22	187	56.2	4.2	130	1 120	165.6	14.9	9	30	1.8	0.4
Colleton	16 836	133	44	487	212.5	11.9	188	1 890	259.4	23.5	36	152	14.3	2.7
Darlington	17 843	185	81	858	728.0	19.1	310	2 715	423.4	36.3	29	93	7.4	1.2
Dillon	6 196	58	29	292	177.3	9.4	151	1 612	196.0	19.6	22	59	5.9	0.7
Dorchester	75 367	708	59	422	97.3	7.9	282	3 450	516.9	46.3	57	187	31.1	3.5
Edgefield	9 597	99	10	D	D	D	79	455	78.8	6.5	11	31	1.4	0.3
Fairfield	8 952	82	8	94	29.5	2.6	70	764	82.8	7.1	7	24	1.0	0.3
Florence	51 265	648	206	2 847	1 017.6	81.6	759	8 935	1 467.3	138.4	114	387	40.7	7.3
Georgetown	119 499	869	56	363	119.6	9.6	346	3 178	481.9	47.6	55	220	16.5	5.0
Greenville	318 551	4 037	930	12 025	10 685.9	451.4	1 852	24 775	4 496.4	380.2	415	2 158	288.9	48.3
Greenwood	38 222	415	52	760	148.1	13.6	339	4 601	606.1	60.7	56	206	22.0	3.5
Hampton	1 826	23	11	D	D	D	131	952	114.1	10.8	9	22	1.7	0.4
Horry	443 216	4 773	230	1 824	481.5	49.5	1 522	14 457	2 505.2	230.7	360	3 026	259.6	59.7
Jasper	7 680	77	12	177	65.5	4.7	79	531	76.9	6.8	9	37	2.9	0.7
Kershaw	29 461	359	24	113	36.9	3.1	221	2 150	296.5	27.2	29	83	6.8	1.0
Lancaster	28 682	245	48	353	136.3	9.2	264	2 608	401.3	36.3	35	108	9.3	1.9
Laurens	19 218	222	40	351	86.5	9.5	200	1 743	296.2	24.4	33	101	6.3	1.3
Lee	3 071	61	15	124	38.5	2.7	74	576	72.4	6.6	5	D	D	D
Lexington	153 378	1 891	301	4 749	2 282.6	152.0	803	10 332	1 803.7	156.6	141	684	86.4	13.6
McCormick	17 191	100	5	D	D	D	41	204	23.5	2.0	2	D	D	D
Marion	8 546	119	31	235	91.6	5.3	178	1 609	215.7	20.9	13	39	3.5	0.8
Marlboro	3 272	36	16	133	54.3	3.8	115	796	122.3	10.6	13	37	2.6	0.5
Newberry	12 925	111	22	D	D	D	152	1 388	198.1	19.4	12	64	3.2	0.9
Oconee	84 436	792	57	D	D	D	276	2 738	403.9	35.1	41	143	12.8	3.1
Orangeburg	16 391	208	103	933	380.9	25.4	461	4 793	704.3	65.2	46	224	15.1	2.9
Pickens	92 330	843	86	D	D	D	372	4 237	655.2	58.1	53	237	22.4	3.9
Richland	280 863	3 609	540	7 346	2 989.4	251.7	1 558	22 311	3 475.6	350.7	392	2 614	310.4	61.3
Saluda	5 377	52	11	102	38.7	1.7	67	415	76.4	5.4	4	12	0.7	0.2
Spartanburg	163 145	2 020	484	6 234	3 965.3	214.8	1 117	13 785	2 311.6	213.5	198	898	90.4	17.9

1. Establishments with payroll.

STATE County	Professional, Scientific, and Technical Services[1], 1997				Manufacturing, 1997				Accommodation and Foodservices, 1997			
	Number of Establishments	Number of Employees	Receipts (mil dol)	Annual Payroll (mil dol)	Number of Establishments	Number of Employees	Receipts (mil dol)	Annual Payroll (mil dol)	Number of Establishments	Number of Employees	Sales (mil dol)	Annual Payroll (mil dol)
	147	148	149	150	151	152	153	154	155	156	157	158
PENNSYLVANIA—Cont'd												
Potter	23	51	4.6	1.0	29	1 166	117.6	28.8	49	270	9.1	1.8
Schuylkill	127	628	44.5	15.6	226	14 370	2 625.1	393.7	297	2 931	85.2	22.8
Snyder	31	130	8.4	3.0	65	4 413	414.2	111.3	78	1 218	36.9	10.3
Somerset	85	471	27.0	8.9	118	4 828	644.1	117.1	168	1 902	54.4	15.4
Sullivan	6	D	D	D	NA	NA	NA	NA	24	105	3.9	0.9
Susquehanna	35	167	8.1	2.6	51	1 160	132.6	22.1	79	693	22.2	5.3
Tioga	45	170	8.6	3.9	46	2 930	415.9	69.4	89	1 091	31.8	7.9
Union	40	146	10.3	4.0	36	3 394	434.5	86.0	90	1 501	46.3	12.1
Venango	45	185	9.3	2.8	89	3 950	1 084.6	137.8	99	1 143	31.5	9.2
Warren	45	162	10.3	4.0	81	4 670	1 116.3	147.8	112	984	27.9	6.7
Washington	297	1 729	197.2	68.1	278	11 725	2 788.4	402.3	351	4 812	133.0	38.8
Wayne	78	329	21.7	8.5	68	1 039	182.3	24.5	172	2 459	106.7	32.2
Westmoreland	611	3 878	398.3	129.6	597	24 404	4 000.2	800.2	710	12 235	320.9	93.5
Wyoming	32	105	8.0	3.3	35	D	D	D	56	722	19.0	4.9
York	502	3 457	268.4	105.2	661	45 754	8 156.9	1 557.5	635	10 721	318.7	91.1
RHODE ISLAND	2 349	14 866	1 418.1	541.5	2 535	75 599	10 482.0	2 288.6	2 617	34 162	1 220.9	340.6
Bristol	59	141	13.5	3.5	100	2 634	267.0	73.0	104	1 386	38.9	10.7
Kent	392	1 573	151.5	52.3	411	12 933	2 115.3	417.1	409	6 904	221.4	61.5
Newport	235	2 401	256.1	92.4	98	2 304	296.1	100.0	328	4 643	207.1	59.8
Providence	1 419	8 957	888.0	345.9	1 774	49 910	6 435.0	1 440.9	1 338	17 307	581.4	162.6
Washington	244	1 794	109.0	47.4	152	7 818	1 368.6	257.6	438	3 922	172.1	45.9
SOUTH CAROLINA	6 576	47 679	6 820.9	1 850.5	4 450	346 142	70 797.0	10 369.4	7 775	150 621	4 835.8	1 313.8
Abbeville	10	30	2.5	1.0	36	3 978	607.5	101.4	26	368	8.3	2.5
Aiken	176	3 782	439.6	166.2	99	19 999	4 256.3	896.7	212	3 618	99.4	26.3
Allendale	7	24	2.3	0.7	14	1 440	310.3	33.6	6	50	1.7	0.4
Anderson	199	777	55.2	16.2	240	20 589	4 180.1	611.4	283	4 919	144.6	37.1
Bamberg	10	35	2.2	0.6	24	1 175	180.4	28.5	24	310	6.5	1.7
Barnwell	19	256	30.9	15.0	22	3 376	450.3	75.9	33	327	10.6	2.6
Beaufort	367	2 006	193.0	85.2	94	1 087	137.5	28.7	353	7 838	337.6	93.2
Berkeley	79	365	24.0	10.2	75	6 396	2 811.2	210.6	135	2 304	63.8	17.4
Calhoun	16	24	2.0	0.5	18	809	97.6	22.9	7	D	D	D
Charleston	950	7 688	732.4	293.3	261	10 530	3 039.4	366.3	847	19 759	710.6	198.0
Cherokee	40	158	9.1	4.0	76	8 195	1 767.1	231.4	85	1 771	40.6	10.8
Chester	22	60	3.4	1.2	54	5 260	964.1	145.8	46	660	19.2	5.0
Chesterfield	29	78	3.6	0.8	58	7 450	1 408.2	196.4	65	882	23.3	6.4
Clarendon	20	89	5.7	3.1	24	1 396	122.4	26.1	50	617	16.2	4.3
Colleton	57	245	18.2	4.4	26	1 779	196.0	46.9	57	856	26.2	7.6
Darlington	60	300	22.1	6.2	63	6 002	2 054.6	185.9	91	964	31.4	8.3
Dillon	21	86	4.8	1.7	25	3 613	394.3	62.9	54	929	26.0	7.1
Dorchester	81	486	27.6	11.1	79	3 669	738.3	110.6	115	2 188	61.8	17.4
Edgefield	17	37	2.0	0.5	28	2 041	333.3	44.6	23	289	6.0	1.7
Fairfield	21	69	3.4	1.2	20	2 239	1 001.9	79.8	21	297	7.8	1.8
Florence	179	1 194	83.8	33.0	139	11 011	2 114.2	328.2	245	4 857	147.1	40.5
Georgetown	103	362	40.3	14.9	78	4 974	1 057.6	141.6	151	2 804	86.9	25.8
Greenville	1 040	11 157	3 374.0	547.5	672	45 372	9 507.5	1 431.8	818	17 006	506.6	141.8
Greenwood	87	467	34.0	12.2	93	11 612	1 875.1	339.6	122	2 320	64.5	17.5
Hampton	18	88	15.5	1.9	20	1 307	196.7	44.2	30	393	10.4	2.9
Horry	400	1 766	135.5	53.8	160	6 687	927.8	173.4	1 044	20 246	881.7	228.5
Jasper	20	55	3.5	0.9	NA	NA	NA	NA	35	769	21.7	5.8
Kershaw	69	266	17.2	5.2	62	4 916	1 637.9	151.8	80	1 197	31.0	8.0
Lancaster	42	128	7.2	2.6	54	5 341	1 561.6	145.5	76	1 112	33.2	8.2
Laurens	33	128	7.8	2.0	72	6 447	834.1	171.7	68	1 218	31.3	8.6
Lee	10	42	2.0	0.9	9	641	172.4	18.3	14	D	D	D
Lexington	330	1 535	115.6	47.2	225	9 964	2 080.7	324.2	338	7 502	203.3	55.4
McCormick	5	12	0.3	0.2	NA	NA	NA	NA	8	127	2.2	0.6
Marion	25	64	4.1	1.5	32	5 007	727.0	112.5	45	610	14.2	3.6
Marlboro	21	58	3.2	0.9	22	2 935	755.2	82.1	36	403	10.5	2.6
Newberry	36	132	8.5	2.0	49	5 553	735.4	130.5	43	697	16.7	4.2
Oconee	77	299	29.0	7.7	80	7 487	1 136.0	202.8	101	1 845	42.2	11.0
Orangeburg	84	459	29.9	12.2	90	9 370	1 700.3	222.9	149	2 583	72.1	18.6
Pickens	110	466	24.5	9.1	134	11 790	1 916.3	305.7	193	3 985	97.9	27.3
Richland	913	7 920	944.2	323.7	235	13 558	3 220.7	460.8	695	13 674	418.6	117.0
Saluda	11	27	0.8	0.3	14	2 565	375.2	46.9	18	D	D	D
Spartanburg	330	2 445	215.8	95.7	481	35 102	7 534.6	1 108.6	465	9 520	244.2	68.7

1. Firms subject to federal tax.

Table B. States and Counties — Health and Other Services and Federal Funds

STATE County	Health Care and Social Assistance[1], 1997				Other Services[1], 1997				Federal funds and grants, fiscal 1999[2] Expenditures (mil dol)			
									Total	Direct payments for individuals[3]		
	Number of Establishments	Number of Employees	Receipts (mil dol)	Annual Payroll (mil dol)	Number of Establishments	Number of Employees	Receipts (mil dol)	Annual Payroll (mil dol)	Total	Social Security and government retirement	Medicare	Food stamps and Supplemental Security Income
	159	160	161	162	163	164	165	166	167	168	169	170
PENNSYLVANIA—Cont'd												
Potter	27	242	13.3	4.8	18	74	5.1	1.0	79.0	37.6	13.8	3.1
Schuylkill	234	3 154	170.2	76.2	203	797	47.0	11.4	751.9	400.0	184.6	17.4
Snyder	51	308	18.2	7.5	50	200	14.2	3.2	119.5	67.4	25.5	3.1
Somerset	133	983	52.9	22.2	125	395	26.3	5.7	374.1	179.0	87.7	12.0
Sullivan	6	116	7.4	3.1	5	8	0.5	0.1	31.6	17.5	6.1	0.4
Susquehanna	47	564	25.1	9.7	53	109	10.7	2.1	159.6	86.7	32.4	5.3
Tioga	70	408	21.2	9.3	48	142	12.8	3.0	213.8	87.2	33.0	6.3
Union	84	704	47.1	20.2	38	105	6.4	1.5	229.7	69.6	23.4	2.4
Venango	112	730	49.0	23.7	94	442	41.1	12.1	273.6	131.9	60.2	12.9
Warren	61	641	37.9	18.5	69	207	12.5	2.6	180.2	95.6	40.6	4.7
Washington	462	4 547	285.1	130.5	331	2 213	167.2	44.3	1 063.0	503.2	277.2	37.3
Wayne	74	710	39.0	17.3	85	260	16.7	4.4	336.6	132.8	45.4	5.3
Westmoreland	851	6 910	432.2	183.6	642	3 158	191.3	52.4	1 747.4	860.7	478.0	49.4
Wyoming	46	340	15.9	7.1	43	124	9.6	2.3	100.7	53.9	22.7	3.8
York	586	6 842	469.4	214.2	585	3 058	202.4	58.0	1 742.3	680.0	225.2	32.1
RHODE ISLAND	2 074	25 368	1 459.3	647.4	1 949	8 602	546.2	167.8	6 036.1	2 062.0	907.8	166.5
Bristol	76	977	49.7	26.1	72	257	15.2	4.0	194.4	106.7	42.4	4.6
Kent	375	4 650	285.3	112.5	341	1 447	87.5	25.8	715.6	364.9	152.9	20.5
Newport	151	1 726	79.3	33.8	156	782	46.1	17.5	1 013.0	210.2	63.4	9.6
Providence	1 223	15 312	909.9	414.2	1 157	5 106	345.3	103.1	3 308.6	1 147.7	566.6	120.9
Washington	249	2 703	135.1	60.8	223	1 010	52.2	17.3	482.6	226.7	82.6	10.8
SOUTH CAROLINA	6 261	78 888	5 318.5	2 361.3	5 672	32 166	1 901.0	563.8	20 833.2	7 634.3	2 382.9	704.7
Abbeville	29	223	8.8	4.3	19	64	3.7	0.9	92.7	46.5	12.4	4.4
Aiken	201	3 163	222.5	87.8	160	937	45.7	12.3	1 969.8	270.7	91.3	22.8
Allendale	5	44	3.6	1.0	10	25	1.2	0.3	60.5	17.0	8.6	5.5
Anderson	244	2 970	183.4	95.2	220	1 123	65.4	22.4	570.4	316.2	104.9	17.5
Bamberg	28	268	13.6	6.0	17	51	3.1	0.9	93.1	28.0	13.3	6.2
Barnwell	36	285	13.1	5.4	28	60	4.8	1.0	118.6	43.8	18.5	9.4
Beaufort	206	1 814	134.8	50.4	181	1 060	58.9	18.3	765.3	287.3	66.4	12.9
Berkeley	87	986	39.6	16.3	111	473	23.6	5.8	404.4	227.4	44.2	19.8
Calhoun	10	138	4.6	2.2	13	56	2.4	0.8	52.7	20.5	6.2	2.6
Charleston	841	9 962	678.6	280.8	628	4 622	268.8	88.5	2 677.1	743.1	216.3	62.6
Cherokee	59	688	50.2	19.6	64	325	18.8	6.3	174.8	83.8	30.4	6.7
Chester	34	187	12.8	6.2	36	154	8.0	1.9	130.4	64.0	26.4	6.2
Chesterfield	46	709	39.8	15.7	35	135	7.6	2.1	178.1	70.3	27.3	10.5
Clarendon	36	468	19.5	8.6	29	135	9.6	2.1	159.1	57.1	22.4	11.5
Colleton	48	829	57.2	19.8	39	201	12.5	3.2	185.5	78.6	34.7	12.1
Darlington	75	1 008	66.8	27.0	80	351	22.7	5.7	259.1	111.5	43.6	17.1
Dillon	56	784	38.4	15.9	36	158	8.2	2.1	147.1	48.7	26.2	13.5
Dorchester	122	1 530	93.9	32.5	124	541	28.6	8.6	342.4	216.3	43.2	13.9
Edgefield	21	206	7.7	3.2	16	46	2.4	0.6	91.3	29.7	10.8	4.4
Fairfield	16	292	9.9	4.5	14	50	2.9	0.8	96.2	41.1	16.8	5.7
Florence	276	5 558	399.9	193.5	191	1 268	73.1	21.7	564.7	220.4	92.7	36.1
Georgetown	125	991	67.4	28.4	97	386	24.0	6.6	290.6	154.6	53.8	13.0
Greenville	673	7 746	575.5	285.4	674	4 537	290.3	86.2	1 346.1	639.9	218.7	46.2
Greenwood	105	1 370	88.1	44.1	96	431	23.8	7.3	250.4	133.8	38.6	10.9
Hampton	22	210	14.4	3.5	25	154	7.0	2.1	121.0	42.1	16.5	6.9
Horry	326	4 036	295.9	117.8	336	1 477	91.5	25.5	729.8	402.5	112.1	27.0
Jasper	21	123	5.8	2.5	22	130	6.0	1.3	70.3	27.7	10.8	4.6
Kershaw	55	588	40.9	18.4	87	308	16.1	4.7	193.8	107.1	32.8	7.6
Lancaster	90	1 530	109.5	40.0	87	344	23.5	4.8	200.4	102.6	40.2	8.7
Laurens	54	532	27.2	13.0	58	217	12.3	3.2	215.1	116.1	37.1	11.4
Lee	14	93	3.0	1.6	16	70	2.8	0.6	87.6	30.0	12.5	7.8
Lexington	281	3 405	193.8	89.3	346	2 257	145.4	41.8	612.1	346.5	93.3	19.9
McCormick	5	47	3.2	1.6	6	20	0.7	0.1	52.5	24.0	5.6	2.3
Marion	65	564	27.6	13.8	38	134	6.9	1.8	218.9	64.8	34.8	12.0
Marlboro	33	507	38.1	13.8	20	73	2.9	0.7	154.8	51.0	25.6	10.2
Newberry	41	441	17.1	8.2	55	252	17.8	4.7	155.2	76.2	24.7	6.7
Oconee	99	777	48.8	24.1	84	362	18.2	5.3	244.4	145.8	44.9	7.0
Orangeburg	146	1 161	73.0	31.2	135	603	27.6	8.7	438.7	170.1	62.8	32.0
Pickens	133	2 019	117.3	61.0	114	441	26.1	7.2	364.3	190.2	55.2	9.2
Richland	686	9 381	723.4	331.4	509	3 641	199.5	62.5	2 621.1	686.5	162.4	52.0
Saluda	17	220	5.7	2.6	14	53	3.5	0.7	59.6	28.1	8.2	3.0
Spartanburg	377	4 899	364.5	167.8	377	2 038	153.4	41.2	865.2	460.8	146.5	34.9

1. Firms subject to federal tax.   2. October 1, 1998 to September 30, 1999.   3. State totals may include programs not allocated by county.

STATE County	Federal funds and grants, fiscal 1999[1] (cont'd)							Local government finances, 1997				
	Expenditures (mil dol) (cont'd)							General revenue				
	Procurement contract awards			Grants[2]							Taxes	
								Total (mil dol)	Intergovern-mental (mil dol)	Total (mil dol)	Per capita[3] (dollars)	
	Salaries and wages	Defense	Other	Medicaid and other health-related	Nutrition and family welfare	Education	Other				Total	Property
	171	172	173	174	175	176	177	178	179	180	181	182
PENNSYLVANIA—Cont'd												
Potter	2.8	0.1	0.8	10.9	2.2	0.8	5.6	40.5	16.3	13.3	778	642
Schuylkill	40.9	3.8	11.2	62.9	12.8	3.6	7.0	285.4	139.2	89.4	591	415
Snyder	4.5	0.0	1.1	10.6	2.0	1.0	2.0	57.2	24.1	24.3	635	384
Somerset	11.9	4.3	3.8	43.9	8.7	3.0	11.6	138.8	66.0	47.9	597	470
Sullivan	1.5	0.0	0.7	3.1	0.4	0.2	1.3	12.9	5.0	6.6	1 089	958
Susquehanna	7.1	0.2	1.8	14.9	3.6	1.3	4.7	81.0	44.5	28.8	683	616
Tioga	8.8	0.2	1.9	22.1	6.4	2.0	42.7	86.3	44.7	27.5	661	519
Union	85.2	0.7	10.7	9.2	5.8	0.7	18.7	79.0	37.5	25.4	608	394
Venango	7.7	0.0	2.5	31.8	7.6	2.4	13.2	136.9	71.0	40.7	701	546
Warren	9.4	3.1	2.7	14.9	4.7	1.7	1.8	88.7	44.2	31.9	720	514
Washington	32.8	3.1	10.2	99.9	25.4	9.8	53.9	404.5	180.0	160.3	779	615
Wayne	7.3	0.4	118.1	13.5	3.7	1.4	6.0	103.2	33.4	54.6	1 203	1 148
Westmoreland	60.0	6.7	16.5	146.9	43.7	10.7	49.2	773.5	317.1	299.8	800	637
Wyoming	3.9	0.0	1.1	9.1	3.1	0.9	1.3	54.8	25.0	23.2	788	630
York	101.2	477.9	58.6	90.9	21.2	6.4	36.2	735.0	264.7	307.6	830	614
RHODE ISLAND	722.5	303.4	117.7	690.9	219.8	109.4	390.9	X	X	X	X	X
Bristol	8.3	1.1	1.6	17.5	3.4	1.7	5.3	103.3	36.6	55.4	1 131	1 116
Kent	42.0	4.0	8.1	57.7	16.0	8.4	26.3	345.5	90.9	225.1	1 392	1 368
Newport	372.5	284.1	11.4	34.0	9.9	7.4	4.9	190.1	46.4	117.1	1 418	1 369
Providence	253.0	6.8	84.0	547.4	181.1	86.4	260.7	1 241.1	445.5	676.3	1 177	1 167
Washington	46.7	7.3	12.5	33.8	9.4	5.4	38.1	250.8	66.2	160.6	1 342	1 319
SOUTH CAROLINA	2 441.2	847.1	1 693.2	2 006.2	557.2	348.6	966.7	X	X	X	X	X
Abbeville	2.6	0.0	0.5	14.7	2.3	1.0	6.8	32.8	16.2	11.7	478	422
Aiken	53.9	0.3	1 427.2	62.1	10.5	5.4	15.5	216.3	98.6	70.7	528	477
Allendale	1.3	0.1	0.3	17.8	2.7	2.0	0.2	21.4	11.1	8.0	695	596
Anderson	22.2	1.1	5.0	56.0	8.9	7.3	18.6	224.3	105.7	84.7	535	466
Bamberg	2.3	0.2	5.5	17.0	3.3	4.5	6.6	27.0	15.3	8.6	518	443
Barnwell	2.5	6.4	0.6	22.2	3.3	1.6	4.9	55.8	31.3	10.1	465	408
Beaufort	249.5	87.4	6.2	29.7	10.0	4.7	6.8	239.9	65.6	101.8	955	864
Berkeley	21.3	8.3	2.2	33.7	17.0	5.3	20.0	183.1	103.7	51.8	385	360
Calhoun	1.6	0.0	0.3	10.0	1.7	0.8	3.5	21.5	9.5	9.5	689	673
Charleston	763.0	445.6	78.0	188.2	31.3	17.5	94.8	762.7	236.2	298.6	1 048	747
Cherokee	4.8	0.0	1.2	20.8	4.1	2.2	16.3	117.1	35.5	30.0	620	551
Chester	3.4	0.0	1.0	17.4	4.1	2.0	4.3	63.2	30.4	23.0	681	592
Chesterfield	4.7	0.0	1.5	41.8	6.4	2.1	10.7	60.3	34.3	19.1	476	428
Clarendon	3.3	0.0	0.7	37.2	5.4	2.3	8.8	63.3	28.7	12.4	404	366
Colleton	5.3	7.0	1.0	33.1	6.9	2.4	0.6	60.2	30.5	23.7	639	555
Darlington	6.5	0.2	1.7	53.4	9.4	3.9	2.9	99.5	49.9	36.0	547	512
Dillon	3.9	0.0	0.7	35.8	5.2	3.6	1.0	46.2	28.3	9.9	334	232
Dorchester	9.8	1.0	2.9	35.0	6.3	3.0	6.9	133.8	70.8	41.4	456	410
Edgefield	23.9	1.7	0.7	14.0	2.2	1.2	1.4	34.4	19.2	11.2	569	513
Fairfield	2.6	0.1	1.0	16.9	3.0	1.8	5.2	52.9	16.8	30.2	1 352	1 333
Florence	36.7	3.3	7.7	104.2	17.8	8.2	20.0	208.8	107.8	62.9	505	339
Georgetown	6.2	11.5	1.1	28.5	5.8	3.2	9.8	122.9	49.3	45.4	868	812
Greenville	95.2	77.9	40.1	109.1	26.3	14.9	55.8	1 037.3	236.3	250.7	719	631
Greenwood	10.5	0.0	2.0	29.1	13.6	4.0	2.2	206.2	45.9	35.7	563	524
Hampton	19.8	0.2	3.0	23.0	3.4	1.6	0.2	42.6	25.4	12.9	680	584
Horry	23.4	11.2	6.1	62.3	15.4	7.7	46.7	409.2	115.7	165.7	980	789
Jasper	1.9	0.1	0.3	18.3	2.6	1.3	2.1	27.2	13.5	10.5	619	503
Kershaw	6.2	0.0	1.3	25.9	3.8	2.1	2.8	128.1	37.5	26.6	557	517
Lancaster	5.6	0.0	3.1	25.1	5.4	2.9	3.3	82.3	44.5	28.1	485	378
Laurens	6.2	0.0	1.3	29.4	4.7	2.3	2.1	107.4	43.1	23.9	386	357
Lee	2.0	0.1	0.6	21.6	3.7	1.7	0.6	27.4	16.8	8.2	407	350
Lexington	29.5	5.2	6.1	40.4	9.1	6.8	48.3	576.2	214.9	134.9	673	636
McCormick	3.7	2.9	0.4	8.9	1.1	2.4	0.2	14.4	7.7	4.5	474	421
Marion	4.9	42.2	1.1	38.5	5.7	3.0	6.1	110.6	36.7	17.2	494	387
Marlboro	4.3	0.0	0.8	36.0	4.9	2.1	12.5	46.2	28.9	12.0	407	307
Newberry	7.4	0.1	1.4	21.2	2.9	1.8	9.1	54.2	26.9	19.4	566	537
Oconee	8.2	0.1	2.1	24.4	2.9	2.3	3.3	96.5	35.7	49.8	785	754
Orangeburg	11.8	0.3	3.0	84.8	18.4	13.2	18.5	220.1	80.0	51.7	591	538
Pickens	14.0	3.2	3.5	24.7	4.2	3.1	51.1	124.7	60.1	43.6	417	337
Richland	699.2	96.0	44.1	209.2	199.2	116.8	281.7	766.6	215.4	160.9	530	444
Saluda	2.6	1.8	0.5	11.5	1.4	1.0	0.3	20.3	12.3	5.7	338	293
Spartanburg	29.9	0.4	14.7	99.5	19.5	10.6	36.0	412.8	192.6	162.1	662	603

1. October 1, 1998 to September 30, 1999.   2. State totals may include programs not allocated by county.   3. Based on the resident population estimated as of July 1 of the year shown.

Table B. States and Counties — Local Government Finances, Government Employment, and Elections

STATE County	Total (mil dol)	Per capita¹ (dollars)	Education	Health and hospitals	Police protection	Public welfare	Highways	Total (mil dol)	Per capita¹ (dollars)	Federal civilian	Federal military	State and local	Democratic	Republican	All other
	183	184	185	186	187	188	189	190	191	192	193	194	195	196	197
PENNSYLVANIA—Cont'd															
Potter	35.8	2 088	56.8	0.0	0.8	6.8	8.8	35.0	2 041	48	58	1 007	NA	NA	NA
Schuylkill	291.3	1 926	53.9	4.8	2.1	6.7	4.8	320.3	2 118	722	501	6 453	NA	NA	NA
Snyder	62.5	1 632	69.8	0.1	1.0	0.8	5.9	26.8	700	93	129	2 497	NA	NA	NA
Somerset	154.5	1 925	62.8	2.9	1.8	0.1	5.5	159.1	1 982	231	271	4 173	NA	NA	NA
Sullivan	12.5	2 053	65.2	0.1	0.6	0.1	9.9	3.7	611	27	21	356	NA	NA	NA
Susquehanna	87.2	2 073	73.9	0.2	0.5	2.4	5.7	61.6	1 463	123	143	1 809	NA	NA	NA
Tioga	87.4	2 101	58.1	5.0	1.2	8.8	6.1	73.0	1 754	169	141	2 864	NA	NA	NA
Union	86.1	2 062	65.9	2.5	1.2	2.3	3.5	106.9	2 559	1 589	145	2 198	NA	NA	NA
Venango	137.3	2 364	54.3	6.4	1.6	2.9	3.4	217.7	3 750	190	195	3 775	NA	NA	NA
Warren	89.3	2 020	48.1	8.4	1.9	13.1	5.9	45.7	1 033	231	148	2 560	NA	NA	NA
Washington	447.1	2 172	60.5	0.2	2.3	4.9	3.9	640.0	3 110	635	701	9 111	NA	NA	NA
Wayne	98.0	2 158	66.1	1.0	0.9	2.7	4.1	142.8	3 145	132	153	2 206	NA	NA	NA
Westmoreland	774.5	2 067	57.6	3.3	2.4	6.6	4.0	1 082.5	2 889	1 123	1 258	15 084	NA	NA	NA
Wyoming	53.1	1 806	65.0	0.1	1.4	0.1	6.5	25.7	875	75	98	1 109	NA	NA	NA
York	690.5	1 864	50.9	3.9	3.7	4.5	3.5	964.9	2 604	3 805	1 689	12 262	NA	NA	NA
RHODE ISLAND	X	X	X	X	X	X	X	X	X	10 591	9 676	54 934	61.0	32.0	7.0
Bristol	105.1	2 147	70.9	0.2	4.7	0.0	5.2	62.1	1 269	114	329	1 682	NA	NA	NA
Kent	316.6	1 958	58.2	0.2	6.7	0.7	3.1	148.0	915	688	1 006	8 006	NA	NA	NA
Newport	174.7	2 115	54.1	0.4	7.5	0.3	2.2	77.5	939	4 246	3 901	3 240	NA	NA	NA
Providence	1 157.0	2 014	52.2	0.1	7.5	0.5	2.7	653.8	1 138	5 015	3 641	31 465	NA	NA	NA
Washington	277.9	2 322	64.7	0.4	6.2	0.0	3.1	171.1	1 430	528	799	10 541	NA	NA	NA
SOUTH CAROLINA	X	X	X	X	X	X	X	X	X	29 258	56 340	278 278	40.9	56.8	2.3
Abbeville	32.9	1 347	62.2	0.6	6.4	0.0	2.8	17.6	720	48	142	1 351	45.0	53.1	1.9
Aiken	207.3	1 547	59.9	4.1	3.1	0.2	2.8	104.5	780	921	772	6 247	32.3	65.4	2.3
Allendale	21.0	1 812	62.1	4.6	4.3	0.5	2.1	17.9	1 548	27	66	1 477	70.0	29.0	1.0
Anderson	226.9	1 434	66.6	0.9	5.0	0.3	4.7	141.6	895	386	927	9 890	34.6	63.2	2.2
Bamberg	25.3	1 520	69.2	1.2	5.4	0.2	1.8	11.2	675	42	95	1 269	62.2	36.9	1.0
Barnwell	49.9	2 285	54.7	14.8	4.2	0.1	1.9	41.6	1 907	51	125	1 677	44.2	54.6	1.1
Beaufort	254.8	2 391	40.8	20.7	4.9	0.1	2.0	258.6	2 426	2 153	11 430	5 769	39.6	57.9	2.5
Berkeley	188.6	1 404	67.7	1.7	4.3	0.3	1.8	264.3	1 968	342	793	6 434	40.9	57.2	1.9
Calhoun	20.4	1 479	75.7	2.7	4.1	0.2	0.0	4.0	290	34	81	938	48.1	50.5	1.5
Charleston	707.7	2 485	35.5	2.6	7.4	0.4	2.3	1 140.0	4 003	8 520	10 282	31 744	44.4	52.2	3.3
Cherokee	83.0	1 716	67.4	1.4	4.6	0.2	2.2	1 403.9	29 033	94	283	2 032	37.6	60.7	1.7
Chester	60.3	1 789	64.7	2.8	4.4	0.3	1.8	82.8	2 455	70	198	2 487	50.2	47.8	2.0
Chesterfield	61.0	1 524	70.8	1.1	5.7	0.4	2.8	23.5	586	97	237	1 963	48.8	50.0	1.2
Clarendon	56.1	1 830	57.9	23.6	3.5	0.1	1.9	21.8	710	71	177	1 952	53.1	45.9	0.9
Colleton	62.2	1 679	61.5	3.4	6.3	0.9	2.3	15.5	419	105	215	2 097	48.2	50.5	1.3
Darlington	93.8	1 426	67.6	1.3	5.1	0.3	2.4	48.8	743	120	382	2 937	46.9	51.6	1.5
Dillon	49.7	1 673	64.2	1.0	4.9	0.2	2.9	15.6	524	86	171	1 458	54.8	44.2	0.9
Dorchester	145.0	1 598	72.9	1.0	3.4	0.4	2.9	106.5	1 174	179	508	4 716	36.2	61.6	2.2
Edgefield	34.5	1 748	64.7	2.7	4.2	0.2	5.4	20.7	1 048	321	115	1 030	44.7	53.9	1.4
Fairfield	53.7	2 398	62.8	2.0	4.5	0.4	1.9	38.4	1 717	43	129	1 460	62.7	35.9	1.5
Florence	195.4	1 571	63.5	1.1	5.0	0.6	1.8	270.0	2 171	707	721	11 233	41.4	57.1	1.5
Georgetown	114.8	2 194	57.4	1.6	5.0	0.2	2.5	181.2	3 462	98	340	3 786	46.4	51.8	1.8
Greenville	1 006.4	2 888	29.9	41.5	3.0	0.0	0.7	631.8	1 813	1 722	2 076	21 976	31.2	66.1	2.7
Greenwood	177.7	2 806	34.3	47.8	2.8	0.1	1.6	87.8	1 386	199	366	6 235	39.0	58.5	2.5
Hampton	42.5	2 231	60.1	3.7	4.6	0.4	2.3	8.7	456	376	111	1 180	63.1	36.1	0.8
Horry	446.4	2 639	45.2	9.2	4.8	0.3	4.0	435.0	2 571	433	1 008	9 429	40.9	56.5	2.6
Jasper	29.2	1 724	51.1	4.0	7.5	0.4	2.6	18.3	1 079	41	98	1 076	56.4	37.3	6.3
Kershaw	127.5	2 671	38.8	38.8	2.1	1.2	0.8	62.9	1 317	111	280	3 193	37.7	60.5	1.7
Lancaster	77.5	1 339	66.7	2.5	6.4	0.2	2.1	72.0	1 244	102	339	2 421	42.4	56.4	1.2
Laurens	107.8	1 741	42.0	27.5	3.7	0.2	2.9	73.3	1 185	103	370	4 251	38.8	59.3	1.9
Lee	24.8	1 226	69.9	0.5	3.2	0.0	1.8	4.9	244	43	117	865	58.7	40.3	1.0
Lexington	576.5	2 877	43.0	38.0	2.9	0.1	0.8	336.6	1 680	497	1 183	11 300	27.5	69.9	2.6
McCormick	15.2	1 600	52.8	2.4	3.8	0.1	2.3	20.4	2 136	90	55	963	51.8	46.5	1.7
Marion	102.0	2 922	36.2	43.1	3.3	0.1	2.6	64.6	1 851	87	199	2 549	60.6	38.6	0.9
Marlboro	50.8	1 717	57.5	0.5	5.2	0.2	1.1	31.8	1 075	81	170	1 742	64.2	34.2	1.6
Newberry	52.0	1 520	69.6	0.7	4.6	0.4	2.3	28.0	818	147	198	1 997	35.8	60.6	3.7
Oconee	103.9	1 637	70.8	0.5	4.5	0.2	4.4	83.0	1 309	163	369	3 338	32.1	65.2	2.7
Orangeburg	232.1	2 653	46.6	33.1	1.7	0.1	1.2	101.2	1 156	234	522	7 130	60.5	38.7	0.8
Pickens	127.5	1 219	64.8	1.2	5.2	0.3	3.3	79.7	762	224	633	7 489	25.8	71.4	2.8
Richland	815.1	2 685	33.6	32.3	4.1	0.2	1.1	676.5	2 228	7 797	11 747	52 685	54.3	43.0	2.6
Saluda	18.7	1 115	63.3	0.7	5.3	0.3	2.5	6.1	363	44	98	826	38.9	59.5	1.6
Spartanburg	407.0	1 662	62.5	1.9	5.1	0.3	2.4	1 121.9	4 579	513	1 433	15 126	35.4	62.4	2.3

1. Based on the resident population estimated as of July 1 of the year shown.

Table B. States and Counties — **Land Area and Population**

STATE/ County code	MSA/ PMSA/ NECMA code[1]	County Type[2]	STATE County	Land area,[3] (sq km) 1990	Total persons	Rank	Per square kilometer	White	Black	Am. Indian, Eskimo, Aleut	Asian and Pacific Islander	Percent Hispanic[4]	Under 5 years	5 to 17 years	18 to 24 years	25 to 34 years	35 to 44 years	45 to 54 years
				1	2	3	4	5	6	7	8	9	10	11	12	13	14	15
			SOUTH CAROLINA— Cont'd															
45 085	8140	3	Sumter	1 724	112 412	469	65.2	54.5	44.1	0.2	1.2	1.8	7.2	19.4	10.7	16.4	15.9	12.3
45 087	...	6	Union	1 332	30 356	1 366	22.8	69.3	30.4	0.1	0.2	0.3	5.4	17.6	8.4	12.6	15.7	14.5
45 089	...	6	Williamsburg	2 419	36 840	1 166	15.2	35.5	64.3	0.1	0.1	0.4	6.5	23.0	9.3	11.7	15.5	12.6
45 091	1520	2	York	1 768	158 180	327	89.5	78.2	20.5	0.6	0.7	1.0	6.7	17.9	10.5	14.1	16.6	14.3
46 000	...	X	SOUTH DAKOTA	196 575	733 133	X	3.7	90.4	0.7	8.2	0.7	1.2	6.8	20.2	10.7	11.7	15.3	12.6
46 003	...	9	Aurora	1 834	3 005	2 988	1.6	98.7	0.0	1.2	0.1	0.3	5.2	22.1	5.7	8.8	13.2	12.8
46 005	...	7	Beadle	3 262	16 637	1 960	5.1	97.9	0.5	1.2	0.4	0.7	6.1	18.3	8.2	10.7	14.9	13.2
46 007	...	9	Bennett	3 070	3 311	2 970	1.1	49.3	0.4	50.2	0.1	1.0	8.9	28.0	9.2	11.3	13.1	10.9
46 009	...	9	Bon Homme	1 459	7 185	2 665	4.9	95.5	0.4	4.0	0.1	0.9	5.3	17.5	8.6	12.4	14.3	12.2
46 011	...	7	Brookings	2 058	25 931	1 497	12.6	97.1	0.5	0.7	1.6	0.5	5.3	16.1	26.0	10.9	13.5	10.5
46 013	...	5	Brown	4 436	35 231	1 218	7.9	95.8	0.2	3.4	0.6	0.5	5.7	18.0	12.8	11.1	15.4	12.7
46 015	...	9	Brule	2 121	5 503	2 807	2.6	91.8	0.2	7.6	0.3	0.8	6.6	24.4	6.6	10.4	13.4	12.5
46 017	...	9	Buffalo	1 219	1 773	3 079	1.5	20.8	0.2	78.7	0.3	0.3	11.4	33.3	10.2	12.7	10.4	10.4
46 019	...	6	Butte	5 824	8 763	2 527	1.5	96.9	0.4	2.3	0.3	4.6	7.1	20.6	7.5	11.1	15.8	13.6
46 021	...	9	Campbell	1 906	1 847	3 072	1.0	99.7	0.1	0.2	0.0	0.5	5.2	15.1	4.8	8.9	11.5	14.1
46 023	...	9	Charles Mix	2 845	9 192	2 493	3.2	74.8	0.1	25.0	0.1	0.5	7.5	23.9	7.2	9.4	12.9	12.9
46 025	...	9	Clark	2 481	4 291	2 886	1.7	99.4	0.1	0.2	0.2	0.3	5.8	20.6	5.8	8.4	14.4	13.0
46 027	...	7	Clay	1 066	13 109	2 205	12.3	94.1	0.6	3.8	1.4	1.1	5.1	14.4	32.7	9.9	12.7	9.6
46 029	...	7	Codington	1 781	25 353	1 519	14.2	98.0	0.1	1.4	0.5	0.5	6.4	20.7	10.5	11.5	15.4	12.7
46 031	...	9	Corson	6 405	4 104	2 906	0.6	49.9	0.0	50.0	0.1	0.9	8.9	26.9	7.4	9.9	10.4	11.0
46 033	...	8	Custer	4 035	7 025	2 675	1.7	96.2	0.3	3.3	0.3	1.5	5.1	20.5	6.0	9.7	17.7	15.7
46 035	...	7	Davison	1 128	17 858	1 879	15.8	97.4	0.2	1.9	0.5	0.4	6.4	19.4	10.7	10.9	14.8	12.5
46 037	...	9	Day	2 664	6 171	2 760	2.3	91.9	0.0	8.0	0.1	0.2	6.2	19.7	6.5	9.0	13.2	12.6
46 039	...	9	Deuel	1 615	4 451	2 874	2.8	99.3	0.0	0.2	0.4	0.6	5.7	19.0	6.3	9.1	13.6	14.6
46 041	...	9	Dewey	5 964	6 002	2 771	1.0	29.3	0.2	70.2	0.3	0.7	11.0	30.4	9.5	13.4	11.6	9.6
46 043	...	9	Douglas	1 123	3 507	2 950	3.1	99.3	0.0	0.7	0.1	0.1	6.7	20.9	6.1	8.6	12.9	13.6
46 045	...	9	Edmunds	2 967	4 191	2 898	1.4	99.3	0.0	0.6	0.1	0.3	5.7	18.8	5.5	8.5	12.5	14.1
46 047	...	7	Fall River	4 506	6 823	2 696	1.5	91.9	0.4	7.1	0.6	2.6	4.2	17.7	5.2	8.1	16.2	14.6
46 049	...	9	Faulk	2 591	2 500	3 022	1.0	99.6	0.0	0.3	0.1	0.4	5.8	18.0	5.8	8.6	12.4	14.7
46 051	...	7	Grant	1 768	7 952	2 604	4.5	98.8	0.3	0.7	0.3	0.5	5.9	21.7	6.8	10.6	15.5	12.4
46 053	...	9	Gregory	2 631	4 909	2 847	1.9	93.6	0.0	6.2	0.1	0.7	5.9	20.3	5.0	8.9	13.0	12.8
46 055	...	9	Haakon	4 696	2 314	3 031	0.5	96.7	0.4	1.6	1.3	0.7	6.1	26.4	6.3	10.3	15.9	11.7
46 057	...	9	Hamlin	1 324	5 414	2 810	4.1	99.4	0.1	0.3	0.3	0.5	6.1	21.5	7.0	8.5	14.2	12.5
46 059	...	9	Hand	3 721	4 141	2 904	1.1	99.2	0.1	0.2	0.4	0.5	5.6	20.1	5.9	8.9	13.7	14.1
46 061	...	9	Hanson	1 126	3 014	2 986	2.7	99.7	0.0	0.3	0.0	0.1	6.2	22.5	7.3	8.8	14.4	13.9
46 063	...	9	Harding	6 917	1 450	3 096	0.2	91.1	3.9	3.1	1.9	6.4	7.1	22.7	7.3	11.4	15.8	12.8
46 065	...	7	Hughes	1 919	15 453	2 037	8.1	91.5	0.2	7.9	0.4	1.1	6.7	21.1	7.2	11.9	18.1	13.9
46 067	...	9	Hutchinson	2 106	8 065	2 591	3.8	99.5	0.0	0.3	0.2	0.2	5.3	18.2	5.9	8.1	13.1	13.3
46 069	...	9	Hyde	2 230	1 585	3 090	0.7	95.8	0.1	3.8	0.3	0.6	5.7	19.4	4.5	9.9	13.8	13.2
46 071	...	9	Jackson	4 841	2 949	2 992	0.6	52.9	0.3	46.5	0.3	0.5	9.0	26.8	8.7	10.0	13.4	11.8
46 073	...	9	Jerauld	1 373	2 127	3 057	1.5	99.4	0.0	0.2	0.3	0.1	4.7	18.9	5.3	7.8	13.7	14.0
46 075	...	9	Jones	2 514	1 204	3 103	0.5	99.4	0.0	0.6	0.0	0.3	7.1	19.3	6.6	9.6	15.0	14.5
46 077	...	9	Kingsbury	2 172	5 735	2 789	2.6	99.7	0.0	0.2	0.1	0.1	5.5	18.7	5.6	8.7	13.9	12.8
46 079	...	6	Lake	1 459	10 685	2 363	7.3	98.7	0.4	0.4	0.4	0.9	5.8	19.1	12.1	10.9	14.7	11.8
46 081	...	6	Lawrence	2 072	21 369	1 688	10.3	96.4	0.2	3.1	0.4	2.6	5.8	19.3	12.7	11.1	16.1	12.1
46 083	7760	3	Lincoln	1 497	21 660	1 673	14.5	98.7	0.3	0.6	0.4	0.3	7.2	22.8	7.7	12.1	18.4	13.8
46 085	...	9	Lyman	4 248	3 783	2 933	0.9	66.6	0.1	33.1	0.2	0.6	8.1	25.3	8.1	11.0	13.5	12.2
46 087	...	8	McCook	1 488	5 556	2 804	3.7	99.2	0.0	0.6	0.2	0.3	6.3	20.3	6.6	9.2	14.0	13.1
46 089	...	9	McPherson	2 945	2 693	3 010	0.9	99.8	0.1	0.1	0.1	0.0	5.1	17.5	5.2	7.7	13.6	14.7
46 091	...	9	Marshall	2 173	4 522	2 870	2.1	93.5	0.1	6.3	0.1	0.2	5.6	19.2	6.1	8.8	13.5	14.0
46 093	...	6	Meade	8 989	21 405	1 685	2.4	93.7	2.9	2.3	1.1	3.0	7.4	22.9	8.8	13.2	17.2	11.1
46 095	...	9	Mellette	3 384	2 043	3 060	0.6	48.0	0.0	51.8	0.2	0.8	9.1	27.8	8.4	10.9	12.7	10.3
46 097	...	9	Miner	1 477	2 684	3 011	1.8	97.3	1.6	0.5	0.6	2.7	6.0	19.0	6.3	9.2	12.9	12.1
46 099	7760	3	Minnehaha	2 096	142 821	370	68.1	96.6	0.9	1.7	0.9	0.9	6.8	18.4	11.6	14.0	17.1	12.9
46 101	...	8	Moody	1 346	6 432	2 738	4.8	89.5	0.2	9.9	0.4	0.3	7.0	22.8	7.6	10.2	15.5	13.3
46 103	6660	3	Pennington	7 191	88 117	569	12.3	87.9	2.2	8.4	1.5	3.4	7.9	19.2	12.1	13.7	16.0	12.2
46 105	...	9	Perkins	7 442	3 466	2 957	0.5	97.6	0.3	2.0	0.1	0.5	5.1	18.8	5.3	10.2	15.1	12.8
46 107	...	9	Potter	2 244	2 838	3 003	1.3	98.7	0.0	1.2	0.0	0.2	4.7	19.8	5.2	7.9	13.8	13.0
46 109	...	9	Roberts	2 852	9 804	2 444	3.4	73.4	0.0	26.4	0.1	0.3	7.2	22.8	8.0	9.5	13.2	12.8
46 111	...	9	Sanborn	1 474	2 680	3 013	1.8	98.5	0.8	0.1	0.5	2.1	6.6	19.9	6.4	10.2	13.6	12.7
46 113	...	7	Shannon	5 423	12 468	2 252	2.3	5.0	0.2	94.6	0.2	1.3	12.8	33.8	12.9	12.2	10.4	8.3
46 115	...	7	Spink	3 895	7 433	2 645	1.9	98.9	0.1	1.0	0.0	0.3	6.1	19.0	7.4	10.2	14.8	13.0
46 117	...	9	Stanley	3 738	2 895	2 997	0.8	92.2	0.1	7.7	0.0	0.7	6.7	23.0	8.0	10.7	15.8	16.9
46 119	...	9	Sully	2 608	1 485	3 093	0.6	98.1	0.4	1.5	0.0	0.3	4.8	20.9	7.2	11.0	13.8	17.2
46 121	...	9	Todd	3 596	9 496	2 472	2.6	15.7	0.3	83.8	0.2	1.3	12.5	33.6	11.2	12.4	11.6	7.8

1. MSA = Metropolitan Statistical Area. PMSA = Primary MSA. NECMA = New England County Metropolitan Area. See Appendix A for explanation of these concepts. See Appendix B for list of metropolitan areas identified by type, with component counties. 2. County typology code from the Economic Research Service of USDA. See Appendix A for definition. 3. Dry land or land partially or temporarily covered by water. 4. Hispanic persons may be of any race.

Table B. States and Counties — **Population and Households**

STATE County	Population, 1999 (cont'd) Age (percent) (cont'd)				Population — change and components of change, 1980-1999							Households, 1990				
					Total persons		Percent change		Components of change, 1990-1999						Percent	
	55 to 64 years	65 to 74 years	75 years and over	Percent female	1990	1980	1980–1990	1990–1999	Births	Deaths	Net migration	Number	Percent change, 1980–1990	Persons per house-hold	Female family house-holder[1]	One person
	16	17	18	19	20	21	22	23	24	25	26	27	28	29	30	31
SOUTH CAROLINA—Cont'd																
Sumter	7.8	5.9	4.5	50.6	101 276	88 243	14.8	11.0	15 692	7 622	-4 765	32 723	20.0	2.91	16.7	19.0
Union	10.6	8.0	7.2	53.6	30 337	30 764	-1.4	0.1	3 624	3 444	-80	11 407	8.0	2.64	16.0	23.6
Williamsburg	8.7	7.2	5.5	53.6	36 815	38 226	-3.7	0.1	5 044	3 471	-1 454	12 108	7.2	3.03	20.5	21.1
York	9.2	6.0	4.6	51.9	131 497	106 720	23.2	20.3	18 857	10 736	18 640	47 006	34.8	2.72	12.7	19.6
SOUTH DAKOTA	8.3	7.0	7.3	50.8	696 004	690 768	0.8	5.3	98 048	62 765	2 009	259 034	6.8	2.59	8.0	26.4
Aurora	10.6	9.5	12.2	49.1	3 135	3 628	-13.6	-4.1	315	412	-26	1 146	-7.9	2.54	4.8	27.6
Beadle	9.4	9.3	9.9	51.3	18 253	19 195	-4.9	-8.9	2 093	1 933	-1 754	7 341	0.1	2.43	6.9	29.3
Bennett	7.5	5.2	5.8	51.3	3 206	3 044	5.3	3.3	681	281	-283	1 030	7.3	3.07	12.8	24.0
Bon Homme	9.4	8.8	11.6	46.9	7 089	8 059	-12.0	1.4	742	803	169	2 647	-7.4	2.44	4.2	28.3
Brookings	6.5	5.4	5.8	48.9	25 207	24 332	3.6	2.9	3 009	1 601	-629	8 910	10.9	2.48	5.9	27.3
Brown	8.4	7.6	8.2	52.1	35 580	36 962	-3.7	-1.0	4 346	3 198	-1 408	13 867	3.8	2.45	7.8	28.4
Brule	8.8	8.4	8.9	50.1	5 485	5 245	4.6	0.3	687	465	-180	1 996	6.3	2.58	5.3	30.1
Buffalo	5.1	4.3	2.2	47.0	1 759	1 795	-2.0	0.8	373	201	-151	446	0.2	3.88	25.8	10.8
Butte	9.4	8.1	6.9	50.1	7 914	8 372	-5.5	10.7	1 169	829	529	3 033	-0.5	2.57	7.4	26.8
Campbell	10.7	15.3	14.4	49.3	1 965	2 243	-12.4	-6.0	197	158	-144	767	-4.6	2.53	3.5	23.6
Charles Mix	8.9	7.8	9.5	50.9	9 131	9 680	-5.7	0.7	1 578	995	-497	3 232	0.1	2.75	8.3	27.6
Clark	11.2	10.7	10.2	49.7	4 403	4 894	-10.0	-2.5	481	525	-56	1 700	-8.4	2.56	3.4	26.8
Clay	6.0	4.5	5.0	51.2	13 186	13 689	-3.7	-0.6	1 372	898	-549	4 433	0.2	2.40	7.7	29.2
Codington	8.1	6.8	7.8	51.1	22 698	20 885	8.7	11.7	3 328	2 067	1 466	8 739	13.9	2.55	7.3	28.1
Corson	7.6	10.0	8.0	49.8	4 195	5 196	-19.3	-2.2	751	385	-450	1 303	-10.1	3.22	13.3	21.3
Custer	10.1	8.0	7.3	49.8	6 179	6 000	3.0	13.7	642	651	883	2 352	11.8	2.52	7.7	24.0
Davison	8.6	7.4	9.3	52.0	17 503	17 820	-1.8	2.0	2 324	1 781	-122	6 948	4.4	2.44	7.3	31.6
Day	10.4	9.8	12.7	50.7	6 978	8 133	-14.2	-11.6	687	1 001	-472	2 732	-8.3	2.50	5.6	28.4
Deuel	11.6	9.2	10.9	48.4	4 522	5 289	-14.5	-1.6	529	484	-95	1 767	-5.6	2.52	4.9	25.1
Dewey	6.5	4.4	3.6	51.6	5 523	5 366	2.9	8.7	1 290	379	-411	1 721	12.4	3.21	21.2	21.6
Douglas	10.0	8.7	12.4	50.7	3 746	4 181	-10.4	-6.4	412	423	-218	1 352	-5.1	2.69	2.8	25.7
Edmunds	11.3	11.0	12.5	50.4	4 356	5 159	-15.6	-3.8	469	536	-87	1 669	-5.8	2.53	3.7	26.1
Fall River	11.9	12.0	11.0	48.1	7 353	8 439	-12.9	-7.2	699	1 062	-136	2 864	-5.3	2.34	8.3	31.6
Faulk	12.6	10.6	11.5	50.3	2 744	3 327	-17.5	-8.9	298	286	-252	1 057	-12.3	2.55	3.1	28.0
Grant	9.2	8.5	9.4	50.4	8 372	9 013	-7.1	-5.0	914	884	-425	3 154	-0.6	2.60	5.0	26.3
Gregory	9.5	11.3	13.4	51.4	5 359	6 015	-10.9	-8.4	488	650	-268	2 139	-4.3	2.47	5.4	32.3
Haakon	7.5	8.1	7.7	51.5	2 624	2 794	-6.1	-11.8	280	217	-373	926	-4.2	2.79	3.7	27.8
Hamlin	10.3	9.1	10.8	50.5	4 974	5 261	-5.5	8.8	704	670	425	1 854	-1.7	2.60	4.5	27.6
Hand	11.8	9.7	10.2	50.8	4 272	4 948	-13.7	-3.1	437	461	-95	1 625	-8.1	2.55	4.5	26.1
Hanson	10.6	8.6	7.8	49.8	2 994	3 415	-12.3	0.7	418	222	-154	1 072	-6.2	2.79	3.5	23.6
Harding	9.3	7.5	6.1	50.1	1 669	1 700	-1.8	-13.1	185	111	-285	592	1.7	2.75	4.6	23.1
Hughes	8.0	6.5	6.5	52.4	14 817	14 220	4.2	4.3	2 074	1 146	-257	5 780	11.6	2.52	8.6	28.9
Hutchinson	11.6	10.9	13.5	50.5	8 262	9 350	-11.6	-2.4	851	1 150	148	3 221	-5.3	2.47	3.6	28.2
Hyde	11.0	9.3	13.1	52.2	1 696	2 069	-18.0	-6.5	187	239	-49	680	-7.4	2.43	3.5	31.3
Jackson	7.5	6.6	6.2	50.4	2 811	3 437	-18.2	4.9	483	253	-78	903	-8.2	3.09	10.5	22.9
Jerauld	10.3	11.7	13.5	50.7	2 425	2 929	-17.2	-12.3	208	316	-182	966	-10.5	2.47	4.0	28.5
Jones	10.8	8.9	8.1	47.8	1 324	1 463	-9.5	-9.1	127	137	-105	519	-6.3	2.55	5.0	25.0
Kingsbury	11.0	10.4	13.4	51.2	5 925	6 679	-11.3	-3.2	581	865	125	2 357	-6.7	2.44	3.6	29.3
Lake	8.8	7.7	9.1	51.2	10 550	10 724	-1.6	1.3	1 086	1 043	124	4 030	2.3	2.50	5.3	28.3
Lawrence	8.0	7.6	7.5	50.8	20 655	18 339	12.6	3.5	2 372	1 750	115	7 926	17.6	2.48	8.1	28.1
Lincoln	8.2	4.3	5.4	49.8	15 427	13 942	10.7	40.4	2 239	1 275	5 234	5 461	14.1	2.77	5.2	20.3
Lyman	9.1	6.8	6.0	49.5	3 638	3 864	-5.8	4.0	616	345	-109	1 268	1.4	2.87	9.9	24.3
McCook	10.3	8.8	11.3	50.6	5 688	6 444	-11.7	-2.3	674	811	18	2 145	-5.2	2.57	4.6	26.6
McPherson	14.4	10.2	11.7	51.3	3 228	4 027	-19.8	-16.6	280	391	-400	1 332	-12.4	2.38	3.5	26.4
Marshall	10.3	10.1	12.5	50.1	4 844	5 404	-10.4	-6.6	452	531	-228	1 919	-2.4	2.49	5.5	28.2
Meade	6.7	6.7	6.0	48.8	21 878	20 717	5.6	-2.2	3 911	1 438	-3 504	7 084	11.3	2.89	7.4	18.3
Mellette	7.8	6.2	6.8	50.2	2 137	2 249	-5.0	-4.4	367	243	-207	681	-0.6	3.06	16.2	22.2
Miner	11.1	10.1	13.4	50.7	3 272	3 739	-12.5	-18.0	297	499	-385	1 276	-7.7	2.50	4.6	28.4
Minnehaha	7.7	5.9	5.6	52.0	123 809	109 435	13.1	15.4	19 287	8 991	9 110	47 681	19.0	2.50	8.8	27.0
Moody	8.5	7.4	7.7	49.9	6 507	6 692	-2.8	-1.2	711	631	-118	2 398	0.5	2.68	6.3	24.3
Pennington	7.2	6.2	5.4	50.7	81 343	70 361	15.6	8.3	13 126	5 567	-1 764	30 553	21.4	2.61	10.2	23.4
Perkins	10.7	11.1	10.9	50.0	3 932	4 700	-16.3	-11.9	396	449	-402	1 586	-9.4	2.44	5.2	28.6
Potter	10.5	11.0	14.0	51.3	3 190	3 674	-13.2	-11.0	303	411	-236	1 249	-5.2	2.50	4.8	28.2
Roberts	9.4	7.3	9.7	49.9	9 914	10 911	-9.1	-1.1	1 540	1 240	-379	3 619	-2.2	2.68	9.7	26.8
Sanborn	11.7	9.4	9.6	49.3	2 833	3 213	-11.8	-5.4	301	270	-167	1 059	-8.5	2.63	3.7	25.2
Shannon	4.7	3.0	1.9	50.3	9 902	11 323	-12.5	25.9	3 095	965	460	2 205	-4.4	4.45	33.3	12.2
Spink	10.6	9.0	9.8	51.6	7 981	9 201	-13.3	-6.9	868	894	-498	3 022	-6.6	2.51	5.7	29.4
Stanley	8.2	5.6	5.1	49.9	2 453	2 533	-3.2	18.0	317	178	312	921	6.8	2.66	10.3	24.1
Sully	10.2	7.7	7.3	48.5	1 589	1 990	-20.2	-6.5	161	103	-157	621	-9.2	2.56	3.5	23.8
Todd	5.1	3.7	2.2	50.7	8 352	7 328	14.0	13.7	2 313	643	-512	2 210	17.7	3.74	28.7	16.7

1. No spouse present.

Table B. States and Counties — Vital Statistics, Health Resources, and Crime

STATE County	Births, average 1996–1998		Deaths, average 1996–1998				Physicians,[4] 1998		Hospitals,[4] 1998			Medicare enrollees 1999	Serious crimes known to police, 1998[6]	
			Number		Rate					Beds			Total	
	Total	Rate[1]	Total	Infant[2]	Total[1]	Infant[3]	Number	Rate[5]	Number	Number	Rate[5]		Number	Rate[7]
	32	33	34	35	36	37	38	39	40	41	42	43	44	45

SOUTH CAROLINA—Cont'd														
Sumter	1 664	15.6	866	24	8.1	14.2	110	103	1	230	215	13 265	4 547	4 211
Union	380	12.4	384	5	12.5	14.0	25	82	2	117	384	5 738	984	3 156
Williamsburg	490	13.2	393	7	10.6	13.6	18	48	1	48	129	5 576	1 097	2 882
York	2 061	13.7	1 234	16	8.2	7.8	173	112	1	276	179	19 888	7 999	5 210
SOUTH DAKOTA	10 311	14.0	6 843	77	9.3	7.5	1 343	182	51	4 195	568	118 979	19 366	2 624
Aurora	32	10.7	42	0	13.8	0.0	0	0	0	0	0	623	2	66
Beadle	204	11.5	198	1	11.1	4.9	25	145	1	95	553	3 636	NA	NA
Bennett	72	21.5	34	0	10.0	4.6	3	89	1	68	2 006	427	NA	NA
Bon Homme	71	9.3	80	0	10.5	4.7	7	91	2	47	611	1 585	NA	NA
Brookings	313	12.0	186	1	7.1	4.3	20	77	1	140	539	3 218	617	2 410
Brown	466	13.0	352	3	9.9	7.2	70	198	1	203	573	6 279	987	2 765
Brule	69	12.4	49	0	8.8	4.8	10	180	1	54	972	1 014	NA	NA
Buffalo	43	24.2	23	1	13.2	15.6	1	58	0	0	0	129	NA	NA
Butte	123	13.7	97	1	10.8	5.4	6	67	1	128	1 419	1 592	NA	NA
Campbell	17	9.0	16	0	8.3	0.0	0	0	0	0	0	679	NA	NA
Charles Mix	170	18.0	101	1	10.7	3.9	7	75	2	87	932	1 717	52	548
Clark	47	10.9	58	0	13.2	7.0	0	0	0	0	0	983	NA	NA
Clay	156	10.2	105	1	6.9	6.4	9	59	1	95	626	1 494	485	3 155
Codington	368	14.5	229	4	9.0	10.9	52	204	1	119	467	4 104	NA	NA
Corson	77	18.2	38	1	9.0	12.9	0	0	0	0	0	935	10	288
Custer	60	8.8	69	0	10.1	0.0	6	87	1	11	159	1 326	NA	NA
Davison	250	13.5	193	2	10.4	8.0	36	200	1	99	550	3 471	577	3 068
Day	70	10.8	108	1	16.7	9.5	2	31	1	28	438	1 587	NA	NA
Deuel	51	11.3	54	1	11.9	26.1	3	66	1	20	443	989	32	703
Dewey	130	22.7	44	2	7.6	12.8	3	52	0	0	0	604	NA	NA
Douglas	37	10.5	45	0	12.6	0.0	2	56	1	9	253	806	1	28
Edmunds	47	11.0	56	0	13.0	7.1	4	95	1	58	1 375	1 005	5	118
Fall River	74	10.4	113	0	15.9	0.0	22	308	1	74	1 037	1 951	NA	NA
Faulk	33	12.9	26	0	10.3	10.1	1	40	1	12	476	717	12	474
Grant	93	11.6	93	1	11.6	10.7	2	25	1	115	1 426	1 603	NA	NA
Gregory	47	9.4	70	1	13.9	21.1	3	61	2	113	2 284	1 324	12	321
Haakon	28	11.3	24	0	9.7	0.0	2	85	1	50	2 125	435	NA	NA
Hamlin	81	15.1	74	0	13.8	4.1	1	19	0	0	0	1 097	NA	NA
Hand	42	10.2	44	0	10.6	0.0	2	48	1	30	724	802	NA	NA
Hanson	50	16.9	20	1	6.7	13.4	0	0	0	0	0	463	NA	NA
Harding	16	11.0	11	0	7.6	0.0	0	0	0	0	0	204	4	267
Hughes	218	14.1	130	1	8.5	4.6	21	137	1	86	559	2 246	614	3 986
Hutchinson	93	11.5	131	0	16.2	3.6	13	162	2	210	2 610	2 125	NA	NA
Hyde	18	10.9	27	0	16.4	0.0	0	0	0	0	0	380	8	485
Jackson	50	17.3	27	1	9.3	20.0	1	34	0	0	0	287	NA	NA
Jerauld	18	8.1	36	0	16.1	18.2	3	135	1	28	1 260	610	5	219
Jones	15	12.0	15	0	12.0	0.0	0	0	0	0	0	232	NA	NA
Kingsbury	67	11.5	87	0	14.9	0.0	4	70	1	17	298	1 573	22	377
Lake	116	10.7	109	0	10.1	2.9	7	63	1	49	440	2 000	205	1 925
Lawrence	230	10.3	198	1	8.9	5.8	33	147	2	64	284	3 504	NA	NA
Lincoln	276	14.2	148	2	7.6	6.0	4	20	1	28	137	1 894	NA	NA
Lyman	63	16.3	37	1	9.7	10.6	2	53	0	0	0	572	NA	NA
McCook	73	12.8	90	0	15.8	4.6	2	36	0	0	0	1 184	35	616
McPherson	24	8.6	39	0	13.9	0.0	2	73	1	25	913	607	NA	NA
Marshall	46	9.9	51	0	11.1	0.0	2	44	1	25	548	1 045	73	1 578
Meade	414	18.6	169	2	7.6	5.6	43	196	1	114	520	3 257	584	2 655
Mellette	40	19.7	19	1	9.3	33.6	0	0	0	0	0	273	NA	NA
Miner	23	8.1	52	0	18.1	0.0	1	36	0	0	0	719	44	1 504
Minnehaha	2 101	14.8	1 012	16	7.1	7.8	499	349	3	821	574	19 073	4 276	3 042
Moody	70	10.7	69	0	10.6	0.0	3	46	1	20	307	970	NA	NA
Pennington	1 322	15.2	630	9	7.2	6.6	251	286	1	328	374	11 859	5 094	5 842
Perkins	43	12.0	42	0	11.7	7.8	0	0	1	56	1 598	889	27	762
Potter	26	8.8	46	0	15.9	13.0	4	140	2	104	3 640	776	60	2 051
Roberts	162	16.4	129	2	13.1	10.3	5	51	1	31	317	1 812	NA	NA
Sanborn	30	10.8	30	0	10.9	0.0	1	36	0	0	0	636	34	1 232
Shannon	328	27.3	112	7	9.3	20.4	11	90	0	0	0	783	NA	NA
Spink	87	11.4	91	0	12.0	0.0	9	119	1	35	462	1 761	91	1 182
Stanley	30	10.2	22	0	7.7	11.2	3	102	0	0	0	369	NA	NA
Sully	15	10.1	11	0	7.0	0.0	0	0	0	0	0	259	7	455
Todd	248	26.9	64	3	7.0	13.4	12	130	0	0	0	544	NA	NA

1. Per 1,000 estimated resident population, average 1996–1998.   2. Deaths of infants under 1 year old.   3. Deaths of infants under 1 year old per 1,000 live births.   4. Data subject to copyright.   5. Per 100,000 resident population as of July 1 of the year shown.   6. Data for serious crimes have not been adjusted for underreporting; this may affect comparability between geographic areas and over time.   7. Per 100,000 population estimated by the FBI.

Table B. States and Counties — Crime, Education, Money Income, and Poverty

STATE County	Serious crimes known to police, 1998[1] (cont'd) Rate[2] Violent	Property	Education — School enrollment and attainment, 1990 Enrollment[3] Total	Percent private	Attainment[4] (percent) High school graduate or more	Bachelor's degree or more	Local government expenditures, fiscal 1997[5] Total current expenditures (mil dol)	Current expenditures per student (dollars)	Money income 1989 Per capita[6] (dollars)	Households Median Dollars	Percent change, 1979–1989 (constant 1989 dollars)	Percent with $100,000 or more	Income and poverty, 1997 Median house-hold income	Percent below poverty level All persons	Persons under 18	Persons 5–17 in families
	46	47	48	49	50	51	52	53	54	55	56	57	58	59	60	61
SOUTH CAROLINA—Cont'd																
Sumter	809	3 402	28 487	12.2	69.8	15.0	91.0	4 790	9 997	22 387	9.6	1.4	29 005	19.7	26.9	25.9
Union	600	2 556	7 089	3.6	55.0	7.2	26.5	5 083	9 669	21 526	-9.4	0.6	28 716	14.2	21.4	20.5
Williamsburg	662	2 220	11 058	9.5	55.6	9.9	34.5	5 033	7 632	18 409	-6.6	1.0	22 448	28.3	39.0	35.3
York	889	4 321	34 511	9.2	67.5	16.9	133.0	5 082	13 306	31 288	9.3	3.0	39 728	11.0	17.0	15.7
SOUTH DAKOTA	154	2 470	185 246	10.4	77.1	17.2	627.0	4 375	10 661	22 503	2.1	1.7	31 354	14.0	19.0	17.1
Aurora	33	33	782	3.3	70.2	11.0	3.0	4 819	8 129	16 497	-5.1	1.0	26 723	15.1	22.6	18.8
Beadle	NA	NA	4 250	14.1	75.7	15.1	15.1	4 729	10 373	22 425	-0.1	0.9	32 620	11.5	14.8	13.8
Bennett	NA	NA	891	2.0	67.7	10.4	3.3	5 320	7 841	16 864	1.6	1.8	22 345	36.1	46.5	42.1
Bon Homme	NA	NA	1 438	12.2	68.0	11.3	6.8	4 348	8 208	17 778	-0.6	0.7	28 703	13.7	17.1	15.0
Brookings	86	2 324	10 655	2.7	82.2	27.3	19.5	4 473	9 926	21 807	-4.3	1.1	35 097	11.1	11.4	10.3
Brown	115	2 650	9 663	10.5	77.9	20.7	26.4	4 640	11 579	22 967	-2.4	1.6	35 046	10.6	13.5	11.6
Brule	NA	NA	1 478	21.4	73.4	14.9	6.3	4 656	9 681	21 184	11.2	1.3	30 971	15.8	21.8	21.6
Buffalo	NA	NA	645	8.2	61.2	4.2	0.0	0	5 067	14 566	-4.4	1.4	18 444	38.9	43.2	41.9
Butte	NA	NA	1 937	3.2	74.5	12.3	8.2	4 118	9 843	19 811	-8.9	1.3	28 585	18.2	26.0	22.8
Campbell	NA	NA	323	0.0	65.5	10.7	1.7	5 012	8 678	17 202	13.6	1.6	24 400	17.0	25.6	21.9
Charles Mix	84	464	2 282	15.6	67.5	9.9	8.5	4 463	7 475	16 541	-2.5	0.8	26 551	23.9	30.5	27.4
Clark	NA	NA	972	10.5	70.4	9.8	3.9	4 192	9 280	19 035	12.2	0.9	28 449	14.2	17.6	17.1
Clay	130	3 025	6 596	3.7	84.4	36.3	7.8	4 843	9 160	19 392	-2.1	0.8	31 147	19.1	21.3	18.5
Codington	NA	NA	5 633	6.7	76.0	12.9	20.7	4 271	10 508	21 816	-4.0	1.5	34 621	10.9	14.0	12.1
Corson	0	288	1 267	0.2	63.3	10.5	5.1	6 306	6 299	14 324	-10.4	0.3	19 878	37.4	45.8	42.8
Custer	NA	NA	1 485	5.5	80.4	17.5	5.8	4 816	10 942	22 662	-10.8	1.5	31 095	13.5	19.7	17.2
Davison	122	2 946	4 616	19.6	75.9	14.8	15.6	4 636	10 105	20 733	-0.2	1.1	33 409	12.7	16.3	14.9
Day	NA	NA	1 568	7.4	69.2	11.3	6.6	5 106	9 191	18 760	4.9	1.1	26 542	18.0	24.0	21.9
Deuel	66	637	988	4.7	69.2	9.7	2.7	4 192	9 117	17 784	4.0	1.1	28 800	12.2	15.8	14.4
Dewey	NA	NA	1 780	2.2	67.1	10.4	5.3	6 667	6 515	14 599	-18.1	1.3	22 027	32.9	36.7	34.4
Douglas	0	28	892	20.9	58.0	11.2	2.4	4 684	7 869	17 067	9.2	0.7	29 365	13.5	16.9	16.7
Edmunds	71	47	894	9.6	64.2	11.3	3.8	4 637	8 792	20 569	19.8	0.8	30 611	11.7	13.9	14.2
Fall River	NA	NA	1 765	3.9	74.1	16.3	6.7	5 079	10 944	20 483	-14.4	1.5	28 440	16.5	22.8	18.7
Faulk	0	474	558	9.1	67.1	10.6	2.4	4 256	8 653	18 709	17.6	0.5	27 522	15.0	18.9	19.2
Grant	NA	NA	2 053	12.8	74.0	9.3	7.7	4 707	10 394	23 431	10.8	1.4	34 381	10.4	13.4	11.7
Gregory	53	268	1 275	0.8	70.3	11.8	5.2	4 687	8 906	16 848	13.0	1.2	24 383	21.1	29.2	24.9
Haakon	NA	NA	736	0.5	83.6	12.7	2.9	4 438	10 117	21 166	4.6	3.5	31 256	13.2	17.4	15.8
Hamlin	NA	NA	1 183	6.5	69.5	11.2	5.8	4 245	9 086	19 949	20.2	1.0	30 161	12.7	16.8	14.9
Hand	NA	NA	940	16.9	73.4	12.8	3.6	5 301	9 305	19 310	11.3	1.0	28 776	14.7	19.4	18.6
Hanson	NA	NA	659	8.6	73.1	15.3	2.6	4 794	9 846	21 920	30.7	0.6	33 830	11.8	14.8	14.4
Harding	0	267	406	3.9	82.8	16.2	1.8	5 097	8 555	20 217	-2.6	1.0	27 927	13.7	17.6	18.1
Hughes	162	3 824	3 750	10.4	84.5	25.6	14.5	4 706	12 263	27 058	-7.5	1.2	40 724	10.4	14.5	12.5
Hutchinson	NA	NA	1 722	7.3	62.6	11.3	8.4	4 599	9 514	18 832	9.4	1.2	30 293	13.2	16.0	14.8
Hyde	121	364	366	0.5	71.2	14.5	1.6	4 974	9 648	19 907	0.6	1.0	29 022	16.7	24.5	21.2
Jackson	NA	NA	767	1.7	68.9	10.9	2.1	4 974	6 947	17 246	-15.5	0.6	23 783	33.5	40.7	38.6
Jerauld	0	219	509	3.1	68.0	11.3	2.8	5 180	9 867	18 588	4.6	1.0	28 026	13.9	18.3	17.0
Jones	NA	NA	277	2.5	75.7	14.4	1.2	3 990	9 592	21 202	6.9	0.8	30 038	14.3	20.4	19.9
Kingsbury	17	360	1 250	3.6	74.0	11.6	6.2	4 510	9 857	20 290	13.5	1.0	30 938	10.6	13.3	12.7
Lake	75	1 850	2 933	5.8	79.6	18.5	10.0	4 384	11 388	23 674	17.4	1.4	34 130	10.9	13.9	12.1
Lawrence	NA	NA	6 024	4.9	81.7	19.2	16.6	4 410	11 378	24 815	8.9	1.4	31 934	12.7	15.9	13.8
Lincoln	NA	NA	4 083	7.9	79.5	16.4	13.4	3 930	12 246	28 543	11.9	3.1	45 830	5.7	7.5	6.7
Lyman	NA	NA	992	11.6	71.0	10.5	2.4	5 705	9 724	21 993	16.7	2.9	27 283	24.3	32.7	30.3
McCook	0	616	1 314	11.0	71.6	11.9	5.3	4 650	9 542	20 764	10.1	1.1	32 417	12.0	15.8	13.6
McPherson	NA	NA	571	2.1	46.0	10.0	2.7	5 106	8 790	15 345	2.0	2.1	23 815	14.5	18.6	18.6
Marshall	22	1 556	942	2.1	65.7	10.2	4.3	4 704	8 799	18 305	6.4	1.0	28 428	13.7	18.6	16.7
Meade	95	2 560	6 198	5.5	81.8	16.4	14.4	4 405	9 725	24 672	-0.9	0.6	34 655	11.4	15.6	13.1
Mellette	NA	NA	641	6.1	68.0	12.3	2.7	5 383	6 964	14 539	-10.3	1.3	20 688	33.4	39.0	37.7
Miner	205	1 299	686	2.0	71.3	10.3	2.7	4 392	9 711	18 750	32.7	1.7	28 085	16.1	20.6	19.1
Minnehaha	255	2 787	31 148	22.4	83.1	21.3	112.7	4 683	13 345	27 764	-1.9	2.6	39 992	8.7	12.1	9.7
Moody	NA	NA	1 589	4.0	74.6	13.9	5.6	4 343	10 169	23 926	12.5	1.2	35 199	10.9	13.8	13.1
Pennington	352	5 490	21 946	9.7	84.8	21.2	81.5	4 471	12 031	25 340	1.5	2.4	34 507	14.3	20.6	18.1
Perkins	28	734	804	2.1	72.5	12.7	4.4	5 940	10 982	19 862	-2.9	2.0	26 543	16.4	23.3	20.2
Potter	68	1 983	730	14.4	71.1	12.3	3.2	5 494	10 177	20 674	9.5	1.7	31 174	12.8	16.8	15.7
Roberts	NA	NA	2 427	7.5	63.5	10.1	10.1	4 977	7 981	17 480	1.2	0.9	25 808	21.9	29.0	26.0
Sanborn	0	1 232	661	3.6	73.9	16.4	2.9	4 551	8 956	19 818	48.3	1.2	28 842	13.6	15.9	17.3
Shannon	NA	NA	3 534	12.7	59.4	10.7	8.1	7 961	3 417	11 105	-33.4	0.0	17 814	42.9	46.2	43.8
Spink	52	1 130	1 678	4.7	72.8	12.7	8.1	4 860	9 674	19 398	-4.2	1.6	28 412	14.3	17.6	17.0
Stanley	NA	NA	661	5.3	77.5	14.6	2.7	4 108	10 759	22 321	-10.1	2.9	33 630	10.9	15.0	13.7
Sully	65	390	383	2.9	78.9	12.9	2.6	6 171	11 559	23 601	18.6	3.8	34 072	10.1	12.4	12.3
Todd	NA	NA	3 124	5.2	67.2	11.8	12.4	5 766	5 043	13 327	-17.7	0.5	18 032	46.1	49.7	49.2

1. Data for serious crimes have not been adjusted for underreporting; this may affect comparability between geographic areas and over time.   2. Per 100,000 population estimated by the FBI.   3. All persons 3 years old and over enrolled in nursery school through college.   4. Persons 25 years old and over.   5. Elementary and secondary education expenditures, local government fiscal years ending between July 1, 1996 and June 30, 1997.   6. Based on population enumerated as of April 1, 1990.

Table B. States and Counties — **Personal Income**

STATE County	Total (mil dol) [62]	Percent change, 1997–1998 [63]	Per capita[1] Dollars [64]	Rank [65]	Wages and salaries[2] (mil dol) [66]	Proprietor's income (mil dol) [67]	Dividends, interest, and rent (mil dol) [68]	Transfer payments Total (mil dol) [69]	Gov't payments to individuals Total (mil dol) [70]	Social Security (mil dol) [71]	Medical payments (mil dol) [72]	Income mainte-nance (mil dol) [73]	Unemploy-ment insurance (mil dol) [74]
SOUTH CAROLINA—Cont'd													
Sumter	1 943	4.7	17 294	2 532	1 341	84	290	363	344	121	133	58	5
Union	548	3.0	17 967	2 353	279	20	77	124	119	56	44	10	3
Williamsburg	559	3.6	15 111	2 922	249	26	72	159	153	47	68	29	4
York	3 710	6.1	24 051	631	1 912	184	534	442	415	205	145	32	9
SOUTH DAKOTA	17 331	5.8	23 715	X	9 599	2 311	3 923	2 430	2 314	1 054	873	176	15
Aurora	58	2.3	19 194	1 985	18	11	18	11	11	5	5	1	0
Beadle	410	-0.8	23 944	654	203	52	108	70	68	31	28	3	0
Bennett	49	4.1	14 403	2 976	19	5	11	14	13	4	5	3	0
Bon Homme	140	6.5	19 356	1 934	49	28	40	27	25	13	10	2	0
Brookings	590	6.6	22 729	909	375	48	131	67	62	29	21	3	0
Brown	919	4.0	25 960	402	497	133	226	125	119	56	47	6	0
Brule	115	7.1	20 883	1 431	43	21	33	20	19	8	8	1	0
Buffalo	21	0.2	11 952	3 087	14	2	3	9	8	1	3	2	0
Butte	147	1.2	16 522	2 706	55	17	41	30	28	14	9	2	0
Campbell	39	13.0	20 639	1 515	10	11	10	8	8	4	3	1	0
Charles Mix	190	0.1	20 467	1 571	72	50	45	39	37	14	15	5	0
Clark	88	0.8	20 331	1 621	23	27	22	16	15	8	5	1	0
Clay	269	4.9	20 427	1 584	123	37	57	38	36	14	13	2	0
Codington	620	5.1	24 393	576	385	73	140	75	71	37	26	4	1
Corson	53	8.0	12 636	3 080	18	5	11	18	18	4	8	4	0
Custer	124	6.2	17 856	2 390	49	9	35	24	23	12	7	1	0
Davison	449	5.2	25 320	460	260	49	113	68	65	30	28	4	0
Day	124	3.4	19 372	1 926	44	21	34	27	26	13	10	2	0
Deuel	99	12.3	21 975	1 108	32	26	21	16	15	8	6	1	0
Dewey	80	5.5	13 650	3 033	48	3	13	20	19	4	6	4	0
Douglas	74	-0.2	21 071	1 369	23	22	16	13	13	6	5	1	0
Edmunds	104	10.6	24 611	545	23	29	29	17	17	8	7	1	0
Fall River	143	3.8	20 765	1 466	76	7	36	35	34	15	11	2	0
Faulk	62	15.7	24 537	554	14	19	17	12	11	6	5	1	0
Grant	188	2.7	23 321	788	88	40	42	29	27	14	10	1	0
Gregory	104	3.8	20 895	1 425	31	23	29	21	21	10	8	2	0
Haakon	56	18.2	23 735	691	19	17	15	7	7	4	2	1	0
Hamlin	106	13.8	19 821	1 774	28	23	23	19	18	9	7	1	0
Hand	90	14.0	21 515	1 250	26	21	29	15	14	7	5	1	0
Hanson	57	18.4	19 458	1 907	11	17	15	8	7	4	2	1	0
Harding	16	-5.6	11 002	3 094	9	-4	8	3	3	2	1	0	0
Hughes	412	6.9	26 857	316	264	38	99	46	43	22	16	2	0
Hutchinson	183	7.6	22 760	903	57	43	52	34	33	17	13	2	0
Hyde	36	18.7	22 232	1 032	11	8	11	6	6	3	2	0	0
Jackson	39	-0.5	13 271	3 055	14	4	11	11	10	3	3	2	0
Jerauld	53	3.7	23 822	676	16	15	12	10	10	5	4	1	0
Jones	30	14.3	24 046	633	10	9	7	4	3	2	1	0	0
Kingsbury	138	8.2	24 041	635	41	36	35	25	24	12	10	1	0
Lake	251	6.7	23 529	738	116	42	50	38	36	18	13	2	0
Lawrence	448	0.6	20 437	1 580	252	45	122	71	67	34	23	4	1
Lincoln	499	7.3	24 417	574	126	76	75	44	41	24	13	2	0
Lyman	78	14.0	20 720	1 477	27	18	16	14	14	5	5	2	0
McCook	123	5.8	21 886	1 130	33	32	27	21	20	10	8	1	0
McPherson	55	12.0	20 046	1 699	13	14	16	11	11	6	3	1	0
Marshall	103	0.8	22 633	943	35	25	27	17	17	9	6	1	0
Meade	501	7.0	23 182	824	158	67	101	60	57	25	19	3	0
Mellette	27	5.6	13 233	3 060	7	3	6	9	9	2	4	2	0
Miner	62	2.7	22 142	1 049	17	16	14	12	11	6	4	1	0
Minnehaha	4 186	7.0	29 817	171	3 037	411	809	393	370	182	142	18	2
Moody	155	6.2	23 904	661	55	38	30	19	18	9	6	1	0
Pennington	2 083	4.6	23 858	671	1 370	160	520	275	262	115	94	20	2
Perkins	73	7.4	20 983	1 399	27	11	23	15	14	8	5	1	0
Potter	81	18.7	28 398	219	21	22	27	12	12	6	4	1	0
Roberts	172	-0.6	17 438	2 500	60	36	39	37	36	15	13	4	0
Sanborn	65	4.6	23 908	660	15	14	21	10	10	4	4	1	0
Shannon	133	11.1	10 885	3 095	86	6	8	51	49	5	19	16	1
Spink	178	-1.1	23 648	713	56	41	40	47	46	15	28	2	0
Stanley	62	14.4	21 186	1 335	23	6	16	7	7	4	2	0	0
Sully	51	34.9	34 804	65	11	23	11	4	4	3	1	0	0
Todd	98	7.4	10 507	3 098	61	1	7	37	35	4	14	11	0

1. Based on the resident population estimated as of July 1 of the year shown. 2. Includes other labor income.

STATE County	Earnings, 1998									Social Security bene- ficiaries, December 1998		Housing units, 1990	
			Percent by selected industries										
			Goods-related[1]		Service-related and other[2]							Supple- mental Security Income recipients, December 1998	
	Total (mil dol)	Farm	Total	Manu- facturing	Total	Retail trade	Finance, insur- ance, and real estate	Services	Govern- ment	Number	Rate[3]		Total	Percent change, 1980– 1990
	75	76	77	78	79	80	81	82	83	84	85	86	87	88
SOUTH CAROLINA—Cont'd														
Sumter	1 425	0.5	D	25.2	D	8.4	3.2	17.0	31.8	16 416	153	4 494	35 016	18.4
Union	299	0.4	D	48.6	D	7.9	2.7	10.1	23.2	7 018	230	962	12 230	7.4
Williamsburg	275	2.3	37.0	31.4	38.0	8.6	3.5	13.6	22.6	7 011	189	2 437	13 265	6.1
York	2 096	0.4	D	24.9	D	10.4	3.5	23.9	13.2	23 904	155	2 434	50 438	36.4
SOUTH DAKOTA	11 910	7.9	20.9	14.2	54.2	10.0	7.0	23.8	17.0	134 728	183	13 172	292 436	5.6
Aurora	29	20.3	4.9	2.3	D	7.9	4.7	D	29.2	733	246	45	1 342	-7.4
Beadle	255	7.5	D	11.8	D	8.7	4.5	24.2	19.0	3 977	231	352	8 093	-1.7
Bennett	25	13.6	D	D	D	14.1	2.0	6.8	40.2	529	156	180	1 292	12.7
Bon Homme	77	22.3	17.3	11.5	D	9.4	D	16.4	19.3	1 756	228	80	3 087	-4.7
Brookings	423	6.3	D	28.1	D	8.2	3.4	11.1	28.0	3 591	138	210	9 824	8.3
Brown	629	5.9	18.3	12.5	61.0	11.1	6.0	29.8	14.9	6 973	197	543	15 101	2.9
Brule	64	14.0	D	2.5	D	15.0	4.5	28.0	15.6	1 103	199	88	2 275	4.8
Buffalo	16	8.5	D	D	D	D	D	35.5	44.6	223	128	106	535	7.2
Butte	73	-2.1	D	3.0	D	15.0	5.0	21.1	21.6	1 845	205	159	3 502	2.9
Campbell	22	39.6	D	D	D	5.1	D	4.7	11.9	546	285	31	944	-1.7
Charles Mix	122	22.3	7.7	3.5	51.8	9.1	3.6	23.1	18.2	1 954	209	286	3 751	-1.3
Clark	49	46.7	D	D	D	5.7	2.3	8.0	12.2	1 112	256	72	2 026	-6.9
Clay	160	10.5	D	2.4	D	8.5	2.6	16.4	45.5	1 704	112	105	4 892	-0.6
Codington	458	4.8	34.3	27.7	49.6	12.7	4.9	19.4	11.4	4 650	183	357	9 539	12.1
Corson	23	14.6	D	D	D	4.1	1.4	19.1	44.6	611	146	241	1 557	-7.5
Custer	57	-7.8	D	3.3	D	14.7	3.1	24.6	39.9	1 560	225	93	3 003	7.8
Davison	309	4.6	D	18.0	D	15.8	4.3	29.8	11.2	3 807	211	384	7 490	3.6
Day	65	20.1	D	13.7	D	7.6	5.4	15.0	16.3	1 775	277	132	3 914	-3.0
Deuel	58	32.7	19.2	13.6	37.8	5.8	4.7	9.5	10.3	1 119	248	65	2 208	-5.2
Dewey	51	-3.4	6.4	1.8	D	6.3	4.1	D	41.8	742	127	314	2 123	13.5
Douglas	44	33.4	D	5.6	D	6.1	2.7	17.2	10.3	865	243	55	1 517	-4.9
Edmunds	52	43.9	7.1	1.1	32.9	7.2	3.1	8.6	16.1	1 084	257	52	2 004	-5.1
Fall River	83	-5.3	D	2.1	D	12.0	2.4	13.8	47.3	2 071	290	195	3 692	-7.6
Faulk	33	51.6	D	D	D	9.4	D	8.6	12.4	738	293	45	1 286	-9.8
Grant	128	22.6	D	12.5	D	7.6	7.4	14.7	8.9	1 811	225	111	3 549	-0.5
Gregory	54	19.9	D	2.8	D	12.9	5.5	20.0	14.2	1 436	290	130	2 595	-0.6
Haakon	36	28.3	D	10.8	D	8.8	4.7	20.4	11.7	451	192	24	1 071	-5.1
Hamlin	51	34.6	D	7.6	D	7.0	3.5	9.3	21.3	1 213	227	61	2 500	-2.1
Hand	47	37.3	D	3.3	D	7.1	4.4	16.2	13.0	995	240	48	2 053	1.7
Hanson	28	48.9	D	8.0	D	4.5	4.3	4.3	12.1	524	179	26	1 232	-1.7
Harding	6	-89.1	D	D	D	16.3	D	48.2	58.9	251	170	9	776	-3.4
Hughes	302	4.0	D	1.3	D	10.3	6.5	24.3	43.3	2 646	172	247	6 255	11.6
Hutchinson	100	35.1	12.5	8.6	41.1	7.5	4.8	17.6	11.4	2 336	290	101	3 657	-5.4
Hyde	19	30.1	7.3	2.2	50.3	12.2	2.5	12.0	12.3	420	262	31	816	-5.4
Jackson	18	10.2	D	2.9	D	15.2	D	15.0	37.0	468	161	36	1 147	-11.5
Jerauld	31	18.4	D	D	D	6.7	3.7	29.0	13.7	658	296	37	1 182	-2.3
Jones	19	26.5	D	D	D	22.8	3.3	13.3	13.5	260	213	13	699	-3.6
Kingsbury	77	36.9	16.8	12.1	35.9	6.2	5.2	11.6	10.4	1 623	284	80	2 765	-9.1
Lake	158	13.6	D	17.7	D	10.1	3.9	16.9	15.7	2 268	204	148	5 148	1.3
Lawrence	297	0.0	29.6	7.7	52.8	11.3	3.1	34.0	17.6	4 014	178	281	9 092	14.3
Lincoln	202	19.6	24.4	13.0	46.3	9.4	2.8	19.2	9.7	2 907	142	96	5 823	8.9
Lyman	45	31.0	D	D	D	9.3	3.6	23.9	16.1	670	178	83	1 523	-3.5
McCook	64	39.3	13.4	10.9	35.4	7.5	3.0	12.1	11.9	1 331	238	58	2 371	-8.3
McPherson	27	33.9	12.7	6.8	D	5.9	5.5	15.9	14.5	924	337	49	1 566	-7.8
Marshall	60	33.7	D	20.2	D	4.3	4.8	9.1	13.6	1 165	255	65	2 640	-4.5
Meade	226	1.9	D	5.2	D	9.5	4.1	16.2	36.8	3 335	152	252	7 592	7.0
Mellette	10	26.0	D	D	D	8.8	D	3.7	35.1	310	153	135	910	4.8
Miner	33	36.7	D	D	D	7.6	2.9	23.9	13.3	778	278	34	1 474	-11.0
Minnehaha	3 448	1.0	D	13.9	D	9.8	12.4	29.3	9.7	21 104	148	1 862	49 780	16.6
Moody	93	31.1	D	D	D	4.0	2.5	18.9	16.1	1 208	186	67	2 666	-2.3
Pennington	1 530	0.3	16.8	8.6	59.2	13.0	6.2	28.2	23.7	14 168	162	1 669	33 741	19.6
Perkins	38	10.8	D	D	D	9.7	5.2	19.1	18.9	1 001	286	75	2 007	-3.6
Potter	44	43.8	D	5.0	D	5.1	4.1	13.5	12.5	815	285	35	1 664	8.5
Roberts	96	25.4	D	4.5	D	8.8	4.4	22.2	19.5	2 106	215	257	4 728	-0.8
Sanborn	29	36.1	D	D	D	6.3	2.0	9.1	13.3	660	241	48	1 326	-7.8
Shannon	92	3.8	3.6	0.0	D	3.6	D	43.9	38.7	1 122	92	1 035	2 699	1.2
Spink	97	31.2	4.6	1.4	37.2	7.3	3.9	12.0	27.0	1 894	250	178	3 545	-6.7
Stanley	29	12.1	41.2	1.0	D	9.2	D	7.7	13.8	438	150	22	1 056	9.1
Sully	34	67.9	D	D	D	6.8	2.7	2.4	9.3	325	221	14	811	-2.4
Todd	63	-1.6	D	D	D	5.2	D	38.6	43.7	689	75	571	2 572	8.7

1. Covers mining, construction, and manufacturing. 2. Covers private sector earnings in agricultural services, forestry, and fisheries; transportation and public utilities; wholesale trade; retail trade; finance, insurance, and real estate; and services. 3. Per 1,000 resident population estimated as of July 1 of the year shown.

Table B. States and Counties — **Housing, Labor Force, and Employment**

	Housing units, 1990 (cont'd)									Civilian labor force, 1999				Civilian employment, 1990[5]		
	Occupied units											Unemployment			Percent	
			Owner-occupied				Renter-occupied									
					Owner cost as a percent of income											
STATE County	Total	Percent	Median value[1]	With a mort-gage	Without a mort-gage	Median rent[2]	Rent as per-cent of income	Sub-stand-ard units[3] (percent)		Total	Percent change, 1998–1999	Total	Rate[4]	Total	Professional, managerial, and technical	Precision production, craft, and repair
	89	90	91	92	93	94	95	96		97	98	99	100	101	102	103

SOUTH CAROLINA—Cont'd																
Sumter	32 723	65.2	56 900	21.0	14.3	356	25.7	7.0		46 955	-0.7	2 585	5.5	37 746	21.8	14.9
Union	11 407	76.9	38 000	16.4	12.7	270	23.4	5.3		15 258	0.9	1 114	7.3	13 728	15.6	15.2
Williamsburg	12 108	79.2	42 600	19.7	13.5	236	24.5	10.5		14 678	0.2	1 903	13.0	14 580	16.0	12.3
York	47 006	71.9	71 300	19.3	12.9	417	24.3	4.2		89 069	2.2	3 680	4.1	67 039	24.5	14.9
SOUTH DAKOTA	259 034	66.1	45 200	19.8	13.3	306	24.6	3.4		399 704	0.5	11 632	2.9	321 891	24.5	10.4
Aurora	1 146	76.7	15 500	19.6	13.7	200	20.8	1.2		1 366	0.4	31	2.3	1 253	20.1	11.5
Beadle	7 341	65.8	34 200	16.3	12.7	279	24.4	1.7		8 469	-5.8	259	3.1	8 553	21.7	13.4
Bennett	1 030	65.0	29 500	20.5	13.8	263	26.1	13.7		1 022	3.0	54	5.3	1 090	17.7	9.9
Bon Homme	2 647	75.8	25 100	17.4	14.2	217	19.2	2.5		3 092	0.2	65	2.1	2 866	18.8	7.7
Brookings	8 910	58.6	51 200	17.5	12.4	293	28.1	2.0		16 492	3.0	260	1.6	12 705	27.4	7.0
Brown	13 867	62.9	46 600	17.5	13.0	292	23.8	1.4		20 710	-0.5	509	2.5	18 016	27.7	10.1
Brule	1 996	72.5	41 300	19.6	14.1	245	22.7	3.4		2 820	0.0	103	3.7	2 637	22.3	7.5
Buffalo	446	42.4	14 999	13.9	14.4	235	21.5	22.6		784	-3.6	90	11.5	512	18.8	6.8
Butte	3 033	68.0	38 700	22.4	14.8	277	23.5	2.3		3 685	-1.1	157	4.3	3 404	20.4	12.1
Campbell	767	82.5	16 400	15.5	14.9	227	20.0	2.2		895	2.9	28	3.1	903	13.8	7.1
Charles Mix	3 232	67.9	27 200	18.0	13.9	199	21.7	5.9		4 420	-1.7	150	3.4	3 532	18.9	9.3
Clark	1 700	78.4	18 700	18.9	13.9	221	22.8	3.1		1 989	2.5	94	4.7	1 843	14.8	9.5
Clay	4 433	52.9	47 800	20.7	13.2	291	32.9	1.8		7 466	8.6	59	0.8	6 384	33.9	6.4
Codington	8 739	67.6	50 600	20.3	12.5	281	25.9	1.2		14 430	-3.2	539	3.7	11 079	22.2	12.1
Corson	1 303	59.2	18 100	16.6	14.7	145	17.6	15.3		1 500	2.3	125	8.3	1 254	19.7	3.7
Custer	2 352	71.9	45 200	21.4	12.6	315	24.2	3.3		3 422	4.5	154	4.5	2 841	27.5	11.1
Davison	6 948	60.5	38 400	18.3	13.7	275	25.0	2.1		10 301	-0.8	238	2.3	8 367	25.4	9.8
Day	2 732	73.8	22 500	16.6	13.3	239	23.0	3.9		3 010	-1.1	219	7.3	2 761	20.6	9.7
Deuel	1 767	78.5	23 100	20.0	15.2	241	24.1	2.8		2 445	0.2	98	4.0	1 986	14.8	9.0
Dewey	1 721	49.2	23 700	13.2	14.0	271	29.5	21.6		2 370	-1.5	324	13.7	1 815	28.4	7.4
Douglas	1 352	78.6	19 600	17.9	15.4	211	23.0	2.8		1 606	-1.5	38	2.4	1 472	17.8	9.0
Edmunds	1 669	79.4	22 700	17.6	14.8	216	21.0	2.4		2 195	0.1	44	2.0	1 972	16.7	11.2
Fall River	2 864	65.6	34 100	19.8	13.0	273	23.8	3.2		3 257	-8.6	131	4.0	3 044	27.5	8.3
Faulk	1 057	80.1	17 900	14.4	13.1	201	21.6	3.7		1 212	3.9	28	2.3	1 199	18.6	4.3
Grant	3 154	73.2	36 600	17.0	13.8	247	22.0	1.8		4 226	-1.2	169	4.0	3 821	17.5	11.1
Gregory	2 139	73.0	26 300	19.2	13.7	208	24.8	3.8		2 570	0.9	114	4.4	2 299	18.1	9.4
Haakon	926	73.2	33 800	22.5	13.8	244	18.8	3.4		1 140	0.1	38	3.3	1 089	17.4	10.7
Hamlin	1 854	77.8	22 800	15.7	15.5	215	20.2	3.4		2 495	-2.5	85	3.4	2 010	17.7	9.8
Hand	1 625	71.1	32 600	14.2	13.0	213	23.9	2.5		2 049	-1.0	44	2.1	1 920	16.6	8.7
Hanson	1 072	74.8	19 900	17.8	14.5	295	17.7	2.9		1 705	4.9	42	2.5	1 451	17.6	10.8
Harding	592	73.3	33 300	20.8	13.2	214	22.8	4.2		761	1.5	31	4.1	800	17.9	5.5
Hughes	5 780	63.2	58 700	16.9	12.2	315	22.7	1.8		9 611	-1.3	213	2.2	7 875	36.1	7.6
Hutchinson	3 221	79.1	25 000	20.0	14.5	220	22.6	0.8		3 859	1.9	103	2.7	3 675	17.2	7.2
Hyde	680	72.2	21 900	15.0	12.7	230	18.2	4.2		915	1.9	23	2.5	781	18.6	10.5
Jackson	903	63.7	22 100	14.0	12.8	256	22.3	13.6		1 111	1.8	71	6.4	1 001	19.1	7.5
Jerauld	966	72.8	18 200	14.9	12.2	186	20.4	2.1		1 294	10.7	32	2.5	1 045	16.8	8.4
Jones	519	76.9	23 400	20.0	13.3	232	23.1	4.2		817	4.2	23	2.8	623	19.3	10.6
Kingsbury	2 357	73.8	22 800	14.9	13.5	205	20.5	1.1		2 596	-5.7	123	4.7	2 549	18.9	8.6
Lake	4 030	67.5	37 600	17.1	11.9	238	20.8	1.6		6 163	-3.0	162	2.6	5 091	24.4	9.7
Lawrence	7 926	64.2	52 300	18.2	12.1	306	25.9	2.5		10 383	-8.8	406	3.9	9 879	23.8	16.7
Lincoln	5 461	79.3	49 100	20.3	13.2	284	20.3	1.8		12 295	2.2	199	1.6	7 909	22.3	11.9
Lyman	1 268	73.3	30 200	17.0	12.3	235	19.9	7.1		2 440	-2.6	119	4.9	1 643	19.8	6.9
McCook	2 145	77.0	22 500	16.6	14.3	222	22.2	2.1		2 430	-3.4	61	2.5	2 555	19.3	10.3
McPherson	1 332	81.3	14 999	21.6	17.3	177	22.1	3.0		1 284	-0.9	33	2.6	1 371	15.9	11.4
Marshall	1 919	73.0	22 900	15.7	13.1	219	24.6	2.2		2 267	-1.0	142	6.3	2 012	18.3	9.8
Meade	7 084	66.8	50 600	23.1	13.2	315	24.6	2.8		13 122	5.3	379	2.9	8 552	22.4	14.4
Mellette	681	65.9	14 999	21.6	15.2	227	27.0	16.5		730	9.1	53	7.3	723	19.6	7.3
Miner	1 276	74.8	19 600	17.6	12.2	200	22.6	2.7		1 431	12.1	52	3.6	1 439	13.8	7.9
Minnehaha	47 681	62.3	58 400	20.0	12.8	377	24.5	1.8		90 137	2.4	1 593	1.8	66 313	27.8	10.0
Moody	2 398	71.2	33 100	15.0	13.1	243	22.4	3.6		3 479	-3.9	195	5.6	3 003	18.3	11.0
Pennington	30 553	61.4	56 600	22.3	13.1	386	26.1	2.9		47 243	0.0	1 192	2.5	36 145	27.9	13.0
Perkins	1 586	76.3	25 700	20.4	12.9	199	20.4	1.8		2 010	4.1	65	3.2	2 068	16.9	8.1
Potter	1 249	75.3	29 300	20.5	13.2	264	23.0	2.3		1 450	-4.3	55	3.8	1 442	19.5	8.5
Roberts	3 619	66.5	24 100	18.8	14.4	215	24.3	5.1		4 808	0.2	270	5.6	3 976	18.8	10.7
Sanborn	1 059	77.2	14 999	14.6	13.4	206	19.6	3.6		1 487	-3.1	43	2.9	1 187	16.6	9.4
Shannon	2 205	44.9	14 999	12.4	16.5	248	26.4	49.8		3 456	1.8	437	12.6	1 977	32.8	10.6
Spink	3 022	70.9	20 300	20.6	13.5	251	21.5	2.8		3 452	-0.8	124	3.6	3 412	19.5	7.2
Stanley	921	73.6	48 300	20.5	15.5	325	30.4	2.5		1 835	-1.2	42	2.3	1 306	23.8	8.7
Sully	621	72.6	28 400	20.8	12.4	250	21.6	2.4		867	-7.8	26	3.0	823	14.7	9.7
Todd	2 210	46.4	14 999	17.8	13.7	243	31.3	24.5		2 931	5.6	219	7.5	2 138	30.5	8.0

1. Specified owner-occupied units. 2. Specified renter-occupied units. 3. Overcrowded or lacking complete plumbing facilities. 4. Percent of civilian labor force. 5. Persons 16 years and older.

Table B. States and Counties — Nonfarm Employment and Agriculture

STATE County	Private nonfarm establishments, employment and payroll, 1998									Agriculture, 1997			
	Number of establish-ments	Employment						Annual payroll		Farms			Farm operators
		Total	Health Care and Social Assistance	Manufac-turing	Retail trade	Finance and Insurance	Professional Scientific and Technical Services	Total (mil dol)	Average per employee (dollars)	Number	Percent with—		Whose principal occu-pation is farming (percent)
											Less than 50 acres	500 acres and over	
	104	105	106	107	108	109	110	111	112	113	114	115	116
SOUTH CAROLINA—Cont'd													
Sumter	1 892	34 515	3 629	12 594	4 954	932	526	774	22 437	396	35.9	16.7	46.2
Union	546	7 962	849	3 565	1 410	190	100	162	20 345	255	23.5	7.5	31.0
Williamsburg	535	8 565	377	3 334	992	268	118	169	19 721	602	28.1	19.8	40.7
York	3 651	50 990	4 685	12 186	7 891	1 172	1 771	1 349	26 454	726	31.8	6.3	34.8
SOUTH DAKOTA	23 521	289 422	48 237	48 082	47 784	20 034	7 499	6 403	22 125	31 284	11.5	52.2	72.6
Aurora	91	442	91	D	D	32	11	7	15 876	421	11.4	54.4	75.3
Beadle	626	6 301	1 233	1 042	1 117	245	93	127	20 120	731	13.1	52.9	68.0
Bennett	68	581	111	D	143	22	6	9	16 050	258	5.8	69.8	75.6
Bon Homme	207	1 635	459	320	223	81	11	27	16 607	672	10.4	34.4	78.3
Brookings	729	10 480	1 083	3 577	1 583	304	245	214	20 412	886	19.4	31.5	59.9
Brown	1 328	16 515	2 633	2 522	3 330	730	418	332	20 113	1 006	15.7	52.0	68.4
Brule	217	1 834	416	28	447	73	33	27	14 611	382	7.6	65.4	82.2
Buffalo	11	D	D	0	D	D	0	D	D	77	3.9	79.2	80.5
Butte	273	1 878	238	175	520	85	79	31	16 276	547	14.1	45.7	59.2
Campbell	53	347	D	D	29	D	2	6	16 801	286	4.5	69.9	75.5
Charles Mix	285	2 487	497	79	473	92	33	40	16 038	735	10.2	57.7	81.6
Clark	120	694	104	D	90	42	14	11	16 117	563	8.2	54.5	75.0
Clay	306	2 619	488	138	673	93	26	35	13 541	397	9.8	43.1	77.1
Codington	997	12 851	1 449	4 098	2 465	352	282	270	21 040	619	19.4	38.8	64.3
Corson	46	268	D	D	63	D	D	3	10 347	425	6.1	74.1	79.8
Custer	222	983	99	42	226	36	38	20	20 032	326	12.9	46.9	63.5
Davison	748	8 995	1 379	1 823	1 625	302	344	190	21 144	429	21.4	37.8	60.1
Day	200	1 565	314	360	254	73	20	25	16 098	693	8.2	49.1	74.6
Deuel	128	837	185	143	137	55	22	15	18 388	564	9.8	38.5	68.4
Dewey	99	1 225	587	D	205	D	9	23	19 137	375	6.1	72.5	66.4
Douglas	122	882	229	114	170	37	6	13	14 236	392	11.5	49.2	80.9
Edmunds	114	721	140	D	170	49	7	12	17 209	449	7.3	69.0	76.4
Fall River	224	2 371	D	D	379	63	44	68	28 604	309	7.4	69.6	83.5
Faulk	68	413	D	6	121	28	5	6	14 971	316	7.9	71.8	83.5
Grant	269	3 107	363	524	427	233	57	60	19 400	534	10.1	42.9	73.0
Gregory	174	1 115	241	78	249	80	30	17	15 669	570	11.1	56.8	78.1
Haakon	95	623	D	D	92	44	11	11	17 226	309	4.9	79.6	80.9
Hamlin	148	728	142	70	168	51	D	12	16 522	413	15.0	44.8	75.8
Hand	133	936	214	D	153	64	22	15	15 907	488	6.6	69.3	80.9
Hanson	50	242	D	D	60	33	9	5	20 479	326	10.7	47.5	77.0
Harding	32	183	D	0	33	D	D	3	14 383	275	7.3	82.9	83.3
Hughes	627	5 927	1 123	64	1 384	383	205	114	19 256	287	11.8	55.1	70.4
Hutchinson	249	2 257	595	477	439	107	29	40	17 903	804	9.5	45.9	80.0
Hyde	44	562	D	D	D	D	8	9	16 423	229	9.2	68.6	79.5
Jackson	64	294	D	D	139	D	D	4	14 741	295	4.7	80.0	82.0
Jerauld	77	493	129	D	135	D	15	8	16 195	276	9.8	56.2	73.9
Jones	58	298	D	D	109	23	1	5	17 178	203	4.4	70.9	76.4
Kingsbury	199	1 377	297	275	235	111	22	24	17 633	580	12.1	49.5	75.9
Lake	351	3 446	574	960	557	108	50	68	19 802	500	15.6	45.4	70.8
Lawrence	821	8 606	995	600	1 249	182	142	166	19 306	270	19.3	31.1	55.9
Lincoln	518	4 510	619	808	740	198	81	102	22 559	806	17.4	28.5	65.5
Lyman	72	589	D	0	155	33	10	9	15 547	414	5.6	74.2	71.7
McCook	173	1 140	257	222	237	48	38	18	15 824	544	13.1	43.4	77.8
McPherson	89	492	148	D	120	57	D	6	13 018	397	3.8	70.5	80.6
Marshall	141	1 270	238	484	145	D	28	26	20 694	490	8.4	57.8	77.8
Meade	493	4 740	D	420	727	175	92	100	21 135	829	11.0	62.2	70.0
Mellette	33	163	D	0	61	D	5	2	13 669	217	3.2	82.5	80.6
Miner	77	395	136	D	88	27	7	19	18 167	369	9.2	46.9	74.0
Minnehaha	5 009	92 181	15 373	12 642	12 620	10 678	2 799	2 276	24 685	1 125	26.3	24.6	56.8
Moody	180	1 520	114	D	220	43	66	30	20 046	549	12.6	35.7	71.9
Pennington	3 178	38 208	6 636	4 264	6 460	2 387	1 328	851	22 266	637	16.2	46.8	64.1
Perkins	130	1 027	149	176	301	72	11	14	13 449	520	6.2	76.3	80.4
Potter	126	927	190	D	295	66	13	16	17 063	285	8.4	67.0	78.6
Roberts	256	1 888	512	99	378	91	24	27	14 461	803	10.8	46.8	73.5
Sanborn	63	550	127	D	D	22	13	8	14 627	382	11.0	51.6	69.9
Shannon	60	1 280	265	D	238	D	5	24	18 661	175	8.0	62.9	70.3
Spink	186	1 227	290	36	282	96	24	21	17 007	647	7.0	66.3	78.1
Stanley	88	658	0	D	124	D	18	15	22 833	194	6.7	78.4	71.1
Sully	53	244	0	D	91	31	3	4	16 258	261	4.6	72.8	80.5
Todd	58	948	262	0	182	D	D	22	23 687	210	2.9	78.1	85.7

Table B. States and Counties — Agriculture, Land, and Water

STATE County	Acreage (1,000)	Percent change, 1992–1997	Average size of farm	Total irrigated (1,000)	Total cropland (1,000)	Average per farm ($1,000)	Average per acre (dollars)	Value of machinery and equipment Average per farm ($1,000)	Total (mil dol)	Average per farm (dollars)	Crops	Livestock and poultry products	$10,000 or more	$100,000 or more	Percent of land owned by Fed. Gov. 1997	Water consumption 1995 (mil gal/ day)
	117	118	119	120	121	122	123	124	125	126	127	128	129	130	131	132
SOUTH CAROLINA—Cont'd																
Sumter	139	0.3	352	5	95	362	994	66	60	151 951	52.0	48.0	38.4	20.2	0.9	32.1
Union	53	-5.1	208	D	22	157	967	29	2	7 125	21.1	78.9	16.5	0.4	18.1	7.2
Williamsburg	189	9.5	315	1	93	364	1 161	61	48	79 522	87.0	13.0	43.4	19.1	0.0	4.6
York	115	-4.6	159	0	56	328	2 365	29	41	56 710	37.3	62.7	22.6	5.0	0.4	216.1
SOUTH DAKOTA	44 355	-1.1	1 418	344	19 355	487	348	91	3 570	114 114	46.3	53.7	76.9	30.2	6.3	460.0
Aurora	343	-9.8	814	D	226	455	472	69	55	130 547	34.1	65.9	79.8	29.9	1.0	0.8
Beadle	707	-2.4	968	8	493	436	434	97	96	131 603	45.4	54.6	75.5	35.8	1.1	9.3
Bennett	797	1.2	3 090	5	234	697	247	125	29	111 521	34.7	65.3	78.7	34.5	2.1	7.1
Bon Homme	311	-3.5	462	6	247	348	723	92	66	97 480	42.1	57.9	81.5	27.7	2.8	4.4
Brookings	408	-8.2	460	13	331	295	703	75	88	98 903	44.0	56.0	67.4	24.6	1.1	6.7
Brown	1 070	4.2	1 063	5	818	586	563	119	146	145 130	63.2	36.8	72.3	34.7	2.3	8.4
Brule	461	-7.3	1 206	2	272	464	380	78	46	119 856	39.3	60.7	83.8	34.6	1.5	4.0
Buffalo	302	8.3	3 923	11	85	904	231	124	22	281 127	37.2	62.8	81.8	42.9	2.6	3.2
Butte	1 166	-6.2	2 132	42	162	454	219	60	41	75 171	13.8	86.2	65.6	17.7	11.1	88.6
Campbell	396	-5.4	1 383	4	212	395	296	82	31	106 695	39.2	60.8	83.9	28.0	2.2	2.7
Charles Mix	680	-1.2	925	15	496	438	486	115	111	151 493	44.6	55.4	85.2	37.1	2.6	10.6
Clark	514	-3.9	913	5	359	333	391	90	73	129 111	43.0	57.0	77.1	29.5	0.9	2.9
Clay	226	-4.7	569	8	208	488	910	122	46	116 222	81.3	18.7	86.6	40.6	0.2	4.5
Codington	385	-2.2	621	4	286	340	550	84	65	104 421	42.1	57.9	71.2	24.6	1.3	11.1
Corson	1 605	-5.7	3 775	3	336	657	171	85	31	71 901	32.1	67.9	80.5	20.9	3.0	2.0
Custer	476	3.1	1 462	6	71	498	345	46	11	34 982	10.4	89.6	54.9	8.6	40.4	4.2
Davison	274	1.3	640	2	215	365	570	79	39	91 464	60.5	39.5	71.8	25.9	0.0	4.0
Day	536	-4.4	774	1	385	335	416	76	49	70 967	61.1	38.9	71.7	19.5	1.5	1.2
Deuel	311	-8.9	551	2	216	300	527	76	47	84 096	41.9	58.1	75.5	23.8	0.7	1.1
Dewey	1 851	-0.4	4 935	D	240	880	177	76	26	70 283	22.9	77.1	74.7	22.1	2.5	1.8
Douglas	247	-2.0	630	1	197	340	560	93	55	139 817	35.6	64.4	88.5	41.6	1.5	1.7
Edmunds	635	-1.0	1 415	1	431	427	327	110	62	137 237	44.3	55.7	77.5	30.7	1.2	1.7
Fall River	978	0.3	3 165	16	119	530	177	43	60	195 411	4.2	95.8	68.3	17.5	26.6	37.6
Faulk	571	2.0	1 808	D	344	603	333	149	53	168 635	53.0	47.0	84.2	41.8	0.3	0.7
Grant	359	-4.0	672	2	271	344	548	95	78	145 766	46.6	53.4	78.7	36.0	1.2	5.6
Gregory	566	-5.9	992	1	264	342	381	63	43	75 621	39.4	60.6	81.8	22.1	1.9	2.1
Haakon	1 325	10.1	4 288	D	428	683	167	95	41	131 994	34.4	65.6	84.1	39.2	0.3	2.1
Hamlin	279	0.6	675	5	232	459	664	120	49	117 660	56.1	43.9	79.4	34.4	0.9	2.7
Hand	811	-5.8	1 662	0	472	468	316	110	66	135 200	44.4	55.6	84.8	35.2	0.3	1.7
Hanson	231	-5.5	710	1	183	359	557	108	43	132 963	49.3	50.7	81.6	36.2	0.2	0.9
Harding	1 702	2.7	6 190	1	193	1 065	169	105	28	101 567	11.0	89.0	83.6	37.1	6.0	1.2
Hughes	391	0.0	1 364	12	237	524	374	105	37	128 599	56.8	43.2	73.2	33.4	2.5	21.7
Hutchinson	479	-4.5	596	2	404	382	653	107	103	128 073	47.4	52.6	84.8	37.8	0.1	2.7
Hyde	532	-2.3	2 324	1	214	590	257	103	30	132 541	40.8	59.2	84.7	36.7	0.1	1.4
Jackson	1 354	-0.5	4 591	1	267	877	188	92	28	95 841	31.7	68.3	77.3	23.1	10.2	2.0
Jerauld	346	3.7	1 255	1	184	359	291	92	37	134 731	30.9	69.1	79.3	27.5	0.4	1.2
Jones	589	0.8	2 900	D	214	626	215	85	19	91 544	28.8	71.2	76.4	25.1	3.2	1.0
Kingsbury	481	4.5	828	2	386	419	503	99	73	126 052	59.0	41.0	79.8	36.7	1.0	3.2
Lake	307	3.1	614	2	260	478	770	107	68	135 773	55.8	44.2	79.6	34.0	1.4	3.4
Lawrence	171	-12.1	635	2	48	454	744	39	9	35 139	12.6	87.4	53.0	7.8	53.5	14.8
Lincoln	319	-1.3	395	1	291	469	1 227	85	100	124 261	61.1	38.9	81.4	35.1	0.1	2.8
Lyman	944	11.5	2 279	8	418	701	333	77	40	97 675	48.8	51.2	77.1	30.7	9.7	5.0
McCook	312	-4.1	574	D	254	378	601	97	64	116 961	60.3	39.7	79.6	39.3	0.9	1.5
McPherson	569	-13.9	1 433	1	311	415	296	142	56	142 123	18.2	81.8	76.3	23.9	2.8	1.9
Marshall	505	3.9	1 030	1	325	454	433	112	80	162 441	37.4	62.6	74.7	31.8	1.9	1.6
Meade	2 074	0.0	2 502	10	432	564	230	55	52	62 803	19.4	80.6	68.3	18.2	3.7	5.2
Mellette	655	-6.6	3 017	0	161	591	201	68	18	81 746	19.9	80.1	82.0	28.6	0.0	1.1
Miner	280	-10.5	760	D	199	399	506	67	40	108 524	48.9	51.1	74.8	30.1	0.4	0.7
Minnehaha	406	-4.4	361	1	352	412	1 149	88	104	92 390	59.6	40.4	68.8	28.4	1.0	24.9
Moody	284	-0.4	517	2	237	507	984	85	68	123 439	56.9	43.1	81.2	33.9	0.7	2.2
Pennington	1 044	-2.1	1 639	9	288	512	325	49	40	62 288	29.2	70.7	61.2	14.1	43.1	30.2
Perkins	1 705	-1.2	3 279	1	454	510	161	77	42	81 322	22.5	77.5	77.3	26.0	7.8	1.5
Potter	530	4.5	1 860	4	352	670	380	128	45	156 802	57.2	42.8	75.8	41.4	0.8	3.8
Roberts	571	-5.5	711	2	441	378	533	85	87	107 883	63.3	36.7	76.2	33.3	0.7	1.6
Sanborn	347	7.3	907	D	220	313	382	76	41	108 247	35.7	64.3	79.3	27.0	0.0	0.8
Shannon	1 474	4.0	8 423		102	2 084	251	55	13	72 515	25.6	74.4	68.0	24.0	10.4	1.2
Spink	849	-4.7	1 313	14	686	583	430	143	117	180 290	63.9	36.1	83.9	46.2	0.3	8.5
Stanley	896	-0.9	4 617	1	243	902	192	113	23	118 250	46.1	53.9	73.2	30.9	7.9	2.5
Sully	599	-2.6	2 295	20	470	1 016	428	180	53	202 026	76.8	23.2	87.0	49.8	5.8	12.9
Todd	1 084	0.5	5 164	15	173	932	173	79	25	119 666	29.4	70.6	81.4	29.5	0.1	8.3

Table B. States and Counties — Residential Construction, Wholesale and Retail Trade, and Real Estate

STATE County	Value of Residential Construction Authorized by Building Permits, 1999		Wholesale Trade, 1997				Retail Trade[1], 1997				Real Estate and Rental and Leasing, 1997			
	New Construction ($1,000)	Number of Housing Units	Number of Establishments	Number of Employees	Sales (mil dol)	Annual Payroll (mil dol)	Number of Establishments	Number of Employees	Sales (mil dol)	Annual Payroll (mil dol)	Number of Establishments	Number of Employees	Receipts (mil dol)	Annual Payroll (mil dol)
	133	134	135	136	137	138	139	140	141	142	143	144	145	146
SOUTH CAROLINA—Cont'd														
Sumter	26 007	271	84	671	208.6	18.1	425	4 841	782.0	72.8	74	277	26.6	4.3
Union	7 211	96	13	38	14.2	1.1	113	1 228	155.2	15.0	17	51	3.1	0.7
Williamsburg	4 120	51	39	367	98.0	7.0	146	1 006	155.6	13.3	6	31	1.0	0.3
York	230 409	1 988	267	3 598	3 001.9	124.2	615	7 155	1 244.4	112.7	120	486	46.0	9.8
SOUTH DAKOTA	329 767	3 672	1 402	15 509	7 874.2	389.8	4 311	45 867	11 707.1	689.6	719	2 951	245.7	45.1
Aurora	85	3	4	38	13.4	1.1	18	D	D	D	3	3	0.1	0.0
Beadle	5 187	72	27	279	183.9	5.8	120	1 082	152.9	15.5	24	99	4.0	1.0
Bennett	482	9	4	59	44.9	0.5	21	D	D	D	1	D	D	D
Bon Homme	540	6	17	129	51.4	1.8	43	D	D	D	5	17	0.6	0.0
Brookings	9 906	152	29	505	265.8	8.3	139	1 513	169.2	17.5	28	80	5.7	0.8
Brown	5 183	71	83	897	637.3	21.5	237	3 128	497.4	47.9	50	123	11.6	2.0
Brule	738	9	9	94	36.5	1.7	51	D	D	D	2	D	D	D
Buffalo	NA	NA	NA	NA	NA	NA	2	D	D	D	2	D	D	D
Butte	255	4	19	139	83.1	2.4	59	402	66.7	6.5	10	D	D	D
Campbell	0	0	6	D	D	D	10	D	D	D	1	D	D	D
Charles Mix	211	3	16	120	63.6	2.3	73	497	63.9	5.7	4	5	0.4	0.0
Clark	612	7	7	76	80.6	1.4	16	D	D	D	3	4	0.1	0.0
Clay	3 101	32	9	44	18.3	1.2	52	493	75.4	6.8	12	24	2.0	0.3
Codington	8 661	101	74	560	320.7	15.8	191	2 382	347.2	32.8	33	94	7.5	1.3
Corson	85	1	5	D	D	D	14	D	D	D	NA	NA	NA	NA
Custer	5 110	70	2	D	D	D	32	D	D	D	9	19	2.6	0.5
Davison	3 765	81	36	504	216.7	12.6	153	1 747	230.7	21.8	27	64	4.0	0.5
Day	605	12	7	85	53.2	1.8	42	D	D	D	5	9	0.7	0.1
Deuel	1 655	13	6	19	7.6	0.2	26	D	D	D	1	D	D	D
Dewey	1 322	21	6	33	12.6	0.7	27	D	D	D	2	D	D	D
Douglas	0	0	9	60	17.4	1.2	18	D	D	D	1	D	D	D
Edmunds	100	1	11	147	101.5	3.3	21	D	D	D	4	8	0.3	0.1
Fall River	371	5	6	31	5.5	0.5	45	D	D	D	5	6	0.9	0.1
Faulk	0	0	6	25	10.6	0.4	11	D	D	D	1	D	D	D
Grant	1 926	19	18	413	106.2	7.4	55	451	68.1	5.3	2	D	D	D
Gregory	270	3	14	88	39.2	1.3	44	D	D	D	3	6	0.2	0.1
Haakon	100	2	10	124	62.4	1.6	20	D	D	D	1	D	D	D
Hamlin	816	13	10	60	38.3	1.4	29	D	D	D	3	3	0.1	0.0
Hand	142	3	12	156	58.5	3.0	22	D	D	D	2	D	D	D
Hanson	NA	NA	9	30	34.3	0.5	10	D	D	D	1	D	D	D
Harding	0	0	2	D	D	D	6	28	4.9	0.5	NA	NA	NA	NA
Hughes	5 672	55	22	159	85.8	4.2	121	1 221	194.7	17.4	19	102	4.0	0.9
Hutchinson	1 570	19	23	245	147.3	5.3	53	D	D	D	2	D	D	D
Hyde	0	0	3	D	D	D	11	D	D	D	NA	NA	NA	NA
Jackson	0	0	2	D	D	D	17	D	D	D	1	D	D	D
Jerauld	78	1	6	D	D	D	16	D	D	D	2	D	D	D
Jones	240	3	9	9	7.5	0.3	13	D	D	D	1	D	D	D
Kingsbury	1 850	18	10	94	69.3	2.4	40	581	115.0	10.4	14	25	1.8	0.3
Lake	4 576	58	12	125	81.0	3.5	67	1 334	226.1	18.6	35	134	8.9	1.2
Lawrence	11 585	87	21	59	12.1	0.9	147	625	150.5	11.1	7	65	2.8	1.6
Lincoln	21 990	206	39	305	200.4	8.0	72	D	D	D	NA	NA	NA	NA
Lyman	300	5	5	D	D	D	18	D	D	D	2	D	D	D
McCook	2 223	26	13	53	33.5	1.0	31	D	D	D	3	4	0.2	0.0
McPherson	82	1	2	D	D	D	16	D	D	D				
Marshall	681	15	10	82	43.0	1.2	23	D	D	D	NA	NA	NA	NA
Meade	9 429	100	22	134	94.8	2.4	81	630	115.9	9.8	16	77	4.1	0.8
Mellette	0	0	NA	NA	NA	NA	9	58	5.1	0.5	1	D	D	D
Miner	495	7	8	39	19.9	0.7	15	D	D	D	NA	NA	NA	NA
Minnehaha	132 125	1 628	356	5 412	2 145.1	163.3	770	12 238	1 999.4	191.7	185	947	97.5	17.4
Moody	308	2	6	32	13.1	0.8	23	D	D	D	5	D	D	D
Pennington	49 524	438	173	2 027	675.7	57.8	581	6 870	1 132.0	112.2	126	530	52.7	9.0
Perkins	0	0	8	62	49.4	1.8	26	159	15.8	1.8	1	D	D	D
Potter	460	4	11	98	57.3	2.3	28	D	D	D	2	D	D	D
Roberts	1 650	14	19	144	202.6	2.6	49	D	D	D	1	D	D	D
Sanborn	100	2	9	39	15.6	0.7	8	D	D	D	1	D	D	D
Shannon	NA	NA	NA	NA	NA	NA	15	D	D	D	1	D	D	D
Spink	270	6	16	146	133.0	3.8	39	261	51.7	4.0	3	6	0.2	0.0
Stanley	2 494	18	5	D	D	D	19	D	D	D	1	D	D	D
Sully	650	3	4	D	D	D	14	D	D	D	1	D	D	D
Todd	0	0	1	D	D	D	17	D	D	D	1	D	D	D

1. Establishments with payroll.

Table B. States and Counties — **Professional, Manufacturing, and Accommodation and Foodservices**

STATE County	Professional, Scientific, and Technical Services[1], 1997				Manufacturing, 1997				Accommodation and Foodservices, 1997			
	Number of Establishments	Number of Employees	Receipts (mil dol)	Annual Payroll (mil dol)	Number of Establishments	Number of Employees	Receipts (mil dol)	Annual Payroll (mil dol)	Number of Establishments	Number of Employees	Sales (mil dol)	Annual Payroll (mil dol)
	147	148	149	150	151	152	153	154	155	156	157	158
SOUTH CAROLINA—Cont'd												
Sumter	116	471	29.1	8.9	84	12 655	2 050.4	303.0	133	2 311	70.0	19.1
Union	21	50	3.3	1.2	43	5 355	679.6	129.2	36	646	13.5	3.6
Williamsburg	27	131	10.1	2.6	34	3 392	533.4	86.8	35	334	10.1	3.1
York	268	1 362	97.5	39.5	222	11 731	2 325.7	391.8	264	5 073	152.9	39.0
SOUTH DAKOTA	1 282	6 228	450.4	161.7	888	46 539	12 305.5	1 162.6	2 258	30 131	888.0	234.4
Aurora	3	10	0.2	0.1	NA	NA	NA	NA	15	49	1.3	0.3
Beadle	25	85	6.0	1.6	21	1 134	263.5	25.7	66	671	17.2	4.8
Bennett	4	5	0.1	0.0	NA	NA	NA	NA	6	47	1.3	0.2
Bon Homme	5	22	5.2	0.7	NA	NA	NA	NA	22	D	D	D
Brookings	41	173	11.3	4.1	31	3 449	902.0	92.4	62	1 236	26.9	7.2
Brown	72	374	22.4	8.0	38	2 492	397.5	61.0	105	1 616	47.4	13.3
Brule	13	31	1.2	0.4	NA	NA	NA	NA	30	276	10.2	2.8
Buffalo	NA	NA	NA	NA	NA	NA	NA	NA	NA	NA	NA	NA
Butte	14	59	4.4	1.1	NA	NA	NA	NA	23	D	D	D
Campbell	2	D	D	D	NA	NA	NA	NA	8	20	0.7	0.1
Charles Mix	12	31	1.7	0.6	NA	NA	NA	NA	27	592	38.8	6.8
Clark	4	7	0.3	0.1	NA	NA	NA	NA	11	56	1.4	0.3
Clay	12	31	1.6	0.3	NA	NA	NA	NA	46	812	15.5	3.8
Codington	53	261	13.7	6.4	63	4 115	395.8	102.6	78	1 185	33.1	9.1
Corson	2	D	D	D	NA	NA	NA	NA	3	5	0.2	0.0
Custer	17	33	1.6	0.6	NA	NA	NA	NA	46	243	14.8	3.9
Davison	33	294	21.3	6.9	36	1 719	365.9	47.2	79	1 190	33.2	9.4
Day	5	17	1.2	0.4	NA	NA	NA	NA	20	125	2.7	0.7
Deuel	4	18	0.7	0.2	NA	NA	NA	NA	12	65	1.6	0.3
Dewey	3	9	0.4	0.1	NA	NA	NA	NA	7	64	1.7	0.5
Douglas	3	2	0.3	0.0	NA	NA	NA	NA	9	28	0.6	0.1
Edmunds	4	2	0.2	0.1	NA	NA	NA	NA	10	61	1.4	0.3
Fall River	11	27	1.2	0.3	NA	NA	NA	NA	35	278	12.4	1.7
Faulk	3	6	0.2	0.1	NA	NA	NA	NA	6	14	0.5	0.1
Grant	12	37	1.6	0.6	6	D	D	D	21	216	5.6	1.5
Gregory	6	20	1.5	0.3	NA	NA	NA	NA	19	91	2.3	0.5
Haakon	3	6	0.3	0.1	NA	NA	NA	NA	9	44	1.3	0.3
Hamlin	5	4	0.3	0.1	NA	NA	NA	NA	13	D	D	D
Hand	5	11	0.5	0.1	NA	NA	NA	NA	9	46	1.2	0.2
Hanson	3	3	0.1	0.0	NA	NA	NA	NA	4	25	0.5	0.1
Harding	2	D	D	D	NA	NA	NA	NA	7	77	1.0	0.2
Hughes	39	197	15.5	5.2	NA	NA	NA	NA	55	894	25.7	7.7
Hutchinson	10	25	1.3	0.5	NA	NA	NA	NA	16	D	D	D
Hyde	2	D	D	D	NA	NA	NA	NA	4	D	D	D
Jackson	NA	NA	NA	NA	NA	NA	NA	NA	17	66	3.8	0.8
Jerauld	3	3	0.2	0.0	NA	NA	NA	NA	7	38	0.8	0.2
Jones	2	D	D	D	NA	NA	NA	NA	12	41	2.4	0.7
Kingsbury	4	12	0.7	0.2	NA	NA	NA	NA	22	98	3.3	0.5
Lake	15	51	3.1	0.8	23	950	167.2	19.7	34	353	8.1	2.2
Lawrence	42	145	8.8	3.5	30	502	88.2	13.1	111	1 728	59.2	15.7
Lincoln	15	56	3.9	1.8	30	D	D	D	33	344	7.8	2.0
Lyman	1	D	D	D	NA	NA	NA	NA	15	96	3.2	0.7
McCook	6	15	0.7	0.3	NA	NA	NA	NA	23	132	2.7	0.6
McPherson	3	8	0.1	0.1	NA	NA	NA	NA	10	D	D	D
Marshall	9	25	1.2	0.4	NA	NA	NA	NA	18	71	1.9	0.5
Meade	21	57	4.9	1.1	NA	NA	NA	NA	54	517	15.7	4.1
Mellette	2	D	D	D	NA	NA	NA	NA	4	14	0.6	0.1
Miner	3	9	0.3	0.1	NA	NA	NA	NA	8	43	1.0	0.2
Minnehaha	366	2 381	182.7	72.6	168	D	D	D	386	8 074	223.4	64.0
Moody	7	54	3.3	1.2	NA	NA	NA	NA	17	D	D	D
Pennington	207	1 119	91.0	30.6	134	4 263	867.3	100.8	326	5 125	163.7	44.3
Perkins	3	10	0.3	0.1	NA	NA	NA	NA	15	91	1.6	0.4
Potter	5	D	D	D	NA	NA	NA	NA	12	79	3.2	0.6
Roberts	10	16	0.6	0.3	NA	NA	NA	NA	29	187	4.6	1.1
Sanborn	6	10	0.6	0.2	NA	NA	NA	NA	6	D	D	D
Shannon	2	D	D	D	NA	NA	NA	NA	6	39	1.2	0.4
Spink	6	17	1.2	0.2	NA	NA	NA	NA	18	191	4.2	1.0
Stanley	4	4	0.4	0.1	NA	NA	NA	NA	8	55	1.5	0.4
Sully	3	2	0.3	0.1	NA	NA	NA	NA	6	87	1.9	0.3
Todd	1	D	D	D	NA	NA	NA	NA	5	40	1.2	0.3

1. Firms subject to federal tax.

STATE County	Health Care and Social Assistance[1], 1997				Other Services[1], 1997				Federal funds and grants, fiscal 1999[2]			
									Expenditures (mil dol)			
									Total	Direct payments for individuals[3]		
	Number of Establishments	Number of Employees	Receipts (mil dol)	Annual Payroll (mil dol)	Number of Establishments	Number of Employees	Receipts (mil dol)	Annual Payroll (mil dol)	Total	Social Security and government retirement	Medicare	Food stamps and Supplemental Security Income
	159	160	161	162	163	164	165	166	167	168	169	170
SOUTH CAROLINA—Cont'd												
Sumter	128	1 347	81.0	40.6	123	827	47.5	14.1	673.0	222.2	55.0	33.4
Union	35	325	17.0	7.4	34	130	5.7	1.5	122.5	65.3	23.6	5.7
Williamsburg	42	342	18.6	7.7	45	220	10.1	3.2	173.8	58.3	25.7	13.8
York	212	4 122	263.1	110.3	223	1 226	66.6	21.9	458.7	249.6	85.1	16.8
SOUTH DAKOTA	1 314	14 080	881.6	414.3	1 356	5 828	344.7	90.7	4 909.0	1 420.0	460.1	90.7
Aurora	4	D	D	D	5	15	1.2	0.1	19.0	6.0	2.8	0.2
Beadle	40	394	19.8	7.9	35	148	6.6	1.9	123.3	40.7	14.8	1.6
Bennett	2	D	D	D	3	7	0.4	0.1	247.7	4.8	1.8	1.7
Bon Homme	7	35	2.0	1.1	7	17	1.4	0.3	37.7	15.2	7.0	0.5
Brookings	37	274	15.8	7.4	40	171	8.2	2.3	100.5	37.0	12.5	1.5
Brown	105	749	54.0	20.8	79	383	21.6	5.5	210.6	72.4	27.6	3.0
Brule	22	239	10.1	3.9	12	36	4.3	0.6	35.5	10.4	4.7	0.8
Buffalo	1	D	D	D	NA	NA	NA	NA	21.4	1.6	1.1	0.5
Butte	17	80	3.3	1.1	20	65	4.0	0.8	37.1	19.4	4.6	1.0
Campbell	1	D	D	D	2	D	D	D	18.5	5.8	2.4	0.1
Charles Mix	15	117	3.3	1.2	22	51	5.0	0.7	72.3	18.2	7.9	1.8
Clark	5	95	2.7	1.4	9	14	0.9	0.1	33.9	9.7	3.5	0.3
Clay	14	120	4.9	2.2	18	70	2.8	0.7	57.6	17.4	6.1	1.2
Codington	46	408	26.0	12.6	63	265	13.9	3.4	101.7	45.3	12.3	2.2
Corson	2	D	D	D	1	D	D	D	37.5	8.8	3.8	1.8
Custer	9	21	1.2	0.3	7	7	0.4	0.1	45.4	20.0	3.6	0.7
Davison	58	507	29.6	12.5	44	158	10.3	2.3	91.9	35.9	16.0	2.3
Day	11	80	3.7	1.1	12	21	2.0	0.4	54.8	15.7	6.8	0.8
Deuel	2	D	D	D	7	11	1.4	0.2	30.3	9.3	3.6	0.3
Dewey	3	D	D	D	1	D	D	D	53.1	7.3	2.3	3.2
Douglas	2	D	D	D	7	38	1.8	0.4	23.0	7.4	3.2	0.3
Edmunds	4	86	2.7	1.5	7	11	0.9	0.1	27.8	9.0	4.3	0.2
Fall River	11	44	1.8	0.7	11	28	2.2	0.3	73.3	30.9	5.6	1.4
Faulk	1	D	D	D	7	14	2.1	0.2	20.3	6.8	2.7	0.2
Grant	13	149	6.5	2.9	19	51	4.0	0.8	40.8	16.9	6.4	0.7
Gregory	8	29	2.1	1.1	9	20	1.4	0.2	33.3	12.5	5.1	0.8
Haakon	2	D	D	D	6	14	1.4	0.2	16.5	4.5	1.6	0.1
Hamlin	5	153	3.5	1.9	7	8	1.0	0.2	29.7	10.7	3.3	0.3
Hand	5	33	2.0	1.0	13	18	1.0	0.2	38.1	7.6	3.1	0.2
Hanson	NA	NA	NA	NA	NA	NA	NA	NA	13.8	4.6	1.4	0.1
Harding	1	D	D	D	NA	NA	NA	NA	9.6	2.3	0.7	0.1
Hughes	41	485	23.9	7.2	33	140	7.8	2.0	238.7	35.9	8.2	1.2
Hutchinson	12	77	3.7	1.3	16	41	3.1	0.6	50.2	19.0	7.8	0.5
Hyde	3	D	D	D	3	6	0.4	0.0	11.9	3.5	1.3	0.2
Jackson	2	D	D	D	NA	NA	NA	NA	16.1	4.1	0.8	0.8
Jerauld	3	5	0.3	0.0	7	9	1.2	0.1	15.2	5.6	2.9	0.2
Jones	1	D	D	D	NA	NA	NA	NA	10.5	2.3	0.9	0.1
Kingsbury	11	172	5.0	2.3	11	44	2.5	0.5	41.4	15.8	6.2	0.4
Lake	12	156	6.3	3.1	19	50	3.5	0.7	53.8	22.0	8.7	0.9
Lawrence	49	255	16.4	5.8	50	154	9.4	2.5	87.4	45.7	12.4	1.2
Lincoln	19	300	17.6	6.2	33	135	10.9	2.5	92.5	21.6	7.1	0.6
Lyman	3	8	0.5	0.3	2	D	D	D	41.9	6.5	2.2	0.7
McCook	14	202	6.0	3.2	9	30	2.2	0.4	39.4	11.7	4.8	0.3
McPherson	5	13	0.6	0.1	4	7	0.7	0.1	16.9	5.2	2.4	0.3
Marshall	7	176	4.3	2.2	11	38	2.5	0.6	35.5	10.4	4.2	0.3
Meade	19	134	6.2	1.8	34	65	5.5	1.1	137.4	45.7	11.3	1.5
Mellette	1	D	D	D	2	D	D	D	12.9	2.4	1.4	0.9
Miner	1	D	D	D	8	22	2.3	0.4	20.2	6.5	3.4	0.3
Minnehaha	284	4 344	347.2	194.3	283	1 858	101.3	31.5	611.4	244.1	69.9	12.3
Moody	7	46	1.2	0.5	8	27	1.7	0.3	42.4	11.7	4.7	0.4
Pennington	226	2 315	163.6	65.6	191	1 049	55.5	17.4	559.1	197.2	42.3	12.9
Perkins	6	8	0.6	0.2	11	22	2.2	0.4	26.3	8.8	3.5	0.3
Potter	5	19	0.6	0.3	6	17	1.9	0.2	26.7	7.4	3.3	0.2
Roberts	11	157	4.9	1.9	15	28	1.8	0.3	71.1	18.8	7.1	1.9
Sanborn	2	D	D	D	7	11	1.1	0.1	24.4	5.9	2.9	0.2
Shannon	1	D	D	D	1	D	D	D	142.6	11.0	4.7	9.4
Spink	8	111	4.1	1.8	9	20	1.8	0.5	62.5	17.7	8.1	0.6
Stanley	NA	NA	NA	NA	6	14	0.7	0.2	15.4	4.6	1.2	0.1
Sully	NA	NA	NA	NA	1	D	D	D	21.2	2.7	1.0	0.0
Todd	2	D	D	D	1	D	D	D	72.9	7.5	3.4	6.1

1. Firms subject to federal tax.   2. October 1, 1998 to September 30, 1999.   3. State totals may include programs not allocated by county.

STATE County	Federal funds and grants, fiscal 1999[1] (cont'd)							Local government finances, 1997				
	Expenditures (mil dol) (cont'd)							General revenue				
	Procurement contract awards			Grants[2]							Taxes	
											Per capita[3] (dollars)	
	Salaries and wages	Defense	Other	Medicaid and other health-related	Nutrition and family welfare	Education	Other	Total (mil dol)	Intergovern-mental (mil dol)	Total (mil dol)	Total	Property
	171	172	173	174	175	176	177	178	179	180	181	182
SOUTH CAROLINA—Cont'd												
Sumter	195.7	30.5	2.7	75.9	18.8	10.0	16.1	163.3	93.2	51.4	482	399
Union	4.7	0.0	0.9	15.7	3.1	1.4	1.4	74.1	25.2	16.1	527	494
Williamsburg	4.5	0.0	1.0	45.9	6.7	3.9	3.5	62.2	35.0	13.1	351	330
York	18.6	0.8	6.3	36.5	12.7	5.3	20.8	266.5	98.7	124.6	828	781
SOUTH DAKOTA	559.0	91.9	431.9	330.7	143.0	131.0	451.1	X	X	X	X	X
Aurora	0.7	0.0	0.2	0.7	0.2	0.1	1.7	5.9	2.2	2.6	875	763
Beadle	19.8	0.0	2.4	9.7	0.9	0.5	12.1	34.9	12.1	16.0	891	668
Bennett	0.9	0.0	227.3	2.3	0.5	2.7	0.5	9.2	2.7	2.4	739	608
Bon Homme	1.4	0.0	0.4	2.8	0.4	0.2	0.7	15.7	4.7	6.7	869	754
Brookings	6.7	0.5	1.0	6.5	1.1	0.7	13.7	62.2	11.2	21.4	817	668
Brown	26.5	1.1	2.7	17.4	2.0	1.2	13.9	63.5	19.0	34.0	952	688
Brule	1.9	0.1	0.9	3.0	0.3	0.5	5.9	11.4	4.4	5.6	1 011	842
Buffalo	4.9	0.1	2.0	1.2	1.5	0.2	6.5	0.4	0.1	0.3	151	145
Butte	2.0	0.0	0.4	2.5	1.6	0.3	1.1	17.8	7.1	6.4	716	568
Campbell	0.6	0.0	0.1	1.6	0.1	0.2	1.0	3.6	1.4	1.7	851	782
Charles Mix	7.7	0.9	1.4	7.8	5.0	4.4	2.4	16.8	7.7	7.2	762	679
Clark	1.2	0.0	1.5	2.5	0.3	0.2	0.3	7.3	2.5	4.0	908	824
Clay	2.9	0.0	0.5	5.7	2.0	1.5	7.5	18.4	4.7	10.1	657	516
Codington	10.1	0.2	6.4	8.3	1.4	0.4	3.5	48.1	10.6	25.7	1 010	680
Corson	3.8	0.0	1.9	3.5	1.0	3.0	3.1	7.8	5.3	1.9	449	365
Custer	6.6	0.0	1.8	2.1	0.3	0.2	9.1	12.8	4.0	6.6	953	787
Davison	5.4	0.1	11.9	8.1	1.3	0.6	2.0	33.0	11.3	16.6	885	577
Day	2.8	0.0	1.2	5.1	0.6	0.4	4.2	13.3	6.1	5.5	856	773
Deuel	1.5	0.5	0.3	2.1	0.2	0.1	0.4	6.6	2.0	3.6	780	674
Dewey	12.5	0.3	4.3	7.9	3.4	3.9	1.9	8.1	5.4	2.2	387	311
Douglas	1.2	0.0	0.5	0.9	0.2	0.2	2.6	5.3	2.0	2.7	757	603
Edmunds	0.9	0.2	0.2	1.6	0.2	0.2	0.0	11.9	2.8	4.3	1 017	947
Fall River	19.5	0.5	5.9	3.7	0.6	0.5	2.9	15.8	5.6	7.2	1 011	846
Faulk	0.8	0.3	0.2	0.9	0.1	0.1	0.0	4.9	1.8	2.6	1 026	958
Grant	2.2	0.0	0.5	3.5	0.4	0.1	0.5	17.4	4.6	8.9	1 106	1 001
Gregory	1.8	0.2	3.2	2.5	0.5	2.5	0.2	10.8	5.0	4.7	930	777
Haakon	0.7	0.0	0.1	0.0	0.1	0.1	0.2	7.5	1.6	2.8	1 151	956
Hamlin	1.3	0.0	0.4	1.4	0.4	0.2	0.2	13.5	4.0	5.8	1 084	977
Hand	0.7	0.0	0.1	1.4	0.2	0.2	13.3	7.8	2.4	4.8	1 157	1 030
Hanson	0.6	0.0	0.2	0.5	0.2	0.1	0.1	4.6	2.0	2.2	769	682
Harding	0.9	0.0	0.2	0.0	0.1	0.1	0.5	3.6	1.1	1.9	1 242	1 018
Hughes	11.0	1.9	4.0	22.0	43.1	30.3	71.7	27.6	7.9	14.4	937	738
Hutchinson	2.2	0.0	0.5	3.7	0.4	0.3	2.0	16.5	6.0	8.2	1 011	907
Hyde	0.2	0.0	0.1	1.7	0.2	0.1	0.0	3.4	1.1	1.9	1 162	988
Jackson	2.4	0.0	1.5	0.5	0.3	0.6	1.4	3.6	1.7	1.6	553	434
Jerauld	0.6	0.0	0.2	0.7	0.2	0.1	0.0	5.0	2.2	2.2	986	888
Jones	0.3	0.1	0.1	0.5	0.0	0.0	1.3	2.9	0.8	1.6	1 267	1 049
Kingsbury	2.0	0.0	0.5	1.4	0.3	0.2	0.9	11.5	4.4	5.6	954	860
Lake	2.8	0.0	1.1	3.5	2.5	0.1	0.9	21.5	7.7	9.7	911	797
Lawrence	7.9	0.0	2.4	6.9	1.4	1.0	5.4	53.4	17.0	25.4	1 149	913
Lincoln	2.0	0.1	0.5	3.0	0.6	0.2	3.5	29.0	12.1	14.2	705	633
Lyman	2.8	2.6	2.5	3.4	0.9	0.9	8.1	5.6	1.6	2.9	739	631
McCook	1.8	0.1	0.4	1.8	0.3	0.1	8.3	11.2	4.4	5.7	1 002	862
McPherson	0.6	0.0	0.1	1.8	0.2	0.1	0.0	5.6	1.8	3.3	1 182	1 097
Marshall	1.2	0.0	0.3	2.3	0.4	0.2	4.5	8.4	2.8	4.5	974	814
Meade	26.5	25.1	5.8	4.2	1.0	4.0	4.3	27.1	9.6	13.5	612	495
Mellette	0.4	0.0	0.1	2.3	0.5	1.2	1.5	5.3	2.9	1.4	685	576
Miner	0.8	0.0	0.2	2.1	0.2	0.1	0.2	6.5	2.2	3.5	1 210	1 042
Minnehaha	106.9	7.3	55.9	45.3	7.9	2.4	32.0	276.2	55.1	166.5	1 185	798
Moody	5.5	0.0	2.6	3.6	0.5	1.0	2.1	13.1	3.9	5.7	874	775
Pennington	168.2	4.5	30.4	25.9	11.1	11.8	31.4	192.8	68.0	91.5	1 050	748
Perkins	1.2	0.0	0.3	2.8	0.2	0.3	0.1	9.0	4.1	3.7	1 056	950
Potter	1.1	0.0	0.2	1.2	0.2	0.1	2.1	8.8	2.7	4.0	1 352	1 237
Roberts	5.8	0.0	2.5	9.4	2.4	1.9	5.2	16.8	8.0	6.7	671	597
Sanborn	0.8	0.0	0.2	1.2	0.2	0.2	5.9	4.6	2.3	1.9	689	593
Shannon	21.1	0.2	6.3	20.2	10.2	13.9	42.1	10.3	9.2	0.6	49	29
Spink	2.6	0.0	0.6	3.7	0.4	0.3	4.7	18.9	5.4	8.3	1 079	932
Stanley	0.3	0.0	0.0	0.2	0.2	0.4	0.6	5.8	2.0	3.1	1 064	868
Sully	0.3	0.0	0.1	0.0	0.1	0.1	4.0	3.8	0.9	2.6	1 701	1 508
Todd	11.3	0.0	0.6	11.2	6.6	11.4	12.9	16.1	13.6	1.7	184	127

1. October 1, 1998 to September 30, 1999.   2. State totals may include programs not allocated by county.   3. Based on the resident population estimated as of July 1 of the year shown.

Table B. States and Counties — Local Government Finances, Government Employment, and Elections

STATE County	Total (mil dol) 183	Per capita[1] (dollars) 184	Education 185	Health and hospitals 186	Police protection 187	Public welfare 188	Highways 189	Total (mil dol) 190	Per capita[1] (dollars) 191	Federal civilian 192	Federal military 193	State and local 194	Democratic 195	Republican 196	All other 197
SOUTH CAROLINA—Cont'd															
Sumter	160.6	1 507	63.3	2.3	6.3	0.5	1.9	82.5	774	1 206	5 499	5 588	46.8	51.9	1.3
Union	69.8	2 286	40.3	35.9	2.0	0.0	1.3	36.5	1 194	94	176	2 268	44.0	54.5	1.5
Williamsburg	64.6	1 731	58.2	17.6	2.8	0.7	2.0	21.3	571	98	214	2 213	59.3	39.9	0.7
York	253.6	1 685	59.4	0.6	5.0	0.3	1.4	439.0	2 917	338	890	8 491	35.4	62.1	2.4
SOUTH DAKOTA	X	X	X	X	X	X	X	X	X	10 767	8 260	50 252	37.6	60.3	2.1
Aurora	5.5	1 834	59.1	0.4	3.4	0.9	19.0	0.0	0	23	21	322	36.3	59.9	3.8
Beadle	36.9	2 054	48.7	0.2	3.9	0.7	8.8	21.1	1 175	370	123	1 034	41.6	56.2	2.3
Bennett	9.0	2 741	39.3	32.8	4.2	0.2	5.8	0.7	204	30	24	361	33.8	63.8	2.4
Bon Homme	14.1	1 836	51.8	0.9	2.0	0.0	12.4	13.5	1 760	35	55	558	37.0	60.6	2.4
Brookings	63.9	2 442	35.5	19.7	3.1	3.0	7.0	19.7	751	139	197	4 887	41.4	56.6	2.1
Brown	64.6	1 811	44.3	0.6	4.8	1.8	14.5	11.3	318	540	254	2 453	43.3	54.7	2.0
Brule	10.7	1 924	64.0	1.7	4.0	0.5	8.4	3.5	626	41	40	350	37.7	58.5	3.7
Buffalo	0.4	202	0.0	0.0	9.8	0.6	56.0	0.0	0	128	12	0	62.7	34.3	2.9
Butte	17.5	1 960	49.5	0.7	3.0	0.1	7.5	5.2	580	57	64	518	22.8	74.8	2.4
Campbell	3.3	1 676	53.8	0.1	1.5	0.5	18.2	0.3	153	10	14	112	16.0	80.6	3.4
Charles Mix	15.9	1 671	56.8	0.4	3.5	0.6	17.0	7.8	825	190	67	511	36.3	61.6	2.1
Clark	7.1	1 636	57.0	1.4	1.9	0.7	17.9	0.6	145	28	31	221	37.5	60.3	2.1
Clay	19.8	1 287	44.0	0.6	7.2	0.5	18.1	9.7	631	54	113	2 986	51.7	46.3	2.0
Codington	52.9	2 080	41.7	0.2	4.1	0.5	8.0	27.3	1 072	172	182	1 445	37.6	60.3	2.0
Corson	6.9	1 606	75.8	0.0	3.7	0.0	9.9	0.0	0	114	30	242	44.2	50.6	5.2
Custer	12.4	1 786	51.2	5.0	7.6	0.5	13.6	6.5	929	190	49	544	26.7	69.8	3.4
Davison	34.6	1 840	48.0	0.8	4.6	0.6	7.5	15.5	824	114	129	1 075	39.0	59.0	2.0
Day	12.9	2 002	55.2	1.5	2.2	0.1	20.3	2.7	422	68	46	373	46.7	50.8	2.6
Deuel	6.3	1 375	47.7	3.7	4.1	1.9	23.7	0.4	95	36	32	234	41.6	56.0	2.4
Dewey	7.4	1 307	75.7	1.1	2.6	0.1	9.0	0.1	21	353	42	257	52.3	45.3	2.4
Douglas	4.9	1 383	52.2	2.5	4.6	1.0	19.4	0.3	89	29	25	164	21.2	76.7	2.0
Edmunds	11.2	2 637	34.4	18.3	3.0	15.1	16.3	0.5	114	24	30	366	34.0	63.3	2.7
Fall River	14.0	1 962	50.4	0.8	3.8	0.3	14.9	1.6	224	542	51	526	33.0	63.7	3.2
Faulk	4.4	1 752	57.5	0.9	1.8	0.9	23.5	0.0	14	20	18	164	29.2	68.0	2.8
Grant	17.2	2 143	46.8	0.8	3.0	0.5	11.1	33.3	4 134	44	58	388	38.5	58.4	3.1
Gregory	10.4	2 059	53.2	0.3	3.3	0.5	13.9	0.5	107	39	35	292	31.8	65.9	2.3
Haakon	7.5	3 025	39.9	0.0	1.8	1.0	13.3	1.0	411	18	17	149	14.5	83.1	2.4
Hamlin	17.4	3 282	67.1	2.2	0.9	10.0	10.7	9.8	1 850	34	38	447	33.9	63.6	2.5
Hand	7.6	1 825	49.5	1.0	3.5	0.3	23.7	2.6	620	22	30	206	27.8	69.9	2.3
Hanson	4.4	1 508	62.5	1.1	2.3	0.5	19.6	0.6	193	11	21	135	32.2	66.4	1.4
Harding	3.5	2 318	53.6	0.3	5.0	0.6	22.2	0.1	69	23	11	116	8.8	88.9	2.3
Hughes	29.5	1 912	54.1	0.5	6.1	0.3	5.9	10.5	684	339	110	3 284	29.4	68.9	1.8
Hutchinson	15.1	1 861	58.7	1.7	2.5	0.7	21.2	3.8	475	43	57	464	29.0	68.9	2.1
Hyde	3.2	1 951	51.5	0.3	3.9	0.2	20.7	0.0	1	0	11	102	26.1	70.9	3.0
Jackson	3.5	1 197	66.2	0.0	2.7	0.8	10.6	0.1	34	90	21	131	30.7	66.1	3.3
Jerauld	5.1	2 256	56.5	0.9	1.8	0.9	13.0	0.4	185	24	16	161	41.7	55.6	2.7
Jones	2.6	2 009	50.4	0.9	4.3	0.0	19.9	0.3	217	11	0	100	20.6	76.7	2.7
Kingsbury	11.1	1 896	60.9	1.3	2.4	0.3	14.6	4.5	764	45	41	281	38.5	59.1	2.4
Lake	19.5	1 830	55.8	0.4	4.0	0.7	12.5	68.5	6 430	64	80	972	45.2	52.9	1.9
Lawrence	51.7	2 334	34.4	0.5	5.9	0.1	8.4	46.0	2 077	207	161	1 708	29.7	67.3	3.0
Lincoln	27.9	1 385	54.5	2.0	2.8	0.0	20.8	17.1	848	49	146	714	36.4	62.0	1.6
Lyman	5.6	1 414	44.7	1.1	5.5	0.2	18.0	0.7	166	73	27	173	34.8	63.1	2.1
McCook	10.8	1 907	51.5	1.3	2.4	0.9	20.5	1.6	275	34	40	282	45.2	52.8	2.1
McPherson	5.7	2 049	50.4	0.9	2.9	0.8	27.3	0.8	274	18	20	171	36.7	61.2	2.1
Marshall	8.1	1 759	55.9	2.0	5.1	0.7	19.8	0.7	143	31	33	326	20.8	75.7	3.5
Meade	27.2	1 237	54.7	0.8	4.0	0.6	9.6	10.2	463	1 219	157	861	24.2	73.4	2.4
Mellette	4.8	2 417	59.1	0.7	3.0	0.2	5.1	0.2	99	14	14	157	30.3	67.5	2.2
Miner	6.0	2 051	45.8	0.8	4.6	0.4	24.2	1.4	467	22	20	163	41.3	57.2	1.5
Minnehaha	259.7	1 848	46.6	1.1	5.3	1.3	9.3	277.8	1 977	2 100	1 057	6 388	44.1	54.5	1.5
Moody	12.6	1 928	46.9	18.2	4.7	0.4	16.6	0.7	110	164	46	322	48.2	49.8	2.0
Pennington	193.4	2 218	44.5	0.9	5.1	0.5	4.9	108.9	1 249	1 260	3 559	5 287	30.4	67.6	2.0
Perkins	8.7	2 457	54.4	0.7	2.5	0.0	17.1	2.1	584	34	25	294	18.4	76.6	5.0
Potter	8.3	2 835	40.0	0.2	3.0	0.5	20.0	1.2	412	28	20	181	23.8	74.4	1.7
Roberts	16.8	1 684	64.3	3.9	2.9	1.0	12.5	1.6	164	143	70	530	41.7	54.9	3.4
Sanborn	4.2	1 504	70.1	0.7	1.5	0.1	13.3	0.3	95	15	20	163	36.9	60.5	2.6
Shannon	9.0	752	95.7	0.1	0.2	0.0	1.8	0.0	0	531	87	335	85.4	12.9	1.7
Spink	18.3	2 376	46.2	21.1	3.7	0.5	11.3	1.8	236	51	54	971	38.8	59.6	1.6
Stanley	5.6	1 922	49.1	0.9	5.4	0.1	19.9	1.6	543	0	21	137	29.1	69.2	1.7
Sully	3.5	2 282	79.1	0.0	1.7	0.5	8.1	0.0	0	11	10	129	24.0	72.7	3.3
Todd	15.2	1 630	91.5	0.0	0.6	0.1	4.3	0.4	48	265	66	562	66.5	32.0	1.5

1. Based on the resident population estimated as of July 1 of the year shown.

Table B. States and Counties — Land Area and Population

| | | | | | Population and population characteristics, 1999 | | | | | | | | | | | | | |
| | | | | | | | | Race (percent) | | | | | Age (percent) | | | | | |
STATE/ County code	MSA/ PMSA/ NECMA code[1]	County Type[2]	STATE County	Land area[3] (sq km) 1990	Total persons	Rank	Per square kilometer	White	Black	Am. Indian, Eskimo, Aleut	Asian and Pacific Islander	Percent Hispanic[4]	Under 5 years	5 to 17 years	18 to 24 years	25 to 34 years	35 to 44 years	45 to 54 years
				1	2	3	4	5	6	7	8	9	10	11	12	13	14	15
			SOUTH DAKOTA—Cont'd															
46 123	...	7	Tripp	4 179	6 622	2 718	1.6	88.4	0.0	11.5	0.2	0.3	6.9	21.7	7.2	10.3	13.6	13.1
46 125	...	8	Turner	1 598	8 660	2 540	5.4	99.5	0.1	0.4	0.1	0.4	5.3	19.9	5.9	9.0	14.8	13.2
46 127	...	8	Union	1 192	12 472	2 251	10.5	98.8	0.3	0.5	0.4	1.2	6.2	21.7	8.0	10.4	16.8	13.2
46 129	...	7	Walworth	1 833	5 614	2 798	3.1	90.0	0.1	9.6	0.3	0.8	6.1	20.1	6.8	9.2	14.8	15.6
46 135	...	7	Yankton	1 351	21 190	1 700	15.7	96.2	0.8	2.6	0.4	0.8	6.3	18.3	10.0	12.6	15.9	13.8
46 137	...	9	Ziebach	5 083	2 165	3 054	0.4	32.1	0.4	67.2	0.2	1.0	11.1	32.7	8.5	13.0	10.1	9.8
47 000	...	X	**TENNESSEE**	106 759	5 483 535	X	51.4	82.1	16.6	0.2	1.0	1.2	6.7	17.8	9.5	14.2	16.4	13.7
47 001	3840	2	Anderson	874	71 004	695	81.2	93.8	4.5	0.4	1.3	1.1	6.0	17.0	7.4	12.6	16.2	14.3
47 003	...	6	Bedford	1 227	34 905	1 231	28.4	87.8	11.2	0.2	0.8	1.1	6.8	18.4	8.4	13.1	15.3	14.3
47 005	...	7	Benton	1 023	16 497	1 972	16.1	96.7	2.8	0.1	0.4	1.0	5.5	16.6	7.5	11.5	14.7	14.7
47 007	...	8	Bledsoe	1 052	10 945	2 347	10.4	95.7	3.8	0.2	0.1	0.8	5.8	17.9	8.7	14.6	17.1	14.7
47 009	3840	2	Blount	1 447	102 785	504	71.0	95.4	3.6	0.2	0.7	0.8	6.1	16.4	8.1	13.5	17.2	15.1
47 011	...	4	Bradley	851	84 126	602	98.9	94.8	4.4	0.3	0.5	1.8	6.2	17.3	11.5	13.8	15.6	14.4
47 013	...	6	Campbell	1 243	38 466	1 121	30.9	98.8	0.5	0.5	0.2	0.7	6.2	18.6	8.7	12.1	15.2	14.4
47 015	...	8	Cannon	688	12 248	2 265	17.8	97.6	2.1	0.1	0.2	0.7	6.3	18.2	8.1	12.5	14.5	14.4
47 017	...	6	Carroll	1 552	29 450	1 395	19.0	87.1	12.7	0.1	0.1	0.8	6.0	17.1	8.3	11.6	14.5	14.3
47 019	3660	2	Carter	883	53 299	861	60.4	98.4	1.0	0.2	0.4	0.7	5.5	15.7	9.4	12.7	15.7	15.0
47 021	5360	2	Cheatham	784	36 128	1 189	46.1	97.1	2.3	0.4	0.2	1.0	7.7	19.7	7.6	16.1	18.1	14.4
47 023	3580	6	Chester	747	14 859	2 075	19.9	87.3	12.3	0.1	0.2	0.6	6.4	17.3	13.9	11.9	14.4	13.1
47 025	...	6	Claiborne	1 125	29 747	1 380	26.4	98.0	1.2	0.2	0.6	0.6	6.1	18.7	9.4	12.7	16.2	14.0
47 027	...	9	Clay	612	7 268	2 657	11.9	97.9	1.8	0.2	0.0	0.7	5.4	17.3	8.2	12.4	15.0	15.6
47 029	...	7	Cocke	1 125	32 291	1 303	28.7	97.2	2.4	0.3	0.1	1.0	5.7	17.4	8.6	13.1	15.9	14.9
47 031	...	5	Coffee	1 111	46 355	962	41.7	94.7	4.1	0.2	1.0	1.2	6.8	18.0	7.7	12.9	14.7	14.4
47 033	...	8	Crockett	687	14 077	2 127	20.5	81.1	18.7	0.1	0.1	0.7	6.2	18.1	7.8	13.2	14.3	14.2
47 035	...	7	Cumberland	1 765	45 326	980	25.7	99.2	0.2	0.4	0.2	0.7	5.8	16.1	7.3	11.6	13.8	13.2
47 037	5360	2	Davidson	1 301	530 050	100	407.4	72.3	25.3	0.2	2.1	1.7	6.9	15.7	10.8	17.2	16.7	12.6
47 039	...	9	Decatur	865	10 788	2 357	12.5	94.9	4.5	0.2	0.3	0.9	5.1	17.0	7.6	11.4	14.6	14.8
47 041	...	6	De Kalb	789	16 174	1 995	20.5	97.9	1.8	0.2	0.2	0.8	6.0	17.6	8.0	12.2	15.1	14.9
47 043	5360	2	Dickson	1 269	43 017	1 023	33.9	93.9	5.6	0.2	0.3	1.0	7.4	19.5	8.5	14.1	15.5	14.0
47 045	...	7	Dyer	1 322	36 725	1 172	27.8	86.4	13.1	0.2	0.3	0.7	6.6	18.8	8.8	13.3	16.0	13.9
47 047	4920	1	Fayette	1 825	31 441	1 333	17.2	53.2	46.5	0.2	0.1	0.9	7.4	22.1	8.4	13.0	15.4	13.4
47 049	...	9	Fentress	1 292	16 357	1 982	12.7	99.6	0.1	0.1	0.2	0.5	6.1	19.0	8.7	12.2	15.9	14.8
47 051	...	7	Franklin	1 433	37 826	1 141	26.4	92.7	6.8	0.2	0.4	1.0	6.0	17.4	9.4	12.1	15.0	14.1
47 053	...	4	Gibson	1 561	48 030	935	30.8	78.6	21.1	0.1	0.1	0.7	6.0	17.4	8.0	12.1	14.5	13.9
47 055	...	6	Giles	1 582	29 036	1 410	18.4	84.7	14.7	0.3	0.3	0.8	6.6	18.0	8.7	12.3	15.3	15.0
47 057	...	8	Grainger	726	20 219	1 751	27.8	99.0	0.7	0.3	0.1	0.5	6.0	17.7	9.1	13.3	15.6	15.6
47 059	...	6	Greene	1 611	60 900	783	37.8	97.2	2.5	0.2	0.2	0.5	5.5	16.3	8.6	12.6	15.7	15.5
47 061	...	6	Grundy	934	14 046	2 132	15.0	99.5	0.2	0.2	0.1	1.0	6.4	20.6	8.5	12.1	14.4	14.6
47 063	...	5	Hamblen	417	54 201	848	130.0	94.5	5.0	0.2	0.4	0.7	6.0	16.8	8.6	12.9	16.0	16.0
47 065	1560	2	Hamilton	1 405	294 720	186	209.8	77.7	20.8	0.2	1.3	1.2	6.4	16.9	9.0	13.4	16.6	13.7
47 067	...	9	Hancock	576	6 767	2 703	11.7	97.9	1.8	0.3	0.0	0.9	6.1	18.5	8.1	12.8	14.4	13.9
47 069	...	6	Hardeman	1 729	24 451	1 554	14.1	59.8	39.7	0.1	0.4	1.2	7.2	20.8	8.6	12.9	14.9	12.3
47 071	...	6	Hardin	1 497	25 247	1 522	16.9	94.6	5.0	0.1	0.3	0.7	6.2	17.8	8.1	11.6	15.4	14.5
47 073	3660	2	Hawkins	1 261	50 109	904	39.7	97.7	1.9	0.2	0.2	0.6	5.8	16.9	8.4	13.2	16.2	15.6
47 075	...	6	Haywood	1 381	19 416	1 793	14.1	47.7	52.0	0.1	0.1	1.3	6.8	22.2	8.6	12.8	15.2	11.8
47 077	...	6	Henderson	1 347	24 767	1 541	18.4	90.4	9.4	0.1	0.1	0.8	6.2	18.1	7.9	12.7	15.5	13.8
47 079	...	7	Henry	1 455	30 091	1 372	20.7	88.5	11.0	0.2	0.3	0.8	5.6	16.7	7.0	11.6	14.4	14.2
47 081	...	6	Hickman	1 587	21 283	1 693	13.4	93.8	5.8	0.3	0.1	0.8	6.4	17.2	8.2	14.9	16.4	14.8
47 083	...	8	Houston	519	7 888	2 612	15.2	95.3	4.4	0.2	0.1	1.2	5.7	17.8	7.4	11.2	14.5	14.6
47 085	...	6	Humphreys	1 379	17 192	1 919	12.5	95.3	3.9	0.2	0.3	0.8	6.0	18.0	7.4	11.8	15.3	15.0
47 087	...	9	Jackson	800	9 643	2 458	12.1	99.3	0.2	0.2	0.3	0.7	5.6	16.7	7.9	12.2	15.7	14.7
47 089	...	6	Jefferson	709	45 104	983	63.6	96.4	3.1	0.3	0.2	0.5	5.3	15.9	10.8	12.4	15.1	16.2
47 091	...	8	Johnson	773	16 736	1 949	21.7	94.9	4.8	0.1	0.2	0.9	5.2	15.6	9.1	13.2	16.6	15.5
47 093	3840	2	Knox	1 317	376 039	151	285.5	88.5	9.7	0.3	1.5	1.1	6.3	15.7	10.9	14.8	16.7	13.4
47 095	...	9	Lake	423	8 131	2 584	19.2	69.0	30.9	0.1	0.0	0.7	4.5	13.1	15.7	17.8	16.1	12.3
47 097	...	6	Lauderdale	1 219	24 234	1 569	19.9	65.9	33.4	0.5	0.1	1.3	6.9	20.3	9.0	14.6	15.0	12.9
47 099	...	6	Lawrence	1 599	39 626	1 097	24.8	97.9	1.6	0.2	0.4	0.8	7.1	18.3	8.6	12.8	14.3	14.1
47 101	...	7	Lewis	731	11 127	2 338	15.2	98.1	1.4	0.3	0.1	1.2	6.6	20.1	7.9	12.6	15.5	13.6
47 103	...	6	Lincoln	1 477	29 773	1 378	20.2	90.0	9.5	0.1	0.3	0.9	6.4	17.7	8.0	12.7	14.7	14.3
47 105	3840	2	Loudon	592	39 892	1 090	67.4	98.1	1.5	0.2	0.3	0.6	5.9	16.2	7.8	12.5	15.8	14.7
47 107	...	7	McMinn	1 114	46 395	959	41.6	93.9	5.4	0.2	0.4	0.8	6.0	17.7	8.5	12.8	15.3	14.9
47 109	...	7	McNairy	1 451	24 312	1 561	16.8	92.5	7.1	0.1	0.3	0.8	5.8	17.7	7.3	11.8	15.1	15.2
47 111	...	6	Macon	796	18 542	1 844	23.3	99.2	0.4	0.1	0.1	0.6	6.8	18.2	8.9	13.3	15.5	14.1
47 113	3580	3	Madison	1 443	86 752	580	60.1	66.0	33.4	0.1	0.5	0.8	6.8	19.0	10.3	13.8	16.3	12.5
47 115	1560	2	Marion	1 295	26 907	1 468	20.8	94.9	4.8	0.1	0.2	0.7	6.4	18.8	8.3	13.0	16.0	14.8

1. MSA = Metropolitan Statistical Area. PMSA = Primary MSA. NECMA = New England County Metropolitan Area. See Appendix A for explanation of these concepts. See Appendix B for list of metropolitan areas identified by type, with component counties.   2. County typology code from the Economic Research Service of USDA. See Appendix A for definition.   3. Dry land or land partially or temporarily covered by water.   4. Hispanic persons may be of any race.

Table B. States and Counties — **Population and Households**

STATE County	55 to 64 years	65 to 74 years	75 years and over	Percent female	Total persons 1990	Total persons 1980	Percent change 1980–1990	Percent change 1990–1999	Births	Deaths	Net migration	Number	Percent change, 1980–1990	Persons per household	Female family householder[1]	One person
	16	17	18	19	20	21	22	23	24	25	26	27	28	29	30	31
SOUTH DAKOTA—Cont'd																
Tripp	9.3	9.3	8.7	50.4	6 924	7 268	-4.7	-4.4	911	644	-552	2 573	0.4	2.65	7.0	25.8
Turner	10.7	9.3	12.0	50.9	8 576	9 255	-7.3	1.0	872	1 118	361	3 332	-4.2	2.51	4.1	26.1
Union	9.6	7.1	7.2	50.5	10 189	10 938	-6.8	22.4	1 313	987	1 983	3 859	-1.8	2.61	6.5	24.8
Walworth	11.9	6.7	9.0	51.9	6 087	7 011	-13.2	-7.8	715	904	-258	2 447	-4.2	2.42	7.0	27.4
Yankton	8.5	7.0	7.6	50.7	19 252	18 952	1.6	10.1	2 727	1 660	945	7 107	7.3	2.51	7.8	28.3
Ziebach	7.0	4.6	3.3	50.7	2 220	2 308	-3.8	-2.5	389	109	-331	630	5.0	3.52	17.1	20.6
TENNESSEE	9.4	6.8	5.7	51.7	4 877 203	4 591 023	6.2	12.4	687 916	463 719	387 196	1 853 725	14.5	2.56	12.6	23.9
Anderson	10.7	9.1	6.7	52.2	68 250	67 346	1.3	4.0	7 746	6 790	2 092	27 384	11.2	2.47	10.8	25.2
Bedford	10.3	7.0	6.4	51.4	30 411	27 916	8.9	14.8	4 369	3 245	3 452	11 608	16.7	2.59	11.1	21.8
Benton	11.9	9.2	8.3	52.4	14 524	14 901	-2.5	13.6	1 667	1 758	2 103	5 784	3.7	2.46	8.0	23.3
Bledsoe	9.7	6.2	5.3	45.5	9 669	9 478	2.0	13.2	1 130	941	1 112	3 261	9.5	2.64	9.2	20.5
Blount	10.1	7.6	6.0	51.8	85 962	77 770	10.5	19.6	10 726	8 400	14 645	33 624	19.3	2.51	9.6	22.0
Bradley	9.3	6.6	5.3	51.8	73 712	67 547	9.1	14.1	10 134	6 256	6 741	27 604	19.9	2.61	10.3	20.7
Campbell	10.4	7.6	6.7	52.1	35 079	34 923	0.4	9.7	4 334	3 726	2 883	13 150	8.8	2.65	12.9	21.2
Cannon	11.1	7.7	7.2	51.3	10 467	10 234	2.3	17.0	1 368	1 147	1 607	3 980	9.8	2.60	8.8	21.9
Carroll	11.0	8.8	8.4	51.9	27 514	28 285	-2.7	7.0	3 437	3 531	2 124	10 727	3.9	2.50	10.2	23.6
Carter	10.6	8.2	7.2	51.5	51 505	50 205	2.6	3.5	5 300	5 410	2 094	20 189	13.0	2.49	10.5	23.7
Cheatham	8.4	4.5	3.6	49.8	27 140	21 616	25.6	33.1	4 194	2 144	6 990	9 515	34.7	2.82	8.2	16.0
Chester	9.9	6.6	6.5	51.8	12 819	12 727	0.7	15.9	1 541	1 270	1 796	4 558	8.3	2.59	9.8	21.1
Claiborne	9.9	7.3	5.8	51.5	26 137	24 595	6.3	13.8	3 260	2 673	3 110	9 629	16.1	2.65	10.5	19.8
Clay	11.4	7.6	7.2	50.5	7 238	7 676	-5.7	0.4	735	891	212	2 855	4.5	2.51	10.5	22.7
Cocke	10.9	7.1	6.4	51.8	29 141	28 792	1.2	10.8	3 791	3 204	2 667	11 191	10.2	2.58	13.4	22.1
Coffee	11.0	8.2	6.3	51.7	40 343	38 311	5.3	14.9	5 680	4 144	4 573	15 500	13.6	2.57	10.0	22.1
Crockett	9.6	8.0	8.6	52.1	13 378	14 941	-10.5	5.2	1 676	1 742	815	5 183	-3.7	2.53	10.9	24.3
Cumberland	11.8	12.0	8.4	51.5	34 736	28 676	21.1	30.5	4 288	3 883	10 370	13 426	35.8	2.55	9.4	20.0
Davidson	8.6	6.2	5.4	52.6	510 786	477 811	6.9	3.8	77 809	45 478	-12 193	207 530	16.8	2.36	14.2	30.3
Decatur	11.3	9.3	8.9	51.6	10 472	10 857	-3.5	3.0	1 195	1 419	574	4 216	3.3	2.45	9.3	24.5
De Kalb	11.1	7.9	7.1	52.1	14 360	13 589	5.7	12.6	1 794	1 679	1 739	5 696	14.9	2.50	10.3	22.7
Dickson	9.5	5.9	5.5	51.4	35 061	30 037	16.7	22.7	5 153	3 441	6 280	13 019	24.4	2.65	11.6	20.3
Dyer	9.4	6.6	6.6	52.4	34 854	34 663	0.6	5.4	4 764	3 833	1 052	13 617	7.3	2.52	12.1	24.7
Fayette	9.0	5.9	5.3	51.3	25 559	25 305	1.0	23.0	3 525	2 457	4 809	8 453	13.8	2.97	15.8	18.6
Fentress	9.9	7.3	6.1	50.9	14 669	14 826	-1.1	11.5	1 849	1 622	1 498	5 511	9.6	2.64	12.1	21.1
Franklin	10.5	8.4	7.2	50.8	34 923	31 983	8.6	8.3	3 905	3 367	2 439	12 660	17.3	2.64	9.0	20.0
Gibson	10.9	8.8	8.3	53.0	46 315	49 467	-6.4	3.7	5 571	5 990	2 305	18 361	0.9	2.48	12.2	24.9
Giles	10.0	7.4	6.8	51.4	25 741	24 625	4.5	12.8	3 189	2 949	3 138	9 832	11.4	2.58	11.4	22.6
Grainger	10.5	6.4	5.8	50.3	17 095	16 751	2.1	18.3	2 204	1 770	2 718	6 394	12.3	2.64	9.2	19.0
Greene	11.3	7.9	6.7	51.6	55 832	54 422	2.6	9.1	6 220	5 915	4 883	21 482	12.1	2.52	10.7	22.1
Grundy	9.2	7.6	6.7	51.4	13 362	13 787	-3.1	5.1	1 771	1 414	380	4 784	6.1	2.75	11.2	20.4
Hamblen	10.7	7.6	5.4	51.9	50 480	49 300	2.4	7.4	6 752	4 918	2 059	19 429	12.6	2.56	11.1	21.3
Hamilton	9.9	7.6	6.5	52.9	285 536	287 643	-0.7	3.2	37 061	27 391	362	111 799	8.2	2.50	13.5	26.0
Hancock	10.9	8.2	7.1	50.6	6 739	6 887	-2.1	0.4	742	750	62	2 484	5.7	2.65	12.9	21.4
Hardeman	9.3	7.4	6.7	52.0	23 377	23 873	-2.1	4.6	3 308	2 462	314	8 276	8.6	2.73	16.4	22.8
Hardin	11.2	7.9	7.3	51.5	22 633	22 280	1.6	11.5	2 742	2 537	2 477	8 726	9.5	2.56	10.1	22.2
Hawkins	10.2	7.4	6.2	51.1	44 565	43 751	1.9	12.4	5 316	4 368	4 732	17 167	12.3	2.58	9.5	21.2
Haywood	8.8	6.8	7.0	53.1	19 437	20 318	-4.3	0.1	2 832	2 096	-697	7 014	7.7	2.74	18.8	24.4
Henderson	11.1	7.8	7.0	51.8	21 844	21 390	2.1	13.4	2 853	2 508	2 650	8 527	10.9	2.54	9.6	22.5
Henry	11.9	9.9	8.6	51.8	27 888	28 656	-2.7	7.9	3 112	3 725	2 909	11 362	4.1	2.42	9.9	25.5
Hickman	10.1	6.9	5.3	48.1	16 754	15 151	10.6	27.0	2 273	1 783	4 054	5 976	17.3	2.63	8.8	20.6
Houston	12.0	8.5	8.2	51.2	7 018	6 871	2.1	12.4	925	893	864	2 683	11.3	2.55	9.7	22.5
Humphreys	11.4	8.4	6.6	50.9	15 813	15 957	-0.9	8.7	1 838	1 763	1 335	6 063	7.6	2.56	9.3	22.6
Jackson	11.7	7.9	7.5	51.0	9 297	9 398	-1.1	3.7	1 054	1 128	453	3 642	8.3	2.52	9.2	22.1
Jefferson	11.2	7.3	5.8	51.0	33 016	31 284	5.5	36.6	4 046	3 320	11 366	12 329	16.1	2.55	9.3	20.5
Johnson	10.2	7.4	7.1	46.8	13 766	13 745	0.2	21.6	1 441	1 625	3 206	5 406	11.7	2.52	11.1	22.8
Knox	9.5	6.9	5.8	52.2	335 749	319 694	5.0	12.0	43 856	30 513	19 523	133 639	13.3	2.42	11.6	27.4
Lake	8.1	6.0	6.4	38.6	7 129	7 455	-4.4	14.1	792	866	1 113	2 418	-6.1	2.50	13.4	25.8
Lauderdale	8.7	6.3	6.4	50.9	23 491	24 555	-4.3	3.2	3 457	2 869	226	8 423	1.7	2.68	14.9	22.5
Lawrence	10.4	7.6	6.7	51.9	35 303	34 110	3.5	12.2	5 139	3 748	3 062	13 338	12.4	2.62	9.7	21.6
Lewis	10.5	6.9	6.5	50.7	9 247	9 700	-4.7	20.3	1 240	1 022	1 685	3 533	15.6	2.58	9.6	24.3
Lincoln	10.7	8.2	7.2	51.7	28 157	26 483	6.3	5.7	3 330	3 132	1 498	10 881	14.1	2.57	10.1	22.6
Loudon	11.0	9.0	7.0	51.7	31 255	28 553	9.5	27.6	4 020	3 425	8 160	12 155	18.1	2.54	10.7	21.7
McMinn	10.5	7.7	6.7	52.2	42 383	41 878	1.2	9.5	5 236	4 334	3 252	16 351	11.0	2.55	10.7	22.0
McNairy	11.0	8.0	7.9	51.6	22 422	22 525	-0.5	8.4	2 871	2 805	1 894	8 834	8.0	2.51	9.3	22.8
Macon	10.3	7.0	5.9	51.2	15 906	15 700	1.3	16.6	2 145	1 667	2 175	6 159	9.1	2.57	8.5	22.0
Madison	8.7	6.6	6.1	52.7	77 982	74 546	4.6	11.2	11 304	7 849	5 530	29 609	10.8	2.55	15.2	25.0
Marion	10.2	6.6	5.8	51.1	24 683	24 416	1.8	9.0	3 102	2 475	1 695	9 215	11.4	2.67	11.2	20.3

1. No spouse present.

Table B. States and Counties — **Vital Statistics, Health Resources, and Crime**

STATE County	Births, average 1996–1998 Total	Rate[1]	Deaths, average 1996–1998 Number Total	Infant[2]	Rate Total[1]	Infant[3]	Physicians,[4] 1998 Number	Rate[5]	Hospitals,[4] 1998 Number	Beds Number	Rate[5]	Medicare enrollees 1999	Serious crimes known to police, 1998[6] Total Number	Rate[7]
	32	33	34	35	36	37	38	39	40	41	42	43	44	45
SOUTH DAKOTA—Cont'd														
Tripp	86	12.6	69	1	10.1	11.7	6	89	1	116	1 722	1 317	NA	NA
Turner	86	10.0	110	0	12.7	3.9	6	70	1	77	892	1 871	NA	NA
Union	160	13.4	101	1	8.5	4.2	14	115	0	0	0	2 109	NA	NA
Walworth	80	14.0	91	0	16.0	4.2	5	90	1	35	627	902	NA	NA
Yankton	280	13.3	184	2	8.7	7.1	77	366	1	271	1 287	3 486	406	1 932
Ziebach	35	15.8	12	0	5.5	9.6	0	0	0	0	0	148	NA	NA
TENNESSEE	75 209	14.0	52 500	633	9.8	8.4	11 512	212	135	21 953	404	815 231	273 420	5 034
Anderson	808	11.3	773	5	10.8	5.8	172	242	1	305	429	13 184	2 738	3 858
Bedford	529	15.4	369	4	10.8	8.2	19	55	1	182	527	5 409	NA	NA
Benton	165	10.2	207	2	12.8	10.1	11	67	1	47	288	3 392	NA	NA
Bledsoe	128	12.0	112	1	10.5	10.4	2	19	1	26	241	1 405	65	606
Blount	1 180	11.8	1 003	6	10.0	5.4	161	159	1	203	200	16 245	2 893	2 849
Bradley	1 107	13.6	739	7	9.1	6.6	123	148	2	266	319	11 788	3 028	3 729
Campbell	464	12.3	431	3	11.4	5.8	26	68	2	200	523	7 924	829	2 286
Cannon	152	12.7	128	2	10.7	10.9	8	66	1	55	453	1 965	95	780
Carroll	377	13.0	393	2	13.5	5.3	19	65	2	92	316	6 382	493	1 686
Carter	568	10.7	609	3	11.5	4.7	36	68	1	100	188	8 542	1 309	2 437
Cheatham	484	14.1	252	3	7.4	6.9	11	31	1	19	54	3 335	395	1 214
Chester	175	12.1	153	2	10.6	9.5	2	14	0	0	0	2 043	NA	NA
Claiborne	355	12.2	301	2	10.3	6.6	16	54	1	110	373	5 725	228	777
Clay	75	10.3	102	1	14.0	17.8	5	69	1	28	386	1 172	28	378
Cocke	410	12.9	364	4	11.5	10.6	20	63	1	109	341	5 791	788	2 465
Coffee	621	13.7	475	4	10.5	5.9	80	175	3	286	625	8 179	1 673	3 633
Crockett	180	13.0	187	1	13.6	3.7	6	43	0	0	0	2 699	391	3 182
Cumberland	502	11.6	470	2	10.9	4.6	69	156	1	160	361	9 940	NA	NA
Davidson	8 370	15.7	5 017	66	9.4	7.9	2 322	435	10	3 405	638	72 553	54 499	10 093
Decatur	125	11.6	162	0	15.1	2.7	7	65	1	40	370	2 140	183	1 715
De Kalb	196	12.5	198	3	12.6	13.6	13	82	1	58	364	2 970	411	2 701
Dickson	567	13.9	377	4	9.2	6.5	29	69	1	114	270	5 940	NA	NA
Dyer	494	13.5	433	4	11.9	8.1	57	155	1	125	340	6 152	NA	NA
Fayette	369	12.6	279	2	9.5	6.3	10	33	1	38	125	3 226	752	2 584
Fentress	200	12.5	189	1	11.8	5.0	10	62	1	71	439	3 188	312	1 939
Franklin	446	12.0	391	5	10.5	10.5	45	120	2	72	192	6 443	NA	NA
Gibson	563	11.7	661	7	13.8	13.0	29	60	3	218	452	9 917	1 769	3 634
Giles	364	12.7	331	2	11.6	4.6	20	69	1	109	377	4 869	NA	NA
Grainger	244	12.5	196	1	10.1	4.1	3	15	0	0	0	3 452	558	2 834
Greene	701	11.8	671	4	11.3	6.2	82	136	2	285	471	11 514	NA	NA
Grundy	195	13.9	156	0	11.2	1.7	9	64	0	0	0	2 587	NA	NA
Hamblen	744	13.8	546	3	10.2	3.6	87	161	2	302	559	8 869	2 127	3 912
Hamilton	3 816	13.0	3 057	34	10.4	9.0	959	325	8	1 589	539	48 809	NA	NA
Hancock	71	10.4	80	0	11.8	4.7	3	44	0	0	0	1 161	98	1 877
Hardeman	336	13.7	284	6	11.6	16.9	17	68	1	48	193	4 434	669	2 936
Hardin	293	11.8	284	3	11.5	10.2	15	60	1	121	485	4 522	NA	NA
Hawkins	589	12.0	509	4	10.4	6.8	24	48	1	50	101	8 115	600	1 258
Haywood	285	14.5	229	5	11.7	16.4	13	67	1	54	277	2 870	950	4 743
Henderson	326	13.6	276	4	11.5	11.3	8	33	1	25	102	4 557	679	2 843
Henry	344	11.5	408	1	13.7	1.9	28	93	1	101	336	6 557	815	2 712
Hickman	266	13.3	218	1	10.9	3.8	7	34	1	18	88	3 198	140	695
Houston	106	13.6	98	0	12.5	3.1	4	51	1	35	446	1 528	88	1 115
Humphreys	208	12.3	185	2	11.0	8.0	13	76	1	42	246	3 026	334	1 965
Jackson	109	11.5	134	0	14.1	0.0	5	52	1	32	332	1 578	NA	NA
Jefferson	472	11.2	401	2	9.5	4.2	28	64	1	67	153	7 878	509	1 196
Johnson	153	9.2	199	1	12.0	8.7	8	48	1	51	304	3 330	NA	NA
Knox	4 716	12.9	3 467	33	9.5	6.9	1 218	332	6	1 897	517	55 675	15 935	4 308
Lake	85	10.3	95	1	11.5	7.8	2	24	0	0	0	1 285	NA	NA
Lauderdale	372	15.4	304	4	12.6	9.9	5	21	1	70	289	4 234	NA	NA
Lawrence	557	14.3	434	6	11.1	10.8	23	58	1	83	211	7 280	1 329	3 358
Lewis	125	11.7	111	1	10.3	5.3	7	64	0	0	0	1 683	140	1 288
Lincoln	352	12.0	351	3	12.0	7.6	22	74	1	63	212	5 362	719	2 433
Loudon	435	11.4	401	4	10.5	9.2	44	113	1	30	77	7 649	1 194	3 087
McMinn	555	12.1	498	3	10.8	6.0	56	121	2	169	365	7 997	2 057	4 430
McNairy	298	12.5	303	3	12.7	11.2	10	42	1	48	200	5 216	235	1 015
Macon	248	14.0	181	3	10.2	13.4	11	61	1	43	237	2 842	287	1 688
Madison	1 230	14.5	868	11	10.2	8.9	284	330	2	710	826	13 115	6 799	7 925
Marion	329	12.4	287	2	10.8	5.1	18	67	2	92	343	4 161	348	1 553

1. Per 1,000 estimated resident population, average 1996–1998.　2. Deaths of infants under 1 year old.　3. Deaths of infants under 1 year old per 1,000 live births.　4. Data subject to copyright.　5. Per 100,000 resident population as of July 1 of the year shown.　6. Data for serious crimes have not been adjusted for underreporting; this may affect comparability between geographic areas and over time.　7. Per 100,000 population estimated by the FBI.

Table B. States and Counties — Crime, Education, Money Income, and Poverty

STATE County	Serious crimes known to police, 1998[1] (cont'd) Rate[2] Violent	Property	Education — School enrollment and attainment, 1990 — Enrollment[3] Total	Percent private	Attainment[4] (percent) High school graduate or more	Bachelor's degree or more	Local government expenditures, fiscal 1997[5] Total current expenditures (mil dol)	Current expenditures per student (dollars)	Money income — 1989 Per capita[6] (dollars)	Households Median Dollars	Percent change, 1979–1989 (constant 1989 dollars)	Percent with $100,000 or more	Income and poverty, 1997 Median household income	Percent below poverty level All persons	Persons under 18	Persons 5–17 in families
	46	47	48	49	50	51	52	53	54	55	56	57	58	59	60	61
SOUTH DAKOTA—Cont'd																
Tripp	NA	NA	1 627	2.8	71.5	9.6	5.9	4 406	10 340	20 082	8.2	1.7	28 631	20.2	27.4	24.3
Turner	NA	NA	1 926	4.5	72.8	12.5	7.2	4 468	9 355	19 926	4.6	0.7	32 510	11.0	13.2	12.1
Union	NA	NA	2 546	7.7	74.2	13.9	11.8	4 507	9 997	22 274	-3.6	0.9	40 373	8.2	10.5	9.7
Walworth	NA	NA	1 275	6.0	71.5	14.5	5.1	4 599	10 518	19 513	-3.1	2.3	28 178	17.6	25.5	22.3
Yankton	119	1 813	4 787	15.0	77.2	18.6	14.8	3 942	10 305	21 798	-9.3	1.4	32 997	11.8	14.5	13.6
Ziebach	NA	NA	765	0.7	62.5	8.5	1.9	6 816	6 132	14 129	-9.0	2.2	20 139	46.4	46.0	51.5
TENNESSEE	715	4 319	1 171 640	12.6	67.1	16.0	4 145.0	4 581	12 255	24 807	4.7	2.6	32 047	13.6	18.9	16.6
Anderson	478	3 380	15 418	5.9	72.4	18.6	71.5	5 559	13 182	26 496	-1.7	1.9	36 006	13.1	19.5	16.4
Bedford	NA	NA	6 666	3.8	57.6	10.5	22.9	3 912	11 311	23 613	2.4	2.1	32 347	11.9	16.4	15.0
Benton	NA	NA	2 888	6.3	56.3	7.4	10.8	4 166	10 046	20 382	0.9	1.2	26 579	16.3	24.1	21.3
Bledsoe	131	475	1 988	6.2	52.1	5.4	7.4	4 300	8 053	18 250	2.5	0.6	25 815	20.2	27.4	24.8
Blount	389	2 460	18 929	8.5	68.5	14.3	75.7	4 824	12 674	25 575	1.3	2.1	35 571	10.9	16.1	14.0
Bradley	310	3 419	17 848	15.9	64.4	11.9	58.2	4 360	11 768	25 678	4.6	1.8	34 368	12.2	16.6	14.7
Campbell	345	1 941	7 499	5.1	47.5	6.6	28.0	4 350	8 098	16 450	-4.5	0.9	23 314	21.3	28.6	26.4
Cannon	82	698	2 223	3.9	54.6	6.9	7.8	3 907	9 863	22 847	16.7	0.4	30 078	12.4	18.7	15.7
Carroll	205	1 481	5 985	7.6	55.3	7.3	21.6	4 144	10 121	20 763	5.3	1.2	29 615	13.4	19.9	16.0
Carter	326	2 111	10 892	10.0	57.5	10.8	38.8	4 574	9 809	19 140	-0.1	1.0	26 736	16.4	23.8	20.4
Cheatham	433	781	6 121	11.1	65.0	10.5	24.2	3 698	11 868	30 778	12.7	1.4	41 036	8.6	11.8	10.8
Chester	NA	NA	3 427	34.2	54.6	8.7	8.8	3 657	8 281	19 413	-1.0	0.3	29 196	14.8	19.5	17.2
Claiborne	140	637	6 178	13.4	50.8	8.0	20.8	4 511	8 371	17 132	9.2	0.8	23 622	20.9	28.8	25.6
Clay	0	378	1 562	3.6	48.5	7.8	5.9	4 807	8 753	17 799	19.6	0.5	22 055	20.4	28.6	25.5
Cocke	231	2 234	5 892	3.1	50.4	5.5	22.6	4 212	8 574	16 818	-3.0	1.1	23 408	20.9	30.2	25.9
Coffee	154	3 479	9 120	5.7	65.1	15.3	40.6	4 632	11 416	24 802	3.3	1.7	32 889	12.8	18.2	16.3
Crockett	301	2 881	2 633	2.9	57.2	6.4	11.0	4 136	10 636	20 296	5.8	1.6	28 276	14.6	21.0	17.9
Cumberland	NA	NA	7 127	5.4	59.8	10.2	25.4	3 957	9 782	20 474	5.5	0.9	27 132	14.7	23.0	20.1
Davidson	1 603	8 490	121 420	28.6	75.9	24.4	393.3	5 627	15 195	28 377	3.2	3.8	39 112	12.5	18.6	16.0
Decatur	197	1 518	2 006	4.3	52.9	4.8	7.5	4 156	9 345	17 925	-1.3	0.7	26 581	14.9	20.8	18.0
De Kalb	394	2 307	2 988	4.0	50.3	8.4	9.7	3 503	9 570	19 388	6.6	1.4	28 036	16.0	23.3	20.2
Dickson	NA	NA	7 792	5.4	61.5	9.2	31.0	4 007	11 162	24 419	2.1	1.6	34 086	12.0	16.3	15.2
Dyer	NA	NA	7 961	3.9	55.3	9.4	32.6	4 794	11 270	22 105	9.0	2.2	31 092	14.9	20.5	17.9
Fayette	536	2 048	6 344	16.8	55.5	8.0	18.3	4 486	9 627	22 199	16.0	1.7	33 062	13.6	17.6	15.9
Fentress	329	1 610	3 319	2.2	44.9	6.6	10.3	5 801	6 927	13 924	0.8	0.4	20 332	23.9	32.5	28.7
Franklin	NA	NA	8 622	18.7	63.5	13.1	24.9	3 748	10 513	23 438	3.7	1.3	32 015	12.9	17.9	16.1
Gibson	493	3 141	9 752	5.5	57.5	8.0	35.2	4 053	10 277	20 938	3.1	0.8	29 587	14.2	20.2	17.2
Giles	NA	NA	5 765	10.1	60.1	8.9	20.1	4 187	10 983	22 078	2.6	1.1	31 855	12.6	17.3	15.6
Grainger	686	2 148	3 465	2.1	46.3	4.8	13.1	4 143	8 415	19 097	4.1	0.6	26 848	17.2	24.6	22.4
Greene	NA	NA	11 364	7.4	58.1	10.3	42.0	4 539	10 161	21 513	5.3	1.1	27 791	14.8	21.4	18.2
Grundy	NA	NA	3 115	5.2	44.7	5.4	10.7	4 404	7 227	16 425	-7.0	0.5	22 502	23.4	32.0	27.6
Hamblen	441	3 471	10 900	7.8	61.6	11.2	42.1	4 713	11 127	23 853	6.7	1.5	32 221	13.1	19.5	16.6
Hamilton	NA	NA	69 981	18.7	72.5	19.7	219.4	5 041	13 619	26 523	0.8	3.5	34 836	12.8	18.8	15.8
Hancock	134	1 743	1 396	1.6	42.4	5.1	6.2	5 074	6 266	11 822	5.4	0.6	18 529	29.1	36.4	35.7
Hardeman	347	2 589	5 578	4.9	53.0	7.6	19.3	4 084	8 650	19 128	5.1	1.0	25 337	20.0	25.5	22.5
Hardin	NA	NA	4 599	4.0	54.8	6.1	16.7	4 137	9 654	17 719	-9.3	1.5	25 852	18.3	25.7	22.8
Hawkins	210	1 048	9 231	5.0	58.0	8.4	32.0	4 332	10 358	21 960	1.5	0.8	31 286	14.8	21.3	18.5
Haywood	1 038	3 705	4 919	2.9	53.0	8.7	17.4	4 436	8 696	17 376	6.0	1.4	25 064	20.9	26.2	23.1
Henderson	247	2 596	4 702	3.6	55.2	6.8	17.2	3 936	9 564	21 099	4.1	0.8	30 665	13.7	18.4	16.6
Henry	329	2 383	5 651	5.9	60.0	8.5	21.2	4 351	10 423	18 891	-5.4	1.3	27 141	15.1	21.5	19.0
Hickman	70	625	3 333	6.2	55.6	7.2	13.7	5 045	9 723	21 567	-1.5	1.8	30 097	15.0	19.9	18.2
Houston	127	988	1 444	4.0	52.8	6.3	5.5	3 943	9 060	20 112	1.1	0.7	25 979	14.9	20.6	18.2
Humphreys	200	1 765	3 550	5.9	63.5	9.2	12.9	4 253	10 614	22 256	-15.9	1.3	30 574	12.5	17.4	15.9
Jackson	NA	NA	1 949	2.2	45.2	6.8	6.8	4 302	9 159	18 081	8.7	1.5	25 871	15.8	23.4	19.3
Jefferson	38	1 158	7 735	22.2	60.5	11.7	25.0	4 058	10 562	22 219	9.2	1.9	29 128	13.7	21.3	17.2
Johnson	NA	NA	2 676	3.9	47.2	5.0	11.4	4 888	7 531	14 967	-9.4	0.7	21 932	22.1	29.1	26.9
Knox	571	3 737	86 906	9.7	74.6	23.9	246.2	4 806	14 007	26 010	5.0	3.5	35 408	11.7	16.2	14.4
Lake	NA	NA	1 545	2.8	49.6	5.0	4.5	4 455	8 285	16 804	0.7	1.2	21 682	30.2	32.8	30.4
Lauderdale	NA	NA	5 304	2.0	52.1	6.0	20.2	4 021	8 607	18 972	3.0	1.1	26 065	18.8	23.7	21.3
Lawrence	286	3 072	7 665	7.9	53.7	6.7	27.5	4 056	10 094	20 842	-3.8	0.9	29 364	13.7	18.5	16.7
Lewis	166	1 122	2 113	7.0	51.5	5.0	7.2	3 629	8 180	17 362	-3.1	0.6	25 354	17.3	23.2	20.6
Lincoln	291	2 142	6 038	4.2	57.5	9.1	20.8	3 902	10 704	21 996	7.9	1.5	30 178	13.6	18.9	16.5
Loudon	318	2 769	6 261	7.0	63.8	9.6	27.1	4 228	12 006	24 258	4.4	2.0	34 382	11.4	18.0	15.9
McMinn	495	3 935	8 816	6.8	57.1	10.5	33.9	4 246	10 508	21 901	-5.0	1.4	30 352	13.9	19.5	17.1
McNairy	225	790	4 667	4.6	57.4	5.2	16.0	3 982	9 185	18 715	-1.1	1.0	26 797	17.0	23.4	20.3
Macon	159	1 529	3 246	2.2	49.2	5.5	12.9	3 855	10 158	19 147	-8.3	1.2	27 332	15.6	21.9	19.9
Madison	1 043	6 882	20 069	19.4	68.3	16.6	72.3	5 303	11 655	23 716	3.3	2.4	32 909	14.8	19.6	17.5
Marion	156	1 397	5 613	3.9	51.9	6.4	19.1	3 972	9 274	20 045	-6.4	0.7	28 563	15.5	21.1	19.2

1. Data for serious crimes have not been adjusted for underreporting; this may affect comparability between geographic areas and over time.   2. Per 100,000 population estimated by the FBI.   3. All persons 3 years old and over enrolled in nursery school through college.   4. Persons 25 years old and over.   5. Elementary and secondary education expenditures, local government fiscal years ending between July 1, 1996 and June 30, 1997.   6. Based on population enumerated as of April 1, 1990.

			Personal income, 1998									
STATE County	Total (mil dol)	Percent change, 1997–1998	Per capita[1] Dollars	Rank	Wages and salaries[2] (mil dol)	Proprietor's income (mil dol)	Dividends, interest, and rent (mil dol)	Transfer payments Total (mil dol)	Government payments to individuals Total (mil dol)	Social Security (mil dol)	Medical payments (mil dol)	Income mainte-nance (mil dol)	Unemploy-ment insurance (mil dol)
	62	63	64	65	66	67	68	69	70	71	72	73	74

STATE County	Total	% chg	Dollars	Rank	Wages	Prop.	Div/int/rent	Transfer Total	Gov Total	Social Sec	Medical	Income maint	Unemp
SOUTH DAKOTA—Cont'd													
Tripp	132	5.5	19 702	1 813	51	27	36	25	24	11	9	2	0
Turner	201	7.5	23 267	803	43	51	42	30	29	16	10	1	0
Union	399	9.1	32 505	101	445	45	90	35	33	17	12	2	0
Walworth	125	8.5	22 361	1 005	49	20	36	24	23	11	7	2	0
Yankton	491	4.3	23 375	777	302	61	113	68	65	31	26	3	0
Ziebach	22	4.5	10 206	3 103	7	3	4	7	7	1	2	2	0
TENNESSEE	132 756	5.3	24 437	X	85 947	12 658	20 598	20 540	19 643	7 712	8 592	1 955	341
Anderson	1 725	2.9	24 337	583	1 398	97	386	304	293	134	114	27	4
Bedford	733	6.0	21 219	1 322	403	76	125	120	114	51	47	9	3
Benton	304	1.3	18 633	2 174	110	27	55	78	75	32	33	6	1
Bledsoe	186	7.4	17 293	2 534	70	30	18	42	40	13	20	5	0
Blount	2 250	4.5	22 227	1 035	1 132	149	400	360	343	163	134	26	5
Bradley	1 935	4.1	23 214	814	1 149	231	281	287	273	116	119	23	4
Campbell	620	2.6	16 249	2 753	247	42	89	211	205	69	89	27	3
Cannon	232	3.8	19 139	2 008	42	15	35	52	50	18	26	4	1
Carroll	575	3.1	19 691	1 822	223	45	96	144	139	55	62	11	3
Carter	916	2.7	17 179	2 570	290	43	132	223	214	88	87	21	4
Cheatham	747	7.0	21 197	1 332	185	79	79	90	84	35	38	6	1
Chester	255	5.8	17 356	2 514	93	16	37	53	51	21	21	5	1
Claiborne	502	4.5	17 010	2 611	197	44	75	147	142	46	65	20	1
Clay	119	2.1	16 368	2 731	46	9	18	38	36	11	18	5	1
Cocke	542	6.1	16 975	2 618	228	31	68	147	142	49	62	21	4
Coffee	1 008	4.8	22 005	1 105	736	86	172	189	182	76	81	14	3
Crockett	285	1.1	20 359	1 616	109	26	49	64	61	23	29	6	1
Cumberland	861	7.4	19 512	1 885	376	101	184	215	208	100	81	15	3
Davidson	17 506	4.2	32 827	89	15 922	2 345	2 986	1 948	1 860	711	859	172	27
Decatur	210	1.3	19 501	1 891	98	15	28	61	60	21	31	4	2
De Kalb	320	2.7	19 964	1 724	126	46	53	73	70	25	34	7	2
Dickson	919	6.0	21 740	1 177	454	87	111	143	136	56	61	11	3
Dyer	777	2.3	21 235	1 312	518	70	113	151	145	58	64	15	2
Fayette	633	8.1	20 828	1 451	175	48	92	99	94	37	39	13	1
Fentress	275	2.8	17 030	2 603	91	45	30	92	89	25	45	12	2
Franklin	759	5.1	20 192	1 655	255	86	122	155	149	64	64	11	2
Gibson	1 007	1.7	20 964	1 404	524	87	158	234	226	90	105	19	4
Giles	616	6.0	21 299	1 293	321	42	94	110	105	44	46	9	2
Grainger	323	5.1	16 328	2 737	102	30	37	81	78	27	37	10	1
Greene	1 256	8.1	20 846	1 439	725	58	183	320	310	102	168	24	6
Grundy	235	4.7	16 744	2 666	46	31	23	74	72	22	35	10	1
Hamblen	1 236	5.3	22 913	868	985	101	188	219	210	91	86	20	4
Hamilton	8 161	3.6	27 712	252	6 260	649	1 481	1 221	1 173	489	494	101	16
Hancock	87	1.9	12 813	3 069	27	6	10	34	33	8	16	7	0
Hardeman	397	0.0	16 352	2 735	184	26	59	117	113	37	53	17	3
Hardin	480	5.7	19 284	1 962	242	41	70	120	116	42	55	12	3
Hawkins	926	3.5	18 703	2 157	400	32	138	195	187	79	76	21	3
Haywood	361	2.1	18 487	2 217	168	37	49	85	82	25	39	13	2
Henderson	486	3.8	19 914	1 738	261	37	68	102	98	36	46	9	4
Henry	627	3.3	20 921	1 415	335	58	123	142	137	61	57	10	3
Hickman	366	6.3	17 719	2 434	102	29	45	74	70	28	32	6	2
Houston	125	4.2	15 902	2 808	37	8	20	40	39	14	19	3	1
Humphreys	324	4.6	19 011	2 053	204	23	55	72	70	30	30	5	2
Jackson	186	4.4	19 326	1 944	50	16	30	49	48	17	23	5	1
Jefferson	779	6.1	17 868	2 387	319	54	127	168	161	65	71	14	3
Johnson	233	6.9	13 973	3 008	92	15	40	77	75	25	33	10	2
Knox	9 911	6.3	26 451	347	6 786	954	1 722	1 314	1 253	539	507	111	17
Lake	94	-2.5	11 495	3 091	37	1	16	37	36	11	19	5	1
Lauderdale	426	2.6	17 624	2 460	252	35	53	109	105	35	50	14	3
Lawrence	750	2.3	19 082	2 029	365	55	106	166	159	62	68	14	9
Lewis	173	1.3	15 901	2 809	62	15	21	49	48	17	24	4	2
Lincoln	585	5.2	19 713	1 806	208	58	93	114	109	46	46	10	2
Loudon	884	6.7	22 648	939	301	63	150	162	155	71	67	9	2
McMinn	882	4.5	19 092	2 026	564	63	136	189	181	75	75	16	4
McNairy	453	5.8	18 883	2 095	213	37	54	119	115	41	55	12	2
Macon	309	3.1	17 115	2 583	97	27	44	74	71	25	35	7	2
Madison	2 130	5.7	24 814	512	1 705	185	298	332	318	121	140	33	5
Marion	521	4.5	19 536	1 874	158	40	57	122	118	42	55	12	2

1. Based on the resident population estimated as of July 1 of the year shown.   2. Includes other labor income.

Table B. States and Counties — Earnings, Social Security, and Housing

STATE County	Earnings, 1998									Social Security bene-ficiaries, December 1998		Housing units, 1990		
			Percent by selected industries											
			Goods-related[1]		Service-related and other[2]							Supple-mental Security Income recipients, December 1998		
	Total (mil dol)	Farm	Total	Manu-facturing	Total	Retail trade	Finance, insur-ance, and real estate	Services	Govern-ment	Number	Rate[3]		Total	Percent change, 1980–1990
	75	76	77	78	79	80	81	82	83	84	85	86	87	88

SOUTH DAKOTA—Cont'd														
Tripp	77	19.2	D	1.6	D	11.2	4.7	24.5	14.2	1 484	220	165	3 023	-0.4
Turner	94	39.2	11.8	5.4	37.1	6.1	5.7	12.5	11.9	2 051	238	98	3 800	-5.5
Union	489	5.3	D	69.2	D	3.4	3.9	8.0	3.5	2 139	175	119	4 286	-3.7
Walworth	69	12.1	D	2.1	D	14.0	4.1	29.5	15.9	1 515	271	147	2 928	-1.2
Yankton	363	5.9	D	23.6	D	11.0	6.4	23.5	15.0	3 948	188	274	7 571	5.6
Ziebach	9	26.5	D	D	D	D	9.1	D	27.4	184	85	98	800	2.4
TENNESSEE	98 605	0.1	27.0	20.4	59.3	10.4	6.8	27.7	13.5	957 642	176	170 156	2 026 067	15.9
Anderson	1 495	0.1	39.2	33.4	D	D	2.3	31.5	14.5	15 404	217	2 330	29 323	13.4
Bedford	479	1.2	50.8	43.0	36.8	8.6	3.9	13.6	11.3	6 314	183	864	12 638	16.9
Benton	137	-1.0	D	24.9	D	12.7	2.9	15.7	16.8	4 034	247	472	7 107	8.9
Bledsoe	100	17.8	25.4	20.2	D	5.3	2.5	D	27.3	1 891	175	401	3 771	10.7
Blount	1 280	0.1	40.4	32.3	46.5	12.4	5.4	18.5	13.2	19 322	191	2 370	36 532	18.5
Bradley	1 381	0.3	D	34.9	D	8.9	4.5	26.4	11.3	14 211	171	2 260	29 562	19.7
Campbell	290	-0.3	29.8	19.5	48.4	14.2	7.6	16.5	22.1	9 649	252	3 011	14 817	11.8
Cannon	56	-5.9	D	16.2	D	13.7	4.1	26.2	21.0	2 448	202	296	4 368	9.1
Carroll	268	-1.0	40.5	34.7	45.1	10.9	4.2	21.1	15.4	7 295	251	1 003	11 783	4.2
Carter	333	-0.2	D	19.9	D	14.2	5.4	23.6	18.9	11 621	218	1 936	21 779	12.8
Cheatham	264	0.1	D	D	D	7.5	3.4	17.4	15.1	4 390	124	414	10 297	37.6
Chester	109	-1.6	D	22.9	D	13.3	D	20.5	18.2	2 867	195	416	4 944	10.6
Claiborne	241	1.5	D	33.3	D	11.6	3.8	15.2	18.6	6 746	228	2 197	10 711	14.1
Clay	55	-1.3	D	38.7	D	9.2	1.8	18.8	20.1	1 771	244	484	3 340	10.8
Cocke	259	1.0	D	34.7	D	16.3	2.6	18.8	15.5	6 946	217	1 980	12 282	8.6
Coffee	822	0.2	D	21.5	D	10.7	3.0	40.2	13.6	9 360	205	1 368	16 786	12.0
Crockett	134	0.4	47.6	38.0	39.0	6.1	3.5	16.2	13.0	3 215	230	579	5 521	-2.4
Cumberland	477	3.2	D	20.2	D	14.6	9.1	25.3	10.4	12 133	274	1 406	15 864	44.2
Davidson	18 267	0.0	16.4	10.2	73.0	10.4	9.0	39.0	10.5	80 421	151	12 538	229 064	22.2
Decatur	112	-2.1	D	26.1	D	8.8	3.4	21.7	15.6	2 869	265	718	5 346	9.6
De Kalb	171	1.1	D	27.2	D	8.0	3.0	30.9	11.2	3 446	216	394	6 694	10.1
Dickson	540	-1.2	D	35.3	D	13.2	4.0	20.2	12.0	6 985	165	953	14 149	27.0
Dyer	588	0.1	44.4	37.2	43.3	10.3	4.5	18.9	12.1	7 395	201	1 502	14 384	7.9
Fayette	223	0.9	44.1	31.7	37.0	7.6	9.3	11.9	18.0	5 150	169	1 194	9 115	11.8
Fentress	137	1.6	D	17.7	D	14.3	4.0	24.0	14.9	3 736	231	1 190	6 120	9.2
Franklin	341	4.7	D	22.2	D	12.3	3.2	30.6	13.0	8 025	214	1 033	13 717	18.4
Gibson	611	0.4	49.3	42.7	38.1	11.1	3.3	15.0	12.2	11 414	237	1 670	19 635	0.3
Giles	363	0.1	D	49.3	D	10.3	3.6	14.4	10.5	5 695	197	797	10 828	13.3
Grainger	132	2.9	D	39.9	D	6.9	1.8	15.4	14.7	3 829	193	1 033	7 501	5.9
Greene	783	0.0	41.4	37.1	45.5	11.0	2.8	20.1	13.1	13 625	225	2 684	23 270	10.1
Grundy	77	8.9	D	12.9	D	16.8	D	15.5	20.2	3 170	224	887	5 155	0.4
Hamblen	1 086	0.0	D	48.0	D	9.2	3.4	15.0	8.9	11 344	210	1 951	20 514	11.1
Hamilton	6 909	0.0	D	18.5	D	10.9	9.3	24.8	16.2	55 485	188	8 004	122 588	11.1
Hancock	32	0.6	D	25.0	D	12.1	D	17.4	27.0	1 381	204	702	2 890	7.6
Hardeman	210	-1.1	42.4	35.0	33.7	9.4	3.7	13.8	25.0	5 197	209	1 678	9 174	9.1
Hardin	283	0.1	D	38.6	D	11.0	3.2	9.8	15.3	5 833	234	1 200	10 275	14.8
Hawkins	433	-1.0	D	55.0	D	7.8	1.6	10.2	15.8	10 162	204	1 887	18 779	10.4
Haywood	205	4.5	40.0	35.2	39.6	8.7	6.9	12.2	15.9	3 671	188	1 181	7 475	6.1
Henderson	298	-1.1	54.3	48.5	36.2	9.7	3.2	15.0	10.7	4 805	197	856	9 278	11.8
Henry	394	0.4	D	32.1	D	13.0	3.5	16.2	15.9	7 596	253	942	13 774	2.1
Hickman	131	-2.7	41.5	31.3	D	11.0	D	15.3	26.5	3 811	185	542	6 662	18.2
Houston	46	-2.7	19.9	11.7	D	11.5	D	43.0	21.8	1 798	229	314	3 085	10.2
Humphreys	226	-1.7	D	41.3	D	8.3	1.8	11.7	21.0	3 661	215	484	7 136	9.6
Jackson	65	-1.9	37.0	27.5	D	8.2	5.6	D	16.1	2 432	253	558	4 219	13.9
Jefferson	372	-0.2	D	26.3	47.3	10.2	2.5	17.6	14.0	8 220	188	1 283	14 170	15.9
Johnson	107	-0.4	D	30.2	D	13.3	3.1	14.5	15.2	3 760	224	989	6 090	13.1
Knox	7 740	0.0	18.9	11.7	64.9	12.8	6.7	30.5	16.2	62 883	171	9 926	143 582	14.1
Lake	39	-4.1	D	D	D	15.0	2.4	19.3	48.1	1 485	182	430	2 610	-13.0
Lauderdale	286	1.0	D	44.5	D	8.3	2.9	11.9	16.5	4 876	201	1 442	9 343	0.8
Lawrence	420	-1.1	D	37.0	D	13.6	3.3	15.0	13.0	8 221	209	1 348	14 229	13.5
Lewis	78	-1.6	D	31.1	D	15.1	3.1	17.8	16.8	2 247	207	337	3 943	21.4
Lincoln	266	1.0	D	30.6	D	12.2	3.5	13.3	20.4	6 266	211	881	11 902	15.6
Loudon	364	5.9	D	30.9	D	10.3	3.8	16.5	15.6	8 333	213	901	12 995	19.9
McMinn	627	0.2	D	50.1	D	9.2	3.6	12.5	11.0	9 605	208	1 544	17 616	11.5
McNairy	250	-0.9	D	34.7	46.2	8.4	2.4	24.8	13.5	5 792	241	1 389	9 734	8.0
Macon	124	0.4	D	25.1	D	12.9	5.3	16.9	17.3	3 714	204	693	6 879	12.8
Madison	1 890	0.2	D	25.7	D	9.3	3.6	23.6	18.1	15 028	175	3 010	31 809	10.3
Marion	198	-0.3	D	29.3	D	16.9	4.0	15.9	15.3	5 339	199	982	10 011	10.9

1. Covers mining, construction, and manufacturing. 2. Covers private sector earnings in agricultural services, forestry, and fisheries; transportation and public utilities; wholesale trade; retail trade; finance, insurance, and real estate; and services. 3. Per 1,000 resident population estimated as of July 1 of the year shown.

Table B. States and Counties — Housing, Labor Force, and Employment

STATE County	Housing units, 1990 (cont'd)								Civilian labor force, 1999		Unemployment		Civilian employment, 1990[5]		
	Occupied units												Percent		
			Owner-occupied			Renter-occupied									
				Owner cost as a percent of income											
	Total	Percent	Median value[1]	With a mortgage	Without a mortgage	Median rent[2]	Rent as percent of income	Substandard units[3] (percent)	Total	Percent change, 1998–1999	Total	Rate[4]	Total	Professional, managerial, and technical	Precision production, craft, and repair
	89	90	91	92	93	94	95	96	97	98	99	100	101	102	103
SOUTH DAKOTA—Cont'd															
Tripp	2 573	73.6	35 600	20.2	13.5	253	25.1	5.6	3 531	3.5	109	3.1	3 033	18.5	9.8
Turner	3 332	76.1	22 800	17.2	14.5	240	20.6	1.8	4 173	-0.8	91	2.2	3 810	18.4	10.8
Union	3 859	72.7	37 600	18.0	12.9	266	22.6	2.0	7 199	2.8	202	2.8	4 724	20.3	11.3
Walworth	2 447	71.5	27 600	16.7	14.1	298	24.6	2.8	3 224	2.9	106	3.3	2 795	22.3	8.9
Yankton	7 107	66.0	48 500	20.6	13.9	286	23.7	1.9	11 070	0.2	252	2.3	9 488	24.9	10.9
Ziebach	630	58.3	14 999	12.7	16.1	251	35.1	25.1	709	4.6	101	14.2	650	21.7	4.6
TENNESSEE	1 853 725	68.0	58 400	20.1	12.6	357	25.0	3.8	2 818 851	2.1	113 503	4.0	2 250 842	26.1	12.2
Anderson	27 384	70.8	55 100	16.7	11.7	342	24.5	3.0	36 246	1.4	1 291	3.6	30 758	32.1	11.4
Bedford	11 608	71.8	48 400	19.5	13.0	307	24.5	3.9	17 911	0.8	914	5.1	14 679	18.3	16.2
Benton	5 784	80.2	39 700	18.6	12.4	270	22.6	3.9	7 547	1.4	616	8.2	6 159	19.9	15.1
Bledsoe	3 261	78.7	36 000	19.0	12.4	232	23.0	4.8	3 911	-3.7	136	3.5	3 662	14.9	15.5
Blount	33 624	74.6	60 200	18.1	11.9	321	23.9	2.2	51 835	3.3	1 923	3.7	38 840	25.9	14.6
Bradley	27 604	68.8	55 000	19.7	12.3	329	24.0	2.8	43 042	2.1	1 537	3.6	36 565	22.2	15.1
Campbell	13 150	73.8	37 900	23.0	12.6	250	27.0	6.9	17 038	-1.1	1 312	7.7	12 298	18.2	18.7
Cannon	3 980	79.3	41 500	17.7	12.7	238	21.1	4.9	5 098	5.2	224	4.4	4 978	14.7	17.4
Carroll	10 727	79.0	35 700	16.8	13.5	262	23.7	3.1	12 680	-4.0	1 183	9.3	12 066	16.3	13.4
Carter	20 189	76.3	43 800	19.4	13.3	282	24.7	3.2	25 802	1.5	1 288	5.0	22 520	21.7	15.0
Cheatham	9 515	83.1	64 000	22.0	13.8	387	24.7	5.3	19 596	3.9	435	2.2	13 449	22.3	17.0
Chester	4 558	77.4	40 200	21.1	13.6	241	23.6	3.5	8 255	3.0	326	3.9	5 615	19.6	13.1
Claiborne	9 629	78.3	41 400	21.7	13.5	248	25.5	7.7	13 207	8.8	569	4.3	10 158	18.8	16.9
Clay	2 855	81.4	37 100	18.6	13.3	215	24.7	8.9	2 734	3.0	324	11.9	3 183	16.1	14.8
Cocke	11 191	72.7	40 300	17.7	12.6	213	25.3	8.6	16 686	2.3	1 127	6.8	12 474	14.4	13.5
Coffee	15 500	70.1	52 800	18.6	12.9	319	23.5	3.6	22 526	-1.3	977	4.3	18 010	23.7	13.5
Crockett	5 183	76.4	38 600	19.7	13.3	258	23.8	3.7	7 343	4.2	398	5.4	5 787	17.5	14.1
Cumberland	13 426	78.4	49 100	22.2	11.7	296	24.3	4.0	21 231	3.6	1 011	4.8	14 009	19.1	14.5
Davidson	207 530	53.8	76 000	20.9	12.6	433	25.3	2.6	311 530	1.5	8 815	2.8	264 680	33.4	8.6
Decatur	4 216	80.5	34 700	21.8	13.6	253	23.6	3.9	5 744	2.9	396	6.9	4 351	14.5	13.5
De Kalb	5 696	76.4	44 200	17.4	13.4	261	24.7	3.8	8 302	0.1	499	6.0	6 571	17.5	14.8
Dickson	13 019	75.7	54 100	20.9	12.5	337	27.0	3.5	21 855	3.9	694	3.2	16 049	21.1	15.5
Dyer	13 617	65.8	44 100	17.3	13.3	310	24.6	3.2	18 508	1.5	885	4.8	15 652	20.1	13.6
Fayette	8 453	74.8	51 400	22.5	12.5	241	23.4	13.5	14 261	3.8	532	3.7	10 569	16.2	15.9
Fentress	5 511	78.6	32 300	23.2	13.2	212	23.1	7.9	6 732	1.3	710	10.5	5 717	17.1	16.6
Franklin	12 660	77.7	48 700	17.6	12.0	296	22.7	2.9	18 239	-0.6	822	4.5	15 307	22.7	15.0
Gibson	18 361	72.6	39 200	16.5	13.3	271	23.7	2.8	21 633	-0.8	1 361	6.3	19 830	16.7	14.4
Giles	9 832	73.0	44 600	18.8	12.1	272	25.9	5.0	16 290	5.6	641	3.9	11 459	17.6	12.9
Grainger	6 394	82.4	40 300	20.4	12.0	246	21.1	9.8	10 207	3.3	436	4.3	7 408	11.0	17.3
Greene	21 482	77.0	44 500	18.0	12.1	272	22.9	4.6	35 229	2.9	2 005	5.7	26 279	20.2	17.1
Grundy	4 784	81.4	29 800	23.3	13.7	211	30.3	7.2	5 414	-4.8	323	6.0	4 946	14.3	15.4
Hamblen	19 429	72.1	51 300	18.0	12.4	291	22.7	3.0	30 614	2.5	1 314	4.3	24 066	19.2	14.4
Hamilton	111 799	64.1	62 000	18.1	12.9	373	24.9	2.8	151 022	3.7	4 944	3.3	134 440	29.8	10.7
Hancock	2 484	78.3	32 200	24.1	11.8	145	28.3	19.2	2 707	-1.5	178	6.6	2 022	12.8	17.3
Hardeman	8 276	73.6	39 200	19.9	13.2	258	24.9	8.3	9 449	0.8	882	9.3	8 962	16.5	13.6
Hardin	8 726	77.4	39 100	20.2	12.4	252	23.5	5.3	12 196	-3.2	853	7.0	9 602	15.4	14.7
Hawkins	17 167	77.1	48 600	16.6	12.0	295	22.7	5.5	23 937	3.7	1 257	5.3	19 335	19.1	16.7
Haywood	7 014	66.4	40 400	21.8	14.3	257	26.0	8.5	8 789	4.1	764	8.7	7 725	17.7	12.4
Henderson	8 527	79.7	42 200	16.4	12.9	266	25.1	3.2	13 997	1.1	872	6.2	10 228	17.4	14.8
Henry	11 362	76.5	41 700	20.9	13.0	270	25.2	3.0	14 592	0.3	948	6.5	11 422	19.0	13.7
Hickman	5 976	80.8	43 200	18.3	13.0	285	23.7	5.2	7 991	-1.8	462	5.8	6 957	19.4	16.7
Houston	2 683	78.7	35 300	18.7	13.4	264	25.5	4.0	2 742	0.1	255	9.3	2 672	17.3	22.0
Humphreys	6 063	77.3	40 700	19.6	12.7	288	22.9	3.5	7 870	2.9	551	7.0	6 613	18.9	17.5
Jackson	3 642	81.6	38 000	17.9	13.1	229	24.4	7.2	4 717	1.6	403	8.5	3 873	14.7	16.3
Jefferson	12 329	77.2	47 900	18.9	11.9	275	25.5	3.9	23 858	5.2	1 008	4.2	15 196	19.8	14.8
Johnson	5 406	80.7	41 300	24.8	12.7	211	25.9	7.1	7 188	-2.4	689	9.6	5 537	13.6	17.3
Knox	133 639	63.9	63 900	19.1	12.8	351	25.5	2.0	200 090	1.6	5 153	2.6	163 586	33.6	9.8
Lake	2 418	58.4	35 100	19.4	13.6	215	27.7	5.0	2 548	1.8	159	6.2	2 484	12.8	9.7
Lauderdale	8 423	66.9	38 700	20.8	14.1	273	24.0	6.8	10 260	2.0	847	8.3	9 071	14.5	14.6
Lawrence	13 338	76.6	43 300	18.0	12.3	255	23.7	3.8	20 878	-3.5	2 326	11.1	15 410	16.6	14.5
Lewis	3 533	75.8	37 200	21.0	12.3	222	26.3	5.1	4 159	-1.8	398	9.6	3 893	16.2	14.5
Lincoln	10 881	73.4	47 100	20.3	12.7	281	24.3	3.5	14 343	1.4	591	4.1	13 260	17.7	14.8
Loudon	12 155	77.6	51 000	20.2	12.2	280	22.8	2.2	20 719	3.8	621	3.0	14 749	21.9	14.5
McMinn	16 351	76.1	45 600	18.7	12.5	269	25.4	3.1	21 849	-0.7	1 270	5.8	18 760	18.6	16.1
McNairy	8 834	79.2	36 400	21.2	13.3	238	24.5	3.8	12 314	3.6	590	4.8	9 509	15.1	17.7
Macon	6 159	78.8	36 600	19.4	13.8	244	22.4	6.5	8 148	3.3	355	4.4	7 369	13.1	17.0
Madison	29 609	65.4	53 500	20.4	12.9	337	24.3	2.8	49 922	3.2	1 687	3.4	35 540	27.9	10.7
Marion	9 215	79.0	42 600	20.7	13.1	263	23.8	3.8	12 666	3.7	611	4.8	10 603	16.2	17.9

1. Specified owner-occupied units.   2. Specified renter-occupied units.   3. Overcrowded or lacking complete plumbing facilities.   4. Percent of civilian labor force.   5. Persons 16 years and older.

Table B. States and Counties — Nonfarm Employment and Agriculture

	Private nonfarm establishments, employment and payroll, 1998								Agriculture, 1997			
		Employment					Annual payroll		Farms			Farm operators
										Percent with—		
STATE County	Number of establish-ments	Total	Health Care and Social Assistance	Manufac-turing	Retail trade	Finance and Insurance	Professional Scientific and Technical Services	Total (mil dol)	Average per employee (dollars)	Number	Less than 50 acres	500 acres and over	Whose principal occu-pation is farming (percent)
	104	105	106	107	108	109	110	111	112	113	114	115	116

SOUTH DAKOTA—Cont'd													
Tripp	236	1 722	386	D	363	100	48	30	17 506	654	7.0	62.5	72.9
Turner	260	1 494	404	125	302	113	28	23	15 642	832	15.3	31.9	71.0
Union	390	11 900	417	D	D	290	116	445	37 414	494	15.0	38.3	69.4
Walworth	236	1 884	397	D	476	76	84	29	15 497	338	10.9	61.8	73.4
Yankton	723	11 038	1 619	2 609	2 091	1 001	249	214	19 387	636	16.7	32.4	68.6
Ziebach	17	203	D	0	13	D	0	5	25 310	259	4.6	81.9	76.4
TENNESSEE	131 110	2 299 348	281 083	482 811	311 720	101 293	86 439	62 441	27 156	76 818	39.5	5.0	36.0
Anderson	1 726	38 946	3 777	11 773	3 917	695	9 539	1 347	34 579	462	47.8	1.9	27.7
Bedford	726	11 816	997	5 654	1 208	257	173	275	23 267	1 408	33.3	5.3	39.3
Benton	347	3 643	399	1 073	774	123	D	70	19 235	433	27.9	4.8	27.0
Bledsoe	142	1 557	400	618	146	31	D	30	19 545	525	24.4	6.7	37.7
Blount	2 132	32 936	3 799	7 108	5 640	1 403	670	901	27 370	1 053	52.9	2.6	32.4
Bradley	1 904	37 841	4 880	12 973	4 282	1 089	890	955	25 234	781	44.6	4.1	37.3
Campbell	646	7 246	1 398	1 832	1 489	278	119	150	20 703	398	45.2	1.3	36.4
Cannon	157	1 488	288	407	189	61	D	26	17 638	754	33.7	2.9	34.2
Carroll	544	8 071	1 128	3 740	878	235	91	147	18 161	851	25.5	8.0	32.5
Carter	772	9 634	1 476	2 149	1 683	334	D	211	21 854	622	64.6	0.8	29.1
Cheatham	485	6 219	405	3 086	750	106	151	146	23 405	556	35.3	3.8	33.6
Chester	238	3 363	250	844	524	81	D	62	18 316	410	24.6	7.3	33.7
Claiborne	470	7 493	987	3 296	724	227	95	144	19 206	1 397	43.7	2.1	41.9
Clay	110	1 629	412	777	157	32	D	31	18 958	503	30.4	3.8	35.8
Cocke	514	6 886	856	2 515	1 160	170	67	145	21 107	886	45.5	1.0	34.5
Coffee	1 214	22 585	2 074	5 678	2 996	613	D	611	27 057	968	41.5	5.6	35.6
Crockett	303	3 015	312	1 048	366	140	D	71	23 712	380	34.2	22.6	52.6
Cumberland	954	11 543	1 780	2 537	2 249	387	219	245	21 248	726	40.8	5.8	31.4
Davidson	19 011	393 097	51 825	30 149	44 853	23 224	18 714	12 408	31 565	533	47.1	2.4	30.0
Decatur	256	3 483	684	1 421	435	100	52	73	21 101	437	19.7	8.7	30.0
De Kalb	317	5 004	511	2 570	426	124	58	112	22 313	806	40.0	3.5	30.8
Dickson	877	12 646	1 426	3 917	2 108	378	147	271	21 446	1 106	32.8	3.8	35.4
Dyer	954	15 779	1 353	6 658	2 104	500	232	367	23 252	526	30.2	25.5	49.8
Fayette	416	4 232	419	1 517	441	154	51	105	24 818	716	28.4	15.6	39.1
Fentress	277	3 775	953	1 290	594	136	D	66	17 408	504	35.9	4.8	40.1
Franklin	692	8 022	1 190	2 186	1 486	217	166	172	21 425	985	45.1	6.1	42.9
Gibson	1 080	16 783	1 677	8 169	2 113	472	199	372	22 178	874	36.5	17.4	45.8
Giles	571	9 290	803	3 926	1 162	373	182	227	24 425	1 570	26.0	5.2	33.8
Grainger	250	2 736	204	1 456	405	D	D	56	20 424	1 095	45.5	1.3	37.1
Greene	1 187	20 966	2 569	7 985	2 719	509	232	465	22 172	3 086	56.3	1.1	38.2
Grundy	190	1 366	266	226	423	D	D	20	14 284	337	49.6	3.9	46.9
Hamblen	1 440	29 270	2 605	14 110	3 619	554	322	706	24 122	667	57.9	1.9	35.2
Hamilton	9 059	165 300	19 340	32 880	21 008	11 273	5 205	4 357	26 356	604	49.2	2.5	29.3
Hancock	63	718	130	D	102	36	D	11	14 822	633	39.5	1.7	43.0
Hardeman	432	5 748	1 165	1 922	777	212	53	141	24 582	559	22.4	15.2	36.3
Hardin	531	6 312	628	2 507	1 013	160	107	134	21 222	594	28.1	7.6	34.7
Hawkins	615	11 152	917	6 284	1 328	193	102	297	26 641	1 813	48.5	0.7	35.7
Haywood	375	5 332	438	2 338	872	256	D	114	21 391	360	24.2	31.1	59.4
Henderson	542	8 790	696	4 176	1 134	251	53	190	21 562	858	21.4	7.1	29.8
Henry	778	10 265	1 402	3 369	1 555	374	198	221	21 498	831	25.5	8.7	36.6
Hickman	301	2 647	456	1 029	309	83	D	58	21 791	678	21.7	7.2	36.1
Houston	123	1 189	329	327	156	29	D	19	16 203	289	23.9	5.2	26.3
Humphreys	323	4 756	346	2 026	684	50	53	140	29 421	577	24.6	9.9	32.4
Jackson	109	1 315	188	646	123	D	D	27	20 902	605	31.7	3.8	37.5
Jefferson	634	9 221	803	2 475	1 332	172	124	195	21 160	1 147	50.2	1.0	38.6
Johnson	239	3 188	239	1 389	423	89	D	62	19 571	679	58.2	1.2	37.4
Knox	11 264	182 606	27 455	19 428	30 153	7 161	9 390	4 740	25 959	1 193	58.1	1.3	33.6
Lake	100	1 043	235	326	173	20	D	16	15 621	80	15.0	51.2	71.2
Lauderdale	379	7 173	503	3 627	865	221	55	141	19 705	505	28.3	18.8	47.3
Lawrence	807	12 038	987	5 827	1 756	259	149	245	20 374	1 617	33.0	3.8	31.2
Lewis	226	2 103	453	634	385	57	D	39	18 610	222	23.0	3.6	32.0
Lincoln	630	6 877	835	2 751	1 290	210	168	142	20 686	1 661	31.7	6.6	37.1
Loudon	748	9 582	1 043	3 123	1 598	256	169	228	23 780	763	51.6	2.4	37.1
McMinn	942	17 708	1 514	9 118	2 053	498	206	440	24 853	1 074	39.9	4.0	35.3
McNairy	483	8 037	718	2 551	712	143	D	161	20 026	720	22.1	7.1	29.7
Macon	314	3 500	445	1 397	573	164	D	64	18 195	1 238	40.0	1.9	33.6
Madison	2 662	49 684	8 031	12 151	7 564	1 337	1 220	1 238	24 912	571	30.8	11.2	38.7
Marion	432	5 391	643	1 657	1 198	170	96	107	19 818	294	37.1	6.5	33.3

Table B. States and Counties — Agriculture, Land, and Water

STATE County	Acreage (1,000)	Percent change, 1992–1997	Average size of farm	Total irrigated (1,000)	Total cropland (1,000)	Average per farm ($1,000)	Average per acre (dollars)	Value of machinery and equipment Average per farm ($1,000)	Total (mil dol)	Average per farm (dollars)	Crops	Live-stock and poultry products	$10,000 or more	$100,000 or more	Percent of land owned by Fed. Gov. 1997	Water consumption 1995 (mil gal/day)
	117	118	119	120	121	122	123	124	125	126	127	128	129	130	131	132
SOUTH DAKOTA—Cont'd																
Tripp	930	-7.6	1 423	2	454	444	330	79	66	100 485	30.8	69.2	79.2	26.8	0.0	5.1
Turner	352	-4.0	424	17	312	383	926	107	97	116 883	53.0	47.0	81.9	34.6	0.2	15.1
Union	254	-2.3	514	31	236	608	1 101	98	86	174 768	58.6	41.4	82.2	43.7	0.3	16.0
Walworth	437	-2.6	1 294	2	246	347	308	88	31	92 349	46.9	53.1	73.4	26.0	1.6	6.5
Yankton	261	-3.7	410	6	219	378	960	71	60	94 970	57.6	42.4	78.9	24.4	0.8	10.5
Ziebach	1 499	6.6	5 788	D	240	912	154	75	23	88 517	41.9	58.1	77.6	25.9	0.2	0.8
TENNESSEE	11 122	-0.4	145	46	7 069	261	1 808	33	2 178	28 358	52.5	47.5	27.7	5.1	4.6	10 076.2
Anderson	41	-2.6	89	0	21	353	3 378	29	5	11 849	49.7	50.3	14.7	1.9	5.1	507.7
Bedford	207	-3.1	147	0	125	225	1 693	34	69	49 041	7.4	92.6	32.3	9.7	0.0	6.5
Benton	69	9.4	159	0	36	189	1 162	27	4	10 079	41.1	58.9	19.9	1.6	2.0	4.2
Bledsoe	96	3.1	183	0	57	239	1 377	37	41	79 044	10.6	89.4	37.1	5.9	0.0	1.7
Blount	93	-2.9	89	0	64	341	3 812	30	19	17 634	45.2	54.8	20.1	2.6	26.7	14.1
Bradley	90	-2.1	115	0	51	300	2 827	35	55	70 283	4.7	95.3	27.8	12.2	0.0	18.7
Campbell	31	2.3	77	D	19	129	1 826	27	3	6 885	48.7	51.3	18.1	0.5	0.0	4.1
Cannon	103	5.9	136	0	53	195	1 533	29	12	16 070	36.0	63.9	21.9	3.7	0.0	1.3
Carroll	172	3.4	202	0	108	245	1 202	35	22	26 126	78.4	21.6	24.9	5.8	3.2	5.0
Carter	39	5.1	63	0	22	149	2 385	22	7	11 730	42.6	57.4	19.0	1.8	36.1	19.8
Cheatham	68	17.5	123	0	38	293	2 469	25	9	15 918	70.5	29.4	32.4	3.8	0.4	2.4
Chester	73	1.5	178	D	42	153	925	25	6	14 302	69.8	30.1	21.7	3.9	0.0	1.6
Claiborne	144	0.7	103	0	73	134	1 372	23	20	14 459	40.6	59.4	31.2	1.5	0.8	2.6
Clay	72	2.3	142	0	34	169	1 181	19	6	12 510	56.4	43.6	33.6	0.6	0.3	1.6
Cocke	75	-10.5	85	1	41	193	2 349	24	14	15 956	46.4	53.6	19.1	2.4	23.2	7.4
Coffee	136	2.7	140	1	89	268	1 837	33	30	30 846	38.0	62.0	30.2	8.0	8.9	5.6
Crockett	151	3.9	396	D	135	567	1 460	99	48	126 462	97.1	2.9	50.8	26.1	0.0	3.4
Cumberland	100	3.5	138	0	57	255	1 818	33	37	51 280	21.4	78.6	22.9	4.5	0.6	7.6
Davidson	52	11.2	98	0	27	371	3 757	31	11	19 974	76.0	24.0	17.3	1.9	0.2	148.4
Decatur	88	1.6	202	D	42	196	960	27	4	9 774	30.6	69.4	24.0	0.7	0.8	6.9
De Kalb	99	3.3	123	0	56	212	1 629	25	26	32 371	80.7	19.3	26.4	2.7	0.6	1.6
Dickson	149	3.2	134	0	77	255	1 788	34	12	10 911	41.5	58.5	26.8	1.3	0.0	4.4
Dyer	234	1.4	445	3	217	570	1 256	90	56	105 750	94.3	5.7	54.6	24.0	0.0	7.1
Fayette	271	4.9	378	1	180	553	1 476	62	51	71 771	70.8	29.2	34.6	12.2	0.0	5.9
Fentress	70	0.2	139	0	34	220	1 572	28	22	43 301	13.9	86.1	35.1	8.7	8.0	19.9
Franklin	132	-2.2	134	1	94	259	1 984	37	63	63 492	27.8	72.2	38.2	14.2	0.3	4.8
Gibson	278	2.2	318	1	249	404	1 250	83	68	78 346	87.0	13.0	41.9	16.5	3.2	8.3
Giles	249	-2.6	159	2	139	199	1 284	27	30	19 287	16.6	83.4	23.5	3.5	0.0	4.8
Grainger	97	-6.9	88	1	52	162	2 046	25	16	14 843	62.3	37.7	27.3	1.7	0.0	1.7
Greene	226	-4.8	73	0	153	177	2 369	28	51	16 595	36.8	63.2	26.2	2.9	9.5	10.4
Grundy	36	-15.6	108	0	18	177	1 454	25	31	91 371	17.2	82.8	43.3	23.4	0.0	1.8
Hamblen	52	-8.8	78	1	37	261	3 165	35	14	20 576	41.3	58.7	19.9	3.3	0.0	8.3
Hamilton	57	-9.8	94	0	30	318	2 710	27	8	13 712	21.8	78.3	17.5	2.6	2.3	1 533.3
Hancock	68	-15.2	107	0	32	117	1 243	19	8	11 947	44.8	55.2	26.4	1.1	0.0	0.6
Hardeman	166	3.9	297	1	91	287	981	32	19	33 490	72.7	27.3	23.4	7.0	0.0	3.2
Hardin	116	5.1	195	0	65	242	1 244	27	10	16 243	65.3	34.7	22.2	4.2	0.9	28.8
Hawkins	147	-5.8	81	0	76	166	1 973	25	16	8 812	54.4	45.6	21.4	0.7	1.8	552.7
Haywood	212	-5.4	589	2	186	684	1 214	116	63	175 142	97.4	2.6	58.1	28.9	2.9	2.9
Henderson	152	3.4	177	0	89	228	1 128	32	18	21 159	33.6	66.4	26.3	4.2	0.0	3.0
Henry	185	-3.0	223	0	118	265	1 103	46	38	45 433	58.0	42.0	40.3	9.1	1.8	4.2
Hickman	128	-1.7	189	0	64	233	1 273	26	9	12 753	22.8	77.2	26.1	1.9	0.6	3.3
Houston	49	10.8	169	0	24	222	1 293	37	4	13 916	22.0	78.0	27.7	2.1	0.0	1.3
Humphreys	122	2.5	211	0	56	250	1 206	36	8	14 152	44.0	56.0	25.0	2.9	1.8	1 220.6
Jackson	83	-4.3	138	0	34	145	1 161	19	5	8 402	50.2	49.8	22.8	0.5	0.1	1.3
Jefferson	98	-0.9	85	1	68	241	3 183	29	20	17 454	30.2	69.8	24.8	2.2	0.0	7.4
Johnson	49	-10.0	73	0	26	174	2 299	23	8	11 205	56.6	43.4	27.8	0.9	26.5	2.7
Knox	88	-6.6	74	0	53	279	3 831	28	15	12 978	57.6	42.4	15.3	1.5	0.0	63.3
Lake	90	-1.5	1 120	3	86	1 655	1 477	227	23	292 546	99.5	0.5	86.2	53.8	1.4	2.1
Lauderdale	192	4.9	380	2	161	439	1 083	85	47	93 649	94.0	6.0	45.1	19.2	5.9	5.0
Lawrence	214	8.6	132	0	134	199	1 535	32	27	16 662	29.2	70.8	24.2	3.4	0.1	6.1
Lewis	37	-0.5	166	0	16	229	1 395	32	2	10 774	37.7	62.3	18.9	0.7	1.5	1.6
Lincoln	276	0.4	166	1	158	228	1 423	34	49	29 737	32.1	67.9	28.6	5.5	0.0	4.5
Loudon	74	0.0	97	0	48	329	2 820	44	45	59 065	D	D	21.1	4.2	0.0	16.6
McMinn	127	2.7	119	0	79	238	2 052	29	34	31 816	10.5	89.5	24.0	6.9	0.8	85.4
McNairy	130	6.7	181	D	70	149	845	30	11	15 439	60.4	39.6	20.0	4.4	0.0	4.3
Macon	135	-2.9	109	0	74	171	1 543	23	20	16 250	71.0	29.0	36.3	2.4	0.0	1.8
Madison	146	3.3	255	D	104	283	1 148	58	29	50 607	79.4	20.6	31.0	10.0	0.0	18.6
Marion	51	0.1	174	D	30	254	1 491	36	11	36 343	15.3	84.7	26.5	7.5	0.0	3.1

Table B. States and Counties — Residential Construction, Wholesale and Retail Trade, and Real Estate

STATE County	Value of Residential Construction Authorized by Building Permits, 1999		Wholesale Trade, 1997				Retail Trade[1], 1997				Real Estate and Rental and Leasing, 1997			
	New Construction ($1,000)	Number of Housing Units	Number of Establishments	Number of Employees	Sales (mil dol)	Annual Payroll (mil dol)	Number of Establishments	Number of Employees	Sales (mil dol)	Annual Payroll (mil dol)	Number of Establishments	Number of Employees	Receipts (mil dol)	Annual Payroll (mil dol)
	133	134	135	136	137	138	139	140	141	142	143	144	145	146
SOUTH DAKOTA—Cont'd														
Tripp	504	13	17	175	82.4	3.1	52	364	52.1	4.5	3	11	0.3	0.1
Turner	2 326	22	14	76	99.5	1.8	42	D	D	D	5	D	D	D
Union	19 557	135	26	210	225.0	6.1	45	D	D	D	7	15	1.6	0.1
Walworth	1 229	12	11	69	34.2	1.5	61	398	54.3	4.9	6	8	0.4	0.1
Yankton	6 570	61	50	428	290.1	8.6	162	1 988	229.6	25.2	19	72	6.4	1.2
Ziebach	NA	NA	2	D	D	D	3	D	D	D	NA	NA	NA	NA
TENNESSEE	3 836 987	37 049	8 234	120 228	82 626.4	3 975.4	24 808	304 452	50 813.2	4 810.3	4 999	29 626	3 732.0	667.3
Anderson	25 942	216	51	342	105.9	9.9	331	3 923	700.9	60.8	74	336	39.2	6.4
Bedford	4 161	64	43	284	72.3	7.7	145	1 298	207.4	18.1	29	70	9.7	1.3
Benton	536	6	14	99	35.2	2.5	78	746	92.5	9.4	11	28	2.1	0.3
Bledsoe	NA	NA	2	D	D	D	31	162	23.6	1.8	2	D	D	D
Blount	17 871	169	97	1 347	655.2	38.2	385	5 590	1 189.1	99.3	80	443	48.3	7.4
Bradley	40 605	549	93	2 328	1 651.3	51.0	392	4 103	745.7	66.1	72	278	29.4	4.9
Campbell	2 461	67	26	477	117.6	15.0	159	1 551	228.9	21.3	18	106	8.9	1.5
Cannon	190	1	8	D	D	D	30	213	33.3	2.9	4	D	D	D
Carroll	1 045	14	26	210	48.2	4.6	121	950	127.4	11.6	14	30	3.1	0.2
Carter	4 747	95	28	D	D	D	156	1 602	265.1	23.2	19	71	5.8	0.8
Cheatham	30 762	371	20	119	29.3	3.1	75	729	130.0	10.5	14	D	D	D
Chester	5 430	75	10	62	34.4	1.3	65	481	99.8	7.8	5	20	0.8	0.3
Claiborne	14 377	274	17	D	D	D	97	736	111.5	10.2	15	78	5.5	0.9
Clay	NA	NA	2	D	D	D	23	127	19.0	1.7	2	D	D	D
Cocke	1 035	36	19	167	68.9	5.3	126	1 361	191.3	16.3	22	96	4.1	0.9
Coffee	11 554	89	50	482	127.4	10.7	283	3 127	490.6	43.8	46	134	13.0	2.2
Crockett	200	3	15	D	D	0.0	58	339	58.4	4.4	3	3	0.5	0.0
Cumberland	9 424	115	35	276	130.5	7.7	222	2 171	368.6	32.4	44	512	43.9	11.2
Davidson	517 342	3 927	1 445	26 012	17 005.2	962.7	3 017	44 452	7 737.6	782.7	866	6 603	1 119.8	173.2
Decatur	90	3	7	36	3.3	0.5	50	371	65.1	5.2	4	7	0.6	0.1
De Kalb	310	4	8	271	96.3	6.6	65	419	67.3	5.7	14	26	1.4	0.3
Dickson	46 515	541	27	471	274.7	11.5	185	2 158	412.9	35.2	32	D	D	D
Dyer	17 367	235	47	572	221.2	15.7	220	2 237	362.4	30.4	33	92	8.0	1.9
Fayette	29 431	233	21	163	102.8	5.1	69	459	77.4	7.0	10	26	2.1	0.4
Fentress	50	4	8	20	4.3	0.4	64	570	77.2	7.1	5	54	3.3	0.8
Franklin	27 952	322	23	145	46.9	3.4	164	1 555	231.0	21.9	20	73	4.2	0.7
Gibson	17 752	214	51	520	333.2	14.4	248	2 221	358.4	33.0	30	76	5.4	0.8
Giles	1 498	26	34	302	93.1	9.5	137	1 218	201.7	16.9	16	78	3.0	0.8
Grainger	0	0	9	46	18.6	1.0	59	385	57.2	4.5	4	11	0.4	0.1
Greene	24 200	310	44	679	283.5	12.4	253	2 871	440.2	39.9	35	97	11.2	1.6
Grundy	NA	NA	4	20	2.1	0.4	57	414	51.5	5.4	8	33	1.1	0.2
Hamblen	29 402	327	70	1 199	460.2	35.1	323	3 595	645.9	54.7	52	184	29.4	3.2
Hamilton	189 224	1 705	694	D	D	D	1 531	20 122	3 269.6	325.8	347	2 045	236.7	58.5
Hancock	105	3	4	25	3.2	0.2	20	100	13.4	1.4	NA	NA	NA	NA
Hardeman	11 950	119	22	D	D	D	103	860	120.7	11.2	10	32	2.6	0.3
Hardin	1 167	36	18	92	35.9	3.0	131	1 079	183.3	15.4	18	50	3.4	0.6
Hawkins	18 932	200	11	D	D	D	138	1 230	194.9	16.0	19	56	4.0	0.7
Haywood	4 083	64	12	135	114.6	3.4	100	830	146.4	12.0	13	33	2.3	0.4
Henderson	4 703	73	20	150	44.1	3.1	124	1 090	177.7	16.0	8	22	1.4	0.2
Henry	2 977	27	41	625	198.0	16.1	167	1 608	244.6	21.9	20	55	5.0	0.5
Hickman	833	10	8	35	9.2	0.5	66	360	48.8	4.5	8	18	1.0	0.2
Houston	388	6	4	D	D	D	29	164	23.7	2.0	2	D	D	D
Humphreys	3 317	35	11	142	52.0	3.0	77	657	110.8	9.5	3	16	0.7	0.2
Jackson	0	0	1	D	D	D	27	145	20.5	1.4	3	5	0.3	0.1
Jefferson	41 684	376	42	246	73.8	6.2	120	1 415	249.5	21.1	18	53	2.6	0.6
Johnson	3 559	71	3	D	D	D	57	417	67.5	6.3	8	D	D	D
Knox	231 279	2 910	950	12 580	7 507.7	449.4	1 946	28 344	5 029.7	478.9	464	2 822	326.5	65.7
Lake	402	23	9	D	D	D	26	172	20.1	2.0	4	13	1.0	0.1
Lauderdale	7 541	98	26	548	364.9	18.4	100	867	123.9	11.4	10	21	2.6	0.5
Lawrence	3 083	46	42	296	174.6	8.7	200	1 822	315.2	27.1	22	77	8.6	1.2
Lewis	504	10	8	67	11.6	1.3	59	367	66.3	5.4	6	5	0.4	0.1
Lincoln	864	8	29	211	102.6	3.9	138	1 360	205.6	18.0	25	92	9.8	1.6
Loudon	25 346	253	41	232	93.1	6.0	137	1 407	271.7	21.0	23	46	7.5	1.2
McMinn	4 402	48	32	D	D	D	209	2 119	361.7	30.3	35	120	12.5	2.2
McNairy	1 978	27	21	D	D	D	100	728	117.2	9.9	14	69	6.8	1.1
Macon	514	12	12	84	19.2	1.2	81	582	89.3	7.8	9	37	1.8	0.4
Madison	82 446	852	161	2 186	756.4	60.5	582	8 169	1 196.5	114.9	90	423	43.2	7.4
Marion	18 436	187	15	D	D	D	111	1 232	186.5	15.2	13	68	3.3	0.7

1. Establishments with payroll.

Table B. States and Counties — Professional, Manufacturing, and Accommodation and Foodservices

STATE County	Professional, Scientific, and Technical Services[1], 1997				Manufacturing, 1997				Accommodation and Foodservices, 1997			
	Number of Establishments	Number of Employees	Receipts (mil dol)	Annual Payroll (mil dol)	Number of Establishments	Number of Employees	Receipts (mil dol)	Annual Payroll (mil dol)	Number of Establishments	Number of Employees	Sales (mil dol)	Annual Payroll (mil dol)
	147	148	149	150	151	152	153	154	155	156	157	158
SOUTH DAKOTA—Cont'd												
Tripp	12	29	1.9	0.5	NA	NA	NA	NA	19	184	4.9	1.4
Turner	10	22	1.2	0.3	NA	NA	NA	NA	17	92	2.2	0.4
Union	31	80	5.7	2.1	26	D	D	D	37	473	15.7	3.8
Walworth	10	63	3.4	1.1	NA	NA	NA	NA	31	218	6.4	1.5
Yankton	41	203	12.9	4.7	30	2 517	452.2	62.3	67	989	23.6	6.2
Ziebach	NA	NA	NA	NA	NA	NA	NA	NA	2	D	D	D
TENNESSEE	8 812	72 225	6 911.8	2 686.6	7 407	483 823	98 503.1	14 351.9	9 604	197 881	6 790.2	1 880.3
Anderson	180	7 960	934.5	384.6	107	8 559	1 336.2	328.0	129	2 384	71.6	19.9
Bedford	36	233	10.9	3.2	64	5 582	1 302.7	146.6	49	727	19.8	4.9
Benton	11	44	2.0	0.5	17	1 150	97.5	23.7	39	339	10.7	2.1
Bledsoe	5	D	D	D	NA	NA	NA	NA	8	82	1.8	0.5
Blount	122	646	55.4	22.5	126	7 027	2 806.9	251.9	167	3 223	97.3	26.5
Bradley	116	699	48.8	17.8	142	12 974	2 931.7	363.8	138	2 533	81.8	21.8
Campbell	27	108	7.6	2.1	53	1 945	243.7	49.1	60	910	26.6	6.7
Cannon	7	19	2.5	0.2	NA	NA	NA	NA	10	119	2.9	0.8
Carroll	24	66	3.8	1.1	50	3 103	456.7	64.1	45	532	12.0	2.9
Carter	36	130	6.8	2.0	48	1 960	273.4	50.7	47	846	21.9	5.8
Cheatham	20	104	23.2	4.1	42	3 060	579.7	81.9	29	348	11.0	2.8
Chester	6	16	1.3	0.2	24	853	76.0	18.7	19	306	6.6	2.1
Claiborne	23	81	3.0	1.2	34	3 584	317.1	67.1	22	412	12.1	3.2
Clay	4	D	D	D	8	771	85.7	13.7	20	73	3.4	0.8
Cocke	20	43	2.7	0.7	40	2 627	382.8	64.6	52	978	30.5	8.3
Coffee	59	D	D	D	67	5 595	1 082.9	178.4	106	1 949	56.5	15.7
Crockett	10	D	D	D	16	1 241	160.8	26.6	16	82	4.8	0.7
Cumberland	42	168	9.7	3.8	47	2 437	442.9	58.9	75	1 300	39.6	11.4
Davidson	1 694	15 055	1 636.8	605.8	752	31 716	6 721.8	1 100.0	1 407	37 523	1 511.7	426.3
Decatur	11	D	D	D	35	1 113	137.0	21.8	21	175	3.9	0.9
De Kalb	14	54	2.4	0.7	28	2 740	333.9	65.7	22	317	6.6	1.7
Dickson	37	120	8.4	2.9	51	3 574	710.3	102.5	70	1 116	37.7	10.6
Dyer	45	179	12.2	3.2	42	6 404	1 121.4	183.5	67	998	30.2	7.6
Fayette	21	50	4.9	1.4	39	1 193	271.6	33.3	18	196	5.0	1.5
Fentress	12	64	3.7	2.1	31	1 471	141.4	22.5	18	225	6.0	1.5
Franklin	38	142	10.7	3.5	43	1 872	438.2	53.1	50	592	16.9	4.4
Gibson	41	176	9.2	2.9	90	7 607	1 085.6	200.7	62	815	22.1	5.9
Giles	28	127	11.5	5.1	48	3 515	679.7	104.6	38	615	14.7	3.7
Grainger	5	D	D	D	35	1 321	180.9	30.6	10	D	D	D
Greene	49	171	13.4	5.5	107	7 990	1 296.7	198.0	102	1 622	42.1	11.9
Grundy	3	D	D	D	NA	NA	NA	NA	8	60	1.9	0.5
Hamblen	68	309	20.2	7.1	129	14 586	2 039.2	369.6	100	2 269	58.3	15.6
Hamilton	664	4 570	401.5	162.7	515	32 559	5 493.2	991.4	711	13 376	453.2	128.2
Hancock	2	D	D	D	NA	NA	NA	NA	2	D	D	D
Hardeman	11	40	2.2	0.7	37	1 957	274.7	51.4	30	291	8.2	1.8
Hardin	26	78	3.5	1.1	52	2 628	530.2	70.0	49	576	17.2	4.4
Hawkins	32	123	7.1	1.9	50	6 534	1 040.9	219.4	45	788	18.0	4.9
Haywood	12	22	1.8	0.6	23	2 477	425.5	64.1	26	350	11.4	2.9
Henderson	24	48	4.2	0.9	47	4 302	710.9	101.6	36	568	13.5	3.7
Henry	32	191	14.5	4.9	66	3 483	506.1	79.7	61	890	22.1	6.0
Hickman	12	66	3.0	1.3	31	1 017	139.5	22.2	23	D	D	D
Houston	4	D	D	D	NA	NA	NA	NA	12	59	1.9	0.4
Humphreys	11	42	2.1	0.8	29	1 976	854.1	75.4	35	358	13.4	3.2
Jackson	5	D	D	D	8	681	104.9	11.8	7	41	1.4	0.3
Jefferson	31	79	5.1	1.3	56	2 880	434.0	59.7	51	790	24.6	6.4
Johnson	7	D	D	D	19	1 392	206.4	29.2	16	197	5.3	1.5
Knox	937	8 000	724.2	280.7	493	20 782	3 245.5	550.3	769	17 252	550.9	157.6
Lake	4	D	D	D	NA	NA	NA	NA	15	140	3.9	1.2
Lauderdale	15	57	2.1	0.6	22	3 525	353.8	74.4	22	283	7.5	1.8
Lawrence	36	110	6.2	1.9	56	5 501	1 063.8	145.8	45	740	21.6	5.8
Lewis	8	27	2.5	0.5	22	600	101.1	16.4	19	D	D	D
Lincoln	34	92	9.4	2.2	43	2 381	455.0	62.9	44	D	D	D
Loudon	43	132	10.2	2.8	45	3 150	806.7	93.0	56	825	26.3	7.3
McMinn	40	160	11.5	3.9	74	8 791	1 572.2	279.4	84	1 303	41.6	10.2
McNairy	14	29	2.1	0.7	48	2 632	328.1	58.2	28	360	6.8	1.7
Macon	12	26	2.6	0.3	38	1 403	80.1	25.9	19	253	6.2	1.5
Madison	142	993	77.8	36.9	138	12 429	3 473.4	382.5	183	4 110	137.7	37.1
Marion	22	53	2.9	0.8	29	1 726	212.8	38.5	41	673	20.4	5.4

1. Firms subject to federal tax.

Table B. States and Counties — Health and Other Services and Federal Funds

	Health Care and Social Assistance[1], 1997				Other Services[1], 1997				Federal funds and grants, fiscal 1999[2]			
									Expenditures (mil dol)			
										Direct payments for individuals[3]		
STATE County	Number of Establishments	Number of Employees	Receipts (mil dol)	Annual Payroll (mil dol)	Number of Establishments	Number of Employees	Receipts (mil dol)	Annual Payroll (mil dol)	Total	Social Security and government retirement	Medicare	Food stamps and Supplemental Security Income
	159	160	161	162	163	164	165	166	167	168	169	170
SOUTH DAKOTA—Cont'd												
Tripp	19	86	4.6	1.9	11	27	1.8	0.4	35.5	13.5	4.6	1.1
Turner	12	84	2.3	1.3	13	24	1.3	0.2	45.6	18.4	6.5	0.4
Union	17	191	9.9	3.3	19	60	4.9	1.3	130.2	22.8	9.3	0.6
Walworth	12	194	7.6	3.9	15	68	4.0	1.1	29.8	10.8	3.6	1.0
Yankton	46	530	37.7	17.8	43	200	11.2	2.8	89.6	37.2	14.7	1.8
Ziebach	NA	NA	NA	NA	1	D	D	D	12.1	1.6	0.6	1.0
TENNESSEE	10 113	155 667	10 753.0	4 659.9	7 767	49 204	2 996.7	918.7	30 866.8	10 382.2	4 384.3	1 136.9
Anderson	156	1 801	117.4	61.3	104	530	26.9	9.4	2 209.7	185.2	63.9	17.0
Bedford	50	439	21.5	8.2	40	378	18.1	5.4	121.2	62.7	24.0	5.2
Benton	20	270	10.7	4.1	15	53	3.4	0.9	82.4	43.4	18.0	3.1
Bledsoe	9	394	19.0	9.3	4	10	0.4	0.1	42.5	15.8	9.9	2.8
Blount	140	1 604	94.2	43.5	140	703	38.6	12.8	673.1	213.0	72.4	15.0
Bradley	201	10 357	442.3	201.0	101	1 304	69.6	26.1	280.3	138.8	63.5	13.5
Campbell	53	590	28.7	11.4	41	144	9.6	2.3	223.8	94.9	43.2	16.2
Cannon	10	192	15.7	6.0	12	33	1.8	0.7	51.5	23.7	15.4	1.8
Carroll	44	687	30.9	12.6	36	112	5.9	1.4	155.0	69.7	33.6	4.9
Carter	68	1 103	58.0	21.4	55	236	14.7	3.4	214.3	104.0	38.6	9.7
Cheatham	26	401	16.0	6.2	17	43	2.9	0.8	81.0	44.4	17.4	2.3
Chester	9	162	6.5	2.7	12	44	2.8	0.6	57.6	22.3	10.6	2.5
Claiborne	30	474	21.5	8.8	27	98	6.1	1.4	166.7	62.5	29.6	11.9
Clay	9	D	D	D	6	18	1.3	0.3	38.9	12.0	8.7	1.1
Cocke	26	324	20.7	6.8	30	103	5.2	1.4	155.7	63.4	28.4	11.9
Coffee	124	2 058	116.4	46.0	83	666	52.0	14.4	538.9	107.8	43.4	9.5
Crockett	15	284	10.2	5.1	22	59	5.4	1.0	74.1	27.7	15.1	2.5
Cumberland	87	764	45.6	18.0	49	179	8.8	2.4	214.3	123.9	41.8	9.1
Davidson	1 462	27 389	2 174.0	925.5	1 092	8 627	530.2	163.9	3 562.8	978.1	444.6	102.2
Decatur	18	527	22.5	10.3	20	98	6.5	1.7	61.7	22.6	18.3	3.0
De Kalb	33	426	24.6	10.8	15	60	3.4	1.0	82.2	32.0	19.7	3.3
Dickson	47	1 305	72.4	29.1	51	233	17.5	4.9	145.7	76.7	31.4	6.4
Dyer	85	746	49.5	19.6	64	324	14.1	4.4	173.5	70.1	33.4	9.4
Fayette	15	222	10.6	4.8	17	63	5.7	1.1	117.6	35.4	18.2	7.8
Fentress	26	886	45.8	17.7	20	52	3.5	0.7	91.9	34.9	23.1	5.5
Franklin	53	911	66.7	22.4	38	121	8.3	1.9	166.2	81.3	37.4	5.0
Gibson	81	1 068	45.6	19.4	64	313	15.6	4.9	268.8	107.6	56.7	10.0
Giles	38	561	27.0	10.6	35	115	8.4	1.6	123.4	56.3	26.9	4.5
Grainger	13	345	9.0	3.5	12	30	2.8	0.6	105.8	37.4	18.0	5.0
Greene	93	996	63.5	24.4	75	271	15.3	4.7	303.3	124.6	46.0	14.9
Grundy	10	44	1.9	0.6	9	20	1.8	0.3	67.5	29.5	15.5	6.0
Hamblen	129	1 760	108.8	41.2	76	429	24.3	8.1	225.2	104.0	45.2	12.0
Hamilton	756	10 787	832.6	371.4	546	3 752	221.0	68.0	2 155.8	674.1	286.2	70.7
Hancock	6	106	3.4	1.6	4	9	0.9	0.2	41.1	10.1	7.5	4.2
Hardeman	23	359	15.7	6.5	26	80	6.4	0.9	153.1	47.1	26.0	10.1
Hardin	35	280	14.7	4.7	29	75	6.0	1.3	141.8	49.7	25.6	7.3
Hawkins	38	402	18.2	7.9	36	120	7.7	2.1	304.7	95.9	36.3	11.6
Haywood	18	245	14.8	5.4	23	140	8.7	2.6	107.6	28.5	20.5	7.8
Henderson	30	375	16.9	6.7	38	102	7.5	1.6	129.8	49.3	26.5	4.2
Henry	62	779	36.8	17.2	46	215	10.7	3.1	171.6	77.6	31.5	5.5
Hickman	13	440	15.2	7.9	20	82	6.7	2.0	73.3	37.3	15.2	3.1
Houston	8	281	14.8	5.6	5	7	0.5	0.1	39.8	20.1	8.0	1.9
Humphreys	18	297	14.6	5.7	16	54	4.0	1.0	177.3	38.0	16.0	2.7
Jackson	8	172	7.4	3.0	5	18	1.2	0.3	47.1	16.2	11.5	2.7
Jefferson	39	581	22.5	9.1	39	119	7.5	1.8	183.8	94.8	34.4	8.4
Johnson	15	139	4.1	1.9	14	47	3.0	0.8	82.2	36.5	17.4	5.0
Knox	925	10 391	963.0	451.7	669	4 539	241.1	76.1	1 821.9	741.4	280.0	66.0
Lake	6	D	D	D	4	D	D	D	47.5	13.2	8.3	2.3
Lauderdale	13	209	11.0	4.1	24	78	6.6	1.6	131.3	44.6	25.2	8.3
Lawrence	59	889	48.9	17.4	36	122	7.6	1.8	170.7	82.6	37.0	7.5
Lewis	15	402	13.7	7.1	9	17	1.9	0.5	44.2	18.7	11.5	2.3
Lincoln	41	369	19.6	7.6	38	126	8.7	1.8	131.0	65.3	22.8	5.3
Loudon	43	622	29.5	12.2	41	211	11.9	3.4	176.3	98.0	35.9	5.8
McMinn	77	1 080	61.3	24.7	48	200	10.0	2.9	198.9	95.5	40.7	8.8
McNairy	34	516	23.4	9.4	33	89	6.4	1.4	162.6	53.9	28.3	7.4
Macon	17	221	11.9	3.9	13	34	2.8	0.6	71.8	27.6	18.1	3.8
Madison	205	3 755	293.3	150.0	170	1 062	57.5	18.4	378.9	155.6	70.5	19.0
Marion	33	658	35.8	13.3	21	101	5.9	1.6	123.4	55.1	30.9	6.7

1. Firms subject to federal tax.   2. October 1, 1998 to September 30, 1999.   3. State totals may include programs not allocated by county.

Table B. States and Counties — Federal Funds and Local Government Finances

	Federal funds and grants, fiscal 1999[1] (cont'd)							Local government finances, 1997				
	Expenditures (mil dol) (cont'd)							General revenue				
	Procurement contract awards			Grants[2]						Taxes		
STATE County	Salaries and wages	Defense	Other	Medicaid and other health-related	Nutrition and family welfare	Education	Other	Total (mil dol)	Intergovernmental (mil dol)	Total (mil dol)	Per capita[3] (dollars) Total	Property
	171	172	173	174	175	176	177	178	179	180	181	182
SOUTH DAKOTA—Cont'd												
Tripp	1.9	0.0	0.4	3.2	0.6	0.6	0.1	11.3	4.3	5.5	805	689
Turner	1.9	0.0	0.6	3.2	0.4	0.2	2.3	13.7	5.0	7.1	823	732
Union	2.1	42.6	29.5	3.9	0.8	0.2	5.7	25.8	7.4	13.6	1 141	961
Walworth	1.7	0.1	0.4	3.0	0.5	0.3	1.0	10.9	4.7	4.7	844	690
Yankton	10.0	2.3	1.2	8.6	1.1	0.5	2.0	34.4	8.8	18.7	889	661
Ziebach	0.2	0.4	0.0	1.6	0.5	1.1	0.1	2.9	1.8	0.9	402	324
TENNESSEE	2 717.9	1 075.8	3 444.6	3 141.6	840.8	389.7	1 528.0	X	X	X	X	X
Anderson	72.3	29.1	1 775.8	39.9	8.0	3.4	11.8	118.4	53.6	38.5	539	413
Bedford	4.4	0.1	0.9	14.8	2.4	1.5	2.2	67.8	22.9	16.9	493	359
Benton	2.6	0.0	0.7	9.6	1.5	0.8	1.2	22.6	12.7	6.2	382	208
Bledsoe	0.9	0.0	0.4	8.3	2.9	0.5	0.3	15.5	10.7	2.9	276	181
Blount	14.6	8.4	276.8	34.2	5.9	4.0	17.7	222.1	55.3	63.0	628	376
Bradley	12.9	0.0	3.8	28.6	7.2	3.5	3.1	190.1	52.9	47.6	594	294
Campbell	4.7	15.1	1.0	32.3	5.5	2.8	3.4	76.2	30.1	17.5	462	261
Cannon	1.3	0.0	0.4	6.8	0.9	0.5	0.1	16.3	9.6	3.8	316	221
Carroll	4.6	3.8	0.9	23.7	2.7	1.3	4.5	42.9	22.5	12.1	418	247
Carter	5.2	0.4	2.6	31.4	4.6	2.4	11.9	73.1	34.4	26.6	501	311
Cheatham	4.1	0.9	0.9	7.0	1.7	1.0	0.5	47.9	21.9	14.8	429	272
Chester	1.7	0.0	0.3	9.4	3.7	0.6	3.3	18.5	10.2	5.3	366	207
Claiborne	3.3	0.1	1.1	28.1	5.9	2.6	20.2	48.7	22.7	9.2	319	194
Clay	1.9	0.5	0.2	10.8	2.8	0.5	1.9	12.3	7.7	2.7	371	305
Cocke	3.7	0.1	0.9	35.1	4.6	1.9	3.7	43.5	24.9	10.9	344	215
Coffee	24.2	292.8	26.1	20.0	3.1	2.1	5.0	76.5	31.3	22.9	503	299
Crockett	2.5	0.9	0.5	13.4	1.7	0.6	0.4	21.4	12.2	6.2	452	262
Cumberland	4.6	0.2	6.6	19.2	3.2	1.7	2.2	59.7	28.4	20.6	478	224
Davidson	439.7	64.0	101.3	427.9	310.0	150.0	451.7	1 487.5	340.7	693.4	1 299	682
Decatur	2.1	0.0	0.5	8.5	0.9	0.5	4.6	17.4	11.5	3.7	341	172
De Kalb	2.1	1.1	0.6	11.3	1.3	0.9	8.4	20.0	11.8	4.9	308	215
Dickson	5.4	0.0	1.3	15.6	3.1	1.8	0.8	67.1	30.0	24.7	603	327
Dyer	6.3	1.4	1.3	29.4	3.3	2.6	3.7	65.1	28.7	20.8	570	293
Fayette	3.0	0.0	0.7	30.8	5.1	1.7	4.7	36.1	20.5	10.7	363	263
Fentress	2.2	0.3	0.7	19.0	2.2	1.0	2.0	20.5	12.7	5.7	359	183
Franklin	7.9	5.2	1.7	18.3	2.7	1.6	0.6	51.3	23.4	20.0	538	340
Gibson	9.3	0.9	1.9	35.8	5.2	2.3	17.6	93.2	42.7	31.4	652	405
Giles	4.2	0.1	1.2	19.9	2.2	1.3	3.8	40.8	19.3	13.8	484	338
Grainger	3.0	0.0	0.6	18.4	1.9	1.0	20.1	22.7	14.6	4.7	243	151
Greene	9.7	6.7	42.4	36.9	4.6	4.0	7.1	86.6	35.9	34.9	587	279
Grundy	1.4	0.0	0.4	10.0	1.9	1.0	1.2	20.0	12.8	4.2	301	222
Hamblen	9.4	0.5	1.5	31.1	9.7	3.3	2.8	90.2	31.4	40.4	753	379
Hamilton	405.1	7.1	419.7	141.0	34.5	17.6	70.7	976.3	233.3	264.1	896	639
Hancock	0.6	0.0	0.2	13.7	1.5	0.7	1.7	11.3	9.0	1.3	195	165
Hardeman	3.2	20.5	0.8	30.9	4.7	1.6	4.0	38.7	21.6	9.2	381	227
Hardin	5.3	0.0	1.0	25.0	2.3	1.3	21.5	47.4	20.5	9.5	383	242
Hawkins	13.6	72.9	26.8	36.3	3.9	2.3	3.1	69.2	28.2	23.1	474	310
Haywood	3.0	0.0	0.5	28.4	4.4	1.3	2.4	33.9	18.3	10.0	506	319
Henderson	2.9	6.5	0.6	19.0	1.8	1.1	15.0	34.1	18.2	9.3	389	161
Henry	7.7	2.4	1.2	18.5	2.5	1.4	16.0	77.8	22.6	15.7	530	276
Hickman	3.2	0.0	0.7	9.8	1.3	0.8	1.1	32.2	15.8	6.6	333	225
Houston	1.3	0.0	0.3	5.6	2.0	0.4	0.1	11.1	7.2	2.6	336	210
Humphreys	21.8	2.8	72.0	10.3	1.4	0.8	10.1	32.8	12.2	10.3	613	369
Jackson	1.3	0.0	0.4	10.6	0.9	0.4	2.0	13.1	8.3	3.3	348	241
Jefferson	5.9	0.2	1.4	19.0	2.8	1.5	12.2	56.0	23.1	16.9	402	242
Johnson	2.1	0.0	0.6	16.3	1.9	0.9	0.8	21.4	12.1	5.2	317	230
Knox	215.1	29.6	118.3	163.2	33.8	19.1	105.8	691.5	192.8	368.3	1 007	536
Lake	1.2	2.7	0.9	9.0	1.4	0.5	2.2	10.2	6.3	2.4	297	186
Lauderdale	3.3	0.6	0.9	29.0	4.4	1.6	1.3	41.7	22.2	8.7	361	271
Lawrence	6.1	0.1	2.2	24.4	2.8	1.7	2.8	57.7	28.1	20.4	522	273
Lewis	1.4	0.0	0.2	6.9	1.0	0.5	1.1	15.4	9.3	3.5	324	186
Lincoln	4.2	0.2	0.8	19.1	6.9	1.2	2.0	62.7	21.6	13.2	453	259
Loudon	8.5	0.3	1.4	16.4	2.6	1.6	3.6	54.3	24.5	17.7	464	340
McMinn	6.0	0.0	4.7	23.3	2.4	2.2	11.0	90.9	28.5	24.3	530	354
McNairy	4.5	0.0	1.0	30.1	6.0	1.1	27.7	36.5	18.8	6.6	277	207
Macon	2.0	0.0	0.5	12.4	4.2	0.8	0.2	26.4	14.8	7.6	429	228
Madison	29.0	0.5	5.5	57.7	5.2	5.5	12.0	365.3	62.6	72.3	852	485
Marion	4.0	0.0	1.0	15.0	3.6	1.5	5.1	37.4	19.9	11.6	436	234

1. October 1, 1998 to September 30, 1999. 2. State totals may include programs not allocated by county. 3. Based on the resident population estimated as of July 1 of the year shown.

Table B. States and Counties — Local Government Finances, Government Employment, and Elections

STATE County	Direct general expenditure Total (mil dol) 183	Per capita¹ (dollars) 184	Education 185	Health and hospitals 186	Police protection 187	Public welfare 188	Highways 189	Debt outstanding Total (mil dol) 190	Per capita¹ (dollars) 191	Federal civilian 192	Federal military 193	State and local 194	Democratic 195	Republican 196	All other 197
SOUTH DAKOTA—Cont'd															
Tripp	12.8	1 858	59.1	0.6	3.4	0.4	14.5	9.6	1 393	41	48	395	28.9	69.0	2.1
Turner	14.2	1 647	62.1	0.8	3.5	1.0	16.6	6.7	779	42	62	440	35.3	62.8	1.9
Union	29.4	2 461	63.9	0.3	3.8	0.2	11.3	17.7	1 483	46	87	604	40.9	56.6	2.6
Walworth	9.8	1 741	53.5	0.3	6.2	1.0	12.3	1.8	328	43	40	397	28.2	68.9	2.9
Yankton	36.0	1 714	53.6	0.8	4.8	0.9	10.7	39.0	1 857	196	150	1 511	41.1	56.1	2.7
Ziebach	2.9	1 285	70.6	0.6	2.5	0.2	12.1	0.0	0	0	16	111	43.6	53.3	3.2
TENNESSEE	X	X	X	X	X	X	X	X	X	50 308	23 782	329 985	47.3	51.1	1.6
Anderson	140.1	1 962	56.9	1.5	4.7	0.1	5.0	180.0	2 519	1 231	284	3 688	47.1	51.0	1.9
Bedford	78.3	2 291	47.5	19.5	3.1	3.9	5.7	41.5	1 215	93	137	1 920	50.3	48.4	1.3
Benton	21.6	1 326	55.6	1.3	5.7	0.0	10.0	12.7	776	72	65	740	58.6	39.4	2.0
Bledsoe	14.2	1 343	58.2	1.2	3.0	1.1	11.2	3.5	326	17	43	1 049	41.8	56.7	1.5
Blount	207.2	2 065	39.4	34.0	4.0	0.2	4.5	112.4	1 120	235	417	5 024	36.1	62.2	1.7
Bradley	187.8	2 341	32.3	35.6	3.6	3.9	3.4	78.5	978	256	333	4 657	29.8	68.5	1.7
Campbell	73.3	1 936	41.6	26.5	2.3	0.1	4.6	33.0	870	84	152	2 123	52.3	46.6	1.1
Cannon	14.7	1 217	56.7	2.5	5.4	0.1	9.9	8.7	726	30	48	411	57.4	41.0	1.6
Carroll	52.8	1 827	69.6	0.2	3.7	0.1	6.7	31.3	1 084	89	116	1 235	48.4	50.5	1.1
Carter	69.5	1 308	58.7	0.8	5.9	0.0	6.3	28.7	541	108	212	2 106	35.2	63.4	1.4
Cheatham	44.5	1 294	62.7	10.3	4.2	0.0	6.3	40.4	1 174	83	141	1 283	48.1	50.4	1.5
Chester	16.7	1 147	58.7	1.8	6.7	0.3	12.3	15.9	1 092	32	59	743	38.3	60.9	0.8
Claiborne	47.3	1 631	48.7	28.9	3.0	0.1	7.9	15.1	522	67	118	1 863	42.7	55.8	1.5
Clay	14.3	1 951	42.8	8.2	12.9	0.1	12.0	5.5	753	48	29	376	56.1	42.6	1.3
Cocke	48.8	1 545	51.2	0.7	4.3	0.0	8.7	21.9	693	69	127	1 364	37.8	60.4	1.8
Coffee	84.4	1 853	56.0	9.4	4.7	0.1	5.2	54.1	1 188	376	289	2 755	49.1	49.4	1.5
Crockett	20.2	1 466	58.3	2.5	3.6	1.3	9.8	19.2	1 390	50	56	608	49.7	49.2	1.1
Cumberland	54.9	1 274	50.6	2.0	5.2	0.5	6.6	32.2	746	90	176	1 616	40.2	57.8	2.0
Davidson	1 604.0	3 005	27.5	7.2	6.0	1.1	2.5	3 185.5	5 969	8 353	2 705	38 449	57.8	40.3	1.9
Decatur	14.3	1 329	58.7	0.3	4.4	0.2	12.0	5.5	512	34	43	699	52.1	46.8	1.1
De Kalb	17.2	1 090	63.0	2.0	6.0	2.5	8.8	15.6	990	40	63	677	60.1	38.5	1.4
Dickson	67.0	1 633	51.1	1.7	5.9	3.3	7.3	74.3	1 811	99	168	2 067	53.6	45.1	1.3
Dyer	79.2	2 172	54.2	1.1	6.3	0.3	9.8	37.0	1 014	113	146	2 332	45.8	53.1	1.1
Fayette	34.2	1 157	54.4	4.6	5.6	0.0	11.2	5.7	192	61	121	1 458	43.7	55.5	0.8
Fentress	20.5	1 291	62.7	2.2	3.1	0.0	11.0	10.9	687	35	64	782	41.9	56.7	1.4
Franklin	46.4	1 249	57.3	0.6	5.5	0.0	8.8	34.5	927	151	149	1 525	53.3	44.7	2.0
Gibson	97.2	2 021	56.2	1.5	5.1	0.1	6.7	52.9	1 100	163	194	2 332	50.6	48.4	1.0
Giles	41.6	1 460	50.8	2.6	5.0	0.1	11.9	24.9	874	77	115	1 266	54.9	43.5	1.6
Grainger	20.2	1 040	68.8	2.2	3.4	0.8	9.0	5.0	255	55	79	651	38.1	60.5	1.4
Greene	85.6	1 440	52.9	2.4	4.1	0.3	11.7	31.6	532	232	241	3 377	38.0	60.2	1.8
Grundy	19.4	1 386	59.6	1.1	3.3	0.2	14.0	18.7	1 341	24	56	617	64.6	33.8	1.6
Hamblen	93.1	1 733	47.9	13.3	5.6	0.2	5.9	41.3	769	170	216	2 922	38.4	60.0	1.6
Hamilton	1 000.3	3 394	23.3	31.0	4.8	4.4	3.3	981.9	3 332	6 472	1 218	19 408	43.0	55.3	1.7
Hancock	11.3	1 655	60.9	3.3	2.6	0.2	14.0	2.6	385	11	27	384	33.3	64.7	2.0
Hardeman	37.8	1 565	54.1	2.8	6.6	0.2	8.8	17.1	709	65	99	1 802	56.3	42.4	1.3
Hardin	43.3	1 748	51.4	20.9	3.4	0.1	5.7	4.6	186	111	99	1 454	42.5	56.4	1.1
Hawkins	64.1	1 315	53.4	13.8	3.9	0.0	8.5	35.3	723	265	198	1 963	39.5	58.9	1.6
Haywood	34.5	1 744	52.5	3.3	4.8	0.0	11.4	8.0	402	52	78	1 039	60.0	39.4	0.6
Henderson	29.6	1 234	60.2	0.3	4.7	0.0	10.7	26.8	1 115	57	97	1 028	37.7	61.4	0.9
Henry	76.3	2 570	35.6	34.7	3.9	0.0	7.4	23.7	798	120	136	2 025	49.5	48.3	2.2
Hickman	30.3	1 524	48.2	21.3	3.7	0.0	8.5	15.2	764	62	82	1 245	58.4	40.1	1.5
Houston	11.1	1 426	57.1	0.2	1.8	0.0	15.1	3.6	464	17	31	430	66.5	31.8	1.7
Humphreys	29.1	1 730	47.4	0.7	3.9	0.0	8.7	84.4	5 027	395	68	901	62.9	35.7	1.4
Jackson	13.3	1 390	55.5	2.9	4.6	0.0	13.7	3.6	372	27	38	376	69.5	29.1	1.4
Jefferson	54.0	1 284	49.3	19.4	4.9	0.6	5.8	28.7	683	119	174	1 871	37.1	61.5	1.4
Johnson	19.7	1 191	63.8	0.8	3.3	0.0	8.3	7.4	445	42	67	607	32.0	66.1	1.9
Knox	771.7	2 111	40.6	2.9	5.2	1.4	6.2	720.8	1 971	3 958	1 558	31 424	40.5	57.7	1.8
Lake	10.9	1 333	43.1	5.9	6.6	0.0	12.4	4.5	553	21	33	663	63.8	35.1	1.1
Lauderdale	40.4	1 672	64.3	0.6	5.2	0.4	7.7	30.0	1 243	66	96	1 699	55.4	43.7	0.9
Lawrence	58.0	1 483	48.7	1.8	6.7	0.1	15.1	60.3	1 543	114	157	1 801	45.9	52.6	1.5
Lewis	13.7	1 275	55.2	0.2	3.6	0.0	4.2	10.0	932	24	43	536	51.6	46.1	2.3
Lincoln	65.0	2 224	36.8	35.2	3.0	0.0	5.4	49.3	1 687	68	118	2 334	47.5	51.0	1.5
Loudon	51.4	1 345	55.0	0.3	6.7	0.0	5.4	96.6	2 526	168	155	1 447	36.0	62.6	1.4
McMinn	88.9	1 937	39.4	22.5	3.1	3.6	6.1	71.2	1 552	138	184	2 140	37.0	61.2	1.8
McNairy	34.9	1 473	48.8	20.9	3.9	0.0	6.9	26.2	1 108	91	96	1 197	44.5	54.5	1.0
Macon	29.8	1 677	63.6	2.8	4.7	0.0	6.2	19.8	1 116	38	72	864	47.1	51.9	1.0
Madison	398.3	4 697	18.5	50.1	2.6	0.0	2.5	226.4	2 670	539	345	9 842	46.5	52.6	0.9
Marion	34.6	1 293	60.0	3.0	6.7	0.0	6.9	10.5	394	77	107	941	53.1	45.4	1.5

1. Based on the resident population estimated as of July 1 of the year shown.

Table B. States and Counties — **Land Area and Population**

STATE/ County code	MSA/ PMSA/ NECMA code[1]	County Type[2]	STATE County	Land area,[3] (sq km) 1990	Total persons	Rank	Per square kilometer	White	Black	Am. Indian, Eskimo, Aleut	Asian and Pacific Islander	Percent Hispanic[4]	Under 5 years	5 to 17 years	18 to 24 years	25 to 34 years	35 to 44 years	45 to 54 years
					1	2	3	4	5	6	7	8	9	10	11	12	13	14	15
			TENNESSEE—Cont'd															
47 117	...	6	Marshall	972	26 423	1 481	27.2	89.5	10.0	0.1	0.4	0.9	6.4	18.9	8.6	13.5	16.2	14.1
47 119	...	4	Maury	1 587	70 440	699	44.4	82.1	17.3	0.2	0.5	1.2	7.0	18.9	8.3	14.1	16.7	13.6
47 121	...	8	Meigs	505	10 134	2 409	20.1	97.9	1.7	0.4	0.1	0.5	5.6	18.5	8.8	12.3	17.3	15.5
47 123	...	6	Monroe	1 645	35 576	1 203	21.6	96.5	3.0	0.2	0.3	0.8	6.5	18.3	8.9	12.4	15.7	14.9
47 125	1660	3	Montgomery	1 396	129 411	404	92.7	77.7	19.1	0.4	2.8	5.6	9.0	18.4	13.1	17.4	15.7	11.4
47 127	...	9	Moore	335	5 140	2 828	15.3	95.7	4.1	0.2	0.1	0.9	5.8	18.7	7.9	11.8	15.8	15.9
47 129	...	8	Morgan	1 352	18 689	1 839	13.8	97.6	1.9	0.3	0.2	0.7	6.1	18.9	8.8	14.9	17.0	13.9
47 131	...	7	Obion	1 411	32 240	1 306	22.8	88.3	11.3	0.1	0.2	0.8	5.7	18.4	8.3	11.9	15.9	14.7
47 133	...	7	Overton	1 122	19 654	1 777	17.5	99.6	0.3	0.1	0.0	0.8	5.7	17.8	8.5	11.9	15.7	15.2
47 135	...	9	Perry	1 075	7 560	2 633	7.0	97.5	2.2	0.1	0.2	1.0	6.8	17.3	6.9	11.1	14.9	14.6
47 137	...	9	Pickett	422	4 711	2 858	11.2	99.9	0.0	0.1	0.1	0.5	6.2	17.7	7.2	11.2	14.9	14.9
47 139	...	9	Polk	1 127	15 094	2 059	13.4	99.1	0.2	0.2	0.5	0.5	5.6	17.5	8.6	11.8	15.5	15.8
47 141	...	5	Putnam	1 039	59 735	796	57.5	96.7	1.9	0.2	1.3	1.1	6.1	15.8	13.2	13.2	15.0	13.5
47 143	...	6	Rhea	818	28 116	1 434	34.4	96.6	2.7	0.3	0.4	1.0	6.1	18.3	9.3	12.4	15.4	14.5
47 145	...	4	Roane	935	50 008	908	53.5	95.6	3.6	0.2	0.6	0.9	5.4	16.7	7.3	11.3	15.7	15.2
47 147	5360	2	Robertson	1 234	54 861	842	44.5	87.5	12.2	0.2	0.2	0.8	7.5	19.5	7.7	14.7	16.4	13.6
47 149	5360	2	Rutherford	1 603	171 401	307	106.9	87.8	9.8	0.2	2.2	1.4	7.7	19.4	12.1	16.5	17.0	12.5
47 151	...	6	Scott	1 378	20 239	1 750	14.7	99.3	0.1	0.5	0.1	0.5	7.0	21.6	9.0	13.1	15.2	13.8
47 153	...	6	Sequatchie	689	10 846	2 356	15.7	99.7	0.1	0.1	0.1	0.6	6.3	18.6	8.9	13.2	16.5	14.6
47 155	3840	2	Sevier	1 534	65 783	729	42.9	98.6	0.5	0.3	0.6	0.9	5.9	17.0	7.9	13.5	16.5	15.4
47 157	4920	0	Shelby	1 955	873 000	43	446.5	52.2	46.2	0.2	1.4	1.4	7.7	19.4	10.1	15.4	17.2	12.4
47 159	...	8	Smith	814	16 771	1 946	20.6	95.9	3.6	0.3	0.2	0.7	6.8	17.9	8.0	13.7	15.4	13.9
47 161	...	8	Stewart	1 185	11 759	2 293	9.9	97.8	1.1	0.6	0.4	1.0	5.1	16.7	7.4	11.7	15.3	15.5
47 163	3660	2	Sullivan	1 070	150 231	348	140.4	97.2	2.0	0.3	0.5	0.7	5.6	15.6	8.1	12.4	15.8	15.6
47 165	5360	2	Sumner	1 371	126 009	416	91.9	93.2	6.0	0.2	0.5	1.1	6.9	19.6	7.9	13.6	17.6	15.1
47 167	4920	1	Tipton	1 190	48 348	932	40.6	73.9	25.4	0.3	0.4	1.2	8.3	21.7	8.5	14.2	15.5	12.8
47 169	...	6	Trousdale	296	6 971	2 678	23.6	83.6	16.0	0.2	0.2	1.0	5.9	18.5	8.2	13.1	16.5	14.2
47 171	3660	2	Unicoi	482	17 310	1 912	35.9	99.6	0.2	0.1	0.1	1.0	5.2	15.5	7.4	12.6	15.2	14.5
47 173	3840	2	Union	579	16 584	1 964	28.6	99.5	0.2	0.3	0.1	0.7	6.9	19.2	9.2	14.5	15.6	14.7
47 175	...	9	Van Buren	708	5 008	2 835	7.1	99.2	0.2	0.5	0.0	0.7	6.4	18.8	8.3	13.8	15.4	14.2
47 177	...	7	Warren	1 121	36 421	1 180	32.5	95.3	3.9	0.2	0.6	1.6	6.3	18.1	8.4	13.0	15.4	14.1
47 179	3660	2	Washington	845	102 814	503	121.7	95.3	3.9	0.2	0.6	1.0	5.8	15.5	10.9	13.7	16.1	13.9
47 181	...	8	Wayne	1 901	16 413	1 978	8.6	93.8	5.9	0.2	0.1	1.4	5.9	16.9	9.4	14.2	16.3	14.6
47 183	...	7	Weakley	1 503	32 952	1 287	21.9	91.1	7.7	0.1	1.1	0.7	5.8	16.1	15.1	12.3	13.7	12.7
47 185	...	7	White	976	22 864	1 617	23.4	97.5	2.2	0.1	0.2	0.7	6.0	17.2	8.1	12.1	15.4	14.5
47 187	5360	2	Williamson	1 509	123 793	423	82.0	91.5	7.4	0.2	0.9	1.3	7.2	20.6	6.3	12.7	21.1	15.5
47 189	5360	2	Wilson	1 478	86 496	583	58.5	91.5	7.7	0.3	0.6	1.1	7.0	19.6	7.6	14.2	18.5	15.5
48 000	...	X	**TEXAS**	678 358	20 044 141	X	29.5	84.3	12.3	0.5	2.9	30.2	8.2	20.4	10.5	13.8	16.3	12.7
48 001	...	6	Anderson	2 774	52 209	875	18.8	74.0	25.0	0.4	0.6	10.9	5.7	17.1	11.8	18.7	15.6	11.5
48 003	...	6	Andrews	3 887	13 738	2 154	3.5	95.1	2.3	0.9	1.7	37.6	9.4	24.9	8.3	11.6	14.0	11.5
48 005	...	5	Angelina	2 076	77 587	644	37.4	82.0	17.0	0.2	0.8	11.5	7.1	21.2	9.7	11.5	15.0	13.7
48 007	...	6	Aransas	653	23 129	1 610	35.4	92.5	1.9	0.8	4.8	24.7	6.8	18.4	6.9	9.7	13.1	13.6
48 009	9080	3	Archer	2 356	8 256	2 574	3.5	99.3	0.2	0.4	0.1	3.3	6.8	20.6	6.7	10.7	15.0	15.3
48 011	...	8	Armstrong	2 366	2 196	3 047	0.9	98.6	0.1	0.6	0.7	4.3	6.2	22.5	5.3	8.7	13.8	13.3
48 013	...	6	Atascosa	3 191	37 442	1 150	11.7	98.6	0.6	0.5	0.3	60.1	9.0	24.0	8.1	11.5	14.6	12.4
48 015	...	6	Austin	1 690	23 843	1 582	14.1	85.5	14.1	0.2	0.2	13.8	6.8	20.4	8.0	10.7	15.5	13.9
48 017	...	7	Bailey	2 141	6 717	2 707	3.1	97.8	1.8	0.1	0.2	45.2	8.3	23.4	7.9	10.7	13.2	12.5
48 019	...	8	Bandera	2 051	16 611	1 962	8.1	98.6	0.3	0.7	0.4	14.6	5.8	17.0	5.1	8.9	15.9	16.3
48 021	0640	2	Bastrop	2 301	52 561	869	22.8	86.2	12.6	0.6	0.6	23.3	8.0	21.4	7.4	12.3	17.4	13.6
48 023	...	7	Baylor	2 255	4 088	2 910	1.8	95.0	4.2	0.2	0.6	10.5	6.1	16.5	5.9	8.8	12.8	13.6
48 025	...	6	Bee	2 280	27 534	1 447	12.1	95.2	3.1	0.4	1.2	59.3	8.2	20.0	11.6	15.8	14.0	11.1
48 027	3810	2	Bell	2 743	222 687	248	81.2	75.1	19.6	0.6	4.7	17.3	9.2	19.7	14.1	15.1	14.8	11.1
48 029	7240	0	Bexar	3 230	1 372 867	23	425.0	90.6	7.0	0.5	1.9	57.0	8.7	20.7	10.8	13.7	15.6	12.1
48 031	...	8	Blanco	1 842	8 511	2 553	4.6	98.2	1.0	0.2	0.6	17.1	6.1	16.6	5.8	8.8	13.3	12.7
48 033	...	9	Borden	2 328	769	3 126	0.3	98.3	0.5	1.0	0.1	19.4	7.9	19.6	5.1	10.0	11.6	17.7
48 035	...	6	Bosque	2 562	16 699	1 952	6.5	96.8	2.4	0.2	0.6	13.0	6.3	18.5	7.0	9.1	13.8	14.2
48 037	8360	3	Bowie	2 300	83 509	606	36.3	75.4	23.5	0.5	0.5	2.2	6.3	20.1	8.4	11.2	16.1	13.8
48 039	1145	1	Brazoria	3 592	234 303	238	65.2	89.2	8.7	0.5	1.7	22.4	8.0	21.3	8.8	14.3	17.3	13.5
48 041	1260	3	Brazos	1 517	134 213	392	88.5	82.6	12.2	0.3	4.9	17.8	6.9	15.4	29.6	13.8	12.3	9.3
48 043	...	7	Brewster	16 040	8 793	2 522	0.5	98.1	0.9	0.2	0.8	50.0	6.9	16.9	13.4	11.0	13.8	12.8
48 045	...	9	Briscoe	2 332	1 825	3 073	0.8	95.1	4.1	0.3	0.5	23.8	7.3	21.4	5.3	8.0	14.6	15.5
48 047	...	7	Brooks	2 443	8 416	2 556	3.4	99.5	0.2	0.2	0.1	91.7	9.7	22.6	8.6	10.9	13.3	12.1
48 049	...	7	Brown	2 445	36 847	1 165	15.1	93.6	5.4	0.5	0.4	14.8	6.9	19.9	9.4	10.1	14.6	13.0
48 051	...	6	Burleson	1 724	15 614	2 026	9.1	79.9	19.3	0.5	0.3	15.9	6.9	20.4	7.9	10.4	14.1	12.7
48 053	...	6	Burnet	2 578	34 120	1 254	13.2	96.4	2.4	0.6	0.6	15.5	6.7	19.4	6.9	10.3	14.8	13.9

1. MSA = Metropolitan Statistical Area. PMSA = Primary MSA. NECMA = New England County Metropolitan Area. See Appendix A for explanation of these concepts. See Appendix B for list of metropolitan areas identified by type, with component counties.   2. County typology code from the Economic Research Service of USDA. See Appendix A for definition.   3. Dry land or land partially or temporarily covered by water.   4. Hispanic persons may be of any race.

STATE County	| Population, 1999 (cont'd) Age (percent) (cont'd) 55 to 64 years (16)	65 to 74 years (17)	75 years and over (18)	Percent female (19)	| Total persons 1990 (20)	1980 (21)	Percent change 1980–1990 (22)	1990–1999 (23)	| Components of change, 1990–1999 Births (24)	Deaths (25)	Net migration (26)	| Households, 1990 Number (27)	Percent change, 1980–1990 (28)	Persons per household (29)	Percent Female family householder[1] (30)	One person (31)
TENNESSEE—Cont'd																
Marshall	9.9	6.8	5.7	51.4	21 539	19 698	9.3	22.7	2 930	2 360	4 361	8 268	15.7	2.57	10.7	23.6
Maury	9.9	6.2	5.4	51.9	54 812	51 095	7.3	28.5	8 021	5 488	13 258	20 608	13.4	2.62	12.7	22.1
Meigs	10.0	7.0	5.1	49.6	8 033	7 431	8.1	26.2	1 046	777	1 852	2 996	18.9	2.64	8.7	19.8
Monroe	10.1	7.4	5.9	51.3	30 541	28 700	6.4	16.5	4 069	3 133	4 156	11 363	17.9	2.63	10.2	21.0
Montgomery	7.6	4.2	3.2	49.8	100 498	83 342	20.6	28.8	20 920	6 769	17 750	34 345	26.3	2.72	10.8	18.1
Moore	10.6	7.6	5.9	49.9	4 696	4 510	4.7	9.5	445	441	457	1 734	13.0	2.72	6.5	18.9
Morgan	9.4	5.9	5.2	46.6	17 300	16 604	4.2	8.0	2 102	1 575	930	5 841	8.4	2.74	11.6	19.2
Obion	10.1	7.6	7.4	52.1	31 717	32 781	-3.2	1.6	3 807	3 533	347	12 412	2.8	2.53	10.3	23.8
Overton	11.1	7.5	6.7	50.8	17 636	17 575	0.3	11.4	2 031	2 039	2 076	6 734	10.0	2.59	9.6	20.3
Perry	12.5	8.4	7.6	51.1	6 612	6 111	8.2	14.3	797	816	987	2 512	12.1	2.57	7.4	22.6
Pickett	12.2	7.6	8.2	51.1	4 548	4 358	4.4	3.6	436	534	268	1 786	15.8	2.52	9.5	24.1
Polk	10.9	7.8	6.6	50.5	13 643	13 602	0.3	10.6	1 671	1 629	1 455	5 092	10.5	2.66	8.9	19.4
Putnam	9.8	7.2	6.2	51.1	51 373	47 690	7.7	16.3	6 806	5 004	6 768	19 753	10.9	2.45	9.7	24.1
Rhea	9.9	7.4	6.6	51.7	24 344	24 235	0.4	15.5	3 268	2 516	3 111	9 185	10.9	2.57	11.8	22.0
Roane	11.5	9.9	6.9	51.8	47 227	48 425	-2.5	5.9	5 219	4 901	2 637	18 453	8.1	2.53	9.9	22.4
Robertson	9.5	5.8	5.2	50.9	41 492	37 021	12.1	32.2	6 506	3 936	10 842	14 801	18.1	2.77	10.4	17.7
Rutherford	7.3	4.2	3.3	50.7	118 570	84 058	41.1	44.6	20 991	7 983	39 854	42 118	50.4	2.69	10.1	20.3
Scott	9.2	5.8	5.2	51.3	18 358	19 259	-4.7	10.2	2 609	1 762	1 096	6 534	5.4	2.78	11.7	20.1
Sequatchie	9.4	6.3	6.3	50.5	8 863	8 605	3.0	22.4	1 205	817	1 595	3 287	13.7	2.67	10.7	20.0
Sevier	10.5	7.7	5.7	51.4	51 050	41 418	23.2	28.9	7 217	4 520	12 209	19 520	32.4	2.58	9.5	19.8
Shelby	7.8	5.6	4.4	52.5	826 330	777 113	6.3	5.6	140 209	72 361	-20 676	303 571	12.8	2.65	18.6	25.7
Smith	10.5	7.0	6.8	51.4	14 143	14 935	-5.3	18.6	1 795	1 654	2 501	5 358	-0.6	2.61	8.3	21.0
Stewart	12.6	8.3	7.4	50.7	9 479	8 665	9.4	24.1	1 183	1 140	2 241	3 678	18.5	2.53	6.8	21.6
Sullivan	11.1	9.1	6.6	52.1	143 596	143 968	-0.3	4.6	16 257	14 201	5 008	56 729	9.0	2.49	9.9	23.0
Sumner	8.6	5.9	4.6	50.9	103 281	85 790	20.4	22.0	14 020	7 921	16 894	36 850	29.0	2.77	9.6	17.3
Tipton	8.3	5.7	5.0	51.2	37 568	32 930	14.1	28.7	6 239	3 465	7 978	13 033	20.9	2.86	13.7	18.5
Trousdale	10.3	6.8	6.6	51.1	5 920	6 137	-3.5	17.8	800	735	1 003	2 261	1.5	2.56	10.7	22.6
Unicoi	11.5	9.7	8.4	52.0	16 549	16 362	1.1	4.6	1 716	1 812	914	6 621	11.3	2.46	9.9	23.6
Union	9.3	5.6	5.0	50.4	13 694	11 707	17.0	21.1	1 746	1 254	2 424	4 932	25.0	2.75	10.3	17.1
Van Buren	10.6	6.8	5.8	50.3	4 846	4 728	2.5	3.3	538	405	60	1 799	13.1	2.69	10.6	17.9
Warren	10.5	7.4	6.7	51.5	32 992	32 653	1.0	10.4	4 322	3 403	2 617	12 681	6.8	2.57	10.8	22.3
Washington	10.1	7.5	6.5	51.6	92 336	88 755	4.0	11.3	11 178	9 022	8 552	35 823	14.9	2.45	10.6	25.1
Wayne	9.6	7.0	6.2	47.0	13 935	13 946	0.0	17.8	1 623	1 481	2 396	5 174	8.0	2.65	9.3	19.5
Weakley	9.6	7.2	7.6	51.7	31 972	32 896	-2.8	3.1	3 456	3 430	1 051	11 992	3.7	2.47	9.0	24.4
White	11.3	8.1	7.4	51.6	20 090	19 567	2.7	13.8	2 462	2 325	2 710	7 722	10.5	2.57	9.9	21.0
Williamson	8.1	4.8	3.8	50.7	81 021	58 108	39.4	52.8	11 623	4 856	35 951	27 928	49.2	2.88	8.0	14.8
Wilson	8.4	5.1	4.1	50.4	67 675	56 064	20.7	27.8	9 541	5 260	14 596	24 070	27.6	2.79	9.3	16.2
TEXAS	8.1	5.5	4.5	50.7	16 986 335	14 225 513	19.4	18.0	3 025 567	1 254 005	1 285 377	6 070 937	23.2	2.73	11.6	23.9
Anderson	8.0	5.6	5.9	40.8	48 024	38 381	25.1	8.7	5 733	4 511	3 086	14 223	14.8	2.67	11.5	22.6
Andrews	8.6	6.8	4.9	50.5	14 338	13 323	7.6	-4.2	2 120	1 013	-1 686	4 758	7.6	2.99	8.1	18.0
Angelina	9.3	6.5	6.0	50.9	69 884	64 172	8.9	11.0	10 963	6 662	3 669	25 004	14.8	2.73	11.1	22.2
Aransas	12.6	11.3	7.6	50.3	17 892	14 260	25.5	29.3	2 182	2 067	5 174	6 938	34.2	2.55	8.2	23.0
Archer	11.2	7.3	6.3	49.8	7 973	7 266	9.7	3.5	862	621	68	2 957	11.8	2.68	6.0	20.5
Armstrong	12.6	7.8	9.7	51.0	2 021	1 994	1.4	8.7	221	247	208	768	2.4	2.56	4.8	24.9
Atascosa	8.4	6.1	5.4	50.4	30 533	25 055	21.9	22.6	4 889	2 435	4 522	9 940	23.7	3.03	11.1	18.7
Austin	10.2	6.7	7.8	50.7	19 832	17 726	11.9	20.2	2 723	2 247	3 581	7 478	16.2	2.62	8.7	25.3
Bailey	9.3	7.5	7.2	50.3	7 064	8 168	-13.5	-4.9	1 092	598	-831	2 454	-8.5	2.86	6.2	20.6
Bandera	14.3	9.6	7.0	49.9	10 562	7 084	49.1	57.3	1 284	1 165	5 923	4 180	49.2	2.46	5.5	23.5
Bastrop	9.3	5.6	5.1	49.3	38 263	24 726	54.7	37.4	6 240	3 387	11 396	13 379	53.4	2.77	10.1	21.5
Baylor	12.3	10.8	13.2	52.7	4 385	4 919	-10.9	-6.8	391	692	19	1 906	-6.0	2.26	5.9	31.7
Bee	7.9	6.0	5.4	46.8	25 135	26 030	-3.4	9.5	3 852	2 052	344	8 592	5.0	2.86	11.6	21.7
Bell	7.2	4.8	4.0	49.7	191 073	157 820	21.1	16.5	45 144	12 784	-7 915	67 240	27.7	2.70	10.6	21.4
Bexar	7.9	6.0	4.5	51.8	1 185 394	988 971	19.9	15.8	211 403	84 047	53 848	409 043	28.1	2.83	14.5	23.2
Blanco	10.2	15.0	11.5	51.9	5 972	4 681	27.6	42.5	814	736	2 526	2 338	28.1	2.48	5.9	25.1
Borden	12.2	9.5	6.4	48.0	799	859	-7.0	-3.8	49	29	-40	294	-1.7	2.72	5.1	16.7
Bosque	11.5	9.0	10.7	50.9	15 125	13 401	12.9	10.4	1 840	2 350	2 168	5 990	8.7	2.46	6.7	25.7
Bowie	9.6	7.7	6.8	51.6	81 665	75 301	8.5	2.3	11 350	8 345	-916	30 595	11.5	2.59	13.2	24.4
Brazoria	8.2	5.1	3.6	48.1	191 707	169 587	13.0	22.2	32 072	12 355	23 227	64 019	18.8	2.86	8.6	18.5
Brazos	5.3	3.8	3.5	48.8	121 862	93 588	30.2	10.1	17 919	5 726	330	43 725	34.6	2.51	9.1	25.2
Brewster	9.6	8.8	6.7	49.7	8 653	7 573	14.3	1.6	1 030	716	-153	3 350	24.4	2.43	9.2	29.2
Briscoe	10.7	8.4	8.8	49.3	1 971	2 579	-23.6	-7.4	237	256	-125	789	-18.4	2.49	5.8	26.7
Brooks	9.2	7.2	6.4	51.8	8 204	8 428	-2.7	2.6	1 457	708	-494	2 673	2.3	3.04	16.1	20.8
Brown	10.3	7.5	8.2	50.8	34 371	33 057	4.0	7.2	4 351	4 120	2 368	13 097	6.4	2.51	10.3	25.8
Burleson	11.7	8.2	7.6	50.8	13 625	12 313	10.7	14.6	1 928	1 598	1 715	5 176	16.1	2.58	10.3	26.4
Burnet	13.1	7.5	7.2	50.6	22 677	17 803	27.4	50.5	3 354	2 954	10 983	9 055	30.3	2.47	7.5	23.9

1. No spouse present.

Table B. States and Counties — **Vital Statistics, Health Resources, and Crime**

STATE County	Births, average 1996–1998 Total	Births, average 1996–1998 Rate¹	Deaths, avg 1996–1998 Number Total	Deaths Number Infant²	Deaths Rate Total¹	Deaths Rate Infant³	Physicians,⁴ 1998 Number	Physicians,⁴ 1998 Rate⁵	Hospitals,⁴ 1998 Number	Hospitals Beds Number	Hospitals Beds Rate⁵	Medicare enrollees 1999	Serious crimes known to police, 1998⁶ Total Number	Serious crimes Total Rate⁷
	32	33	34	35	36	37	38	39	40	41	42	43	44	45
TENNESSEE—Cont'd														
Marshall	333	13.0	260	1	10.1	3.0	14	53	1	96	365	3 877	971	4 029
Maury	926	13.6	611	6	8.9	6.8	127	182	1	302	434	9 946	3 653	5 302
Meigs	131	13.6	89	1	9.2	7.6	4	40	0	0	0	1 674	184	2 252
Monroe	471	13.8	374	3	11.0	7.1	21	60	1	59	169	6 071	718	2 091
Montgomery	2 383	19.2	783	21	6.3	8.7	196	154	1	164	129	11 463	5 856	4 658
Moore	47	9.1	51	0	9.8	0.0	0	0	0	0	0	573	105	1 986
Morgan	226	12.2	177	1	9.5	3.0	7	37	0	0	0	2 417	190	1 068
Obion	401	12.5	409	3	12.7	8.3	39	121	1	133	413	6 059	1 587	4 884
Overton	235	12.3	236	1	12.3	5.7	15	77	1	79	404	3 508	87	449
Perry	97	13.2	92	1	12.5	6.8	4	53	1	74	986	1 418	37	488
Pickett	58	12.4	56	0	12.1	0.0	2	43	0	0	0	808	55	1 181
Polk	184	12.6	180	2	12.3	10.8	15	101	1	40	269	3 092	294	1 976
Putnam	778	13.3	574	5	9.8	6.4	112	189	1	116	196	10 878	2 238	4 105
Rhea	376	13.6	285	2	10.3	6.2	10	36	1	131	471	4 855	664	2 379
Roane	574	11.5	561	4	11.2	6.4	33	66	2	165	330	10 138	1 271	2 517
Robertson	749	14.6	440	7	8.6	9.3	36	68	1	115	217	6 888	2 084	4 102
Rutherford	2 535	15.8	956	19	6.0	7.6	224	135	1	221	133	14 773	NA	NA
Scott	297	15.0	206	1	10.4	2.2	15	75	1	97	484	3 392	294	1 795
Sequatchie	138	13.6	101	0	10.0	0.0	7	68	0	0	0	1 431	322	3 150
Sevier	831	13.2	547	5	8.7	5.6	65	101	1	46	71	10 297	NA	NA
Shelby	14 881	17.2	7 941	189	9.2	12.7	2 420	279	13	4 940	569	105 525	60 319	6 886
Smith	210	13.1	197	1	12.3	3.2	12	73	2	78	477	2 822	NA	NA
Stewart	137	12.1	134	1	11.9	9.7	4	35	0	0	0	2 184	158	1 387
Sullivan	1 718	11.4	1 604	14	10.7	8.3	484	321	3	802	532	29 021	4 995	3 276
Sumner	1 607	13.2	931	8	7.7	4.8	148	119	3	242	195	14 884	4 336	3 518
Tipton	691	15.0	417	8	9.1	12.1	31	65	1	100	211	5 857	NA	NA
Trousdale	85	12.6	77	0	11.5	3.9	5	73	1	26	380	1 069	282	4 096
Unicoi	209	12.1	206	3	12.0	12.7	14	81	1	48	279	3 881	280	1 603
Union	204	12.8	153	2	9.6	9.8	2	12	0	0	0	2 057	231	1 435
Van Buren	56	11.1	49	1	9.6	11.9	1	20	0	0	0	698	28	554
Warren	483	13.5	384	4	10.7	8.3	32	88	1	142	393	6 482	1 073	2 964
Washington	1 265	12.5	1 047	8	10.3	6.3	498	487	3	591	578	18 006	4 138	4 027
Wayne	169	10.3	185	3	11.3	15.8	9	55	1	54	327	2 485	177	1 057
Weakley	380	11.6	365	4	11.2	10.5	33	100	1	65	197	5 414	824	2 689
White	277	12.4	260	3	11.7	9.6	14	62	1	60	264	4 419	663	2 956
Williamson	1 450	13.0	577	6	5.2	3.9	440	374	1	109	93	10 612	3 307	2 935
Wilson	1 079	13.2	642	3	7.9	3.1	78	93	2	395	471	9 165	NA	NA
TEXAS	335 554	17.3	141 781	2 141	7.3	6.4	36 341	184	406	55 695	282	2 223 175	1 010 062	5 112
Anderson	630	12.1	552	7	10.6	11.1	73	139	2	225	430	7 463	1 837	3 440
Andrews	217	15.6	104	2	7.5	9.2	13	93	1	72	515	1 790	362	2 531
Angelina	1 246	16.2	752	8	9.8	6.2	109	141	3	346	447	11 980	3 599	4 610
Aransas	228	10.2	245	3	11.0	11.7	43	188	0	0	0	3 938	1 217	5 302
Archer	105	12.7	60	0	7.3	3.2	1	12	0	0	0	1 062	46	547
Armstrong	21	9.6	25	0	11.6	0.0	0	0	0	0	0	378	29	1 313
Atascosa	557	15.7	277	4	7.8	7.2	20	55	1	30	82	4 147	748	2 086
Austin	330	14.3	241	1	10.5	4.0	22	94	1	30	128	3 882	518	2 225
Bailey	117	17.2	62	1	9.1	8.6	5	72	1	31	449	1 115	181	2 607
Bandera	170	11.3	131	1	8.7	7.8	11	70	0	0	0	2 640	362	2 373
Bastrop	770	15.8	387	6	8.0	7.4	24	48	1	28	56	6 448	1 448	2 905
Baylor	36	8.7	69	0	16.7	9.3	3	72	1	39	939	1 104	122	2 881
Bee	411	14.8	232	2	8.4	4.9	18	65	1	59	213	3 420	888	3 114
Bell	5 141	23.1	1 431	34	6.4	6.5	719	322	4	755	338	21 679	11 344	5 020
Bexar	23 069	17.3	9 431	171	7.1	7.4	3 987	295	16	4 128	305	158 899	87 595	6 467
Blanco	89	10.9	88	1	10.9	11.3	4	48	0	0	0	3 511	104	1 246
Borden	3	4.0	2	0	3.1	0.0	0	0	0	0	0	50	13	1 711
Bosque	211	12.7	265	2	16.0	11.0	14	85	1	72	435	3 648	305	1 800
Bowie	1 181	14.1	941	9	11.2	7.6	206	247	4	711	851	13 845	3 804	4 472
Brazoria	3 514	15.6	1 496	20	6.7	5.8	255	111	4	310	135	22 988	6 819	2 987
Brazos	2 007	15.1	633	10	4.8	5.2	271	203	2	256	192	10 788	7 711	5 703
Brewster	112	12.4	81	1	9.0	9.0	13	146	1	34	382	1 380	216	2 351
Briscoe	27	14.0	25	0	13.3	12.5	0	0	0	0	0	411	33	1 638
Brooks	150	17.8	82	0	9.7	0.0	3	35	0	0	0	1 328	234	2 722
Brown	495	13.5	442	5	12.0	10.8	49	132	1	164	443	6 865	1 742	4 644
Burleson	216	14.0	162	1	10.5	6.2	6	38	1	33	211	2 852	427	2 733
Burnet	420	13.6	339	2	11.0	4.8	37	115	1	42	130	4 850	783	2 505

1. Per 1,000 estimated resident population, average 1996–1998. 2. Deaths of infants under 1 year old. 3. Deaths of infants under 1 year old per 1,000 live births. 4. Data subject to copyright. 5. Per 100,000 resident population as of July 1 of the year shown. 6. Data for serious crimes have not been adjusted for underreporting; this may affect comparability between geographic areas and over time. 7. Per 100,000 population estimated by the FBI.

Table B. States and Counties — Crime, Education, Money Income, and Poverty

STATE County	Serious crimes known to police, 1998[1] (cont'd) Rate[2] Violent	Property	Education — School enrollment and attainment, 1990 — Enrollment[3] Total	Percent private	Attainment[4] (percent) High school graduate or more	Bachelor's degree or more	Local government expenditures, fiscal 1997[5] Total current expenditures (mil dol)	Current expenditures per student (dollars)	Money income 1989 Per capita[6] (dollars)	Households Median Dollars	Percent change, 1979–1989 (constant 1989 dollars)	Percent with $100,000 or more	Income and poverty, 1997 Percent below poverty level Median household income	All persons	Persons under 18	Persons 5–17 in families
	46	47	48	49	50	51	52	53	54	55	56	57	58	59	60	61
TENNESSEE—Cont'd																
Marshall	635	3 394	4 725	2.8	60.0	7.7	20.0	4 278	11 248	23 855	5.3	1.1	33 399	11.0	15.0	13.2
Maury	704	4 598	12 583	8.2	65.2	12.1	47.9	4 030	11 942	26 238	6.3	1.7	36 966	10.9	15.1	13.3
Meigs	86	2 166	1 774	4.4	52.7	6.6	6.9	4 009	9 237	20 181	-14.4	0.6	26 931	18.7	27.0	23.8
Monroe	297	1 794	7 034	8.2	49.9	7.6	25.0	4 043	9 080	19 932	0.9	0.8	27 511	17.2	24.6	21.3
Montgomery	623	4 035	26 250	7.1	77.9	16.5	89.9	4 034	11 056	25 568	8.1	1.2	35 728	11.5	15.5	14.4
Moore	113	1 873	1 152	3.6	66.7	11.7	4.3	4 363	11 545	28 056	14.2	1.6	36 958	9.7	14.8	12.8
Morgan	191	877	4 270	6.7	56.7	3.7	14.2	4 249	7 722	19 280	5.9	0.3	25 982	18.9	25.8	21.4
Obion	431	4 453	7 151	2.7	61.3	8.5	25.5	4 591	11 096	22 344	1.8	1.4	31 911	13.4	18.8	16.5
Overton	57	392	3 670	4.5	44.1	6.9	12.9	4 211	8 622	18 293	6.2	0.9	25 216	16.5	23.6	20.4
Perry	13	475	1 322	4.7	52.7	6.9	5.4	4 323	9 260	19 039	-0.5	1.3	27 209	15.7	22.0	21.1
Pickett	64	1 117	918	1.5	45.8	9.1	4.0	4 767	9 564	14 993	-0.7	1.4	22 027	21.4	29.4	28.3
Polk	249	1 727	2 866	4.2	51.3	5.8	9.9	4 266	9 311	21 663	7.0	0.8	27 703	14.6	20.6	19.1
Putnam	642	3 463	14 821	3.6	63.2	16.8	39.1	4 167	11 004	21 693	5.4	2.0	30 570	13.7	19.1	16.8
Rhea	312	2 067	5 657	12.3	56.0	8.5	17.9	3 854	9 333	19 915	-5.1	0.8	27 479	16.8	23.7	20.8
Roane	299	2 218	10 820	6.2	66.7	13.2	36.0	4 761	12 015	24 210	-4.8	2.2	31 448	14.6	20.7	18.5
Robertson	482	3 620	9 291	8.0	65.5	9.6	39.2	4 050	12 077	28 687	12.7	2.3	38 432	9.7	14.1	12.0
Rutherford	NA	NA	34 747	6.3	73.9	18.7	122.8	4 369	12 536	30 878	15.7	1.8	43 488	7.5	9.6	8.8
Scott	348	1 447	4 705	3.2	51.2	6.6	18.4	4 520	7 803	15 858	-3.8	1.0	21 635	23.6	30.6	28.0
Sequatchie	597	2 553	1 904	7.2	51.4	7.6	7.4	4 250	9 377	19 223	4.5	1.7	27 542	16.5	22.4	21.3
Sevier	NA	NA	10 640	6.3	63.0	10.8	49.8	4 431	10 848	23 042	5.1	1.6	30 189	13.9	21.1	18.3
Shelby	1 114	5 772	220 341	16.4	75.1	20.8	757.5	4 806	13 330	27 132	5.9	4.0	34 583	16.3	22.1	18.6
Smith	NA	NA	2 990	2.6	54.2	6.1	10.6	3 478	10 950	23 255	-0.5	1.6	32 077	12.6	17.5	16.2
Stewart	334	1 053	1 880	2.0	58.9	7.7	7.7	4 001	9 935	20 802	7.7	0.7	28 473	13.2	19.7	17.2
Sullivan	459	2 817	30 972	10.2	66.8	15.6	133.1	5 761	12 725	25 089	-3.6	2.4	33 199	13.0	19.7	16.7
Sumner	373	3 145	25 351	10.3	70.6	14.4	95.8	4 381	13 497	31 795	6.3	3.0	42 845	8.7	11.7	10.4
Tipton	NA	NA	9 449	5.6	61.8	6.7	39.8	3 882	9 796	23 860	8.2	0.9	32 845	14.1	17.9	17.2
Trousdale	479	3 617	1 239	5.2	47.7	7.0	4.6	3 717	9 618	20 127	-19.6	0.7	27 319	15.7	22.0	20.0
Unicoi	344	1 259	3 374	1.6	59.6	9.5	10.9	4 252	10 727	20 536	-0.8	1.5	28 650	14.4	21.2	18.6
Union	106	1 329	2 998	4.3	45.6	4.5	11.1	3 769	8 351	19 595	5.6	0.2	26 692	17.1	23.8	21.4
Van Buren	0	554	1 006	4.3	48.0	4.1	3.5	4 453	8 186	20 676	8.4	0.0	28 361	15.7	20.6	20.4
Warren	224	2 740	6 907	5.9	57.0	8.1	26.6	4 231	10 472	21 019	5.2	1.8	30 135	14.6	20.2	18.0
Washington	430	3 597	23 223	5.8	68.4	18.9	67.1	4 573	11 949	23 698	0.2	2.3	32 651	12.8	17.2	15.8
Wayne	209	848	2 799	2.4	51.0	5.0	11.0	4 013	8 240	18 429	-6.1	0.6	25 053	19.8	25.2	23.1
Weakley	297	2 392	8 923	3.0	56.9	10.3	20.0	3 842	9 857	21 004	8.7	0.9	30 401	13.3	17.1	15.5
White	232	2 724	3 974	4.2	53.2	7.6	13.9	3 625	9 299	19 874	3.6	0.7	27 224	15.8	22.0	20.2
Williamson	382	2 553	21 381	23.1	81.8	34.2	99.5	4 942	19 339	43 615	19.7	10.2	63 959	4.8	5.7	5.3
Wilson	NA	NA	16 337	14.6	71.4	15.6	56.8	4 013	13 681	32 852	7.1	2.8	45 250	7.8	10.7	9.5
TEXAS	565	4 547	4 805 895	10.2	72.1	20.3	20 167.0	5 267	12 904	27 016	-3.5	3.7	34 478	16.7	23.6	22.1
Anderson	586	2 854	11 242	8.4	67.7	9.5	43.8	4 971	9 384	22 737	-0.3	1.5	29 760	20.4	24.0	22.5
Andrews	119	2 412	4 261	4.2	61.2	9.8	21.0	5 882	10 361	26 434	-13.5	1.4	34 638	15.8	20.1	21.1
Angelina	583	4 027	18 706	6.5	65.3	13.2	76.2	4 814	11 248	22 986	-12.3	2.1	30 276	17.3	24.1	22.4
Aransas	279	5 023	4 147	8.6	67.2	14.5	19.2	5 623	11 394	21 315	-9.6	2.8	27 664	22.7	36.0	35.5
Archer	36	511	2 027	4.1	72.5	12.3	11.3	5 567	11 719	25 131	-6.1	2.5	36 394	9.3	13.2	12.7
Armstrong	45	1 268	468	0.6	77.4	14.1	2.5	5 807	11 212	23 081	-11.5	1.2	31 091	11.2	13.7	14.5
Atascosa	131	1 955	8 533	3.2	58.8	8.4	42.9	5 297	8 447	20 048	-6.8	1.3	26 832	23.0	31.2	30.3
Austin	215	2 010	4 836	6.3	62.6	13.8	25.4	4 842	11 837	25 043	3.9	2.2	33 945	13.1	17.7	17.4
Bailey	173	2 434	1 793	0.7	55.4	7.4	9.8	6 068	10 043	19 873	-5.3	4.2	27 005	24.2	33.7	33.5
Bandera	118	2 255	2 199	7.5	76.7	16.9	13.0	5 195	12 798	24 671	10.1	2.2	33 306	13.0	21.6	20.3
Bastrop	259	2 646	9 588	4.9	68.3	13.3	53.1	5 354	10 300	23 967	15.0	1.0	34 006	13.9	19.4	19.4
Baylor	260	2 621	720	3.5	63.6	10.3	4.6	5 756	11 040	17 228	-11.4	1.6	23 287	20.6	29.6	30.3
Bee	256	2 858	7 916	7.0	65.0	12.7	29.2	5 124	8 619	20 614	-3.1	0.9	26 840	26.5	32.3	32.9
Bell	462	4 558	49 611	9.3	79.1	17.2	236.1	4 885	10 908	23 755	8.4	1.9	31 431	14.7	21.3	20.6
Bexar	458	6 009	345 381	13.0	72.7	19.7	1 353.6	5 408	11 827	25 926	2.5	3.0	32 374	18.5	26.4	24.2
Blanco	96	1 150	1 244	7.8	68.9	13.0	8.6	5 541	12 388	22 297	7.0	2.4	29 285	9.1	12.7	13.4
Borden	132	1 579	183	2.7	71.2	17.3	2.4	11 558	17 533	29 375	17.3	11.6	36 730	11.7	14.0	18.2
Bosque	201	1 599	3 006	4.4	64.0	10.8	18.6	5 739	10 992	21 411	9.3	2.1	28 633	16.2	24.8	23.5
Bowie	471	4 001	20 935	4.8	72.1	14.3	80.8	4 918	11 846	24 237	2.2	2.2	32 433	16.9	25.1	22.6
Brazoria	245	2 742	55 183	8.0	75.5	15.1	215.2	4 635	13 468	34 418	-12.0	2.9	43 688	11.0	15.1	14.0
Brazos	393	5 310	58 837	5.3	79.8	35.8	101.5	5 045	10 987	20 411	-1.0	2.6	32 045	18.0	22.1	21.8
Brewster	239	2 112	2 825	2.8	73.2	28.0	9.6	6 113	10 730	17 586	-2.9	3.0	24 952	22.7	31.5	32.4
Briscoe	248	1 390	454	0.7	63.0	11.6	1.7	6 028	10 058	17 696	-3.4	2.0	23 777	23.1	33.3	34.5
Brooks	70	2 652	2 434	3.3	45.6	6.6	9.8	5 233	6 623	13 509	-23.6	1.6	17 701	38.4	50.5	50.9
Brown	456	4 188	8 560	15.1	67.1	13.7	38.9	5 367	9 797	19 291	-8.3	1.6	26 963	19.5	27.0	26.2
Burleson	282	2 451	3 070	6.5	58.2	9.5	18.5	5 638	9 354	19 785	-9.0	1.1	27 802	16.6	23.4	22.3
Burnet	205	2 300	4 711	6.7	69.1	14.0	31.6	5 373	11 530	21 420	5.3	2.0	31 146	13.0	18.3	17.9

1. Data for serious crimes have not been adjusted for underreporting; this may affect comparability between geographic areas and over time.   2. Per 100,000 population estimated by the FBI.   3. All persons 3 years old and over enrolled in nursery school through college.   4. Persons 25 years old and over.   5. Elementary and secondary education expenditures, local government fiscal years ending between July 1, 1996 and June 30, 1997.   6. Based on population enumerated as of April 1, 1990.

Table B. States and Counties — **Personal Income**

STATE County	Personal income, 1998 Total (mil dol)	Percent change, 1997–1998	Per capita[1] Dollars	Per capita[1] Rank	Wages and salaries[2] (mil dol)	Proprietor's income (mil dol)	Dividends, interest, and rent (mil dol)	Transfer payments Total (mil dol)	Government payments to individuals Total (mil dol)	Social Security (mil dol)	Medical payments (mil dol)	Income maintenance (mil dol)	Unemployment insurance (mil dol)
	62	63	64	65	66	67	68	69	70	71	72	73	74
TENNESSEE—Cont'd													
Marshall	567	4.8	21 607	1 221	355	47	87	90	85	37	38	6	1
Maury	1 459	3.4	20 960	1 406	1 354	132	233	240	229	93	103	20	4
Meigs	161	4.3	16 147	2 773	42	16	20	43	41	15	18	4	1
Monroe	619	5.9	17 775	2 412	315	49	84	148	143	57	60	15	3
Montgomery	2 829	5.3	22 245	1 027	981	196	397	329	308	109	119	29	6
Moore	100	3.5	19 343	1 938	45	2	15	17	16	7	7	1	0
Morgan	270	3.8	14 468	2 972	88	22	32	80	77	33	30	9	1
Obion	715	2.7	22 227	1 034	483	64	135	129	124	53	52	11	2
Overton	325	4.3	16 635	2 691	117	31	43	91	87	30	42	10	2
Perry	141	0.2	18 756	2 138	78	11	19	37	36	13	19	2	1
Pickett	82	5.0	17 658	2 450	26	10	11	24	24	8	11	2	0
Polk	270	5.5	18 097	2 322	68	18	36	73	70	29	33	6	1
Putnam	1 321	6.1	22 371	1 003	884	141	234	233	223	90	99	18	4
Rhea	469	5.4	16 847	2 645	327	35	73	122	118	44	52	13	3
Roane	1 033	3.4	20 673	1 495	825	59	139	233	225	93	97	19	4
Robertson	1 193	9.7	22 429	993	388	98	147	167	158	67	69	12	3
Rutherford	4 187	7.8	25 212	468	2 570	559	495	385	358	147	151	25	9
Scott	304	4.2	15 155	2 915	142	24	41	104	101	29	48	16	1
Sequatchie	182	6.1	17 375	2 511	65	13	21	42	40	14	18	4	1
Sevier	1 411	6.1	21 913	1 125	734	165	241	223	213	94	86	17	7
Shelby	25 152	6.7	28 984	195	19 399	2 587	3 567	3 101	2 958	998	1 314	437	42
Smith	330	5.0	20 154	1 666	159	25	53	68	65	24	33	5	1
Stewart	189	4.6	16 427	2 717	69	16	32	49	48	19	20	4	1
Sullivan	3 513	2.7	23 368	780	2 479	227	640	629	604	284	237	49	6
Sumner	2 971	5.6	23 969	649	1 126	260	396	370	350	154	149	23	8
Tipton	891	7.6	18 832	2 115	314	74	99	154	146	54	66	16	3
Trousdale	110	5.1	16 078	2 784	39	12	18	30	29	10	15	2	1
Unicoi	348	3.1	20 198	1 650	150	19	51	86	84	28	35	6	1
Union	240	3.7	14 796	2 951	66	13	28	59	57	24	22	8	1
Van Buren	80	8.1	15 828	2 821	30	4	9	20	19	7	9	2	0
Warren	762	3.6	21 074	1 367	490	79	110	163	157	55	80	14	3
Washington	2 333	3.6	22 830	884	1 633	159	387	401	384	158	159	30	5
Wayne	245	2.0	14 904	2 940	94	11	34	67	64	23	29	7	3
Weakley	641	2.2	19 471	1 903	310	60	105	132	127	52	55	10	2
White	403	6.6	17 733	2 431	186	50	52	99	95	37	43	8	2
Williamson	4 296	9.3	36 508	53	1 920	389	648	238	218	109	86	10	3
Wilson	2 091	6.8	24 914	497	793	180	285	254	240	99	105	14	6
TEXAS	500 087	7.7	25 369	X	327 518	60 795	75 550	59 396	56 106	20 839	24 511	6 306	1 114
Anderson	897	5.4	17 218	2 555	534	79	149	192	183	62	83	18	3
Andrews	244	-1.2	17 351	2 518	138	15	47	47	45	19	18	5	1
Angelina	1 603	4.4	20 735	1 473	998	136	273	317	304	116	143	28	4
Aransas	490	6.9	21 464	1 256	141	25	134	95	91	41	36	9	2
Archer	179	7.0	21 638	1 209	42	26	33	26	25	13	8	2	0
Armstrong	40	0.7	18 489	2 214	11	1	12	9	9	4	4	1	0
Atascosa	622	7.1	17 105	2 585	217	45	82	122	115	39	53	17	2
Austin	527	4.9	22 531	970	253	37	104	83	79	32	37	6	1
Bailey	146	4.2	21 331	1 289	53	37	25	28	27	10	12	4	0
Bandera	355	9.8	22 422	995	50	23	81	53	50	24	17	3	1
Bastrop	1 012	12.1	20 065	1 689	250	65	152	140	131	50	56	13	2
Baylor	81	8.8	19 366	1 928	29	9	20	24	23	10	10	2	0
Bee	432	3.6	15 574	2 868	227	27	68	104	99	29	47	15	1
Bell	5 121	3.6	22 949	861	4 271	247	756	602	574	186	213	67	14
Bexar	32 316	5.5	23 852	673	21 856	4 156	5 467	4 301	4 080	1 311	1 800	556	54
Blanco	172	5.7	20 642	1 511	54	24	36	46	45	23	19	1	0
Borden	9	-30.6	11 140	3 093	4	-3	3	2	2	1	0	0	0
Bosque	319	5.1	19 292	1 960	91	28	77	74	71	32	28	5	1
Bowie	1 811	1.3	21 741	1 176	1 113	145	350	339	325	112	148	37	6
Brazoria	5 228	5.7	22 844	881	2 828	255	770	596	557	231	245	43	16
Brazos	2 674	6.9	20 121	1 673	1 915	163	471	282	260	106	98	31	2
Brewster	165	6.5	18 729	2 150	92	9	39	31	29	11	9	4	0
Briscoe	36	4.0	18 990	2 060	12	6	8	9	9	3	4	1	0
Brooks	115	7.5	13 644	3 034	48	2	17	42	40	9	20	9	0
Brown	693	4.6	18 816	2 118	397	51	116	176	170	61	81	13	2
Burleson	271	2.8	17 441	2 498	88	15	65	63	61	26	23	6	1
Burnet	643	7.6	19 910	1 740	221	77	179	120	115	57	41	8	1

1. Based on the resident population estimated as of July 1 of the year shown. 2. Includes other labor income.

Table B. States and Counties — Earnings, Social Security, and Housing

STATE County	Earnings, 1998									Social Security beneficiaries, December 1998		Supplemental Security Income recipients, December 1998	Housing units, 1990	
			Percent by selected industries											
			Goods-related[1]		Service-related and other[2]									
	Total (mil dol)	Farm	Total	Manufacturing	Total	Retail trade	Finance, insurance, and real estate	Services	Government	Number	Rate[3]		Total	Percent change, 1980–1990
	75	76	77	78	79	80	81	82	83	84	85	86	87	88

TENNESSEE—Cont'd

STATE County	75	76	77	78	79	80	81	82	83	84	85	86	87	88
Marshall	402	-0.3	D	58.7	D	7.5	3.0	9.5	9.3	4 662	177	550	8 909	16.5
Maury	1 486	-0.2	D	48.0	D	6.3	4.6	17.2	11.5	11 397	164	1 763	22 286	14.1
Meigs	57	-0.8	D	31.7	D	9.6	D	13.4	18.2	1 990	200	438	3 689	23.1
Monroe	364	0.0	D	51.0	D	11.4	3.8	12.9	10.8	7 785	224	1 606	12 803	16.4
Montgomery	1 177	0.3	D	19.8	D	15.5	5.3	23.0	18.6	14 292	112	2 312	37 233	25.3
Moore	47	0.6	D	15.1	D	3.5	D	7.6	39.1	827	159	91	1 912	14.6
Morgan	111	-0.7	33.7	26.4	30.4	6.8	1.9	11.5	36.6	4 452	237	621	6 378	7.7
Obion	547	0.9	54.1	49.0	36.3	9.8	2.3	14.3	8.7	6 697	208	1 093	13 359	2.3
Overton	149	0.4	D	29.4	D	11.5	4.2	19.3	18.3	4 402	225	943	7 388	13.2
Perry	89	-1.4	D	56.3	D	5.2	2.9	19.9	10.7	1 786	238	251	3 225	13.5
Pickett	35	4.8	31.7	23.1	D	16.0	4.1	14.7	19.8	1 242	268	258	2 253	20.7
Polk	86	4.7	D	23.3	D	9.3	5.5	20.9	23.0	3 674	247	551	5 659	11.2
Putnam	1 025	-0.3	D	29.0	D	11.3	4.3	17.7	19.1	11 570	196	1 925	21 417	20.3
Rhea	362	0.2	42.1	36.7	22.6	7.2	2.1	9.6	35.2	5 610	202	1 204	10 361	10.4
Roane	884	-0.3	D	27.7	D	D	1.4	43.7	14.6	11 214	224	1 954	20 334	8.6
Robertson	486	2.4	D	33.4	D	11.6	2.7	15.3	16.0	8 383	158	974	15 823	18.9
Rutherford	3 129	0.1	D	30.7	D	8.0	6.0	25.4	12.9	18 020	109	2 126	45 755	49.8
Scott	166	0.1	D	33.6	D	10.9	2.4	17.6	19.0	4 334	216	1 724	7 122	7.8
Sequatchie	78	-0.2	D	31.0	D	10.0	5.4	14.3	16.2	1 943	187	366	3 570	12.9
Sevier	899	-0.4	D	9.0	D	27.5	6.1	34.4	12.2	12 001	186	1 358	24 166	38.1
Shelby	21 986	0.0	D	10.7	D	9.1	8.8	29.1	13.2	122 514	141	32 513	327 796	14.5
Smith	184	-0.6	D	33.6	41.4	12.0	3.6	18.7	11.8	3 264	199	542	6 049	0.0
Stewart	86	0.3	12.8	5.4	D	10.7	4.2	10.5	56.2	2 607	226	426	4 384	22.4
Sullivan	2 706	0.1	43.4	36.0	48.0	9.5	3.4	25.0	8.7	33 601	223	4 537	60 623	10.3
Sumner	1 386	0.0	39.8	30.1	47.0	9.2	4.6	22.6	13.2	18 421	148	2 124	39 807	32.0
Tipton	389	1.2	D	32.5	D	10.2	4.0	17.2	15.4	7 213	152	1 419	14 071	21.6
Trousdale	51	-1.2	D	32.9	D	10.5	5.7	16.5	21.5	1 408	206	253	2 537	1.6
Unicoi	169	0.0	D	43.2	D	5.2	2.2	11.2	16.1	3 862	224	687	7 076	10.6
Union	79	0.2	D	36.6	D	7.3	D	12.3	19.9	3 400	209	651	5 696	22.7
Van Buren	34	0.0	D	D	D	3.2	2.0	8.0	18.6	972	192	194	2 001	14.1
Warren	569	4.2	D	48.1	D	8.2	D	12.5	8.7	7 419	205	1 450	13 802	6.4
Washington	1 792	0.4	D	19.5	D	12.1	3.6	30.1	20.1	19 736	193	3 007	38 378	14.0
Wayne	105	-1.7	D	27.9	D	9.7	3.4	27.6	22.0	3 195	194	536	5 741	10.9
Weakley	370	1.3	31.9	25.4	42.5	8.6	3.2	15.5	24.3	6 554	199	785	12 857	3.2
White	237	-1.5	D	44.6	D	14.4	3.3	13.3	10.9	5 150	227	946	8 369	10.3
Williamson	2 309	0.1	17.9	8.5	74.3	11.7	16.4	35.8	7.8	11 925	101	684	29 875	51.5
Wilson	972	-0.3	33.7	21.0	56.9	16.2	4.5	25.2	9.6	11 782	140	1 230	26 198	30.1
TEXAS	388 314	0.6	25.3	14.1	59.2	8.9	7.4	26.5	14.8	2 547 716	129	409 087	7 008 999	26.3
Anderson	612	-0.6	14.7	5.6	56.5	16.7	3.4	22.1	29.4	7 811	149	1 211	16 909	21.4
Andrews	152	-1.1	41.4	8.7	D	6.8	D	12.6	23.9	2 216	159	265	5 462	17.1
Angelina	1 134	0.2	32.1	26.5	51.6	11.9	4.1	24.2	16.1	14 125	183	2 300	28 796	16.8
Aransas	166	0.0	26.8	7.9	56.0	15.9	4.3	19.9	17.3	4 862	212	422	10 889	37.0
Archer	68	24.4	D	0.6	D	5.2	2.8	11.2	20.7	1 585	190	108	3 680	10.1
Armstrong	12	-5.2	D	D	D	7.3	10.0	22.6	32.4	450	208	31	916	2.2
Atascosa	262	2.4	17.4	4.2	58.7	10.7	3.2	27.0	21.5	5 742	157	804	11 614	24.9
Austin	289	-0.6	37.5	23.0	48.7	7.8	5.0	19.2	14.4	3 925	167	402	8 885	13.3
Bailey	89	33.1	10.3	5.0	38.4	7.0	4.8	6.9	18.1	1 239	179	193	3 109	-1.3
Bandera	73	-1.9	D	3.3	D	11.8	5.2	26.1	24.6	3 061	194	213	6 485	36.3
Bastrop	314	0.2	D	7.0	D	13.9	4.2	18.7	33.8	6 375	127	860	16 301	52.5
Baylor	38	6.3	10.6	1.7	60.1	9.4	3.3	27.7	23.0	1 284	309	125	3 006	-4.3
Bee	254	0.2	15.3	4.0	41.8	8.6	4.0	22.6	42.8	4 092	148	905	10 208	14.0
Bell	4 518	0.0	11.2	7.2	31.9	7.1	2.6	15.8	56.9	24 654	110	3 504	75 957	27.3
Bexar	26 012	0.2	14.0	6.0	60.4	9.8	8.7	25.2	25.4	179 526	133	35 916	455 832	32.0
Blanco	78	7.6	D	2.0	D	9.4	9.9	D	16.6	1 736	207	100	3 135	28.3
Borden	1	-202.8	D	0.0	D	D	D	41.4	183.0	101	133	20	478	-14.5
Bosque	119	6.9	24.5	14.5	47.4	9.3	4.1	21.0	21.1	3 977	240	314	8 074	8.5
Bowie	1 258	1.1	D	9.0	D	12.8	4.1	28.6	27.6	15 212	182	2 671	34 234	14.8
Brazoria	3 083	0.3	51.8	34.4	33.7	7.8	2.5	14.8	14.1	25 557	111	2 771	74 504	23.2
Brazos	2 078	0.0	15.2	7.0	45.4	11.0	5.4	23.0	39.4	12 622	95	1 772	48 799	36.7
Brewster	101	-5.6	D	1.5	D	12.3	2.9	22.7	43.6	1 489	167	225	4 486	38.2
Briscoe	18	18.5	D	6.6	D	7.5	5.7	D	19.1	433	229	43	1 074	-6.3
Brooks	50	-2.7	D	1.6	D	13.8	3.5	23.4	43.9	1 560	184	633	3 104	6.3
Brown	449	0.4	34.6	28.9	47.2	10.8	3.0	24.7	17.9	7 704	208	1 056	16 909	12.6
Burleson	103	-2.5	31.1	5.5	48.1	11.7	4.6	14.8	23.4	3 313	212	410	7 044	12.8
Burnet	299	-1.3	26.0	11.4	56.5	15.6	6.7	22.8	18.8	7 432	231	517	12 801	29.2

1. Covers mining, construction, and manufacturing.   2. Covers private sector earnings in agricultural services, forestry, and fisheries; transportation and public utilities; wholesale trade; retail trade; finance, insurance, and real estate; and services.   3. Per 1,000 resident population estimated as of July 1 of the year shown.

Table B. States and Counties — Housing, Labor Force, and Employment

STATE County	Housing units, 1990 (cont'd) Occupied units Owner-occupied Total	Percent	Median value[1]	Owner cost as a percent of income With a mortgage	Without a mortgage	Renter-occupied Median rent[2]	Rent as percent of income	Sub-standard units[3] (percent)	Civilian labor force, 1999 Total	Percent change, 1998–1999	Unemployment Total	Rate[4]	Civilian employment, 1990[5] Total	Percent Professional, managerial, and technical	Precision production, craft, and repair
	89	90	91	92	93	94	95	96	97	98	99	100	101	102	103
TENNESSEE—Cont'd															
Marshall	8 268	70.8	47 900	17.7	12.7	317	22.9	3.2	12 246	-1.5	448	3.7	10 632	17.5	14.0
Maury	20 608	69.0	60 700	18.7	12.4	366	22.8	3.3	37 127	1.5	1 321	3.6	25 741	21.8	14.2
Meigs	2 996	79.9	44 200	19.5	12.0	268	27.2	8.1	4 636	1.1	368	7.9	3 429	15.0	17.4
Monroe	11 363	79.7	40 200	18.3	12.0	265	22.3	5.0	18 749	7.0	992	5.3	13 059	14.7	16.3
Montgomery	34 345	61.1	58 100	21.3	12.2	373	24.2	3.7	57 559	6.3	1 803	3.1	37 778	25.6	12.1
Moore	1 734	83.7	50 400	16.8	12.9	295	17.5	2.5	2 922	-2.6	65	2.2	2 461	19.1	12.1
Morgan	5 841	82.9	37 800	21.7	13.3	261	26.5	6.3	6 717	0.0	507	7.5	6 129	15.8	18.7
Obion	12 412	70.6	43 500	17.4	13.1	282	23.3	2.8	15 471	1.4	939	6.1	14 176	16.8	11.8
Overton	6 734	80.3	36 700	17.5	12.3	235	23.6	7.4	9 884	1.3	558	5.6	7 820	14.4	15.8
Perry	2 512	83.9	35 600	22.1	12.1	237	22.1	7.0	3 827	2.4	287	7.5	2 776	16.9	12.2
Pickett	1 786	78.8	34 200	19.6	12.8	148	21.3	7.2	2 204	1.9	140	6.4	1 885	14.4	15.1
Polk	5 092	82.9	37 800	20.6	12.2	258	22.6	6.4	6 801	-0.9	346	5.1	5 891	14.1	17.5
Putnam	19 753	66.8	55 000	19.5	12.1	306	25.2	2.9	31 606	2.4	1 426	4.5	24 376	24.8	12.1
Rhea	9 185	74.5	45 300	19.8	12.2	282	23.9	2.8	12 149	4.1	710	5.8	10 324	18.8	16.2
Roane	18 453	76.4	48 700	17.4	12.9	287	22.8	3.2	24 654	-6.0	1 136	4.6	20 183	25.8	15.4
Robertson	14 801	74.9	61 300	20.8	12.8	337	26.1	3.4	28 847	4.1	960	3.3	19 926	20.2	15.6
Rutherford	42 118	66.1	71 800	21.5	12.4	403	26.2	3.2	95 996	4.9	2 563	2.7	60 987	25.7	12.1
Scott	6 534	75.4	33 600	23.9	12.7	230	26.6	8.6	9 050	6.9	763	8.4	6 422	16.9	16.2
Sequatchie	3 287	77.6	39 000	24.1	12.8	288	25.8	5.6	4 908	2.2	195	4.0	3 954	18.1	14.9
Sevier	19 520	75.8	62 400	20.7	11.6	347	24.5	4.9	35 828	4.7	2 324	6.5	24 309	23.0	15.5
Shelby	303 571	59.5	66 500	20.8	13.1	394	26.3	4.8	448 724	1.3	16 745	3.7	376 899	31.0	8.7
Smith	5 358	78.8	45 900	17.4	13.6	258	20.9	5.8	9 867	2.3	373	3.8	6 398	17.5	16.7
Stewart	3 678	82.4	43 700	19.2	12.9	244	21.7	4.1	3 355	5.4	278	8.3	3 952	16.1	16.4
Sullivan	56 729	75.0	55 600	17.7	12.1	308	23.5	2.3	75 287	1.5	3 057	4.1	65 494	26.3	14.0
Sumner	36 850	75.0	73 900	20.7	12.8	418	24.6	2.6	69 497	2.3	1 875	2.7	51 458	26.4	13.6
Tipton	13 033	71.9	56 100	22.8	12.6	323	25.9	6.9	22 422	2.7	750	3.3	15 776	17.1	17.0
Trousdale	2 261	74.7	41 900	20.6	14.3	277	27.0	6.8	2 064	3.6	113	5.5	2 804	13.9	13.2
Unicoi	6 621	77.2	48 100	17.1	12.7	274	25.0	3.4	7 957	1.6	457	5.7	6 857	21.2	14.2
Union	4 932	79.8	45 500	21.0	11.6	265	25.0	9.1	7 878	3.4	278	3.5	5 868	10.6	18.6
Van Buren	1 799	83.8	33 000	21.5	11.9	174	20.4	7.1	2 448	3.5	149	6.1	2 016	10.1	16.2
Warren	12 681	73.2	42 200	18.1	12.7	279	25.0	3.7	19 537	2.1	888	4.5	15 619	16.5	15.5
Washington	35 823	67.4	57 300	18.1	12.1	313	25.4	1.9	52 100	2.2	1 895	3.6	43 126	27.9	11.5
Wayne	5 174	83.6	32 800	17.8	12.3	245	22.2	6.8	7 815	3.7	918	11.7	6 257	12.2	14.7
Weakley	11 992	70.5	39 800	17.0	12.3	258	23.4	2.8	16 822	-1.7	1 042	6.2	14 890	20.6	11.8
White	7 722	81.5	40 300	18.4	13.1	264	24.2	4.8	11 457	3.4	524	4.6	8 988	14.8	18.5
Williamson	27 928	79.5	131 100	21.8	12.0	480	22.9	2.7	66 725	7.0	1 306	2.0	41 207	38.8	9.2
Wilson	24 070	80.5	82 000	21.6	12.4	401	24.6	3.1	47 526	3.9	1 312	2.8	34 063	25.9	14.9
TEXAS	6 070 937	60.9	59 600	20.9	13.1	395	24.6	8.4	10 206 043	0.9	471 630	4.6	7 634 279	30.0	11.7
Anderson	14 223	72.8	42 800	19.4	14.1	368	26.6	5.1	20 491	-1.2	1 252	6.1	15 905	22.1	12.0
Andrews	4 758	76.2	39 200	16.8	11.8	314	21.5	9.3	5 259	-6.2	601	11.4	5 775	23.6	21.5
Angelina	25 004	71.6	43 600	18.7	13.0	338	25.7	6.6	35 557	-1.3	2 123	6.0	28 686	23.8	12.4
Aransas	6 938	73.1	56 700	22.0	13.2	360	23.3	9.9	9 548	-1.7	556	5.8	6 772	26.0	15.7
Archer	2 957	80.4	45 200	21.9	14.0	328	22.7	2.2	4 098	-1.9	130	3.2	3 553	22.0	14.8
Armstrong	768	80.7	43 700	17.7	13.0	289	21.7	3.7	1 035	14.4	17	1.6	842	19.1	10.3
Atascosa	9 940	75.6	37 800	18.8	13.5	280	24.5	15.9	16 768	-0.5	720	4.3	11 306	18.6	17.9
Austin	7 478	74.4	57 400	21.1	13.7	326	22.8	7.9	13 580	11.2	514	3.8	8 489	23.8	14.9
Bailey	2 454	69.7	35 300	19.3	14.0	275	20.3	7.5	3 334	-8.9	171	5.1	3 209	12.0	13.5
Bandera	4 180	79.6	61 900	20.9	11.3	348	26.9	5.5	6 695	5.5	182	2.7	4 583	25.1	14.8
Bastrop	13 379	77.6	53 900	22.4	14.6	355	24.5	9.5	27 951	3.2	704	2.5	16 870	23.1	15.5
Baylor	1 906	70.3	34 000	17.1	16.5	213	20.6	3.5	1 792	-1.0	73	4.1	1 860	18.2	12.6
Bee	8 592	63.8	39 400	22.4	13.1	322	24.8	10.4	10 976	-1.2	660	6.0	8 666	25.7	16.0
Bell	67 240	52.1	56 300	21.5	12.9	374	25.0	5.8	92 938	0.2	3 180	3.4	67 891	28.8	11.7
Bexar	409 043	57.8	56 300	21.4	12.6	379	25.1	9.5	669 947	0.6	21 599	3.2	497 202	30.7	10.6
Blanco	2 338	72.8	56 400	24.1	12.3	296	25.4	5.8	3 912	6.4	83	2.1	2 697	20.4	13.9
Borden	294	69.0	22 800	20.0	11.3	238	14.4	6.2	382	-3.0	9	2.4	376	18.1	13.8
Bosque	5 990	75.8	42 000	17.9	12.6	309	24.0	4.3	7 176	9.6	256	3.6	5 902	21.9	13.6
Bowie	30 595	70.8	48 100	18.0	12.9	354	25.3	4.0	38 912	-1.6	2 270	5.8	34 219	27.0	13.4
Brazoria	64 019	69.2	61 800	18.2	12.3	401	21.6	6.8	104 072	-1.9	7 045	6.8	86 663	28.9	18.1
Brazos	43 725	41.9	66 600	20.1	13.0	411	34.0	6.6	75 447	2.0	1 319	1.7	56 368	38.9	8.2
Brewster	3 350	59.6	45 500	17.2	12.6	277	24.4	10.4	5 175	1.1	128	2.5	3 841	27.6	12.4
Briscoe	789	76.4	22 400	17.3	14.1	271	25.8	5.4	909	-6.4	33	3.6	805	18.4	8.9
Brooks	2 673	71.7	26 700	19.7	12.8	141	24.3	16.7	3 042	5.4	304	10.0	2 706	15.2	12.7
Brown	13 097	71.8	36 500	19.8	13.7	310	26.7	5.2	17 192	2.8	655	3.8	13 564	20.3	11.6
Burleson	5 176	78.8	41 600	24.1	14.4	322	26.4	7.2	6 779	-3.3	308	4.5	5 461	18.7	14.7
Burnet	9 055	75.7	58 400	25.7	13.4	350	29.7	4.8	13 881	3.5	378	2.7	8 717	24.3	15.1

1. Specified owner-occupied units. 2. Specified renter-occupied units. 3. Overcrowded or lacking complete plumbing facilities. 4. Percent of civilian labor force. 5. Persons 16 years and older.

Table B. States and Counties — Nonfarm Employment and Agriculture

	Private nonfarm establishments, employment and payroll, 1998								Agriculture, 1997			
		Employment						Annual payroll		Farms		Farm operators
											Percent with—	
STATE County	Number of establishments	Total	Health Care and Social Assistance	Manufacturing	Retail trade	Finance and Insurance	Professional Scientific and Technical Services	Total (mil dol)	Average per employee (dollars)	Number	Less than 50 acres	500 acres and over	Whose principal occupation is farming (percent)
	104	105	106	107	108	109	110	111	112	113	114	115	116
TENNESSEE—Cont'd													
Marshall	503	11 455	611	7 063	1 169	181	103	280	24 466	1 097	32.1	4.7	33.4
Maury	1 506	29 170	3 557	11 410	3 309	1 290	736	948	32 515	1 532	31.1	5.5	36.9
Meigs	106	1 440	155	730	221	D	D	27	19 091	339	32.2	3.8	33.6
Monroe	654	10 029	852	5 257	1 487	220	76	228	22 752	855	39.8	2.8	33.5
Montgomery	2 319	30 945	3 713	7 019	6 756	945	850	656	21 191	988	35.1	8.4	41.4
Moore	53	784	175	D	D	D	0	19	23 844	371	30.2	3.2	36.4
Morgan	162	1 910	237	942	171	53	D	35	18 505	328	29.6	3.0	32.3
Obion	765	14 187	1 178	6 363	1 901	295	87	371	26 182	705	26.1	18.2	43.5
Overton	297	3 439	806	1 130	482	137	70	65	19 016	889	36.4	4.0	34.1
Perry	121	2 556	385	1 753	120	44	D	53	20 824	235	21.3	9.4	38.7
Pickett	80	1 188	91	672	102	D	D	21	17 767	374	43.3	1.6	34.8
Polk	262	2 245	318	695	324	163	D	41	18 275	255	47.1	1.6	34.9
Putnam	1 677	26 478	2 684	9 181	4 050	602	619	576	21 751	1 120	42.9	2.6	32.8
Rhea	492	7 917	678	4 185	883	142	58	168	21 209	404	31.4	3.7	35.6
Roane	712	8 900	1 597	2 396	1 883	249	118	167	18 753	539	39.5	1.3	33.6
Robertson	942	12 631	1 219	4 754	1 858	226	191	287	22 715	1 474	40.3	6.2	44.9
Rutherford	3 365	69 094	7 669	20 420	9 197	2 884	1 129	1 946	28 169	1 591	39.8	3.6	32.6
Scott	344	6 239	662	3 390	581	151	52	109	17 544	228	34.2	2.6	24.6
Sequatchie	171	2 301	288	850	274	91	D	39	16 801	169	34.6	6.5	40.8
Sevier	2 454	26 160	1 241	2 594	5 922	633	454	502	19 191	801	46.1	1.2	35.7
Shelby	21 376	453 920	51 761	41 641	58 661	20 640	17 918	13 655	30 082	683	53.1	8.8	32.1
Smith	315	5 048	904	2 019	569	139	D	125	24 720	1 045	25.8	3.6	31.8
Stewart	155	1 098	165	314	224	47	D	18	16 127	350	25.4	4.6	34.9
Sullivan	3 655	65 273	9 732	18 388	9 864	1 445	1 689	1 890	28 957	1 315	62.4	1.5	33.8
Sumner	2 523	32 828	3 884	10 559	4 197	747	942	796	24 236	1 703	47.7	2.6	33.7
Tipton	707	8 805	889	2 962	1 624	289	181	189	21 449	592	43.6	13.5	43.9
Trousdale	120	1 617	252	715	164	50	D	34	21 004	405	35.6	4.2	40.5
Unicoi	270	3 944	474	1 713	367	73	D	94	23 799	155	60.6	0.6	33.5
Union	184	2 144	D	1 267	197	65	D	43	20 063	544	44.9	1.8	33.3
Van Buren	49	594	D	D	18	D	D	16	27 626	228	34.2	6.1	37.7
Warren	784	12 924	1 033	6 112	1 696	316	117	302	23 400	1 347	45.1	3.5	41.8
Washington	2 773	51 322	8 444	9 928	7 680	4 452	1 403	1 101	21 462	1 807	62.3	1.2	36.0
Wayne	237	2 941	229	1 262	383	130	D	48	16 419	700	21.7	5.9	29.9
Weakley	669	11 005	1 508	3 983	1 199	300	156	210	19 126	1 010	29.4	10.7	31.8
White	405	6 428	575	3 433	860	123	70	142	22 034	1 034	43.3	3.6	34.3
Williamson	4 020	63 258	8 005	4 898	8 759	6 583	4 513	2 132	33 697	1 410	40.6	4.8	34.0
Wilson	1 846	22 262	2 899	4 984	3 358	631	518	572	25 714	1 676	33.5	2.9	36.0
TEXAS	462 875	7 570 820	911 042	986 892	977 678	360 254	413 798	229 186	30 272	194 301	27.6	21.4	42.9
Anderson	929	11 463	2 080	1 721	1 928	377	314	250	21 833	1 542	30.2	8.9	35.7
Andrews	301	2 995	355	451	377	99	41	66	22 142	142	28.9	43.7	46.5
Angelina	1 822	28 986	4 733	7 184	4 363	732	571	719	24 793	790	41.1	4.8	31.8
Aransas	471	3 499	432	200	811	100	140	65	18 512	54	37.0	18.5	24.1
Archer	154	751	74	17	134	D	17	13	17 537	496	11.5	40.1	51.2
Armstrong	42	316	94	D	D	D	D	7	21 608	235	3.4	59.1	55.3
Atascosa	540	5 182	895	414	1 231	186	151	102	19 623	1 322	21.9	23.2	42.8
Austin	558	5 459	716	980	1 123	261	221	114	20 912	1 820	33.0	8.3	34.8
Bailey	180	1 412	204	100	262	66	41	26	18 198	441	12.0	49.0	67.8
Bandera	323	1 674	141	93	360	60	74	26	15 560	650	22.2	27.5	43.5
Bastrop	737	6 401	897	806	1 426	274	245	117	18 307	1 765	33.1	9.3	39.8
Baylor	140	1 178	609	D	113	D	23	14	12 067	270	13.3	46.3	53.7
Bee	449	4 427	882	341	981	219	131	80	18 041	686	18.1	26.8	44.5
Bell	3 958	72 765	17 497	7 170	10 075	3 258	2 335	1 628	22 378	1 741	36.2	10.9	36.4
Bexar	29 487	529 247	76 591	37 721	68 317	34 544	29 964	13 619	25 732	1 964	46.1	7.8	37.4
Blanco	203	1 805	146	70	271	75	40	37	20 448	617	18.3	30.5	45.4
Borden	2	D	0	0	D	0	0	D	D	107	4.7	72.9	66.4
Bosque	301	2 507	600	597	472	107	43	48	19 198	1 077	16.2	21.7	41.3
Bowie	2 139	29 601	6 989	3 832	5 560	990	667	694	23 454	1 138	31.7	10.5	36.2
Brazoria	3 748	56 950	4 343	14 282	9 050	1 273	1 376	1 841	32 325	1 783	45.4	13.8	33.6
Brazos	3 167	42 899	5 999	3 163	8 002	1 782	3 619	934	21 772	1 084	35.4	11.5	35.1
Brewster	268	2 033	315	D	501	71	51	30	14 751	129	13.2	73.6	51.9
Briscoe	49	181	D	D	D	D	3	3	17 901	232	8.6	50.0	56.0
Brooks	152	1 367	429	D	321	74	20	16	11 745	283	13.4	23.7	40.6
Brown	884	11 944	3 053	3 027	1 852	347	129	252	21 095	1 228	19.5	23.1	42.5
Burleson	304	2 536	239	317	492	133	D	46	18 295	1 337	27.3	11.0	42.0
Burnet	826	5 931	625	712	1 498	219	184	115	19 383	1 110	25.4	24.1	40.2

Table B. States and Counties — Agriculture, Land, and Water

STATE County	Acreage (1,000) [117]	Percent change, 1992–1997 [118]	Average size of farm [119]	Total irrigated (1,000) [120]	Total cropland (1,000) [121]	Average per farm ($1,000) [122]	Average per acre (dollars) [123]	Value of machinery and equipment Average per farm ($1,000) [124]	Total (mil dol) [125]	Average per farm (dollars) [126]	Crops [127]	Livestock and poultry products [128]	$10,000 or more [129]	$100,000 or more [130]	Percent of land owned by Fed. Gov. 1997 [131]	Water consumption 1995 (mil gal/day) [132]
TENNESSEE—Cont'd																
Marshall	167	3.0	152	0	96	244	1 571	28	22	19 710	15.7	84.3	29.1	4.2	0.0	3.5
Maury	243	-1.4	158	0	145	295	1 813	27	27	17 913	29.6	70.4	27.7	3.1	0.3	18.8
Meigs	49	-12.5	144	0	27	206	1 536	27	5	14 110	15.9	84.1	23.0	2.9	0.0	1.4
Monroe	97	-3.1	113	D	66	279	2 333	33	19	22 083	17.2	82.8	23.9	4.4	34.6	4.9
Montgomery	165	-6.0	167	0	109	318	2 033	32	31	31 185	73.4	26.6	38.6	8.5	12.4	25.0
Moore	52	8.5	140	0	29	230	1 563	31	9	25 092	9.8	90.2	25.3	4.6	0.0	0.8
Morgan	46	7.0	140	0	22	266	1 699	35	5	15 997	13.3	86.7	22.6	4.9	2.4	1.4
Obion	242	-5.7	344	1	209	487	1 479	78	64	90 427	78.5	21.5	50.2	19.3	1.7	6.0
Overton	109	3.2	123	0	63	171	1 368	21	12	13 166	30.1	69.9	27.6	1.9	0.0	1.2
Perry	54	2.6	231	0	21	254	1 059	29	4	15 843	41.7	58.3	23.4	2.6	0.0	1.1
Pickett	37	-1.3	100	0	21	184	2 554	17	5	12 564	55.9	44.1	35.0	1.6	3.2	0.6
Polk	32	3.6	126	D	20	362	2 385	44	22	86 858	9.5	90.5	28.2	20.0	52.7	33.3
Putnam	112	-4.2	100	0	59	232	2 259	23	12	10 635	32.9	67.1	19.6	1.2	0.0	10.9
Rhea	56	7.8	139	0	35	223	1 532	31	8	18 751	51.3	48.7	26.2	5.0	0.0	4.1
Roane	53	2.1	99	0	28	255	2 378	28	6	10 707	36.2	63.8	14.7	1.5	9.2	1 254.3
Robertson	236	1.5	160	1	183	340	2 077	45	72	48 781	69.3	30.7	46.7	8.8	0.0	5.8
Rutherford	195	-2.4	123	0	115	294	2 435	24	20	12 471	23.3	76.7	19.5	2.6	0.4	24.5
Scott	30	-9.9	130	D	13	183	1 170	23	5	21 379	D	D	16.2	5.3	17.0	2.5
Sequatchie	26	2.2	151	0	14	251	1 683	28	5	28 781	15.2	84.8	26.6	8.3	0.0	1.0
Sevier	72	-3.1	89	0	41	355	4 230	26	9	11 805	25.0	75.0	18.7	1.4	31.8	9.6
Shelby	128	-11.6	188	5	98	621	3 374	42	29	42 611	91.6	8.4	22.7	7.5	0.7	638.1
Smith	138	-7.8	132	0	73	215	1 543	24	13	12 287	47.8	52.2	26.8	2.1	1.9	3.2
Stewart	57	4.7	161	0	26	231	1 440	23	5	15 137	70.1	29.9	29.7	3.4	8.9	2 196.7
Sullivan	86	-7.1	66	0	55	240	3 142	24	18	13 880	39.1	60.9	22.2	2.0	13.6	543.8
Sumner	182	2.0	107	0	120	280	2 678	31	34	20 166	61.3	38.7	27.4	3.3	1.1	791.8
Tipton	170	-7.2	287	2	149	374	1 386	69	39	65 137	95.2	4.8	35.3	13.0	0.0	5.6
Trousdale	52	-6.1	128	0	31	240	1 687	40	7	17 138	68.1	31.9	42.2	3.2	7.4	0.8
Unicoi	8	-31.8	48	0	4	186	4 517	19	1	6 463	57.3	42.6	10.3	0.6	45.8	2.3
Union	51	4.7	94	0	27	164	2 139	20	4	7 063	43.9	56.2	17.6	0.4	0.0	2.6
Van Buren	32	-4.0	139	0	18	194	1 339	23	3	12 488	21.8	78.2	29.8	1.3	0.0	0.6
Warren	162	-1.8	120	3	112	227	1 796	39	83	61 622	84.7	15.3	42.0	10.2	0.0	6.0
Washington	120	1.4	66	1	88	278	4 159	30	45	24 760	55.1	44.9	27.6	3.4	8.2	21.6
Wayne	130	4.0	186	0	60	178	1 001	21	8	11 724	25.6	74.4	22.3	1.1	0.6	4.5
Weakley	223	9.1	220	0	178	272	1 256	52	55	54 097	63.4	36.6	35.5	12.7	0.0	3.6
White	119	-4.0	115	0	74	217	2 007	27	17	16 332	20.1	79.9	26.8	2.9	0.0	3.2
Williamson	198	-3.0	140	0	110	476	3 641	30	29	20 347	31.8	68.2	26.5	3.8	0.6	4.5
Wilson	211	-1.6	126	0	118	294	2 392	24	17	10 328	17.6	82.4	21.5	1.1	2.1	9.6
TEXAS	131 308	0.3	676	5 485	37 662	398	593	40	13 767	70 852	31.2	68.8	33.4	8.7	1.7	24 332.9
Anderson	354	0.6	230	1	138	205	929	25	24	15 732	14.1	85.9	25.6	1.6	0.0	11.5
Andrews	829	-13.9	5 837	5	70	603	104	51	9	65 340	59.6	40.4	38.7	18.3	0.0	24.3
Angelina	118	14.5	149	0	48	321	1 597	29	16	20 144	4.2	95.8	16.5	2.2	11.0	41.4
Aransas	19	-1.3	347	0	4	326	D	14	0	5 624	13.2	86.5	9.3	0.0	17.5	0.6
Archer	611	-0.3	1 232	0	123	583	505	50	63	127 810	7.8	92.2	61.1	23.8	0.0	22.0
Armstrong	560	11.9	2 385	8	D	729	299	77	28	118 728	19.9	80.1	59.6	19.1	0.0	10.6
Atascosa	708	-7.4	536	29	215	361	675	37	46	34 924	48.9	51.1	29.3	5.7	0.0	55.0
Austin	367	9.0	202	5	161	346	1 730	27	25	13 489	29.3	70.7	22.5	2.3	0.0	12.2
Bailey	409	-5.6	927	70	275	373	367	92	172	389 286	21.3	78.7	62.4	33.8	1.1	173.1
Bandera	364	-8.3	560	1	48	581	1 049	28	5	7 251	16.9	83.1	15.5	0.9	0.0	2.4
Bastrop	392	-0.7	222	3	141	305	1 422	28	28	15 833	26.0	74.0	20.9	2.1	2.1	11.5
Baylor	378	5.6	1 400	2	156	599	401	66	38	140 767	22.2	77.8	61.9	20.7	0.0	3.6
Bee	421	-4.7	614	2	128	357	654	34	28	40 361	36.7	63.3	28.6	6.3	0.3	3.9
Bell	407	-2.5	234	1	214	304	1 102	30	51	29 572	35.7	64.3	24.8	3.9	11.0	48.0
Bexar	448	9.5	228	13	177	297	1 395	28	68	34 767	67.4	32.6	17.4	2.9	6.1	837.5
Blanco	381	2.8	618	0	56	744	1 211	17	13	21 081	D	D	25.3	1.9	0.0	1.8
Borden	515	-18.3	4 810	1	70	1 210	252	80	12	116 226	49.9	50.1	70.1	33.6	0.0	2.2
Bosque	548	0.0	509	3	138	461	873	30	41	38 397	22.1	77.9	28.6	3.2	1.4	5.9
Bowie	281	6.8	247	3	135	308	1 478	30	40	35 288	19.7	80.3	28.0	6.3	6.3	57.6
Brazoria	567	0.5	318	30	203	403	1 293	38	43	23 904	58.9	41.1	22.5	5.0	2.7	286.0
Brazos	265	-10.4	245	6	104	402	1 517	34	41	37 992	18.9	81.1	26.8	3.5	0.0	33.5
Brewster	2 397	-0.3	18 581	D	6	3 130	170	31	9	69 835	D	D	51.9	12.4	19.3	3.7
Briscoe	533	30.3	2 298	28	154	650	282	90	23	97 468	74.4	25.6	57.3	27.6	0.0	26.9
Brooks	458	-19.0	1 620	1	64	723	428	37	9	30 607	13.1	86.9	22.6	5.3	0.0	2.3
Brown	516	0.4	420	6	141	261	643	26	33	26 759	12.3	87.7	30.0	3.0	0.0	19.1
Burleson	322	1.5	241	15	144	341	1 159	28	27	20 485	45.7	54.3	28.0	2.9	2.3	10.8
Burnet	537	-2.0	484	1	95	464	1 054	30	10	9 341	7.7	92.3	22.2	0.9	0.2	134.2

STATE County	Value of Residential Construction Authorized by Building Permits, 1999		Wholesale Trade, 1997				Retail Trade[1], 1997				Real Estate and Rental and Leasing, 1997			
	New Construction ($1,000)	Number of Housing Units	Number of Establishments	Number of Employees	Sales (mil dol)	Annual Payroll (mil dol)	Number of Establishments	Number of Employees	Sales (mil dol)	Annual Payroll (mil dol)	Number of Establishments	Number of Employees	Receipts (mil dol)	Annual Payroll (mil dol)
	133	134	135	136	137	138	139	140	141	142	143	144	145	146
TENNESSEE—Cont'd														
Marshall	14 872	205	17	104	21.4	2.4	122	1 153	180.9	16.7	17	46	3.9	0.7
Maury	71 649	862	54	631	251.3	17.9	306	3 451	572.9	55.7	70	301	31.2	5.9
Meigs	577	8	3	D	D	D	21	163	24.2	2.3	1	D	D	D
Monroe	8 237	173	22	171	48.3	2.8	165	1 505	234.5	19.9	17	38	2.7	0.4
Montgomery	92 243	1 301	93	716	281.8	19.0	523	6 895	1 175.8	108.1	105	378	49.8	5.9
Moore	4 406	50	1	D	D	D	12	51	5.6	0.5	NA	NA	NA	NA
Morgan	100	1	9	D	D	D	41	209	31.2	2.8	2	D	D	D
Obion	12 121	143	43	768	243.7	19.1	183	1 834	296.5	26.8	32	107	6.2	1.5
Overton	376	3	10	D	D	D	64	439	77.1	5.9	8	38	3.2	0.9
Perry	100	1	2	D	D	D	27	145	21.5	1.7	7	10	0.6	0.1
Pickett	NA	NA	2	D	D	D	20	109	17.0	1.3	4	47	1.9	0.5
Polk	0	0	9	D	D	D	53	366	47.0	4.4	6	34	2.0	0.5
Putnam	10 374	164	88	1 188	425.9	31.6	379	3 925	648.6	60.2	56	180	20.7	3.2
Rhea	13 829	146	15	98	26.8	2.7	100	903	137.8	12.3	16	44	3.8	0.4
Roane	3 745	53	22	345	139.8	10.2	176	1 832	308.9	25.9	29	62	5.6	1.2
Robertson	70 782	807	68	785	233.0	19.0	178	1 823	331.4	29.1	28	78	9.2	1.3
Rutherford	243 413	3 222	189	3 908	2 177.0	129.4	594	8 766	1 515.6	144.4	142	725	142.4	17.0
Scott	321	4	20	158	50.1	2.9	74	555	88.0	7.3	7	22	1.4	0.2
Sequatchie	919	16	10	D	D	D	42	288	56.1	4.2	7	13	1.2	0.1
Sevier	39 798	487	50	D	D	D	683	5 554	857.5	86.3	140	727	70.0	14.1
Shelby	883 102	6 842	1 851	34 481	35 419.2	1 214.8	3 574	56 612	8 959.2	891.3	813	7 077	853.1	168.9
Smith	2 453	75	15	105	55.7	2.4	62	642	100.8	8.9	14	34	4.1	0.4
Stewart	800	10	NA	NA	NA	NA	35	260	43.5	3.4	5	26	2.4	0.2
Sullivan	62 880	715	236	2 971	1 268.6	78.9	754	8 945	1 515.6	141.2	127	555	62.5	9.3
Sumner	148 775	1 847	141	1 369	500.2	37.9	403	4 252	665.2	64.4	100	552	60.0	11.9
Tipton	60 996	681	36	229	101.7	4.2	169	1 571	279.7	23.0	21	59	5.1	0.7
Trousdale	1 658	21	8	224	38.6	3.3	28	190	23.4	2.3	2	D	D	D
Unicoi	854	16	9	121	70.3	5.0	50	342	59.1	4.9	11	35	2.1	0.4
Union	8 599	125	9	D	D	D	36	204	28.2	2.3	7	16	0.6	0.1
Van Buren	NA	NA	2	D	D	D	10	30	7.4	0.4	2	D	D	D
Warren	4 930	153	45	339	101.5	8.6	177	1 803	267.0	26.2	28	102	8.1	1.3
Washington	38 377	341	162	2 131	1 192.8	55.5	540	6 873	1 123.1	103.1	118	510	48.3	8.6
Wayne	390	4	8	D	D	D	67	370	45.8	4.2	4	D	D	D
Weakley	13 585	222	49	680	320.2	19.9	153	1 211	171.8	16.1	21	76	5.0	1.0
White	1 262	16	22	190	62.8	4.3	90	856	183.5	13.2	11	20	3.2	0.2
Williamson	343 018	1 721	228	1 749	2 559.9	95.7	540	7 729	1 421.4	142.1	156	1 505	168.7	35.8
Wilson	135 477	1 125	95	1 075	605.8	29.4	290	3 216	566.5	49.6	70	243	42.1	4.5
TEXAS	14 045 115	146 644	33 346	425 744	323 111.7	15 504.9	74 105	950 848	182 516.1	16 197.1	20 753	128 915	15 957.4	3 119.2
Anderson	1 836	21	46	338	166.1	9.7	194	1 877	316.1	27.2	28	111	13.3	2.2
Andrews	1 191	6	20	103	24.6	2.3	52	356	59.7	5.7	10	33	1.9	0.5
Angelina	17 017	171	81	1 237	288.2	31.1	343	4 238	688.8	62.7	77	275	20.7	4.8
Aransas	7 959	68	16	63	24.8	1.7	90	771	124.8	11.8	28	67	7.6	1.1
Archer	1 085	9	18	142	41.5	2.3	27	111	23.4	2.0	1	D	D	D
Armstrong	100	1	2	D	D	D	6	19	2.9	0.2	1	D	D	D
Atascosa	2 839	45	30	227	89.6	6.6	108	1 246	177.2	16.3	15	61	4.1	0.9
Austin	2 567	30	22	390	212.8	11.3	123	1 114	211.4	16.7	19	53	5.9	0.6
Bailey	0	0	20	203	112.1	4.3	36	271	33.9	3.1	2	D	D	D
Bandera	233	4	5	7	0.9	0.1	54	275	50.9	3.9	13	28	2.7	0.4
Bastrop	10 954	145	28	205	69.0	3.4	135	1 450	397.0	20.8	27	64	6.1	1.0
Baylor	0	0	14	D	D	D	21	126	21.4	1.5	2	D	D	D
Bee	115	1	18	128	92.3	3.2	92	1 008	141.8	15.5	22	60	7.0	1.1
Bell	127 532	1 425	150	D	D	D	829	10 409	1 733.5	163.4	240	1 089	93.2	15.9
Bexar	724 821	12 124	1 829	25 191	12 639.2	810.7	4 505	64 928	11 657.5	1 111.1	1 342	8 770	1 115.1	203.5
Blanco	894	12	7	D	D	D	46	231	35.2	3.4	9	25	1.8	0.3
Borden	NA	NA	1	D	D	D	1	D	D	D	NA	NA	NA	NA
Bosque	534	6	11	105	63.3	1.6	73	443	73.2	6.0	10	16	2.2	0.4
Bowie	8 291	121	134	D	D	D	445	5 222	940.7	83.0	88	510	60.2	8.5
Brazoria	200 149	1 983	220	2 524	840.2	102.1	629	8 945	1 534.4	136.0	196	1 231	142.8	29.3
Brazos	115 472	1 599	130	1 655	426.5	41.9	569	7 994	1 336.2	122.2	181	1 090	78.5	17.2
Brewster	746	8	12	62	18.3	1.1	56	460	58.1	6.1	10	26	1.3	0.2
Briscoe	NA	NA	6	D	D	D	9	29	4.3	0.3	1	D	D	D
Brooks	44	1	5	14	3.8	0.2	32	287	38.4	3.8	NA	NA	NA	NA
Brown	2 457	84	42	337	95.7	8.5	194	1 843	302.0	24.6	32	73	7.8	1.2
Burleson	531	6	26	136	133.1	4.3	66	477	81.4	6.5	5	8	1.1	0.1
Burnet	44 255	427	27	163	34.9	4.2	159	1 534	281.0	24.6	52	90	8.6	1.0

1. Establishments with payroll.

STATE County	Professional, Scientific, and Technical Services[1], 1997				Manufacturing, 1997				Accommodation and Foodservices, 1997			
	Number of Establishments	Number of Employees	Receipts (mil dol)	Annual Payroll (mil dol)	Number of Establishments	Number of Employees	Receipts (mil dol)	Annual Payroll (mil dol)	Number of Establishments	Number of Employees	Sales (mil dol)	Annual Payroll (mil dol)
	147	148	149	150	151	152	153	154	155	156	157	158
TENNESSEE—Cont'd												
Marshall	23	72	3.9	1.2	45	7 552	1 349.1	169.4	34	446	12.9	3.2
Maury	87	396	33.4	11.5	75	11 361	4 431.7	532.6	96	2 152	58.3	16.5
Meigs	6	D	D	D	13	764	125.1	14.2	7	83	1.9	0.6
Monroe	26	72	4.0	1.0	84	5 488	834.9	144.8	55	770	27.7	7.0
Montgomery	120	756	41.0	12.3	83	6 519	1 271.6	182.7	237	4 699	132.3	37.3
Moore	1	D	D	D	NA	NA	NA	NA	5	D	D	D
Morgan	5	D	D	D	24	925	98.8	20.1	8	289	3.8	1.1
Obion	25	74	7.0	1.5	46	5 656	1 140.0	195.5	51	927	19.9	5.3
Overton	21	34	2.4	0.7	29	1 249	126.4	23.7	21	263	7.6	1.9
Perry	5	D	D	D	15	1 689	169.8	34.9	6	19	0.7	0.1
Pickett	2	D	D	D	NA	NA	NA	NA	7	D	D	D
Polk	6	D	D	D	22	1 061	72.1	18.3	18	160	4.8	1.2
Putnam	104	554	43.9	14.4	141	9 927	1 757.7	232.3	119	2 960	82.2	22.6
Rhea	18	46	4.6	1.0	40	4 674	434.7	105.6	46	531	17.3	4.3
Roane	34	87	9.2	1.9	42	2 075	256.0	47.1	60	1 083	27.2	7.6
Robertson	48	140	9.2	2.8	74	5 019	730.9	127.2	54	1 213	28.4	7.4
Rutherford	211	888	70.9	24.6	191	19 096	8 851.9	754.7	244	6 157	191.5	56.0
Scott	15	48	3.1	1.5	40	2 915	330.0	56.5	22	292	9.3	2.7
Sequatchie	6	D	D	D	11	948	223.8	18.3	16	D	D	D
Sevier	108	392	25.5	9.1	103	2 611	272.4	64.5	453	8 176	384.1	105.5
Shelby	1 675	15 189	1 503.4	565.4	902	44 145	11 758.7	1 476.9	1 429	35 241	1 362.6	371.5
Smith	11	33	2.1	0.6	23	1 710	396.6	44.9	19	D	D	D
Stewart	4	D	D	D	NA	NA	NA	NA	12	97	3.2	0.7
Sullivan	232	1 319	123.9	59.0	182	18 602	4 245.2	816.7	266	5 599	169.5	48.7
Sumner	157	1 200	54.3	21.3	205	11 852	1 932.0	333.8	144	2 207	67.1	18.6
Tipton	35	160	8.8	2.8	39	3 327	604.8	88.6	44	581	18.2	4.6
Trousdale	5	D	D	D	12	693	63.8	14.4	10	115	2.2	0.6
Unicoi	12	21	1.3	0.4	22	1 518	202.5	36.3	19	337	7.1	1.8
Union	7	18	0.6	0.1	20	1 099	141.1	23.6	10	101	3.0	0.8
Van Buren	2	D	D	D	NA	NA	NA	NA	2	D	D	D
Warren	32	105	7.3	1.9	73	6 610	1 133.3	192.5	56	880	24.0	6.6
Washington	196	1 340	75.9	26.0	151	10 370	1 300.9	257.6	190	4 858	140.6	41.1
Wayne	11	D	D	D	28	1 487	99.6	23.0	19	D	D	D
Weakley	30	73	4.0	1.1	45	3 287	574.0	74.9	55	797	18.7	4.7
White	23	72	5.6	1.5	49	3 442	457.3	81.0	17	D	D	D
Williamson	411	3 425	387.2	161.1	115	4 723	846.6	130.7	189	4 711	160.6	44.9
Wilson	104	346	29.5	9.3	114	5 533	1 122.9	161.1	111	2 225	68.7	19.8
TEXAS	42 492	351 422	42 044.1	15 906.7	21 808	959 665	297 657.0	32 760.8	34 160	638 333	22 698.8	6 175.4
Anderson	61	240	19.4	7.6	41	1 419	287.4	36.1	58	1 031	29.7	8.1
Andrews	14	37	3.0	0.8	NA	NA	NA	NA	20	D	D	D
Angelina	108	508	44.1	14.6	88	7 536	1 363.6	212.8	119	1 908	60.7	17.4
Aransas	32	436	17.6	12.2	NA	NA	NA	NA	72	823	24.9	6.8
Archer	5	16	0.6	0.2	NA	NA	NA	NA	5	31	1.0	0.2
Armstrong	NA	NA	NA	NA	NA	NA	NA	NA	4	21	0.4	0.1
Atascosa	30	312	13.2	4.1	NA	NA	NA	NA	44	450	13.4	3.6
Austin	37	145	8.3	3.4	32	947	153.6	26.8	46	425	15.4	3.8
Bailey	14	31	1.6	0.3	NA	NA	NA	NA	17	D	D	D
Bandera	17	30	4.0	1.0	NA	NA	NA	NA	36	288	10.0	3.0
Bastrop	48	146	10.8	4.1	52	801	78.3	18.5	68	889	25.7	7.3
Baylor	8	22	0.9	0.3	NA	NA	NA	NA	9	74	1.9	0.4
Bee	32	112	6.0	1.7	NA	NA	NA	NA	47	503	14.1	3.7
Bell	193	1 901	166.5	48.2	135	7 365	1 351.3	224.5	376	6 673	202.9	53.5
Bexar	2 841	21 741	2 052.4	805.6	1 101	35 919	5 565.5	986.5	2 558	56 118	2 027.8	563.1
Blanco	11	35	3.1	1.2	NA	NA	NA	NA	22	239	6.2	1.9
Borden	NA	NA	NA	NA	NA	NA	NA	NA	NA	NA	NA	NA
Bosque	15	28	1.6	0.6	18	548	74.9	13.4	19	99	2.8	0.7
Bowie	124	566	53.3	16.0	75	4 056	975.5	128.0	142	2 456	82.9	20.0
Brazoria	246	1 212	93.4	38.8	199	14 149	10 761.0	682.9	295	4 787	148.4	41.8
Brazos	279	2 086	200.9	74.8	101	3 126	382.2	79.6	275	5 668	170.7	48.2
Brewster	17	30	2.0	0.4	NA	NA	NA	NA	45	579	15.1	4.0
Briscoe	4	7	0.2	0.1	NA	NA	NA	NA	2	D	D	D
Brooks	8	25	2.2	0.3	NA	NA	NA	NA	21	201	7.2	2.0
Brown	38	130	7.7	1.8	39	3 055	848.5	98.7	77	1 048	31.7	8.3
Burleson	11	38	1.5	0.4	NA	NA	NA	NA	25	234	6.2	1.6
Burnet	49	125	7.8	3.0	42	714	72.5	16.7	63	878	33.9	10.5

1. Firms subject to federal tax.

Table B. States and Counties — Health and Other Services and Federal Funds

STATE County	Health Care and Social Assistance[1], 1997				Other Services[1], 1997				Federal funds and grants, fiscal 1999[2]			
									Expenditures (mil dol)			
										Direct payments for individuals[3]		
	Number of Establishments	Number of Employees	Receipts (mil dol)	Annual Payroll (mil dol)	Number of Establishments	Number of Employees	Receipts (mil dol)	Annual Payroll (mil dol)	Total	Social Security and government retirement	Medicare	Food stamps and Supplemental Security Income
	159	160	161	162	163	164	165	166	167	168	169	170
TENNESSEE—Cont'd												
Marshall	38	368	16.0	6.4	27	82	5.2	1.3	92.0	43.1	22.7	3.2
Maury	132	1 526	107.5	38.9	98	579	34.1	10.8	252.9	118.5	52.0	12.1
Meigs	5	148	4.2	1.6	4	4	0.7	0.1	43.4	22.0	7.7	2.2
Monroe	42	508	20.8	8.5	33	116	6.0	1.9	154.0	70.5	26.7	9.7
Montgomery	153	2 191	123.6	51.0	172	821	43.1	11.7	496.2	269.6	50.8	16.7
Moore	4	D	D	D	4	2	0.3	0.0	15.0	7.1	3.7	0.3
Morgan	5	38	2.3	0.9	4	D	D	D	73.2	30.6	14.4	4.7
Obion	55	593	34.6	13.8	46	375	18.5	6.2	158.9	69.1	30.8	6.3
Overton	22	524	33.0	13.1	17	71	4.3	0.8	92.5	35.1	24.0	4.9
Perry	12	287	15.3	5.7	6	10	0.7	0.2	37.3	16.0	10.5	1.6
Pickett	4	76	3.6	1.1	4	5	0.4	0.1	24.0	8.5	6.1	1.0
Polk	18	69	6.1	2.2	10	37	2.1	0.5	86.4	37.5	18.4	3.1
Putnam	134	1 325	84.4	34.9	107	451	29.4	7.3	271.0	126.1	54.1	10.9
Rhea	34	208	11.3	5.0	29	90	4.5	1.3	186.5	60.5	26.0	7.4
Roane	65	577	32.7	12.1	40	149	10.3	2.9	306.7	123.2	52.4	12.6
Robertson	60	639	31.8	13.0	69	219	15.1	3.1	169.4	85.1	35.6	7.4
Rutherford	250	3 668	197.6	93.2	203	1 001	67.1	19.6	492.8	212.4	71.4	13.5
Scott	30	637	30.1	14.1	17	408	12.4	6.3	132.5	38.3	23.1	8.4
Sequatchie	16	179	7.6	3.4	11	30	1.6	0.3	47.2	17.1	8.8	2.4
Sevier	76	674	34.7	13.7	110	415	25.4	7.3	219.1	126.5	37.6	8.5
Shelby	1 739	22 689	1 984.1	837.5	1 362	10 783	684.5	219.4	4 822.2	1 425.2	600.3	256.8
Smith	29	568	27.0	9.5	21	61	3.7	1.0	77.6	30.4	21.7	2.8
Stewart	7	115	5.4	2.0	7	29	2.2	0.6	107.7	35.2	9.5	2.1
Sullivan	352	5 392	403.3	190.0	239	1 608	88.0	26.9	661.6	355.6	127.3	28.1
Sumner	210	2 658	162.7	63.9	169	774	39.2	11.6	394.2	192.9	82.2	14.0
Tipton	53	618	28.3	11.9	44	190	12.0	2.6	189.1	87.9	30.9	11.4
Trousdale	14	143	6.4	2.2	5	15	1.2	0.2	31.4	11.0	8.8	1.1
Unicoi	21	259	11.9	5.1	16	55	3.7	0.7	98.5	47.9	18.2	3.9
Union	8	90	3.1	0.9	7	39	2.9	0.6	50.7	22.6	8.8	4.7
Van Buren	5	88	2.6	1.1	NA	NA	NA	NA	22.9	7.0	4.7	0.8
Warren	63	920	67.1	23.7	42	137	10.1	2.5	162.6	69.8	47.1	7.6
Washington	240	3 536	262.5	121.0	178	1 217	54.7	21.5	539.3	237.1	86.2	19.2
Wayne	15	323	13.5	5.6	12	16	1.9	0.3	72.4	26.8	13.3	3.9
Weakley	41	995	60.6	23.1	40	155	11.9	3.7	146.0	61.3	31.4	4.4
White	31	486	28.3	10.3	22	65	4.0	1.1	106.9	47.9	22.1	5.0
Williamson	268	5 184	312.7	154.3	158	1 806	188.3	57.2	247.4	145.2	49.1	3.7
Wilson	145	3 170	205.2	85.3	99	504	22.2	6.5	240.7	122.3	62.2	7.5
TEXAS	37 974	557 007	35 620.9	14 725.4	29 162	197 113	12 477.7	3 785.0	97 987.6	29 869.0	12 506.5	2 904.8
Anderson	112	1 568	90.0	39.4	55	209	14.1	3.6	214.1	94.3	48.3	6.6
Andrews	15	124	9.9	2.5	29	174	11.1	3.1	44.0	21.1	9.7	2.2
Angelina	187	3 211	176.1	76.9	141	692	46.9	13.1	322.6	147.3	72.0	13.2
Aransas	31	362	17.2	6.4	21	76	4.0	1.0	87.7	55.4	17.7	2.7
Archer	5	D	D	D	10	34	2.4	0.5	59.0	17.5	5.0	8.5
Armstrong	1	D	D	D	1	D	D	D	15.1	4.7	2.0	0.0
Atascosa	37	733	34.8	14.9	34	152	7.5	2.2	134.3	57.0	22.4	5.6
Austin	30	484	16.1	8.4	33	84	4.8	1.1	427.1	42.7	21.4	2.3
Bailey	6	27	1.3	0.4	20	78	3.6	0.9	49.0	11.3	6.6	1.1
Bandera	12	144	4.1	2.0	13	33	1.7	0.4	64.1	45.6	8.9	1.1
Bastrop	33	383	15.1	6.1	45	183	12.4	3.7	185.5	88.8	29.6	4.6
Baylor	8	794	6.5	3.6	16	27	3.3	0.3	30.6	12.5	6.5	0.6
Bee	46	493	23.0	10.5	38	164	8.0	2.2	121.9	44.7	25.4	6.2
Bell	292	5 985	414.0	140.2	323	1 765	82.8	26.7	2 622.6	485.0	98.8	23.4
Bexar	2 900	51 908	3 052.9	1 251.8	2 167	15 346	841.4	272.7	9 212.5	2 985.7	921.7	250.1
Blanco	10	158	4.6	3.0	10	30	2.5	0.5	58.5	40.2	12.3	0.4
Borden	NA	NA	NA	NA	NA	NA	NA	NA	3.7	0.5	0.4	0.0
Bosque	11	164	8.4	3.7	12	29	1.9	0.4	78.1	44.2	17.1	1.7
Bowie	233	3 731	231.1	110.2	138	872	55.1	15.5	587.7	224.6	84.6	15.5
Brazoria	306	2 905	155.5	65.8	298	1 312	88.5	24.1	584.2	300.4	120.2	20.0
Brazos	263	2 838	212.1	84.9	196	1 244	64.8	18.4	506.2	148.1	46.3	12.3
Brewster	10	42	2.4	0.9	12	35	1.8	0.3	40.4	17.0	5.3	1.0
Briscoe	NA	NA	NA	NA	3	9	0.2	0.0	19.1	4.3	2.9	0.1
Brooks	9	389	6.0	2.4	10	60	3.1	0.8	59.3	12.3	8.4	4.1
Brown	96	2 526	115.5	44.1	63	292	14.5	4.2	176.2	82.2	43.7	5.8
Burleson	10	136	5.4	2.3	21	90	5.2	1.3	82.7	33.7	12.9	2.6
Burnet	61	454	20.4	7.3	51	126	9.5	2.2	121.1	76.5	21.7	3.3

1. Firms subject to federal tax. 2. October 1, 1998 to September 30, 1999. 3. State totals may include programs not allocated by county.

	Federal funds and grants, fiscal 1999[1] (cont'd)							Local government finances, 1997				
	Expenditures (mil dol) (cont'd)								General revenue			
	Procurement contract awards			Grants[2]							Taxes	
											Per capita[3] (dollars)	
STATE County	Salaries and wages	Defense	Other	Medicaid and other health-related	Nutrition and family welfare	Education	Other	Total (mil dol)	Intergovern-mental (mil dol)	Total (mil dol)	Total	Property
	171	172	173	174	175	176	177	178	179	180	181	182
TENNESSEE—Cont'd												
Marshall	3.3	1.0	1.0	12.2	1.2	0.9	1.5	40.3	16.5	17.0	662	430
Maury	11.1	0.3	6.0	28.9	3.9	2.4	12.9	211.4	44.8	36.4	535	331
Meigs	1.6	0.0	0.3	5.6	2.8	0.5	0.4	12.6	8.7	2.3	242	165
Monroe	4.4	0.1	1.4	24.2	2.1	2.3	11.1	46.5	25.1	13.9	409	209
Montgomery	72.2	4.2	5.9	30.9	9.1	5.4	14.3	266.3	86.5	76.8	618	330
Moore	0.4	0.0	0.1	0.9	1.6	0.2	0.2	5.4	3.5	0.6	112	69
Morgan	4.0	0.0	0.5	12.6	3.2	0.9	1.7	24.0	14.9	6.4	344	280
Obion	6.3	0.1	0.9	19.1	3.0	1.6	7.2	55.5	22.2	21.5	670	328
Overton	2.7	0.0	0.6	19.9	1.7	0.9	1.2	27.9	16.1	5.9	308	186
Perry	1.1	0.0	0.2	6.1	0.5	0.4	0.4	11.9	6.7	3.5	471	341
Pickett	0.4	0.1	0.1	6.2	0.4	0.3	0.1	8.5	5.5	1.7	376	248
Polk	3.9	0.0	0.7	12.2	1.1	0.8	7.5	19.2	11.5	5.9	404	266
Putnam	13.0	3.2	2.8	31.0	7.7	2.3	15.6	147.7	34.1	30.6	525	310
Rhea	59.9	0.0	7.7	18.1	2.8	1.4	1.3	51.4	22.5	10.6	385	233
Roane	27.0	0.3	26.1	31.2	5.4	2.2	18.2	98.7	35.8	26.5	531	332
Robertson	5.1	0.0	1.8	18.1	3.4	1.6	4.7	76.8	33.9	28.0	544	327
Rutherford	86.8	4.8	21.1	33.9	6.8	3.5	17.7	283.8	101.9	121.0	758	456
Scott	3.8	28.0	-2.1	25.4	3.5	1.4	2.4	35.3	23.5	7.7	391	237
Sequatchie	0.9	0.0	10.6	5.3	1.1	0.6	0.2	14.5	8.6	4.0	396	259
Sevier	14.4	0.1	2.5	20.4	3.9	2.1	1.7	162.1	41.6	79.0	1 262	302
Shelby	740.7	440.3	315.0	571.4	148.4	52.8	149.7	2 121.2	671.8	804.3	929	552
Smith	4.7	0.5	0.6	9.8	1.2	0.5	4.0	21.7	12.1	5.6	348	207
Stewart	25.8	0.8	24.5	7.4	0.8	0.5	0.6	15.6	10.9	2.8	253	177
Sullivan	25.4	1.7	7.5	72.0	15.5	6.7	13.3	247.2	80.6	120.1	797	518
Sumner	22.2	1.1	32.3	32.7	5.1	3.2	3.3	200.0	75.1	75.7	621	382
Tipton	5.9	2.4	4.1	28.1	5.6	2.2	2.0	70.2	39.5	20.5	445	291
Trousdale	2.2	0.0	2.4	4.1	0.6	0.2	0.1	10.9	6.1	3.0	439	318
Unicoi	4.2	2.2	6.4	12.3	1.5	0.8	0.8	41.8	12.3	7.2	415	270
Union	1.1	0.0	0.3	9.9	1.7	0.7	0.6	19.4	13.6	3.9	245	176
Van Buren	0.3	0.0	0.1	3.2	0.4	0.3	6.0	8.2	5.6	1.9	377	243
Warren	6.0	0.3	1.2	20.5	2.6	1.6	2.6	52.9	24.7	18.4	515	302
Washington	81.5	0.5	32.8	48.8	7.3	6.1	4.6	160.0	57.6	69.0	679	414
Wayne	1.6	0.0	0.5	12.7	1.2	0.7	11.1	25.0	13.4	5.2	315	198
Weakley	7.3	1.2	1.5	14.6	9.9	1.7	2.3	46.4	22.2	13.6	415	245
White	3.1	1.9	0.7	15.9	1.5	0.9	6.8	27.7	15.2	7.6	342	225
Williamson	15.4	1.8	5.0	17.0	3.2	2.2	2.8	268.9	64.0	119.8	1 076	702
Wilson	10.2	0.1	1.9	22.4	8.4	2.2	0.9	112.1	45.0	46.6	574	319
TEXAS	11 797.8	8 326.0	6 176.5	8 456.4	3 016.6	2 027.6	4 869.3	X	X	X	X	X
Anderson	7.1	0.0	13.5	36.4	2.3	1.5	0.9	72.1	29.3	32.5	618	493
Andrews	1.0	0.0	0.2	4.0	0.7	0.6	0.2	49.5	2.9	31.0	2 204	2 091
Angelina	19.3	0.1	4.5	44.5	5.7	2.9	7.3	172.8	83.2	53.6	698	499
Aransas	1.4	0.0	0.4	5.7	1.5	1.0	0.4	34.4	8.3	19.7	870	734
Archer	20.5	0.0	0.2	2.8	0.2	0.2	0.1	16.4	7.6	7.0	846	665
Armstrong	0.4	0.0	0.1	1.2	0.0	0.0	0.0	3.7	1.7	1.6	721	594
Atascosa	2.8	0.0	0.8	22.5	3.5	2.3	14.2	70.0	39.2	20.5	582	471
Austin	4.8	336.0	1.2	12.0	1.1	0.6	1.3	43.4	15.1	19.9	868	710
Bailey	1.2	0.0	0.3	4.3	0.7	0.4	0.1	22.3	8.4	5.8	843	726
Bandera	3.8	0.0	0.4	3.1	0.4	0.3	0.1	20.2	6.9	10.6	708	618
Bastrop	19.8	0.1	1.5	25.6	4.0	1.5	7.2	97.8	40.7	29.1	593	503
Baylor	0.7	0.0	0.2	3.6	0.5	0.1	0.7	8.7	4.0	3.2	775	668
Bee	2.6	0.0	0.9	20.5	5.6	3.0	2.0	66.9	34.5	14.7	525	406
Bell	1 592.6	224.2	19.7	54.1	14.1	20.7	15.1	537.2	269.8	150.4	676	492
Bexar	2 316.9	1 156.1	284.8	732.3	157.8	85.5	202.9	3 094.4	1 211.1	1 152.0	864	714
Blanco	3.0	0.0	0.2	1.8	0.1	0.1	0.0	13.7	5.8	6.0	725	615
Borden	0.1	0.0	0.0	0.0	0.0	0.0	0.0	5.7	0.2	4.6	6 210	6 148
Bosque	3.1	0.0	0.7	8.2	0.6	0.5	0.4	32.0	16.7	9.6	573	488
Bowie	100.1	22.7	23.2	55.7	8.8	3.6	35.9	170.6	82.0	58.5	699	485
Brazoria	28.7	16.4	7.9	39.7	6.9	4.9	15.1	460.1	111.3	246.4	1 093	978
Brazos	49.8	6.7	27.5	63.1	9.0	8.6	107.8	246.1	60.9	125.8	946	712
Brewster	7.2	0.0	0.4	4.1	0.7	1.2	0.4	30.6	9.3	6.1	675	520
Briscoe	0.5	0.0	0.1	2.3	0.1	0.1	0.0	3.4	1.4	1.6	808	705
Brooks	4.1	3.6	0.2	17.5	1.7	0.7	4.6	17.2	7.3	7.6	895	809
Brown	5.8	4.3	1.3	20.7	2.8	1.3	4.9	75.9	38.9	24.8	673	513
Burleson	2.4	0.5	0.5	13.2	1.4	0.5	10.0	28.0	10.2	14.1	916	775
Burnet	3.4	0.0	0.9	9.5	0.7	0.8	2.3	65.7	16.5	27.1	882	725

1. October 1, 1998 to September 30, 1999.   2. State totals may include programs not allocated by county.   3. Based on the resident population estimated as of July 1 of the year shown.

Table B. States and Counties — Local Government Finances, Government Employment, and Elections

STATE County	Local government finances, 1997 (cont'd)									Government employment, 1998			Presidential election, 2000		
	Direct general expenditure							Debt outstanding					Percent of vote cast —		
			Percent of total for —												
	Total (mil dol)	Per capita¹ (dollars)	Education	Health and hospitals	Police protection	Public welfare	Highways	Total (mil dol)	Per capita¹ (dollars)	Federal civilian	Federal military	State and local	Democratic	Republican	All other
	183	184	185	186	187	188	189	190	191	192	193	194	195	196	197
TENNESSEE—Cont'd															
Marshall	37.7	1 468	54.5	2.7	6.3	0.2	9.1	34.1	1 328	60	105	1 195	54.6	43.9	1.5
Maury	224.4	3 296	22.7	43.8	2.8	0.0	3.2	192.8	2 831	215	277	5 032	47.6	51.0	1.4
Meigs	15.6	1 608	70.2	1.1	2.7	0.0	8.7	6.4	656	20	40	400	45.9	53.0	1.1
Monroe	48.4	1 426	63.6	2.3	4.0	0.1	6.0	23.8	702	97	139	1 293	41.0	57.8	1.2
Montgomery	260.4	2 096	45.8	27.3	4.1	1.2	3.7	215.6	1 736	539	515	6 985	48.2	50.3	1.5
Moore	6.9	1 328	65.8	0.0	8.1	0.0	3.3	0.0	0	0	21	796	48.1	49.8	2.1
Morgan	21.4	1 159	69.5	2.1	2.1	0.0	9.8	6.4	346	39	75	1 486	47.4	51.0	1.6
Obion	52.5	1 635	53.2	0.3	5.9	3.2	8.6	16.3	508	115	129	1 489	48.7	49.6	1.7
Overton	24.9	1 304	55.6	2.4	4.0	0.0	9.3	17.4	907	50	78	1 041	60.1	38.4	1.5
Perry	10.8	1 448	52.9	3.6	4.3	0.0	15.0	4.0	540	18	30	331	57.6	40.6	1.8
Pickett	8.1	1 768	52.6	4.1	3.1	0.0	14.1	4.1	888	0	18	271	41.9	57.2	0.9
Polk	16.6	1 127	63.8	2.7	4.6	0.0	10.7	6.1	416	70	59	691	46.0	52.0	2.0
Putnam	159.3	2 735	29.4	35.1	4.2	0.0	4.3	96.7	1 660	253	241	7 536	48.1	50.1	1.8
Rhea	50.2	1 818	38.8	26.0	3.2	0.0	5.7	25.1	908	940	111	1 376	38.1	60.4	1.5
Roane	89.4	1 791	44.7	27.1	3.6	0.1	5.2	60.4	1 211	521	199	3 506	44.9	53.2	1.9
Robertson	77.2	1 500	52.6	1.5	12.6	0.0	7.3	75.0	1 457	93	211	2 454	50.8	48.0	1.2
Rutherford	268.4	1 682	47.5	3.1	10.2	0.0	5.0	314.1	1 969	1 899	668	9 583	44.0	53.8	2.2
Scott	31.4	1 585	61.8	1.9	4.3	0.0	10.7	38.2	1 929	74	80	1 208	44.9	54.1	1.0
Sequatchie	16.1	1 594	60.7	1.3	3.6	0.0	11.9	15.6	1 541	11	41	446	42.4	55.8	1.8
Sevier	147.0	2 348	40.8	1.3	5.9	0.1	7.3	152.0	2 428	271	257	3 411	32.4	66.0	1.6
Shelby	2 268.1	2 619	36.3	13.0	8.0	0.3	3.2	2 816.8	3 253	14 732	4 714	56 345	56.5	42.1	1.4
Smith	21.7	1 348	53.0	3.5	6.2	0.0	10.6	10.0	623	111	65	658	66.5	32.4	1.1
Stewart	17.0	1 513	69.3	1.8	4.1	0.1	9.7	10.8	958	512	46	547	60.0	38.2	1.8
Sullivan	246.3	1 635	56.1	1.5	5.5	0.2	5.9	255.8	1 698	512	602	6 968	38.3	60.1	1.6
Sumner	174.9	1 436	55.9	1.4	6.2	0.2	5.4	117.3	963	443	494	5 260	43.8	54.7	1.5
Tipton	69.7	1 515	62.3	0.5	9.2	0.0	7.1	63.5	1 380	105	188	1 969	38.1	60.8	1.1
Trousdale	9.6	1 414	51.0	1.1	9.8	0.0	13.0	7.7	1 132	48	27	315	66.8	32.3	0.9
Unicoi	41.8	2 423	27.9	47.5	3.4	0.2	4.4	15.9	924	86	69	930	39.9	58.8	1.3
Union	26.5	1 664	82.2	0.9	2.4	0.0	1.6	10.8	679	21	65	538	44.0	55.0	1.0
Van Buren	8.7	1 743	55.6	2.3	2.4	0.0	16.2	6.6	1 318	0	20	234	58.9	39.7	1.4
Warren	49.5	1 385	57.4	2.7	5.1	0.1	6.2	59.7	1 668	117	144	1 701	56.2	42.3	1.5
Washington	173.7	1 710	50.5	0.8	5.3	0.8	9.1	191.2	1 882	1 906	423	8 759	38.9	59.5	1.6
Wayne	22.6	1 368	52.2	2.1	3.7	12.1	12.8	5.8	353	30	66	900	35.0	63.5	1.5
Weakley	46.6	1 420	46.7	0.5	6.5	8.0	11.6	48.8	1 487	135	135	3 161	47.0	51.6	1.4
White	33.7	1 521	64.6	1.4	3.8	0.3	7.1	20.3	914	57	90	1 021	53.2	45.3	1.5
Williamson	260.2	2 336	45.6	18.5	3.7	0.1	7.4	285.0	2 559	275	468	5 052	32.1	66.6	1.3
Wilson	107.9	1 330	60.3	1.0	6.0	0.0	5.2	108.8	1 341	159	334	2 961	46.1	52.5	1.4
TEXAS	X	X	X	X	X	X	X	X	X	184 577	165 408	1 308 218	38.0	59.3	2.7
Anderson	68.3	1 301	65.4	0.3	5.3	0.0	5.2	36.0	686	132	139	5 766	33.4	65.2	1.4
Andrews	45.1	3 204	49.0	27.7	2.8	0.1	5.4	0.1	11	23	37	1 166	21.8	76.8	1.4
Angelina	181.2	2 360	59.2	14.0	3.5	0.4	4.4	130.4	1 698	400	206	5 839	36.9	61.7	1.4
Aransas	31.8	1 406	61.6	2.8	7.4	0.2	7.5	10.2	451	26	61	968	32.0	65.4	2.7
Archer	15.2	1 832	74.6	0.1	1.2	0.7	7.5	1.1	128	20	23	496	24.8	73.8	1.3
Armstrong	3.7	1 689	69.7	0.3	3.8	0.1	7.5	0.1	55	0	0	138	16.0	82.3	1.7
Atascosa	72.4	2 053	76.6	0.3	2.6	0.8	4.0	13.4	381	51	97	1 940	40.2	58.0	1.8
Austin	50.0	2 185	69.2	0.6	4.9	0.1	4.9	34.2	1 495	105	63	1 264	26.1	72.2	1.7
Bailey	22.2	3 250	46.4	21.5	3.3	6.1	2.8	1.8	257	34	18	573	23.3	76.0	0.6
Bandera	18.8	1 256	71.9	0.9	4.0	0.4	4.4	6.0	400	18	42	636	19.6	77.2	3.2
Bastrop	84.8	1 730	66.2	8.2	3.7	0.6	4.8	82.9	1 692	377	134	2 897	38.1	56.3	5.6
Baylor	8.1	1 954	57.2	2.8	6.0	0.0	9.2	4.4	1 047	20	11	255	33.4	64.8	1.8
Bee	67.9	2 422	72.0	0.5	2.7	0.0	2.9	27.2	969	49	74	3 791	45.6	53.2	1.3
Bell	508.0	2 285	65.0	3.7	3.8	0.5	2.4	618.6	2 783	7 911	42 418	14 341	33.2	65.1	1.7
Bexar	3 120.5	2 342	48.5	11.6	5.8	2.6	3.2	6 604.3	4 956	36 470	36 234	87 053	44.9	52.2	2.9
Blanco	12.0	1 463	71.0	0.2	5.4	0.7	4.2	5.9	719	80	22	367	21.5	73.7	4.8
Borden	4.9	6 505	79.1	0.1	1.5	0.0	9.2	0.0	0	0	0	88	17.6	80.2	2.3
Bosque	30.3	1 816	68.4	11.7	3.1	0.2	3.5	16.0	959	69	44	859	28.5	70.1	1.4
Bowie	166.2	1 987	62.4	3.4	4.5	0.5	2.8	101.4	1 212	3 446	239	5 652	38.5	60.4	1.1
Brazoria	453.6	2 012	61.7	6.0	4.8	0.5	5.1	409.3	1 816	442	653	13 543	31.1	66.8	2.1
Brazos	273.9	2 060	49.1	3.1	4.8	0.3	3.9	325.7	2 448	970	462	28 534	26.3	70.0	3.7
Brewster	30.0	3 317	37.9	41.0	2.3	0.0	2.6	6.7	741	175	24	1 401	37.7	52.2	10.2
Briscoe	2.6	1 334	67.6	0.1	2.2	0.0	7.3	10.5	5 300	14	0	123	29.0	70.5	0.5
Brooks	16.8	1 986	65.5	3.1	4.0	2.2	0.4	0.1	9	99	23	525	76.3	22.9	0.9
Brown	73.9	2 002	59.2	10.2	3.9	0.7	4.4	45.9	1 244	111	99	2 748	24.3	74.4	1.3
Burleson	28.7	1 871	64.8	3.1	4.7	0.1	10.0	6.9	449	53	42	792	38.1	60.4	1.5
Burnet	66.1	2 150	51.8	15.6	4.8	0.3	3.4	71.9	2 338	65	85	1 810	26.9	70.2	2.9

1. Based on the resident population estimated as of July 1 of the year shown.

Table B. States and Counties — Land Area and Population

STATE/County code	MSA/PMSA/NECMA code[1]	County Type[2]	STATE County	Land area,[3] (sq km) 1990	Total persons	Rank	Per square kilometer	White	Black	Am. Indian, Eskimo, Aleut	Asian and Pacific Islander	Percent Hispanic[4]	Under 5 years	5 to 17 years	18 to 24 years	25 to 34 years	35 to 44 years	45 to 54 years
				1	2	3	4	5	6	7	8	9	10	11	12	13	14	15
			TEXAS—Cont'd															
48 055	0640	2	Caldwell	1 414	32 820	1 288	23.2	88.2	11.0	0.3	0.5	45.4	8.2	22.1	11.1	11.9	15.0	11.8
48 057	...	6	Calhoun	1 327	20 426	1 741	15.4	92.8	3.1	0.2	3.9	42.2	7.7	21.2	8.0	11.6	14.2	13.4
48 059	...	6	Callahan	2 328	12 915	2 221	5.5	98.8	0.1	0.4	0.7	5.7	6.4	20.7	6.0	9.5	14.9	14.6
48 061	1240	2	Cameron	2 345	329 131	174	140.4	99.0	0.4	0.2	0.4	85.6	9.8	25.5	10.5	11.7	14.1	10.7
48 063	...	6	Camp	512	10 943	2 348	21.4	73.3	26.1	0.5	0.1	6.8	6.3	19.8	8.4	9.8	14.7	13.5
48 065	...	8	Carson	2 391	6 754	2 704	2.8	98.7	0.3	0.8	0.2	7.3	6.6	23.3	6.1	10.3	14.5	14.1
48 067	...	6	Cass	2 428	30 620	1 357	12.6	77.5	22.0	0.4	0.2	1.9	5.9	20.5	7.6	9.6	14.5	14.3
48 069	...	7	Castro	2 327	8 264	2 572	3.6	96.7	2.9	0.1	0.3	52.5	10.0	26.0	8.4	10.6	13.1	11.8
48 071	3360	1	Chambers	1 552	23 993	1 579	15.5	84.7	14.0	0.4	0.9	7.8	6.5	22.8	8.3	11.1	18.4	14.8
48 073	...	6	Cherokee	2 726	43 653	1 006	16.0	80.2	18.7	0.4	0.7	8.9	6.7	19.2	9.2	11.2	14.5	13.8
48 075	...	7	Childress	1 840	7 543	2 634	4.1	87.0	12.1	0.6	0.4	22.8	5.0	17.8	9.2	13.4	16.7	13.0
48 077	...	6	Clay	2 843	10 511	2 377	3.7	98.0	0.4	1.1	0.4	3.4	6.1	20.1	6.0	10.1	14.5	15.9
48 079	...	7	Cochran	2 008	3 781	2 934	1.9	94.1	5.6	0.2	0.1	47.8	9.2	23.8	8.7	11.2	11.7	12.5
48 081	...	8	Coke	2 328	3 351	2 965	1.4	98.7	0.6	0.5	0.1	16.1	5.6	18.3	5.4	8.5	11.7	13.2
48 083	...	6	Coleman	3 297	9 443	2 477	2.9	96.5	3.0	0.4	0.1	15.6	6.8	17.8	6.3	8.6	12.4	13.3
48 085	1920	0	Collin	2 196	456 612	123	207.9	90.6	4.5	0.5	4.4	9.1	8.2	20.7	8.4	15.3	20.7	15.5
48 087	...	9	Collingsworth	2 380	3 172	2 978	1.3	91.4	6.9	1.3	0.4	20.2	6.6	20.6	6.6	9.3	12.9	10.7
48 089	...	7	Colorado	2 494	19 052	1 817	7.6	81.3	18.2	0.2	0.2	20.0	6.8	19.6	6.7	9.9	13.6	13.3
48 091	7240	1	Comal	1 454	76 770	649	52.8	98.1	1.0	0.4	0.5	28.7	7.0	18.5	7.5	10.3	16.0	14.2
48 093	...	7	Comanche	2 429	13 584	2 169	5.6	99.0	0.4	0.5	0.1	21.2	6.9	17.6	7.3	9.1	12.9	14.4
48 095	...	8	Concho	2 568	3 002	2 989	1.2	99.0	0.5	0.3	0.2	45.9	6.3	18.4	8.3	14.0	14.7	13.1
48 097	...	6	Cooke	2 263	33 391	1 275	14.8	94.2	4.3	0.9	0.7	6.1	7.2	20.7	7.8	10.5	14.8	13.1
48 099	3810	2	Coryell	2 724	73 629	670	27.0	73.6	21.0	0.9	4.5	13.4	8.4	19.3	19.6	18.4	14.0	9.2
48 101	...	9	Cottle	2 334	1 889	3 068	0.8	90.3	9.3	0.2	0.3	19.8	5.6	19.6	5.3	8.8	11.2	12.7
48 103	...	6	Crane	2 035	4 290	2 887	2.1	95.4	4.1	0.2	0.3	40.3	8.8	26.3	8.2	11.4	15.5	12.4
48 105	...	7	Crockett	7 272	4 396	2 879	0.6	98.1	1.5	0.2	0.2	56.7	8.6	22.0	6.9	11.6	15.7	13.7
48 107	...	8	Crosby	2 330	7 056	2 673	3.0	94.4	4.9	0.5	0.1	49.5	8.4	23.1	8.2	10.4	11.6	13.7
48 109	...	7	Culberson	9 875	3 018	2 984	0.3	98.2	0.2	0.5	1.0	75.6	10.1	23.4	9.4	10.5	14.7	12.7
48 111	...	7	Dallam	3 897	6 627	2 716	1.7	95.7	2.7	1.2	0.4	27.1	8.6	22.5	7.2	12.2	14.2	13.2
48 113	1920	0	Dallas	2 279	2 062 100	10	904.8	74.0	21.0	0.7	4.3	21.4	8.3	18.6	10.6	16.3	17.1	13.0
48 115	...	7	Dawson	2 336	14 442	2 103	6.2	92.2	7.5	0.2	0.2	48.5	7.6	21.4	8.6	12.3	14.5	12.1
48 117	...	6	Deaf Smith	3 878	18 800	1 833	4.8	97.5	1.8	0.3	0.4	55.6	10.1	25.6	9.3	11.4	13.3	11.2
48 119	...	8	Delta	718	4 973	2 838	6.9	89.6	9.2	0.9	0.3	2.1	6.1	19.2	8.3	9.2	12.7	14.7
48 121	1920	0	Denton	2 301	404 074	142	175.6	90.0	5.4	0.6	4.0	9.4	8.5	19.1	12.6	17.4	19.0	12.8
48 123	...	6	De Witt	2 355	19 275	1 800	8.2	84.8	14.8	0.2	0.2	31.5	6.4	18.9	7.7	11.7	14.6	11.9
48 125	...	9	Dickens	2 342	2 176	3 052	0.9	94.3	5.1	0.5	0.1	23.6	5.4	19.1	7.2	8.2	12.3	14.0
48 127	...	7	Dimmit	3 447	10 349	2 394	3.0	98.8	0.8	0.1	0.2	86.8	9.4	25.9	9.4	9.9	14.2	11.1
48 129	...	9	Donley	2 408	3 827	2 929	1.6	95.5	4.1	0.4	0.1	5.2	4.8	17.4	10.8	7.7	11.9	14.2
48 131	...	7	Duval	4 643	13 647	2 164	2.9	98.0	1.7	0.1	0.2	88.6	9.0	22.2	9.8	12.1	14.1	12.1
48 133	...	7	Eastland	2 399	17 489	1 901	7.3	97.2	2.2	0.3	0.3	10.1	5.6	18.1	8.9	9.1	12.8	12.8
48 135	5800	3	Ector	2 334	123 748	424	53.0	93.4	5.0	0.7	0.9	37.8	9.3	22.5	9.0	12.9	15.1	11.9
48 137	...	9	Edwards	5 491	3 668	2 937	0.7	99.8	0.0	0.1	0.1	43.3	4.4	11.7	3.3	4.9	6.8	6.7
48 139	1920	1	Ellis	2 435	107 580	488	44.2	88.2	10.8	0.6	0.4	17.2	8.2	22.7	9.2	12.4	16.5	13.9
48 141	2320	2	El Paso	2 624	701 908	71	267.5	94.5	3.4	0.5	1.5	75.4	9.5	22.9	11.1	13.4	14.6	11.4
48 143	...	6	Erath	2 814	31 469	1 331	11.2	98.0	0.9	0.4	0.7	11.7	7.1	17.4	16.8	10.8	13.1	11.5
48 145	...	6	Falls	1 992	17 263	1 913	8.7	69.9	29.3	0.5	0.3	16.2	6.7	19.4	9.9	12.1	13.0	11.6
48 147	...	6	Fannin	2 309	28 677	1 423	12.4	90.3	8.4	0.8	0.4	4.0	5.9	17.9	8.1	10.5	14.6	14.6
48 149	...	7	Fayette	2 461	21 390	1 687	8.7	90.2	9.5	0.2	0.1	11.2	5.9	18.3	6.5	9.7	14.1	12.6
48 151	...	9	Fisher	2 334	4 190	2 899	1.8	94.9	4.2	0.8	0.0	26.1	6.0	20.0	5.9	8.7	13.2	13.8
48 153	...	7	Floyd	2 570	8 112	2 586	3.2	94.1	4.8	0.4	0.7	46.6	9.3	23.1	8.4	10.1	12.3	12.2
48 155	...	9	Foard	1 830	1 631	3 089	0.9	92.1	6.1	1.5	0.3	17.7	6.5	18.3	6.8	9.3	12.8	12.9
48 157	3360	0	Fort Bend	2 266	353 697	162	156.1	69.3	21.1	0.3	9.3	23.8	9.0	23.4	7.6	13.9	21.3	12.8
48 159	...	9	Franklin	740	9 945	2 433	13.4	93.6	4.9	1.1	0.4	6.2	6.4	18.9	6.9	9.6	13.6	14.7
48 161	...	7	Freestone	2 293	17 647	1 893	7.7	77.3	21.8	0.4	0.5	7.7	5.7	19.5	7.8	11.8	15.9	13.2
48 163	...	7	Frio	2 935	15 918	2 010	5.4	90.7	8.7	0.2	0.4	73.4	9.0	22.7	9.5	13.5	16.0	11.3
48 165	...	7	Gaines	3 891	14 767	2 082	3.8	96.4	3.1	0.3	0.2	39.7	10.3	26.2	8.8	11.8	13.1	11.8
48 167	2920	0	Galveston	1 033	248 469	216	240.5	78.4	18.7	0.4	2.5	18.4	7.2	19.9	8.6	13.0	16.8	13.9
48 169	...	6	Garza	2 320	4 515	2 871	1.9	92.4	6.8	0.2	0.5	34.6	8.2	23.5	7.1	10.2	13.1	13.2
48 171	...	7	Gillespie	2 748	20 396	1 743	7.4	98.9	0.4	0.5	0.3	17.8	6.1	17.0	5.6	8.6	12.9	12.7
48 173	...	8	Glasscock	2 333	1 443	3 097	0.6	99.7	0.0	0.3	0.0	36.4	9.8	25.4	8.5	12.8	13.8	14.6
48 175	...	8	Goliad	2 211	7 125	2 669	3.2	92.1	7.4	0.4	0.2	43.4	7.1	20.4	6.7	10.7	15.0	13.4
48 177	...	6	Gonzales	2 766	17 561	1 897	6.3	88.5	10.9	0.4	0.2	42.6	8.1	21.0	8.3	10.6	12.8	12.1
48 179	...	7	Gray	2 404	23 299	1 602	9.7	92.5	5.8	1.0	0.7	11.5	6.2	18.7	7.5	11.4	14.3	13.5
48 181	7640	3	Grayson	2 418	103 728	498	42.9	90.4	7.7	1.2	0.7	4.0	6.5	19.0	8.2	11.0	15.1	14.1
48 183	4420	3	Gregg	710	113 155	464	159.4	78.1	20.6	0.5	0.7	4.3	7.0	19.9	9.4	12.0	15.6	13.3
48 185	...	6	Grimes	2 056	24 033	1 576	11.7	73.5	25.6	0.5	0.4	18.3	6.8	20.3	10.5	13.6	16.2	12.0

1. MSA = Metropolitan Statistical Area. PMSA = Primary MSA. NECMA = New England County Metropolitan Area. See Appendix A for explanation of these concepts. See Appendix B for list of metropolitan areas identified by type, with component counties.   2. County typology code from the Economic Research Service of USDA. See Appendix A for definition.   3. Dry land or land partially or temporarily covered by water.   4. Hispanic persons may be of any race.

Table B. States and Counties — **Population and Households**

STATE County	Age (percent) (cont'd) 55 to 64 years	65 to 74 years	75 years and over	Percent female	Total persons 1990	Total persons 1980	Percent change 1980–1990	Percent change 1990–1999	Components of change, 1990–1999 Births	Deaths	Net migration	Households, 1990 Number	Percent change, 1980–1990	Persons per house-hold	Percent Female family house-holder[1]	One person
	16	17	18	19	20	21	22	23	24	25	26	27	28	29	30	31
TEXAS—Cont'd																
Caldwell	8.5	5.5	5.9	49.3	26 392	23 637	11.7	24.4	3 879	2 441	5 001	8 745	18.8	2.83	11.6	22.5
Calhoun	10.8	7.9	5.2	50.7	19 053	19 574	-2.7	7.2	3 325	1 492	-424	6 777	4.8	2.79	9.1	21.9
Callahan	12.0	7.7	8.3	51.4	11 859	10 992	7.9	8.9	1 223	1 281	1 155	4 565	10.0	2.57	8.1	23.7
Cameron	7.5	5.8	4.4	52.5	260 120	209 727	24.0	26.5	69 548	16 308	16 530	73 278	25.4	3.48	16.1	16.0
Camp	11.2	8.5	7.8	51.7	9 904	9 275	6.8	10.5	1 649	1 290	713	3 773	10.8	2.59	11.6	25.0
Carson	11.1	7.6	6.5	51.0	6 576	6 672	-1.4	2.7	699	590	94	2 402	0.3	2.70	5.6	20.5
Cass	10.6	8.5	8.5	51.9	29 982	29 430	1.9	2.1	3 550	3 625	808	11 320	7.7	2.61	11.1	23.5
Castro	8.6	6.3	5.3	50.6	9 070	10 556	-14.1	-8.9	1 353	611	-1 535	2 877	-8.3	3.13	8.0	19.1
Chambers	8.9	5.5	3.6	49.4	20 088	18 538	8.4	19.4	2 568	1 445	2 816	6 930	10.9	2.88	9.0	18.5
Cherokee	10.4	7.3	7.8	49.5	41 049	38 127	7.7	6.3	5 720	4 625	1 642	14 981	9.9	2.61	11.4	24.9
Childress	10.1	6.0	8.9	44.1	5 953	6 950	-14.3	26.7	821	974	1 732	2 435	-12.3	2.40	9.7	29.8
Clay	12.3	7.2	7.7	50.7	10 024	9 582	4.6	4.9	890	981	613	3 808	5.6	2.60	6.6	21.6
Cochran	8.9	7.1	6.9	50.3	4 377	4 825	-9.3	-13.6	561	347	-807	1 430	-5.6	2.97	7.9	19.2
Coke	14.7	10.0	12.6	51.9	3 424	3 196	7.1	-2.1	312	541	181	1 374	9.3	2.41	6.0	25.9
Coleman	11.5	10.0	13.3	52.0	9 710	10 439	-7.0	-2.7	1 094	1 467	138	4 026	-5.1	2.36	8.0	30.3
Collin	6.1	2.8	2.3	50.1	264 036	144 576	82.6	72.9	52 874	11 826	150 576	95 805	106.6	2.73	7.2	20.8
Collingsworth	10.8	10.1	12.4	51.3	3 573	4 648	-23.1	-11.2	456	506	-346	1 447	-19.2	2.42	7.4	30.1
Colorado	11.4	9.0	9.7	51.8	18 383	18 823	-2.3	3.6	2 363	2 362	744	7 024	1.2	2.57	9.5	26.3
Comal	10.9	8.7	6.9	50.9	51 832	36 446	42.2	48.1	7 900	5 409	22 523	19 315	49.1	2.64	7.9	21.2
Comanche	12.2	8.5	11.1	50.4	13 381	12 617	6.1	1.5	1 446	1 838	651	5 318	6.9	2.45	5.8	26.2
Concho	8.9	7.4	9.0	45.3	3 044	2 915	4.4	-1.4	251	381	102	1 063	-2.6	2.51	7.3	27.5
Cooke	10.2	8.2	7.5	50.8	30 777	27 656	11.3	8.5	3 998	3 020	1 728	11 545	14.6	2.60	8.4	23.8
Coryell	5.3	3.0	2.9	45.4	64 226	56 767	13.1	14.6	8 705	2 799	-1 489	16 687	18.4	2.95	8.2	16.3
Cottle	12.0	11.8	13.1	51.2	2 247	2 947	-23.8	-15.9	189	302	-233	915	-21.4	2.42	7.8	30.8
Crane	7.1	5.9	4.5	50.0	4 652	4 600	1.1	-7.8	590	351	-600	1 537	-1.0	3.00	6.5	18.6
Crockett	9.9	6.3	5.2	49.5	4 078	4 608	-11.5	7.8	539	327	107	1 449	-7.0	2.76	8.4	22.7
Crosby	9.6	7.0	7.9	51.3	7 304	8 859	-17.6	-3.4	1 112	784	-559	2 516	-13.8	2.86	7.3	23.3
Culberson	8.5	6.9	3.8	49.4	3 407	3 315	2.8	-11.4	479	207	-658	1 076	9.0	3.15	12.2	16.8
Dallam	10.7	5.6	5.9	50.8	5 461	6 531	-16.4	21.4	986	572	772	2 122	-11.1	2.56	8.6	27.3
Dallas	7.5	4.8	3.8	50.8	1 852 691	1 556 419	19.0	11.3	347 763	121 324	-12 704	701 686	21.5	2.60	12.7	27.8
Dawson	8.9	7.3	7.1	47.6	14 349	16 184	-11.3	0.6	2 104	1 325	-649	5 084	-7.3	2.80	8.3	23.7
Deaf Smith	7.9	5.6	5.5	50.6	19 153	21 165	-9.5	-1.8	3 631	1 358	-2 600	6 182	-4.7	3.06	9.8	18.7
Delta	11.6	7.9	10.3	51.7	4 857	4 839	0.4	2.4	582	719	284	1 901	-1.6	2.48	8.5	26.5
Denton	5.5	2.7	2.3	50.3	273 644	143 126	91.1	47.7	50 613	12 029	91 493	101 984	107.6	2.61	7.4	24.0
De Witt	10.5	8.4	10.1	49.3	18 840	18 903	-0.3	2.3	2 099	2 593	963	7 195	2.0	2.55	10.3	27.7
Dickens	11.0	10.3	12.5	52.0	2 571	3 539	-27.4	-15.4	241	379	-247	1 073	-21.6	2.36	6.5	32.6
Dimmit	7.6	6.8	5.8	51.6	10 433	11 367	-8.2	-0.8	1 774	760	-1 081	3 072	-2.0	3.38	14.6	15.5
Donley	12.1	9.9	11.2	51.5	3 696	4 075	-9.3	3.5	396	578	327	1 515	-5.8	2.32	6.0	28.0
Duval	8.8	6.3	5.6	49.8	12 918	12 517	3.2	5.6	2 049	1 151	-145	4 159	11.3	3.10	15.4	20.0
Eastland	11.7	9.8	11.2	51.5	18 488	19 480	-5.1	-5.4	2 086	2 657	-356	7 354	-4.9	2.39	7.3	29.2
Ector	8.7	6.2	4.4	51.1	118 934	115 374	3.1	4.0	20 728	8 591	-7 117	42 322	4.6	2.79	11.3	22.5
Edwards	4.6	30.9	26.7	52.4	2 266	2 033	11.5	61.9	306	176	1 440	795	14.1	2.84	7.7	23.3
Ellis	8.0	4.6	4.6	50.2	85 167	59 743	42.6	26.3	14 002	6 794	15 290	28 588	43.9	2.93	9.8	17.3
El Paso	7.7	5.6	3.9	52.3	591 610	479 899	23.3	18.6	141 244	33 295	-2 129	178 366	26.7	3.25	15.8	17.0
Erath	8.9	6.3	8.0	50.3	27 991	22 560	24.1	12.4	3 908	2 820	2 521	10 877	25.0	2.44	7.0	28.4
Falls	10.7	7.6	9.1	48.4	17 712	17 946	-1.3	-2.5	2 226	2 327	-288	6 492	-6.2	2.53	13.2	29.3
Fannin	11.8	7.6	9.0	49.8	24 804	24 285	2.1	15.6	2 838	3 590	4 668	9 691	4.6	2.48	8.2	26.4
Fayette	11.5	10.1	11.3	50.8	20 095	18 832	6.7	6.4	2 336	2 697	1 742	8 101	8.2	2.43	7.3	28.4
Fisher	11.4	9.2	11.7	51.2	4 842	5 891	-17.8	-13.5	434	635	-444	1 892	-14.2	2.52	6.7	25.8
Floyd	9.4	7.2	8.1	51.3	8 497	9 834	-13.6	-4.5	1 308	815	-856	2 982	-9.8	2.81	6.6	22.7
Foard	10.7	9.3	13.4	53.2	1 794	2 158	-16.9	-9.1	205	270	-92	739	-14.1	2.38	8.3	31.0
Fort Bend	5.8	3.9	2.5	49.9	225 421	130 962	72.1	56.9	38 833	9 948	99 298	70 424	76.8	3.14	10.4	13.6
Franklin	12.6	8.7	8.6	51.0	7 802	6 893	13.2	27.5	842	938	2 258	3 017	15.3	2.54	7.4	23.6
Freestone	10.2	7.2	8.8	48.3	15 818	14 830	6.7	11.6	1 730	1 934	2 089	6 063	8.1	2.54	9.9	26.7
Frio	7.5	5.7	4.8	46.6	13 472	13 785	-2.3	18.2	2 567	1 020	927	4 129	2.2	3.20	13.9	18.1
Gaines	8.4	5.2	4.5	49.8	14 123	13 150	7.4	4.6	2 478	844	-962	4 502	7.4	3.13	6.9	18.4
Galveston	9.5	6.5	5.0	50.8	217 396	195 738	11.1	14.3	34 309	18 475	15 692	81 451	17.6	2.64	12.6	24.3
Garza	9.3	7.4	8.0	51.8	5 143	5 336	-3.6	-12.2	649	549	-721	1 822	-1.1	2.79	9.6	22.4
Gillespie	12.3	12.5	12.2	51.7	17 204	13 532	27.1	18.6	1 942	2 338	3 657	6 711	28.6	2.46	5.6	24.2
Glasscock	9.6	3.0	2.7	48.4	1 447	1 304	11.0	-0.3	199	54	-144	456	17.8	3.17	3.5	13.4
Goliad	11.5	8.0	7.2	51.8	5 980	5 193	15.2	19.1	630	617	1 139	2 208	24.3	2.68	7.8	22.9
Gonzales	10.0	8.2	8.8	51.1	17 205	16 949	1.5	2.1	2 388	1 910	-55	6 231	4.7	2.71	10.9	25.8
Gray	11.2	8.3	9.0	50.1	23 967	26 386	-9.2	-2.8	2 893	2 664	-850	9 548	-6.6	2.48	8.1	25.8
Grayson	10.7	7.7	7.7	52.0	95 019	89 796	5.8	9.2	12 785	10 618	6 766	36 847	8.5	2.51	10.2	25.2
Gregg	9.6	6.7	6.4	51.9	104 948	99 495	5.5	7.8	16 389	10 097	2 218	40 027	11.5	2.56	11.7	25.9
Grimes	9.6	5.7	5.4	45.5	18 843	13 580	38.6	27.5	2 698	1 811	4 332	6 040	24.4	2.72	12.6	23.7

1. No spouse present.

STATE County	Births, average 1996–1998 Total	Rate[1]	Deaths, average 1996–1998 Number Total	Number Infant[2]	Rate Total[1]	Rate Infant[3]	Physicians,[4] 1998 Number	Rate[5]	Hospitals,[4] 1998 Number	Beds Number	Beds Rate[5]	Medicare enrollees 1999	Serious crimes known to police, 1998[6] Total Number	Rate[7]
	32	33	34	35	36	37	38	39	40	41	42	43	44	45
TEXAS—Cont'd														
Caldwell	448	14.2	276	2	8.8	5.2	19	59	1	21	65	4 125	761	2 367
Calhoun	348	16.8	166	1	8.1	3.8	12	58	1	75	364	2 871	886	4 189
Callahan	141	11.1	133	1	10.4	4.7	2	16	0	0	0	2 297	100	768
Cameron	7 755	24.2	1 813	29	5.7	3.7	383	117	5	951	291	35 311	16 898	5 182
Camp	185	17.0	150	1	13.7	5.4	2	18	1	41	374	2 251	341	3 056
Carson	75	11.2	65	1	9.8	13.4	0	0	0	0	0	1 033	97	1 425
Cass	391	12.7	393	3	12.8	7.7	12	39	3	114	370	6 001	804	2 592
Castro	135	16.3	64	0	7.7	2.5	5	60	1	30	359	1 018	223	2 641
Chambers	294	12.7	163	3	7.0	11.3	7	29	2	60	253	2 019	595	2 486
Cherokee	680	15.9	496	4	11.6	5.9	62	144	2	148	345	6 729	1 506	3 463
Childress	94	12.3	102	0	13.4	3.6	7	93	1	35	465	1 259	194	2 501
Clay	101	9.6	112	0	10.8	3.3	4	38	1	32	303	1 492	209	1 976
Cochran	54	13.5	38	0	9.5	0.0	3	76	1	30	759	606	144	3 561
Coke	31	9.3	66	0	19.6	10.6	2	59	0	0	0	806	62	1 780
Coleman	116	12.1	163	2	17.0	17.2	13	136	1	25	262	2 387	296	3 037
Collin	6 850	17.1	1 507	30	3.8	4.4	706	165	4	498	116	22 778	16 207	3 972
Collingsworth	45	13.5	54	0	16.2	7.5	2	61	1	20	608	721	90	2 659
Colorado	258	13.7	259	2	13.7	9.0	18	95	3	98	515	3 811	670	3 491
Comal	954	13.5	629	7	8.9	7.3	108	147	1	77	105	12 223	3 143	4 374
Comanche	163	12.1	192	1	14.2	6.1	10	74	2	35	258	2 881	209	1 512
Concho	26	8.4	43	0	14.0	0.0	3	96	1	20	641	565	32	1 014
Cooke	452	13.9	351	4	10.8	8.1	20	61	2	80	244	5 385	897	2 675
Coryell	947	12.3	335	8	4.3	8.1	34	44	1	48	62	4 782	1 765	2 242
Cottle	16	8.0	30	0	15.5	0.0	1	52	0	0	0	510	22	1 106
Crane	59	13.3	42	0	9.5	5.6	4	89	1	28	621	479	113	2 440
Crockett	60	13.3	38	0	8.5	5.6	2	43	1	20	435	539	111	2 417
Crosby	117	16.0	90	1	12.3	5.7	2	28	1	35	485	1 154	71	947
Culberson	36	11.8	20	0	6.5	0.0	1	33	1	25	820	331	33	1 035
Dallam	108	16.9	57	1	9.0	12.3	6	91	1	130	1 969	1 256	161	2 490
Dallas	38 879	19.2	13 361	243	6.6	6.2	4 911	239	27	6 052	295	202 451	144 788	7 040
Dawson	206	13.9	149	2	10.1	8.1	10	68	1	40	272	2 348	408	2 713
Deaf Smith	372	19.4	164	4	8.6	10.7	12	63	1	39	205	2 411	624	3 156
Delta	58	11.9	79	1	16.1	22.9	1	20	0	0	0	1 018	62	1 234
Denton	6 053	16.6	1 472	26	4.0	4.3	438	114	4	605	158	20 533	15 243	4 143
De Witt	215	11.0	293	1	14.9	3.1	11	56	1	49	249	3 463	516	2 580
Dickens	24	10.4	41	0	17.9	0.0	0	0	0	0	0	605	32	1 397
Dimmit	182	17.5	87	1	8.4	7.3	6	58	1	26	251	1 501	363	3 406
Donley	41	10.8	64	1	16.6	24.2	1	26	0	0	0	871	71	1 833
Duval	207	15.3	124	0	9.2	1.6	3	22	0	0	0	2 034	337	2 436
Eastland	220	12.4	286	3	16.1	12.1	7	40	1	36	205	4 287	508	2 996
Ector	2 186	17.6	968	18	7.8	8.1	186	148	2	401	319	15 075	7 256	5 723
Edwards	25	6.9	21	0	5.9	0.0	2	53	0	0	0	2 008	70	1 842
Ellis	1 606	16.0	775	11	7.7	6.6	70	68	2	65	63	11 780	3 962	3 873
El Paso	14 638	21.2	3 793	75	5.5	5.1	1 059	151	6	1 829	260	72 503	38 733	5 431
Erath	435	14.0	323	4	10.4	9.9	30	95	1	75	238	4 804	741	2 331
Falls	230	12.9	245	2	13.7	7.2	33	189	1	29	166	3 023	657	3 642
Fannin	319	11.6	387	2	14.0	6.3	21	75	1	65	231	5 447	667	2 373
Fayette	240	11.3	293	2	13.8	9.7	26	121	1	43	201	5 025	255	1 189
Fisher	43	10.0	64	0	14.9	0.0	3	71	1	23	542	956	65	1 469
Floyd	132	16.2	82	2	10.0	12.6	6	73	1	27	330	1 269	150	1 797
Foard	20	11.7	25	0	14.4	0.0	0	0	0	0	0	392	25	1 425
Fort Bend	4 416	13.8	1 239	23	3.9	5.2	562	166	2	209	62	17 219	8 504	2 605
Franklin	88	9.3	107	1	11.3	7.5	7	72	1	30	310	1 360	172	1 765
Freestone	194	11.0	199	1	11.3	6.9	9	51	1	16	91	2 850	270	1 514
Frio	266	16.9	118	2	7.5	8.8	11	70	2	40	254	1 737	449	2 782
Gaines	241	16.3	106	2	7.2	6.9	6	40	1	33	220	1 497	249	1 635
Galveston	3 612	14.9	2 028	30	8.4	8.2	889	362	2	927	378	30 422	14 757	5 975
Garza	74	15.9	59	1	12.8	9.1	1	22	1	13	282	772	116	2 464
Gillespie	212	10.7	263	1	13.2	6.3	58	289	1	58	289	4 959	417	2 060
Glasscock	18	12.7	6	0	4.3	0.0	0	0	0	0	0	96	15	1 015
Goliad	73	10.8	67	0	9.9	0.0	3	43	0	0	0	1 109	47	682
Gonzales	263	15.0	211	2	12.1	6.3	15	85	1	34	194	3 367	466	2 609
Gray	289	12.2	275	2	11.6	8.1	31	131	1	92	390	4 417	1 221	5 064
Grayson	1 453	14.3	1 213	9	11.9	6.2	177	172	3	540	525	18 340	4 800	4 650
Gregg	1 764	15.6	1 129	17	10.0	9.8	212	187	3	460	406	19 030	6 708	5 832
Grimes	299	13.2	210	2	9.2	7.8	8	34	1	18	77	3 110	862	3 712

1. Per 1,000 estimated resident population, average 1996–1998. 2. Deaths of infants under 1 year old. 3. Deaths of infants under 1 year old per 1,000 live births. 4. Data subject to copyright. 5. Per 100,000 resident population as of July 1 of the year shown. 6. Data for serious crimes have not been adjusted for underreporting; this may affect comparability between geographic areas and over time. 7. Per 100,000 population estimated by the FBI.

Table B. States and Counties — Crime, Education, Money Income, and Poverty

	Serious crimes known to police, 1998[1] (cont'd) Rate[2]		Education						Money income 1989				Income and poverty, 1997 Percent below poverty level		
			School enrollment and attainment, 1990				Local government expenditures, fiscal 1997[5]			Households						
			Enrollment[3]		Attainment[4] (percent)						Median					
STATE County	Violent	Property	Total	Percent private	High school graduate or more	Bach-elor's degree or more	Total current expendi-tures (mil dol)	Current expendi-tures per student (dollars)	Per capita[6] (dollars)	Dollars	Percent change, 1979–1989 (constant 1989 dollars)	Percent with $100,000 or more	Median house-hold income	All persons	Persons under 18	Persons 5–17 in families
	46	47	48	49	50	51	52	53	54	55	56	57	58	59	60	61
TEXAS—Cont'd																
Caldwell	268	2 099	6 947	5.4	60.3	10.9	28.7	4 893	9 242	20 169	1.8	2.1	28 004	19.9	25.3	27.4
Calhoun	336	3 853	5 130	4.3	64.2	10.1	20.0	4 528	10 374	22 706	-25.1	1.3	30 625	18.1	25.7	25.0
Callahan	115	653	2 779	5.2	68.7	9.8	16.2	5 340	10 353	20 712	-10.7	0.9	28 427	16.4	22.5	22.4
Cameron	515	4 667	89 414	5.4	50.0	12.0	429.9	5 241	7 125	17 336	-11.8	1.5	21 699	35.3	45.2	41.4
Camp	314	2 742	2 302	5.2	63.8	10.0	10.3	4 894	9 936	19 673	-15.1	1.2	27 269	17.7	27.9	25.2
Carson	147	1 278	1 805	4.5	76.2	13.9	9.4	6 547	11 710	26 765	-8.9	1.6	38 076	8.7	11.0	11.3
Cass	409	2 183	7 312	4.6	66.5	9.0	34.0	5 345	9 391	19 886	-12.2	0.9	27 929	18.3	26.2	24.0
Castro	320	2 321	2 726	2.5	58.2	10.5	12.8	5 771	7 510	17 838	-17.6	1.5	28 315	26.0	32.6	34.7
Chambers	155	2 331	5 745	5.6	68.1	11.5	28.1	5 863	12 218	31 671	-5.0	2.5	43 345	10.8	16.5	13.3
Cherokee	483	2 980	9 912	11.0	62.7	10.2	40.0	5 120	9 195	19 296	-5.5	1.1	26 928	20.9	29.8	27.3
Childress	335	2 166	1 515	0.5	61.1	10.5	8.2	6 343	9 888	16 091	-12.0	2.3	24 904	26.6	30.7	31.5
Clay	104	1 872	2 328	3.8	68.9	11.1	11.5	5 648	10 978	23 721	-3.5	1.4	32 368	11.6	15.0	15.5
Cochran	124	3 437	1 219	1.1	57.3	10.6	9.9	8 004	8 533	19 301	-9.0	1.5	26 258	26.1	35.5	38.5
Coke	86	1 694	707	2.3	64.6	11.7	5.5	7 162	10 220	19 220	-10.4	1.0	25 700	17.2	25.6	24.8
Coleman	215	2 822	1 884	2.9	59.0	9.6	12.7	6 768	9 353	15 519	-14.7	0.6	21 718	23.9	34.7	35.4
Collin	423	3 549	74 317	13.0	88.3	39.1	362.4	5 063	20 503	46 020	13.5	10.9	65 814	4.7	6.5	6.3
Collingsworth	148	2 511	817	3.8	62.0	12.0	5.2	6 389	9 425	15 421	-13.6	1.7	23 092	25.1	35.4	35.3
Colorado	495	2 996	4 281	11.7	57.9	10.6	20.4	5 405	10 379	20 795	-4.1	2.0	28 966	17.1	23.9	22.9
Comal	251	4 123	12 127	11.0	75.7	20.3	70.7	4 714	13 400	29 457	6.8	3.3	39 600	10.4	15.5	14.8
Comanche	217	1 295	2 475	3.3	57.8	9.2	12.4	4 949	9 679	17 504	-1.1	1.6	23 687	21.8	33.6	30.9
Concho	63	951	625	7.5	54.2	10.3	4.1	7 017	8 126	15 942	-17.6	0.6	23 050	21.9	27.2	28.2
Cooke	119	2 556	7 811	9.3	71.5	11.9	31.0	5 156	11 594	24 525	-6.6	2.1	32 975	14.8	21.8	20.8
Coryell	389	1 853	17 275	6.1	80.3	11.0	52.6	4 898	8 924	23 504	12.0	0.9	33 259	14.4	17.0	17.2
Cottle	151	955	501	0.0	51.8	10.7	2.9	7 079	10 289	15 583	-17.4	1.3	21 187	27.8	38.8	38.7
Crane	108	2 332	1 478	0.3	71.5	9.4	8.4	7 006	10 751	30 659	5.0	2.5	38 169	13.1	16.1	17.5
Crockett	174	2 243	995	2.3	57.8	15.2	6.4	6 392	10 232	19 087	-30.2	2.0	28 647	16.9	21.7	24.8
Crosby	160	787	1 985	3.7	53.1	10.0	12.5	7 262	8 598	17 162	-12.6	1.2	23 177	27.3	37.5	36.9
Culberson	188	847	926	0.3	53.3	12.1	5.0	6 066	7 632	16 559	-13.2	1.6	20 416	32.6	41.5	43.6
Dallam	294	2 196	1 265	5.0	66.0	7.2	9.8	5 485	9 250	19 764	1.1	0.5	30 099	16.3	23.7	23.9
Dallas	907	6 133	479 675	15.2	77.1	26.3	1 828.7	4 896	16 243	31 605	1.5	5.6	40 960	13.5	19.9	18.4
Dawson	625	2 088	3 823	4.0	54.0	9.0	18.6	5 791	9 535	18 920	-20.7	2.0	25 738	26.7	33.0	33.6
Deaf Smith	572	2 584	5 650	9.0	57.5	11.0	23.2	4 991	9 296	21 177	-14.5	3.2	28 490	24.2	30.9	31.4
Delta	100	1 134	1 015	7.0	64.2	12.5	6.2	5 121	9 859	20 208	22.3	1.0	26 362	20.8	30.2	29.8
Denton	362	3 781	84 893	10.1	86.8	32.3	280.4	4 919	16 105	36 914	5.6	4.4	52 242	6.1	7.6	7.6
De Witt	255	2 325	4 394	8.2	55.2	9.2	26.7	5 667	9 564	18 041	-2.4	1.4	25 625	21.5	27.3	26.9
Dickens	349	1 048	557	2.7	60.3	11.2	3.8	7 059	8 465	14 484	-3.1	0.2	21 408	24.2	34.3	34.3
Dimmit	281	3 125	3 333	2.3	39.8	7.8	16.5	6 037	5 386	12 222	-29.9	0.5	16 958	40.2	49.0	48.7
Donley	310	1 523	926	1.7	67.8	11.1	4.5	6 526	9 388	16 747	-13.0	1.1	24 046	21.2	29.5	27.9
Duval	405	2 031	3 995	1.5	47.9	6.4	22.6	6 820	7 126	13 602	-27.8	1.2	19 837	31.9	38.9	40.4
Eastland	259	2 737	4 198	2.4	63.1	11.0	19.4	5 550	8 729	15 774	-11.9	1.9	22 645	21.5	29.5	27.7
Ector	741	4 982	34 687	5.9	66.9	11.4	128.1	4 462	10 897	23 801	-24.3	2.2	31 039	18.7	25.1	24.7
Edwards	105	1 737	667	0.4	58.3	13.8	5.4	6 384	7 537	14 639	-15.4	1.6	19 254	30.8	46.3	49.4
Ellis	253	3 620	22 695	12.4	71.7	13.4	103.2	4 783	12 199	30 553	7.4	2.9	39 855	11.2	15.9	15.0
El Paso	668	4 763	199 118	7.1	63.7	15.2	757.8	4 992	9 150	22 644	-3.5	2.2	25 866	27.8	38.6	34.2
Erath	182	2 149	9 066	2.8	71.3	20.3	26.6	4 780	10 832	19 881	-1.1	1.9	27 882	16.7	23.2	22.4
Falls	604	3 038	4 328	8.8	58.9	8.5	19.2	5 927	8 600	17 227	8.7	1.0	24 285	25.0	32.6	32.5
Fannin	267	2 106	5 125	3.3	64.6	11.2	27.2	5 302	10 298	20 669	2.4	0.9	28 595	16.5	22.2	21.5
Fayette	135	1 054	4 222	7.5	57.6	9.1	19.0	5 062	10 769	19 963	4.2	1.6	29 487	13.8	18.6	18.1
Fisher	158	1 311	1 123	1.8	63.0	11.5	5.4	7 043	9 760	19 368	-20.8	1.9	26 288	20.2	26.4	27.4
Floyd	72	1 725	2 000	1.3	60.7	11.2	13.1	6 278	9 564	19 186	-10.5	2.0	26 587	26.1	36.2	37.9
Foard	57	1 368	360	1.1	62.2	11.2	2.6	6 621	9 228	18 713	0.3	0.7	23 185	23.8	38.0	35.1
Fort Bend	272	2 333	70 286	11.9	80.9	30.2	306.0	4 646	16 056	42 809	-0.2	7.5	55 164	8.0	10.6	10.2
Franklin	164	1 601	1 759	4.7	64.9	11.3	6.9	4 609	12 370	23 103	6.9	3.2	29 822	14.2	21.2	20.1
Freestone	135	1 379	3 829	6.9	65.5	9.2	18.1	5 708	10 735	21 561	9.0	1.2	28 845	18.3	23.2	22.1
Frio	211	2 571	4 032	4.2	50.1	7.5	20.1	5 925	6 629	14 059	-22.2	1.7	20 094	35.0	41.0	42.1
Gaines	184	1 451	4 000	11.2	53.2	9.9	21.8	6 725	9 204	22 335	-6.1	1.9	29 484	20.6	26.0	28.1
Galveston	557	5 418	61 025	8.5	75.8	19.3	317.4	4 908	13 993	29 466	-9.7	3.6	39 119	13.4	19.2	17.9
Garza	446	2 018	1 240	3.9	57.6	9.8	7.8	6 551	9 112	18 994	-15.6	2.3	26 361	23.6	30.5	32.3
Gillespie	44	2 016	3 401	15.9	68.6	17.1	15.7	4 886	12 046	23 722	10.9	2.3	31 497	11.8	18.6	18.5
Glasscock	406	609	467	2.4	64.8	9.8	3.2	7 350	16 219	29 306	13.3	8.4	35 799	11.3	15.1	17.1
Goliad	87	595	1 561	9.2	62.6	9.9	8.3	6 017	10 875	21 411	-2.7	2.3	28 037	18.9	27.8	27.3
Gonzales	554	2 055	4 134	3.3	55.5	8.5	19.5	4 961	9 252	17 500	-3.3	1.5	23 826	25.9	35.7	34.9
Gray	792	4 272	5 760	8.0	71.1	11.9	22.1	5 092	12 771	24 118	-13.6	2.0	32 709	15.2	21.3	20.5
Grayson	302	4 348	23 758	10.3	72.1	14.0	100.5	5 170	12 201	25 241	-1.3	2.3	33 145	13.9	20.4	18.6
Gregg	582	5 250	27 844	12.1	75.8	17.7	111.6	4 715	12 457	25 484	-9.4	2.8	33 594	15.3	22.8	20.5
Grimes	379	3 333	4 687	8.0	59.6	8.6	22.2	5 227	8 920	20 623	8.1	2.2	27 891	21.1	24.6	25.3

1. Data for serious crimes have not been adjusted for underreporting; this may affect comparability between geographic areas and over time. 2. Per 100,000 population estimated by the FBI. 3. All persons 3 years old and over enrolled in nursery school through college. 4. Persons 25 years old and over. 5. Elementary and secondary education expenditures, local government fiscal years ending between July 1, 1996 and June 30, 1997. 6. Based on population enumerated as of April 1, 1990.

Table B. States and Counties — **Personal Income**

STATE County	Total (mil dol) 62	Percent change, 1997-1998 63	Per capita[1] Dollars 64	Per capita[1] Rank 65	Wages and salaries[2] (mil dol) 66	Proprietor's income (mil dol) 67	Dividends, interest, and rent (mil dol) 68	Transfer payments Total (mil dol) 69	Govt payments to individuals Total (mil dol) 70	Social Security (mil dol) 71	Medical payments (mil dol) 72	Income maintenance (mil dol) 73	Unemployment insurance (mil dol) 74
TEXAS—Cont'd													
Caldwell	559	10.0	17 471	2 491	155	26	88	107	102	36	46	13	1
Calhoun	402	6.8	19 535	1 875	472	25	67	71	68	29	28	8	1
Callahan	237	3.6	18 500	2 210	46	16	39	52	49	22	20	4	1
Cameron	4 461	6.3	13 766	3 029	2 521	337	654	1 134	1 080	264	513	232	22
Camp	265	9.1	24 280	593	88	58	50	51	49	19	22	5	1
Carson	173	11.4	25 863	407	212	33	27	22	21	10	8	1	1
Cass	618	3.2	20 105	1 678	256	74	103	145	140	54	62	14	3
Castro	239	3.3	28 778	203	79	110	23	29	27	10	11	6	0
Chambers	564	7.1	23 722	696	255	25	88	69	65	28	27	7	1
Cherokee	941	5.4	21 728	1 181	417	162	168	190	183	69	85	17	2
Childress	116	0.3	15 310	2 901	58	9	26	28	27	10	11	3	0
Clay	210	5.4	19 902	1 747	54	23	39	36	34	17	13	2	0
Cochran	68	-16.9	17 349	2 519	28	10	16	16	16	6	7	3	0
Coke	63	3.1	18 607	2 181	26	0	17	17	16	7	7	1	0
Coleman	176	-1.4	18 550	2 195	52	21	38	59	58	22	27	5	2
Collin	16 542	18.0	38 618	40	6 162	1 223	1 916	617	545	267	210	29	13
Collingsworth	59	-1.3	18 065	2 329	22	6	13	17	17	6	7	3	0
Colorado	427	5.6	22 589	955	151	56	120	89	86	38	35	9	1
Comal	2 026	12.4	27 560	261	684	174	398	241	228	109	90	11	4
Comanche	267	6.8	19 701	1 815	91	28	60	69	66	28	30	5	0
Concho	46	-1.5	14 913	2 938	22	1	13	14	13	5	6	1	0
Cooke	727	6.5	22 099	1 066	313	66	166	126	120	53	48	9	3
Coryell	1 168	2.2	15 824	2 822	310	54	164	125	112	42	48	14	3
Cottle	37	1.0	19 119	2 016	13	3	8	11	10	4	4	1	0
Crane	74	-3.2	16 735	2 669	53	5	12	13	12	5	5	1	0
Crockett	65	2.0	14 340	2 981	39	-1	16	13	12	5	5	1	0
Crosby	128	-8.9	17 670	2 447	45	15	25	37	36	11	19	6	0
Culberson	41	1.7	13 482	3 046	32	2	6	10	9	3	4	2	0
Dallam	183	-7.4	27 935	241	91	73	27	25	24	8	11	3	0
Dallas	68 758	7.1	33 617	73	66 310	12 014	9 940	5 386	5 043	1 987	2 183	514	122
Dawson	259	-5.5	17 705	2 438	119	26	56	67	65	22	34	8	1
Deaf Smith	428	3.0	22 436	990	158	143	61	66	62	21	28	10	1
Delta	102	4.3	20 714	1 483	30	6	15	24	23	9	10	3	0
Denton	10 685	12.1	27 872	243	3 451	532	1 092	625	561	236	240	27	12
De Witt	370	5.1	18 903	2 088	164	24	78	94	90	34	42	11	1
Dickens	44	-1.0	19 698	1 819	16	5	9	16	16	5	8	2	0
Dimmit	125	5.5	12 005	3 085	60	8	14	46	45	11	20	12	1
Donley	66	-5.0	17 091	2 589	21	7	15	19	18	8	7	2	0
Duval	176	2.9	12 942	3 064	92	2	24	68	66	15	36	11	1
Eastland	334	5.7	18 943	2 079	154	25	64	99	96	37	43	8	1
Ector	2 474	6.8	19 824	1 773	1 611	146	386	411	390	153	170	44	11
Edwards	31	3.6	8 401	3 105	10	0	11	10	9	4	3	2	0
Ellis	2 398	8.2	23 119	832	919	182	293	319	302	112	121	22	31
El Paso	11 363	5.3	16 359	2 733	7 421	1 092	1 627	2 071	1 955	549	818	361	17
Erath	661	9.4	21 059	1 372	319	115	117	116	111	40	50	8	1
Falls	287	0.2	16 385	2 725	111	15	56	78	75	26	33	11	1
Fannin	546	5.4	19 263	1 968	233	41	85	129	124	49	56	10	1
Fayette	472	4.1	22 170	1 045	205	41	130	104	100	44	43	7	1
Fisher	73	-15.4	17 143	2 573	27	-5	17	22	21	9	9	2	0
Floyd	181	3.7	22 126	1 058	55	63	29	34	33	12	14	5	0
Foard	33	3.4	19 804	1 780	8	4	9	10	9	4	4	1	0
Fort Bend	8 861	8.5	26 309	363	3 219	639	1 255	512	456	202	188	34	11
Franklin	191	8.4	19 623	1 853	63	23	40	35	34	15	15	2	0
Freestone	288	3.4	16 315	2 739	130	11	60	68	65	28	24	7	1
Frio	214	7.1	13 536	3 042	96	27	29	56	54	14	26	11	1
Gaines	271	4.1	18 191	2 298	123	68	39	44	42	14	21	6	1
Galveston	5 954	4.3	24 303	591	2 983	261	1 007	812	771	305	345	67	18
Garza	84	-1.1	18 198	2 296	30	15	19	22	21	7	11	2	0
Gillespie	464	5.9	23 200	819	165	42	167	88	84	40	36	4	1
Glasscock	18	-26.5	13 325	3 054	10	0	5	2	2	1	1	0	0
Goliad	108	4.2	15 451	2 882	35	3	25	27	26	10	12	3	0
Gonzales	373	8.1	21 311	1 292	130	102	62	79	76	28	32	10	1
Gray	567	4.2	24 021	639	300	56	109	111	107	46	46	7	5
Grayson	2 287	6.4	22 417	997	1 358	114	395	428	410	168	175	27	6
Gregg	2 822	4.5	24 983	493	1 855	289	565	468	449	180	198	39	10
Grimes	366	6.3	15 686	2 853	216	27	61	70	67	24	29	9	1

1. Based on the resident population estimated as of July 1 of the year shown.   2. Includes other labor income.

Table B. States and Counties — Earnings, Social Security, and Housing

STATE County	Total (mil dol)	Farm	Goods-related[1] Total	Manufacturing	Service-related and other[2] Total	Retail trade	Finance, insurance, and real estate	Services	Government	Social Security Number	Rate[3]	Supplemental Security Income recipients, December 1998	Housing units 1990 Total	Percent change, 1980–1990
	75	76	77	78	79	80	81	82	83	84	85	86	87	88
TEXAS—Cont'd														
Caldwell	181	-0.4	D	6.3	D	11.4	3.6	31.2	25.4	4 808	148	828	10 123	23.1
Calhoun	497	0.0	72.5	51.0	18.9	4.4	2.0	7.5	8.5	3 430	167	408	9 559	14.1
Callahan	62	-0.7	24.8	4.3	44.8	10.8	5.4	16.5	31.1	2 798	219	250	5 503	13.3
Cameron	2 857	2.3	D	11.3	D	11.3	5.6	27.6	26.4	40 609	124	15 770	88 759	34.5
Camp	146	30.1	17.9	9.5	42.3	9.3	4.6	12.3	9.8	2 316	211	419	4 530	18.9
Carson	246	9.1	D	7.9	D	1.5	2.1	3.8	11.6	1 118	167	65	2 856	8.4
Cass	329	5.8	38.5	29.6	37.9	9.7	2.9	13.7	17.9	6 942	225	1 007	13 191	12.3
Castro	190	57.9	7.6	6.0	24.2	4.5	2.2	4.8	10.4	1 288	154	179	3 357	-9.0
Chambers	279	4.1	52.1	38.3	27.7	5.3	1.6	8.8	16.0	3 246	137	313	8 061	10.6
Cherokee	579	21.0	20.1	16.3	38.3	12.4	3.5	14.5	20.5	8 768	204	1 129	17 629	12.9
Childress	67	3.0	D	2.7	D	14.3	3.0	14.3	50.1	1 308	174	168	3 046	-0.5
Clay	78	6.9	D	12.3	D	10.1	D	24.8	18.7	2 051	194	110	4 708	7.3
Cochran	39	17.3	D	1.2	D	5.7	2.7	10.6	31.1	721	182	125	1 763	-7.0
Coke	26	-19.6	D	3.4	D	15.9	6.0	22.6	37.3	910	270	61	2 793	33.1
Coleman	73	-2.3	D	3.4	D	15.7	4.1	22.0	28.6	2 827	296	294	5 382	2.7
Collin	7 384	0.1	D	22.2	D	9.4	7.6	35.1	9.1	29 139	68	2 231	103 827	102.9
Collingsworth	28	14.7	4.3	1.4	49.9	8.8	5.8	15.0	31.1	811	247	119	1 952	-9.8
Colorado	207	7.5	25.6	13.1	52.6	11.7	7.0	19.6	14.3	4 672	246	483	8 537	-0.4
Comal	858	-0.2	33.4	17.9	53.4	16.9	4.5	22.7	13.4	13 141	179	811	22 987	47.4
Comanche	119	12.3	13.0	7.0	54.5	10.6	3.3	16.6	20.2	3 586	264	328	6 724	9.9
Concho	23	-0.5	D	D	D	7.5	4.5	37.0	30.2	623	200	107	1 514	6.3
Cooke	380	0.1	36.1	25.3	44.2	12.5	3.8	14.6	19.7	6 224	190	476	13 315	15.6
Coryell	364	-0.6	D	4.4	D	9.6	4.3	15.3	50.4	5 743	74	524	18 970	18.3
Cottle	16	7.6	D	7.8	D	9.4	3.6	20.6	29.2	572	298	74	1 286	-6.3
Crane	57	-3.1	D	D	D	5.1	1.9	9.6	19.8	586	130	75	1 795	6.4
Crockett	38	-15.5	41.3	0.6	D	14.5	D	15.2	27.8	665	145	102	1 897	-4.3
Crosby	60	20.2	D	D	D	5.6	3.9	12.9	24.8	1 412	196	196	3 312	-5.6
Culberson	34	0.3	D	D	D	13.4	D	9.5	32.7	444	146	88	1 286	9.2
Dallam	164	34.6	5.8	1.9	45.4	5.4	3.1	9.7	14.2	975	148	133	2 577	-8.1
Dallas	78 324	0.0	20.8	13.3	71.7	7.6	11.9	31.2	7.4	222 508	108	32 210	795 513	27.3
Dawson	145	5.5	14.7	4.5	53.2	10.0	4.4	13.1	26.5	2 752	187	533	5 969	-3.5
Deaf Smith	301	42.4	13.2	9.7	31.5	4.4	2.7	8.3	12.9	2 732	143	525	7 152	-2.0
Delta	36	5.4	D	D	D	5.5	4.9	24.2	24.9	1 174	237	208	2 305	1.3
Denton	3 983	0.0	29.1	19.6	53.4	12.3	5.0	21.9	17.5	26 419	69	2 092	112 263	104.8
De Witt	188	-1.8	D	17.5	D	10.0	6.0	20.3	32.8	4 582	233	690	8 568	4.1
Dickens	20	14.1	D	D	D	9.9	4.5	16.2	24.5	671	299	92	1 564	-3.1
Dimmit	69	3.0	D	D	D	10.3	3.5	14.0	44.7	1 813	175	721	3 991	9.5
Donley	28	12.2	D	1.7	D	13.3	5.0	16.0	37.7	980	256	86	2 304	9.1
Duval	95	-5.0	D	D	D	4.2	D	18.7	36.9	2 389	175	929	5 127	19.0
Eastland	179	-1.1	41.3	20.6	D	10.0	D	14.6	21.0	4 703	267	504	9 768	4.3
Ector	1 756	-0.2	34.8	12.1	48.8	11.1	3.0	20.2	16.7	17 799	142	2 764	48 789	14.5
Edwards	11	-23.3	D	D	D	11.3	5.8	13.7	49.4	559	148	105	1 550	22.7
Ellis	1 101	-0.2	47.3	38.2	40.2	7.8	3.3	17.2	12.7	13 266	128	21 101	31 314	46.9
El Paso	8 513	0.3	19.7	14.6	52.4	9.8	6.2	22.6	27.7	80 732	115	1 653	187 473	26.7
Erath	433	17.9	24.3	18.9	40.3	9.2	3.2	18.6	17.5	4 973	158	430	12 758	25.7
Falls	126	-3.1	D	7.9	D	7.7	1.9	16.8	47.3	3 655	210	697	7 733	-2.6
Fannin	274	0.0	28.1	21.9	41.1	13.2	5.5	12.5	30.9	6 244	222	732	11 504	10.7
Fayette	246	0.1	22.7	11.4	55.7	11.0	6.0	20.7	21.5	5 814	272	496	10 756	12.9
Fisher	22	-33.9	D	D	D	8.6	8.3	17.0	46.9	1 119	264	107	2 413	-8.7
Floyd	118	41.7	5.9	2.7	36.8	4.1	3.8	7.4	15.6	1 470	179	199	3 535	-8.4
Foard	13	17.3	D	D	D	5.6	D	17.0	26.9	481	283	43	890	-18.4
Fort Bend	3 858	1.3	36.5	17.2	48.0	7.8	8.6	21.1	14.2	23 164	69	2 348	77 075	78.6
Franklin	86	16.1	D	7.8	D	21.8	5.2	23.1	12.2	2 149	222	125	4 219	32.6
Freestone	142	-6.4	28.3	5.6	53.6	13.8	2.9	15.5	24.5	3 548	201	410	7 812	14.2
Frio	123	17.1	11.0	1.9	42.3	8.8	2.6	17.7	29.6	2 233	142	543	4 879	0.4
Gaines	191	30.9	17.6	0.9	34.7	5.4	2.4	6.4	16.9	1 850	123	302	5 221	11.8
Galveston	3 245	0.0	24.4	16.1	44.4	9.3	7.0	18.4	31.2	34 173	139	3 930	99 451	19.9
Garza	44	-3.7	35.8	1.8	46.0	9.1	7.8	19.0	21.8	905	196	119	2 184	7.1
Gillespie	207	0.0	D	10.0	D	17.5	5.6	31.0	14.6	5 202	260	209	8 265	32.8
Glasscock	10	10.4	D	0.0	D	D	D	7.2	39.6	87	62	15	600	4.3
Goliad	38	-4.9	D	0.4	D	10.4	2.9	14.8	32.7	1 378	197	203	2 835	33.8
Gonzales	232	37.6	D	7.3	D	5.9	3.5	13.7	15.0	3 881	221	700	7 810	7.1
Gray	356	3.7	41.6	25.2	41.5	9.0	2.9	18.1	13.2	5 061	214	408	11 532	2.7
Grayson	1 472	0.2	39.3	32.0	48.6	11.1	6.4	23.0	11.9	20 410	199	2 007	44 223	12.0
Gregg	2 144	0.1	32.7	18.0	57.3	12.7	4.2	25.4	10.0	20 841	184	2 972	44 689	13.1
Grimes	243	1.1	43.6	34.5	31.0	6.0	2.1	16.0	24.3	3 116	134	621	7 744	21.3

1. Covers mining, construction, and manufacturing.　2. Covers private sector earnings in agricultural services, forestry, and fisheries; transportation and public utilities; wholesale trade; retail trade; finance, insurance, and real estate; and services.　3. Per 1,000 resident population estimated as of July 1 of the year shown.

Table B. States and Counties — Housing, Labor Force, and Employment

STATE County	Housing units, 1990 (cont'd)								Civilian labor force, 1999				Civilian employment, 1990[5]		
	Occupied units										Unemployment			Percent	
			Owner-occupied				Renter-occupied								
				Owner cost as a percent of income											
	Total	Percent	Median value[1]	With a mortgage	Without a mortgage	Median rent[2]	Rent as percent of income	Substandard units[3] (percent)	Total	Percent change, 1998–1999	Total	Rate[4]	Total	Professional, managerial, and technical	Precision production, craft, and repair
	89	90	91	92	93	94	95	96	97	98	99	100	101	102	103
TEXAS—Cont'd															
Caldwell	8 745	68.4	44 200	22.8	13.9	303	29.3	11.3	16 569	3.2	557	3.4	10 620	21.5	16.3
Calhoun	6 777	71.0	45 000	18.8	11.9	333	28.4	7.6	9 705	7.0	563	5.8	7 766	20.8	17.8
Callahan	4 565	81.0	35 500	20.8	13.6	292	25.9	5.1	6 068	4.3	264	4.4	4 832	20.1	14.6
Cameron	73 278	64.4	38 400	20.7	12.6	295	27.6	25.1	126 602	-1.0	12 463	9.8	86 302	25.4	10.5
Camp	3 773	74.3	42 200	20.4	15.0	324	28.8	7.4	5 293	-4.6	353	6.7	4 058	19.4	17.6
Carson	2 402	81.2	40 200	14.9	12.1	329	19.3	3.5	3 135	0.0	128	4.1	2 775	22.0	16.1
Cass	11 320	77.8	38 700	18.6	13.2	286	25.6	6.5	14 986	-3.8	1 141	7.6	11 628	20.0	17.2
Castro	2 877	66.6	39 900	18.4	13.0	286	24.2	13.9	3 674	-14.1	164	4.5	3 549	15.9	9.9
Chambers	6 930	80.9	57 000	16.7	13.4	391	20.1	7.0	11 847	-0.7	510	4.3	8 924	23.5	17.2
Cherokee	14 981	72.7	39 500	21.6	13.9	291	24.6	7.4	20 961	1.6	865	4.1	16 020	21.6	12.0
Childress	2 435	73.9	31 100	23.8	14.0	271	33.3	5.1	3 022	-4.2	99	3.3	2 284	21.0	11.7
Clay	3 808	82.7	37 500	21.1	14.5	317	22.8	3.2	5 421	2.3	156	2.9	4 330	20.9	15.1
Cochran	1 430	72.7	22 400	18.7	13.1	231	20.9	10.0	1 284	-14.5	73	5.7	1 683	18.1	10.3
Coke	1 374	76.9	37 300	17.9	13.7	238	25.1	3.7	1 544	3.5	43	2.8	1 338	20.2	18.1
Coleman	4 026	73.1	26 300	20.3	14.6	230	27.5	4.7	3 349	-6.1	214	6.4	3 636	19.5	11.5
Collin	95 805	66.6	106 600	22.9	13.3	526	23.4	3.3	268 718	6.6	5 713	2.1	145 946	43.1	8.2
Collingsworth	1 447	78.9	25 100	19.3	15.9	257	29.6	3.7	1 495	-4.0	17	1.1	1 522	18.5	8.3
Colorado	7 024	75.8	45 300	19.6	13.0	277	23.9	7.2	8 211	0.9	313	3.8	7 472	19.2	13.1
Comal	19 315	74.0	76 500	21.5	12.3	420	26.3	6.9	38 505	3.4	979	2.5	23 199	30.5	12.7
Comanche	5 318	77.3	31 700	20.1	14.1	251	26.8	6.2	6 946	2.8	224	3.2	5 434	20.9	9.8
Concho	1 063	70.6	34 300	24.6	15.5	255	27.1	5.6	1 555	0.5	38	2.4	1 246	15.8	9.2
Cooke	11 545	71.4	47 700	21.3	13.3	325	24.1	3.7	17 137	2.1	522	3.0	13 474	21.7	14.6
Coryell	16 687	51.7	51 200	21.8	13.2	402	25.9	4.1	22 313	0.7	805	3.6	15 670	24.2	10.7
Cottle	915	72.1	25 700	19.7	14.8	208	25.0	8.6	860	1.8	43	5.0	915	20.0	9.6
Crane	1 537	80.2	37 500	13.9	11.9	317	19.3	9.3	1 971	-14.2	176	8.9	1 946	24.3	19.9
Crockett	1 449	67.2	43 100	22.7	13.1	259	20.0	7.8	2 025	-2.4	165	8.1	1 674	20.3	15.1
Crosby	2 516	70.9	29 700	19.6	15.1	233	21.1	10.3	2 666	-11.9	175	6.6	2 704	16.9	9.6
Culberson	1 076	65.0	27 500	21.4	12.3	267	23.4	15.5	1 272	4.3	99	7.8	1 419	20.8	7.3
Dallam	2 122	68.7	28 100	18.1	12.3	305	23.7	3.5	3 758	7.7	97	2.6	2 404	12.9	12.4
Dallas	701 686	51.7	79 200	21.3	12.8	448	24.3	8.3	1 224 499	1.0	42 468	3.5	962 376	32.0	9.7
Dawson	5 084	73.4	34 200	18.9	13.2	289	26.7	11.2	5 733	-4.3	395	6.9	5 019	19.5	13.3
Deaf Smith	6 182	66.3	41 700	18.5	12.9	310	24.1	12.2	7 629	-5.8	449	5.9	7 669	18.3	12.2
Delta	1 901	76.0	30 300	19.2	15.1	256	29.0	4.9	3 490	39.4	116	3.3	1 925	20.8	10.1
Denton	101 984	57.4	89 100	23.4	13.1	477	25.6	3.6	243 708	4.9	4 770	2.0	153 373	37.2	9.1
De Witt	7 195	73.9	35 500	22.1	13.6	264	25.3	8.1	8 339	-3.5	379	4.5	7 040	18.9	16.4
Dickens	1 073	75.8	19 100	15.5	17.3	223	23.9	6.2	862	-19.5	47	5.5	993	19.3	12.9
Dimmit	3 072	74.3	21 600	19.5	14.8	253	27.0	21.0	3 648	-0.8	572	15.7	3 075	22.4	13.2
Donley	1 515	72.9	31 000	18.3	15.1	268	33.5	2.7	1 552	3.1	55	3.5	1 508	18.8	10.1
Duval	4 159	79.9	23 400	22.0	13.4	238	29.3	17.1	5 044	-0.5	750	14.9	3 771	18.8	16.6
Eastland	7 354	74.3	27 800	20.5	13.9	255	23.4	4.2	8 802	-1.6	422	4.8	6 970	21.2	14.2
Ector	42 322	65.8	43 400	18.9	12.7	314	22.8	9.1	61 045	-4.1	6 337	10.4	49 951	23.7	17.0
Edwards	795	72.2	30 300	21.9	14.3	225	20.0	14.4	819	-2.3	49	6.0	873	12.4	8.8
Ellis	28 588	72.5	67 900	21.2	14.1	420	25.5	6.2	54 886	2.2	1 715	3.1	39 378	22.8	14.6
El Paso	178 366	58.7	57 300	20.6	12.0	347	26.0	15.3	287 600	-0.7	27 058	9.4	216 790	27.7	11.0
Erath	10 877	62.7	48 600	20.7	14.4	328	28.1	4.2	16 596	0.9	408	2.5	12 635	24.6	10.4
Falls	6 492	70.2	31 400	22.5	14.6	227	25.0	7.9	7 371	-0.3	274	3.7	6 408	19.3	13.1
Fannin	9 691	75.9	35 100	19.8	15.1	302	28.2	4.1	13 255	6.2	707	5.3	9 852	21.2	13.3
Fayette	8 101	75.1	53 100	22.2	13.1	301	23.9	5.3	10 841	4.3	326	3.0	8 800	18.2	14.1
Fisher	1 892	76.4	26 500	17.5	13.2	206	21.6	4.8	1 664	-8.0	65	3.9	1 931	17.2	10.9
Floyd	2 982	69.8	29 200	18.5	12.9	269	24.6	8.8	3 184	-6.9	203	6.4	3 334	13.3	11.6
Foard	739	72.0	20 700	16.7	13.4	254	23.7	4.6	825	-4.0	19	2.3	762	22.8	9.4
Fort Bend	70 424	75.4	71 600	22.1	12.8	524	23.1	7.6	183 186	3.9	5 958	3.3	110 035	38.7	10.3
Franklin	3 017	76.2	46 800	20.8	13.3	324	29.9	5.1	4 341	-2.4	174	4.0	3 054	20.2	16.3
Freestone	6 063	79.5	44 700	17.8	15.6	286	22.8	4.6	7 339	0.6	331	4.5	6 352	20.3	14.7
Frio	4 129	67.6	26 800	23.7	15.4	242	25.6	20.0	6 240	-3.2	453	7.3	4 955	15.9	16.8
Gaines	4 502	72.1	39 800	16.7	12.3	288	21.9	11.4	6 656	-4.9	361	5.4	5 487	20.8	13.4
Galveston	81 451	62.0	59 700	19.6	13.4	401	25.4	5.7	121 984	-2.0	7 965	6.5	99 670	33.1	13.5
Garza	1 822	71.4	30 300	18.6	12.6	237	22.9	9.4	1 886	-8.4	114	6.0	2 018	13.7	14.4
Gillespie	6 711	79.3	63 900	23.4	12.2	376	26.7	5.9	10 328	0.6	223	2.2	7 330	22.5	13.7
Glasscock	456	60.1	47 500	20.0	10.4	150	10.0	10.2	694	6.1	18	2.6	570	14.9	4.4
Goliad	2 208	78.0	39 900	18.8	12.2	275	23.8	9.0	2 670	-1.2	116	4.3	2 389	19.0	15.8
Gonzales	6 231	68.2	36 800	19.1	14.3	246	26.9	10.4	7 383	0.1	239	3.2	7 058	16.0	11.6
Gray	9 548	75.6	35 500	18.0	12.5	337	25.2	3.9	9 447	-10.7	673	7.1	10 055	21.8	15.8
Grayson	36 847	69.3	46 000	18.3	13.5	368	23.8	3.4	50 441	-0.3	2 255	4.5	42 133	26.1	13.8
Gregg	40 027	63.2	56 000	18.4	13.3	348	23.6	4.9	59 175	-1.6	4 408	7.4	46 855	26.2	13.5
Grimes	6 040	74.0	39 300	21.2	15.1	286	25.6	10.6	8 713	-3.4	623	7.2	6 695	18.6	13.0

1. Specified owner-occupied units. 2. Specified renter-occupied units. 3. Overcrowded or lacking complete plumbing facilities. 4. Percent of civilian labor force. 5. Persons 16 years and older.

Table B. States and Counties — Nonfarm Employment and Agriculture

	Private nonfarm establishments, employment and payroll, 1998									Agriculture, 1997			
	Employment						Annual payroll		Farms			Farm operators
STATE County	Number of establishments	Total	Health Care and Social Assistance	Manufacturing	Retail trade	Finance and Insurance	Professional Scientific and Technical Services	Total (mil dol)	Average per employee (dollars)	Number	Less than 50 acres	500 acres and over	Whose principal occupation is farming (percent)
											Percent with—		
	104	105	106	107	108	109	110	111	112	113	114	115	116
TEXAS—Cont'd													
Caldwell	508	4 053	786	516	754	191	84	69	16 923	1 068	26.1	11.8	41.9
Calhoun	420	7 888	462	4 007	793	187	263	298	37 725	257	23.0	36.6	50.2
Callahan	194	1 007	125	95	282	77	21	17	16 822	849	23.4	22.3	38.2
Cameron	5 673	79 534	17 422	11 986	13 157	2 410	1 974	1 432	18 011	902	55.0	16.9	48.1
Camp	256	2 861	442	395	569	120	D	72	25 036	427	32.6	5.4	42.9
Carson	129	795	113	D	145	57	15	16	20 516	348	10.6	60.6	63.5
Cass	617	5 422	1 043	578	1 105	218	115	104	19 214	852	25.1	7.7	37.1
Castro	199	1 450	241	197	237	103	22	28	19 467	489	5.1	59.3	75.9
Chambers	389	5 920	422	1 878	608	117	111	215	36 339	421	33.5	25.4	43.9
Cherokee	827	11 527	2 805	3 419	1 724	272	147	228	19 809	1 429	28.7	7.2	40.6
Childress	171	1 253	298	D	297	58	28	21	17 116	284	7.7	43.3	51.8
Clay	121	996	133	D	195	53	D	18	18 334	818	16.4	28.7	47.1
Cochran	66	522	152	54	88	D	11	9	16 546	276	4.0	63.8	66.7
Coke	80	558	0	D	105	D	D	13	23 203	336	6.5	54.5	46.1
Coleman	223	1 527	506	62	313	96	D	24	15 445	837	10.5	41.3	46.5
Collin	9 598	154 811	11 449	23 699	21 934	7 731	7 663	6 146	39 701	1 407	49.0	8.3	34.5
Collingsworth	71	513	186	D	115	47	21	9	16 938	547	21.0	32.5	44.6
Colorado	538	5 209	828	833	1 032	134	70	106	20 364	1 562	21.3	15.4	42.8
Comal	1 899	22 054	2 666	4 249	3 672	444	490	477	21 646	657	31.1	16.4	40.2
Comanche	318	2 737	634	257	491	132	42	50	18 362	1 438	19.8	18.4	50.3
Concho	63	606	132	D	82	D	5	11	17 759	380	4.5	56.1	63.9
Cooke	846	10 521	954	3 080	2 108	262	153	217	20 646	1 487	29.5	14.2	37.4
Coryell	710	7 488	847	599	1 658	402	356	121	16 169	1 075	17.3	26.2	43.5
Cottle	47	402	82	D	44	D	0	6	16 075	225	3.1	57.8	56.4
Crane	88	1 101	223	D	135	D	D	26	23 916	53	15.1	66.0	47.2
Crockett	133	1 017	14	D	285	D	31	18	17 857	170	6.5	83.5	69.4
Crosby	138	912	165	71	212	52	D	19	20 649	385	5.5	57.9	71.2
Culberson	64	572	46	D	166	D	D	8	13 941	92	6.5	76.1	47.8
Dallam	250	1 642	24	71	275	95	74	32	19 406	414	7.2	69.6	71.3
Dallas	63 998	1 411 913	115 061	162 430	120 471	96 133	105 877	53 229	37 700	768	54.6	8.7	31.9
Dawson	362	2 784	359	240	567	147	87	48	17 090	583	7.7	59.3	69.0
Deaf Smith	444	4 507	643	1 117	599	117	85	89	19 672	647	11.7	62.8	67.1
Delta	75	583	146	D	71	D	9	10	17 516	419	26.3	13.4	37.5
Denton	7 057	94 599	9 735	14 091	18 214	3 311	3 992	2 611	27 603	1 782	52.6	8.6	30.3
De Witt	375	3 713	884	755	613	178	93	68	18 204	1 502	18.7	16.6	43.9
Dickens	60	328	78	0	63	D	D	7	21 070	366	6.6	39.9	47.8
Dimmit	181	1 448	336	D	301	60	28	25	17 392	218	13.8	48.6	46.3
Donley	91	403	52	35	133	27	20	5	13 437	393	6.1	40.2	50.1
Duval	160	1 834	605	D	232	99	D	35	19 184	880	6.7	32.7	38.2
Eastland	495	4 312	634	785	742	141	100	91	20 993	1 137	12.8	20.9	44.6
Ector	3 154	39 079	5 404	3 810	6 239	980	1 076	952	24 352	208	63.9	19.7	36.5
Edwards	41	145	D	0	39	D	D	3	17 724	283	6.4	68.6	53.4
Ellis	1 943	26 556	2 407	9 844	3 364	636	452	653	24 594	1 713	38.1	10.9	33.9
El Paso	12 409	198 571	26 446	37 803	28 757	5 682	5 964	4 358	21 947	415	67.7	11.6	40.7
Erath	811	9 601	1 408	2 024	1 857	230	446	177	18 474	1 787	21.8	18.1	47.1
Falls	293	2 620	809	420	491	128	30	53	20 204	1 027	19.9	17.8	47.0
Fannin	500	6 057	1 179	1 922	952	394	84	140	23 179	1 604	25.7	13.2	39.0
Fayette	705	6 047	847	1 107	1 087	258	153	114	18 821	2 659	27.0	7.7	38.7
Fisher	86	700	150	D	110	53	D	15	21 706	603	9.1	40.5	52.4
Floyd	189	1 207	236	44	196	68	28	22	18 012	517	4.6	57.3	67.5
Foard	43	325	61	D	23	D	6	4	12 142	238	7.1	42.9	42.9
Fort Bend	5 325	72 243	6 347	11 731	13 453	1 665	6 579	2 307	31 938	1 295	40.1	15.1	43.6
Franklin	181	4 834	3 636	D	246	81	37	50	10 241	510	24.5	12.7	45.1
Freestone	330	3 303	496	194	527	123	100	88	26 602	1 205	26.1	14.8	38.5
Frio	265	2 016	408	73	492	112	30	37	18 333	485	9.7	43.5	50.3
Gaines	324	2 526	294	56	445	123	50	51	20 379	712	7.3	59.8	67.3
Galveston	4 769	68 024	13 519	7 529	11 044	3 939	1 812	1 758	25 838	519	59.3	8.3	30.8
Garza	129	893	112	D	128	33	5	13	14 459	259	9.3	56.4	57.9
Gillespie	784	6 228	1 183	718	1 329	224	164	112	17 917	1 462	21.3	26.4	44.4
Glasscock	20	123	0	0	D	6	D	3	21 114	200	3.0	76.0	67.5
Goliad	104	619	91	4	106	35	8	12	19 670	786	17.9	20.5	42.0
Gonzales	388	3 867	660	820	640	152	86	78	20 222	1 629	20.5	19.8	48.4
Gray	698	6 964	1 115	1 135	1 158	195	186	166	23 856	341	10.6	50.7	57.2
Grayson	2 518	38 179	6 828	10 479	6 752	1 841	892	958	25 085	2 080	39.6	8.7	36.6
Gregg	3 910	59 843	8 248	13 968	8 820	1 580	1 630	1 469	24 553	363	42.4	4.4	24.5
Grimes	347	4 412	364	1 849	763	186	129	125	28 430	1 423	30.7	12.2	37.2

Table B. States and Counties — Agriculture, Land, and Water

Table B. States and Counties — Agriculture, Land, and Water

Agriculture, 1997 (cont'd)

STATE County	Land in farms					Value of land and buildings		Value of machinery and equipment Average per farm ($1,000)	Value of products sold				Percent of farms with sales of —		Percent of land owned by Fed. Gov. 1997	Water consumption 1995 (mil gal/day)
	Acreage (1,000)	Percent change, 1992–1997	Acres			Average per farm ($1,000)	Average per acre (dollars)		Total (mil dol)	Average per farm (dollars)	Percent from —		$10,000 or more	$100,000 or more		
			Average size of farm	Total irrigated (1,000)	Total cropland (1,000)						Crops	Livestock and poultry products				
	117	118	119	120	121	122	123	124	125	126	127	128	129	130	131	132

TEXAS—Cont'd

STATE County	117	118	119	120	121	122	123	124	125	126	127	128	129	130	131	132
Caldwell	265	0.5	248	1	105	299	1 303	25	32	30 322	14.5	85.5	25.0	3.6	0.1	5.8
Calhoun	213	2.6	830	3	76	611	732	60	21	79 775	75.4	24.6	55.3	20.6	5.4	85.4
Callahan	489	-0.5	576	1	133	252	417	25	21	24 700	13.6	86.4	32.4	4.4	0.0	3.3
Cameron	369	12.0	409	109	230	446	1 143	62	79	88 042	87.7	12.3	40.7	18.1	4.4	456.5
Camp	63	-7.3	148	0	34	278	1 558	33	151	353 008	0.8	99.2	37.7	15.7	0.0	2.9
Carson	468	-24.8	1 344	74	272	429	317	87	72	208 251	31.1	68.9	64.9	26.7	1.6	71.9
Cass	171	2.2	200	0	72	183	863	28	23	26 662	10.0	90.0	26.6	4.2	1.4	79.9
Castro	559	7.8	1 142	227	409	676	578	160	668	1 366 952	13.4	86.6	80.6	55.8	0.0	400.6
Chambers	242	-3.6	575	25	118	335	642	37	16	37 296	73.9	26.1	39.2	11.9	4.9	123.7
Cherokee	283	5.3	198	1	140	251	1 296	33	103	72 095	58.3	41.7	35.7	7.1	0.0	347.1
Childress	393	-12.6	1 384	6	D	429	312	54	19	67 802	71.2	28.8	50.0	16.9	0.0	6.6
Clay	604	-9.9	738	1	160	429	566	36	38	45 956	13.1	86.9	48.5	10.5	0.0	16.3
Cochran	402	8.4	1 457	69	283	477	318	111	51	185 809	72.2	27.8	57.2	38.4	0.0	54.1
Coke	482	-7.7	1 436	0	55	497	321	26	8	23 781	8.3	91.7	43.8	3.6	0.0	32.0
Coleman	737	8.2	880	2	199	376	470	31	21	24 828	18.4	81.6	47.2	4.9	0.3	3.8
Collin	270	-2.0	192	0	190	447	2 440	34	34	24 162	66.0	34.0	20.3	4.1	0.4	339.1
Collingsworth	488	5.5	893	22	177	443	453	59	31	55 909	65.1	34.9	43.0	13.3	0.0	28.1
Colorado	521	-5.2	333	46	222	399	1 314	32	53	34 106	63.7	36.3	30.2	7.7	1.2	230.8
Comal	183	-11.5	279	0	42	517	1 559	19	5	7 863	32.4	67.6	16.9	1.1	1.1	28.2
Comanche	535	-1.6	372	24	225	292	765	47	94	65 524	18.7	81.3	46.2	9.4	0.7	46.2
Concho	636	11.1	1 673	4	129	666	393	53	20	52 016	36.7	63.3	60.8	12.4	0.0	6.9
Cooke	479	11.4	322	2	188	310	955	32	37	25 075	16.7	83.3	35.1	5.0	1.4	8.1
Coryell	646	6.8	601	1	156	370	569	29	28	26 074	15.9	84.1	32.2	4.3	22.6	1.9
Cottle	507	7.6	2 253	2	127	424	191	48	15	65 567	32.0	68.0	52.9	13.3	0.0	2.8
Crane	491	24.3	9 266	0	28	1 107	119	31	2	38 854	0.0	100.0	54.7	13.2	0.0	3.7
Crockett	1 935	-3.3	11 383	D	D	2 004	177	46	15	89 385	0.5	99.5	72.9	25.3	0.0	5.1
Crosby	563	24.5	1 462	162	368	669	439	134	74	192 877	95.6	4.4	73.0	45.5	0.0	91.5
Culberson	1 569	-0.9	17 057	3	27	1 955	115	43	6	65 497	38.2	61.8	58.7	19.6	2.4	7.9
Dallam	932	19.3	2 250	246	D	1 181	516	153	357	862 291	29.6	70.4	76.6	52.7	10.8	329.2
Dallas	149	20.0	194	1	75	461	2 288	24	22	29 009	73.1	26.9	21.7	4.8	2.3	728.7
Dawson	605	9.5	1 038	65	504	609	529	124	90	153 691	96.9	3.1	68.6	46.1	0.0	45.7
Deaf Smith	880	2.6	1 360	169	572	611	430	136	657	1 014 894	8.2	91.8	71.3	43.4	0.0	278.6
Delta	120	11.2	287	D	82	187	730	28	12	27 647	53.4	46.6	30.3	4.3	3.8	0.8
Denton	363	-0.9	204	1	198	486	2 252	39	54	30 049	24.1	75.9	24.7	3.8	3.4	166.0
De Witt	560	-1.6	373	1	150	289	760	23	23	15 473	9.5	90.5	29.1	2.5	0.0	5.3
Dickens	533	-5.2	1 456	8	140	426	281	46	14	38 645	46.4	53.6	34.4	7.7	0.0	5.1
Dimmit	518	-23.5	2 375	6	44	963	416	54	20	91 295	13.1	86.9	37.2	8.3	0.0	13.5
Donley	643	7.2	1 637	12	93	482	276	42	92	234 013	7.6	92.4	49.9	13.7	0.0	15.5
Duval	844	5.4	959	4	131	459	460	28	13	14 704	35.4	64.6	20.8	2.5	0.0	16.5
Eastland	497	0.8	437	9	172	228	529	28	26	22 763	29.1	70.9	34.4	2.6	0.0	15.4
Ector	462	-10.9	2 223	2	D	300	136	20	3	16 346	5.3	94.7	18.3	3.4	0.0	17.9
Edwards	1 142	2.2	4 035	2	17	1 198	302	23	9	32 103	2.0	98.0	48.1	9.5	0.0	1.0
Ellis	426	0.0	249	1	255	338	1 253	34	40	23 602	61.1	38.9	23.2	4.6	0.4	15.8
El Paso	244	0.0	587	41	47	404	720	72	77	184 754	48.0	52.0	37.6	19.5	13.7	392.6
Erath	613	5.0	343	11	218	353	1 057	41	233	130 339	3.6	96.4	39.6	11.0	0.0	25.1
Falls	362	-4.2	353	3	223	278	798	46	52	50 969	37.4	62.6	43.5	9.7	0.0	8.8
Fannin	445	7.7	277	2	264	296	1 083	27	39	24 451	43.5	56.5	31.3	3.6	3.1	477.5
Fayette	515	3.6	194	1	222	261	1 371	23	60	22 444	9.1	90.9	23.0	2.4	0.0	17.4
Fisher	575	5.3	954	2	222	339	388	68	31	51 157	59.0	41.0	47.8	12.1	0.0	2.8
Floyd	556	-11.6	1 075	170	409	508	460	127	131	252 822	53.6	46.4	63.4	44.7	0.0	226.3
Foard	308	-4.4	1 293	1	128	382	297	56	11	46 674	46.1	53.9	42.4	8.8	0.0	4.7
Fort Bend	432	2.3	333	17	193	503	1 494	51	76	58 994	84.1	15.9	36.7	10.3	0.3	214.9
Franklin	135	4.6	265	0	55	258	995	42	49	96 441	2.5	97.5	40.4	15.9	0.0	4.6
Freestone	423	14.2	351	0	133	313	914	25	20	16 305	7.3	92.7	27.6	1.9	0.0	868.0
Frio	662	-11.7	1 365	47	149	720	531	80	68	140 378	58.3	41.7	41.9	14.8	0.0	100.0
Gaines	772	12.4	1 085	234	591	570	501	134	218	306 599	D	D	63.2	48.0	0.0	549.7
Galveston	105	2.9	202	1	30	251	1 053	28	7	13 112	31.4	68.6	18.3	1.9	0.1	61.1
Garza	514	-10.4	1 986	11	D	426	204	57	15	57 219	67.7	32.3	54.4	18.9	0.0	5.3
Gillespie	694	0.9	475	3	118	630	1 277	25	29	20 014	16.4	83.6	29.8	2.1	0.1	7.3
Glasscock	437	-8.7	2 183	52	132	1 001	439	112	24	118 702	87.9	12.1	71.0	41.5	0.0	52.1
Goliad	434	-6.8	552	0	76	359	665	26	12	15 715	15.7	84.3	28.6	3.1	0.2	8.2
Gonzales	710	6.7	436	3	178	381	797	44	294	180 725	4.7	95.3	40.3	12.3	0.0	8.8
Gray	561	-2.6	1 645	24	D	666	426	69	85	249 747	11.2	88.8	53.4	15.8	0.1	25.2
Grayson	417	1.8	201	2	245	293	1 508	29	35	17 056	44.2	55.8	23.4	3.0	2.9	27.3
Gregg	51	9.3	142	0	26	271	1 377	30	3	7 605	17.5	82.5	17.9	0.6	0.0	24.5
Grimes	370	4.9	260	1	132	299	1 369	29	23	16 406	13.2	86.8	26.9	3.0	0.0	9.1

STATE County	New Construction ($1,000)	Number of Housing Units	Number of Establishments	Number of Employees	Sales (mil dol)	Annual Payroll (mil dol)	Number of Establishments	Number of Employees	Sales (mil dol)	Annual Payroll (mil dol)	Number of Establishments	Number of Employees	Receipts (mil dol)	Annual Payroll (mil dol)
			Wholesale Trade, 1997				Retail Trade[1], 1997				Real Estate and Rental and Leasing, 1997			
	133	134	135	136	137	138	139	140	141	142	143	144	145	146
TEXAS—Cont'd														
Caldwell	3 953	81	25	166	63.1	2.9	92	806	128.4	10.1	19	55	4.9	0.7
Calhoun	5 666	55	29	135	51.9	3.7	77	725	111.1	10.3	16	81	12.7	1.9
Callahan	815	10	8	38	7.2	0.8	36	266	65.4	4.3	3	11	0.5	0.1
Cameron	157 698	2 539	387	3 772	1 218.9	81.6	1 117	13 089	1 904.0	179.3	283	1 208	98.5	18.1
Camp	200	3	11	80	13.2	0.9	58	532	109.6	9.1	7	19	2.2	0.2
Carson	312	2	6	37	20.4	0.8	29	233	25.2	2.3	4	28	0.3	0.1
Cass	754	7	30	222	106.8	6.1	137	1 261	161.5	16.8	18	64	3.5	0.5
Castro	33	1	20	D	D	D	41	208	47.7	3.2	5	D	D	D
Chambers	18 564	213	22	D	D	D	83	648	133.8	9.4	15	84	9.8	2.1
Cherokee	3 145	27	39	250	75.5	8.4	146	1 542	262.6	21.5	32	94	8.2	1.5
Childress	3 494	80	14	101	51.7	2.3	38	309	43.7	3.8	3	7	0.2	0.1
Clay	1 447	18	7	51	17.3	1.2	34	267	53.3	4.1	2	D	D	D
Cochran	0	0	7	26	7.9	0.5	15	87	15.6	1.5	NA	NA	NA	NA
Coke	80	3	3	D	D	D	21	98	24.2	1.3	1	D	D	D
Coleman	290	3	18	102	29.9	1.2	53	324	57.1	4.2	8	15	2.0	0.2
Collin	1 426 882	12 100	737	7 373	7 169.8	326.9	1 301	20 311	4 220.4	407.2	430	1 982	349.3	58.0
Collingsworth	0	0	5	18	7.4	0.4	17	113	17.4	2.1	1	D	D	D
Colorado	1 289	8	40	235	84.9	4.3	113	879	163.3	13.3	12	D	D	D
Comal	112 866	946	99	653	320.1	20.0	317	3 242	633.3	55.7	84	339	28.7	5.0
Comanche	68	2	29	370	124.5	8.5	77	456	79.6	6.4	4	D	D	D
Concho	NA	NA	4	20	2.7	0.4	14	82	14.1	1.2	NA	NA	NA	NA
Cooke	4 072	42	45	354	102.5	6.6	240	2 013	355.6	28.9	18	68	11.7	1.1
Coryell	11 629	128	17	D	D	D	144	1 781	268.7	22.0	44	139	7.4	1.6
Cottle	0	0	1	D	D	D	10	40	10.3	0.6	1	D	D	D
Crane	10	1	6	D	D	D	17	129	21.7	1.8	2	D	D	D
Crockett	NA	NA	6	15	6.7	0.4	31	263	26.6	3.2	2	D	D	D
Crosby	444	8	12	171	65.4	4.8	33	226	41.8	3.2	3	6	0.4	0.1
Culberson	110	2	1	D	D	D	25	162	28.2	1.7	NA	NA	NA	NA
Dallam	2 026	13	22	275	191.7	10.0	43	250	65.3	4.3	7	11	1.3	0.1
Dallas	1 562 205	14 937	6 054	108 131	100 787.3	4 621.7	7 878	117 812	24 538.2	2 400.4	3 352	30 049	4 268.4	932.5
Dawson	449	25	25	122	91.4	2.8	68	553	95.8	8.6	10	39	1.8	0.5
Deaf Smith	284	2	46	368	120.8	10.0	88	595	113.9	8.9	14	37	3.6	0.6
Delta	309	3	2	D	D	D	19	94	16.2	1.2	1	D	D	D
Denton	905 074	6 733	423	3 935	2 762.2	141.4	1 143	16 966	3 180.1	284.9	324	1 540	177.5	29.7
De Witt	1 773	29	22	155	86.4	2.6	81	663	93.0	9.1	14	73	5.0	1.4
Dickens	NA	NA	1	D	D	D	12	54	7.4	0.5	NA	NA	NA	NA
Dimmit	439	9	7	17	6.2	0.4	34	328	50.3	4.5	3	D	D	D
Donley	0	0	2	D	D	D	20	114	23.6	1.7	3	6	0.7	0.1
Duval	NA	NA	6	D	D	D	36	203	35.2	2.6	5	11	1.0	0.2
Eastland	190	3	29	368	255.7	9.1	113	682	116.5	8.8	10	22	3.4	0.4
Ector	11 935	101	355	3 518	1 047.6	117.9	538	6 060	1 139.9	104.4	136	853	87.8	18.1
Edwards	NA	NA	2	D	D	D	9	47	5.8	0.4	1	D	D	D
Ellis	57 151	489	94	751	375.7	19.6	310	3 054	572.7	47.5	86	321	35.2	5.5
El Paso	204 548	4 196	1 000	11 129	6 089.3	309.6	2 134	28 986	4 698.9	430.5	550	2 458	285.3	48.1
Erath	2 446	27	43	378	118.9	6.8	157	1 674	274.1	24.6	26	80	7.8	1.0
Falls	553	12	14	D	D	D	68	435	65.4	5.4	9	31	1.3	0.3
Fannin	3 150	42	26	321	187.8	7.7	101	929	193.8	14.8	15	29	2.4	0.3
Fayette	1 442	14	39	411	318.6	10.6	141	1 063	185.9	15.2	17	63	3.7	0.7
Fisher	0	0	3	D	D	D	17	96	12.4	1.3	2	D	D	D
Floyd	38	1	19	181	58.0	2.7	32	206	47.7	3.2	6	12	0.4	0.1
Foard	0	0	2	D	D	D	6	22	4.3	0.3	1	D	D	D
Fort Bend	144 961	1 160	405	3 793	2 972.1	143.0	825	11 992	2 229.9	196.4	220	763	93.3	17.7
Franklin	163	3	5	19	2.6	0.4	32	220	37.2	3.3	7	18	1.1	0.3
Freestone	1 233	12	15	61	26.4	1.2	63	481	105.9	7.7	6	21	0.9	0.2
Frio	678	27	23	D	D	D	52	461	82.1	6.2	7	10	0.8	0.1
Gaines	685	3	22	182	135.6	5.2	62	470	88.9	7.4	10	24	1.3	0.4
Galveston	234 267	2 107	198	1 522	561.3	46.6	921	10 591	1 786.9	165.8	224	1 160	128.5	25.4
Garza	200	1	8	32	18.7	1.5	29	123	18.3	1.5	3	20	0.8	0.1
Gillespie	10 191	76	36	334	89.8	5.8	153	1 361	172.9	18.6	25	82	5.5	1.0
Glasscock	NA	NA	1	D	D	D	5	D	D	D	NA	NA	NA	NA
Goliad	NA	NA	4	12	2.8	0.2	20	100	17.4	1.3	2	D	D	D
Gonzales	1 753	47	38	353	153.3	6.0	82	728	99.2	8.4	14	41	2.1	0.3
Gray	70	1	42	309	178.7	9.6	130	1 068	169.1	16.0	24	98	18.2	4.2
Grayson	23 160	257	132	958	406.1	25.1	474	6 213	1 092.0	98.5	104	351	32.0	5.8
Gregg	31 906	338	342	3 564	1 863.5	114.0	734	8 825	1 549.7	145.1	134	649	74.8	17.0
Grimes	695	12	19	187	137.0	4.1	73	663	120.5	9.9	12	93	5.7	1.0

1. Establishments with payroll.

STATE County	Professional, Scientific, and Technical Services[1], 1997				Manufacturing, 1997				Accommodation and Foodservices, 1997			
	Number of Establishments	Number of Employees	Receipts (mil dol)	Annual Payroll (mil dol)	Number of Establishments	Number of Employees	Receipts (mil dol)	Annual Payroll (mil dol)	Number of Establishments	Number of Employees	Sales (mil dol)	Annual Payroll (mil dol)
	147	148	149	150	151	152	153	154	155	156	157	158
TEXAS—Cont'd												
Caldwell	28	68	4.3	1.2	18	556	39.2	9.7	36	370	14.1	3.7
Calhoun	30	270	16.6	9.2	20	3 815	2 689.3	208.8	53	524	15.2	4.2
Callahan	9	18	1.5	0.4	NA	NA	NA	NA	15	130	2.9	0.8
Cameron	339	2 278	126.5	42.7	235	12 694	1 732.8	242.4	513	8 349	278.2	71.7
Camp	14	27	3.7	1.2	NA	NA	NA	NA	17	96	3.5	0.9
Carson	3	9	0.6	0.1	NA	NA	NA	NA	10	D	D	D
Cass	26	86	4.8	1.5	26	546	63.9	11.4	47	548	14.7	4.0
Castro	9	28	1.9	0.7	NA	NA	NA	NA	14	D	D	D
Chambers	20	80	6.3	1.9	15	1 499	1 989.7	83.5	31	577	14.9	3.9
Cherokee	47	153	9.5	2.6	91	3 178	327.4	67.0	47	632	20.3	4.9
Childress	9	32	1.6	0.4	NA	NA	NA	NA	24	256	7.2	1.8
Clay	8	12	1.0	0.2	NA	NA	NA	NA	11	61	1.5	0.4
Cochran	4	8	0.3	0.1	NA	NA	NA	NA	5	16	0.5	0.1
Coke	2	D	D	D	NA	NA	NA	NA	7	D	D	D
Coleman	13	34	1.4	0.4	NA	NA	NA	NA	21	173	4.2	1.2
Collin	1 161	6 165	783.9	285.6	318	21 326	6 235.9	972.3	563	11 830	430.9	119.6
Collingsworth	5	25	1.6	0.9	NA	NA	NA	NA	7	43	1.0	0.2
Colorado	28	65	4.0	1.3	29	825	76.0	17.4	48	569	15.3	3.7
Comal	121	382	30.6	11.3	84	4 016	558.6	101.2	172	2 468	80.4	22.8
Comanche	12	28	2.6	0.7	NA	NA	NA	NA	22	165	4.8	1.3
Concho	3	5	0.3	0.1	NA	NA	NA	NA	9	81	2.8	0.6
Cooke	37	112	7.4	2.7	68	3 318	437.7	88.2	64	965	29.0	7.6
Coryell	35	265	16.0	8.2	25	556	52.3	12.0	60	1 201	30.4	9.9
Cottle	NA	NA	NA	NA	NA	NA	NA	NA	5	D	D	D
Crane	4	3	0.4	0.0	NA	NA	NA	NA	7	83	1.9	0.5
Crockett	8	32	2.3	0.8	NA	NA	NA	NA	24	218	6.4	1.7
Crosby	4	6	0.4	0.1	NA	NA	NA	NA	5	34	1.1	0.3
Culberson	2	D	D	D	NA	NA	NA	NA	21	224	6.0	1.5
Dallam	14	D	D	D	NA	NA	NA	NA	27	264	8.7	1.9
Dallas	8 030	90 234	11 406.1	4 676.3	3 383	151 686	29 962.5	5 499.4	4 194	98 652	4 045.9	1 102.7
Dawson	15	60	4.2	1.2	32	1 128	376.7	28.9	30	283	9.8	2.7
Deaf Smith	16	60	3.5	1.4	32	1 128	376.7	28.9	29	D	D	D
Delta	4	4	0.2	0.1	NA	NA	NA	NA	2	D	D	D
Denton	624	5 359	319.1	237.8	305	13 556	2 741.8	459.8	488	9 742	325.0	90.4
De Witt	20	71	3.8	1.2	24	721	87.9	16.4	37	290	8.9	2.6
Dickens	2	D	D	D	NA	NA	NA	NA	7	38	1.5	0.3
Dimmit	10	24	1.7	0.8	NA	NA	NA	NA	12	125	4.0	1.0
Donley	7	11	0.6	0.1	NA	NA	NA	NA	14	79	2.2	0.5
Duval	4	10	0.4	0.1	NA	NA	NA	NA	16	88	2.8	0.7
Eastland	30	86	3.7	1.1	25	713	98.3	17.4	43	382	9.3	2.6
Ector	192	1 005	69.1	26.5	203	3 526	1 286.2	115.6	234	3 806	119.9	32.9
Edwards	2	D	D	D	NA	NA	NA	NA	3	D	D	D
Ellis	96	298	25.2	8.6	174	9 635	2 397.9	285.0	113	1 652	52.5	14.7
El Paso	927	5 777	398.1	161.7	652	36 723	7 966.5	773.9	1 094	19 292	703.3	194.0
Erath	42	320	16.8	7.2	37	2 186	387.7	53.3	68	1 029	30.2	7.9
Falls	10	28	1.4	0.6	NA	NA	NA	NA	20	92	3.7	0.9
Fannin	27	70	4.6	1.8	40	1 784	340.6	43.6	33	281	9.9	2.7
Fayette	34	127	7.1	2.3	39	1 056	148.6	23.2	55	780	20.9	6.0
Fisher	6	8	0.4	0.1	NA	NA	NA	NA	6	D	D	D
Floyd	8	21	1.3	0.3	NA	NA	NA	NA	16	75	2.0	0.6
Foard	3	8	0.2	0.1	NA	NA	NA	NA	3	8	0.2	0.1
Fort Bend	517	4 843	1 024.3	303.6	270	11 923	2 704.9	452.7	319	5 889	205.4	56.2
Franklin	11	31	1.8	0.6	NA	NA	NA	NA	18	198	5.1	1.3
Freestone	23	87	4.8	1.6	NA	NA	NA	NA	24	297	9.2	2.6
Frio	8	28	0.8	0.2	NA	NA	NA	NA	23	168	5.7	1.5
Gaines	9	33	1.9	1.1	NA	NA	NA	NA	21	D	D	D
Galveston	333	1 375	131.6	52.5	160	7 279	9 182.6	392.5	485	9 156	301.5	82.4
Garza	1	D	D	D	NA	NA	NA	NA	13	115	2.7	0.7
Gillespie	48	125	8.2	2.8	45	721	70.7	13.1	67	815	25.9	7.6
Glasscock	1	D	D	D	NA	NA	NA	NA	1	D	D	D
Goliad	7	16	0.9	0.3	NA	NA	NA	NA	13	114	2.6	0.7
Gonzales	26	69	4.3	1.2	19	747	173.6	16.8	26	242	7.1	1.9
Gray	41	181	11.9	3.9	20	1 082	419.9	53.2	55	658	19.0	5.0
Grayson	162	715	52.6	19.6	140	10 223	3 557.3	365.4	200	3 312	104.8	30.7
Gregg	277	1 516	113.5	44.0	205	13 008	3 408.6	447.6	274	4 575	146.3	41.5
Grimes	22	52	4.3	1.1	21	1 910	386.9	63.3	25	D	D	D

1. Firms subject to federal tax.

STATE County	Health Care and Social Assistance¹, 1997				Other Services¹, 1997				Federal funds and grants, fiscal 1999² Expenditures (mil dol)		Direct payments for individuals³	
	Number of Establishments	Number of Employees	Receipts (mil dol)	Annual Payroll (mil dol)	Number of Establishments	Number of Employees	Receipts (mil dol)	Annual Payroll (mil dol)	Total	Social Security and government retirement	Medicare	Food stamps and Supplemental Security Income
	159	160	161	162	163	164	165	166	167	168	169	170
TEXAS—Cont'd												
Caldwell	33	506	19.2	8.2	29	88	4.9	1.1	117.1	51.3	23.9	4.6
Calhoun	25	288	11.9	4.9	31	106	5.7	1.6	82.9	34.1	13.2	3.0
Callahan	8	108	3.6	1.6	8	17	1.4	0.3	54.1	29.4	10.8	0.9
Cameron	509	11 065	498.3	216.2	338	2 279	96.3	30.0	1 281.6	340.5	191.8	111.7
Camp	19	174	6.9	2.9	10	28	1.9	0.4	60.1	27.3	13.8	2.4
Carson	2	D	D	D	9	22	2.0	0.3	38.4	12.2	6.1	0.3
Cass	39	723	28.5	11.6	33	144	10.6	3.5	174.8	75.4	33.5	5.9
Castro	6	58	1.8	0.6	18	55	4.7	1.0	58.8	10.4	5.5	1.2
Chambers	13	135	3.5	1.5	20	78	6.8	2.2	69.8	25.1	17.4	2.1
Cherokee	81	1 155	43.3	20.0	51	105	8.1	1.7	172.4	75.9	43.7	5.8
Childress	10	149	6.5	2.9	5	26	1.1	0.3	44.6	14.2	6.6	1.0
Clay	6	114	4.1	1.8	5	19	1.9	0.3	39.8	19.8	8.0	0.7
Cochran	1	D	D	D	1	D	D	D	34.3	6.6	3.3	0.9
Coke	NA	NA	NA	NA	5	14	0.8	0.1	16.4	8.9	3.5	0.3
Coleman	17	193	7.9	3.0	14	40	5.5	0.5	66.1	26.5	17.1	1.5
Collin	903	9 790	793.9	309.0	480	2 868	169.6	54.3	905.2	344.5	112.1	14.9
Collingsworth	5	133	3.8	2.2	3	7	0.7	0.1	26.7	7.7	4.6	0.7
Colorado	28	349	16.4	6.7	31	91	5.4	1.4	103.6	40.7	19.5	2.8
Comal	151	1 335	69.3	28.7	126	645	37.9	11.5	317.5	188.6	47.8	4.9
Comanche	25	357	13.2	6.0	11	53	3.0	0.8	73.0	31.5	19.2	1.7
Concho	4	D	D	D	2	D	D	D	20.9	6.0	3.9	0.3
Cooke	51	553	24.5	9.7	45	220	11.4	2.9	124.5	66.1	28.3	3.1
Coryell	33	439	18.3	7.9	55	200	11.3	2.9	209.1	129.6	21.3	3.8
Cottle	4	58	1.4	0.6	3	D	D	D	17.8	5.1	2.4	0.4
Crane	8	133	7.0	4.1	4	10	1.1	0.1	11.6	5.9	3.7	0.5
Crockett	2	D	D	D	7	66	2.9	1.0	18.1	6.3	2.1	0.6
Crosby	6	D	D	D	7	11	1.2	0.1	55.1	12.0	10.9	1.5
Culberson	1	D	D	D	1	D	D	D	12.2	3.1	2.5	0.9
Dallam	5	18	1.3	0.6	14	D	D	D	57.6	14.4	6.5	0.7
Dallas	5 123	69 423	5 748.0	2 306.3	3 683	30 022	2 019.0	651.6	8 971.8	2 575.8	1 206.6	258.3
Dawson	20	169	7.6	2.8	27	116	5.3	1.4	101.6	23.9	21.2	3.2
Deaf Smith	17	245	9.5	3.9	36	141	9.5	2.3	90.2	24.0	12.7	4.0
Delta	6	172	5.5	2.5	4	D	D	D	33.5	11.6	6.7	1.0
Denton	599	7 690	531.4	215.6	421	2 850	212.3	58.0	671.1	305.7	109.7	13.6
De Witt	26	407	19.0	6.9	28	83	5.3	1.3	103.4	35.8	21.5	3.6
Dickens	4	54	1.1	0.4	3	5	0.7	0.1	21.8	6.0	6.4	0.4
Dimmit	19	141	6.5	2.6	12	95	5.2	1.4	70.4	12.5	8.5	4.4
Donley	2	D	D	D	4	9	0.7	0.2	22.8	9.7	4.5	0.5
Duval	10	498	21.9	11.3	8	63	2.9	0.9	81.4	19.2	18.1	5.1
Eastland	39	447	19.3	8.5	33	111	6.7	1.7	105.1	49.1	24.9	2.7
Ector	227	3 674	163.7	68.9	233	1 777	194.4	40.8	379.2	177.4	89.3	23.3
Edwards	1	D	D	D	4	D	D	D	13.1	3.3	5.3	0.6
Ellis	113	1 385	73.2	31.0	108	488	31.1	7.9	318.7	147.9	68.0	10.4
El Paso	984	16 524	1 165.3	455.8	824	5 779	265.7	87.6	3 073.8	1 015.1	363.3	162.1
Erath	56	911	46.3	19.3	61	300	14.0	4.1	113.7	58.4	26.1	2.8
Falls	19	395	14.0	6.3	25	61	3.6	0.8	113.0	37.8	17.0	3.9
Fannin	34	699	24.5	12.4	24	82	5.9	1.2	169.6	68.2	30.1	3.0
Fayette	44	589	25.4	9.8	49	168	8.4	2.3	109.8	52.0	25.2	1.9
Fisher	5	57	2.3	0.9	6	16	1.1	0.2	38.7	10.3	5.9	0.4
Floyd	11	103	4.5	1.6	12	44	3.5	0.9	66.4	13.6	8.0	1.5
Foard	3	49	1.7	0.9	2	D	D	D	18.9	4.4	2.3	0.2
Fort Bend	441	4 969	297.4	122.0	337	2 296	141.9	44.5	527.2	233.7	74.1	16.3
Franklin	13	2 632	29.5	18.5	14	31	2.5	0.7	34.7	17.3	8.6	0.8
Freestone	26	310	11.3	4.6	20	83	5.4	1.2	69.6	34.6	12.4	2.3
Frio	22	288	12.7	4.6	13	54	1.9	0.6	62.5	17.6	9.8	4.1
Gaines	11	111	7.5	2.4	31	115	9.1	2.1	81.7	15.7	11.3	2.0
Galveston	360	4 424	215.2	97.2	358	2 159	134.4	39.7	1 044.3	399.5	195.1	33.9
Garza	3	84	2.3	1.1	4	12	0.9	0.2	25.0	8.1	6.4	0.8
Gillespie	56	587	29.5	10.2	47	144	9.7	2.2	95.0	61.7	20.0	0.6
Glasscock	NA	NA	NA	NA	2	D	D	D	16.0	1.1	0.5	0.1
Goliad	5	110	4.7	2.0	4	8	0.4	0.1	30.1	12.7	6.6	1.1
Gonzales	20	202	7.6	3.1	26	119	5.0	1.4	97.6	37.7	16.2	3.6
Gray	47	1 147	58.5	24.1	44	160	10.4	2.7	108.3	51.3	32.2	2.5
Grayson	278	4 362	225.0	104.6	123	649	32.9	9.6	469.8	235.2	96.5	11.8
Gregg	330	5 135	305.2	129.6	232	1 637	105.3	29.9	460.3	236.4	100.8	18.1
Grimes	17	363	13.4	5.8	16	46	3.6	0.7	83.1	35.5	16.9	3.6

1. Firms subject to federal tax.   2. October 1, 1998 to September 30, 1999.   3. State totals may include programs not allocated by county.

Table B. States and Counties — Federal Funds and Local Government Finances

	Federal funds and grants, fiscal 1999[1] (cont'd)							Local government finances, 1997				
	Expenditures (mil dol) (cont'd)							General revenue				
	Procurement contract awards			Grants[2]						Taxes		
											Per capita[3] (dollars)	
STATE County	Salaries and wages	Defense	Other	Medicaid and other health-related	Nutrition and family welfare	Education	Other	Total (mil dol)	Intergovernmental (mil dol)	Total (mil dol)	Total	Property
	171	172	173	174	175	176	177	178	179	180	181	182
TEXAS—Cont'd												
Caldwell	2.9	0.0	0.9	22.8	1.4	1.8	3.4	53.4	26.3	12.9	407	329
Calhoun	3.0	0.2	0.6	8.5	1.6	0.8	8.4	72.9	6.4	33.3	1 601	1 419
Callahan	1.5	0.3	0.4	5.2	0.6	0.6	0.8	22.5	13.4	7.1	552	459
Cameron	102.2	11.2	11.2	273.1	65.8	34.1	96.4	726.9	441.5	157.7	492	367
Camp	1.5	0.2	0.4	11.8	0.6	0.5	0.6	19.7	7.4	8.5	777	663
Carson	0.9	0.5	0.2	1.3	0.2	0.1	3.5	14.3	2.2	10.1	1 510	1 401
Cass	3.8	0.0	1.0	26.1	5.3	1.4	20.1	79.0	27.4	24.7	808	697
Castro	0.8	0.0	0.2	3.0	1.8	0.7	0.1	19.6	10.4	6.3	753	619
Chambers	2.4	2.4	1.4	5.9	1.2	0.4	0.5	69.2	10.8	50.0	2 122	2 002
Cherokee	4.3	0.0	1.2	29.3	3.4	1.9	1.0	64.5	33.2	22.0	514	412
Childress	1.5	0.0	0.3	4.1	0.7	0.5	8.5	18.5	2.4	3.6	477	352
Clay	1.3	0.0	0.4	2.9	0.4	0.2	2.6	36.9	9.5	6.6	636	588
Cochran	0.7	0.0	0.1	2.1	0.3	0.3	0.1	16.3	4.6	8.9	2 241	2 114
Coke	0.7	0.0	0.2	1.0	0.2	0.1	0.4	11.9	3.9	4.1	1 190	1 090
Coleman	2.3	0.3	0.6	7.9	3.2	0.5	2.6	22.9	11.7	5.4	559	432
Collin	46.4	271.9	32.7	34.3	7.9	5.2	20.9	849.2	110.5	539.4	1 344	1 145
Collingsworth	1.2	0.0	0.3	3.0	0.3	0.2	0.1	10.5	5.0	2.4	717	606
Colorado	2.8	0.0	0.7	16.1	1.6	0.7	3.5	41.4	13.6	16.1	854	727
Comal	16.6	6.2	5.2	13.5	3.0	1.6	6.3	134.4	37.2	71.5	1 012	837
Comanche	2.2	0.0	0.5	9.8	0.6	0.5	1.4	34.9	11.3	7.4	545	470
Concho	0.8	0.0	0.2	2.4	0.2	0.1	0.0	15.9	2.6	3.3	1 056	885
Cooke	3.9	0.0	1.0	8.2	1.4	1.0	4.3	93.3	30.4	25.8	782	602
Coryell	10.7	6.7	1.4	11.1	2.8	12.8	3.7	104.4	58.5	24.5	317	235
Cottle	0.6	0.0	0.1	1.8	0.2	0.2	0.0	4.9	2.6	1.8	902	729
Crane	0.3	0.0	0.1	0.7	0.1	0.2	0.0	30.6	0.9	26.9	5 899	5 742
Crockett	0.3	0.0	0.1	2.1	0.4	0.3	5.1	18.7	1.9	12.6	2 799	2 724
Crosby	0.9	0.0	0.2	4.8	0.9	0.6	0.2	17.5	10.3	5.2	707	605
Culberson	2.3	0.2	0.0	1.4	0.1	0.2	0.0	8.8	2.7	4.2	1 330	1 154
Dallam	1.1	0.0	0.7	1.4	0.5	0.4	9.0	15.7	5.9	7.4	1 158	925
Dallas	1 416.6	1 759.5	418.8	653.6	146.8	74.6	347.9	5 985.1	1 174.8	3 078.1	1 521	1 100
Dawson	2.6	0.0	0.5	9.6	4.4	1.1	0.4	38.1	11.2	15.3	1 032	898
Deaf Smith	2.0	0.0	1.1	8.8	2.5	1.4	0.4	36.1	18.4	11.3	580	490
Delta	1.0	1.2	0.3	5.9	0.7	0.2	1.8	11.9	7.1	3.4	688	583
Denton	55.9	85.7	12.5	27.1	6.2	10.1	13.3	536.0	119.8	308.6	845	709
De Witt	2.8	0.0	0.6	19.3	2.4	1.0	12.1	54.5	32.6	11.9	606	522
Dickens	0.6	0.0	0.1	2.3	0.4	0.1	0.0	7.0	3.7	2.5	1 129	786
Dimmit	5.5	0.0	0.2	16.0	5.4	1.5	15.2	32.2	15.7	7.3	697	552
Donley	0.7	0.0	0.1	2.0	0.3	0.1	0.1	16.0	6.3	2.9	769	613
Duval	2.9	0.0	0.2	27.2	2.4	1.2	0.5	40.7	16.7	13.8	1 014	885
Eastland	3.1	0.0	0.9	12.5	0.9	0.7	5.3	49.9	22.2	9.9	555	436
Ector	11.2	0.1	3.3	33.8	13.8	7.5	13.7	415.2	109.5	115.8	929	699
Edwards	0.9	0.0	0.1	1.4	0.3	0.2	0.3	9.1	4.1	3.9	1 039	952
Ellis	10.2	0.5	2.8	30.5	3.5	2.5	25.2	180.3	70.6	82.4	819	679
El Paso	634.5	192.2	56.7	318.6	85.8	53.1	138.2	1 582.9	756.8	507.8	724	557
Erath	4.0	0.0	0.9	11.6	1.2	1.3	0.9	55.0	23.8	22.1	707	523
Falls	10.9	0.0	0.9	23.9	1.9	0.9	5.0	26.9	15.7	7.8	438	336
Fannin	20.0	0.2	1.3	23.9	2.7	0.8	5.2	44.1	24.6	13.5	488	402
Fayette	3.7	0.6	1.4	18.4	1.0	0.6	1.6	37.3	8.4	21.5	1 020	896
Fisher	1.1	0.0	0.2	3.6	0.3	0.3	0.1	14.3	4.7	4.3	991	902
Floyd	1.4	0.0	0.4	5.9	1.3	0.6	0.1	20.9	10.5	5.4	656	565
Foard	0.3	0.0	0.1	1.6	1.3	0.0	2.2	8.4	4.5	1.7	960	852
Fort Bend	29.1	5.8	7.7	28.6	8.2	6.4	69.5	586.7	161.4	339.4	1 057	945
Franklin	0.8	0.0	0.2	3.4	0.3	0.2	1.4	22.5	3.6	7.8	808	694
Freestone	1.9	0.2	0.5	12.3	1.1	0.5	1.0	33.4	6.2	17.5	998	885
Frio	1.0	0.0	0.6	15.8	3.5	1.4	4.5	46.9	16.6	9.0	568	464
Gaines	1.1	0.0	0.2	4.3	1.1	1.1	0.2	57.3	6.0	35.7	2 384	2 311
Galveston	55.5	37.4	96.2	134.3	16.9	9.3	28.3	701.8	155.0	395.5	1 628	1 437
Garza	0.7	0.0	0.2	2.5	0.7	0.2	0.1	13.1	3.8	7.2	1 551	1 386
Gillespie	3.8	0.8	0.7	3.0	1.4	0.4	1.4	32.5	7.7	17.8	895	700
Glasscock	0.1	0.0	0.0	0.5	0.1	0.1	1.5	6.9	0.7	5.8	3 964	3 847
Goliad	0.9	0.0	0.2	5.7	0.6	0.2	0.2	13.9	3.1	8.8	1 294	1 209
Gonzales	7.8	0.1	0.6	19.6	2.2	1.0	2.9	43.1	17.3	10.9	621	544
Gray	3.3	1.2	0.8	8.7	0.8	0.6	0.2	41.9	10.0	23.8	1 004	874
Grayson	15.6	1.4	7.9	44.0	6.7	2.5	33.7	217.3	82.9	85.6	843	680
Gregg	17.4	0.5	3.6	51.4	7.5	3.8	12.8	256.6	84.5	130.5	1 153	878
Grimes	2.3	0.1	0.6	18.9	1.9	0.9	0.2	33.3	13.9	15.4	676	569

1. October 1, 1998 to September 30, 1999.　2. State totals may include programs not allocated by county.　3. Based on the resident population estimated as of July 1 of the year shown.

Table B. States and Counties — **Local Government Finances, Government Employment, and Elections**

STATE County	Local government finances, 1997 (cont'd) Direct general expenditure Total (mil dol)	Per capita[1] (dollars)	Education	Health and hospitals	Police protection	Public welfare	Highways	Debt outstanding Total (mil dol)	Per capita[1] (dollars)	Government employment, 1998 Federal civilian	Federal military	State and local	Presidential election, 2000 Percent of vote cast — Democratic	Republican	All other
	183	184	185	186	187	188	189	190	191	192	193	194	195	196	197
TEXAS—Cont'd															
Caldwell	57.2	1 809	50.8	13.4	3.0	0.3	2.9	22.9	725	60	86	1 660	41.1	55.3	3.6
Calhoun	71.0	3 415	37.1	23.6	3.3	1.4	3.4	78.2	3 759	43	95	1 339	42.1	56.7	1.1
Callahan	21.9	1 711	80.1	0.2	2.9	0.2	1.2	5.0	393	30	34	650	24.0	74.7	1.3
Cameron	693.3	2 161	66.3	1.4	3.8	0.7	2.6	787.6	2 455	1 893	942	21 352	53.5	44.8	1.7
Camp	19.1	1 744	72.4	0.3	3.3	0.0	4.8	14.6	1 329	30	29	482	42.9	56.1	1.0
Carson	14.5	2 165	67.6	0.2	4.0	0.2	10.0	0.0	2	198	18	427	17.5	80.8	1.7
Cass	71.7	2 348	50.7	22.5	3.6	0.2	3.6	27.0	885	73	82	2 055	41.9	57.1	1.0
Castro	18.0	2 168	72.5	1.1	5.4	0.0	5.0	8.5	1 022	25	22	721	30.9	68.3	0.8
Chambers	68.9	2 924	62.0	5.3	4.8	0.5	5.2	37.0	1 569	52	63	1 413	29.5	69.0	1.5
Cherokee	64.6	1 510	66.7	1.3	4.4	0.9	4.9	33.5	783	82	114	3 996	32.7	66.0	1.3
Childress	19.4	2 538	40.6	42.4	4.0	0.0	2.1	0.7	89	37	20	1 131	28.3	70.8	0.8
Clay	37.0	3 552	35.9	0.6	2.0	0.2	4.0	289.0	27 772	28	28	520	31.5	67.1	1.4
Cochran	16.2	4 078	63.7	12.9	2.6	0.7	4.7	1.0	243	17	10	411	29.4	68.9	1.7
Coke	11.4	3 313	52.8	0.1	2.1	25.9	3.9	1.1	332	16	0	407	23.4	75.0	1.5
Coleman	23.7	2 472	59.5	16.9	3.0	0.0	3.3	9.0	939	43	25	765	23.8	75.1	1.1
Collin	891.8	2 222	58.3	2.4	4.0	0.0	4.6	1 401.9	3 493	788	1 140	18 638	24.4	73.1	2.5
Collingsworth	10.7	3 222	49.9	24.5	3.1	0.0	5.5	2.1	629	22	0	300	30.3	68.8	0.8
Colorado	38.3	2 027	59.7	14.7	3.6	0.8	5.4	10.1	532	59	51	1 012	30.7	67.8	1.5
Comal	140.1	1 982	67.5	1.3	4.8	0.3	2.6	136.2	1 927	172	195	3 519	21.8	75.1	3.1
Comanche	30.5	2 246	42.0	37.7	1.4	0.6	4.5	4.2	308	54	36	849	32.6	66.4	1.0
Concho	7.7	2 489	53.5	0.7	2.0	0.5	3.7	15.1	4 854	25	0	255	24.3	74.2	1.5
Cooke	89.2	2 702	56.6	21.3	3.4	0.1	3.3	24.1	731	71	87	2 483	23.4	75.2	1.4
Coryell	88.8	1 146	66.0	11.2	3.6	0.0	2.6	86.5	1 117	314	207	5 733	29.8	68.4	1.8
Cottle	4.8	2 472	67.9	0.9	1.8	0.5	4.3	1.0	501	17	0	160	31.8	66.3	1.8
Crane	19.7	4 313	48.6	13.3	4.8	3.2	2.6	4.4	959	0	12	384	23.4	75.3	1.3
Crockett	18.2	4 029	51.4	14.1	1.8	0.3	6.0	1.7	374	0	12	399	33.4	66.1	0.5
Crosby	17.2	2 338	75.5	1.5	3.0	0.0	5.5	1.2	156	24	19	532	35.2	63.4	1.3
Culberson	8.3	2 636	64.2	0.1	2.8	0.1	3.7	6.2	1 971	54	0	286	57.0	40.8	2.2
Dallam	15.1	2 372	67.0	1.7	6.1	0.1	7.2	1.0	159	27	18	825	19.6	79.4	1.0
Dallas	5 588.5	2 762	41.5	12.0	6.3	0.3	3.5	7 659.5	3 786	27 913	7 182	112 224	44.9	52.6	2.5
Dawson	36.9	2 492	54.1	20.4	3.6	0.5	5.3	76.6	5 176	60	39	1 292	30.2	69.0	0.8
Deaf Smith	35.9	1 845	63.3	9.9	6.6	0.2	3.9	3.2	166	49	51	1 366	24.9	74.0	1.1
Delta	15.0	3 035	79.5	0.0	1.1	0.1	3.7	11.4	2 305	25	13	315	38.2	60.2	1.6
Denton	573.3	1 570	61.9	0.7	5.4	0.3	3.2	938.6	2 571	1 321	1 028	21 068	27.3	69.6	3.0
De Witt	53.6	2 723	52.2	32.3	2.6	0.0	3.2	11.5	582	48	52	2 205	25.4	73.4	1.2
Dickens	8.3	3 678	69.8	0.0	2.7	0.4	3.7	0.4	182	16	0	179	32.2	66.9	0.9
Dimmit	27.8	2 649	60.2	18.3	2.0	0.1	3.2	4.9	464	95	28	945	71.4	27.5	1.1
Donley	16.1	4 228	60.1	0.4	1.6	23.6	3.1	15.2	3 993	18	10	406	20.9	77.5	1.5
Duval	44.1	3 244	51.8	20.0	3.8	1.2	3.7	5.0	366	66	36	1 238	79.3	20.1	0.6
Eastland	47.6	2 664	70.6	12.4	2.0	0.1	2.6	12.1	675	63	47	1 382	27.7	70.6	1.7
Ector	407.7	3 269	39.7	37.2	4.0	0.1	2.1	246.1	1 973	214	336	9 105	28.6	69.6	1.8
Edwards	8.0	2 144	68.4	0.0	4.7	0.8	0.4	3.3	873	17	10	184	27.9	70.8	1.4
Ellis	183.5	1 823	71.1	0.0	4.6	0.3	4.4	174.6	1 735	207	275	4 589	28.5	69.9	1.6
El Paso	1 543.2	2 200	60.6	10.3	5.7	0.6	1.6	1 258.7	1 794	8 643	11 908	43 448	57.8	39.7	2.5
Erath	54.5	1 743	51.1	14.8	6.3	0.0	5.1	24.9	796	88	84	2 904	25.2	73.1	1.7
Falls	27.4	1 543	76.4	0.1	3.2	0.1	2.9	5.2	293	404	46	1 549	42.3	56.7	1.0
Fannin	47.2	1 707	73.7	0.4	4.0	0.0	4.9	23.9	864	551	75	1 808	39.7	58.7	1.6
Fayette	35.2	1 668	58.3	1.6	5.0	0.3	9.8	12.8	608	80	57	1 413	27.1	70.9	2.0
Fisher	14.0	3 221	39.8	31.6	0.0	0.1	5.8	4.5	1 033	27	11	359	47.2	51.7	1.1
Floyd	20.5	2 497	65.8	21.9	2.6	0.0	3.3	0.3	33	38	22	652	24.0	75.6	0.4
Foard	4.9	2 839	52.1	2.5	1.7	0.1	5.2	3.6	2 094	10	0	125	47.3	51.4	1.3
Fort Bend	617.7	1 923	62.7	0.5	5.2	1.0	3.8	706.2	2 199	458	897	16 477	38.5	59.6	1.9
Franklin	20.6	2 146	33.4	29.5	4.3	0.4	7.3	51.7	5 391	16	26	351	29.3	69.7	1.0
Freestone	33.9	1 933	57.5	16.8	3.9	0.0	4.4	4.1	233	38	47	1 165	34.9	64.0	1.2
Frio	49.5	3 119	57.6	1.5	2.8	0.3	3.5	177.1	11 155	27	42	1 289	56.1	43.0	0.9
Gaines	58.4	3 894	56.4	24.8	2.5	0.1	6.7	0.9	63	35	40	1 151	20.9	77.8	1.3
Galveston	704.7	2 900	54.3	7.1	5.3	0.3	3.4	794.6	3 270	918	1 027	28 121	43.0	54.2	2.8
Garza	12.1	2 606	65.1	9.5	6.3	0.3	1.2	0.1	13	17	12	322	25.6	73.6	0.8
Gillespie	30.4	1 529	56.0	1.5	5.7	0.3	4.1	24.9	1 250	78	53	909	15.2	81.6	3.2
Glasscock	5.5	3 770	61.5	0.0	2.1	0.0	14.6	0.0	0	0	0	147	6.8	92.5	0.7
Goliad	13.3	1 962	61.6	2.0	9.7	0.0	9.3	5.6	821	19	19	424	36.4	62.1	1.5
Gonzales	37.7	2 147	55.5	16.4	4.2	0.0	4.9	6.6	378	71	47	1 206	30.9	67.4	1.6
Gray	48.4	2 039	62.9	0.4	4.2	0.2	6.8	19.6	824	65	63	1 534	16.8	82.2	0.9
Grayson	230.0	2 265	63.1	3.3	4.9	1.3	3.6	313.4	3 086	337	274	5 296	34.2	64.1	1.7
Gregg	265.9	2 350	54.8	9.5	6.3	0.9	5.1	206.1	1 821	361	302	6 596	29.3	69.6	1.2
Grimes	36.5	1 596	71.1	1.0	6.7	0.0	5.2	25.0	1 093	45	62	1 818	36.0	61.7	2.3

1. Based on the resident population estimated as of July 1 of the year shown.

Table B. States and Counties — **Land Area and Population**

STATE/ County code	MSA/ PMSA/ NECMA code[1]	County Type[2]	STATE County	Land area,[3] (sq km) 1990	Population and population characteristics, 1999												
					Total persons	Rank	Per square kilometer	White	Black	Am. Indian, Eskimo, Aleut	Asian and Pacific Islander	Percent Hispanic[4]	Under 5 years	5 to 17 years	18 to 24 years	25 to 34 years	35 to 44 years	45 to 54 years
					Race (percent)								Age (percent)					
				1	2	3	4	5	6	7	8	9	10	11	12	13	14	15

			TEXAS—Cont'd															
48 187	7240	1	Guadalupe	1 842	82 808	615	45.0	92.2	6.1	0.5	1.2	36.4	8.1	20.7	9.2	12.1	15.5	13.8
48 189	...	4	Hale	2 602	36 491	1 179	14.0	92.6	6.0	0.6	0.8	48.3	9.3	22.8	10.5	12.3	12.8	11.5
48 191	...	9	Hall	2 339	3 594	2 942	1.5	91.2	8.2	0.4	0.3	23.8	5.9	19.1	6.8	8.1	12.5	13.6
48 193	...	6	Hamilton	2 165	7 609	2 631	3.5	98.9	0.2	0.3	0.6	7.5	6.3	18.3	6.8	9.3	12.9	14.5
48 195	...	7	Hansford	2 382	5 399	2 813	2.3	98.3	0.1	0.7	0.8	25.0	7.8	22.8	7.0	10.5	14.1	13.7
48 197	...	7	Hardeman	1 801	4 389	2 880	2.4	90.8	7.2	1.5	0.5	15.0	6.7	20.2	6.9	9.0	12.3	12.8
48 199	0840	6	Hardin	2 316	49 684	913	21.5	89.8	9.6	0.4	0.3	2.8	6.4	22.5	8.1	10.3	15.7	14.4
48 201	3360	0	Harris	4 478	3 250 404	3	725.9	73.9	19.8	0.4	5.9	27.9	8.5	20.0	10.4	15.4	17.8	13.0
48 203	4420	3	Harrison	2 328	59 797	794	25.7	68.8	30.4	0.3	0.5	3.1	6.4	21.6	9.7	11.0	15.3	13.6
48 205	...	7	Hartley	3 788	5 274	2 821	1.4	88.7	10.4	0.7	0.2	15.5	4.8	17.1	9.3	15.2	19.2	15.3
48 207	...	7	Haskell	2 339	5 970	2 774	2.6	94.3	4.7	0.5	0.4	24.1	6.3	18.7	6.1	9.4	11.8	11.4
48 209	0640	2	Hays	1 756	92 755	545	52.8	94.9	3.7	0.5	0.9	35.1	7.2	18.4	20.2	12.5	16.2	11.3
48 211	...	9	Hemphill	2 356	3 471	2 955	1.5	98.9	0.3	0.6	0.2	14.3	7.5	23.5	5.9	10.8	16.2	14.0
48 213	1920	1	Henderson	2 265	70 673	697	31.2	90.3	8.8	0.4	0.4	5.4	5.9	17.6	7.5	9.1	13.1	14.7
48 215	4880	2	Hidalgo	4 064	534 907	99	131.6	99.1	0.3	0.2	0.4	88.5	10.3	26.3	11.1	11.9	14.0	10.2
48 217	...	6	Hill	2 493	31 060	1 347	12.5	89.1	10.2	0.4	0.3	11.0	6.5	19.0	8.5	9.5	13.7	13.7
48 219	...	6	Hockley	2 353	23 374	1 597	9.9	94.8	4.5	0.5	0.2	38.0	8.8	23.5	10.9	11.7	13.4	11.8
48 221	2800	1	Hood	1 092	38 750	1 118	35.5	98.1	0.3	0.6	1.0	6.0	6.2	17.8	5.8	10.2	14.5	14.0
48 223	...	6	Hopkins	2 033	30 614	1 360	15.1	89.6	9.5	0.5	0.5	6.5	6.9	19.6	8.8	11.0	14.9	14.0
48 225	...	7	Houston	3 188	22 223	1 646	7.0	68.2	31.2	0.2	0.3	6.2	5.7	19.1	7.3	12.3	14.8	12.6
48 227	...	5	Howard	2 339	31 687	1 325	13.5	93.9	4.3	0.9	0.9	32.6	7.8	19.2	8.5	11.8	14.0	13.3
48 229	...	8	Hudspeth	11 840	3 238	2 974	0.3	99.0	0.6	0.3	0.1	72.2	8.7	23.2	8.6	12.4	14.2	12.4
48 231	1920	1	Hunt	2 179	71 717	684	32.9	87.2	11.5	0.5	0.8	6.0	7.0	19.3	9.5	11.3	14.5	15.4
48 233	...	6	Hutchinson	2 298	23 711	1 587	10.3	93.5	3.4	1.9	1.2	13.1	6.9	21.6	7.4	10.7	14.5	12.2
48 235	...	8	Irion	2 724	1 693	3 083	0.6	99.8	0.1	0.1	0.0	29.2	8.5	19.3	7.6	10.5	13.7	15.6
48 237	...	6	Jack	2 376	7 481	2 640	3.1	98.4	1.1	0.3	0.3	4.6	6.9	20.3	6.0	10.2	14.0	14.4
48 239	...	6	Jackson	2 148	13 648	2 163	6.4	89.6	9.7	0.5	0.1	26.8	6.9	21.1	6.9	10.0	14.4	13.1
48 241	...	6	Jasper	2 428	33 494	1 272	13.8	79.0	20.6	0.3	0.2	2.6	6.1	21.6	7.5	9.7	14.1	14.1
48 243	...	9	Jeff Davis	5 865	2 415	3 025	0.4	98.4	0.7	0.7	0.3	47.1	6.2	20.5	6.8	8.8	14.5	15.6
48 245	0840	2	Jefferson	2 340	241 332	228	103.1	62.7	33.8	0.3	3.2	7.1	6.5	19.3	9.2	12.5	15.5	12.9
48 247	...	6	Jim Hogg	2 943	4 972	2 839	1.7	99.6	0.1	0.2	0.1	93.1	10.0	21.9	8.9	11.0	13.6	12.4
48 249	...	4	Jim Wells	2 239	40 212	1 082	18.0	98.5	0.7	0.3	0.5	77.8	9.0	22.8	8.8	11.2	14.5	12.2
48 251	2800	1	Johnson	1 889	122 594	429	64.9	95.5	3.2	0.5	0.8	10.4	7.3	21.4	8.9	12.1	16.7	14.8
48 253	...	6	Jones	2 411	18 846	1 827	7.8	89.1	9.6	0.7	0.6	24.7	5.7	18.4	9.0	12.9	16.2	13.8
48 255	...	6	Karnes	1 943	15 112	2 057	7.8	89.8	9.3	0.7	0.2	51.7	7.0	18.7	9.4	13.7	14.8	11.1
48 257	1920	1	Kaufman	2 036	68 065	712	33.4	84.0	14.8	0.4	0.7	8.5	7.3	21.9	8.2	11.3	16.5	14.7
48 259	...	6	Kendall	1 716	21 865	1 664	12.7	98.6	0.4	0.5	0.5	21.1	7.1	19.1	7.1	10.1	16.0	15.7
48 261	...	9	Kenedy	3 773	436	3 137	0.1	100.0	0.0	0.0	0.0	81.7	8.9	21.6	8.0	13.5	11.9	13.5
48 263	...	9	Kent	2 337	854	3 120	0.4	99.1	0.8	0.1	0.0	15.3	5.7	18.7	4.3	8.1	11.7	14.1
48 265	...	7	Kerr	2 865	43 234	1 018	15.1	96.2	2.6	0.5	0.6	20.8	6.2	16.8	6.7	9.2	12.7	12.1
48 267	...	7	Kimble	3 240	4 238	2 892	1.3	98.7	0.1	0.3	0.8	23.9	6.2	18.9	5.2	8.2	13.6	15.1
48 269	...	9	King	2 363	318	3 139	0.1	100.0	0.0	0.0	0.0	17.9	6.0	23.3	7.5	11.9	17.0	15.1
48 271	...	9	Kinney	3 532	3 465	2 958	1.0	95.8	2.4	1.3	0.5	55.9	6.8	17.0	6.5	9.4	12.2	10.3
48 273	...	4	Kleberg	2 256	29 680	1 386	13.2	94.7	3.2	0.4	1.7	68.0	8.8	20.1	15.2	12.3	13.3	11.6
48 275	...	9	Knox	2 212	4 104	2 906	1.9	91.8	7.7	0.3	0.1	27.9	7.5	20.9	6.1	9.6	12.5	11.8
48 277	...	5	Lamar	2 375	46 050	969	19.4	82.6	16.0	0.9	0.5	1.6	6.5	19.2	9.2	10.2	14.5	14.4
48 279	...	6	Lamb	2 632	14 765	2 083	5.6	93.3	5.6	0.8	0.4	43.3	7.9	22.3	7.9	10.2	12.1	12.4
48 281	...	6	Lampasas	1 844	17 700	1 886	9.6	95.1	2.5	0.7	1.8	17.2	7.6	20.3	7.8	9.9	14.7	14.8
48 283	...	6	La Salle	3 856	5 992	2 772	1.6	91.2	7.9	0.3	0.6	76.5	8.2	21.7	10.6	15.9	13.9	10.8
48 285	...	6	Lavaca	2 512	18 912	1 822	7.5	91.4	8.2	0.2	0.2	11.8	5.9	19.1	6.9	9.2	13.3	13.2
48 287	...	6	Lee	1 628	14 871	2 072	9.1	83.9	15.7	0.2	0.2	14.3	7.1	22.8	7.4	10.9	14.2	12.4
48 289	...	8	Leon	2 777	14 870	2 073	5.4	85.6	13.8	0.4	0.2	5.4	6.3	19.0	6.8	9.7	13.0	13.3
48 291	3360	1	Liberty	3 004	67 161	718	22.4	83.1	15.9	0.5	0.4	8.2	6.7	20.8	9.1	12.9	16.4	13.8
48 293	...	6	Limestone	2 354	20 620	1 732	8.8	77.9	21.5	0.2	0.4	9.4	6.9	19.7	7.2	11.2	14.6	13.0
48 295	...	9	Lipscomb	2 414	3 023	2 983	1.3	98.1	0.1	1.3	0.5	15.2	7.2	21.7	4.8	10.7	13.5	14.3
48 297	...	6	Live Oak	2 684	10 103	2 413	3.8	98.5	0.4	0.5	0.6	41.7	7.1	20.2	6.6	9.7	14.1	14.2
48 299	...	7	Llano	2 421	13 843	2 148	5.7	99.0	0.2	0.4	0.3	5.3	4.2	11.9	4.2	6.2	11.1	12.9
48 301	...	9	Loving	1 743	113	3 140	0.1	100.0	0.0	0.0	0.0	16.8	7.1	20.4	7.1	9.7	13.3	16.8
48 303	4600	3	Lubbock	2 330	227 890	242	97.8	89.5	8.4	0.4	1.8	28.7	7.8	19.0	14.8	13.3	14.4	11.5
48 305	...	6	Lynn	2 310	6 657	2 714	2.9	96.1	3.2	0.4	0.3	49.2	8.8	22.3	8.2	11.6	11.4	13.9
48 307	...	7	McCulloch	2 770	8 802	2 520	3.2	97.4	2.2	0.2	0.1	33.4	7.5	20.8	7.5	9.0	13.6	12.6
48 309	8800	3	McLennan	2 699	204 244	265	75.7	81.7	16.8	0.4	1.1	16.3	7.4	18.9	13.6	11.5	14.3	12.3
48 311	...	9	McMullen	2 883	801	3 124	0.3	99.9	0.0	0.1	0.0	44.8	6.7	16.1	6.4	9.7	14.5	14.4
48 313	...	6	Madison	1 216	11 881	2 286	9.8	74.8	24.3	0.7	0.2	13.2	5.5	16.3	17.2	14.5	11.8	11.6
48 315	...	8	Marion	987	10 998	2 346	11.1	66.6	32.8	0.5	0.1	2.1	5.7	18.6	6.4	9.3	13.7	15.6
48 317	...	6	Martin	2 369	4 988	2 837	2.1	97.5	2.0	0.3	0.1	46.7	9.4	24.6	7.8	10.9	13.5	13.0

1. MSA = Metropolitan Statistical Area. PMSA = Primary MSA. NECMA = New England County Metropolitan Area. See Appendix A for explanation of these concepts. See Appendix B for list of metropolitan areas identified by type, with component counties.   2. County typology code from the Economic Research Service of USDA. See Appendix A for definition.   3. Dry land or land partially or temporarily covered by water.   4. Hispanic persons may be of any race.

Table B. States and Counties — Population and Households

STATE County	55 to 64 years	65 to 74 years	75 years and over	Percent female	Total persons 1990	Total persons 1980	Percent change 1980–1990	Percent change 1990–1999	Births	Deaths	Net migration	Number	Percent change, 1980–1990	Persons per household	Female family householder[1]	One person
	16	17	18	19	20	21	22	23	24	25	26	27	28	29	30	31
TEXAS—Cont'd																
Guadalupe	9.3	6.4	4.9	50.6	64 873	46 708	38.9	27.6	9 139	5 194	13 801	22 663	44.0	2.80	10.0	19.2
Hale	8.6	6.2	6.0	50.5	34 671	37 592	-7.8	5.2	6 105	2 721	-1 523	11 703	-5.5	2.90	9.2	21.6
Hall	11.8	9.6	12.7	52.3	3 905	5 594	-30.2	-8.0	563	613	-250	1 669	-23.3	2.31	7.4	33.7
Hamilton	13.1	7.1	11.7	51.4	7 733	8 297	-6.8	-1.6	953	1 308	281	3 250	-5.1	2.29	7.1	30.4
Hansford	9.9	7.3	6.9	49.9	5 848	6 209	-5.8	-7.7	720	481	-677	2 112	-6.9	2.73	5.5	21.9
Hardeman	10.8	9.2	12.1	51.4	5 283	6 368	-17.0	-16.9	573	734	-711	2 101	-15.1	2.45	7.8	30.3
Hardin	9.9	7.0	5.7	50.6	41 320	40 721	1.5	20.2	5 882	3 663	6 314	14 693	7.0	2.79	9.8	19.2
Harris	7.2	4.5	3.2	50.4	2 818 101	2 409 547	17.0	15.3	541 351	170 070	68 268	1 026 448	18.0	2.72	12.7	26.2
Harrison	9.6	6.6	6.0	51.8	57 483	52 265	10.0	4.0	6 931	5 462	992	20 705	14.7	2.71	13.1	23.0
Hartley	9.0	4.7	5.4	39.9	3 634	3 987	-8.9	45.1	468	279	1 426	1 332	-2.1	2.66	4.0	20.4
Haskell	12.3	11.0	12.9	51.4	6 820	7 725	-11.7	-12.5	649	1 027	-449	2 753	-7.6	2.43	6.8	27.7
Hays	6.5	4.2	3.5	49.5	65 614	40 594	61.6	41.4	9 682	3 686	21 149	22 218	76.6	2.68	7.9	22.3
Hemphill	9.2	5.6	7.2	50.6	3 720	5 304	-29.9	-6.7	337	336	-239	1 348	-26.6	2.72	6.2	22.0
Henderson	13.4	11.2	7.6	51.1	58 543	42 606	37.4	20.7	7 516	7 070	11 812	22 947	42.6	2.51	8.8	22.6
Hidalgo	6.8	5.4	4.0	51.9	383 545	283 323	35.4	39.5	116 653	21 943	58 369	103 479	36.5	3.67	15.0	13.4
Hill	11.4	8.5	9.2	51.5	27 146	25 024	8.5	14.4	3 476	3 595	4 097	10 268	6.0	2.55	9.0	25.7
Hockley	8.1	6.1	5.5	50.6	24 199	23 230	4.2	-3.4	3 303	1 807	-2 284	7 988	6.2	2.96	8.6	18.9
Hood	12.1	12.0	7.2	50.1	28 981	17 714	63.6	33.7	3 661	3 294	9 460	11 137	64.8	2.57	6.3	19.2
Hopkins	9.8	7.2	7.8	50.5	28 833	25 247	14.2	6.2	3 809	3 175	1 237	10 965	15.1	2.59	8.5	24.2
Houston	10.4	8.3	9.4	48.5	21 375	22 299	-4.1	4.0	2 483	2 856	1 295	7 792	8.2	2.51	13.6	26.4
Howard	10.8	7.9	6.7	49.6	32 343	33 142	-2.4	-2.0	4 288	3 415	-1 445	11 477	-4.1	2.63	11.0	23.7
Hudspeth	9.5	5.7	5.4	48.5	2 915	2 728	6.9	11.1	386	173	124	946	15.1	2.97	8.9	22.1
Hunt	10.2	6.6	6.3	50.8	64 343	55 248	16.5	11.5	8 797	6 411	5 101	24 075	18.4	2.61	9.7	23.9
Hutchinson	10.9	8.7	7.0	50.3	25 689	26 304	-2.3	-7.7	3 145	2 387	-2 653	9 642	-2.0	2.63	6.9	22.5
Irion	10.9	7.4	6.5	49.9	1 629	1 386	17.5	3.9	154	129	40	601	18.5	2.71	6.0	19.1
Jack	12.2	7.4	8.5	51.0	6 981	7 408	-5.8	7.2	809	846	556	2 725	-5.8	2.52	6.7	26.1
Jackson	10.5	9.0	8.1	51.5	13 039	13 352	-2.3	4.7	1 734	1 410	351	4 833	3.2	2.67	9.7	23.7
Jasper	11.3	8.3	7.3	51.9	31 102	30 781	1.0	7.7	4 575	3 631	1 567	11 427	6.7	2.69	11.0	21.9
Jeff Davis	11.7	8.9	7.0	48.3	1 946	1 647	18.2	24.1	157	157	474	779	31.6	2.43	5.8	28.6
Jefferson	10.2	7.5	6.4	51.1	239 389	248 652	-3.7	0.8	33 586	23 447	-7 390	90 520	0.3	2.60	14.1	26.1
Jim Hogg	9.0	6.6	6.6	51.6	5 109	5 168	-1.1	-2.7	752	475	-407	1 675	7.1	3.05	14.4	20.4
Jim Wells	9.1	6.5	5.8	51.0	37 679	36 498	3.2	6.7	6 063	2 964	-448	11 979	7.3	3.11	12.1	18.2
Johnson	8.9	5.2	4.8	49.8	97 165	67 649	43.6	26.2	13 907	8 036	19 621	33 462	44.7	2.85	8.8	17.1
Jones	9.5	6.9	7.7	45.5	16 490	17 268	-4.5	14.3	1 770	1 944	2 597	6 180	-2.9	2.60	8.1	24.4
Karnes	9.0	8.4	8.0	44.6	12 455	13 593	-8.4	21.3	1 691	1 437	2 458	4 337	-4.1	2.82	11.5	23.7
Kaufman	9.4	5.6	5.1	50.8	52 220	39 038	33.8	30.3	7 795	5 055	13 163	17 827	35.5	2.86	10.2	19.0
Kendall	10.3	7.5	7.2	50.9	14 589	10 635	37.2	49.9	2 503	1 611	6 472	5 342	40.5	2.66	8.5	19.7
Kenedy	12.8	5.7	3.9	49.1	460	543	-15.3	-5.2	52	42	-33	145	-14.2	3.10	5.5	16.6
Kent	10.4	13.6	13.3	50.9	1 010	1 145	-11.8	-15.4	62	127	-89	399	-7.4	2.47	4.5	26.6
Kerr	11.2	13.1	11.9	52.4	36 304	28 780	26.1	19.1	4 337	5 041	7 813	14 384	28.8	2.38	8.6	27.4
Kimble	12.3	10.2	10.3	50.7	4 122	4 063	1.5	2.8	449	540	219	1 624	3.8	2.50	8.1	24.4
King	9.1	9.1	0.9	47.2	354	425	-16.7	-10.2	34	9	-62	124	-19.5	2.85	3.2	14.5
Kinney	12.7	16.1	9.0	49.2	3 119	2 279	36.9	11.1	357	335	352	1 187	54.0	2.59	6.4	26.7
Kleberg	7.8	5.8	5.1	51.1	30 274	33 358	-9.2	-2.0	5 112	2 001	-3 883	10 058	-2.2	2.89	12.7	21.8
Knox	10.8	9.4	11.4	51.2	4 837	5 329	-9.2	-15.2	541	600	-660	1 887	-7.6	2.51	7.4	28.8
Lamar	10.1	7.7	8.0	52.2	43 949	42 156	4.3	4.8	6 142	5 173	1 303	16 798	6.9	2.56	11.5	25.0
Lamb	10.1	8.2	8.9	51.3	15 072	18 669	-19.3	-2.0	2 181	1 556	-893	5 488	-14.4	2.72	8.3	24.1
Lampasas	11.3	6.3	7.3	51.1	13 521	12 005	12.6	30.9	2 238	1 592	3 481	5 058	14.6	2.64	8.6	23.2
La Salle	7.6	6.3	4.9	46.0	5 254	5 514	-4.7	14.0	819	479	421	1 701	-1.4	3.05	14.2	21.6
Lavaca	11.0	10.0	11.4	51.7	18 690	19 004	-1.7	1.2	2 204	2 539	635	7 349	2.8	2.49	8.0	27.5
Lee	10.2	7.4	7.7	49.2	12 854	10 952	17.4	15.7	1 760	1 288	1 604	4 706	22.0	2.62	8.3	24.5
Leon	12.8	9.9	9.2	51.2	12 665	9 594	32.0	17.4	1 602	1 662	2 300	5 006	30.8	2.51	8.2	26.2
Liberty	9.5	6.2	4.6	47.5	52 726	47 088	12.0	27.4	8 764	5 228	10 957	18 538	14.2	2.79	10.3	21.1
Limestone	10.6	7.8	8.9	52.4	20 946	20 224	3.6	-1.6	2 546	3 016	206	7 722	4.1	2.54	12.1	27.4
Lipscomb	10.8	8.4	8.7	49.4	3 143	3 766	-16.5	-3.8	347	314	-143	1 230	-12.3	2.55	4.7	25.1
Live Oak	11.4	9.0	7.8	51.1	9 556	9 606	-0.5	5.7	1 118	954	428	3 550	7.3	2.67	7.6	22.6
Llano	17.8	16.8	14.8	52.1	11 631	10 144	14.7	19.0	1 083	2 114	3 285	5 278	19.9	2.15	4.6	27.7
Loving	14.2	8.8	2.7	45.1	107	91	17.6	5.6	3	10	16	42	23.5	2.55	0.0	33.3
Lubbock	8.1	6.1	5.1	50.8	222 636	211 651	5.2	2.4	35 266	15 919	-14 386	81 534	12.3	2.61	10.4	25.5
Lynn	10.4	6.7	6.7	50.8	6 758	8 605	-21.5	-1.5	884	668	-295	2 383	-15.8	2.81	8.2	21.8
McCulloch	10.4	7.9	10.7	51.9	8 778	8 735	0.5	0.3	1 045	1 283	301	3 409	0.3	2.52	8.4	28.0
McLennan	9.2	6.6	6.2	51.4	189 123	170 755	10.8	8.0	28 793	17 872	4 781	70 208	14.1	2.58	12.1	25.8
McMullen	11.5	10.7	10.0	49.6	817	789	3.5	-2.0	66	89	11	319	7.4	2.54	3.8	24.1
Madison	8.6	6.4	8.1	41.8	10 931	10 649	2.6	8.7	1 250	1 201	948	3 349	7.8	2.55	11.2	26.8
Marion	13.4	9.5	7.9	50.5	9 984	10 360	-3.6	10.2	982	1 246	1 308	4 048	4.5	2.45	11.9	27.0
Martin	8.4	6.1	6.5	50.4	4 956	4 684	5.8	0.6	684	380	-261	1 632	5.5	3.01	7.0	19.5

1. No spouse present.

Table B. States and Counties — Vital Statistics, Health Resources, and Crime

STATE County	Births, average 1996–1998 Total	Rate[1]	Deaths, average 1996–1998 Number Total	Number Infant[2]	Rate Total[1]	Rate Infant[3]	Physicians,[4] 1998 Number	Rate[5]	Hospitals,[4] 1998 Number	Beds Number	Beds Rate[5]	Medicare enrollees 1999	Serious crimes known to police, 1998[6] Total Number	Rate[7]
	32	33	34	35	36	37	38	39	40	41	42	43	44	45
TEXAS—Cont'd														
Guadalupe	1 059	13.6	601	8	7.8	7.9	66	82	1	77	96	9 588	2 844	3 589
Hale	639	17.5	300	3	8.2	5.2	42	115	2	174	474	5 288	1 297	3 486
Hall	66	17.7	64	0	17.2	5.1	2	55	1	28	768	846	84	2 230
Hamilton	101	13.3	150	1	19.7	13.2	7	92	1	28	368	1 675	147	1 901
Hansford	81	15.2	56	1	10.6	8.2	2	37	1	113	2 113	852	116	2 115
Hardeman	60	12.9	75	0	16.0	0.0	7	152	2	44	958	1 038	57	1 193
Hardin	640	13.3	444	5	9.2	7.3	24	49	1	57	117	6 581	989	2 010
Harris	59 288	18.8	18 879	372	6.0	6.3	7 743	242	43	10 917	341	273 424	181 819	5 664
Harrison	776	13.0	620	8	10.4	10.3	46	77	1	108	181	8 067	2 334	3 847
Hartley	63	12.2	31	1	6.0	15.9	0	0	0	0	0	160	86	1 652
Haskell	66	10.7	104	1	16.9	15.2	3	49	1	32	520	1 580	99	1 595
Hays	1 241	14.6	439	6	5.1	5.1	103	116	1	113	128	7 929	3 853	4 393
Hemphill	36	10.0	36	0	10.0	0.0	4	113	1	19	538	466	73	1 985
Henderson	930	13.8	857	6	12.7	6.1	54	79	1	102	148	9 944	2 308	3 371
Hidalgo	13 265	26.1	2 609	61	5.1	4.6	520	100	5	1 036	198	52 177	30 408	5 874
Hill	392	13.0	402	4	13.4	9.3	21	69	2	140	459	6 024	1 047	3 430
Hockley	345	14.5	205	1	8.6	2.9	12	50	1	44	185	3 004	688	2 828
Hood	411	11.4	417	4	11.6	8.9	41	110	1	55	148	7 736	1 023	2 780
Hopkins	398	13.1	362	2	11.9	5.0	31	102	1	77	252	5 244	753	2 426
Houston	257	11.8	327	3	15.0	10.4	13	59	1	50	228	4 534	NA	NA
Howard	440	13.6	373	2	11.6	5.3	68	212	1	153	477	5 342	1 672	5 051
Hudspeth	29	9.0	18	0	5.6	0.0	0	0	0	0	0	340	45	1 330
Hunt	993	14.3	716	6	10.3	6.4	61	86	2	138	195	10 751	3 962	5 624
Hutchinson	332	13.8	249	3	10.3	9.0	20	83	1	40	166	4 147	765	3 433
Irion	13	7.8	15	0	8.8	0.0	0	0	0	0	0	267	38	2 204
Jack	85	11.7	93	1	12.8	7.8	4	54	1	18	242	1 268	167	2 246
Jackson	190	13.9	167	1	12.2	7.0	8	58	1	31	227	2 289	233	1 678
Jasper	512	15.4	401	5	12.0	9.8	30	90	2	96	287	5 704	741	2 195
Jeff Davis	16	7.2	17	1	7.6	62.5	2	85	0	0	0	364	17	749
Jefferson	3 440	14.2	2 594	26	10.7	7.7	535	221	7	1 589	657	38 347	15 315	6 227
Jim Hogg	82	16.6	56	1	11.2	12.2	1	20	0	0	0	799	67	1 338
Jim Wells	655	16.5	334	6	8.4	8.7	29	72	1	123	307	5 822	2 157	5 326
Johnson	1 644	14.4	925	13	8.1	8.1	97	82	1	102	86	14 898	3 504	3 022
Jones	177	9.5	206	2	11.1	11.3	4	21	3	85	455	2 861	406	2 124
Karnes	179	14.4	163	1	13.1	5.6	3	24	1	34	275	2 495	120	944
Kaufman	865	13.6	572	5	9.0	5.8	40	61	2	173	263	12 479	2 494	3 842
Kendall	297	14.5	195	1	9.5	4.5	80	377	0	0	0	3 857	416	2 007
Kenedy	7	16.9	5	0	12.3	0.0	0	0	0	0	0	52	6	1 382
Kent	7	8.4	14	0	15.6	0.0	8	909	0	0	0	213	3	342
Kerr	464	10.9	575	4	13.6	7.9	161	372	1	123	284	11 170	1 211	2 795
Kimble	55	13.1	57	1	13.6	18.3	3	73	1	18	436	855	65	1 523
King	2	6.7	1	0	2.9	0.0	0	0	0	0	0	35	2	565
Kinney	38	11.1	41	0	12.0	0.0	3	86	0	0	0	734	4	113
Kleberg	530	17.6	224	6	7.4	10.7	24	80	1	90	298	3 516	1 926	6 271
Knox	56	13.0	60	0	13.9	6.0	3	71	1	14	329	988	123	2 808
Lamar	658	14.4	598	3	13.1	4.6	105	228	2	355	771	8 347	3 278	7 045
Lamb	224	15.1	172	1	11.6	4.5	9	61	1	42	285	2 713	353	2 339
Lampasas	244	14.0	185	2	10.6	8.2	9	51	1	22	124	2 660	386	2 171
La Salle	89	14.9	55	1	9.2	11.2	0	0	0	0	0	761	156	2 586
Lavaca	243	12.9	276	1	14.7	2.8	22	117	2	56	298	4 964	268	1 412
Lee	209	14.2	161	1	11.0	6.4	4	27	0	0	0	2 092	261	1 736
Leon	173	12.1	197	1	13.7	5.8	5	35	0	0	0	3 688	289	1 967
Liberty	1 007	15.7	601	8	9.4	7.9	30	46	2	133	204	8 917	2 108	3 243
Limestone	266	12.8	314	1	15.1	5.0	10	48	2	74	354	4 230	906	4 232
Lipscomb	44	14.5	38	0	12.5	0.0	0	0	0	0	0	611	51	1 657
Live Oak	119	11.8	106	0	10.5	2.8	3	30	0	0	0	1 337	129	1 249
Llano	129	9.8	237	1	17.9	10.3	25	185	1	27	200	4 497	281	2 110
Loving	0	0.0	1	0	5.6	0.0	0	0	0	0	0	18	1	926
Lubbock	3 723	16.2	1 801	32	7.8	8.6	705	307	6	1 551	676	29 062	13 786	5 879
Lynn	98	14.9	65	1	9.9	6.8	3	45	1	24	358	1 010	139	2 075
McCulloch	123	14.0	136	1	15.5	10.9	8	91	1	27	309	1 813	214	2 398
McLennan	3 162	15.6	1 924	21	9.5	6.8	368	181	3	638	314	30 158	12 950	6 335
McMullen	7	9.3	10	0	12.3	0.0	0	0	0	0	0	134	2	251
Madison	147	12.4	134	1	11.2	6.8	10	84	1	28	236	1 733	303	2 498
Marion	122	11.5	159	1	14.9	5.5	5	46	0	0	0	1 800	445	4 102
Martin	72	14.5	45	0	9.1	0.0	4	79	1	26	516	634	58	1 124

1. Per 1,000 estimated resident population, average 1996–1998.   2. Deaths of infants under 1 year old.   3. Deaths of infants under 1 year old per 1,000 live births.   4. Data subject to copyright.   5. Per 100,000 resident population as of July 1 of the year shown.   6. Data for serious crimes have not been adjusted for underreporting; this may affect comparability between geographic areas and over time.   7. Per 100,000 population estimated by the FBI.

Table B. States and Counties — Crime, Education, Money Income, and Poverty

	Serious crimes known to police, 1998[1] (cont'd) Rate[2]		School enrollment and attainment, 1990 — Enrollment[3]		Attainment[4] (percent)		Local government expenditures, fiscal 1997[5]		Money income 1989 Per capita[6]	Households Median			Income and poverty, 1997 Percent below poverty level		
STATE County	Violent	Property	Total	Percent private	High school graduate or more	Bachelor's degree or more	Total current expenditures (mil dol)	Current expenditures per student (dollars)	Per capita (dollars)	Dollars	Percent change, 1979–1989 (constant 1989 dollars)	Percent with $100,000 or more	Median household income	All persons	Persons under 18	Persons 5–17 in families
	46	47	48	49	50	51	52	53	54	55	56	57	58	59	60	61
TEXAS—Cont'd																
Guadalupe	218	3 371	17 398	12.6	69.8	13.9	72.9	5 120	11 330	26 801	2.1	1.8	34 874	15.3	21.7	21.6
Hale	277	3 209	9 705	12.5	61.1	12.7	43.4	5 035	9 932	21 183	-6.5	2.3	28 369	22.0	29.1	28.8
Hall	292	1 938	737	0.3	61.3	8.7	5.6	6 108	9 376	13 987	-17.1	1.2	20 045	27.4	40.6	39.7
Hamilton	155	1 746	1 522	7.6	62.9	12.4	9.4	5 960	11 193	18 161	6.9	1.9	25 321	19.6	27.9	27.6
Hansford	164	1 951	1 582	2.4	71.7	15.3	8.9	6 680	12 136	25 787	-13.6	3.1	36 272	10.6	13.4	15.1
Hardeman	251	942	1 220	1.8	62.8	11.0	7.0	6 843	10 502	18 657	-11.8	4.0	25 513	19.4	27.0	28.4
Hardin	187	1 823	11 165	6.6	70.6	9.7	55.2	4 911	11 178	25 289	-21.1	1.2	35 279	13.6	19.0	18.1
Harris	841	4 823	796 212	11.6	74.9	25.4	3 054.3	5 016	15 202	30 970	-11.2	5.5	39 037	15.2	20.9	19.0
Harrison	371	3 476	16 113	10.3	70.4	12.7	61.3	4 783	10 173	22 625	-9.7	1.5	29 805	18.6	24.6	23.7
Hartley	173	1 479	933	7.8	84.6	19.7	2.6	8 246	14 254	28 826	-9.4	4.0	43 504	6.9	5.9	7.7
Haskell	145	1 450	1 396	4.9	58.4	9.0	8.4	6 879	10 099	19 386	-2.3	1.5	23 824	23.9	36.1	34.2
Hays	342	4 051	26 265	6.6	76.9	26.4	86.4	5 151	11 422	25 492	17.3	2.2	37 341	13.1	16.6	16.7
Hemphill	54	1 931	902	1.4	72.9	12.3	8.0	9 096	14 244	28 697	-10.8	4.3	28 383	8.3	9.5	10.7
Henderson	283	3 088	12 997	5.4	64.7	10.3	48.8	4 948	10 692	20 747	-8.8	1.4	28 383	16.3	24.9	22.7
Hidalgo	516	5 358	134 820	4.4	46.6	11.5	709.3	5 403	6 630	16 703	-11.3	1.7	20 034	37.6	47.9	42.9
Hill	206	3 224	6 034	5.4	61.5	10.7	34.6	6 007	10 703	20 067	5.3	1.5	27 481	18.8	27.1	26.4
Hockley	559	2 269	7 763	2.5	64.0	12.4	34.1	6 211	10 648	23 713	-9.3	2.3	31 256	19.5	25.5	25.9
Hood	149	2 631	6 812	10.0	74.7	15.2	29.6	4 321	14 961	31 627	4.2	4.2	38 973	10.5	17.4	16.4
Hopkins	313	2 113	6 524	3.4	62.9	11.2	29.2	4 904	11 049	20 771	-3.3	2.4	28 126	15.7	22.1	21.4
Houston	NA	NA	4 835	7.1	64.0	10.1	22.5	5 495	9 965	18 138	9.7	2.4	25 157	24.1	32.6	31.0
Howard	372	4 679	8 162	4.0	65.2	11.8	31.2	5 114	10 644	23 145	-8.1	1.4	29 347	19.4	26.4	26.8
Hudspeth	236	1 094	831	1.8	48.1	8.0	5.1	6 182	7 994	15 401	-12.6	3.8	19 987	32.9	44.2	43.6
Hunt	620	5 004	16 680	7.3	69.1	15.9	68.4	5 065	11 845	25 317	8.9	1.8	31 542	15.5	23.0	21.2
Hutchinson	256	3 177	7 083	5.8	71.9	13.0	28.5	5 280	11 677	26 717	-15.6	1.6	36 739	12.3	16.6	16.4
Irion	348	1 856	391	6.1	70.5	13.8	2.9	7 650	11 659	24 280	-4.7	1.8	31 533	13.0	18.6	20.9
Jack	161	2 085	1 584	5.3	62.2	11.0	10.6	5 836	11 010	21 627	-5.2	2.1	28 349	16.6	22.4	22.5
Jackson	101	1 577	3 023	5.3	56.6	10.2	19.0	5 535	10 225	20 687	-15.5	2.0	30 345	16.0	22.0	21.6
Jasper	261	1 934	7 854	4.2	64.4	8.3	40.2	5 279	9 659	20 451	-14.6	1.1	28 930	19.2	27.6	24.5
Jeff Davis	396	353	486	4.3	69.5	25.1	3.1	7 794	9 975	18 995	7.8	1.4	25 895	16.6	25.5	28.1
Jefferson	740	5 487	64 519	11.0	74.4	15.5	233.1	5 234	12 348	25 132	-18.6	2.6	32 362	19.1	27.3	24.1
Jim Hogg	260	1 078	1 610	3.5	48.9	11.2	7.8	6 256	6 852	14 704	-23.9	0.5	21 817	30.5	40.1	41.6
Jim Wells	659	4 667	11 238	4.8	55.3	9.4	46.3	5 135	8 080	18 315	-24.4	1.9	24 586	27.0	34.7	33.8
Johnson	277	2 745	25 483	10.6	71.9	11.5	106.1	4 666	12 054	30 612	0.1	2.4	37 768	11.3	16.0	15.2
Jones	225	1 899	4 004	5.2	60.8	10.9	20.7	6 293	9 910	19 270	-8.9	1.5	25 380	23.4	27.5	27.0
Karnes	212	732	3 343	2.4	51.3	8.9	17.4	5 953	8 229	16 155	-21.4	1.5	23 226	30.4	31.8	34.1
Kaufman	394	3 448	13 616	8.3	67.9	10.9	77.4	4 858	11 567	27 280	4.4	2.5	35 477	13.8	19.0	18.1
Kendall	96	1 911	3 614	8.1	80.2	19.9	23.8	4 574	13 426	27 433	0.4	2.7	39 212	10.6	15.1	15.6
Kenedy	230	1 152	129	7.0	43.1	7.8	0.8	17 261	9 212	16 500	-13.2	6.0	23 134	20.1	26.8	32.4
Kent	342	0	212	5.7	63.4	10.3	2.1	10 959	10 087	19 508	-3.5	1.0	28 148	11.4	15.4	17.1
Kerr	143	2 652	7 700	15.4	75.9	20.2	35.5	5 128	12 899	23 205	-5.8	3.7	30 766	14.5	26.5	25.6
Kimble	23	1 500	862	3.8	64.7	12.4	4.7	5 996	11 372	17 553	-15.0	3.5	23 530	18.8	28.3	28.4
King	0	565	104	1.9	78.2	24.5	1.5	17 424	12 027	27 625	31.2	1.6	32 386	9.6	13.1	14.2
Kinney	0	113	729	1.1	56.2	11.0	4.0	6 578	7 931	15 750	-7.8	0.6	21 850	26.0	41.4	42.6
Kleberg	488	5 783	10 824	5.4	63.3	18.9	38.1	5 716	9 580	21 887	-4.4	1.9	27 915	25.5	34.0	34.2
Knox	411	2 397	1 032	2.9	58.6	10.9	7.6	7 314	9 241	17 370	-9.4	1.1	23 780	23.9	35.6	36.0
Lamar	946	6 099	10 887	3.7	67.3	13.0	47.2	5 218	10 511	21 551	7.4	1.7	29 578	19.6	28.5	26.2
Lamb	265	2 074	4 040	2.8	56.7	11.1	22.0	5 991	9 362	19 000	-9.4	1.9	26 129	23.1	30.7	31.4
Lampasas	163	2 008	3 134	6.0	70.7	12.8	17.8	4 981	10 586	22 572	10.1	1.8	28 058	17.4	24.2	25.3
La Salle	514	2 072	1 489	6.1	45.3	10.8	7.9	5 524	8 130	15 615	5.2	1.9	20 054	35.4	42.2	43.5
Lavaca	79	1 333	3 978	17.7	55.7	8.4	11.8	5 241	10 294	19 945	0.3	1.2	27 956	14.6	19.6	19.3
Lee	439	1 297	3 231	9.8	61.1	11.3	16.9	5 646	10 252	21 553	3.5	1.5	30 438	13.2	17.6	19.0
Leon	415	1 552	2 750	2.6	67.4	10.2	16.4	5 501	10 385	20 152	21.1	1.5	27 657	16.5	23.2	23.0
Liberty	238	3 005	13 631	5.4	62.4	7.9	61.7	4 647	9 928	22 637	-19.6	1.5	31 683	17.2	22.9	21.3
Limestone	607	3 625	4 769	3.7	60.2	10.6	24.3	5 847	9 745	19 620	17.2	1.2	25 239	21.4	29.8	28.8
Lipscomb	390	1 267	726	2.5	73.8	14.9	5.8	7 845	11 997	24 648	-3.9	2.8	34 795	11.4	16.2	17.9
Live Oak	68	1 181	2 485	3.5	60.9	12.0	12.5	5 882	10 055	20 898	-20.4	1.5	29 403	18.0	25.5	25.5
Llano	128	1 982	1 573	6.5	71.6	13.3	9.0	5 959	12 448	19 042	-8.0	2.2	26 798	14.5	27.2	25.4
Loving	0	926	24	0.0	56.0	4.0	0.0	0	12 482	26 563	-10.1	0.0	32 152	22.9	23.0	21.9
Lubbock	918	4 961	74 111	7.6	74.2	23.4	223.1	5 195	12 008	24 328	-7.6	2.9	31 961	19.3	27.1	25.5
Lynn	209	1 866	1 695	5.7	54.2	7.5	10.3	6 160	9 909	17 823	-9.6	3.5	26 361	24.3	32.9	35.2
McCulloch	134	2 264	1 991	2.1	62.5	13.8	11.1	6 099	8 847	16 544	-0.1	1.5	23 532	22.7	30.6	32.3
McLennan	687	5 648	57 779	25.3	71.6	16.6	207.1	5 295	11 185	22 665	-0.5	2.0	31 877	18.3	26.3	24.4
McMullen	251	0	167	0.0	64.6	14.6	1.9	9 367	13 485	29 205	4.6	5.3	34 300	13.9	20.2	22.6
Madison	272	2 226	2 726	13.6	58.8	10.1	12.0	5 352	8 767	17 838	-3.0	1.6	25 564	27.4	32.5	31.9
Marion	572	3 530	2 139	5.8	60.2	7.6	8.9	5 406	9 197	15 288	-14.3	1.2	21 444	27.7	36.9	40.0
Martin	0	1 124	1 413	2.3	54.3	6.7	7.5	6 976	9 867	20 596	-24.5	3.4	29 194	20.0	25.8	29.2

1. Data for serious crimes have not been adjusted for underreporting; this may affect comparability between geographic areas and over time.   2. Per 100,000 population estimated by the FBI.   3. All persons 3 years old and over enrolled in nursery school through college.   4. Persons 25 years old and over.   5. Elementary and secondary education expenditures, local government fiscal years ending between July 1, 1996 and June 30, 1997.   6. Based on population enumerated as of April 1, 1990.

Table B. States and Counties — **Personal Income**

	Personal income, 1998												
			Per capita[1]						Transfer payments				
										Government payments to individuals			
STATE County	Total (mil dol)	Percent change, 1997– 1998	Dollars	Rank	Wages and salaries[2] (mil dol)	Proprietor's income (mil dol)	Dividends, interest, and rent (mil dol)	Total (mil dol)	Total (mil dol)	Social Security (mil dol)	Medical payments (mil dol)	Income mainte- nance (mil dol)	Unemploy- ment insurance (mil dol)
	62	63	64	65	66	67	68	69	70	71	72	73	74
TEXAS—Cont'd													
Guadalupe	1 712	7.7	21 282	1 298	609	102	266	237	224	95	86	22	2
Hale	738	3.8	20 107	1 677	381	132	122	140	134	48	59	19	2
Hall	56	-8.6	15 325	2 900	23	3	14	21	20	8	8	3	0
Hamilton	171	4.4	22 415	998	55	27	43	43	42	17	18	4	0
Hansford	179	11.6	33 376	79	61	76	28	18	17	9	6	1	0
Hardeman	94	0.1	20 496	1 559	39	8	23	24	23	9	10	2	0
Hardin	1 001	7.6	20 361	1 614	278	45	142	183	175	68	81	13	3
Harris	102 633	8.5	32 052	113	77 318	19 163	13 083	8 191	7 653	2 732	3 569	842	180
Harrison	1 148	4.0	19 211	1 983	706	87	189	216	206	80	80	24	5
Hartley	143	11.2	27 901	242	29	62	20	8	7	5	1	1	0
Haskell	111	-5.1	18 071	2 327	39	7	26	34	33	14	14	3	0
Hays	1 911	15.4	21 394	1 267	796	123	297	204	189	75	73	16	2
Hemphill	101	3.0	28 621	209	44	25	25	11	11	5	4	1	0
Henderson	1 384	6.9	20 060	1 692	371	119	247	293	281	137	107	18	3
Hidalgo	6 631	6.7	12 759	3 070	3 575	649	941	1 706	1 618	369	776	375	39
Hill	569	3.6	18 609	2 180	208	30	109	138	133	55	56	11	2
Hockley	439	0.8	18 516	2 205	219	47	74	91	87	30	38	11	1
Hood	973	10.0	26 106	390	222	40	190	158	152	79	57	5	2
Hopkins	659	11.0	21 711	1 188	347	90	115	123	118	49	52	9	2
Houston	443	6.1	20 091	1 681	212	40	82	110	107	40	48	14	1
Howard	649	1.2	20 224	1 643	367	40	127	141	135	49	62	14	1
Hudspeth	39	14.0	12 131	3 083	24	1	6	9	9	3	3	2	0
Hunt	1 434	7.4	20 418	1 588	767	80	224	269	258	107	106	24	4
Hutchinson	520	3.2	21 609	1 219	335	34	96	90	86	44	31	6	2
Irion	31	5.9	17 911	2 375	13	0	7	5	5	3	2	0	0
Jack	140	5.1	18 862	2 103	50	14	32	30	29	13	12	2	0
Jackson	288	1.5	21 086	1 361	150	13	55	59	57	23	27	5	1
Jasper	698	5.1	20 867	1 434	324	65	116	162	157	59	73	16	4
Jeff Davis	33	9.3	13 932	3 011	19	-1	9	7	6	3	2	1	0
Jefferson	5 742	5.2	23 802	681	4 429	322	1 039	1 104	1 064	394	498	111	18
Jim Hogg	82	3.8	16 391	2 723	36	3	19	23	22	6	11	4	0
Jim Wells	663	2.7	16 563	2 702	332	46	85	180	174	48	92	26	3
Johnson	2 404	8.3	20 339	1 619	830	183	314	365	345	132	150	20	8
Jones	287	-2.9	15 428	2 886	139	15	53	78	75	29	35	7	1
Karnes	219	1.5	14 417	2 975	103	9	40	60	58	19	28	9	1
Kaufman	1 411	7.6	21 534	1 245	525	102	191	242	231	86	113	18	3
Kendall	584	9.9	27 542	262	168	57	138	72	68	33	28	3	1
Kenedy	9	11.3	20 226	1 642	8	-1	4	1	1	0	0	0	0
Kent	17	9.2	19 662	1 832	7	0	6	5	5	2	2	0	0
Kerr	1 086	5.5	25 448	443	393	114	410	200	193	102	66	10	1
Kimble	72	6.0	17 496	2 485	38	3	21	18	18	8	7	2	0
King	5	-8.8	13 783	3 025	4	0	1	1	1	0	0	0	0
Kinney	45	11.3	13 006	3 063	9	-1	14	15	14	6	5	2	0
Kleberg	537	4.4	17 822	2 401	311	31	83	122	117	29	45	19	2
Knox	83	3.5	19 630	1 848	33	12	16	24	23	8	11	3	0
Lamar	993	3.8	21 648	1 204	569	135	162	201	193	76	83	23	0
Lamb	316	9.6	21 378	1 273	123	85	47	71	68	24	30	9	4
Lampasas	285	6.0	16 052	2 786	87	17	63	71	68	22	31	5	1
La Salle	77	7.5	12 704	3 074	33	6	10	24	23	6	9	5	1
Lavaca	394	4.3	20 918	1 418	133	29	94	97	94	39	43	7	1
Lee	267	3.5	17 909	2 376	135	19	55	51	48	21	20	4	1
Leon	270	5.8	18 665	2 164	140	19	66	72	69	30	29	6	1
Liberty	1 191	4.6	18 281	2 268	440	80	152	252	241	83	124	22	5
Limestone	393	2.4	18 939	2 081	186	22	64	105	101	38	46	11	1
Lipscomb	77	2.5	25 999	396	29	15	21	11	10	5	4	1	0
Live Oak	188	2.5	18 500	2 209	90	7	43	39	37	15	16	4	1
Llano	315	7.5	23 422	762	91	27	103	83	80	42	30	3	0
Loving	4	5.0	32 853	87	2	1	2	0	0	0	0	0	0
Lubbock	5 352	4.8	23 451	755	3 226	634	894	836	798	278	386	78	7
Lynn	119	-14.3	17 743	2 422	44	17	22	27	26	10	11	4	0
McCulloch	159	1.2	18 204	2 294	62	15	40	44	43	16	19	5	1
McLennan	4 435	5.3	21 826	1 150	2 801	410	773	702	668	272	241	75	9
McMullen	19	9.7	24 335	584	8	2	8	3	2	1	1	0	0
Madison	221	2.2	18 623	2 179	91	42	39	46	44	19	18	5	0
Marion	168	3.7	15 403	2 889	46	17	28	50	49	19	17	8	1
Martin	69	-17.3	13 833	3 023	36	1	16	17	16	6	8	2	0

1. Based on the resident population estimated as of July 1 of the year shown.   2. Includes other labor income.

STATE County	Earnings, 1998 Total (mil dol)	Farm	Goods-related[1] Total	Manu-facturing	Service-related and other[2] Total	Retail trade	Finance, insur-ance, and real estate	Services	Govern-ment	Social Security beneficiaries, December 1998 Number	Rate[3]	Supplemental Security Income recipients, December 1998	Housing units, 1990 Total	Percent change, 1980–1990
	75	76	77	78	79	80	81	82	83	84	85	86	87	88
TEXAS—Cont'd														
Guadalupe	711	0.7	42.7	34.0	38.2	10.8	3.7	16.1	18.4	12 418	154	1 366	25 592	42.1
Hale	512	16.8	18.6	14.5	49.8	17.6	2.8	15.2	14.8	5 869	160	912	13 168	-6.2
Hall	26	-2.0	13.3	9.7	D	11.4	5.2	D	36.6	982	269	118	2 189	-16.8
Hamilton	82	10.9	D	8.1	D	13.9	2.6	17.5	19.1	2 199	289	208	4 266	-2.5
Hansford	136	54.7	12.4	1.1	D	3.5	2.6	D	10.8	974	182	56	2 525	-0.4
Hardeman	47	4.3	D	26.4	D	8.4	3.7	12.1	25.9	1 196	261	132	2 678	-6.3
Hardin	323	-0.2	34.6	13.7	46.0	13.1	3.0	18.3	19.6	7 671	157	798	16 486	7.3
Harris	96 481	0.0	29.8	12.5	61.5	7.5	7.0	28.7	8.7	307 209	96	57 522	1 173 808	19.2
Harrison	793	0.5	48.2	35.6	39.8	7.0	4.3	18.4	11.4	9 996	167	1 737	23 481	15.9
Hartley	91	63.0	D	D	D	2.5	D	5.6	12.9	531	104	19	1 541	0.1
Haskell	46	1.9	7.0	1.3	61.8	16.4	6.5	20.9	29.3	1 818	295	169	3 843	5.0
Hays	919	-0.5	25.9	16.3	49.3	16.0	4.6	21.6	25.3	9 110	103	1 189	25 247	74.5
Hemphill	69	25.7	D	1.8	D	5.3	6.2	7.1	15.8	554	157	23	1 712	-15.4
Henderson	490	0.4	23.5	11.9	60.1	15.5	10.0	24.0	16.0	16 207	236	1 150	31 779	35.8
Hidalgo	4 224	2.1	15.0	7.5	55.1	14.0	4.4	24.6	27.8	60 349	116	24 862	128 241	44.0
Hill	238	0.1	D	17.4	D	18.7	4.8	17.4	22.3	6 928	227	671	12 899	8.0
Hockley	266	10.1	D	2.6	D	6.9	3.5	15.3	19.0	3 714	156	484	9 279	10.3
Hood	262	2.5	14.9	4.2	65.1	18.4	9.3	23.4	17.6	8 866	238	393	14 958	67.7
Hopkins	437	9.2	D	23.5	D	11.5	3.4	12.3	13.5	6 219	204	704	12 676	18.3
Houston	252	1.1	24.5	17.0	50.0	8.4	5.3	19.6	24.5	5 185	237	905	10 265	10.9
Howard	407	-1.2	D	12.8	D	9.8	4.3	18.3	31.6	6 098	190	950	13 651	-1.6
Hudspeth	24	7.7	D	D	D	6.0	D	7.4	53.6	456	140	67	1 288	12.5
Hunt	847	0.1	D	37.1	D	9.9	2.8	15.0	21.1	12 959	183	1 686	28 959	20.2
Hutchinson	370	0.8	60.0	31.4	25.7	7.1	1.8	9.8	13.5	4 883	203	333	11 419	4.8
Irion	13	-21.1	D	D	D	9.9	D	14.8	25.1	320	184	23	842	19.9
Jack	64	-4.0	33.3	2.8	46.9	7.3	5.4	22.7	23.7	1 628	219	107	3 497	3.7
Jackson	163	-1.4	53.8	35.3	30.9	7.6	2.3	10.2	16.8	2 792	204	297	5 841	8.5
Jasper	389	-0.5	41.0	32.7	43.4	11.1	3.2	18.9	16.0	7 276	218	1 106	13 824	7.3
Jeff Davis	18	-18.4	D	D	D	10.5	6.1	38.1	40.0	385	163	48	1 348	40.0
Jefferson	4 751	0.2	33.0	21.6	52.7	9.2	3.7	28.7	14.2	44 792	185	6 643	101 289	3.6
Jim Hogg	39	-0.9	19.5	2.1	D	13.2	D	9.3	40.6	955	191	292	2 103	19.1
Jim Wells	379	0.3	28.4	1.9	53.9	11.0	4.0	28.8	17.4	6 653	166	1 919	13 948	14.7
Johnson	1 013	0.7	33.6	22.9	50.9	12.6	3.3	20.5	14.8	15 808	134	1 479	37 029	49.4
Jones	154	-2.2	13.4	6.3	40.6	6.4	4.7	17.5	48.3	3 586	192	360	7 639	2.4
Karnes	113	-4.4	18.8	8.3	42.5	7.9	3.6	20.5	43.1	2 835	229	674	5 117	-3.1
Kaufman	627	0.1	31.3	22.1	48.1	13.4	4.2	20.4	20.7	10 460	159	1 496	20 097	40.6
Kendall	225	-1.8	26.4	8.8	59.8	16.0	10.9	24.5	15.6	4 022	190	172	6 137	30.3
Kenedy	7	-6.8	D	0.0	D	D	0.9	14.9	22.1	51	116	7	213	3.9
Kent	7	-1.2	D	0.0	D	8.6	D	8.4	59.0	244	277	16	603	9.8
Kerr	507	-0.4	18.6	7.9	58.6	12.1	5.3	32.6	23.2	12 075	279	631	17 161	30.6
Kimble	41	-9.2	31.1	19.6	D	15.1	4.6	26.6	22.9	1 023	248	103	2 593	7.4
King	4	13.1	D	1.4	D	D	0.0	D	51.4	38	105	2	191	-11.2
Kinney	15	-14.5	5.6	1.1	D	4.3	D	15.3	69.9	900	258	140	1 821	65.4
Kleberg	343	1.4	12.4	1.9	38.2	10.8	2.9	18.9	48.1	4 103	136	869	12 008	7.1
Knox	45	19.2	16.1	1.0	36.8	5.3	3.6	14.2	27.9	1 088	256	166	2 459	0.9
Lamar	705	-0.9	36.3	30.2	51.7	9.6	3.1	23.4	12.9	9 675	210	1 684	18 964	7.6
Lamb	207	37.8	12.1	9.7	35.8	5.6	2.2	8.0	14.3	3 108	211	431	6 531	-6.6
Lampasas	104	-3.6	30.0	11.4	48.4	13.8	4.2	22.4	25.3	3 039	171	331	6 193	21.6
La Salle	40	9.6	13.4	0.0	34.9	6.4	2.5	16.6	42.1	990	164	292	2 244	3.3
Lavaca	162	-1.9	37.3	29.2	49.4	12.9	3.8	20.6	15.3	5 152	274	582	9 549	9.2
Lee	154	-2.1	36.0	9.5	43.9	8.7	3.9	14.7	22.3	2 748	184	225	5 773	32.0
Leon	159	-4.1	58.0	22.8	33.0	7.6	3.7	10.2	13.1	3 617	250	501	7 019	43.6
Liberty	520	0.5	29.2	17.6	48.5	12.1	3.8	19.8	21.9	9 887	152	1 484	22 243	12.3
Limestone	208	-1.3	16.4	8.5	49.5	10.0	2.6	18.2	35.4	4 970	237	760	9 922	11.4
Lipscomb	43	20.0	D	D	D	3.7	3.7	6.1	20.3	637	214	22	1 683	8.0
Live Oak	97	-7.4	D	D	D	10.7	3.3	13.5	39.5	1 983	196	266	5 519	12.7
Llano	118	-1.5	D	2.3	D	11.4	8.6	28.3	23.4	4 935	366	197	9 773	29.1
Loving	2	6.3	D	0.0	D	0.0	D	D	14.6	19	167	NA	59	18.0
Lubbock	3 860	0.8	15.4	8.7	63.7	13.2	6.5	28.3	20.1	33 249	145	4 759	91 770	14.0
Lynn	61	21.1	3.3	1.5	53.3	3.4	5.2	7.7	22.4	1 231	184	194	2 978	-6.1
McCulloch	78	1.8	D	8.6	D	13.4	5.8	22.1	24.2	2 142	245	313	4 424	8.7
McLennan	3 211	0.2	26.6	20.2	56.3	9.5	11.2	24.3	16.9	33 943	167	4 672	78 857	19.6
McMullen	9	5.8	D	0.0	D	3.3	D	D	33.7	150	190	14	565	16.8
Madison	134	27.8	5.2	1.1	41.3	9.4	5.4	19.9	25.7	2 320	195	267	4 326	10.9
Marion	64	0.6	D	25.3	D	12.5	2.9	19.9	20.6	2 480	228	419	5 729	1.7
Martin	37	-10.3	13.4	2.8	65.5	13.5	5.2	14.1	31.3	776	154	108	2 039	11.1

1. Covers mining, construction, and manufacturing. 2. Covers private sector earnings in agricultural services, forestry, and fisheries; transportation and public utilities; wholesale trade; retail trade; finance, insurance, and real estate; and services. 3. Per 1,000 resident population estimated as of July 1 of the year shown.

Table B. States and Counties — Housing, Labor Force, and Employment

	Housing units, 1990 (cont'd)								Civilian labor force, 1999				Civilian employment, 1990[5]		
	Occupied units							Sub-stand-ard units[3] (percent)			Unemployment			Percent	
	Owner-occupied					Renter-occupied									
STATE County				Owner cost as a percent of income						Percent change, 1998–1999					
	Total	Percent	Median value[1]	With a mort-gage	Without a mort-gage	Median rent[2]	Rent as per-cent of income		Total		Total	Rate[4]	Total	Professional, managerial, and technical	Precision production, craft, and repair
	89	90	91	92	93	94	95	96	97	98	99	100	101	102	103
TEXAS—Cont'd															
Guadalupe	22 663	72.4	60 100	20.4	12.6	369	25.9	7.7	42 567	2.8	1 054	2.5	29 294	23.7	14.6
Hale	11 703	62.4	39 000	18.4	13.0	314	23.9	10.8	17 254	0.9	845	4.9	14 396	20.1	12.8
Hall	1 669	74.7	21 400	20.5	14.2	214	25.7	4.4	1 572	-6.3	83	5.3	1 540	17.1	9.0
Hamilton	3 250	77.2	33 300	17.3	15.9	262	24.3	3.5	4 084	3.9	157	3.8	3 144	19.4	8.6
Hansford	2 112	74.1	43 800	16.7	12.4	325	19.4	7.0	2 456	-1.2	86	3.5	2 515	20.6	13.1
Hardeman	2 101	75.3	25 500	17.1	14.2	240	28.5	4.9	1 903	-5.3	91	4.8	1 981	18.2	8.4
Hardin	14 693	80.5	48 300	16.7	13.4	358	24.8	5.1	23 231	-0.6	1 825	7.9	16 863	22.2	20.1
Harris	1 026 448	52.0	63 500	20.1	13.0	405	23.2	9.8	1 772 281	0.3	82 594	4.7	1 381 829	33.2	11.4
Harrison	20 705	75.3	46 000	18.7	13.8	334	26.7	6.2	27 623	-2.7	1 916	6.9	22 840	22.0	16.3
Hartley	1 332	77.3	60 600	18.3	12.5	300	18.8	1.6	3 004	4.2	39	1.3	1 676	26.4	7.4
Haskell	2 753	76.2	28 200	17.2	13.8	234	27.1	6.1	2 680	1.8	109	4.1	2 640	18.9	12.8
Hays	22 218	58.2	81 300	23.5	13.0	407	34.5	7.5	52 286	3.6	1 421	2.7	30 737	33.8	9.5
Hemphill	1 348	73.5	47 500	14.3	12.9	341	18.7	5.7	1 861	-1.8	55	3.0	1 667	15.0	16.7
Henderson	22 947	79.1	53 600	20.8	14.3	347	26.4	5.4	30 151	1.2	1 058	3.5	22 324	21.8	15.6
Hidalgo	103 479	70.3	35 900	21.5	12.7	282	26.5	28.4	194 414	-0.4	28 124	14.5	122 112	23.3	10.5
Hill	10 268	74.3	37 200	18.6	15.4	309	24.9	5.5	16 236	2.4	571	3.5	10 557	19.0	15.1
Hockley	7 988	72.6	41 900	18.7	12.8	308	25.8	8.5	10 675	-3.6	723	6.8	9 881	21.9	15.8
Hood	11 137	79.1	73 800	19.4	11.8	455	22.5	3.8	17 002	2.0	632	3.7	11 757	29.7	15.3
Hopkins	10 965	70.8	43 600	20.7	14.7	332	25.1	5.2	15 913	0.2	680	4.3	12 530	17.1	12.8
Houston	7 792	74.4	40 000	22.5	14.9	278	29.3	8.3	9 003	2.0	392	4.4	7 699	21.2	12.6
Howard	11 477	70.7	34 900	16.9	12.2	336	23.4	5.2	13 643	-5.1	811	5.9	12 392	25.8	15.2
Hudspeth	946	68.8	23 100	21.3	13.0	391	19.9	17.8	1 439	6.9	50	3.5	1 173	19.3	8.2
Hunt	24 075	70.0	47 300	19.1	14.1	378	27.8	5.0	36 664	1.9	1 392	3.8	28 850	24.7	15.4
Hutchinson	9 642	77.5	38 200	16.7	12.2	333	25.7	4.0	9 251	-3.8	709	7.7	9 903	23.6	20.5
Irion	601	74.0	44 600	19.2	11.3	308	17.2	5.5	701	-7.0	30	4.3	708	18.6	15.0
Jack	2 725	76.9	33 800	20.5	13.0	265	23.9	4.0	3 501	1.4	148	4.2	2 804	20.5	17.3
Jackson	4 833	75.2	42 000	22.1	14.1	314	22.9	6.9	8 460	-1.8	280	3.3	5 079	20.6	19.6
Jasper	11 427	79.1	40 300	18.8	13.6	322	29.9	5.9	14 706	0.3	1 743	11.9	10 766	19.2	17.6
Jeff Davis	779	67.1	43 800	25.0	12.3	292	16.3	5.9	1 455	-6.2	35	2.4	826	28.9	6.4
Jefferson	90 520	66.0	41 800	17.3	13.0	363	25.8	5.2	116 881	-1.4	9 508	8.1	98 779	28.0	13.4
Jim Hogg	1 675	78.1	28 300	21.9	12.8	199	31.8	11.8	2 371	7.9	270	11.4	1 834	21.3	13.1
Jim Wells	11 979	74.3	33 700	22.2	14.1	294	24.8	14.6	17 066	-0.8	1 870	11.0	13 286	20.3	18.8
Johnson	33 462	76.2	61 100	20.8	13.3	411	25.5	5.3	61 160	3.3	2 070	3.4	44 802	23.5	16.2
Jones	6 180	78.1	29 600	20.1	14.3	275	24.0	4.5	9 914	-4.0	342	3.4	6 608	21.9	13.9
Karnes	4 337	74.5	29 600	22.2	13.9	229	24.8	13.0	5 686	-9.3	228	4.0	4 508	20.3	13.7
Kaufman	17 827	76.3	56 600	22.3	14.2	378	28.6	6.3	32 980	2.4	1 313	4.0	22 670	23.6	15.4
Kendall	5 342	74.5	79 000	23.0	13.5	423	27.5	5.5	13 360	6.4	297	2.2	6 851	30.6	13.5
Kenedy	145	20.0	22 500	35.1	10.0	225	14.0	14.9	228	0.4	7	3.1	216	18.1	3.2
Kent	399	74.4	28 100	22.7	13.2	242	16.7	4.5	448	-1.1	12	2.7	429	20.3	8.9
Kerr	14 384	69.5	67 300	22.4	12.9	387	27.1	6.1	17 334	-0.5	373	2.2	14 342	29.6	11.4
Kimble	1 624	73.8	38 900	21.0	14.0	270	26.7	4.2	2 344	-0.6	65	2.8	1 860	12.7	11.5
King	124	35.5	17 500	26.7	15.0	313	15.0	1.6	130	8.3	5	3.8	192	17.7	3.1
Kinney	1 187	68.6	32 400	21.5	13.9	276	23.3	10.5	1 120	0.4	88	7.9	961	17.4	7.8
Kleberg	10 058	59.7	40 800	17.9	13.2	341	27.2	10.7	13 056	-1.8	844	6.5	11 416	29.8	13.1
Knox	1 887	76.0	27 600	21.8	15.2	213	25.5	6.2	1 965	-7.4	106	5.4	1 843	21.1	13.8
Lamar	16 798	68.9	39 000	17.7	13.7	338	28.5	4.0	22 092	6.5	1 322	6.0	17 945	23.2	12.1
Lamb	5 488	73.5	28 900	16.8	13.1	274	24.8	9.0	6 529	0.1	461	7.1	5 595	20.6	12.4
Lampasas	5 058	72.7	49 600	21.6	12.7	330	27.5	6.5	7 819	0.6	253	3.2	5 583	21.7	17.4
La Salle	1 701	67.7	18 300	21.1	13.3	218	29.2	19.8	2 895	-3.4	248	8.6	1 932	17.8	13.5
Lavaca	7 349	78.7	40 700	20.3	13.0	252	21.7	7.2	9 486	3.7	191	2.0	8 005	17.3	16.9
Lee	4 706	77.5	47 800	21.2	12.5	331	24.6	8.0	7 175	0.6	254	3.5	5 481	21.8	17.2
Leon	5 006	81.1	43 500	23.9	14.8	319	27.8	8.7	6 344	8.3	406	6.4	4 656	20.1	17.1
Liberty	18 538	75.5	42 100	20.1	14.2	352	26.1	7.6	29 108	1.1	2 165	7.4	20 309	19.5	19.4
Limestone	7 722	73.1	36 900	21.4	15.0	301	28.6	6.0	9 082	-0.7	391	4.3	8 190	23.9	14.7
Lipscomb	1 230	77.2	35 500	20.9	13.3	317	17.6	4.1	1 532	-5.3	52	3.4	1 361	20.4	17.9
Live Oak	3 550	79.9	42 000	18.9	12.3	272	26.5	9.3	4 409	-1.7	186	4.2	3 740	21.5	17.7
Llano	5 278	79.3	66 700	26.1	13.8	361	27.2	2.7	5 437	2.9	143	2.6	3 558	20.8	15.3
Loving	42	73.8	14 999		10.0	213	12.5	4.7	102	20.0	9	8.8	59	25.4	8.5
Lubbock	81 534	58.2	54 500	20.0	12.6	377	29.5	6.6	123 318	0.1	3 555	2.9	102 790	30.9	9.9
Lynn	2 383	71.0	30 900	21.4	12.9	244	24.7	9.1	2 899	-5.5	129	4.4	2 519	14.2	8.1
McCulloch	3 409	71.8	33 900	22.3	15.1	289	26.4	7.1	3 698	1.2	193	5.2	3 135	21.4	7.6
McLennan	70 208	58.9	50 300	18.6	12.8	360	27.9	5.3	101 622	0.6	3 365	3.3	82 485	27.5	11.6
McMullen	319	75.9	40 000	25.0	11.1	225	12.9	11.6	289	7.4	14	4.8	389	23.4	13.1
Madison	3 349	75.5	41 900	22.9	16.2	351	30.1	8.8	4 240	1.0	150	3.5	3 387	18.8	9.9
Marion	4 048	81.0	34 500	23.6	14.3	255	29.9	12.0	3 883	2.4	347	8.9	3 443	17.7	12.8
Martin	1 632	72.4	40 500	18.0	12.9	233	26.0	9.5	1 734	2.4	98	5.7	1 786	17.0	12.3

1. Specified owner-occupied units. 2. Specified renter-occupied units. 3. Overcrowded or lacking complete plumbing facilities. 4. Percent of civilian labor force. 5. Persons 16 years and older.

Table B. States and Counties — Nonfarm Employment and Agriculture

	Private nonfarm establishments, employment and payroll, 1998								Agriculture, 1997			
	Employment						Annual payroll		Farms			Farm operators
										Percent with—		
STATE County	Number of establishments	Total	Health Care and Social Assistance	Manufacturing	Retail trade	Finance and Insurance	Professional Scientific and Technical Services	Total (mil dol)	Average per employee (dollars)	Number	Less than 50 acres	500 acres and over	Whose principal occupation is farming (percent)
	104	105	106	107	108	109	110	111	112	113	114	115	116
TEXAS—Cont'd													
Guadalupe	1 280	18 791	2 048	6 718	2 773	447	236	392	20 876	1 841	37.9	7.3	40.0
Hale	852	11 567	1 236	2 639	1 623	340	170	238	20 570	840	7.7	50.0	68.7
Hall	93	678	140	D	153	36	4	10	15 409	311	2.3	52.7	61.7
Hamilton	227	1 830	413	299	313	56	48	35	18 858	966	11.5	26.4	45.7
Hansford	186	1 258	D	D	262	97	36	26	21 063	279	5.4	76.3	73.1
Hardeman	104	915	192	D	123	D	12	19	21 200	342	6.1	44.4	50.9
Hardin	754	8 900	1 556	972	1 624	182	272	164	18 388	354	61.0	5.4	35.3
Harris	83 308	1 592 279	153 105	163 834	166 325	74 367	117 133	56 948	35 765	1 727	55.8	7.7	34.7
Harrison	1 226	15 294	1 709	3 417	2 314	902	562	344	22 464	1 107	36.3	10.1	34.1
Hartley	73	733	310	D	138	0	D	14	18 995	245	5.7	69.4	70.2
Haskell	169	989	194	D	243	82	30	16	16 522	611	11.0	40.6	56.8
Hays	2 015	22 634	3 605	3 546	4 328	446	632	466	20 600	816	33.6	16.1	38.1
Hemphill	138	1 008	151	D	132	81	15	22	22 299	230	8.3	62.2	66.1
Henderson	1 125	12 154	1 827	1 911	2 578	412	307	229	18 817	1 630	34.8	8.4	39.3
Hidalgo	7 990	101 510	17 631	11 624	21 758	4 030	3 003	1 885	18 568	1 373	49.5	18.9	45.4
Hill	701	6 296	928	1 293	1 775	180	78	119	18 956	1 563	25.6	14.3	42.7
Hockley	512	5 413	1 353	255	792	204	171	99	18 217	675	15.6	47.7	62.8
Hood	879	7 255	1 229	329	1 731	360	267	137	18 830	799	41.2	12.4	35.8
Hopkins	752	9 758	1 144	1 619	1 702	390	204	203	20 758	1 758	25.3	9.8	47.5
Houston	406	3 969	1 058	604	855	162	106	70	17 727	1 369	21.4	15.6	43.5
Howard	797	9 781	2 357	1 151	1 554	294	156	220	22 459	436	20.0	45.0	50.2
Hudspeth	44	240	D	0	58	D	D	4	17 079	147	7.5	61.9	75.5
Hunt	1 343	20 584	2 942	7 419	2 963	535	608	512	24 861	2 049	38.8	6.4	33.4
Hutchinson	566	7 338	938	1 752	1 027	153	126	212	28 958	190	13.7	53.7	56.3
Irion	43	259	0	D	D	D	D	6	23 857	146	21.9	54.8	50.0
Jack	177	1 278	169	D	160	75	30	24	18 559	730	9.7	31.8	37.8
Jackson	286	5 478	311	D	442	94	57	133	24 236	790	20.5	30.4	50.8
Jasper	749	8 710	1 844	1 712	1 704	272	150	195	22 427	639	55.6	2.0	31.6
Jeff Davis	58	420	103	D	39	D	D	6	14 610	83	7.2	77.1	71.1
Jefferson	6 004	100 900	17 506	14 773	15 203	3 081	4 101	2 990	29 629	562	39.1	25.6	40.0
Jim Hogg	106	892	236	19	221	46	D	13	14 602	188	7.4	61.2	46.8
Jim Wells	790	10 114	3 254	303	1 558	411	333	192	18 942	738	22.6	24.4	43.9
Johnson	2 051	24 652	2 506	6 005	4 017	692	627	527	21 397	2 062	48.6	6.1	33.1
Jones	335	3 344	711	98	519	109	53	60	17 863	867	17.2	27.5	44.6
Karnes	274	2 116	406	158	415	102	68	37	17 457	1 051	12.7	20.3	39.0
Kaufman	1 421	18 713	3 169	4 309	2 487	523	262	416	22 231	1 883	44.6	7.7	33.1
Kendall	672	5 447	568	546	1 021	356	171	115	21 136	730	25.5	22.2	38.8
Kenedy	4	18	0	0	0	0	0	0	14 000	31	3.2	71.0	80.6
Kent	22	122	0	0	13	D	0	4	34 934	171	5.8	51.5	52.6
Kerr	1 257	13 536	3 736	1 104	2 305	272	512	288	21 281	778	23.3	26.9	38.7
Kimble	137	1 148	133	273	196	44	36	19	16 908	485	12.2	52.6	51.8
King	3	D	0	0	0	0	0	D	D	43	2.3	62.8	51.2
Kinney	30	219	D	0	47	0	D	3	13 571	128	6.2	76.6	53.9
Kleberg	545	5 872	1 035	512	1 397	266	112	101	17 214	272	41.5	16.9	32.7
Knox	141	879	261	0	141	58	14	15	16 537	296	8.1	52.0	58.8
Lamar	1 202	18 123	3 207	4 893	2 595	478	300	416	22 938	1 539	24.9	14.4	39.3
Lamb	331	2 737	385	652	492	158	21	60	21 810	865	7.4	42.1	63.6
Lampasas	356	2 912	424	381	530	100	77	52	17 989	746	21.0	26.7	45.2
La Salle	89	702	75	0	161	25	D	11	16 024	280	5.7	53.2	43.6
Lavaca	501	6 217	982	2 414	805	265	74	114	18 281	2 558	26.5	7.7	37.7
Lee	401	3 635	306	470	642	149	87	77	21 290	1 685	26.2	8.5	38.6
Leon	316	3 243	154	D	502	96	55	90	27 885	1 633	24.9	15.5	42.1
Liberty	1 056	10 794	1 705	1 157	2 437	366	267	243	22 541	1 138	44.6	11.5	36.2
Limestone	408	4 437	885	931	771	164	64	79	17 792	1 212	19.7	16.8	41.6
Lipscomb	107	459	10	D	93	50	19	9	19 841	302	7.0	61.3	57.3
Live Oak	209	1 701	176	D	402	92	33	38	22 277	732	15.7	33.2	37.4
Llano	432	3 133	550	64	437	154	83	60	19 109	565	17.0	40.9	43.9
Loving	1	D	0	0	0	0	0	D	D	14	7.1	92.9	50.0
Lubbock	6 480	90 311	17 531	7 514	14 389	3 721	2 885	1 995	22 089	1 068	29.1	32.1	55.3
Lynn	105	817	136	D	139	73	7	18	21 760	490	7.3	60.6	75.9
McCulloch	245	2 116	385	246	452	102	108	39	18 525	545	7.9	43.7	46.2
McLennan	4 742	82 466	12 500	16 100	10 576	3 902	2 350	1 913	23 196	2 006	38.8	11.1	36.8
McMullen	18	88	D	0	D	D	D	3	31 614	210	2.4	74.8	52.4
Madison	217	1 921	482	60	493	93	52	35	18 252	816	24.4	12.5	39.5
Marion	197	1 234	193	282	228	51	10	21	16 812	207	19.3	16.4	42.0
Martin	90	556	151	0	128	35	9	12	22 442	353	8.5	57.2	63.5

Table B. States and Counties — Agriculture, Land, and Water

STATE County	Agriculture, 1997 (cont'd)															
	Land in farms					Value of land and buildings		Value of machinery and equipment Average per farm ($1,000)	Value of products sold				Percent of farms with sales of —		Percent of land owned by Fed. Gov. 1997	Water consumption 1995 (mil gal/day)
	Acreage (1,000)	Percent change, 1992–1997	Acres			Average per farm ($1,000)	Average per acre (dollars)		Total (mil dol)	Average per farm (dollars)	Percent from —		$10,000 or more	$100,000 or more		
			Average size of farm	Total irrigated (1,000)	Total cropland (1,000)						Crops	Live-stock and poultry products				
	117	118	119	120	121	122	123	124	125	126	127	128	129	130	131	132
TEXAS—Cont'd																
Guadalupe	348	0.2	189	1	165	268	1 680	25	31	17 035	44.4	55.6	20.5	2.7	0.2	9.5
Hale	587	4.7	698	310	512	414	568	115	240	285 213	48.7	51.3	69.6	44.4	0.0	354.0
Hall	448	1.1	1 440	9	172	323	235	65	24	75 873	76.2	23.8	55.3	24.1	0.0	11.6
Hamilton	466	1.1	482	1	134	337	779	31	52	54 254	5.6	94.4	37.6	6.8	0.0	3.3
Hansford	582	1.1	2 086	125	314	856	424	140	346	1 241 020	11.4	88.6	77.1	53.8	0.0	166.8
Hardeman	323	2.8	944	5	167	243	285	38	16	46 454	44.1	55.9	48.2	10.2	0.0	10.7
Hardin	65	104.5	185	1	18	209	1 239	23	3	8 116	33.3	66.7	15.5	0.6	8.1	184.3
Harris	311	1.0	180	10	119	343	2 225	29	43	25 073	69.9	30.1	21.2	4.5	2.6	498.9
Harrison	214	6.2	194	0	96	195	1 139	23	12	10 916	14.5	85.5	23.8	1.6	1.5	81.1
Hartley	823	19.8	3 359	126	D	1 240	367	158	350	1 428 449	15.0	85.0	75.1	53.9	0.0	211.4
Haskell	469	-5.1	767	28	292	282	404	58	40	65 033	71.7	28.3	57.4	18.3	0.0	97.5
Hays	298	-35.5	366	1	74	668	1 928	25	11	13 185	41.2	58.8	18.0	2.2	0.0	17.3
Hemphill	624	14.2	2 711	5	D	717	258	42	103	448 302	1.5	98.5	63.0	23.9	0.0	3.8
Henderson	367	3.1	225	1	155	219	1 016	29	29	18 096	34.3	65.7	25.3	2.3	0.0	125.1
Hidalgo	636	-3.7	463	185	439	609	1 360	63	197	143 652	91.8	8.2	41.1	17.3	1.8	932.3
Hill	464	-1.3	297	1	292	247	854	44	58	36 923	59.7	40.3	34.2	6.5	0.6	5.7
Hockley	572	16.4	847	143	430	349	417	107	89	132 319	75.7	24.3	56.7	35.1	0.0	155.9
Hood	225	-0.2	282	5	78	341	1 253	30	18	22 843	47.7	52.3	25.3	2.5	0.0	3 333.4
Hopkins	386	-0.1	220	4	222	211	1 031	38	127	72 298	3.0	97.0	40.4	16.4	1.7	12.4
Houston	440	5.6	322	2	168	279	888	30	27	20 006	14.5	85.5	31.2	2.8	11.9	5.7
Howard	544	11.2	1 247	3	202	480	350	65	31	72 217	69.4	30.6	48.2	19.7	0.0	6.7
Hudspeth	2 503	12.0	17 026	31	40	2 450	144	94	25	170 021	66.2	33.8	72.1	34.7	0.6	157.5
Hunt	353	2.4	172	0	215	200	1 183	24	24	11 754	44.3	55.7	20.8	2.0	0.0	97.2
Hutchinson	400	-0.7	2 106	48	126	671	343	88	43	226 152	31.9	68.1	56.3	28.4	1.0	145.6
Irion	652	-0.8	4 464	1	D	833	193	30	6	40 960	8.8	91.2	51.4	10.3	0.0	3.5
Jack	532	2.5	728	0	71	450	592	23	17	23 177	6.0	94.0	33.4	4.8	0.0	2.4
Jackson	463	0.2	586	22	240	492	809	72	47	59 819	79.6	20.4	40.9	16.3	1.5	87.0
Jasper	87	24.4	136	0	26	190	1 480	29	3	5 446	28.5	71.5	12.4	0.3	5.2	56.7
Jeff Davis	1 482	-2.8	17 851	0	D	2 821	158	53	9	112 582	0.7	99.3	65.1	26.5	0.0	1.2
Jefferson	434	34.7	772	32	181	616	825	42	26	46 187	70.8	29.2	37.2	13.9	7.8	168.5
Jim Hogg	768	4.4	4 086	D	25	1 092	276	26	6	34 577	0.1	99.9	38.8	8.5	0.0	1.6
Jim Wells	496	-4.2	673	3	199	353	612	35	36	48 263	50.1	49.9	28.7	8.3	0.3	4.8
Johnson	333	0.9	161	1	175	301	1 976	25	48	23 336	13.5	86.5	20.7	3.7	0.3	13.3
Jones	459	-10.5	530	4	300	238	426	44	39	45 136	56.2	43.8	42.6	10.5	0.0	285.9
Karnes	417	8.6	397	3	162	251	660	18	16	15 119	23.7	76.3	29.4	2.2	0.0	4.6
Kaufman	389	0.5	206	1	181	262	1 389	24	29	15 412	18.1	81.9	19.4	2.1	0.0	6.7
Kendall	325	-8.3	446	0	49	618	1 426	23	6	8 888	14.2	85.8	19.7	1.2	0.0	4.4
Kenedy	563	1.8	18 159	D	D	5 444	300	49	7	220 380	D	D	74.2	22.6	6.7	0.7
Kent	561	-5.7	3 280	1	51	557	178	42	7	42 565	16.0	84.0	44.4	11.7	0.0	2.1
Kerr	548	3.2	704	2	51	634	886	25	7	9 244	14.6	85.4	21.0	0.9	0.0	7.7
Kimble	773	-0.3	1 594	2	33	800	515	21	7	14 893	11.6	88.4	32.0	2.3	0.0	3.0
King	D	D	D	D	22	1 885	150	54	7	153 438	9.0	91.0	55.8	20.9	0.0	0.7
Kinney	629	-10.0	4 913	3	20	1 576	323	34	6	47 600	D	D	53.1	12.5	0.0	8.5
Kleberg	D	D	D	D	116	2 158	D	94	44	162 712	D	D	25.4	7.0	3.6	7.4
Knox	658	14.1	2 224	31	220	501	233	73	49	165 667	31.5	68.5	65.2	29.1	0.4	26.4
Lamar	431	1.4	280	1	248	217	750	28	35	22 992	31.8	68.2	34.6	5.3	1.6	22.3
Lamb	539	4.1	624	218	439	340	564	96	253	293 022	39.8	60.2	61.8	39.7	0.0	293.3
Lampasas	435	0.6	583	0	71	477	805	27	13	17 361	13.8	86.2	31.8	2.4	0.0	1.7
La Salle	527	-31.2	1 882	4	72	767	424	31	19	66 747	22.1	77.9	38.6	7.1	0.0	6.8
Lavaca	526	-0.4	206	5	220	220	1 017	24	43	16 676	9.8	90.2	22.8	1.6	0.0	16.4
Lee	344	8.0	204	1	130	210	1 116	24	23	13 373	23.9	76.1	28.4	1.0	2.5	4.8
Leon	515	6.8	315	2	183	259	866	27	27	16 572	12.3	87.7	27.7	2.4	0.0	7.1
Liberty	307	-10.3	270	14	160	278	1 152	38	24	20 847	69.6	30.4	19.3	4.2	0.2	611.9
Limestone	443	3.5	365	0	174	274	766	33	26	21 295	11.8	88.2	31.8	3.1	0.0	23.7
Lipscomb	529	-10.2	1 751	22	146	443	256	63	45	150 069	25.0	75.0	58.9	19.9	0.0	17.2
Live Oak	520	-6.9	711	3	128	431	651	34	12	16 077	36.7	63.3	31.0	2.7	0.4	9.3
Llano	532	5.0	942	1	44	752	796	22	10	17 362	5.2	94.8	37.3	2.8	0.0	4.7
Loving	352	1.5	25 148			1 735	69	25	1	62 872	0.0	100.0	71.4	14.3	0.0	0.6
Lubbock	541	12.2	506	212	456	441	808	104	134	125 239	70.6	29.4	53.0	27.7	0.4	217.8
Lynn	563	14.7	1 149	74	421	628	532	120	71	145 749	97.2	2.8	74.7	47.3	0.0	50.9
McCulloch	641	-5.2	1 175	2	135	562	468	47	18	33 089	29.0	71.0	47.5	9.2	0.0	6.4
McLennan	493	4.4	246	2	299	237	968	34	93	46 337	36.7	63.3	24.8	5.4	1.6	57.4
McMullen	521	1.0	2 481	D	26	979	403	30	6	26 439	6.6	93.4	42.4	5.7	1.8	1.3
Madison	224	-8.3	274	0	79	325	1 171	37	43	52 340	D	D	29.7	2.7	0.0	2.8
Marion	62	24.0	299	0	27	300	1 024	26	2	9 896	24.0	76.0	22.7	1.4	1.7	5.1
Martin	539	5.3	1 527	11	272	502	329	95	40	113 116	91.4	8.6	59.5	38.5	0.0	9.2

Table B. States and Counties — Residential Construction, Wholesale and Retail Trade, and Real Estate

STATE County	Value of Residential Construction Authorized by Building Permits, 1999		Wholesale Trade, 1997				Retail Trade[1], 1997				Real Estate and Rental and Leasing, 1997			
	New Construction ($1,000)	Number of Housing Units	Number of Establishments	Number of Employees	Sales (mil dol)	Annual Payroll (mil dol)	Number of Establishments	Number of Employees	Sales (mil dol)	Annual Payroll (mil dol)	Number of Establishments	Number of Employees	Receipts (mil dol)	Annual Payroll (mil dol)
	133	134	135	136	137	138	139	140	141	142	143	144	145	146
TEXAS—Cont'd														
Guadalupe	69 990	628	82	681	366.1	20.6	215	2 665	498.1	41.7	58	205	21.4	3.5
Hale	1 760	16	74	540	294.5	13.3	164	1 566	264.7	23.6	31	111	6.2	1.4
Hall	0	0	6	25	10.1	0.5	22	137	43.1	2.1	NA	NA	NA	NA
Hamilton	160	3	10	118	42.1	2.2	57	301	45.4	4.0	4	D	D	D
Hansford	85	1	23	139	116.1	4.3	38	233	39.0	3.6	3	8	0.5	0.0
Hardeman	0	0	9	41	12.2	0.6	21	115	16.3	1.5	1	D	D	D
Hardin	6 006	35	28	150	33.4	3.3	152	1 630	350.6	24.5	24	90	6.8	0.8
Harris	2 603 777	25 862	7 564	101 357	110 399.7	4 129.7	11 596	168 038	31 045.1	2 921.9	4 039	33 808	4 154.7	829.5
Harrison	3 457	64	65	747	321.2	20.8	220	2 270	378.6	33.2	36	181	13.3	4.0
Hartley	NA	NA	5	D	D	D	10	84	14.4	1.2	7	D	D	D
Haskell	0	0	8	40	23.3	0.6	41	238	58.9	3.3	5	13	1.0	0.3
Hays	98 005	1 010	75	559	174.1	15.9	382	4 056	698.0	61.0	91	312	40.8	7.5
Hemphill	0	0	7	33	10.5	0.8	22	132	19.7	2.0	2	D	D	D
Henderson	16 605	157	42	215	98.3	4.6	221	2 586	381.1	34.3	52	191	18.3	2.8
Hidalgo	323 778	5 700	600	6 395	1 981.7	124.6	1 582	20 862	3 337.6	313.1	346	1 347	116.3	18.5
Hill	2 486	33	26	119	46.8	2.5	229	1 800	331.1	26.4	20	44	4.1	0.4
Hockley	979	10	40	255	81.5	6.3	86	725	150.6	11.3	21	42	3.6	0.6
Hood	7 913	78	29	83	32.5	2.0	159	1 702	346.6	30.3	44	274	14.5	3.6
Hopkins	3 101	36	48	1 088	607.1	27.0	174	1 753	357.2	27.8	23	123	9.2	1.6
Houston	433	5	16	136	49.4	2.4	91	772	122.4	10.6	10	17	1.2	0.2
Howard	614	17	50	559	215.5	22.0	149	1 509	248.6	21.1	37	121	9.5	2.0
Hudspeth	NA	NA	4	7	1.9	0.1	9	52	6.1	0.5	1	D	D	D
Hunt	8 507	129	54	447	263.6	10.1	258	3 013	479.9	41.7	56	214	14.3	3.8
Hutchinson	1 300	6	31	192	163.9	5.5	104	1 028	151.0	13.8	16	47	4.7	0.8
Irion	NA	NA	3	19	5.1	0.4	4	19	1.5	0.1	1	D	D	D
Jack	65	1	7	64	13.0	1.8	35	181	21.3	2.3	6	11	0.5	0.1
Jackson	3 004	29	22	177	58.4	3.3	63	479	90.6	7.6	11	25	1.6	0.2
Jasper	1 018	18	49	247	103.4	6.5	190	1 658	301.0	23.7	23	71	11.7	1.4
Jeff Davis	NA	NA	NA	NA	NA	NA	8	37	3.7	0.5	1	D	D	D
Jefferson	69 240	635	368	4 827	2 081.2	163.7	1 084	14 964	2 570.9	230.1	260	1 597	194.2	34.2
Jim Hogg	NA	NA	5	40	25.3	0.8	34	207	31.4	2.5	1	D	D	D
Jim Wells	2 472	37	56	522	139.8	14.1	160	1 531	258.1	23.4	41	258	35.3	7.5
Johnson	61 207	872	87	762	261.8	18.2	358	3 995	706.8	62.2	69	239	22.7	3.1
Jones	0	0	24	140	145.1	3.4	58	498	163.1	8.0	9	19	0.9	0.2
Karnes	448	15	14	168	45.8	2.4	54	434	59.8	5.1	5	19	1.1	0.1
Kaufman	23 550	362	77	665	189.3	16.8	286	2 693	573.3	43.0	34	103	8.2	1.3
Kendall	63 940	427	31	378	141.1	8.5	93	1 012	305.8	20.1	30	66	7.7	0.8
Kenedy	NA	NA	NA	NA	NA	NA	NA	NA	NA	NA	NA	NA	NA	NA
Kent	NA	NA	1	D	D	D	4	D	D	D	NA	NA	NA	NA
Kerr	12 910	90	48	271	65.6	6.4	210	2 467	436.1	38.4	63	180	18.2	3.2
Kimble	282	3	5	D	D	D	33	201	31.4	2.8	4	7	0.2	0.0
King	NA	NA	NA	NA	NA	NA	NA	NA	NA	NA	NA	NA	NA	NA
Kinney	0	0	2	D	D	D	9	41	4.2	0.4	3	4	0.4	0.0
Kleberg	925	12	10	42	8.2	0.9	113	1 414	214.3	20.0	24	65	7.0	0.8
Knox	NA	NA	13	79	29.8	1.7	31	163	24.7	2.0	1	D	D	D
Lamar	8 889	148	68	519	152.4	12.7	242	2 591	482.5	40.0	46	134	15.3	1.8
Lamb	150	2	25	146	72.6	3.1	63	450	75.4	5.9	5	11	0.5	0.1
Lampasas	425	13	16	79	36.3	0.7	65	562	94.4	7.8	12	32	2.1	0.3
La Salle	0	0	3	D	D	D	27	142	20.0	1.8	3	4	0.2	0.0
Lavaca	1 146	11	30	818	202.6	14.6	108	797	118.1	10.7	11	19	1.3	0.1
Lee	2 821	13	35	324	322.4	7.1	59	665	79.9	9.0	7	16	2.9	0.4
Leon	NA	NA	15	149	56.2	3.2	72	494	77.4	6.0	8	43	2.3	0.5
Liberty	17 608	362	53	D	D	D	204	2 472	441.7	36.5	45	179	17.7	4.2
Limestone	2 897	29	15	D	D	D	91	831	137.6	11.3	10	16	0.8	0.2
Lipscomb	174	2	11	32	12.5	0.6	17	82	10.6	0.8	1	D	D	D
Live Oak	85	2	9	77	25.4	0.9	45	397	75.0	5.1	7	14	1.3	0.2
Llano	1 505	16	15	222	85.5	5.4	77	380	69.1	5.3	17	56	6.0	1.0
Loving	NA	NA	1	D	D	D	NA	NA	NA	NA	NA	NA	NA	NA
Lubbock	100 751	1 041	505	6 628	3 867.8	181.3	1 084	14 538	2 673.0	238.0	296	1 905	133.8	30.7
Lynn	183	3	7	D	D	D	24	122	30.6	2.1	1	D	D	D
McCulloch	90	1	14	91	14.9	1.4	55	473	75.5	5.9	8	40	3.1	0.7
McLennan	58 661	601	315	3 755	1 716.3	102.1	862	10 227	1 797.8	162.7	212	1 086	131.4	21.4
McMullen	NA	NA	NA	NA	NA	NA	5	13	1.9	0.2	NA	NA	NA	NA
Madison	578	12	5	23	12.1	0.8	46	462	137.0	7.5	11	16	1.4	0.2
Marion	60	1	9	31	19.1	1.0	41	246	37.4	2.8	3	2	0.2	0.0
Martin	100	1	10	53	22.2	1.4	17	116	27.9	2.1	NA	NA	NA	NA

1. Establishments with payroll.

STATE County	Professional, Scientific, and Technical Services[1], 1997				Manufacturing, 1997				Accommodation and Foodservices, 1997			
	Number of Establishments	Number of Employees	Receipts (mil dol)	Annual Payroll (mil dol)	Number of Establishments	Number of Employees	Receipts (mil dol)	Annual Payroll (mil dol)	Number of Establishments	Number of Employees	Sales (mil dol)	Annual Payroll (mil dol)
	147	148	149	150	151	152	153	154	155	156	157	158
TEXAS—Cont'd												
Guadalupe	64	204	13.8	4.8	90	5 592	1 320.3	150.4	127	D	D	D
Hale	38	151	9.7	2.7	32	D	D	D	67	923	25.9	6.9
Hall	3	3	0.2	0.0	NA	NA	NA	NA	10	D	D	D
Hamilton	17	37	2.3	0.5	NA	NA	NA	NA	13	103	2.6	0.7
Hansford	6	19	1.3	0.5	NA	NA	NA	NA	11	D	D	D
Hardeman	7	10	0.4	0.1	NA	NA	NA	NA	10	D	D	D
Hardin	38	245	15.3	4.8	37	1 016	173.1	30.0	50	538	16.4	4.5
Harris	9 944	106 124	15 512.9	5 478.2	4 374	158 572	73 227.7	5 991.2	5 470	111 869	4 379.0	1 160.7
Harrison	86	506	83.6	27.3	90	3 128	600.4	83.2	75	1 017	35.1	9.3
Hartley	4	D	D	D	NA	NA	NA	NA	4	15	0.3	0.1
Haskell	7	13	0.6	0.1	NA	NA	NA	NA	8	97	2.3	0.7
Hays	140	459	42.9	14.1	108	3 389	477.0	96.2	177	2 890	88.4	25.4
Hemphill	7	14	1.4	0.2	NA	NA	NA	NA	12	69	1.4	0.3
Henderson	70	220	17.9	6.0	49	1 880	214.3	38.3	95	1 389	40.7	10.3
Hidalgo	482	2 682	193.4	62.7	261	10 284	1 428.2	178.3	626	10 871	352.1	90.1
Hill	29	89	6.2	1.5	37	1 237	174.4	30.7	67	785	25.3	6.4
Hockley	23	148	9.9	3.2	NA	NA	NA	NA	38	544	13.3	3.5
Hood	48	136	11.6	3.0	NA	NA	NA	NA	74	966	28.1	7.6
Hopkins	36	148	11.2	4.2	43	1 463	526.1	41.4	56	747	25.5	7.4
Houston	27	112	4.8	1.5	24	618	131.8	13.3	27	231	7.2	2.0
Howard	41	125	9.3	3.1	27	1 124	726.2	34.6	73	981	24.2	6.7
Hudspeth	NA	NA	NA	NA	NA	NA	NA	NA	5	35	1.4	0.2
Hunt	67	422	24.2	8.4	58	7 223	1 478.9	256.0	117	1 729	50.9	15.1
Hutchinson	24	115	7.4	2.7	30	1 718	1 949.1	89.1	48	578	15.1	4.0
Irion	1	D	D	D	NA	NA	NA	NA	5	D	D	D
Jack	12	27	1.2	0.5	NA	NA	NA	NA	11	D	D	D
Jackson	13	50	2.7	1.2	11	D	D	D	18	205	7.0	1.5
Jasper	32	126	10.3	1.9	29	1 911	543.2	76.6	49	714	21.6	5.6
Jeff Davis	1	D	D	D	NA	NA	NA	NA	12	138	4.5	1.3
Jefferson	469	4 143	490.9	204.3	230	14 471	15 920.2	727.0	426	8 206	261.9	69.9
Jim Hogg	3	14	0.7	0.3	NA	NA	NA	NA	14	106	3.0	0.9
Jim Wells	44	321	23.1	9.9	NA	NA	NA	NA	68	823	25.6	6.6
Johnson	113	499	39.3	12.2	170	5 942	981.4	161.3	134	1 885	60.2	16.6
Jones	13	46	2.2	0.8	NA	NA	NA	NA	24	119	3.7	1.0
Karnes	13	48	2.5	0.6	NA	NA	NA	NA	23	192	5.1	1.3
Kaufman	68	206	14.1	4.8	109	4 274	521.3	120.4	91	1 342	39.9	10.7
Kendall	57	158	11.6	3.9	NA	NA	NA	NA	50	858	27.7	8.5
Kenedy	1	D	D	D	NA	NA	NA	NA	1	D	D	D
Kent	NA	NA	NA	NA	NA	NA	NA	NA	1	D	D	D
Kerr	104	390	35.4	11.6	49	960	92.9	24.9	100	1 417	54.3	15.3
Kimble	7	43	1.7	0.5	NA	NA	NA	NA	27	212	6.7	1.9
King	NA	NA	NA	NA	NA	NA	NA	NA	1	D	D	D
Kinney	1	D	D	D	NA	NA	NA	NA	3	18	0.4	0.1
Kleberg	23	80	4.9	1.4	NA	NA	NA	NA	74	1 048	31.6	8.5
Knox	3	15	0.6	0.2	NA	NA	NA	NA	13	D	D	D
Lamar	52	243	13.6	4.3	60	4 809	2 056.3	161.0	96	1 466	45.9	13.0
Lamb	13	18	1.1	0.2	14	678	123.6	16.7	27	D	D	D
Lampasas	17	65	2.8	1.0	NA	NA	NA	NA	28	D	D	D
La Salle	3	8	0.7	0.1	NA	NA	NA	NA	8	93	3.4	0.9
Lavaca	28	100	19.9	2.2	46	2 127	192.5	37.2	32	375	9.2	2.6
Lee	24	87	6.4	2.5	NA	NA	NA	NA	24	252	8.2	2.1
Leon	15	42	2.4	0.7	NA	NA	NA	NA	24	385	9.3	2.6
Liberty	70	274	24.0	6.9	41	1 220	209.8	36.1	65	984	32.9	8.5
Limestone	22	48	3.4	0.9	17	790	80.1	15.4	33	290	9.7	2.4
Lipscomb	9	18	1.3	0.3	NA	NA	NA	NA	4	D	D	D
Live Oak	13	37	1.9	0.6	NA	NA	NA	NA	29	278	9.5	2.2
Llano	21	72	4.2	1.8	NA	NA	NA	NA	47	298	10.5	2.8
Loving	NA	NA	NA	NA	NA	NA	NA	NA	NA	NA	NA	NA
Lubbock	483	2 516	198.6	67.7	258	7 286	1 566.4	203.8	522	11 154	332.1	87.6
Lynn	4	13	0.4	0.2	NA	NA	NA	NA	7	48	1.0	0.3
McCulloch	17	95	6.7	2.4	NA	NA	NA	NA	23	181	7.1	1.6
McLennan	292	2 039	133.0	57.4	261	16 474	3 855.6	481.7	400	6 900	220.7	59.8
McMullen	1	D	D	D	NA	NA	NA	NA	2	D	D	D
Madison	15	60	4.5	1.3	NA	NA	NA	NA	19	213	7.9	2.1
Marion	4	8	0.8	0.1	NA	NA	NA	NA	35	185	5.0	1.3
Martin	4	11	0.7	0.3	NA	NA	NA	NA	4	28	0.6	0.2

1. Firms subject to federal tax.

Table B. States and Counties — **Health and Other Services and Federal Funds**

STATE County	Health Care and Social Assistance[1], 1997				Other Services[1], 1997				Federal funds and grants, fiscal 1999[2] Expenditures (mil dol)			
										Direct payments for individuals[3]		
	Number of Establishments	Number of Employees	Receipts (mil dol)	Annual Payroll (mil dol)	Number of Establishments	Number of Employees	Receipts (mil dol)	Annual Payroll (mil dol)	Total	Social Security and government retirement	Medicare	Food stamps and Supplemental Security Income
	159	160	161	162	163	164	165	166	167	168	169	170
TEXAS—Cont'd												
Guadalupe	109	1 150	55.9	23.4	76	453	25.7	7.5	358.6	182.2	41.8	8.8
Hale	51	496	26.1	9.1	67	234	13.6	3.5	184.4	56.9	33.3	6.2
Hall	5	89	2.4	0.8	1	D	D	D	35.7	8.6	5.5	0.7
Hamilton	18	306	12.7	6.3	13	27	3.1	0.6	42.8	20.3	12.4	0.8
Hansford	4	D	D	D	14	53	3.6	1.2	37.2	10.0	3.8	0.4
Hardeman	11	83	3.3	1.0	8	22	2.2	0.4	32.4	12.0	6.2	0.7
Hardin	66	1 589	49.3	22.7	46	248	12.9	2.9	164.3	84.6	42.8	6.2
Harris	6 996	92 982	6 784.1	2 802.4	5 209	45 636	3 189.5	978.4	13 997.9	3 412.4	1 769.9	495.4
Harrison	89	946	46.6	19.0	74	369	28.9	7.1	234.1	99.6	44.4	10.3
Hartley	9	42	2.6	0.9	7	42	4.3	0.7	19.4	1.9	0.7	0.1
Haskell	12	163	6.0	2.3	14	65	3.2	0.7	54.9	16.3	8.5	0.9
Hays	135	1 412	77.9	32.7	93	434	22.2	5.9	280.0	117.0	33.7	7.1
Hemphill	3	17	1.1	0.5	6	12	1.5	0.3	11.7	5.2	3.1	0.1
Henderson	86	1 201	63.7	31.8	68	255	13.9	3.7	236.8	122.1	54.8	8.3
Hidalgo	833	15 858	1 167.0	431.0	479	2 465	114.3	30.6	1 810.5	463.1	285.6	178.4
Hill	29	533	30.0	10.4	44	172	9.5	2.5	185.7	73.1	31.4	4.5
Hockley	28	331	14.3	5.9	29	87	5.9	1.3	117.4	35.1	19.6	2.1
Hood	70	595	31.8	14.1	56	319	13.3	4.3	158.4	111.7	30.2	2.3
Hopkins	63	692	35.5	12.0	56	244	13.8	3.5	140.7	59.6	29.7	3.6
Houston	29	880	23.7	11.2	27	126	8.9	2.1	122.6	50.5	25.7	4.7
Howard	60	1 000	63.6	24.7	55	265	11.9	3.4	231.3	71.8	37.1	6.2
Hudspeth	NA	NA	NA	NA	3	5	0.3	0.1	14.0	3.8	1.8	0.3
Hunt	111	1 607	79.5	34.2	90	320	20.4	4.7	598.7	138.3	62.0	9.7
Hutchinson	39	769	31.5	12.5	33	219	17.3	3.8	93.4	50.0	20.4	2.4
Irion	NA	NA	NA	NA	NA	NA	NA	NA	6.4	3.3	1.2	0.1
Jack	7	74	2.8	1.1	9	12	1.1	0.2	27.5	14.3	7.1	0.8
Jackson	13	237	8.5	3.2	20	70	4.4	1.4	75.5	24.9	15.4	1.8
Jasper	65	1 412	42.3	21.7	47	238	12.1	3.6	161.1	68.4	40.3	6.4
Jeff Davis	5	15	0.8	0.2	NA	NA	NA	NA	13.3	4.5	1.4	0.2
Jefferson	707	11 019	681.3	287.9	471	3 318	188.7	56.0	1 350.9	460.4	285.8	47.0
Jim Hogg	3	73	1.4	0.9	3	6	0.5	0.1	30.8	7.2	6.9	1.6
Jim Wells	72	2 680	95.2	42.9	60	320	16.0	4.4	194.6	65.4	41.4	6.4
Johnson	135	1 711	82.7	38.2	145	633	43.2	10.7	350.3	206.3	77.8	10.2
Jones	17	362	13.4	4.9	15	35	2.6	0.5	91.7	33.5	17.9	2.3
Karnes	17	214	7.2	3.0	17	61	3.4	0.7	74.8	24.6	14.8	3.5
Kaufman	120	1 868	91.8	37.5	96	671	56.1	14.7	287.4	154.0	72.0	9.3
Kendall	40	527	19.8	9.2	37	153	8.2	2.7	104.1	72.3	15.4	1.2
Kenedy	NA	NA	NA	NA	NA	NA	NA	NA	1.4	0.4	0.3	0.0
Kent	NA	NA	NA	NA	NA	NA	NA	NA	10.1	2.3	1.0	0.1
Kerr	106	1 446	79.0	31.7	90	458	28.8	8.5	246.6	156.8	43.3	4.3
Kimble	3	D	D	D	7	29	1.6	0.4	18.2	9.8	4.2	0.6
King	NA	NA	NA	NA	NA	NA	NA	NA	2.5	0.4	0.1	0.0
Kinney	1	D	D	D	NA	NA	NA	NA	22.7	10.7	3.3	1.2
Kleberg	52	503	26.4	11.1	48	212	9.8	2.6	253.0	47.2	21.6	7.0
Knox	8	161	5.7	3.0	10	41	3.5	0.8	36.9	10.0	6.3	0.8
Lamar	148	2 772	101.2	46.8	84	394	18.9	5.2	243.3	97.8	42.7	9.3
Lamb	13	178	5.3	2.3	27	62	4.0	0.9	94.9	27.7	16.9	2.4
Lampasas	20	407	15.2	8.5	16	81	4.4	1.3	86.5	55.1	16.9	1.6
La Salle	5	D	D	D	7	24	1.4	0.2	34.5	8.0	4.8	1.9
Lavaca	34	354	15.4	6.2	32	107	6.9	1.7	112.8	51.5	26.1	1.9
Lee	21	178	8.1	2.8	24	75	6.0	1.2	45.8	23.4	9.6	1.2
Leon	16	192	7.8	3.5	20	59	3.2	0.7	94.6	42.5	18.4	2.3
Liberty	87	1 635	90.7	33.2	61	317	15.9	4.5	266.1	107.8	70.1	8.3
Limestone	31	456	17.0	6.6	25	65	4.9	1.2	111.0	46.5	20.0	4.0
Lipscomb	2	D	D	D	5	30	0.7	0.4	15.5	6.1	2.8	0.1
Live Oak	9	170	6.9	2.3	18	49	3.2	0.6	71.6	15.4	9.1	1.7
Llano	21	322	13.5	6.6	13	35	1.6	0.6	87.8	59.9	19.0	1.0
Loving	NA	NA	NA	NA	1	D	D	D	0.9	0.2	0.0	0.0
Lubbock	622	8 383	566.2	239.1	405	3 053	178.4	53.2	951.1	371.2	209.9	35.2
Lynn	4	9	0.5	0.2	7	20	1.3	0.3	54.9	11.3	7.1	1.1
McCulloch	12	261	8.9	4.8	17	63	2.8	0.6	47.1	20.0	10.8	1.9
McLennan	353	4 861	265.9	126.4	329	2 065	114.1	34.4	1 023.7	421.3	113.9	32.2
McMullen	NA	NA	NA	NA	NA	NA	NA	NA	6.7	1.5	0.4	0.1
Madison	13	235	6.8	3.5	10	78	12.4	1.7	42.5	19.6	7.9	1.7
Marion	10	177	4.9	2.4	16	43	2.1	0.5	55.2	22.7	8.8	3.1
Martin	7	92	4.5	1.6	5	D	D	D	37.8	6.9	4.0	0.8

1. Firms subject to federal tax. 2. October 1, 1998 to September 30, 1999. 3. State totals may include programs not allocated by county.

	Federal funds and grants, fiscal 1999[1] (cont'd)							Local government finances, 1997				
	Expenditures (mil dol) (cont'd)							General revenue				
STATE County	Procurement contract awards			Grants[2]						Taxes		
											Per capita[3] (dollars)	
	Salaries and wages	Defense	Other	Medicaid and other health-related	Nutrition and family welfare	Education	Other	Total (mil dol)	Intergovern-mental (mil dol)	Total (mil dol)	Total	Property
	171	172	173	174	175	176	177	178	179	180	181	182
TEXAS—Cont'd												
Guadalupe	11.1	0.2	2.3	28.9	4.8	2.5	9.6	116.9	53.9	47.7	612	504
Hale	5.6	0.4	1.7	23.0	4.4	1.9	2.0	82.0	40.8	27.4	750	527
Hall	1.1	0.0	0.2	4.0	0.5	0.2	2.3	10.3	4.5	3.8	1 037	869
Hamilton	1.5	0.0	0.6	4.5	0.2	0.2	0.7	13.6	7.5	4.4	580	465
Hansford	0.7	0.0	0.2	0.9	0.1	0.2	0.7	24.4	4.3	13.2	2 442	2 299
Hardeman	0.9	0.0	0.2	3.9	0.5	0.2	0.0	14.8	4.2	6.5	1 374	1 155
Hardin	4.2	0.0	1.0	18.1	2.7	1.4	2.3	78.2	41.3	26.3	544	486
Harris	1 371.4	428.1	4 007.6	1 129.8	271.1	138.7	730.5	8 382.8	2 056.8	4 158.1	1 317	1 038
Harrison	7.0	-0.4	2.7	50.6	6.4	4.2	2.8	102.5	29.4	50.4	844	806
Hartley	0.3	0.0	0.1	0.2	0.1	0.1	0.0	4.1	1.2	2.6	511	444
Haskell	1.5	0.0	0.3	4.5	0.5	0.3	3.8	14.8	6.3	5.6	914	783
Hays	8.4	0.6	44.9	27.5	7.6	4.8	15.5	167.7	58.2	70.2	814	633
Hemphill	0.5	0.0	0.1	0.4	0.1	0.1	0.3	15.9	0.7	10.6	2 938	2 750
Henderson	5.1	0.2	1.3	30.9	2.8	2.2	4.6	112.7	47.7	47.6	707	578
Hidalgo	127.1	68.5	34.1	367.8	93.6	54.4	63.7	1 210.8	769.1	282.0	552	421
Hill	4.8	1.3	1.7	21.1	1.7	1.4	30.8	68.4	32.7	20.9	696	490
Hockley	2.4	0.0	0.6	9.6	6.5	1.4	10.5	88.8	28.1	36.8	1 540	1 450
Hood	4.7	0.0	1.3	5.0	1.0	0.5	0.9	69.0	20.0	27.5	760	637
Hopkins	4.7	0.0	1.2	18.8	2.2	0.9	11.9	69.2	20.0	21.1	691	541
Houston	3.6	0.5	1.1	27.2	2.0	1.4	0.2	32.6	16.5	12.6	575	468
Howard	36.0	29.8	3.4	19.8	3.0	1.8	0.5	90.2	28.5	32.3	992	772
Hudspeth	3.9	0.4	0.1	0.4	0.4	0.3	1.1	12.5	4.7	3.3	993	905
Hunt	16.5	257.9	32.3	38.4	4.9	2.7	25.2	165.1	63.7	51.2	739	585
Hutchinson	3.6	0.0	0.7	5.9	0.7	0.7	0.9	60.3	15.4	27.4	1 144	942
Irion	0.3	0.0	0.1	0.5	0.0	0.0	0.2	5.9	0.4	4.5	2 657	2 548
Jack	1.1	0.0	0.3	2.3	0.3	0.3	0.0	19.5	6.5	7.1	974	817
Jackson	1.5	0.0	0.4	7.9	1.4	0.5	0.4	44.4	10.7	13.8	1 014	861
Jasper	3.9	0.6	0.9	25.9	3.5	1.4	7.3	74.4	33.6	29.4	886	751
Jeff Davis	1.0	0.0	0.1	1.1	0.1	0.1	4.3	3.9	1.9	1.8	825	735
Jefferson	140.7	115.1	77.3	129.0	29.4	11.7	19.6	553.3	112.3	332.6	1 375	1 041
Jim Hogg	2.6	0.5	0.1	10.0	0.8	0.4	0.1	12.5	5.3	6.3	1 270	1 218
Jim Wells	6.2	0.0	1.0	43.8	9.2	2.5	8.5	76.4	41.5	24.0	602	425
Johnson	11.4	0.2	3.0	26.1	3.6	2.7	2.4	184.3	83.8	70.6	619	530
Jones	2.6	0.0	0.6	10.0	1.4	0.7	0.8	43.1	21.7	10.0	529	415
Karnes	1.8	0.0	0.5	20.5	3.6	1.1	0.6	33.7	16.1	9.9	792	656
Kaufman	9.5	0.3	2.1	23.0	4.6	2.6	2.0	122.6	64.1	43.7	684	560
Kendall	2.7	6.4	1.0	2.3	0.7	0.6	1.2	38.4	9.5	23.4	1 145	994
Kenedy	0.4	0.0	0.0	0.2	0.0	0.0	0.0	2.7	0.0	2.6	6 077	6 000
Kent	0.4	0.0	0.1	0.7	0.2	0.0	2.5	11.9	0.2	10.7	12 446	12 311
Kerr	24.2	0.5	1.7	8.2	1.8	1.3	2.7	66.9	19.9	35.8	839	654
Kimble	0.7	0.0	0.0	1.6	0.4	0.1	0.4	13.4	3.4	3.0	703	557
King	0.2	0.0	0.0	0.2	0.0	0.0	0.0	3.7	0.0	3.1	8 945	8 546
Kinney	3.7	0.1	0.0	2.3	0.3	0.2	0.1	6.8	3.7	2.3	655	557
Kleberg	44.9	86.3	0.8	21.0	4.5	3.7	3.7	67.6	30.1	26.0	860	710
Knox	1.5	0.1	0.5	4.3	0.5	0.2	2.1	20.2	7.3	3.7	848	715
Lamar	8.2	0.4	2.1	47.2	4.5	2.8	14.8	84.8	37.7	34.6	756	636
Lamb	1.8	0.0	0.4	10.2	1.3	1.1	0.7	41.3	14.7	17.3	1 164	1 055
Lampasas	2.1	0.0	0.5	6.1	1.2	0.7	0.2	27.3	14.7	8.4	482	382
La Salle	2.1	0.0	0.2	10.6	1.2	0.5	2.5	15.9	7.9	4.1	697	586
Lavaca	2.9	0.0	0.8	22.2	1.1	0.6	2.2	24.6	6.6	12.1	649	553
Lee	1.4	0.0	0.5	7.0	0.7	0.5	0.2	25.2	10.1	11.6	786	665
Leon	2.6	0.1	0.7	18.0	0.8	0.5	5.2	25.7	9.1	14.3	988	864
Liberty	6.1	1.5	1.8	29.1	8.4	2.2	15.7	99.2	41.9	44.2	691	586
Limestone	3.2	0.9	1.1	21.4	1.7	0.9	5.0	51.9	15.0	28.3	1 343	1 229
Lipscomb	0.9	0.0	0.2	0.7	0.1	0.1	0.0	10.9	2.0	7.2	2 390	2 240
Live Oak	17.4	14.6	3.3	5.2	0.5	0.5	0.1	20.2	4.3	13.3	1 310	1 216
Llano	2.0	0.0	0.7	3.9	0.1	0.2	0.4	33.5	1.6	14.7	1 125	1 033
Loving	0.2	0.0	0.0	0.0	0.0	0.0	0.3	1.3	0.0	1.1	10 094	9 962
Lubbock	68.6	24.3	13.6	83.7	21.2	11.3	55.2	644.4	274.3	179.0	776	586
Lynn	1.1	0.0	0.3	4.6	0.8	0.5	0.4	17.9	9.1	5.6	849	759
McCulloch	1.7	0.0	0.4	7.7	0.8	0.5	0.3	23.5	10.9	5.6	640	491
McLennan	102.9	109.6	12.5	121.6	16.9	9.6	21.5	607.1	185.8	162.8	802	575
McMullen	0.3	0.0	0.1	0.2	0.1	0.0	3.7	5.3	0.1	4.4	5 589	5 381
Madison	1.1	0.0	0.4	7.5	0.8	0.5	2.1	18.7	7.8	7.2	602	465
Marion	2.3	0.6	0.3	13.4	1.5	0.7	1.5	14.2	6.0	7.0	654	420
Martin	0.8	0.1	0.2	3.4	0.9	0.4	0.3	15.7	6.5	6.8	1 349	1 246

1. October 1, 1998 to September 30, 1999.   2. State totals may include programs not allocated by county.   3. Based on the resident population estimated as of July 1 of the year shown.

Table B. States and Counties — Local Government Finances, Government Employment, and Elections

STATE County	Local government finances, 1997 (cont'd) Direct general expenditure Total (mil dol)	Per capita[1] (dollars)	Education	Health and hospitals	Police protection	Public welfare	Highways	Debt outstanding Total (mil dol)	Per capita[1] (dollars)	Government employment, 1998 Federal civilian	Federal military	State and local	Presidential election, 2000 Percent of vote cast — Democratic	Republican	All other
	183	184	185	186	187	188	189	190	191	192	193	194	195	196	197
TEXAS—Cont'd															
Guadalupe	119.6	1 534	68.7	0.8	4.2	0.1	3.9	75.0	962	177	214	4 196	27.2	70.3	2.5
Hale	76.1	2 079	58.1	10.1	7.9	0.6	3.0	8.7	238	127	97	2 635	23.7	75.4	0.9
Hall	9.4	2 539	62.7	7.2	3.3	0.1	4.3	3.7	1 006	30	10	357	32.6	66.8	0.6
Hamilton	13.2	1 736	79.6	0.0	4.2	0.0	5.3	6.0	789	33	20	511	26.0	72.5	1.5
Hansford	16.3	3 013	53.9	22.5	2.4	0.0	6.3	21.7	4 026	19	14	532	9.5	89.8	0.8
Hardeman	15.0	3 197	46.7	28.4	2.7	0.1	6.4	1.6	350	23	12	431	36.4	62.7	1.0
Hardin	79.8	1 649	77.3	0.7	3.1	0.6	3.9	34.0	703	76	129	2 239	31.4	67.1	1.6
Harris	8 165.3	2 586	44.5	9.4	7.0	0.3	3.5	15 724.2	4 979	24 479	9 568	193 988	42.9	54.3	2.8
Harrison	94.7	1 587	68.3	0.2	4.3	0.6	2.4	83.2	1 395	129	159	2 918	38.7	60.2	1.1
Hartley	4.4	852	66.6	0.1	4.1	0.0	8.9	0.8	151	11	14	459	17.7	81.0	1.3
Haskell	14.7	2 409	60.8	14.5	1.7	0.3	8.0	0.4	60	38	16	457	47.9	50.8	1.3
Hays	185.0	2 144	53.1	0.5	3.6	1.3	5.6	285.0	3 303	141	243	8 894	33.2	58.8	8.0
Hemphill	17.1	4 735	47.9	25.4	3.4	0.0	9.5	2.4	672	16	0	351	17.0	81.6	1.4
Henderson	110.7	1 644	74.0	0.1	5.7	0.3	4.8	63.4	941	99	183	2 795	34.0	64.8	1.2
Hidalgo	1 109.5	2 172	72.7	2.8	3.5	0.7	1.7	572.4	1 120	2 698	1 395	35 353	60.8	37.9	1.3
Hill	75.8	2 523	73.5	5.3	3.0	0.0	3.7	38.4	1 279	92	81	1 923	32.8	65.7	1.5
Hockley	86.2	3 604	73.4	0.6	2.0	0.3	2.4	137.2	5 734	57	63	1 719	21.0	77.8	1.1
Hood	67.9	1 876	52.2	24.8	2.9	0.0	3.2	50.8	1 404	90	99	1 536	26.9	71.0	2.1
Hopkins	65.2	2 136	46.9	28.1	4.3	0.0	4.9	24.1	788	99	81	1 914	33.8	64.9	1.3
Houston	30.2	1 381	73.8	0.1	4.4	0.0	5.2	16.8	769	91	58	2 062	34.4	64.4	1.2
Howard	88.3	2 712	60.6	1.5	3.9	2.4	3.1	224.8	6 904	813	85	2 867	28.7	69.8	1.4
Hudspeth	10.6	3 186	58.5	0.1	4.2	0.1	5.8	2.6	782	77	0	290	41.2	55.7	3.0
Hunt	167.8	2 421	46.8	25.4	3.8	0.0	4.0	109.8	1 585	312	243	5 774	32.1	66.1	1.8
Hutchinson	62.3	2 599	56.1	14.9	3.9	0.4	3.7	9.3	390	72	64	1 694	19.2	79.6	1.2
Irion	3.9	2 301	79.5	0.2	1.5	0.2	4.7	0.0	23	0	0	122	20.4	78.7	0.9
Jack	18.2	2 482	61.7	10.2	3.6	0.0	7.4	11.3	1 543	19	20	525	27.6	70.8	1.5
Jackson	41.3	3 027	50.7	13.7	3.1	0.0	5.3	69.8	5 110	38	36	1 009	29.8	69.3	0.9
Jasper	69.1	2 081	68.4	6.5	3.7	0.2	4.8	26.9	809	82	89	2 033	38.6	60.2	1.2
Jeff Davis	4.1	1 839	76.5	0.1	2.9	1.2	2.8	0.2	76	28	0	210	26.7	66.8	6.5
Jefferson	565.5	2 337	46.5	3.4	6.6	0.5	5.4	777.7	3 214	2 525	770	16 321	52.2	46.4	1.4
Jim Hogg	12.1	2 465	63.2	0.0	6.7	1.9	5.4	7.5	1 516	63	13	437	70.1	28.9	1.0
Jim Wells	70.4	1 767	71.1	0.1	4.1	0.8	3.8	19.6	492	92	142	2 118	61.7	37.4	0.9
Johnson	204.2	1 790	67.1	0.1	3.9	1.3	4.2	154.7	1 357	223	314	4 800	30.4	67.7	1.9
Jones	39.1	2 081	60.1	15.5	4.3	0.0	5.1	6.1	324	91	52	2 545	31.4	67.5	1.1
Karnes	28.5	2 283	65.7	11.3	2.8	0.2	2.2	8.8	707	37	33	1 701	37.5	61.2	1.2
Kaufman	120.4	1 885	76.2	0.0	3.9	0.7	2.6	64.1	1 003	168	175	4 262	32.3	66.3	1.4
Kendall	40.8	2 003	72.0	0.6	4.6	0.1	4.0	30.6	1 501	49	56	1 136	17.2	79.4	3.5
Kenedy	2.1	4 806	93.5	0.1	0.7	0.1	2.1	0.0	0	0	0	81	52.2	46.5	1.3
Kent	11.2	13 006	72.6	1.1	2.4	2.7	9.1	0.0	0	0	0	193	34.5	64.6	0.9
Kerr	60.3	1 415	60.8	0.6	6.3	0.9	4.2	40.5	950	646	115	2 713	20.8	76.1	3.1
Kimble	13.4	3 196	34.9	21.6	2.4	0.1	3.9	1.8	428	17	11	320	19.7	78.8	1.5
King	3.3	9 474	68.7	0.0	2.2	0.0	11.0	0.0	0	0	0	53	10.2	87.6	2.2
Kinney	6.4	1 840	67.7	0.0	1.7	2.2	1.6	2.9	829	66	0	231	33.7	64.5	1.8
Kleberg	67.1	2 219	57.7	1.2	7.4	2.6	3.8	20.9	692	671	716	3 641	48.7	49.2	2.0
Knox	17.7	4 108	48.0	25.2	2.5	0.0	3.0	2.3	542	40	11	419	39.1	60.1	0.8
Lamar	85.1	1 860	74.6	0.6	3.5	0.4	4.0	33.8	739	162	122	2 852	36.0	63.4	0.7
Lamb	39.8	2 678	63.5	16.2	3.8	0.1	3.4	4.0	267	47	39	995	24.2	75.1	0.7
Lampasas	31.2	1 781	71.1	0.4	5.6	0.5	4.7	8.4	481	45	47	881	25.2	72.8	1.9
La Salle	15.4	2 603	56.9	2.3	4.2	0.0	6.9	2.5	424	45	16	502	62.9	36.3	0.8
Lavaca	25.0	1 337	51.9	5.3	6.1	0.4	7.7	6.3	337	58	50	845	28.8	70.1	1.2
Lee	30.7	2 072	70.6	0.5	4.3	0.1	5.4	17.4	1 179	33	40	1 179	31.3	66.8	1.9
Leon	24.3	1 682	73.4	0.0	2.4	0.6	7.0	11.9	823	49	38	689	29.9	69.0	1.1
Liberty	98.3	1 537	64.7	0.2	4.5	0.4	5.8	47.6	745	119	173	3 799	36.4	62.1	1.5
Limestone	48.8	2 320	66.5	9.7	5.0	0.3	4.6	12.0	568	61	56	2 924	39.1	59.5	1.3
Lipscomb	10.5	3 458	59.7	11.7	3.7	0.1	7.5	0.3	87	23	0	321	15.9	82.8	1.2
Live Oak	21.2	2 092	65.5	1.7	7.1	0.4	11.0	5.0	493	329	27	626	27.8	70.6	1.5
Llano	35.0	2 669	33.3	39.0	3.1	0.0	3.6	4.8	366	35	36	887	24.8	73.0	2.2
Loving	1.9	17 943	0.0	0.0	8.2	0.0	3.6	0.0	0	0	0	16	18.6	79.5	1.9
Lubbock	567.6	2 461	42.2	28.0	4.5	0.1	2.5	429.7	1 863	1 206	657	21 124	24.3	73.7	2.0
Lynn	17.3	2 622	67.1	13.7	3.7	0.1	3.3	2.4	359	29	18	530	27.0	72.3	0.7
McCulloch	22.3	2 540	52.7	17.6	3.3	0.8	2.3	13.8	1 569	32	23	676	27.2	71.4	1.4
McLennan	591.5	2 914	40.6	3.6	4.2	0.2	3.0	2 887.4	14 225	3 220	579	11 831	34.1	63.9	2.0
McMullen	3.6	4 564	63.4	0.0	3.2	0.5	17.4	0.0	5	0	0	110	17.5	81.5	0.9
Madison	16.7	1 399	71.7	0.0	4.7	0.4	7.5	15.4	1 293	25	32	1 169	34.3	64.4	1.4
Marion	12.9	1 208	68.8	0.5	6.8	0.0	5.9	4.6	429	37	29	427	47.1	51.9	1.0
Martin	15.2	2 999	51.2	24.7	2.4	0.1	7.7	1.6	321	22	13	381	21.3	78.0	0.7

1. Based on the resident population estimated as of July 1 of the year shown.

Table B. States and Counties — **Land Area and Population**

STATE/ County code	MSA/ PMSA/ NECMA code[1]	County Type[2]	STATE County	Land area,[3] (sq km) 1990	Total persons	Rank	Per square kilometer	White	Black	Am. Indian, Eskimo, Aleut	Asian and Pacific Islander	Percent Hispanic[4]	Under 5 years	5 to 17 years	18 to 24 years	25 to 34 years	35 to 44 years	45 to 54 years
				1	2	3	4	5	6	7	8	9	10	11	12	13	14	15
			TEXAS—Cont'd															
48 319	...	9	Mason	2 414	3 646	2 939	1.5	98.9	0.2	0.6	0.3	25.3	6.3	17.8	5.8	8.6	13.5	14.2
48 321	...	4	Matagorda	2 887	37 828	1 140	13.1	82.2	14.2	0.3	3.4	30.1	8.6	22.6	7.9	12.3	14.9	12.5
48 323	...	5	Maverick	3 316	48 639	929	14.7	97.9	0.2	1.6	0.3	95.0	10.3	26.8	10.1	10.9	14.0	11.0
48 325	...	6	Medina	3 439	37 698	1 144	11.0	96.6	2.4	0.6	0.5	51.6	7.8	20.7	9.0	11.8	15.6	12.8
48 327	...	8	Menard	2 336	2 262	3 039	1.0	99.2	0.4	0.4	0.0	39.6	7.3	18.2	5.7	9.6	12.9	12.2
48 329	5800	3	Midland	2 332	118 490	444	50.8	89.8	8.4	0.5	1.3	26.6	9.2	21.8	8.0	13.4	16.0	11.8
48 331	...	6	Milam	2 633	24 302	1 562	9.2	85.7	13.6	0.4	0.3	19.6	6.9	21.4	7.4	9.7	13.8	13.2
48 333	...	9	Mills	1 938	4 726	2 857	2.4	99.5	0.3	0.2	0.1	14.1	6.2	18.0	5.6	8.3	13.5	12.9
48 335	...	7	Mitchell	2 357	8 782	2 525	3.7	89.7	9.9	0.2	0.1	36.6	5.6	18.3	9.1	13.0	15.6	11.6
48 337	...	6	Montague	2 411	18 753	1 835	7.8	99.3	0.1	0.5	0.1	4.4	6.3	18.7	6.6	9.2	13.1	14.4
48 339	3360	1	Montgomery	2 705	287 644	190	106.3	93.7	4.7	0.4	1.1	9.6	7.6	21.7	8.2	12.0	17.9	15.3
48 341	...	6	Moore	2 330	19 734	1 776	8.5	95.1	1.0	1.1	2.7	38.0	10.2	23.5	9.4	12.7	13.8	11.4
48 343	...	6	Morris	659	13 140	2 201	19.9	73.1	26.1	0.6	0.2	2.6	5.9	20.5	6.8	10.2	14.2	13.5
48 345	...	9	Motley	2 563	1 317	3 102	0.5	93.8	5.4	0.4	0.5	11.4	5.2	17.8	5.7	7.8	12.6	13.6
48 347	...	5	Nacogdoches	2 452	56 147	826	22.9	80.3	18.5	0.3	0.9	6.9	6.3	17.4	20.3	10.9	13.7	11.4
48 349	...	4	Navarro	2 774	41 872	1 044	15.1	78.4	20.2	0.4	1.0	9.6	7.2	19.8	9.6	11.0	14.0	13.6
48 351	...	8	Newton	2 416	14 346	2 109	5.9	75.1	24.5	0.3	0.1	1.5	6.3	22.0	7.9	9.9	14.4	14.3
48 353	...	6	Nolan	2 362	16 253	1 989	6.9	93.8	5.6	0.4	0.3	31.9	7.4	20.7	8.5	10.6	14.3	12.9
48 355	1880	2	Nueces	2 165	315 469	178	145.7	93.8	4.4	0.5	1.3	59.6	8.6	21.8	9.6	13.3	15.7	12.1
48 357	...	7	Ochiltree	2 377	8 683	2 537	3.7	97.9	0.1	1.4	0.6	22.6	8.5	22.4	7.6	12.9	14.9	12.0
48 359	...	8	Oldham	3 887	2 210	3 045	0.6	96.2	0.9	1.8	1.2	10.8	5.8	34.9	5.5	8.2	12.6	11.9
48 361	0840	2	Orange	923	85 240	592	92.4	89.5	9.2	0.3	1.0	3.3	6.5	21.0	8.4	10.9	15.4	15.1
48 363	...	6	Palo Pinto	2 468	26 156	1 488	10.6	95.1	3.4	0.4	1.1	12.0	7.2	19.0	7.9	10.5	14.0	13.7
48 365	...	6	Panola	2 075	22 978	1 613	11.1	79.5	20.1	0.3	0.2	2.9	6.2	21.2	8.2	10.1	15.1	13.9
48 367	2800	1	Parker	2 340	85 427	588	36.5	97.5	1.1	0.7	0.6	5.7	6.9	20.4	7.9	11.0	16.8	15.5
48 369	...	7	Parmer	2 284	10 351	2 393	4.5	97.8	1.4	0.4	0.3	48.0	9.6	24.1	8.4	11.4	13.7	12.6
48 371	...	7	Pecos	12 339	16 066	2 000	1.3	94.5	5.5	0.5	0.4	60.6	7.8	21.6	9.9	13.4	15.4	12.4
48 373	...	6	Polk	2 739	52 520	872	19.2	82.4	15.0	2.2	0.4	8.7	5.5	17.0	7.8	10.2	13.6	12.7
48 375	0320	3	Potter	2 355	109 107	485	46.3	84.8	9.8	1.3	4.1	24.4	8.7	19.4	9.9	13.2	14.0	11.3
48 377	...	7	Presidio	9 987	8 954	2 511	0.9	99.2	0.2	0.2	0.4	85.6	8.5	23.7	8.8	9.9	13.1	12.4
48 379	0320	3	Rains	601	8 957	2 510	14.9	94.5	4.8	0.5	0.2	3.3	5.7	19.1	7.1	9.5	14.2	14.9
48 381	...	3	Randall	2 368	99 584	520	42.1	96.7	1.5	0.6	1.2	9.4	7.3	20.9	10.1	12.8	17.8	14.4
48 383	...	9	Reagan	3 044	3 865	2 926	1.3	96.0	3.6	0.2	0.2	50.2	10.5	28.0	8.6	12.6	15.7	9.9
48 385	...	9	Real	1 813	2 727	3 009	1.5	98.9	0.3	0.8	0.0	27.6	5.8	16.8	7.7	7.0	11.4	14.2
48 387	...	6	Red River	2 720	13 685	2 158	5.0	77.4	21.6	0.8	0.1	2.8	5.3	18.5	7.9	9.2	13.4	14.2
48 389	...	7	Reeves	6 827	14 020	2 137	2.1	97.4	2.1	0.3	0.3	77.1	9.2	23.1	9.3	12.4	13.4	11.7
48 391	...	6	Refugio	1 995	7 735	2 624	3.9	91.2	8.3	0.4	0.1	46.9	6.5	20.2	8.0	10.5	13.5	14.1
48 393	...	9	Roberts	2 394	924	3 113	0.4	99.6	0.0	0.1	0.3	4.1	6.2	22.7	4.4	9.8	16.6	16.6
48 395	...	6	Robertson	2 213	15 762	2 019	7.1	70.9	28.5	0.3	0.3	16.2	7.6	20.7	8.5	10.6	13.0	12.3
48 397	1920	0	Rockwall	334	39 489	1 100	118.2	94.8	3.7	0.4	1.0	7.6	7.0	20.9	6.9	11.5	18.5	16.4
48 399	...	6	Runnels	2 731	11 337	2 319	4.2	98.0	1.7	0.2	0.2	30.5	7.2	20.7	7.2	9.5	13.4	12.8
48 401	...	6	Rusk	2 392	45 819	973	19.2	76.8	22.4	0.5	0.2	5.8	6.3	20.9	7.8	10.8	15.3	13.5
48 403	...	6	Sabine	1 270	10 553	2 374	8.3	87.2	12.4	0.1	0.2	1.8	4.9	15.3	5.9	7.1	10.1	14.5
48 405	...	9	San Augustine	1 367	8 079	2 588	5.9	70.1	29.5	0.2	0.1	2.3	5.5	17.9	7.1	8.8	11.7	13.9
48 407	...	8	San Jacinto	1 478	22 554	1 631	15.3	82.4	16.9	0.5	0.1	3.6	5.8	19.8	6.9	9.3	14.0	15.6
48 409	1880	2	San Patricio	1 792	71 636	686	40.0	96.4	2.4	0.5	0.6	56.9	8.5	22.9	11.3	11.5	14.9	12.6
48 411	...	7	San Saba	2 938	5 812	2 784	2.0	97.6	2.2	0.1	0.1	23.6	6.4	23.9	6.8	7.8	12.4	12.3
48 413	...	8	Schleicher	3 395	2 938	2 993	0.9	98.4	1.4	0.2	0.1	42.6	8.4	24.3	5.7	10.0	14.6	11.5
48 415	...	7	Scurry	2 338	17 649	1 892	7.5	93.0	5.7	0.8	0.5	29.5	7.1	20.4	8.5	13.2	15.3	11.5
48 417	...	8	Shackelford	2 367	3 220	2 976	1.4	98.7	0.6	0.3	0.3	11.0	6.8	20.8	5.2	10.2	14.3	13.1
48 419	...	7	Shelby	2 057	22 685	1 625	11.0	76.6	23.0	0.2	0.2	3.3	6.5	19.5	8.1	9.8	13.4	13.9
48 421	...	9	Sherman	2 391	2 898	2 996	1.2	99.0	0.3	0.4	0.3	22.6	6.6	21.0	6.7	9.8	13.7	14.0
48 423	8640	3	Smith	2 405	169 693	312	70.6	76.4	22.5	0.4	0.7	7.8	6.9	19.2	9.6	11.8	15.5	13.5
48 425	...	8	Somervell	485	6 615	2 719	13.6	98.5	0.3	0.6	0.7	17.9	8.2	23.5	7.8	10.9	16.6	12.8
48 427	...	6	Starr	3 168	56 577	821	17.9	99.7	0.1	0.1	0.1	97.9	10.8	27.7	11.4	11.7	12.9	11.4
48 429	...	7	Stephens	2 317	9 737	2 452	4.2	93.9	5.3	0.3	0.4	12.8	6.5	19.6	7.2	11.0	14.7	13.4
48 431	...	8	Sterling	2 392	1 328	3 101	0.6	98.7	0.2	1.1	0.0	31.6	9.9	24.2	6.6	13.6	13.2	11.0
48 433	...	9	Stonewall	2 380	1 715	3 081	0.7	94.8	4.8	0.0	0.4	14.6	6.2	18.8	5.8	10.4	11.3	13.2
48 435	...	7	Sutton	3 766	4 309	2 884	1.1	90.0	0.3	0.5	0.2	52.6	7.7	22.4	8.1	10.9	16.4	13.1
48 437	...	6	Swisher	2 332	8 262	2 573	3.5	92.2	6.8	0.3	0.7	36.6	7.9	19.9	8.5	11.2	13.1	13.2
48 439	2800	0	Tarrant	2 236	1 382 442	22	618.3	82.6	13.0	0.6	3.9	15.6	8.4	19.0	10.6	15.7	17.1	13.2
48 441	0040	3	Taylor	2 372	122 478	431	51.6	90.6	6.9	0.5	2.0	19.0	8.0	19.2	12.8	12.7	14.3	11.7
48 443	...	9	Terrell	6 107	1 202	3 104	0.2	99.3	0.1	0.5	0.2	59.7	6.7	21.2	5.1	9.3	14.9	15.6
48 445	...	6	Terry	2 305	12 786	2 226	5.5	94.5	4.9	0.3	0.3	45.2	8.5	23.0	8.3	11.3	13.0	12.0
48 447	...	9	Throckmorton	2 363	1 695	3 082	0.7	99.0	0.0	0.4	0.6	10.5	6.5	18.1	5.7	9.7	13.1	15.4
48 449	...	7	Titus	1 063	25 343	1 520	23.8	84.4	14.8	0.5	0.2	13.8	8.2	20.8	9.7	11.6	14.8	12.5

1. MSA = Metropolitan Statistical Area. PMSA = Primary MSA. NECMA = New England County Metropolitan Area. See Appendix A for explanation of these concepts. See Appendix B for list of metropolitan areas identified by type, with component counties.   2. County typology code from the Economic Research Service of USDA. See Appendix A for definition.   3. Dry land or land partially or temporarily covered by water.   4. Hispanic persons may be of any race.

Table B. States and Counties — Population and Households

STATE County	55 to 64 years (16)	65 to 74 years (17)	75 years and over (18)	Percent female (19)	1990 (20)	1980 (21)	1980–1990 (22)	1990–1999 (23)	Births (24)	Deaths (25)	Net migration (26)	Number (27)	Percent change, 1980–1990 (28)	Persons per household (29)	Female family householder[1] (30)	One person (31)
TEXAS—Cont'd																
Mason	12.6	9.4	11.9	51.5	3 423	3 683	-7.1	6.5	304	523	455	1 435	-1.8	2.35	5.6	28.7
Matagorda	8.9	6.7	5.6	50.5	36 928	37 828	-2.4	2.4	5 798	3 057	-1 777	13 164	0.4	2.79	11.7	22.9
Maverick	7.6	5.4	3.9	52.9	36 378	31 398	15.9	33.7	10 158	2 051	4 264	9 756	28.7	3.70	14.5	14.9
Medina	9.5	6.9	5.7	48.3	27 312	23 164	17.9	38.0	4 360	2 517	8 575	9 109	22.2	2.94	9.7	18.4
Menard	12.5	9.8	11.9	49.9	2 252	2 346	-4.0	0.4	235	347	130	937	2.2	2.37	7.2	30.8
Midland	8.9	6.3	4.6	51.6	106 611	82 636	29.0	11.1	18 173	6 912	881	38 920	31.3	2.72	9.8	23.7
Milam	10.4	8.2	9.0	51.3	22 946	22 732	0.9	5.9	3 030	2 618	1 036	8 686	4.7	2.61	10.0	27.0
Mills	12.3	9.8	13.4	51.0	4 531	4 477	1.2	4.3	464	647	400	1 782	0.6	2.39	5.6	27.5
Mitchell	9.7	7.7	9.1	45.3	8 016	9 088	-11.8	9.6	844	1 089	1 033	3 054	-7.6	2.56	8.5	27.2
Montague	12.5	8.8	10.3	51.7	17 274	17 410	-0.8	8.6	1 988	2 663	2 243	6 858	0.3	2.46	7.2	26.2
Montgomery	8.6	5.1	3.6	50.1	182 201	127 222	43.2	57.9	31 979	13 539	86 777	63 563	53.2	2.84	9.1	18.0
Moore	8.4	6.0	4.5	49.8	17 865	16 575	7.8	10.5	3 591	1 296	-389	6 101	9.1	2.90	7.1	18.8
Morris	11.6	8.6	8.7	51.6	13 200	14 629	-9.8	-0.5	1 603	1 572	-55	4 988	-3.8	2.60	13.3	23.3
Motley	12.8	11.2	13.2	50.8	1 532	1 950	-21.4	-14.0	140	226	-121	647	-20.3	2.36	7.3	29.8
Nacogdoches	8.3	6.0	5.9	51.3	54 753	46 786	17.0	2.5	7 607	4 740	-1 339	20 124	22.3	2.49	10.9	26.6
Navarro	10.1	6.6	8.1	51.5	39 926	35 323	13.0	4.9	5 567	4 605	1 093	14 874	11.6	2.60	11.9	25.3
Newton	11.0	7.6	6.5	51.1	13 569	13 254	2.4	5.7	1 630	1 217	393	4 910	9.8	2.75	10.8	21.8
Nolan	10.0	7.3	8.3	51.2	16 594	17 359	-4.4	-2.1	2 150	1 757	-684	6 183	-4.1	2.59	9.3	25.1
Nueces	8.3	6.2	4.5	51.4	291 145	268 215	8.5	8.4	49 459	20 949	-4 146	99 740	14.7	2.87	13.7	21.9
Ochiltree	9.2	6.7	5.7	49.7	9 128	9 588	-4.8	-4.9	1 258	706	-982	3 328	-4.5	2.73	6.9	20.6
Oldham	9.0	6.7	5.4	41.3	2 278	2 283	-0.2	-3.0	238	170	-136	681	1.0	2.76	5.3	20.0
Orange	10.5	7.4	4.9	51.0	80 509	83 838	-4.0	5.9	11 571	7 018	420	29 025	4.0	2.75	10.7	19.5
Palo Pinto	11.3	8.2	8.2	51.4	25 055	24 062	4.1	4.4	3 294	2 959	841	9 531	6.2	2.57	9.4	24.3
Panola	10.4	7.5	7.4	51.7	22 035	20 724	6.3	4.3	2 421	2 281	879	8 241	10.9	2.63	10.0	24.3
Parker	9.7	6.6	5.2	49.8	64 785	44 609	45.2	31.9	8 487	5 280	17 416	23 048	47.4	2.76	7.3	17.8
Parmer	8.0	6.2	6.1	49.2	9 863	11 038	-10.6	4.9	1 730	795	-423	3 241	-7.1	3.01	7.0	18.6
Pecos	8.4	6.1	5.0	45.8	14 675	14 618	0.4	9.5	2 190	1 009	212	4 712	3.2	3.07	9.8	18.3
Polk	12.9	11.6	8.7	48.1	30 687	24 407	25.7	71.1	4 235	4 177	21 777	11 855	33.1	2.55	8.9	23.5
Potter	8.9	7.5	7.1	51.1	97 841	98 637	-0.8	8.6	19 111	10 538	3 007	37 344	-1.1	2.57	12.8	28.3
Presidio	9.9	7.3	6.4	52.0	6 637	5 188	27.9	34.9	1 212	471	1 594	2 255	34.2	2.91	12.3	23.5
Rains	13.0	9.2	7.3	50.4	6 715	4 839	38.8	33.4	689	781	2 325	2 609	36.5	2.53	7.2	23.7
Randall	10.2	3.8	2.8	51.4	89 673	75 062	19.5	11.1	12 030	5 509	3 941	34 553	29.4	2.55	8.2	23.9
Reagan	6.6	4.5	3.7	49.6	4 514	4 135	9.2	-14.4	659	287	-1 034	1 358	4.1	3.29	3.8	15.7
Real	12.4	12.7	12.0	51.5	2 412	2 469	-2.3	13.1	344	365	344	924	2.7	2.55	8.3	23.8
Red River	11.9	9.0	10.5	52.6	14 317	16 101	-11.1	-4.4	1 615	2 002	-184	5 688	-5.9	2.46	11.1	27.9
Reeves	8.2	7.1	5.5	48.3	15 852	15 801	0.3	-11.6	2 238	1 006	-3 061	4 838	1.0	3.14	10.5	19.0
Refugio	10.3	8.6	8.2	52.1	7 976	9 289	-14.1	-3.0	985	812	-397	2 937	-7.3	2.69	12.6	23.8
Roberts	11.6	6.2	6.0	50.8	1 025	1 187	-13.6	-9.9	54	75	-79	391	-8.2	2.62	4.6	22.0
Robertson	10.4	8.4	8.4	51.8	15 511	14 653	5.9	1.6	2 415	1 843	-256	5 793	5.0	2.63	14.1	26.9
Rockwall	8.3	6.0	4.6	50.2	25 604	14 528	76.2	54.2	4 422	1 771	11 297	8 838	81.7	2.87	7.1	15.4
Runnels	10.5	8.3	10.4	50.9	11 294	11 872	-4.9	0.4	1 506	1 464	38	4 346	-3.3	2.56	8.6	26.2
Rusk	10.1	7.3	8.0	51.1	43 735	41 382	5.7	4.8	5 149	4 764	1 839	16 327	8.8	2.64	10.2	24.0
Sabine	16.3	15.0	10.9	51.7	9 586	8 702	10.2	10.1	1 023	1 433	1 414	3 985	19.5	2.37	7.5	24.8
San Augustine	13.1	10.8	11.1	52.6	7 999	8 785	-8.9	1.0	920	1 150	357	3 073	-1.9	2.52	12.9	25.3
San Jacinto	13.9	8.7	6.1	49.5	16 372	11 434	43.2	37.8	1 826	1 640	5 977	6 247	52.8	2.61	9.2	21.6
San Patricio	8.6	5.4	4.4	49.7	58 749	58 013	1.3	21.9	10 363	4 465	7 157	18 776	7.0	3.10	11.7	17.4
San Saba	10.2	8.6	11.6	51.0	5 401	5 841	-7.5	7.6	581	721	555	2 122	-11.0	2.46	7.8	28.0
Schleicher	10.0	7.5	8.0	51.0	2 990	2 820	6.0	-1.7	344	241	-144	1 051	6.4	2.81	6.9	21.5
Scurry	9.4	7.2	7.5	47.6	18 634	18 192	2.4	-5.3	2 239	1 523	-1 662	6 368	-0.1	2.73	7.7	21.9
Shackelford	11.2	7.5	10.6	50.7	3 316	3 915	-15.3	-2.9	327	448	35	1 336	-10.5	2.43	6.7	29.6
Shelby	11.5	8.5	8.9	52.3	22 034	23 084	-4.5	3.0	2 975	3 022	770	8 476	-0.9	2.55	12.0	25.9
Sherman	10.6	9.2	8.4	49.8	2 858	3 174	-10.0	1.4	350	256	-43	1 053	-5.7	2.68	3.6	21.4
Smith	9.7	7.4	6.4	51.7	151 309	128 366	17.9	12.1	22 654	14 200	10 463	56 800	23.4	2.61	11.3	24.3
Somervell	7.8	6.0	6.4	48.3	5 360	4 154	29.0	28.1	717	518	1 070	1 902	24.2	2.74	8.3	22.1
Starr	6.4	4.4	3.3	51.1	40 518	27 266	48.6	39.6	12 721	1 914	5 347	10 331	50.6	3.90	14.2	10.3
Stephens	11.1	8.2	8.3	49.5	9 010	9 926	-9.2	8.1	1 153	1 133	710	3 556	-9.5	2.50	8.8	27.8
Sterling	8.4	6.9	6.3	50.9	1 438	1 206	19.2	-7.6	192	91	-209	494	19.6	2.87	7.1	18.4
Stonewall	12.1	9.4	12.9	51.4	2 013	2 406	-16.3	-14.8	164	254	-205	806	-14.3	2.43	6.7	28.4
Sutton	9.7	6.9	4.8	51.7	4 135	5 130	-19.4	4.2	638	330	-122	1 466	-12.5	2.79	6.6	22.0
Swisher	10.1	8.6	8.2	48.0	8 133	9 723	-16.4	1.6	1 171	826	-200	2 993	-9.1	2.69	7.9	24.4
Tarrant	7.7	4.8	3.6	50.6	1 170 103	860 880	35.9	18.1	205 463	77 414	85 409	438 634	41.4	2.62	10.8	24.7
Taylor	8.6	6.2	6.2	51.6	119 655	110 932	7.9	2.4	18 909	9 909	-7 608	43 301	12.4	2.61	9.3	24.7
Terrell	10.6	8.7	8.1	48.0	1 410	1 595	-11.6	-14.8	131	143	-196	524	-8.1	2.69	7.1	24.6
Terry	9.0	7.7	7.2	49.7	13 218	14 581	-9.3	-3.3	1 863	1 127	-1 136	4 478	-7.5	2.92	9.4	19.7
Throckmorton	12.9	8.0	10.6	51.1	1 880	2 053	-8.4	-9.8	200	239	-137	790	-7.4	2.33	5.2	31.6
Titus	9.2	6.4	6.8	50.7	24 009	21 442	12.0	5.6	4 488	2 561	-534	8 508	9.9	2.75	9.7	21.9

1. No spouse present.

STATE County	Births, average 1996–1998		Deaths, average 1996–1998				Physicians,[4] 1998		Hospitals,[4] 1998				Serious crimes known to police, 1998[6]	
			Number		Rate					Beds			Total	
												Medicare enrollees 1999		
	Total	Rate[1]	Total	Infant[2]	Total[1]	Infant[3]	Number	Rate[5]	Number	Number	Rate[5]		Number	Rate[7]
	32	33	34	35	36	37	38	39	40	41	42	43	44	45
TEXAS—Cont'd														
Mason	33	9.1	53	0	14.6	10.0	2	54	0	0	0	884	2	54
Matagorda	591	15.6	351	6	9.3	10.7	28	74	2	68	179	5 059	1 837	4 767
Maverick	1 071	22.8	242	5	5.2	5.0	34	71	1	60	125	5 622	2 073	4 259
Medina	513	14.0	316	4	8.6	7.1	15	40	1	27	72	4 578	1 037	2 770
Menard	25	10.8	37	0	16.1	13.3	1	43	0	0	0	547	17	717
Midland	1 905	16.2	819	19	7.0	10.0	183	153	2	318	266	13 669	4 709	3 904
Milam	322	13.3	292	1	12.1	3.1	13	54	2	81	334	4 443	542	2 197
Mills	53	11.1	76	0	16.1	6.3	5	106	0	0	0	1 184	40	825
Mitchell	98	10.4	115	0	12.2	0.0	6	62	1	37	381	1 643	271	3 041
Montague	222	12.2	317	0	17.3	1.5	13	70	2	80	432	4 201	608	3 459
Montgomery	3 860	14.9	1 662	24	6.4	6.2	360	132	2	211	78	26 084	9 664	3 683
Moore	401	20.7	151	4	7.8	9.1	13	66	1	111	564	2 132	607	3 061
Morris	173	12.9	180	0	13.5	0.0	5	37	0	0	0	2 795	415	3 458
Motley	17	12.8	23	0	17.9	0.0	1	77	0	0	0	347	7	538
Nacogdoches	844	15.0	558	8	9.9	9.1	107	190	2	293	521	8 111	1 761	3 054
Navarro	634	15.3	502	6	12.1	9.5	50	120	1	134	321	7 382	2 032	4 832
Newton	172	12.0	140	2	9.8	11.6	3	21	0	0	0	2 113	170	1 160
Nolan	229	13.9	195	1	11.9	5.8	9	55	1	54	327	3 054	447	2 667
Nueces	5 270	16.7	2 351	31	7.5	5.8	755	239	8	1 549	490	38 548	23 538	7 294
Ochiltree	139	15.8	78	1	8.9	7.2	3	34	1	44	498	1 095	273	3 017
Oldham	25	11.3	22	0	10.0	0.0	0	0	0	0	0	345	29	1 285
Orange	1 192	14.1	809	10	9.6	8.4	51	60	1	136	160	12 246	3 935	4 573
Palo Pinto	381	14.9	324	5	12.7	12.2	20	78	1	44	171	4 557	960	3 704
Panola	275	12.0	246	1	10.7	3.6	8	35	1	30	130	3 643	541	2 313
Parker	928	11.8	639	9	8.1	9.3	76	93	1	80	98	9 372	1 855	2 316
Parmer	185	17.9	91	3	8.8	14.4	3	29	1	26	252	1 270	163	1 782
Pecos	234	14.5	111	3	6.9	14.3	7	44	2	37	231	1 827	534	3 244
Polk	470	9.9	497	4	10.5	8.5	25	50	1	28	56	11 751	1 045	2 166
Potter	2 075	19.1	1 172	20	10.8	9.6	450	413	3	927	851	22 329	7 938	7 148
Presidio	129	15.6	44	0	5.3	0.0	1	12	0	0	0	1 280	84	963
Rains	82	9.9	91	1	11.0	16.3	2	23	0	0	0	1 304	320	3 833
Randall	1 319	13.4	621	8	6.3	6.1	40	40	2	99	99	4 713	6 173	6 139
Reagan	66	15.9	31	0	7.5	0.0	2	48	1	61	1 451	366	70	1 629
Real	35	12.9	42	0	15.8	0.0	1	37	0	0	0	741	38	1 392
Red River	169	12.2	204	1	14.7	4.0	5	36	1	36	262	3 098	274	1 954
Reeves	215	14.7	113	1	7.7	3.1	5	35	1	46	318	1 829	370	2 450
Refugio	99	12.5	90	0	11.4	0.0	2	25	1	20	253	1 486	118	1 473
Roberts	6	5.9	11	0	11.4	0.0	1	106	0	0	0	126	9	896
Robertson	237	15.3	204	1	13.2	2.8	4	26	0	0	0	2 884	362	2 292
Rockwall	535	15.0	228	2	6.4	4.4	86	231	0	0	0	3 450	992	2 717
Runnels	156	13.7	155	1	13.6	8.6	8	70	2	38	330	2 449	216	1 855
Rusk	546	12.0	536	5	11.8	8.5	28	61	1	96	209	6 770	2 182	4 704
Sabine	104	9.9	165	0	15.6	3.2	5	47	1	36	341	3 210	264	2 458
San Augustine	98	12.2	133	2	16.4	16.9	4	49	1	16	198	1 911	170	2 044
San Jacinto	219	10.5	190	2	9.1	10.6	3	14	0	0	0	2 839	541	2 551
San Patricio	1 124	16.1	508	6	7.3	5.6	31	43	1	68	95	8 540	2 105	2 974
San Saba	58	10.3	76	0	13.4	0.0	1	18	0	0	0	1 214	118	1 807
Schleicher	39	12.9	32	0	10.7	0.0	3	101	1	17	570	470	52	1 679
Scurry	222	12.2	170	0	9.3	1.5	2	11	1	72	398	2 805	385	2 083
Shackelford	31	9.5	50	0	15.3	10.8	1	30	1	24	727	617	16	472
Shelby	330	14.6	339	5	15.0	15.1	11	48	1	48	211	4 579	615	2 671
Sherman	41	14.4	26	0	9.2	0.0	0	0	0	0	0	446	35	1 185
Smith	2 518	15.1	1 670	14	10.0	5.7	519	307	3	558	331	26 726	9 093	5 365
Somervell	91	14.6	61	0	9.9	0.0	4	62	1	58	903	809	146	2 304
Starr	1 385	25.4	206	5	3.8	3.4	9	16	1	44	79	5 013	1 703	3 015
Stephens	129	13.1	122	1	12.3	7.7	5	51	1	35	357	1 752	229	2 275
Sterling	18	12.9	11	0	8.0	0.0	0	0	0	0	0	179	12	852
Stonewall	19	10.9	27	0	15.0	17.2	1	56	1	16	897	426	20	1 089
Sutton	66	15.0	37	0	8.3	0.0	3	67	1	52	1 165	544	141	3 126
Swisher	132	15.8	88	1	10.5	5.0	5	60	1	30	361	1 528	278	3 276
Tarrant	22 765	17.2	8 837	159	6.7	7.0	2 267	167	16	3 465	256	129 679	75 412	5 589
Taylor	1 999	16.5	1 082	16	8.9	8.0	268	220	2	494	405	18 142	5 893	4 773
Terrell	13	10.5	12	0	10.0	0.0	0	0	0	0	0	230	2	165
Terry	203	15.7	120	1	9.3	4.9	7	54	1	42	326	2 018	346	2 618
Throckmorton	17	9.6	26	0	15.2	0.0	3	174	1	20	1 158	371	25	1 443
Titus	515	20.5	283	3	11.2	6.5	38	149	1	145	570	3 749	1 277	4 976

1. Per 1,000 estimated resident population, average 1996–1998.   2. Deaths of infants under 1 year old.   3. Deaths of infants under 1 year old per 1,000 live births.   4. Data subject to copyright.   5. Per 100,000 resident population as of July 1 of the year shown.   6. Data for serious crimes have not been adjusted for underreporting; this may affect comparability between geographic areas and over time.   7. Per 100,000 population estimated by the FBI.

Table B. States and Counties — Crime, Education, Money Income, and Poverty

STATE County	Serious crimes known to police, 1998[1] (cont'd) Rate[2] Violent	Property	Education School enrollment and attainment, 1990 Enrollment[3] Total	Percent private	Attainment[4] (percent) High school graduate or more	Bachelor's degree or more	Local government expenditures, fiscal 1997[5] Total current expenditures (mil dol)	Current expenditures per student (dollars)	Money income 1989 Per capita[6] (dollars)	Households Median Dollars	Percent change, 1979–1989 (constant 1989 dollars)	Percent with $100,000 or more	Income and poverty, 1997 Median house-hold income	Percent below poverty level All persons	Persons under 18	Persons 5–17 in families
	46	47	48	49	50	51	52	53	54	55	56	57	58	59	60	61
TEXAS—Cont'd																
Mason	27	27	646	7.6	65.1	12.9	4.8	7 360	8 575	15 366	-20.6	0.4	22 164	19.9	27.9	28.4
Matagorda	628	4 139	10 030	5.6	67.4	12.6	46.7	5 447	11 374	25 368	-20.7	2.6	31 446	18.1	24.9	24.1
Maverick	273	3 986	12 465	4.3	35.7	7.3	57.0	4 827	5 184	12 262	-24.6	1.2	16 626	39.7	50.7	46.0
Medina	224	2 546	7 048	6.5	61.7	11.0	37.1	4 643	9 820	22 455	4.6	2.3	29 605	19.7	26.2	25.8
Menard	126	591	415	1.0	58.0	11.3	3.9	8 175	9 318	14 271	-12.2	1.6	19 458	28.1	41.8	41.6
Midland	344	3 560	29 324	9.7	76.8	26.4	114.4	4 599	15 417	31 164	-11.7	5.2	38 529	14.3	19.8	19.6
Milam	308	1 889	5 491	3.5	61.0	10.0	24.2	4 987	10 341	18 355	-6.7	1.2	26 537	20.2	27.4	27.0
Mills	82	743	899	4.4	61.6	12.8	7.2	7 184	10 374	17 558	-1.7	1.8	24 013	19.4	28.1	29.4
Mitchell	247	2 794	1 942	3.4	59.3	10.6	11.0	7 190	9 581	17 600	-10.7	1.6	24 925	23.6	28.1	28.3
Montague	222	3 237	3 577	6.0	63.6	10.2	19.4	5 763	10 420	19 054	-5.4	2.0	26 117	16.9	23.5	23.0
Montgomery	437	3 246	49 023	9.7	75.5	19.4	249.4	5 009	14 283	32 254	-14.0	5.0	46 292	10.3	14.6	13.5
Moore	252	2 809	4 438	2.1	61.9	10.8	22.0	4 810	11 195	27 466	-11.3	2.0	35 372	12.7	17.4	17.6
Morris	525	2 933	3 148	1.7	68.6	10.5	17.4	6 152	10 344	19 895	-27.1	1.3	27 513	18.6	25.9	24.7
Motley	0	538	271	0.0	62.2	10.8	1.9	7 607	9 004	16 780	3.7	0.5	22 391	20.1	29.8	32.0
Nacogdoches	340	2 714	21 117	4.8	69.7	20.0	51.7	5 163	9 829	19 340	-3.8	2.0	27 741	20.5	27.9	25.8
Navarro	259	4 573	10 400	5.9	64.6	12.7	42.1	5 136	10 468	21 479	9.1	2.4	28 217	19.0	26.2	25.2
Newton	157	1 003	3 373	2.9	59.1	5.5	15.5	5 464	7 760	16 656	-23.4	0.6	25 358	22.8	29.5	30.4
Nolan	316	2 351	4 305	6.0	62.3	12.0	22.4	6 158	9 738	20 350	-8.4	1.1	26 369	21.8	31.4	30.0
Nueces	688	6 606	87 425	8.0	68.9	17.0	326.7	5 063	11 396	25 337	-8.7	2.6	29 198	21.5	29.2	27.2
Ochiltree	343	2 674	2 245	2.6	71.2	13.8	10.6	5 083	13 325	26 352	-22.7	3.2	36 685	12.6	17.0	17.5
Oldham	133	1 152	919	5.3	73.7	18.6	7.7	9 333	10 577	28 167	23.1	3.7	35 241	13.3	19.2	23.8
Orange	544	4 029	21 996	7.5	72.6	10.4	92.6	5 313	11 493	26 563	-23.2	1.5	35 712	15.2	21.9	20.0
Palo Pinto	390	3 314	5 797	6.0	65.0	11.1	25.7	5 318	9 979	20 389	-9.7	1.6	27 083	18.8	27.1	27.1
Panola	329	1 984	5 679	4.5	67.6	12.0	23.3	5 696	10 695	21 027	-15.1	2.1	30 124	16.4	21.8	21.5
Parker	149	2 167	16 566	8.4	74.5	13.9	66.8	4 733	12 966	30 592	5.8	2.7	40 492	9.0	13.1	12.4
Parmer	164	1 618	2 656	1.9	55.7	8.9	15.4	5 856	9 087	19 742	-16.0	2.0	29 764	16.3	20.2	22.1
Pecos	237	3 007	4 444	2.3	58.0	12.1	24.0	6 596	9 133	21 170	-22.6	1.7	27 309	25.2	28.7	30.1
Polk	205	1 961	6 562	4.1	59.7	8.6	34.1	5 240	9 974	18 968	1.8	1.9	27 404	17.0	28.0	26.7
Potter	691	6 457	24 643	6.5	67.8	11.5	150.3	4 669	10 230	20 472	-14.6	1.7	27 848	20.5	29.3	28.2
Presidio	80	883	1 848	1.8	43.9	11.8	9.6	5 512	6 347	13 016	-9.6	0.5	17 753	35.6	48.1	44.8
Rains	108	3 725	1 493	5.2	62.4	7.5	7.0	5 118	10 711	21 741	6.9	1.3	28 152	14.3	21.6	20.3
Randall	575	5 564	26 739	9.2	85.7	26.4	27.7	3 937	15 369	31 472	-11.6	3.6	44 405	8.5	11.2	11.4
Reagan	442	1 187	1 397	1.6	64.1	10.4	6.5	5 828	10 243	28 586	0.1	2.1	36 158	12.9	15.7	17.3
Real	73	1 319	521	1.7	60.2	10.0	1.9	6 544	8 184	17 428	13.3	0.7	22 319	29.1	49.9	46.4
Red River	214	1 740	3 235	4.7	57.0	7.3	17.2	5 981	8 482	16 217	1.0	0.5	22 035	23.4	33.4	31.3
Reeves	199	2 251	4 346	1.5	45.3	6.9	18.9	5 641	7 765	17 952	-15.3	0.6	22 930	27.5	33.4	34.9
Refugio	175	1 298	2 044	2.4	61.9	11.3	10.3	6 006	10 496	20 733	-14.2	3.0	28 459	19.7	27.2	26.6
Roberts	0	896	260	3.8	81.4	17.4	1.5	7 622	15 679	30 203	3.7	2.3	34 334	9.3	13.1	14.6
Robertson	450	1 842	3 661	8.9	57.2	9.5	20.5	6 215	9 705	17 206	-0.9	1.5	23 600	24.4	33.0	32.8
Rockwall	282	2 435	6 884	11.2	84.1	28.5	33.0	4 155	17 982	42 417	9.8	8.1	57 397	6.7	9.5	9.1
Runnels	155	1 700	2 725	2.4	56.8	10.0	15.7	5 828	9 602	19 348	-4.5	1.6	24 707	19.0	27.9	26.0
Rusk	731	3 973	11 008	4.7	66.6	10.7	44.0	5 674	10 127	22 211	-9.1	1.2	29 418	17.4	22.8	23.0
Sabine	317	2 141	1 762	4.9	60.8	9.5	9.2	5 714	10 539	17 512	7.9	1.3	25 064	18.5	30.9	29.8
San Augustine	180	1 864	1 677	1.9	57.2	8.3	9.4	6 026	8 151	15 134	-12.7	1.0	21 658	23.7	33.6	32.2
San Jacinto	203	2 348	3 706	3.4	58.9	7.7	16.4	4 728	9 657	19 867	0.0	2.2	28 337	19.7	28.4	28.2
San Patricio	249	2 725	17 368	4.1	60.6	11.0	79.1	5 052	9 425	22 864	-20.0	1.9	28 765	23.1	29.7	28.8
San Saba	92	1 715	1 153	5.3	61.7	11.9	7.3	6 240	10 785	14 462	-14.3	1.8	21 722	24.4	35.5	39.6
Schleicher	32	1 647	822	3.0	62.4	13.4	5.1	6 614	10 615	21 696	-10.4	2.7	29 721	17.0	22.2	23.9
Scurry	179	1 904	5 171	5.5	64.3	10.0	20.3	5 570	10 333	24 046	-12.1	1.6	32 307	18.2	23.2	23.9
Shackelford	29	443	790	6.8	66.1	15.0	4.2	6 198	11 487	18 773	-17.1	1.8	28 198	14.7	18.5	20.0
Shelby	343	2 328	5 064	3.7	57.3	8.8	26.6	5 401	9 510	17 446	-5.3	2.2	24 560	21.6	30.0	28.8
Sherman	68	1 117	678	4.3	70.5	13.2	4.8	6 743	10 396	23 005	-17.3	1.3	35 140	11.2	14.5	16.4
Smith	513	4 852	42 179	9.5	75.7	19.8	138.4	4 623	12 742	25 769	-5.9	3.2	34 336	14.9	21.7	20.2
Somervell	110	2 194	1 482	9.5	66.9	13.8	11.9	8 119	11 892	29 539	7.8	1.5	38 415	14.3	20.4	21.2
Starr	331	2 684	15 074	2.2	31.6	6.7	77.8	5 434	4 152	10 182	-20.3	0.5	14 178	46.7	56.4	53.5
Stephens	70	2 205	2 172	7.6	67.5	11.8	9.0	4 561	10 343	19 203	-9.6	2.1	26 079	20.3	27.4	26.7
Sterling	213	639	379	0.5	68.3	13.5	2.8	7 531	12 698	25 208	9.6	3.3	32 781	12.0	14.9	17.5
Stonewall	272	817	417	2.6	65.1	9.8	2.6	7 011	10 240	21 210	4.3	1.3	26 494	17.8	25.3	27.3
Sutton	288	2 838	1 168	3.9	62.0	20.4	6.6	6 379	10 926	20 933	-30.5	5.0	31 567	14.7	20.3	20.6
Swisher	424	2 852	2 069	2.0	61.8	11.5	12.5	6 123	9 692	19 569	-6.3	2.3	28 250	23.0	30.4	31.5
Tarrant	573	5 016	305 649	14.6	79.9	24.0	1 144.2	4 702	15 178	32 335	3.5	4.2	42 927	11.5	16.8	15.5
Taylor	463	4 310	34 059	26.4	75.4	20.7	129.5	5 253	11 791	24 661	-2.4	2.2	31 606	16.8	23.4	22.2
Terrell	83	82	364	1.4	66.3	12.0	2.4	10 377	10 146	21 213	-16.8	0.4	24 682	20.9	26.2	30.4
Terry	325	2 293	3 838	3.4	59.7	9.7	18.9	6 056	10 859	22 392	-6.8	3.0	29 117	24.1	31.3	32.0
Throckmorton	58	1 385	368	2.7	69.8	15.3	2.8	7 598	10 505	18 844	5.0	1.0	25 922	16.4	22.2	22.9
Titus	764	4 212	6 088	5.8	65.4	12.3	26.8	4 873	11 163	22 173	-13.4	2.0	28 873	17.0	23.2	23.0

1. Data for serious crimes have not been adjusted for underreporting; this may affect comparability between geographic areas and over time.   2. Per 100,000 population estimated by the FBI.   3. All persons 3 years old and over enrolled in nursery school through college.   4. Persons 25 years old and over.   5. Elementary and secondary education expenditures, local government fiscal years ending between July 1, 1996 and June 30, 1997.   6. Based on population enumerated as of April 1, 1990.

Table B. States and Counties — **Personal Income**

STATE County	Total (mil dol)	Percent change, 1997–1998	Per capita[1] Dollars	Per capita[1] Rank	Wages and salaries[2] (mil dol)	Proprietor's income (mil dol)	Dividends, interest, and rent (mil dol)	Transfer payments Total (mil dol)	Government payments to individuals Total (mil dol)	Social Security (mil dol)	Medical payments (mil dol)	Income mainte- nance (mil dol)	Unemploy- ment insurance (mil dol)
	62	63	64	65	66	67	68	69	70	71	72	73	74
TEXAS—Cont'd													
Mason	59	1.3	16 105	2 781	18	3	19	16	16	8	6	1	0
Matagorda	736	5.8	19 364	1 929	441	61	125	140	134	59	52	14	5
Maverick	489	7.0	10 258	3 101	255	27	45	170	162	33	79	40	5
Medina	662	7.0	17 939	2 365	197	32	106	122	116	40	55	13	1
Menard	35	0.3	14 958	2 933	12	-1	11	12	11	4	5	1	0
Midland	3 555	4.9	29 846	170	1 903	840	658	341	321	144	135	25	7
Milam	441	3.9	18 234	2 286	222	30	82	102	98	40	39	12	1
Mills	92	3.0	19 460	1 906	32	8	22	26	26	10	12	2	0
Mitchell	138	-1.4	15 588	2 867	64	3	29	40	38	16	16	4	1
Montague	351	5.6	18 873	2 099	107	40	75	92	88	39	38	6	1
Montgomery	7 146	9.6	26 291	366	2 194	530	1 014	703	657	282	293	43	11
Moore	417	4.3	21 278	1 299	243	96	59	51	48	22	20	4	0
Morris	258	1.6	19 334	1 941	176	24	47	67	65	25	28	7	2
Motley	20	-13.4	14 962	2 932	9	-1	5	7	7	3	3	1	0
Nacogdoches	1 098	6.1	19 520	1 881	541	133	217	210	200	73	90	22	2
Navarro	844	5.5	20 294	1 628	434	43	166	179	172	66	75	19	2
Newton	219	4.9	15 357	2 899	57	12	27	57	55	19	24	8	1
Nolan	299	0.5	18 198	2 295	158	25	58	75	72	27	32	8	1
Nueces	7 033	4.9	22 275	1 020	4 658	781	1 126	1 112	1 059	345	490	143	31
Ochiltree	233	16.4	26 480	342	114	63	41	25	23	12	9	2	0
Oldham	50	6.1	23 385	769	22	14	7	6	6	3	2	0	0
Orange	1 829	6.1	21 575	1 232	896	76	288	353	338	132	156	30	10
Palo Pinto	510	6.1	19 682	1 826	210	31	99	108	103	44	44	8	2
Panola	420	5.3	18 242	2 284	167	51	93	92	88	35	37	9	2
Parker	1 979	12.7	24 050	632	441	173	302	224	210	102	77	12	4
Parmer	226	2.1	21 971	1 109	124	78	41	31	29	13	11	4	0
Pecos	213	2.2	13 271	3 056	130	17	35	47	45	16	20	6	1
Polk	862	5.9	17 184	2 565	262	59	234	265	256	125	101	16	2
Potter	2 449	4.5	22 613	949	2 254	420	459	498	480	183	209	41	8
Presidio	88	8.6	10 296	3 100	42	3	16	27	25	8	8	7	2
Rains	141	4.8	16 378	2 728	31	14	25	34	33	16	12	2	0
Randall	2 416	5.5	24 461	565	537	206	410	164	147	78	40	10	2
Reagan	54	-3.5	12 672	3 077	36	-1	11	10	10	4	4	1	0
Real	46	3.6	17 206	2 558	11	3	14	16	16	7	6	2	0
Red River	238	1.6	17 339	2 520	81	15	41	74	72	24	34	10	1
Reeves	195	3.3	13 626	3 035	98	15	27	50	48	15	21	9	1
Refugio	188	4.7	23 766	684	58	19	65	35	34	14	15	4	0
Roberts	17	8.6	17 777	2 411	5	2	3	3	3	1	1	0	0
Robertson	248	2.4	15 904	2 807	101	6	52	72	69	25	28	10	1
Rockwall	1 175	11.2	31 580	126	329	97	161	86	79	38	33	4	1
Runnels	209	4.9	18 118	2 318	91	23	44	52	51	22	22	5	0
Rusk	898	5.5	19 632	1 846	397	104	166	167	160	67	68	15	3
Sabine	211	5.8	20 055	1 694	69	17	48	70	68	29	29	5	1
San Augustine	151	4.2	18 626	2 177	46	16	28	51	50	18	23	6	1
San Jacinto	382	7.4	17 493	2 486	47	20	53	82	78	33	32	9	1
San Patricio	1 209	6.6	17 091	2 590	607	52	154	232	221	75	100	32	5
San Saba	105	5.5	18 061	2 331	43	10	26	28	27	10	13	3	0
Schleicher	45	-11.2	15 075	2 924	22	1	12	11	10	5	4	1	0
Scurry	337	-1.6	18 742	2 143	195	13	73	67	64	27	27	6	1
Shackelford	71	4.8	21 550	1 241	22	12	20	15	14	7	6	1	0
Shelby	489	8.2	21 368	1 276	184	103	76	117	113	40	54	14	2
Sherman	111	14.9	38 754	39	25	66	12	8	8	4	3	1	0
Smith	4 234	6.4	25 190	470	2 573	469	857	633	605	256	252	48	11
Somervell	174	13.0	27 205	285	141	16	27	21	20	8	9	1	0
Starr	456	5.8	8 225	3 106	198	46	42	178	168	28	81	52	3
Stephens	192	3.7	19 743	1 799	83	23	44	44	42	18	20	4	0
Sterling	21	15.7	14 928	2 935	14	0	7	4	4	2	2	0	0
Stonewall	36	8.3	20 273	1 631	15	4	10	9	9	4	4	1	0
Sutton	75	5.6	16 830	2 653	53	1	18	14	13	5	6	2	0
Swisher	205	7.8	24 730	527	60	77	34	33	32	14	12	5	0
Tarrant	37 288	7.7	27 538	263	25 121	2 923	5 256	3 428	3 201	1 301	1 321	256	111
Taylor	2 808	3.7	23 012	851	1 665	376	523	448	428	169	183	37	11
Terrell	21	6.0	18 266	2 278	9	-1	8	5	5	2	2	1	0
Terry	253	-4.4	19 657	1 834	107	37	48	58	56	19	28	7	1
Throckmorton	41	5.6	24 190	609	11	7	12	9	8	3	3	1	0
Titus	535	4.6	21 042	1 377	407	52	85	96	92	35	44	7	2

1. Based on the resident population estimated as of July 1 of the year shown.   2. Includes other labor income.

Table B. States and Counties — Earnings, Social Security, and Housing

STATE County	Earnings, 1998 Total (mil dol)	Farm	Goods-related[1] Total	Manu-facturing	Service-related and other[2] Total	Retail trade	Finance, insur-ance, and real estate	Services	Govern-ment	Social Security bene-ficiaries, December 1998 Number	Rate[3]	Supple-mental Security Income recipients, December 1998	Housing units, 1990 Total	Percent change, 1980–1990
	75	76	77	78	79	80	81	82	83	84	85	86	87	88
TEXAS—Cont'd														
Mason	21	-4.6	D	D	D	13.4	6.3	20.8	31.6	989	268	91	2 356	17.2
Matagorda	501	4.4	17.0	6.5	63.1	8.7	2.3	18.7	15.6	7 034	185	855	18 540	14.4
Maverick	282	0.4	10.9	7.3	47.6	12.0	3.5	16.6	41.0	6 449	134	3 411	11 143	28.5
Medina	229	1.6	16.5	6.4	49.6	13.5	4.4	17.9	32.2	5 719	152	566	10 860	23.9
Menard	11	-35.8	D	D	D	20.0	6.2	12.6	49.6	619	265	86	1 562	10.9
Midland	2 744	0.1	47.7	3.5	42.2	7.3	4.4	18.0	10.2	16 156	135	1 761	45 181	44.1
Milam	251	0.0	50.1	37.3	35.8	8.4	4.1	13.6	14.1	5 141	212	687	10 511	12.0
Mills	40	0.3	12.8	6.9	D	14.3	D	26.2	23.4	1 362	288	160	2 582	13.4
Mitchell	67	-11.5	13.2	2.2	41.8	9.8	2.8	13.7	56.5	1 917	197	231	4 559	4.7
Montague	147	-0.7	D	12.2	D	11.6	4.9	20.1	24.7	4 798	259	421	9 262	8.5
Montgomery	2 724	0.3	26.6	11.1	59.9	11.5	6.2	28.3	13.1	31 500	116	3 122	73 871	48.0
Moore	339	16.3	38.7	30.4	32.9	6.1	1.8	10.0	12.1	2 517	128	185	6 837	12.4
Morris	199	3.2	53.9	50.4	32.0	4.3	2.5	12.2	10.8	3 130	234	443	5 800	2.0
Motley	7	-22.2	D	18.4	D	14.3	5.6	20.5	40.6	369	283	46	1 026	7.1
Nacogdoches	674	6.4	D	20.1	D	11.8	3.5	21.7	23.0	9 035	161	1 552	22 768	24.3
Navarro	477	-0.8	24.2	16.7	59.0	15.6	3.7	26.9	17.6	8 375	201	1 388	17 219	15.2
Newton	69	-1.4	D	32.8	D	6.5	D	18.2	27.2	2 493	175	498	6 378	4.4
Nolan	183	-0.3	27.2	17.8	46.9	9.1	4.0	18.3	26.1	3 410	207	440	7 462	-0.1
Nueces	5 439	0.3	21.7	10.0	56.6	10.2	5.1	28.1	21.4	44 398	140	8 925	114 326	21.1
Ochiltree	177	22.6	35.3	2.0	D	6.6	D	9.4	11.0	1 295	147	95	3 996	3.4
Oldham	36	41.0	D	D	D	3.9	D	D	22.7	350	163	25	861	8.0
Orange	972	0.0	51.6	42.2	34.5	8.4	2.6	16.8	13.9	14 794	174	1 518	32 032	4.5
Palo Pinto	241	-0.6	D	19.4	D	13.3	4.5	19.4	22.1	5 490	213	437	13 349	9.1
Panola	219	7.5	34.9	14.0	37.9	7.3	3.3	15.7	19.7	4 414	191	584	9 700	10.6
Parker	615	0.6	32.3	15.0	48.1	13.1	5.5	19.5	18.9	12 151	148	550	26 044	47.0
Parmer	202	39.8	D	D	D	2.1	1.4	5.8	11.1	1 552	151	168	3 685	-7.4
Pecos	147	1.1	21.2	2.3	40.6	9.3	2.5	15.7	37.2	2 166	135	422	5 841	9.7
Polk	321	-0.3	30.2	21.9	46.9	12.8	3.7	17.5	23.2	14 393	286	1 115	18 662	31.6
Potter	2 674	0.1	19.7	8.3	64.6	11.3	6.9	30.3	15.8	16 572	152	2 499	42 927	4.6
Presidio	45	2.9	D	1.2	D	7.2	3.0	14.0	60.7	1 359	157	605	2 890	36.6
Rains	46	9.6	D	6.7	D	13.4	3.6	19.3	21.1	1 934	224	166	3 533	43.0
Randall	743	3.9	22.4	9.4	55.7	11.0	5.8	22.1	18.1	13 556	136	536	37 807	32.5
Reagan	35	-12.6	D	2.1	D	5.7	3.6	11.8	28.8	456	108	42	1 685	12.4
Real	15	-11.1	D	D	D	10.2	3.7	27.9	34.6	870	324	112	2 049	33.3
Red River	96	0.3	D	30.7	D	10.4	2.3	18.3	23.7	3 396	247	644	6 650	-2.2
Reeves	113	5.6	D	D	D	10.8	2.8	13.3	30.6	2 195	152	540	6 044	7.5
Refugio	77	2.2	36.0	0.6	37.9	11.2	4.1	9.2	23.8	1 675	212	254	3 739	3.5
Roberts	7	23.7	D	D	D	5.3	D	D	32.1	146	155	3	492	0.0
Robertson	107	-6.1	31.8	19.2	49.0	9.3	5.0	13.7	25.3	3 312	213	637	7 338	5.8
Rockwall	426	0.0	22.9	9.9	66.3	11.8	6.3	29.9	10.8	4 138	111	189	9 816	77.6
Runnels	114	4.8	35.8	28.2	38.6	8.7	5.9	14.7	20.8	2 851	248	303	5 345	-3.2
Rusk	502	3.4	38.6	12.2	44.8	7.0	3.0	20.4	13.3	8 088	176	1 000	19 092	12.3
Sabine	86	3.7	D	D	D	8.0	2.8	18.2	19.3	3 485	330	361	6 996	10.7
San Augustine	62	12.2	D	9.6	D	9.7	2.8	21.1	20.4	2 391	296	471	4 168	-2.3
San Jacinto	67	0.9	D	8.8	D	7.9	3.4	22.7	30.8	3 981	183	514	9 823	51.0
San Patricio	659	1.6	30.4	22.5	27.1	6.8	1.9	13.5	41.0	9 750	137	1 929	22 126	13.6
San Saba	53	3.3	D	2.4	D	17.6	D	19.3	34.6	1 386	247	204	3 078	2.1
Schleicher	24	-16.1	D	0.4	D	5.3	3.7	16.4	31.3	562	188	80	1 288	6.4
Scurry	208	-3.8	42.7	4.4	37.0	7.5	3.2	10.5	24.1	3 201	177	334	7 702	6.4
Shackelford	34	-5.2	57.2	1.5	30.2	6.1	4.8	14.6	17.8	748	226	45	1 755	-0.9
Shelby	287	20.4	D	22.5	D	7.9	3.2	15.6	12.6	5 287	232	996	10 616	1.3
Sherman	91	73.0	2.5	0.5	D	2.7	D	4.4	8.1	402	140	19	1 293	0.5
Smith	3 042	0.9	27.5	16.6	58.8	12.1	5.9	30.0	12.8	29 841	177	3 717	64 369	25.8
Somervell	157	-0.4	D	2.9	D	3.0	1.8	17.6	11.1	966	150	101	2 429	29.4
Starr	244	6.8	D	0.5	D	12.6	1.7	20.2	46.8	6 037	108	3 097	12 209	55.9
Stephens	106	-2.9	D	17.8	D	8.9	3.5	15.5	20.8	2 085	213	225	4 982	1.7
Sterling	14	-14.3	D	D	D	9.7	D	14.6	28.1	198	145	27	623	12.7
Stonewall	19	6.4	D	D	D	4.5	D	11.5	26.4	499	280	41	1 085	-4.7
Sutton	54	-12.2	54.5	0.9	D	8.3	4.1	14.2	22.4	642	144	99	1 924	-4.3
Swisher	137	53.8	D	2.9	26.2	4.2	2.2	6.6	15.7	1 676	202	155	3 497	-10.5
Tarrant	28 043	0.0	26.1	17.7	62.1	10.7	6.4	24.9	11.7	148 272	109	17 278	491 152	45.4
Taylor	2 041	0.5	20.5	11.7	52.8	10.5	4.8	27.4	26.2	20 476	168	2 594	49 988	20.1
Terrell	9	-21.4	D	D	D	6.3	3.8	16.5	44.3	207	175	30	810	-14.6
Terry	145	20.4	17.3	1.1	39.2	10.3	3.3	9.6	23.1	2 363	183	342	5 296	-2.7
Throckmorton	18	11.5	D	D	D	3.9	2.5	7.7	26.7	421	244	41	1 106	-0.5
Titus	459	1.4	D	33.2	D	9.7	2.4	12.9	17.5	4 274	168	600	9 357	10.8

1. Covers mining, construction, and manufacturing.   2. Covers private sector earnings in agricultural services, forestry, and fisheries; transportation and public utilities; wholesale trade; retail trade; finance, insurance, and real estate; and services.   3. Per 1,000 resident population estimated as of July 1 of the year shown.

Table B. States and Counties — Housing, Labor Force, and Employment

STATE County	Housing units, 1990 (cont'd)								Civilian labor force, 1999				Civilian employment, 1990[5]		
	Occupied units							Substandard units[3] (percent)		Percent change, 1998–1999	Unemployment			Percent	
	Owner-occupied					Renter-occupied								Professional, managerial, and technical	Precision production, craft, and repair
				Owner cost as a percent of income			Rent as percent of income								
	Total	Percent	Median value[1]	With a mortgage	Without a mortgage	Median rent[2]			Total		Total	Rate[4]	Total		
	89	90	91	92	93	94	95	96	97	98	99	100	101	102	103
TEXAS—Cont'd															
Mason	1 435	77.4	35 200	19.9	15.1	207	22.8	7.0	1 536	5.2	40	2.6	1 424	18.4	14.3
Matagorda	13 164	65.0	53 000	17.3	13.2	352	22.9	10.0	16 681	-1.9	1 678	10.1	14 780	25.3	17.3
Maverick	9 756	67.0	36 200	24.6	13.5	241	27.2	32.0	18 045	0.6	3 898	21.6	10 287	19.7	8.8
Medina	9 109	78.3	45 300	20.7	13.4	288	26.3	11.3	15 885	1.2	541	3.4	10 570	22.3	15.2
Menard	937	73.6	25 700	25.0	14.9	272	28.3	5.5	1 040	-5.6	32	3.1	869	13.3	11.4
Midland	38 920	65.9	62 300	20.2	12.8	367	22.6	6.4	60 859	-5.3	4 217	6.9	48 715	34.3	11.9
Milam	8 686	72.2	40 000	18.6	12.9	278	28.2	8.0	9 483	-0.5	385	4.1	8 494	18.2	13.7
Mills	1 782	79.3	34 100	23.6	14.2	219	22.6	4.6	2 287	-0.5	47	2.1	1 775	14.3	12.1
Mitchell	3 054	76.1	25 700	17.6	13.7	238	28.4	5.0	3 314	-4.5	217	6.5	2 908	18.9	12.4
Montague	6 858	78.1	35 000	20.4	13.6	284	28.5	3.5	7 460	0.8	334	4.5	6 826	17.6	16.5
Montgomery	63 563	71.9	69 400	20.8	13.4	424	23.5	5.7	138 546	3.7	4 763	3.4	83 442	29.7	15.0
Moore	6 101	69.4	46 400	16.2	12.2	334	18.7	9.1	9 345	0.7	283	3.0	7 952	17.4	23.0
Morris	4 988	75.9	35 300	20.1	13.7	292	27.0	6.2	6 306	-4.6	691	11.0	5 044	20.3	14.6
Motley	647	76.7	23 700	20.0	13.1	200	18.6	4.5	531	-11.2	8	1.5	620	14.8	10.6
Nacogdoches	20 124	58.1	54 100	21.3	13.2	343	34.0	4.7	25 425	-4.5	978	3.8	23 595	25.8	10.0
Navarro	14 874	69.5	40 900	20.1	14.5	331	25.8	5.9	21 410	2.1	956	4.5	16 218	22.1	11.4
Newton	4 910	83.2	30 500	21.5	14.0	269	24.3	9.9	5 813	-0.3	794	13.7	4 269	18.0	16.2
Nolan	6 183	70.4	29 300	18.9	13.3	281	27.6	5.0	7 075	-4.0	416	5.9	6 721	20.3	13.8
Nueces	99 740	58.2	54 700	21.3	12.8	369	25.7	10.1	146 001	-1.1	9 582	6.6	121 837	27.6	14.5
Ochiltree	3 328	71.4	45 400	20.8	12.0	349	23.3	4.1	5 332	9.3	217	4.1	4 079	19.0	17.1
Oldham	681	64.9	42 100	17.4	12.4	332	21.1	6.0	1 170	7.8	26	2.2	942	24.8	8.0
Orange	29 025	75.6	44 400	16.1	12.6	347	25.1	4.9	41 525	-1.3	4 249	10.2	32 858	24.3	21.4
Palo Pinto	9 531	72.5	37 400	20.5	13.5	320	26.3	4.8	12 291	-1.6	521	4.2	9 947	22.1	17.2
Panola	8 241	80.4	43 100	20.3	13.4	336	28.6	6.1	7 873	0.2	788	10.0	8 457	19.4	18.9
Parker	23 048	79.0	67 600	20.6	12.8	393	24.5	4.3	41 861	3.7	1 158	2.8	29 647	26.9	16.5
Parmer	3 241	69.9	39 100	19.0	13.2	316	22.8	9.2	4 389	0.6	112	2.6	3 959	12.8	13.7
Pecos	4 712	69.8	38 100	16.8	12.9	280	22.3	13.1	6 684	1.0	558	8.3	5 608	22.3	16.8
Polk	11 855	80.3	39 900	22.4	14.8	331	27.9	6.5	14 978	0.1	848	5.7	10 445	20.3	16.3
Potter	37 344	60.2	39 100	19.0	13.1	332	25.7	7.3	55 297	-0.2	3 217	5.8	41 895	21.4	15.7
Presidio	2 255	69.1	28 200	17.1	15.0	208	24.4	15.9	3 854	6.9	1 070	27.8	2 028	19.4	13.9
Rains	2 609	81.6	42 500	23.0	14.3	340	27.1	3.9	3 672	-1.6	142	3.9	2 670	19.0	15.6
Randall	34 553	68.4	64 800	20.3	12.0	381	24.0	2.7	57 783	0.4	831	1.4	45 900	32.4	10.1
Reagan	1 358	73.0	44 000	19.6	11.1	322	20.4	13.2	1 852	-7.0	164	8.9	1 788	14.8	22.6
Real	924	77.7	38 300	25.2	14.5	268	21.1	6.2	1 351	10.5	46	3.4	832	17.8	12.0
Red River	5 688	75.6	25 700	18.2	14.2	224	25.4	7.6	5 934	-1.0	292	4.9	5 153	17.3	14.2
Reeves	4 838	74.5	25 800	17.8	13.9	261	25.1	11.0	7 133	7.4	818	11.5	5 406	18.2	15.4
Refugio	2 937	71.4	39 300	17.3	13.3	283	23.1	8.5	2 824	-4.3	157	5.6	3 100	19.6	19.0
Roberts	391	71.9	42 200	19.5	12.1	330	16.0	3.0	422	-17.9	11	2.6	507	18.3	13.2
Robertson	5 793	71.1	37 400	21.8	15.4	258	24.1	8.8	6 166	-0.7	292	4.7	5 716	19.4	14.6
Rockwall	8 838	77.4	97 900	23.1	12.6	535	23.7	3.8	21 796	3.2	465	2.1	13 241	37.0	11.1
Runnels	4 346	75.7	30 300	20.1	14.6	281	21.4	4.9	5 055	-2.0	242	4.8	4 722	17.1	12.1
Rusk	16 327	79.0	41 800	19.0	13.8	316	24.9	7.1	20 222	-1.6	1 207	6.0	17 073	20.8	16.9
Sabine	3 985	84.5	36 200	24.6	12.9	258	33.8	5.0	4 056	0.9	393	9.7	3 023	19.0	13.0
San Augustine	3 073	79.2	35 200	21.6	14.2	210	33.9	8.7	3 218	-5.3	205	6.4	2 705	15.5	10.2
San Jacinto	6 247	84.6	40 300	21.1	15.2	309	27.3	10.5	8 484	14.1	338	4.0	5 505	21.3	17.8
San Patricio	18 776	68.3	47 000	19.2	13.4	336	23.7	12.8	29 886	1.4	1 911	6.4	22 339	22.1	17.3
San Saba	2 122	73.0	33 100	17.8	16.5	220	25.1	6.2	2 607	3.0	123	4.7	1 991	17.5	8.7
Schleicher	1 051	71.6	33 300	19.1	11.8	285	23.2	5.4	1 499	-1.4	85	5.7	1 144	17.9	21.3
Scurry	6 368	73.3	38 100	19.4	13.3	329	22.4	7.1	7 332	-10.9	588	8.0	7 171	22.6	17.1
Shackelford	1 336	75.4	32 800	19.8	14.2	302	21.9	4.2	1 327	-6.2	69	5.2	1 406	23.0	14.3
Shelby	8 476	77.7	35 200	22.2	14.1	258	29.5	6.1	9 138	-2.0	637	7.0	7 846	16.8	13.9
Sherman	1 053	70.1	36 900	16.6	12.5	322	20.1	3.4	1 368	-2.6	19	1.4	1 301	16.0	12.9
Smith	56 800	66.5	59 900	20.2	13.2	372	25.9	5.4	89 602	-0.4	3 828	4.3	67 128	28.2	10.6
Somervell	1 902	70.9	55 300	15.9	13.0	338	26.7	8.3	1 702	-14.0	105	6.2	2 009	27.1	17.9
Starr	10 331	78.8	21 900	26.7	13.3	224	34.9	35.5	21 390	-0.6	5 227	24.4	11 273	17.3	12.4
Stephens	3 556	74.8	35 900	22.7	14.7	308	26.5	3.1	4 126	-2.1	184	4.5	3 465	16.9	17.3
Sterling	494	69.2	48 100	21.6	11.7	313	22.8	5.9	661	-4.6	28	4.2	608	18.3	20.1
Stonewall	806	76.9	29 600	20.2	13.7	238	19.2	4.5	682	-12.9	39	5.7	809	17.7	13.3
Sutton	1 466	67.5	39 500	21.2	14.6	299	22.5	8.5	2 035	-9.6	147	7.2	1 847	20.5	11.6
Swisher	2 993	68.4	34 200	19.7	13.0	284	23.6	8.7	3 599	0.0	140	3.9	3 396	16.9	10.0
Tarrant	438 634	58.1	72 900	21.5	12.6	430	23.9	5.4	776 710	1.8	24 092	3.1	598 945	32.2	11.2
Taylor	43 301	62.2	45 500	20.5	12.9	379	25.8	4.4	59 572	-3.3	2 214	3.7	50 278	30.6	10.6
Terrell	524	65.5	27 200	18.8	13.7	235	18.0	6.9	686	44.1	29	4.2	605	22.5	12.7
Terry	4 478	72.6	38 600	21.6	12.3	304	27.8	10.6	5 576	0.9	395	7.1	5 047	20.0	13.0
Throckmorton	790	76.2	28 700	17.7	13.9	240	24.8	2.7	756	2.7	22	2.9	803	20.7	10.2
Titus	8 508	72.3	44 400	19.4	14.5	349	24.4	7.9	12 440	-3.1	716	5.8	10 066	19.8	19.0

1. Specified owner-occupied units.   2. Specified renter-occupied units.   3. Overcrowded or lacking complete plumbing facilities.   4. Percent of civilian labor force.   5. Persons 16 years and older.

Table B. States and Counties — Nonfarm Employment and Agriculture

STATE County	Private nonfarm establishments, employment and payroll, 1998									Agriculture, 1997			
	Number of establishments	Employment						Annual payroll		Farms			Farm operators
		Total	Health Care and Social Assistance	Manufacturing	Retail trade	Finance and Insurance	Professional Scientific and Technical Services	Total (mil dol)	Average per employee (dollars)	Number	Percent with—		Whose principal occupation is farming (percent)
											Less than 50 acres	500 acres and over	
	104	105	106	107	108	109	110	111	112	113	114	115	116
TEXAS—Cont'd													
Mason	109	631	124	34	112	42	14	8	13 236	565	11.5	48.5	50.6
Matagorda	778	9 612	1 028	765	1 512	231	224	331	34 479	768	24.1	31.2	48.4
Maverick	755	7 344	1 071	1 205	1 755	333	187	120	16 285	169	28.4	33.1	46.2
Medina	572	4 854	866	530	1 069	173	351	92	18 994	1 570	26.2	22.7	42.2
Menard	49	249	D	D	68	D	D	4	14 273	291	12.4	53.3	54.3
Midland	4 147	48 297	5 374	2 506	6 700	1 534	2 510	1 288	26 674	411	44.5	24.1	40.1
Milam	408	5 064	650	1 712	700	215	105	139	27 473	1 655	24.4	14.4	44.7
Mills	131	878	303	73	169	50	14	16	18 562	731	12.7	32.7	48.6
Mitchell	147	1 261	367	0	249	57	39	23	18 189	378	12.4	42.9	46.8
Montague	450	3 314	772	498	625	178	90	60	18 143	1 234	18.4	18.4	39.1
Montgomery	5 372	73 544	5 447	7 386	12 919	1 891	3 262	1 883	25 599	1 163	56.1	6.0	31.2
Moore	447	6 584	562	2 900	713	148	80	150	22 750	263	8.0	69.6	67.3
Morris	274	4 406	370	2 267	345	129	69	118	26 718	372	29.6	9.1	38.2
Motley	47	180	D	D	36	D	D	3	17 811	214	4.7	62.1	59.3
Nacogdoches	1 297	17 139	3 226	3 906	3 226	495	385	339	19 805	1 200	27.2	7.3	44.8
Navarro	905	13 216	1 814	2 274	2 355	363	359	257	19 447	1 513	22.5	15.5	40.9
Newton	162	1 659	138	619	193	D	7	35	20 803	294	49.7	3.1	33.3
Nolan	397	4 742	837	1 138	787	176	111	96	20 347	445	10.3	42.7	47.6
Nueces	7 960	117 288	22 383	8 605	16 808	3 629	5 000	2 792	23 802	569	30.4	32.9	49.6
Ochiltree	295	2 495	271	133	389	107	113	52	20 734	361	5.3	68.7	64.3
Oldham	49	481	D	D	66	D	D	9	18 214	140	1.4	76.4	62.9
Orange	1 462	20 120	2 410	5 860	3 226	551	508	569	28 272	334	65.3	8.7	30.8
Palo Pinto	631	6 307	1 000	1 251	1 085	168	98	132	20 950	830	25.8	24.0	38.6
Panola	476	5 031	600	1 087	709	177	130	103	20 379	866	23.7	12.1	40.2
Parker	1 503	14 326	1 574	2 421	3 063	434	520	304	21 235	2 301	50.8	8.2	32.9
Parmer	203	3 234	96	D	321	93	D	70	21 585	599	7.2	57.9	74.1
Pecos	335	3 141	411	94	584	120	59	64	20 272	284	14.1	70.8	54.9
Polk	686	7 449	842	1 491	1 862	244	252	161	21 592	551	35.4	9.3	34.3
Potter	3 627	58 880	10 306	10 338	8 284	2 803	2 524	1 536	26 087	214	28.0	33.6	34.6
Presidio	101	508	D	D	134	42	12	8	15 390	138	11.6	73.2	54.3
Rains	125	840	73	94	205	38	D	14	16 544	493	36.5	8.5	45.8
Randall	1 925	20 804	1 636	1 573	4 752	827	509	436	20 962	583	22.3	39.5	44.4
Reagan	98	824	115	D	111	32	8	21	24 933	123	3.3	79.7	69.1
Real	73	389	161	D	55	D	7	6	14 761	207	8.7	60.4	44.9
Red River	220	2 702	526	1 175	463	77	D	45	16 719	1 088	19.4	17.9	43.8
Reeves	242	2 775	278	D	458	132	143	53	19 199	176	12.5	59.7	44.9
Refugio	168	1 257	185	D	246	58	40	27	21 816	230	17.0	33.5	53.5
Roberts	15	78	D	0	27	D	0	1	17 872	96	1.0	85.4	71.9
Robertson	233	2 230	287	408	350	145	32	47	21 238	1 289	23.0	15.4	40.3
Rockwall	871	8 572	953	935	2 011	301	396	192	22 453	265	47.9	5.3	27.2
Runnels	282	3 018	367	1 403	397	110	29	56	18 712	896	12.4	34.8	50.0
Rusk	764	8 878	1 097	1 307	1 266	312	231	225	25 316	1 296	24.2	9.0	38.0
Sabine	186	1 978	433	D	284	65	18	37	18 573	194	36.1	4.6	36.6
San Augustine	161	1 425	423	154	313	57	D	24	16 912	291	26.8	10.3	48.1
San Jacinto	151	1 181	213	D	201	26	22	22	18 853	398	43.5	7.0	36.2
San Patricio	1 003	11 691	1 218	2 815	1 923	667	311	288	24 663	496	30.2	36.9	57.3
San Saba	176	1 472	457	94	261	D	D	26	17 862	653	11.2	42.4	50.4
Schleicher	66	546	D	D	66	D	3	11	21 038	284	7.4	69.0	52.1
Scurry	426	5 066	528	304	777	162	59	106	20 841	606	15.0	35.6	48.2
Shackelford	118	585	53	D	78	D	16	11	18 619	250	7.6	48.8	45.6
Shelby	537	5 798	635	1 971	1 016	245	126	110	18 952	1 047	24.6	7.0	50.0
Sherman	69	380	7	D	58	D	D	9	22 408	293	5.8	70.3	70.0
Smith	4 854	70 510	14 856	10 417	10 229	2 723	2 919	1 821	25 823	1 844	43.0	4.6	31.3
Somervell	151	3 346	468	D	200	40	16	105	31 288	245	32.7	17.1	29.0
Starr	414	4 626	1 932	44	1 398	160	86	59	12 750	609	8.5	33.2	37.1
Stephens	300	2 484	316	612	437	97	56	49	19 649	454	7.5	42.3	39.2
Sterling	41	181	15	0	D	D	4	3	15 729	67	9.0	73.1	68.7
Stonewall	62	436	104	0	34	D	D	9	20 278	305	4.9	49.8	58.0
Sutton	147	1 127	118	D	218	23	D	24	21 011	211	5.2	80.6	58.3
Swisher	187	1 210	195	186	260	73	25	22	17 772	529	7.2	53.9	59.9
Tarrant	32 593	591 128	61 167	92 642	77 340	22 988	24 810	16 958	28 688	1 048	60.6	6.5	33.0
Taylor	3 558	48 503	9 720	3 462	7 342	1 877	1 201	974	20 074	1 048	27.5	23.8	35.4
Terrell	23	65	0	0	D	D	D	1	12 631	85	4.7	88.2	54.1
Terry	252	2 204	406	15	432	114	43	43	19 626	562	13.0	52.5	67.1
Throckmorton	67	314	75	D	39	37	4	5	16 519	249	4.0	57.0	61.0
Titus	674	13 301	1 928	5 533	1 456	254	158	302	22 705	722	30.3	8.4	38.4

Table B. States and Counties — Agriculture, Land, and Water

STATE County	Land in farms — Acreage (1,000) [117]	Percent change, 1992–1997 [118]	Acres — Average size of farm [119]	Acres — Total irrigated (1,000) [120]	Acres — Total cropland (1,000) [121]	Value of land and buildings — Average per farm ($1,000) [122]	Value of land and buildings — Average per acre (dollars) [123]	Value of machinery and equipment Average per farm ($1,000) [124]	Value of products sold — Total (mil dol) [125]	Value of products sold — Average per farm (dollars) [126]	Percent from — Crops [127]	Percent from — Livestock and poultry products [128]	Percent of farms with sales of — $10,000 or more [129]	Percent of farms with sales of — $100,000 or more [130]	Percent of land owned by Fed. Gov. 1997 [131]	Water consumption 1995 (mil gal/day) [132]
TEXAS—Cont'd																
Mason	595	8.8	1 054	6	65	674	709	25	20	34 647	21.0	79.0	45.5	6.9	0.0	12.7
Matagorda	551	-2.2	717	37	240	494	770	67	58	75 547	73.1	26.9	44.3	18.9	0.3	123.7
Maverick	470	-30.7	2 783	25	29	909	322	82	20	115 837	29.7	70.3	49.1	13.6	0.0	133.9
Medina	750	13.9	477	44	226	453	940	31	60	38 177	43.7	56.3	29.0	5.8	0.0	50.1
Menard	496	1.6	1 704	2	25	684	439	28	13	44 177	6.0	94.0	49.1	6.5	0.0	6.3
Midland	863	19.0	2 100	12	69	508	236	47	19	45 602	44.8	55.2	29.2	10.9	0.0	51.0
Milam	545	-1.1	329	1	248	267	780	29	63	37 815	29.7	70.3	32.1	5.1	0.0	50.1
Mills	425	-0.6	582	4	91	369	585	27	23	31 330	20.0	80.0	39.5	3.3	0.0	3.9
Mitchell	541	-7.8	1 432	1	162	336	269	58	20	53 758	63.4	36.6	42.1	13.5	0.0	4.7
Montague	494	-0.3	400	1	163	292	756	29	30	23 953	11.8	88.2	35.2	4.9	0.1	4.6
Montgomery	193	-0.3	166	0	48	322	2 157	28	16	13 479	59.3	40.7	17.5	1.2	8.0	37.6
Moore	555	-5.4	2 112	120	258	804	385	132	294	1 118 443	15.2	84.8	70.7	50.2	0.9	311.8
Morris	66	-10.2	179	D	36	206	1 136	32	15	39 323	3.0	97.0	32.5	5.6	0.0	85.9
Motley	590	22.9	2 757	6	D	540	199	54	19	87 109	49.5	50.5	55.1	20.1	0.0	5.9
Nacogdoches	372	69.3	310	0	102	299	1 004	35	167	139 076	0.7	99.3	38.7	15.8	2.1	13.9
Navarro	516	-1.8	341	0	237	236	795	39	34	22 190	37.3	62.7	29.9	3.8	0.8	8.6
Newton	62	107.0	211	0	10	209	1 027	23	1	4 917	25.9	74.2	13.3	0.0	0.3	3.9
Nolan	520	-3.0	1 169	7	153	412	358	43	32	72 858	37.8	62.2	40.0	12.1	0.0	4.2
Nueces	438	-1.1	770	1	351	673	910	93	66	116 440	95.3	4.7	48.9	24.1	0.4	155.7
Ochiltree	564	-5.0	1 563	73	348	717	435	116	104	288 089	25.2	74.8	67.6	29.1	0.0	84.9
Oldham	842	-0.7	6 014	8	D	1 305	220	70	88	632 073	4.7	95.3	65.7	33.6	0.0	6.4
Orange	88	54.2	263	2	26	317	1 095	24	3	9 933	42.8	57.2	12.0	2.4	0.8	80.0
Palo Pinto	524	1.4	632	0	83	418	642	28	15	18 038	10.9	89.1	29.5	3.1	0.0	461.8
Panola	202	3.7	234	2	84	196	899	31	46	53 000	1.8	98.2	32.2	7.5	0.0	11.4
Parker	480	15.3	209	1	170	386	1 760	21	44	19 051	24.6	75.4	20.3	2.5	0.7	18.9
Parmer	547	4.0	913	216	434	564	621	141	551	919 706	18.2	81.8	82.1	57.9	0.0	342.3
Pecos	2 943	1.8	10 363	25	D	1 662	160	48	40	141 659	41.8	58.2	56.7	18.7	0.0	70.2
Polk	136	-3.6	247	0	42	222	869	32	4	8 097	10.0	90.0	20.3	0.7	2.3	8.9
Potter	450	11.9	2 102	8	D	494	231	39	19	87 011	14.4	85.6	32.7	14.0	4.6	28.3
Presidio	1 690	-0.3	12 247	5	D	1 588	131	41	14	98 406	36.4	63.6	55.8	21.7	0.0	22.1
Rains	94	-3.6	192	0	46	240	1 323	24	16	32 138	25.7	74.3	31.6	6.3	0.0	1.4
Randall	460	-7.4	789	38	277	493	587	51	203	348 112	9.4	90.6	48.2	16.0	1.4	54.5
Reagan	624	0.9	5 072	24	57	1 028	197	87	12	101 615	65.9	34.1	73.2	32.5	0.0	30.4
Real	378	4.1	1 826	0	10	914	525	20	2	11 994	5.9	94.1	28.0	1.0	0.0	1.0
Red River	445	4.6	409	3	173	300	714	34	39	36 205	16.6	83.4	34.7	4.9	0.0	4.8
Reeves	1 014	-34.8	5 760	18	D	771	131	56	42	239 071	31.1	68.9	51.7	21.0	0.0	97.4
Refugio	550	-17.5	2 392	D	111	961	416	71	24	103 622	68.5	31.5	46.5	18.7	0.1	1.5
Roberts	566	11.0	5 896	8	51	1 256	217	74	14	146 505	13.1	86.9	72.9	34.4	0.0	5.6
Robertson	425	8.3	329	15	177	281	1 016	40	31	24 421	35.6	64.4	32.0	4.2	0.0	23.0
Rockwall	46	-2.1	174	0	32	410	1 979	29	4	14 093	53.8	46.2	17.4	1.9	0.0	0.2
Runnels	581	1.4	649	2	293	289	506	41	27	30 581	56.7	43.3	45.1	8.4	0.0	6.2
Rusk	267	-0.2	206	0	131	207	955	24	29	22 416	29.0	71.0	27.9	2.2	0.0	24.6
Sabine	25	-26.2	129	D	13	173	1 232	30	11	56 395	2.1	97.9	21.6	2.6	26.0	1.9
San Augustine	65	18.6	224	0	26	283	1 337	37	25	86 347	4.0	96.0	36.4	10.3	18.9	1.5
San Jacinto	85	2.0	213	0	28	276	1 148	23	5	11 590	22.8	77.2	21.4	2.3	14.9	2.3
San Patricio	406	13.3	818	3	265	686	797	92	74	149 866	77.0	23.0	51.8	30.4	0.0	11.7
San Saba	733	-1.5	1 122	3	139	714	634	32	25	38 488	18.6	81.4	47.5	7.0	0.0	5.3
Schleicher	739	-3.4	2 601	1	45	744	290	29	12	41 138	15.1	84.9	60.6	9.9	0.0	2.9
Scurry	479	-7.6	790	1	210	309	373	53	24	40 190	57.7	42.3	41.1	11.1	0.0	18.9
Shackelford	516	-8.5	2 063	1	54	604	292	34	11	45 085	17.3	82.7	44.4	12.4	0.0	1.3
Shelby	201	7.1	192	0	86	273	1 520	40	181	173 107	1.2	98.8	41.1	20.9	15.0	6.4
Sherman	607	19.8	2 072	162	355	1 166	584	183	295	1 006 870	17.4	82.6	73.4	56.0	0.0	244.0
Smith	251	1.2	136	1	127	223	1 794	25	38	20 798	52.0	48.0	23.1	2.6	0.0	37.9
Somervell	72	13.8	293	0	20	301	1 235	19	2	8 955	17.1	82.9	23.3	0.4	0.0	6.0
Starr	636	0.5	1 044	10	127	534	506	31	51	83 019	41.8	58.2	28.6	5.1	1.0	49.6
Stephens	465	-13.5	1 024	0	60	402	455	19	8	17 586	7.3	92.7	36.6	2.9	0.0	6.3
Sterling	706	-15.5	10 532	0	14	3 110	295	48	9	127 336	2.0	98.0	58.2	25.4	0.0	1.7
Stonewall	484	-5.6	1 585	0	109	339	215	37	11	34 890	30.4	69.6	43.3	9.5	0.0	1.5
Sutton	925	-0.1	4 383	0	9	1 067	247	35	9	43 525	2.1	97.9	60.7	11.4	0.0	3.2
Swisher	516	2.2	975	115	355	445	437	98	364	688 268	12.8	87.2	64.7	37.4	0.0	181.3
Tarrant	184	9.6	176	1	70	387	2 298	22	21	19 914	50.5	49.5	21.8	3.4	1.3	175.7
Taylor	492	-3.4	469	2	207	280	582	31	53	50 446	17.9	82.1	27.8	4.1	0.9	25.1
Terrell	1 291	-7.5	15 186	D	D	2 238	147	46	5	54 119	D	D	52.9	15.3	0.0	1.1
Terry	468	2.0	833	137	378	424	489	132	92	164 214	95.0	5.0	61.7	42.5	0.1	150.7
Throckmorton	562	-3.4	2 257	0	115	717	312	55	20	82 204	28.9	71.1	65.9	15.7	0.0	1.1
Titus	174	-3.1	242	0	73	242	1 170	28	41	57 331	2.0	98.0	27.1	6.1	0.0	1 420.4

Table B. States and Counties — Residential Construction, Wholesale and Retail Trade, and Real Estate

STATE County	Value of Residential Construction Authorized by Building Permits, 1999		Wholesale Trade, 1997				Retail Trade[1], 1997				Real Estate and Rental and Leasing, 1997			
	New Construction ($1,000)	Number of Housing Units	Number of Establishments	Number of Employees	Sales (mil dol)	Annual Payroll (mil dol)	Number of Establishments	Number of Employees	Sales (mil dol)	Annual Payroll (mil dol)	Number of Establishments	Number of Employees	Receipts (mil dol)	Annual Payroll (mil dol)
	133	134	135	136	137	138	139	140	141	142	143	144	145	146
TEXAS—Cont'd														
Mason	810	8	9	56	38.3	1.1	20	107	10.9	1.0	2	D	D	D
Matagorda	7 970	82	33	D	D	D	152	1 443	224.7	21.7	30	109	6.6	1.6
Maverick	11 368	216	35	165	85.3	3.7	184	1 716	233.3	21.1	29	184	10.3	2.0
Medina	2 882	35	28	241	75.7	4.4	117	955	215.2	18.0	16	37	2.9	0.4
Menard	NA	NA	4	34	13.9	1.0	11	60	10.2	0.7	1	D	D	D
Midland	14 245	127	297	2 708	1 938.6	93.9	549	6 649	1 226.3	108.5	185	899	90.0	17.8
Milam	1 817	15	22	177	119.8	3.2	82	701	106.8	9.8	16	31	1.7	0.3
Mills	NA	NA	7	75	28.2	0.4	36	159	32.3	2.4	3	3	0.1	0.0
Mitchell	29	1	9	93	5.2	0.8	38	226	35.8	3.5	4	11	1.2	0.2
Montague	405	9	30	118	53.7	1.9	86	640	97.9	8.0	11	16	0.9	0.2
Montgomery	587 787	4 919	337	3 271	2 129.7	118.8	835	11 926	2 224.8	187.4	184	861	140.5	24.9
Moore	1 699	18	26	187	137.7	6.0	83	724	127.5	11.0	19	43	3.3	0.5
Morris	271	3	15	230	100.2	6.9	53	342	38.9	4.2	6	7	2.3	0.3
Motley	0	0	3	24	2.4	0.4	11	37	6.1	0.5	1	D	D	D
Nacogdoches	137	2	57	593	161.6	14.1	279	3 036	501.2	45.0	59	174	18.5	3.0
Navarro	3 454	39	45	409	227.5	10.7	196	2 007	347.9	29.4	34	99	9.9	1.6
Newton	0	0	3	22	9.4	0.5	36	185	26.8	2.1	4	13	0.3	0.1
Nolan	504	6	24	171	48.7	4.5	83	786	121.1	10.2	11	32	2.3	0.3
Nueces	91 321	1 002	493	5 029	1 803.1	154.0	1 286	17 018	2 783.5	265.9	388	2 526	334.1	63.2
Ochiltree	545	0	33	175	78.3	4.3	44	377	63.3	5.5	6	15	1.2	0.1
Oldham	0	0	5	27	5.2	0.5	11	60	8.0	0.8	NA	NA	NA	NA
Orange	23 138	221	49	316	61.6	7.4	290	3 310	546.1	44.8	61	337	20.2	4.9
Palo Pinto	527	6	30	223	62.4	4.7	132	1 072	171.9	14.5	23	87	8.8	1.4
Panola	1 254	16	25	161	135.3	3.9	90	696	97.1	8.1	13	37	2.6	0.4
Parker	27 388	294	75	579	231.6	15.6	236	2 657	602.3	49.3	58	144	17.9	2.4
Parmer	1 999	19	28	186	122.0	4.1	42	279	48.3	3.8	6	5	0.4	0.1
Pecos	497	6	15	101	28.2	2.8	75	576	84.1	8.3	7	28	2.2	0.3
Polk	1 434	13	26	214	114.6	3.7	132	1 701	272.1	24.8	21	79	3.9	1.2
Potter	69 771	680	247	3 204	1 209.8	105.5	641	7 939	1 531.3	137.3	159	803	96.0	14.4
Presidio	6 053	67	6	14	4.1	0.2	27	152	21.4	1.6	2	D	D	D
Rains	443	9	5	D	D	D	33	186	22.3	2.4	1	D	D	D
Randall	5 867	28	110	1 620	1 180.9	47.5	346	4 299	838.3	72.4	97	370	34.8	6.9
Reagan	38	3	4	D	D	D	16	84	19.5	1.3	NA	NA	NA	NA
Real	13 694	136	3	D	D	D	19	57	6.3	0.6	2	D	D	D
Red River	349	4	4	D	D	D	59	482	61.2	4.8	4	7	1.8	0.1
Reeves	180	1	13	138	12.0	1.7	43	383	64.2	5.7	6	7	0.3	0.1
Refugio	20	2	12	60	19.3	1.3	38	258	49.6	4.0	6	18	1.2	0.3
Roberts	NA	NA	2	D	D	D	4	20	1.7	0.2	NA	NA	NA	NA
Robertson	1 076	13	11	49	84.2	0.7	55	364	52.0	4.5	9	47	3.2	0.3
Rockwall	127 379	783	58	343	133.2	7.8	112	1 488	266.9	24.1	39	256	17.8	3.9
Runnels	311	4	17	614	64.8	12.6	57	413	69.5	5.5	6	10	0.3	0.1
Rusk	1 705	18	41	516	137.0	11.9	144	1 305	188.0	17.0	21	64	5.0	0.7
Sabine	0	0	5	18	4.0	0.4	47	284	40.6	4.0	6	7	0.7	0.1
San Augustine	165	2	11	67	13.3	1.1	42	312	45.0	3.6	2	D	D	D
San Jacinto	75	1	6	31	4.8	0.5	33	235	29.7	2.9	3	3	0.2	0.0
San Patricio	22 944	248	42	262	105.9	6.8	200	1 988	348.7	29.6	46	150	10.9	1.6
San Saba	0	0	15	105	48.2	1.2	38	254	51.1	3.6	NA	NA	NA	NA
Schleicher	0	0	2	D	D	D	11	45	7.7	0.7	2	D	D	D
Scurry	1 615	45	27	215	50.0	5.9	80	762	135.3	10.9	15	51	3.2	0.7
Shackelford	NA	NA	6	13	2.7	0.3	22	86	14.8	1.0	NA	NA	NA	NA
Shelby	668	7	27	168	99.7	4.3	103	984	155.0	12.4	14	27	4.2	0.3
Sherman	11 537	113	9	40	35.1	0.9	12	47	8.1	0.8	1	D	D	D
Smith	70 090	530	297	3 103	1 237.7	93.9	805	9 773	1 868.6	170.2	189	895	93.2	20.7
Somervell	2 364	48	4	D	D	D	29	220	29.1	2.5	5	10	0.5	0.1
Starr	0	0	21	105	37.2	2.3	131	1 379	201.2	16.3	10	51	2.7	0.5
Stephens	36	1	16	45	10.9	1.2	47	421	56.1	5.8	7	22	0.9	0.2
Sterling	NA	NA	3	8	1.5	0.2	5	38	5.8	0.4	NA	NA	NA	NA
Stonewall	NA	NA	2	D	D	D	10	39	5.7	0.5	1	D	D	D
Sutton	0	0	14	63	18.9	1.7	31	206	56.3	4.0	5	9	0.5	0.1
Swisher	388	3	15	94	42.2	2.1	39	255	41.2	3.2	5	10	0.9	0.1
Tarrant	1 207 997	10 754	2 399	33 372	22 102.4	1 219.5	5 015	71 758	14 097.9	1 326.3	1 384	8 249	1 132.8	196.3
Taylor	25 754	185	219	1 996	933.9	54.1	635	7 211	1 297.7	116.7	168	876	88.4	16.7
Terrell	NA	NA	1	D	D	D	7	26	2.7	0.3	3	3	0.1	0.0
Terry	878	8	22	216	108.6	5.2	46	458	81.3	7.3	6	26	2.3	0.6
Throckmorton	NA	NA	5	8	2.1	0.2	11	37	4.9	0.4	NA	NA	NA	NA
Titus	3 311	59	48	539	203.3	14.2	147	1 483	271.1	23.7	24	85	6.9	1.2

1. Establishments with payroll.

Table B. States and Counties — **Professional, Manufacturing, and Accommodation and Foodservices**

STATE County	Professional, Scientific, and Technical Services[1], 1997				Manufacturing, 1997				Accommodation and Foodservices, 1997			
	Number of Establishments	Number of Employees	Receipts (mil dol)	Annual Payroll (mil dol)	Number of Establishments	Number of Employees	Receipts (mil dol)	Annual Payroll (mil dol)	Number of Establishments	Number of Employees	Sales (mil dol)	Annual Payroll (mil dol)
	147	148	149	150	151	152	153	154	155	156	157	158
TEXAS—Cont'd												
Mason	6	10	0.7	0.1	NA	NA	NA	NA	8	46	1.3	0.3
Matagorda	47	144	8.2	3.4	29	D	D	D	77	804	26.6	7.0
Maverick	28	158	11.7	3.6	19	1 091	78.0	13.2	46	670	23.7	6.1
Medina	34	281	12.1	4.8	23	556	50.5	13.8	46	413	12.9	3.2
Menard	1	D	D	D	NA	NA	NA	NA	9	42	1.9	0.4
Midland	350	2 088	245.0	75.6	135	2 435	326.1	76.5	231	3 814	123.9	34.2
Milam	27	114	8.8	3.7	9	1 559	456.0	65.3	43	342	10.7	2.9
Mills	6	13	1.0	0.1	NA	NA	NA	NA	6	55	1.4	0.4
Mitchell	9	31	1.6	0.4	NA	NA	NA	NA	17	146	3.9	0.9
Montague	30	85	4.9	1.5	21	505	44.1	8.9	38	360	10.4	2.2
Montgomery	498	2 279	251.0	96.4	285	6 706	1 540.8	219.1	284	6 044	230.2	62.6
Moore	20	84	6.0	1.9	19	2 865	2 663.2	72.5	46	630	20.3	5.2
Morris	16	155	18.5	3.4	16	2 224	688.0	95.7	21	D	D	D
Motley	1	D	D	D	NA	NA	NA	NA	3	15	0.3	0.1
Nacogdoches	69	240	18.7	4.6	60	3 475	771.3	99.3	87	1 897	57.1	15.6
Navarro	45	270	13.3	6.2	49	2 191	336.0	58.5	54	878	25.5	6.7
Newton	5	9	0.4	0.1	10	620	133.2	15.8	15	87	3.0	0.8
Nolan	32	104	8.5	3.3	17	1 043	176.7	27.7	35	426	11.7	2.9
Nueces	690	4 415	415.4	150.1	223	8 925	9 988.5	373.8	730	12 846	418.6	111.6
Ochiltree	20	89	5.3	2.4	NA	NA	NA	NA	20	254	7.0	1.8
Oldham	2	D	D	D	NA	NA	NA	NA	3	60	1.2	0.4
Orange	93	442	37.2	14.6	82	6 137	2 893.4	302.4	115	2 096	58.6	16.2
Palo Pinto	29	78	5.4	1.5	37	1 183	134.2	32.6	66	657	21.3	5.6
Panola	35	110	10.2	2.1	12	1 092	125.0	19.7	26	342	10.9	3.2
Parker	104	407	52.2	19.8	101	2 538	310.8	63.5	93	1 316	41.5	10.8
Parmer	10	33	1.7	0.5	6	D	D	D	15	D	D	D
Pecos	15	61	3.1	0.9	NA	NA	NA	NA	32	392	12.7	3.1
Polk	45	248	11.9	4.1	25	1 693	295.8	54.6	55	732	21.5	6.2
Potter	271	2 556	180.1	78.2	145	D	D	D	337	5 864	191.0	51.3
Presidio	5	7	1.3	0.1	NA	NA	NA	NA	15	130	3.3	1.0
Rains	8	19	1.2	0.3	NA	NA	NA	NA	14	87	2.9	0.7
Randall	92	323	19.6	7.1	58	D	D	D	143	2 428	71.6	19.6
Reagan	4	38	1.0	0.8	NA	NA	NA	NA	9	D	D	D
Real	5	10	0.3	0.1	NA	NA	NA	NA	6	42	2.1	0.5
Red River	6	11	1.1	0.3	18	1 171	127.0	24.4	15	D	D	D
Reeves	12	147	6.2	2.2	4	D	D	D	28	285	8.4	2.3
Refugio	7	32	3.1	0.9	NA	NA	NA	NA	23	215	6.1	1.7
Roberts	NA	NA	NA	NA	NA	NA	NA	NA	1	D	D	D
Robertson	9	25	1.5	0.3	NA	NA	NA	NA	18	211	5.9	2.1
Rockwall	72	254	24.1	8.5	56	927	114.8	24.0	44	831	26.7	8.1
Runnels	13	31	1.1	0.3	15	1 453	151.1	28.1	21	119	3.2	0.7
Rusk	40	204	38.7	4.5	51	1 302	170.3	29.4	45	518	15.3	4.3
Sabine	6	14	0.8	0.2	NA	NA	NA	NA	19	166	4.3	1.2
San Augustine	7	15	0.6	0.2	NA	NA	NA	NA	8	57	1.9	0.4
San Jacinto	11	17	1.3	0.5	NA	NA	NA	NA	9	126	4.6	1.1
San Patricio	46	260	20.1	8.6	45	2 510	1 235.3	103.2	109	1 037	31.8	8.3
San Saba	10	19	0.9	0.3	NA	NA	NA	NA	12	D	D	D
Schleicher	2	D	D	D	NA	NA	NA	NA	6	D	D	D
Scurry	18	44	2.5	0.6	NA	NA	NA	NA	36	418	9.5	3.0
Shackelford	9	17	1.4	0.2	NA	NA	NA	NA	8	65	1.8	0.5
Shelby	24	132	10.3	2.0	29	1 989	303.2	39.3	23	243	8.5	2.0
Sherman	2	D	D	D	NA	NA	NA	NA	9	46	0.8	0.2
Smith	392	2 464	284.0	93.0	213	10 969	2 299.1	381.1	294	5 834	175.1	47.8
Somervell	6	15	1.3	0.3	NA	NA	NA	NA	21	197	6.1	1.9
Starr	19	80	5.0	1.4	NA	NA	NA	NA	35	326	10.9	2.4
Stephens	18	36	7.5	0.7	18	562	94.3	13.0	20	158	5.6	1.3
Sterling	4	6	0.3	0.1	NA	NA	NA	NA	4	19	0.7	0.2
Stonewall	1	D	D	D	NA	NA	NA	NA	6	23	0.6	0.1
Sutton	5	11	0.9	0.2	NA	NA	NA	NA	11	151	4.7	1.4
Swisher	4	24	1.2	0.6	NA	NA	NA	NA	12	D	D	D
Tarrant	2 965	19 656	1 912.7	734.6	2 009	95 970	18 621.6	3 583.2	2 330	49 749	1 821.5	499.8
Taylor	229	1 123	93.2	30.4	118	3 062	1 010.7	79.9	269	5 497	151.6	41.8
Terrell	3	3	0.2	0.0	NA	NA	NA	NA	2	D	D	D
Terry	15	43	2.5	0.9	NA	NA	NA	NA	24	272	7.9	2.1
Throckmorton	3	7	0.2	0.1	NA	NA	NA	NA	2	D	D	D
Titus	33	132	7.1	2.6	42	4 792	845.3	102.4	41	689	21.1	5.5

1. Firms subject to federal tax.

Table B. States and Counties — Health and Other Services and Federal Funds

STATE County	Health Care and Social Assistance[1], 1997				Other Services[1], 1997				Federal funds and grants, fiscal 1999[2] Expenditures (mil dol)			
										Direct payments for individuals[3]		
	Number of Establishments	Number of Employees	Receipts (mil dol)	Annual Payroll (mil dol)	Number of Establishments	Number of Employees	Receipts (mil dol)	Annual Payroll (mil dol)	Total	Social Security and government retirement	Medicare	Food stamps and Supplemental Security Income
	159	160	161	162	163	164	165	166	167	168	169	170
TEXAS—Cont'd												
Mason	2	D	D	D	3	D	D	D	18.9	9.6	4.1	0.4
Matagorda	50	434	21.7	8.1	63	288	20.9	7.5	178.6	60.8	25.9	6.7
Maverick	45	358	28.1	8.7	29	83	3.8	0.8	183.7	41.4	29.9	21.7
Medina	41	455	16.8	7.1	34	68	5.1	1.3	141.1	67.7	23.0	4.7
Menard	1	D	D	D	1	D	D	D	13.2	5.9	3.2	0.3
Midland	245	2 971	251.9	102.6	228	1 509	112.2	29.3	332.9	165.8	71.3	12.6
Milam	26	360	12.5	6.2	22	68	4.8	1.1	128.0	51.4	17.8	4.2
Mills	8	153	4.8	2.2	9	15	1.8	0.2	26.5	12.2	6.7	0.7
Mitchell	6	116	3.6	1.6	9	17	2.1	0.3	50.9	18.2	9.2	1.0
Montague	21	438	16.5	8.2	30	88	5.9	1.2	93.9	51.3	21.7	2.3
Montgomery	365	4 857	354.2	139.3	293	2 439	129.1	42.5	657.5	342.1	158.0	23.1
Moore	22	229	11.4	4.8	36	130	12.0	2.5	61.9	25.5	9.0	1.3
Morris	23	392	12.1	5.9	23	91	6.8	2.1	71.8	35.8	15.4	2.8
Motley	NA	NA	NA	NA	4	4	0.1	0.0	14.3	3.6	2.2	0.2
Nacogdoches	159	2 348	133.0	50.1	86	499	23.7	7.2	234.6	95.6	47.7	10.7
Navarro	59	1 510	99.8	34.8	57	278	15.0	3.9	194.3	84.5	36.6	7.7
Newton	3	D	D	D	5	14	1.3	0.2	59.3	25.1	12.7	3.2
Nolan	32	320	15.1	5.7	24	144	7.6	2.4	82.8	35.2	17.1	2.9
Nueces	853	14 979	795.0	357.7	545	3 669	216.3	66.8	1 715.7	532.7	231.7	63.1
Ochiltree	13	59	3.3	1.2	19	103	7.3	2.4	36.3	12.6	5.0	0.6
Oldham	1	D	D	D	4	9	0.3	0.1	11.1	3.9	1.7	0.2
Orange	148	1 622	82.6	35.8	97	509	34.9	10.6	324.7	157.3	86.5	12.3
Palo Pinto	48	406	18.7	7.0	49	190	17.4	3.7	113.2	60.0	25.1	3.3
Panola	33	525	16.9	7.3	28	107	6.1	1.5	96.4	43.1	21.0	2.8
Parker	101	969	46.0	18.4	100	498	30.5	8.9	227.7	148.8	43.0	3.6
Parmer	6	29	1.7	1.0	20	45	4.1	0.8	67.5	14.0	6.1	1.1
Pecos	14	191	6.9	3.2	29	214	9.5	3.4	47.8	18.3	8.1	2.7
Polk	41	590	22.3	8.5	37	128	12.4	2.5	262.5	163.3	50.8	8.2
Potter	357	5 450	440.6	191.7	232	1 524	95.5	27.7	928.9	313.9	104.7	21.8
Presidio	1	D	D	D	5	9	0.7	0.1	39.8	10.3	4.1	3.2
Rains	4	70	0.7	0.3	11	50	3.6	0.4	31.3	16.9	6.6	0.8
Randall	146	1 056	72.4	25.7	147	964	51.1	14.9	102.4	45.1	27.1	2.1
Reagan	5	29	1.2	0.7	11	29	2.9	0.7	13.9	4.5	1.8	0.2
Real	2	D	D	D	1	D	D	D	19.9	9.1	3.1	0.7
Red River	12	372	15.1	6.7	12	63	3.2	1.1	99.5	36.3	18.1	3.0
Reeves	17	163	5.7	1.8	16	36	2.4	0.7	58.3	18.1	9.9	3.4
Refugio	8	124	2.5	1.1	5	17	0.9	0.2	41.7	16.9	9.0	1.3
Roberts	1	D	D	D	NA	NA	NA	NA	4.6	1.6	0.8	0.0
Robertson	14	274	9.9	4.2	16	37	2.7	0.5	89.7	32.8	14.1	4.0
Rockwall	82	736	45.2	19.4	48	211	12.2	3.6	89.1	48.8	15.8	1.4
Runnels	26	242	11.5	5.7	16	38	2.7	0.7	64.3	25.7	12.2	1.4
Rusk	62	756	29.0	11.9	44	201	11.2	3.3	171.4	78.0	36.4	6.1
Sabine	9	338	5.6	2.7	10	19	1.7	0.4	73.0	40.0	17.6	1.6
San Augustine	13	280	11.5	5.3	9	41	1.9	0.4	51.6	20.6	10.9	2.5
San Jacinto	10	50	3.8	1.7	6	25	1.1	0.3	74.3	34.5	16.8	6.0
San Patricio	75	1 085	57.0	23.8	66	229	12.7	3.3	422.4	105.4	50.6	14.4
San Saba	7	165	5.0	2.6	8	21	1.1	0.3	38.1	12.6	7.9	1.0
Schleicher	3	D	D	D	5	10	0.8	0.1	12.5	5.2	2.5	0.4
Scurry	21	236	8.9	3.8	37	174	9.7	2.7	73.8	31.3	15.3	1.9
Shackelford	4	43	1.8	0.8	7	15	1.0	0.2	15.2	8.0	3.2	0.3
Shelby	34	697	32.7	12.8	35	115	7.7	1.8	132.1	51.9	28.9	4.0
Sherman	NA	NA	NA	NA	5	8	0.9	0.1	38.8	5.0	2.3	0.1
Smith	430	5 047	396.8	186.2	288	2 032	116.3	35.4	697.7	333.3	137.1	21.9
Somervell	11	115	5.1	2.6	6	19	0.9	0.3	20.2	9.8	4.6	1.7
Starr	41	1 150	28.2	13.6	32	98	4.2	0.9	193.0	35.0	25.4	22.7
Stephens	15	154	6.1	2.8	12	35	2.1	0.5	40.2	18.7	11.1	1.2
Sterling	2	D	D	D	2	D	D	D	7.1	1.8	1.0	0.1
Stonewall	3	D	D	D	3	13	1.0	0.4	12.2	4.4	2.2	0.2
Sutton	6	30	2.0	0.6	5	38	1.7	0.5	11.4	5.5	2.5	0.5
Swisher	5	61	2.5	1.0	13	34	2.4	0.4	60.2	16.0	7.7	0.8
Tarrant	2 847	35 845	2 381.1	1 039.4	2 145	14 698	948.3	296.2	6 302.0	1 883.7	724.4	128.4
Taylor	314	5 225	310.4	123.2	225	1 892	109.5	34.6	742.5	267.0	89.0	16.8
Terrell	NA	NA	NA	NA	1	D	D	D	11.2	2.9	1.0	0.2
Terry	11	152	7.0	2.7	20	58	4.4	1.2	87.2	21.4	14.6	2.5
Throckmorton	4	46	1.8	0.7	NA	NA	NA	NA	11.6	4.6	2.2	0.2
Titus	76	1 048	48.4	24.4	34	172	9.7	2.2	101.2	45.3	24.1	3.0

1. Firms subject to federal tax.   2. October 1, 1998 to September 30, 1999.   3. State totals may include programs not allocated by county.

Table B. States and Counties — Federal Funds and Local Government Finances

	Federal funds and grants, fiscal 1999[1] (cont'd)							Local government finances, 1997				
	Expenditures (mil dol) (cont'd)							General revenue				
		Procurement contract awards		Grants[2]							Taxes	
											Per capita[3] (dollars)	
STATE County	Salaries and wages	Defense	Other	Medicaid and other health-related	Nutrition and family welfare	Education	Other	Total (mil dol)	Intergovern-mental (mil dol)	Total (mil dol)	Total	Property
	171	172	173	174	175	176	177	178	179	180	181	182
TEXAS—Cont'd												
Mason	0.9	0.0	0.1	2.6	0.2	0.1	0.0	7.3	3.6	2.6	718	640
Matagorda	5.1	11.3	1.2	17.2	11.2	1.8	7.5	141.0	27.6	79.7	2 101	2 008
Maverick	19.7	0.1	2.2	48.6	6.4	5.4	6.4	113.6	55.3	14.8	310	231
Medina	12.4	0.1	0.8	18.2	2.9	1.4	3.6	59.8	33.4	18.3	498	390
Menard	0.5	0.0	0.1	2.1	0.1	0.1	0.0	8.1	2.9	3.1	1 311	926
Midland	27.5	0.0	7.2	18.9	4.7	3.8	13.2	370.5	88.6	123.7	1 043	806
Milam	3.0	0.1	1.0	22.0	1.9	1.1	15.2	43.2	15.1	18.4	757	627
Mills	1.0	0.0	0.2	3.2	0.2	0.3	1.1	9.5	6.0	2.5	530	447
Mitchell	1.2	0.0	0.3	6.1	0.3	0.4	4.5	22.5	5.9	10.7	1 218	1 083
Montague	3.0	0.0	0.8	9.8	0.9	0.5	0.1	46.9	27.9	10.7	587	479
Montgomery	28.5	3.2	7.7	43.5	4.8	5.3	8.9	472.9	155.0	245.3	950	848
Moore	3.7	0.0	0.3	2.3	0.3	0.4	0.4	34.3	5.0	23.5	1 205	1 116
Morris	1.6	0.0	0.4	11.3	1.5	0.7	0.6	24.2	6.6	14.2	1 071	908
Motley	0.4	0.0	0.1	1.3	0.0	0.1	1.6	2.6	1.2	1.3	1 022	896
Nacogdoches	9.7	0.4	2.3	39.5	6.6	3.4	7.0	149.5	57.6	36.2	638	457
Navarro	5.8	0.2	1.3	34.4	4.9	1.7	7.5	94.9	39.5	33.3	804	595
Newton	1.5	0.0	0.4	11.9	1.7	0.7	1.4	22.6	12.3	8.1	560	498
Nolan	2.3	0.0	0.6	9.4	1.9	0.7	1.0	48.5	13.8	17.2	1 041	866
Nueces	291.7	249.8	31.0	171.9	40.8	17.9	29.6	875.9	270.9	343.0	1 080	868
Ochiltree	1.1	0.0	0.3	0.9	0.1	0.2	0.1	23.3	4.9	10.6	1 190	1 037
Oldham	0.4	0.0	0.1	0.4	0.1	0.4	0.1	6.5	2.9	2.7	1 228	1 042
Orange	7.8	9.2	1.9	30.2	6.3	2.8	7.2	192.5	57.0	85.3	1 008	835
Palo Pinto	3.1	0.6	1.0	12.0	4.8	0.9	1.2	67.7	18.2	22.9	897	690
Panola	3.4	0.0	0.7	15.9	1.2	1.0	4.4	60.3	8.8	33.6	1 461	1 432
Parker	8.2	0.4	2.4	11.8	1.8	2.0	2.3	181.7	53.7	46.5	591	491
Parmer	2.4	0.0	0.3	2.9	0.6	0.5	0.1	20.6	11.5	7.5	717	596
Pecos	2.1	0.0	0.4	6.1	2.4	1.1	2.0	70.4	7.5	44.5	2 749	2 587
Polk	3.7	0.0	2.4	21.6	3.4	1.4	5.5	68.1	23.0	31.3	659	549
Potter	91.1	4.7	257.0	37.1	14.1	6.4	47.0	357.8	123.2	146.5	1 341	982
Presidio	9.2	0.0	0.7	9.5	0.8	0.9	0.6	13.4	7.7	3.5	412	312
Rains	0.9	0.0	0.2	3.6	0.3	0.2	0.1	11.2	5.0	5.2	630	531
Randall	2.4	0.0	0.5	5.2	1.3	2.5	1.3	48.2	16.6	24.5	247	219
Reagan	0.4	0.0	0.1	0.4	0.3	0.1	0.0	14.4	2.6	7.8	1 835	1 710
Real	0.4	0.0	0.2	2.5	0.2	0.2	3.2	6.1	1.4	2.0	755	644
Red River	2.2	0.0	0.8	27.0	2.1	0.7	2.9	35.4	13.7	7.2	521	428
Reeves	2.6	0.0	1.1	12.0	2.0	1.1	3.4	50.9	22.7	12.3	831	686
Refugio	1.5	0.0	0.3	5.2	0.8	0.4	0.1	23.0	5.1	11.8	1 492	1 333
Roberts	0.3	0.0	0.1	0.2	0.0	0.0	0.0	4.3	0.1	3.8	3 869	3 761
Robertson	2.4	0.0	0.6	23.8	1.8	1.0	0.3	33.2	13.1	16.0	1 028	958
Rockwall	4.0	0.8	12.1	2.9	0.4	0.3	1.1	61.3	16.1	35.9	998	881
Runnels	2.2	0.0	0.5	8.9	0.8	0.4	0.1	31.2	16.3	7.6	665	579
Rusk	5.2	0.0	1.3	28.2	9.9	1.9	1.8	66.2	26.1	32.3	708	638
Sabine	2.1	0.0	0.4	9.5	0.8	0.4	0.5	19.6	7.1	5.8	550	431
San Augustine	1.1	0.0	0.3	13.0	0.8	0.6	0.7	13.8	7.9	3.8	468	361
San Jacinto	1.5	0.0	0.4	11.3	1.5	0.8	0.6	27.4	10.8	13.2	634	575
San Patricio	105.4	58.4	5.7	41.6	10.1	4.2	2.7	131.1	55.3	54.4	781	702
San Saba	1.2	0.3	0.3	6.8	6.0	0.4	0.4	11.2	6.4	3.4	523	425
Schleicher	0.4	0.0	0.1	1.4	0.3	0.1	0.0	10.4	2.7	5.0	1 629	1 526
Scurry	2.0	0.0	0.5	7.7	1.4	0.7	0.3	40.7	14.9	17.2	947	788
Shackelford	0.6	0.1	0.1	0.9	0.2	0.1	0.0	6.9	3.1	3.1	943	830
Shelby	3.9	0.1	0.8	32.2	4.8	1.1	2.0	41.7	24.7	11.0	487	403
Sherman	0.3	0.1	0.0	0.2	0.1	0.1	7.2	9.3	1.3	5.9	2 036	1 900
Smith	46.3	23.8	13.6	77.7	11.3	6.2	12.9	303.6	114.7	133.3	800	601
Somervell	0.9	0.0	0.2	2.3	0.1	0.2	0.1	79.1	1.3	72.0	11 545	11 462
Starr	12.1	3.7	1.2	49.9	14.3	7.1	14.8	118.3	75.3	25.4	457	396
Stephens	1.2	0.6	0.3	4.5	0.5	0.3	0.4	26.2	8.6	9.3	939	776
Sterling	0.2	0.0	0.0	0.4	0.1	0.0	2.8	5.4	0.2	4.8	3 472	3 364
Stonewall	0.4	0.0	0.1	0.7	0.1	0.1	0.0	5.7	1.1	3.4	1 883	1 726
Sutton	0.4	0.0	0.1	1.4	0.1	0.2	0.0	13.9	2.2	8.7	1 951	1 769
Swisher	1.3	0.0	0.3	3.7	1.6	0.5	0.5	20.9	10.0	6.2	737	619
Tarrant	755.2	2 065.1	153.7	282.3	58.4	34.6	146.1	3 083.7	789.8	1 568.7	1 182	927
Taylor	210.0	53.1	9.0	45.1	11.3	4.3	21.0	242.0	104.8	97.6	804	596
Terrell	0.6	0.0	0.0	0.9	0.1	0.1	5.0	5.1	0.3	3.9	3 305	3 155
Terry	1.6	0.0	0.4	9.1	1.8	0.9	0.3	36.3	11.1	14.2	1 092	989
Throckmorton	0.5	0.0	0.1	1.1	0.0	0.1	0.0	4.2	1.9	1.8	1 076	988
Titus	5.4	0.1	0.8	15.2	2.6	1.2	1.3	113.3	23.2	25.8	1 023	796

1. October 1, 1998 to September 30, 1999.   2. State totals may include programs not allocated by county.   3. Based on the resident population estimated as of July 1 of the year shown.

Table B. States and Counties — Local Government Finances, Government Employment, and Elections

STATE County	Local government finances, 1997 (cont'd) — Direct general expenditure Total (mil dol)	Per capita¹ (dollars)	Education	Health and hospitals	Police protection	Public welfare	Highways	Debt outstanding Total (mil dol)	Per capita¹ (dollars)	Government employment, 1998 Federal civilian	Federal military	State and local	Presidential election, 2000 Percent of vote cast — Democratic	Republican	All other
	183	184	185	186	187	188	189	190	191	192	193	194	195	196	197
TEXAS—Cont'd															
Mason	7.5	2 044	69.9	1.0	2.7	0.3	5.7	0.4	116	16	10	257	23.2	75.1	1.8
Matagorda	137.5	3 626	54.6	17.0	3.2	0.1	4.2	41.1	1 085	92	101	2 781	37.7	60.9	1.4
Maverick	115.7	2 418	57.8	21.6	2.2	0.3	1.3	28.5	595	389	128	3 128	65.0	34.1	1.0
Medina	54.9	1 491	75.9	0.8	3.2	1.3	2.7	27.8	755	59	100	2 578	31.3	66.7	2.0
Menard	7.4	3 168	59.6	1.0	2.1	16.3	6.0	0.8	322	0	0	205	33.7	64.8	1.4
Midland	357.6	3 014	38.6	32.3	4.9	0.0	1.8	210.5	1 774	558	318	7 594	19.0	79.3	1.7
Milam	43.1	1 774	60.8	13.0	4.4	0.1	7.6	11.4	470	66	64	1 239	41.5	56.9	1.6
Mills	9.6	2 006	77.1	1.2	1.2	0.2	4.9	1.2	249	23	13	328	23.7	75.1	1.2
Mitchell	22.3	2 542	57.6	19.8	1.4	0.0	6.7	7.9	895	27	26	1 332	32.5	66.4	1.1
Montague	40.3	2 203	56.7	24.3	3.8	0.3	3.7	23.8	1 299	65	49	1 235	30.8	67.5	1.7
Montgomery	466.6	1 807	59.9	6.9	5.2	0.2	3.0	786.4	3 047	499	723	10 577	21.9	75.9	2.2
Moore	41.2	2 109	71.8	0.1	4.8	0.0	1.3	13.3	683	76	52	1 358	19.7	79.4	0.9
Morris	23.4	1 758	74.3	0.2	5.3	0.5	1.7	2.9	221	31	37	683	50.2	48.7	1.1
Motley	2.4	1 904	77.9	0.0	0.0	0.0	9.1	0.1	90	11	0	101	18.4	80.1	1.6
Nacogdoches	150.2	2 648	38.0	37.6	3.1	0.1	1.8	80.4	1 418	187	157	4 563	31.3	66.4	2.3
Navarro	99.0	2 392	66.4	1.3	4.5	0.0	5.3	46.3	1 120	114	111	2 833	38.6	60.2	1.2
Newton	20.0	1 388	79.9	0.7	4.0	0.5	1.7	2.2	154	26	38	678	50.2	48.6	1.3
Nolan	46.1	2 799	50.4	22.9	4.0	0.8	2.9	14.6	884	49	44	1 758	35.3	62.8	1.9
Nueces	790.2	2 489	49.7	15.7	6.6	0.3	2.1	730.8	2 302	5 451	3 899	21 162	46.6	51.3	2.1
Ochiltree	23.6	2 655	44.3	27.5	4.1	0.0	7.1	1.1	121	32	23	649	8.5	90.7	0.8
Oldham	6.2	2 816	66.7	0.0	6.6	0.0	5.0	0.3	119	0	0	262	14.0	85.1	0.9
Orange	195.3	2 308	50.9	0.3	4.6	0.3	3.6	636.8	7 523	134	236	4 180	40.1	58.4	1.5
Palo Pinto	71.7	2 812	38.9	37.4	3.4	0.2	2.7	31.9	1 250	61	68	1 753	35.8	62.4	1.8
Panola	56.2	2 445	61.4	16.5	2.7	0.2	4.8	12.3	536	74	61	1 374	33.2	65.8	1.0
Parker	149.0	1 891	62.2	13.7	4.0	0.1	4.1	85.1	1 079	161	218	3 692	26.7	71.2	2.1
Parmer	20.1	1 919	77.9	2.5	3.6	0.1	5.7	2.1	197	62	27	801	16.3	82.9	0.8
Pecos	79.7	4 919	50.2	19.1	1.2	0.2	2.5	9.8	602	47	42	1 863	35.8	62.7	1.5
Polk	66.5	1 401	63.3	0.0	1.9	0.0	5.9	263.0	5 542	76	134	2 532	36.2	61.8	2.0
Potter	356.0	3 259	56.4	2.6	6.8	0.0	5.9	440.4	4 032	1 861	324	10 171	28.5	69.5	2.0
Presidio	17.4	2 025	63.4	0.5	3.1	0.1	7.0	11.1	1 297	182	23	521	60.6	35.2	4.3
Rains	9.7	1 185	72.7	0.0	3.1	0.2	6.9	3.0	367	16	23	331	36.8	61.5	1.8
Randall	45.0	455	62.2	0.0	13.9	0.2	3.9	20.3	205	45	265	4 399	17.3	81.2	1.6
Reagan	12.9	3 055	54.2	16.8	3.5	0.0	4.6	1.3	298	13	11	362	22.5	76.4	1.1
Real	5.7	2 137	33.4	0.0	0.8	38.3	1.8	3.6	1 333	0	0	220	21.2	76.9	1.9
Red River	30.2	2 192	59.1	25.6	1.6	0.4	3.9	4.8	348	47	36	793	42.7	56.5	0.8
Reeves	45.0	3 028	44.6	14.3	3.3	0.1	1.8	10.3	692	67	38	1 236	58.9	40.1	1.0
Refugio	21.0	2 667	51.2	22.4	2.3	0.1	4.1	2.1	267	42	21	627	40.1	58.9	1.0
Roberts	3.9	3 947	62.5	0.3	5.3	0.1	11.0	0.3	304	10	0	89	13.1	86.0	0.9
Robertson	35.7	2 299	70.9	0.6	4.8	0.3	3.8	13.3	853	43	41	930	51.5	47.2	1.2
Rockwall	67.4	1 875	62.5	0.3	6.3	0.0	4.9	86.8	2 417	70	99	1 395	20.6	77.4	1.9
Runnels	27.8	2 426	60.5	20.9	2.4	0.0	4.7	9.5	826	46	31	841	23.9	74.6	1.4
Rusk	72.4	1 587	76.2	0.0	3.9	0.5	5.2	29.3	641	108	122	2 035	29.1	69.8	1.1
Sabine	15.0	1 422	64.1	8.8	5.0	0.0	7.1	4.8	458	61	28	494	38.2	60.2	1.6
San Augustine	13.4	1 634	76.0	0.0	4.0	0.1	4.7	0.9	110	24	21	475	43.0	55.6	1.4
San Jacinto	27.4	1 314	71.5	0.1	4.2	1.2	7.6	19.0	909	40	58	713	38.2	59.9	1.9
San Patricio	129.5	1 860	69.4	2.9	4.3	0.0	4.6	45.8	657	352	3 360	3 556	41.9	56.7	1.4
San Saba	11.4	1 776	70.8	0.8	2.3	0.3	6.7	4.6	712	26	15	655	26.5	72.5	1.0
Schleicher	9.6	3 155	52.1	24.4	2.2	0.4	6.2	1.6	527	11	0	279	28.8	70.4	0.8
Scurry	40.1	2 205	68.5	0.7	3.8	0.5	4.9	9.8	540	42	48	1 811	22.4	76.2	1.4
Shackelford	8.2	2 445	75.8	0.0	3.2	0.0	3.7	3.1	942	14	0	217	19.6	79.1	1.3
Shelby	39.8	1 759	78.5	0.0	3.2	0.4	4.3	20.8	919	90	60	1 183	35.8	63.2	1.0
Sherman	8.8	3 019	61.2	13.4	4.8	0.1	8.1	0.8	270	12	0	273	12.4	85.8	1.8
Smith	294.7	1 768	59.4	7.8	5.1	1.8	3.3	248.4	1 490	936	456	10 877	27.2	71.5	1.4
Somervell	76.7	12 298	85.0	3.6	1.1	0.0	3.1	1.3	203	13	17	542	25.8	72.7	1.6
Starr	120.9	2 176	76.9	8.6	2.6	0.2	2.5	23.4	422	286	148	3 847	76.9	22.6	0.6
Stephens	25.9	2 615	38.9	21.2	3.5	0.1	3.4	9.4	948	25	26	757	24.6	73.7	1.7
Sterling	5.4	3 864	68.6	0.2	2.8	7.7	3.4	0.5	383	0	0	157	20.0	78.9	1.1
Stonewall	5.7	3 164	47.8	29.0	3.7	0.0	3.4	0.3	180	12	0	195	36.8	62.1	1.1
Sutton	12.6	2 833	52.6	13.7	7.0	0.6	6.2	0.1	14	10	12	430	30.4	69.0	0.6
Swisher	22.2	2 660	63.8	13.2	2.4	0.1	4.0	0.6	71	35	22	736	34.2	64.5	1.3
Tarrant	3 119.2	2 350	46.9	9.1	6.3	0.3	4.2	6 035.0	4 547	13 515	4 661	68 401	36.8	60.7	2.5
Taylor	240.2	1 978	55.5	5.6	6.1	0.7	4.0	124.8	1 027	1 506	4 970	8 559	24.4	73.7	1.9
Terrell	4.8	4 019	68.6	4.1	1.8	0.0	6.1	0.2	177	11	0	115	45.9	50.9	3.1
Terry	36.6	2 817	51.0	21.9	4.7	2.6	4.6	7.4	570	37	34	1 153	27.3	71.8	0.9
Throckmorton	4.6	2 673	78.7	0.0	0.5	1.6	1.5	0.7	408	12	0	192	27.1	72.2	0.7
Titus	109.6	4 342	36.9	40.8	1.9	0.1	2.5	115.6	4 577	126	68	2 614	37.1	61.6	1.2

1. Based on the resident population estimated as of July 1 of the year shown.

Table B. States and Counties — Land Area and Population

STATE/ County code	MSA/ PMSA/ NECMA code[1]	County Type[2]	STATE County	Land area[3] (sq km) 1990	Total persons	Rank	Per square kilometer	White	Black	Am. Indian, Eskimo, Aleut	Asian and Pacific Islander	Percent Hispanic[4]	Under 5 years	5 to 17 years	18 to 24 years	25 to 34 years	35 to 44 years	45 to 54 years
				1	2	3	4	5	6	7	8	9	10	11	12	13	14	15
			TEXAS—Cont'd															
48 451	7200	3	Tom Green	3 942	102 300	507	26.0	93.4	4.6	0.5	1.5	32.1	7.9	19.4	11.8	12.4	14.7	11.8
48 453	0640	2	Travis	2 563	727 022	64	283.7	83.3	12.1	0.5	4.1	26.9	7.9	17.1	14.9	17.1	17.8	11.5
48 455	...	7	Trinity	1 795	12 713	2 233	7.1	84.0	15.5	0.5	0.3	3.1	5.4	17.0	6.4	8.8	11.9	13.9
48 457	...	6	Tyler	2 391	20 495	1 740	8.6	83.7	15.7	0.5	0.2	5.5	4.8	17.3	8.2	11.1	14.5	15.1
48 459	4420	3	Upshur	1 522	36 541	1 178	24.0	85.6	13.7	0.5	0.2	2.8	6.5	20.4	8.5	10.3	14.6	14.7
48 461	...	8	Upton	3 216	3 552	2 948	1.1	97.0	2.6	0.4	0.1	44.3	8.7	25.9	7.6	10.9	14.5	12.4
48 463	...	7	Uvalde	4 032	26 002	1 494	6.4	98.7	0.4	0.3	0.6	67.0	9.3	22.9	10.5	12.4	13.3	12.0
48 465	...	5	Val Verde	8 212	44 188	998	5.4	96.6	2.1	0.4	0.9	77.0	10.0	24.0	11.4	12.4	13.8	12.9
48 467	...	6	Van Zandt	2 198	44 905	987	20.4	95.1	4.2	0.5	0.3	5.3	6.0	19.2	7.0	9.1	14.4	15.2
48 469	8750	3	Victoria	2 286	82 087	618	35.9	92.1	7.0	0.4	0.4	41.3	8.3	21.7	8.7	12.1	16.0	12.7
48 471	...	4	Walker	2 040	54 988	839	27.0	73.0	25.4	0.5	1.1	14.0	5.1	14.3	18.1	16.1	17.8	12.2
48 473	3360	1	Waller	1 330	28 070	1 436	21.1	61.9	37.4	0.2	0.5	14.4	6.6	19.3	18.3	10.4	14.2	12.7
48 475	...	6	Ward	2 164	11 498	2 308	5.3	95.2	3.8	0.6	0.4	43.9	7.9	24.8	8.1	10.9	14.3	11.6
48 477	...	6	Washington	1 578	29 091	1 407	18.4	76.3	22.4	0.2	1.1	5.9	6.4	18.7	10.8	10.8	14.3	12.0
48 479	4080	3	Webb	8 695	193 180	279	22.2	99.1	0.2	0.2	0.5	95.3	11.1	25.4	11.7	13.0	13.7	10.8
48 481	...	6	Wharton	2 824	40 285	1 079	14.3	83.0	16.3	0.4	0.5	31.2	7.8	21.9	8.6	11.2	14.6	12.7
48 483	...	9	Wheeler	2 368	5 320	2 818	2.2	95.1	3.0	1.2	0.7	8.7	6.0	20.8	5.4	8.8	13.1	14.2
48 485	9080	3	Wichita	1 626	128 237	408	78.9	85.8	10.9	0.9	2.4	11.6	7.1	18.2	12.1	13.3	14.4	12.4
48 487	...	6	Wilbarger	2 515	14 035	2 135	5.6	88.7	9.5	0.7	1.1	19.0	7.3	20.1	8.5	11.0	14.0	12.8
48 489	...	6	Willacy	1 545	19 650	1 778	12.7	99.2	0.5	0.2	0.1	87.3	9.5	26.2	9.3	11.2	12.8	10.6
48 491	0640	2	Williamson	2 912	240 892	229	82.7	91.9	5.6	0.4	2.1	18.9	8.8	22.7	9.0	14.7	19.0	12.7
48 493	7240	1	Wilson	2 091	32 504	1 298	15.5	98.3	1.2	0.3	0.2	43.2	8.3	23.0	8.4	11.4	15.4	13.1
48 495	...	6	Winkler	2 178	7 752	2 623	3.6	96.5	2.4	0.8	0.4	43.7	8.5	25.0	7.5	11.8	13.1	11.8
48 497	...	6	Wise	2 343	46 709	954	19.9	97.5	1.4	0.7	0.4	10.3	7.3	20.8	6.6	11.7	16.0	15.3
48 499	...	6	Wood	1 684	34 443	1 240	20.5	90.2	9.2	0.4	0.2	4.1	5.3	17.9	7.4	9.5	13.2	14.1
48 501	...	7	Yoakum	2 071	7 809	2 620	3.8	98.3	1.0	0.4	0.3	42.3	8.8	25.5	7.6	12.9	14.2	12.1
48 503	...	7	Young	2 389	17 551	1 898	7.3	97.4	1.7	0.1	0.4	8.6	6.9	19.4	6.3	10.5	14.1	13.1
48 505	...	6	Zapata	2 582	11 436	2 309	4.4	99.7	0.0	0.1	0.2	85.7	10.6	25.0	9.4	11.1	13.4	10.9
48 507	...	7	Zavala	3 363	11 889	2 284	3.5	97.1	2.6	0.2	0.1	91.3	10.3	24.7	10.8	11.6	13.3	10.6
49 000	...	X	**UTAH**	212 816	2 129 836	X	10.0	95.1	0.9	1.4	2.6	7.1	9.9	23.3	14.1	13.7	13.1	10.4
49 001	...	9	Beaver	6 708	6 006	2 770	0.9	98.4	0.2	0.8	0.6	3.9	8.4	25.3	8.2	10.0	12.9	10.8
49 003	...	6	Box Elder	14 824	42 782	1 028	2.9	97.2	0.1	1.2	1.6	6.5	10.4	26.5	8.9	12.7	11.9	11.2
49 005	...	4	Cache	3 016	87 328	577	29.0	95.3	0.4	0.8	3.5	3.8	10.7	22.4	19.9	14.3	11.1	8.6
49 007	...	7	Carbon	3 829	20 898	1 720	5.5	97.7	0.6	0.9	0.9	16.0	8.1	23.6	10.7	11.4	14.4	10.4
49 009	...	9	Daggett	1 809	717	3 129	0.4	97.5	0.0	1.5	1.0	3.2	9.8	21.6	7.3	11.3	13.4	14.6
49 011	7160	0	Davis	789	239 364	232	303.4	95.5	1.5	0.6	2.4	5.7	10.5	25.6	12.1	13.6	13.2	11.0
49 013	...	7	Duchesne	8 387	14 759	2 085	1.8	93.9	0.1	5.5	0.5	4.1	10.4	28.5	8.7	11.7	12.9	11.9
49 015	...	9	Emery	11 531	11 052	2 342	1.0	99.0	0.0	0.5	0.5	3.2	9.6	29.0	8.0	11.9	13.9	11.2
49 017	...	9	Garfield	13 402	4 286	2 889	0.3	97.9	0.1	1.8	0.3	1.4	9.1	22.5	8.2	10.0	12.2	11.9
49 019	...	7	Grand	9 536	8 193	2 577	0.9	96.2	0.3	2.9	0.5	6.7	7.6	21.4	7.2	11.9	15.9	13.0
49 021	...	7	Iron	8 543	29 449	1 396	3.4	96.0	0.3	3.0	0.7	2.6	8.9	22.8	18.4	11.0	11.8	10.4
49 023	...	6	Juab	8 785	7 794	2 621	0.9	98.1	0.1	1.6	0.2	1.9	9.4	27.6	9.1	10.6	13.2	11.6
49 025	2620	7	Kane	10 340	6 154	2 762	0.6	97.6	0.2	1.6	0.7	3.0	8.6	23.7	8.4	9.6	13.4	12.0
49 027	...	7	Millard	17 067	12 420	2 255	0.7	96.9	0.2	1.8	1.2	5.2	11.0	28.6	7.4	11.2	12.3	10.4
49 029	...	8	Morgan	1 578	7 204	2 663	4.6	99.3	0.2	0.2	0.4	2.2	8.9	28.1	9.0	10.9	12.5	14.3
49 031	...	9	Piute	1 963	1 484	3 094	0.8	99.2	0.0	0.7	0.1	1.8	6.1	24.2	8.2	6.9	10.1	16.4
49 033	...	9	Rich	2 664	1 918	3 067	0.7	99.3	0.2	0.1	0.5	2.1	11.0	29.0	5.4	11.3	14.7	9.0
49 035	7160	0	Salt Lake	1 910	850 243	47	445.2	94.2	1.2	0.9	3.7	8.9	9.7	22.2	12.8	15.1	14.6	10.9
49 037	...	7	San Juan	20 256	13 603	2 167	0.7	45.7	0.1	53.8	0.4	4.9	10.0	28.8	10.0	12.0	12.9	11.1
49 039	...	6	Sanpete	4 113	22 059	1 656	5.4	96.6	0.3	1.3	1.7	6.0	8.4	26.3	14.7	10.1	12.7	10.1
49 041	...	7	Sevier	4 948	18 645	1 840	3.8	97.6	0.1	2.1	0.2	2.8	8.9	27.1	8.1	10.3	12.5	11.2
49 043	...	6	Summit	4 846	27 692	1 444	5.7	98.6	0.2	0.5	0.7	3.2	9.1	21.7	10.0	16.3	19.4	12.5
49 045	...	6	Tooele	17 990	35 801	1 198	2.0	96.1	1.0	1.7	1.2	15.9	8.9	24.5	11.1	12.8	13.7	12.9
49 047	...	7	Uintah	11 596	25 959	1 496	2.2	88.7	0.1	10.7	0.5	4.5	9.9	27.2	8.7	12.7	13.5	11.2
49 049	6520	2	Utah	5 176	346 997	165	67.0	97.1	0.2	0.7	2.0	4.7	10.7	23.5	22.3	13.2	10.2	8.2
49 051	...	6	Wasatch	3 059	13 767	2 152	4.5	99.0	0.0	0.7	0.3	3.6	9.9	26.3	10.2	12.0	14.2	11.7
49 053	...	4	Washington	6 286	85 406	591	13.6	97.5	0.2	1.4	0.8	2.7	9.3	23.5	12.1	10.1	10.7	9.3
49 055	...	9	Wayne	6 373	2 387	3 026	0.4	97.7	0.6	1.6	0.1	2.6	8.8	26.2	7.2	10.8	14.1	10.9
49 057	7160	0	Weber	1 491	185 469	287	124.4	95.1	2.1	0.8	2.0	10.3	9.1	21.8	12.7	13.4	13.2	11.1
50 000	...	X	**VERMONT**	23 956	593 740	X	24.8	98.4	0.5	0.2	0.8	0.9	5.4	18.1	9.0	14.0	17.6	15.0
50 001	...	6	Addison	1 994	35 440	1 209	17.8	98.4	0.6	0.2	0.8	0.9	5.5	18.5	11.6	13.1	18.1	14.2
50 003	...	6	Bennington	1 752	35 965	1 195	20.5	98.8	0.4	0.1	0.6	0.8	5.3	17.6	7.2	12.6	15.3	15.3
50 005	...	7	Caledonia	1 686	28 821	1 416	17.1	99.0	0.2	0.3	0.4	0.4	5.4	20.0	7.9	12.2	17.2	14.3

1. MSA = Metropolitan Statistical Area. PMSA = Primary MSA. NECMA = New England County Metropolitan Area. See Appendix A for explanation of these concepts. See Appendix B for list of metropolitan areas identified by type, with component counties.   2. County typology code from the Economic Research Service of USDA. See Appendix A for definition.   3. Dry land or land partially or temporarily covered by water.   4. Hispanic persons may be of any race.

STATE County	55 to 64 years (16)	65 to 74 years (17)	75 years and over (18)	Percent female (19)	1990 (20)	1980 (21)	1980–1990 (22)	1990–1999 (23)	Births (24)	Deaths (25)	Net migration (26)	Number (27)	Percent change, 1980–1990 (28)	Persons per household (29)	Female family householder[1] (30)	One person (31)
TEXAS—Cont'd																
Tom Green	8.6	6.9	6.5	51.6	98 458	84 784	16.1	3.9	14 302	8 510	-2 947	35 408	16.6	2.63	10.5	24.8
Travis	6.5	4.1	3.2	50.3	576 407	419 573	37.4	26.1	103 544	31 552	78 534	232 861	47.0	2.39	10.5	31.5
Trinity	14.1	12.5	10.0	51.4	11 445	9 450	21.1	11.1	1 379	1 510	1 455	4 647	27.4	2.43	9.4	25.2
Tyler	12.2	9.4	7.4	46.6	16 646	16 223	2.6	23.1	1 976	2 251	4 174	6 459	10.0	2.54	8.9	23.0
Upshur	10.7	7.2	7.0	51.3	31 370	28 595	9.7	16.5	4 059	3 354	4 540	11 360	12.7	2.69	9.4	21.1
Upton	8.4	6.1	5.6	50.6	4 447	4 619	-3.7	-20.1	547	314	-1 139	1 472	-5.6	3.00	7.0	20.2
Uvalde	8.7	6.3	6.3	51.9	23 340	22 441	4.0	11.4	4 182	1 924	471	7 553	8.5	3.04	12.2	19.3
Val Verde	8.4	4.1	3.1	50.9	38 721	35 910	7.8	14.1	8 671	2 514	-1 082	11 840	14.3	3.21	12.5	16.6
Van Zandt	12.3	8.7	8.0	50.7	37 944	31 426	20.7	18.3	4 671	4 620	7 004	14 349	23.1	2.60	7.6	21.7
Victoria	8.6	6.7	5.3	51.4	74 361	68 807	8.1	10.4	12 059	5 683	1 566	26 228	14.1	2.81	11.1	21.2
Walker	7.5	4.9	4.2	40.3	50 917	41 789	21.8	8.0	5 438	3 247	2 026	14 918	26.3	2.49	10.2	26.7
Waller	8.3	5.4	4.9	50.6	23 374	19 798	18.1	20.1	3 583	2 008	3 174	7 402	29.3	2.76	12.8	22.5
Ward	8.9	7.2	6.1	49.8	13 115	13 976	-6.2	-12.3	1 635	1 007	-2 238	4 444	-6.7	2.88	9.1	20.9
Washington	10.4	8.0	8.7	51.3	26 154	21 998	18.9	11.2	3 228	2 876	2 697	9 619	23.1	2.55	10.6	26.3
Webb	6.9	4.1	3.3	52.5	133 239	99 258	34.2	45.0	44 682	7 445	23 236	34 438	33.0	3.81	17.6	12.7
Wharton	9.3	6.8	7.1	51.0	39 955	40 242	-0.7	0.8	5 640	3 787	-1 412	14 210	2.3	2.77	11.7	23.8
Wheeler	10.9	8.3	12.5	52.1	5 879	7 137	-17.6	-9.5	578	773	-343	2 350	-14.2	2.45	6.6	28.3
Wichita	9.6	6.6	6.3	50.3	122 378	121 082	1.1	4.8	18 087	11 352	-2 862	45 271	5.0	2.55	10.8	25.3
Wilbarger	9.9	7.3	6.7	50.2	15 121	15 931	-5.1	-7.2	1 829	1 727	-1 148	5 741	-4.0	2.50	8.5	28.3
Willacy	8.3	6.6	5.4	51.9	17 705	17 495	1.2	11.0	3 827	1 200	-663	5 049	6.1	3.48	14.2	16.6
Williamson	6.3	3.5	3.3	50.5	139 551	76 521	82.4	72.6	26 883	8 313	82 087	48 792	95.7	2.81	9.6	19.2
Wilson	8.9	5.8	5.6	50.1	22 650	16 756	35.2	43.5	3 312	1 876	8 409	7 481	37.8	3.00	8.1	16.6
Winkler	9.4	7.0	6.0	50.7	8 626	9 944	-13.3	-10.1	1 212	678	-1 390	2 941	-13.8	2.91	7.4	19.3
Wise	9.7	5.8	5.4	48.8	34 679	26 575	30.5	34.7	4 821	3 069	10 239	12 175	29.4	2.77	6.3	19.4
Wood	12.7	10.3	9.6	50.8	29 380	24 697	19.0	17.2	3 678	4 112	5 633	11 426	23.6	2.49	7.5	24.3
Yoakum	7.4	6.4	5.2	49.3	8 786	8 299	5.9	-11.1	1 235	495	-1 724	2 839	5.1	3.08	6.2	15.4
Young	11.4	8.3	10.2	51.9	18 126	19 083	-5.0	-3.2	2 107	2 320	-318	7 101	-3.5	2.51	7.5	25.0
Zapata	7.7	6.8	5.0	51.1	9 279	6 628	40.0	23.2	2 007	747	925	2 862	39.0	3.23	10.3	16.1
Zavala	7.6	6.0	5.0	50.1	12 162	11 666	4.3	-2.2	2 178	832	-1 589	3 356	9.4	3.54	17.3	15.6
UTAH	6.6	4.6	4.1	50.3	1 722 850	1 461 037	17.9	23.6	369 419	98 393	103 356	537 273	19.8	3.15	9.1	18.9
Beaver	10.6	7.0	6.9	50.8	4 765	4 378	8.8	26.0	906	500	848	1 594	11.6	2.95	5.6	21.9
Box Elder	8.2	5.2	5.0	50.1	36 485	33 222	9.8	17.3	6 612	2 286	2 084	10 954	11.7	3.31	6.6	16.6
Cache	5.2	3.6	4.2	49.9	70 183	57 176	22.7	24.4	17 484	3 392	-3 003	21 021	19.7	3.29	6.1	17.0
Carbon	7.9	7.1	6.3	51.1	20 228	22 179	-8.8	3.3	2 858	1 656	-473	6 907	-4.6	2.89	9.5	21.8
Daggett	12.0	3.8	6.3	48.8	690	769	-10.3	3.9	78	41	-6	253	3.7	2.73	4.7	25.7
Davis	6.6	4.4	2.9	49.9	187 941	146 540	28.3	27.4	38 549	7 647	17 783	53 598	34.0	3.45	8.9	13.3
Duchesne	6.7	4.8	4.9	49.4	12 645	12 565	0.6	16.7	2 372	859	642	3 707	5.9	3.40	7.7	15.7
Emery	6.7	4.7	4.9	49.0	10 332	11 451	-9.8	7.0	1 681	600	-329	2 998	-8.5	3.43	6.6	15.4
Garfield	10.5	8.7	6.9	48.8	3 980	3 673	8.4	7.7	624	306	6	1 321	10.5	3.00	5.1	19.8
Grand	10.9	7.3	4.7	51.1	6 620	8 241	-19.7	23.8	1 007	554	1 146	2 489	-9.8	2.63	9.5	24.2
Iron	7.2	5.2	4.4	50.3	20 789	17 349	19.8	41.7	5 143	1 289	4 657	6 269	21.3	3.21	7.4	16.5
Juab	8.3	4.7	5.5	50.0	5 817	5 530	5.2	34.0	1 240	531	1 279	1 801	5.5	3.18	6.6	20.7
Kane	9.0	8.5	6.8	49.6	5 169	4 024	28.5	19.1	793	433	642	1 724	34.1	2.98	5.2	20.4
Millard	7.4	5.5	6.2	49.5	11 333	8 970	26.3	9.6	1 914	855	-105	1 555	14.8	3.55	4.8	11.6
Morgan	8.1	4.1	4.1	49.6	5 528	4 917	12.4	30.3	898	301	1 105	1 555	3.2	3.36	3.6	20.7
Piute	12.1	8.9	7.1	48.1	1 277	1 329	-3.9	16.2	176	143	178	449	-20.3	2.84	3.8	18.4
Rich	7.2	5.9	6.6	48.6	1 725	2 100	-17.9	11.2	244	111	68	521		3.26		
Salt Lake	6.5	4.4	3.9	50.3	725 956	619 066	17.3	17.1	147 859	41 580	9 861	240 680	19.3	2.98	10.1	22.2
San Juan	6.9	4.0	4.2	50.4	12 621	12 253	3.0	7.8	2 690	602	-1 084	3 375	11.8	3.70	14.6	15.6
Sanpete	7.0	5.1	5.6	48.9	16 259	14 620	11.2	35.7	3 049	1 365	4 154	4 859	9.1	3.24	6.5	20.2
Sevier	8.6	6.6	6.7	50.2	15 431	14 727	4.8	20.8	2 664	1 286	1 893	4 877	6.3	3.13	6.5	18.9
Summit	6.1	2.6	2.3	48.6	15 518	10 198	52.2	78.5	3 215	642	9 599	5 271	55.9	2.91	6.2	19.3
Tooele	8.0	4.7	3.3	49.3	26 601	26 033	2.2	34.6	5 192	1 571	5 438	8 581	7.7	3.06	10.0	18.4
Uintah	7.3	5.4	4.1	50.4	22 211	20 506	8.3	16.9	3 909	1 303	1 205	6 670	12.1	3.31	9.7	16.4
Utah	5.3	3.5	3.3	50.7	263 590	218 106	20.9	31.6	72 491	11 997	8 307	70 168	19.9	3.63	7.8	12.2
Wasatch	7.4	4.2	4.1	49.4	10 089	8 523	18.4	36.5	1 973	673	2 391	3 074	18.5	3.26	6.8	16.9
Washington	8.3	9.1	7.5	50.6	48 560	26 065	86.3	75.9	11 897	4 641	28 857	15 256	95.6	3.14	7.9	17.0
Wayne	8.3	7.5	6.3	47.8	2 177	1 911	13.9	9.6	333	182	70	699	13.7	3.07	3.4	19.5
Weber	7.9	5.8	5.0	50.7	158 330	144 616	9.5	17.1	31 568	11 047	5 983	53 253	11.8	2.93	10.4	21.1
VERMONT	8.7	6.4	5.9	50.8	562 758	511 456	10.0	5.5	67 101	44 797	10 574	210 650	18.1	2.57	9.2	23.4
Addison	8.0	6.1	5.0	49.9	32 953	29 406	12.1	7.5	4 019	2 258	826	11 410	21.6	2.68	8.2	20.7
Bennington	9.9	7.7	8.1	51.4	35 845	33 345	7.5	0.3	3 891	3 854	213	13 595	13.7	2.54	10.2	24.3
Caledonia	9.2	7.3	6.6	50.7	27 846	25 808	7.9	3.5	3 034	2 423	451	10 368	12.4	2.60	10.1	23.3

1. No spouse present.

Table B. States and Counties — Vital Statistics, Health Resources, and Crime

STATE County	Births, average 1996–1998 Total	Rate[1]	Deaths, average 1996–1998 Number Total	Infant[2]	Rate Total[1]	Infant[3]	Physicians,[4] 1998 Number	Rate[5]	Hospitals,[4] 1998 Number	Beds Number	Rate[5]	Medicare enrollees 1999	Serious crimes known to police, 1998[6] Total Number	Rate[7]
	32	33	34	35	36	37	38	39	40	41	42	43	44	45
TEXAS—Cont'd														
Tom Green	1 554	15.2	966	9	9.4	6.0	203	198	3	478	465	15 679	5 472	5 244
Travis	12 044	17.3	3 630	72	5.2	6.0	1 837	259	7	1 517	213	60 139	44 957	6 376
Trinity	157	12.5	185	2	14.8	12.8	4	32	1	22	174	3 124	441	3 496
Tyler	217	10.8	245	2	12.1	10.7	10	49	1	36	176	3 809	348	1 703
Upshur	439	12.4	388	2	11.0	5.3	14	39	0	0	0	5 863	904	2 511
Upton	54	14.4	36	0	9.5	0.0	2	53	2	66	1 760	524	60	1 547
Uvalde	445	17.5	220	4	8.7	8.2	23	90	1	64	250	3 788	904	3 471
Val Verde	921	21.3	278	6	6.5	6.9	44	100	1	78	178	3 734	1 887	4 306
Van Zandt	563	13.0	556	3	12.9	5.3	16	36	1	26	59	8 148	1 289	2 949
Victoria	1 332	16.3	638	10	7.8	7.3	189	229	3	588	711	11 171	3 778	4 531
Walker	586	10.7	418	5	7.7	8.5	41	75	1	119	216	5 687	1 758	3 172
Waller	453	16.8	226	3	8.4	6.6	7	26	0	0	0	2 936	957	3 514
Ward	159	13.5	106	1	9.0	8.4	8	68	1	41	347	1 739	408	3 376
Washington	360	12.5	323	4	11.2	10.2	40	137	1	60	206	5 526	881	2 985
Webb	5 188	28.4	870	25	4.8	4.9	170	90	2	377	200	16 260	13 492	7 244
Wharton	599	15.0	407	2	10.2	3.9	53	132	2	221	551	6 256	2 004	4 911
Wheeler	63	11.9	90	1	16.9	15.8	7	132	2	63	1 190	1 245	67	1 241
Wichita	1 941	15.0	1 245	19	9.6	9.8	290	225	3	423	328	18 975	6 526	4 983
Wilbarger	193	13.8	174	0	12.4	1.7	23	168	1	52	379	2 705	660	4 593
Willacy	397	20.4	126	1	6.5	2.5	4	20	0	0	0	2 591	645	3 227
Williamson	3 445	16.3	1 001	17	4.8	4.9	231	103	3	213	95	17 234	4 359	2 037
Wilson	386	12.8	217	1	7.2	1.7	12	38	1	30	95	3 551	478	1 557
Winkler	122	15.5	73	0	9.3	2.7	5	63	1	16	201	1 113	167	2 044
Wise	568	13.4	376	2	8.9	4.1	15	34	1	50	113	5 245	804	1 866
Wood	432	12.7	482	4	14.1	8.5	22	64	2	78	227	7 963	912	2 626
Yoakum	120	14.9	61	1	7.6	5.6	3	37	1	24	300	934	174	2 095
Young	221	12.6	257	1	14.6	6.0	12	68	2	83	469	3 814	616	3 448
Zapata	228	20.3	86	2	7.7	8.8	2	17	0	0	0	1 355	227	1 982
Zavala	209	17.6	92	0	7.7	1.6	2	17	0	0	0	1 590	350	2 880
UTAH	43 437	21.0	11 505	253	5.6	5.8	3 744	178	39	4 269	203	201 217	115 624	5 506
Beaver	118	20.2	54	1	9.2	8.4	5	85	2	70	1 187	915	NA	NA
Box Elder	756	18.4	256	4	6.2	4.8	28	67	2	57	136	4 725	2 074	5 266
Cache	2 074	24.2	377	10	4.4	4.8	127	146	1	139	160	6 812	2 557	2 956
Carbon	324	15.5	189	1	9.1	4.1	22	105	1	88	420	3 301	814	3 813
Daggett	6	8.4	5	0	7.1	0.0	0	0	0	0	0	121	41	5 332
Davis	4 505	19.8	945	22	4.2	5.0	240	103	2	248	106	17 674	5 276	2 288
Duchesne	251	17.6	97	2	6.8	9.3	17	117	1	42	290	1 751	539	3 659
Emery	186	17.2	64	1	5.9	5.4	1	9	0	0	0	1 234	294	2 651
Garfield	76	18.0	39	0	9.3	4.4	3	70	1	20	468	760	NA	NA
Grand	122	15.2	62	1	7.7	10.9	10	124	1	34	421	1 126	656	7 923
Iron	682	24.4	167	4	6.0	5.4	22	77	1	47	164	3 344	1 386	4 898
Juab	172	23.4	60	1	8.1	5.8	4	53	1	20	264	866	NA	NA
Kane	91	15.0	55	1	9.0	7.3	3	48	1	33	532	1 061	154	2 591
Millard	194	15.9	101	1	8.3	5.2	5	41	2	40	327	1 574	323	2 571
Morgan	107	15.6	30	1	4.3	6.2	5	10	142	0	0	641	106	1 505
Piute	19	13.5	19	0	13.2	17.5	0	0	0	0	0	280	57	4 017
Rich	28	15.4	11	0	5.9	11.9	0	0	0	0	0	272	24	1 296
Salt Lake	16 924	20.1	4 809	104	5.7	6.2	2 260	266	9	1 924	226	78 471	66 233	7 856
San Juan	275	20.2	61	1	4.5	3.6	3	22	1	25	182	1 215	151	1 082
Sanpete	370	17.7	148	1	7.1	3.6	16	75	2	41	191	2 621	NA	NA
Sevier	302	16.7	154	4	8.5	14.4	9	49	1	27	146	2 760	945	5 129
Summit	396	15.5	78	3	3.0	7.6	87	325	0	0	0	1 448	1 286	4 896
Tooele	669	21.1	188	3	5.9	4.5	16	48	1	38	114	3 000	1 177	3 674
Uintah	421	16.6	149	3	5.9	6.3	20	78	1	39	152	2 629	954	3 666
Utah	8 776	26.6	1 446	45	4.4	5.1	401	119	4	610	182	25 494	13 261	3 962
Wasatch	247	19.4	78	2	6.1	9.4	18	136	1	40	301	1 316	285	2 185
Washington	1 600	20.2	589	9	7.4	5.6	117	142	1	103	125	13 358	NA	NA
Wayne	41	17.1	22	0	9.1	0.0	1	42	0	0	0	368	63	2 609
Weber	3 704	20.3	1 253	26	6.9	7.0	299	162	2	584	317	21 956	10 634	5 795
VERMONT	6 652	11.3	4 957	45	8.4	6.7	1 651	279	15	1 566	265	86 630	18 552	3 139
Addison	373	10.7	256	3	7.3	8.1	75	213	1	45	128	4 390	915	2 609
Bennington	387	10.7	405	4	11.2	10.3	106	295	1	140	389	6 554	1 097	3 041
Caledonia	298	10.4	260	2	9.1	7.8	48	168	1	37	130	4 817	800	2 911

1. Per 1,000 estimated resident population, average 1996–1998.   2. Deaths of infants under 1 year old.   3. Deaths of infants under 1 year old per 1,000 live births.   4. Data subject to copyright.   5. Per 100,000 resident population as of July 1 of the year shown.   6. Data for serious crimes have not been adjusted for underreporting; this may affect comparability between geographic areas and over time.   7. Per 100,000 population estimated by the FBI.

Table B. States and Counties — Crime, Education, Money Income, and Poverty

STATE County	Serious crimes known to police, 1998[1] (cont'd) Rate[2] Violent	Property	Education School enrollment and attainment, 1990 Enrollment[3] Total	Percent private	Attainment[4] (percent) High school graduate or more	Bachelor's degree or more	Local government expenditures, fiscal 1997[5] Total current expenditures (mil dol)	Current expenditures per student (dollars)	Money income 1989 Per capita[6] (dollars)	Households Median Dollars	Percent change, 1979-1989 (constant 1989 dollars)	Percent with $100,000 or more	Income and poverty, 1997 Median household income	Percent below poverty level All persons	Persons under 18	Persons 5-17 in families
	46	47	48	49	50	51	52	53	54	55	56	57	58	59	60	61
TEXAS—Cont'd																
Tom Green	392	4 852	28 123	5.9	71.0	17.0	102.9	5 150	11 482	24 349	0.1	2.3	31 084	17.2	24.2	22.8
Travis	508	5 868	182 331	10.3	83.4	34.7	525.5	5 035	15 123	27 488	4.2	4.4	40 250	11.7	17.0	16.5
Trinity	507	2 989	2 345	2.1	60.7	9.0	14.3	5 707	9 605	16 963	-3.5	1.3	24 087	21.5	33.6	33.3
Tyler	210	1 493	3 694	3.2	62.2	8.5	22.2	5 597	9 733	20 647	1.5	0.5	27 208	20.3	28.2	25.7
Upshur	181	2 330	8 175	11.7	67.1	8.8	35.3	5 229	10 254	21 889	-13.1	1.7	29 591	16.9	23.4	22.9
Upton	77	1 470	1 325	4.0	62.5	10.3	8.8	8 415	9 500	24 342	-0.9	0.7	31 754	17.2	22.7	23.7
Uvalde	246	3 225	6 905	5.0	56.1	13.5	34.9	5 440	8 625	18 001	-7.2	2.1	22 617	30.0	41.2	40.1
Val Verde	365	3 941	11 484	7.5	56.1	13.0	49.8	4 857	7 904	18 042	-6.6	1.5	23 774	29.5	38.6	38.0
Van Zandt	304	2 645	8 188	4.2	62.1	8.7	41.3	4 594	10 130	21 072	-2.0	1.0	28 901	15.7	22.0	21.1
Victoria	574	3 957	21 249	10.1	70.2	14.1	79.4	5 046	12 196	26 945	-12.4	3.0	36 466	16.0	22.7	22.3
Walker	471	2 701	17 934	7.7	73.3	19.0	39.1	5 047	10 090	21 631	0.0	2.4	30 971	19.9	22.5	21.9
Waller	356	3 158	8 414	7.2	69.6	16.2	31.9	5 069	10 294	22 334	-23.3	2.2	29 832	20.9	26.9	26.2
Ward	290	3 086	3 744	2.6	63.2	10.4	14.8	5 586	9 971	22 270	-17.9	1.8	29 524	19.4	25.8	26.5
Washington	380	2 605	7 103	8.4	62.9	15.1	25.4	4 837	11 036	23 052	-1.0	2.5	32 973	15.5	21.7	20.9
Webb	472	6 772	48 323	7.0	47.8	11.1	224.7	5 010	6 771	18 074	-3.3	2.1	23 386	32.6	42.3	39.4
Wharton	591	4 320	10 781	7.7	61.2	11.8	43.9	4 996	10 911	23 896	-7.2	2.7	30 531	17.4	23.0	23.0
Wheeler	204	1 037	1 439	3.3	65.2	12.7	8.7	8 108	10 370	20 108	-12.4	1.2	28 839	16.6	22.5	22.6
Wichita	608	4 375	30 985	8.7	75.1	16.5	113.5	4 921	11 635	23 899	-7.2	2.2	32 301	15.9	21.0	20.5
Wilbarger	473	4 120	3 525	5.1	62.9	12.7	14.3	4 913	9 823	20 886	3.9	0.9	27 028	19.4	26.9	26.8
Willacy	530	2 697	6 016	1.9	42.9	8.8	30.9	6 069	6 074	14 590	-13.7	1.3	18 616	39.7	50.3	49.7
Williamson	188	1 849	40 989	12.0	81.4	24.6	246.0	4 907	13 490	33 695	2.7	2.7	50 102	6.7	8.6	9.1
Wilson	176	1 381	5 889	8.0	61.2	8.8	30.9	4 764	9 728	23 184	2.8	1.9	33 182	15.2	19.8	20.3
Winkler	184	1 860	2 463	1.7	57.5	10.1	14.3	7 382	9 843	22 366	-20.3	1.3	31 590	16.8	20.3	21.6
Wise	225	1 641	8 369	7.7	67.1	10.0	39.2	5 308	11 307	25 885	-5.7	2.4	36 125	11.2	14.6	14.9
Wood	360	2 266	6 456	8.4	65.7	9.6	31.8	5 191	10 937	20 927	-2.4	2.1	27 395	17.5	24.8	24.8
Yoakum	205	1 890	2 443	1.2	64.0	10.4	16.3	7 052	10 592	26 442	-10.9	4.0	35 414	15.4	19.5	20.8
Young	162	3 286	4 071	6.0	60.7	11.2	19.0	5 029	11 368	21 710	-9.4	2.7	28 514	18.0	25.2	24.6
Zapata	122	1 860	2 943	2.8	50.1	6.9	15.8	5 389	6 541	14 926	-13.4	1.1	20 905	32.1	40.6	43.2
Zavala	354	2 526	3 795	1.7	38.6	6.9	15.7	6 440	4 818	11 822	-20.8	0.8	15 439	45.2	53.5	54.5
UTAH	314	5 192	610 696	11.1	85.1	22.3	1 823.0	3 783	11 029	29 470	-0.5	2.5	38 884	10.0	12.5	10.5
Beaver	NA	NA	1 514	4.4	83.4	9.0	5.9	3 917	8 558	21 092	-1.3	0.6	30 352	12.2	15.7	13.5
Box Elder	124	5 142	12 531	4.2	83.6	17.6	43.0	3 805	11 045	33 468	14.6	1.6	44 570	8.0	9.9	8.5
Cache	101	2 855	29 988	2.7	89.3	30.0	69.9	3 674	9 544	26 949	7.9	1.6	37 084	10.5	11.7	10.5
Carbon	178	3 635	6 750	6.2	74.3	12.5	20.8	4 204	10 225	25 555	-24.3	1.1	35 526	15.7	20.4	16.5
Daggett	910	4 422	213	0.0	75.4	11.7	2.0	9 093	9 575	22 941	-17.0	0.0	35 584	10.8	12.6	13.3
Davis	128	2 160	67 833	6.1	89.9	23.5	217.0	3 664	11 611	35 108	0.4	3.0	48 690	6.6	7.9	6.6
Duchesne	183	3 476	4 591	2.4	74.8	11.8	19.4	4 274	8 197	23 653	-18.6	1.1	31 768	19.3	24.3	20.3
Emery	72	2 579	3 874	2.8	82.4	10.4	15.1	4 549	9 257	30 525	-10.3	0.3	39 838	12.5	15.4	12.6
Garfield	NA	NA	1 141	2.4	79.9	15.0	6.1	5 364	8 248	21 160	2.1	1.1	30 149	13.5	17.8	16.3
Grand	266	7 657	1 835	6.2	79.9	15.4	6.9	4 318	9 899	21 695	-24.6	0.9	28 881	17.8	26.0	21.4
Iron	304	4 594	8 405	2.4	85.8	21.9	25.6	3 918	8 539	23 185	-4.4	1.0	32 911	15.7	21.3	17.1
Juab	NA	NA	1 958	3.4	77.3	8.8	9.8	4 635	8 332	23 569	-6.8	0.0	35 251	11.0	14.1	11.7
Kane	219	2 372	1 602	2.6	82.5	11.8	6.7	4 707	8 721	21 134	3.0	0.6	30 498	16.7	22.4	19.8
Millard	80	2 491	4 160	5.0	84.9	15.9	18.0	4 730	8 574	26 376	21.0	0.3	35 315	14.2	16.9	15.0
Morgan	99	1 406	2 061	4.5	90.1	19.0	8.2	3 981	10 448	33 274	-4.9	2.6	49 084	5.0	5.5	5.4
Piute	423	3 594	407	1.0	79.8	12.5	2.8	6 733	8 160	19 125	-0.1	0.9	25 746	19.2	25.6	21.3
Rich	216	1 080	569	3.5	81.8	15.1	3.5	6 397	8 610	24 940	-7.8	1.0	36 627	11.0	12.4	12.9
Salt Lake	518	7 338	239 033	8.7	85.3	23.8	691.3	3 799	12 222	30 149	-2.3	3.2	44 118	9.1	11.7	9.5
San Juan	172	910	4 755	2.0	59.7	13.1	22.8	6 441	5 907	17 289	-21.9	1.0	26 723	30.0	32.0	29.2
Sanpete	NA	NA	6 532	1.5	82.0	15.6	23.3	4 214	7 585	20 197	-1.4	1.0	30 460	15.7	18.7	15.4
Sevier	233	4 896	5 264	5.1	81.9	12.6	19.7	3 925	8 615	23 300	-11.6	0.5	32 749	15.2	19.3	16.1
Summit	103	4 793	4 785	7.6	91.6	32.9	25.7	4 554	16 739	36 756	12.0	7.4	56 472	5.5	6.7	6.3
Tooele	243	3 431	8 396	4.6	77.3	11.3	29.5	3 828	10 568	30 178	-8.5	0.5	42 277	9.0	11.9	10.1
Uintah	219	3 447	7 622	3.4	73.7	11.2	28.4	4 276	8 379	23 968	-22.9	1.0	32 706	17.4	20.7	18.1
Utah	134	3 828	114 352	30.5	87.9	26.2	273.6	3 571	9 051	27 432	1.1	2.2	41 509	10.3	11.3	9.7
Wasatch	238	1 947	3 158	5.2	83.2	18.5	12.3	3 550	10 722	27 981	7.6	3.5	42 998	7.7	10.0	8.8
Washington	NA	NA	16 064	3.4	84.5	17.7	64.1	3 546	9 450	24 602	8.7	1.9	34 710	12.7	17.9	14.6
Wayne	207	2 402	736	1.4	82.0	20.0	3.5	5 833	7 692	20 000	8.0	0.7	28 100	16.4	22.4	20.3
Weber	351	5 444	50 567	5.6	82.5	18.0	160.4	3 891	11 637	30 125	4.0	1.6	42 764	10.8	14.9	12.2
VERMONT	106	3 033	145 988	17.3	80.8	24.3	718.0	6 753	13 527	29 792	20.2	2.8	35 210	9.7	12.7	10.7
Addison	128	2 481	9 338	29.2	82.0	25.1	43.4	7 191	12 717	30 112	21.8	2.6	37 520	9.8	11.8	10.3
Bennington	169	2 872	8 718	21.9	77.8	23.5	43.2	7 382	13 543	28 485	15.5	3.3	35 779	10.5	13.9	12.0
Caledonia	95	2 816	7 117	18.5	77.4	19.0	30.1	7 301	11 425	25 356	15.2	1.6	31 581	13.0	17.1	14.4

1. Data for serious crimes have not been adjusted for underreporting; this may affect comparability between geographic areas and over time.   2. Per 100,000 population estimated by the FBI.   3. All persons 3 years old and over enrolled in nursery school through college.   4. Persons 25 years old and over.   5. Elementary and secondary education expenditures, local government fiscal years ending between July 1, 1996 and June 30, 1997.   6. Based on population enumerated as of April 1, 1990.

Table B. States and Counties — **Personal Income**

STATE County	Total (mil dol)	Percent change, 1997–1998	Per capita¹ Dollars	Rank	Wages and salaries² (mil dol)	Proprietor's income (mil dol)	Dividends, interest, and rent (mil dol)	Total (mil dol)	Transfer payments — Government payments to individuals Total (mil dol)	Social Security (mil dol)	Medical payments (mil dol)	Income maintenance (mil dol)	Unemployment insurance (mil dol)
	62	63	64	65	66	67	68	69	70	71	72	73	74
TEXAS—Cont'd													
Tom Green	2 273	5.5	22 140	1 052	1 365	175	457	367	351	143	146	30	4
Travis	22 799	14.9	32 148	110	20 589	2 009	3 615	1 586	1 467	592	579	149	29
Trinity	226	5.1	17 938	2 366	54	20	46	70	67	30	27	7	1
Tyler	344	5.4	16 862	2 641	90	26	59	94	91	39	39	8	1
Upshur	645	5.1	18 010	2 339	142	62	102	144	138	59	59	11	3
Upton	64	-0.9	16 952	2 621	41	1	13	13	13	5	5	2	0
Uvalde	433	6.1	16 997	2 614	208	41	91	104	100	30	44	17	2
Val Verde	661	7.5	15 137	2 919	424	28	99	139	132	36	56	30	2
Van Zandt	868	6.7	19 745	1 797	204	67	130	194	187	80	85	12	2
Victoria	1 971	6.2	24 131	617	1 073	159	394	283	269	105	122	26	4
Walker	918	5.3	16 757	2 664	604	43	172	152	143	54	57	14	1
Waller	556	5.9	20 398	1 597	250	28	62	98	93	31	36	9	1
Ward	208	4.9	17 639	2 455	110	11	43	43	41	18	16	5	1
Washington	747	4.5	25 667	421	348	55	247	120	116	49	51	10	1
Webb	2 591	6.3	13 870	3 019	1 690	269	273	526	495	107	237	116	8
Wharton	854	5.5	21 298	1 294	373	94	162	156	150	57	66	16	2
Wheeler	138	4.1	26 061	392	42	38	24	30	29	11	14	2	0
Wichita	2 946	3.4	22 929	865	1 843	323	584	455	435	173	178	41	7
Wilbarger	292	7.8	20 717	1 481	159	24	60	67	65	25	29	7	1
Willacy	235	4.4	11 965	3 086	87	18	29	83	80	19	38	19	3
Williamson	5 849	17.1	26 149	381	2 657	380	641	406	369	171	146	23	6
Wilson	601	9.4	19 185	1 987	103	32	73	89	84	30	39	10	1
Winkler	136	3.8	17 103	2 586	66	11	26	31	30	12	13	3	1
Wise	946	10.1	21 339	1 285	327	71	124	122	115	54	44	8	2
Wood	646	5.4	18 837	2 114	204	81	120	173	167	74	69	10	2
Yoakum	144	-7.9	18 046	2 333	94	18	29	25	24	10	10	3	0
Young	411	5.4	23 384	770	171	65	98	87	84	37	37	6	2
Zapata	139	5.5	12 126	3 084	67	5	28	41	39	10	20	7	1
Zavala	121	4.6	10 215	3 102	50	12	13	49	47	11	21	14	1
UTAH	46 717	6.7	22 240	X	32 201	3 339	8 351	4 857	4 499	1 951	1 620	393	95
Beaver	99	6.8	16 705	2 678	53	16	18	20	19	7	7	1	0
Box Elder	896	7.0	21 359	1 279	701	93	136	97	90	46	30	6	2
Cache	1 560	6.4	17 887	2 381	977	102	283	173	158	68	53	12	3
Carbon	419	3.9	19 930	1 735	269	17	65	86	82	33	30	8	2
Daggett	13	3.5	17 734	2 430	11	0	3	2	2	1	1	0	0
Davis	5 046	7.5	21 603	1 223	2 702	234	809	405	366	163	125	28	8
Duchesne	237	6.0	16 301	2 742	131	16	36	47	45	16	18	7	2
Emery	179	3.6	16 276	2 746	143	11	25	31	29	13	11	3	1
Garfield	76	4.4	17 589	2 470	46	5	14	14	13	7	5	1	1
Grand	157	8.3	19 505	1 887	89	16	37	25	24	12	7	3	1
Iron	492	7.4	17 090	2 591	309	33	84	76	71	31	26	7	1
Juab	113	5.5	14 883	2 943	58	6	18	23	22	9	9	2	1
Kane	128	7.8	20 600	1 529	54	13	26	21	20	10	7	2	0
Millard	193	4.3	15 734	2 838	112	24	37	34	32	15	11	3	1
Morgan	134	6.8	19 066	2 037	46	12	24	12	11	5	3	1	0
Piute	20	7.5	14 428	2 974	6	3	4	5	5	2	2	0	0
Rich	29	2.4	15 526	2 875	12	3	9	5	4	3	1	0	0
Salt Lake	22 079	6.3	26 100	391	17 563	1 576	4 096	1 974	1 828	805	642	155	38
San Juan	173	7.2	12 685	3 075	110	10	26	41	39	10	15	12	0
Sanpete	302	7.2	13 989	3 005	138	32	54	58	54	25	19	5	1
Sevier	304	5.5	16 474	2 711	171	28	55	61	58	27	23	5	1
Summit	1 062	9.2	39 645	34	390	135	208	37	33	16	9	1	2
Tooele	611	10.2	18 244	2 282	398	27	84	65	59	23	23	6	1
Uintah	378	4.8	14 749	2 955	237	30	59	72	67	27	26	8	2
Utah	6 103	7.8	17 956	2 357	4 008	504	894	679	622	260	254	54	12
Wasatch	281	10.1	21 199	1 331	96	23	48	29	26	13	8	2	1
Washington	1 516	8.6	18 428	2 232	760	170	379	262	248	131	86	14	3
Wayne	41	10.2	17 231	2 550	22	6	7	7	7	3	2	1	0
Weber	4 076	5.3	22 178	1 041	2 587	194	815	496	465	169	170	46	13
VERMONT	14 529	5.6	24 602	X	8 772	1 217	3 029	2 047	1 918	847	707	216	47
Addison	776	7.4	22 081	1 075	387	73	166	96	88	43	28	10	4
Bennington	920	5.1	25 599	427	508	74	252	138	130	66	42	13	3
Caledonia	582	4.8	20 394	1 602	283	74	116	105	99	45	30	13	4

1. Based on the resident population estimated as of July 1 of the year shown.   2. Includes other labor income.

Table B. States and Counties — Earnings, Social Security, and Housing

STATE County	Earnings, 1998									Social Security beneficiaries, December 1998		Housing units, 1990		
			Goods-related[1]		Service-related and other[2]							Supplemental Security Income recipients, December 1998		
	Total (mil dol)	Farm	Total	Manufacturing	Total	Retail trade	Finance, insurance, and real estate	Services	Government	Number	Rate[3]		Total	Percent change, 1980–1990
	75	76	77	78	79	80	81	82	83	84	85	86	87	88
TEXAS—Cont'd														
Tom Green	1 540	0.1	20.7	11.4	53.5	10.0	4.9	24.4	25.9	17 746	173	2 288	40 135	22.1
Travis	22 598	0.0	26.4	20.4	56.4	7.5	7.3	29.1	17.2	67 961	96	9 630	264 173	50.9
Trinity	74	4.2	D	13.3	D	11.7	3.7	20.8	24.8	3 606	286	457	7 200	22.8
Tyler	116	-1.1	D	13.8	D	10.6	5.0	15.3	36.0	4 655	228	547	9 047	8.1
Upshur	204	2.1	24.7	10.2	51.9	14.6	5.6	18.0	21.3	7 171	200	763	12 887	12.1
Upton	42	-6.5	D	0.7	D	4.7	3.0	6.9	31.0	652	174	67	1 868	-0.4
Uvalde	249	2.3	14.7	6.4	53.2	11.6	3.5	20.0	29.8	4 370	171	997	9 692	16.1
Val Verde	452	-1.8	D	2.7	D	9.9	2.7	15.2	55.5	6 060	138	2 137	13 905	13.4
Van Zandt	271	4.8	23.2	2.9	52.0	14.2	3.2	21.6	20.0	9 856	224	912	17 013	24.8
Victoria	1 232	-0.8	28.0	12.3	57.1	14.0	5.4	26.3	15.7	12 674	153	1 899	29 162	18.3
Walker	647	-0.2	D	7.3	D	9.3	2.9	13.4	59.3	6 280	114	812	18 349	26.9
Waller	277	-1.6	33.0	23.2	37.1	13.2	3.3	12.1	31.5	3 663	135	497	8 824	31.3
Ward	121	-3.2	D	D	D	8.0	3.1	12.2	27.5	2 139	181	274	5 365	2.0
Washington	403	0.0	D	22.9	D	10.9	9.3	16.2	19.2	6 133	211	879	11 717	21.5
Webb	1 958	0.0	13.7	2.2	61.0	12.0	6.0	19.7	25.3	18 190	97	8 072	37 197	34.0
Wharton	467	11.0	22.0	11.9	48.4	9.4	3.8	21.5	18.6	7 180	179	1 151	16 277	6.4
Wheeler	80	35.1	D	1.8	D	8.0	2.3	15.5	18.1	1 396	264	114	3 071	-4.1
Wichita	2 166	0.3	26.3	14.6	42.8	9.1	3.8	20.3	30.6	20 973	163	2 402	51 413	6.3
Wilbarger	182	4.2	19.1	14.3	37.7	9.4	4.2	13.3	39.0	3 059	223	404	6 812	4.2
Willacy	105	8.0	D	D	D	10.3	3.1	20.2	35.0	3 066	156	1 140	6 072	13.6
Williamson	3 037	-0.2	21.4	11.8	67.8	7.7	4.5	18.5	11.1	20 093	90	1 709	54 466	92.9
Wilson	135	-1.5	23.3	5.8	44.6	11.7	4.1	19.8	33.6	4 295	137	580	8 516	37.2
Winkler	77	-0.6	39.4	0.5	D	7.7	2.5	12.8	23.2	1 376	173	175	3 708	-3.8
Wise	398	-0.6	35.5	17.3	49.1	12.8	3.9	15.7	15.9	6 507	147	405	14 219	29.1
Wood	285	11.1	19.1	8.9	52.2	11.2	4.5	23.7	17.7	8 606	251	785	14 541	27.1
Yoakum	112	3.2	43.8	1.8	33.5	5.2	1.5	9.0	19.5	1 156	144	103	3 372	11.5
Young	236	1.6	D	18.4	D	8.6	4.6	14.8	16.2	4 326	244	398	8 523	3.4
Zapata	72	-1.1	36.6	0.8	D	7.0	3.3	14.3	32.0	1 670	145	446	4 225	38.3
Zavala	62	14.0	D	D	D	6.4	1.9	18.7	34.6	1 988	167	864	4 180	18.4
UTAH	35 540	0.5	23.0	13.9	58.2	10.3	7.9	26.7	18.2	230 745	110	20 242	598 388	22.1
Beaver	68	18.6	D	4.8	D	10.6	2.1	13.0	24.1	927	157	52	2 200	21.1
Box Elder	794	3.8	D	56.8	D	10.1	1.8	8.3	9.3	5 550	132	268	11 890	15.5
Cache	1 080	2.5	D	26.9	D	8.6	3.1	21.7	24.5	7 995	92	449	22 053	16.9
Carbon	287	-1.1	31.9	5.4	47.7	9.5	2.1	21.5	21.5	3 769	180	353	8 713	6.4
Daggett	12	-1.3	D	D	D	3.7	0.5	19.8	64.0	130	176	2	825	11.9
Davis	2 937	0.3	21.2	12.5	42.0	11.4	4.5	18.6	36.5	20 309	87	1 179	55 777	34.2
Duchesne	147	1.8	26.8	5.3	D	9.1	D	12.8	30.5	2 111	146	221	5 860	30.9
Emery	153	1.2	40.5	0.7	D	3.6	0.7	D	17.3	1 515	138	131	3 928	6.1
Garfield	52	-0.9	D	8.4	D	6.8	1.8	32.9	32.3	888	208	31	2 488	40.6
Grand	105	0.0	D	D	D	20.8	D	31.1	24.3	1 380	171	106	2 992	-1.8
Iron	343	3.0	D	14.4	D	12.1	5.6	21.1	28.8	3 767	131	284	8 499	36.0
Juab	64	-0.3	D	19.4	D	14.0	1.6	29.6	23.3	1 069	141	76	2 311	17.4
Kane	67	0.9	D	D	D	13.7	2.7	26.6	26.1	1 261	203	62	3 237	48.1
Millard	136	11.3	D	4.5	D	9.6	D	15.5	22.0	1 847	151	116	4 125	25.4
Morgan	58	10.2	38.1	18.6	D	7.2	2.4	D	17.4	711	101	20	1 681	20.1
Piute	9	31.0	D	D	D	2.9	D	D	37.5	326	233	26	704	13.7
Rich	14	15.2	D	D	D	6.1	D	20.8	36.6	314	171	10	1 859	24.2
Salt Lake	19 139	0.0	19.9	11.6	65.3	10.2	10.6	26.9	14.8	90 524	106	8 883	257 339	19.9
San Juan	120	1.0	25.0	5.7	D	8.2	D	19.4	37.6	1 441	105	695	4 650	24.1
Sanpete	170	10.0	D	13.0	D	8.3	2.4	15.4	33.7	3 205	149	213	6 570	16.5
Sevier	199	6.4	D	7.4	D	11.2	2.4	17.9	23.2	3 327	180	211	6 059	11.7
Summit	525	1.0	17.9	6.0	69.9	14.5	16.7	33.5	11.1	1 786	67	50	11 256	91.5
Tooele	425	0.5	23.2	14.0	38.6	5.7	3.8	13.3	37.8	3 412	102	234	9 510	11.0
Uintah	267	0.5	27.7	1.8	D	10.3	D	22.9	22.6	3 373	131	360	8 142	23.0
Utah	4 512	0.5	D	15.2	D	9.0	4.9	39.7	13.4	30 119	90	2 858	72 820	16.8
Wasatch	119	2.1	D	7.8	D	12.5	4.2	25.2	22.4	1 562	118	73	4 465	-0.2
Washington	929	0.1	23.5	7.2	60.3	15.8	6.4	27.8	16.2	15 283	186	651	19 523	100.8
Wayne	28	12.3	10.7	2.6	D	10.3	D	29.3	32.3	453	190	17	1 061	25.1
Weber	2 781	0.2	29.2	21.6	47.7	10.4	4.8	25.4	22.9	22 381	122	2 502	57 851	14.6
VERMONT	9 989	1.5	27.4	20.2	55.1	10.0	5.6	28.5	16.0	101 159	171	12 683	271 214	21.5
Addison	459	5.2	26.6	19.1	56.0	11.8	3.0	33.8	12.2	5 201	148	611	14 022	16.8
Bennington	582	0.5	D	26.7	D	14.1	4.6	30.6	11.3	7 652	213	823	18 501	18.6
Caledonia	358	3.3	31.8	23.0	49.3	11.0	3.6	24.9	15.7	5 586	196	786	13 449	15.8

1. Covers mining, construction, and manufacturing. 2. Covers private sector earnings in agricultural services, forestry, and fisheries; transportation and public utilities; wholesale trade; retail trade; finance, insurance, and real estate; and services. 3. Per 1,000 resident population estimated as of July 1 of the year shown.

Table B. States and Counties — Housing, Labor Force, and Employment

STATE County	Housing units, 1990 (cont'd)								Civilian labor force, 1999				Civilian employment, 1990[5]		
	Occupied units							Sub-stand-ard units[3] (percent)			Unemployment			Percent	
	Owner-occupied					Renter-occupied								Professional, managerial, and technical	Precision production, craft, and repair
				Owner cost as a percent of income											
	Total	Percent	Median value[1]	With a mortgage	Without a mortgage	Median rent[2]	Rent as percent of income		Total	Percent change, 1998–1999	Total	Rate[4]	Total		
	89	90	91	92	93	94	95	96	97	98	99	100	101	102	103
TEXAS—Cont'd															
Tom Green	35 408	62.3	49 600	19.8	12.8	365	25.1	6.2	50 157	-4.4	2 155	4.3	41 808	26.9	11.2
Travis	232 861	45.7	78 300	23.1	12.5	416	26.8	6.3	468 174	2.9	10 748	2.3	302 536	40.2	7.9
Trinity	4 647	78.9	38 700	23.0	16.5	314	29.7	6.2	5 004	6.7	293	5.9	4 011	18.8	11.0
Tyler	6 459	83.0	37 900	21.0	12.7	313	28.9	7.6	6 520	2.8	571	8.8	5 845	20.3	16.0
Upshur	11 360	80.4	42 100	20.2	13.6	305	27.1	5.8	16 729	-1.5	1 044	6.2	12 668	19.4	15.7
Upton	1 472	75.2	27 600	17.2	12.1	273	13.8	11.6	1 572	-1.5	120	7.6	1 747	20.9	19.9
Uvalde	7 553	69.1	38 600	20.2	12.8	263	24.3	14.2	11 184	-1.9	881	7.9	8 519	23.9	13.2
Val Verde	11 840	61.1	43 400	21.0	12.8	333	25.9	16.6	18 166	2.5	1 515	8.3	12 494	23.0	14.3
Van Zandt	14 349	80.5	45 600	21.2	14.6	341	26.5	5.3	21 349	10.0	682	3.2	14 795	18.8	15.9
Victoria	26 228	64.6	54 700	19.5	12.9	351	26.3	7.3	43 099	-0.7	1 798	4.2	32 462	25.6	15.4
Walker	14 918	57.4	60 300	20.5	16.4	390	31.4	7.3	23 667	0.6	505	2.1	18 228	30.3	7.4
Waller	7 402	68.7	54 300	20.0	15.1	335	27.3	8.6	12 724	1.0	671	5.3	9 636	23.7	11.8
Ward	4 444	76.9	33 300	18.0	12.1	280	22.0	9.8	4 290	-9.0	509	11.9	4 904	23.2	19.7
Washington	9 619	72.4	58 600	20.3	12.5	342	23.8	7.3	14 883	0.0	402	2.7	11 919	23.6	12.1
Webb	34 438	60.6	49 800	22.5	12.7	314	27.6	28.1	72 729	-0.3	6 211	8.5	45 819	23.3	10.0
Wharton	14 210	66.4	49 300	19.5	13.4	313	24.3	9.0	19 072	0.6	1 040	5.5	16 933	20.2	14.7
Wheeler	2 350	78.5	31 200	18.4	13.5	252	23.8	4.3	2 728	-2.3	117	4.3	2 511	24.0	11.0
Wichita	45 271	63.4	46 400	19.8	13.1	362	25.5	3.6	60 335	-2.4	2 857	4.7	51 055	27.6	11.4
Wilbarger	5 741	67.3	36 300	18.9	14.3	312	24.6	4.8	7 496	5.6	185	2.5	6 504	22.1	12.5
Willacy	5 049	75.5	25 800	19.8	13.7	202	22.0	24.7	6 889	-6.3	1 145	16.6	5 521	19.1	12.2
Williamson	48 792	64.0	72 300	23.5	13.3	442	23.8	4.4	142 574	7.1	2 384	1.7	71 243	34.8	11.0
Wilson	7 481	80.6	49 900	23.1	13.0	278	24.5	9.5	15 376	3.4	403	2.6	9 447	19.7	16.7
Winkler	2 941	80.3	29 200	15.7	13.1	290	23.3	8.1	3 071	-3.5	414	13.5	3 102	22.5	23.5
Wise	12 175	79.2	49 700	20.3	13.7	338	24.5	6.7	24 018	4.0	679	2.8	14 453	19.5	16.9
Wood	11 426	79.6	47 400	20.1	13.4	335	28.3	4.7	13 678	1.8	682	5.0	11 309	21.0	14.1
Yoakum	2 839	74.1	45 100	16.4	12.2	371	21.4	10.6	3 403	-3.6	341	10.0	3 546	22.0	18.3
Young	7 101	73.1	41 200	20.9	13.5	300	26.3	3.3	8 158	-0.4	437	5.4	7 839	19.6	16.7
Zapata	2 862	82.0	35 500	24.1	12.6	239	31.8	19.9	4 540	-2.6	602	13.3	2 550	20.0	19.9
Zavala	3 356	69.4	20 300	18.0	13.3	210	31.9	32.1	4 167	-2.3	723	17.4	3 631	18.5	8.3
UTAH	537 273	68.1	68 900	20.9	12.1	369	23.8	5.4	1 083 912	2.0	40 498	3.7	736 059	30.8	11.4
Beaver	1 594	85.1	51 200	21.8	13.8	294	26.5	4.5	2 338	-2.6	91	3.9	1 681	18.3	10.6
Box Elder	10 954	79.0	65 000	16.7	12.0	343	18.3	4.4	18 470	-0.9	858	4.6	14 601	28.1	14.1
Cache	21 021	62.6	67 100	19.7	11.9	335	24.0	6.7	44 065	2.1	1 205	2.7	30 374	31.5	10.7
Carbon	6 907	75.7	51 500	17.8	12.5	313	25.2	3.3	9 710	1.0	682	7.0	7 587	26.5	19.1
Daggett	253	60.1	50 400	25.0	13.1	270	14.2	4.3	417	3.2	16	3.8	295	18.3	15.3
Davis	53 598	74.1	75 700	20.4	11.3	394	22.1	4.6	117 954	3.2	4 083	3.5	77 531	34.1	11.1
Duchesne	3 707	81.5	43 400	21.4	13.2	335	24.4	8.5	5 881	-0.9	555	9.4	4 506	22.8	14.5
Emery	2 998	82.3	48 500	15.8	11.9	311	18.8	6.1	3 961	-3.2	291	7.3	3 702	23.0	22.6
Garfield	1 321	81.9	49 800	21.5	12.8	292	17.8	6.3	2 698	1.5	224	8.3	1 605	16.9	11.7
Grand	2 489	73.6	49 700	21.0	12.8	315	24.5	5.0	5 330	5.3	357	6.7	2 804	23.0	13.3
Iron	6 269	69.8	63 400	21.0	12.2	343	27.9	6.4	14 883	4.8	547	3.7	8 402	25.1	10.5
Juab	1 801	80.1	43 300	17.7	12.2	285	16.3	4.4	3 594	2.5	178	5.0	2 378	16.9	17.3
Kane	1 724	77.4	63 100	24.4	12.3	308	18.8	7.3	2 695	9.2	107	4.0	1 961	21.7	14.4
Millard	3 349	79.3	50 400	19.7	13.8	290	19.4	7.2	4 463	-1.4	200	4.5	4 209	23.2	12.8
Morgan	1 555	82.7	78 000	18.1	12.2	355	14.9	7.6	3 491	-2.9	143	4.1	2 282	25.2	13.5
Piute	449	85.7	45 500	22.3	14.1	242	26.0	6.0	537	5.3	33	6.1	424	21.0	7.3
Rich	521	78.7	45 900	19.0	12.9	304	19.6	4.0	956	0.7	35	3.7	646	18.4	11.8
Salt Lake	240 680	65.1	71 000	21.3	12.1	379	24.0	4.4	476 323	1.5	16 126	3.4	333 193	31.6	10.7
San Juan	3 375	77.3	37 800	15.6	13.2	254	23.1	38.5	4 920	3.2	389	7.9	3 668	30.1	11.7
Sanpete	4 859	79.7	49 000	20.9	14.1	310	26.4	6.9	8 827	0.8	485	5.5	5 417	23.2	14.9
Sevier	4 877	82.4	51 600	20.2	13.0	324	22.1	4.9	8 068	0.7	350	4.3	5 622	22.5	13.7
Summit	5 271	71.2	107 800	22.9	12.6	517	23.2	4.5	14 253	4.0	694	4.9	7 593	37.5	9.1
Tooele	8 581	70.2	60 400	18.0	11.8	351	18.4	5.3	11 794	1.2	657	5.6	11 037	23.2	17.3
Uintah	6 670	75.7	44 400	19.6	13.6	296	24.2	7.5	10 662	1.9	770	7.2	7 563	24.8	17.3
Utah	70 168	62.7	70 000	21.3	11.8	349	25.1	8.0	163 077	2.8	5 148	3.2	105 102	32.1	10.2
Wasatch	3 074	76.0	69 900	21.7	12.9	393	22.6	4.0	6 227	3.7	314	5.0	4 340	23.3	16.7
Washington	15 256	70.8	78 400	25.1	11.9	414	24.9	6.9	37 667	4.4	1 365	3.6	17 224	24.5	11.8
Wayne	699	81.7	54 000	22.8	13.7	257	15.5	5.1	1 419	-2.8	84	5.9	795	22.3	10.4
Weber	53 253	70.7	66 000	20.1	12.0	356	23.3	4.3	99 235	1.3	4 512	4.5	69 127	31.2	12.2
VERMONT	210 650	69.0	95 500	21.9	14.7	446	27.1	2.5	335 778	1.7	10 193	3.0	283 146	31.3	12.3
Addison	11 410	74.2	93 400	22.6	15.3	455	27.5	3.5	20 191	3.1	640	3.2	16 914	29.6	13.0
Bennington	13 595	70.0	97 100	23.0	14.2	434	29.1	2.3	20 039	-1.0	745	3.7	16 995	28.0	14.3
Caledonia	10 368	71.3	72 700	19.8	13.6	349	27.1	2.8	15 307	0.8	625	4.1	13 040	26.6	12.7

1. Specified owner-occupied units.   2. Specified renter-occupied units.   3. Overcrowded or lacking complete plumbing facilities.   4. Percent of civilian labor force.   5. Persons 16 years and older.

Table B. States and Counties — Nonfarm Employment and Agriculture

| | Private nonfarm establishments, employment and payroll, 1998 | | | | | | | | | Agriculture, 1997 | | | |
| | Employment | | | | | | | Annual payroll | | Farms | | | Farm operators |
STATE County	Number of establishments	Total	Health Care and Social Assistance	Manufacturing	Retail trade	Finance and Insurance	Professional Scientific and Technical Services	Total (mil dol)	Average per employee (dollars)	Number	Percent with— Less than 50 acres	500 acres and over	Whose principal occupation is farming (percent)
	104	105	106	107	108	109	110	111	112	113	114	115	116
TEXAS—Cont'd													
Tom Green	2 565	34 098	5 714	4 314	5 394	1 151	1 008	740	21 690	880	34.9	33.2	46.8
Travis	22 483	386 568	40 483	48 149	47 330	20 925	35 639	13 384	34 622	1 038	39.4	12.8	36.8
Trinity	239	1 797	252	191	361	69	87	30	16 661	518	26.8	6.8	40.7
Tyler	310	3 134	512	424	586	73	66	57	18 196	463	50.3	3.9	36.5
Upshur	442	4 063	426	532	882	190	146	71	17 415	1 110	35.9	5.0	35.0
Upton	72	693	196	0	89	D	D	17	23 861	96	10.4	69.8	58.3
Uvalde	579	5 657	1 011	664	1 137	198	107	101	17 926	593	17.5	44.7	50.9
Val Verde	795	8 383	2 300	333	1 818	357	174	133	15 906	238	24.8	63.4	54.2
Van Zandt	731	5 973	965	573	1 322	238	155	115	19 184	2 423	39.7	5.3	40.0
Victoria	2 207	29 345	5 260	3 286	5 206	1 216	861	688	23 458	1 084	32.4	16.6	39.4
Walker	843	9 886	1 801	725	2 195	330	397	169	17 135	826	38.3	8.7	32.9
Waller	489	6 257	513	1 346	1 299	146	230	163	26 081	1 066	43.6	9.3	39.6
Ward	255	2 569	273	38	370	89	55	56	21 795	85	23.5	51.8	41.2
Washington	730	10 274	1 389	2 965	1 622	543	232	225	21 932	1 986	32.2	5.8	38.7
Webb	3 916	46 888	6 734	1 591	9 060	1 859	1 216	927	19 780	453	6.0	61.1	38.4
Wharton	956	11 048	2 287	1 922	1 785	404	198	230	20 816	1 347	24.3	28.1	53.6
Wheeler	185	1 135	308	36	216	52	28	17	15 405	505	9.7	45.0	48.7
Wichita	3 378	46 903	8 815	8 105	7 034	1 564	1 143	1 046	22 297	560	38.4	20.4	34.8
Wilbarger	344	4 622	1 652	702	687	258	62	97	21 024	476	13.9	38.2	54.6
Willacy	207	1 952	366	D	403	109	34	34	17 173	243	21.0	49.4	67.1
Williamson	4 286	60 075	5 511	14 983	10 446	4 709	1 871	2 341	38 972	2 034	36.8	12.7	41.1
Wilson	381	2 805	653	350	662	106	70	45	16 017	1 794	27.5	9.9	37.6
Winkler	172	1 149	166	D	227	56	D	25	21 701	39	28.2	59.0	46.2
Wise	842	8 875	1 007	1 361	1 542	298	228	214	24 083	2 075	41.1	8.4	35.3
Wood	755	5 873	1 013	679	1 227	306	187	107	18 243	1 331	35.8	5.9	43.6
Yoakum	200	1 844	91	77	290	D	20	42	23 026	278	9.4	58.6	61.9
Young	610	5 198	689	1 061	728	223	101	116	22 350	709	12.0	32.4	43.4
Zapata	137	1 337	152	D	225	57	D	25	18 430	323	2.8	57.6	45.2
Zavala	105	1 648	851	D	145	44	19	19	11 445	232	4.3	62.5	53.9
UTAH	52 025	866 146	83 229	124 504	117 336	40 957	43 350	22 200	25 631	14 181	46.3	16.4	42.2
Beaver	141	1 275	251	86	265	38	D	19	15 268	219	31.1	21.5	56.6
Box Elder	750	15 481	1 065	8 543	1 501	335	133	497	32 072	1 077	36.9	26.7	46.8
Cache	2 174	31 339	2 628	11 466	4 647	631	1 228	591	18 872	1 232	42.1	9.5	43.1
Carbon	511	6 647	1 050	433	1 328	113	265	164	24 625	199	48.2	18.1	38.2
Daggett	21	D	0	0	D	D	D	D	D	36	8.3	36.1	58.3
Davis	4 270	56 666	6 283	8 130	10 879	2 933	2 536	1 270	22 409	559	74.4	3.0	35.2
Duchesne	363	2 898	D	88	563	57	93	63	21 674	811	29.6	17.8	44.9
Emery	185	2 651	D	D	356	36	45	97	36 701	450	33.8	19.1	38.4
Garfield	127	950	D	135	131	21	D	20	21 142	285	30.2	18.9	40.7
Grand	360	2 780	193	D	588	D	71	42	15 188	85	52.9	15.3	48.2
Iron	799	8 636	718	1 527	1 641	279	292	153	17 661	375	32.0	34.4	41.6
Juab	147	1 580	D	318	224	D	168	31	19 637	228	22.8	32.5	39.9
Kane	168	1 509	143	359	337	33	13	26	17 035	143	21.0	43.4	46.2
Millard	239	2 573	257	340	556	61	81	61	23 763	650	23.1	30.3	53.8
Morgan	134	1 060	D	299	139	D	16	25	23 931	243	55.1	18.5	39.9
Piute	18	83	0	D	D	D	0	1	12 627	106	12.3	24.5	74.5
Rich	62	322	D	D	52	D	0	6	17 978	162	20.4	53.1	60.5
Salt Lake	24 553	466 200	41 598	54 280	54 046	29 696	25 516	13 160	28 228	593	78.9	3.9	34.1
San Juan	242	2 180	386	235	360	33	67	36	16 464	231	12.6	55.0	49.8
Sanpete	343	3 232	526	535	670	123	24	53	16 407	776	34.9	18.6	49.4
Sevier	463	4 792	590	390	1 050	94	102	99	20 703	478	44.4	9.2	41.4
Summit	1 361	14 351	441	876	2 501	249	525	261	18 180	476	46.6	20.0	38.4
Tooele	438	6 168	442	1 424	1 193	176	320	178	28 822	332	40.7	23.2	43.4
Uintah	692	5 296	527	195	1 163	132	187	118	22 249	795	41.5	15.6	39.5
Utah	6 472	132 096	13 398	16 032	16 601	2 880	8 155	3 063	23 187	1 790	68.2	6.5	37.0
Wasatch	420	2 842	285	253	545	77	107	49	17 340	294	60.9	5.8	33.7
Washington	2 319	23 661	3 059	2 169	5 008	688	720	464	19 622	429	46.9	20.0	38.0
Wayne	79	D	D	D	98	D	D	D	D	191	28.8	9.9	52.4
Weber	4 143	66 954	8 195	16 280	10 850	2 160	2 669	1 593	23 796	936	73.8	2.1	36.2
VERMONT	21 261	239 034	32 784	44 836	37 212	9 370	9 228	5 908	24 716	5 828	25.0	10.0	56.6
Addison	1 028	10 441	1 600	1 993	1 619	279	307	247	23 622	683	20.8	18.7	65.9
Bennington	1 552	16 270	2 449	3 264	3 120	415	329	366	22 466	171	38.0	6.4	50.3
Caledonia	962	9 094	1 304	2 049	1 794	382	264	200	21 995	452	21.5	9.5	54.9

Table B. States and Counties — Agriculture, Land, and Water

STATE County	Acreage (1,000)	Percent change, 1992–1997	Average size of farm	Total irrigated (1,000)	Total cropland (1,000)	Average per farm ($1,000)	Average per acre (dollars)	Value of machinery and equipment Average per farm ($1,000)	Total (mil dol)	Average per farm (dollars)	Crops	Live-stock and poultry products	$10,000 or more	$100,000 or more	Percent of land owned by Fed. Gov. 1997	Water consumption 1995 (mil gal/day)
	117	118	119	120	121	122	123	124	125	126	127	128	129	130	131	132
TEXAS—Cont'd																
Tom Green	959	-6.1	1 089	44	217	554	564	52	86	97 587	31.4	68.6	43.6	14.4	1.2	256.8
Travis	396	19.0	382	3	113	495	1 285	23	16	15 831	58.7	41.3	24.0	3.5	0.5	590.5
Trinity	99	-10.2	191	0	49	245	1 084	33	6	11 744	6.8	93.2	25.7	2.1	14.9	1.9
Tyler	53	-9.8	115	0	25	204	1 954	20	3	6 729	20.8	79.2	17.7	0.4	2.4	2.7
Upshur	175	-9.6	158	1	72	189	1 253	25	31	27 850	3.6	96.4	26.1	5.0	0.0	6.8
Upton	746	7.4	7 774	12	D	1 263	163	79	8	79 714	53.5	46.5	61.5	25.0	0.0	20.1
Uvalde	943	2.8	1 590	53	159	765	488	50	68	115 490	40.9	59.1	40.0	17.7	0.0	60.8
Val Verde	1 748	-3.3	7 345	1	11	1 311	183	24	19	81 723	1.2	98.8	46.2	15.5	0.5	12.4
Van Zandt	361	-4.5	149	2	201	222	1 411	26	56	23 087	36.7	63.3	25.7	3.2	0.0	8.1
Victoria	458	6.3	423	4	155	318	716	33	29	26 419	59.8	40.2	28.0	6.0	0.0	47.4
Walker	184	-14.0	223	0	60	279	1 402	24	11	13 186	25.3	74.7	19.6	1.3	10.5	5.2
Waller	238	-2.0	223	8	116	430	1 958	38	29	27 323	51.5	48.5	27.4	4.2	0.0	24.4
Ward	363	-20.4	4 271	2	D	628	147	32	2	21 181	48.1	51.9	35.3	2.4	0.0	34.7
Washington	336	2.5	169	1	162	274	1 769	23	26	13 135	20.3	79.7	21.6	2.0	1.0	5.7
Webb	2 176	27.1	4 804	6	52	1 594	330	50	28	62 246	9.9	90.1	37.1	6.8	0.0	42.9
Wharton	679	5.3	504	91	443	484	966	73	134	99 146	79.7	20.3	49.4	21.5	0.0	272.0
Wheeler	514	2.4	1 018	6	155	301	275	44	81	159 706	4.7	95.3	46.9	7.3	0.0	5.7
Wichita	339	9.9	605	6	143	443	782	39	22	39 037	33.7	66.3	32.5	6.1	0.9	28.3
Wilbarger	884	2.4	1 857	14	260	545	294	74	33	69 825	57.0	43.0	55.3	13.7	0.0	27.9
Willacy	286	9.7	1 178	18	234	1 171	1 034	166	49	203 689	91.2	8.8	65.0	45.3	2.5	0.1
Williamson	538	-1.4	265	1	296	384	1 569	31	48	23 634	65.8	34.2	27.6	5.3	1.8	25.9
Wilson	446	-6.3	248	19	217	292	1 131	33	46	25 667	30.2	69.8	23.0	3.5	0.0	16.4
Winkler	488	12.6	12 506	D	D	1 311	105	29	2	47 206	D	D	46.2	10.3	0.0	4.0
Wise	412	-10.7	198	1	177	323	1 620	24	34	16 518	12.7	87.3	23.8	3.1	3.4	21.0
Wood	215	5.2	161	3	107	216	1 294	33	75	56 027	17.9	82.1	29.2	8.3	0.0	9.1
Yoakum	343	-0.6	1 234	82	247	616	568	133	52	187 751	93.7	6.3	63.3	39.2	0.0	104.6
Young	553	-1.7	781	0	155	349	452	25	23	32 712	22.6	77.4	41.9	4.7	0.0	7.8
Zapata	403	-16.9	1 249	2	33	434	373	20	7	22 545	D	D	36.5	2.8	0.0	5.8
Zavala	591	-18.3	2 546	20	78	1 021	434	64	45	195 625	40.0	60.0	56.0	22.8	0.0	70.0
UTAH	12 025	24.9	848	1 212	2 070	486	575	51	877	61 864	28.2	71.8	43.6	11.5	63.1	4 301.4
Beaver	131	-31.8	598	35	39	649	1 102	64	59	267 239	11.2	88.8	64.8	26.5	78.0	129.3
Box Elder	1 358	-6.4	1 261	137	344	547	437	80	102	94 868	35.6	64.4	54.0	18.4	31.9	370.9
Cache	266	-0.6	216	93	177	330	1 742	60	105	85 072	13.4	86.6	49.9	18.7	35.1	292.9
Carbon	202	-30.9	1 013	11	17	612	586	35	4	18 200	11.2	88.8	31.7	4.5	49.5	72.0
Daggett	26	20.4	736	8	13	472	641	52	1	40 000	29.7	70.3	63.9	11.1	77.5	15.4
Davis	68	35.8	121	22	27	376	3 296	35	33	59 722	82.2	17.8	31.5	9.5	10.8	159.2
Duchesne	1 328	232.9	1 638	115	125	521	310	44	28	33 992	16.9	83.1	50.8	9.0	44.7	171.5
Emery	159	-34.1	353	41	53	220	683	38	11	24 378	18.3	81.7	38.4	3.1	80.9	152.6
Garfield	121	-12.0	426	25	36	359	762	47	8	26 608	17.7	82.3	48.8	4.2	87.2	70.9
Grand	76	20.3	892	4	6	439	492	42	2	26 935	37.1	62.9	42.4	5.9	71.2	10.3
Iron	405	-6.8	1 079	60	71	609	667	79	42	112 336	66.9	33.1	51.2	17.9	57.3	154.1
Juab	276	-17.2	1 209	22	66	547	467	70	8	36 635	34.5	65.5	44.7	10.1	72.6	110.6
Kane	175	-16.5	1 226	7	15	626	508	33	3	22 590	7.6	92.4	37.8	5.6	80.1	10.0
Millard	458	-5.4	704	99	163	504	668	86	71	109 302	39.7	60.3	66.3	20.0	74.1	284.5
Morgan	179	-23.7	738	9	22	691	941	33	13	54 375	9.1	90.9	46.1	16.5	4.4	107.0
Piute	45	-24.5	420	14	21	377	985	66	7	68 071	9.1	90.8	72.6	14.2	72.3	71.6
Rich	524	6.2	3 233	75	87	854	269	90	16	95 913	7.1	92.9	68.5	20.4	31.7	152.8
Salt Lake	114	5.5	192	15	40	431	2 092	39	23	38 757	55.0	45.0	28.7	7.6	20.4	386.0
San Juan	1 673	414.8	7 243	9	150	1 787	241	60	9	39 381	38.5	61.5	46.8	10.4	59.1	42.1
Sanpete	360	-19.5	464	72	113	339	800	62	83	106 682	9.3	90.7	51.3	18.0	50.5	149.2
Sevier	147	-6.9	308	44	50	235	931	40	40	82 988	16.3	83.7	50.4	12.1	73.7	209.4
Summit	590	57.6	1 239	28	40	740	603	37	17	35 834	5.7	94.3	39.9	9.0	42.9	90.9
Tooele	292	-33.2	879	19	42	586	584	42	17	52 353	13.5	86.5	37.0	6.6	77.7	103.1
Uintah	2 268	75.1	2 853	84	91	695	244	45	21	27 001	26.2	73.8	39.6	5.0	60.2	195.5
Utah	375	-16.7	209	81	150	433	2 244	40	97	54 195	40.4	59.6	32.8	9.4	43.3	298.8
Wasatch	106	-23.6	361	15	17	564	1 544	27	8	26 351	14.4	85.6	29.6	7.8	48.1	96.5
Washington	163	-2.3	380	16	35	418	1 156	37	9	21 777	34.3	65.7	32.9	4.0	73.8	84.2
Wayne	60	-43.8	312	18	18	320	1 080	44	11	58 637	8.9	91.1	59.7	11.0	84.2	58.3
Weber	81	-68.3	87	33	40	328	2 210	44	28	30 420	25.0	75.0	28.8	6.8	15.6	252.1
VERMONT	1 262	-1.3	217	3	617	323	1 520	49	476	81 734	12.5	87.5	50.9	22.9	6.4	565.3
Addison	205	-2.4	300	0	135	389	1 281	75	113	165 034	8.6	91.4	65.6	40.6	17.8	6.7
Bennington	32	-4.8	189	0	12	325	1 833	44	8	47 277	29.0	71.0	40.4	12.3	33.2	8.2
Caledonia	94	-2.8	209	0	43	271	1 475	40	29	64 949	10.6	89.4	49.3	18.4	0.0	6.6

Table B. States and Counties — Residential Construction, Wholesale and Retail Trade, and Real Estate

STATE County	Value of Residential Construction Authorized by Building Permits, 1999		Wholesale Trade, 1997				Retail Trade[1], 1997				Real Estate and Rental and Leasing, 1997			
	New Construction ($1,000)	Number of Housing Units	Number of Establish-ments	Number of Employees	Sales (mil dol)	Annual Payroll (mil dol)	Number of Establish-ments	Number of Employees	Sales (mil dol)	Annual Payroll (mil dol)	Number of Establish-ments	Number of Employees	Receipts (mil dol)	Annual Payroll (mil dol)
	133	134	135	136	137	138	139	140	141	142	143	144	145	146
TEXAS—Cont'd														
Tom Green	32 256	267	159	D	D	D	471	5 404	890.7	84.3	134	550	51.7	8.3
Travis	1 152 292	13 056	1 268	18 345	8 991.9	717.9	2 925	45 335	16 072.8	916.0	1 212	6 484	820.3	159.0
Trinity	48	1	5	D	D	D	60	365	56.1	4.5	4	7	0.9	0.1
Tyler	3 206	103	5	D	D	D	72	612	85.2	7.5	5	10	1.2	0.1
Upshur	1 235	14	17	49	104.5	2.3	101	895	145.1	11.7	9	29	1.5	0.2
Upton	0	0	8	41	24.7	0.9	16	94	14.7	1.1	NA	NA	NA	NA
Uvalde	1 214	30	40	318	165.3	6.2	124	1 054	178.0	15.5	26	85	6.2	0.9
Val Verde	6 773	127	30	291	54.5	5.1	173	1 798	278.1	25.3	31	105	8.5	1.4
Van Zandt	5 103	56	31	179	70.8	4.1	145	1 339	245.2	20.2	23	46	4.6	0.5
Victoria	21 332	198	141	1 665	422.1	46.0	398	5 052	868.7	80.1	91	455	60.5	10.5
Walker	19 199	225	36	247	89.5	4.4	174	2 245	386.7	32.0	47	218	39.1	4.1
Waller	4 538	69	38	D	D	D	80	1 280	480.4	25.6	9	91	3.9	1.3
Ward	63	1	15	103	74.4	2.9	49	381	54.0	5.5	12	83	7.1	2.1
Washington	4 187	61	36	543	289.2	14.6	143	1 565	270.3	22.8	32	155	13.4	2.7
Webb	99 197	1 639	339	2 453	1 105.4	51.1	730	9 051	1 524.6	138.8	155	574	64.3	10.0
Wharton	1 844	17	69	1 005	326.6	23.7	217	1 799	301.0	27.4	34	174	12.8	3.0
Wheeler	0	0	11	80	30.8	1.6	45	226	33.1	2.7	2	D	D	D
Wichita	21 942	201	211	1 906	434.6	44.8	598	7 268	1 198.7	107.3	151	D	D	D
Wilbarger	4 910	117	21	81	30.6	1.9	76	737	111.5	8.9	13	38	3.6	0.6
Willacy	2 552	57	10	68	16.9	1.6	43	386	61.8	4.6	4	28	1.8	0.3
Williamson	475 665	5 605	217	1 723	750.3	57.6	623	8 402	1 582.1	152.9	183	639	73.6	12.8
Wilson	231	0	16	82	36.7	1.6	68	625	109.5	8.9	8	46	3.7	0.6
Winkler	0	0	6	26	7.6	0.9	32	225	43.6	3.3	8	32	3.8	0.9
Wise	14 219	138	38	343	197.2	6.8	122	1 692	689.2	31.3	29	80	13.0	1.7
Wood	1 784	30	47	364	189.5	10.0	146	1 173	211.1	17.3	26	60	3.8	0.9
Yoakum	150	1	22	119	73.4	2.9	42	246	34.0	3.2	7	19	0.7	0.2
Young	880	7	39	194	83.9	3.3	100	737	113.5	10.1	21	53	12.4	1.2
Zapata	NA	NA	3	D	D	D	37	221	26.8	2.3	2	D	D	D
Zavala	546	18	3	42	6.8	0.7	20	178	22.5	2.3	1	D	D	D
UTAH	2 296 384	20 547	3 278	44 319	21 115.5	1 420.5	7 656	114 474	19 964.6	1 856.9	2 169	12 318	1 342.6	236.0
Beaver	5 106	58	3	19	4.0	0.3	30	205	29.4	2.1	1	D	D	D
Box Elder	35 647	486	28	245	73.4	6.1	126	1 452	250.1	19.5	21	67	7.9	1.1
Cache	88 695	705	85	696	146.4	12.4	349	5 242	682.7	70.7	67	439	24.5	6.7
Carbon	11 051	127	46	348	175.3	9.4	94	1 310	174.9	17.6	16	65	5.1	0.9
Daggett	552	6	NA	NA	NA	NA	6	16	1.6	0.3	1	D	D	D
Davis	258 240	2 308	241	2 868	1 184.9	70.7	582	9 488	1 809.7	157.6	165	784	96.1	13.0
Duchesne	8 736	77	20	103	31.1	1.9	62	541	96.3	8.4	9	40	3.8	0.6
Emery	4 069	52	7	15	5.8	0.3	37	359	48.4	3.7	4	8	0.2	0.0
Garfield	5 315	64	3	D	D	D	23	122	16.9	1.4	NA	NA	NA	NA
Grand	6 609	80	11	46	8.8	1.2	74	528	77.0	8.4	20	85	5.8	1.4
Iron	33 786	409	32	266	113.6	6.1	135	1 663	286.9	24.2	43	151	17.0	1.7
Juab	7 294	71	8	52	10.7	0.7	29	267	40.3	3.0	2	D	D	D
Kane	8 384	107	5	D	D	D	42	308	35.0	4.0	9	18	2.0	0.5
Millard	4 954	62	16	82	28.8	1.4	58	495	82.2	6.4	NA	1	D	D
Morgan	10 644	75	7	D	D	D	20	151	24.7	1.9	NA	D	D	NA
Piute	362	5	1	D	D	D	7	25	2.0	0.2	NA	NA	NA	NA
Rich	7 882	90	1	D	D	D	13	43	6.0	0.6	2	D	D	D
Salt Lake	599 174	5 255	2 013	29 521	15 365.4	1 018.0	3 230	53 236	10 139.4	937.0	1 114	7 528	878.2	158.8
San Juan	4 557	55	11	105	12.6	1.2	41	304	33.7	3.4	3	3	0.3	0.0
Sanpete	13 951	167	8	36	15.1	0.6	73	688	90.1	7.3	10	29	1.9	0.3
Sevier	907	8	19	238	78.1	3.9	102	1 067	167.5	14.1	9	47	3.8	1.0
Summit	142 193	994	47	147	116.9	6.0	242	2 520	307.9	32.0	94	634	56.6	11.0
Tooele	102 087	938	9	120	10.3	1.4	74	1 170	182.8	16.7	12	51	4.7	0.8
Uintah	14 376	118	49	291	77.6	7.4	104	1 190	180.4	16.9	23	115	15.4	3.3
Utah	463 313	4 143	320	6 272	2 763.6	190.4	978	15 868	2 486.4	245.1	239	1 085	108.0	16.9
Wasatch	94 075	583	14	65	14.3	2.5	56	454	69.1	6.3	17	29	3.4	0.2
Washington	158 432	1 528	85	641	238.5	18.0	406	4 829	879.4	77.3	102	332	31.8	4.6
Wayne	0	0	1	D	D	D	16	86	9.9	0.8	NA	NA	NA	NA
Weber	205 994	1 976	187	2 025	640.6	57.3	647	10 847	1 753.5	170.3	185	781	74.7	12.7
VERMONT	304 942	2 600	941	10 987	4 731.4	330.6	4 093	36 306	5 898.6	603.3	701	2 362	240.6	42.2
Addison	19 966	182	41	296	90.2	7.7	186	1 523	316.1	30.3	34	87	8.0	1.0
Bennington	23 277	186	49	250	87.0	6.2	359	3 160	553.4	53.0	48	135	13.6	2.3
Caledonia	9 536	93	34	431	179.4	10.2	199	1 644	232.8	24.3	32	81	6.2	1.0

1. Establishments with payroll.

Table B. States and Counties — Professional, Manufacturing, and Accommodation and Foodservices

STATE County	Professional, Scientific, and Technical Services[1], 1997				Manufacturing, 1997				Accommodation and Foodservices, 1997			
	Number of Establishments	Number of Employees	Receipts (mil dol)	Annual Payroll (mil dol)	Number of Establishments	Number of Employees	Receipts (mil dol)	Annual Payroll (mil dol)	Number of Establishments	Number of Employees	Sales (mil dol)	Annual Payroll (mil dol)
	147	148	149	150	151	152	153	154	155	156	157	158
TEXAS—Cont'd												
Tom Green	154	767	60.2	17.2	100	4 452	827.6	105.1	192	3 763	110.8	32.7
Travis	3 128	27 621	3 169.1	1 299.3	774	52 353	14 692.9	1 986.2	1 643	36 951	1 322.6	375.5
Trinity	9	49	3.4	0.9	NA	NA	NA	NA	15	213	7.5	2.5
Tyler	17	41	3.8	0.9	13	565	42.1	8.9	17	D	D	D
Upshur	20	118	9.4	3.1	31	603	81.1	13.2	28	371	11.4	2.9
Upton	2	D	D	D	NA	NA	NA	NA	8	D	D	D
Uvalde	31	70	6.1	1.7	17	710	50.7	9.4	54	636	20.6	5.7
Val Verde	39	122	8.3	2.3	24	522	125.4	10.2	88	1 046	33.3	8.5
Van Zandt	37	120	10.5	3.0	38	622	68.2	16.2	54	586	19.4	5.3
Victoria	141	712	59.5	21.1	71	3 064	1 245.3	119.5	155	2 711	79.6	21.7
Walker	54	208	33.4	4.9	38	677	90.8	14.7	77	1 545	45.4	12.9
Waller	22	45	3.1	0.9	43	1 283	245.6	43.3	40	722	18.0	4.5
Ward	16	69	3.5	1.2	NA	NA	NA	NA	23	198	5.8	1.7
Washington	41	176	12.5	5.0	41	2 982	529.2	81.9	60	767	23.4	6.1
Webb	210	1 029	69.6	23.1	87	1 402	258.6	28.1	253	4 350	144.7	37.4
Wharton	47	169	12.4	4.0	46	2 152	372.3	51.9	59	780	24.8	6.0
Wheeler	10	18	1.5	0.4	NA	NA	NA	NA	17	D	D	D
Wichita	212	1 071	87.6	32.8	153	7 927	1 435.9	254.9	277	5 225	159.6	47.1
Wilbarger	15	46	3.0	0.8	9	681	236.7	19.8	37	444	10.8	3.4
Willacy	10	25	1.3	0.4	NA	NA	NA	NA	20	194	5.7	1.4
Williamson	355	1 874	233.4	73.6	240	11 727	9 637.4	418.8	287	4 499	155.0	41.9
Wilson	20	43	2.1	0.4	NA	NA	NA	NA	26	D	D	D
Winkler	8	19	4.1	0.4	NA	NA	NA	NA	13	100	2.4	0.7
Wise	36	130	8.8	2.7	54	1 340	180.3	37.8	53	861	23.4	6.7
Wood	40	113	7.1	2.0	45	649	143.4	13.5	59	599	16.8	4.3
Yoakum	8	18	1.0	0.3	NA	NA	NA	NA	19	D	D	D
Young	30	87	6.2	2.3	28	1 043	248.4	28.3	38	353	10.0	2.7
Zapata	5	9	0.5	0.1	NA	NA	NA	NA	21	188	7.2	1.6
Zavala	7	19	1.4	0.2	NA	NA	NA	NA	12	66	2.7	0.5
UTAH	4 282	36 468	3 306.1	1 303.1	2 860	119 140	24 014.4	3 726.1	3 780	74 390	2 309.0	648.8
Beaver	4	5	0.1	0.0	NA	NA	NA	NA	34	462	10.3	3.2
Box Elder	33	128	7.4	2.1	51	5 725	1 271.6	270.7	61	1 063	26.0	8.5
Cache	152	905	51.1	20.3	149	8 355	1 785.6	195.0	112	1 991	50.5	13.2
Carbon	27	217	6.8	2.1	NA	NA	NA	NA	54	641	16.9	4.3
Daggett	2	D	D	D	NA	NA	NA	NA	5	72	4.0	1.6
Davis	321	2 158	127.8	56.1	227	7 170	1 592.1	202.8	267	5 752	151.6	42.9
Duchesne	14	97	3.1	1.1	NA	NA	NA	NA	30	274	8.5	1.9
Emery	5	37	1.9	0.9	NA	NA	NA	NA	19	108	4.7	1.3
Garfield	3	5	0.1	0.0	NA	NA	NA	NA	46	425	22.4	7.6
Grand	22	72	4.2	1.3	NA	NA	NA	NA	82	1 141	38.3	9.9
Iron	40	332	10.5	4.2	50	1 520	206.4	37.9	82	1 349	42.0	12.6
Juab	10	D	D	D	NA	NA	NA	NA	22	292	6.8	2.0
Kane	6	18	1.0	0.2	NA	NA	NA	NA	34	328	14.0	3.7
Millard	5	D	D	D	NA	NA	NA	NA	24	328	6.0	1.8
Morgan	7	13	0.7	0.3	NA	NA	NA	NA	9	89	1.9	0.5
Piute	NA	NA	NA	NA	NA	NA	NA	NA	3	38	0.5	0.2
Rich	NA	NA	NA	NA	NA	NA	NA	NA	14	42	2.2	0.6
Salt Lake	2 367	21 993	2 312.1	887.6	1 441	53 424	10 012.2	1 706.4	1 570	35 480	1 200.5	333.7
San Juan	9	67	2.7	2.3	NA	NA	NA	NA	38	382	20.0	3.9
Sanpete	11	24	1.9	0.4	18	908	116.7	16.9	40	439	7.1	1.8
Sevier	25	91	4.9	2.5	NA	NA	NA	NA	43	628	15.7	4.4
Summit	131	479	55.9	22.7	40	861	86.2	21.4	131	3 481	105.1	33.8
Tooele	22	300	25.6	12.8	27	1 737	342.8	56.8	43	475	16.0	3.8
Uintah	43	171	11.7	3.9	NA	NA	NA	NA	52	657	18.1	4.8
Utah	582	6 094	463.3	195.3	390	15 949	2 667.3	461.0	392	8 270	228.0	64.3
Wasatch	31	95	6.4	2.4	NA	NA	NA	NA	36	682	19.7	6.7
Washington	131	605	38.8	15.4	92	1 949	243.4	48.4	195	3 580	113.2	31.6
Wayne	1	D	D	D	NA	NA	NA	NA	22	113	4.0	0.8
Weber	278	2 307	150.3	61.6	210	18 446	5 242.4	635.0	320	5 808	155.1	43.4
VERMONT	1 622	7 792	719.1	279.0	1 226	42 533	7 803.0	1 459.6	1 932	27 088	910.2	277.2
Addison	77	244	17.9	7.4	61	1 871	321.9	59.4	88	948	32.4	11.0
Bennington	86	237	17.2	6.4	88	3 090	504.8	94.1	163	2 044	76.6	21.3
Caledonia	58	229	14.4	7.6	55	1 950	198.0	54.0	72	767	24.4	6.9

1. Firms subject to federal tax.

Table B. States and Counties — Health and Other Services and Federal Funds

STATE County	Health Care and Social Assistance[1], 1997				Other Services[1], 1997				Federal funds and grants, fiscal 1999[2] Expenditures (mil dol)			
									Total	Direct payments for individuals[3]		
	Number of Establishments	Number of Employees	Receipts (mil dol)	Annual Payroll (mil dol)	Number of Establishments	Number of Employees	Receipts (mil dol)	Annual Payroll (mil dol)		Social Security and government retirement	Medicare	Food stamps and Supplemental Security Income
	159	160	161	162	163	164	165	166	167	168	169	170
TEXAS—Cont'd												
Tom Green	186	3 404	208.9	91.7	180	961	58.3	16.1	542.3	214.2	66.7	13.9
Travis	1 705	29 036	1 985.2	805.8	1 336	9 356	590.9	192.2	5 729.2	1 073.3	277.8	72.0
Trinity	5	125	5.1	1.7	18	48	3.1	0.6	74.9	36.7	19.4	1.5
Tyler	22	389	15.5	6.9	10	24	1.8	0.4	90.0	46.1	23.1	3.2
Upshur	22	430	14.6	6.8	24	86	7.5	1.4	139.6	72.8	31.5	3.7
Upton	3	72	2.4	1.5	NA	NA	NA	NA	14.8	5.9	3.4	0.5
Uvalde	43	452	20.4	8.7	39	204	10.4	3.4	110.5	38.4	16.7	7.2
Val Verde	55	2 055	36.6	17.7	49	220	11.4	3.2	310.9	70.6	19.2	13.1
Van Zandt	53	1 004	31.0	15.0	41	238	16.1	4.7	187.4	96.8	47.2	5.2
Victoria	230	3 383	230.0	93.5	151	973	61.8	17.8	315.6	131.3	61.4	12.3
Walker	72	763	31.6	14.0	47	279	13.3	4.2	165.2	72.4	29.1	5.8
Waller	24	442	12.2	6.9	35	125	9.9	2.6	109.7	34.5	17.1	4.2
Ward	11	110	4.3	2.0	16	101	6.1	1.9	52.6	19.7	9.0	2.0
Washington	42	898	30.3	14.8	48	179	11.7	2.7	120.9	58.9	21.8	3.8
Webb	227	4 330	207.1	94.8	190	951	48.0	13.3	721.2	145.2	90.2	52.1
Wharton	55	1 645	84.7	30.6	71	273	17.6	4.4	205.4	69.6	37.7	7.7
Wheeler	13	174	6.1	3.4	7	23	1.3	0.2	43.3	13.5	9.4	0.6
Wichita	273	D	D	D	223	1 518	85.1	28.5	979.9	318.1	95.3	9.8
Wilbarger	29	402	19.8	7.8	18	60	4.0	1.1	78.3	31.0	17.6	2.1
Willacy	17	203	8.8	4.1	13	40	1.8	0.5	96.0	21.7	14.2	5.2
Williamson	293	3 179	180.9	72.2	269	1 508	95.9	29.7	743.9	267.4	65.4	9.1
Wilson	25	327	10.7	4.8	24	91	6.1	1.8	96.1	51.8	15.3	3.3
Winkler	10	108	4.1	1.7	10	37	2.5	0.5	28.2	13.9	8.3	1.3
Wise	51	615	24.2	10.8	51	243	16.5	4.3	120.3	67.5	23.5	3.0
Wood	54	660	25.0	11.2	38	141	7.5	2.1	170.7	96.2	38.1	4.5
Yoakum	5	24	1.2	0.4	12	44	3.5	0.9	40.3	10.7	5.4	0.8
Young	30	364	16.8	6.4	40	107	7.4	1.8	85.9	42.8	20.8	1.9
Zapata	6	75	2.1	1.0	6	15	1.1	0.2	42.9	12.9	11.5	3.6
Zavala	4	689	9.1	6.2	5	10	0.4	0.1	54.2	12.5	8.6	5.3
UTAH	3 851	46 989	2 988.8	1 226.7	2 728	17 612	1 090.5	312.6	9 238.7	3 071.4	796.4	164.5
Beaver	6	20	2.2	0.8	7	13	0.8	0.2	24.0	11.3	4.1	0.4
Box Elder	57	678	39.6	15.4	39	147	7.9	1.5	564.7	76.3	16.6	2.3
Cache	166	1 293	82.5	29.1	125	628	35.4	9.5	248.4	93.9	25.6	4.4
Carbon	53	829	55.8	18.8	34	220	19.3	4.9	160.4	45.8	15.5	3.8
Daggett	NA	NA	NA	NA	NA	NA	NA	NA	8.4	1.9	0.5	0.0
Davis	329	4 717	292.4	127.9	243	1 501	90.6	27.8	1 216.8	374.8	60.4	11.1
Duchesne	21	154	6.6	2.5	19	76	4.9	1.1	47.3	22.5	7.2	2.6
Emery	7	67	3.1	1.3	13	92	11.0	2.9	49.9	16.7	4.7	1.4
Garfield	1	D	D	D	2	D	D	D	23.5	9.8	2.7	0.4
Grand	10	36	2.2	0.7	13	21	1.9	0.3	33.2	15.1	3.2	1.0
Iron	47	343	15.9	5.7	42	136	9.1	2.0	91.7	44.1	11.0	2.9
Juab	8	145	4.6	1.5	7	27	2.6	0.6	26.2	12.4	4.5	0.5
Kane	7	35	1.5	0.7	12	52	2.8	0.7	23.0	13.9	4.1	0.5
Millard	16	70	3.4	1.2	9	28	3.0	0.6	61.6	19.2	6.5	1.1
Morgan	1	D	D	D	1	D	D	D	17.9	13.7	2.1	0.1
Piute	NA	NA	NA	NA	NA	NA	NA	NA	8.4	3.4	1.3	0.1
Rich	1	D	D	D	3	D	D	D	6.1	3.3	0.7	0.1
Salt Lake	1 766	23 094	1 579.6	652.7	1 285	9 616	622.4	185.2	3 505.4	1 097.6	332.5	68.5
San Juan	12	198	8.3	3.1	9	24	1.8	0.4	77.5	12.3	4.3	5.5
Sanpete	23	138	6.5	2.6	23	67	5.9	1.0	68.5	32.5	10.0	1.9
Sevier	33	299	12.2	5.1	28	141	13.1	2.1	69.4	34.9	12.3	1.7
Summit	41	285	14.9	5.4	34	157	8.7	2.2	65.7	22.1	4.4	0.6
Tooele	28	138	6.6	2.4	18	84	4.8	1.5	226.2	78.6	12.8	2.2
Uintah	47	412	26.6	9.3	42	134	16.0	2.6	82.2	34.5	10.1	3.1
Utah	596	7 371	421.0	178.8	340	2 256	103.9	29.1	737.5	339.2	106.3	19.6
Wasatch	17	183	6.6	2.8	15	43	3.7	0.9	40.0	17.2	4.2	0.6
Washington	193	1 722	114.0	41.2	98	433	32.9	8.4	285.9	173.0	42.7	5.6
Wayne	3	D	D	D	3	12	0.7	0.1	11.1	4.5	1.3	0.1
Weber	362	4 431	277.0	113.2	264	1 687	86.2	27.0	1 000.1	445.2	84.9	22.3
VERMONT	1 262	11 481	631.6	273.9	1 171	4 490	304.7	76.4	3 114.3	1 059.9	353.5	79.4
Addison	65	380	19.6	6.7	61	160	11.5	2.2	121.3	50.0	17.3	3.7
Bennington	107	1 132	56.3	26.5	78	282	18.2	4.9	159.4	76.0	26.4	6.0
Caledonia	48	459	21.9	9.8	53	160	11.6	2.7	129.0	57.0	18.9	5.2

1. Firms subject to federal tax. 2. October 1, 1998 to September 30, 1999. 3. State totals may include programs not allocated by county.

Table B. States and Counties — Federal Funds and Local Government Finances

	Federal funds and grants, fiscal 1999[1] (cont'd)							Local government finances, 1997				
	Expenditures (mil dol) (cont'd)							General revenue				
	Procurement contract awards			Grants[2]							Taxes	
											Per capita[3] (dollars)	
STATE County	Salaries and wages	Defense	Other	Medicaid and other health-related	Nutrition and family welfare	Education	Other	Total (mil dol)	Intergovern-mental (mil dol)	Total (mil dol)	Total	Property
	171	172	173	174	175	176	177	178	179	180	181	182
TEXAS—Cont'd												
Tom Green	133.6	18.3	2.1	39.3	10.0	3.5	17.7	174.2	69.8	74.3	724	553
Travis	437.1	180.8	149.6	517.6	1 005.8	628.5	1 324.3	1 773.9	302.8	986.2	1 422	1 086
Trinity	2.1	0.0	0.5	12.2	0.9	0.6	0.2	25.9	11.6	8.4	676	594
Tyler	2.2	0.0	0.5	10.9	1.3	0.7	1.3	34.3	15.3	11.1	551	484
Upshur	3.6	0.0	1.0	18.8	1.7	1.1	4.2	50.3	26.9	18.8	530	459
Upton	0.4	0.0	0.1	1.3	0.3	0.2	0.1	22.8	1.3	16.6	4 350	4 244
Uvalde	5.0	0.0	0.5	18.5	6.3	2.5	3.4	94.5	38.9	14.4	562	401
Val Verde	101.9	43.4	4.2	29.9	8.1	3.6	14.6	87.4	52.8	20.0	463	336
Van Zandt	4.5	0.0	1.2	16.8	1.8	1.4	8.3	65.6	32.2	23.3	542	456
Victoria	11.3	1.6	3.5	35.0	8.3	5.6	28.5	255.3	61.4	85.8	1 046	818
Walker	9.9	0.0	1.9	21.3	2.9	2.7	13.1	167.2	31.9	28.0	514	376
Waller	3.4	4.7	0.8	10.7	2.1	4.8	12.2	51.3	21.5	23.9	893	772
Ward	1.2	0.0	0.3	6.6	0.5	0.6	12.2	31.4	5.0	16.5	1 388	1 273
Washington	4.0	0.0	0.8	26.3	1.2	0.8	0.5	80.2	30.1	27.0	932	852
Webb	88.1	0.5	19.7	149.2	64.0	18.6	81.7	516.1	305.2	128.1	699	543
Wharton	5.0	0.0	1.3	30.4	3.3	2.0	5.5	97.2	40.3	37.6	936	768
Wheeler	1.3	0.0	0.3	2.9	0.3	0.2	10.4	20.1	3.4	10.3	1 949	1 814
Wichita	336.8	83.7	7.0	46.9	11.5	6.6	47.2	224.2	76.2	100.2	778	617
Wilbarger	2.7	0.1	0.5	8.0	1.0	0.5	1.3	52.3	18.3	16.6	1 173	1 069
Willacy	1.7	1.4	0.5	24.3	3.1	2.3	1.0	41.7	26.8	11.4	581	489
Williamson	19.1	195.9	95.1	31.3	6.6	3.0	17.5	421.8	120.5	227.0	1 078	962
Wilson	2.5	0.1	1.4	14.7	0.9	1.0	0.2	47.6	25.0	13.8	458	402
Winkler	0.6	0.0	0.3	2.9	0.2	0.4	0.2	27.0	6.3	13.5	1 680	1 562
Wise	5.5	0.4	2.4	8.0	0.9	0.9	5.8	65.1	27.2	28.3	667	595
Wood	4.9	0.0	1.5	17.2	1.6	2.0	0.8	62.2	18.5	26.3	769	666
Yoakum	0.6	0.0	0.1	2.0	0.8	0.4	0.6	39.1	3.3	29.7	3 630	3 519
Young	2.4	0.0	0.6	9.1	0.9	0.5	1.6	36.7	13.9	12.4	705	550
Zapata	1.4	0.0	0.2	10.7	0.8	1.0	0.4	25.9	7.0	17.3	1 536	1 516
Zavala	0.6	0.0	0.2	17.5	1.7	2.0	0.8	22.6	14.3	6.1	507	333
UTAH	1 469.1	548.1	720.2	713.1	333.7	189.0	757.8	X	X	X	X	X
Beaver	1.4	0.0	0.6	5.0	0.5	0.1	0.3	23.8	11.5	4.9	838	679
Box Elder	9.7	22.6	396.8	8.3	3.3	0.8	15.4	85.1	41.0	27.5	668	537
Cache	15.8	21.6	12.0	18.6	10.0	8.6	24.9	137.6	68.2	39.0	459	308
Carbon	7.3	0.0	63.1	8.4	6.0	1.8	6.7	52.1	26.6	13.7	656	502
Daggett	2.5	0.0	0.7	0.4	0.0	0.1	2.2	3.9	2.1	1.2	1 626	1 405
Davis	504.7	161.1	34.8	26.9	17.5	3.5	13.7	430.4	206.6	125.7	556	408
Duchesne	3.3	0.0	0.9	5.1	1.9	0.8	1.8	55.2	23.5	9.5	655	530
Emery	2.1	0.0	10.9	3.3	1.4	0.3	8.3	67.2	16.8	22.0	2 024	1 876
Garfield	4.4	0.0	3.6	1.9	0.5	0.2	0.1	14.1	8.5	3.5	830	543
Grand	7.9	0.0	0.9	2.4	1.4	0.2	0.9	27.0	13.3	9.3	1 150	670
Iron	13.4	0.0	3.4	4.4	4.9	1.4	2.2	63.6	26.0	22.7	820	602
Juab	1.0	0.0	1.1	2.0	0.6	0.1	2.9	21.5	10.9	5.4	745	620
Kane	2.4	0.0	0.6	0.4	0.6	0.2	0.2	24.9	9.0	5.9	1 019	636
Millard	4.1	1.8	0.5	3.2	1.4	0.5	20.2	48.8	12.8	28.3	2 298	2 177
Morgan	0.6	0.1	0.2	0.8	0.3	0.1	-0.3	13.2	7.3	3.9	571	445
Piute	0.3	0.0	0.3	1.9	0.2	0.1	0.6	4.2	3.3	0.7	523	438
Rich	0.6	0.0	0.2	0.4	0.2	0.1	0.3	6.6	3.5	2.3	1 280	1 132
Salt Lake	474.2	260.4	100.4	382.3	204.5	82.6	445.5	1 905.0	707.6	719.5	857	588
San Juan	6.1	0.0	0.6	26.5	4.1	8.1	6.8	46.7	28.9	9.2	675	551
Sanpete	3.3	0.0	4.5	8.6	2.3	1.9	1.4	47.7	24.5	9.5	452	327
Sevier	7.6	0.1	0.7	6.3	2.5	0.6	0.6	41.0	23.3	10.1	561	405
Summit	5.6	4.1	0.3	1.1	0.7	0.2	26.3	99.0	13.9	54.1	2 102	1 607
Tooele	57.9	42.7	13.4	6.8	3.8	0.9	5.7	95.4	36.5	18.3	584	441
Uintah	15.4	0.0	3.1	6.1	4.5	1.6	2.3	76.6	35.4	18.2	714	564
Utah	52.6	10.1	15.7	81.7	29.0	8.5	55.1	615.9	305.1	185.8	566	405
Wasatch	2.0	0.0	2.7	2.8	0.9	0.2	9.0	31.9	13.5	11.3	882	697
Washington	34.5	0.2	5.2	9.4	4.6	2.3	3.5	158.7	61.8	52.7	670	471
Wayne	3.0	0.0	0.5	1.0	0.3	0.1	0.0	6.4	4.4	1.2	514	364
Weber	225.3	23.2	42.4	86.8	25.7	4.6	24.4	350.5	160.6	116.8	643	463
VERMONT	301.4	213.7	62.5	380.2	134.9	78.9	289.3	X	X	X	X	X
Addison	6.9	4.3	8.6	14.8	4.4	1.6	5.7	70.8	19.1	44.8	1 283	1 276
Bennington	7.0	6.3	1.7	16.9	6.0	2.3	9.0	76.9	23.5	47.9	1 332	1 319
Caledonia	6.1	0.0	1.5	19.4	5.7	1.8	11.6	56.4	20.9	30.8	1 074	1 070

1. October 1, 1998 to September 30, 1999. 2. State totals may include programs not allocated by county. 3. Based on the resident population estimated as of July 1 of the year shown.

Table B. States and Counties — Local Government Finances, Government Employment, and Elections

STATE County	Local government finances, 1997 (cont'd)									Government employment, 1998			Presidential election, 2000		
	Direct general expenditure							Debt outstanding					Percent of vote cast —		
	Total (mil dol)	Per capita[1] (dollars)	Percent of total for —					Total (mil dol)	Per capita[1] (dollars)	Federal civilian	Federal military	State and local	Democratic	Republican	All other
			Education	Health and hospitals	Police protection	Public welfare	Highways								
	183	184	185	186	187	188	189	190	191	192	193	194	195	196	197
TEXAS—Cont'd															
Tom Green	183.4	1 786	59.3	2.9	8.2	0.1	3.4	161.2	1 571	1 323	3 252	7 584	26.8	71.4	1.7
Travis	1 654.7	2 386	40.2	6.4	6.0	1.4	3.7	6 322.5	9 115	9 074	2 099	95 770	41.7	46.9	11.5
Trinity	24.4	1 969	63.3	20.2	2.5	0.1	3.7	7.0	566	50	33	662	40.4	58.4	1.2
Tyler	34.3	1 708	64.9	14.6	2.6	0.1	4.9	6.2	310	48	54	1 481	39.0	59.5	1.5
Upshur	47.5	1 340	78.0	0.3	3.0	0.1	4.3	20.6	581	62	95	1 500	32.6	66.0	1.4
Upton	22.1	5 783	48.1	28.1	2.5	0.0	5.0	1.2	316	0	10	457	20.9	77.1	2.0
Uvalde	93.1	3 635	56.7	33.0	1.9	0.6	1.1	10.5	410	120	68	2 434	40.8	57.7	1.5
Val Verde	86.8	2 012	59.9	3.7	5.3	1.2	3.2	48.4	1 123	1 666	1 441	2 980	44.1	54.2	1.7
Van Zandt	67.2	1 564	72.4	0.1	3.1	0.2	7.5	40.8	948	91	117	1 820	29.3	69.2	1.5
Victoria	239.4	2 918	38.5	31.9	5.6	0.0	3.0	142.9	1 742	234	220	6 067	29.8	68.5	1.6
Walker	153.8	2 821	26.6	3.3	3.6	0.2	2.7	700.2	12 841	192	152	12 091	34.4	63.1	2.5
Waller	57.2	2 133	72.6	0.1	4.0	0.4	6.9	39.3	1 467	55	84	2 987	46.5	52.4	1.2
Ward	32.4	2 728	46.1	21.1	5.3	0.8	4.7	2.8	235	28	31	1 180	32.4	65.4	2.2
Washington	85.0	2 928	79.3	1.0	3.4	0.1	3.4	63.9	2 200	67	77	2 757	25.4	73.2	1.4
Webb	515.0	2 811	67.0	1.2	4.6	0.5	5.3	352.8	1 926	1 761	501	12 491	57.4	41.4	1.2
Wharton	106.4	2 651	67.0	5.4	3.8	0.9	6.0	41.9	1 044	102	107	3 074	36.0	63.0	1.0
Wheeler	18.9	3 555	52.2	26.8	2.3	0.0	6.3	0.4	84	29	14	525	24.2	74.8	1.0
Wichita	228.2	1 771	50.4	4.4	6.2	0.6	4.0	141.7	1 100	2 568	7 802	9 050	33.0	65.1	1.9
Wilbarger	50.5	3 575	47.8	22.3	2.1	0.2	2.6	19.1	1 353	66	36	2 514	29.6	68.6	1.8
Willacy	40.3	2 050	79.2	0.5	3.9	0.1	4.8	7.2	365	36	63	1 341	63.6	35.3	1.1
Williamson	449.3	2 135	69.5	1.2	3.2	0.5	3.4	613.5	2 915	370	595	10 573	27.7	67.8	4.5
Wilson	48.5	1 607	66.8	10.8	2.8	0.0	3.3	23.9	790	52	83	1 552	34.2	64.2	1.6
Winkler	25.6	3 184	58.5	13.6	2.7	0.3	1.5	1.2	144	12	21	652	27.2	71.9	0.9
Wise	65.4	1 542	66.6	1.4	6.4	0.2	5.0	29.4	695	76	117	2 101	29.5	68.6	1.9
Wood	55.1	1 613	59.2	13.3	3.6	0.2	6.1	14.1	413	80	91	1 666	28.0	70.7	1.3
Yoakum	31.4	3 840	56.8	12.3	4.3	0.1	5.9	0.7	85	16	21	738	21.5	77.5	0.9
Young	33.8	1 921	58.9	9.0	4.8	0.3	4.9	12.5	710	49	47	1 355	26.5	72.2	1.3
Zapata	26.5	2 352	61.4	1.0	4.4	1.0	4.1	3.8	336	34	31	906	62.6	36.4	1.0
Zavala	23.4	1 955	68.4	0.6	3.9	0.4	1.9	4.9	410	12	32	873	77.1	22.1	0.7
UTAH	X	X	X	X	X	X	X	X	X	30 620	16 037	145 215	26.3	66.8	6.8
Beaver	17.3	2 945	39.4	13.1	6.6	0.0	10.4	19.0	3 248	31	32	561	24.0	73.4	2.5
Box Elder	87.5	2 130	52.8	0.8	4.1	0.5	5.3	67.9	1 651	220	231	1 929	16.5	79.4	4.1
Cache	134.1	1 581	57.2	3.3	4.8	0.0	4.5	88.1	1 038	298	488	8 109	15.6	78.2	6.2
Carbon	53.3	2 548	42.6	11.5	5.3	0.0	11.0	71.0	3 394	167	114	2 034	44.7	50.9	4.4
Daggett	3.5	4 671	64.3	0.5	5.6	0.0	4.5	2.4	3 180	70	0	131	23.9	72.9	3.2
Davis	412.8	1 826	58.2	1.7	6.4	0.5	3.7	284.0	1 256	9 844	5 329	9 802	21.5	73.3	5.2
Duchesne	55.8	2 811	43.8	28.0	4.4	0.0	5.5	35.8	2 478	83	79	1 527	17.1	79.7	3.2
Emery	66.0	6 066	30.6	1.3	3.2	0.6	9.0	352.5	32 418	47	60	863	21.8	73.8	4.5
Garfield	13.3	3 169	53.1	0.5	2.6	0.0	10.0	15.6	3 715	151	23	348	9.0	87.3	3.6
Grand	30.6	3 766	45.2	3.0	5.3	1.2	7.3	22.3	2 743	201	44	545	32.1	50.4	17.5
Iron	62.1	2 240	54.3	0.2	4.3	0.0	6.6	64.8	2 337	294	156	3 073	14.2	80.3	5.5
Juab	21.0	2 897	51.4	0.5	7.3	0.0	9.5	28.3	3 904	18	41	559	22.2	72.6	5.1
Kane	23.4	4 013	33.9	20.7	5.5	0.0	6.1	26.7	4 582	72	34	530	13.8	80.4	5.7
Millard	39.6	3 215	49.5	2.3	4.5	0.0	7.4	21.8	1 767	81	67	902	14.6	80.6	4.8
Morgan	13.1	1 891	68.4	0.0	5.3	0.0	4.7	7.3	1 053	11	38	330	17.4	77.7	4.8
Piute	3.8	2 708	81.9	0.2	1.6	0.0	4.5	1.9	1 341	0	0	112	17.0	80.2	2.8
Rich	6.6	3 624	64.2	1.1	2.7	0.0	5.4	4.5	2 472	12	10	176	16.9	81.6	1.6
Salt Lake	1 800.5	2 144	43.6	4.5	6.9	0.0	4.7	6 599.9	7 858	8 685	4 973	69 282	35.0	55.9	9.1
San Juan	38.8	2 837	62.7	1.8	2.7	0.0	8.7	24.9	1 820	210	75	1 313	38.8	57.4	3.9
Sanpete	48.8	2 338	52.5	13.5	3.3	0.0	10.1	36.3	1 738	73	117	2 112	16.3	77.8	5.9
Sevier	39.8	2 201	52.6	8.9	5.6	0.0	6.2	35.7	1 974	167	101	1 339	14.8	81.5	3.7
Summit	125.7	4 882	42.5	1.0	4.1	0.0	4.9	123.2	4 783	85	214	1 656	38.0	50.9	11.1
Tooele	88.5	2 818	38.1	15.3	4.9	0.1	5.9	90.5	2 881	1 815	256	1 458	32.1	62.6	5.4
Uintah	76.1	2 982	39.6	5.9	4.9	3.5	13.0	149.1	5 844	398	140	1 363	16.5	80.2	3.3
Utah	592.2	1 805	54.6	1.6	5.2	0.1	3.6	878.7	2 678	1 002	1 849	18 209	13.7	81.7	4.6
Wasatch	28.1	2 193	47.2	3.2	6.5	0.4	5.0	28.2	2 207	55	72	772	26.0	67.3	6.7
Washington	160.9	2 047	51.8	2.0	4.2	0.0	4.1	229.8	2 924	451	447	3 803	16.8	78.5	4.6
Wayne	6.7	2 812	56.5	1.1	3.9	0.0	18.0	1.5	651	100	13	168	16.5	77.9	5.6
Weber	351.9	1 938	51.1	2.0	4.5	3.4	3.2	228.1	1 256	5 973	1 022	12 209	31.7	62.6	5.7
VERMONT	X	X	X	X	X	X	X	X	X	5 478	4 501	39 543	50.6	40.7	8.7
Addison	76.2	2 181	78.1	0.1	1.6	0.2	8.0	27.1	774	134	263	1 634	NA	NA	NA
Bennington	70.2	1 952	65.0	0.1	3.6	0.0	10.6	10.7	298	132	269	1 830	NA	NA	NA
Caledonia	51.6	1 800	64.0	0.4	1.7	0.0	13.9	17.2	599	110	215	1 775	NA	NA	NA

1. Based on the resident population estimated as of July 1 of the year shown.

STATE/ County code	MSA/ PMSA/ NECMA code[1]	County Type[2]	STATE County	Land area,[3] (sq km) 1990	Total persons	Rank	Per square kilometer	White	Black	Am. Indian, Eskimo, Aleut	Asian and Pacific Islander	Percent Hispanic[4]	Under 5 years	5 to 17 years	18 to 24 years	25 to 34 years	35 to 44 years	45 to 54 years
				1	2	3	4	5	6	7	8	9	10	11	12	13	14	15
			VERMONT—Cont'd															
50 007	1303	3	Chittenden	1 396	143 947	366	103.1	97.2	1.0	0.2	1.6	1.2	5.4	16.4	13.3	16.2	17.7	14.5
50 009	...	9	Essex	1 723	6 644	2 715	3.9	99.1	0.4	0.2	0.3	0.5	5.0	19.0	5.3	12.0	16.2	15.8
50 011	1303	3	Franklin	1 650	44 431	994	26.9	98.0	0.4	1.1	0.5	0.7	6.3	21.3	6.8	15.1	17.0	14.5
50 013	1303	3	Grand Isle	214	6 370	2 745	29.8	98.8	0.6	0.4	0.2	0.6	5.7	18.4	5.7	14.2	18.7	16.1
50 015	...	8	Lamoille	1 193	21 935	1 662	18.4	99.1	0.2	0.2	0.5	0.7	5.6	18.5	9.4	14.6	17.7	15.0
50 017	...	9	Orange	1 784	27 871	1 439	15.6	99.1	0.3	0.2	0.4	0.5	5.7	19.8	6.9	13.6	17.5	15.0
50 019	...	7	Orleans	1 805	25 496	1 514	14.1	99.1	0.3	0.3	0.3	0.5	5.2	21.0	6.2	11.7	16.9	15.2
50 021	...	7	Rutland	2 414	62 407	769	25.9	99.1	0.4	0.1	0.5	0.6	5.1	17.1	8.4	13.3	17.2	15.2
50 023	...	6	Washington	1 786	56 289	825	31.5	98.9	0.4	0.1	0.6	1.6	5.2	18.2	8.1	13.1	18.6	15.5
50 025	...	7	Windham	2 043	42 670	1 030	20.9	98.3	0.6	0.1	1.0	0.9	5.3	18.0	6.8	13.8	18.9	14.9
50 027	...	7	Windsor	2 516	55 454	834	22.0	98.7	0.4	0.1	0.7	0.6	5.1	17.5	5.5	13.1	18.0	16.0
51 000	...	X	VIRGINIA	102 558	6 872 912	X	67.0	75.8	20.1	0.3	3.8	3.9	6.6	17.7	9.8	15.2	17.4	13.5
51 001	...	7	Accomack	1 177	32 121	1 309	27.3	61.5	38.1	0.1	0.3	1.9	5.8	17.6	7.1	11.7	14.8	13.0
51 003	1540	3	Albemarle	1 872	80 145	629	42.8	84.8	11.7	0.1	3.4	1.8	6.2	15.8	14.4	15.2	17.2	12.7
51 005	...	6	Alleghany	1 155	12 152	2 269	10.5	96.9	2.6	0.1	0.4	0.8	5.2	18.3	7.2	11.2	16.5	16.5
51 007	...	8	Amelia	924	10 601	2 369	11.5	63.1	36.5	0.2	0.2	0.9	6.1	19.3	7.5	13.0	15.8	15.4
51 009	4640	3	Amherst	1 231	30 351	1 367	24.7	76.0	23.1	0.5	0.4	1.1	5.5	17.2	9.5	12.5	16.5	14.9
51 011	...	8	Appomattox	864	13 317	2 189	15.4	73.6	26.2	0.1	0.1	0.4	5.7	18.7	7.9	12.2	15.3	15.6
51 013	8840	0	Arlington	67	174 848	303	2 609.7	78.7	11.2	0.4	9.6	19.4	5.7	10.9	10.2	22.0	19.7	13.4
51 015	...	4	Augusta	2 517	61 166	781	24.3	95.3	4.2	0.1	0.4	0.7	5.8	18.4	7.2	13.6	17.6	15.5
51 017	...	9	Bath	1 378	4 926	2 845	3.6	93.5	6.1	0.0	0.3	0.8	4.9	15.8	7.9	10.9	14.2	17.6
51 019	4640	3	Bedford	1 955	57 537	815	29.4	90.1	9.4	0.1	0.4	0.6	5.9	17.6	6.9	13.8	17.8	15.6
51 021	...	9	Bland	929	6 795	2 700	7.3	95.6	4.2	0.1	0.2	0.7	4.6	16.9	7.3	13.2	18.0	15.3
51 023	6800	3	Botetourt	1 406	29 184	1 404	20.8	94.1	5.4	0.1	0.5	0.9	5.0	17.1	7.0	12.2	17.9	16.2
51 025	...	8	Brunswick	1 466	18 340	1 851	12.5	36.7	63.2	0.0	0.1	0.5	4.8	16.1	11.5	15.4	17.5	12.1
51 027	...	9	Buchanan	1 305	28 477	1 427	21.8	97.0	2.7	0.1	0.2	1.4	4.6	21.0	8.8	14.2	16.8	14.4
51 029	...	8	Buckingham	1 505	14 754	2 086	9.8	53.0	46.6	0.1	0.2	0.4	5.6	16.0	8.4	16.3	18.0	13.3
51 031	4640	3	Campbell	1 307	50 345	901	38.5	82.5	16.9	0.1	0.5	0.7	5.9	17.7	8.7	13.3	16.1	15.2
51 033	...	8	Caroline	1 379	22 075	1 655	16.0	56.2	42.2	1.2	0.4	0.8	6.6	18.9	8.8	14.0	16.0	14.5
51 035	...	7	Carroll	1 234	27 808	1 440	22.5	99.1	0.6	0.1	0.2	0.9	4.9	16.6	7.6	11.6	15.5	15.1
51 036	6760	2	Charles City County	473	7 240	2 661	15.3	25.3	66.8	7.7	0.2	0.6	5.2	17.6	8.1	13.3	18.2	14.6
51 037	...	8	Charlotte	1 230	12 414	2 256	10.1	59.4	40.3	0.2	0.1	0.6	5.6	18.0	8.2	10.9	13.5	13.5
51 041	6760	2	Chesterfield	1 103	253 365	212	229.7	81.9	15.2	0.3	2.7	1.9	7.3	21.7	7.6	15.0	21.3	14.2
51 043	8840	1	Clarke	457	12 838	2 223	28.1	89.3	10.1	0.2	0.4	1.1	5.6	16.5	7.2	13.1	16.9	14.8
51 045	...	8	Craig	855	4 942	2 841	5.8	99.5	0.2	0.1	0.2	0.2	5.7	17.0	7.4	13.1	16.7	15.4
51 047	8840	1	Culpeper	987	33 562	1 269	34.0	76.7	21.4	0.3	1.5	1.1	6.9	18.7	8.7	15.6	17.0	13.0
51 049	...	8	Cumberland	773	7 876	2 614	10.2	56.9	42.8	0.1	0.2	0.9	6.3	19.6	7.7	12.1	15.2	15.0
51 051	...	9	Dickenson	862	16 716	1 950	19.4	99.1	0.7	0.1	0.1	0.6	5.2	21.3	7.6	12.1	15.9	14.1
51 053	6760	2	Dinwiddie	1 305	25 663	1 508	19.7	58.5	40.9	0.2	0.4	0.9	5.5	17.2	8.2	13.8	16.8	16.0
51 057	...	8	Essex	668	9 121	2 499	13.7	57.3	41.5	0.6	0.6	0.6	5.4	17.9	7.3	12.2	15.7	14.5
51 059	8840	0	Fairfax	1 025	945 717	35	922.7	79.5	8.2	0.3	12.0	9.4	6.6	17.5	8.2	15.9	20.0	15.9
51 061	8840	1	Fauquier	1 684	55 206	837	32.8	85.9	13.0	0.2	0.9	2.0	7.2	19.0	7.3	14.5	18.0	15.3
51 063	...	8	Floyd	988	13 260	2 194	13.4	96.7	2.9	0.1	0.3	0.8	5.1	17.4	7.1	11.6	16.7	15.8
51 065	1540	3	Fluvanna	744	19 622	1 780	26.4	73.0	26.6	0.2	0.2	0.9	6.6	17.9	7.8	14.4	16.5	13.4
51 067	...	6	Franklin	1 793	45 220	981	25.2	87.1	12.5	0.1	0.3	0.5	5.6	16.8	9.4	12.5	16.3	14.4
51 069	...	4	Frederick	1 074	56 555	822	52.7	96.7	2.4	0.2	0.7	1.1	6.9	19.3	7.5	14.8	17.3	15.0
51 071	...	9	Giles	927	16 315	1 983	17.6	97.5	2.2	0.1	0.2	0.6	5.1	16.4	7.9	11.1	15.6	14.9
51 073	5720	1	Gloucester	561	35 463	1 206	63.2	85.7	13.1	0.3	1.0	1.6	6.9	20.0	6.8	14.7	17.8	14.1
51 075	6760	2	Goochland	737	17 651	1 891	23.9	65.8	33.7	0.1	0.4	0.4	5.4	14.6	7.1	15.4	18.8	15.9
51 077	...	9	Grayson	1 146	16 451	1 974	14.4	96.1	3.6	0.1	0.2	0.7	5.1	16.7	7.3	11.4	15.0	14.9
51 079	1540	3	Greene	406	14 685	2 089	36.2	91.7	7.8	0.1	0.4	0.9	7.7	19.3	7.2	15.6	18.3	14.1
51 081	...	6	Greensville	765	11 332	2 321	14.8	35.8	63.4	0.3	0.4	2.1	4.3	14.8	12.2	17.3	19.9	13.3
51 083	...	6	Halifax	2 108	36 920	1 163	17.5	56.5	43.1	0.3	0.2	0.9	5.2	18.6	7.6	11.4	16.2	14.5
51 085	6760	2	Hanover	1 224	85 410	590	69.8	87.2	12.0	0.2	0.6	0.8	6.1	18.5	7.9	13.0	17.7	15.2
51 087	6760	2	Henrico	617	244 652	223	396.5	73.6	23.2	0.3	2.9	1.6	6.3	16.6	8.5	16.1	18.1	13.3
51 089	...	4	Henry	990	55 634	831	56.2	73.3	26.4	0.1	0.3	0.7	5.6	16.7	8.4	12.9	15.7	16.0
51 091	...	9	Highland	1 077	2 480	3 023	2.3	99.8	0.1	0.0	0.1	0.4	5.0	16.2	4.8	12.0	15.6	16.1
51 093	5720	1	Isle of Wight	818	29 632	1 389	36.2	63.6	35.7	0.2	0.4	1.1	6.6	18.7	7.5	14.3	17.0	14.7
51 095	5720	0	James City County	370	45 945	971	124.2	77.8	20.1	0.2	1.9	1.7	6.1	17.2	7.6	13.9	16.9	13.7
51 097	...	8	King and Queen	819	6 540	2 726	8.0	53.0	45.8	1.1	0.2	0.7	6.2	18.2	7.6	12.3	15.5	13.9
51 099	8840	1	King George	466	17 681	1 888	37.9	75.1	23.2	0.3	1.3	1.8	7.6	20.0	8.4	15.4	16.6	13.6
51 101	...	6	King William	713	13 048	2 211	18.3	63.4	34.1	2.1	0.4	1.0	6.7	19.7	7.5	13.4	17.5	14.4
51 103	...	9	Lancaster	345	11 349	2 315	32.9	66.9	32.9	0.1	0.1	1.0	4.3	15.0	4.9	8.9	12.4	12.9
51 105	...	9	Lee	1 132	23 821	1 584	21.0	99.0	0.7	0.1	0.1	0.9	5.7	20.1	7.5	12.0	15.4	14.3
51 107	8840	1	Loudoun	1 347	156 284	330	116.0	87.7	8.4	0.2	3.7	4.0	8.2	18.7	7.7	17.8	19.9	15.0

1. MSA = Metropolitan Statistical Area. PMSA = Primary MSA. NECMA = New England County Metropolitan Area. See Appendix A for explanation of these concepts. See Appendix B for list of metropolitan areas identified by type, with component counties.   2. County typology code from the Economic Research Service of USDA. See Appendix A for definition.   3. Dry land or land partially or temporarily covered by water.   4. Hispanic persons may be of any race.

Table B. States and Counties — Population and Households

STATE County	Age (percent) (cont'd) 55 to 64 years	65 to 74 years	75 years and over	Percent female	Total persons 1990	1980	Percent change 1980–1990	1990–1999	Components of change, 1990–1999 Births	Deaths	Net migration	Households, 1990 Number	Percent change, 1980–1990	Persons per house-hold	Percent Female family householder[1]	One person
	16	17	18	19	20	21	22	23	24	25	26	27	28	29	30	31
VERMONT—Cont'd																
Chittenden	7.4	4.9	4.3	51.3	131 761	115 534	14.0	9.2	16 968	7 569	3 227	48 439	25.7	2.57	8.9	23.0
Essex	11.6	8.3	6.7	50.8	6 405	6 313	1.5	3.7	697	555	118	2 344	7.5	2.61	8.1	21.4
Franklin	8.4	5.7	4.9	50.3	39 980	34 788	14.9	11.1	6 020	3 143	1 702	14 326	23.6	2.76	9.8	19.8
Grand Isle	10.1	6.6	4.5	49.4	5 318	4 613	15.3	19.8	684	401	777	2 018	25.9	2.64	7.5	19.9
Lamoille	8.1	5.9	5.2	49.8	19 735	16 767	17.7	11.1	2 692	1 396	973	7 397	25.4	2.56	8.5	23.5
Orange	8.9	6.7	5.8	49.7	26 149	22 739	15.0	6.6	2 988	2 002	820	9 455	21.8	2.69	8.9	20.1
Orleans	9.4	7.9	6.6	50.5	24 053	23 440	2.6	6.0	2 817	2 308	1 038	8 873	9.6	2.66	9.1	21.2
Rutland	9.3	7.5	6.9	51.3	62 142	58 347	6.5	0.4	6 761	5 731	-554	23 690	15.0	2.52	9.6	24.6
Washington	8.9	5.8	6.5	50.8	54 928	52 393	4.8	2.5	6 142	4 621	41	20 948	12.5	2.50	9.2	26.2
Windham	8.8	6.8	6.8	50.9	41 588	36 933	12.6	2.6	4 788	3 573	3	16 264	17.5	2.49	9.7	25.7
Windsor	9.6	8.1	7.0	50.8	54 055	51 030	5.9	2.6	5 600	4 963	939	21 523	13.0	2.47	8.7	25.1
VIRGINIA	8.6	6.2	5.0	51.1	6 189 197	5 346 797	15.8	11.0	872 681	477 233	242 295	2 291 830	23.0	2.61	11.1	22.9
Accomack	11.2	9.7	9.1	53.0	31 703	31 268	1.4	1.3	3 818	4 055	680	12 653	9.1	2.46	13.1	27.4
Albemarle	8.4	5.6	4.7	51.3	68 177	55 783	22.2	17.6	8 111	4 357	8 319	24 433	29.4	2.53	8.6	23.0
Alleghany	11.8	7.5	5.8	49.9	12 815	14 333	-8.1	-5.2	1 491	1 217	-865	4 942	1.9	2.62	7.9	20.3
Amelia	9.8	6.9	6.3	50.8	8 787	8 405	4.5	20.6	1 146	875	1 568	3 131	13.5	2.80	10.2	19.9
Amherst	10.3	7.3	6.2	52.0	28 578	29 122	-1.9	6.2	3 322	2 466	1 005	9 827	9.7	2.68	10.9	19.5
Appomattox	10.5	7.1	7.0	51.6	12 300	11 971	2.7	8.3	1 567	1 265	761	4 531	11.8	2.68	10.9	19.3
Arlington	7.7	5.4	5.0	51.1	170 895	152 599	12.0	2.3	24 457	10 347	-11 629	78 520	9.6	2.12	7.6	39.3
Augusta	10.4	6.3	5.1	49.4	54 557	47 578	14.9	12.1	6 244	4 202	4 694	19 781	10.0	2.68	8.0	18.2
Bath	12.8	8.1	7.7	49.3	4 799	5 860	-18.1	2.8	486	622	284	1 895	-3.4	2.51	7.9	24.2
Bedford	10.9	6.3	5.1	50.1	45 553	34 927	30.7	26.3	5 760	3 732	10 004	17 292	44.3	2.62	6.4	18.2
Bland	10.8	7.2	6.8	46.5	6 514	6 349	2.6	4.9	578	640	358	2 244	8.0	2.65	8.5	20.9
Botetourt	10.9	7.8	6.0	49.9	24 992	23 270	7.4	16.8	2 501	2 023	3 757	9 148	14.8	2.67	7.3	17.9
Brunswick	9.3	7.5	5.8	45.6	15 987	15 632	2.3	14.7	1 727	1 815	2 438	5 499	9.6	2.67	14.6	25.7
Buchanan	8.6	6.5	5.1	49.4	31 333	37 989	-17.5	-9.1	2 954	2 441	-3 338	11 061	-6.1	2.81	9.3	16.6
Buckingham	9.2	6.9	6.3	45.0	12 873	11 751	9.5	14.6	1 459	1 204	1 671	4 341	12.5	2.71	12.7	23.0
Campbell	10.1	7.5	5.6	50.8	47 499	45 424	4.7	6.0	5 655	3 663	980	17 952	18.7	2.63	10.0	19.9
Caroline	9.4	6.5	5.3	50.7	19 217	17 904	7.3	14.9	2 748	1 666	1 794	6 631	15.9	2.86	12.9	18.7
Carroll	12.3	8.4	8.2	50.7	26 519	27 270	-2.5	4.9	2 641	2 772	1 510	10 463	7.4	2.51	9.1	21.2
Charles City County	10.9	6.6	5.3	51.3	6 282	6 692	-6.1	15.2	750	540	758	2 161	10.7	2.91	14.7	16.9
Charlotte	11.1	10.6	8.5	51.6	11 688	12 266	-4.7	6.2	1 454	1 547	867	4 312	6.5	2.68	12.3	23.0
Chesterfield	7.2	3.5	2.1	51.1	209 599	141 372	48.2	20.9	30 430	10 698	24 282	73 441	60.3	2.82	9.7	16.4
Clarke	11.1	7.4	7.5	50.6	12 101	9 965	21.4	6.1	1 244	1 095	617	4 236	20.5	2.78	9.7	18.8
Craig	11.4	7.0	6.3	49.5	4 372	3 948	10.7	13.0	480	421	527	1 676	15.4	2.59	7.3	19.0
Culpeper	8.6	5.8	5.6	49.3	27 791	22 620	22.9	20.8	3 986	2 565	4 364	9 757	28.3	2.79	10.0	19.0
Cumberland	9.8	7.1	7.1	51.5	7 825	7 881	-0.7	0.7	997	787	-125	2 813	9.9	2.77	12.6	22.2
Dickenson	10.1	7.2	6.5	51.2	17 620	19 806	-11.0	-5.1	1 656	1 596	-940	6 457	0.9	2.71	10.8	19.7
Dinwiddie	10.0	7.4	5.0	50.5	22 279	22 602	-1.3	15.2	2 439	1 818	2 802	7 492	16.7	2.76	12.9	18.8
Essex	10.7	7.6	8.7	52.7	8 689	8 864	-2.0	5.0	1 051	1 033	456	3 258	7.2	2.62	11.3	24.8
Fairfax	8.0	4.9	2.9	50.8	818 310	595 754	37.4	15.6	120 353	33 441	36 662	292 345	42.5	2.75	8.4	18.7
Fauquier	8.8	5.4	4.5	50.0	48 700	35 889	36.1	13.4	6 342	3 453	3 379	16 509	42.2	2.89	7.7	15.3
Floyd	10.8	7.6	8.0	50.4	11 965	11 563	3.5	10.8	1 233	1 187	1 273	4 763	15.0	2.51	8.1	23.0
Fluvanna	10.5	7.4	5.5	50.1	12 429	10 244	21.3	57.9	2 009	1 186	6 356	4 518	32.9	2.73	10.1	18.5
Franklin	10.7	7.5	6.5	50.9	39 549	35 740	10.7	14.6	4 397	3 688	5 063	14 655	23.6	2.59	8.9	20.0
Frederick	9.3	5.8	4.1	49.9	45 723	34 150	33.9	23.7	6 409	3 175	7 643	16 470	43.6	2.76	7.9	16.6
Giles	11.3	9.7	7.8	51.2	16 366	17 810	-8.1	-0.3	1 708	1 847	144	6 461	2.9	2.51	10.4	22.9
Gloucester	8.8	5.8	5.1	50.6	30 131	20 107	49.9	17.7	3 727	2 412	3 903	10 966	53.5	2.72	8.2	19.0
Goochland	10.4	6.4	6.1	51.4	14 163	11 761	20.4	24.6	1 613	1 121	3 034	4 880	32.7	2.70	9.4	17.1
Grayson	11.9	9.2	8.6	51.2	16 278	16 579	-1.8	1.1	1 585	1 761	401	6 468	7.8	2.48	9.3	22.5
Greene	8.7	5.2	3.9	50.5	10 297	7 625	35.0	42.6	1 896	777	3 270	3 749	46.8	2.74	9.9	17.5
Greensville	8.0	5.6	4.4	39.3	8 553	10 903	-20.8	32.5	1 057	848	2 574	3 150	-8.6	2.80	15.5	20.9
Halifax	10.3	8.4	7.8	52.3	36 030	30 599	-5.1	2.5	4 282	4 603	1 327	10 728	5.4	2.66	13.3	22.0
Hanover	9.6	7.2	5.4	51.1	63 306	50 398	25.6	34.9	8 734	4 914	18 325	22 628	39.1	2.73	8.0	16.5
Henrico	9.1	6.5	5.7	53.7	217 878	180 735	20.5	12.3	31 271	19 425	15 488	89 138	33.0	2.41	11.8	26.6
Henry	10.7	7.9	6.2	51.5	56 942	57 654	-1.2	-2.3	6 049	4 611	-2 559	21 771	11.3	2.59	11.7	20.7
Highland	12.5	9.6	8.3	50.2	2 635	2 937	-10.3	-5.9	178	319	1	1 081	-2.5	2.43	6.4	25.3
Isle of Wight	9.5	6.7	5.0	51.5	25 053	21 603	16.0	18.3	3 319	2 118	3 362	9 032	28.2	2.75	12.3	18.6
James City County	9.9	8.7	6.1	51.5	34 779	22 339	55.6	32.1	4 325	2 400	9 210	12 968	69.8	2.60	9.4	19.6
King and Queen	10.6	9.0	6.9	51.4	6 289	5 968	5.4	4.0	750	643	169	2 339	13.8	2.69	13.5	22.0
King George	8.3	5.8	4.3	50.3	13 527	10 543	28.3	30.7	2 148	1 029	2 922	4 736	34.8	2.79	9.3	19.7
King William	9.0	6.0	5.7	51.6	10 913	9 334	16.9	19.6	1 600	1 010	1 568	3 834	24.0	2.82	10.5	19.0
Lancaster	13.6	14.4	13.5	53.4	10 896	10 129	7.6	4.2	1 005	1 783	1 291	4 564	15.9	2.34	10.3	26.3
Lee	10.4	7.3	7.3	51.9	24 496	25 956	-5.6	-2.8	2 482	2 626	-433	9 231	3.7	2.63	11.6	22.4
Loudoun	6.9	3.2	2.7	50.3	86 185	57 427	50.0	81.3	19 799	4 491	54 402	30 490	63.5	2.80	7.9	16.8

1. No spouse present.

Table B. States and Counties — Vital Statistics, Health Resources, and Crime

STATE County	Births avg 1996–1998 Total	Rate¹	Deaths Number Total	Infant²	Deaths Rate Total¹	Infant³	Physicians Number	Rate⁵	Hospitals Number	Beds Number	Rate⁵	Medicare enrollees 1999	Serious crimes Total Number	Rate⁷
	32	33	34	35	36	37	38	39	40	41	42	43	44	45
VERMONT—Cont'd														
Chittenden	1 690	11.9	869	9	6.1	5.1	653	458	2	582	408	15 667	6 033	4 252
Essex	57	8.8	59	1	9.0	11.6	3	46	0	0	0	1 262	NA	NA
Franklin	622	14.2	341	3	7.8	5.4	61	139	1	70	159	5 563	711	1 629
Grand Isle	265	42.0	40	1	6.3	2.5	8	128	0	0	0	860	13 833	
Lamoille	269	12.6	156	2	7.3	6.2	61	282	1	49	227	3 015	1 183	5 498
Orange	243	8.8	221	1	8.0	5.5	50	179	1	42	150	3 956	270	1 063
Orleans	286	11.3	260	2	10.3	7.0	38	150	1	46	182	4 575	495	1 949
Rutland	663	10.6	630	3	10.1	4.5	140	224	1	188	301	11 204	1 223	1 944
Washington	602	10.7	517	8	9.2	13.8	134	238	1	122	217	8 885	1 902	3 356
Windham	458	10.7	401	3	9.4	7.3	95	223	2	81	190	6 863	1 379	3 208
Windsor	439	8.0	542	2	9.8	5.3	179	323	2	164	296	9 879	NA	NA
VIRGINIA	92 856	13.8	53 934	716	8.0	7.7	15 118	223	92	18 211	268	875 799	248 576	3 660
Accomack	402	12.5	444	2	13.8	5.8	29	90	0	0	0	6 706	926	2 861
Albemarle	907	11.7	506	2	6.5	2.6	415	529	0	0	0	8 146	2 342	2 996
Alleghany	155	12.6	118	0	9.6	0.0	17	140	1	174	1 433	424	160	1 289
Amelia	127	12.5	105	1	10.4	10.5	2	19	0	0	0	1 593	133	1 285
Amherst	355	11.8	273	3	9.1	9.4	9	30	0	0	0	4 835	538	1 780
Appomattox	169	13.0	134	2	10.3	9.9	7	53	0	0	0	2 084	183	1 402
Arlington	2 706	15.3	1 130	18	6.4	6.5	566	319	3	690	389	17 665	8 293	4 765
Augusta	679	11.0	506	4	8.2	6.4	55	89	1	131	212	6 451	995	1 596
Bath	47	9.6	64	0	13.1	0.0	8	164	1	25	511	1 044	41	826
Bedford	628	11.3	425	4	7.7	6.9	55	98	0	0	0	8 620	786	1 400
Bland	59	8.7	71	0	10.4	0.0	6	89	0	0	0	1 239	86	1 243
Botetourt	288	10.2	234	1	8.3	3.5	22	77	0	0	0	4 352	362	1 270
Brunswick	180	10.7	195	2	11.7	9.3	3	18	0	0	0	3 063	188	1 109
Buchanan	287	9.8	282	1	9.6	3.5	16	55	1	99	342	6 461	444	1 499
Buckingham	145	10.0	130	1	8.9	4.6	6	41	0	0	0	2 009	185	1 259
Campbell	631	12.6	406	6	8.1	9.5	31	62	0	0	0	6 452	1 153	2 279
Caroline	295	13.6	189	3	8.7	10.2	6	27	0	0	0	3 032	364	1 662
Carroll	290	10.4	318	0	11.4	1.1	13	47	0	0	0	4 455	489	1 733
Charles City County	84	12.1	68	2	9.8	19.8	5	71	0	0	0	812	77	1 096
Charlotte	142	11.7	173	0	14.2	0.0	8	65	0	0	0	3 035	239	1 947
Chesterfield	3 262	13.4	1 319	20	5.4	6.2	553	225	1	284	115	20 277	8 837	3 606
Clarke	116	9.1	112	0	8.8	2.9	23	180	0	0	0	1 743	240	1 843
Craig	47	9.8	47	0	9.8	0.0	0	0	0	0	0	733	41	832
Culpeper	425	13.1	290	3	8.9	6.3	48	145	1	70	212	4 623	747	2 273
Cumberland	106	13.5	97	0	12.4	3.1	3	38	0	0	0	947	121	1 534
Dickenson	172	10.0	182	2	10.6	9.7	11	65	1	50	296	3 699	100	602
Dinwiddie	249	10.1	224	2	9.1	8.0	7	28	0	0	0	2 776	631	2 571
Essex	107	11.7	115	1	12.5	9.3	18	197	1	100	1 096	1 779	291	3 128
Fairfax	13 202	14.4	3 802	67	4.2	5.1	2 543	274	3	507	55	57 092	25 027	2 714
Fauquier	640	12.1	387	5	7.3	7.8	77	142	1	106	196	5 835	910	1 697
Floyd	136	10.5	142	1	11.0	4.9	61	466	0	0	0	2 208	152	1 154
Fluvanna	227	12.8	143	0	8.1	1.5	22	118	0	0	0	2 935	168	938
Franklin	464	10.5	428	2	9.7	4.3	31	70	1	37	83	6 865	820	1 833
Frederick	709	13.0	380	5	7.0	7.5	197	357	0	0	0	5 827	1 299	2 355
Giles	192	11.8	203	1	12.5	5.2	17	105	1	53	326	3 568	225	1 452
Gloucester	370	10.8	275	1	8.0	2.7	42	120	1	71	202	4 360	909	2 616
Goochland	172	9.8	120	1	6.8	7.7	23	129	0	0	0	1 930	258	1 454
Grayson	162	10.0	202	1	12.6	4.1	7	43	0	0	0	2 974	162	994
Greene	209	15.6	86	1	6.4	6.4	6	43	0	0	0	1 595	212	1 566
Greensville	112	9.8	94	1	8.2	8.9	0	0	0	0	0	737	136	1 180
Halifax	442	11.9	503	3	13.6	6.8	65	176	1	192	521	7 229	771	2 061
Hanover	966	12.2	572	7	7.2	6.9	84	102	0	0	0	11 525	1 557	1 956
Henrico	3 380	13.8	2 181	24	8.9	7.2	814	331	4	1 231	500	28 337	11 127	4 525
Henry	633	11.3	568	7	10.2	10.5	8	14	0	0	0	8 087	1 942	3 439
Highland	16	6.2	32	0	12.8	0.0	4	160	0	0	0	532	25	982
Isle of Wight	352	12.3	250	3	8.7	7.6	12	41	0	0	0	3 966	695	2 414
James City County	439	10.2	303	2	7.0	4.6	3	7	0	0	0	1 925	1 119	2 589
King and Queen	69	10.7	73	0	11.2	0.0	2	31	0	0	0	1 063	64	971
King George	242	14.4	116	3	6.9	11.0	36	209	0	0	0	1 707	534	3 126
King William	172	13.8	105	1	8.4	3.9	3	23	0	0	0	1 761	161	1 280
Lancaster	108	9.5	213	0	18.8	3.1	62	545	1	76	668	3 602	167	1 467
Lee	265	11.0	308	3	12.8	10.1	24	101	1	80	336	5 128	350	1 443
Loudoun	2 604	19.5	554	8	4.1	3.2	201	140	1	119	83	9 203	NA	NA

1. Per 1,000 estimated resident population, average 1996–1998. 2. Deaths of infants under 1 year old. 3. Deaths of infants under 1 year old per 1,000 live births. 4. Data subject to copyright. 5. Per 100,000 resident population as of July 1 of the year shown. 6. Data for serious crimes have not been adjusted for underreporting; this may affect comparability between geographic areas and over time. 7. Per 100,000 population estimated by the FBI.

Table B. States and Counties — Crime, Education, Money Income, and Poverty

STATE County	Serious crimes known to police, 1998[1] (cont'd) Rate[2] Violent	Property	Education — School enrollment and attainment, 1990 — Enrollment[3] Total	Percent private	Attainment[4] (percent) High school graduate or more	Bachelor's degree or more	Local government expenditures, fiscal 1997[5] Total current expenditures (mil dol)	Current expenditures per student (dollars)	Money income — 1989 Per capita[6] (dollars)	Households Median Dollars	Percent change, 1979–1989 (constant 1989 dollars)	Percent with $100,000 or more	Income and poverty, 1997 Median household income	Percent below poverty level All persons	Persons under 18	Persons 5–17 in families
	46	47	48	49	50	51	52	53	54	55	56	57	58	59	60	61
VERMONT—Cont'd																
Chittenden	129	4 123	39 777	21.0	86.7	34.0	159.5	6 974	16 096	36 877	25.2	4.5	46 747	7.1	8.7	7.2
Essex	NA	NA	1 511	10.3	68.0	8.5	6.4	6 261	9 854	22 358	7.9	0.3	29 014	13.9	21.1	17.9
Franklin	76	1 553	10 336	7.3	74.8	14.3	48.8	5 883	11 678	28 401	20.8	1.7	35 720	11.2	14.4	12.5
Grand Isle	386	13 447	1 192	11.3	79.0	20.3	5.7	6 933	13 940	30 536	23.4	3.3	39 362	8.9	12.0	11.3
Lamoille	181	5 317	5 265	6.1	80.2	23.9	27.0	6 698	12 519	27 315	23.1	2.4	33 418	10.3	13.3	11.7
Orange	75	988	6 614	9.9	80.4	21.9	37.3	7 004	11 898	28 004	29.9	1.9	35 844	9.6	12.4	10.9
Orleans	94	1 855	6 126	8.9	70.7	14.2	32.6	6 774	10 458	22 809	9.3	1.8	29 184	14.8	20.5	17.0
Rutland	68	1 876	14 714	15.7	79.4	20.6	75.7	6 996	12 780	28 229	14.1	1.9	34 304	10.5	14.1	11.4
Washington	65	3 291	13 391	21.9	81.3	24.4	72.2	6 991	13 547	29 623	22.9	2.6	36 926	9.2	11.8	10.0
Windham	91	3 117	9 743	18.5	81.7	25.2	58.7	8 000	13 134	27 767	21.0	2.2	35 590	9.8	12.6	10.7
Windsor	NA	NA	12 146	11.0	81.3	23.6	71.9	7 254	14 262	29 258	13.7	3.2	36 407	9.4	12.1	10.1
VIRGINIA	326	3 334	1 546 257	13.9	75.2	24.5	6 344.0	5 788	15 713	33 328	13.8	5.2	40 209	11.6	17.0	16.0
Accomack	188	2 673	6 327	9.5	59.5	9.2	29.5	5 350	10 506	20 431	12.1	1.2	25 309	21.9	34.0	30.2
Albemarle	179	2 817	21 567	11.5	81.5	39.4	73.7	6 498	17 448	36 886	23.6	7.3	46 371	8.5	12.6	11.6
Alleghany	81	1 208	3 046	5.4	67.4	9.3	17.3	5 817	11 606	26 486	-0.8	0.9	36 774	11.4	18.2	16.1
Amelia	77	1 208	1 909	9.3	56.3	7.2	9.1	4 983	11 605	26 612	11.4	1.4	33 121	12.3	19.3	17.5
Amherst	106	1 674	6 675	12.5	58.9	10.7	21.7	4 633	11 185	27 771	-0.1	0.8	34 745	12.5	18.9	16.6
Appomattox	153	1 249	2 794	7.2	61.1	8.7	10.8	4 560	10 795	25 612	-6.4	1.1	32 582	13.7	20.4	18.9
Arlington	256	4 509	34 765	31.9	87.5	52.3	158.8	9 051	25 633	44 600	22.6	10.7	57 244	8.1	15.9	15.9
Augusta	111	1 485	12 064	8.2	69.0	11.7	56.1	5 184	12 751	29 474	9.7	1.9	38 934	8.4	12.6	10.9
Bath	141	685	973	4.2	67.3	12.8	7.4	8 574	11 369	24 203	8.6	1.7	32 768	9.8	14.3	14.9
Bedford	146	1 254	10 173	13.7	68.8	15.6	42.8	4 194	14 305	30 712	13.5	2.8	42 540	7.7	12.1	10.6
Bland	14	1 229	1 524	5.1	62.6	4.6	5.5	5 553	9 765	23 587	1.5	0.9	32 199	11.4	14.9	13.0
Botetourt	95	1 175	5 706	10.0	72.9	13.6	23.2	5 030	13 810	33 079	15.1	2.3	45 370	6.5	9.4	8.5
Brunswick	271	838	4 305	15.9	50.5	7.0	13.9	5 350	8 872	19 424	5.8	1.2	25 652	23.1	29.8	28.3
Buchanan	226	1 273	8 251	5.8	42.5	6.4	29.6	5 951	9 621	19 851	-23.3	1.7	25 812	24.7	31.1	29.8
Buckingham	184	1 075	2 838	10.7	53.6	7.9	12.2	5 461	9 165	22 661	18.0	0.9	27 712	22.3	28.5	29.5
Campbell	206	2 073	11 250	17.0	66.1	12.9	40.1	4 786	12 061	27 212	-2.9	1.7	34 895	11.0	18.4	16.4
Caroline	192	1 470	4 244	7.6	58.8	8.3	18.3	4 912	11 837	28 934	19.2	2.7	34 799	14.3	20.7	18.9
Carroll	103	1 630	5 126	4.0	49.7	6.5	20.6	5 128	9 693	21 564	6.4	0.7	28 375	14.4	23.3	20.7
Charles City County	157	939	1 396	10.9	56.4	8.4	7.3	6 974	11 384	29 544	3.0	1.7	37 173	12.3	19.1	18.3
Charlotte	220	1 727	2 572	3.7	52.1	6.5	11.6	5 252	9 008	20 481	10.4	1.2	26 422	18.7	27.0	25.3
Chesterfield	148	3 458	59 331	9.8	84.2	29.2	246.4	4 950	17 423	43 604	8.7	5.7	55 324	6.4	9.4	8.4
Clarke	238	1 605	2 433	15.3	75.0	18.6	10.1	5 440	15 657	34 636	24.1	6.0	43 442	9.2	12.3	13.3
Craig	0	832	860	5.9	68.4	7.7	3.8	5 198	11 186	25 106	10.5	1.4	34 900	8.9	12.9	13.6
Culpeper	228	2 045	6 324	12.1	66.7	14.9	30.2	5 755	14 122	33 523	28.7	4.3	41 324	11.7	17.6	16.3
Cumberland	101	1 433	1 812	16.2	57.6	11.2	7.0	5 765	10 295	22 115	15.8	2.3	28 177	18.0	27.8	25.4
Dickenson	30	572	4 504	4.0	47.1	6.0	17.0	5 488	8 067	16 292	-28.2	1.2	22 941	25.5	32.9	31.9
Dinwiddie	293	2 278	4 535	9.1	59.2	8.4	20.0	4 891	12 212	29 388	5.4	1.8	34 830	12.7	18.7	18.1
Essex	333	2 795	1 816	8.4	64.7	16.4	8.7	5 551	11 529	26 074	10.7	1.6	31 385	14.8	22.6	20.9
Fairfax	105	2 609	217 447	19.0	91.4	49.0	1 013.8	7 076	24 833	59 284	17.9	16.4	71 057	5.3	8.0	7.0
Fauquier	177	1 520	11 380	14.3	78.9	21.5	51.9	5 723	19 195	45 222	39.6	8.9	56 691	7.1	10.5	10.0
Floyd	23	1 131	2 391	5.4	60.2	10.4	9.4	4 886	10 532	22 968	12.1	0.8	31 297	13.4	19.9	18.3
Fluvanna	78	860	2 808	6.6	68.5	16.3	14.6	5 381	12 977	31 378	41.0	2.9	40 134	8.3	12.2	13.3
Franklin	219	1 614	8 923	19.7	59.9	10.1	32.4	4 749	11 936	26 357	5.6	2.0	33 693	12.3	19.4	17.6
Frederick	105	2 250	10 552	10.2	70.1	14.7	52.1	5 234	13 671	32 806	14.4	2.4	42 545	7.8	11.6	10.8
Giles	116	1 336	3 402	2.7	64.5	8.9	13.6	5 297	11 462	24 125	5.9	1.1	32 519	12.7	19.2	19.0
Gloucester	153	2 463	7 335	11.2	74.0	14.7	31.3	4 766	13 122	31 591	16.9	2.3	39 889	10.9	16.3	15.3
Goochland	316	1 138	2 831	21.3	66.7	19.3	11.1	5 759	18 312	36 239	19.2	9.3	50 104	8.0	12.2	11.0
Grayson	61	933	3 087	8.1	51.1	4.2	12.5	5 424	8 966	19 324	-1.7	0.2	26 608	16.5	24.1	22.4
Greene	185	1 381	2 364	8.4	63.5	12.7	13.4	5 494	12 268	29 799	9.1	1.7	37 714	11.2	16.3	17.7
Greensville	373	807	2 124	5.6	50.0	5.3	15.0	5 591	9 504	22 116	13.2	0.9	27 923	20.7	25.6	22.9
Halifax	446	1 615	6 418	4.3	51.6	6.4	33.8	5 261	9 568	22 296	9.2	0.7	28 485	17.2	24.0	21.4
Hanover	113	1 843	15 822	15.2	77.5	18.9	67.3	4 589	16 463	40 683	13.7	4.3	53 618	5.0	6.9	6.5
Henrico	243	4 282	51 199	14.2	81.3	28.0	203.4	5 339	18 019	35 604	5.7	4.7	44 122	7.9	13.2	11.4
Henry	290	3 149	11 443	7.3	53.9	6.7	45.7	5 034	11 491	25 834	-3.0	1.2	30 843	13.0	21.5	19.1
Highland	157	825	477	4.0	61.8	13.0	2.3	6 188	10 828	20 903	-8.1	1.3	28 609	13.7	21.0	21.0
Isle of Wight	236	2 178	5 973	13.4	65.4	10.4	25.8	5 365	12 274	29 168	3.2	1.3	39 331	11.6	17.5	16.6
James City County	169	2 420	8 942	16.8	82.5	32.9	0.0	0	18 139	39 785	26.9	7.4	51 424	7.8	13.4	11.7
King and Queen	228	743	1 247	7.9	57.6	7.5	6.3	7 217	11 278	25 755	27.0	1.3	32 563	16.2	25.4	26.4
King George	427	2 699	3 400	6.8	73.1	20.4	15.1	5 237	15 365	35 556	17.5	3.7	45 575	9.2	14.1	13.3
King William	40	1 240	2 687	6.8	68.5	13.0	13.7	5 650	13 294	33 676	15.0	2.5	43 037	8.9	12.8	12.6
Lancaster	220	1 247	2 000	16.0	64.8	18.9	8.1	5 033	17 698	27 275	23.1	7.4	32 085	16.5	30.2	26.2
Lee	157	1 286	5 684	3.2	48.0	6.5	23.6	5 665	7 837	14 618	-16.4	0.9	21 574	28.5	38.0	36.1
Loudoun	NA	NA	21 224	13.4	86.6	32.7	135.0	6 257	20 757	52 064	27.1	9.3	67 455	3.9	5.5	5.4

1. Data for serious crimes have not been adjusted for underreporting; this may affect comparability between geographic areas and over time.   2. Per 100,000 population estimated by the FBI.   3. All persons 3 years old and over enrolled in nursery school through college.   4. Persons 25 years old and over.   5. Elementary and secondary education expenditures, local government fiscal years ending between July 1, 1996 and June 30, 1997.   6. Based on population enumerated as of April 1, 1990.

Table B. States and Counties — Personal Income

Personal income, 1998

STATE County	Total (mil dol)	Percent change, 1997–1998	Per capita[1] Dollars	Per capita[1] Rank	Wages and salaries[2] (mil dol)	Proprietor's income (mil dol)	Dividends, interest, and rent (mil dol)	Transfer payments Total (mil dol)	Gov. payments to individuals Total (mil dol)	Social Security (mil dol)	Medical payments (mil dol)	Income maintenance (mil dol)	Unemployment insurance (mil dol)
	62	63	64	65	66	67	68	69	70	71	72	73	74
VERMONT—Cont'd													
Chittenden	4 119	6.2	28 909	198	3 273	283	804	402	371	161	141	40	6
Essex	104	5.1	15 805	2 826	51	16	16	23	22	11	4	3	1
Franklin	888	6.5	20 197	1 653	401	87	128	132	123	48	41	20	4
Grand Isle	154	7.9	24 761	521	22	11	31	18	17	9	3	2	1
Lamoille	502	4.8	23 221	811	245	59	108	72	67	28	24	8	4
Orange	570	4.7	20 438	1 579	199	54	123	84	78	38	24	10	1
Orleans	482	5.0	19 010	2 054	224	64	94	108	102	40	39	14	4
Rutland	1 477	4.7	23 617	718	846	105	293	299	285	107	136	27	5
Washington	1 392	4.6	24 787	516	904	115	270	219	206	85	85	22	5
Windham	1 083	5.4	25 368	451	740	87	242	157	147	69	53	15	4
Windsor	1 478	5.4	26 700	329	691	114	386	194	182	98	56	18	2
VIRGINIA	190 528	5.6	28 063	X	128 068	10 190	34 558	18 823	17 596	8 151	6 182	1 632	181
Accomack	614	4.7	19 032	2 044	320	50	147	132	126	59	44	14	2
Albemarle	[3]3 602	[3]6.2	[3]30 947	[3]135	[3]2 574	[3]299	[3]961	[3]329	[3]308	[3]152	[3]112	[3]23	[3]2
Alleghany	[4]513	[4]2.9	[4]21 940	[4]1 115	[4]371	[4]22	[4]83	[4]106	[4]101	[4]43	[4]32	[4]8	[4]1
Amelia	205	7.3	19 687	1 824	63	21	31	33	31	15	12	3	0
Amherst	536	3.1	17 866	2 388	267	27	83	90	85	46	25	7	1
Appomattox	251	3.5	19 093	2 025	101	19	43	43	40	21	13	3	0
Arlington	8 150	6.1	46 677	10	10 575	532	1 751	354	326	147	128	24	3
Augusta	[5]2 342	[5]4.2	[5]22 526	[5]972	[5]1 414	[5]164	[5]450	[5]343	[5]324	[5]179	[5]105	[5]20	[5]3
Bath	108	1.8	22 020	1 099	65	6	28	20	19	9	8	1	0
Bedford	[6]1 537	[6]6.1	[6]24 279	[6]595	[6]433	[6]60	[6]335	[6]190	[6]179	[6]97	[6]50	[6]10	[6]1
Bland	111	3.9	16 357	2 734	53	9	16	24	23	11	6	2	0
Botetourt	684	6.8	23 859	670	209	33	139	84	78	42	21	4	1
Brunswick	268	4.9	15 439	2 885	124	12	42	68	65	27	24	8	0
Buchanan	501	-0.7	17 274	2 540	274	36	96	162	157	71	48	20	3
Buckingham	230	4.7	15 698	2 848	84	20	31	50	47	20	18	6	1
Campbell	[7]2 551	[7]3.8	[7]22 308	[7]1 014	[7]2 276	[7]140	[7]443	[7]463	[7]442	[7]197	[7]173	[7]35	[7]3
Caroline	436	4.1	19 825	1 772	119	26	71	66	62	30	22	6	1
Carroll	[8]633	[8]3.1	[8]18 395	[8]2 240	[8]362	[8]39	[8]104	[8]155	[8]148	[8]63	[8]64	[8]13	[8]2
Charles City County	133	3.7	18 604	2 183	39	7	22	20	19	10	7	2	0
Charlotte	212	5.8	17 206	2 559	87	21	37	53	50	22	18	6	1
Chesterfield	7 577	8.0	30 288	158	3 583	234	1 143	477	432	253	121	26	4
Clarke	351	6.6	27 607	258	113	18	71	31	28	15	10	2	0
Craig	96	6.4	19 697	1 820	14	5	13	15	14	8	4	1	0
Culpeper	847	8.8	25 589	431	385	46	146	91	85	41	32	7	1
Cumberland	144	4.1	18 363	2 248	29	11	24	30	29	13	9	4	0
Dickenson	255	1.9	15 107	2 923	91	17	39	96	93	39	30	12	2
Dinwiddie	[9]1 837	[9]4.1	[9]23 931	[9]657	[9]877	[9]70	[9]248	[9]375	[9]361	[9]125	[9]166	[9]35	[9]2
Essex	185	2.2	20 388	1 607	92	11	43	38	36	16	14	3	0
Fairfax	[10]42 462	[10]6.9	[10]44 303	[10]13	[10]28 317	[10]2 550	[10]7 844	[10]1 576	[10]1 399	[10]682	[10]478	[10]84	[10]11
Fauquier	1 893	7.0	35 104	64	467	110	441	115	105	56	37	7	1
Floyd	218	4.8	16 709	2 677	57	19	44	43	40	21	13	3	0
Fluvanna	390	10.6	20 610	1 525	88	20	77	55	52	28	18	3	0
Franklin	883	6.9	19 787	1 785	349	38	171	135	127	71	35	9	2
Frederick	[11]1 902	[11]6.5	[11]24 362	[11]579	[11]1 355	[11]153	[11]335	[11]204	[11]190	[11]104	[11]61	[11]13	[11]2
Giles	311	2.5	19 176	1 988	180	21	49	67	64	33	22	5	1
Gloucester	743	4.6	21 261	1 303	200	32	141	90	83	41	29	7	1
Goochland	562	4.4	32 265	108	191	30	151	43	40	23	12	3	0
Grayson	274	2.3	16 738	2 668	68	22	47	61	58	30	19	6	1
Greene	267	10.7	18 978	2 065	86	17	31	33	30	15	11	2	0
Greensville	[12]293	[12]3.5	[12]17 615	[12]2 464	[12]225	[12]13	[12]44	[12]63	[12]60	[12]27	[12]24	[12]7	[12]1
Halifax	[13]661	[13]3.7	[13]17 989	[13]2 347	[13]369	[13]41	[13]102	[13]146	[13]139	[13]63	[13]48	[13]17	[13]3
Hanover	2 223	6.5	27 007	302	1 143	123	358	205	190	105	63	8	1
Henrico	7 437	3.0	30 761	143	5 779	246	1 608	651	606	364	181	31	4
Henry	[14]1 457	[14]1.9	[14]20 483	[14]1 566	[14]1 003	[14]79	[14]286	[14]273	[14]259	[14]142	[14]80	[14]20	[14]7
Highland	55	2.3	22 141	1 051	12	8	19	10	9	5	4	1	0
Isle of Wight	719	7.2	24 637	542	459	31	103	90	85	40	32	7	1
James City County	[15]1 791	[15]5.8	[15]31 499	[15]127	[15]1 030	[15]99	[15]470	[15]175	[15]165	[15]88	[15]59	[15]6	[15]1
King and Queen	130	-0.4	20 034	1 702	30	5	22	22	21	9	8	2	0
King George	433	5.9	25 166	473	500	17	81	33	30	13	11	3	0
King William	300	3.7	23 437	759	127	9	54	36	34	18	12	2	0
Lancaster	308	4.1	27 133	293	112	12	132	63	61	33	21	4	1
Lee	378	1.8	15 853	2 816	141	17	51	129	125	45	45	21	2
Loudoun	4 985	14.0	34 495	69	2 754	178	711	195	169	91	58	9	1

1. Based on the resident population estimated as of July 1 of the year shown.   2. Includes other labor income.   3. Charlottesville included with Albemarle County.   4. Clifton Forge and Covington included with Alleghany County.   5. Staunton and Waynesboro included with Augusta County.   6. Bedford City included with Bedford County.   7. Lynchburg included with Campbell County.   8. Galax included with Carroll County.   9. Petersburg and Colonial Heights included with Dinwiddie County.   10. Fairfax City and Falls Church included with Fairfax County.   11. Winchester included with Frederick County.   12. Emporia included with Greensville County.   13. South Boston included with Halifax County.   14. Martinsville included with Henry County.   15. Williamsburg included with James City County.

Table B. States and Counties — Earnings, Social Security, and Housing

STATE County	Earnings, 1998									Social Security beneficiaries, December 1998		Supplemental Security Income recipients, December 1998	Housing units, 1990	
	Total (mil dol)	Farm	Goods-related[1]		Service-related and other[2]					Number	Rate[3]		Total	Percent change, 1980–1990
			Total	Manu-facturing	Total	Retail trade	Finance, insurance, and real estate	Services	Govern-ment					
	75	76	77	78	79	80	81	82	83	84	85	86	87	88
VERMONT—Cont'd														
Chittenden	3 556	0.3	30.6	23.7	55.0	8.5	6.2	29.1	14.1	18 346	129	2 088	52 095	26.0
Essex	67	3.0	62.1	58.3	D	3.5	0.7	7.5	16.2	1 434	218	172	4 403	18.9
Franklin	487	7.3	26.8	21.3	44.0	11.8	3.4	19.5	21.8	6 152	140	1 154	17 250	19.3
Grand Isle	33	9.3	D	4.0	D	10.0	4.1	24.1	22.9	1 134	182	106	4 135	16.3
Lamoille	303	2.1	22.3	12.8	60.2	13.6	3.5	37.1	15.4	3 416	158	461	9 872	31.0
Orange	253	3.7	24.0	12.5	51.7	8.8	3.4	28.1	20.6	4 715	169	551	12 336	17.7
Orleans	288	7.2	27.1	19.8	48.2	10.6	3.8	23.8	17.5	5 315	210	834	12 997	16.3
Rutland	952	0.7	26.8	19.6	57.1	11.5	3.6	29.2	15.4	12 831	205	1 856	31 181	21.0
Washington	1 020	0.3	17.6	11.6	58.0	9.6	11.8	27.0	24.1	10 150	180	1 433	25 328	14.5
Windham	827	0.9	D	15.9	D	9.5	5.7	29.2	10.0	7 972	187	788	25 796	31.9
Windsor	805	0.5	26.1	17.6	51.6	10.1	4.0	28.8	21.8	11 250	203	977	29 849	23.0
VIRGINIA	138 258	0.3	18.2	11.9	57.3	8.1	7.2	29.6	24.3	990 596	146	132 658	2 496 334	23.5
Accomack	370	3.8	D	20.5	D	8.3	3.0	18.6	29.3	7 934	246	1 315	15 840	14.7
Albemarle	(4)2 873	(4)0.3	(4)19.4	(4)10.5	(4)46.0	(4)8.9	(4)7.7	(4)22.9	(4)34.3	10 947	140	774	25 958	27.5
Alleghany	(5)392	(5)0.1	(5)D	(5)D	(5)D	(5)7.5	(5)1.5	(5)15.4	(5)12.4	2 254	186	233	5 481	0.9
Amelia	85	13.2	D	12.6	D	6.7	D	14.2	19.1	1 981	191	302	3 439	14.0
Amherst	293	0.4	35.7	26.5	D	9.5	D	15.2	29.0	5 623	187	717	10 598	9.6
Appomattox	120	0.3	D	D	D	9.4	4.4	11.0	19.4	2 670	203	356	4 913	9.0
Arlington	11 107	0.0	D	2.1	D	4.0	5.4	35.2	39.8	16 779	95	1 889	84 847	12.9
Augusta	(6)1 578	(6)1.6	(6)D	(6)30.2	(6)D	(6)10.4	(6)3.5	(6)17.4	(6)16.8	11 076	179	673	21 202	8.1
Bath	71	0.6	D	D	D	3.4	2.3	48.0	15.9	1 086	222	107	2 596	2.3
Bedford	(7)494	(7)0.3	(7)D	(7)29.0	(7)D	(7)7.5	(7)D	(7)23.5	(7)14.4	9 688	173	710	19 641	41.4
Bland	61	1.4	35.3	31.4	D	4.6	1.0	D	29.1	1 459	216	181	2 706	19.5
Botetourt	242	0.3	41.0	22.7	43.2	8.6	2.8	13.1	15.5	4 949	173	282	9 785	12.3
Brunswick	137	1.2	D	19.0	D	5.6	2.3	20.2	28.3	3 708	222	706	6 456	4.2
Buchanan	310	0.0	44.2	4.1	39.4	7.4	4.4	15.2	16.3	9 192	318	1 718	12 222	-4.3
Buckingham	104	3.5	D	15.3	D	6.0	D	18.4	32.2	2 761	189	513	5 013	10.4
Campbell	(8)2 417	(8)0.1	(8)D	(8)35.8	(8)D	(8)9.1	(8)7.8	(8)22.6	(8)9.8	9 395	187	952	19 008	16.3
Caroline	145	-0.4	D	14.3	D	11.6	5.4	13.5	32.1	3 781	171	390	7 292	11.7
Carroll	(9)402	(9)0.9	(9)D	(9)37.8	(9)D	(9)10.7	(9)2.2	(9)19.3	(9)15.5	6 392	229	860	12 209	4.5
Charles City County	46	0.7	D	20.3	D	4.5	2.2	12.8	22.6	1 242	175	146	2 314	6.5
Charlotte	108	3.2	44.8	38.4	33.0	5.5	2.8	10.9	19.0	3 169	259	668	4 947	8.5
Chesterfield	3 817	0.1	D	18.2	D	11.0	7.1	21.0	18.0	27 808	113	2 320	77 329	58.2
Clarke	130	0.7	D	34.1	D	6.2	4.6	21.1	14.7	1 894	148	152	4 531	14.4
Craig	19	4.6	D	D	D	6.4	4.6	11.6	33.5	990	203	110	1 993	6.4
Culpeper	431	0.7	22.2	14.0	58.1	9.0	5.5	24.9	19.1	5 237	158	674	10 471	26.6
Cumberland	40	7.1	23.5	7.8	44.8	12.3	2.0	17.1	24.6	1 681	214	271	3 170	3.6
Dickenson	107	0.4	32.3	1.5	44.4	8.8	1.5	18.8	23.0	5 075	300	1 028	7 112	3.0
Dinwiddie	(10)947	(10)0.1	(10)D	(10)12.8	(10)D	(10)17.0	(10)4.5	(10)18.9	(10)29.0	4 151	168	789	8 023	17.3
Essex	103	-1.0	31.0	25.7	56.3	18.4	5.0	26.6	13.7	2 066	226	241	4 073	-0.2
Fairfax	(11)30 867	(11)0.0	(11)8.4	(11)3.7	(11)76.6	(11)6.5	(11)6.5	(11)46.2	(11)15.0	73 773	79	5 999	307 966	42.7
Fauquier	577	1.4	D	6.8	D	10.1	7.0	31.8	16.5	6 671	123	443	17 716	41.0
Floyd	76	4.4	30.1	19.7	45.9	10.2	4.1	17.4	19.5	2 783	213	267	5 505	12.0
Fluvanna	107	1.0	23.0	9.2	49.0	5.6	2.8	23.7	27.0	3 238	174	261	5 035	31.5
Franklin	387	2.2	46.7	35.9	37.7	9.1	3.2	16.3	13.4	8 916	200	929	17 526	29.7
Frederick	(12)1 508	(12)0.4	(12)34.6	(12)27.6	(12)54.4	(12)11.4	(12)3.9	(12)28.0	(12)10.6	7 730	140	532	17 864	40.0
Giles	201	0.1	54.9	49.7	D	7.5	D	14.3	11.1	3 935	242	519	7 098	5.4
Gloucester	231	0.1	D	4.3	D	15.3	4.7	24.0	29.1	5 135	146	538	12 451	49.8
Goochland	221	0.3	D	1.7	D	19.4	8.4	22.7	16.8	2 614	147	205	5 203	29.1
Grayson	90	3.8	42.0	36.3	33.4	6.8	3.2	15.5	20.8	4 227	262	561	7 529	10.9
Greene	103	0.6	D	30.0	D	8.0	D	17.2	19.5	1 898	136	221	4 154	35.8
Greensville	(13)238	(13)2.1	(13)D	(13)35.4	(13)D	(13)7.8	(13)D	(13)17.7	(13)23.3	2 016	179	356	3 393	-10.5
Halifax	(14)409	(14)2.5	(14)D	(14)32.4	(14)D	(14)11.5	(14)2.0	(14)18.8	(14)14.7	8 663	235	1 294	11 790	3.9
Hanover	1 266	0.4	D	14.0	D	9.1	4.8	20.5	10.3	11 510	140	523	23 727	37.3
Henrico	6 026	0.1	18.1	12.6	74.0	12.8	20.5	25.6	7.8	38 588	157	1 804	94 539	34.2
Henry	(15)1 082	(15)0.4	(15)D	(15)48.3	(15)D	(15)9.1	(15)3.6	(15)15.9	(15)11.1	12 178	219	1 123	23 169	10.5
Highland	20	10.0	D	23.8	D	4.5	4.4	16.8	18.1	621	248	49	1 759	20.2
Isle of Wight	489	1.1	D	60.6	D	3.7	D	6.8	8.0	4 893	167	557	9 753	26.6
James City County	(16)1 128	(16)0.0	(16)17.2	(16)11.0	(16)59.2	(16)13.6	(16)9.5	(16)32.5	(16)23.6	7 386	167	234	14 330	65.2
King and Queen	35	-6.7	35.3	21.2	D	4.1	D	10.5	43.4	1 215	186	165	2 698	7.5
King George	517	-0.2	4.6	1.9	27.1	1.8	0.9	21.8	68.4	1 833	106	181	5 280	32.1
King William	136	-0.9	54.6	45.1	32.7	7.6	5.4	12.7	13.7	2 136	167	184	4 193	21.9
Lancaster	125	-0.3	13.3	4.2	75.1	12.4	10.7	41.9	11.8	3 804	334	234	5 918	15.9
Lee	157	2.3	28.5	10.9	45.4	8.8	3.8	24.7	23.7	6 557	275	2 011	10 263	6.3
Loudoun	2 931	0.1	17.6	7.1	63.1	8.2	4.0	28.5	19.2	10 374	72	577	32 932	66.8

1. Covers mining, construction, and manufacturing.   2. Covers private sector earnings in agricultural services, forestry, and fisheries; transportation and public utilities; wholesale trade; retail trade; finance, insurance, and real estate; and services.   3. Per 1,000 resident population estimated as of July 1 of the year shown.   4. Charlottesville included with Albemarle County.   5. Clifton Forge and Covington included with Alleghany County.   6. Staunton and Waynesboro included with Augusta County.   7. Bedford City included with Bedford County.   8. Lynchburg included with Campbell County.   9. Galax included with Carroll County.   10. Petersburg and Colonial Heights included with Dinwiddie County.   11. Fairfax City and Falls Church included with Fairfax County.   12. Winchester included with Frederick County.   13. Emporia included with Greensville County.   14. South Boston included with Halifax County.   15. Martinsville included with Henry County.   16. Williamsburg included with James City County.

STATE County	Housing units, 1990 (cont'd)								Civilian labor force, 1999				Civilian employment, 1990[5]		
	Occupied units							Substandard units[3] (percent)		Percent change, 1998–1999	Unemployment			Percent	
	Owner-occupied					Renter-occupied								Professional, managerial, and technical	Precision production, craft, and repair
				Owner cost as a percent of income											
	Total	Percent	Median value[1]	With a mortgage	Without a mortgage	Median rent[2]	Rent as percent of income		Total		Total	Rate[4]	Total		
	89	90	91	92	93	94	95	96	97	98	99	100	101	102	103
VERMONT—Cont'd															
Chittenden	48 439	64.4	117 500	21.8	13.7	526	27.0	1.7	90 240	3.1	1 718	1.9	72 417	39.7	9.4
Essex	2 344	78.3	56 500	18.5	13.9	319	25.0	4.0	2 888	1.3	171	5.9	2 489	18.4	16.5
Franklin	14 326	72.5	81 700	21.4	14.5	412	27.1	3.0	23 761	3.3	725	3.1	19 065	23.5	14.1
Grand Isle	2 018	77.7	105 100	21.6	15.1	462	24.8	1.9	3 452	7.2	171	5.0	2 538	28.6	15.5
Lamoille	7 397	69.8	89 900	23.2	15.8	414	28.2	3.1	12 120	1.8	488	4.0	9 709	29.0	13.0
Orange	9 455	77.6	86 400	22.7	15.2	417	25.6	4.0	15 836	1.7	377	2.4	12 992	28.5	13.9
Orleans	8 873	73.7	66 500	20.5	14.0	326	27.0	2.9	12 288	-2.1	772	6.3	10 627	22.6	13.6
Rutland	23 690	68.5	94 000	22.5	14.9	440	27.6	2.2	32 549	-0.7	1 219	3.7	30 798	27.1	13.4
Washington	20 948	68.7	89 900	21.1	14.8	411	25.6	2.1	31 781	3.3	1 068	3.4	27 345	34.1	11.3
Windham	16 264	64.2	97 200	22.1	15.9	458	27.0	3.2	23 530	-0.4	668	2.8	20 972	29.0	13.3
Windsor	21 523	69.4	97 300	21.8	15.8	457	27.0	2.4	31 797	1.1	806	2.5	27 245	30.4	14.1
VIRGINIA	2 291 830	66.3	91 000	21.9	12.5	495	25.8	4.1	3 521 965	1.0	97 964	2.8	3 028 362	33.8	11.5
Accomack	12 653	74.8	52 700	22.4	14.2	335	25.1	9.8	14 725	3.0	939	6.4	13 690	19.6	12.6
Albemarle	24 433	64.1	111 200	20.4	11.7	530	24.1	3.7	39 518	0.1	453	1.1	34 422	42.3	9.6
Alleghany	4 942	82.1	50 100	14.7	12.2	293	22.6	6.0	6 397	-3.8	378	5.9	6 060	18.7	15.8
Amelia	3 131	80.5	54 900	18.7	11.6	327	18.6	8.9	5 190	2.0	129	2.5	4 213	15.6	15.9
Amherst	9 827	78.6	56 900	16.2	11.7	327	19.9	4.9	14 539	1.7	257	1.8	13 342	19.7	13.9
Appomattox	4 531	81.1	51 000	15.9	11.8	295	23.9	5.2	5 476	-4.2	214	3.9	5 810	19.0	16.2
Arlington	78 520	44.6	231 000	21.5	11.7	703	25.9	5.4	109 319	2.5	1 692	1.5	105 584	55.0	5.1
Augusta	19 781	80.5	70 500	17.9	11.8	357	21.8	4.5	32 466	1.6	751	2.3	27 611	20.8	15.3
Bath	1 895	76.6	46 700	18.6	11.3	312	18.4	7.0	2 366	1.2	111	4.7	2 177	22.9	12.8
Bedford	17 292	85.8	75 800	18.0	11.3	346	20.3	3.6	29 774	1.8	612	2.1	23 433	24.7	14.8
Bland	2 244	84.8	43 800	19.7	11.2	235	14.7	6.5	3 462	-1.9	158	4.6	2 751	15.9	14.8
Botetourt	9 148	85.7	73 400	18.0	12.1	329	18.2	4.1	16 268	-1.3	299	1.8	12 895	25.0	13.3
Brunswick	5 499	74.8	42 900	17.2	13.6	232	22.1	11.6	7 707	5.5	311	4.0	6 421	15.8	13.6
Buchanan	11 061	80.8	41 700	21.7	11.8	270	22.1	6.6	8 364	-7.7	1 161	13.9	9 887	17.8	28.0
Buckingham	4 341	78.2	44 900	18.0	13.5	266	24.9	11.7	6 003	-2.9	247	4.1	5 178	17.3	14.4
Campbell	17 952	77.5	61 800	16.5	11.6	330	21.0	4.2	26 517	2.0	581	2.2	24 048	23.0	15.5
Caroline	6 631	80.0	64 700	21.8	13.4	400	21.4	11.8	10 629	4.9	348	3.3	9 055	18.1	16.0
Carroll	10 463	82.7	44 000	16.1	11.8	268	22.3	6.4	13 910	0.8	956	6.9	12 641	15.9	15.5
Charles City County	2 161	86.2	52 100	20.9	12.2	358	16.9	9.6	3 694	0.5	104	2.8	3 152	14.4	14.1
Charlotte	4 312	77.9	43 100	21.6	12.3	224	19.4	11.4	5 961	0.8	188	3.2	5 182	13.3	12.9
Chesterfield	73 441	79.5	87 200	20.5	12.1	541	24.3	1.3	137 430	0.3	2 723	2.0	113 694	36.1	11.9
Clarke	4 236	74.2	104 300	22.3	12.4	441	21.3	5.7	6 522	-1.6	96	1.5	6 190	22.8	16.6
Craig	1 676	83.1	49 500	17.1	12.6	278	17.2	5.8	1 980	-11.9	87	4.4	2 111	17.0	17.7
Culpeper	9 757	67.3	95 200	22.3	13.0	514	24.0	5.4	16 171	1.3	323	2.0	13 524	25.0	15.5
Cumberland	2 813	79.3	50 600	18.5	11.4	338	25.7	13.1	3 835	1.2	75	2.0	3 637	20.1	12.2
Dickenson	6 457	81.4	39 300	24.1	12.2	262	29.5	8.0	5 599	-3.9	669	11.9	5 076	19.5	22.2
Dinwiddie	7 492	80.1	56 900	17.0	12.5	352	23.0	5.5	11 704	0.5	308	2.6	10 218	19.6	16.8
Essex	3 258	78.9	68 200	21.5	12.7	376	22.2	8.2	4 498	1.6	199	4.4	4 022	21.6	15.8
Fairfax	292 345	70.7	213 800	23.4	11.7	834	26.4	3.4	532 775	1.5	8 415	1.6	468 776	51.9	6.3
Fauquier	16 509	73.3	146 500	23.5	12.3	634	24.1	3.5	28 240	1.3	416	1.5	25 531	31.9	14.0
Floyd	4 763	84.1	51 000	20.1	12.7	270	25.4	7.5	6 735	3.9	296	4.4	5 637	17.3	16.9
Fluvanna	4 518	79.8	75 100	20.7	12.7	429	24.6	6.8	9 228	3.1	110	1.2	6 178	24.5	16.3
Franklin	14 655	81.2	63 400	19.4	11.6	281	18.1	5.0	25 783	5.3	1 045	4.1	20 091	18.0	15.5
Frederick	16 470	79.1	90 100	21.4	12.0	456	21.3	5.6	32 210	-1.8	675	2.1	23 845	25.2	16.5
Giles	6 461	80.5	46 300	16.9	11.4	282	22.9	4.8	8 442	1.1	517	6.1	7 652	18.5	16.1
Gloucester	10 966	80.5	84 000	23.5	13.5	444	27.6	4.0	17 977	1.9	419	2.3	14 091	27.6	18.5
Goochland	4 880	84.2	90 100	20.1	13.2	461	21.5	5.8	9 211	0.2	152	1.7	7 028	29.6	13.0
Grayson	6 468	82.5	39 700	17.1	11.7	241	22.0	7.1	8 061	-0.3	472	5.9	7 843	13.6	14.2
Greene	3 749	76.8	73 700	21.6	13.3	419	24.0	7.4	7 436	3.2	110	1.5	5 473	23.1	19.3
Greensville	3 150	78.6	45 200	20.0	12.8	258	16.8	11.4	5 479	-2.0	163	3.0	3 939	15.8	13.9
Halifax	10 728	76.9	45 200	16.6	13.1	227	19.2	12.9	18 622	2.5	1 176	6.3	13 568	14.5	14.6
Hanover	22 628	83.5	91 300	18.6	12.1	526	23.9	2.6	45 728	2.9	707	1.5	34 407	30.2	14.5
Henrico	89 138	63.8	83 900	20.4	12.6	509	24.4	1.5	139 926	0.0	2 698	1.9	120 294	35.5	9.8
Henry	21 771	77.9	51 800	16.0	11.7	314	19.7	4.4	27 738	-0.7	1 787	6.4	29 513	15.0	14.1
Highland	1 081	81.2	51 400	20.4	11.5	269	17.1	9.0	1 290	1.0	34	2.6	1 293	15.4	13.8
Isle of Wight	9 032	79.5	83 200	21.4	13.0	363	24.3	5.4	15 056	2.2	405	2.7	11 740	23.6	18.5
James City County	12 968	73.3	119 500	22.2	11.5	528	25.8	2.2	24 330	3.5	486	2.0	17 537	38.1	10.9
King and Queen	2 339	81.9	55 600	17.5	13.6	375	18.4	8.7	2 984	1.1	91	3.0	2 919	15.8	18.1
King George	4 736	69.6	90 000	22.2	12.0	491	23.1	5.3	8 507	1.1	165	1.9	6 603	36.7	15.4
King William	3 834	81.2	70 200	21.2	13.4	364	18.5	7.7	6 304	2.9	150	2.4	5 504	26.0	14.3
Lancaster	4 564	81.7	90 000	22.4	13.0	431	23.7	6.7	5 208	3.1	484	9.3	4 236	23.1	13.5
Lee	9 231	75.7	34 400	20.4	12.7	267	29.7	10.4	9 631	-2.1	849	8.8	7 927	17.2	15.7
Loudoun	30 490	73.3	170 200	25.4	13.5	813	25.6	2.0	84 158	7.5	1 010	1.2	50 525	42.4	10.1

1. Specified owner-occupied units. 2. Specified renter-occupied units. 3. Overcrowded or lacking complete plumbing facilities. 4. Percent of civilian labor force. 5. Persons 16 years and older.

Table B. States and Counties — Nonfarm Employment and Agriculture

STATE County	Number of establishments	Total	Health Care and Social Assistance	Manufacturing	Retail trade	Finance and Insurance	Professional Scientific and Technical Services	Total (mil dol)	Average per employee (dollars)	Number	Less than 50 acres	500 acres and over	Whose principal occupation is farming (percent)
	104	105	106	107	108	109	110	111	112	113	114	115	116
VERMONT—Cont'd													
Chittenden	5 257	76 889	9 667	15 441	11 240	3 318	4 577	2 198	28 584	456	35.7	7.2	49.6
Essex	142	1 343	D	884	56	D	8	33	24 672	79	15.2	17.7	70.9
Franklin	1 045	10 508	1 838	2 961	1 715	253	215	255	24 234	740	18.5	12.8	64.6
Grand Isle	172	521	D	28	131	D	29	10	19 395	107	29.0	13.1	64.5
Lamoille	970	8 932	1 203	715	1 399	195	201	161	17 985	297	31.0	6.1	46.8
Orange	746	6 423	1 486	1 303	1 029	180	211	134	20 809	537	20.9	6.9	55.3
Orleans	820	6 870	1 267	1 572	1 209	220	108	141	20 556	569	18.5	11.8	66.3
Rutland	2 259	25 956	3 357	4 605	4 426	729	747	596	22 950	530	23.4	12.8	55.3
Washington	2 226	23 672	3 227	2 876	3 773	2 017	806	563	23 791	344	28.8	3.5	51.7
Windham	1 827	22 321	2 490	3 587	2 897	895	487	534	23 945	305	34.8	4.6	47.9
Windsor	2 255	19 794	2 804	3 558	2 804	467	939	471	23 809	558	30.8	5.4	46.1
VIRGINIA	172 182	2 700 589	293 642	368 397	381 550	131 159	252 923	81 261	30 090	41 095	32.0	9.0	44.8
Accomack	825	8 587	751	3 154	1 345	249	506	146	16 954	268	38.1	21.3	64.2
Albemarle	1 788	20 733	1 850	2 234	3 940	719	1 160	468	22 559	747	30.4	10.4	44.2
Alleghany	162	2 703	730	732	414	D	13	64	23 646	160	22.5	5.6	27.5
Amelia	253	1 681	117	292	251	D	48	34	19 946	336	24.1	11.6	44.9
Amherst	578	8 613	D	1 523	1 371	165	116	190	22 069	406	21.4	9.9	36.5
Appomattox	268	2 911	150	1 241	524	77	D	54	18 411	353	16.1	8.8	40.2
Arlington	5 141	110 040	6 621	520	9 453	2 070	26 263	4 811	43 723	1	100.0	0.0	100.0
Augusta	1 189	16 609	2 521	5 412	1 760	205	308	456	27 473	1 499	36.6	9.1	48.3
Bath	138	721	115	D	111	D	D	20	27 178	129	14.7	28.7	51.9
Bedford	805	7 039	277	1 776	706	74	387	172	24 391	1 198	27.4	6.1	39.6
Bland	106	1 479	93	703	97	D	D	38	25 513	346	21.7	11.6	46.2
Botetourt	585	6 395	283	1 191	795	144	145	168	26 286	505	26.9	7.9	43.4
Brunswick	337	3 730	151	796	440	D	D	69	18 539	294	20.1	13.9	50.3
Buchanan	657	7 055	913	366	1 015	212	326	198	27 995	70	42.9	1.4	21.4
Buckingham	229	1 887	453	305	257	29	58	37	19 629	370	20.8	8.4	45.4
Campbell	1 025	14 341	496	5 197	2 085	200	304	318	22 190	621	18.4	10.8	44.9
Caroline	359	2 672	130	404	644	184	D	55	20 683	179	31.3	18.4	44.1
Carroll	477	5 631	471	2 441	914	57	81	102	18 093	913	33.8	3.0	34.9
Charles City County	108	1 312	D	171	18	D	12	35	26 571	59	30.5	37.3	47.5
Charlotte	246	2 643	110	1 271	267	58	D	51	19 199	493	20.5	12.4	47.5
Chesterfield	5 516	74 635	4 957	10 363	14 946	3 250	3 317	2 054	27 523	159	47.8	7.5	32.7
Clarke	287	2 865	200	1 199	272	87	77	71	24 889	325	31.1	10.5	47.4
Craig	60	404	D	D	25	D	5	6	15 433	176	17.6	11.9	44.3
Culpeper	808	9 723	1 261	1 509	1 877	509	763	250	25 682	521	32.4	10.6	46.4
Cumberland	131	811	103	81	229	D	26	15	18 617	248	20.6	12.5	44.0
Dickenson	279	2 091	206	93	451	62	60	48	23 163	102	39.2	2.0	29.4
Dinwiddie	274	4 152	D	320	439	115	D	97	23 354	351	25.9	11.7	43.9
Essex	320	3 727	546	1 180	815	169	78	72	19 345	114	21.1	36.0	63.2
Fairfax	24 581	444 700	30 425	12 857	48 276	21 603	103 579	19 940	44 839	121	60.3	4.1	43.0
Fauquier	1 485	12 364	1 758	966	2 058	535	759	307	24 860	957	35.2	10.3	47.6
Floyd	240	1 788	176	578	331	D	57	30	16 623	731	25.4	5.6	43.4
Fluvanna	302	1 964	221	71	252	25	62	42	21 195	256	19.5	9.0	42.2
Franklin	935	10 780	574	4 616	1 701	220	185	237	21 984	890	23.5	7.8	47.2
Frederick	1 175	17 176	1 376	4 298	2 414	285	527	424	24 700	568	31.0	7.9	42.8
Giles	320	5 000	466	2 677	649	89	78	133	26 628	341	20.8	8.2	41.6
Gloucester	766	6 199	1 010	423	1 451	157	218	105	16 876	108	45.4	12.0	50.9
Goochland	422	3 211	234	D	398	286	112	82	25 513	229	35.8	10.5	40.6
Grayson	183	1 793	65	1 009	181	73	15	37	20 864	854	35.6	7.1	37.6
Greene	238	1 512	188	D	284	29	80	31	20 443	198	22.2	6.6	49.0
Greensville	128	1 897	D	767	119	0	D	38	20 292	134	20.1	23.9	61.2
Halifax	798	11 535	1 349	4 140	1 569	180	101	250	21 634	940	21.7	11.1	53.7
Hanover	2 590	30 817	1 536	3 777	4 162	824	914	797	25 847	501	39.1	8.6	45.5
Henrico	7 199	138 869	15 888	10 309	19 294	19 676	6 609	4 331	31 188	154	49.4	6.5	35.1
Henry	916	15 315	605	7 699	2 179	309	112	331	21 587	288	27.4	6.2	38.5
Highland	98	405	16	D	32	D	D	6	15 684	283	11.0	17.0	53.7
Isle of Wight	532	9 369	412	4 536	975	140	181	248	26 465	190	24.7	32.6	65.8
James City County	1 017	10 880	696	1 119	1 998	178	671	252	23 183	58	48.3	10.3	46.6
King and Queen	97	592	22	139	47	D	22	11	18 475	127	15.7	18.1	52.8
King George	349	3 984	210	269	342	93	1 693	121	30 278	139	29.5	11.5	40.3
King William	293	3 118	238	1 108	482	132	78	101	32 426	123	17.9	26.0	48.0
Lancaster	479	3 629	915	139	655	234	165	77	21 334	70	25.7	14.3	60.0
Lee	366	3 867	856	763	610	186	57	76	19 690	1 106	37.9	2.9	43.9
Loudoun	3 920	50 489	3 684	3 459	7 256	1 753	4 903	1 696	33 585	1 032	53.3	7.4	38.3

Table B. States and Counties — **Agriculture, Land, and Water**

STATE County	Agriculture, 1997 (cont'd)														
	Land in farms					Value of land and buildings		Value of machinery and equipment Average per farm ($1,000)	Value of products sold				Percent of farms with sales of —		Percent of land owned by Fed. Gov. 1997	Water consumption 1995 (mil gal/day)
	Acreage (1,000)	Percent change, 1992–1997	Average size of farm	Total irrigated (1,000)	Total cropland (1,000)	Average per farm ($1,000)	Average per acre (dollars)		Total (mil dol)	Average per farm (dollars)	Crops (Percent from)	Livestock and poultry products (Percent from)	$10,000 or more	$100,000 or more		
	117	118	119	120	121	122	123	124	125	126	127	128	129	130	131	132
VERMONT—Cont'd																
Chittenden	83	0.4	183	0	42	443	2 214	42	26	56 017	28.9	71.1	41.4	16.2	3.1	20.1
Essex	25	41.7	323	D	9	303	939	54	7	85 687	19.2	80.8	54.4	19.0	0.0	2.5
Franklin	190	-6.8	257	0	99	328	1 247	63	100	134 608	4.3	95.7	66.6	40.4	1.5	7.7
Grand Isle	21	-15.9	197	0	16	474	2 463	89	10	89 766	11.2	88.8	48.6	28.0	0.0	7.0
Lamoille	49	19.4	165	0	20	252	1 626	28	15	52 087	14.1	85.9	43.4	17.2	0.0	4.2
Orange	98	5.8	183	D	42	256	1 509	40	26	48 565	16.9	83.1	46.0	17.9	0.2	3.2
Orleans	144	-3.9	253	0	74	285	1 193	60	60	104 607	6.4	93.6	61.7	29.0	0.0	4.6
Rutland	126	-5.4	237	0	53	295	1 278	41	28	53 504	11.3	88.7	50.0	18.5	11.6	15.8
Washington	56	-4.6	164	0	23	306	1 853	37	15	43 724	21.4	78.6	40.4	11.0	1.4	7.9
Windham	47	6.4	154	0	19	337	2 177	53	20	66 775	44.8	55.2	42.6	16.1	6.8	460.3
Windsor	90	0.0	161	0	30	324	2 098	27	20	35 520	22.6	77.4	33.5	6.6	4.0	10.6
VIRGINIA	8 228	-0.8	200	85	4 322	385	1 920	42	2 344	57 027	33.3	66.7	39.3	10.0	9.8	5 466.9
Accomack	92	0.5	345	9	75	560	1 722	93	85	316 601	41.4	58.6	70.9	41.4	2.2	8.9
Albemarle	172	-8.9	231	1	75	841	3 605	41	21	28 715	21.6	78.4	34.5	3.7	(1)2.9	16.5
Alleghany	31	19.5	194	D	13	239	1 185	38	2	13 323	10.6	89.4	22.5	1.2	(2)59.0	57.1
Amelia	78	12.1	234	1	37	312	1 367	37	58	171 259	7.1	92.9	39.3	18.5	0.0	2.3
Amherst	93	3.0	228	D	34	318	1 240	33	5	12 575	29.4	70.6	25.4	1.0	21.6	18.2
Appomattox	77	-3.0	217	0	39	224	1 014	30	7	19 161	27.9	72.1	34.8	4.2	0.6	1.9
Arlington	D	D	D	D	D	D	D	D	D	D	D	100.0	100.0	(3)NA	0.1
Augusta	282	-1.7	188	3	147	479	2 509	41	139	92 510	9.9	90.1	47.8	15.1	(4)34.9	17.5
Bath	58	24.0	452	D	21	577	1 333	32	2	15 586	13.7	86.2	35.7	3.1	56.9	2.1
Bedford	195	-3.0	163	1	102	283	1 877	33	20	16 490	12.6	87.4	25.0	3.3	(5)5.3	17.0
Bland	83	1.7	241		28	218	862	26	7	20 486	6.8	93.2	35.5	3.8	39.9	1.2
Botetourt	91	-6.7	179	0	41	333	1 870	37	11	21 253	16.5	83.5	27.9	4.2	39.6	18.4
Brunswick	79	-6.9	269	2	33	331	1 136	51	18	61 439	67.9	32.1	45.2	13.9	1.7	4.0
Buchanan	6	-30.0	90	D	2	D	D	26	0	4 874	58.7	41.3	11.4	0.0	0.0	3.6
Buckingham	76	14.9	205	D	38	329	1 576	27	18	48 876	4.8	95.2	30.8	7.8	0.0	2.3
Campbell	141	5.0	227	1	63	300	1 272	36	15	23 531	40.9	59.1	32.7	5.3	0.0	11.3
Caroline	55	6.5	310	1	39	524	1 706	62	12	64 799	86.4	13.6	40.8	15.6	21.7	3.1
Carroll	110	-2.5	121	0	63	170	1 466	28	18	20 108	24.7	75.3	32.6	3.6	(6)4.4	3.5
Charles City County	D	D	D	0	D	737	1 471	106	7	112 597	89.9	10.1	49.2	32.2	0.4	1.7
Charlotte	132	16.4	267	2	54	317	1 170	42	17	33 504	57.4	42.6	39.1	9.5	0.3	1.9
Chesterfield	20	18.5	127	0	10	374	2 952	44	9	53 730	60.1	39.9	27.0	8.2	(7)0.7	1 007.8
Clarke	71	5.0	220	0	48	877	4 171	38	13	40 174	33.6	66.4	40.9	8.9	0.0	2.0
Craig	46	1.5	260	0	20	365	1 251	34	3	14 970	10.1	89.9	38.6	2.3	62.1	0.6
Culpeper	115	0.0	221	1	72	539	2 598	50	22	41 424	35.3	64.7	38.2	7.5	0.0	3.8
Cumberland	61	-1.5	246	0	29	341	1 510	44	25	100 689	7.7	92.3	36.7	16.1	0.0	0.9
Dickenson	9	0.0	89	D	5	88	1 013	15	0	4 790	33.5	66.5	11.8	0.0	7.2	3.3
Dinwiddie	89	4.0	254	2	44	356	1 395	54	18	51 691	76.3	23.7	36.8	11.7	4.5	4.2
Essex	62	9.9	540	D	43	686	1 282	110	10	90 239	95.1	4.9	61.4	28.9	0.1	1.1
Fairfax	12	-23.0	102	0	4	375	3 403	35	5	43 245	68.5	31.5	18.2	5.8	(3)6.3	76.7
Fauquier	239	1.3	250	3	122	969	3 787	53	47	49 607	28.4	71.6	36.3	7.6	1.1	6.6
Floyd	123	4.8	168	0	61	227	1 523	41	30	41 126	38.7	61.3	37.6	4.9	2.0	1.6
Fluvanna	59	1.6	230	0	26	433	1 937	39	6	24 536	12.5	87.5	27.0	2.7	0.0	117.6
Franklin	159	-4.4	178	2	82	282	1 534	46	41	45 982	18.4	81.6	37.6	11.8	0.7	5.7
Frederick	100	2.0	176	0	60	466	2 640	40	21	36 144	69.6	30.4	30.5	7.2	(8)1.8	5.5
Giles	67	-7.9	197	0	28	300	1 183	38	4	12 089	13.0	87.0	30.5	1.2	32.9	309.3
Gloucester	23	-3.3	215	0	17	524	2 598	59	5	46 928	95.5	4.5	43.5	13.9	0.0	2.8
Goochland	47	-8.3	204	0	26	591	3 136	58	7	29 942	29.3	70.6	29.3	4.4	0.0	2.9
Grayson	136	0.2	160	0	65	233	1 462	22	19	22 616	21.1	78.9	38.4	4.7	19.0	2.1
Greene	34	-9.0	170	0	18	471	2 599	37	4	22 475	9.2	90.8	39.9	3.0	14.8	1.6
Greensville	58	14.4	435	0	40	423	963	69	14	107 949	88.9	11.1	65.7	31.3	(9)0.0	3.4
Halifax	228	-2.2	242	4	92	253	1 015	41	40	42 743	81.7	18.3	54.6	11.8	1.5	7.1
Hanover	98	2.3	196	3	61	570	2 678	49	29	57 338	75.6	24.4	39.9	10.8	0.1	26.4
Henrico	26	10.0	171	0	14	478	2 724	42	10	63 866	64.3	35.7	37.0	8.4	0.4	8.0
Henry	48	-1.2	168	1	24	242	1 384	36	8	27 834	39.2	60.8	23.3	3.5	(10)0.0	41.6
Highland	91	-5.8	323	D	35	374	1 247	36	12	43 308	2.2	97.8	54.1	7.8	21.9	5.9
Isle of Wight	88	2.4	463	2	61	740	1 558	106	41	215 922	51.9	48.1	77.9	38.4	0.0	56.3
James City County	9	-11.4	153	0	6	527	3 448	48	2	32 615	79.5	20.5	34.5	8.6	(11)3.4	33.0
King and Queen	51	-4.1	400	0	34	442	1 077	66	10	80 083	80.9	19.1	55.1	16.5	0.0	0.7
King George	34	-10.1	246	1	20	572	2 334	50	5	33 719	89.4	10.6	33.8	5.0	3.5	3.7
King William	56	-4.8	457	0	38	705	1 500	84	12	94 780	78.4	21.6	48.0	22.0	0.0	22.4
Lancaster	17	-14.0	246	D	14	539	2 193	57	3	47 016	97.5	2.5	68.6	15.7	0.0	2.3
Lee	127	-1.2	115	0	63	137	1 184	29	13	11 844	50.8	49.2	32.5	1.1	6.9	3.8
Loudoun	185	-5.1	179	1	117	918	4 746	49	26	25 173	42.5	57.5	31.9	5.0	0.1	18.2

1. Charlottesville included with Albemarle County.   2. Clifton Forge and Covington included with Alleghany County.   3. Arlington County, Alexandria City, Fairfax, and falls Church City included with Fairfax County.   4. Staunton and Waynesboro included with Augusta County.   5. Bedford City included with Bedford County.   6. Galax included with Carroll County.   7. Colonial Heights included with Chesterfield County.   8. Winchester included with Frederick County.   9. Emporia included with Greensville County.   10. Martinsville included with Henry County.   11. Williamsburg included with James City County.

Table B. States and Counties — Residential Construction, Wholesale and Retail Trade, and Real Estate

STATE County	Value of Residential Construction Authorized by Building Permits, 1999		Wholesale Trade, 1997				Retail Trade[1], 1997				Real Estate and Rental and Leasing, 1997			
	New Construction ($1,000)	Number of Housing Units	Number of Establishments	Number of Employees	Sales (mil dol)	Annual Payroll (mil dol)	Number of Establishments	Number of Employees	Sales (mil dol)	Annual Payroll (mil dol)	Number of Establishments	Number of Employees	Receipts (mil dol)	Annual Payroll (mil dol)
	133	134	135	136	137	138	139	140	141	142	143	144	145	146
VERMONT—Cont'd														
Chittenden	93 957	779	303	4 167	1 834.9	140.4	958	11 254	1 863.7	189.6	208	913	118.7	19.4
Essex	1 044	15	3	D	D	D	18	D	D	D	3	10	0.3	0.1
Franklin	27 313	285	49	582	381.6	15.8	237	1 734	324.4	28.6	37	102	7.8	1.3
Grand Isle	3 941	36	7	D	D	D	33	D	D	D	3	3	0.5	0.1
Lamoille	20 393	129	30	270	57.7	8.3	183	1 380	169.6	19.8	25	61	5.8	1.0
Orange	6 099	58	33	D	D	D	109	798	145.8	15.6	19	58	2.6	0.7
Orleans	5 943	69	36	D	D	D	174	1 161	220.4	19.9	18	27	2.7	0.3
Rutland	13 353	130	97	934	218.3	22.0	502	4 344	646.3	66.6	71	243	21.8	4.5
Washington	25 306	226	99	D	D	D	421	3 614	542.4	58.9	66	213	14.0	3.3
Windham	21 444	162	73	1 920	1 244.0	62.5	342	2 950	444.8	50.0	61	210	21.1	3.5
Windsor	33 370	250	87	704	242.9	19.1	372	2 559	415.5	44.7	76	219	17.5	3.7
VIRGINIA	5 142 222	53 151	7 868	106 365	61 046.7	3 784.4	29 032	379 039	62 569.9	6 202.6	6 717	43 976	5 749.2	1 028.4
Accomack	14 526	153	36	250	47.1	5.5	208	1 335	180.5	18.6	31	76	7.8	1.2
Albemarle	133 272	721	64	547	181.6	20.5	314	4 270	718.0	67.4	86	389	38.0	8.2
Alleghany	2 418	29	8	31	2.8	0.7	38	430	65.3	6.1	4	10	1.4	0.2
Amelia	9 247	91	9	167	41.1	4.8	36	226	41.0	4.0	3	6	0.9	0.1
Amherst	17 531	187	18	D	D	D	104	1 082	190.2	18.0	15	49	2.7	0.6
Appomattox	6 364	64	9	50	5.7	0.9	60	536	75.5	8.3	9	17	1.0	0.2
Arlington	56 523	970	110	1 208	819.8	57.2	665	10 098	1 819.4	188.7	257	3 137	690.6	84.2
Augusta	51 632	489	54	622	153.8	16.8	214	1 925	310.8	29.4	48	200	16.0	4.0
Bath	7 079	52	2	D	D	D	25	105	10.8	1.2	5	9	2.0	0.3
Bedford	71 445	560	34	170	281.9	4.8	92	604	83.9	10.0	28	55	6.9	0.9
Bland	1 831	39	6	D	D	D	18	145	19.8	1.4	NA	NA	NA	NA
Botetourt	29 781	231	34	464	213.9	12.5	81	796	130.2	11.0	17	47	2.6	0.5
Brunswick	4 507	51	7	54	27.6	1.3	60	455	49.6	5.3	4	D	D	D
Buchanan	3 281	58	34	296	140.3	8.7	130	1 018	135.2	13.7	14	32	2.4	0.9
Buckingham	3 726	45	5	16	6.6	0.3	42	254	34.4	3.7	7	D	D	D
Campbell	20 608	197	53	D	D	D	209	2 169	338.0	31.3	33	88	9.1	1.2
Caroline	10 925	117	16	74	27.8	2.0	69	608	118.4	8.5	10	26	2.0	0.3
Carroll	15 068	164	25	164	42.9	3.2	114	957	162.6	13.8	14	42	2.3	0.5
Charles City County	3 045	30	1	D	D	D	6	24	3.3	0.3	5	16	2.7	0.3
Charlotte	6 174	94	10	108	18.4	2.4	46	286	42.2	3.7	3	6	0.2	0.1
Chesterfield	254 184	2 753	372	3 154	1 447.5	116.3	938	15 275	2 412.6	230.7	201	1 151	183.9	27.9
Clarke	18 577	123	13	D	D	D	44	297	44.8	3.7	8	D	D	D
Craig	3 640	40	3	5	0.5	0.1	8	25	3.7	0.3	6	8	0.4	0.1
Culpeper	37 209	357	24	287	122.5	7.6	153	1 812	307.0	28.4	28	84	10.2	2.0
Cumberland	3 240	34	6	22	2.1	0.3	29	230	31.4	3.6	1	D	D	D
Dickenson	1 500	25	6	30	4.7	1.2	71	447	64.2	6.1	2	D	D	D
Dinwiddie	16 615	136	9	D	D	D	44	514	64.5	6.0	4	4	0.9	0.1
Essex	6 547	67	7	46	21.4	1.2	68	787	126.0	12.1	13	44	2.6	0.6
Fairfax	625 926	7 494	1 142	18 462	15 659.4	944.7	3 025	48 037	9 261.0	980.6	1 050	9 310	1 481.0	273.7
Fauquier	76 169	466	45	434	171.6	13.8	223	2 052	353.1	36.6	46	150	14.8	3.0
Floyd	8 175	102	6	18	10.7	0.4	45	364	55.3	4.3	7	8	0.8	0.1
Fluvanna	33 729	300	10	D	D	D	33	196	24.5	2.6	9	D	D	D
Franklin	62 363	387	33	186	85.4	5.2	180	1 707	257.7	23.4	20	99	9.8	1.8
Frederick	45 630	452	82	1 246	302.0	33.2	211	2 574	464.7	46.1	35	160	14.6	3.2
Giles	7 041	74	6	D	D	D	71	563	91.2	8.2	10	18	1.7	0.2
Gloucester	21 254	203	30	360	42.5	5.6	134	1 505	228.1	20.7	33	102	8.1	1.5
Goochland	38 845	260	25	168	72.8	4.9	50	391	72.5	6.7	11	15	2.7	0.4
Grayson	9 407	141	3	5	0.9	0.1	38	176	33.4	2.3	9	9	0.3	0.1
Greene	17 729	210	5	D	D	D	37	254	33.8	4.1	7	D	D	D
Greensville	5 232	109	10	45	18.4	0.9	26	179	23.0	1.9	4	21	1.1	0.2
Halifax	8 856	96	24	262	76.9	5.3	164	1 570	215.9	20.6	26	74	7.1	1.0
Hanover	113 269	1 119	240	4 199	3 044.5	150.2	309	4 693	830.0	80.6	72	249	33.0	5.2
Henrico	227 974	2 347	474	7 602	5 902.5	310.0	1 148	19 119	2 974.4	302.4	323	2 167	285.9	54.1
Henry	15 286	129	45	408	136.4	9.8	240	2 263	346.3	30.7	21	67	6.0	1.1
Highland	766	12	5	D	D	D	18	36	4.1	0.3	NA	NA	NA	NA
Isle of Wight	34 828	280	28	D	D	D	97	1 049	141.9	12.4	27	141	12.6	2.5
James City County	137 431	965	27	71	27.0	2.2	190	2 064	303.8	31.0	50	517	29.6	8.8
King and Queen	2 351	24	1	D	D	D	9	40	5.2	0.5	1	D	D	D
King George	19 187	174	7	46	7.3	0.9	48	306	53.2	4.8	15	D	D	D
King William	11 135	136	7	D	D	D	58	485	88.8	8.9	5	7	0.7	0.3
Lancaster	15 188	109	26	171	38.4	3.4	89	687	98.5	10.9	14	24	3.1	0.4
Lee	7 456	133	18	171	47.0	1.5	90	578	86.4	7.7	9	16	0.8	0.1
Loudoun	560 146	6 071	177	1 773	1 301.3	70.8	478	6 933	1 282.0	129.0	143	770	241.5	20.9

1. Establishments with payroll.

STATE County	Professional, Scientific, and Technical Services[1], 1997				Manufacturing, 1997				Accommodation and Foodservices, 1997			
	Number of Establishments	Number of Employees	Receipts (mil dol)	Annual Payroll (mil dol)	Number of Establishments	Number of Employees	Receipts (mil dol)	Annual Payroll (mil dol)	Number of Establishments	Number of Employees	Sales (mil dol)	Annual Payroll (mil dol)
	147	148	149	150	151	152	153	154	155	156	157	158
VERMONT—Cont'd												
Chittenden	514	3 854	429.4	157.5	234	14 302	3 942.1	624.0	392	6 211	207.7	61.1
Essex	4	3	0.7	0.3	11	883	86.0	25.7	21	D	D	D
Franklin	50	174	11.7	5.1	68	2 603	546.6	78.8	93	854	25.1	7.1
Grand Isle	9	16	0.9	0.3	NA	NA	NA	NA	21	D	D	D
Lamoille	78	166	11.3	4.3	51	697	85.2	18.0	112	3 415	122.2	36.5
Orange	56	164	12.0	5.0	58	1 220	128.5	29.3	58	626	20.8	6.4
Orleans	39	105	5.9	2.5	45	1 565	138.1	37.2	68	867	23.8	7.4
Rutland	155	580	42.7	19.8	123	4 635	542.2	150.5	234	3 358	108.6	31.7
Washington	191	729	54.3	21.9	152	2 901	446.2	84.7	176	2 200	63.0	20.2
Windham	124	442	29.1	10.8	120	3 473	442.8	99.5	218	3 194	106.1	36.6
Windsor	181	849	71.7	30.1	155	3 300	417.1	103.2	216	2 458	92.6	28.9
VIRGINIA	17 539	212 632	24 151.7	9 729.8	5 986	370 595	83 814.0	11 557.8	12 343	233 639	8 281.2	2 320.7
Accomack	42	476	49.7	16.0	32	3 209	244.5	52.6	100	892	32.9	9.0
Albemarle	178	1 030	80.9	32.2	54	D	D	D	140	3 054	114.8	35.1
Alleghany	3	7	0.5	0.2	NA	NA	NA	NA	15	199	6.9	2.3
Amelia	7	24	0.8	0.3	NA	NA	NA	NA	7	78	2.2	0.6
Amherst	27	80	4.7	2.0	44	1 678	395.1	53.8	44	615	19.3	4.9
Appomattox	10	34	2.3	0.5	18	1 216	112.7	28.5	19	185	5.6	1.5
Arlington	1 197	25 914	3 024.7	1 298.6	57	509	59.5	16.3	473	11 365	617.7	164.6
Augusta	56	280	15.6	6.0	66	5 372	1 312.4	175.1	66	1 112	33.0	10.0
Bath	7	13	1.3	0.2	3	D	D	D	16	81	2.6	0.9
Bedford	53	270	24.5	9.2	45	1 489	262.0	49.7	27	D	D	D
Bland	3	8	0.3	0.1	7	656	85.5	15.8	3	D	D	D
Botetourt	28	101	5.9	2.7	23	1 422	210.4	39.3	34	723	27.6	7.6
Brunswick	13	34	1.5	0.7	19	937	84.3	18.7	12	D	D	D
Buchanan	32	310	9.4	3.4	NA	NA	NA	NA	25	304	9.8	2.6
Buckingham	10	116	4.2	2.0	NA	NA	NA	NA	4	D	D	D
Campbell	51	243	29.5	9.4	62	5 098	1 383.7	123.5	55	D	D	D
Caroline	12	24	1.7	0.5	NA	NA	NA	NA	28	292	11.9	3.2
Carroll	20	64	3.3	1.0	35	2 430	286.3	45.3	41	498	15.6	4.0
Charles City County	2	D	D	D	10	680	62.2	16.0	6	D	D	D
Charlotte	8	33	1.2	0.3	15	1 178	143.6	25.4	13	117	3.1	1.0
Chesterfield	499	2 644	218.8	93.0	164	10 166	2 671.2	412.6	326	6 966	222.5	61.7
Clarke	18	47	4.4	1.5	13	1 167	190.3	33.7	20	D	D	D
Craig	2	D	D	D	NA	NA	NA	NA	4	D	D	D
Culpeper	50	620	46.6	17.0	28	1 484	278.9	45.3	52	629	22.0	5.9
Cumberland	7	14	0.6	0.2	NA	NA	NA	NA	4	19	0.4	0.1
Dickenson	11	65	2.8	1.6	NA	NA	NA	NA	13	99	3.0	0.8
Dinwiddie	7	D	D	D	NA	NA	NA	NA	16	154	5.9	1.3
Essex	17	66	2.9	1.2	18	1 140	119.4	24.8	23	356	12.4	3.8
Fairfax	4 748	88 929	11 813.4	4 743.6	478	13 181	2 594.5	551.9	1 523	31 596	1 368.8	382.6
Fauquier	131	561	53.4	23.7	36	867	107.8	25.7	70	1 415	47.6	13.9
Floyd	13	23	1.8	0.6	22	547	48.0	11.2	14	D	D	D
Fluvanna	22	47	2.3	0.9	NA	NA	NA	NA	9	107	5.0	1.5
Franklin	43	128	7.4	2.2	66	4 677	519.6	113.0	52	560	16.4	4.8
Frederick	50	441	13.1	5.9	69	3 416	741.1	97.0	72	1 317	45.6	12.8
Giles	11	65	2.8	1.6	15	2 731	538.6	90.5	17	187	6.1	1.7
Gloucester	46	172	9.7	3.8	NA	NA	NA	NA	43	686	19.3	5.1
Goochland	30	49	3.4	1.3	NA	NA	NA	NA	15	173	3.9	1.1
Grayson	7	34	0.8	0.4	18	1 085	123.4	25.8	14	65	1.8	0.6
Greene	9	37	4.7	1.7	NA	NA	NA	NA	10	134	4.5	1.3
Greensville	3	D	D	D	5	733	120.3	15.0	14	221	6.6	1.8
Halifax	32	102	5.6	1.9	42	4 707	652.9	113.8	61	773	23.7	5.9
Hanover	194	769	69.7	24.6	150	3 803	579.7	111.8	110	2 053	69.0	19.2
Henrico	726	5 767	519.4	238.5	216	10 857	2 432.3	379.0	458	9 892	350.6	96.8
Henry	29	97	4.5	1.2	70	7 970	858.4	189.1	73	1 105	31.6	8.4
Highland	3	3	0.1	0.0	NA	NA	NA	NA	6	50	1.0	0.3
Isle of Wight	22	145	8.6	4.0	17	4 698	1 546.8	106.6	34	D	D	D
James City County	106	541	40.2	16.7	26	D	D	D	77	1 715	74.6	21.0
King and Queen	1	D	D	D	NA	NA	NA	NA	2	D	D	D
King George	66	1 401	159.2	56.9	NA	NA	NA	NA	18	D	D	D
King William	17	55	2.5	0.9	13	1 114	357.2	56.5	10	136	3.9	1.1
Lancaster	36	117	9.5	4.0	NA	NA	NA	NA	25	452	17.4	6.2
Lee	20	49	2.6	0.8	17	784	70.8	10.8	18	200	5.7	1.5
Loudoun	530	3 624	618.6	187.5	128	3 459	480.8	132.8	212	3 877	154.8	45.8

1. Firms subject to federal tax.

Table B. States and Counties — Health and Other Services and Federal Funds

STATE County	Health Care and Social Assistance[1], 1997				Other Services[1], 1997				Federal funds and grants, fiscal 1999[2] Expenditures (mil dol)			
										Direct payments for individuals[3]		
	Number of Establishments	Number of Employees	Receipts (mil dol)	Annual Payroll (mil dol)	Number of Establishments	Number of Employees	Receipts (mil dol)	Annual Payroll (mil dol)	Total	Social Security and government retirement	Medicare	Food stamps and Supplemental Security Income
	159	160	161	162	163	164	165	166	167	168	169	170
VERMONT—Cont'd												
Chittenden	372	3 978	242.3	105.6	284	1 439	96.3	28.3	777.7	202.3	63.5	13.7
Essex	3	D	D	D	4	D	D	D	31.9	14.8	4.8	1.2
Franklin	72	746	32.1	14.4	73	219	13.6	3.7	189.1	67.6	23.9	7.0
Grand Isle	6	D	D	D	5	D	D	D	23.6	12.2	3.7	0.6
Lamoille	49	468	23.5	8.9	53	143	10.1	2.4	83.7	35.9	12.3	2.7
Orange	34	D	D	D	46	134	11.4	2.5	101.1	47.7	15.5	3.5
Orleans	30	390	14.2	7.0	60	131	10.7	2.1	120.8	51.6	17.1	5.4
Rutland	147	1 376	77.7	34.7	132	737	30.3	9.0	286.5	128.7	47.1	10.5
Washington	134	1 062	60.6	27.0	124	354	26.3	5.8	463.7	111.1	34.0	8.1
Windham	103	591	34.1	14.1	84	345	33.9	6.3	165.1	81.6	29.0	4.9
Windsor	92	621	36.5	13.9	114	365	26.9	6.4	315.5	122.0	40.1	6.7
VIRGINIA	12 014	150 797	9 859.6	4 417.9	11 301	68 807	4 397.2	1 360.3	57 842.2	14 903.1	3 854.8	843.6
Accomack	29	160	7.7	2.7	49	133	7.9	1.8	276.8	84.6	29.5	7.4
Albemarle	130	1 393	79.6	35.6	90	572	35.7	12.4	187.9	97.5	42.2	3.4
Alleghany	28	752	51.8	20.3	9	46	2.3	0.7	31.5	11.2	2.4	1.4
Amelia	8	110	3.5	1.8	23	44	2.6	0.6	37.6	19.5	5.3	1.6
Amherst	27	462	16.0	5.5	54	169	9.7	2.6	102.8	60.0	15.8	3.0
Appomattox	15	129	3.9	1.5	19	47	2.8	0.7	45.9	26.1	6.8	1.7
Arlington	321	5 064	393.6	160.4	355	1 996	141.4	40.0	5 669.1	424.3	96.8	13.3
Augusta	70	756	61.4	24.9	62	235	15.3	4.5	144.9	81.2	28.0	3.4
Bath	5	16	1.2	0.6	2	D	D	D	25.8	12.5	6.1	0.4
Bedford	28	224	11.3	5.4	25	111	5.4	1.9	178.4	122.1	25.4	5.0
Bland	7	89	4.4	1.7	5	26	3.6	0.7	26.4	14.5	6.0	0.7
Botetourt	28	280	10.0	4.1	49	175	10.5	2.5	92.4	58.5	15.2	1.4
Brunswick	9	120	4.1	1.9	23	94	3.7	1.2	74.6	35.1	14.0	3.8
Buchanan	35	470	22.1	8.7	40	140	8.8	2.3	157.8	90.7	28.6	10.1
Buckingham	10	332	12.8	5.3	14	34	2.4	0.5	51.2	23.0	9.9	2.7
Campbell	46	330	15.1	5.2	72	321	16.8	5.6	166.1	75.9	19.9	5.8
Caroline	11	118	4.3	1.9	27	130	10.2	2.5	88.9	46.6	13.8	2.5
Carroll	29	435	17.5	8.3	26	100	8.5	1.9	92.8	47.7	18.7	4.8
Charles City County	1	D	D	D	5	22	0.9	0.2	22.3	10.9	4.2	0.9
Charlotte	4	99	3.1	1.2	13	40	1.8	0.4	69.9	34.0	11.1	3.1
Chesterfield	383	4 392	241.1	118.4	342	2 383	175.8	50.1	414.1	239.2	65.0	13.3
Clarke	14	192	6.9	3.6	17	58	3.6	1.2	40.7	24.0	7.0	0.8
Craig	4	D	D	D	2	D	D	D	20.7	9.8	2.7	0.6
Culpeper	43	456	29.6	12.7	40	436	24.5	8.7	116.3	64.9	21.4	3.6
Cumberland	4	58	1.2	0.7	9	25	1.1	0.3	26.9	11.6	4.2	1.3
Dickenson	14	389	24.1	8.2	24	65	4.5	1.1	100.9	51.5	17.0	5.9
Dinwiddie	10	73	4.2	1.9	18	54	3.6	0.6	80.8	38.0	13.3	5.7
Essex	25	274	13.4	4.5	24	63	3.0	0.9	44.5	22.4	11.2	1.1
Fairfax	1 867	19 772	1 643.6	709.8	1 329	9 204	772.7	225.8	10 257.1	1 625.4	202.3	44.9
Fauquier	93	890	46.8	20.4	89	450	30.2	9.3	190.4	87.3	25.1	3.5
Floyd	15	155	5.0	2.2	13	34	2.3	0.4	44.2	25.3	9.0	1.4
Fluvanna	8	72	2.4	1.2	13	48	3.0	0.7	64.3	43.2	11.5	1.2
Franklin	35	503	21.9	9.8	75	224	13.0	3.3	140.7	82.7	24.8	4.6
Frederick	47	766	42.7	23.8	74	367	25.5	7.4	112.8	76.3	16.8	3.8
Giles	24	226	9.2	4.0	28	96	5.7	1.4	75.9	41.4	15.8	2.3
Gloucester	44	552	21.8	10.2	52	247	11.8	3.7	123.7	84.1	19.6	3.4
Goochland	18	100	4.5	2.4	18	43	3.4	0.8	46.4	23.1	7.4	1.2
Grayson	10	71	3.2	1.6	16	87	3.1	1.2	61.2	29.9	12.4	3.3
Greene	7	171	4.5	2.5	22	71	3.3	1.2	37.3	21.0	7.1	1.7
Greensville	4	D	D	D	5	11	1.3	0.3	20.7	8.6	2.8	1.6
Halifax	59	558	33.1	18.0	62	230	11.6	3.1	181.8	79.6	30.0	7.0
Hanover	124	1 273	70.8	35.3	180	1 032	64.0	20.6	229.7	149.0	43.1	3.0
Henrico	565	8 260	559.3	280.5	411	3 156	199.2	64.6	454.9	220.2	124.6	10.3
Henry	48	591	24.8	12.9	62	229	11.2	3.6	157.0	94.3	33.1	5.9
Highland	3	D	D	D	5	16	0.8	0.1	11.6	6.4	3.0	0.1
Isle of Wight	20	218	12.1	6.2	49	194	10.6	3.1	107.7	62.1	18.4	3.5
James City County	66	556	28.4	13.3	43	288	14.1	6.5	93.3	62.4	10.1	1.5
King and Queen	2	D	D	D	8	14	0.9	0.3	25.7	13.5	4.8	0.9
King George	16	188	10.2	3.4	24	91	6.2	1.5	596.1	38.9	7.5	1.4
King William	16	118	4.0	1.8	26	64	5.6	1.2	42.7	23.2	8.7	0.9
Lancaster	37	358	19.5	10.1	26	125	7.3	2.6	82.0	56.1	15.3	1.5
Lee	31	560	37.3	14.1	22	82	3.7	1.0	256.8	59.2	27.3	10.5
Loudoun	245	2 035	140.4	54.9	200	1 341	105.5	32.6	750.4	183.8	34.0	3.2

1. Firms subject to federal tax.   2. October 1, 1998 to September 30, 1999.   3. State totals may include programs not allocated by county.

	Federal funds and grants, fiscal 1999[1] (cont'd)							Local government finances, 1997				
	Expenditures (mil dol) (cont'd)							General revenue				
	Procurement contract awards		Grants[2]								Taxes	
												Per capita[3] (dollars)
STATE County	Salaries and wages	Defense	Other	Medicaid and other health-related	Nutrition and family welfare	Education	Other	Total (mil dol)	Intergovernmental	Total (mil dol)	Total	Property
	171	172	173	174	175	176	177	178	179	180	181	182
VERMONT—Cont'd												
Chittenden	103.2	193.5	14.3	98.3	16.3	8.6	40.8	279.6	48.0	177.9	1 258	1 224
Essex	3.4	0.0	1.3	4.2	1.3	0.3	0.7	12.2	5.0	6.2	939	920
Franklin	36.3	4.6	4.2	29.6	7.7	2.0	3.4	77.6	34.2	36.4	837	830
Grand Isle	1.2	0.1	0.3	2.6	0.7	0.2	1.5	11.1	1.7	8.5	1 375	1 363
Lamoille	3.8	0.0	1.0	13.1	2.8	1.4	7.4	43.2	11.4	27.5	1 285	1 279
Orange	5.4	0.1	1.8	15.3	3.7	1.5	5.2	54.2	19.3	31.4	1 131	1 125
Orleans	9.4	0.4	1.4	20.2	7.0	1.5	4.7	48.8	20.7	24.1	954	939
Rutland	17.3	0.5	3.8	47.7	10.1	2.2	13.3	122.3	34.2	73.8	1 177	1 166
Washington	19.4	1.2	3.9	49.5	54.2	34.1	137.6	113.9	35.3	65.5	1 161	1 156
Windham	9.3	0.8	3.8	18.1	8.0	2.3	5.6	100.5	19.7	70.8	1 653	1 643
Windsor	72.7	1.7	15.0	26.8	6.9	1.7	19.8	114.5	27.0	74.9	1 358	1 347
VIRGINIA	12 050.1	12 388.3	6 656.1	1 780.3	822.8	521.9	1 623.8	X	X	X	X	X
Accomack	38.1	10.8	70.8	19.2	5.6	1.7	4.6	63.8	30.3	25.0	778	599
Albemarle	3.6	1.8	1.8	10.5	2.1	2.1	21.8	134.9	41.9	78.4	1 011	737
Alleghany	0.3	1.2	0.2	4.4	1.6	0.7	8.1	33.0	14.3	12.5	1 012	830
Amelia	1.4	0.1	0.4	4.2	0.9	0.5	2.4	15.9	8.3	5.1	494	377
Amherst	2.7	0.1	8.3	8.1	1.6	0.9	1.7	39.6	21.1	14.5	485	333
Appomattox	2.0	0.0	0.4	5.3	1.0	0.5	1.1	18.5	11.0	6.3	486	339
Arlington	2 578.4	1 527.4	875.9	19.4	55.3	28.2	42.6	939.6	248.3	347.4	2 013	1 408
Augusta	5.5	0.2	2.1	10.6	2.3	1.7	6.9	93.9	43.2	36.7	594	392
Bath	1.7	0.0	0.3	1.8	0.4	0.2	2.3	13.9	3.3	9.4	1 900	1 768
Bedford	5.7	1.2	3.0	7.8	2.5	1.2	2.6	72.8	38.3	27.3	490	405
Bland	0.9	0.2	0.4	2.5	0.5	0.3	0.2	10.7	7.6	2.5	371	298
Botetourt	3.1	0.0	4.4	3.9	0.8	0.7	3.7	42.6	19.0	19.7	698	501
Brunswick	2.3	0.3	0.7	9.8	2.4	2.2	0.7	24.4	15.0	7.9	473	366
Buchanan	3.0	1.7	0.8	15.1	5.4	2.0	0.2	49.6	27.6	18.7	636	363
Buckingham	1.3	0.0	0.3	9.6	1.9	0.7	1.2	19.2	13.1	4.8	330	263
Campbell	6.0	0.8	2.8	11.8	3.4	2.1	36.1	74.0	37.6	27.0	537	402
Caroline	11.2	4.4	0.7	5.1	1.9	0.9	-0.2	32.5	17.4	13.5	623	477
Carroll	2.5	0.0	0.7	12.1	2.1	1.3	1.5	35.4	22.0	10.2	366	259
Charles City County	1.0	0.0	0.2	2.5	0.9	0.4	0.3	16.3	6.0	7.8	1 117	475
Charlotte	2.4	0.0	8.3	7.0	1.9	0.6	0.0	18.9	12.3	5.8	477	391
Chesterfield	21.2	5.6	6.5	8.4	6.7	6.2	39.5	509.3	174.1	257.0	1 058	826
Clarke	1.8	0.0	2.8	2.8	0.4	0.3	0.0	20.0	6.5	11.7	905	774
Craig	1.0	3.5	0.9	1.0	0.3	0.2	0.2	6.5	3.9	2.0	404	317
Culpeper	6.4	0.1	1.5	9.0	2.6	1.0	2.5	56.0	23.1	26.1	801	604
Cumberland	0.7	0.3	0.2	4.5	2.7	0.4	0.2	14.4	10.0	3.9	495	391
Dickenson	2.1	3.4	2.8	8.8	2.2	1.3	4.9	33.3	19.8	8.6	499	335
Dinwiddie	1.9	6.8	0.5	8.7	2.1	0.9	1.2	38.9	20.8	14.3	586	461
Essex	1.3	0.0	0.7	3.4	0.6	0.4	0.1	14.8	6.9	7.2	779	557
Fairfax	882.7	4 265.2	2 674.9	77.4	31.5	27.9	103.7	2 373.5	425.7	1 537.6	1 682	1 330
Fauquier	8.8	34.3	10.0	6.0	2.4	1.2	10.1	104.8	27.8	66.4	1 248	1 019
Floyd	2.1	0.0	0.9	3.8	0.7	0.5	0.1	16.3	8.7	6.6	504	384
Fluvanna	1.8	0.0	0.5	4.5	0.9	0.5	0.0	23.2	11.3	10.0	561	476
Franklin	5.5	0.3	1.3	11.2	2.9	1.7	2.4	59.4	29.8	24.1	543	394
Frederick	2.5	0.7	0.8	5.9	1.9	1.8	1.3	97.4	33.9	46.7	855	652
Giles	2.1	0.0	0.6	6.4	1.1	0.7	5.2	26.0	12.6	10.2	634	502
Gloucester	4.0	0.4	0.9	4.0	1.6	0.9	3.7	52.9	26.5	23.2	672	516
Goochland	1.4	0.0	0.5	2.9	0.7	0.7	3.3	24.3	7.9	14.2	807	654
Grayson	1.8	0.8	0.7	9.2	1.2	0.6	0.6	19.8	12.9	5.5	338	254
Greene	1.7	0.0	0.3	3.2	0.6	0.6	0.9	24.3	12.4	8.2	612	482
Greensville	0.1	0.0	0.1	3.2	2.1	0.7	-0.3	22.1	14.0	5.5	483	362
Halifax	5.2	3.5	18.0	26.7	5.1	1.7	2.0	57.6	35.2	18.8	506	320
Hanover	8.2	4.3	3.4	6.1	1.7	1.5	4.8	130.3	44.9	74.5	944	726
Henrico	33.7	10.1	2.3	14.7	7.6	5.0	13.6	522.3	154.0	267.3	1 096	759
Henry	3.6	0.6	0.9	11.7	3.5	2.2	0.4	77.7	40.4	28.3	506	321
Highland	0.5	0.0	0.1	1.0	0.2	0.1	0.1	4.6	2.2	1.8	710	600
Isle of Wight	4.4	0.4	3.5	7.5	2.8	0.9	0.7	50.0	19.2	27.8	973	775
James City County	1.1	2.1	0.1	3.4	2.7	1.1	8.0	78.2	12.7	56.4	1 316	998
King and Queen	0.9	0.0	0.3	1.7	0.8	0.3	0.5	11.6	6.3	4.5	681	612
King George	282.7	260.2	0.6	2.2	0.8	0.5	0.1	24.5	11.2	11.3	669	521
King William	1.7	0.1	0.7	2.7	1.3	0.4	0.7	24.3	10.1	12.5	1 000	838
Lancaster	2.2	0.1	1.2	3.1	1.2	0.4	0.1	18.8	6.6	8.8	783	656
Lee	2.6	0.0	120.8	25.0	5.4	1.9	2.1	36.9	26.5	8.3	347	241
Loudoun	221.2	130.6	155.4	5.8	2.5	2.1	7.0	294.1	55.3	194.5	1 457	1 190

1. October 1, 1998 to September 30, 1999.   2. State totals may include programs not allocated by county.   3. Based on the resident population estimated as of July 1 of the year shown.

Table B. States and Counties — Local Government Finances, Government Employment, and Elections

STATE County	Total (mil dol) 183	Per capita¹ (dollars) 184	Education 185	Health and hospitals 186	Police protection 187	Public welfare 188	Highways 189	Total (mil dol) 190	Per capita¹ (dollars) 191	Federal civilian 192	Federal military 193	State and local 194	Democratic 195	Republican 196	All other 197
VERMONT—Cont'd															
Chittenden	284.3	2 011	60.3	0.2	5.0	0.0	4.9	295.9	2 093	1 694	1 103	10 554	NA	NA	NA
Essex	10.1	1 549	69.6	0.4	0.4	0.0	12.8	0.6	94	70	49	290	NA	NA	NA
Franklin	68.5	1 574	77.2	0.2	1.6	0.0	8.1	49.0	1 126	681	329	2 132	NA	NA	NA
Grand Isle	8.3	1 343	75.5	0.0	0.4	0.0	8.7	6.9	1 119	19	47	229	NA	NA	NA
Lamoille	45.6	2 128	67.4	0.5	3.3	0.0	11.2	19.6	915	72	162	1 440	NA	NA	NA
Orange	50.1	1 801	75.7	0.6	1.3	0.0	11.7	10.6	382	97	209	1 667	NA	NA	NA
Orleans	45.3	1 787	75.4	0.1	1.6	0.0	10.4	22.1	874	196	189	1 421	NA	NA	NA
Rutland	123.4	1 968	65.7	0.2	2.5	0.1	9.2	50.9	811	379	468	4 190	NA	NA	NA
Washington	121.4	2 150	70.4	0.5	2.7	0.0	7.9	56.6	1 001	311	457	6 754	NA	NA	NA
Windham	101.1	2 359	62.6	0.6	2.5	0.1	10.8	26.1	609	187	319	2 426	NA	NA	NA
Windsor	114.8	2 082	67.3	0.3	3.3	0.2	9.2	27.4	496	1 396	422	3 201	NA	NA	NA
VIRGINIA	X	X	X	X	X	X	X	X	X	163 596	164 865	450 499	44.4	52.5	3.1
Accomack	66.0	2 057	55.8	0.8	2.5	10.9	0.7	29.9	933	679	376	1 679	42.7	53.3	4.0
Albemarle	148.0	1 909	64.3	2.7	5.5	3.4	1.1	95.5	1 232	(3)1 233	(3)691	(3)23 650	44.1	49.6	6.2
Alleghany	31.6	2 567	57.9	0.7	2.7	4.5	0.0	25.5	2 075	(4)104	(4)91	(4)1 601	43.2	54.8	2.0
Amelia	15.0	1 458	64.6	0.9	7.1	5.4	0.0	7.1	692	25	40	496	36.6	61.6	1.8
Amherst	42.8	1 428	63.5	0.1	4.2	5.5	0.0	19.1	638	51	116	2 932	41.1	56.9	2.1
Appomattox	17.8	1 372	71.5	0.7	6.5	4.7	0.9	7.0	543	49	51	746	36.0	61.7	2.4
Arlington	1 165.3	6 752	15.7	2.5	3.2	3.8	2.0	1 847.7	10 707	32 302	16 742	9 038	60.2	34.2	5.7
Augusta	104.1	1 684	66.0	0.5	2.5	2.0	0.2	72.6	1 175	(5)302	(5)402	(5)8 244	26.3	70.2	3.5
Bath	13.0	2 640	57.3	1.1	4.7	3.5	0.0	11.0	2 232	49	19	340	37.2	59.3	3.5
Bedford	80.3	1 443	65.8	1.2	3.2	6.6	0.6	65.7	1 180	(6)171	(6)240	(6)2 154	31.2	65.9	2.9
Bland	8.4	1 227	70.0	1.0	6.9	4.6	0.8	3.0	430	16	26	567	31.7	65.4	2.9
Botetourt	41.0	1 450	65.9	0.1	6.6	2.7	0.1	30.1	1 066	59	111	1 117	33.4	64.1	2.5
Brunswick	24.2	1 438	63.2	0.2	4.1	6.6	0.0	3.3	199	42	65	1 370	56.5	42.7	0.8
Buchanan	52.1	1 776	59.0	0.7	3.3	6.4	7.8	27.0	921	63	112	1 847	58.3	39.2	2.5
Buckingham	20.1	1 382	65.4	0.4	3.4	3.9	0.0	4.6	317	44	57	1 053	47.0	50.2	2.8
Campbell	71.5	1 425	63.1	2.1	3.7	4.2	1.2	44.3	883	(7)994	(7)462	(7)6 526	32.8	64.8	2.5
Caroline	30.6	1 408	64.0	1.1	0.6	6.0	0.0	25.8	1 188	298	128	1 011	51.7	46.4	2.0
Carroll	33.8	1 207	67.0	0.9	5.3	6.6	0.5	22.2	794	(8)90	(8)135	(8)2 183	33.1	64.9	2.0
Charles City County	15.8	2 264	54.9	1.3	3.5	8.1	0.0	27.1	3 883	20	27	348	64.6	33.4	2.0
Charlotte	17.1	1 407	70.9	0.7	2.1	8.7	0.3	7.8	639	59	47	747	40.4	57.2	2.4
Chesterfield	532.4	2 191	54.5	3.3	5.6	5.1	0.9	546.7	2 250	3 441	953	14 798	34.8	63.0	2.2
Clarke	18.2	1 406	63.8	1.5	5.1	3.4	1.5	6.9	537	35	50	638	41.0	54.6	4.5
Craig	6.0	1 224	64.0	1.1	6.8	4.3	0.2	2.0	404	29	19	185	34.1	63.4	2.5
Culpeper	62.9	1 931	62.4	0.5	5.1	5.3	3.4	30.0	920	107	128	2 461	35.6	60.8	3.6
Cumberland	15.2	1 941	47.9	1.1	3.3	5.0	0.0	12.7	1 628	14	30	357	40.1	56.3	3.7
Dickenson	32.6	1 893	55.7	4.8	5.2	6.2	4.4	12.8	747	44	65	871	54.7	43.2	2.1
Dinwiddie	46.5	1 912	64.5	0.3	4.2	3.4	0.1	14.1	579	(9)299	(9)306	(9)8 551	43.8	54.3	1.9
Essex	15.9	1 722	56.8	0.5	8.7	3.6	0.6	10.2	1 106	23	35	403	45.7	52.1	2.2
Fairfax	2 500.1	2 735	46.4	4.6	4.8	5.8	2.2	2 582.1	2 824	(10)35 169	(10)7 037	(10)48 524	47.5	48.9	3.7
Fauquier	99.1	1 863	60.0	0.5	7.4	4.1	1.5	77.4	1 456	172	210	2 641	35.3	61.6	3.1
Floyd	14.2	1 086	72.4	2.0	3.0	0.2	0.4	4.6	349	52	51	456	34.1	59.6	6.3
Fluvanna	20.5	1 155	71.6	1.1	3.4	5.6	0.0	7.2	405	37	72	910	39.4	57.0	3.6
Franklin	63.4	1 428	71.4	3.2	4.0	2.7	1.0	35.1	791	109	173	1 534	38.0	59.6	2.4
Frederick	98.1	1 794	66.8	0.7	3.8	3.2	0.0	77.0	1 408	(11)473	(11)308	(11)4 166	32.0	65.1	2.9
Giles	25.3	1 567	57.9	0.9	7.2	5.2	1.0	11.2	695	50	63	788	44.1	52.4	3.6
Gloucester	55.6	1 613	70.1	0.7	4.1	3.4	0.0	56.6	1 642	88	136	2 385	33.2	63.6	3.1
Goochland	22.5	1 280	53.0	12.8	2.8	4.3	2.7	9.0	513	26	69	1 191	36.4	61.3	2.3
Grayson	19.5	1 209	66.9	1.1	5.9	7.7	0.5	3.2	198	34	62	572	36.0	61.8	2.2
Greene	21.8	1 627	66.2	0.6	5.0	3.3	0.0	25.3	1 888	50	54	678	32.8	62.4	4.9
Greensville	26.0	2 274	66.3	0.4	2.8	0.2	0.1	21.1	1 845	(12)30	(12)65	(12)1 853	59.2	40.1	0.7
Halifax	64.6	1 741	55.1	0.9	6.5	4.6	2.3	17.2	463	(13)105	(13)143	(13)1 978	42.4	55.0	2.7
Hanover	154.2	1 953	53.0	2.9	6.8	1.6	0.8	169.0	2 141	146	318	3 829	29.0	68.8	2.2
Henrico	551.9	2 263	43.1	2.9	6.4	2.1	6.3	538.0	2 206	797	957	11 747	42.6	55.0	2.4
Henry	83.9	1 498	62.0	0.9	3.8	5.4	0.3	104.0	1 857	(14)148	(14)277	(14)3 656	41.5	55.3	3.2
Highland	6.8	2 707	74.6	0.8	5.6	2.8	0.1	2.5	991	10	10	148	31.5	65.6	2.9
Isle of Wight	46.5	1 627	63.8	0.7	4.6	4.9	2.2	34.8	1 220	99	113	1 133	39.9	58.6	1.6
James City County	67.9	1 584	43.5	1.6	5.6	3.8	0.0	143.7	3 353	(15)289	(15)548	(15)7 415	37.1	59.7	3.2
King and Queen	12.6	1 932	61.6	0.0	2.1	4.8	0.0	10.0	1 529	17	190	257	48.5	49.8	1.7
King George	24.3	1 434	66.2	1.0	5.6	4.7	2.3	43.3	2 555	3 763	847	673	35.4	61.4	3.3
King William	22.5	1 807	69.3	0.2	4.9	3.0	0.5	9.2	738	24	49	623	36.8	61.5	1.7
Lancaster	17.0	1 506	48.5	1.9	5.7	5.0	0.0	40.4	3 578	43	44	456	35.5	62.5	2.0
Lee	36.3	1 509	70.4	0.9	4.1	7.4	1.6	13.9	577	49	92	1 226	46.1	52.0	1.9
Loudoun	314.5	2 356	52.7	3.4	5.7	4.3	1.9	331.3	2 482	3 953	574	7 265	40.9	56.1	3.0

1. Based on the resident population estimated as of July 1 of the year shown. 3. Charlottesville included with Albemarle County. 4. Clifton Forge and Covington included with Alleghany County. 5. Staunton and Waynesboro included with Augusta County. 6. Bedford City included with Bedford County. 7. Lynchburg included with Campbell County. 8. Galax included with Carroll County. 9. Petersburg and Colonial Heights included with Dinwiddie County. 10. Fairfax City and Falls Church included with Fairfax County. 11. Winchester included with Frederick County. 12. Emporia included with Greensville County. 13. South Boston included with Halifax County. 14. Martinsville included with Henry County. 15. Williamsburg included with James City County.

Table B. States and Counties — **Land Area and Population**

STATE/ County code	MSA/ PMSA/ NECMA code[1]	County Type[2]	STATE County	Land area,[3] (sq km) 1990	Population and population characteristics, 1999			Race (percent)					Age (percent)					
					Total persons	Rank	Per square kilometer	White	Black	Am. Indian, Eskimo, Aleut	Asian and Pacific Islander	Percent Hispanic[4]	Under 5 years	5 to 17 years	18 to 24 years	25 to 34 years	35 to 44 years	45 to 54 years
				1	2	3	4	5	6	7	8	9	10	11	12	13	14	15
			VIRGINIA—Cont'd															
51 109	...	8	Louisa	1 289	25 029	1 530	19.4	69.8	29.6	0.3	0.3	0.8	6.2	19.0	7.6	13.5	16.7	14.4
51 111	...	9	Lunenburg	1 118	11 789	2 291	10.5	54.9	44.7	0.1	0.3	1.4	5.2	17.6	7.8	12.9	17.1	13.4
51 113	...	8	Madison	833	12 627	2 238	15.2	82.8	16.7	0.3	0.2	0.5	5.9	18.6	6.8	12.5	15.9	14.2
51 115	5720	1	Mathews	222	9 255	2 488	41.7	83.5	16.1	0.1	0.3	1.0	4.2	15.9	6.0	9.7	14.6	15.2
51 117	...	7	Mecklenburg	1 616	30 991	1 348	19.2	57.3	42.4	0.1	0.2	0.6	5.2	17.5	7.3	12.0	15.4	13.4
51 119	...	8	Middlesex	337	9 771	2 449	29.0	71.9	27.9	0.1	0.2	1.0	4.8	14.7	5.6	10.7	13.6	14.5
51 121	...	4	Montgomery	1 006	76 997	648	76.5	90.0	4.6	0.1	5.3	1.6	5.2	13.1	27.8	14.3	13.5	10.7
51 125	...	8	Nelson	1 223	14 186	2 121	11.6	77.9	21.7	0.1	0.3	1.3	5.7	17.7	6.5	11.9	16.7	13.7
51 127	6760	2	New Kent	543	13 218	2 197	24.3	73.3	24.8	1.3	0.6	1.2	6.1	17.6	7.0	14.4	20.4	15.2
51 131	...	9	Northampton	537	12 810	2 225	23.9	50.5	49.2	0.1	0.2	2.7	5.7	19.0	6.0	11.6	13.6	11.6
51 133	...	9	Northumberland	498	11 668	2 297	23.4	67.3	32.4	0.1	0.2	0.8	4.5	14.7	5.1	9.6	12.0	13.4
51 135	...	6	Nottoway	815	15 291	2 049	18.8	53.7	45.5	0.3	0.4	0.8	4.9	16.7	7.9	13.8	16.0	13.2
51 137	...	6	Orange	885	25 759	1 503	29.1	82.3	17.2	0.2	0.3	1.1	5.6	17.7	7.0	12.6	15.6	13.9
51 139	...	6	Page	806	23 165	1 608	28.7	96.8	2.5	0.1	0.5	0.8	5.8	17.2	7.6	12.3	15.3	14.6
51 141	...	9	Patrick	1 251	18 529	1 846	14.8	91.1	8.6	0.1	0.2	1.1	4.7	16.5	7.4	11.5	14.6	15.9
51 143	1950	3	Pittsylvania	2 515	56 760	820	22.6	69.2	30.6	0.1	0.2	0.7	5.4	18.4	7.6	12.9	16.8	15.0
51 145	6760	2	Powhatan	677	22 409	1 643	33.1	76.4	23.1	0.2	0.3	0.6	5.6	17.6	8.3	16.2	19.8	15.6
51 147	...	7	Prince Edward	914	19 245	1 806	21.1	59.4	39.8	0.2	0.6	1.0	5.0	15.7	23.9	10.0	12.7	10.5
51 149	6760	2	Prince George	688	28 812	1 418	41.9	64.7	31.8	0.4	3.2	5.9	7.0	19.6	11.7	16.6	18.0	13.4
51 153	8840	0	Prince William	877	270 841	203	308.8	81.8	13.3	0.4	4.5	6.9	8.5	21.7	9.2	17.5	19.7	13.5
51 155	...	7	Pulaski	830	34 401	1 241	41.4	92.5	7.0	0.1	0.3	0.7	5.2	16.4	8.8	11.9	16.5	14.7
51 157	...	8	Rappahannock	690	7 664	2 627	11.1	87.1	12.4	0.2	0.3	1.6	5.7	15.0	7.4	13.1	18.0	16.7
51 159	...	9	Richmond	496	8 745	2 528	17.6	59.2	40.2	0.2	0.4	1.2	4.6	14.8	11.5	15.9	16.2	11.4
51 161	6800	3	Roanoke	649	81 163	624	125.1	95.6	3.0	0.1	1.2	0.9	4.9	17.1	7.5	11.8	18.6	15.7
51 163	...	6	Rockbridge	1 553	19 542	1 786	12.6	95.6	3.7	0.2	0.4	0.5	5.4	16.6	7.6	12.0	15.5	15.3
51 165	...	5	Rockingham	2 205	63 078	759	28.6	97.7	1.8	0.1	0.4	1.5	6.2	18.0	8.9	13.3	16.3	14.2
51 167	...	6	Russell	1 229	28 728	1 421	23.4	98.5	1.4	0.1	0.1	0.5	5.1	19.7	7.9	13.3	16.7	14.9
51 169	3660	2	Scott	1 390	22 506	1 634	16.2	99.1	0.8	0.1	0.1	0.5	4.7	16.9	7.8	11.1	14.8	15.7
51 171	...	6	Shenandoah	1 327	35 141	1 223	26.5	98.0	1.4	0.1	0.5	1.5	5.6	16.0	7.5	12.2	15.4	14.9
51 173	...	6	Smyth	1 171	32 692	1 293	27.9	97.3	2.2	0.1	0.3	0.5	5.2	17.2	8.2	11.9	14.8	14.9
51 175	...	6	Southampton	1 555	17 678	1 889	11.4	49.4	50.3	0.1	0.1	0.6	5.4	17.3	10.4	14.5	14.8	13.4
51 177	8840	0	Spotsylvania	1 038	87 361	576	84.2	85.3	12.7	0.4	1.6	2.4	8.0	22.1	7.7	15.6	19.1	13.0
51 179	8840	1	Stafford	699	93 160	543	133.3	89.4	8.3	0.4	1.9	3.4	8.1	22.0	9.3	15.3	19.2	14.1
51 181	...	8	Surry	723	6 484	2 733	9.0	40.1	59.8	0.1	0.0	0.5	6.3	19.5	7.7	13.3	16.1	13.7
51 183	...	8	Sussex	1 271	12 345	2 261	9.7	37.7	62.0	0.1	0.1	0.3	4.8	14.5	10.3	15.1	18.5	14.6
51 185	...	7	Tazewell	1 346	46 343	963	34.4	95.8	3.3	0.1	0.8	0.5	5.1	19.5	7.4	11.8	16.6	14.2
51 187	8840	1	Warren	554	30 620	1 357	55.3	93.4	6.0	0.2	0.5	1.6	7.1	17.4	8.2	14.5	15.9	14.4
51 191	3660	2	Washington	1 461	49 791	910	34.1	97.9	1.8	0.1	0.2	0.5	4.9	16.8	8.7	11.8	16.4	15.7
51 193	...	6	Westmoreland	594	16 259	1 986	27.4	62.6	36.6	0.2	0.6	1.0	6.0	16.9	6.9	11.3	14.2	14.2
51 195	...	7	Wise	1 045	40 194	1 083	38.5	96.5	3.0	0.1	0.5	0.5	5.3	19.9	9.2	12.7	16.3	13.4
51 197	...	7	Wythe	1 200	26 511	1 479	22.1	95.3	4.2	0.1	0.4	0.4	5.3	17.5	8.2	11.9	15.6	14.5
51 199	5720	0	York	274	58 433	808	213.3	78.6	17.8	0.3	3.4	2.6	6.2	22.1	6.9	12.9	19.0	15.4
	...		Independent Cities															
51 510	8840	NA	Alexandria City	40	117 390	449	2 934.8	70.1	23.5	0.4	6.0	13.4	5.4	10.5	9.7	21.9	19.2	12.8
51 515	4640	NA	Bedford City	18	6 676	2 712	370.9	74.6	24.5	0.1	0.7	1.4	5.6	15.0	6.9	12.2	13.0	11.9
51 520	3660	NA	Bristol City	30	16 709	1 951	557.0	92.5	6.7	0.1	0.6	0.5	5.1	15.0	8.6	11.1	13.4	13.1
51 530	...	NA	Buena Vista City	18	6 467	2 737	359.3	94.4	5.1	0.1	0.4	0.3	4.5	16.1	11.8	10.4	14.5	13.7
51 540	1540	NA	Charlottesville City	27	36 815	1 168	1 363.5	72.3	24.4	0.1	3.2	1.7	5.5	12.4	20.4	16.1	13.4	9.7
51 550	5720	0	Chesapeake City	882	202 759	268	229.9	66.5	31.3	0.3	1.8	1.9	7.4	20.8	8.4	15.8	18.2	13.1
51 560	...	NA	Clifton Forge City	8	4 205	2 895	525.6	82.3	17.4	0.1	0.2	0.8	5.1	15.9	7.1	11.2	12.8	12.8
51 570	6760	NA	Colonial Heights City	19	16 235	1 991	854.5	95.4	1.0	0.3	3.4	1.7	5.0	16.1	7.6	11.1	15.4	15.3
51 580	...	NA	Covington City	11	6 846	2 695	622.4	82.6	16.4	0.1	0.9	0.6	5.3	14.9	8.3	11.8	13.7	13.8
51 590	1950	NA	Danville City	112	50 795	895	453.5	59.4	39.7	0.1	0.7	0.8	5.6	16.2	8.1	11.7	14.8	12.5
51 595	...	NA	Emporia City	18	5 662	2 793	314.6	49.5	49.7	0.3	0.5	1.6	6.7	17.5	7.9	11.9	13.7	12.1
51 600	8840	NA	Fairfax City	16	20 697	1 728	1 293.6	84.1	5.4	0.3	10.3	8.6	5.3	13.7	10.8	16.3	15.6	13.8
51 610	8840	NA	Falls Church City	5	9 944	2 434	1 988.8	88.9	3.6	0.6	6.9	9.5	5.1	13.5	5.7	13.9	20.0	14.1
51 620	...	NA	Franklin City	20	8 139	2 582	407.0	45.6	54.0	0.1	0.3	0.3	6.4	19.7	7.3	12.6	15.7	13.1
51 630	8840	NA	Fredericksburg City	27	18 826	1 830	697.3	73.9	24.5	0.2	1.4	3.5	6.0	12.1	20.4	14.4	12.2	9.9
51 640	...	NA	Galax City	21	6 484	2 733	308.8	92.9	6.7	0.1	0.4	1.4	6.0	14.5	7.3	11.3	13.4	13.3
51 650	5720	NA	Hampton City	134	137 193	383	1 023.8	54.3	42.9	0.3	2.5	2.9	6.9	17.4	11.6	15.9	15.9	12.7
51 660	...	NA	Harrisonburg City	45	34 129	1 253	758.4	89.6	8.1	0.1	2.2	2.4	4.7	11.5	35.0	11.9	11.4	8.9
51 670	6760	NA	Hopewell City	27	22 663	1 627	839.4	68.6	29.2	0.3	1.9	2.8	6.9	18.1	9.7	14.8	14.8	12.2
51 678	...	NA	Lexington City	6	7 359	2 649	1 226.5	84.4	13.7	0.4	1.5	1.2	2.5	9.0	40.0	6.5	8.9	8.9
51 680	4640	NA	Lynchburg City	128	63 926	745	499.4	69.3	29.4	0.2	1.1	1.1	5.9	15.5	13.8	11.6	13.8	11.2

1. MSA = Metropolitan Statistical Area. PMSA = Primary MSA. NECMA = New England County Metropolitan Area. See Appendix A for explanation of these concepts. See Appendix B for list of metropolitan areas identified by type, with component counties. 2. County typology code from the Economic Research Service of USDA. See Appendix A for definition. 3. Dry land or land partially or temporarily covered by water. 4. Hispanic persons may be of any race.

Table B. States and Counties — Population and Households

STATE County	55 to 64 years	65 to 74 years	75 years and over	Percent female	Total persons 1990	1980	Percent change 1980-1990	1990-1999	Births	Deaths	Net migration	Number	Percent change 1980-1990	Persons per house-hold	Female family house-holder[1]	One person
	16	17	18	19	20	21	22	23	24	25	26	27	28	29	30	31
VIRGINIA—Cont'd																
Louisa	10.4	6.6	5.6	50.6	20 325	17 825	14.0	23.1	2 835	2 012	3 904	7 427	24.6	2.71	10.4	20.7
Lunenburg	10.0	9.3	6.6	47.4	11 419	12 124	-5.8	3.2	1 143	1 314	558	4 423	3.9	2.58	10.9	25.4
Madison	10.6	7.5	7.9	50.7	11 949	10 232	16.8	5.7	1 296	1 084	505	4 144	21.5	2.83	8.7	19.2
Mathews	13.7	9.9	10.7	51.8	8 348	7 995	4.4	10.9	739	1 261	1 439	3 530	13.2	2.35	7.6	27.1
Mecklenburg	11.7	9.7	7.8	51.8	29 241	29 444	-0.7	6.0	3 329	3 787	2 325	11 244	10.7	2.52	13.0	25.0
Middlesex	13.5	11.5	11.1	51.7	8 653	7 719	12.1	12.9	720	1 215	1 636	3 530	20.8	2.40	9.0	24.8
Montgomery	6.8	4.4	4.3	48.5	73 913	63 284	16.8	4.2	7 603	4 243	-161	26 241	26.0	2.48	7.7	22.9
Nelson	11.0	9.0	7.9	51.1	12 778	12 204	4.7	11.0	1 377	1 486	1 551	4 807	12.7	2.63	10.5	22.3
New Kent	9.1	6.1	4.0	49.1	10 466	8 781	19.0	26.3	1 470	788	2 060	3 718	26.7	2.77	8.6	14.7
Northampton	11.5	10.8	10.2	53.7	13 061	14 625	-10.7	-1.9	1 542	1 817	78	5 129	-4.9	2.50	16.1	27.8
Northumberland	14.4	14.8	11.3	52.9	10 524	9 828	7.1	10.9	941	1 507	1 741	4 492	17.8	2.34	9.1	26.1
Nottoway	10.1	8.9	8.5	48.5	14 993	14 666	2.2	2.0	1 678	2 016	633	5 244	4.5	2.58	13.9	24.8
Orange	10.8	9.4	7.4	51.0	21 421	18 063	18.6	20.3	2 605	2 299	4 107	7 930	26.8	2.67	9.7	20.0
Page	11.3	8.5	7.4	51.0	21 690	19 401	11.8	6.8	2 393	2 143	1 279	8 055	16.3	2.67	9.4	20.6
Patrick	11.0	9.2	9.2	50.8	17 473	17 647	-1.0	6.0	1 675	1 839	1 313	6 908	11.1	2.50	8.5	21.8
Pittsylvania	10.4	7.6	6.0	50.9	55 672	66 147	-15.8	2.0	5 381	4 975	896	20 613	-6.9	2.68	10.7	19.4
Powhatan	8.7	4.9	3.4	44.8	15 328	13 062	17.3	46.2	2 116	1 029	5 983	4 672	30.5	2.84	8.0	13.5
Prince Edward	8.4	6.7	7.1	51.9	17 320	16 456	5.3	11.1	2 037	1 978	1 911	5 373	8.8	2.59	14.5	26.7
Prince George	7.3	4.0	2.3	47.7	27 390	25 733	6.5	5.2	3 619	1 289	-2 128	8 250	26.8	2.93	10.1	13.5
Prince William	5.3	2.8	1.7	49.3	214 954	144 636	49.1	26.0	40 091	7 649	19 671	69 709	59.2	3.04	8.4	13.2
Pulaski	10.6	8.4	7.5	51.4	34 496	35 229	-2.1	-0.3	3 605	3 614	27	13 349	7.8	2.51	11.1	22.9
Rappahannock	10.4	7.5	6.2	47.5	6 622	6 093	8.7	15.7	673	567	950	2 496	16.4	2.65	7.1	19.7
Richmond	9.5	7.6	8.5	43.4	7 273	6 952	4.6	20.2	709	985	1 767	2 645	9.1	2.62	11.3	23.4
Roanoke	10.9	7.0	6.5	52.7	79 278	72 945	8.7	2.4	6 129	6 684	2 696	30 355	20.3	2.54	8.4	21.2
Rockbridge	12.5	8.9	6.2	50.3	18 350	17 724	3.5	6.5	1 782	1 630	1 086	7 202	13.9	2.52	9.5	21.3
Rockingham	10.2	6.5	6.3	50.6	57 482	52 068	10.4	9.7	7 546	4 762	2 999	20 750	8.8	2.69	7.3	19.0
Russell	10.6	6.2	5.6	50.9	28 667	31 761	-9.7	0.2	2 937	2 671	-112	10 641	0.1	2.66	9.6	19.2
Scott	11.6	8.7	8.7	51.7	23 204	25 068	-7.4	-3.0	2 122	2 588	-164	8 966	2.5	2.57	9.8	21.0
Shenandoah	11.3	8.7	8.4	51.6	31 636	27 559	14.8	11.1	3 693	3 445	3 362	12 452	24.1	2.50	8.9	23.2
Smyth	11.7	8.4	7.6	52.1	32 370	33 345	-2.9	1.0	3 508	3 578	493	12 234	7.1	2.55	11.3	21.5
Southampton	9.5	8.5	6.4	47.5	17 022	18 316	-4.2	3.9	1 747	1 648	570	6 009	4.1	2.69	12.0	22.1
Spotsylvania	7.1	4.3	3.0	50.4	57 397	31 995	79.4	52.2	9 238	3 556	24 088	18 945	74.4	3.01	7.9	13.2
Stafford	6.7	3.1	2.3	48.9	62 255	40 470	53.1	49.6	10 265	3 072	22 529	19 415	59.5	3.05	7.3	12.2
Surry	9.1	8.0	6.5	52.0	6 145	6 046	1.6	5.5	736	597	219	2 283	13.6	2.69	13.4	22.6
Sussex	9.0	6.9	6.4	44.8	10 248	10 874	-5.8	20.5	1 221	1 200	2 018	3 795	6.2	2.65	17.3	24.0
Tazewell	10.5	8.1	6.7	51.8	45 960	50 511	-9.0	0.8	4 903	4 705	315	17 309	1.3	2.62	10.7	21.3
Warren	10.0	6.7	5.7	50.8	26 142	21 200	23.3	17.1	3 933	2 433	3 041	9 879	27.4	2.60	8.9	22.1
Washington	11.3	7.7	6.7	51.4	45 887	46 487	-1.3	8.5	4 445	4 351	3 932	17 483	10.2	2.55	8.8	21.1
Westmoreland	11.8	10.5	8.2	51.9	15 480	14 041	10.2	5.0	1 885	1 893	831	6 057	20.1	2.55	12.3	23.9
Wise	9.7	7.2	6.4	50.4	39 573	43 863	-9.8	1.6	4 841	3 888	-264	14 513	-1.5	2.67	12.1	20.9
Wythe	10.9	8.1	7.8	52.4	25 471	25 522	-0.2	4.1	2 770	2 860	1 210	9 852	9.4	2.55	10.4	22.9
York	8.3	5.8	3.4	50.6	42 434	35 463	19.7	37.7	4 780	2 359	12 706	14 474	32.8	2.90	8.8	15.1
Independent Cities																
Alexandria City	7.4	6.8	6.2	52.9	111 183	103 217	7.7	5.6	17 790	7 337	-4 794	53 280	8.7	2.04	9.1	42.0
Bedford City	10.9	10.0	14.5	53.3	6 176	5 991	1.4	8.1	675	1 100	968	2 475	7.7	2.28	16.2	31.0
Bristol City	11.1	11.2	11.5	56.0	18 426	19 042	-3.2	-9.3	1 923	2 453	-1 158	7 591	4.9	2.33	14.2	30.7
Buena Vista City	10.9	8.9	9.2	55.2	6 406	6 904	-7.2	1.0	739	836	169	2 404	6.0	2.53	14.4	23.7
Charlottesville City	7.3	7.3	7.9	53.7	40 470	39 916	1.4	-9.0	4 948	3 626	-4 943	16 009	3.9	2.37	12.9	30.6
Chesapeake City	7.6	5.2	3.5	51.1	151 982	114 486	32.8	33.4	25 246	10 881	35 438	51 965	42.8	2.87	12.7	16.1
Clifton Forge City	10.8	9.8	14.4	55.1	4 679	5 046	-7.3	-10.1	447	878	-22	1 930	1.8	2.28	13.8	34.5
Colonial Heights City	12.7	10.2	6.7	53.4	16 064	16 509	-2.7	1.1	1 724	1 740	181	6 363	8.4	2.49	10.9	23.0
Covington City	10.8	10.0	11.4	53.2	7 352	9 063	-22.9	-6.9	733	1 021	-187	2 998	-14.6	2.32	12.0	30.4
Danville City	10.8	10.6	9.7	54.6	53 056	45 642	16.2	-4.3	6 646	7 015	-1 768	21 712	24.0	2.38	17.3	30.2
Emporia City	10.3	10.2	9.7	53.3	5 556	4 840	13.2	1.9	751	1 000	383	2 031	15.8	2.51	19.4	27.5
Fairfax City	10.5	8.6	5.1	51.7	19 945	20 537	-4.4	3.8	2 548	1 383	-383	7 362	7.0	2.60	10.2	20.1
Falls Church City	8.5	9.6	9.7	52.9	9 464	9 515	0.0	5.1	899	695	275	4 195	-1.3	2.27	8.4	33.1
Franklin City	10.2	7.6	7.4	54.9	8 392	7 723	1.8	-3.0	1 183	1 154	-253	3 006	16.2	2.57	21.2	25.1
Fredericksburg City	7.5	8.7	8.9	54.5	19 033	17 762	7.1	-1.1	4 433	1 922	-2 690	7 450	25.7	2.24	12.3	34.7
Galax City	11.9	9.7	12.4	54.9	6 745	6 524	2.2	-3.9	855	1 163	93	2 750	4.8	2.32	14.1	29.8
Hampton City	8.3	6.8	4.4	52.1	133 773	122 617	9.1	2.6	20 469	9 737	-10 212	49 673	19.7	2.58	13.5	23.7
Harrisonburg City	6.6	4.7	5.2	53.5	30 707	24 641	24.6	11.1	3 403	2 374	2 496	10 310	73.1	2.40	10.2	28.2
Hopewell City	9.1	7.5	6.8	51.5	23 101	23 397	-1.3	-1.9	3 461	2 362	-1 603	9 014	6.0	2.53	16.3	24.9
Lexington City	8.2	7.4	8.6	41.5	6 959	7 292	-4.6	5.7	586	671	493	2 172	-0.3	2.18	9.5	36.4
Lynchburg City	8.9	9.0	10.3	55.4	66 120	66 743	-1.0	-3.3	8 348	7 482	-2 820	25 143	5.0	2.39	15.6	30.5

1. No spouse present.

Table B. States and Counties — Vital Statistics, Health Resources, and Crime

STATE County	Births, average 1996–1998 Total	Rate[1]	Deaths, average 1996–1998 Number Total	Number Infant[2]	Rate Total[1]	Rate Infant[3]	Physicians,[4] 1998 Number	Rate[5]	Hospitals,[4] 1998 Number	Beds Number	Beds Rate[5]	Medicare enrollees 1999	Serious crimes known to police, 1998[6] Total Number	Rate[7]
	32	33	34	35	36	37	38	39	40	41	42	43	44	45
VIRGINIA—Cont'd														
Louisa	295	12.3	234	3	9.8	9.0	12	49	0	0	0	3 590	242	1 007
Lunenburg	116	9.6	144	1	11.8	8.6	4	33	0	0	0	2 055	180	1 465
Madison	128	10.2	117	1	9.4	10.4	9	71	0	0	0	1 784	128	1 016
Mathews	81	8.9	136	0	14.9	4.1	11	121	0	0	0	2 059	91	990
Mecklenburg	372	12.0	436	3	14.1	7.2	40	129	1	138	444	6 621	1 041	3 336
Middlesex	67	7.0	133	0	14.0	5.0	19	197	0	0	0	2 384	154	1 598
Montgomery	811	10.7	460	3	6.1	3.7	99	130	1	90	119	8 217	2 673	3 487
Nelson	178	12.9	160	1	11.6	5.6	24	172	0	0	0	2 957	389	2 804
New Kent	153	12.1	91	1	7.2	4.3	9	69	0	0	0	1 728	273	2 208
Northampton	157	12.3	189	2	14.8	12.7	44	346	1	158	1 243	2 958	435	3 373
Northumberland	95	8.3	175	1	15.3	14.0	14	122	0	0	0	2 865	189	1 639
Nottoway	176	11.7	219	2	14.5	9.4	21	140	0	0	0	3 091	328	2 241
Orange	296	11.8	275	4	11.0	12.4	23	91	0	0	0	5 258	349	1 386
Page	254	11.1	241	1	10.6	2.6	17	74	1	54	235	4 002	405	1 757
Patrick	197	10.7	215	2	11.8	10.2	17	92	1	61	331	3 485	413	2 255
Pittsylvania	665	11.5	569	6	9.8	8.5	11	19	0	0	0	7 949	655	1 128
Powhatan	238	11.2	131	1	6.2	4.2	19	87	0	0	0	2 163	309	1 444
Prince Edward	216	11.4	218	3	11.6	15.5	42	221	1	108	568	3 590	246	1 292
Prince George	358	11.9	165	1	5.5	2.8	13	43	0	0	0	1 933	568	1 894
Prince William	4 453	17.5	946	35	3.7	7.9	249	96	1	153	59	10 743	8 368	3 261
Pulaski	363	10.6	413	3	12.0	8.3	37	107	1	77	223	6 116	974	2 809
Rappahannock	73	10.2	60	1	8.3	13.6	8	110	0	0	0	1 265	64	900
Richmond	73	8.5	120	1	13.9	18.2	1	12	0	0	0	1 547	75	867
Roanoke	666	8.2	769	2	9.5	3.5	212	262	0	0	0	5 671	1 667	2 033
Rockbridge	211	10.9	196	1	10.1	3.1	7	36	0	0	0	2 225	316	1 614
Rockingham	807	12.7	537	6	8.5	7.4	48	76	0	0	0	8 613	715	1 112
Russell	312	10.7	300	3	10.3	8.6	19	65	1	78	269	5 145	295	1 008
Scott	245	10.8	302	1	13.2	5.4	8	35	0	0	0	4 995	432	1 888
Shenandoah	386	11.3	370	3	10.8	7.8	32	92	1	129	372	6 453	732	2 117
Smyth	354	10.8	418	4	12.7	10.4	50	153	1	176	537	6 645	591	1 781
Southampton	183	10.4	178	2	10.2	9.1	5	29	0	0	0	2 291	262	1 470
Spotsylvania	1 133	14.0	449	6	5.6	5.3	58	69	0	0	0	3 947	2 026	2 479
Stafford	1 209	14.0	378	9	4.4	7.7	26	30	0	0	0	4 003	1 809	2 042
Surry	68	10.7	73	1	11.3	9.8	2	31	0	0	0	962	130	2 004
Sussex	109	10.9	135	1	13.5	6.1	2	20	0	0	0	2 247	262	2 576
Tazewell	488	10.4	529	1	11.3	2.7	108	231	2	243	520	10 344	1 340	2 835
Warren	405	13.5	291	2	9.7	4.9	26	86	1	87	289	4 066	1 026	3 390
Washington	536	10.9	544	3	11.1	5.6	79	161	1	138	281	7 475	964	1 959
Westmoreland	186	11.4	205	2	12.6	12.5	13	80	0	0	0	3 308	379	2 306
Wise	514	13.2	458	3	11.7	6.5	41	106	2	127	329	8 396	775	2 005
Wythe	287	10.9	339	2	12.9	5.8	30	114	1	106	404	5 659	659	2 484
York	524	9.1	286	3	5.0	6.4	354	602	0	0	0	6 629	1 700	2 951
Independent Cities														
Alexandria City	2 099	17.9	817	12	7.0	5.6	391	331	1	347	293	19 467	6 060	5 162
Bedford City	74	11.8	116	0	18.5	0.0	24	380	1	166	2 628	3 182	281	4 426
Bristol City	146	8.4	253	2	14.5	13.7	13	74	0	0	0	5 716	642	3 681
Buena Vista City	73	11.9	94	0	15.2	0.0	3	48	0	0	0	1 430	120	1 939
Charlottesville City	486	12.8	395	6	10.4	11.7	601	1 572	2	734	1 920	7 174	2 700	7 063
Chesapeake City	2 749	14.0	1 260	26	6.4	9.6	445	223	1	260	130	19 357	8 411	4 264
Clifton Forge City	53	12.0	96	0	21.8	6.3	17	392	0	0	0	1 543	107	2 410
Colonial Heights City	318	18.6	212	1	12.4	3.1	41	242	0	0	0	3 685	1 077	6 403
Covington City	76	10.9	108	1	15.6	8.8	NA	NA	0	0	0	2 990	304	4 335
Danville City	630	12.3	756	7	14.8	11.1	155	305	1	336	661	13 339	2 549	4 955
Emporia City	64	11.7	121	2	22.1	36.3	12	219	1	182	3 325	2 060	514	9 235
Fairfax City	297	14.5	206	4	10.1	13.5	251	1 213	0	0	0	8 856	950	4 626
Falls Church City	135	13.7	80	2	8.0	14.8	54	538	1	656	6 533	3 801	483	4 848
Franklin City	95	10.9	125	1	14.3	10.5	32	368	1	208	2 395	2 350	453	5 101
Fredericksburg City	343	16.3	218	4	10.3	11.7	117	540	1	288	1 328	8 259	944	4 439
Galax City	103	15.0	124	1	18.0	6.5	40	583	1	149	2 171	3 241	385	5 544
Hampton City	2 058	14.9	1 089	16	7.9	7.8	204	149	1	289	211	17 277	7 360	5 267
Harrisonburg City	376	11.3	265	4	7.9	10.6	102	305	1	264	790	4 604	1 409	4 169
Hopewell City	351	15.6	257	4	11.4	10.4	31	138	1	140	621	4 042	1 898	8 490
Lexington City	43	5.9	72	1	9.9	15.6	29	394	1	98	1 332	2 532	140	1 929
Lynchburg City	811	12.4	818	7	12.5	8.2	224	342	2	529	808	14 464	3 208	4 869

1. Per 1,000 estimated resident population, average 1996–1998. 2. Deaths of infants under 1 year old. 3. Deaths of infants under 1 year old per 1,000 live births. 4. Data subject to copyright. 5. Per 100,000 resident population as of July 1 of the year shown. 6. Data for serious crimes have not been adjusted for underreporting; this may affect comparability between geographic areas and over time. 7. Per 100,000 population estimated by the FBI.

Table B. States and Counties — Crime, Education, Money Income, and Poverty

STATE County	Serious crimes known to police, 1998[1] (cont'd) Rate[2] Violent	Serious crimes known to police, 1998[1] (cont'd) Rate[2] Property	Education School enrollment and attainment, 1990 Enrollment[3] Total	Education School enrollment and attainment, 1990 Enrollment[3] Percent private	Education Attainment[4] (percent) High school graduate or more	Education Attainment[4] (percent) Bachelor's degree or more	Education Local government expenditures, fiscal 1997[5] Total current expenditures (mil dol)	Education Local government expenditures, fiscal 1997[5] Current expenditures per student (dollars)	Money income 1989 Per capita[6] (dollars)	Money income 1989 Households Median Dollars	Money income 1989 Households Median Percent change, 1979-1989 (constant 1989 dollars)	Money income 1989 Percent with $100,000 or more	Income and poverty, 1997 Median household income	Income and poverty, 1997 Percent below poverty level All persons	Income and poverty, 1997 Percent below poverty level Persons under 18	Income and poverty, 1997 Percent below poverty level Persons 5-17 in families
	46	47	48	49	50	51	52	53	54	55	56	57	58	59	60	61
VIRGINIA—Cont'd																
Louisa	121	886	4 582	7.5	59.8	8.7	20.8	5 212	12 390	26 169	12.6	2.6	34 609	12.6	18.8	17.9
Lunenburg	171	1 294	2 516	3.5	52.2	6.6	10.6	4 927	9 158	19 459	-0.2	0.8	25 500	21.9	29.9	28.4
Madison	63	953	2 652	15.5	62.7	15.4	10.6	5 586	11 145	26 662	19.9	2.3	34 947	12.7	18.2	18.3
Mathews	98	892	1 623	8.9	70.0	15.5	6.4	4 941	13 671	27 428	8.7	1.5	36 385	11.5	18.1	16.8
Mecklenburg	590	2 746	6 072	6.8	58.1	10.0	24.2	4 771	10 508	20 901	-0.7	1.1	27 752	16.2	24.0	22.7
Middlesex	166	1 432	1 515	15.9	66.6	14.7	7.1	5 187	14 834	25 167	23.4	3.8	32 671	13.9	23.4	22.4
Montgomery	342	3 145	32 874	5.0	73.6	31.6	50.2	5 509	10 979	22 949	4.7	1.9	34 498	15.2	17.9	17.9
Nelson	159	2 645	2 699	8.2	57.0	13.4	11.5	5 577	11 419	23 705	15.8	2.8	31 817	13.7	19.7	19.4
New Kent	243	1 965	2 446	7.2	72.8	13.4	10.5	4 879	14 993	38 403	23.0	3.3	49 908	6.3	9.4	9.1
Northampton	326	3 047	2 913	7.3	57.3	12.4	13.1	5 255	10 176	18 117	8.9	2.5	22 912	26.9	37.9	36.0
Northumberland	95	1 544	1 923	12.6	63.9	13.5	8.7	5 472	13 712	23 065	1.3	3.4	30 888	14.3	25.3	24.9
Nottoway	239	2 002	3 031	7.8	53.2	8.8	12.8	5 107	10 036	21 774	-3.2	1.5	27 544	21.2	30.3	27.6
Orange	126	1 247	4 624	8.9	65.9	16.1	21.0	5 549	13 545	31 782	38.2	3.0	39 156	10.6	17.6	15.7
Page	191	1 631	4 181	8.7	55.4	7.9	17.1	4 766	11 304	24 971	17.8	1.7	31 157	12.8	19.5	18.8
Patrick	191	2 064	3 597	3.7	54.1	7.0	13.3	5 018	10 411	22 287	2.2	1.1	29 726	14.8	22.8	20.9
Pittsylvania	121	1 007	12 364	8.1	56.1	7.4	42.7	4 567	11 196	25 585	7.7	1.3	32 384	12.6	19.8	16.7
Powhatan	168	1 276	3 184	18.7	66.3	12.2	15.4	5 196	15 683	37 394	14.4	4.6	49 009	6.6	9.0	9.0
Prince Edward	242	1 050	6 254	21.7	60.5	14.2	13.0	4 972	9 031	21 395	3.8	1.1	27 854	24.0	28.8	28.9
Prince George	127	1 767	7 028	9.5	77.9	16.2	27.5	4 954	12 714	34 825	19.1	1.8	44 845	9.1	13.1	11.8
Prince William	260	3 001	59 451	12.6	87.8	27.6	282.7	5 848	17 833	49 370	15.8	6.5	59 080	6.4	9.6	8.3
Pulaski	228	2 581	7 490	3.9	59.6	11.5	26.5	5 132	11 074	23 319	-3.9	1.1	31 806	14.1	21.0	20.6
Rappahannock	28	872	1 266	10.3	67.2	18.9	5.8	5 560	17 260	32 377	32.5	5.8	40 172	10.4	15.1	16.2
Richmond	173	694	1 491	5.5	56.8	11.8	6.8	5 178	11 036	24 583	5.2	2.2	29 444	18.9	23.9	23.5
Roanoke	243	1 790	19 159	15.5	79.4	22.6	81.5	5 858	16 627	36 886	7.6	4.4	47 838	5.5	8.8	7.2
Rockbridge	82	1 532	3 624	11.5	62.1	12.9	16.7	5 152	11 287	24 955	10.1	1.4	33 687	12.1	18.5	17.4
Rockingham	79	1 033	12 657	16.9	64.7	14.6	54.1	5 206	12 647	29 637	14.0	2.1	37 759	9.4	15.2	12.9
Russell	99	909	6 568	2.5	50.6	6.7	23.9	5 177	8 753	17 853	-22.7	1.0	25 956	20.7	27.6	26.0
Scott	114	1 774	4 676	3.0	51.2	5.9	19.8	5 139	9 100	18 346	0.9	0.4	26 888	18.3	25.8	24.3
Shenandoah	717	1 400	5 774	6.8	65.2	11.2	28.5	5 353	12 686	26 527	17.4	1.7	34 377	11.0	16.6	16.1
Smyth	211	1 570	6 809	3.3	53.3	7.8	26.9	5 050	9 613	20 912	-0.8	0.8	28 367	17.3	25.1	23.4
Southampton	393	1 077	3 940	10.7	58.4	11.4	15.6	5 400	10 948	26 376	13.3	1.4	33 943	17.1	23.5	22.1
Spotsylvania	202	2 277	15 146	9.1	76.6	19.0	82.3	5 131	15 192	41 342	28.3	4.0	51 218	6.8	9.8	8.9
Stafford	120	1 922	16 060	8.2	80.9	21.6	88.3	5 082	15 917	44 661	23.0	5.2	58 005	5.7	7.9	7.3
Surry	385	1 619	1 461	10.7	58.0	11.0	9.9	7 880	11 495	25 027	11.7	1.4	31 097	16.0	23.2	22.5
Sussex	521	2 055	2 139	14.6	54.2	8.6	10.0	6 482	9 856	20 833	-3.2	1.7	27 448	21.0	30.8	29.9
Tazewell	683	2 152	11 338	7.5	57.3	9.1	39.6	5 032	9 995	19 670	-20.0	1.4	27 573	19.6	26.5	25.2
Warren	89	3 301	5 332	14.0	64.6	11.8	21.1	4 507	13 580	31 062	24.2	1.8	39 400	10.9	17.1	15.9
Washington	138	1 821	10 342	12.2	60.4	12.2	37.5	4 977	11 057	22 179	0.7	2.3	31 387	14.3	20.7	19.1
Westmoreland	207	2 099	3 148	9.4	59.0	10.9	13.2	4 830	12 268	24 654	10.1	1.7	30 597	16.1	25.3	24.6
Wise	264	1 741	10 202	3.5	52.1	8.6	39.3	5 097	9 392	19 594	-21.1	1.2	26 593	23.1	30.4	28.7
Wythe	147	2 337	5 751	4.6	61.8	10.0	22.1	5 069	10 404	20 964	-4.8	0.7	29 355	16.2	23.6	23.1
York	686	2 265	12 899	11.7	88.3	28.9	54.2	4 937	15 742	40 363	15.1	4.2	51 898	6.1	8.2	7.9
Independent Cities																
Alexandria City	417	4 745	21 083	28.1	86.9	48.5	92.0	9 056	25 509	41 472	17.7	8.9	51 052	10.2	21.6	21.2
Bedford City	520	3 906	1 149	12.7	60.1	15.0	0.0	0	11 070	22 787	8.8	2.0	29 777	19.0	29.7	27.7
Bristol City	499	3 182	4 103	16.4	60.9	13.8	15.0	6 059	10 290	19 226	-13.6	0.7	27 506	21.1	30.7	31.8
Buena Vista City	259	1 680	1 483	16.6	55.5	8.7	5.8	5 329	10 241	23 929	-0.3	0.9	31 374	15.4	20.3	22.1
Charlottesville City	1 196	5 867	14 747	7.4	75.5	34.1	35.6	8 130	12 928	24 190	3.5	2.6	32 597	21.6	29.6	32.8
Chesapeake City	431	3 833	40 639	12.1	77.1	16.9	187.1	5 257	13 817	35 737	13.2	2.4	45 427	10.1	14.2	13.4
Clifton Forge City	405	2 005	1 050	7.2	69.0	8.9	0.0	0	11 562	20 659	-7.8	3.2	27 604	19.0	27.2	27.5
Colonial Heights City	172	6 231	3 384	6.7	77.8	16.7	17.1	6 127	15 639	34 472	-2.4	2.5	40 923	7.5	11.3	11.2
Covington City	314	4 021	1 365	4.5	64.5	7.0	7.2	7 564	10 814	20 913	-8.7	0.8	27 748	17.2	25.5	28.4
Danville City	463	4 492	10 964	11.4	57.4	12.4	41.9	5 050	11 344	20 413	-11.2	1.3	26 481	22.4	31.0	32.6
Emporia City	1 078	8 157	1 189	9.3	58.1	13.4	0.0	0	10 478	21 009	3.9	1.6	24 255	26.9	36.7	39.1
Fairfax City	200	4 426	5 040	18.2	87.5	41.3	0.3	0	21 929	50 913	17.7	9.0	61 099	5.4	7.4	8.3
Falls Church City	462	4 386	2 281	18.5	91.4	52.8	13.8	9 297	26 709	51 011	24.1	12.4	64 420	3.5	4.4	5.2
Franklin City	394	4 707	1 902	11.5	61.9	14.4	9.7	5 298	11 212	20 357	-9.8	2.7	27 348	23.4	34.4	33.0
Fredericksburg City	282	4 157	5 149	6.4	73.8	26.1	14.7	6 862	13 825	26 614	11.3	2.9	35 484	17.8	27.9	30.5
Galax City	691	4 853	1 204	6.4	56.2	11.3	6.0	4 862	10 490	20 263	7.7	1.6	25 767	22.1	36.2	36.3
Hampton City	383	4 884	36 567	20.8	79.7	19.1	125.6	5 237	13 099	30 144	6.0	1.6	36 297	14.6	22.4	20.7
Harrisonburg City	317	3 852	13 711	11.3	76.8	28.7	22.1	6 129	11 607	25 312	8.8	3.0	35 283	18.3	22.1	22.1
Hopewell City	1 208	7 282	5 223	8.8	67.4	10.0	23.0	5 676	11 897	26 934	-1.5	1.3	32 781	18.4	28.9	29.1
Lexington City	221	1 708	3 415	48.1	72.8	32.1	2.5	5 424	10 077	21 361	4.1	1.9	29 490	20.1	21.0	21.0
Lynchburg City	601	4 268	19 204	37.7	69.5	21.7	53.8	5 663	12 657	23 726	-7.5	2.8	29 105	21.4	30.2	30.5

1. Data for serious crimes have not been adjusted for underreporting; this may affect comparability between geographic areas and over time. 2. Per 100,000 population estimated by the FBI. 3. All persons 3 years old and over enrolled in nursery school through college. 4. Persons 25 years old and over. 5. Elementary and secondary education expenditures, local government fiscal years ending between July 1, 1996 and June 30, 1997. 6. Based on population enumerated as of April 1, 1990.

STATE County	Total (mil dol)	Percent change, 1997–1998	Per capita[1] Dollars	Per capita[1] Rank	Wages and salaries[2] (mil dol)	Proprietor's income (mil dol)	Dividends, interest, and rent (mil dol)	Transfer payments Total (mil dol)	Govt payments to individuals Total (mil dol)	Social Security (mil dol)	Medical payments (mil dol)	Income mainte-nance (mil dol)	Unemploy-ment insurance (mil dol)
	62	63	64	65	66	67	68	69	70	71	72	73	74
VIRGINIA—Cont'd													
Louisa	534	6.9	21 778	1 168	196	56	76	76	71	33	28	6	1
Lunenburg	193	2.7	16 121	2 777	69	12	36	46	44	20	15	5	0
Madison	240	6.6	19 014	2 052	72	17	53	38	36	17	13	3	0
Mathews	232	3.5	25 507	437	33	13	64	38	36	19	13	2	0
Mecklenburg	604	3.6	19 449	1 908	351	34	113	127	121	57	45	13	2
Middlesex	224	3.1	23 255	805	65	11	71	43	41	23	14	2	1
Montgomery	[3]1 711	[3]4.1	[3]18 506	[3]2 208	[3]1 242	[3]92	[3]298	[3]217	[3]200	[3]96	[3]62	[3]17	[3]1
Nelson	273	5.5	19 659	1 833	75	22	61	54	52	23	19	4	0
New Kent	305	5.3	23 705	703	64	13	45	31	29	15	10	2	0
Northampton	242	2.8	18 992	2 059	108	22	55	62	59	28	20	8	1
Northumberland	254	2.0	22 105	1 065	62	21	92	56	53	29	19	2	1
Nottoway	281	4.4	18 522	2 203	155	15	55	68	65	24	28	6	1
Orange	533	5.8	20 988	1 396	197	30	133	92	87	44	32	6	1
Page	422	4.3	18 285	2 267	169	30	75	78	73	36	26	6	1
Patrick	331	2.6	17 945	2 363	131	21	53	66	63	31	22	6	2
Pittsylvania	[4]2 137	[4]3.1	[4]19 738	[4]1 800	[4]1 266	[4]102	[4]364	[4]408	[4]388	[4]196	[4]124	[4]43	[4]9
Powhatan	450	7.3	20 942	1 409	136	30	57	43	39	21	13	2	0
Prince Edward	293	4.5	15 237	2 908	205	22	54	64	61	27	22	8	1
Prince George	[5]1 121	[5]3.4	[5]21 846	[5]1 147	[5]998	[5]40	[5]54	[5]145	[5]136	[5]64	[5]45	[5]15	[5]1
Prince William	[6]8 405	[6]7.1	[6]27 759	[6]247	[6]3 513	[6]320	[6]1 033	[6]427	[6]372	[6]160	[6]133	[6]36	[6]4
Pulaski	662	4.5	19 244	1 975	469	35	94	134	128	62	47	11	1
Rappahannock	184	6.3	25 170	472	37	19	46	21	20	10	8	1	0
Richmond	141	0.8	16 258	2 751	80	4	32	31	29	14	11	2	0
Roanoke	[7]3 341	[7]4.7	[7]31 675	[7]124	[7]1 853	[7]221	[7]797	[7]307	[7]288	[7]176	[7]68	[7]12	[7]2
Rockbridge	[8]655	[8]4.6	[8]19 701	[8]1 816	[8]362	[8]37	[8]146	[8]113	[8]107	[8]58	[8]34	[8]8	[8]1
Rockingham	[9]2 145	[9]6.3	[9]22 072	[9]1 078	[9]1 533	[9]194	[9]378	[9]251	[9]233	[9]131	[9]70	[9]16	[9]1
Russell	487	0.6	16 855	2 643	228	26	66	143	138	59	48	16	3
Scott	365	1.5	16 119	2 778	101	14	52	105	101	43	36	15	1
Shenandoah	726	6.2	20 896	1 424	365	64	143	109	103	58	32	6	1
Smyth	602	4.5	18 360	2 249	392	37	90	128	122	59	42	12	2
Southampton	[10]566	[10]3.0	[10]21 776	[10]1 170	[10]221	[10]28	[10]88	[10]105	[10]100	[10]42	[10]40	[10]13	[10]1
Spotsylvania	[11]2 732	[11]9.2	[11]26 555	[11]337	[11]1 191	[11]137	[11]388	[11]236	[11]217	[11]102	[11]81	[11]14	[11]2
Stafford	2 065	6.1	23 031	848	696	74	293	119	103	53	32	7	1
Surry	115	-0.9	17 682	2 442	101	2	25	21	19	9	7	2	0
Sussex	211	3.4	21 030	1 380	93	7	33	46	44	17	19	6	0
Tazewell	829	1.9	17 766	2 416	413	44	147	223	215	85	72	23	2
Warren	718	7.0	23 857	672	239	41	121	81	75	41	24	5	1
Washington	[12]1 390	[12]4.6	[12]20 877	[12]1 432	[12]889	[12]85	[12]267	[12]258	[12]246	[12]123	[12]75	[12]24	[12]3
Westmoreland	331	3.3	20 313	1 624	74	16	72	65	62	29	24	5	1
Wise	[13]789	[13]2.1	[13]18 277	[13]2 271	[13]522	[13]35	[13]120	[13]232		[13]90	[13]80	[13]29	[13]4
Wythe	513	4.0	19 523	1 877	277	28	80	105	101	48	35	9	1
York	[14]1 727	[14]5.7	[14]25 030	[14]489	[14]525	[14]60	[14]324	[14]138	[14]125	[14]67	[14]38	[14]6	[14]1
Independent Cities													
Alexandria City	5 322	6.6	46 290	11	4 263	328	1 005	314	293	97	134	31	3
Bedford City	[15]	[15]	[15]	[15]	[15]	[15]	[15]	[15]	[15]	[15]	[15]	[15]	[15]
Bristol City	[12]	[12]	[12]	[12]	[12]	[12]	[12]	[12]	[12]	[12]	[12]	[12]	[12]
Buena Vista City	[8]	[8]	[8]	[8]	[8]	[8]	[8]	[8]	[8]	[8]	[8]	[8]	[8]
Charlottesville City	[16]	[16]	[16]	[16]	[16]	[16]	[16]	[16]	[16]	[16]	[16]	[16]	[16]
Chesapeake City	4 707	6.3	23 606	721	2 258	143	600	441	405	181	141	40	5
Clifton Forge City	[17]	[17]	[17]	[17]	[17]	[17]	[17]	[17]	[17]	[17]	[17]	[17]	[17]
Colonial Heights City	[18]	[18]	[18]	[18]	[18]	[18]	[18]	[18]	[18]	[18]	[18]	[18]	[18]
Covington City	[17]	[17]	[17]	[17]	[17]	[17]	[17]	[17]	[17]	[17]	[17]	[17]	[17]
Danville City	[4]	[4]	[4]	[4]	[4]	[4]	[4]	[4]	[4]	[4]	[4]	[4]	[4]
Emporia City	[19]	[19]	[19]	[19]	[19]	[19]	[19]	[19]	[19]	[19]	[19]	[19]	[19]
Fairfax City	[20]	[20]	[20]	[20]	[20]	[20]	[20]	[20]	[20]	[20]	[20]	[20]	[20]
Falls Church City	[20]	[20]	[20]	[20]	[20]	[20]	[20]	[20]	[20]	[20]	[20]	[20]	[20]
Franklin City	[10]	[10]	[10]	[10]	[10]	[10]	[10]	[10]	[10]	[10]	[10]	[10]	[10]
Fredericksburg City	[11]	[11]	[11]	[11]	[11]	[11]	[11]	[11]	[11]	[11]	[11]	[11]	[11]
Galax City	[21]	[21]	[21]	[21]	[21]	[21]	[21]	[21]	[21]	[21]	[21]	[21]	[21]
Hampton City	2 959	6.1	21 646	1 205	2 624	85	490	402	378	156	129	42	4
Harrisonburg City	[9]	[9]	[9]	[9]	[9]	[9]	[9]	[9]	[9]	[9]	[9]	[9]	[9]
Hopewell City	[5]	[5]	[5]	[5]	[5]	[5]	[5]	[5]	[5]	[5]	[5]	[5]	[5]
Lexington City	[8]	[8]	[8]	[8]	[8]	[8]	[8]	[8]	[8]	[8]	[8]	[8]	[8]
Lynchburg City	[22]	[22]	[22]	[22]	[22]	[22]	[22]	[22]	[22]	[22]	[22]	[22]	[22]

1. Based on the resident population estimated as of July 1 of the year shown.   2. Includes other labor income.   3. Radford included with Montgomery County.   4. Danville included with Pittsylvania County.   5. Hopewell included with Prince George County.   6. Manassas and Manassas Park included with Prince William County.   7. Salem included with Roanoke County.   8. Buena Vista and Lexington included with Rockbridge County.   9. Harrisonburg included with Rockingham County.   10. Franklin included with Southhampton County.   11. Fredericksburg included with Spotsylvania County.   12. Bristol included with Washington County.   13. Norton included with Wise County.   14. Poquoson included with York County.   15. Bedford City included with Bedford County.   16. Charlottesville included with Albemarle County.   17. Clifton Forge and Covington included with Alleghany County.   18. Petersburg and Colonial Heights included with Dinwiddie County.   19. Emporia included with Greensville County.   20. Fairfax City and Falls Church included with Fairfax County.   21. Galax included with Carroll County. County.   22. Lynchburg included with Campbell County.

Table B. States and Counties — Earnings, Social Security, and Housing

STATE County	Earnings, 1998									Social Security beneficiaries, December 1998		Supplemental Security Income recipients, December 1998	Housing units, 1990	
		Percent by selected industries												
		Goods-related[1]			Service-related and other[2]									
	Total (mil dol)	Farm	Total	Manu-facturing	Total	Retail trade	Finance, insur-ance, and real estate	Services	Govern-ment	Number	Rate[3]		Total	Percent change, 1980–1990
	75	76	77	78	79	80	81	82	83	84	85	86	87	88
VIRGINIA—Cont'd														
Louisa	252	0.2	D	20.2	D	4.9	3.8	D	12.8	4 335	176	582	9 080	28.6
Lunenburg	81	6.2	33.7	20.9	29.1	7.4	3.0	12.1	31.0	2 742	228	496	5 065	5.3
Madison	89	1.1	30.9	21.7	50.1	13.1	1.5	26.9	17.9	2 244	177	271	4 547	13.8
Mathews	46	2.5	27.4	11.6	46.6	14.7	3.8	17.7	23.6	2 270	250	127	4 725	11.8
Mecklenburg	385	2.5	D	27.8	D	13.1	D	17.6	17.3	7 618	245	1 355	14 589	11.9
Middlesex	76	0.7	21.1	10.8	48.7	12.6	5.8	20.2	29.4	2 727	283	210	5 486	11.1
Montgomery	(4)1 334	(4)0.2	(4)D	(4)22.0	(4)D	(4)10.3	(4)4.5	(4)18.6	(4)35.3	9 173	121	1 017	27 770	24.1
Nelson	97	2.2	D	7.6	D	5.8	3.3	34.2	17.8	3 012	216	400	7 063	28.4
New Kent	77	-0.4	D	4.7	D	11.4	3.7	33.5	22.1	1 738	133	136	3 968	21.9
Northampton	130	11.6	11.3	7.1	52.8	10.4	2.0	31.3	24.3	3 689	290	716	6 183	0.8
Northumberland	83	-0.8	D	30.6	D	7.7	5.9	20.1	15.7	3 447	299	197	6 841	22.5
Nottoway	170	1.9	D	16.0	D	9.5	2.9	12.0	37.9	3 265	218	592	5 732	2.0
Orange	227	2.3	D	24.2	D	12.0	4.9	13.6	21.4	5 406	213	556	9 038	22.8
Page	199	3.1	44.7	35.8	34.6	8.1	2.5	17.2	17.6	4 725	206	565	8 948	7.4
Patrick	153	1.2	50.4	45.8	35.4	7.2	2.1	15.7	13.0	4 126	224	536	8 125	15.2
Pittsylvania	(5)1 368	(5)1.2	(5)D	(5)37.5	(5)D	(5)10.5	(5)3.3	(5)20.5	(5)13.8	13 399	233	1 843	22 861	-5.7
Powhatan	166	0.9	D	2.9	D	7.3	5.6	12.9	40.0	2 491	113	215	4 910	27.9
Prince Edward	226	1.4	D	8.6	D	18.5	3.2	31.1	24.5	3 588	189	836	6 075	9.5
Prince George	(6)1 037	(6)0.1	(6)25.2	(6)18.3	(6)21.5	(6)5.4	(6)1.2	(6)10.8	(6)53.3	3 206	106	306	8 640	24.4
Prince William	(7)3 833	(7)0.0	(7)D	(7)10.2	(7)D	(7)13.8	(7)D	(7)21.4	(7)26.9	16 201	62	1 764	74 759	60.8
Pulaski	505	0.3	D	46.9	D	6.6	1.9	13.5	12.2	7 625	221	1 061	14 740	7.3
Rappahannock	56	1.1	25.5	3.9	56.5	18.5	3.1	25.4	16.9	1 242	171	134	2 964	9.6
Richmond	84	-1.7	D	D	D	7.8	3.2	15.4	32.7	1 763	203	196	3 179	5.7
Roanoke	(8)2 074	(8)0.0	(8)D	(8)21.9	(8)D	(8)9.1	(8)3.3	(8)26.5	(8)15.7	14 981	185	467	31 689	18.2
Rockbridge	(9)399	(9)0.6	(9)D	(9)26.2	(9)D	(9)11.4	(9)3.3	(9)23.6	(9)21.3	3 907	200	345	7 975	11.9
Rockingham	(10)1 727	(10)4.1	(10)D	(10)29.4	(10)D	(10)10.0	(10)3.8	(10)19.9	(10)14.7	13 649	216	798	22 614	8.4
Russell	254	0.9	37.4	20.0	42.7	9.0	2.4	16.1	18.9	7 784	268	1 613	11 558	0.3
Scott	115	1.2	D	15.5	D	15.3	4.4	20.2	27.0	5 971	264	1 586	10 003	2.3
Shenandoah	429	4.3	D	37.9	D	8.9	3.2	15.4	11.7	7 275	210	519	15 160	26.3
Smyth	428	0.5	D	43.9	D	7.2	1.7	16.0	18.1	7 788	238	1 301	13 132	6.7
Southampton	(11)250	(11)4.3	(11)D	(11)13.4	(11)D	(11)9.6	(11)D	(11)22.3	(11)29.9	3 434	197	569	6 560	4.9
Spotsylvania	(12)1 327	(12)0.0	(12)D	(12)9.7	(12)D	(12)16.0	(12)6.9	(12)29.7	(12)16.7	8 992	107	605	20 483	72.9
Stafford	770	0.0	14.5	3.5	55.7	7.3	15.2	18.0	19.8	6 697	77	462	20 529	54.7
Surry	103	-0.2	9.8	3.2	D	1.5	D	6.9	13.4	1 158	179	147	2 982	9.5
Sussex	101	2.2	23.8	15.7	43.3	11.6	2.8	13.9	30.7	2 266	228	559	4 252	7.4
Tazewell	457	0.8	D	11.0	D	16.0	3.3	26.6	19.6	10 706	229	2 092	18 901	3.4
Warren	279	0.2	31.9	19.7	52.1	13.7	4.4	25.9	15.8	4 916	163	391	11 223	17.9
Washington	(13)973	(13)0.9	(13)D	(13)28.0	(13)D	(13)13.0	(13)6.3	(13)18.4	(13)15.1	10 931	222	1 764	19 183	7.3
Westmoreland	90	2.4	D	20.0	D	13.9	5.0	18.6	23.4	3 782	232	382	8 378	12.1
Wise	(14)557	(14)0.1	(14)28.6	(14)3.8	(14)D	(14)11.0	(14)D	(14)22.7	(14)19.9	10 165	263	2 477	15 927	1.7
Wythe	306	0.5	29.5	23.6	50.1	14.0	2.7	21.2	19.9	6 332	241	982	10 659	8.4
York	(15)585	(15)0.1	(15)19.1	(15)5.9	(15)D	(15)10.0	(15)3.3	(15)19.7	(15)40.6	6 742	115	268	15 284	33.8
Independent Cities														
Alexandria City	4 592	0.0	6.1	2.7	69.0	6.9	6.6	46.4	24.9	11 071	94	2 564	58 252	11.9
Bedford City	(16)	(16)	(16)	(16)	(16)	(16)	(16)	(16)	(16)	1 850	293	216	2 625	0.7
Bristol City	(13)	(13)	(13)	(13)	(13)	(13)	(13)	(13)	(13)	4 602	263	844	8 174	5.6
Buena Vista City	(9)	(9)	(9)	(9)	(9)	(9)	(9)	(9)	(9)	1 407	224	201	2 494	3.7
Charlottesville City	(17)	(17)	(17)	(17)	(17)	(17)	(17)	(17)	(17)	6 089	159	1 080	16 785	4.9
Chesapeake City	2 401	0.2	22.9	9.8	54.6	12.9	4.9	22.3	22.4	22 988	115	2 652	55 742	46.5
Clifton Forge City	(18)	(18)	(18)	(18)	(18)	(18)	(18)	(18)	(18)	998	230	214	2 131	3.2
Colonial Heights City	(19)	(19)	(19)	(19)	(19)	(19)	(19)	(19)	(19)	3 638	215	231	6 592	8.5
Covington City	(18)	(18)	(18)	(18)	(18)	(18)	(18)	(18)	(18)	1 873	273	264	3 269	-12.5
Danville City	(5)	(5)	(5)	(5)	(5)	(5)	(5)	(5)	(5)	11 699	230	2 379	23 297	26.6
Emporia City	(20)	(20)	(20)	(20)	(20)	(20)	(20)	(20)	(20)	1 477	270	377	2 178	11.6
Fairfax City	(21)	(21)	(21)	(21)	(21)	(21)	(21)	(21)	(21)	2 398	116	822	7 677	8.9
Falls Church City	(21)	(21)	(21)	(21)	(21)	(21)	(21)	(21)	(21)	1 348	134	402	4 668	3.7
Franklin City	(11)	(11)	(11)	(11)	(11)	(11)	(11)	(11)	(11)	1 954	225	592	3 166	17.8
Fredericksburg City	(12)	(12)	(12)	(12)	(12)	(12)	(12)	(12)	(12)	3 531	163	512	8 063	27.0
Galax City	(22)	(22)	(22)	(22)	(22)	(22)	(22)	(22)	(22)	2 007	292	427	2 943	4.7
Hampton City	2 709	0.0	12.3	8.5	38.3	8.4	2.5	21.4	49.4	19 482	142	2 384	53 623	22.8
Harrisonburg City	(10)	(10)	(10)	(10)	(10)	(10)	(10)	(10)	(10)	2 108	63	494	10 900	76.7
Hopewell City	(6)	(6)	(6)	(6)	(6)	(6)	(6)	(6)	(6)	4 405	196	741	9 625	3.6
Lexington City	(9)	(9)	(9)	(9)	(9)	(9)	(9)	(9)	(9)	1 683	229	221	2 311	-3.3
Lynchburg City	(23)	(23)	(23)	(23)	(23)	(23)	(23)	(23)	(23)	14 060	215	1 953	27 233	7.1

1. Covers mining, construction, and manufacturing. 2. Covers private sector earnings in agricultural services, forestry, and fisheries; transportation and public utilities; wholesale trade; retail trade; finance, insurance, and real estate; and services. 3. Per 1,000 resident population estimated as of July 1 of the year shown. 4. Radford included with Montgomery County. 5. Danville included with Pittsylvania County. 6. Hopewell included with Prince George County. 7. Manassas and Manassas Park included with Prince William County. 8. Salem included with Roanoke County. 9. Buena Vista and Lexington included with Rockbridge County. 10. Harrisonburg included with Rockingham County. 11. Franklin included with Southampton County. 12. Fredericksburg included with Spotsylvania County. 13. Bristol included with Washington County. 14. Norton included with Wise County. 15. Poquoson included with York County. 16. Bedford City included with Bedford County. 17. Charlottesville included with Albemarle County. 18. Clifton Forge and Covington included with Alleghany County. 19. Petersburg and Colonial Heights included with Dinwiddie County. 20. Emporia included with Greensville County. 21. Fairfax City and Falls Church included with Fairfax County. 22. Galax included with Carroll County. 23. Lynchburg included with Campbell County.

	Housing units, 1990 (cont'd)								Civilian labor force, 1999				Civilian employment, 1990[5]		
	Occupied units										Unemployment			Percent	
			Owner-occupied				Renter-occupied								
				Owner cost as a percent of income											
STATE County	Total	Percent	Median value[1]	With a mort-gage	Without a mort-gage	Median rent[2]	Rent as per-cent of income	Sub-stand-ard units[3] (percent)	Total	Percent change, 1998–1999	Total	Rate[4]	Total	Professional, managerial, and technical	Precision production, craft, and repair
	89	90	91	92	93	94	95	96	97	98	99	100	101	102	103

STATE County	89	90	91	92	93	94	95	96	97	98	99	100	101	102	103
VIRGINIA—Cont'd															
Louisa	7 427	79.9	64 400	20.7	12.3	399	24.7	8.8	9 618	3.6	339	3.5	9 646	18.8	19.3
Lunenburg	4 423	77.6	37 600	17.8	13.5	246	20.5	9.0	4 820	5.8	231	4.8	5 121	13.2	14.1
Madison	4 144	77.1	72 200	21.0	12.7	361	17.0	11.3	8 657	6.7	153	1.8	5 511	21.3	12.8
Mathews	3 530	83.3	79 900	23.0	12.3	391	26.8	7.5	4 584	-0.7	101	2.2	3 865	20.9	16.2
Mecklenburg	11 244	71.7	50 700	17.0	13.0	244	18.8	10.3	15 070	2.1	800	5.3	13 355	17.9	13.3
Middlesex	3 530	82.8	77 500	21.1	13.2	338	24.0	6.2	5 046	4.1	109	2.2	3 884	23.0	15.3
Montgomery	26 241	55.4	71 700	19.2	11.6	397	30.0	3.1	37 398	1.8	694	1.9	34 250	37.1	10.3
Nelson	4 807	79.1	53 100	19.2	12.6	308	19.8	11.8	7 317	8.4	157	2.1	5 849	20.3	14.4
New Kent	3 718	87.8	86 500	20.1	12.1	459	18.6	3.8	6 867	5.0	134	2.0	5 326	28.6	16.6
Northampton	5 129	65.7	47 700	19.1	14.7	260	24.8	15.2	5 203	1.1	235	4.5	5 160	24.3	10.9
Northumberland	4 492	87.1	80 300	22.3	12.7	327	22.4	8.1	5 295	2.9	398	7.5	4 192	18.3	13.2
Nottoway	5 244	73.1	43 000	19.3	13.4	294	21.8	6.8	6 587	2.2	184	2.8	6 137	18.9	11.0
Orange	7 930	76.3	83 200	20.8	12.1	419	22.6	4.4	11 194	1.1	279	2.5	10 519	24.3	16.4
Page	8 055	76.9	61 500	20.9	12.8	359	23.8	6.5	11 957	3.3	466	3.9	9 590	14.4	21.5
Patrick	6 908	81.5	51 700	17.6	11.3	230	16.5	4.7	8 980	0.1	487	5.4	8 933	16.3	16.1
Pittsylvania	20 613	79.6	48 800	15.3	12.5	276	18.0	7.7	31 535	0.4	1 842	5.8	27 399	15.6	14.5
Powhatan	4 672	85.1	74 700	20.2	12.0	448	20.5	3.7	10 922	2.9	179	1.6	7 115	26.0	18.2
Prince Edward	5 373	70.9	54 200	18.9	12.7	310	22.3	7.8	8 190	1.3	288	3.5	6 969	23.9	10.0
Prince George	8 250	68.8	75 800	18.3	11.6	434	19.2	5.4	12 775	0.7	345	2.7	10 994	24.1	14.4
Prince William	69 709	71.0	138 500	25.6	12.5	736	26.6	2.4	137 586	1.9	2 707	2.0	112 964	37.3	12.1
Pulaski	13 349	73.0	51 400	16.8	11.9	297	21.7	3.9	17 140	3.0	763	4.5	15 673	21.9	13.6
Rappahannock	2 496	72.2	89 300	22.9	14.9	413	23.2	10.0	4 007	-3.4	80	2.0	3 375	22.6	19.3
Richmond	2 645	81.5	63 100	18.1	12.6	336	17.2	10.8	4 112	4.6	182	4.4	3 215	17.4	14.3
Roanoke	30 355	77.3	80 500	17.5	11.8	420	21.8	1.1	47 545	-2.6	639	1.3	42 577	33.8	9.8
Rockbridge	7 202	74.9	54 700	18.6	12.1	310	21.6	6.8	10 362	4.3	214	2.1	8 679	20.4	14.4
Rockingham	20 750	78.2	71 800	18.8	12.0	362	20.4	5.3	37 823	2.9	474	1.3	30 026	19.7	15.8
Russell	10 641	80.2	45 000	19.3	12.1	269	26.8	6.3	14 378	1.4	1 168	8.1	10 414	16.8	21.0
Scott	8 966	77.8	41 400	15.6	11.9	250	25.5	9.9	9 287	-2.9	609	6.6	8 550	15.8	16.5
Shenandoah	12 452	71.5	73 600	20.8	12.4	359	23.2	5.8	17 566	1.8	492	2.8	15 622	18.7	17.8
Smyth	12 234	74.3	42 600	16.3	11.9	266	20.9	4.8	16 697	0.7	1 013	6.1	14 326	18.4	13.8
Southampton	6 009	71.5	57 000	19.1	13.4	265	20.9	12.3	8 448	8.3	282	3.3	7 316	18.7	14.9
Spotsylvania	18 945	81.9	104 000	22.2	12.5	684	24.1	3.4	43 056	2.9	699	1.6	29 479	29.5	15.3
Stafford	19 415	81.9	125 400	24.3	12.5	669	26.8	2.6	43 953	-1.2	696	1.6	30 440	32.8	15.3
Surry	2 283	76.5	59 400	19.5	13.5	296	24.7	8.8	2 417	-1.5	186	7.7	2 693	17.6	19.9
Sussex	3 795	69.3	48 200	18.2	13.0	293	24.7	10.2	6 403	13.6	184	2.9	4 571	17.3	11.3
Tazewell	17 309	77.0	48 600	19.2	12.1	298	27.6	4.5	19 713	-1.5	1 381	7.0	16 749	24.6	17.7
Warren	9 879	72.3	85 100	21.1	11.9	407	22.5	3.0	14 957	0.0	396	2.6	12 856	23.5	20.7
Washington	17 483	77.1	52 500	18.8	12.2	299	22.2	4.7	24 541	-1.0	1 142	4.7	20 932	22.3	12.9
Westmoreland	6 057	79.3	68 800	19.6	12.7	397	26.3	9.4	7 398	-1.2	376	5.1	6 745	24.4	13.0
Wise	14 513	76.4	43 500	18.8	12.5	302	29.7	5.8	14 712	-0.8	1 357	9.2	13 514	23.9	20.1
Wythe	9 852	77.1	48 900	17.6	11.8	272	23.5	5.1	14 365	-2.1	591	4.1	11 757	20.6	12.8
York	14 474	71.6	121 600	21.9	11.6	513	24.7	2.3	29 155	3.3	581	2.0	18 949	40.7	12.0
Independent Cities															
Alexandria City	53 280	40.5	228 600	22.2	12.0	701	25.4	4.8	75 722	1.5	1 670	2.2	70 756	53.1	4.9
Bedford City	2 475	62.3	55 700	15.6	12.4	251	24.5	1.5	2 713	3.6	59	2.2	2 504	24.2	10.2
Bristol City	7 591	63.1	48 400	19.3	13.6	317	27.9	1.8	8 005	-1.1	276	3.4	7 825	23.0	10.8
Buena Vista City	2 404	72.2	43 300	20.2	13.6	294	20.9	3.6	3 323	6.0	89	2.7	3 006	19.4	12.0
Charlottesville City	16 009	42.4	85 600	20.5	12.6	469	29.7	3.0	19 086	0.1	323	1.7	20 198	38.2	8.4
Chesapeake City	51 965	73.0	88 200	23.9	13.1	494	26.7	2.9	105 309	2.2	2 762	2.6	72 486	30.4	16.1
Clifton Forge City	1 930	62.0	35 200	16.5	12.6	290	29.0	1.5	1 768	-5.4	88	5.0	1 685	22.5	13.5
Colonial Heights City	6 363	72.2	71 000	17.7	12.8	458	23.3	1.1	8 801	0.6	210	2.4	8 063	31.0	13.6
Covington City	2 998	69.2	38 700	17.3	12.9	313	24.2	1.2	3 284	-2.9	247	7.5	2 869	19.2	11.0
Danville City	21 712	59.4	47 000	16.4	12.7	278	23.6	3.0	25 077	0.3	1 653	6.6	23 259	21.9	11.5
Emporia City	2 031	56.7	52 000	19.5	14.6	345	24.1	5.6	2 457	-0.5	118	4.8	2 270	23.7	10.8
Fairfax City	7 362	65.9	184 300	20.5	11.9	823	27.3	2.5	12 429	1.1	112	0.9	11 890	45.0	8.3
Falls Church City	4 195	58.8	226 000	20.7	12.3	809	27.6	4.1	5 937	0.6	76	1.3	5 660	58.5	4.8
Franklin City	3 006	53.8	67 900	18.9	16.5	324	26.0	5.3	4 242	8.5	178	4.2	3 272	24.3	12.2
Fredericksburg City	7 450	37.3	104 900	20.6	12.4	530	27.2	2.7	11 079	2.0	279	2.5	9 629	32.4	12.6
Galax City	2 750	68.3	45 200	17.3	13.2	264	26.9	4.1	3 404	0.5	146	4.3	3 236	21.8	11.3
Hampton City	49 673	59.2	78 200	22.4	13.2	470	26.1	2.6	66 709	-0.7	2 669	4.0	58 561	30.0	15.1
Harrisonburg City	10 310	42.1	89 300	21.3	11.6	410	25.9	1.3	18 398	3.5	240	1.3	14 735	32.0	8.2
Hopewell City	9 014	56.9	54 300	17.3	12.6	389	24.5	3.1	10 633	0.6	440	4.1	10 372	21.8	15.1
Lexington City	2 172	54.9	74 500	19.7	12.5	355	28.8	1.1	3 046	5.7	44	1.4	2 586	34.2	4.9
Lynchburg City	25 143	58.2	56 900	16.9	12.6	346	24.7	2.2	30 396	1.6	632	2.1	29 569	30.7	8.6

1. Specified owner-occupied units.   2. Specified renter-occupied units.   3. Overcrowded or lacking complete plumbing facilities.   4. Percent of civilian labor force.   5. Persons 16 years and older.

Table B. States and Counties — Nonfarm Employment and Agriculture

	Private nonfarm establishments, employment and payroll, 1998								Agriculture, 1997			
STATE County	Number of establish-ments	Employment						Annual payroll		Farms			Farm operators
		Total	Health Care and Social Assistance	Manufac-turing	Retail trade	Finance and Insurance	Professional Scientific and Technical Services	Total (mil dol)	Average per employee (dollars)	Number	Percent with—		Whose principal occu-pation is farming (percent)
											Less than 50 acres	500 acres and over	
	104	105	106	107	108	109	110	111	112	113	114	115	116
VIRGINIA—Cont'd													
Louisa	488	3 950	223	620	533	126	121	123	31 034	385	26.0	10.9	43.4
Lunenburg	209	1 951	80	840	379	68	D	36	18 500	339	20.1	10.0	44.8
Madison	262	2 304	240	515	688	22	D	40	17 230	422	30.6	12.1	46.7
Mathews	198	1 097	115	170	274	D	25	19	16 874	58	50.0	8.6	36.2
Mecklenburg	836	12 115	1 321	4 400	1 970	262	305	239	19 696	604	20.7	14.4	51.7
Middlesex	341	2 199	399	224	449	117	90	39	17 510	67	29.9	19.4	56.7
Montgomery	1 748	22 397	2 186	4 900	4 852	642	1 383	489	21 829	517	32.9	7.4	37.7
Nelson	356	3 077	158	413	237	27	159	50	16 149	357	23.5	8.1	41.2
New Kent	269	2 041	414	154	455	29	49	39	19 314	64	29.7	14.1	42.2
Northampton	329	2 994	877	351	601	54	52	58	19 486	152	30.3	24.3	68.4
Northumberland	316	2 021	72	316	359	100	D	38	18 571	122	26.2	15.6	60.7
Nottoway	366	3 997	764	808	745	115	101	71	17 860	317	15.1	10.1	46.1
Orange	590	6 358	188	2 545	937	100	163	155	24 367	437	28.4	11.2	43.9
Page	448	5 981	493	2 738	698	139	81	109	18 221	541	43.8	4.3	54.0
Patrick	318	4 744	577	2 497	420	96	75	92	19 398	536	32.6	3.4	41.6
Pittsylvania	1 008	11 703	1 069	4 147	1 842	164	227	244	20 840	1 235	20.4	10.3	50.0
Powhatan	461	3 529	153	136	466	86	120	70	19 890	208	33.7	8.7	43.8
Prince Edward	536	7 282	1 872	670	1 487	187	116	133	18 247	312	17.6	10.9	45.2
Prince George	375	4 241	270	312	628	69	169	93	21 878	133	28.6	16.5	43.6
Prince William	4 506	57 514	5 154	3 345	14 200	949	2 863	1 359	23 623	261	47.9	4.6	43.7
Pulaski	677	13 258	1 254	6 653	1 546	173	101	320	24 150	370	31.6	8.9	38.4
Rappahannock	203	1 173	D	D	244	D	87	25	21 258	335	34.6	11.9	43.9
Richmond	219	2 069	328	531	378	80	33	42	20 313	139	27.3	18.7	49.6
Roanoke	1 506	20 847	1 987	2 624	2 720	2 688	708	530	25 438	273	48.7	1.8	42.9
Rockbridge	308	4 500	144	2 184	718	D	43	96	21 439	631	24.1	8.9	41.7
Rockingham	1 165	22 554	1 220	9 887	1 922	226	225	555	24 610	1 834	38.5	3.8	55.8
Russell	579	6 817	691	1 999	916	157	378	150	22 032	1 026	37.0	5.1	43.1
Scott	333	2 942	764	234	770	102	230	54	18 348	1 400	39.5	1.7	35.2
Shenandoah	859	12 326	1 170	5 588	1 690	327	181	268	21 774	841	35.3	5.5	44.2
Smyth	662	12 124	2 024	5 812	1 537	208	200	248	20 461	774	41.7	7.0	38.9
Southampton	292	4 495	218	2 828	347	40	50	161	35 758	277	13.4	41.2	69.3
Spotsylvania	1 386	16 194	955	1 955	3 523	327	641	367	22 651	253	34.4	8.7	42.3
Stafford	1 358	15 278	1 053	781	2 207	2 776	529	377	24 671	158	44.3	4.4	45.6
Surry	76	1 427	D	143	66	D	D	69	48 455	115	27.0	28.7	63.5
Sussex	217	3 196	329	1 291	406	113	D	68	21 411	134	19.4	35.8	70.1
Tazewell	1 227	12 999	1 718	1 442	3 181	362	588	267	20 539	488	30.7	13.3	38.7
Warren	745	7 580	764	1 326	1 289	285	312	169	22 304	259	35.5	9.3	37.1
Washington	1 153	13 808	1 838	2 238	2 492	400	474	305	22 092	1 744	51.3	3.6	36.6
Westmoreland	371	2 549	166	705	505	85	86	40	15 630	160	24.4	23.8	56.9
Wise	938	9 188	968	414	1 933	237	304	213	23 188	137	53.3	5.8	36.5
Wythe	728	8 698	1 154	2 209	1 888	171	138	171	19 605	734	27.9	9.3	42.8
York	1 165	13 577	572	705	2 401	297	483	250	18 435	39	64.1	2.6	35.9
Independent Cities													
Alexandria City	4 571	75 301	6 612	1 888	8 384	3 527	15 368	2 799	37 169	NA	NA	NA	NA
Bedford City	483	5 998	808	2 224	918	144	130	126	21 089	NA	NA	NA	NA
Bristol City	688	13 788	444	6 640	2 291	344	286	318	23 076	NA	NA	NA	NA
Buena Vista City	121	1 953	164	1 029	241	D	17	44	22 428	NA	NA	NA	NA
Charlottesville City	2 209	39 473	9 037	4 606	4 772	4 378	1 905	1 162	29 447	NA	NA	NA	NA
Chesapeake City	4 431	67 765	5 629	4 793	12 649	1 699	3 240	1 545	22 793	201	53.7	15.4	51.7
Clifton Forge City	130	1 214	259	72	324	62	D	19	15 962	NA	NA	NA	NA
Colonial Heights City	656	9 414	694	964	3 887	204	268	164	17 464	NA	NA	NA	NA
Covington City	262	4 667	133	2 591	676	93	47	151	32 265	NA	NA	NA	NA
Danville City	1 494	25 915	3 420	9 404	4 068	974	634	621	23 965	NA	NA	NA	NA
Emporia City	268	4 021	718	1 133	731	81	71	92	22 993	NA	NA	NA	NA
Fairfax City	2 108	32 986	1 896	256	5 341	1 712	12 698	1 349	40 893	NA	NA	NA	NA
Falls Church City	836	13 598	5 425	D	1 663	229	930	488	35 893	NA	NA	NA	NA
Franklin City	223	2 865	873	56	644	131	89	55	19 033	NA	NA	NA	NA
Fredericksburg City	1 484	20 208	4 124	1 031	4 448	790	808	470	23 249	NA	NA	NA	NA
Galax City	316	7 654	1 120	4 379	876	128	91	152	19 850	NA	NA	NA	NA
Hampton City	2 503	46 772	5 921	4 999	9 553	1 605	3 220	1 025	21 907	NA	NA	NA	NA
Harrisonburg City	1 435	23 203	3 703	3 876	4 485	673	819	500	21 543	NA	NA	NA	NA
Hopewell City	474	7 931	1 436	2 892	723	160	165	278	35 067	NA	NA	NA	NA
Lexington City	435	5 573	641	D	1 013	105	152	89	15 975	NA	NA	NA	NA
Lynchburg City	2 391	51 457	7 542	12 747	7 416	2 890	2 758	1 434	27 876	NA	NA	NA	NA

STATE County	Acreage (1,000)	Percent change, 1992–1997	Average size of farm	Total irrigated (1,000)	Total cropland (1,000)	Average per farm ($1,000)	Average per acre (dollars)	Value of machinery and equipment Average per farm ($1,000)	Total (mil dol)	Average per farm (dollars)	Crops	Live-stock and poultry products	$10,000 or more	$100,000 or more	Percent of land owned by Fed. Gov. 1997	Water con-sumption 1995 (mil gal/day)
	117	118	119	120	121	122	123	124	125	126	127	128	129	130	131	132
VIRGINIA—Cont'd																
Louisa	79	-2.4	205	0	41	371	2 056	44	10	24 785	25.8	74.2	36.6	6.0	0.0	2 077.5
Lunenburg	78	-9.6	229	1	31	243	1 086	36	16	48 592	57.4	42.6	36.3	7.7	0.1	1.8
Madison	100	-1.0	237	0	55	478	2 348	45	17	39 773	17.6	82.4	43.8	9.0	15.6	1.8
Mathews	8	40.3	145	D	6	301	2 075	43	4	61 471	95.0	5.0	41.4	8.6	0.0	0.8
Mecklenburg	167	-0.7	276	5	83	300	1 197	54	42	69 450	78.1	21.9	49.2	17.1	2.4	10.7
Middlesex	18	-17.0	273	D	15	458	1 680	81	5	77 441	96.7	3.3	50.7	16.4	0.0	1.1
Montgomery	93	-6.0	180	0	44	325	1 764	38	15	28 610	14.9	85.1	36.6	6.6	(1)12.0	24.6
Nelson	73	0.3	205	1	35	330	1 624	27	7	19 172	58.4	41.6	29.7	2.8	5.4	2.8
New Kent	16	-8.9	256	0	12	496	1 935	51	3	45 955	94.8	5.2	46.9	10.9	0.0	40.1
Northampton	56	8.5	371	9	50	731	1 995	98	39	253 929	70.3	29.7	72.4	35.5	0.4	6.4
Northumberland	38	-6.9	313	D	31	475	1 616	104	10	79 056	98.4	1.6	59.8	20.5	0.0	1.2
Nottoway	69	8.1	218	0	36	286	1 456	38	22	69 579	15.4	84.6	37.5	11.7	12.5	3.2
Orange	101	-6.1	232	0	56	557	2 364	45	26	59 205	39.2	60.8	38.2	8.0	0.3	3.4
Page	68	4.4	125	0	39	335	2 660	44	115	212 955	2.0	98.0	56.9	29.6	32.1	4.6
Patrick	74	-6.1	138	0	36	201	1 710	38	13	24 837	51.8	48.2	28.9	3.9	2.4	2.4
Pittsylvania	267	-10.1	216	7	124	280	1 273	47	59	47 663	75.0	25.0	43.2	13.0	(2)0.0	10.6
Powhatan	43	0.2	207	0	19	445	2 280	35	7	33 014	21.2	78.8	33.2	7.7	0.0	1.7
Prince Edward	73	5.7	234	0	35	283	1 232	31	14	43 336	13.7	86.3	34.3	8.0	0.0	2.8
Prince George	45	-8.2	338	D	21	504	1 373	53	6	43 828	88.0	12.0	42.1	9.8	(3)6.4	22.1
Prince William	36	8.9	138	1	26	568	4 372	43	10	37 290	50.2	49.8	24.9	6.1	(4)17.9	330.1
Pulaski	80	11.7	217	D	40	341	1 414	41	13	35 062	7.5	92.5	38.1	7.0	14.1	8.7
Rappahannock	72	-8.7	215	0	36	728	3 183	38	6	16 535	35.4	64.6	31.9	3.6	18.2	0.9
Richmond	36	-6.8	262	0	26	368	1 395	72	9	63 921	94.5	5.5	56.1	16.5	0.7	2.1
Roanoke	27	6.8	98	0	12	243	2 491	26	5	18 470	51.2	48.8	24.9	4.0	(5)3.6	8.1
Rockbridge	140	-1.3	222	0	64	394	1 911	30	15	24 478	10.8	89.2	37.1	4.9	(6)20.1	7.2
Rockingham	230	-2.4	126	3	145	383	3 069	47	438	238 879	2.7	97.3	61.0	38.2	(7)35.9	29.1
Russell	153	-4.9	149	0	62	189	1 184	26	19	18 128	31.0	69.0	40.9	2.8	0.2	15.7
Scott	138	2.6	98	0	54	119	1 071	28	14	10 147	58.3	41.7	26.2	1.0	12.6	2.7
Shenandoah	127	1.5	151	1	73	371	2 365	32	73	86 853	10.2	89.8	40.5	13.1	23.7	6.9
Smyth	125	4.3	162	0	57	196	1 232	29	20	25 295	18.1	81.9	39.5	5.3	30.8	5.7
Southampton	185	4.2	670	2	103	1 030	1 594	123	55	198 881	76.3	23.7	75.5	44.8	(8)0.0	25.4
Spotsylvania	48	-9.5	190	2	24	526	2 473	39	6	23 988	36.7	63.3	37.2	4.0	(9)2.0	8.0
Stafford	20	-0.5	126	0	11	435	4 413	44	2	12 928	60.1	39.9	21.5	2.5	18.1	10.8
Surry	45	-15.3	390	2	32	606	1 583	94	20	169 878	44.5	55.5	56.5	27.8	0.1	1.3
Sussex	82	-1.8	608	2	45	787	1 284	84	D	D	D	D	61.9	34.3	0.0	1.6
Tazewell	134	-3.9	274	0	50	304	1 015	30	13	26 715	6.1	93.9	38.7	6.4	2.9	6.8
Warren	45	14.8	173	0	23	428	2 808	40	6	21 386	10.8	89.2	27.0	3.5	17.3	8.3
Washington	178	-6.1	102	0	91	213	2 110	30	51	29 134	25.5	74.5	34.8	3.6	(10)8.8	12.5
Westmoreland	63	11.9	392	0	42	640	1 677	99	20	123 397	93.9	6.1	57.5	21.2	0.3	2.6
Wise	16	24.3	118	D	7	223	1 790	25	1	9 228	30.5	69.5	22.6	0.7	(11)18.2	8.3
Wythe	140	6.5	190	0	78	263	1 469	36	24	33 263	7.1	92.9	40.2	7.4	21.5	5.0
York	2	-1.2	51	0	1	577	D	D	2	58 822	D	D	30.8	10.3	(12)11.3	25.2
Independent Cities																
Alexandria City	NA	NA	NA	NA	NA	NA	NA	NA	NA	NA	NA	NA	NA	NA	(13)NA	282.1
Bedford City	NA	NA	NA	NA	NA	NA	NA	NA	NA	NA	NA	NA	NA	NA	(14)NA	0.0
Bristol City	NA	NA	NA	NA	NA	NA	NA	NA	NA	NA	NA	NA	NA	NA	(10)NA	0.0
Buena Vista City	NA	NA	NA	NA	NA	NA	NA	NA	NA	NA	NA	NA	NA	NA	(6)NA	0.4
Charlottesville City	NA	NA	NA	NA	NA	NA	NA	NA	NA	NA	NA	NA	NA	NA	(15)NA	0.0
Chesapeake City	61	12.3	302	1	51	676	2 205	66	36	180 665	90.3	9.7	49.8	20.9	22.9	12.0
Clifton Forge City	NA	NA	NA	NA	NA	NA	NA	NA	NA	NA	NA	NA	NA	NA	(16)NA	0.0
Colonial Heights City	NA	NA	NA	NA	NA	NA	NA	NA	NA	NA	NA	NA	NA	NA	(17)NA	0.0
Covington City	NA	NA	NA	NA	NA	NA	NA	NA	NA	NA	NA	NA	NA	NA	(16)NA	3.4
Danville City	NA	NA	NA	NA	NA	NA	NA	NA	NA	NA	NA	NA	NA	NA	(2)NA	18.9
Emporia City	NA	NA	NA	NA	NA	NA	NA	NA	NA	NA	NA	NA	NA	NA	(18)NA	1.4
Fairfax City	NA	NA	NA	NA	NA	NA	NA	NA	NA	NA	NA	NA	NA	NA	(13)NA	0.1
Falls Church City	NA	NA	NA	NA	NA	NA	NA	NA	NA	NA	NA	NA	NA	NA	(13)NA	0.0
Franklin City	NA	NA	NA	NA	NA	NA	NA	NA	NA	NA	NA	NA	NA	NA	(8)NA	1.2
Fredericksburg City	NA	NA	NA	NA	NA	NA	NA	NA	NA	NA	NA	NA	NA	NA	(9)NA	4.2
Galax City	NA	NA	NA	NA	NA	NA	NA	NA	NA	NA	NA	NA	NA	NA	(19)NA	2.6
Hampton City	NA	NA	NA	NA	NA	NA	NA	NA	NA	NA	NA	NA	NA	NA	(12)NA	1.6
Harrisonburg City	NA	NA	NA	NA	NA	NA	NA	NA	NA	NA	NA	NA	NA	NA	(7)NA	0.0
Hopewell City	NA	NA	NA	NA	NA	NA	NA	NA	NA	NA	NA	NA	NA	NA	(3)NA	156.0
Lexington City	NA	NA	NA	NA	NA	NA	NA	NA	NA	NA	NA	NA	NA	NA	(6)NA	0.0
Lynchburg City	NA	NA	NA	NA	NA	NA	NA	NA	NA	NA	NA	NA	NA	NA	NA	1.4

1. Radford included with Montgomery County. 2. Danville included with Pittsylvania County. 3. Hopewell and Petersburg included with Prince George County. 4. Manassas and Manassas Park included with Prince William County. 5. Roanoke City and Salem included with Roanoke County. 6. Buena Vista and Lexington included with Rockbridge County. 7. Harrisonburg included with Rockingham County. 8. Franklin included with Southhampton County. 9. Fredericksburg included with Spotsylvania County. 10. Bristol included with Washington County. 11. Norton included with Wise County. 12. Hampton, Newport News, and Poquoson included with York County. 13. Arlington County, Alexandria City, Fairfax, and falls Church City included with Fairfax County. 14. Bedford City included with Bedford County. 15. Charlottesville included with Albemarle County. 16. Clifton Forge and Covington included with Alleghany County. 17. Colonial Heights included with Chesterfield County. 18. Emporia included with Greensville County. 19. Galax included with Carroll County.

Table B. States and Counties — Residential Construction, Wholesale and Retail Trade, and Real Estate

STATE County	Value of Residential Construction Authorized by Building Permits, 1999		Wholesale Trade, 1997				Retail Trade[1], 1997				Real Estate and Rental and Leasing, 1997			
	New Construction ($1,000)	Number of Housing Units	Number of Establishments	Number of Employees	Sales (mil dol)	Annual Payroll (mil dol)	Number of Establishments	Number of Employees	Sales (mil dol)	Annual Payroll (mil dol)	Number of Establishments	Number of Employees	Receipts (mil dol)	Annual Payroll (mil dol)
	133	134	135	136	137	138	139	140	141	142	143	144	145	146
VIRGINIA—Cont'd														
Louisa	31 070	303	14	105	29.1	2.9	73	530	77.7	7.4	12	24	2.7	0.3
Lunenburg	2 324	20	11	55	25.9	1.3	56	368	39.7	4.9	2	D	D	D
Madison	12 619	99	9	30	7.6	0.6	48	418	86.9	7.4	4	6	0.3	0.1
Mathews	6 776	50	9	D	D	D	42	287	33.5	3.6	6	13	1.2	0.2
Mecklenburg	18 087	158	38	230	71.1	4.9	200	2 109	272.5	26.3	25	78	6.6	1.3
Middlesex	14 117	107	17	121	26.2	2.7	53	358	48.4	5.4	21	95	3.7	0.8
Montgomery	41 723	374	39	581	169.8	16.6	355	4 976	749.7	74.4	70	497	53.1	10.5
Nelson	21 051	140	7	13	6.1	0.3	51	225	27.6	2.6	11	76	5.9	2.2
New Kent	12 338	133	9	D	D	D	39	412	53.7	4.9	5	11	0.7	0.1
Northampton	7 520	114	22	D	D	D	79	594	73.0	7.5	6	D	D	D
Northumberland	20 399	132	13	D	D	D	54	338	42.4	5.0	10	51	3.2	0.8
Nottoway	5 564	56	14	D	D	D	80	676	86.3	8.8	4	9	0.4	0.2
Orange	28 070	220	23	163	68.4	4.1	104	946	160.1	15.8	20	44	3.1	0.5
Page	6 822	81	13	49	4.5	0.7	83	645	97.2	8.9	8	27	1.9	0.5
Patrick	7 003	78	11	194	24.5	3.7	59	432	66.1	6.1	10	16	1.4	0.2
Pittsylvania	26 698	279	46	D	D	D	213	2 170	300.5	27.9	23	91	11.1	1.8
Powhatan	30 643	298	21	D	D	D	55	391	78.8	7.3	11	45	2.1	0.4
Prince Edward	5 430	58	20	143	30.9	3.4	125	1 703	267.4	24.4	19	80	5.3	1.3
Prince George	24 532	325	16	189	62.4	5.8	66	632	91.8	8.4	14	30	2.8	0.5
Prince William	349 978	3 776	150	1 736	1 191.2	61.7	915	13 936	2 563.1	240.5	160	767	84.0	15.5
Pulaski	12 546	147	21	299	152.0	7.9	133	1 541	250.9	21.6	22	63	4.5	1.0
Rappahannock	5 117	48	6	D	D	D	33	244	49.0	4.3	5	11	1.3	0.2
Richmond	5 493	42	17	89	18.7	2.2	49	460	62.6	5.8	7	25	1.1	0.3
Roanoke	27 871	450	95	796	399.4	24.5	202	2 559	461.8	41.7	52	231	25.2	3.7
Rockbridge	29 487	220	10	D	D	D	79	961	165.3	13.9	11	19	1.8	0.2
Rockingham	47 960	418	57	1 140	539.7	30.6	242	2 075	356.2	35.4	34	452	65.5	12.3
Russell	7 417	89	15	98	93.9	2.6	102	910	154.2	14.5	11	29	3.1	0.7
Scott	5 836	79	11	D	D	D	91	788	143.0	11.0	11	44	11.0	1.1
Shenandoah	24 462	332	24	241	85.9	4.9	158	1 574	279.3	23.6	24	98	16.0	1.3
Smyth	7 422	77	25	237	65.7	6.8	170	1 560	232.1	20.8	16	78	4.3	1.1
Southampton	6 745	72	17	D	D	D	56	378	41.3	4.6	10	19	1.0	0.2
Spotsylvania	197 250	1 631	67	821	686.0	19.5	261	4 038	737.6	66.6	52	455	33.4	7.9
Stafford	149 195	1 228	47	D	D	D	202	2 336	413.5	39.7	42	193	19.8	3.2
Surry	3 985	56	3	52	8.6	0.8	17	84	8.9	1.0	NA	NA	NA	NA
Sussex	1 041	11	14	106	30.7	2.1	47	358	71.5	5.6	5	16	1.9	0.5
Tazewell	6 725	75	81	781	215.1	15.8	267	3 193	565.5	47.2	72	199	29.9	3.4
Warren	20 372	190	18	D	D	D	142	1 354	199.7	19.6	20	44	4.6	0.8
Washington	19 316	312	51	1 125	847.5	29.3	253	2 609	408.9	40.8	41	159	11.9	2.7
Westmoreland	6 399	61	17	64	35.9	1.6	71	546	83.4	8.0	9	18	1.9	0.3
Wise	4 479	68	46	354	177.5	9.7	183	1 961	310.9	28.3	25	89	5.4	1.3
Wythe	10 756	109	21	184	73.0	4.9	204	1 933	346.1	27.2	16	30	3.5	0.5
York	71 673	801	45	415	137.9	10.5	255	2 681	326.9	32.6	41	158	20.8	2.7
Independent Cities														
Alexandria City	98 705	1 090	137	1 830	899.6	75.1	593	7 746	1 507.6	160.0	202	2 023	354.1	57.9
Bedford City	767	9	19	D	D	D	81	975	136.3	13.5	15	34	2.2	0.5
Bristol City	3 094	45	40	D	D	D	155	2 266	331.7	29.2	23	104	11.4	2.2
Buena Vista City	1 499	23	2	D	D	D	32	257	33.2	3.5	6	12	0.8	0.1
Charlottesville City	5 234	70	81	954	265.9	29.7	360	4 345	730.3	73.2	97	458	50.1	9.8
Chesapeake City	170 995	1 635	246	3 833	1 768.2	115.7	779	12 554	1 993.3	184.5	144	704	98.0	15.9
Clifton Forge City	270	4	2	D	D	D	34	321	47.4	4.6	4	7	0.6	0.1
Colonial Heights City	4 549	39	12	D	D	D	205	3 776	496.4	46.5	35	146	15.4	2.8
Covington City	250	3	9	44	15.3	1.1	61	539	90.4	7.9	13	27	1.7	0.3
Danville City	4 239	34	55	964	211.8	22.6	334	3 787	585.5	56.9	59	242	18.1	3.5
Emporia City	1 224	12	8	D	D	D	81	714	97.3	9.7	9	28	2.5	0.4
Fairfax City	7 189	79	48	519	515.2	22.3	305	5 870	1 288.0	115.5	68	345	48.3	9.4
Falls Church City	375	2	22	D	D	D	120	1 536	355.6	34.7	38	137	20.4	3.7
Franklin City	590	5	7	121	48.9	2.3	57	635	95.0	9.3	10	39	3.4	0.6
Fredericksburg City	14 995	247	53	723	427.3	23.3	317	3 701	567.3	60.7	57	297	43.2	6.5
Galax City	1 664	24	6	42	6.0	1.0	71	906	134.6	12.6	10	22	2.0	0.4
Hampton City	25 151	332	94	1 073	370.7	31.3	514	9 930	1 638.9	150.5	113	1 241	89.2	20.6
Harrisonburg City	28 699	590	62	971	749.2	25.5	308	4 161	690.8	64.0	48	263	30.8	5.5
Hopewell City	5 372	84	18	268	92.7	9.5	83	754	100.9	10.6	28	121	10.7	1.8
Lexington City	684	7	5	27	16.9	1.4	68	686	108.9	9.6	20	62	7.4	1.1
Lynchburg City	23 001	187	100	1 292	504.6	43.8	446	7 209	1 228.5	115.8	95	390	37.4	8.2

1. Establishments with payroll.

Table B. States and Counties — **Professional, Manufacturing, and Accommodation and Foodservices**

STATE County	Professional, Scientific, and Technical Services[1], 1997				Manufacturing, 1997				Accommodation and Foodservices, 1997			
	Number of Establish-ments	Number of Employees	Receipts (mil dol)	Annual Payroll (mil dol)	Number of Establish-ments	Number of Employees	Receipts (mil dol)	Annual Payroll (mil dol)	Number of Establish-ments	Number of Employees	Sales (mil dol)	Annual Payroll (mil dol)
	147	148	149	150	151	152	153	154	155	156	157	158
VIRGINIA—Cont'd												
Louisa	33	89	5.7	2.4	29	633	89.3	16.4	20	320	8.9	2.6
Lunenburg	7	27	1.1	0.6	16	900	76.3	16.2	5	41	1.0	0.3
Madison	18	32	1.5	0.5	NA	NA	NA	NA	12	126	5.7	1.7
Mathews	9	21	0.9	0.4	NA	NA	NA	NA	8	D	D	D
Mecklenburg	30	218	7.4	3.0	41	4 589	859.1	102.7	66	1 086	29.1	8.3
Middlesex	21	59	3.7	1.4	NA	NA	NA	NA	22	265	8.8	2.3
Montgomery	150	1 231	115.3	41.9	68	4 836	699.1	153.9	150	3 446	96.1	26.1
Nelson	25	81	5.0	2.2	14	621	41.2	8.7	21	708	23.6	8.3
New Kent	20	34	2.3	0.9	NA	NA	NA	NA	14	121	4.8	1.5
Northampton	14	39	1.6	0.4	NA	NA	NA	NA	29	408	15.6	4.0
Northumberland	11	30	1.7	0.7	19	575	59.6	12.9	16	115	3.1	1.1
Nottoway	15	69	2.2	0.8	18	681	139.9	11.3	29	391	9.7	2.5
Orange	42	145	9.7	3.8	35	2 529	445.6	68.8	34	478	14.6	3.9
Page	20	65	3.1	1.0	16	2 883	461.8	47.5	49	543	21.9	5.8
Patrick	10	37	1.4	0.5	38	2 610	249.7	55.7	22	D	D	D
Pittsylvania	26	182	4.1	1.2	59	D	D	D	56	608	19.7	5.6
Powhatan	30	55	3.8	1.6	NA	NA	NA	NA	9	124	3.9	0.9
Prince Edward	23	83	3.8	1.7	18	D	D	D	44	1 056	27.9	7.6
Prince George	36	277	31.7	13.1	NA	NA	NA	NA	27	674	20.9	5.2
Prince William	403	2 322	189.6	81.8	109	2 974	378.1	115.9	364	7 882	266.0	72.6
Pulaski	30	91	5.7	1.8	41	6 509	1 655.8	169.6	54	749	21.5	5.4
Rappahannock	18	58	6.4	2.3	NA	NA	NA	NA	13	206	8.7	2.9
Richmond	13	30	1.6	0.7	NA	NA	NA	NA	11	D	D	D
Roanoke	117	461	34.2	14.9	64	3 450	598.7	107.6	89	1 302	43.6	12.4
Rockbridge	14	31	2.0	0.7	24	2 090	335.4	50.0	44	525	19.9	5.7
Rockingham	46	214	13.5	5.4	74	9 272	4 112.5	269.7	79	1 706	54.2	14.4
Russell	28	339	9.1	4.6	26	1 614	129.2	28.8	29	339	9.7	2.7
Scott	20	D	D	D	NA	NA	NA	NA	18	D	D	D
Shenandoah	47	176	6.2	2.4	47	5 436	840.5	139.4	72	1 160	30.7	9.3
Smyth	34	165	11.2	4.6	53	4 913	692.6	109.2	47	526	16.5	4.4
Southampton	14	39	3.3	0.9	16	2 874	710.0	131.1	13	147	4.1	1.2
Spotsylvania	80	569	55.7	15.7	40	1 698	304.9	60.4	89	1 741	61.9	16.8
Stafford	96	351	37.9	12.8	47	711	99.2	17.2	95	1 809	57.3	14.9
Surry	5	14	1.0	0.3	NA	NA	NA	NA	5	D	D	D
Sussex	5	7	0.4	0.1	9	1 138	283.5	26.5	14	236	6.8	2.0
Tazewell	64	517	44.7	14.8	58	1 517	161.2	30.6	66	1 091	32.5	8.7
Warren	52	232	28.2	12.1	27	1 540	511.0	37.7	61	763	25.6	7.0
Washington	81	395	26.7	11.1	65	2 031	315.8	53.2	84	1 680	48.5	14.3
Westmoreland	28	73	5.3	1.6	16	694	124.6	13.5	37	253	9.7	2.6
Wise	53	299	18.5	8.6	24	556	64.2	10.1	49	688	20.5	5.6
Wythe	31	159	8.4	3.1	45	2 129	276.9	51.6	65	1 275	38.4	10.1
York	76	241	15.0	5.9	28	D	D	D	93	2 303	77.9	20.7
Independent Cities												
Alexandria City	894	12 710	1 456.2	634.2	114	1 907	328.1	59.4	310	6 616	308.3	92.3
Bedford City	38	114	6.9	2.4	30	2 278	254.3	62.2	24	D	D	D
Bristol City	54	D	D	D	41	6 954	1 222.9	184.4	52	D	D	D
Buena Vista City	8	19	0.6	0.2	10	D	D	D	11	162	4.4	1.4
Charlottesville City	206	1 448	118.7	49.7	67	D	D	D	179	3 521	121.5	34.7
Chesapeake City	263	2 653	198.1	84.5	132	4 558	1 085.0	147.0	305	6 321	187.4	51.6
Clifton Forge City	6	23	0.5	0.1	NA	NA	NA	NA	12	D	D	D
Colonial Heights City	35	219	8.3	3.5	14	838	215.4	20.4	63	1 431	40.8	10.9
Covington City	13	39	2.8	0.9	11	2 615	1 004.9	113.4	16	209	6.7	1.8
Danville City	76	577	27.3	11.6	47	D	D	D	114	2 159	65.7	18.8
Emporia City	13	49	3.1	1.2	13	1 055	158.7	29.0	24	490	16.2	4.4
Fairfax City	504	4 979	887.1	240.3	NA	NA	NA	NA	150	3 029	108.0	29.4
Falls Church City	127	1 600	157.7	68.0	NA	NA	NA	NA	68	D	D	D
Franklin City	12	79	2.6	1.1	NA	NA	NA	NA	18	321	10.1	2.5
Fredericksburg City	134	658	44.7	17.4	41	1 059	240.7	28.6	141	2 748	92.0	24.4
Galax City	13	62	3.3	1.2	24	4 460	380.2	86.8	28	D	D	D
Hampton City	211	3 190	270.9	120.4	80	4 636	971.0	123.4	229	5 002	149.9	41.1
Harrisonburg City	95	618	50.9	19.6	38	3 687	725.8	102.6	109	2 318	70.2	19.0
Hopewell City	25	153	11.5	5.4	19	2 907	1 328.1	147.4	46	D	D	D
Lexington City	34	102	5.1	2.1	NA	NA	NA	NA	57	787	27.4	6.9
Lynchburg City	182	2 715	260.3	107.1	117	12 535	3 096.4	481.1	173	3 808	110.8	30.9

1. Firms subject to federal tax.

Table B. States and Counties — Health and Other Services and Federal Funds

STATE County	Health Care and Social Assistance[1], 1997				Other Services[1], 1997				Federal funds and grants, fiscal 1999[2] Expenditures (mil dol)			
										Direct payments for individuals[3]		
	Number of Establishments	Number of Employees	Receipts (mil dol)	Annual Payroll (mil dol)	Number of Establishments	Number of Employees	Receipts (mil dol)	Annual Payroll (mil dol)	Total	Social Security and government retirement	Medicare	Food stamps and Supplemental Security Income
	159	160	161	162	163	164	165	166	167	168	169	170
VIRGINIA—Cont'd												
Louisa	20	277	14.8	5.1	31	97	5.9	1.6	87.2	50.5	16.9	3.8
Lunenburg	5	13	1.1	0.4	18	57	2.3	0.6	48.8	25.0	9.1	2.6
Madison	10	155	4.9	2.3	9	23	2.3	0.5	44.1	22.3	8.7	1.1
Mathews	9	48	1.6	0.4	11	60	3.9	1.2	52.6	33.1	10.4	0.8
Mecklenburg	50	330	20.1	10.4	74	238	12.7	2.7	164.4	76.3	29.0	5.7
Middlesex	12	140	5.4	2.8	14	41	2.2	0.5	52.1	33.2	9.5	1.1
Montgomery	122	1 973	115.9	47.3	116	655	32.5	10.7	314.5	107.5	33.6	7.9
Nelson	13	131	7.1	2.5	13	30	2.3	0.6	68.1	39.1	12.3	2.1
New Kent	10	315	17.4	9.0	13	22	1.4	0.3	43.9	28.3	8.1	0.8
Northampton	26	286	17.0	7.8	16	49	2.5	0.6	128.6	32.8	11.7	3.7
Northumberland	8	68	3.1	1.3	29	108	6.8	1.8	62.7	39.1	12.9	1.1
Nottoway	17	316	10.8	4.2	36	87	5.8	1.5	90.3	42.0	13.7	3.2
Orange	31	240	17.3	5.6	38	147	10.0	2.4	121.8	79.6	21.7	2.4
Page	26	285	13.2	5.1	36	78	4.6	1.3	102.2	50.9	17.5	2.5
Patrick	21	300	10.6	5.4	16	56	3.8	0.9	65.4	36.8	12.9	2.5
Pittsylvania	46	472	30.8	13.8	81	293	14.2	4.0	186.8	85.2	32.1	11.5
Powhatan	13	99	4.2	2.0	15	42	2.9	0.9	44.9	29.8	7.8	0.6
Prince Edward	62	886	33.7	16.1	42	142	6.8	1.9	80.7	41.7	13.7	4.4
Prince George	11	D	D	D	24	103	6.0	2.2	419.1	44.9	8.0	2.0
Prince William	321	3 036	176.6	85.9	341	2 085	127.7	44.7	1 205.8	407.6	40.0	15.1
Pulaski	55	888	50.5	21.2	45	221	11.2	3.3	134.7	73.5	32.1	4.9
Rappahannock	4	15	1.0	0.2	9	25	2.4	0.5	30.5	18.9	5.8	0.5
Richmond	6	282	9.0	4.1	9	27	2.4	0.8	43.4	19.3	8.8	1.1
Roanoke	102	868	59.2	30.1	90	573	28.9	10.8	125.1	82.0	22.4	3.5
Rockbridge	14	156	5.5	2.9	16	54	3.9	1.0	62.5	27.3	9.0	1.5
Rockingham	51	375	20.7	10.6	95	483	33.1	9.6	178.3	100.0	32.5	4.1
Russell	39	650	28.8	12.8	32	136	6.7	2.3	139.9	65.5	30.1	9.6
Scott	24	506	29.7	10.5	20	88	3.4	1.2	115.3	53.4	23.9	7.5
Shenandoah	62	486	18.3	8.6	62	209	11.5	3.4	137.9	88.5	23.6	3.1
Smyth	48	448	25.6	13.1	45	185	12.6	2.8	164.6	74.0	26.8	6.9
Southampton	18	182	9.3	4.7	22	83	7.9	2.2	65.2	26.6	12.9	3.6
Spotsylvania	67	886	37.2	16.8	108	526	32.5	10.1	105.2	73.6	14.3	3.7
Stafford	89	982	47.1	21.2	120	581	35.1	10.3	213.7	145.9	16.7	3.2
Surry	4	20	1.5	0.7	2	D	D	D	25.8	12.9	4.8	0.8
Sussex	7	247	6.2	3.2	16	57	4.7	0.9	61.9	25.7	12.4	3.8
Tazewell	113	1 454	107.8	40.6	93	709	44.1	13.2	247.7	140.5	48.5	12.4
Warren	46	414	19.8	8.2	52	404	23.8	7.3	103.6	63.2	16.5	2.8
Washington	90	971	49.9	26.7	75	304	15.2	4.7	189.7	91.7	29.7	8.1
Westmoreland	11	63	2.1	1.3	19	62	3.6	0.8	91.1	54.3	18.2	2.5
Wise	58	601	33.1	13.1	72	212	15.2	3.6	258.5	113.4	41.9	15.3
Wythe	42	455	24.0	11.7	46	147	8.0	1.9	118.9	63.9	24.2	5.5
York	53	533	20.9	8.9	98	519	31.9	9.6	308.7	155.0	18.5	3.1
Independent Cities												
Alexandria City	323	2 788	216.5	105.2	267	1 919	122.4	42.9	2 374.0	516.2	104.0	15.6
Bedford City	30	206	10.4	5.0	44	219	14.8	4.4	53.7	39.5	7.8	0.5
Bristol City	26	344	13.6	6.2	44	195	12.0	3.2	126.0	64.8	23.6	4.2
Buena Vista City	5	28	1.5	0.7	9	16	0.9	0.2	28.9	16.5	5.8	1.2
Charlottesville City	162	2 092	138.9	54.6	133	827	41.6	14.5	507.7	105.2	33.8	8.1
Chesapeake City	338	3 228	195.7	87.9	305	2 846	241.4	53.0	797.2	415.9	89.2	19.3
Clifton Forge City	11	216	9.6	4.8	14	49	2.3	0.7	30.4	16.9	8.3	1.0
Colonial Heights City	64	629	39.1	17.1	50	390	19.3	6.7	95.2	71.4	15.4	1.5
Covington City	12	63	3.4	1.7	15	59	5.6	1.1	62.6	36.5	14.2	1.9
Danville City	126	1 459	89.6	42.0	123	735	36.0	10.2	260.4	143.2	49.0	11.1
Emporia City	18	191	13.2	6.1	21	59	2.6	0.7	42.7	21.7	11.4	1.2
Fairfax City	149	1 180	86.4	39.6	126	686	49.5	16.6	2 094.4	239.2	31.6	3.8
Falls Church City	73	915	84.2	35.9	64	323	25.0	8.3	966.7	87.9	30.0	2.5
Franklin City	24	160	13.9	6.8	16	75	4.3	1.2	59.5	28.5	11.4	2.7
Fredericksburg City	140	1 805	132.1	67.2	93	633	37.2	12.3	239.8	151.5	34.2	4.4
Galax City	33	469	24.2	12.0	16	73	4.5	1.3	55.5	33.2	12.2	0.5
Hampton City	192	1 976	106.4	51.9	178	1 129	64.8	20.9	1 704.2	395.2	78.8	19.9
Harrisonburg City	116	1 538	90.7	41.6	84	434	28.1	7.5	103.3	55.4	18.5	3.4
Hopewell City	50	1 444	92.7	40.0	36	409	12.7	4.8	268.6	70.2	20.0	5.1
Lexington City	35	213	11.6	5.0	22	100	3.4	1.1	54.9	31.7	7.0	1.2
Lynchburg City	177	2 893	171.0	86.8	152	933	51.6	15.6	531.9	173.3	55.5	13.0

1. Firms subject to federal tax.   2. October 1, 1998 to September 30, 1999.   3. State totals may include programs not allocated by county.

Table B. States and Counties — Federal Funds and Local Government Finances

STATE County	Federal funds and grants, fiscal 1999[1] (cont'd)							Local government finances, 1997				
	Expenditures (mil dol) (cont'd)							General revenue				
	Procurement contract awards			Grants[2]						Taxes		
											Per capita[3] (dollars)	
	Salaries and wages	Defense	Other	Medicaid and other health-related	Nutrition and family welfare	Education	Other	Total (mil dol)	Intergovern- mental (mil dol)	Total (mil dol)	Total	Property
	171	172	173	174	175	176	177	178	179	180	181	182
VIRGINIA—Cont'd												
Louisa	2.6	0.0	0.7	8.2	1.8	0.9	1.1	41.1	12.4	23.8	999	932
Lunenburg	1.3	1.7	0.3	5.5	1.4	0.6	0.6	17.0	10.4	5.4	441	347
Madison	3.0	0.4	0.5	4.5	1.4	0.5	0.7	16.1	8.5	7.0	557	443
Mathews	2.3	2.4	0.8	1.7	0.5	0.3	0.1	12.3	5.0	6.5	718	617
Mecklenburg	5.9	20.7	1.2	18.8	2.4	1.3	0.5	45.6	26.7	15.2	490	313
Middlesex	1.3	0.1	0.3	1.8	0.7	0.6	1.0	13.2	5.0	7.2	751	611
Montgomery	14.2	20.0	6.3	15.3	5.7	3.6	93.4	110.8	46.1	43.2	569	391
Nelson	3.0	1.0	1.5	6.6	1.1	0.5	0.6	21.0	9.2	10.7	778	631
New Kent	1.6	0.0	0.4	1.9	1.4	0.4	0.4	21.7	10.3	9.7	788	675
Northampton	2.6	4.8	52.1	9.3	2.9	1.6	2.8	70.6	16.1	8.8	689	522
Northumberland	1.5	0.0	0.5	2.5	0.9	0.4	1.2	17.9	7.3	8.7	758	655
Nottoway	17.0	3.1	1.0	6.3	2.0	0.8	0.3	25.7	15.5	7.6	505	347
Orange	2.9	0.8	0.8	7.8	2.1	0.7	1.1	40.3	19.8	18.1	723	589
Page	6.7	5.4	9.0	6.5	1.3	0.8	1.0	34.3	19.9	10.3	451	332
Patrick	2.3	1.1	0.9	6.3	1.2	0.7	0.3	21.5	12.8	7.2	397	276
Pittsylvania	5.0	6.6	1.5	29.8	6.3	2.5	3.0	71.3	44.8	23.2	402	293
Powhatan	2.8	0.2	0.6	1.9	0.4	0.4	0.0	26.3	11.0	14.5	685	470
Prince Edward	3.9	0.2	0.8	8.0	2.1	1.5	0.7	27.3	14.2	10.4	549	305
Prince George	292.1	62.9	3.4	2.4	1.3	0.9	-0.3	46.8	25.5	16.1	543	439
Prince William	393.1	245.8	40.5	9.4	8.3	5.2	36.4	589.9	196.7	309.1	1 215	945
Pulaski	3.2	0.3	1.0	10.2	2.8	1.4	1.8	64.6	29.4	19.6	571	396
Rappahannock	1.6	0.1	0.5	2.2	0.3	0.2	0.0	9.6	3.6	5.5	785	656
Richmond	1.3	2.3	2.7	2.7	0.7	0.6	1.5	13.4	7.7	4.7	553	410
Roanoke	2.4	1.1	0.6	5.7	2.3	1.8	2.2	156.7	51.4	86.2	1 060	788
Rockbridge	2.3	1.6	3.1	5.1	1.2	0.7	10.0	30.9	12.5	13.1	676	450
Rockingham	8.8	3.1	10.3	11.1	1.9	1.7	1.2	103.4	45.4	39.5	620	507
Russell	3.2	2.6	0.6	15.5	3.2	1.8	6.2	45.7	25.5	12.2	419	282
Scott	4.0	0.0	0.7	18.5	3.4	1.3	0.5	31.5	20.9	8.2	361	254
Shenandoah	7.2	0.3	1.5	6.4	1.4	1.1	3.3	49.5	19.1	25.5	744	546
Smyth	4.6	3.8	20.0	16.5	5.1	1.4	4.1	49.6	28.3	15.1	458	288
Southampton	2.1	0.6	0.5	9.3	2.1	0.9	0.1	26.7	15.5	9.4	530	474
Spotsylvania	2.3	0.0	0.8	4.3	2.1	1.5	1.0	136.6	52.3	72.3	892	658
Stafford	8.5	15.8	1.7	3.6	2.8	2.0	12.3	150.6	60.4	75.3	858	692
Surry	1.1	0.0	0.3	2.1	0.8	0.3	0.9	17.0	3.8	12.5	1 939	1 884
Sussex	3.1	0.2	0.4	6.8	2.9	0.6	3.7	21.8	9.2	6.4	636	519
Tazewell	6.4	0.1	1.6	16.0	5.4	4.0	6.1	68.3	40.0	22.2	474	324
Warren	7.8	0.0	5.5	4.6	1.4	0.9	0.6	44.6	19.3	20.7	690	534
Washington	4.8	1.4	4.2	22.2	5.3	2.9	16.0	67.9	34.7	26.5	542	351
Westmoreland	3.2	0.0	0.7	3.9	2.3	0.7	2.6	27.1	14.2	10.8	660	571
Wise	7.1	0.0	43.9	20.5	5.7	3.9	3.3	73.8	40.6	25.9	658	328
Wythe	5.2	0.2	1.1	11.3	2.4	2.4	0.4	46.5	24.2	15.7	595	333
York	90.5	13.8	11.7	3.0	3.0	8.7	0.0	107.3	36.9	52.5	919	683
Independent Cities												
Alexandria City	490.0	901.1	229.0	33.9	11.4	15.6	32.4	355.7	75.8	216.4	1 859	1 338
Bedford City	2.2	0.0	2.1	1.3	0.0	0.2	0.0	7.8	1.2	4.4	700	426
Bristol City	13.8	0.0	3.3	11.0	1.8	0.9	0.2	43.7	18.8	17.8	1 028	594
Buena Vista City	1.3	0.0	0.2	3.0	0.6	0.3	0.0	12.0	6.5	4.1	676	477
Charlottesville City	67.7	111.6	16.7	101.7	6.3	6.8	43.5	83.6	26.0	44.3	1 169	732
Chesapeake City	91.8	91.8	14.0	24.3	11.9	5.4	19.2	547.0	163.4	221.5	1 132	780
Clifton Forge City	0.9	0.0	0.2	1.2	0.5	0.6	0.0	2.9	0.4	1.9	440	167
Colonial Heights City	2.7	0.1	0.7	1.8	0.6	0.6	0.0	35.2	9.9	23.4	1 401	771
Covington City	3.2	0.0	0.4	2.9	0.7	0.4	2.4	14.6	4.8	7.5	1 073	736
Danville City	9.2	0.1	2.1	23.3	7.0	4.4	5.5	106.7	50.0	32.2	631	352
Emporia City	1.3	0.0	0.3	5.8	0.3	0.2	0.3	11.2	2.2	6.4	1 159	578
Fairfax City	42.5	720.3	981.0	17.9	6.5	6.2	36.1	60.2	6.7	45.3	2 227	1 269
Falls Church City	217.1	355.0	149.5	11.4	0.8	0.2	109.7	34.9	4.4	24.1	2 443	1 643
Franklin City	1.2	0.0	0.7	7.4	2.5	0.7	2.1	19.3	9.5	7.6	866	530
Fredericksburg City	12.7	12.0	13.5	4.9	2.9	0.6	0.3	63.8	16.7	30.3	1 436	799
Galax City	2.3	0.1	0.5	3.6	2.0	0.3	0.0	17.6	9.1	6.8	993	461
Hampton City	651.5	242.4	198.7	21.3	13.3	9.9	57.7	299.8	122.3	125.3	904	608
Harrisonburg City	7.7	0.2	4.6	4.1	1.7	1.1	2.2	58.8	14.9	31.7	945	449
Hopewell City	2.1	63.0	91.9	6.4	3.6	1.5	3.3	69.4	23.9	24.3	1 095	824
Lexington City	4.1	0.5	0.5	3.2	0.4	0.1	5.3	10.7	3.7	4.2	590	374
Lynchburg City	42.4	6.2	176.8	21.2	8.5	3.1	21.0	159.2	55.2	68.6	1 049	1 043

1. October 1, 1998 to September 30, 1999. 2. State totals may include programs not allocated by county. 3. Based on the resident population estimated as of July 1 of the year shown.

Table B. States and Counties — Local Government Finances, Government Employment, and Elections

STATE County	Direct general expenditure Total (mil dol)	Per capita[1] (dollars)	Percent of total for — Education	Health and hospitals	Police protection	Public welfare	Highways	Debt outstanding Total (mil dol)	Per capita[1] (dollars)	Government employment, 1998 Federal civilian	Federal military	State and local	Presidential election, 2000 Percent of vote cast — Democratic	Republican	All other
	183	184	185	186	187	188	189	190	191	192	193	194	195	196	197
VIRGINIA—Cont'd															
Louisa	39.6	1 660	60.9	2.2	4.3	4.9	0.2	60.5	2 539	44	96	1 087	42.7	54.1	3.2
Lunenburg	15.8	1 297	70.5	1.7	6.0	4.2	1.0	6.7	550	28	47	864	44.1	54.7	1.2
Madison	15.7	1 259	69.4	1.6	4.0	6.5	0.0	4.0	323	80	49	459	36.7	58.5	4.8
Mathews	11.4	1 250	60.0	10.3	5.7	0.2	0.8	1.4	148	32	64	329	32.5	64.0	3.5
Mecklenburg	44.0	1 421	58.7	0.9	7.3	4.5	3.3	12.4	399	135	120	2 282	41.2	56.6	2.2
Middlesex	12.3	1 292	62.1	1.4	4.7	6.0	0.0	0.3	32	24	37	795	35.6	60.7	3.7
Montgomery	111.7	1 469	49.5	2.2	6.2	3.6	2.3	67.5	888	(3)378	(3)405	(3)14 626	43.2	51.5	5.3
Nelson	19.7	1 435	66.4	1.1	4.1	4.7	0.0	6.1	441	57	54	532	47.3	47.4	5.3
New Kent	18.6	1 521	61.5	0.9	6.5	6.3	3.7	9.3	755	30	51	517	33.6	64.3	2.1
Northampton	137.2	10 728	10.2	0.3	0.7	1.5	72.6	267.8	20 940	47	70	1 155	47.8	47.0	5.2
Northumberland	18.3	1 600	50.0	1.0	3.1	5.2	0.1	6.8	591	30	45	415	37.8	60.0	2.2
Nottoway	23.7	1 579	58.4	0.6	7.0	4.3	1.9	8.6	571	275	59	1 776	44.8	52.3	3.0
Orange	40.2	1 610	57.2	0.7	4.9	4.9	2.2	17.3	694	57	98	1 763	39.4	57.2	3.5
Page	32.2	1 410	55.3	1.1	6.2	6.6	2.6	11.4	500	166	89	968	34.1	63.6	2.3
Patrick	22.7	1 253	61.3	1.6	4.1	4.6	0.2	1.7	95	44	71	650	30.5	66.4	3.1
Pittsylvania	79.7	1 384	71.7	1.1	5.4	6.6	0.0	35.9	624	(4)260	(4)419	(4)5 723	32.3	65.0	2.7
Powhatan	27.8	1 310	74.1	0.6	4.9	4.0	0.0	13.1	619	45	85	2 039	27.9	70.2	1.9
Prince Edward	30.3	1 606	51.6	0.6	6.8	4.2	4.4	27.6	1 463	77	74	1 804	45.9	50.5	3.6
Prince George	70.9	2 383	42.5	0.4	3.1	2.1	0.0	112.5	3 781	(5)3 834	(5)5 605	2 443	38.4	60.4	1.3
Prince William	589.9	2 318	51.9	3.0	5.8	3.4	1.9	846.5	3 327	(6)4 217	(6)6 609	(6)14 108	44.5	52.5	3.0
Pulaski	64.7	1 882	43.6	0.7	7.0	3.5	2.2	57.5	1 672	60	134	2 025	41.4	55.8	2.8
Rappahannock	9.9	1 402	61.1	1.3	3.6	6.5	0.3	2.1	298	43	28	285	41.6	52.7	5.7
Richmond	12.2	1 425	58.7	1.7	6.1	5.6	0.0	1.3	156	23	34	835	36.5	60.5	3.0
Roanoke	157.0	1 930	62.0	0.3	5.3	3.1	0.5	256.8	3 158	(7)2 133	(7)409	(7)6 389	37.7	60.1	2.2
Rockbridge	36.1	1 858	48.5	10.7	2.9	4.0	0.7	26.1	1 342	(8)154	(8)162	(8)2 470	37.7	57.8	4.5
Rockingham	109.7	1 721	67.1	0.6	2.8	5.4	1.4	49.8	781	(9)352	(9)383	(9)8 164	24.3	72.9	2.8
Russell	47.0	1 621	54.2	0.8	2.9	5.4	2.1	84.5	2 913	59	113	1 464	50.4	46.9	2.6
Scott	31.0	1 366	67.2	0.7	5.4	6.1	2.6	7.1	315	62	88	978	38.1	59.3	2.7
Shenandoah	44.5	1 298	66.7	0.8	6.4	3.6	1.5	39.6	1 155	156	134	1 489	30.6	66.7	2.7
Smyth	55.4	1 683	63.7	1.5	5.7	6.8	3.0	30.9	940	97	127	2 667	41.2	56.1	2.8
Southampton	29.7	1 678	56.5	1.3	3.6	5.7	1.2	18.2	1 032	(10)65	(10)102	(10)2 351	50.0	49.1	0.9
Spotsylvania	136.3	1 681	69.3	0.7	3.0	2.8	0.0	136.5	1 684	(11)300	(11)410	(11)6 281	38.4	59.2	2.4
Stafford	153.3	1 745	68.1	0.5	3.5	3.2	0.2	161.2	1 835	155	1 910	3 563	36.8	60.5	2.7
Surry	15.9	2 469	64.8	2.5	3.8	7.6	0.4	7.2	1 121	16	25	473	57.1	40.7	2.2
Sussex	28.4	2 821	37.9	0.6	6.2	5.2	0.2	21.7	2 149	55	38	943	51.4	44.7	4.0
Tazewell	66.8	1 425	62.9	1.2	4.7	5.1	3.1	28.1	600	123	181	3 185	44.2	53.0	2.8
Warren	44.5	1 484	49.4	0.4	7.8	4.5	9.6	34.5	1 150	163	117	1 165	38.6	56.7	4.6
Washington	60.9	1 248	61.4	1.7	5.7	6.0	0.9	29.3	601	(12)395	(12)260	(12)3 971	37.3	59.7	3.0
Westmoreland	26.5	1 626	59.5	1.1	5.7	5.7	0.8	15.0	921	72	63	653	48.5	48.7	2.9
Wise	74.3	1 892	58.3	1.0	4.3	5.8	3.5	26.1	665	(13)276	(13)166	(13)3 151	33.0	64.0	3.0
Wythe	45.3	1 724	50.9	1.3	7.0	7.5	2.6	25.2	959	117	102	1 938	33.9	64.0	2.2
York	121.8	2 133	52.9	0.8	2.4	2.4	0.2	112.4	1 968	(14)1 067	(14)1 942	(14)3 108	35.1	62.3	2.6
Independent Cities															
Alexandria City	344.1	2 956	29.6	6.9	7.9	8.7	6.0	182.9	1 572	7 437	3 263	8 247	60.9	34.5	4.6
Bedford City	8.2	1 295	0.0	1.4	15.7	1.5	12.8	30.2	4 798	(15)	(15)	(15)	44.2	52.0	3.9
Bristol City	44.1	2 552	40.5	0.9	7.2	3.8	5.6	19.2	1 111	(12)	(12)	(12)	42.1	55.7	2.2
Buena Vista City	10.9	1 769	56.4	1.2	6.6	1.6	12.1	5.7	933	(16)	(16)	(16)	47.7	49.6	2.7
Charlottesville City	96.5	2 547	37.9	5.0	7.1	5.6	4.7	52.1	1 374	(16)	(16)	(16)	58.7	30.5	10.8
Chesapeake City	586.2	2 997	42.8	20.7	3.7	1.9	7.1	704.6	3 602	1 170	1 979	12 616	45.0	53.2	1.8
Clifton Forge City	3.5	786	0.0	0.0	21.7	0.0	6.9	0.0	0	(17)	(17)	(17)	56.7	40.0	3.3
Colonial Heights City	33.3	1 997	54.3	0.3	7.1	1.0	3.8	16.7	1 000	(18)	(18)	(18)	27.0	70.9	2.1
Covington City	15.3	2 204	50.4	0.5	7.0	3.7	6.7	11.2	1 605	(17)	(17)	(17)	52.8	43.6	3.6
Danville City	119.6	2 344	38.9	0.5	5.0	4.8	5.4	272.1	5 333	(4)	(4)	(4)	44.9	51.5	3.6
Emporia City	10.1	1 825	25.2	0.0	12.9	2.3	10.9	0.5	87	(19)	(19)	(19)	53.7	45.1	1.3
Fairfax City	54.8	2 692	34.3	0.7	11.5	1.8	12.4	34.0	1 671	(20)	(20)	(20)	45.6	49.8	4.5
Falls Church City	32.7	3 314	49.1	0.4	8.0	3.5	4.7	25.4	2 571	(20)	(20)	(20)	55.6	38.1	6.3
Franklin City	20.8	2 357	51.0	0.8	8.3	4.5	7.9	11.5	1 310	(10)	(10)	(10)	55.3	43.7	1.1
Fredericksburg City	68.9	3 269	23.2	2.7	5.7	4.8	4.8	168.9	8 009	(11)	(11)	(11)	50.3	43.9	5.8
Galax City	13.4	1 948	47.9	1.0	6.9	5.1	11.5	0.0	0	(21)	(21)	(21)	45.0	52.4	2.6
Hampton City	296.8	2 142	45.5	0.0	6.0	4.7	2.4	215.8	1 558	8 146	9 219	8 560	57.4	40.9	1.7
Harrisonburg City	60.0	1 790	38.4	1.7	5.1	0.0	7.9	45.8	1 367	(9)	(9)	(9)	35.0	57.7	7.4
Hopewell City	62.5	2 818	41.7	0.2	5.0	4.8	5.3	66.0	2 976	(5)	(5)	(5)	43.3	53.7	2.9
Lexington City	14.6	2 027	24.8	1.5	6.9	2.9	6.3	20.5	2 843	(8)	(8)	(8)	49.0	44.7	6.3
Lynchburg City	152.7	2 338	37.6	6.2	5.4	1.7	7.9	231.8	3 547	(22)	(22)	(22)	44.1	53.3	2.6

1. Based on the resident population estimated as of July 1 of the year shown. 3. Radford included with Montgomery County. 4. Danville included with Pittsylvania County. 5. Hopewell included with Prince George County. 6. Manassas and Manassas Park included with Prince William County. 7. Salem included with Roanoke County. 8. Buena Vista and Lexington included with Rockbridge County. 9. Harrisonburg included with Rockingham County. 10. Franklin included with Southhampton County. 11. Fredericksburg included with Spotsylvania County. 12. Bristol included with Washington County. 13. Norton included with Wise County. 14. Poquoson included with York County. 15. Bedford City included with Bedford County. 16. Charlottesville included with Albemarle County. 17. Clifton Forge and Covington included with Alleghany County. 18. Petersburg and Colonial Heights included with Dinwiddie County. 19. Emporia included with Greensville County. 20. Fairfax City and Falls Church included with Fairfax County. 21. Galax included with Carroll County. 22. Lynchburg included with Campbell County.

STATE/ County code	MSA/ PMSA/ NECMA code[1]	County Type[2]	STATE County	Land area,[3] (sq km) 1990	Total persons	Rank	Per square kilometer	White	Black	Am. Indian, Eskimo, Aleut	Asian and Pacific Islander	Percent Hispanic[4]	Under 5 years	5 to 17 years	18 to 24 years	25 to 34 years	35 to 44 years	45 to 54 years
					1	2	3	4	5	6	7	8	9	10	11	12	13	14
			VIRGINIA—Cont'd															
51 683	8840	NA	Manassas City	26	33 498	1 271	1 288.4	82.7	12.2	0.3	4.8	8.3	9.0	19.2	10.2	19.5	18.3	11.4
51 685	8840	NA	Manassas Park City	5	7 891	2 611	1 578.2	87.5	8.6	0.1	3.8	7.4	9.0	22.0	9.6	21.1	14.9	10.9
51 690	...	NA	Martinsville City	28	14 996	2 064	535.6	60.0	39.6	0.1	0.2	0.5	5.3	15.5	6.9	11.6	14.3	12.6
51 700	5720	NA	Newport News City	177	179 138	297	1 012.1	59.1	37.1	0.4	3.4	4.1	8.5	18.9	10.8	18.0	15.4	11.0
51 710	5720	NA	Norfolk City	139	225 875	245	1 625.0	52.9	42.8	0.5	3.8	4.1	7.8	16.0	18.5	17.2	13.6	8.8
51 720	5720	NA	Norton City	19	4 008	2 916	210.9	91.1	7.5	0.3	1.1	1.3	5.5	19.9	8.9	12.4	15.6	12.5
51 730	6760	NA	Petersburg City	59	34 398	1 242	583.0	24.4	74.3	0.2	1.1	1.7	6.5	16.5	10.0	13.4	15.1	12.2
51 735	5720	NA	Poquoson City	40	11 571	2 303	289.3	96.6	0.9	0.2	2.2	1.5	5.6	21.7	7.1	11.1	20.4	18.1
51 740	5720	NA	Portsmouth City	86	98 305	525	1 143.1	46.9	51.6	0.3	1.1	1.9	7.4	19.1	9.7	15.0	14.8	11.1
51 750	...	NA	Radford City	25	15 668	2 023	626.7	90.1	7.5	0.1	2.3	1.6	3.4	10.0	43.2	8.5	9.7	8.6
51 760	6760	NA	Richmond City	156	189 700	284	1 216.0	39.8	58.7	0.2	1.2	1.3	5.9	14.2	11.9	15.5	15.7	10.9
51 770	6800	NA	Roanoke City	111	93 357	540	841.1	70.9	27.9	0.2	1.1	1.1	6.3	15.3	8.6	14.5	16.1	11.6
51 775	6800	NA	Salem City	38	24 037	1 575	632.6	93.6	5.2	0.1	1.0	0.7	4.7	14.7	11.2	12.0	15.6	13.9
51 790	...	NA	Staunton City	51	24 496	1 552	480.3	84.6	14.6	0.2	0.6	1.2	4.9	14.7	9.6	12.5	15.1	13.2
51 800	5720	0	Suffolk City	1 036	64 805	736	62.6	50.3	48.8	0.2	0.6	0.9	6.8	20.2	7.8	14.0	16.2	14.1
51 810	5720	0	Virginia Beach City	643	433 461	134	674.1	77.5	15.7	0.4	6.5	4.6	8.2	19.7	10.5	18.4	17.4	14.1
51 820	...	NA	Waynesboro City	36	19 274	1 801	535.4	88.5	10.9	0.2	0.3	1.4	6.1	16.2	7.6	12.4	14.2	14.0
51 830	5720	NA	Williamsburg City	22	12 495	2 249	568.0	77.7	18.5	0.2	3.6	1.8	2.4	6.7	44.9	10.2	7.9	6.4
51 840	...	NA	Winchester City	24	22 477	1 638	936.5	86.7	11.7	0.1	1.5	1.5	6.2	14.5	11.2	14.3	14.7	11.8
53 000	...	X	WASHINGTON	172 447	5 756 361	X	33.4	88.7	3.5	1.8	6.0	6.5	6.8	19.0	9.7	13.7	17.1	14.0
53 001	...	6	Adams	4 986	15 235	2 051	3.1	98.2	0.3	0.4	1.2	44.4	9.5	26.2	8.6	12.3	14.4	12.3
53 003	...	7	Asotin	1 647	21 206	1 697	12.9	97.3	0.3	1.6	0.9	2.6	6.6	20.9	7.5	11.4	14.9	13.7
53 005	6740	3	Benton	4 411	137 844	381	31.3	95.1	1.2	0.9	2.9	11.7	7.5	22.2	8.4	12.8	16.2	14.2
53 007	...	5	Chelan	7 567	60 835	784	8.0	97.7	0.2	1.1	1.1	14.1	7.6	20.6	8.7	12.6	16.5	13.7
53 009	...	5	Clallam	4 520	64 690	737	14.3	92.8	0.7	5.0	1.5	2.9	5.4	17.7	6.7	10.2	15.0	13.1
53 011	6440	1	Clark	1 626	336 268	167	206.8	94.0	1.6	1.0	3.4	3.9	6.9	21.3	8.8	12.7	17.9	14.9
53 013	...	9	Columbia	2 250	4 155	2 903	1.8	98.8	0.1	0.6	0.5	16.8	4.8	19.8	6.6	10.1	15.4	15.1
53 015	...	4	Cowlitz	2 949	91 949	549	31.2	95.8	0.4	1.8	2.0	3.1	6.5	20.2	8.6	11.4	16.0	14.6
53 017	...	7	Douglas	4 715	34 191	1 250	7.3	98.0	0.3	0.9	0.9	14.3	6.9	19.9	8.0	11.3	15.0	12.9
53 019	...	9	Ferry	5 708	7 188	2 664	1.3	80.1	0.4	19.0	0.5	2.0	6.7	23.7	7.8	10.4	17.1	14.1
53 021	6740	3	Franklin	3 217	46 782	952	14.5	91.8	4.3	0.8	3.0	40.5	9.3	26.2	10.6	13.2	14.6	10.3
53 023	...	9	Garfield	1 840	2 339	3 030	1.3	99.0	0.0	0.5	0.5	1.7	4.5	21.2	3.5	8.3	15.5	13.1
53 025	...	5	Grant	6 932	72 019	681	10.4	95.8	1.3	1.2	1.7	24.9	8.2	23.4	8.9	11.8	14.3	12.3
53 027	...	4	Grays Harbor	4 966	67 102	720	13.5	93.7	0.2	4.4	1.6	2.8	6.4	20.0	7.9	11.1	15.4	14.4
53 029	7600	1	Island	540	73 490	671	136.1	90.8	2.3	0.8	6.0	4.9	7.6	18.4	9.4	14.1	15.4	12.3
53 031	...	6	Jefferson	4 685	26 748	1 473	5.7	94.8	0.8	3.0	1.4	2.2	4.8	16.6	5.3	9.0	17.7	14.5
53 033	7600	0	King	5 507	1 664 846	13	302.3	81.8	6.0	1.2	11.0	4.5	6.2	16.2	9.7	15.7	18.6	14.7
53 035	1150	3	Kitsap	1 026	236 560	237	230.6	89.1	2.9	1.8	6.3	4.8	7.3	20.3	9.9	13.2	17.3	13.8
53 037	...	6	Kittitas	5 950	32 021	1 313	5.4	96.3	0.6	0.9	2.2	3.9	5.1	16.3	19.8	10.4	14.6	13.6
53 039	...	7	Klickitat	4 850	19 530	1 787	4.0	95.1	0.2	3.5	1.2	8.2	6.7	22.3	7.1	11.2	17.3	14.2
53 041	...	6	Lewis	6 236	68 621	709	11.0	97.5	0.4	1.2	0.9	3.6	6.3	21.6	7.9	10.5	15.1	14.0
53 043	...	8	Lincoln	5 986	9 759	2 450	1.6	97.7	0.2	1.6	0.5	1.6	5.2	20.5	4.3	9.2	14.9	15.0
53 045	...	6	Mason	2 489	50 357	900	20.2	93.1	1.1	3.9	1.8	3.4	5.5	19.0	7.2	10.9	15.7	14.2
53 047	...	7	Okanogan	13 645	38 432	1 122	2.8	87.4	0.2	11.6	0.7	11.4	7.0	21.2	7.3	11.0	15.7	14.6
53 049	...	7	Pacific	2 524	20 768	1 726	8.2	93.2	0.4	2.9	3.6	3.3	5.6	17.6	6.0	9.1	13.6	13.5
53 051	...	8	Pend Oreille	3 627	11 604	2 299	3.2	96.9	0.2	2.4	0.4	2.2	6.3	22.4	5.5	9.6	16.1	15.8
53 053	8200	2	Pierce	4 340	688 807	72	158.7	83.3	8.2	1.5	7.0	5.4	7.3	19.7	10.7	14.3	16.2	13.3
53 055	...	8	San Juan	453	12 898	2 222	28.5	97.6	0.3	0.9	1.2	2.0	5.0	15.0	3.7	8.3	19.7	16.5
53 057	...	4	Skagit	4 494	101 180	514	22.5	95.8	0.4	2.3	1.4	8.5	6.5	19.7	8.1	11.3	16.3	14.0
53 059	...	8	Skamania	4 290	9 831	2 442	2.3	96.5	0.1	2.5	0.9	3.4	6.8	22.3	7.0	12.1	17.4	15.5
53 061	7600	0	Snohomish	5 414	596 598	86	110.2	92.1	1.3	1.5	5.1	3.6	7.5	19.6	8.9	14.9	18.0	14.1
53 063	7840	2	Spokane	4 568	409 736	140	89.7	94.1	1.7	1.7	2.6	3.1	6.5	19.6	10.3	12.8	16.4	13.5
53 065	...	6	Stevens	6 419	40 137	1 086	6.3	89.2	0.3	6.1	0.8	2.4	6.2	24.3	6.0	9.9	17.2	15.3
53 067	5910	3	Thurston	1 883	205 459	263	109.1	90.8	2.2	1.7	5.3	4.7	6.3	20.2	9.0	12.3	18.0	14.6
53 069	...	9	Wahkiakum	684	3 841	2 927	5.6	97.3	0.1	1.9	0.7	3.4	5.3	19.1	6.1	8.8	15.6	15.7
53 071	...	4	Walla Walla	3 291	53 854	855	16.4	95.0	2.1	1.0	1.8	14.0	6.2	18.5	12.4	12.0	15.0	12.5
53 073	0860	3	Whatcom	5 491	160 310	323	29.2	93.5	0.6	3.3	2.6	4.6	6.1	18.8	12.7	12.1	17.1	13.2
53 075	...	5	Whitman	5 593	38 386	1 123	6.9	90.7	1.4	0.7	7.2	2.6	4.6	13.3	32.7	12.1	11.3	10.2
53 077	9260	3	Yakima	11 127	220 785	249	19.8	90.8	1.7	5.6	1.9	32.9	8.7	23.1	9.9	12.5	14.6	12.3
54 000	...	X	WEST VIRGINIA	62 384	1 806 928	X	29.0	96.3	3.1	0.1	0.5	0.6	5.6	16.8	9.9	12.5	14.9	14.7
54 001	...	7	Barbour	883	15 979	2 007	18.1	97.9	0.9	1.0	0.2	0.7	5.9	17.6	9.8	12.4	14.4	14.7
54 003	8840	3	Berkeley	832	72 846	675	87.6	95.5	3.8	0.2	0.6	0.8	7.0	16.9	9.8	15.0	15.6	14.4
54 005	...	6	Boone	1 303	26 302	1 484	20.2	98.9	0.9	0.1	0.1	0.2	5.4	19.1	8.8	12.5	16.4	15.0

1. MSA = Metropolitan Statistical Area. PMSA = Primary MSA. NECMA = New England County Metropolitan Area. See Appendix A for explanation of these concepts. See Appendix B for list of metropolitan areas identified by type, with component counties.   2. County typology code from the Economic Research Service of USDA. See Appendix A for definition.   3. Dry land or land partially or temporarily covered by water.   4. Hispanic persons may be of any race.

Table B. States and Counties — **Population and Households**

STATE County	Population, 1999 (cont'd) Age (percent) (cont'd) 55 to 64 years	65 to 74 years	75 years and over	Percent female	Population — change and components of change, 1980–1999 Total persons 1990	1980	Percent change 1980–1990	1990–1999	Components of change, 1990–1999 Births	Deaths	Net migration	Households, 1990 Number	Percent change, 1980–1990	Persons per household	Percent Female family householder[1]	One person
	16	17	18	19	20	21	22	23	24	25	26	27	28	29	30	31
VIRGINIA—Cont'd																
Manassas City	5.1	3.9	3.4	49.2	27 757	15 505	80.3	20.7	5 847	1 391	1 342	9 481	87.8	2.88	9.2	17.0
Manassas Park City	6.7	3.8	2.0	50.7	6 798	6 524	3.2	16.1	1 466	290	-69	2 182	17.4	3.09	13.1	13.1
Martinsville City	10.6	12.1	11.0	55.3	16 162	18 149	-10.9	-7.2	1 803	2 494	-411	6 839	3.1	2.35	17.4	31.4
Newport News City	7.4	5.8	4.1	51.5	171 477	144 903	18.3	4.5	31 073	12 570	-14 672	63 952	24.6	2.59	15.1	23.7
Norfolk City	7.0	6.3	5.0	48.4	261 250	266 979	-2.1	-13.5	42 791	20 903	-72 831	89 478	1.9	2.55	16.1	26.8
Norton City	10.1	7.7	7.3	53.8	4 247	4 757	-10.7	-5.6	520	504	-246	1 697	2.7	2.49	16.4	28.4
Petersburg City	9.2	9.6	7.5	54.8	37 071	41 055	-9.8	-7.2	5 635	4 804	-3 583	14 730	-1.3	2.46	23.0	30.3
Poquoson City	9.3	3.2	3.5	50.2	11 005	8 726	26.1	5.1	1 006	766	209	3 769	35.5	2.90	7.6	13.2
Portsmouth City	8.7	8.2	6.0	52.6	103 910	104 577	-0.6	-5.4	16 922	10 344	-13 022	38 741	5.4	2.62	19.3	24.5
Radford City	6.7	5.5	4.4	55.5	15 940	13 457	18.5	-1.7	1 284	890	-650	5 207	31.7	2.48	8.8	25.2
Richmond City	8.4	8.6	8.9	55.0	202 713	219 214	-7.5	-6.4	29 946	23 131	-19 481	85 337	-0.5	2.25	19.8	35.9
Roanoke City	9.8	8.9	9.0	53.8	96 487	100 220	-3.7	-3.2	15 124	11 736	-6 314	41 030	2.5	2.30	15.7	32.3
Salem City	11.5	8.4	7.9	52.5	23 835	23 958	-0.7	0.8	2 485	2 732	523	9 161	6.0	2.37	10.6	26.5
Staunton City	10.8	9.9	9.4	53.2	24 581	24 777	-1.3	-0.4	2 489	2 668	167	9 432	16.5	2.30	11.3	30.7
Suffolk City	9.6	6.4	4.9	52.6	52 143	47 621	9.5	24.3	7 647	5 414	10 257	18 516	17.6	2.78	17.1	20.4
Virginia Beach City	6.6	4.9	3.2	50.3	393 089	262 199	49.9	10.3	64 514	18 874	-19 831	135 566	59.2	2.82	9.5	17.1
Waynesboro City	10.9	10.1	8.5	52.9	18 549	18 563	0.0	3.9	2 422	2 060	414	7 568	28.9	2.40	12.4	26.5
Williamsburg City	5.0	8.7	7.8	53.2	11 600	10 294	10.8	7.7	1 275	1 152	842	3 468	23.0	2.11	8.3	35.0
Winchester City	9.7	9.0	8.7	52.5	21 947	20 217	8.6	2.4	3 144	2 533	14	9 084	14.0	2.31	10.6	32.6
WASHINGTON	8.3	5.8	5.6	50.3	4 866 669	4 132 353	17.8	18.3	729 025	372 964	528 382	1 872 431	21.5	2.53	9.4	25.4
Adams	8.3	4.6	4.0	49.7	13 603	13 267	2.5	12.0	2 780	973	-153	4 586	2.2	2.94	7.3	20.4
Asotin	9.8	7.0	8.2	52.0	17 605	16 823	4.6	20.5	2 461	1 993	3 202	7 003	8.2	2.47	12.6	25.9
Benton	8.3	5.5	4.8	50.3	112 560	109 444	2.8	22.5	18 312	7 551	14 903	42 227	8.3	2.65	9.3	23.5
Chelan	9.5	5.0	5.8	49.8	52 250	45 061	16.0	16.4	9 137	5 183	4 906	20 645	16.0	2.49	8.4	26.8
Clallam	10.4	11.2	10.3	50.0	56 210	51 648	8.8	15.3	6 229	6 652	9 064	22 837	14.2	2.40	8.2	25.8
Clark	8.0	4.9	4.6	50.3	238 053	192 227	23.8	41.3	42 077	18 179	74 500	88 440	28.6	2.66	9.9	22.1
Columbia	10.1	8.7	9.3	50.2	4 024	4 057	-0.8	3.3	446	473	169	1 582	0.3	2.44	7.0	28.4
Cowlitz	9.2	6.6	6.8	50.3	82 119	79 548	3.2	12.0	11 516	7 627	6 199	31 640	7.2	2.56	9.7	23.9
Douglas	8.2	9.6	8.2	49.3	26 205	22 144	18.3	30.5	4 109	1 952	6 091	9 687	21.2	2.68	8.1	20.0
Ferry	8.3	6.4	5.3	47.7	6 295	5 811	8.3	14.2	770	589	743	2 247	15.0	2.70	9.1	22.1
Franklin	6.9	5.0	3.9	48.4	37 473	35 025	7.0	24.8	8 742	2 552	3 184	12 196	1.8	3.03	11.1	19.4
Garfield	12.7	10.1	11.1	51.0	2 248	2 468	-8.9	4.0	180	297	220	922	-2.1	2.39	5.0	27.3
Grant	8.9	6.8	5.5	49.0	54 798	48 522	12.9	31.4	11 513	4 551	10 446	19 745	15.1	2.74	8.4	22.6
Grays Harbor	9.8	7.4	7.6	49.9	64 175	66 314	-3.2	4.6	8 320	6 864	1 664	25 514	1.3	2.48	9.8	26.8
Island	8.9	8.2	5.7	49.5	60 195	44 048	36.7	22.1	9 373	4 228	5 633	21 787	37.4	2.61	6.2	18.7
Jefferson	11.8	11.7	8.5	49.7	20 406	15 965	27.8	31.1	2 046	2 212	6 530	8 627	35.7	2.31	7.9	26.8
King	8.0	5.6	5.4	50.7	1 507 305	1 269 898	18.7	10.5	206 976	104 693	59 017	615 792	23.8	2.40	9.0	29.2
Kitsap	7.5	5.5	5.2	49.2	189 731	147 152	28.9	24.7	31 154	13 605	25 811	69 267	31.2	2.65	8.5	22.1
Kittitas	7.9	5.9	6.4	50.0	26 725	24 877	7.4	19.8	2 920	2 136	4 578	10 460	10.2	2.33	7.2	29.1
Klickitat	8.8	6.1	6.3	49.0	16 616	15 822	5.0	17.5	2 166	1 454	2 244	6 210	7.9	2.64	8.8	22.7
Lewis	9.6	7.1	7.8	50.4	59 358	56 025	5.9	15.6	8 104	6 217	7 624	22 478	8.8	2.60	9.1	23.7
Lincoln	12.0	8.6	10.4	49.8	8 864	9 604	-7.7	10.1	998	989	929	3 605	-2.2	2.43	5.2	26.0
Mason	11.3	9.3	6.8	48.2	38 341	31 184	23.0	31.3	4 834	4 091	11 337	14 565	23.7	2.52	7.9	22.1
Okanogan	9.8	6.5	7.0	49.2	33 350	30 663	8.8	15.2	5 209	3 154	3 145	12 654	11.4	2.59	9.3	24.0
Pacific	12.4	11.3	10.7	50.4	18 882	17 237	9.5	10.0	2 035	2 521	2 427	7 896	13.8	2.35	7.9	27.2
Pend Oreille	10.8	7.1	6.4	50.0	8 915	8 580	3.9	30.2	1 233	901	2 381	3 395	13.1	2.60	8.3	22.8
Pierce	8.1	5.4	5.0	50.4	586 203	485 667	20.7	17.5	90 879	43 373	47 610	214 652	23.2	2.62	10.9	23.4
San Juan	12.2	11.0	8.0	50.0	10 035	7 838	28.0	28.5	983	892	2 785	4 392	31.5	2.25	6.0	27.2
Skagit	9.5	7.4	7.3	50.5	79 545	64 138	24.0	27.2	11 837	7 618	17 608	30 573	24.9	2.55	8.6	23.5
Skamania	9.0	5.0	5.0	48.4	8 289	7 919	4.7	18.6	827	561	1 293	3 066	8.8	2.69	7.8	20.2
Snohomish	7.6	5.0	4.5	49.8	465 628	337 720	37.9	28.1	74 395	29 939	87 277	171 713	42.3	2.68	9.1	20.9
Spokane	8.6	5.9	6.4	51.0	361 333	341 835	5.7	13.4	52 003	31 144	27 257	141 619	10.3	2.47	10.8	27.5
Stevens	8.9	6.0	6.2	49.7	30 948	28 979	6.8	29.7	4 080	2 642	7 883	11 241	14.2	2.73	8.0	21.0
Thurston	8.1	5.8	5.6	51.1	161 238	124 264	29.8	27.4	22 452	12 419	33 898	62 150	34.0	2.55	9.7	24.0
Wahkiakum	10.6	9.4	9.3	50.4	3 327	3 832	-13.2	15.4	331	394	592	1 321	-2.4	2.48	5.5	23.1
Walla Walla	8.5	6.9	8.1	48.7	48 439	47 435	2.1	11.2	6 607	4 627	3 581	17 623	3.8	2.50	9.2	26.9
Whatcom	8.1	5.8	6.1	50.5	127 780	106 701	19.8	25.5	17 787	9 971	25 202	48 543	22.5	2.53	8.0	24.9
Whitman	6.1	4.5	5.1	48.2	38 775	40 103	-3.3	-1.0	3 882	2 048	-2 183	13 546	2.0	2.39	5.2	26.6
Yakima	7.9	5.3	5.9	50.1	188 823	172 508	9.5	16.9	39 322	15 699	8 767	65 985	7.6	2.80	11.3	22.7
WEST VIRGINIA	10.5	8.1	7.0	51.8	1 793 477	1 950 186	-8.0	0.7	198 388	184 750	5 547	688 557	0.3	2.55	10.7	24.5
Barbour	10.4	7.2	7.6	51.7	15 699	16 639	-5.6	1.8	1 617	1 670	382	5 835	2.9	2.60	10.7	24.0
Berkeley	9.8	6.6	4.9	50.5	59 253	46 775	26.7	22.9	8 132	5 295	10 801	22 350	36.0	2.60	9.5	23.2
Boone	9.9	7.5	5.4	51.2	25 870	30 447	-15.0	1.7	3 159	2 429	-221	9 656	-5.2	2.68	11.2	21.2

1. No spouse present.

Table B. States and Counties — **Vital Statistics, Health Resources, and Crime**

STATE County	Births, average 1996–1998 Total	Rate[1]	Deaths, average 1996–1998 Number Total	Infant[2]	Rate Total[1]	Infant[3]	Physicians,[4] 1998 Number	Rate[5]	Hospitals,[4] 1998 Number	Beds Number	Rate[5]	Medicare enrollees 1999	Serious crimes known to police, 1998[6] Total Number	Rate[7]
	32	33	34	35	36	37	38	39	40	41	42	43	44	45
VIRGINIA—Cont'd														
Manassas City	675	19.6	185	3	5.4	4.5	12	34	1	152	430	5 591	1 358	3 926
Manassas Park City	168	19.7	37	1	4.3	7.9	13	149	0	0	0	12	314	3 676
Martinsville City	183	11.6	280	1	17.8	3.6	71	453	1	182	1 162	6 783	929	5 833
Newport News City	3 129	17.7	1 393	40	7.9	12.7	298	167	3	794	445	20 706	9 503	5 359
Norfolk City	4 018	17.8	2 179	57	9.6	14.2	710	330	5	1 321	614	28 999	16 188	6 998
Norton City	38	9.0	51	1	12.2	17.7	36	866	2	121	2 912	1 329	218	5 098
Petersburg City	550	15.8	509	8	14.7	14.6	95	274	1	296	852	8 346	3 369	9 786
Poquoson City	132	11.6	87	0	7.6	2.5	28	244	0	0	0	685	167	1 446
Portsmouth City	1 658	16.6	1 126	23	11.3	13.7	203	205	2	505	510	16 120	7 944	7 917
Radford City	122	7.9	86	1	5.5	8.2	8	51	1	159	1 011	2 281	364	2 356
Richmond City	3 023	15.6	2 464	41	12.8	13.4	998	514	7	1 853	954	38 202	17 684	9 114
Roanoke City	1 499	15.9	1 250	9	13.3	6.2	358	382	2	744	794	24 442	5 364	5 649
Salem City	253	10.2	293	1	11.8	5.3	135	547	1	335	1 357	6 105	701	2 803
Staunton City	258	11.1	295	1	12.7	5.2	69	296	0	0	0	6 293	918	3 902
Suffolk City	865	14.2	577	9	9.5	10.8	135	215	1	185	295	6 851	3 154	5 124
Virginia Beach City	6 416	14.9	2 220	54	5.2	8.5	913	211	2	430	99	37 838	17 665	4 050
Waynesboro City	258	13.9	228	2	12.3	7.8	50	269	0	0	0	5 009	751	4 014
Williamsburg City	136	11.4	130	2	10.9	12.3	11	92	1	105	877	6 209	472	3 966
Winchester City	310	13.9	259	3	11.6	9.7	40	177	1	365	1 611	4 893	1 600	7 072
WASHINGTON	78 599	14.0	42 142	454	7.5	5.8	13 390	235	92	12 093	213	725 018	333 799	5 867
Adams	306	20.0	110	2	7.2	6.5	2	13	2	61	398	1 530	736	4 670
Asotin	270	12.9	218	3	10.4	9.9	30	141	1	41	193	3 745	1 004	4 677
Benton	2 028	15.0	868	13	6.4	6.2	244	179	3	290	213	15 808	6 050	4 605
Chelan	1 000	16.8	558	4	9.4	4.3	191	318	3	246	410	7 452	4 187	6 914
Clallam	659	10.3	761	5	12.0	7.1	170	265	2	198	309	15 182	2 195	3 390
Clark	4 942	15.6	2 139	27	6.8	5.5	446	136	2	310	95	35 921	13 825	4 307
Columbia	47	11.1	47	0	11.1	0.0	3	72	1	18	433	816	NA	NA
Cowlitz	1 207	13.3	888	9	9.8	7.5	154	168	1	209	228	14 477	6 307	6 847
Douglas	446	13.5	227	2	6.9	4.5	23	68	0	0	0	6 688	1 321	3 937
Ferry	80	11.1	71	1	9.8	16.7	3	42	1	25	349	974	112	1 522
Franklin	1 023	22.3	284	5	6.2	4.9	43	93	1	140	301	4 627	1 953	4 095
Garfield	17	7.4	30	0	13.1	0.0	2	86	1	54	2 318	524	74	3 202
Grant	1 339	19.4	536	7	7.8	5.5	70	99	4	201	285	9 977	4 389	6 322
Grays Harbor	875	12.9	747	5	11.0	6.1	73	108	2	188	278	12 474	3 938	5 900
Island	963	13.8	499	6	7.2	5.9	128	182	1	51	73	8 503	1 426	1 990
Jefferson	207	8.0	268	2	10.4	8.0	67	255	1	43	164	5 768	845	3 212
King	21 821	13.3	11 527	114	7.0	5.2	6 141	371	19	4 155	251	197 865	111 627	6 749
Kitsap	3 179	13.7	1 581	16	6.8	4.9	454	195	1	252	108	26 495	9 675	4 067
Kittitas	337	10.7	244	3	7.8	9.9	38	120	1	39	123	4 189	2 002	6 291
Klickitat	239	12.6	149	1	7.9	4.2	15	78	2	58	301	3 015	634	3 279
Lewis	887	13.1	725	6	10.7	6.4	75	110	2	204	299	12 348	3 370	5 033
Lincoln	113	11.6	115	2	11.9	14.8	10	103	2	139	1 428	2 077	276	2 908
Mason	553	11.2	487	5	9.9	9.1	49	98	1	58	116	9 145	3 035	6 049
Okanogan	536	14.1	369	3	9.7	6.2	50	131	3	171	447	6 259	1 172	3 706
Pacific	215	10.3	282	1	13.5	3.1	25	120	2	43	207	5 146	1 009	4 712
Pend Oreille	127	11.2	112	1	9.9	7.9	9	78	2	96	833	2 062	440	4 078
Pierce	9 716	14.6	4 885	67	7.3	6.9	1 376	203	7	1 058	156	79 956	45 446	6 851
San Juan	105	8.6	100	0	8.2	0.0	62	496	0	0	0	2 466	255	2 051
Skagit	1 334	13.7	876	9	9.0	7.0	216	217	3	307	309	16 458	6 044	6 100
Skamania	89	9.3	66	0	6.9	3.8	3	31	0	0	0	946	298	3 763
Snohomish	8 127	14.3	3 482	46	6.1	5.7	790	134	5	621	106	59 825	22 508	3 995
Spokane	5 542	13.6	3 470	31	8.5	5.7	1 025	251	4	1 274	312	58 435	28 463	7 001
Stevens	451	11.5	306	4	7.8	8.1	40	101	2	100	253	5 556	1 310	3 318
Thurston	2 457	12.3	1 473	12	7.4	4.8	461	228	2	437	216	26 187	8 496	4 181
Wahkiakum	37	9.7	52	0	13.5	9.0	3	78	0	0	0	737	90	2 278
Walla Walla	719	13.4	508	7	9.5	9.3	166	309	2	207	385	8 607	3 202	6 023
Whatcom	1 975	12.8	1 151	6	7.5	2.9	325	207	1	228	145	20 976	8 706	5 566
Whitman	408	10.3	218	2	5.5	5.7	47	119	2	90	228	4 102	NA	NA
Yakima	4 225	19.5	1 712	27	7.9	6.3	361	166	4	481	221	27 567	15 464	6 985
WEST VIRGINIA	20 742	11.4	20 689	173	11.4	8.3	3 663	202	56	8 397	464	335 529	46 130	2 547
Barbour	162	10.0	195	1	12.0	8.2	12	74	1	72	446	2 855	159	984
Berkeley	934	13.5	614	7	8.9	7.5	97	137	1	209	294	9 896	2 783	4 040
Boone	318	12.1	295	1	11.2	3.1	9	34	1	38	145	4 695	301	1 142

1. Per 1,000 estimated resident population, average 1996–1998.　2. Deaths of infants under 1 year old.　3. Deaths of infants under 1 year old per 1,000 live births.　4. Data subject to copyright.　5. Per 100,000 resident population as of July 1 of the year shown.　6. Data for serious crimes have not been adjusted for underreporting; this may affect comparability between geographic areas and over time.　7. Per 100,000 population estimated by the FBI.

Table B. States and Counties — Crime, Education, Money Income, and Poverty

STATE County	Serious crimes known to police, 1998 [1] (cont'd) Rate [2] Violent	Property	Education — School enrollment and attainment, 1990 — Enrollment [3] Total	Percent private	Attainment [4] (percent) High school graduate or more	Bachelor's degree or more	Local government expenditures, fiscal 1997 [5] Total current expenditures (mil dol)	Current expenditures per student (dollars)	Money income — 1989 Per capita [6] (dollars)	Households Median Dollars	Percent change, 1979–1989 (constant 1989 dollars)	Percent with $100,000 or more	Income and poverty, 1997 Median household income	Percent below poverty level All persons	Persons under 18	Persons 5–17 in families
	46	47	48	49	50	51	52	53	54	55	56	57	58	59	60	61
VIRGINIA—Cont'd																
Manassas City	269	3 657	6 788	13.8	84.2	25.8	43.0	7 317	18 554	46 674	12.7	6.6	54 608	7.0	10.4	9.6
Manassas Park City	211	3 465	1 781	8.3	74.0	7.9	8.8	5 449	13 428	39 076	12.8	0.6	44 835	9.9	16.5	15.8
Martinsville City	622	5 211	3 279	10.7	62.9	15.8	16.4	5 769	13 742	22 446	-7.8	3.0	28 344	17.3	26.8	26.6
Newport News City	584	4 775	44 002	12.0	79.3	18.4	167.7	5 114	12 711	27 469	2.6	2.0	34 306	16.7	24.4	24.2
Norfolk City	678	6 320	60 528	12.8	72.7	16.8	217.9	5 785	11 643	23 563	12.4	2.2	28 350	24.4	34.0	33.7
Norton City	585	4 513	1 087	5.3	54.3	11.6	4.1	5 325	9 214	15 460	-29.7	1.5	23 171	23.3	31.9	30.4
Petersburg City	1 203	8 583	8 931	10.1	62.2	13.5	31.5	5 091	10 547	21 309	-5.4	1.2	25 428	25.6	39.6	37.0
Poquoson City	165	1 281	3 274	9.0	84.4	29.4	11.4	4 727	16 930	43 236	7.7	4.9	58 371	4.7	6.6	6.3
Portsmouth City	1 004	6 913	25 677	10.6	66.6	11.6	95.6	5 359	11 158	24 601	3.4	1.3	29 815	20.5	31.5	30.3
Radford City	259	2 097	9 233	3.0	75.4	29.1	8.7	5 658	9 704	19 487	-19.4	2.3	30 571	18.9	20.9	19.5
Richmond City	1 445	7 669	49 343	17.9	68.1	24.2	206.9	7 423	13 993	23 551	3.3	3.4	29 234	24.9	38.1	37.5
Roanoke City	570	5 079	19 198	11.1	68.0	15.6	83.1	6 237	12 513	22 591	1.6	2.3	27 492	20.6	31.7	32.4
Salem City	48	2 755	5 665	25.6	76.1	17.8	25.5	6 522	14 467	29 047	7.8	2.7	37 133	10.5	14.4	15.2
Staunton City	217	3 685	5 350	23.6	71.4	17.8	15.9	5 453	12 912	25 366	-5.4	1.8	32 833	15.3	21.1	23.0
Suffolk City	729	4 395	13 002	14.3	63.9	12.3	53.5	4 947	11 831	26 125	2.5	2.5	34 560	16.4	23.6	22.2
Virginia Beach City	227	3 823	105 358	14.5	88.0	25.5	369.7	4 821	15 242	36 271	7.1	4.2	44 714	9.0	13.2	12.4
Waynesboro City	369	3 645	3 679	9.3	71.2	18.2	15.4	5 142	13 469	26 668	-1.1	2.1	33 118	15.9	26.2	26.7
Williamsburg City	277	3 689	6 225	4.8	83.7	42.9	45.4	6 034	11 822	25 393	1.0	4.7	34 657	22.0	23.9	29.0
Winchester City	681	6 391	4 528	17.7	68.8	18.8	23.9	7 166	14 214	26 086	11.5	2.9	33 538	15.8	23.1	24.6
WASHINGTON	429	5 438	1 252 312	12.8	83.8	22.9	5 588.0	5 734	14 923	31 183	1.3	3.7	41 715	10.2	15.2	13.7
Adams	298	4 372	3 707	3.1	66.4	12.3	22.6	6 018	10 083	24 604	-12.8	2.1	32 250	15.4	21.4	20.1
Asotin	265	4 412	4 518	7.2	77.2	12.4	20.6	5 523	11 379	22 897	-10.7	1.5	31 753	15.6	22.9	22.0
Benton	295	4 310	31 738	9.0	83.9	23.3	154.0	5 462	14 027	32 593	-15.1	2.5	46 002	9.3	13.1	12.1
Chelan	286	6 628	12 315	7.3	74.3	16.7	76.1	5 900	12 533	24 312	-6.0	2.2	33 882	13.6	21.0	18.9
Clallam	207	3 183	12 755	9.4	79.7	16.1	60.9	5 681	12 798	25 434	-10.2	1.8	34 376	12.3	19.4	17.5
Clark	380	3 927	62 333	9.9	83.9	16.8	350.2	5 827	13 993	31 800	0.1	2.8	45 890	9.0	13.5	11.7
Columbia	NA	NA	984	2.5	71.8	15.1	5.0	6 102	11 108	22 418	-4.9	0.9	32 009	12.5	17.7	16.8
Cowlitz	378	6 469	20 066	8.3	77.3	11.3	100.6	5 703	12 638	27 866	-10.6	1.7	37 189	12.8	18.4	16.7
Douglas	164	3 773	6 464	5.9	75.9	13.8	35.0	5 452	12 071	27 054	-1.5	2.0	35 999	10.0	14.6	14.2
Ferry	82	1 440	1 745	3.5	72.6	12.0	9.0	6 615	9 860	25 170	2.4	0.3	30 427	19.0	24.4	25.6
Franklin	336	3 759	11 393	6.3	68.1	13.4	58.0	5 814	10 407	24 604	-18.8	2.4	32 276	17.7	24.0	23.2
Garfield	389	2 813	467	3.9	81.8	13.7	3.0	6 884	12 209	25 156	-7.7	1.3	32 363	10.9	13.4	14.9
Grant	432	5 890	14 517	4.6	71.6	11.9	88.8	5 548	10 376	22 372	-12.1	1.6	32 405	14.9	20.6	19.8
Grays Harbor	219	5 681	15 380	6.2	74.0	11.0	78.6	5 664	11 787	23 042	-19.5	1.8	31 091	16.2	23.9	21.7
Island	95	1 895	13 667	10.6	88.3	20.0	49.8	5 036	13 940	29 161	11.1	2.7	41 294	6.6	10.4	10.1
Jefferson	144	3 068	3 782	7.9	82.7	21.8	21.7	5 718	13 551	25 197	-2.1	2.7	35 373	11.4	18.2	17.8
King	474	6 275	369 847	17.1	88.2	32.8	1 431.5	5 860	18 587	36 179	4.2	5.9	51 300	8.0	12.3	10.8
Kitsap	406	6 116	47 813	10.7	86.6	19.8	233.8	5 562	14 311	32 043	0.9	2.7	43 492	8.9	12.6	11.6
Kittitas	176	6 115	10 412	2.9	81.2	22.2	27.7	5 793	10 781	20 489	-3.8	1.5	32 375	13.3	17.1	16.4
Klickitat	248	3 031	4 084	5.3	70.4	10.9	23.8	5 941	10 776	23 012	-13.9	1.6	33 208	15.5	23.0	21.9
Lewis	279	4 754	14 855	7.8	75.4	11.8	75.8	5 681	11 205	24 410	-3.6	1.7	32 557	14.2	20.4	18.4
Lincoln	274	2 634	2 085	8.0	81.9	16.0	18.2	7 716	11 977	24 617	-11.3	1.5	34 888	11.5	15.9	15.1
Mason	341	5 708	8 914	7.8	79.2	13.6	47.3	5 456	12 050	26 304	-2.7	1.6	35 419	12.2	18.8	17.1
Okanogan	310	3 396	8 050	9.6	71.3	12.0	46.9	5 828	10 346	20 303	-12.5	1.3	27 453	18.5	26.9	24.5
Pacific	430	4 282	3 934	10.5	74.2	11.3	24.2	6 893	10 952	20 029	-15.3	1.6	28 131	15.6	25.2	24.4
Pend Oreille	158	3 920	2 199	5.3	74.8	12.0	14.3	5 933	9 556	20 808	1.3	0.7	29 599	17.7	27.8	24.2
Pierce	735	6 116	150 262	14.8	83.2	17.5	687.4	5 704	13 439	30 412	5.4	2.7	41 853	11.0	15.6	14.0
San Juan	56	1 995	1 887	10.5	91.2	33.5	11.4	6 238	21 013	31 278	16.5	8.7	41 610	8.1	14.3	13.6
Skagit	149	5 951	18 837	9.6	81.0	16.3	104.9	5 831	13 804	28 389	2.8	3.1	38 148	11.1	17.7	15.5
Skamania	417	3 346	2 302	12.3	77.4	11.7	9.1	6 295	11 621	28 778	-12.0	1.4	38 915	10.1	14.5	14.1
Snohomish	299	3 696	116 244	12.5	85.7	19.3	525.8	5 462	15 769	36 847	5.9	3.6	49 439	7.2	10.4	9.0
Spokane	554	6 447	100 683	14.3	84.4	20.6	427.5	5 912	12 804	25 769	-3.5	2.4	35 691	12.2	17.1	15.1
Stevens	220	3 098	8 539	6.7	80.9	12.1	39.7	5 718	10 584	24 440	-1.4	1.3	32 387	15.1	21.0	19.4
Thurston	242	3 939	43 319	9.9	86.5	24.7	226.0	6 079	13 901	30 976	3.0	2.2	42 360	9.0	12.8	11.4
Wahkiakum	51	2 227	719	9.3	77.8	10.4	3.0	5 082	12 332	26 969	-17.3	3.1	35 446	10.2	14.6	13.7
Walla Walla	638	5 385	14 390	27.8	79.1	18.8	56.9	6 099	11 508	24 414	-7.0	2.0	34 471	14.5	19.8	18.7
Whatcom	297	5 269	37 132	10.4	83.2	22.0	132.6	5 401	13 753	28 367	5.4	3.4	37 896	11.4	16.3	14.6
Whitman	NA	NA	20 404	3.0	91.0	42.6	35.4	6 990	10 653	21 674	-8.3	1.7	33 952	14.5	15.5	14.8
Yakima	355	6 630	49 580	7.8	66.1	13.7	272.2	5 741	10 735	23 612	-4.7	2.1	30 822	18.3	26.2	23.9
WEST VIRGINIA	249	2 298	436 513	7.5	66.0	12.3	1 848.0	6 076	10 520	20 795	-14.8	1.5	27 432	16.8	24.7	22.7
Barbour	43	941	3 945	15.5	59.8	10.1	16.0	5 528	8 036	15 607	-22.4	0.5	23 259	21.4	29.7	28.6
Berkeley	436	3 604	13 045	9.3	68.4	11.9	68.7	5 761	11 832	27 412	6.3	1.9	35 715	11.2	17.6	16.2
Boone	171	971	6 319	2.4	54.1	6.4	31.8	6 570	9 189	17 073	-37.7	1.0	26 808	19.7	27.9	25.1

1. Data for serious crimes have not been adjusted for underreporting; this may affect comparability between geographic areas and over time.　2. Per 100,000 population estimated by the FBI.　3. All persons 3 years old and over enrolled in nursery school through college.　4. Persons 25 years old and over.　5. Elementary and secondary education expenditures, local government fiscal years ending between July 1, 1996 and June 30, 1997.　6. Based on population enumerated as of April 1, 1990.

Table B. States and Counties — **Personal Income**

STATE County	Total (mil dol)	Percent change, 1997–1998	Per capita¹ Dollars	Per capita¹ Rank	Wages and salaries² (mil dol)	Proprietor's income (mil dol)	Dividends, interest, and rent (mil dol)	Transfer payments Total (mil dol)	Gov't payments to individuals Total (mil dol)	Social Security (mil dol)	Medical payments (mil dol)	Income maintenance (mil dol)	Unemployment insurance (mil dol)
	62	63	64	65	66	67	68	69	70	71	72	73	74
VIRGINIA—Cont'd													
Manassas City	(3)	(3)	(3)	(3)	(3)	(3)	(3)	(3)	(3)	(3)	(3)	(3)	(3)
Manassas Park City	(3)	(3)	(3)	(3)	(3)	(3)	(3)	(3)	(3)	(3)	(3)	(3)	(3)
Martinsville City	(4)	(4)	(4)	(4)	(4)	(4)	(4)	(4)	(4)	(4)	(4)	(4)	(4)
Newport News City	3 812	4.2	21 415	1 262	3 467	146	633	505	473	193	169	61	6
Norfolk City	4 762	-1.4	20 967	1 403	8 039	218	1 042	765	739	248	287	122	8
Norton City	(5)	(5)	(5)	(5)	(5)	(5)	(5)	(5)	(5)	(5)	(5)	(5)	(5)
Petersburg City	(6)	(6)	(6)	(6)	(6)	(6)	(6)	(6)	(6)	(6)	(6)	(6)	(6)
Poquoson City	(7)	(7)	(7)	(7)	(7)	(7)	(7)	(7)	(7)	(7)	(7)	(7)	(7)
Portsmouth City	2 031	3.9	20 502	1 556	1 812	47	330	383	366	129	143	62	5
Radford City	(8)	(8)	(8)	(8)	(8)	(8)	(8)	(8)	(8)	(8)	(8)	(8)	(8)
Richmond City	5 623	2.7	29 439	184	7 311	496	1 139	902	866	293	374	122	7
Roanoke City	2 272	4.8	24 218	603	2 553	118	364	444	426	156	152	44	3
Salem City	(9)	(9)	(9)	(9)	(9)	(9)	(9)	(9)	(9)	(9)	(9)	(9)	(9)
Staunton City	(10)	(10)	(10)	(10)	(10)	(10)	(10)	(10)	(10)	(10)	(10)	(10)	(10)
Suffolk City	1 365	6.1	21 786	1 166	565	46	199	202	190	78	75	25	2
Virginia Beach City	11 613	3.6	26 967	307	5 372	592	1 988	859	780	367	255	64	8
Waynesboro City	(10)	(10)	(10)	(10)	(10)	(10)	(10)	(10)	(10)	(10)	(10)	(10)	(10)
Williamsburg City	(11)	(11)	(11)	(11)	(11)	(11)	(11)	(11)	(11)	(11)	(11)	(11)	(11)
Winchester City	(12)	(12)	(12)	(12)	(12)	(12)	(12)	(12)	(12)	(12)	(12)	(12)	(12)
WASHINGTON	163 348	7.9	28 719	X	104 926	13 207	31 074	19 390	18 262	7 208	6 341	1 734	868
Adams	316	4.3	20 605	1 527	164	25	70	65	62	18	29	6	6
Asotin	443	4.4	20 829	1 450	128	24	101	93	89	37	33	10	2
Benton	3 310	4.6	24 315	587	2 248	189	566	420	392	171	120	36	26
Chelan	1 483	4.4	24 654	536	959	170	331	237	225	98	76	18	16
Clallam	1 465	4.2	22 786	892	582	124	486	310	297	146	95	22	13
Clark	8 802	8.9	26 882	313	3 923	632	1 739	960	895	356	293	92	47
Columbia	84	5.0	20 211	1 647	40	9	22	18	17	8	5	2	1
Cowlitz	1 997	4.7	21 851	1 144	1 253	128	363	380	362	150	124	42	21
Douglas	641	5.3	19 072	2 034	210	15	138	108	102	42	37	8	7
Ferry	115	1.6	16 031	2 789	51	13	22	29	28	9	10	4	2
Franklin	859	4.0	18 479	2 218	576	102	140	166	157	44	66	20	13
Garfield	45	4.0	19 293	1 958	21	2	15	9	9	5	2	1	0
Grant	1 435	7.3	20 301	1 627	771	210	265	256	242	91	86	27	21
Grays Harbor	1 362	3.1	20 186	1 657	700	102	272	327	314	128	117	34	16
Island	1 704	4.8	23 743	690	766	100	488	210	197	105	51	13	6
Jefferson	622	5.1	23 658	711	191	48	210	120	115	59	35	8	4
King	67 671	11.3	40 905	27	53 246	6 850	12 218	5 410	5 079	2 017	1 748	427	193
Kitsap	5 347	2.6	22 957	860	3 155	268	1 230	661	617	228	212	61	33
Kittitas	636	4.7	20 241	1 640	297	75	150	107	100	43	30	7	5
Klickitat	378	2.7	19 535	1 876	190	27	101	76	72	29	24	8	6
Lewis	1 360	2.4	19 969	1 723	731	121	273	300	287	119	103	28	16
Lincoln	208	-0.2	21 269	1 300	80	10	71	42	40	20	13	3	2
Mason	958	4.6	19 220	1 980	359	69	239	211	201	92	68	18	8
Okanogan	751	4.3	19 626	1 851	398	68	148	175	167	59	66	18	14
Pacific	420	4.5	20 139	1 670	154	46	108	112	108	52	36	8	5
Pend Oreille	205	4.1	17 813	2 403	77	21	49	54	52	17	20	8	3
Pierce	16 561	5.8	24 500	560	8 668	870	2 941	2 316	2 185	779	775	251	91
San Juan	446	6.6	35 573	62	116	48	228	46	44	25	12	2	2
Skagit	2 393	5.8	24 079	625	1 167	256	586	393	373	162	133	28	21
Skamania	205	5.7	20 915	1 419	60	7	40	29	27	11	8	3	4
Snohomish	15 817	7.3	27 015	301	8 782	708	2 348	1 618	1 502	618	514	122	60
Spokane	9 573	4.5	23 450	756	6 164	610	1 951	1 573	1 492	554	544	153	60
Stevens	674	5.2	17 028	2 606	292	56	128	154	146	56	51	16	9
Thurston	5 035	5.7	24 895	501	2 766	286	957	683	643	262	203	55	32
Wahkiakum	78	5.1	20 216	1 646	25	5	22	15	14	8	4	1	1
Walla Walla	1 119	4.3	20 845	1 442	696	73	249	203	192	81	65	16	10
Whatcom	3 575	6.0	22 732	908	1 992	393	785	518	487	205	162	44	26
Whitman	724	3.4	18 696	2 159	455	35	175	111	103	42	29	7	4
Yakima	4 533	4.7	20 718	1 480	2 475	413	850	872	828	261	342	106	65
WEST VIRGINIA	36 569	3.8	20 185	X	20 570	2 112	6 369	8 561	8 249	3 255	2 867	775	145
Barbour	238	2.8	14 789	2 952	77	13	46	76	73	27	24	9	3
Berkeley	1 579	7.8	22 234	1 031	796	72	223	232	220	91	63	16	3
Boone	502	4.4	19 193	1 986	311	49	63	128	124	50	36	15	5

1. Based on the resident population estimated as of July 1 of the year shown. 2. Includes other labor income. 3. Manassas and Manassas Park included with Prince William County. 4. Martinsville included with Henry County. 5. Norton included with Wise County. 6. Petersburg and Colonial Heights included with Dinwiddie County. 7. Poquoson included with York County. 8. Radford included with Montgomery County. 9. Salem included with Roanoke County. 10. Staunton and Waynesboro included with Augusta County. 11. Williamsburg included with James City County. 12. Winchester included with Frederick County.

Table B. States and Counties — Earnings, Social Security, and Housing

STATE County	Earnings, 1998									Social Security beneficiaries, December 1998		Supplemental Security Income recipients, December 1998	Housing units, 1990	
	Total (mil dol)	Farm	Goods-related[1]		Service-related and other[2]				Government	Number	Rate[3]		Total	Percent change, 1980–1990
			Total	Manufacturing	Total	Retail trade	Finance, insurance, and real estate	Services						
	75	76	77	78	79	80	81	82	83	84	85	86	87	88
VIRGINIA—Cont'd														
Manassas City	(4)	(4)	(4)	(4)	(4)	(4)	(4)	(4)	(4)	3 148	89	459	10 232	85.7
Manassas Park City	(4)	(4)	(4)	(4)	(4)	(4)	(4)	(4)	(4)	NA	NA	NA	2 252	16.6
Martinsville City	(5)	(5)	(5)	(5)	(5)	(5)	(5)	(5)	(5)	5 019	320	536	7 310	3.3
Newport News City	3 613	0.0	33.9	29.8	39.4	6.5	3.6	22.8	26.7	23 523	132	4 102	69 728	26.8
Norfolk City	8 257	0.0	D	7.0	D	4.5	5.2	17.8	51.4	32 238	150	7 991	98 762	4.1
Norton City	(6)	(6)	(6)	(6)	(6)	(6)	(6)	(6)	(6)	1 436	346	277	1 845	0.3
Petersburg City	(7)	(7)	(7)	(7)	(7)	(7)	(7)	(7)	(7)	7 915	228	2 295	16 196	0.4
Poquoson City	(8)	(8)	(8)	(8)	(8)	(8)	(8)	(8)	(8)	1 410	123	2	3 890	31.7
Portsmouth City	1 859	0.0	D	5.2	D	4.2	1.6	18.5	58.8	18 005	182	4 540	42 283	9.5
Radford City	(9)	(9)	(9)	(9)	(9)	(9)	(9)	(9)	(9)	2 064	131	202	5 496	32.1
Richmond City	7 807	0.0	19.0	15.2	55.7	4.1	13.4	24.3	25.4	34 675	179	8 564	94 141	2.9
Roanoke City	2 671	0.0	D	10.4	D	12.4	8.6	30.0	11.7	19 123	204	3 919	44 384	4.0
Salem City	(10)	(10)	(10)	(10)	(10)	(10)	(10)	(10)	(10)	4 877	198	365	9 609	6.6
Staunton City	(11)	(11)	(11)	(11)	(11)	(11)	(11)	(11)	(11)	5 490	235	611	10 003	15.9
Suffolk City	611	0.5	22.4	15.0	55.0	9.7	3.4	23.8	22.1	10 378	166	2 296	20 011	19.7
Virginia Beach City	5 963	0.1	D	3.0	D	10.8	8.1	29.3	30.6	43 827	101	4 409	147 037	59.8
Waynesboro City	(11)	(11)	(11)	(11)	(11)	(11)	(11)	(11)	(11)	4 598	248	427	7 902	27.4
Williamsburg City	(12)	(12)	(12)	(12)	(12)	(12)	(12)	(12)	(12)	2 317	194	215	3 960	30.2
Winchester City	(13)	(13)	(13)	(13)	(13)	(13)	(13)	(13)	(13)	4 565	201	605	9 808	17.0
WASHINGTON	118 133	1.3	22.5	15.9	58.5	8.9	6.5	29.0	17.8	815 671	143	97 105	2 032 378	20.3
Adams	189	16.0	18.9	15.8	43.6	8.1	2.3	10.3	21.5	2 221	145	271	5 263	4.2
Asotin	152	-1.9	D	7.4	D	15.7	3.2	29.8	21.5	4 320	203	535	7 519	6.8
Benton	2 438	4.3	D	7.8	D	7.8	2.6	31.7	18.1	18 504	136	1 572	44 877	5.2
Chelan	1 129	8.0	D	9.0	D	11.7	4.5	23.4	20.8	11 305	188	940	25 048	13.1
Clallam	707	0.3	D	11.9	D	12.7	4.8	21.4	29.6	16 848	263	1 171	25 225	15.4
Clark	4 554	0.3	32.8	20.7	50.6	9.7	6.1	21.9	16.4	40 622	124	5 010	92 849	27.5
Columbia	49	12.3	D	D	D	6.1	2.2	D	32.4	972	234	130	2 046	12.5
Cowlitz	1 381	0.5	44.1	33.9	41.1	10.1	3.3	18.0	14.3	16 695	182	2 125	33 304	4.9
Douglas	225	8.6	12.2	3.8	50.2	13.8	3.3	15.7	29.0	4 874	145	356	10 640	16.4
Ferry	64	3.7	D	D	D	8.2	2.1	D	34.7	1 210	169	161	3 239	35.3
Franklin	678	17.1	14.7	8.3	47.5	8.3	1.7	18.3	20.6	5 151	111	757	13 664	2.6
Garfield	23	1.4	D	D	D	5.3	3.0	7.8	56.0	560	240	37	1 209	5.9
Grant	981	21.6	D	16.6	D	9.0	D	11.0	21.4	11 115	158	1 374	22 809	12.5
Grays Harbor	802	1.2	D	24.3	D	12.5	D	19.9	21.0	14 647	216	2 006	29 932	4.7
Island	866	0.4	D	3.1	D	7.2	4.5	12.0	61.9	12 112	172	547	25 860	23.9
Jefferson	239	0.9	D	14.7	D	11.5	3.7	21.5	26.2	6 763	258	365	11 014	24.8
King	60 096	0.1	20.0	14.6	69.3	7.8	8.0	36.7	10.6	212 379	128	27 186	647 343	23.2
Kitsap	3 422	0.1	7.6	2.2	35.0	8.4	3.5	19.0	57.3	29 353	126	3 438	74 038	29.2
Kittitas	371	3.8	14.1	8.4	46.1	13.4	2.7	15.2	35.9	4 926	155	379	13 215	12.9
Klickitat	217	4.3	35.0	27.4	36.5	5.5	3.3	9.1	24.2	3 532	183	406	7 213	11.0
Lewis	851	3.2	D	17.4	D	15.6	D	17.5	19.3	13 969	205	1 534	25 487	10.2
Lincoln	90	4.7	6.1	2.1	49.7	8.4	3.7	17.3	39.5	2 265	233	160	4 607	6.2
Mason	429	0.2	D	19.7	D	10.5	4.0	16.3	28.0	10 781	216	871	22 292	27.2
Okanogan	466	10.7	13.5	7.8	45.0	10.8	2.3	20.1	30.9	7 482	196	916	16 629	22.4
Pacific	200	6.5	25.5	21.0	40.4	10.6	3.7	18.1	27.6	5 981	288	503	12 404	13.3
Pend Oreille	97	1.6	D	31.3	D	8.6	2.5	11.9	32.6	2 179	189	418	5 404	15.3
Pierce	9 539	0.3	18.8	11.8	50.2	10.2	6.5	23.0	30.6	91 035	135	14 074	228 842	22.1
San Juan	163	-0.3	D	5.0	D	14.4	7.0	26.9	17.9	2 785	223	87	6 075	14.4
Skagit	1 423	6.1	D	14.2	D	13.0	D	20.3	19.6	18 606	187	1 519	33 580	20.9
Skamania	68	-0.8	D	18.3	D	5.4	2.0	17.4	41.2	1 352	138	146	3 922	14.2
Snohomish	9 489	0.3	46.7	38.9	37.3	8.9	5.1	15.6	15.8	68 596	117	6 847	183 942	40.2
Spokane	6 774	0.2	20.7	13.5	59.1	10.7	7.4	27.1	20.0	64 680	158	8 435	150 105	9.0
Stevens	348	1.6	33.9	26.9	41.5	9.0	2.4	21.6	23.1	7 053	179	772	14 601	16.3
Thurston	3 052	0.9	12.0	6.0	44.4	10.1	4.4	23.1	42.6	30 433	150	3 184	66 464	31.1
Wahkiakum	30	0.8	39.2	35.2	34.9	6.8	2.7	11.9	24.9	866	225	42	1 496	-0.5
Walla Walla	769	5.9	D	18.7	D	9.0	3.7	23.6	24.2	9 517	177	863	19 029	4.9
Whatcom	2 385	3.9	28.2	16.9	53.2	11.7	5.7	22.5	14.7	23 727	151	2 447	55 742	17.4
Whitman	490	0.7	D	3.6	32.2	6.7	2.8	11.3	59.1	4 484	114	267	14 598	1.2
Yakima	2 888	13.7	18.0	12.5	50.7	10.0	3.5	22.5	17.5	31 757	146	5 094	70 852	6.0
WEST VIRGINIA	22 683	0.0	27.3	15.0	51.4	9.5	4.1	25.0	21.3	388 687	215	70 562	781 295	4.5
Barbour	89	-0.6	D	7.1	D	9.7	3.7	26.1	27.4	3 484	216	829	6 956	12.4
Berkeley	868	0.3	D	13.7	D	9.3	4.0	D	32.8	11 066	156	1 417	25 385	36.7
Boone	360	0.0	D	D	D	6.0	D	9.4	12.9	5 835	223	1 227	10 705	-0.5

1. Covers mining, construction, and manufacturing.   2. Covers private sector earnings in agricultural services, forestry, and fisheries; transportation and public utilities; wholesale trade; retail trade; finance, insurance, and real estate; and services.   3. Per 1,000 resident population estimated as of July 1 of the year shown.   4. Manassas and Manassas Park included with Prince William County.   5. Martinsville included with Henry County.   6. Norton included with Wise County.   7. Petersburg and Colonial Heights included with Dinwiddie County.   8. Poquoson included with York County.   9. Radford included with Montgomery County.   10. Salem included with Roanoke County.   11. Staunton and Waynesboro included with Augusta County.   12. Williamsburg included with James City County.   13. Winchester included with Frederick County.

Table B. States and Counties — Housing, Labor Force, and Employment

	Housing units, 1990 (cont'd)								Civilian labor force, 1999				Civilian employment, 1990[5]		
	Occupied units										Unemployment		Percent		
	Owner-occupied					Renter-occupied									
				Owner cost as a percent of income											
STATE County	Total	Percent	Median value[1]	With a mortgage	Without a mortgage	Median rent[2]	Rent as percent of income	Substandard units[3] (percent)	Total	Percent change, 1998–1999	Total	Rate[4]	Total	Professional, managerial, and technical	Precision production, craft, and repair
	89	90	91	92	93	94	95	96	97	98	99	100	101	102	103
VIRGINIA—Cont'd															
Manassas City	9 481	66.1	150 700	25.3	13.7	695	25.5	3.5	20 036	2.6	306	1.5	15 808	37.0	10.5
Manassas Park City	2 182	71.8	101 800	24.4	13.1	739	26.9	3.4	4 743	2.3	54	1.1	3 692	23.6	21.3
Martinsville City	6 839	60.7	52 700	18.9	13.2	320	23.7	2.6	7 156	1.4	698	9.8	7 401	25.4	10.4
Newport News City	63 952	50.0	85 200	22.7	13.0	439	26.2	3.8	84 685	1.8	3 377	4.0	72 950	30.6	14.6
Norfolk City	89 478	44.0	74 500	23.4	13.5	438	28.5	5.7	79 377	-7.3	4 333	5.5	89 580	27.2	12.4
Norton City	1 697	60.9	48 000	18.9	11.7	279	32.0	2.3	1 543	0.3	110	7.1	1 445	28.2	9.3
Petersburg City	14 730	50.9	52 000	21.4	12.7	360	27.7	4.4	15 806	0.3	816	5.2	15 920	21.7	8.2
Poquoson City	3 769	82.7	113 700	22.2	12.2	574	25.6	0.1	6 094	0.3	135	2.2	5 359	39.2	12.8
Portsmouth City	38 741	55.9	67 400	22.9	13.6	416	28.3	4.6	44 809	-0.8	2 214	4.9	42 053	25.1	16.6
Radford City	5 207	47.8	64 500	15.8	12.6	410	35.1	1.2	6 695	4.9	186	2.8	6 319	35.1	8.1
Richmond City	85 337	46.3	66 600	21.4	14.5	413	27.5	3.2	96 039	-0.2	3 234	3.4	96 229	31.0	7.3
Roanoke City	41 030	56.6	54 000	18.8	12.7	336	24.3	2.2	48 874	-2.5	1 256	2.6	45 400	24.6	10.4
Salem City	9 161	67.4	69 100	16.8	11.8	404	25.2	0.4	13 751	-3.0	215	1.6	12 061	28.0	9.6
Staunton City	9 432	61.2	62 700	17.0	12.6	359	24.1	1.6	11 003	1.4	261	2.4	11 161	27.0	10.7
Suffolk City	18 516	67.7	70 700	22.4	14.3	376	28.7	6.9	29 958	2.6	1 060	3.5	22 463	26.1	15.8
Virginia Beach City	135 566	62.5	96 500	24.9	12.2	577	27.0	2.3	212 749	0.1	5 630	2.6	174 616	35.0	11.2
Waynesboro City	7 568	62.3	68 100	18.3	12.7	374	22.4	2.5	8 988	1.5	263	2.9	8 607	28.2	12.4
Williamsburg City	3 468	36.4	121 000	20.3	12.1	492	28.3	1.7	5 920	1.9	350	5.9	4 974	41.6	4.9
Winchester City	9 084	45.4	89 100	19.1	12.7	425	24.2	2.8	13 213	-1.8	325	2.5	11 405	27.6	12.5
WASHINGTON	1 872 431	62.6	93 400	20.4	11.8	445	25.7	4.0	3 075 959	1.2	145 379	4.7	2 293 961	31.7	11.6
Adams	4 586	65.5	45 900	16.2	11.5	284	22.7	10.0	9 002	2.3	919	10.2	5 847	16.8	10.0
Asotin	7 003	65.6	53 900	18.3	11.5	327	28.0	2.7	11 971	-1.6	412	3.4	7 111	23.9	13.7
Benton	42 227	63.1	66 200	16.0	11.4	363	21.5	3.7	72 004	1.6	4 013	5.6	52 440	36.5	10.6
Chelan	20 645	61.9	71 500	19.0	11.2	343	25.4	5.0	35 178	0.4	3 016	8.6	23 004	24.3	10.9
Clallam	22 837	70.2	79 200	19.1	12.0	377	24.8	3.9	24 827	0.6	1 830	7.4	20 874	25.9	10.6
Clark	88 440	64.3	74 200	19.3	11.4	447	24.7	3.2	178 221	1.1	6 962	3.9	110 967	27.5	13.0
Columbia	1 582	67.6	37 400	15.2	12.1	278	18.5	4.6	1 499	0.3	174	11.6	1 570	23.0	6.1
Cowlitz	31 640	65.4	61 300	15.2	11.1	348	24.6	3.8	41 524	-0.3	2 952	7.1	34 306	21.9	14.7
Douglas	9 687	68.7	68 700	17.3	11.0	375	23.0	7.1	19 538	0.4	1 329	6.8	11 664	23.4	10.7
Ferry	2 247	69.8	50 100	14.2	12.1	257	15.9	12.7	2 597	-5.3	289	11.1	2 296	24.7	16.6
Franklin	12 196	59.7	56 000	17.6	11.9	295	25.5	12.6	23 000	0.7	2 170	9.4	15 686	21.0	10.6
Garfield	922	68.8	36 900	15.1	11.9	279	16.6	2.4	1 113	0.1	41	3.7	969	20.5	9.8
Grant	19 745	64.6	51 600	16.9	11.2	281	22.3	7.0	38 335	3.7	3 572	9.3	22 289	20.6	11.8
Grays Harbor	25 514	67.0	49 100	17.2	12.0	322	25.9	3.2	26 951	1.9	2 189	8.1	24 390	21.7	11.0
Island	21 787	65.6	103 400	22.7	11.3	463	25.8	3.8	28 671	-0.7	1 125	3.9	21 236	29.9	16.0
Jefferson	8 627	73.9	88 700	19.6	11.5	384	25.1	6.4	10 701	7.9	634	5.9	7 664	29.7	14.1
King	615 792	58.8	140 100	21.1	11.6	510	25.8	3.4	1 030 378	0.8	32 784	3.2	818 326	38.1	9.7
Kitsap	69 267	64.3	89 100	21.4	11.9	450	24.7	3.9	93 323	2.2	4 679	5.0	78 930	32.9	16.0
Kittitas	10 460	57.2	60 500	18.5	12.7	318	29.9	4.0	14 887	-1.2	831	5.6	11 882	24.5	9.4
Klickitat	6 210	66.0	52 700	16.5	12.3	331	23.0	5.1	9 072	4.2	831	9.2	6 437	20.2	10.0
Lewis	22 478	70.0	57 600	18.0	12.4	348	24.6	4.0	31 006	-6.1	2 552	8.2	23 427	22.0	12.5
Lincoln	3 605	72.6	41 100	17.5	12.2	288	22.6	2.8	4 799	-4.1	239	5.0	3 614	21.4	9.3
Mason	14 565	76.7	70 100	19.5	11.7	382	25.7	5.5	20 781	-1.3	1 243	6.0	14 224	24.6	15.3
Okanogan	12 654	66.7	50 300	17.0	12.2	277	23.0	8.1	23 367	2.5	2 140	9.2	13 632	20.8	9.2
Pacific	7 896	71.9	49 300	17.3	12.9	315	25.0	4.3	8 126	-3.1	675	8.3	6 867	20.4	10.8
Pend Oreille	3 395	73.6	49 500	18.1	11.5	292	26.2	6.3	4 198	-0.4	426	10.1	2 841	22.9	14.5
Pierce	214 652	60.3	82 500	21.1	12.4	436	26.2	4.3	335 293	0.8	15 212	4.5	251 833	28.4	13.2
San Juan	4 392	71.9	166 400	25.1	10.6	475	23.0	6.4	6 337	6.7	239	3.8	4 418	26.1	16.5
Skagit	30 573	69.9	81 500	19.6	11.7	422	25.3	4.3	50 191	4.5	3 179	6.3	34 121	25.3	14.5
Skamania	3 066	73.5	67 100	17.2	11.8	328	17.4	5.3	4 118	-2.6	345	8.4	3 328	21.2	13.7
Snohomish	171 713	66.3	127 200	21.6	11.9	536	25.6	3.7	343 968	4.2	13 525	3.9	235 752	28.6	15.9
Spokane	141 619	63.7	59 000	19.4	12.2	356	26.9	2.7	210 309	0.8	11 029	5.2	157 142	30.9	9.9
Stevens	11 241	76.2	55 900	17.8	11.8	306	23.4	6.2	16 864	-3.5	1 465	8.7	11 583	23.4	12.5
Thurston	62 150	64.7	79 700	21.0	11.7	460	26.0	3.6	101 037	1.9	4 641	4.6	74 539	36.4	9.6
Wahkiakum	1 321	75.5	62 300	16.5	12.6	300	19.3	2.2	1 903	-1.3	125	6.6	1 486	15.6	8.3
Walla Walla	17 623	62.3	56 500	17.4	11.7	319	25.5	4.3	26 224	-0.8	1 771	6.8	21 076	27.2	9.1
Whatcom	48 543	64.3	90 800	19.9	11.9	425	27.1	3.6	81 126	2.5	4 241	5.2	61 657	26.3	13.0
Whitman	13 546	48.2	61 900	16.3	11.5	347	32.0	2.0	19 200	0.1	347	1.8	17 167	41.7	4.9
Yakima	65 985	63.2	55 200	17.9	12.1	339	25.5	10.1	114 301	-0.4	11 233	9.8	77 366	22.9	9.5
WEST VIRGINIA	688 557	74.1	47 900	17.5	12.0	303	26.8	4.0	817 009	2.1	53 909	6.6	671 085	25.4	14.5
Barbour	5 835	77.5	35 200	23.7	13.1	271	30.4	6.0	6 099	0.0	682	11.2	5 170	23.9	14.9
Berkeley	22 350	73.0	70 600	18.0	11.8	368	24.0	3.9	35 672	3.1	1 308	3.7	27 449	22.4	15.4
Boone	9 656	76.3	41 800	16.3	12.0	286	33.3	4.0	8 130	-0.8	907	11.2	7 327	19.2	20.8

1. Specified owner-occupied units. 2. Specified renter-occupied units. 3. Overcrowded or lacking complete plumbing facilities. 4. Percent of civilian labor force. 5. Persons 16 years and older.

Table B. States and Counties — Nonfarm Employment and Agriculture

	Private nonfarm establishments, employment and payroll, 1998									Agriculture, 1997			
		Employment						Annual payroll		Farms			Farm operators
											Percent with—		
STATE County	Number of establishments	Total	Health Care and Social Assistance	Manufacturing	Retail trade	Finance and Insurance	Professional Scientific and Technical Services	Total (mil dol)	Average per employee (dollars)	Number	Less than 50 acres	500 acres and over	Whose principal occupation is farming (percent)
	104	105	106	107	108	109	110	111	112	113	114	115	116

VIRGINIA—Cont'd													
Manassas City	1 568	20 894	2 682	3 272	3 608	562	1 586	720	34 482	NA	NA	NA	NA
Manassas Park City	129	1 983	0	70	150	D	73	60	30 073	NA	NA	NA	NA
Martinsville City	743	18 055	1 699	8 220	1 969	436	258	411	22 745	NA	NA	NA	NA
Newport News City	3 753	85 522	10 218	25 132	9 618	1 890	4 046	2 256	26 379	NA	NA	NA	NA
Norfolk City	5 454	113 834	17 406	D	12 701	9 052	8 180	3 098	27 211	NA	NA	NA	NA
Norton City	287	4 763	1 077	D	857	118	D	123	25 832	NA	NA	NA	NA
Petersburg City	869	13 287	2 912	2 512	1 688	384	1 030	328	24 714	NA	NA	NA	NA
Poquoson City	174	1 226	202	D	188	28	79	21	16 935	NA	NA	NA	NA
Portsmouth City	1 736	24 644	6 328	1 961	3 439	696	1 298	586	23 771	NA	NA	NA	NA
Radford City	348	6 429	1 178	2 690	545	174	167	161	25 091	NA	NA	NA	NA
Richmond City	7 504	159 003	23 417	22 105	12 398	16 511	8 767	5 327	33 505	NA	NA	NA	NA
Roanoke City	4 106	72 622	10 200	8 976	12 015	3 595	2 825	1 788	24 614	NA	NA	NA	NA
Salem City	963	22 047	4 691	5 995	3 065	350	318	599	27 163	NA	NA	NA	NA
Staunton City	863	10 863	1 756	431	2 177	438	254	222	20 441	NA	NA	NA	NA
Suffolk City	1 120	15 043	2 849	2 075	2 512	339	364	359	23 895	218	34.4	20.2	64.2
Virginia Beach City	9 989	132 973	12 605	5 790	23 842	6 944	11 344	2 968	22 322	147	61.9	8.8	48.3
Waynesboro City	583	11 160	567	3 229	1 557	296	125	316	28 276	NA	NA	NA	NA
Williamsburg City	729	15 520	3 047	D	2 200	280	310	374	24 109	NA	NA	NA	NA
Winchester City	1 217	22 007	4 383	5 974	3 843	632	505	584	26 537	NA	NA	NA	NA
WASHINGTON	161 473	2 134 598	269 465	335 467	288 387	96 128	117 463	73 268	34 324	29 011	51.4	16.2	53.3
Adams	403	4 039	477	1 190	590	91	56	84	20 704	628	10.5	56.7	74.4
Asotin	452	3 909	750	342	743	102	152	84	21 549	140	22.1	62.1	53.6
Benton	3 212	47 110	5 203	3 730	7 145	1 142	7 170	1 490	31 629	1 078	67.3	10.4	43.5
Chelan	2 292	24 925	3 985	2 721	4 170	794	655	606	24 324	1 113	71.1	3.3	58.8
Clallam	2 060	15 482	3 052	1 381	2 880	535	517	336	21 683	292	66.8	2.1	43.8
Clark	7 685	93 206	10 877	19 724	12 678	3 855	3 560	2 674	28 687	1 175	71.5	1.6	38.4
Columbia	134	918	167	144	151	27	D	20	21 723	198	20.7	51.5	65.2
Cowlitz	2 402	32 626	4 122	8 181	4 782	863	813	959	29 388	349	59.3	2.6	37.0
Douglas	547	3 892	398	224	1 006	159	106	80	20 520	853	51.3	27.8	64.6
Ferry	149	1 075	117	160	218	16	28	27	24 857	179	18.4	31.3	56.4
Franklin	1 086	13 522	1 744	3 308	2 271	210	201	319	23 602	848	30.8	26.5	68.6
Garfield	54	350	75	0	68	20	D	7	20 071	182	11.0	65.9	73.1
Grant	1 686	16 548	2 085	3 690	3 140	397	463	385	23 260	1 699	28.5	28.0	69.7
Grays Harbor	1 980	17 697	2 606	3 581	2 939	586	462	437	24 714	389	50.9	5.4	46.0
Island	1 551	10 308	1 631	647	2 044	624	339	210	20 402	261	67.8	0.8	42.9
Jefferson	998	5 781	866	880	880	146	135	124	21 471	144	54.9	2.1	34.0
King	58 839	955 805	98 827	140 129	99 494	50 094	70 255	41 614	43 538	1 091	83.9	1.0	43.3
Kitsap	5 071	45 673	8 533	1 366	10 360	1 985	2 482	998	21 859	359	75.4	0.6	34.8
Kittitas	985	6 907	972	462	1 352	117	152	142	20 504	757	50.3	12.2	47.2
Klickitat	509	3 537	446	1 086	430	97	106	102	28 707	530	30.6	30.0	53.0
Lewis	2 022	19 415	2 600	3 467	3 685	440	343	461	23 765	1 117	51.7	1.8	44.6
Lincoln	300	1 996	499	32	310	91	93	42	20 808	707	7.1	73.8	79.8
Mason	1 051	8 552	958	1 435	1 363	315	280	191	22 297	211	75.4	1.9	47.9
Okanogan	1 040	8 204	1 451	649	1 654	195	183	164	19 971	1 270	47.5	18.0	57.2
Pacific	671	4 218	483	801	652	176	72	77	18 235	253	48.6	7.1	59.3
Pend Oreille	232	1 452	274	D	219	38	60	41	27 970	225	30.7	14.7	42.7
Pierce	15 257	190 567	33 411	21 493	29 681	7 833	6 269	5 160	27 078	989	75.4	0.9	42.8
San Juan	804	3 526	121	D	596	114	172	88	24 917	174	56.3	2.9	40.2
Skagit	3 202	32 202	4 971	4 654	6 495	733	957	820	25 449	714	53.8	5.5	52.7
Skamania	178	1 151	126	259	176	D	D	25	21 712	63	52.4	0.0	38.1
Snohomish	14 760	202 949	20 201	61 656	28 887	7 363	6 541	6 422	31 645	1 139	75.9	1.8	45.4
Spokane	11 703	161 001	25 847	21 670	23 451	10 009	7 126	4 285	26 614	1 643	44.1	17.3	43.4
Stevens	793	6 906	1 166	1 621	1 137	170	120	160	23 200	989	27.8	16.8	44.5
Thurston	4 960	49 668	9 070	3 117	9 262	2 055	2 842	1 220	24 565	832	72.7	2.4	39.1
Wahkiakum	107	554	101	D	72	10	D	13	23 451	108	33.3	5.6	43.5
Walla Walla	1 246	16 878	3 640	2 251	2 484	531	344	390	23 124	716	39.0	36.3	60.5
Whatcom	5 317	55 623	6 225	9 279	9 479	2 195	2 582	1 411	25 365	1 228	57.1	2.4	54.3
Whitman	887	7 027	1 229	388	1 537	298	228	136	19 312	1 003	12.4	68.3	80.2
Yakima	4 830	58 832	10 159	9 327	9 906	1 677	1 378	1 442	24 518	3 365	63.0	6.6	55.3
WEST VIRGINIA	41 703	547 234	99 695	74 424	89 474	21 212	18 472	13 279	24 265	17 772	21.1	7.5	40.2
Barbour	269	2 739	568	103	497	78	53	45	16 490	437	14.4	7.8	46.0
Berkeley	1 432	19 735	3 641	3 177	3 925	602	773	486	24 633	509	36.5	3.9	36.7
Boone	404	5 721	583	50	980	169	113	208	36 300	23	39.1	0.0	30.4

STATE County	Acreage (1,000) 117	Percent change, 1992-1997 118	Average size of farm 119	Total irrigated (1,000) 120	Total cropland (1,000) 121	Average per farm ($1,000) 122	Average per acre (dollars) 123	Value of machinery and equipment Average per farm ($1,000) 124	Total (mil dol) 125	Average per farm (dollars) 126	Crops 127	Live-stock and poultry products 128	$10,000 or more 129	$100,000 or more 130	Percent of land owned by Fed. Gov. 1997 131	Water consumption 1995 (mil gal/day) 132
VIRGINIA—Cont'd																
Manassas City	NA	NA	NA	NA	NA	NA	NA	NA	NA	NA	NA	NA	NA	NA	(1)NA	0.1
Manassas Park City	NA	NA	NA	NA	NA	NA	NA	NA	NA	NA	NA	NA	NA	NA	(1)NA	0.4
Martinsville City	NA	NA	NA	NA	NA	NA	NA	NA	NA	NA	NA	NA	NA	NA	(2)NA	0.1
Newport News City	NA	NA	NA	NA	NA	NA	NA	NA	NA	NA	NA	NA	NA	NA	(3)NA	32.6
Norfolk City	NA	NA	NA	NA	NA	NA	NA	NA	NA	NA	NA	NA	NA	NA	6.0	13.6
Norton City	NA	NA	NA	NA	NA	NA	NA	NA	NA	NA	NA	NA	NA	NA	(4)NA	0.9
Petersburg City	NA	NA	NA	NA	NA	NA	NA	NA	NA	NA	NA	NA	NA	NA	(5)NA	0.1
Poquoson City	NA	NA	NA	NA	NA	NA	NA	NA	NA	NA	NA	NA	NA	NA	(3)NA	0.0
Portsmouth City	NA	NA	NA	NA	NA	NA	NA	NA	NA	NA	NA	NA	NA	NA	4.0	2.5
Radford City	NA	NA	NA	NA	NA	NA	NA	NA	NA	NA	NA	NA	NA	NA	(6)NA	3.1
Richmond City	NA	NA	NA	NA	NA	NA	NA	NA	NA	NA	NA	NA	NA	NA	0.0	70.4
Roanoke City	NA	NA	NA	NA	NA	NA	NA	NA	NA	NA	NA	NA	NA	NA	(7)NA	9.2
Salem City	NA	NA	NA	NA	NA	NA	NA	NA	NA	NA	NA	NA	NA	NA	(7)NA	3.4
Staunton City	NA	NA	NA	NA	NA	NA	NA	NA	NA	NA	NA	NA	NA	NA	(8)NA	0.0
Suffolk City	76	-8.2	350	1	57	688	1 869	125	39	177 392	84.1	15.9	67.9	31.7	13.0	88.9
Virginia Beach City	30	-30.3	204	0	25	455	2 529	51	14	92 778	76.8	23.2	46.9	14.3	6.6	8.2
Waynesboro City	NA	NA	NA	NA	NA	NA	NA	NA	NA	NA	NA	NA	NA	NA	(8)NA	11.5
Williamsburg City	NA	NA	NA	NA	NA	NA	NA	NA	NA	NA	NA	NA	NA	NA	(9)NA	1.6
Winchester City	NA	NA	NA	NA	NA	NA	NA	NA	NA	NA	NA	NA	NA	NA	(10)NA	0.2
WASHINGTON	15 180	-3.5	523	1 705	7 914	635	1 192	70	4 768	164 342	68.2	31.8	48.5	23.3	27.1	8 822.5
Adams	1 096	10.0	1 746	148	809	1 307	714	165	202	321 454	92.0	8.0	75.2	47.6	1.0	346.3
Asotin	304	10.7	2 175	0	87	1 003	439	81	10	69 593	65.5	34.5	58.6	25.0	16.1	5.7
Benton	612	-4.4	568	153	440	1 122	2 169	95	301	278 785	97.1	2.9	41.5	22.3	26.6	1 078.1
Chelan	124	10.5	111	31	41	415	3 148	52	146	131 539	99.5	0.5	70.8	35.3	77.2	127.6
Clallam	21	-12.4	72	4	12	400	3 753	26	6	20 584	45.4	54.6	18.8	5.5	45.2	101.6
Clark	73	-12.2	62	4	43	325	5 801	24	43	36 667	39.6	60.4	23.7	5.6	1.7	195.1
Columbia	310	1.7	1 567	4	178	775	514	134	24	123 619	92.0	8.0	61.6	33.3	28.6	17.1
Cowlitz	31	-13.6	89	3	15	365	4 150	34	16	45 612	45.6	54.4	16.9	6.0	3.8	208.4
Douglas	906	-1.3	1 063	21	533	778	668	87	118	137 894	95.5	4.5	69.6	33.2	3.1	63.0
Ferry	810	8.3	4 524	5	22	1 835	400	38	5	28 007	26.5	73.5	44.1	6.7	34.1	13.3
Franklin	564	-15.9	665	221	D	969	1 469	130	333	392 612	86.5	13.5	74.8	51.5	7.3	844.4
Garfield	325	0.0	1 787	1	192	974	543	157	25	135 633	88.9	11.1	75.3	46.7	20.8	2.0
Grant	1 095	0.8	645	446	786	1 001	1 596	149	804	473 368	68.9	31.1	73.4	48.4	14.1	1 795.1
Grays Harbor	42	-5.9	109	3	24	262	2 769	32	15	38 635	32.6	67.4	31.1	8.0	11.4	93.2
Island	16	-20.5	61	1	11	394	6 836	25	11	40 376	14.8	85.2	25.3	5.4	2.9	14.3
Jefferson	13	30.9	91	1	8	270	3 673	19	4	30 007	12.9	87.1	26.4	5.6	56.8	25.6
King	42	-0.8	38	3	24	379	8 839	36	94	85 968	41.1	58.9	28.7	11.0	23.1	291.6
Kitsap	19	91.3	53	0	6	267	5 591	26	12	34 074	32.6	67.4	19.5	2.5	2.5	40.4
Kittitas	178	-49.9	235	76	87	540	2 433	61	80	105 196	60.4	39.6	47.4	15.1	30.1	452.6
Klickitat	589	-14.7	1 111	20	186	627	579	47	33	62 701	71.4	28.6	43.6	12.6	2.9	98.9
Lewis	118	5.1	105	6	62	387	3 635	33	83	74 108	28.3	71.7	28.6	8.7	30.8	54.3
Lincoln	1 376	-6.1	1 946	48	876	1 079	537	139	108	152 486	91.9	8.1	77.2	49.6	0.9	71.6
Mason	20	81.7	95	0	7	302	4 100	17	13	63 340	D	D	26.1	3.3	24.5	18.7
Okanogan	1 179	-8.7	928	48	142	855	808	52	134	105 134	87.1	12.9	54.7	19.9	46.0	139.7
Pacific	40	21.9	159	3	15	368	2 369	35	17	67 052	48.5	51.5	50.2	19.4	1.2	9.8
Pend Oreille	63	14.8	281	2	27	348	1 494	35	3	12 794	40.0	60.0	29.3	1.3	56.5	5.1
Pierce	51	-13.8	51	5	24	336	7 273	30	70	70 612	39.7	60.3	25.5	7.7	28.8	198.3
San Juan	17	-19.6	97	1	12	487	5 419	15	3	15 246	14.1	85.9	21.8	1.1	2.1	3.0
Skagit	93	1.6	131	10	73	610	4 645	71	172	240 463	52.6	47.4	46.4	23.8	43.1	45.9
Skamania	4	5.5	67	0	2	334	4 988	28	2	24 316	86.7	13.3	20.6	4.8	76.7	13.3
Snohomish	61	-18.1	53	4	40	387	6 627	33	113	99 105	30.8	69.2	29.1	11.2	45.4	173.2
Spokane	590	-5.8	359	11	398	469	1 351	52	79	47 903	74.2	25.8	35.2	13.1	1.8	188.7
Stevens	525	-3.8	531	10	123	510	910	37	23	23 069	39.5	60.5	35.0	4.3	18.3	29.4
Thurston	56	-6.2	68	6	27	381	6 278	44	121	145 086	29.9	70.1	23.6	7.1	3.9	49.6
Wahkiakum	13	2.9	124	0	9	348	2 348	31	3	25 135	3.3	96.7	30.6	6.5	1.3	3.3
Walla Walla	715	0.5	998	97	598	891	856	108	257	358 841	D	D	58.7	37.3	0.7	353.6
Whatcom	104	-12.2	84	26	81	449	5 321	56	242	196 778	16.5	83.5	53.3	29.2	61.5	160.8
Whitman	1 301	-7.3	1 297	5	1 067	1 120	874	161	173	172 964	93.5	6.5	80.0	55.1	0.9	15.5
Yakima	1 683	2.6	500	278	D	605	1 220	73	873	259 582	66.5	33.5	61.4	28.9	17.6	1 475.0
WEST VIRGINIA	3 456	5.8	194	3	1 337	213	1 090	24	447	25 176	14.5	85.5	20.7	3.6	7.8	4 618.3
Barbour	87	13.9	198	0	39	168	903	23	4	8 985	11.7	88.3	21.7	0.9	0.4	2.2
Berkeley	73	-0.5	143	0	47	384	2 863	22	18	35 699	64.3	35.7	28.3	7.7	0.1	20.8
Boone	2	-22.2	102		0	116	1 141	19	0	1 944	71.1	28.9	4.3	0.0	0.0	4.0

1. Manassas and Manassas Park included with Prince William County. 2. Martinsville included with Henry County. 3. Hampton, Newport News, and Poquoson included with York County. 4. Norton included with Wise County. 5. Hopewell and Petersburg included with Prince George County. 6. Radford included with Montgomery County. 7. Roanoke City and Salem included with Roanoke County. 8. Staunton and Waynesboro included with Augusta County. 9. Williamsburg included with James City County. 10. Winchester included with Frederick County.

Table B. States and Counties — Residential Construction, Wholesale and Retail Trade, and Real Estate

STATE County	Value of Residential Construction Authorized by Building Permits, 1999		Wholesale Trade, 1997				Retail Trade[1], 1997				Real Estate and Rental and Leasing, 1997			
	New Construction ($1,000)	Number of Housing Units	Number of Establishments	Number of Employees	Sales (mil dol)	Annual Payroll (mil dol)	Number of Establishments	Number of Employees	Sales (mil dol)	Annual Payroll (mil dol)	Number of Establishments	Number of Employees	Receipts (mil dol)	Annual Payroll (mil dol)
	133	134	135	136	137	138	139	140	141	142	143	144	145	146
VIRGINIA—Cont'd														
Manassas City	4 474	64	59	1 008	626.3	41.0	230	3 355	647.5	64.9	51	302	41.1	5.5
Manassas Park City	17 702	247	13	180	36.7	6.4	16	142	28.7	2.9	2	D	D	D
Martinsville City	777	12	23	202	143.7	6.9	142	1 927	248.8	25.3	36	151	18.1	2.5
Newport News City	33 948	628	132	1 634	604.2	50.3	681	9 284	1 488.6	143.6	226	1 720	169.9	35.8
Norfolk City	25 300	233	324	5 845	2 914.6	183.9	918	12 628	1 900.4	207.3	273	2 128	203.8	44.2
Norton City	257	4	15	292	174.9	9.9	66	921	127.8	11.9	9	12	2.3	0.2
Petersburg City	1 550	35	35	538	139.2	16.8	189	1 764	290.0	29.5	28	131	11.1	2.2
Poquoson City	8 495	51	11	D	D	D	28	247	29.8	3.0	6	30	2.8	0.6
Portsmouth City	15 644	247	63	712	167.3	23.6	295	3 291	468.4	51.2	84	457	37.8	7.4
Radford City	2 993	24	8	296	51.7	3.3	58	561	79.2	8.6	21	108	11.3	1.4
Richmond City	19 872	248	464	7 572	5 979.5	283.5	1 013	11 579	1 738.1	193.5	265	2 166	213.5	54.8
Roanoke City	18 215	298	299	3 768	1 292.7	121.0	792	12 425	1 843.7	191.3	158	1 861	114.5	31.8
Salem City	8 309	83	86	1 809	635.8	58.6	174	3 089	452.5	51.8	26	179	13.9	4.0
Staunton City	3 322	45	33	327	132.0	7.4	168	2 213	330.5	32.0	43	214	15.9	3.3
Suffolk City	74 482	942	61	1 305	822.5	43.7	212	2 697	380.0	38.0	43	210	24.1	3.4
Virginia Beach City	214 898	2 205	479	5 642	1 922.8	159.4	1 621	21 987	3 342.7	337.2	472	3 101	333.0	66.8
Waynesboro City	9 760	113	21	D	D	D	115	1 512	216.6	22.2	29	131	9.4	1.9
Williamsburg City	12 984	73	16	D	D	D	163	2 262	330.2	33.7	32	201	40.9	8.3
Winchester City	10 517	91	39	569	301.1	16.4	283	3 667	571.3	58.7	55	208	24.5	5.3
WASHINGTON	4 588 556	42 809	10 039	118 810	75 397.8	4 376.0	22 841	283 653	52 472.9	5 385.9	7 544	41 899	5 352.8	935.3
Adams	1 842	15	36	408	158.5	11.2	71	526	100.2	9.7	11	25	1.8	0.2
Asotin	6 760	58	15	D	D	D	66	714	160.1	13.7	20	80	7.2	1.4
Benton	116 068	770	106	1 050	305.3	22.7	574	7 091	1 208.8	115.6	153	907	102.3	18.9
Chelan	37 259	308	115	1 760	782.5	53.1	415	4 030	697.7	73.3	121	526	38.9	9.2
Clallam	33 962	376	51	358	299.8	11.0	292	2 990	453.6	50.3	70	251	21.9	3.2
Clark	390 895	3 734	458	3 751	2 138.8	137.3	868	12 284	2 214.7	230.9	344	1 910	209.8	39.8
Columbia	2 019	36	14	D	D	D	29	147	23.2	2.5	2	D	D	D
Cowlitz	63 059	589	81	D	D	D	414	4 744	811.5	82.1	98	396	49.8	7.2
Douglas	19 574	165	31	188	81.8	5.6	91	1 109	184.9	17.4	18	99	9.9	1.5
Ferry	1 998	28	2	D	D	D	32	212	33.9	2.9	1	D	D	D
Franklin	27 225	247	93	1 111	550.7	33.0	196	2 205	487.4	45.9	40	219	23.1	4.6
Garfield	328	5	5	D	D	D	12	75	10.9	1.2	1	D	D	D
Grant	38 053	349	109	1 089	365.5	28.5	326	3 291	576.4	58.0	63	178	18.4	2.5
Grays Harbor	25 865	217	68	566	139.0	15.9	324	3 005	473.4	52.0	69	233	16.0	2.9
Island	78 791	592	33	126	40.9	3.2	231	2 000	311.9	33.5	80	226	23.6	3.5
Jefferson	30 956	253	23	D	D	D	149	974	146.0	14.3	34	100	7.9	1.1
King	1 335 439	11 935	4 937	63 696	50 226.1	2 641.6	7 031	99 542	19 399.8	2 025.3	3 119	20 887	3 219.0	560.3
Kitsap	134 085	1 148	135	925	330.9	29.9	773	10 338	1 722.1	179.5	240	1 053	103.4	16.3
Kittitas	27 827	227	36	350	129.9	9.2	178	1 427	230.8	23.0	40	135	12.1	1.7
Klickitat	10 205	92	22	120	33.9	2.2	69	346	47.4	5.4	24	58	5.4	0.6
Lewis	24 480	304	90	D	D	D	388	3 699	597.7	63.5	64	261	19.9	3.9
Lincoln	4 107	42	37	272	131.4	7.3	54	305	57.2	4.9	3	9	0.4	0.1
Mason	28 810	380	35	271	105.1	8.8	148	1 530	233.5	21.9	54	249	15.8	3.4
Okanogan	19 599	196	44	1 472	368.7	20.5	204	1 657	263.2	25.9	39	120	5.1	0.9
Pacific	6 095	69	14	D	D	D	115	680	87.1	11.0	21	37	3.6	0.3
Pend Oreille	6 224	64	5	D	D	D	44	247	35.8	3.3	7	16	0.9	0.2
Pierce	564 536	5 366	781	9 324	4 618.9	327.0	2 289	28 956	5 468.2	550.1	707	4 407	395.8	81.2
San Juan	24 931	311	17	D	D	D	115	561	81.7	10.1	48	92	13.0	1.8
Skagit	75 398	652	122	1 018	344.4	30.2	614	6 096	1 070.7	107.0	114	406	48.3	7.3
Skamania	3 878	45	2	D	D	D	15	137	14.2	1.7	5	10	0.9	0.1
Snohomish	731 387	7 440	755	6 808	3 561.6	232.3	2 027	26 302	5 303.0	524.2	670	3 061	366.2	65.2
Spokane	232 779	2 238	788	11 268	4 878.5	360.9	1 730	22 246	4 122.6	433.9	503	2 674	289.1	47.4
Stevens	14 719	171	28	133	39.8	3.2	141	1 239	184.0	18.6	26	96	10.2	1.3
Thurston	209 908	1 963	201	1 805	580.3	57.5	730	9 008	1 616.8	166.3	218	884	89.7	13.5
Wahkiakum	2 041	23	NA	NA	NA	NA	14	62	7.3	0.9	1	D	D	D
Walla Walla	21 957	173	78	726	318.1	16.4	222	2 426	376.4	41.9	45	187	17.0	2.6
Whatcom	162 338	1 486	308	2 451	1 042.7	76.0	840	9 758	1 673.3	165.7	220	877	91.8	12.3
Whitman	9 670	83	73	D	D	D	156	1 520	243.9	24.0	39	196	13.9	1.9
Yakima	63 487	659	291	4 871	1 853.8	141.9	854	10 174	1 741.6	174.9	212	1 018	99.9	17.0
WEST VIRGINIA	381 091	4 233	1 956	23 805	10 290.4	681.1	8 082	90 087	14 057.9	1 309.3	1 449	5 812	665.0	100.8
Barbour	394	8	9	75	12.7	1.2	57	509	69.3	6.7	4	6	1.9	0.0
Berkeley	84 443	870	52	D	D	D	335	4 000	546.7	52.2	67	241	18.9	3.4
Boone	1 402	20	19	121	52.9	3.5	110	984	146.3	14.4	15	26	4.4	0.3

1. Establishments with payroll.

STATE County	Professional, Scientific, and Technical Services[1], 1997				Manufacturing, 1997				Accommodation and Foodservices, 1997			
	Number of Establishments	Number of Employees	Receipts (mil dol)	Annual Payroll (mil dol)	Number of Establishments	Number of Employees	Receipts (mil dol)	Annual Payroll (mil dol)	Number of Establishments	Number of Employees	Sales (mil dol)	Annual Payroll (mil dol)
	147	148	149	150	151	152	153	154	155	156	157	158
VIRGINIA—Cont'd												
Manassas City	153	1 058	126.9	44.8	34	2 822	791.6	188.5	74	D	D	D
Manassas Park City	7	74	4.9	2.0	NA	NA	NA	NA	5	136	3.2	1.2
Martinsville City	54	223	16.6	7.7	39	8 726	724.1	203.0	46	768	25.1	6.6
Newport News City	286	3 023	218.8	88.6	131	24 707	3 300.5	898.4	312	5 464	170.1	47.7
Norfolk City	439	6 582	468.7	207.0	199	10 996	5 737.3	402.2	539	9 980	299.4	85.1
Norton City	19	188	8.9	4.0	NA	NA	NA	NA	23	D	D	D
Petersburg City	45	1 122	79.8	42.1	43	2 553	409.6	72.4	83	1 194	34.2	10.1
Poquoson City	13	79	5.6	2.8	NA	NA	NA	NA	20	193	4.3	1.2
Portsmouth City	105	1 023	82.1	31.5	71	1 812	368.7	52.0	137	2 040	58.7	15.8
Radford City	31	151	13.9	4.9	21	2 838	393.4	84.6	34	567	14.3	3.6
Richmond City	732	8 113	853.7	356.0	325	21 879	11 748.3	941.2	551	9 087	304.2	91.4
Roanoke City	331	2 632	211.6	88.7	152	8 489	2 156.3	242.9	325	6 380	203.4	58.7
Salem City	65	325	28.8	8.7	73	6 478	1 035.6	202.3	86	1 751	45.2	13.2
Staunton City	45	199	12.5	6.1	NA	NA	NA	NA	72	1 029	34.4	9.4
Suffolk City	59	273	21.4	9.2	52	2 257	1 103.5	63.8	62	1 027	32.8	8.9
Virginia Beach City	895	8 910	726.1	302.6	236	5 806	967.2	139.2	888	18 145	576.3	163.3
Waynesboro City	26	100	5.2	2.4	31	4 558	802.5	160.2	51	838	26.1	7.7
Williamsburg City	34	281	28.5	10.0	14	D	D	D	140	4 581	204.8	55.5
Winchester City	97	479	34.0	15.6	43	6 047	1 431.3	196.1	99	1 713	58.0	18.4
WASHINGTON	13 411	101 848	10 564.8	4 247.3	7 801	328 511	78 852.5	13 004.1	13 105	194 955	6 995.1	1 962.9
Adams	16	54	5.7	1.0	13	1 088	274.7	25.9	37	387	12.2	3.0
Asotin	30	106	7.4	2.7	NA	NA	NA	NA	40	516	16.1	4.9
Benton	274	7 403	926.0	364.4	121	3 672	885.5	139.5	256	4 223	136.1	36.8
Chelan	118	593	45.2	18.6	88	2 535	552.2	76.2	240	2 946	98.8	27.1
Clallam	105	434	33.5	12.0	75	1 481	359.2	49.0	214	2 104	75.9	19.6
Clark	564	2 929	234.2	98.3	421	19 537	3 854.3	715.2	506	8 570	271.7	76.8
Columbia	1	D	D	D	NA	NA	NA	NA	12	D	D	D
Cowlitz	116	677	43.7	18.9	125	8 309	2 496.5	364.4	214	3 208	97.1	28.7
Douglas	23	83	5.1	2.3	NA	NA	NA	NA	46	733	21.6	6.3
Ferry	7	27	1.9	0.8	NA	NA	NA	NA	21	126	5.1	1.1
Franklin	44	134	12.9	4.6	47	3 092	1 160.5	69.1	87	1 105	34.6	9.3
Garfield	1	D	D	D	NA	NA	NA	NA	3	D	D	D
Grant	93	407	25.6	9.5	56	4 090	806.9	111.3	170	1 930	58.8	15.3
Grays Harbor	84	320	22.3	11.1	97	3 792	822.9	125.7	238	2 150	74.2	20.3
Island	98	261	20.0	6.5	49	625	62.5	17.0	122	1 410	44.3	11.9
Jefferson	62	118	7.2	2.3	56	D	D	D	98	1 105	35.1	10.3
King	6 767	61 617	6 900.4	2 784.9	2 993	134 028	26 480.3	5 682.6	4 456	76 070	3 161.2	896.4
Kitsap	443	2 226	169.0	65.5	143	1 441	142.7	36.8	399	5 998	180.2	50.6
Kittitas	37	116	9.5	3.1	32	662	102.4	15.6	125	1 431	45.6	13.0
Klickitat	32	77	5.3	1.9	25	D	D	D	48	297	9.5	2.9
Lewis	81	301	19.9	7.0	115	3 630	648.0	97.1	196	1 919	62.9	17.5
Lincoln	10	78	4.6	2.4	NA	NA	NA	NA	33	154	4.2	1.1
Mason	58	284	17.1	5.9	52	1 664	343.9	51.7	98	953	29.9	7.8
Okanogan	46	150	9.7	3.4	28	794	123.6	20.9	122	1 192	42.4	12.4
Pacific	33	56	4.2	1.6	36	848	112.8	19.0	110	818	26.9	7.6
Pend Oreille	11	56	3.5	1.4	NA	NA	NA	NA	27	167	4.8	1.4
Pierce	974	4 965	444.3	174.0	680	22 283	4 275.9	705.2	1 218	18 808	603.6	169.3
San Juan	53	135	11.8	5.2	NA	NA	NA	NA	99	778	40.1	13.1
Skagit	209	732	55.7	20.6	185	5 026	2 917.7	148.9	277	3 614	118.1	31.5
Skamania	9	13	1.1	0.3	NA	NA	NA	NA	17	221	4.4	1.2
Snohomish	958	4 690	472.5	177.7	837	58 170	19 903.2	2 918.1	1 108	16 699	558.4	153.9
Spokane	886	5 738	444.5	186.9	572	20 892	3 994.6	681.4	904	14 456	453.2	128.5
Stevens	31	93	5.4	2.1	40	1 546	363.6	53.6	82	689	23.5	5.4
Thurston	401	2 571	198.1	86.2	156	3 218	761.0	100.7	406	6 076	193.0	56.6
Wahkiakum	4	D	D	D	NA	NA	NA	NA	13	50	1.5	0.4
Walla Walla	76	314	20.5	8.0	66	2 400	544.7	89.4	113	1 482	42.8	12.0
Whatcom	390	2 615	246.5	109.0	314	9 184	3 947.0	281.4	429	5 926	195.5	52.8
Whitman	43	156	10.3	3.5	NA	NA	NA	NA	110	1 196	30.9	7.6
Yakima	223	1 298	119.4	43.2	239	10 163	2 090.5	264.6	411	5 371	178.6	47.8
WEST VIRGINIA	2 517	15 714	1 166.9	395.2	1 505	72 813	18 293.3	2 460.7	3 290	51 529	1 633.2	462.3
Barbour	15	53	1.8	0.7	NA	NA	NA	NA	22	D	D	D
Berkeley	81	610	55.2	18.1	38	3 093	470.4	85.1	129	1 947	67.6	17.0
Boone	17	104	7.5	2.9	NA	NA	NA	NA	22	259	8.3	2.4

1. Firms subject to federal tax.

Table B. States and Counties — **Health and Other Services and Federal Funds**

STATE County	Health Care and Social Assistance[1], 1997				Other Services[1], 1997				Federal funds and grants, fiscal 1999[2] Expenditures (mil dol)			
									Total	Direct payments for individuals[3]		
	Number of Establishments	Number of Employees	Receipts (mil dol)	Annual Payroll (mil dol)	Number of Establishments	Number of Employees	Receipts (mil dol)	Annual Payroll (mil dol)		Social Security and government retirement	Medicare	Food stamps and Supplemental Security Income
	159	160	161	162	163	164	165	166	167	168	169	170
VIRGINIA—Cont'd												
Manassas City	106	1 161	67.1	34.9	108	832	60.2	22.2	606.6	83.5	20.7	3.2
Manassas Park City	NA	NA	NA	NA	6	72	4.6	1.5	10.0	0.8	0.0	0.3
Martinsville City	78	712	46.8	21.4	40	196	8.8	2.5	124.4	71.8	21.9	4.2
Newport News City	324	3 878	217.6	122.3	306	2 234	116.3	41.1	1 863.8	393.0	98.7	33.9
Norfolk City	400	6 583	451.7	219.1	388	2 569	147.8	49.7	5 110.0	517.4	160.1	60.7
Norton City	35	248	23.3	13.0	19	73	3.6	1.3	38.4	17.9	6.5	1.2
Petersburg City	89	1 438	64.1	32.6	76	620	32.6	12.0	278.2	136.3	48.1	11.7
Poquoson City	10	150	6.0	3.0	16	74	3.1	1.2	23.7	18.0	3.6	0.4
Portsmouth City	170	2 393	134.8	71.8	163	1 364	74.6	27.2	1 360.2	284.4	91.5	32.3
Radford City	47	360	22.1	12.7	19	102	3.5	1.2	88.9	27.4	10.6	1.6
Richmond City	540	14 788	1 111.6	414.8	504	3 887	256.6	82.0	2 852.9	838.3	250.1	72.1
Roanoke City	274	3 623	274.3	127.4	337	2 403	123.8	43.2	742.6	321.0	109.4	23.9
Salem City	64	2 817	224.2	72.7	81	349	19.0	6.2	206.5	82.7	23.5	1.6
Staunton City	63	646	38.4	17.3	53	404	19.7	6.9	128.4	75.0	27.6	3.8
Suffolk City	89	1 334	69.9	34.9	85	453	22.2	6.7	323.4	135.8	41.9	13.9
Virginia Beach City	809	8 315	473.4	223.9	716	4 870	254.7	89.2	2 424.0	973.7	149.2	35.8
Waynesboro City	47	446	26.6	10.6	51	311	19.3	5.2	93.9	61.8	18.9	3.1
Williamsburg City	61	697	45.1	23.5	35	184	7.1	2.6	195.0	116.5	27.6	0.8
Winchester City	126	1 018	98.2	53.5	77	400	21.2	7.3	154.5	74.7	24.0	2.8
WASHINGTON	12 310	122 813	7 797.7	3 390.2	8 771	49 756	3 492.0	1 033.0	31 993.1	10 612.0	3 160.9	731.2
Adams	15	205	8.3	4.2	22	45	4.2	0.8	101.6	18.9	6.8	2.5
Asotin	41	459	18.6	6.7	21	68	3.7	1.1	90.6	46.8	15.4	4.4
Benton	335	2 841	183.0	74.1	178	1 008	55.3	17.2	1 884.6	222.3	62.1	11.4
Chelan	134	1 984	162.8	65.7	118	396	29.1	7.7	269.3	128.9	35.9	7.2
Clallam	173	1 335	72.2	28.6	99	394	27.2	6.8	361.8	208.0	57.2	7.9
Clark	475	6 155	369.2	170.5	414	2 117	141.8	43.3	1 111.8	514.1	144.4	39.6
Columbia	6	21	0.8	0.4	13	33	2.3	0.6	35.1	10.1	3.4	0.7
Cowlitz	168	1 933	110.4	48.6	138	706	43.7	13.4	384.1	183.5	61.7	16.6
Douglas	33	367	23.6	7.8	36	122	9.5	2.5	111.6	48.5	22.4	2.4
Ferry	9	30	0.9	0.2	3	D	D	D	33.9	13.4	3.5	1.2
Franklin	81	669	40.5	15.7	67	343	28.5	7.7	182.6	60.4	21.7	7.4
Garfield	4	9	0.6	0.2	5	8	0.7	0.1	25.1	7.3	2.2	0.2
Grant	84	781	53.0	19.4	88	371	28.8	7.2	294.9	123.9	34.8	9.2
Grays Harbor	147	1 201	69.5	33.2	98	347	22.1	6.0	336.1	160.1	60.7	15.8
Island	115	796	38.3	14.6	62	266	14.8	4.7	576.3	176.9	31.7	4.1
Jefferson	61	715	28.3	13.0	58	220	12.2	3.2	142.3	84.2	21.9	2.7
King	4 360	41 887	2 913.7	1 247.1	3 244	20 986	1 642.9	474.2	8 828.7	2 676.2	959.7	202.3
Kitsap	473	4 466	245.3	104.1	264	1 300	77.7	23.9	2 239.0	573.7	104.8	23.4
Kittitas	51	468	25.4	9.5	55	261	12.6	3.2	123.4	56.5	17.4	2.0
Klickitat	22	165	8.1	3.5	18	64	5.7	1.0	79.9	39.9	11.0	3.3
Lewis	138	1 451	84.3	35.4	84	443	40.2	10.2	315.0	158.8	57.0	11.6
Lincoln	14	60	4.0	1.9	17	24	2.0	0.4	93.8	26.9	8.7	1.1
Mason	60	458	27.2	9.5	51	194	10.5	3.1	231.0	142.1	37.5	5.7
Okanogan	69	594	33.3	14.1	51	138	10.7	2.2	192.9	81.4	23.0	7.2
Pacific	33	209	10.1	3.9	26	72	4.3	1.2	152.2	66.1	21.5	3.8
Pend Oreille	11	70	3.8	1.6	9	28	1.4	0.4	57.1	27.9	6.6	3.2
Pierce	1 439	14 037	865.7	384.0	908	5 430	354.7	114.5	3 715.1	1 446.4	331.1	108.0
San Juan	20	62	3.8	0.9	20	41	3.2	0.8	49.9	34.0	8.4	0.6
Skagit	219	2 291	142.9	67.5	151	880	60.6	18.6	401.9	216.7	72.7	13.1
Skamania	6	23	1.2	0.3	5	9	0.6	0.2	52.7	14.0	3.0	1.0
Snohomish	1 067	10 785	623.5	293.5	827	4 502	292.6	93.7	1 911.8	815.8	255.2	51.1
Spokane	991	11 137	681.4	306.8	699	4 355	258.4	78.5	1 980.0	840.1	278.0	63.0
Stevens	41	475	20.5	9.7	44	189	12.2	3.8	159.0	77.1	21.2	5.3
Thurston	459	4 551	322.8	137.0	264	1 356	79.0	24.2	1 570.7	496.3	106.3	23.4
Wahkiakum	4	72	2.7	1.2	2	D	D	D	16.2	9.7	3.6	0.2
Walla Walla	96	1 183	67.7	29.4	54	256	17.3	4.8	275.1	112.9	35.1	7.1
Whatcom	406	3 627	201.2	82.1	225	1 161	81.3	22.1	670.9	272.4	74.8	17.4
Whitman	59	647	30.7	14.4	56	207	11.4	3.0	235.6	52.5	18.0	2.2
Yakima	391	4 594	298.6	129.8	277	1 408	87.6	26.8	884.7	329.1	120.4	41.7
WEST VIRGINIA	3 266	40 085	2 575.0	1 056.9	2 512	14 805	867.4	255.9	11 028.1	4 386.2	1 588.3	535.7
Barbour	15	124	5.4	1.8	12	29	1.5	0.3	80.4	34.5	14.2	5.4
Berkeley	114	863	55.4	19.8	94	410	22.6	6.8	484.8	152.7	40.4	11.3
Boone	22	209	9.9	4.0	23	101	6.3	1.8	129.0	64.4	20.8	10.5

1. Firms subject to federal tax.   2. October 1, 1998 to September 30, 1999.   3. State totals may include programs not allocated by county.

STATE County	Salaries and wages	Defense	Other	Medicaid and other health-related	Nutrition and family welfare	Education	Other	Total (mil dol)	Intergovernmental (mil dol)	Total (mil dol)	Per capita[3] (dollars) Total	Per capita[3] (dollars) Property
	171	172	173	174	175	176	177	178	179	180	181	182
VIRGINIA—Cont'd												
Manassas City	21.3	386.3	49.7	3.0	2.2	1.3	31.3	76.6	21.7	40.7	1 186	913
Manassas Park City	0.8	1.5	0.2	4.7	0.5	0.3	0.8	22.4	7.6	9.0	1 063	848
Martinsville City	3.6	3.6	3.3	7.5	1.5	1.3	3.7	36.6	15.8	12.7	806	458
Newport News City	453.0	671.6	100.5	36.0	22.4	8.7	20.9	396.2	168.1	171.0	972	663
Norfolk City	2 587.9	1 350.9	165.9	100.0	51.7	27.0	50.8	812.6	302.1	245.3	1 070	627
Norton City	5.2	0.7	0.2	2.4	3.4	0.3	0.2	9.0	4.5	3.6	846	352
Petersburg City	9.4	7.6	9.9	24.1	8.3	4.7	8.9	174.8	43.5	30.5	894	581
Poquoson City	0.8	0.0	0.0	0.3	0.1	0.4	0.0	20.5	7.9	10.6	923	773
Portsmouth City	617.4	227.4	8.6	47.1	18.2	6.7	9.9	245.9	121.8	85.2	856	572
Radford City	6.5	32.6	0.7	3.5	0.7	1.1	1.3	34.3	7.9	19.8	1 291	994
Richmond City	439.0	78.4	97.0	248.3	280.9	151.1	325.6	746.1	299.9	276.1	1 435	951
Roanoke City	89.7	79.1	19.7	45.1	18.2	6.4	13.6	272.3	112.4	114.3	1 214	691
Salem City	78.8	0.0	9.3	5.4	0.8	0.9	0.1	57.7	14.8	33.0	1 332	805
Staunton City	6.9	0.1	1.0	8.5	3.2	0.9	0.5	43.1	17.5	19.4	833	495
Suffolk City	14.0	60.0	5.7	27.5	8.0	2.9	8.1	120.7	59.0	48.9	802	579
Virginia Beach City	867.7	261.3	37.6	23.1	15.9	11.0	18.1	952.8	316.9	437.8	1 012	690
Waynesboro City	2.6	0.2	0.7	3.5	1.6	0.6	0.2	42.7	15.2	20.1	1 083	726
Williamsburg City	20.3	13.8	3.3	1.4	1.3	1.8	6.7	41.9	20.2	18.4	1 558	519
Winchester City	19.8	0.4	22.3	7.0	1.7	0.8	0.0	68.6	18.3	29.4	1 312	623
WASHINGTON	4 868.7	2 296.5	2 317.9	2 709.5	1 052.0	455.4	1 503.4	X	X	X	X	X
Adams	2.0	0.0	10.9	18.2	3.3	0.7	6.8	59.9	35.2	11.6	747	574
Asotin	2.8	1.0	1.1	8.6	4.0	1.5	0.5	53.7	33.7	9.9	469	352
Benton	52.9	16.6	1 442.0	28.3	13.8	4.5	17.2	499.3	238.9	94.8	698	442
Chelan	28.3	1.4	8.7	27.1	9.7	5.8	10.4	178.7	79.6	52.1	872	595
Clallam	26.1	0.7	12.6	22.3	11.2	3.0	9.4	209.5	67.4	40.4	632	457
Clark	131.7	7.5	89.7	86.7	38.7	12.2	24.1	746.4	373.6	225.4	712	524
Columbia	2.4	2.4	0.4	3.2	0.8	0.2	-0.3	20.6	10.9	2.6	610	471
Cowlitz	12.9	0.5	26.0	37.7	17.4	8.3	16.4	237.8	104.7	69.8	769	509
Douglas	6.0	2.9	0.3	7.5	3.2	0.7	1.7	81.0	49.3	18.0	536	434
Ferry	5.1	0.0	0.7	1.9	1.6	0.6	5.3	19.3	14.1	2.9	396	297
Franklin	22.2	4.5	4.9	15.8	11.3	5.2	11.1	142.0	75.3	32.8	697	445
Garfield	3.7	1.4	0.7	0.5	0.3	0.0	-0.7	11.9	7.3	1.7	733	595
Grant	28.8	2.1	15.9	24.0	11.8	5.1	9.7	250.4	115.9	44.2	634	456
Grays Harbor	11.4	10.5	4.3	38.4	14.9	4.7	10.7	190.1	98.2	50.1	737	405
Island	291.3	43.4	2.1	7.8	3.5	4.1	8.6	111.5	61.1	31.9	452	308
Jefferson	8.0	1.0	1.6	7.6	3.7	1.2	9.4	78.8	30.3	21.1	812	591
King	1 128.3	1 387.7	401.7	1 153.9	176.1	61.0	523.7	5 864.6	1 760.6	2 283.7	1 399	804
Kitsap	1 162.9	215.2	21.1	56.2	23.8	21.2	21.2	493.4	253.0	153.2	653	490
Kittitas	6.8	0.2	1.5	8.8	4.1	2.2	16.2	85.7	34.9	20.5	653	391
Klickitat	4.3	2.2	0.9	7.2	3.4	1.1	1.2	64.0	33.3	9.6	506	387
Lewis	12.9	1.7	5.1	34.6	12.0	5.2	11.9	175.7	89.7	48.0	710	443
Lincoln	3.1	0.0	0.9	1.7	1.0	0.3	5.5	54.4	24.4	9.2	943	785
Mason	5.1	0.6	2.9	13.9	7.2	2.7	11.0	130.2	55.6	32.0	646	464
Okanogan	17.9	10.5	9.0	17.2	11.0	3.2	9.4	123.3	58.3	21.7	561	393
Pacific	5.2	1.2	38.7	9.9	3.8	1.1	0.1	65.9	31.8	15.6	740	446
Pend Oreille	3.7	0.0	1.0	5.7	2.0	0.6	5.6	49.3	19.8	10.5	928	731
Pierce	1 033.9	202.3	53.4	300.4	103.4	29.7	65.3	1 692.6	818.3	516.1	776	551
San Juan	3.0	0.5	1.0	0.8	0.6	0.1	0.7	36.8	14.0	16.2	1 324	904
Skagit	17.4	1.5	8.0	30.3	15.0	7.4	12.6	361.1	116.9	77.8	796	560
Skamania	6.8	17.8	5.7	1.9	1.3	0.1	0.3	26.8	16.9	3.7	387	290
Snohomish	289.9	127.0	39.3	147.0	50.0	16.2	88.4	1 440.6	597.1	460.5	816	535
Spokane	311.0	54.3	39.9	196.1	62.7	24.1	53.1	944.3	463.4	295.3	730	456
Stevens	14.6	0.0	9.0	14.2	7.2	1.9	6.3	75.0	50.2	15.4	392	274
Thurston	55.3	9.3	13.4	136.9	276.5	151.5	269.4	505.5	248.5	163.6	817	574
Wahkiakum	0.7	0.0	0.3	1.1	0.3	0.1	0.1	12.6	5.8	2.7	702	492
Walla Walla	34.1	7.6	1.9	19.7	8.4	3.9	9.7	127.7	70.7	33.4	625	450
Whatcom	42.2	128.2	11.6	52.0	20.1	7.5	29.7	363.0	155.4	129.3	838	559
Whitman	11.9	5.0	3.8	23.2	3.1	3.9	39.1	107.3	49.1	23.9	608	421
Yakima	62.1	27.7	25.6	141.3	70.0	19.1	27.1	528.1	328.0	116.2	532	342
WEST VIRGINIA	911.4	108.8	516.5	1 194.9	352.4	207.8	734.8	X	X	X	X	X
Barbour	2.2	0.1	0.8	15.9	2.4	1.2	2.6	26.8	16.6	3.3	205	170
Berkeley	141.6	2.1	79.6	19.3	5.5	2.5	25.1	106.5	55.8	33.1	479	413
Boone	4.7	0.5	1.0	15.8	4.1	2.2	4.7	59.4	27.2	18.0	680	656

1. October 1, 1998 to September 30, 1999. 2. State totals may include programs not allocated by county. 3. Based on the resident population estimated as of July 1 of the year shown.

Table B. States and Counties — Local Government Finances, Government Employment, and Elections

STATE County	Local government finances, 1997 (cont'd) Direct general expenditure Total (mil dol)	Per capita[1] (dollars)	Percent of total for — Education	Health and hospitals	Police protection	Public welfare	High-ways	Debt outstanding Total (mil dol)	Per capita[1] (dollars)	Government employment, 1998 Federal civilian	Federal military	State and local	Presidential election, 2000 Percent of vote cast — Democratic	Republican	All other
	183	184	185	186	187	188	189	190	191	192	193	194	195	196	197
VIRGINIA—Cont'd															
Manassas City	79.5	2 317	56.4	1.7	7.1	3.6	4.0	80.3	2 341	(3)	(3)	(3)	42.4	54.4	3.2
Manassas Park City	22.7	2 679	44.9	1.0	5.9	6.1	2.4	26.9	3 181	(3)	(3)	(3)	40.6	56.6	2.8
Martinsville City	40.6	2 569	41.8	0.5	8.4	4.2	5.9	13.9	880	(4)	(4)	(4)	53.5	45.0	1.5
Newport News City	428.8	2 439	42.5	0.5	7.1	5.5	5.3	545.9	3 104	5 013	8 949	10 491	51.5	46.7	1.8
Norfolk City	850.5	3 708	37.4	5.3	5.2	4.7	2.6	1 485.6	6 476	15 744	57 727	20 245	61.7	35.4	2.9
Norton City	9.0	2 118	49.8	0.0	9.9	7.3	8.4	2.0	474	(5)	(5)	(5)	56.7	41.8	1.6
Petersburg City	152.8	4 476	23.5	49.7	3.8	5.5	2.2	76.9	2 252	(6)	(6)	(6)	79.1	19.1	1.8
Poquoson City	19.0	1 660	61.9	2.1	12.7	0.0	4.4	19.9	1 736	(7)	(7)	(7)	24.7	72.9	2.4
Portsmouth City	298.4	2 998	39.6	3.3	4.1	4.0	2.7	270.8	2 721	10 181	5 149	6 147	62.9	35.6	1.5
Radford City	25.8	1 684	41.8	2.5	10.7	5.4	6.1	0.0	0	(8)	(8)	(8)	46.4	49.2	4.4
Richmond City	808.6	4 203	28.3	4.6	5.5	8.4	3.5	1 010.5	5 252	6 959	1 292	41 045	64.8	30.7	4.5
Roanoke City	259.9	2 761	37.7	0.6	5.0	8.3	3.5	356.2	3 783	1 698	402	6 257	53.6	43.8	2.7
Salem City	77.6	3 129	41.6	0.1	5.5	0.7	4.3	33.3	1 343	(9)	(9)	(9)	40.4	57.5	2.2
Staunton City	39.9	1 709	45.8	0.7	6.4	7.5	7.5	16.1	688	(10)	(10)	(10)	39.0	57.3	3.7
Suffolk City	136.1	2 229	51.3	0.1	4.1	4.8	3.3	162.4	2 660	196	272	3 931	50.6	48.0	1.4
Virginia Beach City	908.1	2 099	46.6	2.4	5.1	1.9	2.4	1 025.9	2 372	4 874	21 552	19 060	41.6	55.9	2.6
Waynesboro City	40.0	2 158	42.5	0.5	6.3	9.6	4.9	22.3	1 202	(10)	(10)	(10)	38.5	57.5	4.0
Williamsburg City	106.2	9 003	65.6	0.3	2.5	0.8	1.3	40.1	3 401	(11)	(11)	(11)	46.3	47.7	6.0
Winchester City	73.8	3 289	41.1	0.3	4.2	2.5	2.3	149.0	6 642	(12)	(12)	(12)	42.1	54.7	3.2
WASHINGTON	X	X	X	X	X	X	X	X	X	66 840	73 524	388 621	50.2	44.6	5.3
Adams	59.9	3 854	52.4	5.4	4.5	0.0	7.4	18.9	1 218	47	57	1 376	28.3	69.2	2.6
Asotin	51.0	2 409	42.0	6.6	4.5	0.1	13.3	21.0	992	66	79	892	34.3	61.5	4.3
Benton	391.1	2 881	44.2	14.6	3.6	0.0	8.3	7 433.4	54 749	815	518	8 906	32.6	64.2	3.2
Chelan	165.9	2 777	50.5	6.0	4.7	0.0	5.3	836.0	14 000	711	224	5 300	31.7	64.0	4.2
Clallam	181.9	2 849	37.0	26.7	4.1	0.0	4.7	92.9	1 455	468	489	4 895	42.7	50.4	6.8
Clark	753.2	2 380	57.1	2.5	3.8	0.2	3.9	981.9	3 102	2 471	1 224	15 754	45.6	49.6	4.8
Columbia	22.2	5 192	23.7	29.0	4.0	0.3	24.4	3.8	885	54	15	464	24.4	72.3	3.3
Cowlitz	261.8	2 882	45.4	2.9	5.1	0.0	8.3	113.5	1 250	271	341	5 406	49.3	45.6	5.0
Douglas	67.1	2 005	54.3	6.8	3.9	0.0	12.5	235.8	7 042	138	125	1 590	29.7	66.2	4.1
Ferry	19.3	2 653	52.7	4.3	3.6	0.0	12.3	11.6	1 604	152	27	566	30.7	62.4	6.9
Franklin	136.2	2 896	48.0	2.1	5.1	0.0	4.3	121.4	2 582	461	173	3 470	34.2	63.1	2.7
Garfield	12.0	5 258	28.6	21.2	3.3	0.0	25.3	1.6	706	109	0	263	22.6	73.9	3.5
Grant	236.1	3 387	47.4	18.6	3.0	1.3	7.3	677.4	9 716	272	269	5 615	29.7	66.5	3.8
Grays Harbor	195.6	2 879	44.8	5.3	5.2	0.1	9.0	76.8	1 130	226	289	4 773	51.2	43.2	5.6
Island	112.8	1 597	53.8	2.8	4.8	0.0	8.1	85.7	1 213	1 444	7 890	2 981	44.8	49.7	5.5
Jefferson	77.6	2 989	30.4	23.9	2.7	0.0	10.6	54.9	2 114	166	107	1 707	52.3	38.5	9.2
King	5 896.8	3 611	29.1	9.5	5.2	0.1	5.5	6 853.8	4 197	20 754	7 441	125 004	60.0	34.4	5.6
Kitsap	491.9	2 097	54.8	4.4	3.4	0.0	3.6	405.8	1 730	14 620	13 716	11 204	49.0	45.3	5.7
Kittitas	86.4	2 752	35.8	20.2	4.2	0.0	12.1	36.0	1 146	164	131	3 993	39.2	54.9	6.0
Klickitat	63.5	3 329	47.9	12.2	2.9	0.0	9.4	63.9	3 351	115	72	1 486	37.5	55.9	6.6
Lewis	172.6	2 553	46.1	5.2	4.5	0.0	13.1	239.7	3 546	322	253	4 627	33.0	61.9	5.1
Lincoln	54.3	5 539	35.0	20.6	2.6	0.0	13.8	12.0	1 227	73	36	1 219	27.3	68.2	4.5
Mason	114.4	2 313	43.4	18.2	3.4	0.0	6.5	77.0	1 556	113	185	3 226	48.4	45.6	6.0
Okanogan	116.8	3 022	43.2	24.6	4.2	0.1	4.3	56.9	1 472	799	142	3 041	29.3	63.4	7.3
Pacific	64.3	3 047	41.7	21.5	4.0	0.0	8.5	19.2	907	61	160	1 569	51.4	42.5	6.1
Pend Oreille	44.8	3 976	32.4	32.5	2.6	0.0	7.9	38.6	3 429	109	43	835	36.3	56.6	7.2
Pierce	1 668.3	2 510	45.9	4.9	5.5	0.3	5.1	1 486.4	2 236	9 703	23 385	37 740	51.5	44.1	4.4
San Juan	35.1	2 861	35.4	3.3	4.7	0.2	8.6	34.8	2 835	64	46	844	52.6	35.7	11.6
Skagit	368.1	3 767	39.5	28.6	3.0	0.0	4.3	237.1	2 427	416	372	7 559	45.2	49.0	5.8
Skamania	23.1	2 398	41.8	3.7	5.0	0.1	15.6	2.7	276	215	36	581	41.3	50.6	8.1
Snohomish	1 424.3	2 523	44.3	9.8	4.0	0.7	6.7	2 008.0	3 557	2 322	7 631	28 391	51.6	43.7	4.7
Spokane	925.5	2 287	51.7	3.3	4.3	0.0	5.1	631.4	1 560	4 300	5 173	25 695	43.3	51.9	4.8
Stevens	70.5	1 798	59.1	3.3	4.5	0.0	10.3	38.7	985	397	147	2 028	30.9	62.8	6.3
Thurston	486.5	2 428	50.4	4.1	3.9	0.1	5.1	353.4	1 764	977	845	31 475	51.8	41.0	7.2
Wahkiakum	10.8	2 784	29.0	9.6	4.4	0.1	19.3	1.9	499	14	14	229	40.7	52.4	6.9
Walla Walla	133.4	2 493	46.6	4.5	4.6	0.0	10.9	79.1	1 479	883	201	3 877	33.6	62.3	4.1
Whatcom	323.7	2 098	48.4	2.7	4.8	0.0	7.8	301.5	1 955	841	605	9 867	46.1	46.5	7.4
Whitman	105.1	2 672	44.2	21.2	3.5	0.0	9.2	29.8	757	274	161	8 140	40.1	55.4	4.5
Yakima	560.2	2 566	57.3	1.2	5.2	0.0	5.8	307.9	1 410	1 433	893	12 033	38.0	58.7	3.4
WEST VIRGINIA	X	X	X	X	X	X	X	X	X	21 583	9 662	118 538	45.6	51.9	2.5
Barbour	25.8	1 590	62.3	4.9	1.8	0.0	1.0	38.5	2 373	44	82	752	41.4	56.4	2.3
Berkeley	108.2	1 567	72.8	1.5	3.1	0.0	0.8	110.2	1 595	2 974	383	3 002	38.2	59.2	2.6
Boone	58.4	2 209	60.3	19.8	1.6	0.0	0.6	5.2	198	95	131	1 403	61.9	36.7	1.4

1. Based on the resident population estimated as of July 1 of the year shown.   3. Manassas and Manassas Park included with Prince William County.   4. Martinsville included with Henry County.   5. Norton included with Wise County.   6. Petersburg and Colonial Heights included with Dinwiddie County.   7. Poquoson included with York County.   8. Radford included with Montgomery County.   9. Salem included with Roanoke County.   10. Staunton and Waynesboro included with Augusta County.   11. Williamsburg included with James City County.   12. Winchester included with Frederick County.

STATE/ County code	MSA/ PMSA/ NECMA code[1]	County Type[2]	STATE County	Land area,[3] (sq km) 1990	Population and population characteristics, 1999															
								Race (percent)					Age (percent)					
					Total persons	Rank	Per square kilometer	White	Black	Am. Indian, Eskimo, Aleut	Asian and Pacific Islander	Percent Hispanic[4]	Under 5 years	5 to 17 years	18 to 24 years	25 to 34 years	35 to 44 years	45 to 54 years
				1	2	3	4	5	6	7	8	9	10	11	12	13	14	15
			WEST VIRGINIA—Cont'd															
54 007	...	9	Braxton	1 330	13 211	2 198	9.9	99.3	0.4	0.1	0.2	0.3	6.3	17.4	8.0	12.0	15.0	14.6
54 009	8080	3	Brooke	230	25 890	1 499	112.6	98.8	0.8	0.1	0.3	0.4	4.6	15.4	10.4	10.8	14.8	14.5
54 011	3400	2	Cabell	729	93 562	538	128.3	95.2	4.1	0.1	0.6	0.5	5.1	14.5	12.8	12.1	13.8	14.5
54 013	...	9	Calhoun	727	7 982	2 599	11.0	99.3	0.0	0.2	0.5	0.3	6.1	18.9	7.8	12.4	15.1	14.6
54 015	...	8	Clay	887	10 609	2 368	12.0	99.5	0.1	0.2	0.2	0.5	6.8	20.5	9.0	12.5	14.9	13.6
54 017	...	9	Doddridge	830	7 447	2 643	9.0	99.3	0.0	0.4	0.2	0.2	5.9	19.2	8.1	13.2	14.7	14.9
54 019	...	6	Fayette	1 720	46 785	951	27.2	93.3	6.3	0.1	0.3	0.6	4.9	18.2	8.9	11.4	14.9	13.7
54 021	...	9	Gilmer	881	7 143	2 667	8.1	98.9	0.5	0.1	0.4	0.3	5.6	15.7	14.1	11.7	12.4	13.9
54 023	...	8	Grant	1 236	11 140	2 337	9.0	98.4	1.1	0.2	0.3	0.4	5.7	16.9	8.8	12.4	15.2	15.7
54 025	...	7	Greenbrier	2 645	35 310	1 214	13.3	95.9	3.7	0.1	0.2	0.5	5.2	16.1	8.1	12.2	14.9	15.2
54 027	...	8	Hampshire	1 662	19 418	1 792	11.7	99.0	0.7	0.1	0.2	0.6	6.6	17.4	9.4	12.5	14.5	14.9
54 029	8080	3	Hancock	215	33 740	1 265	156.9	97.0	2.6	0.1	0.3	0.6	4.7	15.4	7.9	11.8	15.0	14.9
54 031	...	9	Hardy	1 511	11 989	2 277	7.9	97.8	2.0	0.2	0.1	0.6	6.1	15.4	8.9	13.3	14.8	14.8
54 033	...	5	Harrison	1 078	70 329	700	65.2	97.9	1.6	0.1	0.4	1.4	5.6	16.8	9.3	12.2	14.3	14.5
54 035	...	6	Jackson	1 206	28 294	1 432	23.5	99.5	0.1	0.2	0.3	0.3	6.0	17.0	8.0	12.1	13.6	16.6
54 037	8840	1	Jefferson	543	42 271	1 034	77.8	91.9	7.4	0.2	0.5	1.4	6.5	16.5	12.8	13.6	15.7	14.8
54 039	1480	2	Kanawha	2 339	199 263	272	85.2	92.5	6.7	0.1	0.7	0.5	5.4	15.4	8.5	13.0	15.4	14.9
54 041	...	7	Lewis	1 007	17 463	1 903	17.3	99.1	0.3	0.2	0.4	0.5	5.6	16.7	8.9	12.8	14.7	15.1
54 043	...	8	Lincoln	1 133	22 346	1 645	19.7	99.7	0.0	0.1	0.1	0.3	5.8	19.7	9.5	13.0	14.8	15.3
54 045	...	7	Logan	1 176	40 183	1 085	34.2	96.2	3.2	0.1	0.5	0.8	5.2	19.8	9.2	12.4	15.9	13.6
54 047	...	7	McDowell	1 385	29 306	1 398	21.2	86.3	13.4	0.1	0.2	0.7	5.6	20.6	8.4	12.1	14.8	13.5
54 049	...	5	Marion	802	55 939	828	69.7	96.2	3.3	0.1	0.3	0.7	5.0	15.6	10.7	11.2	14.5	14.6
54 051	9000	3	Marshall	795	34 968	1 225	44.0	99.2	0.4	0.1	0.3	0.7	5.7	16.6	8.3	11.8	15.4	15.0
54 053	...	6	Mason	1 119	26 018	1 493	23.3	99.0	0.5	0.1	0.4	0.3	5.4	17.7	7.7	12.5	14.7	15.6
54 055	...	7	Mercer	1 089	64 132	743	58.9	93.1	6.3	0.1	0.5	0.5	5.0	16.5	10.5	11.6	14.8	14.3
54 057	1900	3	Mineral	849	27 069	1 463	31.9	96.8	2.8	0.1	0.3	0.4	5.9	16.6	10.4	11.6	14.6	15.9
54 059	...	7	Mingo	1 095	31 480	1 330	28.7	96.9	2.6	0.2	0.4	0.7	6.3	21.5	10.2	13.8	15.0	13.5
54 061	...	5	Monongalia	935	77 006	647	82.4	95.2	2.5	0.2	2.2	1.0	5.0	13.0	23.2	13.9	13.7	12.0
54 063	...	9	Monroe	1 226	13 296	2 192	10.8	98.3	1.3	0.2	0.1	0.4	5.8	16.7	8.9	11.3	14.8	15.7
54 065	...	8	Morgan	593	13 895	2 143	23.4	98.8	0.8	0.2	0.2	0.4	5.3	14.8	8.1	11.8	14.0	15.2
54 067	...	7	Nicholas	1 680	27 526	1 448	16.4	99.6	0.0	0.1	0.3	0.2	6.1	18.9	8.4	12.3	15.4	14.4
54 069	9000	3	Ohio	275	47 719	941	173.5	95.9	3.3	0.1	0.8	0.3	5.4	14.4	10.4	11.5	14.2	13.9
54 071	...	9	Pendleton	1 808	8 040	2 595	4.4	97.6	2.2	0.0	0.2	0.3	6.1	15.3	8.5	12.7	14.0	13.9
54 073	...	8	Pleasants	339	7 518	2 635	22.2	99.7	0.2	0.1	0.0	0.1	5.5	17.9	8.5	13.0	14.1	15.1
54 075	...	9	Pocahontas	2 435	9 065	2 501	3.7	99.0	0.8	0.1	0.1	0.4	5.6	15.4	7.3	12.3	14.4	15.8
54 077	...	7	Preston	1 679	29 814	1 377	17.8	99.5	0.3	0.1	0.1	0.3	6.0	18.4	8.6	12.7	14.9	14.6
54 079	1480	2	Putnam	897	51 936	880	57.9	99.2	0.3	0.1	0.4	0.4	6.4	17.8	8.1	13.9	16.7	16.1
54 081	...	5	Raleigh	1 572	78 947	636	50.2	91.6	7.6	0.1	0.6	0.5	5.3	18.5	8.3	11.7	16.3	14.4
54 083	...	7	Randolph	2 693	28 654	1 425	10.6	98.6	1.0	0.1	0.3	0.6	5.6	16.2	10.0	13.2	15.2	15.3
54 085	...	8	Ritchie	1 175	10 480	2 381	8.9	99.7	0.1	0.0	0.1	0.1	5.5	17.3	8.7	12.8	14.7	15.6
54 087	...	8	Roane	1 253	15 413	2 044	12.3	99.4	0.1	0.2	0.3	0.3	5.4	19.1	7.9	11.9	15.1	15.8
54 089	...	7	Summers	935	13 863	2 147	14.8	94.8	4.7	0.3	0.3	1.9	4.8	16.2	7.5	12.4	15.2	14.0
54 091	...	7	Taylor	448	15 367	2 045	34.3	98.8	0.8	0.1	0.3	0.5	6.1	16.9	8.8	13.1	14.6	14.5
54 093	...	9	Tucker	1 085	7 513	2 637	6.9	99.7	0.1	0.1	0.2	0.2	5.1	16.3	8.6	11.4	14.6	15.9
54 095	...	9	Tyler	667	9 717	2 454	14.6	99.5	0.1	0.2	0.2	0.3	5.8	17.0	8.1	11.8	14.3	15.7
54 097	...	7	Upshur	919	23 544	1 591	25.6	98.9	0.6	0.2	0.3	0.6	5.9	17.2	13.1	12.0	14.4	14.2
54 099	3400	2	Wayne	1 310	41 860	1 045	32.0	99.6	0.1	0.2	0.1	0.3	5.4	17.5	9.3	12.1	14.8	15.9
54 101	...	9	Webster	1 440	10 036	2 420	7.0	99.7	0.1	0.1	0.1	0.4	6.1	18.9	8.8	12.2	14.9	13.9
54 103	...	6	Wetzel	930	18 220	1 856	19.6	99.6	0.1	0.0	0.3	0.2	5.8	17.0	8.6	11.4	14.1	16.1
54 105	...	8	Wirt	604	5 761	2 788	9.5	99.8	0.1	0.0	0.1	0.1	6.3	18.4	8.0	14.4	13.7	16.4
54 107	6020	3	Wood	951	86 337	585	90.8	98.5	0.9	0.1	0.4	0.3	5.9	16.1	8.6	12.8	14.9	16.2
54 109	...	9	Wyoming	1 297	26 987	1 466	20.8	98.9	0.8	0.1	0.1	0.4	5.5	20.0	8.7	12.4	16.1	14.3
55 000	...	X	**WISCONSIN**	140 672	5 250 446	X	37.3	91.9	5.6	0.9	1.6	2.7	6.3	19.4	9.7	13.1	16.5	13.3
55 001	...	9	Adams	1 678	18 741	1 837	11.2	96.0	2.3	1.0	0.7	2.8	4.7	15.7	5.9	11.5	14.6	14.9
55 003	...	7	Ashland	2 704	16 390	1 981	6.1	89.7	0.3	9.6	0.4	0.9	6.3	20.4	10.1	11.8	15.0	12.1
55 005	...	7	Barron	2 235	44 093	1 000	19.7	98.9	0.2	0.6	0.4	0.6	6.1	20.9	7.7	11.7	15.6	13.1
55 007	...	8	Bayfield	3 824	15 358	2 046	4.0	90.0	0.3	9.5	0.3	0.5	5.6	20.5	5.8	11.1	16.8	14.4
55 009	3080	3	Brown	1 369	216 522	251	158.2	95.2	0.6	2.2	1.9	1.1	6.7	19.7	10.4	14.3	17.3	13.1
55 011	...	8	Buffalo	1 773	14 284	2 114	8.1	99.4	0.1	0.2	0.3	0.5	6.1	20.1	6.9	12.2	15.1	13.6
55 013	...	8	Burnett	2 128	14 913	2 067	7.0	95.0	0.3	4.3	0.3	0.5	5.2	18.8	5.8	9.8	14.7	14.1
55 015	0460	2	Calumet	828	39 029	1 111	47.1	98.5	0.1	0.5	0.9	0.7	7.1	22.8	7.8	14.0	16.9	13.1
55 017	2290	3	Chippewa	2 617	54 722	843	20.9	98.8	0.1	0.3	0.8	0.5	6.3	21.0	7.6	12.2	16.4	13.0
55 019	...	6	Clark	3 149	33 411	1 274	10.6	99.4	0.1	0.3	0.2	0.6	6.6	22.9	7.0	10.9	14.5	12.9
55 021	...	6	Columbia	2 004	51 788	883	25.8	98.5	0.7	0.3	0.5	1.2	5.9	19.6	7.4	12.1	16.8	14.1
55 023	...	7	Crawford	1 483	16 524	1 969	11.1	99.0	0.3	0.2	0.5	0.6	6.2	21.7	6.9	10.6	15.4	13.3

1. MSA = Metropolitan Statistical Area. PMSA = Primary MSA. NECMA = New England County Metropolitan Area. See Appendix A for explanation of these concepts. See Appendix B for list of metropolitan areas identified by type, with component counties.   2. County typology code from the Economic Research Service of USDA. See Appendix A for definition.   3. Dry land or land partially or temporarily covered by water.   4. Hispanic persons may be of any race.

Table B. States and Counties — Population and Households

STATE County	Population, 1999 (cont'd) — Age (percent) (cont'd) 55 to 64 years	65 to 74 years	75 years and over	Percent female	Population — change and components of change, 1980–1999 — Total persons 1990	1980	Percent change 1980–1990	1990–1999	Components of change, 1990–1999 Births	Deaths	Net migration	Households, 1990 Number	Percent change, 1980–1990	Persons per household	Percent Female family householder[1]	One person
	16	17	18	19	20	21	22	23	24	25	26	27	28	29	30	31
WEST VIRGINIA—Cont'd																
Braxton	10.7	7.9	8.1	51.1	12 998	13 894	-6.4	1.6	1 389	1 495	369	4 950	1.0	2.61	10.1	23.3
Brooke	11.6	10.0	7.9	52.0	26 992	31 117	-13.3	-4.1	2 451	2 777	-671	10 131	-4.6	2.56	9.1	23.6
Cabell	10.8	8.5	7.9	53.1	96 827	106 835	-9.4	-3.4	10 985	10 847	-3 098	39 146	-2.7	2.39	11.5	29.0
Calhoun	10.8	7.0	7.4	50.7	7 885	8 250	-4.4	1.2	758	851	222	2 978	2.2	2.64	11.9	22.7
Clay	10.3	6.3	6.1	50.6	9 983	11 265	-11.4	6.3	1 192	1 035	491	3 627	-1.0	2.75	11.8	21.7
Doddridge	11.3	6.8	5.9	50.1	6 994	7 433	-5.9	6.5	764	686	398	2 623	2.0	2.67	8.6	22.8
Fayette	11.1	8.9	8.1	52.1	47 952	57 863	-17.1	-2.4	5 419	5 823	-619	18 292	-7.9	2.55	12.6	25.8
Gilmer	10.2	7.2	9.2	50.3	7 669	8 334	-8.0	-6.9	672	758	-419	2 717	-3.2	2.61	9.3	22.9
Grant	9.9	7.8	7.6	50.6	10 428	10 210	2.1	6.8	1 216	993	530	3 925	11.5	2.62	8.6	21.4
Greenbrier	11.0	8.6	8.7	52.0	34 693	37 665	-7.9	1.8	3 646	4 168	1 277	13 775	1.8	2.48	10.6	25.9
Hampshire	10.8	8.0	5.9	50.5	16 498	14 867	11.0	17.7	2 070	1 573	2 462	6 182	20.0	2.63	8.5	22.3
Hancock	12.0	10.5	7.8	52.2	35 233	41 053	-14.2	-4.2	3 228	3 511	-1 091	13 781	-3.3	2.54	10.5	23.6
Hardy	11.5	8.3	6.9	50.4	10 977	10 030	9.4	9.2	1 254	1 162	948	4 286	19.9	2.55	8.6	22.6
Harrison	10.9	8.4	7.9	52.3	69 371	77 710	-10.7	1.4	7 887	8 127	1 461	27 009	-5.0	2.53	11.0	25.8
Jackson	11.7	7.7	7.2	51.1	25 938	25 794	0.6	9.1	2 914	2 507	2 052	9 645	10.7	2.66	9.2	19.4
Jefferson	8.7	6.6	4.7	50.6	35 926	30 302	18.6	17.7	4 586	2 895	4 726	12 914	29.4	2.68	9.5	21.5
Kanawha	11.1	9.0	7.3	52.8	207 619	231 414	-10.3	-4.0	23 602	21 974	-9 279	84 713	-2.0	2.42	11.8	27.4
Lewis	11.0	7.5	7.8	51.4	17 223	18 813	-8.5	1.4	1 813	2 015	497	6 615	-0.9	2.54	11.1	25.6
Lincoln	9.9	6.5	5.6	50.8	21 382	23 675	-9.7	-4.5	2 602	2 085	517	7 647	0.0	2.79	10.6	18.9
Logan	10.3	7.8	5.9	51.8	43 032	50 679	-15.1	-6.6	4 778	4 233	-3 319	15 425	-5.9	2.77	13.2	20.0
McDowell	10.2	8.2	6.5	52.7	35 233	49 899	-29.4	-16.8	6 024	6 567	-5 586	12 880	-19.7	2.72	14.3	22.8
Marion	10.8	9.0	8.5	53.2	57 249	65 789	-13.0	-2.3	6 024	6 567	-548	22 667	-7.1	2.47	10.8	26.7
Marshall	11.0	9.1	7.2	52.1	37 356	41 608	-10.2	-6.4	3 748	3 708	-2 284	14 051	-2.0	2.59	10.1	23.3
Mason	11.2	8.2	7.0	51.5	25 178	27 045	-6.9	3.3	2 714	2 768	1 000	9 603	2.2	2.59	9.6	22.6
Mercer	10.6	9.1	7.7	53.0	64 980	73 870	-12.0	-1.3	7 543	7 408	-774	25 390	-4.2	2.50	11.7	25.3
Mineral	10.1	8.2	6.7	51.3	26 697	27 234	-2.0	1.4	2 725	2 649	415	9 981	5.8	2.62	9.2	22.4
Mingo	9.0	6.3	4.5	51.2	33 739	37 336	-9.6	-6.7	4 163	3 104	-3 280	11 830	-0.4	2.84	13.4	20.0
Monongalia	7.8	6.1	5.2	50.2	75 509	75 024	0.6	2.0	8 143	5 248	-1 208	29 087	7.3	2.40	8.4	28.7
Monroe	11.6	8.3	7.0	51.2	12 406	12 873	-3.6	7.2	1 275	1 294	959	4 749	7.0	2.58	8.2	23.2
Morgan	12.4	10.4	8.0	51.4	12 128	10 711	13.2	14.6	1 352	1 310	1 762	4 731	24.0	2.52	7.5	22.2
Nicholas	10.4	7.6	6.5	50.9	26 775	28 126	-4.8	2.8	2 747	2 635	729	9 970	5.3	2.67	10.3	21.1
Ohio	11.3	9.9	8.9	53.4	50 871	61 389	-17.1	-6.2	5 189	6 133	-2 008	20 646	-10.0	2.35	11.6	31.9
Pendleton	11.0	9.0	9.4	49.9	8 054	7 910	1.8	-0.2	831	872	48	3 061	8.7	2.58	8.1	21.7
Pleasants	9.9	8.2	7.8	51.7	7 546	8 236	-8.4	-0.4	788	735	-57	2 769	2.3	2.62	9.7	22.9
Pocahontas	11.4	8.5	9.1	49.7	9 008	9 919	-9.2	0.6	939	1 079	240	3 628	1.9	2.44	8.1	26.6
Preston	10.0	7.7	7.0	50.6	29 037	30 460	-4.7	2.7	3 144	2 806	545	10 619	3.6	2.70	8.9	21.2
Putnam	9.4	6.5	5.1	50.9	42 835	38 181	12.2	21.2	5 333	3 524	7 432	15 695	21.0	2.71	8.5	17.6
Raleigh	10.8	8.0	6.2	52.7	76 819	86 821	-11.5	2.8	8 283	8 272	2 390	29 483	-2.2	2.57	11.9	24.3
Randolph	9.3	7.7	7.5	50.1	27 803	28 734	-3.2	3.1	3 004	2 841	785	10 366	7.0	2.55	9.9	25.0
Ritchie	10.5	6.8	8.1	51.0	10 233	11 442	-10.6	2.4	1 035	1 271	512	3 928	-4.8	2.57	9.6	23.1
Roane	10.7	7.1	7.0	50.6	15 120	15 952	-5.2	1.9	1 540	1 630	433	5 740	4.2	2.62	9.1	22.9
Summers	11.5	9.5	8.8	54.8	14 204	15 875	-10.5	-2.4	1 160	1 670	225	5 240	-1.8	2.52	11.0	25.7
Taylor	10.4	7.7	7.9	51.5	14 584	16 584	-8.7	1.5	1 511	1 703	461	5 741	-1.7	2.58	10.6	23.9
Tucker	10.2	8.6	9.2	51.3	7 728	8 675	-10.9	-2.8	715	825	-82	3 017	-2.7	2.51	8.3	25.5
Tyler	11.2	8.1	7.9	51.1	9 796	11 320	-13.5	-0.8	950	1 037	43	3 709	-5.5	2.62	8.2	21.5
Upshur	8.9	6.9	7.4	51.0	22 867	23 427	-2.4	3.0	2 467	2 276	571	8 245	3.1	2.61	9.2	24.0
Wayne	10.6	7.9	6.4	51.6	41 636	46 021	-9.5	0.5	4 634	3 971	-291	15 626	-0.1	2.66	10.5	21.2
Webster	10.2	7.7	7.3	51.1	10 729	12 245	-12.4	-6.5	1 065	1 144	-578	3 996	-4.6	2.67	12.1	21.2
Wetzel	10.9	8.2	8.0	51.8	19 258	21 874	-12.0	-5.4	2 059	2 024	-1 012	7 303	-4.0	2.61	9.8	23.4
Wirt	10.0	6.7	6.1	50.4	5 192	4 922	5.5	11.0	574	490	506	1 942	16.9	2.67	8.4	21.9
Wood	10.2	7.9	7.2	52.4	86 915	93 627	-7.2	-0.7	10 108	8 543	-1 858	34 188	1.0	2.52	10.2	24.2
Wyoming	10.2	7.8	5.1	51.3	28 990	35 993	-19.5	-6.9	2 862	2 409	-2 359	10 474	-8.7	2.76	11.0	19.2
WISCONSIN	8.6	6.7	6.5	50.9	4 891 954	4 705 642	4.0	7.3	637 733	412 353	115 193	1 822 118	10.3	2.61	9.6	24.3
Adams	13.4	11.6	7.8	46.9	15 682	13 457	16.5	19.5	1 557	1 711	3 262	5 972	23.4	2.44	6.4	23.1
Ashland	8.5	7.2	8.7	50.7	16 307	16 783	-2.8	0.5	1 986	1 890	39	6 255	2.5	2.50	9.7	30.6
Barron	9.1	7.5	8.3	50.3	40 750	38 730	5.2	8.2	4 807	4 233	2 919	15 435	12.1	2.60	7.9	24.2
Bayfield	10.7	7.7	7.6	49.0	14 008	13 822	1.3	9.6	1 411	1 465	1 452	5 515	7.9	2.52	7.5	25.6
Brown	7.6	5.5	5.4	51.1	194 594	175 280	11.0	11.3	27 793	13 544	8 384	72 280	20.7	2.62	9.0	24.1
Buffalo	9.9	7.4	8.6	49.5	13 584	14 309	-5.1	5.2	1 471	1 308	602	5 123	2.8	2.61	6.6	23.9
Burnett	11.9	10.6	9.1	50.4	13 084	12 340	6.0	14.0	1 336	1 604	2 134	5 242	15.0	2.45	7.6	25.5
Calumet	8.2	5.2	4.8	50.0	34 291	30 867	11.1	13.8	4 505	2 204	2 555	11 772	21.4	2.89	6.7	17.8
Chippewa	8.9	7.0	7.4	50.5	52 360	52 127	0.4	4.5	6 042	4 737	1 249	19 077	11.0	2.68	7.7	23.0
Clark	9.1	7.4	8.6	49.6	31 647	32 910	-3.8	5.6	4 190	3 110	803	11 209	1.7	2.77	6.2	23.8
Columbia	9.5	7.2	7.3	50.0	45 088	43 222	4.3	14.9	5 692	4 620	5 769	16 868	8.6	2.60	7.1	23.6
Crawford	9.7	8.1	8.2	50.2	15 940	16 556	-3.7	3.7	1 837	1 671	470	5 914	3.4	2.64	7.5	24.9

1. No spouse present.

Table B. States and Counties — Vital Statistics, Health Resources, and Crime

STATE County	Births, average 1996–1998		Deaths, average 1996–1998				Physicians,[4] 1998		Hospitals,[4] 1998				Serious crimes known to police, 1998[6]	
			Number		Rate					Beds			Total	
												Medicare enrollees 1999		
	Total	Rate[1]	Total	Infant[2]	Total[1]	Infant[3]	Number	Rate[5]	Number	Number	Rate[5]		Number	Rate[7]
	32	33	34	35	36	37	38	39	40	41	42	43	44	45
WEST VIRGINIA—Cont'd														
Braxton	148	11.2	166	1	12.5	6.8	5	38	1	30	228	2 630	141	1 063
Brooke	252	9.6	322	2	12.2	7.9	13	50	0	0	0	4 276	296	1 131
Cabell	1 151	12.1	1 217	13	12.8	11.3	423	449	2	738	783	19 795	4 883	5 151
Calhoun	79	10.0	89	1	11.2	8.4	3	38	0	0	0	1 575	75	951
Clay	126	12.0	121	1	11.6	7.9	3	28	0	0	0	1 917	137	1 307
Doddridge	79	10.7	83	0	11.3	4.2	2	26	0	0	0	947	67	910
Fayette	571	11.7	634	3	13.0	4.7	53	111	2	181	378	10 225	939	1 944
Gilmer	76	10.6	88	1	12.2	8.8	3	42	0	0	0	1 297	116	1 620
Grant	137	12.3	108	1	9.7	9.8	12	108	1	65	586	1 920	97	877
Greenbrier	384	10.8	457	3	12.8	7.8	99	280	1	132	373	7 376	469	1 325
Hampshire	212	11.3	189	1	10.1	3.1	12	63	1	47	247	3 139	199	1 056
Hancock	324	9.4	387	3	11.3	8.2	56	165	1	269	792	7 529	574	1 670
Hardy	144	12.2	131	1	11.2	6.9	6	51	0	0	0	2 110	123	1 045
Harrison	807	11.4	899	10	12.7	12.0	150	212	1	309	436	14 013	1 465	2 077
Jackson	319	11.5	281	3	10.2	9.4	17	61	1	72	257	4 961	263	957
Jefferson	489	12.1	334	4	8.3	7.5	51	123	1	56	135	5 334	953	2 384
Kanawha	2 468	12.1	2 487	14	12.2	5.8	659	326	5	1 278	633	39 720	10 510	5 170
Lewis	184	10.5	233	2	13.3	10.8	20	115	1	77	442	3 629	164	937
Lincoln	273	12.3	248	1	11.2	4.9	3	14	0	0	0	3 882	333	1 503
Logan	474	11.4	470	6	11.3	13.4	69	168	3	209	509	8 187	752	1 826
McDowell	348	11.4	416	4	13.6	10.5	15	50	1	124	414	7 353	213	698
Marion	622	10.9	709	6	12.4	9.1	97	172	1	217	385	11 858	827	1 458
Marshall	358	10.0	417	4	11.7	12.1	33	93	1	143	403	5 875	825	2 317
Mason	294	11.4	304	3	11.7	10.2	30	116	1	201	777	4 578	474	1 830
Mercer	820	12.7	808	8	12.6	9.3	153	240	3	555	870	13 940	1 798	2 803
Mineral	292	10.8	303	3	11.2	9.1	22	82	1	63	236	4 713	492	1 839
Mingo	407	12.6	350	4	10.8	9.0	37	116	1	76	238	5 950	333	1 025
Monongalia	846	10.9	608	5	7.8	5.9	517	667	2	562	725	9 503	2 098	2 715
Monroe	134	10.2	143	2	10.9	12.4	6	45	0	0	0	2 943	108	823
Morgan	159	11.7	160	2	11.8	10.5	15	110	1	44	323	2 599	218	1 622
Nicholas	271	9.8	295	3	10.7	12.3	33	120	2	170	616	5 141	555	2 018
Ohio	543	11.1	640	4	13.1	6.8	249	516	2	664	1 375	10 561	1 445	2 966
Pendleton	88	11.0	101	0	12.6	0.0	4	50	0	0	0	1 620	75	940
Pleasants	80	10.8	75	0	10.1	4.2	2	27	0	0	0	1 326	68	911
Pocahontas	95	10.4	111	2	12.2	17.5	10	108	1	40	432	1 888	108	1 198
Preston	317	10.6	307	4	10.3	13.7	31	104	1	58	195	5 177	311	1 076
Putnam	583	11.6	433	3	8.6	5.7	76	149	1	68	133	6 367	1 174	2 345
Raleigh	894	11.3	901	6	11.4	7.1	204	258	3	486	615	15 467	2 532	3 214
Randolph	309	10.7	324	4	11.3	11.9	57	199	1	131	457	5 406	682	2 376
Ritchie	109	10.6	134	2	13.0	15.3	5	48	0	0	0	1 909	87	850
Roane	168	10.9	187	1	12.2	6.0	16	104	1	73	476	2 686	279	1 827
Summers	116	8.5	182	1	13.4	11.5	10	76	1	95	723	2 811	168	1 223
Taylor	161	10.5	183	2	11.9	10.3	7	46	1	131	855	2 658	189	1 235
Tucker	65	8.5	90	0	11.7	5.1	6	79	0	0	0	1 478	77	1 001
Tyler	88	8.9	119	1	12.0	7.5	4	41	1	18	183	1 571	69	688
Upshur	248	10.5	261	3	11.1	12.1	28	119	1	95	404	3 955	278	1 170
Wayne	482	11.4	441	4	10.5	8.3	14	33	0	0	0	6 289	1 084	2 583
Webster	95	9.3	119	1	11.5	14.0	4	39	1	35	342	2 065	112	1 086
Wetzel	217	11.7	213	2	11.5	7.7	17	93	1	58	318	3 812	251	1 360
Wirt	67	11.9	60	0	10.6	5.0	2	35	0	0	0	949	86	1 523
Wood	1 052	12.1	967	8	11.1	7.3	173	199	2	508	585	15 645	2 693	3 103
Wyoming	302	10.9	282	3	10.2	8.8	9	33	0	0	0	5 475	427	1 549
WISCONSIN	67 038	12.9	45 326	471	8.7	7.0	10 943	209	126	17 111	328	777 273	185 093	3 543
Adams	169	9.3	188	3	10.4	15.8	6	32	1	58	314	2 831	NA	NA
Ashland	215	13.0	186	0	11.2	1.6	46	279	1	101	613	3 296	NA	NA
Barron	480	11.0	475	3	10.9	6.2	54	123	3	252	574	8 132	NA	NA
Bayfield	148	9.8	159	1	10.5	9.0	20	132	0	0	0	2 563	NA	NA
Brown	3 077	14.4	1 539	22	7.2	7.3	401	186	3	632	293	26 605	NA	NA
Buffalo	145	10.2	144	0	10.2	2.3	3	21	0	0	0	2 637	NA	NA
Burnett	144	9.9	187	1	12.9	9.3	9	61	1	84	574	3 162	NA	NA
Calumet	466	12.3	241	2	6.3	5.0	16	42	1	47	122	3 608	NA	NA
Chippewa	620	11.4	514	4	9.5	5.9	66	121	3	358	656	9 079	NA	NA
Clark	492	14.9	328	3	9.9	5.4	20	60	1	199	600	5 953	NA	NA
Columbia	623	12.3	501	3	9.9	5.3	54	106	2	213	416	9 279	NA	NA
Crawford	190	11.5	171	1	10.4	7.0	15	90	2	62	374	2 997	NA	NA

1. Per 1,000 estimated resident population, average 1996–1998.   2. Deaths of infants under 1 year old.   3. Deaths of infants under 1 year old per 1,000 live births.   4. Data subject to copyright.   5. Per 100,000 resident population as of July 1 of the year shown.   6. Data for serious crimes have not been adjusted for underreporting; this may affect comparability between geographic areas and over time.   7. Per 100,000 population estimated by the FBI.

Table B. States and Counties — Crime, Education, Money Income, and Poverty

STATE County	Serious crimes known to police, 1998[1] (cont'd) Rate[2]		Education School enrollment and attainment, 1990 Enrollment[3]		Attainment[4] (percent)		Local government expenditures, fiscal 1997[5]		Money income 1989	Households			Income and poverty, 1997 Percent below poverty level		
	Violent	Property	Total	Percent private	High school graduate or more	Bachelor's degree or more	Total current expenditures (mil dol)	Current expenditures per student (dollars)	Per capita[6] (dollars)	Median Dollars	Percent change, 1979–1989 (constant 1989 dollars)	Percent with $100,000 or more	Median household income	All persons	Persons under 18	Persons 5–17 in families
	46	47	48	49	50	51	52	53	54	55	56	57	58	59	60	61
WEST VIRGINIA—Cont'd																
Braxton	68	995	2 723	1.1	56.8	8.1	15.9	5 791	8 249	16 359	-5.1	0.5	23 427	21.5	32.2	30.2
Brooke	149	982	6 967	20.0	71.6	12.2	25.4	6 401	11 656	26 500	-19.3	0.9	32 466	11.6	18.7	16.0
Cabell	333	4 818	25 571	7.3	71.9	18.9	88.1	6 367	12 068	21 255	-11.3	2.5	29 404	16.2	24.6	21.3
Calhoun	152	799	1 851	1.0	56.3	6.8	9.8	6 230	7 223	14 496	-13.5	0.4	22 282	24.2	33.2	33.7
Clay	362	945	2 490	2.5	49.4	6.2	12.6	5 822	6 722	12 855	-22.0	0.2	21 172	26.8	35.2	35.6
Doddridge	109	801	1 546	5.0	64.6	10.3	8.8	6 473	8 297	17 159	-4.4	0.6	26 265	19.2	29.9	27.0
Fayette	145	1 799	12 179	4.8	57.1	8.8	49.5	5 949	8 653	16 774	-20.3	0.8	23 578	21.2	31.2	27.1
Gilmer	307	1 313	2 250	1.0	56.6	14.2	7.6	5 988	7 872	14 539	-13.8	1.0	22 686	25.0	34.0	34.6
Grant	45	832	2 329	4.0	60.2	8.6	10.7	5 611	10 394	20 923	6.9	1.6	27 808	13.6	20.7	18.9
Greenbrier	119	1 206	7 274	6.8	63.0	11.5	33.1	5 547	10 057	19 411	-5.0	1.4	26 800	16.2	24.3	22.3
Hampshire	191	865	3 708	2.7	61.8	9.0	18.2	5 157	9 996	20 753	3.8	1.3	27 976	16.0	26.0	23.9
Hancock	79	1 591	8 220	11.7	72.5	8.9	29.6	6 051	12 464	26 031	-25.0	0.9	32 037	11.8	18.4	16.9
Hardy	178	867	2 156	3.5	55.3	7.3	11.0	5 339	10 096	20 745	6.9	0.5	28 989	16.4	24.9	22.0
Harrison	181	1 896	15 973	9.4	70.6	13.5	74.6	6 075	10 281	20 367	-11.9	1.7	30 739	15.3	21.8	20.5
Jackson	58	899	6 172	4.4	65.4	8.7	31.8	6 219	9 832	21 655	-25.0	0.7	30 941	14.8	21.8	20.5
Jefferson	183	2 201	8 786	7.9	68.2	16.2	37.3	5 501	13 249	30 941	16.8	3.0	39 607	10.0	14.8	13.9
Kanawha	444	4 726	46 753	9.4	72.4	17.6	185.5	5 890	12 887	23 999	-17.2	2.5	32 546	14.3	22.8	19.6
Lewis	189	748	3 605	4.9	62.1	8.2	17.2	6 019	8 561	17 972	-13.4	0.8	24 837	20.2	29.9	28.4
Lincoln	122	1 381	5 108	1.4	49.1	4.7	26.8	6 310	7 224	14 659	-25.8	0.3	22 744	24.9	33.7	32.1
Logan	413	1 413	11 142	3.8	53.4	6.3	45.2	6 330	8 786	17 942	-26.3	1.2	24 600	23.0	30.3	28.3
McDowell	98	600	9 329	3.4	42.3	4.6	38.5	6 337	6 961	13 141	-35.2	0.7	18 592	31.4	39.3	40.0
Marion	95	1 363	13 633	7.0	71.4	12.5	55.5	6 138	10 328	20 386	-15.6	1.0	27 987	15.7	23.5	20.9
Marshall	219	2 098	8 777	14.3	70.9	9.7	39.0	6 572	10 946	22 687	-21.9	1.5	29 284	15.3	23.1	21.1
Mason	274	1 556	5 657	3.1	61.1	6.8	29.1	6 437	9 543	20 135	-20.3	1.0	28 695	17.2	24.3	22.4
Mercer	240	2 563	15 786	4.9	63.1	11.6	62.4	6 172	10 405	19 365	-16.5	1.6	26 279	19.0	29.3	25.7
Mineral	161	1 678	6 555	6.8	72.8	10.4	28.9	5 981	10 398	22 036	-10.3	0.9	29 672	14.3	22.6	20.5
Mingo	216	809	9 089	3.0	50.4	6.6	39.7	6 419	8 328	16 066	-23.6	1.5	24 462	24.9	31.3	29.8
Monongalia	170	2 545	27 645	5.4	75.4	28.1	61.7	6 011	11 772	22 183	-1.0	2.3	32 365	14.4	18.0	17.0
Monroe	69	754	2 682	6.0	62.1	8.0	11.5	5 816	8 959	18 217	-4.6	0.9	26 592	15.9	22.3	21.9
Morgan	67	1 555	2 264	3.1	64.8	11.8	12.3	5 466	11 420	24 372	6.7	1.3	30 915	12.2	21.2	17.9
Nicholas	222	1 796	6 379	3.5	61.2	8.0	31.0	6 230	8 652	18 116	-20.3	0.9	25 872	20.1	28.0	26.4
Ohio	335	2 631	12 437	24.3	75.1	18.4	39.0	6 096	12 348	22 489	-11.0	2.8	31 941	13.5	20.3	18.6
Pendleton	25	915	1 563	2.7	60.6	8.2	8.1	5 550	9 391	19 565	6.6	0.7	27 366	13.4	18.7	18.0
Pleasants	54	857	1 718	5.6	68.7	8.5	11.5	7 765	9 958	20 910	-22.9	1.9	29 723	14.3	19.3	18.5
Pocahontas	211	987	1 732	7.2	60.6	9.7	9.8	6 487	8 860	17 237	-16.8	0.9	24 035	17.5	26.4	25.6
Preston	190	886	6 800	2.8	62.7	8.3	29.8	5 667	9 158	19 940	-8.3	0.9	26 097	17.8	25.4	23.3
Putnam	140	2 205	10 238	7.6	73.8	13.3	49.9	5 680	11 840	27 405	-10.1	1.6	40 649	9.5	12.8	12.6
Raleigh	472	2 742	19 322	10.3	63.2	10.7	80.2	6 123	10 316	19 566	-23.0	1.6	27 864	17.4	25.7	22.9
Randolph	321	2 055	6 365	13.7	65.9	11.9	28.6	5 758	9 009	18 274	-14.8	1.2	25 577	18.3	27.4	25.7
Ritchie	166	684	2 209	1.0	61.5	6.0	11.8	6 442	9 117	17 333	-9.1	0.9	25 126	18.3	27.2	25.7
Roane	157	1 670	3 484	2.4	57.2	6.6	16.9	5 780	7 801	15 375	-21.1	0.5	23 846	21.9	31.5	29.5
Summers	116	1 107	2 974	6.2	58.0	8.5	10.9	5 879	8 203	16 457	-8.6	0.5	21 664	24.2	34.1	32.4
Taylor	59	1 176	3 369	6.4	66.0	8.1	16.2	5 857	8 746	17 963	-15.5	0.4	25 195	19.4	27.1	26.8
Tucker	91	910	1 648	5.7	64.0	8.6	8.0	5 979	8 978	17 949	-7.1	0.9	25 359	15.3	23.7	22.6
Tyler	30	658	2 282	3.8	68.7	9.0	11.0	6 430	9 692	20 360	-19.6	0.4	28 958	15.3	22.4	20.8
Upshur	97	1 073	6 121	22.6	64.3	12.0	23.8	5 628	8 748	18 739	-14.5	1.0	27 150	19.9	27.5	26.3
Wayne	410	2 173	10 322	3.0	63.1	9.0	46.8	5 949	9 430	19 688	-15.8	1.0	28 560	18.6	26.8	25.2
Webster	359	727	2 502	1.7	46.5	5.6	11.4	6 007	6 793	13 371	-18.6	0.5	19 533	28.5	38.9	38.7
Wetzel	87	1 273	4 404	1.7	70.1	10.4	22.1	5 889	10 454	21 545	-20.4	1.2	29 719	17.6	25.8	24.3
Wirt	35	1 488	1 184	1.9	66.2	8.0	7.0	5 753	8 163	16 951	-17.2	0.0	26 155	18.9	29.5	25.7
Wood	233	2 870	20 092	8.3	73.2	13.5	88.9	6 017	12 011	25 161	-9.5	1.6	33 410	13.9	21.8	18.5
Wyoming	178	1 371	7 839	2.1	53.0	6.2	34.2	6 717	8 268	17 248	-35.2	0.8	23 994	23.0	30.3	28.8
WISCONSIN	249	3 294	1 302 230	16.4	78.6	17.7	5 975.0	6 796	13 276	29 442	-0.6	2.6	39 800	9.2	14.3	12.6
Adams	NA	NA	3 057	6.4	67.0	7.4	13.9	6 784	10 926	21 548	-1.0	1.3	30 299	12.9	21.1	18.6
Ashland	NA	NA	4 231	19.2	75.3	12.8	24.0	7 011	9 661	19 012	-2.8	1.3	29 185	15.4	23.5	20.3
Barron	NA	NA	9 716	7.2	73.0	11.7	54.0	6 214	10 377	22 570	0.3	1.3	32 040	10.6	16.1	14.1
Bayfield	NA	NA	3 269	8.9	78.5	18.3	15.8	6 799	9 933	20 666	4.8	0.6	30 043	13.9	22.2	20.8
Brown	NA	NA	51 864	21.1	82.6	17.7	234.3	6 416	13 906	31 303	0.4	2.8	46 319	7.5	11.4	9.6
Buffalo	NA	NA	3 215	7.6	72.6	10.8	16.2	6 521	10 947	23 573	4.8	1.5	32 665	10.9	17.5	15.7
Burnett	NA	NA	2 876	5.0	72.3	8.9	15.0	6 445	9 623	20 153	8.0	0.4	29 356	11.5	18.9	16.8
Calumet	NA	NA	9 075	16.2	79.7	12.9	26.2	5 866	12 904	34 050	-0.7	2.0	48 827	4.4	5.8	5.5
Chippewa	NA	NA	12 967	13.1	74.9	10.8	58.9	6 311	11 170	25 858	1.5	1.7	36 052	9.6	14.4	12.7
Clark	NA	NA	7 738	13.4	67.5	8.6	40.1	6 331	9 810	22 177	3.3	1.5	30 875	11.5	17.5	15.8
Columbia	NA	NA	10 466	13.2	78.3	12.9	68.8	6 105	12 356	28 360	3.3	1.7	39 936	6.4	9.4	8.7
Crawford	NA	NA	3 884	13.9	72.4	10.8	18.3	6 414	9 661	21 436	4.0	0.8	29 849	11.0	15.7	14.9

1. Data for serious crimes have not been adjusted for underreporting; this may affect comparability between geographic areas and over time.　2. Per 100,000 population estimated by the FBI.　3. All persons 3 years old and over enrolled in nursery school through college.　4. Persons 25 years old and over.　5. Elementary and secondary education expenditures, local government fiscal years ending between July 1, 1996 and June 30, 1997.　6. Based on population enumerated as of April 1, 1990.

STATE County	Total (mil dol)	Percent change, 1997–1998	Per capita[1] Dollars	Per capita[1] Rank	Wages and salaries[2] (mil dol)	Proprietor's income (mil dol)	Dividends, interest, and rent (mil dol)	Transfer payments Total (mil dol)	Government payments to individuals Total (mil dol)	Social Security (mil dol)	Medical payments (mil dol)	Income mainte-nance (mil dol)	Unemploy-ment insurance (mil dol)
	62	63	64	65	66	67	68	69	70	71	72	73	74
WEST VIRGINIA—Cont'd													
Braxton	210	3.6	15 880	2 811	95	15	33	63	60	22	20	8	2
Brooke	518	4.2	19 910	1 742	276	26	104	113	108	54	36	6	1
Cabell	2 167	2.3	23 024	850	1 559	98	450	493	477	173	169	41	6
Calhoun	107	4.4	13 454	3 049	33	12	16	37	36	13	12	6	1
Clay	143	4.4	13 561	3 039	58	14	17	46	44	17	11	8	1
Doddridge	118	3.2	15 764	2 831	23	6	21	24	23	12	4	3	1
Fayette	816	2.3	17 318	2 525	349	37	115	278	270	99	98	27	4
Gilmer	121	3.9	16 898	2 630	46	10	26	35	33	12	12	4	1
Grant	198	3.1	17 823	2 399	120	19	36	48	46	17	18	4	1
Greenbrier	662	3.5	18 731	2 149	335	44	126	177	171	63	69	13	3
Hampshire	299	4.8	15 593	2 865	92	22	54	69	66	30	21	7	0
Hancock	762	4.0	22 413	999	530	34	120	170	164	76	63	8	1
Hardy	220	4.5	18 555	2 194	125	15	36	39	37	18	9	4	1
Harrison	1 593	2.7	22 504	977	988	111	310	342	330	134	114	30	8
Jackson	507	4.7	18 128	2 314	287	27	82	116	111	50	37	11	2
Jefferson	1 051	8.9	25 353	454	336	44	160	129	122	52	34	7	1
Kanawha	5 323	3.5	26 421	352	3 816	368	984	1 052	1 017	403	395	73	14
Lewis	284	4.0	16 116	2 779	141	19	59	76	73	31	24	9	1
Lincoln	307	3.3	13 836	3 022	68	20	36	94	90	36	21	18	2
Logan	710	1.8	17 303	2 529	411	28	96	245	238	82	89	26	4
McDowell	414	0.0	13 786	3 024	156	11	66	191	186	70	49	37	3
Marion	1 094	2.2	19 374	1 923	575	64	218	275	265	114	83	22	4
Marshall	666	5.3	18 888	2 093	406	23	110	152	145	62	49	11	3
Mason	437	4.0	16 844	2 646	228	12	66	118	113	45	43	11	3
Mercer	1 312	3.4	20 384	1 611	656	61	250	379	368	125	142	33	3
Mineral	488	3.3	18 035	2 337	158	30	75	122	117	41	43	9	1
Mingo	536	1.3	16 792	2 657	334	50	75	172	166	60	49	27	4
Monongalia	1 763	5.1	22 758	904	1 220	92	337	309	296	99	126	17	3
Monroe	197	2.4	14 917	2 937	53	17	31	55	53	24	16	6	1
Morgan	264	6.0	19 281	1 963	72	20	49	62	59	25	23	3	1
Nicholas	433	2.6	15 713	2 843	207	44	73	128	124	52	42	13	2
Ohio	1 238	3.1	25 677	418	793	89	333	255	247	107	96	16	2
Pendleton	150	3.6	18 563	2 190	61	11	30	33	31	13	12	3	0
Pleasants	151	4.5	20 136	1 671	111	5	23	41	39	14	19	3	1
Pocahontas	174	6.6	19 082	2 028	90	14	29	52	51	17	25	3	1
Preston	453	4.0	15 183	2 913	165	29	77	124	119	48	39	13	3
Putnam	1 182	6.9	23 084	838	559	52	149	168	159	70	43	10	4
Raleigh	1 587	3.9	20 027	1 703	899	76	246	422	408	156	140	35	9
Randolph	517	2.9	18 035	2 336	261	44	91	146	141	46	62	13	3
Ritchie	163	3.7	15 672	2 856	69	11	26	45	43	18	14	5	1
Roane	241	4.3	15 720	2 841	93	25	36	67	64	26	23	8	1
Summers	199	3.7	14 274	2 986	62	6	33	78	76	21	31	8	1
Taylor	229	3.2	14 908	2 939	87	9	35	68	66	23	21	7	2
Tucker	124	0.4	16 351	2 736	60	10	23	37	36	14	14	2	1
Tyler	154	3.2	15 691	2 850	86	8	30	38	36	18	10	3	1
Upshur	369	5.3	15 688	2 851	199	21	69	93	89	36	27	11	3
Wayne	656	2.5	15 638	2 860	299	25	88	156	149	68	28	23	3
Webster	130	1.1	12 723	3 073	68	5	17	50	49	18	13	9	1
Wetzel	351	3.8	19 161	1 996	113	17	62	90	87	36	32	8	2
Wirt	85	4.7	14 872	2 946	15	5	11	20	19	9	5	3	1
Wood	1 979	2.9	22 829	885	1 353	118	346	393	379	160	136	29	6
Wyoming	402	2.1	14 690	2 959	189	14	52	140	136	58	33	20	2
WISCONSIN	137 256	5.8	26 284	X	88 558	7 493	27 517	17 161	16 190	7 766	5 987	1 213	464
Adams	325	4.5	17 629	2 458	112	26	62	76	72	40	21	5	2
Ashland	328	3.5	19 948	1 729	230	24	68	70	67	28	27	5	2
Barron	905	7.0	20 640	1 512	541	81	174	161	152	75	56	10	4
Bayfield	288	4.4	18 963	2 069	81	28	66	58	55	27	18	4	2
Brown	6 043	4.9	28 114	232	4 696	337	1 244	571	530	268	177	33	18
Buffalo	307	8.8	21 558	1 240	155	24	65	49	46	22	18	4	1
Burnett	265	4.8	18 124	2 315	106	21	62	64	61	33	20	4	1
Calumet	940	6.5	24 435	570	368	56	184	88	81	48	23	3	4
Chippewa	1 237	7.8	22 670	932	665	81	246	196	186	85	76	11	6
Clark	617	9.1	18 627	2 176	257	63	131	116	110	50	45	8	4
Columbia	1 190	5.7	23 273	800	538	101	256	172	162	83	60	7	5
Crawford	313	5.7	18 883	2 096	177	16	66	59	56	27	20	4	2

1. Based on the resident population estimated as of July 1 of the year shown.   2. Includes other labor income.

Table B. States and Counties — Earnings, Social Security, and Housing

STATE County	Earnings, 1998									Social Security beneficiaries, December 1998		Supplemental Security Income recipients, December 1998	Housing units, 1990	
			Percent by selected industries											
		Goods-related[1]			Service-related and other[2]									
	Total (mil dol)	Farm	Total	Manufacturing	Total	Retail trade	Finance, insurance, and real estate	Services	Government	Number	Rate[3]		Total	Percent change, 1980–1990
	75	76	77	78	79	80	81	82	83	84	85	86	87	88
WEST VIRGINIA—Cont'd														
Braxton	110	-0.6	D	15.8	D	17.0	2.4	21.3	22.2	3 070	233	788	5 708	2.2
Brooke	302	0.0	D	42.0	D	7.8	1.9	16.8	11.1	5 753	221	425	10 838	-3.2
Cabell	1 657	0.0	21.4	14.8	61.3	10.7	4.5	32.7	17.3	20 047	213	3 929	43 596	0.0
Calhoun	45	-0.5	38.0	4.6	D	8.7	D	16.9	26.0	1 844	232	607	3 446	8.1
Clay	66	0.1	45.1	5.0	D	6.0	1.9	12.9	26.5	2 279	216	711	4 359	5.2
Doddridge	29	-3.6	29.2	9.0	D	7.6	6.6	15.8	34.1	1 538	204	245	3 251	2.0
Fayette	386	0.0	23.7	11.4	49.1	10.6	3.0	25.4	27.2	12 171	254	2 360	20 841	-2.9
Gilmer	56	-1.8	40.8	10.7	D	6.7	1.8	11.3	36.1	1 599	224	391	3 243	2.8
Grant	139	0.5	35.0	18.0	42.6	5.8	3.0	11.5	21.9	2 263	204	431	4 746	15.9
Greenbrier	378	0.5	19.2	10.1	61.8	12.2	3.1	36.8	18.6	7 990	226	1 419	16 757	10.2
Hampshire	113	1.7	D	9.3	D	9.6	4.5	23.2	29.3	3 911	205	717	8 817	26.0
Hancock	565	0.0	D	56.8	D	5.3	1.9	20.0	8.4	8 018	236	591	14 697	-1.8
Hardy	140	2.2	D	53.3	D	7.8	2.7	9.3	13.7	2 458	208	418	5 573	24.6
Harrison	1 100	-0.2	20.5	8.6	50.2	9.5	2.8	21.8	29.5	15 854	224	2 697	29 988	-0.7
Jackson	314	-1.0	D	37.5	D	11.8	2.4	14.4	14.0	5 924	212	1 010	10 571	13.1
Jefferson	380	0.7	D	22.2	D	12.3	3.6	23.8	26.2	6 349	153	631	14 606	26.5
Kanawha	4 185	0.0	20.9	12.2	61.2	8.5	7.0	30.5	17.9	44 936	222	6 380	92 747	2.1
Lewis	160	-0.4	26.3	11.6	47.4	12.0	1.9	21.8	26.7	4 057	233	945	7 454	3.7
Lincoln	88	0.6	28.6	4.8	D	8.3	D	16.8	34.2	4 782	215	1 872	8 429	3.7
Logan	438	0.0	32.3	5.3	52.0	11.1	2.4	27.0	15.6	9 764	238	2 218	16 848	-1.9
McDowell	167	0.0	26.9	1.3	38.6	9.5	4.6	14.7	34.5	9 265	310	3 659	15 330	-11.1
Marion	639	0.1	28.9	9.8	50.5	9.5	4.0	23.7	20.7	12 839	228	1 686	25 491	-2.8
Marshall	429	-0.3	52.6	35.3	D	7.4	1.5	D	14.6	6 954	196	731	15 630	0.8
Mason	240	-0.2	D	23.7	D	6.0	2.1	17.6	19.3	5 410	209	1 078	10 932	6.8
Mercer	716	0.1	14.4	7.8	63.1	12.4	4.2	30.5	22.6	15 404	241	3 230	28 426	-0.1
Mineral	188	0.8	D	22.7	D	12.1	2.7	18.8	25.0	4 859	182	591	10 930	6.7
Mingo	383	0.0	48.5	3.3	37.8	4.7	2.4	13.3	13.7	7 417	232	2 419	13 087	4.3
Monongalia	1 312	-0.2	15.5	8.9	44.0	8.3	3.2	25.4	40.7	11 265	145	1 413	31 563	8.5
Monroe	70	-0.6	26.8	18.8	D	5.9	D	13.1	39.5	3 066	232	708	5 994	15.9
Morgan	91	-0.3	D	14.2	D	10.0	4.0	20.4	24.0	3 011	221	253	6 757	38.3
Nicholas	251	-0.2	34.1	12.1	43.6	12.8	2.7	16.5	22.5	6 294	228	1 115	11 235	7.8
Ohio	882	0.0	D	8.0	D	8.8	6.3	44.5	14.3	11 935	247	1 303	23 229	-4.8
Pendleton	72	3.8	D	15.6	D	6.2	2.5	16.1	38.2	1 839	228	314	4 516	22.2
Pleasants	116	-0.2	50.3	31.3	35.0	4.5	1.7	7.7	14.9	1 569	211	210	3 134	3.4
Pocahontas	104	0.0	D	15.9	D	7.9	2.3	31.2	21.4	2 227	240	373	5 579	1.9
Preston	194	0.0	27.2	13.8	47.4	10.2	3.1	15.9	25.3	6 146	206	1 095	12 137	5.6
Putnam	612	0.1	26.0	10.8	61.5	11.7	3.5	20.7	12.5	7 957	156	899	16 884	22.8
Raleigh	975	0.1	20.1	3.7	58.8	12.8	4.3	29.9	21.2	18 404	233	3 143	33 278	3.7
Randolph	306	0.5	19.8	12.0	57.4	11.0	3.3	30.0	22.3	5 982	209	1 361	12 548	13.4
Ritchie	80	-2.2	D	41.0	D	8.1	3.1	10.5	19.3	2 369	229	487	4 936	1.9
Roane	117	-1.4	D	23.1	D	8.8	4.2	18.3	18.1	3 418	223	818	6 611	9.4
Summers	67	-2.8	D	2.5	D	11.8	4.7	22.3	30.3	2 854	217	807	6 769	3.1
Taylor	96	1.4	D	28.5	D	7.8	1.4	11.1	33.2	2 961	193	635	6 528	0.2
Tucker	70	-0.2	34.6	14.6	41.7	7.6	4.6	22.2	23.9	1 783	234	228	3 900	2.0
Tyler	94	0.5	D	54.5	D	4.6	1.7	8.6	17.0	2 100	214	246	4 441	-3.4
Upshur	221	-1.0	36.0	17.8	47.0	12.1	2.3	24.7	18.0	4 645	197	949	9 506	5.4
Wayne	324	0.0	26.3	12.3	D	7.6	D	13.0	36.6	8 632	206	2 269	16 991	1.0
Webster	73	0.0	43.4	8.7	D	5.2	D	12.1	26.2	2 471	242	780	5 072	6.1
Wetzel	130	-0.3	19.0	5.4	52.6	16.9	3.6	16.5	28.7	4 174	229	748	8 129	-1.3
Wirt	20	-0.9	D	D	D	8.7	4.5	20.5	41.8	1 144	202	258	2 795	38.2
Wood	1 471	0.1	34.7	26.3	49.1	10.5	4.8	24.6	16.2	18 212	210	2 560	37 620	4.0
Wyoming	203	0.0	45.7	4.2	D	8.1	D	11.4	20.6	7 081	259	1 792	11 756	-3.2
WISCONSIN	96 051	0.9	33.6	27.2	51.2	8.7	6.9	23.2	14.4	886 817	170	89 575	2 055 774	10.3
Adams	139	8.9	D	D	D	8.1	1.6	16.7	31.0	4 755	257	317	12 418	23.1
Ashland	255	-0.4	D	22.3	D	D	2.6	29.4	18.6	3 485	212	414	8 371	7.6
Barron	621	4.4	D	32.2	D	10.1	2.7	19.2	16.3	9 487	216	905	19 363	12.9
Bayfield	108	0.1	17.8	7.0	54.8	11.9	3.7	27.7	27.3	3 352	221	242	10 918	13.2
Brown	5 033	0.6	32.7	25.8	56.6	9.1	7.6	23.1	10.1	30 318	141	3 009	74 740	20.0
Buffalo	179	3.9	13.8	9.3	D	5.5	2.4	D	18.3	2 938	205	249	5 586	2.0
Burnett	127	0.1	D	30.2	D	11.7	2.7	21.9	16.8	4 023	275	271	11 743	13.4
Calumet	424	3.5	D	48.6	D	6.6	2.5	10.1	10.2	5 412	141	180	12 465	19.5
Chippewa	746	1.7	46.4	36.7	35.5	9.6	1.7	15.2	16.4	10 544	193	925	21 024	9.5
Clark	320	9.4	D	28.0	D	7.2	2.5	13.5	18.8	6 591	199	585	12 904	4.2
Columbia	638	0.4	D	27.0	D	10.2	5.3	19.0	17.6	9 650	189	562	19 258	8.2
Crawford	193	-0.3	D	35.0	D	15.4	2.7	22.4	14.2	3 524	213	401	7 315	8.1

1. Covers mining, construction, and manufacturing. 2. Covers private sector earnings in agricultural services, forestry, and fisheries; transportation and public utilities; wholesale trade; retail trade; finance, insurance, and real estate; and services. 3. Per 1,000 resident population estimated as of July 1 of the year shown.

Table B. States and Counties — Housing, Labor Force, and Employment

STATE County	Housing units, 1990 (cont'd) Occupied units Owner-occupied Total	Percent	Median value[1]	Owner cost as a percent of income With a mortgage	Without a mortgage	Renter-occupied Median rent[2]	Rent as percent of income	Substandard units[3] (percent)	Civilian labor force, 1999 Total	Percent change, 1998–1999	Unemployment Total	Rate[4]	Civilian employment, 1990[5] Total	Percent Professional, managerial, and technical	Precision production, craft, and repair
	89	90	91	92	93	94	95	96	97	98	99	100	101	102	103
WEST VIRGINIA—Cont'd															
Braxton	4 950	77.9	39 300	21.3	13.3	264	25.3	8.1	5 382	3.8	579	10.8	4 105	20.1	17.2
Brooke	10 131	79.1	44 100	15.5	11.7	306	20.7	2.0	11 479	0.3	720	6.3	10 858	23.7	14.3
Cabell	39 146	64.7	52 800	16.4	11.8	319	28.5	2.1	43 555	2.1	2 243	5.1	38 829	32.4	10.4
Calhoun	2 978	76.7	33 200	19.7	12.3	195	28.1	12.1	2 667	5.7	476	17.8	2 423	21.5	15.1
Clay	3 627	76.0	33 000	21.5	12.0	246	35.1	10.0	4 304	8.1	473	11.0	2 346	21.1	17.4
Doddridge	2 623	82.4	33 800	18.9	11.4	238	27.6	6.4	3 342	1.5	201	6.0	2 387	20.1	18.0
Fayette	18 292	76.4	34 500	19.6	12.4	266	27.2	5.1	18 344	3.5	1 820	9.9	14 337	25.2	16.0
Gilmer	2 717	71.4	42 100	17.0	11.7	282	31.6	9.5	2 741	-1.0	259	9.4	2 370	26.2	17.7
Grant	3 925	81.5	49 900	19.1	11.7	253	22.0	4.7	4 569	0.4	386	8.4	4 486	18.3	18.7
Greenbrier	13 775	75.6	44 000	18.8	12.2	275	25.7	3.7	15 899	5.2	1 298	8.2	13 500	23.0	13.5
Hampshire	6 182	81.1	50 500	18.5	12.6	267	24.4	8.9	8 799	0.2	431	4.9	6 536	19.8	19.6
Hancock	13 781	76.7	45 600	14.0	11.7	320	21.8	1.7	15 274	0.2	970	6.4	14 424	19.6	14.0
Hardy	4 286	82.2	49 300	17.7	13.0	260	23.9	8.6	7 388	7.0	292	4.0	4 861	14.4	17.0
Harrison	27 009	74.0	45 000	19.7	12.5	299	28.1	2.4	34 820	1.2	2 434	7.0	26 011	26.1	13.2
Jackson	9 645	78.4	51 400	16.5	12.0	314	27.8	4.3	12 977	-1.7	973	7.5	9 637	21.4	15.2
Jefferson	0	71.9	84 100	18.1	12.0	376	23.9	3.4	21 845	3.5	625	2.9	17 631	25.0	15.2
Kanawha	84 713	68.5	56 400	16.0	11.5	339	24.1	1.8	107 882	3.0	5 081	4.7	87 615	31.0	11.2
Lewis	6 615	69.8	42 200	18.2	12.4	250	27.5	4.9	7 183	2.5	595	8.3	6 071	21.1	14.9
Lincoln	7 647	77.1	38 200	18.0	11.5	253	35.1	9.9	7 082	1.9	841	11.9	5 891	17.1	19.6
Logan	15 425	73.2	42 100	20.5	12.9	278	27.4	5.0	13 392	-5.1	1 638	12.2	12 253	21.2	20.3
McDowell	12 880	78.7	15 800	22.0	12.9	221	31.6	8.5	7 571	1.0	1 097	14.5	7 398	19.7	21.2
Marion	22 667	75.5	42 300	17.0	12.7	300	29.0	2.0	24 229	2.3	1 946	8.0	20 932	23.5	17.9
Marshall	14 051	77.9	42 700	15.2	11.6	269	26.5	2.3	16 614	1.8	1 046	6.3	14 267	23.0	15.5
Mason	9 603	78.5	44 800	16.8	12.2	262	26.7	5.8	9 177	2.0	1 216	13.3	8 867	17.8	16.4
Mercer	25 390	76.3	44 600	19.1	11.7	280	28.6	3.4	28 620	1.4	1 394	4.9	23 646	25.9	14.7
Mineral	9 981	77.5	49 300	18.3	12.1	270	23.4	2.6	12 487	2.5	897	7.2	10 987	22.6	15.2
Mingo	11 830	72.8	39 400	20.7	12.6	272	34.8	6.6	8 519	-3.9	1 291	15.2	8 396	19.9	22.3
Monongalia	29 087	62.1	64 600	17.4	11.9	359	32.1	2.3	39 122	2.6	1 327	3.4	33 025	36.7	11.3
Monroe	4 749	84.3	42 500	21.1	12.3	261	21.3	6.9	5 411	4.3	235	4.3	4 586	19.0	15.1
Morgan	4 731	83.0	61 900	17.5	11.9	310	27.9	4.6	6 226	2.8	161	2.6	5 142	18.9	18.7
Nicholas	9 970	81.2	42 300	20.0	11.8	288	31.7	5.2	11 099	5.9	1 078	9.7	8 575	21.2	18.2
Ohio	20 646	66.7	48 800	16.9	11.7	280	26.2	1.7	25 095	0.7	1 014	4.0	22 058	30.2	10.9
Pendleton	3 061	79.3	51 600	20.1	11.0	274	24.6	8.4	4 083	8.7	187	4.6	3 391	16.0	16.9
Pleasants	2 769	79.6	51 100	16.0	12.0	259	24.5	5.4	2 871	-14.5	252	8.8	2 792	22.4	18.7
Pocahontas	3 628	79.4	42 000	21.8	12.3	249	26.9	7.4	4 369	2.9	377	8.6	3 465	19.2	10.6
Preston	10 619	81.3	44 200	19.0	12.2	250	25.1	7.1	12 858	2.2	810	6.3	10 525	18.5	20.3
Putnam	15 695	83.3	62 700	16.6	11.6	345	25.4	3.9	27 158	5.8	1 297	4.8	17 954	27.0	13.7
Raleigh	29 483	75.5	44 100	19.8	11.8	296	28.5	3.3	35 518	4.1	2 598	7.3	25 344	26.9	14.7
Randolph	10 366	74.5	46 000	21.1	12.2	274	27.6	5.0	13 791	4.5	1 040	7.5	9 861	24.7	12.9
Ritchie	3 928	80.0	32 400	21.5	12.0	226	27.9	6.3	4 404	5.7	428	9.7	3 740	16.0	16.3
Roane	5 740	78.0	36 600	22.8	11.6	241	27.1	8.5	6 281	-1.0	779	12.4	4 823	18.5	16.5
Summers	5 240	76.7	34 800	19.5	11.5	228	29.9	7.8	4 454	1.9	406	9.1	3 946	21.4	13.8
Taylor	5 741	76.2	34 200	18.6	12.5	254	28.6	4.0	7 049	1.2	563	8.0	5 260	17.3	15.6
Tucker	3 017	80.4	38 200	20.4	11.9	256	23.1	5.4	3 510	-2.1	323	9.2	2 927	20.3	17.4
Tyler	3 709	82.0	43 200	16.2	11.6	283	28.8	4.8	4 311	3.9	320	7.4	3 540	21.2	15.8
Upshur	8 245	75.5	47 900	20.0	12.2	281	27.7	5.5	10 493	-0.8	800	7.6	8 364	23.8	14.9
Wayne	15 626	76.6	46 700	17.3	11.9	288	28.3	5.6	17 148	2.3	1 073	6.3	14 598	24.1	14.5
Webster	3 996	78.4	29 700	23.2	12.6	229	33.1	10.2	3 162	4.5	302	9.6	2 645	15.3	20.3
Wetzel	7 303	77.3	50 200	15.0	12.3	269	24.3	5.5	7 831	6.5	852	10.9	6 556	20.2	18.8
Wirt	1 942	81.3	36 300	18.9	11.6	211	26.9	13.6	2 007	7.3	297	14.8	1 861	18.2	13.9
Wood	34 168	73.8	49 500	15.9	12.4	333	25.6	2.0	44 413	0.4	2 387	5.4	37 725	27.1	12.1
Wyoming	10 474	80.5	34 300	18.1	11.8	257	30.8	5.8	8 306	-2.6	885	10.7	7 372	20.3	24.2
WISCONSIN	1 822 118	66.7	62 500	20.1	13.4	399	24.9	2.6	2 891 982	-2.0	88 101	3.0	2 386 439	26.4	11.5
Adams	5 972	81.4	46 500	21.2	14.1	320	26.0	3.4	7 908	-4.1	293	3.7	5 640	17.2	13.0
Ashland	6 255	70.6	37 300	19.2	15.6	278	27.3	3.9	7 728	-4.3	572	7.4	6 628	24.1	8.6
Barron	15 435	73.5	47 000	20.6	14.3	313	27.5	2.6	23 477	-4.2	910	3.9	18 462	19.0	11.6
Bayfield	5 515	78.8	44 700	20.8	14.9	272	27.0	5.8	7 132	-5.2	412	5.8	5 814	26.4	11.5
Brown	72 280	65.6	62 600	20.3	13.0	373	23.9	2.1	133 352	1.1	3 068	2.3	99 142	26.6	11.2
Buffalo	5 123	75.2	43 000	19.0	13.0	286	22.4	2.7	7 685	-3.4	226	2.9	6 499	17.6	11.3
Burnett	5 242	80.7	44 600	22.0	15.0	276	25.4	4.1	6 906	-1.9	316	4.6	5 243	17.9	16.9
Calumet	11 772	78.6	62 100	20.5	12.1	346	21.0	2.4	24 666	-1.3	559	2.3	17 478	21.3	12.9
Chippewa	19 077	74.2	46 500	18.3	13.5	325	24.9	2.4	30 318	-1.1	1 107	3.7	23 870	20.6	12.0
Clark	11 209	78.7	36 900	20.0	13.9	269	23.5	4.3	15 500	-7.9	764	4.9	13 956	17.0	10.4
Columbia	16 868	72.9	55 700	19.8	13.2	356	23.1	1.6	26 145	-4.7	990	3.8	21 857	21.5	13.2
Crawford	5 914	74.2	42 900	20.5	14.3	298	25.3	3.1	9 717	-7.6	358	3.7	7 142	16.0	10.4

1. Specified owner-occupied units. 2. Specified renter-occupied units. 3. Overcrowded or lacking complete plumbing facilities. 4. Percent of civilian labor force. 5. Persons 16 years and older.

Table B. States and Counties — Nonfarm Employment and Agriculture

STATE County	Number of establish-ments	Total	Health Care and Social Assistance	Manufac-turing	Retail trade	Finance and Insurance	Professional Scientific and Technical Services	Total (mil dol)	Average per employee (dollars)	Number	Less than 50 acres	500 acres and over	Whose principal occupation is farming (percent)
	104	105	106	107	108	109	110	111	112	113	114	115	116
WEST VIRGINIA—Cont'd													
Braxton	331	3 158	556	425	888	84	53	59	18 729	280	11.8	7.9	41.4
Brooke	455	7 529	1 624	1 570	604	123	82	155	20 570	95	25.3	4.2	37.9
Cabell	2 823	44 797	9 660	5 703	7 236	1 928	1 793	1 050	23 433	305	28.9	1.0	37.0
Calhoun	138	1 064	163	235	183	52	D	19	18 073	171	8.2	7.6	38.0
Clay	136	1 312	220	86	236	D	0	34	26 251	100	7.0	3.0	43.0
Doddridge	79	548	162	D	66	D	3	8	14 511	302	10.3	10.3	34.4
Fayette	960	10 150	2 146	876	2 183	339	168	215	21 224	205	25.9	2.0	36.6
Gilmer	132	946	171	165	173	37	D	16	16 551	214	5.1	17.3	37.4
Grant	280	3 380	557	936	398	116	55	76	22 609	375	17.9	22.1	55.2
Greenbrier	1 029	10 041	2 263	998	2 044	313	159	210	20 946	727	23.0	12.1	41.7
Hampshire	338	2 883	825	296	439	128	51	47	16 425	547	21.8	12.4	44.4
Hancock	706	14 430	1 067	7 790	1 607	438	220	421	29 167	64	37.5	1.6	43.8
Hardy	256	4 794	262	3 263	386	117	28	92	19 285	467	22.9	15.8	57.8
Harrison	1 956	25 635	4 788	2 305	4 917	786	864	602	23 480	601	23.5	6.0	35.3
Jackson	530	7 391	941	D	1 408	240	147	195	26 347	730	18.9	4.0	36.0
Jefferson	811	9 756	903	2 089	1 726	352	334	194	19 852	357	40.9	10.4	53.2
Kanawha	5 972	93 918	15 399	6 786	14 395	5 784	5 119	2 554	27 192	154	35.1	1.9	29.9
Lewis	396	4 166	1 074	595	877	104	73	84	20 248	364	16.5	10.2	45.6
Lincoln	244	1 548	211	D	373	64	76	30	19 438	214	30.4	3.3	39.7
Logan	865	10 404	2 046	756	2 351	276	363	264	25 342	10	40.0	0.0	20.0
McDowell	441	3 870	824	D	855	170	114	96	24 933	7	42.9	0.0	57.1
Marion	1 305	15 176	2 655	1 462	2 592	659	732	377	24 833	317	19.6	1.6	34.4
Marshall	589	6 678	1 481	584	1 375	265	135	165	24 696	536	16.2	1.5	32.6
Mason	366	5 113	958	1 201	575	154	85	149	29 058	742	22.6	5.1	38.7
Mercer	1 461	20 307	4 836	1 879	3 793	736	585	456	22 463	409	29.3	3.4	39.4
Mineral	471	4 565	869	999	974	127	72	93	20 310	343	22.2	11.1	38.5
Mingo	674	7 229	758	251	921	261	230	220	30 433	5	80.0	0.0	0.0
Monongalia	2 002	28 921	7 507	2 091	4 825	750	984	679	23 490	430	24.9	2.8	33.0
Monroe	207	1 197	210	D	177	54	29	24	19 785	617	18.0	9.9	41.3
Morgan	249	2 243	458	273	357	98	43	45	19 920	161	21.7	5.0	41.0
Nicholas	687	6 520	1 141	841	1 373	155	232	130	19 964	304	28.9	3.0	38.5
Ohio	1 618	26 099	6 460	1 407	2 599	1 274	1 108	597	22 884	136	14.7	3.7	46.3
Pendleton	171	1 658	312	D	216	D	11	29	17 377	590	19.5	17.3	50.8
Pleasants	132	1 686	219	D	235	68	D	52	30 808	132	15.9	6.1	28.8
Pocahontas	253	3 164	303	438	295	44	D	52	16 305	357	14.0	18.5	44.0
Preston	592	4 855	1 011	753	787	172	127	99	20 305	866	20.3	4.5	40.2
Putnam	1 091	12 325	1 254	1 207	2 027	467	460	311	25 241	454	24.7	0.9	37.7
Raleigh	2 035	23 791	4 698	1 077	4 492	710	836	571	24 021	260	33.8	4.2	36.9
Randolph	772	8 206	1 925	1 164	1 320	242	197	156	18 963	396	18.9	16.4	40.7
Ritchie	238	2 399	228	1 190	272	71	36	50	20 952	352	8.8	11.1	39.5
Roane	293	2 733	520	799	465	124	84	50	18 160	454	12.1	6.6	39.0
Summers	202	1 492	470	56	273	80	52	26	17 656	316	19.0	5.7	40.5
Taylor	227	1 949	603	373	287	56	9	38	19 613	278	29.5	6.5	35.6
Tucker	210	2 412	282	335	303	60	10	36	15 012	191	19.9	5.8	39.3
Tyler	157	1 846	281	910	193	55	D	62	33 810	234	13.7	6.8	43.2
Upshur	523	6 232	921	938	850	144	132	116	18 603	399	23.8	4.5	41.1
Wayne	636	7 746	1 512	1 799	1 074	170	147	205	26 431	151	17.9	7.9	35.1
Webster	199	1 836	425	D	206	47	27	48	26 082	74	28.4	0.0	31.1
Wetzel	460	5 271	609	D	961	D	91	170	32 191	260	9.2	3.8	31.9
Wirt	80	351	23	D	D	22	D	5	13 972	199	15.1	6.0	38.7
Wood	2 350	37 199	5 563	7 796	6 013	1 406	1 035	945	25 404	520	21.5	1.3	36.9
Wyoming	448	4 207	549	110	812	113	72	106	25 088	31	38.7	6.5	32.3
WISCONSIN	138 635	2 319 343	291 781	566 219	309 194	126 572	82 860	64 912	27 987	65 602	19.5	9.2	59.5
Adams	278	2 346	408	494	D	D	D	48	20 369	360	15.3	14.7	53.9
Ashland	580	6 787	1 391	1 424	1 024	191	118	150	22 031	186	10.8	9.7	34.9
Barron	1 274	16 788	2 288	5 839	2 922	395	291	349	20 773	1 384	13.5	7.9	65.8
Bayfield	411	2 171	182	178	348	93	22	36	16 383	325	13.8	12.0	51.4
Brown	6 050	121 799	13 473	24 703	15 578	9 556	3 852	3 543	29 087	1 059	31.4	6.2	62.5
Buffalo	344	3 300	396	323	316	131	50	94	28 531	1 000	11.2	17.7	66.5
Burnett	419	3 323	617	1 004	546	100	68	65	19 567	351	12.5	10.3	51.3
Calumet	791	12 298	819	5 724	1 543	311	260	309	25 097	703	23.0	6.5	67.4
Chippewa	1 207	17 406	2 684	5 652	2 730	385	324	407	23 391	1 471	10.7	10.5	70.5
Clark	802	7 948	1 604	2 889	1 012	257	123	158	19 857	1 883	11.3	6.5	74.0
Columbia	1 453	16 733	1 968	4 892	2 393	427	298	393	23 497	1 359	21.5	12.2	58.0
Crawford	376	5 912	1 153	2 049	1 212	137	55	116	19 653	958	12.8	9.3	59.5

STATE County	Acreage (1,000) 117	Percent change, 1992–1997 118	Average size of farm 119	Total irrigated (1,000) 120	Total cropland (1,000) 121	Average per farm ($1,000) 122	Average per acre (dollars) 123	Value of machinery and equipment Average per farm ($1,000) 124	Total (mil dol) 125	Average per farm (dollars) 126	Crops 127	Livestock and poultry products 128	$10,000 or more 129	$100,000 or more 130	Percent of land owned by Fed. Gov. 1997 131	Water consumption 1995 (mil gal/day) 132
WEST VIRGINIA—Cont'd																
Braxton	67	-8.1	240		24	178	770	24	2	6 182	9.9	90.1	10.0	0.0	9.0	5.7
Brooke	14	13.2	143		7	170	1 187	27	1	11 583	30.9	69.2	15.8	3.2	0.0	50.3
Cabell	32	-11.1	105	0	10	136	1 342	19	2	7 421	81.0	19.0	9.8	1.3	0.8	82.5
Calhoun	38	9.8	225		12	160	654	16	1	4 013	8.9	91.3	9.4	0.0	0.0	1.6
Clay	17	15.3	173	D	5	186	1 078	23	1	5 397	24.6	75.2	12.0	0.0	0.0	1.4
Doddridge	71	19.6	234	D	27	142	647	16	1	3 465	18.1	81.9	6.6	0.0	0.0	0.9
Fayette	23	15.3	113	0	10	122	1 093	16	2	7 673	27.9	72.1	12.2	1.5	5.1	33.5
Gilmer	63	19.5	296	0	25	166	572	23	2	9 110	8.7	91.3	18.7	0.5	0.0	1.2
Grant	122	15.1	325	0	34	422	1 141	28	34	91 766	1.2	98.8	38.9	13.9	6.6	1 005.8
Greenbrier	184	2.4	254	0	62	275	1 070	34	40	55 403	2.7	97.3	38.5	7.2	15.4	11.2
Hampshire	140	3.2	257	1	50	353	1 321	34	16	28 719	18.5	81.5	30.7	4.6	0.8	2.7
Hancock	7	-10.8	112	D	3	137	1 228	28	1	9 038	74.2	25.8	17.2	0.0	0.0	175.8
Hardy	143	0.7	306	0	43	423	1 195	43	109	234 392	1.5	98.5	50.1	26.1	13.0	13.5
Harrison	103	15.9	172	0	48	158	1 062	22	5	7 914	14.3	85.7	12.6	1.3	0.0	59.5
Jackson	117	15.5	160	0	48	152	855	20	4	5 975	30.0	70.0	12.7	0.4	0.1	50.5
Jefferson	73	-1.4	204	0	56	716	3 722	45	19	54 375	42.7	57.3	42.3	13.2	2.1	13.7
Kanawha	19	-3.2	126	D	6	214	1 527	16	1	9 213	74.0	25.9	9.1	1.9	0.0	637.6
Lewis	79	-1.9	218	D	33	208	890	28	3	8 230	15.6	84.4	20.9	0.8	6.9	5.6
Lincoln	27	-8.6	128	0	9	102	825	15	1	5 545	85.5	14.5	14.0	0.0	0.0	2.1
Logan	D	D	D	D	D	243	1 789	11	D	D	D	D	20.0	0.0	0.0	6.2
McDowell	0	-51.2	70		0	97	1 393	21	D	D	D	D	28.6	0.0	0.0	7.3
Marion	39	-4.0	124	0	19	148	1 297	16	2	5 139	43.8	56.3	6.9	0.9	0.0	55.6
Marshall	78	22.0	146	0	32	115	777	19	3	5 453	19.0	81.0	8.8	0.9	0.0	750.5
Mason	121	3.0	162	0	49	179	1 120	29	15	20 340	49.3	50.7	19.5	3.1	0.2	661.7
Mercer	53	-6.2	131	0	18	136	883	22	3	6 207	28.0	72.0	12.5	0.7	0.3	21.9
Mineral	80	6.2	232	0	27	193	926	22	8	24 408	8.5	91.5	21.3	4.7	0.8	5.2
Mingo	D	D	D		D	22	925	11	0	1 211	0.0	100.0	0.0	0.0	1.4	6.5
Monongalia	58	5.6	135	0	28	176	1 141	26	3	6 721	18.5	81.5	14.7	0.9	0.2	132.1
Monroe	139	-6.9	225	0	48	208	1 049	26	19	31 315	9.9	90.1	36.0	5.8	6.3	3.4
Morgan	28	28.1	175	0	11	285	1 433	21	1	8 126	63.1	36.9	13.0	1.9	0.0	2.7
Nicholas	40	20.2	130	D	17	174	1 586	29	3	8 363	12.7	87.3	17.4	1.0	7.2	5.2
Ohio	21	0.5	155	D	13	139	882	23	2	13 159	12.7	87.3	16.9	5.1	0.0	43.8
Pendleton	175	-1.5	297	0	45	356	1 134	31	68	114 667	1.1	98.9	43.1	16.1	29.3	4.9
Pleasants	21	33.4	162	D	6	115	740	19	1	5 800	22.2	77.8	11.4	0.8	0.3	123.4
Pocahontas	129	12.1	361	0	38	289	844	30	5	14 401	11.5	88.5	33.1	2.2	51.8	5.1
Preston	152	9.1	175	D	74	169	987	22	11	12 237	22.1	77.9	20.2	2.3	1.0	147.2
Putnam	57	2.0	126	0	21	167	1 426	19	4	9 629	77.9	22.1	13.4	0.7	0.2	70.1
Raleigh	35	7.4	136	D	14	156	1 091	23	2	7 743	38.6	61.4	18.1	0.8	3.1	14.6
Randolph	104	0.1	263	0	36	214	846	31	6	14 258	13.7	86.3	24.2	2.0	30.1	15.1
Ritchie	87	22.5	247	0	35	153	607	21	2	6 376	17.4	82.7	13.1	0.3	0.0	4.0
Roane	93	13.1	204	0	41	141	646	18	3	5 785	11.5	88.5	16.1	0.0	0.0	3.5
Summers	57	-1.4	181	0	20	192	1 013	25	4	11 526	20.5	79.6	15.2	0.0	10.8	1.6
Taylor	44	4.0	157	0	17	199	1 305	25	4	13 218	42.2	57.7	15.8	2.9	2.2	7.3
Tucker	35	9.7	184	D	11	192	1 067	17	1	5 956	19.0	80.9	14.1	0.0	37.4	16.8
Tyler	48	2.2	205	D	20	107	621	16	1	4 764	16.4	83.6	9.4	0.0	0.1	25.0
Upshur	64	9.0	161	D	28	179	984	19	3	6 345	16.5	83.5	17.5	0.0	0.0	3.9
Wayne	29	-1.3	190	0	8	185	1 115	29	1	9 581	45.7	54.3	19.2	0.0	10.9	20.8
Webster	8	-10.6	109	D	3	94	862	22	0	2 620	23.7	76.3	5.4	0.0	18.6	1.7
Wetzel	48	29.1	184	D	13	117	674	15	1	2 826	25.9	74.1	3.5	0.0	0.0	91.8
Wirt	37	3.0	186	0	15	155	895	19	3	13 231	54.2	45.8	15.1	1.0	0.0	2.5
Wood	67	10.9	128	0	29	142	1 105	18	3	5 454	35.3	64.7	8.8	0.6	0.0	168.6
Wyoming	4	-33.7	128	D	1	91	709	13	0	5 797	58.3	41.7	6.5	0.0	5.1	6.5
WISCONSIN	14 900	-3.6	227	342	10 353	282	1 244	67	5 580	85 056	29.4	70.6	61.4	24.0	5.1	7 251.7
Adams	122	2.2	338	42	84	404	1 263	113	58	161 962	90.4	9.6	52.5	19.2	0.2	38.2
Ashland	47	-8.8	250		24	166	621	37	5	26 458	11.0	89.0	31.2	5.9	31.9	34.5
Barron	325	-7.4	235	9	218	197	866	62	165	118 900	14.1	85.9	66.8	26.3	0.0	16.4
Bayfield	84	-14.1	259	0	48	216	925	45	10	30 275	19.6	80.4	41.5	7.7	31.8	5.4
Brown	196	-4.4	185	0	168	333	1 770	74	128	121 309	13.9	86.1	66.8	31.6	0.0	496.5
Buffalo	309	-4.5	309	5	171	224	746	68	102	102 160	15.1	84.9	67.9	27.1	1.9	178.2
Burnett	83	-1.5	236	0	45	200	692	73	14	40 418	39.0	61.0	41.3	12.3	0.9	2.2
Calumet	144	-11.4	204	0	122	272	1 359	84	76	108 086	17.1	82.9	74.0	34.9	0.0	5.9
Chippewa	373	-3.7	253	2	238	199	765	65	119	80 686	15.8	84.2	68.3	26.1	0.0	11.2
Clark	414	-3.1	220	1	289	175	794	58	159	84 511	9.7	90.3	71.9	30.0	0.0	5.1
Columbia	326	-0.4	240	1	253	362	1 514	71	107	78 639	43.2	56.8	66.1	23.8	0.2	17.1
Crawford	233	-6.2	244	0	114	202	820	42	40	41 736	21.5	78.5	58.5	12.5	2.7	2.8

Table B. States and Counties — Residential Construction, Wholesale and Retail Trade, and Real Estate

STATE County	Value of Residential Construction Authorized by Building Permits, 1999		Wholesale Trade, 1997				Retail Trade[1], 1997				Real Estate and Rental and Leasing, 1997			
	New Construction ($1,000)	Number of Housing Units	Number of Establishments	Number of Employees	Sales (mil dol)	Annual Payroll (mil dol)	Number of Establishments	Number of Employees	Sales (mil dol)	Annual Payroll (mil dol)	Number of Establishments	Number of Employees	Receipts (mil dol)	Annual Payroll (mil dol)
	133	134	135	136	137	138	139	140	141	142	143	144	145	146
WEST VIRGINIA—Cont'd														
Braxton	0	0	17	119	38.8	3.5	87	678	111.1	10.2	6	20	1.7	0.4
Brooke	1 826	24	10	D	D	D	86	684	91.3	8.7	9	27	2.5	0.4
Cabell	14 737	183	169	D	D	D	553	7 592	1 120.1	113.1	113	D	D	D
Calhoun	NA	NA	1	D	D	D	29	168	20.7	1.9	4	5	0.2	0.0
Clay	392	36	1	D	D	D	33	208	37.9	2.6	2	D	D	D
Doddridge	NA	NA	2	D	D	D	15	47	7.0	0.6	1	D	D	D
Fayette	7 656	125	29	402	84.6	11.4	206	2 103	328.6	31.3	25	53	6.3	0.6
Gilmer	0	0	5	16	5.7	0.3	25	164	23.4	2.3	2	D	D	D
Grant	3 457	84	8	D	D	D	54	349	53.0	4.9	7	31	2.0	0.5
Greenbrier	9 159	129	32	211	47.0	5.0	217	2 176	329.0	31.1	33	175	10.2	2.7
Hampshire	18 713	119	14	67	11.5	1.2	59	440	67.8	5.9	5	17	0.7	0.1
Hancock	6 753	87	21	133	42.6	3.5	135	1 682	206.0	20.2	27	85	6.5	1.4
Hardy	6 988	114	5	D	D	D	50	426	53.2	6.0	11	19	1.3	0.3
Harrison	13 821	225	91	1 434	452.2	43.2	391	4 956	766.7	70.2	53	154	15.0	2.3
Jackson	4 153	53	28	394	145.5	8.9	115	1 442	293.5	23.2	13	31	3.3	0.3
Jefferson	49 354	466	19	D	D	D	142	1 291	197.7	21.0	32	73	13.2	1.4
Kanawha	21 385	100	388	4 807	2 162.1	146.8	976	14 450	2 428.6	217.7	285	1 575	204.1	32.0
Lewis	258	7	15	125	26.8	2.9	89	946	143.6	12.7	12	29	3.6	1.0
Lincoln	2 918	52	5	D	D	D	51	358	52.3	4.7	5	12	0.6	0.3
Logan	622	23	46	398	158.7	11.4	204	1 996	335.7	31.0	23	87	7.4	1.7
McDowell	283	9	14	102	157.6	3.0	97	860	108.3	11.9	18	55	5.6	1.0
Marion	1 369	20	67	695	154.8	18.3	236	2 567	421.5	35.7	43	144	9.1	1.6
Marshall	2 951	49	21	D	D	D	114	1 523	204.3	18.3	14	D	D	D
Mason	397	5	6	75	47.9	1.9	80	557	79.5	7.2	15	45	4.8	0.7
Mercer	926	13	72	1 265	354.4	31.1	321	3 683	588.2	53.0	42	134	76.7	3.2
Mineral	36 342	306	18	D	D	D	103	982	142.7	12.6	12	34	2.6	0.3
Mingo	430	7	30	234	54.0	5.7	122	1 006	176.1	15.9	16	38	3.1	0.4
Monongalia	5 440	92	81	688	439.0	19.7	373	4 750	677.2	70.5	108	442	41.8	6.2
Monroe	27	1	10	56	14.1	0.9	37	192	27.7	2.1	3	3	0.2	0.0
Morgan	7 905	94	7	D	D	D	53	355	59.7	6.2	5	11	0.7	0.2
Nicholas	676	8	31	255	64.1	5.9	139	1 333	213.7	18.6	20	35	4.0	0.6
Ohio	3 094	22	110	D	D	D	247	2 706	387.0	43.2	59	D	D	D
Pendleton	2 332	38	5	24	2.9	0.3	33	210	29.4	2.8	2	D	D	D
Pleasants	674	10	5	D	D	D	28	248	41.8	3.5	5	18	1.3	0.2
Pocahontas	0	0	4	25	8.7	0.4	55	373	46.4	4.5	8	41	3.1	0.7
Preston	433	4	26	199	97.3	4.7	87	828	147.0	11.6	20	61	3.5	0.8
Putnam	30 474	304	60	1 255	423.2	43.4	201	2 119	365.0	30.1	27	83	9.2	1.0
Raleigh	8 834	85	131	1 146	378.1	32.8	390	4 889	826.8	75.9	92	335	37.0	6.4
Randolph	1 502	39	37	355	152.5	8.6	149	1 343	201.1	18.4	20	80	4.2	0.8
Ritchie	706	14	8	52	11.2	1.2	48	282	42.0	3.7	4	D	D	D
Roane	270	8	10	D	D	D	58	475	75.1	7.1	4	D	D	D
Summers	1 576	21	10	121	29.5	2.4	45	247	36.0	3.9	2	14	0.4	0.1
Taylor	176	3	5	D	D	D	47	318	55.7	4.5	4			
Tucker	459	8	3	D	D	D	38	266	40.9	3.8	8	77	3.1	0.8
Tyler	0	0	2	D	D	D	32	191	25.6	2.1	1	D	D	D
Upshur	4 013	55	20	310	75.7	3.6	101	837	155.2	14.0	14	33	2.5	0.4
Wayne	3 055	65	31	D	D	D	111	1 127	168.5	15.4	21	D	D	D
Webster	0	0	7	D	D	D	32	212	31.2	2.8	2	D	D	D
Wetzel	227	5	14	69	32.7	1.4	112	1 070	145.5	14.1	17	36	5.2	0.8
Wirt	0	0	2	D	D	D	14	72	10.6	0.7	3	4	0.4	0.1
Wood	18 086	223	116	1 357	489.8	34.0	462	6 058	990.2	91.0	76	400	42.1	7.9
Wyoming	0	0	9	53	47.9	1.7	98	759	108.4	11.3	10	62	3.8	1.0
WISCONSIN	3 868 481	35 620	8 025	110 309	57 192.9	3 764.9	21 717	305 255	50 520.5	4 826.2	4 598	23 924	2 637.5	464.1
Adams	20 423	206	11	146	28.0	2.8	37	327	64.7	5.5	9	D	D	D
Ashland	4 747	44	18	130	40.5	3.3	113	1 041	149.7	13.4	11	36	2.1	0.4
Barron	24 647	294	66	763	153.8	17.6	254	2 812	451.6	41.9	30	84	8.6	1.3
Bayfield	11 873	142	7	36	5.6	0.8	66	328	51.0	4.2	8	25	1.7	0.3
Brown	226 633	1 930	461	6 480	2 848.1	212.1	950	14 976	2 569.1	239.7	197	1 048	116.3	18.7
Buffalo	8 039	80	17	180	47.6	4.2	46	305	45.7	3.8	6	17	0.7	0.1
Burnett	24 827	265	9	20	10.2	0.5	71	530	77.1	7.6	10	D	D	D
Calumet	49 957	482	45	474	98.6	12.1	106	1 615	232.7	20.1	18	56	3.2	0.3
Chippewa	46 681	474	49	654	237.4	21.7	205	2 475	481.3	39.9	26	87	5.2	0.8
Clark	10 953	119	51	278	71.3	6.6	137	1 071	198.0	16.1	13	27	1.9	0.4
Columbia	42 300	389	64	735	352.5	18.5	228	2 434	407.4	37.7	32	55	7.1	1.0
Crawford	2 943	36	19	118	220.9	3.9	88	915	133.6	12.3	16	D	D	D

1. Establishments with payroll.

Table B. States and Counties — Professional, Manufacturing, and Accommodation and Foodservices

STATE County	Professional, Scientific, and Technical Services[1], 1997				Manufacturing, 1997				Accommodation and Foodservices, 1997			
	Number of Establishments	Number of Employees	Receipts (mil dol)	Annual Payroll (mil dol)	Number of Establishments	Number of Employees	Receipts (mil dol)	Annual Payroll (mil dol)	Number of Establishments	Number of Employees	Sales (mil dol)	Annual Payroll (mil dol)
	147	148	149	150	151	152	153	154	155	156	157	158
WEST VIRGINIA—Cont'd												
Braxton	17	49	2.4	0.6	NA	NA	NA	NA	32	444	14.3	4.0
Brooke	18	85	4.5	1.5	22	1 275	637.6	49.6	58	D	D	D
Cabell	179	1 206	76.3	27.7	112	5 766	1 199.5	199.9	253	4 933	140.9	39.3
Calhoun	5	16	0.6	0.2	NA	NA	NA	NA	5	88	3.9	0.7
Clay	3	D	D	D	NA	NA	NA	NA	7	12	0.5	0.1
Doddridge	3	3	0.1	0.0	NA	NA	NA	NA	4	D	D	D
Fayette	46	200	11.9	4.2	34	807	169.4	27.5	65	918	27.9	8.5
Gilmer	6	37	2.1	0.5	NA	NA	NA	NA	11	92	2.5	0.6
Grant	14	34	2.1	0.7	18	929	106.2	15.6	21	166	4.4	1.0
Greenbrier	48	123	8.1	2.4	38	923	99.7	26.2	78	2 098	118.4	41.8
Hampshire	15	48	2.0	0.7	NA	NA	NA	NA	32	311	11.2	3.3
Hancock	47	190	20.1	4.6	37	8 011	2 105.3	330.3	84	D	D	D
Hardy	10	24	1.8	0.3	20	2 940	435.6	57.7	21	341	7.5	2.0
Harrison	115	836	61.4	21.7	68	2 022	394.0	72.7	151	2 340	73.0	20.6
Jackson	25	90	5.8	2.3	16	D	D	D	36	637	20.1	5.2
Jefferson	53	283	16.1	8.4	26	2 172	444.1	60.1	82	1 114	37.6	10.2
Kanawha	525	4 387	384.5	125.5	141	6 590	3 071.3	273.3	420	8 287	280.7	75.9
Lewis	14	77	5.0	1.2	18	538	52.6	13.5	30	341	12.4	3.3
Lincoln	15	78	4.4	2.0	NA	NA	NA	NA	11	D	D	D
Logan	45	341	16.2	7.0	39	853	82.6	20.2	63	751	24.0	6.1
McDowell	22	128	6.4	2.0	NA	NA	NA	NA	17	176	5.6	1.4
Marion	80	581	48.0	17.8	62	1 501	347.0	42.0	96	1 295	36.9	10.5
Marshall	24	100	9.6	3.4	NA	NA	NA	NA	61	661	19.6	5.5
Mason	22	68	3.8	1.1	16	1 173	466.3	47.1	30	307	7.6	2.1
Mercer	81	543	37.7	11.0	56	1 908	298.5	61.8	100	2 010	64.3	17.1
Mineral	20	66	3.1	0.7	16	1 138	136.3	40.4	48	486	13.2	3.4
Mingo	56	248	12.0	4.0	NA	NA	NA	NA	42	346	10.8	3.1
Monongalia	143	902	70.8	23.0	58	2 055	598.0	77.8	207	3 795	95.5	28.4
Monroe	9	10	0.8	0.1	NA	NA	NA	NA	13	D	D	D
Morgan	10	20	1.5	0.4	NA	NA	NA	NA	20	375	11.8	4.2
Nicholas	45	197	9.9	3.4	27	768	123.1	18.2	45	590	18.6	5.3
Ohio	115	923	81.0	23.4	58	D	D	D	148	2 136	60.3	17.5
Pendleton	6	7	0.5	0.1	7	595	47.3	10.4	11	105	2.7	0.7
Pleasants	7	20	0.5	0.1	6	D	D	D	11	127	3.6	1.1
Pocahontas	4	7	0.5	0.1	NA	NA	NA	NA	29	1 011	40.3	11.0
Preston	33	112	5.5	1.9	28	664	69.0	14.1	30	244	6.7	1.7
Putnam	66	414	26.1	9.9	35	1 091	234.0	38.5	67	1 050	32.2	8.5
Raleigh	116	765	53.4	23.2	56	999	164.9	32.6	140	2 489	84.4	23.3
Randolph	47	185	9.2	3.7	29	1 397	169.4	27.3	62	876	23.6	6.6
Ritchie	10	32	1.7	0.3	21	1 035	116.6	27.2	10	97	2.2	0.5
Roane	16	76	3.7	1.3	18	790	170.4	12.9	14	133	4.5	1.3
Summers	8	53	3.2	0.5	NA	NA	NA	NA	18	202	7.4	2.2
Taylor	7	10	0.5	0.1	NA	NA	NA	NA	15	119	3.6	0.9
Tucker	7	17	0.9	0.3	NA	NA	NA	NA	28	326	11.8	3.5
Tyler	7	13	0.6	0.2	12	D	D	D	15	D	D	D
Upshur	32	119	6.9	2.5	26	947	152.5	22.5	42	552	13.7	4.2
Wayne	23	132	8.1	3.3	33	1 770	325.0	47.3	49	443	12.4	3.4
Webster	7	25	1.3	0.3	NA	NA	NA	NA	12	D	D	D
Wetzel	17	87	4.8	1.5	18	D	D	D	42	420	12.3	3.6
Wirt	4	D	D	D	NA	NA	NA	NA	4	13	0.6	0.1
Wood	134	885	59.0	20.6	78	7 010	2 301.9	293.3	198	3 767	110.7	32.1
Wyoming	23	83	4.6	1.6	NA	NA	NA	NA	29	267	8.2	1.8
WISCONSIN	9 281	70 689	6 398.9	2 542.3	9 936	562 479	117 383.0	18 766.4	13 252	190 411	5 641.0	1 548.5
Adams	16	38	1.7	0.7	NA	NA	NA	NA	42	416	14.6	4.0
Ashland	30	102	5.9	2.3	28	1 661	150.7	44.8	73	753	20.8	5.7
Barron	46	230	13.8	5.8	96	5 430	891.5	133.9	146	1 395	39.5	10.4
Bayfield	13	22	1.9	0.5	NA	NA	NA	NA	92	620	22.2	5.5
Brown	373	3 348	270.8	118.7	396	25 825	6 457.4	1 015.7	533	10 183	283.4	81.9
Buffalo	19	39	1.6	0.6	NA	NA	NA	NA	45	D	D	D
Burnett	15	48	2.4	0.9	32	1 106	176.7	30.3	66	D	D	D
Calumet	33	258	18.3	10.2	64	6 078	1 018.9	190.9	75	932	24.9	6.4
Chippewa	54	230	17.0	7.1	112	6 442	989.8	203.7	132	1 322	34.3	8.5
Clark	30	78	4.1	1.5	87	2 863	799.6	70.7	66	D	D	D
Columbia	70	247	20.2	6.0	108	5 311	1 262.4	159.1	190	1 717	62.3	15.1
Crawford	11	38	1.9	1.2	20	2 252	509.1	50.8	54	614	15.7	4.3

1. Firms subject to federal tax.

Table B. States and Counties — **Health and Other Services and Federal Funds**

STATE County	Health Care and Social Assistance[1], 1997				Other Services[1], 1997				Federal funds and grants, fiscal 1999[2] Expenditures (mil dol)			
										Direct payments for individuals[3]		
	Number of Establishments	Number of Employees	Receipts (mil dol)	Annual Payroll (mil dol)	Number of Establishments	Number of Employees	Receipts (mil dol)	Annual Payroll (mil dol)	Total	Social Security and government retirement	Medicare	Food stamps and Supplemental Security Income
	159	160	161	162	163	164	165	166	167	168	169	170
WEST VIRGINIA—Cont'd												
Braxton	12	140	4.4	1.8	14	43	3.1	1.0	83.8	30.0	10.4	5.7
Brooke	50	713	30.7	13.6	30	128	4.8	1.5	100.6	53.4	25.2	5.4
Cabell	238	3 609	273.0	129.9	166	1 249	58.1	20.3	569.6	257.4	86.3	29.8
Calhoun	4	18	1.0	0.3	8	32	1.0	0.3	44.2	16.4	7.5	3.5
Clay	4	75	3.5	1.0	7	45	3.5	1.4	56.2	21.9	8.6	6.3
Doddridge	2	D	D	D	3	D	D	D	26.6	11.8	4.1	2.2
Fayette	64	1 298	62.5	22.6	53	244	17.5	4.6	291.7	137.1	57.3	16.9
Gilmer	6	95	3.9	1.1	6	14	0.8	0.1	135.9	14.7	6.0	3.2
Grant	15	77	4.1	1.3	18	59	3.1	0.9	55.0	21.9	7.6	2.3
Greenbrier	82	1 659	106.4	44.2	65	178	8.5	2.1	196.0	94.6	33.2	9.7
Hampshire	19	327	13.6	5.1	20	49	3.0	0.7	114.9	40.6	13.0	4.2
Hancock	71	814	36.7	16.6	46	218	10.9	2.9	164.2	93.8	46.4	3.9
Hardy	12	104	4.4	1.7	16	40	2.4	0.5	58.1	24.4	7.2	2.0
Harrison	169	1 976	101.3	39.1	115	527	28.0	8.4	400.6	178.1	67.0	21.3
Jackson	35	411	17.7	5.8	34	83	4.5	1.3	125.9	59.4	20.4	7.3
Jefferson	46	297	13.5	5.8	42	187	8.3	2.5	208.5	89.1	22.0	4.7
Kanawha	555	6 286	513.0	210.2	340	2 361	129.6	39.8	1 573.6	541.8	200.4	51.1
Lewis	27	412	29.3	9.4	34	88	5.3	1.3	89.3	41.3	16.7	5.7
Lincoln	8	122	5.5	2.4	20	71	3.7	1.4	116.9	46.8	16.6	12.7
Logan	51	551	31.1	13.4	68	493	43.3	11.9	240.4	115.9	44.2	18.1
McDowell	24	213	10.4	3.9	21	70	5.2	1.4	250.5	98.9	36.1	26.7
Marion	101	1 028	73.3	30.7	105	564	32.2	9.3	345.2	154.7	54.1	16.0
Marshall	57	790	34.0	14.3	31	178	8.8	3.0	144.7	79.0	29.1	6.8
Mason	31	220	13.8	5.1	27	98	5.5	1.6	120.2	55.6	20.9	7.7
Mercer	174	1 620	126.4	55.8	105	997	57.2	19.9	366.9	180.9	71.1	24.0
Mineral	37	548	28.4	10.1	38	128	7.1	2.0	135.2	62.9	27.6	5.5
Mingo	48	574	44.6	14.9	30	149	8.5	2.7	199.5	83.5	27.7	19.3
Monongalia	146	2 716	186.2	92.2	138	1 163	71.2	21.8	426.2	124.9	48.8	12.4
Monroe	5	103	3.6	1.5	8	12	1.4	0.3	83.4	34.7	13.3	4.7
Morgan	11	253	8.8	3.7	12	27	2.1	0.5	56.2	36.3	9.6	2.1
Nicholas	41	365	20.7	6.7	36	167	9.2	2.8	135.8	67.9	22.2	9.1
Ohio	179	1 592	107.0	45.0	104	855	44.7	15.1	300.2	124.5	53.0	11.0
Pendleton	9	56	1.6	0.5	7	19	1.0	0.2	53.4	17.7	6.7	1.4
Pleasants	11	207	5.0	2.2	6	52	4.7	1.1	29.8	15.9	6.1	1.5
Pocahontas	16	174	6.0	2.0	10	19	1.2	0.2	94.4	21.7	9.6	1.9
Preston	25	320	13.6	5.3	40	130	9.0	1.8	142.8	66.3	22.8	7.8
Putnam	63	918	63.5	20.7	49	243	12.9	4.2	154.9	83.7	25.3	6.8
Raleigh	209	3 068	227.3	79.9	120	697	42.8	13.3	474.2	219.8	74.4	25.4
Randolph	71	685	33.7	11.9	35	127	6.2	1.5	185.8	67.4	25.7	8.5
Ritchie	8	156	5.6	2.3	9	24	1.6	0.3	70.9	22.8	8.2	2.9
Roane	13	167	7.1	3.0	7	17	1.5	0.4	75.8	30.8	12.7	6.3
Summers	15	171	7.3	2.5	13	38	2.1	0.7	86.8	36.0	12.3	5.0
Taylor	15	183	7.2	3.8	16	64	3.3	0.8	68.5	34.7	11.4	4.4
Tucker	5	16	0.9	0.2	10	24	1.7	0.3	41.7	18.6	5.4	1.4
Tyler	7	96	2.5	0.8	10	28	1.7	0.4	37.8	19.2	6.7	2.1
Upshur	35	404	18.4	7.2	19	98	4.7	1.6	102.1	48.9	14.8	8.2
Wayne	27	229	10.1	4.3	51	296	20.5	5.3	224.3	75.5	25.1	15.7
Webster	9	108	3.3	1.3	6	18	1.3	0.2	62.0	25.2	9.5	6.0
Wetzel	32	306	13.8	5.0	28	97	4.0	1.0	92.8	46.0	15.3	6.3
Wirt	2	D	D	D	3	D	D	D	26.9	11.5	4.2	2.1
Wood	194	2 376	152.9	64.5	165	1 656	119.1	28.9	490.6	198.5	79.1	20.0
Wyoming	25	220	10.9	4.5	19	86	4.4	1.3	157.4	78.0	24.2	13.7
WISCONSIN	9 315	114 562	6 917.4	3 447.3	8 648	49 101	2 991.3	886.4	22 603.8	9 219.4	3 223.3	519.8
Adams	13	71	3.4	1.4	12	38	2.2	0.6	86.4	33.9	12.0	2.1
Ashland	41	778	33.6	19.7	31	91	5.7	1.4	89.4	38.1	14.5	1.7
Barron	73	879	37.9	17.7	89	303	17.2	4.5	181.2	89.2	27.1	4.4
Bayfield	13	D	D	D	12	28	1.5	0.4	72.1	32.1	10.3	1.8
Brown	380	5 467	359.7	190.1	391	2 650	143.4	46.4	731.8	322.6	94.0	18.0
Buffalo	15	169	10.6	5.1	21	38	3.0	0.5	66.2	27.3	8.4	1.1
Burnett	13	83	3.8	2.1	23	57	4.4	0.9	69.6	36.7	10.2	1.5
Calumet	50	450	21.5	10.2	48	130	8.1	2.1	81.0	42.7	14.3	0.8
Chippewa	77	1 130	46.0	21.5	74	283	20.1	5.0	201.1	99.8	34.6	4.5
Clark	39	364	12.2	5.5	51	127	9.3	1.4	128.2	59.2	25.8	1.8
Columbia	89	846	42.7	17.8	86	320	20.6	5.6	248.7	107.3	38.0	3.3
Crawford	28	590	19.2	9.9	22	87	4.9	1.1	71.8	32.2	10.6	1.6

1. Firms subject to federal tax.   2. October 1, 1998 to September 30, 1999.   3. State totals may include programs not allocated by county.

Table B. States and Counties — Federal Funds and Local Government Finances

	Federal funds and grants, fiscal 1999[1] (cont'd)							Local government finances, 1997				
	Expenditures (mil dol) (cont'd)							General revenue				
	Procurement contract awards			Grants[2]							Taxes	
											Per capita[3] (dollars)	
STATE County	Salaries and wages	Defense	Other	Medicaid and other health-related	Nutrition and family welfare	Education	Other	Total (mil dol)	Intergovern-mental (mil dol)	Total (mil dol)	Total	Property
	171	172	173	174	175	176	177	178	179	180	181	182
WEST VIRGINIA—Cont'd												
Braxton	2.6	0.1	0.5	17.5	2.3	1.1	13.6	23.0	14.1	3.5	266	243
Brooke	2.4	0.0	0.6	7.3	2.0	1.2	1.9	37.7	17.7	13.7	523	458
Cabell	49.4	1.7	15.7	59.3	13.9	5.7	33.5	180.6	76.8	66.4	698	514
Calhoun	1.1	0.0	0.3	12.3	1.1	0.8	0.9	10.5	7.5	1.7	213	208
Clay	1.4	0.0	0.4	13.3	2.6	1.1	0.7	17.1	11.6	2.5	236	231
Doddridge	0.8	0.0	0.2	5.7	0.8	0.5	0.5	10.3	6.4	3.0	412	407
Fayette	14.2	0.3	2.5	40.5	8.4	4.2	7.6	71.5	38.3	20.1	414	362
Gilmer	1.3	0.0	96.8	8.7	1.0	1.0	1.6	10.5	6.6	3.2	452	434
Grant	2.6	4.1	0.4	9.7	2.1	0.5	3.1	44.0	9.1	5.8	521	510
Greenbrier	6.1	6.9	3.3	26.9	3.2	1.7	9.6	56.7	28.0	11.6	326	299
Hampshire	2.5	0.1	35.8	12.1	1.4	0.9	3.2	22.7	15.1	5.5	293	283
Hancock	3.8	0.2	1.1	8.2	2.9	1.3	2.9	61.7	23.1	22.9	665	542
Hardy	2.6	1.1	0.7	12.1	0.8	0.5	6.0	18.0	10.9	4.8	405	383
Harrison	54.4	2.1	15.9	35.8	9.1	4.6	7.7	139.5	61.8	48.5	686	552
Jackson	4.3	0.0	13.4	14.4	2.6	1.5	1.5	49.5	27.0	14.3	517	470
Jefferson	33.2	5.9	20.8	10.4	2.0	1.3	15.6	54.6	24.7	21.8	545	506
Kanawha	140.2	3.0	45.9	144.9	116.1	72.9	235.1	421.7	148.8	169.3	831	606
Lewis	3.3	0.0	0.7	17.3	1.9	1.1	0.9	24.1	14.2	6.5	370	340
Lincoln	2.4	0.0	0.6	29.9	4.8	2.5	0.4	32.1	24.6	5.5	247	244
Logan	6.7	0.0	1.6	32.4	8.1	4.3	6.1	63.5	42.8	16.3	395	368
McDowell	4.7	11.6	1.1	49.0	12.1	4.1	4.8	47.0	33.8	10.1	329	290
Marion	10.5	22.8	26.4	26.3	10.2	6.5	12.4	174.8	45.2	27.7	487	410
Marshall	5.1	0.0	0.9	12.9	3.7	1.9	4.6	78.2	27.9	21.5	604	518
Mason	7.5	4.3	1.1	16.3	3.7	1.6	0.2	46.1	20.4	13.0	500	467
Mercer	14.7	0.0	3.1	47.3	10.5	7.8	3.6	151.9	53.0	24.8	385	301
Mineral	3.2	15.9	1.0	11.4	2.9	1.9	1.4	45.9	32.2	10.0	371	344
Mingo	4.7	5.7	1.5	35.2	9.7	3.0	8.4	58.8	33.9	17.2	529	473
Monongalia	76.9	3.5	60.4	29.6	5.3	7.5	45.5	126.2	47.7	44.2	571	464
Monroe	12.8	0.0	1.0	13.8	1.4	0.8	0.3	13.5	10.2	2.3	174	162
Morgan	1.4	0.0	0.4	4.0	0.7	0.5	1.0	27.3	11.3	5.8	431	407
Nicholas	5.3	0.3	1.1	16.1	4.2	2.0	7.4	64.9	26.8	12.5	454	339
Ohio	23.5	3.3	10.9	23.4	7.3	2.2	34.0	89.5	35.0	29.2	597	390
Pendleton	10.7	4.7	0.5	7.9	0.6	0.5	2.2	12.3	9.5	2.0	255	243
Pleasants	0.8	0.0	0.2	3.5	0.7	0.4	0.1	31.4	6.0	7.9	1 052	1 013
Pocahontas	2.4	1.6	2.0	7.6	0.9	0.5	45.8	18.4	9.1	3.3	360	287
Preston	6.4	0.1	4.5	18.6	3.3	1.9	9.9	38.4	26.1	7.5	251	237
Putnam	7.8	0.1	1.8	14.1	3.0	1.8	9.3	77.2	36.1	23.0	457	430
Raleigh	69.0	0.5	14.8	43.5	10.6	4.5	7.6	146.2	83.1	36.0	455	355
Randolph	11.8	0.0	2.0	24.8	3.1	2.8	37.8	43.2	29.9	6.9	241	193
Ritchie	1.6	0.0	21.9	7.9	0.9	0.9	3.4	13.9	9.0	3.6	350	343
Roane	2.1	0.0	0.5	13.6	2.0	1.6	5.7	21.8	15.8	3.9	254	224
Summers	2.1	1.2	1.5	18.1	2.2	0.9	7.3	16.6	13.1	2.6	190	144
Taylor	2.5	0.6	0.5	10.0	2.0	1.1	0.8	28.0	18.6	5.7	368	322
Tucker	2.6	0.0	0.8	6.4	0.6	0.5	5.3	15.0	8.2	3.4	444	382
Tyler	1.2	0.0	0.3	4.6	1.0	0.6	1.9	20.5	9.6	5.3	524	509
Upshur	4.6	0.8	0.8	13.3	3.3	1.5	4.5	32.9	21.5	5.9	249	227
Wayne	38.4	0.7	1.9	42.9	4.7	2.6	13.7	71.9	44.3	17.2	408	382
Webster	1.1	0.0	0.6	15.7	2.1	1.2	0.2	15.2	10.7	3.5	338	318
Wetzel	2.9	0.4	0.8	13.9	2.3	1.1	2.6	48.6	18.4	10.9	588	504
Wirt	0.8	0.9	0.2	4.7	0.7	0.3	1.4	8.5	6.2	1.6	287	276
Wood	83.3	1.6	12.3	38.5	9.9	4.2	38.8	210.6	64.6	45.3	521	410
Wyoming	5.0	0.1	1.3	21.9	6.9	2.6	2.7	43.2	28.6	11.0	398	372
WISCONSIN	1 513.6	643.8	789.6	2 211.9	984.2	443.2	1 202.5	X	X	X	X	X
Adams	19.7	0.0	1.0	9.9	2.1	0.7	2.3	39.2	18.7	15.8	868	819
Ashland	6.7	4.0	3.5	12.2	3.2	1.6	2.5	55.1	36.3	11.4	694	631
Barron	7.5	0.1	3.1	24.9	10.1	2.2	3.6	123.6	71.0	31.5	720	656
Bayfield	4.8	0.0	3.4	8.8	2.9	2.2	4.2	46.8	25.1	15.4	1 012	954
Brown	56.6	8.4	107.0	56.7	20.5	8.9	24.5	633.5	278.0	208.0	971	946
Buffalo	5.9	0.2	3.6	6.4	1.6	0.5	5.4	34.9	23.1	8.8	622	585
Burnett	1.8	2.5	0.5	8.3	2.2	0.8	3.4	36.8	19.8	12.5	859	806
Calumet	8.2	0.0	1.3	4.6	1.7	0.8	1.3	66.7	33.8	20.6	540	529
Chippewa	10.1	0.9	3.8	22.0	6.7	2.6	8.0	128.7	82.0	32.3	596	541
Clark	5.4	0.2	2.1	15.6	3.3	1.8	4.4	100.2	56.8	20.1	611	600
Columbia	10.0	2.6	49.6	15.3	9.0	1.9	0.7	152.0	73.7	51.8	1 028	949
Crawford	3.6	0.4	1.0	10.6	2.2	1.0	4.8	45.2	27.2	11.5	696	633

1. October 1, 1998 to September 30, 1999.   2. State totals may include programs not allocated by county.   3. Based on the resident population estimated as of July 1 of the year shown.

STATE County	Local government finances, 1997 (cont'd)									Government employment, 1998			Presidential election, 2000		
	Direct general expenditure							Debt outstanding		Federal civilian	Federal military	State and local	Percent of vote cast —		
	Total (mil dol)	Per capita[1] (dollars)	Percent of total for —					Total (mil dol)	Per capita[1] (dollars)				Demo-cratic	Republi-can	All other
			Educa-tion	Health and hospitals	Police protec-tion	Public welfare	High-ways								
	183	184	185	186	187	188	189	190	191	192	193	194	195	196	197
WEST VIRGINIA—Cont'd															
Braxton	22.3	1 674	71.1	1.2	1.0	0.0	0.4	92.7	6 973	57	66	763	51.0	47.5	1.5
Brooke	37.4	1 424	68.7	4.1	3.9	0.0	2.9	24.7	941	44	130	995	49.7	44.6	5.7
Cabell	175.8	1 849	54.8	2.6	4.7	0.0	1.5	127.2	1 338	1 119	507	6 538	46.2	51.0	2.7
Calhoun	13.8	1 751	87.9	0.1	1.0	0.0	0.4	3.9	496	21	40	364	42.5	54.5	3.0
Clay	17.0	1 621	72.5	14.2	0.8	0.0	0.2	1.2	119	28	53	563	45.1	52.7	2.2
Doddridge	10.1	1 363	85.9	3.9	0.6	0.0	0.4	0.0	0	14	38	308	27.5	69.4	3.1
Fayette	70.2	1 449	68.7	0.5	3.5	0.0	1.5	103.2	2 131	290	240	3 345	57.3	40.3	2.4
Gilmer	10.7	1 492	75.6	2.3	2.0	0.0	0.6	0.4	53	27	36	715	39.9	56.9	3.2
Grant	46.0	4 152	23.2	46.5	0.8	0.0	0.2	166.9	15 052	62	56	919	19.7	78.8	1.6
Greenbrier	52.9	1 491	62.3	3.5	3.3	0.0	1.3	69.3	1 953	129	177	2 140	43.9	53.6	2.5
Hampshire	23.2	1 226	82.6	1.2	1.6	0.0	0.7	7.0	373	45	95	1 087	33.9	63.6	2.4
Hancock	58.7	1 703	48.8	0.7	5.3	0.0	4.2	96.2	2 789	76	170	1 366	46.4	47.9	5.7
Hardy	19.6	1 660	78.4	1.4	3.0	0.0	1.7	3.4	291	72	59	530	35.9	62.4	1.7
Harrison	134.7	1 904	58.1	2.1	3.9	0.0	2.2	181.1	2 561	4 236	357	3 575	48.9	48.7	2.3
Jackson	47.1	1 710	68.3	5.8	2.6	0.0	0.4	27.3	991	81	140	1 354	42.9	55.1	2.1
Jefferson	49.3	1 230	73.9	1.5	3.7	0.1	0.6	43.3	1 081	620	207	2 317	47.7	49.0	3.3
Kanawha	398.8	1 958	48.2	3.2	4.7	0.0	2.1	479.0	2 352	2 463	1 106	18 776	50.2	48.0	1.7
Lewis	23.3	1 330	72.7	7.6	2.5	0.0	1.1	1.1	65	65	87	1 427	38.4	58.8	2.8
Lincoln	30.2	1 359	87.4	0.7	0.5	0.0	0.0	7.2	322	49	111	889	52.8	45.4	1.8
Logan	62.2	1 505	83.1	2.5	2.2	0.0	0.7	6.4	154	132	206	2 003	61.8	36.9	1.2
McDowell	45.6	1 490	84.1	0.5	2.1	0.0	0.9	0.4	12	97	150	1 949	53.8	43.6	2.6
Marion	171.4	3 013	33.5	0.9	1.7	0.0	0.9	502.8	8 840	180	282	4 012	44.5	50.8	4.7
Marshall	77.5	2 172	49.8	0.8	2.9	0.0	1.1	318.8	8 929	75	193	1 928	44.2	53.2	2.6
Mason	45.4	1 747	63.4	0.8	2.1	0.0	1.0	73.9	2 845	175	130	1 248	66.3	32.2	1.5
Mercer	159.4	2 478	39.4	34.6	2.0	0.0	0.9	105.9	1 646	296	321	4 463	44.2	54.1	1.7
Mineral	46.2	1 723	79.9	0.9	1.6	0.0	1.0	9.2	342	72	134	1 419	34.2	63.2	2.7
Mingo	55.1	1 693	75.9	1.3	2.3	0.0	0.5	16.5	506	99	160	1 482	60.2	38.5	1.3
Monongalia	123.0	1 587	55.9	4.5	3.7	0.1	1.6	212.0	2 736	1 393	415	14 887	46.1	49.7	4.3
Monroe	13.4	1 019	86.7	1.0	1.9	0.0	0.3	2.9	218	230	66	477	40.7	57.2	2.0
Morgan	27.7	2 056	54.6	29.6	1.2	0.0	0.1	7.9	583	25	68	763	33.6	63.0	3.4
Nicholas	64.3	2 332	48.3	32.9	3.4	0.9	1.5	13.6	492	124	138	1 685	47.3	50.8	1.9
Ohio	79.0	1 616	51.3	1.5	5.7	0.0	3.0	119.2	2 439	457	243	3 592	42.6	53.5	3.9
Pendleton	11.8	1 474	79.6	2.6	1.2	0.0	0.1	1.6	198	173	227	353	36.4	62.0	1.6
Pleasants	31.3	4 186	36.1	0.3	1.0	0.0	0.4	220.0	29 382	14	37	502	39.5	58.7	1.8
Pocahontas	19.7	2 176	49.5	23.2	1.4	0.0	0.5	8.3	917	75	46	763	40.1	56.8	3.0
Preston	38.3	1 287	76.9	1.1	2.6	0.0	0.8	7.4	249	90	149	1 540	33.7	63.3	3.0
Putnam	75.2	1 498	68.8	2.4	2.3	0.0	0.4	144.2	2 873	168	256	2 080	38.6	59.6	1.8
Raleigh	122.5	1 551	69.3	0.7	4.0	0.0	2.1	58.3	738	1 414	596	3 609	45.9	52.3	1.8
Randolph	42.6	1 479	66.2	3.5	1.9	0.0	1.6	10.3	358	292	144	1 816	42.2	55.0	2.8
Ritchie	14.0	1 362	82.9	0.1	1.7	0.0	0.8	0.1	14	31	52	500	26.9	71.3	1.9
Roane	21.8	1 422	79.0	0.1	1.7	0.0	1.0	15.1	987	36	77	643	41.5	56.4	2.2
Summers	16.6	1 208	68.9	1.2	1.7	0.4	0.9	0.5	33	40	66	757	48.8	48.9	2.3
Taylor	26.8	1 747	74.2	3.5	1.4	0.0	1.4	11.9	774	45	77	1 086	43.3	54.7	2.0
Tucker	14.7	1 903	56.7	0.8	1.8	0.0	1.2	3.6	472	67	38	660	39.4	57.8	2.7
Tyler	17.7	1 761	72.4	12.0	1.5	0.0	0.8	10.5	1 044	26	49	506	30.9	65.7	3.4
Upshur	35.1	1 474	67.7	0.7	1.6	0.0	0.9	13.3	558	112	118	1 189	34.1	63.6	2.3
Wayne	70.8	1 682	77.0	1.4	1.5	0.0	0.4	26.4	627	944	210	2 192	48.9	49.2	1.9
Webster	15.0	1 454	76.0	1.4	1.3	0.0	0.8	0.5	45	22	51	627	53.3	44.9	1.8
Wetzel	44.6	2 411	49.6	34.7	2.4	0.0	1.3	33.4	1 807	55	91	1 107	45.3	51.5	3.2
Wirt	8.2	1 454	86.0	0.0	0.6	0.0	0.5	1.3	223	15	28	261	34.3	63.7	1.9
Wood	202.4	2 325	43.4	36.6	3.1	0.0	2.0	118.6	1 362	1 901	436	4 092	37.4	60.3	2.3
Wyoming	42.7	1 543	83.2	0.5	3.0	0.1	0.7	1.3	47	97	137	1 219	54.4	44.1	1.5
WISCONSIN	X	X	X	X	X	X	X	X	X	29 494	19 338	344 990	47.8	47.6	4.6
Adams	47.1	2 595	45.8	3.7	4.8	4.8	14.4	37.0	2 039	359	65	725	52.9	43.0	4.1
Ashland	58.0	3 516	43.9	2.2	3.9	8.1	14.8	44.5	2 696	175	58	1 317	55.2	38.5	6.3
Barron	130.1	2 979	50.6	5.3	3.3	6.8	15.4	77.5	1 776	158	156	3 193	44.9	49.5	5.7
Bayfield	45.7	2 999	39.5	8.2	3.5	3.9	19.6	24.0	1 579	139	65	898	53.6	39.5	6.9
Brown	651.6	3 041	47.2	4.7	5.2	5.1	7.9	515.0	2 404	985	814	12 264	45.6	50.3	4.1
Buffalo	37.0	2 608	50.2	3.6	2.5	5.7	21.3	10.6	748	180	50	773	48.7	45.7	5.5
Burnett	40.0	2 752	44.6	4.8	2.7	6.2	18.0	18.1	1 247	40	52	718	44.5	48.7	6.8
Calumet	75.0	1 971	39.6	4.1	4.4	8.5	14.3	33.5	880	110	135	1 206	41.1	54.3	4.6
Chippewa	131.7	2 428	50.2	6.7	4.8	3.6	15.4	72.1	1 329	215	194	3 479	46.2	49.0	4.7
Clark	107.4	3 256	47.8	6.5	3.2	14.9	10.8	52.3	1 584	113	117	1 973	41.9	52.7	5.4
Columbia	175.5	3 485	53.0	2.1	3.4	7.3	13.6	116.5	2 313	191	181	3 190	49.4	46.8	3.8
Crawford	49.5	2 989	44.5	1.9	6.3	10.2	15.1	44.1	2 662	72	58	832	54.2	40.9	4.9

1. Based on the resident population estimated as of July 1 of the year shown.

STATE/ County code	MSA/ PMSA/ NECMA code[1]	County Type[2]	STATE County	Land area,[3] (sq km) 1990	Total persons	Rank	Per square kilometer	White	Black	Am. Indian, Eskimo, Aleut	Asian and Pacific Islander	Percent Hispanic[4]	Under 5 years	5 to 17 years	18 to 24 years	25 to 34 years	35 to 44 years	45 to 54 years
					1	2	3	4	5	6	7	9	10	11	12	13	14	15
			WISCONSIN—Cont'd															
55 025	4720	2	Dane	3 114	428 563	136	137.6	92.7	3.6	0.4	3.3	2.3	6.1	16.1	14.3	15.8	18.6	12.6
55 027	...	4	Dodge	2 285	83 494	607	36.5	97.4	1.8	0.4	0.4	1.9	6.2	20.0	8.0	13.6	16.6	13.9
55 029	...	7	Door	1 250	27 079	1 461	21.7	98.8	0.2	0.7	0.3	0.9	5.6	19.0	5.9	11.6	16.6	13.4
55 031	2240	3	Douglas	3 391	42 967	1 025	12.7	96.5	0.5	2.1	0.9	0.7	5.9	19.5	8.9	11.9	17.0	13.5
55 033	...	6	Dunn	2 207	39 208	1 105	17.8	96.6	0.6	0.3	2.5	0.8	5.8	18.8	18.2	11.4	15.1	11.4
55 035	2290	3	Eau Claire	1 652	89 741	559	54.3	95.4	0.4	0.6	3.6	0.8	6.2	18.2	16.1	11.6	16.2	12.0
55 037	...	9	Florence	1 264	5 136	2 829	4.1	99.3	0.2	0.3	0.2	0.4	5.5	20.5	5.8	11.5	15.5	15.1
55 039	...	4	Fond du Lac	1 873	94 795	534	50.6	98.5	0.4	0.4	0.8	1.6	6.0	20.2	9.0	12.0	16.3	13.1
55 041	...	9	Forest	2 627	9 667	2 456	3.7	89.2	1.3	9.3	0.2	0.5	6.5	20.2	8.0	10.4	13.5	12.8
55 043	...	6	Grant	2 973	49 328	917	16.6	98.8	0.3	0.2	0.7	0.5	5.8	20.0	13.0	10.9	14.1	12.3
55 045	...	6	Green	1 513	33 847	1 261	22.4	99.3	0.2	0.2	0.4	0.6	6.1	20.4	7.3	12.3	17.0	13.6
55 047	...	6	Green Lake	918	19 561	1 785	21.3	98.8	0.1	0.2	0.8	1.5	5.4	19.8	6.7	10.9	15.5	13.1
55 049	...	6	Iowa	1 976	22 708	1 624	11.5	99.6	0.1	0.1	0.2	0.4	6.6	21.1	7.5	12.7	17.0	12.2
55 051	...	9	Iron	1 961	6 298	2 751	3.2	99.4	0.0	0.5	0.1	0.2	4.4	16.5	5.9	10.1	14.5	13.8
55 053	...	6	Jackson	2 557	17 833	1 881	7.0	95.0	0.4	4.4	0.3	1.1	6.0	20.6	7.5	11.2	15.9	13.4
55 055	...	4	Jefferson	1 443	74 052	666	51.3	98.7	0.3	0.3	0.6	2.5	5.9	19.3	11.0	12.2	16.3	14.1
55 057	...	7	Juneau	1 988	24 091	1 574	12.1	98.3	0.2	0.9	0.6	1.1	6.0	20.2	6.7	11.4	14.2	13.7
55 059	3800	1	Kenosha	707	146 315	359	207.0	93.5	5.3	0.4	0.8	6.5	7.0	19.6	9.7	13.7	16.3	13.9
55 061	...	6	Kewaunee	887	19 966	1 763	22.5	99.3	0.2	0.3	0.2	0.4	6.0	21.3	8.0	11.9	15.5	13.0
55 063	3870	3	La Crosse	1 173	102 438	506	87.3	95.1	0.6	0.4	4.0	1.0	6.2	18.2	14.4	12.7	16.1	12.0
55 065	...	9	Lafayette	1 641	16 020	2 003	9.8	99.5	0.2	0.1	0.2	0.3	6.3	21.6	6.9	12.0	14.6	12.4
55 067	...	6	Langlade	2 260	20 563	1 737	9.1	98.9	0.2	0.7	0.2	0.8	5.8	20.2	6.6	10.9	14.8	13.5
55 069	...	6	Lincoln	2 287	29 949	1 375	13.1	98.6	0.5	0.4	0.5	0.7	5.6	20.5	7.4	11.9	14.7	14.6
55 071	...	4	Manitowoc	1 532	82 726	616	54.0	97.4	0.2	0.4	2.0	1.1	6.0	19.7	7.9	11.8	15.7	13.4
55 073	8940	3	Marathon	4 002	123 584	425	30.9	96.3	0.1	0.5	3.1	0.6	6.4	21.0	8.5	12.7	16.7	13.6
55 075	...	7	Marinette	3 631	43 019	1 022	11.8	99.2	0.1	0.4	0.2	0.6	5.8	20.0	7.2	11.4	15.3	13.7
55 077	...	9	Marquette	1 180	15 344	2 047	13.0	98.9	0.4	0.5	0.3	1.9	5.1	18.5	6.0	10.3	14.0	13.4
55 078	...	NA	Menominee	927	5 033	2 834	5.4	10.4	0.5	88.9	0.2	3.4	9.9	30.4	8.8	13.6	11.8	9.4
55 079	5080	0	Milwaukee	626	906 248	39	1 447.7	72.3	24.6	0.8	2.3	6.6	6.8	18.8	10.2	14.7	15.8	11.8
55 081	...	6	Monroe	2 333	39 725	1 093	17.0	97.9	0.6	0.9	0.6	1.0	6.8	21.8	7.4	11.7	16.3	13.4
55 083	...	6	Oconto	2 585	34 382	1 244	13.3	98.8	0.1	0.8	0.2	0.6	6.2	20.6	7.0	11.9	15.7	13.8
55 085	...	7	Oneida	2 913	36 052	1 193	12.4	98.8	0.2	0.7	0.3	0.5	5.3	17.1	6.4	10.7	15.6	15.2
55 087	0460	2	Outagamie	1 659	158 480	326	95.5	96.1	0.2	1.6	2.1	1.1	7.0	20.7	9.2	14.2	16.8	13.1
55 089	5080	0	Ozaukee	601	82 015	619	136.5	97.8	1.0	0.2	0.9	1.1	6.0	19.0	7.6	11.4	18.2	15.8
55 091	...	8	Pepin	602	7 307	2 650	12.1	99.5	0.1	0.2	0.2	0.4	6.2	22.2	6.5	11.1	15.9	12.9
55 093	5120	1	Pierce	1 493	36 052	1 193	24.1	98.6	0.3	0.3	0.8	0.9	6.3	20.2	14.6	12.8	16.3	12.4
55 095	...	6	Polk	2 376	39 363	1 102	16.6	98.6	0.2	1.0	0.3	0.6	6.3	21.5	6.4	11.9	16.6	13.8
55 097	...	4	Portage	2 088	65 022	735	31.1	97.4	0.4	0.5	1.8	1.4	5.9	19.1	15.6	12.6	15.8	12.2
55 099	...	7	Price	3 244	15 559	2 032	4.8	99.1	0.1	0.5	0.2	0.5	5.6	20.1	6.4	10.8	14.9	13.0
55 101	6600	3	Racine	863	185 777	286	215.3	86.3	12.5	0.4	0.9	7.5	6.7	20.3	8.5	13.4	16.6	13.7
55 103	...	7	Richland	1 518	17 748	1 883	11.7	99.3	0.2	0.2	0.3	0.5	6.1	20.4	7.9	10.9	15.5	13.2
55 105	3620	3	Rock	1 866	151 121	343	81.0	92.5	6.2	0.3	1.1	1.9	6.5	19.7	9.2	12.7	16.2	14.2
55 107	...	7	Rusk	2 365	15 098	2 058	6.4	98.2	0.3	0.6	1.0	0.8	6.0	20.6	7.6	10.9	14.7	12.8
55 109	5120	1	St. Croix	1 870	60 273	791	32.2	99.0	0.3	0.3	0.5	0.6	7.1	22.0	7.9	13.6	18.4	13.9
55 111	...	6	Sauk	2 170	54 282	847	25.0	98.7	0.3	0.7	0.3	0.8	6.4	20.1	7.8	12.5	16.4	13.4
55 113	...	9	Sawyer	3 254	16 230	1 992	5.0	83.4	0.2	16.2	0.2	1.0	5.9	20.1	5.8	10.7	15.0	13.4
55 115	...	6	Shawano	2 312	39 183	1 107	16.9	94.5	0.1	5.1	0.3	0.5	6.0	20.2	7.5	11.6	14.4	13.7
55 117	7620	3	Sheboygan	1 330	110 136	479	82.8	96.0	0.6	0.4	3.0	2.5	6.2	20.0	8.3	12.9	16.5	13.3
55 119	...	6	Taylor	2 525	19 255	1 804	7.6	99.2	0.2	0.2	0.4	0.4	6.8	22.4	7.5	12.4	14.5	12.4
55 121	...	8	Trempealeau	1 901	26 679	1 477	14.0	99.5	0.1	0.1	0.3	0.3	5.9	19.6	7.7	11.4	15.7	13.9
55 123	...	6	Vernon	2 059	27 707	1 443	13.5	99.4	0.1	0.2	0.3	0.6	6.3	20.4	6.3	11.0	15.6	13.4
55 125	...	9	Vilas	2 261	21 703	1 671	9.6	90.4	0.1	9.0	0.4	0.6	5.1	16.3	5.4	9.4	14.3	14.7
55 127	...	4	Walworth	1 438	86 548	581	60.2	97.9	0.8	0.3	1.0	4.1	5.8	17.8	12.7	12.0	16.0	13.7
55 129	...	9	Washburn	2 097	15 770	2 018	7.5	98.5	0.3	0.8	0.4	0.4	5.5	19.6	5.8	10.0	15.6	13.9
55 131	5080	1	Washington	1 116	115 717	456	103.7	99.0	0.2	0.2	0.6	1.1	6.4	20.7	8.3	12.9	17.8	15.0
55 133	5080	0	Waukesha	1 439	358 442	159	249.1	97.9	0.5	0.2	1.4	2.7	5.8	19.6	7.5	11.9	18.6	15.8
55 135	...	6	Waupaca	1 945	50 832	894	26.1	99.2	0.1	0.3	0.3	1.3	6.0	20.2	7.3	11.9	15.6	13.1
55 137	...	8	Waushara	1 622	21 824	1 665	13.5	99.0	0.2	0.4	0.4	2.9	5.4	18.4	6.1	10.4	14.9	13.8
55 139	0460	2	Winnebago	1 136	150 591	347	132.6	96.8	0.7	0.6	1.9	1.2	6.0	17.3	11.4	13.8	16.5	13.5
55 141	...	4	Wood	2 053	76 225	651	37.1	97.6	0.2	0.6	1.5	0.8	6.4	20.4	7.8	12.6	15.8	13.5
56 000	...	X	WYOMING	251 501	479 602	X	1.9	96.0	0.9	2.3	0.9	6.1	6.3	20.1	11.2	11.0	15.5	14.8
56 001	...	5	Albany	11 069	29 060	1 409	2.6	95.6	0.9	0.8	2.6	6.9	5.1	13.4	29.5	12.1	12.7	11.4
56 003	...	9	Big Horn	8 125	11 214	2 332	1.4	99.2	0.0	0.6	0.3	5.7	6.1	20.8	8.2	7.4	13.0	15.9
56 005	...	7	Campbell	12 424	32 727	1 290	2.6	97.9	0.2	1.3	0.5	3.4	7.7	24.8	9.8	13.9	18.1	13.6
56 007	...	7	Carbon	20 452	15 437	2 040	0.8	97.4	0.9	1.0	0.8	14.9	5.6	20.2	9.1	11.6	16.5	15.3

1. MSA = Metropolitan Statistical Area. PMSA = Primary MSA. NECMA = New England County Metropolitan Area. See Appendix A for explanation of these concepts. See Appendix B for list of metropolitan areas identified by type, with component counties. 2. County typology code from the Economic Research Service of USDA. See Appendix A for definition. 3. Dry land or land partially or temporarily covered by water. 4. Hispanic persons may be of any race.

Table B. States and Counties — **Population and Households**

	Population, 1999 (cont'd)				Population — change and components of change, 1980–1999							Households, 1990				
STATE County	Age (percent) (cont'd)				Total persons		Percent change		Components of change, 1990–1999						Percent		
	55 to 64 years	65 to 74 years	75 years and over	Percent female	1990	1980	1980– 1990	1990– 1999	Births	Deaths	Net migration	Number	Percent change, 1980– 1990	Persons per house-hold	Female family house-holder[1]	One person
	16	17	18	19	20	21	22	23	24	25	26	27	28	29	30	31
WISCONSIN—Cont'd																
Dane	6.9	4.9	4.7	50.8	367 085	323 545	13.5	16.7	47 349	21 886	12 394	142 786	18.4	2.46	8.0	26.4
Dodge	8.8	6.3	6.7	48.3	76 559	75 064	2.0	9.1	8 837	7 289	5 614	26 853	8.1	2.71	6.5	21.7
Door	9.3	8.8	9.7	50.6	25 690	25 029	2.6	5.4	2 560	2 799	1 719	10 066	9.3	2.52	6.6	25.1
Douglas	9.0	6.8	7.5	51.0	41 758	44 421	-6.0	2.9	4 932	4 542	950	16 374	-0.6	2.46	11.1	27.8
Dunn	7.6	5.4	6.2	50.0	35 909	34 314	4.6	9.2	4 084	2 382	1 717	12 250	10.9	2.69	6.3	22.9
Eau Claire	7.5	6.2	6.0	51.8	85 183	78 805	8.1	5.4	10 403	6 216	640	31 282	14.5	2.58	8.6	24.9
Florence	9.9	8.3	8.1	48.9	4 590	4 172	10.0	11.9	448	481	600	1 755	17.5	2.57	7.6	22.9
Fond du Lac	8.7	7.2	7.5	51.4	90 083	88 964	1.3	5.2	10 711	7 692	2 002	32 644	9.3	2.67	7.8	23.3
Forest	10.8	9.1	8.8	49.4	8 776	9 044	-3.0	10.2	1 149	1 066	838	3 290	8.8	2.56	9.0	24.6
Grant	8.6	7.4	7.9	49.4	49 266	51 736	-4.8	0.1	5 141	4 480	-409	17 169	2.9	2.69	6.8	23.5
Green	8.8	7.0	7.5	50.8	30 339	30 012	1.1	11.6	3 674	2 828	2 770	11 541	7.3	2.59	7.2	24.2
Green Lake	10.1	8.7	9.6	51.1	18 651	18 370	1.5	4.9	1 903	2 164	1 250	7 189	6.8	2.56	6.7	24.9
Iowa	9.0	7.1	6.8	50.1	20 150	19 802	1.8	12.7	2 603	1 720	1 741	7 406	9.4	2.69	7.5	23.2
Iron	11.9	11.7	11.3	50.3	6 153	6 730	-8.6	2.4	577	917	513	2 602	-2.3	2.32	6.5	29.2
Jackson	9.9	7.8	7.7	48.8	16 588	16 831	-1.4	7.5	1 931	1 719	1 083	6 253	3.0	2.59	8.3	25.5
Jefferson	8.4	6.3	6.4	50.4	67 783	66 152	2.5	9.2	8 157	5 337	3 683	24 019	7.9	2.67	7.8	22.1
Juneau	10.4	8.9	8.4	50.5	21 650	21 037	2.9	11.3	2 648	2 386	2 259	8 265	8.8	2.59	8.1	24.8
Kenosha	8.5	5.9	5.4	50.8	128 181	123 137	4.1	14.1	19 319	10 520	9 644	47 029	9.2	2.67	11.6	23.2
Kewaunee	9.2	7.4	7.8	49.5	18 878	19 539	-3.4	5.8	2 093	1 691	749	6 756	4.4	2.77	6.1	22.4
La Crosse	7.8	6.1	6.5	51.7	97 904	91 056	7.5	4.6	12 137	8 115	866	36 662	14.5	2.54	8.9	26.1
Lafayette	9.9	8.4	8.0	50.5	16 074	17 412	-7.7	-0.3	1 771	1 436	-350	5 876	0.1	2.72	6.8	24.3
Langlade	10.3	8.9	9.1	51.0	19 505	19 978	-2.4	5.4	2 188	2 144	1 104	7 563	7.0	2.55	7.5	26.2
Lincoln	10.0	7.5	7.9	50.1	26 993	26 555	1.6	11.0	3 198	2 795	2 661	10 159	8.4	2.60	7.2	23.4
Manitowoc	9.3	7.9	8.4	50.9	80 421	82 918	-3.0	2.9	9 002	7 642	1 218	30 112	5.6	2.62	7.0	24.9
Marathon	8.3	6.6	6.2	50.4	115 400	111 270	3.7	7.1	15 122	8 221	1 685	41 547	10.2	2.75	7.2	21.0
Marinette	9.6	8.2	8.7	50.8	40 548	39 314	3.1	6.1	4 226	4 568	2 959	15 542	10.0	2.55	7.6	25.8
Marquette	12.9	10.8	9.0	50.2	12 321	11 672	5.6	24.5	1 433	1 423	3 048	4 831	10.8	2.52	5.6	23.4
Menominee	7.2	5.4	3.4	50.1	4 075	3 373	15.3	23.5	933	359	399	1 079	35.0	3.57	29.9	12.6
Milwaukee	8.4	6.8	6.6	52.7	959 212	964 988	-0.6	-5.5	144 100	85 241	-118 434	373 048	2.6	2.50	15.8	29.4
Monroe	8.9	7.1	6.5	49.7	36 633	35 074	4.4	8.4	5 108	3 443	1 523	13 144	10.5	2.70	8.2	23.3
Oconto	10.0	7.6	7.2	49.7	30 226	28 947	4.4	13.7	3 488	2 997	3 738	11 283	13.0	2.65	6.1	22.5
Oneida	11.7	9.6	8.4	50.6	31 679	31 216	1.5	13.8	3 318	3 585	4 746	12 666	10.9	2.44	7.1	24.7
Outagamie	7.9	5.6	5.5	50.4	140 510	128 730	9.2	12.8	20 257	9 926	8 238	50 527	18.2	2.73	7.4	21.4
Ozaukee	9.1	7.1	5.7	50.3	72 894	66 981	8.7	12.5	8 727	5 019	5 646	25 707	18.1	2.79	6.4	17.0
Pepin	9.1	6.8	9.2	50.0	7 107	7 477	-4.9	2.8	770	785	227	2 612	2.4	2.66	6.2	25.0
Pierce	7.0	5.2	5.1	49.9	32 765	31 149	5.2	10.0	3 697	2 180	1 849	11 011	12.1	2.77	7.0	20.7
Polk	8.9	6.9	7.7	49.9	34 773	32 351	7.5	13.2	4 196	3 500	3 988	13 056	14.6	2.62	7.0	23.3
Portage	7.2	5.9	5.8	49.9	61 405	57 420	6.9	5.9	7 536	4 109	437	21 306	16.3	2.71	7.7	22.0
Price	10.5	8.7	10.0	49.6	15 600	15 788	-1.2	-0.3	1 575	1 808	261	6 054	6.1	2.53	6.2	26.2
Racine	8.5	6.6	5.8	51.1	175 034	173 132	1.1	6.1	23 380	14 028	1 947	63 736	7.3	2.70	12.3	22.0
Richland	9.6	7.9	8.5	50.2	17 521	17 476	0.3	1.3	1 852	1 777	230	6 593	5.5	2.62	6.6	24.0
Rock	9.0	6.3	6.2	51.0	139 510	139 420	0.0	8.3	18 810	11 969	5 253	52 252	6.6	2.62	10.6	23.4
Rusk	9.5	8.8	9.1	50.1	15 079	15 589	-3.3	0.1	1 713	1 556	-86	5 693	6.7	2.59	7.6	24.6
St. Croix	7.2	4.6	5.2	49.7	50 251	43 262	16.2	19.9	6 957	3 666	6 868	17 638	24.6	2.81	6.4	19.7
Sauk	8.9	7.2	7.4	50.4	46 975	43 469	8.1	15.6	6 167	4 445	5 735	17 703	14.1	2.61	7.4	23.8
Sawyer	11.9	9.0	8.3	49.3	14 181	12 843	10.4	14.4	1 725	1 740	2 111	5 569	19.3	2.50	9.6	25.0
Shawano	10.1	8.2	8.4	50.1	37 157	35 928	3.4	5.5	4 336	4 071	1 904	13 775	11.6	2.64	6.6	23.1
Sheboygan	8.7	6.9	7.1	50.1	103 877	100 935	2.9	6.0	12 575	8 977	2 989	38 592	8.8	2.63	7.1	23.3
Taylor	8.5	7.4	8.2	49.2	18 901	18 817	0.4	1.9	2 166	1 644	-96	6 692	8.5	2.79	5.7	21.9
Trempealeau	9.1	7.6	9.2	49.9	25 263	26 158	-3.4	5.6	3 163	2 841	1 192	9 495	4.3	2.59	7.4	25.3
Vernon	9.7	8.3	9.1	50.4	25 617	25 642	0.0	8.2	3 224	2 859	1 815	9 725	4.8	2.59	6.8	25.8
Vilas	13.4	11.9	9.8	50.1	17 707	16 535	7.1	22.6	1 706	2 393	4 721	7 294	16.8	2.40	7.2	23.6
Walworth	8.7	6.4	6.8	50.5	75 000	71 507	4.9	15.4	9 161	6 771	9 407	27 620	11.4	2.60	8.0	23.9
Washburn	10.8	9.9	8.8	49.9	13 772	13 174	4.5	14.5	1 423	1 707	2 323	5 456	11.7	2.49	6.9	26.9
Washington	8.0	5.7	5.3	50.1	95 328	84 848	12.4	21.4	13 162	6 614	14 215	32 977	23.4	2.86	7.0	17.2
Waukesha	8.9	6.5	5.3	50.4	304 715	280 203	8.7	17.6	38 051	20 414	37 153	105 990	19.7	2.83	6.7	16.6
Waupaca	9.1	7.7	9.1	50.4	46 104	42 831	7.6	10.3	5 757	5 796	5 010	17 037	13.9	2.62	7.0	23.8
Waushara	11.7	10.0	9.3	50.3	19 385	18 526	4.6	12.6	2 156	2 145	2 490	7 616	10.3	2.52	6.7	23.4
Winnebago	8.6	6.2	6.5	50.5	140 320	131 772	6.5	7.3	17 220	11 159	4 752	53 216	13.5	2.52	8.1	25.1
Wood	8.5	7.4	7.5	51.0	73 605	72 799	1.1	3.6	9 101	6 273	56	27 473	9.6	2.65	8.0	23.5
WYOMING	9.5	6.3	5.4	49.8	453 589	469 557	-3.4	5.7	60 099	32 704	-1 662	168 839	1.9	2.63	8.3	24.5
Albany	6.7	4.9	4.2	48.0	30 797	29 062	6.0	-5.6	3 596	1 487	-3 856	11 957	12.4	2.35	8.0	29.3
Big Horn	12.0	7.7	8.6	49.8	10 525	11 896	-11.5	6.5	1 395	1 125	447	3 905	-5.4	2.65	5.7	25.0
Campbell	6.7	2.9	2.3	48.8	29 370	24 367	20.5	11.4	4 303	1 179	315	9 968	24.5	2.92	7.7	19.1
Carbon	9.6	6.4	5.6	46.5	16 659	21 896	-23.9	-7.3	1 715	1 205	-1 705	6 001	-19.7	2.63	7.6	24.7

1. No spouse present.

STATE County	Births, average 1996–1998 Total	Births, average 1996–1998 Rate[1]	Deaths, average 1996–1998 Number Total	Deaths, average 1996–1998 Number Infant[2]	Deaths, average 1996–1998 Rate Total[1]	Deaths, average 1996–1998 Rate Infant[3]	Physicians,[4] 1998 Number	Physicians,[4] 1998 Rate[5]	Hospitals,[4] 1998 Number	Hospitals,[4] 1998 Beds Number	Hospitals,[4] 1998 Beds Rate[5]	Medicare enrollees 1999	Serious crimes known to police, 1998[6] Total Number	Serious crimes known to police, 1998[6] Total Rate[7]
	32	33	34	35	36	37	38	39	40	41	42	43	44	45
WISCONSIN—Cont'd														
Dane	5 043	12.0	2 485	30	5.9	6.0	1 703	401	4	1 246	293	44 320	NA	NA
Dodge	948	11.5	793	9	9.6	9.5	63	76	3	353	424	9 707	NA	NA
Door	239	8.9	312	1	11.6	5.6	45	167	1	77	285	5 554	NA	NA
Douglas	523	12.2	502	3	11.7	6.4	24	56	1	42	98	7 429	NA	NA
Dunn	459	11.8	260	2	6.7	4.4	23	59	1	55	141	4 968	NA	NA
Eau Claire	1 083	12.2	672	7	7.5	6.2	271	304	2	519	581	12 830	NA	NA
Florence	47	9.1	49	0	9.4	7.0	3	58	0	0	0	856	NA	NA
Fond du Lac	1 132	12.0	856	8	9.1	6.8	156	165	2	220	232	15 813	NA	NA
Forest	101	10.5	114	1	11.9	13.2	3	31	0	0	0	2 024	NA	NA
Grant	511	10.4	471	4	9.6	7.8	39	79	3	260	527	9 012	NA	NA
Green	386	11.7	311	3	9.4	6.9	81	242	1	143	428	5 306	NA	NA
Green Lake	218	11.2	234	1	12.1	3.1	25	129	1	163	839	4 019	NA	NA
Iowa	270	12.2	183	1	8.2	4.9	14	62	1	82	366	3 040	NA	NA
Iron	54	8.4	102	0	15.9	6.2	6	94	0	0	0	1 580	NA	NA
Jackson	200	11.4	182	2	10.4	8.3	13	73	1	38	214	3 068	NA	NA
Jefferson	899	12.3	596	5	8.1	5.2	78	106	1	92	125	12 007	NA	NA
Juneau	271	11.4	268	0	11.2	1.2	17	71	1	95	399	4 759	NA	NA
Kenosha	2 089	14.6	1 168	14	8.2	6.5	185	128	2	307	213	18 393	NA	NA
Kewaunee	220	11.2	179	1	9.1	6.0	12	61	1	17	86	3 347	NA	NA
La Crosse	1 277	12.5	904	9	8.8	6.8	353	344	2	552	538	14 788	NA	NA
Lafayette	173	10.6	164	1	10.0	5.8	6	37	1	28	172	2 678	NA	NA
Langlade	214	10.5	216	1	10.6	4.7	20	98	1	49	239	4 169	NA	NA
Lincoln	324	11.0	309	3	10.5	9.3	32	108	2	125	420	5 708	NA	NA
Manitowoc	922	11.2	830	7	10.1	8.0	111	135	2	354	430	14 530	NA	NA
Marathon	1 559	12.7	889	5	7.3	3.0	219	178	1	270	219	16 844	NA	NA
Marinette	424	9.9	500	5	11.7	11.8	58	135	1	115	267	8 832	NA	NA
Marquette	151	10.2	172	1	11.6	6.6	8	53	0	0	0	3 742	NA	NA
Menominee	92	19.4	41	1	8.7	7.3	3	63	0	0	0	480	NA	NA
Milwaukee	14 635	15.9	8 932	149	9.7	10.2	2 677	294	14	3 537	388	140 462	NA	NA
Monroe	539	13.7	382	5	9.7	9.3	44	111	2	105	266	6 061	NA	NA
Oconto	363	10.9	323	3	9.7	7.3	19	56	2	49	144	5 429	NA	NA
Oneida	334	9.4	389	1	11.0	4.0	117	328	2	132	370	8 112	NA	NA
Outagamie	2 102	13.6	1 147	16	7.4	7.8	295	189	3	426	273	19 657	NA	NA
Ozaukee	930	11.5	581	6	7.2	6.5	278	343	1	82	101	11 023	NA	NA
Pepin	81	11.4	84	0	11.8	4.1	6	84	1	88	1 236	1 388	NA	NA
Pierce	386	11.0	238	2	6.8	6.0	28	79	1	36	101	4 611	NA	NA
Polk	417	10.9	401	3	10.5	6.4	51	131	3	141	364	6 429	NA	NA
Portage	766	11.8	459	4	7.1	5.7	86	133	1	122	188	8 168	NA	NA
Price	154	9.7	202	2	12.8	10.8	14	89	1	42	266	3 241	NA	NA
Racine	2 602	14.0	1 560	21	8.4	8.1	251	135	3	561	301	27 583	NA	NA
Richland	193	10.8	183	1	10.2	6.9	19	106	1	38	212	2 986	NA	NA
Rock	2 001	13.3	1 329	13	8.8	6.7	251	167	3	474	314	21 678	NA	NA
Rusk	160	10.5	178	2	11.7	10.4	13	85	1	142	931	3 069	NA	NA
St. Croix	771	13.4	432	3	7.5	4.3	45	76	3	106	180	5 949	NA	NA
Sauk	694	13.1	486	3	9.2	3.8	70	131	3	186	349	8 713	NA	NA
Sawyer	173	10.8	185	0	11.6	0.0	20	124	1	117	726	3 078	NA	NA
Shawano	455	11.8	439	3	11.4	6.6	28	72	1	53	137	7 057	NA	NA
Sheboygan	1 335	12.2	1 023	6	9.3	4.8	149	135	3	421	382	17 373	NA	NA
Taylor	216	11.2	196	2	10.2	10.8	13	67	1	155	803	3 069	NA	NA
Trempealeau	329	12.5	293	1	11.1	4.0	21	79	3	298	1 126	5 137	NA	NA
Vernon	343	12.6	317	1	11.6	2.9	36	132	2	102	373	5 229	NA	NA
Vilas	171	8.2	264	1	12.6	3.9	29	136	2	114	536	4 948	NA	NA
Walworth	1 033	12.3	757	6	9.0	5.5	99	116	1	88	103	12 242	NA	NA
Washburn	146	9.6	187	1	12.3	4.6	16	104	2	185	1 200	3 960	NA	NA
Washington	1 449	12.9	758	7	6.7	4.8	118	104	2	191	168	14 209	NA	NA
Waukesha	4 140	11.9	2 417	21	6.9	5.2	1 154	327	4	682	193	46 113	NA	NA
Waupaca	595	11.9	637	2	12.7	3.9	41	81	1	40	79	10 359	NA	NA
Waushara	231	10.8	232	2	10.8	10.1	14	65	1	26	120	4 385	NA	NA
Winnebago	1 768	11.8	1 230	9	8.2	5.1	321	214	2	456	304	21 770	NA	NA
Wood	928	12.2	688	3	9.1	3.2	339	446	2	708	931	13 714	NA	NA
WYOMING	6 308	13.1	3 733	41	7.8	6.5	842	175	26	2 309	480	64 448	18 315	3 808
Albany	380	12.7	168	2	5.6	6.2	60	206	1	110	377	3 018	1 260	4 232
Big Horn	149	13.3	129	1	11.4	6.7	8	70	1	118	1 037	2 063	201	1 818
Campbell	457	14.2	135	2	4.2	5.1	43	132	1	119	367	2 073	1 581	4 917
Carbon	178	11.3	136	1	8.6	7.5	19	122	1	50	321	2 171	504	3 378

1. Per 1,000 estimated resident population, average 1996–1998.　2. Deaths of infants under 1 year old.　3. Deaths of infants under 1 year old per 1,000 live births.　4. Data subject to copyright.　5. Per 100,000 resident population as of July 1 of the year shown.　6. Data for serious crimes have not been adjusted for underreporting; this may affect comparability between geographic areas and over time.　7. Per 100,000 population estimated by the FBI.

Table B. States and Counties — Crime, Education, Money Income, and Poverty

STATE County	Serious crimes known to police, 1998[1] (cont'd) — Rate[2] — Violent	Property	Education — Enrollment[3] Total	Percent private	High school graduate or more	Bachelor's degree or more	Total current expenditures (mil dol)	Current expenditures per student (dollars)	Per capita[6] (dollars)	Households Median Dollars	Percent change, 1979–1989 (constant 1989 dollars)	Percent with $100,000 or more	Median household income	All persons	Persons under 18	Persons 5–17 in families
	46	47	48	49	50	51	52	53	54	55	56	57	58	59	60	61
WISCONSIN—Cont'd																
Dane	NA	NA	115 595	9.2	88.9	34.2	450.6	7 345	15 542	32 703	6.6	3.9	47 607	7.2	10.4	9.2
Dodge	NA	NA	18 094	19.3	72.3	10.2	54.8	6 225	12 050	29 166	-4.0	1.8	42 443	6.1	8.2	7.7
Door	NA	NA	5 832	13.0	79.6	16.4	31.9	7 130	12 458	26 259	-0.9	1.9	36 611	8.1	12.3	11.8
Douglas	NA	NA	10 910	6.7	77.2	14.8	47.7	6 409	10 744	22 122	-12.4	0.8	31 510	13.4	21.2	19.2
Dunn	NA	NA	13 694	4.3	77.7	19.4	39.6	6 494	10 364	24 452	5.2	1.6	35 947	11.9	16.3	14.2
Eau Claire	NA	NA	27 624	8.2	82.8	20.9	99.0	6 760	11 801	25 886	0.9	2.0	37 404	11.0	15.2	14.5
Florence	NA	NA	1 110	3.3	75.2	8.9	5.7	5 923	10 352	22 416	12.4	0.7	31 303	10.7	15.2	15.0
Fond du Lac	NA	NA	23 436	21.6	77.5	13.3	98.6	5 984	12 574	29 441	-3.3	2.0	42 700	6.6	9.1	8.3
Forest	NA	NA	2 064	2.7	64.1	7.6	12.9	6 145	8 339	16 907	-10.0	1.0	27 400	13.4	19.0	20.1
Grant	NA	NA	15 331	9.2	77.9	14.7	62.5	6 701	10 704	24 505	-3.3	1.8	33 757	9.7	13.2	12.3
Green	NA	NA	7 284	6.9	76.8	12.0	38.8	6 614	13 006	28 435	1.2	2.0	38 771	6.9	10.2	9.4
Green Lake	NA	NA	4 287	13.9	74.6	11.4	22.5	5 679	11 840	25 708	1.9	1.7	36 015	7.9	11.7	11.1
Iowa	NA	NA	4 836	5.3	80.6	13.3	27.6	7 044	11 339	25 914	7.7	2.1	37 079	8.5	12.4	11.9
Iron	NA	NA	1 162	7.1	74.7	10.5	7.7	7 136	9 280	17 537	5.2	0.7	26 438	11.7	19.7	17.8
Jackson	NA	NA	3 836	2.8	68.8	8.8	20.9	6 271	10 173	21 409	1.6	1.2	31 374	11.6	17.8	16.5
Jefferson	NA	NA	18 627	20.7	77.0	15.1	84.2	6 995	12 770	30 749	0.8	2.4	42 567	5.3	6.9	6.5
Juneau	NA	NA	4 923	10.8	70.6	8.6	29.0	6 375	10 304	22 073	5.1	1.4	31 461	10.5	16.1	14.6
Kenosha	NA	NA	34 027	17.6	75.1	12.7	160.8	6 297	13 265	30 638	-9.0	1.9	42 529	9.1	13.9	12.7
Kewaunee	NA	NA	4 649	17.2	73.5	8.2	21.3	5 783	11 299	26 927	-2.7	1.7	37 356	6.8	8.9	8.7
La Crosse	NA	NA	30 119	13.9	82.6	21.1	107.5	6 911	12 141	26 857	0.8	2.0	38 523	10.0	14.4	13.0
Lafayette	NA	NA	4 035	4.9	77.0	10.1	25.3	6 659	10 641	24 479	-4.1	2.0	32 886	8.8	12.5	11.9
Langlade	NA	NA	4 441	11.7	71.5	8.8	27.2	6 947	10 172	20 703	-3.0	1.8	30 671	11.9	17.8	16.8
Lincoln	NA	NA	6 478	11.7	71.1	10.8	32.7	6 253	11 282	25 175	5.3	1.3	36 694	8.1	11.7	10.9
Manitowoc	NA	NA	19 541	23.4	75.4	12.1	72.5	5 837	12 235	27 467	-7.0	1.9	40 097	6.8	9.6	9.2
Marathon	NA	NA	29 586	13.2	75.9	13.5	128.4	6 439	12 718	30 143	3.7	2.5	42 120	7.8	12.5	10.8
Marinette	NA	NA	10 035	13.6	73.6	10.1	51.3	6 423	10 420	22 396	-4.2	0.8	33 457	9.8	14.4	13.2
Marquette	NA	NA	2 542	10.4	69.7	8.8	13.0	5 514	10 652	22 234	5.4	1.0	29 958	9.9	16.1	14.9
Menominee	NA	NA	1 334	4.0	76.2	3.7	9.6	8 847	5 674	14 122	-36.9	0.4	21 412	25.8	32.9	34.8
Milwaukee	NA	NA	255 180	24.3	76.3	19.3	1 139.0	7 445	13 383	27 867	-8.2	2.4	37 229	16.5	28.4	23.9
Monroe	NA	NA	9 161	15.4	75.7	10.8	40.8	5 759	10 744	24 799	-2.0	1.3	34 392	11.2	17.3	16.0
Oconto	NA	NA	7 069	7.4	69.4	8.5	31.6	5 944	10 375	22 927	1.6	1.4	33 910	8.8	12.3	11.6
Oneida	NA	NA	6 979	8.8	77.6	14.9	44.0	6 809	11 681	23 901	-1.8	1.4	34 713	8.9	14.2	12.8
Outagamie	NA	NA	37 415	20.8	81.5	16.7	178.2	6 199	13 893	33 770	3.8	2.7	47 845	5.4	7.5	6.9
Ozaukee	NA	NA	19 679	26.2	86.9	29.7	91.9	7 214	19 249	42 695	-0.3	9.5	62 427	2.7	3.3	3.1
Pepin	NA	NA	1 745	15.4	71.0	9.6	13.4	7 873	10 751	22 992	-1.3	1.6	32 663	9.6	12.3	12.8
Pierce	NA	NA	10 471	6.8	81.1	17.8	50.5	6 757	12 203	30 520	8.4	2.4	43 666	6.5	8.0	8.0
Polk	NA	NA	8 607	4.5	78.0	11.4	52.1	6 368	11 291	24 267	2.6	1.6	36 282	8.9	12.5	11.9
Portage	NA	NA	20 204	9.2	79.7	19.1	68.9	6 383	11 730	28 686	2.7	1.9	41 782	9.3	12.9	11.3
Price	NA	NA	3 520	8.6	73.3	10.6	18.0	6 255	10 564	22 662	13.2	1.3	33 942	10.4	15.3	13.7
Racine	NA	NA	46 118	18.3	76.4	16.5	199.5	6 612	14 023	32 751	-6.7	2.9	44 675	9.1	14.2	12.6
Richland	NA	NA	4 222	9.2	73.7	10.8	16.1	7 684	10 287	21 946	-1.0	1.4	31 988	11.1	16.7	15.6
Rock	NA	NA	34 529	11.7	78.2	13.3	183.8	6 716	13 428	30 632	-4.6	2.0	41 802	8.9	13.7	12.5
Rusk	NA	NA	3 822	13.6	70.3	10.9	22.3	7 435	9 127	19 617	1.2	1.0	27 772	14.6	21.9	20.1
St. Croix	NA	NA	13 626	9.3	84.4	20.3	64.9	6 237	14 912	36 716	12.0	4.1	51 680	4.7	5.9	5.9
Sauk	NA	NA	10 973	14.0	74.7	12.9	63.4	6 320	11 697	26 217	0.9	1.5	37 657	8.1	12.2	11.3
Sawyer	NA	NA	3 217	6.7	73.7	12.9	17.5	6 871	9 232	18 094	-2.9	1.1	27 130	15.4	23.9	21.1
Shawano	NA	NA	8 349	12.2	69.5	9.4	38.8	6 130	10 586	23 841	2.1	1.4	33 849	9.6	14.0	13.2
Sheboygan	NA	NA	25 856	19.4	77.4	13.8	127.5	6 449	13 425	31 603	0.7	2.3	44 323	5.7	8.0	7.4
Taylor	NA	NA	4 731	10.6	68.8	9.2	23.1	5 948	10 452	24 304	2.0	2.0	33 844	10.6	14.5	14.1
Trempealeau	NA	NA	5 766	9.7	71.7	10.1	39.7	6 769	10 674	23 864	5.0	1.3	31 799	10.5	15.6	13.6
Vernon	NA	NA	5 916	10.3	69.2	11.2	32.7	6 854	10 132	21 548	2.5	1.4	29 853	13.0	19.6	18.8
Vilas	NA	NA	3 637	8.2	76.1	13.7	21.1	8 244	10 866	20 352	-1.9	1.3	29 422	11.7	19.7	19.0
Walworth	NA	NA	21 454	10.2	79.0	17.5	91.8	6 742	13 526	30 345	3.7	2.5	41 584	6.6	9.3	8.6
Washburn	NA	NA	3 153	7.4	74.9	12.8	21.0	6 790	9 847	19 962	-1.1	1.0	28 933	11.7	17.6	17.4
Washington	NA	NA	24 539	20.0	81.3	15.9	124.1	6 470	14 736	38 431	4.3	3.1	53 937	3.5	4.7	4.4
Waukesha	NA	NA	82 751	23.0	88.0	27.1	421.5	7 257	18 148	44 565	3.0	6.8	61 562	3.1	4.0	3.6
Waupaca	NA	NA	10 891	10.3	72.1	11.0	63.8	5 953	11 455	26 083	1.8	1.4	36 842	7.3	10.2	9.6
Waushara	NA	NA	3 979	6.4	70.0	10.0	18.9	5 638	10 408	21 888	2.6	1.1	30 836	12.3	19.8	18.1
Winnebago	NA	NA	37 970	12.3	80.6	18.2	145.5	6 166	13 696	30 007	-0.9	2.5	43 937	6.9	10.2	9.3
Wood	NA	NA	18 911	15.9	78.3	13.5	91.9	6 463	13 130	29 735	1.5	2.5	41 762	8.1	12.0	10.7
WYOMING	248	3 560	134 739	5.6	83.0	18.8	591.0	5 971	12 311	27 096	-19.1	2.0	33 197	12.0	15.3	12.6
Albany	343	3 889	14 368	5.8	89.3	38.5	23.8	5 769	11 825	20 715	-15.6	2.0	32 374	15.1	17.6	14.9
Big Horn	262	1 556	2 944	2.4	77.1	15.0	17.7	6 822	9 717	21 454	-12.8	0.9	31 792	12.4	15.5	13.9
Campbell	317	4 600	9 398	4.4	86.5	15.7	51.4	6 505	13 596	37 055	-15.2	2.5	49 042	7.8	9.0	7.6
Carbon	288	3 090	4 622	3.4	81.7	14.2	21.0	6 460	11 592	27 109	-26.4	1.0	36 124	12.5	14.6	12.2

1. Data for serious crimes have not been adjusted for underreporting; this may affect comparability between geographic areas and over time.   2. Per 100,000 population estimated by the FBI.   3. All persons 3 years old and over enrolled in nursery school through college.   4. Persons 25 years old and over.   5. Elementary and secondary education expenditures, local government fiscal years ending between July 1, 1996 and June 30, 1997.   6. Based on population enumerated as of April 1, 1990.

STATE County	Total (mil dol)	Percent change, 1997–1998	Per capita[1] Dollars	Per capita[1] Rank	Wages and salaries[2] (mil dol)	Proprietor's income (mil dol)	Dividends, interest, and rent (mil dol)	Transfer payments Total (mil dol)	Government payments to individuals Total (mil dol)	Social Security (mil dol)	Medical payments (mil dol)	Income maintenance (mil dol)	Unemployment insurance (mil dol)
	62	63	64	65	66	67	68	69	70	71	72	73	74
WISCONSIN—Cont'd													
Dane	12 831	6.0	30 214	161	9 319	714	2 711	1 016	937	462	340	61	23
Dodge	1 801	6.7	21 702	1 191	1 091	116	362	241	225	123	79	9	6
Door	685	6.0	25 326	458	293	80	223	106	101	57	33	3	5
Douglas	880	4.1	20 396	1 599	489	47	155	178	170	63	64	13	4
Dunn	777	5.5	19 910	1 741	439	46	142	107	100	46	34	8	3
Eau Claire	2 132	6.1	23 896	664	1 508	115	423	283	266	125	95	19	6
Florence	101	5.7	19 428	1 914	24	3	20	19	18	9	6	1	0
Fond du Lac	2 541	6.6	26 867	315	1 540	165	489	305	288	145	104	13	7
Forest	172	4.2	17 757	2 418	70	19	38	42	40	19	13	3	2
Grant	989	6.4	20 062	1 690	456	77	228	171	161	78	60	10	4
Green	759	5.8	22 676	929	380	59	190	103	97	50	37	5	3
Green Lake	458	5.4	23 503	744	203	40	109	74	70	39	24	3	2
Iowa	467	8.2	20 919	1 417	287	29	94	59	55	28	19	3	2
Iron	131	4.5	20 572	1 537	52	15	30	32	31	16	10	2	1
Jackson	362	5.7	20 412	1 590	171	30	82	62	58	27	21	5	2
Jefferson	1 758	5.9	23 888	665	1 040	79	349	241	227	112	95	8	6
Juneau	456	3.8	19 165	1 992	245	35	97	95	90	44	32	6	3
Kenosha	3 730	10.0	25 833	410	1 731	134	569	442	415	202	156	29	8
Kewaunee	419	8.6	21 080	1 365	187	36	90	61	58	31	20	3	2
La Crosse	2 547	5.5	24 862	505	1 966	141	500	318	299	141	105	19	7
Lafayette	293	7.2	18 123	2 316	102	23	73	48	45	24	16	3	1
Langlade	400	3.6	19 503	1 888	202	34	81	83	79	39	27	5	2
Lincoln	611	4.5	20 535	1 545	357	28	117	110	105	52	38	5	4
Manitowoc	2 002	6.8	24 276	596	1 181	113	380	288	273	146	96	11	9
Marathon	3 050	5.0	24 781	518	2 056	164	566	357	334	171	112	23	14
Marinette	886	4.8	20 611	1 524	552	62	170	173	165	82	61	8	5
Marquette	266	4.7	17 594	2 468	95	18	55	62	59	33	19	3	2
Menominee	(3)67	(3)4.4	(3)13 362	(3)3 053	(3)51	(3)3	(3)18	(3)17	(3)16	(3)5	(3)6	(3)2	(3)1
Milwaukee	25 165	4.0	27 607	259	20 179	1 331	4 885	3 945	3 775	1 426	1 601	527	87
Monroe	777	5.1	19 655	1 835	477	57	161	123	116	51	40	8	5
Oconto	626	6.1	18 488	2 216	221	64	127	112	106	56	35	6	3
Oneida	851	5.0	23 803	680	489	52	207	157	150	79	53	6	5
Outagamie	4 267	6.5	27 281	281	3 005	258	783	386	357	194	115	19	14
Ozaukee	3 240	6.2	39 934	32	1 343	125	797	216	201	122	63	5	4
Pepin	139	6.3	19 442	1 910	60	12	29	26	24	12	10	1	1
Pierce	852	8.3	23 978	646	255	40	146	89	82	40	30	4	2
Polk	825	7.1	21 265	1 301	361	64	141	129	122	60	46	7	3
Portage	1 455	5.0	22 452	986	973	75	284	180	168	79	53	10	8
Price	342	3.7	21 737	1 178	192	23	78	65	62	30	24	4	2
Racine	5 142	5.5	27 712	251	2 948	169	976	604	570	284	211	40	19
Richland	333	5.1	18 646	2 169	150	22	73	58	55	28	19	4	2
Rock	3 671	4.1	24 356	580	2 397	141	632	477	449	226	158	31	18
Rusk	270	8.8	17 772	2 414	152	18	52	61	58	27	20	5	2
St. Croix	1 693	9.1	28 731	204	672	76	263	137	126	63	48	5	2
Sauk	1 260	6.7	23 602	722	857	79	266	175	166	83	62	9	6
Sawyer	305	4.9	18 940	2 080	151	25	73	67	64	31	22	5	2
Shawano	(3)773	(3)6.8	(3)19 906	(3)1 745	(3)322	(3)63	(3)136	(3)135	(3)128	(3)68	(3)43	(3)7	(3)3
Sheboygan	2 876	5.9	26 149	382	1 933	164	603	337	317	178	104	14	11
Taylor	375	8.6	19 497	1 893	235	28	73	62	58	28	22	4	2
Trempealeau	543	7.8	20 510	1 551	304	43	96	100	95	43	40	6	2
Vernon	475	6.9	17 352	2 516	175	39	99	96	91	44	33	7	2
Vilas	451	5.9	21 200	1 330	173	47	131	97	93	53	29	5	2
Walworth	2 061	5.9	24 112	619	1 120	112	449	256	240	129	84	10	6
Washburn	294	6.0	19 058	2 038	140	19	68	72	69	32	23	4	2
Washington	3 384	9.2	29 708	175	1 530	152	653	287	266	150	89	9	9
Waukesha	12 848	6.9	36 394	56	8 230	553	2 736	920	855	503	273	22	22
Waupaca	1 186	6.6	23 473	751	598	68	205	210	201	91	84	8	5
Waushara	406	5.4	18 761	2 136	133	28	89	85	81	45	26	5	2
Winnebago	3 987	4.9	26 581	335	3 184	150	835	454	426	229	145	21	12
Wood	2 058	6.7	27 054	298	1 585	117	389	272	258	127	97	14	10
WYOMING	11 671	3.0	24 312	X	6 731	1 074	2 898	1 475	1 382	631	429	101	29
Albany	656	3.5	22 423	994	372	48	163	84	79	29	25	6	1
Big Horn	201	2.7	17 759	2 417	119	16	45	40	38	19	11	3	1
Campbell	801	4.3	24 729	528	644	57	125	62	55	23	18	3	2
Carbon	328	-0.5	21 117	1 351	193	18	79	48	45	20	13	3	1

1. Based on the resident population estimated as of July 1 of the year shown. 2. Includes other labor income. 3. Menominee County included with Shawano County.

Table B. States and Counties — Earnings, Social Security, and Housing

STATE County	Earnings, 1998 Total (mil dol)	Farm	Goods-related[1] Total	Manu-facturing	Service-related and other[2] Total	Retail trade	Finance, insurance, and real estate	Services	Govern-ment	Social Security beneficiaries, December 1998 Number	Rate[3]	Supplemental Security Income recipients, December 1998	Housing units, 1990 Total	Percent change, 1980–1990
	75	76	77	78	79	80	81	82	83	84	85	86	87	88
WISCONSIN—Cont'd														
Dane	10 033	0.4	19.2	12.4	53.6	8.5	10.0	24.3	26.8	49 936	118	5 344	147 851	17.1
Dodge	1 207	2.9	D	41.7	D	6.2	2.5	15.2	12.6	14 077	169	586	28 720	6.4
Door	373	2.9	D	16.5	D	15.5	6.9	26.5	14.0	6 335	234	235	18 037	17.7
Douglas	536	0.1	20.1	11.0	59.9	10.0	2.6	17.6	20.1	7 642	178	1 078	20 610	2.3
Dunn	485	2.7	25.6	18.7	44.6	15.8	2.3	15.5	27.2	5 837	150	639	13 252	11.5
Eau Claire	1 623	0.6	17.5	11.7	64.6	20.0	5.0	27.1	17.3	14 611	164	1 726	32 741	13.0
Florence	27	-1.5	31.5	24.1	36.8	10.7	2.3	13.9	33.2	1 134	218	103	3 775	13.0
Fond du Lac	1 705	1.6	45.8	36.0	41.2	8.0	3.5	16.5	11.3	16 666	176	1 146	34 548	8.9
Forest	89	-0.2	D	18.4	D	9.1	2.6	26.4	24.9	2 391	248	221	7 203	6.7
Grant	532	3.6	D	20.2	D	10.2	4.1	18.1	26.4	10 005	203	856	18 450	1.4
Green	439	3.0	31.1	24.1	52.3	16.8	3.1	22.2	13.6	5 937	178	306	12 087	6.8
Green Lake	242	4.6	37.0	24.2	45.4	9.2	3.3	23.0	13.0	4 573	235	227	9 202	10.6
Iowa	317	1.6	D	7.2	D	D	2.2	13.5	13.5	3 622	162	204	8 220	8.6
Iron	67	-0.3	D	17.1	D	12.9	2.0	28.2	17.2	1 957	308	134	5 243	2.8
Jackson	201	11.2	D	12.8	D	10.1	3.5	D	19.1	3 584	202	417	7 627	9.3
Jefferson	1 118	1.5	D	41.6	D	9.7	2.4	15.4	12.2	12 710	173	713	25 719	7.0
Juneau	279	4.0	42.7	36.7	D	9.2	D	14.6	19.2	5 480	230	500	11 422	14.9
Kenosha	1 866	0.1	D	32.3	D	9.0	3.9	20.2	15.9	22 361	155	2 270	51 262	7.9
Kewaunee	223	7.0	D	34.2	D	6.8	3.1	12.0	14.7	3 717	188	185	7 544	7.4
La Crosse	2 107	0.3	D	20.2	D	10.6	5.2	28.3	14.1	16 568	162	1 798	38 239	14.9
Lafayette	125	9.6	19.3	13.3	43.1	7.1	5.7	11.0	28.1	3 149	194	215	6 313	0.3
Langlade	236	3.6	D	22.1	D	12.3	D	19.7	16.3	4 830	236	414	10 825	10.2
Lincoln	386	0.5	D	38.8	D	8.5	6.3	11.4	16.3	6 308	212	405	13 256	3.7
Manitowoc	1 293	3.0	47.6	40.8	37.8	6.6	2.3	17.7	11.6	16 576	201	1 066	31 843	5.7
Marathon	2 220	1.9	38.0	31.7	48.3	8.1	9.7	16.8	11.8	19 874	161	1 891	43 774	10.1
Marinette	613	1.6	D	44.3	D	8.4	2.3	16.4	12.8	9 766	227	736	25 650	13.7
Marquette	113	1.3	42.4	32.0	37.8	9.1	3.7	14.5	18.4	3 920	260	227	8 035	12.7
Menominee	[4]54	[4]0.0	[4]D	[4]D	[4]D	[4]1.5	[4]D	[4]51.0	[4]20.0	684	143	144	1 742	31.3
Milwaukee	21 511	0.0	25.3	22.2	61.8	7.6	10.7	31.3	12.9	159 135	175	32 978	390 715	3.4
Monroe	534	4.3	D	17.8	D	7.7	2.7	13.5	33.8	6 980	177	689	14 135	10.9
Oconto	284	3.9	D	28.1	D	10.1	2.5	15.3	19.2	6 977	205	451	18 832	11.2
Oneida	541	0.7	D	18.5	D	12.4	4.1	27.3	18.0	9 125	256	562	25 173	8.7
Outagamie	3 263	1.0	D	25.6	D	9.4	9.0	20.4	9.5	21 729	139	1 530	51 923	18.2
Ozaukee	1 469	0.3	D	37.4	D	7.9	7.4	22.5	9.4	12 351	152	285	26 482	17.6
Pepin	72	5.5	17.0	6.8	D	10.3	3.2	16.9	22.4	1 505	211	118	2 919	1.3
Pierce	295	1.5	D	14.7	D	8.9	4.0	17.4	34.5	4 743	133	271	11 536	11.4
Polk	425	2.1	D	31.1	D	9.9	3.7	17.8	16.9	7 491	193	493	18 562	14.4
Portage	1 048	2.1	D	20.8	D	8.9	14.6	16.4	16.8	9 406	145	782	22 910	15.1
Price	215	1.2	D	50.2	D	6.6	2.4	13.0	15.0	3 693	234	329	9 052	3.7
Racine	3 117	0.4	48.6	42.8	39.0	7.2	2.8	20.3	12.0	30 896	166	3 467	66 945	7.0
Richland	172	3.5	D	33.1	D	10.9	3.0	16.3	19.3	3 627	203	341	7 325	4.9
Rock	2 537	0.5	46.6	39.9	40.5	9.2	2.7	18.0	12.4	25 063	166	2 772	54 840	5.3
Rusk	171	3.0	D	36.9	D	9.3	2.1	11.9	21.3	3 488	229	396	7 904	9.9
St. Croix	748	0.8	D	31.8	D	11.3	3.6	21.2	13.7	7 323	124	363	18 519	24.1
Sauk	935	1.1	D	24.6	D	11.7	3.8	23.7	10.5	9 966	187	634	20 439	17.1
Sawyer	176	1.0	25.9	16.7	54.6	13.6	4.9	28.2	13.5	3 769	234	359	13 025	17.8
Shawano	[4]384	[4]7.4	[4]D	[4]21.6	[4]D	[4]12.0	[4]4.1	[4]20.1	[4]16.0	8 312	214	580	16 737	9.8
Sheboygan	2 097	1.0	52.9	46.8	35.7	7.4	4.4	16.8	10.4	19 497	177	1 253	40 695	9.0
Taylor	263	1.0	D	40.6	D	7.9	3.1	14.9	11.4	3 572	185	274	7 710	7.6
Trempealeau	348	3.8	D	40.0	D	6.5	2.6	13.9	17.0	5 664	214	520	10 097	3.6
Vernon	213	2.1	D	12.1	D	11.3	6.5	21.1	23.2	5 878	215	578	10 830	6.8
Vilas	220	1.7	D	9.0	D	17.2	5.1	29.8	14.8	6 064	285	250	20 225	10.0
Walworth	1 231	0.8	D	29.5	D	9.4	3.4	19.3	17.3	14 239	167	750	36 937	10.6
Washburn	158	1.3	24.5	18.1	48.4	12.9	4.7	20.0	25.7	3 972	258	383	9 829	12.8
Washington	1 682	0.4	44.5	36.4	42.0	7.9	5.2	16.6	13.1	16 213	142	566	34 382	21.2
Waukesha	8 783	0.0	37.8	29.2	54.8	7.2	7.4	23.2	7.4	51 543	146	1 567	110 452	19.3
Waupaca	666	2.1	D	36.7	D	9.3	3.3	17.2	15.8	10 852	215	689	20 141	11.0
Waushara	161	9.3	20.3	12.8	50.5	12.1	4.1	16.3	19.9	5 430	251	361	12 246	8.9
Winnebago	3 334	0.1	D	46.6	D	6.0	3.7	18.5	11.5	25 383	169	1 823	56 123	12.9
Wood	1 702	1.7	32.9	27.5	D	8.3	D	33.4	9.8	14 576	192	1 138	28 839	10.1
WYOMING	7 804	0.7	28.6	5.7	46.3	9.7	4.9	18.6	24.3	73 739	153	5 744	203 411	8.1
Albany	420	0.4	15.0	8.7	D	10.3	3.9	22.5	42.5	3 264	112	258	13 844	15.8
Big Horn	136	4.6	34.8	6.8	D	6.7	D	7.5	25.7	2 330	205	184	5 048	4.4
Campbell	701	-0.7	53.1	2.9	34.0	6.7	1.9	12.0	13.5	2 637	81	182	11 538	21.4
Carbon	211	1.6	28.1	10.5	43.5	10.1	2.8	14.4	26.8	2 393	154	148	8 190	-5.4

1. Covers mining, construction, and manufacturing. 2. Covers private sector earnings in agricultural services, forestry, and fisheries; transportation and public utilities; wholesale trade; retail trade; finance, insurance, and real estate; and services. 3. Per 1,000 resident population estimated as of July 1 of the year shown. 4. Menominee County included with Shawano County.

Table B. States and Counties — Housing, Labor Force, and Employment

STATE County	Housing units, 1990 (cont'd)								Civilian labor force, 1999				Civilian employment, 1990[5]		
	Occupied units										Unemployment			Percent	
	Owner-occupied					Renter-occupied									
				Owner cost as a percent of income				Sub-stand-ard units[3] (percent)							
	Total	Percent	Median value[1]	With a mortgage	Without a mortgage	Median rent[2]	Rent as per-cent of income		Total	Percent change, 1998–1999	Total	Rate[4]	Total	Professional, managerial, and technical	Precision production, craft, and repair
	89	90	91	92	93	94	95	96	97	98	99	100	101	102	103
WISCONSIN—Cont'd															
Dane	142 786	55.2	78 400	20.9	13.1	465	26.0	2.6	258 942	-1.2	3 540	1.4	208 069	38.0	7.7
Dodge	26 853	73.1	54 800	20.2	14.1	370	22.6	1.9	47 455	-0.7	1 180	2.5	36 376	18.1	13.1
Door	10 066	77.5	66 500	22.5	14.3	348	23.8	1.6	15 107	-3.6	662	4.4	11 889	22.3	16.7
Douglas	16 374	69.6	38 700	17.9	13.2	300	27.2	2.6	22 269	-2.9	917	4.1	17 697	24.4	10.2
Dunn	12 250	67.2	49 000	18.1	13.2	343	28.7	3.2	21 586	-3.8	655	3.0	16 950	24.0	9.7
Eau Claire	31 282	64.5	53 500	18.9	13.2	356	27.2	2.5	51 377	-1.8	1 358	2.6	40 643	28.6	8.6
Florence	1 755	82.8	45 400	20.0	15.3	302	24.1	4.1	1 779	0.6	112	6.3	1 955	19.8	14.4
Fond du Lac	32 644	71.8	56 000	19.1	12.8	367	23.7	1.5	52 862	-4.1	1 467	2.8	44 902	21.6	13.2
Forest	3 290	76.9	38 400	21.3	15.5	272	25.8	4.1	4 455	-2.6	230	5.2	3 227	18.7	10.9
Grant	17 169	69.5	43 600	17.5	13.2	305	24.0	2.3	23 806	-4.0	824	3.5	23 266	20.9	11.8
Green	11 541	69.3	53 600	20.9	13.1	340	22.5	1.7	18 026	-6.3	575	3.2	15 527	19.4	12.2
Green Lake	7 189	75.1	48 400	20.5	13.6	306	22.5	1.8	10 190	-5.1	413	4.1	8 615	18.2	15.0
Iowa	7 406	72.5	45 900	18.6	14.3	323	23.0	2.8	13 570	-3.4	399	2.9	10 311	18.3	12.1
Iron	2 602	79.2	30 800	19.9	15.1	242	25.7	2.2	3 227	2.5	186	5.8	2 451	21.0	14.5
Jackson	6 253	72.7	39 600	19.0	14.7	290	24.3	3.7	12 625	12.7	396	3.1	7 264	17.2	10.2
Jefferson	24 019	70.6	59 800	19.9	13.5	376	22.1	1.8	40 908	-2.4	996	2.4	35 187	21.9	12.7
Juneau	8 265	75.9	40 700	20.4	14.5	310	23.8	3.0	10 411	-4.6	688	6.6	9 478	18.1	13.9
Kenosha	47 029	68.8	65 100	19.4	12.9	411	24.6	2.8	80 330	-1.1	2 597	3.2	59 827	23.9	14.3
Kewaunee	6 756	80.8	50 000	19.2	14.5	277	20.2	2.2	10 281	-6.6	289	2.8	9 323	15.7	15.3
La Crosse	36 662	62.9	58 400	20.0	13.7	353	25.3	2.4	58 984	-3.1	1 723	2.9	49 988	28.0	9.2
Lafayette	5 876	72.5	39 400	19.8	13.6	308	22.1	2.4	7 534	-7.5	265	3.5	7 808	15.1	12.2
Langlade	7 563	77.5	37 600	19.6	13.8	284	24.5	3.1	9 102	-2.8	469	5.2	8 226	16.9	13.0
Lincoln	10 159	76.3	43 200	18.3	14.5	297	21.0	2.6	14 292	-8.3	653	4.6	12 363	20.5	11.9
Manitowoc	30 112	73.9	49 500	16.6	12.3	295	22.5	2.0	43 594	-4.6	1 555	3.6	38 381	20.2	13.9
Marathon	41 547	74.7	54 600	18.1	13.1	365	23.0	2.6	72 198	-2.0	2 114	2.9	57 719	23.0	11.0
Marinette	15 542	77.4	41 400	18.5	15.0	298	25.0	2.8	20 878	-2.1	964	4.6	17 221	19.4	13.1
Marquette	4 831	80.6	45 600	20.0	14.4	304	22.6	2.4	6 819	-4.4	359	5.3	5 196	16.2	14.3
Menominee	1 079	64.4	48 600	16.8	13.3	226	27.8	16.1	2 508	5.6	190	7.6	971	21.1	9.1
Milwaukee	373 048	52.1	65 300	20.7	14.0	434	26.7	3.5	474 044	-1.7	17 906	3.8	446 630	29.0	10.2
Monroe	13 144	72.8	48 600	20.8	13.8	323	23.1	3.4	19 176	-3.2	745	3.9	16 616	20.3	10.9
Oconto	11 283	81.6	43 200	20.8	16.2	294	23.5	2.7	15 446	-0.5	684	4.4	13 113	18.1	14.5
Oneida	12 666	77.4	52 900	20.3	13.8	332	24.6	2.5	20 128	-0.8	875	4.3	13 958	27.2	12.3
Outagamie	50 527	72.3	64 400	18.8	13.0	385	22.1	1.9	99 987	-0.6	2 494	2.5	71 130	25.5	12.4
Ozaukee	25 707	74.4	100 500	20.8	13.3	495	23.6	1.4	47 675	-1.7	903	1.9	39 100	34.2	12.5
Pepin	2 612	76.4	40 700	20.5	15.4	280	26.1	1.8	3 202	-7.3	127	4.0	3 126	16.9	11.0
Pierce	11 011	70.7	65 500	20.6	13.4	387	24.5	2.2	20 335	-1.4	506	2.5	17 195	22.4	10.3
Polk	13 056	77.9	53 600	20.5	14.3	318	28.0	2.9	21 578	-4.6	787	3.6	15 455	20.0	13.7
Portage	21 306	70.3	58 800	18.4	13.3	372	25.9	3.1	36 219	-3.1	1 187	3.3	30 150	25.4	10.3
Price	6 054	79.6	40 900	20.1	14.4	286	22.4	5.0	6 989	-9.1	476	6.8	6 725	20.8	11.8
Racine	63 736	68.3	64 200	19.3	12.6	402	24.9	2.6	90 572	-3.2	3 993	4.4	84 059	26.3	14.0
Richland	6 593	71.9	40 500	20.4	13.7	299	24.2	3.7	8 271	-7.3	284	3.4	8 003	16.8	13.0
Rock	52 252	68.2	52 300	17.0	12.9	387	24.7	2.0	77 151	-3.6	3 101	4.0	67 826	22.7	12.8
Rusk	5 693	75.0	36 700	19.8	14.3	278	24.4	4.8	7 113	0.5	327	4.6	6 194	19.7	10.8
St. Croix	17 638	74.9	74 400	20.6	14.0	429	24.2	1.8	32 758	0.1	766	2.3	25 705	27.0	11.9
Sauk	17 703	72.3	55 600	20.4	13.5	353	24.3	2.1	33 501	0.3	917	2.7	22 987	20.6	13.3
Sawyer	5 569	74.9	49 500	23.6	16.1	261	26.4	4.0	9 070	-1.1	472	5.2	5 231	24.3	12.8
Shawano	13 775	77.1	45 500	19.8	13.6	305	23.3	3.5	19 928	-5.8	700	3.5	16 708	17.6	12.2
Sheboygan	38 592	70.3	59 400	18.5	13.0	361	21.5	1.7	60 541	-0.9	1 211	2.0	52 159	22.5	12.9
Taylor	6 692	78.9	43 500	17.8	13.8	292	21.3	5.0	10 046	-3.8	393	3.9	8 716	15.7	10.4
Trempealeau	9 495	73.0	40 900	19.8	14.3	276	22.8	3.0	13 831	-4.7	521	3.8	12 039	18.9	11.2
Vernon	9 725	76.2	43 600	20.7	14.4	257	25.8	4.3	13 402	-4.2	530	4.0	11 547	18.0	10.9
Vilas	7 294	79.2	58 900	23.4	14.5	302	26.3	2.9	10 966	0.0	473	4.3	7 129	24.7	14.1
Walworth	27 620	66.9	69 100	20.7	13.6	413	25.0	2.1	52 012	0.2	1 242	2.4	38 093	23.9	13.1
Washburn	5 456	76.3	46 900	21.1	15.0	288	27.3	3.8	7 621	-2.6	433	5.7	5 653	22.6	13.4
Washington	32 977	73.9	83 900	21.2	12.9	455	21.9	1.7	66 338	-1.2	1 500	2.3	50 498	24.9	16.0
Waukesha	105 990	77.3	96 300	21.1	12.8	541	23.5	1.4	209 242	-0.9	4 391	2.1	164 509	34.5	12.0
Waupaca	17 037	76.1	50 000	20.2	14.1	328	23.3	2.6	25 444	-6.6	839	3.3	20 961	20.2	12.4
Waushara	7 616	80.3	45 300	20.3	13.9	307	24.9	3.0	10 097	-5.1	457	4.5	8 089	18.9	13.3
Winnebago	53 216	66.6	60 200	20.0	12.8	382	24.0	1.5	94 737	-2.3	2 102	2.2	70 401	26.5	11.1
Wood	27 473	73.3	50 500	16.7	12.6	343	23.6	2.0	38 919	-3.9	1 411	3.6	34 173	24.2	11.9
WYOMING	168 839	67.8	61 600	18.8	11.9	333	23.7	3.1	262 069	1.6	12 746	4.9	207 868	27.2	13.2
Albany	11 957	49.2	67 300	19.0	11.1	343	32.3	3.0	17 442	2.8	337	1.9	14 927	39.0	7.0
Big Horn	3 905	73.9	44 300	18.4	12.8	289	23.0	4.5	5 806	-0.2	380	6.5	4 277	24.1	11.5
Campbell	9 968	70.5	68 500	16.8	13.6	362	20.5	2.8	19 770	3.1	1 017	5.1	14 531	23.6	17.1
Carbon	6 001	69.1	52 700	16.1	12.0	301	20.0	3.1	8 475	1.3	446	5.3	7 602	20.4	15.3

1. Specified owner-occupied units.   2. Specified renter-occupied units.   3. Overcrowded or lacking complete plumbing facilities.   4. Percent of civilian labor force.   5. Persons 16 years and older.

	Private nonfarm establishments, employment and payroll, 1998								Agriculture, 1997			
STATE County		Employment					Annual payroll		Farms			Farm operators
										Percent with—		Whose principal occupation is farming (percent)
	Number of establishments	Total	Health Care and Social Assistance	Manufacturing	Retail trade	Finance and Insurance	Professional Scientific and Technical Services	Total (mil dol)	Average per employee (dollars)	Number	Less than 50 acres	500 acres and over	
	104	105	106	107	108	109	110	111	112	113	114	115	116
WISCONSIN—Cont'd													
Dane	12 058	214 837	26 791	26 902	30 973	18 580	12 530	6 019	28 018	2 595	30.1	8.1	54.3
Dodge	1 835	29 528	3 390	12 898	3 340	572	538	816	27 639	1 807	20.0	8.7	65.8
Door	1 320	10 311	1 239	2 304	1 615	305	246	219	21 191	702	23.4	4.1	56.0
Douglas	1 101	12 759	1 957	1 503	2 056	337	336	278	21 762	267	15.0	11.6	39.0
Dunn	976	12 852	1 930	2 739	1 911	355	398	288	22 377	1 397	14.3	11.3	58.8
Eau Claire	2 585	41 277	7 475	4 541	7 697	1 837	1 614	936	22 674	927	17.0	5.7	58.8
Florence	104	711	D	238	92	D	10	11	15 792	86	10.5	9.3	51.2
Fond du Lac	2 485	41 813	4 684	11 641	5 931	1 446	1 996	1 079	25 801	1 488	17.6	8.2	62.8
Forest	315	2 295	240	347	340	68	62	45	19 580	111	17.1	8.1	47.7
Grant	1 299	13 337	1 841	3 072	2 328	512	387	249	18 693	2 238	13.7	12.0	65.9
Green	950	12 857	1 777	3 547	3 015	391	243	298	23 189	1 295	17.4	9.8	68.2
Green Lake	622	6 738	1 075	1 980	1 174	177	90	154	22 910	584	17.5	8.7	57.9
Iowa	566	9 397	849	788	D	187	153	216	22 996	1 394	14.1	11.6	59.8
Iron	240	1 974	360	366	347	D	24	36	18 118	38	7.9	10.5	42.1
Jackson	405	4 925	458	880	883	199	118	123	25 012	774	13.2	13.4	58.0
Jefferson	1 850	31 183	3 312	11 908	3 517	730	548	777	24 902	1 240	25.8	7.0	52.2
Juneau	618	7 881	966	2 861	1 034	158	121	167	21 151	654	16.5	10.1	53.7
Kenosha	3 053	46 908	6 155	10 827	6 699	1 188	798	1 295	27 612	388	40.5	12.4	49.5
Kewaunee	484	5 393	401	2 362	694	194	125	130	24 090	795	16.4	6.4	66.2
La Crosse	2 957	55 719	9 902	10 644	8 819	1 972	1 667	1 389	24 929	759	14.9	9.2	53.1
Lafayette	346	2 842	D	662	554	149	57	58	20 412	1 127	16.0	14.2	71.6
Langlade	601	6 251	816	1 423	1 301	212	83	131	21 008	453	19.4	13.0	63.8
Lincoln	800	9 896	1 005	3 385	1 582	231	133	221	22 323	425	15.1	6.4	56.7
Manitowoc	1 857	33 320	4 002	13 830	3 905	727	594	892	26 768	1 227	23.3	8.1	60.1
Marathon	3 371	58 831	6 275	17 188	8 990	4 295	1 548	1 637	27 827	2 703	23.3	6.2	60.6
Marinette	1 070	15 939	2 140	6 627	2 049	420	183	404	25 350	551	15.6	11.1	54.6
Marquette	342	3 220	292	1 233	D	84	35	72	22 466	443	17.8	14.4	50.3
Menominee	98	1 747	D	D	140	D	0	34	19 238	5	60.0	40.0	60.0
Milwaukee	21 384	475 869	71 743	87 619	51 653	38 701	23 116	15 033	31 591	83	67.5	2.4	43.4
Monroe	868	13 017	2 317	4 045	1 668	377	185	301	23 135	1 567	14.3	7.0	61.2
Oconto	841	8 250	921	2 551	960	218	160	182	22 121	940	15.1	8.1	55.7
Oneida	1 541	15 600	3 299	2 514	3 199	405	366	366	23 441	117	25.6	14.5	55.6
Outagamie	4 499	87 805	8 428	21 428	11 647	6 067	2 891	2 533	28 847	1 286	26.4	7.6	59.2
Ozaukee	2 729	36 791	3 465	13 205	4 426	1 418	1 733	1 068	29 025	427	34.7	6.1	49.4
Pepin	195	1 622	286	D	469	72	D	35	21 790	425	15.8	10.4	64.0
Pierce	770	6 239	637	1 031	1 091	274	182	125	19 987	1 265	20.5	7.9	52.4
Polk	1 063	11 625	1 713	3 824	1 598	345	257	246	21 154	1 301	17.6	8.2	51.5
Portage	1 630	26 378	2 367	5 439	3 958	3 954	679	659	24 967	913	14.8	12.2	56.7
Price	464	5 842	871	2 696	796	166	72	147	25 123	370	10.0	10.5	53.0
Racine	4 210	76 877	8 759	20 259	10 083	4 032	2 146	2 261	29 413	554	41.0	9.4	55.1
Richland	348	4 507	514	1 936	860	124	66	103	22 913	1 032	13.2	8.5	57.6
Rock	3 340	60 340	7 290	18 543	8 439	1 606	992	1 736	28 773	1 324	32.6	12.9	52.3
Rusk	360	4 164	675	1 722	484	128	29	95	22 720	578	9.3	10.7	68.9
St. Croix	1 579	20 449	2 395	6 123	3 080	539	902	499	24 392	1 520	23.9	7.4	48.2
Sauk	1 680	24 147	2 792	6 487	4 112	883	645	595	24 636	1 452	16.9	10.6	57.2
Sawyer	625	4 344	542	831	812	161	104	89	20 422	184	16.8	13.6	54.9
Shawano	877	9 952	1 351	2 144	1 736	315	209	203	20 374	1 337	15.3	6.4	65.9
Sheboygan	2 584	53 132	5 050	20 772	5 947	1 764	1 631	1 485	27 948	968	32.2	8.5	61.7
Taylor	481	6 923	840	2 896	885	247	81	168	24 210	887	13.0	10.5	69.3
Trempealeau	719	9 582	1 298	4 422	1 029	292	190	227	23 750	1 408	11.4	9.4	57.7
Vernon	659	5 951	1 429	960	1 142	288	129	109	18 249	1 893	17.9	5.7	59.1
Vilas	810	4 161	403	359	692	146	69	78	18 849	44	31.8	4.5	54.5
Walworth	2 573	35 171	3 102	11 355	3 903	723	902	821	23 346	853	32.6	15.1	56.6
Washburn	569	4 424	719	912	989	156	143	84	18 908	354	17.8	13.0	46.3
Washington	3 053	46 100	4 228	15 880	5 294	2 017	1 239	1 209	26 229	787	30.9	5.6	58.7
Waukesha	12 335	210 582	18 159	50 822	24 285	9 733	10 547	6 813	32 352	630	46.8	7.8	47.5
Waupaca	1 367	16 297	2 179	5 981	2 488	586	250	375	23 003	1 129	19.8	7.2	57.5
Waushara	525	4 009	582	758	847	153	77	76	18 953	634	22.7	12.0	53.0
Winnebago	3 749	80 412	9 144	27 053	8 778	2 368	1 902	2 446	30 415	860	24.0	9.0	57.9
Wood	1 900	36 761	7 689	8 990	5 545	877	645	1 091	29 673	968	16.9	8.6	63.1
WYOMING	17 888	163 791	23 694	8 916	26 974	6 130	6 096	3 980	24 300	9 232	16.9	50.5	60.5
Albany	996	9 255	1 550	548	1 754	376	622	175	18 930	315	10.5	65.1	54.3
Big Horn	287	2 428	303	222	316	80	D	57	23 607	495	17.6	32.7	59.4
Campbell	1 119	13 502	1 176	189	1 618	264	389	434	32 137	531	11.9	72.3	59.7
Carbon	566	4 158	497	381	814	148	91	94	22 534	310	12.9	66.8	69.0

Table B. States and Counties — Agriculture, Land, and Water

STATE County	Land in farms — Acreage (1,000)	Land in farms — Percent change, 1992–1997	Acres — Average size of farm	Acres — Total irrigated (1,000)	Acres — Total cropland (1,000)	Value of land and buildings — Average per farm ($1,000)	Value of land and buildings — Average per acre (dollars)	Value of machinery and equipment Average per farm ($1,000)	Value of products sold — Total (mil dol)	Value of products sold — Average per farm (dollars)	Percent from — Crops	Percent from — Livestock and poultry products	Percent of farms with sales of — $10,000 or more	Percent of farms with sales of — $100,000 or more	Percent of land owned by Fed. Gov. 1997	Water consumption 1995 (mil gal/ day)
	117	118	119	120	121	122	123	124	125	126	127	128	129	130	131	132
WISCONSIN—Cont'd																
Dane	513	-4.8	198	7	414	367	1 853	73	285	109 687	31.1	68.9	59.5	25.6	0.2	112.7
Dodge	392	-5.3	217	1	331	329	1 537	86	194	107 131	26.4	73.6	74.4	32.4	3.4	13.7
Door	122	-6.2	174	1	93	262	1 383	59	38	54 552	31.2	68.8	53.7	17.1	0.2	4.9
Douglas	71	-0.3	265	D	34	177	608	24	6	21 307	21.2	78.8	28.1	4.9	0.2	6.7
Dunn	369	0.4	264	13	235	242	934	71	114	81 872	25.6	74.4	57.1	23.2	0.0	15.1
Eau Claire	191	0.7	206	3	133	196	943	52	58	62 328	30.0	70.0	55.4	19.8	0.0	18.1
Florence	19	-7.8	225	D	11	152	673	44	2	21 513	26.2	73.8	38.4	5.8	26.8	0.6
Fond du Lac	325	-7.7	218	1	273	306	1 388	76	151	101 573	25.5	74.5	71.4	33.3	0.2	17.2
Forest	26	0.6	236	D	12	167	716	36	4	33 313	11.4	88.6	36.9	6.3	51.0	1.0
Grant	600	-3.4	268	D	376	288	1 112	68	204	91 287	17.9	82.1	71.9	33.0	0.5	251.5
Green	305	4.1	235	5	249	313	1 385	74	125	96 813	23.3	76.7	72.0	37.0	0.0	6.5
Green Lake	134	-17.6	230	3	106	306	1 453	62	45	77 493	36.8	63.2	64.6	25.2	0.0	5.3
Iowa	367	1.3	263	8	232	335	1 235	62	111	79 559	20.6	79.4	61.7	25.3	0.0	3.3
Iron	10	-3.7	254	D	5	183	720	41	1	21 553	38.0	62.0	34.2	2.6	0.0	0.8
Jackson	244	11.9	315	4	133	336	1 068	62	78	100 666	53.2	46.8	58.3	22.2	0.3	9.3
Jefferson	242	4.0	195	9	200	375	1 917	67	131	105 860	45.2	54.8	59.3	20.2	0.1	22.7
Juneau	169	-13.2	259	10	110	321	1 288	66	53	80 338	54.3	45.7	56.1	16.5	14.6	8.4
Kenosha	85	-8.9	218	0	74	613	2 961	98	33	85 699	63.9	36.1	59.0	25.5	0.0	35.1
Kewaunee	161	-5.1	203	0	132	288	1 351	88	81	101 548	18.6	81.4	65.2	32.3	0.0	725.9
La Crosse	170	-6.8	223	1	89	233	1 075	51	46	60 287	19.7	80.3	54.8	19.8	3.1	69.0
Lafayette	338	-5.2	300	0	263	345	1 146	84	136	120 859	28.6	71.4	77.4	40.1	0.0	3.2
Langlade	124	3.2	273	13	82	300	1 060	100	51	112 395	57.3	42.7	60.7	23.2	6.2	13.3
Lincoln	84	-2.4	197	0	44	180	928	56	20	47 741	33.4	66.6	49.4	12.5	0.0	10.9
Manitowoc	245	-1.7	200	1	206	256	1 325	72	138	112 841	13.6	86.4	63.0	32.4	0.0	1 260.8
Marathon	516	-2.7	191	6	337	202	1 039	68	204	75 578	24.7	75.3	68.2	24.0	0.0	183.4
Marinette	132	-9.8	239	2	83	217	1 038	48	40	71 845	18.4	81.6	53.5	18.5	0.0	22.3
Marquette	125	-8.2	282	4	86	334	1 137	55	32	72 870	53.5	46.5	51.5	16.9	0.3	1.6
Menominee	0	0.0	77		D	189	2 446	13	0	2 506	D	D	0.0	0.0	0.0	0.3
Milwaukee	6	-30.0	76	0	D	319	4 180	44	7	82 173	D	D	51.8	26.5	0.0	1 974.0
Monroe	330	-4.8	210	3	178	255	1 165	66	102	64 958	33.5	66.5	57.9	17.4	13.2	6.4
Oconto	204	-2.5	217	0	144	225	1 062	63	67	70 870	19.4	80.6	59.4	21.8	21.6	6.2
Oneida	39	22.0	334	2	16	421	1 262	65	13	113 594	85.5	14.5	38.5	17.9	1.3	32.8
Outagamie	252	-4.4	196	0	212	305	1 557	83	142	110 563	23.7	76.3	68.8	33.3	0.0	67.7
Ozaukee	70	-11.5	164	0	59	424	2 509	58	32	75 052	34.5	65.5	52.9	22.7	0.1	223.5
Pepin	104	-8.7	245	1	66	198	879	62	29	69 226	27.0	73.0	70.6	24.0	0.0	1.4
Pierce	268	-2.0	212	0	184	244	1 130	49	76	60 375	30.2	69.8	55.1	21.3	0.0	4.3
Polk	268	-5.1	206	1	171	216	969	49	68	52 225	23.5	76.5	50.8	16.7	0.7	4.8
Portage	263	-1.2	288	76	189	355	1 194	101	115	126 060	67.6	32.4	56.2	22.2	0.0	85.2
Price	93	-2.5	250	D	40	215	739	48	15	40 960	27.6	72.4	43.5	8.9	18.6	9.3
Racine	123	-7.5	222	5	110	520	2 396	77	78	141 584	53.7	46.3	52.5	20.6	0.0	37.7
Richland	238	-12.1	231	2	128	211	922	49	61	59 247	14.9	85.1	51.6	18.5	0.0	2.7
Rock	351	2.3	265	10	308	453	1 727	79	130	97 906	56.9	43.1	58.5	24.7	0.1	152.0
Rusk	159	-5.3	275	0	83	172	615	55	32	56 192	6.9	93.1	59.2	18.0	0.0	4.2
St. Croix	312	1.3	205	4	237	282	1 368	53	92	60 267	28.2	71.8	49.7	17.1	1.0	7.7
Sauk	333	-0.9	229	10	213	286	1 212	77	121	83 487	18.2	81.8	60.9	24.6	1.3	13.2
Sawyer	48	3.1	263	0	27	207	769	55	10	55 544	33.6	66.4	50.0	17.4	14.7	1.5
Shawano	270	-9.2	202	0	184	213	1 082	71	127	94 640	10.0	90.0	67.2	27.0	0.0	6.0
Sheboygan	182	-11.9	188	0	153	313	1 668	78	92	95 254	19.1	80.9	63.8	29.1	0.0	464.7
Taylor	224	-3.2	252	0	122	177	679	51	62	69 621	9.0	91.0	66.3	23.3	18.8	2.2
Trempealeau	341	-2.4	242	4	211	204	829	57	124	88 315	16.2	83.8	57.0	21.2	0.4	5.6
Vernon	344	-6.0	182	0	203	198	1 135	46	86	45 690	16.1	83.9	58.7	13.3	2.1	200.6
Vilas	8	0.0	172	1	D	369	2 143	98	6	140 675	97.9	2.1	43.2	15.9	8.3	1.5
Walworth	220	-3.0	258	1	187	537	2 107	80	93	109 484	48.3	51.7	61.5	28.1	0.0	14.6
Washburn	98	13.8	276	2	46	233	891	51	16	45 010	37.8	62.2	43.8	10.7	0.7	2.5
Washington	127	-13.5	162	0	105	359	2 165	69	61	78 075	33.1	66.9	63.5	21.7	0.0	12.8
Waukesha	106	-7.4	168	1	88	461	2 982	53	42	66 823	64.2	35.8	47.0	16.0	0.0	43.5
Waupaca	227	-6.3	201	9	162	227	1 210	56	86	76 334	26.2	73.8	58.5	22.8	0.0	10.2
Waushara	175	4.5	275	49	127	383	1 308	85	75	118 298	75.3	24.7	49.2	18.6	0.0	25.7
Winnebago	167	-1.5	195	0	136	331	1 722	76	62	71 731	31.7	68.3	57.7	21.7	0.2	68.7
Wood	219	-0.8	227	6	138	320	1 482	77	91	93 834	47.5	52.5	65.8	26.0	0.5	121.9
WYOMING	34 089	3.7	3 692	1 719	2 968	808	222	61	899	97 327	19.3	80.7	62.6	20.6	45.9	7 040.2
Albany	1 922	2.9	6 103	155	133	1 433	243	59	34	108 598	4.9	95.1	61.9	24.8	24.3	179.7
Big Horn	443	0.6	896	116	131	642	666	72	43	87 710	57.9	42.1	63.0	22.4	73.3	740.9
Campbell	2 944	8.9	5 544	5	157	634	119	54	35	65 770	5.8	94.2	65.7	17.1	12.6	52.0
Carbon	2 282	-16.1	7 360	182	158	1 383	191	73	43	140 141	5.8	94.2	65.2	32.9	56.7	786.1

Table B. States and Counties — **Residential Construction, Wholesale and Retail Trade, and Real Estate**

STATE County	Value of Residential Construction Authorized by Building Permits, 1999		Wholesale Trade, 1997				Retail Trade[1], 1997				Real Estate and Rental and Leasing, 1997			
	New Construction ($1,000)	Number of Housing Units	Number of Establish-ments	Number of Employees	Sales (mil dol)	Annual Payroll (mil dol)	Number of Establish-ments	Number of Employees	Sales (mil dol)	Annual Payroll (mil dol)	Number of Establish-ments	Number of Employees	Receipts (mil dol)	Annual Payroll (mil dol)
	133	134	135	136	137	138	139	140	141	142	143	144	145	146
WISCONSIN—Cont'd														
Dane	412 159	3 626	675	10 048	4 350.1	342.7	1 845	30 150	4 860.9	507.2	520	3 519	371.4	71.1
Dodge	35 981	357	86	1 087	528.9	33.7	277	3 220	544.2	49.6	39	161	9.8	1.7
Door	50 133	527	34	159	38.9	3.3	281	1 581	258.9	24.8	55	107	14.5	1.8
Douglas	15 820	240	59	D	D	D	161	2 075	334.1	31.1	40	146	10.0	1.8
Dunn	15 587	196	43	433	98.2	9.5	156	2 060	324.0	30.0	28	50	5.1	0.5
Eau Claire	66 819	624	135	1 463	613.5	42.2	459	7 405	1 036.0	100.7	100	456	45.5	7.1
Florence	0	0	5	D	D	D	12	78	15.1	0.8	5	6	0.5	0.1
Fond du Lac	55 273	470	116	1 204	528.2	36.0	413	5 744	891.2	86.6	73	297	27.9	4.5
Forest	10 035	120	11	76	13.5	1.9	42	345	50.9	4.9	9	30	2.3	0.2
Grant	18 339	199	66	613	174.5	11.2	243	2 310	357.6	32.3	50	126	9.7	1.1
Green	30 444	246	66	588	208.8	14.1	181	3 025	572.9	66.3	18	41	7.0	0.4
Green Lake	13 412	101	19	149	32.6	3.8	113	1 297	161.4	15.7	15	42	3.0	0.4
Iowa	19 737	211	39	331	109.9	10.7	105	4 409	1 211.4	107.7	9	30	2.9	0.2
Iron	10 360	102	8	48	11.9	1.1	38	337	49.4	4.5	11	50	3.2	0.6
Jackson	8 029	102	10	74	8.7	1.1	83	919	124.7	11.6	12	24	3.9	0.6
Jefferson	63 419	551	92	1 483	466.5	42.2	253	3 519	568.2	53.1	54	177	16.5	3.0
Juneau	14 722	172	22	200	77.5	4.5	102	1 056	170.5	15.1	15	31	1.9	0.2
Kenosha	113 775	1 121	135	2 515	1 385.3	91.5	546	6 442	1 072.4	95.7	112	412	43.8	6.6
Kewaunee	16 803	144	20	139	35.5	3.4	72	655	113.6	10.3	8	11	1.0	0.1
La Crosse	72 955	739	154	3 217	1 921.6	102.5	509	9 005	1 452.6	135.6	120	774	59.2	13.3
Lafayette	4 713	46	23	170	62.2	4.0	62	526	94.8	8.8	4	4	0.3	0.0
Langlade	13 434	194	39	348	217.8	11.0	114	1 270	255.7	20.5	10	38	2.0	0.4
Lincoln	21 932	218	25	D	D	D	142	1 504	220.1	20.6	26	82	3.9	0.6
Manitowoc	44 106	402	67	611	257.1	22.0	295	3 856	561.0	55.1	50	183	14.1	2.2
Marathon	89 423	779	221	3 395	1 002.0	102.5	565	9 236	1 421.6	142.6	86	439	39.9	7.1
Marinette	24 064	304	33	485	93.2	14.8	187	2 008	285.9	27.4	26	45	5.3	0.6
Marquette	13 991	148	10	D	D	D	47	444	56.6	5.6	10	32	1.5	0.3
Menominee	2 246	26	2	D	D	D	13	113	15.2	1.2	1	D	D	D
Milwaukee	175 486	2 003	1 393	22 559	13 007.5	845.3	3 224	52 471	8 065.2	839.2	875	6 745	827.5	145.6
Monroe	16 868	201	46	465	241.6	12.2	139	1 618	261.8	22.8	25	85	5.6	1.1
Oconto	41 609	499	28	121	45.1	3.8	118	1 017	178.6	14.2	22	37	2.3	0.4
Oneida	40 571	401	45	441	119.9	12.8	294	3 030	471.5	45.3	63	212	24.9	4.0
Outagamie	150 516	1 300	291	4 066	1 694.0	147.5	712	11 218	1 936.3	182.2	124	702	75.6	15.0
Ozaukee	107 081	771	204	1 314	627.1	49.6	352	4 453	940.1	75.3	78	322	36.7	7.9
Pepin	5 471	54	11	90	27.4	2.1	38	434	88.7	8.6	3	6	0.6	0.1
Pierce	41 908	328	29	D	D	D	112	1 047	151.6	13.6	19	185	27.7	6.0
Polk	41 037	411	38	432	112.5	11.0	183	1 552	221.6	19.7	26	73	7.5	0.6
Portage	39 164	373	93	1 307	380.9	39.8	262	3 916	603.2	56.8	53	191	18.8	2.9
Price	16 553	183	19	211	41.5	3.3	97	726	106.9	9.9	4	12	1.5	0.2
Racine	110 646	910	234	4 560	3 816.9	142.4	664	9 693	1 564.1	142.0	132	746	57.7	12.1
Richland	11 998	115	16	122	32.2	1.6	76	821	128.5	11.4	11	25	1.6	0.2
Rock	92 123	989	152	2 823	1 706.4	95.8	584	8 484	1 599.7	148.4	105	364	52.9	5.6
Rusk	8 398	87	9	35	4.8	0.4	62	486	78.7	6.7	8	23	1.6	0.3
St. Croix	101 817	1 070	80	484	210.3	14.9	224	3 053	590.3	52.2	59	333	21.1	5.1
Sauk	52 323	498	68	1 090	426.4	33.6	295	4 083	582.6	62.2	45	184	22.6	3.4
Sawyer	20 540	249	8	79	23.8	3.4	100	778	133.6	12.0	24	53	5.3	0.6
Shawano	24 405	234	40	450	191.8	12.3	153	1 747	267.5	26.2	20	67	4.4	0.8
Sheboygan	66 007	597	119	2 041	1 185.0	65.4	398	5 831	911.0	88.0	85	400	38.2	6.2
Taylor	7 166	78	19	467	80.8	9.1	88	896	141.8	11.4	11	54	4.3	1.0
Trempealeau	13 651	135	39	215	125.6	5.2	126	1 017	169.4	13.5	18	49	7.3	0.8
Vernon	7 156	78	37	217	75.6	4.5	108	1 139	161.1	16.9	17	32	1.7	0.2
Vilas	30 438	348	20	69	17.0	1.5	150	764	122.8	12.8	24	D	D	D
Walworth	95 255	815	128	1 554	883.1	46.8	371	3 880	627.2	59.2	94	299	33.0	5.2
Washburn	19 515	258	16	90	21.9	2.1	96	975	173.6	15.4	23	70	7.0	0.9
Washington	138 540	1 128	181	2 658	1 107.9	97.0	390	5 184	1 201.5	86.0	76	276	35.0	4.1
Waukesha	486 527	3 271	1 272	16 570	11 523.8	672.1	1 385	24 345	4 094.2	392.4	413	2 432	352.9	65.0
Waupaca	13 923	161	58	406	116.3	9.5	242	2 473	416.3	36.8	34	98	7.2	1.3
Waushara	20 949	269	21	156	54.5	3.6	91	817	148.3	12.9	17	31	3.8	0.5
Winnebago	95 961	1 008	194	3 387	1 088.8	111.9	611	8 712	1 489.6	141.4	148	711	65.2	11.5
Wood	43 143	372	85	1 421	636.9	44.1	355	5 177	950.5	83.0	60	248	19.8	3.3
WYOMING	278 559	1 900	800	5 761	2 547.1	161.9	2 939	26 934	4 530.5	426.7	717	2 463	220.8	39.5
Albany	16 593	205	24	132	84.9	2.7	168	1 663	339.7	27.5	47	129	9.5	1.5
Big Horn	1 024	11	15	64	14.9	1.2	59	340	50.7	5.0	10	D	D	D
Campbell	5 428	40	78	658	235.4	22.9	179	1 733	280.3	28.0	37	142	11.4	1.8
Carbon	1 950	31	18	70	25.5	1.3	103	847	141.2	11.7	22	46	3.5	0.5

1. Establishments with payroll.

STATE County	Professional, Scientific, and Technical Services[1], 1997				Manufacturing, 1997				Accommodation and Foodservices, 1997			
	Number of Establishments	Number of Employees	Receipts (mil dol)	Annual Payroll (mil dol)	Number of Establishments	Number of Employees	Receipts (mil dol)	Annual Payroll (mil dol)	Number of Establishments	Number of Employees	Sales (mil dol)	Annual Payroll (mil dol)
	147	148	149	150	151	152	153	154	155	156	157	158
WISCONSIN—Cont'd												
Dane	1 132	10 748	943.4	412.4	564	26 568	4 840.5	864.4	993	18 607	554.1	156.9
Dodge	64	417	33.6	10.9	164	12 667	3 159.9	413.8	165	1 637	41.6	10.7
Door	64	251	14.7	5.0	63	2 222	267.5	59.7	243	1 796	96.4	25.1
Douglas	52	317	21.5	8.2	56	1 543	500.2	45.4	178	1 818	50.9	13.1
Dunn	43	289	17.5	7.9	60	2 910	875.4	92.0	107	1 383	33.4	9.4
Eau Claire	165	1 485	112.2	48.5	107	4 182	651.3	110.9	247	4 932	115.9	34.6
Florence	4	9	0.3	0.1	NA	NA	NA	NA	16	D	D	D
Fond du Lac	137	630	45.9	18.0	158	11 150	2 115.7	393.2	227	3 584	92.9	25.6
Forest	9	66	3.8	2.0	NA	NA	NA	NA	35	D	D	D
Grant	50	298	18.9	7.8	57	2 996	718.1	68.5	139	1 431	34.7	8.5
Green	43	180	14.2	4.4	77	3 667	840.2	93.5	92	1 182	29.1	8.3
Green Lake	24	89	5.4	1.4	61	2 383	262.0	55.8	62	707	20.0	5.7
Iowa	31	106	5.5	2.2	34	815	156.7	18.4	52	D	D	D
Iron	13	25	1.8	0.6	12	534	64.2	10.5	53	440	11.3	2.7
Jackson	25	103	4.3	2.2	20	810	134.2	17.8	52	685	17.1	4.5
Jefferson	90	598	33.0	13.6	165	12 201	2 431.5	371.8	187	2 098	52.8	13.9
Juneau	26	118	5.7	2.8	47	3 503	522.7	103.0	86	979	34.2	10.1
Kenosha	176	687	47.7	20.4	204	9 526	2 031.0	396.2	340	4 546	133.3	37.1
Kewaunee	23	73	4.3	1.4	45	2 359	314.0	67.1	53	512	11.6	2.8
La Crosse	191	1 531	117.1	52.5	161	10 171	1 382.6	313.7	300	5 533	141.9	41.4
Lafayette	15	23	1.6	0.4	21	661	134.4	14.5	36	256	5.5	1.5
Langlade	15	79	3.8	2.1	39	1 493	184.0	35.9	75	677	18.8	5.2
Lincoln	31	81	5.1	1.6	63	3 637	532.4	101.2	98	894	21.3	6.3
Manitowoc	86	538	41.8	11.9	180	13 474	2 134.1	407.2	179	2 512	59.4	16.4
Marathon	181	1 264	127.4	46.6	232	16 839	3 181.9	502.6	276	3 779	105.2	29.7
Marinette	42	132	9.1	4.0	82	6 766	1 139.1	217.9	140	1 386	36.2	9.9
Marquette	12	27	1.9	0.4	24	996	135.8	27.3	59	D	D	D
Menominee	NA	NA	NA	NA	6	705	51.0	16.6	9	D	D	D
Milwaukee	2 027	20 568	2 101.0	837.7	1 463	86 933	16 535.5	3 213.2	1 838	31 293	1 005.6	280.5
Monroe	36	143	8.7	3.4	58	3 397	745.0	79.9	110	1 186	35.8	9.3
Oconto	33	129	7.0	2.9	61	2 445	297.7	56.6	107	953	26.2	6.3
Oneida	89	363	25.7	10.3	68	2 526	395.3	78.3	209	1 903	61.6	16.9
Outagamie	275	2 371	199.9	86.7	303	21 410	5 315.4	750.7	361	6 755	192.1	53.5
Ozaukee	321	1 443	156.2	55.8	242	13 420	2 763.1	485.8	182	2 900	75.0	22.0
Pepin	6	29	1.4	0.4	NA	NA	NA	NA	26	D	D	D
Pierce	47	158	10.0	4.3	40	942	216.7	24.7	102	994	24.3	6.1
Polk	55	198	11.2	3.8	95	3 912	628.1	90.7	118	904	26.4	7.0
Portage	80	521	33.3	14.6	83	5 534	1 265.8	178.3	202	3 337	86.2	24.6
Price	23	80	4.6	1.8	46	2 957	449.6	91.7	42	D	D	D
Racine	296	1 821	134.3	55.6	379	18 869	5 229.5	664.1	360	5 324	154.7	42.2
Richland	19	67	2.9	1.1	26	1 851	373.3	52.7	32	D	D	D
Rock	182	1 002	65.1	23.5	234	19 547	10 105.6	785.3	343	5 295	151.2	41.3
Rusk	12	30	1.2	0.4	30	1 722	203.1	41.0	42	D	D	D
St. Croix	124	754	93.7	36.0	150	5 867	827.0	174.3	142	1 962	52.9	15.3
Sauk	76	549	37.0	16.8	114	6 570	1 121.2	180.8	241	3 276	123.6	32.9
Sawyer	24	76	4.2	1.6	39	859	137.3	22.4	109	613	24.3	6.1
Shawano	27	144	5.5	3.1	67	1 985	330.3	51.0	109	1 147	32.9	8.6
Sheboygan	150	1 235	92.2	40.5	239	20 047	4 252.7	628.3	237	3 714	105.9	29.1
Taylor	17	59	2.9	1.4	43	2 987	592.7	83.8	39	D	D	D
Trempealeau	29	177	7.7	3.9	62	4 678	799.9	121.8	85	713	17.1	4.9
Vernon	24	103	3.6	1.3	37	970	168.1	20.7	66	D	D	D
Vilas	20	54	3.2	1.1	NA	NA	NA	NA	188	1 451	69.9	17.3
Walworth	158	649	57.3	20.0	218	10 377	1 496.2	311.7	276	5 518	168.1	53.1
Washburn	25	126	7.7	3.2	35	793	94.7	17.1	80	521	17.6	4.3
Washington	162	1 254	102.0	26.3	321	15 660	2 360.2	499.2	217	3 737	93.7	25.7
Waukesha	1 142	9 380	1 031.1	377.8	1 148	49 130	9 434.6	1 760.3	635	11 945	372.6	104.4
Waupaca	51	165	8.7	3.1	105	5 995	1 235.3	176.0	139	1 583	41.8	11.1
Waushara	18	51	2.5	0.9	32	746	79.2	14.9	70	D	D	D
Winnebago	202	1 630	142.9	46.0	316	27 191	6 026.6	976.5	341	5 832	153.7	43.4
Wood	77	518	33.0	12.2	117	9 421	2 535.6	363.3	191	2 468	65.3	17.3
WYOMING	1 264	5 274	388.8	146.9	503	8 448	2 955.1	256.4	1 751	24 950	808.9	219.0
Albany	108	549	40.6	17.1	33	531	89.1	13.5	104	1 922	45.1	12.8
Big Horn	10	33	2.4	1.0	NA	NA	NA	NA	32	215	4.8	1.5
Campbell	80	336	22.3	8.2	NA	NA	NA	NA	77	1 346	41.9	11.1
Carbon	26	73	6.6	1.4	NA	NA	NA	NA	85	781	25.8	6.8

1. Firms subject to federal tax.

Table B. States and Counties — Health and Other Services and Federal Funds

STATE County	Health Care and Social Assistance[1], 1997				Other Services[1], 1997				Federal funds and grants, fiscal 1999[2] — Expenditures (mil dol)			
										Direct payments for individuals[3]		
	Number of Establishments	Number of Employees	Receipts (mil dol)	Annual Payroll (mil dol)	Number of Establishments	Number of Employees	Receipts (mil dol)	Annual Payroll (mil dol)	Total	Social Security and government retirement	Medicare	Food stamps and Supplemental Security Income
	159	160	161	162	163	164	165	166	167	168	169	170
WISCONSIN—Cont'd												
Dane	785	9 899	735.9	320.2	664	4 412	258.5	88.8	2 510.0	620.8	175.8	28.7
Dodge	137	1 252	70.0	34.5	113	402	22.2	6.0	203.1	111.1	39.0	3.0
Door	56	512	23.8	11.2	55	207	12.7	2.8	122.9	65.0	23.3	1.1
Douglas	53	718	33.5	16.0	68	397	22.5	6.0	205.8	98.2	31.3	6.2
Dunn	39	1 003	31.5	16.3	59	268	13.2	3.5	124.0	53.8	15.6	3.4
Eau Claire	180	3 052	196.1	111.8	205	1 242	64.2	19.3	400.2	150.7	50.5	9.7
Florence	4	92	3.3	1.8	3	D	D	D	18.8	10.0	3.5	0.5
Fond du Lac	157	1 748	181.2	54.2	162	945	44.4	13.7	331.9	180.3	58.6	4.9
Forest	10	326	7.5	3.3	10	21	1.4	0.4	55.5	24.4	6.7	1.0
Grant	78	969	35.0	14.4	103	331	18.7	4.2	199.3	92.4	33.5	3.4
Green	52	767	55.7	25.8	73	271	19.0	5.3	110.7	56.9	21.2	1.5
Green Lake	46	334	15.5	7.3	32	104	6.9	1.6	79.0	43.0	15.0	0.8
Iowa	39	303	18.7	7.8	27	81	5.7	1.2	76.0	31.2	10.3	1.1
Iron	10	251	8.2	3.9	10	36	1.2	0.3	33.3	18.1	6.3	0.5
Jackson	18	221	12.3	5.1	25	66	3.4	0.7	76.8	34.5	10.4	1.9
Jefferson	135	1 397	70.7	32.8	129	553	28.3	8.3	251.1	135.8	48.6	2.7
Juneau	31	300	13.9	5.8	40	155	9.4	2.5	125.6	58.4	17.8	1.9
Kenosha	263	2 517	136.9	65.9	222	1 262	68.1	19.3	467.3	231.0	90.7	15.0
Kewaunee	34	251	7.4	3.3	28	76	4.8	1.0	95.3	36.2	12.6	1.0
La Crosse	139	1 013	57.5	26.8	193	1 271	65.1	20.7	378.1	175.1	52.9	10.5
Lafayette	17	79	5.4	1.4	25	68	5.2	1.2	62.2	26.5	10.3	0.9
Langlade	26	374	17.9	8.2	41	150	7.5	1.9	99.6	46.8	16.4	2.2
Lincoln	40	453	22.2	11.8	43	190	10.3	3.1	119.1	65.8	22.0	2.0
Manitowoc	129	1 362	78.1	41.3	129	496	27.9	7.9	288.6	163.4	55.5	4.9
Marathon	200	2 672	188.8	104.9	222	1 201	79.2	20.9	391.2	189.0	64.7	8.6
Marinette	68	1 006	50.0	26.1	53	202	11.8	3.3	241.6	102.8	31.4	3.6
Marquette	18	216	8.8	4.5	21	64	3.9	1.0	77.8	42.7	13.1	1.0
Menominee	1	D	D	D	3	D	D	D	35.9	5.8	1.9	0.6
Milwaukee	2 074	27 274	1 753.0	942.9	1 412	9 778	580.6	187.3	4 534.0	1 670.9	787.1	226.5
Monroe	38	360	15.7	7.6	65	310	14.4	4.6	258.6	92.7	20.0	2.4
Oconto	40	559	19.8	9.7	50	86	6.4	1.1	119.4	61.5	19.6	2.2
Oneida	80	1 272	67.5	30.2	89	336	24.0	6.0	170.4	96.1	29.8	2.7
Outagamie	287	3 049	217.2	111.8	303	2 270	130.9	38.9	416.9	240.1	63.5	7.4
Ozaukee	209	1 958	112.6	53.2	161	877	41.9	13.8	235.5	137.6	42.6	1.3
Pepin	9	117	4.8	2.6	8	29	1.7	0.4	33.2	14.4	5.7	0.4
Pierce	48	646	22.1	11.5	46	168	9.8	2.7	103.9	52.2	16.3	1.3
Polk	58	652	33.8	15.9	63	226	12.3	3.2	138.7	72.2	25.2	2.4
Portage	93	1 220	68.3	39.5	101	554	44.5	10.8	212.4	94.0	29.1	4.4
Price	21	328	10.8	5.2	22	59	3.6	0.8	70.6	37.1	12.3	1.4
Racine	265	3 771	263.8	132.8	291	2 195	125.4	40.3	626.2	329.1	111.1	21.2
Richland	20	156	10.4	5.6	19	58	4.5	0.9	72.9	31.5	11.0	1.5
Rock	223	3 402	196.2	97.5	241	1 052	63.8	16.8	569.5	255.9	89.2	16.6
Rusk	21	248	7.3	3.3	21	44	3.3	0.7	71.9	32.9	9.9	2.0
St. Croix	80	787	44.6	21.7	90	324	21.3	5.6	153.0	74.1	23.2	1.7
Sauk	98	1 358	67.3	33.9	97	345	23.1	5.8	199.3	97.5	34.9	3.6
Sawyer	26	199	8.7	4.3	33	112	6.4	1.7	86.4	37.0	12.1	2.1
Shawano	44	902	28.5	12.7	56	203	13.3	2.9	165.1	77.2	24.6	1.9
Sheboygan	176	2 412	134.3	74.8	172	967	56.5	14.6	372.5	198.7	61.1	6.6
Taylor	23	276	11.4	6.3	31	97	7.1	1.5	69.1	31.7	11.7	1.4
Trempealeau	32	207	7.6	3.6	50	168	10.6	2.4	120.8	52.9	18.1	2.1
Vernon	38	259	12.0	5.8	46	72	4.5	0.9	114.8	53.4	16.0	3.5
Vilas	20	99	4.9	2.0	34	99	6.0	1.4	104.8	58.2	18.9	1.3
Walworth	168	1 504	71.9	33.9	137	496	26.8	7.9	254.8	142.8	50.0	3.3
Washburn	22	264	12.0	6.1	31	95	5.9	1.3	90.6	47.4	12.0	1.9
Washington	168	1 700	82.6	37.6	195	1 374	85.8	24.1	286.7	169.9	52.9	3.0
Waukesha	800	9 241	551.7	274.0	648	5 262	423.2	126.2	1 170.6	585.5	178.2	7.0
Waupaca	80	1 086	53.0	22.2	94	277	18.1	4.6	221.9	119.2	36.7	3.4
Waushara	19	339	10.3	4.7	35	92	6.6	1.5	90.6	50.8	15.6	1.9
Winnebago	318	3 623	264.4	132.3	260	1 778	97.3	28.9	710.0	249.6	93.4	9.7
Wood	121	1 308	69.7	33.1	129	651	54.0	11.4	302.6	158.5	53.1	6.5
WYOMING	1 006	7 875	493.6	210.3	980	4 866	422.8	94.8	2 916.2	911.3	263.9	43.7
Albany	72	601	34.9	16.1	61	358	16.7	5.3	130.5	43.1	15.2	2.3
Big Horn	7	31	2.2	0.9	18	48	2.7	0.5	64.6	25.6	8.9	1.3
Campbell	54	272	21.2	8.8	84	545	48.0	15.1	86.1	28.0	8.4	1.6
Carbon	32	255	11.3	4.9	27	71	4.8	1.2	122.7	28.9	9.9	1.2

1. Firms subject to federal tax. 2. October 1, 1998 to September 30, 1999. 3. State totals may include programs not allocated by county.

STATE County	Federal funds and grants, fiscal 1999[1] (cont'd)							Local government finances, 1997				
	Expenditures (mil dol) (cont'd)							General revenue				
	Salaries and wages	Procurement contract awards		Grants[2]						Taxes		
		Defense	Other	Medicaid and other health-related	Nutrition and family welfare	Education	Other	Total (mil dol)	Intergovern-mental (mil dol)	Total (mil dol)	Per capita[3] (dollars)	
											Total	Property
	171	172	173	174	175	176	177	178	179	180	181	182
WISCONSIN—Cont'd												
Dane	218.5	33.5	54.4	328.6	324.1	156.4	482.4	1 241.6	461.4	558.9	1 406	1 306
Dodge	9.6	0.0	3.2	15.4	4.6	1.8	1.2	188.9	85.1	58.6	711	657
Door	13.8	0.7	2.2	8.5	1.9	1.0	1.9	79.8	28.4	38.8	1 444	1 348
Douglas	8.4	3.7	3.0	24.9	10.4	3.2	9.6	161.7	85.5	47.5	1 099	1 015
Dunn	5.0	0.2	2.0	15.4	4.9	3.9	6.0	106.5	58.5	26.7	690	641
Eau Claire	21.3	3.9	4.5	39.1	10.7	4.9	12.5	268.4	138.2	77.8	872	840
Florence	0.7	0.0	0.1	2.0	0.7	0.3	0.4	14.3	8.5	4.1	780	771
Fond du Lac	12.9	1.2	7.8	26.0	8.5	3.1	8.5	263.9	126.1	87.6	928	908
Forest	3.9	0.1	2.8	9.2	2.5	1.4	0.5	28.2	17.3	8.0	834	789
Grant	8.8	1.1	3.6	21.7	4.2	2.7	7.8	151.0	83.4	36.2	732	723
Green	4.8	0.0	1.2	8.5	2.5	1.3	0.8	86.2	43.2	26.2	789	771
Green Lake	3.0	1.0	0.7	7.1	1.6	0.7	0.5	55.4	26.8	20.7	1 066	1 039
Iowa	4.4	0.0	1.2	7.1	3.1	0.8	7.5	57.1	28.9	19.9	899	839
Iron	1.2	0.0	0.5	4.7	1.0	0.2	0.7	21.0	11.7	6.3	970	900
Jackson	2.9	0.0	0.7	12.4	3.9	1.2	4.8	55.6	31.0	12.6	715	665
Jefferson	10.4	1.0	3.5	22.7	4.8	2.2	7.6	196.3	90.2	65.5	892	830
Juneau	10.6	14.5	1.5	12.5	3.1	1.2	0.3	68.8	39.1	17.4	727	669
Kenosha	15.6	23.2	5.7	40.8	19.0	6.3	6.6	444.2	210.3	169.0	1 183	1 108
Kewaunee	3.4	0.3	28.6	5.0	1.3	0.7	0.9	51.0	27.9	14.7	746	734
La Crosse	26.8	24.5	8.9	35.1	13.5	5.0	12.2	315.8	142.9	97.9	958	867
Lafayette	2.6	0.0	0.7	6.5	1.5	0.7	-0.2	60.5	31.3	15.3	936	928
Langlade	2.7	4.5	0.6	13.3	3.4	1.2	6.4	58.7	32.6	17.5	849	790
Lincoln	4.2	0.0	1.0	12.9	3.5	1.0	5.5	84.1	44.8	22.7	767	716
Manitowoc	10.6	0.3	3.1	26.3	6.7	2.4	2.0	190.5	96.6	52.5	639	619
Marathon	29.4	1.9	9.0	41.0	10.9	4.4	19.1	372.6	180.2	114.2	933	859
Marinette	8.8	0.7	58.3	21.4	4.9	1.7	3.7	113.6	65.3	30.6	710	696
Marquette	2.6	5.0	1.3	4.7	1.4	0.4	2.8	32.0	15.6	12.3	831	786
Menominee	0.3	0.0	5.9	7.7	4.8	5.9	2.7	19.6	16.3	2.6	551	547
Milwaukee	539.4	23.6	93.5	602.0	253.8	81.0	142.0	3 478.1	1 758.8	1 206.8	1 328	1 241
Monroe	78.0	15.2	7.8	19.4	4.4	2.1	8.7	103.6	57.7	26.3	668	606
Oconto	4.9	0.1	2.1	13.0	3.6	1.3	5.4	82.9	50.5	20.0	600	557
Oneida	12.2	0.2	2.0	13.7	6.2	1.4	4.7	114.6	41.0	58.1	1 629	1 530
Outagamie	19.6	1.7	6.2	34.2	10.3	5.5	11.9	483.9	212.7	166.8	1 082	1 054
Ozaukee	8.5	19.9	2.7	7.1	2.0	1.4	5.3	202.6	58.8	101.6	1 258	1 186
Pepin	1.3	0.0	3.4	3.8	0.9	0.3	0.1	25.1	16.1	6.5	908	863
Pierce	5.6	0.1	1.4	11.6	2.6	2.3	1.4	100.3	59.8	27.0	767	724
Polk	6.9	0.3	2.0	15.0	4.7	1.5	1.6	116.6	63.6	30.8	805	755
Portage	11.7	0.0	10.2	19.0	7.6	2.6	19.6	163.0	84.2	52.8	816	742
Price	4.7	0.0	0.8	9.5	2.0	0.5	1.4	44.5	26.5	11.9	758	712
Racine	22.3	8.0	8.7	65.4	28.1	8.4	14.4	476.4	254.7	154.5	833	814
Richland	2.6	0.1	0.6	10.6	2.3	0.7	7.8	47.3	25.3	11.5	643	598
Rock	18.4	63.2	5.5	59.2	22.6	7.4	13.2	445.3	253.4	124.8	830	810
Rusk	2.9	0.0	0.7	10.8	4.5	1.3	4.2	62.0	35.2	9.7	636	540
St. Croix	7.7	0.1	3.4	10.1	3.0	1.3	18.3	146.1	72.3	47.2	824	756
Sauk	8.0	13.9	2.1	17.8	4.6	1.9	3.6	154.7	74.8	54.1	1 021	910
Sawyer	3.4	0.0	4.3	12.2	4.5	1.5	7.6	42.3	21.9	15.7	983	901
Shawano	5.7	0.0	4.1	21.5	4.1	2.1	16.5	93.9	50.8	24.8	643	596
Sheboygan	11.7	8.6	29.9	26.1	9.0	3.1	9.8	334.0	157.6	107.5	978	957
Taylor	3.9	2.2	1.0	6.8	1.8	0.7	4.5	52.4	34.4	11.0	569	559
Trempealeau	5.9	2.0	1.4	17.1	5.8	1.0	4.9	91.2	50.0	20.7	785	746
Vernon	5.0	0.2	1.1	18.4	3.1	1.5	5.9	73.1	42.8	17.3	637	626
Vilas	3.3	0.0	3.7	11.8	2.8	1.3	2.7	52.7	17.8	28.7	1 357	1 277
Walworth	10.1	1.6	2.6	19.0	5.3	2.8	4.1	268.5	80.4	110.9	1 313	1 210
Washburn	6.4	0.1	2.5	10.5	2.6	0.8	3.9	44.3	22.6	16.7	1 090	1 033
Washington	14.3	0.4	3.3	19.7	7.5	2.2	7.0	268.6	107.9	112.9	1 002	970
Waukesha	47.4	103.2	156.5	39.3	12.7	6.8	22.3	948.0	288.9	495.8	1 421	1 377
Waupaca	8.3	5.8	2.1	18.0	4.3	1.6	15.4	133.5	73.5	40.9	818	765
Waushara	3.1	0.0	0.9	10.8	2.4	0.9	1.4	48.5	24.1	18.3	851	806
Winnebago	32.1	232.7	15.7	36.9	13.6	4.3	7.1	400.6	171.7	133.8	892	866
Wood	10.7	0.0	11.4	41.0	7.8	2.9	3.4	226.5	118.0	71.5	943	922
WYOMING	409.7	63.1	136.1	161.1	86.1	82.7	603.5	X	X	X	X	X
Albany	10.7	0.6	5.0	11.5	3.3	4.9	28.1	97.3	36.2	14.5	489	238
Big Horn	4.0	0.0	4.9	5.5	1.2	0.7	10.5	44.9	20.7	11.1	1 003	668
Campbell	4.4	0.0	31.2	2.1	2.4	1.2	3.6	128.1	28.5	76.6	2 389	2 080
Carbon	7.7	10.6	32.3	6.3	2.9	0.8	20.6	58.1	19.1	21.1	1 333	1 069

1. October 1, 1998 to September 30, 1999. 2. State totals may include programs not allocated by county. 3. Based on the resident population estimated as of July 1 of the year shown.

Table B. States and Counties — Local Government Finances, Government Employment, and Elections

STATE County	Direct general expenditure Total (mil dol)	Per capita[1] (dollars)	Education	Health and hospitals	Police protection	Public welfare	Highways	Debt outstanding Total (mil dol)	Per capita[1] (dollars)	Federal civilian	Federal military	State and local	Democratic	Republican	All other
	183	184	185	186	187	188	189	190	191	192	193	194	195	196	197
WISCONSIN—Cont'd															
Dane	1 305.1	3 283	48.5	2.1	5.5	9.8	5.4	1 280.3	3 221	4 261	1 576	67 772	61.1	32.6	6.3
Dodge	205.7	2 495	36.1	3.6	5.1	14.1	11.9	125.6	1 524	188	294	4 203	38.7	57.5	3.8
Door	88.1	3 275	43.0	5.0	4.0	3.1	12.6	61.1	2 271	82	146	1 524	43.1	51.3	5.6
Douglas	157.1	3 638	51.5	5.2	4.8	3.6	7.8	129.7	3 002	119	153	3 189	62.6	31.9	5.5
Dunn	118.7	3 063	44.0	1.5	3.5	14.9	15.9	87.7	2 263	95	138	4 389	47.4	46.1	6.5
Eau Claire	274.0	3 070	51.2	5.3	5.0	7.2	7.8	149.5	1 675	375	315	7 710	50.3	43.7	6.0
Florence	13.6	2 614	44.9	8.5	5.2	0.4	16.7	11.1	2 124	21	18	286	33.9	63.5	2.5
Fond du Lac	269.4	2 856	52.1	7.3	4.2	6.7	7.9	138.9	1 472	247	335	5 164	39.0	57.0	4.0
Forest	33.8	3 528	52.7	2.2	10.4	4.4	13.0	21.4	2 232	123	34	658	45.8	51.0	3.3
Grant	154.7	3 126	53.7	7.0	3.3	8.1	11.2	87.3	1 763	170	174	4 714	48.7	46.6	4.7
Green	95.1	2 869	46.2	3.0	5.1	11.3	14.1	52.5	1 583	95	118	1 800	51.5	44.4	4.1
Green Lake	57.2	2 942	50.8	4.7	5.5	3.8	10.7	44.3	2 276	63	69	1 005	36.2	59.9	3.9
Iowa	63.1	2 847	54.6	0.8	3.2	8.3	14.7	43.7	1 973	86	79	1 296	55.4	40.0	4.5
Iron	19.4	2 995	43.0	6.9	4.6	0.5	19.3	10.6	1 632	22	22	325	46.2	49.4	4.4
Jackson	59.0	3 350	44.2	7.3	3.3	14.2	12.5	28.8	1 633	54	63	1 341	52.0	43.6	4.4
Jefferson	200.0	2 725	47.0	4.4	5.2	9.7	11.0	120.7	1 645	192	260	3 800	42.1	53.2	4.7
Juneau	71.9	2 998	46.2	1.4	3.7	9.5	14.2	43.0	1 792	265	85	1 443	47.1	48.1	4.8
Kenosha	454.2	3 179	51.0	3.9	5.9	7.3	4.9	429.8	3 008	286	534	7 791	50.9	45.3	3.7
Kewaunee	53.9	2 738	46.4	10.1	3.7	1.5	19.9	29.9	1 521	79	70	921	46.3	48.4	5.3
La Crosse	330.5	3 232	49.0	5.0	4.9	7.9	6.8	234.8	2 296	498	379	8 351	51.2	43.8	5.0
Lafayette	65.3	3 988	44.8	7.8	2.6	10.6	16.2	36.3	2 216	62	57	1 144	51.1	45.9	3.0
Langlade	62.9	3 059	45.2	4.0	4.0	5.3	15.9	32.5	1 582	50	72	1 189	43.2	52.7	4.1
Lincoln	88.5	2 987	43.7	4.6	4.9	11.0	13.8	76.3	2 574	72	105	1 800	46.8	47.2	6.0
Manitowoc	210.8	2 564	42.2	3.2	5.2	9.9	12.1	132.7	1 613	187	306	4 102	45.5	49.9	4.6
Marathon	399.6	3 264	46.8	13.0	3.7	3.1	9.5	225.0	1 838	514	437	6 702	45.5	49.5	5.0
Marinette	117.0	2 720	50.0	4.6	4.9	5.1	10.7	73.4	1 707	123	208	2 128	43.6	52.9	3.6
Marquette	44.6	3 009	52.4	5.7	6.9	3.4	13.5	25.6	1 732	53	53	689	47.8	49.0	3.3
Menominee	19.5	4 094	58.6	2.3	3.2	17.2	8.3	1.6	332	(3)0	(3)17	(3)359	77.0	18.2	4.8
Milwaukee	3 337.2	3 672	41.2	5.1	7.1	6.4	4.1	2 732.8	3 007	9 079	3 671	53 672	58.2	37.7	4.1
Monroe	106.1	2 697	43.1	3.0	4.1	13.8	15.4	74.6	1 895	2 468	246	2 083	45.7	50.3	4.0
Oconto	89.8	2 691	42.6	6.4	3.4	4.3	15.6	64.6	1 936	115	120	1 585	43.7	52.5	3.8
Oneida	115.9	3 247	57.0	1.8	4.6	4.1	11.5	80.3	2 248	256	127	2 399	44.1	50.4	5.5
Outagamie	494.5	3 207	50.7	4.4	4.4	5.6	10.4	406.1	2 634	371	551	7 800	43.2	52.1	4.7
Ozaukee	246.2	3 049	41.6	3.4	5.5	5.1	7.5	160.0	1 982	162	286	3 429	31.5	65.2	3.3
Pepin	29.1	4 049	53.9	5.5	3.1	5.5	17.4	14.3	1 992	29	25	521	50.6	44.5	4.9
Pierce	109.5	3 111	51.6	5.4	3.7	2.8	13.7	61.3	1 743	105	126	3 288	47.7	45.5	6.9
Polk	126.9	3 314	54.1	4.5	2.4	7.5	11.9	90.1	2 354	146	137	2 214	45.3	48.4	6.3
Portage	164.5	2 540	45.4	5.7	4.6	6.2	11.2	124.0	1 916	205	234	5 426	53.1	39.1	7.7
Price	43.6	2 771	46.2	2.5	4.2	9.6	17.3	28.9	1 839	127	56	966	43.0	52.2	4.8
Racine	479.1	2 584	43.2	4.4	8.3	10.3	6.1	284.0	1 532	418	658	8 367	46.8	49.5	3.7
Richland	49.0	2 734	37.8	5.6	3.4	14.8	15.7	41.6	2 319	59	63	1 110	46.3	48.2	5.6
Rock	465.5	3 097	46.7	5.1	5.4	12.2	6.5	271.6	1 807	341	532	8 201	57.5	39.0	3.5
Rusk	67.6	4 415	38.2	13.8	2.3	9.7	9.7	33.4	2 181	56	54	1 231	42.9	51.0	6.1
St. Croix	156.3	2 728	49.3	7.1	3.7	5.0	14.8	143.9	2 511	152	208	3 026	50.8	45.2	4.0
Sauk	175.9	3 320	51.0	6.3	4.1	5.5	8.8	130.8	2 469	155	188	2 968	42.9	51.1	5.9
Sawyer	48.8	3 052	45.1	6.2	3.3	5.7	19.3	12.2	763	71	57	1 027	41.7	54.2	4.1
Shawano	116.3	3 020	49.5	3.2	4.0	6.2	14.5	78.2	2 032	(3)113	(3)137	(3)1 985	42.7	53.7	3.6
Sheboygan	354.9	3 229	47.9	4.6	4.4	12.0	7.5	238.9	2 174	234	400	5 784	43.7	50.9	5.5
Taylor	55.5	2 883	47.8	2.3	3.6	7.2	16.3	29.0	1 506	82	68	857	36.2	58.7	5.1
Trempealeau	97.8	3 710	49.4	3.8	2.2	12.9	11.7	61.8	2 345	127	93	1 799	54.9	41.1	4.0
Vernon	77.9	2 865	49.9	0.9	2.7	13.8	14.1	51.3	1 888	110	96	1 684	50.4	43.6	6.0
Vilas	60.3	2 854	51.8	1.9	4.2	3.7	14.4	50.5	2 391	73	75	941	38.2	56.5	5.3
Walworth	283.4	3 357	36.4	15.4	6.8	8.1	7.5	221.9	2 628	203	301	6 193	38.3	56.8	4.9
Washburn	45.6	2 980	50.8	4.7	3.0	4.7	14.1	23.2	1 517	128	54	1 152	45.9	48.6	5.4
Washington	279.4	2 480	49.1	4.8	5.4	6.4	8.2	238.2	2 114	1 112	402	4 713	29.5	67.0	3.5
Waukesha	1 010.6	2 897	51.8	2.5	5.5	3.0	6.0	854.9	2 451	883	1 248	15 334	31.6	65.3	3.1
Waupaca	144.0	2 877	51.7	2.2	5.4	8.6	12.5	118.1	2 360	143	178	3 175	38.5	56.9	4.5
Waushara	56.6	2 631	48.2	6.3	3.2	5.7	14.3	40.2	1 868	65	76	963	41.4	54.4	4.3
Winnebago	434.1	2 895	40.4	4.6	5.1	7.1	9.2	345.0	2 301	575	540	10 361	44.7	50.4	5.0
Wood	223.1	2 944	51.7	7.2	4.7	6.0	9.4	112.9	1 490	205	269	4 363	44.6	49.8	5.7
WYOMING	X	X	X	X	X	X	X	X	X	7 034	6 349	48 207	27.7	67.8	4.5
Albany	89.3	3 005	29.9	34.3	3.9	1.5	2.5	33.0	1 112	235	195	5 944	38.5	59.4	2.1
Big Horn	43.8	3 972	49.2	26.5	3.2	0.2	3.6	27.4	2 486	97	71	1 220	20.6	76.3	3.2
Campbell	143.4	4 469	47.8	3.0	3.5	0.1	5.5	90.7	2 828	85	202	3 072	15.8	81.9	2.3
Carbon	55.6	3 507	43.0	20.0	6.2	0.5	4.5	17.4	1 101	143	97	1 747	32.1	65.5	2.3

1. Based on the resident population estimated as of July 1 of the year shown.   3. Menominee County included with Shawano County.

Table B. States and Counties — **Land Area and Population**

					Population and population characteristics, 1999												
								Race (percent)					Age (percent)				
STATE/ County code	MSA/ PMSA/ NECMA code[1]	County Type[2]	STATE County	Land area,[3] (sq km) 1990	Total persons	Rank	Per square kilometer	White	Black	Am. Indian, Eskimo, Aleut	Asian and Pacific Islander	Percent Hispanic[4]	Under 5 years	5 to 17 years	18 to 24 years	25 to 34 years	35 to 44 years	45 to 54 years
				1	2	3	4	5	6	7	8	9	10	11	12	13	14	15
			WYOMING—Cont'd															
56 009	...	6	Converse	11 020	12 396	2 257	1.1	98.2	0.2	1.1	0.5	5.4	6.5	22.6	8.6	10.3	16.4	15.5
56 011	...	9	Crook	7 404	5 778	2 787	0.8	99.3	0.1	0.6	0.1	0.6	6.5	21.2	7.8	9.6	13.9	16.6
56 013	...	7	Fremont	23 783	36 191	1 187	1.5	80.1	0.2	19.4	0.4	4.0	6.5	21.6	9.4	9.8	14.3	15.1
56 015	...	7	Goshen	5 764	12 651	2 236	2.2	98.9	0.2	0.8	0.1	9.2	5.6	19.0	10.3	9.1	12.9	14.9
56 017	...	7	Hot Springs	5 190	4 475	2 872	0.9	97.5	0.2	2.2	0.1	1.4	4.0	18.7	6.4	8.5	13.7	16.1
56 019	...	7	Johnson	10 791	6 858	2 694	0.6	98.8	0.0	1.1	0.2	1.3	5.0	18.1	8.2	7.8	14.8	16.5
56 021	1580	3	Laramie	6 957	78 877	637	11.3	94.5	3.1	0.8	1.6	10.9	6.7	17.8	12.1	12.1	15.0	15.0
56 023	...	7	Lincoln	10 540	13 998	2 139	1.3	98.7	0.2	0.6	0.5	2.3	7.4	26.4	7.9	9.4	14.4	14.6
56 025	1350	3	Natrona	13 831	63 157	758	4.6	97.7	0.9	0.7	0.7	4.0	6.2	19.0	10.7	10.8	15.2	14.7
56 027	...	9	Niobrara	6 801	2 684	3 011	0.4	98.6	0.4	0.9	0.1	1.6	4.6	16.7	6.6	9.9	13.6	17.1
56 029	...	7	Park	17 982	25 500	1 513	1.4	98.7	0.1	0.6	0.6	3.7	5.9	18.5	10.8	9.6	14.9	15.7
56 031	...	7	Platte	5 400	8 612	2 542	1.6	99.5	0.1	0.3	0.1	5.0	5.8	19.3	8.0	8.2	15.0	16.8
56 033	...	7	Sheridan	6 536	25 090	1 527	3.8	98.3	0.2	0.9	0.6	2.0	4.8	18.6	9.0	8.8	16.4	16.0
56 035	...	9	Sublette	12 643	5 811	2 785	0.5	97.9	0.1	1.6	0.3	1.3	6.1	18.5	8.1	9.8	17.2	17.2
56 037	...	5	Sweetwater	27 003	39 322	1 103	1.5	97.4	0.8	0.8	1.0	9.7	6.9	23.8	10.7	11.7	17.2	14.8
56 039	...	7	Teton	10 381	14 532	2 097	1.4	98.0	0.3	1.0	0.7	1.8	6.6	15.0	10.3	14.7	20.6	16.5
56 041	...	7	Uinta	5 392	20 288	1 747	3.8	98.4	0.2	0.7	0.6	4.8	8.3	28.1	9.5	12.1	16.7	12.2
56 043	...	7	Washakie	5 802	8 541	2 550	1.5	98.0	0.3	1.0	0.8	10.2	5.8	21.0	7.9	9.1	14.4	15.6
56 045	...	7	Weston	6 211	6 403	2 742	1.0	98.3	0.1	1.4	0.2	1.6	5.2	20.2	8.1	9.3	15.2	16.0

1. MSA = Metropolitan Statistical Area. PMSA = Primary MSA. NECMA = New England County Metropolitan Area. See Appendix A for explanation of these concepts. See Appendix B for list of metropolitan areas identified by type, with component counties.   2. County typology code from the Economic Research Service of USDA. See Appendix A for definition.   3. Dry land or land partially or temporarily covered by water.   4. Hispanic persons may be of any race.

STATE County	Population, 1999 (cont'd)				Population — change and components of change, 1980–1999							Households, 1990				
	Age (percent) (cont'd)				Total persons		Percent change		Components of change, 1990–1999						Percent	
	55 to 64 years	65 to 74 years	75 years and over	Percent female	1990	1980	1980–1990	1990–1999	Births	Deaths	Net migration	Number	Percent change, 1980–1990	Persons per household	Female family householder[1]	One person
	16	17	18	19	20	21	22	23	24	25	26	27	28	29	30	31
WYOMING—Cont'd																
Converse	9.7	5.8	4.7	50.6	11 128	14 069	-20.9	11.4	1 391	776	547	4 046	-13.5	2.73	8.9	21.7
Crook	11.0	7.8	5.5	49.6	5 294	5 308	-0.3	9.1	623	379	261	1 892	2.2	2.77	5.3	20.6
Fremont	10.5	7.2	5.8	50.1	33 662	38 992	-13.7	7.5	4 648	2 910	888	12 002	-6.7	2.74	10.7	22.2
Goshen	10.9	8.7	8.4	51.3	12 373	12 040	2.8	2.2	1 374	1 072	1	4 790	7.2	2.54	7.9	25.5
Hot Springs	12.5	9.3	10.7	50.5	4 809	5 710	-15.8	-6.9	390	567	-144	1 943	-10.1	2.38	7.8	29.2
Johnson	11.4	9.8	8.5	50.6	6 145	6 700	-8.3	11.6	677	713	780	2 397	-3.5	2.50	6.4	25.7
Laramie	9.7	6.4	5.1	50.4	73 142	68 649	6.5	7.8	11 110	5 330	-1 018	28 092	11.1	2.55	9.7	25.3
Lincoln	8.6	6.8	4.4	48.7	12 625	12 177	3.7	10.9	1 791	788	402	4 137	7.2	3.05	5.7	19.3
Natrona	10.6	7.6	5.2	51.0	61 226	71 856	-14.8	3.2	8 466	4 596	-1 805	23 837	-7.8	2.54	9.7	25.9
Niobrara	13.3	8.6	9.6	53.8	2 499	2 924	-14.5	7.4	260	303	243	1 032	-10.6	2.31	7.7	31.8
Park	10.2	7.4	6.8	50.6	23 178	21 639	7.1	10.0	2 730	1 926	1 574	8 757	13.2	2.57	7.1	24.2
Platte	10.9	7.9	8.0	50.1	8 145	11 975	-32.0	5.7	832	825	474	3 179	-27.4	2.54	6.0	25.8
Sheridan	11.0	7.7	7.6	50.4	23 562	25 048	-5.9	6.5	2 568	2 349	1 409	9 426	1.1	2.43	8.4	28.3
Sublette	10.8	6.7	5.6	47.7	4 843	4 548	6.5	20.0	612	405	782	1 834	15.3	2.60	4.4	23.4
Sweetwater	7.5	4.1	3.4	49.2	38 823	41 723	-7.0	1.3	5 245	2 085	-2 627	13 616	-3.1	2.83	7.7	22.2
Teton	8.7	4.5	3.1	47.8	11 173	9 355	19.4	30.1	1 692	532	2 234	4 568	21.8	2.43	5.4	26.6
Uinta	6.6	3.7	2.9	49.0	18 705	13 021	43.7	8.5	3 058	893	-566	5 885	44.2	3.12	7.8	18.7
Washakie	10.9	8.2	7.1	49.6	8 388	9 496	-11.7	1.8	964	733	-67	3 156	-3.6	2.61	6.4	24.7
Weston	10.7	8.8	6.4	49.7	6 518	7 106	-8.3	-1.8	659	526	-231	2 419	-4.2	2.65	7.2	22.1

1. No spouse present.

Table B. States and Counties — **Vital Statistics, Health Resources, and Crime**

STATE County	Births, average 1996–1998		Deaths, average 1996–1998				Physicians,[4] 1998		Hospitals,[4] 1998			Medicare enrollees 1999	Serious crimes known to police, 1998[6]	
			Number		Rate					Beds			Total	
	Total	Rate[1]	Total	Infant[2]	Total[1]	Infant[3]	Number	Rate[5]	Number	Number	Rate[5]		Number	Rate[7]
	32	33	34	35	36	37	38	39	40	41	42	43	44	45
WYOMING—Cont'd														
Converse	145	11.9	84	1	6.9	4.6	7	57	1	34	276	1 464	395	3 206
Crook	63	11.0	44	0	7.5	0.0	2	34	1	48	823	866	144	2 702
Fremont	484	13.4	342	6	9.5	12.4	72	200	2	177	491	5 392	1 337	3 718
Goshen	152	11.8	123	1	9.6	6.6	12	93	1	36	279	2 327	332	2 581
Hot Springs	44	9.3	59	0	12.5	0.0	8	169	1	49	1 037	1 048	166	3 539
Johnson	67	9.9	81	0	12.0	0.0	9	132	1	83	1 216	1 363	173	2 544
Laramie	1 153	14.6	606	7	7.7	6.4	197	250	2	266	337	10 500	3 146	3 988
Lincoln	185	13.3	87	1	6.3	5.4	9	65	2	33	238	1 886	263	1 966
Natrona	856	13.5	516	3	8.1	3.5	124	196	1	282	445	9 592	3 126	4 902
Niobrara	29	11.0	31	0	11.7	0.0	3	111	1	52	1 922	510	NA	NA
Park	304	11.9	217	5	8.5	15.4	55	213	2	356	1 381	4 010	809	3 145
Platte	92	10.8	100	1	11.7	7.2	5	58	1	86	997	1 656	226	2 641
Sheridan	274	10.9	276	1	10.9	3.6	60	238	1	64	254	4 501	615	2 436
Sublette	59	10.4	49	0	8.7	5.7	9	157	0	0	0	781	153	2 680
Sweetwater	555	13.9	235	3	5.9	5.4	36	90	1	99	249	3 554	1 941	4 904
Teton	173	12.5	64	1	4.6	5.8	65	459	1	104	734	1 331	532	3 813
Uinta	336	16.5	101	2	5.0	6.9	24	117	1	42	205	1 613	736	3 620
Washakie	100	11.7	91	1	10.6	10.0	10	115	1	30	346	1 448	263	3 041
Weston	73	11.2	61	1	9.3	9.1	5	77	1	71	1 097	1 144	117	1 795

1. Per 1,000 estimated resident population, average 1996–1998.   2. Deaths of infants under 1 year old.   3. Deaths of infants under 1 year old per 1,000 live births.   4. Data subject to copyright.   5. Per 100,000 resident population as of July 1 of the year shown.   6. Data for serious crimes have not been adjusted for underreporting; this may affect comparability between geographic areas and over time.   7. Per 100,000 population estimated by the FBI.

Table B. States and Counties — Crime, Education, Money Income, and Poverty

STATE County	Serious crimes known to police, 1998[1] (cont'd) Rate[2] Violent	Property	Education — School enrollment and attainment, 1990 — Enrollment[3] Total	Percent private	Attainment[4] (percent) High school graduate or more	Bachelor's degree or more	Local government expenditures, fiscal 1997[5] Total current expenditures (mil dol)	Current expenditures per student (dollars)	Money income 1989 Per capita[6] (dollars)	Households Median Dollars	Percent change, 1979–1989 (constant 1989 dollars)	Percent with $100,000 or more	Income and poverty, 1997 Median household income	Percent below poverty level All persons	Persons under 18	Persons 5–17 in families
	46	47	48	49	50	51	52	53	54	55	56	57	58	59	60	61
WYOMING—Cont'd																
Converse	130	3 076	3 240	3.5	83.4	12.7	17.5	6 412	12 023	27 713	-27.1	2.6	37 978	12.6	16.3	14.1
Crook	244	2 458	1 472	7.8	79.7	15.6	9.2	7 143	10 322	23 440	-15.5	1.0	35 003	9.4	11.2	10.9
Fremont	245	3 473	9 450	5.7	77.5	16.5	52.7	7 035	9 806	22 260	-35.1	1.4	29 765	18.7	24.1	19.7
Goshen	194	2 387	3 524	6.9	76.5	14.5	14.9	6 630	10 598	21 750	-7.5	1.6	29 446	16.7	22.0	19.0
Hot Springs	618	2 921	1 227	0.9	76.1	14.3	6.8	7 366	11 940	24 500	-9.5	2.1	29 963	13.6	19.3	14.4
Johnson	132	2 412	1 533	7.2	79.8	17.9	8.2	6 110	11 563	22 157	-19.9	2.5	31 832	13.0	17.9	14.9
Laramie	209	3 779	20 076	7.9	84.2	20.7	79.9	5 391	12 932	27 571	-6.7	1.7	37 168	11.3	15.8	12.8
Lincoln	284	1 682	4 069	2.5	83.2	15.2	22.2	6 056	10 558	28 488	-5.6	1.0	40 589	10.1	12.3	10.3
Natrona	204	4 698	17 410	5.6	85.3	20.4	70.3	5 460	12 992	27 586	-28.0	2.6	34 685	13.1	17.7	14.1
Niobrara	NA	NA	555	1.6	75.7	13.0	3.4	6 827	11 816	20 947	-2.6	2.5	28 740	17.8	22.9	19.4
Park	194	2 951	6 461	6.9	82.6	18.8	24.9	5 087	12 147	25 942	-12.7	2.2	35 150	12.7	17.8	13.5
Platte	199	2 442	2 155	5.7	79.7	11.4	11.1	6 366	10 757	21 822	-33.4	0.9	31 717	13.4	17.2	15.1
Sheridan	135	2 301	6 329	6.0	81.6	17.6	26.5	5 894	12 457	24 772	-18.4	2.1	33 000	12.5	17.7	13.5
Sublette	350	2 330	1 152	2.7	84.2	21.4	9.6	7 390	12 567	26 825	-8.2	3.2	38 194	8.6	12.1	10.7
Sweetwater	318	4 586	12 366	5.7	81.5	13.3	54.9	5 985	13 698	36 210	-10.4	1.9	49 255	8.5	9.9	8.0
Teton	265	3 548	2 182	9.3	91.9	30.0	13.2	5 803	17 234	31 586	2.2	4.3	46 385	4.9	6.0	6.3
Uinta	143	3 477	6 282	2.4	84.1	14.3	32.3	5 613	12 245	33 259	-12.1	2.6	43 939	10.3	12.0	10.1
Washakie	382	2 659	2 130	4.6	78.8	18.4	10.5	5 439	11 017	25 172	-17.7	1.5	36 386	11.0	15.0	11.9
Weston	291	1 504	1 794	5.6	83.2	12.7	8.8	6 116	11 263	26 213	-21.9	1.7	35 667	11.0	13.3	11.4

1. Data for serious crimes have not been adjusted for underreporting; this may affect comparability between geographic areas and over time.   2. Per 100,000 population estimated by the FBI.   3. All persons 3 years old and over enrolled in nursery school through college.   4. Persons 25 years old and over.   5. Elementary and secondary education expenditures, local government fiscal years ending between July 1, 1996 and June 30, 1997.   6. Based on population enumerated as of April 1, 1990.

STATE County	Personal income, 1998												
			Per capita[1]							Transfer payments			
											Government payments to individuals		
	Total (mil dol)	Percent change, 1997–1998	Dollars	Rank	Wages and salaries[2] (mil dol)	Proprietor's income (mil dol)	Dividends, interest, and rent (mil dol)	Total (mil dol)	Total (mil dol)	Social Security (mil dol)	Medical payments (mil dol)	Income mainte- nance (mil dol)	Unemploy- ment insurance (mil dol)
	62	63	64	65	66	67	68	69	70	71	72	73	74
WYOMING—Cont'd													
Converse	245	3.1	19 977	1 720	147	16	59	32	30	15	8	3	1
Crook	119	-4.6	20 553	1 538	49	6	33	16	15	8	4	1	0
Fremont	691	3.9	19 113	2 020	358	46	160	144	137	54	55	16	3
Goshen	247	1.2	19 322	1 945	98	35	60	47	45	22	14	4	1
Hot Springs	100	-1.5	21 488	1 254	44	7	26	24	23	11	9	1	0
Johnson	145	-0.8	21 339	1 286	61	9	50	23	22	13	5	1	0
Laramie	2 013	4.3	25 613	425	1 247	132	462	242	227	95	67	17	3
Lincoln	261	1.1	18 918	2 085	142	19	76	37	34	19	8	3	1
Natrona	1 784	4.1	28 217	229	909	273	428	217	205	100	65	15	3
Niobrara	49	-7.8	18 265	2 280	21	1	16	10	9	5	3	1	0
Park	598	1.5	23 231	810	310	54	178	84	79	41	25	4	2
Platte	172	-1.0	19 999	1 711	100	12	44	31	30	16	8	2	1
Sheridan	648	2.3	25 767	416	292	42	228	92	87	41	26	5	2
Sublette	126	-1.6	21 940	1 116	58	12	42	15	14	8	4	1	0
Sweetwater	1 007	3.7	25 345	455	755	104	168	96	88	37	24	6	3
Teton	748	4.6	52 723	4	409	101	316	31	28	14	8	1	1
Uinta	397	3.2	19 485	1 898	238	24	54	50	46	17	18	3	1
Washakie	185	0.4	21 347	1 282	106	13	50	27	26	14	7	1	1
Weston	147	0.5	22 673	930	58	29	33	22	21	12	6	1	0

1. Based on the resident population estimated as of July 1 of the year shown.   2. Includes other labor income.

Table B. States and Counties — **Earnings, Social Security, and Housing**

STATE County	Earnings, 1998 Total (mil dol)	Farm	Goods-related[1] Total	Manu-facturing	Service-related and other[2] Total	Retail trade	Finance, insurance, and real estate	Services	Govern-ment	Social Security beneficiaries, December 1998 Number	Rate[3]	Supplemental Security Income recipients, December 1998	Housing units, 1990 Total	Percent change, 1980–1990
	75	76	77	78	79	80	81	82	83	84	85	86	87	88
WYOMING—Cont'd														
Converse	163	0.6	37.4	1.8	D	7.3	2.0	D	19.6	1 780	144	105	5 234	-2.2
Crook	55	-3.2	36.1	12.5	D	8.9	2.7	9.9	31.9	1 007	173	38	2 605	7.0
Fremont	404	0.7	20.0	4.1	52.7	14.5	2.9	25.3	26.5	6 481	180	722	14 437	-0.9
Goshen	133	13.5	D	6.7	D	7.9	3.4	17.4	26.8	2 642	205	203	5 551	10.6
Hot Springs	51	0.0	D	D	D	8.7	4.3	27.1	27.4	1 238	262	83	2 429	-4.3
Johnson	70	-5.6	D	4.3	D	13.5	7.3	20.0	30.4	1 559	228	46	3 112	2.7
Laramie	1 378	1.1	11.4	5.1	47.4	9.9	8.0	16.6	40.2	11 354	144	1 097	30 507	11.4
Lincoln	160	0.6	35.6	9.4	40.7	9.4	2.8	9.5	23.1	2 263	163	76	5 409	15.8
Natrona	1 182	0.1	34.7	4.4	50.7	9.1	4.7	22.1	14.6	11 167	176	1 138	29 082	2.1
Niobrara	22	-5.6	D	D	D	11.1	3.3	10.7	44.2	594	220	37	1 456	1.5
Park	365	2.6	22.8	4.3	47.2	10.9	5.0	22.0	27.4	4 718	183	214	10 306	17.5
Platte	113	1.5	D	1.6	D	10.3	D	D	22.9	1 891	219	71	4 026	-20.3
Sheridan	333	0.4	11.9	3.9	57.6	11.4	7.6	24.1	30.1	4 965	197	340	11 154	2.1
Sublette	70	3.8	33.0	1.3	37.6	10.3	3.7	16.3	25.6	896	156	20	2 911	21.6
Sweetwater	858	0.0	53.7	11.2	32.1	7.4	2.9	9.3	14.3	4 092	103	341	15 444	2.2
Teton	510	0.0	18.3	2.8	68.8	14.6	10.8	38.0	12.9	1 475	104	62	7 060	44.3
Uinta	262	-0.4	32.9	3.9	46.1	9.7	2.9	19.9	21.5	1 963	96	204	7 246	61.1
Washakie	119	3.1	31.6	16.6	43.9	8.2	3.1	17.6	21.4	1 658	191	85	3 732	-1.4
Weston	87	2.0	31.8	9.9	D	8.8	3.1	18.7	21.1	1 360	210	54	3 090	6.6

1. Covers mining, construction, and manufacturing. 2. Covers private sector earnings in agricultural services, forestry, and fisheries; transportation and public utilities; wholesale trade; retail trade; finance, insurance, and real estate; and services. 3. Per 1,000 resident population estimated as of July 1 of the year shown.

STATE County	Housing units, 1990 (cont'd)								Civilian labor force, 1999				Civilian employment, 1990[5]		
	Occupied units										Unemployment			Percent	
		Owner-occupied				Renter-occupied									
				Owner cost as a percent of income											
	Total	Percent	Median value[1]	With a mort-gage	Without a mort-gage	Median rent[2]	Rent as per-cent of income	Sub-stand-ard units[3] (percent)	Total	Percent change, 1998–1999	Total	Rate[4]	Total	Professional, managerial, and technical	Precision production, craft, and repair
	89	90	91	92	93	94	95	96	97	98	99	100	101	102	103
WYOMING—Cont'd															
Converse	4 046	71.0	51 000	15.6	11.6	285	20.4	2.2	6 708	2.2	346	5.2	5 071	20.7	17.1
Crook	1 892	78.3	54 400	19.7	12.4	312	17.9	5.3	3 098	3.3	154	5.0	2 411	20.2	11.5
Fremont	12 002	69.6	50 600	17.1	12.3	299	23.9	6.3	18 210	3.7	1 377	7.6	13 745	27.9	12.2
Goshen	4 790	70.1	52 100	21.7	11.6	287	23.7	2.7	6 572	2.0	245	3.7	5 405	21.1	11.0
Hot Springs	1 943	67.1	53 400	20.5	11.6	285	23.8	3.5	2 459	1.7	126	5.1	2 216	26.8	12.5
Johnson	2 397	69.7	56 600	21.1	12.2	298	23.1	3.5	3 958	5.7	136	3.4	2 972	21.2	9.8
Laramie	28 092	65.5	69 800	20.5	11.6	362	24.6	2.1	39 222	-0.3	1 393	3.6	32 914	31.3	9.5
Lincoln	4 137	80.0	60 200	20.1	12.5	339	19.1	4.4	6 577	5.3	405	6.2	5 037	23.6	17.0
Natrona	23 837	68.9	53 100	18.6	11.7	298	23.5	1.9	33 571	1.2	1 833	5.5	28 391	31.0	11.8
Niobrara	1 032	71.4	33 700	19.6	11.9	245	21.1	1.8	1 349	5.6	39	2.9	1 112	24.6	6.7
Park	8 757	67.7	65 600	18.7	12.2	340	21.6	2.4	15 655	3.6	714	4.6	10 781	28.1	12.4
Platte	3 179	75.6	52 100	17.0	12.3	292	23.2	1.7	4 642	3.2	206	4.4	3 572	22.4	13.0
Sheridan	9 426	68.4	58 200	19.7	12.8	326	24.9	2.9	13 851	0.7	674	4.9	10 789	25.8	12.6
Sublette	1 834	69.8	64 400	21.2	13.2	359	19.4	4.2	3 155	3.4	118	3.7	2 330	20.3	16.7
Sweetwater	13 616	70.2	70 900	17.0	11.5	350	18.6	3.4	20 750	-2.9	1 293	6.2	18 115	22.5	20.8
Teton	4 568	58.9	133 400	22.0	12.5	457	23.2	3.9	11 632	6.5	262	2.3	6 633	27.8	16.4
Uinta	5 885	72.2	59 300	20.2	11.9	356	21.5	5.3	10 812	-1.0	742	6.9	8 308	23.6	19.1
Washakie	3 156	71.8	54 600	20.7	11.4	297	21.2	2.8	4 933	0.3	319	6.5	3 752	27.6	12.3
Weston	2 419	78.1	44 700	14.9	11.6	297	21.6	1.8	3 426	2.7	187	5.5	2 977	17.8	15.7

1. Specified owner-occupied units.   2. Specified renter-occupied units.   3. Overcrowded or lacking complete plumbing facilities.   4. Percent of civilian labor force.   5. Persons 16 years and older.

STATE County	Private nonfarm establishments, employment and payroll, 1998									Agriculture, 1997			
	Number of establishments	Employment						Annual payroll		Farms			Farm operators
		Total	Health Care and Social Assistance	Manufacturing	Retail trade	Finance and Insurance	Professional Scientific and Technical Services	Total (mil dol)	Average per employee (dollars)	Number	Percent with—		Whose principal occupation is farming (percent)
											Less than 50 acres	500 acres and over	
	104	105	106	107	108	109	110	111	112	113	114	115	116
WYOMING—Cont'd													
Converse	377	2 809	343	50	426	85	83	67	23 746	348	8.6	69.0	65.5
Crook	190	1 412	156	157	172	43	D	36	25 360	498	6.2	73.3	68.1
Fremont	1 270	9 738	2 133	504	1 722	354	343	189	19 427	983	25.8	29.1	58.7
Goshen	376	2 931	723	251	532	114	62	49	16 853	688	12.9	51.0	67.9
Hot Springs	210	1 595	461	33	237	D	D	25	15 737	147	21.1	35.4	57.8
Johnson	298	1 583	251	31	298	95	54	30	18 888	315	10.5	71.7	68.3
Laramie	2 292	25 338	4 612	1 470	4 873	1 364	1 025	561	22 133	615	10.4	55.9	56.7
Lincoln	478	3 804	316	570	651	106	93	95	24 907	504	27.8	25.4	48.4
Natrona	2 566	24 563	3 453	1 519	3 893	1 162	1 149	599	24 382	311	20.6	48.9	58.5
Niobrara	95	484	107	D	85	D	D	7	14 461	278	3.6	84.9	80.9
Park	1 147	8 401	1 166	568	1 580	396	266	189	22 522	588	24.3	29.3	55.8
Platte	300	2 103	331	74	328	68	50	48	22 893	461	15.2	56.0	68.1
Sheridan	1 065	8 161	1 897	274	1 503	337	365	171	20 896	568	23.2	45.6	53.3
Sublette	311	1 258	134	39	211	44	72	28	22 568	275	18.9	54.2	61.8
Sweetwater	1 124	14 765	1 106	921	2 392	371	286	488	33 022	160	13.8	39.4	48.8
Teton	1 595	13 291	962	270	1 896	334	723	310	23 318	104	27.9	25.0	53.8
Uinta	587	5 680	1 141	262	999	117	143	142	24 964	300	23.0	40.3	55.3
Washakie	379	3 057	637	374	417	129	78	62	20 286	205	28.3	45.9	61.5
Weston	218	1 553	239	D	257	69	D	31	20 117	233	7.7	77.7	57.9

Table B. States and Counties — Agriculture, Land, and Water

STATE County	Acreage (1,000)	Percent change, 1992–1997	Average size of farm	Total irrigated (1,000)	Total cropland (1,000)	Average per farm ($1,000)	Average per acre (dollars)	Value of machinery and equipment Average per farm ($1,000)	Total (mil dol)	Average per farm (dollars)	Crops	Live-stock and poultry products	$10,000 or more	$100,000 or more	Percent of land owned by Fed. Gov. 1997	Water con-sump-tion 1995 (mil gal/day)
	117	118	119	120	121	122	123	124	125	126	127	128	129	130	131	132
WYOMING—Cont'd																
Converse	2 515	6.4	7 228	46	79	836	122	71	27	76 968	6.1	93.9	67.8	25.6	14.3	224.5
Crook	1 690	9.6	3 393	4	181	746	203	70	32	63 345	7.1	92.9	71.3	16.3	13.2	44.6
Fremont	2 619	8.4	2 664	154	D	552	210	47	61	62 560	27.8	72.2	57.9	15.9	51.7	594.0
Goshen	1 266	2.5	1 840	134	289	629	337	65	131	190 197	20.2	79.8	74.1	29.9	1.8	165.5
Hot Springs	944	4.0	6 423	38	36	910	142	52	10	65 035	10.3	89.7	59.2	17.7	41.9	204.4
Johnson	2 132	3.7	6 767	45	61	1 250	192	70	28	88 314	4.9	95.1	73.7	28.3	31.1	299.9
Laramie	1 728	1.7	2 810	61	D	659	241	70	96	156 031	20.8	79.2	59.5	18.5	0.9	112.8
Lincoln	408	-26.9	810	89	115	455	571	54	23	45 574	13.2	86.8	51.4	12.3	71.6	498.7
Natrona	2 807	11.9	9 025	49	52	1 806	190	54	27	86 135	11.7	88.3	54.3	20.3	41.7	190.3
Niobrara	1 608	19.6	5 785	11	91	681	129	59	28	99 876	4.3	95.7	83.1	27.0	7.5	28.4
Park	1 011	26.9	1 720	114	121	632	395	63	66	111 485	47.8	52.2	53.2	21.6	63.6	868.0
Platte	1 285	-5.9	2 787	67	170	645	231	82	68	148 031	16.5	83.5	63.6	20.8	8.1	129.7
Sheridan	1 608	33.0	2 831	60	129	1 019	365	48	38	67 582	9.8	90.2	54.8	13.7	27.2	856.9
Sublette	592	-0.2	2 152	174	169	1 374	673	69	27	98 937	4.7	95.3	58.9	28.4	75.1	448.9
Sweetwater	1 421	-17.4	8 881	34	42	773	87	39	7	43 517	18.7	81.3	61.2	9.4	65.9	73.1
Teton	52	-15.5	504	17	21	444	939	43	5	44 749	29.8	70.2	49.0	13.5	88.9	89.0
Uinta	940	6.8	3 133	110	108	752	254	50	22	74 417	2.5	97.5	62.0	16.3	38.6	180.0
Washakie	450	13.1	2 195	50	58	887	448	85	29	140 201	45.5	54.5	62.9	30.7	66.8	259.0
Weston	1 421	-4.3	6 097	3	96	741	122	44	19	81 191	4.3	95.7	70.8	15.9	20.6	14.0

Note: Agriculture, 1997 (cont'd). Land in farms; Acres; Value of land and buildings; Value of products sold; Percent of farms with sales of —.

Table B. States and Counties — Residential Construction, Wholesale and Retail Trade, and Real Estate

STATE County	Value of Residential Construction Authorized by Building Permits, 1999		Wholesale Trade, 1997				Retail Trade[1], 1997				Real Estate and Rental and Leasing, 1997			
	New Construction ($1,000)	Number of Housing Units	Number of Establishments	Number of Employees	Sales (mil dol)	Annual Payroll (mil dol)	Number of Establishments	Number of Employees	Sales (mil dol)	Annual Payroll (mil dol)	Number of Establishments	Number of Employees	Receipts (mil dol)	Annual Payroll (mil dol)
	133	134	135	136	137	138	139	140	141	142	143	144	145	146
WYOMING—Cont'd														
Converse	606	8	15	128	42.0	2.2	59	430	64.2	5.6	11	19	1.7	0.1
Crook	1 230	10	2	D	D	D	27	180	25.7	2.4	1	D	D	D
Fremont	5 182	62	43	260	85.2	3.9	204	1 735	296.8	27.8	55	217	15.8	3.4
Goshen	675	9	21	240	210.9	4.1	65	509	69.3	7.7	14	33	2.1	0.3
Hot Springs	394	4	3	D	D	D	32	229	20.4	2.2	5	D	D	D
Johnson	2 698	24	12	53	6.9	0.9	56	287	38.5	3.9	11	27	2.4	0.5
Laramie	36 461	323	81	665	267.5	18.6	358	4 851	855.5	77.8	88	321	27.7	5.2
Lincoln	17 830	143	10	23	9.8	0.5	80	623	86.4	7.3	12	29	1.2	0.2
Natrona	19 752	245	206	1 853	984.1	59.2	399	3 985	645.6	65.2	106	414	39.2	8.4
Niobrara	0	0	3	D	D	D	14	84	11.9	1.0	NA	NA	NA	NA
Park	16 159	155	44	178	51.8	4.1	219	1 528	271.3	24.5	35	123	10.8	2.0
Platte	626	8	8	D	D	D	46	374	68.5	4.8	13	24	1.3	0.2
Sheridan	8 389	90	40	246	146.1	6.4	179	1 561	240.8	23.9	76	177	12.5	1.9
Sublette	9 264	75	7	26	10.8	0.6	33	189	26.4	2.7	10	21	2.3	0.4
Sweetwater	5 141	51	82	469	188.5	15.0	212	2 399	402.8	38.6	51	181	15.2	3.0
Teton	122 951	332	35	201	49.3	5.7	242	1 619	300.9	33.7	67	322	46.4	6.0
Uinta	5 269	63	32	226	73.2	7.3	96	1 027	174.5	15.0	29	163	12.7	3.3
Washakie	688	8	15	156	31.8	2.4	70	474	80.7	7.2	12	37	3.2	0.5
Weston	250	3	6	26	4.2	0.9	39	267	38.4	3.3	5	9	0.9	0.1

1. Establishments with payroll.

STATE County	Professional, Scientific, and Technical Services[1], 1997				Manufacturing, 1997				Accommodation and Foodservices, 1997			
	Number of Establishments	Number of Employees	Receipts (mil dol)	Annual Payroll (mil dol)	Number of Establishments	Number of Employees	Receipts (mil dol)	Annual Payroll (mil dol)	Number of Establishments	Number of Employees	Sales (mil dol)	Annual Payroll (mil dol)
	147	148	149	150	151	152	153	154	155	156	157	158
WYOMING—Cont'd												
Converse	21	68	4.1	1.4	NA	NA	NA	NA	45	474	12.7	3.3
Crook	7	14	0.9	0.3	NA	NA	NA	NA	27	120	4.6	1.1
Fremont	78	283	16.7	6.7	41	D	D	D	152	1 397	39.9	11.4
Goshen	18	39	2.9	0.7	NA	NA	NA	NA	35	369	9.0	2.3
Hot Springs	9	28	1.3	0.5	NA	NA	NA	NA	31	234	7.2	1.8
Johnson	21	48	3.1	1.2	NA	NA	NA	NA	35	305	9.7	3.1
Laramie	199	843	64.5	24.7	48	1 349	606.3	45.2	183	3 930	106.3	31.1
Lincoln	24	84	4.2	1.7	20	579	200.8	17.4	53	369	11.5	2.7
Natrona	205	1 213	81.0	30.7	91	1 440	328.3	40.7	172	2 924	79.0	21.8
Niobrara	7	8	0.5	0.1	NA	NA	NA	NA	18	107	3.6	0.8
Park	64	218	12.2	4.3	41	524	66.1	13.9	130	1 283	90.0	21.7
Platte	19	37	3.5	1.0	NA	NA	NA	NA	40	352	9.1	2.4
Sheridan	73	304	24.1	7.4	NA	NA	NA	NA	88	1 199	36.8	10.5
Sublette	17	52	4.5	1.4	NA	NA	NA	NA	46	178	7.6	1.8
Sweetwater	58	236	17.0	7.6	29	696	458.2	36.1	109	1 838	61.3	17.5
Teton	165	577	61.8	23.6	NA	NA	NA	NA	180	4 303	166.3	43.8
Uinta	27	142	10.7	4.3	NA	NA	NA	NA	50	829	24.2	6.5
Washakie	21	70	3.0	1.2	NA	NA	NA	NA	35	320	8.4	2.1
Weston	7	19	0.9	0.3	NA	NA	NA	NA	24	155	4.1	1.1

1. Firms subject to federal tax.

STATE County	Health Care and Social Assistance[1], 1997				Other Services[1], 1997				Federal funds and grants, fiscal 1999[2]			
									Expenditures (mil dol)			
									Total	Direct payments for individuals[3]		
	Number of Establishments	Number of Employees	Receipts (mil dol)	Annual Payroll (mil dol)	Number of Establishments	Number of Employees	Receipts (mil dol)	Annual Payroll (mil dol)	Total	Social Security and government retirement	Medicare	Food stamps and Supplemental Security Income
	159	160	161	162	163	164	165	166	167	168	169	170
WYOMING—Cont'd												
Converse	16	96	4.4	1.4	18	47	3.6	0.7	36.5	18.7	5.2	1.0
Crook	6	D	D	D	7	D	D	D	41.0	10.8	3.3	0.2
Fremont	87	1 144	73.7	28.2	64	219	17.7	4.4	177.3	67.7	25.9	5.9
Goshen	17	60	3.9	1.2	30	71	4.1	0.8	67.8	27.9	8.7	1.0
Hot Springs	11	114	5.2	2.1	14	55	1.9	0.5	25.3	14.0	4.8	0.5
Johnson	12	27	2.5	1.0	12	50	2.5	0.8	28.2	17.0	3.9	0.4
Laramie	153	1 576	105.7	51.0	127	1 122	165.2	24.3	780.7	196.1	43.9	7.5
Lincoln	16	53	2.8	0.6	21	43	3.4	0.7	56.3	25.5	6.7	0.7
Natrona	168	1 524	93.3	40.8	154	808	57.2	15.2	280.2	125.5	38.9	8.5
Niobrara	2	D	D	D	3	D	D	D	12.8	5.7	2.0	0.9
Park	63	293	20.3	9.3	60	248	23.9	5.7	132.0	52.5	15.1	1.8
Platte	15	84	4.3	1.9	19	50	3.3	0.6	48.4	21.5	6.8	0.6
Sheridan	69	537	28.9	11.8	45	214	10.5	2.9	138.7	65.8	15.4	2.5
Sublette	15	52	2.6	1.2	12	18	1.2	0.2	22.1	10.2	2.3	0.2
Sweetwater	61	457	27.5	11.5	76	359	24.0	6.6	132.3	52.3	16.6	2.0
Teton	76	288	28.1	9.1	53	242	14.4	4.6	47.3	18.9	4.9	0.3
Uinta	30	147	9.8	4.3	39	142	8.6	2.1	43.2	23.3	5.4	2.4
Washakie	15	170	6.3	2.0	28	105	6.3	1.8	49.5	17.5	7.3	0.5
Weston	9	70	3.6	1.7	8	30	1.3	0.4	38.4	14.5	4.7	0.3

1. Firms subject to federal tax.   2. October 1, 1998 to September 30, 1999.   3. State totals may include programs not allocated by county.

Table B. States and Counties — Federal Funds and Local Government Finances

STATE County	Federal funds and grants, fiscal 1999[1] (cont'd) Expenditures (mil dol) (cont'd)							Local government finances, 1997 General revenue				
	Procurement contract awards			Grants[2]						Taxes		
											Per capita[3] (dollars)	
	Salaries and wages	Defense	Other	Medicaid and other health-related	Nutrition and family welfare	Education	Other	Total (mil dol)	Intergovern-mental (mil dol)	Total (mil dol)	Total	Property
	171	172	173	174	175	176	177	178	179	180	181	182
WYOMING—Cont'd												
Converse	2.7	0.0	0.6	2.6	1.2	0.5	1.6	39.2	13.4	14.7	1 192	1 003
Crook	2.2	0.0	1.6	1.7	0.3	0.4	18.2	16.5	9.1	5.7	978	837
Fremont	17.9	0.0	6.9	14.2	6.9	17.7	10.2	100.9	62.7	24.3	678	568
Goshen	4.1	0.0	0.7	11.4	2.0	1.0	1.1	34.8	20.2	8.2	639	413
Hot Springs	1.1	0.0	0.3	3.0	0.5	0.2	0.3	13.0	4.9	6.0	1 282	1 096
Johnson	2.8	0.0	0.7	1.7	0.5	0.9	-0.4	30.1	14.9	5.7	846	665
Laramie	216.5	43.3	14.0	46.2	34.9	32.5	130.2	251.1	109.5	42.9	547	361
Lincoln	4.6	0.0	1.2	2.1	1.0	0.7	13.1	59.3	23.0	18.4	1 324	1 187
Natrona	36.3	0.9	6.7	15.4	8.3	3.8	32.7	170.5	100.0	31.4	494	285
Niobrara	1.0	0.0	0.1	0.9	0.2	0.3	0.4	11.5	4.9	2.8	1 057	842
Park	25.8	0.0	17.3	7.1	2.0	0.9	5.6	73.2	32.3	21.3	830	767
Platte	4.9	0.1	0.8	2.9	3.6	0.6	2.3	27.3	10.7	6.9	813	650
Sheridan	24.2	0.0	2.2	11.4	2.6	1.0	9.9	84.6	38.3	15.3	608	315
Sublette	3.8	0.0	0.7	0.4	0.3	0.3	3.8	20.8	4.0	12.5	2 198	2 118
Sweetwater	12.4	0.3	3.1	6.1	4.3	1.3	32.4	170.4	41.1	73.8	1 858	1 604
Teton	11.4	0.6	3.4	1.4	0.4	0.5	5.2	84.5	11.8	31.0	2 228	1 304
Uinta	3.0	0.0	0.6	1.5	2.3	1.1	3.3	67.2	23.3	29.6	1 458	1 272
Washakie	6.2	0.0	1.2	3.6	4.5	0.5	6.3	20.4	11.4	6.2	723	676
Weston	2.0	6.8	0.5	2.1	0.5	0.4	6.0	16.1	9.7	4.9	755	588

1. October 1, 1998 to September 30, 1999.   2. State totals may include programs not allocated by county.   3. Based on the resident population estimated as of July 1 of the year shown.

Table B. States and Counties — **Local Government Finances, Government Employment, and Elections**

STATE County	Local government finances, 1997 (cont'd)							Debt outstanding		Government employment, 1998			Presidential election, 2000		
	Direct general expenditure												Percent of vote cast —		
			Percent of total for —												
	Total (mil dol)	Per capita[1] (dollars)	Educa-tion	Health and hospitals	Police protec-tion	Public welfare	High-ways	Total (mil dol)	Per capita[1] (dollars)	Federal civilian	Federal military	State and local	Demo-cratic	Republi-can	All other
	183	184	185	186	187	188	189	190	191	192	193	194	195	196	197
WYOMING—Cont'd															
Converse	43.2	3 512	46.4	15.5	4.7	0.4	4.4	33.6	2 732	69	77	1 107	20.9	76.2	2.9
Crook	15.6	2 690	65.7	1.7	5.3	0.1	6.9	3.9	674	77	36	560	13.3	84.6	2.1
Fremont	100.5	2 801	67.1	0.7	4.1	0.8	2.4	32.1	894	422	224	3 136	27.6	69.7	2.7
Goshen	34.2	2 664	63.4	4.2	3.4	0.2	2.7	12.3	956	93	80	1 257	26.2	71.4	2.4
Hot Springs	19.4	4 152	71.6	0.5	3.6	0.3	3.5	6.8	1 455	15	29	532	23.3	74.1	2.7
Johnson	23.0	3 393	40.5	35.2	3.6	0.1	4.2	9.4	1 383	62	42	689	15.8	82.1	2.2
Laramie	251.6	3 206	45.0	26.7	3.3	0.2	4.3	114.4	1 458	2 422	3 820	8 667	35.0	62.8	2.2
Lincoln	63.7	4 592	50.6	8.4	3.3	0.2	3.6	147.9	10 666	111	86	1 221	17.5	80.1	2.4
Natrona	176.6	2 775	53.0	1.2	5.0	0.4	3.5	62.0	974	642	398	4 443	31.1	66.3	2.6
Niobrara	10.9	4 154	37.2	24.4	2.7	0.1	2.9	19.6	7 499	25	17	341	17.1	79.9	3.0
Park	73.9	2 880	56.9	9.3	3.8	0.0	3.5	61.9	2 412	785	161	2 373	19.2	78.4	2.4
Platte	27.4	3 206	48.3	1.1	3.3	0.1	3.9	94.3	11 037	99	54	860	29.0	68.0	3.0
Sheridan	84.5	3 353	48.6	26.9	3.8	0.0	4.8	8.2	325	625	157	2 227	27.7	70.0	2.3
Sublette	23.0	4 035	52.1	4.1	6.4	0.7	6.8	34.8	6 117	92	43	465	14.5	82.8	2.7
Sweetwater	195.4	4 917	48.8	17.1	3.9	0.2	3.5	199.8	5 029	260	248	3 695	35.7	60.9	3.4
Teton	79.6	5 715	22.6	43.1	5.2	0.6	2.8	40.5	2 907	393	88	1 440	41.6	56.4	2.0
Uinta	72.5	3 575	57.6	0.5	5.3	0.4	5.5	159.7	7 872	77	127	1 920	22.5	74.5	3.0
Washakie	20.0	2 316	56.8	0.6	5.8	0.4	4.2	13.5	1 563	145	54	663	20.0	78.0	1.9
Weston	16.2	2 486	62.1	2.4	4.6	0.6	6.5	5.4	834	60	43	628	14.8	83.1	2.1

1. Based on the resident population estimated as of July 1 of the year shown.

Metropolitan Areas

(For explanation of symbols, see page xii)

Page

810   Abilene, TX—Columbia, MO
824   Columbia, SC—Harrisburg-Lebanon-Carlisle, PA
838   Hartford, CT—Memphis, TN-AR-MS
852   Merced, CA—Rapid City, SD
866   Reading, PA—Topeka, KS
880   Tucson, AZ—Yuma, AZ

Table C. Metropolitan Areas — **Land Area and Population**

CMSA/ MSA/ PMSA/ NECMA code[1]	Area Name	Land area,[2] (sq km) 1990	Population and population characteristics, 1999														
						Race (percent)						Age (percent)					
			Total persons	Rank	Per square kilometer	White	Black	Am. Indian, Eskimo, Aleut	Asian and Pacific Islander	Percent Hispanic[3]	Under 5 years	5 to 17 years	18 to 24 years	25 to 34 years	35 to 44 years	45 to 54 years
		1	2	3	4	5	6	7	8	9	10	11	12	13	14	15
0040	Abilene, TX	2 372	122 478	270	51.6	90.6	6.9	0.5	2.0	19.0	8.0	19.2	12.8	12.7	14.3	11.7
0120	Albany, GA	1 776	117 421	278	66.1	50.2	48.8	0.3	0.7	1.4	7.6	22.2	10.2	13.4	16.4	11.9
0160	Albany-Schenectady-Troy, NY	8 347	869 474	68	104.2	92.7	5.2	0.2	1.9	2.3	6.3	17.6	9.7	13.6	16.9	13.0
0200	Albuquerque, NM	15 393	678 820	78	44.1	88.2	3.5	6.1	2.2	39.6	7.3	19.1	10.1	13.2	17.1	13.5
0220	Alexandria, LA	3 426	126 775	265	37.0	68.1	30.5	0.4	0.9	1.5	7.0	20.1	9.9	12.8	14.7	13.2
0240	Allentown-Bethlehem-Easton, PA	2 857	618 350	83	216.4	95.6	2.6	0.1	1.6	6.5	5.9	17.2	8.3	13.2	16.5	13.5
0280	Altoona, PA	1 362	129 937	261	95.4	98.4	1.0	0.1	0.4	0.5	5.5	18.9	7.7	11.7	16.0	13.6
0320	Amarillo, TX	4 723	208 691	192	44.2	90.5	5.8	1.0	2.7	17.3	8.0	20.1	10.0	13.0	15.8	12.8
0380	Anchorage, AK	4 397	257 808	167	58.6	80.2	6.3	7.1	6.4	5.2	7.5	21.4	12.7	12.3	17.4	15.6
0450	Anniston, AL	1 576	116 541	281	73.9	79.2	19.7	0.2	0.9	1.9	6.1	17.3	11.2	13.8	15.7	12.9
0460	Appleton-Oshkosh-Neenah, WI	3 623	348 100	138	96.1	96.7	0.4	1.0	1.8	1.1	6.6	19.5	10.0	14.0	16.7	13.3
0480	Asheville, NC	2 864	215 180	188	75.1	91.1	7.8	0.3	0.7	1.5	6.3	17.2	7.6	12.6	16.3	13.7
0500	Athens, GA	1 531	140 372	246	91.7	73.1	23.8	0.2	2.9	2.6	6.5	16.5	19.2	14.6	15.4	11.5
0520	Atlanta, GA	15 867	3 857 097	9	243.1	70.9	25.9	0.2	2.9	3.6	7.6	18.3	9.6	17.1	18.8	13.5
0580	Auburn-Opalika, AL	1 577	102 164	296	64.8	72.0	25.8	0.1	2.1	1.1	6.1	15.1	23.2	14.0	14.2	11.5
0600	Augusta-Aiken, GA-SC	6 342	460 826	106	72.7	64.1	33.3	0.3	2.3	2.5	7.2	19.4	9.7	14.8	16.7	12.7
0640	Austin-San Marcos, TX	10 946	1 146 050	49	104.7	86.3	10.0	0.5	3.2	26.2	8.0	18.7	13.6	15.9	17.8	11.8
0680	Bakersfield, CA	21 087	642 495	80	30.5	87.0	6.6	1.8	4.7	35.9	8.9	23.0	9.2	15.4	15.8	11.3
0733	Bangor, ME	8 796	144 432	242	16.4	97.9	0.4	0.8	0.9	0.6	5.0	17.5	11.1	13.2	17.0	14.4
0743	Barnstable-Yarmouth, MA	1 025	212 519	189	207.3	96.3	2.1	0.7	0.9	1.7	5.4	15.8	4.9	12.0	16.3	12.4
0760	Baton Rouge, LA	4 108	578 946	88	140.9	67.3	31.2	0.2	1.3	1.8	7.1	19.8	12.8	13.7	16.4	12.9
0840	Beaumont-Port Arthur, TX	5 579	376 256	130	67.4	72.4	25.0	0.3	2.3	5.7	6.5	20.1	8.8	11.9	15.5	13.6
0860	Bellingham, WA	5 491	160 310	225	29.2	93.5	0.6	3.3	2.6	4.6	6.1	18.8	12.7	12.1	17.1	13.2
0870	Benton Harbor, MI	1 479	159 709	226	108.0	81.6	16.6	0.4	1.3	2.1	6.4	20.1	8.2	12.5	15.6	13.5
0880	Billings, MT	6 825	127 258	264	18.6	95.5	0.5	3.3	0.6	3.3	6.0	18.6	10.3	11.4	15.5	15.0
0920	Biloxi-Gulfport-Pascagoula, MS	4 622	353 205	137	76.4	77.1	20.1	0.3	2.5	2.2	7.6	19.2	9.9	14.5	15.3	12.8
0960	Binghamton, NY	3 174	247 462	171	78.0	95.5	2.1	0.2	2.3	1.5	6.4	17.7	9.4	13.4	15.4	13.3
1000	Birmingham, AL	8 255	915 077	65	110.9	70.4	28.9	0.2	0.6	0.8	6.7	17.0	9.2	14.9	17.1	13.1
1010	Bismarck, ND	9 219	91 939	304	10.0	96.5	0.1	2.9	0.5	0.8	6.0	19.7	9.2	12.4	16.8	13.9
1020	Bloomington, IN	1 021	116 923	279	114.5	93.4	3.0	0.2	3.3	1.9	5.4	12.9	26.3	14.6	14.1	10.3
1040	Bloomington-Normal, IL	3 066	145 477	240	47.4	93.2	4.8	0.2	1.8	1.9	6.4	17.4	18.3	13.2	16.0	11.4
1080	Boise City, ID	4 260	407 844	120	95.7	97.1	0.6	0.7	1.6	8.4	7.5	19.6	11.9	13.6	16.1	13.2
1123	Boston-Worcester-Lawrence-Lowell-Brockton, MA-NH	16 706	5 901 589	4	353.3	89.9	6.0	0.2	3.9	5.7	6.4	17.6	8.3	15.6	17.4	13.5
1240	Brownsville-Harlingen-San Benito, TX	2 345	329 131	146	140.4	99.0	0.4	0.2	0.4	85.6	9.8	25.5	10.5	11.7	14.1	10.7
1260	Bryan-College Station, TX	1 517	134 213	256	88.5	82.6	12.2	0.3	4.9	17.8	6.9	15.4	29.6	13.8	12.3	9.3
1280	Buffalo-Niagara Falls, NY	4 060	1 142 121	50	281.3	86.1	11.7	0.7	1.4	2.7	6.3	17.6	8.5	13.4	15.7	12.9
1303	Burlington, VT	3 260	194 748	202	59.7	97.5	0.8	0.4	1.3	1.0	5.8	17.5	11.5	15.9	17.5	14.6
1320	Canton-Massillon, OH	2 514	402 460	122	160.1	91.9	7.3	0.3	0.6	1.0	6.2	18.3	8.4	12.6	16.4	13.8
1350	Casper, WY	13 831	63 157	317	4.6	97.7	0.9	0.7	0.7	4.0	6.2	19.0	10.7	10.8	15.2	14.7
1360	Cedar Rapids, IA	1 858	184 891	206	99.5	96.3	2.3	0.2	1.2	1.7	6.4	17.9	10.4	13.5	16.6	14.1
1400	Champaign-Urbana, IL	2 583	170 272	216	65.9	82.8	10.8	0.2	6.3	2.4	6.4	15.1	21.1	15.3	14.8	10.1
1480	Charleston, WV	3 236	251 199	169	77.6	93.9	5.4	0.1	0.6	0.5	5.6	15.9	8.4	13.2	15.7	15.2
1440	Charleston-North Charleston, SC	6 713	552 803	94	82.3	67.0	31.0	0.3	1.7	2.3	7.8	18.3	10.6	16.7	16.2	12.3
1520	Charlotte-Gastonia-Rock Hill, NC-SC	8 751	1 417 217	42	161.9	77.4	20.5	0.4	1.7	2.0	7.4	18.5	8.8	15.4	17.0	13.5
1540	Charlottesville, VA	3 049	151 267	231	49.6	80.9	16.3	0.1	2.7	1.6	6.2	15.6	14.3	15.3	16.3	12.2
1560	Chattanooga, TN-GA	4 726	452 034	110	95.6	84.1	14.7	0.2	1.0	1.1	6.4	17.5	8.7	13.3	16.4	14.1
1580	Cheyenne, WY	6 957	78 877	312	11.3	94.5	3.1	0.8	1.6	10.9	6.7	17.8	12.1	12.1	15.0	15.0
14	Chicago-Gary-Kenosha, IL-IN-WI	17 951	8 885 919	X	495.0	76.4	19.1	0.2	4.3	14.2	7.6	19.1	9.3	14.7	16.8	13.0
1600	Chicago, IL	13 119	8 008 507	3	610.5	75.8	19.3	0.2	4.6	14.8	7.7	19.0	9.3	14.9	16.9	12.9
2960	Gary, IN	2 370	628 377	81	265.1	78.4	20.4	0.2	0.9	11.2	6.9	20.3	8.7	13.4	16.4	13.2
3740	Kankakee, IL	1 755	102 720	294	58.5	82.2	16.6	0.2	1.0	2.9	7.3	21.3	8.9	12.1	15.8	12.8
3800	Kenosha, WI	707	146 315	239	207.0	93.5	5.3	0.4	0.8	6.5	7.0	19.6	9.7	13.7	16.3	13.9
1620	Chico-Paradise, CA	4 247	195 220	201	46.0	92.6	1.5	2.0	4.0	10.5	6.3	18.6	12.3	11.3	15.1	11.6
21	Cincinnati-Hamilton, OH-KY-IN	9 868	1 960 995	X	198.7	87.2	11.5	0.1	1.1	0.7	7.2	19.0	9.6	14.4	16.3	13.0
1640	Cincinnati, OH-KY-IN	8 658	1 627 509	33	188.0	86.0	12.8	0.2	1.0	0.7	7.3	19.1	9.2	14.5	16.3	13.0
3200	Hamilton-Middletown, OH	1 210	333 486	145	275.6	93.4	5.2	0.1	1.3	0.7	6.7	18.9	11.6	13.8	16.6	13.2
1660	Clarksville-Hopkinsville, TN-KY	3 264	201 352	197	61.7	75.9	21.2	0.4	2.5	5.3	8.8	17.9	14.0	17.2	14.9	11.1
28	Cleveland-Akron, OH	9 357	2 910 616	X	311.1	81.6	16.8	0.2	1.4	2.4	6.5	18.0	8.9	13.5	16.3	13.3
0080	Akron, OH	2 344	689 435	76	294.1	87.2	11.2	0.2	1.3	0.8	6.3	17.8	10.3	13.6	16.6	13.1
1680	Cleveland-Lorain-Elyria, OH	7 013	2 221 181	23	316.7	79.8	18.6	0.2	1.4	2.9	6.5	18.1	8.4	13.5	16.2	13.3
1720	Colorado Springs, CO	5 508	499 994	101	90.8	87.7	7.9	0.9	3.5	11.0	7.6	18.9	11.5	13.7	16.3	14.1
1740	Columbia, MO	1 775	130 179	260	73.3	86.8	9.0	0.3	3.8	1.5	6.7	16.2	20.3	15.5	16.3	10.3

1. MSA = Metropolitan Statistical Area. CMSA = Consolidated MSA. PMSA = Primary MSA. NECMA = New England County Metropolitan Area. See Appendix A for explanation of these concepts. See Appendix B for list of metropolitan areas identified by type, with component counties. 2. Dry land or land partially or temporarily covered by water. 3. Hispanic persons may be of any race.

Table C. Metropolitan Areas — **Population and Households**

Area Name	Population, 1999 (cont'd) Age (percent) (cont'd) 55 to 64 years	65 to 74 years	75 years and over	Percent female	Population — change and components of change, 1980–1999 Total persons 1990	Total persons 1980	Percent change 1980–1990	Percent change 1990–1999	Components of change, 1990–1999 Births	Deaths	Net migration	Households, 1990 Number	Percent change, 1980–1990	Persons per household	Percent Female family householder[1]	One person
	16	17	18	19	20	21	22	23	24	25	26	27	28	29	30	31
Abilene, TX	8.6	6.5	6.2	51.6	119 655	110 932	7.9	2.4	18 909	9 909	-7 608	43 301	12.4	2.61	9.3	24.7
Albany, GA	7.9	6.0	4.5	52.6	112 571	112 394	0.2	4.3	17 738	8 655	-4 559	39 362	7.3	2.76	20.8	22.2
Albany-Schenectady-Troy, NY	8.5	7.4	7.1	51.4	861 623	824 729	4.5	0.9	103 805	75 217	-27 171	330 484	11.3	2.51	10.6	26.8
Albuquerque, NM	8.4	6.4	4.9	51.1	589 131	485 430	21.4	15.2	94 961	41 896	36 691	221 619	22.7	2.62	11.8	24.6
Alexandria, LA	9.2	7.0	6.0	52.5	131 556	135 282	-2.8	-3.6	17 927	11 841	-11 228	45 941	2.6	2.73	15.3	23.0
Allentown-Bethlehem-Easton, PA	9.1	8.4	7.9	51.6	595 043	551 052	8.0	3.9	68 740	55 314	11 923	225 831	12.4	2.56	9.3	23.6
Altoona, PA	9.6	8.5	8.6	52.8	130 542	136 621	-4.4	-0.5	14 257	14 253	-120	50 332	2.5	2.54	11.4	25.9
Amarillo, TX	9.5	5.7	5.0	51.3	187 514	173 699	8.0	11.3	31 141	16 047	6 948	71 897	11.5	2.56	10.6	26.2
Anchorage, AK	7.8	3.4	1.9	48.7	226 338	174 431	29.8	13.9	41 771	8 469	-5 075	82 702	36.8	2.68	10.1	22.9
Anniston, AL	9.4	7.7	5.9	51.8	116 032	119 761	-3.1	0.4	15 230	11 208	-4 499	42 983	8.4	2.59	12.4	23.2
Appleton-Oshkosh-Neenah, WI	8.2	5.8	5.9	50.4	315 121	291 369	8.2	10.5	41 982	23 289	15 545	115 515	16.3	2.65	7.7	22.7
Asheville, NC	10.0	8.3	7.9	52.2	191 310	177 761	7.9	12.5	23 603	20 447	21 285	77 290	16.9	2.40	10.6	26.4
Athens, GA	6.9	4.9	4.5	51.8	126 262	104 672	20.6	11.2	16 537	8 192	5 866	47 066	27.4	2.51	12.1	25.5
Atlanta, GA	7.3	4.3	3.4	51.1	2 959 500	2 233 229	32.5	30.3	513 815	202 481	589 331	1 102 578	39.6	2.64	12.9	22.8
Auburn-Opalika, AL	7.2	4.9	3.8	50.5	87 146	76 283	14.2	17.2	12 425	5 963	8 636	33 097	22.7	2.50	11.1	26.1
Augusta-Aiken, GA-SC	8.4	6.3	4.6	51.3	415 220	363 451	14.2	11.0	64 760	35 412	13 834	149 093	23.6	2.69	14.9	22.8
Austin-San Marcos, TX	6.7	4.1	3.4	50.2	846 227	585 051	44.6	35.4	150 228	49 379	198 167	325 995	53.8	2.50	10.2	28.4
Bakersfield, CA	7.0	5.1	4.3	48.3	544 981	403 089	35.2	17.9	112 484	39 666	24 885	181 480	29.8	2.92	12.3	20.3
Bangor, ME	9.0	6.9	5.9	51.1	146 601	137 015	7.0	-1.5	15 137	11 806	-5 153	54 063	17.6	2.57	9.9	22.6
Barnstable-Yarmouth, MA	9.9	11.7	11.5	52.3	186 605	147 925	26.1	13.9	20 283	22 468	28 705	77 586	32.5	2.35	9.8	27.2
Baton Rouge, LA	7.8	5.5	4.0	51.8	528 261	494 151	6.9	9.6	83 240	37 513	5 808	188 377	14.8	2.73	14.4	22.8
Beaumont-Port Arthur, TX	10.2	7.4	5.9	51.0	361 218	373 211	-3.2	4.2	51 039	34 128	-656	134 238	1.8	2.65	12.9	23.9
Bellingham, WA	8.1	5.8	6.1	50.5	127 780	106 701	19.8	25.5	17 787	9 971	25 202	48 543	22.5	2.53	8.0	24.9
Benton Harbor, MI	9.1	7.5	7.0	52.1	161 378	171 276	-5.8	-1.0	21 271	14 324	-8 143	61 025	1.2	2.60	13.3	24.4
Billings, MT	10.1	6.9	6.2	51.4	113 419	108 035	5.0	12.2	15 621	9 206	7 850	44 689	12.0	2.49	9.7	26.5
Biloxi-Gulfport-Pascagoula, MS	9.1	7.0	4.6	50.8	312 368	300 176	4.1	13.1	47 724	26 739	17 030	111 828	14.1	2.71	13.5	22.3
Binghamton, NY	8.9	8.0	7.6	51.3	264 497	263 460	0.4	-6.4	29 762	22 934	-23 222	100 681	7.9	2.55	9.8	25.5
Birmingham, AL	9.1	7.0	5.8	52.5	839 942	815 333	3.0	8.9	117 581	81 447	28 411	319 774	9.3	2.58	14.1	24.9
Bismarck, ND	8.8	6.8	6.3	51.4	83 831	79 988	4.8	9.7	10 799	6 020	3 667	31 361	12.2	2.60	8.5	24.9
Bloomington, IN	6.7	5.0	4.6	51.6	108 978	98 787	10.3	7.3	11 123	6 030	3 170	39 351	15.9	2.39	8.3	28.5
Bloomington-Normal, IL	7.3	4.8	5.2	51.8	129 180	119 149	8.4	12.6	17 454	8 667	7 383	46 796	12.2	2.52	8.3	26.1
Boise City, ID	8.2	5.1	4.9	50.6	295 851	256 881	15.2	37.9	52 993	21 876	81 227	108 759	18.7	2.66	9.2	22.9
Boston-Worcester-Lawrence-Lowell-Brockton, MA-NH	8.1	6.5	6.5	51.6	5 685 769	5 336 242	6.5	3.8	756 673	455 629	-70 166	2 111 440	12.3	2.61	11.6	25.2
Brownsville-Harlingen-San Benito, TX	7.5	5.8	4.4	52.5	260 120	209 727	24.0	26.5	69 548	16 308	16 530	73 278	25.4	3.48	16.1	16.0
Bryan-College Station, TX	5.3	3.8	3.5	48.8	121 862	93 588	30.2	10.1	17 919	5 726	330	43 725	34.6	2.51	9.1	25.2
Buffalo-Niagara Falls, NY	9.6	8.6	7.3	52.0	1 189 340	1 242 826	-4.3	-4.0	145 266	114 966	-74 124	461 803	3.7	2.51	12.9	27.5
Burlington, VT	7.7	5.1	4.5	51.0	177 059	154 935	14.3	10.0	23 672	11 113	5 706	64 783	25.3	2.61	9.1	22.2
Canton-Massillon, OH	9.3	8.0	7.1	52.0	394 106	404 421	-2.6	2.1	49 392	36 656	-3 124	149 240	4.6	2.58	10.7	23.7
Casper, WY	10.6	7.6	5.2	51.0	61 226	71 856	-14.8	3.2	8 466	4 596	-1 805	23 837	-7.8	2.54	9.7	25.9
Cedar Rapids, IA	8.7	6.3	6.0	51.3	168 767	169 775	-0.6	9.6	24 182	12 254	3 832	65 501	6.0	2.51	8.5	25.0
Champaign-Urbana, IL	6.6	5.1	4.9	50.0	173 025	168 392	2.8	-1.6	21 446	9 900	-15 734	63 900	9.4	2.43	8.4	28.7
Charleston, WV	10.8	8.5	6.9	52.4	250 454	269 595	-7.1	0.3	28 935	25 498	-1 847	100 408	1.0	2.46	11.3	25.9
Charleston-North Charleston, SC	7.5	6.3	4.3	51.1	506 877	430 346	17.8	9.1	76 854	35 008	-27 481	177 668	28.9	2.74	13.5	21.3
Charlotte-Gastonia-Rock Hill, NC-SC	8.7	5.9	4.8	51.7	1 161 546	971 447	19.6	22.0	179 003	94 965	172 983	440 670	28.7	2.58	12.0	23.1
Charlottesville, VA	8.4	6.2	5.5	51.6	131 373	113 568	15.7	15.1	16 964	9 946	13 002	48 709	21.0	2.51	10.2	24.6
Chattanooga, TN-GA	10.0	7.4	6.2	52.3	424 176	417 838	1.6	6.6	55 283	40 156	13 995	163 117	10.3	2.55	12.5	24.0
Cheyenne, WY	9.7	6.4	5.1	50.4	73 142	68 649	6.5	7.8	11 110	5 330	-1 018	28 092	11.1	2.55	9.7	25.3
Chicago-Gary-Kenosha, IL-IN-WI	8.3	6.1	5.2	51.3	8 239 820	8 114 844	1.5	7.8	1 355 871	658 862	-158 717	2 969 099	5.1	2.72	13.3	25.3
Chicago, IL	8.2	6.0	5.2	51.3	7 410 858	7 246 048	2.3	8.1	1 238 341	586 589	-161 186	2 671 540	5.4	2.72	13.3	25.6
Gary, IN	8.7	7.2	5.2	51.7	604 526	642 733	-5.9	3.9	83 449	51 944	-8 995	215 907	0.8	2.76	14.3	22.4
Kankakee, IL	8.7	6.7	6.3	51.3	96 255	102 926	-6.5	6.7	14 762	9 809	1 820	34 623	-0.9	2.68	12.5	24.3
Kenosha, WI	8.5	5.9	5.4	50.8	128 181	123 137	4.1	14.1	19 319	10 520	9 644	47 029	9.2	2.67	11.6	23.2
Chico-Paradise, CA	8.5	8.2	8.1	50.3	182 120	143 851	26.6	7.2	23 083	19 097	9 724	71 665	25.9	2.48	9.7	25.4
Cincinnati-Hamilton, OH-KY-IN	8.6	6.1	5.7	51.8	1 817 542	1 726 430	5.3	7.9	260 568	151 850	33 409	679 137	11.5	2.61	12.1	25.3
Cincinnati, OH-KY-IN	8.6	6.2	5.8	51.8	1 526 063	1 467 643	4.0	6.6	219 640	130 311	15 134	574 602	10.3	2.60	12.5	26.1
Hamilton-Middletown, OH	8.5	5.6	5.0	51.5	291 479	258 787	12.6	14.4	40 928	21 539	18 275	104 535	18.6	2.68	10.4	20.8
Clarksville-Hopkinsville, TN-KY	7.5	4.7	3.9	49.0	169 439	150 220	12.8	18.8	34 182	11 851	602	55 981	19.5	2.73	11.6	19.1
Cleveland-Akron, OH	9.1	7.7	6.7	52.2	2 859 662	2 938 277	-2.7	1.8	383 182	261 589	-86 227	1 094 413	3.7	2.56	12.9	26.3
Akron, OH	9.0	7.2	6.1	51.8	657 575	660 328	-0.4	4.8	86 213	56 211	-1 165	249 227	6.5	2.57	11.8	24.7
Cleveland-Lorain-Elyria, OH	9.1	7.9	6.8	52.3	2 202 087	2 277 949	-3.3	0.9	296 969	205 378	-85 062	845 186	2.9	2.56	13.2	26.8
Colorado Springs, CO	8.4	5.1	3.7	50.3	397 014	309 424	28.3	25.9	71 062	22 983	45 852	146 965	36.3	2.60	9.8	23.7
Columbia, MO	5.9	4.5	4.2	51.4	112 379	100 376	12.0	15.8	15 980	6 725	8 922	41 937	18.8	2.42	9.5	27.5

1. No spouse present.

Table C. Metropolitan Areas — Vital Statistics, Health Resources, and Crime

Area Name	Births, average 1996–1998 Total	Rate[1]	Deaths, average 1996–1998 Number Total	Number Infant[2]	Rate Total[1]	Rate Infant[3]	Physicians,[4] 1998 Number	Rate[5]	Hospitals,[4] 1998 Number	Beds Number	Beds Rate[5]	Medicare enrollees 1999	Serious crimes known to police, 1998[6] Total Number	Rate[7]
	32	33	34	35	36	37	38	39	40	41	42	43	44	45
Abilene, TX	1 999	16.5	1 082	16	8.9	8.0	268	220	2	494	405	18 142	5 893	4 773
Albany, GA	1 921	16.3	950	22	8.1	11.5	226	191	2	601	509	15 118	7 751	6 452
Albany-Schenectady-Troy, NY	10 441	11.9	8 157	66	9.3	6.2	2 372	272	12	3 235	371	140 499	26 080	2 970
Albuquerque, NM	10 735	15.3	5 011	66	7.2	6.2	2 065	304	8	1 619	239	87 249	55 689	8 722
Alexandria, LA	1 869	14.8	1 278	21	10.1	11.2	306	241	3	746	588	19 949	8 134	6 747
Allentown-Bethlehem-Easton, PA	7 066	11.5	6 148	56	10.0	8.0	1 498	243	9	2 227	361	110 456	17 050	3 013
Altoona, PA	1 438	11.0	1 558	10	11.9	7.2	283	217	4	593	454	24 773	3 594	2 749
Amarillo, TX	3 394	16.4	1 793	28	8.6	8.2	490	235	5	1 026	492	27 042	14 111	6 669
Anchorage, AK	NA	NA	NA	NA	NA	NA	655	257	2	603	236	16 091	NA	NA
Anniston, AL	1 626	13.9	1 256	21	10.7	12.9	176	150	3	366	313	20 378	6 902	5 850
Appleton-Oshkosh-Neenah, WI	4 336	12.7	2 618	27	7.7	6.4	632	183	6	929	270	45 035	NA	NA
Asheville, NC	2 591	12.2	2 326	20	11.0	7.7	697	326	2	714	334	39 384	7 920	4 064
Athens, GA	1 804	13.1	948	12	6.9	6.7	283	204	2	486	350	15 983	8 440	7 157
Atlanta, GA	59 740	16.4	23 567	467	6.5	7.8	8 138	217	44	9 404	251	345 389	221 718	6 041
Auburn-Opalika, AL	1 389	14.1	682	12	6.9	8.4	137	136	1	289	288	10 319	6 532	6 581
Augusta-Aiken, GA-SC	6 689	14.7	3 953	67	8.7	10.1	1 482	323	7	1 891	413	59 409	24 985	5 363
Austin-San Marcos, TX	17 948	16.7	5 733	103	5.3	5.7	2 214	200	13	1 892	171	95 875	55 378	5 087
Bakersfield, CA	11 459	18.3	4 513	90	7.2	7.8	868	137	11	1 649	261	72 391	30 539	4 899
Bangor, ME	1 541	10.8	1 300	10	9.1	6.3	350	246	4	633	445	23 525	4 814	3 366
Barnstable-Yarmouth, MA	2 054	10.0	2 571	9	12.5	4.2	581	279	2	385	185	55 123	7 294	3 539
Baton Rouge, LA	8 915	15.6	4 256	91	7.5	10.3	1 101	191	8	1 746	304	62 918	45 800	8 220
Beaumont-Port Arthur, TX	5 272	14.1	3 847	41	10.3	7.8	610	162	9	1 782	474	57 174	20 239	5 310
Bellingham, WA	1 975	12.8	1 151	6	7.4	2.9	325	207	1	228	145	20 976	8 706	5 566
Benton Harbor, MI	2 200	13.7	1 543	20	9.6	9.2	242	151	4	733	457	28 086	7 496	4 661
Billings, MT	1 684	13.4	1 055	14	8.4	8.1	357	283	2	520	412	19 040	5 679	4 733
Biloxi-Gulfport-Pascagoula, MS	5 031	14.6	3 094	46	9.0	9.3	762	218	7	1 234	353	46 960	NA	NA
Binghamton, NY	2 859	11.4	2 559	21	10.2	7.6	541	217	3	802	322	45 477	7 127	2 826
Birmingham, AL	12 700	14.1	9 023	134	10.0	10.6	2 756	303	16	4 942	544	134 321	45 517	5 046
Bismarck, ND	1 154	12.7	665	8	7.3	7.2	267	292	3	549	600	13 636	3 146	3 472
Bloomington, IN	1 241	10.7	683	10	5.9	8.3	239	208	1	265	230	12 352	3 965	3 379
Bloomington-Normal, IL	1 937	13.7	944	16	6.7	8.4	264	185	2	322	226	16 265	NA	NA
Boise City, ID	6 367	16.6	2 533	35	6.6	5.5	801	202	5	870	220	45 740	17 062	4 379
Boston-Worcester-Lawrence-Lowell-Brockton, MA-NH	78 717	13.5	49 580	387	8.5	4.9	19 998	341	82	18 725	319	853 150	164 191	3 149
Brownsville-Harlingen-San Benito, TX	7 755	24.2	1 813	29	5.7	3.7	383	117	5	951	291	35 311	16 898	5 182
Bryan-College Station, TX	2 007	15.1	633	10	4.8	5.1	271	203	2	256	192	10 788	7 711	5 703
Buffalo-Niagara Falls, NY	14 444	12.4	12 394	119	10.7	8.2	3 257	283	17	5 074	440	208 202	44 273	3 855
Burlington, VT	2 577	13.5	1 250	13	6.5	4.9	722	374	3	652	338	21 230	7 604	3 965
Canton-Massillon, OH	5 099	12.7	4 022	31	10.0	6.1	792	197	5	1 710	425	69 684	12 011	3 769
Casper, WY	856	13.5	516	3	8.1	3.5	124	196	1	282	445	9 592	3 126	4 902
Cedar Rapids, IA	2 586	14.3	1 355	16	7.5	6.2	354	194	2	877	480	26 037	NA	NA
Champaign-Urbana, IL	2 209	13.1	1 074	14	6.4	6.3	437	260	2	555	331	18 628	NA	NA
Charleston, WV	3 051	12.0	2 920	17	11.5	5.8	735	290	6	1 346	532	46 087	11 684	4 612
Charleston-North Charleston, SC	7 326	13.8	3 975	72	7.5	9.9	1 579	292	8	1 871	346	64 144	33 625	6 486
Charlotte-Gastonia-Rock Hill, NC-SC	20 343	15.1	10 863	144	8.0	7.1	2 645	191	12	3 445	249	172 920	90 424	6 618
Charlottesville, VA	1 829	12.5	1 130	9	7.7	5.3	1 044	700	2	734	492	19 850	136 539	5 517
Chattanooga, TN-GA	5 787	12.9	4 516	45	10.1	7.8	1 053	234	12	1 966	437	71 163	23 082	6 450
Cheyenne, WY	1 153	14.6	606	7	7.7	6.4	197	250	2	266	337	10 500	3 146	3 988
Chicago-Gary-Kenosha, IL-IN-WI	142 657	16.3	70 581	1 262	8.1	8.8	21 849	248	104	28 440	323	1 071 989	NA	NA
Chicago, IL	130 269	16.5	62 701	1 150	7.9	8.8	20 506	258	91	24 995	315	948 937	NA	NA
Gary, IN	8 778	14.1	5 653	86	9.1	9.8	1 000	160	9	2 656	426	88 485	24 621	4 538
Kankakee, IL	1 521	14.9	1 059	12	10.4	8.1	158	155	2	482	472	16 174	NA	NA
Kenosha, WI	2 089	14.6	1 168	14	8.2	6.5	185	128	2	307	213	18 393	NA	NA
Chico-Paradise, CA	2 334	12.1	2 156	17	11.2	7.1	383	197	2	661	340	35 957	8 690	4 421
Cincinnati-Hamilton, OH-KY-IN	27 815	14.4	16 699	228	8.6	8.1	4 409	226	25	6 164	316	264 319	NA	NA
Cincinnati, OH-KY-IN	23 338	14.5	14 215	193	8.8	8.2	4 034	249	20	5 372	332	223 760	NA	NA
Hamilton-Middletown, OH	4 477	13.7	2 484	35	7.6	7.7	375	113	5	792	240	40 559	15 082	4 608
Clarksville-Hopkinsville, TN-KY	3 871	19.6	1 325	31	6.7	8.0	303	152	2	390	195	19 494	NA	NA
Cleveland-Akron, OH	39 446	13.5	28 340	324	9.7	8.2	8 263	284	44	11 528	396	458 068	NA	NA
Akron, OH	9 086	13.2	6 215	60	9.0	6.6	1 535	223	7	2 221	322	101 745	NA	NA
Cleveland-Lorain-Elyria, OH	30 360	13.6	22 125	264	9.9	8.7	6 728	303	37	9 307	419	356 323	NA	NA
Colorado Springs, CO	7 748	16.1	2 693	59	5.6	7.6	1 016	207	4	1 008	206	50 821	24 219	5 088
Columbia, MO	1 736	13.6	752	9	5.9	5.2	813	630	3	931	721	13 703	5 965	4 617

1. Per 1,000 estimated resident population, average 1996–1998.   2. Deaths of infants under 1 year old.   3. Deaths of infants under 1 year old per 1,000 live births.   4. Data subject to copyright.   5. Per 100,000 resident population as of July 1 of the year shown.   6. Data for serious crimes have not been adjusted for underreporting; this may affect comparability between geographic areas and over time.   7. Per 100,000 population estimated by the FBI.

Table C. Metropolitan Areas — Crime, Education, Money Income, and Poverty

Area Name	Serious crimes known to police, 1998[1] (cont'd) Rate[2] Violent	Property	Education — School enrollment and attainment, 1990 Enrollment[3] Total	Percent private	Attainment[4] (percent) High school grad-uate or more	Bach-elor's degree or more	Local government expenditures, fiscal 1997[5] Total current expendi-tures (mil dol)	Current expendi-tures per student (dollars)	Money income 1989 Per capita[6] (dollars)	Households Median Dollars	Percent change, 1979–1989 (constant 1989 dollars)	Percent with $100,000 or more	Income and poverty, 1997 Median house-hold income	Percent below poverty level All persons	Persons under 18	Persons 5–17 in families
	46	47	48	49	50	51	52	53	54	55	56	57	58	59	60	61
Abilene, TX	463	4 310	34 059	26.4	75.4	20.7	129.5	5 253	11 791	24 660	-2.4	2.2	NA	16.8	23.4	22.2
Albany, GA	569	5 883	33 336	11.2	67.9	16.5	126.3	5 523	10 919	24 699	-5.2	2.3	NA	22.1	31.8	29.9
Albany-Schenectady-Troy, NY	276	2 694	221 422	22.8	79.8	23.6	1 105.6	8 242	15 152	32 427	15.8	3.7	NA	10.6	16.8	16.5
Albuquerque, NM	1 090	7 632	162 926	10.6	81.1	24.8	517.8	4 564	13 042	27 317	NA	3.1	NA	14.7	21.4	19.9
Alexandria, LA	835	5 912	34 655	13.5	69.0	14.6	117.1	4 608	10 014	20 810	-7.3	2.1	NA	20.0	29.1	26.8
Allentown-Bethlehem-Easton, PA	264	2 749	137 602	24.4	73.5	17.4	651.7	7 071	14 730	31 875	4.3	3.3	NA	8.0	12.8	11.5
Altoona, PA	203	2 546	29 518	13.6	75.0	10.5	124.2	5 943	11 233	23 270	-6.0	1.3	NA	13.7	19.3	17.5
Amarillo, TX	636	6 033	51 382	7.9	76.4	18.7	178.0	4 538	12 687	25 424	-10.7	2.6	NA	14.7	20.6	19.9
Anchorage, AK	NA	NA	63 357	11.5	90.4	26.9	307.4	6 390	19 620	43 946	-4.2	9.4	NA	9.1	13.2	11.9
Anniston, AL	795	5 055	30 580	7.5	67.4	14.2	85.0	4 311	10 704	23 802	3.9	1.2	NA	16.2	24.5	21.4
Appleton-Oshkosh-Neenah, WI	NA	NA	84 460	16.5	80.9	17.0	349.9	6 159	13 698	31 954	1.0	2.5	NA	5.9	8.3	7.6
Asheville, NC	472	3 592	42 476	14.2	73.0	18.5	165.9	5 230	12 852	25 295	11.5	2.2	NA	12.7	19.4	17.4
Athens, GA	461	6 696	47 163	7.2	73.7	30.7	117.6	5 723	11 999	22 957	6.1	3.2	NA	16.5	22.5	22.4
Atlanta, GA	689	5 352	743 923	15.6	78.7	26.1	3 524.6	5 586	16 670	35 606	18.7	5.8	NA	11.0	17.7	16.4
Auburn-Opalika, AL	924	5 657	35 831	5.3	73.2	25.3	76.7	4 764	11 409	21 227	8.7	2.7	NA	15.0	19.8	18.7
Augusta-Aiken, GA-SC	444	4 919	109 908	12.0	71.4	17.7	422.2	4 800	12 629	28 244	14.7	2.9	NA	16.3	24.5	22.6
Austin-San Marcos, TX	413	4 674	266 120	9.8	81.2	30.7	939.8	5 024	14 166	27 956	6.3	3.8	NA	11.1	15.3	15.2
Bakersfield, CA	599	4 300	153 512	7.7	67.6	13.3	744.5	5 316	12 154	28 633	4.4	3.2	NA	21.0	30.2	29.2
Bangor, ME	104	3 262	41 743	9.7	79.1	17.7	143.8	6 066	12 231	26 630	12.0	2.3	NA	12.1	16.4	14.5
Barnstable-Yarmouth, MA	623	2 916	37 509	13.9	88.4	28.1	215.2	6 832	16 402	31 766	21.9	4.1	NA	8.9	15.5	14.9
Baton Rouge, LA	720	7 500	161 296	17.6	76.8	22.4	454.7	4 588	12 305	26 920	-10.8	3.1	NA	14.9	21.2	19.5
Beaumont-Port Arthur, TX	624	4 686	97 680	9.7	73.6	13.7	380.8	5 203	12 024	25 466	-20.0	2.2	NA	17.5	24.9	22.3
Bellingham, WA	297	5 269	37 132	10.4	83.2	22.0	132.6	5 401	13 753	28 367	5.4	3.4	NA	11.4	16.3	14.6
Benton Harbor, MI	608	4 053	42 700	17.9	74.7	16.7	198.3	6 676	12 636	27 244	-0.1	2.4	NA	14.1	23.0	21.3
Billings, MT	187	4 546	30 202	11.0	83.7	21.5	113.7	5 092	12 416	25 942	-11.3	2.3	NA	12.1	16.8	14.5
Biloxi-Gulfport-Pascagoula, MS	NA	NA	83 588	11.5	73.9	15.4	260.4	4 264	10 708	23 551	-5.4	1.7	NA	14.5	20.6	18.9
Binghamton, NY	161	2 665	69 340	10.9	79.2	20.2	332.9	7 589	13 515	29 245	6.1	2.5	NA	13.2	21.2	20.3
Birmingham, AL	581	4 465	210 978	14.2	73.0	19.7	722.9	4 817	13 322	26 613	1.6	3.5	NA	13.2	19.4	17.6
Bismarck, ND	182	3 290	22 710	14.2	79.4	21.9	70.4	4 320	12 316	27 001	-11.4	2.1	NA	10.2	14.0	11.9
Bloomington, IN	150	3 229	47 386	4.6	82.1	32.9	77.7	5 827	12 017	24 780	7.8	2.9	NA	12.0	14.1	13.5
Bloomington-Normal, IL	NA	NA	45 875	11.4	84.7	29.0	114.8	5 191	14 138	31 366	0.9	3.2	NA	8.8	12.2	11.6
Boise City, ID	310	4 069	82 080	10.3	82.4	21.1	312.8	4 394	12 943	27 790	1.8	2.7	NA	11.0	15.2	12.8
Boston-Worcester-Lawrence-Lowell-Brockton, MA-NH	505	2 644	1 439 096	28.7	80.5	27.8	6 228.8	7 068	17 644	38 529	27.7	7.0	NA	9.8	15.2	14.3
Brownsville-Harlingen-San Benito, TX	515	4 667	89 414	5.4	50.0	12.0	429.9	5 241	7 125	17 335	-11.8	1.6	NA	35.3	45.2	41.4
Bryan-College Station, TX	393	5 310	58 837	5.3	79.8	35.8	101.5	5 045	10 987	20 410	-1.0	2.6	NA	18.0	22.1	21.8
Buffalo-Niagara Falls, NY	425	3 430	301 716	18.2	76.3	18.8	1 513.7	8 350	13 403	28 083	-2.9	2.6	NA	13.6	21.0	20.1
Burlington, VT	125	3 840	51 305	18.0	83.7	29.0	214.1	6 690	15 034	34 663	24.4	3.8	NA	8.1	10.4	8.8
Canton-Massillon, OH	477	3 292	94 853	15.5	75.7	13.9	374.4	5 355	12 848	27 684	-10.6	2.2	NA	10.5	15.8	13.9
Casper, WY	204	4 698	17 410	5.6	85.3	20.4	70.3	5 460	12 992	27 586	-28.0	2.6	NA	13.1	17.7	14.1
Cedar Rapids, IA	NA	NA	44 286	18.3	84.9	21.5	166.3	5 217	14 902	32 137	-4.5	2.8	NA	7.8	11.2	9.6
Champaign-Urbana, IL	NA	NA	67 446	5.9	87.5	34.1	127.5	5 309	13 130	26 540	-3.6	3.0	NA	12.1	16.8	16.7
Charleston, WV	384	4 228	56 991	9.1	72.7	16.9	235.4	5 844	12 708	24 578	-15.8	2.4	NA	13.3	20.5	18.0
Charleston-North Charleston, SC	850	5 636	134 889	14.2	75.7	18.9	419.9	4 807	12 334	28 065	8.3	2.3	NA	15.5	23.6	23.2
Charlotte-Gastonia-Rock Hill, NC-SC	950	5 668	283 880	13.4	72.5	19.6	1 074.7	4 926	14 611	31 124	10.9	3.6	NA	10.2	15.4	14.0
Charlottesville, VA	564	4 953	41 486	9.5	76.9	33.3	137.3	6 578	15 227	31 396	18.1	4.9	NA	12.0	16.4	16.7
Chattanooga, TN-GA	907	5 543	101 482	15.7	68.0	15.9	340.5	4 898	12 558	25 593	0.1	2.7	NA	13.0	19.2	16.9
Cheyenne, WY	209	3 779	20 076	7.9	84.2	20.7	79.9	5 391	12 932	27 571	-6.7	1.8	NA	11.3	15.8	12.8
Chicago-Gary-Kenosha, IL-IN-WI	NA	NA	2 189 520	22.8	76.6	23.4	8 897.7	6 288	16 319	35 771	2.8	6.0	NA	11.0	17.2	15.6
Chicago, IL	NA	NA	1 962 005	23.5	76.7	24.5	7 929.2	6 294	16 683	36 301	4.5	6.5	NA	10.9	17.2	15.7
Gary, IN	567	3 971	167 424	16.0	75.4	14.0	705.5	6 331	13 174	31 628	-13.4	2.4	NA	11.4	17.3	15.2
Kankakee, IL	NA	NA	26 064	17.1	73.1	11.9	102.2	5 580	12 142	28 284	-2.9	1.8	NA	12.9	19.5	18.6
Kenosha, WI	NA	NA	34 027	17.6	75.1	12.7	160.8	6 297	13 265	30 638	-9.0	1.9	NA	9.1	13.9	12.7
Chico-Paradise, CA	336	4 085	56 394	5.7	77.6	19.5	196.9	5 598	12 083	22 775	4.4	2.4	NA	20.9	30.9	30.8
Cincinnati-Hamilton, OH-KY-IN	NA	NA	473 524	19.7	74.6	19.7	1 737.7	5 658	14 329	30 695	1.4	3.8	NA	9.6	13.7	12.3
Cincinnati, OH-KY-IN	NA	NA	392 024	21.2	74.4	19.9	1 458.1	5 759	14 401	30 370	1.7	3.9	NA	9.9	14.2	12.8
Hamilton-Middletown, OH	486	4 122	81 500	12.7	76.0	18.7	279.6	5 184	13 947	32 439	-1.2	3.3	NA	8.1	11.1	9.8
Clarksville-Hopkinsville, TN-KY	NA	NA	42 530	7.1	75.6	14.0	138.8	4 431	10 508	23 730	6.8	1.2	NA	13.5	18.7	17.6
Cleveland-Akron, OH	NA	NA	727 277	20.1	76.2	18.7	2 961.0	6 571	14 462	30 128	-5.4	3.7	NA	11.2	17.1	14.9
Akron, OH	NA	NA	177 922	12.6	78.5	19.3	648.5	5 916	13 997	29 279	-5.4	3.4	NA	10.4	15.7	13.7
Cleveland-Lorain-Elyria, OH	NA	NA	549 355	22.5	75.5	18.5	2 312.5	6 782	14 601	30 350	-5.5	3.7	NA	11.5	17.5	15.2
Colorado Springs, CO	479	4 609	109 787	14.5	88.3	25.8	427.5	4 948	13 664	29 603	8.8	2.9	NA	9.5	13.8	12.2
Columbia, MO	356	4 261	42 951	9.7	84.8	36.5	99.4	4 929	12 707	25 646	-1.4	2.6	NA	11.4	14.3	13.5

1. Data for serious crimes have not been adjusted for underreporting; this may affect comparability between geographic areas and over time. 2. Per 100,000 population estimated by the FBI. 3. All persons 3 years old and over enrolled in nursery school through college. 4. Persons 25 years old and over. 5. Elementary and secondary education expenditures, local government fiscal years ending between July 1, 1996 and June 30, 1997. 6. Based on population enumerated as of April 1, 1990.

Table C. Metropolitan Areas — Personal Income

Area Name	Total (mil dol)	Percent change, 1997–1998	Per capita¹ Dollars	Per capita¹ Rank	Wages and salaries[2] (mil dol)	Proprietor's income (mil dol)	Dividends, interest, and rent (mil dol)	Transfer payments Total (mil dol)	Government payments to individuals Total (mil dol)	Social Security (mil dol)	Medical payments (mil dol)	Income maintenance (mil dol)	Unemployment insurance (mil dol)
	62	63	64	65	66	67	68	69	70	71	72	73	74
Abilene, TX	2 808	3.7	23 012	210	1 665	376	523	448	428	169	183	37	5
Albany, GA	2 546	3.0	21 619	265	1 900	176	409	425	401	134	154	76	8
Albany-Schenectady-Troy, NY	23 884	5.2	27 433	86	15 508	1 368	4 620	3 781	3 604	1 405	1 479	324	53
Albuquerque, NM	16 806	4.5	24 842	146	11 406	954	3 246	2 057	1 938	808	671	225	34
Alexandria, LA	2 790	5.2	22 062	252	1 583	243	484	654	632	163	368	62	4
Allentown-Bethlehem-Easton, PA	17 002	5.1	27 599	82	9 613	1 321	3 253	2 526	2 406	1 124	954	142	81
Altoona, PA	2 900	4.9	22 216	241	1 763	280	483	610	585	197	234	53	17
Amarillo, TX	4 865	5.0	23 495	194	2 791	626	869	663	628	260	249	51	10
Anchorage, AK	8 348	5.0	32 659	23	5 814	672	1 474	989	950	159	219	96	36
Anniston, AL	2 379	4.0	20 315	294	1 577	118	443	445	425	177	157	48	6
Appleton-Oshkosh-Neenah, WI	9 194	5.8	26 659	105	6 557	465	1 802	928	864	471	284	43	29
Asheville, NC	5 405	5.1	25 347	137	3 313	310	1 255	854	816	362	323	71	11
Athens, GA	3 211	6.1	23 160	205	2 216	242	623	375	347	147	129	43	2
Atlanta, GA	115 272	8.7	30 788	35	85 518	10 300	18 022	8 930	8 167	3 508	3 132	918	107
Auburn-Opalika, AL	1 892	3.7	18 831	309	1 134	113	350	254	236	106	78	28	4
Augusta-Aiken, GA-SC	10 379	5.0	22 665	227	7 038	460	1 842	1 576	1 489	575	576	196	21
Austin-San Marcos, TX	32 130	15.1	29 087	54	24 446	2 603	4 792	2 444	2 258	924	900	215	40
Bakersfield, CA	12 407	4.3	19 643	304	7 673	1 369	1 896	2 146	2 029	674	723	407	98
Bangor, ME	3 140	5.2	21 743	262	2 049	237	482	580	556	208	227	61	10
Barnstable-Yarmouth, MA	6 799	6.9	32 612	24	2 653	607	1 964	1 127	1 090	531	430	50	38
Baton Rouge, LA	14 013	6.4	24 403	165	9 671	838	2 285	1 805	1 706	617	764	198	17
Beaumont-Port Arthur, TX	8 571	5.6	22 848	216	5 603	443	1 469	1 640	1 577	594	736	155	31
Bellingham, WA	3 575	6.0	22 732	223	1 992	393	785	518	487	205	162	44	26
Benton Harbor, MI	3 874	2.6	24 235	169	2 347	248	761	636	607	276	222	73	16
Billings, MT	3 083	5.7	24 425	164	1 927	230	663	423	400	182	134	28	8
Biloxi-Gulfport-Pascagoula, MS	7 602	8.6	21 828	256	5 488	394	1 236	1 202	1 141	457	477	112	11
Binghamton, NY	5 919	4.0	23 775	182	3 669	423	1 128	1 080	1 029	462	396	108	15
Birmingham, AL	24 168	4.8	26 582	106	16 676	1 864	4 303	3 248	3 089	1 363	1 187	300	34
Bismarck, ND	2 186	7.1	23 885	179	1 390	144	411	322	306	125	124	16	5
Bloomington, IN	2 639	6.2	22 636	228	1 845	150	544	292	270	128	97	20	5
Bloomington-Normal, IL	3 908	5.8	27 260	90	2 973	199	715	353	325	164	96	28	10
Boise City, ID	10 479	7.9	26 461	108	6 731	1 324	2 014	1 067	1 002	433	348	73	33
Boston-Worcester-Lawrence-Lowell-Brockton, MA-NH	200 107	6.9	34 127	16	136 448	15 959	35 117	23 490	22 453	8 152	10 835	1 899	630
Brownsville-Harlingen-San Benito, TX	4 461	6.3	13 766	317	2 521	337	654	1 134	1 080	264	513	232	22
Bryan-College Station, TX	2 674	6.9	20 121	296	1 915	163	471	282	260	106	98	31	2
Buffalo-Niagara Falls, NY	29 541	3.9	25 654	128	18 461	1 605	5 257	5 564	5 328	2 129	2 168	649	94
Burlington, VT	5 162	6.3	26 787	99	3 695	380	964	553	511	218	186	62	11
Canton-Massillon, OH	9 888	5.5	24 590	159	5 790	550	1 899	1 569	1 487	678	556	111	23
Casper, WY	1 784	4.1	28 217	67	909	273	428	217	205	100	65	15	3
Cedar Rapids, IA	5 421	8.8	29 656	44	4 148	340	1 034	551	513	272	171	34	9
Champaign-Urbana, IL	4 034	3.7	23 753	186	2 840	187	981	410	377	164	123	46	13
Charleston, WV	6 505	4.1	25 745	126	4 376	421	1 133	1 220	1 177	474	438	83	18
Charleston-North Charleston, SC	11 674	6.8	21 529	267	7 616	857	2 131	1 630	1 537	585	637	185	19
Charlotte-Gastonia-Rock Hill, NC-SC	39 795	7.9	28 784	56	29 725	2 925	6 543	4 076	3 833	1 749	1 506	327	64
Charlottesville, VA	4 259	6.9	28 513	63	2 748	336	1 068	417	389	195	142	28	2
Chattanooga, TN-GA	11 071	4.0	24 622	157	7 260	863	1 856	1 763	1 684	716	697	147	24
Cheyenne, WY	2 013	4.3	25 613	129	1 247	132	462	242	227	95	67	17	3
Chicago-Gary-Kenosha, IL-IN-WI	285 768	5.9	32 389	X	191 544	23 641	54 883	29 683	27 960	11 109	11 609	3 439	775
Chicago, IL	263 763	5.9	33 181	21	179 072	22 601	51 284	26 568	25 009	9 778	10 463	3 145	719
Gary, IN	15 963	6.0	25 451	135	9 426	802	2 605	2 264	2 147	969	835	220	34
Kankakee, IL	2 312	3.3	22 596	230	1 314	104	425	409	389	159	155	45	13
Kenosha, WI	3 730	10.0	25 833	123	1 731	134	569	442	415	202	156	29	8
Chico-Paradise, CA	4 050	4.0	20 838	284	1 897	402	911	888	852	336	298	142	19
Cincinnati-Hamilton, OH-KY-IN	54 505	5.8	27 975	X	36 322	3 043	10 796	6 614	6 225	2 650	2 401	512	93
Cincinnati, OH-KY-IN	46 109	5.8	28 507	64	32 172	2 712	9 298	5 605	5 284	2 226	2 060	443	79
Hamilton-Middletown, OH	8 395	6.3	25 372	136	4 150	332	1 498	1 009	941	424	341	69	14
Clarksville-Hopkinsville, TN-KY	4 083	3.4	20 456	291	2 840	273	640	521	493	182	193	53	8
Cleveland-Akron, OH	83 577	4.5	28 694	X	54 528	5 459	16 270	11 921	11 328	4 655	4 568	1 016	177
Akron, OH	18 530	4.8	26 934	96	11 311	810	3 473	2 616	2 475	1 054	962	210	40
Cleveland-Lorain-Elyria, OH	65 047	4.4	29 239	51	43 217	4 649	12 797	9 306	8 853	3 601	3 605	806	137
Colorado Springs, CO	12 873	8.6	26 270	112	8 953	795	2 428	1 256	1 177	461	431	101	18
Columbia, MO	3 302	5.9	25 606	130	2 297	218	653	349	326	132	143	27	2

1. Based on the resident population estimated as of July 1 of the year shown. 2. Includes other labor income.

Table C. Metropolitan Areas — Earnings, Social Security, and Housing

Area Name	Earnings, 1998									Social Security beneficiaries, December 1998		Supplemental Security Income recipients, December 1998	Housing units, 1990	
	Total (mil dol)	Farm	Goods-related[1]		Service-related and other[2]					Number	Rate[3]		Total	Percent change, 1980–1990
			Total	Manu-facturing	Total	Retail trade	Finance, insurance, and real estate	Services	Govern-ment					
	75	76	77	78	79	80	81	82	83	84	85	86	87	88
Abilene, TX	2 041	0.5	20.5	11.7	52.8	10.5	4.8	27.4	26.2	20 476	168	2 594	49 988	20.1
Albany, GA	2 076	1.2	NA	19.5	NA	8.2	NA	25.2	22.6	17 585	149	5 255	42 910	11.1
Albany-Schenectady-Troy, NY	16 876	0.1	NA	11.6	NA	8.8	7.6	29.6	26.2	158 455	182	18 093	361 002	10.4
Albuquerque, NM	12 360	0.2	NA	D	NA	10.3	6.1	32.5	22.0	98 818	146	15 739	241 683	22.8
Alexandria, LA	1 826	0.2	18.5	10.9	56.5	10.1	4.6	30.3	24.9	22 571	178	6 495	51 239	6.2
Allentown-Bethlehem-Easton, PA	10 934	0.1	NA	25.5	NA	8.7	6.4	28.8	10.7	123 850	201	10 236	241 060	12.9
Altoona, PA	2 042	0.5	NA	17.5	NA	13.1	3.2	26.4	14.9	24 079	184	4 185	54 349	4.4
Amarillo, TX	3 417	0.8	20.3	8.5	62.6	11.3	6.6	28.5	16.3	30 128	144	3 035	80 734	16.0
Anchorage, AK	6 486	0.0	15.4	1.5	54.2	9.4	5.3	23.9	30.4	19 039	75	3 549	94 153	33.8
Anniston, AL	1 695	0.8	NA	19.0	NA	9.9	2.7	16.3	36.8	23 521	201	4 389	46 753	9.8
Appleton-Oshkosh-Neenah, WI	7 022	0.7	NA	37.0	NA	7.6	6.1	18.8	10.5	52 524	152	3 533	120 511	15.8
Asheville, NC	3 622	0.9	25.5	18.6	NA	11.1	4.7	30.3	16.1	44 713	209	5 454	85 618	16.8
Athens, GA	2 458	2.4	NA	16.3	NA	9.9	4.3	23.0	30.9	18 037	130	3 563	50 960	32.1
Atlanta, GA	95 817	0.2	NA	11.4	NA	8.4	9.7	29.6	11.3	404 353	108	52 127	1 224 367	45.1
Auburn-Opalika, AL	1 248	0.6	NA	20.3	NA	11.6	4.0	16.8	32.9	13 099	130	2 643	36 636	23.5
Augusta-Aiken, GA-SC	7 498	0.4	NA	25.3	NA	8.7	4.8	20.6	26.4	71 650	156	12 930	165 632	25.6
Austin-San Marcos, TX	27 050	0.0	NA	19.0	NA	7.9	6.9	27.5	17.0	108 347	98	14 216	370 310	56.5
Bakersfield, CA	9 041	4.3	19.4	5.3	50.6	8.8	4.0	20.1	25.7	84 862	134	24 526	198 636	27.6
Bangor, ME	2 286	0.3	NA	16.0	NA	11.8	4.2	27.5	20.1	26 620	187	3 988	61 359	14.9
Barnstable-Yarmouth, MA	3 261	0.2	NA	5.2	NA	17.7	6.8	33.4	17.8	59 558	286	3 727	135 192	35.3
Baton Rouge, LA	10 509	0.1	NA	14.0	NA	8.8	7.1	24.7	18.2	74 768	130	14 755	212 078	19.2
Beaumont-Port Arthur, TX	6 046	0.1	36.1	24.5	49.4	9.2	3.5	26.2	14.4	67 257	179	8 959	149 807	4.2
Bellingham, WA	2 385	3.9	28.2	16.9	53.2	11.7	5.7	22.5	14.7	23 727	151	2 447	55 742	17.4
Benton Harbor, MI	2 595	0.7	42.3	37.0	45.5	8.5	3.5	22.9	11.5	30 943	193	4 882	69 532	1.1
Billings, MT	2 157	0.4	16.2	6.7	68.9	12.4	6.6	31.0	14.5	21 012	167	1 837	48 781	14.1
Biloxi-Gulfport-Pascagoula, MS	5 881	0.0	NA	19.0	NA	8.2	3.2	24.5	29.4	57 840	166	9 663	129 916	14.8
Binghamton, NY	4 092	0.2	NA	28.2	NA	8.6	4.1	25.5	18.1	52 773	212	6 153	108 223	8.3
Birmingham, AL	18 541	0.4	NA	11.3	NA	8.5	9.5	29.3	14.1	159 228	175	26 114	348 470	11.0
Bismarck, ND	1 534	0.7	NA	7.2	NA	10.7	6.0	30.8	20.6	15 206	166	1 206	33 270	10.1
Bloomington, IN	1 996	0.1	25.9	19.6	43.6	9.7	5.0	21.2	30.5	14 110	123	1 255	41 948	15.8
Bloomington-Normal, IL	3 172	0.1	18.7	13.4	68.3	7.9	28.9	21.9	13.1	18 142	127	1 336	49 164	8.3
Boise City, ID	8 055	1.5	32.7	22.8	51.6	9.4	6.6	21.7	14.1	52 023	131	5 689	113 986	15.8
Boston-Worcester-Lawrence-Lowell-Brockton, MA-NH	152 406	0.1	NA	16.9	NA	8.2	10.8	35.2	11.5	937 901	160	141 243	2 270 865	13.3
Brownsville-Harlingen-San Benito, TX	2 857	2.3	NA	11.3	NA	11.3	5.6	27.6	26.4	40 609	124	15 770	88 759	34.5
Bryan-College Station, TX	2 078	0.0	15.2	7.0	45.4	11.0	5.4	23.0	39.4	12 622	95	1 772	48 799	36.7
Buffalo-Niagara Falls, NY	20 066	0.1	NA	22.3	NA	9.0	7.0	26.5	18.1	236 515	205	30 786	492 516	3.9
Burlington, VT	4 076	1.2	NA	23.3	NA	8.9	5.8	27.9	15.1	25 632	133	3 348	73 480	23.8
Canton-Massillon, OH	6 340	0.8	39.6	32.2	48.2	10.6	4.5	22.5	11.4	75 529	188	7 188	158 446	3.2
Casper, WY	1 182	0.1	34.7	4.4	50.7	9.1	4.7	22.1	14.6	11 167	176	1 138	29 082	2.1
Cedar Rapids, IA	4 488	0.3	32.6	25.9	58.0	8.5	7.8	25.9	9.1	29 616	162	2 219	68 357	5.5
Champaign-Urbana, IL	3 027	0.4	18.3	12.7	45.6	8.5	4.8	24.6	35.7	20 244	121	2 204	68 416	9.4
Charleston, WV	4 796	0.0	21.6	12.0	61.2	8.9	6.6	29.3	17.2	52 893	209	7 279	109 631	4.8
Charleston-North Charleston, SC	8 473	0.3	NA	11.1	NA	10.7	6.1	26.6	27.0	76 162	141	13 986	199 879	31.6
Charlotte-Gastonia-Rock Hill, NC-SC	32 650	0.7	NA	18.1	NA	8.7	NA	23.3	10.2	201 572	146	21 390	472 913	29.9
Charlottesville, VA	3 084	0.3	NA	11.1	NA	8.7	NA	22.7	33.6	22 172	149	2 336	51 932	20.1
Chattanooga, TN-GA	8 123	0.3	NA	20.5	NA	11.1	8.5	24.0	16.1	83 212	185	11 751	177 706	12.5
Cheyenne, WY	1 378	1.1	11.4	5.1	47.4	9.9	8.0	16.6	40.2	11 354	144	1 097	30 507	11.4
Chicago-Gary-Kenosha, IL-IN-WI	215 185	0.0	NA	18.1	NA	7.4	11.1	NA	11.7	1 193 786	136	182 628	3 170 271	5.6
Chicago, IL	201 673	0.0	NA	17.4	NA	7.2	11.6	NA	11.6	1 048 325	132	176 431	2 851 754	6.0
Gary, IN	10 228	0.2	NA	28.8	NA	8.6	4.2	24.3	12.3	104 842	168	1 202	230 254	1.0
Kankakee, IL	1 418	1.2	NA	24.7	NA	11.1	4.4	24.1	15.5	18 258	179	2 725	37 001	-1.6
Kenosha, WI	1 866	0.1	NA	32.3	NA	9.0	3.9	20.2	15.9	22 361	155	2 270	51 262	7.9
Chico-Paradise, CA	2 299	1.4	14.4	8.1	62.5	13.0	6.1	32.3	21.7	40 494	208	8 507	76 115	24.0
Cincinnati-Hamilton, OH-KY-IN	39 365	0.1	NA	NA	NA	9.0	8.0	NA	12.1	300 199	154	38 960	722 225	11.2
Cincinnati, OH-KY-IN	34 883	0.1	NA	NA	NA	8.8	8.1	NA	11.7	252 635	156	33 621	611 872	9.9
Hamilton-Middletown, OH	4 482	0.1	33.8	25.4	51.1	10.4	7.1	19.6	15.2	47 564	144	5 339	110 353	19.3
Clarksville-Hopkinsville, TN-KY	3 112	0.5	NA	14.9	NA	8.5	2.9	13.7	49.4	23 888	120	4 410	60 662	19.1
Cleveland-Akron, OH	59 987	0.2	NA	24.7	NA	8.0	7.5	27.9	13.0	509 863	175	64 042	1 163 911	4.1
Akron, OH	12 121	0.1	32.4	26.5	52.7	9.5	5.0	24.0	14.8	115 927	168	13 164	263 776	6.4
Cleveland-Lorain-Elyria, OH	47 866	0.3	NA	24.3	NA	7.6	8.2	28.9	12.6	393 936	177	50 878	900 135	3.4
Colorado Springs, CO	9 748	0.0	18.6	11.6	52.9	8.4	6.1	27.9	28.5	58 499	119	42	165 056	40.4
Columbia, MO	2 515	0.1	14.3	8.5	48.7	9.6	9.1	22.2	36.9	15 455	120	1 789	44 695	19.4

1. Covers mining, construction, and manufacturing. 2. Covers private sector earnings in agricultural services, forestry, and fisheries; transportation and public utilities; wholesale trade; retail trade; finance, insurance, and real estate; and services. 3. Per 1,000 resident population estimated as of July 1 of the year shown.

Table C. Metropolitan Areas — **Housing, Labor Force, and Employment**

Area Name	Housing units, 1990 (cont'd)								Civilian labor force, 1999				Civilian employment, 1990[5]		
	Occupied units							Substandard units[3] (percent)			Unemployment			Percent	
	Owner-occupied					Renter-occupied									
				Owner cost as a percent of income			Rent as percent of income			Percent change, 1998–1999				Professional, managerial, and technical	Precision production, craft, and repair
	Total	Percent	Median value[1]	With a mortgage	Without a mortgage	Median rent[2]			Total		Total	Rate[4]	Total		
	89	90	91	92	93	94	95	96	97	98	99	100	101	102	103
Abilene, TX	43 301	62.2	45 500	20.5	12.9	378	25.8	4.4	59 572	-3.3	2 214	3.7	50 278	30.6	10.6
Albany, GA	39 362	55.7	58 800	18.7	13.2	336	26.1	6.6	57 378	-0.7	4 299	7.5	46 281	27.7	11.9
Albany-Schenectady-Troy, NY	330 484	64.0	99 000	NA	NA	456	NA	1.8	451 445	-0.2	16 082	3.6	424 003	34.0	9.5
Albuquerque, NM	221 619	64.3	82 400	NA	NA	401	NA	6.0	354 615	-2.0	13 961	3.9	271 567	35.1	10.6
Alexandria, LA	45 941	66.5	52 600	19.6	13.4	337	27.6	5.2	61 657	3.2	2 785	4.5	48 788	29.2	10.5
Allentown-Bethlehem-Easton, PA	225 831	71.9	97 500	21.9	13.0	448	26.1	1.8	313 389	0.9	13 144	4.2	286 502	27.9	12.2
Altoona, PA	50 332	72.6	41 100	17.0	13.2	298	26.8	1.6	63 477	1.7	2 880	4.5	55 022	23.0	13.2
Amarillo, TX	71 897	64.2	52 700	19.9	12.7	347	24.8	5.1	113 080	0.1	4 048	3.6	87 795	27.2	12.8
Anchorage, AK	82 702	52.8	109 000	22.6	11.4	563	24.8	4.3	141 119	-0.3	6 360	4.5	111 242	37.5	9.5
Anniston, AL	42 983	70.3	51 600	19.3	12.7	310	23.8	2.3	54 573	-0.3	2 795	5.1	46 899	23.6	14.0
Appleton-Oshkosh-Neenah, WI	115 515	70.3	62 400	19.5	12.8	380	23.0	1.8	219 390	-1.4	5 155	2.3	159 009	25.5	11.9
Asheville, NC	77 290	71.0	63 500	NA	NA	366	NA	2.7	109 810	0.1	2 478	2.3	93 226	27.4	13.3
Athens, GA	47 066	54.8	70 800	NA	NA	387	NA	3.8	73 663	0.1	1 928	2.6	60 422	33.3	10.4
Atlanta, GA	1 102 578	62.7	88 800	NA	NA	524	NA	3.6	2 207 395	4.0	68 051	3.1	1 563 539	32.7	10.4
Auburn-Opalika, AL	33 097	58.1	64 900	16.9	12.4	339	35.1	3.7	48 931	-0.4	1 736	3.5	40 043	30.8	10.5
Augusta-Aiken, GA-SC	149 093	66.7	63 300	NA	NA	383	NA	4.7	208 617	1.2	10 818	5.2	184 471	29.5	13.9
Austin-San Marcos, TX	325 995	51.2	74 800	NA	NA	414	NA	6.3	707 554	3.8	15 814	2.2	432 006	37.7	9.0
Bakersfield, CA	181 480	59.3	82 800	22.5	12.4	439	27.4	10.9	280 491	0.4	31 866	11.4	214 668	26.2	13.3
Bangor, ME	54 063	69.7	69 100	19.3	13.1	396	25.9	3.2	77 866	4.2	3 311	4.3	67 389	28.1	12.8
Barnstable-Yarmouth, MA	77 586	72.4	162 800	NA	NA	645	NA	1.4	106 621	1.6	4 544	4.3	82 526	31.0	12.4
Baton Rouge, LA	188 377	65.3	66 600	18.2	12.5	369	26.5	5.0	305 069	2.3	12 132	4.0	233 090	32.1	12.7
Beaumont-Port Arthur, TX	134 238	69.7	42 900	17.0	13.0	359	25.6	5.1	181 637	-1.3	15 582	8.6	148 500	26.6	15.9
Bellingham, WA	48 543	64.3	90 800	19.9	11.9	424	27.1	3.6	81 126	2.5	4 241	5.2	61 657	26.3	13.0
Benton Harbor, MI	61 025	69.6	52 800	16.9	13.2	367	26.9	2.9	84 718	2.6	3 403	4.0	73 154	27.7	13.5
Billings, MT	44 689	65.7	62 800	21.4	12.0	342	25.5	1.6	73 001	3.7	2 911	4.0	54 760	28.6	9.9
Biloxi-Gulfport-Pascagoula, MS	111 828	67.6	53 200	NA	NA	344	NA	4.8	172 198	3.0	6 277	3.6	123 014	28.8	14.6
Binghamton, NY	100 681	67.9	78 000	19.8	12.9	386	26.7	1.6	124 288	-0.3	5 087	4.1	123 419	34.5	10.9
Birmingham, AL	319 774	68.1	60 600	NA	NA	361	NA	3.2	471 766	-0.2	14 670	3.1	379 295	30.4	11.2
Bismarck, ND	31 361	67.1	63 600	20.6	12.4	339	23.7	2.0	52 934	-2.1	1 582	3.0	42 237	31.5	9.2
Bloomington, IN	39 351	54.8	66 600	18.5	12.0	400	32.2	2.5	60 866	0.2	1 411	2.3	52 564	36.6	9.2
Bloomington-Normal, IL	46 796	63.5	65 900	17.3	11.8	386	24.8	1.5	91 763	7.5	2 027	2.2	68 058	29.5	8.4
Boise City, ID	108 759	69.0	66 300	NA	NA	372	NA	3.6	230 083	3.3	8 485	3.7	143 604	30.9	10.7
Boston-Worcester-Lawrence-Lowell-Brockton, MA-NH	2 111 440	59.3	165 200	NA	NA	595	NA	2.7	3 180 020	0.4	97 946	3.1	2 912 225	36.9	10.0
Brownsville-Harlingen-San Benito, TX	73 278	64.4	38 400	20.7	12.6	294	27.6	25.2	126 602	-1.0	12 463	9.8	86 302	25.4	10.5
Bryan-College Station, TX	43 725	41.9	66 600	20.1	13.0	410	34.0	6.6	75 447	2.0	1 319	1.7	56 368	38.9	8.2
Buffalo-Niagara Falls, NY	461 803	64.5	71 900	NA	NA	380	NA	1.7	569 046	-1.0	30 918	5.4	542 686	29.4	11.0
Burlington, VT	64 783	66.6	109 000	NA	NA	498	NA	2.0	117 453	3.2	2 614	2.2	94 020	36.1	10.5
Canton-Massillon, OH	149 240	70.7	57 100	16.9	12.0	352	24.4	1.5	202 174	0.5	9 150	4.5	175 340	26.4	11.4
Casper, WY	23 837	68.9	53 100	18.6	11.7	297	23.5	1.9	33 571	1.2	1 833	5.5	28 391	31.0	11.8
Cedar Rapids, IA	65 501	70.4	58 500	16.5	12.1	368	23.2	1.4	112 571	1.8	2 047	1.8	87 606	30.8	10.8
Champaign-Urbana, IL	63 900	54.5	67 700	20.1	12.2	410	29.6	2.6	98 270	5.5	2 473	2.5	87 114	39.0	7.4
Charleston, WV	100 408	70.8	57 400	16.1	11.5	339	24.2	2.1	135 040	3.6	6 378	4.7	105 569	30.3	11.6
Charleston-North Charleston, SC	177 668	62.6	72 200	21.8	13.4	432	25.4	4.5	269 631	1.6	9 254	3.4	220 922	28.6	15.1
Charlotte-Gastonia-Rock Hill, NC-SC	440 670	66.8	72 300	19.7	12.6	424	23.6	3.3	773 054	3.6	19 721	2.6	613 891	27.0	12.7
Charlottesville, VA	48 709	59.4	93 800	20.6	12.2	496	26.5	4.1	75 268	0.7	996	1.3	66 271	37.8	10.7
Chattanooga, TN-GA	163 117	68.3	57 300	NA	NA	362	NA	3.0	228 259	3.7	7 946	3.5	197 611	26.2	12.0
Cheyenne, WY	28 092	65.5	69 800	20.5	11.6	361	24.6	2.2	39 222	-0.3	1 393	3.6	32 914	31.3	9.5
Chicago-Gary-Kenosha, IL-IN-WI	2 969 099	61.8	101 900	NA	NA	483	NA	5.1	4 696 619	2.1	191 493	4.1	3 979 255	31.5	10.5
Chicago, IL	2 671 540	61.0	109 900	NA	NA	491	NA	5.3	4 265 257	2.4	174 257	4.1	3 611 434	32.2	10.1
Gary, IN	215 907	69.3	58 100	16.4	13.1	400	24.7	3.6	298 534	-1.9	11 786	3.9	265 789	25.3	14.5
Kankakee, IL	34 623	66.8	54 700	16.9	12.8	375	24.2	3.3	52 498	0.1	2 853	5.4	42 205	25.2	12.1
Kenosha, WI	47 029	68.8	65 100	19.4	12.9	410	24.6	2.8	80 330	-1.1	2 597	3.2	59 827	23.9	14.3
Chico-Paradise, CA	71 665	60.9	94 000	22.4	11.9	438	32.6	5.1	85 763	-0.7	5 830	6.8	70 880	29.6	11.0
Cincinnati-Hamilton, OH-KY-IN	679 137	64.5	70 800	NA	NA	371	NA	2.8	1 034 494	1.7	35 356	3.4	860 318	30.9	10.9
Cincinnati, OH-KY-IN	574 602	63.7	70 400	NA	NA	364	NA	2.9	849 313	1.3	29 398	3.5	723 002	31.1	10.8
Hamilton-Middletown, OH	104 535	69.2	73 000	18.9	12.3	414	25.8	2.0	185 181	3.8	5 958	3.2	137 316	30.0	11.4
Clarksville-Hopkinsville, TN-KY	55 981	58.1	54 000	20.6	12.4	352	24.1	4.2	85 753	5.1	2 872	3.3	59 591	24.7	12.2
Cleveland-Akron, OH	1 094 413	67.0	70 300	NA	NA	398	NA	1.9	1 484 199	1.4	65 525	4.4	1 307 775	30.3	11.4
Akron, OH	249 227	69.0	63 600	18.9	12.6	396	26.7	1.6	364 061	1.6	15 199	4.2	305 611	29.7	11.7
Cleveland-Lorain-Elyria, OH	845 186	66.5	72 100	NA	NA	399	NA	2.0	1 120 138	1.3	50 326	4.5	1 002 164	30.4	11.3
Colorado Springs, CO	146 965	57.4	81 700	22.8	12.2	418	26.0	2.8	258 699	1.5	8 588	3.3	172 530	34.8	10.0
Columbia, MO	41 937	55.0	65 700	17.5	12.0	380	27.3	2.1	81 391	-2.2	1 005	1.2	58 017	38.3	7.8

1. Specified owner-occupied units. 2. Specified renter-occupied units. 3. Overcrowded or lacking complete plumbing facilities. 4. Percent of civilian labor force. 5. Persons 16 years and older.

Table C. Metropolitan Areas — **Nonfarm Employment and Agriculture**

Area Name	Private nonfarm establishments, employment and payroll, 1998							Agriculture, 1997			
	Number of establish-ments	Employment						Annual payroll		Farms		Farm operators
		Total	Health Care and Social Assistance	Manufac-turing	Retail trade	Finance and Insurance	Professional Scientific and Technical Services	Total (mil dol)	Average per employee (dollars)	Number	Percent with— || Whose principal occu-pation is farming (percent)
											Less than 50 acres	500 acres and over	
	104	105	106	107	108	109	110	111	112	113	114	115	116
Abilene, TX	3 558	48 503	9 720	3 462	7 342	1 877	1 201	974	20 081	1 048	27.5	23.8	35.4
Albany, GA	2 827	47 439	7 516	8 714	7 523	1 672	1 354	1 181	24 895	296	36.5	32.8	48.0
Albany-Schenectady-Troy, NY	20 175	323 468	54 961	32 010	48 810	24 572	20 796	9 171	28 352	2 538	27.4	8.1	54.5
Albuquerque, NM	17 590	276 365	36 809	26 064	39 534	12 339	25 154	7 360	26 631	1 460	71.7	9.6	37.9
Alexandria, LA	3 080	45 683	12 419	3 272	7 490	1 741	1 657	1 015	22 218	817	39.4	11.9	46.5
Allentown-Bethlehem-Eas-ton, PA	14 918	249 627	35 585	43 559	30 221	13 486	9 744	7 410	29 684	988	42.9	9.6	56.9
Altoona, PA	3 231	49 527	8 526	9 268	8 207	1 819	2 098	1 151	23 240	422	20.6	10.2	68.5
Amarillo, TX	5 552	79 684	11 942	11 911	13 036	3 630	3 033	1 972	24 748	797	23.8	37.9	41.8
Anchorage, AK	7 786	107 084	15 075	1 718	14 906	4 830	6 892	4 182	39 053	NA	NA	NA	NA
Anniston, AL	2 549	39 928	5 189	11 407	6 418	1 045	892	824	20 637	629	39.1	3.8	35.3
Appleton-Oshkosh-Neenah, WI	9 039	180 515	18 391	54 205	21 968	8 746	5 053	5 288	29 294	2 849	24.9	7.8	60.8
Asheville, NC	6 578	95 337	16 686	19 854	14 098	2 202	2 876	2 321	24 345	1 916	54.6	1.9	42.4
Athens, GA	3 551	51 474	6 953	10 943	9 124	1 546	1 683	1 181	22 944	1 007	37.7	4.7	42.8
Atlanta, GA	108 111	1 894 836	156 075	190 581	230 052	107 425	134 258	63 982	33 767	5 572	48.0	3.5	38.2
Auburn-Opalika, AL	2 008	30 235	4 098	6 598	5 836	832	722	633	20 936	347	32.9	10.7	31.7
Augusta-Aiken, GA-SC	9 740	165 449	26 522	40 870	24 405	4 772	6 785	4 540	27 440	1 492	36.9	8.7	35.7
Austin-San Marcos, TX	30 029	479 731	51 282	68 000	64 284	26 545	38 471	16 377	34 138	6 721	34.1	12.1	39.8
Bakersfield, CA	10 709	142 507	19 216	13 257	23 794	6 615	6 948	3 763	26 406	1 997	35.1	30.3	63.8
Bangor, ME	4 061	53 154	10 778	7 124	9 817	1 670	1 600	1 283	24 137	525	31.0	11.4	47.2
Barnstable-Yarmouth, MA	7 938	66 257	12 080	2 900	13 734	3 052	3 403	1 779	26 850	221	89.6	0.0	49.8
Baton Rouge, LA	14 554	247 957	31 989	21 067	34 707	13 148	14 948	6 763	27 275	1 160	51.2	7.4	35.4
Beaumont-Port Arthur, TX	8 220	129 920	21 472	21 605	20 053	3 814	4 881	3 723	28 656	1 250	52.4	15.4	36.2
Bellingham, WA	5 317	55 623	6 225	9 279	9 479	2 195	2 582	1 411	25 367	1 228	57.1	2.4	54.3
Benton Harbor, MI	4 082	60 344	7 130	16 521	8 212	1 879	1 489	1 630	27 012	1 182	49.1	5.8	54.2
Billings, MT	4 783	53 847	7 789	3 122	8 601	2 591	2 891	1 297	24 087	1 097	32.5	32.0	53.5
Biloxi-Gulfport-Pascagoula, MS	7 411	123 677	18 086	21 484	17 824	3 654	4 434	3 015	24 378	835	49.9	3.2	30.7
Binghamton, NY	5 066	92 610	13 164	25 364	12 641	3 615	3 623	2 590	27 967	1 008	22.7	7.2	53.9
Birmingham, AL	22 956	423 492	57 088	50 136	51 388	29 452	20 777	12 477	29 462	2 646	40.7	3.6	36.4
Bismarck, ND	2 904	40 019	8 559	2 187	6 161	1 950	1 497	908	22 689	1 774	10.9	56.4	62.6
Bloomington, IN	2 874	45 630	6 228	9 088	7 353	1 590	1 622	1 063	23 296	473	33.4	5.5	35.1
Bloomington-Normal, IL	3 523	76 943	7 327	8 323	9 142	19 323	2 050	2 368	30 776	1 475	18.0	35.5	66.0
Boise City, ID	12 150	176 686	20 114	30 881	22 293	8 508	7 772	5 118	28 967	3 119	62.0	6.8	46.0
Boston-Worcester-Law-rence-Lowell-Brockton, MA-NH	161 168	2 878 542	424 828	419 443	337 047	206 516	202 043	105 649	36 702	4 421	57.5	1.9	51.8
Brownsville-Harlingen-San Benito, TX	5 673	79 534	17 422	11 986	13 157	2 410	1 974	1 432	18 005	902	55.0	16.9	48.1
Bryan-College Station, TX	3 167	42 899	5 999	3 163	8 002	1 782	3 619	934	21 772	1 084	35.4	11.5	35.1
Buffalo-Niagara Falls, NY	27 118	466 370	75 644	80 617	64 205	24 465	21 293	12 704	27 240	1 660	38.3	6.4	51.7
Burlington, VT	6 474	87 918	11 505	18 430	13 086	3 571	4 821	2 463	28 015	1 303	25.4	10.9	59.3
Canton-Massillon, OH	9 837	166 770	24 448	42 920	24 195	5 665	4 094	4 322	25 916	1 769	36.2	4.5	43.5
Casper, WY	2 566	24 563	3 453	1 519	3 893	1 162	1 149	599	24 386	311	20.6	48.9	58.5
Cedar Rapids, IA	5 297	110 504	10 971	25 138	13 505	6 171	3 708	3 436	31 094	1 480	28.9	11.6	51.8
Champaign-Urbana, IL	4 065	67 242	9 642	9 776	10 959	2 902	2 981	1 554	23 111	1 371	17.4	31.1	63.8
Charleston, WV	7 063	106 243	16 653	7 993	16 422	6 251	5 579	2 865	26 966	608	27.3	1.2	35.7
Charleston-North Charles-ton, SC	13 544	204 989	30 353	21 200	29 959	6 386	10 524	4 997	24 377	872	47.4	8.5	39.9
Charlotte-Gastonia-Rock Hill, NC-SC	40 611	726 913	65 086	134 067	85 347	42 254	36 411	22 765	31 317	4 253	40.0	4.7	41.3
Charlottesville, VA	4 537	63 682	11 296	6 911	9 248	5 151	3 207	1 703	26 742	1 201	26.7	9.5	44.5
Chattanooga, TN-GA	11 307	198 319	23 430	44 165	26 763	12 191	6 583	5 067	25 550	1 766	41.2	4.5	32.4
Cheyenne, WY	2 292	25 338	4 612	1 470	4 873	1 364	1 025	561	22 141	615	10.4	55.9	56.7
Chicago-Gary-Kenosha, IL-IN-WI	224 871	4 070 483	438 448	657 209	462 579	268 705	276 578	146 902	36 090	7 015	32.8	21.7	56.1
Chicago, IL	206 081	3 741 075	395 358	590 506	416 877	259 023	268 055	137 444	36 739	4 878	34.3	21.2	57.0
Gary, IN	13 433	224 929	31 147	48 662	33 251	7 056	7 034	6 733	29 934	918	32.0	19.9	49.5
Kankakee, IL	2 304	57 571	5 788	7 214	5 752	1 438	691	1 430	24 839	831	21.8	31.0	61.1
Kenosha, WI	3 053	46 908	6 155	10 827	6 699	1 188	798	1 295	27 607	388	40.5	12.4	49.5
Chico-Paradise, CA	4 494	49 894	9 863	5 139	9 021	1 700	2 214	1 062	21 285	1 942	58.7	9.4	54.8
Cincinnati-Hamilton, OH-KY-IN	46 609	892 069	107 310	140 376	113 066	45 840	46 398	27 559	30 893	8 586	38.3	4.0	37.2
Cincinnati, OH-KY-IN	40 412	789 795	95 258	120 309	99 668	39 458	42 818	24 584	31 127	7 737	38.0	3.8	36.4
Hamilton-Middletown, OH	6 197	102 274	12 052	20 067	13 398	6 382	3 580	2 975	29 089	849	40.8	6.6	43.7
Clarksville-Hopkinsville, TN-KY	3 666	52 325	8 514	11 672	9 682	1 669	1 254	1 125	21 500	2 146	29.7	10.5	44.9
Cleveland-Akron, OH	76 762	1 331 079	179 558	257 195	162 747	70 984	66 026	41 190	30 945	4 645	45.3	4.0	44.7
Akron, OH	17 428	287 987	36 198	54 680	38 400	10 143	11 817	8 767	30 442	970	50.7	3.3	42.2
Cleveland-Lorain-Elyria, OH	59 334	1 043 092	143 360	202 515	124 347	60 841	54 209	32 423	31 084	3 675	43.9	4.2	45.4
Colorado Springs, CO	13 057	194 751	21 712	22 293	28 112	10 350	13 975	5 447	27 969	851	32.2	32.0	42.0
Columbia, MO	3 675	58 592	13 754	5 700	8 956	4 822	1 960	1 353	23 092	1 227	28.8	10.8	35.6

Table C. Metropolitan Areas — **Agriculture, Land, and Water**

Area Name	Agriculture, 1997 (cont'd)															
	Land in farms					Value of land and buildings		Value of machinery and equipment Average per farm ($1,000)	Value of products sold				Percent of farms with sales of —		Percent of land owned by Fed. Gov. 1997	Water consumption 1995 (mil gal/day)
			Acres								Percent from —					
	Acreage (1,000)	Percent change, 1992–1997	Average size of farm	Total irrigated (1,000)	Total cropland (1,000)	Average per farm ($1,000)	Average per acre (dollars)		Total (mil dol)	Average per farm (dollars)	Crops	Live-stock and poultry products	$10,000 or more	$100,000 or more		
	117	118	119	120	121	122	123	124	125	126	127	128	129	130	131	132
Abilene, TX	492	-3.4	469	2	207	280	582	31	53	50 446	18.0	82.0	27.8	4.1	0.9	25.1
Albany, GA	221	25.7	747	29	120	1 089	1 422	118	64	217 821	85.0	15.0	49.7	27.7	0.8	160.3
Albany-Schenectady-Troy, NY	493	-0.9	194	3	327	288	1 501	49	156	61 517	28.0	72.0	48.0	16.2	0.4	801.2
Albuquerque, NM	1 628	6.1	1 115	38	67	349	326	24	68	46 311	21.0	79.0	20.3	3.8	29.7	437.3
Alexandria, LA	194	-7.8	238	7	122	333	1 464	56	55	67 534	88.0	12.0	39.8	16.4	11.6	497.7
Allentown-Bethlehem-Easton, PA	190	3.7	192	1	164	645	3 480	64	93	94 080	70.0	30.0	55.4	17.8	0.6	558.1
Altoona, PA	84	10.3	199	0	60	379	2 008	57	51	120 855	14.0	86.0	65.2	38.2	0.1	35.7
Amarillo, TX	910	1.2	1 142	47	D	493	411	48	222	278 004	10.0	90.0	44.0	15.4	3.0	82.8
Anchorage, AK	NA	NA	NA	NA	NA	NA	NA	NA	NA	NA	NA	NA	NA	NA	NA	45.2
Anniston, AL	77	4.6	123	1	39	260	1 896	32	54	85 668	12.0	87.0	22.9	7.6	21.3	26.3
Appleton-Oshkosh-Neenah, WI	564	-5.5	198	1	470	305	1 556	81	280	98 230	24.0	76.0	66.7	30.2	0.1	142.2
Asheville, NC	167	-10.5	87	1	63	263	3 021	20	45	23 243	74.0	26.0	23.7	2.1	15.4	42.0
Athens, GA	134	6.9	133	1	60	320	2 367	29	163	161 742	7.0	93.0	37.1	19.0	0.3	24.3
Atlanta, GA	640	1.4	115	5	283	385	3 514	25	455	81 724	12.0	88.0	27.3	11.2	1.1	1 364.1
Auburn-Opalika, AL	76	11.5	218	1	22	409	1 847	47	20	57 226	86.4	13.6	30.5	3.5	0.0	18.9
Augusta-Aiken, GA-SC	291	3.0	195	D	127	287	1 435	35	98	65 515	D	D	27.4	8.9	9.6	449.4
Austin-San Marcos, TX	1 890	-5.5	281	8	729	401	1 498	26	136	20 175	43.0	57.0	23.7	3.5	1.1	651.0
Bakersfield, CA	2 851	0.4	1 428	913	1 054	2 162	1 605	189	1 969	985 735	91.0	9.0	66.8	45.6	27.9	2 462.7
Bangor, ME	117	-1.2	222	2	49	226	1 058	43	30	57 101	37.0	63.0	40.6	13.5	0.4	21.5
Barnstable-Yarmouth, MA	5	-5.1	21	2	2	329	15 774	32	18	82 466	94.0	6.0	57.9	14.5	15.5	39.5
Baton Rouge, LA	191	-12.2	164	D	106	361	2 047	41	62	53 061	D	D	23.1	6.2	0.0	404.2
Beaumont-Port Arthur, TX	587	42.5	470	34	224	421	912	32	32	25 718	65.0	35.0	24.3	7.0	6.8	432.9
Bellingham, WA	104	-12.2	84	26	81	449	5 321	56	242	196 778	17.0	83.0	53.3	29.2	61.5	160.8
Benton Harbor, MI	174	4.2	147	11	146	283	1 913	63	81	68 846	89.0	11.0	52.9	16.2	0.0	2 195.8
Billings, MT	1 526	4.9	1 391	80	381	524	372	57	96	87 552	31.0	69.0	51.3	16.7	5.2	440.4
Biloxi-Gulfport-Pascagoula, MS	87	20.4	104	0	39	246	2 344	27	10	11 381	49.0	51.0	17.4	1.9	10.6	228.0
Binghamton, NY	195	-8.4	194	1	110	168	929	41	52	51 143	15.0	85.0	39.3	14.3	0.1	141.5
Birmingham, AL	325	0.7	123	4	169	293	2 384	30	217	82 001	10.0	90.0	26.6	10.6	0.0	870.5
Bismarck, ND	2 124	0.6	1 197	7	1 045	388	311	65	96	54 313	39.0	61.0	64.1	15.4	1.0	49.7
Bloomington, IN	62	5.3	131	0	36	296	2 344	27	8	17 772	58.0	42.0	25.8	4.4	8.7	14.6
Bloomington-Normal, IL	697	-1.8	472	1	666	1 278	2 657	130	238	161 521	89.0	11.0	81.9	46.8	0.0	17.0
Boise City, ID	586	-6.1	188	299	325	384	2 093	56	405	129 887	48.0	52.0	44.6	17.3	28.4	1 737.3
Boston-Worcester-Lawrence-Lowell-Brockton, MA-NH	379	-2.0	86	20	D	472	5 771	42	348	78 736	81.0	19.0	45.7	14.6	1.1	916.0
Brownsville-Harlingen-San Benito, TX	369	12.0	409	109	230	446	1 143	62	79	88 042	88.0	12.0	40.7	18.1	4.4	456.5
Bryan-College Station, TX	265	-10.4	245	6	104	402	1 517	34	41	37 993	19.0	81.0	26.8	3.5	0.0	33.5
Buffalo-Niagara Falls, NY	271	-3.7	163	4	214	239	1 474	63	136	81 660	51.0	49.0	47.9	17.0	0.1	1 529.1
Burlington, VT	295	-5.3	226	1	158	380	1 607	58	135	103 422	9.0	91.0	56.3	30.9	1.9	34.8
Canton-Massillon, OH	250	-3.4	141	1	175	304	2 374	43	94	53 293	40.0	60.0	42.6	11.1	1.0	48.2
Casper, WY	2 807	11.9	9 025	49	52	1 806	190	54	27	86 135	12.0	88.0	54.3	20.3	41.7	190.3
Cedar Rapids, IA	339	-2.8	229	0	292	526	2 347	60	113	76 662	66.0	34.0	60.6	20.8	0.0	259.9
Champaign-Urbana, IL	568	-0.8	414	6	549	1 201	2 940	117	190	138 614	96.0	4.0	85.7	42.0	0.3	36.1
Charleston, WV	76	0.6	126	D	27	179	1 452	19	6	9 525	77.0	23.0	12.3	1.0	0.0	707.7
Charleston-North Charleston, SC	161	10.2	184	D	73	301	1 828	40	70	80 835	76.0	24.0	34.4	9.6	16.8	645.1
Charlotte-Gastonia-Rock Hill, NC-SC	591	2.5	139	3	374	383	2 803	37	450	105 711	23.0	77.0	32.1	12.9	0.1	3 504.9
Charlottesville, VA	265	-6.7	221	1	119	693	3 106	40	32	26 795	18.0	82.0	33.8	3.4	3.8	135.7
Chattanooga, TN-GA	241	-6.2	137	1	123	296	1 967	26	81	45 834	8.0	92.0	23.9	6.4	3.0	1 559.7
Cheyenne, WY	1 728	1.7	2 810	61	D	659	241	70	96	156 031	21.0	79.0	59.5	18.5	0.9	112.8
Chicago-Gary-Kenosha, IL-IN-WI	2 310	-4.9	329	43	2 155	1 080	3 374	100	968	137 969	81.0	19.0	69.4	33.0	1.2	13 655.0
Chicago, IL	1 590	-6.0	326	16	1 481	1 169	3 681	101	712	145 893	79.0	21.0	69.4	33.4	1.2	10 738.3
Gary, IN	283	-1.3	309	13	262	789	2 539	68	90	98 098	88.0	12.0	61.8	27.5	2.3	2 852.6
Kankakee, IL	352	-2.1	423	14	338	1 102	2 759	132	133	159 906	89.0	11.0	82.6	40.2	0.0	29.0
Kenosha, WI	85	-8.9	218	1	74	613	2 961	98	33	85 698	64.0	36.0	59.0	25.5	0.0	35.1
Chico-Paradise, CA	404	-10.6	208	224	247	754	3 589	73	286	147 388	97.0	3.0	57.3	26.7	14.1	957.7
Cincinnati-Hamilton, OH-KY-IN	1 109	-6.1	129	5	748	318	2 502	36	217	25 246	75.0	25.0	37.0	5.4	0.5	1 632.8
Cincinnati, OH-KY-IN	974	-6.6	126	4	641	296	2 430	34	182	23 489	78.0	22.0	36.3	4.7	0.6	1 559.0
Hamilton-Middletown, OH	135	-2.5	158	0	108	517	3 024	50	35	41 263	61.0	39.0	43.0	11.7	0.3	73.9
Clarksville-Hopkinsville, TN-KY	474	0.0	221	2	339	346	1 615	47	113	52 827	76.0	24.0	46.0	12.0	7.0	35.4
Cleveland-Akron, OH	571	-5.4	123	7	421	370	3 182	51	294	63 223	75.0	25.0	41.3	9.9	1.7	2 112.9
Akron, OH	105	-9.0	108	1	73	364	3 536	38	33	33 722	64.0	36.0	37.5	8.0	6.3	99.9
Cleveland-Lorain-Elyria, OH	467	-4.6	127	6	348	372	3 103	54	261	71 010	77.0	23.0	42.3	10.4	0.2	2 013.0
Colorado Springs, CO	867	1.2	1 019	15	78	410	443	27	30	35 640	41.0	59.0	36.1	6.2	14.9	134.7
Columbia, MO	250	-8.1	204	4	172	331	1 599	37	40	32 684	42.0	58.0	34.8	5.9	0.8	18.2

Area Name	Value of Residential Construction Authorized by Building Permits, 1999		Wholesale Trade, 1997				Retail Trade[1], 1997				Real Estate and Rental and Leasing, 1997			
	New Construction ($1,000)	Number of Housing Units	Number of Establish-ments	Number of Employees	Sales (mil dol)	Annual Payroll (mil dol)	Number of Establish-ments	Number of Employees	Sales (mil dol)	Annual Payroll (mil dol)	Number of Establish-ments	Number of Employees	Receipts (mil dol)	Annual Payroll (mil dol)
	133	134	135	136	137	138	139	140	141	142	143	144	145	146
Abilene, TX	25 754	185	219	1 996	933.9	54.1	635	7 211	1 297.7	116.7	168	876	88.4	16.7
Albany, GA	70 594	636	191	2 398	1 029.5	70.7	613	8 069	1 208.7	118.3	133	636	83.4	12.5
Albany-Schenectady-Troy, NY	344 709	2 898	1 094	14 639	7 447.2	507.2	3 582	47 672	7 673.7	744.7	669	4 116	580.3	91.5
Albuquerque, NM	523 204	5 311	1 110	13 384	4 880.7	401.0	2 593	38 256	7 107.8	685.0	823	4 808	530.8	89.2
Alexandria, LA	49 451	509	173	1 789	581.1	45.6	586	7 397	1 188.3	108.5	92	660	57.8	12.4
Allentown-Bethlehem-Easton, PA	346 404	3 114	906	12 174	6 826.3	430.3	2 427	31 129	5 657.8	532.3	406	2 388	291.9	51.1
Altoona, PA	24 823	261	160	2 836	1 641.3	82.3	639	8 310	1 331.2	117.7	90	419	34.8	6.9
Amarillo, TX	75 638	708	357	4 824	2 390.8	153.0	987	12 238	2 369.5	209.7	256	1 173	130.8	21.4
Anchorage, AK	205 251	1 265	434	4 748	1 989.1	181.4	1 001	15 115	3 114.9	319.3	356	2 145	322.2	56.8
Anniston, AL	29 152	422	130	1 688	890.9	47.0	578	6 747	982.0	92.5	73	298	24.5	4.4
Appleton-Oshkosh-Neenah, WI	296 434	2 790	530	7 927	2 881.4	271.5	1 429	21 545	3 658.6	343.7	290	1 469	143.9	26.8
Asheville, NC	174 136	1 371	349	4 358	1 369.7	128.4	1 187	13 506	2 242.4	214.4	229	1 053	132.5	21.9
Athens, GA	128 721	1 507	150	D	D	D	669	9 012	1 361.8	130.9	168	661	71.3	11.5
Atlanta, GA	6 124 492	61 046	9 263	140 471	138 768.4	6 098.7	14 631	221 587	40 479.3	3 984.0	4 742	34 506	5 451.9	1 061.2
Auburn-Opalika, AL	58 936	557	86	727	308.0	18.6	425	5 437	774.4	73.7	84	464	35.0	6.9
Augusta-Aiken, GA-SC	272 234	3 242	455	3 774	1 536.8	112.8	1 883	24 355	3 850.6	367.9	415	1 699	179.0	32.3
Austin-San Marcos, TX	1 740 869	19 897	1 613	20 998	10 048.4	797.7	4 157	60 049	18 878.3	1 160.8	1 532	7 554	945.7	180.9
Bakersfield, CA	335 609	3 118	612	7 930	4 313.9	256.4	1 918	22 792	4 224.4	412.1	419	2 479	220.5	43.8
Bangor, ME	29 455	353	196	2 786	938.0	85.6	796	9 433	1 654.6	148.0	146	620	66.9	9.5
Barnstable-Yarmouth, MA	366 137	2 224	259	1 361	462.8	45.5	1 592	13 675	2 518.8	256.5	286	917	138.1	21.4
Baton Rouge, LA	364 493	4 242	951	11 993	4 904.9	404.6	2 402	34 451	5 540.0	516.9	606	4 330	404.0	84.2
Beaumont-Port Arthur, TX	98 383	891	445	5 293	2 176.2	174.5	1 526	19 904	3 467.6	299.4	345	2 024	221.3	39.9
Bellingham, WA	162 338	1 486	308	2 451	1 042.7	76.0	840	9 758	1 673.3	165.7	220	877	91.8	12.3
Benton Harbor, MI	85 886	658	193	1 887	938.3	60.0	674	8 078	1 302.5	125.6	164	627	186.3	10.5
Billings, MT	57 961	591	389	4 915	2 648.9	143.4	717	8 736	1 575.6	144.9	195	770	85.9	12.3
Biloxi-Gulfport-Pascagoula, MS	239 481	2 990	295	2 909	992.3	76.2	1 523	18 255	2 776.7	255.4	342	1 332	113.8	20.1
Binghamton, NY	39 309	372	292	D	D	D	974	13 086	1 981.4	184.3	141	668	86.3	10.7
Birmingham, AL	726 971	5 958	1 971	29 990	18 884.2	1 038.0	3 844	52 390	9 000.7	830.0	815	6 919	945.4	168.8
Bismarck, ND	65 496	568	192	1 983	813.2	52.6	467	6 058	1 010.6	100.9	113	616	52.8	7.4
Bloomington, IN	99 399	1 013	102	D	D	D	514	6 846	1 073.7	97.5	162	869	83.1	15.3
Bloomington-Normal, IL	109 580	1 342	212	2 268	1 348.4	87.1	632	9 242	1 474.6	142.3	134	704	99.8	14.6
Boise City, ID	771 210	6 597	735	9 122	5 917.9	312.0	1 693	21 387	4 177.3	389.9	467	2 128	220.0	37.1
Boston-Worcester-Lawrence-Lowell-Brockton, MA-NH	2 451 197	18 543	10 229	150 552	114 849.2	6 714.1	24 369	331 207	59 245.8	5 820.2	5 656	41 467	5 844.8	1 228.5
Brownsville-Harlingen-San Benito, TX	157 698	2 539	387	3 772	1 218.9	81.6	1 117	13 089	1 904.0	179.3	283	1 208	98.5	18.1
Bryan-College Station, TX	115 472	1 599	130	1 655	426.5	41.9	569	7 994	1 336.2	122.2	181	1 090	78.5	17.2
Buffalo-Niagara Falls, NY	295 007	2 664	1 917	28 285	15 619.1	949.1	4 514	66 786	9 643.8	957.2	849	5 834	769.9	134.2
Burlington, VT	125 211	1 100	359	4 749	2 216.5	156.2	1 228	12 988	2 188.1	218.2	248	1 018	127.0	20.8
Canton-Massillon, OH	210 893	1 485	542	8 422	4 235.3	281.0	1 697	23 989	3 800.8	368.5	281	1 296	127.6	23.1
Casper, WY	19 752	245	206	1 853	984.1	59.2	399	3 985	645.6	65.2	106	414	39.2	8.4
Cedar Rapids, IA	129 371	1 689	375	5 653	2 324.1	166.0	874	13 337	2 040.9	213.9	199	1 135	128.8	25.6
Champaign-Urbana, IL	97 651	999	199	3 737	2 419.0	111.5	675	10 645	1 556.7	151.9	203	1 356	179.7	27.3
Charleston, WV	51 859	404	448	6 062	2 585.3	190.2	1 177	16 569	2 793.6	247.8	312	1 658	213.3	33.0
Charleston-North Charleston, SC	698 276	5 854	606	6 644	4 402.0	209.1	2 424	29 095	4 538.1	441.1	590	3 352	366.3	62.6
Charlotte-Gastonia-Rock Hill, NC-SC	2 221 834	24 475	3 762	50 099	41 925.7	1 956.1	5 866	79 252	14 439.8	1 358.7	1 507	11 445	1 656.4	332.2
Charlottesville, VA	189 964	1 301	160	1 676	525.9	56.6	744	9 065	1 506.7	147.3	199	887	91.9	18.4
Chattanooga, TN-GA	277 112	2 702	814	10 120	4 889.3	302.3	2 048	25 869	4 194.6	404.7	419	2 315	255.9	62.3
Cheyenne, WY	36 461	323	81	665	267.5	18.6	358	4 851	855.5	77.8	88	321	27.7	5.2
Chicago-Gary-Kenosha, IL-IN-WI	5 634 151	44 113	17 360	271 372	237 956.8	11 660.0	30 327	442 052	81 073.8	8 015.9	9 032	63 269	11 824.8	1 933.6
Chicago, IL	5 057 178	39 091	16 373	258 217	230 934.2	11 214.5	27 221	398 282	73 673.5	7 334.5	8 299	59 915	11 431.1	1 866.8
Gary, IN	416 072	3 525	721	8 917	4 818.0	305.8	2 172	31 734	5 420.9	497.2	536	2 594	315.0	54.3
Kankakee, IL	47 125	376	126	1 628	809.3	47.2	388	5 594	907.0	88.5	85	348	34.9	5.9
Kenosha, WI	113 775	1 121	135	2 515	1 385.3	91.5	546	6 442	1 072.4	95.7	112	412	43.8	6.6
Chico-Paradise, CA	117 290	1 028	179	1 792	637.9	56.9	777	9 004	1 502.6	154.0	212	1 012	80.5	13.4
Cincinnati-Hamilton, OH-KY-IN	1 568 611	15 439	3 352	D	D	D	7 287	111 122	18 144.7	1 735.0	1 888	12 308	1 725.1	298.7
Cincinnati, OH-KY-IN	1 253 392	12 031	2 898	48 487	43 669.5	1 817.7	6 365	97 593	15 956.2	1 526.5	1 653	10 984	1 575.4	273.0
Hamilton-Middletown, OH	315 218	3 408	454	D	D	D	922	13 529	2 188.6	208.5	235	1 324	149.7	25.7
Clarksville-Hopkinsville, TN-KY	123 429	1 911	172	1 997	964.3	59.0	824	9 731	1 640.7	151.8	179	644	76.4	9.9
Cleveland-Akron, OH	1 766 593	11 562	5 790	80 340	45 381.4	3 113.1	11 511	162 090	27 129.8	2 668.4	2 725	22 109	2 614.9	468.0
Akron, OH	515 000	3 644	1 253	16 023	9 624.2	598.1	2 637	38 291	6 633.6	639.5	580	3 403	413.2	74.7
Cleveland-Lorain-Elyria, OH	1 251 592	7 918	4 537	64 317	35 757.1	2 515.0	8 874	123 799	20 496.2	2 028.9	2 145	18 706	2 201.7	393.2
Colorado Springs, CO	565 268	5 537	498	6 513	1 417.9	213.3	1 901	27 806	5 015.1	503.6	735	3 064	362.3	62.8
Columbia, MO	119 968	1 216	138	1 651	684.7	49.9	602	8 880	1 469.7	135.3	173	642	75.2	11.0

1. Establishments with payroll.

Table C. Metropolitan Areas — Professional, Manufacturing, Accommodation and Foodservices, Finance and Insurance

Area Name	Professional, Scientific, and Technical Services[1], 1997				Manufacturing, 1997				Accommodation and Foodservices, 1997			
	Number of Establishments	Number of Employees	Sales (mil dol)	Annual Payroll (mil dol)	Number of Establishments	Number of Employees	Sales (mil dol)	Annual Payroll (mil dol)	Number of Establishments	Number of Employees	Sales (mil dol)	Annual Payroll (mil dol)
	147	148	149	150	151	152	153	154	155	156	157	158
Abilene, TX	229	1 123	93.2	30.4	118	3 062	1 011	80	269	5 497	151.6	41.8
Albany, GA	179	1 334	98.7	37.9	98	9 046	4 331	320	201	3 830	120.5	32.4
Albany-Schenectady-Troy, NY	1 768	16 154	1 617.7	636.1	752	31 436	6 970	1 128	1 969	25 692	896.4	251.5
Albuquerque, NM	2 032	23 668	2 619.1	1 054.9	800	25 743	14 171	788	1 374	29 191	952.4	267.3
Alexandria, LA	247	1 956	124.2	42.2	73	3 179	1 166	103	224	3 985	119.8	31.7
Allentown-Bethlehem-Easton, PA	1 136	7 230	677.1	248.9	920	45 167	10 640	1 500	1 258	18 589	649.5	176.0
Altoona, PA	181	1 838	151.6	53.5	157	8 966	1 592	252	254	4 003	108.8	29.6
Amarillo, TX	363	2 879	199.7	85.3	203	11 110	3 625	359	480	8 292	262.6	70.9
Anchorage, AK	907	5 939	767.2	301.3	187	2 022	322	63	640	11 364	574.0	165.8
Anniston, AL	149	702	45.2	13.2	149	10 841	1 505	258	185	4 262	114.4	31.3
Appleton-Oshkosh-Neenah, WI	510	4 259	361.2	142.9	683	54 679	12 361	1 918	777	13 519	370.7	103.3
Asheville, NC	477	2 409	174.9	77.5	347	18 516	3 111	518	530	9 360	340.4	100.8
Athens, GA	258	1 433	116.2	59.3	151	10 960	1 646	275	303	5 537	162.5	44.4
Atlanta, GA	12 807	113 482	13 392.6	5 216.8	4 394	190 720	49 692	6 386	7 296	158 518	6 002.3	1 681.2
Auburn-Opalika, AL	129	589	50.6	16.3	88	7 016	1 233	195	199	4 165	110.3	29.6
Augusta-Aiken, GA-SC	688	6 578	651.3	247.7	364	41 124	10 336	1 561	769	14 593	442.2	119.5
Austin-San Marcos, TX	3 699	30 168	3 460.5	1 392.2	1 192	68 826	24 925	2 529	2 211	45 599	1 605.8	453.9
Bakersfield, CA	753	6 296	525.7	224.6	390	14 306	2 825	379	1 013	14 724	493.2	129.1
Bangor, ME	271	1 388	102.7	45.9	155	8 897	1 659	286	344	4 778	151.3	45.8
Barnstable-Yarmouth, MA	571	1 919	173.7	63.9	226	2 561	349	82	1 144	11 852	624.3	177.3
Baton Rouge, LA	1 548	13 337	1 263.3	475.8	533	21 530	18 449	994	972	20 054	618.6	168.2
Beaumont-Port Arthur, TX	600	4 830	543.3	223.8	349	21 624	18 987	1 059	591	10 840	336.8	90.6
Bellingham, WA	390	2 615	246.5	109.0	314	9 184	3 947	281	429	5 926	195.5	52.8
Benton Harbor, MI	255	1 338	124.6	48.9	397	16 996	2 394	539	383	5 328	163.5	44.0
Billings, MT	404	2 664	199.7	74.9	182	3 223	1 798	110	365	6 691	205.3	58.7
Biloxi-Gulfport-Pascagoula, MS	551	4 266	340.5	140.6	260	21 327	5 786	686	640	13 826	445.5	119.5
Binghamton, NY	369	2 751	244.6	82.7	290	25 484	4 717	1 028	560	7 689	228.5	64.9
Birmingham, AL	2 073	17 463	1 813.0	716.2	1 120	47 970	9 236	1 478	1 505	30 643	961.3	269.4
Bismarck, ND	206	1 890	96.1	40.9	81	2 193	673	74	205	4 065	112.5	31.9
Bloomington, IN	196	1 360	97.0	34.0	122	8 817	2 444	303	302	6 312	176.6	48.8
Bloomington-Normal, IL	234	1 382	111.6	57.9	112	8 388	3 870	358	336	7 104	200.5	58.3
Boise City, ID	933	6 972	938.6	276.9	571	30 667	9 900	1 131	836	14 724	441.5	123.0
Boston-Worcester-Lawrence-Lowell-Brockton, MA-NH	18 317	178 861	23 091.4	9 440.2	9 384	422 764	83 290	16 622	13 151	211 551	8 494.5	2 352.5
Brownsville-Harlingen-San Benito, TX	339	2 278	126.5	42.7	235	12 694	1 733	242	513	8 349	278.2	71.7
Bryan-College Station, TX	279	2 086	200.9	74.8	101	3 126	382	80	275	5 668	170.7	48.2
Buffalo-Niagara Falls, NY	2 043	16 820	1 542.6	563.3	1 561	81 398	18 458	3 259	2 735	38 792	1 143.1	329.9
Burlington, VT	573	4 044	442.0	162.9	302	16 905	4 489	703	506	7 065	232.8	68.2
Canton-Massillon, OH	660	3 662	316.1	110.0	669	41 134	8 525	1 381	806	14 761	400.3	110.3
Casper, WY	205	1 213	81.0	30.7	91	1 440	328	41	172	2 924	79.0	21.8
Cedar Rapids, IA	369	2 936	268.6	106.7	239	22 877	6 376	935	439	7 853	240.1	68.2
Champaign-Urbana, IL	336	2 660	263.2	91.6	152	10 857	2 690	292	449	8 944	248.6	70.6
Charleston, WV	591	4 801	410.6	135.5	176	7 681	3 305	312	487	9 337	312.9	84.3
Charleston-North Charleston, SC	1 110	8 539	784.1	314.6	415	20 595	6 589	688	1 097	24 251	836.2	232.8
Charlotte-Gastonia-Rock Hill, NC-SC	3 302	32 123	3 264.0	1 258.3	2 422	133 983	32 134	4 062	2 651	53 527	1 811.8	491.3
Charlottesville, VA	415	2 562	206.6	84.6	142	6 980	1 163	236	338	6 816	245.8	72.6
Chattanooga, TN-GA	776	4 980	425.2	170.7	707	44 038	7 471	1 266	882	15 946	538.4	149.5
Cheyenne, WY	199	843	64.5	24.7	48	1 349	606	45	183	3 930	106.3	31.1
Chicago-Gary-Kenosha, IL-IN-WI	25 710	244 468	31 494.4	12 091.9	14 080	660 689	145 632	24 785	16 640	292 805	11 833.2	3 195.2
Chicago, IL	24 437	236 655	30 848.6	11 862.4	13 191	594 764	122 696	21 753	14 881	264 904	11 009.9	2 968.9
Gary, IN	965	6 619	565.4	196.4	569	49 462	18 651	2 373	1 190	19 792	589.6	161.9
Kankakee, IL	132	507	32.7	12.7	116	6 937	2 253	264	229	3 563	100.4	27.4
Kenosha, WI	176	687	47.7	20.4	204	9 526	2 031	396	340	4 546	133.3	37.1
Chico-Paradise, CA	308	1 513	130.7	45.0	232	4 944	772	128	380	5 920	156.2	43.3
Cincinnati-Hamilton, OH-KY-IN	4 039	40 006	4 145.8	1 571.7	2 686	139 924	35 239	5 358	3 793	77 902	2 668.8	735.6
Cincinnati, OH-KY-IN	3 595	36 858	3 853.9	1 482.5	2 290	119 533	28 671	4 539	3 274	67 983	2 382.5	655.8
Hamilton-Middletown, OH	444	3 148	291.9	89.2	396	20 391	6 568	819	519	9 919	286.3	79.6
Clarksville-Hopkinsville, TN-KY	199	1 076	66.3	20.0	139	10 988	2 052	298	338	6 907	187.8	55.5
Cleveland-Akron, OH	6 880	57 578	5 971.1	2 393.8	6 021	255 158	53 189	9 468	6 035	106 193	3 316.3	898.4
Akron, OH	1 499	10 377	1 052.4	401.7	1 389	55 296	9 001	1 924	1 423	24 958	736.8	208.1
Cleveland-Lorain-Elyria, OH	5 381	47 201	4 918.7	1 992.1	4 632	199 862	44 188	7 544	4 612	81 235	2 579.5	690.3
Colorado Springs, CO	1 384	10 515	1 199.2	467.1	499	21 593	5 699	701	998	21 480	771.9	216.9
Columbia, MO	272	1 588	112.4	39.1	87	5 703	1 595	165	312	5 983	180.1	48.4

1. Firms subject to federal tax.

Table C. Metropolitan Areas — Health and Other Services and Federal Funds

Area Name	Health Care and Social Assistance[1], 1997				Other Services[1], 1997				Federal funds and grants, fiscal 1999[2] Expenditures (mil dol)			
									Total	Direct payments for individuals		
	Number of Establishments	Number of Employees	Receipts (mil dol)	Annual Payroll (mil dol)	Number of Establishments	Number of Employees	Receipts (mil dol)	Annual Payroll (mil dol)		Social Security and government retirement	Medicare	Food stamps and Supplemental Security Income
	159	160	161	162	163	164	165	166	167	168	169	170
Abilene, TX	314	5 225	310.4	123.2	225	1 892	109.5	34.6	742.5	267.0	89.0	16.8
Albany, GA	257	3 419	243.2	111.9	185	1 214	74.5	23.6	708.7	220.9	78.1	38.2
Albany-Schenectady-Troy, NY	1 578	17 556	1 145.9	515.4	1 228	7 046	494.4	139.2	7 781.1	1 978.2	614.0	109.1
Albuquerque, NM	1 261	17 318	1 181.3	491.2	991	7 049	397.5	128.3	5 421.0	1 398.4	365.4	108.4
Alexandria, LA	335	5 666	306.0	129.1	170	984	55.3	16.7	689.1	261.2	126.6	35.6
Allentown-Bethlehem-Easton, PA	1 461	13 639	946.9	437.7	1 051	6 719	447.8	137.6	2 635.9	1 236.2	633.2	65.8
Altoona, PA	284	2 816	200.5	83.6	251	1 319	72.7	18.9	673.8	309.7	132.0	26.9
Amarillo, TX	503	6 506	513.0	217.3	379	2 488	146.5	42.7	1 031.2	358.9	131.8	24.0
Anchorage, AK	599	5 053	508.6	203.9	393	2 576	185.8	54.8	1 961.4	338.5	63.5	30.8
Anniston, AL	212	2 824	185.1	81.1	206	855	45.3	15.1	865.7	350.2	102.3	29.3
Appleton-Oshkosh-Neenah, WI	655	7 122	503.0	254.4	611	4 178	236.3	69.9	1 208.0	532.4	171.1	17.9
Asheville, NC	478	6 310	440.9	220.4	361	1 873	108.3	34.0	1 092.1	492.7	164.3	33.8
Athens, GA	327	2 530	212.4	103.7	203	1 333	72.2	21.6	572.0	204.9	74.3	23.6
Atlanta, GA	7 456	88 125	6 422.8	2 756.6	6 401	42 758	2 981.9	937.5	17 096.5	4 914.3	1 864.5	489.7
Auburn-Opalika, AL	133	1 478	104.9	51.3	125	661	35.6	10.2	329.9	144.2	47.2	16.6
Augusta-Aiken, GA-SC	892	11 392	824.1	349.9	638	3 889	204.8	63.4	3 843.6	977.9	281.3	93.2
Austin-San Marcos, TX	2 199	34 516	2 278.3	924.9	1 772	11 569	726.2	232.5	7 055.7	1 597.9	430.4	97.4
Bakersfield, CA	938	9 631	755.0	278.5	694	4 192	348.6	92.2	3 150.3	913.6	452.9	139.9
Bangor, ME	310	3 432	209.8	98.2	208	980	82.3	20.4	735.0	289.4	96.2	28.4
Barnstable-Yarmouth, MA	482	5 989	336.5	163.8	439	1 819	124.6	36.0	1 419.8	662.8	300.2	18.9
Baton Rouge, LA	1 166	18 146	1 096.0	481.6	899	6 714	424.2	132.3	2 973.0	839.8	442.3	116.2
Beaumont-Port Arthur, TX	921	14 230	813.2	346.5	614	4 075	236.6	69.4	1 839.9	702.4	415.1	65.5
Bellingham, WA	406	3 627	201.2	82.1	225	1 161	81.3	22.1	670.9	272.4	74.8	17.4
Benton Harbor, MI	281	2 395	154.1	71.3	262	1 452	77.6	25.1	712.0	326.2	131.0	34.2
Billings, MT	334	2 942	228.1	114.5	291	1 788	114.1	34.1	560.6	244.2	75.1	13.4
Biloxi-Gulfport-Pascagoula, MS	657	7 588	551.0	218.8	491	2 594	139.4	43.2	3 491.5	809.9	268.4	65.1
Binghamton, NY	389	4 234	300.8	137.4	346	1 573	103.9	27.5	1 417.0	524.4	187.6	40.5
Birmingham, AL	1 644	27 544	2 153.8	940.2	1 488	11 194	767.4	226.9	4 369.9	1 775.7	842.0	176.6
Bismarck, ND	161	1 589	128.6	59.3	184	1 030	59.7	17.9	677.6	169.4	55.3	8.3
Bloomington, IN	243	2 384	162.1	76.2	160	1 124	64.3	20.0	457.9	158.1	50.7	9.1
Bloomington-Normal, IL	228	2 901	190.8	91.6	226	1 433	85.6	26.8	457.0	192.7	64.6	10.2
Boise City, ID	893	9 685	646.0	303.7	620	3 882	210.0	62.2	1 737.8	649.1	169.8	38.4
Boston-Worcester-Lawrence-Lowell-Brockton, MA-NH	11 498	175 268	10 936.6	5 118.4	10 348	60 832	4 316.8	1 336.9	33 628.0	10 132.8	5 591.1	748.8
Brownsville-Harlingen-San Benito, TX	509	11 065	498.3	216.2	338	2 279	96.3	30.0	1 281.6	340.5	191.8	111.7
Bryan-College Station, TX	263	2 838	212.1	84.9	196	1 244	64.8	18.4	506.2	148.1	46.3	12.3
Buffalo-Niagara Falls, NY	2 275	29 298	1 579.8	703.1	1 908	10 373	664.7	189.8	5 851.7	2 509.4	966.5	208.4
Burlington, VT	450	4 724	274.4	120.0	362	1 658	109.9	32.0	990.4	282.1	91.1	21.3
Canton-Massillon, OH	756	9 782	617.2	296.8	710	4 693	273.9	85.0	1 564.6	808.3	312.9	52.8
Casper, WY	168	1 524	93.3	40.8	154	808	57.2	15.2	280.2	125.5	38.9	8.5
Cedar Rapids, IA	340	3 925	267.5	138.3	350	2 296	143.5	43.3	962.9	320.4	95.0	15.7
Champaign-Urbana, IL	204	4 973	367.9	182.4	244	1 241	65.0	21.0	772.7	231.8	70.9	16.7
Charleston, WV	618	7 204	576.5	230.8	389	2 604	142.4	44.1	1 728.5	625.5	225.8	57.9
Charleston-North Charleston, SC	1 050	12 478	812.1	329.6	863	5 636	320.9	102.9	3 423.9	1 186.8	303.7	96.4
Charlotte-Gastonia-Rock Hill, NC-SC	2 246	31 937	2 226.8	1 004.3	2 417	15 794	1 010.9	315.6	4 407.9	2 147.3	759.0	149.3
Charlottesville, VA	307	3 728	225.4	93.8	258	1 518	83.6	28.8	797.3	266.8	94.6	14.3
Chattanooga, TN-GA	908	12 904	949.7	422.6	690	4 483	267.1	81.0	2 685.0	948.8	412.6	95.0
Cheyenne, WY	153	1 576	105.7	51.0	127	1 122	165.2	24.3	780.7	196.1	43.9	7.5
Chicago-Gary-Kenosha, IL-IN-WI	16 389	181 324	13 092.7	5 736.1	13 631	93 958	6 738.5	2 069.3	35 976.6	12 942.3	6 728.6	1 597.1
Chicago, IL	14 682	164 115	11 992.3	5 225.2	12 268	84 406	6 159.4	1 883.7	32 615.0	11 407.9	6 014.0	1 457.0
Gary, IN	1 276	12 962	856.0	392.0	979	7 336	451.2	148.0	2 473.8	1 115.8	530.2	104.8
Kankakee, IL	168	1 730	107.6	53.0	162	954	59.8	18.3	420.4	187.6	93.7	20.3
Kenosha, WI	263	2 517	136.9	65.9	222	1 262	68.1	19.3	467.3	231.0	90.7	15.0
Chico-Paradise, CA	553	5 261	299.4	114.3	261	1 454	147.1	25.3	935.2	421.3	195.2	44.9
Cincinnati-Hamilton, OH-KY-IN	3 378	46 309	2 770.4	1 377.9	3 009	20 569	1 303.9	410.8	8 643.5	3 228.6	1 321.7	276.2
Cincinnati, OH-KY-IN	2 914	40 680	2 441.3	1 213.4	2 587	17 645	1 111.3	351.2	7 671.0	2 740.7	1 138.8	239.7
Hamilton-Middletown, OH	464	5 629	329.1	164.6	422	2 924	192.6	59.6	972.4	487.9	182.9	36.5
Clarksville-Hopkinsville, TN-KY	249	3 422	188.5	80.6	256	1 141	61.7	16.7	1 671.7	380.0	88.3	30.9
Cleveland-Akron, OH	5 791	69 515	4 290.2	2 062.6	5 032	34 570	2 329.6	666.1	13 341.6	5 388.1	2 695.1	491.0
Akron, OH	1 304	15 741	964.6	484.4	NA	NA	NA	NA	2 786.6	1 172.9	573.3	102.6
Cleveland-Lorain-Elyria, OH	4 487	53 774	3 325.6	1 578.2	3 873	26 825	1 911.5	532.6	10 555.0	4 215.2	2 121.8	388.4
Colorado Springs, CO	1 134	10 522	710.1	311.1	754	4 558	264.9	89.7	3 753.9	1 127.3	210.2	45.0
Columbia, MO	328	4 024	321.4	129.7	230	1 269	67.1	20.6	537.9	177.6	73.4	15.7

1. Firms subject to federal tax. 2. October 1, 1998 to September 30, 1999.

Area Name	Federal funds and grants, fiscal 1999[1] (cont'd)							Local government finances, 1997				
	Expenditures (mil dol) (cont'd)							General revenue				
	Procurement contract awards			Grants[2]							Taxes	
											Per capita[3] (dollars)	
	Salaries and wages	Defense	Other	Medicaid and other health-related	Nutrition and family welfare	Education	Other	Total (mil dol)	Intergovern-mental (mil dol)	Total (mil dol)	Total	Property
	171	172	173	174	175	176	177	178	179	180	181	182
Abilene, TX	210.0	53.1	9.0	45.1	11.3	4.3	21.0	242.0	104.8	97.6	804	596
Albany, GA	147.8	76.7	15.7	58.7	29.8	10.8	7.3	300.2	132.2	109.6	931	552
Albany-Schenectady-Troy, NY	475.1	342.0	116.3	775.3	1 496.8	502.3	1 160.2	2 819.6	930.7	1 368.9	1 562	1 148
Albuquerque, NM	786.6	358.1	1 654.2	313.0	100.0	46.4	228.2	1 492.3	794.3	389.9	578	346
Alexandria, LA	92.6	10.7	26.3	77.0	18.6	8.2	16.1	251.4	107.2	113.8	900	376
Allentown-Bethlehem-Easton, PA	154.5	94.7	46.0	180.2	47.2	13.4	129.2	1 590.8	542.5	657.5	1 071	839
Altoona, PA	45.4	0.5	13.1	73.2	20.3	5.8	38.1	243.5	120.0	78.2	598	430
Amarillo, TX	93.5	4.7	257.4	42.3	15.4	8.9	48.4	406.1	139.8	171.0	822	620
Anchorage, AK	708.2	277.1	81.6	179.3	56.7	25.0	171.4	747.0	306.7	234.7	935	835
Anniston, AL	146.0	151.2	6.7	43.3	9.8	6.3	9.2	301.6	98.5	51.1	436	125
Appleton-Oshkosh-Neenah, WI	59.9	234.4	23.3	75.7	25.7	10.6	20.3	951.2	418.1	321.1	938	914
Asheville, NC	121.5	12.3	54.0	102.9	19.7	12.3	62.2	455.2	204.1	151.4	717	531
Athens, GA	80.1	3.1	19.8	58.5	20.1	9.6	59.1	434.7	108.3	113.0	816	549
Atlanta, GA	2 411.7	3 144.7	770.9	1 125.5	692.9	329.5	1 049.1	9 887.1	3 083.8	4 233.6	1 167	829
Auburn-Opalika, AL	21.0	1.3	7.3	28.2	9.7	4.7	38.5	272.4	66.3	53.8	546	170
Augusta-Aiken, GA-SC	575.3	92.0	1 455.1	201.3	60.3	22.4	48.4	881.1	388.4	309.8	678	437
Austin-San Marcos, TX	487.3	377.3	291.9	624.8	1 025.6	639.5	1 367.8	2 514.5	548.5	1 325.3	1 237	976
Bakersfield, CA	651.1	267.5	63.5	264.7	144.8	45.1	121.9	2 258.4	1 111.7	475.7	757	618
Bangor, ME	82.1	7.4	19.9	104.5	18.8	11.7	60.2	315.8	121.4	137.6	960	908
Barnstable-Yarmouth, MA	118.9	79.4	22.4	68.6	16.5	8.2	105.2	522.1	107.6	331.0	1 614	1 548
Baton Rouge, LA	154.0	73.5	50.1	221.3	386.9	193.5	440.3	1 129.7	383.7	523.9	919	308
Beaumont-Port Arthur, TX	152.7	124.3	80.3	177.3	38.4	16.0	29.0	824.0	210.5	444.2	1 185	923
Bellingham, WA	42.2	128.2	11.6	52.0	20.1	7.5	29.7	363.0	155.4	129.3	838	559
Benton Harbor, MI	22.7	2.0	8.9	98.6	26.9	11.6	35.3	404.7	221.7	101.0	629	610
Billings, MT	92.8	0.4	22.8	44.6	15.2	6.9	15.4	248.1	82.9	83.5	664	613
Biloxi-Gulfport-Pascagoula, MS	795.7	1 117.6	190.3	68.9	33.9	14.6	58.3	948.5	265.3	246.1	717	605
Binghamton, NY	51.7	383.6	17.5	111.1	31.5	11.9	43.7	830.0	324.9	368.8	1 465	1 101
Birmingham, AL	491.0	142.1	132.7	448.7	81.7	43.5	150.8	2 007.8	741.1	841.0	934	359
Bismarck, ND	55.5	0.6	9.5	44.3	58.2	33.1	203.3	177.5	61.2	67.3	739	641
Bloomington, IN	21.9	1.6	12.1	116.3	7.0	7.2	42.7	209.9	67.1	83.6	716	589
Bloomington-Normal, IL	40.5	1.3	8.0	22.1	7.0	4.6	30.4	287.4	91.3	149.2	1 060	903
Boise City, ID	242.5	76.3	60.6	140.6	71.8	47.4	209.0	716.5	297.1	258.9	675	625
Boston-Worcester-Lawrence-Lowell-Brockton, MA-NH	2 721.7	4 526.6	1 129.8	4 463.5	1 029.4	472.9	2 199.8	14 197.1	5 667.3	6 747.6	1 158	1 126
Brownsville-Harlingen-San Benito, TX	102.2	11.2	11.2	273.1	65.8	34.1	96.4	726.9	441.5	157.7	492	367
Bryan-College Station, TX	49.8	6.7	27.5	63.1	9.0	8.6	107.8	246.1	60.9	125.8	946	712
Buffalo-Niagara Falls, NY	514.1	173.1	108.9	739.4	234.6	70.0	202.6	4 038.1	1 458.7	1 737.1	1 491	1 061
Burlington, VT	140.7	198.3	18.8	130.5	24.7	10.8	45.7	368.3	83.9	222.9	1 166	1 139
Canton-Massillon, OH	77.3	17.2	29.6	127.3	48.5	21.7	41.9	837.3	356.8	339.6	843	591
Casper, WY	36.3	0.9	6.7	15.4	8.3	3.8	32.7	170.5	100.0	31.4	494	285
Cedar Rapids, IA	55.1	308.2	38.5	51.7	19.4	5.2	27.8	464.3	173.9	175.0	963	924
Champaign-Urbana, IL	71.6	36.9	14.9	71.3	14.9	14.0	176.4	372.4	147.4	150.3	892	780
Charleston, WV	148.0	3.1	47.7	159.0	119.1	74.7	244.4	498.9	184.9	192.2	757	571
Charleston-North Charleston, SC	794.1	454.9	83.1	256.9	54.6	25.8	121.7	1 079.6	410.7	391.8	768	585
Charlotte-Gastonia-Rock Hill, NC-SC	412.0	50.8	110.1	345.1	126.2	59.6	162.6	4 024.7	1 320.7	1 129.3	836	654
Charlottesville, VA	74.9	113.5	19.3	119.9	9.9	10.0	66.3	266.0	91.6	140.9	961	681
Chattanooga, TN-GA	419.9	7.3	426.1	188.4	51.3	24.0	77.3	1 268.1	347.9	336.3	751	517
Cheyenne, WY	216.5	43.3	14.0	46.2	34.9	32.5	130.2	251.1	109.5	42.9	547	361
Chicago-Gary-Kenosha, IL-IN-WI	4 537.5	829.6	1 791.8	3 607.9	1 064.1	386.8	1 524.7	26 946.9	8 321.0	13 719.7	1 588	1 271
Chicago, IL	4 368.8	779.5	1 747.1	3 254.4	933.5	355.3	1 411.8	24 443.5	7 352.2	12 684.0	1 632	1 284
Gary, IN	131.7	24.2	35.3	274.8	97.5	21.2	95.9	1 832.0	651.5	785.8	1 260	1 235
Kankakee, IL	21.4	2.6	3.7	37.9	14.1	4.0	10.5	227.2	107.0	80.9	793	721
Kenosha, WI	15.6	23.2	5.7	40.8	19.0	6.3	6.6	444.2	210.3	169.0	1 183	1 108
Chico-Paradise, CA	26.9	2.4	18.9	99.7	38.6	11.4	25.0	568.4	340.3	112.7	580	416
Cincinnati-Hamilton, OH-KY-IN	806.4	897.5	524.0	816.3	227.6	85.9	241.4	4 930.2	1 666.8	2 150.3	1 112	754
Cincinnati, OH-KY-IN	774.9	867.9	503.6	724.3	198.0	74.9	206.2	4 256.6	1 415.0	1 867.4	1 162	776
Hamilton-Middletown, OH	31.5	29.6	20.4	92.0	29.5	11.0	35.2	673.7	251.8	283.0	866	645
Clarksville-Hopkinsville, TN-KY	864.1	152.6	12.5	59.7	18.7	9.1	21.3	350.8	127.8	99.2	502	255
Cleveland-Akron, OH	1 161.6	400.0	579.8	1 297.6	428.3	175.6	411.2	8 834.8	2 975.7	4 065.5	1 398	889
Akron, OH	165.2	240.3	48.3	226.3	87.5	40.5	70.7	1 903.2	611.4	866.3	1 269	806
Cleveland-Lorain-Elyria, OH	996.4	159.7	531.5	1 071.3	340.8	135.1	340.5	6 931.6	2 364.3	3 199.2	1 437	914
Colorado Springs, CO	1 194.3	875.0	93.6	82.4	44.5	22.3	29.1	1 187.2	404.2	379.5	791	492
Columbia, MO	92.6	4.8	17.9	55.6	9.5	11.8	60.0	223.9	79.2	93.9	731	424

1. October 1, 1998 to September 30, 1999.   2. State totals may include programs not allocated by county.   3. Based on the resident population estimated as of July 1 of the year shown.

Table C. Metropolitan Areas — Local Government Finances, Government Employment, and Elections

	Local government finances, 1997 (cont'd)									Government employment, 1998			Presidential election, 2000		
	Direct general expenditure							Debt outstanding					Percent of vote cast —		
				Percent of total for —											
Area Name	Total (mil dol)	Per capita[1] (dollars)	Educa-tion	Health and hospitals	Police protec-tion	Public welfare	High-ways	Total (mil dol)	Per capita[1] (dollars)	Federal civilian	Federal military	State and local	Demo-cratic	Republi-can	All other
	183	184	185	186	187	188	189	190	191	192	193	194	195	196	197
Abilene, TX	240.2	1 978	55.5	5.6	6.1	0.7	4.0	124.8	1 027	1 506	4 970	8 559	24.4	73.7	1.9
Albany, GA	301.7	2 564	44.4	11.9	5.0	0.2	2.1	101.4	862	2 876	1 197	9 267	NA	NA	NA
Albany-Schenectady-Troy, NY	2 885.1	3 292	47.4	2.4	3.4	13.7	4.6	2 001.3	2 284	8 201	3 532	98 243	52.8	41.5	5.6
Albuquerque, NM	1 552.0	2 300	44.1	2.2	7.4	0.6	5.4	1 508.3	2 235	13 981	6 868	50 357	NA	NA	NA
Alexandria, LA	250.5	1 981	51.6	0.1	7.9	0.0	4.4	201.5	1 593	2 180	704	11 222	NA	NA	NA
Allentown-Bethlehem-Easton, PA	1 668.2	2 718	48.4	2.4	2.8	8.4	2.9	3 154.0	5 138	2 861	2 117	27 593	NA	NA	NA
Altoona, PA	242.1	1 849	59.3	0.3	2.9	5.5	3.7	328.0	2 505	967	442	7 320	NA	NA	NA
Amarillo, TX	401.0	1 926	57.1	2.3	7.6	0.1	5.6	460.7	2 213	1 906	589	14 570	21.5	76.8	1.7
Anchorage, AK	796.1	3 171	47.4	3.8	5.0	1.1	7.7	1 314.8	5 237	9 954	10 753	17 745	NA	NA	NA
Anniston, AL	295.2	2 521	33.0	36.3	3.6	0.0	3.0	131.3	1 121	4 953	3 881	7 422	40.6	57.3	2.1
Appleton-Oshkosh-Neenah, WI	1 003.6	2 933	45.4	4.5	4.7	6.5	10.2	784.5	2 293	1 056	1 226	19 367	43.6	51.6	4.8
Asheville, NC	461.9	2 186	45.0	9.4	5.3	6.0	2.4	328.8	1 556	2 725	723	13 337	NA	NA	NA
Athens, GA	401.3	2 897	31.4	32.5	5.1	0.8	2.8	253.2	1 828	1 687	859	17 180	NA	NA	NA
Atlanta, GA	9 365.1	2 582	44.2	13.0	4.9	0.8	4.4	13 625.6	3 757	45 179	17 997	215 062	NA	NA	NA
Auburn-Opalika, AL	269.9	2 741	40.6	31.9	3.5	0.0	3.9	317.7	3 225	331	726	12 233	38.1	58.6	3.3
Augusta-Aiken, GA-SC	874.6	1 913	52.7	6.4	4.9	0.3	3.9	663.5	1 451	7 351	11 467	33 675	NA	NA	NA
Austin-San Marcos, TX	2 431.0	2 270	47.7	5.2	5.2	1.1	3.8	7 326.8	6 841	10 022	3 157	119 794	38.0	52.7	9.3
Bakersfield, CA	2 097.2	3 336	42.5	10.0	4.8	11.5	2.4	1 046.2	1 664	9 314	5 637	38 818	36.2	60.7	3.1
Bangor, ME	299.3	2 089	51.8	3.9	3.8	1.9	5.9	139.2	971	1 414	741	11 893	NA	NA	NA
Barnstable-Yarmouth, MA	579.2	2 823	47.9	0.9	5.6	0.5	6.2	414.6	2 021	1 859	1 317	10 894	NA	NA	NA
Baton Rouge, LA	1 136.6	1 993	42.8	3.8	7.2	0.2	5.9	1 190.2	2 088	2 653	3 263	56 484	NA	NA	NA
Beaumont-Port Arthur, TX	840.7	2 242	50.5	2.4	5.8	0.4	4.9	1 448.5	3 863	2 735	1 135	22 740	46.8	51.8	1.4
Bellingham, WA	323.7	2 098	48.4	2.7	4.8	0.0	7.8	301.5	1 955	841	605	9 867	46.1	46.5	7.4
Benton Harbor, MI	397.8	2 475	57.8	7.5	4.1	0.9	4.9	189.4	1 178	442	335	8 313	43.2	54.7	2.1
Billings, MT	245.0	1 948	51.1	3.9	7.0	1.0	3.1	122.8	976	1 713	728	6 857	35.1	58.5	6.4
Biloxi-Gulfport-Pascagoula, MS	1 009.9	2 941	31.4	30.2	4.1	0.6	4.6	1 098.3	3 198	8 945	15 605	22 004	NA	NA	NA
Binghamton, NY	822.1	3 266	47.5	2.6	2.7	13.2	4.9	330.4	1 313	1 016	527	19 443	49.8	44.9	5.3
Birmingham, AL	1 977.5	2 197	40.5	8.3	6.5	1.1	4.7	2 523.5	2 804	9 760	6 079	57 819	40.9	57.1	2.0
Bismarck, ND	169.1	1 857	45.5	1.1	5.1	3.8	8.7	128.0	1 406	1 037	743	8 727	30.0	66.6	3.3
Bloomington, IN	196.8	1 687	48.0	1.2	3.0	4.3	4.4	139.5	1 196	406	420	19 245	47.1	51.4	1.5
Bloomington-Normal, IL	271.8	1 931	47.3	1.5	6.8	1.7	7.9	221.9	1 576	935	330	12 380	40.9	55.8	3.2
Boise City, ID	772.0	2 011	51.5	1.7	5.9	0.9	6.0	331.0	862	4 816	1 856	26 205	30.8	63.4	5.8
Boston-Worcester-Lawrence-Lowell-Brockton, MA-NH	13 277.3	2 278	50.4	2.4	6.4	1.7	4.1	10 295.2	1 767	51 201	22 987	329 592	NA	NA	NA
Brownsville-Harlingen-San Benito, TX	693.3	2 161	66.3	1.4	3.8	0.7	2.6	787.6	2 455	1 893	942	21 352	53.5	44.8	1.7
Bryan-College Station, TX	273.9	2 060	49.1	3.1	4.8	0.3	3.9	325.7	2 448	970	462	28 534	26.3	70.0	3.7
Buffalo-Niagara Falls, NY	4 160.4	3 572	42.5	6.0	4.0	14.0	4.0	2 336.8	2 006	10 266	2 753	74 449	55.6	38.8	5.6
Burlington, VT	361.1	1 890	63.9	0.2	4.2	0.0	5.6	351.8	1 841	2 394	1 479	12 915	NA	NA	NA
Canton-Massillon, OH	817.0	2 029	50.9	6.6	5.7	5.6	5.1	301.7	749	1 266	1 040	18 623	NA	NA	NA
Casper, WY	176.6	2 775	53.0	1.2	5.0	0.4	3.5	62.0	974	642	398	4 443	31.9	68.1	0.0
Cedar Rapids, IA	450.7	2 480	51.4	4.5	6.3	1.2	6.9	272.4	1 499	1 099	869	10 292	53.1	43.9	3.0
Champaign-Urbana, IL	353.7	2 099	49.8	0.6	5.7	2.7	6.9	124.5	739	1 356	453	30 021	47.8	46.6	5.6
Charleston, WV	474.0	1 867	51.4	3.1	4.4	0.0	1.8	623.3	2 455	2 631	1 362	20 856	47.8	50.4	1.7
Charleston-North Charleston, SC	1 041.3	2 042	46.6	2.2	6.3	0.3	2.3	1 510.9	2 963	9 041	11 583	42 894	42.1	55.1	2.8
Charlotte-Gastonia-Rock Hill, NC-SC	3 856.1	2 856	35.1	24.5	4.8	5.2	2.2	4 149.4	3 073	7 866	4 816	85 047	NA	NA	NA
Charlottesville, VA	286.9	1 957	56.1	3.2	5.9	4.3	2.1	180.1	1 228	1 320	817	25 238	45.5	47.8	6.7
Chattanooga, TN-GA	1 296.2	2 897	28.2	31.3	4.6	3.4	3.6	1 091.5	2 439	6 782	1 821	25 429	NA	NA	NA
Cheyenne, WY	251.6	3 206	45.0	26.7	3.3	0.2	4.3	114.4	1 458	2 422	3 820	8 667	35.8	64.2	0.0
Chicago-Gary-Kenosha, IL-IN-WI	25 408.2	2 940	42.4	4.2	7.1	1.7	4.8	25 504.2	2 951	67 903	45 746	476 796	59.0	38.4	2.7
Chicago, IL	22 972.8	2 955	41.8	4.0	7.4	1.1	4.9	24 031.0	3 091	64 700	42 784	428 711	59.3	37.9	2.8
Gary, IN	1 766.0	2 833	45.2	7.7	3.9	8.2	2.9	915.2	1 468	2 580	2 197	34 259	58.3	40.6	1.2
Kankakee, IL	215.3	2 111	58.1	1.3	6.2	0.4	8.2	128.2	1 257	337	231	6 035	47.7	49.9	2.4
Kenosha, WI	454.2	3 179	51.0	3.9	5.9	7.3	4.9	429.8	3 008	286	534	7 791	50.9	45.3	3.7
Chico-Paradise, CA	588.4	3 031	43.5	4.7	3.8	14.3	2.4	196.0	1 010	555	395	13 192	37.4	54.4	8.1
Cincinnati-Hamilton, OH-KY-IN	4 945.0	2 557	40.3	7.0	5.8	4.4	4.8	4 102.2	2 121	16 221	5 561	106 203	NA	NA	NA
Cincinnati, OH-KY-IN	4 260.1	2 650	38.3	7.3	5.8	4.3	4.6	3 343.7	2 080	15 663	4 686	87 542	NA	NA	NA
Hamilton-Middletown, OH	685.0	2 096	52.2	5.4	5.7	5.0	5.6	758.6	2 322	558	875	18 661	NA	NA	NA
Clarksville-Hopkinsville, TN-KY	342.9	1 736	48.5	21.4	4.3	0.9	3.8	337.5	1 709	4 572	24 484	10 362	45.0	53.6	1.4
Cleveland-Akron, OH	8 369.3	2 878	41.7	11.2	6.0	4.7	4.5	6 558.2	2 255	22 748	8 190	167 342	NA	NA	NA
Akron, OH	1 827.7	2 678	39.8	13.2	5.5	4.7	5.7	1 107.3	1 623	3 055	1 825	44 407	NA	NA	NA
Cleveland-Lorain-Elyria, OH	6 541.7	2 939	42.2	10.6	6.1	4.7	4.2	5 450.9	2 449	19 693	6 365	122 935	NA	NA	NA
Colorado Springs, CO	1 144.8	2 385	46.6	14.3	5.3	5.0	5.4	1 299.3	2 707	10 213	29 134	26 203	30.8	63.9	5.3
Columbia, MO	227.7	1 775	52.0	1.3	5.0	2.0	8.3	248.9	1 940	1 971	616	26 701	NA	NA	NA

1. Based on the resident population estimated as of July 1 of the year shown.

Table C. Metropolitan Areas — **Land Area and Population**

CMSA/ MSA/ PMSA/ NECMA code[1]	Area Name	Land area,[2] (sq km) 1990	Population and population characteristics, 1999												
					Race (percent)					Age (percent)					
			Total persons	Rank	Per square kilometer	White	Black	Am. Indian, Eskimo, Aleut	Asian and Pacific Islander	Percent Hispanic[3]	Under 5 years	5 to 17 years	18 to 24 years	25 to 34 years	35 to 44 years	45 to 54 years
		1	2	3	4	5	6	7	8	9	10	11	12	13	14	15

1760	Columbia, SC..............	3 774	516 251	99	136.8	68.7	29.6	0.2	1.5	2.1	6.3	17.3	11.5	16.2	17.5	13.3
1800	Columbus, GA-AL.........	4 066	271 417	163	66.8	56.9	40.7	0.3	2.0	4.9	7.5	18.6	11.7	15.1	15.2	11.8
1840	Columbus, OH..............	8 139	1 489 487	40	183.0	84.3	13.3	0.2	2.1	1.1	6.9	18.0	11.2	15.7	17.1	13.0
1880	Corpus Christi, TX	3 957	387 105	126	97.8	94.3	4.0	0.5	1.2	59.1	8.6	22.0	9.9	13.0	15.6	12.2
1890	Corvallis, OR................	1 752	77 192	315	44.1	91.4	1.1	0.8	6.7	3.9	5.8	16.0	19.6	13.4	14.9	12.6
1900	Cumberland, MD-WV	1 951	98 231	301	50.3	96.5	2.8	0.1	0.6	0.7	5.2	17.5	10.0	10.3	14.5	14.1
31	Dallas-Fort Worth, TX.........	23 582	4 909 523	X	208.2	81.5	14.2	0.6	3.7	16.1	8.2	19.2	10.3	15.5	17.4	13.5
1920	Dallas, TX...................	16 025	3 280 310	10	204.7	79.9	15.6	0.6	3.9	17.0	8.2	19.2	10.3	15.7	17.7	13.5
2800	Fort Worth-Arlington, TX ..	7 557	1 629 213	32	215.6	84.7	11.3	0.6	3.4	14.4	8.2	19.2	10.2	15.0	17.0	13.5
1950	Danville, VA.................	2 627	107 555	289	40.9	64.6	34.9	0.1	0.4	0.7	5.5	17.4	7.8	12.4	15.9	13.8
	Davenport-Moline-Rock															
1960	Island, IA-IL.............	4 423	358 842	133	81.1	92.6	6.1	0.3	1.0	5.8	6.7	19.6	8.7	12.4	16.3	13.6
2000	Dayton-Springfield, OH.......	4 361	958 698	63	219.8	83.7	14.7	0.2	1.4	1.0	6.4	18.1	9.6	13.3	16.2	13.9
2020	Daytona Beach, FL..........	4 120	474 711	103	115.2	87.6	10.8	0.3	1.3	5.8	5.4	15.6	7.9	10.6	14.2	12.1
2030	Decatur, AL.................	3 304	143 460	243	43.4	85.9	12.4	1.3	0.4	1.0	6.7	17.7	8.8	14.4	16.2	14.3
2040	Decatur, IL.................	1 504	113 219	284	75.3	85.9	13.3	0.1	0.6	0.7	6.2	19.2	8.4	11.4	16.3	13.5
	Denver-Boulder-Greeley,															
34	CO......................	22 004	2 417 908	X	109.9	91.0	5.3	0.8	3.0	14.9	7.2	18.8	9.4	13.3	17.8	15.4
1125	Boulder-Longmont, CO	1 923	273 112	162	142.0	95.1	1.0	0.6	3.2	8.3	6.4	16.6	13.6	13.6	18.5	15.2
2080	Denver, CO	9 740	1 978 991	25	203.2	89.8	6.2	0.8	3.1	14.9	7.3	18.9	8.6	13.5	17.9	15.5
3060	Greeley, CO	10 341	165 805	220	16.0	97.5	0.6	0.7	1.2	25.1	7.8	21.2	12.5	11.5	15.2	14.0
2120	Des Moines, IA	4 475	443 496	113	99.1	93.2	4.3	0.3	2.2	3.1	6.9	18.1	10.1	14.7	16.9	13.8
35	Detroit-Ann Arbor-Flint, MI..	17 005	5 469 312	X	321.6	76.5	20.9	0.4	2.1	2.6	6.6	18.9	9.1	14.3	16.8	13.6
0440	Ann Arbor, MI..............	5 255	557 349	92	106.1	88.8	7.2	0.5	3.6	3.1	6.3	18.0	13.1	14.9	18.2	13.5
2160	Detroit, MI.................	10 093	4 474 614	7	443.3	74.9	22.6	0.4	2.0	2.5	6.6	18.9	8.7	14.3	16.7	13.6
2640	Flint, MI....................	1 657	437 349	115	263.9	77.1	21.2	0.7	1.0	2.6	6.7	20.6	8.9	13.6	16.6	14.0
2180	Dothan, AL.................	2 956	135 243	255	45.8	75.8	22.8	0.3	1.1	2.1	7.5	18.6	9.5	15.0	15.6	12.8
2190	Dover, DE..................	1 530	126 048	266	82.4	75.8	21.6	0.6	2.1	3.6	7.6	19.2	9.5	14.9	16.6	12.9
2200	Dubuque, IA................	1 575	88 112	309	55.9	98.7	0.5	0.1	0.7	0.9	6.3	19.5	10.4	11.9	15.0	13.2
2240	Duluth-Superior, MN-WI	19 515	236 400	180	12.1	96.3	0.7	2.1	0.9	0.8	5.4	19.1	9.1	10.7	17.0	13.3
2290	Eau Claire, WI..............	4 269	144 463	241	33.8	96.7	0.2	0.5	2.6	0.7	6.2	19.3	12.9	11.9	16.3	12.4
2320	El Paso, TX.................	2 624	701 908	74	267.5	94.5	3.4	0.5	1.5	75.4	9.5	22.9	11.1	13.4	14.6	11.4
2330	Elkhart-Goshen, IN	1 201	174 680	213	145.4	93.5	5.2	0.3	1.0	2.9	8.2	19.6	9.1	14.0	16.6	13.1
2335	Elmira, NY..................	1 057	91 738	305	86.8	92.1	6.4	0.3	1.2	2.0	6.4	19.2	8.4	12.8	15.9	13.0
2340	Enid, OK...................	2 742	56 954	318	20.8	92.8	3.8	2.1	1.3	2.9	6.7	19.2	8.7	12.3	14.3	12.9
2360	Erie, PA....................	2 077	276 993	161	133.4	92.7	6.4	0.2	0.8	1.8	6.3	19.7	10.1	12.7	15.9	12.7
2400	Eugene-Springfield, OR......	11 795	314 901	151	26.7	95.4	0.9	1.1	2.6	4.0	6.1	17.5	11.6	12.3	15.9	14.4
	Evansville-Henderson, IN-															
2440	KY.....................	3 801	291 181	157	76.6	92.8	6.4	0.2	0.7	0.8	6.7	17.8	9.1	13.8	16.3	13.3
2520	Fargo-Moorhead, ND-MN	7 280	170 122	217	23.4	97.1	0.4	1.2	1.3	1.9	6.2	17.5	16.0	13.3	16.3	12.3
2560	Fayetteville, NC	1 692	283 650	160	167.6	63.3	31.3	1.8	3.6	9.3	9.3	20.5	13.5	17.0	14.4	10.5
	Fayetteville-Springdale-Rog-															
2580	ers, AR................	4 645	285 017	159	61.4	96.8	1.0	1.3	0.9	3.4	7.2	18.0	11.6	13.8	15.0	12.2
2620	Flagstaff, AZ-UT............	58 564	120 652	274	2.1	68.5	1.8	28.6	1.2	12.1	8.2	23.7	14.7	13.2	16.2	11.1
2650	Florence, AL................	3 274	136 879	252	41.8	86.1	13.4	0.2	0.3	0.7	6.1	16.2	9.4	13.0	15.3	14.3
2655	Florence, SC................	2 070	125 229	267	60.5	60.1	39.4	0.1	0.4	0.7	6.4	20.0	9.4	13.3	16.9	14.0
2670	Fort Collins-Loveland, CO ...	6 738	236 849	178	35.2	96.6	0.7	0.7	2.0	8.2	6.7	18.7	13.3	12.5	16.8	14.1
2700	Fort Myers-Cape Coral, FL...	2 081	400 542	124	192.5	90.7	8.1	0.3	1.0	6.8	5.7	15.2	6.3	10.3	13.6	12.0
	Fort Pierce-Port St. Lucie,															
2710	FL......................	2 922	299 967	154	102.7	84.0	14.5	0.4	1.1	6.3	5.9	15.9	6.3	10.7	13.6	11.5
2720	Fort Smith, AR-OK...........	4 676	195 547	200	41.8	87.8	4.4	4.9	2.9	2.9	7.5	19.7	9.0	13.3	15.2	13.4
2750	Fort Walton Beach, FL	2 424	170 049	218	70.2	84.7	10.5	0.7	4.1	4.8	7.3	19.8	8.8	14.4	15.9	13.0
2760	Fort Wayne, IN	6 339	484 320	102	76.4	91.1	7.6	0.3	1.0	2.6	7.6	20.0	8.6	14.3	16.5	12.5
2840	Fresno, CA.................	20 984	879 829	67	41.9	84.1	5.0	1.3	9.6	43.1	8.8	23.2	9.8	14.0	15.5	11.1
2880	Gadsden, AL................	1 385	103 472	293	74.7	84.4	15.0	0.2	0.4	0.6	5.7	17.3	8.7	12.4	15.9	13.7
2900	Gainesville, FL..............	2 264	198 484	199	87.7	73.3	22.7	0.3	3.7	5.3	6.3	17.2	19.5	14.0	15.9	10.6
2975	Glens Falls, NY.............	4 417	121 582	272	27.5	97.3	2.0	0.2	0.6	1.8	6.4	19.3	8.0	13.4	16.5	13.4
2980	Goldsboro, NC..............	1 431	111 711	287	78.1	65.4	33.0	0.3	1.4	2.6	7.4	19.4	8.6	15.9	15.9	12.8
2985	Grand Forks, ND-MN........	8 828	95 461	303	10.8	95.0	1.7	2.0	1.3	3.4	6.8	18.6	15.7	13.7	14.8	11.4
2995	Grand Junction, CO	8 619	115 147	283	13.4	97.8	0.5	0.8	1.0	10.0	6.3	19.9	8.4	10.1	15.1	14.7
	Grand Rapids-Muskegon-															
3000	Holland, MI..............	7 145	1 052 092	58	147.2	90.5	7.5	0.6	1.4	4.1	7.7	20.7	9.5	14.6	16.5	12.3
3040	Great Falls, MT.............	6 988	78 282	313	11.2	92.6	1.6	4.7	1.2	2.1	6.6	18.4	10.2	12.0	14.1	15.0
3080	Green Bay, WI..............	1 369	216 522	187	158.2	95.2	0.6	2.2	1.9	1.1	6.7	19.7	10.4	14.3	17.3	13.1
	Greensboro—Winston-															
3120	Salem—High Point, NC	10 056	1 179 384	47	117.3	79.0	19.5	0.4	1.1	1.6	6.6	17.3	9.0	14.2	16.5	13.9
3150	Greenville, NC	1 688	127 960	262	75.8	64.3	34.3	0.2	1.2	1.8	7.2	18.8	14.3	14.9	15.8	11.4
	Greenville-Spartanburg-															
3160	Anderson, SC...........	8 316	929 565	64	111.8	81.1	17.8	0.2	0.9	1.2	6.1	17.0	10.1	13.8	16.4	14.6
	Harrisburg-Lebanon-Car-															
3240	lisle, PA................	5 157	618 375	82	119.9	90.3	7.9	0.2	1.6	2.5	5.8	17.7	8.6	13.3	17.1	13.8

1. MSA = Metropolitan Statistical Area. CMSA = Consolidated MSA. PMSA = Primary MSA. NECMA = New England County Metropolitan Area. See Appendix A for explanation of these concepts. See Appendix B for list of metropolitan areas identified by type, with component counties. 2. Dry land or land partially or temporarily covered by water. 3. Hispanic persons may be of any race.

Table C. Metropolitan Areas — **Population and Households**

Area Name	Population, 1999 (cont'd) Age (percent) (cont'd)				Population — change and components of change, 1980–1999							Households, 1990				
					Total persons		Percent change		Components of change, 1990–1999						Percent	
	55 to 64 years	65 to 74 years	75 years and over	Percent female	1990	1980	1980–1990	1990–1999	Births	Deaths	Net migration	Number	Percent change, 1980–1990	Persons per house-hold	Female family house-holder[1]	One person
	16	17	18	19	20	21	22	23	24	25	26	27	28	29	30	31
Columbia, SC	8.0	5.7	4.2	51.6	453 847	409 953	10.7	13.8	66 479	33 797	28 308	163 223	22.7	2.61	13.5	23.6
Columbus, GA-AL	8.7	6.5	4.9	50.7	260 862	254 660	2.4	4.0	41 318	22 932	-14 072	92 695	10.9	2.66	17.0	23.6
Columbus, OH	7.9	5.4	4.8	51.2	1 345 460	1 214 291	10.8	10.7	201 690	100 761	46 790	513 498	16.9	2.53	11.6	25.8
Corpus Christi, TX	8.3	6.0	4.5	51.1	349 894	326 228	7.3	10.6	59 822	25 414	3 011	118 516	13.4	2.91	13.4	21.2
Corvallis, OR	7.2	5.4	5.1	49.4	70 811	68 211	3.8	9.0	7 695	3 896	1 633	26 126	9.0	2.47	7.1	25.2
Cumberland, MD-WV	10.7	8.8	8.9	52.1	101 643	107 782	-5.7	-3.4	10 417	11 829	-2 342	39 615	1.3	2.47	10.6	26.4
Dallas-Fort Worth, TX	7.5	4.7	3.7	50.6	4 037 282	3 046 136	32.5	21.6	725 300	266 304	417 934	1 508 031	36.7	2.64	11.0	25.2
Dallas, TX	7.3	4.5	3.6	50.6	2 676 248	2 055 284	30.2	22.6	493 782	172 280	286 028	1 001 750	34.0	2.63	11.3	25.9
Fort Worth-Arlington, TX	8.0	5.1	3.9	50.5	1 361 034	990 852	37.4	19.7	231 518	94 024	131 906	506 281	42.3	2.64	10.4	23.8
Danville, VA	10.6	9.0	7.7	52.7	108 728	111 789	-2.7	-1.1	12 027	11 990	-872	42 325	6.7	2.53	14.1	24.9
Davenport-Moline-Rock Island, IA-IL	8.9	7.0	6.7	51.4	350 855	384 744	-8.8	2.3	45 652	30 914	-6 020	136 269	-1.4	2.52	10.8	26.4
Dayton-Springfield, OH	8.9	7.3	6.2	51.9	951 262	942 083	1.0	0.8	122 736	81 096	-55 372	364 300	7.1	2.55	12.0	24.8
Daytona Beach, FL	10.9	12.5	10.9	51.6	399 438	269 675	48.1	18.8	44 200	52 062	84 327	165 296	50.1	2.33	9.3	25.9
Decatur, AL	9.5	6.9	5.5	51.2	131 556	120 401	9.3	9.0	17 807	11 435	5 933	49 209	19.5	2.63	10.3	21.5
Decatur, IL	9.5	7.7	7.7	52.2	117 206	131 375	-10.8	-3.4	15 070	11 085	-7 708	45 996	-4.8	2.49	11.4	26.4
Denver-Boulder-Greeley, CO	8.6	5.2	4.2	50.8	1 980 140	1 741 899	13.7	22.1	316 773	128 521	251 382	785 276	20.6	2.48	10.1	28.0
Boulder-Longmont, CO	7.5	4.3	4.2	50.0	225 339	189 625	18.8	21.2	30 200	11 546	29 761	88 402	28.2	2.45	7.9	26.3
Denver, CO	8.8	5.4	4.2	50.9	1 622 980	1 428 836	13.6	21.9	264 555	108 076	200 546	649 404	20.4	2.46	10.5	28.7
Greeley, CO	8.4	4.7	4.6	50.3	131 821	123 438	6.8	25.8	22 018	8 899	21 075	47 470	11.0	2.69	9.1	22.3
Des Moines, IA	8.3	5.8	5.5	51.9	392 928	367 561	6.9	12.9	60 888	30 040	19 462	153 100	11.7	2.50	9.9	25.9
Detroit-Ann Arbor-Flint, MI	8.5	6.5	5.5	51.8	5 187 171	5 293 161	-2.0	5.4	737 579	422 042	-169 767	1 916 409	4.7	2.67	14.8	24.3
Ann Arbor, MI	7.0	4.8	4.2	50.2	490 058	454 977	7.7	13.7	64 502	29 376	33 186	175 050	13.4	2.65	8.9	22.7
Detroit, MI	8.7	6.8	5.7	51.9	4 266 654	4 387 735	-2.8	4.9	610 139	358 176	-182 555	1 580 063	3.9	2.67	15.3	24.6
Flint, MI	8.6	6.1	5.3	52.2	430 459	450 449	-4.4	1.6	62 938	34 490	-20 398	161 296	4.3	2.64	16.7	23.9
Dothan, AL	8.6	6.9	5.5	51.9	130 964	122 453	7.0	3.3	18 782	10 672	-4 593	48 418	17.1	2.64	12.7	23.0
Dover, DE	8.0	6.1	5.3	51.3	110 993	98 219	13.0	13.6	17 410	9 006	5 822	39 655	21.1	2.70	11.9	21.2
Dubuque, IA	8.9	7.3	7.4	51.5	86 403	93 745	-7.8	2.0	11 161	7 731	-1 783	30 799	2.6	2.67	8.5	24.4
Duluth-Superior, MN-WI	9.7	7.8	8.1	51.1	239 990	266 650	-10.0	-1.5	24 485	24 949	-2 428	95 275	-2.7	2.44	9.5	28.7
Eau Claire, WI	8.0	6.5	6.5	51.3	137 543	130 932	5.0	5.0	16 445	10 953	1 889	50 359	13.1	2.62	8.3	24.2
El Paso, TX	7.7	5.6	3.9	52.3	591 610	479 899	23.3	18.6	141 244	33 295	-2 129	178 366	26.7	3.25	15.8	17.0
Elkhart-Goshen, IN	8.2	5.8	5.4	50.9	156 198	137 330	13.7	11.8	25 457	11 873	5 434	56 713	17.8	2.71	9.1	21.6
Elmira, NY	9.0	8.0	7.3	50.8	95 195	97 656	-2.5	-3.6	10 843	8 904	-5 095	35 275	2.2	2.56	11.5	25.6
Enid, OK	10.0	7.9	7.9	51.9	56 735	62 820	-9.7	0.4	7 340	5 869	-1 499	22 460	-5.8	2.45	9.1	26.9
Erie, PA	8.3	7.6	6.7	51.3	275 575	279 780	-1.5	0.5	35 734	24 406	-9 120	101 564	4.9	2.61	11.5	25.4
Eugene-Springfield, OR	8.7	6.8	6.6	51.1	282 912	275 226	2.8	11.3	33 949	23 564	22 445	110 799	7.0	2.49	9.4	25.1
Evansville-Henderson, IN-KY	9.1	7.2	6.7	52.1	278 990	276 252	1.0	4.4	35 305	26 414	4 192	108 663	7.0	2.51	10.5	25.8
Fargo-Moorhead, ND-MN	7.7	5.3	5.4	50.6	153 296	137 574	11.4	11.0	20 546	9 883	6 550	57 771	18.4	2.51	7.9	26.7
Fayetteville, NC	6.5	5.1	3.2	49.5	274 713	247 160	11.1	3.3	52 761	16 136	-41 408	91 500	22.1	2.77	14.1	19.4
Fayetteville-Springdale-Rogers, AR	9.7	7.0	5.6	50.7	210 939	178 609	18.1	35.1	35 654	19 639	53 568	80 927	25.1	2.53	7.5	22.4
Flagstaff, AZ-UT	6.3	4.0	2.7	50.0	101 760	79 032	28.8	18.6	17 860	4 534	5 685	31 642	36.6	2.99	11.2	19.9
Florence, AL	10.4	8.7	6.7	52.2	131 327	135 065	-2.8	4.2	16 236	12 902	2 628	51 001	7.6	2.54	10.6	23.2
Florence, SC	8.9	6.5	4.9	53.0	114 344	110 163	3.8	9.5	16 534	11 189	5 873	40 217	12.6	2.78	17.3	21.8
Fort Collins-Loveland, CO	7.9	5.2	4.8	50.5	186 136	149 184	24.8	27.2	25 881	11 288	36 630	70 472	30.3	2.55	7.6	23.0
Fort Myers-Cape Coral, FL	11.3	14.0	11.6	51.5	335 113	205 266	63.3	19.5	40 776	40 166	65 644	140 124	69.8	2.35	8.2	23.0
Fort Pierce-Port St. Lucie, FL	10.6	14.5	11.2	50.2	251 071	151 196	66.1	19.5	31 728	30 346	48 580	101 196	73.4	2.43	8.5	22.3
Fort Smith, AR-OK	9.2	6.7	6.0	51.3	175 911	162 813	8.0	11.2	26 638	17 346	11 004	66 884	13.7	2.59	10.1	23.6
Fort Walton Beach, FL	8.9	7.3	4.6	50.1	143 777	109 920	30.8	18.3	22 365	9 964	10 239	53 313	42.0	2.60	9.5	20.9
Fort Wayne, IN	8.3	6.3	5.9	51.3	456 281	444 772	2.6	6.1	69 295	36 617	-3 194	168 806	8.4	2.66	9.8	23.7
Fresno, CA	6.9	5.6	5.1	49.5	755 569	577 737	30.8	16.4	159 667	54 636	20 861	249 303	25.0	2.97	13.6	20.5
Gadsden, AL	10.7	8.8	6.9	52.6	99 840	103 057	-3.1	3.6	12 188	11 522	850	38 675	4.9	2.55	11.8	24.3
Gainesville, FL	6.4	5.4	4.7	51.0	181 596	151 369	20.0	9.3	23 901	12 754	6 115	71 258	30.5	2.40	12.0	28.1
Glens Falls, NY	8.7	7.3	7.0	50.0	118 539	109 649	8.1	2.6	13 840	10 644	205	42 815	14.8	2.66	10.0	22.9
Goldsboro, NC	8.7	6.6	4.8	50.2	104 666	97 054	7.8	6.7	15 140	8 773	-1 483	36 889	14.2	2.65	14.4	22.4
Grand Forks, ND-MN	7.2	5.6	6.2	49.7	103 272	100 944	2.3	-7.6	14 148	7 656	-15 867	37 324	8.9	2.58	8.0	25.7
Grand Junction, CO	10.6	8.0	7.0	51.4	93 145	81 530	14.2	23.6	12 467	8 831	18 664	36 250	22.2	2.50	9.8	24.8
Grand Rapids-Muskegon-Holland, MI	7.7	5.6	5.4	51.1	937 891	840 824	11.5	12.2	149 977	68 217	28 889	333 911	16.0	2.74	10.8	21.5
Great Falls, MT	10.1	7.0	6.6	50.9	77 691	80 696	-3.7	0.8	11 393	6 596	-5 411	30 133	2.5	2.51	9.3	26.2
Green Bay, WI	7.6	5.5	5.4	51.1	194 594	175 280	11.0	11.3	27 793	13 544	8 384	72 280	20.7	2.62	9.0	24.1
Greensboro—Winston-Salem—High Point, NC	9.4	7.1	6.1	52.2	1 050 304	950 763	10.5	12.3	144 098	92 562	80 629	414 793	20.9	2.47	11.9	25.0
Greenville, NC	7.7	5.6	4.4	52.5	108 480	90 146	20.3	18.0	16 176	8 841	8 506	40 491	34.1	2.53	14.5	25.7
Greenville-Spartanburg-Anderson, SC	9.6	6.7	5.7	51.8	830 499	744 428	11.6	11.9	113 000	73 521	61 682	312 740	21.2	2.58	12.1	23.3
Harrisburg-Lebanon-Carlisle, PA	8.8	7.6	7.3	51.6	587 986	556 242	5.7	5.2	72 135	52 888	12 739	226 353	12.5	2.51	9.6	25.3

1. No spouse present.

Area Name	Births, average 1996–1998		Deaths, average 1996–1998				Physicians,[4] 1998		Hospitals,[4] 1998			Medicare enrollees 1999	Serious crimes known to police, 1998[6]	
			Number		Rate					Beds			Total	
	Total	Rate[1]	Total	Infant[2]	Total[1]	Infant[3]	Number	Rate[5]	Number	Number	Rate[5]		Number	Rate[7]
	32	33	34	35	36	37	38	39	40	41	42	43	44	45
Columbia, SC	7 147	14.1	3 884	58	7.7	8.1	1 339	261	5	1 554	303	60 941	32 510	6 326
Columbus, GA-AL	4 241	15.6	2 533	65	9.3	15.2	507	186	4	991	364	36 585	14 353	5 192
Columbus, OH	22 010	15.1	11 376	185	7.8	8.4	3 497	238	17	4 624	315	174 730	87 611	6 757
Corpus Christi, TX	6 394	16.6	2 859	37	7.4	5.8	786	203	9	1 617	417	47 088	25 643	6 517
Corvallis, OR	829	10.7	444	4	5.7	4.4	188	242	1	124	159	7 996	2 757	3 559
Cumberland, MD-WV	1 070	10.8	1 311	6	13.2	5.6	194	198	3	525	535	20 019	3 068	3 079
Dallas-Fort Worth, TX	82 459	17.6	30 306	514	6.5	6.2	8 847	184	61	11 335	236	455 851	271 750	5 712
Dallas, TX	56 711	18.1	19 488	329	6.2	5.8	6 366	198	42	7 633	238	294 166	189 956	5 983
Fort Worth-Arlington, TX	25 748	16.6	10 818	185	7.0	7.2	2 481	156	19	3 702	232	161 685	81 794	5 170
Danville, VA	1 295	11.9	1 325	13	12.2	9.8	166	153	1	336	310	21 288	3 204	2 925
Davenport-Moline-Rock Island, IA-IL	4 786	13.4	3 306	37	9.3	7.7	624	174	8	1 476	413	55 174	NA	NA
Dayton-Springfield, OH	12 615	13.2	9 044	92	9.5	7.2	2 152	227	13	3 918	413	146 313	44 033	5 364
Daytona Beach, FL	4 734	10.2	6 036	31	13.0	6.5	830	176	9	1 574	334	113 756	27 369	5 771
Decatur, AL	1 879	13.3	1 293	21	9.1	10.8	182	127	4	497	348	20 987	4 901	3 488
Decatur, IL	1 542	13.5	1 212	15	10.6	9.5	198	174	2	581	511	20 007	NA	NA
Denver-Boulder-Greeley, CO	35 465	15.3	14 817	229	6.4	6.4	6 458	273	20	4 997	211	252 173	99 068	4 519
Boulder-Longmont, CO	3 326	12.7	1 348	15	5.1	4.6	754	282	3	360	135	27 015	11 522	4 339
Denver, CO	29 610	15.6	12 440	195	6.5	6.6	5 457	281	16	4 311	222	207 649	80 883	4 542
Greeley, CO	2 529	16.3	1 029	19	6.6	7.5	247	155	1	326	204	17 509	6 663	4 557
Des Moines, IA	6 794	15.7	3 395	49	7.8	7.3	1 086	249	7	1 932	442	56 098	21 273	4 938
Detroit-Ann Arbor-Flint, MI	75 877	13.9	45 994	652	8.4	8.6	14 008	257	67	17 810	326	729 017	301 895	5 661
Ann Arbor, MI	7 003	13.0	3 353	37	6.2	5.4	2 502	457	10	2 047	374	56 266	18 068	3 394
Detroit, MI	62 490	14.0	38 881	537	8.7	8.6	10 678	239	52	13 984	313	611 731	253 202	5 792
Flint, MI	6 384	14.6	3 760	78	8.6	12.2	828	190	5	1 779	408	61 020	30 625	7 142
Dothan, AL	1 963	14.6	1 208	23	9.0	11.7	290	215	3	718	533	20 507	4 038	3 062
Dover, DE	1 821	14.8	996	16	8.1	9.0	181	146	1	190	153	15 837	6 325	5 071
Dubuque, IA	1 164	13.2	828	5	9.4	4.6	187	213	3	670	763	14 454	2 595	2 936
Duluth-Superior, MN-WI	2 547	10.7	2 684	14	11.3	5.8	488	206	9	1 410	596	43 598	7 155	3 639
Eau Claire, WI	1 703	11.9	1 186	11	8.3	6.1	337	234	5	877	610	21 909	NA	NA
El Paso, TX	14 638	21.2	3 793	75	5.5	5.1	1 059	151	6	1 829	260	72 503	38 733	5 431
Elkhart-Goshen, IN	2 876	16.9	1 333	22	7.8	7.6	228	132	2	476	276	21 856	8 634	5 027
Elmira, NY	1 056	11.4	952	5	10.3	4.4	232	252	2	495	538	16 581	3 058	3 278
Enid, OK	798	14.0	675	7	11.9	8.8	121	213	2	298	524	10 223	3 687	6 444
Erie, PA	3 568	12.9	2 702	29	9.7	8.2	631	228	6	1 167	422	44 902	8 634	3 095
Eugene-Springfield, OR	3 669	11.8	2 772	22	8.9	6.0	650	207	4	620	197	47 785	20 623	6 545
Evansville-Henderson, IN-KY	3 733	12.9	2 904	30	10.0	8.0	680	234	5	1 394	479	46 815	10 228	4 529
Fargo-Moorhead, ND-MN	2 263	13.6	1 117	15	6.7	6.6	447	265	3	667	396	20 493	5 177	3 111
Fayetteville, NC	5 602	19.7	1 820	61	6.4	10.9	534	188	2	515	181	28 345	17 688	6 127
Fayetteville-Springdale-Rogers, AR	4 363	16.3	2 283	40	8.5	9.0	483	177	6	735	270	42 086	8 684	3 233
Flagstaff, AZ-UT	1 907	16.0	550	18	4.6	9.3	280	233	3	174	145	13 449	6 802	5 749
Florence, AL	1 734	12.7	1 425	13	10.4	7.7	232	169	4	907	661	25 146	4 456	3 233
Florence, SC	1 787	14.4	1 245	18	10.0	10.1	278	223	4	765	612	18 410	8 201	6 463
Fort Collins-Loveland, CO	2 825	12.5	1 332	17	5.9	6.1	442	191	3	375	162	25 902	9 017	3 911
Fort Myers-Cape Coral, FL	4 526	11.7	4 674	36	12.1	8.0	1 026	261	6	1 707	434	99 107	20 757	5 268
Fort Pierce-Port St. Lucie, FL	3 308	11.4	3 588	28	12.3	8.5	671	227	4	792	268	73 479	14 922	4 959
Fort Smith, AR-OK	2 987	15.5	1 960	22	10.2	7.6	375	193	4	829	427	31 308	8 085	4 193
Fort Walton Beach, FL	2 327	13.9	1 175	22	7.0	9.5	356	210	3	433	256	23 429	6 254	3 666
Fort Wayne, IN	7 457	15.6	4 000	54	8.4	7.2	851	177	9	1 493	310	66 299	18 752	4 705
Fresno, CA	16 397	19.0	6 077	120	7.0	7.3	1 492	171	16	2 242	258	106 105	52 188	5 934
Gadsden, AL	1 337	12.9	1 293	12	12.5	9.2	164	158	2	538	517	19 168	6 371	6 061
Gainesville, FL	2 471	12.5	1 476	27	7.5	10.8	1 325	667	3	1 057	532	25 051	19 116	9 469
Glens Falls, NY	1 305	10.7	1 160	6	9.5	4.6	237	195	2	553	454	20 537	3 351	2 728
Goldsboro, NC	1 670	14.9	1 003	16	9.0	9.8	165	147	1	267	238	16 621	5 869	5 157
Grand Forks, ND-MN	1 419	14.1	808	8	8.0	5.6	204	209	4	665	680	12 817	4 118	4 070
Grand Junction, CO	1 411	12.8	1 030	13	9.3	9.0	312	276	3	422	374	19 622	5 292	4 687
Grand Rapids-Muskegon-Holland, MI	16 245	15.8	7 691	122	7.5	7.6	1 979	191	12	2 465	237	133 028	40 516	4 291
Great Falls, MT	1 107	13.9	739	9	9.3	8.1	201	254	2	402	509	12 698	NA	NA
Green Bay, WI	3 077	14.4	1 539	22	7.2	7.3	401	186	3	632	293	26 605	NA	NA
Greensboro—Winston-Salem—High Point, NC	16 128	14.0	10 379	153	9.0	9.5	2 449	210	13	3 512	301	175 256	67 486	5 774
Greenville, NC	1 833	14.8	996	25	8.0	13.8	559	441	1	571	451	15 761	10 161	8 259
Greenville-Spartanburg-Anderson, SC	12 391	13.7	8 369	98	9.2	7.8	1 628	177	11	2 697	294	139 622	50 190	5 443
Harrisburg-Lebanon-Carlisle, PA	7 393	12.0	5 905	49	9.6	6.7	1 783	289	9	2 203	358	99 371	17 012	2 816

1. Per 1,000 estimated resident population, average 1996–1998. 2. Deaths of infants under 1 year old. 3. Deaths of infants under 1 year old per 1,000 live births. 4. Data subject to copyright. 5. Per 100,000 resident population as of July 1 of the year shown. 6. Data for serious crimes have not been adjusted for underreporting; this may affect comparability between geographic areas and over time. 7. Per 100,000 population estimated by the FBI.

Table C. Metropolitan Areas — Crime, Education, Money Income, and Poverty

Area Name	Serious crimes known to police, 1998[1] (cont'd) Rate[2] — Violent	Property	Education — School enrollment and attainment, 1990 — Enrollment[3] Total	Percent private	Attainment[4] (percent) — High school graduate or more	Bachelor's degree or more	Local government expenditures, fiscal 1997[5] — Total current expenditures (mil dol)	Current expenditures per student (dollars)	Money income — 1989 — Per capita[6] (dollars)	Households Median Dollars	Percent change, 1979–1989 (constant 1989 dollars)	Percent with $100,000 or more	Income and poverty, 1997 — Median household income	Percent below poverty level — All persons	Persons under 18	Persons 5–17 in families
	46	47	48	49	50	51	52	53	54	55	56	57	58	59	60	61
Columbia, SC	868	5 458	127 116	11.9	78.6	25.3	470.9	5 568	13 618	30 473	9.7	3.1	NA	12.5	19.2	17.4
Columbus, GA-AL	377	4 815	64 390	10.8	69.0	15.0	239.1	5 154	11 409	23 622	8.3	2.4	NA	18.2	27.2	25.8
Columbus, OH	537	6 220	358 609	15.1	79.8	23.3	1 420.6	5 959	14 537	30 609	5.3	3.5	NA	10.1	15.1	13.5
Corpus Christi, TX	609	5 908	104 793	7.4	67.6	16.0	405.8	5 061	11 065	24 952	-10.5	2.5	NA	21.8	29.3	27.5
Corvallis, OR	169	3 390	29 624	5.8	89.3	41.3	59.2	5 693	12 994	27 295	0.6	3.3	NA	9.1	10.0	9.1
Cumberland, MD-WV	329	2 750	24 873	8.7	71.4	11.5	99.7	6 228	11 131	21 691	-8.0	1.5	NA	15.5	23.8	22.1
Dallas-Fort Worth, TX	655	5 057	1 066 267	13.8	78.6	25.4	4 149.0	4 836	15 755	32 446	3.7	5.1	NA	11.4	16.4	15.3
Dallas, TX	723	5 260	711 757	13.8	78.4	26.9	2 802.3	4 908	16 218	32 667	4.1	5.7	NA	11.4	16.4	15.2
Fort Worth-Arlington, TX	520	4 650	354 510	13.9	78.9	22.4	1 346.7	4 692	14 845	32 112	3.3	4.0	NA	11.3	16.6	15.3
Danville, VA	281	2 644	23 328	9.7	56.8	9.9	84.6	4 794	11 268	23 086	-1.4	1.3	NA	17.2	24.9	23.8
Davenport-Moline-Rock Island, IA-IL	NA	NA	93 483	16.8	79.1	17.4	346.8	5 582	13 251	27 940	-17.3	2.3	NA	11.2	17.1	15.6
Dayton-Springfield, OH	474	4 890	253 276	18.2	77.6	19.1	918.2	5 954	14 087	30 471	1.9	2.8	NA	10.3	15.4	13.9
Daytona Beach, FL	758	5 013	83 636	20.2	75.7	15.0	317.4	4 984	13 420	25 130	20.2	2.5	NA	13.8	22.1	20.3
Decatur, AL	244	3 244	31 660	7.2	66.2	13.3	129.9	5 092	12 104	26 643	5.6	1.9	NA	12.4	18.2	17.2
Decatur, IL	NA	NA	29 951	15.7	76.2	14.8	98.9	5 127	13 762	28 598	-8.7	2.5	NA	14.0	23.2	21.1
Denver-Boulder-Greeley, CO	389	4 130	533 845	13.7	85.5	29.7	2 065.6	5 288	16 287	32 541	-1.3	4.6	NA	9.1	13.3	12.0
Boulder-Longmont, CO	263	4 076	72 009	9.7	91.3	42.1	215.8	5 006	17 359	35 322	6.6	5.5	NA	7.8	9.9	8.9
Denver, CO	385	4 157	420 586	15.1	85.5	28.9	1 707.2	5 322	16 539	32 851	-2.1	4.7	NA	9.0	13.4	12.1
Greeley, CO	674	3 883	41 250	6.0	74.9	18.4	142.6	5 329	11 350	25 642	-3.2	2.0	NA	12.5	16.8	15.0
Des Moines, IA	312	4 626	99 862	18.5	85.4	22.6	457.8	6 104	14 972	31 181	-1.8	3.3	NA	8.2	12.0	10.3
Detroit-Ann Arbor-Flint, MI	830	4 831	1 423 735	14.0	76.4	18.5	6 433.3	7 154	15 542	34 289	-3.2	4.9	NA	11.6	18.6	17.0
Ann Arbor, MI	335	3 059	162 946	10.5	84.7	30.9	589.8	6 896	16 333	37 097	5.4	5.7	NA	7.5	10.2	10.1
Detroit, MI	870	4 922	1 138 104	14.8	75.4	17.7	5 274.7	7 228	15 649	34 300	-3.3	5.1	NA	11.8	19.1	17.3
Flint, MI	1 032	6 110	122 685	10.5	76.8	12.8	568.8	6 771	13 583	31 029	-11.8	2.5	NA	14.2	23.5	21.5
Dothan, AL	293	2 769	34 718	8.6	70.4	14.5	109.6	4 900	11 535	24 485	8.0	1.8	NA	16.7	25.1	23.8
Dover, DE	701	4 370	29 454	13.8	73.1	15.0	138.8	6 637	12 726	29 497	14.7	2.4	NA	12.1	17.7	16.8
Dubuque, IA	176	2 760	23 997	41.1	77.7	16.8	69.2	5 474	12 331	28 276	-13.0	2.4	NA	9.1	12.1	10.3
Duluth-Superior, MN-WI	275	3 364	64 901	8.2	79.7	16.8	255.2	6 349	11 644	23 690	-16.1	1.3	NA	12.0	17.7	15.1
Eau Claire, WI	NA	NA	40 591	9.8	79.6	16.9	157.9	6 585	11 560	25 875	1.2	1.9	NA	10.5	14.9	13.7
El Paso, TX	668	4 763	199 118	7.1	63.7	15.2	757.8	4 992	9 150	22 643	-3.5	2.2	NA	27.8	38.6	34.2
Elkhart-Goshen, IN	239	4 788	36 915	15.3	72.8	14.2	188.0	6 054	13 825	30 973	5.1	2.0	NA	8.7	14.1	12.6
Elmira, NY	276	3 002	23 886	17.8	77.2	15.4	114.6	8 024	12 069	26 134	2.5	2.0	NA	13.8	21.0	21.0
Enid, OK	654	5 790	13 899	14.1	76.5	17.3	50.6	4 760	11 564	23 243	-16.3	2.2	NA	14.9	22.4	20.2
Erie, PA	312	2 783	74 816	25.9	77.5	16.2	290.2	6 720	12 317	26 581	-5.4	2.3	NA	12.7	18.7	16.7
Eugene-Springfield, OR	384	6 161	80 983	8.3	83.0	22.2	292.6	5 973	12 570	25 267	-7.3	2.4	NA	13.3	18.0	15.2
Evansville-Henderson, IN-KY	325	4 204	68 019	18.6	75.1	14.8	266.7	5 970	13 265	27 228	-4.2	2.6	NA	10.8	16.1	14.6
Fargo-Moorhead, ND-MN	142	2 969	50 047	10.6	85.1	25.0	143.9	5 128	12 449	26 551	-8.2	2.4	NA	10.0	13.1	11.4
Fayetteville, NC	574	5 553	73 885	9.7	80.3	16.6	229.5	4 497	11 100	25 461	13.1	1.6	NA	15.5	21.2	19.7
Fayetteville-Springdale-Rogers, AR	306	2 927	54 023	8.2	74.0	17.3	204.0	4 367	11 925	24 462	9.3	2.1	NA	11.9	17.7	15.6
Flagstaff, AZ-UT	403	5 346	NA	5.8	79.2	23.9	101.0	4 724	10 486	NA	NA	2.3	NA	19.8	25.5	24.7
Florence, AL	236	2 997	31 878	8.5	68.4	14.5	114.3	5 115	11 582	23 106	-9.6	1.9	NA	13.4	20.1	19.1
Florence, SC	980	5 483	32 153	8.9	64.3	14.8	110.1	4 793	11 007	24 264	4.0	2.4	NA	19.4	28.7	25.8
Fort Collins-Loveland, CO	298	3 613	62 261	7.4	88.6	32.3	177.8	4 799	13 968	29 685	3.2	3.0	NA	8.5	10.3	9.5
Fort Myers-Cape Coral, FL	614	4 654	59 636	13.1	76.9	16.4	296.8	5 673	15 623	28 447	16.2	4.0	NA	11.5	19.9	18.6
Fort Pierce-Port St. Lucie, FL	810	4 149	49 320	15.8	75.1	16.1	229.0	5 390	16 177	29 416	19.6	4.7	NA	13.2	21.9	20.8
Fort Smith, AR-OK	391	3 802	42 398	8.0	67.5	11.8	169.7	4 564	11 083	22 400	2.4	2.0	NA	16.1	23.6	21.0
Fort Walton Beach, FL	539	3 127	37 715	7.7	83.8	21.0	138.0	4 591	13 147	27 941	10.0	2.0	NA	10.5	14.7	14.3
Fort Wayne, IN	307	4 398	118 712	17.8	80.0	16.2	486.4	6 067	13 883	31 298	0.0	2.7	NA	8.1	12.5	11.1
Fresno, CA	872	5 062	229 091	6.5	65.9	16.3	1 021.4	5 155	11 711	26 481	0.7	3.5	NA	25.2	37.7	36.0
Gadsden, AL	979	5 082	23 854	8.5	64.1	10.2	77.0	4 638	10 997	22 314	0.0	1.5	NA	16.9	25.5	22.7
Gainesville, FL	1 246	8 223	71 842	7.3	82.7	34.6	146.6	4 943	12 252	22 084	6.7	3.0	NA	18.3	23.0	22.3
Glens Falls, NY	312	2 416	28 933	11.6	76.2	15.5	175.0	7 863	13 298	29 641	20.4	2.4	NA	12.3	19.1	18.8
Goldsboro, NC	641	4 516	27 469	11.4	71.2	12.7	87.8	4 556	10 843	23 559	8.7	1.2	NA	16.6	22.1	20.6
Grand Forks, ND-MN	124	3 946	33 581	5.9	81.2	21.4	89.5	4 808	11 031	24 353	-3.5	1.6	NA	12.2	16.2	14.9
Grand Junction, CO	325	4 362	24 299	7.4	79.5	17.4	94.7	4 789	11 850	23 698	-14.8	1.8	NA	13.0	18.3	16.5
Grand Rapids-Muskegon-Holland, MI	486	3 805	260 702	19.9	78.6	17.8	1 201.4	6 515	13 676	31 796	3.5	3.1	NA	8.7	13.0	12.5
Great Falls, MT	NA	NA	18 971	12.3	82.9	18.4	71.9	4 908	12 011	23 700	-11.9	2.3	NA	14.4	20.1	17.6
Green Bay, WI	NA	NA	51 864	21.1	82.6	17.7	234.3	6 416	13 906	31 302	0.4	2.8	NA	7.5	11.4	9.6
Greensboro—Winston-Salem—High Point, NC	576	5 198	248 233	14.1	71.6	18.7	915.3	5 076	14 454	29 043	8.2	3.4	NA	10.3	15.7	13.9
Greenville, NC	927	7 332	35 790	6.7	71.0	21.9	93.4	4 760	11 642	23 324	7.8	2.3	NA	17.7	23.2	22.1
Greenville-Spartanburg-Anderson, SC	850	4 593	208 948	15.1	66.5	16.7	723.1	4 973	12 653	27 236	4.6	2.3	NA	11.1	17.0	15.6
Harrisburg-Lebanon-Carlisle, PA	246	2 570	134 963	17.1	76.9	18.0	664.0	6 701	14 659	31 637	5.8	2.9	NA	7.6	12.3	11.0

1. Data for serious crimes have not been adjusted for underreporting; this may affect comparability between geographic areas and over time. 2. Per 100,000 population estimated by the FBI. 3. All persons 3 years old and over enrolled in nursery school through college. 4. Persons 25 years old and over. 5. Elementary and secondary education expenditures, local government fiscal years ending between July 1, 1996 and June 30, 1997. 6. Based on population enumerated as of April 1, 1990.

Table C. Metropolitan Areas — **Personal Income**

Area Name	Personal income, 1998												
			Per capita[1]					Transfer payments					
									Government payments to individuals				
	Total (mil dol)	Percent change, 1997–1998	Dollars	Rank	Wages and salaries[2] (mil dol)	Proprietor's income (mil dol)	Dividends, interest, and rent (mil dol)	Total (mil dol)	Total (mil dol)	Social Security (mil dol)	Medical payments (mil dol)	Income mainte-nance (mil dol)	Unemploy-ment insurance (mil dol)
	62	63	64	65	66	67	68	69	70	71	72	73	74
Columbia, SC	13 256	6.8	25 995	120	9 649	775	2 149	1 602	1 513	588	619	136	15
Columbus, GA-AL	6 091	5.2	22 435	235	4 305	309	1 003	924	872	333	299	130	13
Columbus, OH	41 914	6.4	28 454	66	30 070	2 583	7 232	4 539	4 240	1 666	1 626	410	63
Corpus Christi, TX	8 242	5.1	21 326	271	5 265	833	1 280	1 344	1 280	420	590	175	36
Corvallis, OR	2 125	3.7	27 307	88	1 346	106	571	187	173	87	44	14	4
Cumberland, MD-WV	1 961	2.9	19 776	300	1 048	101	347	523	505	178	213	36	13
Dallas-Fort Worth, TX	146 431	8.9	30 541	X	105 448	17 668	20 127	12 012	11 207	4 583	4 718	950	314
Dallas, TX	103 788	9.3	32 406	26	78 834	14 348	14 064	7 836	7 299	2 970	3 113	656	189
Fort Worth-Arlington, TX	42 643	8.0	26 790	98	26 614	3 320	6 063	4 175	3 908	1 613	1 606	293	125
Danville, VA	2 137	3.1	19 738	302	1 266	102	364	408	388	196	124	43	9
Davenport-Moline-Rock Island, IA-IL	9 304	5.0	26 003	119	6 304	624	1 954	1 172	1 100	551	364	107	23
Dayton-Springfield, OH	25 406	3.1	26 422	110	17 662	1 010	5 036	3 514	3 322	1 394	1 283	285	47
Daytona Beach, FL	10 229	4.8	21 869	255	4 154	429	3 034	2 211	2 127	1 105	779	126	16
Decatur, AL	3 248	4.4	22 767	221	1 857	202	497	507	481	200	210	42	8
Decatur, IL	2 918	4.3	25 674	127	2 062	160	579	455	433	200	140	52	12
Denver-Boulder-Greeley, CO	79 121	9.3	33 485	X	54 788	8 206	14 377	6 252	5 846	2 424	2 227	498	83
Boulder-Longmont, CO	9 619	10.0	36 071	13	7 029	711	2 136	556	510	238	161	34	9
Denver, CO	66 024	9.2	34 092	17	45 724	7 097	11 679	5 257	4 924	2 024	1 896	424	68
Greeley, CO	3 478	9.4	21 803	258	2 036	398	562	439	412	163	170	39	6
Des Moines, IA	12 897	6.5	29 527	46	9 753	844	2 256	1 282	1 192	577	434	91	23
Detroit-Ann Arbor-Flint, MI	162 363	5.3	29 775	X	113 503	8 672	28 482	19 867	18 860	7 925	7 747	2 089	516
Ann Arbor, MI	17 316	6.8	31 616	29	10 657	724	3 025	1 390	1 289	633	470	92	31
Detroit, MI	134 613	5.4	30 118	40	95 690	7 605	23 610	16 729	15 903	6 620	6 617	1 780	412
Flint, MI	10 433	1.7	23 947	177	7 155	343	1 847	1 749	1 668	671	660	217	73
Dothan, AL	2 931	4.9	21 790	260	2 243	166	511	461	438	183	157	55	6
Dover, DE	2 757	6.0	22 178	242	1 794	144	455	399	375	159	145	29	15
Dubuque, IA	2 153	4.8	24 499	162	1 525	169	500	293	275	141	99	17	6
Duluth-Superior, MN-WI	5 838	5.8	24 676	153	3 468	441	1 176	1 033	986	400	382	82	25
Eau Claire, WI	3 369	6.7	23 431	197	2 173	196	669	479	452	211	171	31	12
El Paso, TX	11 363	5.3	16 359	315	7 421	1 092	1 627	2 071	1 955	549	818	361	17
Elkhart-Goshen, IN	4 409	7.3	25 527	133	3 965	254	841	482	450	228	162	33	8
Elmira, NY	2 077	4.1	22 524	233	1 278	93	368	423	404	167	165	43	6
Enid, OK	1 294	3.4	22 720	225	720	111	265	254	245	100	113	15	2
Erie, PA	6 570	3.6	23 622	192	4 129	492	1 264	1 099	1 045	451	389	109	36
Eugene-Springfield, OR	7 568	5.4	24 151	173	4 217	638	1 829	1 139	1 084	480	373	102	38
Evansville-Henderson, IN-KY	7 569	5.7	26 079	117	5 070	510	1 552	1 080	1 026	476	402	79	16
Fargo-Moorhead, ND-MN	4 223	7.4	25 073	142	2 843	328	827	489	459	192	162	30	5
Fayetteville, NC	6 851	3.5	24 104	175	5 209	315	997	830	788	253	287	118	13
Fayetteville-Springdale-Rogers, AR	6 384	7.3	22 895	213	4 262	598	1 336	804	756	400	222	49	16
Flagstaff, AZ-UT	2 412	6.3	20 050	297	1 422	199	555	335	314	99	115	47	8
Florence, AL	2 887	0.4	21 054	282	1 590	186	551	538	514	250	178	44	12
Florence, SC	2 757	4.8	22 114	248	1 946	150	393	532	510	153	247	69	7
Fort Collins-Loveland, CO	6 380	9.7	27 607	81	3 857	482	1 280	559	519	240	179	34	8
Fort Myers-Cape Coral, FL	10 860	6.0	27 640	79	4 719	744	3 928	1 919	1 849	984	690	79	11
Fort Pierce-Port St. Lucie, FL	8 485	5.5	28 732	57	2 979	406	3 407	1 547	1 494	761	565	84	24
Fort Smith, AR-OK	4 118	5.3	21 257	274	2 712	437	691	692	658	290	239	65	15
Fort Walton Beach, FL	4 155	5.6	24 655	155	2 826	233	1 000	525	497	201	186	35	5
Fort Wayne, IN	12 830	5.2	26 659	104	9 104	766	2 474	1 445	1 355	691	498	88	17
Fresno, CA	17 345	3.8	19 947	298	9 886	1 943	2 934	3 289	3 126	912	1 182	663	171
Gadsden, AL	2 113	3.8	20 328	293	1 127	128	339	440	422	188	163	42	5
Gainesville, FL	4 887	7.0	24 656	154	3 493	207	949	693	657	223	277	80	8
Glens Falls, NY	2 685	4.5	22 109	250	1 495	239	551	491	466	204	181	45	11
Goldsboro, NC	2 205	3.1	19 710	303	1 410	133	374	405	386	142	164	51	6
Grand Forks, ND-MN	2 243	5.5	22 921	212	1 457	160	421	310	293	115	109	21	4
Grand Junction, CO	2 539	7.0	22 491	234	1 405	194	573	410	390	175	144	28	5
Grand Rapids-Muskegon-Holland, MI	27 727	5.3	26 694	101	20 080	1 710	4 937	3 022	2 831	1 384	970	266	91
Great Falls, MT	1 863	4.3	23 721	190	1 075	133	430	299	285	120	100	23	5
Green Bay, WI	6 043	4.9	28 114	70	4 696	337	1 244	571	530	268	177	33	18
Greensboro—Winston-Salem—High Point, NC	31 857	5.8	27 283	89	21 494	2 015	6 222	3 948	3 743	1 749	1 461	298	67
Greenville, NC	2 884	3.7	22 772	220	1 854	149	502	420	398	140	172	58	6
Greenville-Spartanburg-Anderson, SC	21 787	5.7	23 729	188	15 371	1 371	3 605	2 915	2 753	1 377	957	222	34
Harrisburg-Lebanon-Carlisle, PA	17 132	5.4	27 767	74	12 655	986	3 168	2 160	2 040	934	752	132	64

1. Based on the resident population estimated as of July 1 of the year shown.   2. Includes other labor income.

Table C. Metropolitan Areas — Earnings, Social Security, and Housing

Area Name	Earnings, 1998 Total (mil dol)	Farm	Goods-related[1] Total	Manufacturing	Service-related and other[2] Total	Retail trade	Finance, insurance, and real estate	Services	Government	Social Security beneficiaries, December 1998 Number	Rate[3]	Supplemental Security Income recipients, December 1998	Housing units, 1990 Total	Percent change, 1980–1990
	75	76	77	78	79	80	81	82	83	84	85	86	87	88
Columbia, SC	10 423	0.3	16.0	10.1	56.0	9.3	9.8	24.6	27.7	71 312	139	10 522	177 120	22.5
Columbus, GA-AL	4 614	0.1	NA	NA	NA	8.7	NA	22.0	31.3	42 871	158	8 226	101 457	11.6
Columbus, OH	32 654	0.2	NA	14.0	NA	11.8	11.6	26.2	17.5	194 130	132	29 270	547 847	16.2
Corpus Christi, TX	6 098	0.4	22.7	11.4	53.4	9.8	4.8	26.5	23.5	54 148	140	10 854	136 452	19.8
Corvallis, OR	1 452	1.9	NA	32.6	NA	6.6	2.9	22.3	24.2	9 519	122	592	27 024	7.3
Cumberland, MD-WV	1 148	0.1	NA	19.8	NA	11.7	3.9	25.2	22.5	20 949	214	2 456	43 443	3.1
Dallas-Fort Worth, TX	123 116	0.0	NA	15.5	NA	8.7	9.8	29.2	9.2	520 193	108	81 855	1 702 751	40.8
Dallas, TX	93 182	0.0	NA	14.8	NA	8.1	11.0	30.7	8.3	335 096	104	62 155	1 133 568	38.3
Fort Worth-Arlington, TX	29 933	0.1	26.4	17.7	61.5	10.8	6.3	24.6	12.0	185 097	116	19 700	569 183	46.3
Danville, VA	1 368	1.2	NA	37.5	NA	10.5	3.3	20.5	13.8	25 098	232	4 222	46 158	8.2
Davenport-Moline-Rock Island, IA-IL	6 927	0.5	NA	23.5	NA	9.3	4.9	24.4	16.0	62 536	175	5 888	145 587	0.5
Dayton-Springfield, OH	18 671	0.3	NA	27.2	NA	8.2	4.4	25.4	19.4	162 377	171	20 615	385 420	6.3
Daytona Beach, FL	4 584	1.5	NA	9.7	NA	14.3	6.4	35.3	17.5	128 879	274	8 566	196 187	50.5
Decatur, AL	2 059	2.7	NA	D	NA	9.0	3.8	15.4	13.2	24 919	174	4 365	52 631	17.5
Decatur, IL	2 222	0.2	41.8	32.9	49.0	8.7	3.2	20.6	9.1	22 232	195	3 043	50 049	-3.0
Denver-Boulder-Greeley, CO	62 994	0.4	19.7	11.0	66.9	8.2	9.9	29.7	13.1	281 062	119	30 899	861 909	23.4
Boulder-Longmont, CO	7 740	0.1	28.9	23.2	58.0	7.7	4.9	37.0	12.9	26 998	101	2 339	94 621	26.8
Denver, CO	52 821	0.1	17.8	8.8	69.1	8.3	10.7	29.1	13.0	233 500	120	26 222	716 150	24.0
Greeley, CO	2 433	7.7	31.1	20.3	46.3	8.3	7.1	18.7	14.9	20 564	129	2 338	51 138	10.0
Des Moines, IA	10 597	0.4	NA	10.2	NA	8.9	NA	25.1	13.4	63 597	146	5 595	160 948	10.3
Detroit-Ann Arbor-Flint, MI	122 174	0.0	NA	31.7	NA	7.5	6.2	25.6	11.6	843 976	155	122 895	2 031 519	5.0
Ann Arbor, MI	11 381	0.2	NA	28.3	NA	8.6	4.1	21.9	23.3	66 332	121	5 717	188 223	12.8
Detroit, MI	103 295	0.0	36.6	31.7	53.2	7.3	6.6	26.2	10.2	704 667	158	104 533	1 672 488	4.2
Flint, MI	7 498	0.0	NA	36.7	NA	8.9	3.8	23.7	13.0	72 977	167	12 645	170 808	4.8
Dothan, AL	2 409	0.9	NA	19.1	NA	9.6	3.0	20.1	29.1	24 299	180	5 189	52 628	16.6
Dover, DE	1 938	1.4	NA	12.8	NA	10.5	4.1	18.4	39.4	18 937	153	2 490	42 106	19.1
Dubuque, IA	1 694	2.0	36.4	30.5	54.0	8.7	4.2	28.8	7.6	16 279	185	1 294	32 053	1.7
Duluth-Superior, MN-WI	3 909	0.0	22.2	9.6	58.0	10.1	3.5	26.9	19.8	47 671	202	1 317	116 013	0.5
Eau Claire, WI	2 369	0.9	26.6	19.6	55.4	16.7	3.9	23.4	17.0	25 155	175	2 651	53 765	11.6
El Paso, TX	8 513	0.3	19.7	14.6	52.4	9.8	6.2	22.6	27.7	80 732	115	1 653	187 473	26.7
Elkhart-Goshen, IN	4 220	0.3	NA	55.6	NA	6.3	2.9	13.6	6.0	24 921	145	2 059	60 182	16.0
Elmira, NY	1 371	0.2	32.6	26.4	48.6	9.9	3.7	24.1	18.5	19 413	211	2 870	37 290	1.6
Enid, OK	831	2.5	19.6	8.2	54.0	10.0	4.0	23.6	23.9	11 538	203	1 180	26 502	3.6
Erie, PA	4 621	0.4	38.3	32.5	48.0	9.6	5.4	23.8	13.3	50 878	184	7 024	108 585	4.7
Eugene-Springfield, OR	4 855	0.6	27.2	19.2	54.6	12.0	5.6	26.3	17.7	54 223	173	4 804	116 676	5.0
Evansville-Henderson, IN-KY	5 581	0.2	NA	27.2	NA	9.1	5.4	24.7	9.6	54 135	186	5 850	117 896	9.5
Fargo-Moorhead, ND-MN	3 171	1.7	NA	9.4	NA	9.9	8.2	28.9	15.3	22 489	134	1 963	60 953	14.9
Fayetteville, NC	5 523	0.2	NA	9.2	NA	8.2	3.2	12.5	57.6	34 238	120	7 429	98 360	20.9
Fayetteville-Springdale-Rogers, AR	4 860	3.8	NA	22.2	NA	19.8	4.4	D	12.5	49 402	181	4 380	88 793	25.6
Flagstaff, AZ-UT	1 621	0.3	NA	NA	NA	13.3	4.2	27.6	32.6	12 933	107	2 959	46 151	42.2
Florence, AL	1 776	0.9	NA	23.3	NA	11.1	4.0	19.4	23.6	29 863	218	4 378	55 334	7.8
Florence, SC	2 096	0.3	NA	20.0	NA	10.3	8.5	24.9	18.6	20 311	163	6 072	43 209	10.3
Fort Collins-Loveland, CO	4 339	0.5	35.2	25.4	44.7	10.8	5.5	22.1	19.6	28 846	125	1 920	77 811	25.1
Fort Myers-Cape Coral, FL	5 463	0.8	14.6	4.5	66.7	15.0	9.2	31.5	17.9	110 604	282	5 683	189 051	70.3
Fort Pierce-Port St. Lucie, FL	3 384	2.6	NA	6.8	NA	12.6	8.1	32.2	15.9	85 489	290	5 703	128 042	70.9
Fort Smith, AR-OK	3 149	1.0	NA	27.9	NA	9.2	3.8	27.9	10.6	37 720	194	3 435	74 646	15.2
Fort Walton Beach, FL	3 059	0.0	9.3	4.2	45.9	10.4	6.1	24.0	44.8	26 049	154	2 376	62 569	45.2
Fort Wayne, IN	9 870	0.5	NA	33.9	NA	8.2	7.5	20.7	9.2	76 200	158	5 467	181 864	9.4
Fresno, CA	11 829	5.5	NA	9.7	NA	10.0	NA	24.1	20.9	115 601	133	39 184	266 394	22.1
Gadsden, AL	1 255	1.6	NA	28.9	NA	11.3	3.6	25.7	13.4	23 147	223	4 299	41 787	4.8
Gainesville, FL	3 701	0.5	NA	5.2	NA	9.3	6.5	30.4	38.0	27 353	138	4 752	79 022	34.1
Glens Falls, NY	1 734	0.9	NA	20.2	NA	10.8	5.8	27.2	19.5	23 898	196	2 945	55 953	14.8
Goldsboro, NC	1 543	2.7	NA	15.0	NA	9.4	4.4	18.6	32.9	19 495	174	4 655	39 483	12.7
Grand Forks, ND-MN	1 617	4.8	NA	6.7	NA	10.0	3.5	22.1	32.6	14 040	144	1 058	41 360	5.2
Grand Junction, CO	1 599	0.7	19.9	8.3	60.7	13.5	6.0	28.2	18.7	21 705	192	2 130	39 208	20.4
Grand Rapids-Muskegon-Holland, MI	21 791	0.6	NA	34.9	NA	8.8	5.4	20.7	9.7	153 251	148	18 807	357 679	15.6
Great Falls, MT	1 208	0.6	10.0	3.4	60.1	12.6	7.6	28.3	29.3	14 326	181	1 452	33 063	2.7
Green Bay, WI	5 033	0.6	32.7	25.8	56.6	9.1	7.6	23.1	10.1	30 318	141	3 009	74 740	20.0
Greensboro-Winston-Salem—High Point, NC	23 509	0.7	NA	27.2	NA	9.4	NA	24.6	9.9	202 685	174	21 250	444 316	21.0
Greenville, NC	2 003	0.8	NA	18.0	NA	10.6	4.1	19.5	31.1	18 708	148	4 898	43 070	30.6
Greenville-Spartanburg-Anderson, SC	16 742	0.2	NA	29.4	NA	11.0	5.4	21.2	12.3	163 745	178	18 894	335 792	20.6
Harrisburg-Lebanon-Carlisle, PA	13 641	0.4	NA	15.2	NA	8.6	8.3	24.5	21.7	106 852	173	8 524	241 489	11.6

1. Covers mining, construction, and manufacturing. 2. Covers private sector earnings in agricultural services, forestry, and fisheries; transportation and public utilities; wholesale trade; retail trade; finance, insurance, and real estate; and services. 3. Per 1,000 resident population estimated as of July 1 of the year shown.

Table C. Metropolitan Areas — Housing, Labor Force, and Employment

Area Name	Housing units, 1990 (cont'd) Occupied units — Owner-occupied Total	Percent	Median value[1]	Owner cost as a percent of income With a mortgage	Without a mortgage	Renter-occupied Median rent[2]	Rent as percent of income	Substandard units[3] (percent)	Civilian labor force, 1999 Total	Percent change, 1998–1999	Unemployment Total	Rate[4]	Civilian employment, 1990[5] Total	Percent Professional, managerial, and technical	Precision production, craft, and repair
	89	90	91	92	93	94	95	96	97	98	99	100	101	102	103
Columbia, SC	163 223	65.6	72 600	20.3	12.5	427	24.7	3.7	281 316	0.7	6 897	2.5	226 655	33.9	10.4
Columbus, GA-AL	92 695	56.9	56 600	NA	NA	349	NA	5.0	127 448	1.8	6 511	5.1	101 920	26.1	12.3
Columbus, OH	513 498	59.8	72 300	NA	NA	420	NA	2.1	829 857	2.2	21 894	2.6	675 076	32.7	9.1
Corpus Christi, TX	118 516	59.8	53 600	21.0	12.9	364	25.4	10.5	175 887	-0.7	11 493	6.5	144 176	26.8	14.9
Corvallis, OR	26 126	55.1	72 900	20.1	12.2	387	29.4	3.7	40 782	-2.9	1 195	2.9	32 984	41.2	6.8
Cumberland, MD-WV	39 615	71.8	47 400	17.2	12.7	280	25.5	1.7	44 830	-1.3	3 203	7.1	40 718	25.4	12.5
Dallas-Fort Worth, TX	1 508 031	57.6	77 800	NA	NA	444	NA	6.5	2 810 135	2.2	86 846	3.1	2 073 309	32.5	10.6
Dallas, TX	1 001 750	56.0	81 500	NA	NA	453	NA	7.1	1 913 402	2.3	58 894	3.1	1 388 158	33.1	9.9
Fort Worth-Arlington, TX	506 281	60.7	72 000	NA	NA	428	NA	5.3	896 733	2.0	27 952	3.1	685 151	31.4	11.8
Danville, VA	42 325	69.3	47 900	15.8	12.6	277	22.4	5.3	56 612	0.4	3 495	6.2	50 658	18.5	13.1
Davenport-Moline-Rock Island, IA-IL	136 269	67.8	49 800	16.9	12.6	343	24.8	1.7	190 652	2.7	8 415	4.4	161 975	26.5	11.3
Dayton-Springfield, OH	364 300	65.7	65 000	17.5	12.4	398	25.2	2.0	470 979	0.2	18 058	3.8	438 828	31.9	10.8
Daytona Beach, FL	165 296	72.3	71 000	NA	NA	468	NA	2.4	191 509	1.2	5 944	3.1	166 071	27.4	12.7
Decatur, AL	49 209	73.9	57 700	17.3	12.4	330	22.4	3.3	73 170	0.4	3 432	4.7	60 004	23.9	16.9
Decatur, IL	45 996	70.2	45 400	15.5	12.5	339	25.0	1.6	60 905	5.5	2 940	4.8	52 639	26.3	11.7
Denver-Boulder-Greeley, CO	785 276	61.5	88 400	NA	NA	434	NA	2.9	1 401 341	1.2	35 215	2.5	1 038 930	36.3	9.1
Boulder-Longmont, CO	88 402	61.1	102 800	22.3	12.3	501	28.7	2.4	175 656	1.8	4 662	2.7	124 542	45.0	8.1
Denver, CO	649 404	61.6	87 800	22.6	12.5	431	25.5	2.8	1 139 540	1.1	27 470	2.4	851 275	35.9	9.0
Greeley, CO	47 470	61.2	67 500	22.2	13.0	356	26.6	4.2	86 145	1.8	3 083	3.6	63 113	24.3	12.5
Des Moines, IA	153 100	66.9	59 700	19.5	13.2	426	24.7	2.3	253 831	-0.8	4 750	1.9	210 506	30.4	8.6
Detroit-Ann Arbor-Flint, MI	1 916 409	69.2	67 200	NA	NA	454	NA	3.1	2 801 691	1.8	97 618	3.5	2 344 516	30.3	11.8
Ann Arbor, MI	175 050	65.5	87 300	NA	NA	514	NA	2.8	308 122	4.0	6 747	2.2	250 928	36.7	10.3
Detroit, MI	1 580 063	69.5	67 600	18.2	13.6	453	27.3	3.1	2 295 171	1.8	79 903	3.5	1 914 501	30.0	11.8
Flint, MI	161 296	70.4	50 500	16.0	13.3	400	31.3	3.0	198 398	-1.4	10 968	5.5	179 087	24.6	13.6
Dothan, AL	48 418	65.2	51 400	17.3	12.8	313	22.9	3.9	66 502	0.7	2 736	4.1	57 113	24.8	14.1
Dover, DE	39 655	69.2	80 800	NA	NA	421	NA	3.4	68 139	-0.5	2 601	3.8	51 615	25.9	14.0
Dubuque, IA	30 799	71.2	53 600	16.2	12.1	314	23.8	1.7	48 523	-0.3	1 309	2.7	42 025	25.3	10.5
Duluth-Superior, MN-WI	95 275	73.4	41 600	15.6	12.6	292	28.3	2.3	124 098	-1.1	5 033	4.1	101 011	27.8	12.2
Eau Claire, WI	50 359	68.2	50 600	18.7	13.3	345	26.5	2.5	81 695	-1.5	2 465	3.0	64 513	25.6	9.9
El Paso, TX	178 366	58.7	57 300	20.6	12.0	346	26.0	15.4	287 600	-0.7	27 058	9.4	216 790	27.7	11.0
Elkhart-Goshen, IN	56 713	71.8	62 300	17.0	11.6	404	23.3	2.3	96 605	1.7	2 090	2.2	80 588	22.6	13.8
Elmira, NY	35 275	68.3	53 600	17.5	14.6	360	27.3	1.6	44 683	0.1	2 175	4.9	41 063	28.5	11.8
Enid, OK	22 460	69.1	38 100	19.9	12.3	338	24.0	2.0	27 386	-1.6	827	3.0	24 402	24.7	12.5
Erie, PA	101 564	68.6	54 000	17.5	12.7	328	25.5	1.9	140 809	1.3	7 032	5.0	122 635	26.8	12.4
Eugene-Springfield, OR	110 790	60.8	65 800	20.2	13.3	417	28.5	3.7	163 186	0.5	9 291	5.7	129 698	28.3	10.4
Evansville-Henderson, IN-KY	108 663	68.9	54 500	17.4	12.4	337	24.9	2.3	157 453	0.3	5 086	3.2	132 407	26.2	12.6
Fargo-Moorhead, ND-MN	57 771	58.9	64 500	20.2	12.4	346	26.3	2.1	101 161	-2.1	1 996	2.0	79 205	29.6	8.5
Fayetteville, NC	91 500	57.7	63 500	23.1	13.9	405	26.1	4.3	115 622	2.8	4 409	3.8	96 204	26.5	11.8
Fayetteville-Springdale-Rogers, AR	80 927	66.9	57 600	NA	NA	356	NA	3.6	143 298	3.0	3 409	2.4	99 938	24.6	12.5
Flagstaff, AZ-UT	31 642	61.4	NA	NA	NA	NA	NA	18.6	61 793	3.1	4 110	6.7	43 951	28.2	11.8
Florence, AL	51 001	74.1	49 700	18.1	12.4	295	25.4	2.5	66 853	-2.9	4 446	6.7	56 819	23.1	16.2
Florence, SC	40 217	70.5	54 900	18.6	13.7	341	25.0	6.6	63 202	-1.2	3 465	5.5	51 984	24.7	13.4
Fort Collins-Loveland, CO	70 472	62.9	83 900	22.0	12.5	419	28.4	2.4	140 955	0.1	4 336	3.1	94 102	36.6	10.4
Fort Myers-Cape Coral, FL	140 124	72.1	84 300	22.6	11.8	503	26.2	3.0	179 970	3.2	4 598	2.6	144 465	25.7	13.3
Fort Pierce-Port St. Lucie, FL	101 196	74.0	84 100	21.8	11.7	516	26.4	3.7	125 576	3.4	9 385	7.5	102 436	25.4	14.5
Fort Smith, AR-OK	66 884	69.4	45 200	19.0	12.8	308	24.4	4.3	96 837	1.5	3 589	3.7	77 931	21.9	14.2
Fort Walton Beach, FL	53 313	62.2	70 600	21.6	11.5	412	25.6	2.8	80 527	0.5	2 636	3.3	58 554	31.7	11.4
Fort Wayne, IN	168 806	73.2	57 000	NA	NA	377	NA	2.3	263 192	-0.8	7 542	2.9	228 442	26.3	12.6
Fresno, CA	249 303	55.5	83 900	NA	NA	432	NA	13.5	432 361	0.9	57 227	13.2	303 089	26.6	10.0
Gadsden, AL	38 675	74.0	42 700	17.8	12.9	280	24.0	2.5	49 625	-0.9	3 466	7.0	40 902	20.8	14.4
Gainesville, FL	71 258	54.1	66 000	NA	NA	395	NA	4.7	105 303	2.6	2 248	2.1	85 785	41.8	7.6
Glens Falls, NY	42 815	71.4	81 000	20.5	13.7	432	27.2	2.1	59 558	-1.0	2 945	4.9	52 870	26.0	12.5
Goldsboro, NC	36 889	62.7	58 000	NA	NA	321	NA	4.1	47 881	0.7	1 943	4.1	44 564	23.2	13.1
Grand Forks, ND-MN	37 324	57.1	57 100	NA	NA	352	NA	2.2	51 709	-3.5	1 529	3.0	45 333	29.1	8.8
Grand Junction, CO	36 250	64.9	62 700	21.3	12.2	333	25.4	2.7	58 927	0.4	2 208	3.7	41 219	28.1	11.5
Grand Rapids-Muskegon-Holland, MI	333 911	73.6	65 700	NA	NA	420	NA	2.5	614 660	3.2	19 758	3.2	451 193	25.9	12.4
Great Falls, MT	30 133	63.7	60 200	20.5	11.9	317	25.7	2.5	38 017	-1.4	2 027	5.3	31 669	27.9	10.2
Green Bay, WI	72 280	65.6	62 600	20.3	13.0	372	23.9	2.1	133 352	1.1	3 068	2.3	99 142	26.6	11.2
Greensboro—Winston-Salem—High Point, NC	414 793	67.8	70 700	NA	NA	390	NA	2.6	643 694	1.8	15 216	2.4	559 047	26.0	13.1
Greenville, NC	40 491	58.1	65 300	NA	NA	349	NA	5.4	64 785	2.2	2 897	4.5	53 492	30.0	10.5
Greenville-Spartanburg-Anderson, SC	312 740	70.0	58 700	NA	NA	358	NA	3.2	493 074	-0.4	16 237	3.3	410 204	25.8	13.8
Harrisburg-Lebanon-Carlisle, PA	226 353	68.8	75 400	19.2	12.0	418	23.3	1.9	348 272	-0.4	11 466	3.3	298 729	28.8	10.8

1. Specified owner-occupied units. 2. Specified renter-occupied units. 3. Overcrowded or lacking complete plumbing facilities. 4. Percent of civilian labor force. 5. Persons 16 years and older.

Table C. Metropolitan Areas — Nonfarm Employment and Agriculture

Area Name	Private nonfarm establishments, employment and payroll, 1998									Agriculture, 1997			
		Employment						Annual payroll		Farms			Farm operators
											Percent with—		
	Number of establishments	Total	Health Care and Social Assistance	Manufacturing	Retail trade	Finance and Insurance	Professional Scientific and Technical Services	Total (mil dol)	Average per employee (dollars)	Number	Less than 50 acres	500 acres and over	Whose principal occupation is farming (percent)
	104	105	106	107	108	109	110	111	112	113	114	115	116
Columbia, SC	13 839	233 393	30 037	24 440	33 033	18 805	14 293	5 981	25 626	1 149	43.6	4.6	41.3
Columbus, GA-AL	5 683	101 005	10 519	21 676	14 505	6 546	2 427	2 507	24 821	505	31.1	16.0	36.8
Columbus, OH	36 795	724 046	82 176	80 554	98 394	71 322	38 301	21 802	30 111	4 646	36.0	13.9	48.9
Corpus Christi, TX	8 963	128 979	23 601	11 420	18 731	4 296	5 311	3 080	23 880	1 065	30.3	34.7	53.1
Corvallis, OR	1 968	29 170	3 684	9 055	3 321	545	1 574	922	31 608	726	65.4	7.4	41.5
Cumberland, MD-WV	2 314	29 036	5 486	5 208	5 559	1 086	734	654	22 524	582	22.0	10.0	40.4
Dallas-Fort Worth, TX	124 382	2 385 263	214 019	326 035	260 173	134 056	145 781	81 914	34 342	17 707	46.1	8.1	33.5
Dallas, TX	87 356	1 747 902	147 543	224 638	174 022	109 582	119 557	63 988	36 608	11 497	43.7	8.3	33.7
Fort Worth-Arlington, TX	37 026	637 361	66 476	101 397	86 151	24 474	26 224	17 926	28 125	6 210	50.5	7.7	33.3
Danville, VA	2 502	37 618	4 489	13 551	5 910	1 138	861	865	22 994	1 235	20.4	10.3	50.0
Davenport-Moline-Rock Island, IA-IL	9 360	159 134	18 158	28 441	20 769	6 412	5 212	4 453	27 983	2 761	25.0	21.1	60.2
Dayton-Springfield, OH	21 373	414 619	56 027	87 403	56 137	14 590	20 932	11 915	28 737	3 178	44.0	11.5	43.3
Daytona Beach, FL	11 668	134 415	21 760	11 762	24 649	4 378	5 221	2 745	20 422	1 001	69.9	6.2	50.0
Decatur, AL	3 226	51 824	5 139	14 697	7 177	1 794	1 145	1 350	26 050	2 501	40.9	4.4	31.6
Decatur, IL	2 802	54 225	6 854	10 621	7 048	0	1 105	1 579	29 119	665	24.7	36.7	62.1
Denver-Boulder-Greeley, CO	77 239	1 158 955	111 589	116 265	139 308	74 977	87 686	39 253	33 869	5 537	37.9	21.5	50.6
Boulder-Longmont, CO	10 464	136 146	12 030	26 368	17 624	3 645	17 000	4 827	35 455	657	60.4	6.7	42.0
Denver, CO	63 068	969 914	93 993	78 637	114 549	67 628	69 473	33 005	34 029	1 921	44.5	21.7	43.2
Greeley, CO	3 707	52 895	5 566	11 260	7 135	3 704	1 213	1 421	26 865	2 959	28.6	24.6	57.4
Des Moines, IA	12 900	245 713	30 413	22 575	32 144	37 192	12 001	7 285	29 648	2 932	30.2	18.0	48.0
Detroit-Ann Arbor-Flint, MI	127 218	2 299 686	280 083	423 078	295 425	104 001	141 651	83 278	36 213	8 168	43.2	8.6	45.1
Ann Arbor, MI	13 845	222 798	35 717	49 727	30 613	6 507	13 547	7 450	33 438	2 984	38.1	11.0	45.2
Detroit, MI	104 153	1 927 121	222 241	341 612	239 318	92 360	122 985	71 367	37 033	4 388	45.6	7.3	45.2
Flint, MI	9 220	149 767	22 125	31 739	25 494	5 134	5 119	4 461	29 786	796	49.5	6.4	44.5
Dothan, AL	3 698	56 966	8 635	11 011	9 340	1 486	1 209	1 356	23 804	1 112	28.3	15.9	45.7
Dover, DE	2 966	42 453	5 809	7 256	7 871	2 660	1 387	964	22 707	767	40.3	12.0	59.8
Dubuque, IA	2 599	47 588	6 439	11 250	6 668	1 527	952	1 184	24 880	1 579	17.9	7.3	64.1
Duluth-Superior, MN-WI	6 657	89 666	18 404	6 647	14 828	3 296	2 922	2 177	24 279	980	18.3	9.3	33.7
Eau Claire, WI	3 792	58 683	10 159	10 193	10 427	2 222	1 938	1 343	22 886	2 398	13.1	8.7	66.0
El Paso, TX	12 409	198 571	26 446	37 803	28 757	5 682	5 964	4 358	21 947	415	67.7	11.6	40.7
Elkhart-Goshen, IN	5 030	109 830	7 545	57 042	11 050	1 729	1 675	3 033	27 615	1 335	45.9	6.2	46.7
Elmira, NY	1 933	36 456	6 495	9 262	6 652	908	919	895	24 550	313	23.3	8.0	39.0
Enid, OK	1 669	20 739	3 850	1 396	3 495	686	1 563	433	20 879	1 069	13.5	35.3	55.1
Erie, PA	6 859	116 678	17 158	33 358	16 055	4 714	2 845	3 036	26 020	1 123	37.1	4.2	55.8
Eugene-Springfield, OR	9 726	114 500	14 943	19 059	18 276	4 386	5 794	2 882	25 170	2 104	65.3	4.2	37.2
Evansville-Henderson, IN-KY	7 996	143 201	20 372	28 853	19 114	4 982	4 765	3 847	26 864	1 590	32.1	19.6	50.4
Fargo-Moorhead, ND-MN	5 191	85 860	12 264	8 005	13 240	5 204	2 952	2 067	24 074	1 806	12.3	51.0	75.8
Fayetteville, NC	5 312	86 766	13 542	13 194	15 400	2 993	2 874	1 902	21 921	433	37.9	12.9	43.0
Fayetteville-Springdale-Rogers, AR	7 432	123 754	12 671	28 382	15 694	3 581	3 677	3 097	25 025	4 799	41.1	4.4	45.2
Flagstaff, AZ-UT	3 509	38 488	4 515	2 612	7 470	669	1 025	807	20 968	342	30.4	37.4	44.4
Florence, AL	3 465	49 097	6 397	12 071	8 464	1 466	1 192	1 034	21 060	1 912	39.6	6.7	31.2
Florence, SC	3 281	54 875	9 886	10 924	8 990	4 349	1 382	1 310	23 872	615	33.3	15.4	52.7
Fort Collins-Loveland, CO	7 586	87 930	9 003	14 121	14 193	2 752	5 014	2 235	25 418	1 298	50.5	13.0	39.3
Fort Myers-Cape Coral, FL	11 616	134 701	16 880	5 473	26 249	4 494	8 196	3 144	23 341	509	70.9	10.0	40.3
Fort Pierce-Port St. Lucie, FL	7 933	85 342	14 586	5 612	16 300	3 207	4 208	2 002	23 459	805	53.9	15.8	48.6
Fort Smith, AR-OK	4 952	89 985	12 215	26 699	11 230	2 219	2 777	2 036	22 626	2 655	32.8	7.5	38.5
Fort Walton Beach, FL	4 779	55 450	7 054	3 634	10 844	2 112	3 343	1 153	20 794	342	37.1	6.4	36.5
Fort Wayne, IN	12 778	250 226	27 575	71 295	30 671	11 962	8 714	7 003	27 987	5 416	33.9	12.1	42.5
Fresno, CA	16 941	228 001	31 663	31 242	33 866	9 920	8 982	5 698	24 991	8 265	55.8	11.7	61.5
Gadsden, AL	2 197	33 001	5 097	8 914	4 886	1 017	656	764	23 151	904	47.3	3.1	31.9
Gainesville, FL	5 124	75 584	16 212	5 370	13 469	2 495	4 385	1 771	23 431	1 086	57.9	6.2	40.8
Glens Falls, NY	3 310	41 344	6 051	7 923	7 077	1 655	1 546	1 044	25 252	796	19.5	14.1	63.1
Goldsboro, NC	2 338	36 626	6 382	9 179	6 195	1 256	711	804	21 952	827	39.5	13.1	62.8
Grand Forks, ND-MN	2 586	36 323	7 388	3 189	6 925	1 365	1 265	766	21 089	2 134	8.4	48.6	68.6
Grand Junction, CO	3 528	39 408	6 474	3 884	6 634	1 225	1 901	937	23 777	1 489	64.1	8.3	44.3
Grand Rapids-Muskegon-Holland, MI	26 511	515 774	54 015	153 902	63 192	17 929	17 388	15 555	30 159	4 175	43.9	6.9	47.3
Great Falls, MT	2 522	26 152	5 017	944	5 091	1 613	1 129	534	20 419	903	20.3	44.3	57.5
Green Bay, WI	6 050	121 799	13 473	24 703	15 578	9 556	3 852	3 543	29 089	1 059	31.4	6.2	62.5
Greensboro—Winston-Salem—High Point, NC	32 256	598 402	62 443	149 251	73 095	35 706	20 080	16 537	27 635	6 934	41.0	3.5	45.6
Greenville, NC	3 051	50 143	9 453	8 980	8 409	1 808	1 507	1 175	23 433	474	26.8	23.0	67.1
Greenville-Spartanburg-Anderson, SC	24 418	466 291	37 353	118 861	55 076	14 183	17 015	12 819	27 491	4 043	44.6	3.3	32.5
Harrisburg-Lebanon-Carlisle, PA	15 149	296 313	45 531	38 722	37 303	21 759	11 898	8 102	27 343	3 098	31.6	4.3	57.7

Table C. Metropolitan Areas — **Agriculture, Land, and Water**

Area Name	Land in farms Acreage (1,000)	Percent change, 1992–1997	Acres Average size of farm	Total irrigated (1,000)	Total cropland (1,000)	Value of land and buildings Average per farm ($1,000)	Average per acre (dollars)	Value of machinery and equipment Average per farm ($1,000)	Value of products sold Total (mil dol)	Average per farm (dollars)	Percent from — Crops	Livestock and poultry products	Percent of farms with sales of — $10,000 or more	$100,000 or more	Percent of land owned by Fed. Gov. 1997	Water consumption 1995 (mil gal/day)
	117	118	119	120	121	122	123	124	125	126	127	128	129	130	131	132
Columbia, SC	150	0.7	131	7	77	269	2 381	35	119	103 794	23.0	77.0	31.7	12.7	7.2	683.8
Columbus, GA-AL	156	1.0	308	2	48	399	1 335	31	11	21 513	D	D	23.8	4.6	17.7	97.7
Columbus, OH	1 204	-0.7	259	1	1 038	612	2 392	65	435	93 580	68.0	32.0	53.6	18.7	0.6	251.8
Corpus Christi, TX	844	5.3	792	4	616	679	856	93	141	132 008	86.0	14.0	50.2	27.0	0.2	167.3
Corvallis, OR	131	9.9	180	20	92	413	2 527	55	70	96 697	87.3	12.7	31.5	11.3	17.6	80.9
Cumberland, MD-WV	122	7.6	209	0	47	222	1 167	25	12	20 093	16.0	84.0	22.5	3.8	1.9	50.3
Dallas-Fort Worth, TX	3 585	3.4	202	14	1 795	338	1 668	28	368	20 764	38.0	62.0	21.8	3.1	0.9	5 019.9
Dallas, TX	2 363	1.6	206	6	1 301	330	1 597	30	237	20 578	44.0	56.0	22.1	3.2	1.0	1 478.6
Fort Worth-Arlington, TX	1 222	7.3	197	8	493	352	1 806	24	131	21 108	28.0	72.0	21.3	3.1	0.7	3 541.2
Danville, VA	267	-10.1	216	7	124	280	1 273	47	59	47 663	75.0	25.0	43.2	13.0	0.0	29.5
Davenport-Moline-Rock Island, IA-IL	852	-1.3	309	10	754	705	2 324	89	324	117 332	62.0	38.0	72.6	33.2	0.9	1 034.8
Dayton-Springfield, OH	649	-3.3	204	4	577	529	2 602	62	232	73 093	83.0	17.0	53.9	17.4	0.9	264.6
Daytona Beach, FL	199	4.9	199	18	43	519	2 837	35	148	148 047	95.0	5.0	47.0	19.3	2.3	170.8
Decatur, AL	364	10.5	145	2	234	264	1 811	28	158	63 213	13.0	87.0	25.8	9.1	13.1	202.3
Decatur, IL	323	3.8	486	D	303	1 354	2 803	125	106	158 998	96.0	4.0	74.3	44.1	0.0	46.6
Denver-Boulder-Greeley, CO	3 350	NA	605	470	D	D	D	74	1 480	267 370	24.0	76.0	49.3	17.2	11.9	1 802.2
Boulder-Longmont, CO	128	-18.4	195	39	59	534	2 054	55	44	66 470	64.0	36.0	34.7	7.8	35.0	173.6
Denver, CO	1 309	D	681	38	D	D	D	48	150	78 146	75.0	25.0	38.2	10.5	11.4	466.7
Greeley, CO	1 914	-8.3	647	393	882	567	807	95	1 287	434 821	16.0	84.0	59.8	23.7	8.1	1 161.9
Des Moines, IA	849	0.6	290	1	708	573	2 005	67	248	84 740	71.0	29.0	56.6	21.1	2.0	70.2
Detroit-Ann Arbor-Flint, MI	1 437	-5.1	176	21	1 234	432	2 467	63	505	61 782	78.0	22.0	46.8	13.2	0.1	5 854.0
Ann Arbor, MI	615	-4.5	206	9	531	456	2 166	66	188	62 944	70.0	30.0	49.7	15.4	0.0	103.8
Detroit, MI	704	-4.1	160	11	604	440	2 790	64	289	65 819	84.0	16.0	46.8	12.7	0.1	5 695.8
Flint, MI	118	-13.9	148	1	99	301	2 106	52	28	35 170	73.0	27.0	36.2	7.8	0.0	54.5
Dothan, AL	329	1.0	296	11	200	349	1 143	60	91	81 501	55.0	45.0	45.3	15.2	6.1	133.8
Dover, DE	195	-1.2	254	21	168	647	2 556	74	154	200 379	41.0	59.0	64.4	29.9	3.7	33.9
Dubuque, IA	336	-2.2	213	0	258	336	1 623	69	172	108 709	18.0	82.0	76.0	34.6	0.4	81.5
Duluth-Superior, MN-WI	226	1.0	231	D	121	147	625	25	15	15 682	40.0	60.0	23.2	3.2	16.9	210.3
Eau Claire, WI	564	-2.2	235	4	371	197	825	60	176	73 589	20.0	80.0	63.3	23.7	0.0	29.3
El Paso, TX	244	D	587	41	47	404	720	72	77	184 754	48.0	52.0	37.6	19.5	13.7	392.6
Elkhart-Goshen, IN	183	-4.8	137	24	160	376	2 738	48	124	92 912	28.0	72.0	64.6	24.7	0.0	43.4
Elmira, NY	59	0.5	189	0	36	186	983	41	13	41 208	31.0	69.0	33.9	12.1	0.0	18.2
Enid, OK	615	-7.1	575	0	459	384	693	59	83	77 621	47.0	53.0	66.5	19.0	0.3	6.1
Erie, PA	168	-0.2	149	1	114	290	1 892	63	69	61 366	63.0	37.0	51.0	14.4	0.0	97.2
Eugene-Springfield, OR	224	-7.6	106	23	120	336	3 428	34	87	41 431	62.0	38.0	24.3	6.7	53.5	350.1
Evansville-Henderson, IN-KY	562	-5.7	354	D	491	613	1 761	93	154	97 143	82.0	18.0	58.4	24.7	0.4	875.7
Fargo-Moorhead, ND-MN	1 649	0.7	913	12	1 542	807	900	146	307	169 826	87.0	13.0	76.0	45.8	0.6	26.7
Fayetteville, NC	103	4.2	238	2	57	461	2 205	66	68	156 314	33.0	67.0	45.7	18.9	10.4	35.7
Fayetteville-Springdale-Rogers, AR	631	-2.3	132	2	343	302	2 380	33	697	145 227	1.0	99.0	39.9	19.5	3.8	363.7
Flagstaff, AZ-UT	6 385	3.0	18 669	10	D	2 831	152	33	14	40 693	5.0	95.0	34.8	8.5	46.3	57.4
Florence, AL	327	-3.8	171	3	203	249	1 443	29	62	32 254	42.0	58.0	22.3	6.6	3.3	107.2
Florence, SC	169	-13.5	274	2	114	337	1 230	67	69	112 367	89.0	11.0	53.2	21.5	0.0	50.0
Fort Collins-Loveland, CO	542	0.4	418	78	127	657	1 602	49	100	77 414	38.0	62.0	37.1	10.2	46.9	270.2
Fort Myers-Cape Coral, FL	129	20.6	253	26	34	724	2 664	38	116	228 678	98.0	2.0	39.9	10.6	0.6	134.0
Fort Pierce-Port St. Lucie, FL	411	-16.3	511	201	211	1 348	2 748	77	318	395 230	88.0	12.0	58.9	23.6	0.1	479.9
Fort Smith, AR-OK	547	14.9	206	6	237	228	1 142	29	136	51 215	13.0	87.0	28.7	7.7	14.8	62.3
Fort Walton Beach, FL	51	-10.8	149	0	21	249	1 608	25	9	25 471	61.0	39.0	21.3	3.8	38.8	29.9
Fort Wayne, IN	1 193	0.6	220	3	1 063	458	2 188	58	420	77 504	62.0	38.0	58.8	20.0	0.9	83.0
Fresno, CA	2 363	0.0	305	1 462	1 584	1 009	3 386	77	3 400	411 373	77.0	23.0	72.2	36.7	37.8	4 528.7
Gadsden, AL	95	10.4	105	0	47	207	2 253	28	55	60 779	6.0	94.0	25.3	9.4	0.0	264.5
Gainesville, FL	198	3.8	182	8	75	361	2 209	22	50	46 276	62.0	38.0	32.5	7.7	0.0	48.3
Glens Falls, NY	204	-3.7	256	1	125	318	1 263	61	80	100 156	14.0	86.0	58.7	26.6	0.0	24.3
Goldsboro, NC	229	27.5	277	2	147	542	2 025	83	337	407 605	21.0	79.0	71.0	41.8	0.8	32.0
Grand Forks, ND-MN	1 827	-0.8	856	22	1 656	662	780	151	323	151 481	92.0	8.0	67.4	37.7	1.1	33.9
Grand Junction, CO	417	-0.8	280	88	92	487	2 045	30	50	33 882	40.0	60.0	33.2	5.9	72.1	972.9
Grand Rapids-Muskegon-Holland, MI	667	-2.9	160	42	543	387	2 416	75	652	156 220	54.0	46.0	52.3	22.1	1.0	1 196.3
Great Falls, MT	1 441	1.2	1 596	33	508	620	373	61	67	73 899	48.0	52.0	55.6	16.1	12.5	153.2
Green Bay, WI	196	-4.4	185	0	168	333	1 770	74	128	121 309	14.0	86.0	66.8	31.6	0.0	496.5
Greensboro—Winston-Salem—High Point, NC	800	3.0	115	11	443	307	2 731	35	370	53 405	37.0	63.0	37.7	12.4	0.4	1 140.2
Greenville, NC	193	-0.3	408	2	144	767	1 865	112	196	413 795	50.0	50.0	76.8	49.6	0.8	26.0
Greenville-Spartanburg-Anderson, SC	455	2.2	113	D	248	277	2 730	27	94	23 316	50.0	50.0	17.3	2.6	0.4	351.0
Harrisburg-Lebanon-Carlisle, PA	455	3.2	147	3	367	446	3 070	59	368	118 752	16.0	84.0	61.9	28.6	0.6	205.5

Table C. Metropolitan Areas — Residential Construction, Wholesale and Retail Trade, and Real Estate

Area Name	Value of Residential Construction Authorized by Building Permits, 1999		Wholesale Trade, 1997				Retail Trade[1], 1997				Real Estate and Rental and Leasing, 1997			
	New Construction ($1,000)	Number of Housing Units	Number of Establishments	Number of Employees	Sales (mil dol)	Annual Payroll (mil dol)	Number of Establishments	Number of Employees	Sales (mil dol)	Annual Payroll (mil dol)	Number of Establishments	Number of Employees	Receipts (mil dol)	Annual Payroll (mil dol)
	133	134	135	136	137	138	139	140	141	142	143	144	145	146
Columbia, SC	434 241	5 500	841	12 095	5 272.0	403.7	2 361	32 643	5 279.2	507.3	533	3 298	396.8	74.9
Columbus, GA-AL	150 572	1 549	241	3 382	1 422.4	104.0	1 078	13 800	2 216.0	213.3	271	1 343	158.2	29.1
Columbus, OH	1 533 516	15 847	2 340	41 517	24 477.8	1 572.9	5 710	95 130	16 922.7	1 657.9	1 588	11 553	1 207.6	259.5
Corpus Christi, TX	114 264	1 250	535	5 291	1 909.0	160.7	1 486	19 006	3 132.2	295.5	434	2 676	345.0	64.8
Corvallis, OR	45 900	401	63	681	112.6	15.9	294	3 175	473.9	53.2	111	379	38.9	5.5
Cumberland, MD-WV	45 350	392	89	1 014	291.6	26.8	488	5 701	806.2	76.1	68	232	26.3	3.7
Dallas-Fort Worth, TX	5 431 858	47 688	10 129	156 656	134 407.6	6 404.3	17 277	248 035	49 966.2	4 751.2	5 928	43 562	6 076.9	1 242.8
Dallas, TX	4 127 354	35 690	7 539	121 860	111 779.3	5 149.0	11 509	167 923	34 212.6	3 283.0	4 373	34 656	4 889.0	1 037.6
Fort Worth-Arlington, TX	1 304 505	11 998	2 590	34 796	22 628.3	1 255.3	5 768	80 112	15 753.6	1 468.2	1 555	8 906	1 187.8	205.3
Danville, VA	30 938	313	101	D	D	D	547	5 957	886.0	84.8	82	333	29.2	5.3
Davenport-Moline-Rock Island, IA-IL	138 578	1 176	709	9 840	5 930.7	319.9	1 587	22 573	3 630.9	366.5	329	2 157	230.8	48.2
Dayton-Springfield, OH	408 337	3 699	1 232	17 765	13 286.9	660.9	3 606	57 315	8 873.7	855.1	801	4 371	511.6	92.8
Daytona Beach, FL	483 005	5 265	527	4 586	1 724.3	113.3	1 984	24 859	4 131.8	382.7	599	3 040	305.9	53.3
Decatur, AL	40 498	440	199	2 179	1 337.0	61.2	683	7 147	1 253.1	105.2	104	465	41.4	8.3
Decatur, IL	38 489	265	158	1 815	3 249.3	57.4	506	6 967	1 129.6	110.4	98	515	39.9	8.5
Denver-Boulder-Greeley, CO	3 438 638	29 384	5 324	69 748	54 606.9	2 762.2	9 631	135 043	25 211.0	2 592.2	3 906	25 501	3 610.1	648.6
Boulder-Longmont, CO	368 516	2 992	539	5 558	3 906.0	234.9	1 275	17 269	2 915.0	309.9	486	2 189	287.9	49.2
Denver, CO	2 641 990	22 835	4 538	61 361	49 366.4	2 442.4	7 851	111 579	21 140.5	2 173.1	3 266	22 736	3 256.7	590.0
Greeley, CO	428 133	3 557	247	2 829	1 334.6	84.9	505	6 195	1 155.5	109.2	154	576	65.4	9.5
Des Moines, IA	446 873	3 636	1 008	14 715	9 828.3	507.0	1 927	30 808	4 919.6	503.3	488	3 500	591.5	85.4
Detroit-Ann Arbor-Flint, MI	3 432 605	27 537	8 413	114 303	121 286.3	5 073.5	20 340	288 550	54 531.5	5 178.0	4 743	32 001	4 486.0	783.5
Ann Arbor, MI	642 903	5 361	773	7 322	4 832.0	278.2	2 055	29 758	5 506.6	527.0	512	2 856	271.5	59.7
Detroit, MI	2 505 317	19 370	7 218	101 097	114 554.9	4 578.2	16 476	233 423	44 503.7	4 241.7	3 881	27 532	4 020.9	695.1
Flint, MI	284 384	2 806	422	5 884	1 899.4	217.2	1 809	25 369	4 521.3	409.3	350	1 613	193.6	28.7
Dothan, AL	30 962	534	243	2 686	823.6	62.9	838	9 203	1 490.0	142.7	127	496	43.4	8.6
Dover, DE	81 008	866	110	D	D	D	594	7 864	1 325.4	128.3	128	506	49.4	8.0
Dubuque, IA	42 725	320	157	1 845	926.5	50.8	525	6 583	935.5	100.2	89	341	32.8	4.9
Duluth-Superior, MN-WI	90 515	996	339	3 486	2 263.0	110.8	1 248	14 460	2 226.1	217.3	215	1 064	95.3	16.6
Eau Claire, WI	113 500	1 098	184	2 117	851.0	63.9	664	9 880	1 517.4	140.6	126	543	50.8	7.8
El Paso, TX	204 548	4 196	1 000	11 129	6 089.3	309.6	2 134	28 986	4 698.9	430.5	550	2 458	285.3	48.1
Elkhart-Goshen, IN	124 346	1 127	382	5 031	2 246.1	160.0	751	10 866	1 973.6	179.6	171	884	78.1	13.9
Elmira, NY	22 788	296	107	1 667	447.2	49.2	412	5 963	875.9	82.9	66	345	47.9	7.4
Enid, OK	13 126	85	122	1 967	570.1	48.9	302	3 423	501.7	47.8	70	287	24.6	4.8
Erie, PA	84 051	775	334	4 069	1 277.8	131.9	1 225	16 323	2 562.1	239.0	180	834	75.5	13.8
Eugene-Springfield, OR	195 895	1 830	535	6 144	2 498.6	179.6	1 462	18 145	3 322.6	328.3	463	2 042	226.5	35.0
Evansville-Henderson, IN-KY	172 544	1 716	501	6 301	5 940.7	188.2	1 405	19 403	3 075.6	300.5	306	1 842	202.7	32.8
Fargo-Moorhead, ND-MN	113 696	1 387	433	6 710	3 166.1	200.4	765	12 525	2 127.2	199.1	201	1 194	121.7	18.6
Fayetteville, NC	88 852	1 023	205	2 454	845.3	66.5	1 061	14 929	2 563.3	239.3	272	1 182	137.5	23.4
Fayetteville-Springdale-Rogers, AR	244 175	2 905	445	5 089	9 295.6	154.0	1 310	15 772	2 460.5	234.8	322	1 210	141.8	19.6
Flagstaff, AZ-UT	119 446	1 056	117	1 090	557.8	25.4	695	7 525	1 116.2	116.1	184	680	77.3	13.5
Florence, AL	26 624	313	209	3 132	773.2	75.7	735	8 461	1 308.3	119.9	121	434	41.9	7.5
Florence, SC	51 265	648	206	2 847	1 017.6	81.6	759	8 935	1 467.3	138.4	114	387	40.7	7.3
Fort Collins-Loveland, CO	403 100	3 591	311	2 630	805.6	75.9	1 201	13 810	2 440.5	234.2	360	1 497	190.0	27.8
Fort Myers-Cape Coral, FL	1 021 861	8 816	586	4 593	1 450.3	135.3	1 924	25 417	4 367.0	430.5	642	3 328	461.1	72.2
Fort Pierce-Port St. Lucie, FL	445 289	3 347	372	2 957	1 005.3	77.5	1 322	16 069	2 841.3	272.5	389	1 638	204.5	39.8
Fort Smith, AR-OK	70 101	733	318	2 584	926.2	67.4	989	11 707	1 848.1	167.9	189	828	93.6	14.6
Fort Walton Beach, FL	187 696	1 807	139	959	248.3	23.9	931	11 322	1 754.9	165.7	280	1 582	140.3	29.0
Fort Wayne, IN	498 302	3 900	899	14 048	7 880.4	437.8	2 037	30 121	4 868.8	471.0	455	2 403	302.9	50.4
Fresno, CA	412 027	3 578	1 058	13 627	6 111.0	434.3	2 805	33 404	6 102.0	601.9	653	3 713	398.9	71.1
Gadsden, AL	16 091	195	135	D	D	D	452	4 935	737.8	65.9	68	273	23.9	4.4
Gainesville, FL	181 650	2 728	224	1 824	738.0	54.5	923	12 726	1 934.5	186.2	279	1 630	155.2	28.2
Glens Falls, NY	57 528	549	137	D	D	D	675	6 929	1 115.8	109.9	87	341	45.3	6.1
Goldsboro, NC	39 715	555	151	2 217	891.1	59.4	523	6 169	1 033.0	88.1	81	263	21.0	4.5
Grand Forks, ND-MN	28 765	310	187	1 926	758.7	51.4	503	6 973	1 146.4	101.1	85	590	37.2	7.9
Grand Junction, CO	127 412	1 362	198	1 461	531.1	42.8	600	6 409	1 152.7	115.0	133	658	62.6	11.6
Grand Rapids-Muskegon-Holland, MI	835 151	7 228	1 902	34 712	19 356.4	1 241.3	3 978	63 004	10 419.9	1 042.9	911	5 531	666.6	115.3
Great Falls, MT	11 819	101	141	1 231	1 114.8	32.6	427	5 049	803.0	81.8	100	395	30.4	4.6
Green Bay, WI	226 633	1 930	461	6 480	2 848.1	212.1	950	14 976	2 569.1	239.7	197	1 048	116.3	18.7
Greensboro—Winston-Salem—High Point, NC	994 975	10 487	2 447	34 363	19 221.1	1 285.8	5 511	70 814	12 362.1	1 198.9	1 171	6 626	848.5	140.6
Greenville, NC	104 762	1 189	181	2 153	1 246.8	66.4	643	7 956	1 384.8	124.8	121	495	51.4	7.9
Greenville-Spartanburg-Anderson, SC	699 333	8 290	1 728	21 306	15 790.1	742.7	4 316	53 794	9 178.9	806.8	814	3 818	464.2	78.2
Harrisburg-Lebanon-Carlisle, PA	308 033	3 186	736	15 165	11 751.0	489.4	2 711	38 661	6 706.7	638.6	439	3 066	425.7	69.5

1. Establishments with payroll.

Area Name	Professional, Scientific, and Technical Services[1], 1997				Manufacturing, 1997				Accommodation and Foodservices, 1997			
	Number of Establishments	Number of Employees	Sales (mil dol)	Annual Payroll (mil dol)	Number of Establishments	Number of Employees	Sales (mil dol)	Annual Payroll (mil dol)	Number of Establishments	Number of Employees	Sales (mil dol)	Annual Payroll (mil dol)
	147	148	149	150	151	152	153	154	155	156	157	158
Columbia, SC	1 243	9 455	1 059.8	370.9	460	23 522	5 302	785	1 033	21 176	621.9	172.4
Columbus, GA-AL	325	1 841	163.4	49.3	230	19 930	4 358	597	473	8 942	292.4	84.6
Columbus, OH	3 552	34 157	3 619.4	1 336.2	1 577	77 263	18 153	2 743	3 074	62 081	2 051.6	593.6
Corpus Christi, TX	736	4 675	435.5	158.7	268	11 435	11 224	477	839	13 883	450.3	119.9
Corvallis, OR	210	1 367	116.7	50.1	106	8 547	1 392	495	205	2 807	85.9	24.0
Cumberland, MD-WV	114	581	28.6	14.6	83	5 307	922	180	213	2 920	88.6	23.2
Dallas-Fort Worth, TX	13 418	123 856	14 630.4	6 005.7	6 764	315 240	63 617	11 471	8 336	181 083	6 963.9	1 906.4
Dallas, TX	10 188	103 158	12 614.6	5 236.1	4 452	210 507	43 668	7 655	5 705	127 167	5 012.6	1 371.6
Fort Worth-Arlington, TX	3 230	20 698	2 015.8	769.7	2 312	104 733	19 950	3 816	2 631	53 916	1 951.3	534.7
Danville, VA	102	759	31.4	12.7	106	15 092	2 846	420	170	2 767	85.5	24.4
Davenport-Moline-Rock Island, IA-IL	605	4 308	353.3	134.4	460	26 539	9 412	1 096	864	15 139	428.5	123.1
Dayton-Springfield, OH	1 815	19 167	1 940.4	707.3	1 563	88 330	23 156	3 478	1 803	36 044	1 099.1	309.8
Daytona Beach, FL	914	4 290	366.5	128.2	434	11 776	1 473	309	1 139	21 223	677.9	179.9
Decatur, AL	193	984	74.4	28.9	243	16 307	5 627	610	218	4 276	114.6	32.6
Decatur, IL	156	1 101	90.0	36.1	134	11 616	6 114	479	233	4 105	123.6	35.7
Denver-Boulder-Greeley, CO	9 909	79 903	10 676.2	3 768.9	3 533	115 133	26 466	4 302	5 114	102 537	3 562.3	1 019.0
Boulder-Longmont, CO	1 612	15 458	3 081.9	760.2	686	26 225	5 196	1 052	708	13 824	453.1	131.0
Denver, CO	8 076	63 481	7 522.0	2 980.8	2 639	78 135	16 931	2 905	4 135	84 666	3 002.5	858.5
Greeley, CO	221	964	72.2	27.9	208	10 773	4 339	345	271	4 047	106.8	29.4
Des Moines, IA	1 027	10 837	860.5	350.9	476	22 735	5 543	760	1 010	18 473	565.8	165.1
Detroit-Ann Arbor-Flint, MI	11 780	118 407	12 601.9	5 347.1	8 637	430 461	134 710	19 470	9 532	173 690	5 800.1	1 596.4
Ann Arbor, MI	1 387	9 818	1 081.6	439.9	839	48 754	11 869	2 129	1 002	19 245	619.7	169.0
Detroit, MI	9 733	104 440	11 246.1	4 782.0	7 443	347 293	111 601	15 596	7 736	140 827	4 776.5	1 316.2
Flint, MI	660	4 149	274.3	125.2	355	34 414	11 240	1 745	794	13 618	403.9	111.2
Dothan, AL	224	1 380	84.0	30.9	151	10 487	1 528	255	280	5 149	148.5	38.3
Dover, DE	155	1 091	69.4	30.3	82	7 985	1 966	210	234	3 796	118.4	31.9
Dubuque, IA	117	802	56.4	23.5	133	10 687	3 075	387	233	3 838	94.7	27.4
Duluth-Superior, MN-WI	370	2 503	169.3	74.8	284	6 989	1 380	201	769	10 428	340.6	86.4
Eau Claire, WI	219	1 715	129.2	55.6	219	10 624	1 641	315	379	6 254	150.3	43.1
El Paso, TX	927	5 777	398.1	161.7	652	36 723	7 967	774	1 094	19 292	703.3	194.0
Elkhart-Goshen, IN	246	1 465	111.6	36.0	894	56 087	9 000	1 611	354	6 202	189.4	51.7
Elmira, NY	104	827	56.5	18.3	94	9 098	1 357	278	213	2 965	86.2	24.4
Enid, OK	92	432	33.6	12.1	66	2 389	506	63	123	1 896	51.9	14.7
Erie, PA	379	2 330	177.7	62.4	570	32 813	5 779	1 142	614	9 599	265.2	73.3
Eugene-Springfield, OR	797	4 682	374.3	138.8	624	19 262	3 882	590	809	12 022	387.8	110.5
Evansville-Henderson, IN-KY	579	4 379	307.7	118.6	433	30 411	8 946	1 102	610	11 510	235.7	66.6
Fargo-Moorhead, ND-MN	328	2 625	189.1	75.6	221	7 982	1 742	209	401	8 799	235.7	66.6
Fayetteville, NC	329	2 084	142.1	47.7	121	12 282	2 767	385	495	10 654	318.4	91.2
Fayetteville-Springdale-Rogers, AR	586	2 868	276.9	90.3	387	29 015	4 881	704	602	9 766	282.3	77.8
Flagstaff, AZ-UT	187	795	59.9	21.8	101	2 487	604	82	511	9 737	421.7	109.5
Florence, AL	225	963	67.7	22.5	233	13 126	2 377	376	249	4 324	113.5	31.7
Florence, SC	179	1 194	83.8	33.0	139	11 011	2 114	328	245	4 857	147.1	40.5
Fort Collins-Loveland, CO	711	3 815	336.3	134.2	384	15 840	3 891	645	647	10 779	343.6	95.0
Fort Myers-Cape Coral, FL	997	6 053	458.2	197.4	357	5 363	742	141	824	17 424	699.1	175.2
Fort Pierce-Port St. Lucie, FL	666	3 040	233.4	94.1	296	5 504	1 098	162	503	8 635	315.4	83.0
Fort Smith, AR-OK	309	2 182	134.7	49.1	314	27 144	5 010	675	396	6 530	195.4	52.3
Fort Walton Beach, FL	417	3 181	264.0	113.5	133	3 448	297	82	401	8 450	261.7	73.0
Fort Wayne, IN	838	6 336	512.0	180.1	955	69 514	15 296	2 347	947	18 311	546.4	159.0
Fresno, CA	1 265	11 520	626.4	245.0	790	31 465	6 620	825	1 418	22 022	704.9	188.3
Gadsden, AL	122	621	36.6	13.7	136	8 775	1 577	277	169	3 223	85.0	23.6
Gainesville, FL	570	3 788	292.8	126.4	151	5 251	1 010	157	431	8 981	263.0	67.8
Glens Falls, NY	210	1 239	136.3	42.7	183	7 866	1 463	267	507	4 662	199.4	56.5
Goldsboro, NC	129	596	43.4	16.0	101	9 495	1 418	231	158	2 953	84.4	23.1
Grand Forks, ND-MN	138	925	61.0	28.6	92	3 087	552	75	260	5 253	118.8	33.7
Grand Junction, CO	275	1 283	91.3	39.2	167	3 605	484	99	247	4 555	124.7	36.3
Grand Rapids-Muskegon-Holland, MI	1 958	15 704	1 413.7	596.9	2 334	150 646	28 466	5 649	1 777	34 206	1 010.1	292.2
Great Falls, MT	176	994	69.3	28.6	80	925	229	24	267	3 592	109.7	29.4
Green Bay, WI	373	3 348	270.8	118.7	396	25 825	6 457	1 016	533	10 183	283.4	81.9
Greensboro—Winston-Salem—High Point, NC	2 449	15 760	1 455.7	537.6	2 401	149 443	30 771	4 217	2 279	45 265	1 411.1	404.6
Greenville, NC	219	1 303	88.0	35.3	119	9 305	2 742	281	237	5 342	153.5	41.8
Greenville-Spartanburg-Anderson, SC	1 719	15 003	3 678.6	672.5	1 603	121 048	24 906	3 689	1 844	37 201	1 033.9	285.7
Harrisburg-Lebanon-Carlisle, PA	1 106	9 966	934.3	372.7	674	38 896	8 691	1 241	1 296	21 233	720.4	198.5

1. Firms subject to federal tax.

Table C. Metropolitan Areas — **Health and Other Services and Federal Funds**

Area Name	Health Care and Social Assistance[1], 1997				Other Services[1], 1997				Federal funds and grants, fiscal 1999[2] — Expenditures (mil dol)	Direct payments for individuals		
	Number of Establishments	Number of Employees	Receipts (mil dol)	Annual Payroll (mil dol)	Number of Establishments	Number of Employees	Receipts (mil dol)	Annual Payroll (mil dol)	Total	Social Security and government retirement	Medicare	Food stamps and Supplemental Security Income
	159	160	161	162	163	164	165	166	167	168	169	170
Columbia, SC	967	12 786	917.2	420.7	855	5 898	344.9	104.3	3 233.2	1 032.9	255.6	71.9
Columbus, GA-AL	393	6 141	481.5	186.5	399	2 488	130.3	43.8	2 019.2	650.4	168.0	63.3
Columbus, OH	2 820	37 189	2 339.0	1 159.5	2 091	15 594	940.6	301.6	7 525.1	2 294.3	836.8	211.2
Corpus Christi, TX	928	16 064	852.1	381.5	611	3 898	228.9	70.1	2 138.1	638.1	282.4	77.6
Corvallis, OR	148	1 994	140.5	52.6	88	461	26.3	7.9	308.9	117.3	29.2	4.9
Cumberland, MD-WV	207	1 896	126.8	58.0	173	918	46.3	13.7	610.3	253.5	131.7	18.5
Dallas-Fort Worth, TX	10 290	132 820	9 968.3	4 094.9	7 440	53 833	3 569.9	1 118.6	19 117.3	6 187.7	2 576.5	470.5
Dallas, TX	7 137	93 700	7 426.7	2 984.9	4 994	37 685	2 534.6	798.5	12 078.9	3 837.1	1 701.1	325.9
Fort Worth-Arlington, TX	3 153	39 120	2 541.6	1 110.1	2 446	16 148	1 035.3	320.1	7 038.4	2 350.5	875.4	144.5
Danville, VA	172	1 931	120.4	55.8	204	1 028	50.3	14.1	447.2	228.4	81.1	22.6
Davenport-Moline-Rock Island, IA-IL	664	6 598	445.5	205.5	635	4 097	249.3	73.9	1 697.2	749.5	234.0	50.0
Dayton-Springfield, OH	1 770	22 628	1 413.9	682.0	1 487	13 421	685.8	243.5	5 872.5	2 037.3	704.6	142.1
Daytona Beach, FL	968	10 384	618.1	263.1	754	3 261	173.6	49.9	2 415.9	1 421.6	554.6	60.9
Decatur, AL	262	3 263	197.5	92.1	197	1 417	74.4	23.5	613.0	266.0	103.6	22.4
Decatur, IL	204	2 546	155.6	70.3	189	1 456	86.0	28.7	508.4	240.7	85.9	23.5
Denver-Boulder-Greeley, CO	5 256	55 361	3 951.9	1 728.3	4 199	26 714	1 800.1	540.2	12 591.5	3 538.9	1 252.7	219.0
Boulder-Longmont, CO	715	6 087	405.5	170.7	482	2 945	192.2	60.9	1 348.3	354.2	117.6	15.6
Denver, CO	4 332	46 995	3 408.1	1 501.2	3 502	22 639	1 540.2	461.4	10 756.5	2 978.3	1 055.3	187.6
Greeley, CO	209	2 279	138.2	56.5	215	1 130	67.8	17.9	486.7	206.4	79.9	15.8
Des Moines, IA	876	10 385	694.5	341.4	772	4 934	313.9	94.6	3 301.5	753.4	247.7	42.9
Detroit-Ann Arbor-Flint, MI	11 047	109 879	7 204.7	3 466.6	7 935	56 425	3 827.5	1 208.4	23 067.0	9 021.4	4 755.4	956.4
Ann Arbor, MI	1 132	9 886	694.6	310.5	735	4 342	279.8	91.1	2 080.8	704.2	292.2	39.2
Detroit, MI	8 878	90 527	5 899.6	2 845.4	6 573	47 918	3 292.4	1 042.8	19 166.2	7 559.3	4 076.5	815.2
Flint, MI	1 037	9 466	610.5	310.7	627	4 165	255.2	74.4	1 820.0	757.9	386.7	101.9
Dothan, AL	283	5 213	402.9	184.3	246	1 273	65.8	19.6	841.8	325.8	101.0	32.4
Dover, DE	192	2 157	137.6	59.6	215	1 016	56.0	16.8	902.6	274.0	65.3	16.1
Dubuque, IA	124	2 376	185.8	89.3	172	889	51.2	14.9	322.2	165.7	61.2	7.5
Duluth-Superior, MN-WI	429	6 052	274.1	141.7	395	2 204	146.8	42.0	1 209.7	538.6	181.5	36.1
Eau Claire, WI	257	4 182	242.2	133.2	279	1 525	84.3	24.3	601.3	250.5	85.1	14.2
El Paso, TX	984	16 524	1 165.3	455.8	824	5 779	265.7	87.6	3 073.8	1 015.1	363.3	162.1
Elkhart-Goshen, IN	233	3 281	187.7	78.0	345	2 427	164.1	47.3	462.3	260.0	83.8	14.6
Elmira, NY	162	1 675	123.1	60.7	108	553	36.1	9.8	424.8	197.8	69.3	17.2
Enid, OK	145	1 487	90.8	40.6	104	476	26.0	7.0	369.1	134.6	50.1	8.6
Erie, PA	560	5 498	423.4	190.6	476	2 174	135.0	39.6	1 194.3	531.2	227.4	52.3
Eugene-Springfield, OR	751	7 176	492.8	217.7	473	3 210	194.0	57.1	1 306.4	616.9	184.5	47.1
Evansville-Henderson, IN-KY	586	9 740	603.1	279.5	494	3 863	233.3	73.0	1 191.4	561.6	228.8	41.8
Fargo-Moorhead, ND-MN	300	6 435	499.1	203.1	337	2 358	133.4	41.0	683.2	257.7	73.3	15.1
Fayetteville, NC	407	6 135	366.5	159.9	402	2 631	145.7	45.1	3 103.1	681.4	109.4	52.0
Fayetteville-Springdale-Rogers, AR	497	5 223	314.4	152.2	425	2 583	144.2	44.5	949.6	529.7	146.8	26.2
Flagstaff, AZ-UT	247	1 662	109.0	46.5	195	951	57.5	14.9	575.4	181.6	51.1	21.0
Florence, AL	295	3 607	256.2	110.4	234	1 367	71.5	21.0	731.7	341.7	120.2	23.6
Florence, SC	276	5 558	399.9	193.5	191	1 268	73.1	21.7	564.7	220.4	92.7	36.1
Fort Collins-Loveland, CO	530	4 957	296.2	133.5	384	2 151	127.6	39.0	751.9	331.3	107.4	13.4
Fort Myers-Cape Coral, FL	825	12 968	954.5	408.4	695	3 599	224.9	68.5	2 031.6	1 228.5	505.3	42.9
Fort Pierce-Port St. Lucie, FL	677	10 392	756.4	294.9	517	2 226	138.1	38.8	1 603.5	973.4	408.6	42.1
Fort Smith, AR-OK	391	6 467	419.5	186.5	290	1 749	110.9	28.5	804.4	397.2	144.9	36.4
Fort Walton Beach, FL	356	5 134	412.2	142.7	313	1 531	86.3	25.5	1 764.4	633.9	102.5	14.3
Fort Wayne, IN	774	11 627	744.9	338.4	850	5 707	343.4	107.4	1 821.4	802.5	276.4	43.1
Fresno, CA	1 769	16 742	1 173.5	489.9	1 042	6 412	486.7	127.1	3 446.0	1 155.1	474.4	226.3
Gadsden, AL	199	4 291	312.8	127.9	132	570	34.8	9.5	481.9	236.2	112.4	24.6
Gainesville, FL	502	6 499	435.3	201.2	318	1 631	94.1	28.0	1 038.6	349.5	133.0	34.9
Glens Falls, NY	191	1 985	130.0	64.3	169	668	51.3	14.7	467.8	242.3	81.2	14.5
Goldsboro, NC	181	2 357	114.4	56.0	151	998	58.5	18.5	719.0	238.9	73.6	24.5
Grand Forks, ND-MN	133	1 967	81.4	51.1	168	968	49.3	14.5	614.3	146.7	54.4	8.2
Grand Junction, CO	264	2 504	150.7	69.9	188	1 018	73.9	19.1	539.4	246.5	73.4	13.0
Grand Rapids-Muskegon-Holland, MI	1 777	20 530	1 267.7	640.6	1 680	11 037	745.7	221.2	3 498.0	1 572.1	544.4	123.9
Great Falls, MT	205	1 729	104.2	40.5	153	690	43.3	11.4	1 076.0	199.3	55.3	10.6
Green Bay, WI	380	5 467	359.7	190.1	391	2 650	143.4	46.4	731.8	322.6	94.0	18.0
Greensboro—Winston-Salem—High Point, NC	1 942	27 699	1 973.0	864.1	1 921	12 122	750.9	224.1	4 402.7	2 086.2	739.5	133.3
Greenville, NC	205	3 334	216.7	115.5	158	875	49.1	13.7	467.4	182.6	72.7	27.6
Greenville-Spartanburg-Anderson, SC	1 486	18 322	1 290.9	629.0	1 449	8 464	554.0	163.3	3 320.8	1 690.8	555.7	114.6
Harrisburg-Lebanon-Carlisle, PA	1 209	12 926	855.9	403.4	1 040	5 746	365.7	111.4	5 217.9	1 564.3	464.9	58.1

1. Firms subject to federal tax.   2. October 1, 1998 to September 30, 1999.

Table C. Metropolitan Areas — Federal Funds and Local Government Finances

	Federal funds and grants, fiscal 1999[1] (cont'd)							Local government finances, 1997				
	Expenditures (mil dol) (cont'd)							General revenue				
	Procurement contract awards			Grants[2]						Taxes		
											Per capita[3] (dollars)	
Area Name	Salaries and wages	Defense	Other	Medicaid and other health-related	Nutrition and family welfare	Education	Other	Total (mil dol)	Intergovern-mental (mil dol)	Total (mil dol)	Total	Property
	171	172	173	174	175	176	177	178	179	180	181	182
Columbia, SC	728.7	101.2	50.1	249.5	208.2	123.5	330.0	1 342.7	430.4	295.8	587	520
Columbus, GA-AL	787.0	116.0	11.5	103.4	41.9	17.7	34.6	575.5	246.7	224.9	827	471
Columbus, OH	649.7	356.9	242.5	751.7	950.1	354.5	646.1	3 978.5	1 333.2	1 933.5	1 324	851
Corpus Christi, TX	397.1	308.3	36.7	213.5	50.8	22.1	32.2	1 006.9	326.2	397.3	1 026	838
Corvallis, OR	33.5	2.5	10.5	25.6	5.0	6.1	62.4	158.2	62.1	64.3	841	723
Cumberland, MD-WV	36.0	16.7	14.7	69.3	13.7	6.7	42.2	213.2	112.1	61.2	618	425
Dallas-Fort Worth, TX	2 343.8	4 442.6	675.0	1 165.8	242.0	140.0	591.9	11 531.0	2 614.6	5 900.1	1 260	964
Dallas, TX	1 564.3	2 376.8	514.7	840.6	177.2	100.2	440.2	8 012.2	1 667.2	4 186.8	1 339	1 011
Fort Worth-Arlington, TX ...	779.5	2 065.8	160.4	325.2	64.8	39.8	151.7	3 518.8	947.3	1 713.3	1 101	869
Danville, VA	14.2	6.7	3.6	53.1	13.3	6.8	8.5	178.0	94.8	55.4	510	321
Davenport-Moline-Rock Island, IA-IL	317.0	86.6	25.1	90.4	41.3	11.7	23.3	857.9	355.1	303.6	850	749
Dayton-Springfield, OH	1 098.1	859.4	193.0	384.7	130.5	55.9	139.0	2 594.3	940.4	1 083.1	1 146	728
Daytona Beach, FL	74.6	44.7	24.7	75.6	33.7	21.5	76.8	1 212.8	342.8	406.7	873	709
Decatur, AL	96.5	2.6	7.4	53.5	14.1	6.3	18.9	342.1	119.2	61.9	437	195
Decatur, IL	21.0	9.2	20.8	42.1	12.5	4.9	23.3	270.8	134.0	79.6	697	658
Denver-Boulder-Greeley, CO	1 861.7	1 542.9	1 743.5	816.7	381.1	190.9	827.5	6 873.8	1 940.5	3 063.3	1 321	792
Boulder-Longmont, CO	178.2	77.8	262.9	64.5	14.8	10.3	237.9	657.8	156.2	368.1	1 407	893
Denver, CO	1 652.6	1 462.6	1 471.9	699.8	346.1	170.0	571.3	5 831.1	1 634.8	2 541.1	1 337	782
Greeley, CO	30.9	2.6	8.7	52.4	20.2	10.6	18.2	385.0	149.5	154.2	991	735
Des Moines, IA	311.4	22.8	78.4	187.9	182.4	94.5	306.1	1 211.5	421.8	458.7	1 067	1 019
Detroit-Ann Arbor-Flint, MI	1 851.2	820.9	485.5	2 504.9	871.5	318.0	1 080.4	16 419.3	8 524.2	4 569.9	840	740
Ann Arbor, MI	193.0	91.3	61.1	369.5	42.3	23.1	198.9	1 372.9	640.4	427.0	792	759
Detroit, MI	1 580.5	729.1	392.1	1 932.3	730.0	259.0	799.7	13 579.6	7 093.4	3 886.6	871	754
Flint, MI	77.8	0.5	32.3	203.0	99.2	35.9	81.8	1 466.8	790.4	256.3	589	571
Dothan, AL	221.6	34.9	15.9	53.6	12.9	8.1	15.2	388.3	118.0	72.9	543	182
Dover, DE	203.0	64.3	4.5	61.9	34.1	39.4	122.0	220.2	144.7	37.8	308	280
Dubuque, IA	17.1	0.4	5.2	30.8	8.7	2.2	6.6	195.7	82.2	72.6	824	688
Duluth-Superior, MN-WI	124.7	7.5	34.8	158.8	44.6	15.5	40.6	872.4	421.1	207.7	872	797
Eau Claire, WI	31.4	4.8	34.8	61.1	17.4	7.5	20.5	397.2	220.3	110.1	767	727
El Paso, TX	634.5	192.2	56.7	318.6	85.8	53.1	138.2	1 582.9	756.8	507.8	724	557
Elkhart-Goshen, IN	15.6	3.5	11.0	36.7	9.0	2.6	11.9	350.5	135.9	161.4	946	814
Elmira, NY	25.5	2.1	5.7	59.5	17.4	4.3	13.9	284.8	128.5	107.2	1 151	822
Enid, OK	58.8	66.5	2.5	12.6	4.8	3.1	5.9	99.4	42.6	35.9	633	324
Erie, PA	80.0	25.6	15.9	114.3	44.0	10.2	65.5	628.4	305.3	212.1	759	598
Eugene-Springfield, OR	96.4	5.6	28.7	175.1	45.0	33.1	49.5	846.7	365.1	256.5	824	689
Evansville-Henderson, IN-KY	66.4	55.0	17.4	115.1	28.9	7.0	21.5	615.1	229.1	256.2	887	761
Fargo-Moorhead, ND-MN	106.7	11.6	14.7	52.0	15.5	5.3	52.9	381.8	149.2	125.7	755	657
Fayetteville, NC	1 678.9	298.9	27.9	106.3	46.2	17.9	51.5	709.7	294.8	158.4	558	407
Fayetteville-Springdale-Rogers, AR	75.3	13.2	30.1	39.0	11.9	10.3	48.1	447.9	175.8	167.6	628	370
Flagstaff, AZ-UT	113.7	3.5	34.1	61.6	26.1	22.1	50.3	302.4	131.9	100.1	838	572
Florence, AL	94.8	4.2	34.3	52.0	10.0	7.0	22.1	407.0	118.2	82.9	604	322
Florence, SC	36.7	3.3	7.7	104.2	17.8	8.2	20.0	208.8	107.8	62.9	505	339
Fort Collins-Loveland, CO	102.6	4.3	23.4	59.1	16.0	8.3	66.8	708.1	144.5	250.2	1 107	741
Fort Myers-Cape Coral, FL...	96.0	6.4	22.9	45.9	29.4	17.4	20.6	1 548.2	259.2	458.5	1 184	1 041
Fort Pierce-Port St. Lucie, FL	41.0	21.6	11.4	37.4	25.7	14.3	21.5	767.7	217.5	343.2	1 161	1 037
Fort Smith, AR-OK	67.4	6.9	13.8	65.8	13.8	11.9	32.4	316.5	151.6	106.8	555	309
Fort Walton Beach, FL	480.4	444.5	12.9	26.7	14.5	7.1	12.2	354.9	167.7	108.4	647	548
Fort Wayne, IN	138.4	218.2	75.8	120.3	36.2	9.3	33.5	1 053.1	369.4	459.2	962	878
Fresno, CA	408.1	9.8	97.3	427.7	253.3	79.0	155.7	2 971.1	1 680.2	547.7	630	452
Gadsden, AL	16.0	2.3	4.5	50.1	9.0	6.4	11.1	184.1	91.8	58.4	560	152
Gainesville, FL	143.5	6.1	49.6	132.8	29.8	15.2	99.8	469.0	198.4	135.7	684	581
Glens Falls, NY	23.8	4.2	5.8	59.6	15.3	4.9	6.7	417.1	154.6	192.5	1 570	1 219
Goldsboro, NC	191.9	51.0	3.4	72.3	21.9	8.6	8.9	200.0	123.1	47.0	420	291
Grand Forks, ND-MN	142.8	59.9	8.9	45.5	17.7	10.8	29.6	249.1	114.1	78.7	774	652
Grand Junction, CO	53.5	4.3	79.6	34.6	10.9	5.4	7.8	248.0	103.1	97.9	884	501
Grand Rapids-Muskegon-Holland, MI	224.4	194.2	168.9	299.7	98.4	47.2	155.5	2 725.9	1 425.2	700.6	683	606
Great Falls, MT	181.3	61.8	11.4	48.0	9.2	4.4	21.1	135.2	61.8	42.8	541	514
Green Bay, WI	56.6	8.4	107.0	56.7	20.5	8.9	24.5	633.5	278.0	208.0	971	946
Greensboro—Winston-Salem—High Point, NC	336.0	151.7	110.8	443.0	103.1	55.9	165.5	2 638.1	1 151.6	968.7	840	655
Greenville, NC	20.4	0.9	6.3	82.1	17.7	9.2	25.9	615.5	129.6	64.9	536	396
Greenville-Spartanburg-Anderson, SC	166.0	82.6	64.5	310.1	63.1	38.1	177.8	1 916.2	630.2	571.1	631	556
Harrisburg-Lebanon-Carlisle, PA	630.2	153.0	66.4	369.0	821.6	304.9	699.4	1 450.0	514.7	601.4	978	690

1. October 1, 1998 to September 30, 1999. 2. State totals may include programs not allocated by county. 3. Based on the resident population estimated as of July 1 of the year shown.

Table C. Metropolitan Areas — Local Government Finances, Government Employment, and Elections

Area Name	Local government finances, 1997 (cont'd)									Government employment, 1998			Presidential election, 2000		
	Direct general expenditure							Debt outstanding					Percent of vote cast —		
			Percent of total for —												
	Total (mil dol)	Per capita[1] (dollars)	Education	Health and hospitals	Police protection	Public welfare	Highways	Total (mil dol)	Per capita[1] (dollars)	Federal civilian	Federal military	State and local	Democratic	Republican	All other
	183	184	185	186	187	188	189	190	191	192	193	194	195	196	197
Columbia, SC	1 391.5	2 761	37.5	34.7	3.6	0.2	1.0	1 013.1	2 010	8 294	12 930	63 985	43.1	54.3	2.6
Columbus, GA-AL	544.3	2 001	47.3	9.4	5.8	0.2	3.1	496.9	1 827	5 930	18 487	15 423	NA	NA	NA
Columbus, OH	3 909.7	2 677	41.7	8.2	6.4	4.9	5.1	3 243.4	2 221	14 594	4 456	125 126	NA	NA	NA
Corpus Christi, TX	919.7	2 376	52.5	13.9	6.3	0.2	2.5	776.5	2 006	5 803	7 259	24 718	45.8	52.1	2.0
Corvallis, OR	139.9	1 828	45.9	8.3	9.3	1.7	5.9	27.2	355	658	339	10 280	50.9	41.4	7.7
Cumberland, MD-WV	224.5	2 265	58.5	0.9	2.8	2.7	5.1	108.4	1 093	649	404	6 844	39.4	57.6	3.0
Dallas-Fort Worth, TX	11 243.6	2 401	47.6	9.4	5.9	0.3	3.8	16 824.4	3 593	44 867	15 617	249 174	36.7	60.9	2.4
Dallas, TX	7 703.3	2 464	47.0	9.6	5.8	0.2	3.7	10 498.7	3 358	30 878	10 325	170 745	37.3	60.2	2.5
Fort Worth-Arlington, TX	3 540.3	2 275	48.8	9.0	6.0	0.4	4.2	6 325.6	4 064	13 989	5 292	78 429	35.4	62.2	2.4
Danville, VA	199.3	1 835	52.0	0.7	5.2	5.5	3.2	308.0	2 836	260	419	5 723	37.7	59.2	3.1
Davenport-Moline-Rock Island, IA-IL	832.0	2 329	53.1	4.0	4.4	2.0	7.4	531.8	1 489	7 607	1 373	19 280	53.9	43.3	2.8
Dayton-Springfield, OH	2 485.6	2 630	43.7	4.6	6.5	6.4	4.7	1 406.1	1 488	19 299	8 530	50 970	NA	NA	NA
Daytona Beach, FL	1 156.9	2 483	36.3	21.4	6.4	0.4	4.6	1 058.8	2 272	1 352	1 083	21 465	52.8	45.1	2.2
Decatur, AL	354.2	2 500	40.1	29.3	4.0	0.2	3.4	429.3	3 030	379	886	8 075	40.7	57.3	1.9
Decatur, IL	264.6	2 316	45.5	2.0	5.7	0.6	6.7	167.2	1 463	354	269	6 064	49.0	48.1	2.8
Denver-Boulder-Greeley, CO	6 839.0	2 950	35.4	4.0	5.6	5.4	7.1	11 407.3	4 920	34 008	10 054	153 696	47.1	46.1	6.9
Boulder-Longmont, CO	681.5	2 605	38.9	1.0	6.3	3.5	7.7	620.6	2 372	2 649	915	22 832	50.1	36.4	13.4
Denver, CO	5 769.9	3 035	33.9	4.5	5.5	5.7	7.1	10 581.2	5 566	30 812	8 651	120 258	47.4	46.8	5.8
Greeley, CO	387.6	2 491	51.6	2.0	5.2	5.1	6.7	205.5	1 321	547	488	10 606	36.3	58.0	5.7
Des Moines, IA	1 188.8	2 766	48.3	10.3	4.6	1.3	5.5	1 010.6	2 352	6 088	2 378	28 990	50.6	46.8	2.6
Detroit-Ann Arbor-Flint, MI	16 347.6	3 006	46.8	7.5	5.8	1.2	5.1	11 954.5	2 198	34 932	11 887	299 331	57.2	40.3	2.4
Ann Arbor, MI	1 411.6	2 617	53.7	5.6	4.3	1.3	4.5	1 285.8	2 384	3 201	1 159	72 113	51.4	45.2	3.4
Detroit, MI	13 492.8	3 023	46.0	6.0	6.2	1.2	5.3	10 016.2	2 244	30 322	9 858	204 288	57.5	40.2	2.3
Flint, MI	1 443.2	3 315	47.5	22.9	4.3	1.2	3.6	652.5	1 499	1 409	870	22 930	62.8	34.9	2.3
Dothan, AL	395.1	2 942	30.5	37.3	3.8	0.2	3.9	358.1	2 667	3 348	4 877	9 481	29.9	68.4	1.7
Dover, DE	218.1	1 778	71.3	0.0	5.3	0.2	1.7	105.5	860	1 733	4 558	13 462	47.2	49.9	2.9
Dubuque, IA	191.6	2 175	38.1	5.8	4.4	5.3	10.5	52.5	596	297	440	3 440	55.4	40.8	3.8
Duluth-Superior, MN-WI	867.3	3 641	36.0	7.0	4.9	8.4	11.1	670.5	2 815	2 237	1 056	20 067	60.3	32.8	7.0
Eau Claire, WI	405.7	2 827	50.9	5.7	5.0	6.0	10.3	221.6	1 544	590	509	11 189	48.9	45.6	5.6
El Paso, TX	1 543.2	2 200	60.6	10.3	5.7	0.6	1.6	1 258.7	1 794	8 643	11 908	43 448	57.8	39.7	2.5
Elkhart-Goshen, IN	364.3	2 134	60.9	1.3	4.8	4.8	3.5	157.6	923	292	604	6 815	30.5	68.3	1.2
Elmira, NY	297.6	3 197	43.8	2.8	2.8	17.0	5.2	123.1	1 322	444	198	6 922	46.2	49.8	4.0
Enid, OK	99.7	1 758	54.5	0.6	4.7	0.0	6.7	128.6	2 268	381	1 430	3 675	30.2	30.2	39.6
Erie, PA	657.1	2 352	51.9	5.6	3.9	5.4	3.4	883.8	3 163	1 596	982	14 038	NA	NA	NA
Eugene-Springfield, OR	874.9	2 810	47.8	3.5	4.9	1.1	7.3	757.5	2 433	2 042	1 099	22 585	51.6	40.5	7.9
Evansville-Henderson, IN-KY	592.5	2 051	48.7	1.4	5.4	2.9	4.1	871.8	3 017	1 259	1 030	13 807	43.8	54.9	1.2
Fargo-Moorhead, ND-MN	385.3	2 316	42.4	1.4	4.1	5.2	6.5	483.8	2 908	2 168	1 198	12 723	39.6	56.7	3.7
Fayetteville, NC	746.1	2 627	37.7	26.6	5.8	5.7	1.4	475.3	1 673	10 355	45 494	19 320	NA	NA	NA
Fayetteville-Springdale-Rogers, AR	450.0	1 685	51.9	2.8	5.4	0.0	5.0	355.2	1 331	1 607	1 557	16 589	36.8	60.0	3.2
Flagstaff, AZ-UT	285.8	2 390	43.5	3.2	6.3	5.7	5.4	400.0	3 346	2 859	329	11 684	47.2	45.3	7.5
Florence, AL	396.6	2 889	35.7	37.2	3.2	0.1	4.1	175.3	1 277	1 781	859	10 013	45.5	52.2	2.3
Florence, SC	195.4	1 571	63.5	1.1	5.0	0.6	1.8	270.0	2 171	707	721	11 233	41.4	57.1	1.5
Fort Collins-Loveland, CO	577.9	2 557	34.1	17.4	4.7	4.2	8.5	1 031.1	4 562	2 069	728	20 876	38.9	52.7	8.5
Fort Myers-Cape Coral, FL	1 485.2	3 837	25.8	15.4	3.9	0.4	7.9	2 032.5	5 251	1 821	942	23 544	39.9	57.6	2.5
Fort Pierce-Port St. Lucie, FL	790.7	2 674	43.2	1.4	7.8	0.8	3.8	1 356.0	4 587	764	725	13 560	48.7	49.1	2.2
Fort Smith, AR-OK	298.2	1 550	62.3	0.2	4.9	0.0	8.7	189.7	986	1 291	1 088	8 578	38.9	56.7	4.4
Fort Walton Beach, FL	346.9	2 070	61.9	2.2	5.0	0.4	4.2	155.5	928	6 513	15 163	7 276	24.0	73.7	2.3
Fort Wayne, IN	996.8	2 087	52.5	6.6	4.3	3.6	4.4	402.1	842	2 629	1 699	23 789	34.7	63.8	1.5
Fresno, CA	2 910.7	3 351	40.7	10.4	4.6	13.2	2.9	1 831.8	2 109	9 768	1 827	52 752	42.0	54.1	3.9
Gadsden, AL	177.1	1 698	49.6	1.9	7.7	0.3	6.0	79.1	758	308	646	5 086	44.3	53.6	2.1
Gainesville, FL	479.9	2 420	47.0	1.5	8.0	0.1	2.6	1 023.6	5 161	2 937	632	36 357	55.2	39.8	4.9
Glens Falls, NY	417.8	3 409	50.3	3.6	2.4	11.2	7.6	242.1	1 975	404	255	8 988	41.8	52.9	5.3
Goldsboro, NC	192.4	1 718	58.5	4.8	4.1	6.9	3.0	104.1	929	1 455	4 592	8 236	NA	NA	NA
Grand Forks, ND-MN	260.6	2 562	40.8	1.7	4.0	6.5	8.6	189.7	1 865	1 400	4 080	10 773	39.7	57.1	3.2
Grand Junction, CO	237.6	2 147	45.0	1.3	6.4	8.4	7.7	240.6	2 174	1 170	341	6 556	30.3	63.5	6.3
Grand Rapids-Muskegon-Holland, MI	2 931.3	2 856	55.5	7.5	3.6	1.7	5.3	2 899.8	2 825	4 115	2 163	48 587	37.6	60.1	2.3
Great Falls, MT	145.9	1 843	53.3	1.9	4.1	0.8	3.0	71.9	908	1 474	3 896	3 791	39.0	53.9	7.2
Green Bay, WI	651.6	3 041	47.2	4.7	5.2	5.1	7.9	515.0	2 404	985	814	12 264	45.6	50.3	4.1
Greensboro—Winston-Salem—High Point, NC	2 497.9	2 167	45.2	7.5	5.7	5.6	2.4	1 524.6	1 323	6 355	3 700	63 190	NA	NA	NA
Greenville, NC	538.9	4 452	21.3	56.9	2.9	3.2	1.0	243.6	2 012	373	404	17 018	NA	NA	NA
Greenville-Spartanburg-Anderson, SC	1 850.8	2 046	45.7	23.2	3.9	0.1	1.8	3 378.9	3 735	2 939	5 352	56 513	32.6	64.9	2.5
Harrisburg-Lebanon-Carlisle, PA	1 516.1	2 465	54.6	3.9	2.8	5.9	3.4	2 052.3	3 337	12 292	2 995	55 322	NA	NA	NA

1. Based on the resident population estimated as of July 1 of the year shown.

Table C. Metropolitan Areas — **Land Area and Population**

CMSA/ MSA/ PMSA/ NECMA code[1]	Area Name	Land area[2] (sq km) 1990	Total persons	Rank	Per square kilometer	White	Black	Am. Indian, Eskimo, Aleut	Asian and Pacific Islander	Percent Hispanic[3]	Under 5 years	5 to 17 years	18 to 24 years	25 to 34 years	35 to 44 years	45 to 54 years
		1	2	3	4	5	6	7	8	9	10	11	12	13	14	15
3283	Hartford, CT	3 923	1 113 800	52	283.9	87.6	9.7	0.2	2.6	8.8	6.5	18.4	8.1	13.7	17.3	13.1
3285	Hattiesburg, MS	2 497	113 054	285	45.3	72.5	26.5	0.2	0.8	1.0	7.4	18.7	14.7	14.6	14.6	11.4
3290	Hickory-Morganton-Lenoir, NC	4 244	325 821	147	76.8	91.0	7.7	0.2	1.1	1.3	6.6	18.4	8.0	13.5	16.2	14.5
3320	Honolulu, HI	1 554	864 571	69	556.4	30.9	3.6	0.5	65.0	7.4	6.6	16.8	11.0	12.8	16.3	13.9
3350	Houma, LA	6 061	194 591	203	32.1	79.0	16.4	3.6	1.0	1.9	7.7	21.3	11.1	13.5	15.0	13.1
42	Houston-Galveston-Brazoria, TX	19 960	4 493 741	X	225.1	76.0	18.3	0.4	5.3	25.1	8.3	20.5	9.9	14.8	18.0	13.2
1145	Brazoria, TX	3 592	234 303	181	65.2	89.2	8.7	0.5	1.7	22.4	8.0	21.3	8.8	14.3	17.3	13.5
2920	Galveston-Texas City, TX	1 033	248 469	170	240.5	78.4	18.7	0.4	2.5	18.4	7.2	19.9	8.6	13.0	16.8	13.3
3360	Houston, TX	15 335	4 010 969	8	261.6	75.1	18.9	0.4	5.7	25.7	8.4	20.5	10.0	14.9	18.1	13.1
3400	Huntington-Ashland, WV-KY-OH	5 595	312 447	152	55.8	97.3	2.3	0.1	0.4	0.5	5.5	17.1	9.9	12.1	15.1	15.0
3440	Huntsville, AL	3 556	343 418	141	96.6	77.5	20.3	0.5	1.8	1.9	6.8	16.0	10.4	16.8	15.9	14.1
3480	Indianapolis, IN	9 126	1 536 665	37	168.4	85.0	13.7	0.2	1.1	1.3	7.3	18.5	8.8	15.4	17.0	13.4
3500	Iowa City, IA	1 592	103 813	291	65.2	92.2	2.4	0.2	5.1	2.7	6.1	13.7	23.5	17.2	15.8	10.3
3520	Jackson, MI	1 830	157 271	227	85.9	90.5	8.4	0.4	0.7	2.0	6.4	18.9	8.3	14.0	17.2	13.4
3560	Jackson, MS	6 120	432 647	117	70.7	55.9	43.4	0.1	0.6	0.7	7.3	18.8	11.0	15.4	16.7	12.2
3580	Jackson, TN	2 190	101 611	297	46.4	69.1	30.3	0.1	0.5	0.8	6.7	18.8	10.8	13.5	16.0	12.6
3600	Jacksonville, FL	6 826	1 056 332	57	154.8	74.2	22.7	0.4	2.8	3.8	7.3	20.3	8.9	13.8	17.2	13.0
3605	Jacksonville, NC	1 986	142 480	245	71.7	76.4	19.3	0.7	3.6	9.8	9.9	17.4	21.8	19.5	12.4	7.4
3610	Jamestown, NY	2 751	137 431	249	50.0	96.6	2.4	0.5	0.6	4.0	6.3	19.5	9.2	12.1	15.1	12.7
3620	Janesville-Beloit, WI	1 866	151 121	232	81.0	90.6	6.2	0.3	1.1	1.9	6.5	19.7	9.2	12.7	16.2	14.2
3660	Johnson City-Kingsport-Bristol, TN-VA	7 422	462 769	105	62.4	97.0	2.3	0.2	0.4	0.7	5.5	15.9	9.0	12.6	15.8	15.0
3680	Johnstown, PA	4 566	233 794	182	51.2	97.5	2.0	0.1	0.3	0.8	5.0	18.4	7.7	11.5	15.9	12.9
3700	Jonesboro, AR	1 841	77 668	314	42.2	92.5	6.5	0.3	0.7	1.4	7.0	17.5	13.9	13.6	14.8	12.6
3710	Joplin, MO	3 280	149 981	233	45.7	96.3	1.2	1.7	0.8	1.2	6.4	19.2	9.4	12.2	15.9	13.1
3720	Kalamazoo-Battle Creek, MI	4 874	447 164	112	91.7	87.9	10.0	0.6	1.5	2.7	6.6	19.0	11.0	13.1	16.5	13.2
3760	Kansas City, MO-KS	14 004	1 755 899	28	125.4	84.6	13.4	0.5	1.6	4.0	7.0	19.1	8.8	14.2	17.7	13.4
3810	Killeen-Temple, TX	5 467	296 316	155	54.2	74.8	20.0	0.7	4.6	16.4	9.0	19.6	15.5	15.9	14.6	10.6
3840	Knoxville, TN	6 343	672 087	79	106.0	91.9	6.6	0.3	1.2	1.0	6.2	16.2	9.6	14.1	16.6	14.1
3850	Kokomo, IN	1 433	100 377	299	70.0	93.7	5.3	0.3	0.8	1.9	6.6	18.9	7.7	12.7	16.2	15.1
3870	La Crosse, WI-MN	2 619	121 927	271	46.6	95.7	0.5	0.4	3.4	0.9	6.3	18.7	13.2	12.4	16.1	12.1
3920	Lafayette, IN	2 344	175 439	212	74.8	93.8	1.9	0.3	4.0	2.4	6.5	15.6	21.0	14.0	14.3	11.0
3880	Lafayette, LA	6 717	377 238	128	56.2	69.3	29.7	0.2	0.8	1.5	7.7	20.8	11.0	13.5	15.1	12.6
3960	Lake Charles, LA	2 774	180 607	208	65.1	74.0	25.3	0.2	0.5	1.4	7.0	20.1	10.2	12.8	15.4	13.4
3980	Lakeland-Winter Haven, FL	4 856	457 347	108	94.2	82.7	15.9	0.4	1.0	6.1	6.6	18.9	7.8	10.8	14.3	12.6
4000	Lancaster, PA	2 458	460 035	107	187.2	95.0	3.1	0.1	1.7	5.3	7.0	19.6	8.7	13.5	16.1	13.0
4040	Lansing-East Lansing, MI	4 421	450 789	111	102.0	88.8	7.8	0.6	2.8	5.0	6.6	18.8	13.8	14.1	16.9	12.6
4080	Laredo, TX	8 695	193 180	204	22.2	99.1	0.2	0.2	0.5	95.3	11.1	25.4	11.7	13.0	13.7	10.8
4100	Las Cruces, NM	9 861	170 361	215	17.3	95.9	1.9	0.8	1.3	58.6	8.4	21.3	14.5	11.8	14.2	11.7
4120	Las Vegas, NV-AZ	101 969	1 381 086	43	13.5	84.6	9.3	1.2	4.8	16.7	7.7	18.9	8.5	13.4	15.8	13.4
4150	Lawrence, KS	1 184	98 343	300	83.1	89.2	4.4	2.5	3.9	3.8	5.9	14.6	26.5	14.0	14.6	10.2
4200	Lawton, OK	2 770	106 621	290	38.5	73.9	17.8	4.6	3.7	9.2	8.4	20.5	13.0	14.6	14.2	11.1
4243	Lewiston-Auburn, ME	1 218	101 337	298	83.2	98.4	0.6	0.2	0.7	1.1	5.7	18.1	9.9	13.6	16.1	14.0
4280	Lexington, KY	4 973	455 617	109	91.6	88.2	10.2	0.2	1.5	1.2	6.5	16.0	13.4	15.3	17.0	13.1
4320	Lima, OH	2 087	154 065	229	73.8	90.1	9.0	0.2	0.7	1.3	6.9	20.1	8.8	13.1	15.8	12.5
4360	Lincoln, NE	2 173	237 657	176	109.4	94.3	2.4	0.7	2.5	3.6	6.5	17.0	15.7	13.9	16.6	12.1
4400	Little Rock-North Little Rock, AR	7 534	559 074	91	74.2	77.7	21.1	0.3	0.8	1.9	7.3	18.9	10.4	14.7	16.4	12.7
4420	Longview-Marshall, TX	4 560	209 493	190	45.9	76.8	22.2	0.5	0.6	4.0	6.8	20.5	9.3	11.4	15.4	13.6
49	Los Angeles-Riverside-Orange County, CA	87 970	16 036 587	X	182.3	79.4	8.4	0.7	11.5	39.2	7.9	19.6	10.4	16.0	16.5	12.1
4480	Los Angeles-Long Beach, CA	10 515	9 329 989	1	887.3	74.8	11.2	0.6	13.4	44.4	7.9	19.1	10.8	16.3	16.6	11.9
5945	Orange County, CA	2 045	2 760 948	15	1 350.1	84.2	1.8	0.6	13.5	29.0	7.3	18.1	11.0	16.1	16.7	13.5
6780	Riverside-San Bernardino, CA	70 629	3 200 587	11	45.3	86.5	7.1	1.1	5.2	34.1	8.8	22.2	9.2	15.2	16.1	11.1
8735	Ventura, CA	4 781	745 063	72	155.8	89.8	2.4	0.9	6.9	33.4	7.5	20.5	9.3	14.3	17.4	13.3
4520	Louisville, KY-IN	5 367	1 005 849	61	187.4	85.9	13.0	0.2	0.9	0.9	6.4	17.5	8.9	14.0	17.1	13.7
4600	Lubbock, TX	2 330	227 890	183	97.8	89.5	8.4	0.4	1.8	28.7	7.8	19.0	14.8	13.3	14.4	11.5
4640	Lynchburg, VA	4 639	208 835	191	45.0	79.4	19.8	0.2	0.6	0.9	5.8	16.8	9.8	12.8	15.8	13.9
4680	Macon, GA	3 968	321 586	149	81.0	59.0	39.5	0.2	1.2	1.9	7.3	19.4	9.5	14.5	16.2	13.1
4720	Madison, WI	3 114	428 563	118	137.6	92.7	3.6	0.4	3.3	2.3	6.1	16.1	14.3	15.8	18.6	12.6
4800	Mansfield, OH	2 329	176 617	210	75.8	92.0	7.2	0.2	0.6	0.9	6.2	18.8	8.7	12.7	15.7	14.2
4880	McAllen-Edinburg-Mission, TX	4 064	534 907	98	131.6	99.1	0.3	0.2	0.4	88.5	10.3	26.3	11.1	11.9	14.0	10.2
4890	Medford-Ashland, OR	7 214	175 822	211	24.4	97.0	0.3	1.3	1.3	6.5	6.2	18.1	8.3	10.8	15.2	15.1
4900	Melbourne-Titusville-Palm Bay, FL	2 638	470 365	104	178.3	87.9	9.5	0.5	2.1	4.7	6.0	16.5	7.2	12.4	14.5	13.1
4920	Memphis, TN-AR-MS	7 790	1 105 058	55	141.9	56.3	42.4	0.2	1.2	1.3	7.7	19.7	10.0	15.1	16.9	12.7

1. MSA = Metropolitan Statistical Area. CMSA = Consolidated MSA. PMSA = Primary MSA. NECMA = New England County Metropolitan Area. See Appendix A for explanation of these concepts. See Appendix B for list of metropolitan areas identified by type, with component counties. 2. Dry land or land partially or temporarily covered by water. 3. Hispanic persons may be of any race.

Table C. Metropolitan Areas — Population and Households

Area Name	Population, 1999 (cont'd) Age (percent) (cont'd)				Population — change and components of change, 1980–1999							Households, 1990				
	55 to 64 years	65 to 74 years	75 years and over	Percent female	Total persons 1990	Total persons 1980	Percent change 1980–1990	Percent change 1990–1999	Components of change, 1990–1999 Births	Deaths	Net migration	Number	Percent change, 1980–1990	Persons per household	Female family householder[1]	One person
	16	17	18	19	20	21	22	23	24	25	26	27	28	29	30	31
Hartford, CT	8.5	7.1	7.2	51.5	1 123 678	1 051 606	6.9	-0.9	142 207	92 229	-56 612	423 651	13.9	2.56	11.6	24.4
Hattiesburg, MS	7.9	5.8	4.9	52.7	98 738	89 839	9.9	14.5	14 827	9 036	8 674	36 033	16.9	2.74	15.3	25.1
Hickory-Morganton-Lenoir, NC	9.7	7.2	5.9	51.0	292 405	270 457	8.1	11.4	38 916	25 345	20 608	112 387	18.9	2.55	10.6	21.8
Honolulu, HI	8.7	7.6	6.3	50.2	836 231	762 565	9.7	3.4	129 486	48 642	-69 992	265 304	15.2	3.02	10.5	19.2
Houma, LA	8.4	5.8	4.2	51.2	182 842	176 876	3.4	6.4	27 813	12 991	-2 577	60 672	11.0	2.98	12.3	17.4
Houston-Galveston-Brazoria, TX	7.4	4.7	3.3	50.2	3 731 014	3 118 480	19.6	20.4	693 459	233 068	310 209	1 338 775	21.4	2.75	12.1	24.6
Brazoria, TX	8.2	5.1	3.6	48.1	191 707	169 587	13.0	22.2	32 072	12 355	23 227	64 019	18.8	2.86	8.6	18.5
Galveston-Texas City, TX	9.5	6.5	4.5	50.8	217 396	195 738	11.1	14.3	34 309	18 475	15 692	81 451	17.6	2.64	12.6	24.3
Houston, TX	7.2	4.6	3.2	50.3	3 321 911	2 753 155	20.7	20.7	627 078	202 238	271 290	1 193 305	21.8	2.75	12.3	24.9
Huntington-Ashland, WV-KY-OH	10.6	8.1	6.8	52.1	312 529	336 410	-7.1	0.0	35 801	32 101	-2 809	119 640	0.5	2.56	11.1	23.8
Huntsville, AL	9.1	6.5	4.5	50.8	293 047	242 971	20.6	17.2	43 906	21 495	16 318	110 893	34.5	2.58	10.4	23.4
Indianapolis, IN	8.5	6.0	5.2	51.7	1 380 491	1 305 911	5.7	11.3	216 888	116 151	58 092	529 814	13.1	2.55	11.7	25.4
Iowa City, IA	5.6	3.9	3.9	50.2	96 119	81 717	17.6	8.0	12 184	4 336	89	36 067	19.3	2.41	6.7	27.8
Jackson, MI	8.9	6.7	6.2	49.3	149 756	151 495	-1.1	5.0	19 762	12 930	1 155	53 660	5.3	2.62	11.5	23.2
Jackson, MS	8.0	5.9	4.7	52.5	395 396	362 038	9.2	9.4	61 849	32 770	8 982	140 167	16.5	2.73	17.1	23.8
Jackson, TN	8.9	6.6	6.2	52.6	90 801	87 273	4.0	11.9	12 845	9 119	7 326	34 167	10.5	2.66	12.9	24.5
Jacksonville, FL	8.1	6.3	5.0	51.5	906 727	722 252	25.5	16.5	144 923	76 816	74 440	343 526	32.3	2.57	12.6	24.4
Jacksonville, NC	4.7	4.2	2.7	42.7	149 838	112 784	32.9	-4.9	30 591	6 169	-47 584	40 658	34.2	2.84	9.5	15.4
Jamestown, NY	9.1	7.8	8.2	51.0	141 895	146 925	-3.4	-3.1	16 334	13 917	-6 532	53 696	1.7	2.54	10.3	26.1
Janesville-Beloit, WI	9.0	6.3	6.2	51.0	139 510	139 420	0.1	8.3	18 810	11 969	5 253	52 252	6.6	2.62	10.6	23.4
Johnson City-Kingsport-Bristol, TN-VA	10.8	8.4	7.0	51.8	436 068	433 638	0.6	6.1	48 257	44 205	23 910	170 569	10.6	2.49	10.1	23.4
Johnstown, PA	9.7	9.8	9.1	51.2	241 280	264 506	-8.8	-3.1	23 743	25 254	-5 028	91 578	-0.4	2.55	9.8	25.7
Jonesboro, AR	9.1	6.1	5.5	51.9	68 956	63 239	9.0	12.6	9 879	6 148	6 126	26 285	17.7	2.53	10.5	23.5
Joplin, MO	9.3	7.4	7.0	51.7	134 910	127 513	5.8	11.2	19 634	14 265	10 207	53 020	9.5	2.49	9.1	25.7
Kalamazoo-Battle Creek, MI	8.4	6.1	6.0	51.6	429 453	420 771	2.1	4.1	57 839	34 963	-3 998	160 916	7.5	2.57	11.7	24.3
Kansas City, MO-KS	8.2	6.2	5.3	51.5	1 582 874	1 449 380	9.2	10.9	231 521	127 766	52 191	608 459	13.8	2.55	11.2	26.0
Killeen-Temple, TX	6.7	4.4	3.8	48.6	255 299	214 587	19.0	16.1	53 849	15 583	-9 404	83 927	25.7	2.75	10.1	20.4
Knoxville, TN	9.9	7.4	6.0	52.0	585 960	546 488	7.2	14.7	75 311	54 902	59 053	231 254	15.8	2.47	11.0	25.2
Kokomo, IN	9.5	7.1	6.2	52.0	96 946	103 715	-6.5	3.5	13 200	8 278	-1 223	37 549	1.4	2.55	10.7	24.5
La Crosse, WI-MN	8.1	6.3	6.8	51.5	116 401	109 438	6.4	4.7	14 394	9 829	1 372	43 506	13.4	2.56	8.7	25.7
Lafayette, IN	7.2	5.2	5.1	49.7	161 572	153 247	5.4	8.6	21 274	11 964	2 600	57 068	9.7	2.53	8.0	24.8
Lafayette, LA	8.7	5.8	4.7	52.0	345 053	330 786	4.3	9.3	54 896	26 916	5 204	121 807	13.4	2.78	14.1	22.7
Lake Charles, LA	9.7	6.6	4.9	51.6	168 134	167 223	0.5	7.4	25 632	14 184	1 466	60 328	7.0	2.74	13.2	22.2
Lakeland-Winter Haven, FL	9.7	10.3	8.9	51.3	405 382	321 652	26.0	12.8	58 365	42 914	37 696	155 969	36.3	2.53	10.8	22.4
Lancaster, PA	8.0	6.9	7.2	51.4	422 822	362 346	16.7	8.8	62 474	35 497	11 859	150 956	21.9	2.71	7.9	20.9
Lansing-East Lansing, MI	7.0	5.2	5.0	51.6	432 684	419 750	3.1	4.2	56 918	27 122	-22 321	156 887	9.7	2.62	11.1	24.0
Laredo, TX	6.9	4.1	3.3	52.5	133 239	99 258	34.2	45.0	44 682	7 445	23 236	34 438	33.0	3.81	17.6	12.7
Las Cruces, NM	8.1	5.8	4.2	50.4	135 510	96 340	40.7	25.7	28 576	8 241	14 603	45 043	NA	0.00	12.0	19.6
Las Vegas, NV-AZ	9.8	7.7	4.8	49.4	852 646	528 000	61.5	62.0	171 137	87 169	442 820	330 490	66.5	2.53	10.6	25.1
Lawrence, KS	5.7	4.3	4.2	50.4	81 798	67 640	20.9	20.2	9 909	4 324	7 630	30 138	26.5	2.42	7.6	27.0
Lawton, OK	7.9	5.9	4.3	49.9	111 486	112 456	-0.9	-4.4	19 771	7 642	-22 248	37 569	6.9	2.72	12.1	20.4
Lewiston-Auburn, ME	8.7	7.2	6.7	51.5	105 259	99 509	5.8	-3.7	11 994	9 310	-6 329	40 017	13.6	2.55	10.9	24.4
Lexington, KY	8.3	5.8	4.7	51.9	405 936	370 900	9.4	12.2	56 747	31 601	25 568	154 089	18.0	2.49	11.5	25.3
Lima, OH	8.6	7.2	7.0	50.4	154 340	154 795	-0.3	-0.2	20 347	13 458	-6 646	55 384	3.1	2.69	10.5	22.8
Lincoln, NE	7.3	5.6	5.2	51.0	213 641	192 884	10.8	11.2	29 673	14 365	9 330	82 759	15.3	2.44	8.7	27.5
Little Rock-North Little Rock, AR	8.4	6.2	5.1	52.0	513 026	474 463	8.1	9.0	76 117	43 211	14 085	195 437	15.7	2.56	12.1	24.9
Longview-Marshall, TX	9.8	6.8	6.4	51.8	193 801	180 355	7.5	8.1	27 379	18 913	7 750	72 092	12.6	2.63	11.7	24.3
Los Angeles-Riverside-Orange County, CA	7.1	5.5	4.9	50.1	14 531 529	11 497 549	26.4	10.4	2 757 643	938 140	-326 736	4 900 720	18.3	2.91	12.0	23.0
Los Angeles-Long Beach, CA	7.0	5.5	4.9	50.5	8 863 052	7 477 239	18.5	5.3	1 676 786	563 984	-658 590	2 989 552	9.5	2.91	13.1	25.0
Orange County, CA	7.3	5.3	4.8	49.8	2 410 668	1 932 921	24.7	14.5	458 127	142 260	37 150	827 066	20.5	2.87	9.7	20.7
Riverside-San Bernardino, CA	6.9	5.6	4.8	49.7	2 588 793	1 558 215	66.1	23.6	511 522	193 393	291 165	866 804	57.1	2.91	11.0	19.7
Ventura, CA	7.2	5.5	5.0	49.6	669 016	529 174	26.4	11.4	111 208	38 503	3 539	217 298	25.8	3.02	9.8	17.5
Louisville, KY-IN	9.5	7.0	5.8	52.2	949 012	953 520	-0.5	6.0	129 529	86 885	16 661	366 364	7.8	2.55	13.5	25.3
Lubbock, TX	8.1	6.1	5.1	50.8	222 636	211 651	5.2	2.4	35 266	15 919	-14 386	81 534	12.3	2.61	10.4	25.5
Lynchburg, VA	10.0	7.7	7.3	52.3	193 926	182 207	6.4	7.7	23 760	18 443	10 137	72 689	16.6	2.54	11.4	23.5
Macon, GA	8.8	6.5	4.8	52.5	291 079	272 945	6.6	10.5	44 222	25 310	10 871	106 478	15.3	2.66	16.6	23.5
Madison, WI	6.9	4.9	4.7	50.8	367 085	323 545	13.5	16.7	47 349	21 886	12 394	142 786	18.4	2.46	8.0	26.4
Mansfield, OH	9.4	7.5	6.8	50.6	174 007	181 280	-4.0	1.5	21 951	15 818	-5 953	65 956	2.1	2.69	10.3	24.0
McAllen-Edinburg-Mission, TX	6.8	5.4	4.0	51.9	383 545	283 323	35.4	39.5	116 653	21 943	58 369	103 479	36.5	3.67	15.0	13.4
Medford-Ashland, OR	10.1	8.3	8.0	51.0	146 387	132 456	10.5	20.1	18 979	14 902	25 882	57 238	16.8	2.50	9.1	24.0
Melbourne-Titusville-Palm Bay, FL	10.3	11.6	8.3	50.8	398 978	272 959	46.2	17.9	48 165	38 835	62 789	161 365	58.5	2.43	9.1	23.7
Memphis, TN-AR-MS	7.9	5.6	4.4	52.3	1 007 306	938 777	7.3	9.7	170 172	87 652	15 895	365 450	14.4	2.69	17.9	24.4

1. No spouse present.

Table C. Metropolitan Areas — **Vital Statistics, Health Resources, and Crime**

Area Name	Births, average 1996–1998 Total	Rate[1]	Deaths, average 1996–1998 Number Total	Number Infant[2]	Rate Total[1]	Rate Infant[3]	Physicians,[4] 1998 Number	Rate[5]	Hospitals,[4] 1998 Number	Beds Number	Beds Rate[5]	Medicare enrollees 1999	Serious crimes known to police, 1998[6] Total Number	Rate[7]
	32	33	34	35	36	37	38	39	40	41	42	43	44	45
Hartford, CT	14 933	13.5	10 337	121	9.3	8.1	3 322	299	12	2 690	242	175 658	39 792	4 192
Hattiesburg, MS	1 668	15.2	979	10	8.9	6.0	262	236	3	695	625	15 044	NA	NA
Hickory-Morganton-Lenoir, NC	4 304	13.5	2 935	33	9.2	7.7	497	154	6	812	252	49 217	12 980	4 025
Honolulu, HI	13 057	14.9	5 632	84	6.4	6.4	2 526	290	10	2 316	265	117 980	47 453	5 425
Houma, LA	2 919	15.2	1 426	25	7.4	8.6	249	128	5	647	334	24 961	9 957	5 255
Houston-Galveston-Brazoria, TX	76 444	17.7	26 294	483	6.1	6.3	9 853	224	57	12 767	290	384 009	225 223	5 130
Brazoria, TX	3 514	15.6	1 496	20	6.6	5.8	255	111	4	310	135	22 988	6 819	2 987
Galveston-Texas City, TX .	3 612	14.9	2 028	30	8.4	8.2	889	362	2	927	378	30 422	14 757	5 975
Houston, TX	69 318	18.0	22 770	433	5.9	6.3	8 709	222	51	11 530	293	330 599	203 647	5 202
Huntington-Ashland, WV-KY-OH	3 765	11.9	3 571	35	11.3	9.2	667	212	5	1 460	465	57 861	NA	NA
Huntsville, AL	4 689	14.0	2 501	26	7.5	5.6	538	158	4	960	282	40 554	15 401	4 619
Indianapolis, IN	23 669	15.7	12 983	210	8.6	8.8	4 113	271	24	5 571	367	196 760	62 543	5 246
Iowa City, IA	1 274	12.5	486	10	4.8	7.6	1 063	1 035	2	1 002	975	9 007	3 960	3 857
Jackson, MI	2 062	13.3	1 428	20	9.2	9.7	195	125	2	507	325	23 609	5 955	3 872
Jackson, MS	6 731	15.8	3 697	72	8.7	10.6	1 321	307	9	2 398	558	53 041	25 586	6 915
Jackson, TN	1 405	14.1	1 021	13	10.3	9.0	286	284	2	710	705	15 158	6 799	7 925
Jacksonville, FL	15 640	15.2	8 710	140	8.5	9.0	2 481	237	12	3 177	304	135 572	69 654	6 614
Jacksonville, NC	3 234	22.6	711	24	5.0	7.3	182	128	1	133	93	11 422	5 447	3 748
Jamestown, NY	1 627	11.7	1 467	13	10.5	7.8	193	140	4	687	497	25 821	4 280	3 050
Janesville-Beloit, WI	2 001	13.3	1 329	13	8.8	6.7	251	167	3	474	314	21 678	NA	NA
Johnson City-Kingsport-Bristol, TN-VA	5 276	11.5	5 074	38	11.0	7.2	1 156	250	10	1 729	374	85 751	13 360	2 882
Johnstown, PA	2 398	10.1	2 784	18	11.7	7.2	439	186	7	1 102	466	49 427	3 169	1 460
Jonesboro, AR	1 109	14.5	709	9	9.3	8.1	214	276	2	425	548	11 220	3 508	4 533
Joplin, MO	2 237	15.2	1 604	13	10.9	5.8	287	193	5	759	510	25 309	NA	NA
Kalamazoo-Battle Creek, MI.	6 029	13.6	3 878	53	8.7	8.7	1 015	227	8	1 568	351	64 230	19 604	5 392
Kansas City, MO-KS	25 380	14.8	14 206	185	8.3	7.2	4 205	242	33	6 333	365	224 771	NA	NA
Killeen-Temple, TX	6 088	20.3	1 766	42	5.9	6.8	753	250	5	803	266	26 461	13 109	4 302
Knoxville, TN	8 174	12.5	6 344	55	9.7	6.6	1 662	252	10	2 481	376	105 107	25 149	4 084
Kokomo, IN	1 398	13.9	917	10	9.1	7.6	141	141	3	416	415	15 683	3 486	4 146
La Crosse, WI-MN	1 481	12.2	1 084	9	8.9	6.1	372	305	3	641	526	18 139	NA	NA
Lafayette, IN	2 260	13.2	1 286	13	7.5	5.8	319	185	3	530	308	20 107	5 241	3 767
Lafayette, LA	5 946	16.0	3 033	58	8.2	9.8	620	165	11	1 527	406	49 341	16 726	4 612
Lake Charles, LA	2 795	15.6	1 603	24	8.9	8.7	300	166	6	862	478	25 334	12 791	7 276
Lakeland-Winter Haven, FL..	6 392	14.3	4 932	55	11.0	8.6	725	160	5	1 430	316	88 530	36 322	7 954
Lancaster, PA	6 512	14.4	4 017	47	8.9	7.2	787	172	5	1 118	245	68 534	10 155	2 274
Lansing-East Lansing, MI	5 912	13.1	3 009	37	6.7	6.2	1 061	236	5	1 632	363	51 768	18 951	4 329
Laredo, TX	5 188	28.4	870	25	4.8	4.9	170	90	2	377	200	16 260	13 492	7 244
Las Cruces, NM	3 013	18.1	965	21	5.8	6.9	239	141	1	221	131	19 601	9 671	5 789
Las Vegas, NV-AZ	20 956	16.6	11 026	142	8.7	6.7	2 204	167	13	2 577	195	189 175	76 261	5 809
Lawrence, KS	1 085	11.9	492	8	5.4	7.4	152	163	1	167	179	8 802	NA	NA
Lawton, OK	2 075	18.2	845	19	7.4	9.3	200	176	2	339	299	12 333	6 074	5 282
Lewiston-Auburn, ME	1 173	11.6	1 008	6	9.9	5.4	238	235	2	440	434	17 884	4 082	4 033
Lexington, KY	6 227	14.0	3 566	45	8.0	7.4	1 591	354	11	2 455	546	56 053	NA	NA
Lima, OH	2 091	13.5	1 485	17	9.6	8.1	243	158	4	703	456	25 085	5 395	4 449
Lincoln, NE	3 302	14.1	1 608	24	6.9	7.2	508	216	3	702	298	29 038	15 350	6 555
Little Rock-North Little Rock, AR	8 310	15.0	4 887	76	8.9	9.1	1 792	322	10	2 805	504	73 445	37 222	6 699
Longview-Marshall, TX	2 979	14.3	2 137	27	10.3	9.3	272	130	4	568	272	32 960	9 946	4 698
Los Angeles-Riverside-Orange County, CA	273 887	17.6	102 459	1 620	6.6	5.9	35 766	227	194	45 417	288	1 701 644	641 962	4 063
Los Angeles-Long Beach, CA	163 301	17.9	59 857	965	6.6	5.9	22 895	248	114	30 364	330	975 304	400 975	4 331
Orange County, CA	47 032	17.6	16 114	210	6.0	4.5	6 940	255	37	6 889	253	282 452	82 556	3 050
Riverside-San Bernardino, CA	52 045	17.1	22 022	376	7.2	7.2	4 710	151	35	6 713	216	361 067	138 460	4 464
Ventura, CA	11 509	15.9	4 466	69	6.2	6.0	1 221	167	8	1 451	198	82 821	19 971	2 717
Louisville, KY-IN	13 925	14.0	9 588	107	9.6	7.6	2 596	260	16	4 525	453	151 257	38 270	5 065
Lubbock, TX	3 723	16.2	1 801	32	7.8	8.6	705	307	6	1 551	676	29 062	13 786	5 879
Lynchburg, VA	2 499	12.1	2 038	20	9.8	8.1	343	165	3	695	334	37 553	5 966	2 852
Macon, GA	4 692	14.9	2 746	57	8.7	12.3	676	212	7	1 236	387	43 792	22 659	7 113
Madison, WI	5 043	12.0	2 485	30	5.9	6.0	1 703	401	4	1 246	293	44 320	NA	NA
Mansfield, OH	2 293	13.1	1 764	18	10.1	7.7	225	129	6	653	374	29 284	6 472	3 953
McAllen-Edinburg-Mission, TX	13 265	26.1	2 609	61	5.1	4.6	520	100	5	1 036	198	52 177	30 408	5 874
Medford-Ashland, OR	2 093	12.3	1 756	12	10.3	5.6	429	248	3	471	272	31 590	9 434	5 498
Melbourne-Titusville-Palm Bay, FL	4 871	10.6	4 600	24	10.0	5.0	872	187	5	1 190	255	93 639	23 708	5 053
Memphis, TN-AR-MS	18 297	16.9	9 791	224	9.0	12.3	2 560	234	17	5 330	487	131 219	64 361	6 615

1. Per 1,000 estimated resident population, average 1996–1998.   2. Deaths of infants under 1 year old.   3. Deaths of infants under 1 year old per 1,000 live births.   4. Data subject to copyright.   5. Per 100,000 resident population as of July 1 of the year shown.   6. Data for serious crimes have not been adjusted for underreporting; this may affect comparability between geographic areas and over time.   7. Per 100,000 population estimated by the FBI.

Table C. Metropolitan Areas — Crime, Education, Money Income, and Poverty

	Serious crimes known to police, 1998[1] (cont'd) Rate[2]		Education						Money income 1989				Income and poverty, 1997 Percent below poverty level			
			School enrollment and attainment, 1990				Local government expenditures, fiscal 1997[5]									
			Enrollment[3]		Attainment[4] (percent)					Households						
										Median						
Area Name	Violent	Property	Total	Percent private	High school graduate or more	Bachelor's degree or more	Total current expenditures (mil dol)	Current expenditures per student (dollars)	Per capita[6] (dollars)	Dollars	Percent change, 1979–1989 (constant 1989 dollars)	Percent with $100,000 or more	Median household income	All persons	Persons under 18	Persons 5–17 in families
	46	47	48	49	50	51	52	53	54	55	56	57	58	59	60	61
Hartford, CT	360	3 832	282 344	18.4	79.1	26.5	1 460.2	8 280	18 939	41 428	21.8	7.1	NA	9.1	15.1	14.3
Hattiesburg, MS	NA	NA	32 126	7.7	72.5	20.1	78.8	4 070	10 028	NA	NA	0.7	NA	17.1	22.8	21.0
Hickory-Morganton-Lenoir, NC	323	3 702	64 496	8.1	61.9	11.4	248.3	4 735	12 461	27 177	6.8	1.9	NA	10.5	16.7	14.6
Honolulu, HI	268	5 157	221 821	21.6	81.2	24.6	1 083.5	5 774	16 256	40 580	14.9	7.9	NA	10.2	14.8	13.1
Houma, LA	686	4 569	51 354	12.3	58.0	9.7	169.3	4 310	9 385	21 599	-30.6	1.6	NA	15.8	21.2	21.1
Houston-Galveston-Brazoria, TX	712	4 418	1 059 519	11.0	75.1	24.1	4 263.9	4 958	14 928	31 487	-10.6	5.3	NA	14.1	19.3	17.6
Brazoria, TX	245	2 742	55 183	8.0	75.5	15.1	215.2	4 635	13 468	34 418	-12.0	2.9	NA	11.0	15.1	14.0
Galveston-Texas City, TX	557	5 418	61 025	8.5	75.8	19.3	317.4	4 908	13 993	29 465	-9.7	3.6	NA	13.4	19.2	17.9
Houston, TX	749	4 453	943 311	11.3	75.1	25.0	3 731.3	4 983	15 073	31 473	-10.4	5.5	NA	14.3	19.5	17.8
Huntington-Ashland, WV-KY-OH	NA	NA	78 189	5.7	66.7	12.6	300.5	5 667	10 744	21 057	-14.8	1.7	NA	18.0	27.1	24.1
Huntsville, AL	466	4 153	77 827	12.2	77.1	27.1	260.8	4 884	14 750	31 964	16.2	3.6	NA	11.4	18.1	16.4
Indianapolis, IN	809	4 437	335 267	16.1	78.1	20.2	1 521.4	6 182	14 936	31 314	0.5	3.6	NA	9.3	14.3	12.8
Iowa City, IA	547	3 310	40 420	6.1	90.6	44.0	71.7	5 572	14 113	27 862	2.3	4.6	NA	9.2	9.5	9.0
Jackson, MI	427	3 445	38 772	14.2	77.7	12.9	174.8	6 757	12 556	29 155	-6.1	2.3	NA	11.6	17.3	16.3
Jackson, MS	698	6 217	116 736	19.0	74.4	25.1	295.7	3 998	12 311	26 364	2.9	3.2	NA	15.6	21.6	19.1
Jackson, TN	1 043	6 882	23 496	21.5	66.4	15.5	81.1	5 056	11 179	NA	NA	2.1	NA	14.8	19.6	17.5
Jacksonville, FL	958	5 656	222 340	16.0	77.4	18.6	839.9	4 701	14 141	29 513	15.5	3.2	NA	12.0	16.9	16.0
Jacksonville, NC	309	3 439	33 122	8.6	83.0	13.4	86.7	4 153	10 713	23 385	13.1	1.0	NA	14.6	18.0	18.6
Jamestown, NY	272	2 778	37 059	7.9	74.4	14.2	199.9	7 712	11 287	24 183	-3.2	1.4	NA	16.7	25.4	24.9
Janesville-Beloit, WI	NA	NA	34 529	11.7	78.2	13.3	183.8	6 716	13 428	30 632	-4.6	2.0	NA	8.9	13.7	12.5
Johnson City-Kingsport-Bristol, TN-VA	358	2 524	96 813	8.5	63.1	13.8	354.3	5 055	11 427	22 385	-2.3	· 1.9	NA	14.3	20.6	18.4
Johnstown, PA	200	1 260	54 908	15.9	70.5	10.2	238.8	6 983	10 448	21 529	-16.8	1.3	NA	13.0	18.8	16.9
Jonesboro, AR	341	4 192	19 048	5.2	67.5	16.4	56.5	4 247	11 301	22 150	1.3	2.2	NA	16.6	22.9	20.3
Joplin, MO	NA	NA	32 378	8.5	71.8	13.0	107.9	4 147	10 790	21 393	2.1	1.6	NA	13.6	19.7	17.4
Kalamazoo-Battle Creek, MI	712	4 680	125 496	11.1	79.4	20.3	511.8	6 682	13 431	28 974	-2.4	3.0	NA	12.4	19.1	18.6
Kansas City, MO-KS	NA	NA	402 457	15.9	82.3	23.2	1 639.7	5 611	15 030	31 559	0.1	3.8	NA	9.3	13.6	12.1
Killeen-Temple, TX	443	3 859	66 886	8.5	79.4	15.7	288.7	4 888	10 409	23 698	9.3	1.7	NA	14.6	20.3	19.8
Knoxville, TN	498	3 586	141 152	8.6	71.1	19.5	481.4	4 796	13 201	25 464	3.2	2.8	NA	12.1	17.3	15.2
Kokomo, IN	249	3 897	24 685	9.3	78.2	13.6	109.0	6 325	14 234	31 452	-2.0	2.1	NA	9.2	14.2	13.1
La Crosse, WI-MN	NA	NA	34 739	14.0	81.5	20.0	127.6	6 633	12 053	26 685	1.1	1.9	NA	9.7	13.8	12.6
Lafayette, IN	242	3 525	61 148	7.1	83.2	26.3	145.2	5 842	12 432	27 253	-0.6	2.7	NA	9.9	12.4	11.7
Lafayette, LA	513	4 099	99 048	14.5	63.6	15.2	289.8	4 098	9 817	19 948	-23.0	2.4	NA	18.0	24.4	23.8
Lake Charles, LA	718	6 558	47 034	12.1	70.3	14.7	161.7	4 519	11 233	24 374	-22.3	2.3	NA	14.1	20.0	18.3
Lakeland-Winter Haven, FL	829	7 125	89 009	13.4	68.0	12.9	370.6	4 954	12 392	25 215	5.6	2.4	NA	16.6	25.4	22.7
Lancaster, PA	174	2 100	97 202	22.1	70.5	16.7	451.7	6 691	14 235	33 254	10.6	3.4	NA	7.6	11.8	11.0
Lansing-East Lansing, MI	460	3 869	148 916	9.1	84.2	24.7	539.0	7 110	14 044	32 155	-1.3	3.2	NA	10.8	15.9	15.0
Laredo, TX	472	6 772	48 323	7.0	47.8	11.1	224.7	5 010	6 771	18 074	-3.3	2.1	NA	32.6	42.3	39.4
Las Cruces, NM	526	5 263	46 488	4.4	70.4	21.9	166.3	4 544	9 374	21 858	5.5	1.4	NA	26.6	37.7	34.4
Las Vegas, NV-AZ	730	5 079	190 291	9.1	76.8	13.3	987.4	4 802	14 768	30 022	2.1	3.5	NA	11.8	17.8	15.5
Lawrence, KS	NA	NA	36 059	6.7	88.8	38.4	70.1	5 643	12 003	25 244	6.4	2.7	NA	11.9	14.1	13.5
Lawton, OK	506	4 776	30 373	6.9	81.1	18.4	110.3	4 771	10 602	24 378	5.5	1.5	NA	17.6	25.6	24.0
Lewiston-Auburn, ME	152	3 881	25 878	18.0	71.8	12.6	102.4	6 238	12 397	26 979	19.0	2.0	NA	10.7	14.5	13.7
Lexington, KY	NA	NA	116 334	13.3	74.5	24.5	364.0	5 584	13 390	26 854	5.0	3.3	NA	12.3	17.7	16.8
Lima, OH	469	3 980	39 899	15.2	76.2	10.9	147.2	5 098	11 994	28 141	-3.6	1.8	NA	9.7	13.3	12.2
Lincoln, NE	506	6 049	67 322	12.9	88.1	27.6	204.3	5 823	13 803	28 908	-1.0	2.5	NA	9.0	11.5	8.9
Little Rock-North Little Rock, AR	686	6 013	133 355	15.2	76.6	20.4	454.8	5 047	12 809	26 500	2.0	2.8	NA	13.0	18.8	16.8
Longview-Marshall, TX	453	4 245	52 132	11.5	72.8	14.8	208.2	4 816	11 423	23 969	-10.3	2.3	NA	16.6	23.4	21.9
Los Angeles-Riverside-Orange County, CA	797	3 266	4 089 214	14.7	73.2	22.0	14 163.1	5 185	16 444	36 710	18.4	7.9	NA	17.6	26.4	24.9
Los Angeles-Long Beach, CA	1 017	3 314	2 521 219	15.9	70.0	22.3	8 295.3	5 398	16 149	34 964	18.9	7.9	NA	20.5	30.5	28.7
Orange County, CA	351	2 699	666 355	13.5	81.2	27.8	2 189.7	4 944	19 890	45 921	21.5	11.3	NA	11.0	17.4	16.2
Riverside-San Bernardino, CA	646	3 818	713 348	11.4	74.8	14.8	3 049.0	4 883	13 879	33 278	18.0	4.2	NA	16.5	24.3	23.4
Ventura, CA	316	2 401	188 292	14.7	79.4	23.0	629.0	4 934	17 861	45 612	28.2	9.3	NA	10.3	16.6	15.5
Louisville, KY-IN	791	4 274	237 510	19.0	73.3	17.2	890.4	6 090	13 529	27 435	-2.8	2.9	NA	11.2	17.4	15.5
Lubbock, TX	918	4 961	74 111	7.6	74.2	23.4	223.1	5 195	12 008	24 328	-7.6	2.9	NA	19.3	27.1	25.5
Lynchburg, VA	309	2 543	48 451	23.8	66.6	16.2	158.4	4 834	12 632	26 776	0.0	2.2	NA	13.6	20.5	19.1
Macon, GA	574	6 539	77 090	17.5	71.1	15.8	288.1	5 160	12 731	27 887	7.5	2.7	NA	17.6	27.3	25.8
Madison, WI	NA	NA	115 595	9.2	88.9	34.2	450.6	7 345	15 542	32 703	6.6	3.9	NA	7.2	10.4	9.2
Mansfield, OH	233	3 720	41 131	12.4	73.6	11.0	179.9	5 817	12 208	26 579	-6.0	1.6	NA	11.1	16.1	14.7
McAllen-Edinburg-Mission, TX	516	5 358	134 820	4.4	46.6	11.5	709.3	5 403	6 630	16 702	-11.3	1.7	NA	37.6	47.9	42.9
Medford-Ashland, OR	294	5 204	34 122	9.6	80.1	17.6	166.2	5 866	12 492	25 068	-3.3	2.2	NA	13.8	20.3	16.5
Melbourne-Titusville-Palm Bay, FL	712	4 341	90 909	17.5	82.3	20.4	312.6	4 690	15 093	30 534	8.1	2.8	NA	11.3	17.6	16.2
Memphis, TN-AR-MS	1 081	5 534	267 233	15.5	73.1	18.7	919.2	4 609	12 851	26 899	6.2	3.6	NA	15.7	21.4	18.3

1. Data for serious crimes have not been adjusted for underreporting; this may affect comparability between geographic areas and over time.   2. Per 100,000 population estimated by the FBI.   3. All persons 3 years old and over enrolled in nursery school through college.   4. Persons 25 years old and over.   5. Elementary and secondary education expenditures, local government fiscal years ending between July 1, 1996 and June 30, 1997.   6. Based on population enumerated as of April 1, 1990.

Table C. Metropolitan Areas — **Personal Income**

Area Name	Personal income, 1998 Total (mil dol)	Percent change, 1997–1998	Per capita[1] Dollars	Per capita[1] Rank	Wages and salaries[2] (mil dol)	Proprietor's income (mil dol)	Dividends, interest, and rent (mil dol)	Transfer payments Total (mil dol)	Government payments to individuals Total (mil dol)	Social Security (mil dol)	Medical payments (mil dol)	Income maintenance (mil dol)	Unemployment insurance (mil dol)
	62	63	64	65	66	67	68	69	70	71	72	73	74
Hartford, CT	37 318	5.2	33 647	19	26 843	2 374	6 515	4 773	4 581	1 821	2 058	413	112
Hattiesburg, MS	2 133	4.5	19 130	307	1 332	177	364	385	365	138	147	42	3
Hickory-Morganton-Lenoir, NC	7 637	5.9	23 720	191	5 161	500	1 348	1 089	1 033	486	415	74	19
Honolulu, HI	24 994	1.7	28 670	60	16 730	1 889	4 707	2 646	2 520	1 031	847	403	100
Houma, LA	4 041	7.3	20 861	283	2 465	192	640	671	638	252	284	78	4
Houston-Galveston-Brazoria, TX	132 134	8.2	30 026	X	89 487	20 981	17 431	11 233	10 495	3 894	4 829	1 066	242
Brazoria, TX	5 228	5.7	22 844	217	2 828	255	770	596	557	231	245	43	16
Galveston-Texas City, TX .	5 954	4.3	24 303	167	2 983	261	1 007	812	771	305	345	67	18
Houston, TX	120 951	8.5	30 801	34	83 676	20 465	15 654	9 825	9 167	3 358	4 238	956	208
Huntington-Ashland, WV-KY-OH	6 217	2.8	19 804	299	3 598	274	1 069	1 464	1 407	525	492	162	23
Huntsville, AL	8 610	6.6	25 305	138	7 121	413	1 622	860	800	358	276	83	13
Indianapolis, IN	44 079	6.9	29 022	55	31 953	2 767	7 754	4 714	4 430	2 057	1 725	349	63
Iowa City, IA	2 850	6.4	27 785	72	2 063	194	563	209	188	95	59	13	3
Jackson, MI	3 525	3.1	22 576	231	2 031	214	665	551	523	247	190	50	14
Jackson, MS	10 547	5.6	24 542	160	7 273	786	1 828	1 378	1 300	520	512	165	12
Jackson, TN	2 384	5.7	23 725	189	1 798	202	335	386	369	142	161	38	5
Jacksonville, FL	28 435	6.8	27 244	91	19 739	1 660	5 030	3 376	3 196	1 284	1 263	320	36
Jacksonville, NC	3 170	3.4	22 109	249	2 398	143	428	317	299	99	123	39	4
Jamestown, NY	2 820	4.5	20 387	292	1 633	173	496	642	613	255	247	73	11
Janesville-Beloit, WI	3 671	4.1	24 356	166	2 397	141	632	477	449	226	158	31	18
Johnson City-Kingsport-Bristol, TN-VA	9 791	3.2	21 201	277	5 943	579	1 667	1 897	1 819	804	707	166	24
Johnstown, PA	4 887	3.4	20 729	287	2 358	470	849	1 287	1 241	458	570	84	34
Jonesboro, AR	1 604	3.9	20 771	286	1 071	135	271	253	239	101	90	25	5
Joplin, MO	3 228	4.2	21 691	264	2 105	275	568	573	547	232	236	46	8
Kalamazoo-Battle Creek, MI.	11 030	3.0	24 726	150	7 628	600	1 989	1 555	1 473	667	547	152	36
Kansas City, MO-KS	49 464	5.5	28 473	65	34 330	3 815	8 732	5 443	5 139	2 264	2 086	375	95
Killeen-Temple, TX	6 289	3.3	21 178	278	4 581	302	920	727	686	228	261	81	17
Knoxville, TN	16 420	5.6	24 640	156	10 416	1 440	2 927	2 422	2 313	1 025	929	197	36
Kokomo, IN	2 644	4.3	26 423	109	2 302	113	435	353	334	168	128	23	3
La Crosse, WI-MN	3 011	5.7	24 742	149	2 089	186	594	383	360	170	130	23	8
Lafayette, IN	4 067	5.1	23 312	200	3 024	194	791	451	419	205	138	27	5
Lafayette, LA	8 062	5.3	21 487	268	5 103	578	1 331	1 343	1 278	431	599	167	13
Lake Charles, LA	3 988	3.7	22 139	245	2 759	260	655	664	633	249	283	57	7
Lakeland-Winter Haven, FL ..	10 234	8.2	22 609	229	5 586	812	2 076	1 862	1 782	865	623	171	21
Lancaster, PA	12 012	5.5	26 303	111	7 152	1 227	2 353	1 405	1 316	698	442	86	35
Lansing-East Lansing, MI	10 909	2.1	24 226	170	7 923	552	1 980	1 296	1 213	553	446	123	39
Laredo, TX	2 591	6.3	13 870	316	1 690	269	273	526	495	107	237	116	8
Las Cruces, NM	2 805	6.4	16 599	314	1 512	266	532	495	465	163	173	77	8
Las Vegas, NV-AZ	36 686	8.6	27 780	73	23 827	2 937	7 399	4 277	4 066	1 883	1 398	297	121
Lawrence, KS	1 993	5.7	20 645	289	1 217	101	408	208	192	87	67	14	4
Lawton, OK	2 299	4.0	21 257	273	1 631	116	343	323	306	111	93	42	2
Lewiston-Auburn, ME...........	2 296	3.5	22 671	226	1 319	121	341	446	429	163	191	46	9
Lexington, KY	12 098	6.5	26 912	97	8 677	1 238	2 167	1 321	1 239	533	445	121	14
Lima, OH	3 521	3.6	22 818	219	2 410	185	735	557	526	242	191	40	9
Lincoln, NE	6 474	7.0	27 487	85	4 488	440	1 315	673	633	285	236	40	5
Little Rock-North Little Rock, AR	14 468	5.0	26 105	116	10 253	964	2 447	1 881	1 784	723	706	149	37
Longview-Marshall, TX	4 615	4.5	22 131	246	2 704	438	855	829	794	319	337	75	17
Los Angeles-Riverside-Orange County, CA	422 989	6.6	26 778	X	267 391	46 944	75 047	51 942	48 998	15 467	20 297	9 143	1 111
Los Angeles-Long Beach, CA	246 949	5.9	26 773	100	171 990	28 857	44 226	32 721	30 999	8 515	13 588	6 535	670
Orange County, CA	88 634	8.2	32 541	25	55 033	10 248	16 433	7 140	6 633	2 735	2 455	812	120
Riverside-San Bernardino, CA	66 385	7.5	21 300	272	30 058	5 807	10 409	10 074	9 495	3 439	3 588	1 582	250
Ventura, CA	21 020	6.1	28 711	58	10 310	2 032	3 979	2 007	1 871	778	666	215	71
Louisville, KY-IN	27 717	6.1	27 749	75	18 889	1 544	5 524	3 661	3 477	1 515	1 368	295	51
Lubbock, TX	5 352	4.8	23 451	195	3 226	634	894	836	798	278	386	78	7
Lynchburg, VA	4 624	4.4	22 268	240	2 976	227	861	744	705	340	248	52	4
Macon, GA	7 362	4.4	23 067	209	5 170	435	1 269	1 099	1 035	369	428	152	15
Madison, WI	12 831	6.0	30 214	39	9 319	714	2 711	1 016	937	462	340	61	23
Mansfield, OH	3 853	3.1	21 784	261	2 454	199	704	673	637	290	228	50	14
McAllen-Edinburg-Mission, TX	6 631	6.7	12 759	318	3 575	649	941	1 706	1 618	369	776	375	39
Medford-Ashland, OR	4 022	5.4	23 214	204	1 988	425	1 090	660	629	310	198	51	27
Melbourne-Titusville-Palm Bay, FL	11 043	4.9	23 758	185	6 385	405	2 707	1 937	1 854	928	676	102	22
Memphis, TN-AR-MS...........	30 053	7.3	27 511	84	21 193	2 926	4 111	3 748	3 565	1 250	1 548	517	51

1. Based on the resident population estimated as of July 1 of the year shown.   2. Includes other labor income.

Table C. Metropolitan Areas — Earnings, Social Security, and Housing

Area Name	Earnings, 1998									Social Security beneficiaries, December 1998		Supplemental Security Income recipients, December 1998	Housing units, 1990	
			Goods-related[1]		Service-related and other[2]									
	Total (mil dol)	Farm	Total	Manufacturing	Total	Retail trade	Finance, insurance, and real estate	Services	Government	Number	Rate[3]		Total	Percent change, 1980–1990
	75	76	77	78	79	80	81	82	83	84	85	86	87	88
Hartford, CT	29 217	0.3	NA	18.2	NA	7.2	16.8	26.8	14.7	195 683	176	17 245	450 082	15.4
Hattiesburg, MS	1 509	1.1	18.3	11.2	54.2	13.0	5.0	25.7	26.4	17 573	158	3 747	39 589	NA
Hickory-Morganton-Lenoir, NC	5 661	1.5	NA	44.0	NA	9.1	2.4	15.9	12.0	58 624	182	5 704	121 418	17.6
Honolulu, HI	18 619	0.3	8.7	3.1	57.9	10.1	8.6	26.9	33.1	123 553	142	14 760	281 683	11.8
Houma, LA	2 656	0.4	32.4	12.9	52.0	9.3	2.8	20.2	15.2	31 835	164	8 897	66 748	15.4
Houston-Galveston-Brazoria, TX	110 468	0.1	30.5	13.4	59.5	7.7	6.9	27.6	10.0	438 399	99	71 987	1 537 837	22.6
Brazoria, TX	3 083	0.3	51.8	34.4	33.7	7.8	2.5	14.8	14.1	25 557	111	2 771	74 504	23.2
Galveston-Texas City, TX	3 245	0.0	24.4	16.1	44.4	9.3	7.0	18.4	31.2	34 173	139	3 930	99 451	19.9
Houston, TX	104 140	0.1	30.0	12.7	60.7	7.6	7.0	28.3	9.2	378 669	96	65 286	1 363 882	22.7
Huntington-Ashland, WV-KY-OH	3 871	0.2	NA	18.9	NA	10.4	NA	26.6	18.6	63 657	203	15 573	130 687	2.0
Huntsville, AL	7 534	0.4	NA	24.6	NA	7.1	2.8	27.1	28.8	45 853	135	7 342	119 310	36.2
Indianapolis, IN	34 720	0.2	NA	21.7	NA	9.6	9.7	25.3	12.2	227 843	150	22 742	571 246	13.2
Iowa City, IA	2 256	0.4	NA	8.8	NA	8.4	4.3	19.6	45.7	10 195	99	863	37 210	17.8
Jackson, MI	2 245	0.0	33.2	26.8	50.2	9.1	3.7	22.1	16.6	27 080	173	3 457	57 979	4.0
Jackson, MS	8 059	0.6	16.2	9.3	62.4	9.7	9.3	26.5	20.8	64 576	150	14 759	152 493	17.7
Jackson, TN	1 999	0.1	NA	25.6	NA	9.6	NA	23.5	18.1	17 895	178	3 426	36 753	10.4
Jacksonville, FL	21 399	0.2	NA	7.9	NA	9.2	15.2	27.2	19.5	156 026	149	21 562	384 360	33.7
Jacksonville, NC	2 541	0.7	NA	2.5	NA	6.5	1.7	8.1	73.3	13 802	97	2 383	47 526	34.1
Jamestown, NY	1 806	1.1	34.1	29.7	45.6	10.1	2.6	22.8	19.2	29 745	215	4 156	62 682	2.9
Janesville-Beloit, WI	2 537	0.5	46.6	39.9	40.5	9.2	2.7	18.0	12.4	25 063	166	2 772	54 840	5.3
Johnson City-Kingsport-Bristol, TN-VA	6 522	0.2	NA	30.5	NA	10.8	3.9	23.9	14.3	100 486	217	16 248	183 995	10.3
Johnstown, PA	2 828	0.8	25.5	15.2	55.8	10.8	5.3	27.8	17.9	54 948	232	6 311	103 087	2.5
Jonesboro, AR	1 205	2.6	NA	22.2	54.1	10.8	4.4	27.2	14.9	12 995	168	2 584	28 434	17.8
Joplin, MO	2 380	1.2	NA	25.4	NA	11.1	3.1	22.7	10.1	29 386	198	3 470	57 938	10.8
Kalamazoo-Battle Creek, MI	8 228	0.6	NA	33.8	NA	8.2	NA	21.1	15.8	74 528	167	10 090	176 104	8.1
Kansas City, MO-KS	38 146	0.1	NA	13.0	NA	8.9	9.3	27.9	14.4	254 557	147	22 689	663 910	15.2
Killeen-Temple, TX	4 882	0.0	NA	7.0	NA	7.3	2.7	15.8	56.4	30 397	101	4 028	94 927	25.4
Knoxville, TN	11 857	0.1	NA	17.2	NA	NA	NA	29.1	15.3	121 343	184	17 536	252 294	17.0
Kokomo, IN	2 415	0.7	NA	61.0	NA	6.8	2.7	11.3	9.2	18 273	182	1 668	40 247	2.2
La Crosse, WI-MN	2 275	0.8	NA	19.7	NA	10.3	5.1	27.9	14.4	20 274	166	1 982	45 496	13.9
Lafayette, IN	3 218	0.4	NA	33.3	NA	8.1	5.2	18.9	22.5	22 646	131	1 627	60 234	9.0
Lafayette, LA	5 681	0.6	32.3	9.8	54.1	10.1	4.1	26.1	13.0	59 410	158	12 368	137 601	19.0
Lake Charles, LA	3 019	0.1	39.5	24.3	47.1	7.9	3.2	24.7	13.2	29 737	165	4 977	66 426	9.2
Lakeland-Winter Haven, FL	6 398	2.0	23.0	14.0	61.0	14.5	5.8	26.1	14.0	104 308	230	12 100	186 225	38.1
Lancaster, PA	8 379	1.1	40.2	30.4	50.0	10.1	5.8	21.7	8.7	76 166	167	6 168	156 462	20.9
Lansing-East Lansing, MI	8 475	0.2	24.8	18.8	48.1	8.4	7.4	24.3	26.8	60 567	135	7 954	165 018	10.4
Laredo, TX	1 958	0.0	13.7	2.2	61.0	12.0	6.0	19.7	25.3	18 190	97	8 072	37 197	34.0
Las Cruces, NM	1 777	7.3	NA	4.8	NA	10.4	4.0	21.4	37.8	22 461	133	4 582	49 148	NA
Las Vegas, NV-AZ	26 764	0.1	16.5	3.4	70.0	9.9	9.4	40.7	13.4	217 373	164	19 295	376 083	68.1
Lawrence, KS	1 318	0.2	21.6	14.4	48.2	12.1	5.9	22.0	30.0	9 703	104	935	31 782	24.7
Lawton, OK	1 747	0.4	NA	10.0	NA	7.3	2.8	13.2	57.6	14 701	130	2 125	43 589	9.1
Lewiston-Auburn, ME	1 440	0.4	NA	19.3	62.6	11.5	5.5	33.9	12.1	20 664	204	2 995	43 815	14.2
Lexington, KY	9 915	4.4	NA	23.1	NA	9.1	NA	23.3	16.7	64 756	144	11 698	166 685	18.6
Lima, OH	2 594	0.7	41.6	35.0	43.8	9.3	2.9	21.1	13.9	27 625	179	3 058	59 665	4.0
Lincoln, NE	4 928	0.4	20.2	14.3	58.1	8.1	8.4	27.1	21.4	31 980	136	3 067	86 734	13.6
Little Rock-North Little Rock, AR	11 217	0.4	NA	11.0	NA	9.1	7.8	26.7	21.7	89 214	160	13 402	214 546	18.6
Longview-Marshall, TX	3 142	0.2	36.1	21.9	52.6	11.4	4.3	23.2	11.1	38 008	182	5 472	81 057	13.7
Los Angeles-Riverside-Orange County, CA	314 336	0.5	20.2	15.3	65.9	8.9	9.5	33.6	13.4	1 763 256	112	496 702	5 293 072	19.6
Los Angeles-Long Beach, CA	200 847	0.1	18.8	15.0	68.2	8.2	9.6	36.5	12.9	971 134	105	343 335	3 163 343	10.8
Orange County, CA	65 282	0.3	24.0	18.0	66.0	9.3	12.1	30.0	9.6	293 473	108	52 070	875 072	21.3
Riverside-San Bernardino, CA	35 865	2.1	21.1	12.2	55.2	11.8	5.5	25.3	21.6	408 779	131	87 775	1 026 179	54.3
Ventura, CA	12 342	3.5	20.2	13.3	58.4	9.9	6.6	30.3	17.9	89 870	123	13 522	228 478	24.6
Louisville, KY-IN	20 433	0.1	NA	20.1	NA	9.8	7.3	26.7	12.2	173 109	173	24 209	390 494	8.1
Lubbock, TX	3 860	0.8	15.4	8.7	63.7	13.2	6.5	28.3	20.1	33 249	145	4 759	91 770	14.0
Lynchburg, VA	3 203	0.1	NA	33.9	NA	8.9	D	22.1	12.2	40 616	195	4 548	79 105	16.4
Macon, GA	5 604	0.5	NA	16.5	NA	8.8	6.5	24.2	29.1	49 769	156	10 981	115 154	16.8
Madison, WI	10 033	0.4	19.2	12.4	53.6	8.5	10.0	24.3	26.8	49 936	118	5 344	147 851	17.1
Mansfield, OH	2 654	0.9	NA	36.6	NA	9.4	3.8	19.0	14.3	33 019	189	3 690	69 864	1.7
McAllen-Edinburg-Mission, TX	4 224	2.1	15.0	7.5	55.1	14.0	4.4	24.6	27.8	60 349	116	24 862	128 241	44.0
Medford-Ashland, OR	2 413	0.4	23.1	15.3	60.4	16.4	5.7	26.8	16.1	36 028	208	2 555	60 376	15.5
Melbourne-Titusville-Palm Bay, FL	6 790	0.2	NA	19.9	NA	9.6	4.1	35.9	17.9	108 141	232	7 381	185 150	62.6
Memphis, TN-AR-MS	24 119	0.1	NA	12.1	NA	9.4	8.4	28.2	13.2	155 191	142	39 529	394 329	15.9

1. Covers mining, construction, and manufacturing. 2. Covers private sector earnings in agricultural services, forestry, and fisheries; transportation and public utilities; wholesale trade; retail trade; finance, insurance, and real estate; and services. 3. Per 1,000 resident population estimated as of July 1 of the year shown.

Table C. Metropolitan Areas — Housing, Labor Force, and Employment

Area Name	Housing units, 1990 (cont'd) Occupied units								Civilian labor force, 1999				Civilian employment, 1990[5]		
	Owner-occupied			Owner cost as a percent of income		Renter-occupied					Unemployment			Percent	
	Total	Percent	Median value[1]	With a mortgage	Without a mortgage	Median rent[2]	Rent as percent of income	Substandard units[3] (percent)	Total	Percent change, 1998–1999	Total	Rate[4]	Total	Professional, managerial, and technical	Precision production, craft, and repair
	89	90	91	92	93	94	95	96	97	98	99	100	101	102	103
Hartford, CT	423 651	64.7	169 300	22.0	13.2	576	25.0	2.4	560 207	-0.9	18 130	3.2	590 735	35.4	10.9
Hattiesburg, MS	36 033	65.3	NA	NA	NA	NA	NA	NA	50 329	-1.1	1 619	3.2	41 252	25.6	12.3
Hickory-Morganton-Lenoir, NC	112 387	74.7	57 000	NA	NA	341	NA	3.2	171 143	1.0	3 541	2.1	158 993	19.0	15.6
Honolulu, HI	265 304	52.0	283 600	21.5	10.7	662	27.6	15.9	424 230	-1.1	20 947	4.9	395 811	31.5	9.9
Houma, LA	60 672	74.4	52 600	20.0	12.6	319	26.2	8.3	92 016	-3.5	3 832	4.2	67 524	22.2	17.6
Houston-Galveston-Brazoria, TX	1 338 775	56.2	63 700	NA	NA	405	NA	9.0	2 373 748	0.6	111 671	4.7	1 800 508	32.9	12.0
Brazoria, TX	64 019	69.2	61 800	18.2	12.3	400	21.6	6.9	104 072	-1.9	7 045	6.8	86 663	28.9	18.1
Galveston-Texas City, TX	81 451	62.0	59 700	19.6	13.4	400	25.4	5.7	121 984	-2.0	7 965	6.5	99 670	33.1	13.5
Houston, TX	1 193 305	55.1	64 200	NA	NA	406	NA	9.4	2 147 692	0.9	96 661	4.5	1 614 175	33.1	11.6
Huntington-Ashland, WV-KY-OH	119 640	72.0	46 600	16.6	12.1	305	27.8	3.6	139 307	2.2	9 392	6.7	118 603	26.1	13.4
Huntsville, AL	110 893	67.1	73 900	NA	NA	397	NA	3.1	172 057	0.4	5 754	3.3	144 186	39.3	11.1
Indianapolis, IN	529 814	64.7	64 100	NA	NA	407	NA	2.2	833 848	0.1	20 192	2.4	692 323	29.6	11.4
Iowa City, IA	36 067	52.7	76 900	19.0	12.2	411	28.3	2.9	67 137	2.5	1 363	2.0	54 591	40.8	6.3
Jackson, MI	53 660	73.7	47 900	16.1	12.7	375	25.0	2.1	78 070	2.0	2 658	3.4	64 317	24.7	12.5
Jackson, MS	140 157	65.7	59 900	21.0	13.8	399	27.6	6.3	225 114	0.1	7 614	3.4	180 802	32.0	9.8
Jackson, TN	34 167	67.0	NA	NA	NA	NA	NA	NA	58 177	3.2	2 013	3.5	41 115	NA	11.0
Jacksonville, FL	343 526	64.8	67 800	20.8	12.3	438	25.6	4.1	539 814	1.2	16 091	3.0	422 421	28.9	11.5
Jacksonville, NC	40 658	53.7	62 200	23.4	13.2	397	25.3	4.7	46 631	3.5	1 651	3.5	38 674	24.0	13.8
Jamestown, NY	53 696	68.6	47 800	18.0	13.5	325	28.6	1.6	66 007	-2.3	3 433	5.2	62 263	24.1	12.0
Janesville-Beloit, WI	52 252	68.2	52 300	17.0	12.9	386	24.7	2.0	77 151	-3.6	3 101	4.0	67 826	22.7	12.8
Johnson City-Kingsport-Bristol, TN-VA	170 569	73.7	52 000	17.9	12.3	301	24.4	3.3	226 916	1.3	9 981	4.4	194 639	24.2	13.7
Johnstown, PA	91 578	74.6	40 900	19.1	13.3	277	24.9	2.0	102 543	0.1	5 932	5.8	91 968	23.4	13.3
Jonesboro, AR	26 285	65.4	50 200	19.3	13.1	335	26.8	2.2	42 053	2.1	1 371	3.3	32 772	23.6	11.2
Joplin, MO	53 020	71.7	39 400	17.2	12.0	297	24.5	2.6	81 920	-1.6	2 576	3.1	61 567	22.5	13.0
Kalamazoo-Battle Creek, MI	160 916	68.5	53 800	NA	NA	394	NA	2.5	238 136	2.9	8 385	3.5	199 521	29.4	10.4
Kansas City, MO-KS	608 459	65.6	66 300	NA	NA	424	NA	2.4	978 978	1.3	28 971	3.0	784 951	31.1	10.0
Killeen-Temple, TX	83 927	52.1	57 300	21.5	12.9	378	25.2	5.5	115 251	0.3	3 985	3.5	83 561	27.9	11.5
Knoxville, TN	231 254	68.3	61 100	NA	NA	341	NA	2.6	352 596	2.3	11 590	3.3	278 110	30.3	11.9
Kokomo, IN	37 549	72.8	51 600	14.6	12.1	357	24.5	1.8	50 444	-1.1	1 307	2.6	44 821	23.7	15.9
La Crosse, WI-MN	43 506	65.5	57 500	NA	NA	348	NA	2.4	69 944	-2.7	2 112	3.0	59 030	27.4	9.5
Lafayette, IN	57 068	60.1	59 400	NA	NA	388	NA	3.2	89 853	0.6	1 979	2.2	77 998	32.5	10.3
Lafayette, LA	121 807	67.5	50 500	NA	NA	297	NA	7.4	177 112	-2.3	9 979	5.6	132 264	27.3	13.3
Lake Charles, LA	60 328	70.4	54 700	17.6	12.8	337	26.3	4.5	92 266	0.1	4 481	4.9	67 327	26.2	17.1
Lakeland-Winter Haven, FL	155 969	70.5	61 000	19.7	11.9	385	25.4	4.4	200 286	1.4	9 711	4.8	171 677	23.2	13.3
Lancaster, PA	150 956	69.4	89 400	20.7	11.9	440	23.8	2.9	243 503	0.8	6 602	2.7	215 292	24.0	13.6
Lansing-East Lansing, MI	156 887	64.7	64 500	18.4	13.1	421	26.0	2.6	246 961	1.7	6 373	2.6	216 826	31.6	9.6
Laredo, TX	34 438	60.6	49 800	22.5	12.7	313	27.6	28.1	72 729	-0.3	6 211	8.5	45 819	23.3	10.0
Las Cruces, NM	45 029	NA	67 300	20.7	12.3	346	28.2	9.7	68 148	0.0	5 153	7.6	53 059	32.1	10.5
Las Vegas, NV-AZ	330 490	54.5	91 500	NA	NA	511	NA	6.7	728 750	4.4	32 322	4.4	416 030	23.4	11.5
Lawrence, KS	30 138	52.5	68 000	19.7	12.3	412	33.8	3.0	55 730	1.9	1 789	3.2	41 086	35.1	8.1
Lawton, OK	37 569	60.2	54 000	21.3	12.3	376	25.7	4.8	41 120	-0.2	1 491	3.6	37 640	31.0	8.9
Lewiston-Auburn, ME	40 017	62.2	86 800	21.1	13.9	373	24.9	2.4	59 994	4.2	2 417	4.0	50 588	23.4	14.5
Lexington, KY	154 089	58.4	69 000	NA	NA	370	NA	3.0	262 302	3.7	5 476	2.1	204 827	32.2	9.4
Lima, OH	55 384	73.2	54 200	15.9	11.9	345	23.9	2.1	75 983	3.1	3 410	4.5	67 465	22.8	13.1
Lincoln, NE	82 759	60.5	62 200	18.9	11.9	377	25.6	1.4	142 384	-0.4	3 397	2.4	117 484	32.7	9.5
Little Rock-North Little Rock, AR	195 437	64.8	59 700	19.8	13.0	391	26.3	3.7	298 490	0.8	9 458	3.2	241 622	30.1	10.6
Longview-Marshall, TX	72 092	69.4	51 100	NA	NA	340	NA	5.5	103 527	-1.9	7 368	7.1	82 363	24.0	14.6
Los Angeles-Riverside-Orange County, CA	4 900 720	54.0	211 700	NA	NA	645	NA	15.5	7 968 583	1.6	404 644	5.1	6 912 664	31.1	11.4
Los Angeles-Long Beach, CA	2 989 552	48.2	226 400	25.2	11.6	625	29.5	18.9	4 658 630	0.4	272 818	5.9	4 203 792	30.9	11.0
Orange County, CA	827 066	60.1	252 700	NA	NA	789	NA	10.7	1 471 602	2.5	38 932	2.6	1 292 472	35.0	10.3
Riverside-San Bernardino, CA	866 804	65.2	133 900	25.8	12.2	561	29.7	9.8	1 442 563	4.4	73 964	5.1	1 079 628	26.6	14.4
Ventura, CA	217 298	65.5	245 300	NA	NA	753	NA	10.3	395 788	2.2	18 930	4.8	336 772	33.1	11.7
Louisville, KY-IN	366 364	67.6	56 100	NA	NA	345	NA	2.6	561 682	2.3	19 024	3.4	450 019	27.6	11.6
Lubbock, TX	81 534	58.2	54 500	20.0	12.6	376	29.5	6.6	123 318	0.1	3 555	2.9	102 790	30.9	9.9
Lynchburg, VA	72 689	72.4	61 692	16.6	12.1	335	23.6	3.4	103 939	1.8	2 141	2.1	92 896	25.5	12.8
Macon, GA	106 478	63.1	59 100	NA	NA	361	NA	4.5	152 954	0.3	7 144	4.7	129 317	28.2	13.4
Madison, WI	142 786	55.2	78 400	20.9	13.1	464	26.0	2.6	258 942	-1.2	3 540	1.4	208 069	38.0	7.7
Mansfield, OH	65 956	70.9	49 300	NA	NA	330	NA	2.0	84 347	1.9	5 220	6.2	76 988	22.1	14.7
McAllen-Edinburg-Mission, TX	103 479	70.3	35 900	21.5	12.7	281	26.5	28.4	194 414	-0.4	28 124	14.5	122 112	23.3	10.5
Medford-Ashland, OR	57 238	66.2	74 900	22.0	13.3	412	27.6	4.4	89 158	1.2	5 910	6.6	62 704	25.1	10.7
Melbourne-Titusville-Palm Bay, FL	161 365	69.2	75 200	21.0	11.5	482	26.2	2.2	206 340	1.0	8 019	3.9	183 692	34.7	12.8
Memphis, TN-AR-MS	365 450	61.7	64 600	NA	NA	388	NA	5.3	560 218	1.5	20 343	3.6	456 421	29.0	9.8

1. Specified owner-occupied units. 2. Specified renter-occupied units. 3. Overcrowded or lacking complete plumbing facilities. 4. Percent of civilian labor force. 5. Persons 16 years and older.

Table C. Metropolitan Areas — Nonfarm Employment and Agriculture

Area Name	Private nonfarm establishments, employment and payroll, 1998									Agriculture, 1997			Farm operators
	Number of establishments	Employment						Annual payroll		Farms			
		Total	Health Care and Social Assistance	Manufacturing	Retail trade	Finance and Insurance	Professional Scientific and Technical Services	Total (mil dol)	Average per employee (dollars)	Number	Percent with—		Whose principal occupation is farming (percent)
											Less than 50 acres	500 acres and over	
	104	105	106	107	108	109	110	111	112	113	114	115	116
Hartford, CT	29 955	545 246	76 571	87 974	64 497	70 708	25 677	19 983	36 650	1 270	57.9	2.3	50.2
Hattiesburg, MS	2 859	40 966	7 425	5 983	8 287	1 575	1 200	883	21 554	692	33.7	5.9	38.7
Hickory-Morganton-Lenoir, NC	8 011	158 148	12 611	77 303	18 098	2 433	2 257	3 791	23 971	1 846	44.3	3.0	40.7
Honolulu, HI	20 675	309 487	35 818	10 652	41 597	17 786	14 659	8 744	28 253	880	93.2	1.7	100.0
Houma, LA	4 478	68 532	8 134	7 821	10 813	2 111	2 756	1 847	26 951	535	34.8	18.5	41.9
Houston-Galveston-Brazoria, TX	104 456	1 886 011	185 401	209 143	217 135	83 764	130 770	65 358	34 654	9 112	47.9	11.2	36.3
Brazoria, TX	3 748	56 950	4 343	14 282	9 050	1 273	1 376	1 841	32 327	1 783	45.4	13.8	33.6
Galveston-Texas City, TX	4 769	68 024	13 519	7 529	11 044	3 939	1 812	1 758	25 844	519	59.3	8.3	30.8
Houston, TX	95 939	1 761 037	167 539	187 332	197 041	78 552	127 582	61 759	35 070	6 810	47.7	10.8	37.4
Huntington-Ashland, WV-KY-OH	6 913	98 156	18 918	14 864	17 115	3 597	3 207	2 456	25 021	2 758	30.7	2.9	32.9
Huntsville, AL	8 083	136 188	14 179	33 399	19 216	3 364	16 252	3 910	28 710	2 100	40.1	9.9	35.5
Indianapolis, IN	41 537	762 800	100 034	107 568	96 877	52 182	36 050	24 097	31 590	5 113	40.2	17.3	47.9
Iowa City, IA	2 607	45 266	12 326	3 733	7 536	1 266	1 374	1 073	23 704	1 261	24.0	13.3	55.7
Jackson, MI	3 442	53 517	7 148	12 218	8 471	1 450	1 389	1 470	27 468	987	34.7	8.0	38.0
Jackson, MS	10 971	199 211	32 197	18 877	27 427	12 768	7 932	5 034	25 270	1 746	24.2	14.5	34.0
Jackson, TN	2 900	53 047	8 281	12 995	8 088	1 418	1 220	1 300	24 507	981	28.2	9.6	36.6
Jacksonville, FL	27 902	459 459	54 298	33 960	61 154	49 533	23 160	12 413	27 017	918	62.5	8.6	46.4
Jacksonville, NC	2 599	28 155	4 385	1 930	6 330	928	801	487	17 297	369	40.7	8.4	56.9
Jamestown, NY	3 107	46 937	8 123	13 743	6 862	853	1 060	1 090	23 223	1 557	33.2	5.3	56.0
Janesville-Beloit, WI	3 340	60 340	7 290	18 543	8 439	1 606	992	1 736	28 770	1 324	32.6	12.9	52.3
Johnson City-Kingsport-Bristol, TN-VA	10 259	171 863	24 089	47 574	26 475	7 343	4 184	4 270	24 845	8 856	53.9	1.7	35.1
Johnstown, PA	5 463	70 402	12 389	12 835	11 035	4 184	2 767	1 537	21 832	1 483	19.5	8.0	57.0
Jonesboro, AR	2 289	32 834	5 648	7 187	5 603	1 095	809	755	22 994	754	21.6	33.8	63.8
Joplin, MO	4 051	70 204	10 523	16 678	9 467	1 626	1 117	1 568	22 335	2 977	30.7	7.2	39.3
Kalamazoo-Battle Creek, MI	10 469	186 237	25 399	42 460	25 795	8 268	5 949	5 543	29 763	2 840	34.1	9.6	47.9
Kansas City, MO-KS	47 403	825 691	101 016	95 328	104 439	56 334	52 427	25 670	31 089	9 774	32.1	11.2	40.5
Killeen-Temple, TX	4 668	80 253	18 344	7 769	11 733	3 660	2 691	1 749	21 794	2 816	29.0	16.7	39.1
Knoxville, TN	18 508	292 374	37 315	45 293	47 427	10 213	20 222	7 761	26 545	4 816	51.5	1.8	33.6
Kokomo, IN	2 330	47 828	5 216	20 787	6 367	1 278	603	1 776	37 133	901	28.4	22.1	57.0
La Crosse, WI-MN	3 375	59 931	10 975	11 282	9 326	2 133	1 759	1 468	24 495	1 713	13.0	14.0	57.8
Lafayette, IN	3 817	72 232	8 305	21 416	10 844	3 924	1 704	1 961	27 149	1 250	31.0	25.3	52.5
Lafayette, LA	9 759	136 772	19 717	13 000	21 475	4 683	8 193	3 390	24 786	2 424	45.9	17.7	48.1
Lake Charles, LA	4 285	71 390	10 410	11 154	10 766	2 033	2 878	1 825	25 564	749	35.6	17.5	34.6
Lakeland-Winter Haven, FL	9 625	151 889	18 119	19 335	22 298	8 922	4 620	3 845	25 315	2 464	62.3	8.6	39.3
Lancaster, PA	11 242	201 341	23 726	52 897	30 359	6 663	6 416	5 387	26 756	4 556	39.6	1.3	74.2
Lansing-East Lansing, MI	10 303	166 071	20 478	27 952	27 386	10 838	7 130	4 821	29 030	3 012	34.5	9.9	44.1
Laredo, TX	3 916	46 888	6 734	1 591	9 060	1 859	1 216	927	19 771	453	6.0	61.1	38.4
Las Cruces, NM	3 183	34 739	5 874	2 398	6 604	1 413	2 538	674	19 402	1 290	75.7	7.8	40.4
Las Vegas, NV-AZ	30 446	585 646	43 221	21 666	71 589	20 792	24 007	15 774	26 934	565	49.7	23.0	48.1
Lawrence, KS	2 590	35 809	4 527	4 640	6 189	1 357	1 753	731	20 414	839	30.3	13.8	42.9
Lawton, OK	2 149	27 604	5 158	0	5 182	1 383	1 229	568	20 577	1 030	18.2	25.2	44.3
Lewiston-Auburn, ME	2 763	39 769	7 030	7 880	6 297	2 131	2 064	937	23 561	288	27.4	9.7	52.1
Lexington, KY	12 171	217 622	29 704	43 717	33 792	7 170	9 939	5 839	26 831	6 229	39.7	7.6	47.6
Lima, OH	3 881	68 686	11 081	18 368	9 967	1 730	1 287	1 794	26 119	1 919	27.5	11.4	47.9
Lincoln, NE	6 696	117 339	16 922	15 368	15 904	9 423	8 069	2 928	24 953	1 457	32.3	19.1	46.0
Little Rock-North Little Rock, AR	15 557	266 651	42 420	31 089	36 570	13 207	12 814	6 914	25 929	2 730	30.0	15.2	40.9
Longview-Marshall, TX	5 578	79 200	10 383	17 917	12 016	2 672	2 338	1 884	23 788	2 580	37.0	7.1	33.2
Los Angeles-Riverside-Orange County, CA	362 499	5 952 301	582 722	1 012 299	626 616	289 730	502 153	192 697	32 374	8 292	78.2	4.7	44.6
Los Angeles-Long Beach, CA	219 933	3 693 537	360 703	638 389	349 666	177 067	383 371	123 783	33 513	1 226	84.7	4.7	39.9
Orange County, CA	75 154	1 274 074	105 147	224 709	129 105	78 537	87 038	43 261	33 955	349	74.8	3.2	49.3
Riverside-San Bernardino, CA	50 949	766 953	94 141	115 845	116 004	22 843	19 543	19 310	25 178	4 503	79.2	4.3	44.5
Ventura, CA	16 463	217 737	22 731	33 356	31 841	11 283	12 201	6 343	29 131	2 214	73.3	5.6	46.5
Louisville, KY-IN	26 916	493 737	60 879	79 643	67 763	30 043	19 814	13 910	28 173	3 844	41.6	5.1	38.5
Lubbock, TX	6 480	90 311	17 531	7 514	14 389	3 721	2 885	1 995	22 090	1 068	29.1	32.1	55.3
Lynchburg, VA	5 282	87 448	9 123	23 467	12 496	3 473	3 695	2 240	25 615	2 225	23.8	8.1	40.5
Macon, GA	7 379	118 841	18 997	18 574	19 161	8 157	5 286	3 056	25 715	810	34.1	12.2	36.7
Madison, WI	12 058	214 837	26 791	26 902	30 973	18 580	12 530	6 019	28 017	2 595	30.1	8.1	54.3
Mansfield, OH	4 077	68 412	8 302	22 023	10 223	1 618	1 289	1 708	24 966	1 620	27.2	11.7	49.9
McAllen-Edinburg-Mission, TX	7 990	101 510	17 631	11 624	21 758	4 030	3 003	1 885	18 570	1 373	49.5	18.9	45.4
Medford-Ashland, OR	5 157	58 195	8 568	7 412	9 705	1 823	1 767	1 389	23 868	1 623	66.7	4.7	41.0
Melbourne-Titusville-Palm Bay, FL	11 330	154 136	21 088	20 143	24 865	3 828	13 109	4 171	27 061	470	74.9	8.7	36.2
Memphis, TN-AR-MS	25 213	511 190	57 158	55 163	68 651	21 863	19 394	14 924	29 195	2 717	38.6	17.4	40.9

Table C. Metropolitan Areas — Agriculture, Land, and Water

Area Name	Land in farms Acreage (1,000)	Percent change, 1992–1997	Acres Average size of farm	Acres Total irrigated (1,000)	Acres Total cropland (1,000)	Value of land and buildings Average per farm ($1,000)	Value of land and buildings Average per acre (dollars)	Value of machinery and equipment Average per farm ($1,000)	Value of products sold Total (mil dol)	Value of products sold Average per farm (dollars)	Percent from Crops	Percent from Livestock and poultry products	Percent of farms with sales of $10,000 or more	Percent of farms with sales of $100,000 or more	Percent of land owned by Fed. Gov. 1997	Water consumption 1995 (mil gal/day)
	117	118	119	120	121	122	123	124	125	126	127	128	129	130	131	132
Hartford, CT	108	-6.2	85	5	58	548	6 662	43	173	136 536	83.0	17.0	40.6	13.1	0.2	737.0
Hattiesburg, MS	120	32.1	174	1	41	321	1 739	29	46	65 978	11.0	89.0	27.6	8.5	9.9	50.4
Hickory-Morganton-Lenoir, NC	199	10.9	108	2	115	266	2 630	30	123	66 707	28.0	72.0	32.6	12.7	9.2	853.4
Honolulu, HI	80	-13.1	91	16	29	565	6 225	33	143	162 460	72.0	28.0	57.5	14.5	12.5	278.9
Houma, LA	188	6.2	351	1	100	531	1 419	70	46	86 705	84.0	16.0	43.4	14.0	0.0	62.7
Houston-Galveston-Brazoria, TX	2 395	-1.3	263	106	988	371	1 492	36	253	27 804	69.0	31.0	24.4	5.1	2.6	1 858.4
Brazoria, TX	567	0.5	318	30	203	403	1 293	38	43	23 904	59.0	41.0	22.5	5.0	2.7	286.0
Galveston-Texas City, TX	105	2.9	202	1	30	251	1 053	28	7	13 112	31.0	69.0	18.3	1.9	0.1	61.1
Houston, TX	1 723	-2.2	253	75	754	372	1 584	36	204	29 945	72.0	28.0	25.3	5.4	2.9	1 511.4
Huntington-Ashland, WV-KY-OH	353	-3.9	128	0	131	128	1 084	22	28	10 011	61.0	39.0	22.1	1.1	8.3	211.6
Huntsville, AL	464	7.5	221	8	339	467	2 101	42	82	39 136	49.0	51.0	28.0	7.1	5.8	846.3
Indianapolis, IN	1 423	-4.8	278	D	1 295	758	2 714	73	504	98 523	80.0	20.0	57.5	22.6	0.3	609.7
Iowa City, IA	288	1.1	229	1	249	416	1 816	56	100	79 612	51.0	49.0	64.0	24.0	4.0	62.9
Jackson, MI	181	-14.1	184	3	138	272	1 600	51	44	44 895	54.0	46.0	41.7	9.1	0.0	37.3
Jackson, MS	496	-9.5	284	D	229	370	1 247	42	127	72 737	27.0	73.0	29.1	9.3	0.4	73.2
Jackson, TN	219	2.7	223	0	146	228	1 073	44	35	35 433	78.0	22.0	27.1	7.4	0.0	20.2
Jacksonville, FL	191	-13.1	208	22	50	472	2 319	45	130	141 830	44.0	56.0	31.7	13.7	5.1	257.6
Jacksonville, NC	63	-0.9	172	0	42	291	1 729	48	102	275 201	22.0	78.0	55.6	31.4	15.4	14.8
Jamestown, NY	245	-5.8	157	1	145	172	1 145	46	89	56 951	33.0	67.0	52.0	15.5	0.0	1 204.1
Janesville-Beloit, WI	351	2.3	265	10	308	453	1 727	79	130	97 906	57.0	43.0	58.5	24.7	0.1	152.0
Johnson City-Kingsport-Bristol, TN-VA	715	-3.1	81	2	389	201	2 390	27	152	17 196	43.0	57.0	25.8	2.1	14.6	1 155.4
Johnstown, PA	294	-1.0	198	1	187	259	1 255	55	82	55 241	24.0	76.0	50.5	15.6	0.1	62.7
Jonesboro, AR	363	3.8	482	222	335	612	1 365	119	123	162 763	98.0	2.0	68.4	41.4	0.6	349.6
Joplin, MO	527	-1.9	177	6	348	231	1 272	26	200	67 115	17.0	83.0	35.3	8.9	0.0	33.2
Kalamazoo-Battle Creek, MI	567	-6.4	200	47	444	343	1 658	63	267	94 056	71.0	29.0	51.9	16.2	0.7	274.5
Kansas City, MO-KS	2 256	-1.0	231	13	1 626	359	1 601	41	451	46 160	58.0	42.0	40.6	9.2	1.1	1 459.1
Killeen-Temple, TX	1 053	3.1	374	2	370	329	775	30	80	28 237	29.0	71.0	27.6	4.0	16.7	49.9
Knoxville, TN	419	-2.6	87	1	253	307	3 465	30	98	20 326	D	D	18.0	2.1	14.2	613.8
Kokomo, IN	306	-1.2	340	D	286	921	2 780	97	128	142 536	75.0	25.0	74.1	35.7	0.0	25.1
La Crosse, WI-MN	468	3.0	273	1	276	273	1 086	57	123	72 047	31.0	69.0	61.6	22.4	2.8	72.0
Lafayette, IN	478	-3.1	382	4	443	919	2 389	93	186	148 405	68.0	32.0	71.4	34.6	0.0	51.3
Lafayette, LA	704	-0.8	290	147	604	372	1 399	62	185	76 361	91.0	9.0	38.3	17.0	0.8	235.7
Lake Charles, LA	312	-5.0	416	30	140	500	1 301	33	20	27 307	69.0	31.0	28.8	8.3	0.0	312.0
Lakeland-Winter Haven, FL	621	1.7	252	118	187	532	2 110	31	253	102 865	81.0	19.0	48.0	12.5	2.5	391.9
Lancaster, PA	392	1.0	86	5	331	472	5 578	52	767	168 293	13.0	87.0	82.1	43.5	0.0	165.7
Lansing-East Lansing, MI	666	-2.6	221	6	559	358	1 590	65	200	66 354	57.0	43.0	49.4	14.4	0.0	192.8
Laredo, TX	2 176	27.1	4 804	6	52	1 594	330	50	28	62 247	10.0	90.0	37.1	6.8	0.0	42.9
Las Cruces, NM	581	10.5	451	82	91	541	1 305	65	235	182 546	55.0	45.0	32.7	13.3	76.1	441.4
Las Vegas, NV-AZ	1 153	-47.7	2 041	36	56	908	392	54	62	109 205	35.0	65.0	35.4	9.6	85.8	625.6
Lawrence, KS	219	-1.6	260	2	147	297	1 135	53	39	46 347	56.0	44.0	39.8	10.1	3.1	21.6
Lawton, OK	435	7.0	422	1	194	309	720	39	32	31 380	35.0	65.0	42.1	7.2	23.4	21.1
Lewiston-Auburn, ME	56	-9.8	194	1	23	304	1 715	71	62	216 587	13.0	87.0	47.9	19.4	0.0	14.0
Lexington, KY	1 058	-5.7	170	9	715	416	2 469	37	556	89 301	27.0	73.0	57.4	12.7	1.2	190.4
Lima, OH	403	1.0	210	0	368	456	2 110	74	145	75 525	64.0	36.0	70.0	22.1	0.1	54.4
Lincoln, NE	421	1.5	289	13	344	400	1 410	51	82	56 545	72.0	28.0	51.6	17.4	1.4	21.0
Little Rock-North Little Rock, AR	763	1.6	280	234	551	387	1 364	52	176	64 420	68.0	32.0	34.5	13.6	3.7	480.8
Longview-Marshall, TX	441	-0.4	171	1	193	203	1 212	25	46	17 736	7.0	93.0	24.0	2.9	0.8	112.3
Los Angeles-Riverside-Orange County, CA	1 968	-13.6	237	412	536	705	3 201	56	2 978	359 083	65.0	35.0	48.4	21.9	62.3	4 583.4
Los Angeles-Long Beach, CA	131	-28.9	107	27	49	507	4 475	39	238	193 854	94.0	6.0	37.1	14.1	29.6	1 683.0
Orange County, CA	58	-4.7	167	13	17	871	6 010	90	229	655 819	99.0	1.0	53.0	29.2	13.1	517.3
Riverside-San Bernardino, CA	1 433	-16.2	318	261	338	659	2 087	63	1 665	369 833	39.0	61.0	46.7	20.7	69.5	2 010.4
Ventura, CA	346	7.9	156	111	132	883	6 860	46	846	381 939	98.0	2.0	57.3	27.5	50.0	372.7
Louisville, KY-IN	517	-6.1	135	1	343	325	2 531	35	117	30 382	52.0	48.0	32.1	6.0	3.6	1 246.3
Lubbock, TX	541	12.2	506	212	456	441	808	104	134	125 239	71.0	29.0	53.0	27.7	0.4	217.8
Lynchburg, VA	428	0.8	193	D	199	294	1 540	34	39	17 741	25.0	75.0	27.2	3.4	8.0	47.8
Macon, GA	217	9.7	268	13	115	397	1 474	55	75	92 489	61.0	39.0	34.2	11.6	5.4	168.6
Madison, WI	513	-4.8	198	7	414	367	1 853	73	285	109 687	31.0	69.0	59.5	25.6	0.2	112.7
Mansfield, OH	382	-0.5	236	0	327	438	1 895	67	122	75 524	63.0	37.0	60.2	19.9	0.0	22.0
McAllen-Edinburg-Mission, TX	636	-3.7	463	185	439	609	1 360	63	197	143 653	92.0	8.0	41.1	17.3	1.8	932.3
Medford-Ashland, OR	246	-6.1	152	53	70	353	1 784	32	51	31 397	75.0	25.0	22.1	3.4	47.7	363.6
Melbourne-Titusville-Palm Bay, FL	277	38.3	588	31	27	909	1 474	33	38	80 757	86.0	14.0	36.0	9.8	12.7	135.5
Memphis, TN-AR-MS	1 038	-1.5	382	110	835	594	1 630	69	228	84 060	90.0	10.0	34.3	15.2	1.3	778.7

Table C. Metropolitan Areas — **Residential Construction, Wholesale and Retail Trade, and Real Estate**

Area Name	Value of Residential Construction Authorized by Building Permits, 1999		Wholesale Trade, 1997				Retail Trade[1], 1997				Real Estate and Rental and Leasing, 1997			
	New Construction ($1,000)	Number of Housing Units	Number of Establishments	Number of Employees	Sales (mil dol)	Annual Payroll (mil dol)	Number of Establishments	Number of Employees	Sales (mil dol)	Annual Payroll (mil dol)	Number of Establishments	Number of Employees	Receipts (mil dol)	Annual Payroll (mil dol)
	133	134	135	136	137	138	139	140	141	142	143	144	145	146
Hartford, CT	470 814	3 843	1 676	28 388	17 900.5	1 205.6	4 853	64 199	10 937.9	1 168.5	1 102	7 492	1 142.5	205.4
Hattiesburg, MS	15 010	160	142	D	D	D	597	7 759	1 135.9	106.0	119	477	41.5	6.8
Hickory-Morganton-Lenoir, NC	242 141	2 159	487	7 360	3 606.1	227.1	1 524	17 319	2 935.2	264.7	236	883	103.3	16.8
Honolulu, HI	260 117	1 928	1 463	15 423	6 079.9	487.0	3 269	44 960	8 264.7	823.6	1 221	7 746	1 219.9	208.4
Houma, LA	77 413	741	300	3 189	1 119.0	88.3	805	10 106	1 634.1	143.7	218	2 077	303.7	63.4
Houston-Galveston-Brazoria, TX	3 811 651	36 675	8 837	113 506	117 381.3	4 566.5	15 173	215 892	39 877.0	3 679.1	4 932	38 177	4 691.3	934.5
Brazoria, TX	200 149	1 983	220	2 524	840.2	102.1	629	8 945	1 534.4	136.0	196	1 231	142.8	29.3
Galveston-Texas City, TX	234 267	2 107	198	1 522	561.3	46.6	921	10 591	1 786.9	165.8	224	1 160	128.5	25.4
Houston, TX	3 377 235	32 585	8 419	109 460	115 979.8	4 417.8	13 623	196 356	36 555.7	3 377.3	4 512	35 786	4 420.0	879.8
Huntington-Ashland, WV-KY-OH	23 818	326	361	4 570	1 656.2	125.3	1 456	17 394	2 589.8	247.0	250	942	94.0	16.3
Huntsville, AL	71 851	1 188	520	5 494	3 485.9	189.0	1 479	19 814	3 015.3	291.4	366	1 735	178.2	31.7
Indianapolis, IN	2 084 568	15 862	3 040	42 968	28 933.9	1 613.7	6 203	95 437	16 941.0	1 603.9	1 715	12 032	1 467.6	267.7
Iowa City, IA	122 029	1 072	89	D	D	D	467	6 924	990.9	104.7	120	566	66.7	10.2
Jackson, MI	95 935	1 007	196	2 339	1 047.2	83.7	564	8 108	1 289.4	126.9	96	465	41.9	7.3
Jackson, MS	320 215	3 945	772	11 386	5 390.5	363.6	1 819	27 344	4 249.5	422.9	459	2 224	255.5	38.7
Jackson, TN	87 877	927	171	2 248	790.8	61.8	647	8 650	1 296.3	122.7	95	443	44.0	7.6
Jacksonville, FL	1 216 430	11 604	1 717	23 651	17 396.9	813.0	4 414	59 044	10 329.4	977.0	1 196	7 570	1 092.2	182.3
Jacksonville, NC	69 941	970	69	D	D	D	564	6 542	1 090.1	96.7	129	497	53.0	7.5
Jamestown, NY	23 657	227	159	2 171	748.6	57.6	591	7 096	1 011.1	96.6	86	395	41.9	7.0
Janesville-Beloit, WI	92 123	989	152	2 823	1 706.4	95.8	584	8 484	1 599.7	148.4	105	364	52.9	5.6
Johnson City-Kingsport-Bristol, TN-VA	154 036	1 803	548	7 332	3 732.2	194.4	2 137	24 655	4 041.4	369.4	369	1 534	157.0	25.6
Johnstown, PA	38 234	443	231	2 955	855.2	79.3	1 060	11 916	1 787.9	157.7	115	483	48.4	7.3
Jonesboro, AR	53 189	843	140	1 548	509.7	35.6	480	5 589	854.3	80.8	86	349	41.5	5.9
Joplin, MO	47 169	606	250	2 575	1 092.1	64.3	790	9 302	1 444.4	133.7	151	585	50.4	9.3
Kalamazoo-Battle Creek, MI	238 356	2 072	543	8 329	3 423.0	305.7	1 812	25 894	4 130.9	389.1	373	2 626	236.8	49.6
Kansas City, MO-KS	1 764 620	16 391	3 647	53 535	46 070.8	2 011.0	6 750	98 293	18 112.0	1 723.5	1 930	13 008	1 881.8	311.2
Killeen-Temple, TX	139 161	1 553	167	2 658	1 457.7	81.6	973	12 190	2 002.2	185.4	284	1 228	100.6	17.4
Knoxville, TN	348 836	4 160	1 198	14 821	8 438.0	509.7	3 518	45 022	8 077.2	748.7	788	4 390	492.1	95.0
Kokomo, IN	65 482	567	130	999	958.7	34.8	461	6 556	1 077.7	96.4	95	329	39.7	5.6
La Crosse, WI-MN	84 978	833	185	3 753	1 991.6	112.6	579	9 505	1 528.9	141.6	125	785	61.0	13.4
Lafayette, IN	134 882	1 577	164	1 618	551.3	41.5	690	10 888	1 673.3	156.6	171	818	86.9	13.0
Lafayette, LA	167 287	1 597	666	8 138	3 432.8	266.2	1 637	21 337	3 451.6	320.6	456	3 419	438.9	94.0
Lake Charles, LA	104 796	1 462	244	3 136	1 732.7	90.8	775	10 400	1 606.2	147.1	210	1 164	106.0	20.6
Lakeland-Winter Haven, FL	284 802	3 879	639	8 329	4 176.2	212.7	1 816	22 751	3 844.3	360.9	431	2 001	217.3	39.8
Lancaster, PA	262 112	2 273	663	11 020	10 936.6	341.6	2 012	29 237	4 671.7	480.8	281	1 906	247.2	41.9
Lansing-East Lansing, MI	229 360	2 040	507	7 289	4 509.5	261.8	1 756	26 727	4 317.5	424.4	410	3 493	281.6	63.8
Laredo, TX	99 197	1 639	339	2 453	1 105.4	51.1	730	9 051	1 524.6	138.8	155	574	64.3	10.0
Las Cruces, NM	97 389	920	122	978	283.6	25.0	511	6 266	1 059.1	98.1	175	530	44.8	7.4
Las Vegas, NV-AZ	2 538 389	28 800	1 423	16 654	6 661.7	547.8	4 488	66 198	13 698.9	1 325.7	1 689	12 985	1 726.8	299.7
Lawrence, KS	89 030	896	88	777	248.8	21.0	453	5 664	758.5	80.3	122	434	46.4	6.6
Lawton, OK	15 447	138	84	766	200.6	16.4	436	5 216	691.8	67.8	133	523	48.7	8.1
Lewiston-Auburn, ME	32 092	329	126	1 244	277.8	35.7	533	6 362	1 247.1	96.4	109	418	46.9	7.2
Lexington, KY	409 308	4 459	684	10 214	5 750.8	316.3	2 083	31 088	4 923.7	460.5	517	2 520	358.8	46.9
Lima, OH	52 858	433	236	3 782	3 967.5	107.6	734	10 022	1 632.9	146.1	139	551	47.7	8.1
Lincoln, NE	180 207	1 686	304	D	D	D	996	15 734	2 270.4	232.0	267	1 480	150.3	25.4
Little Rock-North Little Rock, AR	382 641	3 850	1 073	16 315	10 350.4	494.1	2 584	34 803	6 218.0	541.8	618	3 750	430.5	68.9
Longview-Marshall, TX	36 598	416	424	4 360	2 289.3	137.0	1 055	11 990	2 073.4	190.0	179	859	89.7	21.1
Los Angeles-Riverside-Orange County, CA	8 275 968	51 638	32 538	413 546	303 020.6	15 195.0	47 411	616 435	124 135.4	12 079.1	17 465	121 581	20 184.4	3 521.9
Los Angeles-Long Beach, CA	1 900 284	14 060	21 474	259 217	177 244.9	9 450.4	27 577	343 656	69 534.2	6 769.0	10 932	76 904	13 608.6	2 256.3
Orange County, CA	2 013 489	12 239	7 029	103 113	94 403.4	3 999.6	9 084	126 575	26 172.8	2 572.0	3 537	29 156	4 714.8	939.1
Riverside-San Bernardino, CA	3 495 855	20 921	2 947	37 405	20 969.7	1 222.4	8 402	115 373	21 951.8	2 129.4	2 324	12 267	1 452.1	253.0
Ventura, CA	866 340	4 418	1 088	13 811	10 402.7	522.6	2 348	30 831	6 476.6	608.7	672	3 254	409.0	73.4
Louisville, KY-IN	777 975	7 612	1 865	28 299	17 367.6	950.2	4 154	63 200	9 631.4	991.4	1 054	6 823	881.4	143.3
Lubbock, TX	100 751	1 041	505	6 628	3 867.8	181.3	1 084	14 538	2 673.0	238.0	296	1 905	133.8	30.7
Lynchburg, VA	133 352	1 140	224	2 674	1 531.8	79.3	932	12 039	1 977.0	188.5	186	616	58.4	11.3
Macon, GA	184 033	2 337	362	4 127	1 786.2	128.1	1 475	19 930	3 120.1	297.4	298	1 472	201.8	32.6
Madison, WI	412 159	3 626	675	10 048	4 350.1	342.7	1 845	30 150	4 860.9	507.2	520	3 519	371.4	71.1
Mansfield, OH	59 007	591	209	2 422	808.6	67.1	763	10 574	1 549.5	151.3	125	490	49.9	7.4
McAllen-Edinburg-Mission, TX	323 778	5 700	600	6 395	1 981.7	124.6	1 582	20 862	3 337.6	313.1	346	1 347	116.3	18.5
Medford-Ashland, OR	189 945	1 757	284	2 678	1 022.7	69.8	835	9 564	2 075.3	172.2	248	1 003	95.9	15.2
Melbourne-Titusville-Palm Bay, FL	496 714	4 659	577	4 389	1 362.4	136.2	1 856	23 867	3 900.5	370.3	525	2 443	220.0	45.3
Memphis, TN-AR-MS	1 189 734	10 466	2 050	36 575	37 008.2	1 277.5	4 296	65 612	10 476.4	1 012.9	951	7 504	907.3	176.5

1. Establishments with payroll.

Table C. Metropolitan Areas — Professional, Manufacturing, Accommodation and Foodservices, Finance and Insurance

Area Name	Professional, Scientific, and Technical Services[1], 1997				Manufacturing, 1997				Accommodation and Foodservices, 1997			
	Number of Establish-ments	Number of Employees	Sales (mil dol)	Annual Payroll (mil dol)	Number of Establish-ments	Number of Employees	Sales (mil dol)	Annual Payroll (mil dol)	Number of Establish-ments	Number of Employees	Sales (mil dol)	Annual Payroll (mil dol)
	147	148	149	150	151	152	153	154	155	156	157	158
Hartford, CT	2 720	23 268	2 760.9	1 086.4	2 053	89 601	15 058	3 772	2 341	35 958	1 268.8	371.0
Hattiesburg, MS	202	994	75.2	26.2	106	5 940	1 154	133	211	4 755	125.7	33.2
Hickory-Morganton-Lenoir, NC	415	1 921	135.5	50.3	1 012	78 514	9 908	1 925	573	10 632	299.2	84.0
Honolulu, HI	1 917	13 729	1 400.6	546.8	685	11 161	2 692	301	2 125	53 916	3 036.8	852.8
Houma, LA	329	2 597	216.8	78.3	185	6 454	964	202	302	4 687	154.6	42.0
Houston-Galveston-Brazoria, TX	11 650	116 232	17 046.6	5 979.1	5 387	202 631	99 862	7 902	6 989	140 028	5 330.4	1 420.6
Brazoria, TX	246	1 212	93.4	38.8	199	14 149	10 761	683	295	4 787	148.4	41.8
Galveston-Texas City, TX.	333	1 375	131.6	52.5	160	7 279	9 183	393	485	9 156	301.5	82.4
Houston, TX	11 071	113 645	16 821.6	5 887.8	5 028	181 203	79 919	6 826	6 209	126 085	4 880.5	1 296.4
Huntington-Ashland, WV-KY-OH	392	2 314	155.9	63.9	262	15 112	5 602	548	550	9 860	288.5	78.8
Huntsville, AL	835	13 490	1 629.7	619.6	404	35 060	8 313	1 388	584	12 811	391.8	107.5
Indianapolis, IN	3 582	30 739	3 085.3	1 159.3	2 014	106 283	26 773	4 306	3 031	65 908	2 178.1	620.4
Iowa City, IA	164	1 085	81.9	29.3	89	3 639	2 510	121	271	5 496	144.3	40.8
Jackson, MI	200	1 354	90.8	45.5	351	12 248	2 272	422	267	4 467	137.0	37.7
Jackson, MS	912	7 182	721.5	273.1	392	19 717	3 969	522	689	15 039	479.4	134.1
Jackson, TN	148	1 009	79.1	37.1	162	13 282	3 549	401	202	4 416	144.3	39.2
Jacksonville, FL	2 506	19 393	1 727.5	756.1	950	33 883	8 408	1 119	2 047	42 445	1 438.6	385.5
Jacksonville, NC	137	725	34.9	11.9	37	1 829	346	38	249	4 420	127.9	34.5
Jamestown, NY	168	815	48.5	19.2	222	13 084	2 974	409	368	4 323	124.9	35.4
Janesville-Beloit, WI	182	1 002	65.1	23.5	234	19 547	10 106	785	343	5 295	151.2	41.3
Johnson City-Kingsport-Bristol, TN-VA	663	3 861	305.6	117.3	571	48 454	8 653	1 628	721	15 467	445.0	127.7
Johnstown, PA	269	2 090	125.6	51.2	271	12 231	1 994	303	482	6 045	165.7	46.0
Jonesboro, AR	148	675	53.4	19.3	122	6 886	1 258	185	133	2 720	80.2	21.6
Joplin, MO	182	1 092	60.7	25.4	261	16 219	2 847	400	309	5 764	159.5	46.0
Kalamazoo-Battle Creek, MI.	726	4 641	412.0	177.2	748	43 859	9 631	1 587	905	16 004	459.7	135.9
Kansas City, MO-KS	4 407	44 494	4 769.8	1 907.9	2 201	95 231	31 015	3 328	3 270	70 663	2 553.0	731.2
Killeen-Temple, TX	228	2 166	182.5	56.3	160	7 921	1 404	237	436	7 874	233.3	63.3
Knoxville, TN	1 397	17 148	1 750.3	699.9	894	43 228	8 699	1 311	1 584	31 961	1 133.2	317.5
Kokomo, IN	122	503	35.4	11.7	102	20 972	4 931	1 108	207	4 232	124.3	34.3
La Crosse, WI-MN	211	1 584	121.7	53.2	184	10 668	1 433	324	333	5 793	148.7	42.8
Lafayette, IN	242	1 336	110.4	38.2	162	21 654	9 084	840	375	7 475	213.7	61.2
Lafayette, LA	995	6 607	601.0	229.5	363	13 086	3 317	309	568	11 632	344.5	97.8
Lake Charles, LA	348	2 432	183.4	69.2	134	11 274	10 154	542	294	8 019	306.4	75.4
Lakeland-Winter Haven, FL..	712	4 006	347.6	135.4	480	20 627	6 000	634	711	13 383	419.3	113.2
Lancaster, PA	639	5 130	439.8	165.6	918	52 908	10 585	1 752	877	15 724	506.4	145.6
Lansing-East Lansing, MI	897	6 161	598.0	253.6	428	29 104	8 893	1 471	836	17 358	489.7	139.3
Laredo, TX	210	1 029	69.6	23.1	87	1 402	259	28	253	4 350	144.7	37.4
Las Cruces, NM	222	1 334	107.3	45.7	111	2 290	396	47	253	4 278	121.7	32.6
Las Vegas, NV-AZ	2 560	20 871	2 152.4	845.2	990	21 588	3 924	637	2 542	190 873	12 597.4	3 823.1
Lawrence, KS	192	1 280	84.5	33.1	76	4 240	729	120	240	4 627	120.7	34.2
Lawton, OK	127	1 062	63.0	30.5	51	3 325	901	120	203	3 660	96.9	28.9
Lewiston-Auburn, ME	151	1 672	191.6	54.3	183	8 233	1 219	227	180	2 438	77.4	23.3
Lexington, KY	1 040	9 563	1 150.2	316.9	550	44 382	15 908	1 675	957	21 830	706.4	202.0
Lima, OH	217	1 158	77.9	26.6	225	17 765	8 369	697	333	5 793	165.4	43.6
Lincoln, NE	483	7 161	688.0	211.6	267	15 322	3 855	502	545	11 230	318.5	91.8
Little Rock-North Little Rock, AR	1 433	10 922	991.0	428.9	635	31 679	6 195	864	1 049	21 213	644.8	181.1
Longview-Marshall, TX	383	2 140	206.5	74.4	326	16 739	4 090	544	377	5 963	192.8	53.7
Los Angeles-Riverside-Orange County, CA	35 753	449 814	44 285.7	17 310.0	28 102	981 382	171 359	32 251	26 797	473 565	18 990.5	5 116.8
Los Angeles-Long Beach, CA	22 194	346 290	31 678.8	12 767.4	17 915	622 302	106 706	20 311	15 718	267 157	11 074.3	2 991.3
Orange County, CA	8 838	75 635	9 728.8	3 540.6	5 767	215 936	39 134	7 644	5 397	105 298	4 241.7	1 133.2
Riverside-San Bernardino, CA	3 124	17 060	1 648.8	537.2	3 412	109 582	19 355	3 160	4 482	79 231	2 899.1	782.9
Ventura, CA	1 597	10 829	1 229.3	464.9	1 008	33 562	6 163	1 136	1 200	21 879	775.3	209.4
Louisville, KY-IN	2 262	17 402	1 639.8	559.3	1 333	80 938	34 197	2 882	1 882	43 541	1 364.7	395.7
Lubbock, TX	483	2 516	198.6	67.7	258	7 286	1 566	204	522	11 154	332.1	87.6
Lynchburg, VA	351	3 422	325.9	130.0	298	23 078	5 392	770	323	6 030	174.8	48.6
Macon, GA	530	3 737	307.7	109.4	292	18 617	7 022	688	579	11 830	357.8	96.7
Madison, WI	1 132	10 748	943.4	412.4	564	26 568	4 841	864	993	18 607	554.1	156.9
Mansfield, OH	209	1 092	82.5	26.6	310	21 787	3 639	779	366	5 773	170.7	46.4
McAllen-Edinburg-Mission, TX	482	2 682	193.4	62.7	261	10 284	1 428	178	626	10 871	352.1	90.1
Medford-Ashland, OR	341	1 917	99.5	35.4	301	7 428	1 424	202	474	6 253	205.3	60.3
Melbourne-Titusville-Palm Bay, FL	1 073	11 192	1 195.6	455.0	494	20 832	3 451	754	860	16 207	495.3	136.3
Memphis, TN-AR-MS	1 864	16 144	1 555.7	583.1	1 156	58 220	14 625	1 868	1 689	40 218	1 509.6	409.5

1. Firms subject to federal tax.

Table C. Metropolitan Areas — **Health and Other Services and Federal Funds**

Area Name	Health Care and Social Assistance[1], 1997				Other Services[1], 1997				Federal funds and grants, fiscal 1999[2] Expenditures (mil dol)			
									Total	Direct payments for individuals		
	Number of Establishments	Number of Employees	Receipts (mil dol)	Annual Payroll (mil dol)	Number of Establishments	Number of Employees	Receipts (mil dol)	Annual Payroll (mil dol)		Social Security and government retirement	Medicare	Food stamps and Supplemental Security Income
	159	160	161	162	163	164	165	166	167	168	169	170
Hartford, CT	2 490	34 766	2 323.9	1 117.7	2 136	12 552	871.9	269.8	5 997.9	2 093.2	985.0	138.4
Hattiesburg, MS	183	3 307	226.7	121.0	128	860	53.6	15.0	466.0	195.8	78.2	23.6
Hickory-Morganton-Lenoir, NC	498	7 610	491.1	220.8	459	2 462	147.7	45.0	1 061.6	562.9	197.7	34.1
Honolulu, HI	1 730	13 474	1 231.7	563.1	1 097	8 402	560.8	170.7	6 944.7	1 793.4	486.3	184.7
Houma, LA	319	3 564	230.7	110.6	267	2 468	212.0	59.0	875.8	289.0	153.2	46.3
Houston-Galveston-Brazoria, TX	8 592	112 349	7 912.8	3 268.2	6 611	54 362	3 715.9	1 138.4	17 256.8	4 855.4	2 422.1	603.2
Brazoria, TX	306	2 905	155.5	65.8	298	1 312	88.5	24.1	584.2	300.4	120.2	20.0
Galveston-Texas City, TX .	360	4 424	215.2	97.2	358	2 159	134.4	39.7	1 044.3	399.5	195.1	33.9
Houston, TX	7 926	105 020	7 542.1	3 105.2	5 955	50 891	3 493.0	1 074.7	15 628.3	4 155.5	2 106.7	549.3
Huntington-Ashland, WV-KY-OH	554	7 006	474.1	231.8	437	2 595	135.0	41.9	1 677.9	734.8	269.0	106.5
Huntsville, AL	658	7 547	539.0	225.7	530	2 873	152.8	50.8	4 171.7	736.7	172.6	49.8
Indianapolis, IN	2 997	40 791	2 652.3	1 221.8	2 489	18 324	1 094.5	343.4	7 645.6	2 691.5	1 045.3	179.7
Iowa City, IA	181	1 907	97.5	41.4	152	767	43.3	12.5	532.8	115.3	33.6	5.0
Jackson, MI	299	2 649	180.0	85.7	238	1 294	77.2	22.2	575.6	281.5	112.2	24.6
Jackson, MS	769	11 744	878.5	376.6	608	4 229	277.1	80.6	2 633.5	727.6	264.9	99.1
Jackson, TN	214	3 917	299.9	152.7	182	1 106	60.3	18.9	436.5	177.9	81.1	21.6
Jacksonville, FL	2 134	29 760	2 180.5	991.4	1 859	11 003	714.9	217.1	6 172.2	2 248.7	770.3	149.7
Jacksonville, NC	188	2 489	127.1	57.5	195	914	45.5	13.4	1 538.9	283.2	42.5	16.4
Jamestown, NY	243	2 304	109.8	49.9	178	721	45.2	11.3	631.6	290.7	106.5	26.6
Janesville-Beloit, WI	223	3 402	196.2	97.5	241	1 052	63.8	16.8	569.5	255.9	89.2	16.6
Johnson City-Kingsport-Bristol, TN-VA	859	12 513	847.1	388.8	663	3 823	199.5	63.8	2 249.4	1 050.4	383.8	92.3
Johnstown, PA	484	3 732	233.7	114.7	345	1 492	96.1	24.7	1 366.1	584.3	289.7	40.3
Jonesboro, AR	214	3 357	245.4	115.8	118	623	39.5	10.0	301.2	130.9	47.2	12.8
Joplin, MO...........................	298	3 468	204.8	86.7	299	1 411	79.4	21.4	729.6	294.7	117.0	23.8
Kalamazoo-Battle Creek, MI.	861	9 534	618.1	300.4	714	4 577	286.5	88.1	1 892.9	794.9	302.7	69.8
Kansas City, MO-KS...........	3 389	45 900	3 101.9	1 410.5	3 045	19 363	1 217.6	372.6	8 531.2	3 066.5	1 275.7	187.5
Killeen-Temple, TX	325	6 424	432.2	148.1	378	1 965	94.1	29.6	2 831.7	614.6	120.1	27.1
Knoxville, TN	1 348	15 182	1 241.9	583.3	1 071	6 437	346.9	109.6	5 150.8	1 386.7	498.6	117.0
Kokomo, IN	189	2 163	127.5	57.5	152	1 090	51.2	16.4	389.6	202.0	79.7	12.0
La Crosse, WI-MN	156	1 187	65.1	30.1	226	1 348	71.7	22.0	447.0	211.0	64.1	11.5
Lafayette, IN	212	3 067	229.9	107.7	273	1 795	113.7	33.6	619.9	251.1	84.2	12.0
Lafayette, LA	887	11 407	779.2	306.4	552	3 271	215.0	64.4	1 509.2	527.1	283.6	102.2
Lake Charles, LA	405	4 756	319.7	131.7	262	1 914	122.2	35.7	700.6	307.5	155.7	32.2
Lakeland-Winter Haven, FL..	643	9 886	657.7	279.4	611	3 224	199.6	60.6	1 983.0	1 094.6	405.6	84.6
Lancaster, PA	710	8 212	523.8	252.0	808	4 429	276.4	81.6	1 510.9	810.5	278.2	38.7
Lansing-East Lansing, MI	882	7 532	497.6	237.9	612	3 933	212.9	68.2	3 288.5	819.7	261.6	57.9
Laredo, TX	227	4 330	207.1	94.8	190	951	48.0	13.3	721.2	145.2	90.2	52.1
Las Cruces, NM	272	3 149	177.9	75.3	169	1 025	43.9	13.2	925.7	283.1	72.1	43.7
Las Vegas, NV-AZ	2 330	31 173	2 708.3	1 047.0	1 540	12 172	784.8	241.2	5 639.2	2 743.4	861.4	140.8
Lawrence, KS......................	175	1 648	88.7	41.8	132	782	42.5	13.5	290.4	116.1	34.5	5.8
Lawton, OK	208	2 349	141.5	52.8	146	778	36.3	10.9	1 153.6	293.0	52.6	18.3
Lewiston-Auburn, ME............	221	2 542	149.6	68.4	191	714	46.2	12.9	443.3	203.1	79.5	21.7
Lexington, KY......................	925	13 727	946.7	413.5	721	4 533	239.1	75.4	1 962.6	732.8	236.2	76.3
Lima, OH.............................	268	3 440	203.1	103.9	256	1 502	86.6	25.6	709.7	400.6	113.8	23.8
Lincoln, NE..........................	548	6 380	376.7	184.1	418	2 512	134.2	42.0	1 250.5	407.7	101.9	21.5
Little Rock-North Little Rock, AR	1 277	15 592	1 114.6	521.4	913	5 497	333.5	96.2	3 224.6	1 158.8	370.7	92.8
Longview-Marshall, TX	441	6 511	366.4	155.4	330	2 092	141.7	38.4	834.1	408.8	176.7	32.1
Los Angeles-Riverside-Orange County, CA	33 476	327 415	26 324.3	10 252.6	21 477	141 666	10 056.3	2 867.1	67 001.9	18 976.7	12 016.0	2 951.1
Los Angeles-Long Beach, CA	20 278	196 543	15 709.6	6 162.8	13 134	86 614	6 086.4	1 734.3	43 465.6	10 026.1	7 475.1	2 066.9
Orange County, CA............	6 986	66 269	5 571.4	2 170.8	4 249	28 174	2 101.9	600.0	9 292.5	3 335.9	1 833.9	298.5
Riverside-San Bernardino, CA	4 621	51 493	3 956.7	1 505.8	3 219	21 301	1 425.5	406.0	11 053.0	4 533.0	2 230.9	518.2
Ventura, CA......................	1 591	13 110	1 086.6	413.1	875	5 577	442.5	126.7	3 190.8	1 081.6	476.1	67.6
Louisville, KY-IN..................	2 103	33 050	2 164.8	960.4	1 752	11 917	729.2	232.6	5 001.8	1 944.2	794.4	84.3
Lubbock, TX........................	622	8 383	566.2	239.1	405	3 053	178.4	53.2	951.7	371.2	209.9	35.2
Lynchburg, VA	308	4 115	223.8	107.9	347	1 753	98.4	30.1	1 032.8	470.9	124.4	27.4
Macon, GA...........................	695	10 878	806.2	323.2	516	2 660	155.5	47.1	2 368.4	765.4	247.5	75.9
Madison, WI	785	9 899	735.9	320.2	664	4 412	258.5	88.8	2 510.0	620.8	175.8	28.7
Mansfield, OH	333	3 607	192.8	88.8	252	1 838	100.9	37.0	677.4	338.7	132.4	24.4
McAllen-Edinburg-Mission, TX	833	15 858	1 167.0	431.0	479	2 465	114.3	30.6	1 810.5	463.1	285.6	178.4
Medford-Ashland, OR	384	3 810	244.3	110.5	222	1 192	80.6	21.6	763.4	408.8	106.3	23.0
Melbourne-Titusville-Palm Bay,FL..............................	1 017	10 631	783.2	358.0	728	3 778	206.4	63.8	4 132.0	1 520.3	458.9	54.4
Memphis, TN-AR-MS...........	1 960	25 156	2 127.2	896.9	1 599	12 008	763.7	240.1	5 609.8	1 763.1	729.1	303.8

1. Firms subject to federal tax. 2. October 1, 1998 to September 30, 1999.

Area Name	Federal funds and grants, fiscal 1999[1] (cont'd)							Local government finances, 1997				
	Expenditures (mil dol) (cont'd)							General revenue				
	Procurement contract awards			Grants[2]							Taxes	
												Per capita[3] (dollars)
	Salaries and wages	Defense	Other	Medicaid and other health-related	Nutrition and family welfare	Education	Other	Total (mil dol)	Intergovern-mental (mil dol)	Total (mil dol)	Total	Property
	171	172	173	174	175	176	177	178	179	180	181	182
Hartford, CT	411.7	343.3	213.7	696.8	416.0	132.7	434.9	2 831.2	916.6	1 617.2	1 463	1 448
Hattiesburg, MS	45.5	11.2	8.2	34.3	12.2	6.9	28.8	332.0	85.8	55.2	503	463
Hickory-Morganton-Lenoir, NC	46.6	12.4	16.2	91.0	23.9	16.4	46.3	674.7	319.6	161.2	506	383
Honolulu, HI	2 345.6	925.5	114.3	329.4	193.8	123.1	383.8	996.0	150.0	526.9	606	476
Houma, LA	23.6	64.6	163.7	67.4	19.9	13.2	23.6	507.9	165.1	128.6	673	245
Houston-Galveston-Brazoria, TX	1 525.1	499.7	4 131.0	1 421.6	319.7	171.9	880.7	10 824.0	2 713.5	5 502.7	1 274	1 036
Brazoria, TX	28.7	16.4	7.9	39.7	6.9	4.9	15.1	460.1	111.3	246.4	1 093	978
Galveston-Texas City, TX	55.5	37.4	96.2	134.3	16.9	9.3	28.3	701.8	155.0	395.5	1 628	1 437
Houston, TX	1 440.9	445.8	4 026.9	1 247.6	295.9	157.7	837.3	9 662.2	2 447.2	4 860.9	1 262	1 014
Huntington-Ashland, WV-KY-OH	132.7	22.5	28.2	221.0	51.5	20.9	59.3	539.6	284.9	153.1	486	363
Huntsville, AL	732.4	1 695.8	525.0	83.1	17.3	18.6	92.5	607.8	225.3	197.4	593	226
Indianapolis, IN	768.8	919.4	199.1	597.4	373.9	161.7	482.2	3 923.4	1 351.6	1 632.2	1 086	945
Iowa City, IA	63.8	1.0	112.8	137.9	4.6	5.3	29.6	199.1	69.1	84.8	829	768
Jackson, MI	25.5	9.9	6.5	54.6	23.8	6.6	16.0	370.0	218.4	75.9	489	432
Jackson, MS	264.4	147.6	94.6	225.5	251.7	118.2	361.0	825.6	367.6	268.9	632	592
Jackson, TN	30.7	0.5	5.8	67.1	9.0	6.1	15.3	383.8	72.8	77.6	781	444
Jacksonville, FL	1 509.0	552.1	192.2	279.7	122.5	55.6	127.0	2 368.7	882.9	823.9	796	614
Jacksonville, NC	970.1	133.7	5.7	32.2	11.1	5.3	27.3	222.6	130.6	48.8	341	218
Jamestown, NY	23.1	18.9	12.3	79.3	27.8	10.0	28.3	483.0	200.9	189.6	1 354	1 078
Janesville-Beloit, WI	18.4	63.2	5.5	59.2	22.6	7.4	13.2	445.3	253.4	124.8	830	810
Johnson City-Kingsport-Bristol, TN-VA	152.6	79.1	84.3	252.5	43.5	23.4	50.4	734.5	287.5	298.4	648	412
Johnstown, PA	86.6	119.2	14.1	121.5	27.6	8.9	51.4	514.4	239.8	144.0	606	472
Jonesboro, AR	22.6	0.7	4.0	26.9	10.0	7.0	5.1	110.0	53.7	36.3	471	305
Joplin, MO	27.5	18.5	132.9	64.3	15.1	8.4	14.8	247.9	92.5	89.0	605	335
Kalamazoo-Battle Creek, MI.	222.5	34.7	46.6	215.0	71.2	30.6	54.9	1 231.2	646.4	309.6	693	646
Kansas City, MO-KS	1 519.6	259.2	830.6	521.2	175.9	74.9	256.3	4 568.5	1 373.2	1 960.3	1 147	719
Killeen-Temple, TX	1 603.3	230.9	21.1	65.2	16.9	33.5	18.8	641.6	328.3	174.9	584	426
Knoxville, TN	326.1	67.4	2 175.1	283.9	55.9	31.0	141.2	1 267.7	381.3	570.4	872	456
Kokomo, IN	19.4	2.3	5.0	32.7	9.5	2.3	7.8	333.0	91.1	118.9	1 190	1 089
La Crosse, WI-MN	30.1	24.8	9.6	42.7	14.7	5.6	12.1	360.6	170.3	107.4	884	806
Lafayette, IN	32.6	3.0	9.0	56.4	9.8	5.2	109.4	326.4	121.4	139.7	815	716
Lafayette, LA	72.2	15.4	47.8	267.0	48.0	27.1	49.6	571.6	259.4	199.7	537	163
Lake Charles, LA	32.9	13.7	16.0	63.1	18.0	9.1	35.2	480.0	111.0	238.5	1 334	449
Lakeland-Winter Haven, FL.	72.5	19.7	17.5	97.3	55.4	24.0	90.8	896.4	388.5	274.6	612	505
Lancaster, PA	90.4	43.5	45.4	102.9	30.9	11.5	37.8	904.6	306.8	395.6	871	677
Lansing-East Lansing, MI	153.9	22.4	32.8	303.8	670.4	276.9	611.1	1 198.7	633.6	312.9	700	629
Laredo, TX	88.1	0.5	19.7	149.2	64.0	18.6	81.7	516.1	305.2	128.1	699	543
Las Cruces, NM	154.2	136.7	34.4	68.5	27.1	16.8	64.9	371.2	203.5	61.6	365	198
Las Vegas, NV-AZ	637.2	151.0	473.3	234.5	103.4	39.8	201.8	3 791.3	1 416.0	1 173.1	929	545
Lawrence, KS	26.4	4.6	7.2	30.2	6.9	25.4	19.9	214.2	55.5	76.4	839	656
Lawton, OK	562.0	130.8	11.6	27.7	16.8	7.9	12.6	265.5	104.9	49.1	431	208
Lewiston-Auburn, ME	19.9	1.6	4.6	73.1	14.6	6.7	11.2	207.6	72.2	111.1	1 099	1 053
Lexington, KY	232.1	134.1	83.1	188.4	43.1	28.2	143.2	855.7	244.3	337.9	761	339
Lima, OH	29.5	20.7	7.7	46.1	19.5	7.7	14.9	319.8	134.1	123.8	799	527
Lincoln, NE	140.9	19.2	33.7	123.6	127.3	59.0	174.1	605.8	149.9	273.2	1 171	924
Little Rock-North Little Rock, AR	587.0	56.9	61.5	226.3	186.9	101.6	296.9	1 098.3	416.5	360.2	652	394
Longview-Marshall, TX	28.0	0.0	7.2	120.7	15.5	9.0	19.8	409.4	140.9	199.7	959	786
Los Angeles-Riverside-Orange County, CA	5 528.1	9 313.6	3 518.3	6 652.5	3 303.5	926.1	2 945.3	52 345.9	27 358.9	13 323.6	854	578
Los Angeles-Long Beach, CA	2 959.5	7 329.3	2 757.9	5 062.7	2 440.9	632.2	2 108.6	33 598.5	18 386.9	8 143.3	890	573
Orange County, CA	709.3	1 149.1	541.8	599.5	261.8	104.6	342.2	7 098.7	2 844.4	2 392.0	895	637
Riverside-San Bernardino, CA	1 168.1	444.3	171.7	825.4	516.5	160.4	360.5	9 537.1	5 269.0	2 160.1	705	519
Ventura, CA	691.2	390.8	46.9	164.9	84.4	28.9	134.0	2 111.5	858.6	628.3	865	668
Louisville, KY-IN	482.8	812.2	96.0	367.3	110.9	58.3	151.3	2 118.6	657.4	802.6	808	471
Lubbock, TX	68.6	24.3	13.6	83.7	21.2	11.3	55.2	644.4	274.3	179.0	776	586
Lynchburg, VA	58.9	8.3	193.0	50.3	16.0	7.5	61.3	353.5	153.4	141.7	683	595
Macon, GA	698.2	212.1	31.1	124.9	53.1	20.1	98.6	730.1	270.8	257.5	815	528
Madison, WI	218.5	33.5	54.4	328.6	324.1	156.4	482.4	1 241.6	461.4	558.9	1 406	1 306
Mansfield, OH	47.0	6.2	7.8	57.2	20.2	9.4	10.9	397.5	180.7	156.7	896	621
McAllen-Edinburg-Mission, TX	127.1	68.5	34.1	367.8	93.6	54.4	63.7	1 210.8	769.1	282.0	552	421
Medford-Ashland, OR	78.2	1.1	21.2	66.7	20.2	8.1	20.4	386.3	176.3	123.7	724	630
Melbourne-Titusville-Palm Bay, FL	333.1	1 101.5	514.9	48.7	31.6	16.5	31.6	992.6	322.6	330.2	716	569
Memphis, TN-AR-MS	762.6	443.8	323.4	691.9	169.6	62.9	185.4	2 428.3	833.1	903.2	834	507

1. October 1, 1998 to September 30, 1999. 2. State totals may include programs not allocated by county. 3. Based on the resident population estimated as of July 1 of the year shown.

Area Name	Local government finances, 1997 (cont'd)									Government employment, 1998			Presidential election, 2000		
	Direct general expenditure							Debt outstanding					Percent of vote cast —		
						Percent of total for —									
	Total (mil dol)	Per capita[1] (dollars)	Educa-tion	Health and hospitals	Police protec-tion	Public welfare	High-ways	Total (mil dol)	Per capita[1] (dollars)	Federal civilian	Federal military	State and local	Demo-cratic	Republi-can	All other
	183	184	185	186	187	188	189	190	191	192	193	194	195	196	197
Hartford, CT	2 852.3	2 581	54.2	0.9	5.7	1.6	4.2	1 457.8	1 319	7 917	2 861	80 152	NA	NA	NA
Hattiesburg, MS	349.3	3 188	24.1	51.9	2.8	0.2	3.3	161.2	1 471	753	967	12 093	NA	NA	NA
Hickory-Morganton-Lenoir, NC	663.2	2 083	47.1	16.1	4.3	7.3	2.7	262.0	823	884	1 003	20 965	NA	NA	NA
Honolulu, HI	972.6	1 118	0.0	1.3	13.4	0.0	2.6	1 698.5	1 953	28 274	52 170	60 501	50.3	42.6	7.1
Houma, LA	465.6	2 435	38.2	36.9	4.1	0.5	3.8	211.1	1 104	415	1 116	12 897	NA	NA	NA
Houston-Galveston-Brazoria, TX	10 632.2	2 461	48.0	8.3	6.5	0.3	3.6	18 544.6	4 293	27 022	13 188	270 905	40.1	57.3	2.6
Brazoria, TX	453.6	2 012	61.7	6.0	4.8	0.5	5.1	409.3	1 816	442	653	13 543	31.1	66.8	2.1
Galveston-Texas City, TX	704.7	2 900	54.3	7.1	5.3	0.3	3.4	794.6	3 270	918	1 027	28 121	43.0	54.2	2.8
Houston, TX	9 473.9	2 460	46.9	8.5	6.7	0.3	3.5	17 340.7	4 502	25 662	11 508	229 241	40.5	56.9	2.6
Huntington-Ashland, WV-KY-OH	549.5	1 743	59.1	2.9	3.4	1.6	2.6	518.5	1 645	2 921	1 277	17 837	NA	NA	NA
Huntsville, AL	692.9	2 081	42.8	6.5	5.1	0.2	4.9	885.3	2 659	15 265	3 517	23 498	41.8	55.8	2.5
Indianapolis, IN	4 009.2	2 667	45.0	12.7	4.0	2.9	3.5	4 552.1	3 028	14 853	6 274	92 454	39.2	59.2	1.6
Iowa City, IA	217.3	2 124	38.7	3.8	4.5	3.4	13.1	200.7	1 961	1 585	507	25 901	59.1	33.9	7.0
Jackson, MI	396.5	2 552	58.8	7.3	3.4	3.4	5.1	218.2	1 404	439	312	9 123	45.5	51.8	2.8
Jackson, MS	852.7	2 004	48.2	7.8	6.5	0.8	6.2	642.9	1 511	5 359	3 153	43 732	NA	NA	NA
Jackson, TN	414.9	4 178	20.2	48.1	2.8	0.1	2.9	242.3	2 439	571	404	10 585	45.3	53.8	0.8
Jacksonville, FL	2 394.3	2 314	44.3	2.8	6.1	0.5	3.0	5 726.5	5 535	18 502	29 278	45 982	36.6	61.4	1.9
Jacksonville, NC	245.6	1 717	54.8	7.5	4.2	4.9	1.4	93.6	655	5 281	37 705	6 845	NA	NA	NA
Jamestown, NY	511.1	3 650	49.3	1.7	2.8	13.4	7.8	276.8	1 977	414	283	9 312	46.0	49.5	4.5
Janesville-Beloit, WI	465.5	3 097	46.7	5.1	5.4	12.2	6.5	271.6	1 808	341	532	8 201	57.5	39.0	3.5
Johnson City-Kingsport-Bristol, TN-VA	731.5	1 590	53.1	4.9	5.4	1.3	6.3	582.6	1 266	3 334	1 852	25 675	38.3	59.9	1.8
Johnstown, PA	531.5	2 236	51.5	3.4	1.7	6.6	3.8	972.4	4 091	1 350	924	12 586	NA	NA	NA
Jonesboro, AR	111.5	1 449	60.6	0.5	4.6	0.0	6.7	139.4	1 812	437	444	5 252	49.2	48.3	2.5
Joplin, MO	251.2	1 708	53.5	8.0	4.8	0.4	7.8	60.1	408	486	673	7 772	NA	NA	NA
Kalamazoo-Battle Creek, MI	1 306.7	2 925	51.1	8.0	5.1	1.5	5.9	1 083.0	2 424	5 124	939	29 358	48.5	48.2	3.2
Kansas City, MO-KS	4 597.7	2 690	44.8	7.6	6.6	0.6	5.2	5 859.7	3 428	28 102	12 494	104 752	NA	NA	NA
Killeen-Temple, TX	596.8	1 991	65.2	4.8	3.8	0.4	2.5	705.1	2 352	8 225	42 625	20 074	32.5	65.7	1.7
Knoxville, TN	1 343.9	2 054	43.5	7.2	5.0	0.8	5.8	1 272.6	1 945	5 884	2 736	45 532	39.6	58.7	1.8
Kokomo, IN	291.7	2 918	40.0	24.6	3.9	2.0	4.0	126.2	1 263	357	352	6 480	37.2	61.2	1.6
La Crosse, WI-MN	376.5	3 098	49.2	4.4	4.7	7.7	8.0	249.6	2 054	571	458	9 298	50.1	44.7	5.1
Lafayette, IN	322.8	1 882	53.0	5.0	4.4	5.7	4.6	120.6	703	601	642	20 840	38.9	59.2	1.9
Lafayette, LA	561.9	1 510	55.8	8.0	5.5	0.1	4.0	664.8	1 787	1 362	2 088	21 707	NA	NA	NA
Lake Charles, LA	455.7	2 548	39.3	7.7	8.3	0.4	7.4	617.0	3 450	621	1 005	12 267	NA	NA	NA
Lakeland-Winter Haven, FL	895.2	1 995	48.6	2.8	7.8	1.0	4.2	1 182.9	2 637	1 409	1 030	25 237	44.6	53.6	1.8
Lancaster, PA	1 006.5	2 217	55.1	2.5	3.2	4.2	3.5	1 478.9	3 257	1 631	1 541	16 671	NA	NA	NA
Lansing-East Lansing, MI	1 302.0	2 911	57.8	1.7	4.2	2.7	4.2	1 126.7	2 519	2 861	1 327	52 987	52.4	44.6	3.0
Laredo, TX	515.0	2 811	52.4	1.2	4.6	0.5	5.3	352.8	1 926	1 761	501	12 491	57.4	41.4	1.2
Las Cruces, NM	387.8	2 302	44.7	22.3	3.4	1.1	3.6	251.1	1 490	3 608	670	14 177	NA	NA	NA
Las Vegas, NV-AZ	4 067.4	3 223	32.4	8.1	7.3	1.3	7.3	6 394.0	5 066	9 085	9 337	61 924	49.7	46.1	4.2
Lawrence, KS	204.5	2 245	35.9	26.7	5.0	0.3	4.5	182.6	2 004	561	497	14 074	45.8	42.8	11.4
Lawton, OK	259.6	2 278	44.8	33.8	3.9	0.0	2.7	87.0	763	3 810	14 303	7 818	40.8	40.8	18.4
Lewiston-Auburn, ME	206.5	2 044	54.0	0.1	3.8	0.4	5.8	144.9	1 434	366	519	4 628	NA	NA	NA
Lexington, KY	791.7	1 783	50.3	2.5	5.9	0.8	4.0	1 426.0	3 211	5 264	1 622	39 780	41.9	55.0	3.1
Lima, OH	309.6	1 998	52.5	2.7	4.6	5.7	4.7	138.4	893	564	402	9 426	NA	NA	NA
Lincoln, NE	589.1	2 525	45.1	13.3	3.6	2.8	5.0	639.3	2 740	2 577	1 093	26 604	41.7	51.8	6.5
Little Rock-North Little Rock, AR	1 075.8	1 948	45.7	7.6	6.3	0.0	5.3	1 116.7	2 022	9 482	7 721	48 497	48.3	48.9	2.8
Longview-Marshall, TX	408.1	1 960	60.6	6.3	5.4	0.7	4.4	309.9	1 488	552	556	11 014	32.7	66.1	1.2
Los Angeles-Riverside-Orange County, CA	50 639.7	3 244	32.9	7.7	8.2	11.6	2.9	58 476.8	3 746	94 646	61 147	791 376	54.6	41.3	4.1
Los Angeles-Long Beach, CA	31 842.4	3 482	30.2	8.3	8.9	12.9	2.3	36 250.4	3 964	55 490	21 671	485 747	63.5	32.4	4.2
Orange County, CA	6 992.4	2 615	37.4	3.2	8.2	7.5	4.5	9 731.1	3 639	13 070	11 475	122 560	40.4	55.8	3.9
Riverside-San Bernardino, CA	9 723.8	3 174	37.6	8.8	6.1	11.6	3.5	11 158.6	3 642	17 386	21 118	151 493	46.1	50.1	3.9
Ventura, CA	2 081.2	2 867	37.2	8.8	7.1	6.5	3.7	1 336.7	1 841	8 700	6 883	31 576	47.1	48.2	4.7
Louisville, KY-IN	2 204.9	2 220	39.3	9.4	5.0	1.6	2.4	3 522.4	3 546	10 176	3 682	57 283	47.1	50.8	2.1
Lubbock, TX	567.6	2 461	42.2	28.0	4.5	0.1	2.5	429.7	1 863	1 206	657	21 124	24.3	73.7	2.0
Lynchburg, VA	355.5	1 714	51.3	3.4	4.6	3.8	4.0	391.1	1 885	1 216	818	11 612	36.9	60.4	2.6
Macon, GA	722.3	2 285	44.2	16.9	5.7	0.3	4.1	440.1	1 392	13 115	5 640	19 446	NA	NA	NA
Madison, WI	1 305.1	3 283	48.5	2.1	5.5	9.8	5.4	1 280.3	3 221	4 261	1 576	67 772	61.1	32.6	6.3
Mansfield, OH	395.8	2 264	48.5	6.9	5.1	5.2	6.4	89.6	513	790	452	9 822	NA	NA	NA
McAllen-Edinburg-Mission, TX	1 109.5	2 172	72.7	2.8	3.5	0.7	1.7	572.4	1 120	2 698	1 395	35 353	60.8	37.9	1.3
Medford-Ashland, OR	398.8	2 333	49.9	8.6	6.6	0.0	5.7	125.9	736	1 752	596	8 586	39.1	54.3	6.6
Melbourne-Titusville-Palm Bay, FL	964.9	2 093	45.0	7.6	6.9	0.5	4.7	1 111.7	2 412	5 541	3 574	19 592	44.6	52.7	2.7
Memphis, TN-AR-MS	2 572.9	2 375	39.0	11.6	7.9	0.3	3.7	3 054.7	2 820	15 146	5 968	65 651	NA	NA	NA

1. Based on the resident population estimated as of July 1 of the year shown.

Table C. Metropolitan Areas — **Land Area and Population**

CMSA/ MSA/ PMSA/ NECMA code[1]	Area Name	Land area,[2] (sq km) 1990	Total persons	Rank	Per square kilometer	White	Black	Am. Indian, Eskimo, Aleut	Asian and Pacific Islander	Percent Hispanic[3]	Under 5 years	5 to 17 years	18 to 24 years	25 to 34 years	35 to 44 years	45 to 54 years
			1	2	3	4	5	6	7	8	9	10	11	12	13
4940	Merced, CA	4 996	200 746	198	40.2	83.4	4.8	1.1	10.7	40.3	9.9	25.8	9.2	14.2	14.6	10.5
56	Miami-Fort Lauderdale, FL	8 167	3 711 102	X	454.4	78.1	19.6	0.3	2.0	39.0	6.7	17.4	8.4	13.7	16.7	12.7
2680	Fort Lauderdale, FL	3 131	1 535 468	38	490.4	78.9	18.6	0.3	2.2	12.8	6.3	16.6	7.6	13.7	17.3	12.9
5000	Miami, FL	5 036	2 175 634	24	432.0	77.6	20.4	0.3	1.8	57.4	6.9	17.9	9.0	13.8	16.3	12.6
63	Milwaukee-Racine, WI	4 645	1 648 199	X	354.8	82.6	15.1	0.6	1.7	5.2	6.5	19.3	9.2	13.6	16.8	13.3
5080	Milwaukee-Waukesha, WI	3 782	1 462 422	41	386.7	82.1	15.4	0.6	1.8	4.9	6.5	19.2	9.3	13.7	16.8	13.2
6600	Racine, WI	863	185 777	205	215.3	86.3	12.5	0.4	0.9	7.5	6.7	20.3	8.5	13.4	16.6	13.7
	Minneapolis-St. Paul, MN-WI															
5120		15 709	2 872 109	13	182.8	90.3	4.9	1.0	3.8	2.3	7.1	19.4	9.6	14.8	18.2	13.4
5140	Missoula, MT	6 729	89 344	307	13.3	95.8	0.3	2.7	1.2	1.5	5.9	17.4	14.9	12.0	16.6	14.4
5160	Mobile, AL	7 329	535 472	97	73.1	70.5	28.2	0.4	0.9	1.5	7.2	18.8	9.2	14.0	15.9	13.2
5170	Modesto, CA	3 871	436 790	116	112.8	90.0	1.9	1.2	7.0	28.5	8.7	23.3	8.6	14.0	15.8	11.9
5200	Monroe, LA	1 582	146 672	238	92.7	65.6	33.6	0.2	0.7	1.1	7.3	20.5	12.6	12.2	14.5	12.6
5240	Montgomery, AL	5 200	322 441	148	62.0	62.2	36.9	0.2	0.7	1.2	7.1	18.4	10.5	14.8	16.5	13.0
5280	Muncie, IN	1 019	115 472	282	113.3	92.0	7.0	0.3	0.8	1.1	5.8	15.6	16.9	11.5	14.2	13.4
5330	Myrtle Beach, SC	2 936	178 550	209	60.8	81.1	17.5	0.2	1.1	1.4	5.9	16.2	8.7	14.5	15.4	13.2
5345	Naples, FL	5 246	207 029	193	39.5	93.1	5.7	0.5	0.7	18.6	6.0	15.2	6.6	10.6	13.5	11.8
5360	Nashville, TN	10 549	1 171 755	48	111.1	82.5	15.7	0.2	1.5	1.4	7.1	17.9	9.6	15.8	17.4	13.5
5523	New London-Norwich, CT	1 725	246 049	172	142.6	91.5	5.5	0.6	2.3	4.6	7.0	19.1	8.6	14.6	16.5	12.4
5560	New Orleans, LA	8 806	1 305 479	45	148.2	62.6	34.9	0.3	2.2	5.2	7.1	19.3	10.3	13.5	16.4	13.2
70	New York-Northern New Jersey-Long Island, NY-NJ-CT-PA	26 329	20 102 875	X	763.5	73.4	19.4	0.3	6.9	17.6	6.7	17.5	8.4	14.4	17.1	13.6
0875	Bergen-Passaic, NJ	1 086	1 342 116	44	1 235.8	80.7	10.5	0.3	8.5	16.1	6.4	16.8	8.0	13.2	17.4	14.2
2281	Dutchess County, NY	2 076	268 237	164	129.2	87.1	9.2	0.2	3.5	4.9	6.6	17.7	9.1	14.6	17.7	14.1
3640	Jersey City, NJ	121	552 819	93	4 568.8	74.2	15.5	0.4	9.9	41.3	6.8	16.9	9.4	16.4	16.7	12.4
5015	Middlesex-Somerset-Hunterdon, NJ	2 708	1 130 592	51	417.5	82.9	7.9	0.2	9.0	9.6	6.6	16.5	8.9	14.8	18.3	14.0
5190	Monmouth-Ocean, NJ	2 870	1 108 977	53	386.4	89.5	7.0	0.2	3.3	5.4	6.5	18.5	6.9	11.8	17.3	13.2
5380	Nassau-Suffolk, NY	3 103	2 688 904	16	866.5	87.6	8.4	0.2	3.7	8.1	6.1	17.5	8.2	13.3	16.9	14.8
5483	New Haven-Bridgeport-Stamford-Danbury-Waterbury, CT	3 190	1 634 542	31	512.4	85.7	11.3	0.2	2.8	9.8	6.7	18.3	7.6	13.5	17.1	13.5
5600	New York, NY	2 972	8 712 600	2	2 931.6	61.3	28.9	0.4	9.3	25.6	6.9	17.2	8.7	15.4	16.7	13.2
5640	Newark, NJ	4 087	1 954 671	26	478.3	72.3	22.8	0.2	4.6	13.0	6.7	18.1	8.3	13.6	17.9	14.0
5660	Newburgh, NY-PA	3 531	375 556	131	106.4	90.6	7.4	0.3	1.7	8.5	7.8	20.4	8.3	14.2	17.7	13.2
8480	Trenton, NJ	585	333 861	144	570.7	73.4	21.3	0.2	5.1	8.3	6.5	17.4	10.1	13.4	17.6	13.2
	Norfolk-Virginia Beach-Newport News, VA-NC															
5720		6 082	1 562 635	36	256.9	65.6	30.5	0.4	3.6	3.3	7.6	18.9	11.1	16.5	16.3	11.7
5790	Ocala, FL	4 090	245 975	173	60.1	83.9	14.9	0.4	0.8	4.6	5.7	16.9	6.3	9.7	13.2	12.0
5800	Odessa-Midland, TX	4 666	242 238	175	51.9	91.6	6.7	0.6	1.1	32.3	9.3	22.2	8.5	13.2	15.5	11.9
5880	Oklahoma City, OK	11 002	1 046 283	60	95.1	82.2	10.9	4.6	2.3	5.4	7.2	19.2	11.1	13.5	15.9	12.9
5920	Omaha, NE-IA	6 412	698 875	75	109.0	89.0	8.7	0.6	1.7	5.2	7.3	19.9	10.2	13.9	16.6	13.1
5960	Orlando, FL	9 042	1 535 004	39	169.8	82.7	14.2	0.4	2.7	12.0	6.8	18.8	9.3	13.9	16.6	12.6
5990	Owensboro, KY	1 198	91 179	306	76.1	95.1	4.4	0.1	0.4	0.5	7.0	18.3	9.1	13.2	15.5	13.6
6015	Panama City, FL	1 978	147 958	236	74.8	83.3	13.0	1.0	2.8	2.8	6.8	20.0	8.2	13.0	15.8	13.6
	Parkersburg-Marietta, WV-OH															
6020		2 596	149 366	234	57.5	98.2	1.2	0.2	0.5	0.4	5.8	17.3	8.7	12.6	15.4	15.4
6080	Pensacola, FL	4 350	403 384	121	92.7	78.2	17.8	1.2	2.8	2.8	6.8	19.9	9.8	12.8	15.6	13.5
6120	Peoria-Pekin, IL	4 654	346 480	140	74.4	90.5	8.2	0.2	1.1	1.6	6.4	19.6	8.7	11.8	16.5	13.3
77	Philadelphia-Wilmington-Atlantic City, PA-NJ-DE-MD	15 373	5 999 034	X	390.2	77.1	19.6	0.2	3.1	5.2	6.6	18.5	8.6	14.0	16.7	13.1
0560	Atlantic-Cape May, NJ	2 114	337 635	142	159.7	80.3	16.4	0.4	3.0	8.0	6.9	17.4	8.3	13.6	16.2	12.3
6160	Philadelphia, PA-NJ	9 986	4 949 867	5	495.7	76.5	20.1	0.2	3.2	4.7	6.6	18.6	8.5	13.9	16.6	13.2
8760	Vineland-Millville-Bridgeton, NJ	1 267	140 112	247	110.6	77.5	19.7	1.3	1.5	18.3	7.2	20.4	8.4	12.9	16.4	12.5
9160	Wilmington-Newark, DE-MD	2 006	571 420	89	284.9	80.1	17.4	0.2	2.2	3.8	6.6	17.9	9.6	15.3	17.8	13.1
6200	Phoenix-Mesa, AZ	37 746	3 013 696	12	79.8	91.0	4.2	2.4	2.4	21.1	8.3	19.6	9.7	13.9	15.8	12.5
6240	Pine Bluff, AR	2 292	80 785	311	35.2	52.4	46.8	0.2	0.5	1.1	7.1	20.0	12.1	12.7	14.8	12.3
6280	Pittsburgh, PA	11 974	2 331 336	21	194.7	90.3	8.6	0.1	1.0	0.8	5.4	16.8	7.8	12.7	16.2	13.6
6323	Pittsfield, MA	2 412	132 218	258	54.8	96.3	2.4	0.2	1.1	1.5	5.3	17.8	7.6	12.4	16.2	13.5
6340	Pocatello, ID	2 883	74 881	316	26.0	94.7	1.2	2.7	1.4	6.2	7.6	21.8	13.0	12.8	14.7	12.0
6403	Portland, ME	2 164	256 437	168	118.5	97.8	0.8	0.3	1.2	0.8	5.4	16.3	9.6	14.6	18.2	14.2
79	Portland-Salem, OR-WA	18 009	2 180 996	X	121.1	91.8	2.7	1.1	4.4	6.5	6.9	18.8	9.4	13.7	16.9	14.8
6440	Portland-Vancouver, OR-WA	13 021	1 845 840	27	141.8	91.3	3.1	1.0	4.7	5.5	6.9	18.7	9.3	13.9	17.2	14.9
7080	Salem, OR	4 988	335 156	143	67.2	95.0	1.0	1.6	2.4	11.9	7.1	19.5	9.9	12.7	14.9	14.0
6483	Providence-Warwick-Pawtucket, RI	2 436	907 795	66	372.7	91.9	5.1	0.5	2.4	7.3	6.3	18.1	8.6	14.6	16.4	12.6
6520	Provo-Orem, UT	5 176	346 997	139	67.0	97.1	0.2	0.7	2.0	4.7	10.7	23.5	22.3	13.2	10.2	8.2
6560	Pueblo, CO	6 187	136 987	251	22.1	96.0	2.3	0.9	0.8	41.1	6.8	20.0	8.8	10.3	14.3	13.6
6580	Punta Gorda, FL	1 797	136 992	250	76.2	93.8	4.7	0.3	1.2	4.0	4.1	12.6	4.8	7.8	11.3	11.3
6640	Raleigh-Durham-Chapel Hill, NC	9 041	1 105 535	54	122.3	72.9	24.0	0.3	2.8	2.6	7.1	17.3	10.9	17.1	18.1	12.8
6660	Rapid City, SD	7 191	88 117	308	12.3	87.9	2.2	8.4	1.5	3.4	7.9	19.2	12.1	13.7	16.0	12.2

1. MSA = Metropolitan Statistical Area. CMSA = Consolidated MSA. PMSA = Primary MSA. NECMA = New England County Metropolitan Area. See Appendix A for explanation of these concepts. See Appendix B for list of metropolitan areas identified by type, with component counties. 2. Dry land or land partially or temporarily covered by water. 3. Hispanic persons may be of any race.

Table C. Metropolitan Areas — **Population and Households**

Area Name	Population, 1999 (cont'd) Age (percent) (cont'd) 55 to 64 years	65 to 74 years	75 years and over	Percent female	Population — change and components of change, 1980–1999 Total persons 1990	1980	Percent change 1980–1990	1990–1999	Components of change, 1990–1999 Births	Deaths	Net migration	Households, 1990 Number	Percent change, 1980–1990	Persons per house-hold	Female family house-holder[1]	One person
	16	17	18	19	20	21	22	23	24	25	26	27	28	29	30	31
Merced, CA..................	6.9	5.0	4.0	49.5	178 403	134 558	32.6	12.5	37 222	11 419	-4 519	55 331	24.2	3.17	12.5	17.7
Miami-Fort Lauderdale, FL ...	9.1	7.5	7.8	52.1	3 192 725	2 643 766	20.8	16.2	482 322	318 166	343 158	1 220 797	18.8	2.58	12.8	26.9
Fort Lauderdale, FL..........	8.8	7.5	9.3	51.7	1 255 531	1 018 257	23.3	22.3	180 561	145 429	242 062	528 442	26.6	2.35	10.0	29.5
Miami, FL..................	9.3	7.5	6.8	52.4	1 937 194	1 625 509	19.2	12.3	301 761	172 737	101 096	692 355	13.5	2.75	14.9	24.9
Milwaukee-Racine, WI	8.5	6.7	6.1	51.7	1 607 183	1 570 152	2.4	2.6	227 420	131 316	-59 473	601 458	7.4	2.61	12.9	25.1
Milwaukee-Waukesha, WI. ...	8.6	6.7	6.1	51.8	1 432 149	1 397 020	2.5	2.1	204 040	117 288	-61 420	537 722	7.4	2.60	13.0	25.5
Racine, WI..................	8.5	6.6	5.8	51.1	175 034	173 132	1.1	6.1	23 380	14 028	1 947	63 736	7.3	2.70	12.3	22.0
Minneapolis-St. Paul, MN-WI	7.4	5.2	4.8	50.9	2 538 776	2 198 190	15.5	13.1	388 129	165 704	112 640	960 170	21.7	2.59	9.7	24.8
Missoula, MT..................	8.1	5.5	5.3	50.7	78 687	76 016	3.5	13.5	9 976	5 282	6 208	30 782	9.9	2.47	9.5	27.3
Mobile, AL..................	9.1	7.3	5.5	52.3	476 923	443 536	7.5	12.3	73 861	43 802	29 650	173 943	15.9	2.69	15.3	22.9
Modesto, CA..................	7.1	5.5	5.1	50.4	370 522	265 900	39.3	17.9	67 833	28 402	27 664	125 375	32.4	2.91	11.5	19.9
Monroe, LA..................	8.8	6.1	5.4	53.0	142 191	139 241	2.1	3.2	20 944	12 200	-3 935	50 518	6.8	2.72	17.0	24.1
Montgomery, AL..............	8.4	6.2	5.1	52.0	292 517	272 687	7.3	10.2	46 066	26 117	9 296	105 531	13.9	2.67	15.7	24.5
Muncie, IN..................	9.0	7.1	6.6	52.5	119 659	128 587	-6.9	-3.5	13 523	10 483	-6 965	45 177	1.1	2.47	10.6	25.9
Myrtle Beach, SC............	10.8	9.7	5.5	51.5	144 053	101 419	42.0	23.9	19 315	13 557	27 697	55 764	60.3	2.52	11.2	22.3
Naples, FL..................	10.6	14.4	11.2	50.3	152 099	85 971	76.9	36.1	23 017	16 606	49 196	61 703	81.7	2.41	7.1	22.6
Nashville, TN................	8.4	5.6	4.7	51.5	985 026	850 505	15.8	19.0	149 837	81 019	119 214	375 831	24.5	2.54	12.2	24.6
New London-Norwich, CT.....	8.2	7.0	6.7	49.9	254 957	238 409	6.9	-3.5	30 049	17 906	-23 335	93 245	14.0	2.59	9.6	23.1
New Orleans, LA.............	8.7	6.5	4.9	52.4	1 285 262	1 304 212	-1.5	1.6	191 328	110 465	-59 474	469 823	3.7	2.69	17.5	26.1
New York-Northern New Jersey-Long Island, NY-NJ-CT-PA	9.1	6.9	6.3	52.0	19 480 002	18 829 146	3.4	3.2	2 848 641	1 636 018	-536 232	7 126 646	5.3	2.67	14.0	26.3
Bergen-Passaic, NJ..........	9.7	7.4	7.0	51.9	1 296 252	1 292 970	-1.1	3.5	173 295	109 531	-12 987	464 149	2.3	2.71	11.2	22.7
Dutchess County, NY........	8.2	6.2	5.9	49.4	259 462	245 055	5.9	3.4	32 912	19 658	-3 660	89 567	11.1	2.69	9.3	22.2
Jersey City, NJ..............	9.2	6.5	5.7	51.7	553 099	556 972	-0.7	0.1	84 200	47 535	-35 537	208 739	0.4	2.62	16.5	28.7
Middlesex-Somerset-Hunterdon, NJ..................	8.7	6.8	5.4	50.7	1 019 786	886 383	15.1	10.9	144 816	72 924	42 067	365 085	24.8	2.71	9.2	20.8
Monmouth-Ocean, NJ	8.7	8.3	8.9	51.8	986 395	849 211	16.1	12.4	132 418	104 902	96 520	365 717	22.5	2.65	9.3	23.3
Nassau-Suffolk, NY	9.7	7.5	5.9	51.3	2 609 212	2 605 813	0.1	3.1	353 917	203 502	-60 830	856 234	5.8	2.99	10.3	16.5
New Haven-Bridgeport-Stamford-Danbury-Waterbury, CT..................	8.9	7.1	7.3	51.8	1 631 864	1 568 468	4.0	0.2	219 334	136 008	-75 164	609 741	10.4	2.61	11.9	24.4
New York, NY...............	9.1	6.7	6.2	52.8	8 546 846	8 274 961	3.3	1.9	1 338 059	726 757	-425 552	3 252 399	1.7	2.56	17.1	31.6
Newark, NJ..................	8.9	6.5	6.1	51.8	1 915 724	1 963 576	-2.4	2.0	276 148	162 623	-68 639	686 032	1.4	2.74	13.8	23.3
Newburgh, NY-PA	7.6	5.7	5.1	49.6	335 603	277 874	20.8	11.9	50 683	24 918	13 439	112 042	22.6	2.87	9.9	19.7
Trenton, NJ.................	8.7	6.9	6.1	51.5	325 759	307 863	5.8	2.5	42 859	27 660	-5 889	116 941	10.5	2.65	13.2	24.2
Norfolk-Virginia Beach-Newport News, VA-NC	7.6	6.0	4.2	50.8	1 444 710	1 200 998	20.3	8.2	229 529	102 568	-48 993	511 136	27.8	2.69	13.0	21.1
Ocala, FL..................	10.9	14.9	10.4	51.8	194 835	122 488	59.1	26.2	24 659	25 011	52 288	78 177	72.0	2.44	10.3	22.9
Odessa-Midland, TX..........	8.8	6.2	4.5	51.4	225 545	198 010	13.9	7.4	38 901	15 503	-6 236	81 242	15.9	2.76	10.6	23.1
Oklahoma City, OK..........	8.7	6.4	5.1	51.3	958 839	860 969	11.4	9.1	139 333	79 301	27 441	367 775	14.4	2.53	11.4	26.3
Omaha, NE-IA...............	7.9	6.0	4.9	51.4	639 580	605 419	5.6	9.3	99 085	47 148	6 055	240 149	11.4	2.61	11.2	25.2
Orlando, FL..................	8.5	7.3	6.2	51.0	1 224 844	804 774	52.2	25.3	188 797	102 357	222 850	465 275	58.1	2.56	10.6	22.8
Owensboro, KY..............	9.9	7.4	6.1	52.2	87 189	85 949	1.4	4.6	11 608	7 762	418	33 036	9.4	2.58	11.5	24.8
Panama City, FL.............	9.3	7.8	5.6	50.9	126 994	97 740	29.9	16.5	18 904	11 158	11 949	48 938	40.8	2.54	11.1	23.0
Parkersburg-Marietta, WV-OH..................	9.9	7.6	7.3	52.1	149 169	157 893	-5.5	0.1	17 601	14 320	-2 625	57 804	2.9	2.54	9.8	23.9
Pensacola, FL................	8.7	7.3	5.5	51.1	344 406	289 782	18.9	17.1	50 718	29 239	33 726	128 508	28.9	2.59	13.1	22.4
Peoria-Pekin, IL..............	9.2	7.1	7.3	51.3	339 172	365 864	-7.3	2.2	44 228	29 661	-6 223	129 363	-1.1	2.55	10.3	25.4
Philadelphia-Wilmington-Atlantic City, PA-NJ-DE-MD..................	8.6	7.3	6.6	52.0	5 893 019	5 649 031	4.3	1.8	807 018	537 158	-166 602	2 160 142	9.7	2.65	13.5	25.1
Atlantic-Cape May, NJ	9.2	8.0	8.1	51.7	319 416	276 385	15.6	5.7	46 254	34 298	7 182	122 979	18.1	2.53	12.6	26.9
Philadelphia, PA-NJ	8.6	7.3	6.7	52.1	4 922 257	4 781 235	2.9	0.6	667 504	448 766	-187 650	1 801 159	8.4	2.66	13.7	25.3
Vineland-Millville-Bridgeton, NJ..................	8.5	7.1	6.6	50.7	138 053	132 866	3.9	1.5	19 381	13 054	-8 429	47 118	6.4	2.79	15.8	21.6
Wilmington-Newark, DE-MD..................	8.1	6.4	5.2	51.2	513 293	458 545	11.9	11.3	73 879	41 040	22 295	188 886	19.3	2.63	11.8	23.2
Phoenix-Mesa, AZ	8.1	6.4	5.8	50.5	2 238 498	1 600 093	39.9	34.6	424 857	187 173	458 101	846 714	47.7	2.60	10.2	24.8
Pine Bluff, AR	8.3	6.8	5.9	51.9	85 487	90 718	-5.8	-5.5	12 364	8 714	-8 036	30 001	-1.9	2.70	16.0	24.2
Pittsburgh, PA...............	9.8	9.3	8.5	52.6	2 394 811	2 571 223	-6.9	-2.7	263 936	252 101	-65 996	947 248	1.4	2.47	11.5	27.3
Pittsfield, MA................	9.2	8.8	9.2	51.8	139 352	145 110	-4.0	-5.1	14 248	14 047	-6 917	54 315	3.7	2.45	10.8	27.5
Pocatello, ID................	7.8	5.3	4.9	50.3	66 026	65 421	0.9	13.4	11 749	4 546	798	23 412	4.1	2.78	8.8	23.9
Portland, ME................	8.4	6.9	6.3	51.9	243 135	215 789	12.7	5.5	29 475	20 519	4 737	94 512	20.1	2.49	9.8	25.2
Portland-Salem, OR-WA.......	8.4	5.5	5.7	50.7	1 793 476	1 583 518	13.3	21.6	279 036	149 482	263 077	691 102	15.2	2.54	9.8	25.7
Portland-Vancouver, OR-WA..................	8.3	5.3	5.5	50.7	1 515 452	1 333 623	13.6	21.8	234 160	123 783	224 141	589 441	15.7	2.53	9.7	26.0
Salem, OR..................	8.8	6.2	6.9	50.5	278 024	249 895	11.3	20.5	44 876	25 699	38 936	101 661	12.1	2.61	10.1	24.1
Providence-Warwick-Pawtucket, RI..................	7.9	7.6	8.0	52.0	916 270	865 771	5.8	-0.9	115 228	82 581	-38 328	345 290	11.3	2.55	11.9	26.3
Provo-Orem, UT..............	5.3	3.5	3.3	50.7	263 590	218 106	20.9	31.6	72 491	11 997	8 307	70 168	19.9	3.63	7.8	12.2
Pueblo, CO.................	11.1	8.1	7.1	51.5	123 051	125 972	-2.3	11.3	16 439	12 006	9 730	47 057	4.4	2.55	13.7	25.8
Punta Gorda, FL.............	14.2	18.4	15.4	51.8	110 975	58 460	89.8	23.4	9 177	17 013	34 069	48 433	86.8	2.23	6.0	23.0
Raleigh-Durham-Chapel Hill, NC..................	7.4	5.0	4.2	51.5	858 516	664 788	29.1	28.8	135 944	61 682	173 913	334 506	41.5	2.45	11.2	26.2
Rapid City, SD	7.2	6.2	5.4	50.7	81 343	70 361	15.6	8.3	13 126	5 567	-1 764	30 553	21.4	2.61	10.2	23.4

1. No spouse present.

Table C. Metropolitan Areas — **Vital Statistics, Health Resources, and Crime**

Area Name	Births, average 1996–1998 Total	Rate[1]	Deaths, average 1996–1998 Number Total	Infant[2]	Rate Total[1]	Infant[3]	Physicians[4] 1998 Number	Rate[5]	Hospitals[4] 1998 Number	Beds Number	Rate[5]	Medicare enrollees 1999	Serious crimes known to police, 1998[6] Total Number	Rate[7]
	32	33	34	35	36	37	38	39	40	41	42	43	44	45
Merced, CA	3 623	18.7	1 336	25	6.9	6.8	208	105	4	402	203	19 515	10 159	5 117
Miami-Fort Lauderdale, FL	51 926	14.4	34 327	325	9.5	6.3	10 605	290	45	14 195	388	555 395	309 162	8 674
Fort Lauderdale, FL	20 333	13.8	15 819	142	10.7	7.0	3 758	250	20	5 538	368	251 056	95 761	6 397
Miami, FL	31 593	14.8	18 508	183	8.7	5.8	6 847	318	25	8 657	402	304 339	213 401	10 323
Milwaukee-Racine, WI	23 756	14.4	14 248	204	8.6	8.6	4 478	272	24	5 053	307	239 390	NA	NA
Milwaukee-Waukesha, WI.	21 154	14.5	12 688	183	8.7	8.7	4 227	290	21	4 492	308	211 807	NA	NA
Racine, WI	2 602	14.0	1 560	21	8.4	8.1	251	135	3	561	301	27 583	NA	NA
Minneapolis-St. Paul, MN-WI	41 803	14.9	18 433	254	6.6	6.1	6 448	228	32	6 454	228	311 942	132 366	4 862
Missoula, MT	1 035	11.7	617	6	7.0	5.8	273	307	2	336	378	10 947	3 342	4 335
Mobile, AL	7 943	15.1	5 077	95	9.6	12.0	1 083	203	9	1 997	375	79 155	31 291	5 936
Modesto, CA	6 970	16.6	3 277	48	7.8	6.9	642	151	7	1 478	347	53 593	26 165	6 127
Monroe, LA	2 203	15.0	1 340	19	9.1	8.6	332	226	5	1 012	689	19 459	12 707	8 676
Montgomery, AL	4 946	15.5	2 922	60	9.1	12.0	579	180	7	1 346	418	44 686	18 461	5 740
Muncie, IN	1 430	12.2	1 144	13	9.7	9.3	255	218	1	428	366	18 131	NA	NA
Myrtle Beach, SC	2 145	12.7	1 634	20	9.6	9.5	290	166	3	480	275	28 923	18 222	10 557
Naples, FL	2 574	13.4	2 053	19	10.7	7.5	772	387	2	500	251	47 572	10 495	5 268
Nashville, TN	16 841	14.8	9 192	116	8.1	6.9	3 288	284	20	4 620	400	138 150	71 533	7 111
New London-Norwich, CT	2 595	10.5	1 896	17	7.7	6.7	568	231	2	428	174	37 856	NA	NA
New Orleans, LA	19 606	15.0	12 149	159	9.3	8.1	4 280	327	30	6 084	465	176 100	85 328	6 526
New York-Northern New Jersey-Long Island, NY-NJ-CT-PA	299 059	15.0	171 896	1 924	8.6	6.4	68 326	341	209	78 109	390	2 871 592	695 392	3 500
Bergen-Passaic, NJ	18 587	13.9	11 714	91	8.8	4.9	4 808	358	12	5 100	379	205 188	36 725	2 729
Dutchess County, NY	3 367	12.8	2 180	16	8.3	4.7	610	230	3	686	259	39 721	6 592	2 539
Jersey City, NJ	8 781	15.8	4 889	77	8.8	8.8	903	162	9	2 435	437	72 790	25 641	4 614
Middlesex-Somerset-Hunterdon, NJ	15 711	14.2	8 179	77	7.4	4.9	3 278	292	8	2 478	221	141 127	29 877	2 682
Monmouth-Ocean, NJ	14 472	13.4	11 661	73	10.8	5.1	2 460	225	10	3 290	301	202 878	29 679	2 735
Nassau-Suffolk, NY	37 272	14.0	21 966	197	8.2	5.3	10 416	390	28	10 161	380	413 344	39 383	1 474
New Haven-Bridgeport-Stamford-Danbury-Waterbury, CT	23 018	14.1	14 769	146	9.1	6.3	6 015	369	16	4 233	259	254 330	66 521	4 256
New York, NY	138 930	16.0	73 618	956	8.5	6.9	32 328	372	84	37 201	428	1 174 061	356 082	4 127
Newark, NJ	29 160	15.0	17 108	223	8.8	7.6	5 814	298	28	9 797	502	270 024	82 842	4 230
Newburgh, NY-PA	5 306	14.5	2 812	34	7.7	6.4	601	163	6	1 054	285	47 027	8 920	2 506
Trenton, NJ	4 455	13.5	3 000	34	9.1	7.6	1 093	330	5	1 674	505	51 102	13 130	3 951
Norfolk-Virginia Beach-Newport News, VA-NC	23 107	15.0	11 460	239	7.4	10.4	3 377	219	17	3 960	257	175 380	76 038	4 880
Ocala, FL	2 652	11.2	3 013	21	12.8	7.9	385	159	2	534	221	66 595	11 781	4 877
Odessa-Midland, TX	4 091	16.9	1 787	37	7.4	9.0	369	150	4	719	293	28 744	11 965	4 836
Oklahoma City, OK	15 489	15.0	9 123	143	8.8	9.2	2 402	231	19	3 839	369	131 165	70 206	6 758
Omaha, NE-IA	10 740	15.6	5 250	87	7.6	8.2	1 884	272	12	3 380	487	84 892	37 662	5 673
Orlando, FL	20 912	14.3	11 872	131	8.1	6.3	2 925	194	19	4 593	305	221 252	106 453	7 135
Owensboro, KY	1 268	13.9	857	11	9.4	8.9	163	179	2	526	577	14 918	NA	NA
Panama City, FL	1 996	13.7	1 298	19	8.9	9.7	256	174	2	478	325	22 484	8 666	5 822
Parkersburg-Marietta, WV-OH	1 808	12.0	1 622	12	10.8	6.6	259	172	4	758	505	26 335	4 071	2 731
Pensacola, FL	5 391	13.7	3 438	45	8.8	8.3	845	211	6	1 792	448	57 141	20 160	4 988
Peoria-Pekin, IL	4 628	13.4	3 250	39	9.4	8.4	740	215	6	1 262	366	55 521	NA	NA
Philadelphia-Wilmington-Atlantic City, PA-NJ-DE-MD	81 897	13.7	58 880	678	9.8	8.3	19 431	324	89	22 024	368	908 766	274 612	4 596
Atlantic-Cape May, NJ	4 610	13.8	3 750	35	11.2	7.7	652	194	5	1 282	381	59 180	22 561	6 689
Philadelphia, PA-NJ	67 539	13.7	49 065	558	9.9	8.3	17 218	348	75	18 522	374	754 357	214 633	4 351
Vineland-Millville-Bridgeton, NJ	1 942	13.8	1 441	23	10.2	11.8	219	156	3	631	450	22 159	7 216	5 082
Wilmington-Newark, DE-MD	7 806	13.9	4 624	62	8.3	8.0	1 342	237	6	1 589	281	73 070	30 202	5 358
Phoenix-Mesa, AZ	49 845	17.5	22 058	373	7.8	7.5	6 392	218	29	6 561	224	379 791	203 160	7 153
Pine Bluff, AR	1 290	15.7	957	17	11.6	12.9	146	179	1	484	593	12 901	6 180	7 468
Pittsburgh, PA	26 451	11.2	27 433	180	11.6	6.8	7 028	300	37	10 636	453	451 678	58 036	2 628
Pittsfield, MA	1 350	10.1	1 553	7	11.6	5.4	374	281	4	595	447	26 555	3 051	2 578
Pocatello, ID	1 318	17.7	554	10	7.5	7.8	146	195	2	248	331	8 935	2 961	3 947
Portland, ME	3 030	12.0	2 276	14	9.0	4.5	1 007	397	6	1 049	414	40 254	9 431	3 746
Portland-Salem, OR-WA	31 557	14.9	16 820	170	8.0	5.4	5 271	245	22	4 140	193	267 786	124 902	5 841
Portland-Vancouver, OR-WA	26 402	14.8	13 928	138	7.8	5.2	4 710	259	18	3 623	199	218 812	104 585	5 781
Salem, OR	5 155	15.9	2 892	32	8.9	6.1	561	170	4	517	157	48 974	20 317	6 172
Providence-Warwick-Pawtucket, RI	11 590	12.8	8 933	76	9.9	6.5	2 722	301	9	2 614	289	156 769	31 349	3 463
Provo-Orem, UT	8 776	26.6	1 446	45	4.4	5.1	401	119	4	610	182	25 494	13 261	3 962
Pueblo, CO	1 795	13.5	1 339	14	10.1	8.0	324	240	2	563	417	24 749	7 844	5 692
Punta Gorda, FL	1 005	7.6	1 998	5	15.1	5.0	401	297	3	652	483	38 452	3 920	2 881
Raleigh-Durham-Chapel Hill, NC	15 840	15.1	7 213	143	6.9	9.0	4 405	408	13	3 374	312	117 113	60 160	5 706
Rapid City, SD	1 322	15.2	630	9	7.2	6.6	251	286	1	328	374	11 859	5 094	5 842

1. Per 1,000 estimated resident population, average 1996–1998.   2. Deaths of infants under 1 year old.   3. Deaths of infants under 1 year old per 1,000 live births.   4. Data subject to copyright.   5. Per 100,000 resident population as of July 1 of the year shown.   6. Data for serious crimes have not been adjusted for underreporting; this may affect comparability between geographic areas and over time.   7. Per 100,000 population estimated by the FBI.

Area Name	Serious crimes known to police, 1998[1] (cont'd) Rate[2] Violent	Property	Education — School enrollment and attainment, 1990 — Enrollment[3] Total	Percent private	Attainment[4] (percent) High school graduate or more	Bachelor's degree or more	Local government expenditures, fiscal 1997[5] Total current expenditures (mil dol)	Current expenditures per student (dollars)	Money income — 1989 Per capita[6] (dollars)	Households Median Dollars	Percent change, 1979–1989 (constant 1989 dollars)	Percent with $100,000 or more	Income and poverty, 1997 Median household income	Percent below poverty level All persons	Persons under 18	Persons 5–17 in families
	46	47	48	49	50	51	52	53	54	55	56	57	58	59	60	61
Merced, CA	703	4 414	56 282	6.6	63.1	12.0	261.0	5 406	10 606	25 547	3.9	2.8	NA	25.4	37.4	37.3
Miami-Fort Lauderdale, FL	1 190	7 484	778 956	20.6	69.9	18.8	1 134.9	5 191	14 943	28 502	6.2	4.8	NA	17.2	24.9	22.2
Fort Lauderdale, FL	719	5 678	263 345	20.1	76.8	18.8	1 134.9	5 191	16 883	30 570	10.0	4.7	NA	11.7	17.5	15.9
Miami, FL	1 532	8 791	515 611	20.8	65.0	18.8	NA	NA	13 686	26 908	3.1	4.9	NA	21.1	29.6	26.3
Milwaukee-Racine, WI	NA	NA	428 267	23.2	79.3	20.8	1 976.1	7 234	14 702	32 358	-4.4	3.6	NA	11.2	18.6	15.6
Milwaukee-Waukesha, WI	NA	NA	382 149	23.8	79.7	21.3	1 776.6	7 311	14 785	32 315	-4.1	3.6	NA	11.4	19.2	16.0
Racine, WI	NA	NA	46 118	18.3	76.4	16.5	199.5	6 612	14 023	32 750	-6.7	2.9	NA	9.1	14.2	12.6
Minneapolis-St. Paul, MN-WI	414	4 448	673 370	16.6	87.1	26.9	3 150.3	6 537	16 721	36 467	5.6	5.1	NA	7.7	11.7	10.3
Missoula, MT	237	4 098	25 497	6.4	85.4	27.7	75.4	5 223	11 944	23 388	-14.2	2.1	NA	15.3	20.0	17.8
Mobile, AL	604	5 332	128 674	17.4	70.8	15.8	369.5	4 285	11 388	23 644	-3.9	2.4	NA	17.8	26.0	24.1
Modesto, CA	760	5 367	102 957	7.8	68.4	13.0	455.5	5 075	12 731	29 793	10.6	3.5	NA	18.4	27.2	26.6
Monroe, LA	1 204	7 472	42 399	9.1	71.6	18.9	126.8	4 289	10 593	21 129	-9.2	2.3	NA	19.8	29.1	27.2
Montgomery, AL	599	5 141	82 106	15.5	73.2	21.1	229.7	4 237	12 258	26 685	5.5	2.6	NA	16.0	23.7	21.5
Muncie, IN	NA	NA	37 870	5.0	74.5	16.5	110.2	6 424	12 168	24 436	-11.4	2.0	NA	13.8	20.0	17.9
Myrtle Beach, SC	1 156	9 401	33 637	7.7	74.3	16.0	139.4	5 339	12 385	24 959	10.4	2.4	NA	14.4	25.1	23.4
Naples, FL	600	4 668	27 492	11.9	79.0	22.3	170.2	6 039	21 386	34 001	22.1	9.1	NA	11.2	20.5	19.3
Nashville, TN	1 069	6 042	242 440	20.1	74.0	21.4	862.5	4 843	14 567	30 222	7.6	3.7	NA	9.9	13.8	12.0
New London-Norwich, CT	NA	NA	61 393	19.8	80.9	21.8	316.7	8 198	16 702	37 487	23.4	4.7	NA	8.1	12.4	12.5
New Orleans, LA	918	5 608	360 095	29.6	71.9	19.3	1 025.5	4 853	12 005	24 415	-9.7	3.2	NA	18.0	26.4	24.3
New York-Northern New Jersey-Long Island, NY-NJ-CT-PA	647	2 853	4 878 393	25.9	75.1	25.7	26 735.6	9 068	18 864	38 513	26.8	9.4	NA	13.7	22.1	21.1
Bergen-Passaic, NJ	261	2 468	296 616	25.8	77.3	27.3	1 835.0	10 070	21 234	45 039	23.2	12.0	NA	7.9	13.0	12.5
Dutchess County, NY	261	2 278	67 685	24.7	79.8	24.8	363.2	8 369	17 420	42 249	24.4	6.1	NA	8.4	12.9	12.5
Jersey City, NJ	821	3 793	128 644	29.0	64.1	19.7	725.5	9 578	14 480	30 916	28.3	4.2	NA	17.1	28.6	27.1
Middlesex-Somerset-Hunterdon, NJ	215	2 467	250 426	19.0	81.8	30.2	1 479.6	9 489	20 699	48 701	22.7	10.9	NA	5.7	8.9	8.5
Monmouth-Ocean, NJ	211	2 524	229 583	21.9	79.3	22.5	1 454.0	8 921	18 383	39 830	26.8	7.7	NA	7.1	11.4	10.8
Nassau-Suffolk, NY	116	1 358	665 563	23.0	83.2	26.5	4 698.9	11 193	20 884	51 670	27.3	13.9	NA	6.7	10.9	9.8
New Haven-Bridgeport-Stamford-Danbury-Waterbury, CT	432	3 824	395 168	26.5	79.3	29.3	2 090.5	8 434	21 975	43 268	25.7	11.8	NA	9.2	15.4	14.4
New York, NY	1 037	3 090	2 195 241	28.6	70.3	24.6	10 013.6	8 035	17 397	31 658	26.6	7.8	NA	20.4	32.9	31.9
Newark, NJ	670	3 560	472 978	22.6	76.5	26.9	3 042.1	10 168	19 810	42 174	24.4	10.9	NA	10.4	16.4	15.6
Newburgh, NY-PA	303	2 203	90 364	19.0	77.4	19.1	520.3	8 160	15 080	38 161	28.5	5.0	NA	11.0	16.3	15.9
Trenton, NJ	468	3 483	86 125	29.5	77.1	29.5	512.8	10 006	18 936	41 227	25.1	9.0	NA	9.4	14.8	14.3
Norfolk-Virginia Beach-Newport News, VA-NC	459	4 421	375 122	13.6	78.6	19.8	1 408.8	5 179	13 467	30 766	12.0	2.8	NA	13.7	19.7	18.7
Ocala, FL	747	4 130	37 941	11.7	69.6	11.5	173.9	4 798	11 782	22 451	13.6	2.0	NA	16.4	26.7	24.3
Odessa-Midland, TX	548	4 288	64 011	7.6	71.6	18.5	242.5	4 525	13 034	26 744	-19.0	3.6	NA	16.5	22.5	22.3
Oklahoma City, OK	614	6 144	268 693	12.2	79.2	21.6	823.3	4 487	13 269	26 882	-3.7	2.7	NA	14.4	21.5	19.0
Omaha, NE-IA	830	4 843	180 577	19.1	84.4	22.5	658.8	5 537	13 916	30 258	0.6	3.2	NA	8.9	12.3	9.6
Orlando, FL	991	6 144	287 286	14.6	78.6	20.4	1 156.9	4 848	14 591	30 211	18.1	3.6	NA	12.5	19.2	17.0
Owensboro, KY	NA	NA	21 955	22.3	72.3	14.1	77.6	5 533	11 456	24 399	-8.5	1.9	NA	13.2	18.8	17.5
Panama City, FL	566	5 256	32 011	9.5	74.7	15.7	130.8	5 098	12 225	24 684	11.0	2.0	NA	15.1	22.4	21.4
Parkersburg-Marietta, WV-OH	205	2 526	35 570	11.3	75.0	13.4	147.2	5 692	11 772	24 882	-9.5	1.6	NA	13.2	19.8	17.3
Pensacola, FL	798	4 190	89 901	12.3	76.7	18.3	328.0	4 939	12 278	25 735	5.5	2.3	NA	16.0	22.2	21.1
Peoria-Pekin, IL	NA	NA	91 361	18.1	78.4	16.9	300.4	5 318	13 796	29 836	-12.2	2.8	NA	10.9	17.1	16.1
Philadelphia-Wilmington-Atlantic City, PA-NJ-DE-MD	663	3 933	1 463 758	28.9	75.8	22.1	7 268.9	8 156	16 296	35 385	18.2	5.7	NA	11.1	17.0	15.4
Atlantic-Cape May, NJ	533	6 156	69 177	16.5	73.2	16.7	485.3	8 895	15 873	32 407	27.4	4.5	NA	10.9	18.1	17.5
Philadelphia, PA-NJ	667	3 684	1 226 846	30.6	75.9	22.6	5 994.6	8 188	16 354	35 406	17.5	5.9	NA	11.2	17.1	15.4
Vineland-Millville-Bridgeton, NJ	730	4 352	33 115	13.3	63.4	10.8	224.9	8 978	12 560	29 985	16.3	2.6	NA	15.8	24.7	23.9
Wilmington-Newark, DE-MD	690	4 668	134 620	23.6	79.5	23.4	564.1	7 095	17 008	38 216	17.2	5.3	NA	8.7	13.3	11.9
Phoenix-Mesa, AZ	613	6 540	588 764	10.6	80.7	21.4	2 097.8	4 384	14 671	30 350	3.2	4.1	NA	13.1	19.6	18.5
Pine Bluff, AR	1 796	5 672	23 015	6.0	65.9	14.6	77.7	4 797	9 852	21 322	-0.3	1.6	NA	24.9	33.3	29.2
Pittsburgh, PA	317	2 311	554 565	20.1	77.3	18.7	2 581.0	7 621	13 785	26 656	-10.9	3.1	NA	11.7	17.1	15.1
Pittsfield, MA	303	2 275	34 224	21.7	77.9	20.9	153.2	7 133	14 857	30 469	14.5	3.5	NA	11.3	18.2	17.2
Pocatello, ID	309	3 638	23 087	4.3	82.9	19.8	64.7	4 253	10 976	26 275	-10.2	1.6	NA	13.9	17.1	14.5
Portland, ME	182	3 564	58 915	16.5	85.0	27.6	255.8	6 588	15 816	32 285	25.4	4.5	NA	8.1	11.3	9.9
Portland-Salem, OR-WA	513	5 328	456 026	14.4	83.5	22.5	2 123.5	6 020	14 593	30 451	1.0	3.4	NA	9.7	13.7	11.6
Portland-Vancouver, OR-WA	567	5 214	383 949	14.6	84.3	23.3	1 807.4	6 075	15 021	31 037	0.9	3.6	NA	9.2	12.9	11.0
Salem, OR	217	5 955	72 077	13.2	78.9	18.2	316.2	5 723	12 260	26 770	-1.5	2.2	NA	12.7	18.2	15.2
Providence-Warwick-Pawtucket, RI	304	3 159	232 837	24.6	71.0	20.4	999.9	7 380	14 806	31 908	18.8	4.0	NA	11.5	17.8	16.3
Provo-Orem, UT	134	3 828	114 352	30.5	87.9	26.2	273.6	3 571	9 051	27 431	1.1	2.2	NA	10.3	11.3	9.7
Pueblo, CO	875	4 911	32 691	6.1	73.9	14.0	113.5	4 805	10 347	21 552	-16.9	1.3	NA	18.1	25.8	23.1
Punta Gorda, FL	205	2 676	16 107	11.9	75.7	13.4	83.4	5 182	14 431	25 745	16.5	2.7	NA	9.5	17.8	16.9
Raleigh-Durham-Chapel Hill, NC	560	5 146	236 433	16.3	80.0	31.7	809.3	5 049	15 629	32 046	18.0	4.2	NA	9.6	14.1	12.8
Rapid City, SD	352	5 490	21 946	9.7	84.8	21.2	81.5	4 471	12 031	25 340	1.5	2.4	NA	14.3	20.6	18.1

1. Data for serious crimes have not been adjusted for underreporting; this may affect comparability between geographic areas and over time.   2. Per 100,000 population estimated by the FBI.   3. All persons 3 years old and over enrolled in nursery school through college.   4. Persons 25 years old and over.   5. Elementary and secondary education expenditures, local government fiscal years ending between July 1, 1996 and June 30, 1997.   6. Based on population enumerated as of April 1, 1990.

Table C. Metropolitan Areas — Personal Income

Area Name	Personal income, 1998 Total (mil dol)	Percent change, 1997–1998	Per capita[1] Dollars	Per capita[1] Rank	Wages and salaries[2] (mil dol)	Proprietor's income (mil dol)	Dividends, interest, and rent (mil dol)	Transfer payments Total (mil dol)	Government payments to individuals Total (mil dol)	Social Security (mil dol)	Medical payments (mil dol)	Income maintenance (mil dol)	Unemployment insurance (mil dol)
	62	63	64	65	66	67	68	69	70	71	72	73	74
Merced, CA	3 498	4.1	17 732	312	1 684	495	514	756	719	192	295	153	38
Miami-Fort Lauderdale, FL	94 488	5.8	25 826	X	58 161	5 527	20 915	14 922	14 272	4 903	7 066	1 555	263
Fort Lauderdale, FL	43 041	5.9	28 546	62	22 379	1 846	11 427	5 935	5 667	2 539	2 473	332	99
Miami, FL	51 448	5.7	23 919	178	35 782	3 681	9 488	8 987	8 605	2 364	4 594	1 223	163
Milwaukee-Racine, WI	49 779	5.4	30 258	X	34 232	2 331	10 046	5 972	5 666	2 484	2 237	602	141
Milwaukee-Waukesha, WI.	44 637	5.4	30 582	37	31 283	2 162	9 070	5 368	5 096	2 200	2 026	562	122
Racine, WI	5 142	5.5	27 712	77	2 948	169	976	604	570	284	211	40	19
Minneapolis-St. Paul, MN-WI	94 991	7.5	33 561	20	67 999	4 967	19 037	8 350	7 787	3 133	3 270	726	185
Missoula, MT	2 066	5.9	23 234	203	1 314	207	439	273	257	105	86	23	5
Mobile, AL	11 200	4.5	21 062	281	6 866	663	2 015	1 916	1 823	772	701	213	26
Modesto, CA	9 022	6.4	21 136	280	4 689	1 027	1 474	1 546	1 466	489	558	263	71
Monroe, LA	3 117	3.5	21 230	276	1 967	316	532	548	522	176	234	71	5
Montgomery, AL	7 745	4.4	24 084	176	5 275	487	1 380	1 127	1 071	409	412	141	13
Muncie, IN	2 739	4.6	23 545	193	1 741	146	478	434	412	192	149	38	7
Myrtle Beach, SC	4 030	7.2	23 088	207	2 363	403	870	630	599	309	196	51	12
Naples, FL	8 553	5.8	42 813	2	2 991	751	4 087	882	846	500	283	34	7
Nashville, TN	33 910	5.8	29 344	49	23 357	3 997	5 146	3 596	3 405	1 378	1 519	272	59
New London-Norwich, CT	7 392	1.9	29 933	42	5 308	439	1 341	979	938	380	410	78	29
New Orleans, LA	32 955	4.6	25 225	139	21 171	3 265	5 564	5 165	4 941	1 704	2 297	662	40
New York-Northern New Jersey-Long Island, NY-NJ-CT-PA	731 539	5.7	36 582	X	466 339	70 622	133 815	98 966	95 038	29 006	48 596	11 327	2 132
Bergen-Passaic, NJ	53 165	7.6	39 750	6	29 535	5 889	11 206	5 005	4 753	2 202	1 889	296	159
Dutchess County, NY	7 913	9.0	29 812	43	4 059	412	1 440	1 035	981	419	412	80	13
Jersey City, NJ	14 915	4.1	26 970	95	11 111	1 229	1 771	2 421	2 317	670	1 102	313	128
Middlesex-Somerset-Hunterdon, NJ	42 920	6.5	38 414	7	30 878	3 276	7 034	3 501	3 291	1 566	1 266	149	117
Monmouth-Ocean, NJ	34 639	6.0	31 682	28	14 033	1 924	7 410	4 601	4 397	2 106	1 777	177	135
Nassau-Suffolk, NY	99 865	4.7	37 381	9	46 832	6 420	22 215	11 436	10 890	4 513	4 928	722	144
New Haven-Bridgeport-Stamford-Danbury-Waterbury, CT	69 039	5.1	42 346	3	41 263	5 613	12 865	7 306	7 025	2 644	3 286	638	158
New York, NY	315 195	5.7	36 316	12	229 309	39 096	52 440	53 125	51 350	11 054	29 521	7 937	975
Newark, NJ	72 343	5.9	37 136	10	46 296	5 433	13 504	7 781	7 415	2 816	3 248	769	248
Newburgh, NY-PA	9 099	6.1	24 595	158	4 081	485	1 555	1 369	1 296	495	581	132	19
Trenton, NJ	12 447	6.1	37 551	8	8 941	846	2 375	1 386	1 324	520	586	112	36
Norfolk-Virginia Beach-Newport News, VA-NC	36 855	4.0	23 771	183	26 468	1 530	6 448	4 141	3 876	1 629	1 389	448	42
Ocala, FL	5 195	7.1	21 533	266	2 288	356	1 293	1 201	1 158	629	400	85	8
Odessa-Midland, TX	6 029	5.7	24 718	151	3 514	986	1 045	753	712	297	305	69	18
Oklahoma City, OK	24 220	5.1	23 337	199	16 414	2 032	4 168	3 076	2 897	1 258	1 020	277	34
Omaha, NE-IA	20 311	5.4	29 307	50	14 066	1 741	3 764	2 113	1 993	831	800	157	19
Orlando, FL	38 406	8.6	25 555	132	27 254	2 513	6 771	4 978	4 711	2 091	1 880	385	51
Owensboro, KY	2 013	2.9	22 126	247	1 208	117	399	340	324	148	121	30	7
Panama City, FL	3 252	4.3	22 163	243	1 985	228	651	548	522	205	209	50	10
Parkersburg-Marietta, WV-OH	3 346	3.1	22 304	238	2 120	214	590	638	610	262	224	48	12
Pensacola, FL	8 726	4.8	21 719	263	5 315	429	1 648	1 379	1 310	517	503	156	12
Peoria-Pekin, IL	9 231	5.5	26 679	103	6 191	504	1 972	1 222	1 154	570	391	114	33
Philadelphia-Wilmington-Atlantic City, PA-NJ-DE-MD	186 297	5.4	31 119	X	118 317	14 416	34 145	25 813	24 663	9 290	10 937	2 591	737
Atlantic-Cape May, NJ	10 326	5.5	30 735	36	6 284	1 629	1 783	1 545	1 483	590	638	93	98
Philadelphia, PA-NJ	154 763	5.0	31 295	31	96 976	11 597	28 473	21 847	20 895	7 697	9 441	2 276	553
Vineland-Millville-Bridgeton, NJ	3 195	5.1	22 756	222	1 993	232	489	643	617	219	271	63	41
Wilmington-Newark, DE-MD	18 012	8.3	31 885	27	13 064	958	3 400	1 778	1 668	784	588	158	45
Phoenix-Mesa, AZ	78 210	9.5	26 686	102	52 501	5 545	15 091	8 865	8 353	3 816	3 065	669	76
Pine Bluff, AR	1 579	3.2	19 357	306	1 092	79	260	319	305	106	106	49	7
Pittsburgh, PA	66 013	4.0	28 149	69	39 460	5 809	12 432	11 547	11 090	4 544	4 826	824	304
Pittsfield, MA	3 684	4.4	27 731	76	2 077	278	821	694	670	263	319	50	17
Pocatello, ID	1 468	4.6	19 759	301	856	87	237	218	206	78	63	17	6
Portland, ME	7 623	6.5	29 960	41	5 676	488	1 617	940	897	374	375	83	9
Portland-Salem, OR-WA	61 184	5.6	28 453	X	40 010	4 672	12 767	6 483	6 099	2 676	2 133	523	261
Portland-Vancouver, OR-WA	53 563	5.6	29 430	47	35 800	4 014	11 071	5 341	5 015	2 196	1 739	428	223
Salem, OR	7 621	5.3	23 072	208	4 209	658	1 696	1 141	1 084	480	394	95	38
Providence-Warwick-Pawtucket, RI	25 350	5.5	28 007	71	14 619	1 624	4 822	4 369	4 202	1 520	1 895	400	139
Provo-Orem, UT	6 103	7.8	17 956	311	4 008	504	894	679	622	260	254	54	12
Pueblo, CO	2 884	6.2	21 379	269	1 588	135	515	722	699	206	357	75	7
Punta Gorda, FL	3 201	5.2	23 752	187	958	152	1 295	791	767	437	270	20	3
Raleigh-Durham-Chapel Hill, NC	32 804	7.7	30 394	38	24 171	2 304	5 838	2 890	2 701	1 146	1 108	248	36
Rapid City, SD	2 083	4.6	23 858	180	1 370	160	520	275	262	115	94	20	2

1. Based on the resident population estimated as of July 1 of the year shown.   2. Includes other labor income.

Table C. Metropolitan Areas — Earnings, Social Security, and Housing

	Earnings, 1998									Social Security beneficiaries, December 1998			Housing units, 1990	
					Percent by selected industries									
			Goods-related[1]		Service-related and other[2]									
Area Name	Total (mil dol)	Farm	Total	Manu-facturing	Total	Retail trade	Finance, insurance, and real estate	Services	Govern-ment	Number	Rate[3]	Supplemental Security Income recipients, December 1998	Total	Percent change, 1980–1990
	75	76	77	78	79	80	81	82	83	84	85	86	87	88
Merced, CA	2 179	14.6	22.1	17.6	44.2	10.5	3.7	16.4	19.2	25 466	129	8 448	58 410	16.7
Miami-Fort Lauderdale, FL	63 688	0.3	11.6	6.9	72.3	10.9	10.6	32.6	15.8	587 733	161	137 430	1 399 948	21.6
Fort Lauderdale, FL	24 225	0.1	13.6	7.3	71.4	12.8	10.9	33.2	14.9	279 948	186	25 076	628 660	29.3
Miami, FL	39 463	0.4	10.4	6.7	72.9	9.7	10.4	32.2	16.3	307 785	143	112 354	771 288	15.9
Milwaukee-Racine, WI	36 562	0.1	NA	26.9	NA	7.5	8.9	27.4	11.3	270 138	164	38 863	628 976	7.7
Milwaukee-Waukesha, WI.	33 445	0.0	NA	25.4	NA	7.5	9.4	28.0	11.3	239 242	164	35 396	562 031	7.8
Racine, WI	3 117	0.4	48.6	42.8	39.0	7.2	2.8	20.3	12.0	30 896	166	3 467	66 945	7.0
Minneapolis-St. Paul, MN-WI	72 966	0.1	NA	20.4	NA	8.6	10.7	27.3	11.9	348 058	123	35 792	1 015 235	23.0
Missoula, MT	1 521	-0.2	16.5	8.9	64.5	12.5	6.5	29.9	19.3	12 324	138	1 527	33 466	9.6
Mobile, AL	7 529	0.5	25.4	15.7	57.4	11.1	5.9	26.6	16.7	94 234	177	16 894	202 153	22.4
Modesto, CA	5 716	6.1	NA	19.2	NA	10.9	4.2	23.0	16.6	60 448	142	17 431	132 027	28.8
Monroe, LA	2 284	0.3	22.4	16.7	61.2	10.5	8.2	25.6	16.1	21 956	149	5 209	56 300	9.4
Montgomery, AL	5 761	0.4	NA	11.5	NA	9.3	8.1	24.4	29.7	52 230	162	12 907	116 754	14.6
Muncie, IN	1 887	0.7	NA	26.2	NA	9.8	4.3	25.6	17.8	21 374	183	2 699	48 793	2.5
Myrtle Beach, SC	2 766	0.1	17.1	8.6	70.4	20.4	10.2	32.5	12.4	37 571	215	4 288	89 960	63.6
Naples, FL	3 743	3.9	14.8	2.8	71.8	12.7	14.7	35.9	9.5	52 833	265	1 900	94 165	85.6
Nashville, TN	27 354	0.0	NA	NA	NA	10.4	8.6	34.8	10.8	160 327	139	21 043	410 968	28.5
New London-Norwich, CT	5 748	0.6	27.1	22.0	52.5	7.4	2.7	33.6	19.9	42 358	172	3 005	104 461	15.7
New Orleans, LA	24 435	0.0	NA	10.1	NA	8.7	6.6	31.8	16.9	206 638	158	50 724	540 422	9.3
New York-Northern New Jersey-Long Island, NY-NJ-CT-PA	536 961	0.0	NA	11.6	NA	6.3	19.8	31.8	12.6	3 100 861	155	588 220	7 658 812	6.5
Bergen-Passaic, NJ	35 424	0.0	21.7	17.7	69.2	7.8	7.6	32.7	9.1	222 237	165	21 469	487 329	4.5
Dutchess County, NY	4 471	0.1	33.3	28.0	47.8	7.9	4.5	28.4	18.8	45 524	172	5 009	97 632	12.4
Jersey City, NJ	12 340	0.0	13.2	10.5	69.2	7.2	18.2	22.5	17.7	78 508	141	21 300	229 682	3.8
Middlesex-Somerset-Hunterdon, NJ	34 154	0.1	NA	19.1	NA	6.6	10.4	28.4	9.9	158 792	142	11 713	382 814	26.2
Monmouth-Ocean, NJ	15 957	0.2	NA	5.8	NA	11.1	7.4	36.1	19.4	222 263	203	11 413	438 271	22.0
Nassau-Suffolk, NY	53 252	0.1	15.7	10.2	67.8	9.9	10.3	33.4	16.4	460 410	172	38 181	927 609	7.1
New Haven-Bridgeport-Stamford-Danbury-Waterbury, CT	46 877	0.1	NA	20.4	NA	7.5	14.1	31.0	9.0	278 133	170	23 658	651 434	11.9
New York, NY	268 405	0.0	NA	7.7	NA	4.6	28.8	32.5	11.6	1 228 351	141	400 935	3 449 058	2.3
Newark, NJ	51 728	0.0	21.2	17.0	65.4	6.3	11.4	30.0	13.3	295 343	151	39 885	729 651	2.3
Newburgh, NY-PA	4 567	0.4	NA	10.0	NA	11.5	5.5	24.9	28.0	56 279	152	6 716	141 666	27.6
Trenton, NJ	9 786	0.0	16.4	13.1	57.8	5.6	9.3	34.2	25.7	55 021	166	7 941	123 666	10.8
Norfolk-Virginia Beach-Newport News, VA-NC	27 998	0.1	NA	10.6	NA	7.9	NA	22.3	38.5	203 503	132	30 580	558 946	29.8
Ocala, FL	2 644	2.7	23.2	14.6	56.2	13.7	6.1	24.7	17.9	74 980	310	5 824	94 567	70.9
Odessa-Midland, TX	4 500	0.1	42.7	6.8	44.8	8.8	3.8	18.9	12.7	33 955	138	4 525	93 970	27.0
Oklahoma City, OK	18 445	0.1	21.2	12.0	54.7	10.1	6.2	26.4	24.0	151 649	146	17 988	425 043	20.6
Omaha, NE-IA	15 807	0.4	NA	10.7	NA	8.3	9.3	30.6	15.3	95 246	137	9 303	256 489	11.6
Orlando, FL	29 768	0.7	NA	8.3	NA	11.3	8.4	38.3	11.8	251 602	167	29 551	524 197	60.2
Owensboro, KY	1 325	0.5	31.5	20.4	51.9	11.6	5.1	22.2	16.0	17 479	192	2 717	35 041	10.7
Panama City, FL	2 214	0.1	16.2	6.9	55.5	12.7	5.7	26.9	28.3	26 367	179	3 419	65 999	53.8
Parkersburg-Marietta, WV-OH	2 334	0.2	36.1	27.1	48.6	10.2	4.4	24.1	15.1	30 325	202	4 269	63 372	5.4
Pensacola, FL	5 744	0.2	NA	8.7	NA	10.0	4.2	26.8	32.5	66 997	168	9 847	145 061	33.1
Peoria-Pekin, IL	6 695	0.8	35.8	29.4	53.1	8.4	4.9	27.3	10.4	62 487	181	6 599	136 458	-2.6
Philadelphia-Wilmington-Atlantic City, PA-NJ-DE-MD	132 733	0.2	NA	16.8	NA	7.9	10.4	NA	13.0	1 015 408	170	140 453	2 376 423	9.8
Atlantic-Cape May, NJ	7 912	0.4	NA	3.1	NA	8.6	3.8	NA	16.4	66 005	196	6 444	192 414	19.2
Philadelphia, PA-NJ	108 573	0.2	NA	16.8	NA	7.9	10.2	NA	12.8	839 618	170	121 713	1 932 499	8.4
Vineville-Millville-Bridgeton, NJ	2 225	2.1	29.0	22.7	46.0	8.3	4.7	20.7	22.8	25 252	180	4 452	50 294	6.2
Wilmington-Newark, DE-MD	14 022	0.2	NA	24.3	NA	7.4	16.5	25.4	11.2	84 533	150	7 844	201 216	17.3
Phoenix-Mesa, AZ	58 046	0.7	23.1	15.0	63.9	10.2	11.0	28.9	12.3	437 262	149	40 078	1 004 773	55.8
Pine Bluff, AR	1 171	1.3	27.3	24.0	46.8	9.1	3.7	21.0	24.5	14 396	177	3 965	33 311	0.8
Pittsburgh, PA	45 207	0.0	NA	18.4	NA	8.7	7.6	32.0	11.7	503 729	215	56 388	1 015 208	2.6
Pittsfield, MA	2 355	0.1	26.9	20.6	60.7	12.0	4.5	34.7	12.3	29 991	225	3 634	64 324	8.6
Pocatello, ID	944	0.4	NA	11.1	NA	11.9	5.2	19.5	27.0	9 368	125	1 273	25 694	3.5
Portland, ME	6 165	0.0	NA	11.2	NA	12.3	12.5	30.5	14.5	44 664	176	4 588	109 890	19.7
Portland-Salem, OR-WA	44 682	1.1	NA	18.2	NA	9.5	8.0	25.6	14.0	298 903	139	31 053	725 936	13.9
Portland-Vancouver, OR-WA	39 814	0.7	26.8	18.9	60.1	9.5	8.3	25.8	12.4	243 283	134	25 946	620 089	14.8
Salem, OR	4 868	4.1	NA	12.5	NA	10.0	5.5	24.4	27.1	55 620	168	5 107	105 847	8.9
Providence-Warwick-Pawtucket, RI	16 242	0.1	NA	18.5	NA	8.8	8.5	31.4	15.6	175 274	194	24 714	377 097	11.0
Provo-Orem, UT	4 512	0.5	NA	15.2	NA	9.0	4.9	39.7	13.4	30 119	90	2 858	72 820	16.8
Pueblo, CO	1 723	0.1	20.6	12.0	56.9	13.7	7.0	26.0	22.5	27 238	202	4 956	50 872	3.6
Punta Gorda, FL	1 110	1.1	NA	2.7	NA	16.9	6.7	38.4	16.7	49 396	366	1 370	64 641	85.8
Raleigh-Durham-Chapel Hill, NC	26 475	0.7	NA	18.8	NA	8.1	NA	29.5	17.6	135 326	125	19 374	359 310	42.3
Rapid City, SD	1 530	0.3	16.8	8.6	59.2	13.0	6.2	28.2	23.7	14 168	162	1 669	33 741	19.6

1. Covers mining, construction, and manufacturing. 2. Covers private sector earnings in agricultural services, forestry, and fisheries; transportation and public utilities; wholesale trade; retail trade; finance, insurance, and real estate; and services. 3. Per 1,000 resident population estimated as of July 1 of the year shown.

Table C. Metropolitan Areas — Housing, Labor Force, and Employment

Area Name	Housing units, 1990 (cont'd) Occupied units								Civilian labor force, 1999				Civilian employment, 1990[5]		
	Owner-occupied					Renter-occupied		Sub-stand-ard units[3] (percent)		Percent change, 1998–1999	Unemployment			Percent	
	Total	Percent	Median value[1]	With a mortgage	Without a mortgage	Median rent[2]	Rent as per-cent of income		Total		Total	Rate[4]	Total	Professional, managerial, and technical	Precision production, craft, and repair
	89	90	91	92	93	94	95	96	97	98	99	100	101	102	103
Merced, CA	55 331	54.4	90 800	22.7	12.1	429	28.2	15.7	84 759	-0.9	11 238	13.3	66 116	21.7	11.5
Miami-Fort Lauderdale, FL	1 220 797	60.2	88 700	NA	NA	523	NA	12.2	1 815 392	1.2	91 707	5.1	1 500 947	28.6	11.1
Fort Lauderdale, FL	528 442	68.0	91 800	23.6	13.1	574	29.0	5.2	770 374	1.7	31 157	4.0	599 119	29.9	11.7
Miami, FL	692 355	54.3	86 500	23.1	13.0	492	31.3	17.6	1 045 018	0.7	60 550	5.8	901 828	27.8	10.7
Milwaukee-Racine, WI	601 458	60.4	74 800	NA	NA	441	NA	2.9	887 871	-1.6	28 693	3.2	784 796	29.8	11.5
Milwaukee-Waukesha, WI	537 722	59.4	76 900	20.9	13.6	446	26.0	2.9	797 299	-1.5	24 700	3.1	700 737	30.3	11.2
Racine, WI	63 736	68.3	64 200	19.3	12.6	401	24.9	2.6	90 572	-3.2	3 993	4.4	84 059	26.3	14.0
Minneapolis-St. Paul, MN-WI	960 170	68.9	88 300	NA	NA	477	NA	2.3	1 695 747	1.1	37 390	2.2	1 366 976	33.8	9.5
Missoula, MT	30 782	60.1	66 200	20.3	12.2	334	28.0	3.3	52 281	-0.4	1 947	3.7	37 122	30.8	9.1
Mobile, AL	173 943	69.3	55 300	19.1	12.8	328	26.2	4.7	269 492	-0.3	12 571	4.7	198 070	27.2	13.0
Modesto, CA	125 375	60.7	124 300	23.3	11.7	481	28.9	10.5	203 050	0.4	21 435	10.6	151 010	23.8	14.0
Monroe, LA	50 518	64.8	52 800	21.0	13.2	333	28.0	6.3	71 523	0.6	2 790	3.9	58 100	29.7	11.0
Montgomery, AL	105 531	67.1	61 500	19.2	12.6	372	24.5	5.4	164 619	1.6	6 100	3.7	128 656	29.7	10.0
Muncie, IN	45 177	66.8	42 300	15.5	12.7	333	27.5	2.0	61 515	0.0	2 042	3.3	55 097	25.1	12.0
Myrtle Beach, SC	55 764	68.5	75 600	NA	NA	424	NA	4.2	104 862	1.8	4 065	3.9	66 730	24.8	13.6
Naples, FL	61 703	70.2	121 400	22.7	11.7	571	26.5	5.5	93 644	2.0	3 530	3.8	68 449	25.9	12.9
Nashville, TN	375 831	63.2	76 000	21.2	12.6	425	25.3	2.8	661 572	3.0	17 960	2.7	501 819	30.5	10.8
New London-Norwich, CT	93 245	64.7	149 200	22.7	13.0	571	24.8	1.9	129 942	-1.6	4 274	3.3	120 161	33.0	13.6
New Orleans, LA	469 823	58.7	69 800	NA	NA	396	NA	6.4	615 426	-0.9	26 882	4.4	533 656	31.2	10.5
New York-Northern New Jersey-Long Island, NY-NJ-CT-PA	7 126 646	51.9	187 300	NA	NA	546	NA	7.2	9 969 369	0.5	483 824	4.9	9 405 581	35.1	9.1
Bergen-Passaic, NJ	464 149	63.9	214 400	23.6	15.2	645	26.2	4.1	682 847	1.4	31 031	4.5	661 994	35.2	9.8
Dutchess County, NY	89 567	69.1	149 200	NA	NA	599	NA	2.0	119 951	1.3	4 184	3.5	127 925	39.1	10.6
Jersey City, NJ	208 739	32.5	157 000	24.0	15.6	524	25.0	9.9	283 560	0.7	20 534	7.2	268 816	27.2	8.8
Middlesex-Somerset-Hunterdon, NJ	365 085	70.7	173 500	23.7	14.8	679	25.3	2.8	642 206	1.5	20 806	3.2	555 733	38.3	9.5
Monmouth-Ocean, NJ	365 717	77.4	150 600	25.1	16.3	647	29.0	1.9	521 561	1.3	22 037	4.2	456 555	34.4	11.4
Nassau-Suffolk, NY	856 234	80.3	187 000	23.6	16.3	777	29.0	2.7	1 410 693	0.8	47 230	3.3	1 326 668	35.1	10.4
New Haven-Bridgeport-Stamford-Danbury-Waterbury, CT	609 741	65.5	198 400	NA	NA	630	NA	2.7	847 519	-1.2	26 394	3.1	837 868	36.6	10.6
New York, NY	3 252 399	33.3	209 000	22.4	14.5	502	25.7	11.5	4 093 402	0.0	252 766	6.2	3 884 751	34.9	7.7
Newark, NJ	686 032	59.6	188 400	NA	NA	581	NA	5.1	1 023 768	1.4	45 939	4.5	964 896	34.4	9.4
Newburgh, NY-PA	112 042	68.9	139 100	NA	NA	592	NA	3.3	176 677	2.2	6 211	3.5	153 943	30.5	12.5
Trenton, NJ	116 941	66.5	137 900	22.2	14.4	569	25.7	3.1	167 185	0.2	6 692	4.0	166 432	38.8	8.0
Norfolk-Virginia Beach-Newport News, VA-NC	511 136	59.6	86 800	NA	NA	479	NA	3.6	735 598	0.1	24 726	3.4	615 581	31.0	13.7
Ocala, FL	78 177	75.6	61 800	22.0	11.7	385	25.4	4.2	98 169	2.1	3 566	3.6	74 958	23.8	12.9
Odessa-Midland, TX	81 242	65.9	51 700	NA	NA	337	NA	7.8	121 904	-4.7	10 554	8.7	98 666	28.9	14.5
Oklahoma City, OK	367 775	64.3	54 500	20.1	12.5	368	25.6	3.7	549 731	3.0	14 079	2.6	450 696	30.8	10.8
Omaha, NE-IA	240 149	64.6	59 000	NA	NA	399	NA	2.1	385 780	-0.4	9 983	2.6	316 628	30.4	9.5
Orlando, FL	465 275	64.2	82 500	NA	NA	515	NA	4.1	881 568	4.8	23 771	2.7	612 750	29.3	10.8
Owensboro, KY	33 036	68.8	48 000	16.3	11.8	285	24.9	2.7	50 659	2.9	2 572	5.1	39 290	23.9	13.5
Panama City, FL	48 938	65.5	61 600	20.0	12.3	369	25.2	2.9	65 935	0.4	4 037	6.1	53 222	28.3	11.4
Parkersburg-Marietta, WV-OH	57 804	74.1	50 400	16.2	12.2	318	25.0	2.2	76 906	0.3	4 302	5.6	64 976	27.1	12.3
Pensacola, FL	128 508	67.2	59 600	20.2	12.3	383	25.8	3.7	173 086	0.4	6 337	3.7	143 322	29.0	13.5
Peoria-Pekin, IL	129 363	68.0	49 700	15.5	12.3	348	23.1	1.8	187 912	1.8	7 556	4.0	154 817	28.7	10.9
Philadelphia-Wilmington-Atlantic City, PA-NJ-DE-MD	2 160 142	69.4	100 800	NA	NA	517	NA	3.0	3 057 942	1.1	134 103	4.4	2 818 996	32.8	10.5
Atlantic-Cape May, NJ	122 979	66.8	107 700	22.8	15.6	570	27.6	3.5	172 636	-0.3	13 811	8.0	154 687	26.5	10.4
Philadelphia, PA-NJ	1 801 159	69.6	100 400	NA	NA	514	NA	3.0	2 528 749	1.4	104 865	4.1	2 337 323	33.5	10.3
Vineland-Millville-Bridgeton, NJ	47 118	68.5	73 900	20.8	14.4	479	27.9	4.7	64 320	-1.0	5 502	8.6	60 937	22.8	12.6
Wilmington-Newark, DE-MD	188 886	69.1	109 000	20.0	12.2	519	24.7	2.1	292 237	-0.7	9 925	3.4	266 049	32.8	11.3
Phoenix-Mesa, AZ	846 714	63.7	84 200	NA	NA	461	NA	6.3	1 574 891	4.5	48 011	3.0	1 046 251	31.6	11.2
Pine Bluff, AR	30 001	67.1	43 300	17.0	15.0	336	28.1	5.7	35 997	-0.3	2 709	7.5	33 236	25.2	11.6
Pittsburgh, PA	947 248	70.0	55 600	NA	NA	362	NA	1.5	1 153 416	0.2	50 110	4.3	1 041 067	31.3	10.8
Pittsfield, MA	54 315	65.2	114 900	20.8	13.3	436	25.2	1.0	64 717	-1.0	2 428	3.8	65 136	32.0	12.7
Pocatello, ID	23 412	68.7	53 300	18.5	11.6	294	24.3	3.8	40 279	-0.3	2 086	5.2	29 061	30.2	11.0
Portland, ME	94 512	64.3	118 300	22.2	13.2	521	26.2	1.7	142 167	2.1	3 309	2.3	123 322	33.9	10.2
Portland-Salem, OR-WA	691 102	61.9	70 700	NA	NA	430	NA	3.5	1 215 264	-0.2	57 399	4.7	877 443	30.9	10.9
Portland-Vancouver, OR-WA	589 441	61.6	72 400	NA	NA	436	NA	3.3	1 047 177	-0.2	47 114	4.5	754 650	31.2	11.0
Salem, OR	101 661	63.5	60 600	20.7	13.1	394	25.9	4.4	168 087	-0.4	10 285	6.1	122 793	28.8	10.2
Providence-Warwick-Pawtucket, RI	345 290	59.5	131 300	22.2	13.9	480	26.4	2.7	463 780	1.0	19 405	4.2	447 642	29.4	12.1
Provo-Orem, UT	70 168	62.7	70 000	21.3	11.8	348	25.1	8.0	163 077	2.8	5 148	3.2	105 102	32.1	10.2
Pueblo, CO	47 057	67.9	51 300	21.1	12.7	307	27.7	3.7	60 282	-3.6	2 894	4.8	47 431	26.7	10.7
Punta Gorda, FL	48 433	79.6	77 200	NA	NA	499	NA	2.1	46 899	5.1	1 509	3.2	38 468	26.2	13.8
Raleigh-Durham-Chapel Hill, NC	334 506	60.8	89 100	NA	NA	456	NA	3.0	632 966	1.7	9 870	1.6	468 008	37.9	10.1
Rapid City, SD	30 553	61.4	56 600	22.3	13.1	385	26.1	2.9	47 243	0.0	1 192	2.5	36 145	27.9	13.0

1. Specified owner-occupied units.　2. Specified renter-occupied units.　3. Overcrowded or lacking complete plumbing facilities.　4. Percent of civilian labor force.　5. Persons 16 years and older.

Table C. Metropolitan Areas — Nonfarm Employment and Agriculture

Area Name	Private nonfarm establishments, employment and payroll, 1998								Agriculture, 1997			
	Number of establishments	Employment						Annual payroll		Farms		Farm operators
		Total	Health Care and Social Assistance	Manufacturing	Retail trade	Finance and Insurance	Professional Scientific and Technical Services	Total (mil dol)	Average per employee (dollars)		Percent with—	Whose principal occupation is farming (percent)
										Number	Less than 50 acres	500 acres and over	
	104	105	106	107	108	109	110	111	112	113	114	115	116
Merced, CA	2 898	37 537	5 122	8 269	6 471	1 777	725	830	22 112	2 831	52.5	10.8	61.9
Miami-Fort Lauderdale, FL ...	116 068	1 421 571	177 270	100 142	208 568	79 256	78 100	39 910	28 075	1 923	87.0	2.8	53.3
Fort Lauderdale, FL	49 026	585 668	75 472	37 674	94 524	34 526	32 995	16 037	27 382	347	86.2	2.3	55.6
Miami, FL	67 042	835 903	101 798	62 468	114 044	44 730	45 105	23 873	28 560	1 576	87.2	2.9	52.7
Milwaukee-Racine, WI	43 711	846 219	106 354	187 785	95 741	55 901	38 781	26 384	31 179	2 481	39.1	7.0	52.9
Milwaukee-Waukesha, WI.	39 501	769 342	97 595	167 526	85 658	51 869	36 635	24 123	31 355	1 927	38.5	6.3	52.3
Racine, WI	4 210	76 877	8 759	20 259	10 083	4 032	2 146	2 261	29 411	554	41.0	9.4	55.1
Minneapolis-St. Paul, MN-WI	81 314	1 538 957	172 358	226 912	180 081	105 058	92 115	52 910	34 380	10 460	34.3	7.5	46.2
Missoula, MT	3 541	37 491	6 051	2 949	6 877	1 481	1 877	834	22 245	482	53.1	13.9	35.5
Mobile, AL	13 140	200 357	26 523	27 610	29 966	6 532	8 396	4 787	23 892	1 732	49.9	8.1	41.1
Modesto, CA	8 027	113 536	17 086	22 882	17 944	3 504	3 485	2 938	25 877	4 009	65.5	6.5	55.8
Monroe, LA	4 067	61 306	10 387	8 075	9 299	5 234	3 335	1 482	24 174	377	37.9	11.9	42.4
Montgomery, AL	7 934	122 349	14 754	14 774	19 134	8 042	5 943	2 991	24 446	1 562	26.5	15.2	39.1
Muncie, IN	2 762	49 162	7 355	9 357	7 518	1 570	1 421	1 201	24 429	635	38.0	13.7	47.7
Myrtle Beach, SC	6 991	80 708	6 230	6 582	15 240	2 828	2 147	1 615	20 010	896	31.1	9.8	54.9
Naples, FL	7 959	82 383	9 837	2 613	16 562	3 141	3 617	2 054	24 932	235	53.6	23.0	46.8
Nashville, TN	33 069	612 035	77 332	82 767	75 080	34 779	26 305	18 558	30 322	10 049	39.7	3.9	35.6
New London-Norwich, CT.....	5 715	103 413	14 053	19 975	13 539	1 995	4 016	3 212	31 060	610	45.4	3.1	51.0
New Orleans, LA	31 685	534 086	75 477	46 082	69 707	24 701	27 934	14 542	27 228	840	58.7	8.5	43.6
New York-Northern New Jersey-Long Island, NY-NJ-CT-PA	580 009	8 261 846	1 212 367	790 549	900 274	695 705	635 737	353 181	42 748	8 296	64.1	3.7	46.3
Bergen-Passaic, NJ	44 897	611 339	66 075	91 352	75 923	30 117	36 422	23 267	38 059	176	88.6	0.6	47.2
Dutchess County, NY	6 593	82 574	15 020	11 961	13 504	3 315	3 926	2 316	28 048	539	33.0	9.8	54.7
Jersey City, NJ	13 254	210 152	19 391	23 771	21 551	21 835	9 194	7 802	37 126	0	X	X	X
Middlesex-Somerset-Hunterdon, NJ	33 449	568 456	51 066	70 887	60 825	38 534	56 123	24 372	42 874	2 025	66.4	3.7	38.2
Monmouth-Ocean, NJ	28 944	305 726	53 012	19 906	59 141	12 372	19 914	9 403	30 756	1 109	80.7	3.2	44.7
Nassau-Suffolk, NY	87 913	1 019 809	158 789	105 984	152 208	68 471	67 372	34 098	33 436	661	72.6	2.1	65.5
New Haven-Bridgeport-Stamford-Danbury-Waterbury, CT	49 375	759 583	106 923	114 146	99 309	47 454	46 481	32 530	42 826	678	69.9	0.7	52.1
New York, NY	239 690	3 557 965	595 374	216 455	292 463	398 114	312 656	174 547	49 058	179	65.4	1.7	41.9
Newark, NJ	58 022	895 963	111 751	115 721	89 113	62 042	67 276	36 736	41 002	1 980	62.1	3.5	38.3
Newburgh, NY-PA	8 555	93 288	13 465	9 972	18 474	4 213	3 086	2 417	25 909	664	38.9	5.1	68.2
Trenton, NJ	9 317	156 991	21 501	10 394	17 763	9 238	13 287	5 693	36 263	285	64.9	4.6	42.5
Norfolk-Virginia Beach-Newport News, VA-NC	33 971	546 903	67 229	51 803	84 538	23 305	33 659	13 153	24 050	1 105	44.1	18.1	55.3
Ocala, FL	5 383	69 245	10 059	9 922	13 567	2 118	2 354	1 478	21 345	1 669	62.1	5.0	47.0
Odessa-Midland, TX	7 301	87 376	10 778	6 316	12 939	2 514	3 586	2 240	25 636	619	51.1	22.6	38.9
Oklahoma City, OK	29 352	426 425	60 738	52 201	58 206	21 483	20 079	10 497	24 616	6 655	30.5	14.2	40.0
Omaha, NE-IA	18 644	357 254	41 569	36 547	47 312	26 958	17 247	10 303	28 839	3 446	25.1	25.8	61.9
Orlando, FL	43 035	745 905	67 881	47 111	99 221	29 469	39 079	19 558	26 220	3 080	70.6	7.4	46.1
Owensboro, KY	2 395	39 917	5 800	8 175	6 565	1 298	1 030	971	24 325	1 042	43.2	11.8	43.2
Panama City, FL	4 220	54 230	7 311	3 799	9 774	2 836	3 585	1 106	20 395	70	60.0	4.3	40.0
Parkersburg-Marietta, WV-OH	3 915	59 359	8 428	13 172	9 057	2 149	1 521	1 507	25 388	1 420	20.3	3.0	38.1
Pensacola, FL	8 629	125 967	20 915	9 454	19 966	3 907	6 799	2 848	22 609	904	51.5	8.0	45.7
Peoria-Pekin, IL	8 367	157 458	23 200	23 241	19 836	6 457	6 380	4 850	30 802	2 756	25.8	22.8	54.6
Philadelphia-Wilmington-Atlantic City, PA-NJ-DE-MD	153 994	2 586 998	380 829	290 209	320 843	183 508	184 339	87 565	33 848	7 014	56.9	4.9	51.5
Atlantic-Cape May, NJ	10 355	146 021	16 352	5 642	19 805	3 505	4 790	3 916	26 818	573	70.0	1.9	44.5
Philadelphia, PA-NJ	123 490	2 112 593	325 807	244 778	259 624	140 640	162 972	72 104	34 131	5 077	56.7	4.3	52.2
Vineland-Millville-Bridgeton, NJ	3 058	44 863	6 604	11 995	7 188	1 606	1 320	1 250	27 863	573	61.8	4.7	53.1
Wilmington-Newark, DE-MD	17 091	283 521	32 066	27 794	34 226	37 757	15 257	10 295	36 311	791	44.9	10.7	51.5
Phoenix-Mesa, AZ	70 943	1 274 299	121 168	151 900	157 764	78 742	77 637	37 697	29 583	2 184	57.2	20.5	52.4
Pine Bluff, AR	1 640	26 837	4 359	8 004	4 544	828	631	610	22 730	362	25.7	37.0	60.2
Pittsburgh, PA	59 279	1 006 882	154 476	119 805	132 363	57 313	60 480	30 164	29 958	4 894	26.9	3.3	44.6
Pittsfield, MA	4 114	54 752	9 279	8 450	8 548	2 374	2 003	1 524	27 835	387	39.5	7.0	50.1
Pocatello, ID	1 822	23 376	3 299	4 153	4 343	1 403	988	522	22 331	664	44.0	20.6	40.5
Portland, ME	9 934	140 731	22 580	15 313	20 437	11 448	6 974	4 000	28 423	455	47.3	3.5	47.3
Portland-Salem, OR-WA	63 913	939 893	99 983	148 815	117 224	49 564	49 665	29 257	31 128	13 370	70.9	3.4	39.4
Portland-Vancouver, OR-WA	55 436	835 549	85 431	134 710	101 035	43 250	46 081	26 718	31 977	9 677	73.8	2.3	36.8
Salem, OR	8 477	104 344	14 552	14 105	16 189	6 314	3 584	2 539	24 333	3 693	63.5	6.1	46.3
Providence-Warwick-Pawtucket, RI	25 520	375 888	63 877	71 721	43 054	23 289	13 805	10 418	27 716	596	60.4	2.0	47.5
Provo-Orem, UT	6 472	132 096	13 398	16 032	16 601	2 880	8 155	3 063	23 188	1 790	68.2	6.5	37.0
Pueblo, CO	3 178	45 760	9 348	4 362	7 032	1 429	1 189	1 012	22 115	664	31.3	34.2	48.3
Punta Gorda, FL	2 900	30 868	7 036	623	7 115	1 189	1 210	643	20 831	209	47.8	22.0	47.4
Raleigh-Durham-Chapel Hill, NC	31 893	540 152	63 893	73 925	68 239	22 024	39 402	16 826	31 150	4 112	37.4	6.8	50.9
Rapid City, SD	3 178	38 208	6 636	4 264	6 460	2 387	1 328	851	22 273	637	16.2	46.8	64.1

Table C. Metropolitan Areas — **Agriculture, Land, and Water**

Area Name	Land in farms — Acreage (1,000) [117]	Land in farms — Percent change, 1992–1997 [118]	Acres — Average size of farm [119]	Acres — Total irrigated (1,000) [120]	Acres — Total cropland (1,000) [121]	Value of land and buildings — Average per farm ($1,000) [122]	Value of land and buildings — Average per acre (dollars) [123]	Value of machinery and equipment Average per farm ($1,000) [124]	Value of products sold — Total (mil dol) [125]	Value of products sold — Average per farm (dollars) [126]	Percent from — Crops [127]	Percent from — Livestock and poultry products [128]	Percent of farms with sales of — $10,000 or more [129]	Percent of farms with sales of — $100,000 or more [130]	Percent of land owned by Fed. Gov. 1997 [131]	Water consumption 1995 (mil gal/day) [132]
Merced, CA	882	-9.9	311	493	532	951	3 149	96	1 273	449 832	45.0	55.0	72.3	38.6	1.9	1 688.4
Miami-Fort Lauderdale, FL	116	7.4	60	60	74	409	7 180	46	466	242 083	97.0	3.0	52.4	22.8	0.2	856.6
Fort Lauderdale, FL	31	28.7	89	2	7	414	4 791	33	49	141 280	86.0	14.0	57.6	21.3	0.2	287.3
Miami, FL	85	1.3	54	58	68	408	8 047	49	417	264 278	98.0	2.0	51.2	23.2	NA	569.3
Milwaukee-Racine, WI	432	-10.4	174	7	D	431	2 516	64	221	89 016	D	D	54.7	20.4	0.0	2 291.5
Milwaukee-Waukesha, WI	309	-11.5	160	2	D	405	2 563	60	142	73 903	D	D	55.3	20.3	0.0	2 253.8
Racine, WI	123	-7.5	222	5	110	520	2 396	77	78	141 585	54.0	46.0	52.5	20.6	0.0	37.7
Minneapolis-St. Paul, MN-WI	1 906	-4.9	182	85	1 470	358	1 977	62	701	67 014	53.0	47.0	49.0	17.1	1.3	1 554.5
Missoula, MT	262	5.6	544	22	47	494	993	34	8	16 643	27.0	73.0	28.2	3.1	42.1	113.6
Mobile, AL	287	5.5	166	11	178	369	2 354	41	125	72 143	81.0	19.0	31.9	9.7	1.3	1 146.4
Modesto, CA	733	-3.6	183	359	382	779	4 508	61	1 209	301 453	46.0	54.0	63.5	29.4	0.3	1 437.9
Monroe, LA	89	18.8	236	11	60	277	1 239	68	26	68 247	65.0	35.0	35.0	13.3	2.1	111.9
Montgomery, AL	470	6.1	301	2	210	463	1 581	39	64	40 786	47.0	53.0	31.0	7.4	0.3	106.5
Muncie, IN	173	2.6	273	0	160	585	2 219	65	53	82 874	84.0	16.0	57.2	19.8	0.0	18.8
Myrtle Beach, SC	184	-6.3	205	1	117	384	1 943	72	83	92 397	87.0	13.0	55.6	24.0	0.5	94.1
Naples, FL	277	-8.2	1 180	53	69	2 152	1 796	166	277	1 178 400	97.0	3.0	66.8	34.0	35.5	208.2
Nashville, TN	1 291	0.8	128	3	788	324	2 562	31	204	20 266	53.0	47.0	27.5	3.4	0.6	991.4
New London-Norwich, CT	68	2.9	111	0	30	445	4 220	41	126	206 238	44.0	56.0	34.9	12.5	0.3	41.2
New Orleans, LA	163	-9.4	194	D	80	384	2 047	60	55	65 664	84.0	15.0	33.5	11.2	3.8	5 152.3
New York-Northern New Jersey-Long Island, NY-NJ-CT-PA	754	-2.7	91	D	D	D	D	D	D	D	D	D	42.1	13.7	2.2	4 462.1
Bergen-Passaic, NJ	5	21.6	28	0	2	561	18 134	29	13	73 131	95.0	5.0	51.7	14.2	0.0	422.1
Dutchess County, NY	107	-3.0	198	1	63	791	4 619	53	34	63 013	49.0	51.0	53.6	15.2	0.4	39.2
Jersey City, NJ	0	X	X	0	0	X	X	X	0	X	X	X	X	X	1.5	0.2
Middlesex-Somerset-Hunterdon, NJ	180	2.6	89	3	131	652	7 769	40	84	41 698	84.0	16.0	32.4	7.3	0.3	249.4
Monmouth-Ocean, NJ	71	2.6	64	7	52	606	9 241	46	76	68 659	90.0	10.0	39.4	11.5	5.7	139.1
Nassau-Suffolk, NY	37	0.7	56	16	30	671	11 719	70	171	258 664	93.0	7.0	71.0	33.7	0.9	390.1
New Haven-Bridgeport-Stamford-Danbury-Waterbury, CT	36	1.4	54	1	20	640	11 080	36	60	88 674	79.0	21.0	41.7	11.8	0.2	389.0
New York, NY	D	D	D	D	D	D	D	D	D	D	D	D	55.9	20.1	0.9	705.1
Newark, NJ	D	D	D	3	113	624	6 973	34	106	53 716	67.0	33.0	30.4	9.9	4.5	249.0
Newburgh, NY-PA	100	-7.9	151	5	D	573	3 816	74	71	107 277	64.0	36.0	68.2	28.2	4.1	1 372.9
Trenton, NJ	28	-21.1	100	1	23	1 359	13 871	44	13	46 509	92.0	8.0	38.2	10.5	0.0	506.1
Norfolk-Virginia Beach-Newport News, VA-NC	337	-4.0	305	D	258	626	D	D	D	D	D	D	55.9	24.0	7.4	281.3
Ocala, FL	266	-10.3	159	6	100	491	3 094	27	102	60 833	23.0	77.0	31.3	9.3	28.3	52.1
Odessa-Midland, TX	1 325	6.6	2 141	14	D	438	201	38	22	35 771	39.0	61.0	25.5	8.4	0.0	68.9
Oklahoma City, OK	1 775	3.7	267	10	900	271	1 030	33	198	29 688	27.0	73.0	32.5	5.5	0.8	135.4
Omaha, NE-IA	1 271	0.2	369	D	1 115	681	1 943	84	451	130 893	60.0	40.0	70.7	32.4	0.8	1 358.7
Orlando, FL	1 008	-9.5	327	113	181	649	2 037	38	525	170 340	89.0	11.0	45.8	16.9	3.7	493.9
Owensboro, KY	251	0.4	241	3	207	388	1 650	57	71	68 406	82.0	18.0	48.8	15.1	0.0	220.2
Panama City, FL	7	-25.2	96	0	3	179	1 858	23	3	38 171	92.0	8.0	24.3	4.3	5.1	58.9
Parkersburg-Marietta, WV-OH	213	6.5	150	0	102	188	1 312	31	23	16 383	37.0	63.0	21.9	3.2	5.0	859.1
Pensacola, FL	143	4.8	158	7	94	272	1 761	43	46	51 055	81.0	19.0	33.8	13.4	7.2	292.8
Peoria-Pekin, IL	895	0.1	325	34	805	855	2 621	86	308	111 613	79.0	21.0	70.6	31.0	0.0	919.7
Philadelphia-Wilmington-Atlantic City, PA-NJ-DE-MD	839	-0.7	120	85	D	580	4 819	62	950	135 459	D	D	50.7	20.6	1.5	3 118.7
Atlantic-Cape May, NJ	41	-0.7	71	13	25	345	5 113	61	70	122 646	99.0	1.0	43.3	16.8	3.9	71.8
Philadelphia, PA-NJ	569	0.1	112	48	D	594	5 254	60	690	135 846	D	D	51.8	20.6	1.3	2 325.8
Vineland-Millville-Bridgeton, NJ	66	-3.9	116	19	51	421	3 738	77	94	164 314	96.0	4.0	53.8	27.9	0.0	87.4
Wilmington-Newark, DE-MD	163	-2.4	206	4	130	776	3 666	68	96	121 359	51.0	49.0	47.0	17.4	0.8	633.8
Phoenix-Mesa, AZ	2 012	-23.6	921	525	D	1 509	1 529	96	1 028	470 484	56.0	44.0	51.2	32.4	41.2	3 649.2
Pine Bluff, AR	289	2.4	797	147	258	761	976	155	95	263 116	85.0	15.0	60.5	40.3	2.5	454.5
Pittsburgh, PA	642	-6.0	131	2	421	290	2 219	43	132	27 012	45.0	55.0	35.4	6.5	0.2	2 245.7
Pittsfield, MA	63	3.0	162	0	31	547	3 150	35	21	53 553	40.0	60.0	35.9	11.9	0.0	24.0
Pocatello, ID	309	-4.8	466	42	167	257	658	43	25	37 699	62.0	38.0	35.7	8.1	27.4	313.5
Portland, ME	50	-7.7	110	1	26	322	2 600	35	17	38 062	64.0	36.0	38.9	10.5	0.6	36.9
Portland-Salem, OR-WA	1 147	2.0	86	190	799	422	5 002	48	1 264	94 529	81.0	19.0	33.5	11.2	22.0	1 317.3
Portland-Vancouver, OR-WA	670	2.3	69	84	420	393	5 804	38	734	75 891	81.0	19.0	30.5	8.9	22.2	983.4
Salem, OR	478	1.6	129	106	379	499	3 877	75	529	143 369	83.0	17.0	41.2	17.3	21.7	334.0
Providence-Warwick-Pawtucket, RI	45	12.1	75	3	19	410	5 453	37	34	56 525	82.0	18.0	44.1	11.2	0.2	126.1
Provo-Orem, UT	375	-16.7	209	81	150	433	2 244	40	97	54 195	40.0	60.0	32.8	9.4	43.3	298.8
Pueblo, CO	823	-8.3	1 239	36	90	533	471	38	34	50 666	42.0	58.0	45.6	10.5	7.9	246.1
Punta Gorda, FL	290	27.9	1 389	26	45	1 878	1 359	45	50	240 010	89.0	11.0	51.2	22.0	0.0	49.9
Raleigh-Durham-Chapel Hill, NC	669	0.7	163	17	375	423	2 712	44	465	113 039	47.0	53.0	47.6	19.9	1.0	545.3
Rapid City, SD	1 044	-2.1	1 639	9	288	512	325	49	40	62 289	29.0	71.0	61.2	14.1	43.1	30.2

Table C. Metropolitan Areas — Residential Construction, Wholesale and Retail Trade, and Real Estate

Area Name	Value of Residential Construction Authorized by Building Permits, 1999		Wholesale Trade, 1997				Retail Trade¹, 1997				Real Estate and Rental and Leasing, 1997			
	New Construction ($1,000)	Number of Housing Units	Number of Establishments	Number of Employees	Sales (mil dol)	Annual Payroll (mil dol)	Number of Establishments	Number of Employees	Sales (mil dol)	Annual Payroll (mil dol)	Number of Establishments	Number of Employees	Receipts (mil dol)	Annual Payroll (mil dol)
	133	134	135	136	137	138	139	140	141	142	143	144	145	146
Merced, CA	122 639	1 001	117	1 333	699.9	36.4	551	6 122	1 102.1	108.0	121	461	46.0	5.7
Miami-Fort Lauderdale, FL	2 591 074	26 080	13 294	108 664	69 726.6	3 650.6	16 618	199 582	38 700.4	3 635.7	5 641	34 187	5 050.5	817.4
Fort Lauderdale, FL	1 409 811	12 013	4 359	38 614	26 122.2	1 414.7	6 804	89 290	17 979.8	1 639.9	2 263	14 394	2 196.6	351.6
Miami, FL	1 181 263	14 067	8 935	70 050	43 604.4	2 235.9	9 814	110 292	20 720.6	1 995.8	3 378	19 793	2 853.9	465.8
Milwaukee-Racine, WI	1 018 280	8 083	3 284	47 661	30 083.3	1 806.4	6 015	96 146	15 865.1	1 535.0	1 574	10 521	1 309.8	234.6
Milwaukee-Waukesha, WI	907 634	7 173	3 050	43 101	26 266.4	1 664.1	5 351	86 453	14 301.0	1 392.9	1 442	9 775	1 252.1	222.6
Racine, WI	110 646	910	234	4 560	3 816.9	142.4	664	9 693	1 564.1	142.0	132	746	57.7	12.1
Minneapolis-St. Paul, MN-WI	3 019 352	23 173	6 464	98 760	81 849.0	4 106.1	10 519	173 134	31 195.8	2 969.6	3 518	24 708	3 360.5	614.7
Missoula, MT	37 232	422	183	1 991	775.9	50.0	540	6 800	1 069.0	105.7	138	593	46.2	8.2
Mobile, AL	482 474	4 667	850	9 895	3 826.4	295.0	2 482	30 710	4 619.9	452.9	575	3 309	310.5	62.9
Modesto, CA	282 965	2 183	417	5 118	2 264.4	159.1	1 368	17 706	3 282.2	319.2	340	2 033	244.5	42.4
Monroe, LA	62 011	670	248	2 912	1 257.2	82.4	753	9 649	1 483.5	134.0	176	805	79.7	12.7
Montgomery, AL	146 655	1 844	468	5 850	3 095.1	166.2	1 504	19 978	3 146.9	293.6	350	2 365	193.5	42.0
Muncie, IN	43 611	365	119	1 501	653.4	45.8	548	7 340	1 118.7	105.4	119	433	46.9	8.4
Myrtle Beach, SC	443 216	4 773	230	1 824	481.5	49.5	1 522	14 457	2 505.2	230.7	360	3 026	259.6	59.7
Naples, FL	931 569	7 542	350	2 076	813.8	63.0	1 343	15 366	2 627.1	274.1	509	2 874	305.2	66.0
Nashville, TN	1 536 084	13 561	2 213	35 488	23 385.2	1 288.8	5 282	73 125	12 780.5	1 257.9	1 408	9 822	1 557.2	245.4
New London-Norwich, CT	107 116	879	201	2 279	801.6	81.9	1 182	13 923	2 405.0	240.3	188	723	82.4	13.8
New Orleans, LA	558 502	4 933	2 182	27 247	24 973.6	909.6	5 241	69 416	11 032.9	1 073.5	1 320	10 690	1 241.7	231.9
New York-Northern New Jersey-Long Island, NY-NJ-CT-PA	5 824 968	53 542	47 914	D	D	D	85 012	904 682	172 895.5	17 814.0	31 494	168 324	34 036.6	5 390.8
Bergen-Passaic, NJ	286 757	2 194	4 882	68 811	71 520.4	3 315.4	6 127	77 533	15 426.0	1 521.8	1 775	10 482	2 073.1	324.7
Dutchess County, NY	176 919	1 238	274	D	D	D	1 097	13 506	2 259.5	225.7	256	1 502	165.9	28.5
Jersey City, NJ	133 605	1 921	1 065	21 629	11 271.5	864.6	2 327	22 670	3 842.9	384.9	542	3 070	628.1	96.1
Middlesex-Somerset-Hunterdon, NJ	610 012	5 956	2 746	49 781	43 743.1	2 272.7	4 563	61 187	12 124.3	1 171.2	985	5 923	1 050.5	181.7
Monmouth-Ocean, NJ	749 376	7 166	1 626	12 480	7 235.3	505.6	4 793	58 270	11 128.8	1 059.1	985	4 140	634.7	105.0
Nassau-Suffolk, NY	829 618	6 318	7 524	78 508	45 747.2	3 214.0	13 144	149 961	29 993.3	2 968.7	3 438	15 766	2 904.1	453.7
New Haven-Bridgeport-Stamford-Danbury-Waterbury, CT	723 918	4 677	3 084	44 031	56 353.7	2 192.4	7 343	95 954	19 289.1	1 993.9	1 859	11 669	2 225.6	377.2
New York, NY	1 374 396	15 352	21 217	223 228	212 129.3	10 175.2	34 081	293 786	53 828.7	5 967.7	18 735	99 627	21 329.5	3 374.2
Newark, NJ	576 588	5 286	4 407	69 478	58 304.7	3 279.2	8 128	90 246	17 642.9	1 796.1	2 255	12 882	2 533.4	374.2
Newburgh, NY-PA	249 849	2 275	471	D	D	D	1 545	18 334	3 230.3	307.3	305	1 349	196.9	25.6
Trenton, NJ	113 932	1 159	472	8 480	4 403.0	291.5	1 442	18 217	3 183.1	326.1	289	1 685	256.7	43.1
Norfolk-Virginia Beach-Newport News, VA-NC	934 777	8 988	1 585	21 645	8 973.1	649.3	6 010	83 007	12 705.1	1 259.5	1 570	10 833	1 082.8	222.3
Ocala, FL	273 830	2 759	309	3 219	999.6	80.0	1 014	13 159	2 221.4	202.1	244	786	88.4	13.8
Odessa-Midland, TX	26 180	228	652	6 226	2 986.2	211.8	1 087	12 709	2 366.2	212.9	321	1 752	177.8	35.8
Oklahoma City, OK	715 306	6 654	1 844	23 760	16 611.1	703.7	4 394	56 273	10 141.6	905.3	1 276	6 716	734.8	128.5
Omaha, NE-IA	477 912	5 196	1 274	19 950	13 721.6	655.7	2 753	46 740	7 655.9	765.6	738	5 107	622.2	116.8
Orlando, FL	2 612 272	29 593	3 149	36 667	29 509.2	1 201.0	6 795	93 025	16 865.1	1 538.6	2 200	19 964	2 647.1	473.6
Owensboro, KY	34 047	679	141	1 678	872.9	43.7	470	6 011	853.8	84.5	75	476	33.9	7.7
Panama City, FL	98 590	1 044	173	1 406	422.1	34.2	832	9 558	1 496.8	148.1	229	1 018	76.8	15.6
Parkersburg-Marietta, WV-OH	23 526	279	190	2 183	656.4	53.3	741	9 121	1 491.2	136.9	124	546	59.8	10.6
Pensacola, FL	255 386	2 914	470	5 065	1 719.0	135.4	1 620	20 217	3 435.8	305.6	389	1 625	159.4	27.8
Peoria-Pekin, IL	167 301	1 494	494	8 924	9 499.5	372.0	1 375	19 639	3 352.0	311.5	289	1 648	164.0	31.2
Philadelphia-Wilmington-Atlantic City, PA-NJ-DE-MD	2 307 208	22 981	9 964	D	D	D	24 437	320 158	58 373.5	5 869.5	5 373	38 918	10 040.8	1 036.1
Atlantic-Cape May, NJ	216 904	2 627	308	3 219	1 032.5	102.6	2 042	19 298	3 474.2	356.5	444	2 013	329.8	45.9
Philadelphia, PA-NJ	1 788 713	16 658	8 777	119 671	97 035.0	5 011.9	19 454	259 802	47 692.4	4 801.6	3 987	32 530	4 814.3	887.7
Vineland-Millville-Bridgeton, NJ	30 999	371	189	2 230	989.4	69.4	578	7 157	1 226.5	130.1	115	486	52.0	9.4
Wilmington-Newark, DE-MD	270 592	3 325	690	D	D	D	2 363	33 901	5 980.4	581.3	827	3 889	4 844.6	93.1
Phoenix-Mesa, AZ	5 470 726	47 713	4 840	62 284	39 724.9	2 284.0	9 618	149 267	30 011.9	2 856.2	3 502	22 551	3 079.9	558.2
Pine Bluff, AR	10 606	174	77	780	309.8	18.9	393	4 785	726.6	71.8	58	368	23.8	5.8
Pittsburgh, PA	770 422	6 946	3 811	51 132	39 222.1	1 839.2	9 664	132 247	21 462.3	1 998.1	1 909	12 344	1 971.8	292.3
Pittsfield, MA	47 179	327	136	D	D	D	832	8 513	1 280.7	137.7	122	410	43.9	7.5
Pocatello, ID	26 622	308	104	935	282.6	25.2	343	4 177	705.7	65.1	64	255	23.5	3.5
Portland, ME	192 356	1 496	574	8 884	3 673.3	296.8	1 570	20 735	3 825.9	346.5	407	2 731	293.4	63.5
Portland-Salem, OR-WA	1 879 291	17 095	4 494	58 798	48 456.3	2 192.6	8 114	114 249	22 182.9	2 217.8	3 007	17 856	2 175.2	402.1
Portland-Vancouver, OR-WA	1 647 560	15 077	4 127	55 126	47 185.0	2 092.1	6 890	98 020	19 278.0	1 927.3	2 573	15 963	1 966.1	363.9
Salem, OR	231 731	2 018	367	3 672	1 271.3	100.5	1 224	16 229	2 904.9	290.5	434	1 893	209.0	38.2
Providence-Warwick-Pawtucket, RI	299 919	3 123	1 488	18 201	7 360.3	616.4	3 684	41 903	6 879.5	686.1	825	4 298	526.1	95.6
Provo-Orem, UT	463 313	4 143	320	6 272	2 763.6	190.4	978	15 868	2 486.4	245.1	239	1 085	108.0	16.9
Pueblo, CO	135 434	1 437	113	1 101	390.3	27.5	600	7 040	1 180.7	121.7	131	486	58.8	8.2
Punta Gorda, FL	149 416	1 418	103	446	117.2	11.2	515	6 840	1 063.3	100.4	167	601	60.7	10.1
Raleigh-Durham-Chapel Hill, NC	2 310 739	21 472	1 785	25 877	17 143.5	1 049.3	4 906	64 714	11 521.9	1 080.4	1 268	6 834	1 112.6	174.9
Rapid City, SD	49 524	438	173	2 027	675.7	57.8	581	6 870	1 132.0	112.2	126	530	52.7	9.0

1. Establishments with payroll.

Table C. Metropolitan Areas — **Professional, Manufacturing, Accommodation and Foodservices, Finance and Insurance**

Area Name	Professional, Scientific, and Technical Services[1], 1997				Manufacturing, 1997				Accommodation and Foodservices, 1997			
	Number of Establishments	Number of Employees	Sales (mil dol)	Annual Payroll (mil dol)	Number of Establishments	Number of Employees	Sales (mil dol)	Annual Payroll (mil dol)	Number of Establishments	Number of Employees	Sales (mil dol)	Annual Payroll (mil dol)
	147	148	149	150	151	152	153	154	155	156	157	158
Merced, CA	138	668	41.0	15.8	123	8 381	2 432	198	269	3 265	108.4	27.2
Miami-Fort Lauderdale, FL	13 446	70 277	7 580.8	2 959.6	4 998	103 525	14 312	2 779	7 041	136 840	5 673.9	1 493.9
Fort Lauderdale, FL	5 625	27 496	2 940.7	1 103.7	1 967	37 134	5 788	1 115	3 206	61 243	2 474.5	615.5
Miami, FL	7 821	42 781	4 640.0	1 856.0	3 031	66 391	8 524	1 664	3 835	75 597	3 199.5	878.5
Milwaukee-Racine, WI	3 948	34 466	3 524.7	1 353.2	3 553	184 012	36 323	6 623	3 232	55 199	1 701.6	474.9
Milwaukee-Waukesha, WI	3 652	32 645	3 390.4	1 297.6	3 174	165 143	31 094	5 958	2 872	49 875	1 546.9	432.7
Racine, WI	296	1 821	134.3	55.6	379	18 869	5 230	664	360	5 324	154.7	42.2
Minneapolis-St. Paul, MN-WI	9 814	81 621	9 422.4	3 672.8	5 348	234 192	44 600	8 761	5 131	111 217	3 757.3	1 111.4
Missoula, MT	276	1 617	109.7	45.2	136	2 690	562	89	329	4 782	145.6	40.4
Mobile, AL	994	6 930	588.2	235.1	583	27 280	6 304	962	952	19 104	594.5	163.3
Modesto, CA	478	2 974	232.5	81.3	435	25 056	6 887	823	676	9 877	312.7	80.4
Monroe, LA	358	2 042	145.3	50.7	152	8 235	1 983	288	265	5 360	170.1	42.6
Montgomery, AL	646	4 780	445.5	201.4	303	15 813	2 671	426	534	12 217	340.5	94.8
Muncie, IN	153	1 691	87.8	37.3	176	9 972	1 765	403	228	4 981	126.7	35.6
Myrtle Beach, SC	400	1 766	135.5	53.8	160	6 687	928	173	1 044	20 246	881.7	228.5
Naples, FL	743	3 074	414.1	196.5	205	2 305	259	62	518	11 599	536.7	140.8
Nashville, TN	2 682	21 278	2 219.5	832.0	1 544	84 573	21 496	2 792	2 248	55 500	2 076.5	586.4
New London-Norwich, CT	463	3 944	338.9	162.2	237	19 888	2 963	1 035	590	8 652	333.0	95.7
New Orleans, LA	3 406	24 941	2 478.9	967.9	1 022	43 738	26 356	1 673	2 653	60 890	2 369.6	652.8
New York-Northern New Jersey-Long Island, NY-NJ-CT-PA	63 083	569 807	78 862.1	30 606.6	29 610	837 259	164 000	29 316	39 803	494 546	24 535.3	6 816.5
Bergen-Passaic, NJ	5 217	31 665	3 904.1	1 405.8	2 865	94 466	16 884	3 461	2 674	32 527	1 455.9	395.0
Dutchess County, NY	591	3 149	284.3	113.6	210	11 848	3 033	521	558	8 652	252.1	64.4
Jersey City, NJ	977	7 208	931.7	342.8	979	26 470	4 221	788	1 127	10 056	466.5	119.6
Middlesex-Somerset-Hunterdon, NJ	4 676	60 045	6 881.8	2 872.0	1 528	71 336	19 941	3 002	2 173	28 472	1 220.8	332.0
Monmouth-Ocean, NJ	3 026	17 617	1 808.0	768.7	896	19 994	3 258	604	2 323	28 700	1 110.0	303.2
Nassau-Suffolk, NY	9 464	55 636	5 982.3	2 198.9	4 188	113 034	19 126	3 984	5 676	64 915	2 811.1	767.6
New Haven-Bridgeport-Stamford-Danbury-Waterbury, CT	5 719	42 336	5 849.6	2 398.8	2 908	116 940	24 189	4 781	3 416	46 224	1 918.0	532.7
New York, NY	24 511	275 541	43 493.7	16 577.9	11 821	239 106	34 657	6 604	16 261	208 970	12 310.8	3 481.2
Newark, NJ	6 804	62 207	7 958.3	3 214.4	3 261	110 238	32 134	4 341	3 942	48 837	2 219.6	608.6
Newburgh, NY-PA	658	2 780	280.9	100.4	346	D	D	D	778	7 984	305.5	82.2
Trenton, NJ	1 223	10 930	1 407.3	586.2	352	13 537	2 414	580	703	9 870	394.0	109.9
Norfolk-Virginia Beach-Newport News, VA-NC	2 583	27 170	2 097.1	888.0	1 043	62 701	16 721	2 067	2 932	58 484	1 888.0	526.6
Ocala, FL	361	1 882	132.9	52.8	215	9 620	1 288	238	363	6 558	200.9	54.1
Odessa-Midland, TX	542	3 093	314.1	102.1	338	5 961	1 612	192	465	7 620	243.8	67.1
Oklahoma City, OK	2 932	16 522	1 462.5	567.3	1 181	51 318	12 605	1 620	2 161	41 765	1 263.8	349.6
Omaha, NE-IA	1 529	14 710	1 364.3	544.9	709	34 735	8 809	1 100	1 475	26 895	899.4	258.9
Orlando, FL	4 465	34 147	3 378.8	1 344.4	1 564	47 086	8 327	1 628	3 013	103 403	5 399.3	1 274.7
Owensboro, KY	145	857	56.4	23.3	114	8 011	2 938	277	150	3 331	100.6	26.6
Panama City, FL	268	1 730	138.9	56.1	136	3 492	719	109	483	9 268	336.3	84.8
Parkersburg-Marietta, WV-OH	211	1 270	88.8	31.5	182	12 252	4 203	481	320	5 790	176.1	50.7
Pensacola, FL	669	4 446	340.1	143.7	295	9 421	2 642	336	612	13 071	404.6	106.9
Peoria-Pekin, IL	549	5 510	446.9	200.6	350	23 638	7 551	996	822	13 322	381.0	109.1
Philadelphia-Wilmington-Atlantic City, PA-NJ-DE-MD	15 494	164 081	19 882.8	8 074.3	7 571	296 009	78 628	11 145	12 299	216 197	11 327.8	3 047.0
Atlantic-Cape May, NJ	724	4 680	449.9	184.1	242	5 740	711	162	1 727	60 280	5 383.3	1 423.3
Philadelphia, PA-NJ	13 093	147 380	18 002.6	7 343.3	6 606	251 908	66 608	9 483	9 294	133 515	5 134.5	1 395.2
Vineland-Millville-Bridgeton, NJ	200	1 061	88.9	34.1	210	12 985	1 896	398	218	2 554	78.8	21.1
Wilmington-Newark, DE-MD	1 477	10 960	1 341.4	512.8	513	25 376	9 413	1 101	1 060	19 848	731.3	207.4
Phoenix-Mesa, AZ	7 228	58 051	5 136.8	2 141.5	3 438	148 277	35 313	5 200	5 134	116 068	4 335.8	1 207.2
Pine Bluff, AR	85	619	38.1	14.5	84	7 774	1 742	219	131	2 049	57.9	15.0
Pittsburgh, PA	4 925	54 512	6 040.7	2 297.1	3 000	120 793	24 173	4 355	4 875	83 749	2 587.6	728.3
Pittsfield, MA	247	1 420	129.3	50.6	207	9 176	1 423	345	485	7 060	247.3	75.6
Pocatello, ID	108	934	47.4	22.5	62	3 482	775	119	188	2 792	75.3	20.5
Portland, ME	973	6 408	614.6	253.8	382	14 304	2 233	477	792	11 749	429.9	121.3
Portland-Salem, OR-WA	5 923	41 488	3 986.4	1 654.2	3 828	149 132	35 464	5 102	4 639	79 468	2 808.5	795.7
Portland-Vancouver, OR-WA	5 341	38 580	3 762.0	1 565.9	3 363	134 123	32 874	4 684	4 033	69 599	2 496.2	709.8
Salem, OR	582	2 908	224.5	88.3	465	15 009	2 590	418	606	9 869	312.3	85.9
Providence-Warwick-Pawtucket, RI	2 114	12 465	1 162.0	449.1	2 437	73 295	10 186	2 189	2 289	29 519	1 013.8	280.7
Provo-Orem, UT	582	6 094	463.3	195.3	390	15 949	2 667	461	392	8 270	228.0	64.3
Pueblo, CO	192	981	49.7	19.3	107	4 688	1 021	147	321	4 969	142.4	38.1
Punta Gorda, FL	194	1 083	73.3	37.3	74	587	78	14	218	3 935	123.5	31.9
Raleigh-Durham-Chapel Hill, NC	3 560	28 633	3 324.0	1 253.3	1 143	72 443	24 867	2 264	2 219	42 253	1 551.2	432.9
Rapid City, SD	207	1 119	91.0	30.6	134	4 263	867	101	326	5 125	163.7	44.3

1. Firms subject to federal tax.

Table C. Metropolitan Areas — Health and Other Services and Federal Funds

Area Name	Health Care and Social Assistance[1], 1997				Other Services[1], 1997				Federal funds and grants, fiscal 1999[2] Expenditures (mil dol)			
									Total	Direct payments for individuals		
	Number of Establishments	Number of Employees	Receipts (mil dol)	Annual Payroll (mil dol)	Number of Establishments	Number of Employees	Receipts (mil dol)	Annual Payroll (mil dol)		Social Security and government retirement	Medicare	Food stamps and Supplemental Security Income
	159	160	161	162	163	164	165	166	167	168	169	170
Merced, CA	323	2 668	167.8	64.2	171	813	49.2	14.3	734.8	281.5	111.4	52.8
Miami-Fort Lauderdale, FL	10 383	112 426	8 661.5	3 480.5	7 147	41 623	2 788.3	759.1	16 734.5	5 744.2	4 790.4	912.4
Fort Lauderdale, FL	4 226	51 708	3 879.0	1 603.0	3 246	19 188	1 397.3	373.4	6 375.8	2 995.4	2 064.7	178.8
Miami, FL	6 157	60 718	4 782.5	1 877.5	3 901	22 435	1 391.0	385.8	10 358.7	2 748.9	2 725.7	733.6
Milwaukee-Racine, WI	3 516	43 944	2 763.7	1 440.5	2 707	19 486	1 256.9	391.9	6 853.0	2 893.0	1 171.9	258.9
Milwaukee-Waukesha, WI	3 251	40 173	2 499.9	1 307.6	2 416	17 291	1 131.6	351.5	6 226.8	2 563.9	1 060.9	237.6
Racine, WI	265	3 771	263.8	132.8	291	2 195	125.4	40.3	626.2	329.1	111.1	21.2
Minneapolis-St. Paul, MN-WI	5 073	70 207	4 109.1	2 082.1	4 471	41 363	2 493.7	875.8	12 084.7	3 892.6	1 444.4	283.8
Missoula, MT	285	2 305	151.7	70.7	184	956	61.9	17.0	385.9	151.5	43.3	11.4
Mobile, AL	783	12 466	847.7	398.9	838	5 584	354.8	105.8	2 463.6	1 101.6	455.2	129.3
Modesto, CA	805	9 346	656.1	253.2	538	3 154	210.7	58.7	1 539.1	607.0	297.2	93.9
Monroe, LA	355	5 465	339.6	153.9	224	1 332	74.1	22.2	572.4	221.6	133.9	36.6
Montgomery, AL	654	10 312	708.4	290.7	499	3 228	168.3	51.8	2 905.6	793.7	224.9	85.0
Muncie, IN	223	3 304	200.9	94.2	186	1 530	98.7	24.4	445.9	218.3	82.1	19.5
Myrtle Beach, SC	326	4 036	295.9	117.8	336	1 477	91.5	25.5	729.8	402.5	112.1	27.0
Naples, FL	492	5 124	404.9	175.0	431	2 035	109.6	34.8	893.2	551.2	203.7	15.8
Nashville, TN	2 468	44 414	3 172.4	1 370.4	1 858	13 207	882.6	267.5	5 334.0	1 857.1	794.1	157.0
New London-Norwich, CT	490	7 493	521.3	227.8	391	2 113	137.6	37.8	3 278.2	529.6	200.6	22.3
New Orleans, LA	2 910	47 063	3 015.5	1 248.4	1 930	14 036	897.7	271.8	8 112.4	2 177.1	1 344.1	382.0
New York-Northern New Jersey-Long Island, NY-NJ-CT-PA	45 338	432 570	34 143.2	14 472.5	36 922	182 440	12 687.4	3 768.1	102 358.3	33 279.7	19 348.4	4 148.5
Bergen-Passaic, NJ	3 773	33 327	2 974.0	1 226.5	2 911	14 935	1 095.2	345.6	5 601.6	2 452.6	1 147.8	126.9
Dutchess County, NY	583	4 966	347.0	145.8	448	1 802	125.0	33.3	993.5	484.9	176.9	25.2
Jersey City, NJ	1 002	6 936	522.6	213.3	915	4 477	264.3	77.8	2 726.6	726.7	477.3	146.2
Middlesex-Somerset-Hunterdon, NJ	2 365	23 883	2 090.2	825.3	1 959	9 915	752.7	220.5	3 839.1	1 737.7	770.9	66.4
Monmouth-Ocean, NJ	2 682	26 349	1 916.5	825.3	1 944	9 035	567.7	170.4	5 659.8	2 581.8	1 140.0	69.9
Nassau-Suffolk, NY	7 532	77 693	6 073.7	2 540.5	6 187	29 595	2 050.3	608.4	12 405.0	5 193.8	2 503.1	204.7
New Haven-Bridgeport-Stamford-Danbury-Waterbury, CT	3 979	51 826	3 665.7	1 700.5	3 131	17 526	1 230.0	383.8	8 115.9	2 975.1	1 576.1	188.3
New York, NY	16 803	154 220	12 321.5	5 102.1	14 201	67 473	4 595.2	1 320.0	49 534.9	12 537.7	9 287.6	2 923.4
Newark, NJ	4 940	43 453	3 385.6	1 461.0	3 942	21 313	1 546.9	479.1	8 856.8	3 266.0	1 682.7	301.9
Newburgh, NY-PA	697	5 727	383.1	164.4	577	2 679	196.4	52.1	1 664.2	607.2	243.7	43.8
Trenton, NJ	796	7 200	583.3	262.6	538	2 985	210.3	62.1	2 960.9	716.2	342.3	51.8
Norfolk-Virginia Beach-Newport News, VA-NC	2 601	30 528	1 788.9	878.1	2 465	17 087	1 008.4	316.7	14 563.1	3 689.7	827.7	231.3
Ocala, FL	466	6 512	466.6	185.9	369	1 680	93.9	29.4	1 325.7	787.4	272.6	38.6
Odessa-Midland, TX	472	6 645	415.6	171.5	461	3 286	306.6	70.1	712.1	343.2	160.6	35.9
Oklahoma City, OK	2 547	33 079	2 058.9	907.2	1 609	11 495	650.5	196.8	6 697.8	2 157.6	677.5	152.0
Omaha, NE-IA	1 226	15 265	996.6	480.8	1 234	8 294	497.8	156.4	3 756.9	1 264.6	397.6	77.4
Orlando, FL	3 136	38 208	2 746.2	1 240.1	2 626	16 893	1 040.0	314.7	7 505.3	3 048.1	1 201.5	207.5
Owensboro, KY	202	2 568	184.0	76.4	144	829	50.4	14.5	360.4	173.4	67.7	18.6
Panama City, FL	317	4 398	315.8	131.2	246	1 569	85.5	27.6	1 211.3	426.2	119.4	23.4
Parkersburg-Marietta, WV-OH	295	3 795	234.7	100.5	278	2 165	150.8	37.2	752.9	322.4	128.0	31.4
Pensacola, FL	662	11 163	748.8	344.1	557	3 672	210.4	73.6	2 750.7	1 132.4	286.4	69.3
Peoria-Pekin, IL	544	6 673	467.7	239.2	559	3 672	255.1	81.2	1 464.3	652.9	251.1	51.2
Philadelphia-Wilmington-Atlantic City, PA-NJ-DE-MD	12 730	139 603	9 857.3	4 559.7	9 969	58 475	3 898.1	1 202.4	32 678.8	11 656.9	6 207.3	1 103.2
Atlantic-Cape May, NJ	748	6 313	470.8	218.6	597	3 288	173.3	56.8	1 802.2	724.8	370.6	43.6
Philadelphia, PA-NJ	10 631	118 672	8 318.9	3 840.5	8 254	48 485	3 316.7	1 007.5	27 868.7	9 714.0	5 308.0	970.4
Vineland-Millville-Bridgeton, NJ	238	2 191	161.8	74.8	243	1 156	65.2	20.6	670.5	253.6	142.5	29.7
Wilmington-Newark, DE-MD	1 113	12 427	905.7	425.9	875	5 546	342.9	117.5	2 337.4	964.5	386.2	59.5
Phoenix-Mesa, AZ	5 980	65 092	4 618.5	2 016.1	4 168	30 680	2 040.5	606.3	13 693.7	5 118.1	1 952.8	325.1
Pine Bluff, AR	191	1 709	110.3	48.3	110	750	40.7	12.6	536.5	172.1	62.4	29.8
Pittsburgh, PA	5 433	59 633	4 112.6	1 814.6	4 303	25 001	1 652.9	465.3	14 600.8	5 526.4	3 128.4	403.5
Pittsfield, MA	268	4 334	254.6	113.7	231	1 074	62.7	18.7	869.0	295.0	164.9	17.6
Pocatello, ID	157	1 421	79.8	39.1	108	564	33.5	9.5	272.1	125.9	32.3	10.5
Portland, ME	764	9 092	602.3	303.5	503	3 458	226.7	71.3	1 277.1	495.3	168.5	32.8
Portland-Salem, OR-WA	4 608	46 839	3 043.0	1 329.2	3 248	20 378	1 413.9	429.2	8 949.5	3 516.1	1 190.3	251.9
Portland-Vancouver, OR-WA	3 887	40 364	2 663.4	1 162.7	2 817	18 146	1 282.8	388.3	7 125.4	2 865.5	1 005.5	207.6
Salem, OR	721	6 475	379.6	166.5	431	2 232	131.2	40.9	1 824.1	650.6	184.8	44.3
Providence-Warwick-Pawtucket, RI	1 923	23 642	1 380.0	613.6	1 793	7 820	500.2	150.2	4 701.2	1 846.0	844.4	156.9
Provo-Orem, UT	596	7 371	421.0	178.8	340	2 256	103.9	29.1	737.5	339.2	106.3	19.6
Pueblo, CO	299	3 459	203.9	98.4	194	912	47.5	13.9	695.5	327.3	112.2	34.5
Punta Gorda, FL	305	4 286	306.9	134.7	189	674	37.4	10.2	776.7	505.8	217.8	9.7
Raleigh-Durham-Chapel Hill, NC	2 019	28 385	1 734.6	796.4	1 713	10 843	775.0	224.0	5 828.3	1 579.1	557.2	114.0
Rapid City, SD	226	2 315	163.6	65.6	191	1 049	55.5	17.4	559.1	197.2	42.3	12.9

1. Firms subject to federal tax.   2. October 1, 1998 to September 30, 1999.

Table C. Metropolitan Areas — Federal Funds and Local Government Finances

	Federal funds and grants, fiscal 1999[1] (cont'd)							Local government finances, 1997				
	Expenditures (mil dol) (cont'd)							General revenue				
Area Name	Procurement contract awards			Grants[2]						Taxes		
								Total (mil dol)	Intergovern-mental (mil dol)	Total (mil dol)	Per capita[3] (dollars)	
	Salaries and wages	Defense	Other	Medicaid and other health-related	Nutrition and family welfare	Education	Other				Total	Property
	171	172	173	174	175	176	177	178	179	180	181	182
Merced, CA	21.9	10.7	16.3	94.9	62.5	17.1	30.4	764.1	458.6	102.0	520	413
Miami-Fort Lauderdale, FL	1 404.5	179.1	328.2	2 046.8	412.7	191.1	471.9	12 361.3	3 571.4	4 168.9	1 157	890
Fort Lauderdale, FL	386.6	77.6	113.6	199.1	97.0	51.8	128.7	4 746.9	1 168.5	1 714.5	1 166	921
Miami, FL	1 017.9	101.4	214.7	1 847.6	315.7	139.3	343.2	7 614.5	2 402.8	2 454.4	1 151	869
Milwaukee-Racine, WI	631.9	155.0	264.7	733.4	304.1	99.8	191.0	5 373.7	2 469.1	2 071.6	1 266	1 200
Milwaukee-Waukesha, WI.	609.6	147.0	256.0	668.0	276.0	91.4	176.6	4 897.3	2 214.4	1 917.0	1 321	1 249
Racine, WI	22.3	8.0	8.7	65.4	28.1	8.4	14.4	476.4	254.7	154.5	833	814
Minneapolis-St. Paul, MN-WI	1 194.1	1 159.7	401.4	1 153.0	550.8	218.7	764.6	9 216.7	3 517.2	3 108.2	1 113	1 044
Missoula, MT	62.1	1.5	19.5	38.7	10.4	9.3	27.7	158.2	57.6	74.9	843	814
Mobile, AL	161.9	109.5	33.3	166.7	61.4	32.7	90.9	1 040.8	421.0	350.6	665	209
Modesto, CA	60.5	2.4	72.6	200.1	107.3	23.7	36.5	1 342.0	740.0	254.6	604	412
Monroe, LA	26.4	5.6	7.1	76.8	16.2	11.0	14.7	289.6	116.9	136.3	927	353
Montgomery, AL	449.1	233.4	39.8	193.0	228.2	146.1	471.3	524.7	261.1	179.3	562	142
Muncie, IN	21.8	0.2	5.9	55.2	13.9	3.8	7.8	214.2	97.2	86.0	731	670
Myrtle Beach, SC	23.4	11.2	6.1	62.3	15.4	7.7	46.7	409.2	115.7	165.7	980	789
Naples, FL	30.4	0.3	8.9	22.9	20.9	6.1	26.5	502.7	92.3	285.7	1 459	1 257
Nashville, TN	589.0	72.6	165.6	574.6	341.7	165.5	482.4	2 544.2	712.5	1 124.0	991	553
New London-Norwich, CT	363.0	1 943.2	35.3	103.2	24.9	11.3	25.0	663.2	233.3	332.3	1 314	1 285
New Orleans, LA	878.0	1 045.5	825.9	692.9	176.8	88.1	302.4	3 397.8	935.0	1 426.9	1 091	403
New York-Northern New Jersey-Long Island, NY-NJ-CT-PA	8 295.7	4 332.4	4 249.7	16 363.1	4 113.3	1 310.8	4 481.5	89 095.4	28 154.8	44 590.0	2 243	1 519
Bergen-Passaic, NJ	270.8	571.1	224.7	424.7	89.2	31.7	184.0	3 853.6	956.4	2 316.4	1 735	1 715
Dutchess County, NY	62.4	4.7	15.1	152.0	20.7	9.0	21.2	866.8	254.0	462.0	1 745	1 391
Jersey City, NJ	426.7	10.8	147.2	488.7	105.0	31.3	82.0	1 636.7	711.2	666.5	1 209	1 191
Middlesex-Somerset-Hunterdon, NJ	323.8	83.6	258.1	281.4	47.5	20.8	193.8	3 115.4	733.5	1 894.2	1 713	1 687
Monmouth-Ocean, NJ	702.8	652.4	60.1	282.7	63.3	28.8	40.1	3 114.9	869.7	1 752.8	1 628	1 598
Nassau-Suffolk, NY	1 032.7	949.3	698.9	1 121.0	214.7	91.1	182.2	11 467.3	2 675.3	7 405.1	2 777	2 255
New Haven-Bridgeport-Stamford-Danbury-Waterbury, CT	532.3	816.0	244.6	1 078.3	225.0	81.1	271.8	4 423.6	1 263.1	2 670.0	1 643	1 621
New York, NY	3 559.7	682.6	2 218.3	11 073.5	2 683.2	716.7	2 294.1	51 582.0	17 839.5	22 881.7	2 657	1 195
Newark, NJ	840.0	339.1	191.9	976.2	265.4	84.1	706.0	6 260.0	2 008.5	3 389.4	1 744	1 707
Newburgh, NY-PA	391.9	118.8	26.1	144.1	38.4	17.0	16.8	1 562.6	408.8	591.1	1 614	1 309
Trenton, NJ	152.6	104.1	164.7	340.6	361.0	199.2	489.5	1 212.4	434.8	560.9	1 701	1 678
Norfolk-Virginia Beach-Newport News, VA-NC	5 409.0	2 938.2	560.0	305.2	154.6	86.3	204.8	3 778.8	1 398.1	1 550.2	1 003	676
Ocala, FL	33.9	8.6	40.1	51.8	28.7	11.1	36.1	411.8	199.1	119.9	505	446
Odessa-Midland, TX	38.7	0.1	10.5	52.7	18.5	11.3	26.9	785.7	198.1	239.6	984	751
Oklahoma City, OK	1 400.7	748.5	259.9	327.9	321.3	131.0	416.4	2 115.4	693.5	757.3	735	351
Omaha, NE-IA	633.6	168.4	94.9	322.4	82.5	54.7	127.5	1 631.9	529.9	779.2	1 134	864
Orlando, FL	496.4	1 680.1	144.1	220.3	114.2	61.8	253.9	4 004.9	1 175.4	1 502.4	1 024	759
Owensboro, KY	15.7	4.2	7.1	27.2	15.4	3.9	12.7	189.8	66.1	43.6	479	299
Panama City, FL	277.6	129.8	26.1	34.2	18.5	8.5	5.5	460.6	158.6	108.1	739	475
Parkersburg-Marietta, WV-OH	94.6	2.1	15.4	65.5	18.8	9.1	54.5	333.6	115.6	99.8	663	487
Pensacola, FL	713.6	182.9	31.1	116.2	57.2	24.2	84.7	860.9	411.0	238.1	600	400
Peoria-Pekin, IL	158.8	42.1	40.4	76.6	32.4	11.0	74.8	753.4	328.0	282.6	817	692
Philadelphia-Wilmington-Atlantic City, PA-NJ-DE-MD	3 406.2	2 457.5	1 302.9	3 659.4	904.4	262.1	1 202.1	18 746.8	7 421.8	7 916.9	1 326	986
Atlantic-Cape May, NJ	214.2	9.8	136.1	143.0	35.1	12.9	74.2	1 309.3	396.5	729.7	2 180	2 145
Philadelphia, PA-NJ	2 913.3	2 382.4	1 033.1	3 210.0	766.8	215.3	939.4	15 877.0	6 282.1	6 687.3	1 354	962
Vineland-Millville-Bridgeton, NJ	40.6	19.0	8.9	99.2	28.2	7.9	17.3	463.2	280.5	121.7	864	853
Wilmington-Newark, DE-MD	238.0	46.3	124.9	207.2	74.3	26.1	171.3	1 097.3	462.7	378.2	681	533
Phoenix-Mesa, AZ	1 177.5	2 204.8	388.4	846.7	542.7	244.2	647.8	7 142.3	3 011.5	2 452.5	864	594
Pine Bluff, AR	65.0	43.6	18.7	57.9	12.9	8.4	30.2	148.9	72.7	47.6	579	343
Pittsburgh, PA	997.6	1 192.6	610.6	1 471.1	324.2	84.2	518.2	6 449.1	2 682.2	2 479.8	1 050	796
Pittsfield, MA	38.3	86.6	141.0	73.6	20.7	7.4	15.8	303.3	146.3	129.8	967	934
Pocatello, ID	23.0	0.1	12.6	29.9	5.0	3.4	16.1	177.4	69.3	39.1	530	505
Portland, ME	249.1	75.9	33.8	132.1	25.3	11.2	34.9	611.2	131.2	364.6	1 450	1 414
Portland-Salem, OR-WA	1 037.5	209.2	373.6	1 073.4	406.7	190.1	557.0	6 258.0	2 473.3	2 198.5	1 041	810
Portland-Vancouver, OR-WA	950.7	207.8	351.6	881.7	191.8	82.5	266.1	5 514.4	2 115.1	1 978.5	1 107	846
Salem, OR	86.8	1.3	22.0	191.7	214.9	107.6	290.9	743.6	358.3	220.0	676	609
Providence-Warwick-Pawtucket, RI	350.0	19.2	106.2	656.3	209.9	102.0	330.4	1 940.7	639.2	1 117.4	1 235	1 220
Provo-Orem, UT	52.6	10.1	15.7	81.7	29.0	8.5	55.1	615.9	305.1	185.8	566	405
Pueblo, CO	35.9	8.6	12.6	90.7	39.0	10.0	10.8	303.9	144.2	112.1	844	517
Punta Gorda, FL	13.5	1.8	3.7	5.2	7.2	2.9	6.6	268.9	54.4	131.5	984	744
Raleigh-Durham-Chapel Hill, NC	527.3	77.7	409.4	911.9	521.7	240.7	787.9	2 553.7	922.4	879.7	838	642
Rapid City, SD	168.2	4.5	30.4	25.9	11.1	11.8	31.4	192.8	68.0	91.5	1 050	748

1. October 1, 1998 to September 30, 1999. 2. State totals may include programs not allocated by county. 3. Based on the resident population estimated as of July 1 of the year shown.

Area Name	Local government finances, 1997 (cont'd)									Government employment, 1998			Presidential election, 2000		
	Direct general expenditure							Debt outstanding					Percent of vote cast —		
			Percent of total for —												
	Total (mil dol)	Per capita[1] (dollars)	Education	Health and hospitals	Police protection	Public welfare	Highways	Total (mil dol)	Per capita[1] (dollars)	Federal civilian	Federal military	State and local	Democratic	Republican	All other
	183	184	185	186	187	188	189	190	191	192	193	194	195	196	197
Merced, CA	735.8	3 752	44.4	12.9	3.2	14.4	1.7	149.4	762	447	397	11 662	45.1	51.8	3.2
Miami-Fort Lauderdale, FL	12 492.7	3 467	33.3	14.2	7.8	0.7	1.9	14 094.2	3 912	25 221	10 719	192 638	59.7	38.9	1.4
Fort Lauderdale, FL	4 649.6	3 161	31.9	22.2	8.4	0.6	1.9	4 913.8	3 341	7 008	3 749	73 771	67.4	30.9	1.7
Miami, FL	7 843.1	3 679	34.1	9.4	7.5	0.8	1.9	9 180.4	4 306	18 213	6 970	118 867	52.6	46.3	1.1
Milwaukee-Racine, WI	5 352.5	3 271	43.8	4.4	6.8	6.0	5.0	4 269.9	2 609	11 654	6 265	85 515	46.9	49.4	3.7
Milwaukee-Waukesha, WI.	4 873.4	3 358	43.9	4.4	6.6	5.6	4.9	3 985.9	2 747	11 236	5 607	77 148	46.9	49.4	3.7
Racine, WI	479.1	2 584	43.2	4.4	8.3	10.3	6.1	284.0	1 532	418	658	8 367	46.8	49.5	3.7
Minneapolis-St. Paul, MN-WI	9 608.2	3 441	40.3	6.5	4.3	5.7	6.0	12 459.2	4 462	22 162	12 213	191 359	50.0	43.5	6.5
Missoula, MT	163.4	1 839	56.4	4.7	5.4	0.4	3.6	111.4	1 254	1 281	515	7 687	36.7	45.8	17.5
Mobile, AL	1 035.5	1 964	42.0	10.2	5.4	0.3	7.2	1 223.6	2 321	2 742	4 102	32 340	37.0	60.7	2.3
Modesto, CA	1 293.6	3 067	42.7	12.1	4.9	11.6	2.2	1 786.6	4 235	1 241	856	22 055	44.0	52.4	3.6
Monroe, LA	299.4	2 036	48.8	0.7	7.9	0.3	7.7	168.6	1 147	493	819	11 821	NA	NA	NA
Montgomery, AL	531.9	1 667	52.9	4.2	7.4	0.3	7.8	454.4	1 424	7 049	7 008	29 258	42.8	55.7	1.5
Muncie, IN	213.6	1 816	55.4	1.0	4.1	6.3	4.1	77.7	660	413	418	9 633	47.7	50.5	1.8
Myrtle Beach, SC	446.4	2 639	45.2	9.2	4.8	0.3	4.0	435.0	2 571	433	1 008	9 429	40.9	56.5	2.6
Naples, FL	530.4	2 710	46.9	2.9	7.6	0.6	6.7	559.5	2 859	579	451	8 491	32.5	65.6	1.9
Nashville, TN	2 604.2	2 295	36.6	7.0	6.4	0.8	3.9	4 200.4	3 702	11 404	5 189	67 109	48.5	49.8	1.8
New London-Norwich, CT	673.9	2 664	55.5	0.8	5.8	1.1	5.7	441.4	1 745	2 625	9 258	13 885	NA	NA	NA
New Orleans, LA	3 128.0	2 392	35.4	17.2	6.8	0.6	3.3	4 021.4	3 075	16 337	11 583	90 014	NA	NA	NA
New York-Northern New Jersey-Long Island, NY-NJ-CT-PA	86 303.8	4 342	34.3	6.8	6.5	11.8	2.9	79 281.6	3 989	160 387	55 461	1 223 574	NA	NA	NA
Bergen-Passaic, NJ	3 804.9	2 849	47.3	3.9	6.9	5.3	3.2	1 741.2	1 304	5 046	3 241	61 621	NA	NA	NA
Dutchess County, NY	889.0	3 359	48.6	5.3	4.1	9.0	4.7	485.9	1 836	1 443	539	20 265	46.9	47.1	6.0
Jersey City, NJ	1 555.6	2 821	28.9	5.2	7.7	7.3	2.3	1 414.7	2 565	8 293	1 483	35 769	NA	NA	NA
Middlesex-Somerset-Hunterdon, NJ	3 159.1	2 858	54.6	3.3	5.7	3.0	3.4	2 110.6	1 909	6 370	2 832	66 928	NA	NA	NA
Monmouth-Ocean, NJ	3 126.5	2 903	53.2	1.7	5.9	3.4	3.3	2 414.9	2 242	11 954	6 233	49 559	NA	NA	NA
Nassau-Suffolk, NY	11 892.4	4 460	46.2	4.6	7.8	6.9	3.1	8 447.7	3 168	19 790	6 013	155 399	55.7	40.2	4.1
New Haven-Bridgeport-Stamford-Danbury-Waterbury, CT	4 467.2	2 748	50.1	1.3	5.9	2.1	3.7	2 395.7	1 474	11 026	4 164	77 977	NA	NA	NA
New York, NY	48 318.8	5 611	24.4	9.5	6.5	16.6	2.5	55 276.9	6 419	70 533	18 731	563 579	73.8	22.3	3.9
Newark, NJ	6 294.6	3 239	45.3	3.5	6.5	6.5	3.5	3 244.5	1 669	17 152	4 798	122 980	NA	NA	NA
Newburgh, NY-PA	1 595.0	4 355	39.0	1.9	2.8	9.9	3.2	720.9	1 968	5 640	6 585	21 117	NA	NA	NA
Trenton, NJ	1 200.7	3 641	49.0	2.4	5.9	5.8	3.0	1 028.7	3 119	3 140	842	48 380	NA	NA	NA
Norfolk-Virginia Beach-Newport News, VA-NC	3 974.1	2 572	44.6	5.2	4.9	3.4	3.3	4 845.4	3 136	46 946	107 706	96 372	NA	NA	NA
Ocala, FL	416.0	1 753	51.9	0.8	8.5	0.4	9.1	334.0	1 408	649	549	13 640	43.4	53.6	3.1
Odessa-Midland, TX	765.3	3 145	39.2	34.9	4.4	0.1	2.0	456.6	1 876	772	654	16 699	23.3	74.9	1.8
Oklahoma City, OK	2 044.6	1 984	45.7	11.0	7.3	0.2	4.5	2 025.4	1 965	25 454	13 306	76 412	35.8	35.8	28.4
Omaha, NE-IA	1 572.9	2 288	51.2	2.5	5.1	0.5	6.3	1 835.9	2 671	8 545	11 567	41 569	38.6	57.0	4.3
Orlando, FL	4 030.3	2 747	39.7	2.0	6.5	0.7	6.9	8 852.8	6 034	9 472	6 830	76 425	47.0	51.0	2.0
Owensboro, KY	186.5	2 050	40.6	6.7	3.6	0.0	2.8	883.5	9 707	292	346	6 901	39.0	58.9	2.1
Panama City, FL	472.5	3 232	38.8	23.9	6.6	0.0	3.4	247.6	1 693	3 030	4 452	6 836	32.1	65.7	2.2
Parkersburg-Marietta, WV-OH	323.1	2 145	46.5	26.0	3.9	2.1	5.2	142.1	943	2 161	599	7 224	NA	NA	NA
Pensacola, FL	835.6	2 104	51.0	1.4	6.8	0.6	5.1	1 246.6	3 139	7 787	15 754	20 771	32.2	65.5	2.4
Peoria-Pekin, IL	714.0	2 064	51.2	1.4	4.8	1.3	6.5	386.1	1 116	2 179	822	16 944	45.7	51.9	2.4
Philadelphia-Wilmington-Atlantic City, PA-NJ-DE-MD	18 181.9	3 045	45.3	4.6	5.6	4.3	3.7	22 143.6	3 708	65 086	29 100	304 875	NA	NA	NA
Atlantic-Cape May, NJ	1 448.6	4 328	40.1	1.3	7.4	4.3	4.1	1 158.3	3 461	2 870	2 127	25 291	NA	NA	NA
Philadelphia, PA-NJ	15 192.6	3 075	44.6	5.3	5.4	4.5	3.4	19 767.0	4 001	56 546	22 898	235 732	NA	NA	NA
Vineland-Millville-Bridgeton, NJ	441.6	3 134	55.9	3.2	4.0	7.7	4.3	153.1	1 086	759	339	11 204	NA	NA	NA
Wilmington-Newark, DE-MD	1 099.0	1 978	57.8	0.7	6.1	0.1	6.8	1 065.2	1 917	4 911	3 736	32 648	57.8	38.9	3.3
Phoenix-Mesa, AZ	7 125.2	2 509	37.5	3.4	7.1	7.6	4.3	14 214.6	5 006	19 492	13 038	157 158	43.2	53.1	3.7
Pine Bluff, AR	150.9	1 835	53.0	0.3	7.5	0.0	4.3	109.7	1 334	1 609	516	6 134	65.1	32.2	2.6
Pittsburgh, PA	6 382.0	2 703	48.0	5.7	3.7	3.8	3.6	10 199.6	4 320	19 397	8 618	104 435	NA	NA	NA
Pittsfield, MA	324.7	2 418	55.8	0.6	3.7	0.1	6.8	145.7	1 085	456	433	7 239	NA	NA	NA
Pocatello, ID	171.1	2 317	40.7	26.7	5.0	0.7	4.2	43.1	584	520	340	7 800	35.3	59.1	5.6
Portland, ME	569.7	2 266	44.4	0.4	4.8	3.3	5.1	420.3	1 671	3 079	4 245	16 706	NA	NA	NA
Portland-Salem, OR-WA	6 164.3	2 918	43.6	4.6	5.0	0.3	5.3	5 957.7	2 820	19 270	8 086	130 907	51.4	42.4	6.2
Portland-Vancouver, OR-WA	5 392.9	3 017	42.2	4.4	5.0	0.3	5.3	5 508.9	3 082	17 677	6 948	97 872	52.8	41.0	6.2
Salem, OR	771.4	2 372	53.6	6.1	4.9	0.0	5.7	448.9	1 380	1 593	1 138	33 035	43.3	51.1	5.6
Providence-Warwick-Pawtucket, RI	1 856.7	2 052	56.2	0.2	7.0	0.4	3.0	1 035.1	1 144	6 345	5 775	51 694	NA	NA	NA
Provo-Orem, UT	592.2	1 805	54.6	1.6	5.2	0.1	3.6	878.7	2 678	1 002	1 849	18 209	13.5	80.4	6.1
Pueblo, CO	298.9	2 249	43.8	1.9	4.8	12.0	5.9	413.0	3 107	706	408	10 269	53.5	42.3	4.1
Punta Gorda, FL	239.6	1 792	40.7	3.4	7.5	1.5	8.7	365.3	2 732	259	305	4 839	44.3	53.0	2.7
Raleigh-Durham-Chapel Hill, NC	2 454.2	2 337	43.7	12.0	4.9	4.8	2.2	8 587.2	8 178	9 464	4 146	110 506	NA	NA	NA
Rapid City, SD	193.4	2 218	44.5	0.9	5.1	0.5	4.9	108.9	1 249	1 260	3 559	5 287	30.4	67.6	2.0

1. Based on the resident population estimated as of July 1 of the year shown.

Table C. Metropolitan Areas — **Land Area and Population**

CMSA/ MSA/ PMSA/ NECMA code[1]	Area Name	Land area,[2] (sq km) 1990	Population and population characteristics, 1999													
			Total persons	Rank	Per square kilometer	Race (percent)				Percent Hispanic[3]	Age (percent)					
						White	Black	Am. Indian, Eskimo, Aleut	Asian and Pacific Islander		Under 5 years	5 to 17 years	18 to 24 years	25 to 34 years	35 to 44 years	45 to 54 years
		1	2	3	4	5	6	7	8	9	10	11	12	13	14	15
6680	Reading, PA	2 225	358 211	136	161.0	94.7	3.7	0.1	1.4	7.3	6.1	17.7	8.4	13.1	16.2	13.5
6690	Redding, CA	9 805	164 530	222	16.8	93.8	0.8	2.8	2.5	5.5	6.7	21.0	6.9	10.9	16.4	14.3
6720	Reno, NV	16 427	319 816	150	19.5	89.1	2.6	2.3	5.9	14.4	7.8	18.0	9.3	14.2	17.7	13.5
6740	Richland-Kennewick-Pasco, WA	7 628	184 626	207	24.2	94.2	2.0	0.9	2.9	19.0	7.9	23.3	9.0	12.9	15.8	13.2
6760	Richmond-Petersburg, VA	7 628	961 416	62	126.0	67.7	30.0	0.3	2.0	1.6	6.4	17.7	9.0	15.1	18.3	13.4
6800	Roanoke, VA	2 204	227 741	184	103.3	85.1	13.7	0.1	1.0	1.0	5.5	16.1	8.3	13.0	17.2	13.9
6820	Rochester, MN	1 691	119 077	277	70.4	93.7	1.1	0.3	4.9	1.5	7.4	19.6	8.7	14.8	17.1	14.0
6840	Rochester, NY	8 873	1 079 073	56	121.6	87.5	10.1	0.4	2.1	4.0	6.9	18.7	9.1	14.2	16.9	13.3
6880	Rockford, IL	4 026	358 640	134	89.1	90.6	7.7	0.3	1.4	4.9	7.1	19.5	8.2	13.1	16.7	13.7
6895	Rocky Mount, NC	2 707	147 028	237	54.3	58.3	41.1	0.3	0.4	1.2	6.8	20.2	7.8	13.8	16.6	12.9
82	Sacramento-Yolo, CA	13 193	1 741 002	X	132.0	80.9	7.3	1.4	10.5	15.6	7.0	19.7	9.1	14.4	17.4	12.9
6920	Sacramento, CA	10 571	1 585 429	34	150.0	80.5	7.7	1.3	10.4	14.6	7.0	19.8	8.4	14.4	17.6	13.0
9270	Yolo, CA	2 622	155 573	228	59.3	85.3	2.5	1.6	10.6	26.2	7.1	18.4	16.1	14.4	15.5	11.6
6960	Saginaw-Bay City-Midland, MI	4 596	400 753	123	87.2	88.0	10.5	0.6	1.0	5.6	6.6	20.1	8.7	12.7	16.4	13.9
7120	Salinas, CA	8 604	371 756	132	43.2	82.1	6.4	1.0	10.5	41.1	8.3	20.5	10.4	16.2	16.1	10.6
7160	Salt Lake City-Ogden, UT	4 190	1 275 076	46	304.3	94.6	1.4	0.8	3.2	8.5	9.8	22.7	12.6	14.6	14.1	11.0
7200	San Angelo, TX	3 942	102 300	295	26.0	93.4	4.6	0.5	1.5	32.1	7.9	19.4	11.8	12.4	14.7	11.8
7240	San Antonio, TX	8 617	1 564 949	35	181.6	91.2	6.6	0.4	1.8	54.2	8.6	20.6	10.5	13.4	15.6	12.3
7320	San Diego, CA	10 890	2 820 844	14	259.0	81.8	6.5	0.9	10.8	26.5	7.3	18.4	11.5	16.0	16.6	11.6
84	San Francisco-Oakland-San Jose, CA	19 085	6 873 645	X	360.2	71.3	8.9	0.7	19.0	19.7	6.5	17.1	9.0	15.5	18.4	13.9
5775	Oakland, CA	3 776	2 348 723	19	622.0	66.9	15.3	0.8	17.0	17.2	6.7	18.0	9.0	15.0	18.7	14.0
7360	San Francisco, CA	2 630	1 685 647	29	640.9	65.9	7.5	0.5	26.0	18.0	5.3	14.0	8.4	15.9	18.8	14.5
7400	San Jose, CA	3 344	1 647 419	30	492.6	73.4	3.8	0.7	22.1	25.9	6.9	17.5	9.8	17.0	17.3	13.7
7485	Santa Cruz-Watsonville, CA	1 155	245 201	174	212.3	92.5	1.4	1.0	5.2	26.8	6.9	18.4	11.2	14.3	19.9	12.3
7500	Santa Rosa, CA	4 082	439 970	114	107.8	93.2	1.6	1.3	3.9	14.5	6.7	18.8	8.1	13.0	19.5	13.5
8720	Vallejo-Fairfield-Napa, CA	4 098	506 685	100	123.6	73.8	10.9	1.0	14.3	17.7	7.3	20.4	8.4	14.4	18.2	12.8
7460	San Luis Obispo-Atascadero-Paso Robles, CA	8 559	236 953	177	27.7	92.1	2.8	1.2	3.9	17.6	5.9	16.8	12.7	13.2	16.9	11.6
7480	Santa Barbara-Santa Maria-Lompoc, CA	7 093	391 071	125	55.1	89.7	3.1	1.2	6.0	33.6	7.0	17.4	12.8	14.7	15.6	11.7
7490	Santa Fe, NM	5 228	142 509	244	27.3	94.9	0.9	2.9	1.2	46.5	6.6	18.2	8.5	11.1	19.6	16.2
7510	Sarasota-Bradenton, FL	3 401	550 077	95	161.7	91.6	7.2	0.3	0.9	4.8	5.0	13.8	5.8	9.6	13.4	11.9
7520	Savannah, GA	3 527	288 426	158	81.8	60.3	37.8	0.2	1.6	2.1	7.6	19.6	9.5	14.6	16.0	12.4
7560	Scranton—Wilkes-Barre—Hazleton, PA	5 783	611 492	84	105.7	98.1	1.1	0.1	0.7	0.8	5.2	16.7	8.8	11.5	15.3	13.4
91	Seattle-Tacoma-Bremerton, WA	18 710	3 465 760	X	185.2	85.1	5.1	1.4	8.4	4.5	6.8	18.0	9.7	14.9	17.8	14.2
1150	Bremerton, WA	1 026	236 560	179	230.6	89.1	2.9	1.8	6.3	4.8	7.3	20.3	9.9	13.2	17.3	13.8
5910	Olympia, WA	1 883	205 459	194	109.1	90.8	2.2	1.7	5.3	4.7	6.3	20.2	9.0	12.3	18.0	14.6
7600	Seattle-Bellevue-Everett, WA	11 461	2 334 934	20	203.7	84.7	4.7	1.3	9.3	4.3	6.6	17.1	9.5	15.4	18.4	14.4
8200	Tacoma, WA	4 340	688 807	77	158.7	83.3	8.2	1.5	7.0	5.4	7.3	19.7	10.7	14.3	16.2	13.3
7610	Sharon, PA	1 740	121 458	273	69.8	93.5	5.9	0.1	0.5	0.6	5.3	18.0	8.8	11.3	15.2	13.6
7620	Sheboygan, WI	1 330	110 136	288	82.8	96.0	0.6	0.4	3.0	2.5	6.2	20.0	8.3	12.9	16.5	13.3
7640	Sherman-Denison, TX	2 418	103 728	292	42.9	90.4	7.7	1.2	0.7	4.0	6.5	19.0	8.2	11.0	15.1	14.1
7680	Shreveport-Bossier City, LA	6 000	377 673	127	62.9	62.1	36.8	0.3	0.8	1.6	7.1	19.5	9.7	12.4	15.2	13.4
7720	Sioux City, IA-NE	2 944	120 577	275	41.0	93.9	2.0	2.1	2.1	5.9	7.5	20.8	9.4	13.0	15.3	12.2
7760	Sioux Falls, SD	3 593	164 481	223	45.8	96.9	0.8	1.5	0.8	0.9	6.9	19.0	11.1	13.8	17.2	13.0
7800	South Bend, IN	1 185	258 537	166	218.2	87.0	11.2	0.4	1.5	3.2	7.1	17.9	11.4	13.4	15.9	11.7
7840	Spokane, WA	4 568	409 736	119	89.7	94.1	1.7	1.7	2.6	3.1	6.5	19.6	10.3	12.8	16.4	13.5
7880	Springfield, IL	3 063	204 030	196	66.6	90.3	8.5	0.2	1.1	1.0	6.7	18.9	7.6	13.4	17.8	13.3
8003	Springfield, MA	2 972	589 171	87	198.2	89.4	8.2	0.2	2.2	10.8	6.5	18.5	10.3	13.8	16.4	12.3
7920	Springfield, MO	4 744	308 332	153	65.0	96.9	1.7	0.6	0.9	1.1	6.1	17.9	12.4	12.8	16.6	12.7
6980	St. Cloud, MN	4 539	164 913	221	36.3	98.1	0.5	0.3	1.0	0.7	6.8	21.3	15.2	12.2	14.7	11.0
7000	St. Joseph, MO	2 188	97 220	302	44.4	96.0	3.2	0.3	0.4	2.6	6.6	19.3	9.1	12.4	15.6	12.2
7040	St. Louis, MO-IL	16 556	2 569 029	17	155.2	80.8	17.6	0.2	1.3	1.5	7.0	19.3	8.7	13.8	16.8	12.8
8050	State College, PA	2 869	132 190	259	46.1	92.7	2.6	0.2	4.5	1.6	5.1	13.5	25.0	14.3	14.0	11.2
8080	Steubenville-Weirton, OH-WV	1 506	133 292	257	88.5	95.1	4.3	0.2	0.4	0.6	4.9	16.5	8.5	11.0	15.2	14.3
8120	Stockton-Lodi, CA	3 625	563 183	90	155.4	77.2	5.7	1.1	16.0	29.4	8.4	22.5	9.1	14.0	16.1	11.9
8140	Sumter, SC	1 724	112 412	286	65.2	54.5	44.1	0.2	1.2	1.8	7.2	19.4	10.7	16.4	15.9	12.3
8160	Syracuse, NY	7 985	732 920	73	91.8	91.3	6.4	0.6	1.7	1.8	6.8	19.0	10.1	13.9	16.1	12.6
8240	Tallahassee, FL	3 064	260 003	165	84.9	63.6	34.2	0.3	1.9	3.4	6.2	19.1	16.5	13.6	17.1	11.6
8280	Tampa-St. Petersburg-Clearwater, FL	6 617	2 278 169	22	344.3	87.1	10.7	0.4	1.8	10.0	5.9	16.5	7.5	12.0	15.6	12.7
8320	Terre Haute, IN	2 636	148 206	235	56.2	94.2	4.4	0.3	1.1	1.1	6.2	17.4	11.9	12.8	15.3	12.6
8360	Texarkana, TX-Texarkana, AR	3 916	122 886	269	31.4	74.9	24.1	0.5	0.5	2.1	6.7	20.2	8.8	11.7	15.7	13.4
8400	Toledo, OH	3 535	608 976	85	172.3	85.8	12.5	0.3	1.4	4.3	7.0	19.0	11.3	13.6	16.0	12.3
8440	Topeka, KS	1 424	170 773	214	119.9	88.7	9.0	1.1	1.1	7.4	6.5	18.8	9.1	12.7	16.8	13.6

1. MSA = Metropolitan Statistical Area. CMSA = Consolidated MSA. PMSA = Primary MSA. NECMA = New England County Metropolitan Area. See Appendix A for explanation of these concepts. See Appendix B for list of metropolitan areas identified by type, with component counties.   2. Dry land or land partially or temporarily covered by water.   3. Hispanic persons may be of any race.

Table C. Metropolitan Areas — **Population and Households**

Area Name	55 to 64 years	65 to 74 years	75 years and over	Percent female	Total persons 1990	Total persons 1980	Percent change 1980–1990	Percent change 1990–1999	Births	Deaths	Net migration	Number	Percent change, 1980–1990	Persons per household	Female family householder[1]	One person
	16	17	18	19	20	21	22	23	24	25	26	27	28	29	30	31
Reading, PA.................	9.3	7.6	8.0	51.5	336 523	312 509	7.7	6.4	42 701	32 481	11 533	127 649	11.4	2.56	9.1	23.5
Redding, CA.................	9.1	7.9	6.8	50.4	147 036	115 613	27.2	11.9	19 602	14 308	12 637	55 966	30.1	2.58	11.0	22.3
Reno, NV.....................	8.9	6.1	4.6	49.1	254 667	193 623	31.5	25.6	42 608	20 661	43 796	102 294	32.5	2.43	9.4	27.6
Richland-Kennewick-Pasco, WA	8.0	5.4	4.6	49.8	150 033	144 469	3.9	23.1	27 054	10 103	18 087	54 423	6.8	2.74	9.7	22.6
Richmond-Petersburg, VA	8.6	6.3	5.3	52.4	865 640	761 311	13.7	11.1	123 208	73 659	46 118	331 824	23.2	2.53	13.6	25.1
Roanoke, VA.................	10.5	8.0	7.6	52.8	224 592	220 393	1.9	1.4	26 239	23 175	662	89 694	9.5	2.43	11.9	26.5
Rochester, MN...............	7.6	5.2	5.5	51.4	106 470	92 006	15.7	11.8	16 359	6 319	2 858	40 058	22.6	2.59	7.5	24.6
Rochester, NY...............	8.0	6.6	6.3	51.3	1 062 470	1 030 630	3.1	1.6	142 021	84 500	-38 260	396 089	9.3	2.59	11.5	24.7
Rockford, IL.................	8.7	6.7	6.3	51.1	329 676	325 852	1.2	8.8	47 034	27 456	9 135	124 809	8.1	2.60	10.1	23.7
Rocky Mount, NC.............	8.8	7.4	5.8	53.0	133 369	123 141	8.3	10.2	19 571	12 997	7 769	49 360	17.9	2.66	16.7	23.6
Sacramento-Yolo, CA	8.0	6.3	5.2	50.6	1 506 792	1 099 814	34.7	15.5	233 792	108 267	110 240	556 448	33.7	2.60	11.8	23.9
Sacramento, CA...........	8.1	6.4	5.2	50.6	1 365 580	986 440	35.8	16.1	212 959	98 944	106 929	505 476	34.8	2.60	12.0	23.9
Yolo, CA.................	6.9	5.2	4.8	50.0	141 212	113 374	24.6	10.2	20 833	9 323	3 311	50 972	23.4	2.63	10.2	23.1
Saginaw-Bay City-Midland, MI	8.5	6.9	6.3	51.6	399 320	421 518	-5.3	0.4	52 901	31 832	-18 603	148 235	4.4	2.66	12.7	22.9
Salinas, CA.................	6.8	5.8	5.1	48.6	355 660	290 444	22.5	4.5	67 026	20 869	-35 893	112 965	18.0	2.96	10.4	20.4
Salt Lake City-Ogden, UT.....	6.7	4.6	3.9	50.3	1 072 227	910 222	17.8	18.9	217 976	60 274	33 627	347 531	20.1	3.04	10.0	20.6
San Angelo, TX..............	8.6	6.9	6.5	51.6	98 458	84 784	16.1	3.9	14 302	8 510	-2 947	35 408	16.6	2.63	10.5	24.8
San Antonio, TX.............	8.1	6.2	4.7	51.6	1 324 749	1 088 881	21.7	18.1	231 754	96 526	98 581	458 502	29.2	2.82	13.9	22.8
San Diego, CA...............	7.1	6.1	5.4	49.6	2 498 016	1 861 846	34.2	12.9	434 438	167 684	28 193	887 403	32.4	2.69	10.8	22.9
San Francisco-Oakland-San Jose, CA	7.9	6.1	5.6	50.3	6 277 523	5 367 900	16.4	9.5	923 125	440 028	117 504	2 329 808	14.1	2.61	10.7	25.9
Oakland, CA...............	7.8	5.8	5.1	50.8	2 108 078	1 761 710	18.1	11.4	316 016	146 753	73 263	779 806	16.8	2.61	12.1	25.1
San Francisco, CA.........	8.9	7.2	7.0	50.6	1 603 678	1 488 895	7.7	5.1	202 834	132 594	13 949	642 504	4.8	2.43	9.7	32.3
San Jose, CA.............	7.4	5.6	4.6	49.6	1 497 577	1 295 071	15.6	10.0	248 056	79 991	-16 874	520 180	13.4	2.81	10.3	21.7
Santa Cruz-Watsonville, CA	6.6	4.9	5.6	49.8	229 734	188 141	22.1	6.7	34 730	15 587	-3 155	83 566	16.4	2.66	9.6	24.1
Santa Rosa, CA...........	7.4	6.3	6.7	50.4	388 222	299 681	29.5	13.3	52 221	32 871	33 316	149 011	30.2	2.55	9.8	24.6
Vallejo-Fairfield-Napa, CA.	7.3	5.9	5.2	49.4	450 234	334 402	34.6	12.5	69 268	32 232	17 005	154 741	32.2	2.79	10.9	20.2
San Luis Obispo-Atascadero-Paso Robles, CA.........	7.8	7.8	7.2	48.0	217 162	155 435	39.7	9.1	24 733	17 104	12 677	80 281	37.9	2.53	8.5	23.8
Santa Barbara-Santa Maria-Lompoc, CA	7.6	6.5	6.7	49.6	369 608	298 694	23.7	5.8	57 628	25 612	-11 003	129 802	18.7	2.73	9.3	23.0
Santa Fe, NM...............	9.0	6.3	4.6	50.8	117 043	93 118	25.7	21.8	15 925	7 465	17 733	45 053	38.3	2.54	10.5	26.3
Sarasota-Bradenton, FL........	11.3	14.0	15.2	52.6	489 483	350 696	39.6	12.4	50 404	69 429	81 323	216 553	43.7	2.22	7.8	27.4
Savannah, GA................	8.6	6.7	5.1	51.8	257 899	230 728	11.8	11.8	41 952	22 360	9 821	94 940	18.2	2.64	15.3	24.4
Scranton—Wilkes-Barre—Hazleton, PA	9.8	9.4	9.8	52.6	638 524	659 387	-3.2	-4.2	63 286	74 840	-12 838	246 491	3.5	2.50	11.5	27.9
Seattle-Tacoma-Bremerton, WA	8.0	5.5	5.2	50.4	2 970 300	2 408 749	23.3	16.7	435 229	208 257	259 246	1 155 361	27.3	2.51	9.3	26.0
Bremerton, WA............	7.5	5.5	5.2	49.2	189 731	147 152	28.9	24.7	31 154	13 605	25 811	69 267	31.2	2.65	8.5	22.1
Olympia, WA	8.1	5.8	5.6	51.1	161 238	124 264	29.8	27.4	22 452	12 419	33 898	62 150	34.0	2.55	9.7	24.0
Seattle-Bellevue-Everett, WA	8.0	5.5	5.2	50.4	2 033 128	1 651 666	23.1	14.8	290 744	138 860	151 927	809 292	27.7	2.46	8.9	27.1
Tacoma, WA...............	8.1	5.4	5.0	50.4	586 203	485 667	20.7	17.5	90 879	43 373	47 610	214 652	23.2	2.62	10.9	23.4
Sharon, PA.................	9.8	9.1	8.9	51.3	121 003	128 299	-5.7	0.4	12 844	12 427	500	45 591	2.1	2.54	10.3	24.6
Sheboygan, WI..............	8.7	6.9	7.1	50.1	103 877	100 935	2.9	6.0	12 575	8 977	2 989	38 592	8.8	2.63	7.1	23.3
Sherman-Denison, TX	10.7	7.7	7.7	52.0	95 019	89 796	5.8	9.2	12 785	10 618	6 766	36 847	8.5	2.51	10.2	25.2
Shreveport-Bossier City, LA .	9.5	7.1	6.2	53.0	376 330	376 789	-0.1	0.4	53 452	34 823	-17 904	139 815	5.1	2.64	16.7	25.6
Sioux City, IA-NE...........	8.8	6.6	6.5	51.1	115 018	117 457	-2.1	4.8	18 517	10 414	-2 344	42 934	1.4	2.61	10.5	25.5
Sioux Falls, SD.............	7.8	5.7	5.5	51.7	139 236	123 377	12.9	18.1	21 526	10 266	14 344	53 142	18.5	2.53	8.5	26.4
South Bend, IN..............	8.9	7.1	6.7	51.7	247 052	241 617	2.2	4.6	35 286	21 753	-1 061	92 365	7.1	2.54	11.4	26.4
Spokane, WA................	8.6	5.9	6.4	51.0	361 333	341 835	5.7	13.4	52 003	31 144	27 257	141 619	10.3	2.47	10.8	27.5
Springfield, IL..............	8.8	6.5	7.1	52.6	189 550	187 770	0.9	7.6	25 343	17 074	-362	76 345	5.7	2.44	11.1	29.0
Springfield, MA.............	8.0	7.4	7.0	52.3	602 878	581 831	3.6	-2.3	71 880	53 052	-30 689	219 958	8.7	2.58	14.1	25.4
Springfield, MO	8.3	6.8	6.4	51.5	264 346	228 118	15.9	16.6	37 123	24 261	32 025	101 791	21.0	2.49	8.9	25.0
St. Cloud, MN	7.5	5.6	5.6	50.9	149 509	133 348	12.1	10.3	19 838	9 067	5 057	50 711	25.6	2.79	7.5	22.0
St. Joseph, MO	9.2	7.6	7.9	52.1	97 715	101 868	-4.1	-0.5	12 427	10 467	-2 109	37 915	0.2	2.51	10.8	26.7
St. Louis, MO-IL............	8.7	6.9	6.1	51.9	2 492 348	2 414 061	3.2	3.1	348 105	222 545	-46 965	942 119	9.9	2.60	13.5	25.7
State College, PA	6.6	5.3	5.0	48.6	124 812	112 760	10.7	5.9	12 533	6 981	2 114	42 683	18.2	2.55	6.2	23.6
Steubenville-Weirton, OH-WV	11.2	10.2	8.3	52.4	142 523	163 734	-13.0	-6.5	13 589	15 328	-7 009	55 223	-4.1	2.53	10.9	24.7
Stockton-Lodi, CA................	7.3	5.6	5.1	49.2	480 628	347 342	38.4	17.2	84 945	36 647	35 370	158 156	26.9	2.94	12.7	20.9
Sumter, SC	7.8	5.9	4.5	50.6	101 276	88 243	14.8	11.0	15 692	7 622	-4 765	32 723	20.0	2.91	16.7	19.0
Syracuse, NY	8.2	7.0	6.3	51.2	742 237	722 865	2.7	-1.3	95 809	59 130	-44 334	272 974	8.9	2.61	11.2	25.0
Tallahassee, FL	6.6	5.2	4.2	52.1	233 609	190 329	22.7	11.3	32 462	15 778	10 271	88 233	33.3	2.50	13.9	26.2
Tampa-St. Petersburg-Clearwater, FL	10.0	9.9	9.9	52.1	2 067 959	1 613 600	28.2	10.2	255 780	247 374	205 853	869 481	32.4	2.32	9.9	28.0
Terre Haute, IN	9.1	7.3	7.3	51.3	147 585	155 476	-5.1	0.4	18 554	15 552	-1 981	55 824	-1.1	2.48	10.1	27.5
Texarkana, TX-Texarkana, AR	9.5	7.4	6.7	51.8	120 132	113 067	6.2	2.3	16 593	12 101	-1 273	44 868	9.6	2.61	13.8	24.2
Toledo, OH.................	8.2	6.5	6.2	52.1	614 128	616 864	-0.4	-0.8	83 447	52 348	-34 642	230 681	4.7	2.59	12.5	26.1
Topeka, KS	8.9	6.9	6.7	51.8	160 976	154 916	3.9	6.1	21 932	14 493	-2 795	63 768	8.4	2.46	10.5	27.6

1. No spouse present.

Table C. Metropolitan Areas — **Vital Statistics, Health Resources, and Crime**

Area Name	Births, average 1996–1998 Total	Rate[1]	Deaths, average 1996–1998 Number Total	Infant[2]	Rate Total[1]	Infant[3]	Physicians[4] 1998 Number	Rate[5]	Hospitals[4] 1998 Number	Beds Number	Rate[5]	Medicare enrollees 1999	Serious crimes known to police, 1998[6] Total Number	Rate[7]
	32	33	34	35	36	37	38	39	40	41	42	43	44	45
Reading, PA..............	4 433	12.5	3 663	37	10.3	8.3	676	190	3	874	246	60 126	11 878	3 447
Redding, CA..............	1 999	12.3	1 674	13	10.3	6.3	399	243	5	656	399	30 619	7 327	4 435
Reno, NV..............	4 754	15.5	2 450	33	8.0	6.9	801	255	4	1 009	322	38 743	15 576	4 890
Richland-Kennewick-Pasco, WA	3 051	16.8	1 152	18	6.4	5.8	287	157	4	430	235	20 435	8 003	4 469
Richmond-Petersburg, VA	13 104	13.8	8 313	113	8.8	8.6	2 692	281	14	3 804	397	125 756	47 665	5 011
Roanoke, VA..............	2 706	11.9	2 546	13	11.1	5.2	727	319	3	1 079	474	40 570	8 094	3 512
Rochester, MN..............	1 732	15.1	740	7	6.4	4.2	1 438	1 232	3	1 343	1 151	13 725	3 311	2 865
Rochester, NY..............	14 057	13.0	9 315	109	8.6	7.7	3 055	282	16	3 823	353	162 392	42 766	3 936
Rockford, IL..............	5 013	14.1	3 077	37	8.7	7.3	710	199	6	1 068	299	51 449	NA	NA
Rocky Mount, NC..............	2 011	13.9	1 431	24	9.9	11.9	194	133	3	412	282	22 338	8 450	5 744
Sacramento-Yolo, CA	24 165	14.6	12 411	149	7.5	6.2	3 954	235	17	3 841	228	220 087	87 180	5 201
Sacramento, CA..............	22 028	14.6	11 373	135	7.6	6.2	3 449	225	15	3 672	240	203 071	80 468	5 288
Yolo, CA..............	2 137	14.1	1 038	14	6.8	6.4	505	328	2	169	110	17 016	6 712	4 339
Saginaw-Bay City-Midland, MI	5 216	13.0	3 513	42	8.7	8.1	774	193	5	1 496	372	61 617	15 567	4 053
Salinas, CA..............	6 659	18.6	2 286	39	6.4	5.9	743	203	4	675	185	42 526	14 601	3 985
Salt Lake City-Ogden, UT.....	25 133	20.1	7 007	152	5.6	6.1	2 799	221	13	2 756	217	118 101	82 143	6 534
San Angelo, TX..............	1 554	15.2	966	9	9.5	6.0	203	198	3	478	465	15 679	5 472	5 244
San Antonio, TX..............	25 468	16.9	10 878	187	7.2	7.3	4 173	271	19	4 312	280	184 261	94 060	6 122
San Diego, CA..............	43 942	16.1	18 713	236	6.9	5.4	7 405	266	25	6 828	246	336 516	108 908	3 951
San Francisco-Oakland-San Jose, CA..............	96 809	14.4	47 986	498	7.1	5.2	20 681	303	81	20 160	296	829 269	313 907	4 627
Oakland, CA..............	33 168	14.6	16 211	187	7.1	5.6	5 517	238	27	5 829	251	270 633	133 624	5 814
San Francisco, CA..............	20 947	12.5	13 805	94	8.3	4.5	8 054	478	22	6 608	393	243 093	75 775	4 504
San Jose, CA..............	26 600	16.4	8 922	129	5.5	4.9	4 356	265	15	4 488	273	164 906	55 571	3 411
Santa Cruz-Watsonville, CA	3 540	14.8	1 679	19	7.0	5.5	564	232	2	395	163	28 364	9 985	4 101
Santa Rosa, CA..............	5 462	12.8	3 713	25	8.7	4.6	1 142	264	8	889	205	62 630	17 232	3 971
Vallejo-Fairfield-Napa, CA.	7 092	14.5	3 656	44	7.5	6.2	1 048	211	7	1 951	393	59 643	21 720	4 376
San Luis Obispo-Atascadero-Paso Robles, CA	2 453	10.6	1 946	13	8.4	5.4	619	264	6	636	271	38 602	7 357	3 115
Santa Barbara-Santa Maria-Lompoc, CA	5 849	15.1	2 825	27	7.3	4.7	1 083	278	8	1 314	337	54 627	12 393	3 137
Santa Fe, NM..............	1 770	12.7	840	11	6.0	5.8	453	320	2	261	184	16 756	NA	NA
Sarasota-Bradenton, FL.....	5 420	10.1	7 876	29	14.7	5.4	1 723	317	6	2 175	400	156 931	28 192	5 141
Savannah, GA..............	4 352	15.4	2 488	36	8.8	8.2	673	236	4	1 256	440	38 955	17 539	6 048
Scranton—Wilkes-Barre—Hazleton, PA	6 272	10.1	8 176	37	13.2	5.9	1 375	223	14	2 934	477	130 608	NA	NA
Seattle-Tacoma-Bremerton, WA	46 263	13.7	23 447	261	7.0	5.6	9 350	273	35	6 574	192	398 831	199 178	5 870
Bremerton, WA..............	3 179	13.7	1 581	16	6.8	4.9	454	195	1	252	108	26 495	9 675	4 067
Olympia, WA..............	2 457	12.3	1 473	12	7.4	4.7	461	228	2	437	216	26 187	8 496	4 181
Seattle-Bellevue-Everett, WA	30 911	13.6	15 508	166	6.8	5.4	7 059	305	25	4 827	209	266 193	135 561	5 922
Tacoma, WA..............	9 716	14.6	4 885	67	7.3	6.9	1 376	203	7	1 058	156	79 956	45 446	6 851
Sharon, PA..............	1 358	11.1	1 418	7	11.6	5.2	237	194	4	638	523	24 230	2 590	2 173
Sheboygan, WI..............	1 335	12.2	1 023	6	9.3	4.7	149	135	3	421	382	17 373	NA	NA
Sherman-Denison, TX	1 453	14.3	1 213	9	11.9	6.2	177	172	3	540	525	18 340	4 800	4 650
Shreveport-Bossier City, LA .	5 635	14.9	3 811	62	10.1	10.9	1 070	283	12	2 091	552	57 257	26 172	6 883
Sioux City, IA-NE..............	2 050	17.0	1 135	17	9.4	8.6	227	188	2	681	565	18 414	7 432	6 130
Sioux Falls, SD..............	2 377	14.7	1 160	18	7.2	7.6	503	308	4	849	520	20 967	4 336	3 017
South Bend, IN..............	3 847	14.9	2 412	31	9.3	8.1	564	219	4	836	324	40 741	16 159	6 225
Spokane, WA..............	5 542	13.6	3 470	31	8.5	5.7	1 025	251	4	1 274	312	58 435	28 463	7 001
Springfield, IL..............	2 646	13.0	1 888	23	9.3	8.8	674	331	4	1 336	655	30 575	NA	NA
Springfield, MA..............	7 217	12.2	5 724	44	9.7	6.1	1 435	244	9	1 973	335	95 715	26 566	4 676
Springfield, MO..............	4 223	14.0	2 831	29	9.4	7.0	704	231	5	1 657	544	47 670	13 633	4 499
St. Cloud, MN..............	2 121	13.2	1 012	12	6.3	5.5	312	192	5	655	404	21 029	4 662	2 868
St. Joseph, MO..............	1 295	13.3	1 134	8	11.7	6.2	174	179	2	482	495	17 152	5 306	5 691
St. Louis, MO-IL..............	35 573	13.9	24 385	297	9.5	8.4	6 673	260	44	10 556	412	376 668	NA	NA
State College, PA..............	1 262	9.5	782	5	5.9	4.2	235	177	2	232	175	15 106	2 261	1 703
Steubenville-Weirton, OH-WV	1 389	10.2	1 704	17	12.5	11.8	156	116	3	643	478	28 129	1 384	1 193
Stockton-Lodi, CA..............	8 719	16.1	4 099	61	7.6	7.0	750	136	8	1 140	207	66 446	31 889	5 806
Sumter, SC..............	1 664	15.6	866	24	8.1	14.2	110	103	1	230	215	13 265	4 547	4 211
Syracuse, NY..............	9 341	12.7	6 458	63	8.7	6.7	1 951	266	9	2 545	346	111 972	24 247	3 266
Tallahassee, FL..............	3 573	13.7	1 782	32	6.8	9.0	573	220	2	812	311	28 200	20 603	7 767
Tampa-St. Petersburg-Clearwater, FL	27 631	12.4	27 596	225	12.4	8.1	5 762	255	33	8 131	360	464 530	151 536	6 690
Terre Haute, IN..............	1 951	13.1	1 638	16	11.0	8.2	257	173	4	661	445	25 105	NA	NA
Texarkana, TX-Texarkana, AR	1 780	14.4	1 350	14	10.9	8.1	215	174	4	711	576	19 654	6 330	5 064
Toledo, OH..............	8 390	13.8	5 681	54	9.3	6.5	1 647	270	10	2 860	469	88 429	35 181	5 940
Topeka, KS..............	2 365	14.3	1 623	21	9.8	9.0	482	292	2	642	388	27 122	NA	NA

1. Per 1,000 estimated resident population, average 1996–1998.   2. Deaths of infants under 1 year old.   3. Deaths of infants under 1 year old per 1,000 live births.   4. Data subject to copyright.   5. Per 100,000 resident population as of July 1 of the year shown.   6. Data for serious crimes have not been adjusted for underreporting; this may affect comparability between geographic areas and over time.   7. Per 100,000 population estimated by the FBI.

Table C. Metropolitan Areas — Crime, Education, Money Income, and Poverty

Area Name	Serious crimes known to police, 1998[1] (cont'd) Rate[2]		Education — School enrollment and attainment, 1990				Local government expenditures, fiscal 1997[5]		Money income 1989				Income and poverty, 1997			
			Enrollment[3]		Attainment[4] (percent)					Households Median			Percent below poverty level			
	Violent	Property	Total	Percent private	High school graduate or more	Bachelor's degree or more	Total current expenditures (mil dol)	Current expenditures per student (dollars)	Per capita[6] (dollars)	Dollars	Percent change, 1979–1989 (constant 1989 dollars)	Percent with $100,000 or more	Median household income	All persons	Persons under 18	Persons 5–17 in families
	46	47	48	49	50	51	52	53	54	55	56	57	58	59	60	61
Reading, PA	394	3 053	75 295	18.3	70.0	15.1	421.1	6 859	14 604	32 047	9.1	3.1	NA	8.8	14.1	12.3
Redding, CA	679	3 756	39 216	9.9	78.4	13.7	171.3	5 571	12 381	25 581	3.8	2.4	NA	18.1	28.2	27.8
Reno, NV	448	4 442	61 679	8.9	82.5	20.7	246.2	4 956	16 365	31 890	-2.7	4.5	NA	9.8	13.8	12.7
Richland-Kennewick-Pasco, WA	306	4 163	43 131	8.3	80.2	21.0	212.0	5 554	13 123	30 729	-16.0	2.5	NA	11.4	16.2	15.3
Richmond-Petersburg, VA	506	4 505	214 653	13.3	75.8	23.8	887.4	5 506	15 848	33 488	10.4	4.2	NA	11.6	16.9	15.7
Roanoke, VA	338	3 174	49 728	14.3	73.4	18.1	213.2	5 965	14 318	28 943	6.8	3.0	NA	12.4	18.8	17.9
Rochester, MN	266	2 599	28 118	15.4	88.0	29.5	141.6	6 824	16 214	35 788	6.4	5.2	NA	7.0	10.1	9.0
Rochester, NY	276	3 660	279 066	21.6	79.0	22.9	1 540.4	8 097	15 205	34 001	5.0	4.0	NA	11.8	18.5	17.9
Rockford, IL	NA	NA	82 011	16.4	76.4	15.6	352.7	5 815	14 273	31 567	-6.4	2.9	NA	9.4	14.9	14.1
Rocky Mount, NC	636	5 108	33 014	9.3	62.3	11.4	128.1	4 917	11 345	24 020	7.1	1.9	NA	16.8	24.5	21.4
Sacramento-Yolo, CA	601	4 600	418 766	10.8	82.6	23.4	1 547.4	5 119	15 407	32 733	12.7	4.3	NA	15.0	23.5	22.7
Sacramento, CA	589	4 699	367 436	11.2	83.0	22.7	1 413.1	5 113	15 570	33 195	13.0	4.3	NA	15.0	23.5	22.6
Yolo, CA	720	3 619	51 330	7.6	79.1	30.3	134.3	5 178	13 861	28 866	11.9	4.2	NA	15.8	23.6	23.8
Saginaw-Bay City-Midland, MI	539	3 514	113 353	13.2	76.2	15.1	462.6	6 693	13 040	29 156	-12.5	2.7	NA	13.2	21.0	19.6
Salinas, CA	574	3 411	97 096	10.0	72.9	21.5	357.4	5 384	14 578	33 519	13.3	5.3	NA	15.4	24.1	24.0
Salt Lake City-Ogden, UT	422	6 112	357 433	7.7	85.6	22.9	1 068.7	3 784	12 029	30 881	-1.0	2.9	NA	8.9	11.4	9.3
San Angelo, TX	392	4 852	28 123	5.9	71.0	17.0	102.9	5 150	11 482	24 348	0.1	2.3	NA	17.2	24.2	22.8
San Antonio, TX	431	5 691	380 795	12.8	72.5	19.3	1 528.1	5 343	11 828	26 048	2.7	2.9	NA	17.9	25.5	23.6
San Diego, CA	602	3 349	678 445	12.5	81.9	25.3	2 360.8	5 252	16 220	35 021	22.2	6.0	NA	14.2	22.0	21.0
San Francisco-Oakland-San Jose, CA	616	4 011	1 683 435	16.4	82.7	30.9	5 310.9	5 420	19 629	41 458	20.8	9.1	NA	9.9	15.1	14.9
Oakland, CA	739	5 075	565 117	14.8	83.4	29.9	1 830.7	5 195	18 782	40 620	19.6	8.1	NA	10.6	16.0	15.6
San Francisco, CA	630	3 874	395 462	21.3	82.4	34.9	1 108.0	6 094	22 049	40 493	22.6	10.5	NA	9.3	14.2	14.6
San Jose, CA	496	2 915	429 640	17.4	82.0	32.6	1 347.6	5 425	20 423	48 115	22.9	11.4	NA	9.0	13.6	13.5
Santa Cruz-Watsonville, CA	573	3 528	67 978	10.7	81.9	29.7	206.4	5 259	17 347	37 112	31.2	7.5	NA	13.1	21.3	20.7
Santa Rosa, CA	357	3 614	101 892	11.3	84.4	24.5	383.4	5 466	17 239	36 298	22.1	5.2	NA	9.1	13.6	13.2
Vallejo-Fairfield-Napa, CA	648	3 728	123 346	12.5	82.2	19.7	434.8	4 948	15 522	38 453	19.8	4.4	NA	10.7	16.5	15.8
San Luis Obispo-Atascadero-Paso Robles, CA	348	2 767	65 365	9.3	83.3	22.9	192.3	5 325	15 237	31 164	25.6	4.4	NA	12.9	18.5	18.7
Santa Barbara-Santa Maria-Lompoc, CA	474	2 663	109 709	11.8	80.0	26.6	328.9	5 287	17 155	35 676	18.5	7.4	NA	14.6	22.5	22.4
Santa Fe, NM	NA	NA	30 763	16.4	84.5	35.7	90.9	4 790	16 499	32 294	7.9	5.6	NA	10.7	15.5	14.9
Sarasota-Bradenton, FL	634	4 507	81 667	13.6	78.9	19.2	373.3	5 766	16 712	28 124	16.1	4.3	NA	10.0	17.1	16.8
Savannah, GA	570	5 478	66 320	18.4	72.7	17.2	247.7	5 047	12 659	27 038	12.6	2.8	NA	17.4	26.7	25.4
Scranton—Wilkes-Barre—Hazleton, PA	NA	NA	145 217	24.1	72.8	13.6	609.0	7 161	12 004	24 231	2.2	2.0	NA	10.8	16.2	14.5
Seattle-Tacoma-Bremerton, WA	469	5 401	741 152	15.0	86.7	26.4	3 154.3	5 733	16 507	34 421	4.1	4.5	NA	8.5	12.7	11.2
Bremerton, WA	406	3 661	47 813	10.7	86.6	19.8	233.8	5 562	14 311	32 042	0.9	2.7	NA	8.9	12.6	11.6
Olympia, WA	242	3 939	43 319	9.9	86.5	24.7	226.0	6 079	13 901	30 976	3.0	2.2	NA	9.0	12.8	11.4
Seattle-Bellevue-Everett, WA	419	5 503	499 758	15.9	87.7	29.5	2 007.1	5 727	17 804	36 126	4.7	5.3	NA	7.8	11.7	10.3
Tacoma, WA	735	6 116	150 262	14.8	83.2	17.5	687.4	5 704	13 439	30 411	5.4	2.7	NA	11.0	15.6	14.0
Sharon, PA	175	1 998	28 594	20.5	75.1	13.6	145.5	7 437	11 336	24 598	-14.5	1.6	NA	13.2	20.4	18.4
Sheboygan, WI	NA	NA	25 856	19.4	77.4	13.8	127.5	6 449	13 425	31 603	0.7	2.4	NA	5.7	8.0	7.4
Sherman-Denison, TX	302	4 348	23 758	10.3	72.1	14.0	100.5	5 170	12 201	25 240	-1.3	2.3	NA	13.9	20.4	18.6
Shreveport-Bossier City, LA	880	6 003	102 591	9.8	73.5	16.7	354.8	4 605	11 269	22 808	-11.2	2.4	NA	18.4	26.9	25.0
Sioux City, IA-NE	534	5 596	30 460	21.8	77.9	16.0	125.7	5 668	11 988	25 216	-7.2	2.3	NA	10.6	14.8	12.9
Sioux Falls, SD	252	2 765	35 231	20.8	82.7	20.7	126.1	4 590	13 223	27 843	-0.4	2.7	NA	8.3	11.4	9.2
South Bend, IN	637	5 588	67 863	31.6	76.1	19.2	240.6	6 170	13 277	28 235	-4.1	2.6	NA	11.0	16.9	14.8
Spokane, WA	554	6 447	100 683	14.3	84.4	20.6	427.5	5 912	12 804	25 768	-3.5	2.4	NA	12.2	17.1	15.1
Springfield, IL	NA	NA	47 550	17.0	81.5	21.9	174.2	5 518	14 829	30 299	-0.3	2.8	NA	9.9	16.6	15.6
Springfield, MA	1 218	3 458	170 224	22.5	75.7	20.8	682.1	7 167	14 122	31 750	16.3	3.5	NA	14.9	23.6	22.7
Springfield, MO	312	4 187	71 088	14.4	77.5	18.6	211.4	4 356	11 968	24 204	2.0	2.4	NA	12.0	18.0	15.5
St. Cloud, MN	152	2 716	48 493	16.6	78.1	16.9	171.9	5 641	11 498	27 328	2.5	2.3	NA	8.5	11.8	10.7
St. Joseph, MO	308	5 383	23 695	8.9	73.1	13.5	79.3	4 635	11 162	23 494	-2.9	1.7	NA	13.5	18.4	17.1
St. Louis, MO-IL	NA	NA	649 189	24.9	75.9	20.5	2 328.4	5 686	14 847	31 718	2.6	3.9	NA	10.8	16.4	14.6
State College, PA	105	1 598	50 857	5.9	83.6	32.3	111.7	7 868	11 854	26 060	4.6	2.9	NA	9.9	11.8	11.2
Steubenville-Weirton, OH-WV	118	1 075	34 367	17.5	72.0	9.5	122.0	5 757	11 487	24 110	-24.6	1.1	NA	13.8	21.1	19.0
Stockton-Lodi, CA	751	5 055	137 025	11.3	68.6	13.2	547.5	5 046	12 750	30 634	13.7	3.6	NA	18.4	27.3	27.5
Sumter, SC	809	3 402	28 487	12.2	69.8	15.0	91.0	4 790	9 997	22 386	9.6	1.4	NA	19.7	26.9	25.9
Syracuse, NY	298	2 968	203 913	21.3	78.8	20.8	1 022.8	7 785	13 668	30 705	7.7	3.0	NA	12.8	19.4	18.8
Tallahassee, FL	1 121	6 646	82 977	9.8	80.3	32.4	215.2	5 365	13 122	26 208	14.2	3.2	NA	15.8	20.4	19.1
Tampa-St. Petersburg-Clearwater, FL	990	5 700	424 681	16.2	75.1	17.3	1 638.9	5 216	14 374	26 035	14.8	3.0	NA	13.6	21.2	19.2
Terre Haute, IN	NA	NA	40 238	9.3	75.5	15.4	138.8	5 634	11 647	23 368	-7.3	1.8	NA	13.3	19.4	17.4
Texarkana, TX-Texarkana, AR	577	4 487	30 716	5.2	69.6	12.8	115.3	4 886	11 147	22 947	0.4	2.0	NA	18.3	26.6	24.3
Toledo, OH	547	5 393	175 227	16.7	77.6	17.4	604.0	6 157	13 710	29 120	-3.4	3.4	NA	11.8	17.2	15.1
Topeka, KS	NA	NA	40 682	12.8	84.4	22.3	149.8	5 533	14 091	29 878	0.7	2.5	NA	10.7	16.7	14.9

1. Data for serious crimes have not been adjusted for underreporting; this may affect comparability between geographic areas and over time.   2. Per 100,000 population estimated by the FBI.   3. All persons 3 years old and over enrolled in nursery school through college.   4. Persons 25 years old and over.   5. Elementary and secondary education expenditures, local government fiscal years ending between July 1, 1996 and June 30, 1997.   6. Based on population enumerated as of April 1, 1990.

Table C. Metropolitan Areas — Personal Income

Area Name	Personal income, 1998												
		Per capita[1]						Transfer payments					
									Government payments to individuals				
	Total (mil dol)	Percent change, 1997–1998	Dollars	Rank	Wages and salaries[2] (mil dol)	Proprietor's income (mil dol)	Dividends, interest, and rent (mil dol)	Total (mil dol)	Total (mil dol)	Social Security (mil dol)	Medical payments (mil dol)	Income mainte-nance (mil dol)	Unemploy-ment insurance (mil dol)
	62	63	64	65	66	67	68	69	70	71	72	73	74
Reading, PA	9 787	4.6	27 511	83	5 897	806	1 806	1 408	1 339	613	540	89	44
Redding, CA	3 609	4.1	21 986	253	1 744	505	711	779	748	282	281	116	21
Reno, NV	10 342	6.6	33 040	22	6 384	848	2 778	900	850	376	287	56	33
Richland-Kennewick-Pasco, WA	4 170	4.4	22 829	218	2 825	291	706	586	549	215	186	56	38
Richmond-Petersburg, VA	27 267	4.8	28 635	61	20 120	1 289	4 941	2 892	2 717	1 272	991	246	20
Roanoke, VA	6 297	5.0	27 624	80	4 615	372	1 300	834	792	374	241	60	7
Rochester, MN	3 611	9.0	30 880	33	2 980	205	703	334	310	141	125	24	5
Rochester, NY	29 603	3.5	27 390	87	19 394	1 740	5 526	4 601	4 380	1 706	1 820	569	75
Rockford, IL	9 258	5.0	25 938	121	6 253	498	1 780	1 139	1 068	550	355	101	34
Rocky Mount, NC	3 207	2.8	21 979	254	2 019	234	512	555	529	191	222	75	12
Sacramento-Yolo, CA	46 278	7.2	27 102	X	29 525	4 111	8 129	6 252	5 938	1 937	2 341	1 058	138
Sacramento, CA	42 325	7.7	27 232	92	26 467	3 693	7 325	5 768	5 483	1 782	2 173	980	124
Yolo, CA	3 954	2.7	25 791	124	3 058	418	803	484	455	155	168	78	14
Saginaw-Bay City-Midland, MI	10 044	2.8	25 010	143	6 822	454	1 929	1 519	1 445	656	525	166	45
Salinas, CA	10 333	5.8	28 185	68	5 250	1 852	2 316	1 133	1 065	390	379	150	60
Salt Lake City-Ogden, UT	31 201	6.4	24 698	152	22 853	2 004	5 719	2 875	2 659	1 137	936	228	58
San Angelo, TX	2 273	5.5	22 140	244	1 365	175	457	367	351	143	146	30	4
San Antonio, TX	36 655	6.0	23 800	181	23 252	4 464	6 204	4 868	4 616	1 545	2 015	599	61
San Diego, CA	76 502	7.6	27 657	78	47 165	7 219	16 001	8 697	8 196	3 031	3 180	1 174	135
San Francisco-Oakland-San Jose, CA	254 915	7.4	37 414	X	173 311	24 595	50 050	21 565	20 293	7 612	7 601	3 040	452
Oakland, CA	77 940	7.1	33 667	18	44 353	6 866	14 385	7 729	7 296	2 540	2 904	1 164	153
San Francisco, CA	76 080	6.6	45 199	1	55 462	9 843	17 272	5 782	5 467	2 152	1 952	866	98
San Jose, CA	67 034	8.9	40 828	4	57 686	4 843	11 327	4 383	4 076	1 527	1 513	586	92
Santa Cruz-Watsonville, CA	7 613	5.9	31 302	30	3 435	764	1 598	722	677	264	238	85	32
Santa Rosa, CA	13 408	7.8	30 911	32	6 488	1 362	3 163	1 436	1 355	608	478	139	29
Vallejo-Fairfield-Napa, CA	12 841	6.9	25 874	122	5 886	916	2 305	1 513	1 422	522	516	200	48
San Luis Obispo-Atascadero-Paso Robles, CA	5 807	5.7	24 807	147	2 746	783	1 551	792	748	364	225	81	16
Santa Barbara-Santa Maria-Lompoc, CA	11 177	5.2	28 698	59	5 947	1 356	3 193	1 199	1 127	516	355	137	25
Santa Fe, NM	4 145	7.0	29 375	48	2 636	337	1 136	354	329	158	106	29	5
Sarasota-Bradenton, FL	18 558	5.1	34 178	15	7 337	1 165	7 142	2 871	2 774	1 517	1 020	103	15
Savannah, GA	7 170	5.8	25 135	141	4 537	499	1 342	1 000	943	382	355	124	10
Scranton—Wilkes-Barre—Hazleton, PA	14 641	3.4	23 764	184	8 349	1 131	2 850	3 167	3 048	1 223	1 287	188	110
Seattle-Tacoma-Bremerton, WA	112 135	9.1	32 762	X	77 383	9 082	20 182	10 898	10 223	4 009	3 503	930	415
Bremerton, WA	5 347	2.6	22 957	211	3 155	268	1 230	661	617	228	212	61	33
Olympia, WA	5 035	5.7	24 895	145	2 766	286	957	683	643	262	203	55	32
Seattle-Bellevue-Everett, WA	85 191	10.4	36 854	11	62 793	7 658	15 054	7 238	6 778	2 740	2 313	563	259
Tacoma, WA	16 561	5.8	24 500	161	8 668	870	2 941	2 316	2 185	779	775	251	91
Sharon, PA	2 585	4.4	21 231	275	1 414	200	483	557	533	243	211	44	11
Sheboygan, WI	2 876	5.9	26 149	114	1 933	164	603	337	317	178	104	14	11
Sherman-Denison, TX	2 287	6.4	22 417	237	1 358	114	395	428	410	168	175	27	6
Shreveport-Bossier City, LA	8 630	4.3	22 858	214	5 440	640	1 553	1 498	1 434	522	636	171	15
Sioux City, IA-NE	2 909	4.5	24 173	172	1 881	219	526	398	373	175	138	30	6
Sioux Falls, SD	4 686	7.0	29 131	52	3 163	487	884	437	411	206	154	20	2
South Bend, IN	6 657	4.9	25 782	125	4 254	446	1 309	884	836	414	317	68	9
Spokane, WA	9 573	4.5	23 450	196	6 164	610	1 951	1 573	1 492	554	544	153	60
Springfield, IL	5 552	4.3	27 215	94	3 821	396	1 141	684	644	306	220	67	20
Springfield, MA	15 409	4.6	26 131	115	8 805	924	2 666	2 970	2 866	895	1 477	303	74
Springfield, MO	7 130	4.5	23 399	198	4 577	734	1 409	1 045	991	427	394	78	11
St. Cloud, MN	3 670	10.1	22 539	232	2 624	274	723	449	416	174	152	31	13
St. Joseph, MO	2 184	4.4	22 443	236	1 299	137	427	392	374	161	154	30	5
St. Louis, MO-IL	74 516	4.2	29 089	53	49 505	4 059	15 771	9 285	8 821	3 836	3 552	832	155
State College, PA	3 072	4.3	23 272	202	2 078	321	584	358	332	148	103	22	10
Steubenville-Weirton, OH-WV	2 723	3.7	20 224	295	1 579	134	518	668	642	288	244	47	8
Stockton-Lodi, CA	11 440	3.9	20 813	285	6 035	1 132	1 925	2 154	2 051	600	867	399	71
Sumter, SC	1 943	4.7	17 294	313	1 341	84	290	363	344	121	133	58	5
Syracuse, NY	17 797	4.2	24 219	171	11 422	1 137	3 059	3 013	2 863	1 146	1 185	325	45
Tallahassee, FL	6 472	6.6	24 978	144	4 960	326	1 032	751	705	262	255	104	8
Tampa-St. Petersburg-Clearwater, FL	61 373	6.7	27 224	93	36 766	3 196	14 408	10 181	9 781	4 492	3 918	673	90
Terre Haute, IN	3 144	4.6	21 154	279	1 969	175	644	581	553	245	214	43	9
Texarkana, TX-Texarkana, AR	2 535	1.7	20 640	290	1 475	236	468	482	461	165	205	57	8
Toledo, OH	15 907	3.0	26 077	118	11 052	900	3 025	2 419	2 295	877	936	230	41
Topeka, KS	4 345	5.0	25 508	134	3 292	233	870	597	568	251	185	44	10

1. Based on the resident population estimated as of July 1 of the year shown.   2. Includes other labor income.

Table C. Metropolitan Areas — Earnings, Social Security, and Housing

Area Name	Earnings, 1998									Social Security bene-ficiaries, December 1998		Housing units, 1990		
			Percent by selected industries											
			Goods-related[1]		Service-related and other[2]							Supple-mental Security Income recipients, December 1998		
	Total (mil dol)	Farm	Total	Manu-facturing	Total	Retail trade	Finance, insur-ance, and real estate	Services	Govern-ment	Number	Rate[3]		Total	Percent change, 1980–1990
	75	76	77	78	79	80	81	82	83	84	85	86	87	88
Reading, PA	6 703	0.8	35.5	29.4	53.0	9.2	6.4	25.8	10.7	67 215	189	5 281	134 482	12.1
Redding, CA	2 250	0.5	NA	9.2	NA	12.5	4.0	30.3	19.2	34 394	209	7 813	60 552	27.6
Reno, NV	7 232	0.0	18.2	8.3	67.5	9.4	7.3	35.7	14.3	43 543	139	3 656	112 193	30.4
Richland-Kennewick-Pasco, WA	3 116	7.1	NA	7.9	NA	7.9	2.4	28.8	18.6	23 655	129	2 329	58 541	4.6
Richmond-Petersburg, VA	21 409	0.1	NA	14.7	NA	8.9	12.6	22.9	19.7	143 981	150	18 275	355 207	23.9
Roanoke, VA	4 987	0.0	NA	15.7	NA	10.8	8.6	27.7	13.6	43 930	193	5 033	95 467	9.5
Rochester, MN	3 185	0.7	NA	22.3	62.6	7.1	3.6	45.6	9.0	16 213	139	1 360	41 603	21.1
Rochester, NY	21 133	0.5	NA	32.1	NA	8.1	4.9	25.9	13.9	188 114	174	24 222	421 684	8.9
Rockford, IL	6 751	0.6	43.6	37.7	46.1	7.5	5.1	21.3	9.7	59 920	168	5 520	131 195	8.8
Rocky Mount, NC	2 253	4.6	NA	26.5	NA	10.3	D	17.2	15.0	26 096	179	6 366	52 851	14.9
Sacramento-Yolo, CA	33 637	0.6	15.6	8.6	53.8	9.2	8.6	25.7	30.0	235 521	140	58 016	609 904	30.8
Sacramento, CA	30 161	0.3	15.7	8.6	54.1	9.0	9.0	26.7	29.9	216 794	142	53 577	556 904	31.7
Yolo, CA	3 476	3.4	14.6	8.3	51.1	10.7	4.5	16.8	30.9	18 727	122	4 439	53 000	21.5
Saginaw-Bay City-Midland, MI	7 276	0.1	NA	39.1	NA	8.3	3.8	23.0	11.3	72 682	181	10 311	155 508	4.2
Salinas, CA	7 102	15.5	10.2	5.3	53.0	8.8	6.4	22.4	21.3	47 704	130	8 522	121 224	17.1
Salt Lake City-Ogden, UT	24 856	0.1	21.1	12.8	60.6	10.3	9.3	25.8	18.3	133 214	105	12 564	370 967	21.0
San Angelo, TX	1 540	0.1	20.7	11.4	53.5	10.0	4.9	24.4	25.9	17 746	173	2 288	40 135	22.1
San Antonio, TX	27 716	0.2	15.4	7.1	59.5	10.1	8.4	24.9	24.9	209 380	136	38 673	512 927	33.2
San Diego, CA	54 385	0.6	17.8	12.0	57.6	9.4	8.2	30.7	23.9	359 709	129	74 347	946 240	31.4
San Francisco-Oakland-San Jose, CA	197 906	0.3	NA	19.1	NA	7.9	9.5	33.0	11.7	848 201	124	197 797	2 457 201	14.7
Oakland, CA	51 219	0.1	22.3	14.9	62.1	9.0	7.8	30.3	15.6	284 891	123	68 385	820 279	17.8
San Francisco, CA	65 306	0.1	NA	7.3	NA	7.8	17.2	37.6	10.9	233 510	139	62 494	680 010	5.8
San Jose, CA	62 530	0.2	40.4	35.9	52.1	5.9	4.0	32.3	7.3	165 361	101	40 213	540 240	14.0
Santa Cruz-Watsonville, CA	4 200	5.4	21.4	14.5	57.8	11.6	5.1	30.5	15.4	31 012	128	5 354	91 878	13.6
Santa Rosa, CA	7 850	1.5	27.2	17.9	57.6	11.0	8.4	27.3	13.7	68 926	159	9 453	161 062	29.7
Vallejo-Fairfield-Napa, CA.	6 802	1.3	NA	13.3	NA	11.6	4.4	24.5	25.3	64 501	130	11 898	163 732	31.7
San Luis Obispo-Atascad-ero-Paso Robles, CA	3 529	3.2	17.3	8.1	57.7	13.0	6.1	25.8	21.9	42 674	182	4 990	90 200	35.1
Santa Barbara-Santa Maria-Lompoc, CA	7 304	4.6	18.4	11.6	57.9	10.2	6.7	31.4	19.1	59 571	153	8 654	138 149	20.2
Santa Fe, NM	2 973	0.1	8.6	2.7	NA	10.0	7.2	30.1	39.8	18 856	133	1 919	49 029	40.5
Sarasota-Bradenton, FL	8 503	1.7	NA	9.8	NA	12.6	8.6	41.6	10.8	168 123	310	6 514	272 300	38.3
Savannah, GA	5 036	0.0	NA	19.0	NA	9.9	4.6	28.9	18.6	45 155	158	7 954	106 219	21.6
Scranton—Wilkes-Barre—Hazleton, PA	9 480	0.1	NA	NA	NA	10.0	6.2	26.0	14.7	146 898	239	14 370	267 886	2.9
Seattle-Tacoma-Bremerton, WA	86 464	0.1	NA	16.1	NA	8.3	7.2	31.4	16.9	443 908	130	55 276	1 226 489	26.0
Bremerton, WA	3 422	0.1	7.6	2.2	35.0	8.4	3.5	19.0	57.3	29 353	126	3 438	74 038	29.2
Olympia, WA	3 052	0.9	12.0	6.0	44.4	10.1	4.4	23.1	42.6	30 433	150	3 184	66 464	31.1
Seattle-Bellevue-Everett, WA	70 451	0.1	NA	17.8	NA	8.0	7.5	33.5	12.0	293 087	127	34 580	857 145	26.5
Tacoma, WA	9 539	0.3	18.8	11.8	50.2	10.2	6.5	23.0	30.6	91 035	135	14 074	228 842	22.1
Sharon, PA	1 614	0.6	35.5	29.9	51.8	11.3	3.9	26.3	12.1	27 235	223	3 059	48 689	2.2
Sheboygan, WI	2 097	1.0	52.9	46.8	35.7	7.4	4.4	16.8	10.4	19 497	177	1 253	40 695	9.0
Sherman-Denison, TX	1 472	0.2	39.3	32.0	48.6	11.1	6.4	23.0	11.9	20 410	199	2 007	44 223	12.0
Shreveport-Bossier City, LA .	6 080	0.0	24.2	14.3	52.3	9.2	4.2	27.0	23.6	64 844	171	13 972	160 974	11.5
Sioux City, IA-NE	2 100	1.0	NA	D	NA	9.5	5.3	28.1	12.2	20 682	172	2 081	45 557	0.9
Sioux Falls, SD	3 651	2.1	NA	13.8	NA	9.8	11.9	28.7	9.7	24 011	147	1 958	55 603	15.8
South Bend, IN	4 699	0.3	NA	21.7	NA	9.2	6.1	32.3	10.1	45 266	175	3 971	97 956	7.4
Spokane, WA	6 774	0.2	20.7	13.5	59.1	10.7	7.4	27.1	20.0	64 680	158	8 435	150 105	9.0
Springfield, IL	4 217	0.7	NA	3.9	NA	7.4	8.8	32.0	30.5	36 164	177	4 445	81 523	5.2
Springfield, MA	9 730	0.3	22.9	17.6	56.6	9.7	7.3	29.4	20.3	107 423	182	21 569	233 093	9.0
Springfield, MO	5 311	0.1	NA	16.1	NA	13.4	6.3	27.9	12.7	53 354	175	6 097	109 789	20.3
St. Cloud, MN	2 898	2.2	NA	19.0	NA	16.3	4.3	22.2	15.5	22 807	141	1 796	55 327	23.6
St. Joseph, MO	1 435	0.6	NA	22.4	NA	10.1	NA	25.3	15.5	19 282	198	2 248	41 493	-0.5
St. Louis, MO-IL	53 564	0.2	NA	19.9	NA	8.5	8.3	29.0	12.4	432 140	169	49 504	1 027 136	11.2
State College, PA	2 399	0.5	18.7	13.8	41.8	7.7	3.6	21.7	38.9	16 653	125	1 520	46 195	16.8
Steubenville-Weirton, OH-WV	1 713	0.1	NA	37.6	NA	8.2	2.5	22.5	12.3	31 589	235	3 434	59 446	-3.8
Stockton-Lodi, CA	7 166	4.6	20.5	13.6	55.5	10.6	6.6	21.7	19.4	73 894	134	23 644	166 274	22.3
Sumter, SC	1 425	0.5	NA	25.2	NA	8.4	3.2	17.0	31.8	16 416	153	4 494	35 016	18.4
Syracuse, NY	12 559	0.5	NA	20.0	NA	8.6	7.3	25.7	17.1	129 065	176	16 902	299 347	8.9
Tallahassee, FL	5 286	0.9	NA	3.2	NA	8.3	5.4	28.1	42.2	32 674	125	6 532	96 184	31.9
Tampa-St. Petersburg-Clear-water, FL	39 962	0.6	NA	8.5	NA	10.7	10.3	36.3	13.9	528 416	234	47 671	1 025 064	34.2
Terre Haute, IN	2 144	0.0	NA	D	NA	13.3	3.7	23.4	17.2	28 859	194	3 279	62 097	2.1
Texarkana, TX-Texarkana, AR	1 711	1.7	NA	13.9	NA	12.4	3.9	25.7	23.7	22 160	180	4 209	50 406	13.3
Toledo, OH	11 952	0.6	33.1	26.2	NA	8.6	4.6	25.7	15.0	99 065	162	16 157	247 243	4.7
Topeka, KS	3 525	0.2	18.1	12.0	59.0	11.3	8.7	25.2	22.8	29 213	177	3 586	68 991	7.1

1. Covers mining, construction, and manufacturing.
finance, insurance, and real estate; and services.
2. Covers private sector earnings in agricultural services, forestry, and fisheries; transportation and public utilities; wholesale trade; retail trade;
3. Per 1,000 resident population estimated as of July 1 of the year shown.

Table C. Metropolitan Areas — Housing, Labor Force, and Employment

Area Name	Housing units, 1990 (cont'd)								Civilian labor force, 1999				Civilian employment, 1990[5]		
	Occupied units										Unemployment			Percent	
	Owner-occupied					Renter-occupied									
				Owner cost as a percent of income											
	Total	Percent	Median value[1]	With a mortgage	Without a mortgage	Median rent[2]	Rent as percent of income	Substandard units[3] (percent)	Total	Percent change, 1998–1999	Total	Rate[4]	Total	Professional, managerial, and technical	Precision production, craft, and repair
	89	90	91	92	93	94	95	96	97	98	99	100	101	102	103
Reading, PA	127 649	73.9	81 800	19.7	12.5	412	24.7	2.2	182 574	0.1	7 441	4.1	166 292	25.2	13.1
Redding, CA	55 966	64.5	91 300	21.7	11.9	431	29.2	5.1	72 922	1.2	5 113	7.0	58 578	26.8	12.6
Reno, NV	102 294	54.1	111 200	23.4	12.2	508	26.6	5.7	173 249	-1.2	6 423	3.7	140 734	27.7	9.5
Richland-Kennewick-Pasco, WA	54 423	62.4	64 400	16.3	11.5	348	22.1	5.7	95 004	1.4	6 183	6.5	68 126	32.9	10.6
Richmond-Petersburg, VA	331 824	65.0	79 300	20.3	12.9	458	25.5	2.5	509 536	0.5	12 050	2.4	442 812	32.3	10.9
Roanoke, VA	89 694	67.7	67 700	17.9	12.2	363	23.6	1.8	126 438	-2.4	2 409	1.9	112 933	28.5	10.4
Rochester, MN	40 058	72.4	72 300	18.6	11.8	409	23.4	2.1	72 567	3.6	1 457	2.0	57 318	40.1	7.6
Rochester, NY	396 089	67.9	85 500	NA	NA	462	NA	1.7	573 245	-0.3	24 407	4.3	520 469	33.0	11.4
Rockford, IL	124 809	68.8	60 900	NA	NA	373	NA	2.4	201 168	2.7	9 099	4.5	162 794	25.8	13.6
Rocky Mount, NC	49 360	63.3	55 600	NA	NA	327	NA	7.1	67 076	0.2	4 162	6.2	64 829	21.5	12.9
Sacramento-Yolo, CA	556 448	59.0	136 700	NA	NA	530	NA	5.9	878 080	3.9	35 594	4.1	693 136	33.3	10.5
Sacramento, CA	505 476	59.7	136 700	23.4	11.7	532	29.3	5.7	787 880	3.9	31 625	4.0	626 876	32.9	10.7
Yolo, CA	50 972	51.9	137 800	NA	NA	509	NA	7.9	90 200	3.4	3 969	4.4	66 260	37.1	8.8
Saginaw-Bay City-Midland, MI	148 235	73.6	49 100	16.7	13.2	380	29.1	2.5	203 137	1.8	8 581	4.2	169 787	26.9	12.8
Salinas, CA	112 965	50.6	198 200	24.8	11.4	624	28.5	14.6	191 707	3.7	18 137	9.5	146 885	26.8	8.7
Salt Lake City-Ogden, UT	347 531	67.4	71 000	21.0	12.0	377	23.7	4.4	693 512	1.8	24 721	3.6	480 241	31.9	11.0
San Angelo, TX	35 408	62.3	49 600	19.8	12.8	364	25.1	6.2	50 157	-4.4	2 155	4.3	41 808	26.9	11.2
San Antonio, TX	458 502	59.6	57 200	NA	NA	379	NA	9.4	766 305	1.0	24 035	3.1	559 142	30.2	11.0
San Diego, CA	887 403	53.8	186 700	25.9	11.5	610	29.8	9.1	1 358 210	2.9	41 932	3.1	1 145 266	34.5	11.1
San Francisco-Oakland-San Jose, CA	2 329 808	56.5	257 700	NA	NA	689	NA	8.3	3 776 607	1.1	118 487	3.1	3 229 687	37.8	10.0
Oakland, CA	779 806	58.8	224 400	25.3	11.8	641	28.6	7.0	1 211 642	1.7	39 672	3.3	1 042 347	37.7	10.2
San Francisco, CA	642 504	48.3	332 400	25.6	11.7	708	28.0	9.2	956 925	0.9	23 226	2.4	865 380	38.4	7.9
San Jose, CA	520 180	59.1	289 400	24.9	11.5	772	27.4	10.6	962 821	0.0	29 227	3.0	806 917	41.1	10.6
Santa Cruz-Watsonville, CA	83 566	59.9	256 100	27.2	11.7	712	31.4	9.4	140 849	-0.6	8 852	6.3	117 904	36.3	10.7
Santa Rosa, CA	149 011	62.9	201 400	26.2	11.7	644	29.5	4.6	251 168	1.4	6 735	2.7	193 296	31.7	12.3
Vallejo-Fairfield-Napa, CA	154 741	63.3	155 300	25.2	11.8	600	27.9	6.2	253 202	4.1	10 775	4.3	203 843	29.2	13.4
San Luis Obispo-Atascadero-Paso Robles, CA	80 281	59.8	215 300	NA	NA	572	NA	5.7	110 612	1.8	3 615	3.3	97 417	29.3	12.3
Santa Barbara-Santa Maria-Lompoc, CA	129 802	54.7	250 000	25.0	11.3	653	31.3	9.7	199 462	1.9	7 713	3.9	180 217	32.7	10.7
Santa Fe, NM	45 053	68.8	109 900	21.6	11.8	485	26.5	5.8	73 010	-2.1	1 968	2.7	59 394	42.6	9.2
Sarasota-Bradenton, FL	216 553	74.0	84 300	NA	NA	515	NA	2.2	273 833	5.2	5 910	2.2	201 798	28.0	12.5
Savannah, GA	94 940	61.8	63 400	NA	NA	401	NA	4.6	135 962	1.4	5 677	4.2	112 046	27.8	12.8
Scranton—Wilkes-Barre—Hazleton, PA	246 491	69.2	60 400	NA	NA	322	NA	1.6	304 614	-1.3	16 996	5.6	282 064	24.7	12.3
Seattle-Tacoma-Bremerton, WA	1 155 361	61.0	118 100	NA	NA	492	NA	3.7	1 932 670	1.5	71 966	3.7	1 480 616	34.4	11.7
Bremerton, WA	69 267	64.3	89 100	21.4	11.9	449	24.7	3.9	93 323	2.2	4 679	5.0	78 930	32.9	16.0
Olympia, WA	62 150	64.7	79 700	21.0	11.7	459	26.0	3.6	101 037	1.9	4 641	4.6	74 539	36.4	9.6
Seattle-Bellevue-Everett, WA	809 292	60.6	135 900	NA	NA	514	NA	3.5	1 403 017	1.5	47 434	3.4	1 075 314	35.8	11.2
Tacoma, WA	214 652	60.3	82 500	21.1	12.4	435	26.2	4.3	335 293	0.8	15 212	4.5	251 833	28.4	13.2
Sharon, PA	45 591	75.0	41 900	17.1	13.0	320	26.4	2.3	57 899	2.1	2 898	5.0	50 027	23.3	11.8
Sheboygan, WI	38 592	70.3	59 400	18.5	13.0	360	21.5	1.7	60 541	-0.9	1 211	2.0	52 159	22.5	12.9
Sherman-Denison, TX	36 847	69.3	46 600	18.3	13.5	367	23.8	3.4	50 441	-0.3	2 255	4.5	42 133	26.1	13.8
Shreveport-Bossier City, LA	139 815	66.0	55 100	NA	NA	346	NA	5.5	185 313	-1.5	8 864	4.8	149 039	28.3	11.4
Sioux City, IA-NE	42 934	68.5	41 300	17.5	13.1	328	24.8	2.8	63 984	-1.9	1 619	2.5	54 471	24.6	13.0
Sioux Falls, SD	53 142	64.0	57 600	NA	NA	372	NA	1.8	102 432	2.4	1 792	1.7	74 222	27.2	10.2
South Bend, IN	92 365	72.0	50 800	17.1	12.4	401	25.3	2.2	134 879	-1.0	4 164	3.1	117 132	28.9	10.8
Spokane, WA	141 619	63.7	58 900	19.4	12.2	355	26.9	2.7	210 309	0.8	11 029	5.2	157 142	30.9	9.9
Springfield, IL	76 345	67.1	60 200	16.7	12.0	379	23.4	1.8	108 434	1.4	3 918	3.6	97 332	34.4	8.7
Springfield, MA	219 958	60.7	125 600	20.8	13.4	493	26.3	2.9	291 736	0.0	10 395	3.6	287 529	30.5	10.8
Springfield, MO	101 791	66.4	57 200	NA	NA	340	NA	2.5	165 820	1.2	3 932	2.4	127 700	25.6	11.1
St. Cloud, MN	50 711	70.5	61 300	19.8	12.5	389	26.9	2.5	96 433	3.0	2 898	3.0	73 824	24.1	10.7
St. Joseph, MO	37 915	69.5	41 500	NA	NA	303	NA	1.8	50 092	1.2	1 759	3.5	42 597	23.1	11.7
St. Louis, MO-IL	942 119	68.8	69 800	NA	NA	413	NA	3.0	1 321 714	0.0	48 382	3.7	1 176 958	31.3	10.6
State College, PA	42 683	59.8	74 700	20.3	11.8	447	31.3	4.5	65 357	-1.1	1 757	2.7	57 809	35.9	8.1
Steubenville-Weirton, OH-WV	55 223	75.4	43 900	15.3	12.2	300	24.4	2.0	56 635	-1.0	3 738	6.6	54 810	21.0	15.4
Stockton-Lodi, CA	158 156	57.6	121 700	23.3	11.8	488	28.2	12.4	252 954	1.0	22 127	8.7	195 575	24.2	12.5
Sumter, SC	32 723	65.2	56 900	NA	NA	355	NA	7.1	46 955	-0.7	2 585	5.5	37 746	21.8	14.9
Syracuse, NY	272 974	66.7	75 300	NA	NA	426	NA	2.0	362 811	0.0	15 538	4.3	348 527	31.2	11.0
Tallahassee, FL	88 233	59.7	70 500	19.8	12.5	429	29.7	5.1	149 337	2.6	3 890	2.6	119 309	38.7	7.2
Tampa-St. Petersburg-Clearwater, FL	869 481	69.3	71 300	22.6	12.1	447	27.2	3.1	1 201 360	2.4	32 861	2.7	923 652	29.3	11.0
Terre Haute, IN	55 824	72.2	38 100	NA	NA	305	NA	2.8	68 485	-1.6	3 039	4.4	63 645	25.8	11.9
Texarkana, TX-Texarkana, AR	44 868	70.0	46 400	17.8	13.2	344	25.6	4.4	55 987	-0.7	3 020	5.4	49 659	25.1	13.7
Toledo, OH	230 681	66.6	59 700	17.4	13.3	390	25.9	1.9	321 370	1.6	15 354	4.8	279 224	28.8	11.0
Topeka, KS	63 768	66.6	55 700	18.4	12.1	385	24.5	2.2	90 254	-0.5	2 803	3.1	80 143	32.4	8.6

1. Specified owner-occupied units. 2. Specified renter-occupied units. 3. Overcrowded or lacking complete plumbing facilities. 4. Percent of civilian labor force. 5. Persons 16 years and older.

Table C. Metropolitan Areas — **Nonfarm Employment and Agriculture**

Area Name	Number of establishments	Employment Total	Health Care and Social Assistance	Manufacturing	Retail trade	Finance and Insurance	Professional Scientific and Technical Services	Annual payroll Total (mil dol)	Average per employee (dollars)	Farms Number	Percent with— Less than 50 acres	Percent with— 500 acres and over	Farm operators Whose principal occupation is farming (percent)
	104	105	106	107	108	109	110	111	112	113	114	115	116
Reading, PA	8 024	143 449	15 694	41 596	19 416	5 674	6 212	4 139	28 853	1 586	39.0	5.0	63.0
Redding, CA	4 380	44 494	9 019	3 601	8 382	1 371	1 798	1 074	24 138	850	61.3	14.0	41.6
Reno, NV	10 674	161 330	15 048	12 262	19 630	5 470	7 123	4 458	27 633	285	56.1	17.5	36.8
Richland-Kennewick-Pasco, WA	4 298	60 632	6 947	7 038	9 416	1 352	7 371	1 809	29 836	1 926	51.2	17.5	54.6
Richmond-Petersburg, VA	26 717	452 442	51 911	54 015	59 502	41 594	21 532	13 695	30 269	1 858	35.8	10.8	42.2
Roanoke, VA	7 160	121 911	17 161	18 786	18 595	6 777	3 996	3 085	25 305	778	34.6	5.8	43.2
Rochester, MN	2 892	68 663	0	10 989	9 330	1 489	2 350	2 183	31 793	1 317	28.3	10.9	51.3
Rochester, NY	23 893	455 352	64 740	102 583	59 356	16 037	20 449	14 087	30 937	3 609	30.6	14.0	56.8
Rockford, IL	8 743	159 158	18 227	51 103	19 088	5 468	5 144	4 652	29 229	2 276	29.8	20.8	55.3
Rocky Mount, NC	3 237	57 771	6 700	16 739	7 582	2 113	1 247	1 449	25 082	787	31.4	22.9	63.7
Sacramento-Yolo, CA	38 667	558 297	69 033	47 034	76 453	38 145	32 153	16 495	29 545	3 971	63.3	10.9	48.9
Sacramento, CA	35 327	504 427	64 382	41 004	70 395	35 494	29 789	14 963	29 663	3 048	68.7	7.7	46.6
Yolo, CA	3 340	53 870	4 651	6 030	6 058	2 651	2 364	1 532	28 439	923	45.6	21.1	56.4
Saginaw-Bay City-Midland, MI	9 621	158 208	25 017	34 692	26 692	4 250	4 860	5 089	32 167	2 311	30.1	13.2	52.7
Salinas, CA	8 457	101 381	12 257	7 403	16 661	5 001	3 479	2 786	27 480	1 209	40.7	29.9	66.3
Salt Lake City-Ogden, UT	32 966	589 820	56 076	78 690	75 775	34 789	30 721	16 023	27 166	2 088	75.4	2.9	35.3
San Angelo, TX	2 565	34 098	5 714	4 314	5 394	1 151	1 008	740	21 702	880	34.9	33.2	46.8
San Antonio, TX	33 047	572 897	81 958	49 038	75 424	35 541	30 760	14 533	25 368	6 256	36.8	9.2	38.5
San Diego, CA	64 413	961 014	103 808	120 081	121 465	44 864	75 483	29 596	30 797	5 925	90.2	2.0	37.2
San Francisco-Oakland-San Jose, CA	192 225	3 156 939	310 859	468 980	327 321	172 208	261 270	132 862	42 086	8 135	65.3	9.5	49.4
Oakland, CA	56 811	886 967	100 909	115 400	99 287	44 139	57 320	33 030	37 239	1 045	58.0	13.9	45.6
San Francisco, CA	61 677	962 037	87 033	59 883	89 267	92 174	103 300	41 809	43 459	525	47.4	21.7	58.3
San Jose, CA	44 204	946 363	69 613	240 608	81 748	19 746	85 359	47 589	50 286	985	74.5	7.8	47.6
Santa Cruz-Watsonville, CA	6 737	74 213	9 655	8 824	12 368	2 242	4 163	2 113	28 472	722	75.8	3.5	59.8
Santa Rosa, CA	13 017	154 187	21 527	25 915	23 550	9 819	6 684	4 637	30 074	2 745	66.3	7.3	49.0
Vallejo-Fairfield-Napa, CA	9 779	133 172	22 122	18 350	21 101	4 088	4 444	3 684	27 663	2 113	64.3	9.9	47.0
San Luis Obispo-Atascadero-Paso Robles, CA	6 557	69 698	11 648	6 770	11 348	2 087	2 822	1 609	23 085	1 916	49.3	19.7	48.4
Santa Barbara-Santa Maria-Lompoc, CA	10 535	129 260	15 493	15 729	19 489	4 941	7 333	3 708	28 686	1 451	59.0	16.1	52.0
Santa Fe, NM	4 963	50 260	6 993	1 320	9 104	2 132	3 060	1 233	24 532	340	54.4	22.9	37.4
Sarasota-Bradenton, FL	16 280	238 738	30 770	19 394	32 719	7 217	9 475	5 548	23 239	1 012	59.2	12.2	47.2
Savannah, GA	7 407	112 080	15 512	15 972	17 422	3 363	3 760	3 001	26 776	306	35.0	13.4	41.5
Scranton—Wilkes-Barre—Hazleton, PA	15 188	245 900	41 026	50 450	36 013	10 840	7 372	5 786	23 530	1 698	26.7	4.7	52.5
Seattle-Tacoma-Bremerton, WA	100 438	1 454 970	171 673	228 408	179 728	69 954	88 728	55 624	38 230	4 671	77.3	1.4	42.3
Bremerton, WA	5 071	45 673	8 533	1 366	10 360	1 985	2 482	998	21 851	359	84.7	0.6	34.8
Olympia, WA	4 960	49 668	9 070	3 117	9 262	2 055	2 842	1 220	24 563	832	72.7	2.4	39.1
Seattle-Bellevue-Everett, WA	75 150	1 169 062	120 659	202 432	130 425	58 081	77 135	48 246	41 269	2 491	78.6	1.3	44.2
Tacoma, WA	15 257	190 567	33 411	21 493	29 681	7 833	6 269	5 160	27 077	989	75.4	0.9	42.8
Sharon, PA	2 954	44 553	8 393	11 285	7 596	1 089	758	1 016	22 804	1 030	20.4	4.7	51.7
Sheboygan, WI	2 584	53 132	5 050	20 772	5 947	1 764	1 631	1 485	27 949	968	32.2	8.5	61.7
Sherman-Denison, TX	2 518	38 179	6 828	10 479	6 752	1 841	892	958	25 092	2 080	39.6	8.7	38.6
Shreveport-Bossier City, LA	9 073	146 661	25 656	18 295	20 985	4 999	5 049	3 553	24 226	1 186	34.7	14.2	38.5
Sioux City, IA-NE	3 405	60 627	8 286	12 048	8 594	2 499	1 172	1 433	23 636	1 595	19.6	24.8	59.6
Sioux Falls, SD	5 527	96 691	15 992	13 450	13 360	10 876	2 880	2 378	24 594	1 931	22.6	26.3	60.4
South Bend, IN	6 597	120 449	13 954	20 972	17 523	5 338	4 969	3 226	26 783	666	41.3	13.7	45.6
Spokane, WA	11 703	161 001	25 847	21 670	23 451	10 009	7 126	4 285	26 615	1 643	44.1	17.3	43.4
Springfield, IL	5 631	82 178	17 435	3 987	12 567	7 075	3 887	2 106	25 627	1 345	28.8	31.9	60.4
Springfield, MA	13 630	224 710	40 115	37 519	31 433	19 354	7 749	6 193	27 560	957	52.7	2.6	50.9
Springfield, MO	9 229	144 195	22 934	22 896	21 468	6 050	5 274	3 326	23 066	4 897	36.0	5.6	39.1
St. Cloud, MN	4 515	76 696	10 063	15 810	13 003	2 271	1 983	1 938	25 269	3 816	17.9	6.8	63.8
St. Joseph, MO	2 583	36 831	6 135	6 841	5 453	1 565	1 061	888	24 110	1 596	23.3	14.0	48.0
St. Louis, MO-IL	66 394	1 193 331	153 446	178 881	145 681	65 210	66 727	36 695	30 750	8 702	28.6	13.7	45.0
State College, PA	3 116	44 202	5 086	8 711	7 807	1 772	2 649	1 023	23 144	788	26.8	6.1	57.0
Steubenville-Weirton, OH-WV	2 803	42 809	7 123	11 364	6 067	1 420	689	1 068	24 948	569	20.6	5.6	39.2
Stockton-Lodi, CA	9 830	143 285	19 747	22 561	20 891	6 333	3 798	3 785	26 416	3 862	62.6	8.3	59.3
Sumter, SC	1 892	34 515	3 629	12 594	4 954	932	526	774	22 425	396	35.9	16.7	46.2
Syracuse, NY	16 500	287 709	38 973	45 353	40 109	15 576	13 377	8 094	28 133	2 745	22.3	12.2	59.7
Tallahassee, FL	6 863	94 778	15 889	3 961	17 007	4 294	7 502	2 258	23 824	533	44.3	8.4	34.7
Tampa-St. Petersburg-Clearwater, FL	60 694	976 883	124 983	76 151	132 763	61 006	69 113	26 133	26 751	4 151	72.4	4.3	44.4
Terre Haute, IN	3 509	55 704	8 062	10 643	11 540	1 979	1 139	1 333	23 930	1 224	30.2	20.3	50.4
Texarkana, TX-Texarkana, AR	2 858	39 921	8 021	6 123	7 168	1 327	868	926	23 196	1 640	29.9	11.6	38.8
Toledo, OH	15 003	284 220	44 856	55 808	36 587	8 963	12 863	8 161	28 714	2 194	32.8	16.7	49.0
Topeka, KS	4 609	81 210	15 499	7 842	10 790	5 384	3 420	2 173	26 758	823	30.6	14.2	40.8

Table C. Metropolitan Areas — Agriculture, Land, and Water

Area Name	Land in farms Acreage (1,000) [117]	Percent change, 1992–1997 [118]	Acres Average size of farm [119]	Total irrigated (1,000) [120]	Total cropland (1,000) [121]	Value of land and buildings Average per farm ($1,000) [122]	Average per acre (dollars) [123]	Value of machinery and equipment Average per farm ($1,000) [124]	Value of products sold Total (mil dol) [125]	Average per farm (dollars) [126]	Percent from — Crops [127]	Live-stock and poultry products [128]	Percent of farms with sales of — $10,000 or more [129]	$100,000 or more [130]	Percent of land owned by Fed. Gov. 1997 [131]	Water consumption 1995 (mil gal/day) [132]
Reading, PA	222	-0.2	140	1	188	547	3 673	71	248	156 235	48.0	52.0	65.0	29.4	1.0	85.1
Redding, CA	317	-18.4	373	39	59	420	1 021	22	31	36 881	59.0	41.0	29.1	5.1	38.0	310.8
Reno, NV	772	8.6	2 709	35	42	1 326	498	32	23	79 011	67.0	33.0	34.4	7.0	68.9	153.2
Richland-Kennewick-Pasco, WA	1 176	-10.3	610	374	D	1 055	1 833	110	633	328 902	92.0	8.0	56.1	35.2	18.5	1 922.5
Richmond-Petersburg, VA	385	-7.2	207	D	207	492	2 225	51	94	50 799	68.0	32.0	36.6	10.0	1.6	1 341.3
Roanoke, VA	117	-3.9	151	0	53	301	2 011	33	16	20 276	28.0	72.0	26.9	4.1	26.6	39.1
Rochester, MN	304	-0.8	231	0	245	328	1 425	75	106	80 729	48.0	52.0	57.3	22.6	0.0	41.3
Rochester, NY	968	-0.9	268	14	787	348	1 339	84	478	132 497	58.0	42.0	55.5	24.1	0.5	873.6
Rockford, IL	716	-2.0	315	4	651	720	2 524	79	272	119 290	70.0	30.0	67.8	33.0	0.0	83.7
Rocky Mount, NC	347	-3.4	441	19	226	766	1 746	119	317	402 210	47.0	53.0	69.0	43.5	0.0	36.4
Sacramento-Yolo, CA	1 087	-4.5	274	456	615	775	3 038	57	613	154 465	82.0	18.0	40.2	16.1	27.0	2 240.1
Sacramento, CA	550	-11.1	181	162	234	580	3 336	36	268	88 086	64.0	36.0	33.6	11.7	32.5	1 150.1
Yolo, CA	537	3.4	581	294	381	1 420	2 732	126	345	373 666	97.0	3.0	62.1	30.6	4.1	1 090.1
Saginaw-Bay City-Midland, MI	553	-5.9	239	9	493	416	1 668	80	163	70 407	89.0	11.0	59.8	18.5	0.7	746.7
Salinas, CA	1 544	12.5	1 277	260	389	2 685	2 358	226	1 750	1 447 268	98.0	2.0	69.9	44.4	27.5	632.6
Salt Lake City-Ogden, UT	263	-36.6	126	69	107	370	2 439	40	85	40 633	56.0	44.0	29.5	7.8	16.0	797.3
San Angelo, TX	959	-6.1	1 089	44	217	554	564	52	86	97 586	31.0	69.0	43.6	14.4	1.2	256.8
San Antonio, TX	1 425	-1.1	228	33	601	310	1 403	28	151	24 114	50.0	50.0	19.9	2.8	2.5	891.5
San Diego, CA	475	-8.3	80	70	113	407	5 504	23	633	106 790	87.0	13.0	34.7	10.9	22.9	776.5
San Francisco-Oakland-San Jose, CA	2 135	-1.3	262	351	D	1 025	4 217	52	1 602	196 980	82.0	18.0	53.1	22.8	4.2	2 154.8
Oakland, CA	406	-9.6	388	41	85	920	2 172	31	109	104 280	75.0	25.0	43.3	13.0	2.7	758.1
San Francisco, CA	194	-14.0	370	5	D	1 063	2 766	55	193	368 434	73.0	27.0	61.7	25.7	10.8	254.3
San Jose, CA	319	-7.1	324	19	32	606	2 425	50	188	191 355	90.0	10.0	41.5	13.6	1.4	350.3
Santa Cruz-Watsonville, CA	71	34.2	98	21	28	573	6 234	67	248	343 234	95.0	5.0	57.9	29.8	0.1	72.2
Santa Rosa, CA	571	10.4	208	57	145	1 025	5 211	47	464	168 895	69.0	31.0	53.3	23.8	2.5	126.1
Vallejo-Fairfield-Napa, CA	575	-0.3	272	208	284	1 419	5 909	63	400	189 358	92.0	8.0	59.2	27.4	5.5	593.8
San Luis Obispo-Atascadero-Paso Robles, CA	1 302	-1.7	679	61	281	1 046	1 591	49	313	163 335	90.0	10.0	47.2	17.6	16.7	188.4
Santa Barbara-Santa Maria-Lompoc, CA	817	-2.4	563	104	157	1 378	2 716	82	660	454 680	94.0	6.0	52.9	27.0	49.5	322.2
Santa Fe, NM	D	D	D	D	D	D	D	29	D	D	53.0	D	20.0	4.7	28.5	51.0
Sarasota-Bradenton, FL	397	-12.1	392	63	125	915	2 465	57	264	260 643	90.0	10.0	45.4	16.1	0.0	170.6
Savannah, GA	87	27.4	283	D	32	360	1 342	45	13	42 278	79.0	21.0	32.0	8.8	14.2	753.1
Scranton—Wilkes-Barre—Hazleton, PA	258	2.9	152	2	176	303	2 060	51	98	57 551	45.0	55.0	45.7	12.1	0.1	183.3
Seattle-Tacoma-Bremerton, WA	244	-7.8	52	20	132	364	6 991	34	420	89 914	34.0	66.0	26.3	8.7	26.1	767.3
Bremerton, WA	19	91.3	53	0	6	267	5 591	26	12	34 075	33.0	67.0	19.5	2.5	2.5	40.4
Olympia, WA	56	-6.2	68	6	27	381	6 278	44	121	145 087	30.0	70.0	23.6	7.1	3.9	49.6
Seattle-Bellevue-Everett, WA	118	-13.1	47	9	75	384	7 435	33	217	87 198	34.0	66.0	28.5	10.5	31.3	479.0
Tacoma, WA	51	-13.8	51	5	24	336	7 273	30	70	70 612	40.0	60.0	25.5	7.7	28.8	198.3
Sharon, PA	167	3.5	162	0	113	248	1 595	45	46	44 753	39.0	61.0	48.8	11.5	0.3	85.4
Sheboygan, WI	182	-11.9	188	0	153	313	1 668	78	92	95 254	19.0	81.0	63.8	29.1	0.0	464.7
Sherman-Denison, TX	417	1.8	201	2	245	293	1 508	29	35	17 056	44.0	56.0	23.4	3.0	2.9	27.3
Shreveport-Bossier City, LA	335	-1.6	282	3	173	330	1 209	40	42	35 406	56.0	44.0	30.3	7.3	5.2	106.3
Sioux City, IA-NE	639	10.2	401	20	547	506	1 262	78	180	113 027	63.0	37.0	68.0	30.0	0.5	692.8
Sioux Falls, SD	725	-3.1	375	2	643	435	1 183	87	204	105 692	60.0	40.0	74.1	31.2	0.6	27.7
South Bend, IN	154	-10.4	231	13	140	537	2 258	68	55	82 850	73.0	27.0	56.5	18.8	0.0	94.3
Spokane, WA	590	-5.8	359	11	398	469	1 351	52	79	47 903	74.0	26.0	35.2	13.1	1.8	188.7
Springfield, IL	637	4.3	474	1	589	1 112	2 448	112	215	159 810	87.0	13.0	68.3	38.8	0.0	338.9
Springfield, MA	90	-1.6	94	2	43	326	4 176	33	65	67 525	78.0	22.0	41.5	13.0	1.5	258.1
Springfield, MO	777	-1.2	159	1	464	274	1 702	24	106	21 544	9.0	91.0	31.9	4.4	4.5	184.8
St. Cloud, MN	822	-0.7	216	42	623	223	1 075	72	392	102 687	19.0	81.0	67.1	29.0	0.4	46.0
St. Joseph, MO	408	0.1	256	0	323	312	1 193	51	73	45 510	74.0	26.0	51.2	13.0	0.0	60.7
St. Louis, MO-IL	2 159	-2.5	248	11	1 671	474	1 951	58	555	63 769	63.0	37.0	48.7	15.5	0.4	2 951.6
State College, PA	136	-2.9	173	0	93	522	2 761	51	51	64 109	26.0	74.0	58.8	23.2	0.0	33.6
Steubenville-Weirton, OH-WV	92	4.6	162	0	50	156	1 086	27	8	14 729	32.0	68.0	21.4	2.8	0.0	2 372.9
Stockton-Lodi, CA	809	3.2	209	519	559	1 017	4 667	82	1 180	305 465	73.0	27.0	65.3	33.6	0.3	1 816.8
Sumter, SC	139	0.3	352	5	95	362	994	66	60	151 952	52.0	48.0	38.4	20.2	0.9	32.1
Syracuse, NY	687	-2.8	250	3	484	264	1 099	67	284	103 291	30.0	70.0	57.9	24.6	0.1	1 369.5
Tallahassee, FL	125	-21.1	235	8	40	505	2 012	46	96	180 291	90.0	10.0	31.1	7.3	13.3	55.7
Tampa-St. Petersburg-Clearwater, FL	464	-15.9	112	61	183	415	3 788	29	452	108 869	69.0	31.0	38.5	12.1	0.9	474.5
Terre Haute, IN	392	-7.9	321	0	335	554	1 706	75	99	80 928	76.0	24.0	57.8	20.8	1.4	799.8
Texarkana, TX-Texarkana, AR	435	-0.5	265	11	240	295	1 285	34	87	52 898	22.0	78.0	32.7	9.9	3.7	157.9
Toledo, OH	581	-0.2	265	2	548	604	2 275	82	245	111 748	77.0	23.0	72.5	27.3	0.4	771.3
Topeka, KS	224	-1.3	272	12	148	280	1 084	39	29	35 362	74.0	26.0	42.0	9.7	0.6	42.9

Table C. Metropolitan Areas — **Residential Construction, Wholesale and Retail Trade, and Real Estate**

Area Name	Value of Residential Construction Authorized by Building Permits, 1999		Wholesale Trade, 1997				Retail Trade[1], 1997				Real Estate and Rental and Leasing, 1997			
	New Construction ($1,000)	Number of Housing Units	Number of Establishments	Number of Employees	Sales (mil dol)	Annual Payroll (mil dol)	Number of Establishments	Number of Employees	Sales (mil dol)	Annual Payroll (mil dol)	Number of Establishments	Number of Employees	Receipts (mil dol)	Annual Payroll (mil dol)
	133	134	135	136	137	138	139	140	141	142	143	144	145	146
Reading, PA	187 957	1 789	439	7 051	3 121.7	253.0	1 468	19 302	3 330.7	326.2	215	1 324	191.3	28.1
Redding, CA	103 983	804	217	1 786	566.6	51.9	713	8 113	1 354.5	140.3	199	878	80.3	14.6
Reno, NV	442 266	4 424	639	9 339	5 663.6	324.9	1 328	19 418	3 751.1	389.5	614	3 058	444.5	66.1
Richland-Kennewick-Pasco, WA	143 293	1 017	199	2 161	856.0	55.7	770	9 296	1 696.2	161.5	193	1 126	125.4	23.5
Richmond-Petersburg, VA	752 787	7 807	1 696	24 147	16 973.7	910.7	4 145	59 324	9 207.1	927.5	1 002	6 252	765.4	150.7
Roanoke, VA	84 177	1 062	514	6 837	2 541.8	216.7	1 249	18 869	2 888.3	295.7	253	2 318	156.1	40.0
Rochester, MN	164 406	1 385	125	1 176	605.4	37.5	583	9 254	1 431.6	136.5	124	654	72.9	9.7
Rochester, NY	479 885	4 282	1 536	19 113	10 744.4	751.2	3 977	61 350	9 177.5	886.7	815	6 678	754.3	139.4
Rockford, IL	175 847	2 056	607	8 000	3 183.7	256.8	1 331	19 691	3 221.4	313.8	286	1 335	179.6	26.5
Rocky Mount, NC	56 410	790	172	2 806	1 493.1	87.8	720	7 516	1 249.8	114.5	123	758	95.8	15.0
Sacramento-Yolo, CA	2 137 157	14 475	1 960	30 491	15 598.2	1 051.5	5 466	74 401	14 122.4	1 446.5	1 851	12 578	1 359.6	266.0
Sacramento, CA	1 953 264	13 019	1 678	22 662	10 598.1	793.7	5 008	68 625	13 095.7	1 335.9	1 662	11 273	1 181.7	236.0
Yolo, CA	183 892	1 456	282	7 829	5 000.2	257.8	458	5 776	1 026.7	110.6	189	1 305	177.9	30.0
Saginaw-Bay City-Midland, MI	153 490	1 360	465	5 794	2 525.4	190.8	1 995	26 027	4 300.9	405.2	304	1 407	142.7	24.3
Salinas, CA	335 614	2 058	473	7 530	4 747.4	267.9	1 558	16 413	3 035.9	327.9	386	1 837	236.4	38.9
Salt Lake City-Ogden, UT	1 063 408	9 539	2 441	34 414	17 191.0	1 146.0	4 459	73 571	13 702.6	1 264.8	1 464	9 093	1 049.0	184.6
San Angelo, TX	32 256	267	159	D	D	D	471	5 404	890.7	84.3	134	550	51.7	8.3
San Antonio, TX	907 908	13 705	2 026	26 607	13 362.1	852.9	5 105	71 460	12 898.4	1 217.3	1 492	9 360	1 168.9	212.6
San Diego, CA	2 668 332	16 295	4 159	53 589	26 543.9	2 273.7	9 109	119 022	22 215.3	2 241.1	3 742	23 069	3 250.0	573.9
San Francisco-Oakland-San Jose, CA	4 410 585	28 307	13 392	189 537	167 465.4	9 195.8	24 198	319 325	63 219.8	6 608.4	9 220	61 943	10 593.5	1 761.6
Oakland, CA	1 710 039	10 810	4 391	62 404	62 758.8	2 673.7	7 068	96 839	19 781.8	1 980.7	2 721	16 493	2 618.2	438.3
San Francisco, CA	758 343	4 392	4 157	43 484	29 296.5	2 038.6	7 417	88 243	16 906.1	1 888.0	3 167	26 410	4 773.9	834.7
San Jose, CA	993 444	6 880	3 468	66 542	68 095.4	3 891.8	5 278	79 921	16 673.6	1 696.7	1 968	12 585	2 456.4	372.8
Santa Cruz-Watsonville, CA	94 804	465	342	4 472	1 541.8	140.3	986	11 794	1 970.2	215.5	314	1 649	166.5	27.1
Santa Rosa, CA	408 199	3 036	619	7 430	3 069.7	259.4	1 808	22 190	4 146.2	443.7	576	2 394	329.3	48.5
Vallejo-Fairfield-Napa, CA	445 756	2 724	415	5 205	2 703.1	192.0	1 641	20 338	3 742.0	383.8	474	2 412	249.1	40.2
San Luis Obispo-Atascadero-Paso Robles, CA	244 914	1 648	244	1 904	561.5	46.8	1 132	10 917	1 780.7	182.4	319	1 243	149.7	20.9
Santa Barbara-Santa Maria-Lompoc, CA	166 817	810	469	4 282	1 636.0	137.5	1 653	19 187	3 183.5	354.0	557	2 613	357.8	64.3
Santa Fe, NM	81 538	919	176	1 335	381.6	43.4	905	8 423	1 497.0	157.4	216	921	122.6	20.5
Sarasota-Bradenton, FL	769 433	7 008	797	5 470	2 123.5	162.7	2 607	32 476	5 747.5	538.2	836	3 322	449.0	68.3
Savannah, GA	246 957	2 475	374	4 464	2 489.2	146.6	1 413	17 355	2 718.0	267.1	312	1 540	202.1	36.9
Scranton—Wilkes-Barre—Hazleton, PA	135 780	1 331	747	9 994	3 447.2	264.6	2 888	36 815	5 570.9	521.4	410	2 197	206.1	43.1
Seattle-Tacoma-Bremerton, WA	3 054 146	28 444	6 842	82 684	59 358.6	3 291.6	13 081	176 146	33 821.7	3 479.0	5 034	30 518	4 197.7	740.0
Bremerton, WA	134 085	1 148	135	925	330.9	29.9	773	10 338	1 722.1	179.5	240	1 053	103.4	16.3
Olympia, WA	209 908	1 963	201	1 805	580.3	57.5	730	9 008	1 616.8	166.3	218	884	89.7	13.5
Seattle-Bellevue-Everett, WA	2 145 618	19 967	5 725	70 630	53 828.5	2 877.1	9 289	127 844	25 014.6	2 583.0	3 869	24 174	3 608.8	629.0
Tacoma, WA	564 536	5 366	781	9 324	4 618.9	327.0	2 289	28 956	5 468.2	550.1	707	4 407	395.8	81.2
Sharon, PA	32 674	351	124	1 692	656.3	41.9	618	7 852	1 285.0	112.8	84	281	29.6	5.0
Sheboygan, WI	66 007	597	119	2 041	1 185.0	65.4	398	5 831	911.0	88.0	85	400	38.2	6.2
Sherman-Denison, TX	23 160	257	132	958	406.1	25.1	474	6 213	1 092.0	98.5	104	351	32.0	5.8
Shreveport-Bossier City, LA	141 995	1 111	608	7 673	4 066.8	224.1	1 613	20 627	3 465.8	318.9	345	1 628	158.4	29.7
Sioux City, IA-NE	30 066	297	239	D	D	D	603	8 649	1 248.5	127.5	127	747	68.7	12.3
Sioux Falls, SD	154 115	1 834	395	5 717	2 345.5	171.3	842	12 863	2 149.9	202.8	192	1 012	100.3	19.0
South Bend, IN	149 681	1 397	472	7 080	3 389.0	230.7	1 069	16 822	2 782.9	249.0	215	1 274	127.8	25.5
Spokane, WA	232 779	2 238	788	11 268	4 878.5	360.9	1 730	22 246	4 122.6	433.9	503	2 674	289.1	47.4
Springfield, IL	106 483	1 146	274	3 621	1 588.1	122.4	877	12 374	2 050.2	191.6	215	885	87.4	14.7
Springfield, MA	168 651	1 278	682	D	D	D	2 466	31 651	4 884.5	492.2	501	2 352	299.1	48.9
Springfield, MO	257 506	2 520	657	9 379	5 261.8	274.7	1 592	19 993	3 665.7	326.6	397	1 891	162.1	34.1
St. Cloud, MN	121 987	1 217	238	4 771	1 604.2	145.5	763	11 222	1 851.1	170.0	150	733	64.2	11.5
St. Joseph, MO	34 839	359	162	1 673	1 186.0	45.8	446	5 354	884.7	80.5	95	454	33.8	6.0
St. Louis, MO-IL	1 432 857	12 620	4 805	66 406	57 134.3	2 875.6	9 870	141 603	24 122.5	2 499.1	2 612	17 872	2 404.1	427.6
State College, PA	90 262	837	100	D	D	D	617	7 861	1 153.9	108.7	111	704	83.1	14.0
Steubenville-Weirton, OH-WV	11 228	149	100	1 021	335.9	26.1	556	6 335	828.7	81.7	86	310	24.9	5.0
Stockton-Lodi, CA	595 595	4 203	560	9 751	7 651.7	319.3	1 594	19 957	3 679.6	364.7	436	2 602	257.7	52.3
Sumter, SC	26 007	271	84	671	208.6	18.1	425	4 841	782.0	72.8	74	277	26.6	4.3
Syracuse, NY	158 300	1 505	1 206	15 611	11 660.9	571.3	2 895	40 997	6 099.5	606.6	553	4 605	428.2	100.4
Tallahassee, FL	205 437	2 229	281	2 990	1 102.7	88.7	1 195	16 706	2 424.2	245.9	316	1 894	206.4	33.9
Tampa-St. Petersburg-Clearwater, FL	1 963 304	22 980	4 304	53 358	35 721.0	1 808.6	9 142	128 351	24 184.1	2 199.6	2 759	15 239	1 804.9	323.2
Terre Haute, IN	49 115	496	176	1 838	774.7	47.0	675	11 487	2 635.1	184.0	106	545	45.0	9.3
Texarkana, TX-Texarkana, AR	22 095	364	183	2 601	1 212.1	75.5	612	6 734	1 194.8	104.0	112	585	65.1	9.3
Toledo, OH	274 528	2 297	988	13 914	8 164.5	476.7	2 475	37 164	6 083.6	583.4	532	3 298	382.7	72.3
Topeka, KS	102 770	865	204	2 298	947.1	65.9	768	10 625	1 619.6	166.7	199	1 216	88.8	22.4

1. Establishments with payroll.

Table C. Metropolitan Areas — Professional, Manufacturing, Accommodation and Foodservices, Finance and Insurance

Area Name	Professional, Scientific, and Technical Services[1], 1997				Manufacturing, 1997				Accommodation and Foodservices, 1997			
	Number of Establishments	Number of Employees	Sales (mil dol)	Annual Payroll (mil dol)	Number of Establishments	Number of Employees	Sales (mil dol)	Annual Payroll (mil dol)	Number of Establishments	Number of Employees	Sales (mil dol)	Annual Payroll (mil dol)
	147	148	149	150	151	152	153	154	155	156	157	158
Reading, PA	546	5 520	476.6	215.2	587	41 614	7 729	1 511	706	10 091	330.4	90.9
Redding, CA	304	1 636	127.0	51.6	177	3 526	635	119	402	5 070	161.7	41.7
Reno, NV	1 193	6 422	659.7	259.7	418	11 522	1 931	362	778	34 517	1 815.8	583.1
Richland-Kennewick-Pasco, WA	318	7 537	939.0	369.0	168	6 764	2 046	209	343	5 328	170.7	46.1
Richmond-Petersburg, VA	2 381	19 222	1 803.5	780.5	1 004	54 752	19 725	2 123	1 724	32 448	1 082.5	306.1
Roanoke, VA	541	3 519	280.5	115.0	312	19 839	4 001	592	534	10 156	319.8	91.9
Rochester, MN	206	2 145	164.4	84.1	77	10 477	3 085	482	274	5 924	204.3	58.5
Rochester, NY	2 063	17 773	1 826.2	684.7	1 516	106 140	25 984	4 228	2 176	31 670	1 023.5	292.2
Rockford, IL	653	5 722	417.0	202.4	912	51 445	9 929	1 934	702	11 248	352.4	96.0
Rocky Mount, NC	155	989	77.8	27.1	154	17 599	3 328	502	220	4 228	133.8	36.4
Sacramento-Yolo, CA	3 750	27 466	2 973.5	1 121.9	1 489	47 690	14 551	1 689	3 443	56 414	1 878.5	505.7
Sacramento, CA	3 519	25 925	2 769.4	1 062.5	1 314	41 512	13 036	1 477	3 141	52 035	1 738.4	469.5
Yolo, CA	231	1 541	204.1	59.4	175	6 178	1 515	212	302	4 379	140.1	36.2
Saginaw-Bay City-Midland, MI	600	4 439	329.4	138.5	462	33 753	8 792	1 781	781	15 846	455.1	131.5
Salinas, CA	694	2 998	293.1	109.2	302	7 070	1 329	224	905	16 869	835.3	226.0
Salt Lake City-Ogden, UT	2 966	26 458	2 590.2	1 005.3	1 878	79 040	16 847	2 544	2 157	47 040	1 507.2	420.0
San Angelo, TX	154	767	60.2	17.2	100	4 452	828	105	192	3 763	110.8	32.7
San Antonio, TX	3 046	22 370	2 098.8	822.2	1 296	45 807	7 481	1 245	2 883	60 511	2 164.8	600.9
San Diego, CA	7 144	59 761	7 072.3	2 725.7	3 407	118 868	22 234	4 224	5 426	105 069	4 237.9	1 157.4
San Francisco-Oakland-San Jose, CA	24 040	221 672	31 368.0	12 686.9	11 035	479 063	130 727	22 174	15 727	257 563	11 514.6	3 162.4
Oakland, CA	6 345	49 557	6 362.8	2 518.4	3 230	113 175	33 983	4 692	4 288	61 734	2 475.3	656.3
San Francisco, CA	8 849	87 847	13 133.6	5 174.9	2 607	64 080	11 325	2 452	5 433	98 286	5 074.8	1 461.3
San Jose, CA	6 338	71 612	10 440.6	4 424.1	3 464	249 947	72 528	13 094	3 495	60 330	2 590.7	677.7
Santa Cruz-Watsonville, CA	678	3 073	384.1	132.1	387	10 011	2 135	315	591	8 223	305.5	80.8
Santa Rosa, CA	1 171	5 682	565.8	239.1	793	24 209	5 120	969	1 005	13 993	490.2	132.2
Vallejo-Fairfield-Napa, CA	659	3 901	481.0	198.4	554	17 641	5 636	652	915	14 997	578.2	154.1
San Luis Obispo-Atascadero-Paso Robles, CA	529	2 292	212.2	76.7	323	6 322	1 156	182	674	10 534	382.5	101.7
Santa Barbara-Santa Maria-Lompoc, CA	981	6 344	711.2	270.6	502	14 985	2 770	584	952	17 195	633.1	177.1
Santa Fe, NM	531	2 692	282.1	117.1	177	1 501	132	34	403	8 194	325.2	95.4
Sarasota-Bradenton, FL	1 515	7 664	663.0	263.1	663	18 965	2 998	571	1 077	20 531	723.3	196.6
Savannah, GA	528	2 908	224.6	88.4	227	14 606	5 326	609	641	13 513	452.0	123.3
Scranton—Wilkes-Barre—Hazleton, PA	923	6 985	519.3	204.4	849	51 202	9 883	1 421	1 424	20 141	590.3	160.0
Seattle-Tacoma-Bremerton, WA	9 641	76 330	8 204.3	3 294.8	4 858	219 765	51 626	9 460	7 709	125 061	4 740.7	1 338.8
Bremerton, WA	443	2 226	169.0	65.5	143	1 441	143	37	399	5 998	180.2	50.6
Olympia, WA	401	2 571	198.1	86.2	156	3 218	761	101	406	6 076	193.0	56.6
Seattle-Bellevue-Everett, WA	7 823	66 568	7 392.9	2 969.1	3 879	192 823	46 446	8 618	5 686	94 179	3 763.9	1 062.3
Tacoma, WA	974	4 965	444.3	174.0	680	22 283	4 276	705	1 218	18 808	603.6	169.3
Sharon, PA	130	679	49.4	22.0	198	10 457	2 441	327	270	3 953	113.3	32.6
Sheboygan, WI	150	1 235	92.2	40.5	239	20 047	4 253	628	237	3 714	105.9	29.1
Sherman-Denison, TX	162	715	52.6	19.6	140	10 223	3 557	365	200	3 312	104.8	30.7
Shreveport-Bossier City, LA	695	3 908	315.1	116.5	337	16 911	5 397	578	637	13 990	555.8	140.0
Sioux City, IA-NE	204	1 043	79.1	25.7	136	11 977	4 503	301	287	4 468	130.4	36.0
Sioux Falls, SD	381	2 437	186.6	74.4	198	12 978	3 203	340	419	8 418	231.2	66.0
South Bend, IN	520	4 003	369.9	154.8	457	20 435	4 150	699	537	10 620	305.2	86.9
Spokane, WA	886	5 738	444.5	186.9	572	20 892	3 995	681	904	14 456	453.2	128.5
Springfield, IL	489	3 323	280.3	118.8	142	3 986	743	117	521	8 379	255.3	74.6
Springfield, MA	1 003	6 519	492.1	207.9	982	39 110	7 002	1 396	1 263	18 308	578.1	162.5
Springfield, MO	642	4 259	375.1	125.4	516	23 359	4 170	594	695	13 073	382.3	109.1
St. Cloud, MN	249	1 504	113.7	47.4	272	15 406	2 517	441	362	6 520	177.3	47.5
St. Joseph, MO	143	797	65.2	22.0	103	7 382	2 295	235	210	3 357	99.7	27.7
St. Louis, MO-IL	5 911	59 511	6 679.3	2 414.2	3 320	170 766	51 488	6 590	5 065	100 455	3 281.6	943.2
State College, PA	211	2 332	167.5	85.9	159	8 546	1 409	255	287	5 241	154.8	41.2
Steubenville-Weirton, OH-WV	153	627	42.2	13.0	104	11 530	3 226	459	308	3 266	89.9	25.5
Stockton-Lodi, CA	575	3 531	277.7	111.2	553	24 646	5 879	750	826	11 413	376.9	96.5
Sumter, SC	116	471	29.1	8.9	84	12 655	2 050	303	133	2 311	70.0	19.1
Syracuse, NY	1 344	11 797	1 044.2	410.3	787	44 756	9 950	1 681	1 667	22 773	709.3	208.6
Tallahassee, FL	877	6 998	710.4	295.4	159	4 075	745	100	495	10 205	307.5	79.6
Tampa-St. Petersburg-Clearwater, FL	6 398	62 828	6 186.3	2 318.5	2 580	77 098	12 701	2 246	4 138	81 729	2 952.0	780.6
Terre Haute, IN	193	1 072	75.3	23.1	181	10 684	2 922	377	353	6 006	176.3	49.9
Texarkana, TX-Texarkana, AR	162	733	65.9	20.2	100	6 330	1 471	228	221	3 819	128.7	31.6
Toledo, OH	1 152	11 064	1 100.2	385.1	954	55 581	16 347	2 194	1 382	24 590	764.2	205.9
Topeka, KS	405	3 227	233.6	94.7	140	7 722	1 806	265	374	6 745	199.2	54.3

1. Firms subject to federal tax.

Area Name	Health Care and Social Assistance[1], 1997				Other Services[1], 1997				Federal funds and grants, fiscal 1999[2] Expenditures (mil dol)			
										Direct payments for individuals		
	Number of Establishments	Number of Employees	Receipts (mil dol)	Annual Payroll (mil dol)	Number of Establishments	Number of Employees	Receipts (mil dol)	Annual Payroll (mil dol)	Total	Social Security and government retirement	Medicare	Food stamps and Supplemental Security Income
	159	160	161	162	163	164	165	166	167	168	169	170
Reading, PA	601	6 387	412.6	200.5	559	3 102	183.2	56.4	1 343.0	694.7	283.1	38.5
Redding, CA	487	5 441	387.9	156.8	241	1 289	86.4	22.8	845.6	375.9	153.9	41.3
Reno, NV	779	7 430	649.9	288.0	518	3 269	217.6	68.7	1 204.5	547.5	171.0	24.3
Richland-Kennewick-Pasco, WA	416	3 510	223.5	89.8	245	1 351	83.7	24.9	2 067.2	282.7	83.8	18.9
Richmond-Petersburg, VA	1 878	32 981	2 214.3	956.5	1 692	12 163	778.4	245.8	5 251.2	1 899.7	615.2	128.3
Roanoke, VA	468	7 588	567.8	234.3	557	3 500	182.3	62.7	1 166.6	544.3	170.5	30.4
Rochester, MN	168	2 241	102.8	50.7	180	1 363	69.8	20.4	443.8	157.6	59.5	9.6
Rochester, NY	1 771	18 344	1 175.8	491.7	1 502	7 780	513.3	147.9	4 580.1	1 939.7	792.2	161.2
Rockford, IL	525	6 787	503.0	241.5	607	4 163	260.1	82.7	1 199.4	601.2	204.3	43.2
Rocky Mount, NC	205	4 459	279.9	115.3	211	1 247	74.6	20.9	603.8	252.3	101.0	35.9
Sacramento-Yolo, CA	3 549	33 932	2 659.3	1 118.5	2 237	15 481	1 116.3	336.3	14 545.3	3 418.4	1 136.2	348.5
Sacramento, CA	3 282	31 500	2 522.6	1 060.0	2 028	14 340	1 024.1	310.9	13 747.3	3 215.1	1 048.0	324.1
Yolo, CA	267	2 432	136.7	58.6	209	1 141	92.3	25.4	798.0	203.3	88.1	24.4
Saginaw-Bay City-Midland, MI	822	7 512	493.6	243.1	658	3 829	229.0	67.3	1 628.6	741.4	301.8	76.0
Salinas, CA	708	5 613	430.5	177.7	445	2 416	172.1	48.0	1 670.5	635.3	242.6	44.3
Salt Lake City-Ogden, UT	2 457	32 242	2 148.9	893.8	1 792	12 804	799.2	240.0	5 722.3	1 917.7	477.7	101.9
San Angelo, TX	186	3 404	208.9	91.7	180	961	58.3	16.1	542.3	214.2	66.7	13.9
San Antonio, TX	3 185	54 720	3 188.8	1 308.8	2 393	16 535	911.1	293.5	9 984.7	3 408.3	1 026.7	267.0
San Diego, CA	5 508	53 541	4 232.7	1 656.5	3 811	24 273	1 648.1	466.0	17 857.4	4 914.6	2 013.7	409.8
San Francisco-Oakland-San Jose, CA	16 455	150 688	11 833.0	4 863.3	10 604	66 407	5 126.3	1 511.3	34 006.9	10 143.4	4 848.3	1 068.6
Oakland, CA	5 158	51 394	4 144.8	1 697.8	3 365	21 627	1 712.7	503.8	11 382.1	3 369.5	1 713.2	388.5
San Francisco, CA	4 698	35 597	2 870.0	1 193.5	3 151	18 692	1 426.1	414.5	9 145.4	2 727.3	1 425.0	305.7
San Jose, CA	3 742	38 283	3 032.2	1 240.9	2 471	16 850	1 352.9	400.5	8 637.6	1 903.9	881.6	236.4
Santa Cruz-Watsonville, CA	631	4 739	309.8	121.7	330	1 614	112.1	31.3	808.1	325.7	167.1	26.4
Santa Rosa, CA	1 241	11 357	766.6	319.5	676	3 604	252.0	74.0	1 630.5	781.4	350.1	44.4
Vallejo-Fairfield-Napa, CA.	985	9 318	709.6	289.8	611	4 020	270.5	87.2	2 403.2	1 035.6	311.3	67.1
San Luis Obispo-Atascadero-Paso Robles, CA	599	5 083	375.3	161.3	294	1 446	96.2	25.9	882.9	451.4	180.1	23.2
Santa Barbara-Santa Maria-Lompoc, CA	934	6 609	516.9	199.8	536	3 054	192.1	57.4	2 097.6	689.2	266.4	44.1
Santa Fe, NM	346	3 183	184.2	84.0	186	922	58.8	17.3	2 370.3	246.3	60.2	11.4
Sarasota-Bradenton, FL	1 504	21 183	1 513.0	613.1	939	4 701	259.8	81.9	3 129.8	1 938.9	837.4	43.5
Savannah, GA	493	6 733	487.2	243.2	439	2 921	184.2	61.1	2 099.4	562.0	223.0	58.5
Scranton—Wilkes-Barre—Hazleton, PA	1 431	14 933	925.9	408.4	980	4 828	273.8	74.2	3 424.3	1 591.6	778.8	86.7
Seattle-Tacoma-Bremerton, WA	7 913	76 522	5 009.3	2 180.4	5 569	33 840	2 461.7	735.2	18 841.6	6 185.3	1 788.8	412.2
Bremerton, WA	473	4 466	245.3	104.1	264	1 300	77.7	23.9	2 239.0	573.7	104.8	23.4
Olympia, WA	459	4 551	322.8	137.0	264	1 356	79.0	24.2	1 570.7	496.3	106.3	23.4
Seattle-Bellevue-Everett, WA	5 542	53 468	3 575.5	1 555.2	4 133	25 754	1 950.3	572.6	11 316.8	3 668.9	1 246.6	257.5
Tacoma, WA	1 439	14 037	865.7	384.0	908	5 430	354.7	114.5	3 715.1	1 446.4	331.1	108.0
Sharon, PA	303	2 686	162.7	72.5	203	876	44.3	12.9	586.7	299.7	140.9	22.2
Sheboygan, WI	176	2 412	134.3	74.8	172	967	56.5	14.6	372.5	198.7	61.1	6.6
Sherman-Denison, TX	278	4 362	225.0	104.6	123	649	32.9	9.6	469.8	235.2	96.5	11.8
Shreveport-Bossier City, LA .	720	12 092	798.1	351.1	574	3 592	226.4	66.1	2 059.2	775.9	336.2	98.6
Sioux City, IA-NE	243	2 346	198.6	95.1	213	1 594	96.1	29.7	535.4	218.5	81.5	13.3
Sioux Falls, SD	303	4 644	364.8	200.4	316	1 993	112.2	34.0	703.9	265.6	77.0	12.8
South Bend, IN	496	5 999	458.0	212.7	452	3 851	256.3	81.0	1 363.3	481.5	186.4	32.3
Spokane, WA	991	11 137	681.4	306.8	699	4 355	258.4	78.5	1 980.0	840.1	278.0	63.0
Springfield, IL	370	7 740	482.4	206.5	362	2 352	146.2	47.4	2 459.1	506.3	153.7	29.6
Springfield, MA	1 031	15 668	937.6	433.3	937	4 910	334.8	101.3	2 933.7	1 090.4	525.9	126.6
Springfield, MO	528	8 067	559.1	264.0	617	3 887	209.5	62.5	1 224.4	586.8	197.3	40.6
St. Cloud, MN	267	3 669	258.3	130.5	281	1 667	102.7	27.6	545.8	242.0	69.6	11.6
St. Joseph, MO	188	2 366	143.7	65.3	179	855	50.9	14.4	432.1	203.2	87.7	17.8
St. Louis, MO-IL	5 241	62 262	3 946.7	1 806.2	4 472	27 486	1 743.6	554.6	16 068.8	4 972.7	2 143.4	417.9
State College, PA	212	2 520	169.1	72.4	159	958	52.2	14.5	678.4	183.9	68.4	8.8
Steubenville-Weirton, OH-WV	256	3 315	154.3	69.3	197	1 166	54.4	16.8	695.5	352.6	164.9	25.6
Stockton-Lodi, CA	949	9 252	664.0	273.5	690	3 838	265.3	74.2	2 126.5	797.5	349.0	137.9
Sumter, SC	128	1 347	81.0	40.6	123	827	47.5	14.1	673.0	222.2	55.0	33.4
Syracuse, NY	1 236	12 308	887.0	412.5	1 061	6 796	494.7	138.3	3 225.0	1 361.4	478.5	110.2
Tallahassee, FL	467	6 635	470.5	214.0	427	2 712	151.5	49.0	3 189.5	481.8	132.7	46.6
Tampa-St. Petersburg-Clearwater, FL	5 794	80 476	5 822.3	2 384.3	3 972	23 499	1 466.0	441.2	12 470.9	5 945.8	2 942.0	336.5
Terre Haute, IN	302	3 901	264.9	85.3	222	1 560	74.2	22.4	713.4	307.2	135.2	21.8
Texarkana, TX-Texarkana, AR	267	4 304	255.0	119.1	179	1 170	69.3	20.0	784.6	292.2	124.9	27.3
Toledo, OH	1 149	16 531	1 021.8	515.0	1 030	6 734	419.2	125.8	2 456.6	1 018.4	526.2	120.9
Topeka, KS	322	5 720	309.5	159.9	296	1 914	127.2	41.7	1 462.9	422.8	109.4	22.3

1. Firms subject to federal tax. 2. October 1, 1998 to September 30, 1999.

Table C. Metropolitan Areas — **Federal Funds and Local Government Finances**

	Federal funds and grants, fiscal 1999[1] (cont'd)							Local government finances, 1997				
	Expenditures (mil dol) (cont'd)							General revenue				
	Procurement contract awards			Grants[2]						Taxes		
Area Name											Per capita[3] (dollars)	
	Salaries and wages	Defense	Other	Medicaid and other health-related	Nutrition and family welfare	Education	Other	Total (mil dol)	Intergovern-mental (mil dol)	Total (mil dol)	Total	Property
	171	172	173	174	175	176	177	178	179	180	181	182
Reading, PA	64.0	38.5	21.7	98.4	27.1	9.5	45.0	888.2	318.7	394.0	1 113	880
Redding, CA	58.6	3.8	23.1	75.1	42.5	8.8	53.6	535.3	281.8	115.6	709	548
Reno, NV	163.4	22.8	37.1	80.9	23.8	10.7	111.3	874.3	369.6	293.3	959	668
Richland-Kennewick-Pasco, WA	75.1	21.1	1 446.9	44.1	25.1	9.7	28.2	641.4	314.2	127.6	698	442
Richmond-Petersburg, VA	817.0	239.2	217.2	330.1	316.2	174.3	400.7	2 361.6	831.7	1 029.6	1 092	779
Roanoke, VA	174.0	80.2	34.0	60.0	22.2	9.7	19.6	529.4	197.5	253.3	1 108	714
Rochester, MN	50.7	4.8	9.3	109.4	7.6	4.2	13.7	326.5	131.8	102.9	898	812
Rochester, NY	272.9	99.9	96.6	574.2	167.2	103.7	187.4	3 867.0	1 427.1	1 695.6	1 561	1 154
Rockford, IL	70.1	56.2	27.6	79.0	24.6	8.0	26.3	808.4	301.9	367.7	1 036	993
Rocky Mount, NC	30.3	4.3	8.6	96.5	29.4	9.9	10.0	384.5	175.6	74.0	508	391
Sacramento-Yolo, CA	894.3	780.4	295.1	1 151.6	2 608.2	962.6	2 657.9	5 461.0	2 528.5	1 370.8	828	560
Sacramento, CA	754.2	770.8	255.8	1 025.8	2 582.0	953.1	2 573.7	5 015.9	2 309.6	1 249.0	831	567
Yolo, CA	140.1	9.6	39.3	125.8	26.2	9.5	84.2	445.1	218.9	121.8	797	490
Saginaw-Bay City-Midland, MI	95.3	13.6	25.0	164.3	74.4	26.7	65.9	1 109.7	576.4	269.3	668	615
Salinas, CA	376.2	77.0	15.5	106.6	68.1	23.3	66.2	1 447.7	558.4	319.6	883	585
Salt Lake City-Ogden, UT	1 204.2	444.8	177.6	496.1	247.7	90.8	483.6	2 685.9	1 074.8	962.0	771	537
San Angelo, TX	133.6	18.3	2.1	39.3	10.0	3.5	17.7	174.2	69.8	74.3	724	553
San Antonio, TX	2 347.1	1 162.6	293.7	789.4	166.4	90.6	218.9	3 393.4	1 327.2	1 285.0	850	703
San Diego, CA	4 797.3	2 409.3	680.4	1 338.9	441.6	173.5	497.0	8 204.5	3 812.5	2 084.2	766	544
San Francisco-Oakland-San Jose, CA	3 653.3	3 658.8	3 318.0	3 650.6	939.4	308.7	1 821.2	24 707.9	9 596.8	8 138.6	1 215	782
Oakland, CA	1 082.8	300.4	2 031.3	1 211.8	395.9	121.9	584.5	8 708.3	3 468.0	2 600.5	1 145	740
San Francisco, CA	1 373.2	365.3	425.6	1 392.9	187.8	66.0	642.6	6 983.1	2 434.1	2 456.4	1 478	903
San Jose, CA	615.8	2 770.8	776.3	683.3	203.1	67.4	392.5	5 453.7	2 104.5	2 060.5	1 281	826
Santa Cruz-Watsonville, CA	29.0	9.6	26.9	93.0	31.5	15.8	63.7	804.9	339.1	228.5	950	629
Santa Rosa, CA	116.3	15.9	31.1	133.7	54.5	15.8	64.7	1 276.7	511.5	384.6	897	665
Vallejo-Fairfield-Napa, CA	436.1	196.6	26.9	135.8	66.7	21.9	73.3	1 481.1	739.7	408.2	833	591
San Luis Obispo-Atascad-ero-Paso Robles, CA	37.9	7.6	7.8	64.2	36.0	8.1	48.5	676.0	233.4	248.9	1 067	849
Santa Barbara-Santa Maria-Lompoc, CA	276.9	430.2	53.1	120.7	48.6	21.7	120.6	1 210.2	497.5	347.8	891	672
Santa Fe, NM	68.6	5.3	1 445.8	98.3	153.4	62.7	203.2	294.9	154.2	86.6	618	246
Sarasota-Bradenton, FL	103.6	17.8	27.6	57.5	33.6	15.7	40.9	1 556.9	284.1	551.6	1 024	830
Savannah, GA	728.3	259.5	21.4	105.5	49.0	18.2	31.2	769.9	265.0	339.0	1 193	780
Scranton—Wilkes-Barre—Hazleton, PA	224.5	149.5	74.5	286.6	69.2	18.9	87.0	1 249.4	492.3	506.3	814	590
Seattle-Tacoma-Bremerton, WA	3 961.6	1 984.8	531.1	1 802.2	633.3	283.7	976.6	10 108.2	3 738.5	3 609.1	1 072	663
Bremerton, WA	1 162.9	215.2	21.1	56.2	23.8	21.2	21.2	493.4	253.0	153.2	653	490
Olympia, WA	55.3	9.3	13.4	136.9	276.5	151.5	269.4	505.5	248.5	163.6	817	574
Seattle-Bellevue-Everett, WA	1 709.5	1 558.1	443.2	1 308.8	229.6	81.2	620.7	7 416.6	2 418.7	2 776.2	1 224	722
Tacoma, WA	1 033.9	202.3	53.4	300.4	103.4	29.7	65.3	1 692.8	818.3	516.1	776	551
Sharon, PA	17.1	0.7	3.7	48.8	16.9	4.0	19.0	237.6	127.1	74.1	607	449
Sheboygan, WI	11.7	8.6	29.9	26.1	9.0	3.1	9.8	334.0	157.6	107.5	978	957
Sherman-Denison, TX	15.6	1.4	7.9	44.0	6.7	2.5	33.7	217.3	82.9	85.6	843	680
Shreveport-Bossier City, LA	364.6	56.2	35.5	202.9	48.6	24.9	70.7	861.9	332.6	360.4	952	419
Sioux City, IA-NE	48.4	41.7	7.8	52.3	16.4	6.1	18.7	291.0	134.2	102.1	845	776
Sioux Falls, SD	108.9	7.4	56.4	48.3	8.5	2.6	35.5	305.2	67.2	180.7	1 125	777
South Bend, IN	61.5	289.2	103.2	91.6	22.8	6.6	56.8	544.7	219.9	204.9	794	776
Spokane, WA	311.0	54.3	39.9	196.1	62.7	24.1	53.1	944.3	463.4	295.3	730	456
Springfield, IL	111.3	2.7	19.0	230.2	807.9	249.6	296.8	422.5	171.8	174.8	857	755
Springfield, MA	358.1	74.3	90.8	325.6	122.1	44.5	100.7	1 456.0	777.2	488.7	827	814
Springfield, MO	138.8	1.3	33.1	103.7	26.1	12.5	30.0	475.0	179.1	189.8	630	368
St. Cloud, MN	69.6	0.1	25.3	51.3	13.1	6.0	20.9	446.0	221.4	117.6	729	691
St. Joseph, MO	26.9	0.3	4.3	43.9	11.4	4.5	15.9	169.3	68.1	71.6	737	399
St. Louis, MO-IL	1 542.6	4 103.7	495.5	1 266.4	289.7	111.6	455.7	5 706.3	2 031.3	2 564.6	1 003	634
State College, PA	28.9	66.1	7.4	61.3	9.7	6.7	206.4	229.7	80.9	92.8	698	468
Steubenville-Weirton, OH-WV	20.2	2.7	9.2	57.7	19.0	7.5	27.3	239.8	107.2	89.0	651	553
Stockton-Lodi, CA	152.7	35.7	51.0	275.7	145.4	31.3	83.8	1 709.9	922.8	354.1	653	458
Sumter, SC	195.7	30.5	2.7	75.9	18.8	10.0	16.1	163.3	93.2	51.4	482	399
Syracuse, NY	261.5	256.0	70.3	360.3	103.1	37.9	117.4	2 467.2	988.3	1 098.7	1 483	1 172
Tallahassee, FL	96.9	21.9	28.2	355.5	704.2	383.4	850.0	663.8	260.3	207.0	794	539
Tampa-St. Petersburg-Clear-water, FL	1 061.2	734.7	228.5	464.7	213.8	111.7	298.5	5 719.7	1 912.6	2 046.8	919	723
Terre Haute, IN	80.9	16.5	10.7	76.8	14.8	5.0	18.6	273.3	116.2	112.5	758	737
Texarkana, TX-Texarkana, AR	102.8	25.0	24.5	75.1	14.5	6.3	66.6	239.4	115.6	77.9	631	427
Toledo, OH	139.9	31.9	31.8	261.6	87.2	37.5	112.8	1 700.5	608.2	770.7	1 260	758
Topeka, KS	159.6	8.3	25.4	108.5	148.7	70.6	221.8	423.2	144.6	175.0	1 061	836

1. October 1, 1998 to September 30, 1999. 2. State totals may include programs not allocated by county. 3. Based on the resident population estimated as of July 1 of the year shown.

Table C. Metropolitan Areas — Local Government Finances, Government Employment, and Elections

Area Name	Local government finances, 1997 (cont'd) Direct general expenditure		Percent of total for —					Debt outstanding		Government employment, 1998			Presidential election, 2000 Percent of vote cast —		
	Total (mil dol)	Per capita[1] (dollars)	Education	Health and hospitals	Police protection	Public welfare	Highways	Total (mil dol)	Per capita[1] (dollars)	Federal civilian	Federal military	State and local	Democratic	Republican	All other
	183	184	185	186	187	188	189	190	191	192	193	194	195	196	197
Reading, PA	906.5	2 560	55.6	3.1	2.9	6.8	2.9	1 461.7	4 129	1 186	1 223	17 757	NA	NA	NA
Redding, CA	520.3	3 189	42.7	6.9	4.7	11.6	4.8	456.1	2 795	1 194	330	10 104	30.2	65.0	4.7
Reno, NV	877.3	2 869	32.5	2.5	7.8	2.5	5.9	985.2	3 222	3 178	692	18 633	42.6	52.0	5.4
Richland-Kennewick-Pasco, WA	527.3	2 884	45.2	11.4	4.0	0.0	7.2	7 554.8	41 329	1 276	691	12 376	32.9	64.0	3.1
Richmond-Petersburg, VA	2 497.7	2 648	41.3	6.2	5.6	5.1	3.1	2 608.7	2 766	15 597	9 663	86 508	42.8	54.6	2.6
Roanoke, VA	535.5	2 343	47.6	0.4	5.3	5.2	2.5	676.4	2 960	3 890	922	13 763	42.7	54.9	2.4
Rochester, MN	335.5	2 927	51.7	1.4	4.4	7.7	6.8	254.0	2 216	913	477	6 401	43.5	51.6	4.9
Rochester, NY	3 971.1	3 656	46.2	4.1	3.4	14.6	4.1	2 546.4	2 345	5 363	2 284	71 979	47.4	47.9	4.7
Rockford, IL	801.1	2 258	51.9	1.1	6.4	2.5	6.0	527.4	1 487	1 378	811	16 487	45.5	51.4	3.1
Rocky Mount, NC	386.1	2 652	42.5	28.7	4.0	6.5	1.7	50.7	348	585	455	9 930	NA	NA	NA
Sacramento-Yolo, CA	5 417.5	3 272	36.8	3.7	4.7	12.0	4.7	9 522.3	5 751	19 066	6 239	191 964	46.2	48.4	5.4
Sacramento, CA	4 955.2	3 297	37.2	3.6	4.7	12.0	4.4	9 269.2	6 167	16 725	5 919	170 291	45.3	49.5	5.2
Yolo, CA	462.2	3 025	31.9	4.5	5.4	11.7	7.6	253.1	1 657	2 341	320	21 673	54.9	37.5	7.5
Saginaw-Bay City-Midland, MI	1 102.0	2 735	50.4	9.1	4.1	2.0	5.3	856.0	2 124	1 787	843	19 330	51.6	46.2	2.2
Salinas, CA	1 453.5	4 016	30.8	26.3	4.2	6.0	3.2	538.4	1 488	5 214	6 018	23 061	57.5	37.2	5.2
Salt Lake City-Ogden, UT	2 565.2	2 056	47.0	3.7	6.5	0.6	4.3	7 112.0	5 701	24 502	11 324	91 293	31.4	59.1	9.4
San Angelo, TX	183.4	1 786	59.3	2.9	8.2	0.1	3.4	161.2	1 571	1 323	3 252	7 584	26.8	71.4	1.7
San Antonio, TX	3 428.7	2 269	50.3	10.8	5.7	2.3	3.2	6 839.3	4 525	36 871	36 726	96 320	41.9	55.2	2.9
San Diego, CA	8 408.2	3 088	34.2	7.9	5.3	9.5	3.2	7 951.5	2 920	42 919	104 495	150 058	45.7	49.6	4.7
San Francisco-Oakland-San Jose, CA	24 551.2	3 664	28.1	12.0	5.8	8.1	3.5	24 816.0	3 703	63 061	25 549	391 850	64.0	29.9	6.1
Oakland, CA	8 524.0	3 755	27.9	13.3	5.5	8.1	3.8	10 365.9	4 566	19 144	6 755	140 313	64.8	29.8	5.5
San Francisco, CA	7 019.7	4 224	20.3	15.1	6.5	7.6	2.7	7 209.2	4 338	24 405	4 020	108 115	69.4	23.7	6.9
San Jose, CA	5 376.2	3 341	32.6	8.6	5.5	9.2	3.5	4 548.0	2 827	12 508	4 466	75 306	60.7	34.4	4.9
Santa Cruz-Watsonville, CA	812.3	3 378	33.2	9.6	5.4	6.7	3.1	432.9	1 800	538	488	16 185	61.5	27.3	11.2
Santa Rosa, CA	1 357.0	3 166	40.4	10.0	5.3	5.9	4.8	947.4	2 210	1 821	1 424	24 012	59.5	32.2	8.2
Vallejo-Fairfield-Napa, CA.	1 462.0	2 982	36.5	4.8	6.9	10.0	4.2	1 312.6	2 677	4 645	8 396	27 919	56.3	39.4	4.4
San Luis Obispo-Atascadero-Paso Robles, CA	664.8	2 850	39.4	8.4	4.8	8.4	4.4	258.3	1 107	656	490	18 268	40.9	52.2	6.9
Santa Barbara-Santa Maria-Lompoc, CA	1 179.2	3 022	36.8	8.6	6.4	7.4	3.8	516.1	1 323	3 944	4 093	26 460	47.4	46.1	6.5
Santa Fe, NM	317.5	2 266	40.5	1.2	6.3	3.3	8.6	459.8	3 283	1 454	511	23 386	NA	NA	NA
Sarasota-Bradenton, FL	1 508.9	2 801	35.0	18.9	6.1	0.4	4.9	1 511.1	2 805	1 981	1 264	21 210	45.0	52.0	3.0
Savannah, GA	751.7	2 646	41.1	5.8	6.3	0.4	7.0	622.6	2 192	2 767	5 309	17 502	NA	NA	NA
Scranton—Wilkes-Barre—Hazleton, PA	1 320.3	2 124	56.2	0.2	3.0	4.3	3.8	1 676.6	2 697	4 823	2 126	29 902	NA	NA	NA
Seattle-Tacoma-Bremerton, WA	10 080.6	2 993	36.6	8.2	4.9	0.2	5.5	11 193.1	3 323	49 820	60 908	236 795	55.6	39.1	5.3
Bremerton, WA	491.9	2 097	54.8	4.4	3.4	0.0	3.6	405.8	1 730	14 620	13 716	11 204	49.0	45.3	5.7
Olympia, WA	486.5	2 428	50.4	4.1	3.9	0.1	5.1	353.4	1 764	977	845	31 475	51.8	41.0	7.2
Seattle-Bellevue-Everett, WA	7 433.9	3 278	32.4	9.4	5.0	0.2	5.8	8 947.5	3 945	24 520	22 962	156 376	57.6	37.0	5.4
Tacoma, WA	1 668.3	2 510	45.9	4.9	5.5	0.3	5.1	1 486.4	2 236	9 703	23 385	37 740	51.5	44.1	4.4
Sharon, PA	253.9	2 080	63.9	4.1	2.4	1.8	4.2	227.7	1 866	299	412	5 342	NA	NA	NA
Sheboygan, WI	354.9	3 229	47.9	4.6	4.4	12.0	7.5	238.9	2 174	234	400	5 784	42.7	53.7	3.6
Sherman-Denison, TX	230.0	2 265	63.1	3.3	4.9	1.3	3.6	313.4	3 086	337	274	5 296	34.2	64.1	1.7
Shreveport-Bossier City, LA .	818.0	2 160	46.7	7.3	6.9	0.7	3.8	535.2	1 413	4 772	7 481	27 185	NA	NA	NA
Sioux City, IA-NE	301.7	2 497	51.1	2.2	4.8	0.8	6.7	178.4	1 477	904	571	6 185	46.4	50.0	3.6
Sioux Falls, SD	287.6	1 790	47.4	1.2	5.0	1.1	10.4	294.9	1 836	2 149	1 203	7 102	42.9	55.6	1.5
South Bend, IN	554.5	2 149	48.9	1.0	4.1	4.8	4.3	394.6	1 529	1 160	959	12 676	49.4	49.3	1.3
Spokane, WA	925.5	2 287	51.7	3.3	4.3	0.0	5.1	631.4	1 560	4 300	5 173	25 695	43.3	51.9	4.8
Springfield, IL	406.8	1 995	51.1	1.3	7.8	0.9	6.3	458.8	2 250	2 190	480	27 814	41.5	55.5	2.9
Springfield, MA	1 454.4	2 460	52.8	1.4	5.3	1.4	3.6	1 887.7	3 193	6 616	2 024	41 171	NA	NA	NA
Springfield, MO	463.9	1 541	54.5	1.4	4.7	1.7	8.5	441.7	1 468	2 372	1 415	16 861	NA	NA	NA
St. Cloud, MN	444.5	2 757	44.9	3.7	3.5	7.2	10.4	659.0	4 088	1 550	664	10 846	39.8	51.8	8.4
St. Joseph, MO	175.4	1 806	48.3	1.4	5.5	0.2	6.7	32.4	334	563	448	6 334	NA	NA	NA
St. Louis, MO-IL	5 553.1	2 171	50.9	2.8	6.6	0.4	4.8	3 698.2	1 446	30 399	16 990	130 581	NA	NA	NA
State College, PA	225.8	1 698	54.9	3.5	2.9	3.9	3.7	243.4	1 830	476	543	30 627	NA	NA	NA
Steubenville-Weirton, OH-WV	233.2	1 706	53.7	1.5	4.8	7.4	5.1	155.3	1 136	384	493	6 076	NA	NA	NA
Stockton-Lodi, CA	1 703.2	3 139	38.6	10.0	5.4	13.2	3.4	1 050.8	1 937	4 283	1 141	29 290	47.7	48.9	3.4
Sumter, SC	160.6	1 507	63.3	2.3	6.3	0.5	1.9	82.5	774	1 206	5 499	5 588	46.8	51.9	1.3
Syracuse, NY	2 605.4	3 517	46.5	2.5	3.2	12.7	5.6	1 594.1	2 152	4 923	1 847	53 737	51.5	43.5	5.0
Tallahassee, FL	667.4	2 561	43.7	0.5	8.1	0.3	5.1	1 232.8	4 730	1 810	727	57 776	60.4	37.2	2.4
Tampa-St. Petersburg-Clearwater, FL	5 569.8	2 501	38.8	7.6	7.1	1.9	4.0	6 952.0	3 122	18 123	11 621	109 399	48.9	48.1	3.1
Terre Haute, IN	307.8	2 073	63.2	3.7	2.4	2.0	3.7	136.0	916	1 356	551	9 754	46.5	52.1	1.4
Texarkana, TX-Texarkana, AR	233.3	1 891	60.2	2.7	5.5	0.4	3.7	192.2	1 558	3 525	465	7 544	40.7	58.1	1.2
Toledo, OH	1 735.7	2 837	38.3	7.5	5.6	5.0	4.3	1 050.7	1 717	2 485	1 668	45 491	NA	NA	NA
Topeka, KS	418.9	2 540	48.6	4.4	6.2	0.0	5.6	498.3	3 021	2 979	1 066	19 323	46.8	48.3	4.9

1. Based on the resident population estimated as of July 1 of the year shown.

Table C. Metropolitan Areas — **Land Area and Population**

CMSA/MSA/PMSA/NECMA code[1]	Area Name	Land area,[2] (sq km) 1990	Population and population characteristics, 1999													
						Race (percent)					Age (percent)					
			Total persons	Rank	Per square kilometer	White	Black	Am. Indian, Eskimo, Aleut	Asian and Pacific Islander	Percent Hispanic[3]	Under 5 years	5 to 17 years	18 to 24 years	25 to 34 years	35 to 44 years	45 to 54 years
		1	2	3	4	5	6	7	8	9	10	11	12	13	14	15
8520	Tucson, AZ	23 794	803 618	70	33.8	90.2	3.9	3.4	2.4	29.6	7.7	18.4	10.5	13.0	15.6	11.9
8560	Tulsa, OK	12 988	786 117	71	60.5	83.6	8.7	6.6	1.2	3.1	7.2	19.1	9.6	13.0	16.4	13.5
8600	Tuscaloosa, AL	3 432	161 435	224	47.0	70.9	28.0	0.2	0.9	1.0	6.2	16.4	15.7	13.8	15.6	11.9
8640	Tyler, TX	2 405	169 693	219	70.6	76.4	22.5	0.4	0.7	7.8	6.9	19.2	9.6	11.8	15.5	13.5
8680	Utica-Rome, NY	6 798	293 068	156	43.1	93.3	5.3	0.2	1.2	2.8	6.3	18.5	8.9	13.1	15.4	12.8
8750	Victoria, TX	2 286	82 087	310	35.9	92.1	7.0	0.4	0.5	41.3	8.3	21.7	8.7	12.1	16.0	12.7
8780	Visalia-Tulare-Porterville, CA	12 495	358 470	135	28.7	90.7	1.7	1.7	6.0	47.2	9.2	25.6	9.0	13.3	14.9	11.2
8800	Waco, TX	2 699	204 244	195	75.7	81.7	16.8	0.4	1.1	16.3	7.4	18.9	13.6	11.5	14.3	12.3
97	Washington-Baltimore, DC-MD-VA-WV	24 807	7 359 044	X	296.7	68.6	25.9	0.3	5.2	5.6	6.7	17.9	8.6	15.8	18.5	13.9
0720	Baltimore, MD	6 757	2 491 254	18	368.7	69.1	28.0	0.3	2.6	2.0	6.7	18.4	8.3	14.4	17.9	13.4
3180	Hagerstown, MD	1 187	127 791	263	107.7	91.5	7.2	0.3	1.0	1.2	5.8	17.8	8.7	13.8	16.5	13.3
8840	Washington, DC-MD-VA-WV	16 863	4 739 999	6	281.1	67.7	25.3	0.3	6.7	7.6	6.8	17.5	8.8	16.5	18.9	14.2
8920	Waterloo-Cedar Falls, IA	1 469	119 959	276	81.7	91.1	7.6	0.2	1.1	1.3	6.0	18.4	12.7	11.2	15.6	13.1
8940	Wausau, WI	4 002	123 584	268	30.9	96.3	0.1	0.5	3.1	0.6	6.4	21.0	8.5	12.7	16.7	13.6
8960	West Palm Beach-Boca Raton, FL	5 269	1 049 420	59	199.2	83.3	14.8	0.2	1.6	11.2	6.0	15.1	6.7	11.9	15.1	11.7
9000	Wheeling, WV-OH	2 462	153 946	230	62.5	96.4	3.0	0.1	0.4	0.5	5.3	16.1	8.7	11.9	15.6	13.8
9080	Wichita Falls, TX	3 982	136 493	253	34.3	86.6	10.2	0.9	2.2	11.1	7.1	18.3	11.8	13.2	14.4	12.5
9040	Wichita, KS	7 687	548 714	96	71.4	88.2	8.2	1.1	2.5	6.2	7.6	19.8	9.6	13.8	16.4	12.6
9140	Williamsport, PA	3 198	116 709	280	36.5	96.4	2.8	0.2	0.6	0.8	6.0	18.9	8.2	12.5	16.2	13.4
9200	Wilmington, NC	2 729	222 109	185	81.4	79.0	19.9	0.5	0.7	1.6	6.2	17.5	8.7	13.1	16.1	13.6
9260	Yakima, WA	11 127	220 785	186	19.8	90.8	1.7	5.6	1.9	32.9	8.7	23.1	9.9	12.5	14.6	12.3
9280	York, PA	2 343	376 586	129	160.7	94.9	4.0	0.2	1.0	2.2	6.2	18.2	7.7	13.8	17.6	14.5
9320	Youngstown-Warren, OH	4 050	589 236	86	145.5	88.7	10.6	0.2	0.5	1.7	6.0	18.3	8.1	12.0	15.9	13.3
9340	Yuba City, CA	3 194	138 030	248	43.2	82.5	2.9	2.4	12.2	18.8	8.5	22.2	8.6	13.0	14.8	12.9
9360	Yuma, AZ	14 282	135 614	254	9.5	93.0	3.5	1.6	1.9	46.4	9.0	22.0	10.2	12.3	13.1	10.2

1. MSA = Metropolitan Statistical Area. CMSA = Consolidated MSA. PMSA = Primary MSA. NECMA = New England County Metropolitan Area. See Appendix A for explanation of these concepts. See Appendix B for list of metropolitan areas identified by type, with component counties.   2. Dry land or land partially or temporarily covered by water.   3. Hispanic persons may be of any race.

Table C. Metropolitan Areas — **Population and Households**

Area Name	Population, 1999 (cont'd)				Population — change and components of change, 1980–1999							Households, 1990				
	Age (percent) (cont'd)				Total persons		Percent change		Components of change, 1990–1999							Percent	
	55 to 64 years	65 to 74 years	75 years and over	Percent female	1990	1980	1980–1990	1990–1999	Births	Deaths	Net migration	Number	Percent change, 1980–1990	Persons per house-hold	Female family house-holder[1]	One person
	16	17	18	19	20	21	22	23	24	25	26	27	28	29	30	31
Tucson, AZ	8.4	7.7	6.7	51.1	666 957	531 443	25.5	20.5	105 788	60 931	90 365	261 792	33.9	2.49	10.9	27.8
Tulsa, OK	9.2	6.7	5.3	51.4	708 954	657 173	7.9	10.9	105 214	58 945	32 873	277 202	12.5	2.51	10.4	26.3
Tuscaloosa, AL	8.6	6.5	5.4	52.0	150 500	137 541	9.4	7.3	20 094	12 057	3 258	55 354	18.2	2.55	13.0	25.8
Tyler, TX	9.7	7.4	6.4	51.7	151 309	128 366	17.9	12.1	22 654	14 200	10 463	56 800	23.4	2.61	11.3	24.3
Utica-Rome, NY	8.6	8.5	7.9	50.2	316 645	320 180	-1.1	-7.4	36 067	29 847	-30 270	117 498	5.2	2.56	10.9	26.6
Victoria, TX	8.6	6.7	5.3	51.4	74 361	68 807	8.1	10.4	12 059	5 683	1 566	26 228	14.1	2.81	11.1	21.2
Visalia-Tulare-Porterville, CA	6.9	5.1	4.9	49.8	311 932	245 738	26.9	14.9	66 772	23 528	3 888	97 861	21.3	3.12	12.8	18.1
Waco, TX	9.2	6.6	6.2	51.4	189 123	170 755	10.8	8.0	28 793	17 872	4 781	70 208	14.1	2.58	12.1	25.8
Washington-Baltimore, DC-MD-VA-WV	8.1	6.8	4.7	51.3	6 726 395	5 790 555	16.2	9.4	999 235	480 892	99 808	2 491 041	21.2	2.63	12.7	24.4
Baltimore, MD	8.6	6.6	5.7	51.5	2 382 172	2 199 497	8.3	4.6	331 680	207 590	-15 425	880 145	14.9	2.64	14.6	23.5
Hagerstown, MD	9.4	7.3	7.3	49.2	121 393	113 086	7.3	5.3	14 788	10 924	2 687	44 762	12.0	2.53	9.7	23.6
Washington, DC-MD-VA-WV	7.7	5.3	4.2	51.3	4 222 830	3 477 972	21.4	12.2	652 767	262 378	112 546	1 566 134	25.3	2.63	11.8	24.9
Waterloo-Cedar Falls, IA	8.8	7.3	6.8	52.2	123 798	137 961	-10.3	-3.1	15 140	10 822	-7 793	46 932	-2.6	2.51	10.4	25.6
Wausau, WI	8.3	6.6	6.2	50.4	115 400	111 270	3.7	7.1	15 122	8 221	1 685	41 547	10.2	2.75	7.2	21.0
West Palm Beach-Boca Raton, FL	9.2	11.7	12.5	51.7	863 503	576 758	49.7	21.5	116 406	106 994	176 334	365 558	56.0	2.32	8.6	27.5
Wheeling, WV-OH	10.8	9.3	8.5	52.0	159 301	185 566	-14.2	-3.4	15 969	18 275	-2 491	62 858	-6.9	2.47	10.9	27.4
Wichita Falls, TX	9.7	6.6	6.3	50.3	130 351	128 348	1.6	4.7	18 949	11 973	-2 794	48 228	5.4	2.56	10.5	25.0
Wichita, KS	8.2	6.4	5.6	50.9	485 270	442 401	9.7	13.1	78 255	37 857	8 644	186 640	13.3	2.55	9.7	26.0
Williamsport, PA	9.1	7.8	8.0	51.6	118 710	118 416	0.2	-1.7	13 984	11 231	-4 403	44 949	6.8	2.56	9.9	24.1
Wilmington, NC	10.1	8.8	5.8	52.0	171 269	139 248	23.0	29.7	23 839	16 353	43 734	68 208	36.1	2.46	12.3	24.4
Yakima, WA	7.9	5.3	5.9	50.1	188 823	172 508	9.5	16.9	39 322	15 699	8 767	65 985	7.6	2.80	11.3	22.7
York, PA	8.6	6.8	6.6	50.9	339 574	312 963	8.5	10.9	42 025	28 024	20 988	128 666	14.6	2.60	8.4	21.3
Youngstown-Warren, OH	9.9	9.1	7.4	52.1	600 877	644 922	-6.8	-1.9	71 112	61 207	-19 446	227 967	0.6	2.60	12.4	24.3
Yuba City, CA	8.5	6.1	5.4	50.0	122 643	101 979	20.3	12.5	22 138	9 967	2 417	42 887	18.1	2.79	11.8	21.1
Yuma, AZ	8.1	8.8	6.3	49.3	106 895	76 205	40.3	26.9	27 020	8 328	16 417	35 791	19.9	2.87	9.4	19.0

1. No spouse present.

Area Name	Births, average 1996–1998		Deaths, average 1996–1998				Physicians,[4] 1998		Hospitals,[4] 1998			Medicare enrollees 1999	Serious crimes known to police, 1998[6]	
			Number		Rate					Beds			Total	
	Total	Rate[1]	Total	Infant[2]	Total[1]	Infant[3]	Number	Rate[5]	Number	Number	Rate[5]		Number	Rate[7]
	32	33	34	35	36	37	38	39	40	41	42	43	44	45
Tucson, AZ	11 377	14.6	6 979	73	9.0	6.4	2 446	309	9	2 078	263	123 255	60 504	7 566
Tulsa, OK	11 489	15.0	6 693	86	8.7	7.6	1 695	218	14	2 715	349	106 091	39 499	5 121
Tuscaloosa, AL	2 175	13.6	1 336	21	8.3	9.8	333	207	2	680	423	22 174	14 889	9 191
Tyler, TX	2 518	15.1	1 670	14	10.0	5.7	519	307	3	558	331	26 726	9 093	5 365
Utica-Rome, NY	3 363	11.3	3 225	25	10.8	7.4	582	198	6	1 279	434	56 976	8 648	2 887
Victoria, TX	1 332	16.3	638	10	7.8	7.3	189	229	3	588	711	11 171	3 778	4 531
Visalia-Tulare-Porterville, CA	7 011	20.0	2 581	44	7.3	6.3	421	119	7	854	240	40 519	17 579	4 917
Waco, TX	3 162	15.6	1 924	21	9.5	6.7	368	181	3	638	314	30 158	12 950	6 335
Washington-Baltimore, DC-MD-VA-WV	105 039	14.5	53 800	861	7.5	8.2	24 813	341	64	19 722	271	807 100	563 427	4 852
Baltimore, MD	34 142	13.8	23 020	293	9.3	8.6	8 748	352	23	8 330	335	333 809	353 280	5 073
Hagerstown, MD	1 569	12.3	1 218	8	9.5	5.1	236	185	1	320	251	19 944	3 319	2 569
Washington, DC-MD-VA-WV	69 328	15.0	29 562	560	6.4	8.1	15 829	339	40	11 072	237	453 347	206 828	4 578
Waterloo-Cedar Falls, IA	1 609	13.2	1 155	11	9.5	7.0	272	225	3	609	503	19 923	6 305	5 171
Wausau, WI	1 559	12.7	889	5	7.3	3.0	219	178	1	270	219	16 844	NA	NA
West Palm Beach-Boca Raton, FL	12 736	12.6	12 402	79	12.2	6.2	3 403	330	14	3 294	319	239 091	86 639	8 357
Wheeling, WV-OH	1 643	10.7	1 977	14	12.8	8.5	359	235	6	1 198	784	30 624	2 936	2 060
Wichita Falls, TX	2 046	14.9	1 305	19	9.5	9.4	291	212	3	423	308	20 037	6 572	4 716
Wichita, KS	8 368	15.7	4 336	73	8.1	8.8	1 075	197	9	2 225	409	70 904	NA	NA
Williamsport, PA	1 338	11.3	1 205	12	10.2	9.2	250	213	4	612	522	21 386	3 206	2 952
Wilmington, NC	2 619	12.3	1 909	17	9.0	6.5	517	237	4	711	326	36 945	13 611	6 292
Yakima, WA	4 225	19.5	1 712	27	7.9	6.3	361	166	4	481	221	27 567	15 464	6 985
York, PA	4 471	12.1	3 167	24	8.5	5.3	638	171	3	768	206	54 564	11 381	3 146
Youngstown-Warren, OH	7 226	12.2	6 714	68	11.3	9.5	1 079	182	8	2 305	390	109 935	NA	NA
Yuba City, CA	2 213	16.2	1 097	17	8.0	7.7	220	161	2	260	190	18 741	5 882	4 171
Yuma, AZ	3 104	21.5	1 127	19	7.8	6.1	154	116	1	275	208	17 758	NA	NA

1. Per 1,000 estimated resident population, average 1996–1998.   2. Deaths of infants under 1 year old.   3. Deaths of infants under 1 year old per 1,000 live births.   4. Data subject to copyright.   5. Per 100,000 resident population as of July 1 of the year shown.   6. Data for serious crimes have not been adjusted for underreporting; this may affect comparability between geographic areas and over time.   7. Per 100,000 population estimated by the FBI.

Area Name	Serious crimes known to police, 1998[1] (cont'd) Rate[2]		Education — School enrollment and attainment, 1990					Local government expenditures, fiscal 1997[5]		Money income — 1989				Income and poverty, 1997			
			Enrollment[3]			Attainment[4] (percent)					Households Median				Percent below poverty level			
	Violent	Property	Total	Percent private	High school graduate or more	Bachelor's degree or more	Total current expenditures (mil dol)	Current expenditures per student (dollars)	Per capita[6] (dollars)	Dollars	Percent change, 1979–1989 (constant 1989 dollars)	Percent with $100,000 or more	Median household income	All persons	Persons under 18	Persons 5–17 in families
	46	47	48	49	50	51	52	53	54	55	56	57	58	59	60	61
Tucson, AZ............................	746	6 820	188 198	9.8	80.5	23.3	556.1	4 491	13 177	25 400	-4.0	3.1	NA	16.2	24.4	23.4
Tulsa, OK.............................	712	4 409	187 682	17.1	79.4	20.3	628.2	4 606	13 783	26 990	-6.4	3.3	NA	13.1	19.6	17.8
Tuscaloosa, AL	825	8 366	49 658	7.9	69.6	20.0	126.3	4 925	11 406	23 056	4.9	2.5	NA	17.0	24.2	22.2
Tyler, TX	513	4 852	42 179	9.5	75.7	19.8	138.4	4 623	12 742	25 769	-5.9	3.2	NA	14.9	21.7	20.2
Utica-Rome, NY	257	2 630	79 376	13.8	74.6	15.9	405.6	7 887	11 877	25 958	3.3	1.9	NA	14.8	23.0	22.2
Victoria, TX	574	3 957	21 249	10.1	70.2	14.1	79.4	5 046	12 196	26 945	-12.4	3.0	NA	16.0	22.7	22.3
Visalia-Tulare-Porterville, CA	719	4 198	92 825	5.7	60.2	11.8	452.2	5 407	10 302	24 449	3.1	2.6	NA	27.9	39.9	38.5
Waco, TX	687	5 648	57 779	25.3	71.6	16.6	207.1	5 295	11 185	22 664	-0.5	2.0	NA	18.3	26.3	24.4
Washington-Baltimore, DC-MD-VA-WV...............	651	4 201	1 703 511	20.5	80.6	31.6	7 775.7	6 836	19 255	41 921	18.3	8.5	NA	9.1	14.1	13.0
Baltimore, MD.................	730	4 343	593 146	19.8	74.7	23.1	2 591.7	6 573	16 596	36 549	15.2	5.6	NA	10.7	16.6	15.2
Hagerstown, MD..............	379	2 190	25 860	10.8	69.3	11.4	118.8	5 971	12 970	29 632	6.4	2.0	NA	10.1	15.7	14.2
Washington, DC-MD-VA-WV	537	4 041	1 084 505	21.2	84.3	37.0	5 065.2	7 003	20 935	45 900	20.3	10.3	NA	8.2	12.8	11.7
Waterloo-Cedar Falls, IA	386	4 785	37 637	12.4	80.4	17.3	132.1	7 725	12 321	25 682	-21.4	2.0	NA	12.8	18.0	15.9
Wausau, WI	NA	NA	29 586	13.2	75.9	13.5	128.4	6 439	12 718	30 143	3.7	2.5	NA	7.8	12.5	10.8
West Palm Beach-Boca Raton, FL	967	7 390	171 097	20.2	78.8	22.1	733.8	5 333	19 937	32 523	16.4	7.2	NA	11.5	18.6	17.2
Wheeling, WV-OH.................	183	1 877	37 660	15.6	72.9	12.2	132.7	5 905	11 119	21 830	-19.9	1.7	NA	15.2	22.4	20.0
Wichita Falls, TX	573	4 143	33 012	8.4	75.0	16.3	124.8	4 973	11 640	23 982	-7.1	2.2	NA	15.5	20.5	20.0
Wichita, KS	NA	NA	127 866	14.4	82.2	21.5	476.3	5 187	14 303	30 151	-0.8	2.9	NA	10.8	16.1	14.0
Williamsport, PA	232	2 720	27 909	12.3	74.5	12.3	133.0	6 535	11 714	25 552	1.5	1.8	NA	11.9	18.2	16.4
Wilmington, NC	636	5 656	42 226	8.6	75.4	18.0	154.5	4 965	13 215	26 086	5.4	2.6	NA	13.3	20.7	18.7
Yakima, WA	355	6 630	49 580	7.8	66.1	13.7	272.2	5 741	10 735	23 612	-4.7	2.1	NA	18.3	26.2	23.9
York, PA..............................	254	2 892	72 386	15.9	72.8	13.9	320.9	5 870	14 544	32 604	5.8	2.7	NA	6.8	10.7	9.5
Youngstown-Warren, OH......	NA	NA	146 914	12.5	74.3	12.0	559.4	5 751	11 936	25 471	-16.0	1.8	NA	13.0	19.3	17.0
Yuba City, CA	471	3 700	34 454	6.2	70.5	12.7	151.3	5 218	11 391	24 312	6.1	2.4	NA	20.8	31.9	33.7
Yuma, AZ.............................	NA	NA	28 755	5.9	64.9	12.7	121.5	4 368	10 428	23 634	NA	1.8	NA	25.3	40.3	35.1

1. Data for serious crimes have not been adjusted for underreporting; this may affect comparability between geographic areas and over time. 2. Per 100,000 population estimated by the FBI. 3. All persons 3 years old and over enrolled in nursery school through college. 4. Persons 25 years old and over. 5. Elementary and secondary education expenditures, local government fiscal years ending between July 1, 1996 and June 30, 1997. 6. Based on population enumerated as of April 1, 1990.

Table C. Metropolitan Areas — **Personal Income**

										Government payments to individuals			
			Per capita[1]						Transfer payments				
Area Name	Total (mil dol)	Percent change, 1997–1998	Dollars	Rank	Wages and salaries[2] (mil dol)	Proprietor's income (mil dol)	Dividends, interest, and rent (mil dol)	Total (mil dol)	Total (mil dol)	Social Security (mil dol)	Medical payments (mil dol)	Income maintenance (mil dol)	Unemployment insurance (mil dol)
	62	63	64	65	66	67	68	69	70	71	72	73	74
Tucson, AZ	17 959	6.9	22 723	224	10 144	1 068	4 441	2 804	2 666	1 173	1 014	237	19
Tulsa, OK	20 608	6.6	26 533	107	13 163	2 947	3 440	2 408	2 273	1 083	790	181	24
Tuscaloosa, AL	3 547	4.3	22 063	251	2 451	199	602	625	597	219	269	61	6
Tyler, TX	4 234	6.4	25 190	140	2 573	469	857	633	605	256	252	48	11
Utica-Rome, NY	6 573	4.5	22 302	239	3 718	371	1 250	1 431	1 371	538	592	148	21
Victoria, TX	1 971	6.2	24 131	174	1 073	159	394	283	269	105	122	26	4
Visalia-Tulare-Porterville, CA	6 698	6.6	18 893	308	3 259	1 181	978	1 331	1 265	361	493	268	79
Waco, TX	4 435	5.3	21 826	257	2 801	410	773	702	668	272	241	75	9
Washington-Baltimore, DC-MD-VA-WV	244 282	5.9	33 602	X	178 512	14 670	43 543	20 858	19 534	7 445	8 289	1 968	388
Baltimore, MD	73 308	4.9	29 548	45	46 747	4 104	12 966	9 200	8 738	3 330	3 774	937	206
Hagerstown, MD	2 968	5.3	23 282	201	1 921	102	526	453	429	193	162	31	11
Washington, DC-MD-VA-WV	168 006	6.4	36 043	14	129 844	10 465	30 051	11 205	10 367	3 922	4 353	1 000	171
Waterloo-Cedar Falls, IA	2 961	4.2	24 484	163	2 179	166	584	467	442	203	162	41	10
Wausau, WI	3 050	5.0	24 781	148	2 056	164	566	357	334	171	112	23	14
West Palm Beach-Boca Raton, FL	41 361	6.5	40 044	5	17 206	3 142	16 414	5 083	4 900	2 500	1 964	202	71
Wheeling, WV-OH	3 316	5.2	21 348	270	1 777	185	738	751	723	311	275	53	11
Wichita Falls, TX	3 126	3.6	22 851	215	1 885	349	617	481	460	186	185	43	7
Wichita, KS	14 255	5.8	26 211	113	10 099	1 077	2 555	1 654	1 560	730	586	126	24
Williamsport, PA	2 558	4.4	21 791	259	1 562	212	496	469	446	204	157	38	20
Wilmington, NC	5 298	6.0	24 272	168	3 152	428	1 260	860	822	367	323	73	16
Yakima, WA	4 533	4.7	20 718	288	2 475	413	850	872	828	261	342	106	65
York, PA	9 565	4.8	25 596	131	5 577	816	1 729	1 133	1 060	568	327	79	36
Youngstown-Warren, OH	13 693	2.7	23 089	206	7 832	731	2 588	2 676	2 555	1 105	1 012	218	46
Yuba City, CA	2 676	4.9	19 532	305	1 299	294	444	580	555	167	217	102	24
Yuma, AZ	2 411	9.6	18 277	310	1 427	345	367	425	402	153	136	47	34

1. Based on the resident population estimated as of July 1 of the year shown.   2. Includes other labor income.

Table C. Metropolitan Areas — **Earnings, Social Security, and Housing**

Area Name	Earnings, 1998									Social Security beneficiaries, December 1998			Housing units, 1990	
			Percent by selected industries											
			Goods-related[1]		Service-related and other[2]							Supplemental Security Income recipients, December 1998		
	Total (mil dol)	Farm	Total	Manu-facturing	Total	Retail trade	Finance, insurance, and real estate	Services	Govern-ment	Number	Rate[3]		Total	Percent change, 1980–1990
	75	76	77	78	79	80	81	82	83	84	85	86	87	88
Tucson, AZ	11 212	0.1	19.9	12.4	57.3	10.5	6.4	31.5	22.7	137 510	174	13 733	298 207	36.4
Tulsa, OK	16 110	0.0	31.7	21.5	59.5	8.2	6.0	26.3	8.9	121 932	157	12 082	311 890	16.8
Tuscaloosa, AL	2 651	0.2	35.3	21.9	39.5	10.2	3.8	17.5	24.9	26 920	167	5 727	58 740	16.7
Tyler, TX	3 042	0.9	27.5	16.6	58.8	12.1	5.9	30.0	12.8	29 841	177	3 717	64 369	25.8
Utica-Rome, NY	4 089	0.6	NA	16.9	NA	10.0	7.4	27.1	24.7	64 852	220	9 315	132 050	6.2
Victoria, TX	1 232	-0.8	28.0	12.3	57.1	14.0	5.4	26.3	15.7	12 674	153	1 899	29 162	18.3
Visalia-Tulare-Porterville, CA	4 440	14.7	14.3	9.3	50.5	10.8	4.0	15.8	20.5	47 853	135	15 272	105 013	18.3
Waco, TX	3 211	0.2	26.6	20.2	56.3	9.5	11.2	24.3	16.9	33 943	167	4 672	78 857	19.6
Washington-Baltimore, DC-MD-VA-WV	193 183	0.1	NA	5.8	NA	6.8	NA	NA	27.5	NA	NA	NA	2 660 934	21.8
Baltimore, MD	50 851	0.2	NA	9.9	NA	8.3	9.4	31.0	22.3	376 395	152	51 886	938 979	16.0
Hagerstown, MD	2 022	0.4	NA	19.5	NA	10.9	3.4	29.5	15.7	22 057	173	1 997	47 448	11.9
Washington, DC-MD-VA-WV	140 309	0.1	NA	4.1	NA	6.2	NA	NA	29.5	NA	NA	NA	1 674 507	25.6
Waterloo-Cedar Falls, IA	2 345	1.3	NA	30.5	NA	9.1	5.0	23.5	15.9	22 831	188	2 806	49 688	-1.2
Wausau, WI	2 220	1.9	38.0	31.7	48.3	8.1	9.7	16.8	11.8	19 874	161	1 891	43 774	10.1
West Palm Beach-Boca Raton, FL	20 348	1.7	14.9	9.1	72.1	10.0	16.0	34.6	11.3	259 559	251	13 253	461 665	56.1
Wheeling, WV-OH	1 962	0.1	NA	14.7	NA	11.5	4.6	D	16.3	35 341	231	3 908	69 434	-3.3
Wichita Falls, TX	2 235	1.1	NA	14.2	NA	8.9	3.7	20.0	30.3	22 558	164	2 510	55 093	6.6
Wichita, KS	11 176	0.2	39.5	32.3	48.8	8.3	4.1	24.4	11.5	80 192	147	7 868	202 521	16.1
Williamsport, PA	1 773	0.5	31.7	26.0	53.5	10.4	5.0	25.2	14.3	23 785	203	2 999	49 580	4.3
Wilmington, NC	3 580	0.2	NA	16.2	NA	12.6	7.3	24.2	17.5	43 121	198	5 672	94 190	45.2
Yakima, WA	2 888	13.7	18.0	12.5	50.7	10.0	3.5	22.5	17.5	31 757	146	5 094	70 852	6.0
York, PA	6 393	0.2	43.7	36.1	45.7	10.1	4.0	20.5	10.5	62 940	169	5 139	134 761	14.6
Youngstown-Warren, OH	8 564	0.3	37.8	31.7	48.5	10.7	4.2	22.4	13.3	124 520	210	15 247	242 483	1.1
Yuba City, CA	1 593	6.2	14.9	7.7	46.7	10.5	3.6	20.9	32.2	21 461	157	6 337	45 408	14.5
Yuma, AZ	1 771	14.6	NA	3.8	NA	8.9	D	17.0	28.4	20 439	155	2 269	46 541	24.1

1. Covers mining, construction, and manufacturing.   2. Covers private sector earnings in agricultural services, forestry, and fisheries; transportation and public utilities; wholesale trade; retail trade; finance, insurance, and real estate; and services.   3. Per 1,000 resident population estimated as of July 1 of the year shown.

Table C. Metropolitan Areas — **Housing, Labor Force, and Employment**

Area Name	Housing units, 1990 (cont'd)								Civilian labor force, 1999				Civilian employment, 1990[5]		
	Occupied units										Unemployment			Percent	
			Owner-occupied			Renter-occupied										
				Owner cost as a percent of income												
	Total	Percent	Median value[1]	With a mortgage	Without a mortgage	Median rent[2]	Rent as percent of income	Substandard units[3] (percent)	Total	Percent change, 1998–1999	Total	Rate[4]	Total	Professional, managerial, and technical	Precision production, craft, and repair
	89	90	91	92	93	94	95	96	97	98	99	100	101	102	103
Tucson, AZ	261 792	60.9	76 500	22.2	12.0	389	28.7	6.5	384 579	3.4	12 066	3.1	290 058	33.1	10.8
Tulsa, OK	277 202	65.5	58 900	20.2	12.7	360	24.6	3.1	418 851	1.0	13 528	3.2	336 445	30.2	12.6
Tuscaloosa, AL	55 354	61.5	62 100	18.5	12.7	343	29.5	3.8	83 975	0.5	2 492	3.0	65 917	29.2	12.5
Tyler, TX	56 800	66.5	59 900	20.2	13.2	371	25.9	5.4	89 602	-0.4	3 828	4.3	67 128	28.2	10.6
Utica-Rome, NY	117 498	66.5	69 000	18.4	13.9	360	27.0	2.0	143 559	0.8	6 229	4.3	133 749	28.1	11.5
Victoria, TX	26 228	64.6	54 700	19.5	12.9	350	24.5	7.3	43 099	-0.7	1 798	4.2	32 462	25.6	15.4
Visalia-Tulare-Porterville, CA	97 861	60.1	73 900	22.6	12.1	402	29.2	14.5	166 552	1.7	27 308	16.4	118 964	21.8	9.6
Waco, TX	70 208	58.9	50 300	18.6	12.8	359	27.9	5.2	101 622	0.6	3 365	3.3	82 485	27.5	11.6
Washington-Baltimore, DC-MD-VA-WV	2 491 041	62.2	136 098	NA	NA	590	NA	3.9	3 978 354	1.3	121 899	3.1	3 581 926	40.8	9.1
Baltimore, MD	880 145	63.7	101 200	20.7	12.6	489	25.3	2.8	1 300 325	0.1	51 894	4.0	1 192 182	35.1	10.7
Hagerstown, MD	44 762	63.8	83 000	18.7	12.4	357	21.7	2.2	68 018	-2.4	2 318	3.4	56 191	23.0	14.4
Washington, DC-MD-VA-WV	1 566 134	61.3	160 939	NA	NA	658	NA	4.6	2 610 011	2.0	67 687	2.6	2 333 553	44.2	8.2
Waterloo-Cedar Falls, IA	46 932	67.3	44 100	NA	NA	325	NA	2.2	67 372	-3.3	2 621	3.9	56 595	26.2	11.0
Wausau, WI	41 547	74.7	54 800	18.1	13.1	364	23.0	2.6	72 198	-2.0	2 114	2.9	57 719	23.0	11.0
West Palm Beach-Boca Raton, FL	365 558	71.9	98 400	23.4	12.4	586	28.1	4.3	506 543	-0.2	25 472	5.0	387 274	31.4	11.2
Wheeling, WV-OH	62 858	72.4	44 100	16.8	12.0	279	26.6	2.1	73 308	0.7	3 848	5.2	63 304	25.8	13.4
Wichita Falls, TX	48 228	64.5	46 300	NA	NA	360	NA	3.5	64 433	-2.4	2 987	4.6	54 608	27.3	11.7
Wichita, KS	186 640	65.2	57 300	19.5	12.5	391	24.8	3.4	290 160	1.0	9 481	3.3	237 187	30.8	13.9
Williamsport, PA	44 949	69.7	54 900	18.9	12.9	333	25.3	2.2	56 481	-0.9	2 843	5.0	52 566	22.6	12.3
Wilmington, NC	68 208	68.2	71 600	NA	NA	410	NA	2.6	111 007	5.0	3 774	3.4	82 489	27.4	13.5
Yakima, WA	65 985	63.2	55 200	17.9	12.1	338	25.5	10.1	114 301	-0.4	11 233	9.8	77 366	22.9	9.5
York, PA	128 666	74.4	79 700	NA	NA	408	NA	1.7	193 015	0.9	6 921	3.6	176 908	24.0	14.2
Youngstown-Warren, OH	227 967	72.8	49 000	NA	NA	336	NA	1.7	281 453	-0.7	15 488	5.5	249 622	23.6	13.1
Yuba City, CA	42 887	55.9	80 900	21.6	12.0	384	27.7	9.3	56 897	1.0	7 063	12.4	44 688	24.5	13.1
Yuma, AZ	35 791	66.0	64 000	21.3	13.5	435	27.7	14.6	66 773	2.3	19 957	29.9	37 189	24.2	10.2

1. Specified owner-occupied units.   2. Specified renter-occupied units.   3. Overcrowded or lacking complete plumbing facilities.   4. Percent of civilian labor force.   5. Persons 16 years and older.

Table C. Metropolitan Areas — **Nonfarm Employment and Agriculture**

Area Name	Private nonfarm establishments, employment and payroll, 1998									Agriculture, 1997			
	Number of establishments	Employment						Annual payroll		Farms			Farm operators
		Total	Health Care and Social Assistance	Manufacturing	Retail trade	Finance and Insurance	Professional Scientific and Technical Services	Total (mil dol)	Average per employee (dollars)	Number	Percent with—		Whose principal occupation is farming (percent)
											Less than 50 acres	500 acres and over	
	104	105	106	107	108	109	110	111	112	113	114	115	116
Tucson, AZ............................	18 247	268 142	39 133	28 391	39 354	7 942	14 457	6 699	24 983	419	60.1	22.0	45.6
Tulsa, OK.............................	21 874	357 212	41 589	52 578	42 246	20 084	17 134	10 248	28 689	6 006	34.3	13.3	34.9
Tuscaloosa, AL	3 973	65 228	10 317	11 593	10 399	1 790	2 176	1 641	25 158	510	30.8	10.0	37.3
Tyler, TX	4 854	70 510	14 856	10 417	10 229	2 723	2 919	1 821	25 826	1 844	43.0	4.6	31.3
Utica-Rome, NY	6 155	100 353	17 593	20 136	15 072	10 541	2 887	2 307	22 989	1 511	17.5	11.4	65.3
Victoria, TX	2 207	29 345	5 260	3 286	5 206	1 216	861	688	23 445	1 084	32.4	16.6	39.4
Visalia-Tulare-Porterville, CA	5 812	73 205	10 342	11 806	12 637	2 881	1 910	1 672	22 840	5 446	59.7	8.2	55.5
Waco, TX	4 742	82 466	12 500	16 100	10 576	3 902	2 350	1 913	23 197	2 006	38.8	11.1	36.8
Washington-Baltimore, DC-MD-VA-WV	189 293	3 098 996	370 359	180 814	382 760	153 950	409 697	109 190	35 234	12 345	44.5	7.0	46.5
Baltimore, MD..................	61 736	991 749	150 051	90 693	130 815	56 395	75 539	30 481	30 735	3 622	50.9	7.4	48.4
Hagerstown, MD...............	3 222	51 788	7 764	9 502	7 568	5 115	1 095	1 312	25 334	768	34.1	4.7	54.9
Washington, DC-MD-VA-WV	124 335	2 055 459	212 544	80 619	244 377	92 440	333 063	77 397	37 654	7 955	25.1	7.1	44.8
Waterloo-Cedar Falls, IA	3 210	58 478	8 764	13 683	9 021	2 756	1 760	1 490	25 480	1 002	25.1	18.2	52.5
Wausau, WI...........................	3 371	58 831	6 275	17 188	8 990	4 295	1 548	1 637	27 825	2 703	23.3	6.2	60.6
West Palm Beach-Boca Raton, FL	35 287	414 845	59 208	26 764	65 074	21 779	25 345	12 129	29 237	855	76.0	10.4	57.0
Wheeling, WV-OH...................	3 861	52 268	11 565	3 827	9 277	2 418	1 647	1 145	21 906	1 294	16.3	5.6	39.6
Wichita Falls, TX	3 532	47 654	8 889	8 122	7 168	1 564	1 160	1 059	22 223	1 056	25.8	29.6	42.5
Wichita, KS	13 821	256 215	33 943	65 870	29 887	9 012	10 637	7 536	29 413	3 430	25.5	24.9	48.4
Williamsport, PA	2 883	47 148	7 935	12 625	7 407	2 000	1 252	1 070	22 694	841	19.9	4.8	52.3
Wilmington, NC	7 649	88 404	11 872	10 833	15 246	2 851	4 569	2 200	24 886	275	49.8	6.5	47.3
Yakima, WA	4 830	58 832	10 159	9 327	9 906	1 677	1 378	1 442	24 510	3 365	63.0	6.6	55.3
York, PA	8 160	149 419	16 254	45 149	20 317	4 127	3 892	4 167	27 888	1 698	43.9	6.8	50.7
Youngstown-Warren, OH......	13 722	214 495	31 879	55 591	32 592	7 178	5 496	5 620	26 201	2 310	35.9	4.2	43.8
Yuba City, CA	2 423	25 657	5 439	2 663	5 123	892	639	581	22 645	2 020	47.0	12.2	58.9
Yuma, AZ..............................	2 443	30 497	4 179	3 082	6 308	934	717	595	19 510	465	44.7	25.6	59.4

Table C. Metropolitan Areas — **Agriculture, Land, and Water**

Area Name	Acreage (1,000)	Percent change, 1992–1997	Average size of farm	Total irrigated (1,000)	Total cropland (1,000)	Average per farm ($1,000)	Average per acre (dollars)	Value of machinery and equipment Average per farm ($1,000)	Total (mil dol)	Average per farm (dollars)	Crops	Live-stock and poultry products	$10,000 or more	$100,000 or more	Percent of land owned by Fed. Gov. 1997	Water con-sump-tion 1995 (mil gal/ day)
	117	118	119	120	121	122	123	124	125	126	127	128	129	130	131	132
Tucson, AZ	2 914	-16.1	6 954	29	D	2 346	340	38	47	111 840	81.0	19.0	41.1	13.6	29.0	263.8
Tulsa, OK	2 255	6.7	376	6	617	267	716	24	193	32 165	23.0	77.0	27.2	4.3	2.5	143.0
Tuscaloosa, AL	100	4.0	196	1	43	294	1 569	29	21	40 253	30.0	70.0	25.1	6.7	1.5	35.3
Tyler, TX	251	1.2	136	1	127	223	1 794	25	38	20 798	52.0	48.0	23.1	2.6	0.0	37.9
Utica-Rome, NY	358	-11.8	237	1	229	227	970	56	120	79 338	16.0	84.0	61.1	27.5	0.3	55.3
Victoria, TX	458	6.3	423	4	155	318	716	33	29	26 419	60.0	40.0	28.0	6.0	0.0	47.4
Visalia-Tulare-Porterville, CA	1 310	-3.3	240	625	703	835	3 444	68	1 921	352 806	58.0	42.0	67.4	35.7	48.5	2 208.7
Waco, TX	493	4.4	246	2	299	237	968	34	93	46 337	37.0	63.0	24.8	5.4	1.6	57.4
Washington-Baltimore, DC-MD-VA-WV	2 080	-2.4	168	23	1 424	634	3 713	51	669	54 213	45.0	55.0	39.1	11.9	3.8	2 090.0
Baltimore, MD	573	-3.1	158	13	450	633	3 900	60	262	72 398	54.0	46.0	42.7	15.0	3.1	388.8
Hagerstown, MD	126	1.8	164	1	95	454	2 819	68	61	78 911	21.0	79.0	50.5	27.9	4.8	60.0
Washington, DC-MD-VA-WV	1 381	-2.5	174	10	879	651	3 718	46	346	43 548	41.0	59.0	36.3	9.0	4.1	1 641.2
Waterloo-Cedar Falls, IA	286	-4.7	285	1	263	622	2 321	82	128	127 637	60.0	40.0	76.6	35.9	0.0	57.3
Wausau, WI	516	-2.7	191	6	337	202	1 039	68	204	75 578	25.0	75.0	68.2	24.0	0.0	183.4
West Palm Beach-Boca Raton, FL	605	-5.2	707	417	529	2 398	3 404	84	873	1 020 909	100.0	0.0	64.1	33.9	10.1	959.8
Wheeling, WV-OH	247	16.7	191	D	110	165	881	30	17	13 154	18.0	82.0	20.8	3.5	0.0	1 034.0
Wichita Falls, TX	950	3.1	899	6	266	509	604	44	85	80 734	14.0	86.0	45.9	14.4	0.4	50.4
Wichita, KS	1 620	1.5	472	57	1 009	456	976	58	287	83 572	45.0	55.0	54.8	18.0	0.4	144.0
Williamsport, PA	136	1.9	161	2	87	283	1 873	50	43	51 357	37.0	63.0	50.7	15.2	0.3	16.3
Wilmington, NC	42	-1.8	153	1	28	419	2 574	39	35	125 931	D	D	46.2	16.7	1.3	78.5
Yakima, WA	1 683	2.6	500	278	D	605	1 220	73	873	259 582	67.0	33.0	61.4	28.9	17.6	1 475.0
York, PA	261	3.6	154	1	217	472	3 187	57	129	75 748	40.0	60.0	50.0	17.3	0.2	2 350.0
Youngstown-Warren, OH	324	-4.1	140	2	237	285	2 131	50	104	45 189	47.0	53.0	42.0	11.1	1.2	253.4
Yuba City, CA	557	0.7	276	327	394	1 050	3 882	97	386	191 208	95.0	5.0	62.1	32.8	9.1	1 408.6
Yuma, AZ	238	3.8	511	196	215	2 266	4 496	145	522	1 122 716	D	D	68.4	43.0	81.5	1 398.6

Table C. Metropolitan Areas — Residential Construction, Wholesale and Retail Trade, and Real Estate

Area Name	Value of Residential Construction Authorized by Building Permits, 1999		Wholesale Trade, 1997				Retail Trade[1], 1997				Real Estate and Rental and Leasing, 1997			
	New Construction ($1,000)	Number of Housing Units	Number of Establishments	Number of Employees	Sales (mil dol)	Annual Payroll (mil dol)	Number of Establishments	Number of Employees	Sales (mil dol)	Annual Payroll (mil dol)	Number of Establishments	Number of Employees	Receipts (mil dol)	Annual Payroll (mil dol)
	133	134	135	136	137	138	139	140	141	142	143	144	145	146
Tucson, AZ	1 039 225	8 734	929	9 257	2 759.8	266.0	2 785	39 285	6 853.8	693.4	978	6 631	676.6	130.5
Tulsa, OK	537 490	5 355	1 637	20 463	10 168.5	707.8	3 039	41 087	7 293.0	663.9	914	4 836	540.2	99.2
Tuscaloosa, AL	78 356	728	185	1 981	858.1	61.1	790	10 852	1 543.2	151.0	161	1 079	82.6	13.7
Tyler, TX	70 090	530	297	3 103	1 237.7	93.9	805	9 773	1 868.6	170.2	189	895	93.2	20.7
Utica-Rome, NY	43 743	435	278	3 248	1 056.3	86.3	1 225	14 847	2 159.5	210.2	208	748	88.9	12.6
Victoria, TX	21 332	198	141	1 665	422.1	46.0	398	5 052	868.7	80.1	91	455	60.5	10.5
Visalia-Tulare-Porterville, CA	163 030	1 636	343	5 120	2 527.7	135.1	1 107	12 742	2 135.7	211.8	206	809	97.7	12.6
Waco, TX	58 661	601	315	3 755	1 716.3	102.1	862	10 227	1 797.8	162.7	212	1 086	131.4	21.4
Washington-Baltimore, DC-MD-VA-WV	5 143 265	52 205	8 247	123 675	80 810.2	5 174.0	27 318	383 694	66 662.6	7 050.4	7 759	62 797	9 018.8	1 701.0
Baltimore, MD	1 362 269	13 606	3 494	51 526	32 627.0	1 974.6	9 585	132 311	21 687.7	2 340.4	2 331	18 521	2 397.0	476.2
Hagerstown, MD	62 974	642	156	2 184	922.7	62.9	598	7 450	1 220.5	117.3	105	479	43.4	7.3
Washington, DC-MD-VA-WV	3 718 022	37 957	4 597	69 965	47 260.4	3 136.5	17 135	243 933	43 754.3	4 592.6	5 323	43 797	6 578.4	1 217.5
Waterloo-Cedar Falls, IA	32 586	220	169	2 690	952.7	77.0	598	9 386	1 344.8	139.3	126	549	60.9	10.3
Wausau, WI	89 423	779	221	3 395	1 002.0	102.5	565	9 236	1 421.6	142.6	86	439	39.9	7.1
West Palm Beach-Boca Raton, FL	1 111 405	10 008	2 187	17 864	11 544.5	707.0	4 967	61 563	11 731.2	1 126.1	1 716	9 409	1 323.8	248.3
Wheeling, WV-OH	9 322	125	189	2 472	1 734.8	66.7	744	9 588	1 328.9	129.8	121	554	45.0	8.7
Wichita Falls, TX	23 027	210	229	2 048	476.0	47.1	625	7 379	1 222.2	109.3	152	521	51.5	8.0
Wichita, KS	316 080	3 158	900	10 551	6 192.5	352.9	2 154	28 706	4 801.5	471.5	606	2 815	352.3	56.3
Williamsport, PA	30 066	297	137	2 195	481.9	51.4	605	7 600	1 149.3	108.4	78	299	32.2	4.7
Wilmington, NC	377 742	3 840	381	3 895	1 293.9	104.0	1 302	14 842	2 903.0	249.0	338	2 089	182.3	37.3
Yakima, WA	63 487	659	291	4 871	1 853.8	141.9	854	10 174	1 741.6	174.9	212	1 018	99.9	17.0
York, PA	226 495	2 228	450	9 498	3 428.1	275.9	1 447	20 356	3 250.6	315.4	236	1 138	128.3	21.5
Youngstown-Warren, OH	158 325	1 465	749	9 292	3 622.4	282.3	2 568	33 971	5 314.5	497.2	413	2 470	248.8	45.9
Yuba City, CA	44 992	399	130	1 018	453.3	31.9	446	5 129	851.3	86.7	118	592	51.9	7.4
Yuma, AZ	78 808	1 047	132	2 376	512.9	41.3	455	5 984	1 035.7	94.5	113	485	48.4	7.0

1. Establishments with payroll.

Table C. Metropolitan Areas — Professional, Manufacturing, Accommodation and Foodservices, Finance and Insurance

Area Name	Professional, Scientific, and Technical Services[1], 1997				Manufacturing, 1997				Accommodation and Foodservices, 1997			
	Number of Establishments	Number of Employees	Sales (mil dol)	Annual Payroll (mil dol)	Number of Establishments	Number of Employees	Sales (mil dol)	Annual Payroll (mil dol)	Number of Establishments	Number of Employees	Sales (mil dol)	Annual Payroll (mil dol)
	147	148	149	150	151	152	153	154	155	156	157	158
Tucson, AZ	1 811	12 214	1 124.2	430.9	764	26 746	4 455	1 065	1 524	32 305	1 041.9	292.2
Tulsa, OK	2 177	14 688	1 489.2	549.6	1 441	50 859	9 954	1 656	1 593	27 153	873.1	233.0
Tuscaloosa, AL	257	1 733	134.0	51.6	160	10 738	2 558	379	317	7 396	202.5	55.6
Tyler, TX	392	2 464	284.0	93.0	213	10 969	2 299	381	294	5 834	175.1	47.8
Utica-Rome, NY	402	2 504	185.8	65.6	351	20 050	3 148	583	681	7 156	220.7	61.4
Victoria, TX	141	712	59.5	21.1	71	3 064	1 245	120	155	2 711	79.6	21.7
Visalia-Tulare-Porterville, CA	335	1 788	265.6	45.0	282	11 439	3 167	315	510	7 020	232.3	56.8
Waco, TX	292	2 039	133.0	57.4	261	16 474	3 856	482	400	6 900	220.7	59.8
Washington-Baltimore, DC-MD-VA-WV	26 290	346 773	44 475.0	17 623.8	4 979	180 692	39 149	6 730	13 376	263 545	10 802.8	3 067.6
Baltimore, MD	6 666	60 715	6 654.6	2 613.7	2 177	93 594	22 685	3 449	4 492	80 323	2 923.1	808.3
Hagerstown, MD	163	854	63.5	22.7	147	9 173	1 924	294	230	4 135	127.6	36.4
Washington, DC-MD-VA-WV	19 461	285 204	37 757.0	14 987.4	2 655	77 925	14 540	2 987	8 654	179 087	7 752.1	2 222.9
Waterloo-Cedar Falls, IA	193	1 530	100.9	44.9	165	13 542	5 133	556	293	5 544	135.8	39.2
Wausau, WI	181	1 264	127.4	46.6	232	16 839	3 182	503	276	3 779	105.2	29.7
West Palm Beach-Boca Raton, FL	4 211	21 787	2 352.0	985.5	1 051	26 262	6 345	1 138	2 087	41 031	1 659.8	440.9
Wheeling, WV-OH	220	1 350	114.3	34.0	137	3 511	649	90	361	5 078	147.4	41.0
Wichita Falls, TX	217	1 087	88.2	33.0	156	7 939	1 437	255	282	5 256	160.6	47.3
Wichita, KS	1 060	6 705	558.6	225.4	702	66 234	12 218	2 716	1 130	20 170	648.7	184.8
Williamsport, PA	137	1 014	68.8	27.1	208	12 982	2 460	370	283	3 571	106.1	28.5
Wilmington, NC	586	3 404	272.4	110.3	260	10 718	3 711	426	610	10 677	348.7	93.5
Yakima, WA	223	1 298	119.4	43.2	239	10 163	2 091	265	411	5 371	178.6	47.8
York, PA	502	3 457	268.4	105.2	661	45 754	8 157	1 558	635	10 721	318.7	91.1
Youngstown-Warren, OH	831	5 393	370.4	157.0	896	55 718	14 455	2 267	1 195	18 502	529.3	144.2
Yuba City, CA	143	572	37.3	14.3	114	2 792	602	76	187	2 383	75.9	21.9
Yuma, AZ	148	666	48.1	17.3	66	3 041	390	55	245	4 158	130.0	31.3

1. Firms subject to federal tax.

Table C. Metropolitan Areas — Health and Other Services and Federal Funds

Area Name	Health Care and Social Assistance[1], 1997				Other Services[1], 1997				Federal funds and grants, fiscal 1999[2]			
									Expenditures (mil dol)			
										Direct payments for individuals		
	Number of Establishments	Number of Employees	Receipts (mil dol)	Annual Payroll (mil dol)	Number of Establishments	Number of Employees	Receipts (mil dol)	Annual Payroll (mil dol)	Total	Social Security and government retirement	Medicare	Food stamps and Supplemental Security Income
	159	160	161	162	163	164	165	166	167	168	169	170
Tucson, AZ..........................	1 614	19 280	1 283.3	563.9	1 171	7 575	437.9	138.1	5 700.9	1 777.2	593.1	104.5
Tulsa, OK............................	1 747	24 266	1 537.5	681.2	1 202	7 626	526.4	154.2	2 836.2	1 349.6	534.2	97.2
Tuscaloosa, AL	274	3 580	223.9	116.2	248	1 481	79.3	25.1	697.6	277.8	120.2	35.1
Tyler, TX	430	5 047	396.8	186.2	288	2 032	116.3	35.4	697.7	333.3	137.1	21.9
Utica-Rome, NY	484	4 753	312.2	143.5	414	2 245	174.7	44.2	1 571.7	700.3	245.0	55.8
Victoria, TX	230	3 383	230.0	93.5	151	973	61.8	17.8	315.6	131.3	61.4	12.3
Visalia-Tulare-Porterville, CA	588	5 102	334.0	127.8	308	1 544	115.2	28.7	1 317.8	427.2	209.9	85.8
Waco, TX	353	4 861	265.9	126.4	329	2 065	114.1	34.4	1 023.7	421.3	113.9	32.2
Washington-Baltimore, DC-MD-VA-WV...............	15 462	162 986	11 741.6	5 140.1	11 491	79 223	5 341.6	1 668.9	88 661.8	15 294.8	4 732.0	892.0
Baltimore, MD..................	5 234	64 227	4 262.9	1 879.9	3 885	27 412	1 724.4	541.1	17 249.1	4 938.3	2 231.3	403.5
Hagerstown, MD...............	225	3 006	208.0	95.5	207	1 524	81.7	25.4	510.8	259.1	95.0	13.2
Washington, DC-MD-VA-WV	10 003	95 753	7 270.7	3 164.6	7 399	50 287	3 535.4	1 102.3	70 901.9	10 097.4	2 405.7	475.3
Waterloo-Cedar Falls, IA	228	2 173	167.9	83.0	213	1 513	80.2	25.9	511.8	236.5	89.9	20.0
Wausau, WI.........................	200	2 672	188.8	104.9	222	1 201	79.2	20.9	391.2	189.0	64.7	8.6
West Palm Beach-Boca Raton, FL	3 280	39 623	2 981.7	1 257.5	2 113	11 678	726.5	209.6	6 887.8	2 847.6	1 554.2	97.5
Wheeling, WV-OH................	357	4 025	207.0	88.9	228	1 451	75.0	24.4	798.2	381.1	155.4	31.3
Wichita Falls, TX.................	278	3 935	211.8	85.8	233	1 552	87.5	28.9	1 038.9	335.6	100.3	18.3
Wichita, KS	909	17 460	1 261.2	521.8	913	5 640	352.2	107.9	2 775.6	939.1	351.1	59.4
Williamsport, PA..................	218	2 050	134.4	58.6	176	887	57.5	15.2	525.9	245.7	99.0	19.9
Wilmington, NC	496	6 823	440.1	183.2	399	2 128	133.0	39.1	992.4	505.5	149.9	38.7
Yakima, WA	391	4 594	298.6	129.8	277	1 408	87.6	26.8	884.7	329.1	120.4	41.7
York, PA	586	6 842	469.4	214.2	585	3 058	202.4	58.0	1 742.3	680.0	225.2	32.1
Youngstown-Warren, OH......	1 287	15 298	838.1	388.8	889	5 394	299.5	89.6	2 714.6	1 295.5	592.7	114.2
Yuba City, CA	252	2 702	248.1	79.0	148	821	53.9	14.3	790.8	261.4	102.0	34.2
Yuma, AZ	224	2 428	154.1	60.1	158	855	46.5	13.6	775.0	276.7	96.8	20.8

1. Firms subject to federal tax.   2. October 1, 1998 to September 30, 1999.

Table C. Metropolitan Areas — **Federal Funds and Local Government Finances**

Area Name	Federal funds and grants, fiscal 1999[1] (cont'd)							Local government finances, 1997				
	Expenditures (mil dol) (cont'd)							General revenue				
	Procurement contract awards			Grants[2]						Taxes		
											Per capita[3] (dollars)	
	Salaries and wages	Defense	Other	Medicaid and other health-related	Nutrition and family welfare	Education	Other	Total (mil dol)	Intergovern-mental (mil dol)	Total (mil dol)	Total	Property
	171	172	173	174	175	176	177	178	179	180	181	182
Tucson, AZ	576.0	1 658.5	91.8	353.7	106.4	62.5	327.3	1 850.7	837.9	671.3	860	654
Tulsa, OK	267.4	53.8	76.0	172.7	74.0	45.4	97.1	1 518.7	503.4	570.3	746	391
Tuscaloosa, AL	65.1	21.4	13.8	59.5	17.7	11.1	57.0	476.7	141.7	64.7	402	206
Tyler, TX	46.3	23.8	13.6	77.7	11.3	6.2	12.9	303.6	114.7	133.3	800	601
Utica-Rome, NY	128.3	77.9	15.9	204.5	41.5	16.0	48.9	1 032.8	431.1	405.8	1 358	1 004
Victoria, TX	11.3	1.6	3.5	35.0	8.3	5.6	28.5	255.3	61.4	85.8	1 046	818
Visalia-Tulare-Porterville, CA	50.6	5.1	28.8	213.1	111.2	32.0	70.7	1 468.0	786.8	190.2	539	364
Waco, TX	102.9	109.6	12.5	121.6	16.9	9.6	21.5	607.1	185.8	162.8	802	575
Washington-Baltimore, DC-MD-VA-WV	24 949.1	14 240.4	15 442.9	4 630.7	2 128.7	743.8	3 846.6	22 316.2	7 112.1	11 447.2	1 588	885
Baltimore, MD	2 788.6	2 058.6	916.6	2 026.9	632.5	228.0	765.6	5 969.2	2 174.5	2 874.9	1 161	685
Hagerstown, MD	28.1	7.8	11.5	52.2	11.5	3.2	21.3	237.6	87.8	104.0	811	520
Washington, DC-MD-VA-WV	22 132.4	12 174.0	14 514.7	2 551.5	1 484.7	512.5	3 059.6	16 109.4	4 849.8	8 468.4	1 840	1 003
Waterloo-Cedar Falls, IA	32.1	4.6	6.2	56.3	20.1	10.5	9.5	351.5	147.2	104.2	857	735
Wausau, WI	29.4	1.9	9.0	41.0	10.9	4.4	19.1	372.6	180.2	114.2	933	859
West Palm Beach-Boca Raton, FL	290.3	1 501.3	116.2	133.2	72.3	34.2	205.5	3 140.0	632.2	1 523.2	1 495	1 256
Wheeling, WV-OH	38.8	3.6	15.8	66.6	23.8	8.3	59.2	299.2	128.4	93.6	607	437
Wichita Falls, TX	357.3	83.7	7.1	49.7	11.7	6.7	47.2	240.7	83.8	107.2	782	620
Wichita, KS	347.4	631.5	62.2	158.5	65.6	17.5	75.0	1 171.4	484.5	410.3	773	561
Williamsport, PA	36.2	13.6	8.5	46.3	15.2	3.9	24.8	254.6	105.3	97.0	819	555
Wilmington, NC	63.2	37.4	18.2	84.0	22.5	8.4	37.4	693.0	222.8	180.6	846	621
Yakima, WA	62.1	27.7	25.6	141.3	70.0	19.1	27.1	528.1	328.0	116.2	532	342
York, PA	101.2	477.9	58.6	90.9	21.2	6.4	36.2	735.0	264.7	307.6	830	614
Youngstown-Warren, OH	138.0	13.6	29.4	244.1	101.2	36.3	108.9	1 252.6	581.2	476.7	801	570
Yuba City, CA	161.8	7.8	8.3	74.4	37.8	13.1	16.5	406.0	247.5	87.4	627	506
Yuma, AZ	189.7	38.9	17.9	37.8	26.0	11.3	40.6	336.4	182.6	93.8	721	481

1. October 1, 1998 to September 30, 1999.   2. State totals may include programs not allocated by county.   3. Based on the resident population estimated as of July 1 of the year shown.

Area Name	Local government finances, 1997 (cont'd)							Debt outstanding		Government employment, 1998			Presidential election, 2000		
	Direct general expenditure												Percent of vote cast —		
			Percent of total for —												
	Total (mil dol)	Per capita[1] (dollars)	Education	Health and hospitals	Police protection	Public welfare	Highways	Total (mil dol)	Per capita[1] (dollars)	Federal civilian	Federal military	State and local	Democratic	Republican	All other
	183	184	185	186	187	188	189	190	191	192	193	194	195	196	197
Tucson, AZ	2 026.7	2 598	36.8	5.1	5.5	7.0	3.9	2 077.0	2 662	8 619	7 728	56 163	51.3	43.3	5.3
Tulsa, OK	1 522.5	1 992	45.5	2.5	6.0	0.0	3.5	2 364.7	3 094	5 090	3 912	36 785	38.2	38.2	23.6
Tuscaloosa, AL	431.2	2 682	35.6	32.7	3.9	0.0	4.1	333.6	2 075	1 477	1 025	18 547	40.9	56.6	2.5
Tyler, TX	294.7	1 768	59.4	7.8	5.1	1.8	3.3	248.4	1 490	936	456	10 877	27.2	71.5	1.4
Utica-Rome, NY	1 056.5	3 535	46.1	2.4	2.6	11.2	5.6	513.7	1 719	2 334	737	24 897	45.4	49.9	4.7
Victoria, TX	239.4	2 918	38.5	31.9	5.6	0.0	3.0	142.9	1 742	234	220	6 067	29.8	68.5	1.6
Visalia-Tulare-Porterville, CA	1 436.4	4 067	38.3	20.1	3.0	12.0	1.5	565.2	1 600	1 196	713	23 673	36.7	60.2	3.1
Waco, TX	591.5	2 914	40.6	3.6	4.2	0.2	3.0	2 887.4	14 225	3 220	579	11 831	34.1	63.9	2.0
Washington-Baltimore, DC-MD-VA-WV	21 614.3	2 999	40.2	4.4	5.7	7.1	3.5	23 084.2	3 203	418 436	108 699	425 928	56.4	40.0	3.6
Baltimore, MD	5 977.3	2 415	48.0	2.4	6.7	0.5	4.8	5 738.6	2 318	71 478	26 323	162 172	53.9	42.6	3.4
Hagerstown, MD	234.3	1 828	58.6	0.8	3.9	0.3	4.8	230.5	1 799	950	771	6 942	38.4	58.9	2.7
Washington, DC-MD-VA-WV	15 402.7	3 346	36.9	5.2	5.3	9.8	3.0	17 115.1	3 718	346 008	81 605	256 814	58.1	38.2	3.7
Waterloo-Cedar Falls, IA	380.5	3 131	44.8	7.7	4.1	4.2	7.8	232.1	1 910	561	593	10 899	54.7	42.6	2.7
Wausau, WI	399.6	3 264	46.8	13.0	3.7	3.1	9.5	225.0	1 838	514	437	6 702	45.5	49.5	5.0
West Palm Beach-Boca Raton, FL	3 052.6	2 997	32.4	4.1	8.0	0.7	3.8	3 439.3	3 377	5 731	2 409	47 726	62.3	35.3	2.4
Wheeling, WV-OH	284.2	1 843	49.8	4.9	4.4	3.2	4.0	481.4	3 123	699	614	9 471	NA	NA	NA
Wichita Falls, TX	243.4	1 775	51.9	4.1	5.9	0.6	4.2	142.8	1 042	2 588	7 825	9 546	32.3	65.8	1.8
Wichita, KS	1 190.9	2 245	44.2	2.6	5.1	1.2	8.5	1 691.6	3 189	5 004	5 279	29 464	37.3	58.2	4.5
Williamsport, PA	245.0	2 070	56.5	0.1	2.3	3.2	4.7	326.2	2 755	662	402	5 478	NA	NA	NA
Wilmington, NC	702.2	3 288	29.8	36.3	3.6	4.8	1.2	362.3	1 696	1 199	908	16 323	NA	NA	NA
Yakima, WA	560.2	2 566	57.3	1.2	5.2	0.0	5.8	307.9	1 410	1 433	893	12 033	38.0	58.7	3.4
York, PA	690.5	1 864	50.9	3.9	3.7	4.5	3.5	964.9	2 604	3 805	1 689	12 262	NA	NA	NA
Youngstown-Warren, OH	1 219.3	2 049	49.5	5.5	6.1	6.1	4.7	504.0	847	2 652	1 549	30 774	NA	NA	NA
Yuba City, CA	410.8	2 949	46.3	4.4	3.9	12.4	3.8	149.4	1 072	1 414	3 360	8 287	32.7	63.7	3.6
Yuma, AZ	334.0	2 569	46.4	1.4	6.7	2.1	7.3	266.5	2 049	2 399	4 287	6 736	42.1	54.8	3.1

1. Based on the resident population estimated as of July 1 of the year shown.

TABLE D:

Cities of
25,000 or More

(For explanation of symbols, see page xii)

Page

896	**AL**(Anniston)—**CA**(Campbell)
907	**CA**(Carlsbad)—**CA**(Los Altos)
918	**CA**(Los Angeles)—**CA**(San Dimas)
929	**CA**(San Francisco)—**CO**(Littleton)
940	**CO**(Longmont)—**FL**(Miami)
951	**FL**(Miami Beach)—**IL**(Belleville)
962	**IL**(Berwyn)—**IN**(Carmel)
973	**IN**(Columbus)—**KY**(Paducah)
984	**LA**(Alexandria)—**MI**(Burton)
995	**MI**(Dearborn)—**MN**(Winona)
1006	**MS**(Biloxi)—**NJ**(Garfield)
1017	**NJ**(Hackensack)—**NC**(Charlotte)
1028	**NC**(Concord)—**OH**(Upper Arlington)
1039	**OH**(Warren)—**RI**(Woonsocket)
1050	**SC**(Anderson)—**TX**(Laredo)
1061	**TX**(League City)—**VA**(Virginia Beach)
1072	**WA**(Auburn)—**WY**(Laramie)

Table D. Cities — Land Area and Population

STATE Place code	City	Land area, 1990[1] (sq km)	Population, 1999 Total persons	Rank	Per square kilometer	Total persons 1990	Percent change 1990–1999	Total persons 1980	Percent change 1980–1990	White	Black	Am. Indian, Eskimo, Aleut	Asian and Pacific Islander	Other race	His-panic[2]	Foreign born
		1	2	3	4	5	6	7	8	9	10	11	12	13	14	15
01 00000	ALABAMA	131 443.1	4 369 862	X	33	4 040 389	8.2	3 894 025	3.8	73.6	25.3	0.4	0.5	0.1	0.6	1.1
01 01852	Anniston	52.3	25 622	1 176	490	26 638	-3.8	29 523	-9.8	54.5	44.3	0.2	0.7	0.3	0.8	1.4
01 03076	Auburn	84.2	42 601	696	506	33 830	25.9	28 471	18.8	79.9	16.3	0.2	3.4	0.3	0.9	4.2
01 05980	Bessemer	100.2	30 644	989	306	33 581	-8.7	31 729	5.8	41.4	58.4	0.1	0.1	0.0	0.2	0.3
01 07000	Birmingham	384.6	249 459	67	649	265 347	-6.0	284 413	-6.7	36.0	63.3	0.1	0.6	0.1	0.4	1.2
01 20104	Decatur	122.3	54 988	518	450	49 917	10.2	42 002	18.8	82.4	16.5	0.3	0.6	0.2	0.8	1.0
01 21184	Dothan	206.4	58 383	476	283	54 131	7.9	48 750	11.1	71.5	27.3	0.3	0.8	0.1	0.7	1.1
01 26896	Florence	60.9	39 028	774	641	36 426	7.1	37 029	-1.6	82.1	17.1	0.3	0.4	0.1	0.5	0.6
01 28696	Gadsden	92.1	42 120	706	457	42 523	-0.9	47 565	-10.6	70.8	28.2	0.1	0.7	0.1	0.4	1.4
01 35896	Hoover	61.8	61 406	439	994	39 988	53.6	19 792	102.1	95.2	3.3	0.1	1.2	0.2	0.9	2.4
01 37000	Huntsville	425.8	177 893	110	418	159 880	11.3	142 513	12.2	72.6	24.4	0.5	2.1	0.3	1.2	3.9
01 50000	Mobile	305.7	200 206	84	655	199 973	0.1	200 396	-2.1	59.6	38.9	0.2	1.0	0.2	1.0	2.1
01 51000	Montgomery	349.6	195 690	89	560	190 350	2.8	177 857	7.0	56.5	42.3	0.2	0.7	0.2	0.8	1.5
01 59472	Phenix City	52.8	27 550	1 088	522	25 311	8.8	26 941	-6.1	59.4	40.0	0.2	0.3	0.1	0.6	1.0
01 62496	Prichard	65.8	31 881	953	485	34 320	-7.1	39 518	-13.2	20.1	79.4	0.4	0.0	0.0	0.3	0.2
01 77256	Tuscaloosa	122.0	85 171	284	698	77 866	9.4	75 211	3.4	62.8	35.5	0.1	1.3	0.2	0.8	2.1
02 00000	ALASKA	1 477 267.5	619 500	X	0	550 043	12.6	401 851	36.9	75.5	4.1	15.6	3.6	1.2	3.2	4.5
02 03000	Anchorage	4 396.9	257 808	63	59	226 338	13.9	174 431	29.8	80.7	6.4	6.4	4.8	1.6	4.1	5.9
02 24230	Fairbanks	81.1	32 769	923	404	30 843	6.2	22 645	36.2	72.4	13.0	9.2	3.3	2.2	5.4	5.0
02 36400	Juneau	6 717.3	30 192	1 006	4	26 751	12.9	19 528	37.0	80.6	1.1	12.9	4.3	1.0	2.8	4.9
04 00000	ARIZONA	294 333.5	4 778 332	X	16	3 665 339	30.4	2 716 546	34.9	80.8	3.0	5.6	1.5	9.1	18.8	7.6
04 12000	Chandler	123.2	169 053	117	1 372	89 862	88.1	29 720	202.4	85.2	2.6	1.2	2.4	8.7	17.3	7.0
04 23620	Flagstaff	163.8	57 078	493	348	45 857	24.5	34 743	32.0	79.6	2.5	9.2	1.4	7.3	15.2	4.1
04 27400	Gilbert	70.3	97 590	239	1 388	29 149	234.8	NA	NA	90.3	1.6	0.5	1.7	5.9	11.6	4.0
04 27820	Glendale	135.2	201 456	83	1 490	147 070	37.0	97 172	52.2	85.0	3.0	0.9	2.1	8.9	15.5	6.0
04 46000	Mesa	281.3	368 811	45	1 311	289 199	27.5	152 453	89.7	90.1	1.9	1.0	1.5	5.5	10.9	4.9
04 54050	Peoria	159.2	94 170	246	592	51 080	84.4	12 251	313.6	86.9	2.2	0.6	1.4	8.8	15.5	4.3
04 55000	Phoenix	1 087.6	1 211 466	7	1 114	988 015	22.6	789 704	24.6	81.7	5.2	1.9	1.7	9.6	20.0	8.6
04 57380	Prescott	83.9	35 341	849	421	26 592	32.9	20 055	32.6	95.2	0.5	1.2	0.6	2.5	7.1	3.4
04 65000	Scottsdale	477.5	199 943	85	419	130 099	53.7	88 412	47.1	96.0	0.8	0.6	1.2	1.4	4.8	6.3
04 66820	Sierra Vista	368.7	38 468	783	104	32 983	16.6	24 937	32.3	77.4	12.0	0.6	5.2	4.8	11.8	7.0
04 73000	Tempe	102.4	167 740	120	1 638	141 993	18.1	106 743	33.0	86.8	3.2	1.3	4.1	4.6	10.9	7.2
04 77000	Tucson	404.8	466 591	31	1 153	415 444	12.3	330 537	24.5	75.2	4.3	1.6	2.2	16.7	29.3	10.7
04 85540	Yuma	56.6	63 059	428	1 114	56 966	10.7	42 433	34.2	73.0	3.8	1.1	1.7	20.4	35.6	11.9
05 00000	ARKANSAS	134 875.1	2 551 373	X	19	2 350 624	8.5	2 286 357	2.8	82.7	15.9	0.5	0.5	0.3	0.8	1.1
05 15190	Conway	62.4	42 412	700	680	26 481	60.2	20 375	30.0	88.8	10.0	0.3	0.7	0.2	0.5	1.2
05 23290	Fayetteville	104.2	58 163	479	558	42 247	37.7	36 608	15.4	93.1	3.8	1.1	1.6	0.4	1.4	2.3
05 24550	Fort Smith	121.0	74 940	343	619	72 798	3.0	71 626	1.6	86.3	7.7	1.4	4.1	0.6	1.4	4.1
05 33400	Hot Springs	74.7	38 778	777	519	33 095	17.2	35 781	-9.3	83.1	15.5	0.5	0.4	0.5	1.3	2.7
05 34750	Jacksonville	50.9	28 682	1 051	563	29 101	-1.4	NA	NA	79.4	17.0	0.5	2.3	0.8	2.3	3.2
05 35710	Jonesboro	189.8	52 558	546	277	46 535	12.9	31 530	47.6	90.8	8.0	0.3	0.8	0.1	0.5	1.1
05 41000	Little Rock	266.4	176 136	111	661	175 727	0.2	158 461	10.9	64.7	34.0	0.3	0.9	0.2	0.8	2.1
05 50450	North Little Rock	102.9	59 543	461	579	61 829	-3.7	64 288	-3.8	75.3	23.6	0.3	0.4	0.3	0.8	1.1
05 55310	Pine Bluff	109.8	52 249	551	476	57 140	-8.6	56 636	0.9	45.6	53.5	0.2	0.5	0.2	0.4	0.7
05 66080	Springdale	76.8	42 339	702	551	29 945	41.4	23 440	27.8	97.2	0.1	1.1	1.0	0.6	1.5	1.6
05 74540	West Memphis	37.2	26 894	1 121	723	28 259	-4.8	28 138	0.4	56.9	42.1	0.2	0.5	0.2	0.5	0.7
06 00000	CALIFORNIA	403 970.3	33 145 121	X	82	29 785 857	11.3	23 667 765	25.7	69.0	7.4	0.8	9.6	13.2	25.8	21.7
06 00562	Alameda	27.8	75 554	335	2 718	73 979	2.1	63 852	15.9	69.9	6.7	0.7	19.2	3.4	9.1	17.2
06 00884	Alhambra	19.7	84 896	285	4 309	82 087	3.4	64 615	27.0	40.9	2.0	0.4	38.1	18.6	36.1	46.9
06 02000	Anaheim	114.7	300 650	56	2 621	266 406	12.9	219 311	21.5	71.4	2.5	0.5	9.4	16.1	31.4	28.4
06 02252	Antioch	50.7	84 040	288	1 658	62 195	35.1	42 683	45.7	85.4	2.6	1.1	4.8	6.0	15.6	7.7
06 02364	Apple Valley	174.1	58 063	482	334	46 079	26.0	14 305	222.1	86.8	3.9	1.0	2.5	5.9	12.6	5.7
06 02462	Arcadia	28.2	51 223	567	1 816	48 284	6.1	45 994	5.0	71.5	0.8	0.4	23.4	3.9	10.7	27.6
06 03386	Azusa	23.3	42 615	694	1 829	41 203	3.4	29 380	40.2	66.0	3.8	0.7	6.6	22.8	53.4	29.5
06 03526	Bakersfield	237.9	222 352	74	935	176 264	26.1	105 611	66.9	72.7	9.4	1.1	3.6	13.2	20.5	8.0
06 03666	Baldwin Park	17.1	72 786	354	4 256	69 330	5.0	50 554	37.1	55.6	2.4	0.7	12.3	29.0	70.8	43.0
06 04870	Bell	6.6	35 331	851	5 353	34 365	2.8	25 450	35.0	42.0	1.0	0.8	1.4	54.7	86.1	57.0
06 04982	Bellflower	15.7	64 239	418	4 092	61 815	3.9	53 441	15.7	69.8	6.3	0.9	10.1	13.0	23.9	19.0
06 04996	Bell Gardens	6.5	44 703	666	6 877	42 315	5.6	34 117	24.0	38.2	0.5	1.2	1.3	58.8	87.5	52.1
06 06000	Berkeley	27.1	108 319	207	3 997	102 724	5.4	103 328	-0.6	62.1	18.8	0.6	14.8	3.7	8.4	16.5
06 06308	Beverly Hills	14.7	32 653	928	2 221	31 971	2.1	32 367	-1.2	91.3	1.7	0.2	5.5	1.4	5.4	34.8
06 08100	Brea	25.9	36 078	840	1 393	32 873	9.7	27 913	17.8	87.0	1.1	0.4	6.2	5.3	15.4	12.4
06 08786	Buena Park	27.5	74 421	345	2 706	68 784	8.2	64 165	7.2	70.9	2.5	0.7	14.4	11.4	24.5	22.7
06 08954	Burbank	44.9	99 039	229	2 206	93 649	5.8	84 625	10.7	82.6	1.7	0.5	6.8	8.4	22.6	25.7
06 09066	Burlingame	11.3	28 045	1 070	2 482	26 666	5.2	26 173	1.9	87.4	1.0	0.4	8.9	2.3	10.2	19.4
06 10046	Camarillo	47.8	60 951	447	1 275	52 297	16.5	37 797	38.4	86.3	1.6	0.5	6.3	5.2	12.1	11.6
06 10345	Campbell	14.5	38 214	795	2 635	36 088	5.9	27 067	33.3	83.6	2.0	0.6	9.5	4.3	10.6	12.5

1. Dry land or land partially or temporarily covered by water. 2. Hispanic persons may be of any race.

City	Under 5 years	5 to 17 years	18 to 24 years	25 to 34 years	35 to 44 years	45 to 54 years	55 to 64 years	65 to 74 years	75 years and over	Percent female	Number	Percent change, 1980–1990	Persons per house-hold	Female family house-holder[1]	One-person
	16	17	18	19	20	21	22	23	24	25	26	27	28	29	30
ALABAMA	7.0	19.2	11.0	16.0	14.4	10.4	9.0	7.5	5.5	52.1	1 506 790	12.2	2.62	13.4	23.8
Anniston	6.8	19.0	8.2	15.3	14.5	8.6	10.0	10.5	7.1	54.5	10 807	-1.6	2.42	18.6	30.5
Auburn	4.1	10.9	47.3	13.8	8.0	6.4	4.0	3.1	2.4	49.3	13 444	29.3	2.23	8.3	32.5
Bessemer	7.5	19.2	9.8	14.6	12.7	8.9	9.5	9.6	8.1	54.7	12 584	12.4	2.62	23.8	27.8
Birmingham	7.4	18.0	10.5	17.8	14.4	8.4	8.6	8.0	6.8	54.3	105 437	-1.8	2.46	21.7	31.9
Decatur	7.0	18.6	9.1	17.5	14.9	11.7	9.0	7.3	4.9	52.4	19 134	25.7	2.50	12.2	26.1
Dothan	7.4	20.5	9.0	15.9	15.9	9.9	8.8	7.6	5.1	53.1	20 685	19.1	2.55	14.8	26.1
Florence	6.8	15.9	13.6	14.9	12.9	9.9	9.6	9.3	7.1	54.2	14 910	9.0	2.35	13.3	29.6
Gadsden	6.3	16.8	9.6	14.0	12.5	9.5	10.9	11.5	8.8	54.5	17 512	-3.7	2.38	15.6	30.7
Hoover	6.5	17.1	9.1	18.3	18.7	11.7	8.8	6.6	3.3	52.7	16 064	124.6	2.46	7.7	24.6
Huntsville	6.5	16.8	12.0	18.8	14.4	12.0	9.6	6.2	3.8	51.4	63 058	24.2	2.46	11.8	27.1
Mobile	7.5	18.8	10.9	16.8	14.4	9.4	8.6	8.0	5.7	53.6	75 442	5.3	2.53	18.3	28.4
Montgomery	7.8	20.1	10.9	17.2	14.9	9.4	8.0	6.7	5.0	53.5	69 968	11.6	2.59	17.7	27.4
Phenix City	7.5	18.8	9.5	15.9	13.9	10.0	9.8	8.6	5.9	53.7	9 745	0.3	2.55	20.5	27.1
Prichard	8.9	26.3	10.0	14.5	13.7	8.2	7.3	6.7	4.5	54.5	11 121	-7.8	3.03	33.9	20.7
Tuscaloosa	5.6	15.1	23.5	15.7	12.3	8.3	8.0	6.7	4.8	52.2	29 467	12.7	2.35	14.5	31.9
ALASKA	10.0	21.4	10.2	20.5	18.7	9.8	5.4	2.8	1.2	47.3	188 915	42.7	2.80	9.6	22.1
Anchorage	9.4	19.9	10.3	21.6	19.1	10.8	5.3	2.6	1.0	48.6	82 702	36.0	2.68	10.1	22.9
Fairbanks	10.9	18.1	16.4	22.8	14.4	7.5	5.1	3.1	1.9	46.4	10 885	32.7	2.62	10.6	26.4
Juneau	9.0	20.5	7.8	19.1	21.5	11.6	5.3	3.2	2.0	49.3	9 902	39.9	2.66	10.2	23.6
ARIZONA	8.0	18.8	10.7	17.3	14.4	9.5	8.2	7.9	5.1	50.6	1 368 843	42.7	2.62	10.4	24.7
Chandler	10.5	21.3	9.0	24.5	17.1	8.1	4.6	3.3	1.7	50.4	31 490	233.5	2.86	10.4	17.9
Flagstaff	7.0	17.7	26.3	17.7	14.4	8.2	4.3	2.9	1.5	50.4	14 417	41.5	2.75	11.1	20.4
Gilbert	10.9	24.8	10.0	21.4	17.1	8.6	3.9	2.3	0.9	50.1	9 381	NA	3.11	8.8	14.0
Glendale	8.2	20.9	11.1	18.2	16.9	10.4	6.5	4.6	3.3	51.0	53 669	62.5	2.73	11.8	22.0
Mesa	8.7	19.9	10.8	19.0	14.1	8.6	6.6	7.3	5.1	50.9	107 863	99.1	2.65	9.3	24.0
Peoria	9.4	19.6	5.9	20.1	14.3	9.2	7.4	8.2	6.8	52.1	18 254	329.4	2.73	7.5	19.6
Phoenix	8.5	18.6	10.5	19.7	15.5	10.1	7.4	6.0	3.7	50.4	369 921	29.7	2.62	11.8	26.1
Prescott	4.7	12.9	10.0	11.1	11.7	10.6	12.9	15.4	10.7	51.3	11 479	44.0	2.20	7.6	30.4
Scottsdale	5.1	12.7	8.6	17.5	15.2	13.2	11.5	9.9	6.3	52.9	57 583	68.0	2.24	8.4	29.7
Sierra Vista	7.8	18.9	13.9	21.2	14.1	9.8	7.0	5.0	2.2	48.6	11 672	55.0	2.65	8.7	22.3
Tempe	6.5	14.9	20.4	21.4	15.2	9.3	5.8	4.0	2.6	48.6	55 540	48.9	2.47	9.3	26.2
Tucson	7.7	16.7	14.3	19.0	14.0	8.2	7.5	7.3	5.3	51.3	162 685	29.4	2.42	12.4	31.3
Yuma	9.9	20.7	10.5	18.0	13.0	8.5	7.0	7.5	4.9	50.6	19 282	36.2	2.80	10.9	21.2
ARKANSAS	7.0	19.4	10.1	15.3	13.9	10.4	9.1	8.3	6.6	51.8	891 179	9.1	2.57	11.1	24.0
Conway	6.3	14.7	25.8	15.4	12.5	7.5	5.9	6.3	5.5	53.7	9 437	39.1	2.44	10.7	26.1
Fayetteville	6.5	14.0	25.4	18.5	12.5	7.9	5.6	5.1	4.5	50.0	16 894	25.2	2.26	8.8	32.2
Fort Smith	7.5	17.9	9.6	17.0	14.6	10.2	8.4	8.3	6.5	52.2	29 646	6.8	2.41	10.5	29.7
Hot Springs	5.9	14.3	7.8	13.3	12.1	9.6	11.4	12.6	12.8	54.7	14 488	-6.8	2.14	12.2	36.7
Jacksonville	10.3	20.7	13.8	21.9	13.2	8.1	6.1	3.4	2.6	49.7	9 854	NA	2.81	11.2	17.8
Jonesboro	7.1	16.4	17.1	16.8	13.7	9.7	8.2	6.3	4.8	52.1	17 976	58.6	2.46	11.2	25.3
Little Rock	7.3	17.6	10.3	18.9	16.0	9.7	7.7	7.0	5.5	53.6	72 573	18.9	2.37	14.5	32.1
North Little Rock	7.0	18.3	8.9	16.4	14.6	10.5	8.9	9.1	6.3	53.1	24 987	2.4	2.42	15.2	29.0
Pine Bluff	7.8	21.1	11.2	14.8	12.9	8.6	8.5	8.0	7.0	54.3	20 871	4.5	2.64	19.4	27.2
Springdale	7.8	18.8	10.2	17.0	14.3	11.1	8.2	7.1	5.5	52.1	11 432	35.7	2.59	9.3	21.8
West Memphis	9.0	22.0	10.5	16.3	14.5	9.7	7.7	6.3	4.1	53.6	9 879	6.9	2.83	20.8	21.4
CALIFORNIA	8.1	18.0	11.5	19.1	15.6	9.8	7.5	6.2	4.3	49.9	10 381 206	20.1	2.79	11.5	23.4
Alameda	6.4	13.5	12.7	21.2	17.7	9.6	7.1	6.7	5.0	47.2	29 078	9.4	2.36	11.0	31.5
Alhambra	7.2	15.8	11.7	21.3	15.4	8.8	7.1	6.5	6.3	52.4	28 239	8.5	2.83	14.1	24.5
Anaheim	8.6	17.3	13.1	21.2	14.5	9.7	7.5	5.0	3.1	49.4	87 588	9.9	2.99	11.6	19.9
Antioch	10.0	21.1	9.3	19.2	17.6	9.4	5.9	4.5	3.0	50.7	21 401	42.8	2.89	12.2	16.9
Apple Valley	9.6	22.1	8.4	17.1	14.8	10.0	8.1	7.0	3.0	50.6	15 588	206.2	2.95	9.9	14.6
Arcadia	4.5	17.1	8.8	13.6	15.6	14.3	10.2	9.0	6.9	52.9	18 352	2.7	2.60	9.7	23.9
Azusa	9.8	19.2	15.9	22.1	12.6	7.6	6.2	4.0	2.6	49.9	12 651	26.0	3.17	14.8	20.6
Bakersfield	9.8	21.0	10.2	19.2	15.4	8.8	6.4	5.4	3.7	51.4	62 467	57.5	2.75	14.0	23.0
Baldwin Park	10.6	24.8	13.4	18.6	13.4	8.1	5.4	3.5	2.1	49.5	16 614	18.6	4.13	16.3	10.5
Bell	11.8	22.6	14.6	20.4	11.9	7.1	5.3	3.2	3.2	49.0	9 013	1.8	3.78	15.1	17.3
Bellflower	9.3	16.8	11.4	21.1	14.1	9.2	7.4	6.3	4.4	50.9	22 905	5.4	2.67	13.8	25.3
Bell Gardens	12.8	27.6	15.0	18.8	12.3	5.9	3.8	2.4	1.6	48.9	9 244	-1.7	4.52	18.2	9.3
Berkeley	4.5	9.7	22.1	18.8	17.1	10.9	6.0	6.0	4.9	50.3	43 453	-3.1	2.10	10.7	39.8
Beverly Hills	3.2	12.6	8.1	14.4	15.8	14.3	11.5	10.2	9.9	55.5	14 564	-2.3	2.19	8.1	38.1
Brea	6.3	16.5	11.4	18.6	17.5	11.9	8.8	5.8	3.1	50.3	12 224	22.2	2.68	8.0	21.7
Buena Park	8.4	18.1	11.4	20.2	14.5	10.6	8.8	5.2	2.7	49.9	22 210	4.0	3.08	12.8	15.1
Burbank	6.2	13.8	9.8	20.5	15.5	11.4	8.1	8.1	6.5	51.4	39 275	9.1	2.36	10.7	32.0
Burlingame	5.2	10.7	8.0	20.1	16.2	11.5	9.0	9.4	9.9	53.3	12 329	0.0	2.13	7.6	37.3
Camarillo	6.9	17.6	7.9	15.7	16.2	10.7	8.2	9.5	7.2	50.8	18 109	37.1	2.84	7.3	18.1
Campbell	7.3	12.7	10.1	26.4	16.3	10.7	7.2	5.3	4.0	50.5	15 306	30.9	2.35	10.6	29.0

1. No spouse present.

City	Persons in group quarters, 1990 Total	Persons in mental hospitals	Persons in nursing homes	Persons identified as homeless[1]	Serious crimes known to police, 1998[2] Total Number	Total Rate[3]	Violent	Property	Education, 1990 School enrollment Public	Private	Attainment[4] (percent) High school graduate or more	Bachelor's degree or more	Money income, 1989 Per capita (dollars)[5]	Households Median Dollars	Percent change, 1979–1989 (constant 1989 dollars)
	31	32	33	34	35	36	37	38	39	40	41	42	43	44	45
ALABAMA	92 086	2 555	24 031	1 942	200 065	4 597	512	4 085	940 143	116 259	66.9	15.7	11 486	23 597	3.0
Anniston	471	7	34	15	4 204	16 107	2 743	13 364	5 426	866	67.0	17.9	11 371	19 099	-3.3
Auburn	3 842	0	185	0	2 132	5 448	268	5 180	19 968	934	88.1	50.1	10 278	12 931	-11.4
Bessemer	495	0	334	0	4 065	12 961	1 365	11 596	7 261	808	57.8	7.2	8 433	16 331	-15.6
Birmingham	6 444	0	1 641	995	22 533	8 685	1 213	7 472	58 988	9 258	69.3	16.2	10 127	19 193	-4.2
Decatur	914	39	269	7	3 666	6 709	501	6 208	10 803	1 268	74.0	20.5	14 374	30 005	4.5
Dothan	868	0	333	22	2 631	4 611	393	4 218	12 498	1 624	70.5	19.3	13 047	25 790	2.4
Florence	1 423	0	427	29	2 045	5 193	475	4 718	8 578	1 148	70.2	22.6	11 854	21 459	-13.6
Gadsden	822	0	430	15	4 022	9 514	1 970	7 544	8 305	1 072	61.5	10.7	10 772	19 187	-2.0
Hoover	228	0	228	0	1 537	2 760	149	2 611	8 417	2 259	94.2	45.8	21 961	44 747	2.8
Huntsville	4 356	51	553	300	11 716	6 767	719	6 048	38 355	6 335	82.0	33.3	16 204	32 295	8.0
Mobile	5 209	103	1 649	167	18 357	7 486	615	6 871	42 297	11 800	74.8	21.4	12 509	22 446	-8.2
Montgomery	5 680	32	1 063	139	13 908	7 031	757	6 274	45 032	9 062	75.7	24.6	12 755	26 311	5.4
Phenix City	406	0	283	0	1 468	4 635	660	4 635	5 340	658	59.1	10.6	9 954	20 478	10.7
Prichard	583	0	147	0	3 775	11 343	2 485	8 858	10 087	1 096	53.7	5.1	5 820	11 576	-18.3
Tuscaloosa	8 652	1 465	547	17	11 276	13 425	1 005	12 420	27 482	2 546	72.1	27.3	11 469	19 568	1.2
ALASKA	20 643	22	1 202	519	29 331	4 777	654	4 123	141 933	14 424	86.6	23.0	17 610	41 408	-2.8
Anchorage	5 105	0	515	351	13 364	5 256	642	4 614	56 060	7 297	90.4	26.9	19 620	43 946	-4.2
Fairbanks	2 401	8	219	98	1 681	5 025	1 100	3 925	6 876	880	86.2	18.3	14 665	32 033	-9.8
Juneau	445	0	83	8	NA	NA	NA	NA	6 825	813	89.9	30.7	19 920	47 924	-7.3
ARIZONA	79 920	1 004	14 472	4 630	306 985	6 575	578	5 997	896 427	94 695	78.7	20.3	13 461	27 540	-0.1
Chandler	440	38	328	0	8 490	5 617	222	5 395	23 900	2 395	85.8	26.2	14 720	38 124	27.7
Flagstaff	6 297	0	0	9	4 954	8 645	555	8 090	20 097	1 083	86.9	32.7	11 517	28 382	0.4
Gilbert	0	0	0	0	NA	NA	NA	NA	9 173	762	90.8	29.0	14 665	41 081	NA
Glendale	1 366	50	736	29	13 021	6 757	559	6 198	38 015	5 142	82.6	17.7	13 524	31 665	-0.2
Mesa	2 329	0	1 531	266	25 322	6 945	662	6 283	74 891	7 088	84.8	21.0	13 506	30 273	1.2
Peoria	847	0	560	0	3 263	4 058	256	3 802	11 443	1 009	83.5	16.9	14 059	34 205	33.2
Phoenix	14 345	733	3 058	2 509	104 734	8 545	832	7 713	221 676	30 872	78.7	19.9	14 096	29 291	0.3
Prescott	1 140	0	723	0	1 570	4 520	317	4 203	5 012	1 278	83.3	23.5	13 851	22 517	-4.6
Scottsdale	1 080	0	960	0	9 934	5 248	211	5 037	24 551	4 531	90.8	34.5	23 482	39 037	4.8
Sierra Vista	2 242	0	158	0	1 622	4 163	167	3 996	8 273	684	90.1	23.8	13 449	29 590	5.5
Tempe	4 760	0	210	0	15 282	8 882	581	8 301	47 375	4 546	89.9	36.8	15 530	31 885	-4.1
Tucson	11 288	12	2 237	548	45 296	9 685	1 034	8 651	108 663	11 562	78.6	20.7	11 184	21 748	-7.9
Yuma	877	0	440	64	NA	NA	NA	NA	13 405	989	73.6	15.6	11 529	26 753	1.2
ARKANSAS	57 683	617	21 809	645	108 713	4 283	490	3 793	530 045	52 360	66.3	13.3	10 520	21 147	3.3
Conway	3 488	0	314	0	2 098	5 633	499	5 134	8 083	1 696	76.3	27.4	10 457	22 291	-1.9
Fayetteville	3 824	0	231	7	2 551	4 771	348	4 423	15 401	795	84.3	36.0	12 184	21 202	10.4
Fort Smith	1 175	15	774	21	5 203	6 797	584	6 213	14 584	2 112	73.3	16.7	12 994	23 835	2.4
Hot Springs	1 433	0	650	80	NA	NA	NA	NA	5 569	639	64.4	13.2	11 461	15 708	-6.5
Jacksonville	1 369	0	283	0	1 528	5 221	571	4 650	6 929	884	82.9	12.2	10 337	25 009	2.9
Jonesboro	2 256	28	360	0	2 909	5 432	396	5 036	13 083	783	73.3	21.2	12 360	23 318	1.9
Little Rock	3 987	289	1 539	126	18 515	10 497	1 178	9 319	35 746	10 211	82.0	30.3	15 307	26 889	1.6
North Little Rock	1 190	144	543	34	6 294	10 383	1 059	9 324	12 403	1 968	73.0	17.5	12 390	23 958	-5.9
Pine Bluff	1 903	0	800	47	5 430	10 044	2 588	7 456	15 274	1 012	65.5	16.6	9 530	19 143	-5.3
Springdale	283	0	196	0	NA	NA	NA	NA	6 261	555	70.1	13.7	11 837	25 376	0.7
West Memphis	295	0	195	17	1 660	6 113	1 171	4 942	6 755	658	62.5	10.8	10 009	22 052	-2.3
CALIFORNIA	735 442	9 535	148 362	46 834	1 418 674	4 343	704	3 639	7 177 045	1 123 001	76.2	23.4	16 409	35 798	17.1
Alameda	7 831	10	609	34	3 576	4 588	316	4 272	14 112	2 970	88.1	31.3	19 833	38 122	25.7
Alhambra	2 019	0	958	31	2 495	2 927	366	2 561	20 630	3 970	72.1	22.9	13 436	31 368	15.0
Anaheim	3 928	107	1 720	452	10 438	3 495	508	2 987	62 255	8 608	75.4	18.8	15 746	39 620	18.0
Antioch	309	0	252	57	3 293	4 180	771	3 409	16 086	1 775	82.6	14.9	15 153	40 936	16.9
Apple Valley	120	0	52	8	2 255	4 007	368	3 639	11 167	1 479	80.1	14.9	14 643	34 050	-1.9
Arcadia	599	0	410	0	1 596	3 102	282	2 820	10 797	2 325	88.9	36.4	25 441	47 347	13.5
Azusa	1 171	0	0	0	1 386	3 228	461	2 767	10 093	2 518	62.7	12.1	11 038	31 889	15.7
Bakersfield	2 863	101	1 147	550	12 348	5 870	484	5 386	46 179	4 892	77.8	19.6	14 183	32 154	5.0
Baldwin Park	602	0	292	0	1 380	1 896	356	1 540	21 055	1 942	50.5	9.7	8 858	32 684	18.6
Bell	332	0	77	231	777	2 173	551	1 622	9 473	762	33.6	3.7	7 104	22 515	6.3
Bellflower	658	17	549	0	3 035	4 710	1 142	3 568	13 342	2 690	72.3	12.0	14 304	32 711	16.5
Bell Gardens	473	0	328	0	1 626	3 617	1 010	2 607	15 062	466	26.3	1.7	6 125	23 819	17.1
Berkeley	11 019	88	370	1 111	9 274	8 764	886	7 878	33 379	5 963	90.3	58.7	18 720	29 737	31.4
Beverly Hills	70	0	56	0	1 619	4 908	549	4 359	5 389	2 080	89.4	47.0	55 463	54 348	29.5
Brea	50	0	37	5	1 675	4 658	389	4 269	7 779	1 196	87.4	31.0	21 407	51 253	18.6
Buena Park	373	0	297	0	2 447	3 288	445	2 843	16 570	2 440	76.7	15.9	15 176	41 435	11.3
Burbank	808	0	673	45	3 160	3 210	290	2 920	17 715	3 769	79.7	22.9	18 897	35 959	17.8
Burlingame	474	0	393	0	1 071	3 767	359	3 408	4 669	1 087	88.3	33.5	25 031	42 487	25.1
Camarillo	1 070	0	340	0	1 263	2 151	182	1 969	11 591	2 232	87.9	27.2	19 930	48 219	19.6
Campbell	133	0	89	0	NA	NA	NA	NA	7 317	1 296	88.6	31.0	20 759	42 489	28.4

1. Persons in emergency shelters and persons visible in street locations. 2. Data for serious crimes have not been adjusted for underreporting. This may affect comparability between geographic areas and over time. 3. Per 100,000 population estimated by the FBI. 4. Persons 25 years old and older. 5. Based on population enumerated as of April 1, 1990.

Table D. Cities — Income, Poverty, and Housing

City	Percent with $100,000 or more (46)	Persons Total (47)	Persons Percent change in rate, 1979–1989 (48)	Families Total (49)	Total (50)	Percent change, 1980–1990 (51)	Vacant units for sale or rent[1] (52)	Owner Total (53)	Owner Percent (54)	Median value[2] (dollars) (55)	With a mortgage (56)	Without a mortgage (57)	Median rent[3] (dollars) (58)	Rent as percent of income (59)	Substandard units[4] (percent) (60)
ALABAMA	2.3	18.3	-3.0	14.3	1 670 379	13.8	81 774	1 506 790	70.5	53 700	18.4	12.8	325	24.8	4.5
Anniston	2.8	24.4	3.8	19.2	12 100	2.3	815	10 807	60.4	49 700	20.1	13.5	301	24.9	3.0
Auburn	2.9	39.9	18.4	14.8	14 673	34.9	1 009	13 444	37.0	80 900	16.7	11.8	358	35.1	3.4
Bessemer	0.7	29.7	15.1	24.3	13 783	15.8	872	12 584	59.1	40 500	21.9	14.4	270	28.1	5.5
Birmingham	1.4	24.8	12.7	20.8	117 691	2.8	9 178	105 437	53.4	44 500	20.4	13.5	322	26.1	4.3
Decatur	3.0	12.7	-4.5	10.0	20 640	27.1	1 258	19 134	61.7	66 000	16.1	11.8	351	22.6	2.0
Dothan	2.8	17.0	5.6	13.2	22 190	18.1	1 105	20 685	60.9	58 600	16.7	12.7	321	23.5	3.9
Florence	1.9	18.5	18.6	14.3	15 913	11.0	720	14 910	60.5	53 400	17.5	12.6	305	26.2	1.7
Gadsden	1.6	20.4	10.9	16.5	19 146	-2.9	1 088	17 512	64.8	36 300	17.7	13.3	270	24.4	2.3
Hoover	9.0	3.0	-25.0	2.2	17 038	122.3	868	16 064	60.6	112 700	17.0	11.4	488	19.6	0.7
Huntsville	4.6	11.6	-9.4	8.9	67 827	27.3	3 863	63 058	59.8	78 200	16.4	11.7	405	23.3	2.8
Mobile	3.1	22.4	20.4	18.4	82 817	9.6	5 652	75 442	58.1	55 400	19.0	13.0	332	26.5	4.2
Montgomery	2.8	18.1	-6.7	14.4	76 636	13.7	4 987	69 968	60.1	62 200	19.6	12.8	381	24.8	5.0
Phenix City	1.1	22.2	-10.1	18.3	10 813	3.3	798	9 745	55.1	46 900	17.9	12.7	290	26.5	4.5
Prichard	0.4	44.1	13.7	40.4	13 037	-0.2	1 146	11 121	57.4	35 000	24.2	16.7	242	35.1	8.8
Tuscaloosa	3.1	26.7	3.1	17.1	31 194	10.6	1 292	29 467	46.9	62 900	19.0	12.6	342	31.7	3.4
ALASKA	7.7	9.0	-15.9	6.8	232 608	42.9	15 428	188 915	56.1	94 400	21.5	12.2	559	23.8	12.4
Anchorage	9.3	7.1	-4.1	5.4	94 153	33.8	6 731	82 702	52.8	109 700	22.6	11.4	564	24.8	4.3
Fairbanks	3.6	10.4	-1.9	8.1	12 537	29.1	1 003	10 885	31.1	85 400	21.6	10.9	523	26.0	5.3
Juneau	8.6	5.6	36.6	3.7	10 638	38.9	344	9 902	58.2	113 500	20.3	11.6	653	23.9	6.3
ARIZONA	3.4	15.7	19.3	11.4	1 659 430	49.4	143 067	1 368 843	64.2	80 100	22.8	12.4	438	27.5	7.8
Chandler	3.2	9.7	-25.4	7.1	34 967	237.2	2 432	31 490	67.7	90 300	24.2	12.3	517	25.6	6.4
Flagstaff	2.6	17.2	17.0	10.4	16 313	44.1	792	14 417	49.9	90 900	21.0	12.1	470	28.7	8.6
Gilbert	4.3	6.2	NA	5.4	10 655	NA	1 052	9 381	68.9	108 500	25.4	13.2	478	24.1	3.6
Glendale	2.4	11.5	27.8	9.0	61 218	72.6	6 206	53 669	62.1	84 900	23.2	12.2	439	28.3	6.2
Mesa	2.5	9.5	11.8	6.9	140 468	115.1	13 269	107 863	60.9	86 500	23.5	12.0	470	27.0	5.4
Peoria	2.1	7.9	-29.5	5.7	21 944	368.5	2 312	18 254	82.9	85 500	25.3	11.9	590	33.3	3.6
Phoenix	3.9	14.2	27.9	10.5	422 036	36.9	41 553	369 921	59.1	77 100	23.0	13.1	442	27.3	7.2
Prescott	2.9	13.3	5.6	8.1	13 393	47.8	844	11 479	64.6	94 600	23.0	12.2	423	30.7	3.7
Scottsdale	10.9	5.9	5.4	3.5	69 028	64.2	6 118	57 583	64.1	115 200	23.0	11.7	597	27.4	1.4
Sierra Vista	2.6	10.7	33.8	8.7	12 927	57.1	978	11 672	46.0	78 100	20.6	10.7	417	24.7	2.7
Tempe	3.9	13.6	24.8	7.0	61 452	52.8	4 593	55 540	51.6	91 500	21.3	12.1	496	29.5	4.6
Tucson	1.5	20.2	37.4	14.4	183 338	33.6	14 838	162 685	51.4	66 800	21.7	12.5	377	29.6	7.2
Yuma	1.8	16.0	35.6	12.8	22 689	41.1	1 450	19 282	58.5	65 400	21.3	13.5	461	27.6	9.9
ARKANSAS	1.8	19.1	0.4	14.8	1 000 667	11.4	58 062	891 179	69.6	46 300	20.0	13.4	328	26.5	4.9
Conway	1.9	16.9	18.2	10.2	10 139	41.8	562	9 437	55.1	63 100	19.0	13.0	354	28.8	2.2
Fayetteville	2.8	19.8	4.8	10.9	18 835	32.2	1 492	16 894	43.4	66 200	19.1	12.3	351	28.5	2.3
Fort Smith	3.1	13.8	2.2	10.5	33 054	8.8	2 827	29 646	59.2	50 600	17.3	12.6	315	23.8	3.6
Hot Springs	1.3	24.9	23.9	18.5	17 543	-2.5	1 770	14 488	59.9	45 000	20.8	14.9	306	29.9	2.5
Jacksonville	0.8	11.6	33.3	10.6	10 890	NA	885	9 854	47.1	55 100	20.6	12.3	389	24.9	4.2
Jonesboro	2.9	16.5	18.7	12.5	19 537	60.0	1 219	17 976	59.9	58 900	18.7	12.8	344	26.7	1.8
Little Rock	4.4	14.6	3.5	10.8	80 995	25.2	6 639	72 573	56.2	64 200	19.8	13.0	415	26.9	3.2
North Little Rock	2.2	17.2	35.4	12.8	27 255	5.2	1 849	24 987	58.9	56 100	18.5	12.9	370	26.9	3.6
Pine Bluff	1.6	27.7	14.0	22.9	23 189	8.9	1 564	20 871	61.7	41 200	17.5	15.7	333	29.1	5.5
Springdale	2.0	9.4	-16.8	7.1	12 008	32.8	445	11 432	63.9	56 700	19.3	12.1	368	23.4	2.8
West Memphis	1.3	22.9	-12.6	18.4	10 505	9.1	489	9 879	57.7	50 900	20.5	14.1	343	29.0	6.5
CALIFORNIA	7.1	12.5	9.7	9.3	11 182 882	20.5	480 170	10 381 206	55.6	195 500	24.9	11.8	620	29.1	12.0
Alameda	7.7	6.8	-16.0	5.7	30 520	9.8	1 177	29 078	46.3	267 600	26.1	11.3	676	27.0	6.3
Alhambra	3.1	14.8	25.4	11.5	29 604	8.9	1 113	28 239	40.6	231 000	25.4	11.4	636	28.4	21.1
Anaheim	6.2	10.6	37.7	7.4	93 177	12.6	5 016	87 588	49.2	218 700	24.2	11.2	712	29.3	15.1
Antioch	3.6	9.1	24.7	8.1	22 973	46.7	1 418	21 401	64.3	156 900	25.8	11.8	635	30.4	4.2
Apple Valley	4.2	10.7	28.9	9.2	16 672	182.6	742	15 588	69.0	118 100	24.7	12.4	534	29.1	5.1
Arcadia	16.6	5.2	30.0	3.5	19 483	4.6	916	18 352	61.6	440 800	24.0	11.3	716	28.7	5.9
Azusa	2.0	14.3	25.4	10.9	13 232	26.2	502	12 651	48.2	150 800	24.9	11.3	650	29.0	20.7
Bakersfield	4.5	15.0	32.7	12.4	66 175	54.8	3 006	62 467	55.1	91 200	23.0	12.4	468	28.4	7.6
Baldwin Park	2.3	15.7	3.3	12.8	17 179	19.7	423	16 614	60.1	151 100	25.2	11.2	648	30.8	35.0
Bell	0.9	26.1	33.8	22.9	9 401	1.5	277	9 013	30.4	171 200	32.7	12.4	548	31.5	45.6
Bellflower	3.1	9.6	-3.0	7.4	24 117	8.3	1 057	22 905	39.6	195 200	25.0	10.7	630	27.5	13.9
Bell Gardens	1.1	26.1	3.2	23.8	9 546	-2.2	241	9 244	22.5	165 200	29.7	11.7	605	32.3	59.3
Berkeley	8.5	17.5	-16.7	9.4	45 735	-1.3	1 312	43 453	43.6	261 000	25.0	12.3	426	27.1	4.5
Beverly Hills	30.0	6.6	-25.8	4.2	15 723	-0.2	870	14 564	43.8	500 001	24.0	12.2	925	29.5	3.9
Brea	11.4	3.5	2.9	1.7	12 648	12.9	339	12 224	63.5	264 000	23.6	10.8	749	26.8	5.0
Buena Park	5.4	8.0	6.7	5.9	23 200	5.5	886	22 210	56.2	206 000	23.5	11.2	727	28.5	13.6
Burbank	6.1	8.3	7.8	5.9	41 216	11.0	1 607	39 275	45.7	262 500	24.1	11.5	677	28.4	9.8
Burlingame	11.3	4.7	-19.0	2.9	12 914	2.0	443	12 329	47.6	461 500	24.6	11.8	726	25.2	3.8
Camarillo	9.6	4.4	4.8	2.5	18 731	31.6	501	18 109	72.2	249 500	25.5	12.0	845	29.4	4.1
Campbell	7.5	5.8	-23.7	3.8	15 860	32.4	486	15 306	47.0	276 700	23.6	11.9	743	27.2	5.5

1. Includes units rented or sold but not occupied.   2. Specified owner-occupied units.   3. Specified renter-occupied units.   4. Overcrowded or lacking complete plumbing facilities.

City	Civilian labor force, 1999		Unemployment		Civilian employment, 1990[2]	Percent		Disability 1990	Value of residential construction authorized by building permits, 1999		
	Total	Percent change, 1998–1999	Total	Rate[1]	Total	Professional, managerial, and technical	Precision production, craft, and repair	Work disabled persons[3] (percent)	New construction ($1,000)	Number of housing units	Percent single family
	61	62	63	64	65	66	67	68	69	70	71
ALABAMA	2 145 301	-0.3	102 171	4.8	1 741 794	26.1	13.0	9.7	1 883 871	19 037	78.4
Anniston	11 149	-3.3	1 191	10.7	9 510	28.6	10.4	13.4	1 412	22	100.0
Auburn	17 525	-0.4	636	3.6	14 330	43.9	4.8	4.1	48 503	461	57.9
Bessemer	14 164	-0.8	802	5.7	11 903	19.1	11.7	12.7	2 357	33	100.0
Birmingham	130 267	-0.8	6 388	4.9	110 156	27.5	8.6	10.3	15 476	137	100.0
Decatur	27 996	0.5	1 303	4.7	22 815	32.3	13.2	8.3	25 379	201	92.0
Dothan	29 709	1.0	1 153	3.9	25 011	29.5	11.3	8.2	22 900	427	77.0
Florence	19 183	-4.0	1 560	8.1	15 625	29.7	12.3	9.4	14 185	158	73.4
Gadsden	18 748	0.5	1 704	9.1	15 914	21.6	12.3	12.3	1 142	12	100.0
Hoover	26 773	-0.4	330	1.2	22 053	49.6	4.8	3.8	144 250	1 114	56.4
Huntsville	97 395	0.5	3 316	3.4	81 396	44.9	8.2	7.1	18 605	448	100.0
Mobile	103 405	-2.0	5 804	5.6	81 976	33.0	9.1	8.9	31 289	453	62.7
Montgomery	101 669	0.5	3 868	3.8	83 026	32.4	8.1	8.3	92 339	1 067	67.4
Phenix City	13 924	0.9	683	4.9	10 576	21.4	14.5	10.7	16 656	204	81.4
Prichard	12 413	-2.2	866	7.0	10 515	15.1	13.3	12.1	1 563	22	100.0
Tuscaloosa	42 191	0.5	1 575	3.7	32 724	35.0	8.6	7.2	72 633	594	90.7
ALASKA	315 209	-0.5	20 072	6.4	245 379	34.3	11.2	6.6	306 585	2 211	69.6
Anchorage	141 119	-0.3	6 360	4.5	111 242	37.5	9.5	6.7	205 251	1 265	61.9
Fairbanks	15 928	0.2	1 078	6.8	11 445	28.9	10.5	6.5	826	9	100.0
Juneau	16 898	-0.6	844	5.0	14 482	42.0	8.3	5.4	14 888	177	45.2
ARIZONA	2 363 705	4.0	104 158	4.4	1 603 896	30.8	11.4	8.3	7 350 364	65 109	81.8
Chandler	70 669	4.4	1 566	2.2	47 282	36.3	10.8	5.4	430 387	2 857	95.8
Flagstaff	31 756	3.0	1 694	5.3	22 911	30.9	8.5	4.9	55 146	594	53.4
Gilbert	21 835	4.4	453	2.1	14 631	33.9	11.9	4.1	392 392	3 040	90.2
Glendale	110 867	4.5	3 286	3.0	73 610	29.8	11.5	7.9	203 345	1 785	93.1
Mesa	203 173	4.4	5 094	2.5	135 531	31.7	12.3	6.9	720 450	6 905	74.5
Peoria	32 615	4.4	742	2.3	21 809	29.3	13.2	7.3	319 101	3 179	92.5
Phoenix	726 609	4.5	23 702	3.3	480 945	30.4	11.4	8.0	935 766	9 496	55.8
Prescott	17 122	2.8	647	3.8	10 120	32.1	10.6	10.1	75 672	565	63.2
Scottsdale	104 951	4.4	2 234	2.1	70 281	41.3	6.2	5.9	514 487	4 401	73.6
Sierra Vista	14 117	3.1	615	4.4	12 086	38.1	7.8	8.4	18 123	277	98.6
Tempe	119 953	4.4	3 030	2.5	80 002	39.7	8.4	5.6	76 181	711	42.9
Tucson	239 084	3.4	8 298	3.5	179 702	31.0	10.8	9.2	353 785	3 547	76.5
Yuma	34 686	1.4	7 389	21.3	21 684	28.1	9.8	7.7	24 051	275	91.3
ARKANSAS	1 222 213	0.6	54 841	4.5	994 289	23.3	12.5	11.2	965 992	11 502	67.4
Conway	18 746	1.4	598	3.2	12 569	30.3	8.8	6.8	75 088	913	54.3
Fayetteville	28 763	1.8	762	2.6	21 133	37.4	7.2	6.3	66 053	945	40.8
Fort Smith	40 736	1.2	1 376	3.4	33 999	27.1	12.4	9.1	43 675	395	68.1
Hot Springs	NA	0.0	946	NA	12 411	26.4	8.4	14.7	12 845	122	95.9
Jacksonville	12 451	0.1	655	5.3	10 648	26.2	9.0	9.5	10 821	120	55.0
Jonesboro	29 463	2.1	951	3.2	22 968	27.0	9.9	10.0	51 587	813	39.6
Little Rock	100 207	0.2	3 377	3.4	87 408	37.8	6.5	7.9	120 238	1 118	49.4
North Little Rock	31 842	0.2	1 111	3.5	27 741	28.7	10.1	10.2	11 349	82	100.0
Pine Bluff	23 719	-0.4	2 002	8.4	21 683	26.4	9.5	11.1	2 585	80	62.5
Springdale	20 282	2.1	455	2.2	14 898	24.4	12.8	10.1	37 147	453	94.0
West Memphis	13 440	0.1	512	3.8	12 071	22.9	10.4	10.3	8 006	112	44.6
CALIFORNIA	16 585 881	1.6	864 205	5.2	13 996 309	32.3	11.1	7.4	21 030 600	138 039	74.4
Alameda	39 952	1.9	986	2.5	35 523	41.0	8.4	6.6	9 549	62	100.0
Alhambra	42 411	0.5	2 033	4.8	38 702	31.9	9.5	5.4	7 552	54	7.4
Anaheim	162 352	2.5	4 994	3.1	141 959	27.4	12.4	6.2	92 265	540	81.7
Antioch	36 049	1.6	1 462	4.1	29 631	27.1	16.0	8.4	125 015	686	100.0
Apple Valley	23 287	4.1	1 193	5.1	18 185	26.8	16.5	10.4	46 756	363	89.0
Arcadia	25 306	0.8	725	2.9	23 561	45.1	6.2	5.3	68 413	220	100.0
Azusa	21 818	0.3	1 440	6.6	19 532	20.9	13.3	7.1	3 000	22	100.0
Bakersfield	98 099	0.7	8 210	8.4	77 612	31.3	11.4	8.5	218 267	1 936	96.6
Baldwin Park	31 961	0.3	2 151	6.7	28 573	16.3	14.7	6.2	7 767	99	24.2
Bell	14 963	0.1	1 486	9.9	12 918	10.4	15.6	7.5	0	0	0.0
Bellflower	33 223	0.5	1 552	4.7	30 357	24.0	14.1	8.2	2 606	21	100.0
Bell Gardens	17 694	-0.2	1 906	10.8	15 133	8.1	14.8	6.5	325	3	100.0
Berkeley	63 435	1.8	2 018	3.2	55 990	56.4	4.2	7.8	2 303	14	57.1
Beverly Hills	18 079	0.7	541	3.0	16 810	53.8	2.8	3.3	36 942	116	29.3
Brea	21 423	2.6	388	1.8	18 977	40.3	9.7	5.5	2 902	25	12.0
Buena Park	40 401	2.5	1 273	3.2	35 299	27.3	14.4	6.9	45 710	254	100.0
Burbank	54 523	0.6	2 208	4.0	50 144	35.8	10.3	6.4	14 053	48	91.7
Burlingame	16 929	0.7	219	1.3	15 072	38.0	7.9	4.9	12 231	86	14.0
Camarillo	29 036	2.4	1 097	3.8	24 967	39.5	10.1	6.3	108 664	511	97.7
Campbell	25 807	0.1	566	2.2	21 816	40.5	11.0	6.3	12 856	83	75.9

1. Percent of civilian labor force. 2. Persons 16 years and older. 3. Persons 16 to 64 years old.

Table D. Cities — Wholesale Trade, Retail Trade, and Real Estate

City	Wholesale Trade, 1997				Retail Trade[1], 1997				Real Estate and Rental and Leasing, 1997			
	Number of Establishments	Number of Employees	Sales (mil dol)	Annual Payroll (mil dol)	Number of Establishments	Number of Employees	Sales (mil dol)	Annual Payroll (mil dol)	Number of Establishments	Number of Employees	Receipts (mil dol)	Annual Payroll (mil dol)
	72	73	74	75	76	77	78	79	80	81	82	83
ALABAMA	6 315	79 229	40 986.3	2 394.7	20 163	231 665	36 623.3	3 381.7	3 664	20 629	2 130.3	396.7
Anniston	61	873	593.9	25.7	273	3 220	521.5	47.6	46	210	18.0	3.4
Auburn	26	D	D	D	198	2 851	385.1	37.2	53	357	27.0	5.4
Bessemer	70	1 423	922.7	47.8	209	2 773	519.0	45.1	26	96	9.2	1.7
Birmingham	736	14 656	6 744.4	494.1	1 150	16 618	3 085.5	294.7	275	3 000	442.9	81.9
Decatur	138	1 785	868.5	51.9	410	4 920	921.9	74.2	81	404	35.2	7.3
Dothan	180	1 918	643.2	49.1	547	7 148	1 199.2	116.0	84	313	32.8	5.8
Florence	72	1 842	349.0	43.6	353	5 049	710.0	68.7	63	261	25.4	5.3
Gadsden	70	1 031	283.2	28.3	290	3 148	503.5	45.2	43	162	18.7	3.3
Hoover	126	1 240	1 767.6	57.1	203	4 812	874.2	82.0	44	282	28.3	5.2
Huntsville	361	3 968	2 828.5	143.7	945	14 647	2 268.6	219.3	278	1 339	138.7	24.6
Mobile	491	6 314	2 669.0	195.4	1 140	17 003	2 573.2	261.2	291	1 685	175.6	31.9
Montgomery	365	4 733	2 701.0	141.0	1 091	15 619	2 425.3	232.3	287	2 140	175.4	39.3
Phenix City	17	453	91.2	11.6	127	1 470	181.1	18.6	33	109	11.5	1.4
Prichard	27	476	147.7	15.5	77	566	71.1	8.8	8	26	2.7	0.4
Tuscaloosa	117	1 153	516.6	37.2	577	8 496	1 250.9	122.3	129	985	66.6	12.5
ALASKA	784	6 860	2 989.8	256.8	2 866	32 502	6 251.4	670.5	716	4 014	543.2	98.3
Anchorage	434	4 748	1 989.1	181.4	1 001	15 115	3 114.9	319.3	356	2 145	322.2	56.8
Fairbanks	51	590	178.3	21.8	248	3 356	727.0	77.2	64	408	38.9	9.2
Juneau	33	196	96.3	8.2	173	1 807	312.7	37.2	49	249	38.3	4.0
ARIZONA	6 689	80 155	45 763.9	2 748.9	16 283	232 050	43 960.9	4 223.9	5 450	32 529	4 110.1	747.4
Chandler	162	1 952	1 254.0	59.2	283	5 528	1 190.7	127.1	101	449	66.2	9.1
Flagstaff	80	739	505.0	18.2	367	5 011	784.6	79.0	116	439	53.3	9.4
Gilbert	74	301	119.1	9.4	110	1 870	362.7	39.2	54	205	23.0	3.8
Glendale	160	2 130	848.8	57.3	598	11 308	2 311.9	203.3	150	897	101.4	15.5
Mesa	347	2 797	1 280.8	109.0	1 405	23 747	4 348.7	420.2	367	1 576	194.3	28.1
Peoria	25	113	37.6	3.3	149	2 558	454.5	46.6	48	349	31.1	5.5
Phoenix	2 447	37 073	21 861.7	1 383.9	3 807	58 531	11 407.6	1 123.2	1 485	13 109	1 768.6	331.3
Prescott	47	302	113.6	7.8	251	2 822	513.7	52.5	101	272	35.4	5.2
Scottsdale	634	3 997	2 749.3	164.0	1 232	16 189	3 614.6	342.4	570	2 480	430.0	81.2
Sierra Vista	15	D	D	D	145	2 321	371.4	37.1	48	236	18.6	3.4
Tempe	659	10 322	9 609.2	370.2	728	13 575	3 491.9	295.3	293	2 069	274.4	50.3
Tucson	615	6 532	1 801.0	190.1	2 079	30 607	5 370.2	547.7	647	4 879	485.7	98.2
Yuma	65	635	207.9	19.8	300	4 376	697.9	66.2	78	323	24.7	4.2
ARKANSAS	3 619	41 385	27 515.4	1 136.6	12 600	132 335	21 643.7	1 904.4	2 269	9 761	1 001.6	163.2
Conway	54	D	D	D	248	3 111	526.2	47.8	57	133	17.8	2.0
Fayetteville	88	1 202	6 024.6	43.7	401	5 711	790.0	79.9	116	507	61.8	7.9
Fort Smith	219	1 942	660.3	52.1	599	8 197	1 282.6	121.4	120	557	63.9	10.2
Hot Springs	NA	NA	NA	NA	NA	NA	NA	NA	NA	NA	NA	NA
Jacksonville	17	D	D	D	109	1 394	239.8	22.5	35	D	D	D
Jonesboro	111	1 342	458.1	30.6	410	5 146	770.3	73.8	79	D	D	D
Little Rock	555	10 270	4 550.3	332.1	1 101	15 944	2 590.5	236.9	323	2 685	290.6	50.2
North Little Rock	219	3 255	4 712.8	91.6	466	7 671	1 328.5	121.9	68	356	28.8	6.1
Pine Bluff	69	D	D	D	349	4 359	653.5	66.0	52	334	22.8	5.6
Springdale	163	1 775	673.2	51.4	278	3 463	615.0	58.8	57	175	27.9	3.4
West Memphis	41	477	281.9	14.5	151	2 170	402.2	27.0	24	111	12.3	2.2
CALIFORNIA	57 842	755 513	551 230.6	29 900.2	106 357	1 354 797	263 118.3	26 362.7	37 244	243 288	38 288.4	6 570.5
Alameda	68	538	353.4	24.5	204	2 329	408.5	48.5	81	313	49.5	6.5
Alhambra	427	1 972	747.1	46.3	249	3 672	983.2	76.0	95	343	43.4	7.7
Anaheim	962	12 779	15 533.1	457.4	963	13 119	2 773.7	278.2	335	3 019	358.3	88.3
Antioch	32	273	85.6	9.1	197	2 898	500.1	51.4	42	270	35.8	4.2
Apple Valley	21	109	14.8	2.0	68	960	146.6	14.6	35	140	14.9	3.3
Arcadia	309	1 131	569.8	30.2	283	4 000	509.7	59.8	112	492	63.9	10.4
Azusa	56	939	412.9	26.6	89	1 226	307.0	26.7	28	107	14.7	2.4
Bakersfield	291	3 891	2 747.6	144.2	918	12 207	2 382.2	230.0	229	1 333	117.2	23.2
Baldwin Park	152	1 323	744.9	40.7	125	1 041	204.5	21.2	26	94	12.5	1.9
Bell	71	1 287	591.7	39.2	62	483	102.1	10.3	12	90	15.8	2.9
Bellflower	44	316	62.6	6.9	169	2 116	439.4	41.0	84	340	40.8	5.9
Bell Gardens	35	319	147.1	7.9	80	584	104.0	9.5	10	26	2.0	0.2
Berkeley	136	1 389	438.2	61.0	536	6 313	1 238.7	131.9	162	681	108.8	15.4
Beverly Hills	186	1 256	928.6	60.1	414	5 910	1 377.4	170.8	424	2 214	423.9	77.5
Brea	235	2 926	2 548.1	121.4	296	5 094	765.5	75.6	53	351	43.8	9.1
Buena Park	157	2 150	1 322.6	74.7	235	3 793	966.6	88.5	49	398	55.6	12.5
Burbank	261	3 956	5 069.4	162.2	381	5 981	1 306.1	110.6	173	1 853	709.6	81.5
Burlingame	244	1 597	2 062.5	70.2	192	2 282	546.3	59.3	147	966	183.2	24.0
Camarillo	128	1 892	632.8	82.1	249	3 110	607.9	58.9	58	316	41.1	9.3
Campbell	NA	NA	NA	NA	NA	NA	NA	NA	NA	NA	NA	NA

1. Establishments with payroll.

City	Professional, Scientific, and Technical Services, 1997[1]				Manufacturing, 1997				Accommodation and Foodservices, 1997			
	Number of Establishments	Number of Employees	Receipts (mil dol)	Annual Payroll (mil dol)	Number of Establishments	Number of Employees	Receipts (mil dol)	Annual Payroll (mil dol)	Number of Establishments	Number of Employees	Sales (mil dol)	Annual Payroll (mil dol)
	84	85	86	87	88	89	90	91	92	93	94	95
ALABAMA	7 076	54 413	5 295.6	2 051.4	5 444	352 618	67 970.1	10 187.8	6 955	134 719	3 881.8	1 059.6
Anniston	112	570	32.5	9.9	61	4 995	749.2	122.0	86	1 683	48.3	12.7
Auburn	63	340	32.1	11.7	28	1 708	270.3	34.8	125	3 013	76.3	20.2
Bessemer	53	180	10.9	3.9	45	2 164	367.9	70.0	52	1 459	33.3	9.3
Birmingham	815	9 020	991.8	390.3	382	19 057	3 179.5	621.0	524	10 504	346.8	99.6
Decatur	139	822	63.8	25.5	124	8 495	3 219.0	291.1	137	3 117	86.5	25.3
Dothan	160	1 147	69.1	26.4	102	8 269	1 311.0	212.8	176	3 527	111.0	28.3
Florence	136	718	49.3	16.9	83	6 049	743.8	140.9	109	2 242	59.6	17.4
Gadsden	103	468	32.1	12.6	67	6 067	1 241.0	217.5	102	1 953	56.7	15.7
Hoover	168	858	96.1	32.8	NA	NA	NA	NA	90	1 916	60.3	17.2
Huntsville	666	12 461	1 532.3	571.7	240	25 793	6 694.3	1 014.6	400	8 853	282.1	76.6
Mobile	674	5 495	496.7	196.6	213	11 631	1 907.4	445.0	482	10 102	301.6	84.8
Montgomery	540	4 295	407.0	189.2	190	10 312	1 798.7	269.0	411	9 983	277.3	76.5
Phenix City	38	D	D	D	34	2 566	864.2	91.6	60	882	30.4	7.9
Prichard	2	D	D	D	22	1 038	340.1	40.2	26	D	D	D
Tuscaloosa	210	1 556	107.6	44.2	89	6 020	1 058.9	179.1	252	6 355	171.6	47.4
ALASKA	1 437	7 892	945.9	370.8	488	10 770	3 305.0	331.2	1 763	20 587	1 065.5	301.5
Anchorage	907	5 939	767.2	301.3	187	2 022	322.3	62.9	640	11 364	574.0	165.8
Fairbanks	118	592	52.5	21.9	NA	NA	NA	NA	121	1 989	86.7	23.4
Juneau	96	415	44.9	18.5	NA	NA	NA	NA	94	1 117	57.7	16.1
ARIZONA	10 163	75 789	6 669.4	2 724.7	4 917	193 616	43 030.3	6 753.6	9 089	184 323	6 633.0	1 823.2
Chandler	208	746	69.3	25.0	135	9 668	4 744.3	352.0	207	3 846	130.2	35.9
Flagstaff	143	702	53.7	19.9	62	1 798	505.2	67.7	268	5 144	179.7	47.0
Gilbert	111	494	64.8	23.1	78	2 228	311.5	57.4	44	783	24.3	6.3
Glendale	167	768	36.9	14.5	156	6 398	1 075.9	244.0	293	6 042	187.0	51.1
Mesa	628	4 950	282.8	128.5	258	13 921	3 367.1	530.7	577	12 355	411.4	108.9
Peoria	46	430	9.1	3.5	34	558	54.3	13.8	74	1 128	35.4	10.0
Phoenix	3 664	36 761	3 328.5	1 470.5	1 706	69 401	14 649.6	2 532.4	2 223	50 275	2 008.7	555.1
Prescott	144	547	41.0	13.9	65	1 509	178.0	36.7	140	2 037	64.1	17.3
Scottsdale	1 222	6 295	713.2	252.4	257	8 254	1 128.2	192.1	563	18 396	723.5	211.8
Sierra Vista	72	1 196	103.1	43.1	NA	NA	NA	NA	77	1 455	38.4	10.1
Tempe	671	5 531	454.7	160.2	498	24 105	5 414.8	865.2	514	10 694	345.4	95.9
Tucson	1 331	9 883	886.9	349.6	520	20 152	3 483.6	841.2	1 151	23 782	704.4	199.1
Yuma	125	597	44.2	16.1	36	2 481	348.1	44.5	174	3 274	97.4	24.5
ARKANSAS	4 125	23 094	1 825.8	719.6	3 316	230 153	45 186.0	5 778.4	4 663	73 397	2 179.7	589.9
Conway	70	482	40.7	11.6	67	7 242	1 205.9	183.1	91	2 125	61.0	16.8
Fayetteville	217	1 023	80.5	26.7	68	5 962	948.9	144.2	222	3 881	110.7	31.4
Fort Smith	209	1 197	91.6	27.3	206	20 817	3 949.8	521.5	239	4 463	133.1	36.6
Hot Springs	NA	NA	NA	NA	66	2 756	610.0	68.2	NA	NA	NA	NA
Jacksonville	29	99	5.5	2.2	32	1 995	309.5	53.7	52	893	27.3	6.9
Jonesboro	137	652	51.9	18.9	97	6 234	1 126.9	170.7	118	D	D	D
Little Rock	979	8 734	827.9	372.9	251	12 570	2 457.9	365.9	490	10 389	329.0	95.8
North Little Rock	125	898	64.0	24.7	91	4 073	1 095.8	110.4	186	4 378	126.0	34.4
Pine Bluff	79	387	27.2	7.6	75	D	D	D	118	D	D	D
Springdale	97	560	37.4	16.3	106	D	D	D	124	2 099	66.2	17.9
West Memphis	43	292	13.2	4.4	33	D	D	D	65	1 307	45.6	11.7
CALIFORNIA	78 635	805 856	89 555.7	35 258.6	49 418	1 809 667	379 612.4	65 762.8	62 532	1 052 715	42 261.1	11 437.2
Alameda	209	1 576	221.4	89.0	56	2 298	1 009.1	127.3	165	1 908	66.9	17.9
Alhambra	170	1 000	55.7	18.6	125	3 248	308.5	81.8	172	2 627	91.0	24.2
Anaheim	556	4 422	451.5	165.3	896	38 330	6 019.8	1 358.7	689	18 054	818.6	222.9
Antioch	68	254	15.2	5.4	38	577	117.7	20.2	109	1 501	54.1	13.5
Apple Valley	26	69	5.4	2.4	NA	NA	NA	NA	41	612	17.2	4.2
Arcadia	141	804	83.6	29.5	72	971	201.2	29.0	134	2 232	84.4	21.0
Azusa	14	36	2.9	1.4	126	5 017	905.9	197.7	63	894	31.4	7.8
Bakersfield	519	2 793	249.5	89.5	160	4 560	416.0	107.9	472	7 956	272.6	72.8
Baldwin Park	14	122	9.6	3.0	141	2 854	232.1	68.5	60	839	32.6	7.6
Bell	10	192	7.6	3.9	29	940	177.3	28.8	50	684	25.5	5.5
Bellflower	47	227	15.4	5.8	NA	NA	NA	NA	88	1 057	38.9	8.8
Bell Gardens	4	D	D	D	70	1 672	163.3	42.2	37	382	15.7	3.3
Berkeley	464	2 554	332.6	130.2	199	5 247	996.6	212.8	367	4 711	198.6	56.9
Beverly Hills	908	4 940	909.9	319.0	64	501	45.1	10.9	188	6 230	297.9	92.7
Brea	151	1 724	162.6	47.0	187	8 461	1 145.1	316.5	103	2 393	85.0	21.9
Buena Park	67	887	97.0	43.3	126	7 108	1 358.5	227.8	119	2 750	102.0	27.9
Burbank	368	126 307	4 972.4	2 707.5	298	9 355	1 131.2	306.9	236	4 756	201.0	53.0
Burlingame	255	1 802	247.6	108.0	83	2 286	408.5	90.9	123	4 988	287.4	83.8
Camarillo	176	1 468	176.2	68.1	173	8 487	1 513.5	296.9	112	1 846	69.7	17.6
Campbell	NA	NA	NA	NA	156	3 307	613.5	133.6	NA	NA	NA	NA

1. Firms subject to federal tax.

Table D. Cities — Entertainment, Health Care, and Other Services

City	Arts, Entertainment, and Recreation[1], 1997				Health Care and Social Assistance[1], 1997				Other Services[1], 1997			
	Number of Establishments	Number of Employees	Receipts (mil dol)	Annual Payroll (mil dol)	Number of Establishments	Number of Employees	Receipts (mil dol)	Annual Payroll (mil dol)	Number of Establishments	Number of Employees	Receipts (mil dol)	Annual Payroll (mil dol)
	96	97	98	99	100	101	102	103	104	105	106	107
ALABAMA	791	9 381	435.7	105.0	7 121	104 492	7 116.7	3 104.8	6 329	37 061	2 241.7	659.3
Anniston	9	73	1.3	0.6	143	1 806	133.7	59.3	92	429	22.4	7.7
Auburn	12	0	0.0	0.0	48	316	20.2	8.7	53	326	16.0	4.9
Bessemer	5	55	1.6	0.5	71	851	46.3	25.1	65	406	28.7	8.4
Birmingham	41	1 092	58.2	13.1	675	10 682	985.1	442.3	456	4 311	265.4	85.5
Decatur	20	134	4.8	1.1	196	2 088	146.4	67.7	115	1 054	51.5	18.1
Dothan	21	233	8.2	2.6	209	4 502	370.9	170.3	160	921	50.2	14.9
Florence	15	0	0.0	0.0	176	2 120	153.1	64.4	101	673	29.7	10.1
Gadsden	10	103	4.0	1.4	156	3 611	285.8	114.8	79	379	22.4	6.0
Hoover	12	112	3.4	0.9	99	1 628	82.5	36.2	71	512	23.7	8.5
Huntsville	50	884	22.4	6.6	502	5 883	457.4	193.9	358	2 234	120.9	41.1
Mobile	51	849	37.8	7.2	490	9 662	697.9	328.5	429	3 308	215.2	63.1
Montgomery	35	526	19.4	4.8	534	8 898	637.4	262.1	371	2 688	138.6	43.7
Phenix City	3	0	0.0	0.0	36	691	33.7	11.0	63	328	18.2	5.6
Prichard	NA	NA	NA	NA	13	320	13.6	6.1	35	183	7.9	2.4
Tuscaloosa	20	204	4.9	1.7	203	1 920	157.6	84.6	182	1 234	64.9	20.7
ALASKA	320	3 055	168.3	34.9	1 143	8 156	758.1	309.4	852	4 364	331.0	93.4
Anchorage	101	1 455	81.2	16.2	599	5 053	508.6	203.8	393	2 576	185.8	54.8
Fairbanks	26	312	17.4	2.3	99	768	79.0	39.9	83	459	33.5	9.9
Juneau	21	232	14.4	3.0	81	437	40.1	16.6	56	240	15.8	4.5
ARIZONA	1 071	24 416	2 033.3	475.1	9 155	97 091	6 687.9	2 893.3	6 494	43 669	2 794.0	829.6
Chandler	25	0	0.0	0.0	235	2 420	148.7	69.4	157	1 010	54.0	18.5
Flagstaff	24	687	19.7	6.2	205	1 485	98.8	42.9	132	726	44.1	11.7
Gilbert	14	286	14.6	3.5	78	1 255	71.6	31.4	68	321	20.4	8.4
Glendale	21	492	24.4	5.5	373	4 208	288.3	124.4	271	1 442	93.0	25.3
Mesa	59	975	45.4	11.4	799	9 068	585.8	248.8	548	3 686	220.9	71.2
Peoria	8	102	6.0	1.5	106	1 791	112.5	50.6	77	454	24.8	7.6
Phoenix	255	6 004	462.3	158.4	2 677	30 034	2 243.6	994.8	1 836	15 938	1 141.9	321.2
Prescott	12	117	9.0	2.0	175	1 480	86.6	32.9	104	548	27.5	8.2
Scottsdale	113	3 408	276.0	58.8	773	7 095	525.0	226.4	410	2 733	159.9	52.2
Sierra Vista	6	78	1.8	0.5	77	946	59.6	22.7	40	207	8.6	2.7
Tempe	60	1 069	126.1	57.1	369	3 613	262.3	104.7	324	2 511	184.1	57.9
Tucson	116	2 174	109.3	25.6	1 196	14 955	1 045.8	457.0	852	5 858	340.0	107.1
Yuma	20	0	0.0	0.0	195	2 274	140.2	55.0	114	649	32.8	9.8
ARKANSAS	594	5 343	228.7	56.8	4 571	59 960	3 655.1	1 609.7	3 553	18 809	1 113.9	310.5
Conway	13	0	0.0	0.0	122	1 231	72.1	33.2	69	484	25.5	7.5
Fayetteville	23	227	8.0	2.1	167	1 690	121.0	60.1	107	774	33.5	11.1
Fort Smith	19	0	0.0	0.0	263	4 345	326.9	147.4	171	1 225	68.8	19.8
Hot Springs	NA	NA	NA	NA	NA	NA	NA	NA	NA	NA	NA	NA
Jacksonville	6	68	1.5	0.7	44	614	28.3	14.5	42	162	8.1	2.4
Jonesboro	29	181	8.2	2.2	198	3 087	237.9	112.4	103	561	34.7	9.1
Little Rock	55	640	28.6	8.3	704	9 469	777.5	361.7	428	2 983	183.5	52.5
North Little Rock	19	192	10.1	3.6	188	1 610	117.4	52.3	149	960	60.0	18.1
Pine Bluff	12	0	0.0	0.0	181	1 671	108.4	47.5	101	728	39.1	12.3
Springdale	14	90	3.2	0.7	105	1 120	67.0	29.6	97	573	32.1	10.1
West Memphis	9	0	0.0	0.0	55	660	38.1	15.0	52	391	23.0	6.6
CALIFORNIA	12 015	182 004	15 913.8	6 296.6	69 857	664 539	51 968.0	20 619.3	44 642	282 762	20 521.5	5 852.2
Alameda	24	583	95.8	53.9	159	1 631	84.6	36.0	93	479	33.1	9.4
Alhambra	15	103	4.8	1.4	197	2 031	133.4	49.7	100	497	37.5	11.1
Anaheim	50	0	0.0	0.0	730	8 305	726.8	264.4	473	3 487	305.4	77.4
Antioch	19	191	6.7	1.7	136	1 297	102.8	40.3	79	452	32.4	9.7
Apple Valley	1	0	0.0	0.0	142	750	123.3	49.6	21	123	6.9	1.5
Arcadia	45	2 114	105.6	35.4	244	1 806	140.2	62.3	92	303	18.7	4.8
Azusa	4	106	4.3	1.2	34	445	12.5	5.2	53	279	19.1	5.0
Bakersfield	50	1 027	35.6	10.6	639	7 112	600.4	217.4	346	2 300	168.0	45.7
Baldwin Park	3	0	0.0	0.0	56	1 505	85.0	42.7	59	234	15.7	4.7
Bell	NA	NA	NA	NA	23	210	12.9	4.9	34	138	13.2	3.8
Bellflower	9	79	6.0	1.4	115	2 474	255.0	86.3	117	599	42.6	11.9
Bell Gardens	5	0	0.0	0.0	20	371	15.4	7.0	33	240	14.8	4.7
Berkeley	38	447	25.4	6.6	420	2 272	203.9	78.6	203	1 353	84.4	27.3
Beverly Hills	573	2 856	975.1	551.7	769	3 162	443.4	165.8	221	1 546	86.6	28.0
Brea	6	0	0.0	0.0	100	1 059	88.8	30.6	91	941	71.6	26.7
Buena Park	14	3 603	157.3	61.4	80	818	53.1	19.5	66	384	19.5	5.7
Burbank	167	1 831	296.0	190.2	326	2 921	258.4	103.2	218	1 805	146.6	42.0
Burlingame	18	246	17.0	3.0	151	1 441	92.2	40.3	106	587	47.5	14.4
Camarillo	16	194	12.6	3.1	144	826	65.1	24.9	82	719	59.1	18.7
Campbell	NA	NA	NA	NA	NA	NA	NA	NA	NA	NA	NA	NA

1. Firms subject to federal tax.

City	Procurement contracts Defense	Procurement contracts Other	Grants Total[2]	Grants Health and family welfare	Grants Energy and environment	Grants Education	Grants Housing and community development	Direct payments for individuals Educational assistance	Direct payments for individuals Housing assistance	General revenue Total (mil dol)	Intergovernmental Total (mil dol)	Intergovernmental Percent from state government	Taxes Total (mil dol)	Per capita Total	Per capita Property	Per capita Sales and gross receipts
	108	109	110	111	112	113	114	115	116	117	118	119	120	121	122	123
ALABAMA	2 679.0	1 017.5	4 631.8	2 449.8	107.2	434.1	114.2	120.8	61.5	X	X	X	X	X	X	X
Anniston	68.5	0.8	4.2	1.1	0.0	1.0	1.1	0.5	0.4	28.1	2.5	30.9	20.4	792	73	615
Auburn	1.2	3.7	36.1	6.7	1.2	1.3	0.1	5.4	0.0	34.3	2.2	100.0	21.6	575	105	283
Bessemer	0.1	0.3	1.3	0.0	0.0	0.2	0.8	0.7	1.7	20.5	2.1	66.4	15.1	485	34	350
Birmingham	139.9	70.2	291.1	199.6	21.2	5.4	20.6	13.1	15.2	311.3	40.8	34.7	211.9	820	121	345
Decatur	1.3	0.4	6.6	5.4	0.0	0.3	0.3	3.2	3.3	139.7	7.2	10.9	30.0	557	100	405
Dothan	20.1	0.7	7.2	2.6	0.0	1.0	0.9	1.2	0.0	49.9	2.6	60.6	34.5	616	37	552
Florence	0.1	0.6	3.3	0.9	0.0	0.0	1.6	2.0	1.5	54.3	3.2	70.4	37.6	965	609	299
Gadsden	2.2	1.7	8.7	4.1	0.0	2.0	1.2	3.1	0.5	47.4	3.7	53.7	33.7	818	65	367
Hoover	0.0	0.1	1.0	0.0	0.0	0.0	0.1	0.0	0.0	52.0	2.1	47.4	47.5	857	74	670
Huntsville	1 594.9	130.9	65.6	6.0	2.5	5.0	5.1	2.9	3.5	195.3	19.9	30.2	111.9	657	120	475
Mobile	103.0	14.2	61.2	25.7	2.1	5.4	12.2	11.7	7.1	226.8	11.7	81.3	144.6	714	38	561
Montgomery	87.1	21.4	754.0	171.8	67.6	131.1	45.3	12.9	3.6	132.9	11.9	66.5	101.4	517	85	314
Phenix City	0.1	0.1	1.4	0.9	0.0	0.2	0.2	1.1	0.3	42.6	3.7	81.8	12.9	462	73	316
Prichard	0.1	0.5	0.7	0.0	0.0	0.0	0.0	0.0	0.0	13.6	1.2	53.9	8.2	250	66	135
Tuscaloosa	20.9	7.5	36.9	8.2	0.6	4.2	3.6	9.8	2.2	53.9	19.1	9.8	19.6	238	63	64
ALASKA	612.1	233.4	1 929.3	728.3	94.1	222.1	20.9	5.8	19.2	X	X	X	X	X	X	X
Anchorage	154.4	61.6	235.6	105.8	10.7	11.9	11.8	3.1	6.5	741.1	303.5	94.6	234.7	937	837	75
Fairbanks	8.4	19.5	82.9	34.5	3.9	6.2	0.2	0.0	7.0	54.7	4.1	100.0	8.7	263	148	101
Juneau	0.1	2.9	293.0	58.0	71.1	65.9	0.0	0.2	0.0	146.9	41.8	95.4	50.1	1 684	778	834
ARIZONA	4 156.8	624.8	4 537.2	2 236.2	67.4	469.2	101.3	123.1	32.6	X	X	X	X	X	X	X
Chandler	47.5	69.0	3.9	0.0	0.0	0.6	2.3	0.5	1.6	153.7	55.0	74.0	46.3	324	62	240
Flagstaff	2.9	2.0	26.9	11.7	0.8	4.5	1.4	6.4	0.0	60.6	16.5	62.4	23.3	424	162	238
Gilbert	33.6	0.4	1.5	0.0	0.3	0.2	0.2	0.0	0.0	62.3	14.3	95.4	25.6	398	88	175
Glendale	1.9	0.7	4.6	0.0	0.2	0.4	2.4	4.4	4.3	169.6	53.6	77.7	58.3	320	88	199
Mesa	895.0	14.6	16.7	1.2	0.0	0.8	3.2	4.3	2.8	265.7	92.9	87.0	78.3	227	26	173
Peoria	0.1	0.3	1.5	0.0	0.0	0.0	0.9	0.0	0.0	79.2	21.4	80.4	29.6	389	89	245
Phoenix	627.3	114.3	788.2	257.5	36.2	110.5	41.6	44.7	10.1	1 381.1	435.2	67.4	461.4	398	111	261
Prescott	1.6	3.8	3.4	0.6	0.2	1.2	0.0	1.5	0.0	44.2	8.8	94.4	17.0	516	82	398
Scottsdale	208.1	9.6	14.1	3.9	3.4	0.2	1.5	1.4	0.5	263.7	45.0	84.3	129.6	724	163	488
Sierra Vista	45.9	0.1	0.9	0.0	0.0	0.6	0.0	0.1	0.5	25.9	9.5	99.6	8.6	230	34	183
Tempe	307.8	12.4	62.4	12.7	1.8	6.8	1.8	13.5	0.4	193.5	41.4	81.9	87.0	535	116	393
Tucson	1 620.2	50.1	371.8	105.0	6.4	10.7	14.8	20.8	7.9	486.0	202.0	66.8	181.1	403	70	313
Yuma	30.4	6.4	12.3	5.0	0.0	1.4	1.8	2.5	0.7	58.6	23.4	89.4	19.3	319	67	241
ARKANSAS	248.0	218.8	2 614.2	1 488.4	21.0	253.4	42.4	58.0	54.9	X	X	X	X	X	X	X
Conway	1.7	0.1	12.0	4.5	0.0	0.2	0.9	4.4	0.0	21.5	3.0	79.1	7.1	198	24	168
Fayetteville	0.5	5.6	38.1	2.7	0.1	3.2	0.6	4.9	3.3	39.3	5.3	72.4	14.5	278	8	258
Fort Smith	3.8	6.3	10.3	0.1	0.0	0.8	2.1	2.0	3.6	56.7	8.3	91.0	29.6	391	70	309
Hot Springs	0.1	0.1	0.2	0.0	0.0	0.1	0.0	0.6	0.6	38.5	4.2	79.2	16.5	NA	NA	NA
Jacksonville	0.0	0.0	0.9	0.0	0.0	0.0	0.8	0.0	2.4	51.4	6.7	31.6	2.1	72	8	60
Jonesboro	0.0	0.6	11.5	6.1	0.0	3.5	1.4	5.1	2.0	23.0	9.6	29.9	3.0	57	15	24
Little Rock	6.8	17.5	487.0	170.4	20.2	76.8	22.9	5.6	7.3	191.3	63.7	29.5	32.5	185	49	103
North Little Rock	2.9	0.1	2.2	0.1	0.2	0.0	1.1	3.4	4.7	43.3	15.6	32.8	5.5	91	38	35
Pine Bluff	14.1	1.8	16.5	6.0	0.0	2.7	2.0	3.2	6.2	36.8	11.9	42.0	12.7	234	35	186
Springdale	12.2	2.3	1.8	0.1	0.0	0.5	0.3	0.2	1.4	23.7	8.0	28.2	6.4	166	48	106
West Memphis	0.0	0.0	4.3	1.0	0.0	0.5	1.2	0.7	1.4	20.6	5.6	40.7	6.9	257	26	222
CALIFORNIA	17 370.6	8 424.5	36 369.7	21 492.9	291.9	3 008.9	859.8	858.2	665.1	X	X	X	X	X	X	X
Alameda	2.0	29.1	24.8	3.2	15.1	0.4	1.7	1.3	0.0	70.8	13.2	79.6	36.3	477	179	237
Alhambra	0.2	4.2	3.7	0.0	0.0	0.2	3.2	0.3	0.0	56.8	9.4	70.7	28.3	338	113	198
Anaheim	298.1	44.6	7.6	0.0	0.2	0.8	5.6	3.1	2.7	321.4	59.6	46.2	138.4	479	123	327
Antioch	0.1	0.1	1.6	0.0	0.0	0.0	0.9	0.0	1.5	54.6	6.7	88.9	17.3	226	108	95
Apple Valley	0.1	1.2	2.7	0.0	0.0	0.0	0.4	0.0	0.0	17.6	4.4	90.3	6.1	111	23	55
Arcadia	0.9	2.3	0.1	0.0	0.0	0.0	0.0	0.0	0.0	35.0	4.5	91.3	22.2	440	124	253
Azusa	106.8	23.1	1.3	0.3	0.0	1.0	0.0	1.6	0.0	39.9	7.6	89.5	19.4	460	122	196
Bakersfield	2.9	5.7	36.4	14.4	0.0	1.6	13.5	8.7	1.0	148.2	25.0	87.3	63.3	308	92	177
Baldwin Park	0.4	0.1	5.2	0.0	0.4	0.4	3.8	0.2	0.0	27.9	9.2	80.5	13.9	195	97	87
Bell	0.2	2.6	0.0	0.0	0.0	0.0	0.0	0.7	0.0	17.1	4.0	86.8	8.9	254	106	130
Bellflower	0.2	0.2	1.6	0.0	0.0	0.4	1.0	0.1	0.8	20.3	5.5	77.9	11.7	185	28	144
Bell Gardens	0.0	0.0	0.1	0.0	0.0	0.0	0.0	0.0	0.0	20.6	3.8	67.2	10.1	229	49	55
Berkeley	10.7	1 733.5	288.3	118.5	8.5	23.7	7.7	12.7	1.8	168.5	20.0	75.2	72.1	698	194	284
Beverly Hills	1.7	0.8	0.5	0.0	0.2	0.0	0.0	0.0	1.4	126.1	3.9	86.4	69.7	2 153	440	906
Brea	8.7	4.0	6.8	0.0	0.0	0.1	0.0	0.2	0.0	62.9	3.8	74.4	32.6	938	535	374
Buena Park	16.2	0.7	1.6	0.0	0.0	0.0	1.6	0.0	0.0	44.6	8.4	97.5	25.3	351	113	223
Burbank	12.6	0.7	21.6	0.3	0.0	0.2	1.1	0.7	1.4	150.3	24.8	88.8	69.7	722	289	369
Burlingame	16.3	3.7	0.6	0.4	0.1	0.1	0.0	0.0	0.0	37.7	2.3	86.1	24.5	885	152	680
Camarillo	63.8	3.8	1.0	0.2	0.1	0.3	0.5	0.2	0.0	36.5	4.5	93.3	14.0	246	57	146
Campbell	0.3	0.1	1.3	0.1	0.4	0.5	0.0	0.0	4.9	29.9	2.9	90.8	18.4	NA	NA	NA

1. October 1, 1998 to September 30, 1999.   2. Includes program categories not shown separately. State totals include additional categories not allocated by city.   3. Based on population estimated as of July 1 of the year shown.

Table D. Cities — City Government Finances

City	Total (mil dol)	Per capita[1] (dollars) Total	Capital outlays	Public welfare	Highways	Parking facilities	Education	Health and hospitals	Police protection	Sewerage and sanitation	Parks and recreation	Housing and community development	Interest on debt
	124	125	126	127	128	129	130	131	132	133	134	135	136
ALABAMA	X	X	X	X	X	X	X	X	X	X	X	X	X
Anniston	26.9	1 044	162	0.0	11.2	0.0	0.0	1.1	17.8	3.6	11.0	2.5	8.1
Auburn	28.7	762	119	0.0	4.4	0.0	0.0	0.0	12.3	18.7	7.0	1.1	7.6
Bessemer	26.1	834	59	0.0	3.8	0.1	4.5	0.6	23.0	22.3	1.9	0.2	2.2
Birmingham	316.5	1 224	64	0.0	7.2	4.3	0.0	0.6	16.0	3.6	9.2	3.9	20.8
Decatur	128.1	2 381	313	0.0	2.7	0.0	0.0	63.0	5.0	11.7	2.3	0.1	6.5
Dothan	47.0	840	91	0.0	5.4	0.0	0.0	0.4	16.2	19.5	12.0	0.8	5.5
Florence	42.5	1 090	199	0.0	10.7	0.0	4.7	0.2	13.4	12.6	11.9	1.9	1.9
Gadsden	45.7	1 111	184	0.8	9.6	0.0	0.0	0.7	16.6	12.0	10.5	2.2	3.6
Hoover	49.3	890	120	0.0	2.2	0.0	11.9	0.7	15.6	8.5	5.6	0.0	6.8
Huntsville	176.5	1 035	227	0.2	10.2	2.1	0.0	2.9	12.3	23.4	9.4	1.4	10.0
Mobile	197.1	973	122	0.0	9.2	1.8	0.0	3.0	13.9	16.7	10.2	0.0	15.1
Montgomery	128.1	653	61	0.0	18.6	0.1	0.0	1.8	19.6	10.3	14.1	3.0	3.1
Phenix City	32.2	1 149	166	0.0	7.4	0.0	0.0	47.1	8.8	10.9	4.3	3.3	0.8
Prichard	10.7	324	0	0.3	12.0	0.0	0.0	3.8	23.3	18.0	0.9	0.1	1.8
Tuscaloosa	50.5	613	101	0.0	6.3	0.0	0.0	0.3	16.4	17.6	2.4	3.2	2.0
ALASKA	X	X	X	X	X	X	X	X	X	X	X	X	X
Anchorage	790.6	3 156	425	1.1	7.7	0.0	47.7	3.9	5.1	3.4	1.8	0.4	8.6
Fairbanks	47.5	1 443	66	0.0	10.4	0.0	0.0	0.2	11.2	11.7	0.0	0.3	8.6
Juneau	135.4	4 552	639	1.6	5.2	0.2	39.2	23.0	5.1	3.2	3.5	2.4	2.0
ARIZONA	X	X	X	X	X	X	X	X	X	X	X	X	X
Chandler	130.6	914	218	0.0	14.5	0.0	0.0	0.0	18.9	29.2	0.0	6.3	5.7
Flagstaff	48.3	876	7	0.0	13.9	0.0	0.0	0.6	14.8	12.2	9.4	0.9	10.1
Gilbert	52.9	822	280	0.0	8.6	0.0	0.0	0.3	11.4	37.7	7.5	1.9	5.6
Glendale	145.3	797	133	0.1	11.2	0.0	0.0	0.0	16.2	17.0	3.9	6.0	8.0
Mesa	324.9	942	198	0.0	10.7	0.3	0.0	2.4	23.0	15.9	9.3	2.7	7.1
Peoria	64.8	853	129	0.0	6.5	0.0	0.0	0.0	11.8	18.6	15.7	3.3	10.1
Phoenix	1 291.8	1 115	282	0.0	5.8	0.1	0.9	0.1	16.7	11.0	9.8	5.9	10.5
Prescott	30.7	935	217	0.0	15.3	0.0	0.0	0.5	13.8	25.0	11.2	0.0	4.1
Scottsdale	259.9	1 452	444	0.0	9.8	0.0	0.0	0.0	11.8	8.9	7.2	1.4	11.5
Sierra Vista	25.4	678	85	0.0	9.9	0.0	0.0	0.0	15.0	8.2	14.0	1.0	9.5
Tempe	144.9	891	165	0.0	11.3	0.0	0.0	0.0	18.4	11.2	14.5	11.5	5.1
Tucson	426.9	951	203	1.2	12.4	0.1	0.0	0.2	14.8	6.0	13.1	7.2	7.0
Yuma	67.8	1 121	329	0.0	19.8	0.0	0.0	1.9	19.0	14.9	16.6	3.8	3.0
ARKANSAS	X	X	X	X	X	X	X	X	X	X	X	X	X
Conway	23.3	651	76	1.4	6.2	0.0	0.0	0.4	15.3	17.0	2.8	1.7	26.1
Fayetteville	42.7	815	191	0.0	9.2	0.3	0.0	0.0	12.0	33.7	3.4	1.4	5.6
Fort Smith	49.5	653	216	0.0	32.1	0.3	0.0	0.1	13.0	19.8	2.0	1.5	1.0
Hot Springs	34.3	NA	NA	0.0	10.3	0.1	0.0	0.9	22.9	21.9	2.6	1.1	8.9
Jacksonville	51.2	1 753	422	0.0	3.0	0.0	0.0	71.2	4.3	6.3	2.2	1.2	0.8
Jonesboro	24.4	463	88	0.0	18.1	0.3	0.0	2.1	15.0	31.3	4.2	0.0	3.3
Little Rock	227.9	1 297	272	0.0	12.5	0.1	0.0	3.0	12.9	13.6	7.2	1.0	8.9
North Little Rock	50.7	838	19	0.0	8.3	0.0	0.0	1.2	23.1	15.9	5.9	5.9	6.5
Pine Bluff	37.1	686	96	0.0	8.7	0.0	0.0	0.7	20.1	24.4	12.2	3.9	4.3
Springdale	38.9	1 007	547	0.0	9.6	0.0	0.0	0.5	10.6	42.8	9.3	1.6	1.4
West Memphis	20.2	751	150	0.0	6.8	0.0	0.0	1.0	18.4	22.4	2.3	2.9	6.0
CALIFORNIA	X	X	X	X	X	X	X	X	X	X	X	X	X
Alameda	83.4	1 097	70	0.0	14.8	0.0	0.0	0.3	17.3	2.0	8.3	12.6	13.1
Alhambra	57.2	684	112	0.0	8.5	1.2	0.0	2.8	24.2	10.1	9.1	19.3	8.3
Anaheim	360.6	1 248	321	0.0	6.8	0.0	0.0	0.1	15.0	9.1	18.0	11.8	9.7
Antioch	58.3	764	284	0.0	36.1	0.0	0.0	0.7	19.6	2.6	3.1	6.0	16.3
Apple Valley	17.2	313	27	0.0	13.9	0.0	0.0	1.1	25.0	31.0	0.0	2.4	7.2
Arcadia	35.8	710	124	0.0	11.7	0.0	0.0	1.8	24.1	0.9	3.3	6.9	3.2
Azusa	28.8	684	32	0.0	7.1	0.0	0.0	0.4	27.1	5.5	3.0	11.7	19.4
Bakersfield	150.9	734	150	0.0	15.4	0.6	0.0	0.3	20.8	17.1	5.1	5.3	7.0
Baldwin Park	27.0	377	63	0.0	22.2	0.0	0.0	0.7	31.1	0.0	5.0	16.6	10.0
Bell	15.6	446	95	0.0	15.0	0.0	0.0	0.0	24.4	6.2	3.0	16.2	9.7
Bellflower	19.2	304	39	0.0	20.9	0.1	0.0	0.4	35.5	0.0	12.8	5.7	1.9
Bell Gardens	21.2	481	61	0.0	12.3	0.0	0.0	0.0	34.2	0.9	13.3	4.8	4.5
Berkeley	178.3	1 727	262	0.0	6.9	1.4	0.0	13.7	14.8	16.3	3.0	3.4	4.8
Beverly Hills	129.6	4 003	817	0.0	7.8	4.3	0.0	1.7	16.8	12.7	9.6	1.0	10.4
Brea	69.5	1 997	524	0.0	7.2	8.0	0.0	1.4	18.7	2.9	3.1	19.3	21.0
Buena Park	42.5	590	139	0.0	23.0	0.0	0.0	0.0	27.6	5.1	5.7	9.3	7.8
Burbank	162.8	1 685	423	0.0	10.4	0.2	0.0	2.4	14.0	7.7	4.0	27.1	7.6
Burlingame	38.8	1 398	444	0.0	11.8	4.0	0.0	0.0	14.6	8.4	8.5	1.0	3.9
Camarillo	34.3	600	71	0.0	17.2	0.0	0.0	0.4	28.2	23.5	0.0	0.8	3.9
Campbell	28.7	NA	NA	0.0	10.2	0.0	0.0	0.0	21.8	0.5	8.2	8.9	8.1

1. Based on population estimated as of July 1 of the year shown.

Table D. Cities — City Government Finances, City Government Employment, and Climate

City	Debt outstanding Total (mil dol)	Per capita[1] (dollars)	Percent utility	City government employment, 1999	Mean January	Mean July	Limits January[3]	Limits July[4]	Annual precipitation (inches)	Heating degree days	Cooling degree days
	137	138	139	140	141	142	143	144	145	146	147
ALABAMA	X	X	X	X	X	X	X	X	X	X	X
Anniston	33.3	1 291	0.0	371	42.0	79.6	31.6	90.2	52.88	2 854	1 787
Auburn	67.7	1 798	12.1	420	43.1	79.2	32.7	89.3	56.47	2 612	1 865
Bessemer	24.0	768	64.8	454	41.7	79.7	30.5	91.4	59.11	2 893	1 777
Birmingham	809.7	3 132	0.0	3 961	41.5	79.8	31.3	89.9	54.58	2 918	1 797
Decatur	160.7	2 988	8.3	1 657	38.8	79.0	29.2	89.0	57.18	3 323	1 651
Dothan	32.4	579	24.1	992	48.2	80.0	37.2	91.0	55.61	1 903	2 204
Florence	32.1	824	40.5	772	38.7	79.7	29.0	90.3	53.85	3 325	1 736
Gadsden	39.0	947	24.1	651	39.1	78.9	28.7	89.5	55.31	3 317	1 610
Hoover	62.4	1 125	0.0	551	41.5	79.8	31.3	89.9	54.58	2 918	1 797
Huntsville	460.5	2 702	11.3	2 463	38.8	79.0	29.2	89.0	57.18	3 323	1 651
Mobile	660.4	3 260	24.6	2 800	49.9	82.3	40.0	91.3	63.96	1 702	2 627
Montgomery	137.0	698	61.7	2 941	46.1	81.3	35.8	91.1	53.43	2 224	2 212
Phenix City	18.6	664	64.8	865	45.7	81.9	35.2	91.8	51.00	2 261	2 284
Prichard	18.9	576	92.5	NA	49.9	82.3	40.0	91.3	63.96	1 702	2 627
Tuscaloosa	107.1	1 300	84.2	1 013	42.8	81.1	32.4	91.1	54.90	2 661	2 070
ALASKA	X	X	X	X	X	X	X	X	X	X	X
Anchorage	1 307.7	5 220	32.5	8 369	14.9	58.4	8.4	65.2	15.91	10 570	0
Fairbanks	47.8	1 451	0.9	179	10.1	62.5	18.5	72.3	10.87	13 940	84
Juneau	45.0	1 512	0.0	1 162	24.2	56.0	19.0	63.9	54.31	8 897	0
ARIZONA	X	X	X	X	X	X	X	X	X	X	X
Chandler	231.8	1 622	49.9	1 262	51.9	90.2	38.1	104.8	9.04	1 490	3 476
Flagstaff	128.1	2 324	31.1	NA	28.7	66.3	15.2	81.9	22.80	7 131	145
Gilbert	119.6	1 859	58.2	NA	51.9	90.2	38.1	104.8	9.04	1 490	3 476
Glendale	215.4	1 182	16.8	1 420	53.6	93.5	41.2	105.9	7.66	1 350	4 162
Mesa	559.4	1 622	30.9	3 203	52.9	91.2	39.5	105.5	8.50	1 366	3 635
Peoria	144.3	1 897	21.1	766	53.6	93.5	41.2	105.9	7.66	1 350	4 162
Phoenix	2 950.2	2 545	9.3	12 710	53.6	93.5	41.2	105.9	7.66	1 350	4 162
Prescott	29.2	889	8.2	NA	36.2	73.1	21.9	88.1	19.63	4 995	631
Scottsdale	602.4	3 365	3.1	1 666	53.6	93.5	41.2	105.9	7.66	1 350	4 162
Sierra Vista	39.9	1 067	0.0	NA	45.1	78.5	26.8	93.5	18.63	2 928	1 441
Tempe	194.3	1 194	38.1	1 711	52.6	90.6	37.8	106.7	8.88	1 464	3 530
Tucson	748.5	1 667	29.9	5 381	51.3	86.6	38.6	99.4	12.00	1 678	2 954
Yuma	63.6	1 051	22.8	NA	56.5	93.7	44.2	106.6	3.17	927	4 305
ARKANSAS	X	X	X	X	X	X	X	X	X	X	X
Conway	104.1	2 906	32.6	376	39.0	81.4	27.9	93.1	49.36	3 147	1 917
Fayetteville	48.2	921	28.5	536	34.0	78.7	22.9	89.3	44.04	4 141	1 401
Fort Smith	39.7	524	64.0	745	36.9	81.5	25.5	93.0	40.90	3 478	1 894
Hot Springs	73.0	NA	0.0	488	39.3	81.7	28.5	93.3	56.52	3 181	1 958
Jacksonville	18.7	641	9.3	768	38.5	81.4	29.4	91.5	49.25	3 228	1 916
Jonesboro	101.2	1 921	75.8	542	36.6	81.7	27.9	92.3	47.19	3 504	1 940
Little Rock	344.0	1 957	0.0	2 836	39.1	81.9	29.1	92.4	50.86	3 155	2 005
North Little Rock	190.7	3 153	73.9	1 033	38.5	81.4	29.4	91.5	49.25	3 228	1 916
Pine Bluff	26.8	496	0.0	419	40.0	81.8	29.6	92.4	52.36	3 016	2 050
Springdale	7.5	196	0.0	452	34.0	78.7	22.9	89.3	44.04	4 141	1 401
West Memphis	33.0	1 226	54.6	356	37.0	81.1	27.4	90.9	50.77	3 438	1 871
CALIFORNIA	X	X	X	X	X	X	X	X	X	X	X
Alameda	39.1	515	18.7	634	49.9	62.1	43.3	70.0	24.30	2 902	115
Alhambra	90.8	1 085	1.1	473	55.7	75.2	41.7	89.2	17.90	1 433	1 427
Anaheim	1 240.4	4 293	26.9	2 603	57.4	72.6	45.6	82.6	12.27	1 238	1 175
Antioch	172.7	2 263	10.7	327	44.5	73.8	35.9	90.8	12.80	2 837	1 066
Apple Valley	14.4	263	0.0	NA	44.2	79.3	30.0	97.4	5.51	3 127	1 525
Arcadia	17.1	339	0.0	NA	55.7	75.2	41.7	89.2	17.90	1 433	1 427
Azusa	91.1	2 162	0.0	NA	55.8	75.0	43.6	89.0	19.37	1 453	1 394
Bakersfield	177.8	865	4.7	1 254	47.8	84.1	38.6	98.5	5.72	2 182	2 365
Baldwin Park	44.8	628	0.0	NA	55.7	75.2	41.7	89.2	17.90	1 433	1 427
Bell	23.2	663	0.0	NA	58.3	74.3	48.9	84.0	14.77	1 154	1 537
Bellflower	5.3	84	0.0	NA	55.9	73.1	44.9	82.7	11.80	1 430	1 201
Bell Gardens	21.3	483	26.3	NA	58.3	74.3	48.9	84.0	14.77	1 154	1 537
Berkeley	170.0	1 647	0.0	1 578	49.9	62.1	43.3	70.0	24.30	2 902	115
Beverly Hills	219.3	6 774	1.3	829	57.2	70.4	46.5	79.2	13.06	1 391	986
Brea	219.6	6 313	8.5	NA	57.4	72.6	45.6	82.6	12.27	1 238	1 175
Buena Park	35.0	486	0.0	NA	57.4	72.6	45.6	82.6	12.27	1 238	1 175
Burbank	238.4	2 469	16.1	1 290	54.5	75.6	41.3	90.2	15.87	1 609	1 424
Burlingame	26.6	961	0.0	NA	48.7	62.7	41.8	71.6	19.70	3 016	145
Camarillo	13.2	231	1.1	NA	55.3	66.1	44.2	74.4	14.38	1 992	416
Campbell	21.1	NA	0.0	NA	49.4	69.5	40.6	82.4	14.42	2 387	594

1. Based on the population estimated as of July 1 of the year shown.   2. Represents normal values based on the 30-year period, 1961–1990.   3. Average daily minimum.   4. Average daily maximum.

Table D. Cities — Land Area and Population

STATE Place code	City	Land area, 1990¹ (sq km)	Population, 1999			Population				Population characteristics, 1990 — Percent — Race						
			Total persons	Rank	Per square kilometer	Total persons 1990	Percent change 1990–1999	Total persons 1980	Percent change 1980–1990	White	Black	Am. Indian, Eskimo, Aleut	Asian and Pacific Islander	Other race	Hispanic²	Foreign born
		1	2	3	4	5	6	7	8	9	10	11	12	13	14	15
	CALIFORNIA—Cont'd															
06 11194	Carlsbad	97.6	77 192	323	791	63 292	22.0	35 490	78.3	89.8	1.2	0.5	3.2	5.4	13.8	12.7
06 11530	Carson	48.8	89 089	267	1 826	83 995	6.1	81 221	3.4	34.7	26.1	0.6	25.0	13.6	27.9	27.0
06 12048	Cathedral City	49.0	39 168	769	799	30 085	30.2	NA	NA	74.3	2.2	1.0	3.6	18.9	37.2	24.9
06 12524	Ceres	14.4	33 355	911	2 316	26 413	26.3	13 281	98.9	78.0	1.7	1.4	5.0	13.9	22.6	12.4
06 12552	Cerritos	22.3	54 326	523	2 436	53 244	2.0	53 020	0.4	42.3	7.4	0.3	45.2	4.7	12.5	36.3
06 13014	Chico	58.1	51 910	556	893	39 970	29.9	26 603	50.2	89.5	1.8	1.1	4.0	3.6	8.7	6.8
06 13210	Chino	44.2	66 138	400	1 496	59 682	10.8	40 165	48.6	67.3	9.8	0.5	3.4	19.0	36.2	17.2
06 13392	Chula Vista	75.1	164 914	124	2 196	135 160	22.0	83 927	61.0	67.7	4.6	0.6	8.9	18.1	37.3	22.3
06 13756	Claremont	28.5	34 751	872	1 219	32 610	6.6	30 950	5.4	82.2	5.0	0.4	8.5	3.8	10.3	12.2
06 14218	Clovis	37.1	65 737	404	1 772	50 323	30.6	33 021	52.4	83.2	1.7	1.4	5.5	8.3	16.3	7.0
06 14890	Colton	36.6	44 417	670	1 214	40 213	10.5	21 310	89.0	58.2	8.7	0.9	4.3	27.9	49.7	16.9
06 15044	Compton	26.3	92 864	254	3 531	90 454	2.7	81 286	11.3	10.6	54.8	0.3	1.9	32.3	43.7	26.8
06 16000	Concord	76.3	117 891	178	1 545	111 308	5.9	103 255	7.8	84.0	2.4	0.7	8.7	4.2	11.5	14.1
06 16350	Corona	73.8	119 594	175	1 621	75 943	57.5	37 791	101.0	75.9	2.8	0.8	7.1	13.4	30.4	18.7
06 16378	Coronado	20.0	28 168	1 067	1 408	26 540	6.1	16 859	57.4	86.2	6.9	0.6	3.4	2.9	8.3	8.9
06 16532	Costa Mesa	40.3	103 864	211	2 577	96 357	7.8	82 562	16.7	84.3	1.3	0.5	6.6	7.3	20.0	21.6
06 16742	Covina	17.9	44 803	662	2 503	43 332	3.4	33 751	28.4	80.3	4.1	0.5	7.6	7.5	25.6	15.9
06 17568	Culver City	13.2	40 137	749	3 041	38 793	3.5	38 139	1.7	69.2	10.4	0.6	12.0	7.8	19.8	23.5
06 17610	Cupertino	26.7	45 844	644	1 717	39 967	14.7	34 015	17.5	74.4	0.9	0.3	23.0	1.3	4.9	22.1
06 17750	Cypress	17.1	48 330	608	2 826	42 655	13.3	40 391	5.6	79.2	2.0	0.5	13.7	4.6	13.5	15.4
06 17918	Daly City	19.5	99 206	227	5 087	92 088	7.7	78 594	17.2	39.5	7.7	0.4	43.8	8.6	22.4	45.2
06 17946	Dana Point	17.2	34 590	875	2 011	31 896	8.4	10 602	200.8	89.6	0.6	0.6	2.3	7.0	13.9	13.4
06 17988	Danville	45.8	41 122	726	898	31 306	31.4	26 446	18.4	91.6	0.8	0.3	6.5	0.8	4.1	9.1
06 18100	Davis	21.9	56 336	504	2 572	46 322	21.6	36 640	26.4	79.7	3.0	0.7	13.2	3.3	7.4	13.9
06 19192	Diamond Bar	39.1	54 977	519	1 406	53 672	2.4	28 045	91.4	63.7	5.7	0.4	24.9	5.4	17.0	25.7
06 19766	Downey	32.2	94 459	244	2 934	91 444	3.3	82 602	10.7	72.5	3.4	0.6	8.8	14.7	32.0	25.9
06 21712	El Cajon	37.3	94 578	243	2 536	88 918	6.4	73 892	20.3	87.4	2.9	1.0	2.8	5.9	14.0	9.7
06 21782	El Centro	16.2	39 453	764	2 435	31 405	25.6	23 996	30.9	60.0	4.5	0.7	2.5	32.4	65.3	29.2
06 22230	El Monte	24.6	112 885	194	4 589	106 162	6.3	79 494	33.5	62.2	1.0	0.6	11.8	24.5	72.5	48.4
06 22678	Encinitas	46.5	61 263	442	1 317	55 406	10.6	10 796	413.2	89.4	0.6	0.4	2.9	6.7	15.2	13.9
06 22804	Escondido	92.3	122 544	171	1 328	108 648	12.8	64 355	68.8	85.2	1.5	0.8	3.7	8.8	23.4	17.2
06 23042	Eureka	24.5	25 087	1 192	1 024	27 025	-7.2	24 074	12.3	88.2	1.4	4.6	4.4	1.4	4.8	5.6
06 23182	Fairfield	92.9	92 256	256	993	78 650	17.3	58 099	35.4	68.2	13.8	1.0	10.7	6.3	13.2	11.5
06 24638	Folsom	55.5	47 947	614	864	29 802	60.9	11 003	170.9	84.0	9.9	0.7	3.5	2.0	10.9	7.7
06 24680	Fontana	92.3	114 882	188	1 245	87 535	31.2	37 111	135.9	67.7	8.7	0.9	4.5	18.1	36.1	16.5
06 25338	Foster City	9.7	30 361	997	3 130	28 176	7.8	23 287	21.0	73.5	3.2	0.2	22.0	1.1	5.8	22.5
06 25380	Fountain Valley	23.1	57 275	489	2 479	53 691	6.7	55 080	-2.5	78.2	0.9	0.6	17.7	2.5	8.1	19.4
06 26000	Fremont	199.5	208 620	81	1 046	173 339	20.4	131 945	31.4	70.6	3.8	0.7	19.4	5.5	13.3	20.1
06 27000	Fresno	256.8	404 141	39	1 574	354 091	14.1	218 202	62.3	59.2	8.3	1.1	12.5	18.9	29.9	17.1
06 28000	Fullerton	57.3	123 243	169	2 151	114 144	8.0	102 034	11.9	74.7	2.2	0.5	12.2	10.5	21.3	23.6
06 28168	Gardena	13.7	55 374	513	4 042	51 481	7.6	45 165	14.0	32.2	23.5	0.5	33.2	10.6	23.1	29.2
06 29000	Garden Grove	46.5	153 534	128	3 302	142 965	7.4	123 307	15.9	67.3	1.5	0.6	20.5	10.1	23.5	30.5
06 29504	Gilroy	26.6	38 470	782	1 446	31 487	22.2	21 641	45.5	68.2	1.2	0.7	4.0	25.9	47.3	15.5
06 30000	Glendale	79.3	186 903	98	2 357	180 038	3.8	139 060	29.5	74.0	1.3	0.3	14.1	10.2	21.0	45.2
06 30014	Glendora	50.4	50 359	580	999	47 832	5.3	38 654	23.7	88.5	1.1	0.5	5.6	4.2	15.2	12.5
06 31960	Hanford	29.9	37 819	800	1 265	30 463	24.1	20 995	45.1	74.1	5.3	0.8	3.1	16.8	29.6	9.9
06 32548	Hawthorne	15.4	74 187	348	4 817	71 349	4.0	56 447	26.4	42.3	28.3	0.5	11.0	18.0	31.1	29.3
06 33000	Hayward	112.5	131 053	154	1 165	114 705	14.3	94 167	21.8	61.8	9.8	1.0	15.5	11.8	23.9	21.1
06 33182	Hemet	45.5	60 697	451	1 334	43 366	40.0	22 454	93.1	90.9	0.7	0.9	1.2	6.4	14.9	10.0
06 33434	Hesperia	125.1	63 983	420	511	50 418	26.9	13 540	272.4	85.7	2.5	0.9	1.4	9.5	19.0	6.6
06 33588	Highland	35.1	43 220	684	1 231	34 439	25.5	NA	NA	73.1	11.0	1.1	4.8	10.0	22.8	11.6
06 36000	Huntington Beach	68.4	199 618	86	2 918	181 519	10.0	170 505	6.5	86.1	0.9	0.6	8.3	4.0	11.2	14.9
06 36056	Huntington Park	7.9	59 000	469	7 468	56 129	5.1	46 223	21.4	31.2	1.1	0.5	1.8	65.4	91.9	59.4
06 36294	Imperial Beach	11.0	28 881	1 043	2 626	26 512	8.9	22 689	16.8	72.9	4.9	1.2	8.3	12.6	28.3	17.4
06 36448	Indio	44.1	46 768	628	1 060	36 850	26.9	21 611	70.5	54.5	4.0	0.8	1.6	39.1	64.1	31.1
06 36546	Inglewood	23.7	113 607	191	4 794	109 602	3.7	94 245	16.3	17.4	51.9	0.4	2.5	27.8	38.5	28.9
06 36770	Irvine	109.6	142 744	139	1 302	110 330	29.4	62 134	77.6	77.9	1.8	0.2	18.1	2.0	6.3	22.3
06 39248	Laguna Niguel	37.9	54 582	522	1 440	44 723	22.0	12 237	265.5	88.5	1.4	0.3	7.8	2.1	7.8	13.8
06 39290	La Habra	19.0	54 942	520	2 892	51 263	7.2	45 232	13.3	76.6	0.9	0.7	4.1	17.7	33.9	19.9
06 39892	Lakewood	24.3	77 078	324	3 172	73 553	4.8	74 654	-1.5	81.1	3.7	0.7	9.4	5.1	14.6	12.9
06 40004	La Mesa	23.9	56 160	506	2 350	52 911	6.1	50 308	5.2	90.2	3.0	0.5	3.1	3.1	9.0	9.0
06 40032	La Mirada	20.3	45 677	647	2 250	40 452	12.9	40 986	-1.3	81.2	1.4	0.6	8.2	8.5	25.9	15.9
06 40130	Lancaster	230.0	123 962	166	539	97 300	27.4	48 027	102.6	79.4	7.4	0.9	3.7	8.6	15.2	9.1
06 40340	La Puente	9.0	39 110	773	4 346	36 955	5.8	30 882	19.7	63.9	3.5	0.6	7.8	24.1	74.9	37.2
06 40830	La Verne	20.2	32 852	921	1 626	30 843	6.5	23 508	31.2	83.0	3.0	0.6	7.2	6.2	18.4	11.8
06 40886	Lawndale	5.1	29 479	1 022	5 780	27 331	7.9	23 460	16.5	60.6	8.3	0.9	12.1	18.1	34.2	29.4
06 41992	Livermore	50.9	75 515	337	1 484	56 741	33.1	48 349	17.4	89.4	1.5	0.7	4.6	3.8	9.8	6.6
06 42202	Lodi	27.5	56 995	495	2 073	51 874	9.9	35 221	47.3	89.3	0.3	0.9	4.7	4.8	16.9	10.5
06 42524	Lompoc	29.1	41 295	720	1 419	37 649	9.7	26 267	43.3	70.5	7.8	1.3	5.4	14.9	26.8	13.4
06 43000	Long Beach	129.5	435 027	34	3 359	429 321	1.3	361 334	18.8	58.4	13.7	0.6	13.6	13.7	23.6	24.3
06 43280	Los Altos	16.5	27 745	1 084	1 682	26 599	4.3	25 769	3.2	89.0	0.4	0.2	10.0	0.4	3.0	13.2

1. Dry land or land partially or temporarily covered by water.   2. Hispanic persons may be of any race.

City	Under 5 years	5 to 17 years	18 to 24 years	25 to 34 years	35 to 44 years	45 to 54 years	55 to 64 years	65 to 74 years	75 years and over	Percent female	Number	Percent change, 1980–1990	Persons per household	Female family householder[1]	One-person
	16	17	18	19	20	21	22	23	24	25	26	27	28	29	30
CALIFORNIA—Cont'd															
Carlsbad	6.7	14.8	8.9	19.5	17.8	10.7	8.7	8.6	4.4	49.4	24 995	85.0	2.47	8.1	23.2
Carson	7.7	19.7	11.3	17.0	14.5	12.6	9.1	5.4	2.8	50.9	23 808	4.0	3.51	14.2	14.2
Cathedral City	8.9	18.3	9.9	19.6	13.7	8.2	7.8	8.0	5.6	49.5	10 918	NA	2.75	8.8	25.4
Ceres	10.0	23.0	8.9	19.7	15.3	8.3	6.6	5.1	3.1	51.1	8 581	85.1	3.04	11.7	15.7
Cerritos	5.7	22.1	11.1	12.3	18.4	17.5	7.3	3.9	1.6	50.7	15 026	2.6	3.54	9.5	7.4
Chico	5.8	12.6	33.4	17.9	12.7	5.0	3.7	4.6	4.4	49.8	15 508	47.0	2.38	10.5	29.6
Chino	7.9	20.1	20.7	17.0	15.8	8.7	4.9	3.3	1.7	43.2	15 636	43.3	3.27	10.8	14.7
Chula Vista	8.2	18.0	11.1	19.1	14.1	9.6	8.5	7.1	4.3	50.9	47 824	57.2	2.79	12.4	21.8
Claremont	4.6	16.9	18.1	11.8	15.6	11.5	8.9	6.9	5.6	51.5	10 472	10.1	2.68	8.9	21.3
Clovis	9.3	21.4	10.3	20.7	17.3	7.9	5.3	4.3	3.4	51.7	18 259	46.9	2.75	12.7	21.5
Colton	11.2	20.9	12.4	22.8	13.6	7.5	5.1	4.1	2.4	50.6	13 466	81.1	2.96	15.3	21.9
Compton	11.0	25.6	12.8	18.6	11.8	8.1	6.3	4.0	1.8	51.0	22 323	2.8	4.02	27.5	13.6
Concord	7.7	16.8	10.1	20.1	17.0	11.0	7.9	5.9	3.5	50.8	41 940	10.4	2.63	11.1	22.4
Corona	10.7	20.4	11.4	21.9	15.8	9.0	5.1	3.5	2.2	49.3	23 920	99.4	3.16	9.3	14.4
Coronado	3.0	8.7	30.6	18.3	12.6	7.1	6.7	8.1	4.9	34.3	7 327	6.5	2.28	7.5	28.4
Costa Mesa	6.9	12.7	13.4	26.3	16.0	9.3	7.3	5.1	3.0	48.9	37 467	15.1	2.51	9.9	27.2
Covina	7.7	17.5	11.1	18.9	15.6	9.9	8.8	6.6	3.9	52.0	15 531	26.5	2.74	13.0	22.5
Culver City	5.7	12.9	8.5	20.1	18.0	12.1	9.4	8.0	5.3	52.2	16 166	1.7	2.34	11.4	31.6
Cupertino	6.0	15.7	7.8	18.3	20.3	13.7	9.8	5.1	3.3	50.1	15 358	25.3	2.60	8.0	20.0
Cypress	6.6	18.1	11.2	17.4	16.3	13.5	9.6	5.0	2.4	50.8	14 279	12.7	2.98	11.5	15.0
Daly City	7.0	16.7	11.0	19.2	15.5	10.8	9.1	6.5	4.2	51.3	29 010	6.9	3.15	13.5	19.9
Dana Point	6.3	14.2	9.7	19.9	18.9	12.2	8.8	6.7	3.3	49.1	12 701	181.8	2.48	8.3	23.2
Danville	6.1	19.3	6.8	12.2	20.2	17.8	9.1	6.0	2.4	50.8	11 064	31.9	2.82	6.7	12.8
Davis	4.7	11.8	32.3	18.8	13.6	7.6	5.0	3.7	2.5	51.3	17 926	27.5	2.46	7.3	24.3
Diamond Bar	8.0	20.4	9.5	17.7	20.8	13.0	6.3	2.9	1.2	50.3	16 901	100.9	3.18	8.5	11.6
Downey	7.4	17.2	10.4	18.1	14.0	10.8	9.0	8.2	5.1	50.8	33 013	1.0	2.71	12.2	23.0
El Cajon	9.1	17.2	12.6	20.9	13.9	8.4	6.8	6.3	4.8	51.3	32 893	15.6	2.63	14.7	22.9
El Centro	10.1	26.0	9.5	16.8	14.9	8.1	6.2	5.2	3.2	51.0	9 633	24.4	3.21	15.5	18.6
El Monte	10.9	23.2	14.5	19.6	12.8	7.6	5.1	4.0	2.5	48.6	26 131	8.0	4.00	16.3	13.7
Encinitas	6.7	15.2	9.5	21.3	21.3	10.2	6.4	5.2	4.2	48.5	20 782	385.1	2.57	8.9	23.3
Escondido	9.1	17.5	10.9	20.8	14.0	8.3	6.5	6.7	6.2	50.9	39 267	56.6	2.73	10.3	23.3
Eureka	6.9	17.9	9.8	16.3	16.5	9.4	7.9	8.3	7.1	51.4	11 137	9.3	2.35	12.2	32.5
Fairfield	9.5	20.8	11.3	20.5	15.5	9.1	6.9	4.5	2.0	49.7	25 425	38.6	2.92	12.5	16.9
Folsom	6.8	14.0	8.6	25.6	20.2	10.2	5.9	5.2	3.5	40.0	8 757	137.8	2.64	7.5	19.9
Fontana	12.4	23.8	10.3	22.0	14.4	7.3	4.3	3.4	2.3	50.6	26 385	112.6	3.30	13.7	14.6
Foster City	5.2	15.1	8.9	19.7	19.9	15.4	9.1	4.8	2.0	50.1	11 210	26.6	2.50	7.6	23.1
Fountain Valley	5.4	18.4	11.8	14.8	17.0	16.2	9.1	4.7	2.6	50.2	17 407	6.4	3.07	9.6	13.5
Fremont	8.2	17.7	9.3	22.0	18.0	11.2	7.0	4.2	2.3	49.9	60 198	36.1	2.86	9.2	16.8
Fresno	9.9	21.8	11.5	18.2	14.1	8.1	6.4	5.7	4.3	51.4	121 807	48.5	2.84	16.2	24.1
Fullerton	6.7	15.9	13.8	19.9	14.1	10.8	8.6	6.4	3.9	49.9	40 872	7.6	2.74	9.7	22.4
Gardena	7.6	15.9	9.5	21.0	15.0	11.0	9.2	6.8	4.2	50.5	18 126	6.5	2.70	14.4	25.9
Garden Grove	8.7	17.6	11.5	21.1	14.5	9.9	8.1	5.7	3.1	49.3	44 538	6.4	3.17	11.9	16.7
Gilroy	9.4	22.6	11.1	18.5	15.8	9.0	6.0	4.2	3.4	50.0	9 512	38.6	3.27	14.3	15.2
Glendale	6.5	15.2	9.9	19.8	15.7	11.2	8.5	7.0	6.3	51.9	68 604	15.5	2.59	10.5	27.8
Glendora	7.6	18.5	9.2	17.0	15.6	12.1	9.5	6.5	4.0	51.3	16 327	25.8	2.88	9.7	17.5
Hanford	9.4	20.9	10.0	17.4	14.0	9.7	7.4	6.1	5.1	51.5	10 855	47.3	2.80	14.9	21.8
Hawthorne	9.0	16.4	12.7	24.4	15.0	8.7	6.6	4.7	2.6	50.5	27 137	17.9	2.61	16.1	30.1
Hayward	7.8	17.0	10.8	20.7	15.6	9.4	8.3	6.5	3.9	50.8	40 117	16.6	2.75	13.1	22.3
Hemet	6.1	11.3	6.4	12.0	7.6	5.4	9.2	20.5	21.6	54.8	17 397	53.3	2.04	7.9	36.3
Hesperia	9.3	23.3	8.6	16.9	14.6	8.8	7.1	7.2	4.1	50.2	16 551	229.2	3.04	10.0	15.6
Highland	10.2	22.5	10.7	18.9	15.4	8.8	6.9	4.1	2.4	50.8	11 317	NA	3.03	16.1	17.2
Huntington Beach	6.0	14.7	12.2	21.3	16.6	12.9	8.0	5.1	3.1	49.5	68 879	13.0	2.62	9.5	21.5
Huntington Park	11.3	23.1	15.9	20.4	12.2	7.4	4.2	3.3	2.3	49.1	13 903	-7.0	4.01	17.2	13.8
Imperial Beach	10.4	18.5	16.0	23.8	13.7	5.9	5.6	4.2	1.8	48.8	9 080	17.7	2.85	14.6	17.8
Indio	10.6	23.0	13.5	19.1	12.3	7.7	6.1	4.8	2.9	49.3	10 747	61.7	3.35	14.2	18.6
Inglewood	9.8	20.2	12.1	20.9	14.6	10.0	5.6	4.0	2.9	51.5	36 102	-2.2	2.99	21.2	26.9
Irvine	6.8	17.5	13.7	19.2	19.8	11.8	5.6	3.5	2.1	51.6	40 257	88.0	2.69	9.2	19.7
Laguna Niguel	8.4	15.3	8.1	21.7	20.9	12.2	6.5	4.7	2.2	50.7	17 172	275.9	2.58	7.3	18.5
La Habra	8.2	16.8	11.9	20.6	13.3	9.7	8.5	7.1	3.8	50.4	18 112	9.4	2.81	11.5	22.0
Lakewood	7.2	17.4	8.6	18.9	16.0	10.3	9.4	8.5	3.6	50.7	26 102	1.2	2.81	10.3	17.7
La Mesa	5.8	11.4	11.8	20.9	14.8	8.6	8.6	9.6	8.6	52.9	23 206	7.6	2.23	10.7	31.1
La Mirada	6.9	17.3	12.1	16.7	13.8	11.2	10.9	8.0	3.2	50.9	12 731	5.9	3.06	9.1	14.7
Lancaster	9.7	20.3	10.3	21.7	14.5	8.8	6.7	5.0	3.0	49.9	32 901	90.4	2.83	11.1	20.4
La Puente	9.4	22.9	13.8	18.8	12.7	9.6	7.1	3.6	2.1	49.4	9 019	7.0	4.06	16.4	11.5
La Verne	7.2	18.9	10.1	14.8	17.8	11.0	7.4	7.1	5.7	51.8	10 740	29.0	2.82	8.5	19.3
Lawndale	9.3	16.9	13.0	25.3	14.8	9.5	5.5	3.5	2.1	48.4	9 227	12.8	2.95	14.8	21.7
Livermore	8.3	18.9	9.1	20.3	17.5	11.8	7.0	4.4	2.7	50.2	20 643	26.2	2.74	11.3	18.8
Lodi	7.8	17.1	9.5	18.4	14.4	8.9	8.1	7.8	8.0	51.0	19 001	35.7	2.63	11.3	24.0
Lompoc	9.6	19.3	8.5	22.4	15.3	9.3	7.3	5.3	2.9	47.3	12 504	33.3	2.81	13.0	22.1
Long Beach	8.6	16.8	13.0	21.5	14.6	8.5	6.3	4.7	4.7	49.5	158 975	4.6	2.61	13.0	30.8
Los Altos	5.0	15.6	4.6	10.2	16.9	16.8	12.3	11.8	6.8	51.6	9 837	8.0	2.63	5.4	16.3

1. No spouse present.

Table D. Cities — Group Quarters, Crime, Education, and Income

City	Persons in group quarters, 1990 — Total	Persons in mental hospitals	Persons in nursing homes	Persons identified as homeless[1]	Serious crimes known to police, 1998[2] — Total Number	Total Rate[3]	Violent	Property	Education, 1990 — School enrollment Public	Private	Attainment[4] (percent) High school graduate or more	Bachelor's degree or more	Money income, 1989 — Per capita (dollars)[5]	Households Median Dollars	Percent change, 1979–1989 (constant 1989 dollars)
	31	32	33	34	35	36	37	38	39	40	41	42	43	44	45
CALIFORNIA—Cont'd															
Carlsbad	1 268	0	238	959	2 281	3 208	307	2 901	13 006	2 204	89.6	35.8	21 764	45 739	22.1
Carson	342	0	296	0	3 549	4 025	922	3 103	21 574	3 685	71.4	17.1	13 749	43 882	10.0
Cathedral City	92	92	0	0	1 430	3 799	834	2 965	6 530	527	69.6	13.0	13 331	30 908	NA
Ceres	243	20	105	0	2 191	6 852	647	6 205	6 727	596	67.1	8.8	11 603	30 876	17.9
Cerritos	89	83	0	0	3 137	5 737	627	5 110	16 067	2 696	89.2	37.0	18 966	59 076	12.6
Chico	3 063	0	662	118	2 653	5 666	438	5 228	19 251	595	85.6	31.8	10 584	19 005	1.7
Chino	8 205	0	0	0	2 547	3 836	423	3 413	18 730	2 528	74.2	11.8	12 916	41 958	5.3
Chula Vista	1 681	175	531	26	8 150	5 209	747	4 462	33 584	3 926	75.7	17.7	14 102	32 012	6.1
Claremont	4 470	0	470	0	1 071	3 136	199	2 937	6 803	5 675	92.8	51.2	22 161	53 479	18.8
Clovis	242	0	118	41	2 660	4 120	190	3 930	14 762	1 215	81.8	20.1	13 160	31 699	15.1
Colton	362	0	262	100	2 139	4 815	524	4 291	10 697	1 228	70.3	13.4	10 924	28 838	20.4
Compton	531	91	91	44	4 860	5 200	1 595	3 605	26 873	2 917	51.2	6.2	7 842	24 971	10.7
Concord	1 105	0	710	42	6 801	5 735	554	5 181	24 578	4 845	88.1	26.1	17 566	41 675	12.4
Corona	305	0	0	47	4 076	3 926	374	3 552	18 607	2 212	76.1	18.0	15 292	43 555	25.6
Coronado	9 841	0	157	0	608	2 298	204	2 094	3 508	983	94.1	39.3	21 972	47 790	43.6
Costa Mesa	2 260	0	328	267	3 956	3 792	281	3 511	20 013	4 313	83.5	27.3	18 750	40 313	24.6
Covina	604	31	407	97	1 858	4 116	709	3 407	9 773	1 966	82.5	16.4	16 259	38 907	11.2
Culver City	946	151	520	124	1 525	3 808	484	3 324	8 065	1 651	84.1	35.0	21 471	42 971	15.9
Cupertino	313	0	302	0	1 164	2 650	298	2 352	9 609	1 652	94.5	52.1	29 118	64 587	27.1
Cypress	123	0	0	0	1 205	2 479	267	2 212	11 215	1 702	87.5	26.6	19 147	50 981	11.2
Daly City	886	0	561	210	2 779	2 774	327	2 447	21 430	4 887	78.8	24.2	14 744	41 533	14.9
Dana Point	330	0	168	36	757	2 162	189	1 973	6 208	1 128	90.3	35.8	27 986	54 516	44.3
Danville	136	0	136	0	694	1 751	93	1 658	7 660	1 342	95.7	48.3	31 265	74 472	18.9
Davis	2 063	0	256	0	1 700	3 156	323	2 833	22 712	1 171	95.0	63.8	15 269	29 044	18.0
Diamond Bar	0	0	0	0	1 101	1 995	292	1 703	15 049	2 611	90.6	37.0	21 497	60 651	17.5
Downey	1 883	0	723	0	4 146	4 371	459	3 912	20 400	3 645	76.3	16.3	16 696	36 991	9.3
El Cajon	2 055	0	1 196	58	4 818	5 084	828	4 256	20 107	2 486	78.5	14.4	13 518	28 108	10.1
El Centro	521	0	136	49	2 265	5 927	882	5 045	10 192	699	59.5	13.5	9 898	25 147	-8.3
El Monte	1 515	11	725	398	3 920	3 496	1 010	2 486	29 844	2 293	44.3	6.0	8 056	28 034	21.0
Encinitas	1 712	0	455	1 125	NA	NA	NA	NA	11 940	2 248	88.6	39.7	22 451	46 069	56.9
Escondido	1 278	0	708	136	5 670	4 740	606	4 134	23 628	3 293	77.9	18.3	14 647	32 895	28.6
Eureka	1 015	21	367	204	2 591	9 746	715	9 031	6 973	425	79.3	18.0	12 915	21 812	-4.9
Fairfield	2 925	0	247	97	4 878	5 566	690	4 876	20 745	1 753	84.2	15.4	13 713	36 886	22.4
Folsom	6 785	0	116	0	1 244	2 960	209	2 751	6 263	786	84.2	24.2	17 617	46 726	69.5
Fontana	426	57	266	15	4 006	3 750	776	2 974	23 338	2 486	72.0	9.4	11 585	35 558	16.1
Foster City	86	0	86	0	555	1 822	98	1 724	6 224	1 348	95.0	46.7	28 399	60 462	19.7
Fountain Valley	308	0	291	0	1 886	3 271	264	3 007	14 346	2 544	88.7	31.3	20 699	56 255	13.4
Fremont	1 219	125	611	96	7 323	3 805	352	3 453	41 577	6 417	86.6	29.9	20 101	51 231	20.6
Fresno	7 576	0	1 979	725	32 075	7 934	1 052	6 882	104 708	8 198	69.0	19.1	11 528	24 923	3.1
Fullerton	1 858	0	1 022	38	4 482	3 608	345	3 263	28 702	4 867	82.7	29.8	19 098	41 921	15.5
Gardena	813	0	609	0	2 533	4 680	1 120	3 560	11 326	1 695	73.4	16.5	14 601	33 063	6.8
Garden Grove	1 827	93	795	54	5 623	3 646	469	3 177	34 198	4 363	74.4	16.1	13 976	39 882	11.3
Gilroy	385	0	258	88	2 075	5 882	1 097	4 785	9 124	844	68.5	16.2	14 241	40 955	27.7
Glendale	2 601	0	1 983	53	5 346	2 846	297	2 549	39 228	9 304	77.2	28.6	17 966	34 372	19.2
Glendora	818	0	626	0	1 140	2 172	234	1 938	11 726	2 052	83.7	22.2	18 573	46 116	13.6
Hanford	329	0	268	29	1 762	4 766	362	4 404	7 531	765	71.0	11.9	11 283	26 629	8.2
Hawthorne	553	0	229	0	4 310	5 797	1 648	4 149	16 468	3 078	73.9	15.7	13 880	30 967	6.7
Hayward	1 161	0	623	165	7 122	5 713	625	5 088	26 035	3 443	76.3	17.0	15 048	36 058	7.6
Hemet	576	0	503	58	NA	NA	NA	NA	4 873	514	67.3	9.2	12 270	20 382	11.6
Hesperia	70	0	22	0	2 179	3 503	373	3 130	12 993	1 363	71.3	6.7	11 472	30 795	27.3
Highland	99	0	73	0	1 892	4 557	597	3 960	8 762	1 163	74.4	13.7	12 567	31 561	NA
Huntington Beach	525	0	464	7	5 907	2 996	274	2 722	42 235	6 873	89.2	32.1	23 500	50 633	25.8
Huntington Park	224	0	0	80	2 648	4 538	1 210	3 328	16 507	1 399	30.6	5.3	7 238	23 595	24.1
Imperial Beach	676	0	17	0	NA	NA	NA	NA	6 435	449	77.9	12.1	10 731	26 464	21.6
Indio	778	0	88	17	NA	NA	NA	NA	10 010	582	52.0	9.2	9 244	25 976	1.7
Inglewood	1 600	0	578	106	5 069	4 479	1 316	3 163	27 957	5 702	66.0	14.9	11 899	29 881	18.7
Irvine	2 144	0	319	7	3 593	2 719	165	2 554	35 018	3 982	95.1	52.8	25 332	56 307	7.3
Laguna Niguel	15	0	15	0	770	1 441	109	1 332	9 335	2 018	95.9	44.6	28 614	61 501	22.2
La Habra	317	0	254	23	1 787	3 220	400	2 820	11 764	1 965	76.3	18.4	16 196	39 967	13.2
Lakewood	100	0	0	0	3 176	4 129	685	3 444	16 418	2 991	81.4	17.7	17 446	44 700	15.7
La Mesa	1 217	0	1 161	0	2 302	4 077	430	3 647	11 959	1 403	86.7	24.3	16 700	31 171	10.7
La Mirada	1 536	0	262	0	1 162	2 599	385	2 214	8 578	2 929	81.1	17.8	16 415	47 143	7.9
Lancaster	4 574	0	499	45	5 368	4 553	1 136	3 417	22 304	4 222	80.3	16.2	14 842	38 388	13.6
La Puente	262	0	0	0	1 141	2 911	974	1 937	10 440	1 085	50.6	7.5	9 060	33 273	8.4
La Verne	581	0	184	0	777	2 383	* 205	2 178	7 866	1 986	84.6	27.1	18 622	46 587	30.5
Lawndale	89	0	0	36	1 283	4 413	1 262	3 151	6 254	801	69.4	13.1	13 550	34 552	18.7
Livermore	211	0	165	46	1 893	2 857	225	2 632	13 920	1 932	88.2	27.3	19 330	49 149	17.5
Lodi	1 894	0	1 700	194	3 052	5 426	590	4 836	10 743	1 669	72.3	13.9	14 638	30 739	14.4
Lompoc	2 580	0	118	140	1 798	4 281	364	3 917	9 380	1 080	78.4	14.2	13 384	31 702	15.7
Long Beach	14 146	137	3 073	434	19 078	4 437	860	3 577	104 593	13 481	75.5	23.2	15 639	31 938	23.8
Los Altos	411	0	406	5	396	1 393	215	1 178	4 914	1 468	95.7	59.6	37 776	79 579	30.0

1. Persons in emergency shelters and persons visible in street locations. 2. Data for serious crimes have not been adjusted for underreporting. This may affect comparability between geographic areas and over time. 3. Per 100,000 population estimated by the FBI. 4. Persons 25 years old and older. 5. Based on population enumerated as of April 1, 1990.

	Money income, 1989 (cont'd)				Housing units, 1990										
	Households (cont'd)	Percent below poverty, 1989						Occupied units							
		Persons		Families					Owner-occupied units				Renter-occupied units		
											Owner cost as a percent of income				
City	Percent with $100,000 or more	Total	Percent change in rate, 1979–1989	Total	Total	Percent change, 1980–1990	Vacant units for sale or rent[1]	Total	Percent	Median value[2] (dollars)	With a mortgage	Without a mortgage	Median rent[3] (dollars)	Rent as percent of income	Substandard units[4] (percent)
	46	47	48	49	50	51	52	53	54	55	56	57	58	59	60
CALIFORNIA—Cont'd															
Carlsbad	9.4	6.8	-9.3	3.6	27 235	77.4	1 332	24 995	62.2	255 900	27.4	11.6	774	28.9	3.8
Carson	5.7	6.9	-12.7	5.0	24 441	5.1	546	23 808	79.0	188 100	23.1	11.2	721	28.0	20.0
Cathedral City	3.4	13.6	NA	9.6	15 229	NA	1 136	10 918	61.8	113 200	27.7	12.1	649	30.7	13.8
Ceres	1.8	15.5	31.4	12.6	9 075	73.2	421	8 581	64.8	127 700	24.8	12.6	475	29.2	10.6
Cerritos	15.1	4.0	25.0	3.0	15 364	3.0	298	15 026	83.4	300 000	23.2	10.9	1 001	28.6	10.1
Chico	2.0	32.0	22.6	15.9	16 295	47.0	627	15 508	32.9	106 100	23.5	11.7	456	35.1	4.4
Chino	4.6	7.4	-6.3	6.0	16 137	41.9	435	15 636	67.9	172 200	25.2	12.5	656	30.2	11.9
Chula Vista	3.5	9.8	16.7	8.6	49 849	56.3	1 679	47 824	53.3	164 000	24.7	11.3	592	29.5	10.1
Claremont	16.2	5.3	-8.6	2.2	10 831	9.0	306	10 472	69.8	253 900	22.6	10.5	702	28.6	3.5
Clovis	1.9	10.3	12.0	8.6	18 888	41.4	535	18 259	53.2	92 500	22.9	12.1	474	26.6	6.1
Colton	1.5	15.6	11.4	13.4	14 767	77.8	1 154	13 466	52.0	98 500	25.2	12.1	534	29.4	15.0
Compton	1.6	27.5	4.2	24.2	23 239	3.6	778	22 323	56.8	108 000	27.1	13.2	549	34.8	34.5
Concord	4.7	6.7	11.7	4.9	43 715	10.7	1 524	41 940	60.9	195 300	24.4	11.5	677	29.1	4.7
Corona	5.1	8.3	-16.2	5.7	26 538	111.8	2 408	23 920	63.9	186 300	28.6	11.9	659	27.7	11.5
Coronado	15.2	4.1	-28.1	2.6	9 145	8.9	667	7 327	50.2	452 500	27.6	11.4	805	27.9	1.7
Costa Mesa	7.2	9.2	8.2	6.0	39 611	16.4	1 890	37 467	40.2	257 000	24.3	11.3	810	28.6	10.1
Covina	5.0	7.6	20.6	5.3	16 110	27.7	513	15 531	58.1	200 700	24.6	11.1	652	28.3	9.2
Culver City	8.7	6.7	-1.5	4.6	16 943	1.3	654	16 166	55.5	328 900	24.0	11.4	788	28.5	8.7
Cupertino	22.4	3.2	-13.5	2.1	16 055	27.9	593	15 358	63.0	414 300	23.6	11.4	957	24.1	4.2
Cypress	10.3	4.5	-8.2	3.4	14 715	13.9	355	14 279	69.4	252 700	22.3	11.3	811	26.7	6.3
Daly City	5.3	7.2	2.9	5.9	30 162	8.4	965	29 010	58.1	272 100	24.7	11.5	734	27.9	19.3
Dana Point	18.8	7.2	-10.0	4.4	14 666	186.1	1 329	12 701	58.9	336 600	26.9	11.6	898	27.3	3.7
Danville	28.3	2.1	-4.5	1.2	11 466	31.8	327	11 064	87.8	359 200	26.3	11.3	1 001	27.8	0.7
Davis	5.5	25.5	1.6	7.1	18 282	25.6	277	17 926	40.8	191 300	22.0	11.1	588	35.1	5.1
Diamond Bar	13.8	3.5	-5.4	2.4	17 664	98.5	600	16 901	85.7	272 900	27.6	11.5	940	28.7	6.4
Downey	6.5	8.1	15.7	5.7	34 302	1.8	1 052	33 013	52.5	231 600	23.7	11.3	649	26.8	10.8
El Cajon	3.2	12.9	9.3	10.7	34 453	14.5	1 380	32 893	40.7	158 000	23.6	10.8	548	30.8	8.4
El Centro	2.1	23.3	102.6	20.6	10 180	20.2	406	9 633	52.5	79 100	21.4	12.0	431	31.1	21.5
El Monte	1.6	22.5	13.1	18.5	27 167	7.0	867	26 131	40.2	172 100	26.7	11.7	600	30.0	42.5
Encinitas	12.6	8.3	-17.0	3.5	22 123	383.2	827	20 782	61.9	285 700	27.0	12.4	796	28.9	4.7
Escondido	4.1	11.2	0.9	7.8	42 040	54.8	2 389	39 267	51.9	169 500	27.2	11.6	621	30.7	9.7
Eureka	1.8	18.7	34.5	14.6	11 781	9.8	422	11 137	50.7	82 100	21.3	12.0	393	30.1	5.2
Fairfield	2.4	7.4	-21.3	6.3	26 357	39.1	748	25 425	56.2	139 900	24.5	12.0	563	27.0	5.5
Folsom	9.8	5.2	-45.8	4.3	9 418	135.5	558	8 757	74.1	210 600	26.4	12.1	593	29.4	2.5
Fontana	1.7	11.4	-1.7	10.2	29 383	110.5	2 644	26 385	64.2	134 600	27.7	12.0	577	30.3	12.7
Foster City	17.3	2.9	-17.1	1.6	11 747	28.0	474	11 210	60.1	411 700	27.1	11.7	969	24.4	3.6
Fountain Valley	14.5	3.5	-7.9	2.2	18 019	7.5	526	17 407	75.1	287 000	22.3	11.8	893	28.5	5.2
Fremont	9.4	4.3	-10.4	3.0	62 400	37.2	1 983	60 198	64.6	264 300	25.8	11.4	795	27.0	6.7
Fresno	3.0	24.0	52.9	19.3	129 404	45.8	6 274	121 807	48.2	80 300	22.6	12.3	441	30.1	13.0
Fullerton	9.6	9.8	30.7	5.6	42 956	8.7	1 858	40 872	55.1	234 600	23.5	11.3	706	29.4	10.9
Gardena	3.4	9.8	6.5	8.2	19 037	8.4	814	18 126	46.6	200 200	21.7	10.9	646	28.5	16.9
Garden Grove	3.9	10.4	25.3	7.8	45 984	7.3	1 221	44 538	59.6	199 700	24.1	10.9	745	32.2	17.3
Gilroy	6.1	12.9	-0.8	10.7	9 767	35.3	220	9 512	56.8	243 300	27.2	11.5	659	29.4	13.8
Glendale	8.6	14.4	42.6	12.3	72 114	17.0	2 881	68 604	38.7	343 600	25.3	11.6	688	30.5	18.2
Glendora	9.5	5.0	-3.8	3.7	16 876	27.7	462	16 327	73.9	231 600	24.2	11.7	729	27.8	6.0
Hanford	1.8	15.7	-1.9	13.1	11 610	45.2	576	10 855	55.6	73 200	22.3	12.4	421	27.5	9.0
Hawthorne	2.4	13.9	51.1	11.8	29 214	22.2	1 811	27 137	25.5	226 100	24.8	10.8	629	28.2	19.1
Hayward	3.5	9.7	5.4	7.6	42 216	17.7	1 900	40 117	51.5	184 500	24.1	11.5	688	28.8	11.6
Hemet	0.7	14.0	34.6	10.1	19 692	55.4	1 528	17 397	62.3	89 900	25.7	11.4	500	31.4	5.1
Hesperia	1.9	12.5	35.9	10.9	17 359	204.4	570	16 551	73.6	105 400	25.9	12.7	545	32.6	7.3
Highland	3.4	15.8	NA	12.2	12 562	NA	1 123	11 317	61.1	103 300	23.7	11.0	509	29.8	10.6
Huntington Beach	12.3	5.2	-20.0	3.2	72 736	14.2	3 043	68 879	58.5	287 100	23.6	11.6	860	27.6	4.7
Huntington Park	1.1	24.3	3.8	21.7	14 515	-7.0	542	13 903	28.5	163 700	28.9	11.3	521	32.8	51.4
Imperial Beach	1.4	17.7	4.7	14.9	9 525	16.2	317	9 080	29.1	143 300	24.5	11.2	591	31.5	14.6
Indio	1.6	21.2	34.2	17.0	13 028	63.2	961	10 747	49.0	83 600	23.1	11.8	495	28.7	31.4
Inglewood	2.5	16.5	7.1	14.1	38 713	1.3	2 176	36 102	36.3	170 400	26.3	12.8	618	31.2	23.0
Irvine	18.5	6.4	77.8	2.6	42 221	87.5	1 677	40 257	62.5	294 700	26.6	12.3	925	29.3	4.5
Laguna Niguel	22.1	3.1	-3.1	2.2	18 892	273.1	1 430	17 172	74.7	311 800	30.3	11.8	901	29.2	2.0
La Habra	6.4	8.0	31.1	5.9	18 670	8.6	493	18 112	56.4	201 700	23.5	11.8	685	28.4	10.4
Lakewood	5.2	4.9	-5.8	3.2	26 795	2.1	573	26 102	72.1	215 600	23.3	11.1	802	26.6	7.1
La Mesa	3.0	9.2	-7.1	6.0	24 154	6.8	791	23 206	48.2	163 700	22.8	10.7	594	30.1	4.3
La Mirada	6.3	3.9	-20.4	2.4	13 354	6.9	591	12 731	82.4	209 700	22.6	11.2	791	28.5	6.6
Lancaster	4.1	9.9	13.8	7.7	36 217	99.8	2 868	32 901	62.9	133 700	24.4	11.7	610	27.6	5.9
La Puente	1.5	14.0	18.6	12.4	9 285	8.0	244	9 019	60.9	155 400	24.2	11.7	606	31.0	30.3
La Verne	7.8	4.4	-25.4	3.1	11 113	27.7	319	10 740	75.0	255 400	26.5	12.4	675	27.5	4.4
Lawndale	2.2	13.1	2.3	10.4	9 778	14.1	505	9 227	31.4	230 800	26.7	12.3	749	29.2	19.6
Livermore	6.9	5.2	18.2	4.4	21 489	29.2	733	20 643	67.1	217 300	25.9	11.8	762	27.8	2.8
Lodi	3.0	12.6	34.0	10.0	19 676	32.8	553	19 001	54.3	126 300	22.0	11.7	499	26.9	8.5
Lompoc	1.8	15.1	15.3	12.9	13 261	34.3	632	12 504	51.9	144 600	24.3	11.6	514	28.7	9.8
Long Beach	5.5	16.8	18.3	13.5	170 368	6.7	9 632	158 975	41.0	222 900	25.1	11.4	605	30.0	16.6
Los Altos	37.0	1.2	-53.8	0.5	10 107	8.5	194	9 837	87.8	500 001	23.3	11.4	1 001	23.6	1.2

1. Includes units rented or sold but not occupied.   2. Specified owner-occupied units.   3. Specified renter-occupied units.   4. Overcrowded or lacking complete plumbing facilities.

Table D. Cities — Labor Force, Employment, Disability, and Construction

City	Civilian labor force, 1999				Civilian employment, 1990[2]			Disability 1990	Value of residential construction authorized by building permits, 1999		
			Unemployment			Percent					
	Total	Percent change, 1998–1999	Total	Rate[1]	Total	Professional, managerial, and technical	Precision production, craft, and repair	Work disabled persons[3] (percent)	New construction ($1,000)	Number of housing units	Percent single family
	61	62	63	64	65	66	67	68	69	70	71
CALIFORNIA—Cont'd											
Carlsbad	38 889	3.0	961	2.5	33 000	42.2	7.8	6.1	428 381	2 261	74.4
Carson	45 442	0.4	2 597	5.7	41 067	25.4	13.6	7.6	5 410	85	9.4
Cathedral City	19 521	4.8	954	4.9	13 944	21.1	14.9	8.4	30 167	244	92.2
Ceres	14 200	0.3	1 507	10.6	10 554	20.8	16.3	10.8	14 125	118	100.0
Cerritos	30 122	0.8	875	2.9	28 033	42.0	9.8	4.3	0	0	0.0
Chico	22 159	-0.7	1 455	6.6	18 359	29.9	9.0	7.0	66 737	551	99.1
Chino	31 686	4.4	1 093	3.4	25 181	25.7	13.0	6.4	45 249	227	99.1
Chula Vista	71 126	2.9	2 322	3.3	59 865	30.7	12.1	8.0	363 323	2 561	70.7
Claremont	17 967	0.7	598	3.3	16 648	50.0	5.7	5.5	17 563	90	68.9
Clovis	32 777	1.3	2 733	8.3	24 675	30.2	11.0	7.3	65 870	378	95.8
Colton	22 359	3.8	1 387	6.2	17 262	24.5	14.3	7.8	2 251	10	100.0
Compton	35 917	-0.3	4 152	11.6	30 447	15.4	13.4	10.2	1 930	22	90.9
Concord	72 453	1.8	2 029	2.8	60 333	34.2	12.0	7.1	29 813	108	94.4
Corona	52 168	4.9	2 356	4.5	37 410	30.3	13.1	5.9	371 678	1 657	100.0
Coronado	8 512	3.1	176	2.1	7 253	49.5	4.9	5.2	8 808	41	63.4
Costa Mesa	66 789	2.6	1 528	2.3	58 875	34.3	10.0	5.3	8 166	61	96.7
Covina	24 156	0.6	1 023	4.2	22 173	30.0	11.7	7.6	1 226	4	100.0
Culver City	23 712	0.7	773	3.3	21 987	44.1	7.9	5.2	8 772	51	100.0
Cupertino	27 641	0.1	487	1.8	23 469	59.1	5.8	4.5	41 543	133	97.7
Cypress	26 841	2.5	663	2.5	23 616	37.0	11.2	6.2	5 559	43	100.0
Daly City	55 401	0.5	1 416	2.6	48 693	25.1	9.0	6.3	5 346	20	100.0
Dana Point	20 652	2.6	432	2.1	18 241	40.2	9.3	4.4	41 340	153	51.0
Danville	20 412	2.1	296	1.5	17 233	48.8	6.3	3.6	NA	NA	NA
Davis	33 338	3.6	1 109	3.3	24 765	56.0	4.1	4.4	145 631	945	51.7
Diamond Bar	31 613	0.8	886	2.8	29 452	43.7	7.3	4.0	21 694	48	100.0
Downey	48 863	0.6	2 103	4.3	44 819	27.1	12.8	6.5	6 285	40	37.5
El Cajon	47 450	2.8	1 785	3.8	39 732	27.0	15.2	10.5	25 309	181	100.0
El Centro	16 946	-1.4	3 810	22.5	11 165	28.9	9.0	8.5	2 832	36	91.7
El Monte	48 454	0.2	3 638	7.5	42 956	13.4	16.1	6.2	8 226	140	49.3
Encinitas	37 129	3.1	772	2.1	31 633	43.7	8.1	4.4	77 599	311	91.0
Escondido	61 610	2.9	1 966	3.2	51 895	28.9	13.6	8.2	55 313	324	67.9
Eureka	13 299	-1.9	863	6.5	11 220	25.9	10.8	15.7	2 504	26	69.2
Fairfield	41 670	4.4	2 095	5.0	33 008	26.1	14.5	8.4	85 409	686	57.4
Folsom	13 995	3.9	389	2.8	11 741	43.1	7.9	5.9	282 226	1 798	60.5
Fontana	47 032	4.1	2 185	4.6	36 913	21.1	15.9	6.8	244 994	1 323	100.0
Foster City	19 845	0.7	313	1.6	17 617	47.3	6.4	3.5	1 135	4	100.0
Fountain Valley	34 322	2.6	745	2.2	30 291	41.0	10.0	5.6	23 417	458	0.4
Fremont	108 150	1.9	2 558	2.4	96 262	39.0	11.8	5.5	133 494	547	79.5
Fresno	193 357	1.0	23 373	12.1	139 607	31.0	9.2	9.6	197 762	1 727	84.5
Fullerton	70 830	2.5	1 812	2.6	62 264	35.0	9.7	5.9	45 993	199	100.0
Gardena	28 026	0.5	1 308	4.7	25 609	26.0	12.6	7.6	3 385	28	92.9
Garden Grove	82 277	2.4	2 835	3.4	71 668	26.7	14.1	7.3	23 962	173	100.0
Gilroy	17 928	0.1	914	5.1	14 705	26.2	12.6	6.1	94 909	409	96.8
Glendale	96 194	0.4	5 310	5.5	87 112	37.5	9.5	6.5	3 376	32	59.4
Glendora	26 119	0.7	886	3.4	24 186	34.8	12.7	6.9	16 742	50	100.0
Hanford	16 027	-1.1	1 826	11.4	12 400	23.5	10.1	9.5	32 105	275	89.1
Hawthorne	40 818	0.4	2 243	5.5	36 974	26.1	11.9	6.9	2 292	13	38.5
Hayward	63 058	1.7	2 199	3.5	55 481	26.3	13.4	7.8	43 031	344	43.9
Hemet	14 150	4.1	1 096	7.7	9 804	22.5	17.1	14.6	42 616	300	100.0
Hesperia	23 904	3.9	1 401	5.9	18 522	19.7	22.7	11.3	25 296	212	100.0
Highland	18 614	3.9	1 055	5.7	14 453	24.0	14.2	8.3	30 831	136	100.0
Huntington Beach	122 627	2.6	2 436	2.0	108 429	39.5	10.2	5.4	116 456	474	91.1
Huntington Park	26 338	-0.2	2 708	10.3	22 649	10.8	15.0	4.7	0	0	0.0
Imperial Beach	12 203	2.6	647	5.3	10 055	22.3	17.8	9.0	2 411	18	100.0
Indio	21 777	4.1	1 690	7.8	15 086	17.0	11.4	8.4	33 141	285	100.0
Inglewood	56 777	0.1	4 550	8.0	50 059	24.3	10.7	6.7	3 378	25	92.0
Irvine	69 700	2.6	1 278	1.8	61 726	52.8	3.6	3.4	337 429	2 761	46.2
Laguna Niguel	28 914	2.6	450	1.6	25 679	46.5	6.0	3.6	44 004	214	82.7
La Habra	30 670	2.5	933	3.0	26 827	28.4	11.6	6.9	76 842	269	100.0
Lakewood	40 327	0.7	1 384	3.4	37 327	31.6	13.4	6.7	10 300	54	51.9
La Mesa	31 880	3.0	806	2.5	27 037	35.5	10.6	7.5	1 354	6	100.0
La Mirada	22 265	0.7	805	3.6	20 569	29.7	12.6	6.6	12 591	162	30.9
Lancaster	47 275	0.4	2 632	5.6	42 790	33.3	15.7	7.9	55 442	498	68.5
La Puente	17 739	0.2	1 307	7.4	15 750	15.8	15.9	7.3	922	13	23.1
La Verne	16 737	0.7	521	3.1	15 543	37.5	9.1	5.7	11 008	53	100.0
Lawndale	15 447	0.4	925	6.0	13 919	24.5	17.2	6.1	5 027	47	12.8
Livermore	35 130	1.9	829	2.4	31 270	38.1	12.8	6.4	68 284	386	81.9
Lodi	29 759	1.5	1 919	6.4	23 588	24.2	13.2	8.0	38 151	247	96.8
Lompoc	17 883	1.7	957	5.4	15 908	26.0	14.9	9.6	9 700	93	1.1
Long Beach	217 493	0.4	11 840	5.4	197 118	32.5	10.8	8.3	15 281	87	93.1
Los Altos	16 149	0.1	297	1.8	13 701	64.4	4.4	3.5	19 063	56	82.1

1. Percent of civilian labor force.　2. Persons 16 years and older.　3. Persons 16 to 64 years old.

Table D. Cities — Wholesale Trade, Retail Trade, and Real Estate

City	Wholesale Trade, 1997				Retail Trade[1], 1997				Real Estate and Rental and Leasing, 1997			
	Number of Establishments	Number of Employees	Sales (mil dol)	Annual Payroll (mil dol)	Number of Establishments	Number of Employees	Sales (mil dol)	Annual Payroll (mil dol)	Number of Establishments	Number of Employees	Receipts (mil dol)	Annual Payroll (mil dol)
	72	73	74	75	76	77	78	79	80	81	82	83
CALIFORNIA—Cont'd												
Carlsbad	266	4 290	2 140.3	174.8	355	4 855	1 120.5	106.7	139	1 054	134.8	29.7
Carson	338	7 029	5 176.5	273.5	216	4 505	949.5	100.0	70	2 884	544.1	103.7
Cathedral City	35	250	52.5	7.9	169	2 421	574.0	52.6	36	223	25.6	3.9
Ceres	20	D	D	D	81	1 350	222.7	20.9	24	99	8.3	1.4
Cerritos	276	5 313	3 940.4	201.6	279	7 822	1 934.3	159.8	55	282	41.6	6.7
Chico	109	1 300	469.1	44.3	420	5 812	987.8	97.7	101	531	48.9	8.0
Chino	217	2 830	1 296.1	107.0	184	2 963	554.2	55.6	40	209	38.3	4.4
Chula Vista	265	1 717	681.3	46.0	546	7 502	1 276.6	125.7	161	750	93.6	11.9
Claremont	29	210	91.1	7.9	97	1 251	321.6	26.7	28	149	14.2	3.4
Clovis	44	219	89.1	5.6	262	4 319	853.0	78.4	46	256	29.4	3.9
Colton	60	846	279.4	27.3	103	1 682	327.6	33.1	28	144	14.8	3.3
Compton	135	3 114	1 325.1	108.7	148	1 811	375.2	33.5	23	166	25.7	3.6
Concord	203	1 677	1 264.6	68.7	481	7 295	1 654.9	164.3	119	620	123.2	18.4
Corona	220	2 958	2 396.6	102.7	270	4 513	1 066.4	96.0	86	861	69.3	18.4
Coronado	18	82	31.1	1.8	75	529	64.8	8.5	43	221	26.5	5.2
Costa Mesa	373	5 888	7 388.3	289.9	693	12 297	2 343.3	251.8	216	1 751	312.8	58.2
Covina	97	652	333.2	20.4	177	2 632	537.9	52.3	74	358	41.5	7.6
Culver City	201	3 449	1 638.7	160.4	341	4 970	884.9	97.6	100	1 040	91.6	26.0
Cupertino	92	1 464	1 935.2	117.9	248	3 355	509.2	55.0	78	373	67.1	11.7
Cypress	99	3 799	7 999.8	230.9	100	1 254	310.6	25.7	45	152	27.5	3.8
Daly City	47	550	209.7	21.4	240	3 214	524.9	52.3	49	208	43.1	3.9
Dana Point	46	143	136.8	5.1	114	1 295	306.3	27.6	36	158	25.3	3.3
Danville	75	286	328.4	13.2	139	1 599	352.8	31.1	83	597	70.6	12.9
Davis	27	93	29.5	4.1	139	1 885	324.6	37.4	71	487	42.3	8.5
Diamond Bar	174	1 100	1 241.9	31.3	102	1 031	204.3	17.4	54	395	41.2	14.2
Downey	98	1 112	635.1	43.5	295	4 694	1 061.1	103.6	111	533	62.7	10.9
El Cajon	116	1 262	369.2	34.0	497	6 539	1 211.8	123.6	145	656	62.8	12.5
El Centro	47	334	137.5	8.6	172	2 393	417.7	43.0	31	128	10.6	1.4
El Monte	314	3 461	2 389.6	129.8	245	3 320	1 335.3	96.6	46	267	39.5	5.5
Encinitas	81	461	234.6	17.0	224	2 525	493.4	50.6	90	296	51.3	6.8
Escondido	171	1 172	377.2	38.9	600	9 390	1 765.6	186.0	163	964	157.4	20.8
Eureka	56	587	166.3	17.3	271	3 173	539.7	53.9	48	231	14.7	3.8
Fairfield	60	1 016	913.8	37.1	336	5 090	940.9	93.0	84	395	41.4	6.6
Folsom	23	D	D	D	162	2 134	444.9	41.6	34	105	14.2	2.4
Fontana	69	2 432	1 925.2	64.6	209	4 001	773.6	75.1	47	271	42.4	6.2
Foster City	97	1 595	862.6	98.2	60	1 171	246.9	23.9	46	719	115.4	36.6
Fountain Valley	157	1 429	1 951.1	63.4	218	3 242	632.2	57.4	55	327	45.8	9.6
Fremont	656	10 975	15 406.2	477.3	440	6 544	1 705.1	152.1	195	1 168	186.4	26.5
Fresno	655	8 209	3 934.0	269.4	1 546	19 850	3 589.5	362.8	398	2 598	273.1	51.1
Fullerton	225	3 596	2 331.2	134.9	292	4 361	938.6	88.0	122	700	82.1	15.5
Gardena	198	1 708	606.8	51.2	175	2 196	439.3	44.1	49	211	41.2	5.3
Garden Grove	240	3 031	1 469.9	101.4	413	5 618	1 247.9	116.3	103	555	85.0	13.1
Gilroy	43	D	D	D	273	3 118	664.8	60.1	42	136	21.6	2.8
Glendale	315	2 813	1 057.6	101.1	725	9 426	1 844.2	188.1	226	1 421	299.0	43.4
Glendora	50	546	322.9	22.8	133	1 758	341.5	34.7	58	207	22.9	3.5
Hanford	27	218	114.5	4.7	184	2 512	414.6	41.2	38	161	12.4	2.2
Hawthorne	55	821	218.9	28.2	187	2 581	528.4	49.1	56	151	16.9	1.9
Hayward	598	9 655	5 283.1	364.3	438	6 541	1 460.6	147.6	163	1 217	217.4	32.9
Hemet	19	87	49.1	3.3	221	3 349	561.7	60.0	61	328	31.4	5.0
Hesperia	38	187	98.2	4.9	129	1 161	200.2	21.4	30	88	8.4	1.2
Highland	6	148	25.1	3.0	50	578	109.1	9.2	18	61	5.7	0.8
Huntington Beach	477	4 819	2 484.3	171.6	601	8 063	1 700.6	160.6	228	1 188	262.2	38.0
Huntington Park	58	1 167	374.8	35.9	173	1 658	296.2	30.9	12	77	6.4	0.7
Imperial Beach	6	34	6.6	0.5	43	254	34.1	3.5	25	D	D	D
Indio	33	D	D	D	136	1 752	327.0	32.3	32	177	22.9	3.7
Inglewood	102	1 455	509.8	48.9	231	2 567	527.9	47.2	71	636	124.8	15.1
Irvine	894	17 641	29 723.1	881.0	400	6 137	1 368.5	137.1	320	4 308	678.7	157.1
Laguna Niguel	102	337	462.7	14.3	146	2 911	526.8	50.2	61	315	51.6	9.4
La Habra	67	479	175.2	14.8	158	2 378	392.2	43.6	40	163	19.3	2.7
Lakewood	43	315	58.6	7.4	250	4 211	637.0	66.1	40	224	40.7	4.1
La Mesa	36	222	70.3	7.5	281	4 491	872.1	84.6	116	648	65.6	12.2
La Mirada	114	2 755	2 521.4	118.2	95	1 394	287.7	29.0	24	177	25.9	6.4
Lancaster	61	652	198.1	17.2	326	3 906	715.8	75.5	76	420	54.6	8.6
La Puente	18	D	D	D	100	1 125	228.2	19.9	18	122	9.0	1.6
La Verne	45	340	220.7	11.3	84	1 229	212.8	21.1	17	171	15.6	3.5
Lawndale	22	D	D	D	96	1 108	303.9	21.8	27	237	23.4	3.6
Livermore	129	1 708	1 133.7	74.4	188	2 931	593.7	55.4	57	306	46.9	8.9
Lodi	58	1 050	415.4	30.3	218	2 970	529.7	53.8	68	763	51.9	15.2
Lompoc	17	D	D	D	111	1 439	245.7	23.9	33	144	13.2	2.4
Long Beach	402	5 257	8 218.0	200.8	998	11 047	1 939.9	197.4	404	2 934	372.0	62.8
Los Altos	51	D	D	D	115	920	163.6	20.0	78	199	57.1	6.8

1. Establishments with payroll.

Table D. Cities — Professional Services, Manufacturing, Accommodation and Foodservices

City	Professional, Scientific, and Technical Services, 1997[1]				Manufacturing, 1997				Accommodation and Foodservices, 1997			
	Number of Establishments	Number of Employees	Receipts (mil dol)	Annual Payroll (mil dol)	Number of Establishments	Number of Employees	Receipts (mil dol)	Annual Payroll (mil dol)	Number of Establishments	Number of Employees	Sales (mil dol)	Annual Payroll (mil dol)
	84	85	86	87	88	89	90	91	92	93	94	95
CALIFORNIA—Cont'd												
Carlsbad	351	3 377	423.7	136.3	205	12 384	2 418.9	458.0	165	4 176	186.3	50.3
Carson	77	775	94.1	32.4	321	13 958	5 207.9	477.5	118	1 606	63.6	15.7
Cathedral City	30	100	10.5	2.6	NA	NA	NA	NA	86	957	32.4	8.3
Ceres	11	51	2.9	1.2	32	835	131.1	24.0	43	566	20.4	4.8
Cerritos	111	1 627	342.0	111.6	117	5 463	801.1	169.4	99	1 972	72.9	21.6
Chico	171	1 026	99.3	34.4	107	2 455	403.7	63.1	210	3 754	94.1	26.0
Chino	80	585	60.6	17.2	259	9 897	1 294.7	245.8	89	1 816	56.9	14.9
Chula Vista	156	706	57.8	19.4	158	5 626	1 029.2	210.9	280	4 370	157.2	39.9
Claremont	114	726	75.5	22.7	29	1 309	177.6	58.0	70	1 235	40.0	11.5
Clovis	72	355	23.4	8.6	55	2 320	259.4	56.0	133	D	D	D
Colton	31	438	43.6	13.9	54	1 668	278.2	45.4	75	1 021	33.5	8.6
Compton	23	D	D	D	179	8 188	1 108.1	215.3	63	687	23.4	5.5
Concord	256	2 044	246.9	102.2	145	2 554	353.3	97.6	217	3 607	141.2	38.0
Corona	133	733	81.3	25.2	291	10 424	1 817.4	313.2	136	2 311	77.8	19.7
Coronado	48	165	16.5	5.2	NA	NA	NA	NA	69	2 220	125.8	36.7
Costa Mesa	552	6 031	908.1	338.7	310	11 091	1 757.6	429.6	315	6 638	282.7	75.4
Covina	142	783	50.4	18.5	119	3 226	359.5	114.5	106	1 603	63.3	16.0
Culver City	249	2 290	243.0	82.3	119	2 789	253.7	76.1	153	2 491	118.9	33.5
Cupertino	296	2 091	343.7	141.2	49	2 626	295.1	112.9	138	2 657	109.4	30.5
Cypress	75	924	104.5	42.4	40	1 341	200.4	41.8	89	1 400	48.5	12.4
Daly City	69	215	19.9	7.2	NA	NA	NA	NA	115	2 049	82.4	21.4
Dana Point	85	276	31.1	10.2	NA	NA	NA	NA	72	2 515	140.5	34.8
Danville	182	862	104.9	48.0	NA	NA	NA	NA	99	D	D	D
Davis	110	588	95.0	24.7	NA	NA	NA	NA	118	1 930	57.1	14.3
Diamond Bar	135	1 020	133.8	47.2	NA	NA	NA	NA	69	1 021	35.2	9.1
Downey	123	458	38.1	14.0	102	7 464	1 419.0	372.8	183	2 964	116.6	30.0
El Cajon	150	1 481	62.4	27.7	187	6 102	654.3	194.1	211	2 819	103.4	25.4
El Centro	56	334	34.3	11.2	NA	NA	NA	NA	96	1 294	43.0	10.9
El Monte	81	293	38.3	10.4	238	8 068	882.2	211.8	128	1 317	53.2	11.7
Encinitas	213	711	85.6	34.7	NA	NA	NA	NA	148	2 207	73.4	20.7
Escondido	260	1 173	109.1	39.0	190	4 330	563.8	114.5	233	3 505	123.8	32.9
Eureka	107	565	39.8	14.7	44	686	128.5	20.6	146	1 951	64.7	17.1
Fairfield	111	520	41.9	15.6	53	2 955	1 036.1	121.7	133	2 346	79.5	20.2
Folsom	78	329	39.7	16.2	23	648	79.2	26.2	103	D	D	D
Fontana	20	66	3.8	1.2	111	4 811	1 128.7	153.9	119	1 530	55.8	13.5
Foster City	148	1 858	349.2	142.4	26	1 866	563.4	115.8	62	1 206	51.2	13.4
Fountain Valley	164	1 350	191.5	55.5	111	2 645	1 302.2	84.6	128	1 974	74.1	18.0
Fremont	497	4 632	512.0	226.0	464	34 623	10 765.3	1 593.4	290	4 612	176.8	44.2
Fresno	913	10 110	505.0	205.4	412	15 225	3 099.8	395.1	799	13 915	433.4	119.8
Fullerton	260	2 543	427.3	120.0	228	10 916	2 217.1	375.8	199	3 792	137.0	37.0
Gardena	54	227	20.1	6.9	339	7 739	849.2	208.3	162	1 734	68.0	16.8
Garden Grove	184	1 228	95.2	29.2	354	9 710	2 255.3	269.5	278	3 868	138.1	36.5
Gilroy	46	221	18.1	8.4	61	2 538	426.9	76.7	83	1 147	48.3	10.4
Glendale	585	4 637	469.8	186.6	329	7 280	784.7	217.7	304	4 915	191.2	51.4
Glendora	77	329	44.8	12.8	53	1 321	194.4	49.3	78	1 149	39.2	10.4
Hanford	55	274	21.3	7.0	27	1 672	376.3	62.6	91	1 256	40.7	10.3
Hawthorne	33	241	19.1	10.3	114	5 719	1 006.6	234.6	98	1 272	57.8	12.4
Hayward	215	1 525	164.7	64.6	385	11 817	2 287.2	430.1	236	2 959	112.9	27.9
Hemet	72	270	19.8	7.0	25	972	106.5	19.9	106	1 332	44.5	11.2
Hesperia	35	115	10.2	2.1	66	1 212	157.6	26.3	68	873	26.7	7.1
Highland	11	33	1.7	0.5	NA	NA	NA	NA	35	D	D	D
Huntington Beach	460	2 632	258.9	100.8	417	14 927	2 377.3	594.8	378	6 467	237.9	64.3
Huntington Park	18	92	8.0	2.6	163	5 042	575.4	133.5	74	D	D	D
Imperial Beach	7	17	1.1	0.3	NA	NA	NA	NA	47	430	13.9	3.7
Indio	34	85	10.6	2.5	NA	NA	NA	NA	74	1 050	42.0	9.5
Inglewood	51	576	161.8	40.1	74	2 554	384.3	79.7	127	1 694	74.1	15.9
Irvine	1 419	18 430	2 874.4	1 057.0	479	34 067	8 500.6	1 319.0	300	8 073	338.2	91.4
Laguna Niguel	170	575	68.6	29.0	NA	NA	NA	NA	109	D	D	D
La Habra	58	233	22.9	8.8	87	1 371	155.0	39.4	98	1 526	49.8	12.9
Lakewood	57	702	44.4	15.0	NA	NA	NA	NA	147	2 837	91.7	23.5
La Mesa	163	536	46.3	14.9	NA	NA	NA	NA	152	3 516	120.9	35.2
La Mirada	52	256	56.6	10.2	74	4 323	757.0	132.1	72	1 084	44.3	11.0
Lancaster	87	438	42.2	16.5	50	845	79.0	15.3	148	2 716	92.4	23.0
La Puente	10	66	8.0	2.8	NA	NA	NA	NA	57	521	20.7	4.6
La Verne	42	339	36.2	10.2	43	1 062	188.6	35.0	43	744	25.2	6.3
Lawndale	25	184	11.4	4.8	NA	NA	NA	NA	46	594	22.9	5.8
Livermore	120	1 591	200.7	84.7	112	2 897	499.5	89.7	119	1 755	64.8	15.6
Lodi	86	440	24.1	11.1	99	3 149	475.3	88.6	124	1 561	51.1	12.8
Lompoc	26	108	8.1	3.3	NA	NA	NA	NA	77	1 109	37.7	8.9
Long Beach	740	8 083	788.2	308.4	332	27 548	8 786.9	1 400.3	678	11 571	445.8	120.7
Los Altos	213	903	137.2	53.6	NA	NA	NA	NA	60	1 250	47.5	13.3

1. Firms subject to federal tax.

City	Arts, Entertainment, and Recreation[1], 1997				Health Care and Social Assistance[1], 1997				Other Services[1], 1997			
	Number of Establishments	Number of Employees	Receipts (mil dol)	Annual Payroll (mil dol)	Number of Establishments	Number of Employees	Receipts (mil dol)	Annual Payroll (mil dol)	Number of Establishments	Number of Employees	Receipts (mil dol)	Annual Payroll (mil dol)
	96	97	98	99	100	101	102	103	104	105	106	107
CALIFORNIA—Cont'd												
Carlsbad	14	204	15.9	4.0	119	767	51.9	20.3	86	650	38.7	11.0
Carson	7	60	4.0	0.7	116	1 009	63.5	21.6	97	1 177	90.1	29.8
Cathedral City	7	570	46.8	12.3	38	355	26.9	8.2	84	506	35.8	10.4
Ceres	3	0	0.0	0.0	36	311	13.7	4.7	33	139	9.8	1.9
Cerritos	8	202	9.3	2.0	114	1 128	64.9	25.7	63	585	35.2	12.8
Chico	23	479	13.3	4.2	300	3 478	208.1	80.1	136	1 016	112.6	17.6
Chino	9	275	11.2	3.4	102	1 441	110.9	39.4	97	1 159	70.5	23.4
Chula Vista	26	408	27.1	6.6	319	2 169	190.0	68.2	184	1 118	67.0	20.5
Claremont	10	278	12.4	4.4	92	701	40.7	15.8	31	164	6.3	2.2
Clovis	11	0	0.0	0.0	124	1 026	55.5	22.0	102	568	36.6	9.9
Colton	7	10	11.2	1.1	56	838	52.5	21.8	42	514	23.4	7.8
Compton	6	0	0.0	0.0	50	370	24.8	8.3	60	425	23.1	6.6
Concord	15	426	12.5	4.3	327	3 277	213.1	87.4	209	1 382	113.9	35.3
Corona	18	230	14.5	3.3	168	1 720	103.8	40.6	135	1 080	108.0	31.0
Coronado	4	24	3.5	0.4	51	266	26.5	7.8	23	78	4.3	1.4
Costa Mesa	37	686	35.1	11.7	210	1 730	132.4	46.2	292	1 610	117.7	34.6
Covina	8	131	5.5	1.8	181	2 400	163.1	72.9	116	571	40.2	11.4
Culver City	80	174	67.2	37.7	176	3 249	265.2	89.8	132	1 053	77.3	25.7
Cupertino	6	114	5.5	1.4	138	1 158	80.8	27.7	53	277	21.9	4.6
Cypress	16	882	66.3	25.6	72	912	59.7	26.1	82	608	49.0	13.6
Daly City	14	394	12.5	3.9	195	1 623	133.2	53.8	89	428	30.9	8.9
Dana Point	14	120	17.3	2.8	62	338	25.9	10.5	33	130	7.8	2.3
Danville	11	801	20.2	6.9	97	636	45.0	17.9	44	192	11.9	3.7
Davis	12	171	5.8	1.8	132	989	72.5	34.8	48	252	16.9	5.0
Diamond Bar	7	148	7.3	1.6	122	893	74.7	20.5	48	204	16.5	4.9
Downey	10	169	6.6	2.0	239	3 288	228.7	93.4	140	1 475	80.0	25.3
El Cajon	15	270	11.0	2.8	210	2 970	199.4	80.7	170	1 160	84.5	21.6
El Centro	3	58	1.1	0.4	96	1 065	74.4	28.7	43	265	13.8	4.6
El Monte	5	33	1.4	0.5	112	1 448	77.5	30.6	132	738	46.4	12.8
Encinitas	23	163	9.9	2.9	228	1 666	152.1	54.3	92	790	42.4	13.3
Escondido	20	413	17.9	4.7	272	3 026	185.9	79.8	242	1 222	84.7	24.6
Eureka	11	121	3.0	0.8	124	1 164	89.8	32.4	88	504	33.2	9.6
Fairfield	14	284	11.0	3.5	179	1 563	122.5	48.8	118	659	40.1	13.6
Folsom	8	136	4.6	1.5	81	1 137	71.0	30.0	46	244	14.3	3.2
Fontana	3	0	0.0	0.0	71	2 494	233.5	85.1	103	578	37.2	12.6
Foster City	10	165	8.7	2.8	53	356	21.4	9.1	24	141	8.7	4.3
Fountain Valley	11	611	19.1	5.7	259	3 313	312.7	124.0	102	851	52.5	19.0
Fremont	27	782	25.4	7.8	431	4 438	368.1	140.0	293	1 742	129.7	38.1
Fresno	63	1 118	50.3	13.3	1 189	12 047	919.3	385.7	626	4 602	358.9	94.9
Fullerton	17	434	23.8	7.5	268	2 615	229.5	100.3	172	798	68.5	19.0
Gardena	5	0	0.0	0.0	152	2 163	131.7	53.2	136	820	56.0	17.8
Garden Grove	15	0	0.0	0.0	353	3 847	274.8	94.8	228	1 373	94.7	23.8
Gilroy	4	75	1.6	0.5	99	1 235	77.9	34.4	63	733	42.7	12.8
Glendale	70	583	54.6	18.9	618	5 699	422.9	160.7	304	2 164	135.2	49.8
Glendora	5	58	2.1	0.6	147	1 710	101.6	43.4	81	660	34.7	10.2
Hanford	6	83	2.4	0.5	94	1 310	84.7	34.7	50	207	13.8	3.3
Hawthorne	4	16	0.8	0.1	123	1 295	89.7	35.8	112	442	36.6	8.7
Hayward	16	204	9.0	2.5	197	3 352	285.4	128.4	243	2 490	211.8	56.0
Hemet	8	141	5.0	1.5	177	1 973	143.3	55.1	70	399	22.2	6.1
Hesperia	4	39	1.5	0.6	63	308	25.7	6.8	93	466	28.7	7.1
Highland	1	0	0.0	0.0	30	577	37.5	16.8	23	88	4.7	1.7
Huntington Beach	35	843	54.4	14.6	460	3 937	274.7	106.3	344	1 807	138.1	37.3
Huntington Park	4	124	4.2	1.2	116	1 260	96.2	36.3	63	299	20.8	5.8
Imperial Beach	2	0	0.0	0.0	14	339	16.2	6.2	21	116	3.9	1.0
Indio	10	0	0.0	0.0	80	1 011	82.3	30.9	54	288	17.3	5.6
Inglewood	33	2 581	393.7	118.8	274	4 043	314.1	131.0	139	1 037	62.0	17.6
Irvine	45	954	68.6	16.3	364	3 296	292.5	119.6	232	2 270	143.4	49.5
Laguna Niguel	11	177	8.6	3.3	129	563	42.6	17.2	58	411	26.0	7.9
La Habra	2	0	0.0	0.0	75	1 900	160.9	66.0	107	597	37.1	9.8
Lakewood	13	282	9.3	2.7	130	1 546	123.2	52.8	73	740	40.5	16.1
La Mesa	10	170	4.7	1.6	296	3 397	229.7	90.4	99	661	29.0	9.6
La Mirada	7	103	7.3	1.3	76	951	61.3	24.9	36	256	13.3	4.3
Lancaster	13	182	8.4	2.4	266	3 606	307.0	106.5	117	676	51.1	11.9
La Puente	1	0	0.0	0.0	38	206	16.8	4.6	34	100	7.0	1.3
La Verne	1	0	0.0	0.0	35	239	17.1	6.8	28	130	5.8	1.5
Lawndale	3	0	0.0	0.0	59	365	28.2	8.3	85	398	26.0	6.5
Livermore	11	205	8.6	2.0	119	1 159	60.9	31.7	93	734	82.4	26.9
Lodi	9	169	9.2	2.6	145	1 433	100.6	36.7	107	458	32.0	8.0
Lompoc	4	39	0.9	0.2	59	337	26.1	10.5	46	239	13.8	3.7
Long Beach	53	867	56.4	12.3	898	9 999	899.4	383.9	482	3 892	286.5	96.3
Los Altos	7	120	3.5	1.3	112	766	68.9	26.1	54	219	13.4	4.3

1. Firms subject to federal tax.

Table D. Cities — Federal Funds and City Government Finances

City	Selected federal funds, fiscal 1999[1] (mil dol)									City government finances, 1997						
	Procurement contracts		Grants					Direct payments for individuals		General revenue						
										Intergovernmental			Taxes			
														Per capita[3] (dollars)		
	Defense	Other	Total[2]	Health and family welfare	Energy and environment	Education	Housing and community development	Educational assistance	Housing assistance	Total (mil dol)	Total (mil dol)	Percent from state government	Total (mil dol)	Total	Property	Sales and gross receipts
	108	109	110	111	112	113	114	115	116	117	118	119	120	121	122	123
CALIFORNIA—Cont'd																
Carlsbad	28.3	8.5	6.1	5.0	0.1	0.0	0.7	0.1	0.0	95.1	13.9	95.9	36.7	531	184	250
Carson	227.7	0.7	6.4	0.9	0.0	0.9	1.6	0.4	0.6	63.1	10.3	85.4	37.7	436	173	220
Cathedral City	0.0	0.0	0.0	0.0	0.0	0.0	0.0	0.0	0.0	40.5	3.7	72.2	25.2	694	419	163
Ceres	0.0	0.4	0.2	0.0	0.0	0.0	0.1	0.0	1.3	13.8	2.5	96.7	7.1	226	63	137
Cerritos	2.0	0.1	0.0	0.0	0.0	0.0	0.0	0.3	0.0	81.3	4.2	87.5	43.0	802	370	409
Chico	0.0	7.8	6.9	0.3	0.1	1.7	2.5	8.2	1.4	42.3	7.9	59.9	23.2	505	197	299
Chino	4.0	0.2	6.1	0.0	0.0	0.0	1.3	0.0	0.0	49.8	6.1	99.8	19.3	298	129	158
Chula Vista	22.0	2.2	6.7	0.0	0.0	1.4	3.0	3.2	1.4	119.3	16.8	91.6	50.6	333	91	164
Claremont	0.7	0.1	7.7	2.0	0.0	1.3	0.0	3.4	0.0	22.5	3.3	76.0	10.6	317	97	195
Clovis	0.0	8.0	0.3	0.0	0.0	0.0	0.0	0.9	0.0	50.9	5.2	91.1	22.2	351	135	167
Colton	0.2	0.0	0.2	0.0	0.0	0.0	0.0	1.1	1.7	33.5	3.3	94.4	15.0	346	143	174
Compton	10.4	2.1	6.9	0.0	0.0	1.6	4.6	2.7	6.4	89.0	24.9	46.0	40.5	442	239	163
Concord	15.8	1.0	2.0	0.3	0.0	0.4	1.1	0.8	1.5	103.4	17.0	93.5	45.8	399	139	201
Corona	7.1	8.5	1.8	0.7	0.0	0.0	1.0	0.0	0.0	95.3	10.3	89.7	40.3	402	153	134
Coronado	11.4	0.0	1.0	0.0	0.0	0.8	0.0	0.0	0.0	31.8	3.6	49.8	15.0	585	223	344
Costa Mesa	25.6	1.6	3.9	1.0	0.3	0.7	1.8	4.9	0.0	67.9	9.7	70.7	46.1	457	98	335
Covina	1.6	0.8	6.7	0.0	0.0	0.2	0.0	0.0	0.9	36.1	6.5	63.0	19.8	447	164	265
Culver City	7.3	6.3	8.6	2.6	0.0	0.3	0.0	1.3	0.0	95.2	6.7	83.9	52.8	1 343	399	772
Cupertino	1.7	0.9	0.6	0.0	0.0	0.0	0.0	3.3	1.1	32.4	3.0	95.8	19.1	445	65	301
Cypress	2.3	0.2	0.9	0.1	0.0	0.0	0.0	2.1	0.0	29.6	4.0	87.1	17.2	366	130	188
Daly City	0.0	0.1	2.1	0.0	0.0	0.2	1.9	0.4	2.0	66.5	25.4	36.9	23.5	241	79	134
Dana Point	0.0	0.0	0.0	0.0	0.0	0.0	0.0	0.0	0.0	17.5	3.3	97.3	11.7	346	69	246
Danville	0.0	0.0	0.0	0.0	0.0	0.0	0.0	0.0	0.0	18.6	2.5	98.2	10.1	264	87	126
Davis	0.9	3.9	137.8	74.8	16.0	2.5	2.3	9.6	5.5	53.7	7.0	85.2	22.6	432	137	151
Diamond Bar	0.2	0.1	0.1	0.0	0.0	0.0	0.0	0.0	0.0	16.1	6.2	94.1	6.8	125	36	80
Downey	162.5	10.6	151.3	138.7	0.0	9.9	1.9	0.0	0.0	50.2	9.5	83.7	26.7	286	77	190
El Cajon	7.1	0.8	2.0	0.2	0.0	0.2	1.6	5.6	6.4	49.4	8.8	85.4	25.4	276	81	181
El Centro	17.0	3.5	6.2	0.1	0.0	3.1	0.0	0.0	1.7	69.5	5.0	81.9	10.3	277	84	179
El Monte	6.7	1.4	3.9	0.0	0.0	0.0	2.3	1.3	2.7	51.5	13.8	71.2	31.5	287	87	179
Encinitas	2.3	0.2	1.7	0.1	0.0	0.5	0.9	0.0	0.0	33.5	4.2	93.3	18.0	311	180	127
Escondido	4.6	1.1	4.7	0.8	0.0	0.8	2.6	0.0	2.4	80.3	10.7	76.0	36.9	318	96	191
Eureka	0.4	1.1	4.6	1.0	0.2	1.4	0.6	1.8	0.0	25.8	3.5	73.0	13.2	502	144	346
Fairfield	11.5	8.0	15.2	0.0	0.0	4.3	1.1	0.0	1.7	87.7	23.9	63.9	41.8	488	226	191
Folsom	0.6	2.2	3.2	3.1	0.0	0.0	0.0	0.0	1.1	60.6	14.1	99.7	30.6	745	208	274
Fontana	3.5	1.1	2.5	0.0	0.0	0.1	2.4	0.0	0.7	89.0	11.0	71.2	49.5	475	233	161
Foster City	1.9	25.0	5.6	2.2	0.0	0.0	0.0	0.0	0.0	48.6	2.2	100.0	25.1	844	542	268
Fountain Valley	0.0	0.0	1.5	0.0	0.0	0.1	0.5	0.3	0.0	36.3	4.8	85.9	21.4	383	170	189
Fremont	3.1	1.6	7.2	1.3	0.5	0.9	1.5	3.7	0.0	132.0	16.5	92.1	82.7	441	164	172
Fresno	2.4	43.0	80.9	24.5	1.6	5.3	20.3	17.6	17.0	318.0	54.3	82.6	110.5	279	87	154
Fullerton	131.8	8.7	8.6	1.7	0.1	2.0	2.1	10.9	1.4	71.7	11.8	72.9	37.9	316	143	154
Gardena	22.7	2.1	0.4	0.0	0.0	0.0	0.4	1.2	0.3	36.7	7.7	87.1	24.3	457	152	185
Garden Grove	14.1	2.1	7.0	0.8	0.0	0.0	2.7	0.4	0.0	88.4	32.3	36.1	36.8	247	109	116
Gilroy	0.0	0.1	1.5	0.0	0.0	0.2	1.2	0.7	3.1	44.8	5.2	98.5	17.7	516	58	305
Glendale	55.3	7.8	6.4	0.0	0.1	1.4	4.5	7.3	2.7	168.5	32.3	86.5	70.5	383	123	231
Glendora	0.6	0.1	0.2	0.0	0.0	0.0	0.2	2.3	0.0	23.6	4.3	76.4	11.9	231	118	99
Hanford	0.0	0.0	6.8	4.3	0.0	0.3	0.0	0.0	0.4	25.8	6.3	91.4	9.2	254	70	143
Hawthorne	13.0	1.5	17.6	0.1	0.0	0.0	3.6	0.1	0.0	65.4	19.7	89.3	27.9	383	71	261
Hayward	5.5	1.1	20.8	9.0	1.1	5.5	2.8	9.2	3.0	96.3	18.5	64.9	50.2	413	114	232
Hemet	0.3	0.2	1.3	0.0	0.0	0.0	1.2	0.0	1.8	29.0	4.4	91.6	14.3	279	135	119
Hesperia	2.9	0.0	0.5	0.0	0.0	0.2	0.4	0.0	0.0	15.8	6.7	59.2	7.4	122	8	96
Highland	0.1	0.0	0.1	0.0	0.0	0.0	0.0	0.0	0.0	11.8	4.7	88.8	4.7	116	43	43
Huntington Beach	201.4	243.9	4.8	0.0	0.8	1.1	2.0	2.6	0.0	138.0	20.9	73.3	72.5	380	129	209
Huntington Park	0.1	1.9	2.4	0.0	0.0	0.0	2.4	0.0	1.0	36.4	8.6	74.2	15.9	278	146	105
Imperial Beach	0.7	0.0	0.6	0.0	0.0	0.6	0.0	0.0	0.0	12.4	2.1	95.6	3.8	134	52	69
Indio	0.0	0.1	0.1	0.1	0.0	0.0	0.0	0.0	1.4	22.8	4.3	76.5	10.7	246	69	158
Inglewood	14.6	2.5	16.4	0.9	0.0	0.3	5.7	0.2	-3.1	140.3	43.0	93.4	47.9	431	77	291
Irvine	156.6	22.3	105.4	68.0	7.6	2.3	0.4	13.6	0.0	111.4	22.0	88.5	61.3	480	77	343
Laguna Niguel	0.4	2.8	0.4	0.2	0.0	0.0	0.2	0.0	0.0	15.6	4.4	98.6	8.9	172	25	121
La Habra	0.1	0.0	1.3	0.0	0.1	0.5	0.5	0.0	0.0	34.4	9.2	70.1	15.1	282	94	174
Lakewood	23.2	0.2	0.5	0.0	0.0	0.0	0.3	0.0	0.0	37.5	8.4	95.0	19.4	258	84	162
La Mesa	0.2	1.7	1.5	0.0	0.0	0.2	1.0	1.9	1.3	30.1	5.7	92.6	13.7	250	71	166
La Mirada	15.2	2.1	0.0	0.0	0.0	0.0	0.0	1.1	0.0	30.2	3.6	84.2	18.1	413	187	189
Lancaster	5.3	2.3	3.4	0.0	0.0	1.0	2.3	1.9	2.4	90.7	14.6	93.0	42.5	367	227	121
La Puente	1.1	0.1	0.6	0.0	0.0	0.4	0.0	0.6	3.0	8.3	3.4	79.7	3.9	101	15	79
La Verne	1.0	0.4	3.2	0.0	0.0	0.0	0.0	1.2	0.0	22.7	2.6	88.2	10.9	341	197	95
Lawndale	0.0	0.1	0.6	0.0	0.0	0.5	0.0	0.0	0.0	11.1	2.4	83.1	6.9	242	19	207
Livermore	3.8	1.7	8.3	6.9	0.1	0.1	0.4	0.3	0.3	65.5	6.0	97.5	26.7	414	134	184
Lodi	0.3	1.9	0.6	0.0	0.0	0.0	0.0	0.0	0.0	36.0	6.1	86.4	14.3	263	76	167
Lompoc	5.4	0.0	4.4	0.0	0.0	2.8	1.2	0.0	0.0	25.1	4.0	90.5	8.5	207	51	147
Long Beach	2 844.0	44.7	76.7	19.7	1.8	11.5	11.6	23.8	8.9	905.4	181.7	89.2	180.5	428	135	252
Los Altos	0.9	1.5	3.6	2.5	0.0	0.0	0.0	1.0	0.0	19.7	1.9	95.7	8.7	315	128	150

1. October 1, 1998 to September 30, 1999.   2. Includes program categories not shown separately. State totals include additional categories not allocated by city.   3. Based on population estimated as of July 1 of the year shown.

City	City government finances, 1997 (cont'd)												
	General expenditure												
	Per capita[1] (dollars)			Percent of total for —									
	Total (mil dol)	Total	Capital outlays	Public welfare	Highways	Parking facilities	Education	Health and hospitals	Police protection	Sewerage and sanitation	Parks and recreation	Housing and community development	Interest on debt
	124	125	126	127	128	129	130	131	132	133	134	135	136
CALIFORNIA—Cont'd													
Carlsbad	74.8	1 082	180	0.0	10.3	6.0	0.0	1.7	15.1	3.9	7.7	9.2	7.2
Carson	60.6	700	248	0.0	14.4	0.0	0.0	0.1	18.3	0.0	7.8	33.3	6.9
Cathedral City	50.6	1 393	511	0.0	25.6	0.0	0.0	0.4	11.2	0.7	29.4	6.8
Ceres	10.9	351	63	0.0	12.3	0.0	0.0	0.0	35.4	18.3	5.8	7.9	2.7
Cerritos	77.4	1 443	357	0.0	13.1	0.0	0.0	0.1	7.7	2.7	4.3	27.6	15.3
Chico	51.3	1 116	518	0.0	0.1	0.4	0.0	0.3	14.7	3.8	3.1	22.6	6.3
Chino	49.8	769	44	0.0	12.0	0.0	0.0	4.2	24.2	22.4	2.0	8.9	11.1
Chula Vista	112.5	740	39	0.0	10.1	0.3	0.0	0.9	17.9	9.6	7.1	7.7	21.5
Claremont	20.6	615	118	0.0	12.3	0.0	0.0	0.9	26.8	14.4	14.6	9.7	3.1
Clovis	45.2	715	188	0.0	14.7	0.0	0.0	0.3	21.3	25.0	5.0	7.2	4.7
Colton	36.7	848	124	0.0	3.2	0.0	0.0	0.5	19.7	8.3	3.4	13.7	23.0
Compton	83.0	906	167	0.0	15.6	0.0	0.0	2.1	20.6	4.9	1.5	20.5	10.3
Concord	95.4	831	222	0.0	8.8	0.0	0.0	0.4	23.2	9.3	17.4	16.1	8.6
Corona	98.3	981	173	0.0	6.2	0.1	0.0	0.6	18.1	21.7	4.5	11.4	17.0
Coronado	37.3	1 453	488	0.0	18.6	0.3	0.0	0.6	13.2	6.8	23.1	8.1	4.7
Costa Mesa	74.6	739	144	0.0	16.1	0.0	0.0	6.1	32.2	1.4	9.3	1.6	2.5
Covina	33.5	756	147	0.0	9.6	0.1	0.0	4.0	26.2	4.2	11.2	10.4	11.2
Culver City	93.6	2 382	598	0.0	5.9	0.1	0.0	1.4	17.2	14.1	4.8	15.8	11.4
Cupertino	27.9	650	95	0.0	10.5	0.0	0.0	0.2	15.5	6.2	25.5	0.5	11.5
Cypress	22.0	469	77	0.0	22.6	0.0	0.0	0.0	34.0	0.6	5.5	12.0	6.2
Daly City	59.9	614	51	0.0	8.0	0.0	0.0	0.0	20.0	12.5	7.5	17.1	2.6
Dana Point	14.3	421	74	0.0	25.0	0.0	0.0	1.0	32.6	0.2	8.1	3.0	0.0
Danville	17.9	467	72	0.0	17.4	0.0	0.0	0.3	18.2	1.9	19.4	0.6	7.2
Davis	51.4	983	253	0.0	11.4	0.0	0.0	0.2	11.2	21.7	10.6	18.6	1.5
Diamond Bar	11.3	209	36	0.0	21.6	0.0	0.0	0.6	33.8	0.7	15.8	2.6	0.0
Downey	50.6	544	80	0.0	12.4	0.0	0.0	2.3	31.5	0.9	10.9	7.3	2.7
El Cajon	48.5	526	62	0.0	12.8	0.0	0.0	4.8	26.2	15.1	6.2	5.9	7.0
El Centro	67.8	1 813	247	0.0	6.6	0.0	0.0	61.2	5.9	8.1	1.0	2.6	1.6
El Monte	49.2	447	17	0.0	12.8	0.5	0.0	0.3	28.0	0.0	4.9	11.9	2.6
Encinitas	28.0	484	75	0.0	21.8	0.0	0.0	1.3	19.3	0.1	7.9	5.9	7.8
Escondido	79.2	682	151	0.0	14.4	0.0	0.0	1.8	20.7	11.7	7.5	6.9	8.4
Eureka	23.5	898	125	0.0	9.4	0.0	0.0	0.0	23.8	10.5	5.4	15.1	5.8
Fairfield	79.6	930	126	0.0	15.9	0.0	0.0	0.2	15.0	0.2	8.6	18.3	25.1
Folsom	61.4	1 495	556	0.0	21.2	0.0	0.0	0.2	8.7	10.6	10.3	7.9	8.3
Fontana	86.6	832	73	0.0	10.4	0.0	0.0	0.3	17.7	5.4	3.5	16.4	19.6
Foster City	43.9	1 478	290	0.0	4.7	0.0	0.0	0.0	11.5	5.2	7.0	31.7	11.6
Fountain Valley	36.5	655	51	0.0	15.9	0.0	0.0	3.1	24.2	14.0	3.7	7.5	10.7
Fremont	137.9	734	192	0.0	11.0	0.0	0.0	2.2	21.1	0.9	12.6	14.4	10.2
Fresno	318.4	804	145	0.0	7.5	1.0	0.0	0.7	19.6	28.3	5.5	4.4	9.7
Fullerton	69.0	574	93	0.0	12.0	0.0	0.0	1.6	31.7	10.5	5.1	8.2	2.3
Gardena	37.5	707	19	0.0	9.5	0.0	0.0	9.8	29.8	0.0	11.0	0.0	8.0
Garden Grove	89.8	602	113	0.0	12.6	0.0	0.0	3.7	24.7	0.0	2.0	33.6	6.4
Gilroy	35.8	1 040	319	0.0	13.1	0.0	0.0	0.0	23.6	23.1	18.0	0.0	1.7
Glendale	162.2	880	166	0.0	8.9	3.6	0.0	0.5	19.9	14.5	4.5	12.1	3.0
Glendora	22.9	445	78	0.0	10.8	0.0	0.0	1.5	28.6	13.4	13.4	11.4	5.3
Hanford	23.6	651	167	0.0	12.0	0.8	0.0	0.4	18.0	30.1	5.6	3.8	5.5
Hawthorne	56.0	767	52	0.0	7.3	0.0	0.0	0.0	37.9	16.2	4.4	8.4	2.6
Hayward	110.8	911	287	0.0	27.0	0.0	0.0	0.9	20.9	12.5	1.1	1.4	2.4
Hemet	31.4	611	58	0.0	16.9	0.0	0.0	0.2	22.3	16.7	1.0	9.3	3.9
Hesperia	21.9	360	133	0.0	26.8	0.0	0.0	1.9	20.1	0.0	0.0	13.7	11.0
Highland	13.3	329	120	0.0	33.5	0.0	0.0	0.9	23.2	0.0	0.7	4.1	11.0
Huntington Beach	128.2	672	48	0.0	11.6	0.7	0.0	4.2	27.3	6.7	10.0	6.1	4.1
Huntington Park	36.3	634	16	0.0	6.9	2.6	0.0	0.3	30.8	0.5	1.7	12.5	22.0
Imperial Beach	11.8	420	41	0.0	18.9	0.0	0.0	0.6	24.0	24.6	2.9	0.4	0.9
Indio	27.1	619	102	0.0	6.4	0.0	0.0	1.6	21.9	1.5	1.7	13.9	20.8
Inglewood	150.9	1 359	35	0.0	7.5	0.1	0.0	2.1	26.9	9.5	5.0	10.2	2.3
Irvine	103.6	810	148	0.0	25.8	0.0	0.0	1.4	22.8	3.8	11.6	3.1	16.3
Laguna Niguel	12.9	250	54	0.0	29.5	0.0	0.0	1.1	35.1	0.0	0.0	7.7	0.0
La Habra	32.3	602	60	0.0	11.8	0.0	0.0	5.8	25.8	7.0	7.3	5.1	6.6
Lakewood	27.3	362	22	0.0	11.9	0.0	0.0	0.2	24.3	9.8	20.2	9.8	4.4
La Mesa	28.6	521	16	0.0	7.6	0.4	0.0	0.2	21.8	16.1	6.9	16.9	0.9
La Mirada	24.9	567	34	0.0	13.5	0.0	0.0	0.2	16.4	0.0	21.0	13.1	12.3
Lancaster	92.7	801	212	0.0	17.2	0.0	0.0	0.0	15.3	0.1	7.8	31.0	19.5
La Puente	6.9	181	2	0.0	8.4	0.0	0.0	0.6	46.9	1.0	13.6	5.2	0.0
La Verne	19.4	605	64	0.0	15.0	0.0	0.0	2.7	26.6	1.3	2.9	17.2	6.3
Lawndale	7.5	262	21	0.0	8.9	0.0	0.0	0.0	43.0	0.0	5.6	4.5	0.1
Livermore	64.9	1 003	218	0.0	17.0	0.0	0.0	0.7	16.3	11.1	4.7	4.5	11.0
Lodi	41.2	755	204	0.0	12.6	0.0	0.0	0.2	19.5	9.1	9.7	1.9	2.0
Lompoc	23.6	577	53	0.0	15.4	0.0	0.0	0.9	18.4	31.3	5.7	0.6	2.5
Long Beach	962.4	2 281	582	0.0	4.7	0.1	0.0	2.5	12.3	7.1	2.9	11.8	9.4
Los Altos	25.2	908	312	0.0	7.1	0.0	0.0	0.0	16.0	13.2	32.4	0.0	1.9

1. Based on population estimated as of July 1 of the year shown.

Table D. Cities — City Government Finances, City Government Employment, and Climate

City	City government finances, 1997 (cont'd) Debt outstanding — Total (mil dol)	Per capita[1] (dollars)	Percent utility	City government employment, 1999	Climate[2] — Average daily temperature (degrees Fahrenheit) Mean — January	July	Limits — January[3]	July[4]	Annual precipitation (inches)	Heating degree days	Cooling degree days
	137	138	139	140	141	142	143	144	145	146	147
CALIFORNIA—Cont'd											
Carlsbad	72.0	1 043	11.3	NA	54.5	67.6	44.1	73.5	10.93	2 010	555
Carson	83.7	968	0.0	472	56.1	69.7	45.3	78.8	13.57	1 568	794
Cathedral City	113.0	3 111	0.0	NA	56.4	92.0	42.5	108.7	5.31	985	4 014
Ceres	5.2	166	0.0	NA	45.6	77.1	37.4	94.2	12.10	2 605	1 401
Cerritos	137.6	2 565	0.0	389	55.9	73.1	44.9	82.7	11.80	1 430	1 201
Chico	70.6	1 536	0.0	367	44.0	77.4	34.5	94.2	26.32	2 953	1 360
Chino	70.1	1 084	7.8	NA	54.3	74.6	40.7	90.4	16.62	1 713	1 273
Chula Vista	479.8	3 157	0.0	914	55.3	68.2	45.3	73.1	9.34	1 798	638
Claremont	8.5	254	0.0	NA	54.3	74.6	40.7	90.4	16.62	1 713	1 273
Clovis	66.5	1 052	50.6	NA	45.7	81.9	37.4	98.6	10.60	2 556	1 967
Colton	113.5	2 620	0.4	NA	53.6	79.4	40.3	97.0	15.42	1 719	1 804
Compton	126.2	1 376	0.0	721	56.1	69.7	45.3	78.8	13.57	1 568	794
Concord	146.3	1 274	0.0	569	44.5	73.8	35.9	90.8	12.80	2 837	1 066
Corona	305.7	3 050	0.6	714	53.9	75.4	40.5	92.1	11.83	1 747	1 339
Coronado	37.8	1 471	0.0	NA	57.4	71.0	48.9	76.2	9.90	1 256	984
Costa Mesa	21.0	208	0.0	629	55.2	67.1	46.8	71.8	10.85	1 866	500
Covina	50.9	1 148	5.9	NA	54.3	74.6	40.7	90.4	16.62	1 713	1 273
Culver City	174.8	4 449	0.0	693	57.2	70.4	46.5	79.2	13.06	1 391	986
Cupertino	5.3	123	0.0	NA	49.4	69.5	40.6	82.4	14.42	2 387	594
Cypress	6.1	129	0.0	NA	57.4	72.6	45.6	82.6	12.27	1 238	1 175
Daly City	16.6	169	0.0	605	48.7	62.7	41.8	71.6	19.70	3 016	145
Dana Point	0.0	0	0.0	34	53.7	67.2	41.5	75.8	12.19	2 157	493
Danville	20.3	528	0.0	NA	46.1	71.6	35.5	89.8	14.21	2 909	780
Davis	13.3	253	0.0	NA	44.5	74.1	36.3	92.7	18.13	2 911	1 041
Diamond Bar	0.0	0	0.0	NA	54.3	74.6	40.7	90.4	16.62	1 713	1 273
Downey	18.7	201	0.0	495	58.3	74.3	48.9	84.0	14.77	1 154	1 537
El Cajon	48.0	521	0.0	524	56.6	72.5	44.6	83.4	12.80	1 400	1 110
El Centro	24.0	642	5.2	NA	54.6	91.3	39.3	107.5	2.71	1 156	3 741
El Monte	19.3	176	0.0	471	55.7	75.2	41.7	89.2	17.90	1 433	1 427
Encinitas	25.8	445	0.0	NA	54.5	67.6	44.1	73.5	10.93	2 010	555
Escondido	180.6	1 554	4.8	894	55.2	70.5	43.1	81.3	13.04	1 802	868
Eureka	16.5	629	0.0	NA	48.0	57.0	41.5	61.8	37.53	4 496	0
Fairfield	244.2	2 852	27.8	512	45.5	72.0	36.2	88.5	21.38	2 767	898
Folsom	177.0	4 307	1.4	NA	45.6	77.2	37.7	94.2	23.91	2 683	1 422
Fontana	509.9	4 897	0.0	377	56.0	78.6	44.5	94.8	15.63	1 478	1 922
Foster City	59.6	2 006	0.0	NA	48.7	68.7	38.9	83.4	19.74	2 563	486
Fountain Valley	36.0	646	0.0	NA	57.4	72.6	45.6	82.6	12.27	1 238	1 175
Fremont	241.9	1 288	0.0	996	49.0	66.7	41.1	76.1	13.73	2 578	410
Fresno	751.9	1 899	7.1	3 267	45.7	81.9	37.4	98.6	10.60	2 556	1 967
Fullerton	23.5	196	0.0	635	57.4	72.6	45.6	82.6	12.27	1 238	1 175
Gardena	40.0	753	0.0	NA	56.1	69.7	45.3	78.8	13.57	1 568	794
Garden Grove	106.4	713	18.3	697	57.4	72.6	45.6	82.6	12.27	1 238	1 175
Gilroy	47.7	1 387	0.0	NA	47.4	70.9	35.6	88.3	19.77	2 668	719
Glendale	82.6	448	6.7	1 695	54.5	75.6	41.3	90.2	15.87	1 609	1 424
Glendora	21.6	420	0.0	NA	54.3	74.6	40.7	90.4	16.62	1 713	1 273
Hanford	22.4	618	5.2	NA	43.9	78.8	34.3	95.9	7.95	2 816	1 551
Hawthorne	35.6	488	27.7	245	56.8	69.1	47.8	75.3	12.01	1 458	727
Hayward	68.9	566	0.0	822	49.0	66.7	41.1	76.1	13.73	2 578	410
Hemet	15.0	292	40.1	NA	50.2	77.6	39.3	96.2	17.33	2 432	1 451
Hesperia	65.3	1 078	0.0	NA	44.2	79.3	30.0	97.4	5.51	3 127	1 525
Highland	21.3	527	0.0	NA	53.6	79.4	40.3	97.0	15.42	1 719	1 804
Huntington Beach	43.2	227	0.0	1 125	55.2	67.1	46.8	71.8	10.85	1 866	500
Huntington Park	133.0	2 324	0.0	NA	58.3	74.3	48.9	84.0	14.77	1 154	1 537
Imperial Beach	1.3	48	0.0	NA	55.3	68.2	45.3	73.1	9.34	1 798	638
Indio	79.8	1 824	0.0	NA	56.4	92.0	42.5	108.7	5.31	985	4 014
Inglewood	61.9	557	11.3	869	56.8	69.1	47.8	75.3	12.01	1 458	727
Irvine	269.0	2 103	0.0	705	54.5	71.6	41.4	83.7	11.81	1 784	973
Laguna Niguel	0.0	0	0.0	NA	53.7	67.2	41.5	75.8	12.19	2 157	493
La Habra	27.7	517	0.0	NA	57.4	72.6	45.6	82.6	12.27	1 238	1 175
Lakewood	25.5	339	23.0	241	55.9	73.1	44.9	82.7	11.80	1 430	1 201
La Mesa	3.8	69	0.0	NA	56.6	72.5	44.6	83.4	12.80	1 400	1 110
La Mirada	50.4	1 150	0.0	NA	57.4	72.6	45.6	82.6	12.27	1 238	1 175
Lancaster	317.6	2 746	0.0	260	45.1	80.7	31.9	97.1	6.92	2 948	1 720
La Puente	0.0	0	0.0	NA	55.7	75.2	41.7	89.2	17.90	1 433	1 427
La Verne	28.9	903	0.5	NA	54.3	74.6	40.7	90.4	16.62	1 713	1 273
Lawndale	0.2	6	0.0	NA	56.1	69.7	45.3	78.8	13.57	1 568	794
Livermore	118.1	1 826	0.0	393	46.1	71.6	35.5	89.8	14.21	2 909	780
Lodi	1.9	35	0.0	NA	45.1	73.9	36.4	91.4	17.11	2 809	1 020
Lompoc	4.9	121	94.1	NA	52.9	62.9	40.1	72.9	13.95	2 651	265
Long Beach	1 580.8	3 747	3.7	5 522	55.9	73.1	44.9	82.7	11.80	1 430	1 201
Los Altos	6.4	232	0.0	NA	47.5	66.4	37.7	78.4	14.96	2 911	297

1. Based on the population estimated as of July 1 of the year shown.   2. Represents normal values based on the 30-year period, 1961–1990.   3. Average daily minimum.   4. Average daily maximum.

Table D. Cities — Land Area and Population

STATE Place code	City	Land area, 1990[1] (sq km)	Population, 1999 — Total persons	Rank	Per square kilometer	Population — Total persons 1990	Percent change 1990–1999	Total persons 1980	Percent change 1980–1990	Population characteristics, 1990 Percent — Race — White	Black	Am. Indian, Eskimo, Aleut	Asian and Pacific Islander	Other race	His-panic[2]	Foreign born
			1	2	3	4	5	6	7	8	9	10	11	12	13	14	15
	CALIFORNIA—Cont'd															
06 44000	Los Angeles	1 215.6	3 633 591	2	2 989	3 485 557	4.2	2 966 850	17.5	52.8	14.0	0.5	9.8	22.9	39.9	38.4
06 44112	Los Gatos	26.9	29 039	1 037	1 080	27 357	6.1	26 906	1.7	92.8	0.7	0.4	5.0	1.1	5.0	10.9
06 44574	Lynwood	12.6	63 935	421	5 074	61 945	3.2	48 548	27.6	24.0	23.7	0.4	2.2	49.8	70.3	43.9
06 45022	Madera	26.7	37 384	811	1 400	29 283	27.7	21 732	34.7	57.6	4.6	0.9	1.6	35.2	53.8	21.8
06 45400	Manhattan Beach	10.2	34 881	868	3 420	32 063	8.8	31 542	1.7	93.5	0.6	0.3	4.4	1.2	5.1	8.1
06 45484	Manteca	22.8	49 645	586	2 177	40 773	21.8	24 925	63.6	89.5	1.5	1.2	3.5	4.4	17.8	7.1
06 45778	Marina	22.7	17 471	1 662	770	26 512	-34.1	20 647	28.4	53.6	19.0	0.7	20.8	5.9	10.7	18.3
06 46114	Martinez	29.0	36 482	830	1 258	31 800	14.7	22 582	40.9	87.7	3.3	0.8	5.7	2.4	8.4	9.2
06 46492	Maywood	3.0	28 686	1 050	9 562	27 893	2.8	21 810	27.9	31.4	0.4	0.6	0.8	66.9	93.1	58.1
06 46870	Menlo Park	26.1	30 693	987	1 176	28 403	8.1	26 369	7.7	79.1	12.4	0.4	5.9	2.2	9.7	16.0
06 46898	Merced	41.8	60 551	452	1 449	56 155	7.8	36 499	53.9	61.7	6.9	0.9	15.2	15.3	29.9	18.9
06 47766	Milpitas	35.6	61 405	440	1 725	50 690	21.1	37 820	34.0	52.1	5.9	0.9	34.7	6.4	18.6	30.8
06 48256	Mission Viejo	45.2	98 049	237	2 169	79 464	23.4	50 666	43.7	90.3	0.9	0.3	6.3	2.2	7.7	12.5
06 48354	Modesto	78.2	188 253	96	2 407	164 746	14.3	106 602	54.5	80.6	2.7	1.0	7.9	7.8	16.3	12.7
06 48648	Monrovia	34.6	37 876	798	1 095	35 733	6.0	30 531	17.0	69.7	10.1	0.5	4.5	15.1	28.5	19.8
06 48788	Montclair	13.1	30 672	988	2 341	28 434	7.9	22 628	25.7	61.6	9.4	0.8	6.8	21.3	38.2	20.7
06 48816	Montebello	21.4	60 989	446	2 850	59 564	2.4	52 929	12.5	47.0	1.0	0.5	15.1	36.4	67.6	39.0
06 48872	Monterey	21.8	31 804	955	1 459	31 954	-0.5	27 558	16.0	86.6	2.9	0.6	7.3	2.6	7.8	14.7
06 48914	Monterey Park	19.8	63 060	427	3 185	60 738	3.8	54 338	11.8	26.7	0.6	0.3	57.5	14.8	31.3	51.8
06 49138	Moorpark	31.8	30 465	993	958	25 494	19.5	NA	NA	78.9	1.6	0.6	6.6	12.4	22.0	15.4
06 49270	Moreno Valley	127.3	148 895	131	1 170	118 779	25.4	NA	NA	67.4	13.8	0.7	6.6	11.4	22.9	12.3
06 49670	Mountain View	31.2	71 470	362	2 291	67 365	6.1	58 655	14.8	72.7	5.0	0.6	14.7	6.9	16.0	23.0
06 50258	Napa	45.1	67 811	383	1 504	61 865	9.6	50 879	21.6	90.3	0.4	0.8	2.1	6.5	15.2	10.9
06 50398	National City	19.6	55 284	515	2 821	54 249	1.9	48 772	11.2	40.9	8.5	0.7	17.7	32.3	49.6	35.7
06 50916	Newark	36.2	43 619	680	1 205	37 861	15.2	32 126	17.9	68.6	4.3	0.6	15.9	10.5	22.9	21.0
06 51182	Newport Beach	36.3	74 022	349	2 039	66 643	11.1	62 556	6.5	95.8	0.3	0.3	2.9	0.7	4.0	9.1
06 52526	Norwalk	25.3	98 325	233	3 886	94 279	4.3	85 286	10.5	55.8	3.2	0.9	12.4	27.6	47.9	28.3
06 52582	Novato	71.4	48 978	597	686	47 585	2.9	43 916	8.4	89.6	2.8	0.5	5.0	2.1	7.3	11.4
06 53000	Oakland	145.2	365 210	46	2 515	372 242	-1.9	339 337	9.7	32.5	43.9	0.6	14.8	8.3	13.9	19.8
06 53322	Oceanside	105.3	156 538	125	1 487	128 090	22.2	76 698	67.0	74.7	7.9	0.7	6.1	10.6	22.6	15.7
06 53896	Ontario	95.2	148 672	132	1 562	133 179	11.6	88 820	49.9	64.6	7.3	0.7	3.9	23.5	41.7	22.8
06 53980	Orange	60.4	125 686	163	2 081	110 658	13.6	91 788	20.6	83.0	1.4	0.5	7.9	7.2	22.8	20.1
06 54652	Oxnard	63.3	156 372	126	2 470	142 560	9.7	108 195	31.8	58.7	5.2	0.8	8.6	26.7	54.4	31.4
06 54806	Pacifica	32.7	40 731	735	1 246	37 670	8.1	36 866	2.2	76.3	5.2	0.7	13.6	4.2	13.5	14.7
06 55156	Palmdale	201.0	111 272	196	554	73 314	51.8	12 277	472.3	75.7	6.4	0.9	4.4	12.6	22.0	13.4
06 55254	Palm Springs	198.3	44 223	672	223	40 144	10.2	32 271	24.4	83.2	4.5	0.7	3.3	8.3	18.7	20.2
06 55282	Palo Alto	61.3	58 843	471	960	55 900	5.3	55 225	1.2	84.9	2.9	0.3	10.4	1.5	5.0	18.1
06 55520	Paradise	48.3	25 813	1 166	534	25 401	1.6	22 571	12.5	97.1	0.1	0.9	1.0	0.8	3.4	4.1
06 55618	Paramount	12.2	51 828	558	4 248	47 669	8.7	36 407	30.9	48.2	10.7	0.7	5.8	34.6	60.8	37.6
06 56000	Pasadena	59.5	135 698	150	2 281	131 586	3.1	118 550	11.0	57.3	19.0	0.4	8.1	15.2	27.3	27.5
06 56784	Petaluma	31.9	52 799	542	1 655	43 166	22.3	33 834	27.6	92.1	1.3	0.6	3.3	2.7	9.2	8.7
06 56924	Pico Rivera	20.7	61 498	437	2 971	59 177	3.9	53 459	10.7	58.8	0.7	0.6	3.2	36.8	83.2	29.3
06 57456	Pittsburg	28.2	53 849	530	1 910	47 607	13.1	33 034	44.1	58.6	17.6	0.8	12.2	10.9	23.7	18.7
06 57526	Placentia	17.1	48 005	612	2 807	41 259	16.4	35 041	17.7	76.2	1.9	0.5	8.2	13.3	24.7	19.1
06 57764	Pleasant Hill	17.6	33 697	896	1 915	31 583	6.7	25 124	25.7	89.3	1.4	0.6	7.0	1.7	6.6	11.0
06 57792	Pleasanton	42.0	66 482	396	1 583	50 570	31.5	35 160	43.8	90.7	1.4	0.4	5.8	1.7	6.7	7.4
06 58072	Pomona	59.1	137 629	145	2 329	131 700	4.5	92 742	42.0	57.0	14.4	0.6	6.7	21.3	51.3	31.6
06 58240	Porterville	29.1	36 420	831	1 252	29 521	23.4	19 692	49.9	65.0	1.0	1.3	6.5	26.2	34.8	16.4
06 58520	Poway	101.7	50 075	583	492	43 396	15.4	32 263	34.5	89.9	1.4	0.5	6.2	2.0	6.9	9.5
06 59451	Rancho Cucamonga	97.9	123 724	167	1 264	101 409	22.0	55 250	83.5	78.6	5.9	0.6	5.4	9.5	20.0	11.1
06 59514	Rancho Palos Verdes	35.4	43 355	681	1 225	41 667	4.1	36 577	13.9	76.2	1.9	0.2	20.5	1.2	5.3	23.2
06 59920	Redding	132.7	79 742	312	601	66 176	20.5	41 995	58.3	92.6	1.1	2.2	3.3	0.9	4.0	3.8
06 59962	Redlands	63.0	68 326	379	1 085	62 667	9.0	43 619	43.7	79.6	3.8	0.7	4.4	11.4	19.0	10.4
06 60018	Redondo Beach	16.3	64 804	412	3 976	60 167	7.7	57 102	5.4	87.0	1.6	0.5	6.8	4.0	11.5	12.4
06 60102	Redwood City	49.3	74 364	347	1 508	66 072	12.5	54 951	20.2	82.8	3.6	0.5	6.3	6.8	24.1	23.8
06 60466	Rialto	55.0	85 436	283	1 553	72 395	18.0	37 474	93.2	57.9	20.4	0.9	3.5	17.3	31.5	13.0
06 60620	Richmond	77.0	94 100	247	1 222	86 019	9.4	74 676	15.2	36.2	43.8	0.6	11.8	7.6	14.5	15.6
06 60704	Ridgecrest	53.8	30 307	999	563	28 295	7.1	15 929	77.6	87.8	3.2	1.0	4.2	3.8	7.9	7.2
06 62000	Riverside	201.2	265 721	60	1 321	226 546	17.3	170 876	32.6	70.8	7.4	0.8	5.2	15.8	26.0	15.5
06 62546	Rohnert Park	16.6	41 082	728	2 475	36 326	13.1	22 965	58.2	89.2	2.6	1.0	4.8	2.4	8.9	8.7
06 62896	Rosemead	13.3	53 825	531	4 047	51 638	4.2	42 604	21.2	35.4	0.6	0.5	34.3	29.1	49.7	48.4
06 62938	Roseville	77.4	77 048	325	995	44 685	72.4	24 347	83.5	91.5	0.9	1.0	3.3	3.3	10.8	6.5
06 64000	Sacramento	249.4	406 899	38	1 632	369 365	10.2	275 741	34.0	60.1	15.3	1.2	15.0	8.4	16.2	13.7
06 64224	Salinas	48.2	123 607	168	2 564	108 777	13.6	80 479	35.2	54.6	3.0	0.9	8.1	33.4	50.6	26.4
06 65000	San Bernardino	142.7	188 924	95	1 324	170 036	11.1	117 490	44.7	60.6	16.0	1.0	4.0	18.4	34.6	15.5
06 65028	San Bruno	16.7	40 323	745	2 415	38 961	3.5	35 417	10.0	71.6	4.1	0.8	17.9	5.6	18.6	24.1
06 65042	San Buenaventura (Ventura)	53.1	100 152	222	1 886	92 557	8.2	74 393	24.4	86.1	1.7	1.1	2.7	8.5	17.6	9.3
06 65070	San Carlos	14.6	27 854	1 079	1 908	26 382	5.6	24 710	6.8	91.3	0.9	0.3	6.1	1.4	6.5	12.5
06 65084	San Clemente	45.2	47 531	623	1 052	41 100	15.6	27 325	50.4	91.6	0.7	0.4	2.7	4.6	12.9	12.2
06 66000	San Diego	839.2	1 238 974	6	1 476	1 110 623	11.6	875 538	26.9	67.1	9.4	0.6	11.8	11.1	20.7	20.9
06 66070	San Dimas	40.2	35 133	857	874	32 398	8.4	24 014	34.9	81.7	3.8	0.5	8.6	5.5	17.3	14.9

1. Dry land or land partially or temporarily covered by water.　　2. Hispanic persons may be of any race.

Table D. Cities — Population and Households

	Population characteristics, 1990 (cont'd)										Households, 1990				
	Age of population (percent)													Percent	
City	Under 5 years	5 to 17 years	18 to 24 years	25 to 34 years	35 to 44 years	45 to 54 years	55 to 64 years	65 to 74 years	75 years and over	Percent female	Number	Percent change, 1980–1990	Persons per house-hold	Female family house-holder[1]	One-person
	16	17	18	19	20	21	22	23	24	25	26	27	28	29	30
CALIFORNIA—Cont'd															
Los Angeles	8.0	16.7	12.7	21.0	15.0	9.4	7.2	5.8	4.1	49.8	1 217 405	7.0	2.80	13.6	28.5
Los Gatos	5.1	13.3	7.9	17.2	17.2	16.3	10.2	6.9	6.0	52.2	11 273	7.6	2.37	8.3	26.8
Lynwood	11.4	25.9	14.3	18.9	13.0	7.1	4.2	3.1	2.2	49.5	14 158	0.8	4.29	20.3	12.0
Madera	9.9	23.7	10.9	16.6	12.6	8.1	6.8	6.1	5.2	51.4	9 159	21.2	3.15	16.9	20.2
Manhattan Beach	5.6	10.7	8.2	23.3	21.1	13.7	8.9	6.1	2.5	48.9	13 992	6.1	2.29	6.4	27.2
Manteca	9.3	23.1	9.3	19.2	15.7	9.1	6.0	5.3	3.1	49.8	13 440	56.0	3.02	11.9	16.4
Marina	10.5	18.6	16.5	24.2	14.8	5.6	5.4	3.1	1.3	47.2	7 908	38.2	3.05	11.0	12.4
Martinez	6.9	16.0	8.7	20.4	19.8	12.2	7.2	5.3	3.5	50.5	12 515	48.9	2.44	10.4	26.1
Maywood	11.9	24.6	16.5	19.7	12.4	6.9	3.8	2.3	1.9	48.2	6 496	-0.2	4.26	16.1	10.5
Menlo Park	6.3	12.4	6.5	19.9	17.5	9.9	9.1	10.1	8.3	52.5	11 816	5.2	2.28	9.1	33.1
Merced	11.1	23.6	11.0	18.3	13.1	7.6	6.5	5.4	3.5	50.6	18 282	35.3	3.03	15.7	21.7
Milpitas	7.9	18.4	10.6	23.9	18.0	10.7	5.6	3.2	1.6	47.0	14 099	23.8	3.37	10.9	12.0
Mission Viejo	7.8	19.9	8.3	17.4	20.5	12.0	6.4	5.4	2.5	50.5	25 174	57.2	2.88	7.3	14.3
Modesto	9.1	21.1	9.3	18.0	15.6	9.6	6.8	6.2	4.3	51.5	57 958	46.8	2.79	12.1	22.1
Monrovia	8.7	16.8	11.3	21.3	15.2	8.9	6.9	6.1	4.8	51.4	13 242	11.2	2.68	14.1	25.8
Montclair	10.0	20.9	11.6	19.8	13.9	9.2	6.8	4.6	3.3	50.1	8 538	18.4	3.29	14.6	16.5
Montebello	8.3	18.5	12.5	18.5	12.6	9.3	8.4	7.1	4.7	51.6	18 618	4.7	3.17	17.6	18.3
Monterey	6.9	10.9	15.4	24.4	14.6	8.2	6.9	6.9	5.7	49.3	12 693	13.9	2.26	7.6	31.8
Monterey Park	6.2	16.3	11.4	17.4	14.0	10.6	10.3	8.8	5.0	51.3	19 505	5.4	3.10	13.7	17.3
Moorpark	11.4	22.0	8.3	22.6	19.6	8.3	3.9	2.9	1.1	49.1	7 621	NA	3.34	6.7	9.2
Moreno Valley	11.4	25.5	8.5	21.5	17.0	7.7	4.5	2.8	1.1	50.2	34 965	NA	3.40	10.6	10.5
Mountain View	6.7	10.6	10.2	28.5	17.3	9.4	7.5	5.9	3.9	49.0	29 990	8.6	2.23	8.0	35.1
Napa	7.6	17.4	8.8	16.8	16.0	10.5	8.1	8.0	6.8	51.5	23 914	20.9	2.53	10.6	25.9
National City	8.9	18.8	19.0	19.5	12.2	6.0	6.2	5.4	3.9	47.0	14 773	3.9	3.22	19.7	17.9
Newark	8.9	19.5	9.9	21.6	15.3	12.1	7.3	3.5	1.8	49.6	12 015	30.3	3.15	10.4	13.8
Newport Beach	3.9	9.5	9.8	19.6	16.5	14.0	11.3	9.4	6.1	50.6	30 860	11.3	2.14	6.2	31.9
Norwalk	8.7	21.1	11.6	19.2	14.0	9.3	7.7	5.7	2.7	49.8	26 346	4.2	3.48	13.7	13.6
Novato	7.7	17.4	8.4	17.8	18.4	12.5	8.1	6.5	3.3	51.4	18 236	17.6	2.59	9.7	21.3
Oakland	8.0	16.9	10.1	19.2	16.8	9.8	7.0	6.7	5.5	52.0	144 521	1.5	2.52	18.5	33.2
Oceanside	9.5	16.7	11.3	20.8	13.4	7.0	7.2	8.7	5.4	50.4	46 741	60.7	2.72	9.7	20.8
Ontario	10.6	22.1	12.2	21.2	14.7	7.7	5.2	3.7	2.5	49.6	40 277	36.6	3.28	13.3	16.8
Orange	7.8	16.5	12.6	19.9	15.3	11.0	8.1	5.3	3.4	49.6	36 791	15.9	2.90	10.9	18.9
Oxnard	9.3	21.4	12.5	19.0	13.9	9.2	7.2	4.8	2.7	48.9	39 302	18.4	3.56	12.9	15.4
Pacifica	7.6	17.1	9.0	19.4	19.8	11.7	8.0	4.9	2.5	50.5	13 340	4.7	2.81	10.8	18.8
Palmdale	13.0	22.5	8.8	24.0	15.1	7.4	4.6	3.2	1.6	49.6	21 952	366.0	3.13	10.4	14.4
Palm Springs	5.3	11.1	7.9	14.3	13.3	10.8	11.6	13.8	11.9	51.0	18 622	23.2	2.13	8.0	36.6
Palo Alto	4.9	12.5	7.0	19.1	18.3	13.2	9.2	8.9	6.8	51.1	24 206	4.8	2.24	7.5	32.5
Paradise	5.7	15.2	4.1	11.5	13.6	8.9	10.2	16.2	14.5	53.4	11 045	16.2	2.26	8.1	29.3
Paramount	11.3	23.5	13.9	19.9	12.9	7.3	5.0	3.8	2.3	49.8	12 993	16.1	3.64	17.2	17.6
Pasadena	7.3	14.5	11.1	21.5	15.4	9.4	7.7	6.4	6.6	51.2	50 199	6.7	2.53	12.2	32.0
Petaluma	8.0	17.9	8.4	17.7	19.1	10.2	6.9	6.5	5.2	51.4	16 062	31.1	2.66	9.7	22.5
Pico Rivera	8.7	21.4	12.4	17.1	12.9	9.4	8.5	6.3	3.1	50.4	16 002	3.8	3.67	15.2	13.8
Pittsburg	9.8	21.2	10.4	20.8	15.5	8.5	6.2	4.6	3.1	50.3	15 643	40.8	3.02	14.3	17.8
Placentia	7.0	18.7	12.9	17.5	15.6	13.2	8.3	4.3	2.6	49.7	13 369	23.5	3.07	10.9	14.7
Pleasant Hill	6.6	13.8	7.7	21.0	18.8	11.7	8.3	7.6	4.4	51.3	13 004	33.2	2.39	8.3	26.7
Pleasanton	7.4	18.1	9.3	18.1	20.5	14.6	6.5	3.3	2.2	50.4	18 484	62.6	2.73	8.0	16.8
Pomona	11.1	21.8	13.1	20.7	14.1	7.5	5.0	3.7	3.0	48.7	36 443	20.1	3.52	14.2	18.2
Porterville	9.4	22.2	10.5	15.6	14.5	8.0	6.7	6.8	6.2	52.0	9 586	45.1	2.93	16.0	22.5
Poway	7.7	22.3	8.4	15.7	20.1	12.3	6.5	4.5	2.4	50.1	13 888	37.7	3.10	8.4	10.8
Rancho Cucamonga	9.3	22.4	9.7	20.4	18.0	10.2	5.0	3.4	1.6	50.6	33 635	98.0	3.01	9.8	16.1
Rancho Palos Verdes	4.6	16.6	8.0	10.4	15.9	17.9	14.6	8.7	3.3	50.8	14 943	25.8	2.76	6.2	14.0
Redding	8.2	18.6	9.5	16.2	15.4	9.5	8.3	8.3	6.1	51.9	26 105	55.0	2.48	12.2	25.6
Redlands	7.7	19.3	10.4	16.9	15.9	10.7	7.3	6.5	5.3	52.1	21 985	39.9	2.65	11.0	24.4
Redondo Beach	5.7	10.2	9.9	30.0	19.4	10.8	6.8	4.7	2.5	48.8	26 717	8.2	2.25	9.0	29.4
Redwood City	7.9	13.9	9.9	22.5	17.1	9.8	7.4	6.7	4.7	49.6	25 493	10.6	2.52	10.0	27.5
Rialto	10.9	24.8	8.9	19.0	15.4	7.9	6.3	4.5	2.1	51.1	21 893	80.7	3.30	13.9	15.7
Richmond	8.4	17.7	9.6	18.9	15.9	10.3	7.8	7.3	4.2	52.3	32 749	16.1	2.63	20.3	27.2
Ridgecrest	9.7	20.2	9.7	20.1	15.2	10.9	7.2	4.7	2.2	49.1	10 349	79.8	2.67	8.1	23.1
Riverside	8.8	20.0	13.0	19.7	14.5	8.5	6.4	5.3	3.7	50.3	75 463	23.7	2.92	12.5	20.6
Rohnert Park	8.5	18.0	14.2	21.3	17.6	7.8	5.0	4.7	2.8	51.2	13 409	61.0	2.66	10.8	22.0
Rosemead	8.7	21.7	11.8	18.8	13.9	8.8	7.4	4.7	4.2	50.4	13 701	4.2	3.72	15.4	14.3
Roseville	7.9	19.5	7.5	18.6	18.0	10.2	7.2	6.2	5.0	51.7	16 606	80.5	2.65	10.7	20.8
Sacramento	8.2	18.1	10.1	19.6	15.7	9.0	7.3	6.9	5.1	51.6	144 444	27.8	2.50	14.3	30.9
Salinas	10.2	21.8	12.0	20.0	13.9	7.8	6.2	4.8	3.4	50.0	33 360	23.4	3.21	14.2	19.3
San Bernardino	10.7	21.1	11.4	19.9	13.0	7.8	6.3	5.8	4.1	50.5	54 482	26.6	2.90	17.5	23.4
San Bruno	6.6	15.1	9.9	22.1	17.3	10.2	8.5	6.8	3.6	49.2	14 640	6.1	2.58	10.0	27.0
San Buenaventura (Ventura)	7.1	16.2	9.7	19.6	16.7	10.3	8.0	7.1	5.4	50.6	35 408	21.1	2.55	10.7	24.6
San Carlos	6.1	12.5	6.3	17.1	19.6	13.5	9.4	9.0	6.5	52.0	11 044	9.9	2.36	7.5	24.5
San Clemente	7.5	13.3	9.5	20.6	16.3	11.0	9.0	8.1	4.8	49.3	16 701	41.5	2.46	7.0	23.5
San Diego	7.3	15.9	14.4	21.3	15.3	8.8	6.9	6.1	4.0	49.0	406 096	26.3	2.61	11.2	26.3
San Dimas	6.9	19.3	9.6	16.0	17.9	13.3	7.6	5.9	3.5	50.6	10 948	38.0	2.86	10.1	18.3

1. No spouse present.

City	Persons in group quarters, 1990 Total	Persons in mental hospitals	Persons in nursing homes	Persons identified as homeless[1]	Serious crimes known to police, 1998[2] Total Number	Total Rate[3]	Violent	Property	Education, 1990 School enrollment Public	Private	Attainment[4] (percent) High school graduate or more	Bachelor's degree or more	Money income, 1989 Per capita (dollars)[5]	Households Median Dollars	Percent change, 1979–1989 (constant 1989 dollars)
	31	32	33	34	35	36	37	38	39	40	41	42	43	44	45
CALIFORNIA—Cont'd															
Los Angeles	69 284	1 528	17 271	6 462	183 706	5 072	1 359	3 713	806 534	172 104	67.0	23.0	16 188	30 925	17.3
Los Gatos	642	0	502	0	711	2 402	206	2 196	5 803	1 171	93.5	47.9	33 714	57 815	31.0
Lynwood	1 094	131	433	60	2 758	4 301	1 572	2 729	18 255	1 722	40.9	3.9	7 260	25 961	2.6
Madera	377	0	244	25	2 751	7 434	1 454	5 980	8 203	447	52.5	8.9	8 883	21 401	-5.5
Manhattan Beach	0	0	0	0	1 252	3 696	242	3 454	5 141	1 659	96.0	56.4	38 932	67 723	37.4
Manteca	223	0	198	8	2 247	4 793	380	4 413	11 117	979	74.9	10.1	12 813	35 083	15.2
Marina	2 270	0	0	0	600	2 424	202	2 222	6 745	700	84.2	17.0	11 338	29 043	11.6
Martinez	1 338	24	179	56	1 320	3 821	194	3 627	6 891	1 380	88.3	29.3	20 060	45 964	13.8
Maywood	132	0	113	0	739	2 571	508	2 063	8 699	589	27.9	1.6	6 927	25 567	21.5
Menlo Park	1 035	0	377	69	953	3 149	235	2 914	4 338	1 936	89.7	54.8	30 130	50 468	37.4
Merced	845	0	350	74	4 523	7 569	748	6 821	17 527	1 197	69.1	15.8	10 237	24 727	4.4
Milpitas	3 284	0	27	0	2 256	3 752	412	3 340	12 516	2 015	81.0	24.9	17 520	55 730	33.3
Mission Viejo	257	12	219	0	1 490	1 702	133	1 569	19 074	3 242	93.7	39.1	24 160	61 058	19.9
Modesto	2 935	260	1 239	232	12 349	6 737	606	6 131	42 844	4 022	74.8	15.8	13 572	31 701	7.2
Monrovia	188	0	150	0	1 042	2 743	437	2 306	7 520	1 697	77.3	19.7	15 495	35 684	32.6
Montclair	331	0	182	34	2 167	7 031	821	6 210	6 925	919	68.1	10.1	11 530	33 084	8.1
Montebello	422	0	355	0	2 520	4 102	649	3 453	15 222	2 718	60.8	14.6	12 276	31 441	5.8
Monterey	3 310	0	258	30	1 785	6 151	558	5 593	6 250	2 000	88.5	39.8	18 174	34 727	18.0
Monterey Park	224	0	172	0	1 832	2 903	414	2 489	15 474	2 612	70.0	22.4	13 290	32 605	-3.3
Moorpark	0	0	0	0	386	1 301	121	1 180	6 776	1 144	85.3	28.4	19 183	60 368	NA
Moreno Valley	18	0	18	0	7 587	5 196	825	4 371	34 759	3 850	81.8	14.3	13 474	42 186	NA
Mountain View	565	0	381	109	2 484	3 430	646	2 784	12 117	3 071	86.6	40.7	22 436	42 431	27.9
Napa	1 162	0	640	72	2 714	4 063	373	3 690	14 117	1 878	80.8	19.2	16 219	35 479	11.3
National City	6 695	0	631	0	3 122	5 938	1 033	4 905	13 643	1 048	58.9	9.1	8 658	22 129	12.0
Newark	32	0	0	32	2 000	4 886	420	4 466	9 626	1 395	78.6	21.1	16 721	50 471	14.2
Newport Beach	763	78	544	10	2 527	3 510	275	3 235	11 679	2 991	95.3	50.3	45 434	60 374	30.9
Norwalk	2 456	833	579	109	3 554	3 480	848	2 632	24 483	3 547	64.7	9.9	11 713	38 124	16.8
Novato	295	0	241	0	1 382	2 811	309	2 502	10 308	2 009	91.7	31.8	21 518	45 890	11.6
Oakland	7 595	0	2 260	671	36 863	9 794	1 862	7 932	84 860	16 611	74.4	27.2	14 676	27 095	17.3
Oceanside	1 363	0	93	879	5 917	3 938	731	3 207	27 133	3 569	81.2	18.8	14 522	33 453	33.3
Ontario	793	0	459	151	8 328	5 604	723	4 881	33 744	3 830	68.5	11.0	12 120	35 788	12.3
Orange	3 486	0	390	224	3 592	2 899	408	2 491	24 557	6 304	81.7	25.6	19 064	46 539	25.6
Oxnard	1 982	0	536	163	6 378	4 107	601	3 506	36 567	4 356	61.3	13.0	12 096	37 174	25.8
Pacifica	126	0	73	0	891	2 170	424	1 746	8 540	1 376	86.5	22.8	18 553	47 533	17.3
Palmdale	45	0	0	0	4 792	4 413	1 031	3 382	16 749	2 325	79.8	13.3	14 606	41 974	32.8
Palm Springs	536	0	314	97	3 205	7 136	1 040	6 096	5 625	744	77.1	20.4	19 725	27 538	1.7
Palo Alto	845	89	596	7	2 502	4 184	152	4 032	10 227	3 739	94.7	65.2	32 489	55 333	33.4
Paradise	355	0	193	0	1 002	3 838	417	3 421	4 823	415	77.5	15.1	12 887	22 954	9.1
Paramount	265	131	134	0	3 077	5 944	1 188	4 756	13 942	1 353	50.1	6.9	9 429	29 015	15.7
Pasadena	4 355	0	1 820	249	5 889	4 308	620	3 688	25 951	10 994	77.5	36.3	19 588	35 103	28.6
Petaluma	470	0	400	70	1 986	3 980	271	3 709	10 199	1 427	86.4	24.4	17 170	40 926	15.7
Pico Rivera	502	97	389	16	2 080	3 403	1 203	2 200	16 096	1 897	52.3	6.1	10 454	34 383	11.5
Pittsburg	358	0	184	174	2 773	5 285	555	4 730	12 128	1 705	76.5	14.4	13 686	38 532	17.1
Placentia	245	0	192	8	1 147	2 477	482	1 995	11 405	1 215	81.7	30.2	18 924	50 945	13.1
Pleasant Hill	411	0	411	0	1 970	5 936	380	5 556	6 555	1 117	92.4	35.4	21 950	46 885	20.6
Pleasanton	174	0	133	0	1 819	3 099	145	2 954	12 552	1 522	93.0	37.2	24 812	59 458	23.5
Pomona	3 223	268	648	299	6 383	4 649	1 244	3 405	35 026	3 608	59.6	13.1	10 728	32 132	24.6
Porterville	1 439	0	375	103	2 050	5 815	766	5 049	7 677	420	60.8	12.5	9 666	22 168	-3.7
Poway	361	0	316	45	NA	NA	NA	NA	11 751	1 782	91.3	34.4	20 720	53 252	32.0
Rancho Cucamonga	210	0	184	26	3 705	3 097	225	2 872	28 107	4 059	86.0	21.1	17 239	46 193	10.9
Rancho Palos Verdes	370	0	234	0	596	1 381	206	1 175	8 813	2 342	95.2	53.6	36 509	79 797	13.4
Redding	1 672	0	454	758	4 258	5 448	548	4 900	15 928	1 795	81.0	16.6	13 040	25 828	4.3
Redlands	2 098	0	756	201	2 785	4 071	567	3 504	14 150	3 983	84.6	31.3	17 825	37 073	13.7
Redondo Beach	13	0	0	13	2 115	3 327	319	3 008	10 355	2 394	90.4	40.4	26 230	51 913	41.9
Redwood City	1 761	0	365	94	2 577	3 531	454	3 077	13 459	2 652	81.5	27.1	20 292	42 962	31.3
Rialto	82	0	0	0	3 528	4 178	585	3 593	20 166	2 087	73.2	10.2	11 862	36 233	6.1
Richmond	1 047	0	270	268	7 525	8 007	1 378	6 629	20 556	3 009	76.7	22.2	14 630	32 165	23.0
Ridgecrest	121	0	94	0	637	2 032	278	1 754	7 487	725	86.9	26.7	16 258	39 087	1.4
Riverside	6 078	120	1 365	288	12 373	4 682	850	3 832	60 348	9 147	77.8	19.3	14 235	34 801	16.3
Rohnert Park	660	0	0	15	1 820	4 477	266	4 211	10 515	922	87.5	21.8	14 861	36 097	11.3
Rosemead	659	50	450	0	1 824	3 396	802	2 594	14 473	1 577	53.8	10.0	9 796	29 770	13.0
Roseville	686	0	552	134	2 704	4 122	351	3 771	10 563	1 430	86.9	24.0	17 430	39 975	35.1
Sacramento	7 930	176	1 486	1 441	31 620	8 219	878	7 341	92 299	12 126	76.9	23.5	14 087	28 183	15.1
Salinas	1 597	0	547	95	6 374	5 449	1 020	4 429	29 916	2 539	62.3	13.0	11 351	31 271	7.5
San Bernardino	6 036	0	907	969	13 792	7 328	1 263	6 065	41 817	4 451	68.1	12.7	10 865	25 533	8.1
San Bruno	1 147	0	87	5	1 270	3 074	169	2 905	7 977	1 880	84.0	21.3	18 289	42 019	10.6
San Buenaventura (Ventura)	2 168	75	262	52	3 828	3 766	331	3 435	20 228	3 396	84.1	24.6	19 091	40 307	28.0
San Carlos	43	6	34	0	631	2 223	292	1 931	4 088	1 374	91.6	35.8	28 161	54 658	28.9
San Clemente	91	0	27	16	890	1 896	185	1 711	3 841	1 691	90.4	32.4	23 841	46 374	44.4
San Diego	49 228	198	3 221	4 907	54 421	4 514	725	3 789	277 321	42 965	82.3	29.8	16 401	33 686	22.5
San Dimas	1 090	0	359	0	872	2 539	562	1 977	7 466	1 784	85.2	26.7	20 246	50 268	18.6

1. Persons in emergency shelters and persons visible in street locations. 2. Data for serious crimes have not been adjusted for underreporting. This may affect comparability between geographic areas and over time. 3. Per 100,000 population estimated by the FBI. 4. Persons 25 years old and older. 5. Based on population enumerated as of April 1, 1990.

Table D. Cities — Income, Poverty, and Housing

	Money income, 1989 (cont'd)				Housing units, 1990										
	House-holds (cont'd)	Percent below poverty, 1989						Occupied units							
		Persons		Fam-ilies						Owner-occupied units			Renter-occu-pied units		
											Owner cost as a percent of income				
City	Percent with $100,000 or more	Total	Percent change in rate, 1979–1989	Total	Total	Percent change, 1980–1990	Vacant units for sale or rent[1]	Total	Percent	Median value[2] (dollars)	With a mort-gage	Without a mort-gage	Median rent[3] (dol-lars)	Rent as per-cent of income	Sub-standard units[4] (percent)
	46	47	48	49	50	51	52	53	54	55	56	57	58	59	60
CALIFORNIA—Cont'd															
Los Angeles	7.9	18.9	15.2	14.9	1 299 963	9.3	69 406	1 217 405	39.4	244 500	25.3	11.9	600	30.4	22.0
Los Gatos	21.6	4.6	-14.8	2.1	11 822	7.8	399	11 273	64.2	439 900	25.1	11.4	849	27.2	1.6
Lynwood	1.4	21.8	5.8	20.1	14 525	-0.1	299	14 158	48.2	136 000	29.3	12.2	553	32.3	45.7
Madera	1.9	26.9	38.7	21.4	9 530	15.7	290	9 159	50.6	69 400	20.8	12.3	412	29.2	18.6
Manhattan Beach	30.0	3.8	-13.6	1.5	14 695	7.2	528	13 992	62.5	500 001	24.5	11.1	1 001	22.8	1.5
Manteca	2.7	9.9	5.3	8.6	13 981	52.5	474	13 440	58.6	140 500	25.3	12.1	542	25.5	7.3
Marina	1.3	9.7	-28.7	8.5	8 261	38.6	216	7 908	34.5	172 500	23.3	12.3	666	31.6	11.0
Martinez	6.0	5.9	3.5	4.2	12 970	46.7	348	12 515	66.7	203 700	26.2	11.8	676	27.5	2.8
Maywood	1.1	21.3	0.0	19.1	6 680	-2.3	149	6 496	30.5	157 300	29.9	11.2	525	28.3	59.2
Menlo Park	18.6	6.5	-18.8	3.9	12 247	6.1	326	11 816	53.9	463 600	25.8	11.1	853	27.6	4.1
Merced	2.4	25.1	51.2	20.2	18 965	29.1	577	18 282	44.6	91 100	22.6	11.7	438	29.8	15.8
Milpitas	11.6	4.9	-23.4	3.1	14 465	24.1	325	14 099	69.6	255 600	25.7	11.1	869	27.3	16.3
Mission Viejo	17.2	2.0	-39.4	1.0	26 393	52.8	1 086	25 174	80.0	254 500	27.2	11.8	969	30.1	2.7
Modesto	3.5	13.0	26.2	10.5	60 878	43.6	2 542	57 958	58.5	130 700	23.5	11.6	517	29.1	8.7
Monrovia	5.0	12.4	11.7	8.2	13 944	11.2	595	13 242	47.0	234 900	24.7	11.2	654	28.6	11.8
Montclair	2.6	16.7	38.0	13.0	8 915	13.4	336	8 538	61.4	134 700	24.5	11.7	613	33.6	16.3
Montebello	5.5	14.0	17.6	11.6	19 193	3.5	489	18 618	48.4	213 600	23.0	11.0	623	31.3	22.1
Monterey	5.2	6.6	-7.0	3.6	13 497	11.6	564	12 693	35.8	266 600	26.7	11.3	709	28.8	4.9
Monterey Park	5.9	16.4	62.4	13.4	20 298	5.0	627	19 505	54.9	238 800	23.3	11.7	661	31.8	23.1
Moorpark	10.7	4.3	NA	2.6	7 915	NA	266	7 621	80.1	276 800	30.5	12.6	911	28.3	7.8
Moreno Valley	2.9	8.4	NA	6.9	37 945	NA	2 672	34 965	74.0	140 800	28.1	11.2	675	30.5	8.5
Mountain View	8.0	6.2	-10.1	3.8	31 487	10.2	1 246	29 990	37.8	347 000	25.1	11.7	760	26.0	8.3
Napa	4.2	7.7	-11.5	5.2	24 922	23.2	755	23 914	60.0	175 000	23.9	11.5	641	30.0	4.8
National City	0.9	21.3	12.1	20.2	15 243	3.4	371	14 773	35.5	114 700	23.7	10.9	476	29.7	28.2
Newark	6.1	5.0	-5.7	4.1	12 284	29.9	240	12 015	72.2	225 500	24.8	11.3	793	29.8	9.4
Newport Beach	28.7	5.7	-17.4	2.3	34 861	11.0	2 196	30 860	55.8	500 001	25.8	11.7	967	26.3	1.7
Norwalk	2.2	9.3	-11.4	7.2	27 247	5.5	780	26 346	65.0	166 000	24.0	11.3	706	28.4	22.0
Novato	11.1	4.2	-23.6	2.5	18 782	17.6	467	18 236	61.9	279 600	25.0	11.5	818	29.6	3.1
Oakland	4.9	18.8	1.6	16.7	154 737	3.0	7 668	144 521	41.6	177 400	25.3	12.8	538	30.7	12.3
Oceanside	3.2	10.1	-17.9	6.7	51 109	56.1	2 899	46 741	58.4	170 200	28.7	11.6	651	31.9	9.0
Ontario	2.3	13.6	28.3	10.6	42 536	35.7	1 985	40 277	58.6	143 200	25.7	11.6	629	29.8	16.0
Orange	11.2	8.0	19.4	4.7	38 018	15.6	1 039	36 791	61.3	248 700	24.1	11.2	766	28.6	9.5
Oxnard	3.9	12.5	1.6	9.6	41 247	17.6	1 308	39 302	53.7	204 600	25.0	11.1	686	28.5	25.5
Pacifica	6.7	4.5	-22.4	3.2	13 740	4.6	326	13 340	66.7	266 800	25.3	11.7	839	28.2	6.1
Palmdale	3.9	8.9	-15.2	7.7	24 400	389.8	2 157	21 952	70.3	149 700	28.3	11.8	580	28.4	7.2
Palm Springs	7.2	12.6	21.2	8.8	30 517	24.8	2 318	18 622	58.9	141 200	27.2	13.9	563	32.3	7.4
Palo Alto	20.5	4.6	-23.3	1.9	25 188	6.1	808	24 206	56.7	457 800	21.6	10.9	851	25.9	2.8
Paradise	1.5	11.1	11.0	8.2	11 633	14.9	314	11 045	72.5	97 600	24.1	12.0	454	28.9	2.4
Paramount	1.9	17.6	-6.9	15.0	13 726	17.0	631	12 993	42.4	147 200	25.4	11.4	654	30.5	32.4
Pasadena	10.1	14.9	5.7	11.1	53 032	6.6	2 202	50 199	46.3	284 100	25.1	11.8	630	29.8	12.6
Petaluma	4.5	4.2	-33.3	2.7	16 546	31.9	363	16 062	66.9	204 000	24.9	11.7	709	28.2	2.4
Pico Rivera	2.0	11.6	8.4	9.3	16 316	2.7	255	16 002	70.1	165 000	24.6	11.0	613	28.6	26.3
Pittsburg	2.2	10.8	-16.3	8.5	16 709	40.1	915	15 643	61.4	138 900	25.9	12.9	622	27.1	11.2
Placentia	9.9	7.7	51.0	5.2	13 733	20.7	330	13 369	65.2	255 800	22.5	10.9	799	26.7	9.1
Pleasant Hill	8.3	3.6	-20.0	2.1	13 653	34.6	444	13 004	62.2	229 400	25.9	11.5	759	27.9	2.4
Pleasanton	14.6	2.4	-31.4	1.5	19 356	65.9	804	18 484	70.2	297 200	26.4	11.3	836	26.9	1.7
Pomona	3.5	18.4	7.0	14.0	38 466	19.6	1 592	36 443	57.4	134 200	26.8	11.6	592	32.0	24.1
Porterville	1.5	26.8	71.8	22.1	10 073	40.3	389	9 586	55.5	71 500	22.6	12.3	407	30.3	12.1
Poway	13.0	4.0	-23.1	2.9	14 386	37.9	434	13 888	77.6	219 600	26.1	10.8	730	29.1	4.2
Rancho Cucamonga	7.0	5.5	0.0	4.1	36 367	103.9	2 282	33 635	70.3	182 800	26.9	11.8	708	28.2	5.4
Rancho Palos Verdes	37.2	3.2	14.3	2.0	15 468	26.0	416	14 943	81.7	500 001	21.8	11.5	1 001	26.6	2.3
Redding	2.2	14.3	41.6	11.1	27 233	51.9	781	26 105	53.5	95 300	21.9	11.3	439	29.3	4.6
Redlands	6.9	9.0	-7.2	6.4	23 189	35.3	1 008	21 985	59.2	144 300	23.5	11.5	588	26.9	4.7
Redondo Beach	12.3	5.6	-28.2	3.6	28 220	9.1	1 228	26 717	46.4	348 300	27.4	11.8	863	25.4	3.9
Redwood City	9.1	8.3	15.3	6.1	26 847	14.3	1 133	25 493	50.8	349 500	28.2	12.0	728	28.6	10.7
Rialto	2.5	12.1	42.4	9.7	23 836	72.0	1 707	21 893	70.0	125 500	25.0	12.3	583	32.6	11.0
Richmond	3.5	16.1	-2.4	13.5	34 532	18.7	1 390	32 749	54.5	144 300	24.3	12.1	566	29.6	10.4
Ridgecrest	2.5	7.2	16.1	5.3	11 249	68.5	712	10 349	60.5	87 700	19.4	12.9	523	23.7	3.8
Riverside	4.7	11.9	5.3	8.4	80 240	24.8	4 013	75 463	56.3	134 800	23.9	11.3	575	29.6	10.3
Rohnert Park	2.0	8.5	-25.4	4.5	13 915	58.8	438	13 409	55.8	184 000	27.9	12.5	694	30.5	3.3
Rosemead	2.7	20.0	34.2	16.2	14 134	3.6	318	13 701	49.3	193 900	24.8	11.8	648	30.7	35.4
Roseville	5.4	6.8	-35.2	5.2	17 789	81.4	951	16 606	66.0	158 500	24.6	11.5	600	28.9	4.2
Sacramento	3.0	17.2	14.7	13.8	153 362	24.4	6 874	144 444	51.3	115 800	22.6	11.8	495	29.7	8.3
Salinas	2.4	15.6	24.8	12.4	34 577	21.8	1 018	33 360	46.3	161 500	24.4	11.2	580	28.3	21.1
San Bernardino	2.1	22.8	39.9	19.5	58 804	26.6	3 398	54 482	52.3	96 200	22.9	11.5	485	32.1	14.7
San Bruno	6.4	4.8	-4.0	3.8	15 178	3.5	438	14 640	62.5	294 600	25.8	11.5	763	27.6	8.9
San Buenaventura (Ventura)	6.7	6.6	-14.3	4.6	37 343	21.9	1 430	35 408	56.3	242 300	23.9	11.0	723	29.6	6.0
San Carlos	16.5	2.7	-6.9	1.7	11 338	9.5	247	11 044	72.4	407 500	27.7	11.9	810	26.6	1.7
San Clemente	12.1	7.0	-10.3	4.7	18 726	41.5	1 055	16 701	58.6	308 500	28.1	11.8	774	30.5	5.4
San Diego	5.9	13.4	8.1	9.7	431 722	26.3	20 212	406 096	48.3	189 400	25.3	11.4	602	29.8	10.4
San Dimas	10.9	5.4	8.0	3.7	11 479	36.2	464	10 948	76.2	242 800	25.7	11.1	745	29.3	3.9

1. Includes units rented or sold but not occupied.　2. Specified owner-occupied units.　3. Specified renter-occupied units.　4. Overcrowded or lacking complete plumbing facilities.

City	Civilian labor force, 1999				Civilian employment, 1990[2]			Disability 1990	Value of residential construction authorized by building permits, 1999		
			Unemployment			Percent					
	Total	Percent change, 1998–1999	Total	Rate[1]	Total	Professional, managerial, and technical	Precision production, craft, and repair	Work disabled persons[3] (percent)	New construction ($1,000)	Number of housing units	Percent single family
	61	62	63	64	65	66	67	68	69	70	71
CALIFORNIA—Cont'd											
Los Angeles	1 867 057	0.3	124 239	6.7	1 670 488	30.4	10.3	6.7	352 864	4 033	33.3
Los Gatos	18 895	0.1	353	1.9	16 026	53.6	6.0	4.4	15 589	77	79.2
Lynwood	25 564	0.1	2 560	10.0	22 049	13.0	16.4	7.6	1 913	18	100.0
Madera	17 068	0.1	2 853	16.7	10 147	17.2	11.7	10.3	22 492	248	62.9
Manhattan Beach	21 690	0.9	404	1.9	20 403	57.9	4.5	4.0	57 916	194	86.6
Manteca	22 696	1.4	1 585	7.0	17 887	22.5	17.4	9.6	87 343	629	99.7
Marina	11 524	4.2	712	6.2	9 150	23.3	7.7	6.3	140	1	100.0
Martinez	20 860	1.9	513	2.5	17 431	40.5	10.2	6.5	22 519	104	100.0
Maywood	13 062	0.1	1 282	9.8	11 291	8.0	15.5	5.8	367	4	100.0
Menlo Park	16 285	0.7	244	1.5	14 468	57.1	4.7	5.9	9 469	27	100.0
Merced	25 749	-0.9	3 383	13.1	20 113	28.0	11.2	8.8	18 980	172	100.0
Milpitas	31 161	0.0	979	3.1	26 087	37.1	12.3	5.4	40 220	242	27.3
Mission Viejo	44 354	2.6	705	1.6	39 377	43.9	7.5	4.4	142 413	1 015	44.9
Modesto	92 493	0.6	8 711	9.4	69 663	27.5	13.1	9.4	125 804	968	98.9
Monrovia	19 790	0.5	974	4.9	18 035	32.0	10.9	7.3	13 070	81	100.0
Montclair	16 720	4.1	797	4.8	13 106	20.3	14.7	8.5	17 142	103	100.0
Montebello	29 021	0.4	1 552	5.3	26 329	24.7	11.5	6.5	9 731	167	4.2
Monterey	17 231	4.7	589	3.4	14 083	39.7	6.4	5.1	6 400	35	51.4
Monterey Park	29 614	0.5	1 444	4.9	27 001	32.3	8.9	6.2	28 889	282	25.2
Moorpark	15 582	2.4	561	3.6	13 423	39.4	11.8	4.4	9 287	35	100.0
Moreno Valley	73 110	4.5	4 302	5.9	51 676	26.5	15.5	6.8	42 298	259	100.0
Mountain View	49 337	0.1	1 027	2.1	41 755	49.0	7.6	5.5	34 354	294	36.1
Napa	35 732	2.9	1 354	3.8	29 601	30.2	13.2	9.4	70 241	466	73.6
National City	21 741	2.6	1 243	5.7	17 835	17.1	16.0	8.4	0	0	0.0
Newark	23 231	1.8	698	3.0	20 542	29.0	14.9	6.0	20 217	91	100.0
Newport Beach	44 772	2.6	735	1.6	39 728	51.4	4.7	3.9	186 912	1 257	25.9
Norwalk	46 653	0.5	2 461	5.3	42 358	21.0	15.5	6.7	1 005	7	100.0
Novato	27 084	0.2	470	1.7	25 165	37.2	9.4	5.1	98 756	497	100.0
Oakland	188 543	1.3	10 306	5.5	162 488	36.2	7.9	10.4	63 322	760	26.7
Oceanside	65 171	2.8	2 446	3.8	54 576	27.2	13.1	8.0	140 098	755	84.6
Ontario	77 315	4.2	3 559	4.6	60 708	20.9	15.9	6.8	20 447	109	100.0
Orange	68 809	2.5	1 731	2.5	60 514	35.0	9.8	5.2	68 313	544	26.1
Oxnard	80 418	1.8	5 530	6.9	66 922	21.7	13.1	7.5	149 012	1 145	59.3
Pacifica	24 129	0.7	376	1.6	21 424	31.7	13.3	7.5	11 871	54	83.3
Palmdale	34 140	0.4	1 877	5.5	30 924	28.9	18.7	7.0	87 571	840	59.0
Palm Springs	25 908	5.0	1 094	4.2	18 636	30.1	8.8	8.5	23 088	120	100.0
Palo Alto	37 895	0.1	581	1.5	32 251	66.6	3.8	4.5	105 410	783	15.8
Paradise	10 099	-0.4	536	5.3	8 480	28.3	14.7	13.6	6 791	53	100.0
Paramount	22 226	0.1	1 756	7.9	19 620	15.3	15.0	7.7	1 170	10	100.0
Pasadena	72 114	0.5	3 606	5.0	65 665	42.8	7.2	6.9	8 063	52	94.2
Petaluma	29 318	1.5	637	2.2	22 681	33.1	12.7	6.8	76 823	587	67.3
Pico Rivera	28 022	0.3	1 885	6.7	25 052	16.7	13.8	7.5	10 275	71	100.0
Pittsburg	26 659	1.5	1 149	4.3	21 855	24.6	13.2	9.2	53 857	304	100.0
Placentia	26 103	2.5	617	2.4	22 992	36.9	9.5	5.2	28 314	172	90.7
Pleasant Hill	21 568	2.0	417	1.9	18 120	43.8	9.1	6.4	15 477	66	100.0
Pleasanton	33 440	2.1	575	1.7	29 961	42.7	8.3	4.8	121 460	527	43.1
Pomona	62 512	0.2	4 535	7.3	55 571	22.8	13.3	7.7	7 390	73	12.3
Porterville	15 258	1.8	2 960	19.4	10 507	25.1	9.2	12.3	14 775	181	95.0
Poway	25 990	3.1	511	2.0	22 169	40.7	10.2	5.2	35 862	127	100.0
Rancho Cucamonga	63 849	4.5	1 934	3.0	50 962	33.2	12.7	5.7	260 077	1 134	100.0
Rancho Palos Verdes	22 717	0.9	418	1.8	21 373	57.1	3.9	4.4	23 079	43	100.0
Redding	34 631	1.2	2 427	7.0	27 820	30.9	10.3	12.2	55 160	418	100.0
Redlands	35 131	4.4	1 072	3.1	28 034	40.8	9.3	6.9	36 247	208	70.2
Redondo Beach	42 891	0.8	1 153	2.7	40 006	47.2	8.4	4.7	76 450	325	96.3
Redwood City	41 197	0.7	734	1.8	36 496	34.1	11.0	6.7	13 455	66	89.4
Rialto	38 561	4.1	1 984	5.1	30 106	22.6	14.7	8.9	24 522	141	100.0
Richmond	48 129	1.2	2 812	5.8	38 823	32.6	8.8	11.1	25 650	264	27.3
Ridgecrest	16 897	0.9	1 018	6.0	13 710	49.0	11.3	7.8	1 134	10	100.0
Riverside	146 257	4.7	7 958	5.4	103 866	29.9	13.5	7.3	165 866	1 594	47.0
Rohnert Park	25 082	1.3	756	3.0	19 237	28.1	11.9	7.8	4 664	22	100.0
Rosemead	23 676	0.3	1 585	6.7	21 174	19.0	13.5	6.7	12 378	104	28.8
Roseville	31 527	5.5	1 078	3.4	21 763	35.3	11.3	6.5	270 019	1 813	66.4
Sacramento	197 707	3.4	10 193	5.2	161 812	34.7	8.5	10.8	138 950	1 114	82.8
Salinas	63 182	3.3	7 823	12.4	46 848	20.8	9.3	8.9	180 985	1 362	59.4
San Bernardino	80 118	3.7	5 598	7.0	61 337	24.3	13.5	10.7	15 061	120	100.0
San Bruno	23 961	0.6	462	1.9	21 195	29.6	12.9	6.2	3 397	14	100.0
San Buenaventura (Ventura)	55 561	2.4	2 081	3.7	47 791	36.1	12.2	8.4	63 926	362	96.7
San Carlos	16 906	0.8	190	1.1	15 077	43.5	9.1	5.9	4 098	13	100.0
San Clemente	25 031	2.6	510	2.0	22 121	37.0	11.3	5.4	127 513	490	92.0
San Diego	622 793	2.9	19 582	3.1	524 841	37.5	9.4	7.1	793 749	6 579	33.9
San Dimas	18 665	0.8	503	2.7	17 408	38.4	10.0	5.2	7 433	50	100.0

1. Percent of civilian labor force. 2. Persons 16 years and older. 3. Persons 16 to 64 years old.

City	Wholesale Trade, 1997				Retail Trade[1], 1997				Real Estate and Rental and Leasing, 1997			
	Number of Establish-ments	Number of Employees	Sales (mil dol)	Annual Payroll (mil dol)	Number of Establish-ments	Number of Employees	Sales (mil dol)	Annual Payroll (mil dol)	Number of Establish-ments	Number of Employees	Receipts (mil dol)	Annual Payroll (mil dol)
	72	73	74	75	76	77	78	79	80	81	82	83
CALIFORNIA—Cont'd												
Los Angeles	8 327	87 405	49 609.3	3 065.1	10 639	118 117	22 932.8	2 342.9	4 998	39 094	7 382.2	1 219.5
Los Gatos	65	440	272.6	24.2	199	2 216	484.9	53.6	102	402	61.2	12.1
Lynwood	44	747	259.6	23.3	83	925	179.9	17.1	13	78	8.2	1.2
Madera	33	D	D	D	141	1 918	302.5	31.5	19	89	8.9	1.4
Manhattan Beach	54	442	403.3	27.1	159	2 794	612.3	51.1	89	356	46.5	11.3
Manteca	23	D	D	D	147	1 996	359.3	36.2	45	213	19.8	3.8
Marina	9	59	18.7	1.9	41	475	59.9	6.7	22	D	D	D
Martinez	41	446	654.3	20.1	78	1 224	281.7	27.9	33	187	27.6	4.7
Maywood	16	164	54.3	4.7	47	572	86.7	8.9	5	D	D	D
Menlo Park	68	1 674	779.9	107.2	139	1 930	558.1	49.8	91	796	120.8	32.6
Merced	37	576	416.7	18.7	265	3 722	674.7	65.8	67	320	30.5	4.5
Milpitas	224	4 470	3 747.0	206.3	318	4 934	804.5	89.2	45	236	71.9	9.4
Mission Viejo	142	783	465.7	38.5	256	3 702	775.0	67.7	85	862	131.0	29.2
Modesto	164	2 111	870.5	66.9	704	10 008	1 765.7	177.1	171	1 003	136.2	22.0
Monrovia	109	1 020	282.7	32.9	141	2 617	553.2	48.3	26	98	9.6	2.0
Montclair	57	499	129.2	14.1	290	5 363	709.9	84.8	20	144	11.4	2.9
Montebello	123	1 929	1 474.6	77.0	242	3 468	630.0	62.2	60	294	49.3	7.5
Monterey	56	1 324	1 460.5	49.7	264	2 785	381.0	44.5	100	581	60.4	10.6
Monterey Park	268	1 656	864.8	44.3	169	1 683	275.2	26.2	81	350	82.8	7.5
Moorpark	56	773	242.3	31.4	33	452	77.9	9.5	13	43	7.4	1.3
Moreno Valley	25	80	47.0	2.5	277	3 997	691.2	74.9	49	207	18.3	3.1
Mountain View	180	5 479	2 612.0	283.5	296	4 458	977.6	98.8	121	771	102.8	16.4
Napa	84	568	202.5	17.0	319	3 712	648.8	69.6	85	712	53.4	10.5
National City	119	1 302	814.1	39.9	324	5 030	1 052.3	105.7	46	197	30.1	3.7
Newark	83	1 410	683.9	56.6	218	3 470	626.8	60.2	34	224	64.4	5.1
Newport Beach	289	7 136	2 642.8	140.7	440	5 947	1 140.2	125.1	521	5 612	1 233.7	229.0
Norwalk	84	815	610.1	28.7	172	2 810	630.1	57.4	44	206	25.7	4.1
Novato	111	981	423.1	34.9	192	2 619	543.8	59.5	79	434	64.0	10.1
Oakland	526	7 662	3 553.2	285.6	1 030	10 190	2 146.5	213.1	476	2 712	406.9	66.7
Oceanside	125	1 694	925.6	42.1	388	4 916	781.2	82.4	94	445	59.7	7.8
Ontario	371	7 262	5 425.5	251.6	461	7 653	1 769.1	152.1	115	1 008	201.5	25.1
Orange	403	5 751	4 685.5	228.2	484	5 519	1 227.3	123.8	164	947	140.4	24.4
Oxnard	175	2 818	922.9	110.6	487	6 821	1 398.7	135.8	100	464	57.2	9.5
Pacifica	7	14	7.3	0.6	70	721	127.3	12.1	21	58	12.0	1.1
Palmdale	36	268	71.7	8.4	208	2 852	543.0	53.3	58	193	24.7	3.4
Palm Springs	40	D	D	D	225	2 759	438.1	49.1	113	518	91.4	12.3
Palo Alto	104	1 382	1 019.1	126.5	307	6 097	1 337.7	139.9	155	1 336	258.1	44.1
Paradise	8	D	D	D	84	859	120.9	13.3	37	D	D	D
Paramount	200	2 752	888.6	83.4	115	1 515	230.2	24.5	42	232	28.6	4.6
Pasadena	200	2 492	2 219.5	108.6	567	8 330	1 553.1	160.9	239	2 059	244.6	40.8
Petaluma	113	1 948	579.8	60.5	276	3 307	618.6	65.7	71	399	41.9	6.9
Pico Rivera	86	1 532	620.1	51.9	108	1 554	303.9	33.8	24	240	45.9	6.7
Pittsburg	31	378	147.4	14.6	111	2 158	369.0	38.6	22	170	35.4	3.6
Placentia	129	1 264	477.6	45.6	110	1 525	334.6	38.1	36	411	23.4	6.6
Pleasant Hill	35	338	153.9	15.3	159	2 383	382.2	36.2	49	204	26.6	4.8
Pleasanton	253	5 868	13 804.0	331.2	349	5 665	1 068.2	107.5	101	442	92.0	17.7
Pomona	229	2 982	1 184.8	87.3	269	3 216	599.5	63.6	81	424	50.7	9.4
Porterville	23	398	150.5	6.3	165	2 097	340.6	35.1	32	105	16.7	1.3
Poway	60	530	263.4	20.3	139	2 036	442.8	38.9	54	225	25.3	4.1
Rancho Cucamonga	219	2 594	1 529.4	86.3	233	3 947	708.9	70.5	80	460	47.5	9.6
Rancho Palos Verdes	46	101	110.7	5.6	49	595	109.7	10.8	46	127	28.8	3.0
Redding	152	1 311	436.3	40.5	501	6 513	1 128.3	115.6	146	664	59.8	11.1
Redlands	37	496	161.2	16.3	208	3 313	560.8	60.4	67	247	32.5	3.9
Redondo Beach	77	552	366.7	23.2	287	3 968	538.5	62.8	91	295	51.7	5.8
Redwood City	128	1 376	1 099.4	72.6	256	4 199	1 097.2	104.5	88	1 279	114.1	31.6
Rialto	50	553	924.3	21.3	115	1 708	313.9	29.0	41	176	22.1	3.3
Richmond	105	1 396	690.9	47.6	224	2 510	453.7	45.6	54	242	46.7	6.7
Ridgecrest	4	D	D	D	97	1 388	203.0	20.8	18	82	6.9	1.1
Riverside	267	3 395	1 723.0	104.9	800	11 452	2 279.3	219.7	250	1 276	145.0	28.3
Rohnert Park	35	D	D	D	108	2 203	390.8	40.7	42	239	51.8	6.4
Rosemead	100	D	D	D	134	1 155	190.1	18.1	28	126	11.3	2.7
Roseville	77	1 520	668.4	66.1	279	5 514	1 545.9	134.7	79	922	82.3	21.6
Sacramento	594	10 553	5 538.2	369.9	1 296	18 093	3 039.6	329.7	415	3 058	367.3	80.1
Salinas	200	3 802	2 308.0	145.6	496	7 173	1 332.5	146.3	104	546	71.7	11.7
San Bernardino	150	2 728	1 050.2	88.0	640	9 571	1 903.9	181.0	152	556	68.7	11.7
San Bruno	35	244	452.9	10.8	138	2 833	656.6	57.9	29	138	49.6	4.4
San Buenaventura (Ventura)	201	2 816	639.9	98.2	483	6 334	1 249.8	128.2	175	790	94.5	19.4
San Carlos	129	1 504	671.4	57.1	142	1 503	315.9	36.4	52	246	32.1	6.9
San Clemente	144	1 293	748.4	48.7	173	1 587	286.7	27.5	65	236	35.6	4.7
San Diego	2 178	33 766	18 478.4	1 634.8	4 128	54 308	10 018.2	1 020.3	1 954	14 038	2 109.3	386.8
San Dimas	102	970	1 271.8	34.0	101	1 295	210.7	22.3	29	172	27.3	4.0

1. Establishments with payroll.

Table D. Cities — **Professional Services, Manufacturing, Accommodation and Foodservices**

City	Professional, Scientific, and Technical Services, 1997[1]				Manufacturing, 1997				Accommodation and Foodservices, 1997			
	Number of Establishments	Number of Employees	Receipts (mil dol)	Annual Payroll (mil dol)	Number of Establishments	Number of Employees	Receipts (mil dol)	Annual Payroll (mil dol)	Number of Establishments	Number of Employees	Sales (mil dol)	Annual Payroll (mil dol)
	84	85	86	87	88	89	90	91	92	93	94	95
CALIFORNIA—Cont'd												
Los Angeles	10 755	122 686	14 539.9	5 668.2	7 222	186 758	27 378.2	5 302.8	6 215	103 676	4 523.1	1 249.1
Los Gatos	261	1 307	217.4	94.0	61	1 055	136.4	50.2	120	2 282	79.4	23.4
Lynwood	11	48	7.8	1.9	62	2 516	289.0	56.6	56	478	21.0	4.4
Madera	34	204	16.7	6.3	38	1 260	190.9	33.9	64	D	D	D
Manhattan Beach	178	681	97.7	34.4	NA	NA	NA	NA	126	2 782	121.9	33.6
Manteca	28	96	8.5	2.8	28	1 779	208.2	38.4	80	D	D	D
Marina	12	28	1.6	0.6	NA	NA	NA	NA	29	341	13.9	3.1
Martinez	90	311	25.5	10.1	33	D	D	D	77	802	27.9	7.4
Maywood	3	D	D	D	31	514	32.7	9.1	27	278	12.3	2.6
Menlo Park	254	3 754	642.2	268.7	78	6 371	1 478.0	369.8	83	1 352	67.5	17.7
Merced	83	471	29.9	11.4	42	2 326	457.3	64.3	129	1 755	55.2	13.7
Milpitas	140	1 123	188.7	60.4	202	27 550	7 129.6	1 364.6	192	3 839	147.6	37.2
Mission Viejo	178	883	98.7	40.3	46	1 466	272.3	70.3	130	2 184	73.5	18.4
Modesto	328	2 342	181.0	64.2	137	7 462	2 124.8	265.5	334	5 931	182.2	48.3
Monrovia	92	736	79.1	31.7	130	5 150	725.6	199.4	73	1 502	56.7	15.8
Montclair	27	152	8.3	2.7	72	854	95.0	19.9	73	D	D	D
Montebello	57	205	15.5	3.9	112	4 850	642.2	133.7	118	1 579	55.9	13.4
Monterey	222	1 044	114.8	44.9	61	1 317	159.6	44.1	205	4 733	236.7	62.8
Monterey Park	113	334	28.8	8.7	79	1 841	170.4	43.9	128	2 039	84.0	22.8
Moorpark	41	554	82.7	20.5	52	2 578	370.1	79.4	26	D	D	D
Moreno Valley	43	196	10.3	2.5	19	1 095	143.7	20.8	129	2 149	66.6	18.0
Mountain View	446	7 957	1 238.2	497.9	235	20 837	9 372.0	1 298.7	221	3 463	173.7	41.4
Napa	160	1 248	244.0	109.3	104	2 694	591.2	84.7	189	2 720	111.3	30.5
National City	50	554	16.8	8.9	100	1 744	342.7	45.1	148	1 844	63.7	16.5
Newark	67	872	78.2	28.5	84	2 989	597.5	124.1	103	1 684	74.6	17.6
Newport Beach	1 031	7 343	1 120.3	413.7	109	5 136	1 481.8	255.6	339	8 404	371.7	106.7
Norwalk	51	435	13.5	5.6	75	1 234	159.9	28.9	118	1 651	64.4	14.8
Novato	177	1 446	151.4	62.1	82	1 669	263.1	65.2	109	1 341	50.4	13.2
Oakland	1 110	8 673	1 130.3	466.2	574	13 913	2 048.1	426.2	738	9 390	436.3	121.3
Oceanside	169	865	62.3	22.8	157	3 749	416.5	97.5	239	3 893	126.1	33.9
Ontario	119	1 048	121.9	47.2	420	16 296	3 257.5	483.4	210	4 760	217.0	58.8
Orange	497	6 459	611.3	217.4	338	10 463	1 452.6	309.4	246	4 307	171.0	45.5
Oxnard	175	1 069	102.5	35.4	172	6 935	1 440.7	220.8	220	4 487	166.6	47.0
Pacifica	45	97	11.3	4.4	NA	NA	NA	NA	62	575	24.9	6.0
Palmdale	47	227	18.5	6.3	44	D	D	D	111	2 286	74.6	19.2
Palm Springs	130	596	54.3	20.6	37	734	107.6	22.5	220	4 974	197.4	57.4
Palo Alto	731	9 034	1 724.7	720.1	114	7 983	2 232.0	362.6	248	5 211	240.7	72.5
Paradise	28	74	4.5	1.1	NA	NA	NA	NA	52	658	16.3	4.3
Paramount	28	417	26.8	10.3	268	6 401	1 081.7	199.4	55	559	21.7	4.9
Pasadena	872	10 199	1 292.9	484.8	151	2 877	389.0	87.4	364	8 048	313.4	92.9
Petaluma	145	1 158	119.2	51.6	119	4 998	1 403.7	249.8	138	2 010	64.1	17.3
Pico Rivera	16	179	15.3	4.9	81	3 122	518.5	89.0	71	1 004	37.3	9.0
Pittsburg	26	150	12.4	3.5	46	2 362	1 503.1	118.3	66	864	30.3	8.2
Placentia	60	372	41.2	15.5	134	3 438	447.2	85.9	77	1 250	47.3	11.1
Pleasant Hill	116	1 058	104.8	65.0	NA	NA	NA	NA	72	1 268	49.1	12.2
Pleasanton	328	3 797	614.7	185.4	100	1 759	328.4	77.1	187	3 699	152.5	40.7
Pomona	92	555	41.7	16.3	253	9 792	1 551.4	301.9	165	2 603	94.5	23.8
Porterville	38	113	9.0	2.2	35	1 045	161.4	28.1	79	1 143	35.4	8.0
Poway	97	366	51.4	15.6	52	1 397	227.6	41.2	80	1 086	39.5	10.2
Rancho Cucamonga	200	955	100.1	33.7	243	9 913	2 009.1	311.7	153	D	D	D
Rancho Palos Verdes	86	228	25.4	10.8	NA	NA	NA	NA	34	694	26.2	6.4
Redding	261	1 519	115.4	48.6	110	1 351	166.2	38.0	254	3 849	120.5	31.6
Redlands	122	656	56.6	22.4	54	1 803	196.1	41.3	119	1 865	59.1	16.1
Redondo Beach	197	4 408	740.9	278.7	40	D	D	D	161	3 122	126.1	34.8
Redwood City	301	3 687	552.7	232.1	98	4 606	930.1	238.6	173	3 138	130.4	35.2
Rialto	28	164	9.5	3.6	66	1 935	299.0	50.2	64	1 152	32.5	8.0
Richmond	115	923	89.0	43.9	137	4 640	2 979.0	207.8	83	947	29.8	7.4
Ridgecrest	44	1 033	89.3	39.5	NA	NA	NA	NA	48	897	24.9	6.8
Riverside	466	3 195	333.6	101.4	289	10 901	1 687.2	322.4	397	6 281	208.3	56.7
Rohnert Park	53	429	27.5	32.6	48	781	136.2	27.6	74	1 792	60.0	16.4
Rosemead	48	343	21.2	3.7	82	1 759	149.6	38.1	103	1 159	43.0	10.1
Roseville	188	1 357	132.6	55.8	57	D	D	D	167	3 185	102.0	27.2
Sacramento	1 456	11 899	1 355.5	544.8	423	15 763	3 582.7	579.1	877	14 847	528.8	142.9
Salinas	201	1 078	89.1	35.0	97	2 752	641.6	96.0	226	3 118	105.3	27.2
San Bernardino	264	1 877	176.7	66.1	150	4 140	589.5	106.1	322	5 345	177.5	47.7
San Bruno	69	394	41.9	20.0	NA	NA	NA	NA	59	971	38.1	10.2
San Buenaventura (Ventura)	389	2 574	234.3	91.6	157	3 126	374.7	90.9	251	4 544	166.4	47.0
San Carlos	132	805	66.7	27.8	148	3 712	561.6	144.4	83	755	32.0	9.1
San Clemente	157	767	107.0	31.3	91	1 452	189.3	49.3	117	1 269	56.8	14.3
San Diego	4 584	46 351	5 780.7	2 278.2	1 444	65 599	14 315.4	2 562.7	2 776	61 170	2 607.4	706.7
San Dimas	82	1 542	237.8	62.5	99	2 382	321.7	73.1	59	1 156	39.5	10.0

1. Firms subject to federal tax.

City	Arts, Entertainment, and Recreation[1], 1997				Health Care and Social Assistance[1], 1997				Other Services[1], 1997			
	Number of Establishments	Number of Employees	Receipts (mil dol)	Annual Payroll (mil dol)	Number of Establishments	Number of Employees	Receipts (mil dol)	Annual Payroll (mil dol)	Number of Establishments	Number of Employees	Receipts (mil dol)	Annual Payroll (mil dol)
	96	97	98	99	100	101	102	103	104	105	106	107
CALIFORNIA—Cont'd												
Los Angeles	4 229	23 403	4 530.8	2 178.7	7 491	74 565	6 051.2	2 351.7	5 358	33 761	2 397.4	631.4
Los Gatos	17	309	11.8	4.7	269	3 611	227.4	110.8	82	341	21.9	6.0
Lynwood	1	0	0.0	0.0	100	818	71.9	27.6	34	185	9.9	2.3
Madera	6	59	1.4	0.4	93	936	52.3	19.0	48	229	15.9	4.2
Manhattan Beach	23	303	18.6	7.2	129	587	55.4	24.7	67	388	21.7	5.8
Manteca	11	188	8.3	2.0	84	1 024	69.9	28.3	58	657	54.4	14.9
Marina	4	63	1.2	0.5	15	149	7.2	2.7	17	57	4.0	0.8
Martinez	4	12	0.7	0.1	39	1 214	98.8	45.2	42	152	13.3	3.6
Maywood	3	5	0.5	0.0	21	219	13.1	5.0	24	94	6.2	1.8
Menlo Park	15	89	8.3	2.3	114	1 284	109.5	47.2	53	359	27.2	9.0
Merced	13	159	3.4	0.9	204	1 929	127.8	48.7	71	460	25.7	8.2
Milpitas	16	329	14.9	3.1	123	1 065	99.2	35.9	96	721	74.8	18.4
Mission Viejo	19	316	12.8	3.6	268	2 229	207.1	82.7	122	655	70.7	16.5
Modesto	39	693	23.0	6.1	513	6 951	524.4	204.4	245	1 474	95.5	28.5
Monrovia	7	110	4.5	1.8	49	633	47.2	16.5	71	356	22.7	6.5
Montclair	5	124	5.3	1.0	70	1 526	98.6	40.4	67	599	43.1	14.1
Montebello	5	0	0.0	0.0	155	1 300	103.0	39.0	106	813	53.4	15.9
Monterey	25	261	24.0	10.3	230	2 053	168.4	71.8	80	540	30.9	9.2
Monterey Park	6	0	0.0	0.0	203	2 641	201.9	83.2	80	368	22.3	6.2
Moorpark	7	0	0.0	0.0	18	115	7.1	2.5	26	125	9.5	2.4
Moreno Valley	17	246	10.4	3.1	156	1 298	75.0	25.6	94	380	21.2	6.1
Mountain View	15	308	13.0	3.8	236	1 871	175.4	75.8	151	883	74.8	23.1
Napa	14	329	10.2	3.1	259	2 345	151.2	61.4	118	639	44.4	12.3
National City	6	119	7.2	1.3	112	1 088	66.4	27.2	123	838	54.9	17.0
Newark	4	60	1.4	0.3	38	208	14.9	4.6	60	360	29.6	8.1
Newport Beach	61	1 348	77.4	20.8	582	3 923	411.0	175.9	159	1 117	70.3	22.1
Norwalk	6	148	6.6	1.3	97	982	58.1	20.6	74	337	21.9	6.0
Novato	13	220	15.7	5.2	130	998	79.9	34.0	91	646	45.7	14.7
Oakland	62	1 218	183.1	103.0	886	8 669	854.1	338.6	597	3 524	268.3	78.3
Oceanside	14	482	18.2	6.6	215	1 448	131.3	44.8	149	1 022	66.0	18.4
Ontario	12	379	13.6	4.0	114	1 780	196.1	58.1	194	2 069	145.3	47.8
Orange	36	533	19.1	5.6	481	5 069	496.9	201.6	260	1 821	124.6	36.1
Oxnard	34	352	16.9	4.7	309	2 564	194.2	78.7	183	1 011	71.2	17.9
Pacifica	4	67	1.6	0.6	34	249	12.8	5.0	34	119	8.0	2.3
Palmdale	8	181	6.0	1.8	110	926	58.4	21.4	73	366	22.3	5.5
Palm Springs	19	929	42.6	13.6	210	2 790	279.7	98.9	90	563	33.9	9.8
Palo Alto	16	230	16.2	9.2	285	1 900	188.4	70.1	107	964	101.1	29.4
Paradise	4	83	2.3	0.7	96	745	37.6	13.2	35	106	8.0	1.9
Paramount	2	0	0.0	0.0	76	1 199	86.2	30.9	68	677	53.7	16.0
Pasadena	68	853	56.2	19.7	562	6 453	547.7	216.5	300	1 843	133.9	33.9
Petaluma	15	264	11.3	3.7	151	1 375	77.0	33.4	97	543	44.6	12.3
Pico Rivera	3	0	0.0	0.0	80	887	49.0	22.6	59	708	32.7	10.1
Pittsburg	4	21	0.6	0.1	57	500	27.9	10.6	46	289	15.2	6.8
Placentia	5	0	0.0	0.0	67	584	47.0	18.7	60	298	24.5	7.3
Pleasant Hill	10	137	6.4	1.9	98	727	51.0	19.9	50	290	12.4	4.1
Pleasanton	31	531	39.4	15.3	198	1 903	234.6	64.3	107	722	63.5	18.8
Pomona	11	365	47.5	12.0	214	2 315	150.9	60.3	141	813	62.7	16.3
Porterville	5	0	0.0	0.0	95	1 040	61.9	20.0	36	149	11.1	2.2
Poway	13	282	12.8	2.6	140	923	74.5	30.1	65	276	21.4	5.3
Rancho Cucamonga	14	298	15.0	4.3	148	1 524	88.7	31.3	131	1 016	63.7	19.7
Rancho Palos Verdes	4	74	5.3	1.1	71	275	24.1	11.4	24	181	15.4	4.8
Redding	22	261	8.5	2.6	413	4 908	355.9	143.8	171	1 064	69.7	18.6
Redlands	11	279	8.7	2.6	172	2 695	158.5	74.1	89	451	27.8	6.6
Redondo Beach	19	247	11.0	3.8	132	995	85.0	36.7	108	913	83.6	26.1
Redwood City	24	618	28.9	9.0	220	2 232	209.9	96.5	135	804	64.8	19.2
Rialto	4	0	0.0	0.0	78	792	33.1	12.3	58	456	53.0	11.2
Richmond	11	90	9.9	3.0	118	1 345	94.2	42.8	108	547	48.4	13.4
Ridgecrest	2	0	0.0	0.0	42	481	33.1	15.5	37	153	16.1	3.2
Riverside	34	573	23.8	6.5	540	7 486	622.4	244.5	327	2 316	154.0	41.8
Rohnert Park	10	169	6.3	2.3	54	336	18.7	7.4	43	243	15.5	4.8
Rosemead	4	0	0.0	0.0	76	742	44.1	17.6	72	265	15.7	3.6
Roseville	15	205	5.9	1.3	241	2 603	239.9	88.4	107	1 310	132.2	44.7
Sacramento	81	1 285	96.4	18.8	993	10 610	883.1	385.6	572	4 272	335.0	95.0
Salinas	17	247	17.8	2.8	281	2 272	192.3	78.2	155	943	74.0	21.3
San Bernardino	22	406	17.6	4.8	376	3 826	309.9	126.5	211	1 459	96.9	26.2
San Bruno	7	0	0.0	0.0	65	910	103.8	41.3	72	438	36.9	10.2
San Buenaventura (Ventura)	38	474	20.7	5.1	342	2 578	228.6	85.4	162	1 407	132.3	38.8
San Carlos	4	53	1.2	0.6	73	411	30.9	11.1	82	542	47.9	14.8
San Clemente	13	299	11.9	3.2	124	1 032	70.7	28.9	61	335	19.4	5.6
San Diego	267	6 439	479.5	188.9	2 642	28 497	2 464.6	977.0	1 827	12 658	867.9	239.3
San Dimas	15	331	26.4	6.9	78	899	52.2	23.2	62	566	46.6	16.3

1. Firms subject to federal tax.

City	Selected federal funds, fiscal 1999[1] (mil dol)									City government finances, 1997						
	Procurement contracts		Grants					Direct payments for individuals		General revenue						
										Intergovernmental			Taxes			
														Per capita[3] (dollars)		
	Defense	Other	Total[2]	Health and family welfare	Energy and environment	Education	Housing and community development	Educational assistance	Housing assistance	Total (mil dol)	Total (mil dol)	Percent from state government	Total (mil dol)	Total	Property	Sales and gross receipts
	108	109	110	111	112	113	114	115	116	117	118	119	120	121	122	123
CALIFORNIA—Cont'd																
Los Angeles	441.6	227.4	1 514.2	494.2	23.6	43.8	215.6	85.2	111.2	4 706.3	960.1	44.3	1 988.8	560	191	246
Los Gatos	1.5	1.4	0.4	0.3	0.1	0.0	0.0	0.0	0.0	21.0	2.8	89.1	13.2	457	131	243
Lynwood	0.4	0.1	3.1	0.0	0.2	0.1	2.4	0.0	0.0	32.4	5.4	100.0	16.8	268	140	109
Madera	0.0	0.1	4.6	3.1	0.0	0.0	1.2	0.1	0.0	22.2	3.7	87.0	8.5	238	107	108
Manhattan Beach	0.3	0.1	0.1	0.0	0.0	0.0	0.0	0.0	0.0	31.7	2.6	100.0	17.1	515	172	231
Manteca	0.0	0.6	0.7	0.3	0.0	0.1	0.0	0.0	0.0	27.6	3.8	97.2	12.8	282	101	142
Marina	0.7	0.0	9.2	0.0	0.0	0.0	0.3	0.0	0.0	6.8	2.1	83.4	3.3	139	42	93
Martinez	4.9	2.3	28.5	14.7	0.5	0.2	9.9	0.6	0.0	20.6	7.5	83.2	9.0	269	103	116
Maywood	0.0	0.0	0.0	0.0	0.0	0.0	0.0	0.0	0.0	7.2	2.5	82.7	3.9	138	47	78
Menlo Park	50.7	22.7	39.0	12.4	2.4	2.1	0.0	0.0	0.0	35.2	3.2	95.6	21.4	725	319	315
Merced	0.1	0.7	14.6	8.6	0.0	0.5	2.0	4.1	0.7	42.5	9.1	58.8	16.2	278	125	134
Milpitas	8.6	5.5	0.4	0.0	0.0	0.0	0.2	0.9	3.9	70.3	5.5	99.9	44.5	758	351	330
Mission Viejo	0.2	2.8	1.7	0.3	0.8	0.7	0.0	1.4	0.0	35.5	7.3	97.7	23.8	281	112	138
Modesto	0.6	44.8	34.2	24.5	0.0	1.7	4.9	4.3	3.7	111.7	22.4	85.8	50.9	285	45	197
Monrovia	4.5	0.7	0.0	0.0	0.0	0.0	0.0	0.0	1.0	29.4	4.6	67.3	17.6	471	252	194
Montclair	0.0	0.3	0.1	0.0	0.0	0.0	0.0	0.0	1.1	26.5	2.7	81.8	18.0	600	208	364
Montebello	5.1	1.0	2.2	0.0	0.0	0.2	1.8	0.2	0.8	58.0	11.0	79.7	32.1	532	237	258
Monterey	31.3	0.6	14.0	0.1	0.5	1.9	0.0	1.2	0.0	55.2	3.6	91.4	29.1	1 051	236	728
Monterey Park	1.0	0.3	65.8	0.5	0.0	0.7	16.2	4.1	0.0	36.7	7.2	68.0	18.6	300	138	137
Moorpark	3.3	0.0	0.8	0.0	0.0	0.4	0.0	0.0	0.0	14.5	2.3	97.8	6.2	214	92	91
Moreno Valley	0.2	0.0	1.5	0.0	0.0	0.0	1.5	0.0	0.0	59.5	14.4	82.1	28.0	198	65	124
Mountain View	29.8	20.4	22.6	11.1	1.9	0.9	1.9	0.0	0.2	111.4	6.7	92.9	56.6	801	280	433
Napa	0.7	0.1	14.5	6.5	0.0	1.2	2.7	1.0	0.5	48.6	14.9	93.4	23.5	362	129	186
National City	3.4	0.8	8.1	5.9	0.0	0.3	1.8	0.2	1.9	34.6	5.6	79.3	19.8	387	129	216
Newark	0.1	0.1	0.1	0.0	0.0	0.0	0.0	0.0	0.0	26.0	3.8	99.8	15.2	380	106	224
Newport Beach	45.1	6.4	4.7	0.5	0.0	0.0	0.8	0.3	0.0	86.6	11.9	89.4	50.6	726	280	319
Norwalk	6.9	0.6	7.0	0.0	0.0	0.9	2.1	6.2	0.0	45.1	12.7	77.2	20.4	204	63	131
Novato	3.2	3.5	1.4	0.8	0.2	0.1	0.3	0.0	0.0	25.2	4.3	99.9	12.8	267	112	128
Oakland	118.8	52.2	290.9	58.3	1.8	8.0	35.4	8.2	27.8	700.9	121.4	69.5	240.4	655	265	211
Oceanside	6.6	0.3	21.1	0.1	0.0	3.8	2.5	1.2	0.1	136.1	20.3	90.5	33.5	230	107	86
Ontario	21.1	4.5	6.4	0.0	0.0	1.4	4.5	1.1	0.1	148.0	18.8	85.8	68.2	471	198	204
Orange	115.9	1.2	42.7	1.5	0.0	0.6	9.0	3.6	0.4	83.6	10.8	81.5	44.8	374	129	202
Oxnard	18.9	3.5	20.1	7.2	0.0	0.7	7.2	0.4	3.3	110.3	12.6	78.8	42.3	280	115	113
Pacifica	0.2	0.0	10.7	0.0	0.0	0.0	0.0	0.0	3.7	22.2	5.7	98.4	8.4	210	97	92
Palmdale	483.0	10.5	226.5	0.0	0.0	0.7	1.5	0.0	0.7	63.4	13.2	82.7	38.6	362	202	111
Palm Springs	0.5	0.9	15.7	0.0	0.2	0.3	0.0	0.1	1.0	73.2	12.7	92.2	35.4	817	291	493
Palo Alto	60.3	53.4	74.3	4.3	5.0	0.5	2.0	0.1	3.7	114.3	5.1	82.3	41.6	713	130	494
Paradise	0.0	0.0	0.5	0.0	0.0	0.1	0.3	0.0	0.3	8.4	2.8	88.7	4.9	191	95	80
Paramount	0.6	0.1	3.1	0.0	0.0	0.0	1.6	0.1	0.0	31.8	9.7	53.5	15.8	311	128	156
Pasadena	60.8	1 325.5	165.2	52.4	11.3	3.3	4.3	10.0	9.5	224.6	59.7	54.5	94.9	708	213	374
Petaluma	1.4	3.0	1.1	0.4	0.0	0.3	0.4	0.0	1.1	40.5	5.4	94.5	22.4	462	161	189
Pico Rivera	289.2	0.7	6.7	0.0	0.0	0.4	1.4	0.0	0.0	38.4	9.5	87.9	17.2	286	117	147
Pittsburg	0.1	0.0	1.2	0.3	-0.4	0.4	0.7	1.0	7.9	48.5	10.5	93.6	21.3	418	279	125
Placentia	2.4	0.1	0.9	0.0	0.0	0.9	0.0	0.0	0.0	24.0	3.6	88.3	13.6	304	94	157
Pleasant Hill	0.0	0.2	0.2	0.0	0.0	0.2	0.0	2.0	3.4	19.4	3.6	95.9	10.3	322	71	196
Pleasanton	9.4	1.6	1.7	0.2	0.2	0.0	0.4	0.0	0.3	68.0	6.4	83.9	39.1	682	229	334
Pomona	15.7	5.3	10.9	1.6	0.8	1.9	4.8	15.1	-0.2	119.2	24.0	84.5	59.3	440	176	232
Porterville	0.0	3.9	6.7	4.4	0.1	1.0	0.6	2.0	0.0	24.3	5.2	87.6	9.3	270	52	173
Poway	1.4	0.3	0.3	0.1	0.0	0.2	0.0	0.1	0.7	56.2	3.8	82.5	23.3	493	330	128
Rancho Cucamonga	4.5	0.4	1.3	0.0	0.0	0.3	0.8	2.2	0.0	89.2	8.8	91.4	54.4	466	248	174
Rancho Palos Verdes	0.4	0.0	0.4	0.0	0.3	0.0	0.0	0.0	0.0	22.6	10.8	59.4	8.2	194	73	95
Redding	0.9	6.4	19.0	7.1	0.0	0.9	2.9	3.8	1.0	81.7	18.4	58.8	28.5	373	130	206
Redlands	10.2	2.9	0.7	0.0	0.0	0.0	0.0	1.9	1.6	44.3	5.2	94.6	21.8	327	143	155
Redondo Beach	608.1	162.7	3.1	0.1	0.0	0.0	0.8	0.0	0.2	63.4	7.1	84.1	32.0	513	180	286
Redwood City	7.8	7.9	37.1	1.1	0.4	1.5	7.2	0.5	1.5	80.5	11.1	87.8	47.0	660	197	285
Rialto	0.4	0.0	0.8	0.0	0.0	0.0	0.6	0.0	0.0	40.8	6.0	93.6	18.8	228	118	84
Richmond	8.0	7.7	9.2	0.9	0.5	0.0	4.1	0.0	18.4	132.2	31.6	67.8	66.2	727	365	301
Ridgecrest	41.7	0.0	2.2	0.0	0.0	2.1	0.0	1.6	0.0	15.2	2.5	99.5	8.5	278	151	120
Riverside	9.0	2.6	64.4	24.1	2.0	5.2	16.6	17.2	2.7	223.1	32.5	63.3	76.2	299	87	184
Rohnert Park	6.1	0.1	2.1	0.0	0.0	1.8	0.0	2.6	0.1	28.6	3.0	98.0	9.3	235	46	146
Rosemead	0.0	0.8	6.0	0.0	3.0	0.0	2.9	1.7	0.0	20.8	5.4	64.5	10.3	196	87	94
Roseville	10.1	1.4	1.4	0.0	0.0	0.0	1.1	0.0	0.0	100.2	8.3	81.3	41.1	656	118	372
Sacramento	673.2	166.9	5 368.0	1 930.8	66.6	877.2	90.7	22.4	31.7	403.1	36.0	90.6	182.8	486	160	287
Salinas	0.3	2.2	19.6	7.6	0.0	1.6	3.2	2.4	0.4	69.9	13.6	73.8	38.2	341	84	196
San Bernardino	38.5	8.3	81.7	34.7	0.7	7.8	18.2	17.2	8.0	182.5	31.8	62.9	71.9	392	130	231
San Bruno	34.9	0.2	0.7	0.0	0.0	0.7	0.0	1.1	0.0	35.0	4.1	100.0	12.8	317	69	203
San Buenaventura (Ventura)	0.1	0.0	0.8	0.0	0.0	0.0	0.0	0.0	0.0	79.6	12.1	65.4	34.6	356	94	229
San Carlos	16.4	0.4	3.7	0.9	0.0	0.0	0.0	0.0	0.0	33.6	2.3	82.9	12.1	437	164	236
San Clemente	3.9	0.3	0.1	0.0	0.0	0.0	0.0	0.0	0.0	38.7	5.4	85.7	13.5	297	143	105
San Diego	2 051.6	486.3	870.4	591.0	21.4	40.7	40.8	39.8	37.5	1 420.9	377.4	26.1	442.7	378	110	227
San Dimas	12.2	1.0	0.6	0.0	0.0	0.0	0.0	0.2	0.2	16.5	2.7	91.8	9.8	292	114	152

1. October 1, 1998 to September 30, 1999. 2. Includes program categories not shown separately. State totals include additional categories not allocated by city. 3. Based on population estimated as of July 1 of the year shown.

Table D. Cities — City Government Finances

City	City government finances, 1997 (cont'd) General expenditure												
	Per capita[1] (dollars)			Percent of total for —									
	Total (mil dol)	Total	Capital outlays	Public welfare	Highways	Parking facilities	Education	Health and hospitals	Police protection	Sewerage and sanitation	Parks and recreation	Housing and community development	Interest on debt
	124	125	126	127	128	129	130	131	132	133	134	135	136
CALIFORNIA—Cont'd													
Los Angeles	4 935.5	1 389	354	0.0	3.1	0.2	0.3	0.6	18.1	11.6	4.6	5.5	7.0
Los Gatos	17.0	591	84	0.0	11.0	0.0	0.0	0.0	35.3	3.2	7.5	8.5	0.0
Lynwood	36.4	578	62	0.0	12.4	0.0	0.0	0.2	13.1	9.0	9.3	13.9	2.9
Madera	22.6	635	108	0.0	14.0	0.3	0.0	2.1	18.3	19.0	4.2	12.3	4.0
Manhattan Beach	28.8	868	42	0.0	11.1	1.7	0.0	7.6	31.7	12.4	11.9	0.0	0.1
Manteca	26.8	589	91	0.0	16.4	0.0	0.0	0.6	19.9	22.3	9.3	4.7	3.4
Marina	7.7	325	30	0.0	14.5	0.0	0.0	0.0	40.6	0.0	7.1	9.4	1.8
Martinez	18.4	551	164	0.0	38.3	1.1	0.0	0.0	27.0	0.4	11.5	0.0	3.2
Maywood	6.6	233	15	0.0	16.7	0.0	0.0	0.0	55.8	0.0	4.6	8.7	3.8
Menlo Park	34.6	1 172	323	0.0	7.4	0.7	0.0	0.2	19.1	3.3	15.2	28.4	5.6
Merced	48.7	838	224	0.0	4.3	0.0	0.0	0.0	19.8	17.9	6.0	24.3	3.3
Milpitas	69.1	1 178	353	0.0	28.8	0.0	0.0	0.0	17.5	10.5	4.4	11.5	1.0
Mission Viejo	40.1	474	128	0.0	18.9	0.0	0.0	1.4	17.2	0.0	21.4	4.6	0.6
Modesto	114.7	642	142	0.0	12.3	0.2	0.0	3.9	24.9	15.3	12.7	2.9	4.0
Monrovia	29.6	795	76	0.0	7.1	0.0	0.0	1.8	25.9	3.2	8.8	10.5	12.6
Montclair	26.4	880	136	0.0	8.9	0.0	0.0	0.7	24.7	13.0	4.9	14.4	5.9
Montebello	43.2	717	128	0.0	2.8	0.0	0.0	0.0	27.9	4.0	14.1	15.7	10.2
Monterey	47.2	1 702	348	0.0	12.2	5.6	0.0	0.1	14.8	1.0	22.3	1.1	4.0
Monterey Park	37.8	610	54	0.0	9.3	0.0	0.0	0.8	25.6	9.1	6.9	8.3	5.7
Moorpark	13.5	469	131	0.0	31.0	0.0	0.0	0.7	21.2	0.8	9.2	8.7	6.7
Moreno Valley	67.1	476	63	0.0	17.1	0.0	0.0	1.2	34.7	0.0	8.8	3.7	2.2
Mountain View	114.3	1 619	609	0.0	6.0	0.1	0.0	0.0	9.9	17.8	25.4	0.9	4.4
Napa	43.7	672	29	0.0	12.0	0.5	0.0	1.8	18.8	5.6	8.2	16.8	2.7
National City	30.3	594	89	0.0	8.0	0.0	0.0	0.2	29.2	10.8	5.5	13.5	6.3
Newark	26.3	657	23	0.0	12.7	0.0	0.0	9.2	30.6	0.7	11.8	0.0	12.3
Newport Beach	88.4	1 269	243	0.0	17.8	0.0	0.0	1.1	24.7	6.8	7.5	1.2	1.0
Norwalk	46.6	465	35	0.0	7.9	1.0	0.0	0.0	18.0	0.4	7.0	33.4	5.9
Novato	32.6	677	108	0.0	7.1	0.0	0.0	0.8	22.4	0.0	9.9	5.6	22.2
Oakland	786.9	2 143	561	0.0	4.5	0.6	0.0	2.1	12.6	2.3	2.8	10.8	11.4
Oceanside	135.5	929	72	0.0	11.3	0.0	0.0	0.0	16.9	22.6	0.2	2.3	12.2
Ontario	175.4	1 211	379	0.0	7.3	0.0	0.0	2.7	17.8	10.4	4.3	32.5	5.2
Orange	81.9	683	88	0.0	13.6	0.0	0.0	2.0	24.4	9.0	4.6	8.3	9.2
Oxnard	123.8	820	144	0.0	10.6	0.0	0.0	0.0	17.5	29.5	5.5	13.9	6.4
Pacifica	28.8	720	222	0.0	12.6	0.0	0.0	0.2	15.2	33.4	2.5	2.2	1.9
Palmdale	70.8	664	150	0.0	18.6	0.0	0.0	0.6	12.7	0.0	12.0	33.3	6.9
Palm Springs	77.3	1 784	195	0.0	12.6	0.2	0.0	0.3	14.9	6.2	7.6	2.5	14.5
Palo Alto	114.2	1 958	274	0.0	10.7	0.5	0.0	1.5	11.3	30.5	8.7	3.1	1.6
Paradise	6.8	265	15	0.0	13.9	0.0	0.0	1.7	31.5	0.0	0.0	0.0	0.6
Paramount	30.8	606	130	0.0	11.3	0.0	0.0	0.4	20.9	0.0	8.1	19.3	22.5
Pasadena	225.2	1 679	250	0.0	6.0	1.0	0.0	6.5	13.3	3.4	13.3	12.4	8.7
Petaluma	45.8	945	170	0.0	22.1	0.0	0.0	3.1	16.4	12.9	9.1	9.7	3.7
Pico Rivera	32.2	536	46	0.0	5.0	0.0	0.0	0.0	16.4	0.0	13.1	26.7	13.4
Pittsburg	49.2	969	146	0.0	10.0	0.0	0.0	0.3	16.4	1.4	5.3	24.7	27.9
Placentia	26.5	591	98	0.0	14.3	0.0	0.0	0.0	23.7	6.1	11.3	7.5	1.2
Pleasant Hill	18.5	575	39	0.0	23.6	0.0	0.0	0.3	29.1	0.0	0.0	12.5	10.9
Pleasanton	78.1	1 363	295	0.0	12.1	0.0	0.0	0.3	13.5	10.0	13.8	3.4	19.0
Pomona	116.7	866	145	0.0	7.3	0.1	0.0	0.8	23.1	7.2	3.2	25.9	12.4
Porterville	24.6	712	97	0.0	7.8	0.0	0.0	0.3	16.2	23.8	6.6	2.2	12.3
Poway	72.8	1 540	499	0.0	7.0	0.0	0.0	0.8	5.7	5.7	5.0	42.4	20.2
Rancho Cucamonga	92.7	795	118	0.0	15.0	0.0	0.0	0.0	22.4	0.0	5.0	25.3	10.7
Rancho Palos Verdes	19.7	466	222	0.0	20.1	0.0	0.0	0.6	12.6	0.7	44.8	3.0	3.1
Redding	82.0	1 070	275	0.0	13.0	0.4	0.0	0.4	14.5	18.4	5.0	17.3	6.9
Redlands	46.1	692	107	0.0	11.1	0.0	0.0	3.3	18.2	19.6	3.5	4.4	12.7
Redondo Beach	63.2	1 013	23	0.0	5.7	0.0	0.0	5.4	21.3	3.2	8.3	9.8	2.5
Redwood City	79.0	1 111	344	0.0	14.6	0.5	0.0	0.4	15.5	11.9	4.6	9.4	4.5
Rialto	50.5	614	37	0.0	9.7	0.0	0.0	2.8	27.6	12.1	4.5	3.9	11.8
Richmond	136.6	1 500	333	0.0	14.6	0.0	0.0	0.0	20.8	8.3	1.9	10.6	5.0
Ridgecrest	11.9	389	71	0.0	8.9	0.0	0.0	4.6	23.9	4.7	8.7	15.1	12.5
Riverside	207.2	812	105	0.0	12.0	0.1	0.0	0.7	20.6	14.3	7.2	5.1	13.2
Rohnert Park	34.9	885	74	0.0	8.4	0.0	0.0	1.4	16.1	35.7	8.8	7.2	3.9
Rosemead	16.9	320	49	0.0	9.3	0.0	0.0	0.4	28.3	0.3	13.5	16.6	11.8
Roseville	87.8	1 401	339	0.0	11.0	0.0	0.0	0.2	15.9	16.8	10.1	4.3	13.9
Sacramento	337.7	897	107	0.0	10.0	2.5	0.0	0.4	23.0	12.1	7.8	6.9	8.3
Salinas	72.5	649	101	0.0	12.5	0.0	0.0	2.7	25.0	4.4	8.4	11.2	5.3
San Bernardino	200.6	1 093	209	0.0	7.6	0.2	0.0	0.9	16.8	12.3	3.0	21.5	17.6
San Bruno	31.4	779	23	0.0	7.4	0.0	0.0	0.0	18.0	8.7	9.5	0.0	0.3
San Buenaventura (Ventura)	80.7	830	160	0.0	18.2	0.1	0.0	1.2	18.7	8.6	9.2	3.7	6.9
San Carlos	35.5	1 284	479	0.0	3.9	0.0	0.0	0.0	12.4	10.1	6.3	30.6	3.8
San Clemente	39.0	858	186	0.0	24.8	0.0	0.0	1.4	16.3	8.4	12.6	7.5	2.1
San Diego	1 529.2	1 306	499	0.0	6.5	0.3	0.0	0.2	13.0	31.3	13.0	5.9	11.4
San Dimas	16.3	485	71	0.0	17.9	2.7	0.0	0.4	23.1	0.1	12.7	22.2	3.8

1. Based on population estimated as of July 1 of the year shown.

Table D. Cities — City Government Finances, City Government Employment, and Climate

City	City government finances, 1997 (cont'd) Debt outstanding Total (mil dol)	Per capita[1] (dollars)	Percent utility	City government employment, 1999	Climate[2] Average daily temperature (degrees Fahrenheit) Mean January	July	Limits January[3]	July[4]	Annual precipitation (inches)	Heating degree days	Cooling degree days
	137	138	139	140	141	142	143	144	145	146	147
CALIFORNIA—Cont'd											
Los Angeles	9 361.2	2 634	36.0	46 161	58.3	74.3	48.9	84.0	14.77	1 154	1 537
Los Gatos	0.0	0	0.0	NA	49.4	69.5	40.6	82.4	14.42	2 387	594
Lynwood	21.4	340	20.4	NA	58.3	74.3	48.9	84.0	14.77	1 154	1 537
Madera	14.7	411	0.0	NA	44.7	79.7	35.5	97.8	11.15	2 741	1 632
Manhattan Beach	4.8	145	95.9	NA	56.8	69.1	47.8	75.3	12.01	1 458	727
Manteca	17.7	388	0.0	NA	45.0	77.7	37.0	94.4	13.95	2 707	1 470
Marina	5.7	240	0.0	NA	51.7	60.0	43.3	68.1	18.72	3 125	55
Martinez	11.6	347	64.5	NA	49.9	63.2	42.0	71.0	22.20	2 574	199
Maywood	2.8	101	0.0	NA	58.3	74.3	48.9	84.0	14.77	1 154	1 537
Menlo Park	36.7	1 244	0.0	NA	47.5	66.4	37.7	78.4	14.96	2 911	297
Merced	27.3	469	1.9	NA	45.1	78.6	35.7	96.9	12.01	2 692	1 500
Milpitas	46.0	785	0.0	NA	49.4	69.5	40.6	82.4	14.42	2 387	594
Mission Viejo	3.5	41	0.0	110	54.5	71.6	41.4	83.7	11.81	1 784	973
Modesto	135.1	756	20.3	1 206	45.6	77.1	37.4	94.2	12.10	2 605	1 401
Monrovia	58.2	1 562	0.0	NA	55.8	75.0	43.6	89.0	19.37	1 453	1 394
Montclair	24.1	801	0.0	NA	54.3	74.6	40.7	90.4	16.62	1 713	1 273
Montebello	34.7	576	0.0	NA	58.3	74.3	48.9	84.0	14.77	1 154	1 537
Monterey	31.9	1 149	0.0	NA	51.7	60.0	43.3	68.1	18.72	3 125	55
Monterey Park	31.8	513	0.0	393	55.7	75.2	41.7	89.2	17.90	1 433	1 427
Moorpark	9.4	325	0.0	NA	54.6	67.8	41.2	80.8	17.39	2 039	569
Moreno Valley	19.5	138	0.0	298	53.6	76.9	41.2	93.7	10.00	1 796	1 500
Mountain View	130.0	1 841	0.0	NA	47.5	66.4	37.7	78.4	14.96	2 911	297
Napa	31.8	490	42.5	NA	47.1	67.9	37.2	82.1	25.12	2 844	456
National City	23.3	457	0.0	NA	57.4	71.0	48.9	76.2	9.90	1 256	984
Newark	52.7	1 320	0.0	NA	49.0	66.7	41.1	76.1	13.73	2 578	410
Newport Beach	24.8	356	62.3	NA	55.2	67.1	46.8	71.8	10.85	1 866	500
Norwalk	46.8	467	0.0	288	55.9	73.1	44.9	82.7	11.80	1 430	1 201
Novato	109.3	2 272	0.0	NA	46.4	67.0	36.8	82.5	24.60	3 050	335
Oakland	2 271.2	6 185	0.0	4 976	49.9	62.1	43.3	70.0	24.30	2 902	115
Oceanside	164.5	1 127	0.3	882	54.5	67.6	44.1	73.5	10.93	2 010	555
Ontario	216.8	1 496	0.0	1 049	54.3	74.6	40.7	90.4	16.62	1 713	1 273
Orange	140.3	1 170	2.4	696	57.4	72.6	45.6	82.6	12.27	1 238	1 175
Oxnard	102.7	680	7.3	1 182	55.3	66.1	44.2	74.4	14.38	1 992	416
Pacifica	11.4	286	0.0	NA	48.7	62.7	41.8	71.6	19.70	3 016	145
Palmdale	201.1	1 887	0.0	275	45.1	80.7	31.9	97.1	6.92	2 948	1 720
Palm Springs	165.0	3 807	0.0	NA	56.4	92.0	42.5	108.7	5.31	985	4 014
Palo Alto	32.5	557	0.0	NA	47.5	66.4	37.7	78.4	14.96	2 911	297
Paradise	1.1	44	0.0	NA	45.4	77.2	36.9	90.8	52.71	3 214	1 342
Paramount	105.0	2 067	0.4	NA	55.9	73.1	44.9	82.7	11.80	1 430	1 201
Pasadena	377.2	2 813	24.1	1 740	55.8	75.0	43.6	89.0	19.37	1 453	1 394
Petaluma	38.3	791	30.1	NA	46.4	67.0	36.8	82.5	24.60	3 050	335
Pico Rivera	70.0	1 167	28.2	NA	58.3	74.3	48.9	84.0	14.77	1 154	1 537
Pittsburg	225.6	4 441	0.0	NA	44.5	73.8	35.9	90.8	12.80	2 837	1 066
Placentia	32.8	732	0.0	NA	57.4	72.6	45.6	82.6	12.27	1 238	1 175
Pleasant Hill	43.6	1 355	0.0	NA	44.5	73.8	35.9	90.8	12.80	2 837	1 066
Pleasanton	231.7	4 046	0.0	NA	46.1	71.6	35.5	89.8	14.21	2 909	780
Pomona	202.4	1 502	3.6	759	54.3	74.6	40.7	90.4	16.62	1 713	1 273
Porterville	51.1	1 480	18.1	NA	46.4	81.8	36.4	98.3	11.03	2 374	1 998
Poway	182.3	3 857	4.0	NA	56.6	72.5	44.6	83.4	12.80	1 400	1 110
Rancho Cucamonga	239.6	2 055	0.0	432	56.0	78.6	44.5	94.8	15.63	1 478	1 922
Rancho Palos Verdes	10.2	240	0.0	NA	56.1	69.7	45.3	78.8	13.57	1 568	794
Redding	132.1	1 724	49.6	772	45.5	81.5	35.7	98.3	33.30	2 855	1 797
Redlands	114.4	1 716	22.8	469	52.8	78.4	39.6	95.8	12.80	1 875	1 673
Redondo Beach	31.2	500	0.0	NA	56.8	69.1	47.8	75.3	12.01	1 458	727
Redwood City	52.7	741	0.0	NA	48.7	68.7	38.9	83.4	19.74	2 563	486
Rialto	93.3	1 134	0.0	530	53.6	79.4	40.3	97.0	15.42	1 719	1 804
Richmond	124.9	1 372	0.0	981	49.9	63.2	42.0	71.0	22.20	2 574	199
Ridgecrest	23.9	780	0.0	NA	44.9	84.3	29.9	102.9	4.49	2 724	2 231
Riverside	639.3	2 507	38.4	1 842	53.9	77.9	40.5	94.4	9.58	1 678	1 651
Rohnert Park	32.2	814	0.0	197	47.4	67.6	37.0	83.8	30.30	2 883	489
Rosemead	35.9	681	0.0	NA	55.7	75.2	41.7	89.2	17.90	1 433	1 427
Roseville	172.3	2 750	3.2	NA	45.6	77.2	37.7	94.2	23.91	2 683	1 422
Sacramento	339.9	903	1.7	4 295	45.2	75.7	37.7	93.2	17.52	2 749	1 237
Salinas	70.3	629	0.0	657	50.5	62.5	40.0	71.1	12.44	2 964	181
San Bernardino	474.9	2 588	1.8	1 671	53.6	79.4	40.3	97.0	15.42	1 719	1 804
San Bruno	0.6	14	0.0	NA	48.7	62.7	41.8	71.6	19.70	3 016	145
San Buenaventura (Ventura)	80.6	829	21.1	665	55.3	66.1	44.2	74.4	14.38	1 992	416
San Carlos	32.1	1 160	0.0	NA	48.7	68.7	38.9	83.4	19.74	2 563	486
San Clemente	28.1	619	0.0	NA	53.7	67.2	41.5	75.8	12.19	2 157	493
San Diego	2 157.1	1 842	0.0	11 001	57.4	71.0	48.9	76.2	9.90	1 256	984
San Dimas	9.8	291	0.0	NA	54.3	74.6	40.7	90.4	16.62	1 713	1 273

1. Based on the population estimated as of July 1 of the year shown.   2. Represents normal values based on the 30-year period, 1961–1990.   3. Average daily minimum.   4. Average daily maximum.

Table D. Cities — Land Area and Population

STATE Place code	City	Land area, 1990[1] (sq km)	Population, 1999 Total persons	Rank	Per square kilometer	Total persons 1990	Percent change 1990–1999	Total persons 1980	Percent change 1980–1990	White	Black	Am. Indian, Eskimo, Aleut	Asian and Pacific Islander	Other race	His- panic[2]	Foreign born
		1	2	3	4	5	6	7	8	9	10	11	12	13	14	15
	CALIFORNIA—Cont'd															
06 67000	San Francisco	121.0	746 777	12	6 172	723 959	3.2	678 974	6.6	53.6	10.9	0.5	29.1	5.9	13.9	34.0
06 67042	San Gabriel	10.7	37 774	802	3 530	37 120	1.8	30 072	23.4	48.0	1.1	0.5	32.4	18.0	36.3	42.7
06 68000	San Jose	443.6	867 675	11	1 956	782 224	10.9	629 442	24.3	62.8	4.7	0.7	19.5	12.3	26.6	26.5
06 68028	San Juan Capistrano	36.9	31 753	956	861	26 183	21.3	18 959	38.1	89.4	0.4	0.8	2.2	7.3	21.8	19.0
06 68084	San Leandro	34.0	75 084	341	2 208	68 223	10.1	63 952	6.7	74.1	5.8	0.7	13.8	5.6	15.2	17.2
06 68154	San Luis Obispo	24.0	42 891	688	1 787	41 958	2.2	34 252	22.5	88.7	1.9	0.8	5.1	3.6	9.4	8.6
06 68196	San Marcos	60.1	51 756	560	861	38 974	32.8	17 479	123.0	84.7	1.5	0.8	2.9	10.1	27.5	21.2
06 68252	San Mateo	31.6	91 799	257	2 905	85 619	7.2	77 561	10.4	78.6	3.6	0.4	13.3	4.2	15.5	24.0
06 68294	San Pablo	6.7	26 963	1 118	4 024	25 158	7.2	19 750	27.4	49.4	21.3	1.3	17.2	10.8	26.8	26.4
06 68364	San Rafael	43.0	51 046	570	1 187	48 410	5.4	44 800	8.1	83.5	2.9	0.3	5.5	7.7	14.4	21.4
06 68378	San Ramon	29.5	45 926	642	1 557	35 303	30.1	22 356	57.9	87.1	2.0	0.3	9.0	1.5	5.8	10.1
06 69000	Santa Ana	70.2	309 290	54	4 406	293 827	5.3	203 713	44.2	68.0	2.6	0.5	9.7	19.1	65.2	50.9
06 69070	Santa Barbara	48.9	86 290	279	1 765	85 571	0.8	74 414	15.0	77.7	2.2	0.9	2.3	16.8	31.5	22.5
06 69084	Santa Clara	47.4	100 048	224	2 111	93 613	6.9	87 746	6.7	73.7	2.6	0.5	18.6	4.6	15.2	23.0
06 69088	Santa Clarita	104.8	133 887	151	1 278	120 050	11.5	NA	NA	87.3	1.5	0.6	4.2	6.5	13.4	11.5
06 69112	Santa Cruz	34.5	53 511	537	1 551	49 711	7.6	41 483	19.8	85.9	2.3	0.9	4.6	6.3	13.6	12.8
06 69196	Santa Maria	44.5	69 000	375	1 551	61 552	12.1	39 685	55.1	61.6	2.2	0.9	6.1	29.2	45.7	22.2
06 70000	Santa Monica	21.4	91 084	261	4 256	86 905	4.8	88 314	-1.6	82.8	4.5	0.4	6.4	5.9	14.0	25.3
06 70042	Santa Paula	11.9	26 852	1 122	2 256	25 062	7.1	20 552	21.9	59.3	0.3	0.8	1.0	38.5	58.9	24.8
06 70098	Santa Rosa	87.3	136 898	148	1 568	113 261	20.9	83 320	35.9	89.4	1.8	1.2	3.4	4.3	9.5	9.8
06 70224	Santee	41.1	57 915	486	1 409	52 902	9.5	47 080	12.4	91.1	1.7	0.8	3.0	3.4	10.7	5.5
06 70280	Saratoga	31.0	29 799	1 017	961	28 061	6.2	29 261	-4.1	83.7	0.4	0.2	15.0	0.7	3.3	16.0
06 70686	Seal Beach	30.4	26 327	1 144	866	25 098	4.9	25 975	-3.4	93.7	1.0	0.2	4.2	0.9	5.0	9.8
06 70742	Seaside	22.9	28 404	1 058	1 240	38 826	-26.8	36 567	6.2	52.7	23.5	1.0	13.5	9.4	17.4	17.9
06 72016	Simi Valley	85.6	114 247	189	1 335	100 218	14.0	77 500	29.3	88.2	1.5	0.6	5.5	4.2	12.7	11.9
06 73080	South Gate	19.0	88 956	269	4 682	86 284	3.1	66 784	29.2	41.6	1.7	0.4	1.6	54.6	83.1	49.3
06 73262	South San Francisco	23.2	59 059	468	2 546	54 312	8.7	49 393	10.0	61.5	4.0	0.7	24.6	9.2	27.1	30.2
06 73962	Stanton	8.1	33 178	915	4 096	30 491	8.8	23 723	28.5	73.1	2.3	0.5	12.1	12.0	33.5	30.9
06 75000	Stockton	136.2	245 020	68	1 799	210 943	16.2	149 779	40.8	57.5	9.6	1.0	22.8	9.1	25.0	22.6
06 77000	Sunnyvale	56.7	127 324	162	2 246	117 324	8.5	106 618	10.0	71.6	3.4	0.5	19.3	5.1	13.2	22.5
06 78120	Temecula	68.4	46 933	625	686	27 177	72.7	NA	NA	90.7	1.5	0.6	2.8	4.3	14.5	9.6
06 78148	Temple City	10.4	32 323	937	3 108	31 153	3.8	28 972	7.5	71.9	0.6	0.4	19.5	7.6	18.8	24.0
06 78582	Thousand Oaks	128.4	119 192	176	928	104 381	14.2	77 072	35.4	90.4	1.2	0.4	4.8	3.2	9.6	13.5
06 80000	Torrance	53.2	138 999	143	2 613	133 107	4.4	129 881	2.5	73.0	1.5	0.4	21.9	3.3	10.1	22.2
06 80238	Tracy	24.8	51 961	555	2 095	33 558	54.8	18 428	82.1	86.3	2.5	1.0	4.6	5.5	24.3	9.9
06 80644	Tulare	36.9	41 937	711	1 137	33 249	26.1	22 498	47.8	65.6	6.2	1.1	2.5	24.7	33.8	12.0
06 80812	Turlock	24.8	52 429	548	2 114	42 224	24.2	26 278	60.7	82.5	1.2	0.9	4.4	11.0	21.0	18.8
06 80854	Tustin	29.2	64 202	419	2 199	50 689	26.7	32 317	56.8	73.2	5.7	0.5	10.4	10.1	20.7	21.6
06 81204	Union City	48.6	66 012	401	1 358	53 762	22.8	39 406	36.4	43.9	8.6	0.6	33.4	13.5	25.1	32.4
06 81344	Upland	39.1	68 030	382	1 740	63 374	7.3	47 647	33.0	78.3	5.3	0.5	7.0	8.3	17.5	12.8
06 81554	Vacaville	58.6	86 588	277	1 478	71 476	21.1	43 367	64.8	78.8	8.9	1.0	3.8	7.5	15.9	7.8
06 81666	Vallejo	78.3	114 204	190	1 459	109 199	4.6	80 303	36.0	50.5	21.2	0.7	23.0	4.7	10.8	18.1
06 82590	Victorville	108.3	70 386	363	650	50 103	40.5	14 229	252.1	73.1	9.6	1.1	3.7	12.6	23.0	11.4
06 82954	Visalia	60.8	91 762	258	1 509	75 659	21.3	49 729	52.1	74.8	1.5	1.0	6.4	16.3	25.1	11.2
06 82996	Vista	46.5	82 098	298	1 766	71 861	14.2	35 834	100.5	80.7	4.5	0.8	4.0	10.1	24.8	16.8
06 83332	Walnut	23.0	31 531	963	1 371	29 105	8.3	12 478	133.3	48.0	6.6	0.4	37.5	7.5	23.5	34.9
06 83346	Walnut Creek	50.0	65 401	405	1 308	60 569	8.0	53 643	12.9	90.6	1.0	0.3	6.7	1.4	4.7	13.0
06 83668	Watsonville	15.3	36 783	824	2 404	31 099	18.3	23 543	32.1	55.1	0.7	1.0	5.6	37.6	60.9	35.1
06 84200	West Covina	42.0	100 106	223	2 383	96 226	4.0	80 291	19.8	59.8	8.5	0.5	17.2	14.0	34.6	25.3
06 84410	West Hollywood	4.9	36 294	833	7 407	36 118	0.5	35 703	1.2	90.2	3.4	0.4	3.1	2.9	8.7	34.0
06 84550	Westminster	26.0	86 044	281	3 309	78 293	9.9	71 133	10.1	69.6	1.1	0.6	22.5	6.1	19.1	29.1
06 84816	West Sacramento	54.3	30 272	1 001	557	28 898	4.8	10 875	165.7	71.3	2.4	2.0	9.1	15.3	24.4	16.5
06 85292	Whittier	32.5	80 036	310	2 463	77 671	3.0	69 717	11.4	73.4	1.3	0.6	3.3	21.4	39.0	16.0
06 86328	Woodland	23.8	44 131	675	1 854	40 230	9.7	30 235	33.1	77.5	1.3	1.3	3.1	16.9	26.2	10.6
06 86832	Yorba Linda	45.3	61 988	434	1 368	52 422	18.2	28 254	85.5	85.7	1.1	0.4	10.1	2.6	9.4	12.0
06 86972	Yuba City	17.9	35 316	854	1 973	27 385	29.0	18 731	46.2	76.1	2.6	1.7	7.7	11.9	17.9	13.0
06 87042	Yucaipa	68.7	37 327	813	543	32 819	13.7	23 345	40.6	92.6	0.5	0.9	1.0	5.0	11.0	7.4
08 00000	COLORADO	268 659.5	4 056 133	X	15	3 294 473	23.1	2 889 735	14.0	88.2	4.0	0.8	1.8	5.1	12.9	4.3
08 03455	Arvada	57.3	99 444	226	1 735	89 261	11.4	84 619	5.5	94.3	0.6	0.5	2.0	2.6	7.4	3.4
08 04000	Aurora	343.2	252 956	66	737	222 103	13.9	158 588	40.1	82.4	11.4	0.6	3.8	1.7	6.6	5.6
08 07850	Boulder	58.4	91 238	259	1 562	85 127	7.2	76 685	11.0	92.5	1.3	0.5	3.9	1.9	4.8	8.1
08 16000	Colorado Springs	474.5	350 199	48	738	280 430	24.9	215 150	30.3	85.9	7.0	0.8	2.4	3.8	9.1	4.7
08 20000	Denver	397.0	499 775	29	1 259	467 610	6.9	492 365	-5.0	72.1	12.8	1.2	2.4	11.5	23.0	7.4
08 24785	Englewood	16.9	31 844	954	1 884	29 396	8.3	30 021	-2.1	93.8	1.2	0.9	1.5	2.5	8.0	3.7
08 27425	Fort Collins	106.7	113 432	192	1 063	87 491	29.6	65 092	34.4	93.3	1.0	0.5	2.4	2.8	7.1	4.4
08 31660	Grand Junction	38.5	40 876	730	1 062	32 893	24.3	28 144	16.9	91.8	0.8	0.8	1.0	5.5	11.1	3.4
08 32155	Greeley	73.6	72 778	355	989	60 454	20.4	53 006	14.1	89.1	0.7	0.6	1.0	8.6	20.4	4.7
08 43000	Lakewood	105.7	137 916	144	1 305	126 475	9.0	112 860	12.1	93.2	1.0	0.7	1.9	3.2	9.1	4.1
08 45255	Littleton	31.9	41 297	719	1 295	33 711	22.5	28 655	17.6	96.1	0.9	0.6	1.4	1.1	5.2	3.1

1. Dry land or land partially or temporarily covered by water. 2. Hispanic persons may be of any race.

Table D. Cities — Population and Households

City	Under 5 years	5 to 17 years	18 to 24 years	25 to 34 years	35 to 44 years	45 to 54 years	55 to 64 years	65 to 74 years	75 years and over	Percent female	Number	Percent change, 1980–1990	Persons per household	Female family householder[1]	One-person
	16	17	18	19	20	21	22	23	24	25	26	27	28	29	30
CALIFORNIA—Cont'd															
San Francisco	4.9	11.3	9.8	22.2	18.0	10.7	8.6	8.0	6.6	49.9	305 584	1.9	2.29	9.9	39.3
San Gabriel	7.8	16.5	11.3	19.2	14.9	9.9	7.0	7.0	6.4	52.0	12 216	10.1	3.00	13.8	20.5
San Jose	8.3	18.4	11.2	21.6	16.0	10.6	6.7	4.3	2.8	49.2	250 218	19.2	3.08	11.9	18.4
San Juan Capistrano	7.4	19.5	8.5	14.8	18.0	11.3	7.6	7.1	5.8	50.4	9 015	28.8	2.89	8.8	19.1
San Leandro	5.8	13.1	8.2	18.1	15.1	10.1	10.5	11.5	7.6	52.4	29 128	6.5	2.33	10.4	30.8
San Luis Obispo	3.8	9.8	33.1	16.8	12.1	6.5	5.5	6.4	5.9	48.9	16 952	23.5	2.39	7.4	27.9
San Marcos	8.7	18.4	11.7	18.9	13.8	7.8	6.1	8.0	6.6	49.9	13 617	118.8	2.85	9.9	20.2
San Mateo	5.7	12.8	8.7	20.0	16.3	11.3	9.0	8.8	7.4	51.5	35 480	7.9	2.36	9.0	31.1
San Pablo	10.0	20.5	9.9	20.1	14.6	8.1	6.3	5.9	4.7	52.0	8 703	9.3	2.84	19.5	26.6
San Rafael	5.9	11.6	9.1	19.0	18.1	12.9	9.2	8.0	6.2	50.9	20 295	7.6	2.31	8.9	30.8
San Ramon	7.2	19.6	8.9	18.6	23.2	13.0	5.2	3.0	1.3	50.3	12 845	78.3	2.75	7.2	18.0
Santa Ana	10.0	20.4	16.7	22.7	12.7	7.2	4.9	3.4	2.1	46.8	71 611	11.6	4.00	11.8	16.6
Santa Barbara	6.2	12.0	12.5	21.4	16.1	8.4	7.2	7.6	8.6	51.0	34 348	5.5	2.41	9.5	32.4
Santa Clara	6.2	12.6	13.0	24.5	15.7	10.0	8.2	6.3	3.6	49.2	36 545	7.2	2.49	10.2	27.0
Santa Clarita	8.9	19.0	10.2	20.5	18.8	10.6	5.6	4.1	2.2	50.0	38 474	NA	2.84	8.2	18.1
Santa Cruz	5.4	12.6	21.2	18.7	18.3	8.3	5.3	5.4	4.9	50.5	18 121	9.0	2.50	10.1	27.2
Santa Maria	9.8	20.2	11.2	18.9	12.3	8.7	7.3	7.1	4.6	50.4	19 907	42.1	3.04	12.6	19.7
Santa Monica	4.4	9.2	7.3	22.7	20.5	11.1	8.5	8.1	8.2	52.8	44 860	2.1	1.88	7.9	49.6
Santa Paula	9.0	21.1	11.2	18.0	13.0	8.4	7.1	6.6	5.6	49.0	7 664	11.7	3.22	12.0	17.9
Santa Rosa	7.1	16.6	9.6	16.7	17.2	9.3	7.1	8.7	7.6	52.2	45 708	35.0	2.44	10.6	27.5
Santee	8.4	20.5	9.6	20.5	17.6	9.0	6.1	5.0	3.4	50.5	17 770	14.2	2.89	12.1	16.3
Saratoga	4.6	15.8	7.3	9.7	17.2	18.4	13.7	8.4	4.9	50.8	10 050	7.6	2.76	5.4	13.7
Seal Beach	3.3	8.5	6.6	13.2	11.4	10.7	9.4	15.0	21.8	56.0	13 370	0.1	1.86	5.0	46.9
Seaside	9.8	17.3	21.8	21.9	12.5	6.1	5.2	3.9	1.4	43.0	10 641	7.8	3.10	12.3	16.5
Simi Valley	8.0	19.9	10.8	19.0	18.2	12.3	6.5	3.4	1.8	49.7	31 998	46.4	3.12	9.5	12.6
South Gate	10.7	23.8	14.1	18.7	12.6	8.0	4.9	4.4	3.1	50.1	22 428	-1.7	3.84	15.4	15.1
South San Francisco	7.4	16.6	9.6	19.1	15.8	10.4	9.7	7.4	3.8	50.9	18 519	6.0	2.91	12.4	20.9
Stanton	9.3	16.4	12.6	22.5	15.0	8.0	6.5	4.6	5.1	49.8	10 306	20.7	2.92	13.0	23.8
Stockton	9.4	22.3	10.9	16.6	14.6	8.9	6.9	6.0	4.4	50.5	68 794	23.4	3.00	15.5	23.4
Sunnyvale	6.4	12.6	9.7	25.4	15.7	11.0	9.0	6.5	3.7	49.4	48 296	12.9	2.42	9.0	28.1
Temecula	11.2	21.5	9.1	20.9	17.4	7.4	6.3	4.6	1.7	49.1	9 130	NA	2.97	7.4	13.8
Temple City	6.8	16.7	10.1	15.4	15.7	12.1	8.5	7.7	7.0	52.4	11 055	3.5	2.77	12.3	21.9
Thousand Oaks	6.6	18.3	9.9	15.9	18.4	14.0	8.0	5.1	3.9	50.4	36 457	42.0	2.82	8.2	17.2
Torrance	6.0	14.4	8.7	19.7	16.6	12.2	10.4	7.6	4.4	50.9	52 615	6.0	2.51	9.3	25.3
Tracy	10.3	20.7	8.9	22.1	15.8	8.5	5.5	5.2	2.9	49.8	11 208	69.2	2.98	10.5	18.0
Tulare	9.9	24.8	8.7	17.4	13.2	8.6	6.8	6.0	4.5	52.0	10 859	40.7	3.04	16.6	18.5
Turlock	8.9	20.3	11.4	18.0	14.1	8.0	6.7	6.5	6.1	52.0	14 689	48.1	2.81	12.0	21.6
Tustin	8.8	14.9	14.8	24.2	14.3	9.2	6.3	4.5	3.1	49.6	18 332	43.6	2.66	11.6	23.6
Union City	8.3	21.5	10.4	17.9	18.3	11.1	5.7	4.1	2.7	50.5	15 701	31.5	3.39	12.1	12.8
Upland	7.5	19.2	10.8	17.1	15.8	12.5	7.9	5.7	3.5	51.2	23 077	31.1	2.73	11.2	20.9
Vacaville	8.0	18.4	10.4	23.1	17.9	9.7	5.8	4.4	2.4	44.8	22 627	55.5	2.82	10.4	17.3
Vallejo	8.7	19.2	10.4	18.0	16.6	9.5	6.8	6.8	4.1	50.1	37 383	28.3	2.85	13.1	21.7
Victorville	10.0	20.8	9.8	19.8	12.9	7.5	7.5	7.9	3.9	50.4	14 241	166.0	2.83	11.4	20.2
Visalia	9.4	22.1	9.5	16.6	15.3	9.5	6.6	6.0	4.9	51.7	26 111	43.4	2.84	12.3	21.2
Vista	9.6	17.4	12.5	21.2	13.5	7.2	6.2	6.8	5.5	50.1	25 371	84.5	2.78	10.4	20.0
Walnut	8.7	24.0	9.4	14.8	22.6	11.5	5.3	2.5	1.3	50.4	7 846	131.9	3.71	7.0	5.5
Walnut Creek	4.5	12.1	7.0	15.4	16.2	12.0	10.1	10.9	11.8	53.7	28 347	21.1	2.11	6.3	35.8
Watsonville	10.2	20.6	11.2	18.5	12.6	7.5	6.8	6.6	6.0	50.8	9 437	14.5	3.24	13.7	21.3
West Covina	7.8	19.7	11.3	18.4	15.8	10.3	8.1	5.9	2.7	50.9	30 096	13.8	3.18	13.5	14.7
West Hollywood	2.5	4.5	6.6	29.2	20.5	9.5	8.8	8.7	9.8	46.8	22 568	1.7	1.58	4.6	59.3
Westminster	7.4	17.8	12.0	20.0	13.7	11.1	8.9	5.7	3.4	49.3	25 077	4.5	3.10	10.8	17.5
West Sacramento	8.2	19.6	8.5	17.2	13.8	10.0	9.8	8.1	4.8	49.8	11 052	125.3	2.58	14.2	28.4
Whittier	8.4	17.5	10.4	18.9	14.5	8.3	8.0	8.2	5.7	51.1	27 637	2.7	2.72	12.0	22.8
Woodland	8.5	20.5	9.4	18.2	16.2	8.6	7.2	6.1	5.2	51.1	14 198	32.2	2.75	12.1	20.9
Yorba Linda	8.4	21.5	8.5	16.3	20.7	13.1	6.6	3.5	1.5	50.3	16 774	94.0	3.12	7.2	10.8
Yuba City	10.1	18.4	12.2	18.2	13.8	8.8	6.8	6.4	5.3	52.0	10 583	36.0	2.54	15.0	28.1
Yucaipa	6.8	17.8	6.3	14.1	13.5	9.2	8.3	10.8	13.1	53.0	13 319	30.6	2.44	8.3	28.6
COLORADO	7.7	18.5	10.2	18.6	17.2	10.2	7.6	5.9	4.1	50.5	1 282 489	20.7	2.51	9.7	26.6
Arvada	7.4	20.0	8.6	17.2	18.4	12.3	8.4	4.9	2.7	51.0	32 744	16.0	2.71	9.9	19.5
Aurora	8.6	18.8	9.5	22.0	18.5	9.8	6.1	4.3	2.3	51.4	89 132	52.2	2.47	11.8	28.1
Boulder	4.7	10.3	26.3	20.7	17.1	8.0	5.2	4.0	3.8	49.5	34 681	20.3	2.18	7.1	33.4
Colorado Springs	8.5	18.3	10.9	20.2	16.4	9.6	7.0	5.6	3.6	51.1	110 862	36.1	2.49	10.1	26.7
Denver	7.3	14.6	9.5	20.9	16.7	9.3	8.1	7.6	6.1	51.3	210 952	-0.5	2.17	11.5	40.4
Englewood	6.8	14.7	8.9	22.6	15.0	8.3	7.8	8.0	6.9	51.9	13 252	3.7	2.19	10.9	35.9
Fort Collins	6.9	15.5	21.9	19.8	16.0	7.3	4.9	4.3	3.6	50.4	33 689	43.2	2.44	7.6	26.2
Grand Junction	6.5	15.7	11.3	15.3	13.1	9.4	9.5	10.2	9.1	52.7	12 810	9.5	2.15	11.6	37.2
Greeley	7.5	17.1	18.5	16.5	14.2	8.4	6.6	5.8	5.2	51.5	22 647	16.7	2.50	10.1	27.0
Lakewood	6.9	15.3	9.9	19.3	16.3	12.5	9.1	6.5	4.2	51.5	51 657	25.7	2.38	10.7	27.5
Littleton	7.4	16.7	9.1	17.4	16.2	11.7	9.5	7.4	4.5	51.8	13 905	31.0	2.39	9.8	29.5

1. No spouse present.

Table D. Cities — Group Quarters, Crime, Education, and Income

City	Persons in group quarters, 1990 Total	Persons in mental hospitals	Persons in nursing homes	Persons identified as homeless[1]	Serious crimes known to police, 1998[2] Total Number	Total Rate[3]	Violent	Property	Education, 1990 School enrollment Public	Private	Attainment[4] (percent) High school graduate or more	Bachelor's degree or more	Money income, 1989 Per capita (dollars)[5]	Households Median Dollars	Percent change, 1979–1989 (constant 1989 dollars)
	31	32	33	34	35	36	37	38	39	40	41	42	43	44	45
CALIFORNIA—Cont'd															
San Francisco	24 279	220	3 609	5 610	46 139	6 224	990	5 234	139 171	39 838	78.0	35.0	19 695	33 414	25.7
San Gabriel	524	0	502	0	1 164	3 030	742	2 288	8 487	1 648	70.9	21.8	13 733	32 559	14.3
San Jose	11 130	0	2 334	1 068	30 382	3 532	599	2 933	203 672	28 285	77.2	25.3	16 905	46 206	20.5
San Juan Capistrano	152	0	152	0	702	2 340	190	2 150	5 919	1 354	83.6	28.1	23 344	46 250	17.1
San Leandro	280	0	240	18	4 456	6 213	764	5 449	12 810	2 195	79.4	16.9	17 563	35 681	9.8
San Luis Obispo	1 447	0	513	148	2 225	5 106	369	4 737	18 936	918	89.0	34.9	14 760	25 982	18.2
San Marcos	76	0	50	20	NA	NA	NA	NA	9 390	818	76.1	14.8	13 590	31 961	4.7
San Mateo	1 538	0	784	335	3 012	3 256	331	2 925	16 194	3 466	85.3	30.2	22 746	42 894	15.3
San Pablo	430	0	359	71	2 423	8 982	1 512	7 470	6 327	620	65.8	11.6	10 505	25 479	17.7
San Rafael	1 400	0	537	241	2 009	3 898	693	3 205	8 173	2 350	89.0	38.4	24 230	41 922	16.8
San Ramon	4	0	4	0	921	2 237	141	2 096	8 817	1 176	95.4	42.9	25 196	63 607	19.3
Santa Ana	6 394	70	841	435	11 525	3 687	554	3 133	79 865	6 429	49.7	10.6	10 019	35 162	14.3
Santa Barbara	2 279	0	1 542	380	3 385	3 829	572	3 257	17 954	2 887	79.1	33.1	18 934	33 667	30.1
Santa Clara	2 564	0	383	121	3 485	3 442	414	3 028	19 358	6 735	83.5	30.8	19 676	44 707	22.8
Santa Clarita	1 174	0	264	0	2 900	2 273	412	1 861	26 974	5 117	87.9	25.9	21 073	52 970	NA
Santa Cruz	3 677	0	50	287	2 875	5 488	762	4 726	16 742	1 429	85.7	35.2	15 538	31 857	35.5
Santa Maria	710	0	460	116	2 988	4 345	660	3 685	14 912	1 529	65.7	10.7	12 118	29 492	9.9
Santa Monica	2 445	0	1 028	589	5 380	5 966	718	5 248	14 591	4 434	87.5	43.4	29 134	35 997	29.4
Santa Paula	395	0	132	0	1 118	4 107	816	3 291	6 147	705	60.0	9.9	11 650	31 605	19.8
Santa Rosa	1 534	0	657	248	6 868	5 472	465	5 007	25 935	3 540	85.7	26.9	17 259	35 237	21.0
Santee	1 641	8	610	0	NA	NA	NA	NA	13 652	1 353	84.5	13.1	14 179	39 073	14.0
Saratoga	388	0	388	0	356	1 178	73	1 105	5 984	1 486	95.0	57.9	40 660	86 674	25.7
Seal Beach	261	0	184	0	518	1 941	244	1 697	3 834	656	86.3	31.6	25 695	32 834	27.9
Seaside	5 879	0	86	27	1 373	4 177	697	3 480	9 271	717	77.9	14.7	10 409	28 655	17.1
Simi Valley	265	11	104	16	1 788	1 625	145	1 480	25 343	4 393	86.7	21.1	18 630	53 967	21.3
South Gate	115	0	0	20	3 213	3 577	672	2 905	25 757	2 212	40.9	5.3	8 368	27 279	11.4
South San Francisco	465	0	155	66	1 924	3 270	294	2 976	11 736	2 353	77.5	19.7	15 857	42 920	15.1
Stanton	422	0	235	58	1 196	3 548	620	2 928	6 591	899	70.4	14.2	12 803	33 367	14.8
Stockton	4 648	0	1 590	572	17 526	7 311	1 129	6 182	58 278	7 947	66.6	15.0	11 331	26 876	8.4
Sunnyvale	513	0	485	0	3 000	2 337	150	2 187	23 928	4 766	87.1	37.1	22 309	46 403	20.1
Temecula	0	0	0	0	1 638	4 021	405	3 616	6 420	1 221	87.6	21.9	16 895	44 270	NA
Temple City	488	0	488	0	632	1 955	418	1 537	6 971	1 429	83.1	21.9	16 107	38 789	11.5
Thousand Oaks	1 574	14	547	0	1 997	1 713	122	1 591	24 336	6 223	89.8	35.0	23 682	56 856	26.0
Torrance	1 043	9	971	10	5 130	3 696	334	3 362	27 861	5 241	87.6	31.2	22 095	47 204	16.6
Tracy	175	0	161	14	2 046	4 435	321	4 114	8 862	659	77.1	12.1	14 298	40 256	44.4
Tulare	218	0	192	26	2 697	6 613	1 410	5 203	9 321	534	60.8	8.4	9 878	24 686	8.7
Turlock	976	0	824	69	2 936	5 837	515	5 322	10 953	972	69.6	17.1	11 936	27 293	10.7
Tustin	1 832	0	333	44	2 406	3 741	519	3 222	11 382	1 636	86.0	25.5	18 120	38 433	15.9
Union City	408	0	408	0	2 812	4 707	413	4 294	14 557	1 759	77.5	20.6	14 865	46 988	16.4
Upland	429	0	349	53	3 126	4 542	651	3 891	15 433	3 019	84.1	25.4	19 569	41 965	15.3
Vacaville	7 599	0	76	0	2 462	2 956	431	2 525	16 669	1 962	82.4	16.9	14 490	40 679	16.1
Vallejo	2 825	154	467	59	7 563	6 741	1 376	5 365	25 289	4 406	81.0	19.2	14 271	36 605	23.9
Victorville	427	0	256	38	3 348	4 865	484	4 381	9 958	978	75.0	10.5	11 474	28 698	12.8
Visalia	1 602	0	457	149	5 711	6 369	758	5 611	21 504	1 957	75.2	19.7	12 994	29 463	5.1
Vista	1 356	0	763	278	NA	NA	NA	NA	15 666	1 653	79.4	18.4	13 983	32 553	27.1
Walnut	14	0	0	0	607	1 931	280	1 651	9 155	1 704	87.5	35.1	18 749	64 333	27.0
Walnut Creek	762	0	619	0	3 014	4 649	202	4 447	10 716	2 438	94.4	46.9	26 354	45 529	9.5
Watsonville	749	0	316	144	2 175	6 484	1 404	5 080	7 716	673	53.6	10.7	10 422	27 980	15.6
West Covina	400	0	360	0	4 702	4 544	501	4 043	23 760	4 858	80.6	20.2	15 862	42 481	4.0
West Hollywood	402	19	244	119	2 228	5 989	1 038	4 951	3 814	1 232	84.9	37.4	24 386	29 314	27.3
Westminster	278	0	244	0	3 376	3 963	370	3 593	19 479	2 671	75.1	18.1	15 530	41 364	7.6
West Sacramento	356	0	137	15	2 042	6 678	1 789	4 889	6 138	780	66.3	8.9	11 510	23 287	9.1
Whittier	2 537	0	921	83	2 537	3 161	420	2 741	16 509	4 602	79.7	20.8	17 874	38 020	13.7
Woodland	780	23	629	34	1 625	3 738	683	3 055	9 247	1 360	76.2	17.0	13 854	31 671	3.3
Yorba Linda	84	0	6	0	885	1 473	133	1 340	13 803	2 913	92.9	37.0	25 791	67 892	32.9
Yuba City	554	0	219	57	2 027	6 046	537	5 509	6 953	585	74.3	16.4	11 815	23 491	8.3
Yucaipa	303	0	193	45	997	2 694	259	2 435	6 688	1 046	73.9	12.4	14 131	27 182	39.6
COLORADO	78 568	703	18 506	2 879	178 197	4 488	378	4 110	789 735	106 409	84.4	27.0	14 821	30 140	-0.4
Arvada	533	0	240	15	NA	NA	NA	NA	21 923	2 473	88.4	25.0	15 642	39 014	-5.9
Aurora	2 301	21	601	41	NA	NA	NA	NA	51 306	7 402	90.3	26.3	15 255	33 214	-8.7
Boulder	7 554	19	476	231	4 899	5 200	220	4 980	31 418	2 828	94.9	58.9	17 268	29 407	4.8
Colorado Springs	5 355	9	1 641	304	20 922	5 848	540	5 308	62 669	11 837	87.8	27.5	14 243	28 928	8.2
Denver	10 648	261	2 936	1 360	27 027	5 306	573	4 733	86 008	22 991	79.2	29.0	15 590	25 106	-3.4
Englewood	372	0	320	0	2 241	6 825	460	6 365	5 247	1 095	80.2	19.0	13 514	25 422	-2.9
Fort Collins	5 565	19	589	27	4 904	4 521	378	4 143	33 241	2 132	91.5	42.7	13 439	26 826	1.5
Grand Junction	1 435	0	509	62	2 983	8 286	572	7 714	6 862	593	77.1	17.9	11 723	19 042	-13.9
Greeley	3 759	7	604	130	3 997	5 567	419	5 148	19 582	1 372	76.6	25.1	11 461	23 462	-3.5
Lakewood	3 398	38	2 020	82	NA	NA	NA	NA	25 585	4 549	88.2	29.6	16 726	34 054	-12.6
Littleton	483	0	263	0	1 499	3 686	270	3 416	7 242	1 157	89.8	35.7	18 360	34 006	-4.7

1. Persons in emergency shelters and persons visible in street locations.   2. Data for serious crimes have not been adjusted for underreporting. This may affect comparability between geographic areas and over time.   3. Per 100,000 population estimated by the FBI.   4. Persons 25 years old and older.   5. Based on population enumerated as of April 1, 1990.

Table D. Cities — Income, Poverty, and Housing

City	Percent with $100,000 or more	Percent below poverty, 1989 — Persons Total	Percent change in rate, 1979–1989	Families Total	Housing units Total	Percent change, 1980–1990	Vacant units for sale or rent[1]	Occupied units Total	Percent	Median value[2] (dollars)	Owner cost as a percent of income — With a mortgage	Without a mortgage	Median rent[3] (dollars)	Rent as percent of income	Substandard units[4] (percent)
	46	47	48	49	50	51	52	53	54	55	56	57	58	59	60
CALIFORNIA—Cont'd															
San Francisco	7.4	12.7	-7.3	9.7	328 471	3.7	15 836	305 584	34.5	298 900	24.6	11.8	653	28.0	11.4
San Gabriel	4.9	15.2	36.9	12.6	12 736	10.3	431	12 216	48.5	251 600	25.7	11.5	672	30.1	20.2
San Jose	8.0	9.3	13.4	6.5	259 365	19.7	7 715	250 218	61.3	259 100	25.6	11.9	755	28.9	14.4
San Juan Capistrano	15.3	6.2	37.8	3.3	9 612	25.3	457	9 015	76.6	265 000	29.6	10.8	913	31.6	7.3
San Leandro	3.6	5.0	4.2	3.3	30 189	7.5	876	29 128	58.5	193 700	24.0	11.7	650	26.7	5.2
San Luis Obispo	3.8	27.4	17.6	6.7	17 877	23.2	631	16 952	44.1	241 100	26.2	10.8	599	35.1	6.8
San Marcos	3.1	10.9	26.7	7.9	14 476	122.4	738	13 617	62.3	172 200	27.6	10.9	658	29.0	10.8
San Mateo	9.5	6.2	6.9	3.9	36 928	7.8	1 201	35 480	53.2	349 800	25.9	11.1	788	28.2	6.8
San Pablo	1.0	19.0	3.3	17.1	9 417	12.7	569	8 703	47.1	117 900	24.3	11.8	564	33.0	16.8
San Rafael	12.9	8.1	5.2	4.4	21 139	10.1	720	20 295	54.5	342 700	24.0	12.0	730	31.9	6.4
San Ramon	16.9	1.7	6.3	1.1	13 531	75.7	606	12 845	69.2	316 500	28.1	12.1	903	25.5	1.7
Santa Ana	3.0	18.1	29.3	12.5	74 973	11.6	2 878	71 611	48.3	185 400	26.0	11.4	736	31.2	37.0
Santa Barbara	7.6	12.7	15.5	7.8	36 226	6.8	1 296	34 348	42.2	346 900	27.9	11.1	715	31.9	10.4
Santa Clara	6.6	6.2	6.9	3.7	37 873	8.6	1 112	36 545	47.1	270 400	22.5	11.3	779	25.8	8.4
Santa Clarita	10.8	3.7	NA	2.2	41 133	NA	2 276	38 474	75.7	233 300	27.4	13.3	832	27.8	4.5
Santa Cruz	4.9	15.7	-4.8	7.2	19 364	8.4	713	18 121	47.4	263 200	26.2	11.7	707	35.1	7.9
Santa Maria	2.7	16.8	43.6	12.8	21 144	40.8	874	19 907	53.8	141 900	23.9	11.3	548	29.9	15.4
Santa Monica	12.2	9.4	-5.1	5.7	47 753	2.9	1 531	44 860	27.5	500 001	25.5	11.3	532	22.2	4.9
Santa Paula	2.9	12.2	-9.6	10.0	8 062	12.9	290	7 664	58.6	203 600	24.8	11.1	617	30.8	22.5
Santa Rosa	4.7	8.3	-10.8	5.5	47 726	35.6	1 541	45 708	57.9	193 800	24.9	11.3	638	30.5	4.5
Santee	2.1	5.4	-20.6	3.9	18 275	13.0	411	17 770	70.4	144 900	25.6	11.6	667	26.8	4.4
Saratoga	42.0	1.4	-36.4	0.5	10 315	8.1	177	10 050	89.4	500 001	23.5	10.6	1 001	25.4	1.2
Seal Beach	9.5	4.8	-20.0	1.5	14 407	3.4	510	13 370	75.9	353 600	22.6	11.9	821	24.5	1.3
Seaside	1.0	12.2	-17.0	9.9	11 238	8.9	358	10 641	38.0	150 100	24.7	12.3	630	29.7	14.8
Simi Valley	8.9	3.6	-26.5	2.3	33 111	46.2	1 008	31 998	76.4	233 000	26.2	11.2	896	30.7	4.8
South Gate	1.5	17.4	22.5	15.2	22 946	-2.7	420	22 428	48.5	162 500	28.2	11.6	549	30.0	40.0
South San Francisco	4.4	5.9	-4.8	4.7	19 081	5.9	422	18 519	61.4	271 900	24.8	11.7	721	26.7	12.6
Stanton	2.0	13.6	12.4	10.1	10 755	19.9	403	10 306	50.0	171 100	25.8	11.3	718	30.6	15.8
Stockton	3.1	21.4	28.9	16.9	72 525	18.3	2 664	68 794	48.5	107 200	22.2	11.8	476	29.5	16.8
Sunnyvale	9.3	4.7	-2.1	3.3	50 789	15.4	2 231	48 296	48.9	332 700	22.6	10.9	784	25.3	8.0
Temecula	7.2	4.9	NA	3.6	10 659	NA	1 357	9 130	63.6	192 300	29.3	12.4	657	27.6	4.7
Temple City	5.1	5.6	16.7	3.8	11 548	4.6	390	11 055	63.7	255 900	23.1	11.6	716	29.0	10.0
Thousand Oaks	16.5	4.2	-4.5	2.7	37 765	37.4	1 066	36 457	73.7	297 000	26.9	12.3	899	29.6	3.5
Torrance	10.6	5.1	8.5	3.6	54 927	7.7	1 846	52 615	56.3	340 000	23.1	11.2	795	26.9	6.3
Tracy	2.9	7.4	-49.7	5.8	12 174	70.2	872	11 208	60.0	165 400	27.2	11.7	598	26.8	8.1
Tulare	1.9	21.4	22.3	18.3	11 316	38.1	378	10 859	57.0	70 300	23.5	12.3	427	29.7	12.8
Turlock	2.4	13.2	2.3	10.2	15 400	41.1	614	14 689	52.5	123 300	23.2	11.9	460	27.7	10.5
Tustin	6.8	6.8	3.0	4.3	19 300	46.5	858	18 332	40.9	254 500	24.6	11.4	746	28.2	10.9
Union City	5.3	6.5	-8.5	5.1	16 259	31.8	502	15 701	67.4	229 300	25.6	11.9	768	27.6	15.0
Upland	9.9	7.8	14.7	5.8	24 496	31.7	1 203	23 077	60.3	226 500	24.8	11.4	615	28.4	5.7
Vacaville	3.2	6.1	-28.2	4.9	23 660	54.1	890	22 627	64.5	147 900	25.6	12.5	629	27.3	5.0
Vallejo	2.7	8.5	-20.6	6.9	39 902	31.6	2 031	37 383	61.9	140 600	25.5	12.1	578	28.0	8.0
Victorville	1.9	14.8	26.5	11.9	15 627	155.8	1 143	14 241	60.8	102 800	26.2	12.1	508	29.8	9.9
Visalia	3.6	17.6	63.0	14.1	27 154	39.3	842	26 111	60.5	90 300	22.3	12.1	461	31.0	8.5
Vista	3.7	11.7	6.4	8.0	27 418	83.3	1 815	25 371	53.9	183 400	28.2	11.9	631	32.1	10.0
Walnut	14.8	4.1	0.0	3.2	8 091	135.0	219	7 846	90.9	323 000	29.5	12.3	979	29.0	9.8
Walnut Creek	11.7	3.8	-5.0	2.2	29 968	22.8	1 316	28 347	67.7	291 500	23.9	11.9	720	27.3	1.7
Watsonville	1.9	15.3	15.9	11.0	9 909	12.9	270	9 437	47.8	185 000	27.2	11.9	625	30.3	26.6
West Covina	6.7	7.7	45.3	5.7	31 112	13.7	918	30 096	66.7	205 000	25.2	11.5	733	29.4	12.9
West Hollywood	6.4	11.4	-14.9	11.0	23 821	-2.1	1 078	22 568	22.3	351 700	31.7	12.3	608	28.3	5.2
Westminster	6.5	11.4	58.3	7.6	25 852	5.2	693	25 077	62.8	226 100	22.7	11.4	736	31.1	14.2
West Sacramento	1.5	18.5	103.3	15.7	11 652	125.6	426	11 052	55.7	87 600	21.2	11.6	426	30.9	10.3
Whittier	8.1	7.8	5.4	5.5	28 758	3.5	929	27 637	57.7	213 600	24.0	11.1	638	28.4	9.7
Woodland	3.0	9.6	15.7	8.1	14 818	31.7	510	14 198	57.2	131 300	21.8	11.4	484	26.1	8.7
Yorba Linda	22.9	1.9	-36.7	1.3	17 341	91.4	503	16 774	84.3	326 200	27.5	12.0	918	27.4	2.2
Yuba City	2.4	18.6	52.5	15.5	11 068	30.5	407	10 583	40.7	86 300	21.9	11.9	391	27.3	8.2
Yucaipa	2.9	7.6	-15.6	5.8	14 276	33.2	723	13 319	76.8	123 900	23.9	13.1	514	30.5	3.9
COLORADO	3.8	11.7	15.6	8.6	1 477 349	23.7	98 422	1 282 489	62.2	82 700	22.5	12.7	418	26.1	3.0
Arvada	2.9	6.3	61.5	4.9	34 541	17.6	1 462	32 744	72.8	89 800	22.0	12.0	456	25.9	1.7
Aurora	2.3	7.4	37.0	6.1	99 890	59.0	9 494	89 132	58.7	80 200	22.7	11.8	455	24.7	2.8
Boulder	5.6	19.0	16.6	7.5	36 270	19.8	1 306	34 681	46.2	122 700	21.0	11.6	521	31.9	2.2
Colorado Springs	3.0	10.9	5.8	8.6	124 442	41.0	11 451	110 862	54.6	81 900	22.6	12.3	413	25.7	2.9
Denver	3.9	17.1	24.8	13.1	239 636	5.2	22 955	210 952	49.2	79 000	22.4	13.2	386	26.2	4.2
Englewood	1.0	10.9	39.7	7.7	14 908	11.6	1 412	13 252	51.8	72 800	22.6	12.6	424	25.8	2.7
Fort Collins	2.9	17.0	11.1	8.0	35 357	39.3	1 284	33 689	52.7	85 000	21.7	13.0	422	30.8	2.1
Grand Junction	1.8	21.6	63.6	16.8	13 698	7.8	567	12 810	50.4	54 100	21.0	12.2	313	27.1	2.1
Greeley	2.3	19.5	10.8	12.2	23 991	15.7	1 026	22 647	53.9	70 400	21.8	12.4	354	27.4	3.6
Lakewood	3.5	7.6	52.0	5.2	55 678	28.2	3 204	51 657	60.5	91 400	21.3	11.9	465	24.5	1.8
Littleton	5.1	7.3	15.9	5.1	14 778	31.1	777	13 905	60.6	97 700	22.3	11.8	429	27.0	1.5

1. Includes units rented or sold but not occupied.   2. Specified owner-occupied units.   3. Specified renter-occupied units.   4. Overcrowded or lacking complete plumbing facilities.

Table D. Cities — **Labor Force, Employment, Disability, and Construction**

City	Civilian labor force, 1999				Civilian employment, 1990[2]			Disability 1990	Value of residential construction authorized by building permits, 1999		
	Total	Percent change, 1998–1999	Unemployment Total	Rate[1]	Total	Percent Professional, managerial, and technical	Precision production, craft, and repair	Work disabled persons[3] (percent)	New construction ($1,000)	Number of housing units	Percent single family
	61	62	63	64	65	66	67	68	69	70	71
CALIFORNIA—Cont'd											
San Francisco	422 030	1.3	12 793	3.0	386 530	38.5	6.3	8.0	342 967	2 694	5.4
San Gabriel	18 918	0.5	923	4.9	17 248	28.1	9.5	6.0	2 995	15	100.0
San Jose	489 395	0.0	17 503	3.6	407 862	34.4	12.5	6.0	381 108	3 479	45.9
San Juan Capistrano	15 054	2.6	302	2.0	13 308	35.5	10.0	4.6	20 367	53	100.0
San Leandro	38 333	1.8	1 155	3.0	33 893	29.0	12.2	7.8	89 275	377	100.0
San Luis Obispo	23 992	1.7	853	3.6	21 067	34.9	7.1	5.8	17 787	115	70.4
San Marcos	21 025	3.0	623	3.0	17 751	25.3	14.9	6.9	152 835	847	67.9
San Mateo	54 399	0.6	1 081	2.0	48 091	35.3	9.6	4.9	6 125	33	100.0
San Pablo	12 586	1.1	793	6.3	10 103	18.3	14.3	12.7	1 514	12	100.0
San Rafael	28 891	0.0	786	2.7	26 575	41.3	8.3	6.9	26 699	132	85.6
San Ramon	25 003	2.1	416	1.7	21 064	45.1	7.2	3.8	31 780	199	52.3
Santa Ana	163 925	2.3	7 827	4.8	140 823	16.8	13.9	5.2	14 204	62	100.0
Santa Barbara	51 439	2.0	1 682	3.3	46 765	34.8	10.1	6.9	11 784	59	71.2
Santa Clara	64 995	0.0	1 855	2.9	54 573	41.2	10.7	5.5	35 434	526	7.8
Santa Clarita	65 580	0.8	1 815	2.8	61 119	37.5	11.9	5.1	222 351	1 241	63.8
Santa Cruz	31 374	-0.4	1 723	5.5	26 485	38.8	9.0	8.3	8 764	49	87.8
Santa Maria	30 255	1.7	1 693	5.6	26 844	19.8	11.8	8.9	38 264	246	83.3
Santa Monica	54 634	0.6	2 078	3.8	50 375	50.4	5.3	5.9	38 788	282	14.9
Santa Paula	13 559	1.7	1 044	7.7	11 184	20.8	13.0	7.5	2 913	24	41.7
Santa Rosa	71 894	1.4	1 872	2.6	55 373	32.3	11.0	8.1	145 468	1 255	75.1
Santee	30 840	3.0	803	2.6	26 135	27.9	15.7	7.2	26 313	137	100.0
Saratoga	17 014	0.1	311	1.8	14 437	62.8	4.2	4.0	43 612	75	100.0
Seal Beach	11 981	2.6	194	1.6	10 634	47.9	6.4	5.3	1 396	5	100.0
Seaside	16 668	3.9	1 338	8.0	12 973	21.5	9.7	8.3	509	5	100.0
Simi Valley	65 642	2.3	2 717	4.1	56 232	34.6	13.2	6.4	236 968	1 145	82.1
South Gate	39 509	0.0	3 423	8.7	34 588	11.8	17.0	5.7	2 181	19	100.0
South San Francisco	31 921	0.5	790	2.5	28 079	24.7	12.0	5.9	37 323	166	100.0
Stanton	17 666	2.3	835	4.7	15 184	24.6	14.7	6.6	8 144	69	100.0
Stockton	104 179	0.7	10 748	10.3	79 162	27.2	9.7	10.5	170 836	1 354	100.0
Sunnyvale	82 350	0.0	2 121	2.6	69 343	48.4	9.1	5.0	29 001	189	84.1
Temecula	18 119	5.2	620	3.4	13 142	32.3	14.2	5.4	177 360	1 474	86.6
Temple City	16 507	0.7	600	3.6	15 247	32.7	11.2	6.1	5 281	28	82.1
Thousand Oaks	66 852	2.3	2 656	4.0	57 368	42.4	7.9	5.2	208 780	904	96.3
Torrance	78 599	0.7	2 458	3.1	72 981	42.3	10.2	5.2	28 085	110	100.0
Tracy	20 178	1.4	1 470	7.3	15 851	23.5	16.1	8.6	199 132	1 368	99.9
Tulare	17 321	1.5	2 451	14.2	12 704	20.0	12.0	10.8	18 941	277	78.3
Turlock	23 632	0.6	2 191	9.3	17 828	26.0	13.6	8.4	61 578	525	97.0
Tustin	31 069	2.5	837	2.7	27 274	33.9	10.4	5.7	88 827	352	98.6
Union City	31 229	1.9	792	2.5	27 747	26.6	13.2	6.6	57 107	254	100.0
Upland	40 718	4.4	1 317	3.2	32 430	35.5	9.9	6.1	43 618	257	100.0
Vacaville	38 581	4.7	1 431	3.7	30 985	27.0	16.1	7.2	78 327	600	63.8
Vallejo	59 906	4.4	3 045	5.1	47 425	28.3	12.9	9.2	84 800	438	100.0
Victorville	19 284	3.8	1 276	6.6	14 822	23.3	17.1	10.7	43 249	397	79.3
Visalia	41 624	1.3	4 472	10.7	31 741	32.3	9.0	8.3	82 632	649	96.5
Vista	38 200	2.9	1 347	3.5	32 065	28.5	13.7	7.2	27 240	118	100.0
Walnut	16 082	0.7	544	3.4	14 893	43.2	8.1	4.1	1 380	4	100.0
Walnut Creek	36 989	2.0	730	2.0	31 063	49.5	6.0	4.9	16 266	65	96.9
Watsonville	16 933	-1.7	2 235	13.2	13 129	18.1	10.5	6.9	13 233	136	33.8
West Covina	51 828	0.6	2 034	3.9	47 727	29.1	11.5	5.8	16 345	324	1.9
West Hollywood	24 368	0.4	1 363	5.6	22 050	49.6	4.3	6.9	3 385	25	28.0
Westminster	45 598	2.5	1 445	3.2	39 832	30.2	13.1	7.1	20 529	102	100.0
West Sacramento	15 863	3.0	915	5.8	11 486	21.3	13.1	13.2	925	9	77.8
Whittier	40 264	0.6	1 543	3.8	37 114	31.2	11.8	6.2	1 983	11	100.0
Woodland	25 717	3.2	1 247	4.8	18 803	26.9	12.4	7.9	27 368	438	29.5
Yorba Linda	32 747	2.6	486	1.5	29 104	45.1	7.4	4.0	16 051	59	100.0
Yuba City	15 299	0.8	2 298	15.0	11 004	27.0	13.3	12.1	6 467	44	100.0
Yucaipa	16 083	4.4	525	3.3	12 806	26.8	15.7	10.3	31 466	243	100.0
COLORADO	2 264 105	0.8	65 958	2.9	1 633 281	34.3	9.8	7.8	6 035 973	49 313	77.9
Arvada	62 208	0.2	1 566	2.5	48 488	34.3	10.6	7.0	80 848	707	74.1
Aurora	160 927	1.3	3 794	2.4	119 026	33.3	8.3	6.7	251 946	2 770	58.9
Boulder	67 431	1.8	1 930	2.9	47 707	51.0	4.2	4.4	21 800	159	84.3
Colorado Springs	192 189	1.5	6 407	3.3	128 155	36.1	9.3	8.9	NA	NA	NA
Denver	280 667	-1.2	8 620	3.1	233 602	35.4	7.2	9.2	299 673	3 379	50.5
Englewood	20 850	1.3	516	2.5	15 419	27.9	12.8	9.6	2 077	18	100.0
Fort Collins	67 852	-0.2	2 231	3.3	45 199	41.1	7.9	4.7	183 091	1 929	60.0
Grand Junction	17 619	0.1	809	4.6	12 216	29.6	9.8	12.3	NA	NA	NA
Greeley	39 975	1.8	1 437	3.6	29 282	29.0	10.8	7.3	85 818	839	85.5
Lakewood	90 733	0.2	2 113	2.3	70 987	37.3	9.0	7.9	47 274	525	30.3
Littleton	23 966	1.4	551	2.3	17 718	40.5	8.0	7.6	68 764	472	70.3

1. Percent of civilian labor force.   2. Persons 16 years and older.   3. Persons 16 to 64 years old.

Table D. Cities — Wholesale Trade, Retail Trade, and Real Estate

City	Wholesale Trade, 1997				Retail Trade[1], 1997				Real Estate and Rental and Leasing, 1997			
	Number of Establishments	Number of Employees	Sales (mil dol)	Annual Payroll (mil dol)	Number of Establishments	Number of Employees	Sales (mil dol)	Annual Payroll (mil dol)	Number of Establishments	Number of Employees	Receipts (mil dol)	Annual Payroll (mil dol)
	72	73	74	75	76	77	78	79	80	81	82	83
CALIFORNIA—Cont'd												
San Francisco	1 900	17 677	12 219.1	779.8	3 841	39 693	6 795.0	830.6	1 627	14 492	2 721.2	472.9
San Gabriel	156	599	195.5	12.8	173	1 475	306.7	26.7	65	223	29.0	4.5
San Jose	1 423	25 578	27 076.8	1 398.6	2 169	34 278	6 905.0	700.5	794	6 088	1 140.3	179.0
San Juan Capistrano	66	391	212.3	14.1	122	1 427	326.9	32.4	49	212	31.1	8.0
San Leandro	324	4 402	2 533.3	176.1	351	5 952	1 116.7	113.9	120	1 838	242.1	50.5
San Luis Obispo	69	554	161.6	14.4	319	3 845	606.1	62.8	106	501	53.5	7.8
San Marcos	155	1 843	495.5	63.8	229	2 275	525.1	48.7	40	232	25.6	4.4
San Mateo	156	2 138	1 840.2	179.4	400	6 247	1 082.8	120.7	161	1 892	252.5	54.5
San Pablo	13	41	11.5	0.8	139	1 552	315.2	31.7	26	132	22.8	2.7
San Rafael	221	1 775	754.6	66.1	411	4 637	1 075.2	115.7	152	1 458	203.0	41.9
San Ramon	162	2 759	7 459.8	175.5	143	1 962	380.0	38.7	68	548	146.3	24.8
Santa Ana	571	8 899	4 113.4	357.2	876	11 543	2 302.6	232.1	254	2 951	451.6	89.3
Santa Barbara	157	1 145	379.8	35.2	655	7 589	1 220.4	143.3	257	1 397	551.9	45.4
Santa Clara	593	13 779	20 791.0	892.0	414	6 703	1 758.7	187.6	146	973	307.9	30.1
Santa Clarita	75	576	392.6	37.4	297	3 720	736.6	66.9	111	506	74.4	10.9
Santa Cruz	92	888	170.1	23.7	282	3 626	578.9	62.3	80	327	41.9	5.5
Santa Maria	117	1 350	451.7	43.7	353	4 928	810.5	89.5	69	383	32.6	6.3
Santa Monica	234	2 608	3 792.3	124.3	726	8 018	2 200.3	190.0	334	1 932	338.8	70.0
Santa Paula	32	765	265.1	19.4	72	515	124.4	7.4	15	171	10.9	2.0
Santa Rosa	182	2 088	716.2	71.3	758	10 653	2 118.8	220.5	235	959	133.4	20.5
Santee	63	418	106.6	11.2	125	2 234	401.5	40.1	45	173	22.6	3.1
Saratoga	48	D	D	D	64	569	102.7	12.1	55	264	49.4	8.7
Seal Beach	26	159	161.8	9.6	75	749	123.0	12.9	20	126	41.6	4.8
Seaside	15	123	23.6	2.9	83	1 204	353.3	32.5	12	58	7.4	1.0
Simi Valley	146	2 050	843.9	76.9	279	3 806	852.4	69.0	68	341	36.1	6.9
South Gate	86	1 417	1 327.5	41.1	154	1 738	361.1	32.0	27	129	83.2	4.4
South San Francisco	472	7 370	4 778.9	302.0	187	2 558	585.9	56.6	72	1 328	346.3	44.3
Stanton	39	732	127.9	18.7	96	1 136	238.9	21.6	25	101	18.2	2.0
Stockton	262	4 027	2 949.0	125.9	742	9 842	1 771.4	178.2	208	1 223	125.6	25.2
Sunnyvale	386	8 677	7 425.4	574.6	373	6 319	1 659.8	150.3	122	780	131.0	20.6
Temecula	77	973	579.6	37.4	211	2 817	687.7	63.0	51	287	29.9	4.8
Temple City	75	311	90.7	5.9	89	1 033	142.4	14.9	14	58	6.4	0.7
Thousand Oaks	202	1 997	6 480.3	96.3	504	7 185	1 706.4	153.1	145	731	114.8	16.5
Torrance	618	7 802	14 366.0	405.3	794	12 773	3 023.3	265.0	303	1 890	293.5	41.4
Tracy	30	299	219.5	9.7	196	2 464	401.0	38.4	34	115	15.8	1.9
Tulare	40	478	135.9	12.4	154	2 095	315.5	35.4	24	73	10.0	1.0
Turlock	53	409	166.4	12.5	166	1 898	352.6	34.6	33	128	21.5	2.3
Tustin	232	3 233	2 236.2	139.6	235	4 916	1 691.7	138.3	126	652	109.6	17.7
Union City	179	4 640	2 722.5	186.2	88	2 227	510.9	49.6	24	84	15.5	2.1
Upland	108	579	191.3	16.0	224	2 684	528.4	54.3	89	513	44.9	9.3
Vacaville	35	392	110.2	9.9	302	3 830	701.5	67.0	80	312	43.2	6.2
Vallejo	32	387	220.4	12.8	279	4 187	791.0	83.2	68	317	29.8	4.6
Victorville	29	227	63.6	8.3	304	4 766	839.9	81.0	44	221	24.2	5.1
Visalia	137	1 344	1 050.8	44.4	436	6 124	1 042.9	100.7	97	406	52.8	7.9
Vista	110	1 592	426.5	48.7	233	3 212	665.6	61.5	105	590	63.3	9.0
Walnut	247	1 212	1 278.7	33.7	60	553	91.4	9.9	18	106	15.1	3.2
Walnut Creek	121	1 177	2 402.7	64.5	339	5 859	1 240.9	132.8	230	1 342	233.6	42.0
Watsonville	57	1 641	750.6	57.2	142	1 551	302.1	31.5	48	234	19.2	3.4
West Covina	59	199	114.2	6.0	297	5 218	972.8	88.3	48	141	21.0	2.8
West Hollywood	135	862	457.9	34.3	324	2 794	571.2	69.2	97	752	139.3	21.0
Westminster	86	585	202.6	15.4	444	5 042	1 051.9	93.0	73	352	41.4	6.3
West Sacramento	154	4 361	3 109.2	145.5	101	1 098	215.7	23.0	51	435	90.5	14.8
Whittier	90	696	660.3	29.0	247	3 181	618.1	64.6	83	317	33.2	6.4
Woodland	74	2 953	1 561.0	92.8	165	2 372	406.5	43.6	50	291	30.2	4.5
Yorba Linda	157	4 351	1 700.6	65.0	116	1 726	371.3	34.1	54	208	63.8	5.1
Yuba City	48	390	181.5	14.1	231	3 273	528.8	54.7	69	449	36.1	5.7
Yucaipa	23	208	72.1	4.7	79	646	108.6	10.7	35	120	15.9	1.6
COLORADO	7 383	88 364	60 310.4	3 282.0	18 299	225 647	40 536.0	4 163.3	6 663	38 224	4 853.5	883.8
Arvada	122	1 075	282.1	30.2	294	4 106	660.1	70.2	110	558	47.0	9.5
Aurora	289	4 800	4 326.8	189.1	842	13 348	2 335.9	230.7	301	1 921	222.7	48.1
Boulder	251	2 548	1 598.3	100.1	699	9 587	1 544.9	169.8	281	1 425	201.4	35.5
Colorado Springs	417	5 911	1 205.2	200.8	1 644	25 565	4 669.3	466.5	661	2 826	333.1	58.4
Denver	1 681	26 604	16 177.1	972.8	2 410	30 080	5 600.9	628.0	1 201	11 339	1 771.9	287.0
Englewood	220	3 278	4 291.7	137.6	275	3 427	941.1	82.5	70	1 044	147.1	28.4
Fort Collins	110	D	D	D	603	8 644	1 437.0	141.5	194	928	111.6	17.3
Grand Junction	141	1 123	390.4	32.7	467	5 179	965.9	94.4	93	497	46.3	7.9
Greeley	107	1 098	442.2	33.9	297	4 511	764.8	75.3	107	447	50.6	7.5
Lakewood	221	1 326	957.5	53.3	654	9 359	1 801.6	179.4	257	1 330	129.3	28.8
Littleton	114	1 093	875.4	43.9	360	7 383	1 599.0	145.1	89	462	39.6	7.4

1. Establishments with payroll.

City	Professional, Scientific, and Technical Services, 1997[1]				Manufacturing, 1997				Accommodation and Foodservices, 1997			
	Number of Establishments	Number of Employees	Receipts (mil dol)	Annual Payroll (mil dol)	Number of Establishments	Number of Employees	Receipts (mil dol)	Annual Payroll (mil dol)	Number of Establishments	Number of Employees	Sales (mil dol)	Annual Payroll (mil dol)
	84	85	86	87	88	89	90	91	92	93	94	95
CALIFORNIA—Cont'd												
San Francisco	4 984	58 942	9 016.6	3 517.4	1 247	25 037	3 978.9	642.4	3 258	60 113	3 281.1	955.7
San Gabriel	69	211	15.6	4.0	54	628	36.5	11.0	134	1 535	57.2	15.2
San Jose	2 393	24 773	3 370.6	1 426.5	1 225	86 726	26 808.1	4 263.5	1 478	23 699	981.3	249.5
San Juan Capistrano	107	527	72.7	28.8	44	1 108	176.6	40.7	58	932	33.3	9.1
San Leandro	152	1 720	149.5	65.3	257	9 002	2 260.6	310.7	170	2 256	79.3	22.0
San Luis Obispo	236	1 214	120.9	46.8	78	1 521	195.0	43.9	173	3 535	114.4	30.9
San Marcos	69	320	25.1	9.5	227	5 981	872.1	172.1	92	1 555	48.5	14.0
San Mateo	462	2 997	396.6	179.4	77	531	67.5	18.4	235	3 428	148.7	44.0
San Pablo	15	101	11.6	4.6	NA	NA	NA	NA	60	788	29.4	7.0
San Rafael	433	1 893	231.2	94.6	149	1 809	223.2	58.3	198	2 429	93.4	23.8
San Ramon	282	3 271	558.6	203.7	NA	NA	NA	NA	99	D	D	D
Santa Ana	834	7 761	763.3	311.5	961	30 246	4 052.4	878.1	454	6 519	264.5	67.0
Santa Barbara	520	2 950	363.6	133.9	155	2 204	262.6	68.7	385	7 545	294.4	84.9
Santa Clara	583	10 210	1 378.6	588.8	711	46 029	12 884.0	2 398.9	309	6 513	316.3	82.6
Santa Clarita	140	777	79.4	23.1	66	1 136	164.3	39.5	151	2 432	80.8	22.6
Santa Cruz	239	985	109.7	39.1	122	2 969	866.8	101.2	216	3 339	124.5	33.9
Santa Maria	119	848	49.4	21.1	86	2 608	452.4	63.7	146	2 593	79.1	22.8
Santa Monica	995	7 478	1 124.9	444.8	147	4 065	560.6	141.0	375	9 894	461.9	127.1
Santa Paula	28	162	15.0	5.0	NA	NA	NA	NA	38	396	12.8	3.1
Santa Rosa	539	2 613	251.4	95.4	203	9 598	1 784.1	418.2	339	5 122	175.4	47.2
Santee	39	201	13.1	3.8	127	2 356	216.9	61.1	70	D	D	D
Saratoga	152	572	67.1	27.8	NA	NA	NA	NA	42	548	28.6	7.2
Seal Beach	67	371	66.6	21.8	10	D	D	D	62	1 149	41.3	11.3
Seaside	14	40	2.9	1.1	NA	NA	NA	NA	54	953	35.8	9.6
Simi Valley	164	1 228	168.2	55.0	157	4 709	1 208.3	170.5	157	2 789	92.7	23.8
South Gate	21	394	78.9	14.1	200	7 603	1 330.9	214.9	98	966	36.6	8.1
South San Francisco	109	2 634	396.7	127.5	193	10 151	2 011.2	485.9	152	3 819	221.9	64.4
Stanton	13	98	6.5	2.9	64	1 251	117.2	31.4	75	785	29.9	7.2
Stockton	336	2 326	197.4	76.7	191	8 783	1 809.8	256.7	398	5 902	197.7	51.5
Sunnyvale	521	9 031	1 180.3	550.0	438	43 471	11 208.6	2 683.0	293	4 987	226.5	59.8
Temecula	116	1 009	93.7	26.4	107	4 321	1 113.4	145.6	107	2 274	75.3	20.9
Temple City	33	98	6.2	1.8	NA	NA	NA	NA	46	D	D	D
Thousand Oaks	464	2 279	274.0	105.6	137	4 172	602.0	158.9	234	5 150	179.9	47.7
Torrance	684	4 953	655.1	245.7	328	16 065	4 364.1	719.9	400	7 747	296.4	79.5
Tracy	58	299	19.9	7.4	48	2 527	651.2	77.5	88	1 368	43.8	10.8
Tulare	41	187	13.6	5.8	35	1 797	1 331.8	61.0	73	786	27.3	6.4
Turlock	45	229	19.5	6.3	69	3 636	857.2	93.0	87	1 146	35.9	9.2
Tustin	387	2 569	314.1	113.9	141	6 771	1 446.3	282.5	143	2 877	97.9	26.9
Union City	48	257	24.4	7.8	93	3 696	677.5	128.1	69	648	25.1	5.9
Upland	134	753	43.2	16.4	95	1 510	224.1	40.1	114	D	D	D
Vacaville	72	285	21.6	8.2	58	2 382	355.8	71.1	121	2 260	77.0	20.5
Vallejo	88	458	31.0	13.0	40	682	198.2	23.0	172	2 225	73.3	18.7
Victorville	66	355	26.1	9.4	29	773	216.3	27.8	143	2 588	83.8	22.8
Visalia	202	1 171	229.2	31.9	87	3 873	821.2	106.7	204	3 751	123.5	31.7
Vista	143	668	59.5	19.1	153	5 607	743.9	148.9	127	1 380	48.3	11.7
Walnut	54	347	20.8	6.7	48	665	146.7	23.0	30	D	D	D
Walnut Creek	718	5 790	750.6	313.9	45	1 417	355.1	63.5	197	3 719	156.6	42.1
Watsonville	57	333	32.9	12.1	81	3 482	555.6	87.0	81	908	32.9	8.0
West Covina	109	660	42.7	16.2	NA	NA	NA	NA	146	2 285	82.1	23.7
West Hollywood	205	2 868	288.9	123.8	NA	NA	NA	NA	184	4 676	205.4	61.6
Westminster	95	257	16.5	4.6	128	1 984	168.5	43.7	206	2 288	81.2	20.2
West Sacramento	42	571	79.8	23.4	68	2 487	712.9	91.5	66	910	30.5	7.9
Whittier	144	649	55.2	21.6	76	2 733	298.3	69.4	140	2 443	77.7	20.0
Woodland	58	299	24.1	9.5	65	2 309	484.6	77.6	83	1 157	38.1	9.8
Yorba Linda	115	596	63.0	23.3	72	1 523	205.8	70.6	68	1 573	49.7	13.4
Yuba City	90	386	24.7	9.6	35	759	234.1	27.2	79	1 269	39.4	11.4
Yucaipa	28	64	4.0	1.2	NA	NA	NA	NA	40	627	19.1	5.0
COLORADO	14 315	103 008	12 887.7	4 625.1	5 480	173 069	40 012.8	6 176.8	10 064	195 126	6 705.5	1 937.4
Arvada	210	1 123	179.2	40.5	106	3 022	432.0	100.6	150	D	D	D
Aurora	451	3 226	379.3	128.9	139	2 360	342.4	75.3	424	8 844	278.3	76.8
Boulder	948	D	D	D	282	9 940	1 758.8	415.7	363	8 078	272.8	79.0
Colorado Springs	1 227	10 126	1 161.5	451.6	418	17 439	4 204.3	565.9	829	19 464	703.1	199.8
Denver	3 147	29 056	3 640.3	1 455.0	976	26 320	4 867.8	816.2	1 564	33 749	1 335.2	386.0
Englewood	195	898	103.7	38.7	200	4 684	617.2	145.2	96	D	D	D
Fort Collins	410	2 650	243.3	102.6	124	8 117	2 334.6	351.8	311	6 749	190.8	54.6
Grand Junction	210	1 174	80.7	36.3	113	3 212	446.0	91.0	180	3 697	102.8	30.0
Greeley	154	715	53.6	21.1	71	5 073	1 926.5	120.0	153	2 654	70.5	19.3
Lakewood	615	4 788	461.3	193.8	125	1 720	359.0	72.1	317	6 234	202.4	60.1
Littleton	269	1 054	91.8	37.3	67	1 860	279.0	60.0	139	D	D	D

1. Firms subject to federal tax.

Table D. Cities — **Entertainment, Health Care, and Other Services**

City	Arts, Entertainment, and Recreation[1], 1997				Health Care and Social Assistance[1], 1997				Other Services[1], 1997			
	Number of Establish-ments	Number of Employees	Receipts (mil dol)	Annual Payroll (mil dol)	Number of Establish-ments	Number of Employees	Receipts (mil dol)	Annual Payroll (mil dol)	Number of Establish-ments	Number of Employees	Receipts (mil dol)	Annual Payroll (mil dol)
	96	97	98	99	100	101	102	103	104	105	106	107
CALIFORNIA—Cont'd												
San Francisco	332	6 402	632.3	240.8	2 260	14 360	1 209.7	478.5	1 477	8 794	634.9	179.0
San Gabriel	8	44	1.8	0.4	140	1 066	66.2	24.3	78	433	32.4	9.9
San Jose	106	2 907	209.4	82.8	1 701	18 436	1 371.8	567.1	1 146	7 214	546.3	156.7
San Juan Capistrano	14	294	12.9	5.2	71	464	55.4	19.1	43	215	16.3	4.6
San Leandro	11	134	5.2	1.5	198	3 891	242.4	106.2	155	1 057	99.8	29.6
San Luis Obispo	15	121	4.7	1.8	239	2 987	219.4	107.1	92	601	33.5	9.3
San Marcos	15	251	11.1	3.1	66	558	28.3	11.4	97	507	39.9	11.6
San Mateo	39	730	39.1	17.9	343	2 321	179.4	73.0	195	964	67.9	19.8
San Pablo	5	0	0.0	0.0	75	863	60.7	26.7	39	197	12.9	3.3
San Rafael	31	303	23.8	6.0	214	2 269	159.7	72.8	230	1 178	108.8	32.4
San Ramon	12	898	23.1	8.0	153	1 198	109.6	42.4	91	805	61.5	18.4
Santa Ana	28	542	53.0	16.1	677	5 708	426.3	168.0	432	3 105	267.0	79.4
Santa Barbara	43	395	28.3	10.3	416	3 277	286.2	109.5	205	1 130	70.6	20.7
Santa Clara	24	2 699	100.5	28.6	149	2 998	274.6	129.7	229	2 002	206.8	65.9
Santa Clarita	40	369	23.1	8.5	205	1 678	122.1	49.2	146	786	54.5	14.7
Santa Cruz	27	966	35.6	13.1	143	1 195	80.9	28.1	99	522	37.4	10.7
Santa Maria	10	114	4.7	1.0	219	1 706	118.7	45.8	121	750	45.5	12.5
Santa Monica	403	1 697	329.4	170.9	742	5 019	552.4	218.0	300	1 982	135.0	37.9
Santa Paula	1	0	0.0	0.0	33	353	12.0	4.4	28	94	7.5	1.4
Santa Rosa	39	688	36.5	11.7	609	6 325	479.8	208.0	274	1 594	106.0	32.8
Santee	12	207	9.0	2.9	62	401	21.9	9.3	101	517	36.3	10.3
Saratoga	6	95	3.8	1.7	61	410	26.9	10.3	30	215	10.8	4.0
Seal Beach	6	0	0.0	0.0	52	467	35.9	16.8	34	167	6.5	2.2
Seaside	3	8	0.4	0.1	14	68	4.1	1.1	48	235	20.6	5.4
Simi Valley	21	555	18.5	5.7	196	1 283	120.4	46.6	130	659	49.5	13.6
South Gate	5	18	1.2	0.1	89	694	46.1	16.9	84	275	22.8	5.0
South San Francisco	13	153	11.0	2.7	105	1 635	163.0	71.8	137	1 472	106.9	33.6
Stanton	7	0	0.0	0.0	25	107	6.2	1.9	67	231	21.6	4.9
Stockton	42	660	22.4	7.2	558	5 597	432.7	184.4	318	1 733	111.6	34.0
Sunnyvale	20	227	12.7	3.3	235	2 474	249.6	80.0	192	1 459	111.7	34.0
Temecula	13	231	9.2	2.9	102	818	59.0	18.1	81	506	35.7	9.6
Temple City	4	10	0.7	0.2	45	712	27.2	11.1	39	202	9.7	3.7
Thousand Oaks	45	272	23.3	10.5	388	4 125	369.8	135.0	154	970	75.8	23.4
Torrance	37	923	53.4	20.3	795	6 134	520.6	221.2	270	1 467	111.8	31.7
Tracy	10	107	4.9	1.1	70	682	35.4	13.4	48	293	14.7	3.9
Tulare	6	0	0.0	0.0	82	638	45.3	14.4	53	232	17.4	4.3
Turlock	13	83	2.2	0.6	121	1 067	70.4	25.4	75	478	27.7	6.9
Tustin	17	721	34.1	9.0	237	2 551	172.9	68.3	95	771	61.9	17.0
Union City	1	0	0.0	0.0	64	550	50.2	15.0	47	496	63.2	13.2
Upland	14	229	11.4	2.5	244	1 644	132.0	57.0	80	410	28.0	7.5
Vacaville	8	188	4.5	1.6	119	1 115	90.6	31.2	84	423	29.2	7.6
Vallejo	15	484	42.4	6.9	215	2 725	232.6	107.0	134	906	54.7	17.6
Victorville	8	215	6.6	2.3	120	1 606	121.4	37.6	82	497	29.4	8.4
Visalia	15	0	0.0	0.0	283	2 532	183.7	77.2	140	877	67.1	17.3
Vista	9	306	18.8	5.5	167	2 233	174.0	61.7	101	594	38.4	11.8
Walnut	5	18	1.7	0.2	48	549	19.6	6.9	50	423	27.9	10.8
Walnut Creek	25	469	16.2	5.1	353	4 391	369.2	178.9	177	1 051	71.7	21.3
Watsonville	4	167	4.7	1.5	101	774	45.7	16.6	53	188	12.4	3.1
West Covina	6	187	8.0	1.8	272	2 713	223.7	86.1	59	244	13.8	3.6
West Hollywood	254	1 001	264.0	140.7	191	934	139.4	53.3	146	883	47.8	14.7
Westminster	11	0	0.0	0.0	225	1 651	121.9	46.4	154	770	51.3	13.3
West Sacramento	1	0	0.0	0.0	40	408	17.5	8.2	62	372	36.2	9.5
Whittier	16	258	11.0	5.0	266	2 671	250.9	87.3	143	751	62.2	16.7
Woodland	10	0	0.0	0.0	76	913	41.4	13.5	79	379	26.9	7.5
Yorba Linda	6	199	18.6	4.4	108	705	52.1	19.4	76	516	29.4	8.9
Yuba City	10	149	4.6	1.4	169	1 778	198.3	56.5	78	527	31.9	9.2
Yucaipa	2	0	0.0	0.0	48	529	32.5	9.3	41	174	11.5	3.0
COLORADO	1 494	30 541	1 909.6	625.0	8 611	85 370	5 790.8	2 538.1	6 793	39 363	2 571.1	770.0
Arvada	18	234	7.0	2.4	168	1 255	74.0	27.7	158	768	53.8	15.1
Aurora	56	901	40.9	10.5	516	8 108	602.1	236.7	375	2 132	132.3	40.2
Boulder	53	692	34.7	13.5	391	2 990	225.1	93.2	235	1 652	114.9	36.3
Colorado Springs	122	1 522	66.1	18.6	1 048	10 148	690.0	302.8	659	4 163	241.0	82.0
Denver	150	1 772	291.8	146.8	1 478	15 938	1 197.2	562.3	1 101	8 212	604.5	172.8
Englewood	12	274	10.0	2.3	192	1 846	200.2	99.9	164	894	67.2	20.4
Fort Collins	26	529	14.3	4.1	344	3 354	206.7	95.1	184	1 160	70.3	21.7
Grand Junction	18	208	7.2	2.8	229	2 229	138.0	65.0	147	886	67.5	17.3
Greeley	25	260	6.1	2.0	157	1 785	118.2	47.6	123	734	40.2	11.6
Lakewood	44	957	50.7	12.2	350	3 861	227.8	96.5	299	1 550	85.8	27.9
Littleton	14	183	8.7	2.2	170	1 896	125.3	50.2	112	793	57.5	18.5

1. Firms subject to federal tax.

City	Selected federal funds, fiscal 1999[1] (mil dol)									City government finances, 1997						
	Procurement contracts		Grants					Direct payments for individuals		General revenue						
										Intergovernmental			Taxes			
														Per capita[3] (dollars)		
	Defense	Other	Total[2]	Health and family welfare	Energy and environment	Education	Housing and community development	Educational assistance	Housing assistance	Total (mil dol)	Total (mil dol)	Percent from state government	Total (mil dol)	Total	Property	Sales and gross receipts
	108	109	110	111	112	113	114	115	116	117	118	119	120	121	122	123
CALIFORNIA—Cont'd																
San Francisco	208.6	175.6	832.6	408.5	7.4	14.5	47.6	29.1	70.8	3 480.3	1 311.9	88.8	1 080.0	1 469	651	427
San Gabriel	0.2	0.0	0.2	0.1	0.0	0.0	0.0	0.0	0.0	16.3	4.0	72.0	9.9	264	96	148
San Jose	166.0	62.9	130.1	23.2	1.8	9.5	16.4	17.7	32.4	917.5	124.0	48.3	424.7	506	147	228
San Juan Capistrano	1.9	0.6	1.1	0.4	0.0	0.0	0.0	0.1	0.0	23.3	2.3	82.6	13.1	453	232	135
San Leandro	19.6	-0.3	1.3	0.0	0.5	0.0	0.8	0.0	0.2	71.5	7.4	93.9	40.5	578	108	387
San Luis Obispo	2.0	0.1	25.4	17.9	0.0	1.5	1.3	7.7	0.1	38.9	4.7	89.1	18.9	446	91	329
San Marcos	5.8	0.9	6.4	3.4	0.0	1.8	0.0	3.4	0.0	40.1	3.8	85.9	25.7	544	240	246
San Mateo	2.6	4.0	4.4	1.4	0.0	0.1	1.8	0.9	-0.2	72.6	10.4	94.2	39.9	443	169	180
San Pablo	0.0	0.3	3.4	0.0	0.0	2.3	0.0	1.6	1.3	21.7	2.1	92.3	12.9	493	212	114
San Rafael	0.5	2.8	8.0	3.0	0.2	0.2	0.7	0.6	0.8	49.6	10.1	58.6	24.3	483	152	269
San Ramon	27.7	11.0	0.2	0.1	0.1	0.0	0.0	0.0	0.0	41.6	3.2	97.0	25.5	641	189	364
Santa Ana	33.6	74.0	67.0	27.4	0.0	6.0	13.3	4.9	2.0	218.0	45.5	65.7	108.4	359	115	214
Santa Barbara	69.7	14.4	97.1	18.2	5.0	2.0	3.6	13.5	1.0	118.1	14.3	74.0	47.6	553	166	366
Santa Clara	174.8	5.6	24.3	5.2	1.1	0.9	6.2	3.9	2.5	171.9	9.6	83.5	70.2	711	202	475
Santa Clarita	0.0	0.3	0.1	0.0	0.0	0.0	0.0	0.0	0.0	65.5	22.3	88.7	32.8	262	32	195
Santa Cruz	2.8	12.8	54.2	13.8	2.6	4.9	1.5	5.1	4.8	90.7	10.2	91.0	32.5	635	170	351
Santa Maria	20.4	0.8	5.8	0.0	0.0	0.9	1.2	1.4	1.1	50.9	9.6	85.4	19.1	284	55	161
Santa Monica	49.5	7.2	50.3	36.5	0.4	2.5	7.7	5.5	0.6	210.6	28.3	97.9	103.4	1 169	189	719
Santa Paula	7.8	0.7	0.1	0.0	0.0	0.0	0.0	0.0	0.0	11.0	2.1	81.3	4.8	183	87	86
Santa Rosa	3.1	2.1	37.6	8.3	5.4	1.1	1.9	2.9	7.2	130.9	23.3	49.6	50.0	410	86	283
Santee	3.1	0.0	1.2	0.0	0.0	0.1	1.1	0.0	0.8	24.3	4.1	91.3	14.1	251	127	102
Saratoga	0.0	0.0	0.9	0.0	0.9	0.0	0.0	1.5	0.6	14.7	2.4	91.8	6.3	213	75	72
Seal Beach	38.3	4.0	22.4	0.0	0.0	0.0	0.0	0.1	0.0	18.1	2.1	95.6	10.7	415	133	240
Seaside	0.6	0.0	10.5	0.0	0.0	1.5	0.5	1.1	1.5	18.5	3.4	68.9	11.9	379	160	206
Simi Valley	20.8	2.0	4.6	0.0	0.7	0.0	2.4	0.0	0.0	71.5	12.7	74.3	31.3	293	104	151
South Gate	0.9	0.1	3.4	0.0	0.0	0.0	3.4	0.1	1.2	44.6	10.5	79.7	16.6	188	67	102
South San Francisco	2.2	0.7	15.8	5.0	0.0	0.0	0.6	0.0	0.4	68.8	7.4	89.8	31.2	544	180	314
Stanton	0.0	0.0	1.1	0.0	0.0	0.0	0.0	0.0	0.0	13.8	2.7	84.1	8.1	249	89	150
Stockton	26.8	26.2	41.5	18.4	0.5	0.9	14.5	10.8	7.1	166.8	27.3	73.7	72.5	312	63	211
Sunnyvale	2 285.1	15.1	11.1	3.9	0.9	0.7	1.1	0.2	3.4	147.3	21.2	84.5	59.7	477	113	326
Temecula	3.2	0.5	0.1	0.1	0.0	0.0	0.0	0.0	0.1	33.0	3.3	90.1	22.7	576	181	290
Temple City	0.0	0.0	0.1	0.0	0.0	0.1	0.0	0.0	0.0	10.3	2.4	90.4	4.7	148	45	80
Thousand Oaks	29.3	1.2	6.3	0.0	0.5	1.1	1.5	1.1	1.7	88.5	12.3	91.2	46.2	408	122	207
Torrance	175.5	10.4	29.3	16.8	7.7	0.3	0.0	4.8	0.0	166.7	36.5	63.2	90.2	662	124	478
Tracy	3.7	0.7	0.6	0.0	0.0	0.3	0.0	0.0	2.6	47.4	6.5	82.2	12.3	274	133	124
Tulare	1.4	3.3	2.2	0.0	0.0	0.3	1.7	0.0	0.0	27.1	4.9	87.7	10.8	272	77	173
Turlock	0.1	11.2	2.7	0.0	0.0	0.4	2.1	2.7	0.0	26.3	5.4	80.0	10.7	218	41	143
Tustin	12.1	2.0	3.6	0.1	0.1	0.3	0.9	0.0	0.0	38.8	7.4	53.9	25.0	402	120	240
Union City	0.1	4.5	10.9	9.7	0.0	0.3	0.7	0.0	0.6	36.7	7.6	78.1	19.9	342	121	171
Upland	0.1	0.1	2.3	0.0	0.0	0.0	2.0	0.0	0.0	45.7	7.0	76.4	16.1	240	125	87
Vacaville	0.1	0.1	3.6	0.0	0.0	0.0	1.5	0.0	0.0	81.7	16.7	66.1	34.7	426	213	110
Vallejo	3.8	0.7	3.9	0.0	0.0	0.8	1.4	0.3	7.6	109.8	29.9	63.9	29.3	267	71	171
Victorville	0.2	10.9	1.0	0.0	0.1	0.2	0.7	3.1	1.3	41.1	7.1	69.1	19.4	290	127	151
Visalia	0.4	0.9	36.4	12.3	0.0	0.4	4.3	6.9	0.4	68.1	11.0	68.4	23.7	270	84	157
Vista	18.3	5.0	2.0	0.2	0.0	0.3	1.4	1.3	0.0	61.9	7.2	83.5	36.0	458	106	312
Walnut	0.6	0.0	0.9	0.0	0.0	0.6	0.0	5.0	0.0	27.6	2.3	94.8	18.5	600	510	75
Walnut Creek	29.8	13.3	3.4	2.7	0.0	0.0	0.4	0.0	0.0	44.3	4.4	93.0	25.7	409	88	277
Watsonville	2.8	6.3	3.7	0.4	0.1	1.9	1.1	0.0	1.4	49.0	11.4	83.5	17.7	539	184	225
West Covina	4.4	0.0	8.6	4.9	0.0	0.5	2.4	1.3	0.0	62.1	8.4	80.9	33.4	329	119	170
West Hollywood	0.0	0.0	0.0	0.0	0.0	0.0	0.0	0.0	0.0	41.5	3.9	69.2	22.7	621	129	418
Westminster	0.7	0.2	2.1	0.0	0.0	0.4	1.7	0.4	0.0	38.7	7.9	73.8	23.3	283	76	185
West Sacramento	0.2	0.0	1.8	0.6	0.2	0.0	1.0	0.0	0.2	52.6	10.2	95.5	22.3	752	401	296
Whittier	19.1	0.4	2.6	0.0	0.9	0.2	1.3	4.4	1.5	52.4	8.0	77.6	20.8	264	65	183
Woodland	4.2	0.2	3.9	0.0	0.0	0.3	1.6	0.0	2.8	28.7	4.2	86.0	17.3	410	121	187
Yorba Linda	9.2	0.8	0.0	0.0	0.0	0.0	0.0	0.0	0.0	44.1	3.9	90.6	24.3	419	280	99
Yuba City	-0.4	1.1	1.7	0.0	0.0	0.5	0.4	0.0	1.2	21.2	2.7	86.0	11.2	346	123	192
Yucaipa	0.0	0.0	-1.1	0.0	-1.4	0.0	0.0	0.0	0.0	10.4	3.9	86.6	5.1	141	62	47
COLORADO	2 443.1	1 999.4	3 445.7	1 676.7	105.9	296.9	67.4	88.1	70.3	X	X	X	X	X	X	X
Arvada	0.3	6.7	1.0	0.0	0.0	0.0	0.5	0.0	2.0	74.3	10.4	27.5	39.2	407	37	355
Aurora	19.3	18.0	126.8	117.2	0.2	1.2	3.5	1.2	0.9	208.4	17.1	59.4	124.9	495	60	420
Boulder	61.5	237.6	265.5	28.9	14.6	4.4	2.0	6.0	1.0	119.6	13.0	87.2	81.6	897	140	668
Colorado Springs	418.0	66.7	38.4	8.7	0.3	4.6	4.6	7.1	2.4	453.4	39.3	42.4	104.7	303	42	261
Denver	906.7	202.3	833.0	248.4	71.8	105.0	39.7	20.5	26.0	1 637.0	363.8	90.9	501.4	1 007	269	634
Englewood	155.8	56.6	18.8	2.7	1.2	0.9	0.0	0.0	0.0	38.7	2.3	85.2	20.7	656	65	575
Fort Collins	3.4	10.9	88.9	29.8	2.7	3.1	2.2	5.5	5.7	115.9	7.1	54.7	64.8	622	90	519
Grand Junction	4.3	73.0	4.3	0.3	0.1	0.6	0.6	2.1	4.7	41.9	8.3	28.1	24.1	699	81	614
Greeley	1.4	0.8	16.5	4.0	0.0	3.1	1.3	6.0	4.6	49.8	6.6	32.7	29.6	431	64	354
Lakewood	2.5	62.3	11.9	7.7	2.0	0.0	1.6	1.8	0.1	65.0	12.9	41.6	38.7	287	35	239
Littleton	271.6	87.9	3.6	0.1	0.1	0.1	1.8	0.7	0.0	35.9	7.8	20.3	18.4	466	50	402

1. October 1, 1998 to September 30, 1999.   2. Includes program categories not shown separately. State totals include additional categories not allocated by city.   3. Based on population estimated as of July 1 of the year shown.

Table D. Cities — City Government Finances

City	City government finances, 1997 (cont'd)												
	General expenditure												
	Per capita[1] (dollars)			Percent of total for —									
	Total (mil dol)	Total	Capital outlays	Public welfare	Highways	Parking facilities	Education	Health and hospitals	Police protection	Sewerage and sanitation	Parks and recreation	Housing and community development	Interest on debt
	124	125	126	127	128	129	130	131	132	133	134	135	136
CALIFORNIA—Cont'd													
San Francisco	3 594.3	4 888	1 169	10.1	1.2	0.2	1.9	21.8	7.8	4.2	6.4	3.0	7.0
San Gabriel	16.2	430	75	0.0	10.0	0.0	0.0	0.0	31.4	0.0	7.2	4.6	0.1
San Jose	850.6	1 014	188	0.0	6.2	0.5	0.0	0.0	16.3	19.1	8.2	13.5	8.5
San Juan Capistrano	18.6	642	71	0.0	14.0	1.4	0.0	0.2	17.9	12.4	9.8	6.9	19.2
San Leandro	69.4	992	111	0.0	14.8	0.5	0.0	0.7	18.2	15.2	6.8	7.8	2.6
San Luis Obispo	36.2	853	163	0.0	15.0	2.9	0.0	0.0	17.3	10.5	7.4	2.6	8.5
San Marcos	36.7	777	121	0.0	11.7	0.0	0.0	0.0	14.2	0.0	6.4	21.1	22.1
San Mateo	70.1	777	162	0.0	12.3	1.0	0.0	0.0	19.8	17.2	9.6	7.5	3.6
San Pablo	21.2	813	310	0.0	18.1	0.0	0.0	0.2	31.5	0.0	2.4	26.3	11.1
San Rafael	52.6	1 043	272	0.0	14.8	1.4	0.0	3.9	18.2	0.0	9.5	20.2	4.3
San Ramon	42.9	1 076	255	0.0	24.9	0.0	0.0	0.2	17.5	0.2	11.6	3.3	9.1
Santa Ana	255.9	846	197	0.0	9.5	0.4	0.0	1.4	28.4	6.3	5.5	17.8	10.4
Santa Barbara	111.5	1 294	324	0.0	10.3	2.7	0.0	0.4	15.5	4.8	8.2	9.7	4.9
Santa Clara	145.8	1 477	276	0.0	8.5	0.7	0.0	0.2	13.6	17.8	4.7	8.9	9.6
Santa Clarita	50.7	405	105	0.0	25.8	0.0	0.0	0.1	21.5	0.9	13.3	3.2	3.1
Santa Cruz	91.2	1 783	680	0.0	7.6	1.8	0.0	1.2	14.6	32.6	8.8	6.6	2.5
Santa Maria	55.0	821	275	0.0	13.0	0.0	0.0	0.0	18.3	35.9	4.0	1.5	3.4
Santa Monica	176.8	1 998	221	0.0	7.6	1.0	0.0	0.2	20.0	10.5	7.7	10.7	2.8
Santa Paula	12.8	483	118	0.0	15.0	0.0	0.0	0.7	24.0	21.0	3.8	13.2	0.0
Santa Rosa	138.6	1 137	262	0.0	12.8	1.8	0.0	0.4	16.2	25.8	7.3	3.6	9.6
Santee	23.3	417	71	0.0	16.5	0.0	0.0	3.9	26.3	0.0	4.1	11.8	3.7
Saratoga	12.7	431	19	0.0	18.2	0.0	0.0	0.2	22.6	0.0	17.0	1.5	1.2
Seal Beach	16.5	640	10	0.0	8.7	0.4	0.0	15.1	32.1	8.0	10.4	1.8	2.9
Seaside	12.6	400	28	0.0	10.0	0.0	0.0	0.0	33.9	1.6	14.5	7.2	2.3
Simi Valley	60.6	566	72	0.0	11.5	0.0	0.0	1.0	25.3	14.4	0.1	8.9	17.6
South Gate	43.4	493	55	0.0	14.3	0.0	0.0	0.2	29.4	8.8	7.2	20.4	5.6
South San Francisco	70.6	1 230	212	0.0	10.2	0.5	0.0	1.6	13.2	13.6	7.3	5.9	2.7
Stanton	12.5	385	52	0.0	15.2	0.0	0.0	0.5	38.6	1.1	2.8	6.1	2.5
Stockton	186.4	801	38	0.0	6.8	0.1	0.0	0.0	25.2	12.6	4.4	8.1	10.8
Sunnyvale	146.6	1 171	124	0.0	8.4	0.1	0.0	0.2	13.3	27.4	8.6	3.6	3.8
Temecula	39.8	1 012	481	0.0	25.7	0.0	0.0	0.1	11.3	0.0	9.3	30.9	2.3
Temple City	7.5	238	6	0.0	13.3	0.5	0.0	1.7	29.1	0.6	9.4	6.4	3.5
Thousand Oaks	83.7	738	90	0.0	20.3	0.0	0.0	0.1	14.7	12.3	3.1	14.4	5.8
Torrance	140.9	1 034	9	0.0	5.4	0.0	0.0	2.9	25.3	4.6	6.8	1.9	7.2
Tracy	57.8	1 290	407	0.0	19.6	0.1	0.0	0.3	11.6	19.4	7.2	12.7	9.3
Tulare	30.3	759	295	0.0	7.8	0.2	0.0	1.0	15.9	42.0	3.9	7.5	0.0
Turlock	29.4	601	172	0.0	11.9	0.0	0.0	0.4	26.4	29.3	4.7	2.1	1.8
Tustin	43.7	702	110	0.0	12.3	0.0	0.0	0.2	27.0	0.0	7.3	9.5	17.8
Union City	35.3	606	116	0.0	9.2	0.0	0.0	0.1	27.0	0.0	9.2	18.8	5.6
Upland	53.3	794	117	0.0	10.3	0.0	0.0	0.3	18.5	22.8	4.7	4.8	15.9
Vacaville	78.2	961	298	0.0	13.6	0.0	0.0	3.1	15.2	11.6	8.1	16.6	9.4
Vallejo	108.0	985	96	0.0	9.9	0.1	0.0	0.8	19.4	2.1	24.4	19.6	7.3
Victorville	36.3	540	95	0.0	22.6	0.0	0.0	0.9	18.1	19.2	6.4	7.0	8.3
Visalia	60.5	689	122	0.0	3.1	0.0	0.0	0.0	18.4	21.9	10.4	7.4	8.8
Vista	62.5	796	252	0.0	26.5	0.0	0.0	3.0	12.3	10.0	6.6	8.3	9.6
Walnut	25.6	829	115	0.0	10.1	0.0	0.0	0.1	9.5	0.0	5.9	56.4	9.1
Walnut Creek	43.7	696	178	0.0	15.2	1.5	0.0	0.0	25.1	0.0	22.0	3.7	2.3
Watsonville	51.3	1 567	492	0.0	3.9	0.0	0.0	0.9	12.3	31.1	6.6	8.7	3.4
West Covina	61.2	603	130	0.0	14.9	0.4	0.0	3.0	25.5	1.7	5.9	11.2	10.0
West Hollywood	37.4	1 025	99	0.0	15.3	5.1	0.0	0.0	24.3	5.2	6.3	6.4	5.0
Westminster	41.3	502	80	0.0	14.3	0.0	0.0	1.3	39.1	0.0	4.3	9.3	8.6
West Sacramento	62.2	2 094	347	0.0	29.7	0.0	0.0	0.3	13.4	11.8	2.7	18.4	8.3
Whittier	44.9	570	33	0.0	13.5	0.3	0.0	0.1	34.0	11.9	11.3	6.1	5.0
Woodland	27.3	647	118	0.0	13.9	0.0	0.0	0.1	22.6	9.0	13.4	3.6	4.4
Yorba Linda	48.4	832	250	0.0	20.5	0.0	0.0	7.3	12.2	0.0	12.3	21.8	10.1
Yuba City	28.8	888	215	0.0	14.2	0.0	0.0	0.3	18.4	18.1	8.1	4.8	10.2
Yucaipa	6.4	176	31	0.0	20.5	0.0	0.0	1.0	42.2	0.0	19.3	4.5	0.0
COLORADO	X	X	X	X	X	X	X	X	X	X	X	X	X
Arvada	63.0	654	93	3.8	20.2	0.0	0.0	0.0	15.7	8.8	14.8	2.9	10.1
Aurora	193.6	767	91	0.0	7.4	0.0	0.0	0.0	21.6	9.6	8.2	1.3	7.4
Boulder	112.0	1 232	76	0.0	14.0	1.7	0.0	0.0	12.4	5.8	16.8	8.6	6.7
Colorado Springs	379.5	1 099	120	0.0	10.8	0.3	0.0	40.4	12.8	4.4	4.3	2.4	3.9
Denver	1 635.2	3 285	296	11.4	3.6	0.4	0.0	13.9	6.9	5.1	5.2	2.2	19.1
Englewood	36.4	1 154	102	0.0	11.2	0.0	0.0	0.0	14.9	12.7	13.3	4.8	11.0
Fort Collins	110.0	1 056	291	0.3	22.2	0.4	0.0	0.0	12.6	12.0	17.0	0.9	8.0
Grand Junction	43.6	1 263	358	0.0	18.1	0.4	0.0	0.2	17.7	6.7	25.4	4.0	1.3
Greeley	53.9	786	209	0.0	13.7	0.2	0.0	0.3	17.1	18.5	17.4	3.1	0.7
Lakewood	70.0	518	134	0.0	16.3	0.0	0.0	0.9	32.4	3.3	15.6	5.4	6.3
Littleton	33.1	838	14	0.1	10.6	0.0	0.0	0.0	15.3	14.1	2.8	1.1	3.7

1. Based on population estimated as of July 1 of the year shown.

City	City government finances, 1997 (cont'd)			City government employment, 1999	Climate[2]				Annual precipitation (inches)	Heating degree days	Cooling degree days
	Debt outstanding				Average daily temperature (degrees Fahrenheit)						
					Mean		Limits				
	Total (mil dol)	Per capita[1] (dollars)	Percent utility		January	July	January[3]	July[4]			
	137	138	139	140	141	142	143	144	145	146	147
CALIFORNIA—Cont'd											
San Francisco	5 039.7	6 854	7.1	26 656	51.1	59.1	45.8	64.6	19.71	3 005	65
San Gabriel	0.3	8	0.0	NA	55.7	75.2	41.7	89.2	17.90	1 433	1 427
San Jose	1 668.7	1 990	0.0	6 692	49.4	69.5	40.6	82.4	14.42	2 387	594
San Juan Capistrano	45.4	1 566	0.0	NA	53.7	67.2	41.5	75.8	12.19	2 157	493
San Leandro	27.0	385	0.0	306	49.9	62.1	43.3	70.0	24.30	2 902	115
San Luis Obispo	35.9	845	40.0	NA	52.5	65.2	41.5	78.1	23.46	2 498	335
San Marcos	208.6	4 413	0.0	NA	55.2	70.5	43.1	81.3	13.04	1 802	868
San Mateo	44.4	492	0.0	656	48.7	68.7	38.9	83.4	19.74	2 563	486
San Pablo	91.2	3 490	0.0	NA	49.9	63.2	42.0	71.0	22.20	2 574	199
San Rafael	30.9	613	0.0	NA	48.8	67.7	40.6	81.6	35.74	2 581	449
San Ramon	75.6	1 897	0.0	NA	46.1	71.6	35.5	89.8	14.21	2 909	780
Santa Ana	394.5	1 304	5.2	2 121	57.4	72.6	45.6	82.6	12.27	1 238	1 175
Santa Barbara	129.7	1 505	45.3	1 197	52.0	65.4	40.3	73.9	16.25	2 438	289
Santa Clara	402.1	4 073	57.0	1 043	49.4	69.5	40.6	82.4	14.42	2 387	594
Santa Clarita	24.4	195	0.0	294	54.5	75.6	41.3	90.2	15.87	1 609	1 424
Santa Cruz	41.1	803	4.0	NA	49.9	63.5	38.8	75.7	28.99	2 969	148
Santa Maria	33.0	492	0.0	NA	51.1	63.1	38.3	73.3	12.36	2 984	169
Santa Monica	78.2	884	0.0	1 907	57.2	65.5	49.6	69.3	13.21	1 819	446
Santa Paula	25.0	945	100.0	NA	54.6	67.8	41.2	80.8	17.39	2 039	569
Santa Rosa	238.6	1 957	0.0	1 154	47.4	67.6	37.0	83.8	30.30	2 883	489
Santee	16.2	290	0.0	NA	56.6	72.5	44.6	83.4	12.80	1 400	1 110
Saratoga	2.3	79	0.0	NA	49.4	69.5	40.6	82.4	14.42	2 387	594
Seal Beach	7.2	279	1.2	NA	55.9	73.1	44.9	82.7	11.80	1 430	1 201
Seaside	4.4	141	0.0	NA	51.7	60.0	43.3	68.1	18.72	3 125	55
Simi Valley	183.1	1 711	0.0	586	54.6	67.8	41.2	80.8	17.39	2 039	569
South Gate	54.1	614	26.4	370	58.3	74.3	48.9	84.0	14.77	1 154	1 537
South San Francisco	42.5	742	0.0	NA	48.7	62.7	41.8	71.6	19.70	3 016	145
Stanton	19.3	591	0.0	NA	57.4	72.6	45.6	82.6	12.27	1 238	1 175
Stockton	266.4	1 145	6.4	1 865	45.0	77.7	37.0	94.4	13.95	2 707	1 470
Sunnyvale	72.6	580	0.0	895	49.4	69.5	40.6	82.4	14.42	2 387	594
Temecula	25.1	639	0.0	NA	53.9	75.4	40.5	92.1	11.83	1 747	1 339
Temple City	4.4	138	0.0	NA	55.7	75.2	41.7	89.2	17.90	1 433	1 427
Thousand Oaks	107.6	949	0.0	493	55.3	66.1	44.2	74.4	14.38	1 992	416
Torrance	162.4	1 193	5.9	1 521	56.1	69.7	45.3	78.8	13.57	1 568	794
Tracy	81.7	1 825	3.6	NA	45.2	76.2	36.7	92.1	11.85	2 659	1 321
Tulare	14.2	356	0.0	NA	45.4	80.4	37.0	96.0	10.15	2 511	1 762
Turlock	7.5	152	0.0	NA	45.6	77.1	37.4	94.2	12.10	2 605	1 401
Tustin	105.5	1 695	9.7	NA	54.5	71.6	41.4	83.7	11.81	1 784	973
Union City	43.2	741	0.0	NA	49.0	66.7	41.1	76.1	13.73	2 578	410
Upland	93.1	1 388	0.0	NA	54.3	74.6	40.7	90.4	16.62	1 713	1 273
Vacaville	151.1	1 857	0.0	633	45.2	75.2	36.1	94.1	23.84	2 764	1 154
Vallejo	287.3	2 622	19.5	572	49.9	63.2	42.0	71.0	22.20	2 574	199
Victorville	80.4	1 198	0.0	NA	44.2	79.3	30.0	97.4	5.51	3 127	1 525
Visalia	100.8	1 148	0.0	536	45.4	80.4	37.0	96.0	10.15	2 511	1 762
Vista	74.9	954	0.0	263	55.2	70.5	43.1	81.3	13.04	1 802	868
Walnut	37.5	1 215	0.0	NA	54.3	74.6	40.7	90.4	16.62	1 713	1 273
Walnut Creek	9.0	143	0.0	414	44.5	73.8	35.9	90.8	12.80	2 837	1 066
Watsonville	35.5	1 083	18.4	NA	49.4	61.8	38.3	71.3	21.73	3 213	107
West Covina	108.2	1 066	5.4	458	55.7	75.2	41.7	89.2	17.90	1 433	1 427
West Hollywood	29.2	800	0.0	214	58.3	74.3	48.9	84.0	14.77	1 154	1 537
Westminster	55.5	674	9.1	321	57.4	72.6	45.6	82.6	12.27	1 238	1 175
West Sacramento	126.2	4 248	0.0	NA	45.2	75.7	37.7	93.2	17.52	2 749	1 237
Whittier	39.3	500	19.9	524	55.7	75.2	41.7	89.2	17.90	1 433	1 427
Woodland	48.0	1 137	0.0	NA	44.5	76.9	35.9	96.3	19.43	2 777	1 387
Yorba Linda	57.5	989	0.0	NA	57.4	72.6	45.6	82.6	12.27	1 238	1 175
Yuba City	10.2	313	3.9	NA	45.6	78.8	37.2	96.0	21.04	2 524	1 607
Yucaipa	0.0	0	0.0	NA	52.8	78.4	39.6	95.8	12.80	1 875	1 673
COLORADO	X	X	X	X	X	X	X	X	X	X	X
Arvada	103.0	1 070	15.4	586	30.2	71.9	17.1	85.7	15.86	6 158	554
Aurora	346.5	1 373	40.2	2 348	29.7	73.5	16.1	88.2	15.40	6 020	679
Boulder	107.3	1 180	3.4	1 292	32.6	73.0	19.9	87.5	18.58	5 554	649
Colorado Springs	591.5	1 714	56.7	6 584	28.8	70.8	16.1	84.4	16.24	6 415	419
Denver	4 969.5	9 982	6.0	14 006	29.7	73.5	16.1	88.2	15.40	6 020	679
Englewood	49.2	1 559	1.0	487	29.7	73.5	16.1	88.2	15.40	6 020	679
Fort Collins	159.6	1 532	24.7	1 584	27.7	71.5	14.1	85.5	15.07	6 368	479
Grand Junction	9.6	278	8.0	545	25.0	78.8	14.5	93.6	8.64	5 548	1 183
Greeley	25.9	378	84.2	647	26.1	73.5	12.3	89.1	13.97	6 306	645
Lakewood	63.6	471	0.0	1 025	30.2	71.9	17.1	85.7	15.86	6 158	554
Littleton	20.9	530	0.0	347	30.2	71.9	17.1	85.7	15.86	6 158	554

1. Based on the population estimated as of July 1 of the year shown.   2. Represents normal values based on the 30-year period, 1961–1990.   3. Average daily minimum.   4. Average daily maximum.

STATE Place code	City	Land area, 1990[1] (sq km)	Population, 1999			Population				Population characteristics, 1990 — Percent						
												Race				
			Total persons	Rank	Per square kilometer	Total persons 1990	Percent change 1990–1999	Total persons 1980	Percent change 1980–1990	White	Black	Am. Indian, Eskimo, Aleut	Asian and Pacific Islander	Other race	Hispanic[2]	Foreign born
		1	2	3	4	5	6	7	8	9	10	11	12	13	14	15
	COLORADO—Cont'd															
08 45970	Longmont	34.0	64 551	416	1 899	51 976	24.2	42 942	21.0	92.7	0.4	0.7	1.2	4.9	11.1	3.8
08 46465	Loveland	55.4	48 385	607	873	37 357	29.5	30 244	23.5	94.9	0.3	0.5	0.7	3.6	6.8	1.5
08 54330	Northglenn	18.1	31 246	972	1 726	27 195	14.9	29 847	-8.9	90.7	1.6	0.8	2.0	4.8	14.6	3.7
08 62000	Pueblo	93.0	103 852	212	1 117	98 640	5.3	101 686	-3.0	83.0	2.2	0.8	0.6	13.4	39.5	2.3
08 77290	Thornton	53.5	77 589	320	1 450	55 031	41.0	40 343	36.4	89.7	1.3	0.9	1.7	6.5	16.9	2.5
08 83835	Westminster	69.4	97 100	241	1 399	74 619	30.1	50 176	48.7	90.6	1.0	0.6	3.7	4.0	11.5	4.2
08 84440	Wheat Ridge	23.0	30 045	1 012	1 306	29 419	2.1	30 280	-2.8	94.7	0.6	0.6	1.5	2.7	7.3	3.2
09 00000	CONNECTICUT	12 549.6	3 282 031	X	262	3 287 116	-0.2	3 107 564	5.8	87.0	8.3	0.2	1.5	2.9	6.5	8.5
09 08000	Bridgeport	41.5	137 040	147	3 302	141 686	-3.3	142 546	-0.6	58.5	26.6	0.3	2.3	12.3	26.5	14.6
09 08420	Bristol	68.7	59 145	466	861	60 640	-2.5	57 370	5.7	96.0	2.1	0.2	0.8	0.9	2.7	7.0
09 18430	Danbury	109.1	66 965	390	614	65 585	2.1	60 470	8.5	86.8	6.6	0.2	3.9	2.5	7.7	15.0
09 37000	Hartford	44.8	128 367	160	2 865	139 739	-8.1	136 392	2.5	40.0	38.9	0.3	1.4	19.4	31.6	15.3
09 46450	Meriden	61.5	56 365	502	917	59 479	-5.2	57 118	4.1	89.7	4.3	0.2	0.7	5.2	13.7	6.0
09 47290	Middletown	105.9	44 001	677	415	42 762	2.9	39 040	9.5	85.4	11.1	0.2	1.9	1.4	3.3	7.5
09 47500	Milford	58.0	(3)48 231	(3)610	(3)832	(3)48 139	(3)0.2	NA	NA	97.1	1.4	0.1	0.7	0.7	2.0	5.2
09 49880	Naugatuck Borough	42.5	30 150	1 008	709	30 625	-1.6	26 456	15.8	96.2	1.9	0.2	0.9	0.8	3.1	8.9
09 50370	New Britain	34.5	70 010	365	2 029	75 491	-7.3	73 840	2.2	81.6	7.6	0.2	1.8	8.9	16.3	16.5
09 52000	New Haven	48.8	122 195	172	2 504	130 474	-6.3	126 109	3.5	53.9	36.1	0.3	2.4	7.3	13.2	8.1
09 52280	New London	14.3	25 903	1 163	1 811	28 540	-9.2	28 842	-1.0	73.0	16.8	0.7	2.2	7.3	12.1	6.6
09 55990	Norwalk	59.1	78 083	319	1 321	78 331	-0.3	77 767	0.7	79.3	15.5	0.1	1.6	3.5	9.4	13.3
09 56200	Norwich	73.4	34 852	869	475	37 391	-6.8	38 074	-1.8	91.3	5.3	0.6	1.1	1.7	3.1	4.4
09 68100	Shelton	79.2	38 262	794	483	35 418	8.0	31 314	13.1	97.1	1.0	0.2	1.3	0.4	2.5	7.6
09 73000	Stamford	97.7	110 802	198	1 134	108 056	2.5	102 453	5.5	76.3	17.8	0.1	2.6	3.2	9.8	18.6
09 76500	Torrington	103.1	34 583	876	335	33 687	2.7	30 987	8.7	96.7	1.7	0.2	1.2	0.2	1.1	6.8
09 80000	Waterbury	74.0	104 263	210	1 409	108 961	-4.3	103 266	5.5	79.6	13.0	0.3	0.7	6.4	13.4	8.7
09 82800	West Haven	28.1	51 622	562	1 837	54 021	-4.4	53 184	1.6	84.1	12.4	0.2	2.0	1.2	3.6	8.4
10 00000	DELAWARE	5 062.5	753 538	X	149	666 168	13.1	594 338	12.1	80.3	16.9	0.3	1.4	1.1	2.4	3.3
10 21200	Dover	55.2	32 099	948	582	27 630	16.2	23 504	17.6	65.5	30.9	0.5	2.0	1.1	2.8	3.7
10 50670	Newark	22.3	28 318	1 062	1 270	26 463	7.0	25 247	4.8	90.4	5.7	0.1	3.5	0.2	1.5	5.9
10 77580	Wilmington	27.9	71 491	361	2 562	71 529	-0.1	70 195	1.9	42.1	52.4	0.2	0.4	4.9	7.1	3.5
11 00000	DISTRICT OF COLUMBIA	159.1	519 000	X	3 262	606 900	-14.5	638 432	-4.9	29.6	65.8	0.2	1.8	2.5	5.4	9.7
11 50000	Washington	159.1	519 000	24	3 262	606 900	-14.5	638 432	-4.9	29.6	65.8	0.2	1.8	2.5	5.4	9.7
12 00000	FLORIDA	139 852.4	15 111 244	X	108	12 938 071	16.8	9 746 961	32.7	83.1	13.6	0.3	1.2	1.8	12.2	12.9
12 00950	Altamonte Springs	22.1	39 482	763	1 787	35 167	12.3	22 028	59.6	89.9	5.9	0.3	1.8	2.1	8.5	8.0
12 07300	Boca Raton	70.4	72 967	353	1 036	61 486	18.7	49 505	24.2	94.4	2.9	0.1	1.9	0.8	5.6	13.3
12 07875	Boynton Beach	39.2	55 007	517	1 403	46 284	18.8	35 624	29.9	77.7	20.1	0.1	0.6	1.4	6.8	12.5
12 07950	Bradenton	29.7	47 140	624	1 587	43 769	7.7	30 170	45.1	82.9	14.4	0.2	0.6	1.9	5.4	5.7
12 10275	Cape Coral	272.3	93 518	250	343	74 991	24.7	32 103	133.6	97.5	1.0	0.2	0.6	0.7	3.7	6.5
12 12875	Clearwater	64.4	99 936	225	1 552	98 669	1.3	85 528	15.4	89.1	9.0	0.2	1.0	0.6	2.9	8.2
12 13275	Coconut Creek	28.9	39 172	768	1 355	27 269	43.7	NA	NA	97.1	1.5	0.1	0.8	0.5	4.1	10.7
12 14250	Coral Gables	30.6	42 445	699	1 387	40 091	5.9	43 241	-7.3	93.0	3.4	0.1	1.7	1.7	41.8	35.6
12 14400	Coral Springs	60.8	116 136	185	1 910	78 864	47.3	37 349	111.2	93.1	3.5	0.2	2.1	1.1	7.1	11.4
12 16475	Davie	83.7	69 589	369	831	47 143	47.6	20 877	125.8	92.8	3.9	0.2	1.7	1.4	10.0	10.9
12 16525	Daytona Beach	83.5	64 706	413	775	61 991	4.4	54 176	14.4	67.4	30.7	0.2	1.1	0.5	2.5	7.0
12 16725	Deerfield Beach	27.0	51 248	566	1 898	46 997	9.0	39 193	19.9	81.6	16.7	0.1	0.8	0.8	3.9	15.1
12 17100	Delray Beach	38.4	54 117	526	1 409	47 184	14.7	34 325	37.5	72.0	26.3	0.1	0.7	0.9	6.1	14.3
12 18575	Dunedin	26.8	35 680	845	1 331	34 427	3.6	30 203	14.0	98.1	1.1	0.2	0.4	0.2	1.8	7.1
12 24000	Fort Lauderdale	81.2	154 021	127	1 897	149 238	3.2	153 279	-2.6	69.6	28.1	0.2	0.9	1.2	7.2	17.4
12 24125	Fort Myers	56.9	46 254	634	813	44 947	2.9	36 638	22.7	64.2	32.2	0.2	0.8	2.6	7.7	4.6
12 24300	Fort Pierce	31.8	37 076	818	1 166	36 830	0.7	33 802	9.0	53.7	42.4	0.3	0.5	3.1	6.4	9.3
12 25175	Gainesville	90.3	92 291	255	1 022	91 482	0.9	81 371	4.6	73.4	21.4	0.2	3.9	1.1	4.4	8.1
12 28450	Hallandale	10.9	30 452	995	2 794	30 997	-1.8	36 511	-15.1	84.0	14.2	0.1	0.5	1.2	8.8	25.0
12 30000	Hialeah	49.8	212 547	77	4 268	188 008	13.1	145 254	29.4	89.9	1.9	0.1	0.5	7.5	87.6	70.4
12 32000	Hollywood	70.6	131 828	153	1 867	121 720	8.3	121 323	0.3	88.2	8.5	0.2	1.3	1.7	11.9	17.8
12 32275	Homestead	30.1	30 680	980	1 030	26 694	16.1	20 668	29.2	64.8	23.0	0.3	0.9	9.4	35.3	19.8
12 35000	Jacksonville	2 004.0	(4)695 877	(4)14	(4)347	(4)635 042	(4)9.6	NA	NA	72.7	24.4	0.4	1.9	0.7	2.4	3.5
12 36950	Kissimmee	32.2	39 568	760	1 229	30 337	30.4	15 487	95.9	83.6	9.3	0.3	2.4	4.4	14.5	8.2
12 38250	Lakeland	99.4	75 177	340	756	70 576	6.5	47 406	48.9	78.1	20.2	0.2	0.9	0.6	3.3	4.3
12 39075	Lake Worth	14.5	29 040	1 036	2 003	28 564	1.7	27 048	5.6	80.5	14.9	0.3	0.9	3.4	15.7	20.4
12 39425	Largo	36.6	66 831	393	1 826	65 910	1.4	58 977	11.8	97.6	1.0	0.2	0.8	0.4	1.9	6.0
12 39525	Lauderdale Lakes	9.3	28 845	1 046	3 102	27 341	5.5	25 426	7.5	51.6	45.6	0.2	1.4	1.1	6.0	32.4
12 39550	Lauderhill	19.0	50 946	571	2 681	49 015	3.9	37 271	31.5	58.6	38.5	0.1	1.5	1.2	6.8	20.6
12 43125	Margate	22.9	51 604	563	2 253	42 985	20.1	36 044	19.3	93.1	3.7	0.2	1.5	1.5	7.7	13.6
12 43975	Melbourne	74.3	69 779	368	939	60 034	16.2	46 497	29.1	87.4	9.5	0.3	2.1	0.7	3.5	6.3
12 45000	Miami	92.1	369 253	44	4 009	358 648	3.0	346 865	3.4	65.6	27.4	0.2	0.6	6.2	62.5	59.7

1. Dry land or land partially or temporarily covered by water. 2. Hispanic persons may be of any race. 3. 1999 population is for Milford "remainder"; most other items are for Milford Consolidated city; see Appendix A. 4. 1999 population is for Jacksonville "remainder"; most other items are for Jacksonville Consolidated city; see Appendix A.

Table D. Cities — Population and Households

City	Under 5 years	5 to 17 years	18 to 24 years	25 to 34 years	35 to 44 years	45 to 54 years	55 to 64 years	65 to 74 years	75 years and over	Percent female	Number	Percent change, 1980–1990	Persons per household	Female family householder[1]	One-person
	16	17	18	19	20	21	22	23	24	25	26	27	28	29	30
COLORADO—Cont'd															
Longmont	8.7	19.5	8.9	19.1	16.8	11.0	6.5	5.2	4.5	51.1	19 570	26.7	2.61	10.0	23.7
Loveland	8.0	20.5	7.7	17.1	16.6	10.0	7.1	6.9	6.0	51.7	14 049	22.8	2.62	9.4	21.9
Northglenn	7.4	18.9	10.6	17.7	15.6	12.6	10.0	4.9	2.4	50.4	9 829	3.4	2.75	10.9	20.3
Pueblo	7.1	19.1	9.3	15.4	14.2	9.2	9.9	9.0	6.9	52.0	38 324	2.7	2.50	14.9	27.9
Thornton	10.0	22.5	9.5	21.4	18.1	8.4	4.9	3.0	2.1	50.9	19 055	40.2	2.87	12.2	18.4
Westminster	8.9	20.5	9.5	22.5	19.5	8.9	5.4	3.1	1.7	50.8	27 828	63.3	2.67	10.2	21.9
Wheat Ridge	6.6	13.7	7.9	18.0	14.7	10.1	9.6	10.3	9.1	53.1	13 138	3.9	2.20	10.4	33.2
CONNECTICUT	6.9	15.9	10.5	17.8	15.5	10.8	9.0	7.8	5.8	51.5	1 230 479	12.4	2.59	11.4	24.2
Bridgeport	8.1	18.0	11.1	19.7	13.1	8.9	7.5	7.6	6.0	52.5	52 328	0.1	2.63	20.6	29.4
Bristol	7.0	15.0	10.4	20.3	14.5	10.1	9.0	8.0	5.5	51.6	23 956	17.2	2.51	10.3	24.9
Danbury	7.2	14.4	11.6	20.9	14.8	11.2	8.1	6.3	5.4	50.8	24 094	14.2	2.60	10.5	25.8
Hartford	8.3	18.9	15.2	20.3	12.9	8.2	6.5	5.4	4.4	52.3	51 464	0.8	2.55	27.6	32.8
Meriden	7.8	16.4	9.2	19.3	15.1	9.2	8.2	8.4	6.3	52.1	23 240	10.5	2.51	12.8	26.8
Middletown	6.7	12.6	15.9	22.2	14.1	9.3	7.2	6.9	5.1	51.5	16 821	19.0	2.31	11.9	31.0
Milford	6.5	15.3	9.1	18.0	16.1	11.4	9.7	9.0	4.8	51.4	18 826	NA	2.62	9.7	22.5
Naugatuck Borough	8.2	18.1	9.1	20.8	15.8	8.3	7.4	7.2	5.1	51.2	11 330	21.7	2.69	10.4	23.1
New Britain	6.8	14.3	13.3	20.0	12.8	7.1	8.8	10.0	6.9	52.2	30 170	5.6	2.40	14.6	29.9
New Haven	7.8	15.6	16.9	20.5	12.6	8.1	6.4	6.3	5.9	53.0	48 986	4.1	2.41	21.6	34.0
New London	7.1	12.5	23.1	19.2	11.6	7.2	6.5	6.8	6.1	49.7	10 712	2.3	2.29	15.5	34.7
Norwalk	6.8	13.3	9.0	21.7	15.3	11.7	9.6	7.4	5.1	51.8	30 560	8.1	2.53	11.7	25.8
Norwich	7.7	16.2	10.7	18.9	13.7	8.5	8.7	8.9	6.8	52.3	15 018	4.5	2.44	13.0	27.8
Shelton	7.1	16.1	9.0	17.3	16.0	12.7	9.2	7.2	5.4	50.7	12 454	23.6	2.79	8.0	18.1
Stamford	6.8	13.5	9.0	20.7	15.5	11.3	10.1	7.8	5.4	52.2	41 945	9.4	2.54	12.4	26.5
Torrington	6.8	13.9	9.6	18.5	14.7	9.2	8.7	10.0	8.5	51.9	13 883	15.4	2.38	9.8	29.0
Waterbury	7.8	15.6	10.5	19.1	13.1	8.7	8.7	9.1	7.3	52.7	43 164	13.5	2.48	15.4	29.7
West Haven	7.0	14.2	10.9	20.7	14.4	9.5	8.5	9.0	5.8	52.1	21 284	5.2	2.48	13.0	27.5
DELAWARE	7.3	17.2	11.4	17.9	14.8	10.2	9.0	7.4	4.7	51.5	247 497	19.7	2.61	11.8	23.2
Dover	6.9	16.2	18.5	16.8	13.6	9.7	7.4	6.1	4.7	51.5	9 903	29.0	2.48	14.0	27.2
Newark	3.9	10.1	42.7	11.4	10.4	7.0	6.1	4.9	3.6	52.8	7 469	3.0	2.57	7.5	23.4
Wilmington	7.1	17.8	9.7	19.3	14.8	8.9	7.7	8.1	6.7	53.5	28 556	6.3	2.44	21.8	36.4
DISTRICT OF COLUMBIA	6.0	13.2	13.4	20.2	15.7	10.3	8.4	7.4	5.4	53.4	249 634	-1.7	2.26	19.5	41.5
Washington	6.0	13.2	13.4	20.2	15.7	10.3	8.4	7.4	5.4	53.4	249 634	-1.7	2.26	19.5	41.5
FLORIDA	6.6	15.6	9.4	16.4	14.0	10.0	9.8	10.6	7.7	51.6	5 134 869	37.0	2.46	10.7	25.5
Altamonte Springs	5.8	14.3	12.7	25.0	16.0	9.8	7.0	5.6	3.8	52.0	15 432	79.9	2.24	10.0	32.6
Boca Raton	5.0	12.1	8.5	15.3	15.2	11.6	10.7	11.1	10.4	52.0	26 297	29.9	2.27	6.7	28.3
Boynton Beach	5.8	12.3	6.8	15.5	11.9	8.6	9.0	14.0	16.1	53.3	20 292	32.7	2.25	9.5	30.0
Bradenton	5.9	13.4	7.5	14.9	12.4	7.9	9.6	14.4	14.0	53.5	18 871	53.6	2.23	10.1	30.9
Cape Coral	6.2	15.3	6.8	14.7	13.6	9.7	11.7	14.1	8.0	51.8	29 748	128.3	2.50	7.8	17.1
Clearwater	4.8	12.9	7.9	14.6	13.1	10.5	10.7	12.9	12.6	53.9	44 138	18.6	2.17	10.2	33.0
Coconut Creek	4.9	7.2	6.1	16.7	11.0	7.3	10.4	21.9	14.4	54.4	13 575	NA	2.02	6.1	30.2
Coral Gables	4.6	10.8	15.8	15.8	14.3	12.1	9.3	9.6	7.7	52.6	15 460	-5.6	2.33	9.5	31.2
Coral Springs	7.1	23.6	9.5	15.4	20.9	11.9	4.7	3.9	3.0	51.2	27 014	137.4	2.94	9.9	16.5
Davie	7.7	17.1	10.0	20.3	17.6	11.1	7.2	6.1	2.8	51.1	17 907	138.0	2.62	10.9	20.7
Daytona Beach	5.2	11.6	17.1	15.7	11.5	8.1	9.4	11.1	10.3	50.7	27 546	20.2	2.10	12.9	37.6
Deerfield Beach	4.8	8.7	6.5	15.8	11.3	7.7	8.9	15.6	20.7	54.6	23 118	25.4	2.00	7.4	38.1
Delray Beach	5.4	10.2	6.3	15.1	12.0	8.9	10.3	16.5	15.2	53.0	21 390	45.6	2.19	9.2	31.8
Dunedin	4.0	10.8	6.9	12.5	12.1	9.5	11.0	15.5	17.7	55.0	15 888	14.6	2.08	8.0	34.1
Fort Lauderdale	6.0	12.8	8.1	19.1	15.6	10.8	9.6	9.3	8.7	49.6	66 440	-2.2	2.17	11.3	38.2
Fort Myers	8.6	16.9	11.0	18.2	12.8	8.6	7.9	8.0	8.1	51.3	18 144	25.9	2.40	16.5	32.3
Fort Pierce	8.5	17.9	8.7	14.6	11.5	9.0	9.7	12.3	7.7	52.1	14 171	11.2	2.54	18.6	27.8
Gainesville	5.8	13.5	27.1	17.7	13.6	7.1	5.8	5.3	4.0	50.8	31 924	12.4	2.35	12.8	30.0
Hallandale	3.5	6.4	4.7	10.6	7.6	7.2	11.9	19.7	28.5	56.0	17 135	-10.6	1.79	7.2	45.7
Hialeah	6.5	16.8	9.8	15.6	12.5	12.7	12.3	8.1	5.8	52.2	59 381	23.1	3.13	14.9	13.9
Hollywood	5.6	13.4	7.6	15.9	13.6	10.7	10.3	10.7	12.2	52.6	52 904	4.3	2.28	9.9	33.4
Homestead	10.8	20.1	11.9	19.4	12.5	8.7	6.0	6.1	4.5	49.2	9 317	21.0	2.83	18.8	22.6
Jacksonville	8.0	17.9	11.1	19.6	15.1	9.8	7.8	6.5	4.2	51.2	256 768	NA	2.54	13.4	25.3
Kissimmee	8.0	17.2	13.0	20.8	15.0	9.9	7.3	5.0	3.9	51.0	11 318	92.9	2.62	12.5	20.6
Lakeland	6.3	15.0	10.4	14.4	12.1	9.3	9.9	12.1	10.6	53.8	29 656	54.9	2.29	12.3	30.6
Lake Worth	6.8	12.8	8.7	17.8	13.2	8.3	8.1	10.2	14.0	50.7	12 565	-2.0	2.21	9.5	36.7
Largo	4.4	9.5	7.5	15.4	11.2	8.8	10.8	16.4	16.1	54.1	31 921	19.0	2.02	8.0	34.7
Lauderdale Lakes	6.7	14.2	7.6	15.8	11.9	7.7	5.8	10.9	19.4	55.5	11 962	5.5	2.26	13.5	33.8
Lauderhill	7.3	15.0	8.5	18.8	13.8	8.2	7.1	10.7	10.6	53.7	21 131	27.2	2.33	13.0	30.4
Margate	5.2	11.9	7.6	14.9	12.7	9.1	8.4	14.8	15.4	52.8	18 930	29.5	2.26	7.4	28.1
Melbourne	6.1	14.3	11.6	18.7	13.1	9.5	9.8	10.0	6.9	51.1	25 065	44.1	2.32	10.8	29.1
Miami	7.1	15.9	9.1	16.3	13.3	10.8	10.8	9.3	7.5	51.7	130 252	-3.3	2.70	18.6	28.9

1. No spouse present.

City	Persons in group quarters, 1990				Serious crimes known to police, 1998[2]				Education, 1990				Money income, 1989		
					Total		Rate[3]		School enrollment		Attainment[4] (percent)			Households	
														Median	
	Total	Persons in mental hospitals	Persons in nursing homes	Persons identified as home-less[1]	Number	Rate[3]	Violent	Property	Public	Private	High school graduate or more	Bachelor's degree or more	Per capita (dollars)[5]	Dollars	Percent change, 1979–1989 (constant 1989 dollars)
	31	32	33	34	35	36	37	38	39	40	41	42	43	44	45
COLORADO—Cont'd															
Longmont	447	0	398	0	3 349	5 542	405	5 137	12 304	1 105	84.5	20.5	14 037	32 534	-1.2
Loveland	476	0	427	39	1 924	4 114	242	3 872	9 525	938	84.2	18.6	13 345	30 548	4.2
Northglenn	153	0	153	0	1 475	4 847	371	4 476	6 266	806	83.1	13.8	13 619	34 726	-11.3
Pueblo	2 799	227	948	125	6 701	6 514	1 117	5 397	24 669	1 584	73.2	13.8	10 168	20 501	-18.0
Thornton	386	0	379	0	4 134	5 904	493	5 411	13 765	1 478	82.6	14.1	12 799	34 146	-2.3
Westminster	285	0	185	8	NA	NA	NA	NA	18 763	2 462	88.4	23.8	15 456	36 716	-1.2
Wheat Ridge	510	0	441	26	1 799	5 820	375	5 445	4 830	889	82.7	20.6	15 451	28 338	-8.6
CONNECTICUT	101 495	2 806	30 962	5 118	123 971	3 787	366	3 421	626 637	178 849	79.2	27.2	20 189	41 721	24.0
Bridgeport	4 215	55	1 371	260	9 053	6 527	1 438	5 089	26 482	9 076	61.1	12.3	13 156	28 704	23.6
Bristol	563	0	526	13	1 646	2 769	416	2 353	11 180	2 287	75.0	15.4	16 909	38 261	17.9
Danbury	3 036	0	687	125	2 339	3 556	195	3 361	11 815	3 528	76.5	26.9	19 300	43 832	30.2
Hartford	8 360	334	815	838	11 955	9 010	1 244	7 766	33 231	8 323	59.4	14.4	11 081	22 140	14.7
Meriden	1 127	0	802	35	2 005	3 503	257	3 246	10 904	2 736	72.6	15.8	15 618	36 211	19.9
Middletown	3 855	922	179	98	1 490	3 413	94	3 319	6 840	4 492	77.3	26.4	17 814	37 644	29.8
Milford	552	0	395	96	NA	NA	NA	NA	8 725	2 663	81.9	23.4	19 099	44 142	NA
Naugatuck Borough	179	0	116	16	653	2 152	59	2 093	6 559	1 384	78.2	17.0	16 691	39 902	26.9
New Britain	3 025	0	628	69	5 042	7 072	655	6 417	15 222	3 097	64.7	16.7	14 715	30 121	14.0
New Haven	12 435	0	1 187	1 656	13 255	10 622	1 684	8 938	26 285	14 607	71.0	26.7	12 968	25 811	31.8
New London	4 065	0	310	25	1 504	5 999	802	5 197	4 907	3 257	75.4	17.9	12 971	26 336	14.5
Norwalk	892	0	460	141	3 603	4 602	249	4 353	13 496	3 764	79.5	29.5	23 075	48 171	29.8
Norwich	709	0	555	12	1 554	4 327	409	3 918	7 121	1 457	71.8	16.4	14 844	29 354	13.7
Shelton	673	0	673	0	701	1 878	59	1 819	6 140	2 553	83.1	23.9	20 256	49 965	27.5
Stamford	1 346	0	682	338	4 491	4 064	395	3 669	16 930	6 071	81.2	35.1	27 092	49 787	33.2
Torrington	664	0	520	6	684	1 967	106	1 861	5 782	1 109	72.5	15.7	16 407	35 230	28.4
Waterbury	1 936	32	1 292	120	7 187	6 748	727	6 021	18 018	6 124	66.8	14.1	14 209	30 533	22.6
West Haven	1 326	0	528	63	2 348	4 498	128	4 370	8 993	3 440	74.5	17.2	15 810	35 723	24.6
DELAWARE	20 187	0	4 596	335	39 902	5 363	762	4 601	135 362	35 857	77.5	21.4	15 854	34 875	16.6
Dover	3 085	0	318	37	2 834	9 096	912	8 184	6 691	1 537	82.2	26.5	14 105	31 308	9.6
Newark	5 928	0	55	9	1 304	4 560	465	4 095	11 556	2 201	89.6	47.6	14 076	38 584	27.5
Wilmington	1 944	0	534	265	7 816	10 963	1 843	9 120	13 799	3 298	67.7	18.9	14 256	26 389	34.6
DISTRICT OF COLUMBIA	40 949	1 517	7 008	5 482	46 210	8 836	1 719	7 117	97 160	54 088	73.1	33.3	18 881	30 727	13.1
Washington	40 949	1 517	7 008	5 482	46 171	8 828	1 719	7 109	97 160	54 088	73.1	33.3	18 881	30 727	13.1
FLORIDA	304 798	6 208	80 298	8 892	1 027 123	6 886	939	5 947	2 459 541	467 121	74.4	18.3	14 698	27 483	11.7
Altamonte Springs	267	0	267	0	2 217	5 542	447	5 095	6 807	1 402	89.8	30.0	16 284	31 538	1.2
Boca Raton	1 853	0	423	0	3 959	5 553	362	5 191	9 193	4 222	88.4	34.9	28 307	42 314	12.1
Boynton Beach	580	0	453	63	5 786	10 956	1 346	9 610	7 227	1 192	73.1	16.4	16 668	28 824	21.1
Bradenton	1 814	44	1 245	71	2 674	5 484	580	4 904	6 865	862	75.2	15.6	13 815	26 010	20.8
Cape Coral	510	0	474	0	3 329	3 655	272	3 383	12 658	1 591	81.4	15.2	14 934	31 177	8.1
Clearwater	3 176	21	2 154	238	7 382	7 215	1 068	6 147	16 257	2 950	80.2	20.4	16 726	26 473	8.2
Coconut Creek	0	0	0	0	1 203	3 401	280	3 121	2 739	987	84.3	21.7	19 347	33 191	NA
Coral Gables	4 054	0	0	0	3 735	9 161	630	8 531	4 099	7 975	89.6	49.1	30 852	47 506	29.6
Coral Springs	58	0	43	0	4 273	3 906	303	3 603	20 831	3 758	89.2	31.5	18 319	43 428	0.6
Davie	309	56	25	0	4 033	6 615	533	6 082	9 362	2 304	80.7	20.5	16 747	36 843	7.1
Daytona Beach	4 010	61	1 168	107	8 257	12 281	2 026	10 255	9 823	5 895	73.6	16.5	11 901	18 631	8.0
Deerfield Beach	147	0	118	0	2 374	4 616	556	4 060	5 142	1 810	74.3	16.1	17 093	26 950	16.1
Delray Beach	333	0	70	0	5 773	10 936	1 546	9 390	6 357	1 307	74.6	21.5	21 292	31 146	12.7
Dunedin	903	0	872	0	1 198	3 369	315	3 054	4 785	780	81.6	18.9	16 721	25 906	11.4
Fort Lauderdale	5 026	231	992	708	18 260	11 575	1 124	10 451	22 214	6 278	74.2	21.9	19 814	27 239	5.5
Fort Myers	1 584	0	443	68	6 063	12 766	2 306	10 460	8 871	1 230	68.4	16.1	12 329	22 102	10.4
Fort Pierce	846	0	350	251	5 126	13 388	3 424	9 964	7 822	662	56.9	11.3	9 961	18 913	4.3
Gainesville	9 674	0	326	30	9 498	10 641	1 372	9 269	35 803	2 617	84.8	40.5	11 549	21 077	-0.1
Hallandale	275	0	215	0	1 324	4 088	713	3 375	2 862	706	67.9	14.1	16 950	20 841	-9.4
Hialeah	1 951	380	1 083	49	NA	NA	NA	NA	38 812	7 282	46.3	7.3	8 914	23 443	-10.8
Hollywood	1 140	0	732	187	11 017	8 289	815	7 474	18 887	5 667	72.9	15.7	16 303	27 352	3.0
Homestead	521	0	419	33	4 313	18 355	4 000	14 355	5 935	693	55.6	8.5	9 757	20 594	7.9
Jacksonville	18 994	241	3 415	736	NA	NA	NA	NA	136 589	27 199	76.9	18.4	13 857	28 513	NA
Kissimmee	323	20	233	0	4 188	10 863	1 393	9 470	5 924	685	76.1	13.4	11 931	27 591	22.1
Lakeland	2 746	0	1 164	148	8 849	11 707	1 181	10 526	12 241	3 150	74.0	19.3	13 487	24 462	10.5
Lake Worth	745	90	562	30	4 091	13 797	1 592	12 205	4 543	848	67.1	12.5	12 130	21 665	7.6
Largo	1 257	27	918	58	3 425	5 095	653	4 442	8 011	1 877	77.1	13.8	14 539	24 296	4.8
Lauderdale Lakes	365	66	291	0	1 935	6 616	940	5 676	5 155	948	68.1	9.7	11 295	20 731	-12.4
Lauderhill	432	0	403	0	3 172	6 041	996	5 045	8 582	2 143	79.2	19.0	14 953	26 722	-3.1
Margate	141	0	141	0	1 980	3 767	339	3 428	6 294	1 114	74.6	12.3	14 897	28 465	6.3
Melbourne	1 469	0	453	75	5 492	7 866	1 101	6 765	10 843	3 871	79.2	18.8	13 224	25 893	5.8
Miami	7 397	139	1 349	1 069	44 922	12 045	2 549	9 496	74 008	13 310	47.6	12.8	9 799	16 925	-8.8

1. Persons in emergency shelters and persons visible in street locations. 2. Data for serious crimes have not been adjusted for underreporting. This may affect comparability between geographic areas and over time. 3. Per 100,000 population estimated by the FBI. 4. Persons 25 years old and older. 5. Based on population enumerated as of April 1, 1990.

Table D. Cities — Income, Poverty, and Housing

City	Money income, 1989 (cont'd) Households (cont'd) Percent with $100,000 or more	Percent below poverty, 1989 Persons Total	Percent change in rate, 1979–1989	Families Total	Housing units, 1990 Total	Percent change, 1980–1990	Vacant units for sale or rent[1]	Occupied units Total	Owner-occupied units Percent	Median value[2] (dollars)	Owner cost as a percent of income With a mortgage	Without a mortgage	Renter-occupied units Median rent[3] (dollars)	Rent as percent of income	Substandard units[4] (percent)
	46	47	48	49	50	51	52	53	54	55	56	57	58	59	60
COLORADO—Cont'd															
Longmont	2.3	7.8	27.9	6.0	20 480	25.3	771	19 570	62.2	85 900	22.6	13.7	466	25.5	2.7
Loveland	1.9	7.9	8.2	5.7	14 711	20.5	515	14 049	63.8	73 400	21.8	12.2	400	24.2	2.4
Northglenn	1.4	5.3	-5.4	3.7	10 442	6.3	545	9 829	63.5	71 500	21.9	12.4	431	25.2	2.2
Pueblo	1.2	21.6	51.0	18.0	40 862	2.1	1 688	38 324	64.8	48 700	20.8	12.7	303	28.1	3.6
Thornton	1.0	8.2	28.1	6.9	20 974	44.8	1 402	19 055	69.9	75 600	23.5	11.9	469	26.1	3.5
Westminster	2.9	6.6	17.9	5.6	29 868	60.9	1 738	27 828	65.2	85 700	23.1	11.8	477	24.2	2.5
Wheat Ridge	2.8	8.4	20.0	6.0	14 130	8.1	826	13 138	53.5	88 600	22.6	12.6	425	25.3	1.7
CONNECTICUT	9.2	6.8	-14.8	5.0	1 320 850	14.0	55 167	1 230 479	65.6	177 800	22.9	13.7	598	26.6	2.5
Bridgeport	2.7	17.1	-16.2	15.0	57 224	3.5	3 971	52 328	44.2	145 900	26.2	16.9	594	30.3	7.1
Bristol	3.1	4.4	-25.4	2.9	24 989	19.0	780	23 956	62.4	153 500	23.6	13.6	549	24.7	1.7
Danbury	8.4	5.8	-13.4	4.7	25 950	14.9	1 229	24 094	60.1	190 300	24.0	14.5	693	26.5	4.4
Hartford	1.9	27.5	9.1	25.7	56 098	1.5	4 053	51 464	23.6	133 800	23.9	14.8	504	29.1	9.4
Meriden	3.0	7.3	-1.4	6.3	24 826	11.8	1 147	23 240	60.5	146 300	23.8	13.9	533	26.7	2.7
Middletown	4.2	7.0	-27.8	4.9	18 102	22.5	1 057	16 821	50.7	157 000	22.3	13.2	576	24.6	1.6
Milford	6.7	3.7	NA	2.5	20 149	NA	NA	18 851	76.2	171 800	23.3	14.2	748	26.1	1.4
Naugatuck Borough	4.2	4.2	-40.8	3.2	11 930	22.6	519	11 330	67.1	143 100	24.3	14.4	578	23.9	1.6
New Britain	2.2	12.8	8.5	10.7	32 335	8.6	1 679	30 170	43.1	139 200	24.4	14.9	512	24.8	4.5
New Haven	3.7	21.3	-8.2	18.2	54 057	6.8	3 507	48 986	31.8	145 000	23.5	14.9	568	30.0	5.1
New London	2.1	15.1	-10.7	12.0	11 970	4.8	941	10 712	36.9	131 800	27.2	14.6	526	27.7	4.3
Norwalk	12.0	5.2	-25.7	3.8	32 224	9.4	1 341	30 560	62.0	241 300	23.7	15.4	738	26.6	3.7
Norwich	3.2	11.9	-5.6	9.7	16 472	7.9	961	15 018	52.7	126 200	24.0	13.9	524	26.9	2.2
Shelton	9.9	2.5	-28.6	1.6	12 981	24.1	388	12 454	79.5	208 600	22.8	12.7	654	27.1	0.4
Stamford	16.9	6.3	-18.2	3.9	44 279	10.5	1 874	41 945	57.9	295 700	22.8	14.7	794	26.5	4.8
Torrington	3.3	5.2	-24.6	3.1	15 161	18.5	739	13 883	62.7	141 700	24.2	14.0	511	24.6	1.5
Waterbury	2.4	12.1	-14.2	9.9	47 205	15.5	3 387	43 164	49.0	131 800	23.2	13.9	492	26.8	3.6
West Haven	2.7	6.1	-35.1	4.2	22 679	8.4	1 017	21 284	56.1	147 000	23.6	15.0	621	26.4	2.6
DELAWARE	4.5	8.7	-26.8	6.1	289 919	21.5	12 178	247 497	70.2	100 100	19.5	12.0	495	24.7	2.5
Dover	3.5	12.5	-8.8	10.1	10 488	28.6	408	9 903	53.9	88 700	19.5	11.6	470	24.6	2.5
Newark	5.4	17.4	-5.9	1.8	7 860	4.0	320	7 469	56.3	134 600	19.2	10.8	534	32.9	1.6
Wilmington	3.8	18.1	-26.4	15.1	31 244	2.4	1 827	28 556	53.2	77 800	19.7	13.9	450	26.8	4.1
DISTRICT OF COLUMBIA	7.8	16.9	-9.3	13.3	278 489	0.5	19 907	249 634	38.9	123 900	20.5	12.8	479	25.4	8.3
Washington	7.8	16.9	-9.1	13.3	278 489	0.5	19 907	249 634	38.9	123 900	20.5	12.8	479	25.4	8.3
FLORIDA	3.9	12.7	-6.0	9.0	6 100 262	39.3	425 736	5 134 869	67.2	77 100	22.3	12.2	481	28.0	5.7
Altamonte Springs	2.7	7.7	35.1	5.4	17 140	85.1	1 274	15 432	39.1	90 000	22.2	13.1	553	25.2	2.7
Boca Raton	16.2	5.5	7.8	3.6	33 043	27.9	1 981	26 297	74.5	165 300	24.3	12.1	656	28.3	1.9
Boynton Beach	3.1	9.6	-3.0	6.2	25 544	41.1	1 557	20 292	76.5	79 400	23.4	11.9	632	28.1	4.7
Bradenton	1.7	12.8	-11.1	8.8	22 123	46.1	1 530	18 871	61.1	71 700	23.1	12.0	483	27.5	3.6
Cape Coral	3.2	5.9	0.0	4.0	34 486	116.3	1 851	29 748	75.1	91 100	23.6	11.9	533	26.7	1.3
Clearwater	4.1	10.7	24.4	7.5	53 833	21.8	4 707	44 138	61.8	82 100	23.1	11.9	464	28.1	2.0
Coconut Creek	2.9	4.1	NA	2.4	15 773	NA	898	13 575	74.4	109 300	23.4	12.8	744	26.6	1.4
Coral Gables	22.5	6.5	-27.8	4.4	16 561	-6.3	740	15 460	63.6	223 500	22.2	13.3	540	27.2	4.1
Coral Springs	10.2	5.2	26.8	4.3	29 785	133.1	2 117	27 014	62.4	160 200	26.1	13.8	661	27.9	3.3
Davie	4.9	7.8	-8.2	4.8	19 889	141.2	1 085	17 907	73.8	106 600	24.8	11.3	581	26.3	3.7
Daytona Beach	1.7	22.5	-0.9	16.0	32 167	24.0	2 896	27 546	46.8	63 000	24.1	13.1	420	30.4	4.1
Deerfield Beach	3.0	9.9	16.5	5.8	28 796	29.1	1 732	23 118	72.1	97 400	23.5	12.7	611	28.0	4.0
Delray Beach	8.2	11.3	-8.9	7.5	27 527	40.8	2 217	21 390	70.3	92 900	24.2	12.9	599	28.6	5.1
Dunedin	3.0	7.1	18.3	4.6	18 411	17.7	993	15 888	70.5	76 500	22.8	11.7	466	27.8	1.1
Fort Lauderdale	7.1	17.1	20.4	13.1	81 268	1.4	6 119	66 440	54.4	99 200	24.1	13.7	486	29.3	7.8
Fort Myers	2.8	20.7	-4.6	17.2	21 388	30.9	1 987	18 144	42.4	60 500	20.2	12.4	451	27.3	7.3
Fort Pierce	1.8	29.2	5.8	20.1	17 250	13.7	1 584	14 171	51.8	56 100	20.7	12.7	401	33.4	9.1
Gainesville	2.9	26.3	8.7	15.7	34 608	16.1	2 072	31 924	47.1	63 800	19.5	12.1	383	33.2	5.5
Hallandale	3.7	16.0	44.1	10.5	24 798	6.7	1 722	17 135	66.8	76 600	25.0	13.0	517	34.9	4.6
Hialeah	1.0	18.2	37.9	15.5	62 187	23.8	2 394	59 381	49.9	80 100	23.6	12.8	484	32.8	28.9
Hollywood	4.8	11.0	29.4	7.7	63 303	9.0	4 487	52 904	64.7	82 100	23.0	13.5	523	30.7	5.6
Homestead	1.3	29.9	9.9	24.6	10 775	22.3	967	9 317	38.7	67 300	22.2	12.7	410	30.2	17.4
Jacksonville	2.9	12.8	NA	9.8	284 673	NA	NA	257 245	62.0	63 400	20.6	12.4	431	25.6	4.4
Kissimmee	0.8	11.8	-2.5	9.2	13 602	103.5	1 471	11 318	45.7	74 400	22.1	12.1	531	27.5	6.3
Lakeland	2.9	14.0	-8.5	10.2	34 933	60.0	2 484	29 656	59.0	61 600	19.9	12.4	403	25.9	3.3
Lake Worth	1.6	17.1	44.9	13.6	15 632	-1.4	1 221	12 565	55.6	66 900	24.0	12.7	453	29.3	8.7
Largo	1.7	7.4	5.7	4.4	38 711	23.4	2 567	31 921	65.8	71 500	22.0	11.5	473	27.3	1.6
Lauderdale Lakes	0.7	14.2	69.0	10.4	13 921	13.2	918	11 962	66.0	79 600	25.1	12.9	544	31.4	6.4
Lauderhill	3.0	10.3	30.4	7.9	26 274	31.1	2 358	21 131	57.9	93 500	23.7	12.5	575	32.2	6.6
Margate	2.1	7.7	75.0	5.3	21 647	28.0	1 077	18 930	78.3	83 000	23.0	13.6	627	28.2	3.0
Melbourne	1.6	12.8	7.6	8.7	28 070	49.7	2 023	25 065	58.1	65 100	20.6	11.8	467	27.7	3.0
Miami	2.6	31.2	27.3	25.7	144 550	-0.8	10 802	130 252	33.1	79 200	24.3	13.2	404	32.7	25.7

1. Includes units rented or sold but not occupied.   2. Specified owner-occupied units.   3. Specified renter-occupied units.   4. Overcrowded or lacking complete plumbing facilities.

City	Civilian labor force, 1999				Civilian employment, 1990[2]			Disability 1990	Value of residential construction authorized by building permits, 1999		
			Unemployment			Percent					
	Total	Percent change, 1998–1999	Total	Rate[1]	Total	Professional, managerial, and technical	Precision production, craft, and repair	Work disabled persons[3] (percent)	New construction ($1,000)	Number of housing units	Percent single family
	61	62	63	64	65	66	67	68	69	70	71
COLORADO—Cont'd											
Longmont	37 424	1.6	1 276	3.4	26 328	33.2	12.5	7.2	122 519	1 208	80.3
Loveland	26 767	0.1	784	2.9	17 897	29.9	13.7	7.3	97 178	934	79.4
Northglenn	20 023	1.5	439	2.2	14 688	24.4	13.3	7.3	26 113	257	78.2
Pueblo	47 519	-3.7	2 373	5.0	37 313	27.2	9.5	13.1	NA	NA	NA
Thornton	39 056	1.5	880	2.3	28 632	24.0	13.1	6.6	114 834	1 194	90.2
Westminster	55 392	1.0	1 020	1.8	42 000	34.3	11.0	6.2	43 484	330	59.1
Wheat Ridge	19 087	0.1	466	2.4	14 916	32.0	12.2	10.2	5 467	31	54.8
CONNECTICUT	1 691 552	-1.0	53 446	3.2	1 692 874	35.5	11.2	6.4	1 466 185	10 637	87.0
Bridgeport	59 866	-2.7	3 660	6.1	62 443	22.0	11.9	8.8	3 727	63	88.9
Bristol	30 888	-1.4	1 117	3.6	33 112	27.9	15.5	7.0	10 907	92	100.0
Danbury	35 409	-2.6	1 025	2.9	35 764	34.5	11.2	5.7	30 891	321	62.9
Hartford	52 606	-2.5	3 276	6.2	56 870	24.3	9.0	9.7	2 204	44	68.2
Meriden	29 445	-1.2	1 138	3.9	30 347	26.9	14.3	7.6	3 368	43	95.3
Middletown	23 259	-0.4	759	3.3	23 923	36.2	11.7	5.5	6 362	142	61.3
Milford	25 642	-2.3	785	3.1	26 737	32.9	12.7	6.0	20 072	258	58.5
Naugatuck Borough	16 457	-1.4	568	3.5	16 137	29.5	14.5	6.6	6 253	64	100.0
New Britain	33 388	-2.0	1 821	5.5	36 681	26.1	13.2	7.1	569	13	76.9
New Haven	55 981	-1.4	2 200	3.9	58 178	34.7	8.2	8.8	19 220	234	73.9
New London	11 916	-4.4	589	4.9	12 371	26.2	11.0	10.4	0	0	0.0
Norwalk	48 383	-0.7	1 339	2.8	45 360	37.0	11.3	5.8	20 181	151	65.6
Norwich	18 560	-2.2	816	4.4	17 348	27.5	14.9	10.9	3 054	28	100.0
Shelton	19 574	-0.6	637	3.3	19 083	36.6	14.2	5.3	17 610	169	94.1
Stamford	65 615	-0.5	1 643	2.5	60 010	39.9	8.2	5.2	63 692	451	16.4
Torrington	18 560	-0.8	624	3.4	17 531	28.2	14.0	7.9	8 803	110	100.0
Waterbury	52 060	-2.3	2 507	4.8	51 384	26.6	12.7	9.8	3 399	66	97.0
West Haven	27 680	-1.5	981	3.5	28 527	27.6	12.0	7.2	1 518	40	95.0
DELAWARE	388 971	-0.8	13 648	3.5	335 147	31.0	11.9	7.7	492 470	5 285	91.2
Dover	16 849	-0.5	638	3.8	12 767	35.0	9.3	8.4	15 201	208	47.6
Newark	13 809	0.1	366	2.7	12 287	43.9	5.1	3.2	4 505	48	100.0
Wilmington	33 359	-0.7	1 591	4.8	33 188	29.4	7.8	10.6	4 145	116	46.6
DISTRICT OF COLUMBIA	282 119	5.5	17 692	6.3	303 994	44.0	4.5	8.4	53 284	683	46.7
Washington	282 119	5.5	17 692	6.3	303 994	44.0	4.5	8.4	53 284	683	46.7
FLORIDA	7 366 498	1.9	284 168	3.9	5 810 467	28.8	11.5	8.7	16 197 445	165 018	64.6
Altamonte Springs	30 411	4.2	782	2.6	21 224	36.7	6.9	5.2	16 900	415	5.5
Boca Raton	38 984	0.1	1 253	3.2	30 374	41.4	7.2	4.8	84 203	233	64.8
Boynton Beach	25 644	-0.2	1 318	5.1	19 583	28.1	11.2	7.9	40 989	563	31.1
Bradenton	25 105	5.4	637	2.5	18 062	26.8	13.4	9.5	3 586	74	67.6
Cape Coral	41 076	3.2	1 027	2.5	32 991	26.3	13.1	8.4	147 969	2 007	85.7
Clearwater	55 794	1.7	1 595	2.9	45 175	29.4	9.9	8.9	14 696	247	17.4
Coconut Creek	14 943	1.6	706	4.7	11 539	35.4	9.5	7.6	48 096	633	57.0
Coral Gables	23 400	1.1	705	3.0	20 790	52.3	4.5	3.0	18 270	37	100.0
Coral Springs	52 881	1.9	1 536	2.9	41 614	36.8	8.7	4.5	145 882	1 202	89.0
Davie	33 130	1.8	1 167	3.5	25 905	32.0	13.2	6.9	81 302	735	100.0
Daytona Beach	30 284	0.9	1 248	4.1	26 724	26.5	10.0	10.9	31 285	331	34.7
Deerfield Beach	25 148	1.8	910	3.6	19 644	28.4	10.5	7.0	29 517	331	100.0
Delray Beach	26 151	-0.4	1 838	7.0	19 573	29.3	9.5	6.9	39 314	435	70.6
Dunedin	17 901	1.8	413	2.3	14 576	29.6	10.6	7.9	12 495	105	97.1
Fort Lauderdale	94 416	1.6	4 786	5.1	72 643	28.7	10.1	8.0	203 760	1 291	9.1
Fort Myers	25 957	3.0	935	3.6	20 612	25.4	11.7	10.9	58 881	892	13.5
Fort Pierce	18 259	2.1	2 745	15.0	13 474	18.7	10.4	11.5	26 460	407	17.2
Gainesville	47 742	2.5	1 215	2.5	38 730	45.0	5.6	6.4	19 307	252	75.4
Hallandale	13 058	1.5	725	5.6	9 996	27.7	9.5	9.8	2 383	34	47.1
Hialeah	104 300	0.7	6 317	6.1	89 758	15.6	16.1	6.6	17 840	282	20.2
Hollywood	72 903	1.7	3 349	4.6	56 372	28.3	13.6	8.8	24 124	271	64.6
Homestead	13 002	0.8	713	5.5	11 257	16.6	14.4	8.4	3 781	62	100.0
Jacksonville	NA	NA	NA	NA	314 432	28.9	11.1	9.1	549 436	6 156	63.0
Kissimmee	26 445	4.6	841	3.2	16 552	21.8	10.2	7.0	57 300	608	88.2
Lakeland	34 993	1.5	1 551	4.4	30 126	29.7	10.6	8.9	62 958	1 005	23.0
Lake Worth	17 158	-0.3	944	5.5	13 053	21.1	14.4	8.0	1 037	10	100.0
Largo	35 412	1.8	822	2.3	28 831	27.6	11.5	10.0	15 671	141	97.9
Lauderdale Lakes	14 280	1.5	813	5.7	10 915	20.5	11.3	6.5	0	0	0.0
Lauderhill	29 681	1.7	1 247	4.2	23 045	29.3	10.2	6.7	3 244	30	100.0
Margate	24 527	1.7	981	4.0	19 083	24.8	14.8	7.1	7 753	92	52.2
Melbourne	31 279	0.9	1 396	4.5	27 679	32.6	13.5	9.4	60 096	724	57.3
Miami	180 502	0.4	15 178	8.4	151 446	19.7	12.2	8.1	164 593	1 572	3.2

1. Percent of civilian labor force.　2. Persons 16 years and older.　3. Persons 16 to 64 years old.

Table D. Cities — Wholesale Trade, Retail Trade, and Real Estate

City	Wholesale Trade, 1997				Retail Trade[1], 1997				Real Estate and Rental and Leasing, 1997			
	Number of Establishments	Number of Employees	Sales (mil dol)	Annual Payroll (mil dol)	Number of Establishments	Number of Employees	Sales (mil dol)	Annual Payroll (mil dol)	Number of Establishments	Number of Employees	Receipts (mil dol)	Annual Payroll (mil dol)
	72	73	74	75	76	77	78	79	80	81	82	83
COLORADO—Cont'd												
Longmont	79	1 519	1 751.6	81.3	300	4 269	776.4	76.8	78	348	41.1	5.9
Loveland	62	611	186.4	18.0	264	3 101	613.5	52.3	76	303	40.9	4.9
Northglenn	26	145	59.7	4.1	106	1 276	268.0	27.2	40	232	22.7	4.4
Pueblo	90	890	360.3	24.0	532	6 586	1 117.2	114.5	107	450	51.0	7.6
Thornton	47	438	557.6	18.8	158	4 013	729.2	80.0	34	325	20.8	6.2
Westminster	94	688	272.5	26.9	372	6 483	1 093.4	104.6	88	441	60.1	7.2
Wheat Ridge	66	648	268.3	18.1	198	2 747	589.2	57.6	49	226	40.5	4.1
CONNECTICUT	5 283	77 716	75 821.6	3 595.3	14 574	186 935	34 938.9	3 634.3	3 372	20 635	3 522.8	609.3
Bridgeport	131	1 665	601.2	63.7	342	3 755	665.8	81.6	94	342	57.0	8.3
Bristol	58	839	251.9	32.1	215	2 741	556.1	50.7	33	131	22.7	2.9
Danbury	125	2 150	904.0	69.9	497	8 262	1 715.5	166.6	76	1 739	535.3	66.1
Hartford	171	4 575	3 038.6	214.5	419	3 644	764.8	87.0	191	1 708	282.2	62.7
Meriden	67	745	220.4	25.1	256	3 678	570.1	59.6	66	307	36.0	6.4
Middletown	51	672	220.3	22.8	148	2 020	377.6	40.0	52	249	42.7	5.1
Milford	153	1 925	776.7	80.7	342	5 645	1 133.3	106.0	43	193	31.8	4.5
Naugatuck Borough	22	372	152.2	13.0	77	1 139	186.9	18.6	16	78	8.0	1.0
New Britain	41	575	279.0	24.0	203	2 068	435.7	42.8	37	223	26.0	5.6
New Haven	130	1 399	737.6	50.9	390	3 377	506.2	64.4	140	847	113.3	19.1
New London	22	223	63.8	8.3	146	1 799	428.6	43.8	23	147	14.7	3.6
Norwalk	210	4 134	3 682.2	338.1	411	7 133	1 792.5	180.7	94	443	144.3	18.2
Norwich	29	480	175.8	15.2	181	2 749	468.5	47.8	30	128	12.2	2.0
Shelton	47	1 111	921.7	54.0	94	1 626	381.2	30.7	22	473	80.5	18.1
Stamford	354	5 992	22 164.2	430.8	545	6 973	1 798.1	186.7	216	1 816	358.0	74.5
Torrington	52	603	209.8	23.9	201	2 531	454.5	43.5	26	127	10.3	2.1
Waterbury	113	1 462	494.9	51.7	481	5 527	982.0	96.4	100	436	58.5	10.6
West Haven	57	1 000	490.0	41.5	140	1 479	277.2	28.4	43	100	13.1	1.9
DELAWARE	906	13 509	12 585.5	619.5	3 736	47 116	8 237.0	798.7	1 101	5 243	5 006.5	118.3
Dover	40	D	D	D	310	5 026	802.9	77.2	71	294	30.6	4.7
Newark	52	D	D	D	204	3 796	760.8	70.1	60	335	73.9	6.5
Wilmington	106	1 736	1 158.1	70.1	354	3 674	708.5	71.7	269	1 015	2 425.1	24.8
DISTRICT OF COLUMBIA	348	5 008	3 918.6	223.0	2 075	19 608	2 788.8	351.5	934	7 725	1 354.2	275.4
Washington	348	5 008	3 918.6	223.0	2 075	19 608	2 788.8	351.5	934	7 725	1 354.2	275.4
FLORIDA	31 214	296 139	187 079.9	9 678.2	66 643	841 814	151 191.2	14 169.5	20 388	118 086	15 360.4	2 652.2
Altamonte Springs	152	1 137	897.2	51.0	407	6 342	896.6	94.8	102	533	85.6	15.2
Boca Raton	525	6 440	4 325.7	322.1	744	9 092	1 438.2	163.8	344	2 096	378.2	69.8
Boynton Beach	92	498	171.1	14.4	219	2 757	405.0	42.2	76	276	41.3	6.6
Bradenton	37	219	98.3	6.5	241	3 294	519.6	50.1	76	261	39.0	4.9
Cape Coral	94	D	D	D	300	3 747	515.3	52.9	97	287	51.9	5.7
Clearwater	301	2 173	1 020.3	65.6	775	11 505	2 535.5	222.9	201	961	93.6	20.2
Coconut Creek	41	85	61.1	3.9	55	1 016	420.4	27.5	25	85	15.7	2.1
Coral Gables	268	1 981	4 723.1	117.7	315	3 652	795.2	75.6	260	1 266	176.7	35.4
Coral Springs	259	2 588	915.1	88.7	417	6 395	950.0	92.3	136	452	86.7	12.5
Davie	267	2 285	1 406.1	56.1	303	3 690	684.8	71.6	113	401	57.9	10.2
Daytona Beach	90	1 028	393.2	27.6	546	7 481	1 466.9	126.7	151	975	106.9	18.2
Deerfield Beach	211	3 391	6 510.8	153.8	278	4 340	885.8	81.8	84	495	67.3	12.4
Delray Beach	120	569	231.5	19.2	344	4 265	1 467.3	102.4	85	356	41.4	8.0
Dunedin	41	217	81.8	8.4	129	1 346	175.4	20.0	28	107	17.9	2.5
Fort Lauderdale	761	8 279	6 347.6	336.0	1 203	13 080	3 192.2	287.9	495	4 013	799.5	117.2
Fort Myers	207	2 258	557.6	65.2	614	8 593	1 695.1	160.2	151	983	148.9	21.6
Fort Pierce	59	899	260.3	19.1	257	2 844	431.0	39.9	53	236	23.7	4.1
Gainesville	138	1 296	620.9	40.8	498	6 521	1 098.3	104.8	171	876	97.7	17.1
Hallandale	90	524	121.7	12.1	134	1 932	263.0	29.1	50	109	21.0	2.1
Hialeah	576	4 040	1 114.6	99.0	945	10 430	1 530.9	151.2	252	884	199.3	21.1
Hollywood	361	2 408	1 191.1	80.0	556	6 758	1 234.9	121.6	219	1 351	160.8	29.7
Homestead	35	D	D	D	122	1 636	303.0	27.8	25	95	7.4	2.1
Jacksonville	1 394	21 860	16 590.0	760.3	3 134	44 276	8 034.1	761.4	886	6 374	918.5	158.4
Kissimmee	43	D	D	D	309	3 517	531.7	52.3	130	2 347	207.3	47.6
Lakeland	164	2 468	2 191.2	66.1	621	9 559	1 559.9	148.6	139	689	81.7	13.0
Lake Worth	69	D	D	D	183	1 519	274.6	26.4	44	218	20.4	4.8
Largo	179	1 593	526.0	46.4	382	4 358	626.5	66.1	108	648	76.9	11.8
Lauderdale Lakes	19	D	D	D	78	713	142.1	13.2	22	928	123.5	23.3
Lauderhill	51	193	63.6	4.9	159	1 884	534.1	33.3	54	412	30.4	6.2
Margate	97	381	195.8	10.3	198	3 187	848.1	68.2	53	338	40.4	5.8
Melbourne	142	1 124	388.1	38.5	446	6 394	1 137.5	111.6	115	642	63.4	11.4
Miami	1 810	12 885	7 178.4	388.8	2 533	21 675	3 681.5	362.5	729	4 625	719.5	119.7

1. Establishments with payroll.

City	Professional, Scientific, and Technical Services, 1997[1]				Manufacturing, 1997				Accommodation and Foodservices, 1997			
	Number of Establishments	Number of Employees	Receipts (mil dol)	Annual Payroll (mil dol)	Number of Establishments	Number of Employees	Receipts (mil dol)	Annual Payroll (mil dol)	Number of Establishments	Number of Employees	Sales (mil dol)	Annual Payroll (mil dol)
	84	85	86	87	88	89	90	91	92	93	94	95
COLORADO—Cont'd												
Longmont	188	915	74.6	32.4	152	4 688	556.7	136.6	140	2 460	82.6	22.9
Loveland	123	543	38.5	13.0	66	5 214	1 260.8	225.2	103	1 728	53.9	13.6
Northglenn	42	232	21.3	7.4	42	616	102.8	17.4	49	1 128	39.2	10.9
Pueblo	176	939	46.5	17.9	70	2 818	578.4	96.2	280	4 547	131.6	35.3
Thornton	42	264	11.4	3.8	26	1 587	279.3	44.5	109	2 616	85.2	23.5
Westminster	187	968	67.6	28.5	70	2 450	659.3	95.7	170	3 812	118.0	33.9
Wheat Ridge	144	993	93.9	37.8	58	1 413	295.2	53.1	99	1 707	54.2	15.5
CONNECTICUT	9 393	71 058	9 115.8	3 700.1	5 844	252 330	46 938.2	10 452.1	6 903	96 556	3 746.6	1 062.8
Bridgeport	184	1 528	172.6	79.3	249	10 340	1 424.4	375.0	163	D	D	D
Bristol	73	292	20.7	8.2	158	4 542	580.5	159.0	98	D	D	D
Danbury	231	1 744	199.7	81.6	130	6 556	1 302.0	281.0	181	2 803	111.4	30.0
Hartford	405	6 197	891.3	322.3	112	2 183	254.5	60.6	313	4 733	172.8	50.4
Meriden	74	721	60.4	20.2	103	4 353	751.2	162.9	106	1 232	49.6	12.3
Middletown	88	686	76.4	32.5	58	5 256	1 662.2	222.0	103	1 094	44.5	12.0
Milford	158	1 081	126.0	49.3	206	6 100	1 104.5	258.8	168	2 647	99.0	25.6
Naugatuck Borough	32	83	8.5	2.6	63	2 957	737.5	109.8	42	D	D	D
New Britain	71	376	39.4	15.0	141	5 329	845.0	193.2	95	D	D	D
New Haven	418	2 855	339.9	137.1	106	4 177	750.6	147.2	262	3 327	137.8	37.8
New London	100	886	72.4	34.1	NA	NA	NA	NA	95	1 392	48.1	14.0
Norwalk	378	3 173	420.7	174.2	170	6 713	1 420.5	297.7	202	1 944	93.2	25.7
Norwich	75	407	34.1	16.8	48	1 403	254.5	44.8	78	1 379	47.9	13.4
Shelton	108	934	103.6	42.7	77	4 923	728.6	211.8	74	862	40.9	10.2
Stamford	720	10 898	1 713.6	787.5	183	6 126	2 515.3	229.6	281	3 980	198.4	55.0
Torrington	51	176	18.5	4.3	83	3 770	443.8	118.7	72	866	30.9	8.6
Waterbury	152	848	78.7	28.4	219	6 433	1 085.3	220.9	198	2 472	83.9	23.4
West Haven	53	463	25.3	8.8	62	5 258	1 623.1	276.5	97	1 238	42.6	12.1
DELAWARE	1 717	12 382	1 430.4	553.4	675	41 084	13 397.3	1 474.3	1 605	26 969	1 009.0	280.8
Dover	89	820	52.3	23.9	29	3 902	1 338.5	111.5	134	2 689	82.3	22.2
Newark	96	509	57.5	23.1	52	D	D	D	123	2 829	111.2	26.6
Wilmington	450	4 322	690.2	266.2	102	D	D	D	219	3 798	155.9	50.5
DISTRICT OF COLUMBIA	3 760	61 123	10 365.2	3 935.5	200	2 858	320.2	101.1	1 700	42 650	2 263.5	701.4
Washington	3 760	61 123	10 365.2	3 935.5	200	2 858	320.2	101.1	1 700	42 650	2 263.5	701.4
FLORIDA	42 403	276 263	27 231.1	10 803.5	15 992	433 149	77 477.5	13 185.1	28 999	608 834	24 165.3	6 239.5
Altamonte Springs	252	1 411	119.6	45.9	NA	NA	NA	NA	156	4 756	167.2	47.5
Boca Raton	1 029	4 922	612.4	237.1	175	4 828	639.0	211.2	297	5 635	279.0	61.5
Boynton Beach	152	996	56.2	24.5	65	D	D	D	101	2 001	63.0	18.1
Bradenton	196	814	74.5	30.1	34	D	D	D	104	1 652	55.2	13.2
Cape Coral	164	1 469	68.7	36.9	77	549	46.5	12.9	122	1 787	60.0	16.5
Clearwater	634	4 100	397.1	169.3	182	3 191	342.9	84.8	401	7 830	339.3	84.1
Coconut Creek	57	128	15.3	4.6	NA	NA	NA	NA	19	116	5.3	1.3
Coral Gables	1 109	5 707	606.4	248.3	NA	NA	NA	NA	172	3 701	153.3	47.3
Coral Springs	421	1 587	127.9	45.8	82	1 186	139.8	34.5	179	3 218	109.9	27.5
Davie	214	669	68.7	22.8	111	1 447	156.1	39.0	138	D	D	D
Daytona Beach	280	1 761	152.3	53.4	63	1 931	200.4	44.4	321	7 016	247.2	62.6
Deerfield Beach	218	1 350	142.0	67.7	100	2 511	333.9	78.4	140	2 438	105.0	25.5
Delray Beach	180	1 773	197.9	89.0	67	613	84.4	18.2	138	2 233	84.2	21.8
Dunedin	122	2 328	257.0	75.7	NA	NA	NA	NA	77	916	32.0	7.9
Fort Lauderdale	1 656	8 971	1 086.8	448.4	352	7 546	1 001.7	247.2	698	19 971	941.5	221.9
Fort Myers	322	2 093	179.2	80.7	95	1 743	296.7	47.9	213	4 338	145.1	38.1
Fort Pierce	95	848	47.2	21.0	NA	NA	NA	NA	113	1 751	53.8	14.3
Gainesville	371	2 547	199.1	84.0	85	1 688	414.3	57.7	273	4 610	140.2	36.2
Hallandale	66	243	20.8	8.4	55	733	78.3	18.7	67	1 610	46.0	13.3
Hialeah	237	1 710	81.2	31.9	690	18 397	1 822.3	425.4	268	3 248	129.7	31.2
Hollywood	607	3 377	307.9	136.6	169	3 498	769.6	92.6	320	4 871	163.4	44.6
Homestead	38	144	11.1	4.3	NA	NA	NA	NA	67	990	32.8	8.2
Jacksonville	1 959	17 491	1 552.9	690.0	754	28 237	7 231.0	944.1	1 420	28 354	917.2	244.2
Kissimmee	93	382	28.6	9.6	32	526	79.5	15.1	205	6 281	480.2	80.2
Lakeland	256	1 911	172.6	66.6	81	4 007	652.3	127.5	222	5 146	160.4	42.8
Lake Worth	92	382	29.0	12.7	46	523	40.3	10.8	78	852	32.9	9.2
Largo	178	819	90.9	27.9	138	2 544	229.8	60.6	176	2 854	89.8	21.8
Lauderdale Lakes	17	60	5.9	1.9	NA	NA	NA	NA	27	326	11.6	3.0
Lauderhill	103	394	25.4	9.1	NA	NA	NA	NA	63	D	D	D
Margate	100	300	32.1	8.4	NA	NA	NA	NA	97	D	D	D
Melbourne	297	2 072	209.7	87.0	91	4 435	1 282.6	160.6	182	3 407	96.8	28.1
Miami	2 447	16 969	2 231.5	955.7	575	7 490	1 021.7	188.8	912	16 953	764.8	202.7

1. Firms subject to federal tax.

City	Arts, Entertainment, and Recreation[1], 1997				Health Care and Social Assistance[1], 1997				Other Services[1], 1997			
	Number of Establishments	Number of Employees	Receipts (mil dol)	Annual Payroll (mil dol)	Number of Establishments	Number of Employees	Receipts (mil dol)	Annual Payroll (mil dol)	Number of Establishments	Number of Employees	Receipts (mil dol)	Annual Payroll (mil dol)
	96	97	98	99	100	101	102	103	104	105	106	107
COLORADO—Cont'd												
Longmont	22	278	12.6	2.5	151	1 845	103.3	44.4	120	583	33.1	10.5
Loveland	9	73	3.1	0.6	128	1 187	73.6	32.3	78	473	23.0	7.3
Northglenn	5	97	3.0	0.8	33	482	27.1	11.5	45	345	17.5	5.1
Pueblo	26	0	0.0	0.0	282	3 349	199.9	96.5	166	846	43.3	12.9
Thornton	12	194	7.6	1.9	105	1 324	87.0	37.6	67	743	49.5	14.5
Westminster	13	263	8.4	2.8	153	1 486	93.5	42.6	105	493	28.1	9.9
Wheat Ridge	15	96	4.2	1.1	186	1 818	147.9	72.5	105	600	45.3	13.6
CONNECTICUT	1 046	27 236	2 526.8	589.2	7 515	100 363	6 849.7	3 199.3	6 121	34 089	2 370.2	727.8
Bridgeport	20	166	19.6	3.4	252	4 422	332.3	144.2	161	932	71.9	22.1
Bristol	13	178	18.7	3.7	116	1 460	93.5	45.4	92	434	23.8	6.5
Danbury	27	224	11.4	3.2	192	3 359	232.0	129.4	152	853	59.2	17.8
Hartford	16	227	58.9	33.2	324	3 772	466.7	249.5	212	1 129	76.3	21.4
Meriden	6	0	0.0	0.0	113	1 567	107.8	47.3	96	447	29.9	10.2
Middletown	8	21	2.4	0.3	123	1 694	134.3	61.2	87	462	54.6	14.7
Milford	21	441	25.0	9.4	139	2 380	125.7	57.8	130	789	50.9	17.4
Naugatuck Borough	2	0	0.0	0.0	36	520	30.3	11.5	52	261	18.3	5.9
New Britain	7	68	5.2	1.2	118	2 004	154.0	84.7	100	530	40.7	11.5
New Haven	15	282	81.6	5.9	331	3 999	391.2	171.7	254	1 748	119.4	35.9
New London	8	0	0.0	0.0	103	1 953	195.7	71.5	66	409	23.3	8.1
Norwalk	41	314	40.4	7.7	234	2 389	203.9	99.9	179	880	73.9	23.5
Norwich	10	123	6.4	1.9	139	1 971	129.2	68.1	74	422	23.9	7.1
Shelton	4	21	1.1	0.3	61	1 036	70.8	35.5	47	237	14.5	4.7
Stamford	56	752	116.1	25.0	340	2 938	265.5	115.6	219	1 133	83.5	25.5
Torrington	8	68	7.9	0.7	94	1 601	86.9	37.0	76	303	17.5	4.8
Waterbury	22	190	19.0	2.5	248	4 374	316.6	153.6	188	1 001	62.9	19.4
West Haven	8	37	9.1	0.6	60	967	49.3	24.6	111	643	46.4	15.9
DELAWARE	216	4 074	240.1	62.0	1 465	15 980	1 131.6	526.4	1 198	7 006	420.5	140.7
Dover	10	0	0.0	0.0	128	1 428	94.3	42.6	103	678	36.1	11.4
Newark	9	138	5.5	1.4	126	1 456	167.5	73.8	69	473	27.4	11.6
Wilmington	21	754	24.2	7.8	249	2 106	190.5	90.0	166	1 236	72.4	27.0
DISTRICT OF COLUMBIA	171	1 564	161.9	56.1	1 464	13 692	1 054.8	476.7	978	6 218	404.8	111.1
Washington	171	1 564	161.9	56.1	1 464	13 692	1 054.8	476.7	978	6 218	404.8	111.1
FLORIDA	4 763	103 980	7 871.5	1 972.9	35 568	447 117	32 559.1	13 610.7	26 121	146 360	9 123.6	2 665.7
Altamonte Springs	17	164	9.1	2.1	192	2 032	166.3	70.2	110	778	48.9	15.3
Boca Raton	76	1 502	73.6	23.1	547	5 483	470.9	194.5	310	1 823	129.2	37.3
Boynton Beach	15	26	6.6	0.9	190	2 277	165.9	70.6	114	469	27.1	7.1
Bradenton	13	37	4.4	1.4	226	6 301	470.7	176.5	99	531	29.3	8.6
Cape Coral	23	228	12.0	2.6	168	1 330	98.3	41.2	137	550	40.5	11.5
Clearwater	40	512	28.3	7.6	522	6 373	426.7	186.0	259	1 915	159.2	47.9
Coconut Creek	7	21	1.1	0.2	39	351	15.8	7.0	29	131	7.0	2.3
Coral Gables	27	347	25.6	4.9	462	3 479	311.4	121.0	122	752	35.7	12.4
Coral Springs	46	731	33.5	10.0	362	2 500	189.9	76.6	192	747	34.8	9.7
Davie	33	439	99.7	49.5	110	880	48.7	20.9	205	962	84.9	24.5
Daytona Beach	29	1 007	101.0	17.9	221	3 362	202.2	92.9	138	788	36.6	12.6
Deerfield Beach	23	325	120.4	13.0	117	1 398	97.8	32.7	128	918	39.1	14.2
Delray Beach	23	247	9.6	4.3	200	1 880	125.5	55.7	157	860	57.9	16.8
Dunedin	9	121	4.7	1.3	130	1 232	81.0	41.1	62	297	14.7	4.3
Fort Lauderdale	117	1 481	116.7	52.2	699	8 023	570.5	267.4	524	3 508	392.4	73.3
Fort Myers	19	483	14.0	4.4	292	7 275	566.7	252.3	200	1 504	89.5	29.6
Fort Pierce	9	71	5.4	1.6	140	2 991	216.0	88.0	90	497	26.9	8.6
Gainesville	35	523	18.8	4.7	281	2 442	157.1	77.9	209	1 096	69.1	20.5
Hallandale	17	0	0.0	0.0	107	767	59.2	23.1	90	470	28.6	9.3
Hialeah	31	282	30.1	5.8	680	9 124	698.4	233.9	465	1 893	113.4	29.5
Hollywood	72	1 419	103.5	18.3	450	6 097	514.4	211.2	288	2 096	143.6	42.5
Homestead	6	0	0.0	0.0	68	460	29.4	11.2	43	183	10.9	2.9
Jacksonville	173	2 808	187.6	94.3	1 579	23 107	1 729.8	810.5	1 448	9 054	604.7	184.3
Kissimmee	34	1 065	52.9	16.0	182	2 772	195.0	80.6	97	552	29.4	9.7
Lakeland	24	321	12.2	3.5	265	4 898	329.3	133.3	161	941	44.6	14.7
Lake Worth	9	282	10.7	4.4	93	1 055	54.3	22.2	93	343	22.3	5.6
Largo	16	114	5.0	1.3	249	5 499	401.1	156.2	176	771	47.4	14.9
Lauderdale Lakes	2	0	0.0	0.0	81	2 560	219.5	83.6	29	77	3.8	0.9
Lauderhill	11	139	4.1	2.1	111	1 580	76.4	32.8	89	462	21.2	6.1
Margate	19	194	9.2	2.6	143	1 952	136.6	53.2	130	541	34.4	9.6
Melbourne	22	360	15.7	3.6	263	3 690	309.3	141.3	135	809	40.8	13.5
Miami	123	2 733	470.2	146.5	1 319	12 101	980.0	375.5	836	5 045	337.2	85.8

1. Firms subject to federal tax.

Table D. Cities — Federal Funds and City Government Finances

City	Selected federal funds, fiscal 1999[1] (mil dol) — Procurement contracts		Grants					Direct payments for individuals		City government finances, 1997 — General revenue	Intergovernmental		Taxes	Per capita[3] (dollars)		
	Defense	Other	Total[2]	Health and family welfare	Energy and environment	Education	Housing and community development	Educational assistance	Housing assistance	Total (mil dol)	Total (mil dol)	Percent from state government	Total (mil dol)	Total	Property	Sales and gross receipts
	108	109	110	111	112	113	114	115	116	117	118	119	120	121	122	123
COLORADO—Cont'd																
Longmont	4.5	4.3	2.9	0.9	0.5	0.0	0.5	0.0	1.8	58.7	5.8	39.6	33.6	576	100	412
Loveland	0.9	4.2	1.8	0.7	0.0	0.0	0.2	0.0	0.1	39.7	3.6	49.5	16.2	360	63	277
Northglenn	0.0	0.0	0.1	0.0	0.0	0.0	0.0	0.0	0.0	20.4	1.9	78.3	11.5	395	58	325
Pueblo	0.3	7.8	11.7	2.8	0.1	2.5	3.5	4.3	4.7	68.4	11.4	52.6	41.2	414	62	346
Thornton	11.1	1.8	0.6	0.5	0.0	0.0	0.0	0.6	0.5	61.0	3.1	80.9	37.9	564	100	444
Westminster	0.6	5.2	0.8	0.0	0.6	0.2	0.0	2.2	0.7	103.1	15.6	23.2	49.5	531	25	489
Wheat Ridge	4.4	4.6	5.5	0.5	2.0	0.0	0.0	0.0	0.0	19.9	3.0	100.0	14.2	475	31	431
CONNECTICUT	3 126.8	509.6	3 845.7	2 588.4	90.4	251.6	78.2	51.0	71.6	X	X	X	X	X	X	X
Bridgeport	31.1	4.3	22.3	8.8	0.5	2.2	6.0	1.9	7.0	421.6	188.9	93.9	163.4	1 184	1 178	0
Bristol	0.1	0.0	1.6	0.0	0.0	0.0	1.0	0.0	0.9	127.9	42.2	94.7	71.0	1 191	1 179	0
Danbury	48.6	13.9	21.8	1.4	16.4	0.1	2.0	0.1	4.3	145.9	30.6	95.4	90.3	1 379	1 359	0
Hartford	29.6	13.4	561.4	289.0	55.7	76.6	31.4	2.7	9.6	523.5	296.6	84.7	184.9	1 389	1 365	0
Meriden	2.1	24.9	2.9	1.0	0.0	0.2	1.5	0.1	0.0	127.9	53.9	99.6	64.7	1 132	1 131	0
Middletown	1.3	1.3	9.6	3.1	0.0	0.6	0.7	3.3	3.6	116.0	33.1	100.0	54.6	1 263	1 256	0
Milford	2.1	0.7	0.8	0.0	0.0	0.0	0.6	0.0	0.0	NA	NA	NA	NA	NA	NA	NA
Naugatuck Borough	0.5	0.0	0.1	0.0	0.0	0.0	0.0	0.0	0.0	67.5	30.0	99.9	32.7	1 080	1 072	0
New Britain	1.3	0.2	9.8	3.5	0.0	0.3	5.2	2.0	-0.4	159.6	71.0	98.6	75.1	1 050	1 040	0
New Haven	1.4	13.2	326.7	255.2	12.5	8.3	9.1	8.0	13.4	449.1	238.7	94.5	147.8	1 185	1 151	3
New London	5.6	11.1	4.3	0.3	0.0	1.5	1.5	1.4	9.9	70.8	37.0	94.9	24.3	972	960	0
Norwalk	14.0	4.4	4.6	1.1	0.5	0.2	2.5	1.2	1.9	196.8	32.7	94.4	154.9	1 986	1 943	0
Norwich	0.1	0.0	1.6	0.0	0.0	0.0	1.3	0.7	2.1	96.7	41.0	95.7	41.0	1 143	1 033	0
Shelton	6.9	17.2	0.2	0.0	0.0	0.0	0.0	0.0	0.4	63.6	8.2	97.8	48.1	1 293	1 272	0
Stamford	14.4	16.9	16.5	2.1	1.2	0.0	3.2	0.6	-1.5	308.9	34.0	83.6	242.4	2 202	2 170	0
Torrington	2.8	0.0	0.3	0.0	0.0	0.0	0.2	0.0	2.3	70.9	22.2	100.0	43.3	1 255	1 240	0
Waterbury	8.3	0.6	12.5	2.3	0.0	2.9	4.8	1.7	3.2	254.2	119.2	93.5	116.0	1 090	1 079	0
West Haven	2.8	1.1	2.5	1.1	0.0	0.0	0.7	1.1	0.0	106.3	41.6	96.0	61.3	1 175	1 169	0
DELAWARE	92.7	128.5	825.1	390.4	61.6	82.5	11.1	11.5	18.2	X	X	X	X	X	X	X
Dover	2.0	0.5	139.8	8.6	45.7	29.2	5.2	4.5	0.0	18.0	2.3	78.6	8.1	266	180	13
Newark	4.8	3.6	60.0	11.2	4.1	3.8	0.1	3.1	4.6	12.9	1.6	82.9	4.2	151	116	0
Wilmington	16.1	10.4	58.9	19.6	1.1	7.1	5.8	0.8	4.3	106.3	13.8	47.4	58.8	846	291	24
DISTRICT OF COLUMBIA	1 344.1	5 059.3	5 292.8	2 697.0	55.0	347.2	96.2	33.1	91.0	X	X	X	X	X	X	X
Washington	1 344.1	5 059.3	5 292.8	2 697.0	55.0	347.2	96.2	33.1	91.0	5 040.0	1 782.2	0.0	2 637.4	4 855	1 288	1 686
FLORIDA	6 764.2	1 875.1	11 190.9	6 049.0	152.7	1 199.7	239.4	433.3	280.5	X	X	X	X	X	X	X
Altamonte Springs	0.7	0.5	0.1	0.0	0.0	0.0	0.0	0.1	0.0	38.2	3.2	97.5	18.4	478	228	224
Boca Raton	71.5	4.7	8.0	2.4	0.1	0.0	0.2	0.4	0.3	100.7	15.9	36.1	53.1	775	400	318
Boynton Beach	0.0	0.2	0.9	0.0	0.0	0.0	0.4	0.1	0.0	57.6	6.5	86.7	26.1	515	327	140
Bradenton	1.0	0.4	6.1	2.8	0.0	0.0	0.5	2.4	0.2	28.8	7.2	75.5	10.9	230	72	144
Cape Coral	0.2	0.1	1.5	0.0	0.0	0.0	1.0	0.1	0.0	106.1	11.9	70.7	31.6	359	258	81
Clearwater	109.0	11.2	9.4	0.6	0.0	6.1	1.7	2.4	0.0	115.7	14.6	50.8	51.2	512	210	277
Coconut Creek	0.0	0.0	1.5	1.5	0.0	0.0	0.0	0.4	0.0	19.8	3.3	76.1	11.0	323	133	130
Coral Gables	0.0	0.0	91.5	82.6	0.1	1.6	0.0	6.8	0.0	73.0	4.1	91.7	40.7	1 021	605	290
Coral Springs	10.3	12.6	0.8	0.0	0.0	0.0	0.0	0.0	0.8	62.7	7.7	97.0	35.9	341	146	157
Davie	0.6	0.0	1.1	0.0	0.0	0.2	0.2	0.1	0.0	34.9	5.2	81.6	23.6	404	186	179
Daytona Beach	10.6	3.1	17.5	1.2	0.0	0.5	1.8	1.5	2.4	67.2	11.9	46.1	26.0	398	206	170
Deerfield Beach	2.2	3.2	1.0	0.0	0.0	0.0	0.0	0.0	0.0	46.1	5.0	85.7	18.2	367	251	83
Delray Beach	0.0	0.5	1.9	0.4	0.0	0.0	0.8	0.0	0.0	56.1	7.6	62.4	31.1	614	382	185
Dunedin	0.0	0.5	0.1	0.0	0.0	0.0	0.0	0.2	0.0	37.0	3.6	82.8	12.6	362	136	213
Fort Lauderdale	15.9	11.2	62.4	16.3	0.7	2.5	3.5	31.4	8.8	183.9	24.4	53.2	93.9	619	348	232
Fort Myers	0.8	1.5	22.1	7.8	0.2	5.0	3.5	4.3	2.3	76.6	13.2	38.2	23.5	512	213	254
Fort Pierce	7.3	1.4	8.1	0.5	0.0	2.6	2.2	1.6	0.0	32.4	6.4	58.5	11.0	299	174	118
Gainesville	5.4	36.4	160.8	68.7	4.9	5.4	2.6	14.2	18.6	75.1	11.0	84.6	22.4	257	110	130
Hallandale	0.0	0.0	0.1	0.0	0.0	0.0	0.0	0.0	0.0	36.5	3.7	65.5	15.7	505	287	196
Hialeah	0.0	0.0	9.7	0.0	0.0	1.7	7.6	13.0	0.0	146.4	20.6	28.4	78.6	384	168	195
Hollywood	10.3	0.3	6.3	1.3	1.7	0.0	2.0	0.8	1.0	125.3	18.0	59.1	56.3	440	222	181
Homestead	0.0	0.0	3.5	0.5	2.6	0.0	0.0	0.0	1.0	35.7	14.8	33.9	5.9	255	178	48
Jacksonville	335.8	111.2	55.5	19.2	1.1	4.1	5.7	16.2	68.2	898.6	119.9	57.0	379.3	526	323	185
Kissimmee	6.1	0.0	1.9	0.0	0.0	0.7	0.0	0.1	1.9	36.3	11.9	33.7	13.3	365	124	224
Lakeland	1.1	0.5	8.2	0.0	0.0	0.1	2.9	2.2	0.6	95.0	12.4	59.4	18.4	252	81	150
Lake Worth	2.4	0.1	0.2	0.0	0.0	0.2	0.0	2.7	0.0	34.4	9.2	29.6	10.3	360	226	116
Largo	37.7	1.4	2.7	0.0	0.3	0.0	0.8	0.0	0.3	55.8	12.4	53.8	20.9	317	89	213
Lauderdale Lakes	0.0	0.0	0.2	0.0	0.0	0.0	0.0	0.8	6.1	10.3	2.3	96.7	5.3	189	67	112
Lauderhill	0.0	0.0	2.5	0.1	0.0	0.0	1.7	0.8	0.0	20.0	4.4	98.8	12.5	247	83	145
Margate	0.0	0.0	1.2	0.0	0.0	0.0	0.1	0.3	0.0	25.1	4.7	80.5	16.8	332	157	144
Melbourne	674.5	8.3	6.1	0.3	0.2	0.6	0.8	1.5	3.3	58.1	9.0	59.7	21.1	312	114	175
Miami	0.0	0.0	289.3	78.1	9.4	17.9	43.9	48.9	17.9	379.7	66.2	44.4	193.1	529	345	165

1. October 1, 1998 to September 30, 1999.   2. Includes program categories not shown separately. State totals include additional categories not allocated by city.   3. Based on population estimated as of July 1 of the year shown.

City	City government finances, 1997 (cont'd)												
	General expenditure												
	Per capita[1] (dollars)			Percent of total for —									
	Total (mil dol)	Total	Capital outlays	Public welfare	Highways	Parking facilities	Education	Health and hospitals	Police protection	Sewerage and sanitation	Parks and recreation	Housing and community development	Interest on debt
	124	125	126	127	128	129	130	131	132	133	134	135	136
COLORADO—Cont'd													
Longmont	59.0	1 012	245	0.0	15.6	0.0	0.0	0.1	14.1	19.2	16.5	1.2	2.4
Loveland	40.1	892	189	1.2	13.3	0.0	0.0	3.6	16.9	13.6	22.5	1.5	2.2
Northglenn	20.6	705	160	0.0	14.1	0.0	0.0	0.0	21.7	21.1	12.2	3.6	6.7
Pueblo	61.3	617	105	0.4	14.0	0.0	0.0	0.7	17.2	7.0	8.4	4.4	11.2
Thornton	49.3	733	160	0.0	20.0	0.0	0.0	0.0	16.1	18.9	11.8	0.0	5.3
Westminster	85.0	913	203	0.0	16.6	0.0	0.0	0.0	12.0	5.4	12.5	0.7	23.6
Wheat Ridge	19.7	657	243	0.0	15.3	0.0	0.0	0.0	32.6	0.0	9.6	0.0	1.1
CONNECTICUT	X	X	X	X	X	X	X	X	X	X	X	X	X
Bridgeport	407.2	2 951	71	3.5	1.0	0.0	38.7	2.2	7.2	6.5	1.0	3.0	2.8
Bristol	129.0	2 163	63	2.4	3.7	0.0	51.5	2.2	6.7	6.2	1.6	0.3	1.7
Danbury	142.7	2 178	225	0.9	3.6	0.3	48.7	1.5	6.7	2.4	2.1	0.6	2.9
Hartford	534.5	4 016	174	3.5	3.6	0.5	46.3	1.5	6.3	2.8	1.3	9.6	1.9
Meriden	147.8	2 585	395	1.1	1.9	0.1	44.9	1.2	4.7	3.9	1.2	1.1	3.5
Middletown	115.7	2 675	294	0.7	6.7	0.3	39.6	1.2	6.7	14.8	1.8	0.6	9.1
Milford	NA	NA	NA	NA	NA	NA	NA	NA	NA	NA	NA	NA	NA
Naugatuck Borough	64.2	2 116	60	0.3	4.1	0.0	59.8	1.9	4.8	0.2	1.6	0.4	2.9
New Britain	130.1	1 819	8	1.2	2.2	0.3	59.8	0.6	6.5	7.1	3.0	0.2	4.5
New Haven	458.9	3 681	371	4.8	2.9	1.7	41.4	0.7	5.1	3.7	2.6	1.9	3.0
New London	73.9	2 952	169	2.5	8.3	0.4	42.6	2.0	9.9	9.0	3.0	3.1	1.7
Norwalk	163.4	2 096	10	1.6	12.0	0.0	59.5	1.4	7.8	0.1	2.8	0.1	3.2
Norwich	107.9	3 008	241	1.3	2.7	0.4	57.2	0.1	5.6	7.0	2.9	1.6	2.5
Shelton	64.8	1 743	69	2.6	3.8	0.0	60.5	0.4	4.6	5.3	0.9	0.2	1.9
Stamford	332.6	3 022	278	3.8	2.2	0.4	38.9	3.6	6.3	3.7	1.3	0.7	2.9
Torrington	64.4	1 866	30	0.2	4.6	0.1	52.9	0.2	6.9	9.7	1.3	0.0	3.6
Waterbury	231.8	2 178	99	4.4	2.0	0.4	54.7	2.0	9.3	5.7	2.5	1.2	0.9
West Haven	96.6	1 852	10	1.6	1.8	0.0	60.1	0.3	11.5	7.3	0.7	0.5	2.6
DELAWARE	X	X	X	X	X	X	X	X	X	X	X	X	X
Dover	23.4	770	184	0.0	7.9	0.0	0.0	0.0	37.6	29.9	1.7	1.1	2.8
Newark	17.0	611	14	1.5	7.2	0.0	0.0	0.0	23.3	30.0	7.9	0.0	1.9
Wilmington	102.0	1 468	128	0.0	1.5	2.2	0.0	0.0	20.7	25.1	4.7	8.1	10.2
DISTRICT OF COLUMBIA	X	X	X	X	X	X	X	X	X	X	X	X	X
Washington	4 517.7	8 317	569	26.3	2.6	0.0	14.9	9.8	6.2	3.8	1.6	2.6	6.7
FLORIDA	X	X	X	X	X	X	X	X	X	X	X	X	X
Altamonte Springs	32.6	850	118	0.0	6.8	0.0	0.0	1.1	20.0	16.8	6.7	0.0	2.3
Boca Raton	104.7	1 528	211	0.0	8.9	0.0	0.0	0.0	12.5	7.3	14.0	3.6	9.4
Boynton Beach	47.1	929	43	0.0	1.8	0.0	0.0	0.2	20.8	22.9	14.4	0.0	4.7
Bradenton	25.2	533	1	0.0	4.7	0.4	0.0	0.0	18.6	25.1	10.0	9.4	7.8
Cape Coral	67.0	761	31	0.0	11.0	0.0	0.0	0.0	14.2	5.9	12.5	0.3	17.5
Clearwater	117.8	1 176	236	0.0	8.2	1.8	0.0	2.2	19.6	16.9	14.3	1.2	0.9
Coconut Creek	17.2	505	41	0.0	8.4	0.0	0.0	0.2	32.2	14.7	12.5	0.0	5.1
Coral Gables	81.3	2 037	342	0.0	4.8	3.1	0.0	0.0	29.7	12.2	11.6	0.0	1.3
Coral Springs	63.6	604	153	0.0	7.6	0.0	0.0	2.1	28.4	8.0	22.6	0.0	4.1
Davie	34.7	593	88	0.0	8.4	0.0	0.0	0.0	37.1	0.0	15.4	0.0	5.6
Daytona Beach	63.1	968	81	0.0	7.7	0.0	0.0	0.0	27.2	16.0	17.5	4.5	2.2
Deerfield Beach	43.3	874	61	0.0	4.5	0.1	0.0	0.1	13.8	25.2	7.3	0.6	2.8
Delray Beach	63.7	1 255	109	0.0	5.1	0.1	0.0	10.0	20.9	8.4	15.7	1.8	5.8
Dunedin	35.7	1 025	129	0.0	4.2	0.0	0.0	0.0	9.4	25.9	10.7	0.0	14.1
Fort Lauderdale	180.0	1 186	84	0.0	4.1	2.4	0.0	0.0	30.0	8.0	11.0	10.0	3.3
Fort Myers	68.6	1 495	114	0.0	5.6	3.0	0.0	0.0	16.4	12.7	15.3	11.4	12.4
Fort Pierce	30.4	824	64	0.0	6.6	0.0	0.0	0.0	23.6	24.6	7.5	4.1	2.6
Gainesville	86.5	991	77	0.0	5.8	0.0	0.0	0.0	20.6	16.5	5.4	3.8	7.6
Hallandale	34.4	1 105	187	0.0	3.9	0.0	0.0	0.0	23.8	17.4	9.2	0.0	0.5
Hialeah	139.2	680	75	0.0	4.7	0.0	0.0	0.0	19.2	25.2	4.8	5.0	6.1
Hollywood	117.5	919	24	0.0	7.3	1.4	0.0	0.0	30.6	19.5	7.6	0.8	0.5
Homestead	32.8	1 424	235	0.0	6.5	0.0	0.0	0.0	26.2	17.1	14.9	14.4	5.8
Jacksonville	1 018.9	1 413	295	0.8	3.9	0.2	0.0	4.9	9.8	13.0	6.9	3.8	20.2
Kissimmee	30.0	821	117	0.0	19.3	0.0	0.0	0.0	24.3	4.7	10.5	5.5	1.9
Lakeland	104.8	1 433	383	0.0	5.7	0.5	0.0	0.0	15.5	20.9	21.7	1.3	6.1
Lake Worth	32.8	1 150	145	0.0	6.2	0.2	0.0	0.0	23.1	24.6	10.6	0.0	3.5
Largo	58.3	885	209	0.0	1.9	0.0	0.0	0.0	16.0	23.2	16.3	2.0	2.8
Lauderdale Lakes	11.8	418	9	0.6	5.6	0.0	0.0	12.4	27.3	0.0	12.2	0.0	12.5
Lauderhill	21.9	434	13	0.0	4.1	0.0	0.0	0.0	20.9	18.2	12.2	0.0	1.1
Margate	25.4	501	60	0.0	2.9	0.0	0.0	0.0	30.1	0.0	10.5	0.0	1.6
Melbourne	43.5	644	46	0.0	9.3	0.0	0.0	0.0	27.0	13.7	9.3	1.7	3.4
Miami	416.4	1 140	187	0.0	4.6	3.8	0.0	0.0	23.9	10.2	11.1	3.8	9.2

1. Based on population estimated as of July 1 of the year shown.

Table D. Cities — City Government Finances, City Government Employment, and Climate

City	City government finances, 1997 (cont'd) Debt outstanding Total (mil dol)	Per capita[1] (dollars)	Percent utility	City government employment, 1999	Climate[2] Average daily temperature (degrees Fahrenheit) Mean January	July	Limits January[3]	July[4]	Annual precipitation (inches)	Heating degree days	Cooling degree days
	137	138	139	140	141	142	143	144	145	146	147
COLORADO—Cont'd											
Longmont	37.0	634	37.1	779	26.6	72.4	11.7	88.7	13.60	6 443	562
Loveland	23.0	511	55.4	630	27.7	71.5	14.1	85.5	15.07	6 368	479
Northglenn	63.8	2 182	72.2	NA	29.7	73.5	16.1	88.2	15.40	6 020	679
Pueblo	113.2	1 138	16.6	900	29.8	77.1	14.2	93.0	11.19	5 413	973
Thornton	252.9	3 762	53.9	549	29.7	73.5	16.1	88.2	15.40	6 020	679
Westminster	298.3	3 203	8.2	808	30.2	71.9	17.1	85.7	15.86	6 158	554
Wheat Ridge	3.0	101	0.0	NA	30.2	71.9	17.1	85.7	15.86	6 158	554
CONNECTICUT	X	X	X	X	X	X	X	X	X	X	X
Bridgeport	188.9	1 369	0.0	4 815	28.9	73.7	21.9	81.7	41.66	5 537	724
Bristol	44.4	745	28.3	NA	24.6	73.7	15.8	85.0	44.14	6 151	677
Danbury	66.8	1 020	19.7	1 776	23.8	71.3	13.2	83.6	44.50	6 492	486
Hartford	244.3	1 836	0.0	2 356	24.6	73.7	15.8	85.0	44.14	6 151	677
Meriden	85.1	1 489	5.8	1 650	27.1	72.8	19.2	83.3	49.72	5 945	633
Middletown	200.9	4 645	0.0	NA	27.1	72.8	19.2	83.3	49.72	5 945	633
Milford	NA	NA	NA	NA	NA	NA	NA	NA	NA	NA	NA
Naugatuck Borough	29.6	975	0.0	919	27.1	72.8	19.2	83.3	49.72	5 945	633
New Britain	126.2	1 764	0.8	1 938	24.6	73.7	15.8	85.0	44.14	6 151	677
New Haven	227.8	1 828	0.0	4 454	28.9	73.7	21.9	81.7	41.66	5 537	724
New London	31.0	1 238	18.8	856	27.7	71.4	18.5	80.7	48.16	5 951	472
Norwalk	81.5	1 045	0.0	2 112	27.5	72.9	17.9	83.5	46.80	5 865	613
Norwich	34.3	957	0.0	1 170	27.6	72.2	17.5	82.7	50.01	5 869	551
Shelton	22.2	598	0.0	NA	28.9	73.7	21.9	81.7	41.66	5 537	724
Stamford	210.6	1 913	0.0	3 428	27.4	72.6	17.6	84.4	49.43	5 778	613
Torrington	52.2	1 513	0.0	NA	23.6	70.7	13.5	82.0	49.28	6 636	418
Waterbury	68.6	644	17.5	3 404	27.1	72.8	19.2	83.3	49.72	5 945	633
West Haven	43.2	827	0.0	NA	28.9	73.7	21.9	81.7	41.66	5 537	724
DELAWARE	X	X	X	X	X	X	X	X	X	X	X
Dover	51.1	1 680	84.0	356	33.8	77.2	25.0	87.7	44.14	4 337	1 199
Newark	9.2	331	0.0	247	31.3	76.0	22.3	87.2	42.61	4 825	1 033
Wilmington	192.8	2 774	15.0	1 281	30.6	76.4	22.4	85.6	40.84	4 937	1 046
DISTRICT OF COLUMBIA	X	X	X	X	X	X	X	X	X	X	X
Washington	3 973.3	7 314	0.1	34 885	34.6	80.0	26.8	88.5	38.63	4 047	1 549
FLORIDA	X	X	X	X	X	X	X	X	X	X	X
Altamonte Springs	28.7	748	63.6	NA	59.7	82.3	48.6	91.5	48.11	686	3 381
Boca Raton	183.0	2 671	26.4	1 204	66.2	82.5	56.8	91.2	59.15	262	4 038
Boynton Beach	88.9	1 751	51.5	NA	65.1	82.2	55.7	89.9	60.75	323	3 891
Bradenton	28.0	594	0.0	NA	60.2	81.4	49.0	90.8	53.71	678	3 186
Cape Coral	306.6	3 482	46.5	1 045	63.8	82.8	53.2	91.1	53.37	418	3 855
Clearwater	122.7	1 226	87.7	1 700	59.9	82.1	50.0	90.2	43.92	726	3 396
Coconut Creek	12.2	358	0.0	NA	66.2	82.5	56.8	91.2	59.15	262	4 038
Coral Gables	22.8	571	0.0	834	67.2	82.6	59.2	89.0	55.91	200	4 198
Coral Springs	71.7	681	56.2	591	66.2	82.5	56.8	91.2	59.15	262	4 038
Davie	81.9	1 400	66.8	NA	67.2	82.6	57.9	90.1	60.64	205	4 124
Daytona Beach	72.3	1 108	74.0	NA	57.5	81.2	46.9	89.8	47.89	909	2 919
Deerfield Beach	32.6	658	36.5	NA	66.2	82.5	56.8	91.2	59.15	262	4 038
Delray Beach	97.0	1 913	48.2	NA	66.2	82.5	56.8	91.2	59.15	262	4 038
Dunedin	86.5	2 487	26.8	NA	59.9	82.1	50.0	90.2	43.92	726	3 396
Fort Lauderdale	110.4	727	25.8	2 375	67.2	82.6	57.9	90.1	60.64	205	4 124
Fort Myers	193.7	4 218	39.5	NA	63.8	82.8	53.2	91.1	53.37	418	3 855
Fort Pierce	117.6	3 189	91.0	NA	62.5	81.4	51.6	90.4	50.06	490	3 441
Gainesville	507.7	5 816	77.7	1 913	53.7	80.7	42.5	90.7	51.81	1 316	2 570
Hallandale	3.7	118	2.0	NA	67.2	82.6	57.9	90.1	60.64	205	4 124
Hialeah	68.9	336	7.1	1 449	66.3	82.4	56.8	89.8	63.01	273	4 012
Hollywood	120.3	941	94.4	1 560	67.2	82.6	57.9	90.1	60.64	205	4 124
Homestead	26.8	1 166	0.0	322	65.3	81.1	54.5	90.1	58.74	277	3 603
Jacksonville	4 790.4	6 643	55.8	NA	NA	NA	NA	NA	NA	NA	NA
Kissimmee	284.5	7 792	97.4	NA	61.0	81.7	48.7	91.4	46.11	603	3 324
Lakeland	654.6	8 947	72.9	2 040	61.1	82.5	50.4	92.2	47.54	588	3 546
Lake Worth	61.9	2 174	59.4	NA	65.1	82.2	55.7	89.9	60.75	323	3 891
Largo	25.8	393	0.0	NA	59.9	82.1	50.0	90.2	43.92	726	3 396
Lauderdale Lakes	16.5	585	0.0	NA	67.2	82.6	57.9	90.1	60.64	205	4 124
Lauderhill	17.4	344	54.0	NA	67.2	82.6	57.9	90.1	60.64	205	4 124
Margate	19.0	375	69.4	NA	66.2	82.5	56.8	91.2	59.15	262	4 038
Melbourne	91.7	1 355	72.1	NA	60.9	81.1	50.7	90.0	45.49	644	3 193
Miami	576.4	1 579	0.0	3 341	67.2	82.6	59.2	89.0	55.91	200	4 198

1. Based on the population estimated as of July 1 of the year shown.   2. Represents normal values based on the 30-year period, 1961–1990.   3. Average daily minimum.   4. Average daily maximum.

Table D. Cities — **Land Area and Population**

STATE Place code	City	Land area, 1990[1] (sq km)	Population, 1999				Population				Population characteristics, 1990						
														Percent			
														Race			
			Total persons	Rank	Per square kilo-meter		Total persons 1990	Percent change 1990–1999		Total persons 1980	Percent change 1980–1990	White	Black	Am. Indian, Eskimo, Aleut	Asian and Pacific Islander	Other race	His-panic[2]	Foreign born
		1	2	3	4		5	6		7	8	9	10	11	12	13	14	15
	FLORIDA—Cont'd																
12 45025	Miami Beach	18.2	97 855	238	5 377		92 639	5.6		96 298	-3.8	88.3	5.2	0.2	1.2	5.2	46.8	51.3
12 45975	Miramar	76.9	61 425	438	799		40 663	51.1		32 813	23.9	79.3	15.7	0.2	2.3	2.6	17.3	20.1
12 49425	North Lauderdale	10.0	30 244	1 004	3 024		26 473	14.2		NA	NA	80.1	14.5	0.2	2.9	2.3	12.1	18.6
12 49450	North Miami	21.8	50 584	578	2 320		50 001	1.2		42 566	17.5	62.4	31.9	0.2	2.4	3.1	24.6	37.2
12 49475	North Miami Beach	12.9	35 020	860	2 715		35 361	-1.0		36 553	-3.3	71.6	21.8	0.2	3.4	3.1	22.1	35.0
12 50575	Oakland Park	16.5	28 228	1 065	1 711		26 326	7.2		23 035	14.3	83.2	12.9	0.2	1.7	2.1	11.9	16.6
12 50750	Ocala	74.7	47 926	616	642		42 045	14.0		37 161	13.1	74.9	23.8	0.3	0.6	0.4	2.2	2.7
12 53000	Orlando	174.2	180 308	105	1 035		164 674	9.5		128 291	28.4	68.8	26.9	0.3	1.6	2.5	8.7	6.9
12 53150	Ormond Beach	65.3	35 321	853	541		29 721	18.8		21 378	39.0	95.1	3.5	0.1	1.0	0.2	1.7	6.0
12 54000	Palm Bay	164.8	78 649	317	477		62 543	25.8		18 560	237.0	89.3	7.5	0.3	1.8	1.2	5.3	7.4
12 54700	Panama City	40.1	39 869	756	994		34 396	15.9		33 346	3.1	75.5	21.8	0.6	1.7	0.4	1.3	2.8
12 55775	Pembroke Pines	82.7	121 279	174	1 466		65 566	85.0		35 776	83.3	91.3	5.3	0.2	2.0	1.3	11.5	15.0
12 55925	Pensacola	58.6	57 112	492	975		59 198	-3.5		57 619	2.7	65.7	31.9	0.5	1.6	0.3	1.6	2.7
12 56975	Pinellas Park	35.9	44 388	671	1 236		43 571	1.9		32 811	32.8	96.1	1.0	0.3	1.9	0.8	3.3	6.3
12 57425	Plantation	56.3	82 134	297	1 459		66 814	22.9		48 501	37.8	90.7	6.2	0.1	1.8	1.2	8.1	13.9
12 58050	Pompano Beach	52.7	76 342	329	1 449		72 411	5.4		52 618	37.6	70.0	28.5	0.1	0.6	0.8	5.4	14.2
12 58575	Port Orange	52.1	45 452	653	872		35 399	28.4		18 756	88.7	97.7	1.0	0.3	0.8	0.2	2.0	5.3
12 58715	Port St. Lucie	196.6	81 845	299	416		55 761	46.8		14 690	279.6	94.2	3.8	0.3	0.9	0.9	4.0	6.3
12 60975	Riviera Beach	19.4	29 655	1 019	1 529		27 646	7.3		26 473	4.4	28.7	69.7	0.2	0.8	0.7	2.6	8.1
12 63000	St. Petersburg	153.3	234 647	70	1 531		240 318	-2.4		238 647	0.7	78.0	19.6	0.2	1.7	0.5	2.6	7.2
12 63650	Sanford	44.8	37 142	816	829		32 387	14.7		23 176	39.7	68.8	28.5	0.4	0.9	1.4	4.9	3.7
12 64175	Sarasota	37.9	50 763	575	1 339		50 897	-0.3		48 876	4.1	82.0	16.2	0.2	0.7	0.9	4.7	6.5
12 69700	Sunrise	47.2	82 174	296	1 741		65 683	25.1		39 681	65.5	89.3	7.4	0.1	1.9	1.3	8.6	16.3
12 70600	Tallahassee	163.9	135 938	149	829		124 773	8.9		81 548	53.0	68.2	29.1	0.2	1.8	0.7	3.0	4.5
12 70675	Tamarac	29.8	53 485	538	1 795		44 822	19.3		29 376	52.6	96.0	2.3	0.1	0.9	0.7	5.4	13.6
12 71000	Tampa	281.5	290 973	58	1 034		280 015	3.9		271 523	3.1	70.9	25.0	0.3	1.4	2.4	15.0	8.0
12 71900	Titusville	50.5	41 586	715	823		39 394	5.6		31 910	23.5	87.3	11.0	0.4	0.8	0.5	2.8	3.2
12 76600	West Palm Beach	127.8	76 970	326	602		67 764	13.6		63 305	7.0	63.4	32.6	0.1	0.9	2.9	14.2	18.7
13 00000	**GEORGIA**	150 009.5	7 788 240	X	52		6 478 149	20.2		5 462 982	18.6	71.0	27.0	0.2	1.2	0.7	1.7	2.7
13 01052	Albany	143.6	75 929	331	529		78 804	-3.6		74 059	6.4	44.2	55.0	0.2	0.4	0.2	0.8	1.0
13 03436	Athens	43.0	89 361	265	2 078		86 522	3.3		42 549	103.3	66.4	29.6	0.1	3.3	0.5	1.6	5.6
13 04000	Atlanta	341.3	401 726	40	1 177		393 929	2.0		425 022	-7.3	31.0	67.1	0.1	0.9	0.9	1.9	3.4
13 04196	Augusta	50.9	186 206	99	3 658		186 177	0.0		47 532	-6.1	43.0	56.0	0.2	0.6	0.2	0.8	1.7
13 19000	Columbus	560.0	(3)181 547	(3)103	(3)324		(3)178 685	(3)1.6		NA	NA	59.0	38.0	0.3	1.4	1.4	2.9	3.4
13 25720	East Point	35.6	34 595	917	929		34 595	-4.4		37 486	-7.7	31.6	66.3	0.2	0.7	1.1	1.9	3.2
13 44340	La Grange	67.2	24 973	1 199	372		25 574	-2.4		24 163	5.8	56.7	42.3	0.1	0.8	0.1	0.6	1.6
13 49000	Macon	124.0	113 336	193	914		107 365	5.6		116 903	-8.2	47.1	52.2	0.1	0.4	0.1	0.6	0.8
13 49756	Marietta	52.8	51 055	569	967		44 129	15.7		30 829	43.1	76.3	20.5	0.3	1.8	1.1	3.2	5.1
13 66668	Rome	62.7	32 677	926	521		30 425	7.4		29 609	2.4	68.8	29.7	0.2	0.7	0.6	1.7	1.8
13 67284	Roswell	84.4	57 952	485	687		47 986	20.8		23 337	105.6	92.2	4.9	0.1	1.8	1.1	2.7	6.3
13 69000	Savannah	162.1	129 556	158	799		137 812	-6.0		141 378	-2.5	46.8	51.3	0.2	1.1	0.5	1.4	1.9
13 71492	Smyrna	29.5	37 685	805	1 277		32 453	16.1		20 312	59.8	80.2	15.9	0.3	2.3	1.4	3.5	5.9
13 78800	Valdosta	68.6	42 462	697	619		40 038	6.1		37 533	6.7	55.2	43.5	0.2	0.9	0.2	1.1	1.8
13 80508	Warner Robins	43.2	49 396	590	1 143		43 861	12.6		39 879	10.0	72.7	25.0	0.3	1.4	0.6	1.8	3.0
15 00000	**HAWAII**	16 636.5	1 185 497	X	71		1 108 229	7.0		964 691	14.9	33.4	2.5	0.5	61.8	1.9	7.3	14.7
15 14650	Hilo CDP	140.6	NA	NA	NA		NA	NA		35 269	7.2	26.6	0.6	0.6	70.2	2.1	8.5	5.2
15 17000	Honolulu CDP	214.5	395 327	41	1 843		377 059	4.8		365 048	3.3	26.7	1.3	0.3	70.5	1.2	4.6	21.4
15 23150	Kailua CDP	17.2	NA	NA	NA		NA	NA		35 812	2.8	57.7	1.4	0.5	39.1	1.3	5.5	5.5
15 28250	Kaneohe CDP	17.0	NA	NA	NA		NA	NA		29 919	18.5	31.2	1.2	0.4	65.6	1.6	6.9	6.1
15 51050	Mililani CDP	10.1	NA	NA	NA		NA	NA		21 365	37.4	34.2	2.9	0.3	61.2	1.4	5.4	8.5
15 62600	Pearl City CDP	12.9	NA	NA	NA		NA	NA		42 575	-27.2	21.4	2.5	0.3	74.1	1.7	6.6	10.1
15 77750	Waimalu CDP	15.3	NA	NA	NA		NA	NA		NA	NA	28.1	2.3	0.4	67.8	1.4	5.6	12.7
15 79700	Waipahu CDP	6.7	NA	NA	NA		NA	NA		29 139	7.9	11.6	2.0	0.5	83.8	2.2	11.5	26.6
16 00000	**IDAHO**	214 325.0	1 251 700	X	6		1 006 734	24.3		944 127	6.6	94.4	0.3	1.4	0.9	3.0	5.3	2.9
16 08830	Boise City	119.5	168 370	118	1 409		126 685	32.9		102 451	23.7	96.4	0.6	0.6	1.6	0.8	2.7	2.3
16 39700	Idaho Falls	37.6	48 627	601	1 293		43 973	10.6		39 590	11.1	95.3	0.6	0.6	1.2	2.3	4.2	2.5
16 46540	Lewiston	42.6	30 597	992	718		28 082	9.0		27 986	0.3	97.4	0.1	1.4	0.7	0.4	1.2	1.5
16 56260	Nampa	28.0	46 125	636	1 647		28 365	62.6		25 112	13.0	89.5	0.3	1.0	1.1	8.2	12.8	4.2
16 64090	Pocatello	71.5	52 781	543	738		46 117	14.5		46 340	-0.5	94.1	0.9	1.4	1.3	2.4	4.5	1.9
16 82810	Twin Falls	27.3	34 316	882	1 257		27 634	24.2		26 209	5.4	94.8	0.2	0.7	1.6	2.8	6.8	2.9
17 00000	**ILLINOIS**	143 986.6	12 128 370	X	84		11 430 602	6.1		11 427 409	0.0	78.3	14.8	0.2	2.5	4.2	7.9	8.3
17 00243	Addison	22.3	34 259	884	1 536		32 053	6.9		29 759	7.7	87.9	1.7	0.1	5.9	4.4	13.4	19.5
17 01114	Alton	38.9	31 072	977	799		33 060	-6.0		34 171	-3.2	75.6	23.1	0.5	0.3	0.5	1.1	0.9
17 02154	Arlington Heights	41.9	76 242	330	1 820		75 463	1.0		66 116	14.1	94.0	0.3	0.1	3.7	0.8	2.7	9.3
17 03012	Aurora	86.7	129 371	159	1 492		99 672	29.8		81 293	22.6	74.1	11.9	0.2	1.3	12.5	23.0	12.0
17 04845	Belleville	36.2	40 429	742	1 117		42 806	-5.6		41 580	2.9	92.1	6.8	0.2	0.6	0.3	1.3	1.6

1. Dry land or land partially or temporarily covered by water.   2. Hispanic persons may be of any race.   3. 1999 population is for Columbus "remainder"; most other items are for Columbus Consolidated city; see Appendix A.

Table D. Cities — **Population and Households**

City	Population characteristics, 1990 (cont'd)										Households, 1990				
	Age of population (percent)													Percent	
	Under 5 years	5 to 17 years	18 to 24 years	25 to 34 years	35 to 44 years	45 to 54 years	55 to 64 years	65 to 74 years	75 years and over	Percent female	Number	Percent change, 1980–1990	Persons per house-hold	Female family house-holder[1]	One-person
	16	17	18	19	20	21	22	23	24	25	26	27	28	29	30
FLORIDA—Cont'd															
Miami Beach	4.6	9.6	7.5	16.1	12.6	9.4	10.0	11.8	18.5	53.4	49 305	-11.4	1.85	9.1	50.7
Miramar	8.0	18.3	8.8	20.6	16.2	10.6	8.1	5.7	3.7	51.8	14 395	23.8	2.82	13.3	17.7
North Lauderdale	8.7	19.5	10.8	24.0	17.8	8.0	4.7	4.0	2.4	50.3	9 071	NA	2.92	12.0	15.1
North Miami	7.2	15.5	9.9	19.9	15.4	9.0	8.1	7.7	7.3	52.7	20 127	3.1	2.44	13.9	33.2
North Miami Beach	6.3	15.6	7.3	17.1	15.5	10.3	8.6	9.1	10.2	53.5	13 968	-11.6	2.47	13.9	29.2
Oakland Park	6.8	10.9	10.0	25.2	16.3	9.3	8.6	7.2	5.8	49.8	12 097	13.7	2.14	10.7	34.9
Ocala	6.9	16.6	9.0	14.2	12.0	10.6	9.9	11.5	9.3	53.7	17 393	28.3	2.34	15.3	31.3
Orlando	6.8	14.2	16.1	22.7	13.7	8.2	7.0	6.4	4.9	49.7	65 703	37.0	2.29	14.2	33.0
Ormond Beach	4.6	13.6	6.6	12.1	13.5	11.5	13.0	14.8	10.3	52.6	12 703	54.3	2.32	8.7	24.9
Palm Bay	8.6	18.4	8.7	21.8	14.7	8.2	8.3	7.9	3.5	50.2	23 328	233.6	2.67	8.8	17.9
Panama City	6.8	17.6	9.3	16.5	13.3	10.2	9.4	9.5	7.4	53.2	14 053	8.6	2.38	15.0	30.5
Pembroke Pines	6.2	14.1	7.7	18.4	15.5	9.8	9.0	11.6	7.9	53.2	26 722	110.2	2.40	8.5	24.6
Pensacola	6.5	17.3	9.5	15.3	14.7	10.1	9.9	9.9	6.7	53.6	23 983	10.5	2.40	16.6	29.8
Pinellas Park	6.5	13.9	8.6	17.0	12.7	9.6	8.5	12.3	10.8	53.0	18 185	40.0	2.34	10.3	26.4
Plantation	5.5	15.5	8.9	16.5	16.8	13.4	9.1	7.6	6.7	52.1	26 489	57.4	2.50	8.7	22.9
Pompano Beach	5.9	11.2	7.4	17.3	13.0	9.3	10.6	12.9	12.4	51.9	32 157	32.3	2.17	10.5	34.7
Port Orange	5.2	14.2	7.0	15.3	15.1	9.3	11.4	14.7	7.8	51.8	14 964	97.1	2.35	8.0	23.1
Port St. Lucie	7.5	17.3	6.4	18.3	14.5	8.5	10.4	12.2	4.8	50.6	20 675	298.1	2.69	6.9	13.2
Riviera Beach	8.9	19.4	8.8	15.5	11.9	10.7	9.2	9.3	6.2	52.7	10 333	10.5	2.65	21.8	25.7
St. Petersburg	5.9	13.8	8.3	16.4	14.0	9.7	9.6	10.9	11.3	53.6	105 703	1.2	2.19	12.4	35.1
Sanford	8.6	18.0	10.9	19.7	14.7	7.5	7.6	7.6	5.5	51.2	12 119	43.6	2.58	16.0	26.9
Sarasota	5.9	12.3	9.1	15.9	12.6	9.6	9.5	12.1	13.1	53.0	22 822	5.3	2.14	12.6	34.2
Sunrise	6.9	14.8	7.4	17.9	15.1	8.2	6.6	11.9	11.1	53.0	26 314	64.3	2.43	8.9	25.1
Tallahassee	5.5	13.8	26.4	18.1	13.8	7.9	5.7	5.2	3.5	52.4	50 442	63.0	2.26	13.2	31.6
Tamarac	3.0	5.7	5.3	11.9	8.3	6.8	11.4	25.0	22.6	54.6	22 906	64.3	1.94	5.2	31.4
Tampa	7.4	15.5	10.8	19.0	14.0	9.9	8.8	8.3	6.3	52.0	114 800	8.6	2.35	15.5	32.3
Titusville	7.0	16.1	8.1	18.1	12.7	10.8	11.4	9.8	6.0	51.6	16 207	40.0	2.42	10.9	25.6
West Palm Beach	6.8	13.5	9.5	19.6	14.1	9.5	8.8	9.4	8.9	52.2	28 787	8.3	2.27	13.3	35.2
GEORGIA	7.6	19.0	11.4	18.1	15.7	10.3	7.7	6.0	4.1	51.5	2 366 615	26.4	2.66	13.9	22.7
Albany	8.6	22.3	12.0	15.5	13.9	9.0	7.8	6.5	4.2	53.6	27 926	12.9	2.69	24.1	25.0
Athens	5.2	10.7	39.2	15.2	8.9	5.7	5.0	5.4	4.8	53.7	17 012	12.4	2.25	14.7	34.7
Atlanta	7.6	16.5	13.0	19.4	15.4	9.7	7.2	6.0	5.3	52.3	155 752	-4.4	2.40	23.4	35.0
Augusta	7.8	16.5	10.7	16.9	11.9	8.7	8.6	10.3	8.5	55.1	18 819	-2.2	2.26	23.1	39.2
Columbus	8.2	18.9	12.1	18.3	14.0	9.2	8.5	6.7	4.1	51.4	65 942	NA	2.61	17.1	24.5
East Point	8.0	18.8	10.4	19.0	15.7	9.8	6.7	7.1	4.5	53.7	13 373	-9.0	2.55	22.5	28.2
La Grange	7.9	19.6	11.4	15.4	12.4	8.7	8.9	8.3	7.4	55.0	9 772	13.4	2.54	20.2	28.9
Macon	7.7	18.8	11.4	16.5	13.6	8.7	8.8	8.5	6.1	54.7	41 175	-2.5	2.50	22.7	29.6
Marietta	7.4	12.4	15.9	25.7	13.8	7.8	6.3	5.9	4.7	51.7	19 866	54.6	2.17	11.3	35.8
Rome	6.8	17.1	10.8	15.2	13.0	9.9	9.5	9.6	8.3	54.4	12 008	7.2	2.39	17.1	32.0
Roswell	7.0	18.2	9.3	17.9	20.2	14.1	6.5	4.3	2.5	51.0	18 189	124.9	2.62	8.3	20.5
Savannah	8.2	18.6	11.8	17.3	13.0	9.3	8.1	8.2	5.6	52.9	51 938	2.3	2.55	19.8	29.5
Smyrna	5.7	11.4	12.3	29.4	15.4	10.3	7.1	5.0	3.4	52.5	14 835	85.1	2.06	9.5	38.8
Valdosta	8.5	19.5	16.7	16.1	12.9	8.6	6.8	6.2	4.6	53.6	14 143	10.0	2.65	19.6	24.8
Warner Robins	8.4	19.7	9.6	20.0	14.7	10.8	8.6	5.9	2.3	51.7	16 721	21.4	2.60	14.0	24.2
HAWAII	7.5	17.8	10.9	18.1	16.1	9.8	8.5	7.1	4.2	49.1	356 267	20.8	3.01	10.5	19.4
Hilo CDP	6.8	20.7	8.4	13.9	15.8	10.2	9.7	8.9	5.6	51.2	13 324	19.2	2.79	13.9	22.1
Honolulu CDP	5.4	13.7	9.8	17.8	16.2	10.8	10.3	9.8	6.1	50.6	134 563	5.7	2.63	11.0	27.4
Kailua CDP	6.6	17.5	9.9	16.5	17.0	12.0	9.6	7.6	3.3	49.5	11 843	10.6	3.11	10.3	11.4
Kaneohe CDP	7.3	17.7	9.9	18.8	15.4	10.5	9.5	6.4	4.5	50.2	10 610	29.3	3.26	10.8	11.7
Mililani CDP	8.3	24.3	7.9	17.4	22.3	11.4	4.4	2.7	1.0	49.6	8 776	38.4	3.35	6.9	8.1
Pearl City CDP	6.8	17.5	12.1	17.2	13.0	13.1	11.6	6.5	2.2	49.5	8 876	-20.6	3.49	9.1	8.2
Waimalu CDP	6.9	16.8	10.8	20.9	19.9	11.1	7.5	4.9	1.2	49.5	10 372	NA	2.87	8.3	17.3
Waipahu CDP	8.4	20.9	12.7	16.6	12.2	9.6	9.1	6.7	3.8	49.9	7 567	9.0	4.13	17.7	9.2
IDAHO	8.0	22.7	9.8	15.2	14.8	9.8	7.7	6.9	5.1	50.2	360 723	11.0	2.73	8.0	22.4
Boise City	7.4	18.1	11.2	18.4	16.9	9.1	7.0	6.7	5.2	51.7	50 852	25.8	2.42	9.7	27.8
Idaho Falls	9.2	22.7	10.0	16.7	14.8	8.8	7.6	6.1	4.1	50.0	16 017	15.1	2.71	8.4	24.6
Lewiston	6.4	17.9	10.0	15.4	15.1	9.9	9.2	9.0	7.0	51.2	11 515	6.7	2.40	8.2	27.8
Nampa	9.0	19.6	12.6	16.2	11.3	8.4	6.6	8.3	8.1	52.1	10 213	13.7	2.61	11.7	26.7
Pocatello	8.5	21.6	12.4	16.8	14.7	8.2	6.9	6.5	4.5	50.9	17 183	2.3	2.62	9.5	26.5
Twin Falls	8.0	20.6	9.5	15.4	13.8	9.2	8.0	8.2	7.3	52.0	10 472	7.4	2.55	9.7	26.3
ILLINOIS	7.4	18.4	10.6	17.4	14.9	10.2	8.5	7.2	5.4	51.4	4 202 240	3.8	2.65	12.0	25.7
Addison	8.1	18.9	11.7	19.6	14.0	12.8	8.4	4.5	2.0	50.0	10 722	13.0	2.98	10.3	17.5
Alton	8.1	18.0	9.2	17.3	13.3	8.2	8.6	8.4	8.8	53.3	12 969	-0.1	2.47	15.4	30.5
Arlington Heights	6.8	15.9	8.2	18.0	16.3	12.5	10.0	6.9	5.3	51.9	28 810	29.7	2.58	6.2	23.7
Aurora	10.5	20.6	11.3	21.1	13.9	8.5	5.6	4.7	3.8	50.6	33 710	21.8	2.90	12.2	22.7
Belleville	6.7	16.2	8.6	17.8	14.3	8.1	9.3	9.5	9.6	53.3	17 739	9.6	2.32	11.6	33.5

1. No spouse present.

Table D. Cities — Group Quarters, Crime, Education, and Income

City	Persons in group quarters, 1990 — Total	Persons in mental hospitals	Persons in nursing homes	Persons identified as homeless[1]	Serious crimes known to police, 1998[2] — Total — Number	Total — Rate[3]	Rate[3] — Violent	Rate[3] — Property	Education, 1990 — School enrollment — Public	Private	Attainment[4] (percent) — High school graduate or more	Bachelor's degree or more	Money income, 1989 — Per capita (dollars)[5]	Households — Median — Dollars	Median — Percent change, 1979–1989 (constant 1989 dollars)
	31	32	33	34	35	36	37	38	39	40	41	42	43	44	45
FLORIDA—Cont'd															
Miami Beach	1 444	0	1 029	95	15 189	15 729	1 443	14 286	12 727	4 088	65.5	21.2	16 504	15 312	7.4
Miramar	0	0	0	0	2 912	5 499	693	4 806	8 394	2 231	77.9	14.9	13 820	35 794	2.5
North Lauderdale	0	0	0	0	1 623	5 523	650	4 873	6 342	1 051	82.7	14.9	13 440	36 297	NA
North Miami	863	0	778	0	5 258	10 142	1 668	8 474	10 969	2 549	69.3	17.9	13 297	24 898	-2.1
North Miami Beach	861	0	539	72	2 554	7 177	770	6 407	7 195	1 596	68.7	14.9	13 531	24 963	3.0
Oakland Park	348	0	173	0	3 552	12 148	1 556	10 592	3 678	1 177	78.3	17.5	15 273	27 708	6.0
Ocala	1 292	69	577	46	5 617	11 969	1 355	10 614	7 851	836	71.6	16.7	12 783	21 766	7.7
Orlando	14 236	147	677	915	25 421	14 004	2 252	11 752	30 232	4 687	78.1	22.6	13 879	26 119	18.8
Ormond Beach	272	0	272	0	1 556	4 677	334	4 343	4 713	1 273	84.2	26.2	18 875	32 704	8.4
Palm Bay	270	21	190	0	4 220	5 452	813	4 639	12 924	2 745	82.1	16.7	12 645	30 287	5.9
Panama City	907	13	502	63	3 036	8 200	718	7 482	7 685	887	70.3	16.7	12 169	21 881	11.6
Pembroke Pines	1 360	491	79	0	4 289	4 100	282	3 818	11 439	3 041	81.8	20.9	16 747	36 431	-6.5
Pensacola	644	18	516	35	3 757	6 129	825	5 304	12 794	2 073	79.1	28.1	14 795	25 066	5.1
Pinellas Park	776	0	681	24	2 973	6 615	483	6 132	6 818	1 440	73.8	10.8	12 734	26 109	11.7
Plantation	492	0	472	0	5 252	6 424	352	6 072	11 895	3 782	87.7	31.7	21 702	41 832	-1.2
Pompano Beach	2 445	0	598	13	7 475	9 644	1 564	8 080	10 047	2 605	73.7	18.4	17 382	29 683	5.2
Port Orange	175	0	114	0	1 158	2 714	80	2 634	6 514	1 018	79.8	15.3	13 391	26 472	21.5
Port St. Lucie	184	0	117	0	NA	NA	NA	NA	10 499	1 824	80.6	13.2	14 018	32 553	2.5
Riviera Beach	194	0	73	10	5 941	19 940	2 346	17 594	6 396	829	67.1	15.7	14 674	24 847	5.9
St. Petersburg	6 676	28	3 980	292	22 833	9 469	1 937	7 532	40 870	8 716	75.1	18.6	14 132	23 577	19.2
Sanford	1 158	0	196	63	3 648	9 841	1 486	8 355	7 106	732	70.8	11.9	11 115	25 029	27.8
Sarasota	2 019	0	944	83	4 617	8 800	1 367	7 433	7 874	1 266	76.4	21.0	16 151	24 884	13.5
Sunrise	474	35	405	0	6 162	7 642	418	7 224	11 575	2 564	79.2	16.7	14 593	31 540	13.5
Tallahassee	10 700	0	507	152	14 507	10 380	1 279	9 101	48 511	3 552	85.5	40.7	13 247	23 453	19.1
Tamarac	242	0	242	0	1 767	3 329	273	3 056	4 030	1 156	76.0	14.2	18 012	26 703	7.7
Tampa	10 024	88	1 384	460	35 960	12 189	2 557	9 632	54 676	11 045	70.6	18.7	13 277	22 772	10.3
Titusville	122	0	10	24	2 285	5 328	765	4 563	7 868	1 279	80.7	18.9	14 274	28 425	2.6
West Palm Beach	2 467	45	1 193	149	12 803	15 512	1 902	13 610	11 038	3 175	71.7	20.4	15 712	26 504	18.3
GEORGIA	172 721	3 640	36 549	4 288	417 479	5 463	573	4 890	1 433 862	209 997	70.9	19.3	13 631	29 021	15.2
Albany	2 852	8	636	70	6 527	8 183	758	7 425	20 885	2 449	66.4	17.8	10 496	21 885	-4.3
Athens	7 501	0	337	12	NA	NA	NA	NA	22 535	993	72.2	36.1	9 252	14 286	-14.9
Atlanta	20 491	5	1 706	2 501	NA	NA	NA	NA	83 204	19 991	69.9	26.6	15 279	22 275	17.7
Augusta	1 983	0	328	108	NA	NA	NA	NA	9 311	1 419	57.2	17.4	10 367	15 315	6.5
Columbus	7 567	168	910	238	NA	NA	NA	NA	39 810	4 829	71.5	16.6	11 949	24 056	NA
East Point	258	0	160	0	4 001	11 349	1 084	10 265	7 203	1 217	72.3	18.0	12 508	26 787	7.9
La Grange	784	0	422	8	2 664	10 235	484	9 751	5 457	1 093	57.7	16.2	12 181	21 851	9.2
Macon	3 442	18	888	146	12 750	10 962	893	10 069	22 027	5 648	63.9	15.3	11 502	21 038	-3.4
Marietta	1 093	0	414	57	3 809	7 144	756	6 388	8 009	2 067	81.3	28.2	15 808	27 371	7.4
Rome	1 624	108	388	29	3 370	11 417	2 070	9 347	5 500	1 509	63.4	17.5	11 973	21 078	4.3
Roswell	194	0	194	0	2 587	4 519	272	4 247	10 090	2 521	92.3	45.6	24 080	52 205	11.9
Savannah	5 298	229	475	247	11 597	8 328	790	7 538	28 821	6 439	70.1	16.6	10 978	22 102	5.6
Smyrna	360	71	104	0	2 444	6 699	540	6 159	5 001	968	84.7	34.1	19 158	33 863	6.1
Valdosta	2 239	0	413	3	5 300	12 399	1 006	11 393	11 884	1 009	69.5	21.1	11 329	21 864	10.0
Warner Robins	288	0	186	11	3 950	8 301	681	7 620	10 021	1 190	80.7	14.8	12 531	29 722	-5.1
HAWAII	36 745	289	3 225	1 691	63 623	5 333	247	5 086	233 972	56 606	80.1	22.9	15 770	38 829	13.2
Hilo CDP	640	0	249	114	NA	NA	NA	NA	9 899	979	79.2	20.9	13 373	30 014	-1.4
Honolulu CDP	10 599	27	1 767	829	47 453	5 425	268	5 157	66 403	21 760	79.5	27.7	18 554	37 190	11.5
Kailua CDP	9	0	0	0	NA	NA	NA	NA	6 560	3 007	88.6	33.5	20 008	55 259	19.4
Kaneohe CDP	837	195	425	9	NA	NA	NA	NA	6 924	2 501	83.8	24.9	16 479	49 770	9.5
Mililani CDP	0	0	0	0	NA	NA	NA	NA	7 978	2 088	92.5	33.0	17 898	55 337	19.1
Pearl City CDP	8	0	0	0	NA	NA	NA	NA	6 803	1 604	83.9	15.9	15 580	50 752	3.2
Waimalu CDP	157	24	0	0	NA	NA	NA	NA	6 041	1 945	88.6	31.7	20 426	51 985	NA
Waipahu CDP	51	0	21	0	NA	NA	NA	NA	7 546	933	65.7	7.6	10 875	38 380	7.9
IDAHO	21 516	233	6 318	539	45 653	3 715	282	3 433	268 404	27 234	79.7	17.7	11 457	25 257	-1.4
Boise City	2 676	81	1 215	151	8 518	5 356	369	4 987	31 126	3 154	88.6	27.8	15 208	29 121	2.9
Idaho Falls	491	0	303	34	3 013	6 107	588	5 519	11 614	1 114	84.2	25.7	13 107	29 887	-3.9
Lewiston	412	0	184	0	1 556	5 026	129	4 897	6 830	480	80.9	16.3	12 828	25 711	-4.6
Nampa	1 708	0	609	37	2 588	6 548	476	6 072	6 158	1 285	70.4	10.7	8 810	19 696	-4.7
Pocatello	968	10	195	21	2 086	3 974	290	3 684	15 104	831	83.1	22.2	11 385	24 955	-12.2
Twin Falls	871	0	384	159	2 601	7 875	590	7 285	6 737	487	76.5	13.7	11 329	23 206	-6.6
ILLINOIS	285 237	4 408	93 662	9 551	586 923	4 873	808	4 065	2 440 505	591 168	76.2	21.0	15 201	32 252	-0.4
Addison	146	0	0	0	NA	NA	NA	NA	6 866	1 627	74.7	16.1	15 944	41 375	-1.1
Alton	818	214	329	12	NA	NA	NA	NA	6 926	1 079	72.4	11.6	10 904	22 948	-5.0
Arlington Heights	1 136	0	964	17	NA	NA	NA	NA	13 402	4 757	89.8	39.5	22 864	51 331	1.4
Aurora	1 780	48	647	257	5 966	4 921	618	4 303	21 198	6 097	71.2	18.6	13 335	35 039	3.5
Belleville	1 568	0	1 023	32	NA	NA	NA	NA	8 058	1 895	75.6	15.2	13 117	26 668	-4.5

1. Persons in emergency shelters and persons visible in street locations. 2. Data for serious crimes have not been adjusted for underreporting. This may affect comparability between geographic areas and over time. 3. Per 100,000 population estimated by the FBI. 4. Persons 25 years old and older. 5. Based on population enumerated as of April 1, 1990.

Table D. Cities — Income, Poverty, and Housing

City	Money income, 1989 (cont'd) Households (cont'd) Percent with $100,000 or more	Percent below poverty, 1989 Persons Total	Persons Percent change in rate, 1979-1989	Families Total	Housing units, 1990 Total	Percent change, 1980-1990	Vacant units for sale or rent[1]	Occupied units Total	Owner-occupied units Percent	Median value[2] (dollars)	Owner cost as a percent of income With a mortgage	Without a mortgage	Renter-occupied units Median rent[3] (dollars)	Rent as percent of income	Substandard units[4] (percent)
	46	47	48	49	50	51	52	53	54	55	56	57	58	59	60
FLORIDA—Cont'd															
Miami Beach	5.0	25.2	42.4	19.9	62 413	-3.3	8 028	49 305	28.5	191 300	25.2	13.7	427	35.1	15.5
Miramar	1.9	8.4	42.4	6.5	15 243	25.5	602	14 395	77.8	81 200	22.9	13.7	610	29.1	6.2
North Lauderdale	1.7	6.7	NA	4.7	9 800	NA	532	9 071	66.2	78 500	23.3	13.8	658	27.2	8.4
North Miami	2.4	15.5	47.6	12.4	22 107	7.7	1 466	20 127	48.7	71 800	24.2	12.5	489	28.5	15.8
North Miami Beach	3.1	12.9	43.3	9.0	15 821	-6.9	846	13 968	61.0	72 700	25.6	12.4	514	31.2	12.0
Oakland Park	1.8	10.4	10.6	7.8	13 875	17.9	937	12 097	49.3	89 200	22.8	13.0	541	27.7	6.0
Ocala	2.9	19.9	-5.2	15.4	19 478	32.7	1 403	17 393	57.2	62 900	21.5	12.6	392	26.4	5.3
Orlando	2.7	15.8	-11.2	12.2	73 425	42.5	6 200	65 703	41.1	74 300	21.4	12.6	506	27.3	5.4
Ormond Beach	6.2	6.7	-6.9	4.5	14 190	52.8	814	12 703	76.9	91 500	21.8	12.7	544	28.3	1.1
Palm Bay	1.5	8.7	26.1	6.1	26 273	232.7	1 842	23 328	66.8	67 500	22.2	11.1	510	24.8	2.3
Panama City	2.0	19.6	-5.3	16.4	15 928	12.6	1 314	14 053	58.3	49 800	19.3	13.1	364	26.3	2.8
Pembroke Pines	3.4	5.1	45.7	3.5	29 546	105.4	1 196	26 722	76.8	93 800	22.1	13.7	685	27.0	2.7
Pensacola	3.8	18.9	-3.1	14.2	26 366	13.1	1 626	23 983	60.5	63 600	20.0	12.6	388	26.8	3.5
Pinellas Park	1.0	9.3	4.5	6.9	20 593	41.0	1 171	18 185	73.6	61 900	22.2	12.1	498	26.7	2.6
Plantation	9.3	3.5	-7.9	2.1	29 399	61.3	1 824	26 489	72.6	130 100	23.2	12.5	705	27.1	2.9
Pompano Beach	5.0	16.0	42.9	10.7	42 719	29.4	2 434	32 157	63.3	99 300	23.5	12.9	542	29.3	7.8
Port Orange	0.9	8.2	-16.3	5.1	17 019	92.2	1 063	14 964	78.8	78 900	24.3	11.8	547	28.7	1.1
Port St. Lucie	2.1	5.4	-16.9	4.2	24 241	278.2	2 084	20 675	76.4	79 800	22.7	11.6	639	25.2	2.2
Riviera Beach	4.5	22.6	39.5	17.9	14 078	17.6	1 105	10 333	58.6	61 600	21.7	14.6	495	32.8	11.0
St. Petersburg	2.8	13.6	-2.9	9.5	125 452	5.0	10 299	105 703	63.0	63 000	22.3	13.1	417	28.3	3.4
Sanford	1.2	16.3	-25.9	12.1	13 834	53.1	1 290	12 119	56.3	59 300	22.0	13.2	458	27.1	5.2
Sarasota	4.4	13.3	-10.7	10.3	26 974	6.4	1 776	22 822	56.9	71 600	23.0	12.2	492	28.6	3.6
Sunrise	1.6	6.5	30.0	4.5	29 295	68.0	1 504	26 314	75.6	89 100	24.1	13.7	651	27.8	3.2
Tallahassee	2.7	22.3	-7.1	11.9	55 221	63.8	3 941	50 442	45.2	72 400	19.4	12.8	444	31.2	4.2
Tamarac	3.2	5.8	28.9	3.4	26 141	68.4	1 393	22 906	78.2	77 600	23.3	12.4	633	29.3	1.6
Tampa	3.4	19.4	3.7	15.0	129 681	13.6	11 234	114 800	55.5	59 000	21.9	13.0	408	27.2	6.0
Titusville	1.5	10.6	-16.5	7.9	18 183	45.6	1 308	16 207	64.2	66 100	18.1	12.0	458	25.5	2.5
West Palm Beach	3.8	16.2	2.5	12.7	34 971	16.5	3 090	28 787	50.3	72 000	22.8	13.2	517	28.0	7.1
GEORGIA	3.8	14.7	-11.7	11.5	2 638 418	30.1	173 937	2 366 615	64.9	71 300	20.9	12.8	433	25.8	4.7
Albany	2.6	27.5	13.2	22.1	30 603	16.9	2 324	27 926	47.2	56 200	18.6	13.1	332	26.8	7.5
Athens	2.4	39.3	47.7	22.5	18 499	19.1	1 121	17 012	33.4	64 900	20.0	13.7	347	34.1	4.3
Atlanta	6.3	27.3	-0.7	24.6	182 754	2.2	21 547	155 752	43.1	71 200	22.6	14.7	422	28.7	6.8
Augusta	2.4	33.3	9.5	27.9	21 588	3.7	1 476	18 819	42.9	49 000	19.9	12.9	300	29.3	6.4
Columbus	2.6	18.6	NA	14.9	70 902	NA	NA	65 858	53.9	58 100	19.8	12.2	358	25.5	4.5
East Point	1.7	16.9	28.0	14.5	15 671	-1.0	2 019	13 373	49.7	64 500	20.4	12.5	461	27.6	6.4
La Grange	3.3	21.3	7.0	16.8	10 949	21.5	948	9 772	48.8	52 300	21.3	13.7	361	25.6	5.4
Macon	2.6	24.4	8.9	20.8	45 499	2.5	3 308	41 175	49.7	49 300	18.8	12.9	336	27.5	5.0
Marietta	3.6	14.2	8.4	9.4	23 158	68.2	2 999	19 866	33.4	87 500	20.5	12.3	539	27.1	2.5
Rome	2.2	18.7	-3.1	15.4	13 099	9.5	773	12 008	51.4	51 300	17.8	13.2	294	25.5	3.9
Roswell	14.4	3.3	-10.8	2.2	20 318	129.8	1 973	18 189	67.8	142 000	23.4	12.5	586	24.4	1.2
Savannah	1.8	22.6	0.9	18.5	58 762	8.2	4 386	51 938	50.7	54 800	21.8	13.6	390	28.6	4.9
Smyrna	3.5	6.6	11.9	4.1	16 822	98.2	1 809	14 835	43.1	78 100	20.2	13.3	562	24.4	2.5
Valdosta	2.8	23.8	3.5	19.1	15 608	14.2	1 046	14 143	50.1	59 600	19.9	13.2	359	26.5	5.2
Warner Robins	0.9	11.8	14.6	10.0	18 086	22.4	1 222	16 721	57.1	56 000	16.8	11.1	405	23.4	3.6
HAWAII	7.1	8.3	-16.6	6.0	389 810	16.6	14 817	356 267	53.9	245 300	21.4	10.8	650	27.4	15.6
Hilo CDP	3.7	14.5	4.3	11.3	14 134	20.0	471	13 324	60.1	111 800	17.8	10.7	417	27.5	10.3
Honolulu CDP	9.0	8.4	-16.0	5.5	145 796	2.5	6 669	134 563	47.0	353 900	20.1	10.8	623	26.9	16.0
Kailua CDP	12.8	3.4	-52.1	2.1	12 225	9.9	196	11 843	70.0	318 900	22.6	10.6	883	31.0	7.1
Kaneohe CDP	7.9	4.9	-5.8	2.9	10 849	27.2	147	10 610	70.2	242 700	21.0	10.6	845	30.2	10.4
Mililani CDP	7.0	1.7	-48.5	1.4	8 900	38.8	82	8 776	77.7	285 300	25.3	10.4	1 001	30.8	9.1
Pearl City CDP	8.1	3.5	-2.8	2.4	8 999	-20.8	81	8 876	67.8	252 300	15.0	10.1	753	30.3	15.2
Waimalu CDP	10.4	3.1	NA	1.9	10 613	NA	181	10 372	64.2	325 500	23.8	10.9	882	29.4	10.8
Waipahu CDP	5.9	13.4	-2.2	12.8	7 739	8.7	155	7 567	51.5	234 800	18.6	10.7	617	28.3	30.9
IDAHO	2.1	13.3	5.2	9.7	413 327	10.2	16 815	360 723	70.1	58 200	19.3	11.8	330	23.8	4.5
Boise City	3.3	9.4	6.8	6.3	53 271	22.9	1 916	50 852	63.1	67 700	19.8	11.5	404	25.2	2.4
Idaho Falls	2.1	10.5	32.9	8.8	16 845	11.9	605	16 017	64.8	63 400	16.8	11.6	364	22.9	3.6
Lewiston	1.8	11.3	-1.7	8.1	12 054	5.0	367	11 515	65.0	56 900	16.3	11.6	304	22.9	1.1
Nampa	0.7	18.5	6.9	13.6	10 760	10.0	367	10 213	60.6	45 600	21.3	11.5	308	23.4	6.0
Pocatello	1.8	15.3	59.4	11.1	18 768	1.7	1 118	17 183	64.0	51 300	18.3	11.5	289	24.5	3.3
Twin Falls	2.2	14.4	24.1	10.3	11 009	4.1	394	10 472	62.8	51 600	17.7	11.5	313	23.7	3.8
ILLINOIS	4.9	11.9	8.2	9.0	4 506 275	4.3	208 467	4 202 240	64.2	80 900	20.2	12.7	445	25.9	4.2
Addison	5.4	4.7	23.7	3.7	11 025	9.8	265	10 722	63.6	126 000	21.5	12.6	531	24.3	6.8
Alton	1.0	19.9	26.8	16.6	14 212	2.5	834	12 969	64.8	37 500	15.7	13.1	330	27.5	3.9
Arlington Heights	12.1	2.4	-7.7	1.4	30 428	31.1	1 268	28 810	72.6	169 100	20.0	11.5	711	25.9	0.9
Aurora	2.9	10.5	20.7	8.1	35 621	21.1	1 539	33 710	61.4	81 900	21.4	13.1	499	25.8	7.3
Belleville	1.6	9.0	15.4	5.9	19 080	11.4	1 014	17 739	61.3	58 500	19.4	12.5	393	27.8	1.9

1. Includes units rented or sold but not occupied.   2. Specified owner-occupied units.   3. Specified renter-occupied units.   4. Overcrowded or lacking complete plumbing facilities.

Table D. Cities — **Labor Force, Employment, Disability, and Construction**

City	Civilian labor force, 1999 Total	Civilian labor force, 1999 Percent change, 1998–1999	Unemployment Total	Unemployment Rate[1]	Civilian employment, 1990[2] Total	Percent Professional, managerial, and technical	Percent Precision production, craft, and repair	Disability 1990 Work disabled persons[3] (percent)	Value of residential construction authorized by building permits, 1999 New construction ($1,000)	Value of residential construction authorized by building permits, 1999 Number of housing units	Value of residential construction authorized by building permits, 1999 Percent single family
	61	62	63	64	65	66	67	68	69	70	71
FLORIDA—Cont'd											
Miami Beach	44 337	0.6	3 000	6.8	37 867	32.2	6.6	8.6	27 348	477	1.7
Miramar	27 319	1.8	991	3.6	21 338	30.7	14.3	6.5	214 186	2 079	89.0
North Lauderdale	18 797	1.8	715	3.8	14 655	24.5	16.5	5.4	0	0	0.0
North Miami	28 698	0.7	1 790	6.2	24 649	26.8	10.4	6.6	0	0	0.0
North Miami Beach	18 781	0.9	891	4.7	16 388	27.7	11.1	7.9	1 934	9	55.6
Oakland Park	19 522	1.8	678	3.5	15 273	24.8	13.1	7.2	24 588	361	13.6
Ocala	22 661	2.1	874	3.9	17 263	28.9	9.9	12.4	23 692	286	53.5
Orlando	115 180	5.0	3 363	2.9	82 176	30.9	8.9	8.4	176 986	2 889	14.9
Ormond Beach	14 197	1.1	305	2.1	12 786	41.2	8.1	7.4	40 183	286	100.0
Palm Bay	33 626	0.9	1 356	4.0	29 890	31.1	15.8	8.4	74 328	863	64.8
Panama City	17 724	0.2	1 301	7.3	14 121	29.6	10.2	11.7	18 493	190	64.2
Pembroke Pines	40 908	1.9	1 083	2.6	32 277	35.0	10.2	6.1	177 005	1 924	61.4
Pensacola	26 948	-0.4	1 042	3.9	24 099	38.7	7.5	9.3	12 775	116	87.9
Pinellas Park	24 737	1.8	615	2.5	20 106	24.3	16.2	11.4	5 864	63	100.0
Plantation	46 082	1.9	1 357	2.9	36 249	41.4	8.2	5.3	29 610	136	100.0
Pompano Beach	41 288	1.6	1 983	4.8	31 856	27.7	11.6	8.8	3 921	49	91.8
Port Orange	17 861	1.1	416	2.3	16 056	28.6	11.5	10.1	62 980	469	99.6
Port St. Lucie	30 874	3.5	2 156	7.0	24 942	24.6	17.5	8.9	122 893	1 121	100.0
Riviera Beach	16 094	-0.6	1 426	8.9	11 808	22.7	12.3	10.4	22 658	483	15.5
St. Petersburg	135 705	1.7	4 229	3.1	109 586	30.8	10.5	10.7	80 194	700	25.6
Sanford	21 440	4.2	722	3.4	14 841	24.2	14.9	9.8	42 342	717	32.2
Sarasota	31 620	4.9	836	2.6	23 554	28.4	11.0	9.0	13 454	222	33.3
Sunrise	38 221	1.8	1 406	3.7	29 838	31.2	10.8	6.1	29 904	397	100.0
Tallahassee	82 768	3.1	2 531	3.1	65 373	42.4	5.0	5.4	118 137	1 559	50.9
Tamarac	21 053	1.7	927	4.4	16 312	28.7	9.9	8.9	16 953	275	3.3
Tampa	173 239	2.9	5 667	3.3	129 830	29.2	9.8	10.9	247 109	3 158	39.5
Titusville	20 499	1.0	787	3.8	18 258	35.4	12.5	9.4	9 199	78	93.6
West Palm Beach	44 401	-0.4	2 822	6.4	33 472	28.6	10.1	8.5	58 834	550	93.8
GEORGIA	4 088 008	1.7	162 571	4.0	3 090 276	28.2	11.9	8.8	8 749 615	89 600	79.9
Albany	36 254	-1.7	3 241	8.9	30 689	27.9	10.6	9.8	21 135	244	91.8
Athens	46 998	NA	1 307	2.8	19 344	33.0	6.0	6.4	56 439	889	60.4
Atlanta	226 446	2.7	11 785	5.2	175 126	32.4	6.8	10.0	237 197	3 888	19.5
Augusta	81 275	0.1	5 110	6.3	15 760	27.4	9.7	14.8	NA	NA	NA
Columbus	87 085	2.0	4 756	5.5	71 922	28.4	10.9	10.3	83 992	1 022	56.2
East Point	21 344	2.9	1 020	4.8	16 519	24.7	8.4	9.2	1 217	12	100.0
La Grange	13 503	0.4	903	6.7	10 975	24.4	11.9	11.2	24 749	381	23.4
Macon	50 114	-1.3	3 054	6.1	44 111	25.4	10.8	12.5	38 081	390	97.7
Marietta	34 243	3.6	1 169	3.4	24 226	33.0	10.3	6.4	46 886	350	100.0
Rome	15 317	-4.0	977	6.4	12 928	27.8	8.3	11.4	NA	NA	NA
Roswell	34 785	3.2	496	1.4	27 870	43.0	5.8	3.4	49 127	319	96.2
Savannah	64 368	0.6	3 350	5.2	55 865	27.4	10.7	10.3	12 755	187	65.8
Smyrna	27 778	3.6	691	2.5	19 841	37.8	7.3	5.0	135 172	899	100.0
Valdosta	22 288	-0.8	1 190	5.3	16 688	29.2	7.6	10.2	10 734	192	84.9
Warner Robins	25 092	2.0	1 050	4.2	19 757	30.5	16.4	9.5	33 824	744	51.1
HAWAII	594 810	-0.4	33 326	5.6	529 059	29.9	10.5	6.6	632 743	4 211	79.8
Hilo CDP	NA	NA	NA	NA	17 062	29.5	10.1	9.3	NA	NA	NA
Honolulu CDP	424 230	-1.1	20 947	4.9	191 891	33.6	8.0	5.9	NA	NA	NA
Kailua CDP	NA	NA	NA	NA	19 234	38.6	10.4	5.7	NA	NA	NA
Kaneohe CDP	NA	NA	NA	NA	18 426	33.3	11.5	5.5	NA	NA	NA
Mililani CDP	NA	NA	NA	NA	14 815	38.0	12.0	4.2	NA	NA	NA
Pearl City CDP	NA	NA	NA	NA	15 592	26.4	12.2	5.9	NA	NA	NA
Waimalu CDP	NA	NA	NA	NA	16 661	37.9	11.4	4.3	NA	NA	NA
Waipahu CDP	NA	NA	NA	NA	14 233	16.0	12.3	8.5	NA	NA	NA
IDAHO	655 272	0.3	33 913	5.2	443 703	27.1	11.3	9.0	1 366 527	12 309	86.3
Boise City	105 515	3.4	3 396	3.2	66 115	36.0	9.0	7.5	150 743	1 391	71.3
Idaho Falls	28 846	2.1	1 088	3.8	19 741	41.4	9.6	7.7	29 001	489	45.8
Lewiston	20 043	0.3	691	3.4	13 120	25.5	13.2	9.8	9 071	79	64.6
Nampa	19 362	3.0	1 006	5.2	11 925	22.5	14.1	14.3	123 307	1 347	94.7
Pocatello	28 838	-0.3	1 470	5.1	20 824	31.9	10.1	9.2	13 152	139	82.7
Twin Falls	16 876	-6.7	860	5.1	12 714	25.0	10.2	10.0	18 616	197	89.3
ILLINOIS	6 385 420	2.6	273 628	4.3	5 417 967	30.0	10.7	6.9	6 537 643	53 974	72.7
Addison	20 790	0.3	861	4.1	17 774	24.4	14.0	4.1	8 316	35	100.0
Alton	14 159	0.1	868	6.1	13 004	24.3	12.9	12.1	2 257	30	40.0
Arlington Heights	45 948	0.6	1 133	2.5	41 977	43.3	7.1	3.6	24 999	215	26.0
Aurora	68 083	5.1	2 996	4.4	49 137	25.6	11.5	6.5	195 551	2 378	54.0
Belleville	20 879	-0.5	1 634	7.8	18 942	29.0	10.3	8.6	10 746	144	62.5

1. Percent of civilian labor force.   2. Persons 16 years and older.   3. Persons 16 to 64 years old.

City	Wholesale Trade, 1997				Retail Trade[1], 1997				Real Estate and Rental and Leasing, 1997			
	Number of Establish-ments	Number of Employees	Sales (mil dol)	Annual Payroll (mil dol)	Number of Establish-ments	Number of Employees	Sales (mil dol)	Annual Payroll (mil dol)	Number of Establish-ments	Number of Employees	Receipts (mil dol)	Annual Payroll (mil dol)
	72	73	74	75	76	77	78	79	80	81	82	83
FLORIDA—Cont'd												
Miami Beach	136	470	255.9	12.5	466	3 680	504.2	62.1	313	1 909	189.7	33.1
Miramar	84	1 479	712.8	57.9	115	2 063	341.1	29.3	33	131	18.4	2.8
North Lauderdale	13	27	8.8	0.6	48	950	121.2	11.7	9	30	2.6	0.5
North Miami	108	574	183.1	16.2	235	3 402	705.8	83.2	95	535	57.7	10.7
North Miami Beach	96	379	180.7	11.3	217	2 775	541.4	47.8	69	242	33.5	4.8
Oakland Park	223	1 500	489.7	49.2	275	2 719	517.4	53.6	72	286	38.8	5.7
Ocala	198	2 243	680.8	54.6	602	8 560	1 470.4	136.7	145	487	57.5	8.5
Orlando	676	9 637	4 389.2	315.3	1 406	18 296	3 786.5	334.3	457	6 995	991.3	194.8
Ormond Beach	58	622	207.6	17.9	170	2 231	257.1	30.2	79	412	43.9	8.1
Palm Bay	46	264	117.5	11.0	150	2 174	307.1	28.1	47	335	25.2	6.3
Panama City	88	686	246.5	18.1	415	5 461	916.9	88.6	86	363	32.4	6.0
Pembroke Pines	135	417	233.3	13.9	375	7 362	1 650.7	125.8	95	422	77.8	9.4
Pensacola	151	1 992	552.8	53.9	470	6 415	991.4	93.9	115	511	52.2	9.5
Pinellas Park	115	1 234	391.7	33.0	241	5 235	1 530.8	104.9	37	157	18.6	3.0
Plantation	229	878	629.3	35.0	441	6 511	1 137.4	109.9	145	788	94.2	15.4
Pompano Beach	503	5 616	2 386.7	177.8	587	6 828	1 571.8	140.1	190	953	141.1	24.3
Port Orange	38	207	62.0	5.6	109	1 572	207.5	21.8	38	223	16.6	3.2
Port St. Lucie	NA	NA	NA	NA	NA	NA	NA	NA	NA	NA	NA	NA
Riviera Beach	101	1 627	1 088.9	55.3	114	847	157.3	17.9	42	136	24.3	3.1
St. Petersburg	293	3 147	2 221.3	112.5	933	12 942	2 128.7	208.2	287	1 531	177.4	31.2
Sanford	84	1 046	249.6	28.1	303	3 960	628.4	57.7	32	276	24.1	4.6
Sarasota	123	890	329.3	23.9	512	5 601	931.6	93.9	184	864	124.4	20.4
Sunrise	246	2 713	1 728.5	123.1	448	7 971	1 355.2	133.7	74	706	78.1	13.3
Tallahassee	204	2 181	602.2	62.6	864	13 270	1 721.2	188.5	241	1 659	179.5	30.0
Tamarac	95	706	433.5	24.9	208	2 516	350.8	38.4	62	452	43.7	10.1
Tampa	1 048	18 497	15 906.4	630.9	1 792	25 054	4 756.7	428.9	526	4 489	599.8	110.6
Titusville	29	186	42.3	4.0	182	2 602	386.5	37.1	36	127	10.3	1.4
West Palm Beach	188	1 897	1 356.4	68.4	615	9 261	1 968.5	188.4	203	1 508	142.6	39.8
GEORGIA	13 978	191 078	163 647.5	7 519.7	33 073	420 676	72 212.5	6 943.6	7 794	47 669	6 912.9	1 308.8
Albany	171	2 151	971.2	63.8	548	7 595	1 134.8	112.6	122	618	79.3	12.1
Athens	NA	NA	NA	NA	NA	NA	NA	NA	NA	NA	NA	NA
Atlanta	1 164	15 406	17 285.9	636.9	2 044	26 738	4 229.8	491.1	832	8 689	1 485.7	318.5
Augusta	NA	NA	NA	NA	NA	NA	NA	NA	NA	NA	NA	NA
Columbus	208	2 884	1 316.5	91.3	845	11 718	1 950.9	186.6	224	1 197	142.7	27.3
East Point	39	673	396.0	17.0	91	1 160	155.4	16.8	35	542	32.6	8.9
La Grange	42	397	189.3	12.9	202	2 809	445.6	43.5	34	135	14.1	2.5
Macon	210	2 776	984.0	81.8	765	10 586	1 630.2	159.5	157	986	137.1	24.3
Marietta	342	4 471	2 719.7	190.6	409	7 391	1 948.2	167.1	149	1 091	132.6	23.7
Rome	76	795	309.9	25.5	343	4 389	707.0	65.8	40	266	20.6	4.5
Roswell	309	2 912	6 033.5	151.9	321	4 720	1 298.8	118.4	132	716	126.5	21.2
Savannah	220	2 737	1 487.2	90.9	962	12 394	1 894.3	188.8	194	974	115.7	23.0
Smyrna	117	1 906	3 411.0	82.4	226	4 820	927.2	81.0	92	527	158.0	18.5
Valdosta	109	1 027	408.0	27.5	379	4 892	758.2	72.7	73	438	31.4	6.9
Warner Robins	31	310	184.1	10.5	238	3 790	607.1	58.0	61	254	36.6	3.9
HAWAII	1 872	18 532	7 147.5	576.0	5 088	64 218	11 317.8	1 161.8	1 753	12 446	1 824.1	311.9
Hilo CDP	87	811	314.2	22.0	261	3 696	552.2	63.0	78	378	37.1	6.5
Honolulu CDP	1 114	11 332	4 537.5	354.2	2 258	27 812	5 483.5	534.7	973	6 707	968.4	179.3
Kailua CDP	26	81	58.4	3.9	104	1 758	227.9	27.5	30	114	15.6	2.7
Kaneohe CDP	22	84	23.1	1.9	137	2 171	371.8	37.7	30	114	10.2	2.4
Mililani CDP	14	115	37.5	6.3	50	1 181	176.8	19.5	12	36	3.4	0.6
Pearl City CDP	37	517	176.1	14.8	50	1 062	239.7	18.8	15	49	6.2	1.1
Waimalu CDP	18	86	10.0	1.5	84	1 259	251.7	27.0	22	151	10.2	3.3
Waipahu CDP	60	1 246	364.7	41.3	119	1 908	378.3	39.6	25	113	14.7	3.1
IDAHO	1 980	22 828	10 127.8	628.0	5 848	63 732	11 649.6	1 079.7	1 236	4 870	450.3	73.9
Boise City	367	5 235	4 637.4	200.1	939	12 880	2 505.9	230.0	294	1 536	167.7	28.2
Idaho Falls	125	1 529	572.0	38.9	398	4 758	790.0	76.9	65	365	18.9	3.5
Lewiston	55	557	183.1	14.7	220	2 749	453.6	47.2	39	178	11.5	2.5
Nampa	70	890	377.1	23.8	216	2 664	563.2	49.0	48	103	12.8	1.5
Pocatello	89	883	270.6	24.2	239	2 809	538.4	48.8	59	221	21.4	3.1
Twin Falls	109	1 190	330.7	26.9	299	4 013	726.7	65.6	58	218	24.6	3.5
ILLINOIS	21 956	325 847	275 978.4	13 325.5	44 568	610 790	108 002.2	10 596.0	11 411	73 819	12 830.0	2 101.4
Addison	257	4 566	2 649.9	182.1	123	2 754	801.0	63.9	34	239	39.6	8.4
Alton	27	327	79.2	11.6	207	2 404	392.6	36.8	33	121	14.3	2.1
Arlington Heights	326	3 664	4 427.1	192.3	326	4 970	1 302.5	92.7	104	913	139.9	27.2
Aurora	140	2 212	5 262.0	93.8	463	7 942	1 171.5	121.0	90	486	51.8	10.0
Belleville	42	D	D	D	231	3 073	543.4	55.4	58	247	22.8	4.1

1. Establishments with payroll.

City	Professional, Scientific, and Technical Services, 1997[1]				Manufacturing, 1997				Accommodation and Foodservices, 1997			
	Number of Establishments	Number of Employees	Receipts (mil dol)	Annual Payroll (mil dol)	Number of Establishments	Number of Employees	Receipts (mil dol)	Annual Payroll (mil dol)	Number of Establishments	Number of Employees	Sales (mil dol)	Annual Payroll (mil dol)
	84	85	86	87	88	89	90	91	92	93	94	95
FLORIDA—Cont'd												
Miami Beach	298	1 048	107.2	36.4	NA	NA	NA	NA	466	12 714	551.0	160.3
Miramar	59	368	37.7	13.6	36	729	124.9	25.1	44	425	15.6	3.4
North Lauderdale	25	249	27.5	12.4	NA	NA	NA	NA	36	431	14.0	3.3
North Miami	123	716	36.8	14.5	63	529	44.6	10.3	107	1 952	66.6	16.7
North Miami Beach	185	722	72.7	34.4	48	647	100.9	16.0	74	911	32.8	8.4
Oakland Park	156	1 520	145.8	49.0	166	1 855	193.8	48.8	115	1 729	70.7	17.5
Ocala	252	1 557	112.0	47.1	138	7 680	1 023.1	185.3	203	4 763	141.2	39.0
Orlando	1 348	14 678	1 505.2	630.4	281	12 168	2 390.5	522.5	581	18 872	753.5	214.0
Ormond Beach	119	573	47.5	15.2	47	1 039	100.1	26.4	113	2 485	70.5	19.8
Palm Bay	76	306	27.3	11.5	61	8 325	1 171.6	358.6	80	1 152	35.5	9.4
Panama City	155	840	63.1	25.0	63	2 255	514.8	74.8	175	3 471	129.5	33.3
Pembroke Pines	226	785	65.6	23.6	54	632	80.0	15.7	190	4 009	134.3	34.4
Pensacola	372	3 047	234.9	106.7	75	1 865	475.7	62.9	183	4 156	130.5	35.3
Pinellas Park	85	622	40.3	17.7	190	7 653	1 136.3	209.6	92	1 565	60.4	14.1
Plantation	489	2 583	280.2	77.4	53	D	D	D	164	3 601	136.1	35.5
Pompano Beach	278	1 367	142.4	41.3	284	6 711	783.8	187.8	229	3 035	124.9	34.1
Port Orange	43	267	23.2	8.8	NA	NA	NA	NA	66	1 403	40.7	11.4
Port St. Lucie	NA	NA	NA	NA	NA	NA	NA	NA	NA	NA	NA	NA
Riviera Beach	58	240	31.1	13.2	73	1 439	213.2	42.1	41	741	33.1	8.2
St. Petersburg	842	10 581	792.7	373.1	203	7 389	1 237.3	227.1	432	7 827	268.8	76.2
Sanford	63	342	24.8	12.6	61	2 270	253.6	50.2	81	1 594	51.4	13.8
Sarasota	483	2 969	329.2	137.7	89	1 529	136.6	35.5	241	4 628	183.5	49.5
Sunrise	187	643	94.5	22.1	71	2 405	201.3	50.6	163	3 065	115.9	27.8
Tallahassee	704	6 304	654.0	277.3	102	D	D	D	401	8 819	268.9	69.8
Tamarac	175	724	74.5	28.6	NA	NA	NA	NA	102	D	D	D
Tampa	1 780	26 172	3 145.2	1 112.8	463	13 213	2 442.1	364.2	842	20 303	782.8	212.3
Titusville	79	286	25.2	11.4	46	614	49.9	12.3	80	2 005	52.8	15.8
West Palm Beach	758	6 079	644.2	305.8	154	7 014	2 269.2	402.8	294	5 797	223.0	60.1
GEORGIA	17 810	138 198	15 266.4	5 908.8	9 083	533 830	124 526.8	15 534.1	13 829	274 322	9 689.9	2 695.1
Albany	164	1 286	94.6	36.6	76	D	D	D	188	3 688	116.6	31.2
Athens	NA	NA	NA	NA	90	9 388	1 368.5	234.9	NA	NA	NA	NA
Atlanta	2 573	38 245	5 305.7	1 969.6	499	21 497	5 822.0	688.7	1 361	37 792	1 604.8	478.7
Augusta	NA	NA	NA	NA	NA	NA	NA	NA	365	D	D	D
Columbus	264	1 607	146.2	43.6	158	D	D	D	365	D	D	D
East Point	31	159	12.2	4.8	41	1 199	286.7	40.6	48	1 084	45.3	12.6
La Grange	50	221	15.8	6.9	70	8 540	1 634.0	257.6	59	1 026	31.3	7.9
Macon	308	1 792	163.4	51.7	154	10 650	5 388.6	419.5	273	5 786	175.0	47.3
Marietta	419	3 087	267.4	99.7	158	4 886	924.1	169.1	235	4 203	163.2	45.4
Rome	108	579	53.9	17.4	88	5 342	1 070.6	154.1	118	2 246	78.9	20.2
Roswell	500	2 323	268.8	103.2	58	759	164.3	24.7	151	3 072	115.8	33.6
Savannah	367	2 239	188.1	75.7	131	4 579	1 279.7	139.3	413	9 619	334.6	90.1
Smyrna	173	1 327	153.2	75.6	50	1 032	136.8	36.6	142	3 028	109.5	30.7
Valdosta	117	674	41.6	16.9	70	4 816	1 272.4	118.9	138	2 787	83.0	23.6
Warner Robins	89	969	89.0	35.3	34	D	D	D	120	2 510	69.5	18.6
HAWAII	2 480	15 743	1 574.0	606.5	921	15 109	3 192.5	405.0	3 081	88 083	5 007.9	1 507.5
Hilo CDP	124	573	35.6	13.8	58	716	80.2	17.5	116	1 881	64.7	18.5
Honolulu CDP	1 650	12 014	1 282.5	503.2	491	7 639	904.9	187.7	1 503	42 549	2 604.0	733.4
Kailua CDP	67	202	20.4	7.8	NA	NA	NA	NA	83	D	D	D
Kaneohe CDP	25	97	7.6	2.6	NA	NA	NA	NA	60	1 009	36.9	9.5
Mililani CDP	14	87	11.1	5.7	NA	NA	NA	NA	27	D	D	D
Pearl City CDP	12	91	6.4	2.6	NA	NA	NA	NA	42	734	27.9	7.2
Waimalu CDP	22	380	12.3	6.1	NA	NA	NA	NA	43	884	39.8	10.2
Waipahu CDP	15	49	3.7	1.4	NA	NA	NA	NA	77	1 287	48.7	12.6
IDAHO	2 364	19 669	2 046.1	756.2	1 647	66 184	16 952.9	2 099.8	2 978	42 067	1 232.5	345.7
Boise City	675	5 927	868.9	252.1	210	16 823	5 780.6	753.4	511	10 138	316.3	89.0
Idaho Falls	187	7 210	740.5	334.8	79	2 107	217.8	44.9	170	3 335	88.6	25.4
Lewiston	65	D	D	D	44	D	D	D	97	1 415	42.0	12.3
Nampa	54	306	19.9	7.6	71	5 798	3 008.7	179.9	96	1 701	46.1	12.3
Pocatello	97	885	44.5	21.2	52	2 315	385.7	70.4	133	2 031	56.4	15.4
Twin Falls	119	493	35.2	12.4	64	2 400	512.1	51.8	125	2 160	58.3	17.1
ILLINOIS	30 378	274 714	33 855.1	13 105.4	17 953	887 350	200 020.0	31 837.9	23 984	397 300	14 826.8	4 018.7
Addison	99	1 146	77.9	21.4	388	10 598	1 461.1	346.9	53	990	39.2	8.7
Alton	63	350	25.8	11.0	31	1 716	358.4	66.1	99	1 821	57.1	15.0
Arlington Heights	430	4 523	446.5	146.0	120	10 976	3 052.9	645.6	147	2 953	124.2	32.5
Aurora	204	1 937	115.4	53.1	148	8 759	2 743.1	387.4	192	3 122	110.3	29.1
Belleville	177	1 119	101.2	43.2	60	2 239	307.7	65.7	132	2 260	61.8	17.0

1. Firms subject to federal tax.

City	Arts, Entertainment, and Recreation[1], 1997				Health Care and Social Assistance[1], 1997				Other Services[1], 1997			
	Number of Establishments	Number of Employees	Receipts (mil dol)	Annual Payroll (mil dol)	Number of Establishments	Number of Employees	Receipts (mil dol)	Annual Payroll (mil dol)	Number of Establishments	Number of Employees	Receipts (mil dol)	Annual Payroll (mil dol)
	96	97	98	99	100	101	102	103	104	105	106	107
FLORIDA—Cont'd												
Miami Beach	56	409	51.0	10.8	330	3 313	292.4	123.4	163	1 023	41.7	13.6
Miramar	7	25	1.0	0.4	65	956	102.1	36.3	53	228	18.3	5.7
North Lauderdale	2	0	0.0	0.0	19	123	5.2	2.0	34	232	20.9	5.6
North Miami	23	117	8.1	1.8	115	2 044	132.1	63.0	116	418	20.3	5.6
North Miami Beach	16	344	28.1	6.9	194	3 116	237.7	113.8	105	514	27.0	8.4
Oakland Park	13	155	24.9	3.6	138	2 503	200.5	76.2	205	766	55.9	13.7
Ocala	16	204	7.7	1.8	346	5 464	416.1	167.4	223	1 171	65.7	21.0
Orlando	122	0	0.0	0.0	676	7 391	683.5	321.8	440	4 650	289.2	89.0
Ormond Beach	23	277	9.0	2.8	180	2 294	144.4	62.9	58	305	14.0	4.0
Palm Bay	13	119	5.2	1.2	121	1 032	70.3	31.2	81	286	17.5	5.1
Panama City	24	271	10.4	2.6	200	3 295	257.7	104.1	112	798	38.6	11.9
Pembroke Pines	37	392	19.8	5.0	298	1 916	139.4	55.0	159	1 096	54.0	17.8
Pensacola	31	392	25.4	4.5	315	3 553	287.5	145.0	115	952	52.3	15.0
Pinellas Park	15	135	7.5	2.0	83	1 293	64.0	33.9	135	840	50.6	14.8
Plantation	33	320	17.9	4.6	505	7 694	649.6	267.0	154	1 178	71.7	21.8
Pompano Beach	35	513	38.2	7.4	195	2 304	140.5	60.9	270	2 338	163.6	52.6
Port Orange	7	30	1.3	0.4	77	568	34.0	11.8	55	215	9.1	2.8
Port St. Lucie	NA	NA	NA	NA	NA	NA	NA	NA	NA	NA	NA	NA
Riviera Beach	11	58	5.3	1.5	29	145	6.7	2.4	51	220	19.5	4.9
St. Petersburg	50	825	20.2	11.6	783	9 333	656.0	289.4	412	2 116	125.0	40.0
Sanford	13	145	5.5	2.0	72	1 964	140.0	55.9	86	319	20.6	5.9
Sarasota	39	757	42.2	9.1	380	3 285	288.3	136.3	179	1 186	61.0	22.2
Sunrise	21	443	19.5	3.4	193	2 942	196.5	74.7	127	558	33.7	10.0
Tallahassee	42	385	13.5	3.7	393	5 607	405.0	189.0	322	2 179	121.6	40.2
Tamarac	12	141	8.2	2.0	207	3 294	225.5	86.0	99	469	24.7	6.9
Tampa	114	5 723	471.6	167.7	1 014	14 076	1 178.9	467.3	785	5 358	358.9	109.7
Titusville	14	151	7.5	1.9	119	1 302	85.5	39.5	81	388	23.4	7.3
West Palm Beach	45	630	44.5	13.0	421	5 793	389.8	187.5	220	1 476	97.8	31.1
GEORGIA	1 653	23 437	1 533.7	408.9	13 960	173 768	12 065.1	5 158.0	11 482	69 422	4 580.7	1 407.5
Albany	11	156	7.4	1.6	245	3 266	238.2	109.6	159	1 110	66.0	21.3
Athens	NA	NA	NA	NA	NA	NA	NA	NA	NA	NA	NA	NA
Atlanta	157	3 937	379.9	88.0	1 134	12 059	1 040.0	480.2	903	7 202	498.6	149.4
Augusta	NA	NA	NA	NA	NA	NA	NA	NA	NA	NA	NA	NA
Columbus	37	D	D	D	343	5 225	439.9	171.6	305	2 004	104.7	35.8
East Point	4	51	1.2	0.4	87	981	62.3	28.0	51	443	41.0	14.6
La Grange	3	60	1.0	0.4	62	970	65.0	32.3	61	320	19.7	6.3
Macon	25	275	8.2	2.2	430	7 536	627.8	247.8	247	1 385	82.9	26.7
Marietta	25	454	24.5	6.5	284	3 777	303.5	137.1	213	1 640	108.2	37.9
Rome	10	56	4.7	0.8	147	3 735	330.8	125.1	73	642	35.9	12.4
Roswell	24	259	12.1	3.7	204	2 257	217.3	78.6	172	1 241	137.7	29.0
Savannah	42	475	21.0	5.8	370	5 400	405.8	216.0	270	1 877	110.5	37.2
Smyrna	13	241	13.1	2.4	121	1 458	104.3	38.3	75	491	34.4	10.4
Valdosta	15	120	5.1	1.1	165	2 399	148.0	65.9	107	572	30.1	8.6
Warner Robins	8	102	2.5	1.0	128	1 370	98.0	41.5	107	563	27.3	8.3
HAWAII	386	6 925	409.6	116.6	2 360	18 221	1 646.3	730.8	1 476	10 375	683.2	206.4
Hilo CDP	11	129	4.2	1.0	180	1 643	155.4	53.9	76	476	28.6	8.9
Honolulu CDP	159	2 592	143.5	43.2	1 194	9 866	925.5	427.4	748	5 786	395.5	117.0
Kailua CDP	9	248	11.8	3.4	108	526	44.1	20.8	36	229	13.3	4.7
Kaneohe CDP	6	72	4.1	1.4	63	587	37.6	16.3	55	729	37.0	12.2
Mililani CDP	3	149	6.8	2.2	25	169	15.6	7.2	18	91	3.6	1.2
Pearl City CDP	5	37	2.2	0.6	29	296	26.4	9.1	27	197	15.6	4.6
Waimalu CDP	9	208	11.2	3.0	66	463	49.1	25.3	28	220	13.5	4.3
Waipahu CDP	1	0	0.0	0.0	53	239	22.7	10.2	55	291	22.9	7.4
IDAHO	457	4 425	174.1	45.2	2 551	26 365	1 548.3	680.1	1 858	9 461	550.6	151.7
Boise City	56	825	28.2	8.2	587	5 728	433.0	204.9	319	2 584	132.7	39.8
Idaho Falls	19	203	3.8	1.2	225	3 094	226.9	90.4	112	591	38.1	10.4
Lewiston	11	0	0.0	0.0	109	0	0.0	0.0	82	527	27.7	8.0
Nampa	9	97	4.1	0.8	98	1 580	86.4	45.5	87	412	20.6	5.9
Pocatello	18	206	4.4	1.5	145	1 280	72.5	35.8	89	475	29.3	8.3
Twin Falls	19	96	4.0	0.9	127	2 028	108.7	49.4	83	542	26.3	7.9
ILLINOIS	3 097	46 972	3 640.3	1 040.6	21 122	248 667	16 870.2	7 441.8	18 806	118 317	8 296.8	2 503.0
Addison	9	57	2.8	0.8	40	233	16.1	7.0	110	855	74.8	22.4
Alton	11	0	0.0	0.0	111	1 344	93.1	47.7	70	393	25.8	7.5
Arlington Heights	23	398	35.7	9.1	269	3 153	246.5	121.9	149	1 055	56.5	19.9
Aurora	20	0	0.0	0.0	191	3 113	253.8	111.8	154	949	58.8	19.5
Belleville	13	220	7.1	2.0	198	2 228	147.3	75.6	119	652	38.1	13.2

1. Firms subject to federal tax.

Table D. Cities — Federal Funds and City Government Finances

City	Procurement contracts Defense	Other	Grants Total[2]	Health and family welfare	Energy and environment	Education	Housing and community development	Direct payments for individuals Educational assistance	Housing assistance	Intergovernmental Total (mil dol)	Total (mil dol)	Percent from state government	Taxes Total (mil dol)	Per capita[3] (dollars) Total	Property	Sales and gross receipts
	108	109	110	111	112	113	114	115	116	117	118	119	120	121	122	123
FLORIDA—Cont'd																
Miami Beach	0.0	0.0	10.8	5.9	0.0	0.0	4.4	0.1	8.2	246.3	71.2	10.3	99.6	1 054	548	223
Miramar	0.2	0.1	0.2	0.1	0.0	0.0	0.0	0.0	0.0	35.9	5.5	78.4	17.1	335	140	125
North Lauderdale	0.0	0.0	0.0	0.0	0.0	0.0	0.0	0.0	0.0	14.5	2.5	90.3	6.4	227	103	107
North Miami	0.0	0.0	1.7	0.4	0.0	0.0	1.1	0.0	0.0	47.6	5.9	82.5	15.3	302	169	109
North Miami Beach	0.0	0.0	0.9	0.2	0.0	0.0	0.0	1.8	1.3	46.3	7.8	69.5	17.8	510	294	191
Oakland Park	25.7	1.2	0.5	0.5	0.0	0.0	0.0	0.0	0.0	28.5	3.0	74.3	11.6	414	204	181
Ocala	6.7	1.0	7.0	4.6	0.2	0.0	0.6	0.0	9.4	40.8	10.2	47.0	12.3	273	174	76
Orlando	1 616.6	58.4	126.5	17.9	13.9	3.0	5.5	16.7	10.8	319.6	72.6	52.1	102.5	590	259	294
Ormond Beach	1.3	0.2	0.2	0.0	0.0	0.0	0.0	0.0	0.7	29.2	3.1	77.7	11.3	350	139	194
Palm Bay	74.8	1.7	1.1	0.0	0.1	0.0	0.8	0.1	0.0	37.7	6.5	84.0	21.6	288	125	147
Panama City	18.6	17.2	3.5	3.4	0.0	0.4	0.8	2.3	8.3	33.0	6.2	61.0	15.7	435	123	148
Pembroke Pines	0.2	0.0	0.9	0.0	0.0	0.0	0.4	0.0	0.0	74.2	7.6	88.6	38.1	378	117	161
Pensacola	103.2	9.2	20.2	3.2	0.7	1.1	1.9	6.6	8.0	70.9	17.3	37.9	28.0	474	135	317
Pinellas Park	10.3	0.2	6.1	1.0	0.0	5.0	0.0	0.1	0.0	32.2	4.5	72.4	17.6	400	137	237
Plantation	0.6	0.9	0.5	0.2	0.0	0.0	0.0	0.0	0.0	50.2	5.9	95.2	30.6	390	175	173
Pompano Beach	5.3	1.7	18.6	0.0	0.0	0.0	1.2	0.0	3.7	84.1	10.0	73.8	45.2	606	360	208
Port Orange	0.1	0.0	0.4	0.0	0.0	0.0	0.0	0.0	0.0	28.7	3.3	93.5	9.4	227	102	114
Port St. Lucie	0.0	0.2	0.4	0.0	0.0	0.0	0.0	0.0	0.0	38.9	5.3	82.1	16.5	NA	NA	NA
Riviera Beach	0.3	0.5	0.2	0.0	0.0	0.0	0.0	0.1	3.1	31.9	3.8	64.9	18.0	628	433	176
St. Petersburg	365.9	8.8	23.5	10.9	0.4	0.2	4.2	1.7	5.3	265.4	50.8	44.5	94.0	398	228	151
Sanford	3.5	0.8	12.1	1.1	0.0	2.4	3.2	2.0	2.3	26.4	3.8	82.7	11.6	326	149	159
Sarasota	5.9	1.3	9.7	2.0	0.1	0.0	4.8	0.1	0.0	79.9	8.3	67.2	35.9	705	342	329
Sunrise	0.0	0.5	0.8	0.0	0.0	0.0	0.5	0.0	0.0	86.7	7.0	88.4	34.9	450	210	189
Tallahassee	15.2	17.6	1 836.4	634.6	11.8	367.3	46.6	23.8	10.1	178.8	23.3	49.4	47.3	346	92	230
Tamarac	0.0	0.0	0.1	0.0	0.0	0.0	0.1	0.0	0.0	30.7	4.3	98.5	13.5	264	163	76
Tampa	75.3	48.4	119.3	56.1	0.9	8.7	6.1	22.7	18.9	347.1	63.7	49.5	141.2	495	217	236
Titusville	23.9	2.0	6.8	0.0	0.0	0.0	4.5	0.0	0.0	25.5	4.1	80.7	10.7	259	97	150
West Palm Beach	1 376.9	64.5	56.3	20.1	2.5	0.4	1.5	3.0	3.0	102.1	15.0	46.7	55.7	702	419	236
GEORGIA	4 095.8	1 054.3	6 751.5	3 749.2	106.4	640.7	160.3	147.1	183.7	X	X	X	X	X	X	X
Albany	54.4	10.7	12.8	5.5	0.0	2.4	3.5	6.5	5.0	62.7	14.0	2.8	21.5	273	139	108
Athens	0.1	0.6	27.0	22.8	0.0	0.0	0.0	0.0	0.9	120.8	24.5	25.2	53.6	NA	NA	NA
Atlanta	290.6	397.7	1 788.5	693.3	76.1	206.1	107.4	36.2	64.6	813.9	128.0	4.1	241.2	600	271	220
Augusta	7.6	17.0	38.1	26.2	1.1	1.2	2.5	6.6	4.5	199.7	27.6	73.0	104.3	2 496	685	1 725
Columbus	1.1	2.5	15.7	5.1	0.1	1.6	6.9	3.5	4.3	NA	NA	NA	NA	NA	NA	NA
East Point	0.0	0.2	1.3	0.5	0.0	0.0	0.0	0.1	0.0	25.7	8.2	2.4	9.0	265	152	95
La Grange	1.9	1.8	5.1	4.0	0.0	0.0	0.6	0.6	1.6	83.1	5.4	32.1	3.6	142	12	102
Macon	7.5	9.9	11.1	4.0	0.7	1.1	1.3	8.5	6.1	83.0	31.7	1.9	30.2	266	134	108
Marietta	2 652.3	22.5	20.2	0.3	0.0	1.1	4.7	2.6	0.0	60.1	8.0	1.5	22.8	448	158	192
Rome	0.2	1.2	1.1	0.0	0.0	0.0	0.0	2.4	2.2	31.1	6.9	16.5	13.2	459	234	158
Roswell	5.4	2.5	1.3	0.1	0.0	0.0	0.5	0.0	0.0	45.3	11.4	1.2	19.8	357	252	69
Savannah	176.5	9.4	29.7	8.4	0.4	3.7	6.4	10.2	4.6	155.8	40.8	10.9	55.2	405	246	126
Smyrna	0.8	5.4	0.0	0.0	0.0	0.0	0.0	0.0	0.6	28.9	3.7	4.7	13.9	400	249	113
Valdosta	41.0	0.3	6.6	4.6	0.0	0.7	0.1	4.9	1.9	30.1	7.7	15.9	13.4	320	96	195
Warner Robins	81.9	0.9	7.1	5.0	0.0	0.0	0.5	0.6	0.0	24.8	1.4	100.0	12.2	268	153	92
HAWAII	992.7	148.6	1 334.6	603.1	33.1	162.7	44.1	17.5	25.6	X	X	X	X	X	X	X
Hilo CDP	NA	NA	NA	NA	NA	NA	NA	NA	NA	NA	NA	NA	NA	NA	NA	NA
Honolulu CDP	89.2	40.7	362.8	109.3	1.3	108.6	29.6	11.3	14.7	975.4	146.5	48.9	526.9	1 244	977	238
Kailua CDP	NA	NA	NA	NA	NA	NA	NA	NA	NA	NA	NA	NA	NA	NA	NA	NA
Kaneohe CDP	NA	NA	NA	NA	NA	NA	NA	NA	NA	NA	NA	NA	NA	NA	NA	NA
Mililani CDP	NA	NA	NA	NA	NA	NA	NA	NA	NA	NA	NA	NA	NA	NA	NA	NA
Pearl City CDP	NA	NA	NA	NA	NA	NA	NA	NA	NA	NA	NA	NA	NA	NA	NA	NA
Waimalu CDP	NA	NA	NA	NA	NA	NA	NA	NA	NA	NA	NA	NA	NA	NA	NA	NA
Waipahu CDP	NA	NA	NA	NA	NA	NA	NA	NA	NA	NA	NA	NA	NA	NA	NA	NA
IDAHO	156.3	713.8	1 176.8	534.1	59.3	114.8	18.4	26.1	10.0	X	X	X	X	X	X	X
Boise City	13.0	25.8	249.9	52.4	44.9	40.2	10.7	5.1	0.6	130.9	22.7	79.4	49.6	325	269	21
Idaho Falls	4.3	535.2	3.3	1.4	0.4	0.1	0.0	0.3	0.2	35.0	8.6	56.0	13.1	273	257	4
Lewiston	0.3	9.4	3.3	2.2	0.1	0.2	0.0	1.3	2.8	24.6	6.1	61.7	9.8	325	287	5
Nampa	27.2	4.7	4.5	2.4	0.0	0.3	0.7	0.7	0.1	23.8	5.1	67.4	7.6	202	159	13
Pocatello	0.1	2.3	9.5	2.5	0.5	1.8	0.4	6.0	-0.6	31.0	8.3	65.8	12.8	249	224	12
Twin Falls	0.0	7.7	7.3	4.2	0.0	0.4	0.0	1.8	0.1	21.4	6.8	87.6	7.2	224	197	10
ILLINOIS	1 310.5	2 169.8	10 586.2	6 221.4	141.6	1 027.0	319.9	244.9	182.1	X	X	X	X	X	X	X
Addison	1.5	0.1	0.0	0.0	0.0	0.0	0.0	0.0	0.0	26.4	8.7	98.5	5.5	163	100	19
Alton	0.6	1.3	7.2	5.2	0.0	0.6	0.7	0.0	0.7	28.4	15.2	100.0	5.2	165	115	43
Arlington Heights	9.0	0.6	0.5	0.0	0.0	0.0	0.4	0.0	-0.4	52.8	20.3	97.3	25.9	337	275	53
Aurora	1.3	2.4	3.9	0.0	0.1	0.0	2.4	0.6	0.1	82.6	32.7	94.8	36.0	309	212	61
Belleville	13.9	1.4	5.7	0.0	0.1	0.4	4.4	2.7	0.3	28.7	4.9	100.0	15.5	371	167	191

1. October 1, 1998 to September 30, 1999.   2. Includes program categories not shown separately. State totals include additional categories not allocated by city.   3. Based on population estimated as of July 1 of the year shown.

City	Total (mil dol)	Per capita[1] (dollars)		Percent of total for —									
		Total	Capital outlays	Public welfare	Highways	Parking facilities	Education	Health and hospitals	Police protection	Sewerage and sanitation	Parks and recreation	Housing and community development	Interest on debt
	124	125	126	127	128	129	130	131	132	133	134	135	136
FLORIDA—Cont'd													
Miami Beach	204.5	2 163	385	0.0	1.5	5.8	0.0	3.4	18.8	11.1	13.7	9.4	10.5
Miramar	36.7	721	41	0.0	3.1	0.0	0.0	0.0	25.7	21.0	8.5	0.0	11.9
North Lauderdale	13.1	465	7	0.0	5.2	0.0	0.0	0.0	34.2	18.3	13.0	0.5	0.5
North Miami	44.3	872	213	0.0	4.1	0.0	0.0	0.0	37.3	17.0	4.9	0.0	6.9
North Miami Beach	45.1	1 295	241	0.0	6.1	0.0	0.0	0.0	24.0	22.5	11.6	1.7	2.3
Oakland Park	27.3	972	20	0.0	1.8	0.0	0.0	1.8	24.5	33.5	6.9	0.0	0.0
Ocala	54.6	1 215	176	0.0	14.9	0.1	0.0	0.0	21.7	15.8	9.2	1.3	3.6
Orlando	277.0	1 593	99	0.0	7.5	2.6	0.0	0.0	20.1	14.9	14.8	1.5	8.4
Ormond Beach	24.9	773	77	0.0	8.0	0.0	0.0	0.0	16.8	29.9	16.5	0.0	3.3
Palm Bay	34.5	460	74	0.0	17.2	0.0	0.0	0.4	25.7	6.8	7.8	3.1	3.5
Panama City	29.2	810	152	0.0	11.7	0.0	0.0	0.6	18.8	10.1	14.4	1.6	4.7
Pembroke Pines	104.6	1 039	105	0.0	2.7	0.0	0.0	2.2	14.2	5.7	10.4	0.7	4.7
Pensacola	76.1	1 287	182	0.0	7.3	0.0	0.0	0.2	14.5	6.1	13.2	6.4	37.1
Pinellas Park	30.4	691	96	0.0	14.9	0.0	0.0	0.1	20.6	10.5	12.1	0.0	4.9
Plantation	45.1	573	55	0.0	5.4	0.0	0.0	0.0	36.7	10.3	14.2	0.0	5.1
Pompano Beach	80.2	1 075	39	0.0	2.7	0.3	0.0	6.1	30.6	13.8	9.3	3.8	5.0
Port Orange	25.7	620	40	0.0	7.4	0.0	0.0	0.0	16.4	17.6	9.5	0.0	7.3
Port St. Lucie	42.8	NA	NA	0.0	10.9	0.0	0.0	0.8	21.8	18.9	6.5	1.0	29.8
Riviera Beach	28.8	1 006	85	0.0	6.3	0.0	0.0	3.5	27.6	9.0	11.7	1.0	2.0
St. Petersburg	246.4	1 044	101	0.0	6.1	0.5	0.0	2.4	19.8	16.8	19.6	0.3	13.6
Sanford	23.8	669	53	0.0	16.0	0.0	0.0	0.0	21.2	11.3	9.8	2.7	3.3
Sarasota	69.8	1 371	99	0.0	7.4	0.5	0.0	0.0	24.4	20.3	12.5	2.1	5.1
Sunrise	92.6	1 194	255	0.0	2.9	0.0	0.0	0.0	14.0	27.0	19.5	0.0	7.8
Tallahassee	194.3	1 420	6	0.0	9.3	0.3	0.0	0.1	14.0	22.8	7.8	5.4	5.9
Tamarac	25.6	501	32	0.0	7.4	0.0	0.0	0.0	24.4	13.9	5.6	0.0	1.8
Tampa	322.7	1 132	77	0.0	6.3	1.8	0.0	1.7	23.9	21.7	8.9	2.0	12.0
Titusville	22.0	530	20	0.0	9.2	0.0	0.0	0.1	24.5	14.8	2.9	3.0	5.5
West Palm Beach	90.9	1 146	109	0.0	5.4	1.5	0.0	1.9	26.6	7.2	9.2	4.8	6.6
GEORGIA	X	X	X	X	X	X	X	X	X	X	X	X	X
Albany	62.7	798	71	0.0	3.0	0.0	0.0	0.0	15.5	20.1	6.5	4.5	2.1
Athens	105.4	NA	NA	2.4	5.7	0.6	0.0	5.2	17.4	13.5	6.5	2.3	0.6
Atlanta	887.7	2 209	475	0.1	5.3	0.0	0.0	0.0	11.2	14.6	7.2	1.6	10.2
Augusta	190.3	4 555	1 084	0.5	8.6	0.1	0.0	6.3	12.5	10.1	3.8	1.4	5.8
Columbus	NA	NA	NA	NA	NA	NA	NA	NA	NA	NA	NA	NA	NA
East Point	26.8	786	29	0.0	4.4	0.0	0.0	0.0	23.5	16.8	2.6	1.0	5.1
La Grange	87.5	3 436	269	0.1	2.2	0.0	0.5	70.6	4.6	6.6	1.5	4.4	0.1
Macon	84.6	746	98	0.0	5.1	0.0	0.0	0.2	18.5	6.2	5.0	7.2	3.0
Marietta	75.4	1 479	534	4.0	7.3	0.0	0.0	0.0	10.6	10.4	3.2	2.9	3.7
Rome	29.4	1 021	227	0.0	11.2	0.0	0.0	0.3	14.1	24.6	2.6	2.6	3.5
Roswell	46.0	830	227	0.0	10.4	0.0	0.0	0.0	13.7	11.4	12.3	1.2	5.3
Savannah	165.4	1 214	267	0.6	7.6	1.2	0.0	0.0	14.7	20.1	6.9	4.6	4.7
Smyrna	32.0	919	317	0.0	5.8	0.0	0.0	0.0	32.2	18.0	5.7	0.9	2.1
Valdosta	31.8	760	249	0.0	20.9	0.0	0.0	0.5	19.9	17.1	6.5	0.1	0.2
Warner Robins	26.8	589	58	0.0	6.9	0.0	0.0	0.0	20.6	23.1	4.6	3.9	0.4
HAWAII	X	X	X	X	X	X	X	X	X	X	X	X	X
Hilo CDP	NA	NA	NA	NA	NA	NA	NA	NA	NA	NA	NA	NA	NA
Honolulu CDP	958.1	2 262	263	0.0	2.6	0.0	0.0	1.3	13.6	20.2	7.3	7.1	12.8
Kailua CDP	NA	NA	NA	NA	NA	NA	NA	NA	NA	NA	NA	NA	NA
Kaneohe CDP	NA	NA	NA	NA	NA	NA	NA	NA	NA	NA	NA	NA	NA
Mililani CDP	NA	NA	NA	NA	NA	NA	NA	NA	NA	NA	NA	NA	NA
Pearl City CDP	NA	NA	NA	NA	NA	NA	NA	NA	NA	NA	NA	NA	NA
Waimalu CDP	NA	NA	NA	NA	NA	NA	NA	NA	NA	NA	NA	NA	NA
Waipahu CDP	NA	NA	NA	NA	NA	NA	NA	NA	NA	NA	NA	NA	NA
IDAHO	X	X	X	X	X	X	X	X	X	X	X	X	X
Boise City	137.6	901	305	0.0	0.4	1.3	0.0	0.3	12.5	25.9	5.7	0.4	1.9
Idaho Falls	37.7	784	129	0.0	6.9	0.0	0.0	3.5	17.6	15.9	12.4	0.0	0.5
Lewiston	25.3	837	81	0.0	14.6	0.0	0.0	0.0	12.9	23.0	9.0	0.0	0.0
Nampa	24.8	661	176	0.0	8.5	0.0	0.0	0.0	15.6	17.5	11.7	2.7	1.6
Pocatello	28.2	548	61	0.0	10.6	0.0	0.0	4.1	16.8	21.0	10.3	1.8	1.7
Twin Falls	25.8	807	297	0.0	22.2	0.1	0.0	0.0	15.5	14.2	3.7	5.3	1.2
ILLINOIS	X	X	X	X	X	X	X	X	X	X	X	X	X
Addison	30.7	914	77	0.0	13.7	0.0	0.0	0.0	19.0	13.3	0.0	5.7	18.1
Alton	25.7	815	11	0.0	11.0	0.0	0.0	0.3	15.6	13.6	10.7	0.0	12.8
Arlington Heights	44.9	585	9	0.0	4.3	1.2	0.0	2.7	21.2	0.0	0.0	1.2	8.1
Aurora	98.7	848	206	0.0	14.1	0.9	0.0	0.4	20.4	5.6	2.6	1.0	9.5
Belleville	26.9	645	118	0.0	7.5	0.9	0.0	0.0	16.9	23.6	4.0	0.0	11.5

1. Based on population estimated as of July 1 of the year shown.

Table D. Cities — City Government Finances, City Government Employment, and Climate

City	City government finances, 1997 (cont'd) Debt outstanding Total (mil dol)	Per capita[1] (dollars)	Percent utility	City government employment, 1999	Climate[2] Average daily temperature (degrees Fahrenheit) Mean January	July	Limits January[3]	July[4]	Annual precipitation (inches)	Heating degree days	Cooling degree days
	137	138	139	140	141	142	143	144	145	146	147
FLORIDA—Cont'd											
Miami Beach	291.9	3 088	0.0	1 581	68.1	82.6	62.3	86.9	45.35	139	4 157
Miramar	102.2	2 006	41.9	NA	66.3	82.4	56.8	89.8	63.01	273	4 012
North Lauderdale	2.5	87	60.4	NA	66.2	82.5	56.8	91.2	59.15	262	4 038
North Miami	61.1	1 204	12.0	527	66.3	82.4	56.8	89.8	63.01	273	4 012
North Miami Beach	17.0	489	15.9	NA	68.1	82.6	62.3	86.9	45.35	139	4 157
Oakland Park	0.1	4	0.0	NA	67.2	82.6	57.9	90.1	60.64	205	4 124
Ocala	124.3	2 765	69.3	NA	57.5	81.5	45.1	92.2	51.59	930	3 046
Orlando	322.4	1 854	0.0	3 395	59.7	82.3	48.6	91.5	48.11	686	3 381
Ormond Beach	44.6	1 381	74.8	NA	57.5	81.2	46.9	89.8	47.89	909	2 919
Palm Bay	57.5	767	71.4	NA	60.9	81.1	50.7	90.0	45.49	644	3 193
Panama City	41.5	1 154	52.1	NA	50.7	80.8	39.1	90.0	65.06	1 681	2 409
Pembroke Pines	88.5	879	30.5	NA	66.3	82.4	56.8	89.8	63.01	273	4 012
Pensacola	139.5	2 358	8.6	NA	50.6	82.1	41.4	89.9	62.25	1 617	2 636
Pinellas Park	31.4	714	37.5	NA	60.7	83.1	52.9	89.8	48.62	603	3 626
Plantation	72.6	923	57.3	755	67.2	82.6	57.9	90.1	60.64	205	4 124
Pompano Beach	78.7	1 056	29.8	922	66.2	82.5	56.8	91.2	59.15	262	4 038
Port Orange	90.2	2 180	69.7	NA	57.5	81.2	46.9	89.8	47.89	909	2 919
Port St. Lucie	294.7	NA	0.0	NA	62.5	81.4	51.6	90.4	50.06	490	3 441
Riviera Beach	11.4	397	39.7	NA	65.1	82.2	55.7	89.9	60.75	323	3 891
St. Petersburg	599.4	2 540	10.6	2 845	60.7	83.1	52.9	89.8	48.62	603	3 626
Sanford	45.2	1 270	76.7	NA	58.2	81.5	46.8	91.6	48.81	831	3 004
Sarasota	119.4	2 346	58.6	NA	60.2	81.4	49.0	90.8	53.71	678	3 186
Sunrise	288.9	3 723	71.2	861	67.2	82.6	57.9	90.1	60.64	205	4 124
Tallahassee	290.0	2 119	47.0	2 760	50.5	81.3	38.1	91.3	65.71	1 705	2 518
Tamarac	28.2	551	78.2	NA	66.2	82.5	56.8	91.2	59.15	262	4 038
Tampa	605.2	2 122	9.0	4 099	59.9	82.1	50.0	90.2	43.92	726	3 396
Titusville	71.3	1 717	76.5	NA	58.6	81.3	47.3	91.4	54.07	803	3 057
West Palm Beach	127.0	1 601	21.7	1 254	65.1	82.2	55.7	89.9	60.75	323	3 891
GEORGIA	X	X	X	X	X	X	X	X	X	X	X
Albany	64.4	819	68.0	1 388	46.5	80.8	33.8	91.9	51.48	2 205	2 206
Athens	45.6	NA	0.0	NA	41.8	79.6	32.0	89.6	49.74	2 893	1 709
Atlanta	1 339.1	3 332	18.5	8 204	41.0	78.8	31.5	88.0	50.77	2 991	1 667
Augusta	243.2	5 820	38.6	2 423	43.9	80.8	32.0	91.7	44.66	2 565	1 948
Columbus	NA	NA	NA	NA	NA	NA	NA	NA	NA	NA	NA
East Point	34.1	998	42.4	542	41.0	78.8	31.5	88.0	50.77	2 991	1 667
La Grange	44.7	1 756	99.3	407	43.4	79.0	31.9	90.1	54.52	2 667	1 696
Macon	44.6	394	0.0	1 479	45.4	81.2	34.2	91.9	44.63	2 334	2 125
Marietta	90.9	1 785	0.0	678	41.0	78.8	31.5	88.0	50.77	2 991	1 667
Rome	39.8	1 384	65.5	649	38.4	76.9	27.0	87.3	55.33	3 467	1 337
Roswell	44.1	796	1.8	NA	41.0	78.8	31.5	88.0	50.77	2 991	1 667
Savannah	212.4	1 558	36.8	2 123	48.9	81.8	38.1	91.1	49.22	1 847	2 365
Smyrna	26.0	747	13.3	379	41.0	78.8	31.5	88.0	50.77	2 991	1 667
Valdosta	13.7	328	74.8	575	49.0	80.7	36.7	92.1	52.24	1 844	2 350
Warner Robins	34.1	749	96.1	459	45.4	81.2	34.2	91.9	44.63	2 334	2 125
HAWAII	X	X	X	X	X	X	X	X	X	X	X
Hilo CDP	NA	NA	NA	NA	71.7	75.8	63.6	83.0	129.19	0	3 284
Honolulu CDP	1 698.5	4 011	2.7	NA	71.4	78.9	62.4	87.7	21.53	0	3 845
Kailua CDP	NA	NA	NA	NA	71.3	77.0	65.5	82.2	79.91	0	3 482
Kaneohe CDP	NA	NA	NA	NA	71.3	77.0	65.5	82.2	79.91	0	3 482
Mililani CDP	NA	NA	NA	NA	71.4	78.9	62.4	87.7	21.53	0	3 845
Pearl City CDP	NA	NA	NA	NA	71.4	78.9	62.4	87.7	21.53	0	3 845
Waimalu CDP	NA	NA	NA	NA	71.4	78.9	62.4	87.7	21.53	0	3 845
Waipahu CDP	NA	NA	NA	NA	71.4	78.9	62.4	87.7	21.53	0	3 845
IDAHO	X	X	X	X	X	X	X	X	X	X	X
Boise City	51.9	340	0.0	1 231	29.0	74.0	21.6	90.2	12.11	5 861	754
Idaho Falls	59.4	1 235	94.4	588	18.2	68.6	10.0	86.0	10.88	8 063	305
Lewiston	1.5	49	100.0	273	33.6	74.1	27.6	89.0	12.43	5 270	814
Nampa	11.4	302	0.0	355	29.0	74.0	21.6	90.2	12.11	5 861	754
Pocatello	23.8	464	0.0	513	23.3	70.6	14.4	88.1	12.14	7 180	421
Twin Falls	4.9	154	3.5	219	26.9	68.8	18.6	85.0	10.40	6 769	329
ILLINOIS	X	X	X	X	X	X	X	X	X	X	X
Addison	84.1	2 504	0.0	244	21.0	73.2	12.9	83.7	35.82	6 536	752
Alton	40.0	1 268	0.0	NA	27.0	78.5	17.9	88.4	38.43	5 214	1 346
Arlington Heights	72.2	941	16.1	593	21.0	73.2	12.9	83.7	35.82	6 536	752
Aurora	126.4	1 086	10.5	1 155	19.7	73.1	10.7	84.2	36.88	6 699	702
Belleville	46.2	1 111	0.0	NA	29.9	77.4	20.3	89.4	38.37	4 774	1 271

1. Based on the population estimated as of July 1 of the year shown. 2. Represents normal values based on the 30-year period, 1961–1990. 3. Average daily minimum. 4. Average daily maximum.

Table D. Cities — Land Area and Population

STATE Place code	City	Land area, 1990[1] (sq km)	Population, 1999			Population				Population characteristics, 1990 — Percent						
			Total persons	Rank	Per square kilometer	Total persons 1990	Percent change 1990–1999	Total persons 1980	Percent change 1980–1990	Race					His-panic[2]	Foreign born
										White	Black	Am. Indian, Eskimo, Aleut	Asian and Pacific Islander	Other race		
		1	2	3	4	5	6	7	8	9	10	11	12	13	14	15
	ILLINOIS—Cont'd															
17 05573	Berwyn	10.1	42 894	686	4 247	45 426	-5.6	46 849	-3.0	95.6	0.1	0.1	1.7	2.4	7.9	12.0
17 06613	Bloomington	43.3	60 872	449	1 406	51 889	17.3	44 189	17.4	90.9	6.7	0.2	1.5	0.8	1.6	2.2
17 07133	Bolingbrook	29.1	56 156	507	1 930	40 843	37.5	37 245	9.7	76.8	15.6	0.3	5.0	2.3	5.9	7.9
17 09447	Buffalo Grove	20.7	42 624	693	2 059	36 417	17.0	22 238	63.8	94.2	1.0	0.1	4.4	0.4	2.0	7.9
17 09642	Burbank	10.7	27 834	1 080	2 601	27 600	0.8	28 462	-3.0	97.5	0.0	0.2	1.1	1.2	4.7	10.2
17 10487	Calumet City	18.8	36 994	820	1 968	37 840	-2.2	39 697	-4.7	73.3	23.7	0.1	0.6	2.3	6.4	5.1
17 11163	Carbondale	26.4	27 228	1 107	1 031	27 033	0.7	26 287	2.8	74.3	17.4	0.1	7.1	1.0	2.5	10.1
17 11332	Carol Stream	20.2	37 738	803	1 868	31 759	18.8	15 514	104.7	88.4	3.4	0.2	5.8	2.1	5.7	9.8
17 12385	Champaign	33.5	65 226	408	1 947	63 502	2.7	58 133	9.2	80.7	14.2	0.2	4.1	0.8	1.9	5.4
17 14000	Chicago	588.5	2 799 050	3	4 756	2 783 726	0.6	3 005 078	-7.4	45.4	39.1	0.3	3.7	11.5	19.6	16.9
17 14026	Chicago Heights	23.4	31 726	957	1 356	32 966	-3.8	37 026	-11.0	55.0	35.1	0.2	0.3	9.4	15.0	6.4
17 14351	Cicero	15.1	70 344	364	4 659	67 436	4.3	61 232	10.1	75.2	0.2	0.4	1.6	22.6	37.0	23.9
17 18563	Danville	39.3	32 938	919	838	33 828	-2.6	39 019	-13.3	78.3	19.1	0.2	1.1	1.3	2.1	1.3
17 18823	Decatur	96.0	80 945	305	843	83 900	-3.5	94 081	-10.8	82.5	16.7	0.1	0.5	0.2	0.5	0.9
17 19161	De Kalb	20.8	39 329	767	1 891	35 076	12.1	33 099	6.0	88.9	4.7	0.1	4.5	1.8	4.1	7.3
17 19642	Des Plaines	36.8	57 068	494	1 551	53 414	6.8	53 568	-0.3	92.0	0.6	0.1	4.7	2.5	6.6	13.5
17 20591	Downers Grove	35.3	51 856	557	1 469	47 464	9.3	42 572	10.0	93.2	1.7	0.1	4.2	0.8	2.4	6.9
17 22255	East St. Louis	36.4	36 656	829	1 007	40 944	-10.5	55 200	-25.8	1.6	98.1	0.1	0.1	0.1	0.4	0.0
17 23074	Elgin	56.8	89 408	264	1 574	77 014	16.1	63 798	20.7	77.8	7.3	0.2	3.5	11.2	18.9	12.9
17 23256	Elk Grove Village	27.8	35 058	859	1 261	33 429	4.9	28 907	15.6	91.5	0.8	0.1	6.8	0.8	3.6	9.4
17 23620	Elmhurst	26.3	44 153	674	1 679	42 029	5.1	44 276	-5.1	95.9	0.4	0.1	3.0	0.6	2.7	6.8
17 24582	Evanston	20.1	71 679	359	3 566	73 233	-2.1	73 706	-0.6	70.6	22.9	0.2	4.8	1.5	3.7	11.5
17 27884	Freeport	26.7	26 031	1 158	975	25 840	0.7	26 266	-1.6	87.1	11.6	0.2	0.9	0.3	0.8	1.8
17 28326	Galesburg	43.7	32 888	920	753	33 530	-1.9	35 305	-5.0	88.6	8.4	0.2	0.9	2.0	3.8	2.0
17 29730	Glendale Heights	13.3	30 170	1 007	2 268	27 915	8.1	23 163	20.5	81.7	2.8	0.2	13.3	2.1	6.2	15.3
17 29938	Glenview	31.0	41 208	724	1 329	38 436	7.2	32 060	19.9	91.0	0.8	0.1	7.4	0.7	2.4	11.3
17 30926	Granite City	32.4	31 041	978	958	32 766	-5.3	36 815	-11.0	98.4	0.2	0.4	0.5	0.5	1.8	1.4
17 32746	Hanover Park	15.7	36 099	838	2 299	32 918	9.7	28 850	14.1	85.5	3.6	0.2	7.4	3.3	11.0	13.7
17 33383	Harvey	16.0	29 167	1 030	1 823	29 771	-2.0	35 779	-16.8	15.1	80.0	0.2	0.3	4.4	6.5	4.4
17 34722	Highland Park	31.2	31 343	968	1 005	30 575	2.5	30 611	-0.1	93.7	2.6	0.1	2.4	1.3	4.7	10.9
17 35411	Hoffman Estates	48.4	48 521	603	1 003	46 363	4.7	37 272	24.4	87.2	2.9	0.2	8.0	1.7	5.5	12.4
17 38570	Joliet	72.0	97 308	240	1 352	77 217	26.0	77 956	-0.9	69.2	21.6	0.2	1.0	8.0	12.7	7.3
17 38934	Kankakee	26.5	26 717	1 128	1 008	27 541	-3.0	30 141	-8.6	62.0	36.1	0.2	0.5	1.2	2.4	1.9
17 42028	Lansing	17.0	28 612	1 053	1 683	28 131	1.7	29 039	-3.1	95.7	3.0	0.1	0.4	0.8	2.8	3.5
17 44407	Lombard	24.1	43 099	685	1 788	39 408	9.4	37 295	5.7	93.4	1.3	0.1	4.4	0.7	2.8	6.8
17 47774	Maywood	7.0	25 743	1 172	3 678	27 139	-5.1	27 998	-3.1	12.0	83.8	0.1	0.5	3.6	6.6	5.1
17 49867	Moline	38.9	42 720	690	1 098	43 080	-0.8	45 709	-5.8	94.1	2.0	0.2	0.9	2.8	6.8	3.6
17 51089	Mount Prospect	26.7	53 613	536	2 008	53 168	0.8	52 634	1.0	90.2	1.1	0.1	6.4	2.1	6.4	16.2
17 51622	Naperville	72.4	122 993	170	1 699	85 806	43.3	42 346	102.6	92.6	2.1	0.1	4.8	0.4	1.8	6.3
17 53000	Niles	15.1	30 004	1 013	1 987	28 375	5.7	30 363	-6.5	91.6	0.4	0.1	7.0	0.9	3.6	21.8
17 53234	Normal	31.5	45 623	649	1 448	40 023	14.0	35 672	12.2	92.4	5.0	0.1	1.9	0.6	1.5	2.7
17 53481	Northbrook	32.7	33 645	901	1 029	32 565	3.3	30 778	5.8	93.0	0.2	0.0	6.4	0.3	1.6	10.1
17 53559	North Chicago	19.2	36 097	839	1 880	34 978	3.2	38 774	-9.8	56.7	34.4	0.5	3.6	4.7	9.2	6.2
17 54638	Oak Forest	14.0	28 866	1 044	2 062	26 202	10.2	26 096	0.4	97.1	0.6	0.2	1.5	0.6	2.5	3.7
17 54820	Oak Lawn	21.7	58 002	484	2 673	56 182	3.2	60 590	-7.3	98.3	0.1	0.1	1.1	0.5	2.4	7.5
17 54885	Oak Park	12.2	53 787	532	4 409	53 648	0.3	54 887	-2.3	77.0	18.3	0.1	3.3	1.3	3.6	6.6
17 56640	Orland Park	34.6	51 548	564	1 490	35 720	44.3	23 045	55.0	95.4	0.4	0.1	3.6	0.6	2.3	7.4
17 57225	Palatine	25.5	53 768	533	2 109	41 554	29.4	32 166	29.2	94.2	0.9	0.1	3.2	1.5	3.6	8.3
17 57875	Park Ridge	17.8	37 866	799	2 127	37 075	2.1	38 704	-4.2	97.4	0.1	0.1	2.2	0.2	1.3	10.5
17 58447	Pekin	28.3	33 261	914	1 175	32 254	3.1	33 967	-5.0	99.2	0.1	0.2	0.4	0.1	0.6	0.8
17 59000	Peoria	105.9	111 127	197	1 049	113 508	-2.1	124 160	-8.6	76.5	20.9	0.2	1.7	0.7	1.6	3.0
17 62367	Quincy	32.9	40 108	751	1 219	39 682	1.1	42 554	-6.7	94.9	4.1	0.2	0.5	0.2	0.4	0.7
17 65000	Rockford	116.5	143 831	137	1 235	142 815	0.7	139 712	1.5	81.1	15.0	0.3	1.5	2.1	4.2	4.9
17 65078	Rock Island	39.2	38 389	787	979	40 630	-5.5	47 036	-13.6	80.7	17.2	0.2	0.6	1.2	3.8	2.4
17 68003	Schaumburg	48.7	75 242	339	1 545	68 586	9.7	53 303	28.7	90.6	2.1	0.1	6.5	0.6	2.7	9.6
17 70122	Skokie	26.0	58 573	474	2 253	59 432	-1.4	60 278	-1.4	81.2	2.2	0.1	15.6	0.9	4.1	27.9
17 72000	Springfield	110.2	117 876	179	1 070	105 412	11.8	99 637	5.8	85.6	13.0	0.2	1.0	0.3	0.8	1.8
17 73157	Streamwood	17.6	35 746	842	2 031	31 197	14.6	23 456	33.0	91.2	2.0	0.2	4.2	2.4	7.4	9.2
17 75484	Tinley Park	27.1	47 929	615	1 769	37 115	29.1	26 169	41.8	96.2	1.6	0.1	1.4	0.7	2.5	3.4
17 77005	Urbana	20.2	36 744	825	1 819	36 383	1.0	35 978	1.1	75.7	11.4	0.2	11.7	0.9	2.7	14.4
17 79293	Waukegan	57.4	76 425	328	1 331	69 481	10.0	67 653	2.7	64.3	19.8	0.4	3.1	12.4	23.7	15.5
17 81048	Wheaton	28.7	56 225	505	1 959	51 441	9.3	43 043	19.5	93.0	2.5	0.1	3.8	0.6	2.0	6.5
17 81087	Wheeling	21.0	30 262	1 003	1 441	29 911	1.2	23 270	28.5	90.1	1.7	0.2	4.6	3.4	8.4	12.7
17 82075	Wilmette	13.9	26 345	1 143	1 895	26 694	-1.3	28 229	-5.4	92.4	0.5	0.0	6.9	0.2	1.7	13.2
17 83245	Woodridge	19.5	29 836	1 015	1 530	26 359	13.2	22 322	18.1	86.4	6.1	0.0	6.2	1.2	4.1	9.0
18 00000	INDIANA	92 903.7	5 942 901	X	64	5 544 156	7.2	5 490 214	1.0	90.6	7.8	0.2	0.7	0.7	1.8	1.7
18 01468	Anderson	98.1	58 317	477	594	59 518	-2.0	64 714	-8.0	84.9	14.2	0.3	0.4	0.3	0.6	0.9
18 05860	Bloomington	39.1	66 743	395	1 707	62 735	6.4	52 044	19.2	91.2	4.0	0.2	4.0	0.6	1.6	6.8
18 10342	Carmel	32.6	46 274	632	1 419	25 380	82.3	18 272	38.9	97.0	0.5	0.1	2.3	0.2	0.9	3.5

1. Dry land or land partially or temporarily covered by water.   2. Hispanic persons may be of any race.

Table D. Cities — Population and Households

City	Age of population (percent) Under 5 years	5 to 17 years	18 to 24 years	25 to 34 years	35 to 44 years	45 to 54 years	55 to 64 years	65 to 74 years	75 years and over	Percent female	Households, 1990 Number	Percent change, 1980–1990	Persons per household	Percent Female family householder[1]	One-person
	16	17	18	19	20	21	22	23	24	25	26	27	28	29	30
ILLINOIS—Cont'd															
Berwyn	6.3	12.9	8.3	18.4	13.7	9.3	9.7	11.3	10.1	53.5	19 298	-2.3	2.34	10.7	34.0
Bloomington	7.5	16.6	13.2	20.0	15.0	8.6	7.1	6.1	5.9	53.1	21 480	17.3	2.31	9.6	33.7
Bolingbrook	9.3	25.2	9.7	18.7	20.4	9.7	3.7	2.1	1.2	50.2	12 387	13.4	3.30	9.9	13.2
Buffalo Grove	9.5	19.2	6.4	21.8	21.1	10.1	6.2	4.0	1.7	51.0	13 335	88.8	2.73	5.8	20.7
Burbank	6.5	18.2	9.9	16.5	13.4	11.2	10.6	8.8	4.9	51.3	9 171	8.0	2.98	10.9	17.0
Calumet City	6.7	16.3	8.9	18.8	13.7	10.7	9.2	10.0	5.5	52.7	15 434	-1.1	2.45	14.6	29.5
Carbondale	4.2	8.1	49.3	15.5	7.9	4.3	3.8	3.6	3.4	46.3	9 606	9.2	2.12	9.0	38.0
Carol Stream	11.3	19.5	9.6	27.4	18.0	5.8	3.2	2.6	2.5	50.6	11 333	92.8	2.79	7.4	19.4
Champaign	5.9	12.1	31.8	17.6	12.2	6.8	5.5	4.9	3.3	48.2	24 173	13.7	2.30	8.8	34.2
Chicago	7.7	18.3	11.3	19.3	13.9	9.5	8.1	7.0	4.9	52.1	1 025 174	-6.3	2.67	19.6	32.1
Chicago Heights	9.1	21.2	10.8	15.9	12.4	9.5	8.5	7.6	5.0	52.5	10 932	-9.3	2.97	22.0	21.1
Cicero	8.9	19.5	10.7	18.5	13.0	8.3	7.5	7.9	5.7	50.2	23 179	-3.9	2.85	14.3	26.5
Danville	7.4	19.1	8.3	14.2	13.6	9.8	10.1	9.9	7.6	53.6	13 791	-10.5	2.40	14.0	32.4
Decatur	6.9	18.1	9.7	15.2	14.3	9.8	9.8	8.9	7.2	53.2	34 013	-5.2	2.39	13.4	29.9
De Kalb	4.7	10.0	43.9	14.7	9.1	6.0	4.8	3.8	3.1	51.1	10 557	9.5	2.43	8.1	29.5
Des Plaines	6.3	14.3	8.6	17.3	14.4	12.0	11.7	9.0	6.2	51.7	19 990	6.4	2.61	8.2	23.6
Downers Grove	7.7	17.2	7.8	18.0	17.8	11.0	8.3	6.9	5.2	51.7	17 660	15.2	2.63	6.4	23.8
East St. Louis	9.4	25.2	11.7	13.8	12.2	8.7	8.1	6.3	4.6	55.0	13 059	-22.4	3.12	39.7	25.4
Elgin	9.2	19.3	10.9	20.7	14.6	8.7	6.3	5.6	4.7	50.6	26 865	13.3	2.79	10.9	24.2
Elk Grove Village	8.0	18.2	8.7	20.3	17.1	11.4	8.9	4.7	2.6	50.9	12 002	29.0	2.77	7.2	20.0
Elmhurst	7.2	16.6	8.6	16.5	15.8	11.2	10.0	8.5	5.7	51.7	15 135	2.6	2.72	7.6	20.3
Evanston	5.6	12.3	18.0	19.5	15.4	9.6	7.2	5.8	6.6	53.1	27 954	-0.2	2.31	10.7	34.2
Freeport	7.2	17.0	9.7	16.2	12.0	10.5	8.9	9.8	8.7	53.6	10 843	1.9	2.33	10.9	32.1
Galesburg	6.3	16.0	10.8	15.8	14.8	8.5	9.6	9.5	8.5	51.1	13 272	-1.9	2.30	11.2	33.3
Glendale Heights	8.6	20.3	11.3	24.0	17.0	10.3	4.5	2.4	1.5	49.4	9 613	28.7	2.91	8.5	19.7
Glenview	7.1	17.2	8.0	13.6	16.5	13.8	11.1	8.6	4.3	51.3	13 348	24.7	2.75	7.0	18.7
Granite City	6.9	18.0	9.2	16.7	12.9	10.6	10.4	9.1	6.1	52.1	13 008	-3.9	2.50	12.9	26.6
Hanover Park	10.3	22.3	10.7	23.3	16.7	9.7	4.1	2.2	0.7	48.6	10 053	15.1	3.27	9.5	12.0
Harvey	9.6	24.6	11.5	16.3	13.7	8.9	7.0	5.1	3.1	52.0	9 052	-17.6	3.25	28.9	21.6
Highland Park	7.3	17.2	7.3	13.2	17.7	14.0	11.0	7.5	4.9	51.1	11 023	7.9	2.73	6.1	17.0
Hoffman Estates	8.6	20.2	10.0	21.9	18.4	11.1	5.6	2.8	1.6	49.8	15 924	30.3	2.91	8.0	17.4
Joliet	8.1	19.2	11.3	17.2	13.0	8.8	7.9	7.6	6.8	51.4	26 779	-1.6	2.71	14.7	27.0
Kankakee	8.8	20.4	9.6	16.0	13.0	8.9	7.7	8.2	7.4	53.0	10 397	-6.1	2.52	19.3	32.5
Lansing	6.5	16.4	9.0	17.2	15.1	10.7	10.2	9.7	5.1	52.3	10 881	4.6	2.58	8.8	23.8
Lombard	7.5	16.1	9.3	20.9	14.8	10.4	8.5	7.0	5.6	51.5	15 046	16.0	2.60	7.7	24.4
Maywood	7.8	22.8	11.1	16.0	13.5	11.6	8.6	5.1	3.5	53.0	8 036	-4.9	3.35	26.6	18.4
Moline	7.1	17.9	8.4	15.9	14.9	10.2	9.6	9.2	6.8	52.8	18 265	1.0	2.35	10.7	31.0
Mount Prospect	6.5	14.5	10.3	19.3	13.5	12.4	11.3	7.9	4.2	50.3	20 281	7.4	2.62	6.8	22.3
Naperville	9.0	21.5	8.1	18.0	21.4	11.2	5.4	3.2	2.2	50.8	29 101	123.5	2.89	5.5	17.6
Niles	4.6	10.9	8.6	14.0	11.3	12.2	13.9	13.3	11.2	53.1	10 776	5.6	2.48	8.1	25.5
Normal	4.8	12.4	41.9	13.1	10.3	6.3	4.7	3.8	2.6	53.1	11 856	22.5	2.64	8.2	21.0
Northbrook	6.2	18.1	6.7	10.1	16.2	15.2	13.0	8.8	5.8	51.3	11 391	19.6	2.78	5.6	15.8
North Chicago	7.9	15.4	35.9	18.1	9.7	4.3	3.7	3.1	1.8	34.8	7 142	0.8	3.10	18.3	19.0
Oak Forest	7.8	20.6	10.5	17.6	16.8	12.5	6.9	5.1	2.2	50.7	8 865	15.6	2.95	8.8	17.8
Oak Lawn	5.6	14.5	9.2	14.8	12.3	10.6	12.7	11.8	8.4	53.5	21 459	3.5	2.59	9.6	26.2
Oak Park	7.1	16.1	8.0	20.9	19.5	10.4	6.7	5.6	5.7	53.4	22 607	0.6	2.35	12.0	34.3
Orland Park	7.1	19.8	9.3	15.2	17.0	12.8	8.9	6.9	2.9	51.2	12 096	73.7	2.95	6.9	15.6
Palatine	6.9	16.9	9.6	20.2	16.6	12.5	8.5	5.3	3.5	51.2	15 158	42.8	2.58	7.6	24.8
Park Ridge	5.5	15.1	7.8	12.3	14.6	12.9	12.8	10.7	8.2	53.1	13 466	1.9	2.63	8.2	21.0
Pekin	7.1	18.8	9.1	15.5	13.5	10.6	9.9	8.7	6.9	52.9	13 078	0.7	2.43	10.4	28.4
Peoria	7.4	18.5	12.1	15.5	14.0	9.6	8.6	7.9	6.5	52.8	44 976	-3.3	2.42	14.7	31.6
Quincy	6.7	17.3	9.9	14.6	12.4	9.6	9.3	10.2	9.9	53.7	16 086	-3.4	2.33	11.1	33.4
Rockford	8.1	17.8	9.7	17.6	14.4	9.2	8.4	8.2	6.5	52.5	54 839	5.6	2.47	13.4	28.6
Rock Island	6.9	17.8	12.3	13.7	13.6	8.8	9.3	9.5	8.0	53.2	16 239	-7.7	2.37	13.8	32.6
Schaumburg	6.5	17.0	10.4	22.6	18.8	11.8	5.6	4.0	3.2	51.2	27 589	41.3	2.48	7.8	28.4
Skokie	5.1	15.1	7.0	13.0	15.2	11.5	12.4	12.3	8.4	53.2	22 708	1.0	2.58	8.5	22.2
Springfield	7.3	17.0	9.3	18.2	15.6	9.4	8.5	7.7	7.1	54.0	45 006	10.0	2.29	12.7	35.0
Streamwood	10.1	19.5	10.3	24.9	16.4	10.0	5.5	2.1	1.2	50.0	9 931	55.9	3.12	7.7	10.9
Tinley Park	8.5	20.3	8.1	20.0	18.5	9.5	6.3	5.8	3.0	51.3	12 678	53.7	2.84	7.9	20.2
Urbana	5.9	10.3	32.7	20.2	11.0	5.6	5.2	4.7	4.4	51.1	13 210	8.2	2.20	8.3	35.4
Waukegan	8.2	18.8	11.3	19.9	14.0	9.4	7.6	6.1	4.6	50.7	24 545	2.0	2.75	13.3	25.7
Wheaton	7.8	18.3	11.3	16.8	17.4	11.5	7.6	5.3	4.1	51.7	17 770	24.2	2.74	7.2	20.6
Wheeling	8.4	14.5	8.3	27.0	16.9	9.2	7.4	5.0	3.2	51.2	12 468	37.7	2.39	8.4	29.9
Wilmette	6.9	17.7	6.1	10.0	17.4	13.7	12.0	9.5	6.7	52.6	9 720	-0.5	2.71	7.4	18.6
Woodridge	9.4	18.6	10.8	23.9	18.4	10.0	5.1	2.9	1.0	50.2	9 622	25.4	2.73	9.7	21.4
INDIANA	7.2	19.1	10.9	16.5	14.8	10.3	8.7	7.3	5.3	51.5	2 065 355	7.1	2.61	10.5	24.1
Anderson	6.9	17.3	11.7	15.3	13.4	10.0	9.3	9.1	7.0	53.3	24 311	-1.7	2.36	14.2	30.8
Bloomington	4.0	8.4	45.2	16.5	9.6	5.1	4.5	3.7	3.1	52.5	20 983	24.2	2.19	8.5	35.5
Carmel	7.1	21.5	7.2	13.4	20.4	13.1	8.3	5.0	4.0	51.9	9 111	52.7	2.75	6.7	18.7

1. No spouse present.

Table D. Cities — Group Quarters, Crime, Education, and Income

City	Persons in group quarters, 1990				Serious crimes known to police, 1998[2]				Education, 1990				Money income, 1989		
					Total		Rate[3]		School enrollment		Attainment[4] (percent)			Households	
														Median	
	Total	Persons in mental hospitals	Persons in nursing homes	Persons identified as homeless[1]	Number	Rate[3]	Violent	Property	Public	Private	High school graduate or more	Bachelor's degree or more	Per capita (dollars)[5]	Dollars	Percent change, 1979–1989 (constant 1989 dollars)
	31	32	33	34	35	36	37	38	39	40	41	42	43	44	45
ILLINOIS—Cont'd															
Berwyn	161	0	112	35	NA	NA	NA	NA	7 075	2 268	73.1	15.0	15 097	31 326	3.9
Bloomington	2 300	0	649	60	NA	NA	NA	NA	10 713	3 423	83.9	31.7	15 667	29 354	9.1
Bolingbrook	0	0	0	0	NA	NA	NA	NA	11 265	1 982	85.6	23.1	14 766	46 166	3.7
Buffalo Grove	0	0	0	0	NA	NA	NA	NA	7 729	1 951	94.5	47.4	23 718	56 011	9.9
Burbank	276	0	198	0	NA	NA	NA	NA	5 572	1 456	70.1	7.5	13 294	37 449	-10.8
Calumet City	0	0	0	0	NA	NA	NA	NA	6 810	2 046	73.0	10.4	13 569	30 138	-17.0
Carbondale	6 660	0	188	60	NA	NA	NA	NA	17 690	456	87.5	46.2	8 037	11 821	-23.3
Carol Stream	45	0	45	0	NA	NA	NA	NA	6 868	1 475	89.3	32.1	16 697	45 141	26.1
Champaign	7 969	0	224	78	NA	NA	NA	NA	27 633	1 534	88.2	40.0	13 025	22 967	-8.0
Chicago	46 903	819	13 174	7 036	249 302	9 063	2 179	6 884	544 092	200 101	66.0	19.5	12 899	26 301	2.6
Chicago Heights	578	213	335	11	NA	NA	NA	NA	7 689	1 533	65.1	11.6	11 047	27 551	-11.5
Cicero	1 289	0	468	30	NA	NA	NA	NA	13 991	3 295	56.3	7.1	10 687	27 170	-3.1
Danville	695	0	379	17	NA	NA	NA	NA	7 238	1 129	74.1	15.0	12 401	22 315	-13.6
Decatur	2 652	302	1 007	25	NA	NA	NA	NA	17 067	3 711	74.0	15.7	13 348	25 451	-12.5
De Kalb	9 155	0	174	65	NA	NA	NA	NA	18 692	866	87.0	39.5	10 826	25 387	-2.3
Des Plaines	1 158	5	952	0	NA	NA	NA	NA	9 395	2 294	83.1	21.6	18 231	42 176	-1.2
Downers Grove	410	0	230	0	NA	NA	NA	NA	9 015	3 159	89.7	40.0	20 891	48 226	3.0
East St. Louis	228	0	136	56	NA	NA	NA	NA	12 182	892	55.7	7.3	6 421	12 627	-2.3
Elgin	2 076	995	481	25	NA	NA	NA	NA	16 733	3 505	74.0	18.3	13 929	35 554	7.4
Elk Grove Village	130	38	0	0	NA	NA	NA	NA	6 956	1 437	87.8	26.5	19 262	48 863	3.3
Elmhurst	777	0	261	0	NA	NA	NA	NA	7 626	3 134	87.8	36.2	21 005	49 611	7.2
Evanston	8 692	0	1 480	48	NA	NA	NA	NA	10 640	14 218	89.2	58.0	22 346	41 115	13.0
Freeport	575	37	430	0	NA	NA	NA	NA	5 090	587	74.3	14.4	12 631	24 758	-8.4
Galesburg	3 054	0	605	12	NA	NA	NA	NA	6 842	1 670	75.0	13.9	11 982	22 469	-17.2
Glendale Heights	0	0	0	0	NA	NA	NA	NA	6 900	1 203	84.2	23.9	15 715	42 822	-0.1
Glenview	452	0	139	0	NA	NA	NA	NA	7 067	2 576	92.2	46.2	30 531	59 020	6.5
Granite City	299	69	186	8	NA	NA	NA	NA	7 132	857	69.9	8.6	12 326	25 598	-14.6
Hanover Park	0	0	0	0	NA	NA	NA	NA	8 531	902	83.7	19.0	14 770	44 237	0.3
Harvey	434	100	151	59	NA	NA	NA	NA	8 670	957	66.7	8.0	8 690	23 201	-23.2
Highland Park	433	0	182	0	NA	NA	NA	NA	6 231	1 737	92.3	55.9	43 394	71 905	11.3
Hoffman Estates	209	49	160	0	NA	NA	NA	NA	10 808	2 156	90.3	33.5	19 072	49 475	6.6
Joliet	4 392	0	1 337	71	NA	NA	NA	NA	15 170	4 827	71.1	14.6	13 091	30 967	-2.6
Kankakee	1 385	30	402	12	NA	NA	NA	NA	6 196	1 199	65.9	11.6	10 349	20 328	-18.3
Lansing	47	0	47	0	NA	NA	NA	NA	4 875	1 783	81.9	15.5	16 112	36 641	-9.4
Lombard	301	0	176	26	NA	NA	NA	NA	6 865	2 967	88.3	30.4	18 281	44 210	1.8
Maywood	156	0	141	0	NA	NA	NA	NA	6 653	1 574	66.0	10.2	10 698	30 780	-4.3
Moline	245	0	141	0	NA	NA	NA	NA	9 196	1 631	81.2	19.3	14 939	27 512	-18.0
Mount Prospect	12	0	0	12	NA	NA	NA	NA	8 939	2 956	85.0	30.9	20 345	46 508	2.4
Naperville	1 192	0	378	0	2 346	2 139	60	2 079	20 702	5 738	95.5	54.4	23 934	60 979	6.6
Niles	1 488	0	1 467	0	NA	NA	NA	NA	3 718	1 541	75.0	20.2	17 422	38 718	-8.5
Normal	8 678	0	291	0	NA	NA	NA	NA	21 090	1 143	92.1	40.4	12 101	31 376	-7.6
Northbrook	637	0	561	0	NA	NA	NA	NA	6 536	2 188	90.3	55.1	38 100	73 362	9.6
North Chicago	12 948	0	637	17	NA	NA	NA	NA	6 501	1 152	79.2	10.2	9 165	25 500	-4.0
Oak Forest	0	0	0	0	NA	NA	NA	NA	5 619	1 677	87.2	17.8	15 745	43 387	-1.5
Oak Lawn	522	0	522	0	NA	NA	NA	NA	7 904	4 407	80.0	17.6	16 852	38 665	-4.7
Oak Park	464	0	273	52	NA	NA	NA	NA	10 100	3 876	90.9	51.2	21 269	40 453	17.2
Orland Park	0	0	0	0	NA	NA	NA	NA	7 862	2 367	88.5	28.8	20 521	51 748	4.5
Palatine	197	0	181	0	NA	NA	NA	NA	7 850	2 046	90.6	37.6	22 098	48 668	-4.5
Park Ridge	777	0	620	0	NA	NA	NA	NA	5 828	2 750	89.4	37.4	26 150	52 817	1.5
Pekin	488	0	389	0	NA	NA	NA	NA	7 055	678	75.7	10.5	12 246	25 198	-17.8
Peoria	4 745	238	1 255	201	10 971	9 673	814	8 859	23 270	9 717	77.9	23.6	14 039	26 074	-14.5
Quincy	2 130	0	1 377	1	NA	NA	NA	NA	7 166	2 613	73.6	14.5	11 708	21 325	-10.2
Rockford	3 954	101	2 005	344	13 709	9 390	983	8 407	27 221	6 684	74.8	18.7	14 109	28 282	-8.4
Rock Island	2 083	22	525	59	NA	NA	NA	NA	7 987	3 257	76.3	17.0	12 381	24 131	-19.0
Schaumburg	214	0	209	5	NA	NA	NA	NA	15 125	2 669	90.5	34.2	20 826	47 029	6.8
Skokie	718	0	645	0	NA	NA	NA	NA	10 550	3 511	85.5	36.7	20 595	42 276	-7.9
Springfield	2 071	0	1 116	253	8 843	7 734	1 043	6 691	20 012	5 644	81.7	24.9	14 813	27 995	0.2
Streamwood	0	0	0	0	NA	NA	NA	NA	6 857	1 110	83.4	19.9	16 416	48 758	10.1
Tinley Park	1 151	498	0	0	NA	NA	NA	NA	8 162	1 961	82.3	18.2	15 518	43 198	3.0
Urbana	7 476	0	400	14	NA	NA	NA	NA	17 462	653	89.2	53.8	11 439	21 705	-11.0
Waukegan	1 786	0	623	0	NA	NA	NA	NA	16 320	2 389	71.1	14.1	13 060	31 315	-2.1
Wheaton	2 842	0	893	0	NA	NA	NA	NA	10 537	5 328	92.2	49.4	22 433	52 208	11.3
Wheeling	102	0	102	0	NA	NA	NA	NA	5 085	1 114	85.9	30.0	18 480	39 848	1.2
Wilmette	353	0	148	0	NA	NA	NA	NA	4 965	1 931	95.1	63.7	38 465	71 274	15.0
Woodridge	0	0	0	0	NA	NA	NA	NA	5 940	1 252	91.6	32.4	17 730	44 570	1.3
INDIANA	162 133	3 015	50 845	2 507	245 952	4 169	431	3 738	1 233 973	202 215	75.6	15.6	13 149	28 797	-2.3
Anderson	1 922	0	563	24	NA	NA	NA	NA	11 127	2 876	71.3	12.0	12 161	23 221	-12.1
Bloomington	14 685	10	199	63	2 829	4 204	214	3 990	34 145	1 322	86.5	47.9	10 616	18 393	0.4
Carmel	296	0	296	0	919	2 367	33	2 334	5 906	1 320	95.0	51.3	24 956	54 505	5.0

1. Persons in emergency shelters and persons visible in street locations. 2. Data for serious crimes have not been adjusted for underreporting. This may affect comparability between geographic areas and over time. 3. Per 100,000 population estimated by the FBI. 4. Persons 25 years old and older. 5. Based on population enumerated as of April 1, 1990.

Table D. Cities — Income, Poverty, and Housing

City	Money income, 1989 (cont'd) Households Percent with $100,000 or more	Percent below poverty, 1989 — Persons Total	Persons Percent change in rate, 1979–1989	Families Total	Housing units, 1990 Total	Percent change, 1980–1990	Vacant units for sale or rent[1]	Occupied units Total	Percent	Owner-occupied units Median value[2] (dollars)	Owner cost as a percent of income With a mortgage	Without a mortgage	Renter-occupied units Median rent[3] (dollars)	Rent as percent of income	Sub-standard units[4] (percent)
	46	47	48	49	50	51	52	53	54	55	56	57	58	59	60
ILLINOIS—Cont'd															
Berwyn	1.9	5.7	5.6	3.8	20 044	-2.1	488	19 298	61.9	90 200	21.3	13.8	448	23.6	2.2
Bloomington	3.6	10.0	1.0	7.1	22 640	12.9	850	21 480	58.3	66 100	18.7	11.7	375	23.5	2.0
Bolingbrook	2.8	3.2	-3.0	2.4	12 889	9.5	433	12 387	79.4	94 300	23.1	12.3	558	26.2	2.8
Buffalo Grove	12.8	1.5	-46.4	1.0	13 866	76.3	458	13 335	83.8	163 600	22.7	12.3	754	24.4	0.7
Burbank	2.1	4.3	7.5	2.6	9 298	7.1	88	9 171	82.9	89 600	20.2	12.3	509	28.3	3.2
Calumet City	1.1	9.8	63.3	7.8	16 587	2.1	992	15 434	62.4	64 300	19.6	12.8	458	25.0	3.5
Carbondale	0.8	46.1	32.9	24.0	10 416	11.2	676	9 606	29.0	54 800	19.2	13.3	319	35.1	3.6
Carol Stream	2.2	3.5	-38.6	2.7	12 098	88.4	688	11 333	65.0	128 700	26.1	11.6	620	26.3	2.7
Champaign	3.2	22.7	22.7	9.6	25 996	15.3	1 516	24 173	47.2	66 500	20.3	12.6	422	35.1	2.4
Chicago	3.5	21.6	6.4	18.3	1 133 039	-3.5	83 759	1 025 174	41.5	78 700	21.1	13.7	445	27.3	9.2
Chicago Heights	2.4	20.1	36.7	17.1	11 620	-8.7	412	10 932	62.5	62 500	20.6	13.4	402	28.8	7.3
Cicero	1.0	13.9	56.2	11.2	24 841	-4.0	1 091	23 179	53.3	73 200	22.1	13.2	415	23.8	8.5
Danville	2.4	19.3	44.0	15.3	15 326	-7.4	972	13 791	63.1	38 800	17.1	12.9	325	27.1	2.4
Decatur	2.5	15.9	34.7	12.3	37 470	-2.6	2 586	34 013	65.9	42 800	16.1	12.7	339	26.3	1.6
De Kalb	2.7	24.4	26.4	8.7	10 915	10.3	277	10 557	42.5	78 500	20.6	13.2	436	31.9	4.0
Des Plaines	5.8	2.2	-31.3	1.5	20 509	6.3	419	19 990	79.8	130 000	20.1	11.8	577	25.0	2.4
Downers Grove	9.1	2.5	0.0	1.5	18 166	14.4	386	17 660	78.5	143 900	20.8	12.3	566	24.9	1.0
East St. Louis	0.4	43.9	1.4	39.5	15 622	-17.3	1 506	13 057	50.5	26 400	20.0	16.3	320	35.1	11.0
Elgin	3.0	7.8	2.6	5.9	27 936	12.2	807	26 865	62.3	96 800	22.2	13.7	501	23.7	6.8
Elk Grove Village	6.3	2.7	58.8	2.0	12 416	27.0	378	12 002	76.6	137 900	21.0	11.9	647	24.1	2.2
Elmhurst	10.3	1.4	-53.3	0.9	15 486	3.2	252	15 135	83.6	135 600	20.4	12.3	605	26.1	1.1
Evanston	12.1	9.8	38.0	5.3	29 164	-0.4	1 001	27 954	51.1	184 800	20.8	12.9	636	27.9	2.6
Freeport	1.2	12.5	58.2	9.6	11 722	5.4	687	10 843	64.9	46 800	17.5	12.0	315	24.9	1.1
Galesburg	1.9	17.9	90.4	12.9	14 322	-1.3	754	13 272	63.0	37 100	16.5	13.2	296	27.1	0.9
Glendale Heights	3.4	2.7	0.0	2.0	10 210	29.6	422	9 613	69.5	105 500	23.4	12.4	623	24.3	2.9
Glenview	24.7	1.7	-5.6	0.9	13 763	25.2	306	13 348	85.4	235 600	20.3	12.0	777	24.2	1.1
Granite City	1.3	13.2	23.4	10.5	13 886	-1.9	657	13 008	68.4	42 700	16.1	13.2	351	28.5	2.3
Hanover Park	3.9	2.8	-22.2	2.1	10 405	11.2	314	10 053	79.9	101 900	23.4	12.2	593	25.9	5.5
Harvey	1.0	25.6	40.7	23.1	10 286	-10.2	982	9 052	58.8	49 900	22.3	13.3	453	35.1	12.2
Highland Park	34.7	2.8	33.3	1.6	11 436	8.4	260	11 023	80.4	257 000	21.4	12.6	696	25.6	1.3
Hoffman Estates	8.3	2.0	-28.6	1.3	16 608	25.7	626	15 924	73.8	133 800	21.8	11.5	693	25.9	3.1
Joliet	2.5	13.0	8.3	9.6	29 043	-2.6	1 650	26 779	63.1	64 500	18.3	13.5	403	26.3	5.2
Kankakee	1.1	23.5	30.6	20.3	11 380	-3.3	582	10 397	50.7	40 000	17.5	13.9	355	27.6	4.6
Lansing	2.6	2.7	-6.9	2.0	11 184	4.8	261	10 881	73.0	77 900	18.2	12.3	509	23.4	1.6
Lombard	4.3	2.6	4.0	1.6	15 848	17.9	716	15 046	73.0	118 000	21.5	12.3	668	26.7	1.4
Maywood	2.3	15.2	12.6	11.4	8 547	-2.6	405	8 036	62.6	67 900	21.1	13.6	483	32.9	9.8
Moline	3.4	10.3	51.5	8.1	19 235	3.3	709	18 265	64.3	49 600	16.5	12.2	350	23.5	1.5
Mount Prospect	7.7	3.3	26.9	2.1	20 994	7.4	581	20 281	69.1	155 100	19.3	11.5	615	24.3	3.2
Naperville	16.8	1.5	-21.1	0.9	30 906	119.8	1 617	29 101	76.1	176 500	23.2	12.0	698	24.1	0.8
Niles	5.3	3.7	15.6	2.5	11 052	3.0	231	10 776	75.6	140 700	19.1	12.3	591	27.4	3.0
Normal	3.0	21.7	26.2	5.7	12 300	18.6	325	11 856	55.0	74 000	16.6	11.5	433	29.5	1.0
Northbrook	34.2	1.8	-10.0	1.1	11 673	17.5	200	11 391	90.6	271 000	18.0	11.5	916	32.7	0.6
North Chicago	1.1	14.9	58.5	12.4	7 925	6.2	545	7 142	33.0	64 000	19.3	13.0	485	27.9	6.9
Oak Forest	3.7	3.0	25.0	2.1	9 058	12.7	172	8 865	78.0	104 300	20.2	12.8	544	24.0	2.0
Oak Lawn	4.4	3.4	3.0	2.4	21 835	3.0	282	21 459	81.9	108 100	19.4	12.4	534	26.4	1.7
Oak Park	8.3	4.6	-9.8	3.1	23 571	0.6	711	22 607	53.5	138 700	21.1	12.7	535	23.0	1.6
Orland Park	10.6	2.4	-11.1	1.5	12 484	64.8	313	12 096	84.9	152 700	21.8	12.5	620	24.4	1.2
Palatine	10.4	2.5	25.0	1.8	15 851	42.9	605	15 158	69.4	149 600	20.6	11.8	665	24.0	1.2
Park Ridge	16.3	1.3	-31.6	0.9	13 821	2.1	230	13 466	87.3	185 700	19.2	12.2	640	25.9	1.1
Pekin	1.5	13.9	63.5	10.9	13 776	-0.1	436	13 078	63.7	41 200	15.4	12.6	307	22.6	2.1
Peoria	3.9	18.9	53.7	15.1	48 260	-5.1	2 445	44 976	56.5	49 200	16.6	12.8	360	24.4	2.3
Quincy	2.0	15.0	26.1	11.7	17 530	-2.5	1 080	16 086	64.1	41 800	16.4	12.5	276	25.0	2.0
Rockford	3.1	13.4	30.1	10.5	58 146	6.4	2 189	54 839	59.6	56 300	17.5	13.1	367	24.6	2.8
Rock Island	2.2	19.3	56.9	13.9	17 901	-2.4	1 076	16 239	62.0	44 100	17.0	12.8	313	27.0	2.3
Schaumburg	6.5	2.7	3.8	2.2	29 499	40.9	1 606	27 589	65.2	133 500	21.5	12.3	739	25.2	1.4
Skokie	9.6	3.9	56.0	2.7	23 170	1.6	341	22 708	75.3	149 400	21.1	12.0	645	26.9	2.3
Springfield	2.5	12.6	20.0	9.7	48 534	10.2	2 692	45 006	58.3	59 200	16.2	11.9	379	23.7	1.9
Streamwood	3.1	2.6	13.0	1.7	10 324	54.9	361	9 931	86.5	107 100	22.7	12.8	891	24.6	2.4
Tinley Park	2.9	2.5	-35.9	1.4	13 222	53.3	495	12 678	79.0	115 900	22.6	13.3	560	25.9	1.6
Urbana	2.8	21.8	23.2	12.7	14 006	9.8	649	13 210	39.5	69 000	20.3	12.4	413	30.3	4.0
Waukegan	2.4	9.5	0.0	6.5	25 800	0.5	972	24 545	53.6	72 600	21.4	13.2	490	25.2	7.5
Wheaton	13.7	5.1	54.5	1.8	18 630	22.3	767	17 770	74.5	148 700	22.3	12.1	646	26.8	1.2
Wheeling	3.4	3.2	0.0	2.0	12 998	35.2	457	12 468	64.6	113 400	23.3	12.0	679	24.8	2.7
Wilmette	33.7	2.1	-25.0	1.2	10 046	0.6	235	9 720	85.9	280 800	19.8	11.8	818	25.8	0.6
Woodridge	4.2	2.9	-12.1	2.1	10 198	19.6	519	9 622	64.9	120 500	23.7	11.7	581	23.7	2.0
INDIANA	2.5	10.7	10.1	7.9	2 246 046	7.4	97 102	2 065 355	70.2	53 900	16.7	12.3	374	24.3	2.6
Anderson	1.4	18.0	41.7	15.2	26 362	-0.9	1 175	24 311	63.8	37 000	15.1	12.2	338	26.3	1.9
Bloomington	3.0	31.5	35.2	15.3	22 025	24.4	820	20 983	34.2	76 300	18.1	11.7	403	34.9	3.0
Carmel	17.0	1.6	-44.8	1.0	9 645	50.0	486	9 111	71.2	142 500	18.7	11.1	560	23.0	0.4

1. Includes units rented or sold but not occupied.   2. Specified owner-occupied units.   3. Specified renter-occupied units.   4. Overcrowded or lacking complete plumbing facilities.

City	Civilian labor force, 1999		Unemployment		Civilian employment, 1990[2]	Percent		Disability 1990	Value of residential construction authorized by building permits, 1999		
	Total	Percent change, 1998–1999	Total	Rate[1]	Total	Professional, managerial, and technical	Precision production, craft, and repair	Work disabled persons[3] (percent)	New construction ($1,000)	Number of housing units	Percent single family
	61	62	63	64	65	66	67	68	69	70	71
ILLINOIS—Cont'd											
Berwyn	23 031	-0.3	1 039	4.5	22 052	26.7	12.3	6.8	4 810	75	8.0
Bloomington	38 911	7.4	934	2.4	28 115	31.8	8.1	6.2	59 078	665	75.6
Bolingbrook	31 700	2.6	1 214	3.8	21 789	31.2	11.8	4.0	51 131	554	100.0
Buffalo Grove	25 920	1.2	602	2.3	21 071	46.6	6.3	2.6	7 557	60	33.3
Burbank	15 001	0.9	560	3.7	13 615	18.7	16.8	7.0	4 898	50	96.0
Calumet City	19 194	-0.4	1 051	5.5	17 664	22.8	12.1	6.9	1 619	18	100.0
Carbondale	11 901	3.6	457	3.8	11 098	38.6	3.9	4.8	5 556	109	9.2
Carol Stream	22 519	-0.2	665	3.0	17 773	35.1	10.9	3.3	13 831	77	100.0
Champaign	38 462	5.4	934	2.4	32 714	41.8	5.5	4.9	43 518	512	35.7
Chicago	1 351 912	3.6	72 695	5.4	1 207 108	28.1	8.9	8.4	556 994	5 400	15.5
Chicago Heights	14 726	0.2	1 018	6.9	13 612	22.3	10.6	9.1	1 042	12	100.0
Cicero	34 272	1.5	2 183	6.4	28 832	15.0	14.0	7.0	0	0	0.0
Danville	14 282	0.1	1 148	8.0	13 627	28.3	9.2	11.1	8 153	130	15.4
Decatur	41 447	5.0	2 450	5.9	36 125	27.3	10.3	9.7	6 316	64	75.0
De Kalb	20 500	1.2	652	3.2	18 203	34.0	7.9	3.3	21 539	309	43.7
Des Plaines	33 408	1.4	1 420	4.3	29 257	30.9	12.2	5.4	17 502	349	18.3
Downers Grove	30 296	2.5	819	2.7	25 318	44.7	8.2	3.9	14 306	65	100.0
East St. Louis	11 726	-0.9	1 116	9.5	10 888	19.7	6.0	15.6	0	0	0.0
Elgin	49 619	0.2	2 650	5.3	39 227	26.5	11.9	5.9	34 617	319	100.0
Elk Grove Village	21 447	1.4	546	2.5	19 167	35.0	10.0	3.7	1 417	8	100.0
Elmhurst	25 165	-0.2	611	2.4	22 486	40.3	8.6	4.8	26 677	308	82.5
Evanston	43 299	1.4	1 510	3.5	40 413	52.2	3.7	4.8	8 512	68	4.4
Freeport	12 790	2.0	977	7.6	11 926	23.0	13.4	7.9	5 779	48	39.6
Galesburg	16 230	1.1	732	4.5	14 086	25.9	11.1	10.0	3 275	31	100.0
Glendale Heights	19 306	-1.1	653	3.4	16 336	30.6	11.5	2.8	18 945	250	100.0
Glenview	21 789	2.6	507	2.3	18 805	47.8	5.8	3.4	33 911	181	83.4
Granite City	15 156	-0.2	991	6.5	14 010	22.3	11.7	12.3	2 623	49	14.3
Hanover Park	21 897	1.4	883	4.0	18 209	25.7	12.4	4.9	350	3	100.0
Harvey	12 475	-0.7	1 099	8.8	11 187	20.1	10.7	11.6	255	2	100.0
Highland Park	17 460	-0.8	316	1.8	16 059	52.2	4.0	2.9	22 680	73	79.5
Hoffman Estates	30 185	0.5	810	2.7	26 782	36.7	9.4	3.8	5 597	48	100.0
Joliet	44 359	2.4	2 952	6.7	32 754	24.2	12.3	7.1	142 327	1 732	98.4
Kankakee	12 003	-3.1	1 083	9.0	10 322	27.8	8.7	11.9	180	4	50.0
Lansing	16 060	0.3	555	3.5	14 507	28.0	15.7	5.3	1 606	22	100.0
Lombard	25 492	0.1	750	2.9	21 895	37.5	11.0	3.6	9 558	149	24.2
Maywood	13 036	-0.6	1 053	8.1	11 957	21.2	6.8	9.8	227	3	100.0
Moline	22 753	3.2	1 257	5.5	19 779	30.8	9.7	7.5	6 632	30	100.0
Mount Prospect	33 334	0.1	847	2.5	30 621	36.2	9.5	4.4	5 427	69	10.1
Naperville	67 756	8.4	1 733	2.6	45 705	51.4	5.4	2.3	235 635	1 849	62.3
Niles	16 202	2.4	481	3.0	14 316	29.8	11.3	4.0	2 193	12	100.0
Normal	28 594	8.9	565	2.0	21 262	32.9	5.2	2.9	24 381	474	57.4
Northbrook	18 400	1.5	417	2.3	16 669	51.4	3.9	3.4	36 480	132	92.4
North Chicago	8 160	-0.8	787	9.6	7 688	21.8	9.2	9.0	3 529	35	85.7
Oak Forest	16 448	1.9	543	3.3	14 282	29.6	14.3	5.0	11 600	131	67.9
Oak Lawn	30 968	0.9	1 014	3.3	27 689	29.1	13.2	5.9	11 672	116	74.1
Oak Park	33 835	5.5	894	2.6	31 041	54.1	4.5	3.9	4 215	32	100.0
Orland Park	26 636	5.8	782	2.9	18 330	38.2	10.0	4.0	89 708	572	81.1
Palatine	29 167	3.2	1 192	4.1	22 917	40.7	7.4	3.6	32 769	225	72.4
Park Ridge	20 895	2.0	458	2.2	18 781	45.6	7.1	3.8	24 873	119	73.1
Pekin	16 770	0.9	969	5.8	13 941	25.1	11.9	8.0	10 894	95	82.1
Peoria	57 721	1.3	2 712	4.7	49 082	35.1	7.2	9.0	55 700	541	65.6
Quincy	20 845	1.3	961	4.6	17 362	27.1	10.0	9.2	12 622	90	71.1
Rockford	78 245	1.4	5 194	6.6	65 168	28.3	11.6	8.5	20 993	358	57.3
Rock Island	19 309	2.5	1 063	5.5	17 063	26.1	9.3	9.5	2 311	17	100.0
Schaumburg	49 464	1.1	1 295	2.6	42 148	37.7	8.1	3.7	4 918	27	77.8
Skokie	32 883	0.9	877	2.7	30 818	41.6	7.2	4.7	14 935	117	28.2
Springfield	62 227	5.1	2 699	4.3	53 528	37.6	7.1	7.7	57 920	635	54.5
Streamwood	22 096	3.1	833	3.8	17 889	28.5	13.5	5.0	31 206	358	98.3
Tinley Park	24 571	5.3	791	3.2	18 592	30.9	15.2	4.2	93 206	688	85.5
Urbana	20 493	10.6	602	2.9	18 293	50.5	4.6	4.1	11 567	132	29.5
Waukegan	40 665	-0.2	2 352	5.8	33 556	24.4	12.0	7.6	36 406	304	46.7
Wheaton	32 041	1.4	702	2.2	27 643	49.2	5.7	3.8	12 346	42	100.0
Wheeling	20 216	2.1	637	3.2	18 200	33.9	9.4	4.0	2 503	17	100.0
Wilmette	13 955	1.7	244	1.7	13 257	58.9	3.6	3.6	15 433	46	100.0
Woodridge	19 012	0.5	565	3.0	15 715	39.6	9.6	3.9	15 373	102	100.0
INDIANA	3 077 612	-0.3	93 028	3.0	2 628 695	25.6	12.9	7.9	4 786 192	41 844	80.7
Anderson	29 470	-2.2	1 199	4.1	26 407	20.9	12.2	10.9	16 731	157	79.6
Bloomington	31 705	0.1	903	2.8	27 232	42.8	4.4	4.3	NA	NA	NA
Carmel	21 659	4.0	237	1.1	13 477	46.7	4.7	3.5	250 234	1 117	84.6

1. Percent of civilian labor force.   2. Persons 16 years and older.   3. Persons 16 to 64 years old.

Wholesale Trade, Retail Trade, and Real Estate

City	Wholesale Trade, 1997				Retail Trade[1], 1997				Real Estate and Rental and Leasing, 1997			
	Number of Establish-ments	Number of Employees	Sales (mil dol)	Annual Payroll (mil dol)	Number of Establish-ments	Number of Employees	Sales (mil dol)	Annual Payroll (mil dol)	Number of Establish-ments	Number of Employees	Receipts (mil dol)	Annual Payroll (mil dol)
	72	73	74	75	76	77	78	79	80	81	82	83
ILLINOIS—Cont'd												
Berwyn	29	141	98.1	4.7	147	1 578	272.8	27.8	25	106	9.1	1.5
Bloomington	109	1 137	566.5	50.5	364	5 300	905.1	85.6	78	323	43.1	5.5
Bolingbrook	54	1 076	1 102.0	34.9	102	2 786	456.9	43.9	29	158	15.2	2.2
Buffalo Grove	190	2 251	2 784.6	111.8	123	1 705	357.6	40.9	45	324	36.0	9.0
Burbank	10	84	9.1	1.4	91	1 794	290.2	26.0	12	68	5.5	1.0
Calumet City	20	D	D	D	194	4 775	715.1	72.1	22	108	9.8	1.3
Carbondale	19	173	42.6	4.7	206	3 170	443.4	44.5	52	318	22.6	4.3
Carol Stream	103	3 552	4 950.8	157.4	80	1 349	299.7	26.6	20	105	14.5	2.4
Champaign	76	1 414	689.0	38.3	379	6 227	825.3	82.6	108	859	106.3	18.2
Chicago	3 312	50 029	31 971.1	1 970.1	7 885	86 703	13 882.1	1 553.2	2 971	25 827	5 226.4	899.1
Chicago Heights	51	890	371.9	25.6	93	1 165	308.7	26.4	21	132	11.5	2.4
Cicero	45	669	403.7	29.5	133	1 869	347.4	32.3	22	115	10.8	1.5
Danville	60	1 802	1 004.0	55.1	214	3 212	434.2	44.2	48	D	D	D
Decatur	129	1 609	3 119.0	50.6	372	5 334	882.6	87.8	88	498	38.7	8.3
De Kalb	20	D	D	D	130	2 153	297.9	32.1	36	200	26.4	3.1
Des Plaines	224	5 611	4 724.2	258.4	197	2 592	562.6	51.8	85	1 293	691.3	40.4
Downers Grove	171	3 009	3 195.4	143.0	267	5 969	1 591.6	135.1	67	397	73.5	10.5
East St. Louis	23	D	D	D	73	617	71.2	8.6	20	69	6.2	1.3
Elgin	169	2 985	2 158.1	129.4	226	3 887	862.8	82.4	78	433	68.5	10.9
Elk Grove Village	621	10 899	8 110.0	479.7	152	3 039	550.1	68.2	55	467	86.9	14.7
Elmhurst	197	6 605	2 264.9	341.4	188	2 898	850.4	74.0	68	472	73.1	15.8
Evanston	95	992	403.3	30.0	292	4 370	746.0	87.1	128	603	101.5	15.1
Freeport	25	230	80.1	5.6	135	2 155	346.3	34.9	23	97	9.0	1.5
Galesburg	42	527	210.5	14.5	198	3 304	409.3	45.9	35	148	11.0	1.8
Glendale Heights	79	2 417	1 337.5	96.7	63	1 390	332.8	29.7	8	82	16.1	1.4
Glenview	146	1 753	866.8	77.3	166	1 909	515.6	45.4	54	178	29.7	4.4
Granite City	36	578	859.5	19.2	110	1 456	250.2	22.7	31	186	14.6	3.5
Hanover Park	26	558	333.7	26.0	76	1 094	157.6	18.5	15	71	13.3	1.1
Harvey	30	659	277.7	26.5	66	777	141.1	15.8	10	38	3.4	0.7
Highland Park	106	410	1 106.1	22.0	180	2 419	570.5	52.4	58	125	27.0	4.0
Hoffman Estates	107	1 094	1 790.1	67.9	104	1 657	332.8	36.7	35	158	24.1	3.1
Joliet	90	952	216.2	28.9	405	7 042	1 281.5	119.9	74	304	34.9	5.4
Kankakee	40	403	205.9	13.6	115	1 289	212.3	24.5	27	163	16.3	2.8
Lansing	43	589	310.3	23.1	158	3 073	472.9	48.1	42	163	17.5	3.0
Lombard	180	3 003	3 228.9	137.2	282	5 138	858.2	91.3	63	703	75.2	24.6
Maywood	10	68	21.3	1.7	45	332	90.3	7.0	9	41	5.5	1.1
Moline	73	1 072	766.8	43.6	325	5 164	805.5	81.6	61	370	52.8	9.1
Mount Prospect	136	2 164	3 162.7	109.9	232	4 285	573.1	66.2	46	224	31.0	5.2
Naperville	310	3 398	12 942.4	192.8	396	7 212	1 506.7	143.3	139	606	105.6	16.2
Niles	95	2 178	661.9	72.5	234	5 190	1 147.9	91.2	32	254	31.5	5.8
Normal	35	D	D	D	152	2 843	398.2	39.8	40	336	48.9	7.9
Northbrook	375	4 107	3 172.5	190.8	269	4 258	723.0	86.2	126	659	144.6	25.6
North Chicago	22	777	269.7	37.9	37	343	69.2	11.3	12	D	D	D
Oak Forest	31	323	173.7	12.4	58	549	155.3	14.3	21	86	6.9	2.2
Oak Lawn	39	139	71.2	3.9	239	4 298	1 039.9	92.0	60	271	29.5	4.5
Oak Park	57	242	146.1	9.4	181	1 624	240.0	26.7	59	383	40.5	7.3
Orland Park	73	476	150.1	16.4	374	7 389	1 244.9	117.8	64	253	57.9	6.5
Palatine	167	799	689.3	36.4	217	2 943	554.5	54.6	75	439	67.8	9.7
Park Ridge	108	457	605.4	18.1	117	1 432	305.0	29.0	54	318	59.0	9.3
Pekin	28	D	D	D	152	2 429	463.8	41.5	23	134	12.7	3.0
Peoria	231	3 831	5 321.3	138.6	566	9 434	1 501.0	149.3	154	753	92.9	16.8
Quincy	82	1 175	403.4	34.0	275	4 308	607.1	62.0	50	209	17.0	2.7
Rockford	320	4 838	1 812.5	167.6	679	11 718	1 875.3	185.9	150	806	104.7	18.1
Rock Island	80	1 728	543.6	53.9	128	1 365	201.1	20.0	41	185	17.1	3.1
Schaumburg	431	9 640	12 007.5	536.1	523	12 331	2 262.6	227.5	132	1 130	299.0	39.4
Skokie	234	3 921	6 222.6	230.0	413	7 088	981.6	118.7	116	756	351.9	46.4
Springfield	162	2 370	963.3	80.0	618	9 812	1 634.3	154.7	145	624	69.8	11.3
Streamwood	32	184	93.9	7.3	64	891	163.7	12.4	13	107	3.5	1.0
Tinley Park	41	350	172.7	12.9	130	2 456	494.0	44.1	23	129	9.7	2.0
Urbana	32	D	D	D	109	1 836	287.3	30.4	36	138	48.3	4.1
Waukegan	73	2 423	1 016.1	94.6	288	4 373	735.2	78.2	61	335	47.8	8.0
Wheaton	115	369	408.2	15.1	217	2 919	513.3	51.7	59	253	40.1	6.7
Wheeling	203	3 111	1 473.3	134.3	101	1 707	366.7	31.7	36	307	41.6	13.2
Wilmette	47	134	214.6	6.8	133	1 571	241.0	27.0	56	242	31.7	6.4
Woodridge	33	1 109	536.7	41.0	64	1 308	203.3	19.3	30	160	20.6	3.1
INDIANA	8 896	112 705	66 350.1	3 737.8	24 954	337 867	57 241.6	5 273.8	5 427	28 948	3 269.1	572.6
Anderson	60	885	247.7	23.1	346	5 079	833.0	77.0	68	307	23.2	5.0
Bloomington	72	868	284.5	26.7	443	6 424	1 010.6	91.4	140	822	75.7	14.2
Carmel	175	1 670	2 788.6	90.4	184	3 663	720.9	69.9	74	519	82.6	13.8

1. Establishments with payroll.

Table D. Cities — Professional Services, Manufacturing, Accommodation and Foodservices

City	Professional, Scientific, and Technical Services, 1997[1]				Manufacturing, 1997				Accommodation and Foodservices, 1997			
	Number of Establishments	Number of Employees	Receipts (mil dol)	Annual Payroll (mil dol)	Number of Establishments	Number of Employees	Receipts (mil dol)	Annual Payroll (mil dol)	Number of Establishments	Number of Employees	Sales (mil dol)	Annual Payroll (mil dol)
	84	85	86	87	88	89	90	91	92	93	94	95
ILLINOIS—Cont'd												
Berwyn	59	128	10.3	3.3	22	585	79.5	23.6	101	D	D	D
Bloomington	173	1 005	89.4	38.2	59	D	D	D	192	4 221	124.7	37.1
Bolingbrook	78	291	24.9	10.2	21	2 453	807.9	153.8	57	988	34.4	8.7
Buffalo Grove	219	1 244	154.1	67.5	54	3 889	652.1	138.3	74	D	D	D
Burbank	17	85	4.3	1.1	NA	NA	NA	NA	69	D	D	D
Calumet City	34	119	7.1	2.0	19	757	155.3	23.4	106	1 674	51.4	12.8
Carbondale	57	457	24.3	9.5	NA	NA	NA	NA	107	1 945	52.1	14.1
Carol Stream	62	319	26.4	12.0	91	5 123	973.3	190.8	50	864	29.5	7.8
Champaign	183	1 654	202.0	67.0	67	2 846	393.2	74.8	252	5 728	152.1	42.5
Chicago	8 115	118 842	17 205.3	6 757.5	3 195	130 372	26 745.9	4 178.4	5 148	92 348	4 481.9	1 194.1
Chicago Heights	42	327	27.5	12.4	71	4 061	982.5	149.0	54	762	23.5	6.2
Cicero	30	305	16.3	6.2	123	5 613	973.2	190.7	89	914	37.8	9.3
Danville	77	287	25.8	7.7	60	4 864	1 363.4	160.5	116	1 893	53.3	15.5
Decatur	144	1 026	81.1	33.4	98	D	D	D	196	D	D	D
De Kalb	49	149	12.5	3.5	47	2 648	535.3	71.2	94	1 719	45.4	11.1
Des Plaines	281	5 785	649.1	213.5	164	12 021	1 849.6	411.0	144	2 408	104.6	26.8
Downers Grove	272	1 843	182.2	69.8	104	5 174	692.7	203.0	117	3 415	126.4	35.1
East St. Louis	8	D	D	D	22	564	134.9	20.9	37	476	18.6	4.1
Elgin	185	1 437	164.1	53.8	175	9 955	1 779.0	345.8	129	2 019	76.4	20.2
Elk Grove Village	146	2 803	339.3	115.5	550	23 239	3 916.5	864.4	85	1 442	63.6	16.6
Elmhurst	229	1 044	107.7	47.0	85	2 882	421.0	103.1	83	D	D	D
Evanston	357	2 085	227.6	80.7	67	2 310	321.7	74.4	177	2 491	110.1	30.1
Freeport	49	223	16.3	6.5	40	7 645	1 058.2	280.7	78	1 108	31.4	7.5
Galesburg	47	257	19.3	7.0	48	D	D	D	104	D	D	D
Glendale Heights	41	176	23.8	6.6	48	2 304	327.2	87.7	43	D	D	D
Glenview	214	523	82.3	23.8	68	1 481	222.9	54.2	104	1 842	76.3	21.7
Granite City	45	278	33.1	15.8	28	5 632	1 857.1	234.5	72	937	28.6	7.5
Hanover Park	30	79	6.3	2.9	NA	NA	NA	NA	47	626	23.3	6.0
Harvey	9	57	7.2	2.8	48	2 361	699.2	110.4	38	504	13.7	3.6
Highland Park	226	576	83.5	26.3	44	D	D	D	71	968	41.6	10.9
Hoffman Estates	160	1 676	268.0	89.1	23	971	191.2	45.6	83	1 653	72.1	18.4
Joliet	172	1 047	93.5	40.7	104	7 268	3 814.8	323.6	191	3 300	107.9	28.1
Kankakee	67	305	20.8	8.2	32	2 502	673.5	96.0	69	900	26.5	7.2
Lansing	56	220	35.3	8.8	34	870	171.4	29.7	75	1 331	46.3	12.5
Lombard	212	1 630	192.4	85.6	102	1 718	246.3	62.2	95	2 231	87.6	24.3
Maywood	8	52	4.2	1.6	28	603	74.0	19.1	33	363	19.3	4.7
Moline	91	576	43.1	18.6	61	2 150	500.4	89.7	163	3 304	90.5	25.7
Mount Prospect	181	849	95.0	29.3	46	3 457	553.4	134.8	101	D	D	D
Naperville	588	3 513	404.3	173.6	84	2 334	348.9	80.4	233	4 972	184.8	53.0
Niles	97	745	50.2	23.1	102	6 376	1 023.3	242.4	102	1 774	59.9	16.4
Normal	30	172	5.8	2.3	19	D	D	D	93	2 250	60.2	16.8
Northbrook	569	7 553	695.5	379.1	123	4 672	840.3	161.1	112	1 602	75.1	21.1
North Chicago	19	135	14.7	6.2	28	1 606	356.6	51.7	56	934	31.3	8.9
Oak Forest	46	188	13.6	5.1	22	519	85.7	16.1	36	532	16.1	4.5
Oak Lawn	110	271	23.9	8.2	31	527	57.1	17.5	96	2 205	74.4	20.2
Oak Park	226	915	88.4	34.4	43	679	82.8	22.3	81	1 458	49.3	14.6
Orland Park	167	632	58.3	19.9	55	2 195	477.7	92.4	127	2 676	98.7	26.2
Palatine	225	1 039	113.0	43.5	76	2 830	453.6	91.9	115	1 887	69.5	17.6
Park Ridge	229	1 517	150.3	64.9	NA	NA	NA	NA	61	755	25.9	6.3
Pekin	55	223	12.8	5.2	28	D	D	D	75	1 319	34.6	10.0
Peoria	299	4 031	337.5	154.2	113	5 666	1 381.6	197.3	344	6 592	203.4	59.1
Quincy	96	442	36.7	11.6	57	2 995	774.0	96.6	117	2 098	62.9	17.5
Rockford	440	4 666	258.8	107.6	477	26 100	4 467.4	998.8	347	6 984	223.7	61.1
Rock Island	101	1 022	69.1	30.6	58	1 927	238.5	47.7	92	1 178	33.6	8.3
Schaumburg	457	4 468	592.6	238.8	190	8 709	1 448.1	404.8	210	5 836	239.2	62.7
Skokie	351	2 378	326.6	114.3	212	9 083	1 815.5	310.1	138	2 572	101.0	27.8
Springfield	398	3 008	255.1	108.9	84	2 850	462.9	82.2	373	6 820	209.9	62.0
Streamwood	38	62	5.0	2.0	45	918	148.4	36.8	38	612	24.2	6.3
Tinley Park	83	287	22.7	7.4	33	1 140	197.1	40.2	62	1 037	34.9	9.4
Urbana	61	534	27.1	11.4	33	D	D	D	104	2 038	62.9	18.4
Waukegan	143	1 293	116.9	59.9	95	6 037	986.8	213.6	152	2 101	79.5	19.7
Wheaton	381	1 859	191.9	82.1	34	508	63.1	19.0	84	2 007	62.2	16.6
Wheeling	144	1 022	124.4	45.4	186	10 194	2 306.9	415.8	57	D	D	D
Wilmette	146	258	36.6	15.6	NA	NA	NA	NA	45	D	D	D
Woodridge	49	208	22.9	11.6	16	741	192.6	30.5	25	466	15.3	4.5
INDIANA	9 795	69 393	5 974.2	2 207.5	9 303	625 692	142 270.7	22 121.4	11 705	215 710	6 646.3	1 865.3
Anderson	126	889	49.2	26.2	59	8 999	1 769.1	456.0	160	4 055	116.4	32.8
Bloomington	167	1 285	91.2	31.3	61	5 013	1 751.3	159.4	275	6 020	165.8	45.1
Carmel	235	2 517	251.2	105.1	53	1 304	177.8	44.2	79	1 636	57.7	16.3

1. Firms subject to federal tax.

City	Arts, Entertainment, and Recreation[1], 1997				Health Care and Social Assistance[1], 1997				Other Services[1], 1997			
	Number of Establishments	Number of Employees	Receipts (mil dol)	Annual Payroll (mil dol)	Number of Establishments	Number of Employees	Receipts (mil dol)	Annual Payroll (mil dol)	Number of Establishments	Number of Employees	Receipts (mil dol)	Annual Payroll (mil dol)
	96	97	98	99	100	101	102	103	104	105	106	107
ILLINOIS—Cont'd												
Berwyn	6	65	5.1	1.7	107	763	67.2	30.6	66	333	25.0	6.2
Bloomington	19	226	8.3	1.8	145	1 814	129.6	64.1	136	965	60.2	19.1
Bolingbrook	7	54	1.9	0.5	54	673	30.0	12.1	56	351	25.7	6.8
Buffalo Grove	15	76	5.6	1.1	108	1 102	91.4	39.7	59	547	40.8	12.4
Burbank	3	0	0.0	0.0	25	469	27.8	11.6	31	124	9.5	2.7
Calumet City	5	98	6.0	1.1	57	917	42.6	14.9	45	224	14.1	4.0
Carbondale	7	16	1.9	0.3	84	1 406	81.7	39.7	49	219	11.6	2.8
Carol Stream	9	201	5.1	2.1	62	513	43.7	21.7	47	471	35.6	10.2
Champaign	22	280	6.9	2.5	121	2 269	161.7	67.1	127	741	38.0	13.0
Chicago	563	7 547	864.0	361.1	4 019	43 898	3 217.3	1 284.8	3 333	23 886	1 820.5	502.9
Chicago Heights	2	0	0.0	0.0	46	1 130	95.3	40.8	52	349	17.4	5.4
Cicero	24	575	79.9	10.9	33	1 063	51.6	18.6	72	465	34.4	11.4
Danville	8	80	2.8	0.7	82	1 285	78.7	36.8	77	487	23.3	7.8
Decatur	16	213	5.6	2.0	185	2 354	147.7	67.0	144	1 278	73.6	25.6
De Kalb	5	0	0.0	0.0	34	385	26.5	13.2	58	282	13.0	3.8
Des Plaines	11	87	3.5	1.1	182	2 088	175.4	69.1	145	1 042	88.7	27.7
Downers Grove	15	192	5.9	1.8	180	2 091	192.7	81.9	117	1 153	104.3	37.9
East St. Louis	2	0	0.0	0.0	41	419	26.1	7.5	28	177	10.0	2.8
Elgin	17	0	0.0	0.0	178	1 864	135.5	71.5	126	1 292	78.5	28.4
Elk Grove Village	8	65	5.8	1.2	105	1 228	120.3	57.9	97	918	77.7	28.0
Elmhurst	8	123	4.8	1.8	144	2 235	208.5	91.9	103	892	64.7	21.9
Evanston	29	157	8.4	3.0	237	2 145	220.7	114.5	98	529	32.2	11.1
Freeport	3	7	0.5	0.1	58	574	32.9	17.2	58	295	13.5	4.0
Galesburg	12	77	3.1	0.5	63	1 119	68.1	25.5	64	330	20.4	5.7
Glendale Heights	7	189	9.5	1.7	25	1 178	52.7	25.9	24	127	11.5	3.9
Glenview	31	206	15.9	7.2	123	1 032	74.8	37.5	101	752	38.0	13.6
Granite City	7	62	3.1	1.1	80	898	61.2	23.6	62	390	20.8	6.9
Hanover Park	2	0	0.0	0.0	35	429	25.0	12.4	36	261	14.3	6.9
Harvey	1	0	0.0	0.0	53	819	61.8	34.9	29	278	30.3	11.5
Highland Park	15	188	6.0	2.4	158	1 238	97.1	52.1	79	453	30.1	8.9
Hoffman Estates	15	194	10.0	2.8	169	3 590	305.3	121.8	45	277	14.8	4.4
Joliet	16	0	0.0	0.0	232	2 607	225.9	108.3	128	888	59.2	16.9
Kankakee	8	102	5.9	1.2	86	777	58.3	28.7	60	361	23.8	7.1
Lansing	9	68	3.9	1.0	39	259	14.2	6.1	78	678	38.4	13.6
Lombard	16	380	49.8	5.0	104	1 475	91.6	38.9	117	1 049	104.5	35.9
Maywood	1	0	0.0	0.0	23	121	9.0	3.6	19	86	5.8	1.6
Moline	16	103	6.6	1.2	137	1 515	113.0	54.2	105	681	51.2	13.4
Mount Prospect	6	92	5.7	1.4	82	1 053	62.3	24.8	84	365	24.9	6.1
Naperville	33	650	22.0	6.9	309	3 625	247.7	100.3	173	1 311	72.4	24.0
Niles	9	98	3.1	0.8	90	1 405	78.5	31.7	70	639	52.5	16.2
Normal	2	0	0.0	0.0	52	701	44.0	21.4	51	337	16.3	5.3
Northbrook	25	551	20.2	9.7	168	1 935	133.6	71.2	69	686	47.3	17.4
North Chicago	1	0	0.0	0.0	10	71	5.1	2.8	11	94	4.7	1.8
Oak Forest	4	18	1.2	0.3	49	397	34.8	16.5	43	315	31.8	7.5
Oak Lawn	6	77	5.4	1.3	214	2 249	207.2	109.4	111	656	39.3	12.5
Oak Park	19	88	4.6	1.3	219	1 964	144.5	64.3	90	585	40.4	12.6
Orland Park	16	515	18.1	5.6	170	1 408	91.9	39.3	104	833	44.0	14.0
Palatine	26	209	11.5	2.9	103	842	58.5	28.5	127	915	68.7	20.2
Park Ridge	9	88	5.3	2.4	179	1 523	189.6	84.4	73	402	21.0	7.0
Pekin	7	59	1.5	0.5	67	803	45.2	21.4	66	352	18.5	5.4
Peoria	33	690	28.7	9.6	311	4 072	349.3	186.0	202	1 996	146.6	48.0
Quincy	16	173	3.7	1.1	106	1 490	93.2	49.4	113	636	36.2	11.6
Rockford	45	429	16.7	4.2	349	4 885	397.9	196.2	293	2 654	165.0	54.3
Rock Island	12	530	24.6	8.1	77	816	46.1	19.7	79	618	33.8	10.0
Schaumburg	15	326	16.9	3.4	171	2 134	177.9	67.5	188	1 498	109.8	35.5
Skokie	34	266	11.3	2.6	252	3 679	218.6	91.4	172	1 403	81.8	26.3
Springfield	45	553	39.7	7.8	307	7 266	466.0	199.5	248	1 813	112.8	37.3
Streamwood	5	93	2.9	1.0	35	399	24.7	8.3	47	241	16.4	4.7
Tinley Park	14	208	29.9	4.2	75	529	31.8	13.0	52	311	17.5	5.7
Urbana	6	0	0.0	0.0	32	0	0.0	0.0	48	296	14.8	4.9
Waukegan	18	312	9.5	3.1	124	1 448	93.4	46.1	111	493	33.7	9.7
Wheaton	9	194	8.0	2.7	137	1 520	133.1	50.5	95	551	30.8	10.3
Wheeling	7	29	1.9	0.5	38	342	23.7	8.5	65	545	72.3	14.7
Wilmette	18	21	2.6	0.9	95	467	43.0	20.8	53	400	27.8	9.9
Woodridge	8	249	9.8	3.0	56	404	26.3	11.3	27	148	8.5	2.3
INDIANA	1 500	24 903	1 918.3	516.1	10 236	132 416	8 132.3	3 675.3	9 243	60 711	3 701.4	1 127.8
Anderson	21	0	0.0	0.0	158	1 520	91.5	41.3	127	784	43.3	14.2
Bloomington	17	56	7.9	0.7	200	2 054	148.2	69.9	119	725	35.1	11.3
Carmel	21	246	11.9	3.5	131	1 520	123.2	53.3	79	552	44.6	13.2

1. Firms subject to federal tax.

Table D. Cities — Federal Funds and City Government Finances

City	Selected federal funds, fiscal 1999[1] (mil dol)									City government finances, 1997						
	Procurement contracts		Grants					Direct payments for individuals		General revenue						
											Intergovernmental		Taxes			
														Per capita[3] (dollars)		
	Defense	Other	Total[2]	Health and family welfare	Energy and environment	Education	Housing and community development	Educational assistance	Housing assistance	Total (mil dol)	Total (mil dol)	Percent from state government	Total (mil dol)	Total	Property	Sales and gross receipts
	108	109	110	111	112	113	114	115	116	117	118	119	120	121	122	123
ILLINOIS—Cont'd																
Berwyn	0.0	0.1	0.5	0.0	0.0	0.3	0.0	0.0	0.0	26.6	3.0	100.0	13.8	316	93	149
Bloomington	0.9	0.1	11.0	4.1	0.1	0.0	1.5	1.6	0.0	46.6	11.6	91.0	25.9	451	200	231
Bolingbrook	0.4	0.2	0.6	0.0	0.0	0.0	0.0	0.0	0.0	39.1	10.7	95.2	16.9	329	144	154
Buffalo Grove	9.9	3.5	0.1	0.1	0.0	0.0	0.0	0.0	0.0	32.1	13.8	99.7	8.7	211	172	11
Burbank	0.0	0.0	0.0	0.0	0.0	0.0	0.0	0.0	0.0	14.9	5.6	100.0	8.4	304	197	66
Calumet City	0.0	1.3	0.0	0.0	0.0	0.0	0.0	0.0	0.0	25.6	14.2	100.0	8.5	229	166	46
Carbondale	3.5	0.0	12.1	6.9	0.5	2.4	0.0	9.5	0.3	23.4	11.9	93.8	3.7	138	48	90
Carol Stream	0.5	0.1	0.9	0.0	0.0	0.0	0.8	0.0	3.1	18.2	6.5	97.5	6.5	176	40	116
Champaign	15.5	3.1	136.5	2.3	13.8	1.1	0.6	4.4	-0.6	58.6	28.5	93.6	19.8	310	212	71
Chicago	135.5	290.1	1 531.4	485.9	15.4	98.6	178.6	82.9	119.7	4 172.9	1 195.5	71.2	1 742.1	640	230	367
Chicago Heights	0.0	0.3	0.0	0.0	0.0	0.2	0.0	0.9	0.0	27.9	7.1	100.0	15.8	494	377	87
Cicero	0.5	0.2	3.0	0.0	0.0	0.0	2.2	0.7	0.0	55.7	17.5	98.4	26.1	368	229	88
Danville	3.0	44.3	4.7	2.1	0.0	0.4	2.1	1.0	-0.6	23.4	9.9	96.2	6.8	210	193	0
Decatur	6.6	16.9	10.8	2.9	0.0	1.1	2.5	1.8	0.7	50.1	29.0	89.1	12.0	147	104	35
De Kalb	0.0	0.0	6.6	1.2	0.2	2.2	0.9	5.3	0.0	32.0	4.3	88.4	16.4	460	113	338
Des Plaines	0.9	8.6	6.8	0.0	5.0	0.2	0.8	0.8	0.0	43.0	13.6	98.4	20.2	368	229	88
Downers Grove	18.8	1.7	1.0	1.0	0.0	0.0	0.0	0.0	-0.7	34.6	15.1	100.0	9.6	191	115	63
East St. Louis	0.2	1.3	9.7	3.6	-0.2	0.4	5.7	0.0	2.6	33.3	23.7	99.5	8.3	214	86	111
Elgin	5.8	0.8	1.9	0.0	0.0	0.1	1.4	0.0	-0.3	83.3	37.7	95.8	24.3	282	251	18
Elk Grove Village	1.8	1.4	3.4	3.4	0.0	0.0	0.0	0.0	0.0	32.9	11.7	95.1	16.7	486	281	152
Elmhurst	5.4	0.4	0.1	0.0	0.0	0.0	0.0	0.8	0.0	40.4	15.3	98.4	12.5	288	154	114
Evanston	8.1	1.3	162.7	111.4	4.9	1.5	2.2	12.1	0.0	80.7	16.3	86.3	44.3	618	394	173
Freeport	0.4	0.1	2.0	0.9	0.0	0.5	0.4	0.5	0.0	17.0	7.6	98.8	3.1	119	81	32
Galesburg	0.0	0.0	2.0	0.0	0.0	0.7	1.0	1.4	-0.8	25.4	8.1	94.5	8.7	263	124	134
Glendale Heights	0.3	0.4	0.0	0.0	0.0	0.0	0.0	0.0	0.0	21.6	8.1	100.0	5.9	195	110	75
Glenview	8.4	0.1	0.0	0.0	0.0	0.0	0.0	0.0	0.0	36.0	11.7	73.7	14.9	381	256	109
Granite City	9.2	0.3	1.6	0.0	0.0	0.0	1.5	0.4	0.7	27.2	19.3	99.5	6.7	214	86	111
Hanover Park	0.0	0.0	-0.2	0.0	0.0	0.0	0.0	0.0	0.0	14.4	3.4	100.0	8.8	246	110	94
Harvey	0.5	0.2	0.8	0.2	0.0	0.3	0.0	0.0	0.0	17.6	4.4	100.0	11.6	398	271	110
Highland Park	0.0	0.2	0.2	0.0	0.0	0.1	0.0	0.0	-0.3	42.9	9.0	100.0	21.3	686	401	175
Hoffman Estates	0.1	1.1	0.0	0.0	0.0	0.0	0.0	0.0	0.0	47.4	9.0	100.0	28.6	588	545	29
Joliet	6.3	1.4	8.6	3.7	0.0	0.5	2.8	1.5	0.2	100.4	25.0	94.0	54.0	622	135	452
Kankakee	2.4	0.2	4.8	1.8	0.0	0.6	1.4	2.0	-0.3	25.1	7.4	93.2	8.4	310	161	98
Lansing	0.0	0.1	0.1	0.0	0.0	0.0	0.0	0.0	0.0	20.8	12.9	100.0	4.4	153	78	61
Lombard	7.0	2.0	0.3	0.0	0.1	0.0	0.2	3.1	0.0	31.6	13.0	96.2	11.1	264	97	133
Maywood	0.3	0.0	1.2	0.2	0.9	0.0	0.0	0.0	0.0	15.3	4.8	100.0	8.8	336	221	104
Moline	10.0	1.5	3.9	0.0	0.0	0.2	1.5	1.1	0.6	31.2	7.9	86.0	13.8	322	200	99
Mount Prospect	0.9	0.6	0.2	0.0	0.0	0.0	0.2	0.0	1.5	32.3	11.9	96.3	17.1	317	214	64
Naperville	3.7	0.2	1.2	0.5	0.0	0.0	0.5	0.7	0.4	96.0	27.4	97.0	36.8	344	208	113
Niles	1.2	0.1	0.0	0.0	0.0	0.0	0.0	0.0	0.0	25.7	3.3	80.2	19.4	665	102	548
Normal	0.0	0.0	5.7	0.5	0.0	2.7	0.4	5.0	-0.3	28.8	12.5	92.5	8.4	196	97	76
Northbrook	1.7	1.5	0.3	0.0	0.0	0.1	0.0	0.0	0.0	44.9	17.8	86.5	13.4	407	329	51
North Chicago	2.8	5.8	15.0	4.6	0.0	8.8	0.5	0.2	3.4	12.6	6.4	100.0	4.6	144	54	61
Oak Forest	0.0	0.0	0.0	0.0	0.0	0.0	0.0	0.2	0.0	12.1	4.1	100.0	5.5	199	171	14
Oak Lawn	0.1	0.1	0.5	0.1	0.0	0.0	0.3	0.8	0.0	34.4	17.0	97.4	11.1	193	145	36
Oak Park	0.1	0.0	4.4	0.6	0.1	0.0	3.4	0.0	0.0	44.2	11.1	82.0	22.8	441	316	104
Orland Park	2.6	0.0	0.0	0.0	0.0	0.0	0.0	0.0	0.0	34.1	16.1	100.0	6.7	147	107	6
Palatine	0.8	0.7	0.7	0.0	0.0	0.4	0.0	0.0	0.7	32.6	10.6	100.0	13.1	295	234	31
Park Ridge	0.1	0.4	0.5	0.3	0.0	0.0	0.0	0.0	0.0	25.3	6.9	100.0	16.6	449	267	163
Pekin	0.0	0.5	1.4	0.0	0.0	0.7	0.4	0.0	-0.5	23.0	11.0	95.1	5.1	158	141	12
Peoria	4.2	6.0	28.4	4.0	2.9	0.6	6.6	2.3	11.6	100.9	42.8	81.3	41.8	373	101	196
Quincy	3.8	0.0	9.0	1.2	0.0	0.4	0.5	2.0	0.2	31.6	14.1	90.4	7.9	195	104	82
Rockford	45.5	4.1	21.5	6.0	0.2	0.9	7.5	1.8	7.0	109.6	51.3	80.2	41.2	287	228	37
Rock Island	3.4	0.8	10.2	3.5	0.0	0.3	3.8	1.1	2.4	41.2	8.8	79.9	12.8	322	212	97
Schaumburg	16.9	2.5	2.0	0.1	0.0	0.0	0.3	0.0	0.0	61.7	7.9	99.9	42.3	569	13	527
Skokie	4.2	8.7	1.7	0.0	0.0	0.1	0.8	0.1	0.0	45.3	17.4	91.0	24.1	411	292	102
Springfield	1.0	4.0	1 464.0	686.6	85.7	246.2	46.9	1.9	-1.4	82.7	37.4	91.4	27.3	242	94	132
Streamwood	0.0	0.0	0.2	0.0	0.0	0.0	0.0	0.0	0.0	16.5	6.1	94.6	8.4	245	139	76
Tinley Park	0.0	0.0	0.9	0.0	0.0	0.7	0.0	0.0	0.3	22.8	9.3	96.3	8.6	199	150	13
Urbana	4.5	0.9	80.1	41.9	0.4	9.5	1.2	14.3	0.3	24.7	5.1	72.9	13.1	396	147	234
Waukegan	2.2	2.1	11.9	3.8	0.0	0.2	5.5	0.2	3.9	57.7	19.8	83.9	21.5	290	161	99
Wheaton	0.0	0.1	8.3	0.0	0.0	0.0	7.1	1.1	0.1	34.0	10.9	99.5	12.7	235	161	64
Wheeling	2.1	0.3	0.7	0.4	0.0	0.0	0.0	0.0	0.0	20.2	8.6	98.5	6.8	220	209	0
Wilmette	0.0	0.0	0.1	0.0	0.0	0.0	0.1	0.0	0.0	21.0	6.5	82.6	10.3	396	241	110
Woodridge	0.0	0.1	0.3	0.0	0.0	0.0	0.0	0.0	0.0	16.9	5.6	96.5	5.2	181	80	78
INDIANA	1 643.8	578.0	4 705.8	2 776.3	72.4	429.9	131.5	166.1	164.0	X	X	X	X	X	X	X
Anderson	0.0	0.6	4.9	1.4	0.0	0.3	2.4	1.2	2.6	44.4	10.2	82.7	22.2	376	299	10
Bloomington	1.6	3.7	132.6	91.7	5.4	5.9	2.3	23.7	3.3	48.6	13.8	54.3	19.2	288	195	0
Carmel	0.0	0.0	0.6	0.6	0.0	0.0	0.0	0.0	0.0	32.2	6.7	53.1	16.3	441	239	0

1. October 1, 1998 to September 30, 1999.   2. Includes program categories not shown separately. State totals include additional categories not allocated by city.   3. Based on population estimated as of July 1 of the year shown.

Table D. Cities — City Government Finances

	City government finances, 1997 (cont'd)											
	General expenditure											
	Per capita[1] (dollars)			Percent of total for —								
City	Total (mil dol)	Total	Capital outlays	Public welfare	Highways	Parking facilities	Education	Health and hospitals	Police protection	Sewerage and sanitation	Parks and recreation	Housing and community development	Interest on debt
	124	125	126	127	128	129	130	131	132	133	134	135	136

ILLINOIS—Cont'd													
Berwyn	28.4	649	101	0.0	13.2	0.0	0.0	0.0	19.2	14.4	3.5	0.0	6.2
Bloomington	49.6	865	219	0.0	14.9	1.6	0.0	0.0	21.7	8.7	8.0	2.2	3.7
Bolingbrook	39.9	778	67	0.0	25.9	0.0	0.0	1.4	19.8	10.6	2.1	0.0	12.2
Buffalo Grove	28.4	691	65	0.0	11.6	0.2	0.0	0.0	21.3	12.7	6.9	0.0	8.1
Burbank	13.7	494	217	0.0	6.1	0.0	0.0	0.0	24.3	0.0	0.0	0.2	1.2
Calumet City	32.9	884	216	0.0	16.8	0.0	0.0	0.9	15.9	3.0	0.5	1.3	5.8
Carbondale	22.5	845	170	0.0	5.8	1.7	0.0	0.0	17.2	10.2	0.7	0.0	15.4
Carol Stream	20.2	549	172	0.0	34.0	0.0	0.0	0.0	20.7	7.2	0.0	0.0	4.1
Champaign	50.1	783	71	0.0	11.3	5.1	0.0	0.2	14.8	11.0	8.3	4.5	0.9
Chicago	4 144.0	1 523	251	3.4	9.8	0.0	0.0	3.0	20.7	7.2	1.0	4.4	11.8
Chicago Heights	30.8	964	61	0.0	5.7	0.0	0.0	0.7	18.8	13.8	0.0	0.0	14.8
Cicero	50.8	716	173	0.3	19.5	0.8	0.0	0.0	20.5	6.3	0.7	0.6	1.1
Danville	25.1	780	181	0.0	5.9	0.7	0.0	0.0	22.2	8.7	1.7	25.2	5.4
Decatur	54.2	667	86	0.0	16.6	0.8	0.0	0.0	21.9	1.6	0.0	4.7	8.5
De Kalb	32.3	909	385	0.0	14.6	0.1	0.0	0.0	10.2	2.9	5.3	2.9	3.2
Des Plaines	43.4	792	173	0.3	17.6	0.8	0.0	0.0	18.5	5.7	0.7	0.5	10.6
Downers Grove	33.1	661	109	0.0	15.2	1.7	0.0	0.0	19.0	3.0	0.0	1.5	11.8
East St. Louis	31.6	820	23	0.0	12.8	0.0	0.0	0.0	23.4	8.7	0.0	3.7	6.4
Elgin	84.5	982	252	0.0	14.9	0.4	0.0	0.0	29.3	6.1	8.9	7.3	5.4
Elk Grove Village	32.8	951	122	0.0	16.0	0.0	0.0	0.8	19.9	5.1	0.2	0.0	3.7
Elmhurst	33.8	781	110	0.3	24.9	0.8	0.0	0.5	19.9	12.4	0.8	6.2	6.9
Evanston	121.9	1 703	740	1.2	2.8	1.8	0.0	1.8	10.2	44.8	6.1	5.3	7.8
Freeport	15.7	598	74	0.0	12.1	0.0	0.0	0.3	16.6	26.9	0.0	6.2	1.2
Galesburg	25.2	760	98	0.7	12.2	0.0	0.0	0.0	16.3	6.0	9.8	0.0	10.9
Glendale Heights	17.7	583	0	0.0	18.8	0.0	0.0	0.0	20.4	8.9	11.6	2.2	4.3
Glenview	35.8	913	110	0.0	12.6	0.3	0.0	0.4	15.7	5.7	0.2	0.0	12.1
Granite City	24.1	767	23	0.0	13.7	0.0	0.0	0.0	25.0	9.3	0.0	4.0	0.0
Hanover Park	11.1	311	0	0.0	24.7	2.0	0.0	1.0	35.2	0.0	0.0	0.0	11.1
Harvey	15.5	533	0	0.0	4.8	2.4	0.0	0.0	26.4	10.7	0.0	0.0	3.8
Highland Park	41.6	1 342	347	0.0	19.5	0.8	0.0	0.0	12.3	1.8	19.6	0.0	2.3
Hoffman Estates	50.2	1 030	247	0.0	7.1	0.0	0.0	0.8	16.4	2.6	0.4	0.4	28.9
Joliet	88.9	1 024	296	0.0	15.1	0.7	0.0	0.0	17.9	7.6	0.3	2.5	4.1
Kankakee	23.4	859	2	0.0	10.7	0.0	0.0	0.1	17.5	23.6	0.2	7.4	13.7
Lansing	21.7	757	134	0.0	9.9	0.0	0.0	0.0	21.2	10.2	0.0	1.0	15.9
Lombard	32.5	777	265	0.0	7.4	0.1	0.0	0.0	15.7	3.4	0.0	0.0	5.7
Maywood	16.8	642	0	1.4	9.8	0.0	0.0	0.0	36.5	0.0	2.2	0.0	10.9
Moline	31.5	736	3	0.0	9.9	1.5	0.0	0.0	19.3	12.6	6.1	3.2	8.7
Mount Prospect	32.7	605	46	1.8	20.3	0.3	0.0	0.9	31.6	11.3	0.5	1.3	3.5
Naperville	85.5	799	164	0.0	23.3	0.6	0.0	0.0	18.7	11.7	2.0	0.6	5.6
Niles	27.8	957	182	3.0	1.7	0.0	0.0	0.0	16.4	5.0	0.0	0.0	6.9
Normal	26.8	627	130	0.0	17.4	0.0	0.0	0.0	12.5	3.6	15.4	1.1	8.1
Northbrook	34.2	1 039	273	0.0	18.1	0.6	0.0	0.0	19.5	7.0	0.0	2.3	1.6
North Chicago	9.7	305	3	0.0	9.0	0.0	0.0	0.0	37.1	10.6	0.0	6.8	0.0
Oak Forest	11.8	430	112	0.0	13.9	1.4	0.0	0.0	26.4	2.7	0.0	21.1	7.0
Oak Lawn	30.3	526	0	0.5	8.8	0.1	0.0	0.0	28.1	10.1	0.0	1.4	4.1
Oak Park	45.1	875	154	0.0	10.6	2.5	0.0	1.9	21.8	4.4	0.0	11.2	3.4
Orland Park	29.7	651	87	0.0	6.6	0.0	0.0	0.0	24.5	15.5	10.0	0.0	3.1
Palatine	31.0	698	39	0.0	8.5	0.2	0.0	1.1	24.0	14.0	0.0	0.0	15.8
Park Ridge	23.7	640	56	0.0	13.4	1.0	0.0	0.5	18.8	12.1	1.7	0.9	1.9
Pekin	20.5	631	39	0.0	10.4	0.2	0.0	0.0	17.0	11.7	0.1	9.8	17.5
Peoria	103.4	920	74	0.0	11.6	0.0	0.0	0.0	14.3	5.0	3.5	21.3	7.0
Quincy	29.4	726	103	0.0	16.5	0.2	0.0	0.5	16.6	16.1	0.0	0.6	15.9
Rockford	106.9	745	106	5.8	17.7	0.7	0.0	0.3	21.2	8.4	0.0	5.1	3.8
Rock Island	35.8	902	43	0.0	12.4	1.0	0.0	0.0	17.5	8.4	13.8	7.0	7.6
Schaumburg	57.8	777	155	0.0	18.1	0.2	0.0	2.8	24.9	2.1	6.1	0.7	4.5
Skokie	59.2	1 009	355	0.0	6.9	0.0	0.0	1.2	12.7	5.1	0.0	7.3	2.9
Springfield	83.2	737	91	0.0	14.0	0.8	0.0	3.6	21.7	5.9	5.6	3.5	6.9
Streamwood	14.7	429	86	0.0	27.7	0.0	0.0	0.0	29.1	0.0	2.6	2.0	5.2
Tinley Park	17.9	413	75	0.0	17.7	4.6	0.0	0.0	32.3	5.6	0.0	0.0	2.4
Urbana	26.4	796	174	0.3	18.5	1.8	0.0	0.0	20.7	7.4	0.0	13.1	9.2
Waukegan	57.7	778	120	0.0	18.7	0.9	0.0	0.5	22.7	7.6	0.6	2.5	10.5
Wheaton	31.3	577	102	0.3	13.4	1.1	0.0	0.0	18.7	7.4	1.4	0.0	3.5
Wheeling	19.6	650	194	0.7	15.2	13.4	0.0	0.0	25.7	3.4	0.0	5.4	2.8
Wilmette	22.1	848	158	0.4	16.5	0.6	0.0	0.5	17.7	28.9	0.3	2.5	1.6
Woodridge	20.4	707	268	0.0	12.7	0.0	0.0	0.0	20.8	1.0	6.2	0.0	2.4
INDIANA	X	X	X	X	X	X	X	X	X	X	X	X	X
Anderson	52.3	884	57	0.0	6.1	0.4	0.0	0.9	14.8	17.0	6.1	6.5	3.8
Bloomington	45.9	690	148	0.4	9.6	2.5	0.0	2.7	8.7	30.9	10.4	5.7	3.9
Carmel	25.8	700	54	0.0	7.9	0.0	0.0	0.1	19.7	13.9	0.0	0.0	2.2

1. Based on population estimated as of July 1 of the year shown.

City	City government finances, 1997 (cont'd) Debt outstanding Total (mil dol)	Per capita[1] (dollars)	Percent utility	City government employment, 1999	Climate[2] Average daily temperature (degrees Fahrenheit) Mean January	July	Limits January[3]	July[4]	Annual precipitation (inches)	Heating degree days	Cooling degree days
	137	138	139	140	141	142	143	144	145	146	147
ILLINOIS—Cont'd											
Berwyn	33.6	768	0.0	317	21.0	73.2	12.9	83.7	35.82	6 536	752
Bloomington	49.3	860	11.1	475	23.9	75.9	15.4	86.7	37.10	5 759	1 117
Bolingbrook	56.1	1 092	0.0	325	19.7	73.1	10.7	84.2	36.88	6 699	702
Buffalo Grove	44.4	1 079	11.7	258	21.0	73.2	12.9	83.7	35.82	6 536	752
Burbank	1.6	57	0.0	NA	22.4	75.1	14.9	84.4	37.38	6 176	940
Calumet City	43.4	1 165	0.0	369	23.7	74.1	15.2	85.5	36.82	6 043	857
Carbondale	50.8	1 905	0.0	NA	29.5	77.6	19.1	89.0	44.40	4 865	1 271
Carol Stream	19.1	520	0.0	NA	21.0	73.2	12.9	83.7	35.82	6 536	752
Champaign	5.5	85	0.0	NA	23.8	75.0	16.0	85.3	39.71	5 854	985
Chicago	8 216.1	3 019	3.9	41 932	22.4	75.1	14.9	84.4	37.38	6 176	940
Chicago Heights	67.1	2 103	0.0	410	20.6	73.7	12.2	83.8	37.12	6 541	780
Cicero	16.3	231	0.0	536	22.4	75.1	14.9	84.4	37.38	6 176	940
Danville	24.4	760	0.0	304	25.1	75.2	16.1	86.8	40.18	5 610	1 005
Decatur	104.6	1 286	35.3	574	25.2	76.2	16.0	87.9	40.16	5 522	1 120
De Kalb	5.4	153	0.0	233	17.7	73.0	8.9	83.8	36.35	7 034	682
Des Plaines	69.6	1 270	5.9	466	21.0	73.2	12.9	83.7	35.82	6 536	752
Downers Grove	48.7	973	0.0	385	21.0	73.2	12.9	83.7	35.82	6 536	752
East St. Louis	47.3	1 227	0.0	345	28.4	78.4	18.9	89.6	37.86	5 001	1 329
Elgin	135.1	1 570	37.3	622	18.3	71.9	9.3	82.7	35.19	7 084	603
Elk Grove Village	24.9	724	0.0	395	21.0	73.2	12.9	83.7	35.82	6 536	752
Elmhurst	28.7	663	0.0	414	21.0	73.2	12.9	83.7	35.82	6 536	752
Evanston	214.7	2 999	6.7	890	21.0	73.2	12.9	83.7	35.82	6 536	752
Freeport	5.8	221	28.2	NA	17.1	72.9	7.8	84.2	33.08	7 169	645
Galesburg	36.3	1 095	0.0	NA	21.1	75.1	12.5	85.3	36.55	6 314	925
Glendale Heights	22.6	746	34.6	NA	21.0	73.2	12.9	83.7	35.82	6 536	752
Glenview	81.3	2 077	5.1	366	21.0	73.2	12.9	83.7	35.82	6 536	752
Granite City	0.0	0	0.0	NA	28.4	78.4	18.9	89.6	37.86	5 001	1 329
Hanover Park	15.8	443	0.0	NA	21.0	73.2	12.9	83.7	35.82	6 536	752
Harvey	10.2	352	12.4	NA	20.6	73.7	12.2	83.8	37.12	6 541	780
Highland Park	32.8	1 058	24.5	400	21.0	73.2	12.9	83.7	35.82	6 536	752
Hoffman Estates	252.3	5 179	0.0	347	18.3	71.9	9.3	82.7	35.19	7 084	603
Joliet	66.3	764	40.7	775	20.7	73.8	11.8	84.6	36.26	6 463	776
Kankakee	62.1	2 283	0.0	407	21.1	74.6	12.3	85.2	35.31	6 322	921
Lansing	61.7	2 152	2.0	NA	23.7	74.1	15.2	85.5	36.82	6 043	857
Lombard	18.6	444	0.0	311	21.0	73.2	12.9	83.7	35.82	6 536	752
Maywood	24.3	927	0.3	NA	21.0	73.2	12.9	83.7	35.82	6 536	752
Moline	36.6	855	0.0	414	19.9	75.2	11.3	85.9	39.08	6 474	911
Mount Prospect	7.6	141	0.0	366	21.0	73.2	12.9	83.7	35.82	6 536	752
Naperville	137.6	1 286	37.7	1 031	19.7	73.1	10.7	84.2	36.88	6 699	702
Niles	36.4	1 253	24.9	NA	21.0	73.2	12.9	83.7	35.82	6 536	752
Normal	28.8	676	0.0	286	23.9	75.9	15.4	86.7	37.10	5 759	1 117
Northbrook	21.1	641	52.8	NA	21.0	73.2	12.9	83.7	35.82	6 536	752
North Chicago	10.2	321	100.0	NA	19.3	71.2	10.8	81.1	34.20	7 136	542
Oak Forest	16.8	613	4.8	NA	20.6	73.7	12.2	83.8	37.12	6 541	780
Oak Lawn	29.0	502	41.7	479	22.4	75.1	14.9	84.4	37.38	6 176	940
Oak Park	34.3	665	9.0	418	22.4	75.1	14.9	84.4	37.38	6 176	940
Orland Park	14.4	315	5.6	327	20.6	73.7	12.2	83.8	37.12	6 541	780
Palatine	73.6	1 655	0.1	332	21.0	73.2	12.9	83.7	35.82	6 536	752
Park Ridge	9.0	244	0.0	283	21.0	73.2	12.9	83.7	35.82	6 536	752
Pekin	58.8	1 812	0.0	NA	21.6	75.5	13.2	85.7	36.25	6 148	982
Peoria	138.4	1 233	0.0	1 007	21.6	75.5	13.2	85.7	36.25	6 148	982
Quincy	37.6	927	0.3	433	23.9	76.7	15.6	86.8	39.66	5 763	1 106
Rockford	98.3	685	32.9	1 182	18.2	73.2	9.8	83.8	36.28	6 969	702
Rock Island	42.5	1 071	30.8	440	19.9	75.2	11.3	85.9	39.08	6 474	911
Schaumburg	24.1	324	0.0	706	21.0	73.2	12.9	83.7	35.82	6 536	752
Skokie	75.7	1 291	1.1	562	21.0	73.2	12.9	83.7	35.82	6 536	752
Springfield	260.3	2 305	51.4	1 686	24.2	76.5	15.9	86.9	35.25	5 688	1 141
Streamwood	16.1	471	35.6	NA	18.3	71.9	9.3	82.7	35.19	7 084	603
Tinley Park	14.4	333	29.5	218	20.6	73.7	12.2	83.8	37.12	6 541	780
Urbana	34.4	1 037	0.0	281	23.8	75.0	16.0	85.3	39.71	5 854	985
Waukegan	92.8	1 251	6.3	593	19.3	71.2	10.8	81.1	34.20	7 136	542
Wheaton	19.3	356	0.0	NA	21.1	73.9	12.3	86.0	36.68	6 354	818
Wheeling	16.4	542	0.0	227	21.0	73.2	12.9	83.7	35.82	6 536	752
Wilmette	42.3	1 627	31.8	210	21.0	73.2	12.9	83.7	35.82	6 536	752
Woodridge	26.8	930	27.7	NA	19.7	73.1	10.7	84.2	36.88	6 699	702
INDIANA	X	X	X	X	X	X	X	X	X	X	X
Anderson	35.5	601	15.1	1 190	24.8	73.5	17.4	83.7	38.47	5 916	812
Bloomington	50.8	765	27.5	701	27.3	75.8	18.1	85.9	43.14	5 309	1 068
Carmel	17.4	472	32.6	393	25.5	75.4	17.2	85.5	39.94	5 615	1 014

1. Based on the population estimated as of July 1 of the year shown. 2. Represents normal values based on the 30-year period, 1961–1990. 3. Average daily minimum. 4. Average daily maximum.

Table D. Cities — Land Area and Population

STATE Place code	City	Land area, 1990[1] (sq km)	Population, 1999 Total persons	Rank	Per square kilometer	Total persons 1990	Percent change 1990–1999	Total persons 1980	Percent change 1980–1990	White	Black	Am. Indian, Eskimo, Aleut	Asian and Pacific Islander	Other race	Hispanic[2]	Foreign born
		1	2	3	4	5	6	7	8	9	10	11	12	13	14	15
	INDIANA—Cont'd															
18 14734	Columbus	52.4	37 198	815	710	33 948	9.6	30 614	10.9	95.4	2.5	0.2	1.6	0.3	0.9	2.5
18 19486	East Chicago	31.0	30 457	994	982	33 892	-10.1	39 786	-14.8	38.0	33.6	0.2	0.2	28.0	47.8	11.6
18 20728	Elkhart	44.4	43 336	682	976	44 661	-3.0	41 305	8.1	84.0	14.0	0.4	0.8	0.9	2.0	2.7
18 22000	Evansville	105.4	121 864	173	1 156	126 272	-3.5	130 496	-3.2	89.6	9.5	0.2	0.6	0.2	0.6	0.9
18 25000	Fort Wayne	162.3	196 708	88	1 212	195 680	0.5	172 196	11.4	80.5	16.7	0.3	1.0	1.5	2.7	2.2
18 27000	Gary	130.1	110 271	202	848	116 646	-5.5	151 953	-23.2	16.3	80.6	0.2	0.2	2.8	5.7	1.4
18 29898	Greenwood	28.0	34 951	863	1 248	26 507	31.9	19 327	37.2	98.5	0.1	0.2	1.1	0.2	0.8	2.5
18 31000	Hammond	59.4	77 363	321	1 302	84 236	-8.2	93 714	-10.1	84.8	9.2	0.2	0.4	5.3	11.8	4.4
18 36000	Indianapolis	950.0	(3)738 907	(3)13	(3)778	(3)731 726	(3)1.0	NA	NA	76.2	22.3	0.2	0.9	0.4	1.0	1.9
18 40392	Kokomo	37.3	45 218	657	1 212	44 996	0.5	47 808	-5.9	89.5	8.9	0.3	0.7	0.6	1.7	1.4
18 40788	Lafayette	34.7	49 104	596	1 415	45 933	6.9	43 011	3.7	95.8	2.1	0.3	1.1	0.6	1.7	2.5
18 42426	Lawrence	52.0	34 912	867	671	26 849	30.0	25 591	4.9	86.7	10.7	0.3	1.7	0.7	1.7	2.7
18 46908	Marion	32.3	30 046	1 011	930	32 607	-7.9	35 874	-9.1	82.6	14.8	0.4	0.7	1.4	3.2	0.9
18 48528	Merrillville	80.3	31 290	970	390	27 257	14.8	27 677	-1.5	91.7	5.0	0.1	0.9	2.3	6.9	7.0
18 48798	Michigan City	50.8	32 752	924	645	33 822	-3.2	36 833	-8.2	75.8	22.5	0.3	0.7	0.7	1.8	2.0
18 49932	Mishawaka	36.0	46 096	638	1 280	42 635	8.1	40 201	6.1	97.1	1.6	0.4	0.7	0.3	1.1	2.6
18 51876	Muncie	59.0	66 916	391	1 134	71 170	-6.0	77 216	-7.8	89.1	9.5	0.3	0.7	0.4	0.9	1.4
18 52326	New Albany	34.6	40 273	746	1 164	36 322	10.9	37 103	-2.1	93.2	6.2	0.2	0.3	0.2	0.5	1.0
18 61092	Portage	53.9	33 477	905	621	29 062	15.2	27 409	6.0	97.1	0.4	0.2	0.5	1.7	6.4	2.4
18 64260	Richmond	47.6	38 282	792	804	38 705	-1.1	41 327	-6.3	89.6	9.2	0.3	0.6	0.3	0.7	0.8
18 71000	South Bend	94.3	98 941	230	1 049	105 511	-6.2	109 727	-3.8	76.0	20.9	0.4	0.9	1.8	3.4	3.4
18 75428	Terre Haute	71.6	52 664	545	736	57 475	-8.4	61 125	-6.0	88.6	9.4	0.4	1.1	0.4	1.3	2.5
18 82862	West Lafayette	12.7	30 406	996	2 394	26 144	16.3	21 247	23.0	88.7	2.2	0.2	8.3	0.7	2.0	11.5
19 00000	**IOWA**	144 716.0	2 869 413	X	20	2 776 831	3.3	2 913 808	-4.7	96.6	1.7	0.3	0.9	0.5	1.2	1.6
19 01855	Ames	50.9	48 777	599	958	47 198	3.3	45 775	3.1	89.9	2.4	0.1	6.9	0.6	1.6	9.3
19 06355	Bettendorf	55.0	31 552	961	574	28 139	12.1	27 376	2.8	96.8	1.4	0.2	1.0	0.7	2.2	1.8
19 09550	Burlington	34.3	26 585	1 131	775	27 208	-2.3	29 529	-7.9	94.1	4.5	0.2	0.7	0.5	1.3	1.2
19 11755	Cedar Falls	73.7	34 542	877	469	34 298	0.7	36 310	-5.5	96.9	1.1	0.2	1.4	0.4	0.8	2.6
19 12000	Cedar Rapids	138.5	115 777	186	836	108 772	6.4	110 217	-1.3	95.5	2.9	0.2	1.0	0.4	1.1	2.0
19 14430	Clinton	91.9	27 812	1 081	303	29 201	-4.8	32 828	-11.0	96.5	2.4	0.3	0.5	0.3	0.7	1.0
19 16860	Council Bluffs	95.3	57 365	488	602	54 315	5.6	56 449	-3.8	97.8	0.8	0.3	0.4	0.7	2.4	1.0
19 19000	Davenport	158.9	98 256	236	618	95 333	3.1	103 264	-7.7	89.1	7.9	0.4	1.0	1.5	3.5	2.5
19 21000	Des Moines	194.9	190 958	92	980	193 189	-1.2	191 003	1.1	89.2	7.1	0.4	2.4	0.9	2.4	3.1
19 22395	Dubuque	59.7	56 742	498	950	57 538	-1.4	62 321	-7.7	98.4	0.6	0.1	0.6	0.3	0.6	1.5
19 28515	Fort Dodge	37.3	25 593	1 178	686	26 057	-1.8	29 423	-12.0	95.4	3.3	0.3	0.5	0.5	1.5	1.2
19 38595	Iowa City	57.0	61 298	441	1 075	59 735	2.6	50 508	18.3	91.1	2.5	0.2	5.6	0.6	1.7	7.2
19 49755	Marshalltown	39.1	25 941	1 161	663	25 178	3.0	26 938	-6.5	97.1	1.0	0.3	1.1	0.5	1.0	1.6
19 50160	Mason City	66.3	28 690	1 049	433	29 040	-1.2	30 144	-3.7	97.3	0.9	0.1	0.5	1.2	2.9	1.1
19 73335	Sioux City	140.6	82 843	292	589	80 505	2.9	82 003	-1.8	92.6	2.3	2.0	1.5	1.6	3.3	3.1
19 82425	Waterloo	156.9	62 800	430	400	66 467	-5.5	75 985	-12.5	86.6	12.1	0.2	0.7	0.4	0.8	0.9
19 83910	West Des Moines	46.4	44 636	667	962	31 702	40.8	21 894	44.8	96.3	1.3	0.1	1.6	0.6	1.9	1.7
20 00000	**KANSAS**	211 921.6	2 654 052	X	13	2 477 588	7.1	2 364 236	4.8	90.1	5.8	0.9	1.3	2.0	3.8	2.5
20 21275	Emporia	23.8	24 897	1 209	1 046	25 512	-2.4	25 287	0.9	89.3	2.8	0.6	2.6	4.8	7.8	4.5
20 33625	Hutchinson	53.6	39 561	761	738	39 308	0.6	40 284	-2.4	91.5	4.1	0.6	0.4	3.4	5.4	1.8
20 36000	Kansas City	279.2	139 971	142	501	151 521	-7.6	161 093	-5.9	65.0	29.3	0.7	1.2	3.8	7.1	2.7
20 38900	Lawrence	59.4	78 911	316	1 328	65 608	20.3	52 738	24.4	87.1	4.9	3.0	3.9	1.2	3.0	6.2
20 39000	Leavenworth	58.8	39 123	771	665	38 495	1.6	33 656	14.4	79.8	15.8	0.7	2.0	1.7	4.7	4.3
20 39350	Lenexa	75.2	40 518	741	539	34 110	18.8	18 639	83.0	94.6	2.4	0.4	2.0	0.5	1.7	2.6
20 44250	Manhattan	28.6	41 499	717	1 451	43 081	-3.7	32 645	32.0	90.1	5.0	0.5	3.3	1.2	2.8	5.4
20 52575	Olathe	109.5	88 152	272	805	63 402	39.1	37 258	70.2	94.3	3.0	0.4	1.7	0.6	1.8	2.0
20 53775	Overland Park	144.2	142 783	138	990	111 790	27.7	81 784	36.7	95.4	1.8	0.3	1.9	0.5	2.0	3.8
20 62700	Salina	54.4	44 077	676	810	42 299	4.2	41 843	1.1	93.1	3.5	0.5	1.2	1.6	2.7	2.0
20 64500	Shawnee	108.2	46 364	631	429	37 962	22.1	29 625	28.1	94.9	2.1	0.4	1.7	0.9	2.6	2.5
20 71000	Topeka	142.9	124 529	165	871	119 883	3.9	115 266	4.0	84.7	10.6	1.3	0.8	2.6	5.8	1.6
20 79000	Wichita	298.2	335 562	50	1 125	304 017	10.4	279 272	8.9	82.3	11.3	1.2	2.6	2.7	5.0	4.0
21 00000	**KENTUCKY**	102 906.8	3 960 825	X	38	3 686 892	7.4	3 660 324	0.7	92.0	7.1	0.2	0.5	0.2	0.6	0.9
21 08902	Bowling Green	75.0	45 550	650	607	41 688	9.3	40 450	3.1	86.4	12.2	0.2	1.1	0.1	0.7	1.5
21 17848	Covington	34.3	40 099	752	1 169	43 646	-8.1	49 569	-11.9	91.5	7.7	0.2	0.4	0.2	0.7	0.6
21 28900	Frankfort	37.7	26 762	1 127	710	26 535	0.9	25 973	2.2	87.4	11.7	0.2	0.6	0.2	0.6	1.0
21 35866	Henderson	33.7	26 566	1 133	788	25 945	2.4	24 834	4.5	88.9	10.5	0.2	0.3	0.1	0.4	0.5
21 37918	Hopkinsville	52.7	32 270	942	612	29 809	8.3	27 318	9.2	69.9	29.0	0.2	0.6	0.3	0.9	1.6
21 46027	Lexington-Fayette	736.9	243 785	69	331	225 366	8.2	204 165	10.4	84.5	13.4	0.2	1.6	0.3	1.1	2.9
21 48000	Louisville	160.9	253 128	65	1 573	269 555	-6.1	298 455	-9.7	69.2	29.7	0.2	0.7	0.2	0.7	1.5
21 58620	Owensboro	38.8	54 010	528	1 392	53 577	0.8	54 450	-1.6	93.0	6.4	0.1	0.3	0.1	0.4	0.5
21 58836	Paducah	45.5	25 777	1 169	567	27 256	-5.4	29 315	-7.0	78.4	20.9	0.2	0.3	0.2	0.6	1.0

1. Dry land or land partially or temporarily covered by water.   2. Hispanic persons may be of any race.   3. 1999 population is for Indianapolis "remainder"; most other items are for Indianapolis Consolidated city; see Appendix A.

Table D. Cities — Population and Households

	Population characteristics, 1990 (cont'd)										Households, 1990				
	Age of population (percent)													Percent	
City	Under 5 years	5 to 17 years	18 to 24 years	25 to 34 years	35 to 44 years	45 to 54 years	55 to 64 years	65 to 74 years	75 years and over	Percent female	Number	Percent change, 1980–1990	Persons per house-hold	Female family house-holder[1]	One-person
	16	17	18	19	20	21	22	23	24	25	26	27	28	29	30
INDIANA—Cont'd															
Columbus	7.2	17.6	9.7	16.2	15.2	11.1	9.0	7.8	6.1	52.8	12 850	9.7	2.42	11.1	27.7
East Chicago	7.5	23.7	9.7	15.6	12.3	8.5	9.8	8.3	4.5	52.5	12 122	-10.8	2.78	25.8	27.4
Elkhart	9.2	17.9	10.5	18.7	13.9	9.0	7.7	7.3	5.9	52.5	17 519	9.3	2.45	14.0	29.7
Evansville	6.9	16.1	10.3	17.5	13.3	9.4	9.3	9.4	7.7	53.6	52 948	3.0	2.30	12.8	32.9
Fort Wayne	8.0	18.4	10.9	18.8	14.2	8.4	7.9	7.4	6.0	52.4	69 627	5.6	2.43	13.8	31.0
Gary	8.0	23.7	9.4	14.5	13.5	10.2	9.4	7.4	4.0	54.0	40 968	-17.3	2.83	29.1	25.6
Greenwood	7.0	17.7	10.5	18.8	16.0	10.4	7.6	6.1	5.9	53.0	10 594	50.6	2.44	9.4	27.4
Hammond	7.4	19.2	9.6	18.1	13.5	8.9	9.1	9.1	5.2	51.6	32 146	-6.9	2.61	14.4	27.7
Indianapolis	7.9	17.7	10.4	20.2	14.6	9.4	8.2	6.8	4.8	52.5	296 599	NA	2.46	13.6	29.1
Kokomo	7.5	18.7	9.3	17.0	14.6	10.3	9.1	7.8	5.7	53.5	18 664	2.0	2.37	13.9	31.0
Lafayette	7.4	16.9	11.2	18.9	14.5	9.7	8.2	7.5	5.7	51.6	18 074	5.5	2.37	9.6	31.1
Lawrence	8.6	18.0	9.6	23.2	15.0	8.8	7.8	5.6	3.4	51.2	10 612	13.3	2.47	12.0	25.6
Marion	6.5	17.8	10.5	14.7	12.8	11.0	10.1	9.1	7.4	52.4	12 693	-2.6	2.42	15.0	30.1
Merrillville	6.0	17.1	8.9	15.5	15.1	11.3	10.3	9.3	6.5	52.1	10 006	9.1	2.69	9.1	21.2
Michigan City	7.2	18.2	9.5	18.4	14.6	9.3	8.9	8.3	5.5	50.2	12 562	-0.9	2.51	15.9	29.3
Mishawaka	7.4	18.0	10.8	18.4	14.4	8.5	7.9	8.1	6.7	53.2	18 001	10.2	2.33	11.7	33.3
Muncie	6.1	13.4	26.0	13.6	11.1	8.4	8.1	7.7	5.5	53.4	27 188	-1.2	2.34	12.7	31.0
New Albany	7.2	17.5	9.6	16.8	13.4	9.7	9.4	9.3	7.1	53.8	14 691	4.7	2.41	16.0	28.3
Portage	7.0	21.1	9.2	16.9	16.2	11.0	8.4	6.7	3.5	51.3	10 520	14.8	2.74	10.8	19.9
Richmond	7.1	17.4	12.1	15.3	12.8	9.5	9.3	9.2	7.3	53.4	15 579	-1.4	2.38	14.3	30.2
South Bend	8.1	17.8	9.8	17.4	13.9	7.7	8.7	9.3	7.4	52.8	42 260	0.1	2.45	14.9	30.7
Terre Haute	6.3	14.8	18.2	15.9	12.0	8.0	7.9	9.0	7.8	51.1	21 488	-6.8	2.32	13.4	33.5
West Lafayette	3.5	7.4	49.7	14.0	7.9	5.1	4.0	4.4	3.9	46.2	9 153	25.9	2.36	4.4	29.5
IOWA	7.0	18.9	10.2	15.4	14.2	9.9	9.0	8.2	7.2	51.6	1 064 325	1.1	2.52	8.0	25.9
Ames	5.1	10.1	40.8	16.3	10.7	5.4	4.9	3.6	3.1	46.8	15 613	10.8	2.36	5.3	26.9
Bettendorf	6.8	21.1	7.5	14.9	18.4	12.6	8.6	6.4	3.7	51.5	10 663	13.7	2.62	8.2	22.1
Burlington	7.0	18.8	8.4	14.9	14.6	10.0	9.1	9.3	7.8	53.1	10 986	-2.6	2.43	11.7	29.4
Cedar Falls	5.1	15.6	27.5	11.9	13.5	8.4	6.9	6.0	5.1	53.0	11 689	-0.1	2.50	8.1	23.8
Cedar Rapids	7.0	17.2	11.3	17.8	15.0	10.0	8.5	7.4	5.8	52.0	43 674	4.9	2.43	9.2	27.5
Clinton	7.0	18.4	8.5	15.4	13.6	10.0	9.5	9.6	8.0	52.9	11 667	-4.5	2.44	11.2	28.0
Council Bluffs	8.0	18.9	9.5	17.7	13.7	8.9	9.6	7.8	5.9	52.8	21 131	1.4	2.52	13.4	26.1
Davenport	8.1	19.3	10.6	17.6	14.8	8.8	8.1	7.1	5.6	52.1	37 205	-2.5	2.50	12.9	28.0
Des Moines	7.8	16.4	11.9	18.9	14.4	9.1	8.1	7.3	6.0	52.9	78 453	4.0	2.38	11.9	30.7
Dubuque	6.6	18.4	11.5	15.1	14.1	9.3	9.0	8.4	7.6	52.9	21 437	1.4	2.52	9.6	27.7
Fort Dodge	7.6	17.8	9.1	14.7	14.3	8.1	9.5	9.4	9.4	53.5	10 502	-5.5	2.35	11.2	31.2
Iowa City	5.6	11.2	33.7	19.7	13.1	5.8	4.3	3.4	3.1	50.5	21 951	18.2	2.34	6.8	29.7
Marshalltown	6.4	17.7	8.5	14.7	14.3	10.8	9.2	9.6	8.7	51.5	9 974	-2.6	2.40	9.8	29.1
Mason City	7.0	17.3	10.3	16.0	13.5	8.9	9.7	8.8	8.4	53.5	12 027	1.5	2.32	9.5	31.5
Sioux City	7.7	19.8	10.5	15.9	14.0	8.7	8.7	8.1	6.7	52.1	30 488	1.0	2.55	11.4	27.1
Waterloo	7.1	19.0	9.2	15.0	14.8	9.9	9.3	9.0	6.7	52.8	27 037	-4.6	2.42	12.4	28.9
West Des Moines	6.6	16.8	10.2	19.7	16.3	11.9	7.9	6.2	4.4	52.7	12 974	56.1	2.41	7.0	27.1
KANSAS	7.6	19.1	10.3	16.7	14.6	9.5	8.4	7.5	6.4	51.0	944 726	8.2	2.53	8.6	25.9
Emporia	7.8	18.1	19.5	16.9	12.8	7.3	5.7	5.6	6.3	51.8	9 753	2.8	2.42	8.8	31.5
Hutchinson	7.0	16.9	10.5	16.8	14.1	9.3	8.8	8.7	7.8	50.9	15 656	-1.3	2.36	9.8	30.3
Kansas City	8.4	20.2	9.4	17.7	13.6	9.0	8.7	7.4	5.5	52.4	57 146	-4.4	2.59	16.9	28.0
Lawrence	6.0	12.9	31.8	18.5	12.1	6.6	4.9	3.9	3.3	50.2	24 513	30.3	2.35	8.0	28.8
Leavenworth	7.3	18.6	8.3	20.5	21.3	8.8	6.0	5.3	3.9	43.6	11 475	8.9	2.70	10.7	24.5
Lenexa	8.5	19.8	10.0	19.9	21.2	10.6	4.6	2.7	2.9	51.3	12 713	97.2	2.66	7.9	21.8
Manhattan	6.3	13.8	30.5	17.9	12.4	6.3	4.7	4.4	3.7	48.4	14 689	14.6	2.39	6.7	28.2
Olathe	10.1	22.2	9.8	22.5	18.7	7.4	4.2	2.7	2.4	50.9	21 445	77.9	2.89	8.7	17.4
Overland Park	7.2	17.5	8.3	19.1	18.2	11.2	8.6	6.5	3.4	52.3	44 936	51.5	2.47	7.9	25.6
Salina	7.6	18.7	9.7	17.4	14.1	9.7	8.4	7.8	6.6	52.1	17 287	6.6	2.40	10.1	28.9
Shawnee	7.5	18.8	9.3	19.6	18.1	11.5	7.9	4.8	2.4	50.8	14 567	39.3	2.60	8.1	22.8
Topeka	7.4	17.2	9.8	18.1	14.4	9.3	9.1	8.0	6.7	52.4	49 936	7.8	2.33	11.9	32.0
Wichita	8.6	18.0	10.2	19.5	14.6	8.7	8.0	7.3	5.1	51.4	123 249	11.6	2.43	11.1	30.0
KENTUCKY	6.8	19.1	10.9	16.6	14.9	10.4	8.8	7.3	5.4	51.6	1 379 782	9.2	2.60	11.6	23.3
Bowling Green	5.9	15.1	21.5	15.5	12.3	8.7	7.8	7.3	5.8	53.9	15 973	11.3	2.29	13.3	31.8
Covington	8.4	18.6	10.3	19.0	13.5	7.9	7.9	7.7	6.7	52.5	17 319	-7.6	2.43	16.7	34.0
Frankfort	6.6	15.9	10.9	17.1	15.4	10.6	9.3	8.1	6.2	53.0	11 037	5.9	2.26	13.9	32.9
Henderson	6.9	18.5	9.5	16.7	14.5	9.8	8.8	8.3	7.0	53.8	10 548	9.7	2.41	14.1	28.3
Hopkinsville	7.3	18.8	9.9	15.5	14.3	10.0	9.0	8.0	7.2	54.1	11 402	15.3	2.50	17.4	26.7
Lexington-Fayette	6.7	15.6	14.5	20.3	16.1	9.5	7.3	5.8	4.1	52.2	89 529	18.9	2.38	12.2	29.1
Louisville	6.8	16.7	9.9	17.9	14.1	8.8	9.4	9.1	7.5	53.7	113 065	-3.4	2.31	18.3	30.0
Owensboro	7.2	18.1	10.2	15.9	13.9	10.2	9.6	8.5	6.5	53.7	21 672	7.7	2.39	13.8	30.1
Paducah	6.1	16.7	7.4	15.0	12.7	9.6	10.3	11.3	10.9	55.3	11 955	-1.2	2.21	15.4	35.7

1. No spouse present.

Table D. Cities — **Group Quarters, Crime, Education, and Income**

City	Persons in group quarters, 1990				Serious crimes known to police, 1998[2]				Education, 1990				Money income, 1989		
					Total		Rate[3]		School enrollment		Attainment[4] (percent)			Households	
															Median
	Total	Persons in mental hospitals	Persons in nursing homes	Persons identified as home-less[1]	Number	Rate[3]	Violent	Property	Public	Private	High school grad-uate or more	Bach-elor's degree or more	Per capita (dollars)[5]	Dollars	Percent change, 1979–1989 (constant 1989 dollars)
	31	32	33	34	35	36	37	38	39	40	41	42	43	44	45
INDIANA—Cont'd															
Columbus	677	0	463	12	NA	NA	NA	NA	6 697	767	76.1	20.3	14 366	28 859	-4.4
East Chicago	167	0	117	0	NA	NA	NA	NA	9 030	1 359	57.7	6.6	9 090	19 391	-32.7
Elkhart	742	19	517	57	NA	NA	NA	NA	8 362	1 006	71.7	13.7	13 331	25 291	-1.0
Evansville	4 293	381	1 957	80	7 812	6 302	426	5 876	21 814	6 538	72.4	14.6	12 564	22 936	-6.0
Fort Wayne	3 984	77	1 593	157	14 163	7 570	447	7 123	34 842	9 109	77.1	15.7	12 726	26 344	-2.0
Gary	881	26	524	130	7 487	6 702	1 208	5 494	32 701	2 915	64.8	8.8	8 994	19 390	-32.9
Greenwood	462	0	456	0	1 464	4 641	149	4 492	5 045	876	82.7	18.7	16 367	32 994	-2.0
Hammond	438	0	124	180	6 633	8 228	1 229	6 999	17 236	3 488	69.3	9.2	11 576	26 883	-19.6
Indianapolis	13 605	592	5 966	586	NA	NA	NA	NA	142 850	33 552	76.5	21.9	14 605	29 083	NA
Kokomo	689	55	368	66	2 874	6 259	390	5 869	9 749	1 074	74.0	13.0	12 619	26 272	-4.3
Lafayette	937	64	548	109	3 096	6 933	495	6 438	9 452	1 461	80.5	21.4	13 468	27 023	1.9
Lawrence	537	56	190	0	NA	NA	NA	NA	5 451	799	78.9	17.3	14 011	29 652	1.6
Marion	1 911	24	1 187	86	2 461	8 215	277	7 938	6 450	1 187	66.5	10.8	11 188	22 006	-12.1
Merrillville	359	0	316	0	1 051	3 415	166	3 249	5 645	1 060	80.2	15.1	15 131	36 221	-15.3
Michigan City	2 273	0	359	0	2 849	8 602	722	7 880	7 025	1 111	69.1	9.4	10 868	23 127	-19.0
Mishawaka	737	71	246	0	NA	NA	NA	NA	8 434	1 893	74.2	14.8	12 823	24 302	-6.3
Muncie	7 332	0	355	81	NA	NA	NA	NA	24 616	1 155	70.1	16.0	10 686	19 353	-14.2
New Albany	883	0	706	18	2 325	5 976	573	5 403	7 474	846	68.3	12.9	11 781	23 933	-6.0
Portage	213	0	213	0	1 367	4 134	136	3 998	6 797	780	74.5	9.3	13 057	33 118	-19.6
Richmond	1 565	7	446	14	NA	NA	NA	NA	7 798	1 723	68.0	13.0	10 975	20 585	-12.0
South Bend	2 088	0	1 386	275	9 168	8 901	761	8 140	19 506	6 035	72.0	18.5	11 949	24 131	-8.2
Terre Haute	7 780	0	802	72	5 013	9 225	322	8 903	15 758	1 731	72.3	15.8	10 527	19 118	-11.3
West Lafayette	4 311	0	179	0	393	1 436	139	1 297	16 117	578	95.7	68.4	13 169	21 786	-10.0
IOWA	99 528	1 347	36 455	1 290	100 188	3 501	312	3 189	626 759	110 970	80.1	16.9	12 422	26 229	-6.8
Ames	10 336	0	213	14	1 051	2 195	79	2 116	25 919	790	95.1	54.1	11 347	24 636	-8.7
Bettendorf	180	0	180	0	989	3 168	291	2 877	6 778	1 030	90.1	34.2	17 747	40 174	-8.6
Burlington	490	0	344	0	1 503	5 616	695	4 921	5 950	665	77.8	14.0	12 025	25 105	-7.6
Cedar Falls	5 110	0	605	0	1 207	3 469	285	3 184	14 217	858	88.5	31.4	12 114	28 003	-16.6
Cedar Rapids	2 692	0	1 066	135	NA	NA	NA	NA	22 774	5 248	84.5	23.3	15 246	31 458	-3.3
Clinton	741	11	441	12	NA	NA	NA	NA	6 273	924	76.2	14.4	11 830	23 562	-22.0
Council Bluffs	1 002	18	484	83	NA	NA	NA	NA	11 712	1 301	73.9	10.0	11 318	25 014	-6.5
Davenport	2 304	50	917	121	7 156	7 328	1 410	5 918	20 270	6 047	78.8	20.1	12 557	26 218	-16.9
Des Moines	6 369	170	1 281	448	14 204	7 310	488	6 822	36 096	10 629	81.0	18.9	13 710	26 703	-4.7
Dubuque	3 547	0	929	145	2 174	3 790	232	3 558	8 542	7 146	78.4	19.4	12 377	27 027	-13.6
Fort Dodge	1 158	0	836	15	1 804	7 322	666	6 656	4 884	1 248	78.3	16.1	11 639	22 783	-14.5
Iowa City	8 352	36	126	15	2 485	4 036	737	3 299	28 991	1 516	93.9	53.7	13 277	24 565	1.7
Marshalltown	1 262	34	1 048	17	1 390	5 459	1 001	4 458	5 630	515	80.8	17.8	13 424	27 325	-7.1
Mason City	1 107	0	490	59	2 118	7 287	664	6 623	6 226	924	79.7	16.3	12 229	24 146	-7.1
Sioux City	2 653	0	575	97	6 492	7 749	702	7 047	15 735	5 393	77.9	17.5	12 339	25 045	-7.3
Waterloo	924	0	572	6	4 535	6 993	535	6 458	13 639	2 776	77.9	14.1	12 475	23 578	-24.2
West Des Moines	493	0	389	0	1 640	4 034	253	3 781	5 959	1 792	94.8	41.8	21 503	41 045	3.9
KANSAS	82 791	1 822	26 155	1 242	127 737	4 859	397	4 462	593 376	74 989	81.3	21.1	13 300	27 291	-0.5
Emporia	1 949	0	220	0	NA	NA	NA	NA	8 755	405	83.1	24.7	11 159	22 621	-13.6
Hutchinson	2 494	0	593	33	NA	NA	NA	NA	8 499	1 021	77.2	14.3	11 849	23 557	-8.0
Kansas City	1 514	0	817	85	NA	NA	NA	NA	34 012	4 776	69.3	10.1	10 478	23 307	-8.6
Lawrence	7 876	0	378	72	NA	NA	NA	NA	30 002	1 450	90.9	44.0	11 760	22 900	3.7
Leavenworth	7 444	0	917	0	NA	NA	NA	NA	8 880	1 609	85.4	29.3	12 827	30 156	5.9
Lenexa	266	0	266	0	NA	NA	NA	NA	7 892	1 907	95.8	45.5	20 202	46 935	0.4
Manhattan	2 602	0	209	12	NA	NA	NA	NA	17 017	607	92.6	42.2	11 273	21 531	-1.4
Olathe	1 465	0	699	69	NA	NA	NA	NA	16 435	3 078	90.9	31.2	14 696	39 742	5.6
Overland Park	644	59	488	0	NA	NA	NA	NA	23 677	5 233	94.1	44.8	21 214	44 246	1.4
Salina	841	0	432	38	NA	NA	NA	NA	8 348	1 609	81.9	17.6	13 044	25 084	-5.7
Shawnee	101	0	61	0	NA	NA	NA	NA	8 176	1 880	90.0	29.5	17 268	39 206	-3.3
Topeka	3 685	252	1 137	288	NA	NA	NA	NA	24 726	4 120	82.7	22.1	13 680	26 774	-0.4
Wichita	4 581	152	1 919	395	23 303	7 079	665	6 414	65 447	12 134	81.9	22.7	14 516	28 024	-2.9
KENTUCKY	100 731	1 690	27 874	1 360	113 725	2 889	284	2 605	807 842	110 473	64.6	13.6	11 153	22 534	-3.7
Bowling Green	3 992	63	582	25	3 245	7 206	879	6 327	12 816	489	71.5	23.4	11 760	20 043	-1.9
Covington	1 113	29	639	69	NA	NA	NA	NA	7 859	1 788	62.4	9.8	10 293	21 003	5.3
Frankfort	980	0	214	0	NA	NA	NA	NA	5 488	686	77.1	22.7	13 100	25 670	-2.0
Henderson	528	0	400	19	NA	NA	NA	NA	5 349	641	66.3	11.8	11 828	22 085	-13.7
Hopkinsville	1 239	530	525	9	NA	NA	NA	NA	6 528	487	69.4	13.4	10 440	21 352	-4.4
Lexington-Fayette	12 403	333	1 214	128	NA	NA	NA	NA	56 571	8 444	80.2	30.6	14 962	28 056	5.2
Louisville	7 949	69	2 772	836	17 896	6 820	943	5 877	51 805	13 390	67.2	17.2	11 527	20 141	-2.1
Owensboro	1 660	27	807	37	2 576	4 691	240	4 451	9 906	2 944	71.8	15.3	11 492	21 952	-10.4
Paducah	768	0	496	17	2 144	7 998	653	7 345	5 214	565	69.0	14.6	11 918	17 196	-13.4

1. Persons in emergency shelters and persons visible in street locations. 2. Data for serious crimes have not been adjusted for underreporting. This may affect comparability between geographic areas and over time. 3. Per 100,000 population estimated by the FBI. 4. Persons 25 years old and older. 5. Based on population enumerated as of April 1, 1990.

Table D. Cities — Income, Poverty, and Housing

City	Money income, 1989 (cont'd) Households (cont'd) Percent with $100,000 or more	Percent below poverty, 1989 Persons Total	Percent change in rate, 1979–1989	Families Total	Housing units, 1990 Total	Percent change, 1980–1990	Vacant units for sale or rent[1]	Occupied units Total	Owner-occupied units Percent	Median value[2] (dollars)	Owner cost as a percent of income With a mortgage	Without a mortgage	Renter-occupied units Median rent[3] (dollars)	Rent as percent of income	Substandard units[4] (percent)
	46	47	48	49	50	51	52	53	54	55	56	57	58	59	60
INDIANA—Cont'd															
Columbus	2.7	10.9	2.8	7.7	13 458	9.4	455	12 850	61.8	59 900	17.8	12.2	405	24.4	1.8
East Chicago	0.8	25.6	52.4	24.5	13 484	-9.7	957	12 122	45.4	42 600	15.9	12.8	286	25.0	7.8
Elkhart	2.9	12.5	4.2	10.3	19 147	8.3	1 316	17 519	55.9	49 200	17.0	12.0	388	24.4	1.9
Evansville	2.2	14.6	19.7	11.2	58 188	7.3	3 865	52 948	59.0	45 500	17.9	12.8	340	25.8	2.0
Fort Wayne	1.5	11.5	4.5	8.3	77 166	9.3	5 408	69 627	59.6	47 800	16.2	12.0	382	24.4	2.3
Gary	0.7	29.4	44.1	26.4	47 082	-13.5	4 009	40 968	58.6	31 700	18.5	15.4	335	29.9	7.3
Greenwood	2.9	6.1	32.6	4.4	11 399	51.5	657	10 594	58.5	74 400	18.7	11.5	444	24.3	1.7
Hammond	0.9	13.5	45.2	11.8	33 924	-6.0	1 316	32 146	64.1	45 500	16.0	13.5	377	24.1	4.1
Indianapolis	3.3	12.5	NA	9.7	324 530	NA	NA	296 297	56.8	60 400	17.6	12.3	409	24.3	2.6
Kokomo	1.1	16.4	45.1	14.2	20 340	4.2	1 179	18 664	62.7	42 400	15.3	12.7	357	26.1	2.1
Lafayette	2.3	8.9	-1.1	5.7	19 259	5.1	908	18 074	59.4	51 700	17.4	11.9	385	22.9	2.2
Lawrence	1.2	7.4	0.0	5.9	11 621	15.3	873	10 612	62.7	64 400	19.4	12.0	424	22.8	2.0
Marion	1.3	18.9	39.0	15.4	14 000	-1.9	764	12 693	58.6	34 500	16.4	12.9	317	26.0	2.8
Merrillville	2.6	3.6	12.5	2.9	10 322	11.1	270	10 006	73.6	62 300	16.0	12.2	530	26.4	2.4
Michigan City	1.2	16.4	36.7	13.8	13 995	2.4	752	12 562	59.8	43 700	18.1	14.4	363	25.9	2.9
Mishawaka	1.5	9.1	-2.2	6.5	19 028	10.1	755	18 001	59.6	46 800	17.5	12.2	363	25.2	1.8
Muncie	1.6	23.8	34.5	14.3	29 828	1.3	1 462	27 188	57.5	34 500	16.3	13.3	325	29.5	2.5
New Albany	1.3	15.5	32.5	13.0	15 593	5.1	682	14 691	59.3	48 100	17.1	12.6	348	25.4	2.0
Portage	1.7	7.9	54.9	7.3	10 864	13.2	245	10 520	70.7	62 000	15.3	12.4	432	23.0	2.4
Richmond	1.8	20.5	44.4	16.3	16 942	0.3	906	15 579	58.8	38 800	16.3	13.1	294	25.1	2.1
South Bend	1.6	14.4	19.0	11.2	45 757	2.1	2 641	42 260	65.9	40 300	17.3	13.2	410	26.3	2.9
Terre Haute	1.3	20.4	48.9	15.5	24 077	-2.1	1 496	21 488	62.1	32 300	16.6	12.9	282	27.4	2.7
West Lafayette	5.0	34.2	62.9	7.3	9 465	25.8	241	9 153	33.5	94 900	16.2	10.8	482	35.1	3.0
IOWA	2.1	11.5	13.7	8.4	1 143 669	1.1	41 387	1 064 325	70.0	45 900	17.3	12.8	336	24.1	1.9
Ames	2.8	24.1	52.5	10.5	16 058	8.4	337	15 613	44.1	72 500	18.0	11.5	404	30.0	3.0
Bettendorf	5.5	4.7	74.1	3.2	11 063	14.4	314	10 663	73.7	67 500	17.3	12.0	415	21.0	0.8
Burlington	1.2	13.7	45.7	11.3	11 777	-2.6	477	10 986	69.6	38 700	16.2	12.5	319	23.7	1.6
Cedar Falls	2.5	16.8	102.4	9.1	12 066	-1.0	241	11 689	63.7	56 600	14.8	11.9	329	28.5	1.5
Cedar Rapids	3.0	10.0	31.6	6.6	45 473	4.4	1 386	43 674	67.2	56 900	16.5	12.1	379	23.5	1.3
Clinton	1.1	12.7	67.1	10.2	12 584	-2.4	649	11 667	68.4	36 700	15.0	12.6	302	24.7	1.3
Council Bluffs	1.3	12.2	18.4	10.0	22 244	1.3	865	21 131	66.2	44 500	19.0	13.6	378	25.2	2.6
Davenport	1.8	15.6	57.6	12.4	40 343	0.1	2 137	37 205	61.2	48 800	17.3	13.1	351	26.3	1.8
Des Moines	2.3	12.9	21.7	9.5	83 289	4.2	3 450	78 453	62.0	49 500	20.2	13.6	408	27.0	3.0
Dubuque	2.2	10.9	32.9	7.6	22 377	1.0	690	21 437	66.1	51 600	16.1	12.1	315	24.2	1.6
Fort Dodge	1.2	12.8	24.3	9.5	11 212	-3.6	524	10 502	64.7	38 500	17.3	12.6	301	24.8	1.2
Iowa City	4.7	23.4	18.8	9.3	22 464	16.8	352	21 951	44.7	79 000	18.3	12.3	414	31.1	3.2
Marshalltown	1.7	9.5	15.9	6.8	10 630	-1.3	506	9 974	68.3	43 500	17.0	12.8	327	23.4	1.3
Mason City	1.7	9.6	2.1	7.2	12 669	0.4	515	12 027	65.8	44 100	16.8	12.9	322	25.2	1.0
Sioux City	2.6	13.8	21.1	10.5	32 177	0.5	1 192	30 488	67.0	41 000	17.2	13.2	326	25.4	2.6
Waterloo	2.0	16.9	62.5	14.3	29 023	-1.8	1 391	27 037	65.4	39 800	16.2	13.5	326	25.6	2.4
West Des Moines	9.2	3.3	-21.4	1.9	13 668	53.1	578	12 974	62.2	90 400	19.6	12.8	526	22.7	0.9
KANSAS	2.8	11.5	13.7	8.3	1 044 112	9.3	60 956	944 726	67.9	52 200	19.1	12.6	372	24.5	2.7
Emporia	1.9	16.7	46.5	11.1	10 732	5.5	617	9 753	54.2	47 400	18.8	13.5	303	24.3	3.3
Hutchinson	1.6	12.0	23.7	9.1	17 163	0.4	1 082	15 656	64.5	39 000	16.2	12.2	310	23.2	2.1
Kansas City	0.7	17.9	24.3	14.6	64 457	0.0	5 980	57 146	61.9	41 200	19.8	13.9	374	26.9	4.7
Lawrence	2.8	24.1	26.2	11.5	25 893	28.3	1 107	24 513	46.2	69 400	19.8	12.3	415	34.6	3.1
Leavenworth	1.3	9.5	-19.5	7.4	12 568	10.0	887	11 475	51.7	57 500	20.9	13.1	427	22.3	2.5
Lenexa	7.9	4.3	19.4	2.9	13 496	90.2	729	12 713	63.6	104 000	20.7	11.4	500	23.8	1.1
Manhattan	1.7	24.6	43.0	10.1	15 558	14.0	685	14 689	44.3	65 900	20.4	12.2	396	33.4	3.2
Olathe	2.4	4.1	-22.6	3.3	22 497	72.6	948	21 445	66.3	83 300	22.2	12.2	470	24.4	1.4
Overland Park	8.6	2.8	0.0	1.9	48 043	53.8	2 495	44 936	64.4	95 300	19.2	11.6	549	23.1	0.8
Salina	2.5	12.2	45.2	8.6	18 411	4.2	850	17 287	64.1	45 100	17.1	12.5	329	24.1	1.7
Shawnee	4.6	4.1	5.1	3.3	15 217	36.6	555	14 567	67.2	84 800	19.0	11.7	462	23.8	1.5
Topeka	2.2	12.3	32.3	9.3	54 664	8.5	3 527	49 936	60.8	48 800	18.3	12.2	380	24.6	2.3
Wichita	2.8	12.5	22.5	9.5	135 069	15.8	9 508	123 249	58.9	56 700	19.8	12.7	395	25.4	3.7
KENTUCKY	2.0	19.0	8.1	16.0	1 506 845	10.1	65 649	1 379 782	69.6	50 500	18.0	12.3	319	24.9	4.7
Bowling Green	2.4	23.9	29.9	18.1	17 501	15.3	1 265	15 973	50.6	58 200	20.0	12.3	332	27.9	2.6
Covington	1.0	19.8	13.8	17.7	19 117	-6.3	1 164	17 319	50.8	41 600	17.5	12.7	305	26.1	4.3
Frankfort	1.2	13.0	18.2	10.4	11 880	5.9	659	11 037	53.9	61 500	16.1	11.6	345	23.5	1.7
Henderson	1.5	17.0	34.9	14.9	11 355	13.2	544	10 548	58.3	50 200	16.1	12.7	315	24.4	2.9
Hopkinsville	1.5	21.8	15.3	17.1	12 236	16.2	567	11 402	57.3	43 500	18.1	12.4	305	24.1	3.9
Lexington-Fayette	4.2	14.1	4.4	10.2	97 742	19.6	6 427	89 529	53.0	73 900	18.4	11.7	394	24.9	2.5
Louisville	1.9	22.6	17.1	18.6	124 018	-1.7	6 928	113 065	54.9	44 300	17.8	12.9	308	26.4	3.6
Owensboro	1.8	18.9	37.0	15.3	23 074	9.1	1 042	21 672	60.1	46 100	15.8	12.0	280	25.4	2.5
Paducah	2.5	23.8	27.3	19.1	13 150	3.1	907	11 955	54.4	37 800	17.0	12.6	257	25.9	2.0

1. Includes units rented or sold but not occupied. 2. Specified owner-occupied units. 3. Specified renter-occupied units. 4. Overcrowded or lacking complete plumbing facilities.

City	Civilian labor force, 1999				Civilian employment, 1990[2]			Disability 1990	Value of residential construction authorized by building permits, 1999		
			Unemployment			Percent					
	Total	Percent change, 1998–1999	Total	Rate[1]	Total	Professional, managerial, and technical	Precision production, craft, and repair	Work disabled persons[3] (percent)	New construction ($1,000)	Number of housing units	Percent single family
	61	62	63	64	65	66	67	68	69	70	71
INDIANA—Cont'd											
Columbus	19 381	0.1	442	2.3	15 417	32.7	10.7	9.2	NA	NA	NA
East Chicago	12 998	-2.2	949	7.3	11 490	16.9	11.7	10.7	1 023	10	100.0
Elkhart	26 449	1.6	772	2.9	21 893	20.0	14.8	10.1	4 203	47	87.2
Evansville	67 858	0.3	2 423	3.6	58 474	25.8	10.3	8.8	16 045	193	79.3
Fort Wayne	97 877	-0.8	3 610	3.7	85 039	26.8	10.9	8.9	23 324	244	75.4
Gary	45 481	-2.2	3 938	8.7	39 616	21.3	9.6	12.8	547	5	100.0
Greenwood	19 467	1.2	258	1.3	14 531	30.8	13.0	5.4	60 388	507	92.5
Hammond	39 246	-2.3	1 744	4.4	35 762	20.0	15.0	9.3	3 797	48	47.9
Indianapolis	416 577	-1.2	11 685	2.8	372 602	31.1	9.8	8.2	593 192	5 576	71.1
Kokomo	22 254	-1.6	728	3.3	19 652	24.0	14.6	10.8	27 371	237	79.7
Lafayette	26 165	0.9	550	2.1	22 767	28.5	11.1	7.9	37 088	564	47.2
Lawrence	15 267	-1.2	383	2.5	13 697	27.9	12.9	6.1	51 740	443	100.0
Marion	13 410	-1.4	757	5.6	13 607	21.1	13.8	12.8	NA	NA	NA
Merrillville	14 297	-2.4	288	2.0	13 359	25.7	14.8	6.6	10 292	108	68.5
Michigan City	16 295	-0.8	800	4.9	14 582	20.4	11.4	9.5	7 150	105	88.6
Mishawaka	24 630	-1.0	727	3.0	21 419	24.7	11.7	6.6	17 692	241	55.2
Muncie	35 138	-0.3	1 493	4.2	31 169	24.7	9.7	9.7	8 784	139	46.8
New Albany	21 190	0.3	595	2.8	16 476	26.4	11.9	9.6	11 836	179	49.7
Portage	16 142	-0.7	632	3.9	13 161	20.6	17.0	10.1	19 801	262	87.8
Richmond	19 632	-2.9	808	4.1	16 804	25.8	11.2	10.9	4 595	44	95.5
South Bend	55 380	-0.8	2 368	4.3	47 503	29.0	9.4	8.2	NA	NA	NA
Terre Haute	24 815	-1.7	1 326	5.3	23 222	27.2	9.4	10.2	10 491	153	66.0
West Lafayette	13 783	0.9	383	2.8	11 910	55.8	2.6	2.1	20 317	374	7.8
IOWA	1 574 269	0.3	40 138	2.5	1 340 242	25.3	10.5	7.6	1 405 608	13 491	71.9
Ames	29 544	0.7	686	2.3	25 307	46.7	4.0	3.2	30 236	654	27.2
Bettendorf	16 914	0.3	366	2.2	14 582	38.9	8.9	5.2	29 344	208	75.0
Burlington	14 264	-1.8	512	3.6	12 348	26.2	13.9	9.0	2 972	29	44.8
Cedar Falls	20 196	-3.4	658	3.3	17 077	31.7	7.8	5.5	13 062	78	93.6
Cedar Rapids	72 193	1.8	1 408	2.0	56 107	32.0	10.2	6.8	54 948	817	45.9
Clinton	14 896	-1.0	630	4.2	12 754	23.2	12.6	8.9	4 537	39	89.7
Council Bluffs	30 632	-0.2	716	2.3	25 915	20.9	11.6	11.3	20 058	245	72.7
Davenport	51 869	0.5	1 891	3.6	44 039	27.9	10.4	7.8	33 275	296	85.1
Des Moines	119 785	-0.9	2 888	2.4	99 816	26.9	9.2	9.1	43 529	437	78.9
Dubuque	32 014	-0.4	963	3.0	27 639	27.9	9.7	7.2	8 080	84	65.5
Fort Dodge	13 037	1.2	381	2.9	11 551	26.9	10.2	9.6	3 523	32	81.2
Iowa City	41 202	2.5	882	2.1	33 465	43.1	4.6	4.1	44 751	395	50.4
Marshalltown	13 177	-1.2	310	2.4	12 086	28.6	11.5	8.0	4 512	44	45.5
Mason City	15 964	-1.9	367	2.3	14 045	25.5	8.8	9.5	6 684	48	79.2
Sioux City	44 280	-1.9	1 193	2.7	38 030	26.4	12.4	9.2	9 855	91	95.6
Waterloo	34 253	-3.2	1 599	4.7	28 541	25.6	11.7	10.2	9 535	69	76.8
West Des Moines	21 760	-0.8	297	1.4	18 327	46.1	3.9	4.1	89 178	627	88.0
KANSAS	1 434 249	1.7	42 726	3.0	1 172 214	28.7	11.5	7.2	1 668 027	15 688	72.1
Emporia	14 424	-0.7	485	3.4	12 074	25.4	15.4	5.6	8 255	162	17.3
Hutchinson	20 892	1.6	705	3.4	17 962	23.8	12.2	8.7	12 281	121	52.1
Kansas City	71 726	-0.9	4 031	5.6	64 557	19.9	11.5	9.6	14 810	142	98.6
Lawrence	44 793	1.8	1 568	3.5	32 924	37.7	6.5	5.1	69 679	698	56.2
Leavenworth	14 886	1.9	556	3.7	11 601	32.6	9.0	8.6	7 253	109	48.6
Lenexa	27 040	4.1	482	1.8	19 682	44.4	5.7	3.3	83 671	590	51.9
Manhattan	21 397	-0.8	559	2.6	18 236	39.5	6.6	4.3	14 790	135	68.1
Olathe	47 336	3.9	1 017	2.1	34 327	37.3	8.7	4.3	216 871	2 364	63.4
Overland Park	87 475	4.1	1 474	1.7	63 736	45.0	4.8	3.8	300 345	2 738	43.0
Salina	26 217	1.5	656	2.5	20 957	25.3	12.4	8.6	14 258	115	93.0
Shawnee	29 924	3.9	657	2.2	21 690	34.5	10.1	4.4	86 094	797	83.9
Topeka	65 953	-0.7	2 373	3.6	58 267	32.2	7.7	9.2	34 876	404	44.6
Wichita	182 088	0.6	6 667	3.7	149 768	31.7	13.1	8.5	113 836	1 404	91.8
KENTUCKY	1 969 791	2.4	88 032	4.5	1 563 960	24.7	12.9	11.4	1 909 051	21 581	76.4
Bowling Green	24 840	1.1	467	1.9	19 291	30.5	8.0	9.3	38 359	532	41.7
Covington	19 548	-1.3	681	3.5	18 636	22.6	12.4	12.2	11 059	250	62.4
Frankfort	14 870	2.2	432	2.9	13 236	36.4	7.7	8.0	9 734	159	54.7
Henderson	14 422	-0.4	712	4.9	11 710	23.4	13.0	11.4	12 465	239	43.1
Hopkinsville	15 159	13.0	558	3.7	11 985	26.0	11.5	10.8	14 186	290	35.9
Lexington-Fayette	146 093	3.2	2 846	1.9	117 906	37.2	7.8	7.4	211 830	2 205	80.9
Louisville	131 774	0.2	5 520	4.2	115 546	28.1	9.7	11.5	22 545	376	69.1
Owensboro	29 660	1.6	1 602	5.4	23 746	25.9	11.5	10.1	19 842	427	51.8
Paducah	11 803	-1.4	326	2.8	10 489	26.5	9.7	14.0	5 450	70	50.0

1. Percent of civilian labor force.   2. Persons 16 years and older.   3. Persons 16 to 64 years old.

Table D. Cities — Wholesale Trade, Retail Trade, and Real Estate

City	Wholesale Trade, 1997				Retail Trade[1], 1997				Real Estate and Rental and Leasing, 1997			
	Number of Establishments	Number of Employees	Sales (mil dol)	Annual Payroll (mil dol)	Number of Establishments	Number of Employees	Sales (mil dol)	Annual Payroll (mil dol)	Number of Establishments	Number of Employees	Receipts (mil dol)	Annual Payroll (mil dol)
	72	73	74	75	76	77	78	79	80	81	82	83
INDIANA—Cont'd												
Columbus	81	698	588.1	22.4	286	3 941	566.8	55.6	50	228	30.5	4.8
East Chicago	60	1 115	953.8	39.0	60	610	83.6	10.6	14	128	21.2	4.0
Elkhart	168	2 457	1 147.6	80.3	330	5 168	920.2	82.5	89	371	42.5	7.0
Evansville	296	4 051	1 480.3	123.3	870	13 655	2 092.6	211.3	198	1 327	148.7	23.5
Fort Wayne	531	8 532	4 041.7	281.3	1 058	17 653	2 859.6	283.0	238	1 582	193.2	35.5
Gary	65	1 480	534.5	52.1	218	2 361	359.8	30.8	62	272	32.2	4.5
Greenwood	61	501	552.5	19.7	258	4 847	728.5	70.1	46	208	26.9	3.8
Hammond	95	1 366	961.1	44.5	251	3 388	556.3	52.0	62	553	77.2	17.6
Indianapolis	1 863	D	D	D	3 405	56 872	10 305.6	990.4	1 048	D	D	D
Kokomo	73	601	553.3	22.3	346	5 564	878.7	81.5	73	281	35.3	5.2
Lafayette	83	1 027	218.2	26.3	410	6 608	1 060.4	100.8	87	411	45.4	7.0
Lawrence	34	346	110.7	11.0	116	1 418	241.4	25.6	33	149	12.6	2.7
Marion	43	431	118.8	13.4	233	3 131	524.9	46.2	39	154	11.4	2.2
Merrillville	63	681	284.0	24.3	308	5 485	965.6	87.5	60	302	26.7	4.6
Michigan City	55	726	248.0	22.7	299	3 759	562.4	57.1	35	148	13.4	2.2
Mishawaka	87	1 278	667.0	41.4	393	8 081	1 479.9	116.8	56	248	29.7	4.6
Muncie	80	1 151	444.0	37.6	406	5 648	863.3	83.7	90	341	37.4	6.6
New Albany	69	D	D	D	174	1 886	265.7	30.0	43	214	17.2	3.4
Portage	27	612	364.5	18.3	80	1 185	197.2	17.5	26	148	22.3	3.0
Richmond	68	1 362	1 148.3	45.7	249	3 582	585.7	54.6	48	187	20.7	3.4
South Bend	250	4 759	2 191.4	155.5	440	6 597	939.1	98.6	104	853	80.4	18.0
Terre Haute	114	1 390	592.3	36.6	411	7 586	1 963.8	129.8	68	404	30.9	7.2
West Lafayette	9	D	D	D	79	1 660	188.4	17.2	45	D	D	D
IOWA	5 399	63 596	35 453.7	1 820.1	14 695	175 694	26 723.8	2 633.4	2 518	12 619	1 457.5	249.0
Ames	50	380	129.6	10.8	246	3 922	510.8	54.6	48	304	20.7	5.0
Bettendorf	78	665	516.4	26.3	124	1 821	252.2	28.9	42	182	27.4	3.7
Burlington	33	330	152.2	7.9	132	2 108	259.3	31.0	37	394	46.6	9.7
Cedar Falls	38	723	420.6	22.3	180	2 611	429.5	41.4	35	96	13.1	1.7
Cedar Rapids	285	4 914	1 986.5	139.7	640	10 952	1 638.6	172.0	154	996	110.4	22.1
Clinton	36	277	77.4	6.0	153	1 883	321.5	34.3	35	141	9.4	1.3
Council Bluffs	68	1 155	836.3	36.0	287	4 400	717.2	67.5	52	273	24.8	4.5
Davenport	252	3 458	2 372.4	111.8	545	8 810	1 416.2	147.5	107	1 184	111.3	28.4
Des Moines	408	6 500	2 459.9	221.1	897	13 577	2 103.9	231.6	235	1 848	263.9	43.8
Dubuque	97	1 164	656.2	32.3	382	5 537	734.3	80.4	80	322	30.0	4.5
Fort Dodge	53	D	D	D	216	2 932	374.4	40.5	45	D	D	D
Iowa City	38	D	D	D	333	5 448	775.2	79.8	89	438	50.3	7.8
Marshalltown	39	D	D	D	155	2 296	295.0	31.8	27	239	20.2	6.1
Mason City	55	657	344.1	19.1	218	3 451	519.7	47.4	38	126	13.3	1.9
Sioux City	188	D	D	D	469	7 174	1 049.7	108.3	105	D	D	D
Waterloo	102	1 750	389.1	49.3	347	6 030	807.8	88.5	84	438	47.1	8.5
West Des Moines	118	1 665	3 625.2	68.3	274	5 081	608.2	68.4	87	853	163.2	23.4
KANSAS	5 085	59 954	42 209.9	1 946.8	12 271	140 412	22 571.9	2 191.1	2 602	13 005	1 525.8	259.6
Emporia	35	535	182.9	13.3	163	1 870	274.3	26.6	31	D	D	D
Hutchinson	60	955	345.4	28.8	238	2 966	510.3	50.7	41	142	52.1	2.0
Kansas City	293	6 566	3 864.7	216.5	404	4 622	851.0	83.3	119	684	82.4	14.7
Lawrence	77	644	207.0	18.7	413	5 420	731.5	77.8	111	409	45.6	6.4
Leavenworth	13	D	D	D	128	1 638	272.0	24.3	25	113	13.0	1.8
Lenexa	383	6 605	3 410.9	248.5	226	3 574	634.4	70.7	62	441	48.4	9.1
Manhattan	41	517	141.7	12.7	294	3 570	484.4	47.8	73	241	19.1	3.0
Olathe	181	3 333	1 536.1	130.5	319	4 695	1 106.9	97.8	75	381	46.9	8.1
Overland Park	513	5 130	12 533.4	244.3	745	13 018	2 208.7	222.6	281	2 692	430.0	72.1
Salina	81	989	421.4	28.4	302	4 285	663.4	62.7	64	268	32.3	4.1
Shawnee	75	593	376.5	18.7	165	2 439	459.1	44.2	49	226	29.1	4.2
Topeka	177	1 900	706.5	56.7	706	10 166	1 559.8	160.2	186	1 187	87.3	22.0
Wichita	682	8 221	4 005.0	274.3	1 580	22 657	3 834.5	381.9	480	2 483	317.6	50.4
KENTUCKY	5 051	69 309	37 242.9	2 071.2	17 369	212 189	33 332.7	3 128.1	3 227	16 284	1 961.6	314.3
Bowling Green	128	1 795	1 276.6	50.3	458	6 764	1 048.2	96.3	92	379	36.2	5.5
Covington	35	312	159.3	11.2	173	1 869	310.1	32.4	36	301	19.1	5.7
Frankfort	26	D	D	D	179	2 893	382.0	34.9	32	D	D	D
Henderson	59	D	D	D	192	2 203	415.4	36.1	39	172	15.2	3.3
Hopkinsville	66	D	D	D	241	2 498	406.0	39.6	57	212	23.3	3.4
Lexington-Fayette	NA	NA	NA	NA	NA	NA	NA	NA	NA	NA	NA	NA
Louisville	677	14 614	8 597.4	488.2	1 166	15 744	2 069.0	240.0	332	2 698	331.7	60.0
Owensboro	105	1 272	564.7	33.6	393	4 356	656.1	63.4	61	433	30.8	7.3
Paducah	112	D	D	D	432	5 688	914.3	81.8	63	373	56.9	10.5

1. Establishments with payroll.

City	Professional, Scientific, and Technical Services, 1997[1]				Manufacturing, 1997				Accommodation and Foodservices, 1997			
	Number of Establish-ments	Number of Employees	Receipts (mil dol)	Annual Payroll (mil dol)	Number of Establish-ments	Number of Employees	Receipts (mil dol)	Annual Payroll (mil dol)	Number of Establish-ments	Number of Employees	Sales (mil dol)	Annual Payroll (mil dol)
	84	85	86	87	88	89	90	91	92	93	94	95
INDIANA—Cont'd												
Columbus	123	694	50.7	22.3	96	11 647	2 273.1	366.2	110	2 721	88.6	24.6
East Chicago	17	135	14.0	5.5	51	16 068	4 894.2	812.3	57	494	16.0	3.6
Elkhart	136	898	67.3	20.7	349	17 947	3 023.5	554.5	184	3 093	94.5	26.9
Evansville	359	3 237	231.8	89.9	213	15 029	3 446.0	528.1	396	D	D	D
Fort Wayne	505	4 954	412.1	144.6	390	22 830	4 258.9	846.3	506	11 413	350.9	103.0
Gary	46	403	54.8	12.6	62	10 066	3 377.4	511.3	120	1 465	43.7	11.4
Greenwood	96	506	31.2	12.3	45	1 013	289.6	36.1	107	2 419	66.4	19.3
Hammond	101	1 364	79.7	30.2	76	4 195	1 468.0	171.4	164	2 024	71.3	17.3
Indianapolis	2 174	22 189	2 356.5	875.1	1 094	D	D	D	1 751	D	D	D
Kokomo	87	393	30.1	10.1	66	D	D	D	160	3 637	109.6	29.9
Lafayette	134	972	79.1	27.8	71	D	D	D	152	3 092	94.7	27.6
Lawrence	39	146	14.8	4.3	30	626	61.9	19.6	52	802	23.2	6.6
Marion	53	320	14.5	4.9	56	8 037	1 537.0	356.6	92	1 901	54.9	15.3
Merrillville	177	1 609	167.0	56.3	35	641	82.1	17.7	134	3 640	118.2	33.5
Michigan City	64	406	21.3	7.4	69	4 621	946.9	153.3	106	1 679	55.1	15.0
Mishawaka	113	1 067	99.9	40.6	128	5 253	636.5	162.9	164	3 655	104.8	29.8
Muncie	111	1 480	65.3	27.6	109	7 185	1 305.6	302.4	174	4 337	109.2	30.4
New Albany	114	877	69.8	25.3	100	6 779	1 168.7	188.2	87	1 408	44.5	12.8
Portage	43	228	22.7	10.1	22	2 172	1 124.5	112.6	56	951	28.1	8.0
Richmond	54	343	24.4	11.3	95	8 093	1 500.2	250.1	103	2 158	63.6	18.4
South Bend	292	2 564	235.7	99.2	200	10 066	1 850.1	361.8	257	4 868	142.8	40.8
Terre Haute	133	836	55.2	16.9	92	5 998	1 398.4	200.3	217	4 308	126.8	36.2
West Lafayette	38	137	16.5	5.4	20	D	D	D	86	1 860	47.0	13.5
IOWA	4 670	31 115	2 435.6	887.9	3 749	235 880	62 413.7	7 573.3	6 830	99 148	2 762.8	769.5
Ames	104	808	88.3	31.2	44	2 344	824.1	75.3	168	3 173	79.0	21.7
Bettendorf	65	356	33.3	12.3	28	1 127	130.9	34.3	72	1 712	49.5	15.8
Burlington	49	219	15.8	5.0	37	4 089	891.2	142.0	89	D	D	D
Cedar Falls	61	627	35.3	16.8	50	1 911	261.7	61.5	99	2 182	47.9	15.3
Cedar Rapids	296	2 391	229.8	89.3	164	21 491	6 194.2	890.3	350	6 760	209.8	59.5
Clinton	41	156	9.8	3.2	28	3 649	1 780.1	126.9	91	1 184	32.1	9.0
Council Bluffs	78	458	39.1	12.5	41	D	D	D	146	3 338	174.2	45.1
Davenport	229	1 571	138.5	44.1	121	6 380	2 984.9	248.0	262	5 707	167.0	48.5
Des Moines	450	6 867	527.9	218.0	234	11 168	2 841.7	375.8	514	9 234	293.7	86.7
Dubuque	98	733	51.9	22.3	86	D	D	D	179	3 220	80.1	23.7
Fort Dodge	61	309	21.9	8.2	44	1 976	911.3	61.3	78	1 274	35.5	10.3
Iowa City	125	761	62.2	21.0	48	2 945	2 339.2	102.7	178	3 743	89.2	25.5
Marshalltown	45	193	12.6	4.7	38	D	D	D	70	981	27.3	7.9
Mason City	53	321	23.0	9.6	37	3 308	677.9	88.8	88	1 495	39.1	11.1
Sioux City	169	907	71.3	23.1	94	6 018	1 853.7	160.2	214	3 544	103.2	28.4
Waterloo	122	876	64.9	27.6	93	11 413	4 848.1	487.4	163	3 120	82.1	22.2
West Des Moines	214	1 911	167.4	74.8	43	1 390	194.6	43.6	118	2 641	78.4	24.8
KANSAS	5 345	39 534	3 559.3	1 396.0	3 309	193 742	46 296.4	6 532.5	5 677	91 173	2 685.7	757.1
Emporia	37	D	D	D	30	D	D	D	96	1 593	36.2	9.7
Hutchinson	75	407	23.9	10.3	47	2 365	364.0	71.2	103	1 927	56.7	14.6
Kansas City	146	1 098	86.1	32.4	249	14 624	7 562.1	623.8	212	2 962	102.6	28.7
Lawrence	175	1 216	77.4	30.1	56	3 439	541.6	86.2	222	4 511	117.9	33.6
Leavenworth	51	637	73.1	19.4	NA	NA	NA	NA	63	1 104	27.6	8.3
Lenexa	216	3 229	299.5	121.2	133	7 703	1 506.0	232.7	89	1 994	69.7	19.2
Manhattan	87	665	55.5	20.9	NA	NA	NA	NA	153	3 003	75.3	21.2
Olathe	182	636	62.0	22.4	117	4 902	842.3	181.4	128	2 785	79.2	23.7
Overland Park	795	11 091	1 306.2	527.1	106	1 632	226.4	50.7	340	8 788	316.7	93.8
Salina	80	697	51.6	20.2	68	5 496	985.3	160.7	127	2 357	66.1	20.0
Shawnee	95	201	19.2	7.7	42	D	D	D	77	D	D	D
Topeka	376	3 131	224.9	91.5	124	D	D	D	353	D	D	D
Wichita	865	6 100	518.0	210.6	496	52 170	8 579.6	2 158.6	852	15 891	528.1	151.1
KENTUCKY	6 189	41 991	3 820.3	1 260.1	4 218	288 405	86 636.1	9 198.1	6 546	129 442	4 056.1	1 140.6
Bowling Green	130	869	53.1	18.4	88	D	D	D	182	4 306	134.0	39.5
Covington	100	754	77.0	31.4	45	1 491	321.1	40.7	133	2 283	87.5	24.3
Frankfort	95	655	59.5	24.7	28	2 760	504.5	79.1	85	D	D	D
Henderson	62	265	17.1	5.4	62	6 189	1 557.8	192.9	75	1 392	40.8	11.8
Hopkinsville	71	272	21.4	6.6	48	4 406	775.0	114.5	72	1 713	42.4	14.9
Lexington-Fayette	NA	NA	NA	NA	283	17 403	4 313.9	654.0	NA	NA	NA	NA
Louisville	1 024	9 645	948.4	334.6	456	29 078	17 225.4	1 076.2	648	15 529	507.6	147.7
Owensboro	127	809	53.2	22.3	86	D	D	D	121	2 865	87.4	23.2
Paducah	120	886	62.7	20.4	40	1 634	300.9	51.9	167	3 808	117.5	33.3

1. Firms subject to federal tax.

City	Arts, Entertainment, and Recreation[1], 1997				Health Care and Social Assistance[1], 1997				Other Services[1], 1997			
	Number of Establishments	Number of Employees	Receipts (mil dol)	Annual Payroll (mil dol)	Number of Establishments	Number of Employees	Receipts (mil dol)	Annual Payroll (mil dol)	Number of Establishments	Number of Employees	Receipts (mil dol)	Annual Payroll (mil dol)
	96	97	98	99	100	101	102	103	104	105	106	107
INDIANA—Cont'd												
Columbus	10	59	2.7	0.5	133	1 519	102.0	54.9	81	574	34.0	12.1
East Chicago	3	0	0.0	0.0	28	253	11.6	5.2	40	492	41.3	15.8
Elkhart	14	140	4.3	1.5	114	1 500	106.4	41.7	145	1 163	69.1	20.6
Evansville	43	1 804	140.5	31.4	368	7 358	475.3	227.9	304	2 787	161.4	51.7
Fort Wayne	58	674	28.1	8.8	434	7 242	424.5	191.2	447	3 741	237.4	74.6
Gary	9	0	0.0	0.0	127	1 160	71.5	31.8	78	558	31.0	9.7
Greenwood	18	229	9.5	2.4	83	1 232	76.2	31.9	85	681	39.9	14.4
Hammond	10	0	0.0	0.0	69	558	44.4	17.7	120	937	54.0	19.1
Indianapolis	230	4 451	428.7	175.8	1 752	26 194	1 802.7	829.6	1 320	11 727	702.1	221.8
Kokomo	21	279	8.6	2.6	150	1 761	110.3	50.7	107	849	37.6	12.3
Lafayette	13	220	5.8	1.7	129	2 390	188.5	94.0	146	1 118	78.2	22.4
Lawrence	10	0	0.0	0.0	30	0	0.0	0.0	48	256	15.0	4.6
Marion	8	73	3.0	0.6	96	1 531	67.5	33.1	67	335	15.5	4.8
Merrillville	13	313	12.9	3.6	251	2 761	197.2	95.3	91	654	43.8	15.0
Michigan City	10	0	0.0	0.0	93	1 164	87.5	40.3	76	465	26.2	9.7
Mishawaka	17	270	7.5	2.3	102	1 129	73.3	32.3	102	693	43.4	13.3
Muncie	18	255	6.8	1.8	182	2 555	173.4	81.1	141	1 346	87.8	21.3
New Albany	11	69	2.1	0.8	135	1 730	103.1	43.7	82	543	28.8	10.0
Portage	8	43	1.8	0.4	46	494	24.6	10.6	52	357	21.4	7.0
Richmond	12	89	3.5	0.8	86	985	51.5	27.0	82	423	20.6	6.5
South Bend	16	178	7.1	1.7	303	4 038	344.7	165.3	220	2 470	172.6	55.3
Terre Haute	18	144	4.2	1.1	211	3 023	226.9	71.1	129	1 162	54.9	16.3
West Lafayette	5	26	0.9	0.2	31	329	21.8	6.2	38	216	8.1	3.0
IOWA	875	14 169	919.8	220.3	4 876	56 374	3 183.2	1 540.6	5 234	24 383	1 486.5	411.3
Ames	15	289	9.0	2.7	62	1 142	76.9	41.1	78	472	27.8	7.7
Bettendorf	11	0	0.0	0.0	66	480	35.2	11.9	52	396	21.0	7.5
Burlington	8	96	3.4	0.7	79	643	45.2	19.6	44	222	12.1	3.3
Cedar Falls	6	0	0.0	0.0	62	616	33.4	16.9	50	308	18.4	6.0
Cedar Rapids	30	544	14.0	4.3	266	3 172	226.4	116.5	251	1 651	95.8	29.4
Clinton	11	0	0.0	0.0	69	646	39.8	15.0	59	248	14.4	3.9
Council Bluffs	19	0	0.0	0.0	93	1 220	71.4	40.2	100	536	31.8	9.6
Davenport	39	0	0.0	0.0	228	2 501	196.1	97.8	206	1 376	79.7	25.7
Des Moines	41	495	45.1	6.0	409	4 536	403.6	201.9	368	2 531	153.5	49.1
Dubuque	20	1 106	73.7	19.1	104	2 146	179.0	85.8	130	773	40.3	12.7
Fort Dodge	5	46	1.2	0.3	79	674	49.2	23.6	68	374	18.9	6.0
Iowa City	20	213	6.0	1.7	124	1 312	76.7	30.6	104	569	32.4	9.6
Marshalltown	8	0	0.0	0.0	48	532	29.0	14.2	50	236	13.9	3.7
Mason City	11	0	0.0	0.0	62	1 118	74.0	46.3	72	371	16.8	5.7
Sioux City	28	0	0.0	0.0	209	1 986	181.2	87.3	155	1 195	59.0	18.9
Waterloo	17	184	8.4	2.1	156	1 494	131.2	64.7	132	1 121	55.1	18.5
West Des Moines	16	275	10.3	3.6	158	2 146	121.3	63.7	75	586	26.7	8.5
KANSAS	652	7 618	374.5	91.0	4 793	66 613	4 116.1	1 771.8	4 604	24 081	1 548.4	452.9
Emporia	9	67	1.6	0.4	60	696	32.4	16.4	64	289	14.5	4.2
Hutchinson	5	69	1.3	0.3	73	1 172	93.1	45.3	79	403	20.0	6.3
Kansas City	23	0	0.0	0.0	199	3 705	288.5	101.4	215	1 325	74.0	24.2
Lawrence	33	263	8.9	2.3	159	1 399	80.1	37.2	119	738	38.7	13.0
Leavenworth	7	39	1.0	0.3	56	429	21.7	10.5	50	241	11.9	4.0
Lenexa	14	212	7.3	2.0	95	2 157	161.8	55.9	94	925	99.5	25.2
Manhattan	12	0	0.0	0.0	92	936	55.1	22.0	83	439	18.0	5.8
Olathe	15	96	4.7	1.5	154	1 897	106.9	53.2	141	814	49.1	15.5
Overland Park	56	1 105	45.0	13.5	447	7 629	570.2	243.5	261	1 823	109.3	38.1
Salina	11	0	0.0	0.0	123	0	0.0	0.0	99	526	31.9	9.9
Shawnee	13	110	3.7	1.1	58	661	31.9	13.5	71	384	26.1	8.7
Topeka	34	546	17.2	4.1	308	5 637	307.4	159.0	277	1 782	120.3	39.3
Wichita	78	0	0.0	0.0	701	14 506	1 103.3	450.4	675	4 622	283.2	89.0
KENTUCKY	906	10 580	550.2	126.3	6 805	94 720	5 936.2	2 620.3	5 383	31 164	1 870.3	551.4
Bowling Green	21	136	4.0	0.9	218	3 778	259.3	103.6	116	976	40.7	13.6
Covington	10	114	5.8	1.4	38	695	24.0	13.1	76	391	26.0	8.3
Frankfort	6	84	2.8	1.1	84	1 234	87.2	36.1	55	385	20.5	8.6
Henderson	7	0	0.0	0.0	89	680	48.3	19.2	57	475	30.2	10.0
Hopkinsville	10	38	1.6	0.4	91	0	0.0	0.0	67	247	16.0	4.0
Lexington-Fayette	NA	NA	NA	NA	NA	NA	NA	NA	NA	NA	NA	NA
Louisville	94	1 991	130.7	21.1	799	14 394	998.1	472.7	580	4 014	240.6	73.6
Owensboro	17	147	5.4	1.3	178	2 374	174.7	73.5	119	747	43.7	12.8
Paducah	15	142	4.9	1.7	157	1 927	167.2	85.5	93	645	43.7	10.8

1. Firms subject to federal tax.

Table D. Cities — Federal Funds and City Government Finances

City	Procurement contracts Defense [108]	Other [109]	Grants Total[2] [110]	Health and family welfare [111]	Energy and environment [112]	Education [113]	Housing and community development [114]	Direct payments for individuals Educational assistance [115]	Housing assistance [116]	Intergovernmental Total (mil dol) [117]	Total (mil dol) [118]	Percent from state government [119]	Taxes Total (mil dol) [120]	Per capita[3] (dollars) Total [121]	Property [122]	Sales and gross receipts [123]
INDIANA—Cont'd																
Columbus	13.5	0.2	10.6	1.8	6.5	0.2	0.4	0.0	3.0	32.7	11.6	46.0	10.4	317	309	0
East Chicago	0.7	0.0	2.7	0.0	0.0	0.0	2.5	0.0	4.4	72.2	13.3	74.6	32.3	1 016	992	17
Elkhart	2.5	7.0	1.8	0.0	0.0	0.0	1.2	0.0	2.7	39.6	15.1	49.9	18.1	410	351	0
Evansville	54.2	1.3	14.6	4.5	0.0	0.0	5.8	3.4	7.7	110.3	31.5	70.1	38.1	309	219	0
Fort Wayne	195.6	49.3	13.0	4.1	0.0	1.0	3.3	1.7	7.7	110.5	28.6	74.4	44.7	242	203	0
Gary	10.6	0.1	23.6	0.2	0.0	1.6	9.2	0.0	5.8	105.3	23.5	87.9	46.6	420	415	0
Greenwood	0.0	0.0	0.2	0.0	0.0	0.0	0.0	0.1	0.2	18.3	6.5	39.2	4.5	146	140	0
Hammond	1.5	0.6	8.8	2.6	0.2	0.0	5.6	0.5	0.0	88.2	19.6	73.7	31.1	389	379	0
Indianapolis	906.9	89.3	787.2	263.8	45.9	130.1	69.2	47.1	37.5	1 187.8	289.4	85.6	520.7	688	551	36
Kokomo	0.0	0.1	3.3	1.7	0.0	0.0	1.5	0.0	0.3	43.4	11.2	62.1	19.9	434	346	0
Lafayette	1.1	1.2	33.4	3.0	1.3	0.0	1.3	0.1	7.0	39.2	10.8	51.1	16.6	375	246	0
Lawrence	0.0	0.0	0.1	0.0	0.0	0.0	0.0	0.0	0.0	12.1	2.9	83.9	5.0	153	118	0
Marion	0.0	2.2	5.6	1.3	0.0	0.4	1.0	1.6	5.0	22.0	4.7	78.7	10.4	347	238	0
Merrillville	0.0	0.8	0.2	0.0	0.0	0.2	0.0	1.0	0.0	8.9	2.7	95.5	5.1	167	153	0
Michigan City	0.3	0.7	2.8	1.4	0.0	0.4	0.6	0.0	2.5	34.7	8.5	66.6	12.6	382	366	0
Mishawaka	162.0	85.8	1.7	0.7	0.0	0.0	0.7	0.6	6.0	25.1	5.8	89.1	11.8	261	253	0
Muncie	0.0	0.9	8.4	1.4	0.0	0.9	3.8	4.7	1.9	37.7	11.4	69.2	17.9	258	209	0
New Albany	0.7	0.3	3.0	1.3	0.0	0.1	1.4	0.0	0.8	23.5	5.6	69.7	8.8	229	200	0
Portage	0.0	0.0	0.5	0.0	0.1	0.0	0.0	0.0	0.8	21.4	6.3	95.4	6.1	189	179	0
Richmond	0.5	2.3	2.3	1.6	0.0	0.0	0.3	1.0	4.7	29.6	10.0	56.9	11.0	295	273	0
South Bend	125.4	5.2	27.7	4.0	1.7	0.3	6.5	0.1	7.5	105.4	25.1	71.6	39.2	384	370	0
Terre Haute	15.0	2.7	12.7	1.9	0.0	1.6	3.4	5.7	0.3	36.7	10.0	75.2	17.6	322	316	0
West Lafayette	1.9	1.6	69.6	23.1	9.2	3.3	0.4	12.3	1.4	15.9	2.9	84.3	6.7	246	171	0
IOWA	413.9	484.0	2 595.3	1 490.8	32.4	239.8	61.2	80.5	48.6	X	X	X	X	X	X	X
Ames	6.6	29.7	75.1	11.1	5.4	2.7	0.1	12.2	0.0	117.1	11.3	76.0	13.8	289	225	53
Bettendorf	0.2	0.4	0.7	0.1	0.0	0.0	0.0	0.0	0.5	30.6	5.6	63.9	16.4	530	344	173
Burlington	4.2	0.1	2.6	1.8	0.0	0.0	0.2	0.0	0.1	21.4	5.5	55.8	9.4	349	262	87
Cedar Falls	3.9	0.0	6.5	0.6	0.6	4.8	0.3	3.8	1.1	58.2	11.8	32.8	12.5	357	242	103
Cedar Rapids	307.6	27.9	20.5	5.1	1.0	1.4	1.7	5.9	2.3	136.7	25.1	51.4	48.8	430	394	22
Clinton	0.0	0.0	0.2	0.0	0.0	0.0	0.1	0.3	0.0	25.2	5.3	84.8	11.6	411	296	109
Council Bluffs	0.0	0.1	3.4	0.5	0.0	0.5	1.9	1.2	5.3	55.0	12.3	49.7	28.8	518	329	178
Davenport	11.1	0.5	12.1	5.9	0.0	1.1	2.6	5.4	2.9	100.5	23.7	69.6	42.9	442	344	86
Des Moines	5.3	19.0	460.6	152.9	21.0	76.0	40.6	3.2	9.8	236.7	44.5	58.2	100.3	519	476	34
Dubuque	0.4	1.7	7.4	1.3	0.0	0.2	1.1	2.2	0.8	60.7	15.0	36.6	23.3	407	264	124
Fort Dodge	3.5	0.1	1.7	1.2	0.0	0.3	0.0	1.1	1.0	18.4	5.1	48.9	7.7	311	304	0
Iowa City	0.6	94.3	150.4	122.5	2.0	3.5	3.4	5.2	3.3	67.0	17.1	52.8	20.9	343	325	8
Marshalltown	0.0	19.9	10.1	0.0	0.0	0.4	0.0	0.5	0.0	19.0	4.4	60.9	9.3	368	351	10
Mason City	0.6	2.3	2.4	1.6	0.0	0.2	0.3	1.0	-0.3	24.5	5.4	61.1	11.3	390	257	119
Sioux City	12.7	0.9	16.8	3.7	0.2	1.7	1.6	2.8	2.0	93.0	28.4	46.5	36.8	439	370	62
Waterloo	0.7	0.1	7.0	1.6	0.0	0.6	1.9	1.7	2.0	88.4	31.4	25.5	32.8	505	374	121
West Des Moines	7.2	9.6	1.3	1.1	0.0	0.1	0.0	0.0	0.0	40.9	8.3	62.6	22.3	553	517	21
KANSAS	939.3	323.9	2 182.8	1 159.4	42.4	254.8	47.0	53.7	23.3	X	X	X	X	X	X	X
Emporia	0.2	0.0	2.3	0.5	0.0	1.5	0.0	2.0	0.9	16.3	2.5	59.5	6.7	270	172	92
Hutchinson	0.0	0.1	1.5	0.9	0.0	0.3	0.1	0.9	0.0	30.8	6.1	37.8	14.9	381	216	160
Kansas City	5.2	18.4	50.7	34.8	0.2	2.2	4.5	1.7	6.8	220.6	36.0	26.0	64.6	453	305	146
Lawrence	4.6	4.5	57.9	17.2	0.5	23.2	1.6	4.7	0.0	102.8	18.0	61.0	21.9	305	147	148
Leavenworth	1.0	10.8	0.8	0.0	0.0	0.1	0.6	0.2	0.0	20.9	4.8	49.6	10.3	262	158	97
Lenexa	2.0	4.3	2.0	0.9	0.0	0.0	0.0	0.0	0.1	46.7	9.6	27.1	22.6	605	344	238
Manhattan	1.7	7.9	38.4	5.9	4.3	4.3	0.1	6.0	0.0	26.0	6.5	43.0	10.9	258	154	98
Olathe	15.6	1.7	5.4	0.7	0.0	0.0	3.3	0.9	1.6	76.2	15.5	32.7	25.1	319	167	140
Overland Park	2.2	19.1	17.7	15.5	0.0	0.2	1.2	1.4	1.9	86.6	15.1	52.6	54.6	417	114	274
Salina	0.4	3.7	2.9	2.2	0.0	0.3	0.4	1.7	-0.7	40.1	12.6	25.3	9.9	224	161	55
Shawnee	0.9	0.2	0.2	0.0	0.0	0.0	0.0	0.0	0.9	28.4	8.3	19.0	12.5	291	154	121
Topeka	8.3	9.3	406.8	116.1	34.5	66.0	26.9	2.6	3.3	132.8	22.5	48.5	63.4	530	281	242
Wichita	606.5	23.8	37.4	12.2	0.4	3.2	5.4	4.9	0.5	323.6	123.4	48.4	80.3	251	148	92
KENTUCKY	1 364.7	910.2	4 395.1	2 678.0	61.1	416.9	97.4	87.8	52.8	X	X	X	X	X	X	X
Bowling Green	0.9	0.6	17.1	7.8	0.0	3.3	0.4	5.3	3.2	51.5	4.7	28.7	24.9	564	118	11
Covington	0.1	9.1	16.7	3.4	0.2	0.3	4.1	0.0	0.9	50.2	12.9	24.1	23.5	573	97	44
Frankfort	1.1	0.7	644.7	190.9	48.3	127.1	34.3	2.1	3.3	21.2	3.1	71.0	11.8	441	80	2
Henderson	0.5	0.2	0.8	0.0	0.0	0.0	0.5	0.0	1.6	21.3	4.4	36.0	7.2	271	108	27
Hopkinsville	-0.2	3.5	2.5	0.0	0.0	0.3	1.1	0.0	1.0	21.9	2.5	69.9	10.7	378	81	11
Lexington-Fayette	111.1	20.6	129.8	61.2	4.5	8.0	4.2	28.6	1.2	296.7	20.2	65.0	121.0	NA	NA	NA
Louisville	726.9	33.2	125.0	40.6	1.5	14.4	25.0	11.0	18.3	320.1	76.3	46.4	169.3	649	178	8
Owensboro	4.2	3.9	13.8	7.6	0.0	0.2	2.4	1.2	5.1	44.5	4.5	63.4	14.8	273	96	7
Paducah	19.7	279.2	3.8	1.6	0.0	0.3	1.0	0.1	2.2	37.1	6.8	28.1	18.7	703	178	10

1. October 1, 1998 to September 30, 1999.   2. Includes program categories not shown separately. State totals include additional categories not allocated by city.   3. Based on population estimated as of July 1 of the year shown.

Table D. Cities — City Government Finances

City	Total (mil dol)	Per capita¹ (dollars) Total	Capital outlays	Public welfare	Highways	Parking facilities	Education	Health and hospitals	Police protection	Sewerage and sanitation	Parks and recreation	Housing and community development	Interest on debt
	124	125	126	127	128	129	130	131	132	133	134	135	136
INDIANA—Cont'd													
Columbus	29.0	880	107	0.0	8.2	0.3	0.0	1.7	12.0	17.7	15.9	0.0	3.4
East Chicago	64.2	2 021	157	0.0	5.9	0.0	0.0	4.3	9.8	20.5	7.8	8.2	19.5
Elkhart	36.0	813	96	0.0	6.5	0.0	0.0	0.3	16.6	19.0	9.4	3.4	4.1
Evansville	85.1	689	37	0.1	5.3	0.4	0.0	2.5	19.7	16.8	10.4	5.3	3.6
Fort Wayne	109.9	595	32	0.0	9.6	0.8	0.0	1.0	22.0	13.4	12.3	6.1	5.0
Gary	104.3	940	112	0.0	4.6	0.0	0.0	2.0	10.5	17.6	9.8	0.4	10.7
Greenwood	18.8	613	39	0.0	5.8	0.0	0.0	0.0	14.2	22.8	4.1	0.0	1.6
Hammond	91.8	1 146	26	0.0	6.4	0.0	0.0	0.9	12.9	21.1	4.8	4.4	3.4
Indianapolis	1 222.9	1 615	352	6.3	5.2	0.4	0.1	21.7	8.3	7.6	6.5	5.4	11.9
Kokomo	42.7	932	131	0.0	9.4	0.0	0.0	0.0	14.0	18.6	3.6	2.5	4.4
Lafayette	33.5	756	50	0.0	10.5	1.0	0.0	0.0	14.6	16.3	8.1	5.3	0.5
Lawrence	12.0	367	32	0.0	12.9	0.0	0.0	2.6	20.1	19.7	6.7	0.0	0.6
Marion	20.1	670	41	0.0	9.0	0.1	0.0	0.0	18.8	17.1	3.4	1.5	1.8
Merrillville	8.6	281	13	0.0	13.0	0.0	0.0	8.0	27.6	0.0	2.1	0.0	0.8
Michigan City	32.5	985	159	0.0	5.0	0.0	0.0	0.4	11.4	40.1	10.5	0.4	3.3
Mishawaka	25.8	573	64	0.0	7.6	0.0	0.0	2.8	14.7	13.5	10.8	4.3	6.5
Muncie	37.5	543	7	0.0	6.5	0.2	0.0	0.3	13.5	31.6	3.2	6.6	0.2
New Albany	21.8	570	75	0.3	8.2	0.1	0.0	1.2	18.0	27.4	5.1	1.6	5.1
Portage	16.6	512	133	0.0	10.4	0.0	0.0	0.3	13.4	21.1	25.0	0.0	1.9
Richmond	29.9	802	101	0.0	7.1	0.4	0.0	0.0	15.3	20.8	9.8	0.1	0.3
South Bend	98.1	960	96	0.0	7.9	0.6	0.0	2.6	14.0	11.2	11.5	12.3	4.4
Terre Haute	33.9	621	46	0.0	6.2	0.2	0.0	0.0	12.3	14.3	8.3	8.2	3.8
West Lafayette	12.0	440	26	0.0	8.1	0.0	0.0	0.0	18.5	30.6	10.2	2.4	0.0
IOWA	X	X	X	X	X	X	X	X	X	X	X	X	X
Ames	110.4	2 314	461	0.6	7.9	0.3	0.0	64.5	3.8	6.6	2.9	0.8	3.7
Bettendorf	31.0	999	378	0.0	28.3	0.0	0.0	0.0	10.8	6.3	7.9	1.3	6.4
Burlington	21.8	812	190	1.1	20.4	0.5	0.0	3.5	13.8	14.3	8.7	0.1	5.7
Cedar Falls	50.3	1 443	239	0.0	18.4	0.3	0.0	41.8	5.2	6.3	5.2	3.2	2.9
Cedar Rapids	134.3	1 183	361	0.0	13.0	4.2	0.0	0.7	15.8	22.4	6.9	5.9	6.3
Clinton	26.2	927	251	0.8	28.6	0.1	0.0	1.9	13.7	9.6	6.2	0.9	14.5
Council Bluffs	61.0	1 098	446	0.0	14.8	0.2	0.0	1.4	10.3	28.9	7.6	2.9	7.5
Davenport	100.8	1 040	250	2.1	20.7	0.9	0.0	0.0	4.3	10.2	8.2	7.6	15.8
Des Moines	220.9	1 142	171	0.0	8.6	2.2	0.0	0.9	13.1	22.5	3.9	9.1	9.0
Dubuque	66.1	1 154	424	0.2	17.2	1.0	0.0	1.5	9.0	14.5	6.6	7.9	4.2
Fort Dodge	17.6	709	150	0.7	18.3	0.4	0.0	5.8	12.4	15.2	7.5	4.7	6.7
Iowa City	71.3	1 171	488	0.0	13.9	2.9	0.0	0.4	7.2	35.5	4.5	8.8	5.7
Marshalltown	19.4	766	247	0.1	15.9	0.3	0.0	0.2	15.8	29.5	5.8	4.6	4.3
Mason City	19.7	681	112	0.4	14.9	0.4	0.0	0.6	15.0	13.1	9.0	7.2	9.5
Sioux City	100.5	1 199	359	0.0	10.9	0.7	0.0	0.2	10.1	8.9	9.7	9.1	7.3
Waterloo	94.7	1 457	596	0.2	16.2	1.9	0.0	2.7	8.9	29.9	4.8	10.1	9.4
West Des Moines	37.1	918	276	0.9	25.4	0.0	0.0	2.9	12.0	10.8	8.9	6.1	7.3
KANSAS	X	X	X	X	X	X	X	X	X	X	X	X	X
Emporia	17.9	722	57	0.0	15.0	0.2	0.0	0.3	16.1	19.8	10.3	0.6	4.2
Hutchinson	28.1	720	26	0.0	8.3	0.0	0.0	0.7	14.3	17.6	7.6	0.0	3.7
Kansas City	209.0	1 465	116	0.0	6.2	0.2	0.0	2.0	13.5	6.1	1.7	2.5	44.9
Lawrence	98.2	1 366	213	0.2	4.7	0.4	0.0	53.3	7.9	6.7	4.5	7.5	2.8
Leavenworth	22.8	579	145	0.0	21.3	0.1	0.0	0.0	12.3	10.7	5.0	9.7	4.0
Lenexa	45.4	1 211	292	0.0	21.5	0.0	0.0	0.3	13.3	0.5	6.5	0.0	29.9
Manhattan	31.2	741	228	2.2	5.4	0.0	0.0	0.6	14.9	22.0	9.5	0.2	11.3
Olathe	68.9	876	178	0.0	14.3	0.0	0.0	0.1	12.8	13.8	4.3	0.6	22.6
Overland Park	85.9	655	185	0.7	30.6	0.0	0.0	0.7	20.2	0.0	10.9	0.2	4.1
Salina	37.0	837	265	0.0	6.4	0.0	0.0	1.1	9.3	9.8	8.5	0.7	5.3
Shawnee	27.7	644	210	0.3	32.1	0.0	0.0	0.0	19.0	8.1	6.1	0.0	16.6
Topeka	134.6	1 125	186	0.0	11.5	1.6	0.0	10.8	14.4	11.5	5.8	5.0	12.7
Wichita	340.7	1 063	381	2.4	19.7	0.0	0.0	2.2	11.5	13.0	6.6	5.1	9.0
KENTUCKY	X	X	X	X	X	X	X	X	X	X	X	X	X
Bowling Green	47.0	1 063	137	0.8	9.0	0.0	0.0	0.0	12.3	9.0	9.5	4.9	24.5
Covington	45.3	1 106	114	0.0	11.1	1.1	0.0	0.0	18.5	4.3	1.1	28.0	11.4
Frankfort	18.5	695	85	0.0	7.4	0.1	0.0	4.9	15.4	18.0	9.1	1.7	1.8
Henderson	20.2	763	112	1.7	6.8	0.0	0.0	0.0	14.1	24.2	7.4	7.8	5.4
Hopkinsville	19.5	689	24	0.0	8.2	0.0	0.0	0.0	14.3	17.7	2.8	9.9	16.2
Lexington-Fayette	204.1	NA	NA	2.7	9.5	0.0	0.0	0.0	15.6	1.2	5.1	1.6	7.9
Louisville	310.8	1 192	205	2.7	6.8	1.8	0.0	0.0	14.5	4.5	7.6	9.9	7.0
Owensboro	44.4	816	127	0.0	6.6	0.2	0.0	0.0	13.4	10.7	5.3	2.6	17.9
Paducah	34.8	1 306	132	0.0	9.7	0.0	0.0	0.0	14.4	18.4	4.3	15.4	1.3

1. Based on population estimated as of July 1 of the year shown.

Table D. Cities — City Government Finances, City Government Employment, and Climate

City	City government finances, 1997 (cont'd) Debt outstanding Total (mil dol)	Per capita[1] (dollars)	Percent utility	City government employment, 1999	Climate[2] Average daily temperature (degrees Fahrenheit) Mean January	July	Limits January[3]	July[4]	Annual precipitation (inches)	Heating degree days	Cooling degree days
	137	138	139	140	141	142	143	144	145	146	147
INDIANA—Cont'd											
Columbus	24.7	750	45.6	453	22.0	72.1	13.6	83.6	37.50	6 576	644
East Chicago	124.3	3 915	0.0	551	23.7	74.1	15.2	85.5	36.82	6 043	857
Elkhart	32.0	723	32.2	593	23.3	72.9	16.1	82.9	39.14	6 331	728
Evansville	54.9	445	1.7	1 231	30.1	78.4	21.2	89.1	43.14	4 708	1 376
Fort Wayne	81.4	440	24.4	1 852	22.9	74.0	15.3	84.6	34.75	6 273	824
Gary	94.9	855	0.0	1 998	23.7	74.1	15.2	85.5	36.82	6 043	857
Greenwood	16.8	549	0.0	NA	25.5	75.4	17.2	85.5	39.94	5 615	1 014
Hammond	56.7	708	0.0	1 358	23.7	74.1	15.2	85.5	36.82	6 043	857
Indianapolis	2 373.7	3 135	0.5	NA	NA	NA	NA	NA	NA	NA	NA
Kokomo	27.2	594	0.0	540	22.1	73.1	13.6	84.4	39.89	6 429	770
Lafayette	13.7	310	65.0	641	22.5	73.5	13.9	84.4	36.05	6 228	806
Lawrence	5.1	155	80.9	NA	25.5	75.4	17.2	85.5	39.94	5 615	1 014
Marion	16.0	534	59.8	410	23.1	73.3	14.7	84.4	37.56	6 260	760
Merrillville	1.8	58	0.0	NA	23.7	74.1	15.2	85.5	36.82	6 043	857
Michigan City	51.4	1 560	24.5	437	23.7	74.1	15.2	85.5	36.82	6 043	857
Mishawaka	35.5	789	2.7	540	23.3	72.9	16.1	82.9	39.14	6 331	728
Muncie	1.4	20	0.0	656	23.6	74.4	15.7	84.4	37.88	6 027	878
New Albany	19.5	511	0.0	NA	31.7	77.2	23.2	87.0	44.39	4 514	1 288
Portage	9.5	294	0.0	NA	23.7	74.1	15.2	85.5	36.82	6 043	857
Richmond	1.0	27	0.0	568	24.9	73.1	15.9	84.5	39.95	5 963	759
South Bend	60.0	588	7.5	1 669	23.3	72.9	16.1	82.9	39.14	6 331	728
Terre Haute	30.4	558	0.0	592	25.3	75.6	16.2	86.6	41.19	5 581	1 025
West Lafayette	0.0	0	0.0	NA	23.8	74.9	15.8	86.0	35.80	5 940	935
IOWA	X	X	X	X	X	X	X	X	X	X	X
Ames	95.2	1 997	20.8	567	18.2	74.2	8.8	85.3	32.94	6 776	816
Bettendorf	35.3	1 138	0.0	229	19.9	75.2	11.3	85.9	39.08	6 474	911
Burlington	21.6	805	8.7	255	21.8	75.7	13.1	85.8	36.06	6 158	992
Cedar Falls	43.6	1 250	18.5	667	14.6	73.1	5.4	83.9	33.70	7 406	702
Cedar Rapids	189.8	1 672	0.0	1 235	17.6	74.2	9.2	84.6	33.72	6 924	788
Clinton	57.1	2 016	0.0	236	20.3	75.1	11.3	86.1	35.21	6 324	941
Council Bluffs	79.4	1 430	5.3	454	21.1	76.9	10.9	87.9	29.86	6 300	1 072
Davenport	236.2	2 435	0.0	871	19.9	75.2	11.3	85.9	39.08	6 474	911
Des Moines	375.3	1 940	8.0	2 197	19.4	76.6	10.7	86.7	33.12	6 497	1 036
Dubuque	41.5	724	0.0	566	15.9	72.3	7.7	82.4	38.36	7 327	593
Fort Dodge	17.7	715	0.2	221	16.2	73.8	6.6	85.1	33.93	7 261	768
Iowa City	133.4	2 190	0.0	522	20.6	76.3	11.5	87.5	36.31	6 227	1 047
Marshalltown	25.8	1 021	0.0	206	16.9	73.3	7.2	84.8	34.43	7 170	695
Mason City	31.7	1 094	8.8	192	13.2	72.5	4.2	83.6	32.74	7 837	623
Sioux City	113.0	1 349	9.5	861	17.7	75.7	7.7	86.5	25.86	6 893	907
Waterloo	142.1	2 185	0.0	599	14.6	73.1	5.4	83.9	33.70	7 406	702
West Des Moines	65.6	1 624	19.9	311	19.4	76.6	10.7	86.7	33.12	6 497	1 036
KANSAS	X	X	X	X	X	X	X	X	X	X	X
Emporia	25.0	1 004	32.5	261	28.7	79.3	17.9	91.3	36.84	4 856	1 414
Hutchinson	25.5	653	24.1	381	28.1	80.7	16.4	93.6	29.22	5 103	1 489
Kansas City	1 369.4	9 599	0.0	2 896	25.7	78.5	16.7	88.7	37.62	5 393	1 288
Lawrence	80.7	1 123	6.3	1 281	29.2	80.3	19.2	91.3	39.28	4 734	1 565
Leavenworth	20.1	511	11.1	304	27.0	78.5	16.7	90.1	40.54	5 192	1 313
Lenexa	190.0	5 071	0.0	360	28.0	78.2	18.3	88.7	39.56	5 029	1 308
Manhattan	51.0	1 211	0.0	297	27.8	80.0	17.3	91.4	33.82	5 043	1 478
Olathe	282.3	3 589	8.2	684	28.0	78.2	18.3	88.7	39.56	5 029	1 308
Overland Park	59.9	457	0.0	669	28.0	78.2	18.3	88.7	39.56	5 029	1 308
Salina	72.1	1 631	48.4	529	28.1	80.9	17.6	92.6	29.82	5 101	1 534
Shawnee	79.1	1 840	0.0	193	28.0	78.2	18.3	88.7	39.56	5 029	1 308
Topeka	311.6	2 604	4.3	1 696	26.7	78.5	16.3	89.3	35.23	5 265	1 304
Wichita	634.8	1 981	5.1	3 178	29.5	81.4	19.2	92.8	29.33	4 791	1 628
KENTUCKY	X	X	X	X	X	X	X	X	X	X	X
Bowling Green	202.6	4 583	10.5	609	32.9	77.9	23.6	88.7	50.93	4 328	1 370
Covington	85.9	2 097	0.0	411	28.1	75.1	19.5	85.5	41.33	5 248	996
Frankfort	14.4	538	2.8	484	29.8	75.5	19.4	87.3	42.52	5 002	1 038
Henderson	118.5	4 479	89.0	431	32.2	77.8	23.4	88.6	44.80	4 323	1 393
Hopkinsville	55.0	1 941	29.4	378	32.0	77.7	22.1	89.5	50.79	4 437	1 365
Lexington-Fayette	358.2	NA	0.0	NA	30.8	75.8	22.4	85.8	44.55	4 783	1 140
Louisville	349.6	1 341	20.1	4 558	31.7	77.2	23.2	87.0	44.39	4 514	1 288
Owensboro	346.1	6 368	68.8	843	32.2	77.9	23.1	89.3	46.65	4 334	1 415
Paducah	23.7	892	61.8	554	32.6	78.8	23.5	89.0	49.31	4 279	1 475

1. Based on the population estimated as of July 1 of the year shown.   2. Represents normal values based on the 30-year period, 1961–1990.   3. Average daily minimum.   4. Average daily maximum.

Table D. Cities — Land Area and Population

STATE Place code	City	Land area, 1990[1] (sq km)	Population, 1999			Population				Population characteristics, 1990 — Percent						
										Race						
			Total persons	Rank	Per square kilo-meter	Total persons 1990	Percent change 1990–1999	Total persons 1980	Percent change 1980–1990	White	Black	Am. Indian, Eskimo, Aleut	Asian and Pacific Islander	Other race	His-panic[2]	Foreign born
		1	2	3	4	5	6	7	8	9	10	11	12	13	14	15
22 00000	LOUISIANA	112 836.0	4 372 035	X	39	4 221 826	3.6	4 206 116	0.3	67.3	30.8	0.4	1.0	0.5	2.2	2.1
22 00975	Alexandria	64.1	45 959	641	717	49 049	-6.3	51 565	-4.9	49.6	49.3	0.2	0.7	0.2	1.0	1.1
22 05000	Baton Rouge	191.5	210 667	80	1 100	219 531	-4.0	219 419	0.1	53.9	43.9	0.1	1.7	0.3	1.6	3.0
22 08920	Bossier City	98.5	56 413	501	573	52 721	7.0	50 861	3.7	79.3	18.1	0.4	1.5	0.7	2.6	2.5
22 36255	Houma	35.1	32 541	930	927	30 495	6.7	32 608	-6.5	71.0	25.0	3.0	0.8	0.2	1.4	0.8
22 39475	Kenner	39.2	71 567	360	1 826	72 033	-0.6	66 382	8.5	77.4	18.1	0.3	1.7	2.5	10.1	7.7
22 40735	Lafayette	106.0	116 806	182	1 102	101 865	14.7	81 961	24.3	70.8	27.2	0.2	1.3	0.5	1.7	2.7
22 41155	Lake Charles	83.1	72 173	357	869	70 580	2.3	75 226	-6.2	57.3	41.6	0.2	0.5	0.3	1.1	0.9
22 51410	Monroe	67.8	52 114	553	769	54 909	-5.1	57 597	-4.7	43.3	55.6	0.1	0.8	0.2	0.8	1.4
22 54035	New Iberia	26.3	33 317	913	1 267	31 828	4.7	32 766	-2.9	64.2	33.3	0.2	2.0	0.3	2.3	2.4
22 55000	New Orleans	467.9	460 913	32	985	496 938	-7.2	557 515	-10.9	34.9	61.9	0.2	1.9	1.1	3.5	4.2
22 70000	Shreveport	255.4	187 393	97	734	198 518	-5.6	205 776	-3.5	54.3	44.8	0.2	0.5	0.2	1.1	1.1
23 00000	MAINE	79 939.2	1 253 040	X	16	1 227 928	2.0	1 125 043	9.1	98.4	0.4	0.5	0.5	0.1	0.6	3.0
23 02795	Bangor	89.2	32 662	927	366	33 181	-1.6	31 643	4.9	97.1	0.9	0.7	1.0	0.2	0.6	3.4
23 38740	Lewiston	88.3	36 193	835	410	39 757	-9.0	40 481	-1.8	98.2	0.7	0.2	0.7	0.2	0.7	5.7
23 60545	Portland	58.6	61 925	435	1 057	64 157	-3.5	61 572	4.2	96.6	1.1	0.4	1.7	0.2	0.8	5.1
24 00000	MARYLAND	25 316.3	5 171 634	X	204	4 780 753	8.2	4 216 933	13.4	71.0	24.9	0.3	2.9	0.9	2.6	6.6
24 01600	Annapolis	16.4	33 125	916	2 020	33 195	-0.2	31 740	4.6	64.9	33.0	0.2	1.3	0.4	1.5	3.7
24 04000	Baltimore	209.3	632 681	16	3 023	736 014	-14.0	786 775	-6.5	39.1	59.2	0.3	1.1	0.3	1.0	3.2
24 08775	Bowie	33.3	41 091	727	1 234	37 642	9.2	33 695	11.7	91.4	5.7	0.3	2.3	0.4	2.2	4.9
24 30325	Frederick	47.1	48 710	600	1 034	40 186	21.2	28 086	43.1	84.3	12.8	0.3	1.9	0.7	2.1	3.3
24 31175	Gaithersburg	23.6	48 395	606	2 051	39 676	22.0	26 424	50.2	72.2	12.9	0.4	10.2	4.4	9.3	20.3
24 36075	Hagerstown	25.7	34 611	874	1 347	35 306	-2.0	34 132	3.4	92.5	6.3	0.1	0.7	0.3	0.8	1.3
24 67675	Rockville	31.4	48 160	611	1 534	44 830	7.4	43 811	2.3	79.2	8.3	0.3	9.8	2.5	8.6	22.0
25 00000	MASSACHUSETTS	20 300.3	6 175 169	X	304	6 016 425	2.6	5 737 093	4.9	89.8	5.0	0.2	2.4	2.6	4.8	9.5
25 02690	Attleboro	71.3	39 902	754	560	38 383	4.0	34 196	12.2	95.5	1.0	0.2	2.4	0.9	2.9	8.6
25 05595	Beverly	40.0	39 113	772	978	38 195	2.4	37 655	1.4	97.6	0.9	0.1	1.0	0.4	1.1	5.0
25 07000	Boston	125.4	555 249	21	4 428	574 283	-3.3	562 994	2.0	62.8	25.6	0.3	5.3	6.0	10.8	20.0
25 09000	Brockton	55.6	93 653	249	1 684	92 788	0.9	95 172	-2.5	80.2	13.0	0.3	1.7	4.8	6.3	11.2
25 11000	Cambridge	16.7	92 942	253	5 565	95 802	-3.0	95 322	0.5	75.3	13.5	0.3	8.4	2.5	6.8	22.3
25 13205	Chelsea	5.7	27 425	1 094	4 811	28 710	-4.5	25 431	12.9	69.7	5.2	0.3	5.0	19.8	31.4	21.8
25 13660	Chicopee	59.3	53 751	534	906	56 632	-5.1	55 112	2.8	95.4	1.8	0.1	0.6	2.1	3.6	6.5
25 21990	Everett	8.8	34 773	871	3 951	35 701	-2.6	37 195	-4.0	93.5	3.2	0.3	1.8	1.3	3.8	11.3
25 23000	Fall River	80.3	90 555	262	1 128	92 703	-2.3	92 574	0.1	97.2	1.0	0.1	1.3	0.4	1.7	20.7
25 23875	Fitchburg	71.9	40 407	743	562	41 194	-1.9	39 580	4.1	89.4	3.4	0.2	2.6	4.3	9.6	7.6
25 26150	Gloucester	67.3	29 744	1 018	442	28 716	3.6	27 717	3.6	99.3	0.2	0.1	0.3	0.1	0.9	6.1
25 29405	Haverhill	86.3	55 525	512	643	51 418	8.0	46 865	9.7	94.9	2.0	0.2	0.8	2.1	5.3	5.7
25 30840	Holyoke	55.1	40 677	737	738	43 704	-6.9	44 678	-2.2	73.1	3.6	0.2	0.8	22.3	31.1	5.6
25 34550	Lawrence	18.0	69 794	367	3 877	70 207	-0.6	63 175	11.1	65.0	6.4	0.5	1.9	26.2	41.6	20.9
25 35075	Leominster	74.8	40 358	744	540	38 145	5.8	34 508	10.5	93.1	2.3	0.2	1.6	2.8	8.3	7.6
25 37000	Lowell	35.7	101 103	219	2 832	103 439	-2.3	92 418	11.9	81.1	2.4	0.2	11.1	5.3	10.1	16.4
25 37490	Lynn	28.0	80 985	302	2 892	81 245	-0.3	78 471	3.5	83.1	8.1	0.3	3.7	4.9	9.1	13.8
25 37875	Malden	13.2	52 507	547	3 978	53 884	-2.6	53 386	0.9	89.4	4.2	0.2	5.2	1.0	2.6	13.6
25 38715	MarlBorough	54.6	33 408	908	612	31 813	5.0	30 617	3.9	94.8	1.8	0.2	1.9	1.3	4.2	8.9
25 39835	Medford	21.1	55 559	511	2 633	57 407	-3.2	58 076	-1.2	93.4	4.1	0.1	2.0	0.4	1.7	11.8
25 40115	Melrose	12.2	27 241	1 104	2 233	28 150	-3.2	30 055	-6.3	98.1	0.6	0.1	1.1	0.1	0.8	5.6
25 45000	New Bedford	52.2	94 780	242	1 816	99 922	-5.1	98 478	1.5	87.6	4.1	0.4	0.4	7.6	6.7	20.9
25 45560	Newton	46.8	80 143	309	1 712	82 585	-3.0	83 622	-1.2	92.8	2.1	0.1	4.6	0.5	2.0	13.0
25 46330	Northampton	89.3	28 412	1 055	318	29 289	-3.0	29 286	0.0	93.0	1.8	0.2	2.9	2.2	4.1	6.4
25 52490	Peabody	42.5	49 212	593	1 158	47 264	4.1	45 976	2.8	96.8	1.2	0.0	1.1	0.9	2.9	11.4
25 53960	Pittsfield	105.5	45 296	656	429	48 622	-6.8	51 974	-6.4	95.5	3.1	0.2	0.8	0.4	1.1	4.2
25 55777	Quincy	43.5	85 777	282	1 972	84 985	0.9	84 743	0.3	91.7	1.1	0.2	6.6	0.5	1.4	11.2
25 56585	Revere	15.3	41 747	713	2 729	42 786	-2.4	42 423	0.9	93.2	1.4	0.2	3.7	1.5	3.8	12.5
25 59105	Salem	21.0	38 341	789	1 826	38 091	0.7	38 220	-0.3	93.0	2.7	0.3	1.4	2.7	6.7	8.9
25 62535	Somerville	10.6	73 872	350	6 969	76 210	-3.1	77 372	-1.5	88.7	5.6	0.1	3.7	1.8	6.3	22.3
25 67000	Springfield	83.2	147 216	135	1 769	156 983	-6.2	152 319	3.1	68.6	19.2	0.2	1.0	11.0	16.9	7.4
25 69170	Taunton	120.7	53 107	540	440	49 832	6.6	45 001	10.7	95.3	2.0	0.2	0.5	2.1	4.7	11.7
25 72600	Waltham	32.9	58 634	473	1 782	57 878	1.3	58 200	-0.6	91.4	3.1	0.1	3.6	1.9	5.6	15.1
25 76030	Westfield	120.7	37 615	807	312	38 372	-2.0	36 465	5.2	96.5	0.9	0.1	0.8	1.7	4.1	4.1
25 81035	Woburn	32.8	37 419	810	1 141	35 943	4.1	36 626	-1.9	96.6	1.0	0.2	1.5	0.8	2.3	6.1
25 82000	Worcester	97.3	167 132	121	1 718	169 759	-1.5	161 799	4.9	87.1	4.5	0.3	2.8	5.3	9.6	8.9
26 00000	MICHIGAN	147 135.8	9 863 775	X	67	9 295 287	6.1	9 262 044	0.4	83.4	13.9	0.6	1.1	0.9	2.2	3.8
26 01380	Allen Park	18.2	31 401	966	1 725	31 092	1.0	34 196	-9.1	98.0	0.5	0.2	0.7	0.6	3.2	6.1
26 03000	Ann Arbor	67.1	109 750	203	1 636	109 608	0.1	107 960	1.5	82.0	9.0	0.4	7.7	0.9	2.6	10.9
26 05920	Battle Creek	110.9	53 699	535	484	53 516	0.3	35 724	49.8	80.7	16.5	0.6	1.3	0.8	1.8	2.3
26 06020	Bay City	26.9	34 800	870	1 294	38 936	-10.6	41 593	-6.4	93.6	2.4	0.8	0.4	2.7	5.6	0.9
26 12060	Burton	60.8	27 328	1 100	449	27 437	-0.4	29 976	-8.5	95.2	2.6	1.0	0.5	0.8	2.1	1.8

1. Dry land or land partially or temporarily covered by water.　2. Hispanic persons may be of any race.

Table D. Cities — **Population and Households**

City	Population characteristics, 1990 (cont'd) Age of population (percent)										Households, 1990			Percent	
	Under 5 years	5 to 17 years	18 to 24 years	25 to 34 years	35 to 44 years	45 to 54 years	55 to 64 years	65 to 74 years	75 years and over	Percent female	Number	Percent change, 1980–1990	Persons per house-hold	Female family house-holder[1]	One-person
	16	17	18	19	20	21	22	23	24	25	26	27	28	29	30
LOUISIANA	7.9	21.2	11.0	16.7	14.4	9.6	8.1	6.5	4.6	51.9	1 499 269	6.1	2.74	15.6	23.7
Alexandria	7.8	21.5	10.0	15.6	13.1	9.3	8.5	7.8	6.4	54.3	18 134	-1.3	2.63	21.1	28.0
Baton Rouge	7.1	17.8	16.4	16.5	13.8	9.2	7.8	7.0	4.5	52.7	83 340	5.9	2.51	17.7	29.7
Bossier City	8.8	20.3	11.2	19.1	14.1	9.8	7.9	5.6	3.3	51.7	19 032	13.4	2.67	13.8	22.4
Houma	8.5	22.7	9.1	16.8	14.3	9.0	8.0	7.4	4.3	52.4	10 658	-3.6	2.82	16.7	22.2
Kenner	8.1	21.7	10.6	18.3	17.5	10.6	6.9	3.8	2.7	51.8	25 056	19.6	2.85	14.0	21.8
Lafayette	7.5	19.1	13.6	18.1	14.8	9.2	8.2	5.9	3.6	51.9	36 326	26.4	2.50	13.8	28.9
Lake Charles	7.5	20.2	10.8	16.1	13.5	9.4	9.4	8.0	5.2	52.7	26 815	0.8	2.57	17.2	27.7
Monroe	8.8	21.9	14.9	14.2	12.1	7.1	7.6	7.0	6.4	54.8	19 131	-2.7	2.67	24.2	29.7
New Iberia	8.7	22.9	10.2	15.9	12.8	8.9	8.2	7.5	4.8	52.6	11 143	5.2	2.82	18.0	23.1
New Orleans	7.7	19.8	11.1	17.1	14.4	9.1	7.9	7.4	5.6	53.5	188 235	-9.1	2.55	24.1	32.2
Shreveport	7.9	20.6	9.6	15.9	14.2	9.4	8.6	7.7	6.0	53.9	75 645	1.4	2.57	19.9	28.7
MAINE	7.0	18.2	10.1	16.7	15.7	10.2	8.8	7.5	5.8	51.3	465 312	17.7	2.56	9.5	23.3
Bangor	7.2	14.8	14.0	19.1	14.1	9.3	7.9	7.0	6.7	53.1	13 392	14.1	2.31	12.7	31.1
Lewiston	7.0	15.5	14.1	15.7	12.4	9.5	9.4	9.0	7.4	52.9	15 823	5.9	2.37	12.6	29.7
Portland	6.7	13.1	12.8	21.7	14.8	8.2	7.7	7.6	7.4	53.5	28 235	10.9	2.21	12.2	35.3
MARYLAND	7.5	16.8	10.6	18.8	16.3	10.9	8.3	6.6	4.2	51.5	1 748 991	19.7	2.67	13.3	22.6
Annapolis	6.8	14.6	10.7	20.0	15.4	11.6	8.7	7.2	5.0	53.5	14 061	12.6	2.33	16.7	31.8
Baltimore	7.7	16.7	11.1	18.8	14.1	9.5	8.4	7.9	5.7	53.3	276 484	-1.9	2.59	24.6	30.5
Bowie	7.6	16.4	9.8	20.5	15.7	13.8	9.9	4.9	1.4	49.9	12 891	35.8	2.92	8.0	12.7
Frederick	8.5	15.4	12.5	21.8	15.1	8.4	6.4	6.3	5.7	53.2	15 671	48.2	2.45	12.4	27.3
Gaithersburg	9.1	15.4	10.7	26.4	16.9	10.3	4.7	3.0	3.5	51.6	15 202	47.7	2.57	11.6	25.7
Hagerstown	8.2	15.2	10.8	18.6	13.6	8.8	8.7	9.1	6.9	53.9	15 063	7.7	2.30	14.4	32.3
Rockville	6.7	16.3	9.2	18.4	17.5	12.3	9.2	6.3	4.1	50.8	15 660	8.2	2.77	9.9	20.0
MASSACHUSETTS	6.9	15.6	11.8	18.3	15.3	10.0	8.6	7.6	6.0	52.0	2 247 110	10.6	2.58	12.1	25.8
Attleboro	8.8	16.3	10.0	20.7	13.9	10.2	8.2	7.0	5.0	51.2	14 180	19.5	2.66	10.6	23.1
Beverly	6.9	14.4	10.7	18.5	15.7	9.8	9.0	8.3	6.7	53.2	14 796	7.7	2.48	11.2	26.7
Boston	6.2	12.8	17.3	23.2	13.6	8.2	7.1	6.3	5.2	51.9	228 464	4.3	2.37	16.8	35.5
Brockton	8.4	17.9	11.1	18.5	14.1	9.7	7.9	6.7	5.7	51.9	32 850	-0.6	2.76	17.4	24.6
Cambridge	4.8	9.3	19.6	25.1	16.0	8.8	6.0	5.8	4.6	51.4	39 405	1.2	2.08	10.7	42.3
Chelsea	9.1	16.7	11.8	21.3	11.9	7.6	8.2	7.5	5.9	51.1	10 553	2.3	2.65	20.7	30.4
Chicopee	6.3	15.5	10.9	17.0	13.4	9.7	10.0	10.7	6.5	52.6	22 625	11.2	2.44	13.4	28.3
Everett	6.7	12.8	10.8	20.5	13.3	9.1	10.2	9.1	7.5	53.5	14 528	3.3	2.43	14.8	29.7
Fall River	7.4	16.8	11.3	16.9	11.7	9.0	8.8	10.2	8.0	53.8	37 303	7.0	2.44	14.8	30.1
Fitchburg	8.0	16.0	14.3	18.1	12.3	7.8	8.0	8.3	7.2	52.6	15 363	7.6	2.54	14.0	27.6
Gloucester	6.6	14.8	9.1	17.0	17.0	10.0	10.2	8.5	6.9	51.8	11 579	10.2	2.46	11.2	28.2
Haverhill	8.4	15.6	10.4	21.5	13.7	9.2	7.1	7.5	6.7	52.3	19 575	13.6	2.55	12.8	25.8
Holyoke	9.3	19.3	10.5	16.0	11.4	8.7	7.8	8.6	8.4	53.8	15 850	-4.3	2.65	23.0	28.2
Lawrence	9.9	21.8	11.0	18.4	12.6	7.5	6.3	6.8	5.6	52.2	24 270	2.1	2.83	24.2	26.2
Leominster	7.6	15.5	10.2	20.7	14.6	9.9	8.5	7.5	5.5	51.7	14 834	17.9	2.54	10.4	24.5
Lowell	8.6	17.6	14.1	20.5	12.1	7.6	7.2	7.1	5.1	51.3	37 019	13.3	2.68	17.0	27.5
Lynn	8.2	16.4	10.4	19.0	13.9	9.0	8.2	8.2	6.8	52.2	31 554	3.3	2.53	16.9	31.1
Malden	6.7	12.8	11.1	22.1	14.2	8.9	8.9	8.3	7.1	52.7	21 921	5.9	2.43	12.4	31.1
MarlBorough	7.7	14.4	10.4	22.4	16.7	9.6	7.3	6.5	4.9	50.8	12 152	11.5	2.55	10.0	25.1
Medford	5.5	11.9	13.6	19.6	13.6	9.2	9.7	9.2	7.6	53.4	21 829	8.3	2.54	12.2	26.0
Melrose	6.1	14.7	9.1	16.9	16.6	10.8	9.1	8.4	8.4	53.7	10 941	3.0	2.54	10.0	27.7
New Bedford	7.5	17.5	10.4	16.8	12.4	8.9	9.2	9.6	7.8	53.1	38 788	3.8	2.51	17.1	28.1
Newton	5.5	13.1	13.5	16.5	16.6	10.9	8.9	7.9	7.1	53.9	29 455	3.9	2.60	9.0	22.4
Northampton	4.7	12.8	17.3	17.7	17.4	8.0	7.3	7.5	7.2	56.3	11 164	9.1	2.28	10.5	33.5
Peabody	6.3	15.1	9.2	17.7	15.2	11.1	11.1	8.8	5.4	52.0	17 556	11.6	2.65	10.8	22.4
Pittsfield	6.8	15.9	9.5	16.8	14.3	9.5	9.9	9.7	7.6	52.5	19 916	2.4	2.41	12.7	29.1
Quincy	5.8	10.9	12.2	21.8	13.3	10.0	9.3	9.1	7.6	53.5	35 678	6.1	2.34	12.1	33.6
Revere	6.0	12.6	10.8	18.7	13.6	10.3	10.8	9.7	7.4	51.7	17 438	6.2	2.43	13.6	29.9
Salem	6.5	12.1	13.1	21.7	14.3	8.9	8.3	8.5	6.7	53.7	15 806	5.3	2.34	12.7	31.6
Somerville	5.0	10.2	16.8	26.6	13.8	7.7	7.7	6.8	5.4	52.2	30 319	2.3	2.44	12.3	30.1
Springfield	8.5	18.5	12.2	18.2	13.0	8.3	7.6	7.9	5.8	52.9	57 769	4.7	2.60	21.2	27.8
Taunton	7.5	16.9	10.2	19.4	14.6	9.2	8.2	8.2	6.0	52.2	18 849	20.2	2.59	13.5	24.9
Waltham	4.9	10.6	19.4	20.9	13.8	8.5	8.6	7.3	5.9	51.5	20 728	0.6	2.42	10.6	30.4
Westfield	6.8	16.2	14.7	16.2	14.6	9.9	8.0	8.2	5.6	52.4	13 823	11.4	2.60	11.4	23.7
Woburn	6.5	14.4	10.8	21.7	14.6	9.9	10.5	8.1	4.5	51.3	13 485	9.5	2.54	11.5	24.4
Worcester	7.2	15.1	14.8	18.6	12.2	8.0	8.0	8.6	7.4	52.4	63 884	8.6	2.46	15.7	30.1
MICHIGAN	7.6	18.9	10.8	16.9	15.1	10.2	8.5	7.1	4.9	51.5	3 419 331	6.9	2.66	12.9	23.7
Allen Park	6.0	14.8	7.3	16.2	14.4	9.9	11.4	13.1	6.9	51.9	12 030	-0.2	2.55	9.2	23.5
Ann Arbor	5.7	11.4	27.1	20.9	14.8	7.4	5.4	4.1	3.2	50.5	41 657	6.5	2.32	8.1	31.4
Battle Creek	8.4	19.3	8.9	16.7	14.9	9.2	8.3	7.9	6.5	53.0	21 457	52.5	2.45	16.4	29.3
Bay City	7.7	18.4	10.1	17.3	14.4	8.5	8.4	8.9	6.4	52.5	15 570	0.0	2.48	14.4	29.9
Burton	7.4	19.5	9.8	17.5	14.3	11.1	9.4	7.1	3.9	51.8	10 447	1.0	2.64	14.2	22.4

1. No spouse present.

City	Persons in group quarters, 1990				Serious crimes known to police, 1998[2]				Education, 1990				Money income, 1989		
					Total		Rate[3]		School enrollment		Attainment[4] (percent)			Households	
														Median	
	Total	Persons in mental hospitals	Persons in nursing homes	Persons identified as homeless[1]	Number	Rate[3]	Violent	Property	Public	Private	High school graduate or more	Bachelor's degree or more	Per capita (dollars)[5]	Dollars	Percent change, 1979–1989 (constant 1989 dollars)
	31	32	33	34	35	36	37	38	39	40	41	42	43	44	45
LOUISIANA	112 452	1 728	32 072	1 795	266 435	6 098	780	5 318	979 200	206 559	68.3	16.1	10 635	21 949	-14.0
Alexandria	1 542	0	701	38	5 341	11 510	1 289	10 221	11 442	1 664	68.6	18.4	10 887	18 546	-7.9
Baton Rouge	10 699	0	1 508	126	24 291	11 235	1 153	10 082	58 990	11 453	76.8	28.3	12 398	21 898	-13.8
Bossier City	1 801	0	513	9	3 815	6 762	892	5 870	13 180	1 207	81.4	15.9	11 326	25 918	-5.6
Houma	419	37	120	65	2 959	9 653	1 592	8 061	7 138	1 211	62.6	12.6	9 790	19 397	-35.0
Kenner	554	0	554	0	4 574	6 330	643	5 687	13 205	7 665	77.5	21.3	12 884	30 389	-12.2
Lafayette	3 480	100	672	54	8 806	8 243	853	7 390	24 506	4 497	75.2	27.3	12 925	23 430	-17.3
Lake Charles	1 601	64	511	17	5 562	7 721	923	6 798	17 200	2 627	69.4	18.4	11 475	21 225	-24.8
Monroe	3 914	0	756	33	7 986	14 551	2 270	12 281	16 657	1 650	68.7	23.7	10 037	16 223	-7.5
New Iberia	413	0	314	0	825	2 508	207	2 301	7 560	966	57.1	9.9	8 740	18 506	-31.3
New Orleans	16 942	23	3 084	888	40 811	8 662	1 462	7 200	104 217	42 298	68.1	22.4	11 372	18 477	-6.7
Shreveport	3 813	0	2 308	202	NA	NA	NA	NA	49 670	5 988	74.1	19.6	11 663	22 079	-12.4
MAINE	37 222	805	9 855	476	37 826	3 041	126	2 915	267 445	37 423	78.8	18.8	12 957	27 854	20.3
Bangor	2 327	299	391	51	2 139	6 776	196	6 580	7 145	1 616	83.5	24.4	13 418	24 674	16.5
Lewiston	2 319	0	723	62	1 814	4 943	174	4 769	6 752	2 842	63.7	9.7	12 277	24 051	16.2
Portland	2 086	0	728	244	3 657	5 751	530	5 221	11 762	2 375	83.2	29.6	14 914	26 576	29.9
MARYLAND	113 272	3 049	26 884	3 061	275 527	5 366	797	4 569	982 507	229 826	78.4	26.5	17 730	39 386	15.9
Annapolis	412	0	80	0	2 904	8 580	1 690	6 890	6 147	1 899	80.2	32.8	18 358	35 516	19.8
Baltimore	20 538	55	5 266	1 478	72 498	10 947	2 420	8 527	142 587	38 971	60.7	15.5	11 994	24 045	12.0
Bowie	5	0	0	5	NA	NA	NA	NA	7 605	2 319	92.4	37.6	21 876	59 622	9.9
Frederick	1 671	0	761	30	2 475	5 200	1 034	4 166	7 673	1 684	77.9	24.0	15 410	34 891	18.7
Gaithersburg	473	0	459	14	NA	NA	NA	NA	8 554	1 316	86.7	39.6	18 845	43 644	23.3
Hagerstown	769	9	335	65	1 870	5 320	740	4 580	6 230	599	65.0	9.9	11 742	22 859	9.1
Rockville	1 507	98	576	138	NA	NA	NA	NA	9 056	2 437	86.4	45.4	21 484	52 073	11.4
MASSACHUSETTS	214 886	3 386	55 662	7 128	211 203	3 436	621	2 815	1 100 827	429 307	80.0	27.2	17 224	36 952	25.4
Attleboro	623	34	436	30	NA	NA	NA	NA	6 703	2 078	75.3	20.2	14 970	36 631	23.0
Beverly	1 506	0	448	60	837	2 144	64	2 080	6 747	2 776	87.1	28.0	18 436	39 603	25.9
Boston	33 003	166	5 129	2 716	34 981	6 251	1 327	4 924	87 567	78 941	75.7	30.0	15 581	29 180	39.0
Brockton	2 308	127	1 136	367	5 094	5 428	1 112	4 316	19 297	3 424	74.4	12.9	13 455	31 712	23.6
Cambridge	14 172	0	682	302	4 362	4 616	634	3 982	10 994	23 172	84.4	54.2	19 879	33 140	39.1
Chelsea	690	0	586	0	NA	NA	NA	NA	4 867	1 899	63.2	12.0	11 559	25 144	33.9
Chicopee	1 326	0	410	0	NA	NA	NA	NA	9 156	3 376	66.3	10.4	13 525	28 905	11.6
Everett	393	0	211	0	1 137	3 220	748	2 472	5 369	2 151	72.9	11.3	14 220	30 786	17.9
Fall River	1 733	16	1 217	66	4 012	4 381	702	3 679	17 693	3 208	46.7	8.4	10 966	22 452	16.4
Fitchburg	2 225	6	608	40	2 475	6 125	1 703	4 422	8 714	1 671	68.8	13.1	12 140	27 101	14.4
Gloucester	239	0	141	49	623	2 104	277	1 827	4 850	1 075	75.6	20.4	16 044	32 690	24.7
Haverhill	1 446	0	881	70	2 408	4 413	590	3 823	9 533	2 324	78.0	21.0	15 464	36 945	46.5
Holyoke	1 646	0	1 166	76	NA	NA	NA	NA	8 634	2 083	68.0	15.2	11 088	22 858	10.4
Lawrence	1 543	0	596	81	2 439	3 504	881	2 623	15 852	3 437	57.0	9.7	9 686	22 183	10.5
Leominster	431	0	284	12	1 394	3 501	266	3 235	6 801	1 958	75.2	19.3	15 960	35 974	29.7
Lowell	4 090	65	1 214	152	4 005	3 933	1 021	2 912	23 926	5 033	65.8	15.5	12 701	29 351	21.5
Lynn	1 408	0	817	355	4 817	5 911	1 140	4 771	15 162	3 558	73.2	14.3	13 026	28 553	18.6
Malden	683	0	365	115	756	1 421	380	1 041	8 111	3 760	77.9	20.1	15 820	34 344	28.6
Marlborough	831	0	449	50	761	2 288	144	2 144	5 418	1 396	83.0	26.6	18 471	41 315	28.3
Medford	1 970	0	248	25	1 464	2 583	206	2 377	7 219	5 878	79.0	23.7	16 941	38 859	26.9
Melrose	320	0	320	0	442	1 598	58	1 540	4 722	1 494	87.7	31.4	20 202	44 109	24.5
New Bedford	2 363	16	1 206	82	3 926	4 020	1 040	2 980	19 739	2 854	49.7	9.7	10 923	22 647	16.1
Newton	6 013	0	832	120	1 336	1 651	89	1 562	11 272	11 642	91.7	57.2	28 840	59 719	33.6
Northampton	3 838	267	719	49	763	2 624	399	2 225	5 383	3 457	81.9	32.9	14 623	31 097	24.8
Peabody	526	0	376	103	1 531	3 129	131	2 998	7 650	2 813	79.2	20.9	17 002	39 800	14.8
Pittsfield	622	0	338	17	1 506	3 248	203	3 045	9 230	1 636	78.1	11.9	15 426	29 987	12.9
Quincy	1 528	21	564	70	2 669	3 096	283	2 813	11 658	6 183	82.7	23.2	17 436	35 858	23.1
Revere	356	0	242	114	NA	NA	NA	NA	6 255	2 076	73.9	12.3	14 723	30 659	20.7
Salem	1 157	0	45	85	1 306	3 397	107	3 290	6 835	1 756	78.2	24.5	16 155	32 645	28.6
Somerville	2 243	43	307	62	2 303	3 070	375	2 695	9 543	9 759	75.2	30.9	15 179	32 455	34.5
Springfield	6 842	36	1 490	380	12 072	8 021	2 728	5 293	31 044	11 959	69.6	15.0	11 584	25 656	15.0
Taunton	899	336	313	0	1 650	3 152	449	2 703	9 135	1 732	66.8	12.1	13 613	32 315	22.8
Waltham	7 677	440	618	89	1 349	2 338	213	2 125	7 457	8 422	79.0	26.5	16 777	38 514	23.4
Westfield	2 367	0	349	44	1 130	2 999	709	2 290	9 515	1 445	78.7	19.3	14 225	33 498	11.1
Woburn	173	0	162	0	553	1 497	92	1 405	6 176	1 901	86.4	23.7	18 155	42 679	23.4
Worcester	12 660	263	3 013	517	10 152	6 018	1 093	4 925	30 317	15 786	72.9	21.1	13 393	28 955	22.4
MICHIGAN	210 686	4 747	57 622	4 458	459 720	4 683	621	4 062	2 242 239	338 803	76.8	17.4	14 154	31 020	-3.7
Allen Park	425	104	213	0	955	3 040	223	2 817	5 507	1 776	78.7	16.5	17 013	39 925	-11.4
Ann Arbor	12 621	0	522	189	4 372	3 952	421	3 531	45 196	4 204	93.9	64.2	17 786	33 344	8.6
Battle Creek	800	0	438	159	NA	NA	NA	NA	12 557	1 335	76.6	15.8	12 963	25 306	13.7
Bay City	360	0	21	25	1 979	5 404	560	4 844	8 932	1 529	70.0	9.4	10 782	21 380	-18.0
Burton	0	0	0	0	2 187	7 961	641	7 320	6 743	674	72.7	6.7	12 940	29 961	-14.6

1. Persons in emergency shelters and persons visible in street locations.   2. Data for serious crimes have not been adjusted for underreporting. This may affect comparability between geographic areas and over time.   3. Per 100,000 population estimated by the FBI.   4. Persons 25 years old and older.   5. Based on population enumerated as of April 1, 1990.

Table D. Cities — Income, Poverty, and Housing

City	Money income, 1989 (cont'd) — Households (cont'd) — Percent with $100,000 or more	Percent below poverty, 1989 — Persons — Total	Persons — Percent change in rate, 1979–1989	Families — Total	Housing units, 1990 — Total	Percent change, 1980–1990	Vacant units for sale or rent[1]	Occupied units — Total	Owner-occupied units — Percent	Median value[2] (dollars)	Owner cost as a percent of income — With a mortgage	Without a mortgage	Renter-occupied units — Median rent[3] (dollars)	Rent as percent of income	Substandard units[4] (percent)
	46	47	48	49	50	51	52	53	54	55	56	57	58	59	60
LOUISIANA	2.4	23.6	26.8	19.4	1 716 241	10.8	120 665	1 499 269	65.9	58 500	20.6	13.3	352	27.9	6.5
Alexandria	3.3	28.8	19.0	24.0	20 348	3.6	1 543	18 134	56.6	54 300	19.3	14.0	332	30.6	5.7
Baton Rouge	4.0	26.2	40.1	20.3	97 115	15.5	9 376	83 340	52.8	67 900	18.2	12.5	354	28.5	5.3
Bossier City	1.4	16.0	37.9	12.8	21 815	21.5	1 971	19 032	57.4	58 400	20.1	12.0	376	26.6	4.3
Houma	2.3	26.4	52.6	22.0	11 476	-0.5	647	10 658	64.5	53 700	20.9	13.0	319	28.6	7.8
Kenner	3.5	14.2	44.9	12.2	27 259	22.2	1 721	25 056	58.8	74 200	22.0	11.9	449	26.6	5.3
Lafayette	4.1	21.9	42.2	17.0	40 379	35.3	2 824	36 326	53.3	66 000	18.0	13.1	333	24.2	4.7
Lake Charles	2.8	23.6	54.2	20.3	29 844	6.0	2 178	26 815	58.4	52 200	18.5	13.1	339	27.3	4.5
Monroe	3.3	37.8	27.7	31.6	21 610	2.3	1 707	19 131	51.9	50 100	22.3	13.0	300	30.5	9.0
New Iberia	1.6	28.7	72.9	23.6	12 426	10.0	866	11 143	61.1	46 700	19.4	13.3	291	27.2	8.8
New Orleans	3.6	31.6	19.7	27.3	225 573	-0.4	26 583	188 235	43.7	69 600	23.2	14.2	379	31.2	8.5
Shreveport	3.0	25.3	42.9	20.2	87 473	9.3	8 730	75 645	60.5	54 800	20.7	13.5	351	28.1	5.2
MAINE	2.4	10.8	-16.9	8.0	587 045	17.2	22 097	465 312	70.5	87 400	21.4	13.4	419	26.8	3.1
Bangor	3.5	15.0	2.7	11.5	14 366	12.3	719	13 392	48.5	76 800	18.8	14.2	411	26.5	1.8
Lewiston	2.0	13.9	4.5	11.0	17 118	7.9	1 126	15 823	47.0	87 200	20.6	14.3	361	25.8	1.6
Portland	2.9	14.0	-9.1	10.6	31 293	11.9	1 764	28 235	42.1	112 200	23.2	14.9	504	28.1	1.7
MARYLAND	6.9	8.3	-15.6	6.0	1 891 917	20.4	77 134	1 748 991	65.0	116 500	21.1	12.4	548	25.4	3.3
Annapolis	6.3	12.1	-21.4	9.9	15 252	14.0	647	14 061	47.8	138 500	21.0	13.3	602	27.1	2.2
Baltimore	2.4	21.9	-4.4	17.8	303 706	0.3	19 025	276 484	48.6	54 700	19.4	13.7	413	27.3	4.9
Bowie	10.0	1.1	-35.3	0.5	13 066	36.6	139	12 891	84.2	143 200	20.3	11.5	960	24.4	0.6
Frederick	2.4	8.0	-22.3	6.1	16 611	47.1	754	15 671	45.5	113 400	22.1	13.0	582	25.5	2.3
Gaithersburg	5.7	6.0	-6.3	5.1	16 059	48.3	781	15 202	49.6	147 300	22.8	11.1	678	26.4	5.4
Hagerstown	1.1	15.8	-1.9	13.1	16 361	10.3	949	15 063	41.2	68 200	18.9	13.8	330	22.8	1.5
Rockville	14.3	5.8	18.4	3.7	16 238	9.1	480	15 660	66.2	180 900	20.7	11.4	798	28.1	4.4
MASSACHUSETTS	6.7	8.9	-6.9	6.7	2 472 711	12.0	103 550	2 247 110	59.3	162 800	22.3	13.8	580	26.8	2.7
Attleboro	2.9	6.4	-8.6	4.3	15 045	20.3	631	14 180	61.3	143 200	23.4	13.4	538	25.9	2.7
Beverly	7.1	6.6	-9.6	5.3	15 652	11.1	667	14 796	58.9	177 200	22.0	13.1	640	27.6	1.0
Boston	4.8	18.7	-7.4	15.0	250 863	3.9	17 557	228 464	30.9	161 400	22.6	14.1	625	28.4	7.0
Brockton	3.1	13.6	7.9	11.7	35 376	1.9	2 049	32 850	53.3	131 700	22.9	15.0	571	29.3	4.5
Cambridge	7.8	10.7	-29.1	7.2	41 979	1.6	1 518	39 405	30.3	263 800	21.3	13.8	538	24.3	4.3
Chelsea	2.3	24.1	12.6	22.9	11 574	10.5	865	10 553	28.1	142 000	24.6	14.5	594	29.2	10.0
Chicopee	1.6	9.8	11.4	8.1	23 690	12.3	765	22 625	58.1	113 800	20.3	13.9	452	24.1	2.0
Everett	2.0	9.6	-7.7	8.2	15 416	5.1	679	14 528	41.3	156 100	24.2	13.7	611	25.1	2.5
Fall River	0.9	14.3	-3.4	12.3	40 375	9.1	2 434	37 303	33.0	127 800	21.8	14.1	351	24.5	2.6
Fitchburg	1.8	14.0	8.5	11.7	16 665	8.6	934	15 363	48.3	124 000	22.3	14.1	521	27.4	3.8
Gloucester	5.3	7.5	-23.5	6.8	13 125	9.0	555	11 579	57.8	177 100	25.7	15.9	571	26.4	1.4
Haverhill	3.3	8.8	-16.2	7.4	21 321	15.1	1 405	19 575	58.6	140 100	24.5	14.0	586	27.4	1.4
Holyoke	2.2	25.7	33.2	22.9	16 917	-6.1	883	15 850	38.9	116 800	19.2	12.2	436	28.5	7.1
Lawrence	1.1	27.5	42.5	25.6	26 915	3.6	2 230	24 270	32.0	129 600	23.7	15.1	559	31.6	11.3
Leominster	3.7	7.2	-22.6	5.8	15 533	19.6	541	14 834	57.6	137 200	22.6	13.9	524	24.8	3.0
Lowell	2.4	18.0	33.3	15.1	40 302	15.5	2 733	37 019	41.9	131 100	22.3	13.7	561	28.4	7.2
Lynn	1.8	15.9	15.2	13.9	34 670	6.3	2 614	31 554	46.2	139 200	24.3	14.9	574	29.4	5.3
Malden	2.7	7.5	-20.2	5.5	23 217	8.2	1 054	21 921	43.2	162 900	22.1	14.7	651	26.7	2.7
Marlborough	7.0	5.7	-21.9	4.3	13 027	13.2	749	12 152	58.2	166 300	22.2	12.8	705	26.1	1.9
Medford	5.3	6.9	-9.2	4.9	22 650	9.7	596	21 829	57.1	182 400	23.1	14.1	665	25.4	1.3
Melrose	8.0	4.2	-6.7	2.9	11 297	3.0	280	10 941	65.4	196 100	21.5	13.2	628	25.7	1.1
New Bedford	1.0	16.8	3.7	14.6	41 760	5.7	2 178	38 788	43.8	115 900	22.3	14.5	404	27.2	3.5
Newton	23.8	4.3	-25.9	2.3	30 497	4.7	673	29 455	68.9	293 400	20.9	13.1	884	25.2	1.1
Northampton	3.0	11.5	-9.4	6.9	11 747	10.2	355	11 164	50.9	132 900	21.0	13.6	530	24.9	2.7
Peabody	5.6	4.6	-22.0	3.8	18 240	12.3	532	17 556	70.4	177 100	21.9	14.3	603	26.4	1.2
Pittsfield	3.3	9.7	-5.8	7.8	21 272	3.8	857	19 916	59.6	111 100	20.8	13.1	461	26.6	1.1
Quincy	4.5	6.8	-17.1	5.3	37 732	9.8	1 572	35 678	48.8	161 100	21.1	14.2	657	26.4	2.2
Revere	3.1	11.6	9.4	8.6	18 726	9.0	1 055	17 438	48.9	160 500	24.8	16.1	620	31.1	2.8
Salem	4.1	11.7	11.4	9.6	17 161	8.1	1 129	15 806	46.0	163 600	24.2	14.2	608	27.2	2.7
Somerville	3.2	11.5	-7.3	7.6	31 786	2.7	1 137	30 319	31.0	165 800	21.6	15.4	677	27.2	3.7
Springfield	1.5	20.1	12.9	17.7	61 320	4.5	2 833	57 769	49.4	105 500	21.3	13.5	495	29.5	4.7
Taunton	1.8	8.3	-21.0	6.7	20 281	20.9	1 105	18 849	57.7	138 900	22.3	13.5	523	26.4	2.6
Waltham	5.5	6.5	-19.8	4.2	21 723	2.4	823	20 728	45.9	191 100	21.0	13.0	707	25.3	3.0
Westfield	2.9	8.0	2.6	7.2	14 470	11.3	465	13 823	65.4	136 000	21.1	13.8	529	27.5	1.5
Woburn	6.2	5.1	-12.1	4.5	14 105	10.9	494	13 485	61.1	172 600	22.0	12.6	710	24.0	1.4
Worcester	2.6	15.3	6.3	12.2	69 336	12.5	4 116	63 884	43.3	128 900	21.2	13.7	527	26.9	3.4
MICHIGAN	3.8	13.1	26.1	10.2	3 847 926	7.2	134 958	3 419 331	71.0	60 600	18.0	13.5	423	27.2	2.9
Allen Park	3.8	3.3	57.1	2.2	12 233	0.8	164	12 030	87.2	67 400	15.9	13.8	492	25.1	1.5
Ann Arbor	7.8	16.1	9.5	6.0	44 010	9.6	2 051	41 657	43.2	116 400	20.4	12.9	568	30.0	2.6
Battle Creek	2.3	18.3	2.2	14.1	23 252	54.0	1 151	21 457	62.9	39 300	16.9	13.8	381	30.3	2.2
Bay City	0.9	18.1	37.1	14.8	16 372	0.3	527	15 570	67.5	32 600	17.3	14.3	312	29.2	2.0
Burton	1.6	14.3	60.7	11.0	10 840	1.9	278	10 447	76.1	44 400	16.2	13.6	388	32.4	2.9

1. Includes units rented or sold but not occupied.　2. Specified owner-occupied units.　3. Specified renter-occupied units.　4. Overcrowded or lacking complete plumbing facilities.

Table D. Cities — Labor Force, Employment, Disability, and Construction

City	Civilian labor force, 1999				Civilian employment, 1990[2]			Disability 1990	Value of residential construction authorized by building permits, 1999		
			Unemployment			Percent					
	Total	Percent change, 1998–1999	Total	Rate[1]	Total	Professional, managerial, and technical	Precision production, craft, and repair	Work disabled persons[3] (percent)	New construction ($1,000)	Number of housing units	Percent single family
	61	62	63	64	65	66	67	68	69	70	71
LOUISIANA	2 051 621	-0.6	103 966	5.1	1 641 614	28.1	12.5	10.3	1 766 666	17 836	81.6
Alexandria	22 768	2.8	1 378	6.1	17 726	32.6	7.7	12.4	10 776	81	100.0
Baton Rouge	120 195	1.4	5 089	4.2	95 679	35.6	8.1	7.6	33 491	414	74.6
Bossier City	28 206	0.1	1 272	4.5	21 090	28.6	11.1	8.0	33 756	259	100.0
Houma	15 107	-3.4	685	4.5	10 860	27.2	13.2	14.2	NA	NA	NA
Kenner	39 424	-0.9	1 498	3.8	34 952	30.8	11.0	7.5	15 857	90	91.1
Lafayette	56 974	-1.9	2 807	4.9	41 441	37.2	8.8	8.6	NA	NA	NA
Lake Charles	38 282	0.1	2 269	5.9	27 620	29.4	12.7	10.7	48 560	800	14.8
Monroe	24 101	0.1	1 331	5.5	19 247	34.2	5.9	8.9	6 742	52	80.8
New Iberia	15 177	-4.6	1 483	9.8	11 288	21.0	15.8	11.9	4 780	33	100.0
New Orleans	198 011	-2.3	10 003	5.1	186 036	34.1	7.0	10.7	122 234	1 151	32.1
Shreveport	95 213	-2.1	4 531	4.8	78 900	30.4	9.3	9.1	57 841	408	88.2
MAINE	671 973	3.2	27 549	4.1	571 842	27.8	13.4	10.2	623 269	5 695	94.5
Bangor	17 916	2.5	535	3.0	16 086	35.1	9.0	10.3	2 958	45	28.9
Lewiston	21 363	3.0	798	3.7	18 827	21.5	13.2	12.4	2 135	18	100.0
Portland	36 682	0.1	935	2.5	33 378	35.1	8.1	9.7	11 187	115	80.9
MARYLAND	2 765 644	0.3	97 909	3.5	2 481 342	37.0	10.3	7.0	3 102 361	29 757	81.2
Annapolis	21 164	0.9	1 042	4.9	18 188	40.2	7.3	7.9	7 517	100	92.0
Baltimore	295 128	-2.9	21 069	7.1	314 688	27.6	9.3	11.7	13 396	191	24.1
Bowie	23 918	0.7	460	1.9	22 649	45.4	8.7	5.4	NA	NA	NA
Frederick	26 549	1.4	699	2.6	21 423	34.2	12.0	6.6	72 915	1 032	54.7
Gaithersburg	26 066	1.4	594	2.3	23 627	44.3	8.0	5.5	54 345	577	80.2
Hagerstown	20 185	-2.4	724	3.6	16 644	20.6	12.5	10.3	3 048	55	96.4
Rockville	27 397	1.4	594	2.2	24 862	49.5	8.5	6.3	23 273	452	36.5
MASSACHUSETTS	3 277 898	0.1	104 780	3.2	3 027 950	36.2	10.0	7.2	2 666 006	18 967	81.5
Attleboro	21 591	-0.2	755	3.5	19 917	28.7	15.6	8.4	13 475	193	80.3
Beverly	21 744	0.6	530	2.4	20 256	36.2	10.1	6.8	12 572	58	100.0
Boston	295 886	-1.0	9 760	3.3	288 704	37.1	6.4	8.0	168 271	1 147	11.1
Brockton	46 386	0.0	1 944	4.2	42 921	24.0	11.7	10.4	4 273	46	100.0
Cambridge	55 073	-0.7	1 058	1.9	54 097	55.0	4.5	5.5	20 433	95	11.6
Chelsea	12 404	-0.7	676	5.4	11 981	22.3	10.8	11.3	120	3	100.0
Chicopee	26 969	-0.5	1 024	3.8	27 373	21.9	13.3	8.2	4 808	65	96.9
Everett	18 561	-0.4	725	3.9	17 794	24.4	11.2	8.7	350	4	50.0
Fall River	42 573	-1.5	2 642	6.2	40 226	18.5	12.9	11.2	9 192	169	77.5
Fitchburg	17 743	-2.4	799	4.5	17 948	26.0	10.7	9.1	3 042	31	100.0
Gloucester	16 011	0.0	698	4.4	14 470	30.1	13.0	8.5	17 576	115	72.2
Haverhill	29 200	2.0	1 136	3.9	25 492	33.7	12.5	6.9	15 013	183	91.3
Holyoke	16 088	-1.4	779	4.8	16 446	28.0	11.1	12.6	1 560	20	60.0
Lawrence	28 246	0.4	2 300	8.1	25 644	22.2	13.4	9.8	751	8	75.0
Leominster	20 839	-0.4	827	4.0	19 533	32.5	11.3	7.7	7 519	67	100.0
Lowell	50 774	0.2	2 152	4.2	45 912	28.2	13.1	9.3	7 015	97	75.3
Lynn	38 424	0.3	1 558	4.1	36 053	25.8	12.6	10.0	2 297	26	84.6
Malden	29 688	-0.5	986	3.3	28 671	33.5	9.3	8.3	1 462	39	53.8
MarlBorough	19 963	0.8	594	3.0	18 070	40.3	10.4	5.8	12 258	135	95.6
Medford	31 225	-0.8	798	2.6	30 450	34.5	9.6	6.4	595	8	100.0
Melrose	15 162	-0.5	358	2.4	14 855	43.0	9.4	6.0	1 775	7	71.4
New Bedford	40 909	-2.9	3 043	7.4	40 185	19.7	11.9	12.0	4 494	78	87.2
Newton	47 075	-0.3	781	1.7	46 439	57.0	4.4	4.0	19 745	113	54.9
Northampton	15 734	0.1	354	2.2	15 816	39.0	7.0	8.0	10 127	64	100.0
Peabody	27 389	1.1	775	2.8	24 949	31.2	11.9	7.5	14 907	186	12.9
Pittsfield	20 986	-1.1	903	4.3	22 379	31.9	11.7	10.1	3 313	31	100.0
Quincy	49 534	-0.3	1 432	2.9	46 523	33.3	9.9	7.4	10 329	163	17.2
Revere	21 234	-0.4	886	4.2	20 393	25.6	10.8	9.9	3 560	59	25.4
Salem	21 300	0.4	710	3.3	19 958	34.5	10.6	7.0	4 480	41	100.0
Somerville	44 513	-0.8	997	2.2	43 677	38.0	7.5	6.8	0	0	0.0
Springfield	64 423	-0.7	3 248	5.0	65 274	26.8	9.9	10.6	5 325	76	89.5
Taunton	27 453	0.5	949	3.5	24 527	24.6	12.1	9.0	17 478	204	91.2
Waltham	34 359	1.8	829	2.4	32 353	35.6	10.9	5.8	9 923	172	43.6
Westfield	19 048	0.8	643	3.4	18 929	29.3	12.1	7.0	18 251	126	92.1
Woburn	22 230	0.8	582	2.6	20 485	35.8	11.3	6.1	8 011	118	26.3
Worcester	77 990	-2.4	2 850	3.7	75 836	31.0	9.2	9.0	18 349	269	84.4
MICHIGAN	5 136 130	2.1	193 841	3.8	4 166 196	28.3	12.0	9.0	6 204 660	54 257	83.7
Allen Park	15 562	1.1	274	1.8	13 873	31.2	12.9	8.3	557	5	100.0
Ann Arbor	69 795	3.6	1 067	1.5	59 668	55.3	3.7	4.2	53 928	345	63.5
Battle Creek	26 442	2.5	1 290	4.9	21 874	27.0	10.2	12.7	17 326	241	46.1
Bay City	18 492	1.8	1 181	6.4	15 458	23.1	12.5	11.3	8 088	154	6.5
Burton	12 576	-1.4	778	6.2	11 273	18.7	15.4	10.6	11 586	143	100.0

1. Percent of civilian labor force.　　2. Persons 16 years and older.　　3. Persons 16 to 64 years old.

Table D. Cities — **Wholesale Trade, Retail Trade, and Real Estate**

City	Wholesale Trade, 1997				Retail Trade[1], 1997				Real Estate and Rental and Leasing, 1997			
	Number of Establishments	Number of Employees	Sales (mil dol)	Annual Payroll (mil dol)	Number of Establishments	Number of Employees	Sales (mil dol)	Annual Payroll (mil dol)	Number of Establishments	Number of Employees	Receipts (mil dol)	Annual Payroll (mil dol)
	72	73	74	75	76	77	78	79	80	81	82	83
LOUISIANA	6 390	76 350	46 972.3	2 375.2	17 863	224 412	35 807.9	3 307.9	4 151	28 571	3 342.1	642.2
Alexandria	101	1 255	427.5	32.5	362	5 064	777.6	76.3	61	375	34.5	5.4
Baton Rouge	594	7 871	2 925.2	283.0	1 408	20 737	3 382.5	328.9	388	3 279	271.4	64.5
Bossier City	77	1 023	1 111.3	28.2	305	4 370	761.7	67.0	54	238	23.5	3.8
Houma	102	1 276	429.7	38.6	246	3 088	437.5	42.4	70	1 269	199.9	43.9
Kenner	170	D	D	D	350	5 765	968.9	86.5	71	1 404	128.2	25.5
Lafayette	321	4 159	1 864.0	137.4	818	12 689	2 104.3	198.9	252	1 850	238.5	51.0
Lake Charles	141	2 039	533.0	56.0	483	6 705	1 019.8	96.4	137	714	62.3	12.3
Monroe	139	1 867	680.8	56.9	470	6 314	1 058.1	94.4	113	628	58.0	9.7
New Iberia	82	1 139	279.8	36.2	214	2 748	505.3	43.3	62	998	175.9	36.4
New Orleans	484	6 086	2 450.5	210.2	1 871	20 405	2 771.3	315.6	481	3 538	407.4	72.3
Shreveport	422	5 186	1 723.0	154.9	930	12 010	2 056.5	198.3	213	1 069	110.4	20.4
MAINE	1 726	19 932	7 305.6	616.2	7 074	72 897	12 737.1	1 164.2	1 343	5 929	601.7	114.2
Bangor	92	1 600	620.5	49.2	335	5 340	999.7	87.9	81	347	47.2	6.1
Lewiston	60	D	D	D	202	2 548	593.1	40.1	50	172	16.4	2.7
Portland	233	3 538	1 477.5	113.0	422	5 380	1 292.3	97.5	172	1 618	163.4	37.3
MARYLAND	6 283	92 458	54 906.6	3 656.3	19 798	274 260	46 428.2	4 914.0	5 065	39 502	4 764.7	971.3
Annapolis	89	646	419.0	28.6	466	6 238	1 032.9	111.3	80	530	74.4	14.9
Baltimore	792	14 152	6 171.2	499.2	2 256	23 159	3 438.4	414.7	597	4 807	568.2	124.9
Bowie	26	D	D	D	104	2 284	339.1	35.5	39	175	34.0	3.4
Frederick	123	2 088	634.0	68.4	464	7 724	1 308.2	132.7	111	617	73.2	14.9
Gaithersburg	76	D	D	D	333	6 573	1 340.1	128.7	84	D	D	D
Hagerstown	79	967	301.6	28.3	305	4 123	689.7	62.4	54	D	D	D
Rockville	131	2 656	2 937.3	150.0	305	4 250	983.6	97.4	74	1 172	183.4	32.7
MASSACHUSETTS	9 993	146 827	112 792.4	6 484.8	26 209	335 736	58 578.0	5 894.8	5 834	41 233	5 925.4	1 214.1
Attleboro	40	394	172.1	16.7	158	2 973	476.3	38.8	33	153	23.1	4.4
Beverly	46	331	210.8	18.0	146	1 820	350.5	34.2	36	140	20.4	3.2
Boston	770	9 857	7 574.9	437.2	2 262	26 624	4 255.7	472.0	826	12 736	1 550.8	426.5
Brockton	84	1 666	604.2	58.1	359	5 414	932.4	106.4	53	257	35.3	5.4
Cambridge	145	3 696	1 457.9	183.4	538	7 290	1 113.4	124.6	143	1 144	206.7	36.8
Chelsea	116	D	D	D	98	1 260	241.4	24.6	29	98	13.3	2.4
Chicopee	57	D	D	D	183	2 372	382.8	34.0	34	165	26.5	3.5
Everett	75	1 269	925.6	59.8	85	595	123.9	11.4	13	85	7.6	1.8
Fall River	87	1 079	401.8	27.4	349	3 408	592.4	61.1	76	302	33.2	5.3
Fitchburg	45	D	D	D	170	2 011	349.8	39.2	36	161	12.1	3.1
Gloucester	66	318	227.8	11.0	123	1 300	227.6	23.7	33	99	10.9	3.1
Haverhill	71	703	157.7	19.4	158	2 202	420.7	39.3	35	176	19.5	3.9
Holyoke	47	765	245.6	24.3	218	3 305	451.3	46.8	37	271	18.3	3.9
Lawrence	72	1 119	344.5	37.1	158	1 255	328.4	29.9	38	206	20.7	3.7
Leominster	56	602	408.7	22.4	209	3 166	494.2	45.4	46	193	23.9	4.2
Lowell	88	1 159	353.9	41.5	256	2 514	472.4	44.1	63	466	41.9	7.3
Lynn	61	856	419.5	31.4	213	2 658	429.8	43.9	47	254	31.0	5.5
Malden	48	845	463.8	29.8	161	1 869	364.6	31.9	44	264	31.6	4.5
Marlborough	104	3 725	2 244.5	201.3	219	3 074	494.3	59.0	31	174	35.6	4.6
Medford	64	1 146	386.2	40.2	185	2 918	547.4	50.3	23	183	35.5	4.8
Melrose	18	238	67.3	5.8	73	818	130.2	14.2	13	30	4.6	0.6
New Bedford	146	2 111	782.7	59.4	325	3 273	499.4	52.2	64	238	25.1	4.7
Newton	175	2 587	1 857.5	109.0	390	5 701	978.1	113.9	140	1 506	281.6	49.2
Northampton	22	D	D	D	206	2 525	380.0	41.5	52	152	22.2	2.3
Peabody	109	2 817	2 689.7	132.4	282	4 899	886.4	86.4	42	263	20.8	4.9
Pittsfield	51	D	D	D	243	3 362	527.9	56.0	55	218	22.0	4.2
Quincy	89	859	384.8	28.0	271	5 146	822.5	84.0	72	691	158.6	18.2
Revere	30	D	D	D	140	1 882	302.8	31.3	26	152	18.3	3.3
Salem	49	456	175.3	20.7	172	1 880	292.7	32.1	36	157	20.7	4.3
Somerville	80	1 020	352.0	35.0	208	3 307	559.0	53.0	35	158	20.9	2.8
Springfield	166	2 524	1 989.4	116.4	565	7 313	1 123.3	120.1	119	688	101.4	18.0
Taunton	73	1 364	644.5	56.2	252	3 261	417.2	44.5	35	180	35.3	3.8
Waltham	158	4 158	4 387.3	279.2	258	3 185	587.5	64.8	96	779	227.7	30.8
Westfield	51	879	765.3	23.9	152	2 191	335.8	32.2	33	118	13.0	2.2
Woburn	288	4 495	2 780.6	216.5	223	3 640	754.3	86.2	57	1 245	165.4	33.7
Worcester	216	2 085	803.4	70.0	722	8 854	1 530.5	157.3	139	1 313	201.7	33.8
MICHIGAN	13 936	189 057	158 757.3	7 629.6	39 564	529 441	93 706.1	8 922.3	8 302	50 941	6 492.7	1 126.2
Allen Park	30	399	272.4	27.0	104	852	115.4	13.5	26	109	14.0	1.7
Ann Arbor	174	1 767	1 399.0	80.6	647	9 645	1 369.5	154.4	147	1 414	107.4	33.2
Battle Creek	59	976	1 139.7	37.5	266	3 825	632.7	58.2	53	270	32.0	5.2
Bay City	63	938	409.2	27.0	221	2 081	400.1	36.6	42	175	14.7	3.3
Burton	31	560	136.3	17.7	228	3 754	513.5	56.3	28	152	14.7	3.9

1. Establishments with payroll.

City	Professional, Scientific, and Technical Services, 1997[1]				Manufacturing, 1997				Accommodation and Foodservices, 1997			
	Number of Establishments	Number of Employees	Receipts (mil dol)	Annual Payroll (mil dol)	Number of Establishments	Number of Employees	Receipts (mil dol)	Annual Payroll (mil dol)	Number of Establishments	Number of Employees	Sales (mil dol)	Annual Payroll (mil dol)
	84	85	86	87	88	89	90	91	92	93	94	95
LOUISIANA	9 077	63 642	5 754.6	2 159.0	3 545	165 777	80 424.0	6 054.5	7 151	147 016	5 259.9	1 408.9
Alexandria	173	1 114	90.1	31.3	32	D	D	D	138	2 717	80.7	22.2
Baton Rouge	1 114	9 708	856.1	330.0	265	5 598	1 444.6	201.2	594	13 431	409.5	113.6
Bossier City	72	286	19.3	6.7	57	1 915	211.4	45.4	150	5 379	292.7	67.9
Houma	118	737	65.4	24.7	57	2 086	269.5	74.5	86	1 262	41.8	13.2
Kenner	116	599	42.9	17.0	68	1 693	161.2	45.6	160	3 712	148.4	35.4
Lafayette	703	5 264	502.4	194.3	125	3 434	538.4	89.1	329	8 380	250.9	73.3
Lake Charles	273	1 738	127.6	45.4	66	D	D	D	183	6 092	239.5	59.7
Monroe	251	1 593	115.8	40.6	58	3 061	408.0	76.1	172	3 734	116.9	29.5
New Iberia	100	427	29.5	10.7	51	1 427	209.0	46.8	71	1 186	29.6	7.7
New Orleans	1 420	12 469	1 401.8	551.5	261	10 453	2 305.0	362.2	1 105	32 081	1 371.8	377.5
Shreveport	531	3 033	274.8	102.6	177	D	D	D	374	7 150	219.3	61.2
MAINE	2 552	13 747	1 215.6	474.8	1 812	82 288	14 097.6	2 591.1	3 714	39 624	1 509.3	428.8
Bangor	147	869	70.4	33.0	46	D	D	D	144	2 709	88.4	27.2
Lewiston	73	1 215	153.4	38.2	79	D	D	D	77	1 032	32.2	9.7
Portland	436	3 645	363.9	152.7	119	3 905	624.9	107.0	275	4 084	147.4	42.4
MARYLAND	14 115	146 814	15 940.2	6 483.8	3 996	163 992	36 505.9	5 840.5	9 049	161 273	5 972.5	1 644.7
Annapolis	370	2 142	253.7	95.2	NA	NA	NA	NA	166	4 426	169.2	49.5
Baltimore	1 395	14 695	1 645.0	666.3	688	30 216	9 822.2	1 006.2	1 328	20 021	849.9	232.0
Bowie	113	1 662	66.9	39.8	NA	NA	NA	NA	44	1 031	33.4	9.1
Frederick	255	3 129	224.7	105.5	79	3 097	505.1	100.3	178	3 687	123.2	33.4
Gaithersburg	278	6 826	1 197.7	432.5	42	1 993	318.0	89.8	144	3 327	129.5	35.1
Hagerstown	107	607	36.3	15.4	64	3 361	593.1	96.9	124	2 604	78.5	22.3
Rockville	673	14 867	1 598.6	673.9	68	1 438	166.2	52.9	183	2 703	104.9	28.1
MASSACHUSETTS	18 086	177 345	22 744.1	9 261.4	9 554	417 135	77 876.6	16 379.0	14 800	227 476	9 269.9	2 575.6
Attleboro	50	169	17.0	5.7	143	9 714	1 412.0	333.5	81	1 697	53.9	15.0
Beverly	91	325	43.0	15.9	83	3 861	726.1	168.1	79	909	33.3	8.8
Boston	3 053	49 765	7 871.3	2 949.9	536	18 944	3 941.5	671.5	1 907	39 831	2 049.1	576.1
Brockton	138	1 181	78.6	30.8	121	3 009	378.0	92.0	150	2 658	88.2	24.9
Cambridge	738	20 339	2 751.9	1 341.2	106	3 050	585.2	98.1	413	7 766	404.3	111.9
Chelsea	34	342	37.6	14.6	62	2 084	341.4	66.0	62	D	D	D
Chicopee	35	131	10.7	3.9	109	4 974	990.0	184.6	125	1 608	52.8	14.0
Everett	29	251	16.3	7.4	77	2 216	297.0	82.1	55	D	D	D
Fall River	145	586	48.2	16.7	199	12 366	1 364.5	337.3	181	2 276	78.3	20.9
Fitchburg	67	259	19.1	6.9	89	3 896	653.6	145.3	101	1 370	46.9	12.7
Gloucester	69	215	26.2	9.5	64	3 948	846.8	137.2	101	1 031	42.4	13.0
Haverhill	99	631	45.4	19.0	119	3 885	545.9	130.8	123	D	D	D
Holyoke	51	459	25.4	9.1	88	4 223	886.8	139.0	81	1 153	39.7	10.0
Lawrence	63	424	23.9	9.0	120	6 252	1 052.4	207.9	84	D	D	D
Leominster	68	323	31.4	11.3	135	6 003	1 256.0	196.3	95	1 344	42.5	11.6
Lowell	144	1 389	138.2	48.3	101	5 709	888.1	193.3	174	D	D	D
Lynn	80	233	18.9	7.0	67	6 870	2 101.8	325.2	131	D	D	D
Malden	71	715	29.5	12.7	63	1 929	309.2	63.8	89	938	36.5	9.5
MarlBorough	138	2 020	338.4	125.5	90	4 959	1 592.9	258.0	115	2 024	80.0	23.4
Medford	85	429	52.3	20.2	52	924	98.3	24.9	87	1 201	42.6	11.4
Melrose	76	336	29.9	11.9	NA	NA	NA	NA	30	364	13.9	3.8
New Bedford	165	653	49.0	19.1	151	9 839	1 259.9	273.8	209	2 019	70.7	17.4
Newton	540	4 235	451.7	209.0	87	2 999	542.6	110.2	163	3 699	172.1	49.1
Northampton	107	468	33.0	12.7	39	1 471	264.5	46.3	97	1 873	57.9	17.4
Peabody	114	836	85.6	35.3	98	4 028	690.1	164.5	135	2 408	97.9	27.4
Pittsfield	112	821	70.1	30.3	59	D	D	D	125	2 083	61.6	18.0
Quincy	222	1 972	209.5	84.6	72	753	127.3	25.9	201	2 943	115.2	30.9
Revere	35	102	10.1	3.7	NA	NA	NA	NA	84	D	D	D
Salem	154	511	46.3	15.4	70	1 733	190.2	54.9	116	1 556	51.5	14.9
Somerville	140	776	94.8	33.6	83	2 574	433.0	96.2	154	D	D	D
Springfield	321	2 198	188.1	82.4	174	7 199	1 161.1	258.9	278	4 770	146.3	43.3
Taunton	80	591	31.4	13.3	71	4 465	709.0	174.4	101	D	D	D
Waltham	308	5 834	737.4	329.4	161	7 431	1 217.2	351.5	172	2 852	123.3	30.9
Westfield	48	308	30.5	13.7	105	3 786	634.7	132.6	73	1 095	29.8	7.8
Woburn	195	2 113	243.4	99.7	195	5 778	876.7	226.8	77	1 528	74.5	18.0
Worcester	445	2 718	232.7	93.3	278	13 475	2 139.5	528.5	415	6 202	200.3	54.7
MICHIGAN	18 614	162 971	16 231.7	6 882.9	16 045	833 429	214 900.7	34 418.9	18 958	320 014	10 158.7	2 835.8
Allen Park	50	492	52.2	19.3	20	D	D	D	62	1 276	34.5	8.7
Ann Arbor	621	6 371	809.0	320.8	131	4 330	599.8	160.0	344	8 266	273.7	75.9
Battle Creek	96	568	51.6	22.3	81	10 194	3 337.7	409.4	162	3 033	91.4	26.9
Bay City	95	621	46.5	22.6	79	4 174	794.7	198.3	111	1 629	41.3	11.1
Burton	29	437	24.6	8.9	41	D	D	D	82	1 445	43.2	12.1

1. Firms subject to federal tax.

Table D. Cities — **Entertainment, Health Care, and Other Services**

City	Arts, Entertainment, and Recreation[1], 1997				Health Care and Social Assistance[1], 1997				Other Services[1], 1997			
	Number of Establishments	Number of Employees	Receipts (mil dol)	Annual Payroll (mil dol)	Number of Establishments	Number of Employees	Receipts (mil dol)	Annual Payroll (mil dol)	Number of Establishments	Number of Employees	Receipts (mil dol)	Annual Payroll (mil dol)
	96	97	98	99	100	101	102	103	104	105	106	107
LOUISIANA	1 016	22 828	1 958.1	412.9	8 580	129 773	7 967.6	3 341.5	5 998	39 764	2 595.2	767.2
Alexandria	15	79	7.9	1.1	236	4 053	243.9	101.7	109	629	38.1	11.9
Baton Rouge	59	2 688	273.4	46.0	769	11 992	793.7	364.8	539	4 223	249.6	80.1
Bossier City	21	0	0.0	0.0	90	1 461	81.0	32.3	123	701	36.8	10.7
Houma	14	130	6.9	1.6	112	1 181	102.1	53.3	94	857	87.0	22.1
Kenner	18	0	0.0	0.0	100	1 821	95.6	37.3	157	815	49.3	14.4
Lafayette	44	990	44.7	8.2	558	6 842	564.7	218.9	263	1 938	116.5	37.6
Lake Charles	25	0	0.0	0.0	299	3 622	268.0	111.3	165	1 213	68.5	20.8
Monroe	18	127	10.0	1.7	233	3 869	253.0	112.0	114	828	40.2	12.5
New Iberia	12	0	0.0	0.0	126	1 566	106.3	38.7	79	414	28.3	8.2
New Orleans	117	3 609	271.8	61.7	1 022	19 447	1 245.4	530.6	605	4 684	257.7	77.8
Shreveport	66	1 832	234.5	33.6	532	8 680	612.4	274.1	332	2 328	153.6	45.8
MAINE	524	5 456	254.4	64.0	2 727	28 944	1 608.4	766.3	1 923	8 820	612.3	169.6
Bangor	20	212	39.9	1.9	181	2 230	154.4	74.5	87	553	47.2	11.8
Lewiston	10	148	4.4	1.4	133	1 460	97.3	45.2	75	0	0.0	0.0
Portland	38	353	19.1	5.0	284	3 230	245.0	125.1	179	1 171	84.8	24.3
MARYLAND	1 460	19 398	1 412.4	494.8	10 841	116 241	8 060.7	3 538.0	7 871	55 241	3 561.3	1 129.2
Annapolis	34	296	16.5	4.4	146	1 678	124.1	63.5	141	1 411	66.6	23.4
Baltimore	107	2 147	338.7	168.5	1 220	16 856	1 093.8	486.1	891	6 733	426.4	131.5
Bowie	18	209	17.9	6.6	111	652	43.3	18.3	47	244	10.9	3.7
Frederick	26	401	17.3	4.1	230	2 439	167.0	79.5	157	1 030	79.2	22.1
Gaithersburg	20	458	15.3	4.3	108	875	61.5	27.3	124	884	59.9	18.6
Hagerstown	13	135	7.2	1.2	143	1 748	146.0	67.0	108	717	30.5	10.0
Rockville	32	828	63.9	14.8	196	1 863	136.1	59.5	186	1 753	166.0	54.8
MASSACHUSETTS	1 781	22 598	1 578.5	518.6	11 887	182 902	11 361.4	5 310.5	10 806	61 557	4 359.8	1 338.6
Attleboro	5	57	5.8	1.2	74	1 003	66.1	29.0	55	238	15.0	4.3
Beverly	13	123	7.6	2.2	108	2 108	125.3	74.5	55	294	19.0	5.9
Boston	165	3 463	433.2	186.3	963	19 284	1 437.5	701.5	1 021	7 625	519.3	150.1
Brockton	15	177	4.3	1.3	188	3 962	271.5	132.7	142	754	45.8	12.1
Cambridge	40	529	46.2	7.5	201	2 433	219.3	93.9	148	1 024	91.0	21.6
Chelsea	2	0	0.0	0.0	23	577	26.8	11.9	31	153	15.2	4.4
Chicopee	6	63	2.6	0.8	51	1 145	53.3	23.1	89	476	31.6	9.7
Everett	4	32	1.1	0.2	51	327	20.2	9.8	69	403	31.1	9.3
Fall River	11	34	1.9	0.3	202	2 493	154.3	80.8	154	730	39.8	12.1
Fitchburg	5	0	0.0	0.0	90	1 051	63.0	28.4	70	331	22.4	6.8
Gloucester	11	74	5.1	1.6	45	432	26.1	12.3	55	201	12.6	4.1
Haverhill	15	464	15.9	4.7	76	1 858	100.4	54.5	85	466	26.3	8.5
Holyoke	11	58	6.4	1.7	95	1 287	86.0	40.7	59	294	16.0	5.2
Lawrence	4	0	0.0	0.0	57	0	0.0	0.0	94	842	56.3	19.1
Leominster	9	68	3.2	0.9	68	708	55.2	18.1	71	362	21.2	6.5
Lowell	10	154	6.1	2.2	145	2 311	146.5	69.6	149	738	46.4	13.6
Lynn	8	40	1.9	0.7	131	1 835	104.8	51.6	110	527	33.1	10.4
Malden	9	85	4.2	0.9	88	1 525	60.6	30.5	106	536	38.7	9.6
MarlBorough	11	158	4.6	1.3	59	881	54.8	22.5	77	696	91.1	23.3
Medford	3	61	2.7	0.6	93	1 051	70.9	31.3	96	698	55.3	18.8
Melrose	3	0	0.0	0.0	76	1 035	69.9	40.1	42	170	11.1	3.5
New Bedford	14	87	4.3	1.0	153	3 383	163.6	80.5	142	890	66.6	17.8
Newton	37	347	22.4	6.8	338	4 519	247.4	118.9	159	1 057	73.4	21.7
Northampton	14	85	3.5	0.9	104	1 389	84.1	41.8	67	286	21.3	6.0
Peabody	7	77	3.6	1.6	90	1 792	84.5	41.2	110	543	34.8	10.7
Pittsfield	18	0	0.0	0.0	128	2 115	144.5	60.0	102	0	0.0	0.0
Quincy	20	217	11.8	3.0	203	3 576	180.9	80.6	161	934	62.8	19.6
Revere	3	0	0.0	0.0	50	710	34.3	15.1	78	285	19.5	5.2
Salem	16	67	5.3	1.5	122	1 187	79.8	41.1	76	330	26.3	6.7
Somerville	19	264	18.4	4.8	60	577	37.3	14.5	112	920	58.4	20.6
Springfield	16	191	8.5	2.9	333	5 394	358.0	168.0	223	1 636	108.0	35.0
Taunton	9	57	2.1	0.5	88	1 425	93.0	45.2	77	355	24.5	6.6
Waltham	18	225	12.7	2.7	131	1 759	177.9	60.2	137	710	70.2	19.0
Westfield	9	63	3.5	1.1	56	661	32.9	13.3	71	329	19.5	6.5
Woburn	13	109	6.8	2.9	79	2 458	140.1	55.1	101	765	62.5	26.3
Worcester	21	521	13.9	5.0	385	8 418	651.3	280.7	310	2 203	134.8	42.2
MICHIGAN	2 693	34 161	2 202.8	664.6	18 943	186 954	11 811.5	5 696.8	14 705	93 792	6 159.1	1 893.8
Allen Park	11	325	18.1	8.9	85	885	52.1	24.4	58	300	13.0	4.5
Ann Arbor	43	533	18.8	5.6	305	2 913	242.0	88.6	168	1 129	73.0	23.1
Battle Creek	15	187	7.6	2.0	181	1 988	113.0	53.0	94	892	52.8	16.2
Bay City	10	107	6.6	1.5	98	1 092	70.1	37.3	90	541	31.7	9.8
Burton	7	39	1.7	0.4	75	462	28.2	13.7	57	402	24.3	7.2

1. Firms subject to federal tax.

Table D. Cities — Federal Funds and City Government Finances

City	Selected federal funds, fiscal 1999[1] (mil dol)									City government finances, 1997						
	Procurement contracts		Grants					Direct payments for individuals		General revenue						
										Intergovernmental			Taxes			
														Per capita[3] (dollars)		
	Defense	Other	Total[2]	Health and family welfare	Energy and environment	Education	Housing and community development	Educational assistance	Housing assistance	Total (mil dol)	Total (mil dol)	Percent from state government	Total (mil dol)	Total	Property	Sales and gross receipts
	108	109	110	111	112	113	114	115	116	117	118	119	120	121	122	123
LOUISIANA	1 449.9	1 216.7	5 227.9	3 111.9	107.7	513.5	144.4	130.8	80.9	X	X	X	X	X	X	X
Alexandria	4.4	12.9	14.5	4.8	0.0	0.0	1.4	1.4	0.0	49.2	13.8	23.1	23.4	508	97	374
Baton Rouge	43.3	5.3	880.1	205.4	52.3	166.3	59.7	18.7	12.8	481.0	64.1	73.4	267.7	1 240	309	835
Bossier City	0.5	0.2	3.2	2.1	0.0	0.0	1.0	1.3	2.3	107.6	4.4	29.4	37.0	665	95	540
Houma	0.6	1.1	4.3	0.0	0.0	0.2	4.0	0.3	0.0	194.5	30.0	56.5	45.5	1 511	734	730
Kenner	0.9	0.2	2.8	0.0	0.0	0.0	0.6	0.6	0.0	58.6	30.7	9.0	17.7	244	70	55
Lafayette	7.0	18.6	28.5	9.6	3.1	2.0	2.8	10.3	1.8	99.3	10.4	49.2	54.4	519	100	382
Lake Charles	7.8	10.1	11.2	4.8	0.0	0.4	2.6	3.7	1.9	60.3	5.2	70.3	43.2	604	64	503
Monroe	5.5	2.3	8.9	3.7	0.0	2.0	1.5	6.0	5.9	79.8	15.1	17.4	48.7	893	137	713
New Iberia	1.2	0.6	3.0	0.5	0.0	0.0	0.3	0.3	2.3	17.2	2.3	37.9	11.4	352	66	251
New Orleans	865.8	489.6	320.6	151.4	7.4	14.1	51.5	35.6	12.5	756.0	165.5	51.6	332.7	698	305	350
Shreveport	12.8	19.0	42.1	17.1	1.0	2.5	6.2	4.4	8.9	217.2	36.8	36.1	123.2	643	210	403
MAINE	681.4	121.2	1 664.3	1 059.9	22.3	131.1	28.9	41.8	-6.9	X	X	X	X	X	X	X
Bangor	2.6	8.1	38.0	2.8	0.4	3.4	1.3	8.5	0.1	97.6	34.6	51.2	34.4	1 088	984	92
Lewiston	0.0	0.2	4.2	1.8	0.0	0.0	1.5	0.9	2.3	67.3	21.6	100.0	38.1	1 034	1 027	0
Portland	46.8	4.4	24.7	7.6	0.4	2.4	2.4	6.3	-2.1	171.6	30.3	92.9	88.8	1 407	1 378	0
MARYLAND	5 438.4	5 145.2	5 744.0	3 728.3	131.4	397.8	122.2	78.7	129.5	X	X	X	X	X	X	X
Annapolis	262.3	28.8	142.7	4.7	8.7	1.5	5.4	0.8	6.9	38.3	6.6	43.5	19.5	587	501	12
Baltimore	753.5	352.7	1 423.3	810.7	85.7	136.7	77.0	23.7	59.0	1 953.0	1 046.9	88.4	698.2	1 034	700	69
Bowie	1.9	6.5	5.8	0.7	0.0	1.9	0.0	2.7	0.0	19.7	7.0	33.8	8.7	217	192	6
Frederick	13.2	18.9	12.8	8.6	0.5	0.1	0.4	1.1	-0.6	44.3	13.0	43.8	18.8	408	379	10
Gaithersburg	119.1	147.7	25.2	16.3	5.9	0.0	0.0	0.1	0.2	24.7	6.5	23.7	13.0	287	234	15
Hagerstown	3.7	4.6	5.6	2.3	0.5	0.0	1.3	1.0	2.7	29.8	6.9	42.7	12.2	352	329	7
Rockville	354.8	1 124.7	255.8	149.0	6.1	9.7	18.2	4.4	9.5	42.6	8.2	25.9	18.6	405	374	9
MASSACHUSETTS	4 449.9	1 303.4	8 838.2	5 664.7	408.5	554.2	210.0	229.7	222.6	X	X	X	X	X	X	X
Attleboro	0.4	3.3	4.3	0.0	0.0	0.0	0.5	0.0	-0.3	66.4	28.4	98.5	30.3	776	763	0
Beverly	11.8	2.4	3.3	2.4	0.0	0.0	0.3	0.6	0.5	68.8	16.7	93.1	42.7	1 107	1 100	2
Boston	128.7	139.3	2 119.9	998.4	271.8	42.6	93.9	48.6	95.3	1 995.4	925.9	94.2	802.3	1 437	1 344	57
Brockton	2.0	5.3	7.5	0.0	0.6	3.2	2.0	3.5	200.7	116.3	96.7	67.5	731	715	2
Cambridge	236.4	166.9	642.8	373.3	73.1	11.3	16.1	14.8	9.2	246.6	42.2	72.2	162.1	1 730	1 610	54
Chelsea	4.9	0.1	5.8	1.6	0.0	0.4	0.5	0.0	0.1	89.1	57.8	96.9	20.2	733	712	0
Chicopee	7.6	12.0	2.0	0.0	0.0	0.0	1.3	0.4	1.1	95.1	45.5	96.6	39.1	717	707	3
Everett	-1.4	-0.2	0.2	0.0	0.0	0.0	0.0	0.0	0.0	75.6	23.7	83.3	46.5	1 328	1 320	0
Fall River	7.3	0.1	11.2	3.1	0.2	0.6	6.5	1.6	3.8	174.0	122.6	90.7	39.5	435	427	1
Fitchburg	0.9	0.4	3.4	0.1	0.0	0.8	1.8	1.1	-0.4	76.9	44.2	94.5	23.6	592	582	2
Gloucester	0.5	0.8	2.2	1.2	0.0	0.0	0.8	0.0	0.0	60.7	15.6	85.8	36.2	1 236	1 213	7
Haverhill	0.1	0.3	8.6	1.1	0.0	0.3	1.4	2.9	2.2	139.7	46.4	94.0	44.0	815	801	3
Holyoke	0.1	0.7	17.3	8.5	0.0	1.0	2.9	1.5	4.4	135.3	84.5	96.1	30.2	729	718	3
Lawrence	2.3	0.1	14.9	5.5	0.5	0.9	4.9	0.0	4.5	179.3	138.1	93.0	30.2	439	428	1
Leominster	0.0	1.0	3.7	3.2	0.1	0.0	0.6	0.0	2.5	64.2	28.1	97.2	31.1	792	779	6
Lowell	8.9	2.1	27.8	9.1	4.9	2.1	4.8	4.7	-1.9	224.9	144.2	99.7	62.6	620	607	2
Lynn	662.3	0.3	6.9	2.5	0.5	0.0	3.5	0.0	11.5	179.4	105.7	93.8	52.2	648	638	0
Malden	1.9	0.8	143.0	1.1	0.0	137.1	4.7	0.4	0.1	93.2	39.0	90.5	41.2	782	764	0
MarIborough	244.3	4.4	1.5	0.2	0.7	0.0	0.0	0.0	2.3	65.5	12.7	95.1	47.7	1 448	1 412	16
Medford	0.4	0.1	15.0	0.3	1.3	0.2	5.0	2.8	0.0	93.7	31.2	93.3	52.2	928	917	0
Melrose	0.0	0.0	0.1	0.0	0.0	0.0	0.0	0.0	1.7	49.9	14.6	96.9	28.8	1 050	1 042	0
New Bedford	12.9	1.1	19.0	3.0	2.3	0.5	7.1	0.4	2.8	210.1	130.0	85.7	53.4	551	544	0
Newton	3.4	12.5	38.5	13.1	0.0	3.3	3.6	1.5	-0.2	197.0	25.4	85.1	148.0	1 844	1 801	14
Northampton	38.5	1.0	3.9	1.8	0.0	0.0	0.7	1.7	0.0	49.6	17.9	93.9	23.7	823	799	7
Peabody	2.1	0.9	4.4	0.6	1.3	0.7	1.1	0.0	3.1	90.2	27.7	86.4	44.3	916	893	10
Pittsfield	84.3	2.1	4.9	1.7	0.0	0.4	1.9	0.5	2.0	90.3	46.8	90.3	38.0	821	812	5
Quincy	151.7	26.2	7.1	2.6	0.0	0.0	4.3	1.9	5.6	241.7	53.7	93.6	88.9	1 039	1 022	0
Revere	4.5	0.0	0.5	0.0	0.0	0.0	0.2	0.0	4.3	75.4	36.4	97.3	37.2	891	874	5
Salem	1.8	0.1	7.8	0.1	0.1	6.2	1.4	2.3	0.0	80.7	26.6	91.8	44.2	1 162	1 151	4
Somerville	5.3	0.9	49.7	44.1	0.1	0.2	4.4	0.5	9.9	124.8	66.2	92.1	50.4	678	666	2
Springfield	3.0	6.9	37.5	2.0	0.1	9.8	8.7	6.7	20.5	437.2	284.2	83.7	101.5	677	663	4
Taunton	321.2	1.3	3.5	1.3	0.2	0.0	1.4	0.0	0.4	88.5	42.2	89.4	36.8	709	696	2
Waltham	37.4	14.1	55.6	41.1	3.9	0.4	1.3	5.2	0.0	115.8	24.1	96.3	78.0	1 363	1 308	21
Westfield	0.7	0.3	6.1	0.9	0.0	0.2	0.5	1.3	0.0	73.3	35.2	92.2	31.0	825	816	0
Woburn	20.0	9.3	6.4	3.2	1.3	0.0	0.3	0.0	0.0	68.5	13.1	99.4	45.1	1 230	1 190	24
Worcester	14.3	22.2	116.3	82.4	2.0	4.5	9.8	9.1	12.4	378.1	213.6	94.4	128.8	774	762	4
MICHIGAN	1 167.8	897.0	9 764.0	5 944.9	235.2	899.0	281.3	180.1	212.0	X	X	X	X	X	X	X
Allen Park	0.0	0.0	0.3	0.0	0.0	0.1	0.0	0.0	0.0	27.4	5.1	91.3	12.0	382	362	0
Ann Arbor	59.3	42.2	391.1	247.7	15.0	7.2	4.2	11.9	2.0	126.3	29.0	65.9	50.1	460	444	0
Battle Creek	25.2	7.3	11.0	4.9	0.5	2.0	2.5	1.4	0.2	86.3	18.0	66.9	36.8	689	472	0
Bay City	0.5	1.4	3.4	0.0	0.0	0.0	2.1	0.0	0.5	34.6	11.3	66.2	12.2	333	322	0
Burton	0.0	0.0	0.0	0.0	0.0	0.0	0.0	0.0	0.5	12.7	3.8	94.8	4.2	154	139	0

1. October 1, 1998 to September 30, 1999. 2. Includes program categories not shown separately. State totals include additional categories not allocated by city. 3. Based on population estimated as of July 1 of the year shown.

Table D. Cities — City Government Finances

City	City government finances, 1997 (cont'd)												
	General expenditure												
	Per capita[1] (dollars)			Percent of total for —									
	Total (mil dol)	Total	Capital outlays	Public welfare	Highways	Parking facilities	Education	Health and hospitals	Police protection	Sewerage and sanitation	Parks and recreation	Housing and community development	Interest on debt
	124	125	126	127	128	129	130	131	132	133	134	135	136
LOUISIANA	X	X	X	X	X	X	X	X	X	X	X	X	X
Alexandria	56.0	1 217	189	0.0	7.6	1.0	0.0	0.0	14.3	23.0	2.2	11.1	2.1
Baton Rouge	500.1	2 317	424	0.3	9.8	0.1	0.0	1.9	12.6	18.6	3.5	5.7	11.6
Bossier City	90.3	1 621	95	0.0	3.3	0.0	0.0	57.2	9.0	5.5	1.5	3.1	5.1
Houma	174.5	5 787	860	1.2	7.5	0.0	0.0	58.2	6.8	4.4	1.2	2.2	1.3
Kenner	47.2	652	79	1.5	10.6	0.0	0.0	0.2	22.6	13.6	7.9	2.1	5.8
Lafayette	87.4	833	30	0.1	11.3	0.3	0.0	0.8	11.4	14.9	8.6	5.4	11.9
Lake Charles	61.1	856	265	0.4	10.3	0.0	0.0	0.3	10.9	8.9	8.8	16.8	0.9
Monroe	76.9	1 408	327	0.0	21.4	0.0	0.0	0.0	10.4	11.1	11.3	15.1	2.8
New Iberia	18.0	555	136	2.2	11.9	0.0	0.0	0.0	16.0	35.3	4.8	5.2	6.5
New Orleans	703.2	1 475	295	0.4	2.7	0.6	0.0	3.9	9.9	12.2	2.5	10.3	9.2
Shreveport	187.6	979	163	0.1	6.4	0.2	0.0	0.2	13.5	14.7	4.3	11.4	6.3
MAINE	X	X	X	X	X	X	X	X	X	X	X	X	X
Bangor	83.5	2 637	72	5.6	6.3	0.4	31.0	0.0	5.3	3.2	3.3	2.7	2.7
Lewiston	63.5	1 725	26	1.0	0.5	0.3	45.7	0.0	5.5	11.8	2.5	4.4	2.7
Portland	177.3	2 809	115	9.7	4.9	0.0	31.9	0.4	4.5	6.1	2.7	0.2	4.3
MARYLAND	X	X	X	X	X	X	X	X	X	X	X	X	X
Annapolis	40.5	1 217	231	0.0	10.4	1.4	0.0	0.0	17.2	23.2	3.5	1.2	4.4
Baltimore	1 842.0	2 727	427	0.0	7.5	0.5	38.6	4.5	11.1	7.8	3.0	3.5	4.1
Bowie	17.0	424	3	0.0	9.9	0.0	0.0	0.3	2.1	28.4	14.3	0.7	5.4
Frederick	43.1	932	212	0.0	17.9	1.4	0.0	0.0	18.0	12.8	10.9	5.9	9.6
Gaithersburg	20.7	457	65	0.0	12.6	0.1	0.0	0.7	21.6	5.8	25.7	0.0	0.0
Hagerstown	32.1	927	180	0.0	7.1	1.7	0.0	0.0	20.6	23.2	15.2	2.7	2.6
Rockville	36.5	794	81	0.0	10.7	0.0	0.0	0.5	7.9	13.4	27.0	0.9	7.6
MASSACHUSETTS	X	X	X	X	X	X	X	X	X	X	X	X	X
Attleboro	74.4	1 903	374	0.4	3.0	0.0	58.8	0.3	5.0	13.5	1.2	0.0	2.6
Beverly	64.9	1 683	63	0.1	3.6	0.1	50.0	0.6	6.9	9.9	1.1	0.9	1.0
Boston	1 859.2	3 330	324	5.6	3.4	0.2	30.7	5.3	11.2	7.6	1.5	3.9	2.5
Brockton	177.3	1 921	73	0.2	3.4	0.1	56.2	0.3	6.6	6.7	0.4	1.7	0.3
Cambridge	246.7	2 632	277	0.1	2.8	0.3	36.8	0.0	6.8	4.1	1.3	1.2	1.3
Chelsea	95.9	3 474	833	0.1	2.6	0.0	60.0	0.3	5.0	2.3	0.0	2.1	6.3
Chicopee	92.7	1 700	116	1.0	4.1	0.0	53.6	2.8	6.0	5.5	1.9	1.5	0.9
Everett	74.3	2 122	174	0.2	5.3	0.1	41.9	0.6	7.6	2.6	1.7	0.0	1.3
Fall River	161.8	1 781	112	0.4	2.8	0.0	50.9	1.2	11.4	4.6	0.4	2.8	0.5
Fitchburg	73.9	1 855	199	0.2	3.8	0.0	50.7	0.4	6.4	6.7	0.5	2.2	1.5
Gloucester	65.5	2 238	442	0.1	4.3	0.0	51.8	0.5	5.9	10.8	1.0	3.2	2.2
Haverhill	139.4	2 584	303	2.6	1.9	0.1	39.6	23.5	4.7	3.9	0.7	1.9	2.4
Holyoke	132.8	3 204	326	9.3	3.0	0.0	51.6	0.6	10.8	4.5	0.6	1.8	3.0
Lawrence	156.4	2 272	36	0.1	2.5	0.3	59.4	0.1	4.5	4.9	0.3	2.1	2.4
Leominster	59.1	1 506	186	0.2	4.6	0.0	54.1	0.4	6.7	11.8	0.5	0.8	2.9
Lowell	214.3	2 122	235	0.2	1.6	0.4	54.9	0.5	6.4	5.5	1.1	0.0	4.8
Lynn	168.3	2 089	61	3.2	4.0	0.3	52.9	0.4	5.9	4.8	0.4	3.6	0.7
Malden	96.0	1 820	111	1.9	3.1	1.7	40.7	0.2	6.2	2.9	0.1	1.5	1.0
MarlBorough	58.6	1 776	161	0.1	6.9	0.0	56.6	0.5	7.5	7.9	1.0	1.1	1.4
Medford	90.7	1 615	102	0.3	3.0	0.0	42.0	0.3	7.7	4.2	0.6	2.6	0.3
Melrose	49.1	1 789	140	0.1	3.0	0.0	51.7	0.4	5.8	10.4	1.8	0.6	0.3
New Bedford	190.5	1 965	137	0.3	2.8	0.0	50.8	1.2	6.9	13.6	0.8	2.0	0.6
Newton	198.1	2 468	309	0.1	5.3	0.0	55.8	0.6	4.9	3.6	2.3	1.6	0.6
Northampton	54.2	1 878	290	0.3	4.5	0.6	50.4	1.6	5.4	3.7	1.2	1.6	3.2
Peabody	89.7	1 855	120	0.1	4.2	0.0	47.3	0.5	5.9	4.3	1.3	7.8	0.3
Pittsfield	92.8	2 005	247	0.2	3.4	0.3	51.2	0.4	5.5	6.8	0.5	2.6	0.6
Quincy	256.4	2 998	139	0.1	2.7	0.0	28.9	29.9	6.2	3.5	0.8	1.0	2.0
Revere	82.3	1 970	47	0.4	3.2	0.0	47.9	0.3	6.4	3.0	0.8	1.2	0.4
Salem	75.8	1 994	45	0.2	2.8	0.6	46.1	1.0	7.1	3.4	2.1	3.2	2.8
Somerville	138.8	1 866	181	0.2	4.0	0.2	43.7	0.6	7.0	2.2	0.4	3.9	1.3
Springfield	458.4	3 057	411	0.1	1.1	0.1	54.4	2.7	5.6	7.0	1.2	3.0	1.0
Taunton	95.3	1 835	209	5.3	4.1	0.1	51.9	0.5	6.6	3.6	1.1	1.2	1.2
Waltham	106.7	1 864	241	0.2	5.1	0.2	47.7	0.4	8.2	10.8	0.8	0.9	0.9
Westfield	73.7	1 963	331	0.1	4.9	0.1	56.3	0.3	5.0	5.8	0.8	1.7	2.1
Woburn	66.4	1 812	57	0.2	5.8	0.0	44.4	0.3	7.6	2.6	0.7	0.0	1.0
Worcester	365.9	2 199	305	0.1	3.7	0.0	52.0	1.1	6.7	4.4	1.1	1.2	2.6
MICHIGAN	X	X	X	X	X	X	X	X	X	X	X	X	X
Allen Park	24.6	784	87	0.2	14.1	0.0	0.0	0.0	13.8	25.0	4.4	1.0	1.2
Ann Arbor	115.8	1 065	120	1.3	8.0	2.7	0.0	0.0	10.9	14.0	2.6	0.0	4.8
Battle Creek	118.5	2 219	893	0.0	11.1	0.7	0.0	0.0	9.9	9.8	2.1	0.0	8.6
Bay City	33.1	905	117	0.0	19.3	0.2	0.0	0.0	16.4	21.4	2.8	0.0	3.6
Burton	13.3	485	69	0.0	16.3	0.0	0.0	0.0	24.0	29.3	0.3	0.0	3.6

1. Based on population estimated as of July 1 of the year shown.

Table D. Cities — City Government Finances, City Government Employment, and Climate

| City | City government finances, 1997 (cont'd) Debt outstanding | | | City government employment, 1999 | Climate[2] Average daily temperature (degrees Fahrenheit) | | | | Annual precipitation (inches) | Heating degree days | Cooling degree days |
| | Total (mil dol) | Per capita[1] (dollars) | Percent utility | | Mean January | Mean July | Limits January[3] | Limits July[4] | | | |
	137	138	139	140	141	142	143	144	145	146	147
LOUISIANA	X	X	X	X	X	X	X	X	X	X	X
Alexandria	84.6	1 837	75.4	863	46.8	82.4	36.4	92.5	58.50	2 003	2 477
Baton Rouge	849.5	3 935	0.0	NA	49.8	82.3	39.6	91.4	60.89	1 669	2 690
Bossier City	75.3	1 353	20.2	1 392	45.1	82.7	34.8	93.0	46.11	2 264	2 368
Houma	117.0	3 879	29.4	1 351	52.1	81.6	42.0	90.4	62.91	1 429	2 668
Kenner	52.1	720	0.0	657	51.3	81.9	41.8	90.6	61.88	1 513	2 655
Lafayette	330.1	3 147	50.1	2 233	50.6	82.1	41.2	90.6	58.36	1 587	2 673
Lake Charles	9.2	128	0.0	834	50.4	82.2	41.1	90.8	54.84	1 616	2 650
Monroe	44.4	814	0.0	1 350	44.2	82.3	34.6	92.4	51.48	2 407	2 323
New Iberia	15.9	490	0.0	NA	50.4	81.7	40.5	90.7	59.56	1 609	2 596
New Orleans	1 178.4	2 472	0.8	10 655	51.3	81.9	41.8	90.6	61.88	1 513	2 655
Shreveport	316.6	1 653	39.6	3 019	45.1	82.7	34.8	93.0	46.11	2 264	2 368
MAINE	X	X	X	X	X	X	X	X	X	X	X
Bangor	25.8	814	0.0	1 346	17.5	68.2	8.2	78.1	41.23	7 930	251
Lewiston	45.6	1 238	16.5	1 102	20.2	70.7	11.1	80.7	45.30	7 244	398
Portland	104.1	1 649	0.0	2 489	20.8	68.6	11.4	78.8	44.34	7 378	268
MARYLAND	X	X	X	X	X	X	X	X	X	X	X
Annapolis	29.8	898	20.0	514	33.6	77.6	24.6	87.6	41.81	4 382	1 271
Baltimore	1 323.3	1 959	12.1	29 493	31.8	77.0	23.4	87.2	40.76	4 707	1 137
Bowie	11.3	281	26.5	NA	33.6	77.6	24.6	87.6	41.81	4 382	1 271
Frederick	75.3	1 628	17.3	459	31.4	74.7	23.1	85.3	40.25	4 810	925
Gaithersburg	0.0	0	0.0	NA	30.7	74.7	21.4	85.8	41.11	5 093	889
Hagerstown	20.0	578	22.4	431	28.7	74.9	20.3	85.8	38.60	5 293	909
Rockville	34.4	748	5.1	582	30.7	74.7	21.4	85.8	41.11	5 093	889
MASSACHUSETTS	X	X	X	X	X	X	X	X	X	X	X
Attleboro	93.3	2 387	30.5	1 178	25.9	71.2	15.5	82.3	46.68	6 346	457
Beverly	21.2	550	12.9	925	28.6	73.5	21.6	81.8	41.51	5 641	678
Boston	1 091.4	1 954	0.0	21 330	28.6	73.5	21.6	81.8	41.51	5 641	678
Brockton	21.5	233	31.4	2 941	26.9	71.2	16.9	82.2	45.50	6 225	461
Cambridge	79.1	844	15.4	5 007	28.6	73.5	21.6	81.8	41.51	5 641	678
Chelsea	103.6	3 753	0.0	NA	28.6	73.5	21.6	81.8	41.51	5 641	678
Chicopee	32.2	591	6.0	1 851	26.8	74.1	17.6	85.4	43.88	5 754	751
Everett	18.0	513	0.0	NA	28.6	73.5	21.6	81.8	41.51	5 641	678
Fall River	34.4	379	0.0	2 729	30.6	73.5	23.4	81.3	47.34	5 426	729
Fitchburg	23.8	598	5.8	NA	23.4	71.3	13.4	81.5	47.02	6 698	485
Gloucester	72.7	2 484	3.0	1 000	28.6	73.5	21.6	81.8	41.51	5 641	678
Haverhill	96.1	1 782	0.7	2 084	24.7	72.5	15.2	83.8	44.43	6 413	575
Holyoke	79.6	1 920	30.9	2 113	26.8	74.1	17.6	85.4	43.88	5 754	751
Lawrence	66.2	962	0.0	NA	24.7	72.5	15.4	82.6	42.80	6 322	555
Leominster	32.3	824	0.0	NA	23.4	71.3	13.4	81.5	47.02	6 698	485
Lowell	196.0	1 941	3.7	3 272	24.3	73.3	14.7	84.8	42.07	6 339	610
Lynn	110.2	1 368	52.4	2 705	28.6	73.5	21.6	81.8	41.51	5 641	678
Malden	20.7	392	0.2	1 375	28.6	73.5	21.6	81.8	41.51	5 641	678
MarlBorough	27.5	835	12.5	1 012	23.4	71.3	13.4	81.5	47.02	6 698	485
Medford	9.4	167	15.0	1 281	28.6	73.5	21.6	81.8	41.51	5 641	678
Melrose	9.0	328	0.0	815	28.6	73.5	21.6	81.8	41.51	5 641	678
New Bedford	175.4	1 810	2.9	3 522	30.6	73.5	23.4	81.3	47.34	5 426	729
Newton	37.4	466	0.0	3 047	28.6	73.5	21.6	81.8	41.51	5 641	678
Northampton	43.1	1 495	18.4	NA	23.6	71.8	12.2	84.6	42.50	6 404	522
Peabody	46.2	955	45.7	1 485	24.5	71.0	14.3	82.7	46.64	6 573	425
Pittsfield	25.9	559	31.6	NA	21.4	68.9	11.0	81.5	43.47	7 060	293
Quincy	109.3	1 278	2.9	3 051	27.4	71.5	18.5	81.5	47.69	6 072	450
Revere	15.4	370	12.9	NA	28.6	73.5	21.6	81.8	41.51	5 641	678
Salem	42.0	1 104	3.3	NA	28.6	73.5	21.6	81.8	41.51	5 641	678
Somerville	53.3	716	0.0	1 838	28.6	73.5	21.6	81.8	41.51	5 641	678
Springfield	104.5	697	0.0	7 549	26.8	74.1	17.6	85.4	43.88	5 754	751
Taunton	40.4	778	44.8	1 757	25.9	71.2	15.5	82.3	46.68	6 346	457
Waltham	10.5	184	7.8	1 419	28.6	73.5	21.6	81.8	41.51	5 641	678
Westfield	51.7	1 377	30.8	1 503	26.8	74.1	17.6	85.4	43.88	5 754	751
Woburn	17.8	485	0.0	NA	24.5	71.0	14.3	82.7	46.64	6 573	425
Worcester	289.6	1 741	21.3	5 743	22.8	69.7	15.0	79.3	47.75	6 979	333
MICHIGAN	X	X	X	X	X	X	X	X	X	X	X
Allen Park	4.5	144	0.0	NA	22.9	72.9	15.5	83.8	32.71	6 500	677
Ann Arbor	104.6	962	32.3	1 393	23.2	73.0	16.2	83.7	32.81	6 379	713
Battle Creek	142.8	2 673	13.0	686	22.5	71.7	14.9	83.2	35.70	6 677	575
Bay City	42.1	1 153	55.1	430	22.0	72.2	14.7	84.1	29.51	6 763	599
Burton	8.3	303	9.0	NA	21.5	70.6	14.2	81.5	30.28	6 979	483

1. Based on the population estimated as of July 1 of the year shown.　2. Represents normal values based on the 30-year period, 1961–1990.　3. Average daily minimum.　4. Average daily maximum.

Table D. Cities — Land Area and Population

STATE Place code	City	Land area, 1990[1] (sq km)	Population, 1999			Population				Population characteristics, 1990 — Percent						
												Race				
			Total persons	Rank	Per square kilometer	Total persons 1990	Percent change 1990–1999	Total persons 1980	Percent change 1980–1990	White	Black	Am. Indian, Eskimo, Aleut	Asian and Pacific Islander	Other race	His-panic[2]	Foreign born
		1	2	3	4	5	6	7	8	9	10	11	12	13	14	15
	MICHIGAN—Cont'd															
26 21000	Dearborn	63.1	88 215	271	1 398	89 286	-1.2	90 660	-1.5	97.6	0.6	0.3	0.9	0.6	2.8	16.5
26 21020	Dearborn Heights	30.3	57 753	487	1 906	60 838	-5.1	67 706	-10.1	97.3	0.5	0.4	1.3	0.5	2.3	9.3
26 22000	Detroit	359.3	965 084	10	2 686	1 027 974	-6.1	1 203 339	-14.6	21.6	75.7	0.4	0.8	1.5	2.8	3.4
26 24120	East Lansing	24.6	46 565	630	1 893	50 677	-8.1	51 392	-1.4	84.6	6.9	0.3	7.0	1.2	2.5	10.7
26 24290	Eastpointe	13.2	33 702	894	2 553	35 283	-4.5	38 280	-7.8	98.7	0.2	0.4	0.6	0.1	0.8	6.8
26 27440	Farmington Hills	86.2	79 693	313	925	74 614	6.8	58 056	28.5	93.9	1.9	0.2	3.8	0.2	1.2	9.7
26 27880	Ferndale	10.0	24 131	1 240	2 413	25 084	-3.8	26 227	-4.4	95.8	1.4	0.9	1.4	0.6	1.7	6.7
26 29000	Flint	87.6	130 853	155	1 494	140 925	-7.1	159 611	-11.7	49.6	47.9	0.7	0.5	1.2	2.9	1.6
26 31420	Garden City	15.2	32 185	945	2 117	31 846	1.1	35 640	-10.6	98.6	0.2	0.4	0.5	0.3	1.5	3.5
26 34000	Grand Rapids	114.6	185 009	100	1 614	189 126	-2.2	181 843	4.0	76.4	18.5	0.8	1.1	3.1	5.0	3.9
26 38640	Holland	36.7	33 652	900	917	30 745	9.5	26 281	17.0	87.7	1.1	0.3	3.2	7.7	14.1	6.9
26 40680	Inkster	16.2	30 872	982	1 906	30 772	0.3	35 190	-12.6	36.1	62.4	0.4	0.7	0.4	1.1	2.1
26 41420	Jackson	28.6	35 151	856	1 229	37 425	-6.1	39 739	-5.8	80.2	17.7	0.6	0.4	1.2	2.5	1.7
26 42160	Kalamazoo	63.6	75 660	334	1 190	80 277	-5.8	79 722	0.7	77.3	18.8	0.6	1.9	1.5	2.7	4.7
26 42820	Kentwood	54.5	42 893	687	787	37 826	13.4	30 438	24.3	91.3	5.6	0.4	2.0	0.8	2.0	4.7
26 46000	Lansing	87.8	127 716	161	1 455	127 321	0.3	130 414	-2.4	73.9	18.6	1.0	1.8	4.7	7.9	3.1
26 47800	Lincoln Park	15.1	41 898	712	2 775	41 832	0.2	45 105	-7.3	97.3	0.9	0.5	0.4	0.8	3.8	4.0
26 49000	Livonia	92.5	100 160	220	1 083	100 850	-0.7	104 814	-3.8	98.0	0.3	0.2	1.3	0.2	1.3	6.8
26 50560	Madison Heights	18.6	31 573	959	1 697	32 196	-1.9	35 375	-9.0	95.9	0.9	0.5	2.4	0.2	1.2	8.0
26 53780	Midland	71.5	40 769	733	570	38 053	7.1	37 257	2.1	95.6	1.7	0.4	1.9	0.5	1.7	4.4
26 56320	Muskegon	37.2	39 401	766	1 059	39 809	-1.0	40 823	-2.5	69.9	27.1	1.0	0.3	1.7	3.5	1.5
26 59440	Novi	78.9	45 474	651	576	32 998	37.8	22 525	46.5	96.0	0.8	0.3	2.6	0.2	1.1	6.2
26 59920	Oak Park	13.0	29 095	1 031	2 238	30 468	-4.5	31 537	-3.4	62.8	34.3	0.1	2.4	0.4	1.5	14.9
26 65440	Pontiac	51.8	68 149	381	1 316	71 136	-4.2	76 715	-7.3	51.3	42.2	0.8	1.4	4.4	8.0	2.3
26 65560	Portage	83.4	43 992	678	527	41 042	7.2	38 157	7.6	94.3	2.8	0.4	2.1	0.5	1.4	3.2
26 65820	Port Huron	20.7	32 337	936	1 562	33 694	-4.0	33 981	-0.8	90.1	6.8	0.8	0.6	1.7	3.5	2.7
26 69035	Rochester Hills	85.1	67 412	386	792	61 766	9.1	NA	NA	95.0	1.4	0.2	3.2	0.3	1.4	7.2
26 69800	Roseville	25.4	50 852	572	2 002	51 412	-1.1	54 311	-5.3	97.3	1.0	0.5	1.1	0.2	1.2	5.7
26 70040	Royal Oak	30.6	63 700	424	2 082	65 410	-2.6	70 893	-7.7	97.9	0.5	0.4	1.1	0.2	1.1	6.4
26 70520	Saginaw	45.2	62 422	431	1 381	69 512	-10.2	77 508	-10.3	52.3	40.3	0.5	0.4	6.4	10.5	1.8
26 70760	St. Clair Shores	29.9	65 333	406	2 185	68 107	-4.1	76 210	-10.6	98.7	0.2	0.3	0.6	0.1	0.9	6.6
26 74900	Southfield	67.9	74 725	344	1 101	75 727	-1.3	75 568	0.2	67.9	29.1	0.3	2.4	0.4	1.7	14.1
26 74960	Southgate	17.8	32 476	932	1 824	30 771	5.5	32 058	-4.0	96.5	1.2	0.5	1.1	0.7	2.8	5.6
26 76460	Sterling Heights	94.9	124 571	164	1 313	117 810	5.7	108 999	8.1	96.3	0.4	0.2	2.9	0.2	1.1	9.9
26 79000	Taylor	61.2	72 029	358	1 177	70 811	1.7	77 568	-8.7	93.2	4.2	0.6	1.3	0.7	2.8	3.9
26 80700	Troy	86.9	79 074	315	910	72 884	8.5	67 102	8.6	91.5	1.3	0.2	6.8	0.2	1.3	11.6
26 84000	Warren	88.8	141 008	141	1 588	144 864	-2.7	161 134	-10.1	97.3	0.7	0.5	1.3	0.1	1.1	8.1
26 86000	Westland	53.0	86 369	278	1 630	84 724	1.9	84 603	0.1	94.7	3.3	0.6	1.0	0.5	1.9	4.4
26 88900	Wyandotte	13.7	31 641	958	2 310	30 938	2.3	34 006	-9.0	98.2	0.2	0.6	0.4	0.6	2.1	3.9
26 88940	Wyoming	62.9	69 275	374	1 101	63 891	8.4	59 616	7.2	93.5	2.7	0.5	1.5	1.7	3.5	3.5
27 00000	MINNESOTA	206 207.1	4 775 508	X	23	4 375 665	9.1	4 075 970	7.4	94.4	2.2	1.1	1.8	0.5	1.2	2.6
27 01900	Apple Valley	44.9	46 905	626	1 045	34 598	35.6	21 818	58.6	96.7	0.9	0.2	1.9	0.3	1.0	2.2
27 06382	Blaine	87.9	46 268	633	526	38 975	18.7	28 558	36.5	97.2	0.3	0.8	1.4	0.4	1.0	1.5
27 06616	Bloomington	92.0	86 226	280	937	86 335	-0.1	81 831	5.5	94.7	1.6	0.3	3.1	0.3	0.9	4.0
27 07948	Brooklyn Center	20.6	27 743	1 085	1 347	28 887	-4.0	31 230	-7.5	90.9	5.2	0.9	2.3	0.6	1.3	2.4
27 07966	Brooklyn Park	67.5	63 758	423	945	56 381	13.1	43 332	30.1	90.6	4.9	0.6	3.4	0.4	1.2	3.6
27 08794	Burnsville	64.4	60 308	454	936	51 288	17.6	35 674	43.8	94.8	2.3	0.3	2.3	0.3	1.0	2.8
27 13114	Coon Rapids	59.1	63 479	425	1 074	52 978	19.8	35 826	47.9	97.3	0.5	0.8	1.1	0.3	0.9	1.3
27 17000	Duluth	175.1	80 980	303	462	85 493	-5.3	92 811	-7.9	95.9	0.9	2.1	0.9	0.2	0.6	2.4
27 17288	Eagan	83.5	59 972	458	718	47 409	26.5	20 700	129.0	93.7	2.4	0.3	3.1	0.5	1.3	3.5
27 18116	Eden Prairie	83.9	48 518	604	578	39 311	23.4	16 263	141.7	96.4	1.1	0.2	2.1	0.2	0.7	2.6
27 18188	Edina	40.8	45 710	646	1 120	46 075	-0.8	46 073	0.0	97.2	0.7	0.1	1.7	0.2	0.7	3.7
27 22814	Fridley	26.2	27 935	1 076	1 066	28 335	-1.4	30 228	-6.3	95.7	1.0	0.7	2.2	0.4	1.0	3.3
27 39878	Mankato	30.0	31 305	969	1 044	31 459	-0.5	28 650	9.8	96.3	0.7	0.3	2.3	0.5	1.1	3.4
27 40166	Maple Grove	85.1	48 874	598	574	38 736	26.2	20 525	88.7	97.1	0.9	0.3	1.6	0.2	0.8	1.7
27 40382	Maplewood	44.9	34 920	866	778	30 954	12.8	26 990	14.7	94.4	2.5	0.6	2.0	0.5	1.5	2.6
27 43000	Minneapolis	142.3	353 395	47	2 483	368 383	-4.1	370 951	-0.7	78.4	13.0	3.3	4.3	0.9	2.1	6.1
27 43252	Minnetonka	70.2	51 813	559	738	48 370	7.1	38 683	25.0	97.1	0.9	0.2	1.6	0.3	0.8	2.6
27 43864	Moorhead	26.1	33 395	909	1 280	32 295	3.4	29 998	7.7	95.3	0.5	1.4	1.1	1.7	2.8	2.5
27 51730	Plymouth	85.3	62 152	432	729	50 889	22.1	31 614	61.0	95.7	1.6	0.4	2.0	0.3	1.0	2.6
27 54214	Richfield	17.8	33 699	895	1 893	35 710	-5.6	37 851	-5.7	93.5	2.6	0.6	2.8	0.5	1.1	3.9
27 54880	Rochester	76.3	80 768	307	1 059	70 729	14.2	57 890	22.2	94.2	1.0	0.3	4.1	0.3	1.2	5.2
27 55852	Roseville	34.3	34 391	880	1 003	33 485	2.7	35 820	-6.5	95.1	1.6	0.3	2.6	0.4	1.1	3.8
27 56896	St. Cloud	37.6	58 099	480	1 545	48 812	19.0	42 566	14.7	96.8	1.0	0.6	1.3	0.3	0.6	1.3
27 57220	St. Louis Park	27.7	42 456	698	1 533	43 787	-3.0	42 931	2.0	95.3	1.9	0.4	2.1	0.3	1.0	6.5
27 58000	St. Paul	136.7	256 213	64	1 874	272 235	-5.9	270 230	0.7	82.3	7.4	1.4	7.1	2.0	4.2	7.3
27 71032	Winona	30.7	24 965	1 200	813	25 435	-1.8	25 075	1.4	97.6	0.7	0.2	1.2	0.3	0.9	1.8

1. Dry land or land partially or temporarily covered by water.   2. Hispanic persons may be of any race.

Table D. Cities — **Population and Households**

City	Population characteristics, 1990 (cont'd)										Households, 1990				
	Age of population (percent)													Percent	
	Under 5 years	5 to 17 years	18 to 24 years	25 to 34 years	35 to 44 years	45 to 54 years	55 to 64 years	65 to 74 years	75 years and over	Percent female	Number	Percent change, 1980–1990	Persons per house-hold	Female family house-holder[1]	One-person
	16	17	18	19	20	21	22	23	24	25	26	27	28	29	30
MICHIGAN—Cont'd															
Dearborn	7.1	16.0	8.9	17.4	13.9	9.5	9.4	10.8	7.2	51.6	35 442	1.6	2.51	10.4	29.0
Dearborn Heights	6.0	14.6	9.0	17.2	13.0	10.8	12.6	11.1	5.7	52.0	23 432	1.0	2.58	10.6	23.4
Detroit	9.0	20.4	11.0	16.6	14.1	8.8	7.9	7.3	4.9	53.6	374 057	-13.8	2.71	30.3	29.8
East Lansing	3.3	7.3	57.0	12.8	8.0	4.6	2.7	2.5	1.9	51.5	13 500	5.8	2.43	6.5	28.7
Eastpointe	7.0	15.7	8.2	18.4	13.1	8.2	10.6	11.9	6.9	52.7	13 443	0.5	2.62	11.5	23.0
Farmington Hills	6.6	16.1	8.3	18.8	17.1	11.9	9.4	7.4	4.4	51.3	29 234	43.7	2.52	6.0	25.5
Ferndale	8.4	17.9	9.1	22.5	14.9	8.2	6.8	6.8	5.4	50.9	9 858	-0.9	2.54	13.9	28.5
Flint	9.4	21.1	11.2	17.6	13.4	8.8	7.8	6.2	4.5	53.2	53 894	-6.6	2.56	26.3	29.3
Garden City	6.9	18.4	9.4	19.1	13.9	10.7	11.7	7.3	2.6	50.6	11 213	0.6	2.84	11.1	17.6
Grand Rapids	9.4	18.2	12.5	19.6	13.3	7.1	6.9	6.8	6.2	52.5	69 029	5.3	2.60	16.1	27.2
Holland	8.6	18.2	15.6	17.4	12.4	7.4	6.7	6.9	6.7	52.9	10 572	15.9	2.71	9.6	23.4
Inkster	8.1	20.6	11.1	17.0	14.5	9.3	8.0	7.5	3.8	52.9	11 201	-4.9	2.73	24.2	26.8
Jackson	9.7	18.7	10.7	18.4	12.7	7.8	7.8	7.5	6.5	53.1	14 723	-2.2	2.47	18.7	31.4
Kalamazoo	7.4	14.7	24.4	17.9	12.0	7.0	6.0	5.5	5.2	52.9	29 409	3.5	2.41	15.2	31.1
Kentwood	7.9	18.5	11.1	21.6	15.2	9.3	6.8	5.6	4.0	52.2	15 247	32.7	2.47	9.7	28.3
Lansing	9.2	18.4	11.7	21.4	15.0	7.9	6.7	5.8	3.9	52.6	50 635	2.3	2.50	16.6	29.1
Lincoln Park	7.0	17.2	9.4	18.8	14.6	8.9	9.7	9.5	4.9	51.7	16 257	-1.5	2.57	12.6	25.2
Livonia	6.6	16.3	8.6	16.2	15.8	11.5	11.8	8.3	4.8	51.4	35 916	10.0	2.77	7.7	17.7
Madison Heights	7.2	15.7	10.4	21.5	13.7	10.1	10.0	6.9	4.5	51.7	12 850	0.2	2.49	11.1	28.7
Midland	7.1	17.9	11.2	16.7	15.6	11.0	8.5	6.7	5.2	51.7	14 812	13.2	2.49	7.7	25.4
Muskegon	8.7	17.9	11.8	19.4	13.2	7.4	7.1	7.7	6.9	50.5	14 770	-2.9	2.46	20.2	31.6
Novi	7.7	18.1	8.1	21.7	18.2	11.1	7.1	5.1	2.8	51.7	12 699	58.3	2.58	8.2	23.2
Oak Park	8.2	20.0	8.3	17.4	15.6	10.1	7.9	8.0	4.4	52.1	10 885	-3.1	2.80	15.9	22.0
Pontiac	9.8	20.6	12.5	19.3	13.3	9.1	6.6	5.2	3.5	51.6	24 777	-3.7	2.76	25.5	26.3
Portage	7.4	19.4	9.3	17.2	18.3	11.1	8.6	5.7	2.9	51.5	15 467	18.1	2.64	8.6	21.6
Port Huron	8.7	19.8	10.7	17.7	13.1	8.3	7.8	7.4	6.5	53.4	13 158	2.3	2.51	18.2	28.5
Rochester Hills	7.2	19.1	8.4	17.1	19.8	11.8	7.8	4.8	3.9	51.4	22 353	NA	2.73	6.8	19.5
Roseville	7.2	16.8	9.8	20.1	13.8	8.8	9.9	8.9	4.8	52.1	19 537	7.3	2.62	12.6	24.7
Royal Oak	6.8	13.9	7.6	22.5	16.1	8.5	8.8	9.3	6.4	52.8	28 344	0.6	2.29	9.2	32.3
Saginaw	9.7	22.3	10.3	16.9	13.5	8.0	7.4	6.9	5.0	53.9	26 179	-4.8	2.61	26.0	28.1
St. Clair Shores	5.7	14.1	8.1	16.5	13.3	10.4	13.3	11.4	7.2	52.6	27 218	1.9	2.49	9.8	26.3
Southfield	5.7	14.4	8.7	17.9	15.9	11.0	9.5	8.8	8.0	53.2	32 112	8.2	2.34	9.7	32.3
Southgate	6.0	16.0	10.0	17.9	16.2	10.0	10.6	9.2	4.1	51.5	12 128	10.0	2.52	9.5	26.9
Sterling Heights	6.5	19.5	11.1	16.3	17.3	12.7	7.3	5.9	3.3	51.2	40 835	20.4	2.87	8.4	19.1
Taylor	8.2	19.5	11.6	18.5	14.2	11.1	8.9	5.2	2.7	51.4	24 861	1.3	2.82	16.4	18.2
Troy	6.7	19.8	8.5	15.4	19.7	13.4	8.1	5.2	3.1	51.0	26 167	13.7	2.78	6.3	20.5
Warren	6.2	14.8	10.4	17.7	12.2	11.7	12.0	9.5	5.4	51.4	54 602	1.6	2.63	11.4	22.7
Westland	7.3	16.4	11.3	21.0	13.6	10.7	8.9	6.3	4.5	52.0	33 110	14.1	2.53	11.7	27.1
Wyandotte	7.1	17.0	9.0	18.4	14.9	8.2	9.1	10.3	5.9	51.7	12 319	-4.4	2.50	12.4	28.3
Wyoming	8.8	18.9	11.1	21.4	14.1	8.1	7.8	6.1	3.6	51.5	24 168	9.8	2.63	10.4	23.6
MINNESOTA	7.7	19.0	10.1	17.8	15.2	9.8	7.9	6.7	5.8	51.0	1 647 853	13.9	2.58	8.6	25.1
Apple Valley	9.3	25.5	7.6	18.4	21.0	12.1	3.5	1.5	1.1	50.1	11 145	74.5	3.09	8.1	12.7
Blaine	9.7	22.6	9.9	22.0	17.4	10.3	5.0	2.3	0.8	49.8	12 825	49.5	3.04	10.0	12.8
Bloomington	6.2	15.2	9.9	18.9	15.7	13.1	10.9	6.6	3.7	51.6	34 488	20.9	2.47	8.2	23.4
Brooklyn Center	7.2	16.2	10.3	18.5	13.8	9.6	12.1	8.0	4.4	51.9	11 226	3.9	2.56	12.8	21.8
Brooklyn Park	9.2	20.6	11.2	22.9	18.2	9.5	5.0	2.5	0.8	50.8	20 386	32.9	2.76	11.7	19.2
Burnsville	9.1	19.2	10.9	22.3	16.7	12.0	6.1	2.7	1.1	50.5	19 127	58.6	2.67	9.2	19.5
Coon Rapids	9.2	22.2	10.0	20.5	16.7	10.9	5.7	2.8	1.9	50.6	17 449	68.2	3.01	10.6	13.3
Duluth	6.4	16.5	13.7	15.0	14.3	8.9	8.0	8.8	8.4	52.9	34 563	-2.5	2.36	11.1	31.7
Eagan	11.2	18.6	9.1	28.7	18.5	8.5	3.4	1.3	0.6	50.4	17 427	155.2	2.72	7.9	19.0
Eden Prairie	10.5	18.8	7.6	25.1	21.9	8.9	4.1	2.2	0.9	51.0	14 447	168.8	2.71	7.3	18.0
Edina	5.3	14.7	6.2	12.1	16.3	12.4	12.5	11.3	9.1	54.6	19 860	10.7	2.30	6.2	29.7
Fridley	6.6	16.8	11.9	18.6	14.6	13.1	10.7	5.2	2.5	50.7	10 909	5.1	2.58	11.7	20.6
Mankato	5.4	12.6	33.7	14.8	10.4	6.4	5.8	5.8	5.1	50.8	11 220	12.2	2.46	8.7	27.2
Maple Grove	10.1	24.4	6.5	21.9	21.3	10.0	3.7	1.5	0.6	50.1	12 531	99.0	3.09	6.8	11.3
Maplewood	8.0	17.2	9.2	18.9	15.0	10.7	9.4	6.7	5.1	51.5	11 496	31.2	2.62	11.0	21.5
Minneapolis	7.3	13.3	13.3	23.5	15.7	7.9	6.2	6.3	6.6	51.5	160 682	-0.9	2.19	12.7	38.5
Minnetonka	6.7	17.5	7.6	17.5	19.3	12.3	9.3	6.5	3.3	51.5	18 687	47.8	2.56	6.7	21.3
Moorhead	6.8	15.6	26.6	14.1	11.8	7.2	6.7	5.9	5.2	53.5	11 063	11.7	2.56	10.3	24.8
Plymouth	8.0	19.5	9.2	19.7	19.1	13.0	6.6	3.6	1.3	50.3	18 361	75.3	2.72	7.5	17.7
Richfield	6.2	13.1	10.0	20.6	14.2	9.3	9.7	10.8	6.1	52.3	15 551	2.0	2.29	9.8	29.8
Rochester	8.7	17.1	10.0	21.7	14.9	9.7	7.0	5.4	5.6	52.3	27 913	27.2	2.45	8.3	29.1
Roseville	5.5	13.8	11.3	16.3	13.2	11.8	11.3	9.8	7.0	53.2	13 562	5.7	2.37	7.8	27.0
St. Cloud	6.2	14.3	28.0	17.5	11.3	6.3	6.2	5.5	4.7	50.9	17 926	28.1	2.46	10.4	27.9
St. Louis Park	6.4	11.4	9.5	24.3	14.8	9.2	8.3	8.6	7.5	53.6	19 925	12.9	2.16	8.4	33.4
St. Paul	8.4	16.1	12.2	20.4	14.6	7.6	6.9	7.0	6.8	52.8	110 249	3.8	2.37	13.0	34.7
Winona	5.3	13.7	26.1	13.0	11.8	7.1	7.0	7.4	8.8	53.1	9 334	7.1	2.36	8.3	32.3

1. No spouse present.

Table D. Cities — Group Quarters, Crime, Education, and Income

City	Persons in group quarters, 1990 — Total	Persons in mental hospitals	Persons in nursing homes	Persons identified as homeless[1]	Serious crimes known to police, 1998[2] — Total Number	Total Rate[3]	Rate[3] Violent	Property	Education, 1990 — School enrollment Public	Private	Attainment (percent) High school graduate or more	Bachelor's degree or more	Money income, 1989 Per capita (dollars)[5]	Households Median Dollars	Percent change, 1979–1989 (constant 1989 dollars)
	31	32	33	34	35	36	37	38	39	40	41	42	43	44	45
MICHIGAN—Cont'd															
Dearborn	272	18	0	16	6 869	7 517	812	6 705	19 659	3 603	75.9	21.7	16 852	34 909	-5.9
Dearborn Heights	480	0	298	0	2 247	3 655	286	3 369	10 888	3 045	74.1	13.7	16 493	36 771	-13.3
Detroit	15 381	245	5 574	1 312	117 911	11 791	2 443	9 348	244 105	46 262	62.1	9.6	9 443	18 742	-20.0
East Lansing	17 913	0	97	56	1 798	3 725	265	3 460	34 848	1 206	96.6	71.2	11 212	24 716	-1.7
Eastpointe	12	0	0	0	NA	NA	NA	NA	6 854	1 377	69.5	8.9	14 156	34 069	-5.8
Farmington Hills	975	0	589	22	2 818	3 489	215	3 274	15 282	3 967	89.2	42.0	25 499	51 986	0.7
Ferndale	71	0	71	0	1 351	5 459	497	4 962	5 390	817	73.8	13.0	12 704	28 964	-1.8
Flint	2 644	0	653	98	16 216	11 973	2 463	9 510	37 455	4 565	69.3	10.3	10 415	20 176	-29.9
Garden City	0	0	0	0	833	2 577	133	2 444	7 066	812	75.0	7.1	14 257	38 717	-9.6
Grand Rapids	9 590	11	3 261	758	14 502	7 619	1 224	6 395	36 852	16 614	76.4	20.8	12 070	26 809	3.5
Holland	2 087	0	398	46	NA	NA	NA	NA	5 831	3 495	73.6	22.5	13 344	30 689	6.6
Inkster	178	0	89	74	NA	NA	NA	NA	7 486	1 106	66.7	7.3	10 723	25 198	-18.3
Jackson	1 029	0	75	59	2 722	7 300	968	6 332	8 316	1 675	71.5	10.8	10 410	20 830	-14.6
Kalamazoo	9 437	259	718	237	5 461	7 014	1 055	5 959	27 289	3 454	79.6	29.8	11 956	23 207	-5.3
Kentwood	224	0	157	0	2 046	4 839	274	4 565	8 264	1 861	83.9	26.0	15 453	34 324	4.7
Lansing	884	31	285	93	NA	NA	NA	NA	33 276	4 581	78.3	18.3	12 232	26 398	-7.2
Lincoln Park	55	28	18	0	2 496	5 922	505	5 417	7 879	1 962	67.6	6.8	13 338	30 638	-14.0
Livonia	1 344	0	1 003	0	3 381	3 218	196	3 022	21 482	4 718	84.7	23.8	19 145	48 645	-3.4
Madison Heights	140	0	140	0	1 715	5 211	307	4 904	6 754	838	72.4	11.0	14 912	31 757	-12.0
Midland	1 206	0	402	13	NA	NA	NA	NA	8 979	2 626	88.4	41.9	19 255	38 747	-1.8
Muskegon	4 076	21	574	63	3 558	8 906	869	8 037	9 468	1 290	68.7	8.2	8 890	18 748	-7.1
Novi	261	0	261	0	1 885	4 275	338	3 937	7 912	1 152	89.5	33.9	20 752	47 518	5.4
Oak Park	0	0	0	0	938	3 097	201	2 896	7 084	2 000	80.8	22.2	14 544	36 090	-3.1
Pontiac	2 867	778	510	163	NA	NA	NA	NA	17 191	1 642	62.4	7.9	9 847	21 962	-19.0
Portage	149	0	149	0	1 915	4 398	202	4 196	10 380	1 512	88.6	31.3	17 602	39 045	3.1
Port Huron	647	0	353	3	1 739	5 200	616	4 584	8 167	712	71.2	10.6	11 210	21 522	-13.1
Rochester Hills	795	0	577	0	NA	NA	NA	NA	14 788	2 863	89.4	39.5	23 209	54 996	NA
Roseville	130	0	130	0	2 564	4 948	367	4 581	10 659	1 959	69.4	6.9	13 437	32 337	-8.8
Royal Oak	428	0	292	69	2 214	3 373	210	3 163	12 168	3 049	86.0	28.4	18 065	36 835	-1.6
Saginaw	1 206	21	310	46	4 964	7 619	1 932	5 687	19 417	1 885	68.6	9.3	8 944	17 736	-27.2
St. Clair Shores	447	0	403	0	2 108	3 256	204	3 052	12 145	2 586	77.9	13.7	16 690	36 929	-9.4
Southfield	708	0	603	0	6 332	8 224	1 069	7 155	14 392	4 153	84.8	34.7	21 098	40 579	-8.5
Southgate	267	0	86	0	1 342	4 270	630	3 640	6 140	1 106	73.8	9.5	15 485	36 526	-13.6
Sterling Heights	692	0	634	33	4 576	3 815	219	3 596	31 317	4 132	80.7	18.5	17 084	46 470	0.4
Taylor	772	48	677	0	4 550	6 327	478	5 849	15 295	2 857	68.2	6.8	12 955	32 659	-12.9
Troy	16	0	16	0	3 020	3 777	155	3 622	18 495	3 217	88.9	39.9	23 249	55 407	7.0
Warren	1 363	41	1 224	49	7 634	5 471	973	4 498	29 107	4 142	71.7	10.3	15 224	35 980	-10.0
Westland	1 108	290	767	0	5 033	5 545	499	5 046	18 382	2 031	75.7	11.4	15 079	34 995	-8.6
Wyandotte	157	85	7	0	965	3 036	164	2 872	6 203	1 202	68.9	7.8	13 190	28 312	-13.1
Wyoming	261	0	106	0	2 925	4 345	618	3 727	13 538	2 949	78.6	13.2	13 271	31 103	-0.5
MINNESOTA	117 261	1 738	47 051	2 434	191 197	4 047	310	3 737	1 006 375	168 652	82.4	21.8	14 389	30 909	3.8
Apple Valley	202	0	202	0	1 254	2 831	108	2 723	9 791	1 171	95.4	36.6	18 173	49 981	7.9
Blaine	14	0	0	0	2 498	5 627	205	5 422	10 419	894	87.3	14.6	13 841	40 404	0.5
Bloomington	1 070	0	798	0	5 155	5 901	230	5 671	16 656	3 691	91.2	31.7	20 032	41 736	-4.5
Brooklyn Center	115	0	95	0	2 356	8 308	406	7 902	6 128	438	83.8	14.1	14 645	34 168	-8.5
Brooklyn Park	35	0	0	0	3 148	5 092	450	4 642	14 211	1 464	90.7	20.9	15 541	40 018	7.7
Burnsville	199	0	118	14	2 470	4 196	163	4 033	11 925	1 810	94.5	34.3	18 523	43 620	-2.5
Coon Rapids	473	0	387	0	2 938	4 557	189	4 368	13 297	1 729	88.8	16.5	14 669	42 069	0.3
Duluth	4 094	0	1 380	335	4 085	4 832	433	4 399	22 227	2 868	81.4	22.5	12 484	23 370	-8.5
Eagan	52	0	0	0	1 692	2 864	117	2 747	10 643	1 872	96.0	39.2	18 662	46 612	15.4
Eden Prairie	155	0	79	0	1 461	3 043	108	2 935	8 759	1 825	97.0	46.8	23 898	52 956	5.5
Edina	366	0	366	0	1 474	3 156	105	3 051	8 318	2 306	94.7	52.6	32 301	48 936	-3.3
Fridley	193	17	176	0	1 777	6 207	231	5 976	5 977	875	87.1	20.5	16 347	36 855	-3.8
Mankato	3 858	54	171	72	1 828	5 806	168	5 638	13 745	985	84.9	29.2	10 376	22 480	-7.1
Maple Grove	0	0	0	0	1 406	3 090	123	2 967	10 837	1 266	95.4	28.5	17 481	50 611	8.8
Maplewood	820	0	486	0	1 925	5 602	169	5 433	5 677	1 541	85.4	20.3	16 459	37 856	-3.3
Minneapolis	16 577	78	5 427	1 069	34 621	9 561	1 525	8 036	78 444	17 368	82.6	30.3	14 830	25 324	5.3
Minnetonka	604	0	364	0	1 564	3 090	61	3 029	9 565	2 619	94.3	43.2	25 221	50 659	0.0
Moorhead	3 943	19	357	46	1 278	3 796	276	3 520	10 617	2 760	83.5	27.9	10 550	24 265	-11.8
Plymouth	907	0	85	0	1 708	2 819	124	2 695	11 725	2 332	94.4	41.4	21 908	51 314	10.0
Richfield	159	0	108	0	1 694	4 887	352	4 535	6 273	1 002	88.1	20.9	15 992	32 405	-5.3
Rochester	2 480	0	918	62	2 837	3 672	333	3 339	14 746	3 275	89.1	33.2	16 533	34 922	6.0
Roseville	1 338	0	617	0	1 934	5 596	203	5 393	5 869	2 480	88.6	34.5	18 593	37 862	-9.8
St. Cloud	4 571	148	407	42	NA	NA	NA	NA	17 215	1 828	84.4	25.4	11 736	24 004	-6.8
St. Louis Park	687	7	625	0	1 697	3 931	148	3 783	6 788	1 714	90.6	35.3	19 212	34 778	-2.9
St. Paul	10 274	0	2 199	585	20 265	7 720	909	6 811	52 372	21 353	81.1	26.5	13 727	26 498	-1.4
Winona	3 429	0	507	0	1 188	4 766	60	4 706	7 844	1 962	76.9	22.6	10 756	22 497	-2.0

1. Persons in emergency shelters and persons visible in street locations, areas and over time.　3. Per 100,000 population estimated by the FBI.　2. Data for serious crimes have not been adjusted for underreporting. This may affect comparability between geographic　4. Persons 25 years old and older.　5. Based on population enumerated as of April 1, 1990.

City	Money income, 1989 (cont'd)				Housing units, 1990										
	House-holds (cont'd)	Percent below poverty, 1989						Occupied units							
		Persons		Fam-ilies						Owner-occupied units			Renter-occu-pied units		
											Owner cost as a percent of income				
	Percent with $100,000 or more	Total	Percent change in rate, 1979–1989	Total	Total	Percent change, 1980–1990	Vacant units for sale or rent[1]	Total	Percent	Median value[2] (dollars)	With a mort-gage	Without a mort-gage	Median rent[3] (dol-lars)	Rent as per-cent of income	Sub-standard units[4] (percent)
	46	47	48	49	50	51	52	53	54	55	56	57	58	59	60
MICHIGAN—Cont'd															
Dearborn	5.2	10.8	80.0	8.2	36 929	3.5	1 069	35 442	74.4	69 600	16.9	13.3	465	26.2	3.6
Dearborn Heights	4.6	5.5	44.7	4.0	23 939	1.9	352	23 432	84.3	64 500	16.3	12.9	532	24.5	1.9
Detroit	1.2	32.4	47.9	29.0	410 027	-13.0	23 665	374 057	52.9	25 600	17.7	14.8	372	35.1	5.9
East Lansing	7.0	33.8	24.3	11.4	14 403	9.8	775	13 500	33.2	97 000	17.8	12.5	451	34.0	6.0
Eastpointe	1.8	4.9	8.9	3.7	13 684	1.7	204	13 443	87.5	55 300	18.2	13.0	467	27.7	2.2
Farmington Hills	15.6	3.0	-16.7	1.7	31 171	44.6	1 678	29 234	65.6	145 900	20.2	12.6	660	23.4	1.1
Ferndale	1.0	10.7	24.4	8.4	10 207	0.3	260	9 858	68.1	38 400	17.4	14.4	467	25.0	2.9
Flint	1.0	30.6	81.1	27.6	58 724	-3.7	3 277	53 894	58.1	33 900	16.7	14.2	375	35.1	4.7
Garden City	1.6	4.3	19.4	3.0	11 374	0.4	104	11 213	86.3	59 700	16.5	12.4	470	26.3	1.8
Grand Rapids	1.9	16.1	19.3	12.6	73 716	5.5	3 316	69 029	59.9	58 300	19.0	13.8	414	28.3	2.8
Holland	4.0	11.8	37.2	8.2	11 243	16.4	477	10 572	68.0	68 200	18.2	13.0	453	25.4	3.6
Inkster	1.4	23.2	50.6	19.6	12 045	-1.7	602	11 201	58.6	36 500	16.5	14.2	436	29.1	7.6
Jackson	1.0	24.7	55.3	21.2	15 689	-1.6	688	14 723	55.8	32 100	17.3	13.7	338	27.6	2.5
Kalamazoo	3.1	26.2	33.7	19.3	31 488	4.2	1 557	29 409	47.4	48 600	17.8	14.4	403	30.1	3.5
Kentwood	2.7	5.0	-26.5	3.7	16 337	34.9	997	15 247	57.7	78 100	18.7	13.4	475	22.7	2.3
Lansing	1.2	19.4	48.1	16.5	53 919	3.8	2 487	50 635	54.8	48 400	18.0	13.5	399	26.8	3.2
Lincoln Park	1.7	8.5	70.0	6.2	16 763	-0.5	409	16 257	78.5	44 500	16.3	13.8	432	23.8	2.2
Livonia	7.6	2.6	18.2	1.7	36 641	11.0	615	35 916	88.9	94 800	17.7	12.5	606	26.7	1.2
Madison Heights	1.5	8.4	35.5	6.9	13 220	1.5	285	12 850	69.5	59 800	17.7	12.6	481	25.2	2.1
Midland	8.3	9.5	66.7	6.1	15 447	12.0	469	14 812	69.1	74 200	16.8	11.3	422	25.2	1.1
Muskegon	0.5	26.5	37.3	23.0	16 019	-2.0	873	14 770	54.6	32 400	17.0	13.6	343	30.2	4.7
Novi	8.9	3.3	17.9	2.2	13 557	56.4	772	12 699	73.0	127 900	21.4	14.2	680	21.7	1.3
Oak Park	2.5	10.9	55.7	8.4	11 344	0.4	263	10 885	73.8	48 000	18.6	14.1	567	24.6	5.2
Pontiac	0.8	26.7	51.7	24.1	26 593	-4.2	1 263	24 777	49.7	36 300	17.2	14.0	436	30.5	7.0
Portage	5.8	4.2	16.7	2.8	16 133	18.1	532	15 467	71.6	71 800	17.3	12.4	434	22.6	1.4
Port Huron	2.0	22.1	38.1	20.0	14 026	4.7	630	13 158	54.5	41 400	18.6	15.0	387	31.7	3.0
Rochester Hills	14.2	2.6	NA	1.7	23 535	NA	947	22 353	77.7	137 900	21.3	13.2	643	23.2	1.4
Roseville	1.5	6.2	3.3	4.9	20 025	8.3	396	19 537	74.6	55 400	17.5	13.5	476	25.4	2.2
Royal Oak	3.4	4.6	9.5	2.9	29 163	1.3	609	28 344	70.0	75 600	17.9	13.3	497	23.6	1.3
Saginaw	0.7	31.7	52.4	28.5	27 986	-2.6	1 166	26 179	57.5	32 800	17.0	14.8	343	35.1	5.0
St. Clair Shores	3.4	3.6	2.9	2.6	27 929	2.9	543	27 218	84.7	69 700	17.9	13.5	504	27.0	1.4
Southfield	6.9	5.8	56.8	3.5	35 054	12.0	2 320	32 112	53.9	85 100	19.4	13.6	672	25.3	2.4
Southgate	2.1	4.6	48.4	3.3	12 504	10.4	319	12 128	70.2	58 700	16.4	13.4	503	21.8	2.1
Sterling Heights	4.5	3.6	12.5	2.8	42 317	22.6	1 333	40 835	77.6	97 000	18.3	13.1	533	23.5	1.9
Taylor	1.8	11.9	40.0	11.0	25 727	1.5	688	24 861	67.7	48 400	15.9	12.8	457	23.2	4.0
Troy	13.4	2.8	0.0	2.0	27 197	14.5	896	26 167	74.7	128 900	19.6	12.3	620	22.7	1.6
Warren	2.9	6.5	32.7	5.1	56 189	3.0	1 296	54 602	79.5	69 500	16.7	13.2	492	25.2	2.5
Westland	1.7	7.1	36.5	5.6	34 514	15.2	1 210	33 110	60.2	63 400	16.2	12.7	512	24.2	2.7
Wyandotte	1.4	9.7	26.0	8.0	12 822	-3.5	324	12 319	70.0	49 400	15.7	14.8	412	24.8	1.9
Wyoming	1.5	7.1	20.3	5.4	25 056	10.4	700	24 168	67.4	57 700	17.8	12.7	429	23.0	2.1
MINNESOTA	3.6	10.2	7.6	7.3	1 848 445	14.6	67 710	1 647 853	71.8	74 000	20.4	12.4	422	26.7	2.4
Apple Valley	8.8	3.5	40.0	2.6	11 538	70.2	349	11 145	87.4	101 100	22.3	12.0	592	28.6	1.2
Blaine	1.3	5.2	13.0	4.1	13 176	51.4	320	12 825	90.2	80 600	21.0	11.6	539	27.0	1.8
Bloomington	7.4	3.7	23.3	2.3	35 815	21.1	1 083	34 488	70.3	97 500	20.0	11.3	574	25.8	1.3
Brooklyn Center	1.9	7.1	31.5	5.8	11 713	6.7	435	11 226	69.5	79 400	19.5	11.1	509	28.9	2.6
Brooklyn Park	2.3	7.5	25.0	7.0	21 265	34.6	805	20 386	67.4	88 400	21.4	11.5	475	26.4	2.7
Burnsville	5.7	4.2	35.5	3.5	20 244	57.6	998	19 127	64.9	108 100	20.8	10.5	576	24.7	2.3
Coon Rapids	2.6	4.8	17.1	3.8	18 098	68.6	591	17 449	80.0	82 500	21.3	11.6	556	27.2	1.9
Duluth	2.1	16.6	38.3	10.5	36 022	-2.9	947	34 563	64.4	46 300	15.5	12.4	312	29.4	1.3
Eagan	4.8	2.8	-22.2	2.2	18 450	156.0	949	17 427	68.8	104 300	22.8	11.6	604	22.7	1.5
Eden Prairie	12.7	3.1	14.8	2.4	15 405	169.8	866	14 447	72.5	121 600	22.5	11.5	657	23.1	0.9
Edina	19.7	3.2	28.0	1.8	20 983	12.5	774	19 860	76.4	156 700	20.3	11.7	654	27.4	0.5
Fridley	3.5	6.1	45.2	4.9	11 418	7.1	456	10 909	67.5	86 000	17.8	10.8	485	25.4	2.1
Mankato	1.1	25.2	59.5	11.0	11 688	10.0	385	11 220	51.5	62 100	18.2	11.9	385	29.9	2.7
Maple Grove	5.4	2.3	-14.8	1.8	12 968	91.7	392	12 531	89.8	96 000	22.5	11.4	710	24.5	0.9
Maplewood	3.0	6.2	55.0	5.6	12 120	34.0	530	11 496	75.9	87 800	21.2	12.0	512	26.9	1.8
Minneapolis	3.2	18.5	37.0	14.1	172 666	2.3	9 494	160 682	49.7	71 700	20.7	13.0	424	28.4	3.8
Minnetonka	14.6	2.1	-4.5	1.1	20 119	52.1	1 299	18 687	76.6	121 000	20.7	11.5	660	23.9	0.8
Moorhead	1.5	19.9	73.0	10.8	11 511	8.8	384	11 063	60.2	62 000	17.8	11.9	343	33.6	2.9
Plymouth	12.5	3.4	21.4	2.4	19 616	77.7	1 125	18 361	73.6	127 400	21.7	11.5	611	22.9	0.8
Richfield	1.4	5.5	48.6	3.9	16 094	4.3	478	15 551	66.9	84 800	20.3	11.4	457	27.0	1.4
Rochester	4.7	7.8	14.7	4.8	28 961	25.3	822	27 913	66.2	71 900	18.6	11.7	416	23.6	2.0
Roseville	5.7	3.7	19.4	2.6	14 216	8.0	593	13 562	68.4	97 000	18.6	11.5	507	26.8	0.8
St. Cloud	2.0	19.6	39.0	9.3	18 828	30.0	783	17 926	51.3	59 400	18.3	12.3	399	28.8	1.9
St. Louis Park	4.4	5.1	15.9	3.1	20 678	14.5	632	19 925	62.6	87 100	20.4	12.3	544	25.1	1.3
St. Paul	2.5	16.7	53.2	12.4	117 583	6.0	5 905	110 249	53.9	70 900	21.3	13.2	424	28.4	4.3
Winona	1.1	17.2	26.5	7.2	9 682	5.2	239	9 334	63.6	50 400	17.3	12.6	320	27.8	1.7

1. Includes units rented or sold but not occupied.   2. Specified owner-occupied units.   3. Specified renter-occupied units.   4. Overcrowded or lacking complete plumbing facilities.

Table D. Cities — Labor Force, Employment, Disability, and Construction

City	Civilian labor force, 1999				Civilian employment, 1990[2]			Disability 1990	Value of residential construction authorized by building permits, 1999		
	Total	Percent change, 1998–1999	Unemployment		Total	Percent		Work disabled persons[3] (percent)	New construction ($1,000)	Number of housing units	Percent single family
			Total	Rate[1]		Professional, managerial, and technical	Precision production, craft, and repair				
	61	62	63	64	65	66	67	68	69	70	71
MICHIGAN—Cont'd											
Dearborn	43 838	1.1	885	2.0	38 978	36.0	10.3	7.9	17 010	108	57.4
Dearborn Heights	31 883	1.1	605	1.9	28 383	27.3	13.3	8.6	16 015	97	67.0
Detroit	397 697	0.9	28 024	7.0	335 462	22.1	8.8	13.8	41 690	440	35.9
East Lansing	29 350	1.6	906	3.1	26 344	41.5	2.1	2.0	2 540	22	90.9
Eastpointe	19 869	NA	561	2.8	16 006	23.0	15.0	9.5	454	7	100.0
Farmington Hills	49 394	2.4	843	1.7	40 703	48.6	7.8	4.9	27 486	207	67.1
Ferndale	15 151	2.4	458	3.0	12 318	25.2	13.4	10.4	1 167	14	100.0
Flint	54 474	-1.6	5 268	9.7	47 016	21.2	11.0	14.4	9 432	134	6.7
Garden City	17 770	1.1	338	1.9	15 819	18.5	17.0	9.8	2 761	27	100.0
Grand Rapids	116 280	3.2	5 086	4.4	85 877	27.2	9.6	9.2	26 972	313	77.0
Holland	21 538	3.7	706	3.3	14 823	26.9	9.7	7.1	5 384	51	54.9
Inkster	13 885	1.0	656	4.7	12 005	21.8	9.9	14.1	581	8	100.0
Jackson	18 315	1.9	917	5.0	14 838	22.5	9.6	15.2	1 952	18	100.0
Kalamazoo	43 173	3.4	1 896	4.4	36 210	33.0	6.8	8.1	9 786	72	16.7
Kentwood	27 836	3.1	557	2.0	21 068	30.9	9.1	5.9	18 870	264	79.9
Lansing	67 420	1.5	2 331	3.5	60 089	27.8	9.2	10.7	11 539	212	17.9
Lincoln Park	21 254	1.1	541	2.5	18 796	18.3	14.3	10.6	215	2	100.0
Livonia	57 418	1.1	825	1.4	51 356	36.4	12.0	6.2	16 280	129	92.2
Madison Heights	20 284	2.4	666	3.3	16 447	24.1	14.3	9.2	1 213	16	100.0
Midland	22 750	2.8	493	2.2	18 103	49.4	8.1	5.8	15 695	136	61.0
Muskegon	18 582	2.8	1 160	6.2	13 970	21.4	11.0	15.5	5 235	53	100.0
Novi	22 066	2.4	409	1.9	18 156	41.2	9.4	5.0	36 658	227	100.0
Oak Park	17 527	2.4	521	3.0	14 257	32.8	8.8	9.1	2 705	39	100.0
Pontiac	33 902	2.3	2 463	7.3	26 357	17.7	11.9	14.5	15 481	208	97.6
Portage	25 779	3.2	478	1.9	22 195	37.1	8.3	6.0	29 970	195	97.9
Port Huron	16 993	2.6	983	5.8	13 281	22.7	11.2	11.9	5 676	56	75.0
Rochester Hills	39 274	2.4	762	1.9	32 287	48.2	7.8	4.5	56 913	485	53.0
Roseville	31 084	2.1	1 251	4.0	24 731	20.2	15.9	9.8	3 478	67	58.2
Royal Oak	42 667	2.4	886	2.1	35 027	38.9	9.6	7.0	1 290	23	100.0
Saginaw	27 804	1.3	2 198	7.9	22 721	20.6	9.2	12.6	307	5	100.0
St. Clair Shores	41 036	2.1	1 227	3.0	33 001	28.8	12.9	8.1	6 291	45	100.0
Southfield	48 733	2.4	1 348	2.8	39 725	44.1	6.6	7.2	11 086	120	35.8
Southgate	16 963	1.1	333	2.0	15 091	23.0	14.3	9.2	25 528	249	35.7
Sterling Heights	77 462	2.1	2 064	2.7	62 504	32.8	12.8	5.9	47 055	581	100.0
Taylor	36 233	1.0	1 061	2.9	31 917	17.6	16.2	10.5	11 721	141	100.0
Troy	47 586	2.4	718	1.5	39 292	48.6	8.1	3.9	69 828	589	49.2
Warren	86 759	2.1	3 318	3.8	69 172	24.6	14.8	8.7	8 351	118	78.0
Westland	49 336	1.1	998	2.0	43 865	23.0	14.6	8.7	12 138	119	98.3
Wyandotte	15 045	1.1	398	2.6	13 291	21.5	14.5	11.8	3 173	30	66.7
Wyoming	44 838	3.1	1 357	3.0	33 581	20.9	12.6	7.7	34 199	437	52.4
MINNESOTA	2 698 511	0.6	75 453	2.8	2 192 417	30.3	10.1	7.4	4 052 938	33 344	80.0
Apple Valley	27 806	2.6	460	1.7	19 122	39.4	8.7	4.7	57 511	644	45.7
Blaine	28 150	2.1	567	2.0	21 899	23.8	14.9	7.1	86 347	703	100.0
Bloomington	57 106	-0.5	1 014	1.8	51 813	36.2	7.8	5.9	4 079	31	100.0
Brooklyn Center	16 392	-0.6	388	2.4	15 306	26.9	11.3	8.1	2 697	18	100.0
Brooklyn Park	40 642	3.2	924	2.3	32 716	30.1	11.0	5.8	59 644	548	74.6
Burnsville	39 520	0.9	718	1.8	30 795	36.6	7.6	5.0	45 109	462	24.5
Coon Rapids	39 521	-0.3	810	2.0	29 489	28.2	12.2	6.7	31 966	353	66.6
Duluth	44 016	-2.2	1 580	3.6	37 139	33.0	7.9	8.8	18 543	287	28.2
Eagan	40 312	1.7	591	1.5	28 797	42.8	7.8	4.1	51 460	282	97.2
Eden Prairie	40 465	5.6	522	1.3	23 463	45.9	5.8	4.0	51 093	280	67.1
Edina	25 800	-0.7	420	1.6	23 495	52.5	2.8	3.7	18 019	60	68.3
Fridley	18 303	-1.4	422	2.3	16 583	30.6	10.0	6.7	8 719	131	2.3
Mankato	20 171	1.5	507	2.5	16 806	25.7	8.4	6.9	11 488	116	43.1
Maple Grove	29 821	4.2	475	1.6	22 334	36.8	10.3	4.5	134 135	991	80.3
Maplewood	20 173	2.7	334	1.7	16 170	31.9	11.1	7.6	26 601	264	36.4
Minneapolis	205 140	-1.8	5 805	2.8	192 508	36.4	6.3	9.8	103 908	1 141	12.6
Minnetonka	32 464	1.7	562	1.7	27 926	45.2	5.8	4.2	21 272	115	53.0
Moorhead	19 624	-1.1	389	2.0	15 987	30.2	6.2	6.7	16 750	176	55.1
Plymouth	39 745	2.6	657	1.7	29 820	43.6	6.6	4.0	81 659	734	62.3
Richfield	21 429	-0.7	416	1.9	20 327	29.9	8.5	6.3	15 781	154	7.8
Rochester	48 730	4.0	1 029	2.1	38 108	43.5	6.3	6.0	119 958	1 119	56.9
Roseville	21 064	0.6	334	1.6	18 546	43.4	7.4	4.7	6 894	33	100.0
St. Cloud	36 736	0.9	1 093	3.0	25 283	28.9	6.9	7.0	25 553	231	89.6
St. Louis Park	28 187	-0.7	478	1.7	26 394	39.1	5.9	6.3	8 193	66	93.9
St. Paul	141 033	-1.1	4 138	2.9	133 383	33.6	7.2	9.5	18 047	152	73.0
Winona	13 736	-8.0	445	3.2	12 437	26.9	10.1	5.8	7 515	48	100.0

1. Percent of civilian labor force. 2. Persons 16 years and older. 3. Persons 16 to 64 years old.

Table D. Cities — Wholesale Trade, Retail Trade, and Real Estate

City	Wholesale Trade, 1997 Number of Establish-ments	Number of Employees	Sales (mil dol)	Annual Payroll (mil dol)	Retail Trade[1], 1997 Number of Establish-ments	Number of Employees	Sales (mil dol)	Annual Payroll (mil dol)	Real Estate and Rental and Leasing, 1997 Number of Establish-ments	Number of Employees	Receipts (mil dol)	Annual Payroll (mil dol)
	72	73	74	75	76	77	78	79	80	81	82	83
MICHIGAN—Cont'd												
Dearborn	156	1 822	1 104.2	78.4	557	9 607	1 752.5	170.9	81	1 132	375.6	44.8
Dearborn Heights	30	237	101.6	8.4	187	2 455	391.6	38.8	35	192	19.2	2.6
Detroit	740	12 878	14 616.4	541.3	2 253	17 886	3 188.7	289.1	380	2 279	233.2	47.2
East Lansing	22	D	D	D	119	2 471	304.0	32.3	59	367	32.6	10.0
Eastpointe	NA	NA	NA	NA	NA	NA	NA	NA	NA	NA	NA	NA
Farmington Hills	416	5 457	7 318.4	266.7	328	4 696	1 100.4	104.2	206	3 754	429.5	89.1
Ferndale	69	808	289.5	31.0	109	1 363	341.4	32.9	27	92	10.8	1.4
Flint	139	1 970	728.3	62.0	531	5 157	864.6	86.3	101	476	59.8	8.7
Garden City	18	139	24.1	4.2	111	1 300	392.1	31.5	16	49	5.8	0.7
Grand Rapids	485	8 890	4 426.2	345.5	795	11 578	2 018.1	214.8	225	1 461	162.6	30.9
Holland	64	1 011	549.2	35.3	230	3 525	612.3	58.7	54	258	32.6	5.6
Inkster	8	79	27.0	3.0	55	470	86.7	7.9	8	47	4.7	0.7
Jackson	100	1 311	633.6	52.1	237	3 671	567.5	56.3	43	160	19.4	2.5
Kalamazoo	155	2 389	687.3	84.8	337	4 265	727.2	70.5	110	1 317	113.6	27.7
Kentwood	121	3 845	3 354.0	142.9	267	5 718	855.4	84.4	62	504	51.8	11.0
Lansing	190	3 186	933.4	103.9	523	8 178	1 486.6	150.2	105	1 730	103.8	27.5
Lincoln Park	22	187	40.0	5.2	159	2 644	352.5	35.9	26	100	11.8	1.4
Livonia	424	8 691	6 430.2	337.7	644	9 668	1 591.2	167.7	120	799	149.1	21.5
Madison Heights	141	2 960	2 722.8	152.0	193	3 744	717.8	66.4	48	510	57.3	9.6
Midland	54	478	240.4	19.6	256	3 673	584.7	59.4	45	168	22.1	2.8
Muskegon	53	669	237.7	22.3	176	2 571	413.0	42.5	26	134	13.1	1.9
Novi	163	3 940	2 851.9	185.1	323	6 100	1 177.8	105.4	53	254	34.7	6.3
Oak Park	91	1 178	627.7	44.3	182	2 510	401.9	55.2	34	374	30.3	7.1
Pontiac	76	D	D	D	228	2 548	502.3	44.6	45	299	27.5	5.6
Portage	83	2 431	692.7	94.7	338	6 404	879.0	85.9	55	354	30.1	6.9
Port Huron	30	285	173.1	11.4	168	1 936	375.7	40.3	36	131	17.7	2.7
Rochester Hills	175	1 405	1 302.5	66.9	240	4 340	968.3	92.3	51	223	41.0	6.1
Roseville	78	973	383.6	39.0	293	5 807	966.3	91.2	47	179	20.6	2.8
Royal Oak	118	915	590.0	37.8	297	4 193	773.9	85.4	67	212	44.2	4.6
Saginaw	76	1 182	317.9	39.0	206	1 898	260.6	30.5	33	176	10.9	2.6
St. Clair Shores	86	548	605.4	23.5	234	3 306	547.8	58.4	47	244	40.0	4.1
Southfield	440	6 838	15 374.8	426.0	566	8 925	1 987.7	182.6	292	3 001	356.3	89.2
Southgate	17	D	D	D	171	3 836	888.7	70.3	19	87	8.8	2.1
Sterling Heights	155	2 409	952.0	106.0	495	9 680	1 598.9	160.0	87	410	64.3	9.7
Taylor	86	1 931	1 872.1	66.3	343	6 038	1 037.0	102.3	56	627	128.3	21.0
Troy	521	7 489	11 690.9	384.1	607	12 184	2 410.8	226.9	169	1 527	191.3	41.2
Warren	274	4 379	2 802.5	169.5	563	8 524	1 730.7	172.0	108	682	105.2	15.4
Westland	76	738	280.8	27.9	335	6 533	1 160.5	101.2	54	410	51.2	7.5
Wyandotte	31	286	59.5	9.4	107	753	122.2	13.3	13	99	4.3	2.3
Wyoming	223	7 193	3 330.3	272.5	308	5 510	934.6	101.4	63	851	150.2	23.3
MINNESOTA	9 348	131 787	99 444.5	5 024.0	20 883	282 282	48 077.7	4 525.7	5 051	30 172	3 886.4	687.2
Apple Valley	49	244	245.7	12.9	112	2 761	529.3	46.5	37	152	18.3	2.7
Blaine	59	964	316.5	33.0	199	3 100	504.4	45.5	36	282	33.9	4.6
Bloomington	485	8 222	10 687.5	402.2	587	12 036	2 079.0	201.3	191	2 224	211.3	67.1
Brooklyn Center	54	540	329.1	20.1	133	3 435	675.0	58.0	33	216	21.5	4.0
Brooklyn Park	97	1 270	580.1	52.7	154	4 656	1 220.1	93.6	41	283	28.3	5.5
Burnsville	225	2 563	1 605.0	88.5	372	7 850	1 272.9	123.4	90	507	69.6	10.0
Coon Rapids	39	456	172.3	19.7	151	3 412	573.7	49.3	58	293	25.8	4.7
Duluth	129	1 611	778.7	49.3	536	7 277	1 037.1	110.8	109	694	54.9	11.3
Eagan	163	3 496	2 059.3	144.7	140	3 251	555.1	57.4	69	367	56.3	8.3
Eden Prairie	319	6 208	5 447.1	303.0	188	3 597	676.4	61.9	96	1 562	399.5	68.4
Edina	300	2 906	5 783.3	145.7	377	8 123	1 182.9	132.6	199	1 253	166.9	33.6
Fridley	94	1 593	817.6	61.3	107	2 863	482.5	47.0	27	177	31.9	3.5
Mankato	74	1 179	415.5	32.9	266	4 823	702.4	66.1	57	333	28.5	6.1
Maple Grove	95	1 606	1 252.8	86.2	97	1 569	277.6	24.9	31	130	14.6	1.6
Maplewood	41	421	126.1	12.1	254	4 936	854.6	77.5	52	234	25.8	3.9
Minneapolis	841	14 152	13 527.1	644.3	1 333	15 860	2 344.0	287.7	518	4 246	587.8	121.4
Minnetonka	288	4 016	7 374.9	189.6	352	7 410	1 157.6	116.5	98	786	188.8	24.1
Moorhead	36	507	220.1	12.0	138	2 113	361.6	28.7	33	D	D	D
Plymouth	350	11 437	6 950.7	412.4	165	4 057	1 460.4	109.5	93	427	93.4	11.9
Richfield	37	322	110.1	11.6	148	2 746	438.7	46.2	36	367	34.4	5.2
Rochester	88	843	443.4	28.6	502	8 675	1 311.7	126.4	111	617	71.2	9.4
Roseville	151	2 334	1 227.2	89.6	350	8 031	1 210.6	122.9	81	824	133.2	19.8
St. Cloud	98	2 835	985.2	100.4	373	6 530	1 065.3	99.1	101	568	52.6	9.6
St. Louis Park	229	2 817	2 204.8	118.5	232	3 851	671.5	69.7	155	1 346	180.9	26.8
St. Paul	456	7 746	4 075.5	323.5	872	12 246	1 907.3	225.7	304	2 507	235.6	53.0
Winona	57	508	360.7	13.4	173	2 135	313.6	30.4	35	D	D	D

1. Establishments with payroll.

City	Professional, Scientific, and Technical Services, 1997[1]				Manufacturing, 1997				Accommodation and Foodservices, 1997			
	Number of Establish-ments	Number of Employees	Receipts (mil dol)	Annual Payroll (mil dol)	Number of Establish-ments	Number of Employees	Receipts (mil dol)	Annual Payroll (mil dol)	Number of Establish-ments	Number of Employees	Sales (mil dol)	Annual Payroll (mil dol)
	84	85	86	87	88	89	90	91	92	93	94	95
MICHIGAN—Cont'd												
Dearborn	215	2 747	252.8	127.1	119	13 098	5 533.8	764.4	267	5 771	221.3	62.0
Dearborn Heights	67	348	20.3	10.9	NA	NA	NA	NA	104	1 814	57.0	14.3
Detroit	718	12 794	1 594.4	604.3	825	47 487	19 778.5	2 312.2	1 108	15 426	576.0	150.4
East Lansing	110	687	57.9	24.9	NA	NA	NA	NA	113	2 372	62.9	17.0
Eastpointe	NA	NA	NA	NA	NA	NA	NA	NA	NA	NA	NA	NA
Farmington Hills	656	7 600	829.1	359.6	155	5 109	993.8	225.3	181	3 779	131.4	38.2
Ferndale	41	369	49.2	12.6	89	2 278	403.7	85.1	50	615	20.0	5.1
Flint	253	1 497	101.8	46.6	94	D	D	D	266	3 824	112.9	29.8
Garden City	13	28	2.7	1.6	NA	NA	NA	NA	54	740	26.4	6.1
Grand Rapids	661	6 066	647.4	257.7	459	30 971	5 140.1	1 309.1	386	8 134	262.6	78.5
Holland	76	682	55.4	26.3	117	16 130	3 246.8	615.7	87	2 258	57.3	19.1
Inkster	9	30	1.8	0.7	NA	NA	NA	NA	28	164	8.9	2.0
Jackson	109	966	60.6	30.8	143	4 453	826.1	149.8	111	1 769	57.9	14.6
Kalamazoo	227	1 861	169.7	76.7	153	7 499	1 450.5	253.8	206	4 217	112.1	33.8
Kentwood	95	1 096	80.8	35.4	99	9 998	1 550.8	332.1	102	2 798	84.7	24.7
Lansing	279	2 201	240.7	108.0	131	D	D	D	260	5 620	159.8	47.7
Lincoln Park	24	530	62.4	27.5	NA	NA	NA	NA	79	D	D	D
Livonia	384	6 668	553.6	224.0	350	17 012	4 243.0	826.7	266	6 399	213.6	57.1
Madison Heights	118	2 302	235.2	95.6	227	6 683	1 060.2	282.2	102	2 250	77.9	19.6
Midland	108	603	61.6	19.9	49	5 289	1 671.1	278.9	93	2 330	68.0	20.5
Muskegon	90	568	52.1	23.1	108	6 918	1 231.0	236.7	82	D	D	D
Novi	126	1 436	166.9	66.6	87	2 448	378.8	104.4	96	2 778	90.9	28.7
Oak Park	47	368	43.3	12.5	78	1 632	208.1	63.4	45	743	22.4	5.9
Pontiac	54	510	28.4	12.4	58	8 474	4 570.2	378.7	130	D	D	D
Portage	114	953	85.2	38.4	78	5 667	902.2	239.4	110	2 752	78.6	23.4
Port Huron	75	397	30.2	14.2	74	5 789	1 355.6	184.8	69	1 143	38.4	10.3
Rochester Hills	184	2 952	190.4	81.8	140	7 936	1 264.0	285.9	103	2 592	76.7	22.4
Roseville	58	846	28.6	14.0	202	6 582	930.5	257.1	111	2 563	83.2	22.3
Royal Oak	207	1 903	300.2	75.8	98	2 397	531.4	96.3	143	3 071	107.0	32.9
Saginaw	116	1 023	73.2	32.0	78	7 667	2 289.5	420.8	123	1 928	55.5	15.2
St. Clair Shores	160	862	59.9	31.4	68	2 756	335.0	76.7	128	D	D	D
Southfield	938	13 035	1 584.8	696.8	115	4 564	748.8	211.7	283	4 739	195.6	54.5
Southgate	26	335	15.8	9.3	NA	NA	NA	NA	74	D	D	D
Sterling Heights	234	2 657	302.7	136.2	314	21 628	6 777.9	1 241.7	202	4 083	126.3	36.7
Taylor	63	893	45.3	17.4	90	2 662	652.4	94.2	154	2 789	84.4	22.9
Troy	843	15 151	1 644.7	822.1	396	11 872	1 678.0	470.9	225	5 330	202.4	57.3
Warren	193	4 180	391.2	203.1	518	23 404	8 065.3	1 157.2	301	5 435	193.3	51.4
Westland	69	415	41.5	16.6	79	2 533	402.6	91.5	154	3 022	94.1	25.1
Wyandotte	43	161	9.9	4.0	49	2 227	511.1	96.0	68	901	26.8	7.2
Wyoming	80	967	63.4	25.6	185	11 933	2 055.0	539.2	131	2 557	78.1	21.9
MINNESOTA	12 391	96 677	10 447.9	4 091.3	8 091	382 530	76 244.9	13 126.1	9 982	179 487	5 934.2	1 688.8
Apple Valley	107	266	21.5	9.6	NA	NA	NA	NA	37	1 011	33.8	9.0
Blaine	81	334	27.6	11.3	134	3 147	368.3	106.2	52	1 568	43.9	12.7
Bloomington	578	7 762	967.6	376.6	209	10 538	1 655.5	420.8	246	9 049	383.3	106.7
Brooklyn Center	70	386	31.4	13.8	44	1 723	242.3	66.6	45	1 456	44.5	14.1
Brooklyn Park	116	865	86.2	41.8	109	5 406	860.9	226.8	68	D	D	D
Burnsville	212	956	96.4	33.9	113	4 055	723.6	148.1	108	3 101	92.2	27.0
Coon Rapids	95	452	35.0	13.4	61	2 613	379.1	102.8	77	1 705	53.7	15.5
Duluth	197	1 446	98.3	43.4	97	2 751	534.2	88.9	241	4 872	156.3	43.1
Eagan	214	879	105.8	42.2	85	4 169	3 294.1	169.5	102	2 541	82.7	26.6
Eden Prairie	330	3 902	441.0	170.8	146	9 873	1 528.6	412.6	106	2 189	85.9	24.6
Edina	522	4 975	699.1	238.0	93	3 007	479.4	109.4	89	D	D	D
Fridley	84	389	37.6	17.1	159	9 797	1 673.7	382.5	45	1 145	28.2	8.8
Mankato	81	569	46.1	15.7	62	3 721	1 476.4	116.6	111	2 295	62.4	17.1
Maple Grove	138	356	36.0	14.9	105	5 685	1 028.2	227.8	55	1 552	42.1	12.5
Maplewood	81	501	47.7	23.4	32	712	110.2	21.6	87	2 249	64.1	18.8
Minneapolis	1 977	27 509	3 565.9	1 384.7	699	25 906	3 953.5	951.1	921	20 653	828.9	246.8
Minnetonka	363	1 994	212.8	90.0	118	7 462	1 457.8	296.9	110	2 804	108.4	32.9
Moorhead	44	268	21.4	9.0	26	926	205.3	29.1	65	1 349	32.2	9.7
Plymouth	303	2 114	286.5	101.0	207	12 651	2 096.5	498.1	72	2 130	107.4	31.6
Richfield	60	423	19.8	7.7	NA	NA	NA	NA	52	1 414	45.4	12.6
Rochester	184	2 082	155.3	81.8	64	D	D	D	247	5 624	196.7	56.4
Roseville	217	2 022	222.0	71.0	88	5 238	604.9	196.0	103	3 362	102.3	31.1
St. Cloud	141	1 012	78.1	33.8	75	7 189	981.7	194.0	142	3 759	100.5	27.5
St. Louis Park	384	3 228	321.2	135.2	113	4 241	707.5	159.9	89	2 255	66.5	20.6
St. Paul	803	6 333	646.5	290.9	375	20 215	5 536.6	737.5	599	10 532	350.9	105.5
Winona	57	197	12.9	4.1	83	5 992	921.5	170.7	85	1 501	40.0	10.6

1. Firms subject to federal tax.

Table D. Cities — Entertainment, Health Care, and Other Services

City	Arts, Entertainment, and Recreation[1], 1997				Health Care and Social Assistance[1], 1997				Other Services[1], 1997			
	Number of Establishments	Number of Employees	Receipts (mil dol)	Annual Payroll (mil dol)	Number of Establishments	Number of Employees	Receipts (mil dol)	Annual Payroll (mil dol)	Number of Establishments	Number of Employees	Receipts (mil dol)	Annual Payroll (mil dol)
	96	97	98	99	100	101	102	103	104	105	106	107
MICHIGAN—Cont'd												
Dearborn	23	764	25.0	6.5	330	2 666	238.9	111.3	180	1 200	76.3	28.2
Dearborn Heights	9	107	3.9	1.2	95	791	46.9	20.9	98	619	37.1	12.2
Detroit	66	1 773	173.5	73.6	900	12 747	730.3	371.9	829	7 518	467.3	149.6
East Lansing	8	314	6.0	2.2	101	1 098	75.5	34.8	36	268	11.2	4.1
Eastpointe	NA	NA	NA	NA	NA	NA	NA	NA	NA	NA	NA	NA
Farmington Hills	34	374	24.2	6.6	313	2 982	224.2	97.7	155	1 205	69.4	24.3
Ferndale	8	42	3.0	0.8	31	260	13.1	6.0	54	315	23.4	7.8
Flint	10	107	3.6	1.1	292	2 900	206.0	100.9	199	1 384	84.1	23.4
Garden City	3	16	0.9	0.2	73	549	44.1	22.4	65	333	21.9	6.4
Grand Rapids	44	679	25.6	7.3	462	5 625	413.0	221.3	334	2 478	168.6	53.8
Holland	8	162	4.9	1.8	86	1 412	83.0	42.1	87	603	37.1	12.5
Inkster	2	0	0.0	0.0	20	104	3.9	1.7	19	93	6.2	1.7
Jackson	11	196	6.5	1.5	168	1 384	114.9	52.8	97	669	38.2	10.6
Kalamazoo	23	529	14.3	4.7	191	2 875	216.5	112.9	174	1 469	92.2	30.2
Kentwood	14	315	11.6	2.9	57	669	40.9	16.6	79	1 026	75.0	20.8
Lansing	25	462	41.7	6.3	254	2 316	184.3	95.5	204	1 413	77.6	24.2
Lincoln Park	11	119	3.4	1.0	68	965	58.8	27.1	87	523	30.1	9.5
Livonia	35	697	92.1	12.7	371	3 919	264.2	113.0	245	2 467	232.2	71.0
Madison Heights	15	245	14.6	3.9	82	703	56.9	24.3	85	956	62.6	20.9
Midland	13	181	8.6	3.2	176	1 599	105.1	52.8	83	556	37.3	9.9
Muskegon	15	220	7.1	2.0	126	1 370	97.5	52.2	51	380	19.2	6.7
Novi	15	138	10.1	2.2	96	974	59.9	29.1	72	694	47.8	17.8
Oak Park	8	84	4.1	0.8	62	364	21.4	10.4	41	172	13.0	3.5
Pontiac	9	0	0.0	0.0	90	792	65.6	30.0	105	775	47.1	14.1
Portage	13	250	7.0	1.9	109	1 077	62.2	28.6	100	692	40.8	12.8
Port Huron	10	115	5.4	1.0	131	978	87.3	46.6	62	383	20.2	5.8
Rochester Hills	16	142	16.7	2.7	197	1 885	111.0	52.5	76	491	41.5	12.0
Roseville	12	254	10.2	2.4	96	789	59.5	27.6	110	559	38.9	13.1
Royal Oak	17	110	6.9	1.5	171	1 157	89.9	42.5	129	1 014	65.2	24.7
Saginaw	7	72	5.5	1.2	128	1 243	81.3	42.2	93	507	28.1	8.4
St. Clair Shores	25	218	12.6	3.2	202	1 473	119.8	58.6	136	778	36.6	11.5
Southfield	29	566	22.1	8.1	602	8 302	533.1	276.2	170	1 565	99.6	32.3
Southgate	9	31	1.2	0.3	69	795	58.0	27.3	56	546	54.1	13.6
Sterling Heights	21	173	14.1	4.0	210	2 114	140.7	61.6	169	1 217	82.0	29.2
Taylor	13	188	6.6	2.0	102	1 411	68.3	33.0	96	623	54.2	14.3
Troy	32	362	66.8	8.6	324	3 065	211.4	113.5	185	1 951	169.6	50.8
Warren	21	396	15.6	4.3	314	4 053	286.7	139.7	278	2 122	152.3	47.3
Westland	14	193	8.9	2.4	132	1 848	103.3	44.5	107	913	60.7	20.4
Wyandotte	8	79	2.9	0.7	46	317	28.4	12.7	62	422	21.0	7.1
Wyoming	12	191	6.7	2.1	75	1 097	57.9	23.4	165	1 161	75.3	24.5
MINNESOTA	1 593	27 958	1 469.7	477.9	8 033	106 839	5 864.5	2 946.0	7 614	55 723	3 394.6	1 103.6
Apple Valley	5	73	2.3	0.6	54	837	38.6	19.7	48	353	19.4	6.3
Blaine	9	133	4.4	1.1	56	576	27.0	11.5	63	429	26.3	9.3
Bloomington	37	1 896	87.3	26.0	153	2 105	112.1	66.5	177	5 563	200.1	136.3
Brooklyn Center	9	242	5.7	2.2	53	758	44.6	23.2	45	404	16.3	5.7
Brooklyn Park	12	261	7.6	2.2	70	1 017	41.0	18.4	84	679	39.6	12.3
Burnsville	20	461	7.2	3.0	121	2 359	106.4	50.8	120	1 019	55.4	19.1
Coon Rapids	17	423	12.3	2.7	110	2 280	121.4	64.0	70	431	26.2	7.5
Duluth	31	279	9.7	2.3	224	2 800	137.0	72.6	186	1 122	71.5	21.4
Eagan	16	426	14.2	3.8	98	855	47.9	18.4	95	1 634	102.7	41.9
Eden Prairie	23	1 837	125.7	68.0	86	1 349	113.6	36.7	83	1 777	155.9	61.0
Edina	26	114	10.4	2.7	327	4 058	301.4	154.4	104	1 356	63.3	25.6
Fridley	8	256	5.1	2.1	56	793	60.6	34.1	59	512	44.2	10.9
Mankato	15	86	3.2	0.7	102	1 840	91.5	46.8	82	579	30.5	9.2
Maple Grove	8	103	4.4	1.7	66	666	32.7	16.0	51	311	16.5	6.1
Maplewood	14	137	5.6	1.4	78	967	67.5	34.6	74	541	28.0	8.2
Minneapolis	139	2 506	233.4	77.4	672	9 019	622.7	318.0	672	7 965	499.0	155.1
Minnetonka	33	320	23.6	6.9	111	2 170	114.0	54.6	76	738	42.2	17.3
Moorhead	4	57	1.1	0.4	43	380	20.2	9.2	59	264	15.6	4.5
Plymouth	17	98	8.8	2.6	120	1 207	83.9	47.9	71	566	45.6	13.9
Richfield	7	69	2.9	0.6	63	686	33.7	14.2	59	396	27.1	9.0
Rochester	22	322	14.1	4.0	145	2 151	97.4	48.7	145	1 221	60.3	18.0
Roseville	12	152	10.3	1.7	97	1 407	66.0	33.8	100	1 166	89.1	29.3
St. Cloud	26	251	11.9	3.0	179	2 765	213.6	111.4	121	1 006	60.7	18.8
St. Louis Park	24	937	38.7	8.4	164	2 542	165.7	83.5	111	775	52.2	16.5
St. Paul	72	764	32.1	9.4	578	9 286	622.3	349.4	420	3 054	177.5	55.7
Winona	10	134	7.3	2.1	57	498	31.4	13.9	51	260	14.1	3.7

1. Firms subject to federal tax.

Table D. Cities — Federal Funds and City Government Finances

City	Selected federal funds, fiscal 1999[1] (mil dol)									City government finances, 1997						
	Procurement contracts		Grants					Direct payments for individuals		General revenue						
											Intergovernmental		Taxes			
														Per capita[3] (dollars)		
	Defense	Other	Total[2]	Health and family welfare	Energy and environment	Education	Housing and community development	Educational assistance	Housing assistance	Total (mil dol)	Total (mil dol)	Percent from state government	Total (mil dol)	Total	Property	Sales and gross receipts
	108	109	110	111	112	113	114	115	116	117	118	119	120	121	122	123
MICHIGAN—Cont'd																
Dearborn	0.3	0.6	16.7	0.1	7.4	1.4	4.8	8.3	0.8	115.7	18.5	86.0	54.7	598	567	0
Dearborn Heights	0.0	0.0	0.2	0.0	0.0	0.0	0.0	0.0	0.0	42.6	13.4	66.8	14.9	242	232	0
Detroit	14.0	83.4	505.1	158.5	7.4	7.0	108.0	26.1	35.5	1 971.3	911.4	72.1	635.7	636	237	51
East Lansing	1.3	2.1	118.8	29.4	6.6	4.0	1.0	9.8	-0.4	32.6	11.2	74.0	9.8	202	190	0
Eastpointe	NA	NA	NA	NA	NA	NA	NA	NA	NA	25.1	6.5	82.7	10.1	NA	NA	NA
Farmington Hills	2.2	1.0	0.5	0.0	0.0	0.0	0.4	0.3	1.3	57.3	11.3	90.1	30.0	375	356	0
Ferndale	1.5	0.0	1.0	0.0	0.0	0.0	0.8	0.1	0.0	24.3	5.6	88.2	10.9	444	432	0
Flint	0.7	8.7	46.1	14.0	1.2	5.5	11.4	10.5	11.1	395.3	116.6	90.6	54.7	406	395	0
Garden City	0.1	0.0	0.0	0.0	0.0	0.0	0.0	0.0	-0.2	28.5	10.3	46.7	8.4	261	245	0
Grand Rapids	30.5	30.6	37.9	9.9	0.0	2.3	12.7	8.2	7.1	188.6	51.1	64.4	71.2	378	119	0
Holland	9.8	38.8	5.2	2.0	0.0	1.2	0.7	1.1	1.7	35.2	8.3	69.0	10.8	324	316	0
Inkster	0.1	0.0	1.4	0.1	0.0	0.0	1.3	0.0	3.3	18.2	5.4	92.5	6.3	204	193	0
Jackson	9.6	0.5	9.2	5.3	0.2	0.0	2.6	1.4	3.6	34.2	11.0	71.1	13.8	384	194	0
Kalamazoo	8.7	1.5	22.8	6.1	0.4	6.7	0.1	7.6	10.9	101.6	27.9	65.1	26.2	339	322	0
Kentwood	0.0	0.0	0.6	0.0	0.0	0.0	0.0	0.0	3.9	18.8	4.9	98.3	8.0	191	164	0
Lansing	7.6	3.8	1 132.2	506.7	104.1	255.7	66.2	7.0	3.8	166.1	35.6	82.5	58.3	464	259	0
Lincoln Park	0.0	0.0	0.7	0.1	0.0	0.0	0.6	0.0	0.2	32.9	9.9	74.4	13.5	320	305	0
Livonia	5.4	0.7	1.5	0.0	0.0	0.6	0.6	2.6	1.9	87.2	17.6	92.1	39.4	375	353	0
Madison Heights	0.5	0.1	0.0	0.0	0.0	0.0	0.0	0.1	0.9	31.9	7.6	80.5	14.4	442	415	0
Midland	1.8	0.9	4.9	0.0	0.5	0.1	0.4	1.6	0.4	44.2	6.9	93.4	20.9	524	511	0
Muskegon	88.9	8.6	11.3	4.5	0.4	0.6	3.7	1.1	1.4	32.9	11.3	75.8	12.4	314	151	0
Novi	1.3	1.1	0.3	0.0	0.0	0.0	0.0	0.0	0.0	37.0	6.5	78.3	17.6	403	368	0
Oak Park	0.1	0.1	0.2	0.1	0.0	0.0	0.0	0.7	1.1	30.8	6.1	95.8	12.1	404	395	0
Pontiac	6.3	0.5	36.1	6.5	0.0	0.0	10.8	0.0	12.4	98.6	30.6	75.8	38.0	540	322	0
Portage	0.0	0.0	0.4	0.0	0.0	0.0	0.2	0.0	0.0	31.3	6.5	95.8	14.1	325	309	0
Port Huron	3.6	1.5	5.7	1.8	1.2	0.1	1.9	0.9	0.0	42.6	14.8	44.0	17.3	527	348	0
Rochester Hills	6.2	0.0	0.0	0.0	0.0	0.0	0.0	0.0	0.0	47.1	8.7	98.3	17.7	262	237	0
Roseville	9.5	2.0	0.2	0.0	0.0	0.0	0.2	0.0	1.2	39.0	11.5	71.5	15.9	309	297	0
Royal Oak	0.0	0.2	2.5	0.3	0.0	0.0	2.2	0.0	0.6	55.2	11.1	90.5	24.1	371	324	0
Saginaw	10.9	4.4	20.3	7.1	0.0	0.0	8.1	1.0	2.9	72.0	25.4	57.9	21.8	335	104	0
St. Clair Shores	3.1	0.0	2.7	0.0	0.0	0.1	2.5	0.1	0.0	48.0	10.5	91.0	18.2	283	267	0
Southfield	10.4	1.3	3.6	3.2	-0.7	0.2	0.7	1.2	1.6	95.4	15.6	79.4	44.3	582	557	0
Southgate	0.0	0.0	2.2	0.0	0.0	0.0	0.0	0.9	0.2	25.3	4.9	96.1	11.6	369	350	0
Sterling Heights	413.2	0.3	0.9	0.0	0.0	0.1	0.7	0.0	3.8	78.5	17.7	92.7	38.9	328	307	0
Taylor	0.3	0.6	1.8	0.0	0.0	0.0	1.5	0.1	18.7	61.7	13.6	97.5	30.3	422	404	0
Troy	6.5	15.6	5.7	0.0	2.3	0.0	0.0	0.3	0.5	69.5	10.3	95.7	35.8	452	424	0
Warren	142.4	1.4	12.8	0.0	0.0	0.1	2.4	1.7	0.0	123.1	27.7	97.3	57.9	419	407	0
Westland	1.3	0.1	2.5	0.0	0.0	0.0	1.7	0.0	0.0	57.9	14.7	80.5	20.4	225	210	0
Wyandotte	0.0	0.0	0.0	0.0	0.0	0.0	0.0	0.0	0.3	45.2	12.6	67.5	14.5	457	443	0
Wyoming	0.1	0.0	0.8	0.0	0.0	0.0	0.4	0.0	0.0	43.2	11.1	83.0	16.0	241	222	0
MINNESOTA	1 198.0	609.3	4 498.5	2 779.5	86.3	354.4	91.7	141.3	91.6	X	X	X	X	X	X	X
Apple Valley	0.0	0.0	0.2	0.1	0.0	0.0	0.0	0.0	1.6	32.6	6.5	84.5	10.9	253	225	4
Blaine	0.0	0.0	2.6	2.6	0.0	0.0	0.0	0.0	0.0	25.4	5.1	93.4	8.2	189	169	6
Bloomington	63.8	2.1	0.7	0.1	0.0	0.2	0.2	0.7	0.0	100.7	16.2	70.1	50.6	584	460	89
Brooklyn Center	0.0	1.1	0.0	0.0	0.0	0.0	0.0	0.0	0.0	28.8	6.0	99.0	9.3	329	300	15
Brooklyn Park	3.6	0.2	0.1	0.0	0.0	0.0	0.0	0.0	1.2	51.6	5.2	89.7	23.3	380	350	0
Burnsville	10.1	0.8	0.8	0.7	0.1	0.0	0.0	0.0	2.6	57.5	6.2	94.1	15.5	272	242	10
Coon Rapids	0.0	0.0	1.0	0.5	0.0	0.5	0.0	0.9	2.7	46.0	8.0	95.5	12.4	197	158	28
Duluth	0.6	12.6	23.3	4.2	0.2	2.1	8.1	5.0	2.0	131.6	40.7	81.7	29.3	350	195	150
Eagan	55.3	5.2	0.0	0.0	0.0	0.0	0.0	0.2	0.0	41.9	4.9	96.4	14.0	244	217	0
Eden Prairie	11.7	3.2	1.9	0.0	0.4	0.0	0.0	0.0	1.7	47.9	2.8	86.7	17.7	373	328	0
Edina	74.8	0.6	0.6	0.6	0.0	0.0	0.0	0.0	1.7	38.7	3.9	91.5	17.7	382	347	5
Fridley	1.6	0.0	0.6	0.0	0.0	0.0	0.0	0.0	-0.2	21.3	4.3	93.4	7.7	277	256	4
Mankato	0.5	0.2	4.0	2.2	0.0	1.0	0.1	3.8	1.2	32.6	9.9	97.5	10.3	328	313	0
Maple Grove	0.5	0.1	0.5	0.5	0.0	0.0	0.0	0.0	0.0	41.5	5.3	81.9	13.5	299	259	0
Maplewood	0.0	0.1	0.0	0.0	0.0	0.0	0.0	0.0	2.2	31.9	3.8	96.8	9.4	276	248	0
Minneapolis	459.5	106.3	362.4	224.9	9.4	16.8	22.6	16.6	18.9	663.7	156.9	82.9	225.4	628	441	153
Minnetonka	10.3	26.8	0.5	0.1	0.2	0.0	0.0	0.2	1.1	33.0	4.7	93.8	16.0	319	272	5
Moorhead	0.0	0.1	4.3	2.8	0.0	0.3	0.4	3.9	0.0	30.4	9.8	87.4	3.1	92	92	0
Plymouth	16.1	0.7	0.2	0.0	0.0	0.0	0.2	0.8	0.1	45.2	7.0	95.9	16.4	274	238	0
Richfield	0.0	0.0	0.1	0.1	0.0	0.0	0.0	0.3	0.0	30.1	9.4	77.2	10.4	304	280	8
Rochester	4.8	4.1	91.4	86.5	0.0	0.9	0.4	1.5	1.3	73.5	17.3	84.9	27.3	360	244	95
Roseville	5.0	1.1	15.6	0.0	6.2	0.0	0.0	1.1	0.0	36.1	3.1	91.9	14.4	422	365	14
St. Cloud	0.0	2.3	6.7	2.1	0.0	0.7	1.4	4.3	0.5	67.4	14.3	90.5	16.9	332	252	60
St. Louis Park	3.4	2.7	0.8	0.9	0.0	0.0	0.0	0.9	0.0	58.5	8.3	92.8	14.4	335	301	5
St. Paul	177.2	30.8	839.8	192.4	61.8	114.7	48.7	13.9	21.7	466.2	157.6	86.6	107.8	415	273	109
Winona	3.6	0.4	0.9	0.3	0.0	0.6	0.0	2.9	0.1	21.8	8.8	96.5	5.9	239	187	37

1. October 1, 1998 to September 30, 1999.   2. Includes program categories not shown separately. State totals include additional categories not allocated by city.   3. Based on population estimated as of July 1 of the year shown.

Table D. Cities — City Government Finances

	City government finances, 1997 (cont'd)												
	General expenditure												
	Per capita[1] (dollars)			Percent of total for —									
City	Total (mil dol)	Total	Capital outlays	Public welfare	Highways	Parking facilities	Education	Health and hospitals	Police protection	Sewerage and sanitation	Parks and recreation	Housing and community development	Interest on debt
	124	125	126	127	128	129	130	131	132	133	134	135	136
MICHIGAN—Cont'd													
Dearborn	100.2	1 096	0	0.7	11.4	0.0	0.0	0.4	17.4	14.2	5.4	2.5	4.3
Dearborn Heights	41.2	669	78	0.0	15.1	0.0	0.0	0.0	20.8	29.0	2.5	0.0	1.3
Detroit	1 789.0	1 789	232	0.0	8.6	0.4	0.3	5.6	16.8	18.8	5.7	5.4	5.2
East Lansing	39.6	822	167	0.5	8.1	2.2	0.0	0.0	15.9	26.1	3.0	0.0	6.4
Eastpointe	24.1	NA	NA	0.0	11.9	0.0	0.0	0.0	20.1	20.9	5.4	0.0	1.9
Farmington Hills	52.5	657	145	0.0	14.3	0.0	0.0	0.0	21.4	5.2	6.9	0.0	2.1
Ferndale	27.2	1 109	283	0.5	22.0	0.9	0.0	0.0	16.5	25.5	1.5	0.0	2.6
Flint	376.1	2 789	169	0.0	2.6	0.0	0.0	66.3	7.4	4.4	2.1	1.7	1.9
Garden City	28.7	888	293	0.0	9.7	0.0	0.0	0.0	12.4	17.6	4.4	0.0	6.1
Grand Rapids	194.7	1 034	42	0.0	9.8	2.7	0.0	0.0	15.7	13.2	4.2	10.2	6.8
Holland	39.5	1 188	377	0.5	19.1	0.0	0.0	0.0	9.5	16.1	8.0	0.0	4.6
Inkster	18.2	587	10	0.0	17.2	0.0	0.0	0.0	19.6	24.9	2.8	1.1	1.5
Jackson	35.2	979	253	0.0	20.1	3.4	0.0	0.0	19.0	14.5	5.0	0.0	0.6
Kalamazoo	97.7	1 262	145	0.1	12.9	0.0	0.0	0.0	23.7	20.5	2.1	0.1	21.2
Kentwood	18.7	446	42	0.0	19.2	0.0	0.1	0.0	22.9	7.0	4.6	0.0	0.2
Lansing	169.3	1 346	269	1.0	5.7	2.5	0.0	0.0	9.8	12.9	3.2	0.1	11.1
Lincoln Park	28.4	674	34	0.9	13.5	0.0	0.0	0.0	23.8	22.0	4.7	2.1	0.8
Livonia	74.3	707	0	0.1	10.7	0.0	0.0	0.0	20.5	19.9	4.1	0.8	7.6
Madison Heights	33.2	1 019	140	1.3	9.3	0.0	0.0	0.0	19.3	37.2	2.3	0.0	1.2
Midland	36.7	922	95	0.0	13.9	0.2	0.0	0.0	11.3	17.1	7.9	4.9	2.1
Muskegon	40.1	1 014	280	0.0	19.2	0.0	0.0	0.0	15.0	17.1	4.1	0.8	3.6
Novi	43.7	1 001	297	0.0	22.1	0.0	0.0	0.0	14.9	20.4	6.4	0.0	10.1
Oak Park	30.0	999	38	0.3	7.1	0.0	0.0	0.0	23.6	20.6	3.9	0.0	7.5
Pontiac	97.8	1 388	145	0.0	7.5	1.4	0.0	0.2	15.6	9.2	12.2	7.3	5.6
Portage	33.0	762	115	1.4	15.8	0.0	0.0	0.0	16.4	16.8	5.5	0.0	6.8
Port Huron	42.1	1 280	288	0.1	10.6	0.4	0.0	0.0	12.4	23.0	6.2	12.2	0.4
Rochester Hills	55.6	824	150	0.0	12.2	0.0	0.0	0.0	15.5	38.5	2.4	0.0	4.3
Roseville	38.8	757	87	0.0	17.1	0.0	0.0	0.0	21.0	24.5	3.0	0.9	1.4
Royal Oak	51.2	789	87	0.0	6.7	4.3	0.0	0.4	18.0	22.0	4.7	0.0	3.8
Saginaw	71.2	1 095	117	0.4	9.6	0.7	0.0	0.0	18.0	18.2	5.0	17.0	8.6
St. Clair Shores	46.7	729	72	0.0	12.1	0.0	0.0	0.0	18.5	31.0	8.0	0.0	1.8
Southfield	93.2	1 223	131	0.4	9.7	3.3	0.0	0.0	15.6	17.1	9.0	5.3	1.8
Southgate	23.0	731	71	0.4	15.6	0.0	0.0	0.0	18.9	25.8	2.9	0.0	0.3
Sterling Heights	80.7	680	85	0.0	12.6	0.0	0.0	0.0	22.4	10.2	1.9	0.0	2.3
Taylor	55.4	770	77	0.4	17.1	0.0	0.0	0.0	13.8	0.6	11.9	0.0	4.3
Troy	68.1	861	88	0.0	18.0	0.0	0.0	0.0	23.2	20.0	8.6	0.0	0.8
Warren	116.6	844	69	0.0	10.8	0.0	0.0	0.0	19.9	23.3	3.5	1.5	1.9
Westland	58.0	639	56	0.8	12.9	0.0	0.0	0.0	16.8	32.1	2.5	0.8	1.3
Wyandotte	34.9	1 096	0	0.7	6.4	3.8	0.0	0.0	9.4	14.8	2.5	0.0	17.2
Wyoming	51.6	776	259	0.0	17.7	0.0	0.0	0.0	17.1	22.6	5.0	4.2	0.9
MINNESOTA	X	X	X	X	X	X	X	X	X	X	X	X	X
Apple Valley	23.8	555	93	0.0	22.3	0.0	0.0	0.1	16.1	16.8	14.4	0.0	10.6
Blaine	20.4	471	90	0.0	3.8	0.0	0.0	0.0	13.7	20.3	6.0	9.3	9.5
Bloomington	76.1	878	135	0.0	12.9	0.0	0.0	4.0	12.6	11.8	12.5	0.0	28.4
Brooklyn Center	31.9	1 134	365	0.0	19.1	0.0	0.0	0.0	12.6	18.1	17.3	3.5	13.8
Brooklyn Park	63.6	1 037	491	0.0	12.2	0.0	0.0	0.0	11.3	22.8	13.5	26.0	2.7
Burnsville	52.7	923	148	0.0	16.7	0.0	0.0	0.0	10.7	7.2	6.9	0.0	43.2
Coon Rapids	39.2	625	109	0.0	5.8	0.0	0.0	0.6	10.0	11.6	7.4	2.3	30.6
Duluth	119.0	1 421	226	0.0	16.7	0.0	0.0	0.0	9.3	10.8	12.4	3.1	11.3
Eagan	34.9	610	202	0.0	7.8	0.0	0.0	0.0	15.8	11.9	7.4	3.9	10.7
Eden Prairie	38.5	809	127	0.0	8.9	0.0	0.0	0.0	10.3	21.3	10.5	1.6	32.4
Edina	36.6	789	136	0.0	14.9	0.0	0.0	1.1	11.8	13.1	17.5	7.5	18.4
Fridley	18.9	679	113	0.0	16.0	0.0	0.0	0.0	17.3	21.4	4.0	2.8	10.0
Mankato	37.4	1 195	388	0.0	21.7	0.7	0.0	0.0	9.0	15.6	10.0	5.4	7.4
Maple Grove	43.0	952	495	0.0	46.9	0.0	0.0	0.0	8.2	9.2	6.4	0.4	7.9
Maplewood	30.5	899	99	0.0	5.8	0.0	0.0	2.0	12.2	16.1	5.4	0.0	33.9
Minneapolis	667.7	1 861	396	0.0	5.0	3.8	0.0	1.6	10.8	8.9	9.4	4.6	19.1
Minnetonka	34.2	682	245	0.0	12.1	0.0	0.0	0.4	14.3	14.4	12.9	10.9	4.4
Moorhead	36.3	1 090	314	0.0	16.0	0.2	0.0	0.6	10.6	19.9	7.8	8.8	11.9
Plymouth	38.9	647	161	0.0	31.5	0.0	0.0	0.0	11.9	14.3	6.0	0.4	14.8
Richfield	23.5	684	69	0.0	7.2	0.0	0.0	0.7	19.0	12.3	16.4	3.0	13.5
Rochester	71.0	939	261	0.0	13.3	2.2	0.0	0.2	13.8	10.1	11.8	0.5	8.0
Roseville	29.5	862	165	0.0	13.4	0.0	0.0	0.0	10.4	11.3	10.8	3.0	24.2
St. Cloud	63.9	1 259	287	0.0	17.4	0.8	0.0	1.5	10.0	12.3	5.7	1.1	30.1
St. Louis Park	58.4	1 363	276	0.0	4.4	0.0	0.0	0.1	8.4	10.9	12.1	1.0	40.5
St. Paul	433.1	1 668	316	0.0	14.6	0.7	0.0	2.5	11.4	9.4	15.6	9.7	13.9
Winona	19.8	798	157	0.5	18.6	0.1	0.0	0.5	12.6	6.7	9.9	3.8	14.1

1. Based on population estimated as of July 1 of the year shown.

Table D. Cities — City Government Finances, City Government Employment, and Climate

City	City government finances, 1997 (cont'd) Debt outstanding Total (mil dol)	Per capita[1] (dollars)	Percent utility	City government employment, 1999	Climate[2] Mean January	July	Limits January[3]	July[4]	Annual precipitation (inches)	Heating degree days	Cooling degree days
	137	138	139	140	141	142	143	144	145	146	147
MICHIGAN—Cont'd											
Dearborn	115.1	1 259	0.0	1 003	22.9	72.9	15.5	83.8	32.71	6 500	677
Dearborn Heights	6.1	98	0.0	NA	22.9	72.9	15.5	83.8	32.71	6 500	677
Detroit	2 213.8	2 213	22.2	18 107	24.7	74.2	18.7	83.3	32.09	6 167	805
East Lansing	45.1	935	0.0	NA	20.1	70.5	12.4	81.9	29.68	7 228	458
Eastpointe	5.6	NA	0.0	NA	24.7	74.2	18.7	83.3	32.09	6 167	805
Farmington Hills	23.0	288	0.0	445	22.2	72.4	14.8	83.8	30.56	6 653	647
Ferndale	13.0	532	0.0	NA	24.7	74.2	18.7	83.3	32.09	6 167	805
Flint	102.0	756	0.0	3 786	21.5	70.6	14.2	81.5	30.28	6 979	483
Garden City	48.7	1 505	0.0	NA	22.9	72.9	15.5	83.8	32.71	6 500	677
Grand Rapids	394.4	2 095	38.8	1 985	21.8	71.6	14.7	82.8	36.04	6 973	534
Holland	48.0	1 445	59.7	443	23.3	70.8	16.8	81.9	36.25	6 747	529
Inkster	4.7	152	0.0	NA	22.9	72.3	15.6	83.3	32.62	6 569	626
Jackson	6.8	190	29.3	NA	21.5	72.2	14.3	83.2	29.73	6 791	621
Kalamazoo	435.1	5 617	3.3	905	23.7	73.5	16.4	84.9	37.03	6 230	764
Kentwood	1.7	40	68.2	NA	21.8	71.6	14.7	82.8	36.04	6 973	534
Lansing	304.3	2 420	10.1	2 026	20.9	70.8	13.3	82.6	30.62	7 101	490
Lincoln Park	9.5	225	44.5	NA	22.9	72.9	15.5	83.8	32.71	6 500	677
Livonia	94.6	900	4.9	755	22.9	72.9	15.5	83.8	32.71	6 500	677
Madison Heights	6.0	183	21.3	NA	24.7	74.2	18.7	83.3	32.09	6 167	805
Midland	41.0	1 028	39.1	402	22.0	72.2	14.7	84.1	29.51	6 763	599
Muskegon	31.8	804	16.7	NA	23.3	70.3	17.7	80.3	32.56	6 924	431
Novi	78.2	1 791	0.0	NA	21.0	71.0	13.6	81.4	29.95	7 064	515
Oak Park	37.7	1 258	11.1	NA	24.7	74.2	18.7	83.3	32.09	6 167	805
Pontiac	127.9	1 815	2.7	1 979	22.2	72.4	14.8	83.8	30.56	6 653	647
Portage	37.8	872	0.0	NA	23.7	73.5	16.4	84.9	37.03	6 230	764
Port Huron	4.0	120	0.0	NA	22.4	71.7	15.4	81.5	30.34	6 898	544
Rochester Hills	36.2	537	0.0	280	22.2	72.4	14.8	83.8	30.56	6 653	647
Roseville	11.6	227	0.0	NA	24.7	74.2	18.7	83.3	32.09	6 167	805
Royal Oak	24.5	378	0.0	451	24.7	74.2	18.7	83.3	32.09	6 167	805
Saginaw	120.7	1 857	10.5	665	22.7	73.0	15.7	84.4	30.89	6 538	675
St. Clair Shores	23.9	373	0.0	NA	24.7	73.5	17.4	83.7	33.23	6 185	737
Southfield	24.2	317	0.0	827	22.2	72.4	14.8	83.8	30.56	6 653	647
Southgate	4.2	135	79.4	NA	22.9	72.3	15.6	83.3	32.62	6 569	626
Sterling Heights	32.1	270	0.0	664	23.1	71.3	16.7	81.3	31.36	6 777	526
Taylor	38.5	535	0.0	581	22.9	72.3	15.6	83.3	32.62	6 569	626
Troy	8.3	104	0.0	524	22.2	72.4	14.8	83.8	30.56	6 653	647
Warren	45.5	329	0.0	1 038	24.7	74.2	18.7	83.3	32.09	6 167	805
Westland	20.7	228	0.0	373	22.9	72.3	15.6	83.3	32.62	6 569	626
Wyandotte	155.3	4 882	43.1	NA	22.9	72.9	15.5	83.8	32.71	6 500	677
Wyoming	22.5	338	25.2	470	21.8	71.6	14.7	82.8	36.04	6 973	534
MINNESOTA	X	X	X	X	X	X	X	X	X	X	X
Apple Valley	49.2	1 145	2.7	190	11.3	72.4	0.9	84.5	32.42	8 048	590
Blaine	38.9	899	4.8	NA	11.8	73.6	2.8	84.0	28.32	7 981	682
Bloomington	225.2	2 599	0.0	567	11.8	73.6	2.8	84.0	28.32	7 981	682
Brooklyn Center	60.6	2 153	0.0	NA	11.8	73.6	2.8	84.0	28.32	7 981	682
Brooklyn Park	59.3	968	13.0	488	11.8	73.6	2.8	84.0	28.32	7 981	682
Burnsville	334.2	5 855	0.0	285	11.8	73.6	2.8	84.0	28.32	7 981	682
Coon Rapids	186.5	2 969	5.7	258	11.8	73.6	2.8	84.0	28.32	7 981	682
Duluth	253.2	3 026	2.9	1 166	7.0	66.1	-2.2	77.1	30.00	9 818	180
Eagan	80.5	1 405	22.9	230	11.8	73.6	2.8	84.0	28.32	7 981	682
Eden Prairie	203.9	4 282	10.5	280	11.8	73.6	2.8	84.0	28.32	7 981	682
Edina	107.8	2 327	0.4	301	11.8	73.6	2.8	84.0	28.32	7 981	682
Fridley	35.0	1 255	13.8	169	11.8	73.6	2.8	84.0	28.32	7 981	682
Mankato	61.2	1 957	4.0	241	11.7	73.1	1.2	84.7	29.51	8 005	670
Maple Grove	88.7	1 965	4.5	195	11.8	73.6	2.8	84.0	28.32	7 981	682
Maplewood	148.6	4 373	0.0	334	11.8	73.6	2.8	84.0	28.32	7 981	682
Minneapolis	1 808.6	5 041	2.0	6 276	11.8	73.6	2.8	84.0	28.32	7 981	682
Minnetonka	17.3	345	0.0	253	11.8	73.6	2.8	84.0	28.32	7 981	682
Moorhead	91.1	2 733	25.8	314	5.9	71.1	-3.6	83.4	19.45	9 254	537
Plymouth	89.5	1 490	4.2	255	11.8	73.6	2.8	84.0	28.32	7 981	682
Richfield	52.5	1 528	0.0	348	11.8	73.6	2.8	84.0	28.32	7 981	682
Rochester	89.2	1 180	0.0	787	11.5	70.9	2.6	81.8	29.66	8 250	472
Roseville	114.1	3 338	0.0	166	11.8	73.6	2.8	84.0	28.32	7 981	682
St. Cloud	327.3	6 442	13.9	454	8.1	70.1	-2.4	82.6	27.43	8 928	415
St. Louis Park	353.7	8 259	0.0	267	11.8	73.6	2.8	84.0	28.32	7 981	682
St. Paul	891.8	3 435	2.3	3 156	11.8	73.6	2.8	84.0	28.32	7 981	682
Winona	46.4	1 870	5.9	193	14.1	73.2	4.0	85.0	32.57	7 694	662

1. Based on the population estimated as of July 1 of the year shown.   2. Represents normal values based on the 30-year period, 1961–1990.   3. Average daily minimum.   4. Average daily maximum.

Table D. Cities — **Land Area and Population**

STATE Place code	City	Land area, 1990[1] (sq km)	Population, 1999 Total persons	Rank	Per square kilo-meter	Population Total persons 1990	Percent change 1990–1999	Total persons 1980	Percent change 1980–1990	White	Black	Am. Indian, Eskimo, Aleut	Asian and Pacific Islander	Other race	His-panic[2]	Foreign born
		1	2	3	4	5	6	7	8	9	10	11	12	13	14	15
28 00000	MISSISSIPPI	121 506.4	2 768 619	X	23	2 575 475	7.5	2 520 770	2.2	63.5	35.6	0.3	0.5	0.1	0.6	0.8
28 06220	Biloxi	50.9	47 759	619	938	46 319	3.1	49 311	-6.1	74.6	18.6	0.3	5.7	0.7	2.8	5.4
28 29180	Greenville	67.6	41 731	714	617	45 226	-7.7	40 613	11.4	39.8	59.6	0.1	0.4	0.1	0.6	0.6
28 29700	Gulfport	58.6	64 679	414	1 104	64 045	1.0	39 676	61.4	69.9	28.6	0.3	0.9	0.3	1.5	2.1
28 31020	Hattiesburg	65.8	49 233	592	748	45 325	8.6	40 829	11.0	58.2	40.4	0.1	1.1	0.2	1.0	2.3
28 36000	Jackson	282.3	180 664	104	640	202 062	-10.6	202 893	-0.4	43.6	55.7	0.1	0.5	0.1	0.4	1.0
28 46640	Meridian	92.3	41 266	721	447	41 036	0.6	46 577	-11.9	54.0	45.4	0.1	0.4	0.1	0.6	0.5
28 55360	Pascagoula	39.3	27 345	1 098	696	25 899	5.6	29 318	-11.7	77.2	21.5	0.2	0.9	0.2	1.0	1.1
28 74840	Tupelo	132.5	36 817	822	278	30 685	20.0	23 905	28.4	75.2	24.4	0.1	0.3	0.1	0.5	0.5
29 00000	MISSOURI	178 446.0	5 468 338	X	31	5 116 901	6.9	4 916 766	4.1	87.7	10.7	0.4	0.8	0.4	1.2	1.6
29 06652	Blue Springs	41.7	45 982	639	1 103	40 103	14.7	25 927	54.7	95.6	2.4	0.4	1.1	0.5	1.6	1.6
29 11242	Cape Girardeau	59.6	36 687	828	616	34 475	6.4	34 361	0.3	90.2	8.0	0.2	1.3	0.2	0.6	1.8
29 13600	Chesterfield	77.6	44 216	673	570	42 325	4.5	NA	NA	93.7	2.4	0.1	3.6	0.2	1.2	5.9
29 15670	Columbia	114.8	80 500	308	701	69 133	16.4	62 061	11.4	85.1	9.9	0.3	4.1	0.5	1.3	6.0
29 24778	Florissant	26.4	50 060	584	1 896	51 038	-1.9	55 372	-7.8	95.0	4.1	0.2	0.5	0.2	1.0	1.4
29 27190	Gladstone	20.8	28 364	1 061	1 364	26 243	8.1	24 990	5.0	97.1	1.0	0.5	0.8	0.7	2.5	1.6
29 35000	Independence	202.5	117 545	180	580	112 301	4.7	111 806	0.4	96.2	1.4	0.6	1.0	0.8	2.0	1.6
29 37000	Jefferson City	68.9	35 406	848	514	35 517	-0.3	33 618	5.6	88.8	10.1	0.3	0.5	0.3	0.8	1.4
29 37592	Joplin	76.9	45 016	659	585	41 175	9.3	38 869	5.1	95.0	2.1	1.9	0.6	0.3	1.2	1.4
29 38000	Kansas City	806.9	437 764	33	543	434 829	0.7	448 154	-3.0	66.8	29.6	0.5	1.2	1.9	3.9	2.8
29 39044	Kirkwood	23.4	27 107	1 112	1 158	28 318	-4.3	27 987	1.2	93.1	5.9	0.1	0.7	0.1	0.7	2.1
29 41348	Lee's Summit	153.1	68 961	376	450	46 418	48.6	28 742	61.5	96.9	1.7	0.3	0.6	0.4	1.0	1.4
29 46586	Maryland Heights	54.3	23 761	1 262	438	25 440	-6.6	NA	NA	93.5	3.6	0.2	2.4	0.3	1.1	3.6
29 60788	Raytown	25.7	28 911	1 042	1 125	30 601	-5.5	31 759	-3.6	95.3	3.2	0.4	0.5	0.5	1.4	1.1
29 64082	St. Charles	42.9	59 276	463	1 382	50 634	17.1	37 379	35.5	95.9	2.8	0.3	0.7	0.3	1.0	1.2
29 64550	St. Joseph	112.3	69 577	371	620	71 852	-3.2	76 691	-6.3	95.0	3.6	0.3	0.4	0.7	2.2	0.8
29 65000	St. Louis	160.4	333 960	51	2 082	396 685	-15.8	453 085	-12.4	50.9	47.5	0.2	0.9	0.4	1.3	2.5
29 65126	St. Peters	40.9	52 411	549	1 281	40 660	28.9	15 700	159.0	96.4	2.2	0.2	1.0	0.3	1.1	1.4
29 70000	Springfield	176.0	142 669	140	811	140 494	1.5	133 116	5.5	95.7	2.5	0.7	0.9	0.3	1.0	1.5
29 75220	University City	15.2	36 874	821	2 426	40 087	-8.0	42 738	-6.2	49.1	48.2	0.1	2.2	0.4	1.1	6.3
30 00000	MONTANA	376 990.9	882 779	X	2	799 065	10.5	786 690	1.6	92.7	0.3	6.0	0.5	0.5	1.5	1.7
30 06550	Billings	84.4	92 988	252	1 102	81 125	14.6	66 798	21.4	94.6	0.5	3.2	0.6	1.1	3.1	1.6
30 11390	Butte-Silver Bow	1 860.0	(3)33 325	(3)912	(3)18	(3)33 252	(3)0.2	NA	NA	97.4	0.0	1.1	0.6	0.8	2.2	1.8
30 32800	Great Falls	40.0	56 340	503	1 409	55 125	2.2	56 725	-2.8	93.1	1.0	4.6	0.8	0.5	1.7	3.0
30 50200	Missoula	43.1	58 460	475	1 356	42 918	36.2	33 387	28.5	95.5	0.3	2.4	1.4	0.3	1.3	2.8
31 00000	NEBRASKA	199 113.2	1 666 028	X	8	1 578 417	5.6	1 569 825	0.5	93.8	3.6	0.8	0.8	1.0	2.3	1.8
31 03950	Bellevue	20.8	44 730	664	2 150	39 240	14.0	21 813	79.9	89.4	6.5	0.4	2.4	1.3	3.9	4.2
31 19595	Grand Island	53.2	41 950	710	789	39 487	6.2	33 180	19.0	96.0	0.3	0.3	1.3	2.0	4.8	2.4
31 28000	Lincoln	163.9	215 928	75	1 317	191 972	12.5	171 932	11.7	94.5	2.4	0.6	1.7	0.9	2.0	2.7
31 37000	Omaha	260.7	386 742	42	1 483	344 463	12.3	314 267	9.1	83.9	13.1	0.7	1.0	1.3	3.1	2.8
32 00000	NEVADA	284 397.2	1 809 253	X	6	1 201 675	50.6	800 508	50.1	84.3	6.6	1.6	3.2	4.4	10.4	8.7
32 09700	Carson City	371.8	50 046	585	135	40 443	23.7	32 022	26.3	90.7	1.7	2.7	1.4	3.4	7.7	6.6
32 31900	Henderson	185.3	166 399	123	898	64 948	156.2	NA	NA	91.4	2.7	1.0	2.0	2.9	8.1	5.3
32 40000	Las Vegas	215.7	418 658	37	1 941	258 877	61.7	164 674	56.8	78.4	11.4	0.9	3.6	5.7	12.5	10.3
32 51800	North Las Vegas	157.9	101 841	217	645	47 849	112.8	42 739	12.0	45.2	37.4	1.0	2.4	14.0	22.2	14.0
32 60600	Reno	148.9	166 650	122	1 119	134 230	24.2	100 756	32.8	86.1	2.9	1.4	4.9	4.8	11.1	11.9
32 68400	Sparks	36.9	64 338	417	1 744	53 367	20.6	40 780	30.9	88.4	2.4	1.4	4.5	3.3	8.6	7.9
33 00000	NEW HAMPSHIRE	23 230.7	1 201 134	X	52	1 109 252	8.3	920 610	20.5	98.0	0.6	0.2	0.8	0.3	1.0	3.7
33 14200	Concord	166.5	38 981	776	234	36 006	8.3	30 400	18.4	98.2	0.6	0.3	0.7	0.2	1.0	3.0
33 18820	Dover	69.2	26 586	1 130	384	25 042	6.2	22 387	11.9	97.4	1.1	0.2	1.1	0.2	1.0	3.8
33 45140	Manchester	85.5	102 830	214	1 203	99 332	3.5	90 936	9.2	97.0	1.0	0.2	1.1	0.8	2.1	6.8
33 50260	Nashua	80.1	82 677	294	1 032	79 662	3.8	67 865	17.4	95.2	1.6	0.2	1.9	1.1	3.0	7.0
33 62900	Portsmouth	40.4	25 798	1 167	639	25 925	-0.5	26 254	-1.3	92.6	4.6	0.3	1.7	0.8	2.0	4.0
33 65140	Rochester	117.0	28 241	1 064	241	26 630	6.0	21 560	23.5	98.7	0.3	0.2	0.6	0.2	0.7	2.5
34 00000	NEW JERSEY	19 214.8	8 143 412	X	424	7 747 750	5.1	7 365 011	5.0	79.3	13.4	0.2	3.5	3.6	9.6	12.5
34 02080	Atlantic City	29.4	37 708	804	1 283	37 986	-0.7	40 199	-5.5	35.4	51.3	0.5	4.0	8.8	15.3	9.9
34 03580	Bayonne	14.6	60 189	457	4 123	61 464	-2.1	65 047	-5.5	90.4	4.7	0.1	1.8	2.9	9.5	12.0
34 10000	Camden	22.8	82 402	295	3 614	87 492	-5.8	84 910	3.0	19.0	56.4	0.4	1.3	22.9	31.2	3.9
34 13690	Clifton	29.3	75 669	333	2 583	71 984	5.1	74 388	-3.2	92.8	1.4	0.1	3.5	2.2	6.8	19.0
34 19390	East Orange	10.2	69 801	366	6 843	73 552	-5.1	77 690	-5.3	7.2	89.9	0.4	0.6	1.8	4.1	13.0
34 21000	Elizabeth	31.9	110 586	200	3 467	110 002	0.5	106 201	3.6	65.5	19.8	0.3	2.7	11.6	39.1	36.9
34 22470	Fair Lawn Borough	13.4	31 098	976	2 321	30 548	1.8	32 229	-5.2	96.0	0.6	0.1	2.9	0.4	3.5	16.6
34 24420	Fort Lee Borough	6.6	33 854	892	5 129	31 997	5.8	32 449	-1.4	77.2	1.3	0.1	20.3	1.1	5.6	35.1
34 25770	Garfield	5.5	27 236	1 105	4 952	26 727	1.9	26 803	-0.3	93.8	2.2	0.1	1.7	2.2	9.0	24.3

1. Dry land or land partially or temporarily covered by water. 2. Hispanic persons may be of any race. 3. 1999 population is for Butte-Silver Bow "remainder"; most other items are for Butte-Silver Bow Consolidated city; see Appendix A.

Table D. Cities — Population and Households

City	\	\	Age of population (percent)	\	\	\	\	\	\	Percent female	Number	Percent change, 1980–1990	Persons per house-hold	Female family house-holder[1]	One-person
	Under 5 years	5 to 17 years	18 to 24 years	25 to 34 years	35 to 44 years	45 to 54 years	55 to 64 years	65 to 74 years	75 years and over						
	16	17	18	19	20	21	22	23	24	25	26	27	28	29	30
MISSISSIPPI	7.6	21.4	11.4	15.5	13.6	9.6	8.3	7.0	5.5	52.2	911 374	10.0	2.75	15.9	23.4
Biloxi	8.6	16.9	16.9	19.6	11.5	7.0	8.0	6.9	4.6	48.4	16 644	3.7	2.50	13.0	28.9
Greenville	8.5	25.2	9.6	14.5	13.5	8.6	7.9	6.9	5.4	53.8	15 322	16.0	2.91	24.8	24.3
Gulfport	7.4	17.9	10.8	17.4	12.9	9.6	9.5	8.9	5.6	51.0	15 797	7.5	2.45	16.5	29.6
Hattiesburg	7.1	16.5	22.6	16.5	11.2	7.1	6.4	6.6	6.1	54.2	15 911	9.4	2.36	19.0	33.4
Jackson	7.7	19.8	12.1	17.9	14.4	8.8	7.7	6.6	5.0	53.7	71 865	0.3	2.64	20.4	27.5
Meridian	7.5	19.7	9.8	15.3	14.1	8.2	8.9	9.2	7.2	54.5	16 170	-6.8	2.46	20.7	31.0
Pascagoula	8.1	20.0	10.8	16.7	13.4	10.9	8.6	6.8	4.7	51.2	9 774	-2.3	2.59	16.3	25.7
Tupelo	7.9	20.0	8.7	17.4	14.7	11.1	8.0	6.6	5.6	53.4	11 705	32.1	2.56	14.5	26.1
MISSOURI	7.2	18.5	10.1	16.7	14.4	10.2	8.9	7.7	6.3	51.8	1 961 206	9.3	2.54	10.6	26.0
Blue Springs	8.6	24.5	8.7	17.9	19.5	9.8	4.8	3.5	2.6	51.2	13 529	63.1	2.95	9.5	14.9
Cape Girardeau	6.2	15.2	19.5	15.2	12.2	9.3	8.0	7.5	7.0	53.1	13 442	8.0	2.34	10.1	30.5
Chesterfield	5.8	21.3	8.2	11.4	19.7	15.8	8.6	4.9	4.3	51.1	13 115	NA	2.83	5.1	17.4
Columbia	6.0	12.6	30.0	18.5	12.2	6.9	5.1	4.5	4.1	52.0	25 841	20.7	2.27	9.7	32.2
Florissant	6.8	16.8	8.8	18.5	12.7	10.6	12.1	8.9	4.8	52.2	19 177	8.2	2.61	9.8	21.6
Gladstone	6.4	16.3	9.8	16.6	15.4	13.3	10.8	7.6	3.8	52.3	10 535	14.8	2.46	8.8	24.0
Independence	7.1	16.9	9.4	17.6	13.4	11.3	9.9	8.6	5.7	52.5	45 322	7.0	2.46	10.3	26.1
Jefferson City	6.0	15.5	10.8	17.5	15.9	9.7	8.9	8.0	7.7	51.0	14 162	13.3	2.28	9.5	34.4
Joplin	7.1	15.8	11.5	16.8	13.1	9.6	8.9	9.2	8.0	53.7	17 474	9.1	2.26	10.9	32.7
Kansas City	7.7	17.1	9.8	19.7	14.5	9.8	8.6	7.4	5.6	52.4	177 607	1.2	2.40	15.1	32.5
Kirkwood	6.6	16.4	6.0	15.5	17.2	10.3	9.8	9.6	8.6	54.2	11 212	4.6	2.41	8.8	28.6
Lee's Summit	8.6	19.8	8.1	19.1	17.2	10.1	6.4	4.3	6.4	52.7	17 632	59.4	2.60	8.6	23.4
Maryland Heights	6.5	13.5	12.0	26.1	15.2	12.2	7.5	4.2	2.8	50.5	10 667	NA	2.35	7.8	30.0
Raytown	6.2	15.2	7.9	16.3	14.6	9.9	12.0	11.0	6.9	53.4	12 697	4.8	2.39	9.3	26.0
St. Charles	7.7	17.1	11.2	21.3	15.1	9.9	7.9	5.6	4.3	51.2	21 670	59.7	2.45	9.2	27.6
St. Joseph	7.3	18.8	9.6	16.0	13.1	9.1	9.1	8.9	8.1	53.1	28 411	-2.1	2.44	12.2	29.1
St. Louis	8.0	17.3	10.3	18.4	12.8	8.1	8.5	8.5	8.2	54.5	164 931	-7.6	2.34	20.5	39.2
St. Peters	10.6	23.0	7.1	21.8	20.6	8.3	4.1	3.1	1.4	50.6	15 223	211.8	3.00	7.1	14.4
Springfield	6.2	14.4	17.8	16.4	12.9	8.9	8.1	8.1	7.2	52.7	57 353	10.7	2.28	10.1	31.5
University City	7.1	16.4	10.4	18.1	15.7	10.5	8.0	7.1	6.8	54.1	16 556	-1.6	2.40	16.2	30.1
MONTANA	7.4	20.4	8.8	15.4	15.9	10.3	8.6	7.6	5.7	50.5	306 163	7.4	2.53	8.6	26.3
Billings	7.4	18.4	9.4	17.4	15.3	10.0	8.6	7.8	5.7	52.3	33 181	26.4	2.39	10.5	29.4
Butte-Silver Bow	6.8	18.2	9.0	14.5	14.7	10.3	9.5	9.4	7.6	50.9	13 825	NA	2.39	8.8	31.5
Great Falls	7.4	18.7	8.5	16.5	14.7	10.6	9.1	8.2	6.3	52.1	22 639	3.6	2.39	10.4	29.5
Missoula	6.6	16.0	16.8	17.8	16.0	8.2	6.3	6.3	6.0	51.6	17 677	29.0	2.28	10.2	33.3
NEBRASKA	7.6	19.6	9.9	16.3	14.5	9.5	8.6	7.5	6.7	51.3	602 363	5.2	2.54	8.3	26.5
Bellevue	7.8	19.6	12.7	19.2	15.2	10.8	7.9	4.6	2.3	50.0	11 429	49.9	2.70	9.9	20.7
Grand Island	7.9	20.3	8.5	16.6	14.5	9.1	8.4	7.9	6.8	51.9	15 244	19.7	2.51	9.3	27.8
Lincoln	7.2	16.2	16.6	18.8	14.9	8.4	7.0	5.9	5.1	51.4	75 402	15.9	2.40	9.1	28.8
Omaha	7.6	17.9	10.9	18.5	14.2	9.5	8.6	7.2	5.6	52.2	133 842	12.9	2.45	13.3	30.6
NEVADA	7.7	17.0	9.9	18.5	16.0	11.3	9.0	7.1	3.5	49.1	466 297	52.9	2.53	10.2	25.7
Carson City	6.9	15.4	8.3	16.6	16.1	12.3	9.7	9.4	5.4	48.9	15 895	30.9	2.39	9.6	27.2
Henderson	8.1	20.1	9.0	19.2	16.9	10.7	7.6	5.8	2.6	50.3	23 237	NA	2.77	9.7	18.0
Las Vegas	8.2	16.6	9.9	19.8	15.5	10.9	8.8	7.0	3.3	49.3	99 735	59.8	2.55	12.0	26.2
North Las Vegas	10.6	23.5	11.7	18.1	13.2	9.7	6.5	4.6	2.2	50.5	14 525	11.2	3.24	23.2	17.1
Reno	7.1	13.4	12.6	20.2	16.0	10.7	8.3	7.3	4.4	49.2	57 286	30.9	2.26	9.6	33.7
Sparks	7.8	17.3	10.1	19.5	17.1	10.9	8.0	5.6	3.7	50.7	20 561	35.7	2.56	11.2	23.7
NEW HAMPSHIRE	7.6	17.5	10.6	18.5	16.5	10.1	8.0	6.4	4.8	51.0	411 186	27.1	2.62	8.5	22.0
Concord	7.1	16.1	9.8	20.8	16.4	8.3	7.5	6.8	7.2	51.5	14 222	24.2	2.35	9.9	30.4
Dover	6.4	13.6	15.3	20.8	13.2	9.5	8.3	7.2	5.8	52.2	10 345	23.5	2.36	9.5	27.7
Manchester	7.8	15.2	11.9	20.9	14.0	8.5	8.0	7.8	5.8	52.1	40 338	17.3	2.40	11.1	29.2
Nashua	8.0	16.1	10.2	21.8	15.7	10.1	7.9	5.9	4.2	50.9	31 051	26.5	2.53	9.3	24.8
Portsmouth	8.0	14.4	12.0	23.9	14.7	7.8	7.2	6.5	5.7	50.7	10 329	9.4	2.39	9.9	28.6
Rochester	8.5	17.8	9.3	19.3	15.1	8.9	8.5	7.4	5.4	51.4	10 221	32.0	2.58	10.0	22.5
NEW JERSEY	6.9	16.4	10.1	17.6	15.5	10.9	9.3	7.9	5.5	51.7	2 794 711	9.6	2.70	12.1	23.1
Atlantic City	7.4	15.2	10.1	17.0	12.9	8.6	9.8	9.7	9.3	52.8	15 731	-5.7	2.30	22.8	40.6
Bayonne	5.5	14.3	8.9	17.4	13.6	10.7	10.6	11.9	7.0	52.8	25 309	-0.5	2.42	13.7	31.4
Camden	10.7	24.9	12.1	17.5	11.8	8.3	6.4	5.3	3.1	52.4	26 626	-6.1	3.15	36.9	23.6
Clifton	5.4	12.4	8.6	17.6	14.3	10.0	11.0	12.1	8.6	52.7	29 041	0.4	2.44	10.3	28.1
East Orange	7.9	17.9	10.8	18.6	14.0	11.0	8.1	6.6	5.1	54.7	27 210	-5.7	2.63	26.4	35.1
Elizabeth	7.5	17.2	10.7	20.0	14.0	10.2	8.5	6.8	5.2	51.3	39 101	0.4	2.76	17.2	26.7
Fair Lawn Borough	5.6	14.8	7.0	13.5	15.3	11.4	12.2	12.2	7.9	52.3	11 493	-0.7	2.64	8.7	20.4
Fort Lee Borough	5.8	9.8	5.1	20.2	16.1	10.6	12.1	11.6	8.9	52.9	15 236	2.7	2.10	6.6	38.6
Garfield	6.5	13.1	10.0	20.6	14.0	8.9	9.2	10.4	7.0	52.2	10 946	2.0	2.44	11.8	28.9

1. No spouse present.

City	Persons in group quarters, 1990				Serious crimes known to police, 1998[2]				Education, 1990				Money income, 1989		
					Total		Rate[3]		School enrollment		Attainment[4] (percent)			Households	
														Median	
	Total	Persons in mental hospitals	Persons in nursing homes	Persons identified as home-less[1]	Number	Rate[3]	Violent	Property	Public	Private	High school grad-uate or more	Bach-elor's degree or more	Per capita (dollars)[5]	Dollars	Percent change, 1979–1989 (constant 1989 dollars)
	31	32	33	34	35	36	37	38	39	40	41	42	43	44	45
MISSISSIPPI	69 113	2 245	15 803	546	120 647	4 384	411	3 973	646 850	80 636	64.3	14.7	9 648	20 136	-0.7
Biloxi	4 727	0	176	27	NA	NA	NA	NA	9 631	1 458	75.2	18.0	10 036	19 824	-3.3
Greenville	530	0	377	6	5 436	12 596	992	11 604	11 422	2 229	61.5	15.6	9 081	18 060	3.2
Gulfport	2 083	328	603	68	5 528	8 428	427	8 001	8 387	1 482	74.8	18.3	11 451	21 174	-0.6
Hattiesburg	4 380	0	583	46	3 920	8 074	461	7 613	14 774	1 303	74.0	27.0	10 013	15 576	-15.4
Jackson	6 698	0	1 235	123	20 674	10 690	1 166	9 524	47 579	11 800	75.0	26.9	12 216	23 270	-6.2
Meridian	1 229	452	327	66	2 237	5 446	523	4 923	9 418	965	68.6	15.8	10 670	18 004	-8.8
Pascagoula	616	0	62	40	2 293	8 376	712	7 664	6 437	767	73.9	16.3	11 778	24 986	-7.3
Tupelo	709	0	507	25	2 875	8 021	379	7 642	7 350	634	76.1	21.9	14 083	27 871	11.1
MISSOURI	144 393	2 172	52 060	2 550	262 506	4 826	556	4 270	1 060 947	231 676	73.9	17.8	12 989	26 362	1.0
Blue Springs	260	0	239	0	2 080	4 606	250	4 356	11 237	1 473	90.1	23.8	14 793	39 904	-3.9
Cape Girardeau	3 064	0	538	0	2 326	6 489	220	6 269	9 984	1 223	77.0	24.3	12 254	22 634	-4.0
Chesterfield	923	0	493	0	1 075	2 348	118	2 230	8 336	3 537	92.9	53.7	28 019	66 930	NA
Columbia	10 334	17	845	38	4 403	5 592	478	5 114	28 099	3 008	87.2	45.0	12 452	22 059	-3.6
Florissant	857	33	591	0	1 556	3 062	118	2 944	8 923	3 334	80.3	16.3	14 914	36 809	-5.9
Gladstone	294	0	294	0	1 100	3 845	252	3 593	5 215	1 003	87.9	23.0	17 786	37 302	-6.7
Independence	1 060	14	804	0	8 813	7 904	606	7 298	21 019	3 436	78.3	13.7	13 208	28 242	-12.5
Jefferson City	3 186	0	585	50	1 853	5 053	281	4 772	6 801	1 653	78.1	27.5	15 701	27 597	-4.7
Joplin	1 446	0	353	33	2 642	6 463	340	6 123	8 315	1 294	73.0	16.5	11 296	19 420	-1.4
Kansas City	8 983	291	3 571	700	NA	NA	NA	NA	85 407	20 508	78.8	22.0	13 799	26 713	0.5
Kirkwood	305	0	258	0	649	2 348	152	2 196	4 447	2 049	88.2	42.9	22 058	42 113	8.5
Lee's Summit	557	0	539	0	NA	NA	NA	NA	11 021	1 603	89.9	27.3	16 658	38 800	13.8
Maryland Heights	414	0	409	5	1 240	5 113	260	4 853	4 672	1 268	86.4	33.5	17 785	39 211	NA
Raytown	319	0	294	0	1 319	4 434	313	4 121	5 705	904	84.8	18.1	14 914	32 002	-13.4
St. Charles	1 378	64	462	30	2 274	3 866	231	3 635	9 326	4 357	79.9	22.9	15 626	34 336	4.2
St. Joseph	2 429	306	1 129	19	4 907	6 950	324	6 626	15 759	1 651	71.5	13.3	11 044	22 303	-3.7
St. Louis	10 575	402	3 786	818	51 459	14 952	2 571	12 381	67 583	29 211	62.8	15.3	10 798	19 458	0.9
St. Peters	134	0	123	0	1 870	3 705	180	3 525	10 707	3 288	89.8	25.5	15 468	45 298	8.0
Springfield	9 830	12	1 828	353	11 313	7 789	507	7 282	32 620	7 043	77.0	20.7	11 878	21 577	-1.8
University City	327	0	167	12	2 344	7 038	420	6 618	7 138	4 369	83.6	41.2	17 260	32 150	6.4
MONTANA	23 792	282	7 764	424	35 822	4 071	139	3 932	197 360	18 399	81.0	19.8	11 213	22 988	-11.1
Billings	1 788	33	756	136	NA	NA	NA	NA	18 669	2 487	84.2	23.5	12 834	25 639	-7.8
Butte-Silver Bow	699	0	347	98	NA	NA	NA	NA	7 508	1 019	78.3	17.9	11 364	21 216	NA
Great Falls	901	0	692	39	NA	NA	NA	NA	11 351	1 764	82.2	19.3	12 603	23 113	-15.3
Missoula	2 700	0	724	30	NA	NA	NA	NA	14 246	838	87.2	33.4	11 759	21 033	-10.0
NEBRASKA	47 586	979	19 171	569	73 259	4 405	451	3 954	368 874	64 535	81.8	18.9	12 452	26 016	-2.5
Bellevue	137	0	111	11	1 400	3 186	84	3 102	8 040	1 567	89.4	24.1	13 540	31 923	-2.5
Grand Island	1 112	0	832	10	3 629	8 754	446	8 308	8 677	862	79.0	14.6	11 246	25 019	-4.9
Lincoln	10 831	0	1 518	179	14 226	6 711	549	6 162	53 203	8 151	88.3	28.5	13 720	28 056	-2.1
Omaha	8 191	325	3 477	333	26 409	7 171	1 315	5 856	69 339	21 515	82.6	23.1	13 957	26 927	-1.9
NEVADA	24 226	262	3 605	1 611	92 250	5 281	644	4 637	256 041	24 370	78.8	15.3	15 214	31 011	1.6
Carson City	2 432	0	171	22	NA	NA	NA	NA	8 859	666	82.7	16.3	15 131	31 570	0.9
Henderson	596	0	333	54	6 539	4 855	411	4 444	15 309	1 190	82.5	17.3	16 427	38 802	NA
Las Vegas	4 148	114	570	767	NA	NA	NA	NA	51 242	6 457	76.3	13.4	14 737	30 590	4.5
North Las Vegas	556	0	404	17	6 022	6 953	1 429	5 524	12 338	584	58.3	4.0	8 565	23 917	-8.4
Reno	4 171	84	754	652	10 075	6 075	506	5 569	28 714	2 951	81.9	22.4	16 091	28 388	-3.4
Sparks	665	69	373	54	3 222	5 077	391	4 686	12 119	898	82.3	16.0	14 453	32 420	-7.8
NEW HAMPSHIRE	32 074	383	8 202	380	28 675	2 420	107	2 313	219 482	57 283	82.2	24.4	15 959	36 329	27.4
Concord	2 528	331	509	51	NA	NA	NA	NA	6 766	1 677	84.5	28.1	15 981	32 733	22.6
Dover	606	0	382	35	NA	NA	NA	NA	4 543	1 179	83.1	24.3	15 413	31 507	20.7
Manchester	2 732	21	817	147	4 018	3 876	226	3 650	15 971	5 932	74.9	19.6	15 111	31 911	22.0
Nashua	971	0	495	34	NA	NA	NA	NA	14 699	4 765	82.7	28.8	18 010	40 505	25.3
Portsmouth	1 216	50	316	64	NA	NA	NA	NA	4 563	932	88.8	26.6	15 557	30 591	26.5
Rochester	313	0	239	0	NA	NA	NA	NA	4 845	1 017	75.0	14.1	13 395	30 807	14.4
NEW JERSEY	171 399	4 725	47 054	9 466	296 527	3 654	440	3 214	1 453 475	413 927	76.7	24.9	18 714	40 927	23.3
Atlantic City	1 771	0	902	627	8 785	22 577	1 781	20 796	6 257	997	58.3	9.5	12 017	20 309	23.6
Bayonne	248	0	0	0	1 342	2 199	356	1 843	9 090	3 502	70.1	16.6	16 159	31 954	12.9
Camden	3 590	0	358	331	8 499	9 977	2 468	7 509	22 739	3 405	49.7	6.4	7 276	17 386	11.7
Clifton	942	0	356	0	2 501	3 459	227	3 232	11 339	3 127	72.9	20.4	18 950	39 905	20.0
East Orange	2 081	0	775	386	5 383	7 616	1 698	5 918	14 771	4 573	69.3	14.7	12 376	26 810	19.6
Elizabeth	2 265	0	297	129	8 138	7 319	905	6 414	21 337	6 015	58.5	11.5	12 112	27 631	6.9
Fair Lawn Borough	142	0	142	0	514	1 643	125	1 518	5 059	1 786	81.3	30.3	22 418	49 658	19.2
Fort Lee Borough	0	0	0	0	912	2 717	173	2 544	3 651	1 847	84.9	42.2	31 758	46 395	23.2
Garfield	0	0	0	0	794	2 896	215	2 681	3 790	1 261	60.1	11.5	14 963	31 649	19.8

1. Persons in emergency shelters and persons visible in street locations. 2. Data for serious crimes have not been adjusted for underreporting. This may affect comparability between geographic areas and over time. 3. Per 100,000 population estimated by the FBI. 4. Persons 25 years old and older. 5. Based on population enumerated as of April 1, 1990.

City	Money income, 1989 (cont'd)				Housing units, 1990										
	Households (cont'd)	Percent below poverty, 1989						Occupied units							
		Persons		Families						Owner-occupied units			Renter-occupied units		
											Owner cost as a percent of income				
	Percent with $100,000 or more	Total	Percent change in rate, 1979–1989	Total	Total	Percent change, 1980–1990	Vacant units for sale or rent[1]	Total	Percent	Median value[2] (dollars)	With a mortgage	Without a mortgage	Median rent[3] (dollars)	Rent as percent of income	Substandard units[4] (percent)
	46	47	48	49	50	51	52	53	54	55	56	57	58	59	60
MISSISSIPPI..................	1.7	25.2	5.5	20.2	1 010 423	10.8	49 635	911 374	71.5	45 600	20.8	13.5	309	27.1	7.2
Biloxi..........................	1.3	21.4	32.9	16.4	18 864	5.3	1 655	16 644	43.8	55 400	18.5	12.2	331	24.9	4.3
Greenville.....................	2.2	32.0	2.9	26.9	16 492	19.7	934	15 322	58.3	42 500	21.1	15.0	332	32.3	10.2
Gulfport........................	2.1	20.3	18.7	17.1	18 236	13.3	1 883	15 797	56.7	52 100	21.5	12.4	343	25.9	3.8
Hattiesburg...................	2.4	35.9	44.8	28.3	17 675	10.3	1 329	15 911	46.1	47 100	20.3	12.9	304	28.9	5.4
Jackson.........................	3.7	22.7	23.4	18.0	79 374	4.9	5 977	71 865	57.3	54 600	21.8	14.0	388	28.8	6.5
Meridian........................	2.7	27.8	21.9	23.3	17 740	-4.1	1 063	16 170	57.7	45 900	18.3	12.9	284	26.5	4.9
Pascagoula....................	1.9	19.7	60.2	17.5	11 053	-2.9	956	9 774	59.3	49 100	16.5	13.1	333	25.7	5.3
Tupelo..........................	3.9	12.6	-9.4	9.2	12 335	30.8	473	11 705	61.1	62 400	18.1	12.6	337	22.8	2.6
MISSOURI.....................	2.8	13.3	9.3	10.1	2 199 129	10.6	124 286	1 961 206	68.8	59 800	18.4	12.3	368	25.2	3.0
Blue Springs..................	3.0	4.7	27.0	3.8	14 246	61.7	634	13 529	72.0	76 700	20.1	11.8	507	23.6	1.8
Cape Girardeau..............	2.5	18.0	29.5	12.3	14 627	9.0	953	13 442	57.4	58 300	17.1	13.1	331	28.4	1.9
Chesterfield..................	24.2	2.1	NA	1.4	14 019	NA	779	13 115	79.5	172 800	18.9	10.8	682	24.6	0.4
Columbia.......................	2.9	22.4	28.0	12.4	27 551	21.4	1 417	25 841	43.8	73 400	17.9	11.9	382	29.0	2.2
Florissant......................	1.4	3.3	32.0	2.2	19 797	9.7	542	19 177	79.0	67 200	15.6	11.4	492	24.3	1.5
Gladstone.....................	3.7	3.5	29.6	2.2	11 076	15.3	478	10 535	68.8	72 700	16.6	11.4	431	22.8	1.4
Independence................	1.4	9.5	43.9	6.9	48 262	8.7	2 347	45 322	67.1	56 000	16.9	11.7	387	25.1	1.8
Jefferson City................	2.9	9.7	36.6	6.8	15 437	14.5	977	14 162	59.5	61 500	16.8	12.0	326	22.8	1.0
Joplin..........................	1.8	17.0	13.3	12.7	19 367	11.5	1 311	17 474	60.4	41 100	16.6	12.1	317	25.7	2.0
Kansas City...................	2.9	15.3	15.9	11.7	201 789	5.2	18 091	177 607	56.9	56 100	18.4	12.7	404	25.0	3.3
Kirkwood.......................	9.8	2.8	-9.7	1.3	11 699	5.3	381	11 212	78.0	100 500	17.6	11.8	558	22.9	0.7
Lee's Summit.................	4.6	4.8	-7.7	3.4	18 755	57.3	1 024	17 632	65.9	84 700	20.8	11.6	506	26.2	1.5
Maryland Heights...........	2.2	3.6	NA	2.4	11 469	NA	689	10 667	61.6	82 200	17.8	11.6	525	20.1	1.0
Raytown........................	1.5	4.8	92.0	3.4	13 216	6.4	434	12 697	75.0	63 900	17.3	11.4	427	23.1	0.8
St. Charles....................	2.5	6.5	8.3	4.4	23 246	62.1	1 322	21 670	59.7	80 700	18.2	11.7	477	22.7	1.8
St. Joseph.....................	1.6	16.7	41.5	13.2	31 276	-2.1	1 681	28 411	65.8	39 800	15.1	11.9	303	24.3	1.9
St. Louis.......................	1.3	24.6	12.8	20.6	194 919	-3.6	19 858	164 931	45.1	50 700	19.1	13.6	342	27.9	5.8
St. Peters......................	1.9	2.6	73.3	2.2	15 773	198.4	471	15 223	83.8	86 000	20.8	11.4	529	22.6	1.6
Springfield....................	2.3	17.8	24.5	11.6	62 472	11.4	3 874	57 353	55.5	53 900	17.3	11.7	340	26.4	2.4
University City...............	6.8	12.8	24.3	8.8	17 706	1.9	997	16 556	58.8	75 200	19.1	12.0	488	26.7	2.4
MONTANA.....................	1.7	16.1	30.7	12.0	361 155	10.0	20 004	306 163	67.3	56 600	20.2	12.5	311	25.0	3.2
Billings.........................	2.4	12.5	23.8	9.2	35 964	28.4	2 132	33 181	61.2	63 600	21.4	12.2	346	25.7	1.4
Butte-Silver Bow............	1.6	14.7	NA	11.3	15 474	NA	NA	13 899	70.8	43 800	17.4	13.4	265	25.6	2.2
Great Falls....................	2.3	14.7	53.1	11.2	24 157	0.7	1 081	22 639	62.8	60 600	20.2	11.7	310	27.1	2.4
Missoula.......................	1.9	19.0	26.7	12.9	18 488	27.1	542	17 677	49.5	64 500	20.8	12.7	324	28.4	3.1
NEBRASKA....................	2.2	11.1	4.2	8.0	660 621	5.7	28 503	602 363	66.5	50 400	19.4	12.6	348	23.7	1.9
Bellevue.......................	1.6	5.7	26.7	4.3	11 960	53.4	419	11 429	59.8	62 100	20.3	12.3	445	24.6	2.7
Grand Island..................	1.2	11.2	62.3	7.8	15 855	15.6	448	15 244	60.8	47 600	17.7	12.5	319	22.8	2.1
Lincoln.........................	2.3	11.3	27.0	6.5	79 079	14.4	2 826	75 402	58.1	61 700	19.0	12.0	379	25.7	1.5
Omaha..........................	3.3	12.6	10.5	9.6	143 612	14.5	6 845	133 842	59.2	54 600	19.4	12.7	386	25.1	2.2
NEVADA.......................	3.8	10.2	16.7	7.3	518 858	52.6	32 551	466 297	54.8	95 700	22.4	11.9	509	26.8	6.4
Carson City...................	2.8	8.0	14.3	5.6	16 628	24.4	550	15 895	60.3	99 300	20.9	10.6	480	27.4	3.0
Henderson.....................	5.2	7.1	NA	5.0	25 400	NA	1 827	23 237	64.3	100 700	23.4	11.7	616	25.6	4.7
Las Vegas.....................	3.5	11.5	9.5	8.2	109 670	63.4	8 370	99 735	50.4	89 200	22.2	11.6	490	27.3	8.0
North Las Vegas.............	1.0	21.4	48.6	18.6	15 837	12.1	981	14 525	49.9	58 100	21.0	12.4	426	27.7	17.4
Reno............................	4.1	11.5	42.0	7.6	61 384	29.6	3 341	57 286	42.6	109 600	23.3	12.2	492	26.9	6.9
Sparks..........................	2.1	7.2	26.3	4.8	21 660	33.9	764	20 561	54.2	97 300	22.9	12.8	537	26.5	4.5
NEW HAMPSHIRE...........	4.5	6.4	-24.4	4.4	503 904	30.4	28 301	411 186	68.2	129 400	24.4	14.7	549	26.4	2.1
Concord........................	3.4	6.7	-25.6	4.2	15 697	29.4	1 261	14 222	52.3	112 400	24.5	14.7	555	26.6	1.3
Dover...........................	2.4	9.4	-17.5	5.6	11 307	29.1	803	10 345	50.2	119 900	24.6	16.2	523	26.7	1.4
Manchester....................	2.5	9.0	-13.5	6.3	44 361	23.7	3 485	40 338	46.0	118 600	23.4	15.1	537	26.3	2.0
Nashua.........................	5.3	6.5	0.0	4.7	33 383	31.2	2 057	31 051	57.7	138 800	23.2	14.8	645	26.0	1.6
Portsmouth....................	3.1	6.7	-28.0	5.1	11 369	15.1	780	10 329	41.9	137 600	23.7	13.8	553	26.4	2.3
Rochester......................	1.2	6.3	-16.0	5.0	11 076	35.9	699	10 221	69.0	105 200	23.6	14.6	519	27.9	1.3
NEW JERSEY.................	8.8	7.6	-20.2	5.6	3 075 310	10.9	146 561	2 794 711	64.9	162 300	23.4	15.1	592	26.3	4.1
Atlantic City..................	1.8	25.0	0.4	20.6	21 626	0.5	2 456	15 731	30.4	73 400	19.7	15.8	434	28.2	9.4
Bayonne........................	4.2	8.8	-8.3	6.3	26 468	0.4	872	25 309	40.5	168 500	21.9	14.5	479	22.4	3.4
Camden.........................	0.5	36.6	-0.8	34.1	30 138	-7.5	2 026	26 626	48.4	31 300	20.6	16.2	414	32.5	15.4
Clifton..........................	6.3	4.7	6.8	3.1	29 999	1.9	766	29 041	60.8	185 000	23.4	14.3	613	24.0	2.2
East Orange...................	3.0	17.7	-11.9	15.6	28 987	-6.7	1 539	27 210	27.5	116 200	23.7	15.6	534	28.2	11.3
Elizabeth......................	2.1	16.1	1.9	13.7	41 315	1.7	1 757	39 101	31.7	145 400	25.3	14.6	520	26.2	11.4
Fair Lawn Borough..........	11.6	2.9	-17.1	2.3	11 759	0.7	198	11 493	81.0	199 000	22.9	15.4	594	28.3	1.1
Fort Lee Borough............	16.9	6.0	30.4	3.9	16 847	8.8	1 388	15 236	58.4	283 000	25.1	16.0	728	25.0	4.8
Garfield........................	2.0	7.4	8.8	5.1	11 458	3.1	366	10 946	42.6	172 900	27.3	19.3	615	24.4	3.1

1. Includes units rented or sold but not occupied.   2. Specified owner-occupied units.   3. Specified renter-occupied units.   4. Overcrowded or lacking complete plumbing facilities.

City	Civilian labor force, 1999				Civilian employment, 1990[2]			Disability 1990	Value of residential construction authorized by building permits, 1999		
			Unemployment			Percent					
	Total	Percent change, 1998–1999	Total	Rate[1]	Total	Professional, managerial, and technical	Precision production, craft, and repair	Work disabled persons[3] (percent)	New construction ($1,000)	Number of housing units	Percent single family
	61	62	63	64	65	66	67	68	69	70	71
MISSISSIPPI..................	1 269 955	0.1	64 666	5.1	1 028 773	24.6	12.9	11.0	989 518	12 871	74.5
Biloxi...........................	19 262	-0.2	869	4.5	14 916	33.3	9.7	11.3	16 848	169	89.3
Greenville	17 670	-5.9	1 567	8.9	16 429	26.5	10.0	10.5	5 193	31	87.1
Gulfport	31 562	1.4	1 135	3.6	15 870	30.4	9.8	13.5	37 888	426	95.3
Hattiesburg	21 492	-2.0	861	4.0	16 896	34.1	6.8	9.3	11 777	101	74.3
Jackson	98 475	-1.0	4 442	4.5	87 485	31.7	8.6	9.3	53 616	1 068	17.2
Meridian	17 615	-1.3	1 100	6.2	15 769	27.8	10.6	10.3	5 208	61	93.4
Pascagoula	14 655	1.6	679	4.6	11 039	32.7	15.1	10.0	4 291	30	100.0
Tupelo	19 198	0.1	548	2.9	14 994	31.3	8.3	7.8	11 708	119	84.9
MISSOURI	2 847 386	-0.3	95 947	3.4	2 367 395	27.8	11.1	8.5	2 742 784	26 881	77.0
Blue Springs..............	23 786	0.2	475	2.0	20 770	33.0	10.4	4.4	39 295	383	92.4
Cape Girardeau	20 688	1.6	655	3.2	16 549	30.6	8.4	7.5	18 673	244	27.9
Chesterfield	20 380	-0.8	282	1.4	19 254	52.4	3.1	3.0	NA	NA	NA
Columbia	48 793	-2.2	647	1.3	34 748	41.7	4.9	5.7	73 482	773	76.7
Florissant	28 392	-1.0	610	2.1	26 616	29.3	12.9	6.3	124	1	100.0
Gladstone	18 553	0.5	329	1.8	14 623	30.6	10.0	5.9	7 958	66	100.0
Independence	64 968	0.0	1 892	2.9	56 201	24.2	12.8	8.7	36 279	349	100.0
Jefferson City	21 660	-1.2	474	2.2	17 033	38.8	7.2	7.4	26 879	199	81.4
Joplin.........................	24 660	-1.9	800	3.2	18 536	26.7	9.8	11.4	19 015	196	98.0
Kansas City	254 988	0.1	9 875	3.9	211 817	30.4	8.5	8.2	235 499	2 427	55.5
Kirkwood	14 640	-0.9	280	1.9	13 757	46.7	6.2	5.2	6 040	81	45.7
Lee's Summit	27 601	0.2	518	1.9	24 084	35.0	10.1	5.2	125 540	1 232	68.2
Maryland Heights	17 116	-0.9	279	1.6	16 130	41.2	7.9	4.9	NA	NA	NA
Raytown	18 030	0.2	373	2.1	15 732	31.6	11.1	7.0	6 152	91	20.9
St. Charles	40 717	2.2	883	2.2	29 966	33.8	11.0	7.1	31 884	302	98.0
St. Joseph	35 538	0.9	1 359	3.8	30 501	23.8	11.1	9.8	24 481	245	58.4
St. Louis	153 394	-2.2	10 005	6.5	161 434	27.3	7.7	11.1	37 522	487	31.6
St. Peters	32 923	2.3	628	1.9	24 295	36.3	11.7	3.8	24 566	241	90.5
Springfield	83 146	0.4	2 124	2.6	67 529	27.0	9.5	8.1	56 620	568	69.4
University City............	22 258	-1.3	893	4.0	20 468	48.8	3.8	5.8	6 015	31	74.2
MONTANA	474 006	1.3	24 645	5.2	350 723	26.9	10.4	9.7	226 260	2 566	62.6
Billings.......................	52 785	3.7	2 058	3.9	39 632	30.6	9.0	9.2	57 518	584	65.4
Butte-Silver Bow	16 967	-6.1	982	5.8	13 935	29.6	10.6	12.5	6 801	79	72.2
Great Falls	27 996	-1.4	1 548	5.5	23 273	29.7	9.6	11.5	11 819	101	88.1
Missoula	28 749	-0.4	1 176	4.1	20 335	35.6	6.7	8.1	37 232	422	68.7
NEBRASKA.................	911 100	-0.6	26 055	2.9	772 813	26.2	10.3	7.1	827 968	8 696	76.2
Bellevue	19 024	0.7	467	2.5	14 403	31.9	8.9	7.0	58 075	665	63.6
Grand Island	24 931	-0.2	908	3.6	19 662	23.2	12.4	8.6	12 244	129	73.6
Lincoln.......................	128 757	-0.4	3 217	2.5	106 117	33.3	9.2	6.5	164 689	1 555	69.5
Omaha	202 155	-0.7	6 407	3.2	167 866	30.8	9.1	8.2	221 461	2 654	74.6
NEVADA	941 600	2.4	41 863	4.4	607 437	24.8	11.4	8.3	2 976 683	32 643	74.4
Carson City	21 970	-3.1	902	4.1	19 360	30.6	12.4	8.4	34 883	327	90.8
Henderson	56 282	4.3	2 020	3.6	32 372	27.6	11.9	7.9	710 879	5 837	89.8
Las Vegas	229 594	4.3	10 010	4.4	131 001	23.5	11.2	8.6	599 646	7 367	74.3
North Las Vegas	35 402	4.6	2 699	7.6	19 510	11.5	12.6	11.1	200 125	2 654	68.7
Reno	91 946	-1.2	3 696	4.0	74 448	28.3	8.0	7.8	211 465	2 543	52.2
Sparks	36 803	-1.2	1 243	3.4	29 998	25.6	8.9	7.3	89 139	780	83.2
NEW HAMPSHIRE	665 927	2.1	18 068	2.7	574 237	32.6	12.5	7.3	781 944	6 326	90.0
Concord......................	21 908	2.7	426	1.9	17 890	37.6	9.8	7.0	9 785	89	95.5
Dover..........................	14 640	-0.4	304	2.1	13 701	33.2	11.0	7.8	17 436	149	78.5
Manchester	57 100	0.8	1 421	2.5	51 828	28.0	11.2	8.9	18 343	183	85.2
Nashua.......................	47 253	1.4	1 407	3.0	43 728	37.3	10.4	7.3	11 899	160	85.0
Portsmouth.................	12 519	0.4	258	2.1	12 401	35.4	8.5	9.8	2 310	23	78.3
Rochester...................	14 080	-1.1	379	2.7	12 967	25.1	15.3	9.8	8 159	92	100.0
NEW JERSEY.................	4 206 799	1.2	193 300	4.6	3 868 698	34.0	10.0	6.2	3 162 436	31 976	78.6
Atlantic City	19 865	-0.7	2 474	12.5	16 812	17.0	5.2	10.9	9 423	81	100.0
Bayonne	30 186	0.8	1 464	4.8	29 354	28.3	10.9	7.7	1 861	27	11.1
Camden	32 706	1.9	4 320	13.2	27 306	17.0	8.8	12.2	733	13	100.0
Clifton........................	38 425	1.2	1 573	4.1	37 633	30.7	11.8	4.9	406	4	50.0
East Orange	35 045	0.9	2 687	7.7	33 853	25.4	7.5	9.1	843	8	75.0
Elizabeth	55 608	1.4	4 389	7.9	50 977	18.2	11.5	7.1	5 468	92	15.2
Fair Lawn Borough	15 788	1.5	490	3.1	15 493	40.3	8.0	5.7	3 430	113	2.7
Fort Lee Borough.........	17 072	1.5	673	3.9	16 608	50.2	5.3	3.6	9 157	52	50.0
Garfield......................	14 160	1.5	744	5.3	13 587	21.5	14.0	6.2	1 864	33	21.2

1. Percent of civilian labor force. 2. Persons 16 years and older. 3. Persons 16 to 64 years old.

Table D. Cities — Wholesale Trade, Retail Trade, and Real Estate

City	Wholesale Trade, 1997				Retail Trade[1], 1997				Real Estate and Rental and Leasing, 1997			
	Number of Establishments	Number of Employees	Sales (mil dol)	Annual Payroll (mil dol)	Number of Establishments	Number of Employees	Sales (mil dol)	Annual Payroll (mil dol)	Number of Establishments	Number of Employees	Receipts (mil dol)	Annual Payroll (mil dol)
	72	73	74	75	76	77	78	79	80	81	82	83
MISSISSIPPI	3 173	36 520	18 445.2	1 012.1	12 791	138 372	20 774.5	1 935.3	2 125	8 354	794.2	132.1
Biloxi	44	551	175.3	14.0	259	3 162	403.2	44.9	61	281	26.9	3.9
Greenville	55	610	333.9	19.9	252	3 048	413.2	41.6	63	264	23.4	3.6
Gulfport	98	1 147	286.1	27.6	395	4 958	861.5	77.8	101	418	39.5	7.3
Hattiesburg	93	1 266	1 119.3	28.4	385	5 542	818.7	78.7	89	364	32.9	5.5
Jackson	404	6 820	2 828.5	218.4	968	15 841	2 595.6	265.7	263	1 455	147.7	23.6
Meridian	94	1 770	942.1	48.0	434	5 009	753.0	72.8	66	242	22.5	3.5
Pascagoula	30	271	173.1	8.6	186	2 632	499.8	41.5	34	156	11.7	2.9
Tupelo	156	1 721	670.7	46.5	431	5 785	895.2	84.7	58	268	23.1	4.5
MISSOURI	9 522	125 929	91 411.9	4 639.8	24 181	297 556	51 269.9	4 945.0	5 500	31 301	3 991.1	698.1
Blue Springs	61	372	195.0	12.7	171	2 833	534.3	51.2	43	211	26.1	3.4
Cape Girardeau	111	1 183	539.0	31.9	359	4 893	780.6	73.0	73	238	26.1	4.6
Chesterfield	243	2 023	3 024.1	98.0	218	3 564	380.5	47.5	120	555	73.7	13.4
Columbia	106	1 466	596.4	44.5	491	7 836	1 270.8	116.7	147	566	69.9	10.0
Florissant	48	415	95.1	11.7	227	4 432	688.2	68.7	33	125	24.5	3.2
Gladstone	22	101	31.0	2.8	104	1 828	317.2	31.3	38	300	20.2	7.1
Independence	106	981	410.8	30.2	507	8 120	1 278.4	128.0	114	425	48.9	7.9
Jefferson City	83	D	D	D	260	4 191	694.0	64.4	65	172	20.8	3.3
Joplin	142	1 495	651.9	38.6	438	6 287	970.6	89.8	85	394	32.4	6.2
Kansas City	898	18 053	12 630.3	702.2	1 843	27 774	5 773.0	511.0	516	4 660	816.0	126.5
Kirkwood	97	637	286.6	22.4	140	1 994	437.9	44.9	39	184	26.6	5.3
Lee's Summit	101	975	907.8	31.0	195	2 709	475.3	46.3	82	307	40.7	5.5
Maryland Heights	258	4 975	2 687.7	187.6	127	3 459	717.3	80.0	31	454	55.7	16.2
Raytown	53	487	342.5	22.6	137	2 804	498.7	49.2	28	121	12.0	1.8
St. Charles	109	1 055	354.2	31.2	300	3 815	650.0	61.3	76	624	254.7	15.8
St. Joseph	139	1 556	1 106.3	42.9	382	4 733	777.6	71.2	85	D	D	D
St. Louis	902	16 599	10 582.9	646.4	1 241	14 511	2 361.7	282.4	401	3 520	402.9	76.7
St. Peters	67	594	666.2	19.6	308	5 619	1 000.8	95.7	39	197	20.0	3.7
Springfield	488	8 326	4 908.2	249.7	1 106	16 060	2 937.4	266.7	283	1 570	136.4	29.6
University City	54	615	180.3	20.7	105	1 366	164.1	20.6	43	395	26.8	6.9
MONTANA	1 577	14 381	7 709.5	372.3	5 042	48 337	7 779.1	746.5	1 186	4 265	353.4	58.1
Billings	314	4 128	2 295.1	121.1	642	8 103	1 432.0	133.8	170	712	77.8	11.4
Butte-Silver Bow	55	534	192.0	10.7	220	2 147	333.1	32.0	39	134	11.3	2.0
Great Falls	111	1 030	1 039.8	27.8	389	4 895	782.9	79.8	90	357	26.8	4.2
Missoula	145	1 675	515.4	42.7	463	6 166	990.0	97.1	124	536	42.7	7.1
NEBRASKA	3 157	41 002	38 015.4	1 170.2	8 295	102 684	16 529.3	1 554.6	1 587	8 240	891.1	160.8
Bellevue	12	15	3.4	0.3	124	2 335	379.2	34.6	30	146	12.9	2.1
Grand Island	94	D	D	D	307	4 256	658.5	63.6	56	170	19.6	2.9
Lincoln	270	D	D	D	952	15 326	2 197.5	225.2	254	1 460	147.6	25.0
Omaha	932	15 973	10 907.3	533.0	1 786	33 724	5 479.3	572.3	511	4 278	524.0	103.2
NEVADA	2 253	27 251	12 806.9	918.5	6 222	89 452	18 220.8	1 798.2	2 460	16 890	2 276.5	381.5
Carson City	88	557	222.4	18.7	262	3 383	678.4	66.1	102	343	51.2	7.4
Henderson	85	729	301.2	21.7	321	5 824	1 252.6	113.6	111	1 335	161.1	31.9
Las Vegas	500	6 266	2 208.8	209.2	1 516	24 600	5 811.5	535.7	608	4 009	498.6	83.6
North Las Vegas	91	1 903	735.5	67.5	138	2 277	433.9	39.7	49	451	79.8	16.6
Reno	286	3 487	3 043.4	118.6	928	14 619	2 865.8	294.2	419	2 266	342.9	47.6
Sparks	290	5 391	2 376.7	188.2	256	3 559	640.2	71.2	86	495	63.0	11.8
NEW HAMPSHIRE	2 033	22 631	11 371.1	875.0	6 645	84 170	15 890.1	1 428.2	1 399	6 639	719.4	151.1
Concord	63	848	268.7	28.8	331	4 578	943.6	75.7	62	D	D	D
Dover	44	329	114.9	9.2	119	1 603	270.1	27.6	36	114	15.6	1.9
Manchester	226	3 185	1 368.2	115.0	561	7 594	1 547.6	140.5	143	821	86.2	19.2
Nashua	160	2 028	1 527.4	102.3	492	9 611	1 848.8	161.2	119	541	62.9	14.0
Portsmouth	101	1 270	1 263.7	58.4	273	3 784	881.0	67.0	70	235	33.5	5.9
Rochester	26	829	88.8	20.1	143	2 154	371.2	35.4	26	79	10.8	1.5
NEW JERSEY	17 812	266 944	227 366.7	11 886.1	34 837	420 724	79 914.9	7 926.0	8 292	47 558	8 881.9	1 376.5
Atlantic City	24	203	63.5	7.0	255	1 832	296.5	31.8	63	773	112.1	13.2
Bayonne	57	1 127	1 081.0	45.7	224	1 588	232.1	31.8	40	208	25.3	4.9
Camden	92	1 184	480.5	40.8	158	1 212	241.7	24.1	32	285	18.9	5.2
Clifton	215	2 474	2 579.4	104.8	286	4 075	767.8	79.0	94	346	46.7	10.1
East Orange	17	D	D	D	131	939	149.1	17.0	78	346	52.8	7.5
Elizabeth	158	3 181	2 119.1	120.3	396	3 947	723.8	65.1	129	505	58.1	9.2
Fair Lawn Borough	83	715	1 264.7	31.1	116	1 199	241.7	24.1	30	99	14.6	2.5
Fort Lee Borough	250	1 942	4 352.2	119.2	158	1 588	300.7	28.9	139	462	112.2	12.6
Garfield	61	D	D	D	81	817	137.5	17.4	15	36	10.0	1.1

1. Establishments with payroll.

Table D. Cities — **Professional Services, Manufacturing, Accommodation and Foodservices**

City	Professional, Scientific, and Technical Services, 1997[1]				Manufacturing, 1997				Accommodation and Foodservices, 1997			
	Number of Establish-ments	Number of Employees	Receipts (mil dol)	Annual Payroll (mil dol)	Number of Establish-ments	Number of Employees	Receipts (mil dol)	Annual Payroll (mil dol)	Number of Establish-ments	Number of Employees	Sales (mil dol)	Annual Payroll (mil dol)
	84	85	86	87	88	89	90	91	92	93	94	95
MISSISSIPPI	3 627	21 671	1 761.6	662.1	3 008	227 800	39 658.3	5 599.4	4 050	84 834	3 064.8	814.5
Biloxi	100	618	53.3	20.0	36	D	D	D	144	4 911	183.2	51.8
Greenville	66	299	31.7	8.8	49	4 313	904.0	105.3	80	1 400	44.7	11.7
Gulfport	182	909	75.7	28.5	67	1 885	259.3	50.4	156	3 017	87.4	23.0
Hattiesburg	156	827	63.3	20.9	62	4 625	942.4	103.4	161	3 502	101.1	26.5
Jackson	619	5 424	552.0	219.2	173	9 337	1 709.3	236.9	396	9 427	293.3	85.0
Meridian	106	452	32.5	9.8	70	D	D	D	138	2 777	85.8	23.5
Pascagoula	81	648	72.4	31.1	39	D	D	D	59	1 272	36.0	9.9
Tupelo	131	838	62.7	26.3	109	8 813	1 470.7	231.3	134	2 662	78.3	21.7
MISSOURI	10 601	93 792	9 953.3	3 643.6	7 497	371 448	93 115.5	11 647.0	11 150	203 849	6 780.8	1 933.3
Blue Springs	94	344	21.7	9.2	41	978	127.5	28.2	83	1 868	52.0	14.9
Cape Girardeau	91	639	41.3	14.6	52	3 602	1 246.9	111.3	103	2 468	77.0	21.5
Chesterfield	252	2 513	252.1	116.2	42	1 489	207.7	47.8	78	D	D	D
Columbia	232	1 242	88.8	29.9	62	4 277	1 376.1	120.7	278	5 731	173.6	46.6
Florissant	61	579	24.2	10.2	NA	NA	NA	NA	131	D	D	D
Gladstone	71	305	25.8	13.0	NA	NA	NA	NA	52	D	D	D
Independence	183	1 079	73.1	29.2	108	3 711	812.5	129.1	221	4 577	143.1	41.5
Jefferson City	157	881	73.1	29.5	39	3 603	1 046.8	114.9	118	2 619	80.6	23.6
Joplin	109	750	45.4	19.6	108	5 585	849.8	148.2	187	4 118	116.1	33.9
Kansas City	1 317	17 551	1 907.7	806.7	575	27 888	7 155.5	998.5	1 053	26 879	1 042.5	312.3
Kirkwood	111	482	48.9	20.4	41	1 272	136.5	41.1	55	1 113	30.2	9.6
Lee's Summit	156	691	65.3	27.1	77	2 577	456.7	72.1	89	1 798	53.6	15.6
Maryland Heights	119	2 918	301.1	105.3	132	4 858	980.3	171.6	75	3 097	126.7	38.8
Raytown	69	427	21.0	9.4	33	663	58.0	17.5	60	921	25.4	7.1
St. Charles	194	1 805	119.8	37.2	83	2 565	360.2	78.7	176	3 783	113.6	31.9
St. Joseph	130	D	D	D	91	D	D	D	189	3 133	94.2	26.1
St. Louis	963	13 915	1 819.8	663.7	802	33 836	8 605.5	1 243.6	954	18 843	686.6	195.8
St. Peters	64	607	37.2	16.5	69	3 822	1 489.7	126.4	111	2 492	65.0	19.2
Springfield	509	3 691	338.6	111.7	310	18 260	3 673.5	488.3	545	11 243	335.8	96.2
University City	98	452	49.3	20.2	NA	NA	NA	NA	67	D	D	D
MONTANA	2 082	10 735	769.4	297.7	1 160	19 611	4 866.3	560.1	3 278	38 533	1 198.9	325.4
Billings	367	2 502	186.2	69.9	141	D	D	D	303	6 137	186.2	53.7
Butte-Silver Bow	88	861	60.2	25.7	NA	NA	NA	NA	130	1 354	47.8	12.3
Great Falls	162	962	66.8	27.7	64	853	221.2	22.1	223	3 277	95.8	27.0
Missoula	250	1 553	103.7	43.7	94	1 103	151.0	28.1	259	4 322	129.7	36.4
NEBRASKA	3 076	25 720	2 273.4	838.0	1 960	106 690	27 859.2	3 040.5	4 070	61 048	1 726.6	488.2
Bellevue	61	1 166	128.7	48.7	10	1 070	146.1	20.9	78	1 196	35.1	10.1
Grand Island	90	401	31.3	11.7	59	5 107	1 714.9	139.1	139	2 702	67.7	20.2
Lincoln	464	D	D	D	234	D	D	D	518	10 856	309.7	89.2
Omaha	1 121	11 882	1 075.5	447.0	497	24 767	6 528.1	787.2	960	18 796	590.8	176.1
NEVADA	4 171	28 963	2 974.4	1 171.1	1 615	37 849	6 361.8	1 178.0	3 632	241 672	15 322.7	4 665.3
Carson City	233	806	86.2	30.2	186	4 157	514.5	120.8	133	2 404	93.1	27.7
Henderson	166	691	72.1	28.8	60	3 131	939.0	96.8	167	3 736	206.8	55.0
Las Vegas	1 344	13 489	1 308.4	563.5	274	3 884	493.8	114.1	872	43 124	2 283.7	836.1
North Las Vegas	35	580	73.6	19.4	74	2 071	363.6	63.0	53	2 276	127.6	37.4
Reno	860	4 999	486.1	197.6	192	6 086	1 076.3	191.6	565	26 468	1 406.6	462.7
Sparks	111	881	86.2	33.8	182	4 477	684.6	136.2	117	5 118	253.5	71.8
NEW HAMPSHIRE	3 341	18 268	1 626.6	713.1	2 328	98 934	19 813.1	3 361.4	3 029	43 942	1 543.5	449.8
Concord	216	1 340	132.0	60.7	56	3 016	372.7	89.6	119	2 266	73.5	21.6
Dover	71	415	20.8	9.5	58	3 300	525.2	111.4	61	D	D	D
Manchester	339	3 297	314.8	144.4	191	8 952	1 394.5	289.7	230	4 115	140.2	38.4
Nashua	333	1 454	168.5	70.9	179	11 164	1 990.4	521.2	182	3 677	131.1	39.3
Portsmouth	220	1 389	128.0	55.4	50	1 497	279.3	46.2	154	2 978	124.0	35.5
Rochester	35	354	29.4	12.6	38	2 694	1 218.0	74.8	61	761	24.6	6.7
NEW JERSEY	25 849	220 238	25 943.8	10 441.0	11 812	409 788	97 060.8	15 430.2	16 974	251 872	13 407.4	3 608.2
Atlantic City	82	758	74.4	37.7	NA	NA	NA	NA	205	48 506	4 717.1	1 246.0
Bayonne	66	278	13.7	4.8	52	1 747	556.1	60.6	114	D	D	D
Camden	42	308	30.7	13.0	81	2 757	557.8	117.6	84	583	25.2	5.8
Clifton	271	2 605	232.0	83.8	211	9 631	1 780.5	374.9	142	D	D	D
East Orange	66	1 368	187.4	60.2	NA	NA	NA	NA	59	955	37.2	9.4
Elizabeth	115	401	40.0	14.1	129	5 983	1 143.6	191.0	227	2 132	117.9	30.0
Fair Lawn Borough	210	1 075	175.6	56.9	62	3 146	589.3	116.4	59	566	22.5	6.1
Fort Lee Borough	260	1 658	230.9	70.9	NA	NA	NA	NA	96	1 062	53.6	15.0
Garfield	37	122	11.8	3.3	105	3 293	521.4	90.8	48	305	12.2	3.1

1. Firms subject to federal tax.

Table D. Cities — Entertainment, Health Care, and Other Services

City	Arts, Entertainment, and Recreation[1], 1997				Health Care and Social Assistance[1], 1997				Other Services[1], 1997			
	Number of Establish-ments	Number of Employees	Receipts (mil dol)	Annual Payroll (mil dol)	Number of Establish-ments	Number of Employees	Receipts (mil dol)	Annual Payroll (mil dol)	Number of Establish-ments	Number of Employees	Receipts (mil dol)	Annual Payroll (mil dol)
	96	97	98	99	100	101	102	103	104	105	106	107
MISSISSIPPI................	483	21 239	1 394.0	371.7	4 139	55 529	3 632.3	1 547.0	3 491	17 449	1 057.1	299.6
Biloxi........................	32	8 696	587.8	164.3	118	2 554	192.8	77.2	66	468	21.7	6.7
Greenville.................	12	0	0.0	0.0	106	1 108	74.5	29.0	91	438	24.5	7.1
Gulfport....................	23	0	0.0	0.0	190	2 279	181.5	68.3	137	918	48.9	16.7
Hattiesburg..............	13	118	5.4	2.2	125	2 489	177.6	100.1	75	653	40.3	11.9
Jackson....................	22	312	21.7	4.4	506	7 381	584.0	263.4	342	2 848	166.8	52.3
Meridian...................	12	53	2.1	0.6	142	1 932	160.2	80.5	115	609	30.8	9.2
Pascagoula...............	4	8	0.3	0.1	103	821	65.0	29.5	60	349	19.9	5.3
Tupelo......................	8	0	0.0	0.0	136	1 928	162.5	91.1	97	780	47.0	20.6
MISSOURI	1 493	29 484	1 803.9	684.2	10 213	131 485	7 885.4	3 596.7	9 427	52 060	3 203.3	963.1
Blue Springs.............	14	178	4.1	1.7	111	1 126	64.5	24.4	102	662	25.9	9.3
Cape Girardeau.........	12	75	6.4	0.9	162	1 850	146.5	67.9	82	442	26.9	8.4
Chesterfield..............	23	161	9.4	2.5	197	2 562	183.9	88.4	67	517	20.6	8.0
Columbia..................	25	473	14.4	4.3	287	3 639	308.7	123.8	183	1 155	59.4	19.0
Florissant.................	11	159	4.4	1.6	160	1 701	94.4	44.6	106	582	32.7	11.3
Gladstone.................	4	72	2.0	0.6	79	898	51.8	23.0	68	311	19.5	5.8
Independence............	20	238	11.9	2.7	214	3 759	233.7	110.8	215	1 180	59.9	20.3
Jefferson City...........	9	100	9.2	1.6	149	1 863	122.2	69.6	84	498	23.9	7.4
Joplin.......................	18	147	4.4	1.1	208	2 049	146.1	66.6	150	929	50.2	14.7
Kansas City..............	97	3 530	296.5	174.0	949	13 404	1 011.8	508.2	793	6 083	420.5	123.3
Kirkwood..................	10	79	2.4	0.9	109	776	70.4	31.8	46	294	20.1	6.8
Lee's Summit............	19	202	5.8	1.8	98	872	49.9	22.3	94	507	27.1	9.1
Maryland Heights.......	8	91	19.0	1.3	36	1 834	135.9	49.8	51	485	40.4	12.7
Raytown...................	6	107	3.6	1.3	59	582	21.6	9.3	69	525	36.8	10.2
St. Charles...............	22	2 085	157.1	46.5	155	2 052	180.6	91.7	141	711	40.9	12.5
St. Joseph................	17	0	0.0	0.0	173	0	0.0	0.0	151	755	44.4	12.7
St. Louis..................	68	3 603	378.4	209.4	581	9 806	612.5	263.9	673	4 693	334.1	101.2
St. Peters................	21	262	7.3	2.2	121	1 339	82.0	34.9	111	816	38.0	13.6
Springfield................	45	536	16.5	5.0	411	6 608	509.0	244.3	438	3 184	166.0	51.8
University City..........	5	0	0.0	0.0	64	676	23.1	10.5	66	680	37.2	14.1
MONTANA	639	5 638	306.5	62.2	2 034	15 673	928.6	412.6	1 612	6 986	449.1	117.0
Billings.....................	75	882	57.1	9.5	310	2 685	216.0	109.3	238	1 477	94.4	26.8
Butte-Silver Bow........	25	185	9.8	2.1	114	1 055	53.4	24.7	71	282	16.6	4.3
Great Falls...............	41	349	18.0	4.2	201	1 721	103.9	40.5	127	606	36.6	9.7
Missoula...................	48	505	34.2	7.7	251	2 112	143.4	67.2	155	805	49.9	14.5
NEBRASKA................	517	5 957	258.6	58.1	3 057	34 763	2 027.7	970.3	3 288	16 940	1 039.2	297.1
Bellevue...................	9	136	6.6	1.4	42	531	21.2	10.5	58	268	15.8	5.0
Grand Island.............	13	314	15.7	2.4	103	0	0.0	0.0	107	639	36.8	10.4
Lincoln.....................	51	1 035	36.3	9.7	531	6 264	373.5	182.5	395	2 466	130.8	41.3
Omaha......................	116	1 870	70.3	17.3	865	10 874	793.5	374.4	817	6 339	367.5	119.9
NEVADA....................	811	23 960	1 667.5	465.8	3 226	39 476	3 406.5	1 358.9	2 175	16 185	1 061.7	328.0
Carson City..............	39	1 001	51.0	13.7	172	1 274	86.7	39.8	104	634	42.2	13.5
Henderson................	48	2 654	150.3	43.6	186	1 694	125.9	49.9	108	975	55.9	18.7
Las Vegas................	193	4 384	374.3	84.0	1 021	17 184	1 624.8	605.1	594	5 323	328.7	105.8
North Las Vegas........	10	1 636	62.1	25.8	47	1 937	110.6	36.8	56	843	55.7	19.5
Reno........................	80	2 854	139.7	44.3	589	5 514	509.3	234.4	326	2 230	137.3	45.9
Sparks.....................	28	1 173	65.6	19.7	115	1 657	117.1	43.5	140	874	68.1	19.3
NEW HAMPSHIRE...........	460	6 545	365.0	99.6	2 373	28 889	1 734.1	836.3	2 159	11 379	794.5	236.6
Concord....................	17	0	0.0	0.0	136	2 141	156.5	84.4	103	589	50.4	12.9
Dover.......................	4	14	1.1	0.1	102	1 425	73.1	34.7	40	226	16.0	4.8
Manchester...............	24	342	13.6	4.0	231	2 887	195.4	99.0	222	1 642	116.4	39.2
Nashua.....................	19	252	19.0	6.9	197	2 922	197.4	93.0	153	1 197	90.9	28.8
Portsmouth...............	15	214	9.0	3.4	142	2 756	172.4	73.2	64	432	26.3	8.9
Rochester.................	8	92	3.7	1.1	62	643	34.9	18.6	47	231	16.3	4.4
NEW JERSEY................	2 393	27 187	1 981.2	602.2	18 905	172 723	13 702.4	5 900.2	15 077	78 644	5 434.8	1 665.1
Atlantic City.............	16	100	11.2	2.7	57	624	34.1	17.3	68	725	27.7	9.2
Bayonne...................	9	66	3.1	1.1	130	791	70.7	30.5	100	315	26.2	10.1
Camden....................	2	0	0.0	0.0	74	1 020	74.7	39.6	64	673	36.8	11.0
Clifton.....................	19	123	7.9	1.8	271	2 248	355.8	98.4	160	661	57.4	18.7
East Orange.............	2	0	0.0	0.0	113	1 707	85.6	36.1	61	388	57.1	12.8
Elizabeth..................	7	30	9.5	5.4	174	1 037	80.6	34.7	175	1 114	84.3	25.8
Fair Lawn Borough	11	68	3.4	0.8	171	1 203	124.0	54.6	77	840	55.6	23.3
Fort Lee Borough	14	70	16.2	4.1	162	1 724	96.8	44.6	94	469	26.3	8.2
Garfield....................	4	13	0.5	0.2	22	80	5.8	1.5	62	200	17.9	4.3

1. Firms subject to federal tax.

Table D. Cities — Federal Funds and City Government Finances

City	Selected federal funds, fiscal 1999[1] (mil dol)									City government finances, 1997						
	Procurement contracts		Grants					Direct payments for individuals		General revenue						
										Intergovernmental			Taxes			
														Per capita[3] (dollars)		
	Defense	Other	Total[2]	Health and family welfare	Energy and environment	Education	Housing and community development	Educational assistance	Housing assistance	Total (mil dol)	Total (mil dol)	Percent from state government	Total (mil dol)	Total	Property	Sales and gross receipts
	108	109	110	111	112	113	114	115	116	117	118	119	120	121	122	123
MISSISSIPPI	1 528.1	411.2	3 387.3	1 909.2	56.0	327.0	69.3	102.2	96.3	X	X	X	X	X	X	X
Biloxi	1.5	1.5	10.4	3.9	0.0	0.0	5.0	0.0	3.5	55.7	22.4	96.5	23.7	490	278	200
Greenville	2.7	1.2	7.6	5.3	0.0	0.0	0.1	0.1	3.5	26.7	10.5	87.5	6.6	155	133	18
Gulfport	49.6	5.8	12.4	6.1	0.0	0.1	1.7	0.2	3.9	181.6	16.0	84.2	21.3	329	233	83
Hattiesburg	4.0	4.0	19.7	4.9	0.1	1.4	1.7	8.6	6.0	37.4	14.9	80.3	12.7	266	195	66
Jackson	18.5	19.8	621.0	198.1	39.8	90.5	51.0	9.4	17.6	154.7	57.2	71.0	52.1	270	239	24
Meridian	9.4	1.2	6.3	1.8	0.0	0.1	2.0	1.4	1.3	31.4	11.6	94.2	11.9	291	249	36
Pascagoula	804.8	2.7	3.2	0.0	0.0	0.2	0.5	0.0	0.6	18.8	5.9	84.7	5.9	220	180	36
Tupelo	0.1	2.5	4.2	3.5	0.0	0.0	0.0	0.1	3.5	38.7	19.6	81.3	8.5	243	221	7
MISSOURI	4 318.6	1 386.7	5 478.5	3 353.5	44.9	458.2	150.2	150.3	86.6	X	X	X	X	X	X	X
Blue Springs	0.0	0.1	0.2	0.0	0.0	0.0	0.0	0.0	0.3	22.5	3.2	60.8	12.8	286	66	212
Cape Girardeau	0.9	2.3	2.9	1.0	0.0	0.8	0.0	2.8	0.0	32.0	5.0	85.6	17.6	497	43	429
Chesterfield	28.5	2.0	0.3	0.3	0.0	0.0	0.0	0.7	0.0	18.0	8.2	85.6	6.3	138	34	90
Columbia	4.8	10.2	86.6	30.1	1.6	7.6	1.6	10.5	1.4	61.0	6.4	58.2	26.3	342	58	277
Florissant	0.0	0.3	0.6	0.1	0.1	0.0	0.3	0.1	0.0	16.3	9.2	24.2	5.0	98	6	77
Gladstone	0.0	0.1	0.0	0.0	0.0	0.0	0.0	0.1	0.0	14.7	1.5	69.2	9.0	325	48	259
Independence	1.7	7.2	4.3	0.0	0.0	1.3	2.1	0.1	0.0	57.6	7.5	62.0	28.2	255	44	194
Jefferson City	5.3	3.9	780.1	268.2	28.5	124.8	38.9	1.6	1.5	30.4	5.3	71.6	18.0	497	88	400
Joplin	8.2	121.1	5.8	3.4	0.0	0.2	1.1	2.7	0.8	31.3	3.6	52.4	18.5	424	13	399
Kansas City	49.3	566.8	109.9	42.0	6.7	8.5	0.0	14.1	32.1	723.7	82.4	20.1	412.8	936	158	437
Kirkwood	0.0	0.1	0.2	0.0	0.0	0.0	0.0	0.0	-0.3	14.4	5.5	20.4	5.4	197	61	108
Lee's Summit	0.2	0.1	0.8	0.0	0.0	0.0	0.5	0.0	1.5	50.3	6.1	75.0	22.5	363	181	172
Maryland Heights	7.7	-1.6	0.6	0.0	0.0	0.0	0.0	0.0	0.0	14.3	9.5	16.8	3.9	163	0	137
Raytown	0.0	0.0	0.0	0.0	0.0	0.0	0.0	0.0	0.2	12.2	1.0	82.8	6.8	230	39	181
St. Charles	1.3	0.9	6.3	4.9	0.1	0.0	1.4	1.2	0.0	51.9	8.2	32.7	34.4	609	110	483
St. Joseph	0.3	0.5	7.1	2.3	2.3	0.0	3.0	2.1	2.6	50.9	10.5	53.8	27.3	388	99	271
St. Louis	3 837.5	172.4	525.8	319.7	4.0	11.7	61.9	27.6	24.7	655.7	83.5	45.7	373.4	1 062	161	480
St. Peters	1.9	0.6	0.4	0.0	0.0	0.0	0.0	0.7	0.0	30.0	2.5	16.7	19.2	395	98	289
Springfield	1.1	15.6	17.8	8.4	0.2	2.2	2.6	9.7	5.5	137.3	21.3	67.9	58.1	405	63	321
University City	0.0	0.0	12.7	0.2	0.0	0.0	0.0	0.0	1.1	21.0	8.4	48.3	7.6	199	79	108
MONTANA	99.2	420.8	1 399.4	507.6	145.1	145.9	21.2	26.3	36.9	X	X	X	X	X	X	X
Billings	0.4	12.6	17.5	8.6	0.1	2.2	1.0	2.7	4.8	64.3	9.1	79.4	17.2	189	166	0
Butte-Silver Bow	1.0	28.8	5.0	1.6	1.3	0.4	0.2	1.0	1.6	33.5	7.4	90.5	12.0	347	263	11
Great Falls	3.9	7.1	8.6	2.9	0.0	1.3	1.7	1.5	7.3	31.5	5.4	73.3	9.1	158	135	0
Missoula	1.5	10.7	26.3	7.4	0.3	5.9	1.1	4.7	2.9	27.5	4.9	92.5	13.0	253	221	4
NEBRASKA	226.8	243.6	1 651.2	921.5	33.2	171.0	32.2	38.0	31.0	X	X	X	X	X	X	X
Bellevue	38.9	6.3	19.4	0.0	0.1	19.3	0.0	0.8	2.1	24.0	3.8	78.3	14.0	328	198	122
Grand Island	-0.7	4.9	4.0	0.7	0.0	0.2	0.4	1.4	2.4	40.4	5.2	80.7	15.1	367	150	205
Lincoln	15.0	21.4	353.6	96.9	30.8	50.1	18.3	8.9	3.7	229.0	35.0	69.1	77.4	370	149	165
Omaha	22.0	43.6	75.1	36.2	0.6	5.5	9.0	9.8	9.5	270.9	41.9	71.2	175.8	483	200	262
NEVADA	273.7	527.9	1 249.0	511.6	117.1	102.3	28.2	14.8	8.2	X	X	X	X	X	X	X
Carson City	9.9	3.5	286.4	62.6	78.7	37.4	0.1	0.6	0.0	118.8	20.6	78.2	15.4	327	172	97
Henderson	0.5	0.1	7.7	0.0	0.0	0.0	0.7	0.0	0.0	137.0	46.0	87.4	33.7	275	145	57
Las Vegas	37.9	408.9	91.7	20.4	9.5	3.4	11.4	10.9	1.1	433.8	162.1	76.2	102.2	271	125	63
North Las Vegas	0.3	2.3	5.2	1.6	0.0	0.0	0.0	0.0	4.0	88.9	33.3	66.5	20.6	262	148	47
Reno	3.1	16.3	100.3	22.0	7.4	3.1	3.5	3.0	1.7	158.2	48.6	73.2	61.9	398	212	60
Sparks	16.5	0.6	2.1	0.0	0.0	0.3	0.7	0.0	0.0	55.7	18.9	87.8	21.5	361	198	44
NEW HAMPSHIRE	359.7	122.0	1 120.0	614.0	27.5	85.6	25.1	31.3	23.7	X	X	X	X	X	X	X
Concord	0.6	1.6	205.5	58.6	23.7	31.4	13.5	1.1	5.2	36.3	3.1	54.0	21.6	583	557	0
Dover	0.6	0.0	1.3	0.0	0.0	0.0	0.6	0.7	0.6	48.3	8.0	66.5	34.0	1 321	1 283	0
Manchester	10.0	3.8	19.7	3.4	0.0	0.4	7.6	3.3	2.0	181.6	24.2	84.4	119.6	1 184	1 144	0
Nashua	213.7	21.1	5.2	0.7	0.2	0.0	1.0	1.2	2.0	150.3	13.9	94.4	117.7	1 451	1 440	0
Portsmouth	42.1	5.9	5.8	1.1	0.0	0.0	0.8	0.0	1.1	53.4	9.1	79.7	34.1	1 362	1 341	0
Rochester	0.8	0.1	1.9	1.0	0.0	0.0	0.7	0.0	0.5	48.7	7.4	96.2	37.2	1 343	1 309	0
NEW JERSEY	2 838.0	1 368.1	7 261.6	4 273.5	155.1	616.3	220.2	135.7	197.1	X	X	X	X	X	X	X
Atlantic City	0.2	95.6	22.7	5.0	0.0	0.0	4.9	0.2	8.8	133.6	16.9	100.0	106.1	2 767	2 680	0
Bayonne	0.3	0.2	8.0	0.9	0.0	0.1	4.7	0.0	2.7	132.2	39.9	88.5	76.5	1 265	1 251	0
Camden	77.9	7.5	54.0	14.9	-0.4	0.6	13.1	0.1	13.7	113.1	69.6	85.2	25.4	300	293	0
Clifton	64.1	1.2	2.5	0.0	0.0	0.2	1.9	0.2	2.0	54.7	17.7	99.3	33.3	467	455	0
East Orange	8.4	7.4	5.9	4.0	0.0	0.0	1.9	0.2	14.0	207.9	134.9	98.5	56.3	798	794	0
Elizabeth	1.2	5.9	17.0	0.3	0.0	0.0	15.6	0.2	-3.7	129.6	56.7	82.4	49.3	447	409	0
Fair Lawn Borough	0.7	0.5	0.4	0.0	0.4	0.0	0.0	0.0	0.0	23.8	6.6	100.0	16.2	523	507	0
Fort Lee Borough	0.9	0.0	1.0	0.5	0.0	0.0	0.0	0.0	4.9	27.0	2.9	97.5	19.4	585	567	0
Garfield	0.0	0.0	0.5	0.0	0.0	0.0	0.0	0.0	0.0	67.5	32.0	82.4	25.7	949	873	50

1. October 1, 1998 to September 30, 1999. 2. Includes program categories not shown separately. State totals include additional categories not allocated by city. 3. Based on population estimated as of July 1 of the year shown.

Table D. Cities — **City Government Finances**

City	City government finances, 1997 (cont'd) — General expenditure												
	Per capita[1] (dollars)			Percent of total for —								
	Total (mil dol)	Total	Capital outlays	Public welfare	Highways	Parking facilities	Education	Health and hospitals	Police protection	Sewerage and sanitation	Parks and recreation	Housing and community development	Interest on debt
	124	125	126	127	128	129	130	131	132	133	134	135	136
MISSISSIPPI	X	X	X	X	X	X	X	X	X	X	X	X	X
Biloxi	43.2	893	50	7.1	18.9	0.0	0.0	0.0	19.7	16.6	6.1	1.3	2.8
Greenville	25.9	604	134	0.6	9.7	0.0	0.0	0.0	21.5	25.3	3.6	0.0	2.8
Gulfport	184.8	2 850	372	0.1	1.9	0.1	0.0	71.0	5.3	3.7	1.1	0.4	2.2
Hattiesburg	38.4	804	224	0.0	10.7	0.5	0.0	1.1	14.9	19.0	4.8	3.1	10.4
Jackson	148.7	771	136	2.5	12.9	0.0	0.0	0.6	15.1	12.7	3.4	2.7	6.9
Meridian	25.3	619	22	0.0	10.8	0.0	0.0	0.0	18.4	15.9	6.9	3.9	7.2
Pascagoula	19.3	714	85	0.4	19.0	0.0	0.0	0.0	18.2	22.1	3.8	2.2	2.3
Tupelo	33.3	946	204	0.0	29.9	0.0	0.0	0.0	16.8	9.0	13.8	3.1	5.5
MISSOURI	X	X	X	X	X	X	X	X	X	X	X	X	X
Blue Springs	21.3	478	154	0.0	17.7	0.0	0.0	3.0	19.6	11.0	13.5	1.3	3.2
Cape Girardeau	29.6	834	264	0.0	11.8	0.0	0.0	0.5	13.0	27.4	7.9	1.1	3.2
Chesterfield	23.2	510	203	0.0	33.8	0.0	0.0	0.0	18.5	3.2	12.9	10.8	10.2
Columbia	62.9	820	129	1.1	11.2	2.4	0.0	4.2	13.2	19.4	9.8	0.6	6.6
Florissant	15.4	306	21	0.0	22.6	0.0	0.0	1.9	35.6	0.0	20.4	2.7	1.6
Gladstone	14.7	528	131	0.0	22.9	0.0	0.0	0.0	20.9	8.9	11.1	2.6	1.3
Independence	62.6	568	36	0.0	7.2	0.0	0.0	1.5	27.4	14.4	2.7	2.3	7.0
Jefferson City	28.2	781	191	0.0	25.2	2.4	0.0	1.1	17.3	14.4	11.3	0.0	1.0
Joplin	40.2	919	338	0.7	11.5	0.1	0.0	1.7	10.6	32.2	4.0	1.7	2.9
Kansas City	783.9	1 776	414	0.0	5.6	0.1	0.0	7.0	13.4	8.1	7.8	7.2	7.4
Kirkwood	18.2	662	140	0.0	11.8	0.0	0.0	0.0	19.4	7.3	7.6	0.0	0.8
Lee's Summit	38.2	617	56	0.0	12.9	0.0	0.0	0.0	18.3	14.9	4.9	2.3	9.8
Maryland Heights	13.4	556	82	0.0	38.2	0.0	0.0	0.0	32.1	0.0	12.9	0.0	0.0
Raytown	12.2	414	28	0.0	16.7	0.0	0.0	6.5	26.0	17.7	0.0	0.0	0.1
St. Charles	48.8	863	317	0.0	15.3	0.1	0.0	0.3	18.6	5.6	5.8	10.9	3.3
St. Joseph	57.1	813	295	0.5	12.0	1.2	0.0	2.3	10.9	21.9	5.4	5.4	1.6
St. Louis	630.8	1 794	356	0.0	2.3	0.9	0.0	4.8	17.6	3.0	2.8	6.5	6.2
St. Peters	31.0	640	179	0.0	32.2	0.0	0.0	1.0	12.4	12.4	18.2	0.0	5.0
Springfield	126.4	881	206	2.5	13.7	0.0	0.0	4.1	11.6	16.5	13.2	2.1	5.8
University City	21.7	568	29	0.0	12.1	0.0	0.0	0.0	22.4	10.8	9.1	0.0	7.5
MONTANA	X	X	X	X	X	X	X	X	X	X	X	X	X
Billings	56.7	622	68	0.0	7.4	0.9	0.0	0.0	12.9	15.1	4.1	2.8	7.1
Butte-Silver Bow	42.9	1 238	461	2.3	6.9	0.3	0.0	4.4	9.4	6.7	4.2	29.5	1.0
Great Falls	31.5	546	21	0.0	8.3	1.0	0.0	0.7	12.8	11.5	11.5	10.7	3.3
Missoula	30.5	595	133	0.0	7.2	2.1	0.0	4.4	15.1	10.3	5.6	0.8	10.8
NEBRASKA	X	X	X	X	X	X	X	X	X	X	X	X	X
Bellevue	21.0	491	72	1.0	15.7	0.0	0.0	1.0	19.1	22.7	5.0	2.6	0.9
Grand Island	31.9	774	58	0.0	15.3	0.3	0.0	0.5	12.9	16.2	6.6	2.2	3.5
Lincoln	212.4	1 015	232	0.0	9.9	0.6	0.0	33.8	7.8	9.4	5.5	2.8	2.8
Omaha	268.2	736	106	0.0	17.3	1.4	0.0	0.0	16.8	14.1	8.6	3.2	3.0
NEVADA	X	X	X	X	X	X	X	X	X	X	X	X	X
Carson City	103.9	2 199	117	1.0	4.8	0.0	0.0	53.1	7.8	2.8	4.7	0.0	2.1
Henderson	142.4	1 164	405	0.0	5.5	0.0	0.0	0.0	11.5	15.1	8.8	1.5	13.2
Las Vegas	384.7	1 021	223	0.2	12.5	0.7	0.0	0.6	14.9	11.5	5.9	3.0	2.6
North Las Vegas	85.3	1 084	216	0.0	9.8	0.0	0.0	0.5	21.1	9.1	4.6	3.4	2.2
Reno	153.7	989	208	0.0	11.6	1.5	0.0	0.7	23.8	9.0	6.7	4.9	7.4
Sparks	68.0	1 144	368	0.5	9.7	0.1	0.0	0.0	14.1	15.2	8.9	10.6	4.0
NEW HAMPSHIRE	X	X	X	X	X	X	X	X	X	X	X	X	X
Concord	35.7	963	179	3.2	11.0	1.8	0.0	1.0	12.6	10.4	6.2	0.0	2.4
Dover	48.2	1 870	125	1.1	3.2	0.8	43.8	0.3	6.3	8.7	2.4	1.6	2.2
Manchester	179.6	1 779	146	0.6	7.8	0.9	44.3	1.4	6.9	4.8	2.7	1.1	3.0
Nashua	150.8	1 860	184	0.3	4.4	1.2	57.0	1.1	6.4	5.6	1.0	0.6	1.6
Portsmouth	49.4	1 975	32	1.0	4.6	0.6	44.2	5.6	9.6	10.3	1.2	0.0	1.5
Rochester	38.4	1 387	82	1.0	3.4	0.0	62.5	0.7	6.5	3.9	1.3	0.0	2.1
NEW JERSEY	X	X	X	X	X	X	X	X	X	X	X	X	X
Atlantic City	148.7	3 877	527	1.4	7.4	0.2	0.0	4.2	25.0	3.5	6.1	1.1	3.2
Bayonne	140.2	2 317	90	4.1	2.8	0.5	47.3	1.0	7.6	8.4	2.6	3.7	3.0
Camden	99.7	1 175	23	2.4	2.9	0.0	0.0	0.3	22.3	9.3	3.7	10.5	2.1
Clifton	52.0	729	58	1.2	7.4	0.0	0.0	1.8	18.9	17.6	2.7	0.2	4.1
East Orange	196.5	2 786	85	2.6	0.9	0.0	58.9	1.7	7.1	4.6	1.2	1.7	1.8
Elizabeth	129.7	1 178	63	0.3	4.9	0.0	0.0	1.4	19.5	15.2	3.3	11.6	6.0
Fair Lawn Borough	23.7	768	132	0.6	9.0	0.0	0.0	1.5	19.5	18.9	5.8	0.0	3.2
Fort Lee Borough	28.8	870	97	0.3	16.0	0.1	0.0	3.0	18.2	18.2	1.7	0.0	0.0
Garfield	68.1	2 518	154	1.1	1.1	7.3	52.7	0.3	9.2	5.5	0.9	9.2	0.0

1. Based on population estimated as of July 1 of the year shown.

City	City government finances, 1997 (cont'd) Debt outstanding Total (mil dol)	Per capita[1] (dollars)	Percent utility	City government employment, 1999	Climate[2] Average daily temperature (degrees Fahrenheit) Mean January	July	Limits January[3]	July[4]	Annual precipitation (inches)	Heating degree days	Cooling degree days
	137	138	139	140	141	142	143	144	145	146	147
MISSISSIPPI	X	X	X	X	X	X	X	X	X	X	X
Biloxi	16.1	333	4.2	490	51.0	82.3	42.3	90.0	61.76	1 507	2 666
Greenville	23.0	536	45.6	496	41.2	81.9	31.0	92.5	53.38	2 778	2 153
Gulfport	82.0	1 265	9.3	2 657	50.7	82.3	41.2	91.3	62.72	1 551	2 645
Hattiesburg	64.3	1 345	25.9	723	46.0	81.3	34.3	91.8	60.58	2 180	2 265
Jackson	180.9	937	42.6	2 159	44.1	81.5	32.7	92.4	55.37	2 467	2 215
Meridian	50.1	1 226	46.9	546	45.0	81.0	33.4	92.1	56.71	2 444	2 138
Pascagoula	16.9	624	3.4	314	48.9	82.1	39.3	90.3	63.72	1 761	2 617
Tupelo	47.6	1 353	23.3	501	39.9	80.6	30.9	90.7	55.87	3 079	1 908
MISSOURI	X	X	X	X	X	X	X	X	X	X	X
Blue Springs	11.8	265	22.7	264	25.7	78.5	16.7	88.7	37.62	5 393	1 288
Cape Girardeau	65.4	1 843	18.6	464	31.7	79.6	22.6	90.2	46.31	4 386	1 543
Chesterfield	33.9	746	0.0	165	29.3	79.8	20.8	89.3	37.51	4 758	1 534
Columbia	134.7	1 755	37.2	935	27.6	77.4	18.5	88.6	39.05	5 212	1 189
Florissant	4.3	85	0.0	288	29.3	79.8	20.8	89.3	37.51	4 758	1 534
Gladstone	10.7	386	60.4	154	25.7	78.5	16.7	88.7	37.62	5 393	1 288
Independence	148.2	1 343	51.2	1 204	25.7	78.5	16.7	88.7	37.62	5 393	1 288
Jefferson City	10.2	281	0.0	NA	27.4	77.4	15.3	90.1	38.43	5 302	1 175
Joplin	20.0	458	0.0	389	32.3	80.0	22.7	90.2	43.23	4 303	1 560
Kansas City	1 078.6	2 444	11.7	6 555	25.7	78.5	16.7	88.7	37.62	5 393	1 288
Kirkwood	12.3	448	15.9	263	29.3	79.8	20.8	89.3	37.51	4 758	1 534
Lee's Summit	91.2	1 474	34.1	527	28.0	78.3	17.5	90.2	39.84	4 993	1 316
Maryland Heights	0.0	0	0.0	NA	29.3	79.8	20.8	89.3	37.51	4 758	1 534
Raytown	0.8	27	0.0	392	25.7	78.5	16.7	88.7	37.62	5 393	1 288
St. Charles	25.4	449	0.0	442	27.5	77.6	17.2	89.2	37.74	5 179	1 226
St. Joseph	23.1	330	0.0	634	24.6	78.1	14.7	88.9	35.69	5 590	1 254
St. Louis	775.3	2 205	6.3	8 139	28.4	78.4	18.9	89.6	37.86	5 001	1 329
St. Peters	36.5	752	32.5	440	27.5	77.6	17.2	89.2	37.74	5 179	1 226
Springfield	273.6	1 908	59.0	2 854	31.1	78.1	20.4	89.6	43.04	4 638	1 320
University City	25.2	661	0.0	319	29.3	79.8	20.8	89.3	37.51	4 758	1 534
MONTANA	X	X	X	X	X	X	X	X	X	X	X
Billings	73.5	806	19.0	730	22.8	72.5	13.7	86.7	15.08	7 164	652
Butte-Silver Bow	62.0	1 789	41.5	NA	NA	NA	NA	NA	NA	NA	NA
Great Falls	40.4	699	58.9	479	21.2	68.2	11.6	83.3	15.21	7 741	388
Missoula	49.0	956	0.0	328	22.7	66.8	15.4	83.4	13.46	7 792	280
NEBRASKA	X	X	X	X	X	X	X	X	X	X	X
Bellevue	7.3	170	0.0	185	21.1	76.9	10.9	87.9	29.86	6 300	1 072
Grand Island	59.0	1 433	57.8	510	21.9	76.7	11.1	88.5	24.90	6 421	997
Lincoln	429.5	2 053	77.5	2 477	21.3	78.2	10.1	90.0	28.26	6 278	1 134
Omaha	202.5	556	0.0	2 861	21.1	76.9	10.9	87.9	29.86	6 300	1 072
NEVADA	X	X	X	X	X	X	X	X	X	X	X
Carson City	65.9	1 394	23.8	1 452	33.6	69.9	20.7	89.5	10.87	5 691	401
Henderson	328.4	2 684	17.0	1 361	45.5	91.1	33.6	105.9	4.13	2 407	3 201
Las Vegas	170.7	453	0.0	2 457	45.5	91.1	33.6	105.9	4.13	2 407	3 201
North Las Vegas	62.9	800	54.3	1 028	45.5	91.1	33.6	105.9	4.13	2 407	3 201
Reno	160.7	1 033	0.0	1 312	32.9	71.6	20.7	91.9	7.53	5 674	508
Sparks	62.3	1 046	0.0	637	32.9	71.6	20.7	91.9	7.53	5 674	508
NEW HAMPSHIRE	X	X	X	X	X	X	X	X	X	X	X
Concord	43.1	1 165	47.1	424	18.6	69.5	7.4	82.4	36.37	7 554	328
Dover	35.2	1 365	55.5	845	22.2	69.8	11.0	82.9	42.18	7 002	347
Manchester	186.4	1 846	20.8	2 817	18.6	69.5	7.4	82.4	36.37	7 554	328
Nashua	55.5	685	0.0	2 589	21.4	70.2	10.0	82.4	43.00	7 110	382
Portsmouth	32.7	1 306	61.0	735	22.2	69.8	11.0	82.9	42.18	7 002	347
Rochester	20.5	742	57.3	730	21.5	70.2	10.4	83.2	46.85	7 052	397
NEW JERSEY	X	X	X	X	X	X	X	X	X	X	X
Atlantic City	69.0	1 798	0.0	1 719	30.9	74.7	21.4	84.5	40.29	5 169	826
Bayonne	83.8	1 385	0.0	2 061	29.5	74.9	23.3	82.2	43.50	5 362	874
Camden	31.3	368	4.8	1 345	31.8	76.6	23.7	86.6	45.56	4 725	1 085
Clifton	21.7	304	0.0	NA	28.3	74.9	19.4	85.9	49.79	5 486	838
East Orange	62.9	891	0.0	2 786	30.6	77.8	23.4	87.0	43.97	4 888	1 201
Elizabeth	160.9	1 460	15.0	1 435	30.6	77.8	23.4	87.0	43.97	4 888	1 201
Fair Lawn Borough	18.4	595	9.8	400	28.3	74.9	19.4	85.9	49.79	5 486	838
Fort Lee Borough	0.0	0	0.0	NA	29.5	74.9	23.3	82.2	43.50	5 362	874
Garfield	0.0	0	0.0	NA	28.3	74.9	19.4	85.9	49.79	5 486	838

1. Based on the population estimated as of July 1 of the year shown.   2. Represents normal values based on the 30-year period, 1961–1990.   3. Average daily minimum.   4. Average daily maximum.

Table D. Cities — Land Area and Population

STATE Place code	City	Land area, 1990[1] (sq km)	Population, 1999 Total persons	Rank	Per square kilometer	Total persons 1990	Percent change 1990–1999	Total persons 1980	Percent change 1980–1990	White	Black	Am. Indian, Eskimo, Aleut	Asian and Pacific Islander	Other race	Hispanic[2]	Foreign born
		1	2	3	4	5	6	7	8	9	10	11	12	13	14	15
	NEW JERSEY—Cont'd															
34 28680	Hackensack	10.7	37 656	806	3 519	37 049	1.6	36 039	2.8	66.4	24.8	0.2	3.7	5.0	15.1	23.5
34 32250	Hoboken	3.3	33 413	907	10 125	33 397	0.0	42 460	-21.3	79.0	5.5	0.2	4.4	10.9	30.1	16.8
34 36000	Jersey City	38.5	230 458	72	5 986	228 517	0.8	223 532	2.2	48.2	29.7	0.3	11.4	10.4	24.2	24.6
34 36510	Kearny	23.7	34 997	861	1 477	34 874	0.4	35 735	-2.4	90.5	1.2	0.2	4.7	3.4	17.1	27.0
34 40350	Linden	28.0	37 040	819	1 323	36 701	0.9	37 836	-3.0	76.8	20.0	0.1	1.5	1.6	7.4	16.0
34 41310	Long Branch	13.5	29 303	1 026	2 171	28 658	2.3	29 819	-3.9	73.5	19.5	0.2	1.5	5.3	13.6	10.6
34 46680	Millville	109.7	26 582	1 132	242	25 992	2.3	24 815	4.7	86.6	8.4	0.4	0.6	3.9	7.6	3.3
34 51000	Newark	61.7	263 087	61	4 264	275 221	-4.4	329 248	-16.4	28.6	58.5	0.2	1.2	11.5	26.1	18.7
34 51210	New Brunswick	13.5	41 578	716	3 080	41 711	-0.3	41 442	0.6	57.4	29.6	0.3	4.0	8.8	19.3	16.8
34 55950	Paramus Borough	27.1	25 877	1 164	955	25 004	3.5	26 474	-5.6	88.2	0.8	0.0	10.5	0.5	3.6	18.4
34 56550	Passaic	8.0	61 173	444	7 647	58 041	5.4	52 463	10.6	45.3	20.6	0.5	7.1	26.5	50.0	36.2
34 57000	Paterson	21.9	148 645	133	6 787	140 891	5.5	137 970	2.1	41.2	36.0	0.3	1.4	21.1	41.0	25.1
34 58200	Perth Amboy	12.4	42 274	703	3 409	41 967	0.7	38 951	7.7	59.8	11.8	0.4	1.6	26.4	55.5	25.0
34 59190	Plainfield	15.6	46 235	635	2 964	46 577	-0.7	45 555	2.2	26.5	65.7	0.5	1.1	6.3	15.0	15.1
34 61530	Rahway	10.3	25 208	1 186	2 447	25 325	-0.5	26 723	-5.2	75.4	20.2	0.2	2.4	1.9	7.5	10.6
34 65790	Sayreville Borough	41.8	38 626	779	924	34 998	10.4	29 969	16.8	93.1	3.2	0.1	3.0	0.5	4.0	8.0
34 74000	Trenton	19.8	84 398	286	4 263	88 675	-4.8	92 124	-3.7	42.2	49.3	0.3	0.7	7.7	14.1	7.6
34 74630	Union City	3.3	56 946	496	17 256	58 012	-1.8	55 593	4.4	74.7	5.1	0.2	2.1	17.9	75.6	55.1
34 76070	Vineland	177.9	55 360	514	311	54 780	1.1	53 753	1.9	73.0	11.5	0.3	0.9	14.3	23.6	5.9
34 79040	Westfield	17.4	29 265	1 028	1 682	28 870	1.4	30 447	-5.2	91.5	4.6	0.1	3.5	0.3	2.0	9.2
34 79610	West New York	2.6	39 407	765	15 157	38 125	3.4	39 194	-2.7	76.7	4.0	0.4	1.9	17.0	73.3	60.4
35 00000	**NEW MEXICO**	314 334.1	1 739 844	X	6	1 515 069	14.8	1 303 302	16.2	75.6	2.0	8.9	0.9	12.6	38.2	5.3
35 01780	Alamogordo	44.3	28 411	1 056	641	27 596	3.0	24 024	14.9	82.7	6.0	0.8	1.9	8.5	25.0	6.1
35 02000	Albuquerque	342.4	420 578	36	1 228	384 915	9.3	331 767	16.0	78.2	3.0	3.0	1.7	14.0	34.5	5.5
35 16420	Clovis	35.8	31 504	964	880	30 954	1.8	31 194	-0.8	72.8	7.0	0.7	1.7	17.7	26.8	3.5
35 25800	Farmington	60.9	40 599	739	667	33 997	19.4	31 222	8.9	77.1	0.8	13.8	0.4	7.9	16.0	1.6
35 32520	Hobbs	48.9	26 898	1 120	550	29 121	-7.6	29 153	-0.1	78.7	7.4	0.6	0.5	12.8	30.1	6.1
35 39380	Las Cruces	97.1	75 786	332	780	62 360	21.5	45 060	38.4	88.2	1.9	0.9	1.1	7.9	46.9	9.5
35 63460	Rio Rancho	118.3	52 012	554	440	32 512	60.0	NA	NA	84.1	2.6	2.1	1.2	9.9	21.8	4.6
35 64930	Roswell	75.5	47 644	620	631	44 260	7.6	39 676	11.6	81.7	2.6	0.7	0.6	14.5	36.5	6.4
35 70500	Santa Fe	94.8	69 299	373	731	56 537	22.6	48 953	15.5	81.2	0.6	2.2	0.6	15.3	47.4	4.5
36 00000	**NEW YORK**	122 309.7	18 196 601	X	149	17 990 778	1.1	17 558 165	2.5	74.4	15.9	0.3	3.9	5.5	12.3	15.9
36 01000	Albany	55.4	93 994	248	1 697	100 031	-6.0	101 727	-1.7	75.5	20.6	0.3	2.3	1.3	3.1	7.7
36 03078	Auburn	21.7	29 058	1 035	1 339	31 258	-7.0	32 501	-3.8	91.9	6.8	0.3	0.5	0.4	2.2	3.9
36 06607	Binghamton	26.9	46 674	629	1 735	53 008	-11.9	55 860	-5.1	91.9	4.9	0.3	2.1	0.8	1.8	5.9
36 11000	Buffalo	105.2	295 619	57	2 810	328 175	-9.9	357 870	-8.3	64.7	30.7	0.8	1.0	2.8	4.9	4.5
36 24229	Elmira	19.0	31 270	971	1 646	33 724	-7.3	35 327	-4.5	85.4	12.3	0.3	0.6	1.3	2.7	2.0
36 27485	Freeport	11.9	39 892	755	3 352	39 894	0.0	38 272	4.2	56.5	32.3	0.4	1.3	9.6	21.2	21.5
36 33139	Hempstead	9.5	46 778	627	4 924	45 982	1.7	40 404	13.8	32.4	58.8	0.5	1.7	6.7	19.1	23.4
36 38077	Ithaca	14.1	29 401	1 024	2 085	29 541	-0.5	28 732	2.8	81.8	6.5	0.3	10.0	1.4	3.6	11.5
36 38264	Jamestown	22.9	32 229	943	1 407	34 681	-7.1	35 775	-3.1	94.9	2.6	0.5	0.5	1.5	3.0	2.9
36 42554	Lindenhurst	9.7	26 477	1 137	2 730	26 879	-1.5	26 919	-0.1	97.9	0.5	0.1	1.0	0.6	4.1	8.4
36 43335	Long Beach	5.5	34 367	881	6 249	33 510	2.6	34 073	-1.7	87.0	7.8	0.3	1.7	3.3	10.8	13.9
36 49121	Mount Vernon	11.4	66 898	392	5 868	67 153	-0.4	66 713	0.7	39.8	55.3	0.4	1.8	2.7	7.8	21.8
36 50034	Newburgh	9.9	26 153	1 152	2 642	26 454	-1.1	23 438	12.9	51.2	34.8	0.3	0.5	13.1	23.2	12.1
36 50617	New Rochelle	26.8	67 545	385	2 520	67 265	0.4	70 794	-5.0	76.0	18.1	0.1	2.9	2.8	10.8	21.8
36 51000	New York	800.2	7 428 162	1	9 283	7 322 564	1.4	7 071 639	3.5	52.3	28.7	0.4	7.0	11.6	24.4	28.4
36 51055	Niagara Falls	36.4	55 928	509	1 536	61 840	-9.6	71 384	-13.4	82.2	15.6	1.6	0.3	0.3	1.2	6.4
36 53682	North Tonawanda	26.2	32 443	934	1 238	34 989	-7.3	35 760	-2.2	98.9	0.2	0.3	0.4	0.2	0.8	3.4
36 59641	Poughkeepsie	13.3	27 748	1 083	2 086	28 844	-3.8	29 757	-3.1	65.4	31.5	0.4	1.5	1.3	3.8	10.0
36 63000	Rochester	92.7	214 470	76	2 314	230 356	-6.9	241 741	-4.7	61.1	31.5	0.5	1.8	5.1	8.7	6.2
36 63418	Rome	194.1	39 696	759	205	44 350	-10.5	43 826	1.2	89.4	8.0	0.2	1.3	1.1	3.9	4.5
36 65255	Saratoga Springs	73.6	25 770	1 170	350	25 001	3.1	23 906	4.6	95.5	3.3	0.2	0.7	0.3	1.4	3.0
36 65508	Schenectady	28.1	60 784	450	2 163	65 566	-7.3	67 972	-3.5	88.6	8.7	0.3	1.1	1.4	2.7	5.6
36 73000	Syracuse	65.0	150 563	129	2 316	163 860	-8.1	170 105	-3.7	75.0	20.3	1.3	2.2	1.3	2.9	6.5
36 75484	Troy	27.0	51 201	568	1 896	54 269	-5.7	56 638	-4.2	88.3	7.6	0.2	3.0	0.8	2.1	6.2
36 76540	Utica	42.3	58 750	472	1 389	68 637	-14.4	75 632	-9.2	86.7	10.5	0.3	1.1	1.5	3.4	5.4
36 76705	Valley Stream	8.9	33 881	891	3 807	33 946	-0.2	35 769	-5.1	94.9	0.4	0.0	3.6	1.0	4.5	11.2
36 78608	Watertown	22.5	27 440	1 093	1 220	29 429	-6.8	27 861	5.6	93.8	3.8	0.5	0.8	1.1	2.0	3.6
36 81677	White Plains	25.4	50 240	582	1 978	48 718	3.1	46 999	3.7	73.7	19.0	0.2	3.1	4.1	14.2	21.2
36 84000	Yonkers	46.8	191 458	91	4 091	188 082	1.8	195 351	-3.7	76.2	14.1	0.2	3.0	6.5	16.7	20.2
37 00000	**NORTH CAROLINA**	126 179.9	7 650 789	X	61	6 632 448	15.4	5 880 095	12.8	75.6	22.0	1.2	0.8	0.5	1.2	1.7
37 02140	Asheville	90.5	65 974	402	729	63 379	4.1	53 583	18.3	79.1	19.8	0.3	0.6	0.2	0.9	2.0
37 09060	Burlington	52.7	42 169	705	800	39 498	6.8	37 324	5.8	76.3	22.6	0.2	0.8	0.1	0.6	1.3
37 10740	Cary	80.7	91 213	260	1 130	44 394	105.5	21 708	104.5	89.8	5.5	0.3	3.8	0.6	1.6	5.7
37 11800	Chapel Hill	42.8	43 336	682	1 013	38 711	11.9	32 461	19.3	82.3	12.5	0.3	4.3	0.5	1.6	8.3
37 12000	Charlotte	451.3	520 829	23	1 154	419 558	24.1	314 447	33.4	65.6	31.8	0.4	1.8	0.4	1.4	3.8

1. Dry land or land partially or temporarily covered by water.   2. Hispanic persons may be of any race.

Table D. Cities — **Population and Households**

	Population characteristics, 1990 (cont'd)										Households, 1990				
	Age of population (percent)													Percent	
City	Under 5 years	5 to 17 years	18 to 24 years	25 to 34 years	35 to 44 years	45 to 54 years	55 to 64 years	65 to 74 years	75 years and over	Percent female	Number	Percent change, 1980–1990	Persons per house-hold	Female family house-holder[1]	One-person
	16	17	18	19	20	21	22	23	24	25	26	27	28	29	30
NEW JERSEY—Cont'd															
Hackensack	5.1	10.6	9.8	23.7	16.1	11.2	8.9	8.0	6.6	50.7	16 464	4.8	2.16	11.9	39.7
Hoboken	4.8	11.9	13.3	29.8	14.7	7.9	6.5	6.6	4.5	50.9	15 036	-2.7	2.17	12.8	37.8
Jersey City	7.3	17.1	11.4	21.0	14.9	9.7	7.7	6.4	4.5	51.4	82 381	1.8	2.73	20.4	28.7
Kearny	6.2	15.2	10.5	19.8	14.3	11.7	9.5	7.9	5.0	50.6	12 470	-3.7	2.77	12.2	22.1
Linden	5.7	14.1	8.9	17.1	14.5	10.3	10.2	11.4	7.7	52.4	14 369	1.5	2.53	13.1	26.9
Long Branch	7.1	15.6	9.5	20.3	13.8	9.4	8.9	8.5	6.9	53.0	11 544	-1.1	2.44	15.5	32.1
Millville	7.6	19.0	10.7	16.2	14.5	9.8	8.7	8.4	5.1	52.6	9 640	6.7	2.67	15.0	23.8
Newark	7.9	20.7	12.5	18.5	13.5	9.9	7.7	5.7	3.6	52.2	91 552	-17.8	2.91	28.6	27.5
New Brunswick	5.8	11.0	33.9	18.3	10.5	5.8	5.3	5.4	3.9	52.5	12 711	-4.3	2.70	17.5	28.3
Paramus Borough	4.7	15.3	9.1	12.7	14.4	13.2	13.8	11.2	5.7	51.6	7 776	1.7	3.07	8.3	11.3
Passaic	8.8	18.7	12.2	19.0	14.1	9.7	7.1	5.7	4.6	51.0	18 735	-2.4	3.06	20.2	23.3
Paterson	8.8	20.3	12.1	18.5	13.8	9.8	7.1	5.5	4.0	51.9	43 946	-4.8	3.14	23.7	21.3
Perth Amboy	7.5	18.4	11.3	17.9	14.1	9.5	7.6	7.8	5.8	51.6	14 207	5.3	2.91	17.6	24.2
Plainfield	8.0	17.9	11.7	19.3	15.3	10.3	7.6	5.6	4.2	52.1	15 146	-0.4	3.02	21.5	21.8
Rahway	6.6	14.2	9.6	18.9	16.2	9.9	9.5	9.7	5.5	51.9	9 623	-1.9	2.62	12.8	24.9
Sayreville Borough	7.0	14.5	9.7	20.4	14.8	11.0	10.0	8.8	3.8	51.3	12 749	35.0	2.72	9.9	19.7
Trenton	8.5	18.0	10.9	19.1	14.5	8.3	7.8	7.7	5.2	51.5	30 744	-5.3	2.76	24.6	28.8
Union City	7.3	16.8	10.8	19.7	14.4	11.2	9.7	6.3	4.0	51.0	20 612	-0.7	2.80	18.5	23.7
Vineland	7.0	18.5	10.1	16.0	14.4	10.5	9.0	8.4	6.1	52.9	18 732	8.1	2.81	15.2	21.1
Westfield	6.9	17.0	7.1	14.6	18.0	12.2	10.9	8.0	5.4	52.0	10 289	0.2	2.78	7.3	17.2
West New York	6.6	14.9	10.3	18.4	12.7	12.1	11.4	8.1	5.5	52.0	14 419	-6.6	2.64	16.2	26.6
NEW MEXICO	8.3	21.2	10.0	16.9	15.0	9.7	8.0	6.4	4.3	50.8	542 709	22.5	2.74	11.9	23.0
Alamogordo	8.6	20.2	9.7	18.3	14.7	9.3	8.8	6.6	3.9	50.5	10 482	20.8	2.60	10.1	23.1
Albuquerque	7.3	17.7	10.4	19.0	16.3	10.3	7.9	6.7	4.4	51.5	153 818	23.9	2.46	12.1	28.2
Clovis	8.3	21.2	10.1	17.6	12.5	9.8	8.2	6.5	5.7	52.0	11 676	2.2	2.62	12.5	23.9
Farmington	9.1	24.1	7.4	18.1	16.4	8.7	7.7	5.7	2.8	51.0	11 979	9.9	2.83	10.1	20.6
Hobbs	9.0	24.4	9.1	16.2	13.9	7.9	8.3	6.6	4.5	51.6	10 242	0.6	2.81	12.6	22.2
Las Cruces	7.6	19.1	13.9	17.6	13.2	9.4	7.9	6.7	4.6	51.0	23 797	47.3	2.59	12.7	25.1
Rio Rancho	10.1	20.0	6.1	22.0	16.1	7.3	6.5	8.0	4.0	51.3	11 658	NA	2.77	8.7	17.1
Roswell	8.1	22.0	9.5	14.7	12.6	9.0	8.4	8.6	7.1	51.6	16 195	10.9	2.67	12.8	24.9
Santa Fe	6.4	16.7	8.9	15.8	18.5	12.5	8.6	7.4	5.1	52.5	22 789	26.7	2.39	12.3	31.0
NEW YORK	7.0	16.7	10.9	17.4	15.1	10.6	9.1	7.5	5.6	52.1	6 639 322	4.6	2.63	13.8	27.2
Albany	6.0	12.1	19.8	18.8	13.2	7.4	7.2	7.4	8.0	53.5	42 121	3.1	2.17	14.7	38.6
Auburn	7.2	16.1	10.0	18.3	14.2	7.7	8.1	9.7	8.7	51.1	11 936	1.5	2.41	14.5	32.2
Binghamton	6.6	13.2	13.9	17.2	12.9	8.5	8.6	9.9	9.1	53.4	22 617	-0.7	2.25	13.2	36.2
Buffalo	7.8	16.5	12.5	18.5	13.0	8.3	8.5	8.5	6.4	53.4	136 436	-3.1	2.33	20.2	35.6
Elmira	8.5	17.8	14.0	16.9	12.5	7.5	7.8	8.3	6.6	51.5	12 428	-0.7	2.46	17.2	32.1
Freeport	7.4	16.5	11.3	18.4	15.2	11.9	9.1	6.2	3.9	51.6	13 240	4.3	3.00	15.4	22.4
Hempstead	7.1	16.6	18.0	18.6	13.8	10.5	7.2	4.8	3.5	53.2	14 586	4.0	3.11	22.6	23.5
Ithaca	2.9	7.0	51.4	14.6	8.7	4.0	3.7	3.7	3.9	48.3	9 617	4.9	2.26	8.3	36.5
Jamestown	8.1	17.3	10.4	16.7	13.0	8.4	8.8	8.5	8.7	53.2	14 269	0.8	2.37	13.3	31.9
Lindenhurst	7.8	16.2	10.4	19.8	15.1	10.2	9.6	7.2	3.8	51.2	8 600	1.2	3.11	10.9	14.6
Long Beach	6.2	11.4	8.3	20.9	14.7	10.4	9.5	8.2	10.5	52.4	13 592	2.0	2.35	10.2	34.3
Mount Vernon	6.9	16.0	9.8	17.9	14.4	11.2	8.8	8.1	6.9	54.8	25 175	-0.3	2.64	20.5	29.0
Newburgh	10.0	20.3	13.3	17.3	12.7	8.5	7.1	6.2	4.5	53.3	9 008	7.1	2.83	23.2	27.0
New Rochelle	6.1	14.0	9.8	16.3	14.6	11.5	10.6	8.9	8.2	53.2	25 317	-1.7	2.57	11.8	28.8
New York	6.9	16.1	10.3	18.7	15.2	10.9	8.9	7.3	5.7	53.1	2 819 401	1.0	2.54	18.0	32.9
Niagara Falls	7.3	16.5	9.3	16.6	12.7	8.2	10.3	11.3	7.8	53.8	25 970	-5.1	2.35	16.5	33.1
North Tonawanda	7.1	17.8	9.3	17.0	16.1	8.6	9.7	9.1	5.4	52.1	13 635	5.7	2.56	10.6	26.0
Poughkeepsie	8.4	14.9	10.3	20.0	13.9	8.3	8.3	8.0	7.8	52.9	11 874	-3.6	2.36	17.1	33.8
Rochester	9.5	16.6	13.0	21.7	13.4	7.8	6.1	6.1	5.9	52.8	93 607	-1.3	2.37	20.6	35.3
Rome	7.8	16.6	12.7	20.0	13.0	8.6	7.5	8.0	5.8	48.2	15 754	4.1	2.55	11.8	27.2
Saratoga Springs	5.7	14.7	18.3	15.4	15.0	10.2	7.1	6.7	7.0	52.4	9 688	13.7	2.36	9.7	32.1
Schenectady	7.9	14.1	13.0	19.2	12.6	8.1	8.0	9.0	8.0	52.9	27 748	-0.6	2.26	14.6	36.0
Syracuse	7.6	15.0	17.8	18.4	12.0	7.6	7.0	7.6	7.1	53.4	64 945	-3.2	2.33	16.9	35.8
Troy	7.0	14.5	19.8	17.8	11.6	7.1	8.0	7.4	6.8	50.7	20 761	1.1	2.37	14.8	33.7
Utica	7.2	15.5	11.6	16.6	11.7	8.8	9.3	10.5	8.8	53.2	28 358	-2.1	2.31	15.4	35.6
Valley Stream	5.9	15.3	9.2	15.2	15.9	9.8	11.7	11.0	6.0	52.3	11 851	-1.6	2.86	9.9	18.4
Watertown	8.8	17.7	11.6	18.8	12.1	8.3	7.8	7.3	7.6	53.4	11 430	8.2	2.50	13.6	29.3
White Plains	5.3	12.5	8.9	20.0	15.6	11.7	10.1	8.1	7.7	53.4	19 432	2.8	2.39	11.7	33.9
Yonkers	6.7	14.7	9.6	17.9	13.8	10.2	10.6	9.3	7.2	53.4	72 101	-2.4	2.57	15.3	28.3
NORTH CAROLINA	6.9	17.3	11.8	17.3	15.2	10.5	8.9	7.3	4.8	51.5	2 517 026	23.0	2.54	12.3	23.7
Asheville	6.1	14.6	9.1	15.5	15.1	9.5	9.8	11.2	9.1	54.6	27 027	23.0	2.19	13.9	35.2
Burlington	6.4	15.2	9.5	15.9	13.7	11.1	11.0	10.2	6.9	53.9	16 627	15.3	2.35	13.7	28.9
Cary	8.1	17.8	8.8	24.0	19.7	11.4	5.8	2.9	1.5	50.6	16 908	125.5	2.59	6.8	21.1
Chapel Hill	3.9	10.2	36.3	17.1	11.4	7.5	4.9	4.9	3.8	54.3	13 780	36.9	2.18	8.1	32.8
Charlotte	7.5	16.8	10.6	21.1	16.3	10.3	7.7	5.9	3.8	52.5	158 991	34.2	2.45	14.0	28.0

1. No spouse present.

Table D. Cities — Group Quarters, Crime, Education, and Income

	Persons in group quarters, 1990				Serious crimes known to police, 1998[2]				Education, 1990				Money income, 1989		
					Total		Rate[3]		School enrollment		Attainment[4] (percent)			Households	
														Median	
City	Total	Persons in mental hospitals	Persons in nursing homes	Persons identified as home-less[1]	Number	Rate[3]	Violent	Property	Public	Private	High school grad-uate or more	Bach-elor's degree or more	Per capita (dollars)[5]	Dollars	Percent change, 1979–1989 (constant 1989 dollars)
	31	32	33	34	35	36	37	38	39	40	41	42	43	44	45
NEW JERSEY—Cont'd															
Hackensack	1 470	0	216	83	1 667	4 390	469	3 921	5 178	1 603	74.4	25.7	20 217	38 976	29.2
Hoboken	799	0	0	78	1 225	3 664	395	3 269	4 539	2 763	69.8	39.7	20 020	34 873	78.8
Jersey City	4 049	0	950	681	13 240	5 730	1 418	4 312	38 426	18 260	65.7	21.4	13 060	29 054	35.6
Kearny	360	0	0	0	1 611	4 547	418	4 129	6 166	2 098	68.5	15.3	15 735	37 840	19.8
Linden	284	0	237	0	2 109	5 668	392	5 276	6 110	1 428	68.2	12.2	16 308	35 911	9.8
Long Branch	415	0	254	0	1 505	5 109	601	4 508	4 756	1 401	71.8	20.1	16 104	30 693	32.8
Millville	259	0	162	43	1 590	5 998	822	5 176	5 768	709	69.8	11.6	13 748	31 266	14.9
Newark	8 902	0	385	2 982	23 045	8 560	2 094	6 466	64 085	12 541	51.2	8.5	9 424	21 650	27.7
New Brunswick	7 340	0	125	144	3 255	7 715	652	7 063	16 133	1 514	66.0	23.4	11 252	28 289	24.2
Paramus Borough	1 216	76	902	18	2 907	11 226	417	10 809	4 598	1 440	85.4	31.2	22 202	58 995	18.2
Passaic	601	0	193	8	3 147	5 441	1 093	4 348	11 197	3 442	55.6	14.2	11 057	26 669	29.7
Paterson	2 949	0	101	472	6 588	4 323	839	3 484	28 935	8 211	54.9	8.7	10 518	26 960	34.1
Perth Amboy	611	0	415	0	1 854	4 319	669	3 650	8 811	1 672	50.2	8.2	11 351	28 377	17.1
Plainfield	820	0	418	0	2 997	6 419	1 480	4 939	9 386	2 979	71.4	18.9	14 742	38 463	25.8
Rahway	152	0	106	0	1 027	4 033	377	3 656	4 265	1 209	77.2	17.8	17 383	40 776	13.9
Sayreville Borough	238	0	184	0	1 026	2 704	232	2 472	5 981	1 446	78.3	17.0	18 297	46 057	11.3
Trenton	3 797	129	425	450	5 960	6 932	1 314	5 618	16 369	5 161	58.2	10.5	11 018	25 719	26.0
Union City	194	0	0	178	2 254	3 910	404	3 506	10 978	3 510	50.5	10.7	11 089	25 655	22.4
Vineland	2 282	0	604	142	3 402	6 053	687	5 366	10 891	2 241	61.3	12.6	12 963	30 733	14.9
Westfield	243	0	217	0	515	1 752	37	1 715	5 833	1 510	91.2	53.6	30 748	66 760	31.9
West New York	0	0	0	0	1 763	4 636	634	4 002	6 725	1 735	49.9	12.4	12 047	26 361	23.8
NEW MEXICO	28 810	321	6 276	874	116 711	6 719	961	5 758	400 077	35 912	75.1	20.4	11 246	24 087	-1.9
Alamogordo	352	0	192	0	1 504	5 164	343	4 821	6 917	664	82.0	16.7	11 255	24 579	2.8
Albuquerque	5 952	105	1 811	306	45 648	10 806	1 317	9 489	94 742	11 923	83.9	28.4	14 013	27 555	-0.4
Clovis	310	0	206	0	2 105	6 194	809	5 385	8 510	341	74.1	13.8	10 002	21 222	-5.8
Farmington	118	0	56	22	2 640	6 843	2 146	4 697	9 771	580	79.9	14.8	12 302	28 911	-13.8
Hobbs	292	0	198	0	1 975	7 034	1 079	5 955	8 103	650	66.4	13.4	10 230	22 807	-25.7
Las Cruces	580	0	244	58	7 041	9 131	702	8 429	19 862	1 078	79.1	29.2	11 175	23 648	3.8
Rio Rancho	158	0	119	0	NA	NA	NA	NA	7 475	648	87.4	19.6	12 345	31 512	NA
Roswell	1 355	0	268	20	NA	NA	NA	NA	11 187	1 077	69.3	15.1	10 830	21 870	4.4
Santa Fe	1 491	28	326	80	NA	NA	NA	NA	10 888	2 973	84.0	36.1	16 554	30 023	12.2
NEW YORK	543 722	20 035	126 175	43 085	652 202	3 589	638	2 951	3 538 249	1 117 969	74.8	23.1	16 501	32 965	18.2
Albany	9 545	352	1 761	498	7 392	7 165	972	6 193	22 598	8 263	77.7	29.5	13 742	25 152	20.0
Auburn	2 571	0	704	0	1 256	4 212	235	3 977	6 179	778	68.3	11.9	10 638	22 271	-1.0
Binghamton	1 917	474	709	95	2 581	5 398	301	5 097	11 617	1 685	73.9	19.8	12 106	20 891	2.3
Buffalo	9 871	335	2 582	339	22 321	7 232	1 129	6 103	73 144	15 883	67.3	16.0	10 445	18 482	-4.9
Elmira	3 211	150	316	0	1 773	5 558	288	5 270	6 828	1 872	71.4	11.1	10 949	18 548	-7.4
Freeport	152	0	100	0	1 573	3 902	675	3 227	8 330	1 812	77.2	21.4	17 018	43 948	31.3
Hempstead	3 963	0	404	99	1 463	3 127	667	2 460	9 452	6 029	70.2	16.0	13 294	36 715	29.0
Ithaca	7 649	0	235	13	1 063	3 702	153	3 549	5 648	12 862	86.7	50.2	9 213	17 738	2.8
Jamestown	870	14	658	16	1 468	4 453	473	3 980	7 384	856	71.2	13.4	10 731	20 582	1.4
Lindenhurst	134	0	0	27	NA	NA	NA	NA	5 190	1 111	77.4	12.1	16 116	46 615	32.6
Long Beach	1 539	0	1 334	0	637	1 849	177	1 672	4 724	1 499	83.0	28.7	20 993	41 495	51.8
Mount Vernon	781	0	449	132	2 559	3 793	940	2 853	12 743	4 004	70.8	20.4	15 835	34 850	30.0
Newburgh	946	0	23	215	1 256	4 735	1 018	3 717	6 446	1 045	57.9	11.4	9 989	22 224	21.4
New Rochelle	2 182	0	1 253	52	2 199	3 247	315	2 932	9 476	5 836	78.2	33.3	23 745	43 482	24.1
New York	166 549	4 903	43 265	33 579	323 150	4 392	1 167	3 225	1 357 534	528 124	68.3	23.0	16 281	29 823	28.4
Niagara Falls	805	0	580	156	728	1 250	170	1 080	11 748	2 479	67.7	9.7	10 904	20 641	-16.8
North Tonawanda	83	0	45	0	732	2 171	128	2 043	7 031	1 366	79.8	15.2	12 722	29 576	0.3
Poughkeepsie	784	0	348	47	1 479	5 273	670	4 603	5 549	1 209	68.5	21.8	14 936	27 606	33.1
Rochester	9 902	499	2 182	320	18 713	8 449	866	7 583	42 973	17 061	68.8	19.0	11 704	22 785	-0.3
Rome	4 247	0	441	4	844	2 076	123	1 953	9 775	1 167	74.3	15.4	11 171	24 234	0.3
Saratoga Springs	2 221	42	408	0	898	3 542	177	3 365	4 285	2 980	83.5	30.8	15 876	30 938	19.7
Schenectady	2 877	0	469	355	3 463	5 509	778	4 731	10 770	4 361	74.8	17.3	12 569	24 316	10.7
Syracuse	12 583	58	2 319	474	9 949	6 422	919	5 503	30 062	20 398	71.2	22.0	11 351	21 242	2.9
Troy	5 175	7	656	41	369	706	101	605	8 999	8 003	71.5	18.4	11 704	23 362	16.7
Utica	3 083	631	1 100	183	3 185	5 232	396	4 836	13 047	3 276	67.4	12.3	10 726	19 950	0.5
Valley Stream	21	0	0	0	NA	NA	NA	NA	5 753	2 081	81.8	19.2	19 089	47 287	19.6
Watertown	880	0	626	26	1 023	3 583	343	3 240	5 285	1 012	76.8	16.1	11 616	22 765	10.7
White Plains	2 165	368	391	493	2 282	4 572	309	4 263	7 567	3 342	80.3	37.5	24 330	44 004	30.5
Yonkers	2 896	0	741	244	7 185	3 756	529	3 227	27 270	16 321	73.6	21.9	17 484	36 376	15.9
NORTH CAROLINA	223 900	2 500	47 014	2 946	401 615	5 322	579	4 743	1 444 680	180 233	70.0	17.4	12 885	26 647	9.8
Asheville	2 264	93	753	178	5 005	7 628	980	6 648	11 961	1 545	75.1	23.0	13 079	22 267	10.5
Burlington	446	0	279	0	3 150	7 575	866	6 709	6 742	1 193	70.3	19.2	14 635	26 500	3.8
Cary	65	0	65	0	2 145	2 699	151	2 548	10 139	1 702	94.9	48.8	20 595	46 259	10.3
Chapel Hill	8 658	61	228	13	2 865	6 272	447	5 825	18 120	1 560	93.4	71.2	16 288	30 489	15.5
Charlotte	5 945	0	2 251	663	52 502	8 852	1 455	7 397	81 623	16 104	81.0	28.4	16 793	31 873	12.4

1. Persons in emergency shelters and persons visible in street locations. 2. Data for serious crimes have not been adjusted for underreporting. This may affect comparability between geographic areas and over time. 3. Per 100,000 population estimated by the FBI. 4. Persons 25 years old and older. 5. Based on population enumerated as of April 1, 1990.

	Money income, 1989 (cont'd)				Housing units, 1990										
	House-holds (cont'd)	Percent below poverty, 1989						Occupied units							
		Persons		Fam-ilies						Owner-occupied units			Renter-occu-pied units		
											Owner cost as a percent of income				
City	Percent with $100,000 or more	Total	Percent change in rate, 1979–1989	Total	Total	Percent change, 1980–1990	Vacant units for sale or rent[1]	Total	Percent	Median value[2] (dollars)	With a mort-gage	Without a mort-gage	Median rent[3] (dol-lars)	Rent as per-cent of income	Sub-standard units[4] (percent)
	46	47	48	49	50	51	52	53	54	55	56	57	58	59	60
NEW JERSEY—Cont'd															
Hackensack	5.7	7.0	-19.5	4.8	17 705	8.6	1 087	16 464	34.6	186 300	24.8	18.9	693	25.5	5.8
Hoboken	7.2	16.4	-30.2	15.9	17 421	3.6	1 874	15 036	21.6	250 000	25.6	23.4	560	25.1	6.3
Jersey City	3.5	18.9	-10.8	16.6	90 723	3.1	6 831	82 381	29.6	127 700	24.6	16.0	527	25.6	12.0
Kearny	4.6	6.1	-24.7	4.0	13 435	1.0	749	12 470	49.6	165 700	22.9	16.0	619	24.2	3.3
Linden	3.2	5.6	-20.0	4.0	14 917	2.2	430	14 369	61.2	151 800	23.5	15.4	594	25.1	3.0
Long Branch	5.0	14.7	-25.8	10.8	13 632	3.5	1 351	11 544	44.1	149 100	27.1	18.0	601	28.2	4.8
Millville	2.2	11.5	3.6	9.2	10 150	7.6	366	9 640	63.2	70 500	20.5	13.8	478	27.4	3.0
Newark	1.5	26.3	-19.8	22.8	102 473	-15.6	8 054	91 552	23.1	110 000	24.4	15.2	445	26.9	14.9
New Brunswick	2.9	22.0	-6.4	15.7	13 556	-4.1	703	12 711	32.3	126 700	28.0	18.9	640	29.9	12.2
Paramus Borough	17.8	3.0	0.0	1.6	7 892	2.5	103	7 776	91.1	246 200	21.5	13.4	1 001	23.9	1.4
Passaic	3.5	17.0	-27.7	14.6	19 619	-1.2	742	18 735	28.1	165 100	27.2	14.9	532	28.0	17.2
Paterson	2.5	18.5	-26.6	15.7	46 138	-4.2	1 776	43 946	33.6	138 700	24.2	18.1	524	28.4	14.3
Perth Amboy	1.8	15.2	-14.1	12.5	15 017	6.4	607	14 207	42.0	125 500	24.5	17.1	568	28.3	12.4
Plainfield	6.8	12.2	-6.2	9.5	16 063	-0.6	770	15 146	51.0	141 400	25.0	15.2	627	27.0	10.7
Rahway	5.0	6.4	6.7	4.9	9 989	-0.7	307	9 623	65.7	151 100	24.6	17.0	611	25.6	3.7
Sayreville Borough	7.6	3.1	0.0	2.4	13 347	38.2	541	12 749	71.3	156 800	22.3	14.2	658	22.8	1.1
Trenton	1.5	18.1	-14.6	15.1	33 578	-6.3	1 887	30 744	51.1	71 300	21.1	15.2	451	26.9	8.0
Union City	2.0	18.2	-10.3	16.7	22 592	5.1	1 560	20 612	21.8	150 400	28.5	13.0	505	27.5	16.8
Vineland	3.5	10.9	-21.6	8.6	19 548	7.9	635	18 732	67.0	83 600	21.6	15.3	511	28.7	5.1
Westfield	27.9	1.8	-41.9	1.2	10 588	1.2	244	10 289	81.3	257 300	22.2	13.8	814	24.3	0.5
West New York	2.4	16.4	-10.4	12.8	15 794	-0.2	1 069	14 419	22.7	162 000	26.3	15.0	439	25.4	15.4
NEW MEXICO	2.5	20.6	17.1	16.5	632 058	24.5	38 093	542 709	67.4	70 100	21.6	12.5	372	26.5	8.8
Alamogordo	0.9	13.5	-10.0	11.4	11 974	26.1	1 239	10 482	63.7	58 200	21.2	11.5	364	25.3	4.0
Albuquerque	3.3	14.0	12.9	10.3	166 870	25.7	9 707	153 818	57.3	85 900	22.1	12.2	402	27.3	4.8
Clovis	1.1	21.4	31.3	17.1	12 978	2.8	961	11 676	64.2	51 300	20.6	12.5	331	26.9	6.1
Farmington	2.8	15.2	67.0	12.2	13 119	9.2	755	11 979	65.1	66 100	20.1	12.2	378	24.1	6.9
Hobbs	2.3	24.8	100.0	20.9	12 327	10.4	1 327	10 242	66.0	41 600	17.2	12.0	324	25.1	7.4
Las Cruces	1.4	22.6	11.3	16.6	25 676	44.9	1 532	23 797	56.2	68 300	19.9	11.9	366	28.9	5.5
Rio Rancho	1.0	4.6	NA	3.4	12 325	NA	516	11 658	82.8	69 900	23.8	11.7	541	26.4	3.2
Roswell	2.4	21.6	21.3	17.7	18 242	12.0	1 487	16 195	69.1	44 600	19.4	12.8	343	28.5	6.5
Santa Fe	5.3	12.3	-12.8	9.2	24 681	29.7	1 006	22 789	59.6	99 000	22.3	12.0	496	27.7	5.1
NEW YORK	6.8	13.0	-2.8	10.0	7 226 891	5.2	276 872	6 639 322	52.2	131 600	21.5	14.4	486	26.3	6.8
Albany	2.6	18.3	4.6	12.1	46 199	0.0	2 850	42 121	38.3	101 800	19.7	13.0	456	26.9	2.6
Auburn	0.8	13.8	7.8	11.9	12 682	3.3	510	11 936	52.0	53 600	21.1	16.0	386	28.7	1.6
Binghamton	1.8	20.0	29.0	12.0	24 626	1.6	1 436	22 617	44.4	71 500	19.7	13.3	361	29.3	2.1
Buffalo	1.4	25.6	23.7	21.7	151 971	-2.9	8 513	136 436	43.1	46 700	17.9	14.2	352	31.8	2.5
Elmira	1.2	22.2	26.9	19.4	13 301	-3.0	586	12 428	48.1	43 600	17.6	15.9	343	29.5	1.7
Freeport	8.5	7.4	-40.8	5.4	13 660	4.0	344	13 240	65.2	170 800	24.5	16.9	625	27.9	9.9
Hempstead	5.7	12.4	-13.9	10.4	15 117	1.6	447	14 586	45.4	156 600	23.3	16.1	655	28.7	15.8
Ithaca	2.5	39.4	22.0	15.0	10 075	5.8	322	9 617	28.9	95 600	22.2	13.8	493	35.1	2.0
Jamestown	1.1	18.7	37.5	14.6	15 461	-0.1	937	14 269	51.9	43 300	16.6	13.2	311	28.6	1.2
Lindenhurst	6.5	3.5	-18.6	2.6	8 847	2.1	173	8 600	80.5	156 800	25.3	17.2	737	29.1	1.5
Long Beach	9.9	8.3	-37.6	5.4	15 358	1.0	869	13 592	56.0	187 600	23.3	16.9	758	27.9	6.6
Mount Vernon	5.8	11.8	-19.2	8.9	26 232	0.2	865	25 175	36.8	227 200	23.6	16.6	532	24.5	7.9
Newburgh	2.1	26.2	-1.9	23.6	9 995	1.0	739	9 008	35.4	103 100	25.8	17.1	533	33.2	9.0
New Rochelle	15.7	7.6	-5.0	4.7	26 398	0.7	908	25 317	51.6	321 400	23.1	15.8	578	26.3	5.3
New York	6.4	19.3	-3.5	16.3	2 992 169	1.6	130 092	2 819 401	28.6	189 600	21.8	14.1	496	25.7	12.7
Niagara Falls	0.7	18.6	35.8	15.5	28 635	-2.9	1 277	25 970	56.0	45 100	17.9	15.0	330	30.8	1.9
North Tonawanda	1.0	6.1	-12.9	4.8	14 001	5.8	224	13 635	67.9	68 100	19.1	14.0	388	24.6	1.2
Poughkeepsie	3.8	14.7	-14.5	11.6	13 112	-0.4	730	11 874	40.2	128 700	21.0	15.4	522	28.1	4.3
Rochester	1.4	23.5	34.3	21.1	101 154	-1.4	5 833	93 607	44.0	65 200	22.1	15.7	442	32.3	3.1
Rome	1.7	12.1	12.0	9.7	16 661	5.4	646	15 754	53.4	69 200	19.2	14.6	393	27.3	2.2
Saratoga Springs	4.2	8.9	-21.2	6.0	10 751	13.4	604	9 688	53.7	108 800	18.9	12.8	475	27.6	1.2
Schenectady	1.3	14.9	3.5	11.4	30 232	-0.1	1 618	27 748	46.6	82 100	22.0	14.0	428	28.1	1.4
Syracuse	1.7	22.7	23.4	17.0	71 502	-2.3	5 148	64 945	41.1	67 600	20.1	14.7	409	29.6	3.1
Troy	1.6	17.2	-5.5	12.7	22 871	1.3	1 364	20 761	39.6	84 400	20.6	13.5	396	24.9	2.6
Utica	1.2	21.7	29.2	16.6	31 127	-2.1	1 791	28 358	48.9	65 900	20.6	14.4	338	28.7	2.2
Valley Stream	9.0	3.2	-13.5	2.2	12 165	-0.6	228	11 851	81.1	187 300	23.6	16.6	753	27.2	1.4
Watertown	1.7	15.8	12.1	13.1	12 405	9.6	672	11 430	45.5	60 100	20.0	15.3	400	27.9	2.2
White Plains	14.6	7.7	-1.3	4.3	20 714	7.9	1 092	19 432	51.6	296 000	20.9	13.9	589	25.9	6.1
Yonkers	6.9	11.0	12.2	9.0	75 562	-0.5	2 690	72 101	43.5	228 100	22.9	15.1	522	25.4	7.1
NORTH CAROLINA	2.6	13.0	-12.3	9.9	2 818 193	23.9	136 083	2 517 026	68.0	65 800	20.5	12.9	382	24.4	3.9
Asheville	2.2	15.9	-4.8	11.4	29 713	27.9	1 764	27 027	56.6	57 000	21.3	14.0	365	26.3	2.1
Burlington	3.2	9.9	-14.7	6.5	17 696	17.6	887	16 627	61.8	66 000	19.6	12.6	393	24.5	2.1
Cary	7.7	3.2	3.2	2.1	18 008	126.6	1 014	16 908	67.4	108 800	21.9	12.3	538	21.6	1.0
Chapel Hill	9.3	16.1	-1.2	5.8	14 850	41.7	906	13 780	40.5	141 100	22.0	11.5	489	28.8	1.8
Charlotte	5.1	10.8	-12.9	8.5	170 430	37.4	9 616	158 991	55.0	81 300	20.1	12.6	462	24.3	3.4

1. Includes units rented or sold but not occupied. 2. Specified owner-occupied units. 3. Specified renter-occupied units. 4. Overcrowded or lacking complete plumbing facilities.

City	Civilian labor force, 1999				Civilian employment, 1990[2]				Disability 1990	Value of residential construction authorized by building permits, 1999		
			Unemployment			Percent						
	Total	Percent change, 1998–1999	Total	Rate[1]	Total	Professional, managerial, and technical	Precision production, craft, and repair		Work disabled persons[3] (percent)	New construction ($1,000)	Number of housing units	Percent single family
	61	62	63	64	65	66	67	68	69	70	71
NEW JERSEY—Cont'd											
Hackensack	21 917	1.5	1 051	4.8	21 132	31.9	8.5	6.1	2 233	31	48.4
Hoboken	19 782	0.8	998	5.0	19 197	44.4	5.1	5.5	23 644	266	0.0
Jersey City	112 403	0.7	10 061	9.0	104 595	27.5	7.7	7.2	94 596	1 242	2.0
Kearny	18 586	0.8	948	5.1	18 026	24.8	10.8	5.6	649	12	0.0
Linden	18 952	1.3	1 001	5.3	17 866	23.8	12.0	7.2	3 613	98	6.1
Long Branch	15 899	1.1	1 059	6.7	13 759	30.1	10.9	8.8	5 369	61	70.5
Millville	12 708	-0.9	941	7.4	12 191	24.6	13.6	8.6	3 843	63	100.0
Newark	111 749	0.9	10 858	9.7	105 553	16.7	10.3	10.7	41 579	711	13.6
New Brunswick	23 698	1.3	1 584	6.7	20 422	28.3	6.6	5.6	932	16	43.8
Paramus Borough	12 891	1.5	391	3.0	12 659	38.7	8.6	4.7	6 802	34	94.1
Passaic	28 665	1.6	2 751	9.6	26 463	18.6	9.7	7.2	8	2	0.0
Paterson	67 812	1.6	6 566	9.7	62 543	16.0	10.9	8.0	393	12	100.0
Perth Amboy	23 094	1.3	1 910	8.3	19 563	17.5	10.9	7.5	6 386	207	22.2
Plainfield	25 607	1.3	1 757	6.9	23 738	26.0	7.9	7.4	996	10	100.0
Rahway	13 919	1.3	588	4.2	13 268	29.1	11.2	5.9	1 363	20	100.0
Sayreville Borough	21 364	1.2	642	3.0	19 137	28.6	12.1	5.2	17 573	167	80.8
Trenton	39 661	0.0	3 387	8.5	37 616	21.1	8.7	9.9	680	19	100.0
Union City	29 618	0.7	2 661	9.0	27 550	17.2	10.1	6.1	285	6	0.0
Vineland	26 120	-1.0	2 171	8.3	24 812	24.9	11.9	9.7	13 216	135	98.5
Westfield	15 749	1.4	370	2.3	15 306	52.9	5.1	3.4	3 416	24	100.0
West New York	19 741	0.7	1 394	7.1	18 751	17.8	10.7	6.3	4 642	77	41.6
NEW MEXICO	809 713	-2.6	45 520	5.6	629 272	31.6	12.0	8.8	1 079 858	9 716	88.5
Alamogordo	11 615	-0.5	449	3.9	10 377	31.0	15.5	9.3	12 311	100	98.0
Albuquerque	233 663	-2.4	8 759	3.7	187 575	37.6	9.1	8.2	360 873	4 010	90.4
Clovis	14 469	-3.5	622	4.3	11 757	25.7	13.7	10.9	3 833	37	100.0
Farmington	21 450	-3.5	1 003	4.7	14 691	31.5	14.3	6.9	13 951	104	100.0
Hobbs	12 255	-6.0	1 196	9.8	11 071	24.8	18.5	9.7	996	1	100.0
Las Cruces	34 427	0.0	2 468	7.2	26 918	38.6	8.4	7.0	41 991	380	92.4
Rio Rancho	23 415	NA	728	3.1	14 892	31.2	11.7	7.2	40 276	449	100.0
Roswell	18 808	-7.0	1 643	8.7	17 322	26.7	11.5	10.8	3 186	36	94.4
Santa Fe	36 914	-2.0	955	2.6	29 117	39.7	7.9	6.4	61 993	781	48.4
NEW YORK	8 883 034	0.1	459 191	5.2	8 370 718	33.5	9.4	7.4	4 414 787	42 619	58.1
Albany	52 766	-0.3	2 165	4.1	49 915	38.0	5.0	8.0	4 900	83	9.6
Auburn	13 462	-0.6	890	6.6	12 641	24.3	10.2	9.4	335	4	100.0
Binghamton	23 200	-0.2	1 403	6.0	22 939	31.8	8.9	11.4	901	8	100.0
Buffalo	141 838	-0.8	12 510	8.8	131 001	27.2	8.5	11.7	8 947	285	24.2
Elmira	14 009	0.2	1 038	7.4	12 530	24.0	11.2	13.0	679	21	9.5
Freeport	22 710	0.4	792	3.5	21 601	27.8	10.3	6.7	685	6	100.0
Hempstead	27 385	0.5	1 366	5.0	25 643	24.0	7.3	6.3	773	16	100.0
Ithaca	14 445	1.4	470	3.3	13 088	47.6	3.4	3.7	8 274	159	0.6
Jamestown	15 723	-2.3	906	5.8	14 743	25.4	10.0	11.0	50	1	100.0
Lindenhurst	14 991	1.2	613	4.1	13 815	23.3	15.1	6.5	1 230	21	52.4
Long Beach	18 008	0.4	729	4.0	17 029	35.9	7.9	6.1	1 558	20	20.0
Mount Vernon	33 260	-0.2	1 787	5.4	32 498	30.9	9.1	8.0	1 862	21	33.3
Newburgh	12 390	2.0	922	7.4	10 628	21.7	9.0	11.7	45	1	100.0
New Rochelle	35 253	-0.2	1 307	3.7	35 052	40.0	8.1	5.6	3 120	21	71.4
New York	3 444 159	0.0	230 613	6.7	3 257 637	33.7	7.5	8.0	808 124	12 421	11.8
Niagara Falls	27 870	-1.6	2 713	9.7	24 888	21.7	11.2	11.9	598	8	75.0
North Tonawanda	18 428	-1.3	931	5.1	17 310	26.4	12.7	7.2	1 175	13	100.0
Poughkeepsie	12 917	1.4	752	5.8	13 443	34.7	9.1	9.8	972	11	27.3
Rochester	113 906	0.2	7 980	7.0	101 942	29.4	10.4	11.2	9 799	176	21.6
Rome	16 849	1.2	718	4.3	15 900	30.1	10.3	10.9	430	7	100.0
Saratoga Springs	13 536	0.7	528	3.9	11 763	41.6	7.2	5.5	27 696	200	89.5
Schenectady	31 110	-1.3	1 608	5.2	29 832	28.2	10.0	10.8	206	3	100.0
Syracuse	73 340	0.0	4 143	5.6	70 288	32.6	7.6	10.4	511	9	100.0
Troy	26 073	-0.7	1 497	5.7	24 502	29.6	8.0	8.2	2 913	54	40.7
Utica	29 760	1.1	1 724	5.8	27 634	26.0	10.4	12.5	1 012	5	100.0
Valley Stream	17 515	0.4	594	3.4	16 676	30.6	13.4	4.7	230	2	100.0
Watertown	12 226	0.8	1 183	9.7	11 286	30.0	9.5	9.3	510	5	60.0
White Plains	26 687	-0.3	964	3.6	26 561	44.2	5.9	5.7	4 904	41	100.0
Yonkers	90 892	-0.2	4 256	4.7	89 458	32.4	10.0	7.2	7 121	74	24.3
NORTH CAROLINA	3 874 423	2.1	122 153	3.2	3 238 414	25.7	13.3	8.7	8 616 858	84 754	75.6
Asheville	33 724	0.1	996	3.0	28 410	31.2	8.7	11.2	28 527	282	62.1
Burlington	23 555	1.6	600	2.5	20 579	26.6	12.9	8.7	26 435	271	81.5
Cary	38 050	2.4	367	1.0	26 644	52.4	5.9	3.1	243 958	1 874	63.8
Chapel Hill	24 158	0.4	315	1.3	19 269	54.9	3.1	3.0	87 346	881	47.8
Charlotte	279 518	4.1	6 137	2.2	216 696	32.5	8.8	6.5	NA	NA	NA

1. Percent of civilian labor force.   2. Persons 16 years and older.   3. Persons 16 to 64 years old.

City	Wholesale Trade, 1997				Retail Trade[1], 1997				Real Estate and Rental and Leasing, 1997			
	Number of Establishments	Number of Employees	Sales (mil dol)	Annual Payroll (mil dol)	Number of Establishments	Number of Employees	Sales (mil dol)	Annual Payroll (mil dol)	Number of Establishments	Number of Employees	Receipts (mil dol)	Annual Payroll (mil dol)
	72	73	74	75	76	77	78	79	80	81	82	83
NEW JERSEY—Cont'd												
Hackensack	279	2 902	2 434.3	131.5	284	3 895	719.8	82.1	155	2 624	487.4	77.0
Hoboken	83	575	742.6	25.7	152	974	130.0	12.7	61	306	41.8	7.3
Jersey City	278	5 701	2 510.8	202.7	809	8 787	1 536.0	144.6	212	1 082	188.2	25.3
Kearny	98	1 231	539.9	56.3	131	1 550	237.3	28.5	32	320	62.1	13.1
Linden	131	1 475	1 861.5	56.8	195	2 303	502.4	50.3	44	279	36.8	6.5
Long Branch	41	394	523.2	14.7	73	785	147.5	15.1	31	72	14.7	1.5
Millville	25	D	D	D	100	1 621	257.7	26.4	10	27	3.4	0.5
Newark	426	5 393	2 319.3	192.0	832	5 920	912.8	101.5	193	3 108	502.7	75.5
New Brunswick	63	908	249.1	28.8	136	1 208	149.7	18.5	37	185	36.0	3.8
Paramus Borough	167	2 785	2 943.1	157.9	623	13 648	2 438.3	249.3	60	575	139.4	18.1
Passaic	95	919	296.4	29.4	218	1 961	440.1	38.5	50	215	34.8	5.4
Paterson	211	2 804	1 105.6	104.4	382	2 513	409.3	48.1	77	419	45.6	9.9
Perth Amboy	62	871	514.8	32.8	152	1 302	215.5	21.8	20	109	15.6	2.6
Plainfield	35	381	97.9	11.3	122	813	136.3	16.0	31	123	18.4	2.8
Rahway	56	912	444.9	38.1	86	609	166.1	13.3	21	117	15.8	2.5
Sayreville Borough	48	335	117.6	12.0	104	1 673	243.0	24.8	23	98	17.7	1.9
Trenton	81	987	317.6	32.9	240	2 039	353.9	41.1	56	447	56.2	8.8
Union City	88	509	166.2	15.8	319	1 504	265.0	25.5	47	135	17.5	1.9
Vineland	123	1 184	542.7	38.8	308	3 680	643.8	69.6	79	362	41.9	7.1
Westfield	53	280	327.2	20.4	170	1 338	234.3	25.8	39	137	53.7	7.6
West New York	64	413	160.7	14.8	217	1 028	150.4	17.0	45	185	34.6	4.2
NEW MEXICO	2 182	21 344	7 397.6	601.1	7 421	86 300	14 984.5	1 455.5	1 887	8 844	893.9	165.2
Alamogordo	17	94	25.2	2.0	164	1 996	287.6	28.5	34	140	9.9	1.8
Albuquerque	919	10 636	3 630.1	330.3	2 004	30 720	5 914.6	568.7	677	4 251	480.0	80.6
Clovis	33	268	95.3	5.9	221	2 352	330.5	33.3	51	D	D	D
Farmington	115	1 002	276.8	28.5	359	4 854	806.9	79.0	62	403	29.4	14.0
Hobbs	85	708	253.8	20.6	175	1 914	336.1	34.8	38	279	34.3	8.2
Las Cruces	79	656	194.2	17.8	407	5 655	955.6	89.1	138	448	40.6	6.4
Rio Rancho	NA	NA	NA	NA	NA	NA	NA	NA	NA	NA	NA	NA
Roswell	61	514	196.9	12.0	243	2 542	384.3	37.7	72	D	D	D
Santa Fe	146	1 207	319.7	37.7	782	7 504	1 368.3	143.1	174	798	99.9	18.1
NEW YORK	37 499	414 249	319 697.6	17 185.8	75 241	805 208	139 303.9	14 329.8	27 214	145 326	27 770.1	4 447.8
Albany	164	2 401	1 438.6	90.4	492	6 830	1 074.2	113.2	124	1 000	142.7	22.4
Auburn	44	424	131.5	12.1	183	2 671	412.1	41.4	35	130	16.3	2.4
Binghamton	80	1 018	305.7	26.6	202	3 239	452.3	45.2	46	283	21.1	3.3
Buffalo	468	7 225	3 273.0	235.5	916	10 187	1 243.9	154.3	217	1 635	279.0	48.1
Elmira	46	552	136.6	15.1	119	1 685	234.8	23.8	24	D	D	D
Freeport	120	969	350.6	30.6	162	1 964	431.1	39.9	39	189	27.2	4.7
Hempstead	58	547	191.9	21.0	208	1 584	570.3	43.1	40	203	40.8	5.4
Ithaca	42	268	166.9	9.2	273	3 581	491.0	52.8	50	357	29.9	6.3
Jamestown	65	583	172.1	15.3	149	2 638	425.1	39.0	34	148	18.4	3.0
Lindenhurst	65	389	310.4	12.2	102	991	170.4	20.4	12	43	5.5	0.7
Long Beach	26	23	29.3	1.1	93	549	88.4	10.0	42	99	19.0	2.4
Mount Vernon	123	1 708	673.5	65.0	240	1 739	303.5	38.0	109	504	85.5	16.1
Newburgh	57	683	199.7	21.5	121	1 277	197.7	21.8	34	142	19.3	2.8
New Rochelle	147	1 221	614.1	55.8	256	2 581	609.4	51.0	146	552	80.6	11.1
New York	18 482	185 407	182 107.1	8 614.3	28 456	232 494	41 912.2	4 731.1	16 530	90 795	19 526.3	3 086.7
Niagara Falls	60	708	204.4	16.8	255	3 437	438.9	45.0	37	226	23.4	4.4
North Tonawanda	38	D	D	D	103	1 159	134.6	15.3	8	46	4.2	0.4
Poughkeepsie	50	D	D	D	172	1 475	195.6	23.7	49	490	28.6	6.5
Rochester	441	7 329	5 193.4	308.2	756	8 251	1 140.8	131.9	203	1 511	188.9	34.8
Rome	24	146	31.4	3.5	164	2 177	321.6	29.9	36	162	14.6	2.7
Saratoga Springs	28	294	188.3	8.8	183	2 348	375.0	35.9	35	128	13.1	2.0
Schenectady	57	1 060	425.5	41.3	235	2 169	338.4	35.5	27	118	11.7	2.1
Syracuse	262	3 569	1 529.4	124.9	708	8 860	1 346.8	147.4	167	2 595	172.7	59.6
Troy	55	482	201.7	13.5	168	2 258	330.2	34.3	39	166	20.3	3.7
Utica	94	1 341	448.8	37.7	218	2 461	346.5	36.0	54	193	26.0	3.4
Valley Stream	119	779	592.1	35.9	251	2 873	586.8	51.2	56	191	37.6	5.0
Watertown	52	554	168.3	15.4	273	3 743	519.4	52.6	44	222	27.2	3.5
White Plains	139	1 781	3 222.7	127.4	497	6 946	1 176.7	133.4	179	641	167.5	21.0
Yonkers	228	2 460	1 037.6	84.2	620	8 171	1 533.4	144.8	336	1 106	227.8	29.4
NORTH CAROLINA	12 284	157 774	98 080.1	5 574.1	35 563	416 287	72 356.8	6 697.4	7 346	39 349	5 026.0	900.6
Asheville	211	2 134	777.0	64.8	794	10 637	1 762.0	170.8	149	829	107.1	17.9
Burlington	89	1 080	332.4	35.6	419	5 403	829.4	82.3	58	292	60.6	5.7
Cary	132	1 260	1 728.9	57.9	410	7 311	1 218.3	108.2	99	397	74.4	12.8
Chapel Hill	33	123	254.9	5.2	223	3 347	480.6	58.4	83	D	D	D
Charlotte	2 150	32 325	30 244.7	1 319.9	2 306	35 463	6 830.3	662.5	859	8 677	1 285.6	272.3

1. Establishments with payroll.

City	Professional, Scientific, and Technical Services, 1997[1]				Manufacturing, 1997				Accommodation and Foodservices, 1997			
	Number of Establishments	Number of Employees	Receipts (mil dol)	Annual Payroll (mil dol)	Number of Establishments	Number of Employees	Receipts (mil dol)	Annual Payroll (mil dol)	Number of Establishments	Number of Employees	Sales (mil dol)	Annual Payroll (mil dol)
	84	85	86	87	88	89	90	91	92	93	94	95
NEW JERSEY—Cont'd												
Hackensack	512	3 354	367.9	142.3	140	2 551	391.7	85.2	108	D	D	D
Hoboken	146	871	126.0	53.6	69	1 655	311.0	47.5	132	1 150	46.9	12.6
Jersey City	353	3 553	522.8	184.9	190	5 770	1 039.2	179.8	345	2 789	121.3	32.5
Kearny	58	199	17.9	5.4	69	2 068	361.9	62.7	74	D	D	D
Linden	53	318	20.9	9.5	164	8 202	6 332.5	364.1	103	987	39.2	11.1
Long Branch	36	109	8.7	3.3	24	505	58.5	15.2	77	941	39.2	12.5
Millville	38	112	8.5	2.7	52	4 684	609.5	154.4	44	408	14.3	3.8
Newark	281	4 559	722.5	245.1	439	14 960	3 353.1	491.9	454	5 346	335.0	88.5
New Brunswick	127	634	74.6	29.6	78	2 689	689.9	114.0	131	1 614	67.3	19.5
Paramus Borough	211	2 181	273.1	115.2	32	1 541	238.2	70.8	128	2 306	98.4	25.4
Passaic	49	344	26.7	11.1	144	4 687	433.2	108.6	68	418	19.3	4.4
Paterson	75	477	34.7	11.7	340	8 436	1 748.4	277.2	154	861	39.9	10.3
Perth Amboy	35	146	11.7	3.9	53	2 408	865.6	85.9	71	448	18.9	3.8
Plainfield	40	247	21.5	8.7	42	1 128	154.9	30.9	46	D	D	D
Rahway	35	270	22.0	13.9	68	3 316	1 153.8	167.4	66	572	24.5	6.3
Sayreville Borough	71	217	19.7	10.8	24	2 272	860.7	101.2	45	414	15.5	3.8
Trenton	109	730	83.2	40.4	89	2 790	370.8	104.7	187	1 131	51.8	13.3
Union City	78	207	18.8	5.3	133	1 563	102.3	29.4	143	D	D	D
Vineland	112	718	64.1	24.5	105	6 223	913.0	186.9	100	1 531	44.8	12.3
Westfield	191	1 086	119.2	47.5	NA	NA	NA	NA	64	D	D	D
West New York	63	168	18.9	6.7	172	1 970	142.2	34.3	66	502	17.5	4.2
NEW MEXICO	3 702	31 535	3 243.4	1 307.3	1 593	39 664	17 906.1	1 135.8	3 825	67 134	2 144.9	599.1
Alamogordo	45	187	8.3	3.2	18	562	92.1	10.1	73	1 068	29.3	7.7
Albuquerque	1 746	D	D	D	592	D	D	D	1 082	24 747	813.2	228.8
Clovis	60	210	11.6	4.4	NA	NA	NA	NA	79	1 605	45.7	13.0
Farmington	125	768	42.8	17.2	47	695	74.1	16.9	121	2 783	79.8	21.7
Hobbs	51	283	17.1	7.3	NA	NA	NA	NA	78	1 152	33.5	8.9
Las Cruces	184	970	66.1	27.1	65	1 433	253.4	28.6	208	3 396	103.2	27.2
Rio Rancho	NA	NA	NA	NA	30	D	D	D	NA	NA	NA	NA
Roswell	84	456	37.3	13.6	40	D	D	D	106	1 859	51.5	13.7
Santa Fe	408	1 864	194.8	81.9	136	1 155	95.2	23.7	329	7 045	288.9	84.5
NEW YORK	45 619	416 892	57 475.0	21 773.1	23 908	785 891	146 720.2	26 515.8	38 045	473 327	21 671.1	6 101.1
Albany	377	3 579	433.5	151.9	86	1 933	420.5	62.6	365	4 395	152.2	41.1
Auburn	61	458	32.0	14.0	64	3 087	556.3	92.6	94	1 266	34.3	10.0
Binghamton	138	909	76.2	26.3	79	5 994	1 266.4	199.6	157	2 278	64.8	18.9
Buffalo	592	5 811	608.6	217.4	466	20 307	4 527.2	748.4	678	8 280	252.3	70.5
Elmira	58	411	37.8	11.0	30	2 531	334.5	70.3	80	D	D	D
Freeport	98	345	33.5	13.2	122	3 330	392.4	92.7	71	586	27.2	8.1
Hempstead	88	633	56.1	18.5	38	674	84.1	20.3	53	709	30.8	8.1
Ithaca	137	1 215	111.1	42.5	61	2 775	515.3	97.0	213	2 718	81.3	23.3
Jamestown	75	394	27.9	10.8	83	5 056	666.9	150.2	96	897	26.1	6.9
Lindenhurst	42	168	13.5	4.9	68	802	82.0	20.5	65	684	24.8	6.2
Long Beach	50	122	16.8	5.8	NA	NA	NA	NA	43	269	12.5	3.2
Mount Vernon	80	313	34.5	10.1	147	4 405	602.1	142.3	63	376	15.8	3.9
Newburgh	57	578	86.7	26.2	48	1 467	116.9	28.5	62	D	D	D
New Rochelle	175	1 416	61.5	22.9	61	1 167	138.5	36.8	123	D	D	D
New York	19 790	249 961	40 075.3	15 355.4	10 569	207 975	27 735.8	5 504.1	13 726	182 381	11 000.4	3 119.7
Niagara Falls	79	320	32.0	8.2	69	3 942	1 234.0	183.7	221	3 253	104.6	28.4
North Tonawanda	37	150	9.2	3.9	61	2 131	522.2	72.6	60	477	12.4	3.3
Poughkeepsie	121	858	91.1	36.9	38	D	D	D	91	894	39.8	9.7
Rochester	718	6 970	706.4	277.6	533	51 405	12 269.7	2 218.8	516	6 498	222.5	63.9
Rome	55	467	51.0	16.2	49	2 278	547.5	72.9	85	957	28.2	7.9
Saratoga Springs	97	508	26.9	8.8	28	1 782	374.0	59.5	121	2 107	87.7	26.4
Schenectady	130	1 112	136.9	44.9	66	3 401	1 302.9	154.9	182	1 453	51.5	14.3
Syracuse	486	5 183	484.7	185.4	163	10 193	1 958.1	409.5	414	5 253	167.9	50.7
Troy	102	946	70.3	29.9	41	1 727	196.9	53.2	127	1 590	46.1	13.6
Utica	157	1 046	75.2	27.0	102	4 095	509.2	118.7	149	1 625	50.4	14.1
Valley Stream	139	781	73.2	32.6	NA	NA	NA	NA	89	1 133	41.7	10.4
Watertown	65	452	27.1	13.0	41	1 855	279.9	56.0	122	1 642	57.2	15.1
White Plains	579	3 165	450.5	169.2	NA	NA	NA	NA	180	2 103	113.8	29.2
Yonkers	217	948	96.3	30.3	131	4 074	742.6	132.6	249	2 103	102.2	25.2
NORTH CAROLINA	14 351	101 610	9 760.9	3 693.5	11 306	773 548	161 900.5	21 297.9	14 579	262 848	8 625.0	2 393.2
Asheville	353	2 115	152.3	70.5	142	6 168	1 405.3	164.7	356	7 242	268.0	81.4
Burlington	91	475	36.6	16.3	110	8 811	1 435.6	208.6	151	3 553	103.7	28.3
Cary	385	2 538	309.3	135.9	65	2 767	384.7	89.3	187	3 765	132.8	37.5
Chapel Hill	228	1 541	128.5	55.1	NA	NA	NA	NA	211	3 566	130.1	38.0
Charlotte	1 958	23 207	2 648.9	1 044.1	787	31 811	6 504.0	1 058.5	1 277	27 598	1 008.7	279.1

1. Firms subject to federal tax.

City	Arts, Entertainment, and Recreation[1], 1997				Health Care and Social Assistance[1], 1997				Other Services[1], 1997			
	Number of Establish-ments	Number of Employees	Receipts (mil dol)	Annual Payroll (mil dol)	Number of Establish-ments	Number of Employees	Receipts (mil dol)	Annual Payroll (mil dol)	Number of Establish-ments	Number of Employees	Receipts (mil dol)	Annual Payroll (mil dol)
	96	97	98	99	100	101	102	103	104	105	106	107
NEW JERSEY—Cont'd												
Hackensack	12	149	16.9	3.3	250	2 583	233.5	113.0	157	1 230	84.2	27.6
Hoboken	13	78	3.6	1.0	80	389	42.3	14.4	75	238	15.3	4.2
Jersey City	27	227	17.4	6.6	329	2 776	214.8	89.8	303	2 357	114.2	32.8
Kearny	2	0	0.0	0.0	62	266	19.6	8.4	80	245	15.3	4.1
Linden	3	0	0.0	0.0	54	543	38.4	15.0	113	699	60.2	19.5
Long Branch	7	41	2.8	0.8	88	650	61.3	29.2	63	287	16.3	5.0
Millville	2	0	0.0	0.0	41	452	32.1	13.0	40	270	14.2	4.8
Newark	5	59	2.2	0.6	310	2 971	198.3	91.9	400	2 826	185.4	60.6
New Brunswick	2	0	0.0	0.0	94	1 271	241.9	64.0	66	433	20.5	6.7
Paramus Borough	17	304	9.7	2.7	137	1 230	102.1	40.2	68	893	60.0	21.7
Passaic	4	9	1.4	0.2	82	718	55.5	24.5	73	395	24.9	8.4
Paterson	5	12	1.4	0.3	157	800	78.2	36.4	193	1 182	83.5	28.1
Perth Amboy	2	0	0.0	0.0	66	794	52.8	21.8	75	399	29.3	9.3
Plainfield	1	0	0.0	0.0	69	668	53.3	23.2	48	192	13.8	4.5
Rahway	4	0	0.0	0.0	41	281	28.7	16.5	62	251	22.8	7.2
Sayreville Borough	3	0	0.0	0.0	49	481	30.0	12.2	52	260	13.4	3.9
Trenton	3	0	0.0	0.0	100	1 298	83.0	40.6	102	552	40.6	11.0
Union City	7	22	2.8	0.6	136	1 186	59.7	24.7	106	341	20.5	5.5
Vineland	8	56	2.2	0.5	130	1 081	81.3	37.9	140	647	34.2	11.8
Westfield	5	13	1.4	0.3	151	1 423	106.3	50.4	80	426	24.4	8.4
West New York	6	15	3.8	1.2	75	493	31.3	11.6	71	227	12.1	3.0
NEW MEXICO	440	8 679	520.4	115.4	2 923	32 824	2 057.3	864.3	2 318	13 448	759.1	227.2
Alamogordo	10	80	1.4	0.5	61	491	27.0	11.6	46	215	10.3	2.7
Albuquerque	121	2 980	150.1	39.2	1 073	15 510	1 085.5	450.0	788	6 073	339.0	111.0
Clovis	10	0	0.0	0.0	94	0	0.0	0.0	67	302	15.5	4.2
Farmington	10	108	2.3	0.7	143	1 122	75.4	34.5	122	900	54.6	15.6
Hobbs	9	0	0.0	0.0	68	966	64.5	20.3	68	432	34.4	9.7
Las Cruces	17	134	7.0	1.9	246	2 587	157.4	65.5	132	688	33.4	9.5
Rio Rancho	NA	NA	NA	NA	NA	NA	NA	NA	NA	NA	NA	NA
Roswell	5	46	1.4	0.3	112	772	44.8	21.3	67	309	17.4	4.6
Santa Fe	67	878	136.9	16.3	286	2 785	161.9	73.3	159	825	52.0	15.1
NEW YORK	7 311	77 057	7 029.0	2 284.6	36 054	358 075	26 008.3	10 970.9	30 104	146 365	10 014.6	2 858.7
Albany	23	600	11.9	5.0	239	3 154	263.9	134.2	147	1 060	98.5	27.8
Auburn	16	98	4.9	1.4	119	879	56.2	23.9	55	313	24.5	5.6
Binghamton	14	254	9.3	1.6	145	1 672	100.6	47.0	89	452	27.2	8.4
Buffalo	55	1 170	68.7	40.9	436	7 567	431.0	218.8	440	2 527	155.8	47.1
Elmira	4	28	2.2	0.6	92	813	70.5	36.2	37	195	16.3	4.1
Freeport	17	46	5.1	1.1	85	804	66.2	23.3	95	343	29.3	7.7
Hempstead	9	0	0.0	0.0	109	3 294	167.8	75.5	91	1 284	72.7	26.9
Ithaca	20	210	6.6	2.0	95	681	52.1	21.5	62	382	20.6	5.7
Jamestown	8	56	2.8	0.7	114	1 335	61.6	29.7	55	256	18.8	4.5
Lindenhurst	9	0	0.0	0.0	44	259	21.6	8.9	92	345	28.6	7.7
Long Beach	11	104	5.3	1.8	104	1 180	85.0	32.1	51	203	9.4	2.7
Mount Vernon	13	43	4.9	1.9	109	951	53.8	22.3	133	674	48.7	15.7
Newburgh	3	0	0.0	0.0	80	822	52.9	24.8	49	194	14.3	4.1
New Rochelle	34	580	32.2	8.5	202	1 459	125.3	51.5	141	508	38.0	9.9
New York	3 332	32 475	4 458.9	1 527.7	13 210	125 076	9 746.8	3 988.2	11 623	56 487	3 779.9	1 088.6
Niagara Falls	9	108	3.5	0.9	101	1 341	49.7	21.4	81	329	19.7	5.1
North Tonawanda	11	100	3.5	0.8	54	214	13.4	5.3	57	186	12.5	3.4
Poughkeepsie	13	149	6.0	1.8	126	1 365	102.7	45.7	70	273	21.4	4.8
Rochester	53	703	40.8	10.2	396	6 278	415.2	186.7	387	2 530	184.8	55.0
Rome	13	48	1.9	0.5	87	1 003	57.0	27.7	50	237	13.7	3.7
Saratoga Springs	14	0	0.0	0.0	85	882	64.1	25.9	46	224	12.5	3.2
Schenectady	13	0	0.0	0.0	171	2 027	127.2	60.1	113	798	54.6	15.1
Syracuse	28	290	18.9	3.6	356	4 374	375.4	196.5	260	1 995	129.8	42.1
Troy	14	50	2.9	0.4	152	1 924	110.4	49.4	75	367	25.3	6.8
Utica	10	79	2.9	0.6	172	1 534	119.3	50.0	98	713	33.5	10.7
Valley Stream	12	33	6.7	2.7	113	749	67.4	26.9	119	998	37.6	13.0
Watertown	13	97	3.9	1.0	100	888	67.8	37.6	59	323	21.3	6.2
White Plains	28	231	22.2	7.6	327	3 565	283.3	139.9	115	735	48.8	15.1
Yonkers	32	536	49.1	10.5	375	3 612	261.6	107.8	278	961	64.7	18.6
NORTH CAROLINA	2 090	23 481	1 632.6	470.5	12 582	173 770	10 708.8	4 859.6	11 483	64 802	4 060.6	1 204.0
Asheville	38	788	51.3	15.6	366	4 785	376.6	192.9	214	1 324	78.2	25.6
Burlington	11	114	3.8	1.1	143	3 022	261.9	94.6	109	744	38.7	12.5
Cary	25	472	22.1	7.0	206	2 223	138.9	62.2	151	1 114	76.4	22.9
Chapel Hill	20	165	5.1	1.4	157	1 694	98.5	48.5	65	429	20.2	7.0
Charlotte	154	1 896	341.5	123.0	1 001	15 218	1 208.9	543.4	1 045	8 575	557.9	177.1

1. Firms subject to federal tax.

Table D. Cities — Federal Funds and City Government Finances

	Selected federal funds, fiscal 1999[1] (mil dol)									City government finances, 1997						
	Procurement contracts		Grants					Direct payments for individuals		General revenue						
										Intergovernmental			Taxes			
														Per capita[3] (dollars)		
City	Defense	Other	Total[2]	Health and family welfare	Energy and environment	Education	Housing and community development	Educational assistance	Housing assistance	Total (mil dol)	Total (mil dol)	Percent from state government	Total (mil dol)	Total	Property	Sales and gross receipts
	108	109	110	111	112	113	114	115	116	117	118	119	120	121	122	123
NEW JERSEY—Cont'd																
Hackensack	0.3	0.1	18.3	3.5	0.0	0.3	13.8	0.5	4.1	51.9	11.9	74.5	34.2	912	893	0
Hoboken	3.1	0.3	10.7	1.7	0.2	0.8	5.0	1.8	0.0	67.0	24.3	70.9	20.2	610	587	8
Jersey City	0.8	1.7	37.3	11.5	0.5	2.3	21.8	13.1	25.1	404.1	197.3	75.8	117.0	511	491	0
Kearny	0.4	0.0	0.2	0.0	0.0	0.0	0.0	0.0	0.0	55.9	29.3	98.7	21.8	620	614	0
Linden	0.4	0.4	1.5	0.0	0.0	0.0	0.1	0.0	2.6	56.3	28.2	99.8	22.3	605	600	0
Long Branch	15.5	0.0	1.2	0.0	0.0	0.0	0.9	0.0	0.0	58.4	21.2	70.9	17.7	610	587	8
Millville	0.0	0.0	0.5	0.0	0.0	0.0	0.4	0.0	6.0	23.6	10.0	99.3	8.3	315	299	0
Newark	26.1	19.6	603.7	69.1	1.0	6.8	54.1	7.0	58.8	522.8	233.2	74.0	151.8	565	416	39
New Brunswick	6.0	5.0	99.1	37.3	1.8	5.3	4.7	24.9	0.1	103.6	49.1	82.4	39.4	949	873	50
Paramus Borough	0.3	1.2	2.0	0.0	0.0	0.0	0.0	4.3	0.0	36.3	7.1	96.4	20.1	786	734	0
Passaic	1.5	0.0	10.4	1.3	4.3	0.0	4.4	0.0	0.3	57.9	28.2	38.1	21.4	376	364	0
Paterson	1.5	9.7	24.4	12.4	0.0	0.6	6.7	4.6	15.4	156.1	67.3	67.9	67.4	449	449	0
Perth Amboy	0.0	0.7	1.7	0.0	0.0	0.3	1.3	0.2	0.0	46.2	19.2	73.2	17.3	409	401	0
Plainfield	0.3	0.6	4.4	3.0	0.0	0.4	0.4	0.2	0.2	46.3	12.9	95.7	24.9	538	534	0
Rahway	0.3	0.2	1.7	0.0	0.8	0.0	0.1	0.0	-1.4	29.8	10.8	91.5	13.7	543	543	0
Sayreville Borough	0.1	0.0	0.4	0.0	0.0	0.0	0.2	0.0	0.0	27.3	17.2	100.0	6.1	163	142	0
Trenton	18.5	22.4	1 012.6	318.3	79.6	166.0	24.0	2.9	8.0	297.2	191.0	93.3	76.4	894	869	0
Union City	0.4	0.0	4.7	0.0	0.0	0.4	1.5	0.0	0.0	146.5	90.8	98.8	47.0	822	817	0
Vineland	14.2	0.3	6.9	0.0	0.7	0.4	1.4	1.8	5.1	42.5	21.6	92.6	14.1	252	247	0
Westfield	0.0	0.1	0.1	0.0	0.0	0.0	0.0	0.0	-0.4	20.2	4.2	97.4	11.4	390	370	0
West New York	0.1	0.0	5.1	3.6	0.0	0.0	0.2	0.2	0.0	94.7	50.6	96.3	36.2	961	953	0
NEW MEXICO	615.0	3 316.0	2 750.0	1 269.6	122.9	344.3	44.1	55.3	52.4	X	X	X	X	X	X	X
Alamogordo	15.1	0.1	3.5	0.5	0.0	2.4	0.2	0.1	0.0	23.1	7.6	88.6	8.7	301	67	222
Albuquerque	269.5	1 602.8	248.9	65.6	23.6	12.5	12.8	14.7	15.8	618.3	220.5	73.8	168.4	401	148	232
Clovis	0.2	0.0	2.1	0.0	0.0	0.7	0.6	1.6	2.1	19.9	6.3	94.8	8.5	246	16	227
Farmington	0.0	6.2	2.4	0.0	0.0	1.4	0.0	2.3	2.2	78.0	14.6	97.2	16.1	423	18	388
Hobbs	0.0	0.2	2.9	1.6	0.1	1.0	0.0	1.4	4.2	30.0	13.3	96.2	9.8	350	32	316
Las Cruces	32.6	29.4	40.7	8.5	6.6	3.2	1.8	9.7	4.6	49.6	6.4	73.7	21.6	288	48	233
Rio Rancho	0.0	2.9	0.0	0.0	0.0	0.0	0.0	0.0	0.0	27.5	3.6	100.0	13.7	NA	NA	NA
Roswell	0.2	5.6	1.5	0.0	0.2	1.0	0.0	0.4	1.6	33.1	10.7	87.1	12.3	258	40	213
Santa Fe	1.7	3.8	394.2	104.7	72.8	58.2	21.4	3.4	4.8	102.8	35.6	81.2	35.7	537	18	483
NEW YORK	3 217.6	3 555.2	28 869.9	20 476.1	362.9	1 870.1	927.8	936.4	624.4	X	X	X	X	X	X	X
Albany	5.3	37.2	3 029.4	1 131.1	236.2	469.7	32.0	114.8	5.3	125.1	53.5	31.8	39.5	381	339	23
Auburn	0.8	0.1	8.7	1.4	0.5	1.9	1.3	1.8	0.6	32.3	12.1	40.1	8.8	296	261	25
Binghamton	46.3	2.5	24.4	6.9	7.1	0.5	3.5	1.3	4.5	51.3	24.1	33.6	18.8	389	365	18
Buffalo	62.9	22.4	146.0	66.7	1.2	5.9	32.5	12.7	24.4	836.8	562.3	75.1	117.3	378	304	53
Elmira	1.0	0.0	5.9	2.1	0.0	0.0	2.0	1.3	6.0	28.5	12.5	37.2	8.6	269	241	21
Freeport	0.7	0.1	2.6	0.5	0.0	1.4	0.3	0.0	0.0	29.3	1.8	71.8	17.6	438	417	7
Hempstead	0.0	1.1	7.3	5.3	0.1	0.6	0.0	0.0	7.0	37.4	6.9	36.0	26.8	575	551	13
Ithaca	6.2	2.6	153.4	39.1	4.7	2.8	2.3	11.8	1.1	36.2	9.7	47.1	15.4	540	260	267
Jamestown	17.6	1.4	4.3	0.0	0.0	0.3	1.8	1.7	0.0	47.6	19.1	67.9	10.4	314	297	9
Lindenhurst	1.6	0.1	0.0	0.0	0.0	0.0	0.0	0.0	0.0	8.9	1.0	82.3	5.7	215	193	12
Long Beach	0.1	0.1	0.6	0.0	0.0	0.2	0.2	0.2	2.6	44.1	11.3	34.8	21.0	611	562	27
Mount Vernon	2.0	0.0	6.9	3.4	0.0	0.3	2.8	0.1	3.2	59.2	17.2	56.4	34.5	514	351	140
Newburgh	1.2	0.8	12.4	2.6	0.0	0.5	1.2	0.8	2.7	30.5	12.9	33.7	9.8	374	319	41
New Rochelle	0.5	0.2	8.2	0.7	0.0	3.0	4.1	0.8	1.1	83.2	24.8	41.7	47.5	706	450	226
New York	457.5	2 079.5	15 816.1	12 564.6	18.8	663.9	639.6	381.3	402.9	43 756.2	16 752.9	84.1	19 368.2	2 624	1 001	544
Niagara Falls	9.3	0.4	6.5	0.1	0.0	0.1	4.7	0.1	2.4	95.3	33.2	54.3	28.4	487	342	133
North Tonawanda	2.4	0.3	0.3	0.0	0.0	0.0	0.1	0.0	0.1	31.6	11.1	35.7	14.5	430	343	75
Poughkeepsie	0.1	0.7	8.6	1.6	0.0	0.8	4.5	5.4	7.5	41.6	17.5	29.0	11.8	426	396	18
Rochester	83.8	20.8	267.6	110.4	33.8	51.4	24.1	17.0	12.4	640.5	400.3	73.8	152.9	690	616	61
Rome	58.0	0.1	4.4	0.0	0.0	0.0	1.9	0.0	0.3	47.1	19.2	51.8	18.9	462	286	168
Saratoga Springs	1.0	0.2	1.9	0.0	0.3	0.1	1.2	1.3	0.0	26.0	11.5	24.3	8.6	344	279	31
Schenectady	313.7	8.5	34.1	3.3	23.3	0.2	5.0	2.4	2.9	64.9	30.5	29.0	20.2	321	282	25
Syracuse	214.6	23.9	85.8	31.1	3.4	2.1	18.5	13.9	10.7	353.0	260.6	74.7	31.5	202	164	20
Troy	4.3	0.8	30.2	4.8	2.7	0.5	2.5	5.5	2.9	62.9	40.5	25.0	16.1	306	275	17
Utica	12.0	1.3	15.5	6.2	0.3	0.2	5.2	4.4	2.6	62.3	23.5	43.7	25.9	422	241	174
Valley Stream	0.1	0.4	0.0	0.0	0.0	0.0	0.1	0.0	0.0	18.4	1.0	78.2	15.2	446	414	16
Watertown	0.5	0.5	6.3	1.4	0.2	0.1	2.9	1.4	3.7	33.7	17.3	19.8	8.5	295	265	20
White Plains	106.9	1.5	26.3	8.5	0.3	0.3	12.0	2.0	1.4	102.7	11.0	50.1	64.7	1 303	600	650
Yonkers	20.4	0.6	19.3	1.7	0.5	5.0	12.1	0.0	9.6	450.4	172.2	93.5	242.7	1 275	846	230
NORTH CAROLINA	1 045.5	1 004.3	7 608.0	4 842.2	98.1	599.1	125.9	146.7	96.2	X	X	X	X	X	X	X
Asheville	9.5	37.4	13.3	4.4	0.5	0.5	2.4	1.7	3.2	71.8	24.9	37.0	24.6	384	339	8
Burlington	3.1	0.1	0.6	0.0	0.0	0.0	0.6	0.0	5.0	38.5	11.7	49.1	11.3	279	256	4
Cary	6.0	11.1	3.8	0.2	0.0	0.0	0.0	0.0	0.0	77.8	15.4	36.8	33.8	447	387	12
Chapel Hill	0.8	20.0	226.0	195.8	1.9	2.0	1.1	0.0	0.2	38.9	16.9	28.3	15.5	351	313	20
Charlotte	32.8	35.3	88.3	19.1	1.8	8.1	13.5	8.6	6.6	718.1	179.2	35.9	207.7	471	360	78

1. October 1, 1998 to September 30, 1999.   2. Includes program categories not shown separately. State totals include additional categories not allocated by city.   3. Based on population estimated as of July 1 of the year shown.

City	City government finances, 1997 (cont'd) General expenditure												
	Per capita[1] (dollars)			Percent of total for —									
	Total (mil dol)	Total	Capital outlays	Public welfare	Highways	Parking facilities	Education	Health and hospitals	Police protection	Sewerage and sanitation	Parks and recreation	Housing and community develop-ment	Interest on debt
	124	125	126	127	128	129	130	131	132	133	134	135	136
NEW JERSEY—Cont'd													
Hackensack	47.3	1 264	101	0.3	3.2	1.5	0.0	1.7	17.7	17.2	2.0	6.7	3.4
Hoboken	58.5	1 767	87	2.0	1.1	3.1	0.0	1.1	15.6	6.3	1.5	14.3	9.0
Jersey City	329.1	1 437	144	1.2	4.6	0.9	0.0	1.8	12.4	12.7	3.0	22.4	7.1
Kearny	38.9	1 109	0	0.5	4.5	0.0	0.0	1.7	21.4	6.3	2.3	0.0	10.3
Linden	45.1	1 224	85	0.2	7.5	0.5	0.0	1.4	19.0	11.3	6.3	0.1	2.6
Long Branch	46.9	1 621	87	2.1	1.2	3.4	0.0	1.2	17.0	6.8	1.6	15.5	0.8
Millville	15.8	598	96	2.5	10.5	0.0	0.0	1.7	15.6	27.9	4.8	0.0	0.7
Newark	492.5	1 834	82	9.9	1.8	0.3	0.0	3.6	16.9	11.0	2.1	14.3	1.8
New Brunswick	105.0	2 528	154	1.1	1.1	7.2	52.5	0.3	9.1	5.5	0.9	9.2	0.4
Paramus Borough	32.6	1 276	139	0.2	4.2	0.0	4.1	1.3	28.3	18.3	6.1	1.7	3.6
Passaic	57.1	1 000	98	0.4	2.9	0.0	0.0	2.0	11.6	12.4	0.4	30.2	4.3
Paterson	156.2	1 040	52	9.4	4.9	1.4	0.0	1.3	18.7	16.5	1.4	4.9	3.9
Perth Amboy	45.3	1 072	146	2.1	2.7	1.0	0.0	0.8	19.7	27.4	2.7	2.8	6.4
Plainfield	42.7	924	61	9.8	7.6	0.3	0.0	1.6	21.1	5.0	1.2	0.5	1.9
Rahway	26.6	1 053	105	0.0	12.1	0.0	0.0	3.3	22.2	11.8	1.6	0.7	4.1
Sayreville Borough	24.7	662	21	0.2	4.5	0.0	0.0	0.7	27.3	17.4	3.5	0.0	7.1
Trenton	294.4	3 446	197	1.3	0.8	0.4	48.2	0.9	9.5	6.3	1.1	8.3	1.6
Union City	141.0	2 468	134	0.5	0.7	0.5	61.1	0.5	8.1	3.4	0.8	2.0	2.9
Vineland	42.5	761	51	2.9	13.3	0.0	0.0	8.5	16.3	1.1	1.5	8.0	1.9
Westfield	22.9	787	0	0.3	6.2	0.0	0.0	1.5	20.3	8.9	4.4	0.0	0.6
West New York	98.8	2 621	133	0.3	1.6	0.0	56.6	0.6	7.5	4.6	0.5	3.6	4.8
NEW MEXICO	X	X	X	X	X	X	X	X	X	X	X	X	X
Alamogordo	23.4	806	246	0.0	14.3	0.0	0.0	0.8	17.1	14.7	18.3	2.5	3.3
Albuquerque	623.2	1 485	409	0.5	8.2	0.5	0.0	1.5	12.7	12.1	14.3	4.2	8.6
Clovis	21.2	612	130	0.0	13.9	0.0	0.0	6.1	19.4	18.6	6.4	0.0	5.9
Farmington	80.9	2 131	253	0.0	9.6	0.0	0.0	0.1	8.4	8.1	11.2	0.0	41.0
Hobbs	28.9	1 033	224	0.3	16.1	0.0	0.0	1.1	29.0	10.4	5.6	0.0	4.1
Las Cruces	63.2	844	118	0.0	14.5	0.0	0.0	0.1	12.5	14.1	11.1	3.2	12.2
Rio Rancho	27.8	NA	NA	0.0	18.9	0.0	0.0	0.0	29.3	12.6	10.0	0.0	4.8
Roswell	25.7	541	87	0.0	15.3	1.1	0.0	0.1	18.7	17.3	6.4	0.0	0.4
Santa Fe	116.6	1 753	476	7.1	14.9	2.1	0.0	0.0	8.6	16.1	12.9	5.0	7.0
NEW YORK	X	X	X	X	X	X	X	X	X	X	X	X	X
Albany	117.4	1 134	46	0.0	6.4	1.0	0.0	0.1	20.2	9.3	5.4	2.3	15.6
Auburn	39.9	1 340	325	0.0	8.2	0.4	0.0	0.0	8.6	30.2	3.4	5.2	14.7
Binghamton	52.3	1 082	160	2.2	9.3	1.0	0.0	0.1	13.5	15.2	4.7	6.4	3.9
Buffalo	931.0	2 998	149	0.0	3.6	0.3	47.7	0.2	6.1	4.7	0.6	3.9	4.0
Elmira	29.5	921	163	0.0	9.9	1.2	0.0	0.0	14.5	3.7	4.1	16.2	4.4
Freeport	34.7	865	94	0.0	6.9	0.1	0.0	0.0	26.7	9.7	6.6	1.5	5.1
Hempstead	47.2	1 013	109	0.0	7.6	0.4	0.0	0.0	21.8	5.2	4.0	13.0	3.1
Ithaca	34.4	1 206	87	0.0	7.9	0.9	0.0	0.0	14.0	13.0	11.4	5.5	8.0
Jamestown	54.4	1 642	101	0.0	4.3	0.1	45.1	0.0	7.0	7.7	2.6	4.0	6.8
Lindenhurst	9.0	339	21	0.0	15.3	0.6	0.0	0.0	0.0	9.7	6.3	0.0	2.4
Long Beach	50.7	1 476	403	0.1	8.3	0.1	0.0	0.0	19.7	13.6	7.3	0.4	7.5
Mount Vernon	57.5	857	55	8.6	2.5	0.0	0.0	1.2	18.6	6.8	2.8	5.4	3.9
Newburgh	29.8	1 134	81	5.5	7.2	0.2	0.0	0.0	19.9	14.5	2.8	6.3	8.5
New Rochelle	92.7	1 377	150	0.6	5.1	0.6	0.0	1.3	16.4	4.4	4.4	3.9	11.3
New York	41 433.6	5 614	873	18.0	1.7	0.0	22.8	9.8	6.9	5.3	1.5	6.8	4.6
Niagara Falls	97.3	1 667	85	3.7	3.8	0.5	0.0	0.1	10.8	15.7	8.6	3.0	16.9
North Tonawanda	32.6	965	89	0.0	10.2	0.0	0.0	0.1	10.6	18.2	8.4	1.5	8.3
Poughkeepsie	36.3	1 305	142	7.8	5.2	1.4	0.0	0.1	15.9	15.6	2.0	2.7	6.6
Rochester	674.1	3 042	287	0.3	3.0	0.3	55.7	0.0	6.8	2.6	3.4	3.5	3.6
Rome	45.3	1 105	155	0.0	13.7	0.8	0.0	0.1	9.9	11.8	2.4	12.7	11.5
Saratoga Springs	27.6	1 100	145	0.0	8.9	0.0	0.0	0.2	13.2	14.5	10.2	8.2	1.9
Schenectady	66.6	1 058	197	0.0	9.2	0.7	0.0	0.0	14.5	17.6	3.5	9.8	7.1
Syracuse	391.4	2 511	91	0.0	4.0	1.4	54.4	0.0	6.4	2.3	0.7	2.7	7.6
Troy	65.7	1 251	49	0.0	4.4	0.5	0.0	0.2	11.2	5.7	1.8	33.9	10.7
Utica	75.2	1 225	125	3.2	4.1	0.6	0.0	0.0	11.6	6.9	3.1	6.1	9.3
Valley Stream	18.9	553	31	0.0	14.2	0.6	0.0	0.1	0.9	21.3	9.8	0.0	4.4
Watertown	32.2	1 123	115	0.0	10.5	0.2	0.0	0.0	12.5	9.4	4.0	5.7	15.8
White Plains	94.3	1 900	122	4.4	6.6	7.3	0.0	0.0	18.9	7.2	5.5	2.1	7.5
Yonkers	476.5	2 504	179	0.0	3.1	0.5	52.2	0.0	8.6	2.1	1.2	0.0	3.4
NORTH CAROLINA	X	X	X	X	X	X	X	X	X	X	X	X	X
Asheville	63.6	993	102	0.0	12.5	0.9	0.0	0.1	16.6	15.8	10.6	5.8	3.6
Burlington	33.9	839	87	0.0	8.3	0.0	0.0	1.1	18.4	27.4	14.0	1.3	2.6
Cary	44.4	587	87	0.0	5.2	0.0	0.0	0.0	11.4	22.4	8.7	0.0	3.7
Chapel Hill	31.8	718	77	0.0	5.4	5.2	0.0	0.0	19.4	8.2	4.8	8.6	5.1
Charlotte	527.2	1 195	239	0.3	9.1	0.1	0.0	0.5	16.7	10.2	5.3	3.8	14.7

1. Based on population estimated as of July 1 of the year shown.

Table D. Cities — City Government Finances, City Government Employment, and Climate

City	City government finances, 1997 (cont'd) Debt outstanding — Total (mil dol)	Per capita[1] (dollars)	Percent utility	City government employment, 1999	Climate[2] — Average daily temperature (degrees Fahrenheit) Mean January	Mean July	Limits January[3]	Limits July[4]	Annual precipitation (inches)	Heating degree days	Cooling degree days
	137	138	139	140	141	142	143	144	145	146	147
NEW JERSEY—Cont'd											
Hackensack	25.4	677	0.0	462	28.3	74.9	19.4	85.9	49.79	5 486	838
Hoboken	81.4	2 456	0.2	598	29.5	74.9	23.3	82.2	43.50	5 362	874
Jersey City	371.9	1 624	14.1	3 764	29.5	74.9	23.3	82.2	43.50	5 362	874
Kearny	38.3	1 091	3.4	NA	30.6	77.8	23.4	87.0	43.97	4 888	1 201
Linden	10.9	296	0.0	585	30.6	77.8	23.4	87.0	43.97	4 888	1 201
Long Branch	4.4	150	0.0	NA	30.6	73.7	22.3	82.3	47.13	5 253	746
Millville	1.4	54	0.0	NA	31.1	75.9	22.5	85.3	42.28	4 946	983
Newark	189.4	705	27.7	5 240	30.6	77.8	23.4	87.0	43.97	4 888	1 201
New Brunswick	113.6	2 735	10.1	3 700	29.0	74.6	20.6	84.9	47.02	5 340	804
Paramus Borough	18.0	705	0.0	NA	28.3	74.9	19.4	85.9	49.79	5 486	838
Passaic	29.1	510	0.0	719	28.3	74.9	19.4	85.9	49.79	5 486	838
Paterson	94.9	631	0.0	1 484	28.3	74.9	19.4	85.9	49.79	5 486	838
Perth Amboy	94.0	2 224	9.3	474	29.0	74.6	20.6	84.9	47.02	5 340	804
Plainfield	13.6	295	0.0	NA	29.4	75.0	21.5	86.4	49.00	5 227	891
Rahway	18.6	735	5.9	325	30.6	77.8	23.4	87.0	43.97	4 888	1 201
Sayreville Borough	29.3	784	23.8	NA	29.0	74.6	20.6	84.9	47.02	5 340	804
Trenton	130.2	1 524	37.8	3 884	29.6	75.4	20.5	87.3	45.43	5 172	937
Union City	65.1	1 140	0.0	1 958	29.5	74.9	23.3	82.2	43.50	5 362	874
Vineland	20.9	373	28.4	859	31.1	75.9	22.5	85.3	42.28	4 946	983
Westfield	3.2	110	0.0	NA	29.7	74.8	20.3	86.6	48.75	5 239	841
West New York	137.9	3 659	0.0	1 166	29.5	74.9	23.3	82.2	43.50	5 362	874
NEW MEXICO	X	X	X	X	X	X	X	X	X	X	X
Alamogordo	23.3	803	0.0	350	42.6	80.4	28.3	94.9	12.74	2 908	1 764
Albuquerque	1 121.0	2 671	22.2	7 053	34.2	78.5	21.7	92.5	8.88	4 425	1 244
Clovis	17.5	504	0.0	345	36.5	76.9	22.3	90.5	17.51	4 068	1 156
Farmington	968.3	25 524	14.6	685	28.6	75.0	15.7	92.3	8.26	5 495	803
Hobbs	16.8	602	0.0	412	42.5	79.8	28.0	92.8	16.78	2 851	1 790
Las Cruces	145.5	1 946	3.6	1 190	41.8	80.4	26.4	94.2	9.40	3 155	1 618
Rio Rancho	101.8	NA	0.0	745	34.2	78.5	21.7	92.5	8.88	4 425	1 244
Roswell	49.7	1 046	0.0	602	39.5	80.7	24.7	94.6	12.58	3 267	1 776
Santa Fe	224.1	3 368	34.5	1 165	30.4	69.0	13.7	84.9	16.37	6 138	324
NEW YORK	X	X	X	X	X	X	X	X	X	X	X
Albany	185.6	1 792	0.0	1 475	20.6	71.8	11.0	84.0	36.17	6 894	507
Auburn	81.7	2 743	1.0	NA	23.1	71.5	15.1	81.7	36.57	6 782	501
Binghamton	25.0	517	18.0	653	21.1	69.2	14.3	78.6	36.99	7 273	337
Buffalo	541.5	1 744	21.4	10 699	23.6	71.1	17.0	80.2	38.58	6 747	477
Elmira	28.1	879	60.1	NA	22.8	69.7	13.4	82.7	33.32	6 982	373
Freeport	17.8	442	8.0	341	31.2	75.5	24.9	82.8	41.59	5 027	921
Hempstead	25.3	543	6.7	NA	31.0	74.4	25.0	82.6	44.68	5 316	853
Ithaca	31.0	1 089	2.1	NA	21.5	68.6	12.9	79.8	35.40	7 207	288
Jamestown	33.4	1 006	46.2	819	24.3	70.5	17.8	78.7	45.82	6 591	461
Lindenhurst	1.5	58	0.0	NA	31.2	75.5	24.9	82.8	41.59	5 027	921
Long Beach	50.3	1 466	4.5	NA	31.2	75.5	24.9	82.8	41.59	5 027	921
Mount Vernon	19.6	292	0.0	814	28.7	74.1	19.7	85.7	46.01	5 470	779
Newburgh	25.6	976	9.1	NA	27.4	75.2	19.3	86.5	47.51	5 550	896
New Rochelle	92.8	1 377	0.0	734	28.7	74.1	19.7	85.7	46.01	5 470	779
New York	46 925.8	6 358	27.4	416 400	31.5	76.8	25.3	85.2	47.25	4 805	1 096
Niagara Falls	199.4	3 417	39.7	847	23.6	71.1	17.0	80.2	38.58	6 747	477
North Tonawanda	24.5	725	12.2	370	23.6	71.1	17.0	80.2	38.58	6 747	477
Poughkeepsie	31.4	1 131	12.6	NA	23.8	72.2	14.2	83.8	40.72	6 391	566
Rochester	371.1	1 675	10.3	10 518	23.6	70.2	16.3	80.7	31.96	6 734	425
Rome	48.9	1 192	8.3	418	20.1	70.2	12.7	80.3	45.09	7 305	423
Saratoga Springs	12.7	506	6.5	NA	20.1	71.1	9.3	84.1	40.88	6 998	452
Schenectady	48.4	769	9.1	700	21.8	71.7	13.2	82.6	36.46	6 881	537
Syracuse	424.9	2 726	1.3	6 307	22.4	70.4	14.2	81.7	38.93	6 834	438
Troy	69.4	1 321	3.5	621	21.3	73.0	11.6	83.8	36.18	6 758	599
Utica	58.4	951	0.0	788	20.1	70.2	12.7	80.3	45.09	7 305	423
Valley Stream	9.4	276	0.0	NA	31.2	75.5	24.9	82.8	41.59	5 027	921
Watertown	53.6	1 866	35.4	375	17.9	68.6	8.3	79.6	32.04	7 753	299
White Plains	92.2	1 857	3.6	1 024	27.2	73.3	20.2	82.1	48.92	5 832	691
Yonkers	270.7	1 422	5.1	5 327	28.7	74.1	19.7	85.7	46.01	5 470	779
NORTH CAROLINA	X	X	X	X	X	X	X	X	X	X	X
Asheville	92.6	1 445	61.7	1 032	35.7	72.8	24.8	83.0	47.59	4 308	787
Burlington	22.5	557	37.3	672	37.5	78.2	27.0	88.9	44.96	3 680	1 408
Cary	40.9	540	30.6	886	38.9	78.1	28.8	88.0	41.43	3 457	1 417
Chapel Hill	21.9	495	0.0	539	37.2	76.8	25.7	88.7	46.02	3 802	1 233
Charlotte	1 331.1	3 016	17.6	4 925	39.3	79.3	29.6	88.9	43.09	3 341	1 582

1. Based on the population estimated as of July 1 of the year shown. 2. Represents normal values based on the 30-year period, 1961–1990. 3. Average daily minimum. 4. Average daily maximum.

Table D. Cities — Land Area and Population

STATE Place code	City	Land area, 1990[1] (sq km)	Population, 1999			Population				Population characteristics, 1990 Percent						
			Total persons	Rank	Per square kilometer	Total persons 1990	Percent change 1990–1999	Total persons 1980	Percent change 1980–1990	White	Black	Am. Indian, Eskimo, Aleut	Asian and Pacific Islander	Other race	His-panic[2]	Foreign born
		1	2	3	4	5	6	7	8	9	10	11	12	13	14	15
	NORTH CAROLINA—Cont'd															
37 14100	Concord	56.5	50 258	581	890	29 591	69.8	16 942	74.7	78.6	20.6	0.2	0.5	0.1	0.5	1.2
37 19000	Durham	179.4	179 212	108	999	138 894	29.0	100 847	37.7	51.7	45.7	0.2	2.0	0.4	1.2	3.8
37 22920	Fayetteville	105.1	106 970	208	1 018	75 850	41.0	59 507	27.5	57.6	38.3	1.3	1.5	1.3	3.1	3.5
37 25580	Gastonia	78.7	62 106	433	789	54 725	13.5	47 285	15.7	74.0	24.9	0.2	0.7	0.2	0.5	1.1
37 26880	Goldsboro	54.5	44 580	668	818	40 736	9.4	31 895	27.6	50.3	47.4	0.3	1.3	0.6	1.5	1.9
37 28000	Greensboro	206.7	199 562	87	965	185 125	7.8	155 684	18.1	63.9	33.9	0.5	1.4	0.3	1.0	2.6
37 28080	Greenville	46.7	58 035	483	1 243	46 274	25.4	35 740	29.6	64.2	34.1	0.2	1.2	0.3	0.8	1.7
37 31060	Hickory	52.6	33 368	910	634	28 474	17.2	20 753	37.2	81.4	17.1	0.3	1.0	0.3	0.8	2.0
37 31400	High Point	111.4	76 955	327	691	69 428	10.8	63 355	9.6	68.1	30.2	0.5	0.9	0.2	0.8	1.5
37 34200	Jacksonville	33.7	68 554	377	2 034	78 031	-12.1	17 056	357.5	67.6	26.7	0.5	3.0	2.2	5.2	4.2
37 35200	Kannapolis	40.7	35 328	852	868	31 592	11.8	34 564	-8.6	81.3	18.0	0.1	0.2	0.3	0.6	0.5
37 35920	Kinston	34.0	24 832	1 213	730	25 295	-1.8	25 234	0.2	41.6	57.8	0.1	0.4	0.1	0.5	0.9
37 55000	Raleigh	228.3	261 205	62	1 144	218 859	19.3	150 255	41.2	69.2	27.6	0.3	2.5	0.5	1.4	5.0
37 57500	Rocky Mount	64.7	58 084	481	898	53 078	9.4	41 283	19.8	49.6	49.6	0.2	0.4	0.1	0.5	0.8
37 74440	Wilmington	76.9	65 255	407	849	55 530	17.5	44 000	26.2	64.9	33.9	0.3	0.6	0.3	0.9	1.8
37 74540	Wilson	47.9	41 258	722	861	38 400	7.4	34 424	11.6	52.4	46.9	0.1	0.3	0.3	0.7	0.9
37 75000	Winston-Salem	184.2	168 086	119	913	162 292	3.6	131 885	14.5	59.5	39.3	0.2	0.8	0.3	0.9	2.1
38 00000	**NORTH DAKOTA**	178 695.2	633 666	X	4	638 800	-0.8	652 717	-2.1	94.6	0.6	4.1	0.5	0.3	0.7	1.5
38 07200	Bismarck	63.0	55 109	516	875	49 272	11.8	44 485	10.8	96.7	0.1	2.6	0.4	0.2	0.7	1.2
38 25700	Fargo	77.2	88 128	273	1 142	74 084	19.0	61 383	20.7	97.1	0.4	1.1	1.3	0.2	0.7	2.0
38 32060	Grand Forks	37.4	45 967	640	1 229	49 417	-7.0	43 765	12.9	95.5	0.8	2.3	1.1	0.4	1.2	2.2
38 53380	Minot	34.3	35 673	846	1 040	34 544	3.3	32 843	5.2	95.8	1.1	2.1	0.8	0.2	0.8	2.2
39 00000	**OHIO**	106 067.2	11 256 654	X	106	10 847 115	3.8	10 797 603	0.5	87.8	10.6	0.2	0.8	0.5	1.3	2.4
39 01000	Akron	161.1	211 822	78	1 315	223 019	-5.0	237 177	-6.0	73.8	24.5	0.3	1.2	0.3	0.7	3.1
39 03828	Barberton	19.7	27 360	1 096	1 389	27 623	-1.0	29 751	-7.2	94.1	5.3	0.3	0.3	0.1	0.3	1.4
39 04720	Beavercreek	66.7	40 861	731	613	33 626	21.5	31 589	6.4	96.3	0.9	0.2	2.3	0.2	1.0	3.4
39 07972	Bowling Green	20.5	29 168	1 029	1 423	28 303	3.1	25 728	10.0	93.9	2.6	0.2	2.1	1.2	2.2	3.7
39 09680	Brunswick	29.8	32 849	922	1 102	28 218	16.4	28 104	0.4	98.6	0.4	0.1	0.8	0.2	0.8	3.1
39 12000	Canton	52.4	78 582	318	1 500	84 161	-6.6	94 730	-11.2	80.7	18.2	0.5	0.3	0.3	1.1	2.2
39 15000	Cincinnati	200.0	330 914	52	1 655	364 114	-9.1	385 457	-5.5	60.5	37.9	0.2	1.1	0.3	0.7	2.8
39 16000	Cleveland	199.5	501 662	28	2 515	505 616	-0.8	573 822	-11.9	49.5	46.6	0.3	1.0	2.6	4.6	4.1
39 16014	Cleveland Heights	21.0	53 277	539	2 537	54 052	-1.4	56 438	-4.2	60.2	37.1	0.2	2.1	0.4	1.1	7.2
39 18000	Columbus	494.5	671 247	15	1 357	632 945	6.1	564 866	12.1	74.4	22.6	0.2	2.4	0.4	1.1	3.7
39 19778	Cuyahoga Falls	66.1	49 193	594	744	48 950	0.5	43 890	11.5	98.1	1.1	0.1	0.6	0.1	0.4	2.7
39 21000	Dayton	142.5	169 338	116	1 188	182 011	-7.0	203 371	-10.5	58.4	40.4	0.2	0.6	0.3	0.7	1.4
39 23380	East Cleveland	8.0	29 077	1 034	3 635	33 096	-12.1	36 957	-10.4	5.3	93.7	0.1	0.7	0.2	0.6	1.7
39 25256	Elyria	50.3	55 826	510	1 110	56 746	-1.6	57 538	-1.4	85.0	13.7	0.2	0.5	0.6	1.5	1.6
39 25704	Euclid	27.7	49 498	588	1 787	54 875	-9.8	59 999	-8.5	82.9	16.0	0.1	0.9	0.2	0.8	6.3
39 25914	Fairborn	29.0	33 775	893	1 165	31 300	7.9	29 702	5.4	92.4	4.1	0.4	2.6	0.5	1.3	3.6
39 25970	Fairfield	54.0	42 242	704	782	39 709	6.4	30 777	29.0	95.0	3.3	0.1	1.4	0.2	0.7	1.9
39 27048	Findlay	35.1	38 509	781	1 097	35 703	7.9	35 594	0.3	95.9	1.3	0.2	0.8	1.8	3.4	2.0
39 29106	Gahanna	34.1	30 050	1 010	881	23 898	25.7	18 001	32.8	90.3	7.9	0.1	1.3	0.3	0.8	1.8
39 29428	Garfield Heights	18.7	28 390	1 059	1 518	31 739	-10.6	34 938	-9.2	84.4	14.8	0.1	0.5	0.2	0.8	3.6
39 33012	Hamilton	51.7	60 901	448	1 178	61 438	-0.9	63 189	-2.8	91.9	7.3	0.2	0.4	0.2	0.5	0.7
39 36610	Huber Heights	53.9	42 607	695	790	38 696	10.1	35 480	9.1	90.7	6.9	0.2	1.7	0.4	1.5	2.4
39 39872	Kent	22.6	25 780	1 168	1 141	28 835	-10.6	26 164	10.2	89.9	7.1	0.2	2.5	0.3	0.9	4.8
39 40040	Kettering	48.3	57 156	490	1 183	60 569	-5.6	61 186	-1.0	97.8	0.7	0.1	1.2	0.1	0.8	3.0
39 41664	Lakewood	14.4	54 222	524	3 765	59 718	-9.2	61 963	-3.6	97.5	0.8	0.2	1.0	0.4	1.5	6.9
39 41720	Lancaster	40.5	36 714	827	907	34 507	6.4	34 953	-1.3	98.8	0.5	0.2	0.4	0.1	0.5	0.8
39 43554	Lima	32.8	42 635	692	1 300	45 553	-6.4	47 381	-3.9	74.5	24.0	0.2	0.5	0.7	1.5	0.8
39 44856	Lorain	62.3	67 377	387	1 081	71 245	-5.4	75 416	-5.5	78.2	13.8	0.4	0.3	7.3	16.9	2.8
39 47138	Mansfield	72.3	51 326	565	710	50 627	1.4	53 927	-6.1	80.7	18.1	0.2	0.6	0.3	0.9	2.7
39 47306	Maple Heights	13.4	24 636	1 219	1 839	27 089	-9.1	29 735	-8.9	83.8	14.7	0.1	1.1	0.4	0.7	3.7
39 47754	Marion	20.8	36 362	832	1 748	34 075	6.7	37 040	-8.0	94.7	4.2	0.3	0.5	0.3	0.8	0.8
39 48244	Massillon	34.2	30 634	990	896	30 969	-1.1	30 557	1.3	89.4	9.8	0.2	0.2	0.3	0.9	1.2
39 49056	Mentor	69.3	51 686	561	746	47 491	8.8	42 065	12.9	98.6	0.3	0.1	0.9	0.1	0.6	2.4
39 49840	Middletown	52.3	52 922	541	1 012	46 758	13.2	43 719	5.3	88.3	11.0	0.1	0.4	0.1	0.4	0.9
39 54040	Newark	46.7	47 612	621	1 020	44 396	7.2	41 200	7.8	96.0	3.2	0.2	0.4	0.2	0.7	0.7
39 56882	North Olmsted	29.8	32 978	918	1 107	34 204	-3.6	36 486	-6.3	97.1	0.7	0.1	1.7	0.3	1.2	6.4
39 61000	Parma	51.8	81 207	301	1 568	87 876	-7.6	92 548	-5.0	97.9	0.7	0.1	1.1	0.2	0.9	8.6
39 66390	Reynoldsburg	24.3	30 282	1 000	1 246	25 748	17.6	20 661	24.6	93.9	4.1	0.3	1.5	0.3	0.9	2.5
39 70380	Sandusky	26.0	27 932	1 077	1 074	29 764	-6.2	31 360	-5.1	79.7	18.9	0.2	0.3	0.9	2.3	1.3
39 71682	Shaker Heights	16.3	28 297	1 063	1 736	30 955	-8.6	32 487	-4.7	66.9	30.7	0.2	1.9	0.3	1.1	6.6
39 74118	Springfield	50.6	65 154	409	1 288	70 487	-7.6	72 563	-2.9	81.6	17.4	0.2	0.5	0.3	0.6	1.1
39 74944	Stow	44.4	32 162	946	724	27 998	14.9	25 303	10.7	97.1	1.1	0.1	1.6	0.1	0.5	3.5
39 75098	Strongsville	63.8	40 132	750	629	35 308	13.7	28 577	23.6	96.6	0.8	0.1	2.4	0.2	1.0	5.4
39 77000	Toledo	208.7	307 946	55	1 476	332 943	-7.5	354 635	-6.1	77.0	19.7	0.3	1.0	2.0	4.0	2.8
39 79002	Upper Arlington	24.9	31 553	960	1 267	34 128	-7.5	35 648	-4.3	97.3	0.3	0.1	2.3	0.1	0.7	4.8

1. Dry land or land partially or temporarily covered by water.   2. Hispanic persons may be of any race.

Table D. Cities — Population and Households

City	Under 5 years (16)	5 to 17 years (17)	18 to 24 years (18)	25 to 34 years (19)	35 to 44 years (20)	45 to 54 years (21)	55 to 64 years (22)	65 to 74 years (23)	75 years and over (24)	Percent female (25)	Number (26)	Percent change, 1980-1990 (27)	Persons per household (28)	Female family householder[1] (29)	One-person (30)
NORTH CAROLINA—Cont'd															
Concord	6.6	15.5	11.4	16.3	14.3	9.9	9.3	9.3	7.3	53.5	10 807	70.7	2.44	13.8	27.4
Durham	7.3	14.8	14.9	21.9	15.1	8.2	6.6	6.1	5.2	53.5	56 001	46.5	2.30	16.1	32.6
Fayetteville	7.7	17.4	13.4	18.3	13.9	9.7	9.1	6.9	3.7	52.7	29 639	37.2	2.47	16.8	26.3
Gastonia	7.1	18.5	10.0	16.1	14.8	9.8	9.4	8.3	6.1	53.4	20 983	21.2	2.56	17.0	24.5
Goldsboro	8.5	17.2	11.7	22.7	13.9	7.9	7.7	6.5	3.9	48.8	13 423	22.5	2.56	20.0	26.8
Greensboro	6.4	15.2	14.8	18.5	15.3	9.8	8.2	7.0	4.8	53.6	74 905	31.7	2.33	13.8	30.5
Greenville	5.8	14.0	29.8	15.9	12.4	7.4	6.5	5.0	3.2	52.7	17 017	47.2	2.35	14.4	30.6
Hickory	6.1	14.6	13.6	17.4	14.3	10.3	9.2	8.3	6.3	53.5	11 800	44.1	2.28	13.2	31.5
High Point	7.3	17.1	10.5	17.4	14.9	9.9	8.8	7.5	6.6	53.7	27 529	18.3	2.46	16.6	27.0
Jacksonville	10.3	19.2	13.9	21.9	13.0	7.4	6.7	5.0	2.6	52.2	10 916	76.1	2.69	13.1	18.4
Kannapolis	6.9	15.9	10.0	16.5	12.8	9.4	10.1	10.8	7.8	53.7	12 018	-6.8	2.44	14.1	26.2
Kinston	6.4	19.0	8.4	14.2	15.1	9.2	10.8	10.3	6.7	55.9	9 987	9.9	2.42	23.0	31.6
Raleigh	6.2	13.4	17.5	22.7	16.0	9.0	6.6	5.3	3.5	51.5	85 822	56.2	2.26	11.3	32.2
Rocky Mount	7.7	20.0	9.4	16.5	15.9	9.3	8.3	7.6	5.2	54.7	18 871	24.3	2.58	19.9	26.4
Wilmington	6.3	15.5	15.1	16.3	13.3	8.8	8.7	9.4	6.5	54.7	23 557	34.8	2.26	18.0	32.8
Wilson	6.9	19.6	11.0	15.3	14.1	9.9	9.4	8.5	5.4	54.8	14 461	15.9	2.44	20.5	29.4
Winston-Salem	6.7	15.1	12.8	18.4	14.3	9.9	8.9	7.9	6.2	54.1	59 919	18.8	2.27	16.7	33.8
NORTH DAKOTA	7.5	20.0	10.6	16.3	14.1	8.9	8.4	7.4	6.8	50.2	240 878	5.4	2.55	7.3	26.5
Bismarck	7.3	19.7	9.7	18.0	16.1	9.5	8.2	6.2	5.2	52.2	19 315	16.6	2.48	9.5	27.5
Fargo	7.1	15.2	18.2	20.1	14.8	7.7	6.8	5.4	4.7	50.4	30 149	27.4	2.32	7.7	31.4
Grand Forks	7.5	15.8	21.6	19.2	12.8	7.8	6.0	4.9	4.3	50.0	18 531	18.8	2.43	9.5	29.1
Minot	7.2	18.0	12.5	17.3	14.5	8.4	8.1	7.1	6.8	52.3	13 965	14.7	2.39	9.9	30.8
OHIO	7.2	18.6	10.5	16.5	14.9	10.3	9.0	7.6	5.3	51.8	4 087 546	6.6	2.59	11.7	25.0
Akron	7.5	17.0	12.1	17.5	14.1	8.4	8.5	8.6	6.2	52.8	89 923	-0.8	2.42	16.6	30.8
Barberton	7.1	18.2	9.2	16.9	13.3	8.6	9.9	9.9	6.9	53.2	11 082	-1.1	2.47	14.3	28.2
Beavercreek	5.8	20.1	8.2	13.2	19.6	14.2	9.8	5.9	3.3	50.3	11 693	18.4	2.84	5.5	13.6
Bowling Green	3.8	9.1	50.6	12.0	8.4	5.2	4.3	3.7	3.1	54.7	8 502	19.3	2.39	6.8	29.0
Brunswick	7.2	22.7	10.4	16.8	18.3	12.0	6.5	4.1	2.1	50.6	9 032	12.4	3.09	8.1	12.7
Canton	7.9	18.2	9.9	16.5	13.8	8.5	8.8	9.2	7.2	53.8	33 452	-8.1	2.44	17.0	31.2
Cincinnati	8.4	16.7	12.8	19.6	13.0	7.9	7.8	7.2	6.7	53.5	154 342	-2.3	2.26	18.2	39.5
Cleveland	8.7	18.2	10.4	18.1	12.6	8.9	9.1	8.2	5.8	53.1	199 787	-8.6	2.48	22.7	33.5
Cleveland Heights	6.6	18.4	9.1	18.0	18.0	9.6	7.3	6.8	6.0	53.5	21 012	0.9	2.52	13.0	29.5
Columbus	7.9	15.8	15.5	22.3	14.4	8.0	7.0	5.4	3.7	51.7	256 996	18.2	2.38	14.2	31.3
Cuyahoga Falls	6.8	16.0	8.8	19.4	14.9	9.2	9.6	9.4	5.9	52.6	20 383	21.3	2.38	9.7	29.1
Dayton	8.5	17.4	13.1	18.0	12.9	8.3	8.6	8.0	5.2	52.9	72 670	-6.6	2.41	20.6	33.4
East Cleveland	8.4	20.5	10.2	16.6	14.8	10.0	9.1	6.3	4.1	56.4	13 362	-9.8	2.45	31.4	34.3
Elyria	8.3	19.3	10.2	18.3	14.7	9.2	8.2	7.3	4.5	52.0	21 423	3.7	2.61	13.9	24.8
Euclid	6.2	13.6	7.5	18.2	13.3	9.2	9.9	12.3	9.8	54.4	24 894	-2.2	2.17	11.9	37.1
Fairborn	7.0	15.8	17.2	18.8	12.9	9.8	8.8	6.8	2.9	50.8	12 673	14.7	2.43	11.4	26.1
Fairfield	7.3	18.1	10.3	20.4	16.8	10.7	7.9	5.2	3.2	51.5	15 289	41.9	2.56	8.3	22.9
Findlay	7.6	17.5	11.1	17.6	14.3	9.9	8.5	7.6	6.0	52.3	14 117	4.3	2.46	9.2	28.0
Gahanna	9.0	20.6	8.7	18.4	18.3	10.6	6.7	4.9	2.8	51.8	9 453	62.3	2.88	10.3	16.5
Garfield Heights	6.4	15.9	8.5	16.9	13.6	8.9	10.3	12.5	7.0	53.6	12 483	-1.3	2.52	13.7	26.0
Hamilton	8.2	19.2	9.3	17.8	13.1	8.9	9.4	8.2	6.0	53.0	23 992	1.0	2.52	14.9	26.7
Huber Heights	8.0	20.8	9.4	19.3	17.0	11.7	7.9	4.4	1.6	50.7	13 509	18.2	2.85	9.9	15.5
Kent	5.1	11.7	41.9	14.6	10.3	5.1	4.5	4.1	2.9	53.9	8 808	1.4	2.46	12.9	28.0
Kettering	6.2	15.1	8.5	17.7	14.3	10.2	11.1	10.3	6.6	52.7	26 098	7.4	2.30	8.5	30.0
Lakewood	6.6	16.6	9.4	22.2	15.5	8.7	7.4	7.2	6.4	53.6	26 999	0.1	2.20	10.7	41.0
Lancaster	7.3	17.6	9.8	16.5	13.8	10.0	9.3	8.6	7.1	53.2	13 981	4.8	2.44	12.4	27.4
Lima	8.2	19.4	11.1	18.5	13.2	8.4	7.9	7.5	5.8	49.5	16 311	-6.7	2.57	17.9	28.3
Lorain	8.1	20.9	9.2	16.6	13.4	9.4	9.1	8.3	5.0	52.6	26 198	1.4	2.69	16.7	24.5
Mansfield	7.3	16.9	11.3	17.1	13.2	10.4	8.9	8.5	6.4	51.1	20 197	-2.1	2.36	13.8	32.1
Maple Heights	6.7	16.0	8.0	17.6	14.0	8.5	10.4	11.9	6.9	52.8	10 551	-2.0	2.55	12.0	25.2
Marion	8.4	19.9	9.8	16.6	14.4	9.4	8.5	7.7	5.4	52.5	13 179	-4.4	2.56	13.3	26.5
Massillon	7.1	17.8	9.3	16.8	13.3	9.9	9.7	8.9	7.2	52.6	12 110	5.6	2.49	13.2	27.5
Mentor	7.5	19.9	8.2	16.5	18.5	11.8	8.3	6.4	3.0	51.2	16 730	23.4	2.82	8.4	17.2
Middletown	7.9	17.9	10.0	16.9	14.1	9.0	9.6	8.7	5.9	52.7	18 362	8.9	2.48	14.4	26.4
Newark	7.9	18.0	9.7	17.8	13.4	9.4	8.6	8.1	7.2	53.1	17 802	10.3	2.44	12.3	29.1
North Olmsted	6.2	18.3	8.9	15.0	16.0	12.6	10.1	8.1	4.8	52.1	12 657	3.4	2.68	8.9	22.4
Parma	6.3	15.0	8.0	17.7	13.2	9.9	10.9	12.2	6.9	52.6	34 685	3.5	2.50	10.0	24.7
Reynoldsburg	7.1	19.1	10.5	18.2	18.4	10.7	8.3	5.3	2.4	52.0	9 981	35.8	2.58	9.7	23.1
Sandusky	8.0	18.9	9.6	17.5	14.1	8.1	9.1	9.1	5.6	53.0	12 059	1.1	2.44	14.7	31.8
Shaker Heights	5.8	18.0	6.4	14.2	17.9	12.3	10.7	8.4	6.3	53.9	12 648	-1.0	2.43	11.2	27.7
Springfield	7.8	18.1	12.6	15.5	13.6	8.8	8.2	8.3	7.0	53.4	27 247	-1.0	2.47	15.7	29.5
Stow	7.6	19.2	8.5	18.1	18.6	10.2	8.2	5.9	3.6	51.5	10 086	18.8	2.72	8.2	19.6
Strongsville	7.1	20.2	8.1	14.9	20.1	13.4	8.2	5.7	2.2	50.8	12 284	32.9	2.87	6.0	16.7
Toledo	8.1	18.0	11.7	17.7	13.5	8.9	8.5	7.9	5.7	52.6	130 883	-1.8	2.50	15.7	29.7
Upper Arlington	5.8	16.6	5.7	11.6	17.5	12.4	11.8	10.5	8.2	53.5	13 956	3.1	2.43	6.8	25.6

1. No spouse present.

City	Persons in group quarters, 1990				Serious crimes known to police, 1998[2]				Education, 1990				Money income, 1989		
					Total		Rate[3]		School enrollment		Attainment[4] (percent)			Households	
														Median	
	Total	Persons in mental hospitals	Persons in nursing homes	Persons identified as homeless[1]	Number	Rate[3]	Violent	Property	Public	Private	High school graduate or more	Bachelor's degree or more	Per capita (dollars)[5]	Dollars	Percent change, 1979–1989 (constant 1989 dollars)
	31	32	33	34	35	36	37	38	39	40	41	42	43	44	45
NORTH CAROLINA—Cont'd															
Concord	1 010	0	539	33	NA	NA	NA	NA	4 963	656	66.2	14.8	13 452	25 473	7.8
Durham	7 909	0	1 049	194	16 433	10 641	1 130	9 511	28 098	12 204	78.5	35.4	14 498	27 256	26.6
Fayetteville	2 392	64	459	102	9 038	11 156	849	10 307	17 968	2 408	79.1	23.8	12 825	24 354	12.8
Gastonia	1 084	0	722	83	7 503	12 961	1 644	11 317	11 601	1 260	62.4	16.0	12 684	25 910	4.8
Goldsboro	6 296	599	339	25	3 728	8 976	1 209	7 767	9 550	1 342	74.9	16.0	10 726	19 955	6.7
Greensboro	8 683	0	1 173	166	17 653	8 807	972	7 835	44 080	6 205	79.2	29.9	15 644	29 184	9.0
Greenville	4 877	0	181	75	6 412	11 370	1 098	10 272	17 981	1 138	79.0	33.7	12 206	22 661	0.4
Hickory	1 404	10	475	29	3 261	10 380	716	9 664	5 155	1 456	72.1	23.4	15 433	27 212	15.1
High Point	1 799	0	764	110	6 998	9 169	1 030	8 139	13 569	2 288	68.2	18.1	13 324	25 035	6.8
Jacksonville	603	0	433	11	2 621	3 687	397	3 290	7 284	891	84.5	18.2	11 566	25 698	2.2
Kannapolis	372	0	302	0	1 040	2 803	299	2 504	5 392	370	58.7	7.7	11 031	22 369	-5.7
Kinston	1 169	0	245	0	2 549	9 923	1 078	8 845	6 016	297	61.5	15.4	10 490	18 253	-6.5
Raleigh	13 923	936	720	321	17 985	7 023	826	6 197	48 512	10 640	86.6	40.6	16 896	32 451	13.7
Rocky Mount	329	0	289	0	NA	NA	NA	NA	11 044	1 349	66.9	16.7	12 593	24 055	5.1
Wilmington	2 260	15	432	104	6 899	10 649	1 273	9 376	13 966	1 161	73.1	20.7	12 077	20 609	13.7
Wilson	1 611	0	578	24	3 815	9 315	1 309	8 006	8 501	1 658	63.1	18.4	12 028	21 881	-0.9
Winston-Salem	7 244	0	1 530	265	16 243	10 337	1 252	9 085	27 405	9 202	77.0	27.2	15 696	26 488	12.0
NORTH DAKOTA	24 315	302	8 159	276	17 105	2 681	89	2 592	164 233	13 310	76.7	18.1	11 051	23 213	-9.4
Bismarck	1 292	0	550	56	2 242	4 155	89	4 066	10 955	1 891	83.4	26.4	13 339	28 223	-12.9
Fargo	4 053	47	877	107	2 983	3 523	128	3 395	21 535	1 924	88.7	30.2	13 554	25 326	-11.5
Grand Forks	4 336	0	465	87	2 903	5 872	125	5 747	17 482	854	85.8	29.3	11 902	25 456	-5.1
Minot	1 169	0	421	24	1 676	4 750	142	4 608	9 440	675	81.6	21.1	11 934	23 727	-13.1
OHIO	260 938	4 773	93 769	4 646	485 066	4 328	363	3 965	2 338 126	460 100	75.7	17.0	13 461	28 706	-3.5
Akron	5 025	154	1 545	166	NA	NA	NA	NA	51 202	6 897	72.9	14.9	12 015	22 279	-9.6
Barberton	240	0	240	0	1 380	5 037	402	4 635	5 845	596	68.8	7.9	10 366	21 688	-11.7
Beavercreek	407	0	384	0	1 720	5 534	148	5 386	7 915	2 037	89.0	37.2	18 362	49 143	4.7
Bowling Green	7 850	0	262	0	1 110	3 862	136	3 726	16 517	532	88.6	41.6	10 354	21 766	-4.0
Brunswick	314	0	206	12	NA	NA	NA	NA	6 916	1 321	81.6	13.1	13 821	40 950	-3.4
Canton	2 428	28	1 479	150	6 482	7 988	1 575	6 413	16 943	2 915	67.0	9.7	10 133	19 807	-15.0
Cincinnati	14 790	528	4 444	1 028	NA	NA	NA	NA	75 004	20 862	69.6	22.2	12 547	21 006	-1.1
Cleveland	9 691	191	3 397	543	34 593	6 981	1 308	5 673	94 499	29 944	58.8	8.1	9 258	17 822	-13.4
Cleveland Heights	972	0	713	0	1 024	1 896	37	1 859	10 361	5 859	88.1	45.0	18 228	36 043	3.6
Columbus	20 693	375	3 484	649	62 608	9 468	817	8 651	151 248	25 510	78.7	24.6	13 151	26 651	7.2
Cuyahoga Falls	334	180	124	6	1 744	3 089	193	2 896	9 278	2 186	85.2	21.5	14 472	30 895	-5.3
Dayton	6 699	410	1 564	402	18 021	10 476	1 048	9 428	37 015	13 248	68.3	12.3	9 946	19 779	-2.8
East Cleveland	296	0	287	0	NA	NA	NA	NA	8 399	967	62.6	7.1	9 020	16 378	-18.0
Elyria	779	14	433	42	NA	NA	NA	NA	12 560	1 987	75.2	11.0	11 980	26 923	-12.0
Euclid	776	0	625	0	2 614	5 009	276	4 733	8 578	2 856	74.8	17.3	14 447	26 904	-10.8
Fairborn	525	0	243	0	1 345	4 402	200	4 202	8 988	793	77.8	21.0	13 053	27 558	-2.9
Fairfield	652	0	469	0	2 117	4 959	307	4 652	7 501	2 008	85.2	25.9	16 789	38 531	-6.7
Findlay	1 007	0	363	29	NA	NA	NA	NA	6 796	1 749	82.0	22.1	14 814	30 445	5.2
Gahanna	551	0	117	0	972	3 081	155	2 926	6 548	1 508	84.3	28.6	15 713	42 015	7.5
Garfield Heights	317	0	92	0	NA	NA	NA	NA	4 983	1 808	71.7	8.5	12 491	28 694	-12.4
Hamilton	812	0	449	57	4 969	7 936	1 720	6 216	11 827	2 056	66.6	9.9	11 108	22 886	-10.9
Huber Heights	207	0	115	0	1 577	4 072	194	3 878	9 805	1 249	84.1	18.3	14 323	37 912	2.3
Kent	7 178	0	113	10	1 050	3 842	293	3 549	15 595	559	85.9	33.6	9 191	21 463	-7.8
Kettering	575	0	402	0	2 373	4 099	142	3 957	11 125	3 250	86.8	28.6	18 988	34 506	-0.5
Lakewood	319	18	239	0	1 423	2 567	117	2 450	11 180	3 845	84.1	29.0	16 258	28 791	-0.1
Lancaster	439	0	376	8	1 861	5 148	985	4 163	6 381	923	72.8	11.6	11 307	22 430	-12.3
Lima	3 674	0	255	109	3 536	8 263	858	7 405	9 919	2 036	69.3	8.4	9 535	21 061	-11.3
Lorain	760	36	503	19	2 530	3 603	433	3 170	16 225	2 299	67.5	7.7	10 676	24 123	-20.0
Mansfield	2 993	0	415	43	3 501	6 875	567	6 308	9 455	1 642	69.7	13.0	11 774	22 591	-2.4
Maple Heights	235	0	205	0	210	813	108	705	4 771	1 185	72.2	8.1	12 792	29 568	-11.7
Marion	379	0	270	0	2 256	6 784	192	6 592	7 519	699	69.7	9.4	10 365	22 439	-10.4
Massillon	860	285	133	16	NA	NA	NA	NA	5 776	1 027	69.4	8.2	10 952	23 819	-8.6
Mentor	182	0	92	0	1 707	3 384	87	3 297	10 104	2 592	86.0	22.3	16 717	42 095	-0.8
Middletown	418	0	315	24	3 199	6 579	282	6 297	8 664	1 300	71.4	12.8	12 988	25 714	-6.3
Newark	1 014	0	827	0	2 642	5 331	309	5 022	8 581	1 011	72.8	11.3	11 680	23 062	-6.1
North Olmsted	289	0	273	0	NA	NA	NA	NA	6 848	2 203	85.9	25.0	16 567	39 657	-5.2
Parma	1 053	0	892	0	NA	NA	NA	NA	14 456	4 843	76.9	15.3	14 702	33 281	-8.9
Reynoldsburg	0	0	0	0	NA	NA	NA	NA	5 393	1 115	88.2	24.7	15 758	37 169	2.8
Sandusky	329	0	136	39	2 512	8 656	451	8 205	5 726	1 274	71.2	9.5	11 620	22 532	-16.2
Shaker Heights	88	0	0	0	821	2 827	227	2 600	6 069	2 576	92.6	61.0	32 708	51 128	7.7
Springfield	3 112	10	968	6	6 595	9 825	1 749	8 076	14 616	3 597	68.3	10.9	10 648	21 407	-5.7
Stow	334	0	300	0	741	2 388	39	2 349	6 254	1 229	86.0	30.4	16 310	39 638	-2.2
Strongsville	104	0	95	0	1 163	2 834	29	2 805	7 735	2 358	89.5	30.2	20 217	50 916	6.4
Toledo	5 764	326	1 994	259	25 571	8 046	905	7 141	70 649	18 325	73.2	14.1	11 894	24 819	-8.6
Upper Arlington	277	0	277	0	811	2 452	100	2 352	6 853	1 523	95.7	59.2	30 388	53 140	7.7

1. Persons in emergency shelters and persons visible in street locations. 2. Data for serious crimes have not been adjusted for underreporting. This may affect comparability between geographic areas and over time. 3. Per 100,000 population estimated by the FBI. 4. Persons 25 years old and older. 5. Based on population enumerated as of April 1, 1990.

City	Money income, 1989 (cont'd)				Housing units, 1990										
	Households (cont'd)	Percent below poverty, 1989						Occupied units							
		Persons		Families				Owner-occupied units					Renter-occupied units		
											Owner cost as a percent of income				
	Percent with $100,000 or more	Total	Percent change in rate, 1979–1989	Total	Total	Percent change, 1980–1990	Vacant units for sale or rent[1]	Total	Percent	Median value[2] (dollars)	With a mortgage	Without a mortgage	Median rent[3] (dollars)	Rent as percent of income	Substandard units[4] (percent)
	46	47	48	49	50	51	52	53	54	55	56	57	58	59	60
NORTH CAROLINA— Cont'd															
Concord	2.9	12.1	11.0	8.7	11 616	70.4	555	10 807	61.0	59 600	20.1	13.1	389	23.0	3.1
Durham	3.2	14.9	-22.0	11.3	60 607	52.4	3 639	56 001	44.2	80 600	22.5	13.8	440	24.8	2.9
Fayetteville	2.9	18.8	-13.8	15.3	31 712	37.6	1 468	29 639	54.2	67 900	22.6	14.0	405	27.2	3.2
Gastonia	2.6	14.2	4.4	11.5	22 196	24.6	982	20 983	58.2	60 200	19.2	13.0	378	24.0	3.4
Goldsboro	1.1	21.2	-1.4	17.4	14 345	24.8	600	13 423	40.2	55 300	22.4	13.6	332	24.9	3.9
Greensboro	4.4	11.6	-9.4	8.2	80 411	34.3	4 297	74 905	53.7	78 500	21.1	12.9	437	24.9	2.4
Greenville	3.0	26.6	8.6	15.9	18 054	46.0	840	17 017	42.1	73 300	20.6	12.9	374	30.8	4.1
Hickory	4.3	11.3	-8.1	7.7	12 701	47.2	725	11 800	51.8	66 900	20.3	12.5	384	21.5	2.6
High Point	3.3	12.7	-9.3	9.9	29 408	20.9	1 489	27 529	54.4	65 200	21.7	13.7	390	24.4	2.3
Jacksonville	1.8	11.9	-15.6	10.3	11 810	77.3	687	10 916	48.7	66 100	22.5	13.1	443	27.1	4.4
Kannapolis	0.6	11.8	9.3	9.4	12 717	-6.6	485	12 018	63.5	46 700	17.8	12.7	339	23.2	4.1
Kinston	2.1	25.2	7.7	20.8	10 826	11.5	550	9 987	52.0	54 000	21.6	16.1	281	27.8	4.8
Raleigh	4.7	11.8	-3.3	7.7	92 643	60.1	5 891	85 822	46.9	96 600	22.1	12.6	479	24.6	2.9
Rocky Mount	3.1	18.1	-8.1	15.6	20 173	24.9	1 064	18 871	52.6	60 300	19.2	14.7	364	25.4	4.2
Wilmington	2.3	22.1	-9.4	16.8	26 469	37.8	2 117	23 557	47.1	63 300	21.3	13.9	392	28.0	2.3
Wilson	2.8	23.5	19.3	19.4	15 383	18.0	704	14 461	49.3	64 500	20.7	14.5	333	28.1	3.1
Winston-Salem	4.8	15.2	-7.3	11.6	65 631	22.5	4 697	59 919	51.8	69 600	19.1	12.7	385	24.7	2.3
NORTH DAKOTA	1.6	14.4	14.1	10.9	276 340	6.8	15 360	240 878	65.6	50 800	20.3	13.0	313	23.9	2.5
Bismarck	2.5	9.7	47.0	7.4	20 038	15.1	548	19 315	60.7	67 900	20.5	12.0	347	23.3	1.7
Fargo	2.9	13.7	41.2	7.9	31 711	25.7	1 338	30 149	48.1	70 300	20.7	12.8	355	25.2	1.7
Grand Forks	2.0	14.5	20.8	9.9	19 589	14.1	924	18 531	48.7	64 700	20.5	12.1	367	26.1	2.5
Minot	1.8	14.3	53.8	11.0	15 040	14.7	843	13 965	60.2	56 200	20.9	12.8	322	25.5	1.5
OHIO	2.9	12.5	21.7	9.7	4 371 945	6.4	178 706	4 087 546	67.5	63 500	18.2	12.5	379	25.3	2.2
Akron	2.0	20.5	36.7	16.5	96 372	-0.3	4 480	89 923	58.7	43 800	19.8	13.1	360	28.4	1.7
Barberton	0.6	16.9	55.0	14.9	11 731	0.2	369	11 082	64.3	44 000	17.0	13.1	340	26.6	2.2
Beavercreek	5.0	3.5	59.1	2.6	12 148	19.2	398	11 693	86.1	97 100	19.1	11.6	577	22.9	0.2
Bowling Green	3.5	27.0	3.8	6.2	8 964	20.7	413	8 502	42.2	81 700	17.7	11.6	393	33.8	2.3
Brunswick	2.0	4.2	44.8	3.2	9 444	11.6	280	9 032	81.0	83 700	20.6	12.4	474	22.9	1.6
Canton	0.9	21.9	41.3	18.8	36 527	-6.9	2 202	33 452	57.3	37 700	16.9	12.4	298	26.7	1.9
Cincinnati	2.6	24.3	23.4	20.7	169 088	-2.1	11 558	154 342	38.3	61 900	18.9	13.0	329	25.8	4.3
Cleveland	0.7	28.7	29.9	25.2	224 311	-6.4	17 358	199 787	47.9	40 900	19.3	13.6	322	29.3	3.5
Cleveland Heights	6.2	8.5	13.3	5.4	21 862	2.1	693	21 012	62.6	71 500	19.5	13.0	489	25.9	1.4
Columbus	1.9	17.2	4.2	12.6	278 084	17.5	16 781	256 996	46.6	66 000	19.6	12.3	422	25.0	2.5
Cuyahoga Falls	2.0	6.6	53.5	5.5	21 269	22.4	595	20 383	66.6	61 500	16.5	12.3	427	24.4	0.8
Dayton	0.5	26.5	27.4	22.0	80 370	-7.4	5 699	72 670	51.0	43 200	17.8	13.7	329	29.3	3.4
East Cleveland	0.7	27.8	23.0	25.9	15 168	-4.5	1 353	13 362	32.3	42 200	22.7	15.8	362	30.0	2.7
Elyria	1.4	13.7	35.6	11.7	22 544	2.4	854	21 423	62.9	56 300	18.3	12.8	374	24.3	2.1
Euclid	1.2	7.8	30.0	5.3	26 586	0.6	1 513	24 894	58.7	65 000	18.6	12.9	434	25.8	1.2
Fairborn	1.9	15.4	33.9	10.9	13 288	14.1	532	12 673	51.3	61 800	16.9	11.8	431	27.7	4.7
Fairfield	3.6	3.8	31.0	2.7	16 281	43.9	904	15 289	64.0	86 300	18.3	11.6	509	21.9	0.5
Findlay	2.7	8.5	16.4	6.7	15 003	5.2	624	14 117	67.7	62 700	16.9	11.7	363	23.2	1.8
Gahanna	4.2	5.0	35.1	3.6	9 921	62.4	379	9 453	76.0	87 600	20.1	12.4	475	22.8	1.3
Garfield Heights	0.8	5.9	0.0	4.0	13 000	0.8	398	12 483	80.8	58 500	20.7	13.4	408	23.6	1.2
Hamilton	1.1	16.8	25.4	14.0	25 362	1.6	1 046	23 992	60.5	53 700	18.1	12.4	363	27.9	2.5
Huber Heights	1.8	4.3	-15.7	3.2	14 306	18.1	733	13 509	70.8	65 900	17.6	11.7	556	22.2	1.1
Kent	2.1	27.5	28.5	17.2	9 275	0.8	374	8 808	38.6	68 400	17.6	12.0	401	31.3	2.6
Kettering	4.7	4.2	0.0	2.8	27 096	6.9	822	26 098	65.9	77 900	16.8	11.7	453	23.3	1.1
Lakewood	3.3	8.5	34.9	6.1	28 521	0.2	1 104	26 999	44.5	73 200	20.6	13.7	409	23.0	1.3
Lancaster	1.5	14.1	42.4	11.0	14 754	5.4	483	13 981	59.9	51 700	17.9	12.4	362	24.5	1.6
Lima	1.0	21.6	27.8	18.6	18 666	-2.0	1 468	16 311	59.1	38 900	15.4	12.3	329	27.6	2.6
Lorain	0.8	19.8	47.8	16.6	27 544	-0.2	879	26 198	61.1	52 300	16.9	12.8	363	27.5	3.8
Mansfield	1.6	17.8	30.9	14.5	21 909	-2.5	1 210	20 197	58.0	42 300	17.0	12.9	336	25.3	1.6
Maple Heights	1.2	4.0	-16.7	2.9	10 791	-1.2	180	10 551	85.0	57 900	19.6	12.8	405	24.2	1.7
Marion	1.0	16.8	13.5	13.9	14 243	-3.6	628	13 179	61.5	34 500	16.3	12.9	337	25.6	2.5
Massillon	0.9	14.4	44.0	12.2	12 814	4.3	481	12 110	67.3	43 600	17.5	13.0	345	26.0	2.0
Mentor	4.0	2.9	3.6	2.3	17 172	21.4	352	16 730	85.9	89 800	19.6	12.3	558	24.5	1.1
Middletown	2.4	15.4	20.3	13.1	19 385	8.7	774	18 362	60.0	57 600	17.6	13.0	376	26.1	2.5
Newark	1.6	15.6	34.5	13.3	18 967	10.7	897	17 802	56.8	49 500	17.1	12.2	351	26.5	1.9
North Olmsted	3.1	3.1	10.7	2.5	13 081	3.7	341	12 657	79.0	94 700	19.4	13.0	504	23.2	1.0
Parma	1.9	4.1	36.7	3.1	35 589	3.8	702	34 685	77.8	74 200	17.9	12.3	462	23.8	1.3
Reynoldsburg	2.7	4.4	57.1	2.5	10 587	37.4	549	9 981	61.1	78 700	20.2	11.1	510	22.7	0.9
Sandusky	1.3	15.4	40.0	12.9	13 416	1.9	784	12 059	57.5	48 800	16.8	12.9	340	24.4	2.1
Shaker Heights	21.5	3.5	2.9	2.3	13 374	0.9	618	12 648	64.9	138 100	18.4	12.7	591	23.8	0.6
Springfield	1.3	20.9	18.8	16.6	29 562	0.7	1 613	27 247	55.8	42 000	17.1	13.1	351	27.6	2.5
Stow	2.9	3.1	10.7	2.3	10 462	17.9	312	10 086	72.2	83 700	20.8	12.6	521	21.8	0.9
Strongsville	8.0	2.3	9.5	1.9	13 099	34.3	734	12 284	82.4	117 300	20.2	11.6	457	24.6	0.9
Toledo	1.6	19.1	40.4	15.4	142 125	-0.8	7 550	130 883	60.7	48 900	17.0	13.9	378	27.2	2.1
Upper Arlington	18.5	1.4	-41.7	0.7	14 376	3.4	293	13 956	81.7	141 800	18.3	11.6	578	23.2	0.3

1. Includes units rented or sold but not occupied. 2. Specified owner-occupied units. 3. Specified renter-occupied units. 4. Overcrowded or lacking complete plumbing facilities.

Table D. Cities — **Labor Force, Employment, Disability, and Construction**

City	Civilian labor force, 1999				Civilian employment, 1990[2]			Disability 1990	Value of residential construction authorized by building permits, 1999		
			Unemployment			Percent					
	Total	Percent change, 1998–1999	Total	Rate[1]	Total	Professional, managerial, and technical	Precision production, craft, and repair	Work disabled persons[3] (percent)	New construction ($1,000)	Number of housing units	Percent single family
	61	62	63	64	65	66	67	68	69	70	71
NORTH CAROLINA— Cont'd											
Concord	17 459	4.6	388	2.2	13 753	23.3	13.8	9.2	NA	NA	NA
Durham	85 699	0.3	1 952	2.3	71 211	41.0	7.5	6.8	306 310	3 092	50.3
Fayetteville	36 138	2.8	1 388	3.8	30 060	33.1	8.6	10.8	27 010	359	54.3
Gastonia	29 372	2.2	1 137	3.9	26 232	24.2	12.4	10.5	47 727	565	37.5
Goldsboro	14 262	0.6	756	5.3	13 102	26.4	9.6	10.7	8 149	235	91.5
Greensboro	115 846	2.1	2 909	2.5	100 100	31.7	8.2	6.7	143 848	2 021	53.8
Greenville	27 528	2.3	1 513	5.5	22 486	37.9	6.1	5.8	51 395	788	47.3
Hickory	16 981	1.0	467	2.8	15 448	26.3	9.0	7.4	40 480	274	84.3
High Point	41 104	2.0	1 209	2.9	35 360	23.4	10.9	8.8	126 760	1 247	74.0
Jacksonville	12 799	3.5	435	3.4	10 631	30.2	10.0	7.3	24 898	428	45.3
Kannapolis	17 507	4.1	621	3.5	13 850	19.3	15.8	10.0	NA	NA	NA
Kinston	11 783	1.7	1 059	9.0	10 155	29.2	11.0	12.1	5 259	53	100.0
Raleigh	169 403	2.3	2 730	1.6	117 849	42.1	6.7	5.7	533 924	5 784	59.1
Rocky Mount	24 494	0.2	1 736	7.1	23 032	26.8	10.2	9.4	25 672	341	61.3
Wilmington	34 132	4.2	1 273	3.7	25 805	27.9	10.8	9.8	NA	NA	NA
Wilson	18 817	3.8	1 798	9.6	16 203	26.9	8.9	10.6	30 633	387	79.8
Winston-Salem	78 423	1.0	2 325	3.0	69 563	34.2	8.2	7.5	96 588	1 060	71.2
NORTH DAKOTA	336 822	-2.9	11 456	3.4	287 558	26.4	9.8	7.0	223 249	2 579	56.0
Bismarck	32 708	-2.3	852	2.6	25 729	36.2	7.6	7.2	30 009	261	53.6
Fargo	52 346	-2.4	957	1.8	40 254	33.6	7.2	6.1	62 082	867	44.3
Grand Forks	28 073	-4.7	684	2.4	25 076	34.1	7.8	6.0	15 292	179	35.8
Minot	18 623	-4.1	606	3.3	15 535	29.0	7.8	6.8	12 916	174	51.1
OHIO	5 749 099	1.2	245 754	4.3	4 931 357	28.5	11.6	9.0	6 401 999	55 888	71.6
Akron	113 736	1.8	6 695	5.9	94 103	25.2	10.6	11.1	33 752	369	77.8
Barberton	13 297	1.8	752	5.7	11 029	18.6	15.7	12.5	15 578	139	98.6
Beavercreek	19 228	4.8	409	2.1	16 960	49.5	8.5	6.3	NA	NA	NA
Bowling Green	17 110	2.5	703	4.1	14 118	39.9	4.9	3.4	NA	NA	NA
Brunswick	18 796	3.2	749	4.0	14 521	23.5	16.7	7.2	52 745	329	100.0
Canton	38 129	0.7	2 709	7.1	32 336	22.2	9.6	12.1	8 963	105	75.2
Cincinnati	174 341	0.1	8 860	5.1	158 881	33.6	7.8	11.5	17 702	212	82.5
Cleveland	206 255	1.1	18 133	8.8	182 225	20.3	10.7	13.7	40 870	451	79.6
Cleveland Heights	29 070	1.0	843	2.9	27 342	50.4	5.0	6.5	100	1	100.0
Columbus	390 279	2.0	11 487	2.9	325 088	33.6	7.5	8.9	512 584	8 009	35.8
Cuyahoga Falls	28 711	1.7	839	2.9	24 503	33.5	10.3	7.5	27 819	295	50.8
Dayton	76 324	-1.1	5 090	6.7	70 730	25.7	10.0	12.9	6 500	43	100.0
East Cleveland	14 354	1.2	1 464	10.2	12 486	19.0	5.4	14.5	0	0	0.0
Elyria	30 440	1.0	1 589	5.2	26 257	24.2	13.4	8.5	15 463	126	90.5
Euclid	27 530	1.0	984	3.6	25 714	31.0	10.5	7.7	1 329	12	100.0
Fairborn	16 135	4.8	724	4.5	13 889	33.4	9.9	10.6	19 325	288	33.0
Fairfield	29 363	3.8	649	2.2	22 000	36.9	8.9	8.2	23 917	182	100.0
Findlay	23 048	1.9	739	3.2	17 483	31.0	11.0	7.8	19 092	148	73.6
Gahanna	16 816	2.0	312	1.9	14 167	38.9	8.7	7.2	23 963	122	100.0
Garfield Heights	15 485	1.0	554	3.6	14 463	23.7	14.2	7.8	784	8	100.0
Hamilton	34 693	3.7	1 691	4.9	25 285	21.5	12.8	13.6	13 607	130	83.1
Huber Heights	20 240	-0.8	606	3.0	19 495	31.4	11.3	8.0	NA	NA	NA
Kent	16 824	1.0	775	4.6	13 891	30.0	6.5	5.3	10 993	70	100.0
Kettering	31 964	-0.8	612	1.9	31 130	40.7	8.9	7.0	7 461	47	48.9
Lakewood	33 712	1.0	991	2.9	31 695	38.1	8.0	6.7	30	2	0.0
Lancaster	20 979	3.6	788	3.8	15 362	24.4	12.2	10.6	18 635	134	100.0
Lima	18 906	2.7	1 434	7.6	16 656	19.8	12.0	11.5	1 084	14	35.7
Lorain	32 824	0.9	2 319	7.1	27 762	21.4	12.9	10.1	11 087	96	95.8
Mansfield	23 094	2.1	1 873	8.1	20 519	23.7	11.8	11.9	9 133	183	15.3
Maple Heights	13 695	1.0	435	3.2	12 884	23.1	11.6	7.1	1 843	17	100.0
Marion	16 321	-2.0	809	5.0	14 086	20.7	13.8	12.7	3 616	65	95.4
Massillon	14 540	0.6	817	5.6	12 528	22.5	11.0	10.9	18 681	155	91.0
Mentor	28 002	1.7	951	3.4	24 672	34.1	12.2	6.1	25 187	123	100.0
Middletown	NA	NA	NA	NA	19 913	24.9	12.5	11.5	10 389	117	85.5
Newark	23 605	-0.4	1 151	4.9	19 187	27.0	10.8	9.0	132 007	993	96.5
North Olmsted	18 663	0.9	393	2.1	17 697	33.9	10.1	5.9	10 376	74	51.4
Parma	44 661	0.9	966	2.2	42 325	29.2	12.2	7.1	8 294	66	92.4
Reynoldsburg	17 447	1.9	269	1.5	14 742	34.5	9.2	6.0	44 220	569	49.4
Sandusky	15 961	0.4	1 001	6.3	13 137	21.3	11.1	10.9	9 696	85	22.4
Shaker Heights	16 710	0.9	396	2.4	15 803	61.6	2.8	4.9	418	2	100.0
Springfield	30 907	-0.5	1 716	5.6	28 636	24.5	10.4	12.5	8 235	91	100.0
Stow	16 820	1.6	338	2.0	14 490	40.2	9.3	5.2	41 486	319	58.0
Strongsville	19 843	0.9	428	2.2	18 806	39.3	9.3	3.8	51 573	485	53.4
Toledo	160 871	1.1	9 877	6.1	141 298	26.6	10.7	10.2	12 599	251	42.6
Upper Arlington	19 980	2.0	182	0.9	16 994	60.3	2.8	4.4	10 734	29	100.0

1. Percent of civilian labor force.   2. Persons 16 years and older.   3. Persons 16 to 64 years old.

Wholesale Trade, Retail Trade, and Real Estate

City	Wholesale Trade, 1997				Retail Trade[1], 1997				Real Estate and Rental and Leasing, 1997			
	Number of Establish-ments	Number of Employees	Sales (mil dol)	Annual Payroll (mil dol)	Number of Establish-ments	Number of Employees	Sales (mil dol)	Annual Payroll (mil dol)	Number of Establish-ments	Number of Employees	Receipts (mil dol)	Annual Payroll (mil dol)
	72	73	74	75	76	77	78	79	80	81	82	83
NORTH CAROLINA— Cont'd												
Concord	74	1 000	691.7	28.7	228	3 734	667.0	61.3	51	297	38.7	6.4
Durham	182	2 736	1 652.9	80.4	909	12 206	1 833.1	195.7	213	1 162	146.0	27.8
Fayetteville	140	1 653	549.5	45.8	755	12 055	2 089.9	193.4	197	867	90.5	16.9
Gastonia	127	1 197	726.9	41.8	442	6 895	1 128.1	103.3	67	308	27.1	5.1
Goldsboro	101	1 799	738.2	47.8	371	4 996	812.4	70.5	69	242	18.1	4.3
Greensboro	783	14 701	9 531.0	629.7	1 294	19 942	3 390.0	350.0	361	2 807	324.3	63.6
Greenville	122	1 196	527.2	30.2	474	6 729	1 144.5	105.3	100	431	44.7	6.9
Hickory	194	4 048	1 990.6	127.8	493	7 484	1 291.3	122.2	100	489	65.5	10.5
High Point	315	2 996	1 885.3	102.7	501	6 575	1 173.9	117.6	90	500	51.6	9.6
Jacksonville	28	156	36.4	3.7	321	4 561	758.4	69.2	75	365	41.2	5.8
Kannapolis	16	D	D	D	189	2 223	350.9	33.3	29	156	15.3	3.3
Kinston	50	1 017	357.7	18.1	258	2 935	462.0	42.0	38	154	12.9	2.2
Raleigh	778	11 873	8 296.7	553.2	1 618	22 689	4 568.5	414.5	494	3 291	624.6	95.0
Rocky Mount	99	1 744	896.0	58.6	392	4 833	825.3	76.4	75	395	48.5	7.2
Wilmington	209	2 748	994.0	74.1	743	9 566	1 952.2	163.6	159	755	85.8	14.6
Wilson	93	1 075	422.1	29.1	319	3 975	663.1	60.4	52	181	17.5	2.7
Winston-Salem	331	4 649	2 543.7	149.8	1 101	15 734	2 769.2	260.4	280	1 527	252.2	34.5
NORTH DAKOTA	1 604	16 992	8 618.4	454.4	3 569	40 685	6 702.1	616.1	657	3 325	287.0	46.3
Bismarck	134	1 472	591.2	42.0	356	5 081	808.4	82.0	90	D	D	D
Fargo	246	4 603	2 168.8	148.5	486	9 166	1 588.9	153.0	144	1 017	107.3	16.6
Grand Forks	97	D	D	D	312	5 345	889.2	77.5	63	494	31.8	6.7
Minot	62	D	D	D	292	4 534	711.7	69.8	55	D	D	D
OHIO	17 322	254 226	158 310.2	9 192.2	44 521	630 098	102 938.8	9 924.5	9 692	62 628	7 243.7	1 334.6
Akron	334	4 956	2 808.5	175.7	908	11 912	1 731.7	192.5	163	1 276	112.6	27.8
Barberton	42	401	122.2	15.0	93	873	123.8	12.6	10	60	4.1	1.1
Beavercreek	41	289	287.2	12.0	230	4 947	707.4	64.8	31	138	26.4	3.1
Bowling Green	23	164	63.3	4.4	124	1 895	262.5	23.7	33	156	13.4	2.1
Brunswick	44	464	155.8	13.3	102	1 285	307.8	24.9	15	71	10.6	1.5
Canton	141	2 493	1 072.0	75.1	391	5 050	775.7	78.8	82	375	32.5	6.7
Cincinnati	705	15 388	10 660.8	671.6	1 334	18 093	3 017.0	308.7	512	3 571	431.5	99.0
Cleveland	921	16 936	7 155.4	622.5	1 607	15 454	2 378.3	276.7	346	3 159	328.8	76.0
Cleveland Heights	27	58	52.7	1.7	154	1 594	278.7	28.8	56	267	26.9	3.5
Columbus	1 092	24 483	13 539.2	1 002.5	2 717	51 028	8 595.5	897.7	788	7 701	770.2	179.2
Cuyahoga Falls	79	530	157.2	16.8	207	3 683	760.3	64.7	49	305	25.3	5.3
Dayton	287	5 256	3 296.5	209.5	529	6 801	1 045.2	113.7	155	1 017	115.7	25.7
East Cleveland	12	D	D	D	69	515	54.3	6.7	21	116	11.9	1.8
Elyria	65	647	183.1	19.0	272	4 415	705.6	66.1	46	233	26.7	3.7
Euclid	72	2 532	1 342.3	174.3	169	2 418	314.7	32.5	49	358	29.4	6.5
Fairborn	15	253	138.1	8.3	101	1 326	224.4	19.0	27	121	14.3	1.9
Fairfield	93	1 683	1 279.8	60.5	182	3 254	710.6	60.6	45	387	38.1	8.2
Findlay	61	607	336.0	17.8	259	3 665	569.3	52.3	55	D	D	D
Gahanna	49	421	278.9	19.3	89	1 296	189.2	17.6	22	81	14.0	1.6
Garfield Heights	51	1 487	810.2	71.4	78	1 287	179.9	18.6	13	46	6.5	0.6
Hamilton	75	1 404	890.5	51.2	233	2 755	375.3	40.3	55	303	23.7	5.6
Huber Heights	21	295	160.1	13.1	129	2 150	276.6	26.1	24	212	27.0	6.4
Kent	28	189	61.0	6.1	74	1 215	338.1	26.3	28	154	14.8	1.9
Kettering	73	924	595.4	43.1	228	4 821	756.0	71.2	66	348	38.3	6.1
Lakewood	62	617	255.7	22.8	155	1 767	300.6	30.9	47	282	31.4	5.3
Lancaster	40	364	97.7	12.2	270	3 868	540.0	57.9	47	200	18.5	3.0
Lima	89	1 197	436.2	32.8	188	2 143	361.9	33.5	48	201	15.3	3.1
Lorain	40	877	199.0	23.6	175	2 148	314.9	29.5	55	212	16.2	3.3
Mansfield	96	1 344	445.3	36.2	273	3 186	486.6	53.1	53	214	25.8	3.7
Maple Heights	27	709	250.5	20.3	135	1 750	197.9	23.0	18	79	5.4	1.2
Marion	32	287	84.7	8.8	156	2 482	397.7	37.4	38	150	12.9	3.1
Massillon	33	1 158	833.3	45.5	128	1 831	296.6	28.1	14	54	4.1	0.8
Mentor	138	1 828	477.5	56.8	401	7 492	1 316.3	120.6	48	308	29.9	5.4
Middletown	40	876	302.2	29.0	193	2 232	327.0	33.5	59	245	27.5	4.4
Newark	43	447	178.5	14.8	192	2 038	323.3	32.9	45	199	16.9	3.5
North Olmsted	57	D	D	D	324	5 444	935.6	76.9	27	127	19.9	3.4
Parma	73	981	290.8	34.1	366	5 440	794.1	80.8	55	438	47.3	7.9
Reynoldsburg	33	432	147.9	8.9	101	1 214	151.7	16.6	48	221	26.6	3.6
Sandusky	47	498	147.8	15.1	224	3 016	419.7	43.4	37	165	13.7	2.7
Shaker Heights	34	245	337.0	8.8	89	1 187	203.9	19.6	29	162	19.0	2.7
Springfield	69	1 126	657.6	30.5	328	4 983	724.2	70.6	49	223	21.2	3.8
Stow	46	727	451.2	23.7	99	1 971	266.4	29.2	27	144	16.3	2.1
Strongsville	85	1 516	632.2	62.8	226	4 434	511.3	57.4	39	199	18.7	3.3
Toledo	487	7 731	3 692.8	259.5	1 281	18 732	2 513.1	280.4	255	1 729	192.4	37.6
Upper Arlington	48	366	242.9	12.3	124	1 511	156.7	21.3	48	D	D	D

1. Establishments with payroll.

City	Professional, Scientific, and Technical Services, 1997[1]				Manufacturing, 1997				Accommodation and Foodservices, 1997			
	Number of Establishments	Number of Employees	Receipts (mil dol)	Annual Payroll (mil dol)	Number of Establishments	Number of Employees	Receipts (mil dol)	Annual Payroll (mil dol)	Number of Establishments	Number of Employees	Sales (mil dol)	Annual Payroll (mil dol)
	84	85	86	87	88	89	90	91	92	93	94	95
NORTH CAROLINA—Cont'd												
Concord	80	510	36.8	16.7	78	6 253	6 968.6	225.4	89	1 915	66.4	18.0
Durham	470	4 648	689.2	204.0	123	D	D	D	386	7 800	295.9	81.9
Fayetteville	272	1 849	122.9	42.9	78	9 100	2 170.0	295.1	354	8 134	246.8	67.2
Gastonia	139	648	52.1	20.6	211	12 666	2 385.8	360.0	166	3 346	107.0	29.1
Goldsboro	101	519	38.7	14.2	64	4 644	579.8	116.1	125	2 553	73.0	19.9
Greensboro	763	5 741	542.0	192.7	411	21 305	5 903.6	711.5	653	15 531	489.3	142.7
Greenville	177	1 131	75.6	30.9	60	4 006	1 827.2	143.5	198	4 854	138.7	38.1
Hickory	172	939	73.6	26.6	253	17 501	2 235.8	441.1	195	4 498	127.5	37.4
High Point	206	1 579	127.6	51.5	288	17 182	2 247.9	465.0	184	3 023	97.1	27.9
Jacksonville	92	590	26.6	9.1	NA	NA	NA	NA	137	2 729	76.7	20.4
Kannapolis	46	229	12.3	5.6	21	D	D	D	58	909	31.0	8.4
Kinston	50	351	23.1	12.0	51	3 832	904.5	98.1	75	1 517	46.5	13.2
Raleigh	1 465	12 856	1 424.1	566.8	328	7 954	2 147.1	241.5	780	16 886	606.2	171.3
Rocky Mount	89	610	52.6	19.1	65	7 886	1 475.0	220.3	118	2 549	81.2	22.1
Wilmington	347	2 508	198.9	81.7	139	5 257	1 241.1	202.0	289	6 562	203.5	56.9
Wilson	79	D	D	D	70	7 534	2 821.1	238.5	115	2 463	76.2	20.5
Winston-Salem	575	4 515	465.8	179.4	241	17 789	4 449.7	583.0	479	10 328	327.7	94.0
NORTH DAKOTA	1 077	7 076	418.0	175.7	704	21 956	5 115.9	604.8	1 827	26 330	684.9	189.0
Bismarck	174	D	D	D	48	D	D	D	149	3 444	95.7	27.6
Fargo	246	2 129	147.9	58.0	133	5 206	1 057.5	131.2	242	6 616	178.7	51.5
Grand Forks	102	710	48.4	23.2	43	1 536	231.9	33.7	152	3 941	88.4	26.1
Minot	80	797	37.0	17.1	41	D	D	D	131	2 678	68.0	19.8
OHIO	21 182	182 805	18 294.7	6 948.0	17 974	984 201	241 902.9	35 950.5	22 631	401 206	12 411.0	3 444.2
Akron	480	4 837	564.6	203.3	370	12 822	2 020.4	451.8	489	7 364	223.9	62.6
Barberton	27	112	7.3	2.5	77	4 140	535.5	122.5	57	692	22.5	5.8
Beavercreek	141	2 040	231.2	92.4	31	826	167.7	31.4	69	D	D	D
Bowling Green	48	331	34.0	8.8	41	3 107	429.8	96.6	87	1 808	39.7	11.0
Brunswick	41	228	18.2	5.9	29	658	93.6	21.0	48	824	21.4	6.0
Canton	198	1 160	105.8	42.3	182	13 120	3 233.5	461.9	208	3 620	100.1	27.0
Cincinnati	1 282	18 517	2 137.0	830.5	604	28 917	6 540.2	1 021.8	829	16 006	564.1	158.1
Cleveland	1 284	19 671	2 502.5	987.2	1 270	44 400	8 675.8	1 662.2	1 099	17 757	674.4	176.9
Cleveland Heights	109	235	19.9	7.1	NA	NA	NA	NA	83	D	D	D
Columbus	1 825	20 837	2 377.4	875.1	685	32 243	8 409.3	1 173.3	1 508	32 807	1 160.0	334.7
Cuyahoga Falls	109	964	44.7	20.5	88	3 220	531.9	111.4	123	2 695	79.8	23.5
Dayton	407	4 535	550.6	181.8	350	20 112	3 579.4	811.2	327	5 098	180.7	48.0
East Cleveland	4	10	0.7	0.1	NA	NA	NA	NA	29	454	14.1	3.8
Elyria	97	506	43.8	18.5	132	7 704	1 610.8	260.2	124	2 278	68.6	17.6
Euclid	60	378	31.3	15.3	108	8 223	1 627.6	326.0	83	D	D	D
Fairborn	65	1 932	200.6	84.2	14	779	139.5	27.0	79	1 656	50.5	14.6
Fairfield	69	461	33.8	13.7	84	3 096	492.8	95.9	81	1 727	48.5	13.6
Findlay	91	445	31.8	12.7	66	7 559	1 397.3	271.5	143	2 766	74.7	22.3
Gahanna	70	568	53.0	23.9	28	517	74.4	16.1	64	1 272	38.2	11.5
Garfield Heights	42	435	42.6	19.4	48	1 502	189.3	48.1	54	D	D	D
Hamilton	102	756	38.9	17.8	86	3 717	692.2	136.9	130	2 184	62.1	17.0
Huber Heights	26	246	14.7	7.0	34	D	D	D	79	1 524	45.2	12.5
Kent	41	145	8.8	2.6	72	2 412	343.0	70.2	84	1 328	33.3	9.9
Kettering	142	1 360	132.7	53.2	51	5 025	831.9	269.9	115	D	D	D
Lakewood	110	526	36.0	16.6	41	1 128	182.1	44.1	112	1 356	41.3	10.7
Lancaster	79	337	22.9	8.8	78	4 282	625.1	134.0	100	2 249	66.3	18.4
Lima	98	556	38.5	14.2	48	3 856	1 743.7	209.3	93	1 427	43.7	11.7
Lorain	66	782	39.2	20.8	64	7 745	6 669.5	340.4	99	D	D	D
Mansfield	111	673	42.7	17.4	126	7 844	1 256.5	265.4	143	2 289	74.0	20.3
Maple Heights	12	47	3.1	1.2	31	576	77.9	19.0	47	575	19.3	5.0
Marion	56	313	17.7	6.7	48	2 723	784.9	92.6	67	1 395	41.6	10.8
Massillon	42	253	15.0	6.6	64	4 737	975.6	144.7	79	1 107	31.0	7.5
Mentor	140	659	62.8	23.7	244	8 617	1 450.4	274.8	127	3 338	86.5	24.9
Middletown	73	557	92.8	20.6	71	7 187	3 662.9	353.0	97	2 370	69.5	20.0
Newark	88	821	40.5	16.6	49	4 017	770.2	133.4	102	1 335	40.6	11.1
North Olmsted	70	466	33.4	15.7	NA	NA	NA	NA	117	2 617	72.3	20.6
Parma	102	1 001	42.6	14.8	58	5 002	972.8	278.8	189	2 778	76.2	20.4
Reynoldsburg	80	497	42.9	21.3	15	591	213.0	16.0	75	1 043	33.6	9.0
Sandusky	62	336	26.9	13.6	66	5 206	799.0	223.4	123	2 853	104.9	28.8
Shaker Heights	97	489	56.5	18.8	NA	NA	NA	NA	38	779	22.6	6.1
Springfield	91	532	27.4	11.2	115	D	D	D	169	3 258	95.0	26.3
Stow	64	229	14.5	4.9	72	2 527	342.5	89.4	44	886	23.6	6.2
Strongsville	117	447	35.4	16.2	76	3 286	650.9	122.7	95	2 151	51.4	13.4
Toledo	584	5 500	569.5	183.3	462	25 446	9 282.3	1 101.0	737	13 187	424.0	112.3
Upper Arlington	128	552	46.9	18.3	NA	NA	NA	NA	53	1 016	29.6	9.2

1. Firms subject to federal tax.

City	Arts, Entertainment, and Recreation[1], 1997				Health Care and Social Assistance[1], 1997				Other Services[1], 1997			
	Number of Establishments	Number of Employees	Receipts (mil dol)	Annual Payroll (mil dol)	Number of Establishments	Number of Employees	Receipts (mil dol)	Annual Payroll (mil dol)	Number of Establishments	Number of Employees	Receipts (mil dol)	Annual Payroll (mil dol)
	96	97	98	99	100	101	102	103	104	105	106	107
NORTH CAROLINA— Cont'd												
Concord	19	248	34.7	6.8	104	1 710	118.0	61.0	96	489	26.4	8.4
Durham	31	363	17.3	4.8	341	5 018	276.0	137.4	294	2 088	111.5	39.6
Fayetteville	35	601	18.7	6.1	336	5 054	328.7	142.6	239	1 835	98.5	31.9
Gastonia	16	179	5.0	1.4	189	2 807	189.2	91.8	131	926	50.3	14.6
Goldsboro	11	111	3.4	1.0	144	1 798	98.1	48.2	108	844	49.6	16.0
Greensboro	76	727	29.0	9.0	567	8 420	596.2	293.4	476	3 853	270.4	77.9
Greenville	29	410	12.2	4.2	167	2 805	194.9	105.4	114	742	39.2	11.6
Hickory	18	194	9.0	2.1	169	3 752	296.4	125.9	138	919	51.1	17.6
High Point	23	347	47.7	4.5	180	1 913	170.1	75.5	154	813	42.7	13.7
Jacksonville	16	123	4.0	1.1	138	2 078	109.3	49.0	107	596	27.5	9.1
Kannapolis	10	155	7.5	2.6	37	422	19.4	7.2	65	295	19.6	5.8
Kinston	11	50	2.4	0.6	107	1 359	85.8	36.8	67	530	23.0	7.5
Raleigh	95	899	39.9	10.6	731	10 956	833.0	387.7	575	4 540	371.6	97.6
Rocky Mount	15	100	3.8	1.3	132	2 849	192.4	77.9	114	830	49.8	14.3
Wilmington	38	467	16.4	5.0	329	5 047	344.8	146.6	224	1 496	90.8	28.3
Wilson	11	89	2.9	0.8	110	1 740	93.3	46.0	75	614	28.2	9.6
Winston-Salem	45	451	18.0	5.6	446	6 048	555.7	225.7	352	2 623	135.0	47.3
NORTH DAKOTA	248	3 154	164.3	32.6	1 013	13 181	904.1	386.4	1 281	6 294	364.3	101.3
Bismarck	15	0	0.0	0.0	131	1 437	121.0	55.4	132	808	44.1	13.6
Fargo	29	452	18.8	4.0	205	5 753	466.9	187.7	206	1 813	98.9	31.0
Grand Forks	19	166	4.8	1.0	75	1 414	62.9	43.4	94	673	33.7	10.8
Minot	26	170	6.1	1.6	97	1 010	88.6	27.8	87	510	22.6	7.1
OHIO	2 902	37 210	2 308.6	706.6	20 399	261 520	15 440.1	7 477.0	17 314	116 165	7 087.5	2 165.7
Akron	48	777	47.8	10.9	415	5 418	410.5	229.6	368	2 522	138.9	45.3
Barberton	4	42	1.1	0.3	63	755	48.6	20.7	51	322	17.4	5.7
Beavercreek	9	177	9.0	2.7	72	948	64.1	31.7	63	351	21.4	6.2
Bowling Green	5	66	1.7	0.5	45	533	26.3	12.7	40	281	14.4	4.7
Brunswick	5	77	1.6	0.6	45	660	27.5	13.2	49	283	17.0	4.9
Canton	16	155	8.2	2.0	185	2 703	196.6	107.3	153	1 009	66.1	21.5
Cincinnati	84	1 340	181.4	100.3	862	12 504	869.7	469.4	609	4 476	297.6	92.4
Cleveland	84	2 738	354.1	143.9	531	9 272	590.9	300.6	749	5 448	377.6	103.4
Cleveland Heights	13	88	2.8	0.8	112	736	48.6	20.5	65	457	28.9	8.8
Columbus	133	2 316	93.4	23.3	1 325	18 567	1 299.0	675.2	998	8 317	509.7	163.0
Cuyahoga Falls	7	68	2.8	0.7	155	1 311	77.7	39.9	92	532	28.7	9.3
Dayton	27	329	14.4	3.8	319	4 624	307.4	167.5	279	2 613	171.8	56.8
East Cleveland	1	0	0.0	0.0	21	288	16.0	7.1	22	96	3.7	1.1
Elyria	9	120	4.3	1.2	124	1 188	91.7	49.0	75	479	28.8	8.0
Euclid	9	90	2.1	0.6	95	1 712	97.0	56.3	98	566	34.8	10.3
Fairborn	5	39	0.7	0.2	33	276	15.8	5.5	60	524	24.7	11.7
Fairfield	15	195	6.2	1.7	110	1 602	96.2	44.0	102	616	42.5	13.1
Findlay	8	56	2.2	0.6	105	1 183	77.0	39.2	74	566	30.3	10.0
Gahanna	6	133	6.5	2.7	72	562	32.4	14.4	43	576	34.6	10.1
Garfield Heights	NA	NA	NA	NA	61	416	37.7	15.7	48	266	15.0	4.8
Hamilton	10	93	2.4	0.6	115	1 128	70.0	37.5	83	421	27.3	6.9
Huber Heights	6	61	1.5	0.5	64	671	35.6	15.1	51	286	14.5	4.4
Kent	2	0	0.0	0.0	40	385	22.2	8.7	35	201	9.5	3.1
Kettering	16	213	7.1	2.5	177	2 267	149.1	76.6	88	707	31.9	11.6
Lakewood	8	43	1.9	0.5	138	1 479	100.2	58.4	72	431	26.5	8.5
Lancaster	12	84	9.8	1.7	141	1 458	84.7	41.5	73	437	23.8	8.0
Lima	4	29	0.7	0.2	142	1 633	122.7	67.6	75	489	21.9	6.4
Lorain	15	168	8.2	1.9	139	1 775	115.6	65.1	85	689	37.6	12.4
Mansfield	15	260	4.7	1.5	176	1 887	111.4	53.7	112	955	47.1	20.2
Maple Heights	7	51	2.5	0.5	57	504	31.6	12.1	49	270	22.8	5.2
Marion	8	66	2.2	0.4	106	1 678	96.8	48.6	62	298	15.3	4.8
Massillon	4	45	0.7	0.2	49	742	39.0	17.2	61	318	15.3	4.7
Mentor	19	166	9.1	2.3	106	1 248	65.1	27.3	138	1 002	67.1	21.7
Middletown	11	130	5.6	2.3	109	1 157	82.7	43.1	91	578	28.8	9.5
Newark	10	139	3.9	1.2	118	2 582	114.3	60.0	80	518	29.1	9.5
North Olmsted	9	86	1.9	0.6	77	760	42.5	19.1	99	634	29.1	10.8
Parma	16	355	4.5	1.3	209	2 058	161.8	69.5	160	1 313	67.3	22.2
Reynoldsburg	6	71	2.5	1.2	67	396	23.7	10.8	63	283	17.5	5.0
Sandusky	18	0	0.0	0.0	119	877	62.2	31.9	73	384	16.0	5.2
Shaker Heights	4	11	0.6	0.2	68	1 248	42.2	22.9	40	294	14.1	4.9
Springfield	8	80	3.2	0.9	190	2 001	130.6	64.6	125	1 053	50.4	14.8
Stow	11	114	4.2	1.3	59	747	47.7	20.0	48	350	13.5	5.1
Strongsville	8	91	3.2	0.8	72	468	29.0	12.3	64	524	44.6	13.6
Toledo	80	1 230	66.2	16.3	596	8 240	543.8	267.6	571	3 880	247.0	74.5
Upper Arlington	6	10	0.3	0.1	78	714	39.9	17.8	36	237	11.0	3.6

1. Firms subject to federal tax.

	Selected federal funds, fiscal 1999[1] (mil dol)									City government finances, 1997						
										General revenue						
	Procurement contracts		Grants					Direct payments for individuals			Intergovernmental		Taxes			
														Per capita[3] (dollars)		
City	Defense	Other	Total[2]	Health and family welfare	Energy and environment	Education	Housing and community development	Educational assistance	Housing assistance	Total (mil dol)	Total (mil dol)	Percent from state government	Total (mil dol)	Total	Property	Sales and gross receipts
	108	109	110	111	112	113	114	115	116	117	118	119	120	121	122	123
NORTH CAROLINA— Cont'd																
Concord	0.0	0.0	2.4	0.9	0.0	0.6	0.7	0.9	0.0	43.5	12.8	35.9	14.5	441	423	6
Durham	24.6	162.9	313.7	263.3	8.4	8.3	4.2	8.6	1.5	182.6	49.9	28.1	54.8	366	331	13
Fayetteville	7.5	5.1	18.3	4.7	0.0	3.4	7.1	6.8	3.2	102.5	31.9	33.4	27.4	344	317	3
Gastonia	2.4	0.3	1.4	0.0	0.0	0.0	1.5	0.0	0.0	55.0	18.4	37.5	14.4	254	227	12
Goldsboro	1.3	0.0	6.0	3.3	0.0	0.4	0.7	1.1	0.1	28.4	12.1	38.0	7.7	188	167	6
Greensboro	126.1	9.9	63.6	6.8	0.6	11.5	4.7	8.0	4.1	222.1	62.7	41.0	88.5	453	405	20
Greenville	0.8	2.8	16.1	4.2	0.0	0.6	0.0	6.8	0.0	42.1	15.6	38.6	13.3	243	206	12
Hickory	0.5	3.7	3.8	0.2	0.0	0.0	0.7	1.4	0.7	48.9	19.6	56.3	16.4	537	469	34
High Point	1.4	1.9	1.5	0.0	0.0	0.0	1.1	1.7	3.2	86.1	28.0	54.1	30.1	404	354	17
Jacksonville	7.0	0.5	2.8	0.8	0.0	0.3	0.4	0.8	3.1	31.6	15.0	30.4	7.1	102	91	0
Kannapolis	0.0	0.1	1.8	0.9	0.0	0.0	0.8	0.0	2.9	15.3	6.6	44.9	6.0	167	160	3
Kinston	0.9	0.1	8.3	0.4	0.0	0.3	0.0	1.0	0.6	30.2	16.1	68.1	5.8	229	202	11
Raleigh	23.2	16.6	1 237.8	381.7	61.5	179.0	64.6	12.4	5.0	240.5	78.3	35.4	97.4	400	315	51
Rocky Mount	4.0	0.2	5.6	3.7	0.0	0.5	0.7	1.2	2.6	43.4	15.7	51.7	12.1	230	212	3
Wilmington	21.9	10.1	18.3	5.8	0.1	0.0	3.3	3.3	6.5	66.6	24.1	33.7	18.0	289	263	6
Wilson	3.1	1.5	0.8	0.5	0.0	0.2	0.1	1.2	1.6	40.2	11.6	44.2	10.4	261	233	7
Winston-Salem	3.9	6.2	102.7	78.2	4.2	3.4	4.2	6.3	2.4	247.2	73.3	35.3	67.3	439	397	11
NORTH DAKOTA	149.4	105.1	1 009.5	387.7	30.1	96.6	10.9	31.3	12.8	X	X	X	X	X	X	X
Bismarck	0.4	3.3	199.5	43.5	12.4	31.4	5.0	3.5	1.5	50.8	6.6	58.5	17.4	325	166	145
Fargo	10.0	4.5	30.6	4.4	0.2	1.1	2.2	5.0	2.9	74.5	12.7	50.5	24.7	295	106	174
Grand Forks	3.2	3.8	25.4	8.1	6.3	1.9	0.2	4.7	4.1	46.2	6.9	66.8	17.4	343	127	200
Minot	1.1	9.0	6.2	2.3	0.0	1.5	0.2	1.9	1.3	23.8	3.2	91.5	11.1	310	177	119
OHIO	2 596.7	1 910.8	10 254.4	6 644.5	93.5	911.0	292.7	359.1	342.4	X	X	X	X	X	X	X
Akron	219.0	3.7	47.7	14.1	0.3	2.0	18.4	9.0	7.7	270.5	49.7	60.7	144.2	665	104	46
Barberton	9.3	0.0	1.5	0.0	0.2	0.0	1.0	0.1	0.0	22.2	4.4	98.9	10.1	372	31	0
Beavercreek	175.4	3.2	0.1	0.0	0.0	0.0	0.0	0.0	0.0	11.9	3.0	97.1	6.7	216	192	6
Bowling Green	0.1	0.9	4.5	1.2	0.0	1.9	0.8	3.8	0.0	21.0	3.2	74.3	10.6	376	46	0
Brunswick	0.1	0.5	0.0	0.0	0.0	0.0	0.0	0.0	0.0	14.4	3.2	76.3	7.0	221	75	5
Canton	5.8	3.4	23.2	5.7	3.3	0.4	8.9	2.4	10.5	79.5	16.2	70.2	39.4	486	27	0
Cincinnati	817.1	68.8	203.5	125.7	4.8	5.5	27.6	19.2	54.0	658.2	161.6	34.1	286.1	827	136	16
Cleveland	90.6	341.9	387.8	223.7	12.4	8.8	41.1	28.0	28.7	684.8	162.6	53.0	338.3	679	109	44
Cleveland Heights	0.8	0.9	1.3	0.4	0.0	0.0	0.8	0.2	2.5	42.5	7.9	45.5	25.8	475	128	10
Columbus	219.8	147.6	1 817.8	733.1	53.4	285.5	92.8	28.1	46.9	770.2	116.4	60.5	383.7	584	41	13
Cuyahoga Falls	3.2	0.0	1.6	0.0	0.0	1.6	0.0	0.6	1.7	40.3	5.3	97.9	18.5	376	133	6
Dayton	227.2	32.5	83.7	23.4	0.9	5.9	24.9	10.8	20.8	257.3	37.0	51.5	120.7	698	93	3
East Cleveland	0.0	0.0	0.7	0.0	0.0	0.0	0.7	0.0	7.1	19.9	5.4	64.9	9.4	303	71	3
Elyria	2.4	0.5	3.0	0.1	0.0	0.1	0.9	2.6	0.8	48.0	7.8	91.5	24.6	434	84	4
Euclid	0.8	0.0	1.6	0.0	0.0	0.4	1.0	0.0	1.4	49.8	4.4	64.0	28.1	535	146	2
Fairborn	25.0	4.8	1.5	0.9	0.0	0.0	0.6	0.1	4.3	20.3	3.7	69.5	7.7	252	78	0
Fairfield	28.2	12.2	3.2	3.1	0.0	0.0	0.0	0.1	0.4	30.2	3.8	98.3	14.7	349	57	6
Findlay	0.1	0.1	4.5	2.0	0.0	0.5	0.2	1.5	0.9	25.5	3.8	100.0	12.1	328	58	0
Gahanna	0.3	0.4	0.2	0.0	0.0	0.0	0.1	0.0	0.0	25.6	3.3	97.9	11.8	376	133	6
Garfield Heights	0.0	0.0	0.6	0.6	0.0	0.0	0.0	0.0	0.0	20.6	3.9	100.0	13.2	437	187	0
Hamilton	0.1	0.1	7.3	0.2	0.0	0.0	3.7	0.2	2.3	73.7	8.7	69.3	23.0	371	53	6
Huber Heights	-0.2	0.0	0.1	0.0	0.0	0.0	0.0	0.0	0.0	19.8	4.6	96.5	10.8	278	77	0
Kent	3.1	0.5	12.6	2.1	0.3	3.9	0.7	8.0	4.0	19.3	3.4	81.9	10.1	373	61	0
Kettering	1.2	0.0	5.2	0.4	0.0	0.0	0.5	0.2	0.0	47.5	9.1	93.4	28.2	484	115	0
Lakewood	0.0	0.2	2.5	0.0	0.0	0.0	2.5	0.2	0.6	41.7	9.8	70.6	23.0	413	198	0
Lancaster	0.0	0.6	2.2	0.9	0.0	0.0	1.1	0.0	2.6	26.9	4.6	85.5	10.3	292	41	0
Lima	12.8	1.1	5.4	1.8	0.0	0.0	1.9	2.0	1.5	29.0	4.8	57.8	14.8	346	23	8
Lorain	0.2	0.1	9.6	5.4	0.0	1.1	2.8	0.4	4.3	45.6	9.3	83.9	22.4	320	48	4
Mansfield	5.6	0.1	5.0	0.4	0.0	0.1	2.1	1.3	0.4	41.3	9.3	63.4	22.0	432	49	4
Maple Heights	0.2	0.0	0.0	0.0	0.0	0.0	0.0	0.2	0.0	18.5	5.5	96.4	10.7	414	159	4
Marion	1.9	0.0	5.4	4.7	0.0	0.0	0.3	0.0	2.3	28.6	6.6	66.5	10.3	309	31	4
Massillon	0.6	0.0	1.8	0.0	0.0	0.5	0.8	0.0	0.1	21.8	4.4	70.8	10.1	330	41	0
Mentor	3.9	0.9	1.1	0.3	0.0	0.0	0.2	1.3	0.0	41.2	6.6	96.3	27.6	550	99	11
Middletown	-0.6	0.0	2.5	0.0	0.0	0.0	0.9	0.0	0.0	25.5	4.2	97.7	19.1	397	108	0
Newark	92.3	0.1	6.3	2.5	0.0	0.0	1.3	0.7	0.2	70.1	30.1	94.8	24.1	493	243	0
North Olmsted	0.0	2.6	0.0	0.0	0.0	0.0	0.0	0.0	0.0	34.4	9.3	58.5	17.2	497	240	1
Parma	0.0	0.0	1.0	0.0	0.0	0.0	1.0	0.0	0.0	45.0	10.5	86.4	30.0	353	88	2
Reynoldsburg	0.2	0.3	4.1	0.0	3.1	0.1	0.0	0.0	0.0	12.7	1.4	100.0	6.3	215	22	11
Sandusky	0.7	7.8	2.2	1.4	0.0	0.0	0.2	0.1	0.9	20.4	2.9	100.0	11.5	395	62	82
Shaker Heights	0.0	2.9	0.2	0.0	0.0	0.0	0.1	0.0	0.0	36.3	3.4	79.6	24.0	820	183	0
Springfield	7.0	0.5	8.4	0.0	0.0	1.3	4.7	2.4	7.5	46.4	10.1	84.4	21.9	324	27	2
Stow	0.1	0.0	0.6	0.0	0.0	0.0	0.0	0.0	-0.2	16.1	2.7	94.0	12.3	397	108	0
Strongsville	0.1	2.0	0.4	0.0	0.0	0.0	0.0	0.0	0.0	30.5	4.6	51.5	15.5	376	46	0
Toledo	28.3	3.4	64.9	22.9	0.4	0.9	15.9	9.4	17.1	289.8	51.0	58.5	162.9	513	41	7
Upper Arlington	0.0	0.0	0.0	0.0	0.0	0.0	0.0	0.0	0.0	24.8	3.1	100.0	16.5	501	158	13

1. October 1, 1998 to September 30, 1999.   2. Includes program categories not shown separately. State totals include additional categories not allocated by city.   3. Based on population estimated as of July 1 of the year shown.

Table D. Cities — **City Government Finances**

City	City government finances, 1997 (cont'd)												
	General expenditure												
	Per capita[1] (dollars)			Percent of total for —									
	Total (mil dol)	Total	Capital outlays	Public welfare	Highways	Parking facilities	Education	Health and hospitals	Police protection	Sewerage and sanitation	Parks and recreation	Housing and community development	Interest on debt
	124	125	126	127	128	129	130	131	132	133	134	135	136
NORTH CAROLINA— Cont'd													
Concord	42.8	1 299	229	0.0	7.0	0.0	0.0	0.0	11.3	22.8	5.2	1.2	4.7
Durham	144.1	962	108	0.0	10.0	0.4	0.0	0.0	18.3	24.8	6.2	4.7	8.5
Fayetteville	91.2	1 145	212	0.0	10.5	0.2	0.0	0.0	27.6	21.4	7.5	1.9	6.7
Gastonia	67.4	1 192	287	0.0	20.2	0.0	0.0	0.0	14.6	18.5	4.3	2.4	6.9
Goldsboro	24.9	611	47	0.0	19.8	0.0	0.0	0.4	19.2	17.0	6.3	0.6	0.5
Greensboro	207.0	1 059	129	0.0	10.1	0.3	0.0	0.0	18.1	15.2	16.0	3.4	5.9
Greenville	41.0	750	156	0.0	9.4	0.1	0.0	0.3	20.2	25.5	8.6	2.1	2.0
Hickory	47.5	1 556	482	0.0	21.2	0.0	0.0	0.1	10.6	17.4	5.3	1.4	0.8
High Point	75.5	1 014	73	0.0	7.5	0.4	0.0	0.0	14.8	21.7	7.5	2.6	4.5
Jacksonville	30.2	432	68	0.0	9.7	0.0	0.0	0.3	17.2	24.6	8.1	1.9	6.6
Kannapolis	13.4	376	74	0.0	10.3	0.0	0.0	0.0	28.9	22.2	0.1	5.9	2.1
Kinston	25.7	1 025	20	0.0	5.7	0.0	41.4	0.2	5.3	18.4	3.7	10.9	0.9
Raleigh	193.7	795	158	0.6	11.8	0.2	0.0	0.1	15.6	14.5	16.1	3.6	3.9
Rocky Mount	43.3	823	112	0.0	11.0	0.0	0.0	0.0	17.0	22.8	7.2	2.9	2.5
Wilmington	50.5	813	38	0.0	6.4	0.3	0.0	0.0	17.8	18.8	8.2	1.7	4.6
Wilson	34.3	859	75	0.0	7.0	0.3	0.0	0.0	15.5	23.5	9.6	5.2	0.2
Winston-Salem	175.9	1 145	150	0.0	9.4	1.6	0.0	0.1	17.8	24.3	8.2	11.4	4.0
NORTH DAKOTA	X	X	X	X	X	X	X	X	X	X	X	X	X
Bismarck	44.8	837	193	0.0	16.5	1.3	0.0	1.4	11.5	9.5	3.3	1.8	12.5
Fargo	76.3	911	401	0.3	3.5	0.3	0.0	3.4	6.6	6.7	6.3	3.3	9.2
Grand Forks	48.0	948	274	0.0	7.3	1.6	0.0	2.6	9.0	14.9	7.8	4.5	8.8
Minot	16.9	471	36	1.9	9.6	0.5	0.0	0.0	18.4	8.9	5.0	0.0	14.1
OHIO	X	X	X	X	X	X	X	X	X	X	X	X	X
Akron	264.0	1 217	318	0.0	10.8	4.0	0.0	7.5	14.3	16.2	12.0	2.0	2.1
Barberton	21.4	786	73	0.0	13.3	0.0	0.0	5.0	15.9	14.6	5.8	3.7	10.1
Beavercreek	13.9	447	129	0.0	20.3	0.0	0.0	0.6	34.0	0.0	22.4	0.0	5.0
Bowling Green	22.2	785	201	0.0	8.9	0.5	0.0	0.0	22.5	29.6	2.7	4.1	7.1
Brunswick	11.4	362	59	0.0	14.0	0.0	0.0	0.3	19.3	16.4	11.0	0.9	4.9
Canton	77.1	951	121	0.0	10.4	0.0	0.0	4.4	17.7	15.1	2.9	5.6	2.1
Cincinnati	647.9	1 874	445	0.0	9.6	1.1	0.0	5.3	11.7	24.1	7.1	4.1	2.6
Cleveland	643.3	1 291	127	0.5	7.0	0.8	0.0	4.6	22.8	6.1	7.6	10.8	4.1
Cleveland Heights	38.6	712	20	0.0	9.7	1.2	0.0	1.1	15.1	9.2	5.5	11.5	3.4
Columbus	757.3	1 153	220	0.0	8.9	0.1	0.0	4.0	20.1	18.9	7.0	2.2	8.0
Cuyahoga Falls	41.4	839	127	0.0	7.2	0.0	0.0	0.0	30.1	23.3	8.6	2.1	2.3
Dayton	269.5	1 558	307	0.1	9.6	0.7	0.0	0.0	16.8	9.5	2.0	5.8	7.1
East Cleveland	17.3	556	0	0.0	4.9	0.3	0.0	0.0	23.6	25.1	1.4	9.8	0.0
Elyria	45.1	796	88	0.0	13.7	0.0	0.0	3.0	19.8	19.0	4.5	1.2	7.4
Euclid	47.6	906	55	0.0	7.0	0.0	0.0	1.7	16.4	23.0	6.9	4.5	2.3
Fairborn	18.6	608	40	0.0	1.7	0.0	0.0	0.4	21.0	20.3	1.7	4.0	3.7
Fairfield	26.6	630	129	0.0	18.6	0.0	0.0	3.0	18.1	17.6	7.6	0.2	10.1
Findlay	27.8	753	231	0.0	12.9	0.4	0.0	1.8	19.8	23.4	2.8	0.0	3.8
Gahanna	22.9	730	96	0.0	8.3	0.0	0.0	0.0	34.7	14.5	9.9	2.5	0.0
Garfield Heights	17.8	589	11	0.0	7.2	0.0	0.0	0.4	21.4	11.2	4.5	0.9	4.9
Hamilton	63.4	1 025	64	0.0	6.7	1.1	0.0	1.8	11.4	34.4	4.3	3.7	7.5
Huber Heights	21.0	540	116	0.0	11.8	0.0	0.0	0.0	21.9	13.0	1.1	0.4	4.7
Kent	23.3	861	284	0.5	18.8	0.0	0.0	2.6	9.5	12.7	3.6	5.4	1.5
Kettering	38.4	660	64	0.0	21.0	0.0	0.0	0.0	20.2	1.0	20.0	1.5	2.3
Lakewood	36.3	652	14	0.0	4.9	0.8	0.0	4.3	14.9	17.9	5.8	7.2	5.3
Lancaster	27.1	764	14	0.0	8.7	0.0	0.0	3.2	18.8	23.9	4.0	2.7	5.4
Lima	27.4	638	36	0.0	4.1	0.2	0.0	1.0	21.8	31.3	3.5	0.9	2.3
Lorain	42.1	604	82	0.0	6.1	0.0	0.0	3.1	22.1	12.9	3.7	5.7	8.2
Mansfield	39.6	778	127	0.3	19.8	0.2	0.0	0.2	19.8	4.2	2.3	5.7	2.1
Maple Heights	17.9	689	142	1.7	8.2	0.0	0.0	1.4	16.8	25.7	4.5	0.5	3.6
Marion	27.0	812	113	0.0	8.9	0.1	0.0	3.0	15.7	27.2	3.5	11.4	1.0
Massillon	21.9	714	135	0.0	11.2	0.1	0.0	1.9	14.3	21.5	2.2	0.7	3.7
Mentor	37.9	755	173	0.0	19.3	0.0	0.0	1.6	17.5	1.4	11.0	0.7	5.9
Middletown	22.5	468	20	0.0	13.2	0.0	0.0	0.0	17.5	0.8	8.3	0.0	0.0
Newark	62.1	1 271	14	21.5	9.1	0.0	0.0	19.3	4.6	5.6	0.8	4.5	0.9
North Olmsted	30.2	873	291	0.3	22.2	0.0	0.0	0.4	11.9	12.6	3.0	1.3	6.7
Parma	46.4	546	121	0.5	21.0	0.0	0.0	1.0	20.3	1.8	4.2	2.4	1.4
Reynoldsburg	12.7	437	132	0.0	21.8	0.0	0.2	0.0	27.5	22.2	8.9	0.0	4.1
Sandusky	20.4	703	115	0.0	6.0	0.0	0.0	0.0	15.3	15.0	3.8	4.8	1.3
Shaker Heights	37.3	1 279	202	0.0	11.6	0.0	0.0	0.9	17.4	11.6	10.1	7.9	0.1
Springfield	45.0	667	10	0.1	5.3	0.0	0.0	2.4	20.4	15.6	7.8	4.5	3.4
Stow	12.8	413	7	0.0	15.1	0.0	0.0	1.4	19.8	0.9	9.5	0.0	3.5
Strongsville	24.6	595	79	0.0	11.8	0.7	0.0	0.0	29.7	15.2	3.5	5.4	0.0
Toledo	300.9	948	180	0.0	6.2	0.3	0.0	3.3	19.1	15.9	2.8	4.5	4.9
Upper Arlington	21.2	646	19	0.0	9.0	3.9	0.0	0.7	19.2	10.4	10.8	0.0	3.8

1. Based on population estimated as of July 1 of the year shown.

City	City government finances, 1997 (cont'd) Debt outstanding — Total (mil dol)	Per capita[1] (dollars)	Percent utility	City government employment, 1999	Climate[2] — Average daily temperature (degrees Fahrenheit) Mean January	Mean July	Limits January[3]	Limits July[4]	Annual precipitation (inches)	Heating degree days	Cooling degree days
	137	138	139	140	141	142	143	144	145	146	147
NORTH CAROLINA— Cont'd											
Concord	74.5	2 262	56.4	718	38.5	78.8	27.2	90.0	45.70	3 497	1 541
Durham	252.4	1 685	17.6	1 978	37.1	77.1	25.1	88.8	48.10	3 867	1 278
Fayetteville	207.4	2 604	46.8	1 801	40.3	79.4	29.1	89.7	46.72	3 169	1 623
Gastonia	98.6	1 744	23.0	1 012	39.8	78.2	29.1	88.9	46.63	3 338	1 464
Goldsboro	35.0	857	43.4	NA	41.0	79.8	30.5	89.9	49.27	3 040	1 689
Greensboro	262.1	1 341	4.1	3 465	36.7	76.9	26.6	86.9	42.62	3 865	1 253
Greenville	42.3	775	47.1	1 060	40.6	78.8	29.6	89.5	49.00	3 129	1 561
Hickory	26.0	852	49.1	636	37.7	76.8	27.8	86.6	49.38	3 728	1 258
High Point	61.4	825	13.7	1 255	38.9	77.9	29.0	88.3	44.52	3 420	1 400
Jacksonville	26.9	385	0.0	NA	44.9	79.5	35.0	86.8	54.75	2 506	1 815
Kannapolis	17.1	479	11.2	NA	38.5	78.8	27.2	90.0	45.70	3 497	1 541
Kinston	21.1	843	81.6	414	40.6	78.1	29.5	89.0	51.20	3 196	1 465
Raleigh	225.1	923	21.9	2 938	38.8	78.6	28.9	88.3	44.97	3 397	1 493
Rocky Mount	27.3	519	40.8	897	39.9	78.4	29.4	88.9	45.69	3 321	1 447
Wilmington	78.1	1 256	50.7	804	44.9	80.1	34.4	88.5	54.27	2 470	1 926
Wilson	6.9	173	79.5	651	39.4	78.5	28.4	89.4	46.96	3 371	1 519
Winston-Salem	197.7	1 287	49.7	2 524	38.9	77.9	29.0	88.3	44.52	3 420	1 400
NORTH DAKOTA	X	X	X	X	X	X	X	X	X	X	X
Bismarck	86.6	1 617	3.1	487	9.2	70.4	-1.7	84.4	15.47	8 968	488
Fargo	184.6	2 203	36.6	687	5.9	71.1	-3.6	83.4	19.45	9 254	537
Grand Forks	90.1	1 779	0.1	593	4.3	69.1	-5.3	81.6	18.34	9 733	453
Minot	12.8	356	56.8	343	9.0	69.9	0.4	82.0	18.57	9 193	492
OHIO	X	X	X	X	X	X	X	X	X	X	X
Akron	232.4	1 071	26.1	2 748	24.8	71.9	16.9	82.3	36.82	6 160	625
Barberton	38.4	1 408	8.7	NA	24.8	71.9	16.9	82.3	36.82	6 160	625
Beavercreek	16.1	519	0.0	NA	26.0	74.2	17.9	84.9	36.64	5 708	886
Bowling Green	12.9	456	0.0	NA	22.7	73.0	14.4	84.6	32.77	6 482	694
Brunswick	7.4	233	0.0	NA	24.8	71.9	17.6	82.4	36.63	6 201	621
Canton	32.3	399	37.8	1 121	24.8	71.9	16.9	82.3	36.82	6 160	625
Cincinnati	245.7	711	29.8	6 295	29.8	76.4	21.2	86.6	40.70	4 928	1 135
Cleveland	1 502.3	3 015	64.4	9 294	24.8	71.9	17.6	82.4	36.63	6 201	621
Cleveland Heights	14.9	274	0.0	536	24.8	71.9	17.6	82.4	36.63	6 201	621
Columbus	1 402.5	2 134	27.4	8 599	26.4	73.2	18.5	83.7	38.09	5 708	797
Cuyahoga Falls	23.1	468	14.9	715	24.8	71.9	16.9	82.3	36.82	6 160	625
Dayton	277.4	1 604	19.1	2 992	26.0	74.2	17.9	84.9	36.64	5 708	886
East Cleveland	0.0	0	0.0	NA	24.8	71.9	17.6	82.4	36.63	6 201	621
Elyria	24.3	429	3.2	597	26.2	73.3	17.9	85.0	35.95	5 818	779
Euclid	23.9	455	0.0	537	24.8	71.9	17.6	82.4	36.63	6 201	621
Fairborn	8.8	287	33.3	NA	26.0	74.2	17.9	84.9	36.64	5 708	886
Fairfield	38.3	909	6.7	NA	26.1	73.9	15.8	86.2	41.79	5 791	830
Findlay	50.6	1 370	40.8	NA	23.6	72.8	16.5	82.7	34.26	6 302	720
Gahanna	0.0	0	0.0	NA	26.4	73.2	18.5	83.7	38.09	5 708	797
Garfield Heights	16.9	558	0.0	NA	24.8	71.9	17.6	82.4	36.63	6 201	621
Hamilton	326.3	5 277	88.8	667	26.1	73.9	15.8	86.2	41.79	5 791	830
Huber Heights	26.6	684	46.1	NA	26.0	74.2	17.9	84.9	36.64	5 708	886
Kent	8.6	317	11.3	NA	24.8	71.9	16.9	82.3	36.82	6 160	625
Kettering	16.4	281	0.0	734	26.0	74.2	17.9	84.9	36.64	5 708	886
Lakewood	40.0	717	19.6	600	24.8	71.9	17.6	82.4	36.63	6 201	621
Lancaster	7.2	202	0.0	412	25.4	72.8	16.0	84.7	36.32	5 988	724
Lima	19.3	450	50.0	455	23.6	73.6	15.2	84.4	35.94	6 253	810
Lorain	66.1	948	19.4	507	26.2	73.3	17.9	85.0	35.95	5 818	779
Mansfield	17.9	352	28.8	610	24.5	72.1	16.8	82.1	39.66	6 258	666
Maple Heights	9.7	372	0.0	NA	24.8	71.9	17.6	82.4	36.63	6 201	621
Marion	7.6	227	0.0	NA	23.4	72.6	14.3	84.5	36.91	6 407	692
Massillon	12.6	409	0.0	NA	24.8	71.9	16.9	82.3	36.82	6 160	625
Mentor	34.9	695	0.0	450	26.6	71.9	19.3	81.2	35.93	5 929	636
Middletown	0.0	0	0.0	655	26.6	74.3	17.5	85.5	39.26	5 694	897
Newark	7.5	154	0.0	NA	26.7	73.2	18.2	85.0	41.48	5 657	767
North Olmsted	60.8	1 758	0.0	500	24.8	71.9	17.6	82.4	36.63	6 201	621
Parma	7.0	82	0.0	537	24.8	71.9	17.6	82.4	36.63	6 201	621
Reynoldsburg	10.7	368	23.8	NA	26.4	73.2	18.5	83.7	38.09	5 708	797
Sandusky	9.2	317	26.8	NA	24.8	73.6	17.5	82.4	34.05	6 131	752
Shaker Heights	0.6	22	0.0	NA	24.8	71.9	17.6	82.4	36.63	6 201	621
Springfield	12.7	188	36.4	672	24.3	72.2	15.3	83.7	38.31	6 254	649
Stow	9.2	298	0.0	NA	24.8	71.9	16.9	82.3	36.82	6 160	625
Strongsville	0.0	0	0.0	NA	24.8	71.9	17.6	82.4	36.63	6 201	621
Toledo	254.4	801	14.0	3 005	22.5	72.1	14.9	83.4	32.97	6 579	610
Upper Arlington	14.4	439	27.8	NA	26.4	73.2	18.5	83.7	38.09	5 708	797

1. Based on the population estimated as of July 1 of the year shown.   2. Represents normal values based on the 30-year period, 1961–1990.   3. Average daily minimum.   4. Average daily maximum.

Table D. Cities — Land Area and Population

STATE Place code	City	Land area, 1990[1] (sq km)	Population, 1999 — Total persons	Rank	Per square kilometer	Population — Total persons 1990	Percent change 1990–1999	Total persons 1980	Percent change 1980–1990	Population characteristics, 1990 Percent — Race: White	Black	Am. Indian, Eskimo, Aleut	Asian and Pacific Islander	Other race	Hispanic[2]	Foreign born
		1	2	3	4	5	6	7	8	9	10	11	12	13	14	15
	OHIO—Cont'd															
39 80892	Warren	41.4	47 845	617	1 156	50 793	-5.8	56 629	-10.3	77.9	21.3	0.2	0.3	0.3	0.7	2.6
39 83342	Westerville	27.3	34 295	883	1 256	30 269	13.3	23 416	29.3	96.8	1.7	0.1	1.2	0.2	0.7	1.8
39 83622	Westlake	41.2	29 570	1 020	718	27 018	9.4	19 483	38.7	96.3	0.6	0.1	2.9	0.2	0.9	6.8
39 88000	Youngstown	87.5	82 757	293	946	95 732	-13.6	115 435	-17.1	59.3	38.1	0.2	0.3	2.0	4.0	3.0
39 88084	Zanesville	27.0	26 989	1 117	1 000	26 778	0.8	28 655	-6.6	88.3	10.8	0.5	0.2	0.2	0.4	0.8
40 00000	**OKLAHOMA**	177 877.5	3 358 044	X	19	3 145 576	6.8	3 025 487	4.0	82.1	7.4	8.0	1.1	1.3	2.7	2.1
40 04450	Bartlesville	54.7	33 693	897	616	34 256	-1.6	34 568	-0.9	88.6	3.3	6.4	1.1	0.6	1.8	2.2
40 09050	Broken Arrow	104.5	75 336	338	721	58 082	29.7	35 761	62.3	91.7	3.1	3.6	1.0	0.7	2.1	2.0
40 23200	Edmond	220.9	66 757	394	302	52 310	27.6	34 637	51.0	91.8	3.1	2.5	2.0	0.6	1.8	3.1
40 23950	Enid	187.0	45 196	658	242	45 309	-0.2	50 363	-10.0	89.1	4.4	2.3	1.3	1.0	2.1	1.6
40 41850	Lawton	132.5	79 927	311	603	80 561	-0.8	80 054	0.6	70.8	19.3	3.3	3.3	3.3	6.3	5.8
40 48350	Midwest City	63.5	54 172	525	853	52 267	3.6	49 559	5.5	77.1	16.3	3.9	1.7	1.0	2.7	2.4
40 49200	Moore	55.7	45 431	654	816	40 318	12.7	35 063	15.0	90.2	1.8	5.3	1.3	1.5	3.4	2.2
40 50000	Muskogee	89.3	38 432	786	430	37 708	1.9	40 011	-5.8	69.0	18.9	11.0	0.5	0.6	1.5	1.0
40 52500	Norman	458.5	94 193	245	205	80 071	17.6	67 996	17.8	87.5	3.6	4.8	3.2	0.9	2.4	4.3
40 55000	Oklahoma City	1 575.1	475 322	30	302	444 724	6.9	403 243	10.3	74.8	16.0	4.2	2.4	2.7	5.0	4.2
40 59850	Ponca City	45.0	26 052	1 157	579	26 359	-1.2	26 238	0.5	90.2	2.9	5.5	0.7	0.7	1.9	1.2
40 66800	Shawnee	108.2	27 979	1 073	259	26 017	7.5	26 506	-1.8	82.6	3.4	12.5	0.8	0.7	2.0	1.1
40 70300	Stillwater	70.6	38 444	785	545	36 676	4.8	38 268	-4.2	87.6	3.7	3.4	4.6	0.6	1.8	7.2
40 75000	Tulsa	475.3	381 579	43	803	367 302	3.9	360 919	1.8	79.3	13.6	4.7	1.4	1.0	2.6	3.0
41 00000	**OREGON**	248 646.7	3 316 154	X	13	2 842 337	16.7	2 633 156	7.9	92.8	1.6	1.4	2.4	1.8	4.0	4.9
41 01000	Albany	29.7	38 773	778	1 305	33 523	15.7	26 544	26.3	96.1	0.3	1.1	1.3	1.1	3.0	2.0
41 05350	Beaverton	35.8	64 563	415	1 803	53 307	21.1	30 582	74.3	89.4	1.0	0.5	7.7	1.4	3.3	9.7
41 15800	Corvallis	33.5	50 784	574	1 516	44 757	13.5	40 960	9.3	89.1	1.2	0.7	8.0	1.0	2.8	10.2
41 23850	Eugene	98.5	130 501	156	1 325	112 733	15.8	105 624	6.7	93.4	1.3	0.9	3.5	1.0	2.7	5.1
41 31250	Gresham	57.1	87 106	276	1 525	68 285	27.6	33 005	106.8	93.8	1.1	1.0	2.7	1.4	3.3	5.1
41 34100	Hillsboro	49.9	65 835	403	1 319	37 598	75.1	27 664	35.9	88.6	0.5	0.6	2.2	8.2	11.2	9.2
41 40550	Lake Oswego	24.7	34 952	862	1 415	30 576	14.3	22 909	33.5	96.2	0.5	0.3	2.7	0.3	1.6	6.2
41 47000	Medford	47.3	59 937	459	1 267	47 021	27.5	39 603	18.7	94.8	0.3	1.2	1.2	2.6	5.1	3.7
41 59000	Portland	322.9	503 637	26	1 560	485 975	3.6	366 423	26.5	84.6	7.7	1.2	5.3	1.2	3.2	7.7
41 64900	Salem	107.6	129 650	157	1 205	107 793	20.3	89 233	20.8	91.2	1.5	1.6	2.4	3.3	6.1	5.6
41 69600	Springfield	34.8	50 744	576	1 458	44 664	13.6	41 621	7.3	95.4	0.7	1.5	1.5	0.9	2.9	2.7
41 73650	Tigard	26.4	38 212	796	1 447	29 435	29.8	14 286	106.0	94.3	0.7	0.6	3.4	0.9	2.4	5.0
42 00000	**PENNSYLVANIA**	116 082.8	11 994 016	X	103	11 882 842	0.9	11 864 720	0.2	88.5	9.2	0.1	1.2	1.0	2.0	3.1
42 02000	Allentown	45.9	100 160	220	2 182	105 301	-4.9	103 758	1.5	86.2	5.0	0.2	1.3	7.3	11.7	5.8
42 02184	Altoona	25.3	49 363	591	1 951	51 881	-4.9	57 078	-9.1	98.0	1.5	0.1	0.3	0.1	0.4	1.1
42 06064	Bethel Park Borough	30.3	32 627	929	1 077	33 823	-3.5	34 755	-2.7	98.1	1.0	0.1	0.8	0.1	0.5	2.3
42 06088	Bethlehem	49.9	69 511	372	1 393	71 427	-2.7	70 419	1.4	87.6	2.9	0.1	1.7	7.7	13.0	5.2
42 13208	Chester	12.5	40 148	748	3 212	41 856	-4.1	45 794	-8.6	32.0	65.2	0.2	0.4	2.2	3.8	2.0
42 21648	Easton	11.0	25 292	1 183	2 299	26 276	-3.7	26 027	1.0	86.8	9.4	0.2	1.7	1.9	4.4	5.7
42 24000	Erie	56.9	101 474	218	1 783	108 718	-6.7	119 123	-8.7	86.1	12.0	0.2	0.5	1.2	2.4	2.3
42 32800	Harrisburg	21.0	48 619	602	2 315	52 376	-7.2	53 264	-1.7	42.6	50.6	0.3	1.8	4.8	7.7	2.9
42 38288	Johnstown	15.2	24 998	1 197	1 645	28 124	-11.1	35 496	-20.8	90.3	8.9	0.1	0.2	0.5	1.3	1.4
42 41216	Lancaster	19.1	52 712	544	2 760	55 551	-5.1	54 725	1.5	70.9	12.2	0.2	2.0	14.7	20.6	4.1
42 46256	McKeesport	13.0	22 698	1 306	1 746	26 016	-12.8	31 012	-16.1	81.9	17.2	0.2	0.2	0.5	1.2	2.1
42 52330	Monroeville Borough	51.2	27 667	1 086	540	29 169	-5.1	NA	NA	90.2	6.6	0.1	2.9	0.2	0.7	4.7
42 53368	New Castle	22.1	25 841	1 165	1 169	28 334	-8.8	33 621	-15.7	91.5	8.0	0.1	0.2	0.2	0.5	2.0
42 54656	Norristown	9.1	29 276	1 027	3 217	30 754	-4.8	34 684	-11.3	70.8	26.4	0.2	1.7	0.9	2.7	5.2
42 60000	Philadelphia	350.0	1 417 601	5	4 050	1 585 577	-10.6	1 688 210	-6.1	53.5	39.9	0.2	2.7	3.7	5.6	6.6
42 61000	Pittsburgh	144.1	336 882	49	2 338	369 879	-8.9	423 938	-12.8	72.1	25.8	0.2	1.6	0.3	0.9	4.6
42 61536	Plum Borough	74.2	26 465	1 138	357	25 609	3.3	25 390	0.9	97.1	2.0	0.0	0.8	0.2	0.6	2.0
42 63624	Reading	25.3	73 778	351	2 916	78 380	-5.9	78 686	-0.4	78.6	9.7	0.1	1.4	10.1	18.5	4.3
42 69000	Scranton	65.3	73 766	352	1 130	81 805	-9.8	88 117	-7.2	97.2	1.6	0.1	0.9	0.2	0.7	2.6
42 73808	State College Borough	11.6	39 017	775	3 364	38 981	0.1	36 130	7.9	88.5	3.4	0.1	7.3	0.6	2.0	9.0
42 85152	Wilkes-Barre	17.7	42 358	701	2 393	47 523	-10.9	51 551	-7.8	96.1	2.9	0.1	0.6	0.3	0.7	2.0
42 85312	Williamsport	23.0	29 922	1 014	1 301	31 933	-6.3	33 401	-4.4	82.3	6.7	0.2	0.5	0.2	0.8	1.1
42 87048	York	13.5	39 704	758	2 941	42 192	-5.9	44 619	-5.4	72.5	21.3	0.2	1.1	4.9	7.7	1.7
44 00000	**RHODE ISLAND**	2 706.5	990 819	X	366	1 003 464	-1.3	947 154	5.9	91.4	3.9	0.4	1.8	2.5	4.6	9.5
44 19180	Cranston	74.0	75 009	342	1 014	76 060	-1.4	71 992	5.7	95.1	2.4	0.2	1.8	0.5	2.0	7.3
44 22960	East Providence	34.7	47 835	618	1 379	50 380	-5.1	50 980	-1.2	92.1	4.4	0.5	0.6	2.5	1.7	14.7
44 49960	Newport	20.6	24 242	1 237	1 176	28 227	-14.2	29 258	-3.5	88.6	8.1	0.7	1.4	1.1	2.8	5.2
44 54640	Pawtucket	22.6	67 662	384	2 994	72 644	-6.9	71 204	2.0	89.3	3.6	0.3	0.6	6.2	7.2	17.7
44 59000	Providence	47.8	149 887	130	3 136	160 728	-6.7	156 804	2.5	69.9	14.8	0.9	5.9	8.4	15.5	19.6
44 74300	Warwick	92.0	83 994	289	913	85 427	-1.7	87 123	-1.9	98.0	0.8	0.2	0.8	0.2	1.0	4.2
44 80780	Woonsocket	20.0	41 409	718	2 070	43 877	-5.6	45 914	-4.4	93.3	2.6	0.2	3.0	0.9	2.6	7.0

1. Dry land or land partially or temporarily covered by water. 2. Hispanic persons may be of any race.

City	Under 5 years	5 to 17 years	18 to 24 years	25 to 34 years	35 to 44 years	45 to 54 years	55 to 64 years	65 to 74 years	75 years and over	Percent female	Number	Percent change, 1980–1990	Persons per house-hold	Female family house-holder[1]	One-person
	16	17	18	19	20	21	22	23	24	25	26	27	28	29	30
OHIO—Cont'd															
Warren	8.0	18.0	8.4	15.8	13.4	9.3	10.1	10.1	6.9	53.9	20 314	-3.4	2.45	17.2	29.6
Westerville	6.8	22.3	9.9	13.5	21.0	11.8	6.5	4.1	3.9	52.7	10 178	42.2	2.85	8.8	17.6
Westlake	6.0	17.7	7.0	15.2	17.2	12.3	9.1	8.1	7.4	52.5	10 262	51.0	2.55	6.1	26.9
Youngstown	7.4	18.9	9.3	15.0	12.3	8.7	10.1	11.0	7.2	53.7	37 037	-11.9	2.52	21.5	29.5
Zanesville	8.4	18.8	10.1	15.7	12.3	9.0	8.9	8.9	7.8	54.7	10 819	-3.2	2.42	17.4	32.3
OKLAHOMA	7.2	19.4	10.2	16.2	14.4	10.3	8.9	7.5	6.0	51.3	1 206 135	7.9	2.53	10.4	25.6
Bartlesville	6.8	19.0	7.5	14.1	14.1	11.6	10.0	9.6	7.2	52.7	14 013	1.5	2.41	8.3	26.8
Broken Arrow	9.4	24.3	6.8	20.0	19.8	9.0	5.1	3.3	2.2	50.7	19 256	66.1	2.99	8.4	13.3
Edmond	8.1	20.9	11.1	18.3	17.4	11.1	6.3	3.8	3.2	51.4	18 756	58.3	2.71	9.3	19.1
Enid	6.9	18.1	9.1	17.1	13.9	9.0	9.9	8.1	7.9	52.1	18 215	-5.9	2.40	9.7	28.6
Lawton	8.9	20.5	12.2	19.4	13.2	9.1	7.6	5.5	3.6	51.3	29 566	5.8	2.66	13.2	21.9
Midwest City	8.1	19.6	10.1	18.6	14.5	9.2	8.8	7.8	3.4	52.2	20 390	11.3	2.54	13.7	25.7
Moore	8.2	24.1	9.1	19.4	17.0	11.1	6.1	3.2	1.8	51.1	13 567	24.2	2.96	11.5	14.3
Muskogee	7.0	19.6	8.5	14.9	12.9	9.2	9.1	9.9	8.8	53.9	15 088	-4.1	2.42	14.5	30.7
Norman	6.5	15.7	21.0	18.8	15.0	8.5	6.3	4.8	3.4	50.1	31 907	28.7	2.34	9.2	30.3
Oklahoma City	7.7	18.2	9.9	19.0	14.9	10.2	8.3	6.8	5.0	51.8	178 662	11.4	2.44	12.6	30.0
Ponca City	7.7	18.9	7.7	15.4	14.6	9.6	9.2	8.9	8.1	52.7	10 733	1.1	2.41	8.4	28.9
Shawnee	7.1	17.6	12.7	14.8	12.2	8.9	8.6	8.8	9.3	54.0	10 337	-0.3	2.39	12.1	30.9
Stillwater	5.3	11.9	36.3	17.8	10.0	6.0	4.4	4.0	4.2	49.3	14 172	10.0	2.19	7.2	32.9
Tulsa	7.3	17.0	10.7	18.4	15.1	10.2	8.7	7.4	5.3	52.2	155 447	7.1	2.31	11.8	32.7
OREGON	7.1	18.4	9.4	15.9	16.7	10.4	8.3	7.9	5.9	50.8	1 103 313	11.1	2.52	9.2	25.3
Albany	8.0	18.1	11.0	17.0	14.7	10.1	7.1	7.7	6.4	51.9	11 786	13.7	2.46	11.5	26.8
Beaverton	7.9	17.1	9.8	22.3	18.0	9.8	6.1	5.0	4.0	52.1	22 100	81.2	2.39	9.4	28.7
Corvallis	5.8	12.6	29.5	17.2	13.3	7.1	4.9	5.3	4.3	49.1	16 743	14.0	2.30	7.3	30.4
Eugene	5.9	15.2	16.7	16.6	17.5	8.9	6.5	6.9	5.8	51.9	46 274	9.5	2.30	9.2	31.0
Gresham	7.9	19.6	9.9	17.7	17.3	10.6	7.0	5.7	4.3	51.5	25 705	119.4	2.62	10.3	22.5
Hillsboro	8.8	22.1	9.4	18.0	18.0	9.1	6.0	4.7	3.9	50.5	12 849	34.0	2.87	10.8	19.4
Lake Oswego	5.7	18.0	6.1	14.5	21.2	14.9	8.4	6.8	4.5	52.0	12 487	46.9	2.43	7.1	25.3
Medford	7.7	17.4	8.7	15.7	15.7	9.4	8.2	9.2	8.0	52.5	18 867	20.8	2.44	10.7	26.8
Portland	7.0	15.0	10.0	18.9	18.1	9.2	7.3	7.8	6.7	51.5	187 268	17.8	2.27	11.0	34.9
Salem	7.3	17.0	10.5	18.0	16.3	9.1	7.1	7.8	7.0	50.3	40 936	19.6	2.41	11.2	29.9
Springfield	8.8	18.8	12.2	19.1	15.3	8.6	6.3	4.7	5.1	51.7	17 447	8.2	2.54	13.5	24.9
Tigard	8.0	16.3	8.5	21.5	18.4	9.3	6.6	6.2	5.1	52.0	12 055	109.2	2.42	8.5	26.0
PENNSYLVANIA	6.7	16.8	10.3	16.1	14.7	10.2	9.8	9.0	6.4	52.1	4 495 966	6.5	2.57	11.3	25.6
Allentown	7.2	14.7	11.3	18.7	13.2	8.8	9.2	9.3	7.6	52.7	42 775	3.6	2.36	12.7	31.7
Altoona	6.6	17.9	9.2	15.0	13.3	9.6	9.8	10.7	8.0	54.2	20 684	-1.7	2.47	14.0	28.9
Bethel Park Borough	7.0	16.6	7.1	15.8	15.8	12.9	11.1	8.8	4.8	52.0	12 692	9.7	2.65	7.5	20.5
Bethlehem	6.1	14.9	14.8	15.6	13.0	8.9	9.5	10.5	6.7	52.0	27 268	4.1	2.44	12.0	27.9
Chester	9.3	18.7	13.0	16.4	12.6	8.6	7.8	8.2	5.4	54.0	14 537	-8.1	2.74	29.4	27.8
Easton	7.5	15.9	16.8	18.0	12.3	8.1	7.5	7.2	6.6	51.0	9 397	-0.2	2.51	14.3	29.8
Erie	7.9	17.4	12.1	16.6	13.2	8.2	8.6	9.5	6.6	52.8	42 131	-3.2	2.47	15.6	30.8
Harrisburg	8.9	17.8	10.4	18.7	15.5	8.4	7.2	6.8	6.2	53.5	21 520	-2.4	2.39	23.1	37.9
Johnstown	6.2	15.4	8.3	14.2	12.3	9.3	11.3	13.2	9.9	55.0	12 536	-12.2	2.22	15.8	37.6
Lancaster	8.4	18.0	14.0	18.7	13.6	7.6	7.4	7.2	5.1	51.9	21 189	2.7	2.49	16.4	32.5
McKeesport	6.4	15.2	9.1	14.0	12.2	8.1	11.5	12.6	10.9	54.7	10 543	-14.2	2.36	18.7	32.8
Monroeville Borough	5.9	15.1	8.2	16.9	15.9	12.0	11.7	9.1	5.2	52.2	11 828	NA	2.44	8.5	26.4
New Castle	6.8	15.3	8.8	14.3	12.6	9.0	10.5	12.5	10.2	54.8	11 374	-10.0	2.42	15.6	30.9
Norristown	8.0	15.3	9.1	21.0	14.6	8.2	9.2	8.7	5.8	52.9	12 187	-0.8	2.44	15.0	35.2
Philadelphia	7.3	16.6	11.4	17.4	13.4	9.5	9.1	8.7	6.5	53.5	603 075	-2.8	2.56	20.3	31.6
Pittsburgh	6.1	13.8	13.7	17.1	13.2	8.5	9.6	10.2	7.8	53.6	153 483	-7.8	2.27	17.2	36.2
Plum Borough	7.4	18.4	9.0	18.9	16.9	12.4	8.9	5.5	2.4	50.6	9 067	14.4	2.82	8.4	16.2
Reading	8.2	17.2	11.7	17.1	11.6	8.6	8.8	8.9	7.8	53.1	31 403	-2.2	2.44	16.4	32.6
Scranton	6.0	15.0	11.8	14.4	11.9	9.0	10.0	12.0	10.0	54.2	32 637	-2.8	2.37	13.8	34.0
State College Borough	2.2	4.1	65.8	12.2	5.5	3.1	2.7	2.8	1.9	46.0	10 938	11.1	2.43	3.4	27.4
Wilkes-Barre	5.6	14.4	13.1	14.3	12.4	8.6	10.7	11.5	9.5	54.0	19 435	-2.9	2.31	14.5	36.1
Williamsport	7.7	17.4	13.7	16.9	12.6	8.4	8.2	8.6	6.4	52.8	12 588	1.5	2.42	15.1	31.3
York	8.8	17.6	11.9	18.8	13.0	8.8	7.6	7.5	6.0	52.9	16 887	-5.5	2.47	17.9	31.9
RHODE ISLAND	6.7	15.8	12.0	17.3	14.7	9.6	8.9	8.5	6.5	52.0	377 977	11.7	2.55	11.7	26.2
Cranston	5.7	13.6	9.6	17.8	15.2	9.4	10.1	10.7	7.9	51.9	29 349	12.4	2.46	11.2	27.1
East Providence	6.0	14.9	9.1	17.1	13.9	9.9	10.0	10.7	8.4	53.5	19 950	7.4	2.48	11.0	28.5
Newport	6.4	13.9	16.6	19.4	14.1	9.2	7.0	7.4	6.0	51.7	11 196	4.1	2.31	14.0	33.8
Pawtucket	7.4	15.3	10.4	19.6	12.8	8.9	9.2	9.4	7.0	53.0	29 711	5.8	2.42	13.7	30.6
Providence	7.8	16.1	17.6	18.1	12.0	7.7	7.0	7.1	6.5	52.4	58 905	-2.1	2.52	18.4	31.8
Warwick	6.0	15.5	8.7	16.9	15.1	10.9	10.1	10.0	6.8	52.5	33 437	8.5	2.52	9.6	26.5
Woonsocket	7.7	16.7	10.9	17.6	12.9	9.1	8.9	8.9	7.4	52.9	17 572	2.7	2.45	14.1	29.3

1. No spouse present.

Table D. Cities — Group Quarters, Crime, Education, and Income

City	Persons in group quarters, 1990				Serious crimes known to police, 1998[2]				Education, 1990				Money income, 1989		
					Total		Rate[3]		School enrollment		Attainment[4] (percent)			Households	
														Median	
	Total	Persons in mental hospitals	Persons in nursing homes	Persons identified as homeless[1]	Number	Rate[3]	Violent	Property	Public	Private	High school graduate or more	Bachelor's degree or more	Per capita (dollars)[5]	Dollars	Percent change, 1979–1989 (constant 1989 dollars)
	31	32	33	34	35	36	37	38	39	40	41	42	43	44	45
OHIO—Cont'd															
Warren	1 012	0	789	16	NA	NA	NA	NA	10 265	1 615	71.3	10.0	11 508	22 637	-17.9
Westerville	1 244	0	367	7	1 093	3 221	115	3 106	7 196	2 363	91.5	40.1	17 835	48 212	16.0
Westlake	882	0	798	0	519	1 737	100	1 637	5 062	1 865	89.9	37.7	24 000	47 629	5.5
Youngstown	2 352	85	1 076	95	6 886	7 925	1 283	6 642	20 621	4 137	65.6	8.3	8 544	17 060	-24.3
Zanesville	544	33	295	13	2 018	7 347	561	6 786	5 505	642	62.2	9.4	9 504	17 658	-3.3
OKLAHOMA	93 760	1 586	29 666	2 698	167 479	5 004	539	4 465	754 928	83 883	74.6	17.8	11 893	23 577	-4.6
Bartlesville	483	0	265	0	1 540	4 515	569	3 946	7 497	1 035	82.4	31.6	16 411	30 366	-10.8
Broken Arrow	507	0	340	0	1 939	2 746	204	2 542	15 539	3 001	89.6	24.7	13 931	37 601	-2.4
Edmond	1 400	0	270	0	2 098	3 277	102	3 175	15 678	2 147	90.3	43.5	17 215	37 644	2.7
Enid	1 677	0	414	0	3 532	7 679	798	6 881	9 045	1 714	75.8	17.8	11 812	22 746	-17.0
Lawton	1 957	0	747	92	5 605	6 785	583	6 202	21 442	1 574	81.5	19.0	10 772	24 200	5.4
Midwest City	492	0	463	29	3 170	5 793	322	5 471	13 054	1 121	82.3	16.8	12 687	27 042	-8.0
Moore	186	0	173	0	1 724	3 774	346	3 428	11 522	1 175	82.2	13.9	11 739	32 984	-5.7
Muskogee	1 193	0	549	76	3 207	8 377	943	7 434	8 327	786	68.9	16.0	10 436	19 507	-1.3
Norman	5 412	250	639	37	3 806	4 107	221	3 886	29 231	1 670	87.1	38.1	13 690	25 165	-3.5
Oklahoma City	9 395	88	3 305	1 320	NA	NA	NA	NA	96 535	16 593	78.2	21.6	13 528	25 741	-3.4
Ponca City	496	4	304	62	1 870	7 131	404	6 727	5 417	610	80.0	21.9	13 776	26 405	-5.9
Shawnee	1 383	0	418	3	2 083	7 684	450	7 234	5 105	1 700	69.5	14.0	10 301	19 002	-7.3
Stillwater	5 608	7	338	15	1 585	4 058	335	3 723	19 050	505	89.5	44.3	10 747	18 501	-0.6
Tulsa	8 832	306	2 343	415	NA	NA	NA	NA	71 945	22 270	82.3	25.8	15 434	25 708	-9.1
OREGON	65 268	1 565	18 200	3 682	185 323	5 647	420	5 227	639 167	85 066	81.5	20.6	13 418	27 250	-3.1
Albany	437	0	265	8	3 239	8 315	198	8 117	6 739	554	81.1	12.4	11 444	24 474	-7.6
Beaverton	456	0	310	0	3 226	4 926	283	4 643	11 487	2 141	91.5	36.0	17 107	33 951	-1.4
Corvallis	6 283	0	375	12	2 231	4 601	167	4 434	20 972	971	92.1	49.0	11 921	23 212	1.7
Eugene	6 250	0	815	490	11 463	9 013	546	8 467	35 773	3 269	88.6	34.9	13 886	25 369	1.2
Gresham	750	0	589	22	5 150	6 203	506	5 697	15 782	1 973	83.6	15.9	13 526	31 833	-10.9
Hillsboro	574	0	228	23	2 978	5 479	421	5 058	9 352	1 132	81.7	19.3	13 125	31 125	-0.2
Lake Oswego	249	0	90	0	944	2 634	142	2 492	6 626	1 551	96.6	53.9	27 946	51 499	6.6
Medford	935	0	363	105	4 973	8 633	398	8 235	8 533	1 333	81.7	17.9	13 791	25 677	-1.9
Portland	11 325	225	3 059	1 627	NA	NA	NA	NA	84 548	19 773	82.9	25.5	14 478	25 592	3.3
Salem	9 051	0	969	220	9 302	8 376	311	8 065	22 513	4 774	81.5	21.7	12 641	25 236	-0.1
Springfield	298	0	152	47	5 246	10 324	423	9 901	10 414	830	77.7	10.8	10 222	21 932	-11.9
Tigard	139	20	25	20	2 878	7 794	322	7 472	6 005	1 066	90.9	30.1	16 946	35 669	6.1
PENNSYLVANIA	348 263	7 535	106 454	9 350	392 788	3 273	421	2 852	2 161 247	668 306	74.7	17.9	14 068	29 069	2.8
Allentown	4 136	461	952	99	6 022	5 887	662	5 225	17 369	5 851	69.4	15.3	12 822	25 983	1.1
Altoona	753	0	432	50	1 945	3 900	347	3 553	9 865	1 818	73.3	9.5	10 398	20 695	-8.9
Bethel Park Borough	174	0	154	0	329	988	63	925	6 005	2 215	89.7	33.2	17 603	41 149	-5.1
Bethlehem	5 066	0	594	41	NA	NA	NA	NA	11 083	8 370	71.1	20.2	13 684	28 375	-1.5
Chester	1 881	0	310	115	4 206	10 429	3 923	6 506	7 617	3 741	62.2	7.7	9 115	20 864	8.1
Easton	2 666	0	347	162	NA	NA	NA	NA	4 748	2 511	68.6	12.7	11 319	26 365	23.0
Erie	4 519	0	1 007	297	4 786	4 564	599	3 965	15 980	11 501	72.3	14.0	10 715	22 032	-10.7
Harrisburg	958	6	276	210	2 547	5 014	931	4 083	10 667	1 701	67.2	14.0	11 037	20 329	1.4
Johnstown	348	0	160	40	948	3 659	421	3 238	4 506	974	64.2	7.2	8 500	14 839	-24.8
Lancaster	2 743	0	212	354	2 198	4 074	623	3 451	10 943	2 931	61.4	13.5	10 693	22 210	-6.0
McKeesport	1 166	0	819	0	1 206	5 221	693	4 528	4 677	773	66.6	6.8	9 024	16 427	-24.4
Monroeville Borough	300	0	300	0	959	3 390	406	2 984	5 355	1 273	87.0	31.7	17 753	36 422	NA
New Castle	824	0	460	79	1 357	5 078	625	4 453	5 136	529	67.8	8.6	9 298	17 103	-22.9
Norristown	1 047	613	133	140	2 265	7 522	1 162	6 360	4 699	1 916	67.3	12.9	13 527	28 643	16.7
Philadelphia	43 963	504	9 337	4 199	106 078	7 319	1 464	5 855	251 843	143 190	64.3	15.2	12 091	24 603	11.5
Pittsburgh	20 579	8	3 081	781	21 492	6 067	891	5 176	67 147	29 963	72.4	20.1	12 580	20 747	-7.7
Plum Borough	0	0	0	0	NA	NA	NA	NA	5 548	1 120	86.8	22.8	14 413	36 782	-0.7
Reading	1 786	0	184	169	6 291	8 275	1 165	7 110	13 831	3 624	58.4	8.5	11 041	22 112	8.8
Scranton	4 268	0	838	34	NA	NA	NA	NA	11 828	7 380	70.4	13.6	11 108	21 060	0.4
State College Borough	12 241	0	23	10	330	631	25	606	28 108	1 283	96.0	68.2	8 694	18 257	11.5
Wilkes-Barre	2 614	0	451	93	2 126	4 841	419	4 422	7 318	3 633	69.5	12.9	10 513	19 525	-1.1
Williamsport	1 421	0	172	61	1 819	5 996	478	5 518	6 951	1 592	72.3	13.1	10 276	20 290	-0.1
York	524	0	216	129	3 235	7 889	1 136	6 753	7 573	1 550	62.8	9.9	10 485	21 812	8.8
RHODE ISLAND	38 774	265	10 156	494	34 756	3 518	312	3 206	191 802	62 833	72.0	21.3	14 981	32 181	19.3
Cranston	3 786	0	248	80	2 104	2 845	166	2 679	12 779	3 270	74.0	21.1	15 922	34 528	18.9
East Providence	957	0	826	0	915	1 900	260	1 640	8 500	2 338	66.9	16.0	14 387	31 007	10.6
Newport	2 399	0	239	88	1 814	7 473	873	6 600	5 103	2 407	84.1	32.2	16 358	30 534	28.3
Pawtucket	594	0	465	23	2 701	3 930	428	3 502	12 198	3 781	61.6	13.1	12 865	26 541	16.2
Providence	12 070	15	1 961	210	11 190	7 393	692	6 701	29 887	20 234	62.8	21.6	11 838	22 147	15.5
Warwick	1 128	0	770	0	2 911	3 450	215	3 235	15 203	3 661	77.8	21.3	16 371	35 786	13.9
Woonsocket	748	0	632	59	1 056	2 538	370	2 168	8 535	1 081	56.2	9.1	11 997	25 363	20.9

1. Persons in emergency shelters and persons visible in street locations. 2. Data for serious crimes have not been adjusted for underreporting. This may affect comparability between geographic areas and over time. 3. Per 100,000 population estimated by the FBI. 4. Persons 25 years old and older. 5. Based on population enumerated as of April 1, 1990.

	Money income, 1989 (cont'd)				Housing units, 1990										
	Households (cont'd)	Percent below poverty, 1989						Occupied units							
		Persons		Families					Owner-occupied units				Renter-occupied units		
											Owner cost as a percent of income				
City	Percent with $100,000 or more	Total	Percent change in rate, 1979–1989	Total	Total	Percent change, 1980–1990	Vacant units for sale or rent[1]	Total	Percent	Median value[2] (dollars)	With a mortgage	Without a mortgage	Median rent[3] (dollars)	Rent as percent of income	Substandard units[4] (percent)
	46	47	48	49	50	51	52	53	54	55	56	57	58	59	60
OHIO—Cont'd															
Warren	1.3	20.0	43.9	16.9	21 785	-2.6	1 150	20 314	58.6	42 900	16.2	12.4	331	25.6	2.0
Westerville	7.5	2.8	-26.3	1.8	10 521	39.5	290	10 178	76.5	109 000	20.0	11.9	505	25.4	0.6
Westlake	13.8	2.1	0.0	1.6	11 014	52.5	651	10 262	75.1	133 400	20.0	11.4	624	21.7	0.3
Youngstown	0.6	29.0	59.3	24.4	40 802	-9.5	2 407	37 037	64.6	31 000	18.8	14.5	300	33.8	2.1
Zanesville	1.6	25.9	38.5	22.7	11 770	-3.5	670	10 819	56.3	34 600	17.0	12.8	289	28.7	2.5
OKLAHOMA	2.3	16.7	24.7	13.0	1 406 499	13.7	112 149	1 206 135	68.1	48 100	20.0	12.8	340	25.4	3.7
Bartlesville	4.7	11.1	73.4	8.7	15 908	7.4	1 212	14 013	71.4	55 300	16.2	11.3	365	24.7	1.5
Broken Arrow	2.4	6.5	47.7	5.2	20 420	61.3	894	19 256	74.3	67 700	20.7	11.5	482	24.8	2.0
Edmond	7.0	7.3	0.0	5.2	20 598	61.7	1 429	18 756	67.8	80 000	20.6	12.1	423	26.2	1.8
Enid	2.3	14.3	68.2	11.1	21 680	4.3	2 188	18 215	65.6	38 400	19.6	12.2	340	24.0	1.9
Lawton	1.3	15.9	4.6	13.4	34 622	8.5	3 898	29 566	57.9	55 000	21.4	12.2	378	26.6	4.6
Midwest City	1.3	11.2	51.4	8.9	22 846	17.2	2 007	20 390	63.0	48 300	19.3	11.4	388	24.5	3.5
Moore	0.7	8.0	37.9	6.7	14 824	26.1	1 014	13 567	74.1	51 200	20.1	12.3	465	24.7	4.0
Muskogee	1.4	22.5	16.0	18.0	17 674	1.6	1 851	15 088	63.7	40 300	19.6	13.5	298	27.7	2.5
Norman	3.1	15.0	20.0	8.2	35 650	32.7	3 044	31 907	51.0	65 600	19.3	12.1	362	28.9	2.4
Oklahoma City	2.8	15.9	32.5	12.0	212 367	19.9	23 602	178 662	59.5	54 900	20.6	12.5	364	25.1	4.4
Ponca City	2.1	10.7	46.6	8.1	12 294	7.8	974	10 733	70.0	48 600	16.8	11.7	346	24.2	1.9
Shawnee	1.1	21.2	17.8	16.5	11 784	3.6	930	10 337	64.3	40 200	19.5	13.0	322	28.3	2.6
Stillwater	1.7	26.4	27.5	12.5	15 771	12.4	1 219	14 172	39.7	64 900	18.7	11.8	354	35.1	1.8
Tulsa	4.6	15.0	44.2	11.5	176 211	12.7	15 096	155 447	55.8	60 500	19.8	12.8	358	24.4	2.9
OREGON	2.8	12.4	16.1	8.7	1 193 567	10.2	40 232	1 103 313	63.1	67 100	20.4	13.4	408	25.5	3.9
Albany	0.9	14.7	1.4	11.3	12 322	9.5	410	11 786	51.9	52 000	17.6	13.2	396	25.4	2.8
Beaverton	4.0	6.4	-12.3	5.2	24 083	77.8	1 853	22 100	47.0	89 800	20.7	13.5	508	24.5	2.3
Corvallis	2.6	21.0	18.6	10.0	17 307	12.6	403	16 743	43.2	71 000	20.8	12.2	385	31.1	3.5
Eugene	3.3	17.0	15.6	9.0	47 991	6.8	1 315	46 274	50.7	73 200	20.4	13.1	425	30.6	2.6
Gresham	1.7	8.3	29.7	6.0	26 978	118.0	850	25 705	58.4	71 100	20.6	14.1	446	26.1	2.6
Hillsboro	1.7	8.3	6.4	6.2	13 347	32.0	398	12 849	58.6	71 900	20.9	13.6	480	24.7	5.5
Lake Oswego	16.4	3.7	-19.6	1.8	13 110	44.9	503	12 487	67.4	142 600	21.2	12.8	641	23.8	0.6
Medford	2.9	14.4	19.0	11.5	19 684	18.9	613	18 867	56.7	71 500	21.4	13.4	431	28.6	3.9
Portland	3.0	14.5	11.5	9.7	198 368	18.1	7 344	187 268	53.0	59 200	20.2	14.3	397	25.8	3.7
Salem	2.2	14.5	22.9	10.5	42 601	14.8	1 311	40 936	54.7	60 300	20.4	13.7	387	25.9	3.8
Springfield	0.9	16.5	8.6	13.2	18 121	3.7	505	17 447	49.3	51 000	20.2	13.4	423	28.3	5.3
Tigard	3.0	4.8	-31.4	3.7	12 599	106.1	491	12 055	57.8	90 400	21.7	11.6	484	24.1	1.8
PENNSYLVANIA	3.6	11.1	6.0	8.2	4 938 140	7.4	195 284	4 495 966	70.6	69 700	20.2	13.3	404	26.1	2.3
Allentown	1.8	12.9	10.3	9.3	45 636	4.3	2 324	42 775	56.6	76 600	21.8	13.5	434	27.1	3.5
Altoona	1.1	18.0	46.3	14.0	22 698	0.9	1 383	20 684	66.1	31 600	16.4	13.7	285	28.6	1.4
Bethel Park Borough	5.4	3.8	58.3	3.0	12 997	8.4	220	12 692	80.8	82 200	20.1	12.9	509	25.3	0.4
Bethlehem	3.2	13.0	17.1	8.8	28 486	4.0	877	27 268	61.0	90 600	20.8	12.5	453	27.5	2.7
Chester	0.7	25.2	-2.7	20.6	16 512	-7.4	1 377	14 537	53.1	38 400	20.4	17.0	392	29.3	6.2
Easton	1.2	13.7	-12.2	9.4	10 309	2.2	684	9 397	52.1	80 500	23.2	13.5	460	27.4	2.4
Erie	1.0	19.3	44.0	15.2	45 424	-3.0	2 064	42 131	56.6	43 300	17.6	13.5	314	26.6	2.5
Harrisburg	1.5	27.0	16.9	23.9	24 590	-5.5	1 630	21 520	42.4	38 400	18.0	13.8	363	26.3	5.5
Johnstown	0.3	26.9	63.0	22.5	14 667	-3.3	1 623	12 536	47.7	26 600	17.2	13.6	239	26.3	1.6
Lancaster	1.1	20.9	23.7	16.3	22 468	2.3	1 012	21 189	47.2	59 200	20.1	12.5	390	27.5	5.7
McKeesport	0.6	24.2	68.1	20.6	12 535	-5.0	1 051	10 543	60.1	27 800	21.6	15.9	280	29.6	2.3
Monroeville Borough	4.9	4.3	NA	3.2	12 644	NA	750	11 828	69.5	66 700	19.6	13.1	536	24.1	0.7
New Castle	0.1	19.7	27.1	16.1	12 463	-6.5	774	11 374	63.3	29 100	19.0	14.5	274	28.9	1.9
Norristown	2.0	9.5	-19.5	7.0	13 080	-1.2	661	12 187	55.0	80 600	22.5	14.9	504	28.2	2.8
Philadelphia	2.2	20.3	-1.5	16.1	674 899	-1.6	44 060	603 075	61.9	49 400	19.3	14.8	452	29.8	5.1
Pittsburgh	2.9	21.4	29.7	16.6	170 159	-5.0	12 288	153 483	52.3	41 200	19.2	14.3	368	28.7	2.3
Plum Borough	2.3	4.3	13.2	3.5	9 289	11.6	155	9 067	79.4	63 700	20.6	12.3	511	21.7	0.8
Reading	1.2	19.4	12.8	15.2	34 276	0.4	1 976	31 403	55.9	37 700	17.4	13.5	352	26.7	4.4
Scranton	1.6	15.2	17.8	11.1	35 357	-2.2	1 708	32 637	53.7	57 100	18.7	14.3	320	26.1	1.7
State College Borough	2.8	45.4	15.8	7.9	11 623	14.7	544	10 938	23.8	115 800	18.6	10.6	490	35.1	11.5
Wilkes-Barre	1.0	15.4	14.1	10.4	20 734	-3.1	839	19 435	52.7	44 200	17.7	14.1	317	27.0	1.5
Williamsport	1.5	21.1	27.1	16.4	13 326	-2.7	463	12 588	46.5	44 900	19.9	13.8	322	27.2	2.5
York	0.9	20.3	16.0	16.4	18 407	-4.7	1 222	16 887	49.8	41 600	18.4	12.5	357	27.3	3.4
RHODE ISLAND	4.1	9.6	-6.7	6.8	414 572	11.2	19 071	377 977	59.5	133 500	22.7	13.9	489	27.5	2.6
Cranston	3.8	6.5	-11.0	4.9	30 516	11.9	843	29 349	66.4	129 700	22.4	14.6	534	27.1	1.3
East Providence	2.2	6.8	-4.2	5.0	20 808	7.2	621	19 950	60.3	122 500	22.7	13.9	470	26.3	2.1
Newport	4.7	12.5	-22.4	10.0	13 094	10.2	1 018	11 196	41.6	155 000	24.4	15.5	593	27.7	2.0
Pawtucket	1.6	10.6	-9.4	8.1	31 615	6.2	1 413	29 711	45.8	112 500	22.7	14.4	437	25.8	3.4
Providence	3.5	23.0	12.7	18.3	66 794	-1.1	5 760	58 905	36.2	113 000	22.1	14.3	469	30.2	6.5
Warwick	4.6	4.8	-27.3	3.2	35 141	8.3	1 119	33 437	74.4	116 600	22.7	14.1	570	27.3	1.2
Woonsocket	1.4	13.9	-2.8	11.6	18 739	2.1	1 058	17 572	35.5	118 800	21.5	15.6	439	26.7	2.7

1. Includes units rented or sold but not occupied. 2. Specified owner-occupied units. 3. Specified renter-occupied units. 4. Overcrowded or lacking complete plumbing facilities.

City	Civilian labor force, 1999				Civilian employment, 1990[2]			Disability 1990	Value of residential construction authorized by building permits, 1999		
			Unemployment			Percent					
	Total	Percent change, 1998–1999	Total	Rate[1]	Total	Professional, managerial, and technical	Precision production, craft, and repair	Work disabled persons[3] (percent)	New construction ($1,000)	Number of housing units	Percent single family
	61	62	63	64	65	66	67	68	69	70	71
OHIO—Cont'd											
Warren	22 483	-1.0	1 834	8.2	19 323	21.7	11.3	12.7	521	6	66.7
Westerville	18 813	2.2	234	1.2	15 802	43.0	4.7	3.6	23 448	166	81.9
Westlake	14 350	0.9	260	1.8	13 648	48.0	6.6	4.1	73 572	286	84.6
Youngstown	34 761	-1.7	3 403	9.8	30 086	20.8	10.4	14.7	4 033	60	76.7
Zanesville	12 611	2.7	1 243	9.9	9 860	22.6	10.5	13.9	1 296	14	85.7
OKLAHOMA	1 647 638	1.3	56 693	3.4	1 369 138	27.9	12.0	10.2	1 430 600	14 186	78.0
Bartlesville	13 869	6.0	538	3.9	15 068	40.2	9.9	7.0	3 997	56	55.4
Broken Arrow	35 443	1.0	738	2.1	29 037	34.8	10.1	6.0	95 514	749	100.0
Edmond	31 619	3.1	474	1.5	26 930	42.9	7.0	5.2	96 983	578	97.2
Enid	21 513	-1.7	724	3.4	19 100	25.7	12.1	9.3	11 916	74	83.8
Lawton	31 919	-0.2	1 179	3.7	29 197	32.2	7.9	10.6	14 350	119	96.6
Midwest City	27 890	2.5	766	2.7	23 453	28.4	11.9	9.1	18 887	184	100.0
Moore	26 208	4.4	460	1.8	20 364	25.3	14.1	8.7	38 244	428	92.5
Muskogee	17 964	2.7	691	3.8	14 782	25.8	10.2	13.2	5 651	63	100.0
Norman	52 324	4.0	1 222	2.3	40 417	40.5	8.1	6.9	89 532	827	77.3
Oklahoma City	252 388	2.7	7 066	2.8	209 496	30.7	10.0	9.7	344 793	3 285	87.3
Ponca City	12 228	-3.1	751	6.1	11 952	33.0	12.9	7.7	8 614	70	57.1
Shawnee	12 406	2.0	492	4.0	10 266	29.8	10.8	11.8	8 413	81	100.0
Stillwater	22 971	5.0	301	1.3	17 425	39.6	5.7	4.5	17 417	215	62.3
Tulsa	220 442	0.9	7 644	3.5	179 327	34.1	10.4	8.3	173 092	2 053	33.4
OREGON	1 760 442	0.1	100 361	5.7	1 319 960	28.8	10.7	10.0	2 652 791	23 249	71.4
Albany	17 805	-0.8	1 249	7.0	13 441	22.4	13.2	10.7	29 554	380	39.7
Beaverton	44 227	0.2	1 670	3.8	30 118	39.0	7.6	5.8	34 447	371	64.4
Corvallis	25 153	-2.9	782	3.1	20 306	45.1	4.9	5.6	31 254	303	43.2
Eugene	68 348	0.5	3 498	5.1	54 654	36.7	7.4	7.8	124 642	1 269	51.7
Gresham	43 275	-0.8	1 683	3.9	34 938	25.4	11.7	8.6	74 080	760	58.3
Hillsboro	27 350	0.2	1 116	4.1	18 566	28.3	13.1	9.3	88 271	713	86.7
Lake Oswego	22 435	-0.8	641	2.9	16 632	52.7	3.2	4.3	21 492	115	100.0
Medford	29 633	1.2	1 856	6.3	20 922	26.3	8.8	11.2	63 613	766	53.5
Portland	275 766	-0.7	15 149	5.5	218 750	32.7	9.4	10.4	205 419	2 453	37.9
Salem	63 559	-0.4	4 021	6.3	46 474	33.1	8.7	10.8	74 740	752	76.2
Springfield	25 700	0.6	1 636	6.4	20 281	18.1	11.8	13.1	32 966	279	82.4
Tigard	23 406	0.2	934	4.0	15 904	37.0	9.7	6.3	51 399	364	100.0
PENNSYLVANIA	5 968 988	0.6	262 336	4.4	5 434 532	28.9	11.6	8.3	4 634 786	42 662	85.7
Allentown	50 775	-1.2	2 631	5.2	49 821	25.1	11.0	8.1	12 005	104	100.0
Altoona	23 183	0.1	1 215	5.2	21 061	22.5	12.9	11.9	1 857	27	92.6
Bethel Park Borough	18 105	0.3	501	2.8	16 761	41.2	9.3	5.1	12 163	76	34.2
Bethlehem	32 956	-0.9	1 470	4.5	32 127	30.1	9.9	7.2	3 108	53	92.5
Chester	16 492	1.0	1 082	6.6	15 715	20.2	9.2	14.0	295	0	0.0
Easton	11 894	-0.7	560	4.7	11 644	22.5	10.6	9.0	295	1	100.0
Erie	49 933	-1.3	2 785	5.6	46 064	25.6	11.0	10.9	4 273	64	50.0
Harrisburg	24 345	-3.1	1 149	4.7	22 901	26.2	7.8	12.3	393	5	100.0
Johnstown	9 461	-2.8	672	7.1	9 106	20.9	8.6	13.5	840	14	100.0
Lancaster	25 421	-2.6	990	3.9	25 188	21.9	10.5	10.2	1 068	17	100.0
McKeesport	8 779	0.1	575	6.5	8 553	21.6	11.6	12.4	388	7	100.0
Monroeville Borough	17 179	NA	516	3.0	14 930	43.4	7.3	7.3	3 826	35	91.4
New Castle	10 108	0.6	830	8.2	9 906	22.7	9.5	13.5	262	5	100.0
Norristown	15 337	-4.2	668	4.4	15 384	24.7	10.1	9.8	87	1	100.0
Philadelphia	640 912	0.1	38 314	6.0	651 621	28.6	9.0	11.0	27 003	367	26.4
Pittsburgh	160 105	-1.0	6 886	4.3	153 991	33.1	7.4	10.7	26 487	367	48.5
Plum Borough	15 634	3.1	515	3.3	13 535	34.0	12.0	5.9	13 019	130	100.0
Reading	34 390	-2.7	2 035	5.9	34 188	19.0	10.8	10.3	3 511	52	7.7
Scranton	34 926	-2.0	1 908	5.5	34 256	24.4	10.6	11.5	2 464	29	100.0
State College Borough	16 442	-1.5	191	1.2	15 632	44.0	1.7	2.3	3 733	64	76.6
Wilkes-Barre	20 520	-3.1	1 266	6.2	20 211	23.7	9.5	10.8	294	5	100.0
Williamsport	13 446	-1.2	883	6.6	13 018	22.9	10.4	11.5	2 381	43	44.2
York	18 150	-2.4	1 056	5.8	18 903	18.5	11.7	12.1	280	4	100.0
RHODE ISLAND	503 778	1.1	20 890	4.1	487 913	30.1	12.0	8.6	336 166	3 414	79.1
Cranston	37 208	1.5	1 533	4.1	36 461	32.2	11.9	7.7	22 627	266	80.1
East Providence	24 981	0.0	1 095	4.4	25 166	24.9	12.5	10.3	4 106	60	96.7
Newport	11 695	2.9	508	4.3	12 899	35.2	9.2	7.0	3 057	16	100.0
Pawtucket	35 716	-0.9	1 646	4.6	36 356	21.7	13.6	9.7	1 368	22	100.0
Providence	68 548	0.1	3 671	5.4	69 200	28.9	10.7	9.8	6 516	180	42.8
Warwick	44 673	0.7	1 645	3.7	43 769	31.7	11.7	8.6	13 915	137	86.9
Woonsocket	19 540	-0.8	971	5.0	19 882	20.3	14.1	12.1	1 252	20	100.0

1. Percent of civilian labor force.   2. Persons 16 years and older.   3. Persons 16 to 64 years old.

Table D. Cities — Wholesale Trade, Retail Trade, and Real Estate

City	Wholesale Trade, 1997				Retail Trade[1], 1997				Real Estate and Rental and Leasing, 1997			
	Number of Establish- ments	Number of Employees	Sales (mil dol)	Annual Payroll (mil dol)	Number of Establish- ments	Number of Employees	Sales (mil dol)	Annual Payroll (mil dol)	Number of Establish- ments	Number of Employees	Receipts (mil dol)	Annual Payroll (mil dol)
	72	73	74	75	76	77	78	79	80	81	82	83
OHIO—Cont'd												
Warren	62	728	265.2	19.2	281	4 639	761.2	82.1	57	267	28.4	5.0
Westerville	74	963	831.9	35.1	136	1 989	283.7	28.1	44	293	29.7	5.3
Westlake	174	2 482	2 050.2	123.6	148	2 532	401.0	41.4	55	592	76.8	15.4
Youngstown	153	2 251	702.1	69.5	347	3 442	487.4	56.3	60	436	32.3	6.4
Zanesville	41	813	337.3	22.0	266	3 226	506.9	46.6	46	172	20.1	3.5
OKLAHOMA	5 191	59 641	32 132.3	1 756.1	14 352	161 613	27 065.6	2 406.9	3 344	15 354	1 576.0	284.5
Bartlesville	28	112	24.1	2.4	183	2 431	409.8	36.6	41	D	D	D
Broken Arrow	113	1 218	420.4	42.5	217	2 956	616.0	48.5	52	189	21.3	3.4
Edmond	96	399	156.0	11.9	274	3 549	522.6	50.4	91	789	106.8	12.4
Enid	96	D	D	D	282	3 333	488.6	46.9	65	277	23.8	4.6
Lawton	80	751	173.1	15.9	392	5 005	664.4	65.5	123	500	47.1	7.9
Midwest City	28	D	D	D	220	4 401	742.7	60.8	60	257	25.6	3.7
Moore	40	350	93.5	6.7	114	1 592	237.5	22.3	25	84	6.2	1.1
Muskogee	65	830	231.7	21.2	281	3 221	505.6	48.0	50	208	16.0	3.1
Norman	79	987	397.6	27.0	399	5 268	968.0	82.5	132	514	40.7	7.8
Oklahoma City	1 307	19 128	14 323.2	572.8	2 145	28 167	5 337.0	490.8	705	4 136	464.1	87.2
Ponca City	32	226	145.7	6.3	158	1 963	280.5	27.0	30	78	9.4	1.2
Shawnee	25	D	D	D	221	2 535	358.3	33.9	47	165	17.4	2.3
Stillwater	30	399	135.1	8.8	193	2 639	370.6	34.2	55	236	12.1	2.7
Tulsa	1 237	16 094	8 372.1	577.7	1 905	28 474	5 100.5	484.1	684	3 904	451.4	84.0
OREGON	5 943	74 790	53 679.1	2 578.7	14 467	178 349	33 396.8	3 308.8	4 556	23 058	2 704.0	470.9
Albany	55	731	214.6	21.7	198	2 773	461.9	45.4	47	218	21.4	3.4
Beaverton	271	3 919	5 353.3	189.0	399	6 830	1 584.6	146.0	169	1 115	124.7	16.4
Corvallis	29	387	45.4	7.4	236	2 792	413.7	46.7	87	322	33.1	4.4
Eugene	356	3 977	1 687.8	125.2	826	11 203	2 036.4	209.4	276	1 408	165.7	24.9
Gresham	64	722	507.8	23.5	277	4 397	905.4	79.6	102	461	53.3	8.1
Hillsboro	83	1 007	325.5	41.7	225	3 704	884.3	78.6	60	203	28.6	3.6
Lake Oswego	166	1 448	2 076.1	70.5	151	1 357	251.4	28.3	105	880	100.6	22.4
Medford	149	1 216	462.5	38.3	499	6 687	1 306.9	121.6	117	640	60.7	10.3
Portland	1 700	26 464	23 728.9	948.6	2 621	34 060	6 190.4	683.9	945	7 255	926.8	189.9
Salem	171	2 083	694.8	60.3	665	10 054	1 826.2	181.9	225	1 232	136.8	29.0
Springfield	53	642	242.0	15.7	248	3 141	504.6	47.6	65	282	28.2	4.5
Tigard	246	3 515	3 212.5	157.4	335	7 330	1 429.4	139.7	110	667	117.5	19.8
PENNSYLVANIA	17 138	237 567	159 354.2	8 588.2	50 208	650 144	109 948.5	10 561.9	8 684	57 519	7 668.6	1 360.5
Allentown	203	2 749	1 531.9	92.2	452	5 234	1 037.1	99.6	115	645	80.2	12.0
Altoona	85	2 011	1 090.2	61.7	326	5 126	814.4	71.5	48	244	20.4	4.8
Bethel Park Borough	56	483	157.2	15.7	122	2 087	335.8	31.4	25	116	17.4	2.6
Bethlehem	111	1 344	858.8	55.4	228	2 856	486.2	49.9	52	320	43.4	7.7
Chester	30	311	96.2	10.3	79	657	156.2	16.0	10	47	5.5	1.0
Easton	46	1 235	624.2	52.6	129	1 071	167.2	19.3	16	41	7.2	1.1
Erie	128	1 861	487.4	57.8	494	5 859	772.3	83.3	74	386	34.7	8.1
Harrisburg	91	3 726	2 544.3	110.2	229	2 977	591.3	57.6	52	348	52.5	8.4
Johnstown	43	932	281.5	29.8	149	1 632	227.9	23.1	20	138	13.3	1.9
Lancaster	97	953	420.9	29.4	311	4 582	750.2	82.5	60	586	39.4	13.5
McKeesport	29	357	95.9	8.5	80	779	168.5	14.1	12	44	3.3	0.6
Monroeville Borough	81	824	331.7	31.8	335	7 123	1 173.7	108.9	55	435	50.9	8.8
New Castle	51	515	231.5	14.3	176	2 650	379.3	38.8	26	167	17.3	3.7
Norristown	77	1 416	549.7	50.9	106	1 337	225.5	25.8	27	155	25.4	3.5
Philadelphia	1 403	22 298	12 004.0	848.4	4 782	51 398	8 118.2	887.1	964	9 550	1 158.1	253.5
Pittsburgh	742	12 740	12 543.4	517.2	1 544	19 790	2 734.1	311.3	492	3 974	786.2	107.1
Plum Borough	46	515	257.2	20.7	60	673	103.4	10.6	18	55	6.5	1.4
Reading	95	1 851	583.5	61.0	310	2 919	502.8	55.7	50	298	36.9	7.8
Scranton	130	1 835	464.3	44.8	473	6 503	902.8	91.5	55	339	31.0	5.4
State College Borough	29	384	69.0	10.0	271	3 665	424.5	43.2	65	442	54.3	8.7
Wilkes-Barre	77	1 379	417.8	35.9	319	5 659	894.0	80.8	54	330	36.5	8.4
Williamsport	58	1 181	238.7	28.8	175	2 081	321.0	34.4	28	D	D	D
York	98	1 612	549.1	48.1	190	1 861	338.4	38.8	36	238	27.0	4.8
RHODE ISLAND	1 590	18 762	7 602.7	635.2	4 169	45 747	7 505.8	752.1	922	4 649	573.4	105.4
Cranston	153	2 776	961.9	97.3	305	4 031	689.4	61.3	70	301	29.3	5.7
East Providence	128	1 981	966.3	75.6	189	2 134	393.1	39.2	49	251	36.0	5.4
Newport	31	119	89.5	4.3	247	1 442	200.5	21.3	40	184	21.1	4.7
Pawtucket	92	953	231.7	27.8	233	2 489	434.7	49.7	57	275	31.0	5.0
Providence	295	3 589	1 462.4	125.9	611	5 155	772.6	92.2	175	1 374	125.8	29.5
Warwick	206	1 924	782.6	66.6	519	8 920	1 446.6	137.5	100	1 030	152.0	27.2
Woonsocket	45	683	161.6	19.6	152	1 806	245.0	24.1	30	94	13.4	1.5

1. Establishments with payroll.

City	Professional, Scientific, and Technical Services, 1997[1]				Manufacturing, 1997				Accommodation and Foodservices, 1997			
	Number of Establishments	Number of Employees	Receipts (mil dol)	Annual Payroll (mil dol)	Number of Establishments	Number of Employees	Receipts (mil dol)	Annual Payroll (mil dol)	Number of Establishments	Number of Employees	Sales (mil dol)	Annual Payroll (mil dol)
	84	85	86	87	88	89	90	91	92	93	94	95
OHIO—Cont'd												
Warren	127	715	50.3	21.1	69	12 471	3 247.4	629.7	137	2 415	67.9	18.4
Westerville	148	864	68.2	30.3	37	1 206	191.5	49.8	62	D	D	D
Westlake	162	1 047	85.6	37.5	55	1 662	308.7	54.8	70	1 936	61.5	16.9
Youngstown	126	906	80.2	35.5	148	4 658	954.0	166.5	177	2 467	79.3	19.9
Zanesville	54	344	27.1	10.0	53	4 194	599.0	112.2	105	2 097	61.4	16.9
OKLAHOMA	7 009	40 633	3 543.0	1 323.7	4 087	164 060	37 453.2	4 963.2	6 534	105 934	3 151.3	856.8
Bartlesville	68	762	73.5	23.0	31	930	139.7	40.2	83	1 443	47.1	13.1
Broken Arrow	141	484	42.5	12.9	129	4 191	614.9	136.8	101	1 789	49.3	14.0
Edmond	219	687	68.6	19.9	39	929	91.0	23.2	124	2 603	76.9	22.2
Enid	89	D	D	D	54	D	D	D	117	1 889	51.6	14.6
Lawton	119	1 008	60.2	29.1	45	D	D	D	179	3 391	89.1	25.0
Midwest City	68	625	47.2	20.2	18	D	D	D	98	1 973	56.3	16.0
Moore	35	190	11.0	3.5	NA	NA	NA	NA	68	1 107	31.7	8.7
Muskogee	63	326	23.0	7.2	61	3 476	760.7	117.4	109	1 959	54.9	14.2
Norman	288	1 239	106.8	37.2	83	2 442	679.6	71.6	225	4 779	139.9	38.6
Oklahoma City	1 848	12 251	1 100.3	449.3	759	38 354	9 658.1	1 251.1	1 071	21 553	684.2	188.8
Ponca City	57	776	33.7	14.0	45	D	D	D	62	1 054	29.5	7.8
Shawnee	61	269	20.3	6.1	41	2 799	545.5	96.3	111	2 439	70.0	19.2
Stillwater	85	550	40.1	15.9	28	2 195	814.6	68.4	114	2 398	56.0	15.6
Tulsa	1 688	12 883	1 355.7	504.0	872	29 436	5 526.1	986.6	1 035	19 183	643.9	172.6
OREGON	8 117	52 514	4 734.6	1 925.0	5 768	213 111	47 666.0	7 095.3	8 363	124 425	4 385.7	1 236.6
Albany	82	431	30.1	13.6	68	3 538	630.7	124.2	98	1 633	50.9	14.6
Beaverton	280	1 804	195.5	75.6	135	9 717	2 310.1	383.4	200	3 738	146.2	41.7
Corvallis	149	1 051	80.9	39.8	51	6 510	895.8	420.5	177	2 545	78.8	22.0
Eugene	605	3 899	333.5	123.5	340	9 524	1 330.3	277.1	452	7 351	234.5	68.1
Gresham	106	262	19.1	6.6	82	5 338	795.6	183.2	166	3 321	105.0	30.3
Hillsboro	143	1 165	143.7	69.9	173	8 734	1 977.3	339.4	130	2 613	82.3	23.1
Lake Oswego	253	1 559	185.0	74.1	54	1 083	127.8	36.3	88	1 404	47.0	12.8
Medford	212	1 377	76.5	26.4	74	2 007	344.8	61.9	213	3 634	119.0	35.3
Portland	2 478	22 439	2 245.3	931.2	1 144	39 059	7 385.1	1 310.6	1 679	28 839	1 134.9	322.8
Salem	395	2 357	178.2	70.4	224	7 085	1 226.0	211.4	335	5 642	186.1	52.4
Springfield	44	347	13.7	6.1	87	3 334	915.3	123.3	136	2 369	82.0	22.2
Tigard	247	2 528	234.0	108.3	110	3 706	566.4	125.5	130	2 541	88.4	25.5
PENNSYLVANIA	23 184	235 025	26 240.3	10 448.3	17 128	826 521	172 193.2	27 641.3	24 465	365 158	12 227.2	3 364.1
Allentown	258	1 624	136.1	54.9	238	8 310	4 060.0	325.0	230	3 665	132.1	36.5
Altoona	100	1 149	104.9	35.6	68	2 622	424.7	62.7	152	2 419	65.8	17.6
Bethel Park Borough	71	275	33.4	9.6	49	527	71.3	15.7	64	D	D	D
Bethlehem	177	1 388	175.9	55.3	109	6 650	1 063.1	237.3	182	2 120	81.1	21.7
Chester	9	52	4.2	1.8	34	2 372	782.6	101.3	51	335	12.7	3.1
Easton	92	290	43.6	8.8	53	3 748	639.5	112.4	89	884	33.8	9.6
Erie	207	1 486	121.7	43.3	203	10 286	1 789.0	357.2	238	2 926	81.0	21.5
Harrisburg	265	2 426	290.6	99.4	58	2 299	478.9	69.9	174	1 958	71.1	18.5
Johnstown	73	476	30.3	11.6	49	4 264	989.4	112.4	78	680	22.2	5.7
Lancaster	179	1 502	145.2	59.6	108	9 758	2 038.5	382.2	129	1 932	68.4	19.2
McKeesport	28	208	7.0	2.1	24	827	111.0	30.7	41	386	10.9	2.7
Monroeville Borough	104	2 796	416.0	124.2	26	687	82.2	19.6	109	3 260	98.5	28.3
New Castle	57	358	23.9	9.6	89	2 483	436.9	76.0	86	1 333	34.3	9.2
Norristown	117	834	89.6	33.3	63	1 517	196.6	48.8	68	D	D	D
Philadelphia	2 444	49 894	6 317.4	2 690.5	1 342	47 928	11 098.1	1 582.4	2 989	38 521	1 691.6	461.1
Pittsburgh	1 488	21 926	2 700.8	1 091.7	479	13 924	2 395.0	471.6	1 065	19 012	677.3	188.2
Plum Borough	36	297	49.0	15.6	36	1 523	194.2	48.1	29	470	13.0	3.8
Reading	132	925	88.6	46.2	160	16 969	3 654.2	737.4	164	D	D	D
Scranton	188	1 235	118.7	42.9	124	4 567	591.2	114.1	201	2 913	86.6	22.4
State College Borough	100	1 160	84.6	38.6	38	2 140	251.8	66.0	139	2 908	84.1	22.2
Wilkes-Barre	148	982	93.1	39.5	69	3 390	422.4	81.3	143	2 487	73.7	20.2
Williamsport	76	593	41.9	17.5	72	6 023	1 284.3	182.7	98	854	24.7	6.4
York	177	1 390	122.6	50.4	123	9 253	1 924.0	332.3	111	D	D	D
RHODE ISLAND	2 349	14 866	1 418.1	541.5	2 535	75 599	10 482.0	2 288.6	2 617	34 162	1 220.9	340.6
Cranston	185	1 072	107.0	34.3	252	7 160	949.0	213.3	162	D	D	D
East Providence	123	1 161	113.6	42.5	133	4 397	555.5	129.2	108	D	D	D
Newport	91	432	46.1	15.1	NA	NA	NA	NA	182	2 938	144.4	43.1
Pawtucket	94	355	30.2	11.4	205	9 766	1 535.2	294.3	122	D	D	D
Providence	689	4 672	517.3	206.2	570	12 465	1 294.1	337.1	443	6 216	237.6	63.7
Warwick	277	1 266	121.0	43.4	260	6 751	1 154.8	206.0	232	4 899	155.0	43.7
Woonsocket	43	199	15.0	5.8	84	2 700	317.3	80.5	89	D	D	D

1. Firms subject to federal tax.

City	Arts, Entertainment, and Recreation[1], 1997				Health Care and Social Assistance[1], 1997				Other Services[1], 1997			
	Number of Establishments	Number of Employees	Receipts (mil dol)	Annual Payroll (mil dol)	Number of Establishments	Number of Employees	Receipts (mil dol)	Annual Payroll (mil dol)	Number of Establishments	Number of Employees	Receipts (mil dol)	Annual Payroll (mil dol)
	96	97	98	99	100	101	102	103	104	105	106	107
OHIO—Cont'd												
Warren	13	110	5.3	1.7	211	1 996	122.0	53.0	104	481	30.0	7.5
Westerville	10	559	13.8	4.2	140	1 904	121.1	56.2	50	321	17.5	5.9
Westlake	14	155	4.3	1.3	161	2 122	111.7	49.3	58	485	31.1	10.3
Youngstown	12	161	4.1	1.0	216	2 964	190.2	91.1	144	1 145	70.6	24.4
Zanesville	5	73	1.6	0.4	116	1 203	96.1	45.4	79	750	40.7	13.8
OKLAHOMA	746	8 904	531.4	110.3	6 991	91 803	5 061.4	2 244.0	4 572	26 308	1 599.4	458.5
Bartlesville	10	0	0.0	0.0	99	819	59.4	29.8	61	335	19.7	6.6
Broken Arrow	18	403	15.3	5.1	123	1 822	73.7	35.3	111	698	37.7	12.9
Edmond	25	263	13.0	4.5	186	2 148	120.0	53.7	102	598	30.0	9.6
Enid	14	0	0.0	0.0	143	0	0.0	0.0	91	446	23.2	6.5
Lawton	19	0	0.0	0.0	196	2 295	139.0	51.9	135	709	33.5	9.8
Midwest City	16	134	2.7	0.8	127	2 273	161.3	62.4	69	393	19.3	5.4
Moore	8	85	2.2	0.5	53	617	23.4	10.7	45	255	15.6	4.7
Muskogee	10	0	0.0	0.0	150	2 195	97.7	44.1	61	362	21.0	6.4
Norman	34	348	22.9	3.8	236	2 426	148.1	66.7	112	679	32.3	9.7
Oklahoma City	109	2 521	104.8	31.3	1 474	18 208	1 308.1	586.6	892	7 677	445.6	135.6
Ponca City	11	0	0.0	0.0	84	593	35.1	14.9	49	226	13.8	3.9
Shawnee	6	0	0.0	0.0	84	1 273	62.3	27.0	49	214	11.8	3.4
Stillwater	11	87	1.7	0.5	88	1 012	51.0	23.6	67	372	16.1	4.8
Tulsa	106	1 305	92.5	19.0	1 240	17 228	1 244.7	553.7	794	5 621	399.7	115.3
OREGON	968	16 098	875.8	260.6	7 328	68 285	4 431.4	1 899.6	4 794	28 185	1 897.5	561.9
Albany	13	169	6.1	1.3	92	887	53.7	25.1	64	397	22.3	7.8
Beaverton	29	575	34.9	8.7	184	1 521	103.3	36.6	140	924	62.5	17.8
Corvallis	14	213	7.1	2.5	129	1 925	137.8	51.3	66	371	18.7	5.9
Eugene	48	641	20.7	6.5	489	4 929	373.8	162.3	260	2 135	130.9	38.7
Gresham	20	300	10.9	3.6	176	1 477	92.0	37.9	117	732	45.5	14.8
Hillsboro	12	151	3.8	1.3	146	1 197	79.4	33.7	103	493	36.9	11.5
Lake Oswego	16	89	6.3	1.9	138	1 006	58.0	22.4	76	387	33.9	8.8
Medford	17	207	12.6	3.3	219	2 920	196.6	92.9	118	798	52.8	14.8
Portland	167	2 453	179.1	72.9	1 430	15 676	1 098.2	489.0	1 094	8 597	621.8	189.4
Salem	43	646	37.6	8.3	442	4 213	269.5	120.0	230	1 433	81.6	26.9
Springfield	18	197	4.6	1.4	124	1 280	77.1	36.0	85	604	34.2	10.4
Tigard	12	129	5.9	1.7	139	1 413	112.6	40.2	91	607	48.5	15.8
PENNSYLVANIA	2 883	40 892	2 439.3	810.6	24 888	262 603	17 633.5	7 994.9	19 754	107 502	7 085.7	2 049.0
Allentown	25	225	10.5	3.1	268	2 036	145.4	66.5	216	1 528	97.0	31.0
Altoona	20	245	6.2	1.9	182	2 033	160.9	67.5	138	719	37.7	10.5
Bethel Park Borough	8	155	6.3	1.1	67	781	42.9	17.2	84	428	21.9	7.1
Bethlehem	8	84	2.8	0.8	196	1 642	133.8	53.5	108	947	51.8	20.1
Chester	NA	NA	NA	NA	43	568	36.1	15.6	29	110	6.6	2.2
Easton	8	87	4.1	1.3	51	639	31.1	15.3	69	440	31.7	11.0
Erie	25	225	13.4	3.5	301	3 261	286.6	138.2	193	936	64.8	17.6
Harrisburg	17	86	6.2	1.7	117	970	74.6	37.0	104	638	48.6	14.0
Johnstown	3	55	2.8	0.8	125	1 007	89.3	51.3	41	191	11.7	3.9
Lancaster	17	276	14.6	4.2	138	1 711	156.0	88.1	97	697	40.1	14.9
McKeesport	5	11	1.0	0.5	51	464	26.3	10.7	41	220	14.2	4.0
Monroeville Borough	15	265	9.2	3.0	168	2 369	186.6	78.0	87	594	29.9	10.0
New Castle	12	152	6.8	1.6	84	893	52.9	24.2	77	347	18.6	4.9
Norristown	5	31	3.2	1.1	90	2 402	243.1	102.2	41	258	20.4	6.4
Philadelphia	160	4 595	413.7	224.1	2 574	27 295	1 931.1	899.0	1 913	10 971	737.4	199.6
Pittsburgh	84	2 331	237.3	128.5	1 070	15 743	1 402.7	622.3	722	4 725	317.6	91.7
Plum Borough	6	64	2.3	0.6	26	144	8.2	3.5	35	176	9.4	2.7
Reading	13	180	32.0	6.8	120	1 168	65.7	30.9	106	943	52.6	16.0
Scranton	21	135	6.6	1.5	249	2 599	202.0	93.8	151	998	57.0	16.7
State College Borough	13	228	5.5	1.4	120	1 214	82.8	37.5	53	533	25.7	8.2
Wilkes-Barre	5	0	0.0	0.0	140	1 709	125.5	57.7	95	441	25.1	6.9
Williamsport	2	0	0.0	0.0	108	1 042	76.1	36.3	63	324	27.9	6.3
York	10	0	0.0	0.0	65	667	46.6	25.6	63	414	27.5	8.1
RHODE ISLAND	307	3 877	234.8	58.1	2 074	25 368	1 459.3	647.4	1 949	8 602	546.2	167.8
Cranston	23	219	16.5	3.7	198	1 735	113.4	49.0	177	838	51.5	17.3
East Providence	18	509	13.7	4.1	102	1 611	96.8	43.0	115	466	36.2	10.6
Newport	18	441	20.2	6.3	57	499	32.6	13.5	52	210	12.8	4.5
Pawtucket	13	90	7.2	2.3	112	1 167	72.3	32.1	132	822	51.2	16.2
Providence	29	274	25.8	5.5	401	4 950	336.8	160.2	284	1 466	107.9	32.3
Warwick	31	202	14.8	3.4	271	3 314	223.8	86.0	199	918	58.2	17.5
Woonsocket	5	76	2.1	0.7	68	1 287	60.5	28.2	81	275	14.0	4.2

1. Firms subject to federal tax.

Table D. Cities — Federal Funds and City Government Finances

City	Selected federal funds, fiscal 1999[1] (mil dol)									City government finances, 1997						
	Procurement contracts		Grants					Direct payments for individuals		General revenue						
										Intergovernmental			Taxes			
														Per capita[3] (dollars)		
	Defense	Other	Total[2]	Health and family welfare	Energy and environment	Education	Housing and community development	Educational assistance	Housing assistance	Total (mil dol)	Total (mil dol)	Percent from state government	Total (mil dol)	Total	Property	Sales and gross receipts
	108	109	110	111	112	113	114	115	116	117	118	119	120	121	122	123
OHIO—Cont'd																
Warren	0.2	0.2	8.0	3.6	0.1	0.0	2.9	0.6	4.2	42.4	8.0	35.0	16.4	339	27	8
Westerville	0.6	0.4	0.9	0.2	0.3	0.4	0.0	1.1	1.4	33.9	3.8	100.0	17.4	515	190	3
Westlake	3.2	0.6	0.3	0.0	0.0	0.0	0.0	0.0	0.0	32.0	4.3	95.4	19.0	632	254	0
Youngstown	3.8	3.1	34.6	5.6	0.0	0.5	9.6	4.6	2.1	69.6	20.3	36.1	30.0	343	22	5
Zanesville	0.5	0.1	2.3	1.4	0.0	0.0	0.3	1.0	1.3	27.4	4.7	100.0	12.7	465	71	9
OKLAHOMA	1 197.7	471.8	3 230.7	1 725.5	68.6	355.6	79.9	87.8	74.5	X	X	X	X	X	X	X
Bartlesville	0.0	0.8	3.6	1.6	0.5	0.4	0.2	0.8	3.2	26.6	0.6	98.0	14.8	438	62	371
Broken Arrow	0.1	1.6	2.4	0.0	0.4	0.1	0.9	0.1	0.0	32.5	0.9	66.9	19.4	281	53	223
Edmond	0.2	6.0	1.3	0.0	0.0	0.5	0.3	3.5	1.1	34.7	1.7	57.9	16.8	264	0	254
Enid	0.0	0.1	3.0	0.0	0.0	0.2	1.1	0.0	1.7	36.8	4.5	63.0	17.0	372	0	369
Lawton	6.4	7.5	8.1	2.3	0.1	1.2	3.1	2.8	3.3	41.2	2.8	31.1	25.0	303	6	293
Midwest City	171.3	0.6	2.3	0.0	0.0	1.2	1.0	2.3	3.3	104.8	1.2	13.7	19.9	367	11	345
Moore	0.3	0.1	1.0	0.0	0.0	0.5	0.0	0.0	0.7	19.3	0.5	95.5	10.9	244	34	206
Muskogee	0.1	4.6	6.9	1.5	0.0	1.5	0.5	0.8	0.4	84.6	0.9	80.7	16.6	437	8	417
Norman	41.1	4.4	52.3	11.2	3.1	4.8	1.5	6.6	0.0	147.4	10.6	80.5	29.6	328	15	306
Oklahoma City	303.7	173.4	615.6	226.3	32.7	70.1	34.3	7.3	11.5	511.5	46.4	48.8	288.0	613	57	542
Ponca City	63.3	0.6	2.6	0.3	0.1	0.3	1.2	0.2	0.8	19.9	1.9	19.3	8.3	317	14	300
Shawnee	0.6	0.5	15.4	11.2	0.0	1.1	2.1	1.1	0.0	41.9	2.2	40.3	12.3	457	14	433
Stillwater	8.4	5.9	44.6	2.7	1.6	17.7	0.0	5.6	0.8	61.5	2.0	100.0	13.5	351	31	317
Tulsa	46.1	30.4	39.5	11.5	1.6	4.3	7.4	12.3	18.9	480.4	29.5	33.2	203.9	539	65	463
OREGON	303.8	461.7	3 518.3	2 015.4	45.2	308.9	68.0	70.8	39.0	X	X	X	X	X	X	X
Albany	0.0	0.0	0.6	0.2	0.0	0.0	0.0	2.2	0.6	34.4	5.8	53.0	14.9	393	318	72
Beaverton	24.9	2.9	31.3	18.3	0.0	0.4	0.9	0.0	0.3	38.5	7.4	52.4	16.4	260	176	41
Corvallis	2.3	8.0	70.3	9.2	1.7	4.0	0.2	9.3	0.2	47.0	6.4	68.3	22.5	474	317	75
Eugene	2.9	4.8	91.5	42.2	2.2	19.6	4.8	11.2	4.4	155.5	32.7	32.4	61.8	500	414	29
Gresham	0.0	0.2	3.5	2.4	0.0	0.0	0.5	1.8	0.2	55.1	12.5	47.6	28.6	350	194	40
Hillsboro	0.4	1.3	4.0	0.0	0.0	0.0	2.8	0.0	0.3	64.1	3.1	100.0	27.4	522	348	57
Lake Oswego	0.8	0.2	0.0	0.0	0.0	0.0	0.0	0.0	0.0	35.6	3.7	19.5	22.2	640	455	47
Medford	0.5	2.6	5.0	2.0	0.1	0.0	0.7	0.1	1.0	47.6	5.1	53.1	25.4	453	328	67
Portland	148.0	138.0	334.4	163.7	19.4	16.9	26.8	20.3	15.2	645.4	94.1	35.0	320.8	667	430	89
Salem	0.3	8.0	458.5	65.8	14.2	87.8	21.9	4.5	4.1	116.7	14.3	56.4	53.5	437	347	53
Springfield	0.0	0.1	4.5	3.5	-0.2	0.0	0.8	0.1	0.0	58.4	12.9	61.8	12.0	243	198	29
Tigard	0.0	0.3	0.0	0.0	0.0	0.0	0.0	0.0	0.0	24.1	3.9	54.9	15.1	425	216	61
PENNSYLVANIA	3 841.1	2 092.6	13 140.7	8 437.5	137.2	977.6	444.6	350.6	314.6	X	X	X	X	X	X	X
Allentown	85.1	9.0	34.6	1.0	12.3	0.6	3.1	2.6	0.9	75.0	16.4	44.5	32.5	318	197	0
Altoona	0.1	1.4	8.8	2.3	-1.6	1.0	3.3	0.5	3.2	20.9	6.8	81.6	10.7	213	143	0
Bethel Park Borough	0.2	0.1	0.0	0.0	0.0	0.0	0.0	0.0	0.0	15.4	1.9	61.5	8.0	236	70	2
Bethlehem	2.5	0.9	23.5	6.7	0.8	1.7	4.1	4.0	5.2	51.5	8.0	68.7	20.8	296	193	0
Chester	2.0	0.1	7.5	1.3	0.0	0.2	4.5	2.3	0.8	23.7	4.3	78.5	16.3	400	192	0
Easton	4.0	0.2	3.2	0.0	0.0	0.0	2.0	0.6	0.0	24.2	5.9	65.5	6.0	234	149	0
Erie	22.1	2.9	40.9	6.2	13.0	0.9	9.5	4.5	7.2	78.1	25.3	60.0	30.3	288	218	0
Harrisburg	3.2	17.2	1 807.0	707.6	42.3	293.6	69.8	4.8	4.1	64.8	12.5	48.9	17.3	340	224	0
Johnstown	106.9	2.2	15.1	2.5	1.9	0.0	2.6	2.4	1.4	30.3	9.7	40.2	8.7	334	211	10
Lancaster	21.1	5.8	14.3	5.5	-0.6	0.1	6.6	1.6	5.6	39.5	12.1	70.1	14.0	262	183	0
McKeesport	0.1	0.1	3.2	0.0	0.0	0.4	2.3	0.0	3.5	15.1	3.8	29.2	5.7	243	98	0
Monroeville Borough	NA	NA	NA	NA	NA	NA	NA	NA	NA	21.3	1.8	51.0	15.2	531	141	0
New Castle	0.5	0.2	3.0	1.9	0.0	0.0	0.8	0.1	5.1	13.9	2.1	99.6	7.7	287	150	0
Norristown	2.8	0.9	8.7	0.2	0.2	0.0	7.6	0.0	0.0	18.5	3.6	72.6	11.6	388	128	0
Philadelphia	725.2	343.0	1 128.3	636.8	14.2	24.4	147.6	56.3	39.5	3 722.6	1 402.7	61.0	1 715.3	1 161	242	96
Pittsburgh	303.3	256.1	589.0	300.4	29.4	7.6	77.7	36.1	75.1	483.8	136.0	50.9	247.4	706	358	81
Plum Borough	0.0	0.0	0.0	0.0	0.0	0.0	0.0	0.0	0.0	6.3	1.1	92.0	4.2	157	67	0
Reading	2.7	6.2	16.6	4.0	0.1	0.6	7.9	2.9	3.5	55.6	13.6	51.6	23.1	304	206	0
Scranton	7.8	3.4	18.9	4.3	0.0	0.0	4.1	3.5	2.6	46.6	10.1	66.8	30.7	398	126	0
State College Borough	63.5	0.5	76.8	36.3	2.2	2.6	1.4	0.4	0.0	20.2	2.1	67.3	6.1	154	46	0
Wilkes-Barre	8.1	13.3	23.4	7.5	1.6	1.4	10.0	4.0	2.3	30.0	6.2	44.9	17.5	395	129	0
Williamsport	10.5	2.4	11.7	2.2	4.0	0.2	2.1	3.0	2.8	16.6	4.7	97.2	8.9	292	155	0
York	446.9	1.2	15.4	3.5	-0.2	0.4	8.7	1.2	0.0	35.8	6.7	97.8	12.0	293	169	0
RHODE ISLAND	303.4	117.7	1 411.0	861.8	23.0	109.4	30.6	42.7	6.7	X	X	X	X	X	X	X
Cranston	0.6	1.7	25.9	19.0	0.0	1.0	0.8	0.0	0.0	162.1	38.3	96.5	105.1	1 414	1 398	0
East Providence	0.2	1.1	3.3	0.8	0.0	0.0	0.9	0.1	2.6	82.9	23.7	88.4	53.9	1 113	1 105	0
Newport	48.6	7.7	3.7	2.3	0.0	0.6	0.5	0.7	0.0	73.2	16.6	64.5	43.0	1 770	1 656	17
Pawtucket	0.2	4.2	8.6	3.7	0.0	1.0	3.5	1.1	2.6	118.8	50.4	90.9	60.6	877	870	0
Providence	1.9	19.4	328.7	112.4	20.5	48.0	20.1	18.9	-7.0	390.0	162.6	92.2	179.8	1 178	1 166	0
Warwick	2.1	1.2	23.8	2.6	0.4	1.6	1.3	7.4	0.0	180.8	35.8	95.8	132.9	1 573	1 546	9
Woonsocket	0.3	0.3	4.5	2.2	0.0	0.0	2.0	0.0	8.3	81.1	35.8	94.4	38.6	923	916	0

1. October 1, 1998 to September 30, 1999.   2. Includes program categories not shown separately. State totals include additional categories not allocated by city.   3. Based on population estimated as of July 1 of the year shown.

City	City government finances, 1997 (cont'd)											
	General expenditure											
	Per capita[1] (dollars)			Percent of total for —								
	Total (mil dol)	Total	Capital outlays	Public welfare	Highways	Parking facilities	Education	Health and hospitals	Police protection	Sewerage and sanitation	Parks and recreation	Housing and community development	Interest on debt
	124	125	126	127	128	129	130	131	132	133	134	135	136
OHIO—Cont'd												
Warren	55.4	1 147	410	0.0	7.1	21.8	0.0	1.3	9.5	14.6	1.5	7.4	3.4
Westerville	32.4	960	274	0.0	17.0	0.0	0.0	0.1	14.5	15.7	11.0	1.0	0.8
Westlake	26.8	893	121	0.0	14.0	0.0	0.0	1.2	12.3	9.4	8.9	0.0	15.9
Youngstown	72.1	825	0	0.0	7.9	0.1	0.0	1.6	18.2	16.4	2.5	20.6	2.5
Zanesville	24.2	883	29	0.4	6.5	0.2	0.0	0.7	28.2	21.4	5.8	9.9	0.0
OKLAHOMA	X	X	X	X	X	X	X	X	X	X	X	X	X
Bartlesville	23.5	697	155	0.0	9.3	0.0	0.0	0.0	14.5	26.3	11.6	0.0	5.1
Broken Arrow	30.2	437	130	0.0	10.0	0.0	0.0	3.1	19.2	21.6	11.9	0.9	9.3
Edmond	41.8	659	129	0.0	12.1	0.0	0.0	0.0	16.2	13.9	11.8	0.2	2.8
Enid	37.8	828	238	0.0	9.2	0.0	0.0	0.0	10.3	31.2	3.6	3.2	8.8
Lawton	37.7	456	31	0.1	7.0	0.0	0.0	0.3	24.1	17.2	6.5	3.4	0.2
Midwest City	92.2	1 699	101	0.0	3.2	0.0	0.0	64.8	7.7	4.5	2.7	1.0	2.6
Moore	23.8	534	51	0.3	4.5	0.0	0.0	0.0	13.8	6.7	0.5	0.0	13.7
Muskogee	83.1	2 194	72	0.0	4.9	0.0	0.0	65.6	5.4	3.7	2.7	0.0	3.4
Norman	138.9	1 540	242	0.0	6.5	0.0	0.0	63.9	6.7	6.9	2.8	1.1	1.3
Oklahoma City	441.0	939	136	0.0	8.6	0.4	0.0	0.0	19.8	12.3	14.0	3.5	8.9
Ponca City	23.5	897	64	0.0	5.9	4.0	0.0	0.6	13.0	14.0	10.3	5.7	1.6
Shawnee	37.9	1 411	162	0.0	8.0	0.0	0.0	57.0	6.8	4.7	3.8	1.9	0.4
Stillwater	56.9	1 479	129	0.1	4.3	0.0	0.0	58.7	8.7	7.0	5.1	0.0	1.2
Tulsa	511.7	1 352	395	0.1	2.8	0.2	0.0	3.3	12.9	20.8	4.9	1.1	14.9
OREGON	X	X	X	X	X	X	X	X	X	X	X	X	X
Albany	30.0	792	186	0.0	24.6	0.0	0.0	4.0	15.1	10.2	11.6	0.3	2.8
Beaverton	29.2	462	71	0.5	18.8	0.0	0.0	0.0	25.5	6.2	0.5	0.7	1.4
Corvallis	38.0	799	123	0.0	9.9	0.3	0.0	0.0	17.4	17.8	7.1	3.1	2.1
Eugene	147.5	1 192	278	0.0	5.4	2.3	0.0	3.1	15.3	12.3	11.1	4.7	1.7
Gresham	79.9	979	508	0.0	5.2	0.0	0.0	0.0	14.9	13.9	2.0	3.3	1.8
Hillsboro	41.9	798	176	0.0	10.8	0.2	0.0	0.0	14.7	29.7	7.9	0.0	1.5
Lake Oswego	34.9	1 006	296	1.0	17.2	0.0	0.5	0.0	11.1	11.7	14.3	2.6	3.4
Medford	40.6	724	197	0.0	14.1	0.2	0.0	0.0	23.2	17.9	6.4	3.9	1.4
Portland	686.4	1 427	329	0.0	10.0	1.0	0.0	0.0	14.5	26.8	8.8	6.4	8.3
Salem	113.3	925	158	0.0	15.8	0.9	0.0	1.9	14.6	17.3	10.4	3.3	4.6
Springfield	56.0	1 133	342	0.0	8.1	0.0	0.0	5.9	11.9	20.6	0.4	1.2	2.1
Tigard	17.5	492	110	0.5	17.2	0.0	0.0	0.0	27.0	5.5	3.9	0.0	2.6
PENNSYLVANIA	X	X	X	X	X	X	X	X	X	X	X	X	X
Allentown	69.8	683	68	0.0	10.2	0.0	0.0	4.7	17.2	20.2	7.1	7.5	5.2
Altoona	20.6	411	92	0.0	14.6	0.1	0.0	0.0	19.6	0.3	2.8	14.4	1.1
Bethel Park Borough	15.5	460	94	0.0	14.8	0.0	0.0	0.0	20.5	23.1	12.8	0.0	7.3
Bethlehem	62.2	885	161	0.0	4.0	0.0	0.0	1.4	11.9	22.4	2.8	3.6	5.1
Chester	24.6	606	24	0.0	10.1	0.0	0.0	3.4	32.0	6.3	4.9	0.0	5.5
Easton	24.7	959	82	0.0	4.1	1.1	0.0	0.2	12.0	24.2	2.1	6.6	4.5
Erie	76.2	724	62	0.0	8.7	0.0	0.0	0.1	22.5	19.0	5.9	5.5	2.0
Harrisburg	79.6	1 564	241	0.0	8.9	0.0	0.0	0.0	13.9	15.9	8.4	10.6	5.6
Johnstown	26.6	1 016	70	0.0	6.0	1.2	0.0	0.0	6.8	16.9	1.8	23.6	8.3
Lancaster	42.3	788	17	0.0	4.6	0.0	0.0	0.5	18.8	25.6	2.0	8.2	0.7
McKeesport	15.3	657	14	0.0	8.1	2.2	0.0	0.0	22.4	17.8	6.2	8.5	0.6
Monroeville Borough	20.6	720	82	0.0	13.5	0.0	0.0	0.0	29.5	16.0	5.6	1.0	1.7
New Castle	12.3	457	7	0.0	9.0	0.1	0.0	0.1	14.4	13.6	4.9	2.0	2.6
Norristown	17.1	568	5	0.0	9.1	0.0	0.0	1.4	26.2	7.1	3.3	2.0	2.2
Philadelphia	3 445.5	2 331	244	8.7	2.9	0.0	0.5	14.1	11.8	7.3	2.4	5.2	3.7
Pittsburgh	493.9	1 410	225	0.0	6.8	0.0	0.0	2.6	12.9	4.9	2.4	14.3	12.8
Plum Borough	8.0	303	11	0.0	26.2	0.0	0.0	0.0	22.7	9.3	0.8	0.3	2.1
Reading	52.4	693	38	0.0	5.3	0.0	0.0	0.0	19.3	10.8	3.7	4.8	8.7
Scranton	50.8	658	24	0.0	11.2	1.5	0.0	0.1	19.5	5.3	2.3	6.9	0.8
State College Borough	18.4	467	42	0.0	7.3	2.1	0.0	1.1	20.7	31.8	6.2	3.8	2.9
Wilkes-Barre	27.4	616	6	0.0	9.0	1.3	0.0	1.1	18.5	8.8	5.9	8.0	1.2
Williamsport	17.4	571	51	0.0	8.8	1.4	0.0	0.0	20.2	1.5	2.3	0.0	0.7
York	42.3	1 037	47	0.0	5.1	1.4	0.0	2.1	15.0	20.8	5.3	6.3	6.3
RHODE ISLAND	X	X	X	X	X	X	X	X	X	X	X	X	X
Cranston	148.1	1 993	56	0.1	3.5	0.0	53.3	0.0	10.1	8.1	1.5	1.1	3.2
East Providence	79.9	1 651	5	0.1	3.0	0.0	56.6	0.2	8.2	7.3	2.4	1.8	0.9
Newport	64.1	2 637	217	0.7	1.1	0.4	43.2	0.0	10.3	15.8	3.2	2.0	1.8
Pawtucket	115.5	1 672	61	2.6	2.9	0.0	55.0	0.7	9.5	0.1	0.3	4.5	3.3
Providence	358.7	2 351	141	0.1	0.8	0.0	51.8	0.0	7.3	1.5	3.3	3.9	2.4
Warwick	176.4	2 088	88	0.8	2.2	0.0	56.5	0.1	6.1	4.6	1.4	0.9	2.1
Woonsocket	86.6	2 071	17	1.2	1.8	0.0	49.8	0.0	6.1	6.7	0.6	2.4	1.7

1. Based on population estimated as of July 1 of the year shown.

Table D. Cities — City Government Finances, City Government Employment, and Climate

City	City government finances, 1997 (cont'd) — Debt outstanding — Total (mil dol)	Per capita[1] (dollars)	Percent utility	City government employment, 1999	Climate[2] — Average daily temperature (degrees Fahrenheit) — Mean — January	July	Limits — January[3]	July[4]	Annual precipitation (inches)	Heating degree days	Cooling degree days
	137	138	139	140	141	142	143	144	145	146	147
OHIO—Cont'd											
Warren	34.7	718	15.4	501	24.4	70.5	15.3	83.2	36.11	6 402	491
Westerville	10.7	317	70.6	337	25.9	73.2	16.5	85.5	39.32	5 719	786
Westlake	64.5	2 146	0.0	NA	24.8	71.9	17.6	82.4	36.63	6 201	621
Youngstown	33.4	382	5.2	880	23.6	70.3	16.4	81.3	37.32	6 544	497
Zanesville	8.7	319	100.0	NA	26.8	72.7	18.3	83.5	39.42	5 714	716
OKLAHOMA	X	X	X	X	X	X	X	X	X	X	X
Bartlesville	21.6	641	10.4	336	34.7	82.1	22.5	94.7	35.91	3 777	1 868
Broken Arrow	53.2	769	6.7	703	35.2	83.3	24.9	93.7	40.59	3 691	2 017
Edmond	25.7	405	49.7	513	35.9	82.0	25.2	93.4	33.36	3 659	1 859
Enid	120.3	2 631	48.4	534	35.1	83.3	24.7	95.2	32.35	3 788	2 008
Lawton	0.7	9	0.0	779	36.8	83.5	23.7	95.8	29.27	3 457	2 069
Midwest City	42.3	781	0.0	493	35.9	82.0	25.2	93.4	33.36	3 659	1 859
Moore	39.9	897	0.8	218	35.9	82.0	25.2	93.4	33.36	3 659	1 859
Muskogee	45.5	1 202	0.0	449	37.3	82.2	26.6	93.8	41.74	3 413	1 937
Norman	37.8	419	7.6	2 126	37.8	82.2	25.6	94.8	35.41	3 295	1 967
Oklahoma City	736.1	1 567	18.1	4 773	35.9	82.0	25.2	93.4	33.36	3 659	1 859
Ponca City	34.7	1 325	82.3	426	32.4	82.5	22.1	93.8	34.24	4 226	1 865
Shawnee	26.1	974	92.9	260	38.3	82.0	25.9	94.9	38.27	3 222	1 954
Stillwater	28.1	730	83.8	1 079	33.6	81.6	21.4	93.1	33.85	4 028	1 755
Tulsa	1 444.5	3 817	7.9	4 357	35.2	83.3	24.9	93.7	40.59	3 691	2 017
OREGON	X	X	X	X	X	X	X	X	X	X	X
Albany	37.7	993	41.2	293	38.3	64.3	31.6	78.4	66.42	5 287	172
Beaverton	37.7	597	80.8	389	38.9	65.8	32.5	79.7	37.57	5 011	232
Corvallis	14.7	309	75.5	402	39.3	65.6	33.0	80.2	42.70	4 923	203
Eugene	249.5	2 017	80.1	2 266	40.8	67.3	35.2	81.7	49.37	4 546	300
Gresham	59.7	732	20.4	527	39.6	68.2	33.7	79.9	36.30	4 522	371
Hillsboro	11.8	225	10.0	361	38.9	65.8	32.5	79.7	37.57	5 011	232
Lake Oswego	25.4	733	4.5	291	39.6	68.2	33.7	79.9	36.30	4 522	371
Medford	13.1	234	4.9	443	38.1	72.9	30.4	90.5	18.86	4 611	725
Portland	1 238.8	2 576	11.1	5 260	39.6	68.2	33.7	79.9	36.30	4 522	371
Salem	134.7	1 099	20.9	1 490	39.6	66.3	32.7	81.6	39.16	4 927	247
Springfield	19.8	401	20.2	512	40.8	67.3	35.2	81.7	49.37	4 546	300
Tigard	9.8	273	0.0	236	38.9	65.8	32.5	79.7	37.57	5 011	232
PENNSYLVANIA	X	X	X	X	X	X	X	X	X	X	X
Allentown	164.1	1 605	36.1	964	26.6	74.1	18.8	84.5	43.52	5 785	773
Altoona	2.2	43	0.0	280	26.0	71.3	19.1	81.5	36.81	6 140	582
Bethel Park Borough	19.4	577	0.0	NA	26.1	72.1	18.5	82.6	36.85	5 968	654
Bethlehem	150.6	2 144	60.5	655	26.6	74.1	18.8	84.5	43.52	5 785	773
Chester	23.5	577	0.0	NA	32.4	78.3	26.4	87.3	42.45	4 586	1 291
Easton	15.5	602	0.0	NA	26.6	74.1	18.8	84.5	43.52	5 785	773
Erie	29.5	280	0.0	805	25.4	71.3	18.2	79.9	41.53	6 279	550
Harrisburg	72.7	1 429	0.0	787	28.6	75.7	21.2	85.8	40.50	5 347	962
Johnstown	34.8	1 333	0.0	189	28.0	73.2	19.6	85.9	47.75	5 649	739
Lancaster	23.6	440	0.0	532	27.9	74.1	19.2	84.9	41.22	5 584	780
McKeesport	1.7	72	0.0	373	26.1	72.1	18.5	82.6	36.85	5 968	654
Monroeville Borough	9.5	333	0.0	NA	26.1	72.1	18.5	82.6	36.85	5 968	654
New Castle	4.3	159	0.0	146	24.1	70.6	15.0	83.2	37.38	6 542	489
Norristown	15.5	515	0.0	167	29.8	75.9	21.4	86.5	44.38	5 114	1 022
Philadelphia	3 422.8	2 316	50.5	29 374	30.4	76.7	22.8	86.1	41.41	4 954	1 101
Pittsburgh	797.6	2 277	0.0	4 310	26.1	72.1	18.5	82.6	36.85	5 968	654
Plum Borough	1.8	67	0.0	NA	26.1	72.1	18.5	82.6	36.85	5 968	654
Reading	92.4	1 220	31.9	778	26.6	74.0	17.0	85.1	44.71	5 796	759
Scranton	4.7	61	0.0	637	24.7	71.7	17.5	81.8	36.18	6 291	539
State College Borough	8.3	210	0.0	193	24.7	71.3	16.7	82.0	37.48	6 364	529
Wilkes-Barre	5.0	113	0.0	389	24.7	71.7	17.5	81.8	36.18	6 291	539
Williamsport	2.2	73	0.0	NA	25.2	72.3	17.1	83.1	40.72	6 087	622
York	43.3	1 063	0.0	404	29.0	74.5	19.4	86.9	40.40	5 256	860
RHODE ISLAND	X	X	X	X	X	X	X	X	X	X	X
Cranston	64.2	863	1.6	2 239	27.9	72.7	19.1	82.1	45.53	5 884	606
East Providence	10.9	225	0.0	1 361	27.9	72.7	19.1	82.1	45.53	5 884	606
Newport	34.1	1 405	49.8	771	30.3	70.7	22.6	78.3	44.81	5 659	464
Pawtucket	75.1	1 088	4.5	1 889	27.9	72.7	19.1	82.1	45.53	5 884	606
Providence	284.0	1 861	8.7	5 442	27.9	72.7	19.1	82.1	45.53	5 884	606
Warwick	62.4	738	2.7	2 761	27.9	72.7	19.1	82.1	45.53	5 884	606
Woonsocket	14.9	357	25.3	NA	27.9	72.7	19.1	82.1	45.53	5 884	606

1. Based on the population estimated as of July 1 of the year shown.   2. Represents normal values based on the 30-year period, 1961–1990.   3. Average daily minimum.   4. Average daily maximum.

Table D. Cities — Land Area and Population

STATE Place code	City	Land area, 1990[1] (sq km)	Population, 1999			Population				Population characteristics, 1990 — Percent						
												Race				
			Total persons	Rank	Per square kilometer	Total persons 1990	Percent change 1990–1999	Total persons 1980	Percent change 1980–1990	White	Black	Am. Indian, Eskimo, Aleut	Asian and Pacific Islander	Other race	Hispanic[2]	Foreign born
		1	2	3	4	5	6	7	8	9	10	11	12	13	14	15
45 00000	SOUTH CAROLINA	77 987.8	3 885 736	X	50	3 486 310	11.5	3 120 729	11.7	69.0	29.8	0.2	0.6	0.3	0.9	1.4
45 01360	Anderson......................	32.1	26 166	1 151	815	26 385	-0.8	27 313	-3.4	65.1	34.3	0.2	0.3	0.2	0.5	0.7
45 13330	Charleston.....................	111.9	89 063	268	796	88 256	0.9	69 510	15.0	57.2	41.6	0.1	0.9	0.2	0.8	2.4
45 16000	Columbia.......................	303.4	111 821	195	369	110 734	1.0	101 208	9.4	53.7	43.7	0.3	1.4	0.9	2.0	3.3
45 25810	Florence........................	38.2	30 053	1 009	787	29 913	0.5	30 104	-0.6	52.3	47.0	0.1	0.5	0.1	0.6	1.5
45 30850	Greenville.....................	65.0	56 873	497	875	58 256	-2.4	58 242	0.0	63.6	35.2	0.1	0.8	0.2	1.0	2.0
45 48535	Mount Pleasant.............	56.4	44 785	663	794	30 108	48.7	13 838	117.6	89.9	9.2	0.1	0.6	0.1	0.9	2.3
45 50875	North Charleston............	129.6	84 106	287	649	70 304	19.6	62 534	12.4	62.7	34.3	0.5	1.6	0.9	2.5	2.3
45 61405	Rock Hill......................	60.0	48 474	605	808	42 112	15.1	35 386	17.6	60.4	38.1	0.4	0.8	0.2	0.6	1.3
45 68290	Spartanburg..................	46.9	40 704	736	868	43 479	-6.4	43 838	-0.8	53.1	45.6	0.1	0.9	0.2	0.8	2.4
45 70405	Sumter.........................	58.9	46 111	637	783	40 977	12.5	24 896	64.6	59.8	38.2	0.3	1.2	0.5	1.6	1.8
46 00000	SOUTH DAKOTA............	196 575.2	733 133	X	4	696 004	5.3	690 768	0.8	91.6	0.5	7.3	0.4	0.2	0.8	1.1
46 52980	Rapid City.....................	91.5	58 268	478	637	54 523	6.9	46 492	17.3	88.2	1.3	8.9	1.0	0.7	2.2	2.1
46 59020	Sioux Falls	116.7	116 720	183	1 000	100 836	15.8	81 341	24.0	96.8	0.7	1.6	0.7	0.2	0.6	1.7
47 00000	TENNESSEE	106 758.5	5 483 535	X	51	4 877 203	12.4	4 591 023	6.2	83.0	16.0	0.2	0.7	0.2	0.7	1.2
47 03440	Bartlett.........................	37.3	37 117	817	995	27 038	37.3	17 170	57.2	96.4	2.4	0.1	1.0	0.1	0.7	1.6
47 14000	Chattanooga..................	306.7	147 110	136	480	152 393	-3.5	169 550	-10.1	65.0	33.7	0.2	1.0	0.2	0.6	1.7
47 15160	Clarksville.....................	189.3	99 049	228	523	75 542	31.1	54 777	37.9	75.0	20.9	0.4	2.2	1.5	3.9	3.7
47 15400	Cleveland......................	51.4	36 138	837	703	32 236	12.1	26 432	22.0	91.6	7.2	0.3	0.5	0.5	1.4	1.5
47 16540	Columbia.......................	76.2	32 308	939	424	28 583	13.0	26 372	8.4	78.5	20.6	0.2	0.4	0.3	0.7	0.6
47 28960	Germantown..................	39.8	37 781	801	949	33 159	13.9	20 459	61.4	95.2	1.9	0.2	2.7	0.1	0.8	3.9
47 33280	Hendersonville..............	57.2	39 728	757	695	32 188	23.4	26 561	21.2	96.7	2.3	0.2	0.6	0.2	0.8	1.9
47 37640	Jackson........................	104.5	54 036	527	517	49 145	10.0	49 131	0.0	59.1	40.3	0.1	0.4	0.1	0.5	0.7
47 38320	Johnson City	79.2	59 160	465	747	50 354	17.5	39 738	26.7	93.1	5.9	0.2	0.7	0.2	0.6	1.6
47 39560	Kingsport......................	83.8	42 769	689	510	40 457	5.7	32 027	26.3	94.8	4.4	0.1	0.6	0.1	0.3	1.4
47 40000	Knoxville.......................	200.1	174 860	112	874	169 761	3.0	175 030	-3.0	82.7	15.8	0.2	1.0	0.2	0.7	2.0
47 48000	Memphis.......................	663.2	606 109	18	914	618 652	-2.0	646 356	-4.3	44.0	54.8	0.2	0.8	0.2	0.7	1.4
47 51560	Murfreesboro.................	78.6	61 177	443	778	44 922	36.2	32 845	36.8	82.3	14.5	0.2	2.8	0.2	0.8	2.9
47 52004	Nashville-Davidson	1 301.0	(3)506 385	(3)25	(3)389	(3)488 188	(3)3.7	NA	NA	74.8	23.4	0.3	1.3	0.3	0.8	2.5
47 55120	Oak Ridge.....................	221.6	26 788	1 126	121	27 310	-1.9	27 662	-1.3	89.4	8.0	0.4	2.1	0.2	1.0	3.5
48 00000	TEXAS	678 357.8	20 044 141	X	30	16 986 335	18.0	14 225 513	19.4	75.2	11.9	0.4	1.9	10.6	25.5	9.0
48 01000	Abilene.........................	267.0	108 995	205	408	106 707	2.1	98 312	8.5	82.4	7.0	0.4	1.3	8.9	15.5	4.0
48 03000	Amarillo........................	227.8	171 959	114	755	157 571	9.1	149 230	5.6	82.7	6.0	0.8	1.9	8.7	14.7	4.1
48 04000	Arlington.......................	240.9	311 962	53	1 295	261 717	19.2	160 113	63.5	82.6	8.4	0.5	3.9	4.5	8.9	7.6
48 05000	Austin..........................	564.0	587 873	19	1 042	472 020	24.5	345 544	36.6	70.6	12.4	0.4	3.0	13.6	23.0	8.5
48 06128	Baytown........................	81.1	69 588	370	858	63 843	9.0	56 923	12.2	73.0	12.0	0.3	0.8	13.9	23.2	9.9
48 07000	Beaumont......................	207.3	109 697	204	529	114 323	-4.0	118 102	-3.2	55.0	41.3	0.2	1.7	1.9	4.3	3.2
48 07132	Bedford.........................	25.9	50 451	579	1 948	43 762	15.3	20 821	110.2	92.8	2.6	0.4	2.5	1.6	4.6	4.1
48 10768	Brownsville....................	72.3	147 701	134	2 043	107 027	38.0	84 997	25.9	84.8	0.2	0.1	0.3	14.6	90.1	28.9
48 10912	Bryan...........................	84.6	58 920	470	696	55 002	7.1	44 337	24.1	69.9	17.2	0.2	1.5	11.1	19.8	6.6
48 13024	Carrollton......................	90.0	103 311	213	1 148	82 169	25.7	40 587	102.5	83.1	4.9	0.4	6.8	4.8	10.2	11.4
48 15976	College Station..............	76.3	61 121	445	801	52 443	16.5	37 272	40.7	83.0	6.3	0.2	6.5	4.0	8.9	9.1
48 16432	Conroe.........................	54.2	38 517	780	711	27 675	39.2	18 034	53.5	74.5	13.4	0.3	0.9	11.0	17.4	10.2
48 17000	Corpus Christi...............	349.6	281 791	59	806	257 428	9.5	231 999	11.0	76.1	4.4	0.4	0.9	17.7	50.4	5.3
48 19000	Dallas..........................	886.8	1 076 214	9	1 214	1 007 618	6.8	904 074	11.5	55.3	29.5	0.5	2.2	12.6	20.9	12.5
48 19624	Deer Park......................	26.9	30 804	983	1 145	27 424	12.3	22 648	21.1	92.2	1.1	0.4	1.2	5.1	10.8	3.0
48 19792	Del Rio.........................	38.2	35 728	843	935	30 705	16.4	30 034	2.2	65.5	1.4	0.4	0.4	32.3	77.2	21.3
48 19972	Denton.........................	136.3	79 208	314	581	66 270	19.5	48 063	37.9	82.0	9.5	0.5	2.8	5.3	9.0	7.1
48 20092	DeSoto.........................	55.9	36 139	836	646	30 544	18.3	15 538	96.6	76.0	20.8	0.3	1.1	1.7	5.0	2.9
48 21628	Duncanville....................	29.2	35 939	841	1 231	35 008	2.7	27 781	26.0	82.5	12.1	0.3	2.1	2.9	6.7	3.4
48 22660	Edinburg.......................	36.6	45 454	652	1 242	31 091	46.2	24 075	29.1	74.3	0.5	0.2	0.4	24.7	85.9	18.5
48 24000	El Paso.........................	635.5	612 070	17	964	515 342	18.9	425 259	21.2	76.9	3.4	0.4	1.2	18.1	69.0	23.4
48 24768	Euless..........................	41.5	45 911	643	1 106	38 149	20.3	24 002	58.9	86.5	4.6	0.6	5.1	3.3	7.9	7.7
48 27000	Fort Worth.....................	728.0	502 369	27	690	447 619	12.2	385 166	16.2	63.8	22.0	0.4	2.0	11.8	19.5	9.0
48 28068	Galveston......................	119.6	59 790	460	500	59 067	1.2	61 902	-4.6	61.5	29.1	0.2	2.3	6.9	21.4	7.7
48 29000	Garland........................	148.5	193 272	90	1 301	180 635	7.0	138 857	30.1	79.7	8.9	0.5	4.5	6.5	11.6	8.8
48 30464	Grand Prairie.................	177.4	114 906	187	648	99 606	15.4	71 457	39.4	75.8	9.7	0.8	3.0	10.7	20.5	7.8
48 30644	Grapevine.....................	81.0	42 106	707	520	29 407	43.2	11 801	147.4	94.7	1.8	0.5	1.1	1.9	5.7	2.6
48 31928	Haltom City....................	32.0	37 510	809	1 172	32 856	14.2	29 014	13.2	89.8	1.3	0.7	4.8	3.3	8.5	7.1
48 32372	Harlingen......................	69.7	57 139	491	820	48 746	17.2	43 543	11.9	80.1	0.8	0.2	0.4	18.5	71.0	13.9
48 35000	Houston........................	1 398.3	1 845 967	4	1 320	1 654 348	11.6	1 595 167	2.7	52.7	28.1	0.3	4.1	14.9	27.6	17.8
48 35528	Huntsville......................	54.3	32 148	947	592	30 628	5.0	23 936	16.7	64.7	26.7	0.4	0.9	7.2	13.0	5.2
48 35576	Hurst...........................	25.6	37 240	814	1 455	33 574	10.9	31 420	6.9	93.4	2.6	0.5	1.2	2.3	5.2	3.7
48 37000	Irving...........................	175.1	179 520	107	1 025	155 037	15.8	109 943	41.0	78.7	7.5	0.6	4.6	8.5	16.3	12.6
48 39148	Killeen.........................	71.7	81 405	300	1 135	63 535	28.1	46 296	37.2	58.1	30.1	0.5	5.8	5.5	14.0	8.5
48 39352	Kingsville......................	32.9	24 820	1 214	754	25 276	-1.8	28 808	-12.3	66.8	3.8	0.3	1.6	27.6	62.4	5.2
48 41440	La Porte	49.9	33 442	906	670	27 923	19.8	14 062	98.6	85.3	7.1	0.5	1.0	6.1	14.3	4.4
48 41464	Laredo..........................	85.1	183 160	102	2 152	122 893	49.0	91 449	34.4	70.8	0.1	0.2	0.4	28.5	93.9	24.4

1. Dry land or land partially or temporarily covered by water.   2. Hispanic persons may be of any race.   3. 1999 population is for Nashville-Davidson "remainder"; most other items are for Nashville-Davidson Consolidated city; see Appendix A.

Table D. Cities — Population and Households

City	Under 5 years	5 to 17 years	18 to 24 years	25 to 34 years	35 to 44 years	45 to 54 years	55 to 64 years	65 to 74 years	75 years and over	Percent female	Number	Percent change, 1980–1990	Persons per household	Female family householder[1]	One-person
	Age of population (percent)										Households, 1990			Percent	
	16	17	18	19	20	21	22	23	24	25	26	27	28	29	30
SOUTH CAROLINA	7.4	19.0	11.7	17.0	15.0	10.2	8.4	7.1	4.3	51.6	1 258 044	22.1	2.68	14.0	22.4
Anderson	6.7	16.4	11.1	14.8	12.5	8.3	9.6	10.8	9.7	55.8	10 509	1.7	2.36	18.0	33.3
Charleston	7.1	15.1	17.3	18.1	13.8	8.2	7.6	8.0	4.9	52.8	30 753	22.1	2.43	17.0	30.8
Columbia	6.1	13.8	22.7	20.0	12.8	7.0	5.8	6.5	5.2	50.8	33 919	11.2	2.31	16.5	34.0
Florence	7.4	19.0	10.0	16.4	14.7	9.7	8.5	8.7	5.6	54.6	11 074	6.4	2.57	20.7	27.7
Greenville	6.8	15.4	13.5	18.3	14.0	8.5	7.7	9.0	6.8	54.5	24 101	8.8	2.25	16.7	36.6
Mount Pleasant	7.7	16.7	9.0	22.2	19.5	8.9	6.8	5.8	3.4	51.1	11 788	135.9	2.52	9.2	23.0
North Charleston	10.0	16.4	20.9	24.2	11.4	6.6	4.7	3.4	2.3	45.6	23 499	31.0	2.59	16.6	24.9
Rock Hill	7.6	17.1	17.0	17.2	12.7	8.9	6.9	6.8	5.7	54.5	14 669	25.3	2.64	18.4	24.6
Spartanburg	7.8	17.3	12.7	16.0	13.4	9.5	8.0	8.7	6.6	55.2	16 712	4.8	2.45	21.0	31.2
Sumter	8.2	18.5	13.0	22.2	13.9	7.4	6.4	6.4	4.0	48.6	12 737	47.1	2.78	18.2	22.0
SOUTH DAKOTA	7.8	20.7	9.8	15.7	13.7	9.0	8.6	7.8	6.9	50.8	259 034	6.4	2.59	8.0	26.4
Rapid City	8.5	19.1	11.4	18.1	14.8	8.7	7.8	6.4	5.2	51.1	21 152	22.6	2.51	11.3	26.4
Sioux Falls	7.9	17.9	11.4	19.9	14.9	8.6	7.7	6.5	5.2	52.4	39 790	28.9	2.43	9.4	28.7
TENNESSEE	6.8	18.1	10.8	16.7	15.2	10.8	8.9	7.3	5.4	51.8	1 853 725	14.5	2.56	12.6	23.9
Bartlett	6.8	25.3	7.9	14.4	23.3	11.0	6.0	3.6	1.6	51.0	8 456	68.2	3.15	7.9	8.4
Chattanooga	6.8	16.5	10.8	16.5	14.1	10.2	9.9	8.5	6.8	53.8	62 177	0.3	2.37	17.1	31.1
Clarksville	8.9	17.1	18.1	20.9	13.8	7.8	6.2	4.2	3.0	48.3	25 442	42.7	2.70	11.4	19.4
Cleveland	6.1	16.0	13.3	15.5	13.6	11.0	9.7	8.2	6.6	53.5	11 996	20.2	2.41	12.1	27.4
Columbia	7.3	17.5	9.4	16.9	13.8	10.1	9.9	8.5	6.5	53.5	11 267	16.5	2.48	15.2	26.3
Germantown	6.0	25.1	6.8	8.7	23.4	17.0	7.6	4.0	1.4	50.7	10 713	72.7	3.07	5.9	10.9
Hendersonville	6.6	20.1	9.5	16.3	17.8	13.5	7.7	5.1	3.3	51.7	11 441	36.1	2.77	9.3	16.7
Jackson	7.2	17.9	12.8	15.8	13.6	8.8	8.6	7.9	7.5	54.4	19 206	6.0	2.43	18.8	29.2
Johnson City	5.2	14.5	15.1	15.6	13.3	10.6	9.8	8.9	6.9	52.4	19 675	39.5	2.30	12.0	30.7
Kingsport	6.1	15.6	8.3	13.3	13.0	12.5	11.4	11.5	8.4	54.9	15 629	22.8	2.28	12.6	30.1
Knoxville	5.9	13.9	16.5	18.0	13.1	8.7	8.5	8.6	6.8	53.3	69 973	2.2	2.20	14.3	35.5
Memphis	8.1	18.8	11.2	18.1	14.2	9.2	8.4	7.1	5.1	53.3	229 829	-0.2	2.59	21.9	28.3
Murfreesboro	6.4	16.1	21.8	17.5	13.4	8.1	6.8	5.6	4.2	52.3	17 110	48.4	2.38	12.0	29.9
Nashville-Davidson	7.0	15.8	11.4	20.6	15.4	10.0	8.2	6.6	5.0	52.5	207 497	NA	2.36	14.0	30.1
Oak Ridge	5.3	16.9	6.9	13.5	16.1	11.3	11.6	12.1	6.3	52.9	11 763	6.4	2.30	10.4	29.8
TEXAS	8.2	20.3	11.1	18.2	14.9	9.6	7.6	5.9	4.2	50.7	6 070 937	23.0	2.73	11.6	23.9
Abilene	8.3	18.7	14.0	17.8	13.3	8.5	7.7	6.5	5.1	51.3	38 395	13.2	2.60	9.6	25.0
Amarillo	8.3	19.7	9.7	17.7	14.9	9.0	8.7	6.9	5.1	52.1	61 137	9.2	2.54	11.0	27.2
Arlington	8.8	18.1	12.4	23.9	16.8	9.5	5.4	3.2	1.7	49.9	100 651	71.9	2.58	9.4	24.8
Austin	7.5	15.6	17.2	23.0	15.7	8.0	5.6	4.2	3.1	50.1	192 148	43.1	2.33	11.0	34.1
Baytown	8.9	22.0	10.9	17.7	15.1	9.0	6.8	5.5	4.1	50.7	22 422	11.7	2.82	12.5	22.0
Beaumont	7.4	19.5	10.1	16.8	14.3	9.5	8.7	7.7	6.0	52.4	43 357	0.8	2.55	15.9	28.1
Bedford	7.1	18.7	10.1	20.7	20.2	12.5	6.1	3.0	1.7	51.0	17 586	153.1	2.48	7.8	27.3
Brownsville	9.0	27.5	11.7	15.0	13.0	8.2	6.9	5.3	3.4	52.8	26 322	14.5	3.70	20.3	15.2
Bryan	8.5	18.4	16.4	20.3	12.8	8.0	5.9	5.3	4.5	50.4	20 705	28.7	2.61	12.2	25.5
Carrollton	9.5	18.8	8.0	25.0	20.3	10.3	4.8	2.2	1.1	50.8	30 452	112.6	2.69	9.0	19.2
College Station	4.5	9.2	54.3	14.8	8.0	4.3	2.1	1.4	1.3	46.4	17 878	49.4	2.31	6.3	26.7
Conroe	8.5	20.5	12.0	18.7	13.9	9.3	6.9	5.4	4.9	50.5	10 016	48.7	2.68	13.7	25.5
Corpus Christi	8.2	21.9	9.7	18.0	14.8	9.5	7.9	6.1	3.9	51.2	89 468	16.6	2.83	13.8	22.5
Dallas	8.0	17.0	11.4	22.8	14.8	9.3	7.2	5.6	4.0	50.8	402 060	13.1	2.46	13.9	34.2
Deer Park	7.6	24.8	8.8	17.0	18.9	11.8	6.3	3.1	1.6	49.8	8 822	26.4	3.11	9.0	10.9
Del Rio	8.6	24.8	10.6	14.7	13.7	9.3	8.0	6.3	4.0	51.4	9 465	6.8	3.23	14.2	17.8
Denton	6.4	13.7	27.1	19.0	12.9	7.6	5.1	4.3	3.9	52.0	25 719	47.1	2.31	8.6	32.5
DeSoto	7.6	21.5	8.6	17.5	19.1	12.6	6.5	3.8	2.8	51.6	10 754	121.2	2.81	10.3	16.8
Duncanville	7.1	22.3	9.1	15.9	18.5	13.0	7.5	4.3	2.3	51.4	12 509	42.4	2.85	11.7	16.9
Edinburg	8.9	24.5	13.9	16.5	12.7	8.0	6.4	5.6	3.5	52.1	8 474	26.0	3.39	19.9	15.7
El Paso	8.7	23.1	11.6	17.1	13.8	9.4	7.7	5.5	3.2	52.0	160 545	25.0	3.17	16.4	17.9
Euless	8.6	16.8	10.8	26.8	15.6	11.2	6.1	2.8	1.3	50.3	15 456	74.7	2.46	9.6	28.0
Fort Worth	8.6	17.9	11.7	20.8	13.9	8.5	7.4	6.5	4.7	50.8	168 274	16.8	2.58	13.3	29.0
Galveston	7.1	17.8	9.8	19.6	14.0	9.4	8.7	7.9	5.7	51.7	24 157	0.8	2.37	16.6	34.3
Garland	9.3	20.5	9.9	20.9	17.5	10.5	6.0	3.5	2.0	50.6	63 193	37.8	2.85	11.3	18.4
Grand Prairie	9.3	20.8	10.6	20.8	17.0	8.9	6.2	4.2	2.2	50.3	34 958	46.5	2.83	11.4	20.6
Grapevine	9.2	19.1	8.0	23.3	21.6	10.1	4.5	2.3	2.1	50.0	10 969	151.5	2.64	7.6	20.8
Haltom City	8.1	17.1	11.3	19.5	14.1	9.6	8.2	7.4	4.6	50.8	12 756	21.5	2.55	11.2	25.7
Harlingen	9.1	23.4	9.9	15.6	13.0	8.0	8.0	7.1	6.0	52.5	15 398	17.2	3.09	14.6	20.1
Houston	8.3	18.4	11.6	21.1	15.3	9.8	7.3	5.1	3.1	50.4	616 877	2.2	2.60	14.6	31.0
Huntsville	5.1	10.8	28.5	22.0	14.8	6.8	4.6	3.5	4.0	39.7	7 853	19.4	2.33	11.9	32.8
Hurst	7.2	17.8	10.1	17.4	14.8	13.4	10.4	6.2	2.8	51.1	12 779	15.2	2.61	10.5	20.1
Irving	8.3	13.3	13.3	26.6	14.3	10.0	6.3	3.4	1.9	49.8	63 236	57.6	2.44	9.9	30.1
Killeen	11.5	18.8	18.3	22.9	12.2	7.3	5.0	2.6	1.4	49.6	23 248	39.3	2.72	11.3	20.3
Kingsville	8.3	20.1	17.2	15.7	12.3	9.4	6.8	6.1	4.0	50.6	8 529	-6.2	2.85	13.5	22.8
La Porte	9.2	23.2	8.9	19.4	18.0	9.8	6.3	3.3	2.0	50.2	9 144	102.9	3.03	9.4	15.3
Laredo	9.9	26.1	12.2	16.2	12.5	8.4	6.6	4.8	3.2	52.2	32 029	33.8	3.78	18.2	12.9

1. No spouse present.

Table D. Cities — Group Quarters, Crime, Education, and Income

City	Persons in group quarters, 1990				Serious crimes known to police, 1998[2]				Education, 1990				Money income, 1989		
					Total		Rate[3]		School enrollment		Attainment[4] (percent)			Households	
														Median	
	Total	Persons in mental hospitals	Persons in nursing homes	Persons identified as home-less[1]	Number	Rate[3]	Violent	Property	Public	Private	High school graduate or more	Bach-elor's degree or more	Per capita (dollars)[5]	Dollars	Percent change, 1979–1989 (constant 1989 dollars)
	31	32	33	34	35	36	37	38	39	40	41	42	43	44	45
SOUTH CAROLINA	115 740	2 152	18 228	982	221 607	5 777	903	4 874	807 539	105 471	68.3	16.6	11 897	26 256	6.5
Anderson.......................	1 405	0	676	10	2 285	8 371	1 191	7 180	4 761	1 240	62.6	17.0	10 866	19 433	-7.1
Charleston...................	5 588	0	265	186	7 690	10 510	1 303	9 207	20 313	4 266	76.5	29.4	14 093	25 153	11.3
Columbia.....................	19 602	1 028	953	201	11 463	9 938	1 248	8 690	27 583	4 420	76.0	31.7	12 210	23 216	11.8
Florence......................	1 292	0	338	15	3 715	11 958	1 828	10 130	6 826	815	69.1	22.5	12 831	24 906	2.8
Greenville....................	4 092	0	501	109	5 973	10 141	1 469	8 672	9 860	5 723	72.5	29.3	14 708	23 963	12.8
Mount Pleasant.............	424	0	424	0	1 674	4 745	312	4 433	5 835	1 733	90.3	41.8	18 931	38 605	2.2
North Charleston..........	9 445	26	489	15	NA	NA	NA	NA	13 770	2 177	73.9	11.4	10 315	21 824	6.4
Rock Hill.....................	3 089	0	661	41	7 005	7 005	1 211	5 794	11 694	915	62.9	17.7	11 481	26 615	9.7
Spartanburg.................	2 606	158	413	131	5 677	13 091	2 253	10 838	8 701	2 683	65.9	23.4	12 142	22 423	4.8
Sumter........................	6 570	93	196	33	2 982	7 604	1 313	6 291	10 066	1 658	77.9	20.6	11 495	21 221	6.0
SOUTH DAKOTA............	25 955	427	9 356	515	19 366	2 624	154	2 470	165 993	19 253	77.1	17.2	10 661	22 503	2.1
Rapid City	1 465	0	340	157	3 128	5 409	427	4 982	13 173	1 553	84.9	23.4	12 469	25 740	-1.4
Sioux Falls..................	4 171	49	1 086	118	3 915	3 464	288	3 176	18 482	6 481	83.4	22.9	13 677	27 286	-2.7
TENNESSEE	128 828	2 849	35 192	2 151	273 420	5 034	715	4 319	1 023 651	147 989	67.1	16.0	12 255	24 807	4.7
Bartlett........................	365	163	81	0	1 000	2 763	500	2 263	7 493	1 461	90.9	23.5	16 080	47 346	7.4
Chattanooga.................	4 953	272	1 702	175	15 960	10 468	1 799	8 669	29 855	6 383	69.0	18.2	12 332	22 197	-2.4
Clarksville...................	6 958	12	379	0	5 051	5 122	676	4 446	18 542	1 498	81.3	18.5	11 252	25 341	9.6
Cleveland....................	1 317	0	382	0	1 952	5 698	528	5 170	5 836	1 686	66.2	17.1	12 265	22 894	4.0
Columbia.....................	589	0	462	0	2 540	7 664	957	6 707	5 612	619	66.7	14.2	12 558	25 238	4.0
Germantown.................	0	0	0	0	771	2 396	78	2 318	8 084	3 084	97.2	53.5	28 087	69 019	12.5
Hendersonville	421	0	101	0	1 041	2 707	127	2 580	7 279	1 112	83.3	21.1	16 010	38 068	-1.1
Jackson.......................	2 269	0	643	15	5 711	11 111	1 488	9 623	9 711	2 744	67.4	17.1	11 268	21 063	-4.3
Johnson City	3 987	65	1 443	38	3 072	5 385	563	4 822	12 861	862	71.1	25.9	13 071	23 053	10.9
Kingsport.....................	686	0	544	36	2 487	5 903	722	5 181	6 525	625	67.9	20.3	13 825	22 750	-8.1
Knoxville.....................	11 055	472	1 285	474	10 165	5 965	866	5 099	41 467	3 478	70.8	21.7	12 108	19 923	-0.7
Memphis......................	15 979	282	3 895	349	53 214	8 807	1 499	7 308	134 579	24 065	70.4	17.5	11 682	22 674	-3.6
Murfreesboro................	4 253	0	241	58	2 616	4 626	495	4 131	14 856	693	77.0	27.2	12 983	26 394	10.2
Nashville-Davidson	21 116	568	3 329	793	NA	NA	NA	NA	86 713	34 707	75.9	24.4	15 195	28 377	NA
Oak Ridge....................	269	41	120	0	1 455	5 578	406	5 172	5 777	519	85.6	35.5	17 661	32 615	-1.6
TEXAS	391 134	5 315	101 005	8 968	1 010 062	5 112	565	4 547	4 313 852	492 043	72.1	20.3	12 904	27 016	-3.5
Abilene........................	6 730	100	996	32	NA	NA	NA	NA	22 076	8 601	76.0	22.0	11 857	24 725	-2.3
Amarillo.......................	2 152	80	1 101	294	NA	NA	NA	NA	38 082	3 383	75.7	17.8	12 744	24 915	-11.7
Arlington......................	2 006	50	859	46	19 520	6 380	608	5 772	63 396	9 712	87.8	30.0	16 239	35 048	-1.1
Austin	18 042	586	2 422	471	39 194	7 002	541	6 461	136 404	15 087	82.3	34.4	14 295	25 414	3.1
Baytown.......................	529	11	398	31	3 383	4 816	347	4 469	16 749	1 112	71.2	14.7	12 963	30 151	-16.7
Beaumont.....................	3 519	43	1 105	146	9 294	8 245	1 088	7 157	27 247	4 513	75.2	19.7	12 751	24 495	-13.9
Bedford........................	218	0	218	0	1 574	3 068	257	2 811	10 534	1 441	93.0	34.3	19 847	42 453	-5.4
Brownsville...................	1 696	0	515	24	7 860	5 727	659	5 068	34 454	2 204	45.5	12.2	6 284	15 890	-18.9
Bryan..........................	906	0	307	84	4 056	6 772	636	6 136	16 906	1 454	73.7	26.9	11 691	22 577	-2.5
Carrollton.....................	195	0	195	0	NA	NA	NA	NA	18 429	3 305	89.9	37.4	19 065	45 787	6.6
College Station..............	11 218	47	105	0	2 531	4 189	217	3 972	35 207	1 269	93.8	58.9	9 262	14 481	-11.7
Conroe	762	0	188	10	2 392	6 632	735	5 897	6 562	661	69.8	18.3	11 477	23 634	-17.5
Corpus Christi	4 250	73	1 346	165	22 510	7 833	729	7 104	70 472	6 576	70.9	17.8	11 755	25 773	-8.5
Dallas.........................	16 589	131	5 259	1 480	NA	NA	NA	NA	207 066	38 835	73.5	27.1	16 300	27 489	1.1
Deer Park.....................	190	0	87	0	607	1 949	116	1 833	8 267	719	84.3	15.3	15 645	46 199	-4.0
Del Rio........................	172	0	172	0	1 719	4 871	442	4 429	8 824	629	52.8	11.1	7 522	17 394	-8.1
Denton.........................	6 994	0	509	0	3 568	4 565	406	4 159	26 259	1 443	81.9	36.4	12 013	23 156	-4.7
DeSoto	339	0	339	0	1 461	4 049	349	3 700	7 572	1 388	88.0	29.4	18 093	45 550	-2.2
Duncanville...................	70	0	63	0	1 601	4 312	431	3 881	9 306	1 423	87.0	29.0	17 060	41 028	-4.8
Edinburg......................	1 107	0	117	0	3 526	8 902	737	8 165	10 025	744	56.2	19.4	7 474	18 956	-5.6
El Paso........................	6 140	192	1 072	434	35 787	5 730	700	5 030	160 046	12 978	65.3	16.2	9 603	23 460	-1.6
Euless.........................	87	0	72	0	1 692	3 917	264	3 653	8 026	1 144	86.2	25.8	16 635	34 950	2.0
Fort Worth....................	13 883	328	3 029	1 036	35 491	7 129	870	6 259	92 695	20 327	71.6	21.5	13 162	26 547	3.5
Galveston.....................	1 857	0	254	222	5 310	8 600	591	8 009	14 619	1 699	70.0	21.1	12 399	20 825	-14.0
Garland........................	440	0	421	0	8 870	4 526	258	4 268	44 069	6 388	82.6	24.3	15 056	37 274	-1.9
Grand Prairie................	698	0	358	0	6 484	6 189	490	5 699	24 379	3 092	76.3	19.4	13 752	34 507	5.0
Grapevine.....................	246	0	152	0	1 383	3 554	118	3 436	6 557	833	89.4	35.1	19 526	48 901	29.6
Haltom City	299	38	227	95	1 694	4 593	488	4 105	6 333	771	69.6	9.8	11 764	25 392	-12.8
Harlingen......................	1 257	0	260	0	3 838	6 492	516	5 976	13 775	1 156	59.3	14.8	9 183	20 858	3.1
Houston.......................	23 483	448	4 335	1 850	127 817	7 112	1 123	5 989	387 704	57 424	70.5	25.1	14 261	26 261	-15.2
Huntsville.....................	9 820	0	303	0	1 247	4 204	583	3 621	10 930	747	73.4	21.4	9 273	17 876	-4.5
Hurst...........................	211	0	211	0	2 136	5 638	272	5 366	7 400	945	86.1	22.4	16 621	37 473	-6.5
Irving..........................	993	0	430	0	9 454	5 180	431	4 749	31 464	6 880	80.7	26.2	16 424	31 767	-6.1
Killeen.........................	334	55	156	24	5 304	6 659	719	5 940	15 510	1 084	85.8	14.4	9 582	22 468	13.3
Kingsville.....................	1 071	0	104	0	1 619	6 298	556	5 742	8 871	516	64.2	20.4	9 338	22 053	-2.4
La Porte.......................	159	0	159	0	647	1 965	246	1 719	7 960	472	81.6	14.4	14 349	41 733	2.4
Laredo.........................	1 840	0	274	5	13 135	7 571	482	7 089	41 001	3 279	48.8	11.6	6 981	18 395	3.5

1. Persons in emergency shelters and persons visible in street locations. 2. Data for serious crimes have not been adjusted for underreporting. This may affect comparability between geographic areas and over time. 3. Per 100,000 population estimated by the FBI. 4. Persons 25 years old and older. 5. Based on population enumerated as of April 1, 1990.

City	Money income, 1989 (cont'd)				Housing units, 1990										
	Households (cont'd)	Percent below poverty, 1989						Occupied units							
		Persons		Families						Owner-occupied units			Renter-occupied units		
											Owner cost as a percent of income				
	Percent with $100,000 or more	Total	Percent change in rate, 1979–1989	Total	Total	Percent change, 1980–1990	Vacant units for sale or rent[1]	Total	Percent	Median value[2] (dollars)	With a mortgage	Without a mortgage	Median rent[3] (dollars)	Rent as percent of income	Substandard units[4] (percent)
	46	47	48	49	50	51	52	53	54	55	56	57	58	59	60
SOUTH CAROLINA	2.3	15.4	-7.4	11.9	1 424 155	23.4	78 102	1 258 044	69.8	61 100	19.8	13.0	376	24.4	5.0
Anderson	1.7	19.9	0.5	14.8	11 503	5.8	710	10 509	52.3	53 100	20.6	13.5	327	24.6	3.7
Charleston	4.5	21.6	-0.9	16.3	34 322	25.9	2 025	30 753	48.1	86 600	22.0	13.4	428	28.6	4.1
Columbia	3.8	21.2	1.4	15.7	36 928	13.4	2 082	33 919	45.0	72 600	20.6	12.1	392	27.8	4.7
Florence	4.1	21.8	8.5	17.8	11 790	7.3	475	11 074	57.4	59 200	18.9	13.4	367	25.8	4.8
Greenville	4.6	17.7	-9.7	13.7	26 453	12.6	1 820	24 101	46.8	68 700	19.7	12.6	367	23.7	3.3
Mount Pleasant	5.4	5.8	-14.7	4.2	12 443	135.5	492	11 788	62.1	96 900	22.0	12.9	537	22.1	1.5
North Charleston	0.5	21.7	7.4	19.2	26 608	31.6	1 997	23 499	37.5	60 100	21.4	13.4	410	26.2	5.3
Rock Hill	2.1	16.4	11.6	12.1	15 682	27.4	747	14 669	53.9	56 300	19.6	13.9	438	25.1	5.5
Spartanburg	3.3	21.8	4.3	17.1	17 950	4.6	1 009	16 712	48.2	58 300	19.7	12.7	341	25.7	4.5
Sumter	2.5	20.7	-8.8	16.6	13 650	48.2	458	12 737	47.4	59 000	20.6	13.8	354	25.8	5.1
SOUTH DAKOTA	1.7	15.9	-6.2	11.6	292 436	5.6	13 361	259 034	66.1	45 200	19.8	13.3	306	24.6	3.4
Rapid City	2.5	13.6	22.5	10.6	22 530	20.4	1 112	21 152	57.3	56 800	21.8	12.9	396	26.6	2.6
Sioux Falls	2.7	8.5	-1.2	5.5	41 568	26.0	1 306	39 790	58.8	59 100	20.1	12.5	380	24.7	1.7
TENNESSEE	2.6	15.7	-4.8	12.4	2 026 067	15.9	104 351	1 853 725	68.0	58 400	20.1	12.6	357	25.0	3.8
Bartlett	4.0	2.3	-28.1	2.1	8 807	64.0	324	8 456	90.9	91 200	21.4	11.7	607	23.9	1.1
Chattanooga	2.7	18.2	1.7	14.4	69 601	4.5	5 765	62 177	54.2	54 100	19.5	13.7	360	25.7	3.2
Clarksville	1.5	13.3	3.9	11.0	27 642	42.4	1 832	25 442	54.7	59 000	21.4	11.7	377	24.4	3.6
Cleveland	2.3	17.4	4.8	13.8	13 050	23.1	841	11 996	55.1	60 900	20.0	12.9	319	24.8	2.6
Columbia	1.9	14.3	-6.5	11.6	12 142	18.8	645	11 267	61.3	61 500	17.7	12.4	379	23.3	2.6
Germantown	24.3	1.1	-31.3	1.0	11 131	63.4	375	10 713	89.6	145 100	20.4	10.8	631	23.0	0.3
Hendersonville	4.6	4.5	12.5	3.0	12 472	42.7	901	11 441	72.8	86 300	21.2	11.9	496	25.3	0.7
Jackson	2.3	21.0	16.0	17.9	20 739	7.0	1 315	19 206	55.9	50 600	20.6	13.2	334	25.0	2.1
Johnson City	3.4	17.3	3.0	11.7	21 241	41.3	1 028	19 675	56.8	60 000	17.7	12.0	313	25.7	1.3
Kingsport	3.5	18.1	26.6	14.3	16 742	26.0	738	15 629	62.9	55 400	17.0	12.4	297	23.6	1.5
Knoxville	2.3	20.8	6.1	15.3	76 453	4.4	4 788	69 973	49.9	49 800	20.4	13.6	332	26.5	2.1
Memphis	2.9	23.0	5.5	18.7	248 531	1.7	15 120	229 829	55.1	55 700	20.3	13.4	373	27.1	5.8
Murfreesboro	2.4	16.0	0.6	9.9	18 708	50.4	1 335	17 110	47.6	78 200	20.9	13.1	388	27.2	2.5
Nashville-Davidson	3.8	13.0	NA	10.0	229 064	NA	NA	207 530	53.8	75 600	20.9	12.6	433	25.3	2.6
Oak Ridge	4.1	9.5	13.1	7.0	12 664	10.5	769	11 763	66.5	64 100	15.8	11.4	378	23.5	1.7
TEXAS	3.7	18.1	23.1	14.1	7 008 999	26.3	541 918	6 070 937	60.9	59 600	20.9	13.1	395	24.6	8.4
Abilene	2.3	15.3	26.4	11.0	44 436	21.8	3 957	38 395	59.5	45 800	20.5	12.9	380	25.6	4.4
Amarillo	2.6	16.8	69.7	13.1	68 592	13.8	5 645	61 137	62.6	50 700	19.9	12.8	348	24.7	5.3
Arlington	4.4	8.2	39.0	5.7	112 767	72.6	10 112	100 651	51.8	82 800	22.0	11.8	444	23.7	4.7
Austin	3.5	17.9	13.3	11.5	217 054	48.2	20 339	192 148	40.6	72 600	22.6	12.6	410	27.3	6.7
Baytown	3.3	16.1	56.3	13.4	25 020	14.6	2 010	22 422	56.7	50 400	17.6	12.5	385	22.9	9.6
Beaumont	3.5	21.1	34.4	16.6	49 021	4.2	3 466	43 357	60.0	44 500	17.7	13.5	370	26.7	5.1
Bedford	6.6	3.6	12.5	2.3	18 848	141.1	1 136	17 586	55.0	95 900	21.4	11.7	456	21.6	1.9
Brownsville	1.3	43.9	31.8	38.5	28 992	18.7	1 488	26 322	55.8	39 900	21.2	13.1	292	28.6	29.8
Bryan	2.2	22.0	17.6	16.1	23 007	32.3	1 664	20 705	48.3	58 400	19.2	13.3	391	28.3	7.6
Carrollton	6.8	4.5	55.2	3.2	32 992	113.5	2 178	30 452	60.7	99 700	22.7	13.0	542	23.4	5.1
College Station	2.4	38.0	17.6	16.6	19 845	52.8	1 555	17 878	24.0	79 500	21.2	11.8	428	35.1	5.9
Conroe	2.4	18.8	35.3	15.1	11 500	47.8	1 152	10 016	46.9	59 600	20.5	13.7	369	24.1	10.5
Corpus Christi	2.7	20.0	27.4	16.4	100 205	22.8	7 550	89 468	56.6	56 500	21.3	12.6	373	25.7	9.4
Dallas	6.2	18.0	26.8	14.7	465 600	19.3	50 329	402 060	44.1	78 800	21.1	13.0	426	24.2	9.8
Deer Park	3.9	5.2	40.5	3.6	9 127	23.2	238	8 822	75.0	66 800	16.4	11.7	467	20.2	4.7
Del Rio	0.9	38.3	18.9	31.3	10 691	10.1	866	9 465	61.5	43 600	20.2	12.8	319	27.7	17.1
Denton	2.4	20.7	46.8	9.9	28 791	49.3	2 077	25 719	39.1	77 300	22.8	12.9	423	33.8	4.4
DeSoto	6.7	4.0	100.0	2.7	11 650	130.5	751	10 754	69.4	95 700	23.2	12.9	497	23.5	2.1
Duncanville	5.5	3.8	18.8	2.6	13 358	46.2	783	12 509	67.7	86 200	19.9	11.3	529	26.2	2.4
Edinburg	1.9	33.8	20.7	30.8	9 206	26.5	418	8 474	57.3	44 700	19.8	13.8	311	26.2	19.9
El Paso	2.4	25.3	19.3	21.2	168 625	25.5	6 103	160 545	57.6	58 500	20.6	12.0	349	26.1	13.9
Euless	3.2	5.4	3.8	4.0	17 117	75.8	1 469	15 456	45.3	76 300	21.1	11.5	455	22.0	4.0
Fort Worth	3.2	17.4	25.2	13.6	194 429	24.6	19 335	168 274	54.5	59 900	21.4	13.1	403	24.6	7.8
Galveston	3.1	24.2	52.2	20.0	30 898	10.9	3 522	24 157	42.0	57 200	20.7	14.6	381	27.1	6.5
Garland	3.6	7.8	52.9	5.8	69 595	44.0	5 687	63 193	64.2	73 100	21.7	12.4	494	24.9	6.5
Grand Prairie	2.3	10.0	14.9	7.7	38 721	54.3	3 051	34 958	60.9	68 400	21.3	12.1	439	24.2	8.6
Grapevine	7.1	4.2	-12.5	2.5	11 907	135.7	780	10 969	62.6	111 000	22.6	11.4	484	22.6	2.4
Haltom City	1.4	12.1	28.7	9.3	14 030	26.6	970	12 756	59.2	52 300	20.7	12.4	390	24.8	4.7
Harlingen	1.6	29.9	13.3	25.3	17 798	22.5	1 229	15 398	59.0	42 700	19.2	12.8	332	25.8	16.0
Houston	4.8	20.7	63.0	17.2	726 435	7.1	84 106	616 877	44.6	58 000	19.9	13.4	390	23.6	11.9
Huntsville	2.0	30.0	22.4	17.4	9 136	25.3	924	7 853	36.4	62 700	18.0	16.4	389	32.4	6.8
Hurst	4.4	7.8	110.8	5.3	13 801	12.3	921	12 779	62.7	82 800	18.4	11.8	445	24.3	3.2
Irving	3.8	10.5	75.0	7.7	71 059	64.9	6 474	63 236	37.1	79 400	20.0	12.2	485	23.0	8.0
Killeen	0.6	14.5	-19.0	11.8	26 439	34.0	2 742	23 248	41.5	58 600	23.7	12.8	385	25.4	7.1
Kingsville	1.6	27.3	25.8	21.9	10 100	1.5	1 035	8 529	56.9	40 800	17.7	13.0	343	27.6	10.2
La Porte	2.9	8.8	4.8	7.1	9 966	98.9	463	9 144	71.0	56 600	18.9	13.0	465	22.4	5.8
Laredo	2.2	37.3	8.1	32.2	33 998	34.6	1 091	32 029	59.0	52 500	22.6	12.8	315	27.6	26.1

1. Includes units rented or sold but not occupied. 2. Specified owner-occupied units. 3. Specified renter-occupied units. 4. Overcrowded or lacking complete plumbing facilities.

Table D. Cities — **Labor Force, Employment, Disability, and Construction**

City	Civilian labor force, 1999				Civilian employment, 1990[2]			Disability 1990	Value of residential construction authorized by building permits, 1999		
	Total	Percent change, 1998–1999	Unemployment Total	Rate[1]	Total	Percent Professional, managerial, and technical	Precision production, craft, and repair	Work disabled persons[3] (percent)	New construction ($1,000)	Number of housing units	Percent single family
	61	62	63	64	65	66	67	68	69	70	71
SOUTH CAROLINA	1 961 962	0.2	87 782	4.5	1 603 425	25.4	13.8	9.1	3 614 665	36 161	75.1
Anderson	13 823	-0.6	641	4.6	11 321	26.0	10.1	10.5	7 597	80	95.0
Charleston	45 302	5.9	1 511	3.3	36 988	35.9	8.6	6.6	138 351	1 825	39.3
Columbia	48 451	0.5	1 835	3.8	40 661	38.3	6.6	7.9	59 735	467	82.4
Florence	15 859	-1.0	1 007	6.3	12 924	31.6	8.5	10.3	NA	NA	NA
Greenville	34 373	-0.4	1 053	3.1	28 677	33.6	7.3	8.0	6 300	54	81.5
Mount Pleasant	19 856	5.7	247	1.2	16 563	46.8	9.3	4.3	187 441	1 695	91.6
North Charleston	31 746	5.9	1 384	4.4	25 645	22.8	16.1	8.8	25 635	218	100.0
Rock Hill	27 172	2.3	1 519	5.6	20 140	25.2	11.2	6.7	65 851	746	74.5
Spartanburg	23 270	0.0	1 384	5.9	19 079	29.2	7.7	10.3	13 353	142	16.9
Sumter	15 820	-0.6	932	5.9	12 665	28.3	10.6	9.7	NA	NA	NA
SOUTH DAKOTA	399 704	0.5	11 632	2.9	321 891	24.5	10.4	7.8	329 767	3 672	78.3
Rapid City	32 242	0.0	797	2.5	24 681	29.7	12.2	8.4	21 759	214	63.6
Sioux Falls	74 677	2.4	1 377	1.8	54 787	28.9	9.4	8.3	96 687	1 200	72.5
TENNESSEE	2 818 851	2.1	113 503	4.0	2 250 842	26.1	12.2	9.7	3 836 987	37 049	80.7
Bartlett	16 496	1.2	201	1.2	14 217	36.6	9.9	4.5	44 633	305	100.0
Chattanooga	76 797	3.6	3 046	4.0	67 875	28.2	9.1	11.1	65 104	683	59.3
Clarksville	40 827	6.2	1 430	3.5	26 694	27.5	10.7	8.7	60 649	937	90.6
Cleveland	16 967	2.1	672	4.0	14 355	27.6	11.7	9.9	16 789	216	69.0
Columbia	19 090	1.5	703	3.7	13 218	24.2	12.2	9.5	9 565	115	100.0
Germantown	19 341	1.2	221	1.1	16 682	51.9	2.9	3.2	NA	NA	NA
Hendersonville	23 481	2.5	472	2.0	17 509	34.2	9.5	4.8	68 404	789	69.6
Jackson	30 712	3.2	1 186	3.9	21 755	28.0	8.9	10.0	55 133	552	90.6
Johnson City	27 253	2.2	1 064	3.9	22 533	33.8	8.7	9.8	35 502	309	81.2
Kingsport	17 174	1.7	752	4.4	14 829	31.2	12.1	11.6	16 125	221	55.7
Knoxville	92 844	1.4	3 086	3.3	75 323	31.3	8.4	11.0	40 328	970	43.5
Memphis	320 761	1.3	14 537	4.5	267 179	27.7	8.8	9.2	NA	NA	NA
Murfreesboro	36 875	4.9	1 257	3.4	23 249	31.2	8.5	7.6	122 350	1 591	67.3
Nashville-Davidson	311 530	1.5	8 815	2.8	264 680	33.4	8.6	7.3	466 652	3 706	65.7
Oak Ridge	14 852	0.5	409	2.8	12 673	50.0	8.5	8.8	5 817	35	100.0
TEXAS	10 206 043	0.9	471 630	4.6	7 634 279	30.0	11.7	7.6	14 045 115	146 644	69.5
Abilene	52 723	-3.3	2 056	3.9	44 317	31.9	10.0	8.3	25 348	179	96.6
Amarillo	94 451	0.1	3 652	3.9	73 106	27.0	12.9	8.5	69 771	680	75.0
Arlington	188 984	1.8	5 113	2.7	146 327	35.4	9.8	5.1	252 181	2 914	70.2
Austin	378 981	2.9	9 274	2.4	244 056	39.8	7.5	5.9	619 046	8 385	39.4
Baytown	35 484	0.4	1 895	5.3	27 419	25.1	20.3	7.4	13 557	124	100.0
Beaumont	57 477	-1.5	4 533	7.9	48 706	31.6	9.9	9.5	31 628	283	100.0
Bedford	33 823	1.8	639	1.9	26 408	40.1	7.4	4.1	5 530	44	100.0
Brownsville	47 582	-1.4	5 414	11.4	31 884	26.3	9.9	7.7	66 213	926	90.2
Bryan	35 812	2.0	635	1.8	26 749	33.8	10.1	6.8	35 190	640	50.9
Carrollton	69 507	3.2	1 316	1.9	48 713	41.1	7.9	3.6	156 913	1 529	47.5
College Station	30 043	2.0	553	1.8	22 425	47.8	3.8	2.1	80 282	959	44.9
Conroe	20 922	3.7	760	3.6	12 575	26.3	12.8	7.8	5 869	77	94.8
Corpus Christi	131 213	-1.1	8 546	6.5	109 555	28.4	14.1	8.6	83 361	948	67.5
Dallas	669 482	1.3	27 143	4.1	511 202	31.8	8.4	7.2	386 492	5 724	30.6
Deer Park	17 370	0.2	615	3.5	13 702	30.6	17.1	6.2	21 110	391	14.1
Del Rio	15 080	2.4	1 311	8.7	10 332	22.7	14.7	9.1	6 773	127	96.1
Denton	54 694	4.8	1 558	2.8	34 108	35.5	7.9	5.5	165 975	1 580	66.1
DeSoto	21 428	1.0	480	2.2	17 055	38.7	9.3	4.7	39 137	282	100.0
Duncanville	23 945	1.0	599	2.5	19 008	36.1	9.3	4.9	4 864	51	100.0
Edinburg	16 714	0.0	2 147	12.8	10 697	33.9	9.1	8.4	29 028	631	51.5
El Paso	258 293	-0.6	23 312	9.0	195 521	29.1	10.5	7.9	185 128	3 770	80.8
Euless	29 717	1.8	661	2.2	23 123	33.0	10.4	4.6	10 710	94	100.0
Fort Worth	271 226	1.7	11 157	4.1	206 967	29.3	11.5	8.5	345 788	4 041	78.6
Galveston	32 355	-2.0	2 739	8.5	25 889	34.0	7.9	9.4	14 817	101	100.0
Garland	124 053	1.0	3 323	2.7	98 295	32.0	12.0	5.9	95 777	1 337	38.0
Grand Prairie	64 786	1.1	2 115	3.3	50 781	27.8	12.5	6.4	113 399	920	100.0
Grapevine	21 343	1.9	353	1.7	16 704	41.6	9.5	4.3	19 380	188	100.0
Haltom City	21 009	1.8	636	3.0	16 213	18.2	16.8	9.6	19 313	186	100.0
Harlingen	26 066	0.1	1 841	7.1	18 317	29.3	10.7	7.0	29 650	571	46.4
Houston	1 026 091	0.5	56 740	5.5	788 520	32.1	10.4	7.0	917 084	9 014	45.4
Huntsville	12 761	0.6	321	2.5	9 790	30.9	4.7	5.0	7 515	69	100.0
Hurst	23 704	1.8	699	2.9	18 308	32.8	10.6	5.9	10 990	140	61.4
Irving	115 583	1.0	3 315	2.9	91 405	31.4	10.1	5.3	74 595	342	100.0
Killeen	27 303	-0.4	1 512	5.5	19 508	25.4	12.7	8.3	74 207	951	75.0
Kingsville	11 061	-1.8	726	6.6	9 661	31.4	12.6	8.1	925	12	100.0
La Porte	17 339	0.2	605	3.5	13 685	28.6	18.7	5.9	44 794	486	61.3
Laredo	68 006	-0.3	5 651	8.3	42 951	24.1	9.6	6.4	99 197	1 639	81.5

1. Percent of civilian labor force.   2. Persons 16 years and older.   3. Persons 16 to 64 years old.

Table D. Cities — Wholesale Trade, Retail Trade, and Real Estate

City	Wholesale Trade, 1997				Retail Trade[1], 1997				Real Estate and Rental and Leasing, 1997			
	Number of Establishments	Number of Employees	Sales (mil dol)	Annual Payroll (mil dol)	Number of Establishments	Number of Employees	Sales (mil dol)	Annual Payroll (mil dol)	Number of Establishments	Number of Employees	Receipts (mil dol)	Annual Payroll (mil dol)
	72	73	74	75	76	77	78	79	80	81	82	83
SOUTH CAROLINA	5 035	58 910	34 179.8	1 866.8	18 481	209 256	33 634.3	3 107.2	3 541	18 760	2 012.6	377.1
Anderson	57	685	241.9	17.0	378	5 272	718.7	69.6	59	204	22.1	3.1
Charleston	111	1 064	455.5	34.9	793	9 394	1 351.2	137.8	195	D	D	D
Columbia	276	3 637	1 584.9	136.6	827	11 608	1 917.3	190.5	240	1 132	162.2	35.3
Florence	93	D	D	D	415	5 954	926.9	89.6	74	244	29.9	5.0
Greenville	288	3 975	6 613.6	162.4	812	12 028	2 011.1	186.8	202	1 047	137.6	24.2
Mount Pleasant	52	178	161.2	7.5	234	2 625	357.2	38.0	66	280	28.5	5.3
North Charleston	203	3 211	2 237.3	107.6	507	7 214	1 341.4	125.7	93	724	71.9	14.6
Rock Hill	100	1 137	415.4	41.5	330	4 249	699.1	64.1	68	267	25.8	5.7
Spartanburg	105	D	D	D	440	6 349	1 017.1	96.4	102	435	47.7	9.9
Sumter	56	D	D	D	340	4 355	654.1	62.8	60	233	22.1	3.6
SOUTH DAKOTA	1 402	15 509	7 874.2	389.8	4 311	45 867	11 707.1	689.6	719	2 951	245.7	45.1
Rapid City	144	1 897	633.9	54.2	486	6 368	1 040.6	102.1	108	487	50.3	8.6
Sioux Falls	313	5 146	2 073.5	157.5	696	11 676	1 913.6	184.8	176	919	95.3	17.2
TENNESSEE	8 234	120 228	82 626.4	3 975.4	24 808	304 452	50 813.2	4 810.3	4 999	29 626	3 732.0	667.3
Bartlett	50	D	D	D	144	3 110	466.7	44.4	24	136	15.6	3.2
Chattanooga	602	8 378	3 688.8	255.1	1 150	16 191	2 707.0	268.0	264	1 740	209.6	52.7
Clarksville	86	D	D	D	485	6 674	1 143.3	105.4	100	370	49.6	5.9
Cleveland	73	2 213	1 616.1	47.1	355	3 937	721.6	63.9	65	248	25.4	3.8
Columbia	43	556	205.2	16.1	247	3 119	528.0	51.7	63	248	27.5	4.3
Germantown	66	472	1 417.2	28.3	186	3 200	368.0	37.7	55	205	32.6	4.2
Hendersonville	71	437	218.2	16.4	139	1 552	238.5	23.6	49	183	29.9	3.2
Jackson	143	1 975	702.1	55.1	547	7 771	1 152.3	110.0	78	394	38.0	6.8
Johnson City	126	1 843	1 086.4	47.4	435	6 118	1 012.9	91.9	103	459	45.5	8.1
Kingsport	102	1 167	464.7	31.1	415	5 841	996.0	92.4	71	320	32.2	5.1
Knoxville	671	8 791	4 595.8	309.0	1 431	22 302	4 031.1	386.5	332	2 227	243.7	51.7
Memphis	1 470	27 381	24 961.4	948.4	2 535	37 267	6 358.3	635.4	609	5 875	691.5	144.7
Murfreesboro	92	935	477.6	28.3	433	6 874	1 187.9	113.8	102	358	44.0	5.5
Nashville-Davidson	1 445	26 012	17 005.2	962.7	3 017	44 452	7 737.6	782.7	866	6 603	1 119.8	173.2
Oak Ridge	30	180	52.7	6.1	192	2 625	455.4	41.1	54	277	36.0	5.7
TEXAS	33 346	425 744	323 111.7	15 504.9	74 105	950 848	182 516.1	16 197.1	20 753	128 915	15 957.4	3 119.2
Abilene	200	1 861	653.2	50.5	586	6 820	1 223.1	112.4	165	867	88.2	16.6
Amarillo	307	3 565	1 466.5	115.7	910	11 528	2 196.0	195.4	232	1 113	125.1	20.5
Arlington	519	6 347	4 614.2	226.9	1 152	18 925	3 806.7	368.2	322	1 787	217.8	43.8
Austin	1 065	16 673	8 086.0	661.5	2 604	40 259	7 561.4	749.7	1 022	5 751	725.1	140.4
Baytown	46	D	D	D	268	4 289	755.0	69.2	67	474	46.1	7.3
Beaumont	271	3 246	1 379.4	107.6	656	9 662	1 674.4	150.7	182	1 113	139.3	24.2
Bedford	84	332	335.6	17.8	141	2 039	448.9	36.3	52	293	33.7	7.3
Brownsville	220	1 952	585.7	37.3	518	6 661	985.0	91.5	131	525	39.3	6.3
Bryan	90	1 097	278.4	28.8	281	3 555	657.5	58.5	77	582	33.6	9.5
Carrollton	431	7 788	14 382.2	312.8	320	5 405	1 230.5	124.8	129	1 198	128.7	29.4
College Station	22	368	79.5	7.8	268	4 342	653.6	62.1	93	471	42.1	6.7
Conroe	103	D	D	D	360	5 170	1 146.7	92.0	59	273	36.5	5.3
Corpus Christi	453	4 708	1 656.2	144.5	1 183	16 289	2 666.6	255.7	358	2 379	327.1	61.4
Dallas	3 470	49 621	35 859.7	2 128.0	4 365	60 881	12 436.0	1 266.1	2 139	19 869	2 751.0	670.4
Deer Park	31	529	157.0	24.1	73	768	112.0	11.4	21	163	21.2	4.8
Del Rio	30	291	54.5	5.1	166	1 777	275.5	25.0	31	105	8.5	1.4
Denton	101	1 152	796.3	32.0	374	5 476	966.8	87.2	110	543	51.0	10.0
DeSoto	42	194	68.0	6.3	88	1 287	256.3	22.3	37	291	22.7	6.0
Duncanville	51	309	132.6	9.9	126	2 015	365.8	34.9	38	161	20.7	3.0
Edinburg	45	1 145	204.9	15.9	99	1 699	254.1	22.2	39	144	13.8	2.3
El Paso	950	10 705	5 954.5	300.9	2 006	28 171	4 588.9	420.2	533	2 400	282.0	46.9
Euless	69	606	294.5	25.1	83	1 076	191.3	16.6	32	159	21.0	2.8
Fort Worth	843	14 840	9 968.1	524.9	1 856	23 572	4 703.3	449.2	535	3 489	445.1	92.6
Galveston	55	606	212.3	16.5	252	2 777	362.0	37.8	73	282	34.8	7.3
Garland	283	4 671	2 727.3	170.5	543	7 133	1 426.8	135.5	168	883	110.7	19.3
Grand Prairie	326	6 538	5 025.1	236.1	305	4 760	920.0	92.9	93	1 052	165.9	22.6
Grapevine	60	411	425.5	21.7	206	2 205	573.7	48.2	34	169	35.4	4.2
Haltom City	116	1 305	431.6	42.4	149	1 527	291.9	28.2	44	203	30.9	4.9
Harlingen	96	1 170	359.9	27.4	326	4 106	611.4	59.0	74	349	39.4	7.3
Houston	5 750	82 917	99 680.2	3 389.1	7 871	112 989	21 778.4	2 078.3	2 912	27 355	3 223.5	680.8
Huntsville	25	D	D	D	157	2 122	371.1	30.7	43	207	38.5	4.0
Hurst	63	416	183.4	14.6	282	4 233	685.2	69.8	52	215	26.2	3.9
Irving	522	16 189	22 890.4	741.9	651	13 102	3 255.9	277.4	276	3 529	532.3	87.7
Killeen	25	206	54.3	3.9	329	3 879	660.3	61.2	123	614	50.6	8.2
Kingsville	9	D	D	D	105	1 385	209.2	19.7	22	D	D	D
La Porte	38	378	144.4	16.5	72	977	212.0	18.3	30	230	20.4	5.2
Laredo	335	D	D	D	723	9 027	1 520.8	138.5	155	574	64.3	10.0

1. Establishments with payroll.

City	Professional, Scientific, and Technical Services, 1997[1]				Manufacturing, 1997				Accommodation and Foodservices, 1997			
	Number of Establishments	Number of Employees	Receipts (mil dol)	Annual Payroll (mil dol)	Number of Establishments	Number of Employees	Receipts (mil dol)	Annual Payroll (mil dol)	Number of Establishments	Number of Employees	Sales (mil dol)	Annual Payroll (mil dol)
	84	85	86	87	88	89	90	91	92	93	94	95
SOUTH CAROLINA	6 576	47 679	6 820.9	1 850.5	4 450	346 142	70 797.0	10 369.4	7 775	150 621	4 835.8	1 313.8
Anderson	125	501	36.8	10.3	73	9 005	2 141.4	285.6	130	2 792	87.3	23.4
Charleston	482	4 132	412.8	185.0	84	1 985	602.9	65.7	388	9 484	346.4	97.6
Columbia	699	6 453	771.7	256.8	105	7 137	1 648.3	253.4	387	7 826	242.4	69.7
Florence	129	1 006	70.5	28.6	52	4 653	701.2	148.6	162	3 838	113.0	31.5
Greenville	617	8 440	3 116.3	437.3	159	14 641	4 021.7	504.2	342	7 560	238.0	68.3
Mount Pleasant	153	607	52.1	19.5	NA	NA	NA	NA	103	2 181	72.8	19.8
North Charleston	190	2 160	203.1	65.0	108	5 292	1 237.0	188.6	211	4 297	135.1	35.1
Rock Hill	144	721	50.6	20.6	75	4 658	901.1	151.9	134	3 179	92.2	24.4
Spartanburg	197	1 296	121.5	43.6	93	8 867	2 339.5	311.4	194	4 282	109.8	31.9
Sumter	101	423	26.6	8.3	59	10 009	1 522.3	234.4	107	2 148	65.3	17.7
SOUTH DAKOTA	1 282	6 228	450.4	161.7	888	46 539	12 305.5	1 162.6	2 258	30 131	888.0	234.4
Rapid City	195	1 104	88.7	30.2	109	3 513	756.2	77.3	234	4 643	135.5	37.6
Sioux Falls	343	2 341	181.1	72.6	133	11 605	2 995.2	301.9	352	7 691	215.0	61.8
TENNESSEE	8 812	72 225	6 911.8	2 686.6	7 407	483 823	98 503.1	14 351.9	9 604	197 881	6 790.2	1 880.3
Bartlett	66	320	25.1	10.8	31	1 327	242.8	29.5	53	D	D	D
Chattanooga	529	4 252	370.0	151.8	389	23 272	4 091.4	739.9	528	10 682	366.7	103.6
Clarksville	113	736	39.7	11.7	70	6 047	1 190.7	169.5	221	D	D	D
Cleveland	108	678	47.0	17.5	122	11 978	2 618.5	322.0	130	2 476	80.2	21.3
Columbia	74	350	27.9	9.8	42	D	D	D	81	1 836	48.3	13.1
Germantown	97	509	62.6	25.0	NA	NA	NA	NA	61	D	D	D
Hendersonville	87	621	24.9	9.5	62	1 917	307.2	52.7	61	1 135	34.8	10.4
Jackson	136	974	76.9	36.6	123	D	D	D	177	4 079	137.1	36.9
Johnson City	166	1 231	66.9	24.2	101	8 801	1 074.1	211.5	160	4 131	125.2	36.0
Kingsport	123	734	70.2	39.8	61	D	D	D	155	3 545	115.0	33.0
Knoxville	650	6 376	551.0	209.5	318	14 827	2 429.9	394.5	586	12 873	405.9	117.2
Memphis	1 300	13 282	1 328.0	496.3	688	32 938	8 888.5	1 104.8	1 071	25 344	920.6	254.9
Murfreesboro	150	622	48.1	17.7	87	5 660	1 415.5	170.8	171	4 785	151.0	44.6
Nashville-Davidson	1 694	15 055	1 636.8	605.8	752	31 716	6 721.8	1 100.0	1 407	37 523	1 511.7	426.3
Oak Ridge	142	7 814	926.4	382.3	59	5 669	897.3	247.3	79	1 504	48.1	13.3
TEXAS	42 492	351 422	42 044.1	15 906.7	21 808	959 665	297 657.0	32 760.8	34 160	638 333	22 698.8	6 175.4
Abilene	223	1 116	92.7	30.2	106	2 798	977.5	74.0	246	5 225	143.9	39.5
Amarillo	344	2 794	194.5	83.6	176	D	D	D	442	7 732	247.9	67.1
Arlington	649	3 950	342.5	130.0	323	13 408	2 909.8	481.6	548	13 989	521.9	139.3
Austin	2 699	25 127	2 897.0	1 179.9	596	46 780	13 235.1	1 892.1	1 491	33 899	1 215.7	348.8
Baytown	83	652	53.3	28.0	44	D	D	D	124	1 960	72.3	18.8
Beaumont	336	3 370	432.1	181.8	131	5 882	5 041.5	250.9	265	5 794	182.0	49.1
Bedford	148	731	59.7	23.3	24	D	D	D	82	1 850	67.6	18.5
Brownsville	185	940	72.4	24.5	110	6 511	963.3	123.6	221	3 035	105.3	26.4
Bryan	157	814	52.8	21.9	73	2 527	309.3	63.4	115	1 743	53.1	14.4
Carrollton	278	1 963	195.8	79.7	227	13 714	2 502.0	532.5	164	2 974	106.0	28.8
College Station	102	1 229	144.8	51.9	NA	NA	NA	NA	156	3 909	117.4	33.7
Conroe	127	478	39.2	15.0	91	2 544	806.8	86.4	98	1 963	73.7	19.6
Corpus Christi	678	4 376	413.8	149.6	205	D	D	D	647	11 822	382.5	102.0
Dallas	5 564	68 907	8 686.8	3 694.5	1 762	77 920	15 722.9	2 884.1	2 374	58 031	2 354.8	663.2
Deer Park	35	440	37.0	14.8	31	4 364	7 583.0	260.7	30	485	17.1	4.3
Del Rio	34	111	7.0	1.8	NA	NA	NA	NA	80	1 010	31.8	8.2
Denton	163	1 115	62.7	25.0	73	4 187	1 350.0	143.7	171	3 395	110.9	30.6
DeSoto	54	207	12.0	4.8	NA	NA	NA	NA	47	1 109	40.2	11.6
Duncanville	59	151	18.1	4.8	40	2 452	237.3	50.3	57	1 231	40.8	11.5
Edinburg	66	469	32.3	12.5	26	2 134	471.5	32.5	78	1 034	34.4	8.3
El Paso	909	5 633	389.3	158.9	599	33 212	7 602.1	716.2	1 040	18 828	687.2	189.6
Euless	63	269	25.1	9.3	41	1 060	107.1	31.0	54	871	35.0	9.1
Fort Worth	1 297	9 539	1 064.3	404.8	821	56 215	11 198.3	2 337.9	881	17 152	614.7	172.6
Galveston	104	438	48.0	17.3	32	592	56.3	15.8	190	4 240	141.4	41.2
Garland	256	1 439	222.5	59.6	377	16 285	2 944.6	556.5	301	4 471	165.6	42.4
Grand Prairie	130	768	59.1	22.8	232	12 709	2 014.2	464.0	151	2 236	88.0	21.6
Grapevine	106	307	45.9	14.0	36	1 539	310.4	47.6	92	3 629	180.8	51.8
Haltom City	35	136	9.2	3.1	138	3 292	361.3	89.7	52	664	26.5	6.4
Harlingen	105	731	43.4	14.7	65	4 480	562.4	86.1	126	2 269	77.1	21.0
Houston	7 763	91 030	14 150.3	4 922.5	2 969	104 218	32 595.8	3 599.3	3 902	83 796	3 398.9	903.4
Huntsville	48	D	D	D	NA	NA	NA	NA	73	1 477	44.0	12.2
Hurst	150	1 666	102.3	52.0	43	716	104.7	17.5	84	1 262	39.4	10.6
Irving	542	9 262	1 086.1	415.1	240	11 146	2 590.9	435.9	397	11 448	575.3	140.2
Killeen	64	929	87.6	16.6	NA	NA	NA	NA	174	3 022	90.5	23.9
Kingsville	22	D	D	D	NA	NA	NA	NA	66	923	28.0	7.6
La Porte	43	553	63.7	21.7	35	2 442	1 819.1	132.5	46	660	19.5	5.2
Laredo	206	973	64.8	21.3	86	D	D	D	249	4 341	144.2	37.3

1. Firms subject to federal tax.

City	Arts, Entertainment, and Recreation[1], 1997				Health Care and Social Assistance[1], 1997				Other Services[1], 1997			
	Number of Establish-ments	Number of Employees	Receipts (mil dol)	Annual Payroll (mil dol)	Number of Establish-ments	Number of Employees	Receipts (mil dol)	Annual Payroll (mil dol)	Number of Establish-ments	Number of Employees	Receipts (mil dol)	Annual Payroll (mil dol)
	96	97	98	99	100	101	102	103	104	105	106	107
SOUTH CAROLINA	1 325	18 499	1 107.1	251.9	6 261	78 888	5 318.5	2 361.3	5 672	32 166	1 901.0	563.8
Anderson....................	14	108	4.2	0.8	169	2 358	154.2	81.7	83	563	29.4	10.2
Charleston.................	50	614	30.0	6.2	356	2 858	222.6	101.5	174	1 409	51.5	19.6
Columbia...................	44	662	33.7	7.8	490	7 599	621.7	288.1	235	2 020	103.6	34.8
Florence....................	20	379	13.9	2.4	206	4 637	360.9	175.9	84	746	37.7	11.8
Greenville..................	43	601	31.5	8.3	297	2 931	237.8	113.5	233	2 135	123.3	37.8
Mount Pleasant...........	18	244	14.2	3.5	139	1 710	94.6	41.7	90	537	35.2	10.6
North Charleston.........	29	262	27.4	3.9	233	4 631	321.2	122.9	211	1 976	139.8	45.0
Rock Hill...................	27	243	8.5	2.5	144	3 527	222.1	97.3	121	700	42.8	13.9
Spartanburg	18	155	8.0	2.4	166	2 617	209.1	94.3	119	772	44.4	13.2
Sumter......................	16	136	6.0	1.6	115	1 165	75.4	37.4	87	676	38.3	11.4
SOUTH DAKOTA	432	4 647	299.2	60.2	1 314	14 080	881.6	414.3	1 356	5 828	344.7	90.7
Rapid City	63	485	23.9	5.1	217	2 295	162.4	65.3	170	940	49.1	15.7
Sioux Falls	67	746	48.1	10.0	269	4 275	351.5	194.4	246	1 786	95.6	30.4
TENNESSEE	1 755	18 263	1 228.7	394.3	10 113	155 667	10 753.0	4 659.9	7 767	49 204	2 996.7	918.7
Bartlett.....................	4	84	3.2	1.0	74	646	45.7	17.2	65	345	17.6	6.3
Chattanooga...............	55	648	27.3	9.3	611	9 114	727.1	332.2	385	2 809	167.9	53.5
Clarksville.................	28	0	0.0	0.0	143	1 979	115.0	48.0	157	755	39.7	10.8
Cleveland	18	0	0.0	0.0	195	10 316	437.6	199.4	91	1 239	63.5	24.1
Columbia...................	16	90	4.6	1.6	117	1 411	102.5	36.3	80	500	26.8	8.6
Germantown...............	5	96	4.5	2.0	101	1 056	84.1	36.3	45	428	17.1	7.5
Hendersonville	22	241	16.6	5.8	108	1 526	101.1	40.2	83	451	22.7	6.6
Jackson	20	162	5.2	1.5	198	3 728	290.1	147.4	151	995	51.1	16.7
Johnson City	13	116	2.9	1.0	211	3 117	247.7	115.2	133	965	44.4	17.1
Kingsport	15	147	6.1	2.1	213	3 881	288.1	132.9	127	1 014	48.7	18.1
Knoxville...................	71	869	31.0	10.1	700	8 146	798.6	378.2	497	3 653	188.1	60.9
Memphis...................	99	2 062	90.7	24.4	1 364	17 644	1 635.3	695.0	1 039	8 210	534.1	166.8
Murfreesboro.............	18	158	6.4	1.8	189	3 057	166.6	83.2	132	701	41.4	12.2
Nashville-Davidson	545	6 077	560.4	211.3	1 462	27 389	2 174.0	925.5	1 092	8 627	530.2	163.9
Oak Ridge	6	53	1.8	0.5	113	1 243	93.1	51.2	63	337	16.6	6.1
TEXAS	3 894	65 218	3 743.8	1 143.4	37 974	557 007	35 620.9	14 725.4	29 162	197 113	12 477.7	3 785.0
Abilene	41	312	19.2	4.2	305	5 117	306.6	121.2	208	1 767	98.3	32.3
Amarillo....................	40	403	15.3	4.3	476	6 338	506.8	215.0	336	2 310	133.7	39.8
Arlington...................	65	4 831	246.8	107.3	702	8 890	618.9	257.8	438	3 628	216.4	70.4
Austin.......................	171	2 810	126.8	45.5	1 550	27 475	1 894.7	770.0	1 210	8 761	558.0	183.2
Baytown....................	14	135	5.5	1.5	178	1 905	124.8	53.0	115	1 151	59.8	21.8
Beaumont..................	28	232	10.4	2.4	450	7 396	426.4	193.3	286	2 024	123.7	34.7
Bedford.....................	14	250	6.6	2.5	176	2 119	161.4	62.2	68	395	19.4	6.2
Brownsville................	21	235	8.9	2.6	230	4 623	272.4	109.4	144	1 217	50.0	15.9
Bryan.......................	10	0	0.0	0.0	166	1 402	102.8	46.5	126	782	45.3	12.5
Carrollton..................	29	306	11.6	2.9	203	2 265	156.4	65.5	201	1 592	101.3	34.6
College Station...........	17	300	8.9	3.4	94	1 432	109.2	38.4	56	408	15.8	4.9
Conroe	15	122	6.1	1.7	152	2 793	219.6	83.0	113	822	41.6	12.1
Corpus Christi	56	579	30.5	7.6	831	14 413	768.8	343.7	510	3 465	205.2	63.8
Dallas.......................	313	4 772	393.1	123.6	3 009	40 422	3 923.9	1 567.6	1 973	16 667	1 070.5	341.7
Deer Park	4	31	0.5	0.2	36	216	13.8	4.2	55	516	30.4	11.7
Del Rio	8	0	0.0	0.0	53	0	0.0	0.0	47	0	0.0	0.0
Denton......................	18	211	5.3	1.7	216	3 437	247.9	99.7	137	806	83.9	15.5
DeSoto......................	6	100	3.4	1.0	138	1 837	97.5	42.4	49	317	19.3	5.2
Duncanville	8	107	3.0	0.9	124	1 399	68.5	30.5	85	489	38.4	10.7
Edinburg	4	69	1.4	0.3	97	3 396	320.8	95.0	56	182	11.7	2.1
El Paso.....................	73	1 710	94.0	23.4	970	16 345	1 159.2	453.7	791	5 613	258.7	85.7
Euless	4	0	0.0	0.0	74	674	51.4	22.1	49	330	23.8	6.6
Fort Worth	81	1 342	70.0	19.7	1 159	14 987	1 053.0	487.1	783	5 483	355.5	111.6
Galveston...................	34	280	15.5	5.8	104	1 048	49.4	17.2	97	472	23.8	6.7
Garland.....................	37	632	30.3	7.5	342	5 525	261.5	111.7	316	1 901	118.2	34.9
Grand Prairie	20	311	76.3	5.9	157	1 633	85.4	34.8	154	1 133	88.5	28.4
Grapevine..................	14	295	3.9	1.4	112	1 036	74.3	33.4	74	388	28.7	8.2
Haltom City	8	0	0.0	0.0	34	804	22.8	12.2	83	455	30.7	9.3
Harlingen...................	9	48	2.4	0.5	207	5 611	184.3	90.6	116	719	33.0	10.3
Houston.....................	361	8 000	654.1	203.5	4 768	66 288	5 075.2	2 087.9	3 429	32 465	2 289.5	694.0
Huntsville..................	4	0	0.0	0.0	70	0	0.0	0.0	42	245	10.1	3.3
Hurst........................	8	128	5.4	1.1	98	856	55.2	23.0	102	549	29.0	10.0
Irving	36	1 182	271.6	102.8	382	4 602	347.3	148.3	306	2 356	146.5	50.5
Killeen	16	162	5.9	1.3	101	866	46.3	15.1	151	731	35.6	11.1
Kingsville	3	0	0.0	0.0	51	0	0.0	0.0	46	0	0.0	0.0
La Porte	3	0	0.0	0.0	24	323	14.0	6.6	46	913	109.6	36.8
Laredo......................	17	0	0.0	0.0	226	0	0.0	0.0	189	0	0.0	0.0

1. Firms subject to federal tax.

City	Procurement contracts		Grants					Direct payments for individuals		Intergovernmental			Taxes			
														Per capita³ (dollars)		
	Defense	Other	Total²	Health and family welfare	Energy and environment	Education	Housing and community development	Educational assistance	Housing assistance	Total (mil dol)	Total (mil dol)	Percent from state government	Total (mil dol)	Total	Property	Sales and gross receipts
	108	109	110	111	112	113	114	115	116	117	118	119	120	121	122	123
SOUTH CAROLINA..........	847.1	1 693.2	3 878.7	2 302.1	92.3	348.6	67.5	104.8	79.3	X	X	X	X	X	X	X
Anderson..........................	0.5	0.4	8.4	0.1	0.2	0.6	1.8	0.9	5.9	18.8	3.3	49.8	8.5	322	211	0
Charleston.......................	195.9	35.9	98.4	45.0	7.1	3.1	5.9	9.9	7.6	123.3	23.4	38.7	56.8	800	413	141
Columbia..........................	45.0	16.8	633.1	182.0	66.0	105.4	40.0	20.2	6.4	110.1	16.3	28.6	43.0	381	227	48
Florence..........................	2.9	0.8	11.5	5.5	0.0	0.9	0.9	3.9	1.3	20.3	2.5	51.2	10.8	357	59	168
Greenville........................	76.9	12.2	26.2	9.3	0.0	2.6	6.4	4.1	2.7	62.5	6.4	55.8	37.4	656	366	64
Mount Pleasant................	3.7	0.3	0.6	0.0	0.0	0.0	0.0	0.0	0.4	25.9	2.6	56.8	13.9	405	184	109
North Charleston.............	80.6	2.6	2.6	0.0	0.5	0.0	1.2	0.0	6.0	50.4	10.4	34.2	27.9	465	214	140
Rock Hill..........................	0.3	1.8	6.9	4.9	0.0	0.8	0.5	2.6	0.7	22.5	4.0	46.4	11.9	271	191	0
Spartanburg.....................	0.2	2.8	10.6	4.3	0.0	1.3	2.9	4.1	1.5	34.0	6.9	47.1	16.3	388	222	52
Sumter.............................	1.3	0.3	13.3	5.2	0.0	3.6	1.8	2.8	1.8	19.1	4.7	35.8	8.6	222	125	33
SOUTH DAKOTA............	91.9	431.9	1 055.8	415.8	28.5	131.0	13.6	68.5	21.8	X	X	X	X	X	X	X
Rapid City........................	4.2	25.8	17.7	4.9	0.3	0.9	1.0	3.1	9.1	59.7	11.5	27.5	29.2	507	102	389
Sioux Falls.......................	6.9	43.3	15.5	3.9	0.1	1.0	1.8	2.2	3.0	103.8	8.5	51.3	62.4	551	162	372
TENNESSEE	1 075.8	3 444.6	5 900.0	3 664.7	93.1	389.7	119.2	108.8	186.9	X	X	X	X	X	X	X
Bartlett.............................	1.6	0.0	0.2	0.0	0.0	0.0	0.0	0.0	0.0	24.7	7.5	47.3	9.2	257	175	40
Chattanooga.....................	6.4	328.1	33.6	8.4	0.4	4.9	5.8	5.6	9.0	347.6	159.2	52.5	94.7	629	462	151
Clarksville........................	2.2	0.2	6.8	1.1	0.0	1.3	1.8	4.3	1.6	47.9	19.3	52.3	13.6	144	87	48
Cleveland.........................	0.0	2.0	3.2	2.5	0.0	0.0	0.2	2.4	1.2	55.1	24.1	67.8	14.0	418	196	211
Columbia..........................	0.3	3.6	0.7	0.0	0.0	0.0	0.0	2.0	0.5	24.1	10.0	36.7	6.0	186	122	56
Germantown.....................	0.2	0.0	0.0	0.0	0.0	0.0	0.0	0.0	0.0	29.1	8.9	45.5	11.6	364	320	41
Hendersonville	0.6	0.2	0.3	0.0	0.0	0.0	0.0	0.0	0.5	15.8	3.8	84.7	7.8	210	90	97
Jackson............................	0.5	1.4	4.8	0.0	0.0	1.9	1.7	4.1	3.5	61.2	20.2	44.7	19.4	384	298	73
Johnson City	0.1	5.5	8.7	4.1	0.1	2.1	0.7	4.2	4.2	103.1	52.6	44.5	25.3	455	375	70
Kingsport..........................	0.1	3.2	6.6	5.4	0.0	0.2	0.6	0.0	4.0	87.9	49.3	43.1	23.4	567	499	62
Knoxville..........................	29.2	91.5	82.0	14.0	5.1	5.9	4.7	7.5	13.4	194.2	32.1	42.6	100.7	601	330	262
Memphis...........................	42.1	238.1	184.8	87.3	0.5	9.0	41.7	14.1	44.0	1 165.0	774.8	52.2	228.5	383	305	74
Murfreesboro....................	3.2	16.3	4.2	0.0	0.0	0.2	0.7	4.6	3.0	82.2	45.5	43.6	20.9	388	321	52
Nashville-Davidson	63.9	55.8	987.2	378.6	74.3	130.8	45.6	15.6	33.7	1 337.7	273.6	96.0	690.5	1 291	679	484
Oak Ridge........................	28.5	1 737.5	9.7	1.9	6.0	0.1	1.0	0.0	1.5	55.2	33.3	52.7	12.0	434	353	76
TEXAS............................	8 326.0	6 176.5	18 369.8	9 975.7	236.0	2 027.6	459.1	491.2	362.1	X	X	X	X	X	X	X
Abilene.............................	26.9	0.3	17.9	3.4	0.1	0.7	3.1	4.1	1.7	68.7	4.9	54.3	41.4	381	181	195
Amarillo............................	4.7	247.4	15.2	5.8	0.0	1.4	3.5	1.7	0.4	109.3	11.8	16.3	49.8	293	74	214
Arlington...........................	115.4	8.0	14.2	1.2	1.3	2.0	5.7	6.0	1.9	183.6	6.8	38.4	103.2	350	157	184
Austin...............................	180.2	109.4	2 956.8	799.4	108.4	612.9	125.0	19.8	11.2	631.3	77.7	42.9	253.8	469	236	206
Baytown...........................	0.0	0.0	2.2	0.0	0.0	0.4	1.7	1.3	1.4	48.6	4.9	11.7	25.9	380	255	122
Beaumont.........................	108.5	57.2	9.7	2.5	0.0	1.3	2.7	3.4	0.3	94.5	7.2	34.2	63.4	570	184	268
Bedford............................	0.2	2.2	0.1	0.0	0.0	0.0	0.0	0.0	0.0	61.6	0.9	100.0	32.7	661	284	360
Brownsville.......................	8.7	5.5	38.6	14.3	0.0	3.6	5.8	2.2	4.0	57.6	9.4	28.1	25.0	189	87	98
Bryan...............................	0.4	4.9	10.0	2.6	0.0	0.0	2.5	0.0	0.6	41.4	2.2	24.6	18.6	319	157	155
Carrollton.........................	13.5	4.1	0.0	0.0	0.0	0.0	0.0	0.0	0.0	79.8	3.1	19.8	49.6	513	303	200
College Station.................	6.3	17.5	130.4	30.6	9.6	5.2	1.8	7.8	0.0	39.9	1.7	9.3	21.8	372	146	217
Conroe.............................	1.3	1.9	2.7	0.8	0.0	0.0	0.2	0.1	3.0	26.7	0.7	53.8	19.1	565	141	414
Corpus Christi..................	175.7	13.8	26.6	6.0	0.0	3.1	12.2	5.4	14.7	202.6	10.7	23.3	90.3	322	165	151
Dallas...............................	727.1	188.2	297.9	153.3	0.7	8.0	46.3	16.1	30.4	1 452.3	137.5	20.3	575.3	546	280	254
Deer Park.........................	198.8	0.1	0.1	0.0	0.0	0.1	0.0	0.0	0.0	14.8	0.0	**********	14.4	476	379	97
Del Rio.............................	2.1	3.2	1.6	1.3	0.0	0.0	0.2	0.0	0.1	17.3	3.2	83.5	6.7	194	63	128
Denton.............................	1.1	2.5	12.9	2.3	0.6	5.7	2.4	7.4	0.1	59.3	3.9	32.1	24.6	335	152	175
DeSoto.............................	0.2	0.7	0.1	0.0	0.0	0.0	0.0	0.2	0.0	28.6	0.3	1.6	13.7	393	234	155
Duncanville.......................	0.0	0.5	0.0	0.0	0.0	0.0	0.0	0.0	0.0	21.6	1.8	92.3	11.9	330	144	174
Edinburg...........................	0.2	0.8	29.1	19.6	0.0	4.9	1.0	14.8	1.0	19.6	2.6	100.0	10.1	268	141	122
El Paso............................	134.5	34.7	119.3	28.5	0.2	8.4	23.7	25.6	7.3	355.2	40.9	24.6	181.2	302	162	130
Euless.............................	3.4	1.0	0.1	0.0	0.0	0.0	0.0	0.0	0.0	25.0	0.3	100.0	12.9	311	158	142
Fort Worth........................	1 887.8	56.8	75.4	24.0	0.2	2.5	9.9	9.7	16.2	482.4	41.8	100.0	239.8	500	297	138
Galveston.........................	24.5	88.2	70.1	55.8	0.7	1.5	6.6	1.0	4.7	71.6	3.4	12.6	28.3	472	180	268
Garland............................	84.6	1.3	3.4	0.0	0.0	0.0	3.3	0.1	1.4	128.9	13.0	79.9	58.4	307	197	104
Grand Prairie....................	690.7	28.0	3.0	0.0	0.0	0.0	2.4	0.9	2.5	91.5	7.3	4.1	46.0	421	242	171
Grapevine.........................	0.7	2.9	0.0	0.0	0.0	0.0	0.0	0.0	0.0	50.0	0.7	100.0	24.4	650	330	295
Haltom City......................	0.0	0.0	0.0	0.0	0.0	0.0	0.0	0.0	0.3	16.2	0.3	47.9	10.0	281	97	171
Harlingen..........................	0.5	0.9	10.3	5.4	0.0	0.0	2.8	3.0	0.9	45.1	4.2	9.7	17.2	302	93	203
Houston...........................	221.6	3 830.9	844.4	375.6	96.8	24.7	56.1	46.8	69.4	1 733.8	148.3	25.5	891.8	511	254	241
Huntsville.........................	0.0	0.0	2.5	0.0	0.0	1.5	0.0	3.2	1.3	13.5	0.1	75.9	6.4	221	49	165
Hurst...............................	14.8	0.9	0.5	0.0	0.0	0.2	0.0	0.7	0.0	25.9	0.1	100.0	18.8	516	176	330
Irving...............................	95.9	4.3	2.4	0.0	0.1	0.7	0.0	2.8	2.1	132.3	4.1	21.0	89.0	503	241	243
Killeen.............................	2.6	4.1	16.0	0.0	0.0	13.5	2.1	5.7	0.0	37.6	1.5	6.3	21.1	270	104	158
Kingsville.........................	82.4	0.2	3.8	1.0	0.1	2.1	0.0	4.5	2.5	11.1	0.0	100.0	6.5	254	112	131
La Porte...........................	0.6	0.1	0.6	0.0	0.0	0.0	0.0	0.0	0.2	26.3	0.1	100.0	10.9	342	248	82
Laredo.............................	0.4	14.5	68.1	43.1	0.1	3.5	6.1	7.4	1.2	197.4	100.9	6.5	36.8	223	114	99

1. October 1, 1998 to September 30, 1999.   2. Includes program categories not shown separately. State totals include additional categories not allocated by city.   3. Based on population estimated as of July 1 of the year shown.

Table D. Cities — City Government Finances

	City government finances, 1997 (cont'd)												
	General expenditure												
	Per capita[1] (dollars)			Percent of total for —									
City	Total (mil dol)	Total	Capital outlays	Public welfare	Highways	Parking facilities	Education	Health and hospitals	Police protection	Sewerage and sanitation	Parks and recreation	Housing and community development	Interest on debt
	124	125	126	127	128	129	130	131	132	133	134	135	136
SOUTH CAROLINA	X	X	X	X	X	X	X	X	X	X	X	X	X
Anderson......................	19.3	729	115	0.0	6.6	0.0	0.0	1.2	16.6	19.7	4.4	9.5	5.2
Charleston....................	94.6	1 332	216	0.7	2.3	1.5	0.0	0.0	17.1	17.7	5.7	3.2	3.5
Columbia......................	98.8	876	115	0.2	6.1	1.4	0.0	0.5	17.2	20.4	6.0	4.3	1.2
Florence......................	17.7	588	30	0.0	7.5	0.0	0.0	0.0	23.3	17.4	8.6	3.5	7.6
Greenville....................	55.3	970	85	0.0	5.5	0.7	0.0	1.0	18.3	8.9	11.2	3.9	1.4
Mount Pleasant	20.1	586	90	0.0	3.0	0.0	0.0	0.0	20.2	28.1	8.4	0.8	2.3
North Charleston...........	52.9	883	211	0.0	3.1	0.0	0.0	0.0	26.5	6.0	17.3	3.5	4.5
Rock Hill.....................	31.3	711	17	0.0	3.7	0.0	0.0	0.0	16.9	9.2	9.1	0.0	11.3
Spartanburg	25.1	596	93	0.0	11.9	0.2	0.0	0.7	23.2	12.8	0.4	7.4	1.0
Sumter........................	17.5	454	59	0.0	3.9	1.2	0.0	0.0	26.5	22.1	5.0	0.9	0.5
SOUTH DAKOTA..............	X	X	X	X	X	X	X	X	X	X	X	X	X
Rapid City	69.8	1 211	572	0.0	4.0	0.4	0.0	0.3	9.9	16.7	21.2	1.0	5.2
Sioux Falls	93.6	826	201	0.0	19.3	1.0	0.0	2.9	10.7	8.6	24.7	3.7	2.3
TENNESSEE	X	X	X	X	X	X	X	X	X	X	X	X	X
Bartlett.......................	26.0	728	171	0.0	15.8	0.0	0.0	0.0	28.8	10.2	13.5	0.0	4.4
Chattanooga.................	366.1	2 434	477	3.0	6.1	0.0	31.9	0.5	7.5	18.0	3.8	0.8	5.0
Clarksville...................	36.7	387	27	0.0	12.3	0.8	0.0	0.9	21.0	12.0	6.5	4.8	4.4
Cleveland	52.5	1 566	176	0.3	5.5	0.0	44.4	0.6	8.1	19.3	2.4	0.3	2.9
Columbia......................	20.6	644	28	0.4	11.3	0.4	0.0	0.0	17.7	30.6	3.8	0.0	2.0
Germantown..................	31.5	991	250	0.0	5.0	0.0	0.0	0.3	13.5	11.7	14.5	0.0	5.4
Hendersonville	15.5	416	13	0.7	17.1	0.0	0.0	0.0	23.1	13.7	4.1	0.0	2.8
Jackson.......................	60.8	1 205	193	0.2	7.7	0.2	0.0	1.0	13.4	32.3	10.0	2.2	4.3
Johnson City	106.3	1 914	470	1.2	10.5	0.0	42.9	0.0	6.4	11.7	4.8	4.4	6.2
Kingsport.....................	77.5	1 876	86	0.0	5.0	0.1	49.4	0.0	7.4	7.4	3.0	0.5	7.5
Knoxville......................	241.6	1 442	590	0.9	12.9	0.6	0.0	0.0	10.4	17.7	4.9	7.1	5.6
Memphis......................	1 187.9	1 991	251	0.0	4.3	0.0	50.3	0.6	11.1	7.0	6.2	2.3	2.3
Murfreesboro.................	75.0	1 389	191	0.0	6.1	0.0	36.6	0.1	8.7	10.0	11.0	2.1	3.6
Nashville-Davidson	1 355.8	2 534	440	1.3	2.9	0.0	32.6	8.5	6.9	7.2	8.5	0.0	8.5
Oak Ridge	60.3	2 175	326	0.2	6.1	0.0	57.2	0.2	5.2	9.7	2.9	1.3	1.7
TEXAS	X	X	X	X	X	X	X	X	X	X	X	X	X
Abilene........................	65.5	604	44	0.1	11.3	0.0	0.0	4.9	16.3	11.8	7.6	3.7	5.2
Amarillo.......................	110.3	650	103	0.0	17.9	0.0	0.0	1.5	15.6	14.5	7.1	7.7	10.4
Arlington......................	176.0	597	99	0.0	14.7	0.0	0.0	0.9	20.9	14.1	13.0	3.4	5.6
Austin.........................	629.4	1 163	153	1.2	6.2	0.3	0.1	10.2	12.2	11.9	7.1	1.6	18.9
Baytown.......................	51.8	760	139	0.1	12.5	0.0	0.0	0.7	22.1	12.3	10.8	2.1	6.2
Beaumont.....................	104.5	939	157	0.0	16.4	0.0	0.0	3.7	17.6	9.3	3.6	3.5	6.2
Bedford.......................	56.9	1 152	250	0.0	8.9	0.0	0.0	0.8	16.8	15.9	8.8	0.0	1.7
Brownsville...................	62.7	474	84	0.3	8.7	0.8	0.0	3.4	18.4	12.5	5.7	8.7	5.4
Bryan..........................	42.4	727	46	0.2	7.4	0.0	0.0	0.0	14.1	20.7	4.1	3.4	6.5
Carrollton.....................	63.2	654	144	0.0	16.9	0.0	0.0	2.0	16.9	10.9	10.2	0.0	6.4
College Station..............	44.0	748	177	0.0	5.3	0.0	0.0	0.0	10.4	21.2	11.1	4.6	3.8
Conroe........................	22.3	661	151	0.0	8.5	0.0	0.0	0.0	19.1	12.7	6.9	2.6	5.5
Corpus Christi...............	165.2	590	17	0.0	6.1	0.1	0.0	4.3	21.5	11.2	7.7	1.1	3.7
Dallas.........................	1 194.4	1 134	159	0.1	6.7	0.2	0.0	1.9	15.7	13.9	8.1	2.0	20.5
Deer Park.....................	13.0	431	0	0.0	5.3	0.0	0.0	0.0	24.7	12.2	13.6	4.2	8.7
Del Rio........................	19.9	576	58	5.0	10.2	0.0	0.0	1.7	19.7	15.6	5.2	0.0	6.0
Denton........................	52.0	708	49	0.0	9.2	0.0	0.0	0.6	16.8	21.7	6.1	3.6	5.3
DeSoto........................	41.1	1 176	450	0.0	2.7	0.0	0.0	0.0	8.9	5.0	2.2	0.0	23.8
Duncanville...................	24.1	670	49	0.0	12.6	0.0	0.0	0.0	19.1	27.8	5.0	0.0	8.0
Edinburg......................	17.1	454	38	0.6	7.7	0.0	0.0	4.3	15.4	16.3	12.6	11.8	4.3
El Paso........................	316.8	528	76	0.6	6.6	0.0	0.0	7.5	22.7	12.6	6.4	1.7	8.5
Euless.........................	46.9	1 126	432	0.0	2.1	0.0	0.0	0.4	11.5	7.9	27.8	0.0	3.4
Fort Worth....................	433.5	904	93	0.0	11.7	0.1	0.0	1.9	19.7	22.0	7.9	3.3	4.4
Galveston.....................	60.6	1 009	41	0.0	4.2	0.0	0.0	0.8	11.3	11.7	12.1	3.2	20.5
Garland.......................	130.3	686	93	0.0	20.2	0.0	0.0	1.1	17.3	17.8	6.5	6.0	3.5
Grand Prairie.................	79.6	729	34	0.0	7.0	0.0	0.2	0.9	19.4	15.9	8.1	10.7	12.0
Grapevine.....................	75.5	2 012	684	0.0	15.1	0.0	0.0	0.0	6.8	4.5	5.9	0.0	18.9
Haltom City	15.3	430	32	0.0	6.7	0.0	0.0	0.6	31.7	20.9	4.3	0.0	5.5
Harlingen.....................	44.0	773	31	0.9	8.1	0.0	0.0	5.6	12.6	18.9	8.0	2.8	7.1
Houston.......................	1 907.2	1 094	270	0.0	8.7	0.2	0.0	4.1	19.9	20.8	5.4	2.6	9.8
Huntsville.....................	11.8	405	10	0.0	14.4	0.0	0.0	0.0	18.7	20.7	5.8	0.0	6.2
Hurst..........................	41.2	1 128	537	0.0	8.1	0.0	0.0	0.0	14.1	9.3	39.5	0.0	3.3
Irving..........................	139.7	789	88	0.0	11.2	0.0	0.0	3.5	12.2	17.5	6.1	0.6	3.5
Killeen.........................	32.7	419	30	0.2	8.1	0.0	0.0	0.7	23.8	21.6	7.0	4.6	3.9
Kingsville.....................	10.5	416	18	0.0	0.0	0.0	1.6	1.8	22.7	31.2	1.9	0.0	0.8
La Porte.......................	23.3	728	47	0.0	8.5	0.0	0.0	3.6	18.2	13.7	13.2	0.0	5.4
Laredo.........................	182.3	1 105	246	0.0	13.6	0.1	0.0	3.2	9.5	6.4	3.1	3.5	3.7

1. Based on population estimated as of July 1 of the year shown.

Table D. Cities — City Government Finances, City Government Employment, and Climate

City	City government finances, 1997 (cont'd) — Debt outstanding — Total (mil dol)	Per capita[1] (dollars)	Percent utility	City government employment, 1999	Climate[2] — Average daily temperature (degrees Fahrenheit) — Mean January	Mean July	Limits January[3]	Limits July[4]	Annual precipitation (inches)	Heating degree days	Cooling degree days
	137	138	139	140	141	142	143	144	145	146	147
SOUTH CAROLINA..........	X	X	X	X	X	X	X	X	X	X	X
Anderson......................	21.2	800	0.0	352	42.1	79.8	32.2	89.9	46.38	2 891	1 807
Charleston...................	294.2	4 141	84.3	1 878	47.8	81.5	37.7	90.2	51.53	2 013	2 266
Columbia.....................	158.2	1 403	86.8	1 860	43.8	80.8	32.1	91.6	49.91	2 649	1 966
Florence......................	35.1	1 164	38.3	364	43.8	80.6	33.4	90.4	43.84	2 585	1 993
Greenville...................	25.3	443	0.0	967	40.1	78.2	30.0	88.2	51.27	3 272	1 473
Mount Pleasant...........	35.0	1 021	79.9	NA	47.8	81.5	37.7	90.2	51.53	2 013	2 266
North Charleston.........	41.0	683	0.0	794	47.8	81.5	37.7	90.2	51.53	2 013	2 266
Rock Hill.....................	86.4	1 961	27.2	675	40.9	79.1	30.9	89.2	48.65	3 054	1 624
Spartanburg................	78.1	1 854	96.3	665	41.9	79.4	31.5	90.6	49.87	2 887	1 688
Sumter.......................	17.0	442	79.6	463	44.0	80.0	32.4	91.1	48.14	2 609	1 888
SOUTH DAKOTA..............	X	X	X	X	X	X	X	X	X	X	X
Rapid City...................	68.7	1 192	9.1	872	22.3	72.2	10.7	86.2	16.64	7 301	611
Sioux Falls..................	137.5	1 215	9.4	937	13.8	74.3	3.3	86.3	23.86	7 809	744
TENNESSEE	X	X	X	X	X	X	X	X	X	X	X
Bartlett.......................	33.3	932	39.2	NA	39.7	82.6	30.9	92.3	52.10	3 082	2 118
Chattanooga................	289.2	1 922	0.0	3 107	37.4	78.7	28.0	89.0	53.46	3 587	1 544
Clarksville..................	83.7	883	45.1	905	34.0	78.1	23.3	90.0	50.75	4 159	1 417
Cleveland....................	32.2	960	7.9	1 318	36.5	76.6	25.8	88.0	54.65	3 884	1 236
Columbia.....................	17.9	560	46.5	NA	34.4	77.1	23.2	88.8	54.26	4 206	1 281
Germantown................	25.5	802	4.8	NA	39.7	82.6	30.9	92.3	52.10	3 082	2 118
Hendersonville............	8.5	229	0.0	NA	36.2	79.3	26.5	89.5	47.30	3 729	1 616
Jackson......................	78.9	1 566	75.4	1 136	37.0	80.1	27.3	90.9	52.88	3 540	1 744
Johnson City...............	155.2	2 795	31.4	1 779	34.0	74.4	24.3	84.6	40.72	4 406	972
Kingsport...................	133.7	3 234	12.3	1 645	36.1	75.8	26.4	87.1	43.79	3 901	1 167
Knoxville.....................	295.7	1 765	43.0	2 730	36.0	76.6	26.0	87.1	47.14	3 937	1 266
Memphis......................	846.3	1 418	31.7	25 190	39.7	82.6	30.9	92.3	52.10	3 082	2 118
Murfreesboro...............	84.3	1 562	30.9	1 577	35.2	77.9	24.5	89.3	53.17	3 992	1 406
Nashville-Davidson............	2 739.4	5 120	28.8	NA	NA	NA	NA	NA	NA	NA	NA
Oak Ridge...................	71.5	2 577	28.5	1 089	35.0	75.8	25.1	86.7	53.77	4 183	1 156
TEXAS	X	X	X	X	X	X	X	X	X	X	X
Abilene.......................	55.0	507	31.4	1 121	42.8	84.0	30.8	95.2	24.40	2 584	2 451
Amarillo......................	186.8	1 102	18.1	1 638	35.1	78.6	21.2	91.7	19.56	4 258	1 354
Arlington....................	378.7	1 285	28.9	2 561	43.4	85.3	32.7	96.5	33.70	2 407	2 603
Austin........................	3 866.5	7 143	70.3	10 119	48.8	84.5	38.6	95.0	31.88	1 688	3 016
Baytown......................	87.9	1 290	37.5	538	50.5	83.1	40.6	91.4	51.85	1 550	2 809
Beaumont....................	135.5	1 218	26.5	1 323	49.6	82.3	39.5	91.9	55.58	1 677	2 581
Bedford......................	17.5	353	9.3	NA	43.4	85.3	32.7	96.5	33.70	2 407	2 603
Brownsville.................	263.1	1 992	69.8	1 285	59.4	84.5	49.9	93.3	26.61	635	3 888
Bryan..........................	78.5	1 348	52.1	801	48.5	83.6	38.7	93.8	39.08	1 788	2 776
Carrollton...................	133.1	1 375	22.1	950	43.4	85.3	32.7	96.5	33.70	2 407	2 603
College Station............	62.0	1 056	31.7	674	48.5	83.6	38.7	93.8	39.08	1 788	2 776
Conroe.......................	35.4	1 049	17.2	NA	48.8	83.1	37.9	94.0	47.33	1 774	2 676
Corpus Christi.............	488.1	1 742	31.5	3 225	55.1	84.1	45.3	93.3	30.13	1 016	3 439
Dallas........................	3 603.2	3 421	9.6	15 042	44.6	85.9	34.5	95.7	36.08	2 259	2 763
Deer Park...................	22.7	750	26.6	NA	52.2	83.5	42.9	92.3	50.83	1 371	3 012
Del Rio......................	46.5	1 348	52.1	NA	50.2	85.2	38.5	96.2	18.24	1 506	3 142
Denton.......................	175.6	2 390	75.3	1 024	41.9	83.2	30.3	94.0	37.27	2 665	2 225
DeSoto.......................	100.7	2 877	7.7	NA	44.6	85.9	34.5	95.7	36.08	2 259	2 763
Duncanville.................	27.9	774	7.5	NA	44.6	85.9	34.5	95.7	36.08	2 259	2 763
Edinburg.....................	17.2	457	16.5	NA	58.5	85.4	48.5	95.8	22.83	693	4 076
El Paso.......................	576.8	961	24.9	6 081	42.8	82.3	29.4	96.1	8.81	2 708	2 094
Euless........................	49.1	1 179	10.0	362	43.4	85.3	32.7	96.5	33.70	2 407	2 603
Fort Worth..................	927.5	1 933	34.0	6 076	43.4	85.3	32.7	96.5	33.70	2 407	2 603
Galveston....................	190.2	3 168	10.5	774	52.7	83.3	47.1	87.3	42.28	1 263	2 994
Garland......................	224.6	1 182	10.2	1 909	44.6	85.9	34.5	95.7	36.08	2 259	2 763
Grand Prairie..............	157.8	1 444	20.3	933	43.4	85.3	32.7	96.5	33.70	2 407	2 603
Grapevine...................	205.5	5 479	7.6	473	41.6	83.7	30.0	94.9	33.68	2 683	2 328
Haltom City.................	19.3	544	17.1	NA	43.4	85.3	32.7	96.5	33.70	2 407	2 603
Harlingen....................	60.8	1 069	34.8	721	57.3	83.9	46.7	94.4	27.53	813	3 662
Houston......................	4 996.3	2 865	22.0	22 729	52.2	83.5	42.9	92.3	50.83	1 371	3 012
Huntsville...................	24.0	827	51.5	NA	47.6	83.3	37.6	94.4	44.96	1 862	2 654
Hurst.........................	20.6	565	28.7	NA	43.4	85.3	32.7	96.5	33.70	2 407	2 603
Irving.........................	148.2	838	36.9	1 669	44.6	85.9	34.5	95.7	36.08	2 259	2 763
Killeen.......................	47.0	602	45.2	691	45.4	84.0	34.5	95.2	34.87	2 153	2 623
Kingsville...................	9.7	380	100.0	NA	56.4	84.3	44.7	95.0	27.60	911	3 590
La Porte.....................	33.0	1 033	41.6	NA	52.2	83.5	42.9	92.3	50.83	1 371	3 012
Laredo........................	169.0	1 025	6.2	1 841	54.4	86.9	42.9	98.8	21.42	1 025	3 915

1. Based on the population estimated as of July 1 of the year shown.   2. Represents normal values based on the 30-year period, 1961–1990.   3. Average daily minimum.   4. Average daily maximum.

Table D. Cities — Land Area and Population

STATE Place code	City	Land area, 1990[1] (sq km)	Population, 1999			Population				Population characteristics, 1990 Percent						
												Race				
			Total persons	Rank	Per square kilometer	Total persons 1990	Percent change 1990–1999	Total persons 1980	Percent change 1980–1990	White	Black	Am. Indian, Eskimo, Aleut	Asian and Pacific Islander	Other race	His-panic[2]	Foreign born
		1	2	3	4	5	6	7	8	9	10	11	12	13	14	15
	TEXAS—Cont'd															
48 41980	League City	133.1	44 966	660	338	30 159	49.1	16 575	82.0	88.1	5.1	0.3	2.3	4.1	11.7	5.9
48 42508	Lewisville	93.3	77 355	322	829	46 521	66.3	24 273	91.7	88.6	4.6	0.6	1.9	4.2	8.7	4.8
48 43888	Longview	135.5	75 534	336	557	70 311	7.4	62 762	12.0	76.6	19.9	0.4	0.6	2.4	4.1	2.4
48 45000	Lubbock	269.7	190 002	93	704	186 206	2.0	173 979	7.0	77.6	8.6	0.3	1.4	12.1	22.5	3.3
48 45072	Lufkin	61.1	33 482	904	548	30 210	10.8	28 562	5.8	65.2	27.2	0.2	0.8	6.6	9.6	5.2
48 45384	McAllen	84.0	110 292	201	1 313	84 021	31.3	66 281	26.8	70.9	0.3	0.2	0.7	27.8	77.0	26.4
48 47892	Mesquite	110.9	116 179	184	1 048	101 484	14.5	67 053	51.3	87.2	5.8	0.5	2.6	3.8	8.8	4.7
48 48072	Midland	170.5	98 293	235	576	89 343	10.0	70 525	26.8	79.8	9.1	0.4	1.0	9.7	21.3	6.3
48 48768	Mission	36.0	43 947	679	1 221	28 653	53.4	22 551	27.1	75.4	0.2	0.2	0.1	24.1	80.1	21.9
48 48804	Missouri City	60.1	66 341	397	1 104	36 143	83.6	24 533	47.5	60.6	29.4	0.3	6.3	3.4	9.2	9.6
48 50256	Nacogdoches	64.6	30 804	983	477	30 872	-0.2	27 149	13.7	73.5	22.5	0.2	0.9	2.9	5.1	3.9
48 50820	New Braunfels	65.9	38 281	793	581	27 334	40.0	22 404	22.0	85.5	1.3	0.2	0.3	12.7	34.8	5.0
48 52356	North Richland Hills	47.2	56 151	508	1 190	45 895	22.3	30 592	50.0	93.6	1.8	0.5	1.6	2.4	5.8	3.3
48 53388	Odessa	91.6	89 293	266	975	89 699	-0.5	90 027	-0.4	77.6	6.0	0.5	0.7	17.5	31.1	7.6
48 56000	Pasadena	113.4	133 660	152	1 179	119 604	11.8	112 560	6.3	83.7	1.0	0.5	1.6	13.2	28.8	10.9
48 57200	Pharr	40.9	45 844	644	1 121	32 921	39.3	21 381	54.0	70.2	0.1	0.2	0.1	29.4	88.4	26.1
48 58016	Plano	171.6	232 904	71	1 357	127 885	82.1	72 329	76.8	88.5	4.1	0.3	4.0	3.0	6.2	7.5
48 58820	Port Arthur	200.0	56 574	499	283	58 551	-3.4	61 251	-4.4	49.3	42.2	0.3	4.8	3.4	8.2	6.8
48 61796	Richardson	73.2	87 517	274	1 196	74 840	16.9	72 480	3.3	86.8	4.7	0.3	6.6	1.6	4.3	9.8
48 63500	Round Rock	49.5	67 173	389	1 357	30 923	117.2	11 762	162.9	84.6	5.5	0.4	1.1	8.3	18.7	4.6
48 64472	San Angelo	124.0	88 244	270	712	84 462	4.5	73 240	15.3	78.8	4.8	0.4	1.1	14.9	28.0	5.4
48 65000	San Antonio	862.6	1 147 213	8	1 330	976 514	17.5	785 809	24.2	72.2	7.0	0.4	1.1	19.2	55.6	9.4
48 65600	San Marcos	45.1	40 538	740	899	28 738	41.1	23 420	22.7	78.4	5.3	0.2	0.9	15.2	37.4	4.6
48 67496	Sherman	96.8	34 105	888	352	31 584	8.0	30 413	3.9	83.2	12.6	0.9	0.8	2.4	4.4	3.0
48 72176	Temple	111.3	52 154	552	469	46 150	13.0	42 483	8.6	72.8	17.1	0.4	0.9	8.8	13.7	2.8
48 72368	Texarkana	54.5	32 285	940	592	32 294	0.0	31 271	3.3	63.0	35.9	0.4	0.5	0.3	1.1	0.8
48 72392	Texas City	160.9	42 701	691	265	40 822	4.6	41 403	-1.4	67.1	25.1	0.4	1.1	6.2	15.9	3.4
48 74144	Tyler	102.7	83 796	290	816	75 450	11.1	70 501	7.0	66.1	28.2	0.3	0.5	4.9	8.9	5.3
48 75428	Victoria	78.0	61 699	436	791	55 076	12.0	50 695	8.6	76.9	7.4	0.3	0.4	14.5	37.9	3.2
48 76000	Waco	196.3	108 520	206	553	103 590	4.8	101 262	2.3	67.6	23.1	0.3	0.9	8.1	16.3	4.6
48 79000	Wichita Falls	140.2	98 919	231	706	96 259	2.8	94 201	2.2	80.4	11.2	0.7	1.8	5.8	10.0	4.3
49 00000	**UTAH**	212 815.5	2 129 836	X	10	1 722 850	23.6	1 461 037	17.9	93.8	0.7	1.4	1.9	2.2	4.9	3.4
49 07690	Bountiful	27.6	41 169	725	1 492	37 544	9.7	32 877	14.2	98.2	0.1	0.3	0.9	0.5	1.6	2.1
49 43660	Layton	47.3	56 469	500	1 194	41 784	35.1	22 862	82.8	92.7	2.1	0.7	2.3	2.3	5.6	2.8
49 45860	Logan	36.6	40 778	732	1 114	32 771	24.4	26 844	22.1	91.4	0.6	1.3	5.1	1.7	3.1	7.8
49 53230	Murray	24.7	32 449	933	1 314	31 274	3.8	25 750	21.5	95.8	0.7	0.5	1.5	1.5	4.2	3.2
49 55980	Ogden	67.6	68 210	380	1 009	63 943	6.7	64 407	-0.7	87.4	2.7	1.1	1.8	7.0	12.0	3.9
49 57300	Orem	46.5	82 965	291	1 784	67 561	22.8	52 399	28.9	96.4	0.1	0.8	1.5	1.2	3.0	3.0
49 62470	Provo	100.0	110 690	199	1 107	86 835	27.5	74 108	17.2	94.1	0.3	1.1	2.7	1.9	4.2	5.4
49 65330	St. George	148.9	47 994	613	322	28 572	68.0	11 350	151.7	96.8	0.2	1.6	0.7	0.7	2.0	2.1
49 67000	Salt Lake City	282.4	171 151	115	606	159 928	7.0	163 033	-1.9	87.0	1.7	1.6	4.7	4.9	9.7	8.3
49 67440	Sandy	51.8	101 853	216	1 966	75 240	35.4	50 546	48.9	97.1	0.2	0.3	1.7	0.8	2.5	2.9
49 82950	West Jordan	69.5	65 139	410	937	42 915	51.8	27 192	57.8	94.0	0.3	0.6	1.9	3.1	6.5	2.2
49 83470	West Valley City	88.1	102 718	215	1 166	86 969	18.1	72 378	20.2	90.8	0.8	1.1	4.0	3.2	7.1	4.3
50 00000	**VERMONT**	23 955.7	593 740	X	25	562 758	5.5	511 456	10.0	98.6	0.3	0.3	0.6	0.1	0.7	3.1
50 10675	Burlington	27.3	38 332	790	1 404	39 127	-2.0	37 712	3.8	96.8	1.0	0.3	1.5	0.4	1.2	4.2
51 00000	**VIRGINIA**	102 558.3	6 872 912	X	67	6 189 197	11.0	5 346 797	15.8	77.4	18.8	0.2	2.6	0.9	2.6	5.0
51 01000	Alexandria	39.6	117 390	181	2 964	111 182	5.6	103 217	7.7	69.1	21.9	0.3	4.2	4.6	9.7	16.2
51 07784	Blacksburg	48.6	34 458	878	709	34 590	-0.4	30 638	12.9	84.7	4.3	0.1	7.7	0.5	1.8	10.8
51 14968	Charlottesville	26.6	36 815	823	1 384	40 475	-9.0	39 916	1.4	76.1	21.2	0.1	2.3	0.3	1.2	3.6
51 16000	Chesapeake	882.4	202 759	82	230	151 982	33.4	114 486	32.8	70.7	27.4	0.3	1.2	0.4	1.3	1.7
51 21344	Danville	111.5	50 795	573	456	53 056	-4.3	45 642	16.2	62.7	36.6	0.1	0.5	0.1	0.5	0.7
51 35000	Hampton	134.2	137 193	146	1 022	133 811	2.5	122 617	9.1	58.4	38.9	0.3	1.7	0.7	2.0	2.9
51 35624	Harrisonburg	45.5	34 129	887	750	30 707	11.1	19 671	56.1	91.1	6.6	0.1	1.5	0.7	1.6	2.4
51 47672	Lynchburg	127.9	63 926	422	500	66 049	-3.2	66 743	-1.0	72.5	26.4	0.2	0.8	0.2	0.7	1.7
51 48952	Manassas	25.9	33 498	902	1 293	27 957	19.8	15 438	81.1	83.5	10.3	0.3	3.1	2.8	5.7	7.6
51 56000	Newport News	177.0	179 138	109	1 012	171 439	4.5	144 903	18.3	62.6	33.6	0.3	2.3	1.2	2.8	4.1
51 57000	Norfolk	139.2	225 875	73	1 623	261 250	-13.5	266 979	-2.1	56.7	39.1	0.4	2.6	1.2	2.9	3.7
51 61832	Petersburg	59.3	34 398	879	580	37 027	-7.1	41 055	-9.8	26.6	72.1	0.2	0.8	0.3	1.2	1.8
51 64000	Portsmouth	85.8	98 305	234	1 146	103 910	-5.4	104 577	-0.6	51.2	47.3	0.3	0.8	0.4	1.3	1.3
51 67000	Richmond	155.7	189 700	94	1 218	202 798	-6.5	219 214	-7.5	43.4	55.2	0.2	0.9	0.3	0.9	1.8
51 68000	Roanoke	111.1	93 357	251	840	96 509	-3.3	100 220	-3.7	74.6	24.3	0.2	0.7	0.2	0.7	1.6
51 76432	Suffolk	1 036.2	64 805	411	63	52 143	24.3	47 621	9.5	54.7	44.6	0.2	0.4	0.1	0.6	0.8
51 82000	Virginia Beach	643.2	433 461	35	674	393 089	10.3	262 199	49.9	80.5	13.9	0.4	4.3	0.9	3.1	5.2

1. Dry land or land partially or temporarily covered by water.   2. Hispanic persons may be of any race.

Table D. Cities — **Population and Households**

City	Under 5 years	5 to 17 years	18 to 24 years	25 to 34 years	35 to 44 years	45 to 54 years	55 to 64 years	65 to 74 years	75 years and over	Percent female	Number	Percent change, 1980–1990	Persons per house-hold	Female family house-holder[1]	One-person
	16	17	18	19	20	21	22	23	24	25	26	27	28	29	30
TEXAS—Cont'd															
League City	8.9	21.3	8.0	22.5	17.7	11.5	5.4	3.0	1.6	49.9	10 586	98.9	2.84	7.9	17.1
Lewisville	9.3	17.7	12.5	25.9	16.2	9.4	4.5	2.5	1.9	50.0	17 683	123.8	2.61	8.8	23.3
Longview	7.9	19.1	10.2	17.3	14.4	9.6	8.4	7.2	5.8	52.1	27 206	18.8	2.52	12.3	26.7
Lubbock	7.6	18.0	17.4	18.2	13.2	8.6	7.3	5.6	4.1	50.9	69 143	13.4	2.56	10.7	26.8
Lufkin	7.7	20.3	9.8	15.9	13.0	9.3	8.8	7.9	7.3	52.9	11 222	10.6	2.61	13.6	27.1
McAllen	8.2	25.2	10.5	15.6	14.3	9.1	6.8	6.0	4.3	52.4	24 905	27.7	3.34	15.0	17.4
Mesquite	9.3	21.1	9.7	22.1	16.3	9.8	6.4	3.2	2.0	51.6	35 856	68.2	2.81	11.7	19.1
Midland	9.8	21.2	8.6	18.5	15.0	9.0	8.5	5.9	3.6	51.8	33 169	30.7	2.67	10.3	25.0
Mission	8.6	25.1	11.1	13.5	12.4	7.7	7.4	9.0	5.3	52.2	8 315	29.9	3.42	15.4	14.4
Missouri City	8.5	23.2	7.3	16.8	23.2	11.1	5.7	3.0	1.1	50.9	11 544	50.2	3.12	10.1	10.4
Nacogdoches	5.4	14.4	33.2	13.3	11.2	6.4	5.3	5.4	5.5	52.6	11 306	21.4	2.34	12.6	30.8
New Braunfels	7.4	19.8	8.0	15.0	14.0	8.8	9.0	9.2	8.8	52.8	9 997	26.9	2.66	10.5	24.1
North Richland Hills	8.7	19.2	10.1	20.3	17.5	10.4	6.9	4.6	2.2	51.0	16 901	61.3	2.71	9.5	18.6
Odessa	9.0	21.9	9.6	17.6	13.9	9.7	8.3	6.2	3.8	51.6	32 826	1.3	2.71	12.2	24.2
Pasadena	8.9	21.0	11.3	19.5	14.6	9.6	7.6	4.9	2.7	50.1	42 044	8.3	2.82	11.5	21.6
Pharr	8.9	27.4	12.1	13.6	11.4	8.3	7.1	7.0	4.3	51.9	8 659	56.8	3.78	16.1	12.0
Plano	8.6	21.6	8.2	19.9	21.4	12.3	4.4	2.2	1.4	50.1	44 352	100.1	2.89	7.6	15.7
Port Arthur	8.0	20.2	8.4	15.5	12.2	8.9	9.8	9.7	7.2	52.8	22 326	1.1	2.60	17.2	28.6
Richardson	7.1	19.6	7.3	16.3	18.9	14.3	9.2	4.9	2.6	51.3	27 220	12.8	2.73	9.9	17.1
Round Rock	9.9	23.3	9.3	23.2	17.8	7.6	3.9	2.7	2.2	50.8	10 568	190.4	2.90	11.1	18.1
San Angelo	7.8	19.1	13.1	16.9	13.4	8.6	8.0	7.1	5.9	51.9	30 661	15.6	2.59	11.3	26.1
San Antonio	8.4	20.7	11.5	18.2	14.2	9.1	7.6	6.3	4.1	51.8	326 761	26.1	2.80	15.7	25.0
San Marcos	4.9	12.8	42.3	15.1	8.3	5.5	4.1	3.5	3.5	51.1	9 849	48.7	2.40	10.0	30.3
Sherman	6.9	17.8	12.3	15.9	12.9	8.8	8.5	8.8	7.9	53.2	12 454	6.1	2.42	12.6	29.4
Temple	7.9	18.1	9.3	17.1	13.8	8.9	8.5	8.7	7.7	51.9	18 153	11.9	2.45	12.8	29.2
Texarkana	7.4	20.1	8.9	15.1	14.5	8.6	8.3	9.5	7.6	54.4	12 475	3.9	2.47	17.6	29.1
Texas City	7.3	21.2	9.1	15.6	15.7	10.5	9.5	6.9	4.1	51.4	15 110	8.6	2.68	14.7	23.7
Tyler	7.2	18.4	12.0	16.1	13.6	9.4	8.5	7.6	7.1	53.0	29 381	13.3	2.49	13.5	30.1
Victoria	8.1	22.2	9.2	16.9	14.7	10.0	7.9	6.6	4.5	51.9	19 777	15.3	2.75	12.7	23.3
Waco	7.6	16.8	18.8	15.7	11.0	7.4	7.9	7.9	6.9	52.2	39 482	4.7	2.45	14.9	30.8
Wichita Falls	8.0	18.1	13.3	18.0	13.3	8.4	8.3	6.9	5.7	50.9	35 470	5.6	2.53	11.6	26.6
UTAH	9.8	26.6	11.6	16.0	13.0	8.0	6.2	5.1	3.6	50.3	537 273	19.5	3.15	9.1	18.9
Bountiful	8.4	26.8	9.6	12.5	11.0	11.2	9.6	6.9	3.9	51.1	11 152	22.4	3.25	8.3	14.8
Layton	11.4	28.3	9.5	18.2	14.3	8.3	5.5	3.3	1.2	49.9	12 730	94.4	3.28	9.7	14.9
Logan	10.7	17.4	25.8	19.3	9.3	4.4	4.2	4.0	4.8	50.1	11 034	19.7	2.87	6.5	21.7
Murray	8.9	21.7	10.0	18.4	13.3	9.6	7.7	6.8	3.5	51.6	11 712	28.2	2.66	10.8	25.6
Ogden	9.2	19.7	11.9	16.9	11.7	7.8	8.1	8.0	6.6	51.2	24 239	0.5	2.57	12.5	28.8
Orem	12.6	31.7	11.3	15.2	11.2	7.0	4.9	3.8	2.3	50.6	17 584	25.9	3.82	8.7	10.8
Provo	9.4	16.3	36.4	17.1	5.9	4.5	3.8	3.5	3.0	51.5	23 805	18.6	3.32	7.6	12.8
St. George	9.1	23.5	12.3	12.1	10.1	6.7	8.2	10.8	7.3	51.4	9 450	162.6	2.96	8.4	18.0
Salt Lake City	8.3	16.7	12.3	19.8	13.9	7.5	6.9	7.5	7.0	50.7	66 657	-1.7	2.33	10.2	35.8
Sandy	10.7	33.5	7.5	14.6	18.9	8.2	3.2	2.1	1.4	49.8	19 423	50.8	3.85	7.1	8.1
West Jordan	12.2	34.4	8.5	18.1	15.2	6.3	2.8	1.8	0.8	49.8	11 143	64.4	3.83	10.3	10.0
West Valley City	10.7	28.9	10.8	17.6	14.4	8.5	4.9	2.7	1.4	50.1	25 933	28.1	3.35	12.7	14.3
VERMONT	7.3	18.1	11.2	16.9	16.4	10.2	8.0	6.6	5.2	51.0	210 650	18.1	2.57	9.2	23.4
Burlington	5.3	10.7	30.5	17.9	12.1	6.7	6.2	5.5	5.1	53.4	14 680	12.3	2.29	10.2	32.1
VIRGINIA	7.2	17.2	11.6	18.4	16.0	10.7	8.1	6.5	4.3	51.0	2 291 830	22.9	2.61	11.1	22.9
Alexandria	5.5	9.8	10.9	27.6	18.0	10.8	7.1	5.9	4.3	52.6	53 280	8.2	2.04	9.1	42.0
Blacksburg	3.5	7.3	53.8	15.0	8.5	4.5	3.3	2.6	1.5	44.8	11 175	23.1	2.37	5.4	24.5
Charlottesville	6.0	11.9	23.5	19.7	12.9	7.2	6.7	6.4	5.8	53.1	16 009	4.0	2.37	12.9	30.6
Chesapeake	8.2	20.7	9.3	19.1	16.8	10.3	7.2	5.6	2.8	51.0	51 965	42.1	2.87	12.7	16.1
Danville	6.5	16.0	9.3	14.4	13.6	10.7	10.8	10.9	7.7	54.4	21 712	23.9	2.38	17.3	30.2
Hampton	7.9	17.1	13.3	19.8	14.0	10.5	7.9	6.4	3.1	51.2	49 673	19.2	2.58	13.5	23.7
Harrisonburg	4.7	10.9	37.0	14.1	10.1	7.1	5.7	5.4	5.0	53.8	10 310	73.9	2.40	10.2	28.2
Lynchburg	6.9	15.8	15.5	14.7	13.0	9.0	8.6	8.8	7.7	55.0	25 143	5.3	2.39	15.6	30.5
Manassas	9.7	18.6	12.0	23.5	17.6	9.4	4.4	2.9	2.0	49.0	9 481	86.7	2.88	9.2	17.0
Newport News	9.2	18.2	12.1	21.7	13.9	8.6	7.0	5.9	3.4	51.0	63 952	23.8	2.59	15.1	23.7
Norfolk	8.3	14.7	21.6	20.1	11.7	6.6	6.5	6.3	4.1	46.7	89 478	1.2	2.55	16.1	26.8
Petersburg	7.4	15.9	11.8	17.0	13.8	9.7	9.5	9.0	6.0	53.8	14 730	-1.4	2.46	23.0	30.3
Portsmouth	8.4	18.2	11.1	18.0	12.9	9.1	8.5	8.7	5.0	52.4	38 741	5.3	2.62	19.3	24.5
Richmond	6.9	14.0	12.9	19.5	14.4	8.6	8.4	8.5	6.8	54.3	85 337	-0.8	2.25	19.8	35.9
Roanoke	7.1	15.2	9.4	18.0	14.6	9.2	9.4	9.5	7.6	53.7	41 030	2.5	2.30	15.7	32.3
Suffolk	7.7	19.4	8.5	16.8	14.2	11.3	9.1	8.0	5.0	52.6	18 516	17.5	2.78	17.1	20.4
Virginia Beach	8.9	19.0	12.8	22.6	15.8	9.1	6.0	3.9	2.0	49.2	135 566	58.9	2.82	9.5	17.1

1. No spouse present.

City	Persons in group quarters, 1990				Serious crimes known to police, 1998[2]				Education, 1990				Money income, 1989		
					Total		Rate[3]		School enrollment		Attainment[4] (percent)			Households	
														Median	
	Total	Persons in mental hospitals	Persons in nursing homes	Persons identified as homeless[1]	Number	Rate[3]	Violent	Property	Public	Private	High school graduate or more	Bachelor's degree or more	Per capita (dollars)[5]	Dollars	Percent change, 1979–1989 (constant 1989 dollars)
	31	32	33	34	35	36	37	38	39	40	41	42	43	44	45
TEXAS—Cont'd															
League City	135	0	135	0	1 197	2 865	117	2 748	8 090	877	89.2	32.3	17 932	45 043	· 3.6
Lewisville	319	0	165	0	3 237	4 947	237	4 710	11 127	1 490	84.7	25.5	15 316	36 006	-6.0
Longview	1 654	21	855	19	4 950	6 469	652	5 817	15 714	2 684	77.4	18.9	12 761	25 377	-12.4
Lubbock	9 215	0	904	62	12 299	6 270	1 021	5 249	58 505	5 047	75.6	26.0	12 322	24 130	-8.5
Lufkin	853	7	660	47	2 402	7 056	643	6 413	7 361	641	68.9	18.8	12 527	22 357	-11.8
McAllen	768	0	432	43	8 003	7 379	298	7 081	26 121	2 017	57.9	19.1	9 814	22 068	-9.2
Mesquite	695	0	695	0	5 898	5 109	343	4 766	25 110	3 195	81.2	18.3	14 115	35 934	-1.2
Midland	776	0	403	64	4 050	4 002	352	3 650	21 706	2 534	78.3	29.0	16 201	31 544	-11.4
Mission	250	0	0	0	2 794	7 048	202	6 846	9 069	472	52.6	12.2	6 887	17 489	-8.5
Missouri City	104	0	104	0	1 113	2 174	166	2 008	10 253	1 713	92.3	39.8	18 764	51 984	-8.6
Nacogdoches	4 370	0	446	33	1 020	3 186	375	2 811	13 908	606	72.8	26.0	9 478	15 917	-18.9
New Braunfels	722	0	487	20	2 241	6 233	248	5 985	6 066	688	68.4	18.5	11 777	26 409	5.2
North Richland Hills	121	0	97	0	2 321	4 203	237	3 966	10 401	1 916	86.4	22.0	15 912	38 354	-2.4
Odessa	868	0	477	70	5 647	6 072	890	5 182	24 136	1 668	69.5	13.6	12 402	24 346	-23.0
Pasadena	875	14	607	12	6 390	4 711	781	3 930	30 795	2 089	69.8	10.9	12 402	28 729	-20.7
Pharr	161	0	27	40	3 012	7 100	740	6 360	11 037	323	41.6	8.4	5 561	15 605	-11.6
Plano	446	53	368	6	8 182	3 894	392	3 502	33 450	5 413	93.2	46.6	21 820	53 905	11.5
Port Arthur	537	0	413	23	3 122	4 517	666	3 851	14 491	1 094	65.5	10.0	9 706	18 548	-28.9
Richardson	572	0	549	0	NA	NA	NA	NA	18 315	2 913	93.3	45.9	21 335	50 240	3.2
Round Rock	328	0	216	0	1 130	1 997	198	1 799	8 471	937	85.0	22.1	12 764	33 228	-14.5
San Angelo	5 026	0	1 175	223	5 095	5 655	366	5 289	23 095	1 477	70.9	17.6	11 353	23 534	-1.0
San Antonio	20 603	624	5 104	742	77 408	7 032	451	6 581	236 083	34 802	69.1	17.8	10 884	23 584	2.2
San Marcos	5 079	110	210	0	2 099	5 658	453	5 205	14 937	482	67.8	27.5	8 103	14 816	-16.2
Sherman	1 500	0	554	0	2 302	6 747	513	6 234	6 920	1 598	75.1	19.2	12 929	24 763	-6.3
Temple	1 561	0	1 309	57	3 466	6 606	425	6 181	10 107	1 176	73.8	20.4	12 914	23 194	-2.6
Texarkana	767	0	610	0	2 636	8 033	893	7 140	7 550	453	70.2	17.5	11 931	21 745	2.5
Texas City	331	0	216	0	4 196	9 632	1 015	8 617	10 678	633	71.4	9.9	11 794	26 144	-26.5
Tyler	2 347	11	1 111	6	6 123	7 238	622	6 616	19 461	2 109	77.1	24.7	13 400	23 661	-12.3
Victoria	703	0	506	4	3 283	5 264	686	4 578	14 265	1 639	70.7	15.8	12 332	25 576	-12.3
Waco	6 819	131	1 472	67	9 535	8 589	1 014	7 575	21 923	12 251	68.4	17.0	10 195	17 852	-11.3
Wichita Falls	6 521	424	1 255	78	5 891	5 811	714	5 097	22 298	2 267	75.5	18.0	11 686	23 560	-5.9
UTAH	28 825	462	6 222	912	115 624	5 506	314	5 192	543 194	67 502	85.1	22.3	11 029	29 470	-0.5
Bountiful	343	66	246	0	462	1 115	155	960	11 691	859	91.6	30.5	14 399	38 346	-5.4
Layton	12	0	0	0	1 139	1 963	107	1 856	13 578	881	88.2	19.7	11 545	34 466	3.0
Logan	1 090	0	247	6	1 281	3 155	113	3 042	14 662	379	90.4	36.8	9 394	21 312	0.2
Murray	103	0	103	0	3 650	10 651	531	10 120	8 158	931	84.2	20.4	13 216	28 950	-6.1
Ogden	1 558	0	452	248	6 067	8 909	634	8 275	16 644	1 211	75.1	16.2	10 754	23 487	-0.9
Orem	416	0	180	0	4 005	4 806	68	4 738	23 570	3 841	90.0	30.4	9 726	31 262	6.8
Provo	7 689	328	241	70	3 902	3 748	146	3 602	17 547	27 699	89.8	34.5	8 408	21 162	-0.2
St. George	483	0	228	6	NA	NA	NA	NA	8 736	332	86.3	19.9	10 520	25 947	14.2
Salt Lake City	4 346	14	886	489	19 337	10 828	820	10 008	42 020	5 084	83.0	30.4	13 482	22 697	2.5
Sandy	335	0	224	0	NA	NA	NA	NA	26 947	2 680	93.1	29.4	12 840	43 971	10.1
West Jordan	247	34	90	0	2 592	4 345	183	4 162	15 733	1 221	86.3	15.9	9 434	33 273	-2.5
West Valley City	231	0	129	0	NA	NA	NA	NA	27 447	1 565	79.7	11.6	9 511	29 510	-11.4
VERMONT	21 576	129	4 809	305	18 552	3 139	106	3 033	120 725	25 263	80.8	24.3	13 527	29 792	20.2
Burlington	5 431	0	444	106	2 505	6 345	248	6 097	11 397	2 954	82.4	34.8	13 918	25 523	16.7
VIRGINIA	208 772	3 931	37 762	2 814	248 576	3 660	326	3 334	1 331 800	214 457	75.2	24.5	15 713	33 328	13.8
Alexandria	2 312	0	1 124	388	6 060	5 162	417	4 745	15 153	5 930	86.9	48.5	25 509	41 472	17.7
Blacksburg	8 100	0	0	0	872	2 515	179	2 336	22 450	835	91.8	61.6	9 750	18 592	-1.4
Charlottesville	2 235	0	474	28	2 700	7 063	1 196	5 867	13 659	1 088	75.5	34.1	12 928	24 190	3.5
Chesapeake	2 644	0	1 022	0	8 411	4 264	431	3 833	35 713	4 926	77.1	16.9	13 817	35 737	13.2
Danville	1 422	0	667	61	2 549	4 955	463	4 492	9 712	1 252	57.4	12.4	11 344	20 413	-11.2
Hampton	5 609	0	938	6	7 360	5 267	383	4 884	28 947	7 620	79.7	19.1	13 099	30 144	6.0
Harrisonburg	6 102	0	499	0	1 409	4 169	317	3 852	12 155	1 556	76.8	28.7	11 607	25 312	8.8
Lynchburg	5 928	0	864	47	3 208	4 869	601	4 268	11 962	7 242	69.5	21.7	12 657	23 726	-7.5
Manassas	695	22	297	5	1 358	3 926	269	3 657	5 850	938	84.2	25.8	18 554	46 674	12.7
Newport News	4 646	167	946	116	9 503	5 359	584	4 775	38 723	5 279	79.3	18.4	12 711	27 469	2.6
Norfolk	33 165	125	1 040	255	16 188	6 998	678	6 320	52 797	7 731	72.7	16.8	11 643	23 563	12.4
Petersburg	2 027	1 327	465	64	3 369	9 786	1 203	8 583	8 028	903	62.2	13.5	10 547	21 309	-5.4
Portsmouth	2 490	125	690	0	7 944	7 917	1 004	6 913	22 950	2 727	66.6	11.6	11 158	24 601	3.4
Richmond	11 105	93	2 614	288	17 684	9 114	1 445	7 669	40 511	8 832	68.1	24.2	13 993	23 551	3.3
Roanoke	1 938	0	698	237	5 364	5 649	570	5 079	17 074	2 124	68.0	15.6	12 513	22 591	1.6
Suffolk	654	0	481	0	3 154	5 124	729	4 395	11 145	1 857	63.9	12.3	11 831	26 125	2.5
Virginia Beach	11 499	264	701	294	17 665	4 050	227	3 823	90 065	15 293	88.0	25.5	15 242	36 271	7.1

1. Persons in emergency shelters and persons visible in street locations.　2. Data for serious crimes have not been adjusted for underreporting. This may affect comparability between geographic areas and over time.　3. Per 100,000 population estimated by the FBI.　4. Persons 25 years old and older.　5. Based on population enumerated as of April 1, 1990.

Table D. Cities — Income, Poverty, and Housing

City	Money income, 1989 (cont'd)				Housing units, 1990										
	House-holds (cont'd)	Percent below poverty, 1989						Occupied units							
		Persons		Fam-ilies					Owner-occupied units				Renter-occu-pied units		
											Owner cost as a percent of income				
	Percent with $100,000 or more	Total	Percent change in rate, 1979–1989	Total	Total	Percent change, 1980–1990	Vacant units for sale or rent[1]	Total	Percent	Median value[2] (dollars)	With a mort-gage	Without a mort-gage	Median rent[3] (dol-lars)	Rent as per-cent of income	Sub-standard units[4] (percent)
	46	47	48	49	50	51	52	53	54	55	56	57	58	59	60
TEXAS—Cont'd															
League City	5.3	4.9	36.1	3.6	11 381	91.4	624	10 586	71.0	69 100	20.6	12.0	555	22.1	5.1
Lewisville	2.1	6.0	46.3	3.9	19 724	126.9	1 674	17 683	51.9	81 600	23.1	13.2	486	23.8	4.2
Longview	2.6	17.0	44.1	13.7	30 293	20.7	2 199	27 206	58.1	56 700	18.0	12.8	346	23.8	4.6
Lubbock	3.1	19.6	36.1	13.3	77 852	16.3	7 303	69 143	55.3	55 500	20.1	12.6	381	29.9	6.4
Lufkin	3.0	20.9	28.2	15.4	12 488	14.0	916	11 222	60.5	47 800	18.6	13.6	350	25.0	6.6
McAllen	3.9	32.7	23.9	27.7	28 597	31.0	1 498	24 905	60.3	56 300	20.1	12.8	340	25.3	20.1
Mesquite	1.8	7.7	48.1	6.3	39 251	76.4	2 699	35 856	63.5	68 700	21.3	12.7	469	24.3	4.7
Midland	5.7	14.4	65.5	11.3	38 453	42.7	4 435	33 169	62.5	62 300	20.1	12.8	368	22.6	6.1
Mission	1.2	37.3	18.8	30.3	10 658	32.0	539	8 315	71.5	40 100	21.6	12.7	247	27.4	21.2
Missouri City	9.4	3.4	36.0	2.0	12 346	50.9	680	11 544	83.0	79 000	21.7	12.4	706	22.6	3.8
Nacogdoches	1.8	31.5	40.0	18.4	12 253	21.8	721	11 306	41.8	59 100	20.3	13.7	346	35.1	4.4
New Braunfels	2.6	14.9	40.6	11.6	11 065	29.5	630	9 997	63.8	65 500	21.1	12.6	420	27.5	8.8
North Richland Hills	3.2	5.1	24.4	3.8	18 121	60.4	1 087	16 901	62.8	82 500	21.9	12.3	478	24.0	3.9
Odessa	2.5	19.4	68.7	15.5	37 751	12.9	3 854	32 826	61.3	43 700	18.7	12.8	313	22.7	8.2
Pasadena	2.3	14.1	83.1	11.1	47 539	7.2	4 020	42 044	51.5	49 000	18.2	12.3	383	23.0	10.7
Pharr	1.1	44.5	18.7	37.7	11 031	80.9	707	8 659	72.8	29 700	22.6	13.1	254	27.4	31.7
Plano	12.9	3.3	-13.2	2.2	47 370	95.3	2 500	44 352	70.1	114 100	22.6	12.0	586	23.3	2.7
Port Arthur	1.5	28.1	58.8	24.0	25 746	6.7	2 022	22 326	65.0	30 400	18.1	13.5	320	26.9	7.3
Richardson	10.7	4.4	41.9	3.1	28 734	13.2	1 342	27 220	70.3	110 000	19.9	11.3	597	24.3	2.8
Round Rock	1.7	9.0	26.8	7.3	11 699	182.5	911	10 568	54.0	69 800	24.0	13.8	446	23.7	5.4
San Angelo	2.3	18.5	42.3	13.7	34 619	22.2	2 688	30 661	59.2	48 300	20.2	13.0	365	25.4	6.2
San Antonio	2.4	22.6	8.1	18.7	365 414	31.5	29 506	326 761	54.0	49 700	20.9	12.7	369	25.3	10.6
San Marcos	0.8	37.1	19.3	21.7	10 923	52.7	888	9 849	31.6	58 200	20.6	13.5	398	35.1	8.8
Sherman	3.0	15.6	64.2	10.8	14 261	10.6	1 381	12 454	57.8	49 800	17.1	12.9	380	23.8	3.4
Temple	3.3	19.2	27.2	14.8	20 718	19.4	2 062	18 153	52.9	55 800	19.1	13.2	354	25.2	4.3
Texarkana	3.2	21.8	5.3	16.7	14 313	9.6	1 433	12 475	57.7	46 000	19.0	13.5	361	26.1	4.0
Texas City	1.6	16.8	64.7	14.6	16 676	11.0	1 159	15 110	61.9	50 300	17.6	13.1	365	24.8	4.2
Tyler	3.7	19.5	44.4	15.2	32 860	15.7	2 840	29 381	52.8	60 000	18.8	13.2	366	26.9	5.9
Victoria	3.2	18.9	33.1	15.7	21 802	19.6	1 546	19 777	58.2	54 400	20.0	12.9	354	24.7	7.3
Waco	1.9	28.7	32.9	19.7	45 088	12.7	4 451	39 482	46.5	43 100	19.4	13.0	353	29.6	6.2
Wichita Falls	2.4	16.6	28.7	13.2	40 364	6.4	3 379	35 470	59.4	47 700	20.3	13.0	365	25.6	3.9
UTAH	2.5	11.4	10.3	8.6	598 388	22.1	28 928	537 273	68.1	68 900	20.9	12.1	369	23.8	5.4
Bountiful	5.9	4.9	19.5	4.2	11 488	21.8	248	11 152	76.4	87 100	17.5	11.1	397	21.9	2.7
Layton	2.0	7.1	34.0	6.1	13 462	93.3	609	12 730	72.2	72 700	21.2	11.1	394	22.2	5.7
Logan	1.4	21.6	19.3	12.7	11 440	15.6	286	11 034	43.2	67 900	19.9	11.6	328	25.2	8.6
Murray	2.6	8.0	3.9	5.9	12 347	27.1	534	11 712	61.0	74 900	20.6	11.7	392	21.8	2.8
Ogden	1.3	16.8	28.2	13.1	27 194	5.9	2 183	24 239	58.8	54 700	20.2	12.4	330	24.6	5.1
Orem	2.9	9.0	-21.7	7.9	17 965	21.2	260	17 584	67.9	73 100	20.9	11.2	362	23.0	6.0
Provo	2.2	29.6	7.2	17.4	24 578	15.5	531	23 805	39.9	74 000	20.7	12.0	336	27.5	11.8
St. George	2.3	12.7	-21.1	7.9	11 766	183.4	731	9 450	65.8	85 100	24.2	11.3	423	25.7	5.8
Salt Lake City	3.4	16.4	15.5	11.9	73 762	1.3	5 494	66 657	49.4	67 200	21.0	12.7	333	24.9	4.3
Sandy	4.7	4.2	-22.2	3.2	20 110	47.0	518	19 423	87.3	87 500	21.9	11.4	500	22.8	2.9
West Jordan	1.2	7.0	2.9	6.6	11 640	64.8	405	11 143	78.8	67 600	22.2	13.4	401	25.7	6.6
West Valley City	0.6	11.5	66.7	10.1	27 367	28.7	1 237	25 933	67.3	58 300	20.8	11.9	390	24.6	6.4
VERMONT	2.8	9.9	-18.5	6.9	271 214	21.5	10 000	210 650	69.0	95 500	21.9	14.7	446	27.1	2.5
Burlington	3.7	19.3	19.1	11.2	15 480	12.5	507	14 680	40.2	113 500	21.9	12.8	493	30.1	2.2
VIRGINIA	5.2	10.2	-13.2	7.7	2 496 334	23.5	118 944	2 291 830	66.3	91 000	21.9	12.5	495	25.8	4.1
Alexandria	8.9	7.1	-21.1	4.7	58 252	11.9	4 099	53 280	40.5	228 600	22.2	12.0	701	25.4	4.8
Blacksburg	2.1	37.4	17.6	12.8	11 857	21.2	595	11 175	31.6	94 300	18.6	11.0	417	35.1	2.1
Charlottesville	2.6	23.7	12.9	10.0	16 785	4.9	487	16 009	42.4	85 600	20.5	12.6	469	29.7	3.0
Chesapeake	2.4	9.0	-19.6	7.0	55 742	46.5	2 988	51 961	73.0	88 200	23.9	13.1	494	26.7	2.9
Danville	1.3	19.0	37.7	15.0	23 297	26.6	1 012	21 712	59.4	47 000	16.4	12.7	278	23.6	3.0
Hampton	1.6	10.8	-7.7	8.8	53 623	22.8	3 288	49 673	59.2	78 200	22.4	13.2	470	26.1	2.6
Harrisonburg	3.0	21.5	31.1	8.4	10 900	76.7	478	10 310	42.1	89 300	21.3	11.6	410	25.9	1.3
Lynchburg	2.8	16.4	25.2	12.8	27 233	7.1	1 483	25 143	58.2	56 900	16.9	12.6	346	24.7	2.2
Manassas	6.6	3.8	-50.6	2.7	10 232	85.7	647	9 481	66.1	150 700	25.3	13.7	695	25.5	3.5
Newport News	2.0	14.0	3.7	12.2	69 728	26.8	4 688	63 952	50.0	85 200	22.7	13.0	439	26.2	3.8
Norfolk	2.2	19.3	-6.8	15.1	98 762	4.1	7 825	89 478	44.0	74 500	23.4	13.5	438	28.5	5.7
Petersburg	1.2	20.3	0.0	15.4	16 196	0.4	985	14 730	50.9	52 000	21.4	12.7	360	27.7	4.4
Portsmouth	1.3	17.7	-7.8	14.9	42 283	9.5	2 961	38 741	55.9	67 400	22.9	13.6	416	28.3	4.6
Richmond	3.4	20.9	8.3	17.4	94 141	2.9	6 457	85 337	46.3	66 600	21.4	14.5	413	27.5	3.2
Roanoke	2.3	16.1	-1.2	12.8	44 384	4.0	2 558	41 030	56.6	54 000	18.8	12.7	336	24.3	2.2
Suffolk	2.5	17.3	0.0	13.9	20 011	19.7	897	18 516	67.7	70 700	22.4	14.3	376	28.7	6.9
Virginia Beach	4.2	5.9	-33.7	4.3	147 037	59.8	8 805	135 566	62.5	96 500	24.9	12.2	577	27.0	2.3

1. Includes units rented or sold but not occupied.   2. Specified owner-occupied units.   3. Specified renter-occupied units.   4. Overcrowded or lacking complete plumbing facilities.

Table D. Cities — Labor Force, Employment, Disability, and Construction

City	Civilian labor force, 1999				Civilian employment, 1990[2]			Disability 1990	Value of residential construction authorized by building permits, 1999		
	Total	Percent change, 1998–1999	Unemployment Total	Rate[1]	Total	Percent Professional, managerial, and technical	Precision production, craft, and repair	Work disabled persons[3] (percent)	New construction ($1,000)	Number of housing units	Percent single family
	61	62	63	64	65	66	67	68	69	70	71
TEXAS—Cont'd											
League City	18 973	-2.0	552	2.9	16 151	43.4	11.7	5.1	117 581	1 160	62.8
Lewisville	43 352	4.9	756	1.7	27 666	34.2	9.5	5.8	78 361	851	57.5
Longview	40 112	-1.6	3 077	7.7	31 711	26.9	12.8	7.8	25 560	277	48.0
Lubbock	104 177	0.1	3 021	2.9	86 820	32.5	9.1	7.3	92 439	969	78.9
Lufkin	15 612	-1.3	888	5.7	12 633	28.4	7.5	8.8	14 535	140	91.4
McAllen	48 052	0.6	4 987	10.4	31 624	31.9	7.7	7.2	62 842	927	90.3
Mesquite	68 596	1.0	1 777	2.6	54 402	29.7	12.8	6.5	97 186	1 289	52.1
Midland	51 282	-5.4	3 517	6.9	41 080	36.1	10.5	7.2	14 245	127	100.0
Mission	13 748	0.1	1 687	12.3	8 857	21.1	10.4	9.1	45 027	732	93.3
Missouri City	31 501	3.4	681	2.2	19 676	45.6	7.9	3.6	64 267	583	100.0
Nacogdoches	14 372	-4.6	643	4.5	13 251	29.5	6.7	6.7	137	2	100.0
New Braunfels	19 487	3.4	485	2.5	11 759	29.3	10.6	8.3	24 214	294	95.9
North Richland Hills	32 826	1.8	775	2.4	25 507	33.3	11.2	5.1	42 620	302	89.1
Odessa	46 828	-4.2	4 784	10.2	38 514	25.9	15.8	8.7	11 935	101	100.0
Pasadena	70 037	0.4	3 489	5.0	54 423	22.2	18.9	7.7	54 910	729	46.8
Pharr	15 502	-1.1	2 660	17.2	9 430	19.4	10.5	9.0	18 541	402	92.3
Plano	132 083	6.6	2 400	1.8	71 973	48.2	5.9	3.4	554 514	5 247	44.0
Port Arthur	25 723	-0.6	3 313	12.9	20 616	20.4	14.3	11.0	6 991	72	100.0
Richardson	55 127	2.0	1 220	2.2	41 250	46.7	5.2	4.3	118 731	636	76.4
Round Rock	32 513	7.1	503	1.5	16 267	32.0	10.9	5.7	209 416	2 969	52.1
San Angelo	42 589	-4.3	1 951	4.6	35 394	27.3	10.8	8.8	32 256	267	100.0
San Antonio	526 726	0.6	18 466	3.5	389 772	29.0	10.7	8.8	564 618	10 891	54.1
San Marcos	22 132	3.6	877	4.0	12 844	29.3	6.9	4.4	21 319	335	23.6
Sherman	17 072	-0.4	838	4.9	14 195	32.2	10.8	9.8	8 558	86	81.4
Temple	27 092	0.4	680	2.5	19 977	32.7	9.4	10.1	25 748	232	98.3
Texarkana	14 428	-2.1	997	6.9	12 543	28.2	10.8	10.2	6 825	93	95.7
Texas City	21 825	-2.0	1 672	7.7	17 617	25.0	18.9	9.1	11 038	120	100.0
Tyler	44 815	-0.6	2 257	5.0	33 307	31.3	8.2	8.0	60 200	408	77.9
Victoria	32 044	-0.7	1 416	4.4	24 073	27.9	13.2	8.8	21 332	198	99.0
Waco	51 587	0.3	2 236	4.3	41 429	27.4	9.7	8.6	28 063	301	67.1
Wichita Falls	46 670	-2.4	2 259	4.8	39 448	28.6	10.6	10.3	18 793	165	100.0
UTAH	1 083 912	2.0	40 498	3.7	736 059	30.8	11.4	7.3	2 296 384	20 547	81.4
Bountiful	24 525	3.2	677	2.8	16 319	39.1	7.3	5.8	21 934	95	91.6
Layton	27 510	3.2	1 002	3.6	18 139	32.2	12.8	6.8	47 855	558	96.1
Logan	22 038	2.0	742	3.4	15 092	34.0	8.4	5.0	18 811	162	88.9
Murray	21 868	1.5	505	2.3	15 467	30.9	11.2	6.6	24 720	130	100.0
Ogden	39 346	1.1	2 564	6.5	26 843	27.7	11.8	11.8	57 803	617	56.9
Orem	40 368	2.8	1 056	2.6	26 162	35.6	10.2	4.9	43 961	531	70.4
Provo	58 913	2.8	2 087	3.5	37 818	34.6	6.8	4.9	49 866	532	32.7
St. George	23 529	4.4	929	3.9	10 723	26.0	10.4	7.3	82 763	760	82.4
Salt Lake City	108 874	1.5	4 322	4.0	75 698	37.4	7.4	9.5	62 281	377	62.1
Sandy	46 210	NA	1 164	2.5	32 614	35.7	9.2	4.9	25 266	174	95.4
West Jordan	26 062	1.5	677	2.6	18 379	26.3	14.4	7.1	149 049	1 465	51.7
West Valley City	57 516	1.5	2 581	4.5	39 774	22.4	15.6	8.7	40 286	511	93.7
VERMONT	335 778	1.7	10 193	3.0	283 146	31.3	12.3	7.9	304 942	2 600	84.1
Burlington	23 698	0.3	545	2.3	20 862	36.2	7.8	7.0	4 918	51	21.6
VIRGINIA	3 521 965	1.0	97 964	2.8	3 028 362	33.8	11.5	7.5	5 142 222	53 151	79.1
Alexandria	75 722	1.5	1 670	2.2	70 756	53.1	4.9	4.9	98 705	1 090	59.3
Blacksburg	15 493	1.8	352	2.3	14 129	51.5	4.6	2.8	9 577	90	71.1
Charlottesville	19 086	0.1	323	1.7	20 198	38.2	8.4	5.6	5 234	70	62.9
Chesapeake	105 309	2.2	2 762	2.6	72 486	30.4	16.1	7.4	170 995	1 635	93.1
Danville	25 077	0.3	1 653	6.6	23 259	21.9	11.5	10.4	4 239	34	100.0
Hampton	66 709	-0.7	2 669	4.0	58 561	30.0	15.1	8.4	25 151	332	100.0
Harrisonburg	18 398	3.5	240	1.3	14 735	32.0	8.2	5.0	28 699	590	31.9
Lynchburg	30 396	1.6	632	2.1	29 569	30.7	8.6	8.7	23 001	187	90.4
Manassas	20 036	2.6	306	1.5	15 808	37.0	10.5	4.7	4 474	64	93.8
Newport News	84 685	1.8	3 377	4.0	72 950	30.6	14.6	8.7	33 948	628	100.0
Norfolk	79 377	-7.3	4 333	5.5	89 580	27.2	12.4	9.2	25 300	233	82.0
Petersburg	15 806	0.3	816	5.2	15 920	21.7	8.2	12.5	1 550	35	100.0
Portsmouth	44 809	-0.8	2 214	4.9	42 053	25.1	16.6	10.7	15 644	247	100.0
Richmond	96 039	-0.2	3 234	3.4	96 229	31.0	7.3	9.3	19 872	248	53.6
Roanoke	48 874	-2.5	1 256	2.6	45 400	24.6	10.4	11.2	18 215	298	61.7
Suffolk	29 958	2.6	1 060	3.5	22 463	26.1	15.8	10.8	74 482	942	86.5
Virginia Beach	212 749	0.1	5 630	2.6	174 616	35.0	11.2	6.0	214 898	2 205	59.0

1. Percent of civilian labor force.   2. Persons 16 years and older.   3. Persons 16 to 64 years old.

City	Wholesale Trade, 1997				Retail Trade[1], 1997				Real Estate and Rental and Leasing, 1997			
	Number of Establishments	Number of Employees	Sales (mil dol)	Annual Payroll (mil dol)	Number of Establishments	Number of Employees	Sales (mil dol)	Annual Payroll (mil dol)	Number of Establishments	Number of Employees	Receipts (mil dol)	Annual Payroll (mil dol)
	72	73	74	75	76	77	78	79	80	81	82	83
TEXAS—Cont'd												
League City	31	161	49.9	4.5	116	1 339	279.8	25.5	34	202	17.5	3.6
Lewisville	95	1 348	773.7	43.6	402	6 554	1 412.4	125.0	72	300	35.8	5.6
Longview	245	2 772	847.9	87.5	583	7 436	1 252.4	121.7	107	452	56.1	10.5
Lubbock	446	6 118	3 705.7	170.6	992	13 893	2 519.8	226.6	285	1 883	132.4	30.5
Lufkin	59	919	193.3	22.6	291	3 824	626.6	57.9	65	229	18.5	4.0
McAllen	295	2 443	966.8	54.6	757	10 916	1 665.7	165.9	168	577	62.4	8.9
Mesquite	88	1 505	1 384.1	48.8	476	8 899	1 572.8	147.3	99	670	55.5	11.4
Midland	223	1 921	1 304.9	67.5	516	6 500	1 199.4	105.6	171	821	77.5	14.5
Mission	36	264	96.7	6.0	136	1 963	314.9	28.8	28	161	8.5	1.6
Missouri City	33	117	35.8	4.2	85	1 163	145.3	15.0	29	168	18.6	3.0
Nacogdoches	37	355	118.3	10.0	230	2 749	431.0	40.4	51	163	17.3	2.6
New Braunfels	65	506	301.5	16.8	262	2 979	584.0	51.9	62	285	20.3	4.2
North Richland Hills	57	270	218.4	11.0	236	4 647	993.9	87.3	41	165	26.3	3.3
Odessa	234	2 279	738.8	73.7	489	5 614	1 063.4	98.2	120	697	64.3	12.4
Pasadena	110	1 583	589.6	56.5	422	5 739	878.2	88.1	120	811	99.9	19.9
Pharr	55	713	201.6	14.0	160	1 587	208.8	21.9	17	76	6.7	0.9
Plano	443	4 766	5 038.9	194.4	804	14 928	3 167.2	290.9	224	1 332	261.6	41.9
Port Arthur	33	1 053	355.0	34.5	215	2 585	399.6	39.0	22	205	22.1	4.5
Richardson	478	10 306	8 145.8	565.8	417	6 096	1 597.7	141.5	159	667	101.7	21.2
Round Rock	70	767	433.2	27.9	162	D	D	D	54	171	17.7	2.6
San Angelo	141	1 282	346.5	29.6	446	5 246	874.8	82.8	128	535	50.6	8.0
San Antonio	1 650	23 198	12 097.5	756.4	3 848	55 174	9 723.6	947.0	1 170	8 005	974.7	187.0
San Marcos	35	D	D	D	285	3 449	599.1	50.5	55	208	28.3	3.5
Sherman	67	569	206.6	15.7	250	4 231	749.1	67.8	63	250	23.0	4.0
Temple	76	2 081	1 271.7	69.5	305	4 196	730.0	71.3	69	325	28.1	5.6
Texarkana	102	1 411	879.6	44.5	331	4 263	768.3	69.6	65	351	42.0	6.1
Texas City	40	223	109.0	9.0	184	3 127	460.0	42.5	37	318	26.0	6.2
Tyler	186	2 189	990.8	71.3	643	8 822	1 692.9	154.3	142	690	73.5	15.5
Victoria	125	D	D	D	379	4 913	846.3	77.9	89	D	D	D
Waco	210	2 956	1 481.1	82.1	601	8 053	1 393.7	128.1	170	938	120.8	19.1
Wichita Falls	176	1 771	391.2	41.0	514	6 450	1 070.1	96.4	129	467	48.3	7.5
UTAH	3 278	44 319	21 115.5	1 420.5	7 656	114 474	19 964.6	1 856.9	2 169	12 318	1 342.6	236.0
Bountiful	51	221	95.9	6.7	142	2 425	510.2	45.7	46	153	18.5	3.2
Layton	41	401	121.1	8.3	208	3 631	676.9	58.0	56	322	28.3	4.6
Logan	53	409	74.9	8.1	248	3 895	500.8	53.8	55	401	22.3	6.4
Murray	186	2 103	967.7	64.1	343	6 445	1 418.9	128.5	103	632	71.0	12.6
Ogden	127	1 654	504.5	45.5	408	6 090	922.8	94.7	96	479	44.9	8.9
Orem	103	1 047	481.7	31.4	420	7 352	1 170.3	116.2	77	349	36.9	5.7
Provo	91	3 704	1 748.9	114.1	252	3 782	638.1	60.9	99	489	49.9	7.6
St. George	66	559	216.8	16.4	332	4 151	784.5	68.4	86	277	28.9	4.0
Salt Lake City	714	13 524	7 479.4	471.0	1 039	15 539	3 041.0	278.5	362	3 606	380.2	80.9
Sandy	NA	NA	NA	NA	NA	NA	NA	NA	NA	NA	NA	NA
West Jordan	53	626	262.3	17.7	97	2 173	330.7	32.8	33	127	14.5	1.5
West Valley City	NA	NA	NA	NA	NA	NA	NA	NA	NA	NA	NA	NA
VERMONT	941	10 987	4 731.4	330.6	4 093	36 306	5 898.6	603.3	701	2 362	240.6	42.2
Burlington	58	678	331.5	24.6	261	3 041	354.9	42.6	62	323	42.0	7.7
VIRGINIA	7 868	106 365	61 046.7	3 784.4	29 032	379 039	62 569.9	6 202.6	6 717	43 976	5 749.2	1 028.4
Alexandria	137	1 830	899.6	75.1	593	7 746	1 507.6	160.0	202	2 023	354.1	57.9
Blacksburg	8	D	D	D	127	1 773	191.3	21.2	37	345	39.7	7.9
Charlottesville	81	954	265.9	29.7	360	4 345	730.3	73.2	97	458	50.1	9.8
Chesapeake	246	3 833	1 768.2	115.7	779	12 554	1 993.3	184.5	144	704	98.0	15.9
Danville	55	964	211.8	22.6	334	3 787	585.5	56.9	59	242	18.1	3.5
Hampton	94	1 073	370.7	31.3	514	9 930	1 638.9	150.5	113	1 241	89.2	20.6
Harrisonburg	62	971	749.2	25.5	308	4 161	690.8	64.0	48	263	30.8	5.5
Lynchburg	100	1 292	504.6	43.8	446	7 209	1 228.5	115.8	95	390	37.4	8.2
Manassas	59	1 008	626.3	41.0	230	3 355	647.5	64.9	51	302	41.1	5.5
Newport News	132	1 634	604.2	50.3	681	9 284	1 488.6	143.6	226	1 720	169.9	35.8
Norfolk	324	5 845	2 914.6	183.9	918	12 628	1 900.4	207.3	273	2 128	203.8	44.2
Petersburg	35	538	139.2	16.8	189	1 764	290.0	29.5	28	131	11.1	2.2
Portsmouth	63	712	167.3	23.6	295	3 291	468.4	51.2	84	457	37.8	7.4
Richmond	464	7 572	5 979.5	283.5	1 013	11 579	1 738.1	193.5	265	2 166	213.5	54.8
Roanoke	299	3 768	1 292.7	121.0	792	12 425	1 843.7	191.3	158	1 861	114.5	31.8
Suffolk	61	1 305	822.5	43.7	212	2 697	380.0	38.0	43	210	24.1	3.4
Virginia Beach	479	5 642	1 922.8	159.4	1 621	21 987	3 342.7	337.2	472	3 101	333.0	66.8

1. Establishments with payroll.

Table D. Cities — Professional Services, Manufacturing, Accommodation and Foodservices

City	Professional, Scientific, and Technical Services, 1997[1]				Manufacturing, 1997				Accommodation and Foodservices, 1997			
	Number of Establishments	Number of Employees	Receipts (mil dol)	Annual Payroll (mil dol)	Number of Establishments	Number of Employees	Receipts (mil dol)	Annual Payroll (mil dol)	Number of Establishments	Number of Employees	Sales (mil dol)	Annual Payroll (mil dol)
	84	85	86	87	88	89	90	91	92	93	94	95
TEXAS—Cont'd												
League City	58	176	15.9	5.6	NA	NA	NA	NA	46	966	34.2	9.4
Lewisville	106	640	62.7	20.9	85	5 347	930.8	219.5	134	3 713	122.2	35.0
Longview	246	1 416	110.8	43.0	135	10 208	3 074.3	374.8	213	3 927	128.0	37.0
Lubbock	474	2 495	197.1	67.2	210	6 357	1 465.0	182.3	488	10 760	321.1	84.3
Lufkin	99	487	43.0	14.2	52	5 006	763.2	120.1	102	1 781	56.8	16.4
McAllen	302	1 677	124.3	38.6	100	3 709	511.4	69.5	253	6 005	188.6	50.0
Mesquite	121	514	36.2	13.0	72	3 338	1 147.3	111.1	168	4 278	148.4	40.5
Midland	323	1 898	228.7	70.7	73	901	119.1	32.4	225	D	D	D
Mission	16	52	3.9	1.3	27	1 176	177.9	22.1	70	923	30.8	8.0
Missouri City	54	D	D	D	18	675	163.4	28.3	39	531	17.9	4.4
Nacogdoches	46	174	12.7	3.1	36	3 101	719.6	92.5	78	1 789	54.0	14.9
New Braunfels	89	302	23.5	7.3	59	3 525	449.9	86.2	128	2 762	72.7	20.7
North Richland Hills	81	573	38.1	18.0	33	1 980	405.3	59.4	91	2 570	76.8	21.3
Odessa	181	949	65.4	25.1	120	1 886	758.9	62.1	217	3 704	117.9	32.4
Pasadena	137	1 410	176.9	69.1	100	5 905	4 893.4	270.7	174	3 081	108.6	28.8
Pharr	30	112	8.5	2.2	NA	NA	NA	NA	48	678	25.1	5.9
Plano	683	3 535	535.3	179.3	124	8 614	2 547.5	448.6	347	8 108	298.8	83.9
Port Arthur	50	355	27.5	10.2	33	3 915	6 712.2	234.9	86	1 265	44.5	12.2
Richardson	521	4 020	459.1	191.2	179	11 246	3 350.5	444.5	205	3 633	149.7	39.4
Round Rock	83	870	152.9	40.6	69	D	D	D	102	2 130	77.2	21.5
San Angelo	149	735	58.1	16.2	85	4 323	803.4	101.8	184	3 706	108.6	32.0
San Antonio	2 507	19 099	1 831.9	729.7	953	32 870	5 199.7	911.6	2 237	50 503	1 844.1	509.4
San Marcos	61	251	20.5	6.1	42	1 972	245.7	54.0	131	2 444	74.6	20.6
Sherman	108	484	34.6	12.9	58	6 992	2 672.0	274.4	95	1 921	63.6	17.6
Temple	77	602	49.1	20.6	59	5 515	1 164.7	183.0	130	2 497	77.5	20.8
Texarkana	108	503	50.5	15.1	49	2 717	608.3	90.3	102	2 081	70.2	17.1
Texas City	53	304	20.9	9.3	27	5 408	8 922.0	327.2	82	1 471	42.8	11.5
Tyler	325	2 173	256.0	83.9	115	9 228	2 068.8	339.0	228	5 027	152.5	41.6
Victoria	135	705	58.4	21.0	60	2 765	1 195.5	111.0	147	2 680	78.5	21.5
Waco	241	1 910	125.0	54.7	177	14 884	3 608.3	444.3	276	5 511	177.4	48.3
Wichita Falls	200	1 037	83.4	30.6	121	6 090	1 069.6	206.0	234	D	D	D
UTAH	4 282	36 468	3 306.1	1 303.1	2 860	119 140	24 014.4	3 726.1	3 780	74 390	2 309.0	648.8
Bountiful	115	516	31.3	12.1	37	504	54.1	12.3	57	1 026	26.6	7.6
Layton	56	340	21.4	10.5	NA	NA	NA	NA	94	2 520	66.1	18.6
Logan	101	777	42.4	16.9	79	5 455	909.8	124.5	85	1 561	41.9	10.5
Murray	198	2 165	255.9	93.1	148	2 680	247.3	61.9	95	2 186	62.1	18.2
Ogden	200	1 932	123.4	53.2	130	13 226	2 696.5	410.9	183	3 153	84.0	24.2
Orem	188	2 031	112.8	46.3	99	2 359	272.6	61.3	103	2 253	59.3	15.8
Provo	199	2 966	268.1	114.6	93	3 367	346.7	79.8	142	3 759	105.8	31.6
St. George	105	552	33.7	14.0	60	1 377	191.3	35.5	133	2 961	83.9	24.4
Salt Lake City	1 123	12 408	1 400.3	558.4	512	25 306	4 894.8	813.8	638	15 653	572.6	157.4
Sandy	NA	NA	NA	NA	92	2 662	309.5	82.1	NA	NA	NA	NA
West Jordan	31	74	5.1	1.5	76	2 567	433.5	91.1	61	1 054	30.7	8.3
West Valley City	NA	NA	NA	NA	170	6 627	1 199.4	230.8	NA	NA	NA	NA
VERMONT	1 622	7 792	719.1	279.0	1 226	42 533	7 803.0	1 459.6	1 932	27 088	910.2	277.2
Burlington	203	1 597	147.9	62.4	55	D	D	D	136	1 862	66.4	19.1
VIRGINIA	17 539	212 632	24 151.7	9 729.8	5 986	370 595	83 814.0	11 557.8	12 343	233 639	8 281.2	2 320.7
Alexandria	894	12 710	1 456.2	634.2	114	1 907	328.1	59.4	310	6 616	308.3	92.3
Blacksburg	99	1 046	105.0	38.0	23	1 910	225.3	57.8	72	1 689	42.9	11.6
Charlottesville	206	1 448	118.7	49.7	67	D	D	D	179	3 521	121.5	34.7
Chesapeake	263	2 653	198.1	84.5	132	4 558	1 085.0	147.0	305	6 321	187.4	51.6
Danville	76	577	27.3	11.6	47	D	D	D	114	2 159	65.7	18.8
Hampton	211	3 190	270.9	120.4	80	4 636	971.0	123.4	229	5 002	149.9	41.1
Harrisonburg	95	618	50.9	19.6	38	3 687	725.8	102.6	109	2 318	70.2	19.0
Lynchburg	182	2 715	260.3	107.1	117	12 535	3 096.4	481.1	173	3 808	110.8	30.9
Manassas	153	1 058	126.9	44.8	34	2 822	791.6	188.5	74	D	D	D
Newport News	286	3 023	218.8	88.6	131	24 707	3 300.5	898.4	312	5 464	170.1	47.7
Norfolk	439	6 582	468.7	207.0	199	10 996	5 737.3	402.2	539	9 980	299.4	85.1
Petersburg	45	1 122	79.8	42.1	43	2 553	409.6	72.4	83	1 194	34.2	10.1
Portsmouth	105	1 023	82.1	31.5	71	1 812	368.7	52.0	137	2 040	58.7	15.8
Richmond	732	8 113	853.7	356.0	325	21 879	11 748.3	941.2	551	9 087	304.2	91.4
Roanoke	331	2 632	211.6	88.7	152	8 489	2 156.3	242.9	325	6 380	203.4	58.7
Suffolk	59	273	21.4	9.2	52	2 257	1 103.5	63.8	62	1 027	32.8	8.9
Virginia Beach	895	8 910	726.1	302.6	236	5 806	967.2	139.2	888	18 145	576.3	163.3

1. Firms subject to federal tax.

City	Arts, Entertainment, and Recreation[1], 1997				Health Care and Social Assistance[1], 1997				Other Services[1], 1997			
	Number of Establish-ments	Number of Employees	Receipts (mil dol)	Annual Payroll (mil dol)	Number of Establish-ments	Number of Employees	Receipts (mil dol)	Annual Payroll (mil dol)	Number of Establish-ments	Number of Employees	Receipts (mil dol)	Annual Payroll (mil dol)
	96	97	98	99	100	101	102	103	104	105	106	107
TEXAS—Cont'd												
League City	16	188	10.9	2.6	69	843	42.4	19.1	77	697	40.7	13.9
Lewisville	14	163	8.0	2.6	142	2 024	151.4	57.4	122	816	57.9	16.8
Longview	22	266	8.8	2.8	288	4 662	285.4	120.5	176	1 336	85.5	23.5
Lubbock	56	503	29.8	6.6	586	8 074	556.8	235.6	354	2 842	163.8	48.8
Lufkin	9	0	0.0	0.0	170	2 914	162.7	69.7	115	594	40.5	11.1
McAllen	16	282	13.7	2.5	436	8 354	663.1	251.5	179	1 169	52.9	15.7
Mesquite	25	514	17.3	4.9	235	3 408	238.2	90.9	167	1 020	65.0	19.6
Midland	28	0	0.0	0.0	238	2 931	248.9	101.2	186	1 226	84.8	21.7
Mission	5	172	5.5	1.5	83	1 148	54.6	26.5	62	320	13.9	3.9
Missouri City	3	0	0.0	0.0	80	1 196	76.1	29.2	44	228	11.6	3.6
Nacogdoches	10	0	0.0	0.0	148	2 224	127.6	48.3	63	397	15.9	5.4
New Braunfels	20	111	3.5	1.0	128	1 220	63.5	26.3	88	455	25.2	7.2
North Richland Hills	13	277	7.1	2.5	91	1 616	109.9	44.2	95	525	30.1	9.7
Odessa	32	231	8.1	1.6	220	3 646	164.0	69.1	175	1 168	128.6	24.1
Pasadena	18	195	6.9	2.2	308	4 293	298.3	116.7	184	1 502	87.4	33.6
Pharr	4	21	1.1	0.2	54	1 030	32.1	12.0	53	314	11.6	3.5
Plano	57	979	49.6	13.2	582	6 465	591.2	227.3	280	1 758	108.0	34.1
Port Arthur	7	79	2.8	0.9	126	1 934	153.4	59.0	63	396	21.3	6.0
Richardson	24	433	19.8	6.0	330	3 203	195.2	80.3	183	1 408	99.3	33.6
Round Rock	12	111	4.1	1.6	103	1 208	87.1	34.6	81	670	39.7	12.5
San Angelo	16	0	0.0	0.0	180	3 316	207.7	91.1	167	912	53.8	15.3
San Antonio	233	8 152	343.9	104.2	2 525	47 329	2 859.8	1 165.6	1 821	13 038	723.0	233.0
San Marcos	10	72	2.9	0.8	101	1 129	66.8	29.2	64	343	14.0	4.2
Sherman	10	60	1.8	0.5	160	2 632	147.5	68.3	66	317	15.0	4.4
Temple	19	256	7.4	2.4	139	4 347	333.1	111.0	112	613	28.8	9.5
Texarkana	12	0	0.0	0.0	194	3 204	208.9	101.9	92	616	34.9	10.3
Texas City	9	53	2.0	0.5	82	1 712	77.9	40.7	56	248	13.3	3.6
Tyler	23	386	33.3	6.2	374	4 539	375.6	176.6	194	1 722	90.1	28.7
Victoria	15	0	0.0	0.0	228	0	0.0	0.0	132	900	53.7	15.8
Waco	29	431	18.9	6.7	293	4 296	238.5	115.2	210	1 389	73.9	24.1
Wichita Falls	23	319	14.4	3.7	235	3 396	193.7	77.9	182	1 296	70.8	22.9
UTAH	480	9 444	412.4	137.7	3 851	46 989	2 988.8	1 226.7	2 728	17 612	1 090.5	312.6
Bountiful	10	98	2.7	0.9	157	1 892	108.3	46.9	67	372	17.5	5.2
Layton	7	79	2.8	0.9	68	1 164	103.1	43.3	44	341	16.0	4.5
Logan	13	190	4.3	1.8	139	1 207	77.1	26.6	83	425	23.4	6.3
Murray	15	64	3.0	0.8	185	2 209	149.7	71.9	135	901	55.4	16.3
Ogden	24	471	9.5	3.2	216	2 855	197.0	76.6	156	1 097	58.0	17.8
Orem	24	258	7.9	2.3	143	2 013	97.0	39.2	107	849	37.3	10.7
Provo	21	609	11.8	4.4	233	2 874	177.7	82.2	121	863	36.7	11.0
St. George	18	0	0.0	0.0	166	1 501	104.0	37.7	75	356	27.3	7.2
Salt Lake City	71	1 709	150.4	60.6	567	8 700	668.8	265.0	445	3 886	262.3	80.8
Sandy	NA	NA	NA	NA	NA	NA	NA	NA	NA	NA	NA	NA
West Jordan	5	88	2.9	0.7	78	971	60.9	25.2	52	255	15.2	4.1
West Valley City	NA	NA	NA	NA	NA	NA	NA	NA	NA	NA	NA	NA
VERMONT	293	5 450	226.9	61.4	1 262	11 481	631.6	273.9	1 171	4 490	304.7	76.4
Burlington	15	96	21.3	4.3	112	1 937	120.0	55.7	74	469	34.4	11.3
VIRGINIA	1 613	26 624	1 397.9	392.9	12 014	150 797	9 859.6	4 417.9	11 301	68 807	4 397.2	1 360.3
Alexandria	35	357	32.1	13.4	323	2 788	216.5	105.2	267	1 919	122.4	42.9
Blacksburg	6	0	0.0	0.0	60	1 216	84.7	31.6	42	246	9.4	3.6
Charlottesville	21	292	27.9	9.6	162	2 092	138.9	54.6	133	827	41.6	14.5
Chesapeake	29	482	17.6	4.4	338	3 228	195.7	87.9	305	2 846	241.4	53.0
Danville	12	61	2.0	0.6	126	1 459	89.6	42.0	123	735	36.0	10.2
Hampton	29	251	10.6	2.6	192	1 976	106.4	51.9	178	1 129	64.8	20.9
Harrisonburg	12	147	3.5	1.3	116	1 538	90.7	41.6	84	434	28.1	7.5
Lynchburg	22	212	5.6	1.5	177	2 893	171.0	86.8	152	933	51.6	15.6
Manassas	10	174	5.7	1.7	106	1 161	67.1	34.9	108	832	60.2	22.2
Newport News	31	516	17.2	4.3	324	3 878	217.6	122.3	306	2 234	116.3	41.1
Norfolk	49	707	27.3	7.4	400	6 583	451.7	219.1	388	2 569	147.8	49.7
Petersburg	9	79	5.1	0.9	89	1 438	64.1	32.6	76	620	32.6	12.0
Portsmouth	17	108	7.1	1.3	170	2 393	134.8	71.8	163	1 364	74.6	27.2
Richmond	45	840	25.1	10.0	540	14 788	1 111.6	414.8	504	3 887	256.6	82.0
Roanoke	34	674	17.4	5.4	274	3 623	274.3	127.4	337	2 403	123.8	43.2
Suffolk	4	0	0.0	0.0	89	1 334	69.9	34.9	85	453	22.2	6.7
Virginia Beach	131	1 656	89.3	18.7	809	8 315	473.4	223.9	716	4 870	254.7	89.2

1. Firms subject to federal tax.

Table D. Cities — Federal Funds and City Government Finances

City	Selected federal funds, fiscal 1999[1] (mil dol)									City government finances, 1997						
	Procurement contracts		Grants					Direct payments for individuals		General revenue						
										Intergovernmental			Taxes			
														Per capita[3] (dollars)		
	Defense	Other	Total[2]	Health and family welfare	Energy and environment	Education	Housing and community development	Educational assistance	Housing assistance	Total (mil dol)	Total (mil dol)	Percent from state government	Total (mil dol)	Total	Property	Sales and gross receipts
	108	109	110	111	112	113	114	115	116	117	118	119	120	121	122	123
TEXAS—Cont'd																
League City	0.0	0.8	1.8	1.7	0.0	0.0	0.0	0.0	0.0	25.8	0.0	**********	16.8	414	282	118
Lewisville	73.8	2.4	1.8	0.1	0.0	0.9	0.7	0.0	1.4	45.8	0.7	87.8	30.0	487	205	249
Longview	0.4	0.1	3.7	0.2	0.0	0.0	1.9	1.2	2.7	49.1	3.9	12.8	33.4	448	203	238
Lubbock	8.4	4.4	35.3	11.1	1.0	3.2	6.1	8.8	14.0	165.3	60.5	83.7	51.1	264	113	146
Lufkin	0.0	0.9	0.3	0.0	0.0	0.0	0.1	1.6	0.9	26.4	0.8	100.0	16.3	493	191	296
McAllen	67.4	4.4	7.2	0.4	0.0	0.3	3.7	12.0	3.0	88.7	5.7	25.4	39.7	384	135	244
Mesquite	1.1	0.0	3.4	0.0	0.0	1.6	1.1	1.1	1.2	75.2	4.0	11.2	45.6	408	162	238
Midland	0.0	0.6	9.4	1.4	0.0	0.2	1.9	1.4	0.0	71.7	1.9	40.7	36.8	379	184	188
Mission	0.0	0.5	3.1	0.0	0.0	0.3	1.4	0.0	1.0	21.3	0.5	100.0	12.0	317	138	173
Missouri City	0.1	0.0	0.1	0.0	0.0	0.0	0.1	0.0	0.0	16.6	1.5	5.7	14.0	251	165	68
Nacogdoches	0.4	0.5	6.2	3.6	0.0	1.4	0.2	3.7	4.2	18.9	1.6	7.7	10.3	331	154	170
New Braunfels	5.6	3.5	2.3	0.5	0.0	0.0	0.5	0.0	0.5	22.6	0.7	85.5	11.1	326	118	196
North Richland Hills	0.0	0.5	0.0	0.0	0.0	0.0	0.0	0.0	0.1	37.6	1.4	100.0	24.5	461	176	269
Odessa	0.1	0.6	9.6	4.3	0.0	1.6	2.2	2.3	2.4	55.8	3.8	17.1	24.1	265	109	154
Pasadena	1.0	0.0	5.3	0.0	0.0	0.0	4.0	5.3	4.0	73.5	5.7	9.9	47.1	358	146	205
Pharr	0.0	0.1	2.9	0.0	0.0	1.0	1.5	0.0	0.0	16.9	2.3	100.0	7.6	188	80	102
Plano	52.5	6.8	5.0	1.4	0.0	0.2	1.4	0.0	0.1	153.3	2.3	15.0	96.9	504	252	227
Port Arthur	3.5	0.3	7.2	2.7	0.0	0.0	3.3	1.0	7.7	35.6	4.7	58.7	13.5	234	120	112
Richardson	124.1	9.8	10.2	5.2	0.7	0.5	0.0	2.9	0.0	101.2	1.5	100.0	53.6	661	284	360
Round Rock	194.4	89.5	0.2	0.0	0.0	0.0	0.2	0.3	0.0	28.9	0.2	46.5	18.8	359	139	205
San Angelo	0.2	0.2	8.5	4.3	0.0	0.3	0.8	2.4	3.4	47.1	4.4	25.7	27.4	311	174	132
San Antonio	779.2	206.9	257.8	147.4	0.1	24.5	41.6	36.3	13.9	776.9	131.0	55.0	317.2	297	147	139
San Marcos	0.5	43.0	13.7	6.2	1.0	2.9	1.1	4.8	0.3	24.1	1.7	81.3	12.1	345	36	299
Sherman	0.5	4.6	1.2	0.1	0.0	0.0	0.7	0.7	0.6	28.4	0.9	29.8	15.6	469	196	264
Temple	7.2	8.1	4.1	0.6	1.9	0.0	1.2	0.9	3.6	42.1	3.3	53.0	22.6	439	149	285
Texarkana	2.2	18.0	2.6	0.0	0.0	0.7	1.5	1.4	4.0	28.7	2.6	47.6	15.0	463	151	308
Texas City	3.4	0.0	1.7	0.0	0.0	0.2	0.7	0.7	0.8	40.1	0.7	20.7	20.1	475	284	186
Tyler	23.8	3.5	7.9	3.6	0.0	0.7	2.6	5.2	4.5	62.9	6.5	4.4	29.3	357	118	232
Victoria	1.1	1.2	6.6	2.6	0.0	2.4	0.9	1.6	0.3	42.7	3.6	55.5	25.1	410	193	210
Waco	99.0	2.1	31.0	20.5	2.5	2.0	2.8	8.4	12.8	96.2	10.6	49.8	46.7	431	173	253
Wichita Falls	2.1	1.6	9.1	3.3	0.0	2.1	2.1	1.6	5.2	64.4	8.1	28.8	33.9	338	168	163
UTAH	548.1	720.2	1 993.7	923.5	49.1	189.0	31.0	69.5	13.6	X	X	X	X	X	X	X
Bountiful	0.8	0.8	0.0	0.0	0.0	0.0	0.0	0.1	0.0	16.2	1.7	47.7	8.3	211	52	147
Layton	0.5	1.5	1.1	0.0	0.0	0.0	0.0	0.0	1.9	25.1	1.3	70.4	13.0	255	77	160
Logan	21.3	6.4	39.4	8.8	0.3	7.3	0.0	7.7	0.0	25.8	1.7	48.8	9.3	238	43	172
Murray	0.7	0.2	4.7	0.1	0.0	0.0	0.0	0.1	0.0	25.6	3.3	21.9	15.2	458	117	321
Ogden	20.6	37.2	21.0	2.3	1.0	1.5	1.7	6.3	3.6	57.0	6.5	24.9	31.2	474	199	247
Orem	0.4	0.3	7.6	0.6	0.0	0.9	0.8	3.7	0.0	38.2	2.8	49.4	21.2	266	68	183
Provo	4.4	2.5	19.2	5.6	1.2	1.4	3.8	8.8	0.0	48.0	5.6	32.4	23.6	237	64	156
St. George	0.2	1.4	4.4	0.0	0.0	0.9	0.0	1.8	0.7	33.7	1.1	88.5	14.6	340	113	206
Salt Lake City	242.8	50.9	632.8	206.9	43.4	67.7	21.4	13.9	1.8	314.4	55.5	9.4	121.0	701	362	300
Sandy	0.1	0.1	0.9	0.5	0.0	0.0	0.0	0.0	0.0	38.2	3.4	55.9	23.9	NA	NA	NA
West Jordan	0.6	0.0	0.1	0.0	0.0	0.0	0.0	0.0	0.0	26.3	1.4	80.1	13.5	235	63	141
West Valley City	0.0	0.6	1.6	0.0	0.0	0.0	0.0	0.0	0.0	43.5	5.5	42.6	26.9	NA	NA	NA
VERMONT	213.7	62.5	883.2	482.0	35.5	78.9	17.1	31.7	3.0	X	X	X	X	X	X	X
Burlington	185.7	3.6	75.4	49.4	2.0	3.9	1.1	6.2	1.2	47.3	6.4	27.3	16.1	412	352	42
VIRGINIA	12 388.3	6 656.1	4 748.8	2 307.8	93.8	521.9	115.3	436.1	108.6	X	X	X	X	X	X	X
Alexandria	900.0	211.6	58.6	14.5	3.9	12.9	3.0	11.9	5.2	367.7	87.8	69.3	216.4	1 840	1 324	362
Blacksburg	10.9	4.3	65.1	4.1	4.2	1.3	0.0	4.1	1.2	15.9	5.6	59.3	4.8	141	51	46
Charlottesville	111.5	8.2	137.0	90.7	2.5	5.0	2.1	3.6	0.2	82.6	25.2	86.8	44.3	1 087	681	383
Chesapeake	91.8	9.1	2.1	0.0	0.0	0.0	3.2	0.0	7.2	424.5	163.4	95.7	221.5	1 152	793	256
Danville	0.1	0.4	7.3	1.0	0.0	1.9	3.1	1.2	2.8	106.7	50.0	95.5	32.2	602	336	184
Hampton	30.0	191.6	59.0	3.1	1.1	4.6	3.4	5.2	1.7	294.8	118.5	92.2	125.3	903	607	231
Harrisonburg	0.2	3.4	2.4	0.2	0.0	0.2	0.0	2.8	1.0	57.7	14.9	98.0	31.7	947	450	381
Lynchburg	6.2	166.0	8.8	2.3	3.7	0.1	1.2	4.1	3.9	159.2	55.2	99.4	68.6	1 019	1 013	0
Manassas	386.3	47.0	35.1	4.3	0.7	0.6	0.0	0.1	1.2	76.4	21.7	98.3	40.7	1 225	943	220
Newport News	555.0	92.6	12.1	4.1	0.5	0.6	4.3	2.9	9.8	397.6	169.5	86.9	171.0	971	662	240
Norfolk	1 346.0	137.3	58.1	19.7	3.7	12.8	10.1	9.8	2.8	687.8	279.6	81.2	245.3	1 051	616	352
Petersburg	7.6	8.2	10.2	0.3	0.0	2.4	1.5	3.4	0.5	78.5	43.5	88.4	30.5	798	518	200
Portsmouth	192.9	6.2	8.9	0.8	0.0	0.6	5.5	7.9	1.6	243.6	122.8	88.4	85.2	841	561	226
Richmond	78.2	50.9	824.4	277.6	59.0	139.1	41.8	8.7	4.3	727.0	301.3	81.7	276.1	1 393	923	354
Roanoke	79.1	5.6	23.0	8.3	0.0	1.6	3.4	2.4	7.2	264.9	111.1	82.0	114.3	1 197	681	396
Suffolk	44.0	4.3	1.5	0.6	0.0	0.0	0.7	0.1	0.0	120.7	59.0	90.7	48.9	831	600	164
Virginia Beach	247.3	28.3	7.0	0.1	0.0	0.0	4.0	7.2	9.8	859.9	317.1	96.2	437.8	1 017	693	257

1. October 1, 1998 to September 30, 1999.   2. Includes program categories not shown separately. State totals include additional categories not allocated by city.   3. Based on population estimated as of July 1 of the year shown.

Table D. Cities — City Government Finances

City	City government finances, 1997 (cont'd)												
				General expenditure									
	Per capita[1] (dollars)			Percent of total for —									
	Total (mil dol)	Total	Capital outlays	Public welfare	Highways	Parking facilities	Education	Health and hospitals	Police protection	Sewerage and sanitation	Parks and recreation	Housing and community development	Interest on debt
	124	125	126	127	128	129	130	131	132	133	134	135	136
TEXAS—Cont'd													
League City	26.0	640	94	0.0	17.0	0.0	0.0	2.1	15.1	11.7	2.6	0.0	6.8
Lewisville	37.6	612	127	0.2	11.7	0.0	0.0	2.1	20.0	16.6	9.2	0.0	6.3
Longview	53.5	718	111	4.4	15.8	0.0	0.0	5.8	17.8	15.2	6.0	2.4	8.8
Lubbock	123.2	637	120	0.0	9.4	0.0	0.0	3.0	17.2	19.5	6.9	3.2	7.3
Lufkin	24.8	749	109	0.0	24.0	1.1	0.0	3.1	18.3	19.2	3.0	0.0	2.8
McAllen	38.9	376	16	1.4	4.9	0.5	0.0	1.1	25.7	6.3	12.9	3.8	4.2
Mesquite	90.0	804	149	0.0	14.2	0.0	0.1	1.5	18.0	10.6	7.9	3.9	8.4
Midland	72.9	750	127	0.0	6.2	0.0	0.0	3.4	15.6	24.5	6.1	1.8	3.8
Mission	18.9	500	8	0.0	11.9	0.0	0.0	0.1	22.1	22.4	8.5	1.9	0.2
Missouri City	21.3	381	138	0.0	16.4	0.0	0.0	0.0	28.7	11.7	7.2	0.0	8.8
Nacogdoches	20.7	664	178	0.0	2.5	1.8	0.0	1.2	13.3	28.7	4.4	15.0	4.2
New Braunfels	20.5	605	8	0.0	6.9	0.0	0.0	5.0	18.6	22.1	11.0	0.0	3.4
North Richland Hills	20.1	378	0	0.0	8.0	0.0	0.0	2.9	29.1	0.0	6.9	4.3	6.4
Odessa	52.5	578	48	0.6	12.0	0.1	0.0	0.0	23.1	17.9	4.5	3.6	5.4
Pasadena	65.0	494	92	0.6	7.9	0.0	0.0	1.6	26.9	10.8	8.6	8.0	7.0
Pharr	16.4	407	14	0.0	9.9	0.0	0.0	0.0	21.3	15.0	2.9	5.0	17.3
Plano	148.9	774	143	0.0	11.2	0.0	0.2	1.0	13.0	16.1	8.6	2.4	10.3
Port Arthur	46.4	805	46	0.0	12.2	0.0	0.0	2.2	16.9	17.9	1.5	4.5	15.9
Richardson	96.2	1 185	250	0.0	8.7	0.0	0.0	0.8	16.4	15.4	8.5	0.0	4.5
Round Rock	26.6	507	121	0.2	14.8	0.0	0.0	0.8	17.4	7.4	11.7	0.0	9.8
San Angelo	46.5	528	67	0.0	9.9	0.0	0.0	8.6	23.5	7.7	13.6	2.3	4.9
San Antonio	856.9	802	153	3.6	9.1	0.5	2.9	4.3	17.8	13.1	9.6	2.2	6.6
San Marcos	35.7	1 020	337	3.8	14.6	0.0	0.0	0.9	11.7	14.2	12.2	1.3	16.2
Sherman	21.1	636	54	0.0	9.1	0.1	0.0	0.0	19.9	19.6	5.0	1.1	4.9
Temple	41.7	812	179	0.0	7.8	0.0	0.0	2.2	15.2	11.4	7.1	3.2	0.8
Texarkana	27.6	849	103	0.0	8.0	0.0	0.0	5.0	17.6	21.0	3.9	2.5	3.9
Texas City	39.6	934	71	0.0	13.8	0.0	0.0	0.6	15.3	14.1	11.8	1.6	21.3
Tyler	54.3	660	7	7.3	9.5	0.0	0.0	0.0	20.5	14.2	4.3	1.9	18.5
Victoria	34.8	570	38	0.0	11.9	0.0	0.0	1.6	22.9	14.9	5.2	1.4	8.6
Waco	90.4	834	125	0.5	9.7	0.0	0.0	4.7	16.5	16.6	10.9	1.4	13.3
Wichita Falls	67.1	670	57	0.0	8.7	0.0	0.0	5.0	16.5	16.0	4.9	6.7	2.0
UTAH	X	X	X	X	X	X	X	X	X	X	X	X	X
Bountiful	21.0	530	218	0.0	10.4	0.0	0.0	0.0	37.5	11.0	14.5	0.6	1.1
Layton	23.9	470	139	0.0	20.0	0.0	0.0	0.0	19.2	20.4	18.5	0.0	1.9
Logan	27.7	704	74	0.0	9.6	0.0	0.0	2.7	12.6	22.3	10.1	0.6	3.7
Murray	23.9	723	143	0.0	19.5	0.0	0.0	0.0	25.9	6.7	16.0	2.2	1.2
Ogden	49.1	747	172	0.0	8.0	0.0	0.0	3.0	11.2	12.4	13.7	5.7	8.0
Orem	38.5	483	112	0.0	18.6	0.0	0.0	0.0	15.1	16.0	4.9	5.0	1.5
Provo	56.1	564	147	0.0	4.0	0.0	0.0	0.0	15.2	7.5	6.6	6.9	7.5
St. George	32.5	759	244	0.0	11.8	0.0	0.0	0.0	12.9	18.5	35.1	0.1	3.9
Salt Lake City	275.8	1 598	447	0.0	10.4	0.0	0.0	0.0	12.4	7.7	5.5	5.8	7.6
Sandy	42.3	NA	NA	0.0	17.5	0.0	0.0	0.0	17.6	5.7	11.2	3.0	5.2
West Jordan	26.4	458	125	0.0	9.1	0.0	0.0	0.0	20.4	12.8	16.2	0.6	3.0
West Valley City	85.1	NA	NA	0.0	8.0	0.0	0.0	0.0	10.5	0.9	53.6	8.2	1.1
VERMONT	X	X	X	X	X	X	X	X	X	X	X	X	X
Burlington	47.6	1 220	190	0.0	4.8	3.8	0.0	0.1	12.3	10.0	5.9	12.9	10.3
VIRGINIA	X	X	X	X	X	X	X	X	X	X	X	X	X
Alexandria	348.0	2 959	250	8.6	5.9	1.4	29.2	6.8	7.8	7.2	4.3	2.9	3.9
Blacksburg	14.8	431	77	0.0	5.6	0.0	0.0	0.0	21.0	20.0	6.9	0.0	2.7
Charlottesville	91.9	2 254	69	5.8	4.9	0.1	39.8	5.3	7.5	5.8	4.6	3.1	2.3
Chesapeake	474.7	2 468	519	2.3	8.7	0.1	52.9	2.8	4.5	3.4	1.6	1.7	4.4
Danville	119.6	2 236	266	4.8	5.4	0.0	38.9	0.5	5.0	8.5	2.2	3.9	6.7
Hampton	284.7	2 052	172	4.9	2.5	0.5	45.1	0.0	6.2	5.3	5.8	3.0	4.2
Harrisonburg	59.5	1 780	257	0.0	8.0	0.4	38.7	1.7	5.1	19.5	3.3	1.1	4.7
Lynchburg	152.1	2 262	228	1.7	7.9	0.0	36.9	6.2	5.4	6.0	1.5	2.0	5.8
Manassas	72.1	2 170	39	4.0	4.5	0.0	49.0	1.8	7.8	9.0	1.7	0.2	4.8
Newport News	428.8	2 435	410	5.5	5.3	0.1	42.5	0.5	7.1	4.8	4.8	6.2	4.8
Norfolk	703.4	3 013	376	5.7	3.1	1.4	33.9	4.4	6.3	4.3	4.9	9.5	7.8
Petersburg	77.1	2 017	34	10.8	4.4	0.0	46.6	2.0	7.5	1.7	0.7	1.8	2.5
Portsmouth	256.0	2 527	369	4.6	3.2	0.3	46.1	3.8	4.8	5.1	2.7	6.2	3.9
Richmond	779.9	3 934	621	8.7	2.3	0.0	29.4	4.7	5.7	8.2	2.6	17.5	1.8
Roanoke	252.0	2 637	246	8.5	3.6	0.4	38.9	0.6	5.2	6.3	2.4	6.6	8.4
Suffolk	134.5	2 283	571	4.9	3.3	0.0	50.8	0.1	4.2	6.3	1.0	3.5	5.5
Virginia Beach	823.9	1 914	297	2.1	2.6	0.1	51.4	2.7	5.6	4.6	3.1	0.4	5.4

1. Based on population estimated as of July 1 of the year shown.

Table D. Cities — City Government Finances, City Government Employment, and Climate

City	City government finances, 1997 (cont'd) Debt outstanding Total (mil dol)	Per capita[1] (dollars)	Percent utility	City government employment, 1999	Climate[2] Average daily temperature (degrees Fahrenheit) Mean January	Mean July	Limits January[3]	Limits July[4]	Annual precipitation (inches)	Heating degree days	Cooling degree days
	137	138	139	140	141	142	143	144	145	146	147
TEXAS—Cont'd											
League City	25.9	637	0.0	NA	52.2	83.5	42.9	92.3	50.83	1 371	3 012
Lewisville	75.2	1 222	57.9	568	41.9	83.2	30.3	94.0	37.27	2 665	2 225
Longview	78.7	1 055	50.8	720	44.0	82.6	32.7	93.2	47.27	2 433	2 249
Lubbock	292.1	1 509	36.4	1 795	38.8	80.0	24.6	91.9	18.65	3 431	1 689
Lufkin	25.0	754	45.3	NA	47.6	82.8	36.9	93.2	42.40	1 951	2 551
McAllen	239.9	2 322	2.1	1 149	58.5	85.4	48.5	95.8	22.83	693	4 076
Mesquite	147.5	1 317	15.4	942	44.6	85.9	34.5	95.7	36.08	2 259	2 763
Midland	99.0	1 018	39.7	896	43.6	81.4	28.5	94.6	15.21	2 570	2 132
Mission	7.5	199	95.2	NA	57.1	85.5	45.8	96.7	22.82	829	3 985
Missouri City	16.6	297	0.0	NA	52.2	83.5	42.9	92.3	50.83	1 371	3 012
Nacogdoches	38.7	1 242	15.6	NA	47.6	82.8	36.9	93.2	42.40	1 951	2 551
New Braunfels	25.4	749	64.5	NA	48.2	83.7	36.5	95.3	34.27	1 790	2 791
North Richland Hills	82.0	1 541	17.1	NA	43.4	85.3	32.7	96.5	33.70	2 407	2 603
Odessa	120.1	1 321	64.7	836	42.5	82.0	28.5	95.4	14.96	2 751	2 163
Pasadena	92.0	699	20.9	946	52.2	83.5	42.9	92.3	50.83	1 371	3 012
Pharr	43.3	1 071	18.6	NA	58.5	85.4	48.5	95.8	22.83	693	4 076
Plano	251.2	1 306	9.4	1 694	43.4	85.3	32.7	96.5	33.70	2 407	2 603
Port Arthur	94.4	1 635	0.0	680	50.9	82.8	41.5	91.9	57.18	1 499	2 764
Richardson	91.1	1 122	11.2	944	44.6	85.9	34.5	95.7	36.08	2 259	2 763
Round Rock	69.9	1 332	16.5	NA	48.8	84.5	38.6	95.0	31.88	1 688	3 016
San Angelo	46.1	523	6.3	1 109	43.7	82.7	30.6	96.2	20.45	2 414	2 400
San Antonio	4 353.9	4 077	69.8	15 338	49.3	85.0	37.9	95.0	30.98	1 644	2 996
San Marcos	100.2	2 862	38.5	441	48.1	83.2	36.2	94.7	34.55	1 818	2 712
Sherman	52.6	1 588	68.8	NA	40.5	83.3	29.8	94.6	40.39	2 890	2 209
Temple	60.3	1 173	52.0	587	45.4	84.0	34.5	95.2	34.87	2 153	2 623
Texarkana	54.7	1 684	49.0	558	44.5	82.8	35.0	93.0	46.89	2 295	2 380
Texas City	58.9	1 391	0.0	500	52.7	83.3	47.1	87.3	42.28	1 263	2 994
Tyler	163.6	1 990	7.0	1 013	46.4	83.2	35.0	95.2	39.74	2 105	2 490
Victoria	62.2	1 019	23.0	650	52.7	84.1	42.5	93.5	37.41	1 296	3 118
Waco	225.8	2 082	23.1	1 379	45.2	85.6	34.2	96.8	31.96	2 179	2 816
Wichita Falls	72.7	726	73.4	1 167	39.8	85.0	27.6	97.2	28.90	3 042	2 340
UTAH	X	X	X	X	X	X	X	X	X	X	X
Bountiful	4.5	114	0.0	315	27.9	77.9	19.3	92.2	16.18	5 765	1 047
Layton	9.4	185	4.1	245	28.6	76.2	19.6	92.0	22.09	5 799	927
Logan	24.9	634	43.5	442	23.6	73.0	15.5	86.7	19.52	6 854	623
Murray	11.5	348	43.6	380	27.9	77.9	19.3	92.2	16.18	5 765	1 047
Ogden	58.5	890	0.0	641	28.9	77.8	19.8	92.3	22.59	5 557	1 096
Orem	14.5	182	0.0	455	28.0	74.5	18.3	90.2	17.04	5 907	745
Provo	107.3	1 078	51.7	663	28.0	74.5	18.3	90.2	17.04	5 907	745
St. George	70.4	1 647	42.4	436	32.2	73.5	19.8	88.8	18.23	5 452	687
Salt Lake City	381.5	2 210	8.4	2 965	27.9	77.9	19.3	92.2	16.18	5 765	1 047
Sandy	55.2	NA	0.0	543	27.9	77.9	19.3	92.2	16.18	5 765	1 047
West Jordan	26.5	460	7.8	328	27.9	77.9	19.3	92.2	16.18	5 765	1 047
West Valley City	76.5	NA	0.0	451	27.9	77.9	19.3	92.2	16.18	5 765	1 047
VERMONT	X	X	X	X	X	X	X	X	X	X	X
Burlington	180.5	4 628	57.7	590	16.3	70.5	7.5	81.2	34.47	7 771	388
VIRGINIA	X	X	X	X	X	X	X	X	X	X	X
Alexandria	183.0	1 556	0.0	4 423	34.6	80.0	26.8	88.5	38.63	4 047	1 549
Blacksburg	9.9	287	26.7	NA	29.6	70.6	19.0	82.3	40.91	5 574	514
Charlottesville	52.1	1 277	16.2	1 696	34.5	76.4	25.5	86.7	47.29	4 224	1 156
Chesapeake	641.4	3 335	16.9	7 537	39.1	78.2	30.9	86.4	44.64	3 495	1 422
Danville	272.1	5 088	11.8	2 421	36.1	78.0	25.4	89.6	43.18	3 944	1 381
Hampton	205.1	1 478	0.0	5 121	39.1	78.2	30.9	86.4	44.64	3 495	1 422
Harrisonburg	45.8	1 369	31.1	1 054	31.3	74.3	20.5	86.7	35.24	4 908	876
Lynchburg	231.8	3 446	10.5	2 657	34.2	75.6	24.7	86.0	40.88	4 340	1 048
Manassas	80.3	2 418	29.5	1 240	33.0	77.2	22.9	88.7	36.13	4 447	1 198
Newport News	545.9	3 099	20.6	8 384	39.1	78.2	30.9	86.4	44.64	3 495	1 422
Norfolk	1 188.1	5 090	21.9	11 975	39.1	78.2	30.9	86.4	44.64	3 495	1 422
Petersburg	46.1	1 206	55.8	1 744	38.6	78.9	27.8	90.3	43.53	3 408	1 533
Portsmouth	187.8	1 853	23.9	4 471	39.1	78.2	30.9	86.4	44.64	3 495	1 422
Richmond	810.8	4 090	31.7	7 744	35.7	78.0	25.7	88.4	43.16	3 963	1 348
Roanoke	349.4	3 657	7.2	4 518	34.5	75.6	25.0	86.4	41.13	4 360	1 052
Suffolk	162.4	2 756	17.5	2 428	39.1	78.2	30.9	86.4	44.64	3 495	1 422
Virginia Beach	828.6	1 925	11.1	15 992	39.1	78.2	30.9	86.4	44.64	3 495	1 422

1. Based on the population estimated as of July 1 of the year shown.   2. Represents normal values based on the 30-year period, 1961–1990.   3. Average daily minimum.   4. Average daily maximum.

Table D. Cities — Land Area and Population

STATE Place code	City	Land area, 1990[1] (sq km)	Population, 1999			Population				Population characteristics, 1990 — Percent						
			Total persons	Rank	Per square kilometer	Total persons 1990	Percent change 1990–1999	Total persons 1980	Percent change 1980–1990	Race — White	Black	Am. Indian, Eskimo, Aleut	Asian and Pacific Islander	Other race	Hispanic[2]	Foreign born
		1	2	3	4	5	6	7	8	9	10	11	12	13	14	15
53 00000	WASHINGTON	172 447.2	5 756 361	X	33	4 866 669	18.3	4 132 353	17.8	88.5	3.1	1.7	4.3	2.4	4.4	6.6
53 03180	Auburn	51.0	38 460	784	754	33 650	14.3	26 417	27.4	92.4	1.4	2.1	3.0	1.2	3.1	5.0
53 05210	Bellevue	68.4	105 521	209	1 543	95 213	10.8	73 883	17.6	86.5	2.2	0.4	9.9	0.9	2.5	13.3
53 05280	Bellingham	57.0	63 019	429	1 106	52 179	20.8	45 805	13.9	93.8	0.8	1.8	2.8	0.9	2.4	7.1
53 07695	Bremerton	51.5	40 612	738	789	38 142	6.5	36 209	5.3	83.9	7.1	1.7	5.3	2.0	4.8	4.6
53 20750	Edmonds	18.9	40 751	734	2 156	30 743	32.6	27 679	11.1	93.5	0.9	0.9	4.0	0.6	2.0	8.1
53 22640	Everett	77.4	87 352	275	1 129	70 937	23.1	54 413	30.4	91.7	1.7	1.7	3.9	1.0	2.8	6.4
53 35275	Kennewick	52.1	50 727	577	974	42 148	20.4	34 397	22.5	89.9	1.1	0.8	2.0	6.2	8.7	4.7
53 35415	Kent	49.0	66 233	398	1 352	37 960	74.5	23 152	64.0	89.2	3.8	1.4	4.4	1.2	3.9	4.9
53 35940	Kirkland	27.7	45 635	648	1 647	40 059	13.9	18 779	113.3	92.8	1.5	0.6	4.3	0.8	2.4	7.1
53 40245	Longview	31.1	34 256	885	1 101	31 499	8.8	31 041	1.5	94.7	0.5	1.5	2.1	1.1	2.0	3.5
53 40840	Lynnwood	18.0	34 034	889	1 891	28 637	18.8	22 641	26.5	88.5	2.0	1.1	7.6	0.9	3.0	10.6
53 51300	Olympia	41.8	39 904	753	955	33 729	18.3	27 447	22.9	92.0	1.2	1.2	4.8	0.7	2.6	6.1
53 57535	Redmond	37.4	44 708	665	1 195	35 800	24.9	23 318	53.5	91.1	1.3	0.5	6.3	0.8	2.5	9.6
53 57745	Renton	42.1	47 540	622	1 129	41 688	14.0	30 612	36.2	83.5	6.6	1.2	7.7	1.1	3.0	7.8
53 58235	Richland	83.0	37 553	808	452	32 315	16.2	33 578	-3.8	93.0	1.4	0.7	3.3	1.6	3.0	3.9
53 63000	Seattle	217.3	537 150	22	2 472	516 259	4.0	493 846	4.5	75.3	10.1	1.4	11.8	1.4	3.6	13.1
53 67000	Spokane	144.8	184 323	101	1 273	177 165	4.0	171 300	3.4	93.3	1.9	2.0	2.1	0.7	2.1	3.9
53 70000	Tacoma	124.4	180 020	106	1 447	176 664	1.9	158 501	11.5	78.1	11.4	2.0	6.9	1.5	3.8	7.7
53 74060	Vancouver	36.6	118 743	177	3 244	62 065	91.3	42 834	27.6	92.3	2.3	1.3	3.2	1.0	3.0	4.8
53 75775	Walla Walla	26.7	28 862	1 045	1 081	26 482	9.0	25 631	3.3	88.1	2.2	1.0	1.3	7.4	10.2	6.4
53 80010	Yakima	38.7	72 483	356	1 873	58 427	24.1	49 826	17.3	82.5	2.4	2.0	1.3	11.8	16.3	8.8
54 00000	WEST VIRGINIA	62 384.2	1 806 928	X	29	1 793 477	0.7	1 950 186	-8.0	96.2	3.1	0.1	0.4	0.1	0.5	0.9
54 14600	Charleston	76.3	54 598	521	716	57 287	-4.7	63 968	-10.4	84.1	14.2	0.2	1.3	0.2	0.6	1.8
54 39460	Huntington	38.6	52 273	550	1 354	54 844	-4.7	63 684	-13.9	92.5	6.7	0.1	0.5	0.1	0.5	1.2
54 55756	Morgantown	20.0	29 017	1 038	1 451	25 879	12.1	27 605	-6.3	92.0	3.5	0.1	4.1	0.4	1.1	5.7
54 62140	Parkersburg	28.9	32 212	944	1 115	33 862	-4.9	39 967	-15.3	97.7	1.7	0.2	0.3	0.1	0.3	0.8
54 86452	Wheeling	35.7	32 526	931	911	34 882	-6.8	43 067	-19.0	94.7	4.5	0.1	0.7	0.1	0.3	1.6
55 00000	WISCONSIN	140 672.5	5 250 446	X	37	4 891 769	7.3	4 705 642	4.0	92.2	5.0	0.8	1.1	0.9	1.9	2.5
55 02375	Appleton	44.4	67 178	388	1 513	65 695	2.3	59 040	11.3	96.6	0.2	0.4	2.4	0.3	0.9	2.8
55 06500	Beloit	41.9	35 728	843	853	35 571	0.4	35 207	1.0	81.8	15.7	0.3	1.2	1.1	1.9	2.4
55 10025	Brookfield	69.5	38 290	791	551	35 184	8.8	34 035	3.4	96.9	0.4	0.2	2.4	0.2	0.7	6.0
55 22300	Eau Claire	71.7	60 223	456	840	56 806	6.0	51 516	10.3	95.1	0.4	0.6	3.8	0.2	0.6	3.5
55 26275	Fond du Lac	33.1	40 987	729	1 238	37 755	8.6	35 863	5.3	97.8	0.3	0.5	0.8	0.6	1.5	1.5
55 31000	Green Bay	113.5	98 362	232	867	96 466	2.0	87 899	9.7	94.2	0.5	2.5	2.3	0.5	1.1	2.4
55 31175	Greenfield	29.9	35 246	855	1 179	33 403	5.5	31 467	6.2	97.6	0.4	0.4	1.0	0.7	2.0	4.3
55 37825	Janesville	60.9	60 255	455	989	52 210	15.4	51 071	2.2	98.1	0.6	0.2	0.8	0.3	1.1	1.9
55 39225	Kenosha	55.8	89 447	263	1 603	80 426	11.2	77 685	3.5	89.8	6.4	0.4	0.6	2.9	5.9	5.0
55 40775	La Crosse	47.5	49 409	589	1 040	51 140	-3.4	48 347	5.8	93.8	0.7	0.4	4.9	0.2	0.9	4.2
55 48000	Madison	149.6	210 674	79	1 408	190 766	10.4	170 616	11.8	90.7	4.2	0.4	3.9	0.7	2.0	5.7
55 48500	Manitowoc	37.3	33 491	903	898	32 521	3.0	32 547	-0.1	96.4	0.2	0.5	2.5	0.4	1.1	2.7
55 51000	Menomonee Falls	86.2	31 925	950	370	26 840	18.9	27 845	-3.6	98.8	0.3	0.2	0.5	0.1	0.6	2.9
55 53000	Milwaukee	248.8	572 424	20	2 301	628 088	-8.9	636 212	-1.3	63.4	30.5	0.9	1.9	3.4	6.3	4.7
55 56375	New Berlin	95.4	38 360	788	402	33 592	14.2	30 529	10.0	98.4	0.2	0.2	1.0	0.2	0.8	2.9
55 60500	Oshkosh	46.5	60 333	453	1 297	55 006	9.7	49 620	10.9	96.3	0.8	0.5	2.2	0.3	0.8	2.8
55 66000	Racine	40.0	80 902	306	2 023	84 298	-4.0	85 730	-1.7	76.4	18.4	0.3	0.5	4.3	8.1	3.8
55 72975	Sheboygan	34.3	49 558	587	1 445	49 587	-0.1	48 085	3.1	94.4	0.2	0.4	3.9	1.1	2.5	5.0
55 78650	Superior	95.7	27 339	1 099	286	27 134	0.8	29 571	-8.2	96.1	0.5	2.4	0.8	0.1	0.5	1.7
55 84250	Waukesha	44.8	63 261	426	1 412	56 894	11.2	50 319	13.1	95.4	0.6	0.3	1.3	2.5	5.9	3.1
55 84475	Wausau	36.5	36 726	826	1 006	37 060	-0.9	32 426	14.3	93.1	0.1	0.7	6.0	0.1	0.7	5.2
55 84675	Wauwatosa	34.3	45 405	655	1 324	49 366	-8.0	51 308	-3.8	97.3	1.2	0.2	1.0	0.2	1.0	3.9
55 85300	West Allis	29.3	59 332	462	2 025	63 221	-6.2	63 982	-1.2	98.2	0.3	0.5	0.6	0.4	1.5	2.8
56 00000	WYOMING	251 500.8	479 602	X	2	453 589	5.7	469 557	-3.4	94.2	0.8	2.1	0.6	2.3	5.7	1.7
56 13150	Casper	53.4	48 233	609	903	46 765	3.1	51 016	-8.3	96.5	0.9	0.5	0.5	1.5	3.9	1.6
56 13900	Cheyenne	48.7	53 925	529	1 107	50 008	7.8	47 283	5.8	89.6	3.1	0.7	1.2	5.4	11.8	2.4
56 45050	Laramie	28.8	24 905	1 207	865	26 687	-6.7	24 410	9.3	93.1	0.9	0.8	2.3	2.9	6.7	3.5

1. Dry land or land partially or temporarily covered by water.   2. Hispanic persons may be of any race.

Table D. Cities — **Population and Households**

City	\[Age of population (percent)\] Under 5 years	5 to 17 years	18 to 24 years	25 to 34 years	35 to 44 years	45 to 54 years	55 to 64 years	65 to 74 years	75 years and over	Percent female	\[Households, 1990\] Number	Percent change, 1980–1990	Persons per house-hold	Female family house-holder[1]	One-person
	16	17	18	19	20	21	22	23	24	25	26	27	28	29	30
WASHINGTON	7.5	18.4	10.0	17.6	16.5	10.3	7.8	6.9	4.9	50.4	1 872 431	21.4	2.53	9.4	25.4
Auburn	8.4	17.2	10.7	20.3	14.6	9.5	7.8	6.6	4.9	51.2	13 357	28.1	2.43	12.8	27.6
Bellevue	5.7	15.3	9.9	18.2	16.6	13.9	10.0	6.8	3.6	51.1	35 756	27.8	2.41	7.9	26.0
Bellingham	5.4	13.8	21.1	15.8	15.5	7.7	6.6	6.8	7.3	52.4	21 189	15.7	2.27	9.1	31.6
Bremerton	9.4	14.1	19.2	19.6	11.3	6.9	6.1	7.1	6.4	46.9	14 718	4.1	2.34	10.9	32.6
Edmonds	5.9	15.0	8.5	15.2	16.5	13.3	10.9	9.0	5.6	52.7	12 628	22.1	2.41	8.7	25.1
Everett	8.6	16.4	11.1	20.9	14.3	9.0	6.7	6.9	6.3	50.4	28 679	27.9	2.38	12.2	30.1
Kennewick	9.1	21.5	10.2	18.6	15.7	9.4	6.4	5.5	3.7	51.0	16 074	24.2	2.61	11.5	25.7
Kent	8.7	15.7	13.5	24.4	14.8	9.9	6.4	4.0	2.6	49.8	16 246	69.3	2.33	11.2	30.8
Kirkland	6.7	14.0	10.9	23.3	18.3	10.4	6.7	5.6	4.0	52.1	17 211	117.5	2.28	9.0	30.1
Longview	7.5	18.6	9.1	15.5	15.6	10.2	8.6	8.0	6.9	51.7	12 875	4.8	2.40	10.7	29.2
Lynnwood	8.0	16.8	11.1	21.3	15.4	10.3	7.4	5.8	3.9	51.3	11 331	28.8	2.50	11.9	26.6
Olympia	6.3	16.2	10.3	16.9	18.4	9.7	7.6	8.0	6.5	52.6	14 951	28.7	2.22	10.0	34.5
Redmond	6.9	18.3	9.8	21.1	19.9	11.4	5.8	3.7	3.1	50.8	14 153	74.0	2.50	8.8	25.1
Renton	7.2	14.8	10.9	23.3	15.9	10.0	7.3	6.3	4.2	50.3	18 219	45.1	2.27	9.9	32.5
Richland	7.2	19.1	8.1	16.2	15.6	11.8	9.5	7.9	4.7	51.2	13 162	6.0	2.44	8.4	28.0
Seattle	5.6	10.7	11.9	21.9	18.0	9.2	7.4	8.2	7.0	51.2	236 702	7.7	2.09	9.0	39.8
Spokane	7.5	16.9	10.8	17.7	14.4	8.7	7.8	8.6	7.7	52.3	75 147	5.5	2.29	12.4	33.8
Tacoma	8.2	17.7	10.9	18.9	14.6	8.7	7.3	7.2	6.4	51.6	69 939	10.3	2.44	13.3	31.3
Vancouver	7.9	15.4	11.4	18.4	14.1	8.7	7.8	8.7	7.7	52.2	20 138	6.9	2.22	13.2	35.7
Walla Walla	6.7	17.2	12.8	16.1	14.2	8.7	7.3	8.4	8.6	48.9	9 912	2.8	2.38	10.5	32.1
Yakima	8.8	17.8	10.4	16.7	13.7	8.4	7.8	8.2	8.2	51.8	21 596	6.8	2.47	12.1	30.7
WEST VIRGINIA	5.9	18.8	10.0	14.6	15.1	10.7	9.9	8.7	6.3	52.0	688 557	0.3	2.55	10.7	24.5
Charleston	6.0	15.7	8.0	16.0	15.2	10.2	10.6	10.2	8.1	54.5	25 306	-4.4	2.21	13.9	35.7
Huntington	4.9	14.5	15.0	13.3	12.3	9.6	10.4	10.9	9.0	54.6	23 419	-8.3	2.21	13.2	35.6
Morgantown	3.8	8.1	43.0	12.5	9.6	5.7	5.9	6.5	4.9	50.3	9 588	-0.8	2.21	6.9	34.8
Parkersburg	6.0	16.1	8.7	14.5	14.0	10.3	10.7	10.4	9.3	54.3	14 463	-8.1	2.30	13.0	31.5
Wheeling	5.6	15.3	8.6	13.3	13.3	10.6	11.4	12.3	9.7	54.6	15 038	-12.5	2.24	12.5	36.3
WISCONSIN	7.4	19.0	10.5	16.8	14.8	9.8	8.5	7.3	6.0	51.1	1 822 118	10.1	2.61	9.6	24.3
Appleton	8.1	19.3	9.9	19.0	15.2	9.3	7.3	6.3	5.7	51.8	24 818	17.6	2.57	8.6	24.8
Beloit	8.8	19.8	11.6	16.4	12.9	9.0	8.0	7.4	6.1	53.2	13 307	4.5	2.58	16.1	26.3
Brookfield	6.3	19.5	6.8	11.2	17.0	13.7	12.9	8.3	4.3	50.7	11 939	15.6	2.92	5.1	11.3
Eau Claire	7.0	16.1	21.6	15.2	13.6	7.3	6.6	6.9	5.8	53.1	21 118	15.3	2.49	9.4	27.8
Fond du Lac	7.2	18.9	9.7	16.5	14.5	8.6	8.2	8.3	8.0	53.0	14 637	12.7	2.49	9.9	28.4
Green Bay	8.1	17.8	11.2	19.5	14.8	8.6	7.4	6.9	5.8	52.2	38 383	15.0	2.45	10.8	29.1
Greenfield	5.3	13.7	9.6	17.3	15.9	10.3	10.7	9.7	7.4	53.0	13 785	14.2	2.36	8.0	28.6
Janesville	8.1	18.3	9.6	17.9	14.6	10.7	8.8	6.7	5.3	51.5	20 388	10.2	2.54	10.0	25.2
Kenosha	8.3	18.8	10.5	17.9	14.2	8.9	7.9	7.4	6.1	51.9	29 919	6.4	2.61	14.0	25.7
La Crosse	6.6	13.7	22.4	15.7	11.7	6.8	7.6	7.8	7.9	53.7	19 970	11.3	2.34	10.1	33.2
Madison	6.2	12.3	22.2	20.3	15.2	8.3	6.3	5.0	4.2	51.3	77 361	16.2	2.30	8.3	31.2
Manitowoc	6.6	17.3	8.1	15.9	14.0	8.9	9.3	9.7	10.1	52.7	13 144	5.5	2.39	8.4	31.1
Menomonee Falls	6.7	17.1	8.1	16.5	13.7	13.5	12.8	7.4	4.3	50.7	9 817	11.7	2.71	7.0	17.9
Milwaukee	8.6	18.8	12.0	19.1	13.5	8.0	7.6	6.9	5.5	52.7	240 540	-0.8	2.53	19.8	30.5
New Berlin	6.7	19.0	7.9	15.8	17.7	13.6	10.7	5.8	2.7	50.1	11 695	25.6	2.86	5.4	13.7
Oshkosh	6.6	14.6	19.0	17.2	13.1	7.8	7.6	7.1	6.9	52.3	20 957	14.8	2.39	9.2	29.7
Racine	8.8	20.4	9.4	18.1	14.1	8.2	8.1	7.2	5.8	52.6	31 767	0.0	2.62	17.0	26.1
Sheboygan	7.5	18.1	9.0	17.5	13.9	8.6	8.4	8.8	8.2	52.0	19 703	8.4	2.47	8.7	28.3
Superior	7.0	18.0	11.0	15.4	14.3	8.8	8.0	8.9	8.6	52.8	11 001	-3.4	2.36	13.5	31.6
Waukesha	8.0	18.6	11.4	20.2	15.9	9.2	6.7	5.2	4.7	51.7	21 235	20.4	2.59	10.0	25.4
Wausau	7.6	17.1	10.0	16.7	14.3	8.1	8.8	9.0	8.4	53.2	14 718	15.3	2.45	9.4	29.0
Wauwatosa	6.7	15.4	6.0	17.3	15.5	9.5	9.8	9.5	10.3	53.8	19 848	2.7	2.39	7.7	29.0
West Allis	6.6	15.0	9.0	20.0	13.5	8.8	9.2	9.7	8.2	52.7	26 797	4.0	2.32	10.0	31.7
WYOMING	7.7	22.2	9.1	16.4	16.4	10.0	7.8	6.1	4.3	50.0	168 839	1.2	2.63	8.3	24.5
Casper	7.7	21.3	8.3	16.8	16.4	9.6	8.7	7.1	4.2	51.6	18 504	-1.8	2.49	10.2	27.6
Cheyenne	7.6	18.8	9.2	17.6	16.5	9.9	8.6	7.0	4.8	51.1	20 243	11.2	2.44	10.3	28.4
Laramie	6.2	14.4	28.1	18.2	12.8	7.4	5.3	4.3	3.3	48.4	10 400	15.6	2.31	8.3	30.6

1. No spouse present.

City	Persons in group quarters, 1990				Serious crimes known to police, 1998[2]				Education, 1990				Money income, 1989		
					Total		Rate[3]		School enrollment		Attainment[4] (percent)			Households	
														Median	
	Total	Persons in mental hospitals	Persons in nursing homes	Persons identified as home-less[1]	Number	Rate[3]	Violent	Property	Public	Private	High school grad-uate or more	Bach-elor's degree or more	Per capita (dollars)[5]	Dollars	Percent change, 1979–1989 (constant 1989 dollars)
	31	32	33	34	35	36	37	38	39	40	41	42	43	44	45
WASHINGTON	119 736	2 928	32 840	5 226	333 799	5 867	429	5 438	1 091 450	160 862	83.8	22.9	14 923	31 183	1.3
Auburn	602	63	401	8	3 930	10 523	613	9 910	6 396	952	82.0	12.9	13 866	30 007	-3.1
Bellevue	566	0	384	10	4 570	4 826	171	4 655	17 391	3 831	94.2	45.7	23 816	43 800	1.2
Bellingham	4 221	0	953	149	4 736	7 550	316	7 234	16 420	1 148	85.2	28.2	13 698	24 714	9.0
Bremerton	3 793	41	507	35	2 759	6 447	825	5 622	6 978	790	82.0	12.6	11 418	22 610	-6.0
Edmonds	290	0	248	10	1 249	3 712	134	3 578	5 776	1 271	90.2	31.0	20 868	40 515	1.0
Everett	1 669	0	787	228	6 321	7 419	730	6 689	13 420	1 694	81.0	14.2	13 829	28 415	6.7
Kennewick	241	0	122	0	3 670	7 006	426	6 580	10 920	1 041	82.5	19.8	12 767	28 261	-20.3
Kent	157	0	0	75	NA	NA	NA	NA	7 449	1 164	86.4	21.0	15 993	32 341	-5.4
Kirkland	790	0	381	0	1 680	3 739	120	3 619	7 464	1 955	91.9	36.6	21 200	38 437	9.2
Longview	677	0	394	138	3 519	10 175	567	9 608	6 861	597	77.9	13.0	12 908	25 535	-14.0
Lynnwood	365	0	326	0	2 778	8 430	300	8 130	6 155	895	86.1	18.5	13 984	30 512	-7.7
Olympia	597	21	326	44	3 003	7 453	372	7 081	7 414	925	88.9	33.1	15 502	27 785	5.5
Redmond	388	0	388	0	1 558	3 604	197	3 407	8 007	1 379	94.0	40.9	20 037	42 299	-4.2
Renton	327	0	165	99	4 019	8 673	481	8 192	7 968	1 186	85.5	21.8	16 298	32 393	-3.1
Richland	132	0	104	0	1 272	3 319	164	3 155	7 830	934	90.3	34.7	17 085	36 626	-13.9
Seattle	20 995	127	4 004	2 553	52 870	9 825	832	8 993	93 394	26 830	86.4	37.9	18 308	29 353	7.8
Spokane	5 210	65	2 211	322	17 664	9 314	832	8 482	37 985	7 857	83.2	21.0	12 375	22 192	-4.4
Tacoma	5 745	43	2 232	418	19 319	10 480	1 442	9 038	35 474	8 010	79.3	15.8	12 272	25 333	3.9
Vancouver	1 768	0	709	193	NA	NA	NA	NA	9 242	947	80.0	15.0	12 606	21 552	-5.3
Walla Walla	2 880	0	572	73	2 433	8 414	923	7 491	6 052	1 797	78.9	16.3	11 247	21 301	-9.6
Yakima	1 491	0	753	154	7 220	10 824	607	10 217	12 197	1 219	70.9	16.5	11 593	22 189	-3.2
WEST VIRGINIA	36 412	599	12 591	576	46 130	2 547	249	2 298	403 602	32 911	66.0	12.3	10 520	20 795	-14.8
Charleston	1 462	71	345	229	5 752	10 268	1 014	9 254	10 603	1 894	77.2	28.6	16 067	23 584	-11.9
Huntington	3 002	94	509	90	3 059	6 244	502	5 742	13 996	1 235	72.4	20.8	12 005	18 276	-13.0
Morgantown	4 763	0	88	97	1 059	3 967	281	3 686	13 480	604	85.2	44.2	10 533	18 022	-2.2
Parkersburg	486	0	394	0	1 526	4 695	298	4 397	6 386	653	69.2	12.8	11 269	20 461	-11.9
Wheeling	1 193	0	482	0	1 282	3 893	416	3 477	5 395	2 337	74.7	18.4	12 665	21 053	-9.7
WISCONSIN	133 151	2 659	50 345	1 471	185 093	3 543	249	3 294	1 088 366	213 864	78.6	17.7	13 276	29 442	-0.6
Appleton	1 882	8	586	9	NA	NA	NA	NA	13 920	3 790	85.3	23.7	14 735	33 006	3.2
Beloit	1 287	0	305	18	NA	NA	NA	NA	7 875	1 640	72.4	11.3	11 435	25 859	-7.6
Brookfield	316	0	316	0	NA	NA	NA	NA	6 632	2 813	91.0	41.7	24 814	57 132	6.0
Eau Claire	4 284	0	581	10	NA	NA	NA	NA	18 887	1 526	84.8	23.3	11 426	24 735	2.1
Fond du Lac	1 338	135	718	4	NA	NA	NA	NA	7 587	1 981	78.2	14.1	12 472	26 826	-7.3
Green Bay	2 442	145	902	158	4 749	4 566	288	4 278	20 116	4 192	80.9	16.7	12 969	26 770	-1.7
Greenfield	878	0	862	0	NA	NA	NA	NA	5 258	1 905	80.9	19.2	16 102	35 082	-5.4
Janesville	435	0	266	26	NA	NA	NA	NA	10 745	1 448	81.2	15.5	14 447	31 583	-4.7
Kenosha	2 384	0	1 028	30	NA	NA	NA	NA	17 341	4 022	73.2	12.2	12 284	27 770	-12.5
La Crosse	4 170	0	622	19	NA	NA	NA	NA	14 873	2 406	80.7	21.4	10 898	21 947	-2.7
Madison	13 046	0	1 069	210	8 349	4 149	366	3 783	63 473	5 938	90.6	42.0	15 143	29 420	6.3
Manitowoc	1 141	0	1 044	0	NA	NA	NA	NA	5 537	1 854	74.5	14.5	12 286	24 202	-10.4
Menomonee Falls	233	0	233	0	NA	NA	NA	NA	4 912	1 361	84.9	19.9	17 074	42 315	-5.8
Milwaukee	18 333	205	5 888	486	46 144	7 843	1 002	6 841	132 933	43 700	71.5	14.8	11 106	23 627	-12.0
New Berlin	161	0	144	0	NA	NA	NA	NA	6 588	2 234	90.3	28.7	18 245	49 394	3.2
Oshkosh	4 824	0	516	0	NA	NA	NA	NA	15 619	1 675	78.6	19.6	11 843	25 168	-1.4
Racine	1 129	0	508	35	NA	NA	NA	NA	19 115	3 626	72.0	14.9	11 858	26 540	-14.1
Sheboygan	1 003	0	884	13	NA	NA	NA	NA	9 400	2 253	75.4	13.2	12 740	27 647	-3.5
Superior	1 107	0	546	12	NA	NA	NA	NA	6 780	571	77.3	15.9	10 769	20 905	-13.6
Waukesha	2 095	0	551	18	NA	NA	NA	NA	12 120	3 749	85.1	25.3	14 915	36 192	2.0
Wausau	934	157	506	54	NA	NA	NA	NA	7 456	1 257	75.4	17.4	13 169	25 505	-1.8
Wauwatosa	1 991	855	755	0	NA	NA	NA	NA	8 411	3 104	88.7	38.5	19 065	40 041	2.6
West Allis	1 080	48	953	0	NA	NA	NA	NA	10 678	2 965	79.2	12.4	13 978	29 622	-5.4
WYOMING	10 298	285	2 679	189	18 315	3 808	248	3 560	127 228	7 511	83.0	18.8	12 311	27 096	-19.1
Casper	777	0	345	29	2 457	5 025	211	4 814	12 529	767	86.4	23.0	13 424	27 698	-28.5
Cheyenne	564	0	357	38	2 503	4 640	191	4 449	12 385	1 133	84.6	22.1	13 351	28 117	-5.3
Laramie	2 676	0	140	13	930	3 591	293	3 298	12 463	743	90.0	40.4	11 652	19 642	-15.6

1. Persons in emergency shelters and persons visible in street locations.   2. Data for serious crimes have not been adjusted for underreporting. This may affect comparability between geographic areas and over time.   3. Per 100,000 population estimated by the FBI.   4. Persons 25 years old and older.   5. Based on population enumerated as of April 1, 1990.

City	Percent with $100,000 or more (46)	Persons Total (47)	Percent change in rate, 1979–1989 (48)	Families Total (49)	Total (50)	Percent change, 1980–1990 (51)	Vacant units for sale or rent[1] (52)	Total (53)	Percent (54)	Median value[2] (dollars) (55)	With a mortgage (56)	Without a mortgage (57)	Median rent[3] (dollars) (58)	Rent as percent of income (59)	Substandard units[4] (percent) (60)
WASHINGTON	3.7	10.9	11.5	7.8	2 032 378	20.3	72 094	1 872 431	62.6	93 400	20.4	11.8	445	25.7	4.0
Auburn	1.6	10.8	9.1	8.1	13 977	23.2	494	13 357	48.8	91 500	19.9	12.0	467	24.5	4.0
Bellevue	11.2	5.6	14.3	3.4	37 428	27.7	1 373	35 756	58.2	192 800	19.3	11.4	610	27.2	2.1
Bellingham	3.0	16.7	-1.8	8.0	22 114	12.0	660	21 189	50.9	89 100	19.4	11.9	426	29.1	2.7
Bremerton	0.7	18.1	40.3	15.5	15 693	4.9	610	14 718	39.1	64 200	19.5	12.5	390	24.7	5.6
Edmonds	7.8	4.7	6.8	2.9	12 945	20.9	251	12 628	67.0	160 100	19.1	11.1	534	26.7	2.2
Everett	2.0	12.0	-0.8	9.9	30 795	28.8	1 675	28 679	45.5	98 000	21.4	13.2	484	25.7	4.4
Kennewick	1.3	13.9	51.1	12.1	17 209	19.0	575	16 074	53.1	64 800	16.4	11.2	345	23.1	4.3
Kent	1.9	8.8	20.5	6.6	17 484	58.8	1 076	16 246	36.0	107 100	20.0	11.8	519	23.4	5.6
Kirkland	6.4	5.7	18.8	3.6	18 061	118.7	659	17 211	55.2	160 200	20.9	11.7	630	24.6	2.0
Longview	2.1	16.0	36.8	13.0	13 441	2.5	332	12 875	57.2	61 100	14.6	10.9	352	26.3	3.5
Lynnwood	1.4	9.3	31.0	7.5	11 871	28.8	453	11 331	49.5	122 400	20.6	11.5	529	28.3	4.6
Olympia	2.4	13.0	13.0	8.4	15 928	26.8	730	14 951	52.0	77 800	20.1	11.8	456	27.5	3.5
Redmond	6.6	3.6	-26.5	1.9	14 972	71.5	663	14 153	57.6	168 600	20.5	11.9	661	24.7	1.7
Renton	2.1	7.0	-15.7	5.6	19 243	41.6	748	18 219	48.5	106 300	20.0	11.9	489	24.4	3.6
Richland	3.9	7.8	56.0	5.8	13 872	3.6	396	13 162	62.0	69 200	14.7	11.4	382	19.2	1.4
Seattle	4.8	12.4	10.7	7.4	249 032	8.3	9 058	236 702	48.9	137 900	21.1	11.7	463	26.9	4.2
Spokane	2.2	17.3	24.5	12.5	79 875	5.0	3 470	75 147	57.2	51 100	19.3	12.6	344	28.2	3.1
Tacoma	1.7	16.8	19.1	12.5	75 147	10.9	3 753	69 939	52.7	66 200	21.1	13.2	413	28.1	4.9
Vancouver	2.0	17.1	31.5	13.3	21 025	5.7	646	20 138	43.1	61 300	18.1	11.7	393	27.2	3.2
Walla Walla	2.0	19.3	54.4	14.3	10 649	4.7	490	9 912	56.6	50 800	17.5	11.7	315	25.6	4.8
Yakima	2.2	20.2	33.8	15.7	22 968	7.5	961	21 596	53.3	56 700	17.6	12.4	346	26.8	7.3
WEST VIRGINIA	1.5	19.7	31.1	16.0	781 295	4.5	39 062	688 557	74.1	47 900	17.5	12.0	303	26.8	4.0
Charleston	5.3	18.8	49.2	15.0	28 111	0.3	1 987	25 306	55.5	66 100	15.9	11.4	329	24.7	1.0
Huntington	3.0	23.2	51.6	16.7	26 674	-3.5	2 081	23 419	57.1	46 700	17.2	12.1	311	30.9	1.4
Morgantown	2.5	30.7	26.3	10.4	10 422	0.9	617	9 588	44.4	69 500	16.5	11.7	355	35.1	1.4
Parkersburg	1.4	19.0	33.8	15.2	16 341	-4.3	1 224	14 463	62.9	42 600	16.3	13.3	330	27.1	0.7
Wheeling	3.0	16.9	33.1	13.6	17 128	-6.6	1 335	15 038	61.3	47 000	16.9	11.8	274	26.5	1.7
WISCONSIN	2.6	10.7	23.0	7.6	2 055 774	10.3	55 030	1 822 118	66.7	62 500	20.1	13.4	399	24.9	2.6
Appleton	3.1	6.8	15.3	5.1	25 528	18.0	528	24 818	66.3	64 400	20.0	13.3	391	23.1	1.8
Beloit	1.2	17.5	50.9	14.5	14 033	4.6	506	13 307	60.2	37 900	16.1	13.3	381	28.8	3.2
Brookfield	18.0	1.1	-47.6	0.8	12 254	16.3	220	11 939	91.5	121 900	20.5	12.1	781	23.9	0.8
Eau Claire	1.7	18.6	25.7	10.1	21 880	13.8	504	21 118	57.5	52 600	18.3	13.3	352	27.3	2.4
Fond du Lac	1.5	9.6	39.1	7.1	15 176	12.1	400	14 637	62.5	51 700	19.6	12.9	378	25.0	1.5
Green Bay	1.8	13.4	39.6	10.0	39 726	15.3	1 065	38 383	56.6	55 500	20.6	13.3	363	25.1	2.5
Greenfield	1.8	3.4	25.9	2.4	14 301	15.4	445	13 785	62.5	80 300	21.7	14.6	531	23.2	1.2
Janesville	2.2	8.3	48.2	6.5	21 153	9.6	484	20 388	65.6	56 000	17.0	12.7	408	24.1	1.5
Kenosha	1.3	12.7	58.8	9.9	31 197	6.1	898	29 919	62.0	58 700	19.4	13.0	400	25.4	3.2
La Crosse	1.4	21.0	50.0	10.2	20 897	11.4	705	19 970	49.6	53 500	19.8	14.3	344	27.1	3.3
Madison	3.7	16.1	20.1	6.6	80 047	16.0	2 143	77 361	47.0	75 200	20.7	13.2	472	28.3	3.2
Manitowoc	1.9	10.7	67.2	7.2	13 728	6.7	421	13 144	66.0	48 100	17.1	12.3	294	23.5	1.9
Menomonee Falls	4.6	2.8	100.0	2.0	10 043	10.8	176	9 817	79.6	87 600	19.8	13.5	507	24.4	0.9
Milwaukee	1.0	22.2	60.9	18.5	254 204	0.3	9 278	240 540	44.8	53 500	20.6	14.2	418	28.0	4.8
New Berlin	5.1	1.7	-5.6	1.3	12 102	26.8	374	11 695	84.6	96 700	20.9	12.7	631	20.9	0.9
Oshkosh	1.4	12.6	40.0	6.7	21 827	14.6	612	20 957	57.0	53 800	20.4	13.0	379	25.7	1.6
Racine	1.3	15.9	69.1	13.2	33 156	0.5	976	31 767	59.6	52 500	18.2	13.1	383	27.2	3.5
Sheboygan	1.5	9.3	63.2	6.5	20 588	9.4	534	19 703	61.6	53 500	18.6	13.3	364	23.0	2.0
Superior	1.0	17.1	61.3	12.9	11 684	-2.5	349	11 001	61.2	37 300	18.4	13.4	295	27.5	1.1
Waukesha	2.2	6.1	19.6	4.5	22 065	20.3	683	21 235	55.5	81 600	21.4	12.8	525	25.0	2.7
Wausau	2.7	11.7	34.5	7.8	15 318	15.2	402	14 718	63.0	51 000	18.9	13.5	360	24.5	2.8
Wauwatosa	5.8	3.3	26.9	1.8	20 289	3.4	308	19 848	68.7	89 300	20.6	13.4	526	25.5	0.8
West Allis	0.8	5.3	17.8	4.3	27 502	4.6	471	26 797	59.4	63 100	21.6	14.9	446	23.5	1.8
WYOMING	2.0	11.9	50.1	9.3	203 411	8.1	15 866	168 839	67.8	61 600	18.8	11.9	333	23.7	3.1
Casper	2.7	11.4	90.0	9.6	21 700	7.1	2 326	18 504	66.3	53 100	18.4	11.5	296	23.5	1.5
Cheyenne	1.6	10.3	32.1	8.6	21 859	11.5	1 289	20 243	63.9	68 700	20.3	11.7	365	25.0	1.7
Laramie	1.9	21.0	28.8	10.6	11 076	16.1	514	10 400	45.8	66 900	18.8	11.2	343	32.4	3.0

1. Includes units rented or sold but not occupied. 2. Specified owner-occupied units. 3. Specified renter-occupied units. 4. Overcrowded or lacking complete plumbing facilities.

City	Civilian labor force, 1999				Civilian employment, 1990[2]			Disability 1990	Value of residential construction authorized by building permits, 1999		
			Unemployment			Percent					
	Total	Percent change, 1998–1999	Total	Rate[1]	Total	Professional, managerial, and technical	Precision production, craft, and repair	Work disabled persons[3] (percent)	New construction ($1,000)	Number of housing units	Percent single family
	61	62	63	64	65	66	67	68	69	70	71
WASHINGTON	3 075 959	1.2	145 379	4.7	2 293 961	31.7	11.6	9.1	4 588 556	42 809	65.8
Auburn	21 232	0.8	805	3.8	16 756	24.0	16.6	11.5	19 143	119	86.6
Bellevue	62 254	0.7	1 447	2.3	49 880	44.3	6.2	5.2	112 977	1 019	23.0
Bellingham	34 726	2.5	1 786	5.1	26 416	29.9	10.4	7.8	72 313	787	35.1
Bremerton	15 711	2.1	1 238	7.9	12 887	26.0	17.0	13.4	3 650	33	100.0
Edmonds	24 248	4.0	756	3.1	16 760	38.3	9.6	5.8	29 413	161	44.7
Everett	48 695	4.6	2 956	6.1	32 632	24.8	16.6	11.2	35 536	374	43.3
Kennewick	26 869	1.5	1 725	6.4	19 393	33.1	10.5	9.6	35 976	277	100.0
Kent	27 507	0.8	914	3.3	21 814	30.4	12.6	7.6	90 878	1 075	28.1
Kirkland	30 182	0.7	799	2.6	24 103	38.0	8.5	5.6	75 482	418	50.2
Longview	16 193	-0.3	1 198	7.4	13 337	24.6	13.1	11.9	14 562	165	75.8
Lynnwood	22 501	4.2	974	4.3	15 358	26.5	15.5	10.2	23 139	230	65.2
Olympia	22 230	1.9	1 002	4.5	16 415	43.3	6.9	10.4	35 339	499	40.3
Redmond	26 296	0.7	575	2.2	21 099	43.3	7.7	4.5	33 049	187	58.3
Renton	29 219	0.8	1 032	3.5	23 122	34.5	12.7	7.3	47 984	447	38.9
Richland	21 764	1.8	1 006	4.6	16 010	50.4	7.7	7.4	40 391	233	83.7
Seattle	359 989	0.8	13 579	3.8	284 160	41.1	7.0	8.4	256 784	3 545	13.5
Spokane	101 282	0.9	6 028	6.0	75 112	30.9	8.9	13.1	54 977	588	58.7
Tacoma	100 378	0.8	5 255	5.2	74 841	27.0	11.9	12.4	79 989	607	71.0
Vancouver	32 671	1.0	1 682	5.1	20 079	25.5	12.1	13.1	114 625	1 436	57.7
Walla Walla	13 275	-0.8	1 138	8.6	10 461	27.9	7.8	10.9	2 579	17	88.2
Yakima	32 729	-0.4	3 263	10.0	22 118	28.0	9.5	10.6	6 433	109	26.6
WEST VIRGINIA	817 009	2.1	53 909	6.6	671 085	25.4	14.5	12.6	381 091	4 233	84.5
Charleston	30 204	3.0	1 502	5.0	24 462	40.1	6.9	11.3	18 132	71	100.0
Huntington	23 402	2.1	1 491	6.4	20 534	35.9	7.6	13.6	7 435	101	24.8
Morgantown	12 724	2.6	473	3.7	10 705	45.7	4.9	4.2	4 283	69	21.7
Parkersburg	16 533	0.2	1 091	6.6	13 862	26.5	10.7	12.0	2 400	36	88.9
Wheeling	16 946	0.7	658	3.9	14 920	31.9	9.3	9.7	2 543	18	88.9
WISCONSIN	2 891 982	-2.0	88 101	3.0	2 386 439	26.4	11.5	7.3	3 868 481	35 620	69.8
Appleton	42 285	-3.2	1 252	3.0	33 379	32.4	10.1	6.1	39 370	230	89.1
Beloit	16 831	-4.9	932	5.5	15 920	24.1	13.1	9.6	4 858	86	69.8
Brookfield	20 737	-3.2	385	1.9	17 654	44.8	7.2	4.1	31 998	133	100.0
Eau Claire	34 029	-1.6	1 047	3.1	26 961	30.4	7.8	7.1	37 991	393	47.8
Fond du Lac	21 297	-4.0	757	3.6	17 928	24.4	11.5	7.6	19 505	209	44.5
Green Bay	59 483	-4.3	2 087	3.5	47 686	25.0	10.7	7.5	48 647	501	44.3
Greenfield	20 282	-0.5	372	1.8	17 941	30.5	12.1	7.2	20 531	215	60.5
Janesville	31 302	-3.5	1 375	4.4	26 143	23.8	11.9	7.9	39 577	422	65.4
Kenosha	47 241	-2.1	1 951	4.1	35 935	23.6	12.7	9.1	36 130	417	56.8
La Crosse	27 051	-5.4	1 033	3.8	24 796	28.1	7.4	7.0	8 656	136	23.5
Madison	127 997	-2.6	1 912	1.5	108 284	42.3	5.5	5.6	145 140	1 444	38.2
Manitowoc	16 538	-5.3	721	4.4	14 554	24.5	12.0	8.5	9 283	110	69.1
Menomonee Falls	18 880	-0.3	307	1.6	14 781	31.2	13.9	5.1	40 984	326	53.7
Milwaukee	285 613	-2.7	14 257	5.0	274 237	24.8	10.2	10.2	20 631	204	45.6
New Berlin	23 187	-0.9	402	1.7	19 132	36.6	10.8	4.5	55 081	461	44.5
Oshkosh	36 272	-2.6	992	2.7	27 170	26.6	9.3	6.4	22 773	383	41.0
Racine	33 894	-4.8	2 620	7.7	37 407	24.4	12.6	9.1	3 586	27	100.0
Sheboygan	26 566	-2.5	633	2.4	24 283	22.9	11.0	7.7	8 068	98	46.9
Superior	14 032	-3.7	573	4.1	11 492	25.5	8.8	9.6	3 840	52	59.6
Waukesha	37 903	-0.7	1 141	3.0	31 399	32.6	10.6	7.2	61 141	558	40.7
Wausau	20 108	-4.2	710	3.5	17 387	29.0	9.7	7.8	12 739	95	83.2
Wauwatosa	25 109	-2.4	483	1.9	24 674	45.7	6.5	4.7	273	2	100.0
West Allis	33 931	-1.2	850	2.5	32 452	24.3	13.0	7.3	2 191	26	15.4
WYOMING	262 069	1.6	12 746	4.9	207 868	27.2	13.2	7.3	278 559	1 900	76.6
Casper	25 544	1.2	1 293	5.1	21 694	33.5	10.8	7.0	16 037	217	29.5
Cheyenne	27 544	-0.3	965	3.5	23 126	33.3	8.5	8.4	18 573	204	83.3
Laramie	15 013	2.8	281	1.9	12 856	40.0	6.7	4.6	9 842	140	25.7

1. Percent of civilian labor force. 2. Persons 16 years and older. 3. Persons 16 to 64 years old.

Table D. Cities — **Wholesale Trade, Retail Trade, and Real Estate**

City	Wholesale Trade, 1997				Retail Trade[1], 1997				Real Estate and Rental and Leasing, 1997			
	Number of Establishments	Number of Employees	Sales (mil dol)	Annual Payroll (mil dol)	Number of Establishments	Number of Employees	Sales (mil dol)	Annual Payroll (mil dol)	Number of Establishments	Number of Employees	Receipts (mil dol)	Annual Payroll (mil dol)
	72	73	74	75	76	77	78	79	80	81	82	83
WASHINGTON	10 039	118 810	75 397.8	4 376.0	22 841	283 653	52 472.9	5 385.9	7 544	41 899	5 352.8	935.3
Auburn	135	2 935	1 409.5	90.0	297	4 494	931.4	92.9	57	264	32.7	6.1
Bellevue	579	6 532	11 707.9	316.2	789	13 580	2 745.9	266.2	458	4 723	685.5	151.0
Bellingham	154	1 264	570.4	38.9	502	6 902	1 126.8	115.3	134	529	60.7	8.1
Bremerton	24	289	86.9	10.0	182	2 149	463.6	48.3	48	288	25.6	4.1
Edmonds	70	316	325.1	11.4	160	1 788	361.2	38.5	70	175	27.9	5.8
Everett	144	1 570	592.6	56.1	473	6 518	1 340.0	133.5	138	787	108.4	14.5
Kennewick	59	419	193.2	11.3	378	5 236	890.7	83.8	86	678	82.9	16.1
Kent	454	9 062	5 480.1	346.8	315	4 399	929.9	94.4	95	677	120.6	17.9
Kirkland	206	2 341	2 421.9	135.7	250	3 984	1 012.9	86.1	129	800	102.8	18.3
Longview	46	488	108.0	12.9	224	3 019	554.5	56.4	66	315	35.9	5.7
Lynnwood	87	835	726.1	29.7	404	7 637	1 374.9	139.4	94	519	56.3	10.4
Olympia	74	647	204.8	23.7	371	4 670	853.5	86.5	108	465	50.1	7.7
Redmond	344	4 489	4 405.2	202.9	271	3 061	543.6	65.2	73	441	82.7	12.3
Renton	126	3 117	1 709.3	121.8	228	4 662	1 417.5	121.1	76	801	176.5	22.7
Richland	22	D	D	D	131	1 338	203.0	21.8	41	143	13.4	2.0
Seattle	1 860	23 635	16 085.6	978.1	2 698	34 886	6 146.2	717.7	1 391	8 567	1 302.0	228.0
Spokane	521	7 028	2 709.8	214.1	1 054	13 757	2 389.8	263.0	291	1 800	202.8	33.8
Tacoma	318	4 790	2 819.6	181.7	832	11 432	2 180.3	226.6	237	1 695	152.4	36.9
Vancouver	248	2 277	1 237.4	86.5	440	6 900	1 298.4	137.9	206	1 376	154.5	30.6
Walla Walla	56	D	D	D	190	2 233	348.4	38.9	40	170	14.9	2.4
Yakima	152	2 984	1 047.5	87.5	443	6 123	1 053.7	107.1	115	659	72.8	11.9
WEST VIRGINIA	1 956	23 805	10 290.4	681.1	8 082	90 087	14 057.9	1 309.3	1 449	5 812	665.0	100.8
Charleston	179	2 738	1 386.6	84.0	466	7 135	961.8	102.2	172	907	118.7	17.5
Huntington	136	1 803	551.4	50.0	313	4 091	637.5	65.4	101	464	39.6	7.1
Morgantown	36	D	D	D	267	3 650	505.5	54.9	60	246	20.8	2.8
Parkersburg	78	917	350.0	23.9	291	3 667	617.1	58.5	61	363	36.6	7.3
Wheeling	89	1 694	1 361.1	47.1	223	2 342	354.3	39.2	58	D	D	D
WISCONSIN	8 025	110 309	57 192.9	3 764.9	21 717	305 255	50 520.5	4 826.2	4 598	23 924	2 637.5	464.1
Appleton	94	1 631	583.2	56.7	329	4 683	691.0	73.9	61	345	30.6	5.9
Beloit	17	288	185.9	13.7	141	1 994	385.6	32.3	24	82	17.9	1.3
Brookfield	226	3 092	1 541.1	141.5	349	6 557	939.4	94.0	118	796	92.6	22.0
Eau Claire	100	1 629	754.4	52.3	372	6 849	1 007.5	95.3	86	391	42.2	6.2
Fond du Lac	66	848	361.7	27.2	270	4 084	635.9	61.5	49	222	22.2	3.3
Green Bay	201	2 733	1 316.0	88.9	515	8 419	1 395.5	135.8	107	618	61.0	10.5
Greenfield	36	D	D	D	184	4 012	707.8	65.8	35	160	39.1	3.1
Janesville	68	1 829	1 270.6	60.4	310	5 461	992.1	98.4	52	217	29.1	3.6
Kenosha	66	853	208.6	27.3	313	4 549	699.7	66.4	80	336	34.3	5.0
La Crosse	92	2 701	1 746.4	88.7	336	5 685	905.3	90.9	80	683	47.5	11.8
Madison	324	4 530	1 621.6	149.1	1 078	18 263	2 761.0	282.4	328	2 523	277.3	51.3
Manitowoc	34	370	192.3	15.3	162	2 411	357.3	34.4	27	114	8.1	1.5
Menomonee Falls	151	1 762	1 051.2	74.2	152	3 142	535.1	56.1	30	191	21.2	6.5
Milwaukee	753	14 029	8 379.2	531.4	1 700	22 655	3 381.2	360.6	484	3 899	462.3	90.6
New Berlin	166	2 918	1 064.5	107.1	92	1 481	213.6	24.3	25	123	40.9	4.4
Oshkosh	72	1 078	323.1	32.7	332	4 744	841.5	83.3	87	485	41.6	7.5
Racine	101	1 974	2 300.4	67.7	362	5 297	710.0	70.1	68	388	31.0	6.8
Sheboygan	57	1 173	712.8	38.1	210	3 565	523.9	54.7	47	212	24.0	3.4
Superior	48	D	D	D	128	1 884	309.2	28.6	34	113	8.5	1.5
Waukesha	203	2 738	3 554.5	114.7	242	4 556	970.8	82.6	83	620	72.7	12.5
Wausau	71	873	306.1	27.8	251	5 060	745.9	77.5	33	174	14.2	2.9
Wauwatosa	140	2 622	1 773.5	89.9	289	6 903	942.9	121.4	76	510	65.9	11.6
West Allis	128	1 797	578.4	66.2	311	5 485	1 013.5	93.2	66	1 011	113.6	21.4
WYOMING	800	5 761	2 547.1	161.9	2 939	26 934	4 530.5	426.7	717	2 463	220.8	39.5
Casper	122	921	687.1	25.6	346	3 702	595.2	59.6	91	329	29.3	5.6
Cheyenne	56	457	178.2	13.4	308	4 496	761.4	71.9	77	300	26.1	5.0
Laramie	19	101	81.5	2.3	158	1 607	332.6	26.9	44	125	9.0	1.4

1. Establishments with payroll.

City	Professional, Scientific, and Technical Services, 1997[1]				Manufacturing, 1997				Accommodation and Foodservices, 1997			
	Number of Establishments	Number of Employees	Receipts (mil dol)	Annual Payroll (mil dol)	Number of Establishments	Number of Employees	Receipts (mil dol)	Annual Payroll (mil dol)	Number of Establishments	Number of Employees	Sales (mil dol)	Annual Payroll (mil dol)
	84	85	86	87	88	89	90	91	92	93	94	95
WASHINGTON	13 411	101 848	10 564.8	4 247.3	7 801	328 511	78 852.5	13 004.1	13 105	194 955	6 995.1	1 962.9
Auburn	73	310	18.9	8.3	167	13 946	1 875.8	605.2	112	1 894	55.3	15.5
Bellevue	1 073	12 563	1 645.8	651.9	163	2 740	681.8	93.3	332	6 369	272.5	73.9
Bellingham	254	1 909	187.7	80.7	130	3 457	583.9	91.5	264	3 793	112.0	31.9
Bremerton	71	976	65.6	27.1	NA	NA	NA	NA	108	1 613	49.4	13.6
Edmonds	146	555	53.5	20.5	NA	NA	NA	NA	92	1 167	41.6	11.4
Everett	221	1 390	119.7	51.0	130	D	D	D	263	4 184	143.5	37.7
Kennewick	118	D	D	D	46	D	D	D	141	2 339	77.2	20.2
Kent	162	1 387	140.7	51.6	295	26 894	3 997.4	1 274.8	181	2 744	96.2	25.7
Kirkland	302	4 454	330.1	148.9	93	1 941	315.8	63.2	168	3 838	150.1	45.2
Longview	79	466	29.1	12.8	46	2 556	824.3	115.2	94	1 642	45.7	13.3
Lynnwood	120	618	58.5	28.2	61	1 526	145.9	40.8	150	3 142	106.4	29.1
Olympia	253	1 248	90.1	39.2	47	1 368	387.0	47.3	202	3 426	106.9	32.9
Redmond	278	3 426	269.9	125.3	227	11 807	2 183.7	448.5	134	2 062	79.7	22.3
Renton	122	627	67.1	26.1	70	D	D	D	165	2 468	84.4	24.0
Richland	127	3 310	278.2	166.8	28	1 449	294.2	65.6	79	1 483	47.2	13.4
Seattle	3 235	31 669	3 703.6	1 489.6	1 213	33 935	5 021.1	1 132.7	2 105	34 197	1 550.6	445.9
Spokane	635	4 413	357.4	151.9	315	6 862	927.5	210.0	568	9 847	306.0	88.5
Tacoma	434	2 722	278.6	108.7	276	10 894	2 625.6	363.5	425	6 735	220.6	61.9
Vancouver	333	2 070	158.3	68.3	193	13 073	2 515.9	494.0	254	4 169	137.0	39.9
Walla Walla	59	265	17.5	6.8	43	1 137	154.7	31.2	96	1 287	38.2	10.7
Yakima	158	1 038	102.6	37.0	102	4 624	747.7	124.0	219	3 445	115.8	31.9
WEST VIRGINIA	2 517	15 714	1 166.9	395.2	1 505	72 813	18 293.3	2 460.7	3 290	51 529	1 633.2	462.3
Charleston	371	3 413	326.8	103.7	44	2 152	278.2	85.5	210	3 967	147.6	38.9
Huntington	140	992	67.8	24.1	72	5 111	1 034.8	176.3	187	3 573	102.1	28.6
Morgantown	98	647	52.5	17.4	20	D	D	D	150	2 726	72.4	21.0
Parkersburg	97	668	44.0	15.0	30	1 103	113.6	31.6	129	2 367	69.1	19.6
Wheeling	107	836	74.4	20.9	53	D	D	D	130	1 837	51.6	15.0
WISCONSIN	9 281	70 689	6 398.9	2 542.3	9 936	562 479	117 383.0	18 766.4	13 252	190 411	5 641.0	1 548.5
Appleton	165	1 457	130.3	52.9	120	8 235	2 168.1	314.7	168	3 336	94.0	28.1
Beloit	41	185	9.4	3.5	52	4 896	1 257.5	198.9	91	1 360	37.8	10.9
Brookfield	314	3 071	321.0	139.2	90	2 873	456.6	102.5	99	2 519	93.9	24.5
Eau Claire	136	1 328	100.5	43.3	93	4 353	623.5	115.6	200	4 659	108.4	32.9
Fond du Lac	91	468	36.3	14.8	93	7 301	1 609.5	297.4	134	2 525	69.3	19.4
Green Bay	209	1 763	140.9	66.2	200	16 692	4 634.5	695.3	286	5 153	137.9	40.1
Greenfield	65	676	38.4	18.0	NA	NA	NA	NA	74	2 176	58.4	17.3
Janesville	99	564	39.6	15.2	104	12 380	8 390.6	504.2	154	3 107	88.3	24.2
Kenosha	126	544	36.7	16.2	126	5 949	1 287.7	280.6	207	2 787	78.6	21.8
La Crosse	139	1 403	105.9	49.4	91	7 001	1 110.3	246.2	208	3 799	98.3	29.2
Madison	702	8 705	759.2	341.9	228	11 464	2 573.9	370.4	602	12 763	390.8	110.9
Manitowoc	53	441	35.9	9.5	88	9 202	1 478.9	280.1	92	1 480	38.2	10.6
Menomonee Falls	89	585	45.3	21.3	211	9 784	1 476.3	354.1	56	868	24.5	7.4
Milwaukee	1 092	14 871	1 570.3	628.8	848	46 467	8 392.4	1 643.5	1 143	17 743	606.5	170.4
New Berlin	91	1 062	215.1	45.7	150	6 647	1 299.8	259.0	54	D	D	D
Oshkosh	94	774	85.7	20.9	114	8 692	1 860.5	291.8	177	3 591	93.5	27.3
Racine	139	898	59.3	24.8	219	9 065	1 845.0	322.3	166	2 653	78.4	21.8
Sheboygan	83	786	57.8	24.6	99	7 887	1 415.6	260.6	136	1 809	49.3	13.3
Superior	45	300	19.7	7.4	45	D	D	D	111	1 447	37.6	10.5
Waukesha	186	1 971	199.1	75.7	195	9 902	2 578.4	394.2	127	2 688	79.9	23.3
Wausau	103	727	64.5	27.9	83	8 190	1 192.1	228.8	101	1 496	39.7	11.5
Wauwatosa	281	1 880	196.1	70.9	81	7 766	1 388.8	342.8	114	2 559	82.0	23.1
West Allis	135	843	73.8	29.5	145	7 537	864.7	226.4	159	D	D	D
WYOMING	1 264	5 274	388.8	146.9	503	8 448	2 955.1	256.4	1 751	24 950	808.9	219.0
Casper	182	798	66.6	23.9	NA	NA	NA	NA	138	2 644	69.9	19.7
Cheyenne	186	807	61.9	23.7	35	D	D	D	156	3 423	90.4	26.9
Laramie	98	527	39.2	16.8	NA	NA	NA	NA	92	1 866	42.5	12.0

1. Firms subject to federal tax.

City	Arts, Entertainment, and Recreation[1], 1997				Health Care and Social Assistance[1], 1997				Other Services[1], 1997			
	Number of Establishments	Number of Employees	Receipts (mil dol)	Annual Payroll (mil dol)	Number of Establishments	Number of Employees	Receipts (mil dol)	Annual Payroll (mil dol)	Number of Establishments	Number of Employees	Receipts (mil dol)	Annual Payroll (mil dol)
	96	97	98	99	100	101	102	103	104	105	106	107
WASHINGTON	1 680	27 971	1 620.1	544.6	12 310	122 813	7 797.7	3 390.2	8 771	49 756	3 492.0	1 033.0
Auburn	19	1 406	106.7	32.1	126	2 433	125.2	60.5	115	653	50.4	15.8
Bellevue	59	1 186	62.5	18.1	560	4 476	340.0	147.2	320	2 011	173.5	48.4
Bellingham	32	225	11.1	3.7	305	3 076	176.5	72.4	133	770	49.7	13.4
Bremerton	15	129	4.4	1.0	148	2 235	115.0	56.8	65	376	22.8	6.9
Edmonds	9	238	10.5	2.6	151	1 271	96.3	43.4	83	343	21.8	6.8
Everett	25	352	17.8	4.5	253	3 407	216.0	117.4	197	1 591	105.4	36.7
Kennewick	19	327	12.3	2.9	149	1 329	88.3	34.1	113	642	32.0	10.4
Kent	13	183	8.5	2.2	133	1 620	110.3	44.2	179	1 507	120.9	38.4
Kirkland	20	356	82.1	58.2	225	2 116	132.9	57.7	154	914	65.0	21.1
Longview	11	79	2.3	0.6	131	1 564	93.8	41.6	76	402	24.4	7.6
Lynnwood	12	152	5.7	1.9	125	1 069	66.0	24.9	113	560	42.3	13.7
Olympia	22	314	14.3	3.0	288	3 199	258.6	111.4	111	505	32.7	10.3
Redmond	21	310	16.5	5.1	126	1 491	95.3	36.5	116	879	75.2	23.6
Renton	16	231	27.6	2.4	174	1 763	115.1	50.8	118	786	54.5	17.7
Richland	9	133	5.1	1.5	148	1 108	79.9	32.9	45	313	20.9	6.2
Seattle	263	3 786	308.8	151.4	1 643	17 217	1 318.7	574.4	1 266	9 352	756.9	207.1
Spokane	59	863	47.1	8.8	622	8 079	505.9	234.3	444	2 938	180.0	54.2
Tacoma	44	1 260	116.1	30.2	598	7 046	461.2	215.1	318	2 360	154.4	52.2
Vancouver	36	537	21.1	4.7	293	4 380	286.1	135.3	224	1 319	84.7	26.0
Walla Walla	8	0	0.0	0.0	81	958	59.7	26.3	49	240	16.5	4.6
Yakima	24	419	18.9	5.3	243	3 102	209.0	96.9	153	918	59.3	18.5
WEST VIRGINIA	408	4 996	273.3	56.6	3 266	40 085	2 575.0	1 056.9	2 512	14 805	867.4	255.9
Charleston	24	252	11.6	3.0	314	3 898	365.3	151.4	141	1 196	64.5	20.1
Huntington	20	118	4.4	1.2	199	3 237	254.2	121.2	113	808	44.3	14.6
Morgantown	15	122	4.6	1.3	74	1 887	133.2	68.6	83	590	37.8	11.1
Parkersburg	10	113	3.8	1.3	145	1 819	118.3	51.8	109	1 365	106.1	24.6
Wheeling	17	328	34.7	4.3	175	1 572	105.7	44.6	96	755	39.7	13.8
WISCONSIN	1 730	22 339	1 327.5	384.3	9 315	114 562	6 917.4	3 447.3	8 648	49 101	2 991.3	886.4
Appleton	18	195	8.7	2.0	185	2 058	164.6	85.6	158	1 218	72.0	20.5
Beloit	4	57	2.6	0.7	54	1 153	55.7	30.6	55	222	11.2	2.9
Brookfield	17	429	10.7	3.6	162	1 696	115.7	53.9	110	1 153	86.9	29.4
Eau Claire	20	230	14.9	3.8	148	2 706	179.9	105.4	150	1 026	51.0	15.8
Fond du Lac	19	180	5.3	1.9	106	1 325	162.2	45.2	98	709	31.2	10.4
Green Bay	31	0	0.0	0.0	223	3 256	240.5	131.0	191	1 332	76.5	24.8
Greenfield	13	163	6.1	1.7	94	2 414	103.1	55.5	78	537	26.1	9.0
Janesville	16	242	7.9	2.2	104	1 618	116.7	55.0	107	542	32.7	8.8
Kenosha	25	703	37.8	9.0	217	2 182	120.3	58.6	159	931	46.9	14.0
La Crosse	23	465	9.5	3.9	90	629	40.3	18.5	123	882	47.4	15.9
Madison	75	1 475	49.2	14.2	431	6 355	549.7	235.5	343	2 911	162.8	57.6
Manitowoc	10	86	3.8	0.7	91	1 058	61.7	32.4	55	257	14.1	4.3
Menomonee Falls	9	105	8.0	1.8	62	1 647	108.1	57.0	70	964	113.6	28.4
Milwaukee	90	1 781	368.8	90.7	915	11 854	781.1	426.7	755	5 080	307.4	97.3
New Berlin	10	184	4.3	1.5	70	674	39.8	18.2	61	741	71.0	19.9
Oshkosh	22	212	8.6	1.9	143	1 518	99.6	47.1	101	711	31.6	9.4
Racine	14	150	6.1	1.4	123	1 629	150.1	69.4	141	979	52.7	18.5
Sheboygan	9	99	2.4	0.6	117	1 904	110.6	62.9	97	685	41.0	10.5
Superior	10	90	5.1	0.9	47	583	29.3	14.0	61	357	20.9	5.5
Waukesha	21	236	7.8	2.4	185	2 249	134.2	73.3	126	774	41.2	13.3
Wausau	14	289	6.4	1.5	118	1 795	147.9	85.2	84	477	19.9	5.9
Wauwatosa	12	184	5.6	1.6	436	4 766	378.0	216.5	89	822	43.9	14.1
West Allis	15	284	16.3	2.9	170	2 274	139.8	74.1	164	1 167	77.2	25.1
WYOMING	262	2 108	93.3	23.3	1 006	7 875	493.6	210.3	980	4 866	422.8	94.8
Casper	23	123	7.3	1.6	165	0	0.0	0.0	117	627	37.1	11.2
Cheyenne	18	0	0.0	0.0	142	1 524	103.7	50.3	103	1 046	159.5	22.7
Laramie	14	0	0.0	0.0	70	0	0.0	0.0	56	338	15.5	4.9

1. Firms subject to federal tax.

City	Selected federal funds, fiscal 1999[1] (mil dol)									City government finances, 1997						
	Procurement contracts		Grants					Direct payments for individuals		General revenue						
											Intergovernmental		Taxes			
														Per capita[3] (dollars)		
	Defense	Other	Total[2]	Health and family welfare	Energy and environment	Education	Housing and community development	Educational assistance	Housing assistance	Total (mil dol)	Total (mil dol)	Percent from state government	Total (mil dol)	Total	Property	Sales and gross receipts
	108	109	110	111	112	113	114	115	116	117	118	119	120	121	122	123
WASHINGTON	2 296.5	2 317.9	5 720.3	3 459.1	90.1	455.4	108.0	109.6	115.5	X	X	X	X	X	X	X
Auburn	1.0	13.2	3.6	2.0	0.0	0.8	0.4	1.5	2.5	52.7	7.6	79.6	23.6	649	260	367
Bellevue	13.4	11.1	4.4	0.5	0.5	0.0	0.3	2.0	5.7	153.1	17.5	50.2	90.9	985	256	544
Bellingham	3.1	2.3	18.3	4.5	0.1	3.2	2.1	6.2	1.0	67.6	9.2	70.6	33.9	556	132	296
Bremerton	115.2	2.7	7.7	3.8	0.0	1.1	1.7	1.6	2.9	33.3	3.5	79.6	15.7	378	112	216
Edmonds	0.0	9.0	1.1	0.9	0.0	0.2	0.0	0.1	1.6	28.1	5.9	60.8	12.9	402	186	205
Everett	62.5	1.9	19.4	1.2	0.1	0.2	1.8	4.5	10.4	116.2	10.8	68.2	67.6	834	276	397
Kennewick	6.6	2.4	6.1	0.0	4.5	0.3	0.9	0.0	2.8	43.4	12.9	93.5	20.2	396	104	265
Kent	75.9	4.9	2.6	0.0	0.4	0.1	0.0	0.0	2.2	85.5	13.2	48.5	41.0	959	343	586
Kirkland	2.5	2.3	1.0	0.0	0.0	0.0	0.4	1.0	1.9	46.8	4.0	87.1	25.1	574	193	362
Longview	0.1	0.3	3.0	1.9	0.0	0.3	0.3	1.3	0.3	31.9	5.4	68.3	15.5	460	136	270
Lynnwood	9.4	1.8	5.1	3.3	0.0	0.0	0.9	1.3	0.9	46.2	13.8	94.2	20.1	642	205	408
Olympia	2.0	4.5	707.4	229.1	41.2	133.5	19.4	4.3	1.1	61.8	10.3	26.3	26.1	669	211	377
Redmond	53.7	4.5	1.3	1.3	0.0	0.0	0.0	0.0	0.0	62.1	8.4	52.6	33.5	796	238	493
Renton	8.6	9.0	2.5	1.2	0.2	0.4	0.0	0.9	4.7	80.2	10.9	82.4	38.3	848	292	470
Richland	9.8	1 436.5	4.9	2.5	0.2	0.0	0.9	0.0	0.0	39.9	7.6	49.4	16.0	428	142	256
Seattle	1 201.9	223.3	902.6	514.2	26.0	20.1	35.1	25.8	15.9	940.1	117.4	74.4	474.0	903	302	385
Spokane	7.4	14.8	32.0	7.0	0.0	7.2	9.8	10.3	14.1	192.1	22.5	77.2	77.4	415	159	228
Tacoma	33.2	21.7	46.6	14.3	0.2	3.8	9.3	10.3	7.0	243.6	22.8	65.8	97.2	543	184	240
Vancouver	7.1	79.7	11.1	6.4	0.0	1.5	0.4	2.1	4.7	83.6	16.4	41.4	33.9	565	195	284
Walla Walla	1.0	0.4	4.5	0.7	0.0	0.9	0.0	2.1	1.6	26.0	5.8	75.6	7.9	278	69	177
Yakima	1.7	8.1	19.2	12.5	0.0	1.8	1.4	1.7	2.5	59.4	12.6	73.0	28.8	442	120	307
WEST VIRGINIA	108.8	516.5	2 489.9	1 431.9	59.6	207.8	46.0	42.2	20.9	X	X	X	X	X	X	X
Charleston	1.1	23.4	394.2	92.3	43.2	62.0	34.6	2.2	5.5	80.0	4.7	21.2	42.1	750	185	64
Huntington	1.7	10.3	19.6	4.9	0.0	1.0	4.5	5.7	5.5	42.4	7.2	12.1	18.1	335	86	44
Morgantown	3.3	58.0	47.6	12.6	3.2	4.8	0.0	7.8	0.2	23.5	1.9	19.0	9.3	347	108	41
Parkersburg	1.0	9.1	9.7	2.6	0.0	0.0	2.0	1.9	0.9	89.2	0.9	65.3	10.0	305	83	6
Wheeling	1.0	8.2	22.8	3.2	0.4	0.0	3.6	2.0	1.1	26.6	2.4	4.5	11.8	353	80	56
WISCONSIN	643.8	789.6	4 841.7	2 933.6	112.6	443.2	114.1	131.1	121.1	X	X	X	X	X	X	X
Appleton	1.7	1.5	8.1	0.2	0.0	1.2	1.6	1.8	1.1	73.1	21.6	86.7	26.4	401	376	3
Beloit	1.7	0.3	2.9	0.6	0.0	0.7	1.3	0.6	0.0	43.9	22.2	88.8	7.8	218	196	7
Brookfield	1.0	0.9	0.0	0.0	0.0	0.0	0.0	0.0	0.0	40.1	4.9	75.7	19.0	505	436	44
Eau Claire	3.9	0.4	5.3	0.6	0.0	1.2	1.5	4.8	0.5	52.0	21.4	76.2	14.3	243	206	14
Fond du Lac	1.2	0.8	2.5	1.5	0.0	0.2	0.7	0.9	4.1	37.8	13.0	92.2	13.9	351	324	8
Green Bay	8.2	95.9	11.5	3.7	0.0	1.2	2.6	1.1	2.6	105.0	36.6	90.0	32.4	318	299	7
Greenfield	0.0	0.0	0.0	0.0	0.0	0.0	0.0	0.5	2.7	28.0	6.4	90.6	14.7	428	409	1
Janesville	38.9	0.5	2.7	0.0	0.0	0.0	1.9	0.6	0.2	51.1	16.3	78.5	14.8	250	231	7
Kenosha	22.6	1.9	5.4	2.5	0.0	0.4	1.4	2.0	6.7	76.6	28.2	83.1	28.4	327	304	3
La Crosse	24.4	0.5	8.5	2.2	0.0	1.5	1.7	4.3	0.0	56.8	20.2	83.8	17.2	342	309	16
Madison	32.1	28.0	1 111.6	421.5	104.3	135.4	43.1	16.6	10.2	233.4	85.4	76.6	92.7	469	423	24
Manitowoc	0.2	0.4	0.4	0.1	0.0	0.0	0.3	0.4	2.2	32.7	11.2	91.5	7.4	223	195	9
Menomonee Falls	0.8	0.3	0.0	0.0	0.0	0.0	0.0	0.0	0.0	34.1	4.2	100.0	15.0	493	436	1
Milwaukee	0.0	0.0	181.8	92.5	1.8	15.4	34.2	22.8	38.5	697.9	371.3	80.2	165.0	279	262	0
New Berlin	0.4	0.1	0.1	0.0	0.0	0.0	0.0	0.0	0.0	28.0	3.1	97.3	11.5	317	283	0
Oshkosh	201.4	7.7	5.2	2.9	0.0	0.4	0.9	2.6	1.9	54.4	20.6	82.7	15.0	258	231	8
Racine	6.7	0.8	15.3	2.7	0.0	1.1	3.7	0.0	2.2	96.4	44.1	83.6	33.4	404	392	2
Sheboygan	4.7	3.6	4.1	0.7	0.0	0.0	2.6	0.0	1.6	47.8	19.6	89.2	16.2	324	299	9
Superior	3.5	1.1	4.7	2.4	0.1	0.6	1.2	1.4	2.9	40.4	17.3	83.1	9.0	330	278	12
Waukesha	40.6	1.0	5.3	1.7	0.0	0.0	2.4	1.3	0.4	52.8	11.4	87.7	25.9	430	395	9
Wausau	0.2	0.5	4.7	1.7	0.0	0.9	1.5	0.9	1.0	37.1	14.7	71.1	12.2	331	309	13
Wauwatosa	0.0	0.0	2.6	0.5	0.0	0.0	1.7	0.0	0.6	44.7	9.2	71.8	24.3	519	485	14
West Allis	0.0	0.1	2.1	0.0	0.0	0.3	1.8	0.0	1.1	58.4	19.5	79.2	24.6	406	379	1
WYOMING	63.1	136.1	933.4	217.7	36.1	82.7	11.7	12.5	7.0	X	X	X	X	X	X	X
Casper	0.8	1.6	8.4	0.2	0.2	0.3	4.0	1.0	0.5	49.8	27.9	63.8	3.1	63	33	20
Cheyenne	2.5	8.5	181.8	26.4	31.3	29.5	6.4	0.9	0.5	46.8	25.5	60.9	5.2	96	43	36
Laramie	0.6	3.8	26.7	3.8	4.7	3.6	0.0	4.4	0.1	25.1	18.4	81.9	1.7	65	38	16

1. October 1, 1998 to September 30, 1999.   2. Includes program categories not shown separately. State totals include additional categories not allocated by city.   3. Based on population estimated as of July 1 of the year shown.

Table D. Cities — City Government Finances

	City government finances, 1997 (cont'd)												
	General expenditure												
	Per capita[1] (dollars)			Percent of total for —									
City	Total (mil dol)	Total	Capital outlays	Public welfare	Highways	Parking facilities	Education	Health and hospitals	Police protection	Sewerage and sanitation	Parks and recreation	Housing and community development	Interest on debt
	124	125	126	127	128	129	130	131	132	133	134	135	136
WASHINGTON	X	X	X	X	X	X	X	X	X	X	X	X	X
Auburn	41.2	1 132	246	0.0	14.2	0.0	0.0	1.0	17.1	22.7	8.1	0.7	0.5
Bellevue	144.4	1 565	412	0.2	16.0	0.0	0.0	4.4	10.4	11.2	11.0	4.4	4.8
Bellingham	57.0	934	191	0.0	15.0	0.6	0.0	1.3	12.9	10.9	11.0	2.3	4.7
Bremerton	38.3	922	239	0.0	8.3	0.2	0.0	2.6	12.9	27.3	9.0	1.6	5.8
Edmonds	23.5	734	90	0.0	12.9	0.0	0.0	4.4	17.9	5.5	7.5	0.0	6.0
Everett	117.9	1 455	165	0.1	11.0	0.2	0.0	2.3	12.5	12.0	7.1	0.8	5.3
Kennewick	41.7	815	308	0.0	34.4	0.0	0.0	2.1	13.0	7.6	7.5	0.6	0.9
Kent	93.8	2 197	665	0.2	11.1	0.0	0.0	2.0	10.9	14.9	13.7	0.3	6.1
Kirkland	48.0	1 096	143	0.1	11.3	0.9	0.0	0.1	10.1	24.4	7.1	0.0	3.9
Longview	33.2	983	218	0.0	14.6	0.0	0.0	0.1	17.1	18.4	8.9	13.8	1.4
Lynnwood	51.1	1 629	760	0.0	42.3	0.0	0.0	1.1	9.0	6.0	7.9	0.0	5.5
Olympia	53.0	1 360	114	0.0	5.8	0.0	0.0	1.4	11.7	19.8	7.5	1.4	4.5
Redmond	57.4	1 363	319	0.0	22.1	0.0	0.0	3.4	8.9	20.9	6.5	0.8	2.4
Renton	74.1	1 640	328	0.0	19.7	0.0	0.0	0.2	12.6	19.9	9.8	2.0	2.2
Richland	52.8	1 411	612	0.0	19.3	0.0	0.0	4.2	6.6	11.0	4.0	2.4	6.4
Seattle	1 117.9	2 130	573	0.0	9.4	0.0	0.0	1.6	12.6	17.2	13.5	4.8	2.7
Spokane	189.0	1 013	163	0.0	7.7	0.1	0.0	1.4	12.2	28.8	9.1	1.7	9.5
Tacoma	236.6	1 321	100	0.3	8.4	0.2	0.0	2.7	15.7	24.3	3.7	2.5	9.6
Vancouver	83.4	1 390	374	0.0	8.1	1.4	0.0	0.3	10.1	18.1	20.7	0.9	5.4
Walla Walla	29.1	1 020	403	0.0	13.1	0.0	0.0	4.3	9.1	28.4	3.9	0.0	7.0
Yakima	63.0	968	300	0.0	13.3	0.0	0.0	0.5	16.1	20.5	5.2	2.8	3.3
WEST VIRGINIA	X	X	X	X	X	X	X	X	X	X	X	X	X
Charleston	77.7	1 386	161	0.0	5.3	3.2	0.0	3.4	13.1	10.8	16.8	8.3	8.9
Huntington	42.3	783	17	0.0	4.7	1.9	0.0	0.3	13.8	13.4	6.2	15.1	9.8
Morgantown	21.2	789	200	0.1	7.2	3.9	0.0	0.2	14.3	27.1	8.6	0.0	4.6
Parkersburg	86.8	2 648	43	0.0	4.0	0.1	0.0	78.3	4.0	5.3	0.3	0.7	0.3
Wheeling	19.9	597	20	0.0	10.7	3.3	0.0	0.5	17.6	22.8	3.4	1.4	0.4
WISCONSIN	X	X	X	X	X	X	X	X	X	X	X	X	X
Appleton	63.1	958	137	0.0	17.2	3.1	0.0	1.4	13.7	19.1	6.3	1.0	8.0
Beloit	42.3	1 180	126	0.0	13.4	1.0	0.0	7.9	17.2	17.3	7.1	0.8	6.7
Brookfield	35.0	927	124	0.0	16.3	0.9	0.0	0.6	15.6	22.6	6.0	0.0	6.7
Eau Claire	55.3	940	214	0.0	20.6	0.5	0.0	6.2	14.1	13.4	9.5	4.5	4.7
Fond du Lac	36.8	928	179	0.0	20.2	1.1	0.0	2.6	14.7	17.3	5.6	2.4	8.7
Green Bay	107.0	1 048	187	0.0	20.0	2.1	0.0	0.2	15.3	18.3	7.6	0.8	9.3
Greenfield	23.2	673	62	0.0	15.7	0.0	0.0	5.7	23.9	12.2	3.3	0.0	8.0
Janesville	58.3	988	245	9.1	15.7	0.8	0.0	2.2	12.1	17.5	6.4	2.2	5.2
Kenosha	74.8	861	85	0.0	11.0	0.0	0.0	4.4	18.6	13.8	5.7	1.6	13.4
La Crosse	57.2	1 138	145	0.1	12.7	1.0	0.0	0.1	13.2	10.6	11.1	2.2	9.3
Madison	212.3	1 074	162	0.0	10.7	2.6	0.0	4.0	15.6	12.4	11.7	5.2	5.3
Manitowoc	32.5	974	127	0.0	19.0	0.2	0.0	0.7	12.9	16.1	6.4	1.4	8.6
Menomonee Falls	40.4	1 328	381	0.0	19.3	0.0	0.0	0.1	12.5	30.4	2.1	0.1	8.1
Milwaukee	720.6	1 220	199	0.0	8.0	1.2	0.0	3.4	21.6	15.3	1.3	9.8	3.3
New Berlin	63.4	1 751	952	0.0	8.3	0.0	0.0	0.0	8.5	20.5	2.2	0.0	3.8
Oshkosh	50.7	875	156	0.0	21.6	0.3	0.0	3.0	13.7	15.0	6.2	1.8	8.6
Racine	88.8	1 075	15	0.0	11.4	1.6	0.0	3.0	24.2	13.4	8.2	2.6	6.2
Sheboygan	48.6	973	166	0.0	15.2	0.9	0.0	0.1	14.8	15.6	6.6	3.9	8.3
Superior	34.3	1 252	104	0.0	14.9	0.0	0.0	0.0	13.2	14.4	6.1	3.7	18.1
Waukesha	54.7	909	149	0.0	17.6	0.8	0.0	2.2	16.1	16.1	6.6	0.5	9.3
Wausau	35.9	976	156	0.0	23.2	1.6	0.0	3.4	14.4	12.5	5.1	11.5	5.9
Wauwatosa	51.2	1 095	176	0.0	16.4	0.0	0.0	3.3	18.1	19.4	1.2	1.8	7.8
West Allis	59.0	974	82	3.3	16.2	0.1	0.0	7.2	20.8	13.1	1.2	5.4	6.8
WYOMING	X	X	X	X	X	X	X	X	X	X	X	X	X
Casper	41.9	858	132	0.0	9.6	0.1	0.0	1.9	15.4	20.4	14.5	1.1	0.7
Cheyenne	39.9	743	168	0.1	21.5	0.5	0.0	1.9	13.4	14.2	10.5	2.5	4.8
Laramie	23.4	880	380	4.8	7.0	0.0	0.0	3.1	10.8	44.6	4.0	0.0	0.4

1. Based on population estimated as of July 1 of the year shown.

	City government finances, 1997 (cont'd)				Climate[2]						
	Debt outstanding			City government employment, 1999	Average daily temperature (degrees Fahrenheit)						
					Mean		Limits				
City	Total (mil dol)	Per capita[1] (dollars)	Percent utility		January	July	January[3]	July[4]	Annual precipitation (inches)	Heating degree days	Cooling degree days
	137	138	139	140	141	142	143	144	145	146	147
WASHINGTON	X	X	X	X	X	X	X	X	X	X	X
Auburn	2.1	57	41.8	NA	39.7	64.7	33.1	78.0	39.39	4 996	139
Bellevue	96.0	1 041	20.3	1 417	40.1	65.2	35.2	75.2	37.19	4 908	190
Bellingham	57.5	943	52.0	752	37.6	62.2	31.8	70.9	36.17	5 609	51
Bremerton	34.9	838	0.0	NA	39.1	64.1	33.7	75.0	51.65	5 119	134
Edmonds	30.7	959	0.0	NA	40.1	65.2	35.2	75.2	37.19	4 908	190
Everett	123.6	1 526	0.0	956	39.1	62.9	33.3	72.2	36.51	5 311	80
Kennewick	12.8	249	33.8	NA	33.1	74.7	26.1	90.3	7.49	4 895	830
Kent	99.6	2 332	14.9	754	39.7	64.7	33.1	78.0	39.39	4 996	139
Kirkland	36.2	828	0.0	NA	40.1	65.2	35.2	75.2	37.19	4 908	190
Longview	17.7	523	46.7	NA	39.0	63.8	32.7	76.4	46.54	5 094	132
Lynnwood	33.1	1 056	41.6	NA	40.1	65.2	35.2	75.2	37.19	4 908	190
Olympia	20.3	519	0.0	544	38.0	62.9	31.6	76.5	50.59	5 655	101
Redmond	33.3	791	15.1	553	40.1	65.2	35.2	75.2	37.19	4 908	190
Renton	51.5	1 140	52.2	652	40.1	65.2	35.2	75.2	37.19	4 908	190
Richland	93.5	2 497	37.8	NA	33.4	74.4	25.9	89.4	6.99	4 882	822
Seattle	1 758.7	3 352	64.2	9 609	40.1	65.2	35.2	75.2	37.19	4 908	190
Spokane	270.6	1 450	3.0	2 227	27.1	68.8	20.8	83.1	16.49	6 842	398
Tacoma	675.8	3 773	63.2	4 793	40.1	65.2	35.2	75.2	37.19	4 908	190
Vancouver	108.7	1 812	77.0	923	38.1	64.6	31.2	77.1	41.30	5 196	183
Walla Walla	33.3	1 167	0.0	NA	34.1	75.1	28.4	89.4	19.49	4 958	889
Yakima	33.6	516	5.0	667	29.7	69.9	21.8	86.7	7.97	5 967	458
WEST VIRGINIA	X	X	X	X	X	X	X	X	X	X	X
Charleston	101.2	1 804	0.0	848	32.1	75.1	23.0	85.7	42.53	4 646	1 031
Huntington	56.7	1 051	0.0	503	32.0	74.7	23.2	84.3	41.49	4 665	1 005
Morgantown	20.3	754	20.0	351	29.0	72.9	20.8	83.2	41.21	5 363	785
Parkersburg	35.1	1 072	89.0	1 604	29.9	74.4	21.7	84.2	41.51	5 063	953
Wheeling	22.8	683	94.2	875	27.7	73.3	17.6	85.4	40.81	5 598	788
WISCONSIN	X	X	X	X	X	X	X	X	X	X	X
Appleton	100.3	1 523	12.0	702	15.5	71.9	7.2	81.9	30.75	7 693	539
Beloit	51.2	1 429	0.6	477	17.6	72.7	8.8	83.7	33.05	7 161	636
Brookfield	55.7	1 478	20.1	335	19.9	73.6	12.3	84.3	31.11	6 804	725
Eau Claire	50.8	864	15.1	855	10.7	71.5	0.8	83.2	31.61	8 330	507
Fond du Lac	50.2	1 266	20.0	503	16.1	72.0	7.9	82.0	29.39	7 541	562
Green Bay	177.4	1 738	17.9	1 024	14.3	69.7	5.8	80.5	28.83	8 089	381
Greenfield	28.5	828	0.0	242	18.9	70.9	11.6	79.9	32.93	7 324	479
Janesville	59.1	1 003	14.3	NA	17.6	72.7	8.8	83.7	33.05	7 161	636
Kenosha	155.7	1 792	3.5	794	20.0	69.7	11.7	78.7	33.21	7 195	410
La Crosse	72.1	1 437	4.3	676	14.4	73.5	5.3	84.5	30.55	7 491	692
Madison	273.6	1 385	7.6	2 449	16.0	71.0	7.2	82.4	30.88	7 673	485
Manitowoc	44.3	1 326	63.3	431	17.9	69.8	9.7	80.1	29.11	7 597	374
Menomonee Falls	94.2	3 099	16.8	253	18.9	70.9	11.6	79.9	32.93	7 324	479
Milwaukee	552.5	936	0.0	7 875	19.9	73.6	12.3	84.3	31.11	6 804	725
New Berlin	55.0	1 519	10.2	231	19.8	73.6	12.3	83.0	32.33	6 795	708
Oshkosh	101.6	1 753	13.1	790	14.8	71.8	5.4	82.5	31.15	7 852	522
Racine	104.3	1 264	21.2	961	19.4	71.0	11.2	79.7	34.37	7 167	509
Sheboygan	97.4	1 948	2.1	550	20.3	70.9	12.8	80.4	31.19	7 087	472
Superior	83.9	3 061	0.0	399	10.0	65.9	0.1	77.5	28.91	9 483	206
Waukesha	99.7	1 657	10.0	573	18.6	72.3	10.8	82.8	32.55	7 117	600
Wausau	42.3	1 149	9.3	344	12.0	70.0	2.8	80.8	32.82	8 427	402
Wauwatosa	73.3	1 568	9.1	428	19.9	73.6	12.3	84.3	31.11	6 804	725
West Allis	68.9	1 137	3.8	631	19.8	73.6	12.3	83.0	32.33	6 795	708
WYOMING	X	X	X	X	X	X	X	X	X	X	X
Casper	7.7	157	17.0	538	22.4	70.8	12.0	87.6	12.52	7 682	445
Cheyenne	69.1	1 287	65.7	570	26.5	68.4	15.2	82.2	14.40	7 326	285
Laramie	13.7	514	10.1	223	20.0	64.1	8.0	80.4	10.88	9 008	74

1. Based on the population estimated as of July 1 of the year shown.   2. Represents normal values based on the 30-year period, 1961–1990.   3. Average daily minimum.   4. Average daily maximum.

Congressional Districts of the 105th Congress

(For explanation of symbols, see page xii)

Page

1084	**AL**(District 1)—**CA**(District 44)
1088	**CA**(District 45)—**GA**(District 11)
1092	**HI**(District 1)—**LA**(District 6)
1096	**LA**(District 7)—**MO**(District 3)
1100	**MO**(District 4)—**NY**(District 24)
1104	**NY**(District 25)—**PA**(District 7)
1108	**PA**(District 8)—**TX**(District 27)
1112	**TX**(District 28)—**WY**(At-Large)

STATE District	Land area, 1990[1] (sq km)	Total persons	Per square kilometer	White	Black	Am. Indian, Eskimo, Aleut	Asian and Pacific Islander	Other race	Hispanic[2]	Foreign born	U.S. citizen	Under 5 years	5 to 17 years	18 to 24 years	25 to 34 years	35 to 44 years	45 to 54 years	55 to 64 years
	1	2	3	4	5	6	7	8	9	10	11	12	13	14	15	16	17	18
ALABAMA	131 443	4 040 587	30.7	73.6	25.3	0.4	0.5	0.1	0.6	1.1	99.5	7.0	19.2	11.0	16.0	14.4	10.4	9.0
District 1	17 574	577 226	32.8	69.9	28.5	0.9	0.7	0.1	0.8	1.3	99.4	7.5	20.7	10.0	15.8	14.3	10.3	8.8
District 2	26 241	577 227	22.0	74.8	24.1	0.3	0.6	0.2	0.8	1.2	99.5	7.2	19.5	10.5	16.2	14.6	10.3	8.7
District 3	22 583	577 227	25.6	73.1	26.0	0.2	0.5	0.2	0.6	0.9	99.5	6.7	18.9	13.4	15.2	13.8	10.1	9.0
District 4	23 671	577 227	24.4	92.5	6.6	0.6	0.2	0.1	0.4	0.4	99.8	6.4	18.8	9.8	14.8	14.2	11.3	10.0
District 5	11 419	577 227	50.5	83.4	14.9	0.6	0.9	0.2	0.8	1.6	99.2	6.9	18.0	10.7	17.7	14.8	11.4	9.2
District 6	7 372	577 226	78.3	89.7	9.2	0.2	0.8	0.1	0.6	1.6	99.1	6.6	16.9	11.4	17.7	16.1	10.5	8.8
District 7	22 583	577 227	25.6	32.1	67.5	0.1	0.2	0.1	0.3	0.4	99.8	7.8	21.7	10.9	15.0	13.3	8.8	8.6
ALASKA	1 477 268	550 043	0.4	75.5	4.1	15.6	3.6	1.2	3.2	4.5	97.9	10.0	21.4	10.2	20.5	18.7	9.8	5.4
At Large	1 477 268	550 043	0.4	75.5	4.1	15.6	3.6	1.2	3.2	4.5	97.9	10.0	21.4	10.2	20.5	18.7	9.8	5.4
ARIZONA	294 333	3 665 228	12.5	80.8	3.0	5.6	1.5	9.1	18.8	7.6	95.4	8.0	18.8	10.7	17.3	14.4	9.5	8.2
District 1	546	610 872	1 119.7	86.9	3.2	1.7	2.3	5.9	13.2	6.9	95.8	8.0	17.0	13.2	21.5	15.5	9.1	6.5
District 2	45 869	610 871	13.3	60.1	6.8	4.5	1.3	27.3	50.5	17.3	87.5	9.8	22.4	12.2	17.3	13.1	8.4	7.2
District 3	107 783	610 871	5.7	87.6	1.9	3.3	1.1	6.1	11.8	5.1	97.4	7.3	17.9	7.8	15.1	13.5	9.2	9.4
District 4	501	610 871	1 220.2	92.1	1.9	1.2	1.0	1.8	3.0	5.5	97.1	7.0	17.0	10.2	17.9	16.3	11.7	8.7
District 5	32 870	610 871	18.6	88.0	3.0	0.9	1.9	6.3	16.5	7.0	96.4	6.9	16.9	11.0	16.5	14.9	9.9	9.0
District 6	106 765	610 872	5.7	70.3	1.3	21.7	0.7	5.9	13.0	3.8	98.1	8.9	21.5	9.9	15.7	13.2	9.0	8.3
ARKANSAS	134 875	2 350 725	17.4	82.7	15.9	0.5	0.5	0.3	0.8	1.1	99.5	7.0	19.4	10.1	15.3	13.9	10.4	9.1
District 1	42 989	588 588	13.7	81.3	17.9	0.3	0.3	0.2	0.6	0.5	99.7	7.2	20.5	9.6	14.5	13.3	10.4	9.3
District 2	15 343	587 412	38.3	81.2	17.6	0.4	0.6	0.2	0.8	1.3	99.3	7.2	18.9	10.8	17.1	15.0	10.3	8.4
District 3	29 810	589 523	19.8	95.9	1.6	1.1	1.0	0.4	1.1	1.5	99.2	6.8	18.5	10.3	15.1	13.9	10.4	9.3
District 4	46 733	585 202	12.5	72.4	26.6	0.4	0.2	0.4	0.8	0.9	99.6	6.8	19.8	9.7	14.3	13.4	10.2	9.4
CALIFORNIA	403 971	29 760 021	73.7	69.0	7.4	0.8	9.6	13.2	25.8	21.7	85.1	8.1	18.0	11.5	19.1	15.6	9.8	7.5
District 1	27 981	573 082	20.5	84.5	3.9	2.7	3.6	4.7	11.2	8.1	95.1	7.4	18.7	9.4	16.6	16.7	10.2	8.2
District 2	73 595	573 322	7.8	91.6	1.5	2.4	2.4	2.0	6.0	4.5	97.3	7.2	18.6	9.7	14.5	15.4	10.0	9.1
District 3	19 827	571 374	28.8	82.2	3.2	1.4	5.5	7.7	14.2	10.3	93.1	8.0	18.9	11.6	17.8	14.9	9.7	8.1
District 4	27 990	571 033	20.4	92.7	1.8	1.3	2.1	2.1	7.4	5.2	97.3	7.0	18.3	8.0	16.7	18.0	11.2	8.8
District 5	391	573 684	1 467.7	65.6	12.8	1.2	13.2	7.2	14.7	12.7	91.9	8.3	18.2	10.6	19.4	15.6	9.0	7.4
District 6	4 121	571 227	138.6	90.0	2.4	0.8	3.4	3.4	8.9	10.7	93.8	6.7	15.6	8.5	17.0	19.3	11.9	8.1
District 7	903	572 773	634.0	62.7	16.6	0.8	14.4	5.6	13.3	16.3	90.9	8.3	18.1	9.9	18.9	17.0	10.1	7.4
District 8	89	573 247	6 432.2	52.0	12.8	0.5	27.8	6.9	15.7	33.7	79.3	4.9	11.1	10.5	22.8	18.2	10.3	8.5
District 9	189	573 458	3 037.3	45.4	31.8	0.6	15.7	6.6	12.0	19.2	87.5	7.1	14.9	13.0	19.2	17.4	9.6	6.9
District 10	2 651	572 008	215.8	87.9	2.3	0.6	6.4	2.9	8.7	9.5	95.3	7.1	17.5	8.5	17.0	18.3	13.0	8.2
District 11	4 731	571 772	120.9	74.9	5.8	1.1	11.5	6.7	21.1	15.1	89.4	8.7	20.5	10.4	17.5	15.0	9.5	7.6
District 12	277	571 535	2 060.2	65.2	4.1	0.4	25.7	4.5	14.3	29.8	84.7	6.1	14.2	9.6	18.8	16.9	11.2	9.3
District 13	619	572 441	924.7	64.2	7.4	0.8	19.4	8.2	18.4	21.5	87.4	8.0	17.5	9.9	20.4	16.6	10.3	7.8
District 14	1 236	571 131	462.0	78.1	4.9	0.4	12.2	4.4	13.5	20.7	86.5	6.5	13.6	10.8	20.8	16.8	11.5	8.5
District 15	1 172	572 485	488.5	82.2	2.3	0.6	11.3	3.6	10.8	15.0	91.2	6.8	15.5	10.0	20.2	17.2	12.4	8.4
District 16	2 452	571 551	233.1	55.1	5.2	0.8	21.1	17.8	36.8	30.4	78.9	8.9	19.5	12.3	21.2	15.8	9.1	6.1
District 17	12 657	570 981	45.1	69.5	4.4	0.9	6.3	18.9	31.6	19.7	86.0	8.3	18.2	13.1	18.8	15.6	8.6	6.9
District 18	10 719	571 393	53.3	75.7	2.8	1.0	6.0	14.4	26.0	16.3	87.8	9.4	22.1	10.2	17.6	14.2	9.0	7.2
District 19	19 793	573 043	29.0	73.5	3.3	1.3	7.4	14.6	23.6	12.0	91.3	8.6	20.8	10.4	16.7	15.1	9.5	7.7
District 20	17 760	573 282	32.3	48.7	6.4	1.0	5.5	38.4	55.4	25.4	80.8	10.4	24.4	11.9	17.7	12.5	7.8	6.3
District 21	23 093	571 300	24.7	77.7	4.0	1.5	3.2	13.6	20.3	8.8	94.0	9.0	21.3	9.6	17.6	14.8	9.5	7.5
District 22	15 638	572 891	36.6	81.7	2.8	1.0	3.9	10.7	21.3	13.3	91.0	7.0	15.7	14.6	17.7	15.0	9.1	7.8
District 23	4 616	571 483	123.8	76.9	2.5	0.8	5.2	14.6	30.0	17.8	87.5	8.3	19.5	10.9	18.5	16.1	10.0	7.2
District 24	786	572 563	728.1	84.6	2.1	0.4	6.4	6.5	13.5	22.4	85.9	6.5	14.8	10.3	18.7	17.3	12.3	9.1
District 25	5 330	573 105	107.5	80.0	4.5	0.7	6.5	8.4	16.4	15.4	90.9	8.8	18.8	10.6	20.3	16.5	10.3	7.2
District 26	181	571 523	3 158.7	53.5	6.2	0.6	7.3	32.4	52.7	42.2	67.8	9.4	18.9	13.4	21.6	14.5	8.2	6.0
District 27	789	572 594	725.7	70.9	8.3	0.4	10.5	9.8	20.6	30.5	78.7	6.8	15.4	10.0	19.4	16.2	11.0	8.2
District 28	1 203	572 927	476.4	70.9	5.7	0.5	13.0	9.8	24.1	20.9	86.9	7.5	18.6	10.8	16.9	16.1	10.9	8.3
District 29	305	571 566	1 871.4	83.8	3.5	0.3	7.7	4.7	13.2	30.7	80.9	4.3	8.8	11.4	21.9	17.8	11.0	8.9
District 30	96	572 538	5 935.1	43.6	3.5	0.5	21.3	31.1	61.5	58.5	53.9	9.0	18.4	14.1	21.1	14.6	8.4	6.2
District 31	195	572 643	2 931.5	48.3	1.7	0.5	22.8	26.7	58.5	45.2	66.6	9.1	20.4	13.6	19.5	13.4	8.2	6.8
District 32	122	572 595	4 695.2	32.2	40.3	0.4	7.9	19.2	30.2	30.1	77.7	7.9	16.2	12.2	20.4	15.1	9.4	7.5
District 33	124	570 943	4 609.9	35.7	4.5	0.6	4.3	55.0	83.7	56.0	53.2	10.6	22.2	16.3	20.1	12.7	6.9	4.8
District 34	234	573 047	2 448.6	56.7	1.9	0.6	9.3	31.4	62.3	31.1	77.3	8.9	20.9	12.6	18.1	13.5	9.2	7.9
District 35	113	570 882	5 061.5	21.3	42.7	0.4	6.0	29.7	43.1	32.8	74.4	10.4	21.4	13.1	20.0	13.3	8.3	6.1
District 36	600	573 663	956.5	77.7	3.2	0.5	12.5	6.1	14.9	19.4	88.2	6.2	13.3	10.0	21.4	17.3	12.1	9.3
District 37	187	572 049	3 059.7	26.2	33.6	0.6	10.8	28.9	45.1	32.5	76.4	10.8	23.6	13.1	18.4	12.9	8.2	6.2
District 38	192	572 657	2 977.6	69.2	7.7	0.7	9.1	13.2	25.7	21.5	84.9	8.1	15.9	12.5	20.8	14.8	8.9	7.2
District 39	271	573 574	2 112.7	72.8	2.6	0.5	13.8	10.2	22.8	21.8	86.3	7.2	17.8	12.1	17.8	15.0	11.6	9.1
District 40	77 473	573 625	7.4	82.1	5.4	1.5	3.5	7.5	16.1	8.5	94.9	8.9	20.1	10.3	17.5	14.6	9.0	7.7
District 41	595	572 663	962.9	68.0	6.8	0.5	10.1	14.6	31.5	21.9	84.9	9.3	20.9	11.8	19.4	16.9	9.8	5.9
District 42	543	571 844	1 052.4	66.0	11.1	0.9	4.0	18.1	34.3	15.2	89.0	10.8	22.6	10.8	20.0	14.7	8.1	5.7
District 43	1 936	571 231	295.1	75.7	5.9	0.8	4.3	13.2	25.0	14.0	90.5	9.4	20.4	11.1	19.6	15.3	9.1	6.7
District 44	16 470	571 583	34.7	76.5	5.1	1.1	2.9	14.4	28.1	16.0	88.8	8.5	18.5	8.7	16.5	12.7	8.2	8.7

1. Dry land or land partially or temporarily covered by water.   2. Hispanic persons may be of any race.

Table E. Congressional Districts 105th Congress — **Population, Households, Group Quarters, and Education**

STATE District	Population and population characteristics, 1990 (cont'd) Percent (cont'd) Age (cont'd) 65 to 74 years	75 years and over	Percent female	Households, 1990 Number	Persons per house-hold	Percent Female family house-holder[1]	One person	Persons in mental hospitals, 1990	Persons in nursing homes, 1990	Persons identified as homeless, 1990[2]	Education, 1990 School enrollment Public	Private
	19	20	21	22	23	24	25	26	27	28	29	30
ALABAMA	7.5	5.5	52.1	1 506 790	2.62	13.4	23.8	2 555	24 031	1 942	940 143	116 259
District 1	7.4	5.2	52.2	209 370	2.71	15.1	22.8	898	3 036	171	130 928	24 463
District 2	7.4	5.7	51.7	215 137	2.61	12.6	24.2	39	3 177	122	133 381	17 952
District 3	7.5	5.4	51.6	212 651	2.63	13.0	23.2	14	3 739	90	145 948	12 298
District 4	8.4	6.3	51.9	220 788	2.59	9.9	22.2	23	4 237	21	122 944	6 690
District 5	6.8	4.4	51.2	219 452	2.58	10.4	22.9	189	2 524	377	132 398	14 574
District 6	7.0	5.1	52.0	223 443	2.50	9.0	24.9	1 053	4 408	61	128 956	22 950
District 7	7.7	6.3	54.1	205 949	2.74	24.4	26.1	339	2 910	1 100	145 588	17 332
ALASKA	2.8	1.2	47.3	188 915	2.80	9.6	22.1	22	1 202	519	141 933	14 424
At Large	2.8	1.2	47.3	188 915	2.80	9.6	22.1	22	1 202	519	141 933	14 424
ARIZONA	7.9	5.1	50.6	1 368 843	2.62	10.4	24.7	1 004	14 472	4 630	896 427	94 695
District 1	5.3	3.9	50.3	241 398	2.49	10.0	27.6	83	2 823	244	158 476	17 856
District 2	6.0	3.7	49.7	196 480	3.02	15.5	22.4	692	2 057	3 083	163 163	10 830
District 3	11.8	8.0	50.9	234 162	2.55	7.9	22.7	82	3 041	316	128 856	13 315
District 4	6.9	4.3	51.3	246 345	2.47	10.1	26.5	62	2 099	69	130 917	23 503
District 5	9.0	5.9	50.9	242 990	2.43	9.2	27.3	33	2 647	239	149 618	16 837
District 6	8.5	5.1	50.5	207 468	2.86	10.5	20.3	52	1 805	679	165 397	12 354
ARKANSAS	8.3	6.6	51.8	891 179	2.57	11.1	24.0	617	21 809	645	530 045	52 360
District 1	8.4	6.8	52.1	220 333	2.63	12.1	23.3	62	5 837	125	137 897	8 892
District 2	7.1	5.2	51.9	224 233	2.55	11.6	24.8	450	4 605	165	126 639	23 950
District 3	8.9	6.8	51.2	227 700	2.53	8.2	23.1	36	5 059	41	130 270	10 621
District 4	8.9	7.4	52.0	218 913	2.59	12.6	24.8	69	6 308	314	135 239	8 897
CALIFORNIA	6.2	4.3	49.9	10 381 206	2.79	11.5	23.4	9 535	148 362	46 834	7 177 045	1 123 001
District 1	7.6	5.2	49.4	208 711	2.62	10.3	22.9	1 277	3 460	1 103	141 281	15 223
District 2	9.4	6.0	50.3	219 020	2.54	9.9	23.4	8	3 225	1 518	146 553	11 082
District 3	6.7	4.3	50.8	209 586	2.67	11.2	22.0	90	3 148	246	152 376	14 398
District 4	7.6	4.4	49.1	210 045	2.62	8.6	19.9	36	2 680	201	130 707	15 478
District 5	6.7	4.7	51.6	223 134	2.53	13.8	28.9	212	2 253	1 491	144 846	18 983
District 6	7.4	5.6	50.9	226 960	2.45	9.4	26.5	12	3 032	625	118 862	22 489
District 7	6.3	4.0	50.9	208 202	2.71	13.6	22.9	179	2 274	799	132 051	21 511
District 8	7.5	6.1	49.3	245 820	2.25	10.0	41.7	167	2 744	5 587	108 929	29 675
District 9	6.5	5.4	51.1	227 756	2.40	15.4	34.4	26	3 368	1 813	138 801	26 478
District 10	6.3	4.2	50.6	213 366	2.63	8.1	20.5	116	2 809	237	127 426	23 447
District 11	6.4	4.4	49.8	192 038	2.90	12.5	20.5	0	4 170	1 148	143 398	18 398
District 12	7.9	6.0	51.5	215 787	2.61	10.0	26.1	0	3 960	643	117 876	29 648
District 13	5.9	3.5	50.4	198 910	2.85	11.2	19.4	115	2 786	314	134 510	19 992
District 14	6.9	4.5	49.5	223 976	2.46	8.3	27.2	210	3 431	614	110 734	41 810
District 15	5.8	3.7	50.2	214 252	2.64	9.6	21.5	0	2 983	126	129 080	27 549
District 16	4.2	2.9	48.4	168 563	3.30	12.8	17.6	134	1 693	1 419	155 284	17 494
District 17	6.0	4.5	49.0	189 099	2.87	10.4	21.8	49	2 730	872	145 568	16 303
District 18	6.1	4.2	50.0	186 489	3.00	11.7	19.1	258	3 339	573	152 875	12 256
District 19	6.7	4.5	51.2	202 858	2.79	12.3	21.6	0	2 567	390	157 759	13 495
District 20	5.1	3.7	48.0	158 379	3.46	15.4	16.0	116	2 429	881	164 046	7 916
District 21	6.5	4.3	50.3	199 642	2.80	11.7	21.3	9	2 110	622	147 377	12 895
District 22	7.5	5.5	49.3	205 198	2.65	9.0	23.3	662	3 941	890	153 080	18 518
District 23	5.6	3.9	49.4	183 312	3.05	10.1	17.8	762	1 790	397	137 882	21 842
District 24	6.7	4.3	50.6	219 354	2.57	8.9	24.8	321	3 587	144	111 175	36 752
District 25	4.9	2.6	49.1	190 996	2.90	9.2	17.6	3	1 511	45	130 990	27 888
District 26	4.8	3.2	48.9	177 447	3.18	12.9	23.1	475	2 992	950	139 415	22 546
District 27	7.0	6.0	51.4	219 623	2.56	11.0	28.3	0	5 605	401	117 406	35 243
District 28	6.5	4.6	51.3	192 695	2.91	11.3	19.7	123	5 187	254	134 410	33 286
District 29	8.3	7.7	50.6	278 690	1.99	6.6	44.1	108	4 581	1 283	95 817	35 631
District 30	4.6	3.5	49.1	177 284	3.18	15.1	24.7	226	2 347	655	150 278	23 524
District 31	5.2	3.7	50.3	158 775	3.53	15.4	16.7	88	3 122	486	156 835	20 202
District 32	6.5	4.9	52.1	212 744	2.65	18.1	31.0	557	2 707	491	131 294	30 735
District 33	3.6	2.9	47.5	145 328	3.78	16.5	19.9	14	2 475	3 127	166 671	15 978
District 34	5.8	3.2	50.3	162 272	3.49	14.6	14.8	943	2 286	231	151 796	22 076
District 35	4.5	2.9	50.9	174 747	3.24	22.5	23.8	81	1 581	426	152 935	20 363
District 36	6.7	3.7	49.8	233 720	2.42	8.7	28.0	5	2 555	573	108 621	29 419
District 37	4.3	2.6	50.4	153 884	3.68	21.6	16.8	321	2 071	598	162 935	17 288
District 38	6.9	4.9	49.8	215 601	2.57	12.1	29.0	274	4 453	306	130 772	20 280
District 39	6.1	3.3	50.3	190 832	2.97	10.5	17.3	96	2 777	112	143 061	24 737
District 40	7.1	4.7	49.7	201 282	2.76	10.5	20.9	190	2 660	507	135 036	19 737
District 41	3.8	2.2	49.2	172 941	3.22	11.0	15.2	193	983	416	153 316	22 104
District 42	4.4	2.8	50.5	181 408	3.12	14.2	18.3	50	1 971	1 246	151 431	17 026
District 43	5.4	3.1	49.4	182 767	3.04	10.2	17.0	174	2 285	483	143 130	19 040
District 44	10.6	7.6	50.6	209 956	2.68	9.2	24.1	37	2 423	252	124 652	13 310

1. No spouse present. 2. Persons in emergency shelters and persons visible in street locations.

STATE District	High school graduate or more	Bach-elor's degree or more	Per capita[2]	Median	Percent with $100,000 or more	Persons Total	Families Total	Total	Total	Percent	Median value[3] (dollars)	With a mortgage	Without a mortgage
	31	32	33	34	35	36	37	38	39	40	41	42	43
ALABAMA	66.9	15.7	11 486	23 597	2.3	18.3	14.3	1 670 379	1 506 790	70.5	53 700	18.4	12.8
District 1	68.9	14.7	10 961	22 881	2.2	20.9	16.7	242 227	209 370	70.9	53 000	19.1	12.8
District 2	68.2	16.7	11 636	24 374	2.2	17.0	13.0	238 839	215 137	70.5	54 200	18.3	12.6
District 3	61.5	12.3	10 204	21 594	1.4	19.3	14.2	238 911	212 651	71.9	47 400	18.5	12.9
District 4	57.7	8.1	10 170	20 877	1.3	17.6	14.2	243 265	220 788	77.0	43 000	19.0	12.8
District 5	71.6	20.4	13 268	28 364	2.7	12.9	10.0	236 764	219 452	70.4	63 500	17.5	12.2
District 6	78.9	26.3	16 033	31 864	5.1	9.4	6.5	238 873	223 443	69.7	73 100	17.3	12.1
District 7	60.5	10.6	8 135	16 560	0.8	31.2	26.2	231 500	205 949	62.4	40 700	20.9	14.1
ALASKA	86.6	23.0	17 610	41 408	7.7	9.0	6.8	232 608	188 915	56.1	94 400	21.5	12.2
At Large	86.6	23.0	17 610	41 408	7.7	9.0	6.8	232 608	188 915	56.1	94 400	21.5	12.2
ARIZONA	78.7	20.3	13 461	27 540	3.4	15.7	11.4	1 659 430	1 368 843	64.2	80 100	22.8	12.4
District 1	86.1	27.6	15 144	31 288	3.4	11.5	7.6	275 479	241 398	55.1	88 700	22.6	12.4
District 2	59.1	9.2	8 424	20 258	1.1	27.9	22.6	231 083	196 480	57.9	54 900	22.5	13.8
District 3	79.0	16.2	13 185	27 627	2.3	12.1	8.6	295 941	234 162	74.4	80 100	23.8	11.9
District 4	86.7	26.3	18 331	33 681	6.9	8.6	6.2	280 302	246 345	62.8	91 100	22.7	12.5
District 5	84.4	25.0	14 361	27 047	3.4	13.2	9.0	278 234	242 990	63.1	81 200	22.0	11.8
District 6	73.8	15.9	11 322	25 710	2.8	21.3	16.1	298 391	207 468	72.2	76 400	23.5	12.3
ARKANSAS	66.3	13.3	10 520	21 147	1.8	19.1	14.8	1 000 667	891 179	69.6	46 300	20.0	13.4
District 1	58.3	9.5	9 148	18 180	1.4	24.6	19.4	246 976	220 333	68.0	40 100	20.6	14.0
District 2	74.4	19.0	12 334	25 142	2.5	14.4	10.8	248 354	224 233	66.3	56 800	19.9	13.1
District 3	68.8	13.3	10 876	21 903	1.8	14.9	11.3	253 952	227 700	71.2	49 000	20.2	12.5
District 4	63.9	11.4	9 723	19 621	1.4	22.4	17.6	251 385	218 913	72.7	40 400	19.1	14.0
CALIFORNIA	76.2	23.4	16 409	35 798	7.1	12.5	9.3	11 182 882	10 381 206	55.6	195 500	24.9	11.8
District 1	79.6	18.2	14 298	30 943	3.7	11.4	8.6	231 913	208 711	63.2	136 400	23.9	12.0
District 2	78.3	16.4	12 458	24 807	2.5	15.1	11.1	248 607	219 020	64.4	94 300	22.7	12.2
District 3	79.0	19.1	13 786	30 296	3.2	12.9	9.3	221 030	209 586	59.1	118 400	22.7	11.7
District 4	85.1	21.1	16 263	35 772	5.3	7.5	5.7	264 760	210 045	69.3	152 400	24.6	12.2
District 5	79.5	24.0	14 661	29 974	3.4	15.7	12.4	237 135	223 134	53.0	122 500	22.8	11.7
District 6	87.8	33.0	21 603	40 564	10.0	6.7	4.2	242 255	226 960	62.0	257 400	25.9	11.7
District 7	82.0	23.2	16 006	38 608	4.1	9.6	7.5	219 422	208 202	62.0	168 100	24.9	11.8
District 8	76.3	33.8	19 377	31 659	6.9	14.1	11.5	266 127	245 820	29.0	274 700	25.3	12.0
District 9	80.2	35.4	16 833	30 067	6.6	16.5	13.4	242 284	227 756	43.0	223 900	25.2	12.3
District 10	90.1	35.8	23 972	52 378	14.5	4.4	3.2	224 187	213 366	71.5	275 100	26.0	11.6
District 11	71.5	14.7	13 299	31 605	3.9	14.7	11.3	202 059	192 038	58.1	124 000	23.2	11.8
District 12	84.4	31.6	20 984	44 720	9.8	6.0	4.0	224 724	215 787	59.4	324 100	25.2	11.5
District 13	80.6	22.4	17 335	43 877	6.4	6.4	4.7	206 484	198 910	62.0	223 700	25.1	11.5
District 14	88.0	44.2	26 047	50 078	15.8	6.1	3.6	233 781	223 976	54.7	404 400	24.5	11.5
District 15	88.3	34.8	22 833	50 823	12.4	5.0	3.2	223 320	214 252	63.2	291 500	24.6	11.6
District 16	69.7	19.4	14 614	42 223	6.5	11.6	8.4	174 940	168 563	60.9	234 500	26.9	12.0
District 17	74.5	23.0	15 006	33 911	5.5	11.7	8.0	204 376	189 099	52.8	220 800	25.5	11.6
District 18	66.4	12.5	12 013	28 324	3.3	16.0	12.7	196 560	186 489	58.7	114 800	23.1	11.8
District 19	74.4	20.2	13 516	29 153	4.1	16.4	12.6	219 589	202 858	58.9	90 800	22.4	12.1
District 20	47.9	6.4	8 097	21 140	1.8	27.9	23.2	167 455	158 379	51.3	64 000	22.9	12.4
District 21	72.7	15.0	12 983	29 943	3.4	15.1	12.1	218 942	199 642	61.3	85 000	22.3	12.3
District 22	81.4	25.3	16 458	33 680	6.2	13.0	7.3	222 918	205 198	56.7	230 100	26.0	11.3
District 23	77.1	20.5	16 617	42 989	7.5	7.9	5.5	193 300	183 312	63.3	235 600	25.9	11.3
District 24	86.2	33.4	25 767	48 433	16.2	6.2	4.0	232 664	219 354	62.5	305 700	26.3	11.9
District 25	82.8	22.9	18 849	46 480	10.0	7.2	5.1	205 124	190 996	71.5	214 100	26.5	12.1
District 26	60.6	15.4	12 198	32 134	3.6	15.8	12.1	187 617	177 447	44.5	186 600	26.1	11.8
District 27	80.2	31.4	20 344	37 929	10.4	11.5	8.8	230 676	219 623	49.3	296 000	24.7	11.6
District 28	82.5	25.6	18 064	43 508	9.0	7.1	4.9	200 651	192 695	67.4	233 700	25.1	11.4
District 29	86.3	43.5	34 253	37 540	16.8	11.7	7.3	300 369	278 690	35.3	500 001	24.3	11.9
District 30	52.8	16.1	9 637	23 435	2.4	24.1	20.7	190 029	177 284	24.4	189 000	25.2	11.5
District 31	56.4	13.3	10 264	30 667	2.9	18.1	14.7	165 006	158 775	48.2	180 100	25.8	11.5
District 32	69.9	23.3	14 520	28 332	5.6	19.2	15.8	226 524	212 744	36.4	234 800	25.1	12.1
District 33	33.6	5.3	6 997	20 708	1.2	28.0	24.9	153 629	145 328	24.7	156 200	28.2	11.6
District 34	61.7	12.0	12 012	36 224	4.2	11.6	9.1	167 247	162 272	62.8	174 400	23.9	11.1
District 35	57.1	10.1	9 761	25 481	1.9	24.6	21.4	186 648	174 747	36.4	150 500	25.8	12.5
District 36	86.7	36.8	25 534	48 522	14.8	6.8	4.5	247 623	233 720	52.8	371 100	24.5	11.4
District 37	54.8	9.2	9 104	27 127	2.3	23.3	20.6	161 398	153 884	50.4	142 800	25.8	12.1
District 38	76.5	21.0	16 497	34 364	5.6	12.5	9.5	228 531	215 601	45.7	224 700	24.4	11.3
District 39	81.6	25.4	18 190	46 196	9.5	7.0	4.6	198 048	190 832	64.6	239 000	23.0	11.2
District 40	78.3	16.0	13 568	30 408	3.7	12.5	10.2	259 542	201 282	64.1	110 300	24.2	12.5
District 41	76.8	21.4	16 002	44 607	8.5	9.9	7.2	182 322	172 941	67.8	204 600	26.6	11.7
District 42	72.2	12.7	12 308	33 737	2.9	14.2	11.8	196 432	181 408	62.1	127 000	25.4	11.7
District 43	76.4	15.7	14 449	37 806	5.0	10.2	7.2	200 134	182 767	66.5	153 700	26.6	11.9
District 44	71.3	13.2	14 417	29 049	4.2	13.1	9.7	272 645	209 956	68.3	121 800	26.4	12.5

1. Persons 25 years old and older. 2. Based on the population enumerated as of April 1, 1990. 3. Specified owner-occupied units.

	Housing units, 1990 (cont'd)			Civilian labor force, 1990			Civilian employment, 1990[4]			Disability, 1990
	Occupied units (cont'd)				Unemployment			Percent		
	Renter-occupied									
STATE District	Median rent[1] (dollars)	Rent as a percent of income	Substandard units[2] (percent)	Total	Total	Rate[3]	Total	Professional, managerial, and technical	Precision production, craft, and repair	Work disabled persons[5] (percent)
	44	45	46	47	48	49	50	51	52	53
ALABAMA	325	24.8	4.5	1 870 381	128 587	6.9	1 741 794	26.1	13.0	9.7
District 1	322	25.8	5.2	257 686	21 704	8.4	235 982	25.9	13.2	9.5
District 2	329	23.5	4.8	266 730	15 580	5.8	251 150	26.5	11.9	9.4
District 3	296	26.3	4.9	263 608	19 051	7.2	244 557	21.8	14.4	10.3
District 4	262	24.5	3.5	263 925	18 362	7.0	245 563	17.9	16.7	11.8
District 5	361	23.1	3.0	286 996	16 482	5.7	270 514	31.9	13.4	8.6
District 6	405	23.4	2.1	293 669	11 810	4.0	281 859	36.1	10.6	6.9
District 7	276	28.6	8.5	237 767	25 598	10.8	212 169	19.9	11.1	11.5
ALASKA	559	23.8	12.4	268 966	23 587	8.8	245 379	34.3	11.2	6.6
At Large	559	23.8	12.4	268 966	23 587	8.8	245 379	34.3	11.2	6.6
ARIZONA	438	27.5	7.8	1 727 798	123 902	7.2	1 603 896	30.8	11.4	8.3
District 1	478	27.4	5.4	344 059	18 082	5.3	325 977	36.1	9.8	6.4
District 2	366	29.7	17.0	256 524	29 410	11.5	227 114	19.3	13.7	10.0
District 3	457	27.7	5.7	258 645	16 502	6.4	242 143	25.9	13.7	9.4
District 4	473	26.9	3.4	338 605	17 744	5.2	320 861	35.7	9.6	6.9
District 5	404	27.6	3.9	283 981	18 856	6.6	265 125	35.4	10.0	8.8
District 6	426	25.0	14.1	245 984	23 308	9.5	222 676	27.7	13.0	8.9
ARKANSAS	328	26.5	4.9	1 066 368	72 079	6.8	994 289	23.3	12.5	11.2
District 1	290	27.6	5.8	253 428	21 349	8.4	232 079	19.6	12.9	12.6
District 2	383	26.4	3.8	286 980	16 691	5.8	270 289	28.9	11.0	9.7
District 3	328	24.9	4.2	275 250	14 541	5.3	260 709	22.6	13.5	10.9
District 4	299	27.4	5.7	250 710	19 498	7.8	231 212	21.5	12.9	11.6
CALIFORNIA	620	29.1	12.0	14 992 811	996 502	6.6	13 996 309	32.3	11.1	7.4
District 1	512	28.8	6.2	264 821	17 741	6.7	247 080	27.8	12.8	10.5
District 2	429	30.0	5.3	241 522	21 393	8.9	220 129	27.7	12.1	12.2
District 3	498	28.8	6.7	278 111	19 874	7.1	258 237	29.5	11.4	9.3
District 4	569	28.1	4.2	277 140	14 713	5.3	262 427	31.7	12.6	8.5
District 5	505	29.7	7.5	278 768	19 446	7.0	259 322	34.4	8.8	10.1
District 6	709	29.8	3.8	308 961	12 877	4.2	296 084	37.9	10.3	7.3
District 7	625	28.8	7.4	293 836	18 738	6.4	275 098	32.5	11.9	8.8
District 8	631	28.0	12.6	329 403	22 199	6.7	307 204	37.3	6.2	8.6
District 9	538	29.3	9.5	289 473	22 017	7.6	267 456	42.6	6.9	9.0
District 10	746	27.7	2.5	313 157	12 063	3.9	301 094	42.0	9.6	5.7
District 11	499	28.1	11.1	261 968	21 496	8.2	240 472	25.7	12.2	9.5
District 12	780	27.5	8.5	323 495	13 774	4.3	309 721	35.5	9.1	5.6
District 13	726	27.8	9.3	314 374	16 014	5.1	298 360	32.2	12.8	6.8
District 14	777	26.4	6.9	332 677	12 107	3.6	320 570	49.7	7.7	5.2
District 15	794	27.4	5.6	336 280	12 835	3.8	323 445	43.6	9.8	5.5
District 16	718	29.5	19.6	298 455	19 890	6.7	278 565	29.0	14.3	6.4
District 17	643	29.3	13.1	274 605	20 389	7.4	254 216	29.0	9.7	7.3
District 18	462	28.6	12.2	250 269	25 598	10.2	224 671	23.0	13.2	9.6
District 19	450	28.7	8.9	267 363	19 488	7.3	247 875	30.8	10.2	8.7
District 20	379	28.6	23.5	224 242	35 244	15.7	188 998	14.9	9.8	9.8
District 21	454	28.0	7.8	254 789	19 280	7.6	235 509	28.1	13.0	9.9
District 22	621	31.5	8.1	285 521	15 435	5.4	270 086	31.6	11.2	7.3
District 23	733	29.2	11.8	297 601	14 679	4.9	282 922	31.0	12.5	7.2
District 24	779	29.7	6.4	334 603	15 232	4.6	319 371	41.3	8.8	5.3
District 25	690	28.7	6.5	299 582	15 602	5.2	283 980	35.5	13.4	6.6
District 26	624	30.1	26.3	302 105	24 212	8.0	277 893	23.4	14.3	6.3
District 27	671	29.2	12.3	306 541	17 886	5.8	288 655	40.5	9.0	6.5
District 28	705	28.7	9.2	299 246	14 540	4.9	284 706	35.3	10.6	6.3
District 29	678	28.4	7.6	341 150	20 037	5.9	321 113	51.0	4.4	5.2
District 30	525	30.1	41.0	290 735	29 044	10.0	261 691	20.7	11.7	6.2
District 31	622	29.6	30.9	265 665	21 809	8.2	243 856	21.3	12.8	6.3
District 32	592	31.0	17.8	294 698	26 007	8.8	268 691	31.5	8.8	8.0
District 33	484	30.9	50.9	252 675	30 937	12.2	221 738	10.5	14.0	6.6
District 34	637	29.4	22.1	275 183	20 216	7.3	254 967	22.1	13.6	6.9
District 35	573	31.6	27.7	262 143	29 948	11.4	232 195	19.6	12.3	8.6
District 36	812	26.8	6.5	341 509	14 426	4.2	327 083	44.5	8.7	5.4
District 37	548	32.2	32.7	242 189	27 933	11.5	214 256	18.0	14.3	9.0
District 38	636	28.7	12.8	293 538	17 626	6.0	275 912	31.4	11.6	7.8
District 39	736	28.2	10.1	317 414	14 955	4.7	302 459	34.0	11.0	6.0
District 40	507	28.3	6.9	239 718	18 831	7.9	220 887	28.8	15.1	9.8
District 41	656	29.8	12.2	292 909	16 494	5.6	276 415	31.5	11.4	5.8
District 42	562	30.4	12.6	263 898	22 251	8.4	241 647	24.8	14.7	8.4
District 43	595	29.5	9.5	270 568	17 826	6.6	252 742	27.6	15.2	7.6
District 44	545	30.7	10.0	240 511	18 297	7.6	222 214	24.1	13.6	9.5

1. Specified renter-occupied units. 2. Overcrowded or lacking complete plumbing facilities. 3. Percent of total civilian labor force. 4. Persons 16 years old and older. 5. Persons 16 to 64 years of age.

Table E. Congressional Districts 105th Congress — **Land Area and Population**

STATE District	Land area, 1990[1] (sq km)	Total persons	Per square kilometer	Race White	Black	Am. Indian, Eskimo, Aleut	Asian and Pacific Islander	Other race	Hispanic[2]	Foreign born	U.S. citizen	Under 5 years	5 to 17 years	18 to 24 years	25 to 34 years	35 to 44 years	45 to 54 years	55 to 64 years
	1	2	3	4	5	6	7	8	9	10	11	12	13	14	15	16	17	18
CALIFORNIA—Con.																		
District 45	237	570 874	2 411.9	82.1	1.2	0.6	11.0	5.1	14.8	19.2	87.8	6.5	14.7	12.4	21.1	15.4	11.5	8.4
District 46	163	571 380	3 510.2	66.5	2.5	0.6	12.3	18.2	50.0	42.7	66.0	9.7	19.3	15.4	22.1	13.1	7.6	5.9
District 47	788	571 518	725.2	83.6	1.8	0.4	9.6	4.6	13.1	17.7	89.2	6.9	15.8	11.3	18.7	17.0	11.8	7.6
District 48	3 931	572 928	145.8	83.3	4.0	1.1	4.5	7.1	17.2	14.1	91.1	8.7	16.9	12.8	19.6	15.8	9.0	6.9
District 49	306	573 362	1 874.1	82.1	5.3	0.7	6.6	5.3	12.8	14.0	91.4	5.3	10.9	17.7	22.7	14.7	8.6	7.6
District 50	350	573 463	1 638.9	46.5	14.4	0.6	14.8	23.6	40.6	30.1	79.2	9.6	20.9	13.3	19.4	13.7	8.0	6.6
District 51	1 285	572 982	446.1	84.6	1.8	0.6	8.2	4.9	13.6	15.7	90.7	7.6	17.0	10.1	19.1	17.7	10.1	6.9
District 52	16 665	573 203	34.4	83.6	3.1	1.1	3.0	9.2	22.6	12.4	92.2	8.3	19.2	10.9	18.3	15.3	9.4	7.7
COLORADO	268 658	3 294 394	12.3	88.2	4.0	0.8	1.8	5.1	12.9	4.3	97.7	7.7	18.5	10.2	18.6	17.2	10.2	7.6
District 1	565	549 068	971.1	73.0	12.9	1.1	2.4	10.5	21.9	7.1	95.8	7.6	15.1	10.0	20.4	16.2	9.1	8.2
District 2	3 963	549 072	138.6	92.7	0.8	0.6	2.4	3.4	9.5	4.4	97.6	7.6	18.2	11.3	19.4	18.1	10.6	7.1
District 3	147 743	549 062	3.7	91.7	0.7	1.4	0.5	5.7	17.4	2.6	98.7	7.1	19.3	9.2	16.3	16.7	10.1	8.7
District 4	104 338	549 070	5.3	91.3	0.7	0.6	1.1	6.3	14.7	3.4	98.1	7.7	20.0	11.3	16.8	16.0	9.7	7.5
District 5	10 961	549 066	50.1	88.8	5.6	0.7	2.2	2.8	7.4	4.3	98.3	8.4	19.8	10.5	18.9	17.7	10.4	6.9
District 6	1 087	549 056	504.9	91.7	3.5	0.5	2.3	1.9	6.4	4.2	98.0	7.5	18.4	8.9	19.6	18.8	11.4	7.5
CONNECTICUT	12 550	3 287 116	261.9	87.0	8.3	0.2	1.5	2.9	6.5	8.5	95.9	6.9	15.9	10.5	17.8	15.5	10.8	9.0
District 1	1 223	548 016	448.0	78.3	14.2	0.2	1.7	5.6	10.1	10.6	95.0	6.8	15.9	10.4	17.6	15.4	10.5	8.9
District 2	4 414	548 041	124.2	93.3	3.7	0.4	1.4	1.3	3.0	4.7	98.0	7.1	16.1	12.8	18.6	15.8	10.2	8.1
District 3	1 101	547 765	497.4	84.1	11.9	0.2	1.5	2.2	4.9	6.4	97.2	6.7	15.4	11.0	17.5	15.4	10.4	9.0
District 4	657	547 765	834.1	80.0	13.1	0.1	2.2	4.5	11.1	13.9	92.2	6.9	15.3	9.8	17.6	15.0	11.5	10.0
District 5	1 519	547 764	360.7	91.2	4.8	0.2	1.4	2.4	6.2	8.1	96.3	7.3	16.7	9.5	17.6	16.1	11.3	8.7
District 6	3 635	547 765	150.7	95.0	2.3	0.1	1.1	1.5	3.5	7.2	96.9	6.8	15.8	9.5	17.6	16.2	11.1	9.2
DELAWARE	5 062	666 168	131.6	80.3	16.9	0.3	1.4	1.1	2.4	3.3	98.5	7.3	17.2	11.4	17.9	14.8	10.2	9.0
At Large	5 062	666 168	131.6	80.3	16.9	0.3	1.4	1.1	2.4	3.3	98.5	7.3	17.2	11.4	17.9	14.8	10.2	9.0
DISTRICT OF COLUMBIA	159	606 900	3 815.7	29.6	65.8	0.2	1.8	2.5	5.4	9.7	93.1	6.2	13.1	13.6	20.0	15.7	10.2	8.4
Delegate	159	606 900	3 815.7	29.6	65.8	0.2	1.8	2.5	5.4	9.7	93.1	6.2	13.1	13.6	20.0	15.7	10.2	8.4
FLORIDA	139 853	12 937 926	92.5	83.1	13.6	0.3	1.2	1.8	12.2	12.9	92.7	6.6	15.6	9.4	16.4	14.0	10.0	9.8
District 1	11 597	562 518	48.5	84.0	12.8	0.9	1.8	0.5	2.1	3.0	98.8	7.4	18.0	10.9	17.8	14.4	10.7	9.4
District 2	30 610	562 518	18.4	74.0	24.1	0.5	0.9	0.5	1.9	2.5	98.5	6.8	18.4	13.6	16.5	14.5	10.0	8.4
District 3	4 717	562 518	119.3	50.4	47.0	0.3	1.0	1.4	3.4	3.8	97.7	8.3	19.6	10.9	17.0	13.5	9.4	8.7
District 4	4 740	562 519	118.7	91.0	6.4	0.3	1.7	0.6	2.7	4.7	98.1	6.9	15.9	10.3	18.2	15.8	10.2	9.0
District 5	9 380	562 518	60.0	89.6	8.5	0.2	1.1	0.5	2.7	5.7	97.8	5.4	13.6	11.2	13.3	11.8	8.8	11.1
District 6	12 369	562 518	45.5	87.1	11.0	0.3	0.9	0.7	2.8	3.1	98.7	6.7	17.1	8.5	15.2	13.1	10.4	10.4
District 7	2 510	562 518	224.1	93.2	4.0	0.3	1.3	1.2	5.5	5.9	97.4	6.4	16.1	9.2	17.4	15.5	10.3	9.4
District 8	2 185	562 518	257.5	88.8	5.2	0.3	2.3	3.3	11.4	7.8	95.7	6.9	15.6	13.1	20.5	15.1	9.5	8.1
District 9	2 321	562 518	242.4	94.6	3.4	0.3	1.0	0.7	4.1	6.4	97.5	5.8	14.5	7.5	15.4	14.9	10.0	10.0
District 10	391	562 518	1 440.2	88.6	9.4	0.2	1.3	0.4	2.3	6.9	97.2	5.3	12.5	7.6	14.9	13.4	9.7	10.5
District 11	655	562 519	859.2	78.7	17.2	0.3	1.4	2.3	13.9	8.0	95.5	7.3	16.1	11.6	19.6	14.7	10.2	8.5
District 12	9 072	562 519	62.0	84.1	12.6	0.3	0.6	2.3	6.1	4.2	97.8	7.2	18.2	9.3	14.8	13.6	10.1	9.8
District 13	3 989	562 518	141.0	92.8	5.4	0.2	0.5	1.0	4.3	6.3	97.6	5.1	12.2	6.7	12.5	11.7	9.0	11.9
District 14	9 049	562 518	62.2	91.9	5.7	0.2	0.5	1.7	6.6	6.6	96.8	5.7	13.2	7.2	13.8	12.2	9.6	12.7
District 15	8 114	562 519	69.3	90.2	7.6	0.3	1.1	0.7	3.4	5.4	97.6	6.5	15.2	8.4	16.5	13.4	10.3	11.2
District 16	13 657	562 519	41.2	93.0	4.0	0.4	0.8	1.8	6.3	8.0	96.1	6.1	14.3	7.1	15.1	13.4	9.4	10.8
District 17	272	562 519	2 069.8	36.6	58.4	0.2	1.3	3.6	23.0	29.5	79.1	9.2	21.3	10.8	17.1	14.4	9.7	7.6
District 18	298	562 519	1 887.6	48.7	4.2	0.1	1.2	5.8	66.7	56.8	64.1	5.8	14.2	10.0	16.0	13.6	11.8	11.3
District 19	681	562 519	825.5	94.8	2.7	0.1	1.4	0.9	6.2	12.1	94.8	5.4	12.5	6.9	15.0	13.8	8.8	9.3
District 20	8 961	562 518	62.8	92.1	4.4	0.3	1.6	1.6	12.3	14.0	92.1	6.4	15.3	8.1	17.0	16.4	11.2	9.3
District 21	615	562 519	914.0	87.6	4.1	0.1	1.5	6.7	69.6	55.8	64.4	7.5	17.1	10.4	19.4	15.1	11.5	9.0
District 22	331	562 519	1 700.9	94.2	3.0	0.1	1.1	1.7	12.8	20.9	89.5	4.1	8.6	6.6	14.8	14.8	10.2	11.6
District 23	3 187	562 519	176.5	44.8	51.6	0.2	0.9	2.4	9.4	18.1	87.8	8.6	18.9	10.2	18.4	14.1	9.2	7.4
GEORGIA	150 010	6 478 216	43.2	71.0	27.0	0.2	1.2	0.7	1.7	2.7	98.4	7.6	19.0	11.4	18.1	15.7	10.3	7.7
District 1	21 143	588 541	27.8	67.6	30.6	0.2	0.8	0.8	1.7	1.7	99.1	8.1	19.4	12.8	17.4	14.0	9.4	7.7
District 2	29 683	587 583	19.8	59.5	39.2	0.2	0.4	0.6	1.7	1.4	99.0	7.9	21.4	11.8	15.6	13.7	9.5	8.0
District 3	7 947	589 630	74.2	73.2	24.7	0.2	1.2	0.6	1.8	2.4	98.9	8.0	20.0	10.7	17.5	15.7	10.7	8.0
District 4	772	589 322	763.2	58.4	36.6	0.2	3.6	1.2	3.2	7.5	95.1	7.2	16.3	11.9	22.4	17.2	10.2	7.1
District 5	1 033	589 359	570.4	35.7	62.0	0.2	1.3	0.9	1.9	3.8	97.4	7.7	17.2	12.7	19.6	16.0	9.6	6.9
District 6	1 528	589 600	386.0	91.0	6.4	0.2	1.9	0.6	2.1	4.5	97.1	7.6	17.7	9.8	21.9	20.1	11.6	6.1
District 7	9 589	589 405	61.5	85.6	13.2	0.2	0.6	0.4	1.1	1.4	99.3	7.7	18.9	11.1	17.7	15.1	10.5	8.2
District 8	29 791	587 912	19.7	67.9	31.1	0.2	0.5	0.4	1.0	1.1	99.5	7.5	20.2	10.5	16.2	14.3	10.3	8.7
District 9	15 088	589 420	39.1	94.7	3.7	0.3	0.4	1.0	1.7	1.7	98.8	7.0	18.5	10.7	16.6	15.0	11.3	9.1
District 10	25 111	588 046	23.4	60.9	37.5	0.2	1.0	0.4	1.1	1.7	99.3	7.7	20.3	10.8	16.9	14.8	10.0	8.2
District 11	8 324	589 398	70.8	86.5	11.8	0.2	1.2	0.4	1.3	2.2	98.6	7.7	19.4	12.6	17.8	16.4	10.5	6.9

1. Dry land or land partially or temporarily covered by water.   2. Hispanic persons may be of any race.

Table E. Congressional Districts 105th Congress — Population, Households, Group Quarters, and Education

STATE District	Population and population characteristics, 1990 (cont'd) Percent (cont'd) Age (cont'd)			Households, 1990		Percent		Persons in mental hospitals, 1990	Persons in nursing homes, 1990	Persons identified as homeless, 1990[2]	Education, 1990 School enrollment	
	65 to 74 years	75 years and over	Percent female	Number	Persons per household	Female family householder[1]	One person				Public	Private
	19	20	21	22	23	24	25	26	27	28	29	30
CALIFORNIA—Con.												
District 45	5.8	4.4	49.7	213 006	2.65	9.6	23.7	48	3 415	462	129 212	21 484
District 46	4.3	2.7	47.6	155 659	3.58	12.0	17.7	239	2 423	805	145 927	14 110
District 47	5.8	5.1	51.0	212 084	2.64	8.6	22.4	31	2 914	397	134 293	25 071
District 48	6.5	3.9	48.4	200 215	2.75	8.2	18.8	47	1 480	1 409	122 723	20 171
District 49	7.3	5.2	47.1	233 952	2.23	8.8	33.1	110	2 373	3 410	118 532	26 356
District 50	5.3	3.2	49.9	175 606	3.18	17.0	18.1	261	1 899	358	162 685	13 956
District 51	6.7	4.6	49.8	207 876	2.71	8.3	20.0	0	2 058	4 274	130 907	22 227
District 52	6.5	4.3	50.7	199 359	2.81	12.0	19.7	82	4 719	224	149 489	15 581
COLORADO	5.9	4.1	50.5	1 282 489	2.51	9.7	26.6	703	18 506	2 879	789 735	106 409
District 1	7.5	5.8	51.2	242 791	2.21	12.0	38.9	285	3 514	1 435	103 373	25 128
District 2	4.7	3.1	50.4	210 000	2.56	9.1	23.9	12	2 220	394	141 214	16 453
District 3	7.4	5.2	50.1	210 794	2.54	9.4	24.5	212	3 809	355	133 296	10 140
District 4	6.2	4.8	50.5	202 437	2.64	8.6	22.7	81	3 831	290	154 377	11 309
District 5	4.6	2.7	49.7	199 048	2.66	9.1	21.5	75	2 036	312	132 360	22 223
District 6	5.1	2.9	51.0	217 419	2.50	9.7	25.7	38	3 096	93	125 115	21 156
CONNECTICUT	7.8	5.8	51.5	1 230 479	2.59	11.4	24.2	2 806	30 962	5 118	626 637	178 849
District 1	8.0	6.3	52.2	208 723	2.54	13.9	25.8	635	7 473	1 321	108 930	26 157
District 2	6.8	5.0	50.3	200 769	2.58	9.5	23.3	1 226	4 603	389	117 463	24 803
District 3	8.4	6.1	52.2	207 515	2.55	12.4	25.7	94	4 817	2 045	99 326	37 858
District 4	8.0	5.9	52.3	204 373	2.63	12.7	24.2	267	4 505	898	91 527	37 542
District 5	7.4	5.5	51.2	201 115	2.67	10.5	22.6	584	5 322	330	103 010	29 976
District 6	8.1	5.8	51.1	207 984	2.58	9.3	23.2	0	4 242	135	106 381	22 513
DELAWARE	7.4	4.7	51.5	247 497	2.61	11.8	23.2	0	4 596	335	135 362	35 857
At Large	7.4	4.7	51.5	247 497	2.61	11.8	23.2	0	4 596	335	135 362	35 857
DISTRICT OF COLUMBIA	7.3	5.5	53.4	249 634	2.26	19.5	41.5	1 517	7 008	5 482	97 160	54 088
Delegate	7.3	5.5	53.4	249 634	2.26	19.5	41.5	1 517	7 008	5 482	97 160	54 088
FLORIDA	10.6	7.7	51.6	5 134 869	2.46	10.7	25.5	6 208	80 298	8 892	2 459 541	467 121
District 1	7.3	4.1	50.6	211 725	2.57	11.7	22.3	118	2 673	109	129 082	15 103
District 2	6.9	4.8	50.9	207 532	2.57	13.2	24.2	1 274	3 562	386	151 482	13 592
District 3	7.6	5.0	51.9	204 394	2.65	19.8	25.7	152	3 055	1 596	125 092	17 463
District 4	8.3	5.4	50.8	224 605	2.44	8.8	25.5	250	3 747	180	102 743	24 538
District 5	15.2	9.6	52.1	237 502	2.30	8.8	25.7	198	3 703	119	122 401	11 198
District 6	11.5	6.9	50.6	214 281	2.54	9.6	21.3	747	2 956	129	107 364	12 865
District 7	9.6	6.2	51.3	222 116	2.50	8.7	22.5	112	2 983	50	107 556	23 368
District 8	6.8	4.3	50.3	216 066	2.51	9.4	23.9	117	3 337	192	110 278	20 900
District 9	12.6	9.2	52.2	233 442	2.36	7.8	25.0	104	5 948	300	96 621	18 455
District 10	13.2	12.9	53.3	253 213	2.16	10.0	33.2	174	7 805	828	84 608	18 419
District 11	7.1	4.9	51.6	225 942	2.43	13.7	28.4	141	3 269	481	113 733	23 386
District 12	10.4	6.8	51.3	209 945	2.61	10.8	21.5	853	3 755	331	111 587	16 538
District 13	17.4	13.5	52.8	247 257	2.23	7.6	27.0	45	5 191	211	80 825	12 392
District 14	16.0	9.6	51.3	234 797	2.35	7.5	22.8	397	3 298	393	84 730	12 380
District 15	11.9	6.7	50.7	226 294	2.44	8.7	23.2	154	2 676	336	102 294	20 246
District 16	14.3	9.5	51.6	233 951	2.38	7.1	23.7	0	2 384	96	90 314	19 403
District 17	5.7	4.2	51.9	182 462	3.02	23.4	23.5	75	3 293	1 218	148 820	22 330
District 18	9.4	7.9	51.9	209 846	2.63	12.5	27.0	29	1 809	103	99 203	35 799
District 19	15.7	12.5	52.6	244 747	2.27	6.5	26.2	100	3 248	117	84 064	22 223
District 20	9.4	6.8	51.1	222 030	2.50	8.6	23.6	571	1 483	342	98 338	27 960
District 21	6.1	3.9	51.7	188 480	2.94	13.2	17.1	399	1 844	49	121 234	34 017
District 22	14.3	16.6	53.2	284 067	1.96	6.9	40.1	74	3 211	480	59 776	26 809
District 23	6.7	6.4	51.1	200 175	2.72	18.5	26.2	124	5 068	846	127 396	17 737
GEORGIA	6.0	4.1	51.5	2 366 615	2.66	13.9	22.7	3 640	36 549	4 288	1 433 862	209 997
District 1	6.7	4.4	50.8	209 008	2.69	14.2	22.8	194	3 777	257	133 708	18 076
District 2	7.0	5.2	52.0	203 783	2.76	18.1	22.6	6	4 513	215	145 566	13 658
District 3	5.8	3.7	51.3	208 344	2.77	14.1	19.3	105	2 865	258	130 897	15 908
District 4	4.8	2.9	51.8	228 142	2.54	13.6	25.3	498	1 827	112	119 734	30 347
District 5	5.7	4.7	52.4	231 179	2.45	21.5	32.2	6	2 689	2 523	124 151	27 503
District 6	3.5	1.8	50.7	226 407	2.60	7.8	21.7	74	570	36	120 706	27 610
District 7	6.4	4.5	51.5	214 189	2.70	11.8	20.6	318	3 949	378	125 421	15 074
District 8	7.2	5.1	52.3	214 046	2.67	15.7	23.5	9	5 370	172	132 407	17 971
District 9	7.1	4.7	50.8	217 009	2.67	9.7	19.7	182	3 423	141	119 177	12 059
District 10	6.7	4.6	51.5	206 840	2.72	16.6	22.8	2 091	4 821	124	134 957	16 350
District 11	5.2	3.6	51.1	207 668	2.78	10.3	18.4	157	2 745	72	147 138	15 441

1. No spouse present. 2. Persons in emergency shelters and persons visible in street locations.

STATE District	Education, 1990 (cont'd) Attainment[1] (percent)		Money income, 1989			Percent below poverty level, 1989		Housing units, 1990					
				Households		Persons	Families		Occupied units				
											Owner-occupied		
												Owner cost as a percent of income	
	High school graduate or more	Bachelor's degree or more	Per capita[2]	Median	Percent with $100,000 or more	Total	Total	Total	Total	Percent	Median value[3] (dollars)	With a mortgage	Without a mortgage
	31	32	33	34	35	36	37	38	39	40	41	42	43
CALIFORNIA—Con.													
District 45	84.5	27.7	21 046	45 074	10.2	7.4	4.8	226 144	213 006	56.4	266 300	23.4	11.6
District 46	59.8	12.5	11 297	35 416	3.0	15.5	10.7	163 094	155 659	48.2	188 500	24.9	11.2
District 47	89.7	37.1	25 268	51 554	16.1	5.6	3.0	224 182	212 084	65.6	280 800	25.9	11.5
District 48	86.3	27.7	19 435	42 389	10.5	7.7	5.0	220 694	200 215	63.9	237 300	28.9	11.9
District 49	87.7	33.9	19 184	32 562	6.9	10.9	6.6	250 763	233 952	42.2	226 000	23.1	11.3
District 50	67.9	13.9	10 577	27 655	2.1	18.5	16.2	183 673	175 606	47.9	137 300	25.5	11.4
District 51	87.6	34.5	20 586	45 186	10.2	7.0	4.1	223 276	207 876	65.0	231 000	27.1	11.6
District 52	77.9	17.1	14 075	33 046	4.0	11.9	9.1	212 029	199 359	59.5	155 400	24.9	11.5
COLORADO	84.4	27.0	14 821	30 140	3.8	11.7	8.6	1 477 349	1 282 489	62.2	82 700	22.5	12.7
District 1	78.9	26.8	14 942	24 870	3.5	17.1	13.3	277 331	242 791	49.7	75 500	22.4	13.1
District 2	87.7	29.5	15 823	35 117	3.7	8.7	5.6	227 757	210 000	65.4	89 900	22.6	12.3
District 3	79.8	20.5	12 115	24 521	2.4	15.9	12.3	287 282	210 794	66.0	62 300	21.9	12.9
District 4	79.7	21.5	12 387	26 577	2.6	13.8	9.7	226 424	202 437	65.4	70 200	22.3	13.1
District 5	89.5	30.1	15 370	33 348	5.0	8.9	6.9	223 409	199 048	64.0	90 600	22.9	12.2
District 6	91.1	33.4	18 289	37 333	5.5	5.7	4.0	235 146	217 419	65.0	92 400	22.4	11.9
CONNECTICUT	79.2	27.2	20 189	41 721	9.2	6.8	5.0	1 320 850	1 230 479	65.6	177 800	22.9	13.7
District 1	77.9	26.6	18 644	39 961	7.3	9.3	7.3	220 374	208 723	61.0	172 000	22.3	13.3
District 2	79.7	23.2	16 946	38 524	4.8	6.2	4.4	222 167	200 769	65.8	151 300	22.9	13.0
District 3	79.7	26.8	18 243	39 815	6.9	7.7	5.5	223 071	207 515	64.7	173 800	22.9	14.3
District 4	79.3	34.0	27 130	47 636	17.7	7.5	5.6	217 000	204 373	63.5	277 400	23.2	14.6
District 5	79.2	26.9	20 316	44 056	10.6	5.6	4.5	214 744	201 115	68.7	183 900	23.5	13.8
District 6	79.5	25.3	19 863	42 817	7.8	4.6	3.1	223 494	207 984	70.1	166 400	22.8	13.5
DELAWARE	77.5	21.4	15 854	34 875	4.5	8.7	6.1	289 919	247 497	70.2	100 100	19.5	12.0
At Large	77.5	21.4	15 854	34 875	4.5	8.7	6.1	289 919	247 497	70.2	100 100	19.5	12.0
DISTRICT OF COLUMBIA	73.1	33.3	18 881	30 727	7.8	16.9	13.3	278 489	249 634	38.9	123 900	20.5	12.8
Delegate	73.1	33.3	18 881	30 727	7.8	16.9	13.3	278 489	249 634	38.9	123 900	20.5	12.8
FLORIDA	74.4	18.3	14 698	27 483	3.9	12.7	9.0	6 100 262	5 134 869	67.2	77 100	22.3	12.2
District 1	77.5	18.4	12 505	25 866	2.3	14.9	11.6	258 132	211 725	67.0	62 400	20.6	12.1
District 2	70.9	19.1	11 341	22 839	2.1	19.5	14.1	239 932	207 532	68.1	57 400	19.8	12.7
District 3	64.7	10.3	10 047	21 306	1.3	22.0	17.5	233 261	204 394	59.9	50 500	21.0	12.9
District 4	82.4	23.0	16 718	31 676	4.7	7.9	5.4	254 229	224 605	66.7	80 900	21.1	12.1
District 5	71.8	15.8	11 876	21 434	1.8	15.8	10.0	279 405	237 502	73.6	61 700	22.2	11.7
District 6	72.0	12.5	12 026	25 036	1.9	12.3	9.1	252 176	214 281	76.0	66 500	21.5	11.7
District 7	81.3	20.5	15 132	30 921	3.5	7.7	5.2	252 429	222 116	71.3	80 600	22.7	11.8
District 8	81.4	22.7	15 464	31 251	3.9	8.7	5.7	242 521	216 066	60.0	85 100	22.3	11.8
District 9	79.9	19.8	15 797	29 293	3.8	8.0	5.6	276 822	233 442	74.4	85 300	23.4	11.7
District 10	76.0	17.3	15 124	25 145	3.0	10.4	6.8	306 396	253 213	68.6	69 000	22.2	12.5
District 11	74.5	19.4	13 578	26 166	2.9	15.2	11.2	255 548	225 942	56.7	66 600	21.6	12.7
District 12	67.0	13.0	12 277	25 315	2.5	14.0	10.2	248 234	209 945	71.6	62 200	20.5	12.0
District 13	77.8	18.5	16 254	27 616	4.0	8.8	5.7	309 680	247 257	74.9	81 800	23.2	11.8
District 14	77.4	17.7	17 165	29 620	5.3	9.3	6.0	329 550	234 797	72.8	90 900	22.8	11.8
District 15	79.8	18.9	15 225	29 755	3.3	9.1	6.3	266 306	226 294	71.1	75 500	21.2	11.6
District 16	77.9	18.4	16 952	30 582	4.9	8.3	5.6	300 042	233 951	75.7	88 500	22.5	11.8
District 17	57.7	11.0	9 157	21 899	1.5	26.6	22.6	202 033	182 462	50.4	64 100	23.1	12.9
District 18	62.3	21.2	14 779	25 537	6.2	17.9	13.5	228 069	209 846	50.3	95 600	22.8	13.1
District 19	82.7	22.8	20 029	34 396	6.6	5.5	3.5	296 389	244 747	76.4	107 600	24.2	12.2
District 20	80.9	21.9	18 285	35 378	6.5	7.1	4.7	258 189	222 030	74.8	103 200	23.3	12.9
District 21	67.7	19.4	13 173	32 043	3.6	12.2	9.9	203 185	188 480	59.3	91 300	23.4	12.8
District 22	79.5	24.1	24 663	29 595	8.8	9.8	6.4	376 377	284 067	62.9	118 200	23.6	13.2
District 23	61.4	11.0	10 511	23 039	1.6	21.5	17.3	231 357	200 175	54.9	67 600	23.1	13.1
GEORGIA	70.9	19.3	13 631	29 021	3.8	14.7	11.5	2 638 418	2 366 615	64.9	71 300	20.9	12.8
District 1	70.1	15.0	11 429	24 779	2.2	18.4	14.3	236 195	209 008	63.4	59 400	20.9	13.2
District 2	61.5	12.3	9 804	20 938	1.7	24.2	19.5	226 367	203 783	64.8	47 700	19.4	13.5
District 3	71.4	14.9	13 217	30 672	3.0	12.5	9.8	225 222	208 344	67.5	70 100	20.9	12.4
District 4	85.5	33.1	17 461	36 523	5.4	8.1	5.8	253 656	228 142	56.0	91 800	21.3	12.1
District 5	72.8	24.9	15 003	25 547	5.3	22.0	19.1	269 275	231 179	45.5	73 600	22.1	13.8
District 6	90.2	39.5	22 297	46 148	10.9	4.1	2.6	249 786	226 407	65.9	118 100	22.1	12.0
District 7	64.6	12.4	12 446	28 898	2.2	11.7	8.9	233 609	214 189	70.4	64 800	20.1	12.7
District 8	63.7	12.2	11 038	23 577	2.0	19.3	15.7	235 779	214 046	67.6	50 000	18.5	13.1
District 9	60.9	11.4	12 062	26 631	2.3	11.8	9.2	247 670	217 009	75.5	62 700	20.5	12.5
District 10	64.8	13.8	11 159	24 666	2.3	18.5	15.0	235 187	206 840	68.5	55 600	20.1	12.8
District 11	72.7	20.8	14 001	32 761	3.7	11.4	7.6	225 672	207 668	71.7	83 500	21.6	12.4

1. Persons 25 years old and older.   2. Based on the population enumerated as of April 1, 1990.   3. Specified owner-occupied units.

STATE District	Housing units, 1990 (cont'd) Occupied units (cont'd) Renter-occupied Median rent[1] (dollars)	Rent as a percent of income	Substandard units[2] (percent)	Civilian labor force, 1990 Total	Unemployment Total	Rate[3]	Civilian employment, 1990[4] Total	Percent Professional, managerial, and technical	Precision production, craft, and repair	Disability, 1990 Work disabled persons[5] (percent)
	44	45	46	47	48	49	50	51	52	53
CALIFORNIA—Con.										
District 45	815	28.3	7.6	338 389	15 191	4.5	323 198	36.4	10.7	5.7
District 46	719	31.0	28.1	298 519	22 785	7.6	275 734	19.8	14.0	6.2
District 47	845	28.4	5.4	323 619	11 702	3.6	311 917	43.0	7.4	4.5
District 48	696	29.9	6.8	280 497	13 599	4.8	266 898	35.7	10.6	5.9
District 49	607	29.1	5.9	300 179	16 123	5.4	284 056	41.3	8.4	7.2
District 50	540	31.7	20.0	246 477	21 805	8.8	224 672	24.4	13.3	8.5
District 51	730	28.9	6.0	306 434	14 427	4.7	292 007	41.1	9.3	5.6
District 52	566	29.6	8.4	275 286	19 471	7.1	255 815	29.6	13.5	8.7
COLORADO	418	26.1	3.0	1 732 719	99 438	5.7	1 633 281	34.3	9.8	7.8
District 1	382	26.4	4.3	290 621	20 548	7.1	270 073	33.5	7.9	9.4
District 2	477	26.9	2.4	313 860	15 458	4.9	298 402	36.8	10.3	6.5
District 3	361	26.2	3.9	267 934	18 036	6.7	249 898	28.0	11.9	9.1
District 4	379	26.8	3.3	277 284	15 215	5.5	262 069	28.4	11.5	7.6
District 5	432	25.9	2.4	266 620	16 662	6.2	249 958	38.6	8.9	8.1
District 6	473	24.5	1.8	316 400	13 519	4.3	302 881	39.1	8.6	6.5
CONNECTICUT	598	26.6	2.5	1 788 693	95 819	5.4	1 692 874	35.5	11.2	6.4
District 1	572	27.0	3.2	294 722	15 651	5.3	279 071	35.9	9.6	6.5
District 2	564	25.6	1.9	291 699	15 610	5.4	276 089	33.1	13.2	7.2
District 3	623	28.1	2.3	297 972	16 659	5.6	281 313	35.3	11.0	6.8
District 4	706	27.6	3.7	298 189	17 371	5.8	280 818	39.0	8.9	5.7
District 5	574	26.1	2.2	300 164	16 043	5.3	284 121	35.6	12.0	6.3
District 6	571	24.7	1.7	305 947	14 485	4.7	291 462	34.2	12.7	5.9
DELAWARE	495	24.7	2.5	349 092	13 945	4.0	335 147	31.0	11.9	7.7
At Large	495	24.7	2.5	349 092	13 945	4.0	335 147	31.0	11.9	7.7
DISTRICT OF COLUMBIA	479	25.4	8.2	327 436	23 442	7.2	303 994	44.0	4.5	8.4
Delegate	479	25.4	8.2	327 436	23 442	7.2	303 994	44.0	4.5	8.4
FLORIDA	481	28.0	5.7	6 167 236	356 769	5.8	5 810 467	28.8	11.5	8.7
District 1	390	25.6	3.5	249 851	16 569	6.6	233 282	29.2	12.9	11.0
District 2	373	27.9	5.4	264 289	15 740	6.0	248 549	30.6	10.0	10.2
District 3	389	28.3	7.4	255 498	19 880	7.8	235 618	20.7	11.7	12.0
District 4	481	25.6	2.4	283 222	12 441	4.4	270 781	33.1	11.1	8.0
District 5	398	30.2	3.0	224 822	13 909	6.2	210 913	30.9	11.7	10.9
District 6	400	25.4	3.8	236 437	13 800	5.8	222 637	24.1	13.1	11.2
District 7	529	26.8	2.3	290 119	14 411	5.0	275 708	31.8	11.4	7.8
District 8	531	26.9	4.1	311 293	13 491	4.3	297 802	30.4	10.4	7.0
District 9	485	26.5	1.9	268 022	12 559	4.7	255 463	31.9	10.7	8.3
District 10	448	28.2	2.4	263 277	11 940	4.5	251 337	29.8	11.4	10.3
District 11	439	26.6	5.0	299 580	17 375	5.8	282 205	29.2	10.0	9.7
District 12	381	25.6	5.1	255 685	17 489	6.8	238 196	23.8	12.7	10.1
District 13	512	27.9	2.4	237 154	10 307	4.3	226 847	27.3	12.5	9.1
District 14	519	26.1	3.5	248 732	10 664	4.3	238 068	25.8	13.2	9.0
District 15	485	26.4	2.5	266 793	15 265	5.7	251 528	31.8	13.0	9.0
District 16	575	25.8	3.1	258 165	12 321	4.8	245 844	29.4	13.3	8.1
District 17	426	30.7	22.0	260 046	28 131	10.8	231 915	20.9	11.0	8.3
District 18	460	31.9	17.5	290 069	20 399	7.0	269 670	29.2	11.1	6.4
District 19	672	27.8	2.2	262 333	11 455	4.4	250 878	33.4	10.3	6.2
District 20	624	28.3	4.2	293 791	12 525	4.3	281 266	33.3	11.5	6.8
District 21	592	30.1	19.3	308 196	19 292	6.3	288 904	28.4	11.4	4.9
District 22	545	30.6	4.2	268 636	13 337	5.0	255 299	34.3	9.5	7.1
District 23	486	30.6	13.3	271 226	23 469	8.7	247 757	20.4	12.6	8.8
GEORGIA	433	25.8	4.7	3 278 378	188 102	5.7	3 090 276	28.2	11.9	8.8
District 1	375	26.7	5.3	259 372	17 076	6.6	242 296	25.6	13.1	10.1
District 2	298	26.0	7.3	258 595	18 703	7.2	239 892	22.7	11.8	10.8
District 3	412	25.7	4.3	289 932	17 441	6.0	272 491	25.5	13.5	9.1
District 4	561	25.9	3.8	353 265	18 058	5.1	335 207	37.0	7.8	5.7
District 5	456	27.9	6.2	302 906	24 994	8.3	277 912	30.6	7.9	9.0
District 6	598	23.9	1.4	355 591	12 093	3.4	343 498	41.4	7.7	4.3
District 7	405	25.3	3.7	303 726	17 082	5.6	286 644	23.0	15.2	9.7
District 8	315	25.4	5.6	271 715	17 974	6.6	253 741	23.3	13.7	11.8
District 9	365	23.5	4.0	302 602	14 005	4.6	288 597	20.8	15.0	10.1
District 10	338	25.7	6.5	269 381	16 581	6.2	252 800	25.3	13.4	10.3
District 11	443	26.6	3.5	311 293	14 095	4.5	297 198	28.8	13.3	7.8

1. Specified renter-occupied units.   2. Overcrowded or lacking complete plumbing facilities.   3. Percent of total civilian labor force.   4. Persons 16 years old and older.   5. Persons 16 to 64 years of age.

Table E. Congressional Districts 105th Congress — Land Area and Population

Population and population characteristics, 1990

STATE District	Land area, 1990[1] (sq km)	Total persons	Per square kilometer	Race White	Race Black	Race Am. Indian, Eskimo, Aleut	Race Asian and Pacific Islander	Race Other race	Hispanic[2]	Foreign born	U.S. citizen	Age Under 5 years	Age 5 to 17 years	Age 18 to 24 years	Age 25 to 34 years	Age 35 to 44 years	Age 45 to 54 years	Age 55 to 64 years
	1	2	3	4	5	6	7	8	9	10	11	12	13	14	15	16	17	18
HAWAII	16 636	1 108 229	66.6	33.4	2.5	0.5	61.8	1.9	7.3	14.7	93.4	7.5	17.8	10.9	18.1	16.1	9.8	8.5
District 1	470	554 119	1 178.6	29.1	2.5	0.3	66.6	1.5	5.5	18.1	91.7	6.6	15.6	10.9	18.7	16.2	10.3	9.2
District 2	16 166	554 110	34.3	37.6	2.4	0.6	57.1	2.3	9.2	11.2	95.1	8.5	20.0	10.9	17.5	15.9	9.3	7.8
IDAHO	214 325	1 006 749	4.7	94.4	0.3	1.4	0.9	3.0	5.3	2.9	98.3	8.0	22.7	9.8	15.2	14.8	9.8	7.7
District 1	102 441	503 357	4.9	94.9	0.2	1.3	1.0	2.5	4.6	2.7	98.5	7.4	21.3	9.1	15.0	15.5	10.5	8.2
District 2	111 884	503 392	4.5	93.9	0.4	1.4	0.9	3.4	5.9	3.1	98.2	8.5	24.0	10.4	15.4	14.1	9.2	7.3
ILLINOIS	143 987	11 430 602	79.4	78.3	14.8	0.2	2.5	4.2	7.9	8.3	95.4	7.4	18.4	10.6	17.4	14.9	10.2	8.5
District 1	144	571 530	3 976.0	27.3	69.7	0.1	1.0	1.9	3.6	4.7	97.5	7.8	18.9	10.7	16.8	13.2	9.5	9.2
District 2	322	571 530	1 772.8	27.1	68.5	0.1	0.6	3.7	6.6	4.3	97.8	8.0	21.6	11.1	16.2	14.0	10.8	8.7
District 3	328	571 531	1 744.3	93.3	1.9	0.1	1.4	3.2	7.4	9.9	95.6	6.7	15.9	9.4	17.2	14.1	10.4	10.1
District 4	102	571 530	5 586.7	48.6	6.3	0.4	2.6	42.1	65.0	32.5	76.5	10.1	22.8	13.4	19.3	13.1	7.7	5.9
District 5	137	571 530	4 181.4	86.8	1.5	0.3	5.9	5.6	13.3	23.1	87.1	5.8	12.4	10.3	21.8	15.2	10.1	9.2
District 6	477	571 530	1 198.8	91.8	1.5	0.1	4.9	1.6	5.3	11.4	94.8	7.2	16.3	9.9	18.6	15.5	11.1	9.4
District 7	132	571 530	4 345.1	29.0	65.6	0.1	3.2	2.0	4.3	6.0	97.0	8.5	20.3	11.6	18.6	14.2	9.2	7.6
District 8	1 118	571 530	511.3	92.2	1.7	0.2	4.0	1.9	5.5	9.1	94.9	8.1	18.3	9.7	20.4	17.4	11.4	7.3
District 9	139	571 530	4 106.4	73.1	12.1	0.3	10.0	4.5	9.7	24.4	87.0	5.8	12.5	11.2	20.2	15.0	9.8	9.1
District 10	633	571 530	903.1	86.5	6.2	0.2	4.1	3.1	7.1	10.7	94.5	7.7	17.9	10.4	16.6	16.3	11.5	9.1
District 11	6 729	571 528	84.9	87.4	8.6	0.2	0.7	3.2	6.5	4.0	98.1	7.3	19.6	9.6	16.5	14.7	10.4	8.8
District 12	9 082	571 530	62.9	81.5	17.0	0.2	0.9	0.4	1.3	1.4	99.2	7.3	18.9	11.6	16.5	13.8	9.4	8.8
District 13	1 046	571 531	546.5	91.6	3.2	0.1	4.2	0.9	3.0	7.0	97.1	8.1	19.7	9.2	18.6	18.3	11.4	6.9
District 14	6 352	571 530	90.0	88.8	4.2	0.2	1.7	5.1	9.8	6.9	95.8	8.5	20.2	11.5	18.0	16.0	9.8	6.9
District 15	19 404	571 532	29.5	89.7	7.4	0.2	1.9	0.8	1.6	2.8	98.3	6.8	17.4	15.4	16.6	13.8	9.2	8.0
District 16	8 013	571 530	71.3	92.9	4.7	0.2	0.9	1.4	3.1	3.5	98.4	7.8	19.5	9.0	17.0	15.7	10.8	8.2
District 17	21 571	571 530	26.5	94.7	3.3	0.2	0.6	1.4	3.0	1.7	99.2	6.5	18.6	10.1	14.4	14.0	10.4	9.5
District 18	15 989	571 580	35.7	93.7	5.1	0.2	0.7	0.3	0.9	1.5	99.5	6.8	19.4	9.3	15.2	15.2	10.8	9.2
District 19	27 798	571 530	20.6	95.5	3.9	0.2	0.3	0.1	0.5	0.7	99.7	6.5	18.3	9.8	14.5	13.6	10.4	9.5
District 20	24 473	571 480	23.4	95.0	4.2	0.2	0.4	0.2	0.7	1.0	99.6	6.9	18.8	9.1	15.9	14.2	10.1	9.3
INDIANA	92 904	5 544 159	59.7	90.6	7.8	0.2	0.7	0.7	1.8	1.7	99.2	7.2	19.1	10.9	16.5	14.8	10.3	8.7
District 1	1 683	554 416	329.4	74.2	21.1	0.2	0.6	3.9	8.5	3.8	98.7	7.0	20.8	9.8	15.8	15.0	10.5	9.1
District 2	10 071	554 416	55.1	95.0	4.1	0.2	0.4	0.2	0.6	0.8	99.5	6.6	18.3	11.7	15.0	14.3	11.0	9.3
District 3	4 703	554 416	117.9	90.7	7.4	0.3	0.8	0.8	1.9	2.4	98.9	7.6	18.9	11.0	16.3	14.9	9.8	8.6
District 4	9 342	554 416	59.3	92.9	5.5	0.3	0.6	0.7	1.6	1.4	99.4	8.0	20.5	9.8	16.8	15.0	9.8	8.1
District 5	18 033	554 415	30.7	96.7	2.2	0.4	0.3	0.4	1.3	1.1	99.6	7.1	20.0	9.3	15.4	14.6	10.9	9.3
District 6	5 278	554 416	105.0	97.7	1.1	0.2	0.9	0.2	0.8	1.7	99.2	7.3	19.1	8.5	17.6	16.8	11.2	8.4
District 7	12 308	554 416	45.0	96.3	2.0	0.2	1.2	0.3	0.8	2.0	98.7	6.7	17.9	14.5	15.9	14.3	10.1	8.3
District 8	13 538	554 416	41.0	95.8	3.1	0.2	0.8	0.2	0.6	1.3	99.1	6.5	17.4	13.5	15.8	14.1	9.9	8.8
District 9	17 439	554 416	31.8	97.7	1.7	0.2	0.3	0.1	0.4	0.6	99.8	6.9	20.1	9.3	16.0	15.1	10.8	8.9
District 10	509	554 416	1 088.7	68.6	29.8	0.2	0.9	0.5	1.2	1.9	99.1	8.2	17.7	11.4	20.5	13.8	8.8	8.1
IOWA	144 716	2 776 755	19.2	96.6	1.7	0.3	0.9	0.5	1.2	1.6	99.2	7.0	18.9	10.2	15.4	14.2	9.9	9.0
District 1	11 605	555 229	47.8	95.0	2.6	0.2	1.3	0.8	2.0	2.4	98.6	7.1	18.4	12.4	17.2	15.1	9.9	8.0
District 2	31 757	555 494	17.5	97.3	1.7	0.2	0.5	0.2	0.7	0.9	99.6	6.8	19.6	9.8	14.3	13.7	10.0	9.3
District 3	35 828	555 299	15.5	97.5	0.9	0.2	1.1	0.3	0.8	1.7	98.9	6.5	18.3	11.3	14.5	14.0	9.9	9.1
District 4	19 421	555 276	28.6	95.3	2.8	0.2	1.2	0.5	1.5	1.7	99.2	7.3	18.5	9.6	17.1	14.9	10.1	8.8
District 5	46 106	555 457	12.0	98.0	0.6	0.4	0.6	0.4	0.9	1.2	99.5	7.0	19.9	8.0	14.1	13.4	9.4	9.9
KANSAS	211 922	2 477 574	11.7	90.1	5.8	0.9	1.3	2.0	3.8	2.5	98.6	7.6	19.1	10.3	16.7	14.6	9.5	8.4
District 1	145 674	619 370	4.3	94.2	1.3	0.4	0.8	3.2	5.2	2.6	98.3	7.3	19.6	8.8	15.0	13.4	9.4	9.3
District 2	36 195	619 391	17.1	90.1	6.3	1.2	1.1	1.3	3.0	2.0	98.9	7.3	18.7	11.8	16.2	14.2	9.2	8.2
District 3	4 017	619 439	154.2	87.2	8.9	0.7	1.7	1.5	3.3	2.9	98.4	7.8	18.6	11.3	18.3	16.1	9.9	7.6
District 4	26 036	619 374	23.8	88.8	6.6	1.2	1.6	1.9	3.7	2.6	98.6	8.0	19.4	9.2	17.1	14.6	9.5	8.6
KENTUCKY	102 907	3 685 296	35.8	92.0	7.1	0.2	0.5	0.2	0.6	0.9	99.5	6.8	19.1	10.9	16.6	14.9	10.4	8.8
District 1	29 089	614 265	21.1	91.4	7.8	0.2	0.3	0.3	0.7	0.7	99.7	6.5	18.5	10.6	15.4	14.0	10.6	9.2
District 2	20 098	614 794	30.6	93.4	5.5	0.2	0.6	0.3	0.8	1.1	99.5	7.1	20.0	11.2	16.7	14.7	10.5	8.4
District 3	618	613 603	992.9	80.6	18.3	0.2	0.7	0.2	0.7	1.5	99.2	6.8	17.4	9.7	17.4	15.3	10.1	9.5
District 4	14 258	602 896	42.3	97.3	2.2	0.1	0.3	0.1	0.4	0.7	99.7	7.1	19.6	10.3	16.6	15.2	10.5	8.7
District 5	26 746	624 837	23.4	98.7	0.9	0.1	0.2	0.0	0.3	0.2	99.9	6.7	21.4	10.4	15.8	14.9	10.4	8.5
District 6	12 098	614 901	50.8	90.8	8.1	0.1	0.8	0.2	0.7	1.4	99.1	6.6	17.7	12.8	17.5	15.5	10.3	8.2
LOUISIANA	112 836	4 219 973	37.4	67.3	30.8	0.4	1.0	0.5	2.2	2.1	98.8	7.9	21.2	11.0	16.7	14.4	9.6	8.1
District 1	6 177	602 842	97.6	85.5	12.1	0.3	1.1	0.9	4.3	4.1	97.9	7.0	19.2	9.6	16.9	15.9	10.6	8.8
District 2	696	602 877	866.1	35.8	60.7	0.3	2.2	1.1	3.6	4.2	97.5	8.2	21.3	11.5	17.0	14.5	9.0	7.5
District 3	17 893	602 839	33.7	73.6	23.6	1.5	0.9	0.4	2.2	1.4	99.2	8.6	22.8	10.4	17.4	14.2	9.6	7.8
District 4	26 407	602 876	22.8	66.0	32.5	0.4	0.7	0.5	1.8	1.2	99.4	8.1	20.7	11.2	16.1	13.6	9.5	8.5
District 5	33 948	602 933	17.8	68.1	31.1	0.2	0.4	0.2	0.9	0.8	99.6	7.6	21.6	11.5	15.0	13.1	9.5	8.6
District 6	10 121	602 774	59.6	66.9	31.8	0.2	0.9	0.3	1.4	1.8	98.8	7.8	20.7	12.5	17.7	15.3	9.6	7.2

1. Dry land or land partially or temporarily covered by water.   2. Hispanic persons may be of any race.

Table E. Congressional Districts 105th Congress — Population, Households, Group Quarters, and Education

STATE District	Population and population characteristics, 1990 (cont'd) Percent (cont'd) Age (cont'd) 65 to 74 years	75 years and over	Percent female	Households, 1990 Number	Persons per house-hold	Percent Female family house-holder[1]	One person	Persons in mental hospitals, 1990	Persons in nursing homes, 1990	Persons identified as homeless, 1990[2]	Education, 1990 School enrollment Public	Private
	19	20	21	22	23	24	25	26	27	28	29	30
HAWAII	7.1	4.2	49.1	356 267	3.01	10.5	19.4	289	3 225	1 691	233 972	56 606
District 1	7.9	4.6	49.7	188 969	2.83	10.3	22.5	61	1 748	837	110 167	31 711
District 2	6.3	3.7	48.5	167 298	3.20	10.8	15.8	228	1 477	854	123 805	24 895
IDAHO	6.9	5.1	50.2	360 723	2.73	8.0	22.4	233	6 318	539	268 404	27 234
District 1	7.4	5.5	50.4	185 172	2.65	8.2	22.3	75	3 759	149	125 535	12 577
District 2	6.5	4.7	50.1	175 551	2.82	7.8	22.5	158	2 559	390	142 869	14 657
ILLINOIS	7.2	5.4	51.4	4 202 240	2.65	12.0	25.7	4 408	93 662	9 551	2 440 505	591 168
District 1	8.2	5.7	54.2	210 872	2.67	25.6	31.1	273	2 758	966	115 893	44 975
District 2	6.1	3.6	53.0	183 227	3.09	25.6	20.6	321	2 874	458	141 490	26 853
District 3	9.8	6.4	52.0	214 647	2.64	10.8	25.1	0	3 383	76	90 948	39 716
District 4	4.7	3.0	48.7	170 646	3.30	18.7	22.2	7	916	522	134 500	32 138
District 5	8.6	6.6	51.9	243 577	2.32	9.9	35.6	28	3 212	134	72 418	47 205
District 6	7.1	4.9	51.1	210 552	2.67	8.1	22.5	67	4 818	414	107 651	34 041
District 7	6.0	4.0	53.0	204 386	2.72	25.8	32.3	533	2 231	3 682	133 073	32 324
District 8	4.6	2.8	50.3	205 605	2.76	7.7	20.0	69	1 880	46	121 377	26 743
District 9	8.5	7.9	51.9	245 104	2.24	9.4	38.2	91	9 888	1 170	83 762	55 974
District 10	6.3	4.1	50.1	199 839	2.75	8.3	20.4	0	5 125	54	114 762	32 749
District 11	7.7	5.4	51.1	204 630	2.73	10.6	22.4	0	5 430	71	119 295	27 332
District 12	7.6	6.0	51.5	213 212	2.59	13.5	25.8	800	5 207	280	142 993	19 274
District 13	4.8	2.9	50.5	197 921	2.84	7.0	18.9	390	2 318	13	124 678	36 129
District 14	5.2	4.0	50.3	192 838	2.86	8.6	19.6	991	3 983	370	142 639	25 434
District 15	7.1	5.8	51.0	213 068	2.50	9.1	27.0	57	6 069	284	163 016	14 983
District 16	6.9	5.1	50.9	210 646	2.68	9.0	21.8	215	4 539	379	123 118	21 750
District 17	9.0	7.6	51.6	221 563	2.48	9.2	27.1	22	7 522	72	130 850	18 213
District 18	7.8	6.4	51.7	217 008	2.55	9.3	25.0	227	6 719	322	124 593	25 584
District 19	9.3	8.1	52.0	223 161	2.47	9.0	26.7	302	8 302	64	132 299	10 356
District 20	8.5	7.3	51.6	219 738	2.53	9.3	25.9	15	6 488	174	121 150	19 395
INDIANA	7.3	5.3	51.5	2 065 355	2.61	10.5	24.1	3 015	50 845	2 507	1 233 973	202 215
District 1	7.4	4.5	52.0	198 750	2.75	14.8	22.8	52	3 210	336	129 239	24 866
District 2	7.8	5.8	51.7	209 961	2.55	10.2	24.0	418	4 975	162	128 116	12 726
District 3	7.5	5.5	51.0	203 314	2.62	10.4	24.1	124	5 118	421	109 890	32 012
District 4	6.8	5.1	51.2	202 849	2.69	9.4	23.0	95	5 100	197	118 376	24 487
District 5	7.8	5.6	51.3	205 013	2.65	8.8	22.3	549	5 118	169	121 805	15 570
District 6	6.5	4.7	51.7	209 027	2.62	7.7	21.9	171	5 395	37	114 881	22 308
District 7	7.0	5.3	50.4	200 596	2.59	8.5	23.2	235	5 795	235	146 172	16 048
District 8	7.8	6.2	51.9	211 519	2.50	9.2	26.2	439	6 185	162	136 877	17 801
District 9	7.3	5.5	51.2	202 651	2.68	9.6	21.5	412	5 466	202	120 627	12 971
District 10	6.6	4.8	52.6	221 675	2.45	16.4	30.8	520	4 483	586	107 990	23 426
IOWA	8.2	7.2	51.6	1 064 325	2.52	8.0	25.9	1 347	36 455	1 290	626 759	110 970
District 1	6.6	5.3	51.2	211 466	2.53	8.9	25.2	303	4 777	283	140 148	21 722
District 2	8.7	7.6	51.7	209 760	2.55	7.6	25.5	260	7 994	239	121 393	26 324
District 3	8.6	7.9	51.1	212 356	2.48	7.4	25.9	342	8 704	62	134 632	17 202
District 4	7.5	6.3	52.1	216 874	2.50	9.4	26.0	249	6 025	531	116 217	20 867
District 5	9.5	8.7	51.8	213 869	2.51	6.7	26.7	193	8 955	175	114 369	24 855
KANSAS	7.5	6.4	51.0	944 726	2.53	8.6	25.9	1 822	26 155	1 242	593 376	74 989
District 1	8.7	8.5	51.0	239 568	2.50	6.7	27.0	597	9 183	129	145 568	13 957
District 2	7.5	6.8	50.1	230 344	2.53	8.4	25.8	495	7 110	476	155 428	14 431
District 3	6.1	4.3	51.6	235 450	2.57	10.0	24.7	438	3 778	242	152 418	25 649
District 4	7.5	6.0	51.2	239 364	2.54	9.3	26.4	292	6 084	395	139 962	20 952
KENTUCKY	7.3	5.4	51.6	1 379 782	2.60	11.6	23.3	1 690	27 874	1 360	807 842	110 473
District 1	8.5	6.8	51.2	232 764	2.54	10.2	23.6	515	6 572	109	132 226	8 906
District 2	6.6	4.8	50.8	222 235	2.69	10.1	20.6	211	4 393	62	137 126	16 468
District 3	8.1	5.8	53.0	246 351	2.45	14.8	28.4	388	4 950	836	115 452	35 838
District 4	7.0	5.0	51.4	220 240	2.68	10.7	22.3	90	4 075	124	132 266	20 867
District 5	7.0	5.0	51.2	225 010	2.74	12.0	19.8	150	3 858	84	145 258	9 850
District 6	6.6	4.9	51.9	233 182	2.52	11.3	24.4	336	4 026	145	145 514	18 544
LOUISIANA	6.5	4.6	51.9	1 499 269	2.74	15.6	23.7	1 728	32 072	1 795	979 200	206 559
District 1	7.3	4.8	52.0	228 470	2.60	11.9	25.5	390	3 736	145	108 597	49 215
District 2	6.3	4.5	53.0	217 170	2.70	24.3	28.9	51	3 227	974	134 896	46 987
District 3	5.7	3.6	51.3	200 349	2.98	13.8	18.1	51	3 215	124	138 324	27 104
District 4	7.0	5.4	51.6	217 133	2.68	15.4	24.4	0	5 674	216	147 134	13 332
District 5	7.4	5.7	52.3	211 252	2.74	15.6	23.4	512	7 583	71	154 590	15 522
District 6	5.6	3.6	51.1	210 773	2.75	14.7	22.7	569	3 541	126	147 842	32 109

1. No spouse present. 2. Persons in emergency shelters and persons visible in street locations.

STATE District	Education, 1990 (cont'd) Attainment[1] (percent) High school graduate or more	Bachelor's degree or more	Money income, 1989 Per capita[2]	Households Median	Percent with $100,000 or more	Percent below poverty level, 1989 Persons Total	Families Total	Housing units, 1990 Total	Occupied units Total	Percent	Owner-occupied Median value[3] (dollars)	Owner cost as a percent of income With a mortgage	Without a mortgage
	31	32	33	34	35	36	37	38	39	40	41	42	43
HAWAII	80.1	22.9	15 770	38 829	7.1	8.3	6.0	389 810	356 267	53.9	245 300	21.4	10.8
District 1	81.4	26.6	17 508	40 257	8.3	7.0	4.7	201 204	188 969	50.4	311 200	21.1	10.7
District 2	78.6	18.8	14 032	37 247	5.8	9.5	7.4	188 606	167 298	57.8	190 900	21.6	10.9
IDAHO	79.7	17.7	11 457	25 257	2.1	13.3	9.7	413 327	360 723	70.1	58 200	19.3	11.8
District 1	78.8	16.7	11 530	25 086	2.0	13.0	9.4	212 660	185 172	71.3	60 300	19.7	11.7
District 2	80.7	18.7	11 384	25 446	2.3	13.5	10.0	200 667	175 551	68.7	55 900	18.8	12.0
ILLINOIS	76.2	21.0	15 201	32 252	4.9	11.9	9.0	4 506 275	4 202 240	64.2	80 900	20.2	12.7
District 1	70.7	18.4	11 709	24 140	2.6	23.8	19.8	235 969	210 872	44.7	73 100	19.6	13.3
District 2	70.1	13.1	11 468	30 217	2.6	18.0	15.1	197 780	183 227	62.9	65 000	20.7	13.3
District 3	74.5	15.7	15 854	36 250	4.0	5.4	3.9	221 318	214 647	73.8	92 800	20.5	12.8
District 4	46.5	8.4	8 352	23 083	1.1	23.8	21.5	189 130	170 646	36.0	64 900	21.4	13.6
District 5	73.6	26.1	19 242	33 262	5.9	8.0	5.3	258 537	243 577	48.8	109 900	22.2	13.5
District 6	85.1	28.6	19 405	44 216	7.6	3.3	2.0	218 595	210 552	73.7	130 400	21.4	12.3
District 7	66.6	20.9	13 056	25 220	4.9	29.5	25.9	233 596	204 386	36.9	89 500	21.3	13.3
District 8	87.1	30.2	20 488	47 374	9.5	3.3	2.3	217 242	205 605	74.2	132 300	21.9	12.4
District 9	81.1	36.6	18 691	32 183	6.4	11.9	8.3	261 802	245 104	45.8	145 800	21.4	13.0
District 10	87.6	40.4	26 405	50 355	18.5	4.4	3.0	208 089	199 839	74.4	181 400	21.2	12.4
District 11	75.8	13.4	13 838	33 632	2.5	8.2	6.3	215 470	204 630	73.7	67 400	18.8	12.5
District 12	71.9	13.9	11 547	25 032	1.7	17.4	13.1	231 781	213 212	66.6	48 000	18.4	13.1
District 13	89.0	35.0	20 912	50 087	10.5	2.5	1.8	207 243	197 921	77.4	140 300	22.3	12.5
District 14	80.4	22.7	15 769	39 815	5.5	6.9	4.5	200 903	192 838	71.1	100 600	21.6	12.6
District 15	79.7	21.1	12 709	26 760	2.3	13.6	8.6	228 106	213 068	64.0	52 500	17.8	12.3
District 16	78.9	17.1	15 107	34 668	3.8	7.6	5.7	223 666	210 646	72.5	73 700	20.0	12.6
District 17	76.3	13.3	12 052	25 195	1.7	12.8	9.7	240 317	221 563	70.0	41 600	16.4	12.5
District 18	79.0	17.5	13 792	30 189	2.6	10.6	8.0	230 713	217 008	70.3	52 000	16.1	12.3
District 19	70.7	11.1	11 333	22 979	1.5	15.3	11.7	245 810	223 161	74.6	38 800	17.2	12.9
District 20	73.9	13.2	12 289	26 173	1.9	12.2	9.3	240 208	219 738	73.1	47 200	17.9	12.9
INDIANA	75.6	15.6	13 149	28 797	2.5	10.7	7.9	2 246 046	2 065 355	70.2	53 900	16.7	12.3
District 1	75.0	14.2	13 161	31 300	2.5	12.8	10.7	212 239	198 750	68.6	57 000	16.4	13.1
District 2	73.1	12.3	12 311	26 185	1.8	12.7	9.3	224 937	209 961	71.2	43 400	15.5	12.4
District 3	74.8	16.1	13 385	29 470	2.7	8.8	6.5	219 701	203 314	72.5	55 500	16.9	12.3
District 4	78.2	15.0	13 436	30 859	2.4	7.8	5.5	226 688	202 849	74.3	56 500	16.1	11.7
District 5	75.1	10.9	12 252	27 893	1.6	9.8	7.6	228 884	205 013	75.1	46 700	15.8	12.4
District 6	85.3	26.7	17 971	38 644	6.0	4.5	3.1	220 193	209 027	72.8	81 400	17.7	11.7
District 7	78.8	17.4	12 536	28 080	2.3	10.7	6.9	216 510	200 596	71.4	54 700	16.7	12.2
District 8	74.5	15.7	12 153	25 242	2.1	13.4	9.2	230 924	211 519	70.1	49 200	17.3	12.5
District 9	69.9	10.2	11 727	26 900	1.5	10.7	8.3	219 460	202 651	76.0	49 300	17.2	12.3
District 10	71.6	16.9	12 562	25 304	1.9	15.8	12.6	246 510	221 675	52.0	46 200	17.7	12.7
IOWA	80.1	16.9	12 422	26 229	2.1	11.5	8.4	1 143 669	1 064 325	70.0	45 900	17.3	12.8
District 1	82.8	22.7	13 660	29 544	2.7	11.5	7.8	223 842	211 466	66.7	55 800	17.0	12.5
District 2	77.9	13.8	11 611	25 010	1.7	12.3	9.4	226 600	209 760	72.2	42 600	16.3	12.9
District 3	79.3	15.7	11 567	24 767	1.6	12.7	9.1	229 322	212 356	71.2	41 400	16.9	12.7
District 4	82.5	18.9	13 813	28 591	2.7	9.8	7.4	230 124	216 874	68.3	52 900	19.2	13.2
District 5	78.0	13.4	11 461	24 150	1.8	11.3	8.3	233 781	213 869	71.7	37 200	16.8	12.8
KANSAS	81.3	21.1	13 300	27 291	2.8	11.5	8.3	1 044 112	944 726	67.9	52 200	19.1	12.6
District 1	77.9	15.2	11 328	23 433	1.6	12.3	9.0	273 364	239 568	71.2	38 200	17.7	12.6
District 2	80.7	18.4	11 662	24 903	1.7	13.4	9.8	255 015	230 344	67.7	44 500	18.6	12.6
District 3	85.9	31.5	16 585	34 275	5.6	9.4	6.4	252 929	235 450	65.7	75 800	20.1	12.7
District 4	80.6	19.6	13 623	28 308	2.5	10.9	8.2	262 804	239 364	67.0	52 500	19.3	12.7
KENTUCKY	64.6	13.6	11 153	22 534	2.0	19.0	16.0	1 506 845	1 379 782	69.6	50 500	18.0	12.3
District 1	62.0	9.5	10 238	20 331	1.3	19.0	15.4	258 606	232 764	73.4	40 500	17.6	12.6
District 2	65.1	11.2	10 609	23 212	1.5	16.8	14.0	243 599	222 235	72.8	48 200	18.1	12.2
District 3	74.1	19.7	14 072	26 614	3.3	14.3	11.4	264 057	246 351	63.3	57 000	16.9	12.3
District 4	68.0	13.5	11 935	26 569	2.3	14.6	12.2	238 483	220 240	71.8	57 300	17.5	12.1
District 5	48.1	7.6	7 725	15 061	1.0	32.7	29.2	249 968	225 010	74.5	35 500	21.1	12.5
District 6	70.0	19.9	12 413	25 364	2.7	16.3	12.8	252 132	233 182	62.7	61 900	18.5	12.1
LOUISIANA	68.3	16.1	10 635	21 949	2.4	23.6	19.4	1 716 241	1 499 269	65.9	58 500	20.6	13.3
District 1	76.4	22.2	13 755	27 413	4.1	15.2	11.9	253 541	228 470	67.3	75 500	20.7	12.7
District 2	65.9	17.6	9 918	18 585	2.4	31.0	27.0	259 749	217 170	46.6	62 400	23.1	14.4
District 3	61.4	9.4	9 614	22 948	1.5	22.6	18.7	225 323	200 349	75.1	56 700	20.2	12.9
District 4	71.2	14.7	10 218	20 920	1.9	23.7	19.1	255 542	217 133	67.1	51 000	20.8	13.6
District 5	63.8	13.7	9 153	18 258	1.8	27.9	22.8	242 121	211 252	70.3	44 100	21.0	13.8
District 6	74.2	20.6	11 790	26 001	2.9	20.0	15.8	239 278	210 773	66.6	65 000	18.5	12.7

1. Persons 25 years old and older.   2. Based on the population enumerated as of April 1, 1990.   3. Specified owner-occupied units.

STATE District	Housing units, 1990 (cont'd) Occupied units (cont'd) Renter-occupied Median rent[1] (dollars)	Rent as a percent of income	Substandard units[2] (percent)	Civilian labor force, 1990 Total	Unemployment Total	Rate[3]	Civilian employment, 1990[4] Total	Percent Professional, managerial, and technical	Precision production, craft, and repair	Disability, 1990 Work disabled persons[5] (percent)
	44	45	46	47	48	49	50	51	52	53
HAWAII	650	27.4	15.6	548 347	19 288	3.5	529 059	29.9	10.5	6.6
District 1	659	27.4	15.2	284 477	8 520	3.0	275 957	33.1	9.0	5.7
District 2	633	27.3	16.0	263 870	10 768	4.1	253 102	26.3	12.1	7.5
IDAHO	330	23.8	4.5	472 773	29 070	6.1	443 703	27.1	11.3	9.0
District 1	332	24.3	4.2	238 745	16 266	6.8	222 479	26.7	11.8	9.9
District 2	327	23.2	4.9	234 028	12 804	5.5	221 224	27.4	10.9	8.1
ILLINOIS	445	25.9	4.2	5 803 007	385 040	6.6	5 417 967	30.0	10.7	6.9
District 1	425	29.5	6.7	259 745	35 334	13.6	224 411	30.2	7.7	10.0
District 2	449	28.2	7.8	273 582	36 478	13.3	237 104	24.5	9.1	9.0
District 3	489	24.0	3.0	296 879	15 121	5.1	281 758	26.2	13.2	6.3
District 4	393	25.3	18.1	258 181	30 076	11.6	228 105	14.6	12.4	7.5
District 5	514	24.3	4.3	332 958	18 538	5.6	314 420	32.3	10.6	5.6
District 6	605	25.3	2.5	326 767	10 872	3.3	315 895	35.2	10.3	4.3
District 7	449	29.3	9.3	259 036	36 625	14.1	222 411	32.5	6.7	9.7
District 8	667	24.7	2.3	333 760	10 669	3.2	323 091	35.5	10.5	4.3
District 9	508	27.1	6.0	323 326	17 631	5.5	305 695	40.6	6.7	6.1
District 10	605	25.7	2.7	300 033	9 761	3.3	290 272	41.9	7.4	4.3
District 11	414	23.7	2.8	282 360	17 879	6.3	264 481	24.8	14.1	6.8
District 12	360	28.8	3.7	259 924	24 269	9.3	235 655	25.6	11.5	9.8
District 13	619	23.7	1.4	316 857	10 206	3.2	306 651	40.2	9.7	3.8
District 14	484	24.4	3.8	304 148	13 112	4.3	291 036	29.7	12.3	5.3
District 15	372	26.7	2.2	286 446	15 319	5.3	271 127	29.3	9.6	6.7
District 16	392	23.6	2.1	301 095	13 933	4.6	287 162	26.8	14.1	6.4
District 17	309	24.6	1.7	272 048	17 235	6.3	254 813	22.9	12.0	7.8
District 18	352	22.8	1.7	281 996	14 028	5.0	267 968	28.8	10.8	7.4
District 19	295	26.1	2.5	258 530	20 309	7.9	238 221	22.0	13.3	9.4
District 20	337	24.7	2.6	275 336	17 645	6.4	257 691	25.1	11.9	8.4
INDIANA	374	24.3	2.6	2 788 838	160 143	5.7	2 628 695	25.6	12.9	7.9
District 1	399	24.7	3.7	263 391	20 854	7.9	242 537	25.6	14.1	8.5
District 2	331	24.6	2.0	273 968	18 463	6.7	255 505	22.6	13.2	8.9
District 3	395	24.1	2.3	282 049	14 037	5.0	268 012	25.3	12.5	7.2
District 4	373	23.1	2.6	289 381	13 914	4.8	275 467	24.7	13.1	7.0
District 5	335	23.2	2.1	270 180	16 031	5.9	254 149	20.2	15.2	8.3
District 6	452	23.2	1.2	300 474	9 257	3.1	291 217	34.4	10.8	5.6
District 7	358	24.9	2.9	275 124	13 471	4.9	261 653	27.1	12.9	7.2
District 8	341	26.7	2.6	271 217	16 901	6.2	254 316	26.6	12.6	8.0
District 9	325	23.6	3.4	273 762	17 437	6.4	256 325	20.6	14.5	9.0
District 10	394	24.5	3.3	289 292	19 778	6.8	269 514	27.2	10.4	9.4
IOWA	336	24.1	1.9	1 403 883	63 641	4.5	1 340 242	25.3	10.5	7.6
District 1	365	24.6	1.8	294 488	15 106	5.1	279 382	29.7	10.3	6.6
District 2	300	23.6	1.9	271 182	13 261	4.9	257 921	22.2	11.2	7.5
District 3	315	24.6	2.0	276 177	13 080	4.7	263 097	24.6	10.9	8.1
District 4	405	24.6	2.1	296 650	11 956	4.0	284 694	27.7	9.3	7.9
District 5	285	22.7	1.6	265 386	10 238	3.9	255 148	21.7	11.0	7.9
KANSAS	372	24.5	2.7	1 229 986	57 772	4.7	1 172 214	28.7	11.5	7.2
District 1	297	22.4	2.6	301 308	10 355	3.4	290 953	21.8	12.7	7.2
District 2	344	25.2	2.8	284 824	15 891	5.6	268 933	27.6	10.8	8.1
District 3	454	25.4	2.3	332 705	15 632	4.7	317 073	35.8	8.3	5.7
District 4	376	24.6	3.1	311 149	15 894	5.1	295 255	29.0	14.2	8.0
KENTUCKY	319	24.9	4.7	1 688 314	124 354	7.4	1 563 960	24.7	12.9	11.4
District 1	278	24.5	4.0	269 270	21 778	8.1	247 492	19.9	14.3	12.0
District 2	310	24.5	4.5	284 214	20 406	7.2	263 808	20.9	13.8	10.5
District 3	344	24.8	2.5	309 313	19 413	6.3	289 900	29.9	10.3	9.1
District 4	337	24.1	4.4	288 295	16 579	5.8	271 716	25.4	12.6	10.0
District 5	243	27.7	9.1	221 371	27 962	12.6	193 409	20.4	17.6	18.2
District 6	352	24.9	3.9	315 851	18 216	5.8	297 635	29.0	10.6	8.8
LOUISIANA	352	27.9	6.5	1 816 917	175 303	9.6	1 641 614	28.1	12.5	10.3
District 1	416	25.3	3.9	287 863	19 040	6.6	268 823	33.7	10.7	9.0
District 2	372	31.5	9.2	257 514	33 025	12.8	224 489	29.2	8.9	11.0
District 3	330	26.1	8.2	252 431	23 449	9.3	228 982	22.1	16.6	11.2
District 4	336	27.7	6.2	246 496	28 011	11.4	218 485	26.7	12.2	10.3
District 5	302	28.9	6.4	241 803	24 747	10.2	217 056	25.8	11.9	11.2
District 6	365	26.7	5.6	279 794	23 400	8.4	256 394	31.0	12.9	8.0

1. Specified renter-occupied units.　2. Overcrowded or lacking complete plumbing facilities.　3. Percent of total civilian labor force.　4. Persons 16 years old and older.　5. Persons 16 to 64 years of age.

Table E. Congressional Districts 105th Congress — Land Area and Population

Population and population characteristics, 1990 — Percent

STATE District	Land area, 1990¹ (sq km)	Total persons	Per square kilometer	White	Black	Am. Indian, Eskimo, Aleut	Asian and Pacific Islander	Other race	Hispanic²	Foreign born	U.S. citizen	Under 5 years	5 to 17 years	18 to 24 years	25 to 34 years	35 to 44 years	45 to 54 years	55 to 64 years
	1	2	3	4	5	6	7	8	9	10	11	12	13	14	15	16	17	18
LOUISIANA—Con.																		
District 7	17 595	602 832	34.3	75.1	23.8	0.2	0.5	0.3	1.2	1.0	99.4	8.2	21.9	10.3	16.7	13.9	9.6	8.5
MAINE	79 939	1 227 928	15.4	98.4	0.4	0.5	0.5	0.1	0.6	3.0	98.8	7.0	18.2	10.1	16.7	15.7	10.2	8.8
District 1	9 368	613 961	65.5	98.5	0.5	0.3	0.7	0.1	0.6	2.9	98.8	7.1	17.6	9.7	17.2	16.3	10.1	8.6
District 2	70 572	613 967	8.7	98.3	0.4	0.7	0.4	0.1	0.5	3.0	98.7	6.9	18.7	10.4	16.2	15.2	10.2	9.1
MARYLAND	25 316	4 781 468	188.9	71.0	24.9	0.3	2.9	0.9	2.6	6.6	96.1	7.5	16.8	10.6	18.8	16.3	10.9	8.3
District 1	9 004	597 684	66.4	83.4	15.0	0.2	1.0	0.3	1.1	2.3	99.0	7.1	16.8	10.6	17.1	15.5	11.1	9.3
District 2	2 341	597 683	255.3	91.7	5.9	0.3	1.8	0.3	1.2	3.3	98.6	7.2	16.4	9.9	17.7	16.1	11.3	9.5
District 3	553	597 680	1 081.7	79.5	17.5	0.3	2.2	0.5	1.7	5.5	97.4	7.5	15.7	9.8	19.6	15.8	10.0	8.2
District 4	500	597 690	1 196.0	33.5	58.5	0.3	4.6	3.2	6.4	13.5	90.5	7.9	17.3	11.4	21.1	17.4	10.8	6.8
District 5	4 059	597 681	147.2	77.2	18.6	0.4	3.0	0.8	2.4	5.6	96.9	7.6	17.1	12.6	20.0	16.4	11.4	7.4
District 6	7 389	597 688	80.9	93.8	4.5	0.2	1.3	0.2	0.9	2.1	99.0	7.3	17.7	10.0	17.3	16.5	11.2	8.4
District 7	282	597 680	2 119.7	27.2	71.0	0.3	1.3	0.2	0.9	2.9	98.3	7.8	17.2	11.5	18.9	14.7	9.4	8.4
District 8	1 189	597 682	502.5	81.5	8.2	0.2	8.0	2.0	6.3	17.2	89.0	7.5	16.4	8.6	18.8	17.6	12.1	8.5
MASSACHUSETTS	20 300	6 016 425	296.4	89.8	5.0	0.2	2.4	2.6	4.8	9.5	94.8	6.9	15.6	11.8	18.3	15.3	10.0	8.6
District 1	7 854	601 643	76.6	94.2	1.7	0.2	1.3	2.6	4.8	4.8	97.8	7.1	16.8	12.8	16.5	15.2	9.4	8.2
District 2	2 294	601 642	262.3	89.6	5.6	0.2	1.0	3.6	6.0	5.8	97.3	7.2	17.2	11.1	17.2	15.0	9.7	8.5
District 3	1 869	601 642	322.0	94.4	1.8	0.2	1.8	1.9	3.7	7.6	96.2	7.2	16.7	11.4	17.4	15.3	10.0	8.5
District 4	1 974	601 642	304.7	93.5	2.2	0.2	2.1	2.0	2.5	11.2	94.1	6.7	16.6	11.4	16.8	16.1	10.5	8.2
District 5	1 518	601 643	396.3	89.4	2.3	0.2	3.6	4.5	8.1	9.9	94.1	7.9	17.8	10.9	18.4	15.9	10.7	7.9
District 6	1 289	601 643	466.9	95.3	1.9	0.1	1.5	1.2	2.9	6.9	96.8	6.9	15.6	9.9	17.5	16.1	10.9	9.3
District 7	447	601 642	1 344.9	93.8	2.3	0.1	2.8	1.0	3.0	10.3	95.0	6.1	13.2	11.4	19.3	15.0	10.2	9.7
District 8	115	601 643	5 224.2	65.5	23.3	0.3	5.6	5.3	10.6	21.3	85.8	5.9	11.9	19.3	23.7	13.7	8.0	6.7
District 9	658	601 643	913.8	87.6	6.7	0.2	2.8	2.7	4.6	12.1	93.6	6.8	14.6	10.5	19.3	14.9	10.1	9.2
District 10	2 282	601 642	263.7	95.1	2.1	0.4	1.5	0.9	1.4	5.4	97.6	6.7	15.8	9.3	17.0	15.6	10.4	9.3
MICHIGAN	147 136	9 295 297	63.2	83.4	13.9	0.6	1.1	0.9	2.2	3.8	98.3	7.6	18.9	10.8	16.9	15.1	10.2	8.5
District 1	58 963	580 956	9.9	96.2	0.8	2.4	0.4	0.2	0.6	1.6	99.5	6.8	18.9	9.6	15.1	14.7	9.9	9.4
District 2	14 165	580 956	41.0	92.9	4.4	0.6	0.6	1.5	3.0	2.1	99.1	8.1	20.5	9.6	16.3	14.8	10.0	8.4
District 3	4 312	580 956	134.7	89.6	7.5	0.5	1.0	1.5	2.8	2.8	98.7	8.6	19.7	11.0	18.5	14.8	9.1	7.4
District 4	22 469	580 956	25.9	97.1	1.1	0.7	0.4	0.7	1.8	1.4	99.4	7.1	19.6	12.3	15.1	14.1	10.5	9.0
District 5	14 127	580 956	41.1	88.9	8.4	0.6	0.5	1.7	3.4	1.6	99.5	7.5	20.4	9.4	15.6	14.6	10.5	9.1
District 6	7 530	580 956	77.1	88.1	9.5	0.5	0.9	0.8	1.8	2.8	98.7	7.4	19.1	11.6	16.1	14.9	10.2	8.5
District 7	10 716	580 957	54.2	92.3	5.6	0.4	0.5	1.1	2.4	1.6	99.4	7.3	19.7	9.8	16.1	15.6	10.7	8.7
District 8	5 029	580 956	115.5	90.4	5.8	0.6	1.7	1.4	2.9	3.5	98.2	7.2	18.5	14.1	17.2	16.2	10.5	7.3
District 9	2 112	580 956	275.0	79.4	17.8	0.6	1.0	1.2	2.8	2.9	98.7	8.1	19.4	10.8	18.3	15.8	10.7	7.7
District 10	2 926	580 956	198.6	96.5	2.0	0.4	0.7	0.4	1.3	4.8	98.2	7.2	18.1	9.9	17.8	15.3	10.5	9.1
District 11	984	580 956	590.1	93.0	4.1	0.3	2.4	0.2	1.3	8.0	96.9	6.8	16.7	8.3	17.5	16.7	11.7	9.9
District 12	386	580 956	1 505.6	93.3	3.7	0.4	2.4	0.2	1.2	8.8	96.3	6.8	17.0	9.7	18.1	15.4	11.1	9.1
District 13	1 179	580 956	492.7	85.2	11.0	0.4	2.9	0.5	1.7	5.6	96.9	7.1	16.7	15.1	19.5	15.7	9.9	7.4
District 14	207	580 956	2 809.2	29.2	69.1	0.3	1.0	0.4	1.1	3.9	98.2	8.9	20.7	11.1	16.4	14.6	9.0	7.7
District 15	219	580 956	2 656.5	26.4	70.0	0.4	0.7	2.4	4.3	3.9	97.9	8.8	19.2	10.9	16.2	13.8	8.6	8.6
District 16	1 811	580 956	320.7	96.6	1.4	0.4	1.0	0.6	2.4	6.1	97.5	7.1	18.1	9.7	17.0	15.1	10.4	9.5
MINNESOTA	206 207	4 375 099	21.2	94.4	2.2	1.1	1.8	0.5	1.2	2.6	98.6	7.7	19.0	10.1	17.8	15.2	9.8	7.9
District 1	24 061	546 887	22.7	97.8	0.3	0.3	1.2	0.4	1.0	1.7	99.0	7.4	19.6	11.2	15.9	14.1	9.6	8.1
District 2	42 181	546 888	13.0	98.5	0.1	0.4	0.5	0.5	1.0	1.0	99.6	7.7	21.0	8.2	15.4	13.9	9.7	8.5
District 3	1 284	546 888	425.8	95.4	1.8	0.4	2.1	0.3	0.9	2.8	98.6	8.2	18.4	9.1	20.3	17.7	11.3	7.5
District 4	476	546 887	1 148.6	89.0	4.2	0.9	4.6	1.2	2.9	5.3	96.5	7.9	16.7	11.3	19.1	15.0	9.3	8.0
District 5	277	546 887	1 972.8	83.9	9.4	2.4	3.5	0.7	1.8	5.5	96.6	7.1	13.4	12.0	22.1	15.4	8.5	7.4
District 6	2 880	546 887	189.9	96.8	0.9	0.6	1.4	0.4	1.1	1.9	99.1	9.1	22.0	9.0	20.4	17.7	10.7	5.9
District 7	68 167	546 901	8.0	96.7	0.2	2.2	0.5	0.3	0.8	1.0	99.6	7.3	20.4	11.8	14.6	13.2	9.1	8.5
District 8	66 874	546 874	8.2	97.0	0.4	2.1	0.4	0.2	0.5	1.5	99.6	6.9	20.4	8.4	14.6	14.8	10.1	9.1
MISSISSIPPI	121 506	2 573 216	21.2	63.5	35.6	0.3	0.5	0.1	0.6	0.8	99.6	7.6	21.4	11.4	15.5	13.6	9.6	8.3
District 1	26 926	514 548	19.1	76.8	22.8	0.1	0.3	0.1	0.5	0.5	99.8	7.2	20.1	11.5	15.2	13.7	10.4	8.6
District 2	31 730	514 845	16.2	36.6	63.0	0.1	0.3	0.1	0.5	0.4	99.8	8.3	24.5	11.4	14.3	12.5	8.6	7.6
District 3	25 910	515 314	19.9	67.0	31.3	1.1	0.5	0.1	0.6	0.7	99.6	7.4	20.7	11.7	15.9	14.1	9.6	8.3
District 4	20 293	513 853	25.3	58.8	40.7	0.1	0.3	0.1	0.4	0.7	99.6	7.4	21.0	10.8	15.8	13.7	9.4	8.6
District 5	16 647	514 656	30.9	78.3	20.0	0.2	1.2	0.2	1.1	1.8	99.0	7.7	20.7	11.7	16.5	13.9	10.1	8.5
MISSOURI	178 446	5 117 073	28.7	87.7	10.7	0.4	0.8	0.4	1.2	1.6	99.3	7.2	18.5	10.1	16.7	14.4	10.2	8.9
District 1	377	568 285	1 506.3	46.3	52.3	0.2	1.0	0.3	0.9	2.1	99.0	7.7	18.6	10.8	17.6	13.7	9.0	8.7
District 2	1 391	568 306	408.5	94.2	3.7	0.2	1.6	0.2	1.0	2.8	98.9	7.3	18.6	8.6	17.6	16.9	11.8	8.7
District 3	3 264	568 326	174.1	96.3	2.3	0.2	0.8	0.3	1.1	2.3	99.1	7.3	17.3	8.8	18.1	14.7	9.9	9.1

1. Dry land or land partially or temporarily covered by water.   2. Hispanic persons may be of any race.

Table E. Congressional Districts 105th Congress — **Population, Households, Group Quarters, and Education**

	Population and population characteristics, 1990 (cont'd)			Households, 1990				Persons in mental hospitals, 1990	Persons in nursing homes, 1990	Persons identified as homeless, 1990[2]	Education, 1990	
	Percent (cont'd)					Percent					School enrollment	
	Age (cont'd)											
STATE District	65 to 74 years	75 years and over	Percent female	Number	Persons per house-hold	Female family house-holder[1]	One person				Public	Private
	19	20	21	22	23	24	25	26	27	28	29	30
LOUISIANA—Con.												
District 7	6.4	4.5	51.7	214 122	2.76	13.5	22.6	155	5 096	139	147 817	22 290
MAINE	7.5	5.8	51.3	465 312	2.56	9.5	23.3	805	9 855	476	267 445	37 423
District 1	7.5	5.9	51.6	235 671	2.54	9.5	23.9	515	4 371	302	125 381	22 305
District 2	7.4	5.8	51.0	229 641	2.58	9.6	22.7	290	5 484	174	142 064	15 118
MARYLAND	6.6	4.2	51.5	1 748 991	2.67	13.3	22.6	3 049	26 884	3 061	982 507	229 826
District 1	7.6	4.8	50.8	221 366	2.62	11.3	21.8	456	3 527	155	122 228	21 549
District 2	7.6	4.4	51.2	222 476	2.64	9.8	20.9	258	2 853	65	116 671	27 909
District 3	7.8	5.5	52.4	232 681	2.52	13.3	25.9	2	3 700	322	108 060	37 227
District 4	4.6	2.8	52.4	216 758	2.72	18.1	23.5	44	2 122	640	130 430	30 266
District 5	4.9	2.7	49.9	204 414	2.82	10.1	18.2	333	2 530	80	136 510	26 994
District 6	6.7	4.7	50.7	214 745	2.70	8.7	20.0	968	4 121	248	126 395	21 506
District 7	7.1	5.0	53.1	216 574	2.68	26.1	28.5	707	4 564	1 207	127 649	26 366
District 8	6.3	4.1	51.6	219 977	2.69	8.5	21.2	281	3 467	344	114 564	38 009
MASSACHUSETTS	7.6	6.0	52.0	2 247 110	2.58	12.1	25.8	3 386	55 662	7 128	1 100 827	429 307
District 1	7.9	6.2	51.7	222 811	2.57	11.5	25.1	76	6 269	255	136 410	27 658
District 2	8.2	5.9	52.4	222 230	2.62	13.2	24.2	359	5 791	452	115 664	36 960
District 3	7.7	5.9	51.6	220 174	2.63	11.3	23.7	587	6 049	547	115 245	38 702
District 4	7.5	6.2	52.4	218 092	2.64	11.1	23.9	193	5 585	327	112 568	45 466
District 5	6.1	4.4	50.7	209 525	2.79	12.1	20.9	72	4 216	283	124 398	32 039
District 6	7.8	6.0	52.0	225 496	2.61	11.0	24.4	525	5 446	814	108 322	34 197
District 7	8.3	6.8	52.7	232 429	2.51	10.9	27.1	454	5 445	480	93 609	44 595
District 8	5.9	4.9	51.9	238 103	2.34	15.3	35.3	527	4 444	1 485	89 945	95 976
District 9	8.0	6.6	52.3	226 665	2.59	13.2	27.2	568	6 802	1 921	96 541	44 845
District 10	9.0	6.9	52.2	231 585	2.55	10.9	25.5	25	5 615	564	108 125	28 869
MICHIGAN	7.1	4.9	51.5	3 419 331	2.66	12.9	23.7	4 747	57 622	4 458	2 242 239	338 803
District 1	8.9	6.8	50.1	219 934	2.55	8.6	24.8	116	4 984	129	141 202	10 208
District 2	7.2	5.2	50.8	206 301	2.75	9.6	20.4	40	4 646	122	136 535	21 779
District 3	6.1	4.7	51.1	208 512	2.70	11.2	22.6	213	5 432	799	125 240	34 953
District 4	7.4	4.9	50.6	207 299	2.71	9.0	20.2	0	3 527	56	155 564	15 753
District 5	7.6	5.4	51.6	214 348	2.68	12.5	22.4	532	3 188	90	142 201	16 336
District 6	7.0	5.2	51.6	216 367	2.62	11.5	23.4	533	4 327	266	144 530	19 892
District 7	7.1	5.1	50.5	210 201	2.65	10.8	22.5	711	4 450	320	136 113	20 856
District 8	5.3	3.7	51.2	208 151	2.67	10.3	22.1	214	3 040	161	171 559	17 147
District 9	5.4	3.7	51.5	213 603	2.67	15.3	23.6	502	2 649	261	143 213	19 014
District 10	7.4	4.6	51.4	214 512	2.69	10.3	22.1	58	2 667	102	132 964	18 247
District 11	7.6	4.8	51.3	220 558	2.61	7.8	22.3	0	3 876	81	121 979	27 812
District 12	7.7	5.1	51.8	220 490	2.62	10.4	24.6	44	2 707	151	129 810	21 323
District 13	5.2	3.4	51.2	215 487	2.59	11.2	25.0	951	3 162	475	162 931	19 505
District 14	6.9	4.6	53.9	206 555	2.79	28.0	25.3	384	2 781	163	136 841	31 412
District 15	8.2	5.8	53.2	220 864	2.58	29.1	34.1	198	3 531	1 221	135 115	21 008
District 16	8.1	4.9	51.4	216 149	2.67	11.4	22.9	251	2 655	61	126 442	23 558
MINNESOTA	6.7	5.8	51.0	1 647 853	2.58	8.6	25.1	1 738	47 051	2 434	1 006 375	168 652
District 1	7.3	6.8	51.0	201 475	2.61	6.9	24.5	23	6 791	143	132 798	21 838
District 2	8.0	7.6	50.6	200 523	2.66	6.0	23.7	878	7 603	0	122 315	19 628
District 3	4.7	2.8	51.0	205 269	2.64	8.2	20.6	0	2 506	14	119 766	21 890
District 4	6.9	5.8	52.3	215 257	2.47	11.2	29.0	47	5 526	613	108 657	36 614
District 5	7.3	6.9	52.0	235 878	2.23	11.5	35.3	172	8 334	1 079	109 395	23 613
District 6	3.3	2.0	49.9	184 815	2.93	9.0	15.6	244	2 241	22	137 283	17 939
District 7	7.8	7.2	50.4	198 065	2.65	7.2	24.2	283	7 380	122	142 435	16 630
District 8	8.6	7.1	50.6	206 571	2.58	8.1	25.1	91	6 670	441	133 726	10 500
MISSISSIPPI	7.0	5.5	52.2	911 374	2.75	15.9	23.4	2 245	15 803	546	646 850	80 636
District 1	7.3	5.9	51.9	186 772	2.69	12.5	22.2	0	3 219	89	123 001	10 407
District 2	7.0	6.0	53.2	170 188	2.95	23.3	24.2	0	3 285	41	141 705	18 117
District 3	6.7	5.5	52.0	184 721	2.71	14.3	23.1	1 951	2 869	105	128 182	16 617
District 4	7.4	5.8	52.8	185 716	2.69	16.6	24.9	0	3 496	130	123 559	21 636
District 5	6.6	4.3	51.0	183 977	2.71	13.7	22.5	294	2 934	181	130 403	13 859
MISSOURI	7.7	6.3	51.8	1 961 206	2.54	10.6	26.0	2 172	52 060	2 550	1 060 947	231 676
District 1	7.6	6.3	53.9	220 470	2.51	20.3	32.0	20	3 838	746	115 400	39 729
District 2	6.1	4.2	51.4	210 097	2.66	8.1	21.4	293	5 411	101	107 468	44 375
District 3	8.0	6.8	52.2	225 237	2.49	9.8	28.0	560	5 298	104	88 946	43 811

1. No spouse present. 2. Persons in emergency shelters and persons visible in street locations.

STATE District	Education, 1990 (cont'd) Attainment[1] (percent)		Money income, 1989			Percent below poverty level, 1989		Housing units, 1990					
				Households		Persons	Families		Occupied units				
										Owner-occupied			
												Owner cost as a percent of income	
	High school graduate or more	Bach-elor's degree or more	Per capita[2]	Median	Percent with $100,000 or more	Total	Total	Total	Total	Percent	Median value[3] (dollars)	With a mortgage	Without a mortgage
	31	32	33	34	35	36	37	38	39	40	41	42	43
LOUISIANA—Con.													
District 7	64.6	14.1	9 999	20 595	2.2	24.7	21.2	240 687	214 122	69.0	49 400	19.5	13.4
MAINE	78.8	18.8	12 957	27 854	2.4	10.8	8.0	587 045	465 312	70.5	87 400	21.4	13.4
District 1	81.8	22.6	14 453	31 124	3.2	8.4	5.9	288 000	235 671	69.0	107 700	22.3	13.2
District 2	75.8	14.9	11 462	24 718	1.7	13.2	10.0	299 045	229 641	72.0	66 700	20.0	13.6
MARYLAND	78.4	26.5	17 730	39 386	6.9	8.3	6.0	1 891 917	1 748 991	65.0	116 500	21.1	12.4
District 1	74.7	19.9	16 104	35 115	5.2	8.4	6.1	269 162	221 366	70.3	101 300	21.0	12.9
District 2	78.1	22.3	17 931	40 120	6.1	5.2	3.9	233 772	222 476	70.5	110 900	20.3	12.0
District 3	75.1	27.2	17 779	35 970	5.8	9.0	6.5	247 292	232 681	63.3	91 000	20.3	13.0
District 4	83.0	27.7	17 251	41 081	5.7	6.5	4.8	228 160	216 758	52.8	124 000	22.1	11.7
District 5	83.2	25.4	18 178	46 936	6.9	4.9	2.9	215 948	204 414	71.9	132 100	21.6	11.9
District 6	77.6	20.9	15 979	36 883	5.2	7.0	5.3	230 013	214 745	71.9	113 700	21.4	12.3
District 7	64.0	16.1	11 718	25 684	2.1	21.4	17.4	237 408	216 574	46.9	60 100	19.4	13.3
District 8	91.3	51.1	26 900	56 789	18.2	3.7	2.3	230 162	219 977	72.8	207 200	22.0	11.5
MASSACHUSETTS	80.0	27.2	17 224	36 952	6.7	8.9	6.7	2 472 711	2 247 110	59.3	162 800	22.3	13.8
District 1	78.0	21.4	14 200	31 903	3.3	10.2	7.7	245 899	222 811	62.8	123 700	21.8	13.4
District 2	74.7	18.8	14 652	33 401	3.5	9.9	7.9	235 845	222 230	63.9	129 100	21.7	13.5
District 3	76.6	24.2	15 917	36 873	5.0	7.9	5.9	234 772	220 174	61.7	150 800	22.0	13.6
District 4	77.5	30.9	18 963	39 005	10.0	7.7	5.8	235 024	218 092	63.8	170 600	22.7	14.0
District 5	79.9	28.8	18 293	42 701	9.3	8.9	7.0	222 166	209 525	64.4	174 200	22.2	13.5
District 6	83.3	27.4	18 549	40 836	8.0	6.8	5.2	242 831	225 496	65.5	181 100	22.8	13.9
District 7	84.0	30.6	19 825	41 318	8.6	5.9	4.2	243 218	232 429	57.4	193 600	21.9	13.9
District 8	76.7	36.0	16 327	30 417	5.5	17.4	13.5	257 784	238 103	29.1	189 700	22.2	14.4
District 9	81.6	27.8	17 980	38 646	7.6	8.9	6.7	241 312	226 665	57.4	172 800	21.6	13.5
District 10	86.7	26.4	17 535	37 489	6.2	6.3	4.9	313 860	231 585	68.7	163 700	23.5	14.4
MICHIGAN	76.8	17.4	14 154	31 020	3.8	13.1	10.2	3 847 926	3 419 331	71.0	60 600	18.0	13.5
District 1	77.0	14.5	10 846	22 788	1.5	13.3	9.9	324 094	219 934	75.8	44 900	19.9	14.3
District 2	75.9	13.6	12 305	28 905	2.3	11.4	8.8	251 114	206 301	78.7	58 400	18.2	13.2
District 3	79.9	19.1	13 924	31 917	3.3	9.4	7.2	221 593	208 512	70.8	66 000	18.5	13.0
District 4	76.2	13.5	11 549	25 898	1.9	15.2	11.3	272 679	207 299	78.1	49 300	17.8	13.4
District 5	73.8	10.7	11 891	26 312	1.7	15.0	12.5	251 888	214 348	75.7	47 400	17.3	13.7
District 6	77.2	18.6	13 043	28 453	2.8	13.8	10.2	244 821	216 367	70.0	54 600	17.3	13.3
District 7	78.2	13.9	12 900	29 976	2.2	11.4	8.8	230 242	210 201	74.0	50 700	16.9	13.1
District 8	84.0	24.1	15 455	35 911	4.5	10.6	7.2	220 922	208 151	70.1	72 100	18.5	13.1
District 9	78.0	17.7	15 132	34 737	4.5	14.2	11.8	227 038	213 603	67.9	65 200	18.5	13.6
District 10	77.3	12.8	15 603	36 536	3.9	6.6	5.2	225 686	214 512	76.8	71 500	18.8	13.7
District 11	87.7	34.4	24 466	49 021	13.7	3.4	2.2	232 727	220 558	77.9	111 100	19.3	12.8
District 12	78.6	19.9	16 796	38 760	4.4	6.0	4.5	227 981	220 490	73.9	76 200	18.0	13.3
District 13	81.6	27.3	16 267	36 596	4.9	10.1	6.5	226 392	215 487	61.6	77 500	18.2	13.0
District 14	69.2	12.5	11 462	25 079	2.5	24.6	21.9	219 109	206 555	64.9	29 800	17.4	14.2
District 15	58.6	11.1	9 650	15 264	2.1	36.6	32.6	247 821	220 864	45.2	23 200	19.0	15.3
District 16	74.0	12.9	15 175	35 315	3.6	8.4	6.8	223 819	216 149	75.4	62 400	16.2	13.5
MINNESOTA	82.4	21.8	14 389	30 909	3.6	10.2	7.3	1 848 445	1 647 853	71.8	74 000	20.4	12.4
District 1	79.9	18.5	12 688	28 403	2.5	9.8	6.4	213 303	201 475	75.0	58 800	18.1	12.4
District 2	75.6	13.3	12 043	26 937	2.3	10.0	7.5	220 151	200 523	77.5	54 700	19.6	12.5
District 3	92.2	32.9	20 805	44 329	9.1	4.0	3.0	216 358	205 269	72.5	102 900	21.5	11.6
District 4	85.0	28.1	15 937	32 287	4.2	10.8	7.6	227 007	215 257	62.8	84 100	20.9	12.6
District 5	84.9	30.3	16 099	28 880	3.8	14.0	9.9	250 444	235 878	55.9	80 100	20.4	12.5
District 6	89.1	22.1	15 922	42 161	4.3	4.6	3.6	192 441	184 815	81.4	89 500	21.6	11.7
District 7	74.7	14.6	10 341	23 146	1.3	15.3	10.9	246 080	198 065	74.8	50 900	18.8	12.8
District 8	77.1	13.8	11 279	24 472	1.3	13.5	9.9	282 661	206 571	78.7	49 000	17.9	12.7
MISSISSIPPI	64.3	14.7	9 648	20 136	1.7	25.2	20.2	1 010 423	911 374	71.5	45 600	20.8	13.5
District 1	59.6	10.8	9 639	20 867	1.3	20.1	15.8	203 963	186 772	77.2	43 900	20.5	13.0
District 2	55.3	13.5	7 771	15 530	1.4	37.7	31.0	186 579	170 188	64.4	40 200	22.0	15.0
District 3	66.6	16.1	10 303	21 625	1.8	22.0	17.6	201 965	184 721	74.0	47 100	20.0	13.1
District 4	67.7	18.1	10 411	20 234	2.3	25.3	20.4	207 200	185 716	71.3	47 900	21.6	13.8
District 5	71.6	15.1	10 116	21 702	1.6	20.8	17.1	210 716	183 977	70.0	49 700	20.4	12.8
MISSOURI	73.9	17.8	12 989	26 362	2.8	13.3	10.1	2 199 129	1 961 206	68.8	59 800	18.4	12.3
District 1	70.6	19.5	12 632	24 963	2.7	19.1	15.1	250 456	220 470	56.6	55 800	18.5	12.8
District 2	86.4	33.6	20 654	43 957	9.3	3.7	2.5	222 053	210 097	75.5	95 300	18.3	11.5
District 3	73.1	17.2	14 272	30 863	2.4	7.9	6.0	243 430	225 237	70.0	72 100	18.2	12.2

1. Persons 25 years old and older.   2. Based on the population enumerated as of April 1, 1990.   3. Specified owner-occupied units.

Table E. Congressional Districts 105th Congress — Housing, Labor Force, and Employment

STATE District	Housing units, 1990 (cont'd) Occupied units (cont'd) Renter-occupied Median rent[1] (dollars)	Rent as a percent of income	Substandard units[2] (percent)	Civilian labor force, 1990 Total	Unemployment Total	Rate[3]	Civilian employment, 1990[4] Total	Percent Professional, managerial, and technical	Precision production, craft, and repair	Disability, 1990 Work disabled persons[5] (percent)
	44	45	46	47	48	49	50	51	52	53
LOUISIANA—Con.										
District 7	299	27.1	6.4	251 016	23 631	9.4	227 385	26.5	14.8	11.6
MAINE	419	26.8	3.1	612 564	40 722	6.6	571 842	27.8	13.4	10.2
District 1	476	26.8	2.2	319 148	18 082	5.7	301 066	30.7	12.9	9.0
District 2	365	26.7	3.9	293 416	22 640	7.7	270 776	24.6	14.0	11.3
MARYLAND	548	25.4	3.3	2 592 878	111 536	4.3	2 481 342	37.0	10.3	7.0
District 1	487	25.0	2.9	316 881	12 955	4.1	303 926	29.9	12.9	7.6
District 2	507	23.4	1.7	321 422	11 456	3.6	309 966	34.4	12.6	6.8
District 3	506	25.1	2.2	318 100	13 866	4.4	304 234	38.8	9.4	7.4
District 4	643	26.3	6.9	350 723	16 220	4.6	334 503	36.8	8.2	6.0
District 5	674	25.0	3.4	339 228	10 991	3.2	328 237	37.5	12.2	6.5
District 6	448	23.7	1.9	313 112	11 234	3.6	301 878	33.1	13.2	6.6
District 7	432	27.1	5.2	287 190	26 314	9.2	260 876	28.5	8.3	11.2
District 8	777	26.0	2.6	346 222	8 500	2.5	337 722	53.9	6.2	4.6
MASSACHUSETTS	580	26.8	2.7	3 245 950	218 000	6.7	3 027 950	36.2	10.0	7.2
District 1	479	26.7	2.4	309 808	20 952	6.8	288 856	31.8	12.0	8.0
District 2	497	26.1	2.3	312 166	20 992	6.7	291 174	29.7	11.8	8.1
District 3	515	25.4	2.0	319 569	21 468	6.7	298 101	33.9	11.0	7.4
District 4	512	25.7	1.9	319 762	21 540	6.7	298 222	38.6	9.4	7.3
District 5	603	27.3	3.5	322 110	23 599	7.3	298 511	39.9	10.5	6.6
District 6	617	26.9	1.7	330 930	19 978	6.0	310 952	36.9	10.6	6.8
District 7	685	25.8	1.9	343 166	20 105	5.9	323 061	39.9	8.7	6.4
District 8	636	27.8	6.4	340 921	25 903	7.6	315 018	41.2	5.9	7.1
District 9	616	27.0	3.3	327 990	22 017	6.7	305 973	36.7	8.7	7.4
District 10	651	27.9	1.7	319 528	21 446	6.7	298 082	32.7	11.5	7.1
MICHIGAN	423	27.2	2.9	4 540 537	374 341	8.2	4 166 196	28.3	12.0	9.0
District 1	328	26.2	2.8	258 970	22 749	8.8	236 221	24.4	13.1	9.7
District 2	383	26.6	2.8	279 389	19 378	6.9	260 011	23.7	13.7	9.3
District 3	425	24.9	2.4	297 820	16 566	5.6	281 254	26.4	11.7	7.8
District 4	360	28.0	2.7	267 165	23 811	8.9	243 354	24.2	13.4	9.4
District 5	366	29.4	2.7	262 224	27 850	10.6	234 374	22.4	13.6	9.9
District 6	385	27.0	2.8	291 458	20 633	7.1	270 825	27.7	12.0	8.8
District 7	382	25.2	2.2	280 617	20 589	7.3	260 028	24.9	12.6	9.7
District 8	435	26.0	2.4	307 202	18 386	6.0	288 816	32.4	11.2	7.1
District 9	448	28.4	3.2	288 004	26 855	9.3	261 149	29.4	12.3	9.5
District 10	471	25.4	2.0	299 272	19 666	6.6	279 606	27.0	14.9	8.2
District 11	638	23.9	1.4	317 353	13 676	4.3	303 677	42.4	9.3	5.6
District 12	512	24.3	2.3	310 557	17 788	5.7	292 769	32.6	12.0	7.5
District 13	519	26.2	3.2	317 717	18 356	5.8	299 361	34.2	10.5	7.4
District 14	421	32.8	5.4	255 943	39 271	15.3	216 672	24.6	9.0	11.6
District 15	337	35.1	5.6	221 076	49 314	22.3	171 762	24.0	8.4	15.1
District 16	456	24.4	2.5	285 770	19 453	6.8	266 317	25.3	14.1	9.0
MINNESOTA	422	26.7	2.4	2 311 336	118 919	5.1	2 192 417	30.3	10.1	7.4
District 1	343	24.9	2.1	283 587	12 701	4.5	270 886	27.3	10.6	7.0
District 2	306	24.6	2.1	270 553	11 727	4.3	258 826	22.6	12.2	7.2
District 3	569	25.1	1.5	327 353	11 687	3.6	315 666	37.4	8.6	5.2
District 4	455	27.4	3.0	298 090	14 387	4.8	283 703	35.6	7.9	7.6
District 5	446	27.9	3.0	310 203	17 689	5.7	292 514	36.5	6.8	8.8
District 6	513	26.0	1.6	311 414	13 466	4.3	297 948	30.9	11.9	6.2
District 7	321	27.5	3.0	260 477	16 556	6.4	243 921	23.7	10.5	8.0
District 8	303	28.1	3.2	249 659	20 706	8.3	228 953	24.7	13.5	9.5
MISSISSIPPI	309	27.1	7.2	1 123 485	94 712	8.4	1 028 773	24.6	12.9	11.0
District 1	277	25.3	5.5	240 550	16 136	6.7	224 414	19.7	14.3	10.6
District 2	267	30.2	12.0	201 161	23 852	11.9	177 309	23.1	11.0	11.4
District 3	324	25.1	6.8	234 720	16 044	6.8	218 676	25.7	13.0	9.8
District 4	344	27.9	6.7	225 917	19 907	8.8	206 010	26.9	11.3	11.5
District 5	329	26.3	5.2	221 137	18 773	8.5	202 364	27.7	14.7	11.7
MISSOURI	368	25.2	3.0	2 522 783	155 388	6.2	2 367 395	27.8	11.1	8.5
District 1	391	28.3	4.8	274 940	26 323	9.6	248 617	31.1	7.9	9.0
District 2	519	22.8	1.2	312 487	10 326	3.3	302 161	40.3	8.5	5.1
District 3	390	24.2	2.3	292 360	15 899	5.4	276 461	28.5	12.2	7.5

1. Specified renter-occupied units.   2. Overcrowded or lacking complete plumbing facilities.   3. Percent of total civilian labor force.   4. Persons 16 years old and older.   5. Persons 16 to 64 years of age.

Table E. Congressional Districts 105th Congress — **Land Area and Population**

STATE District	Land area, 1990[1] (sq km)	Total persons	Per square kilometer	White	Black	Am. Indian, Eskimo, Aleut	Asian and Pacific Islander	Other race	Hispanic[2]	Foreign born	U.S. citizen	Under 5 years	5 to 17 years	18 to 24 years	25 to 34 years	35 to 44 years	45 to 54 years	55 to 64 years
	1	2	3	4	5	6	7	8	9	10	11	12	13	14	15	16	17	18
MISSOURI—Con.																		
District 4	36 523	569 146	15.6	95.4	3.2	0.5	0.6	0.4	1.1	1.1	99.5	7.1	19.0	10.4	15.8	13.7	10.2	9.2
District 5	968	569 130	587.9	73.2	23.7	0.5	1.0	1.6	3.2	2.4	98.9	7.6	17.2	9.8	18.5	14.4	9.9	9.0
District 6	35 149	569 131	16.2	96.5	2.1	0.4	0.5	0.5	1.5	1.1	99.5	7.0	19.0	9.6	14.7	14.6	10.6	8.7
District 7	24 065	568 017	23.6	97.3	0.9	1.0	0.5	0.2	0.8	0.9	99.6	6.6	17.9	11.2	15.1	13.8	10.4	9.4
District 8	45 248	568 385	12.6	94.8	4.4	0.3	0.4	0.1	0.5	0.7	99.7	6.8	19.6	9.7	14.4	13.2	10.4	9.7
District 9	31 461	568 347	18.1	95.0	3.7	0.3	0.8	0.2	0.7	1.4	99.1	7.5	19.1	12.1	16.7	14.2	9.8	7.9
MONTANA	376 991	799 065	2.1	92.7	0.3	6.0	0.5	0.5	1.5	1.7	99.4	7.4	20.4	8.8	15.4	15.9	10.3	8.6
At Large	376 991	799 065	2.1	92.7	0.3	6.0	0.5	0.5	1.5	1.7	99.4	7.4	20.4	8.8	15.4	15.9	10.3	8.6
NEBRASKA	199 113	1 578 385	7.9	93.8	3.6	0.8	0.8	1.0	2.3	1.8	99.2	7.6	19.6	9.9	16.3	14.5	9.5	8.6
District 1	34 705	526 297	15.2	96.4	1.1	1.1	0.9	0.6	1.4	1.7	99.1	7.2	18.7	11.4	16.0	14.2	9.3	8.5
District 2	1 551	526 567	339.5	87.5	9.7	0.6	1.2	1.2	2.8	2.6	98.9	8.3	19.7	10.4	18.8	15.6	9.5	7.6
District 3	162 857	525 521	3.2	97.6	0.2	0.7	0.3	1.2	2.9	1.0	99.5	7.2	20.4	7.8	14.1	13.7	9.6	9.6
NEVADA	284 396	1 201 833	4.2	84.3	6.6	1.6	3.2	4.4	10.4	8.7	94.9	7.7	17.0	9.9	18.5	16.0	11.3	9.0
District 1	598	600 957	1 004.8	79.5	10.5	0.8	3.8	5.4	12.2	10.5	93.7	7.5	16.6	10.3	18.3	15.4	11.5	9.4
District 2	283 798	600 876	2.1	89.0	2.7	2.4	2.6	3.4	8.5	6.9	96.1	7.8	17.5	9.5	18.6	16.6	11.1	8.6
NEW HAMPSHIRE	23 231	1 109 252	47.7	98.0	0.6	0.2	0.8	0.3	1.0	3.7	98.3	7.6	17.5	10.6	18.5	16.5	10.1	8.0
District 1	6 493	554 360	85.4	98.0	0.7	0.2	0.8	0.3	1.0	3.6	98.4	7.7	17.2	10.8	19.3	16.3	9.8	7.7
District 2	16 738	554 892	33.2	98.1	0.6	0.2	0.9	0.3	1.0	3.8	98.3	7.5	17.8	10.4	17.6	16.6	10.4	8.2
NEW JERSEY	19 215	7 730 188	402.3	79.3	13.4	0.2	3.5	3.6	9.6	12.5	93.6	6.9	16.4	10.1	17.6	15.5	10.9	9.3
District 1	832	594 630	714.5	78.4	15.8	0.2	1.7	3.9	6.3	3.5	98.4	8.0	18.7	10.0	18.6	15.2	9.7	8.2
District 2	4 952	594 630	120.1	80.7	14.1	0.4	1.2	3.5	6.6	4.1	98.4	7.1	17.2	10.1	17.1	14.5	10.0	9.3
District 3	2 503	594 630	237.6	88.9	8.0	0.2	2.1	0.9	2.6	5.4	98.3	6.6	17.4	9.3	15.5	15.4	11.0	9.7
District 4	1 811	594 630	328.4	83.7	12.5	0.2	1.5	2.1	5.2	6.8	97.5	7.4	16.6	9.0	17.2	16.0	9.6	8.5
District 5	2 787	594 630	213.4	93.5	1.3	0.2	4.5	0.5	2.8	10.4	95.3	6.8	17.1	8.8	15.4	16.6	12.7	10.1
District 6	523	594 630	1 137.8	81.8	11.2	0.2	4.8	2.0	6.1	11.1	94.4	6.8	14.9	12.4	19.3	15.1	10.3	9.0
District 7	708	594 629	839.7	83.6	10.2	0.1	4.6	1.5	5.0	12.5	94.3	6.6	14.8	8.9	17.9	16.0	11.5	10.5
District 8	271	594 629	2 197.2	74.7	13.0	0.2	3.6	8.6	17.8	18.4	89.8	6.8	15.6	10.6	17.3	14.9	10.5	9.6
District 9	240	594 630	2 481.0	83.7	6.5	0.1	6.6	3.1	11.4	22.4	88.6	5.9	13.2	9.4	18.7	15.2	10.9	10.6
District 10	142	594 630	4 179.6	32.6	60.2	0.3	2.4	4.5	12.3	16.2	90.1	7.4	17.9	11.6	18.6	14.5	10.1	8.3
District 11	1 651	594 630	360.1	92.3	2.7	0.1	3.9	1.0	4.1	10.2	95.4	6.6	16.3	9.5	16.9	17.1	13.3	9.6
District 12	2 647	594 630	224.6	89.6	5.2	0.1	4.4	0.7	2.7	9.0	96.2	6.6	16.7	10.0	16.2	17.6	12.4	8.9
District 13	148	594 630	4 019.3	67.4	13.7	0.3	4.6	14.1	41.5	32.5	80.0	7.0	16.6	11.4	20.0	14.1	9.9	8.8
NEW MEXICO	314 334	1 515 069	4.8	75.6	2.0	8.9	0.9	12.6	38.2	5.3	96.8	8.3	21.2	10.0	16.9	15.0	9.7	8.0
District 1	12 203	505 491	41.4	77.6	2.7	2.7	1.5	15.6	38.1	5.2	97.0	7.8	18.7	10.3	18.6	16.2	10.1	7.9
District 2	174 423	504 659	2.9	83.9	2.1	3.7	0.7	9.5	42.1	8.0	94.9	8.3	22.2	10.5	15.8	13.5	9.2	8.6
District 3	127 709	504 919	4.0	65.4	1.2	20.1	0.6	12.6	34.6	2.7	98.5	8.8	22.7	9.3	16.4	15.4	9.9	7.6
NEW YORK	122 310	17 990 455	147.1	74.4	15.9	0.3	3.9	5.5	12.3	15.9	91.4	7.0	16.7	10.9	17.4	15.1	10.6	9.1
District 1	1 651	580 338	351.6	93.0	4.1	0.3	1.7	0.9	4.7	6.8	97.2	7.1	18.3	10.7	16.7	16.3	11.3	7.9
District 2	491	580 337	1 181.9	85.5	9.8	0.2	1.7	2.9	9.7	9.1	95.6	7.2	17.4	11.1	18.3	14.9	11.9	9.5
District 3	401	580 337	1 448.1	94.4	2.0	0.1	2.6	1.0	4.4	10.1	96.2	6.1	15.4	9.7	16.1	15.6	11.7	12.0
District 4	218	580 338	2 659.9	78.3	16.2	0.2	3.2	2.2	7.5	15.0	92.9	6.3	16.0	10.5	15.9	14.9	11.1	10.7
District 5	393	580 337	1 475.9	84.0	3.5	0.1	10.6	1.7	7.3	22.3	89.3	5.7	14.6	9.0	16.1	15.7	12.1	11.4
District 6	97	580 337	5 970.5	29.3	56.2	0.6	6.3	7.5	16.9	28.9	83.0	7.3	18.3	11.4	17.6	14.3	11.1	8.9
District 7	67	580 337	8 679.6	70.0	10.1	0.3	11.5	8.1	21.3	36.0	79.7	5.7	12.9	9.8	19.0	14.7	10.7	10.1
District 8	40	580 337	14 349.5	80.4	8.6	0.2	6.3	4.6	12.7	25.1	87.7	5.2	11.0	9.6	21.0	18.3	10.8	8.9
District 9	97	580 338	5 970.2	87.6	3.3	0.1	6.2	2.7	8.5	24.4	89.5	5.8	13.2	8.7	16.9	14.7	10.1	10.8
District 10	44	580 335	13 266.0	26.8	60.7	0.4	2.3	9.7	19.7	20.5	88.5	8.3	20.2	11.6	17.9	14.4	10.1	7.7
District 11	26	580 337	22 392.1	18.7	74.0	0.4	2.8	4.1	11.5	39.6	74.3	8.3	20.2	11.1	18.6	16.1	10.2	7.1
District 12	36	580 340	16 276.5	33.8	13.7	0.5	19.7	32.3	57.9	42.7	69.8	8.2	19.7	12.4	19.1	14.7	9.8	7.5
District 13	169	580 337	3 440.1	86.7	5.6	0.2	5.5	2.1	7.5	16.6	92.4	6.8	15.8	10.2	17.7	15.4	10.9	9.3
District 14	35	580 337	16 756.3	85.9	4.6	0.2	5.6	3.8	10.9	24.2	86.7	3.8	7.3	8.6	23.1	18.3	13.0	10.4
District 15	28	580 337	20 568.4	27.6	46.9	0.7	2.4	22.4	46.4	29.6	80.1	7.5	17.1	12.1	19.1	14.5	10.0	8.0
District 16	40	580 338	14 504.8	20.0	42.2	0.6	2.1	35.1	60.2	21.3	85.2	10.5	23.1	12.4	17.6	13.2	9.5	6.6
District 17	56	580 337	10 392.9	40.3	41.9	0.4	3.7	13.7	29.1	26.2	84.8	7.5	16.9	11.0	17.6	14.0	10.1	6.6
District 18	243	580 337	2 384.1	81.1	7.5	0.1	8.2	3.1	10.4	26.4	86.2	5.8	13.6	9.4	16.8	15.1	11.4	10.8
District 19	2 797	580 337	207.5	89.0	7.3	0.2	2.3	1.3	5.2	9.8	95.7	7.1	16.4	10.6	17.5	16.8	11.8	8.8
District 20	3 336	580 338	174.0	86.6	8.2	0.2	3.4	1.6	6.1	12.2	94.4	7.5	18.5	9.5	16.1	16.1	12.0	9.2
District 21	2 816	580 337	206.1	91.3	6.3	0.2	1.5	0.8	2.1	5.2	98.1	6.7	15.5	12.6	16.7	14.7	9.5	9.0
District 22	16 861	580 337	34.4	96.6	2.2	0.2	0.7	0.4	1.5	3.4	98.9	7.1	18.0	9.8	16.6	16.0	10.9	8.8
District 23	15 504	580 337	37.4	95.8	2.9	0.2	0.6	0.5	1.5	2.8	99.1	6.9	17.9	12.0	15.3	14.0	10.1	8.9
District 24	32 098	580 338	18.1	95.4	2.6	0.8	0.6	0.7	1.6	2.8	98.8	7.5	19.0	13.3	16.9	14.0	9.4	8.1

1. Dry land or land partially or temporarily covered by water.   2. Hispanic persons may be of any race.

Table E. Congressional Districts 105th Congress — **Population, Households, Group Quarters, and Education**

STATE District	Population and population characteristics, 1990 (cont'd) Percent (cont'd) Age (cont'd) 65 to 74 years	75 years and over	Percent female	Households, 1990 Number	Persons per household	Percent Female family householder[1]	One person	Persons in mental hospitals, 1990	Persons in nursing homes, 1990	Persons identified as homeless, 1990[2]	Education, 1990 School enrollment Public	Private
	19	20	21	22	23	24	25	26	27	28	29	30
MISSOURI—Con.												
District 4	8.0	6.6	50.3	211 458	2.57	7.9	23.5	293	5 867	148	123 315	14 345
District 5	7.6	6.1	52.6	230 604	2.42	14.1	30.9	352	4 808	770	112 021	24 521
District 6	7.7	6.6	51.5	216 556	2.55	8.3	24.6	308	7 237	120	127 126	15 818
District 7	8.6	7.0	51.8	222 201	2.47	8.3	25.1	43	5 964	407	121 800	17 539
District 8	8.9	7.3	51.7	216 430	2.55	10.0	24.5	205	7 199	42	127 929	9 638
District 9	6.8	5.9	51.2	208 153	2.61	8.2	23.5	98	6 438	112	136 942	21 900
MONTANA	7.6	5.7	50.5	306 163	2.53	8.6	26.3	282	7 764	424	197 360	18 399
At Large	7.6	5.7	50.5	306 163	2.53	8.6	26.3	282	7 764	424	197 360	18 399
NEBRASKA	7.5	6.7	51.3	602 363	2.54	8.3	26.5	979	19 171	569	368 874	64 535
District 1	7.6	7.2	51.1	200 847	2.51	7.2	26.6	418	6 783	189	126 322	21 364
District 2	5.8	4.3	51.4	197 804	2.61	11.5	25.8	387	4 267	344	120 640	31 272
District 3	9.0	8.6	51.3	203 712	2.51	6.3	27.1	174	8 121	36	121 912	11 899
NEVADA	7.1	3.5	49.1	466 297	2.53	10.2	25.7	262	3 605	1 611	256 041	24 370
District 1	7.5	3.5	49.4	236 070	2.51	11.8	26.9	103	1 661	821	122 181	12 717
District 2	6.8	3.4	48.7	230 227	2.54	8.5	24.4	159	1 944	790	133 860	11 653
NEW HAMPSHIRE	6.4	4.8	51.0	411 186	2.62	8.5	22.0	383	8 202	380	219 482	57 283
District 1	6.4	4.7	51.1	206 495	2.61	8.6	22.1	66	4 025	265	108 795	27 677
District 2	6.5	5.0	50.9	204 691	2.63	8.3	21.8	317	4 177	115	110 687	29 606
NEW JERSEY	7.9	5.5	51.7	2 794 711	2.70	12.1	23.1	4 725	47 054	9 466	1 453 475	413 927
District 1	7.2	4.5	51.8	211 962	2.76	14.4	23.2	1 176	3 474	544	121 179	27 161
District 2	8.6	6.2	51.7	218 043	2.64	13.1	24.3	16	5 349	1 135	118 911	20 237
District 3	9.3	5.8	51.4	212 334	2.73	9.3	19.8	226	4 017	345	118 014	25 163
District 4	9.2	7.5	52.0	220 574	2.64	11.3	24.5	108	4 689	809	105 910	31 063
District 5	7.3	5.2	51.4	206 078	2.85	8.2	17.0	163	5 285	75	114 256	32 717
District 6	7.2	4.9	51.5	215 093	2.66	11.1	24.0	0	3 463	470	119 669	29 649
District 7	8.5	5.3	51.5	215 596	2.71	9.7	20.2	91	3 491	84	105 574	31 184
District 8	8.4	6.3	52.4	212 344	2.74	13.6	23.8	335	3 945	480	107 175	32 572
District 9	9.5	6.6	52.1	234 586	2.51	10.9	28.0	0	1 520	142	87 249	37 900
District 10	6.8	4.8	53.0	212 001	2.74	23.3	29.2	26	3 019	2 515	118 547	33 831
District 11	6.4	4.4	51.0	209 150	2.79	7.9	18.5	1 182	3 895	233	110 964	36 420
District 12	7.0	4.5	50.9	209 601	2.73	7.2	19.6	1 402	2 994	542	115 923	40 705
District 13	7.2	4.9	51.2	217 349	2.69	17.3	27.4	0	1 913	2 092	110 104	35 325
NEW MEXICO	6.4	4.3	50.8	542 709	2.74	11.9	23.0	321	6 276	874	400 077	35 912
District 1	6.4	4.1	51.1	194 425	2.56	11.8	25.7	114	1 897	393	124 601	15 151
District 2	7.0	4.8	50.4	175 354	2.81	11.3	21.2	0	2 518	92	141 133	8 293
District 3	5.9	4.0	50.9	172 930	2.87	12.7	21.8	207	1 861	389	134 343	12 468
NEW YORK	7.5	5.6	52.1	6 639 322	2.63	13.8	27.2	20 035	126 175	43 085	3 538 249	1 117 969
District 1	6.6	5.2	51.1	192 807	2.93	9.6	18.1	1 348	3 788	852	133 496	23 533
District 2	5.9	3.8	51.2	178 664	3.18	11.8	14.2	3 367	3 164	478	121 559	27 597
District 3	8.8	4.7	51.3	195 063	2.94	9.0	15.5	99	2 739	26	100 484	39 607
District 4	9.1	5.5	52.1	191 210	2.98	11.8	18.1	0	2 391	179	102 986	43 339
District 5	9.2	6.2	52.0	212 262	2.70	9.2	21.8	791	4 943	25	99 371	39 835
District 6	6.8	4.4	53.2	180 632	3.16	21.5	19.7	1 221	3 596	1 996	126 323	37 043
District 7	9.1	8.0	52.7	235 147	2.43	13.5	31.9	633	4 186	1 121	86 113	39 436
District 8	8.0	7.2	51.2	282 170	1.98	8.0	48.4	259	2 832	5 523	65 486	59 934
District 9	10.6	9.1	52.8	238 905	2.40	9.9	32.4	0	4 859	402	80 709	44 746
District 10	5.8	3.9	54.0	202 579	2.78	27.4	29.9	368	2 805	4 303	133 230	38 274
District 11	5.0	3.5	54.7	199 404	2.87	27.8	26.7	643	2 853	2 182	143 756	41 960
District 12	5.1	3.3	51.2	184 010	3.12	25.0	22.1	113	750	3 315	138 501	27 828
District 13	7.9	6.1	52.2	215 118	2.66	11.8	25.9	374	4 252	501	95 709	45 244
District 14	8.4	7.2	53.5	316 747	1.78	6.4	52.3	330	3 397	4 650	44 272	53 840
District 15	6.5	5.2	52.9	214 632	2.55	27.5	35.6	1 093	1 767	5 559	122 630	42 579
District 16	4.3	2.7	54.3	188 194	3.04	38.0	23.8	103	1 215	3 367	157 515	26 041
District 17	7.3	7.0	54.6	217 580	2.59	22.8	30.6	318	8 955	950	114 575	42 483
District 18	9.3	7.7	52.8	222 962	2.55	10.3	27.5	167	4 637	606	85 083	49 269
District 19	6.2	4.9	50.1	199 080	2.74	8.7	21.0	1 439	4 267	963	110 589	39 430
District 20	6.3	4.8	51.0	192 825	2.91	9.4	19.2	1 118	4 802	2 147	111 535	45 346
District 21	8.5	6.9	52.3	228 409	2.43	11.6	29.4	369	6 001	907	110 479	38 735
District 22	7.3	5.5	50.3	210 874	2.65	8.9	22.1	861	3 987	92	120 436	23 835
District 23	8.5	6.4	51.0	211 591	2.60	10.0	25.0	1 580	5 921	209	133 239	20 197
District 24	6.8	5.1	49.7	202 380	2.69	9.6	22.7	446	3 965	243	138 790	17 759

1. No spouse present.　2. Persons in emergency shelters and persons visible in street locations.

Table E. Congressional Districts 105th Congress — Education, Money Income, Poverty, and Housing

STATE District	Education, 1990 (cont'd) Attainment[1] (percent) High school graduate or more	Bach-elor's degree or more	Money income, 1989 Per capita[2]	Households Median	Percent with $100,000 or more	Percent below poverty level, 1989 Persons Total	Families Total	Housing units, 1990 Total	Occupied units Total	Owner-occupied Percent	Median value[3] (dollars)	Owner cost as a percent of income With a mortgage	Without a mortgage
	31	32	33	34	35	36	37	38	39	40	41	42	43
MISSOURI—Con.													
District 4	72.0	12.7	10 984	23 064	1.5	13.7	10.3	260 130	211 458	72.8	49 600	19.9	12.5
District 5	78.8	20.0	13 650	26 968	2.6	13.9	10.4	257 319	230 604	60.0	56 700	18.1	12.4
District 6	78.4	16.0	12 641	27 165	2.2	11.4	8.7	239 346	216 556	70.8	55 300	17.7	12.3
District 7	72.9	14.6	11 029	21 712	1.9	15.2	11.1	249 377	222 201	70.7	48 400	18.2	12.0
District 8	59.0	9.5	9 300	18 207	1.2	22.4	18.1	243 493	216 430	71.3	37 900	18.5	12.9
District 9	73.6	16.6	11 741	26 055	1.9	12.9	9.2	233 525	208 153	72.3	55 400	18.3	12.4
MONTANA	81.0	19.8	11 213	22 988	1.7	16.1	12.0	361 155	306 163	67.3	56 600	20.2	12.5
At Large	81.0	19.8	11 213	22 988	1.7	16.1	12.0	361 155	306 163	67.3	56 600	20.2	12.5
NEBRASKA	81.8	18.9	12 452	26 016	2.2	11.1	8.0	660 621	602 363	66.5	50 400	19.4	12.6
District 1	81.4	18.5	12 088	25 763	1.7	10.9	7.3	216 569	200 847	66.9	50 100	18.5	12.4
District 2	85.6	24.8	14 322	30 889	3.5	9.5	7.2	211 302	197 804	62.8	61 300	20.7	12.6
District 3	78.5	13.8	10 942	22 344	1.5	13.0	9.5	232 750	203 712	69.6	38 300	17.7	12.7
NEVADA	78.8	15.3	15 214	31 011	3.8	10.2	7.3	518 858	466 297	54.8	95 700	22.4	11.9
District 1	75.9	13.3	14 837	29 611	3.5	11.4	8.2	257 734	236 070	50.1	89 300	22.1	11.8
District 2	81.7	17.3	15 592	32 413	4.0	8.9	6.4	261 124	230 227	59.6	104 100	22.6	11.9
NEW HAMPSHIRE	82.2	24.4	15 959	36 329	4.5	6.4	4.4	503 904	411 186	68.2	129 400	24.4	14.7
District 1	82.4	23.8	16 044	36 511	4.2	6.3	4.3	256 621	206 495	66.3	132 500	24.8	14.6
District 2	81.9	24.9	15 874	36 145	4.8	6.5	4.4	247 283	204 691	70.1	125 800	24.0	14.9
NEW JERSEY	76.7	24.9	18 714	40 927	8.8	7.6	5.6	3 075 310	2 794 711	64.9	162 300	23.4	15.1
District 1	74.2	16.9	14 502	35 250	3.3	9.9	7.8	224 858	211 962	69.1	94 100	22.3	14.9
District 2	71.3	14.9	14 732	32 410	3.7	9.9	7.3	293 580	218 043	69.0	93 900	22.1	14.9
District 3	80.5	24.1	18 138	41 257	7.5	4.3	3.1	258 262	212 334	82.3	129 200	23.3	15.2
District 4	75.9	18.7	16 107	36 888	4.4	6.9	5.0	241 499	220 574	73.6	130 500	24.3	15.8
District 5	85.4	32.6	23 942	53 433	16.3	3.2	2.2	219 632	206 078	80.8	214 400	24.3	15.0
District 6	79.5	24.9	18 135	42 309	7.4	6.4	4.3	233 776	215 093	63.1	160 600	23.7	15.5
District 7	82.7	32.4	23 253	50 996	13.9	3.4	2.2	222 996	215 596	74.6	186 900	23.1	14.7
District 8	72.4	24.5	18 527	39 944	9.5	8.7	6.4	221 064	212 344	57.2	193 600	23.4	15.1
District 9	74.9	24.7	20 012	40 816	8.1	6.0	4.4	250 771	234 586	54.6	195 700	23.3	15.8
District 10	65.7	14.6	12 833	28 849	3.2	17.1	14.1	229 399	212 001	35.7	137 600	24.3	16.0
District 11	87.3	37.4	25 454	57 219	18.0	2.6	1.7	219 540	209 150	76.4	215 600	23.3	14.0
District 12	87.5	39.7	24 615	54 630	16.9	2.9	1.7	222 475	209 601	78.3	205 700	23.9	14.3
District 13	58.0	15.9	13 028	28 721	3.3	17.1	14.4	237 458	217 349	31.0	143 900	24.5	15.6
NEW MEXICO	75.1	20.4	11 246	24 087	2.5	20.6	16.5	632 058	542 709	67.4	70 100	21.6	12.5
District 1	81.6	26.0	13 373	27 074	3.3	14.8	11.2	211 995	194 425	61.9	84 600	22.4	12.4
District 2	69.5	15.0	9 672	21 456	1.6	23.5	18.9	212 793	175 354	69.4	52 700	20.2	12.4
District 3	73.7	19.7	10 689	23 610	2.4	23.6	19.3	207 270	172 930	71.7	68 600	21.6	12.7
NEW YORK	74.8	23.1	16 501	32 965	6.8	13.0	10.0	7 226 891	6 639 322	52.2	131 600	21.5	14.4
District 1	82.3	22.8	17 614	45 464	8.7	5.2	3.7	239 124	192 807	79.1	159 000	24.5	17.0
District 2	80.2	18.9	17 515	50 076	10.1	4.9	3.4	187 197	178 664	79.6	159 600	23.8	16.6
District 3	86.4	29.9	23 702	56 060	17.3	3.0	2.0	201 470	195 063	83.8	205 300	22.9	15.7
District 4	81.3	26.2	20 349	50 887	13.3	4.5	3.1	197 348	191 210	78.1	197 800	23.4	16.4
District 5	83.9	34.8	24 296	50 103	16.2	4.8	3.3	221 098	212 262	66.6	256 900	22.4	14.8
District 6	69.0	14.6	13 150	36 223	4.5	11.4	8.9	187 044	180 632	54.5	159 600	21.7	14.3
District 7	67.9	18.0	14 905	30 324	3.3	12.2	9.3	245 730	235 147	32.5	206 100	23.1	14.5
District 8	78.6	42.1	26 168	32 784	11.8	16.8	13.3	305 736	282 170	22.9	223 000	25.7	15.8
District 9	75.2	24.2	17 918	34 758	6.1	9.4	6.9	251 674	238 905	42.9	212 300	21.1	13.6
District 10	61.9	16.8	11 479	23 164	3.7	28.3	24.6	217 709	202 579	23.6	167 900	22.0	15.4
District 11	67.0	17.5	11 706	26 148	3.3	21.7	19.1	208 896	199 404	18.5	183 900	20.9	13.8
District 12	47.4	10.5	8 534	20 444	1.4	30.4	28.3	193 414	184 010	15.3	176 300	25.2	14.8
District 13	74.2	19.3	17 143	38 437	7.0	9.0	7.2	228 476	215 118	52.4	190 700	21.6	13.9
District 14	84.9	51.4	41 151	42 184	18.3	9.4	5.6	351 475	316 747	25.8	235 700	22.0	13.1
District 15	56.9	17.6	10 367	19 238	2.3	33.0	29.8	229 718	214 632	6.4	186 600	17.4	15.7
District 16	47.0	6.1	7 102	15 060	0.8	41.8	39.5	195 891	188 194	8.2	144 300	24.4	13.0
District 17	66.6	17.1	13 155	27 227	3.2	18.3	15.8	226 051	217 580	21.8	176 400	22.8	14.9
District 18	80.3	33.4	24 392	43 754	14.3	6.1	4.2	232 883	222 962	53.7	288 500	22.2	15.2
District 19	83.4	32.4	22 458	50 239	14.4	4.8	3.1	215 634	199 080	71.0	199 200	23.2	14.6
District 20	81.7	29.6	19 680	47 107	12.7	7.1	4.4	211 857	192 825	71.8	193 600	23.1	15.4
District 21	79.3	24.2	15 304	31 489	3.7	9.8	6.5	244 635	228 409	59.1	99 200	20.1	13.2
District 22	79.0	20.4	14 646	33 306	3.6	7.4	5.2	258 294	210 874	73.6	99 600	20.9	13.6
District 23	75.4	15.9	11 792	26 155	1.9	11.9	8.4	243 283	211 591	70.0	67 900	19.4	13.9
District 24	73.8	13.7	11 060	25 687	1.5	13.6	10.0	261 036	202 380	68.3	56 700	18.3	13.6

1. Persons 25 years old and older.   2. Based on the population enumerated as of April 1, 1990.   3. Specified owner-occupied units.

STATE District	Housing units, 1990 (cont'd)			Civilian labor force, 1990			Civilian employment, 1990[4]			Disability, 1990
	Occupied units (cont'd)				Unemployment			Percent		
	Renter-occupied									
	Median rent[1] (dollars)	Rent as a percent of income	Substandard units[2] (percent)	Total	Total	Rate[3]	Total	Professional, managerial, and technical	Precision production, craft, and repair	Work disabled persons[5] (percent)
	44	45	46	47	48	49	50	51	52	53
MISSOURI—Con.										
District 4	319	24.4	3.1	260 703	16 491	6.3	244 212	22.7	13.3	9.7
District 5	398	25.6	2.9	296 982	20 157	6.8	276 825	29.2	9.6	8.5
District 6	362	23.4	2.2	283 964	14 874	5.2	269 090	25.6	11.5	7.6
District 7	315	24.8	2.9	274 984	15 482	5.6	259 502	23.2	11.9	9.7
District 8	268	27.2	4.3	244 026	20 097	8.2	223 929	20.5	12.9	12.7
District 9	338	25.2	2.9	282 337	15 739	5.6	266 598	26.3	12.6	7.6
MONTANA	311	25.0	3.2	376 940	26 217	7.0	350 723	26.9	10.4	9.7
At Large	311	25.0	3.2	376 940	26 217	7.0	350 723	26.9	10.4	9.7
NEBRASKA	348	23.7	1.9	802 139	29 326	3.7	772 813	26.2	10.3	7.1
District 1	338	23.8	1.8	274 624	9 385	3.4	265 239	25.7	11.1	6.8
District 2	405	24.5	2.1	272 303	11 290	4.1	261 013	32.1	8.9	7.1
District 3	284	22.4	2.0	255 212	8 651	3.4	246 561	20.5	10.8	7.6
NEVADA	509	26.8	6.4	647 520	40 083	6.2	607 437	24.8	11.4	8.3
District 1	505	27.7	7.3	324 969	23 003	7.1	301 966	22.9	10.6	9.0
District 2	515	25.6	5.5	322 551	17 080	5.3	305 471	26.7	12.1	7.6
NEW HAMPSHIRE	549	26.4	2.1	612 345	38 108	6.2	574 237	32.6	12.5	7.3
District 1	555	26.3	1.9	307 846	19 587	6.4	288 259	32.1	12.7	7.4
District 2	541	26.5	2.3	304 499	18 521	6.1	285 978	33.1	12.4	7.1
NEW JERSEY	592	26.3	4.1	4 104 673	235 975	5.7	3 868 698	34.0	10.0	6.2
District 1	514	27.1	3.6	301 618	18 014	6.0	283 604	30.2	12.0	7.7
District 2	525	27.5	3.5	298 490	18 467	6.2	280 023	25.9	12.0	7.9
District 3	651	27.8	1.6	295 827	13 571	4.6	282 256	35.5	10.6	6.4
District 4	583	27.6	2.7	293 829	16 755	5.7	277 074	31.1	11.2	7.0
District 5	717	27.5	1.4	321 606	12 413	3.9	309 193	39.5	10.4	4.8
District 6	645	26.5	3.4	330 769	18 000	5.4	312 769	33.9	10.3	6.1
District 7	699	25.4	2.2	335 075	13 983	4.2	321 092	40.0	9.0	4.9
District 8	595	26.4	5.8	321 203	20 653	6.4	300 550	32.0	9.8	6.1
District 9	640	25.1	4.1	331 373	18 679	5.6	312 694	33.9	9.5	5.4
District 10	520	26.8	9.9	302 157	32 441	10.7	269 716	23.9	8.9	8.6
District 11	730	25.0	1.7	341 973	11 598	3.4	330 375	42.1	8.9	4.4
District 12	696	25.4	1.2	323 319	11 416	3.5	311 903	46.2	7.8	4.2
District 13	505	25.5	11.7	307 434	29 985	9.8	277 449	23.4	10.2	7.2
NEW MEXICO	372	26.5	8.8	684 160	54 888	8.0	629 272	31.6	12.0	8.8
District 1	400	27.4	5.4	254 244	17 144	6.7	237 100	35.7	10.2	8.5
District 2	325	26.1	8.3	208 524	18 671	9.0	189 853	26.4	13.8	9.4
District 3	372	25.5	13.2	221 392	19 073	8.6	202 319	31.8	12.5	8.6
NEW YORK	486	26.3	6.8	8 989 621	618 903	6.9	8 370 718	33.5	9.4	7.4
District 1	782	31.2	2.0	296 385	14 163	4.8	282 222	33.2	12.2	6.1
District 2	817	30.2	3.5	313 560	15 807	5.0	297 753	28.7	12.7	6.6
District 3	811	27.8	1.8	315 140	12 489	4.0	302 651	37.7	9.1	5.1
District 4	705	27.7	3.9	307 030	13 667	4.5	293 363	35.0	9.0	5.3
District 5	660	25.2	5.2	310 388	14 322	4.6	296 066	41.8	8.0	4.6
District 6	565	26.1	12.5	293 135	25 862	8.8	267 273	25.2	8.8	7.5
District 7	520	24.8	10.5	299 744	22 708	7.6	277 036	27.4	9.9	6.7
District 8	544	24.3	8.7	325 148	22 614	7.0	302 534	52.5	4.4	6.9
District 9	534	24.7	5.7	284 285	17 787	6.3	266 498	36.7	8.6	6.6
District 10	441	27.2	14.8	251 627	30 858	12.3	220 769	30.6	6.6	9.8
District 11	482	25.7	19.8	284 039	31 195	11.0	252 844	28.4	7.0	7.4
District 12	454	28.9	26.3	257 574	29 928	11.6	227 646	17.2	9.4	9.3
District 13	553	25.5	4.4	285 756	18 640	6.5	267 116	31.6	9.8	6.8
District 14	678	22.6	5.8	371 386	19 360	5.2	352 026	55.8	3.9	5.3
District 15	402	26.3	17.8	244 974	33 674	13.7	211 300	29.5	6.0	10.6
District 16	398	29.8	24.4	210 473	34 894	16.6	175 579	15.8	8.7	13.2
District 17	483	25.1	13.3	276 890	25 718	9.3	251 172	28.5	8.4	8.9
District 18	594	24.6	6.4	312 392	15 333	4.9	297 059	40.3	8.0	5.0
District 19	653	26.6	2.1	306 422	12 426	4.1	293 996	41.4	9.9	5.5
District 20	659	27.6	3.8	301 878	13 084	4.3	288 794	38.6	9.9	6.0
District 21	453	25.2	1.7	301 022	15 194	5.0	285 828	34.7	8.5	7.4
District 22	465	26.0	2.0	291 866	15 815	5.4	276 051	31.6	11.9	7.5
District 23	366	27.0	2.1	270 258	17 453	6.5	252 805	27.5	12.0	9.1
District 24	368	27.2	2.8	257 903	22 901	8.9	235 002	25.3	12.5	8.8

1. Specified renter-occupied units.   2. Overcrowded or lacking complete plumbing facilities.   3. Percent of total civilian labor force.   4. Persons 16 years old and older.   5. Persons 16 to 64 years of age.

STATE District	Land area, 1990[1] (sq km)	Population and population characteristics, 1990																
									Percent									
				Race								Age						
		Total persons	Per square kilometer	White	Black	Am. Indian, Eskimo, Aleut	Asian and Pacific Islander	Other race	Hispanic[2]	Foreign born	U.S. citizen	Under 5 years	5 to 17 years	18 to 24 years	25 to 34 years	35 to 44 years	45 to 54 years	55 to 64 years
	1	2	3	4	5	6	7	8	9	10	11	12	13	14	15	16	17	18
NEW YORK—Con.																		
District 25	4 761	580 337	121.9	91.0	6.6	0.6	1.3	0.5	1.4	4.1	98.4	7.5	17.4	12.1	17.1	14.7	9.7	8.7
District 26	7 985	580 338	72.7	90.6	5.7	0.2	2.0	1.5	4.3	6.1	97.3	6.9	16.2	13.5	17.0	14.6	10.0	8.7
District 27	9 308	580 337	62.3	95.5	2.5	0.3	1.1	0.5	1.3	3.5	98.6	7.1	18.1	10.6	16.1	15.6	10.7	9.0
District 28	714	580 337	812.6	81.5	14.0	0.3	2.0	2.3	4.3	6.7	97.3	7.7	16.6	11.2	17.9	15.2	10.0	8.2
District 29	3 060	580 337	189.6	92.6	4.5	0.8	0.7	1.4	2.8	4.8	98.3	7.0	16.9	10.6	17.0	14.6	9.8	9.4
District 30	1 877	580 337	309.2	81.5	16.7	0.6	0.6	0.7	1.5	3.4	98.9	7.1	16.9	10.7	16.5	13.9	10.1	9.9
District 31	17 061	580 337	34.0	95.9	2.3	0.6	0.6	0.6	1.5	2.1	99.2	7.2	19.0	10.7	15.1	14.3	10.0	9.2
NORTH CAROLINA	126 180	6 628 637	52.5	75.6	22.0	1.2	0.8	0.5	1.2	1.7	99.0	6.9	17.3	11.8	17.3	15.2	10.5	8.9
District 1	21 110	552 394	26.2	41.6	57.3	0.6	0.2	0.3	0.7	0.7	99.8	7.4	20.2	10.2	15.6	13.9	9.6	9.2
District 2	10 709	552 378	51.6	76.2	21.9	0.6	0.7	0.5	1.2	1.8	98.9	6.8	17.2	10.8	17.2	14.5	10.5	9.0
District 3	19 510	552 387	28.3	76.6	21.5	0.4	0.7	0.7	1.6	1.6	99.1	7.3	17.9	12.0	17.2	14.6	10.2	9.2
District 4	4 755	552 387	116.2	77.2	20.1	0.3	1.9	0.5	1.3	4.0	97.5	6.9	15.5	14.4	20.8	17.0	10.1	6.9
District 5	10 990	552 386	50.3	83.9	15.2	0.2	0.4	0.3	0.8	1.0	99.4	6.2	16.2	11.6	16.5	15.0	11.1	9.5
District 6	6 368	552 385	86.7	91.3	7.5	0.4	0.6	0.2	0.7	1.3	99.3	6.3	16.2	11.0	16.8	15.9	11.7	9.6
District 7	9 361	552 386	59.0	71.5	18.7	7.3	1.1	1.5	2.9	2.2	98.9	7.7	17.3	17.6	18.5	13.7	8.9	7.5
District 8	11 496	552 387	48.1	72.8	23.2	2.5	0.8	0.6	1.4	1.5	99.2	7.6	17.4	10.7	16.6	14.9	10.5	8.6
District 9	2 700	552 387	204.6	89.1	8.9	0.3	1.3	0.3	1.1	2.9	98.3	7.0	16.6	10.7	19.3	16.7	10.9	8.4
District 10	11 309	552 386	48.8	93.7	5.5	0.2	0.4	0.3	0.7	1.0	99.4	6.3	17.4	9.8	16.3	16.1	12.2	9.7
District 11	15 724	552 387	35.1	90.9	7.2	1.4	0.3	0.2	0.7	1.2	99.5	5.9	16.2	9.8	14.2	14.4	11.3	10.6
District 12	2 148	552 387	257.2	41.8	56.6	0.4	0.9	0.3	0.9	1.6	98.8	7.7	17.7	12.7	18.1	14.6	9.4	8.0
NORTH DAKOTA	178 695	638 800	3.6	94.6	0.6	4.1	0.5	0.3	0.7	1.5	99.4	7.5	20.0	10.6	16.3	14.1	8.9	8.4
At Large	178 695	638 800	3.6	94.6	0.6	4.1	0.5	0.3	0.7	1.5	99.4	7.5	20.0	10.6	16.3	14.1	8.9	8.4
OHIO	106 067	10 847 115	102.3	87.8	10.6	0.2	0.8	0.5	1.3	2.4	99.0	7.2	18.6	10.5	16.5	14.9	10.3	9.0
District 1	458	570 900	1 246.8	68.6	30.1	0.2	0.9	0.2	0.6	2.4	98.9	8.1	18.2	11.7	17.7	13.3	8.9	8.7
District 2	5 045	570 902	113.2	96.7	2.3	0.1	0.8	0.1	0.5	1.8	99.2	7.5	19.3	8.9	17.3	16.0	10.7	8.7
District 3	1 117	570 901	511.1	80.7	17.8	0.2	1.0	0.3	0.8	2.0	99.2	7.4	17.5	10.6	17.5	14.8	10.5	9.3
District 4	11 738	570 901	48.6	94.4	4.6	0.2	0.4	0.4	0.9	1.1	99.6	7.2	19.7	9.7	15.7	14.6	10.6	9.2
District 5	13 470	570 901	42.4	95.9	2.1	0.2	0.3	1.5	3.1	1.1	99.6	7.3	20.7	9.3	15.6	14.9	10.3	8.9
District 6	16 502	570 901	34.6	97.1	2.1	0.2	0.5	0.1	0.4	0.9	99.5	6.8	19.5	11.5	15.3	14.2	10.5	9.1
District 7	8 996	570 902	63.5	93.6	5.3	0.2	0.7	0.2	0.7	1.3	99.4	6.9	19.3	10.7	15.6	15.5	11.3	8.8
District 8	7 066	570 901	80.8	96.2	2.8	0.1	0.7	0.2	0.5	1.1	99.4	7.4	19.8	11.1	16.1	15.0	10.4	8.7
District 9	2 845	570 901	200.6	84.9	12.2	0.2	1.0	1.7	3.4	2.5	98.9	7.6	18.6	12.3	16.6	14.4	9.4	8.4
District 10	403	570 903	1 416.0	94.1	2.1	0.2	1.4	2.2	4.0	6.5	97.6	7.1	16.6	9.3	17.9	14.6	10.0	9.3
District 11	270	570 901	2 117.5	39.8	58.6	0.2	1.0	0.5	1.1	4.2	98.5	7.7	17.9	10.0	16.8	13.9	9.4	9.4
District 12	2 648	570 902	215.6	74.8	23.2	0.2	1.4	0.3	0.8	2.5	98.7	8.0	19.1	11.2	18.4	16.1	10.1	7.8
District 13	4 370	570 894	130.7	93.6	4.5	0.2	0.5	1.1	2.9	2.4	99.2	7.4	20.2	9.5	15.9	16.2	11.3	8.7
District 14	1 293	570 900	441.6	87.7	10.9	0.2	1.0	0.2	0.6	2.9	98.7	6.9	17.2	12.1	16.4	15.0	9.8	9.2
District 15	2 262	570 902	252.4	92.4	4.9	0.2	2.2	0.3	1.0	3.5	97.8	7.0	15.4	14.8	20.8	15.1	9.2	7.7
District 16	5 528	570 902	103.3	94.4	4.8	0.2	0.4	0.1	0.6	1.5	99.4	7.3	19.2	9.9	15.4	14.9	10.4	9.2
District 17	3 484	570 900	163.9	89.2	9.8	0.2	0.4	0.5	1.3	2.3	99.5	6.7	18.3	8.9	14.7	14.7	10.4	10.4
District 18	15 725	570 900	36.3	97.1	2.4	0.2	0.2	0.1	0.3	0.8	99.8	6.8	19.3	8.8	15.0	14.5	10.6	9.9
District 19	2 848	570 901	200.4	96.8	1.8	0.1	1.0	0.3	0.9	4.7	98.7	6.4	17.1	8.6	15.7	15.2	11.1	10.5
OKLAHOMA	177 877	3 145 585	17.7	82.1	7.4	8.0	1.1	1.3	2.7	2.1	98.8	7.2	19.4	10.2	16.2	14.4	10.3	8.9
District 1	1 745	524 264	300.4	83.2	9.6	5.1	1.2	0.9	2.3	2.5	98.6	7.7	18.6	10.0	18.0	15.8	10.2	8.3
District 2	30 294	524 264	17.3	77.1	5.1	17.2	0.2	0.4	1.1	0.6	99.7	6.9	20.1	8.9	14.1	13.9	11.2	9.8
District 3	46 526	524 264	11.3	83.4	4.0	11.4	0.6	0.5	1.4	1.1	99.3	6.5	19.4	11.1	14.2	13.1	10.2	9.4
District 4	20 945	524 265	25.0	84.2	7.2	4.8	1.7	2.1	4.0	2.8	98.6	7.4	19.8	12.3	17.5	14.4	9.8	7.9
District 5	12 076	524 264	43.4	86.6	5.6	4.6	1.7	1.5	3.2	3.0	98.2	7.4	18.6	9.5	17.4	15.5	10.2	8.5
District 6	66 291	524 264	7.9	78.3	13.2	4.9	1.0	2.6	4.4	2.4	98.6	7.3	19.9	9.5	15.8	13.5	10.0	9.2
OREGON	248 646	2 842 321	11.4	92.8	1.6	1.4	2.4	1.8	4.0	4.9	97.2	7.1	18.4	9.4	15.9	16.7	10.4	8.3
District 1	7 663	568 461	74.2	93.2	0.8	0.8	3.4	1.8	4.0	6.5	96.2	7.2	17.9	9.2	17.8	18.1	10.7	7.4
District 2	182 842	568 464	3.1	93.7	0.3	2.3	0.9	2.8	5.4	3.6	97.8	7.1	19.4	8.1	14.0	15.7	10.6	9.4
District 3	2 109	568 465	269.6	87.3	5.9	1.2	4.5	1.2	3.2	6.6	96.3	7.4	17.2	9.7	17.7	17.3	9.7	7.6
District 4	41 649	568 465	13.6	96.0	0.5	1.4	1.4	0.8	2.4	2.7	98.6	6.8	18.5	9.7	14.7	16.1	10.6	8.9
District 5	14 383	568 466	39.5	93.6	0.6	1.2	2.0	2.5	5.0	5.1	96.9	7.0	18.9	10.4	15.2	16.3	10.5	8.2
PENNSYLVANIA	116 083	11 881 643	102.4	88.5	9.2	0.1	1.2	1.0	2.0	3.1	98.7	6.7	16.8	10.3	16.1	14.7	10.2	9.8
District 1	136	565 842	4 175.2	37.7	52.4	0.2	2.4	7.3	9.9	4.6	97.8	8.3	18.8	12.0	17.3	13.3	9.2	8.5
District 2	118	565 650	4 807.7	34.7	62.2	0.3	2.2	0.7	1.6	5.1	97.2	6.9	15.5	12.9	18.0	13.7	9.3	8.8
District 3	147	565 866	3 846.8	89.3	4.9	0.2	3.2	2.5	4.7	9.4	95.9	6.9	15.8	9.8	17.3	13.3	9.4	9.7
District 4	3 427	565 792	165.1	96.3	3.2	0.1	0.4	0.1	0.5	1.9	99.6	6.4	17.3	8.4	15.2	15.0	10.6	10.8
District 5	27 142	565 813	20.8	97.8	1.0	0.2	0.9	0.2	0.6	1.8	98.9	6.4	18.4	14.5	15.0	13.7	10.0	9.3
District 6	4 925	565 760	114.9	95.2	2.5	0.1	0.6	1.7	3.3	2.0	99.3	6.5	16.6	9.5	15.6	14.4	10.2	10.3
District 7	786	565 746	719.7	93.8	3.8	0.1	2.1	0.2	0.9	5.2	97.9	6.6	15.5	10.3	16.9	14.8	10.5	10.3

1. Dry land or land partially or temporarily covered by water.   2. Hispanic persons may be of any race.

Table E. Congressional Districts 105th Congress — Population, Households, Group Quarters, and Education

STATE District	Population and population characteristics, 1990 (cont'd) — Percent (cont'd) — Age (cont'd)		Percent female	Households, 1990		Percent		Persons in mental hospitals, 1990	Persons in nursing homes, 1990	Persons identified as homeless, 1990[2]	Education, 1990 — School enrollment	
	65 to 74 years	75 years and over		Number	Persons per house-hold	Female family house-holder[1]	One person				Public	Private
	19	20	21	22	23	24	25	26	27	28	29	30
NEW YORK—Con.												
District 25	7.4	5.5	52.0	217 749	2.57	11.4	25.7	259	5 094	585	122 707	36 605
District 26	7.4	5.7	50.9	213 391	2.56	10.5	25.8	612	4 584	811	127 068	35 531
District 27	7.3	5.5	50.9	206 855	2.69	8.7	21.3	271	5 149	0	129 008	23 859
District 28	7.3	5.8	52.2	225 411	2.49	13.3	27.8	550	5 298	369	108 608	41 717
District 29	8.6	6.0	52.1	225 954	2.51	11.5	27.7	335	4 459	394	123 226	23 985
District 30	9.0	5.9	52.3	223 708	2.54	15.0	27.1	399	3 472	309	119 465	27 468
District 31	8.2	6.4	51.1	213 009	2.60	10.2	24.7	569	6 047	21	131 301	20 914
NORTH CAROLINA	7.3	4.8	51.5	2 517 026	2.54	12.3	23.7	2 500	47 014	2 946	1 444 680	180 233
District 1	8.3	5.7	53.5	202 736	2.65	20.8	25.2	15	5 275	343	134 868	9 663
District 2	7.9	5.1	51.9	212 833	2.52	11.6	24.3	573	4 841	77	112 324	21 898
District 3	7.3	4.3	50.9	205 941	2.59	11.4	22.1	652	3 196	53	129 274	11 719
District 4	5.1	3.4	51.4	215 806	2.44	10.0	25.9	826	2 676	341	134 932	22 232
District 5	7.9	5.9	52.1	217 545	2.46	11.2	25.4	15	5 735	106	115 289	14 789
District 6	7.5	4.9	51.6	216 882	2.49	8.9	23.2	0	3 653	46	109 667	17 488
District 7	5.7	3.1	47.1	184 729	2.67	12.0	20.7	137	2 638	68	122 876	11 369
District 8	7.1	4.7	51.6	200 750	2.70	13.0	20.9	0	3 798	179	123 772	12 733
District 9	6.2	4.0	51.5	215 438	2.52	9.1	23.4	0	2 773	143	112 566	21 466
District 10	7.4	4.8	51.1	212 320	2.57	9.1	20.6	53	3 413	35	111 122	11 321
District 11	10.2	7.5	52.2	221 168	2.43	10.3	24.8	97	5 227	240	109 507	11 071
District 12	6.7	4.9	53.2	210 878	2.54	21.2	27.5	132	3 789	1 315	128 483	14 484
NORTH DAKOTA	7.4	6.8	50.2	240 878	2.55	7.3	26.5	302	8 159	276	164 233	13 310
At Large	7.4	6.8	50.2	240 878	2.55	7.3	26.5	302	8 159	276	164 233	13 310
OHIO	7.6	5.3	51.8	4 087 546	2.59	11.7	25.0	4 773	93 769	4 646	2 338 126	460 100
District 1	7.4	6.0	52.9	223 619	2.48	16.4	31.9	580	6 137	1 162	115 474	36 735
District 2	6.7	4.8	51.4	211 251	2.66	9.4	22.4	29	4 694	70	116 047	27 010
District 3	7.6	5.0	52.1	225 198	2.49	13.2	27.1	492	4 779	402	118 751	30 101
District 4	7.7	5.6	51.0	210 326	2.63	9.7	22.9	62	5 412	181	122 355	20 107
District 5	7.5	5.4	50.9	206 472	2.72	8.5	21.6	20	5 804	86	128 740	19 363
District 6	7.5	5.6	51.5	209 760	2.63	10.7	22.8	209	5 530	134	142 204	10 518
District 7	7.0	4.9	50.9	205 376	2.67	9.9	20.8	237	5 829	53	129 801	19 770
District 8	6.8	4.7	51.3	204 772	2.72	9.2	20.6	13	4 961	104	134 813	16 069
District 9	7.2	5.3	52.2	214 332	2.59	12.8	26.2	336	4 489	259	133 634	27 818
District 10	9.0	6.2	52.1	228 377	2.46	11.3	29.7	188	4 090	178	92 667	39 890
District 11	8.6	6.3	54.2	227 289	2.45	21.7	32.6	30	4 795	365	117 640	33 157
District 12	5.6	3.8	52.1	215 958	2.58	14.5	25.4	363	3 953	305	122 945	28 490
District 13	6.7	4.1	51.1	198 819	2.82	9.7	18.7	818	3 876	150	125 213	26 719
District 14	8.0	5.4	52.1	219 388	2.53	12.2	25.7	316	3 748	195	136 173	18 719
District 15	5.9	4.1	50.4	223 084	2.44	9.5	27.9	206	3 288	512	137 714	20 879
District 16	8.0	5.7	51.8	209 545	2.65	10.0	23.1	325	7 150	322	114 809	25 217
District 17	9.8	6.1	52.4	217 693	2.59	12.6	24.6	93	5 428	111	122 075	17 330
District 18	8.7	6.4	52.1	216 909	2.59	10.2	23.9	406	5 424	44	120 210	14 266
District 19	9.4	5.9	52.0	219 378	2.57	9.2	24.0	50	4 382	13	106 861	27 942
OKLAHOMA	7.5	6.0	51.3	1 206 135	2.53	10.4	25.6	1 586	29 666	2 698	754 928	83 883
District 1	6.6	4.7	51.8	209 563	2.45	11.0	28.3	377	3 576	438	111 763	27 971
District 2	8.5	6.5	51.3	196 048	2.61	10.0	23.0	546	5 052	348	124 837	8 422
District 3	8.5	7.5	51.4	199 724	2.53	10.1	25.4	64	6 561	176	135 126	7 125
District 4	6.2	4.7	50.2	192 106	2.61	9.9	22.8	258	4 257	151	140 823	10 035
District 5	7.1	5.8	52.0	209 157	2.45	9.8	27.6	60	4 732	304	118 145	19 701
District 6	7.9	6.8	51.4	199 537	2.54	11.6	26.5	281	5 488	1 281	124 234	10 629
OREGON	7.9	5.9	50.8	1 103 313	2.52	9.2	25.3	1 565	18 200	3 682	639 167	85 066
District 1	6.5	5.1	50.7	225 335	2.47	8.0	27.3	126	3 155	1 451	123 228	23 901
District 2	9.2	6.5	50.5	219 958	2.54	8.5	23.7	78	4 095	495	125 701	10 824
District 3	7.4	6.1	51.6	226 909	2.46	11.6	28.5	170	4 005	503	115 597	21 627
District 4	8.6	5.9	50.9	221 212	2.52	9.0	23.7	55	3 007	785	135 962	11 644
District 5	7.7	5.7	50.6	209 899	2.60	8.9	22.8	1 136	3 938	448	138 679	17 070
PENNSYLVANIA	9.0	6.4	52.1	4 495 966	2.57	11.3	25.6	7 535	106 454	9 350	2 161 247	668 306
District 1	7.6	5.0	53.5	202 744	2.72	26.3	29.2	0	2 304	2 687	111 794	35 826
District 2	8.3	6.6	54.5	222 487	2.45	21.9	35.3	243	4 127	1 400	94 112	56 504
District 3	10.2	7.6	52.4	218 642	2.54	13.1	29.1	262	3 907	242	64 818	59 711
District 4	10.0	6.4	52.2	215 984	2.58	10.0	23.3	27	4 613	159	110 439	19 718
District 5	8.0	5.9	50.5	205 789	2.58	8.2	23.8	576	4 696	111	142 367	16 431
District 6	9.7	7.2	51.8	218 537	2.53	9.4	25.1	510	4 616	368	99 996	21 176
District 7	9.1	6.0	52.0	211 077	2.60	9.4	24.6	423	4 812	494	81 651	58 663

1. No spouse present. 2. Persons in emergency shelters and persons visible in street locations.

Table E. Congressional Districts 105th Congress — **Education, Money Income, Poverty, and Housing**

STATE District	High school graduate or more	Bachelor's degree or more	Per capita[2]	Median	Percent with $100,000 or more	Persons Total	Families Total	Housing units Total	Occupied Total	Owner-occupied Percent	Median value[3] (dollars)	With a mortgage	Without a mortgage
	31	32	33	34	35	36	37	38	39	40	41	42	43
NEW YORK—Con.													
District 25	79.9	22.7	14 148	31 080	3.2	10.3	7.1	234 546	217 749	64.9	78 100	20.5	13.9
District 26	77.4	22.5	13 786	30 335	3.3	12.2	7.4	245 650	213 391	63.9	94 500	20.8	13.6
District 27	80.3	22.0	14 934	34 573	4.3	6.9	4.6	223 052	206 855	75.8	81 300	20.3	13.7
District 28	79.5	27.4	16 205	33 899	4.9	11.7	9.0	237 546	225 411	62.3	90 700	21.1	13.9
District 29	77.2	17.8	13 350	28 951	2.1	10.9	8.2	240 237	225 954	64.5	71 600	19.7	13.8
District 30	72.7	14.6	12 176	26 263	1.6	13.7	10.7	240 455	223 708	63.5	68 300	19.0	14.1
District 31	75.5	15.0	11 382	25 124	1.7	13.1	9.6	249 732	213 009	70.9	48 500	18.1	13.6
NORTH CAROLINA	70.0	17.4	12 885	26 647	2.6	13.0	9.9	2 818 193	2 517 026	68.0	65 800	20.5	12.9
District 1	57.8	9.3	8 918	18 226	0.9	26.1	22.1	226 602	202 736	62.2	46 100	21.4	14.6
District 2	70.5	18.1	13 172	27 271	2.6	12.7	9.6	231 097	212 833	68.4	67 600	20.8	13.3
District 3	71.6	14.4	11 567	24 553	1.9	14.5	11.1	252 022	205 941	69.4	63 100	21.5	13.2
District 4	84.0	35.9	16 708	34 569	5.1	9.3	5.7	231 012	215 806	61.0	96 000	21.9	12.6
District 5	65.3	14.8	12 716	25 543	2.4	12.3	9.0	241 796	217 545	70.3	59 500	18.7	12.6
District 6	72.1	19.0	14 942	30 628	3.8	7.5	5.3	232 020	216 882	73.7	73 300	19.4	12.2
District 7	74.9	15.8	11 663	24 708	2.1	14.4	11.4	225 714	184 729	65.2	64 000	21.6	13.4
District 8	65.8	11.4	11 462	26 180	1.7	12.2	9.3	216 877	200 750	73.0	57 100	20.3	13.2
District 9	78.5	26.2	17 234	35 346	5.1	6.6	4.6	231 164	215 438	69.0	83 600	20.1	12.3
District 10	65.4	13.6	13 434	28 511	2.8	8.8	6.5	235 030	212 320	78.9	64 000	18.9	12.1
District 11	68.2	15.3	11 923	23 564	1.8	13.7	10.1	266 453	221 168	74.3	59 700	19.7	12.6
District 12	65.6	14.3	10 878	23 068	1.2	17.7	14.5	228 406	210 878	50.0	58 400	20.5	13.6
NORTH DAKOTA	76.7	18.1	11 051	23 213	1.6	14.4	10.9	276 340	240 878	65.6	50 800	20.3	13.0
At Large	76.7	18.1	11 051	23 213	1.6	14.4	10.9	276 340	240 878	65.6	50 800	20.3	13.0
OHIO	75.7	17.0	13 461	28 706	2.9	12.5	9.7	4 371 945	4 087 546	67.5	63 500	18.2	12.5
District 1	72.2	18.7	12 616	25 405	2.3	17.4	14.0	240 036	223 619	52.2	65 100	18.7	12.5
District 2	76.9	23.7	16 813	34 688	6.3	8.0	6.5	223 177	211 251	71.6	79 400	18.9	12.2
District 3	77.8	20.1	14 500	30 083	3.0	12.7	9.8	239 785	225 198	62.8	65 000	17.7	12.6
District 4	75.3	11.3	12 009	27 312	1.6	11.1	8.7	226 597	210 326	73.0	50 600	16.3	12.2
District 5	77.0	12.4	12 755	30 117	2.2	8.6	6.4	227 819	206 472	76.0	58 000	16.6	12.1
District 6	68.3	11.4	10 349	21 761	1.5	20.1	16.3	228 672	209 760	71.3	46 600	18.0	12.8
District 7	76.2	15.3	12 919	30 364	2.3	11.0	8.5	216 324	205 376	70.8	62 900	17.7	12.3
District 8	75.4	14.8	13 355	31 171	2.7	9.4	7.0	216 423	204 772	72.3	66 300	17.8	12.1
District 9	76.9	16.3	13 477	28 856	3.1	14.1	10.7	229 932	214 332	66.3	58 700	17.3	13.4
District 10	75.5	19.5	14 813	30 323	3.2	10.4	8.2	241 919	228 377	65.6	73 700	19.0	12.7
District 11	68.5	18.2	12 629	22 459	3.0	22.1	18.7	251 169	227 289	51.7	58 800	20.1	13.7
District 12	80.2	23.5	14 723	30 859	4.1	13.4	10.6	232 495	215 958	57.6	75 800	19.8	12.3
District 13	78.6	16.5	14 307	34 725	3.8	8.5	6.7	207 670	198 819	76.9	77 000	19.7	12.3
District 14	78.2	19.7	13 931	28 184	3.4	12.9	9.7	231 833	219 388	67.1	60 600	18.6	12.6
District 15	81.0	27.0	15 076	31 020	3.3	10.8	6.3	236 234	223 084	58.0	73 200	19.5	12.0
District 16	74.0	13.7	12 413	27 524	2.2	11.7	9.1	220 757	209 545	70.6	58 200	17.3	12.0
District 17	74.4	12.3	11 938	25 220	1.8	14.4	11.7	231 698	217 693	72.5	48 600	17.7	12.9
District 18	71.4	8.5	10 531	22 808	1.1	15.5	12.6	239 127	216 909	74.1	44 400	17.2	12.3
District 19	79.8	19.4	16 609	34 385	4.9	6.1	4.5	230 278	219 378	75.4	77 900	18.9	12.6
OKLAHOMA	74.6	17.8	11 893	23 577	2.3	16.7	13.0	1 406 499	1 206 135	68.1	48 100	20.0	12.8
District 1	81.7	23.4	14 695	27 472	3.9	13.0	9.9	235 405	209 563	61.3	61 100	20.1	12.7
District 2	67.9	11.6	9 914	20 633	1.3	19.7	15.9	233 834	196 048	75.3	41 300	20.1	12.9
District 3	66.7	13.3	9 635	18 394	1.3	22.4	17.8	233 844	199 724	71.7	36 100	20.3	13.3
District 4	77.5	18.7	11 554	25 391	1.8	14.6	11.2	218 365	192 106	66.6	51 200	20.4	12.6
District 5	81.8	26.4	15 024	28 348	3.8	11.9	8.8	241 632	209 557	65.7	58 700	19.5	12.2
District 6	71.8	13.3	10 540	21 797	1.5	18.8	14.7	243 419	199 537	68.4	40 000	19.5	12.9
OREGON	81.5	20.6	13 418	27 250	2.8	12.4	8.7	1 193 567	1 103 313	63.1	67 100	20.4	13.4
District 1	87.3	30.8	17 120	33 227	5.4	8.6	5.5	239 642	225 335	59.7	84 800	20.4	13.1
District 2	77.6	15.2	11 704	23 949	2.0	14.7	11.0	250 107	219 958	66.8	62 600	20.7	13.4
District 3	81.5	19.0	13 167	27 150	2.0	12.5	9.0	240 658	226 909	58.7	59 800	20.2	14.0
District 4	79.4	17.1	11 919	24 593	2.0	14.4	10.1	235 820	221 212	64.4	60 600	20.2	13.4
District 5	81.6	20.7	13 180	28 608	2.8	11.8	7.9	227 340	209 899	66.2	69 200	20.7	12.9
PENNSYLVANIA	74.7	17.9	14 068	29 069	3.6	11.1	8.2	4 938 140	4 495 966	70.6	69 700	20.2	13.3
District 1	58.1	10.4	9 703	20 372	1.3	28.0	23.6	233 392	202 744	59.4	37 600	20.2	15.7
District 2	69.2	21.9	13 121	24 880	3.0	20.9	16.1	252 645	222 487	55.6	42 800	19.6	15.2
District 3	66.6	12.7	13 429	29 157	2.1	10.9	8.4	232 906	218 642	71.1	65 800	19.0	14.0
District 4	77.5	15.3	12 684	26 792	2.1	10.6	8.6	228 328	215 984	76.0	55 700	19.6	13.2
District 5	75.7	15.3	10 946	23 934	1.8	14.6	9.5	256 769	205 789	72.2	47 900	18.3	12.7
District 6	69.8	12.6	13 349	28 766	2.4	8.9	6.1	232 771	218 537	74.1	66 500	19.1	13.0
District 7	84.6	31.0	20 175	41 710	9.3	4.6	3.0	219 919	211 077	74.3	134 500	21.3	13.6

1. Persons 25 years old and older.　2. Based on the population enumerated as of April 1, 1990.　3. Specified owner-occupied units.

STATE District	Median rent[1] (dollars)	Rent as a percent of income	Substandard units[2] (percent)	Total	Total	Rate[3]	Total	Professional, managerial, and technical	Precision production, craft, and repair	Work disabled persons[5] (percent)
	44	45	46	47	48	49	50	51	52	53
NEW YORK—Con.										
District 25	433	27.1	1.8	295 657	16 051	5.4	279 606	33.1	9.9	7.7
District 26	449	28.6	2.6	287 824	16 557	5.8	271 267	35.2	10.6	7.7
District 27	434	25.6	1.4	295 849	14 218	4.8	281 631	31.6	12.1	6.7
District 28	477	28.9	1.7	299 372	15 925	5.3	283 447	37.1	9.6	7.6
District 29	383	27.4	1.7	289 569	18 917	6.5	270 652	28.5	11.8	8.2
District 30	374	29.3	1.8	280 120	21 909	7.8	258 211	26.0	11.6	8.7
District 31	341	27.4	2.3	271 955	19 434	7.1	252 521	26.2	12.4	9.2
NORTH CAROLINA	382	24.4	3.9	3 401 495	163 081	4.8	3 238 414	25.7	13.3	8.7
District 1	290	27.9	8.3	246 996	19 288	7.8	227 708	17.9	13.2	12.0
District 2	376	23.9	4.3	286 505	12 648	4.4	273 857	28.0	13.7	8.7
District 3	359	25.2	4.2	261 335	14 393	5.5	246 942	24.5	14.4	9.6
District 4	477	24.8	2.6	321 449	11 137	3.5	310 312	40.2	9.1	5.8
District 5	348	23.7	3.7	291 264	12 969	4.5	278 295	23.7	14.1	9.0
District 6	403	23.0	2.2	314 266	9 836	3.1	304 430	26.0	14.1	7.2
District 7	391	25.6	4.1	225 060	14 888	6.6	210 172	25.2	14.0	10.0
District 8	359	24.0	4.7	273 784	13 889	5.1	259 895	20.7	15.1	9.3
District 9	472	23.0	2.2	317 014	10 931	3.4	306 083	32.1	11.0	6.3
District 10	352	21.5	3.1	305 379	10 821	3.5	294 558	21.6	15.0	8.3
District 11	333	24.5	3.0	267 899	14 052	5.2	253 847	23.3	14.8	10.4
District 12	381	25.3	4.8	290 544	18 229	6.3	272 315	21.1	11.7	9.4
NORTH DAKOTA	313	23.9	2.5	303 641	16 083	5.3	287 558	26.4	9.8	7.0
At Large	313	23.9	2.5	303 641	16 083	5.3	287 558	26.4	9.8	7.0
OHIO	379	25.3	2.2	5 279 995	348 638	6.6	4 931 357	28.5	11.6	9.0
District 1	336	25.6	3.7	276 732	18 124	6.5	258 608	31.4	9.3	10.1
District 2	409	23.8	2.2	288 646	13 058	4.5	275 588	33.2	11.2	8.0
District 3	403	25.1	2.1	281 876	17 378	6.2	264 498	33.2	10.0	9.4
District 4	337	23.8	2.1	272 753	19 257	7.1	253 496	22.3	13.9	8.9
District 5	351	22.9	2.0	281 396	17 929	6.4	263 467	22.1	14.5	7.7
District 6	315	28.7	4.3	244 376	22 384	9.2	221 992	24.8	13.3	12.7
District 7	376	24.5	2.2	274 824	16 857	6.1	257 967	27.4	12.4	9.2
District 8	389	24.4	2.0	283 594	14 807	5.2	268 787	26.3	12.6	8.4
District 9	392	25.9	1.9	279 761	22 284	8.0	257 477	28.1	11.2	8.6
District 10	388	24.7	1.6	283 444	16 978	6.0	266 466	30.7	10.8	8.5
District 11	376	28.6	2.8	258 249	29 251	11.3	228 998	31.0	7.7	11.3
District 12	417	24.7	2.4	299 109	16 298	5.4	282 811	33.4	8.3	8.5
District 13	403	24.2	2.3	285 963	15 637	5.5	270 326	27.9	13.8	7.3
District 14	394	27.0	1.5	281 368	18 754	6.7	262 614	30.2	11.2	8.9
District 15	438	24.5	1.7	312 928	13 894	4.4	299 034	34.5	8.6	7.6
District 16	353	24.2	2.1	274 286	17 411	6.3	256 875	24.9	11.7	8.4
District 17	337	26.4	1.7	258 333	21 757	8.4	236 576	24.0	12.9	10.3
District 18	298	26.0	2.8	251 720	22 498	8.9	229 222	20.7	14.2	10.4
District 19	464	24.9	1.3	290 637	14 082	4.8	276 555	31.4	12.7	7.3
OKLAHOMA	340	25.4	3.7	1 470 069	100 931	6.9	1 369 138	27.9	12.0	10.2
District 1	366	24.4	2.9	270 670	15 413	5.7	255 257	32.6	11.2	8.0
District 2	289	27.2	4.5	227 519	16 708	7.3	210 811	22.3	14.7	12.5
District 3	294	27.8	4.1	224 304	19 054	8.5	205 250	24.3	12.8	12.6
District 4	364	25.5	3.5	238 390	17 348	7.3	221 042	29.4	11.7	9.7
District 5	370	24.4	3.0	268 490	14 305	5.3	254 185	33.9	9.9	7.9
District 6	323	25.5	4.2	240 696	18 103	7.5	222 593	22.5	12.5	10.6
OREGON	408	25.5	3.9	1 407 143	87 183	6.2	1 319 960	28.8	10.7	10.0
District 1	453	24.4	3.2	306 224	13 194	4.3	293 030	36.6	9.7	7.7
District 2	363	25.3	4.8	262 274	20 950	8.0	241 324	23.4	10.9	10.9
District 3	414	25.5	3.5	295 378	17 481	5.9	277 897	27.5	11.2	10.3
District 4	390	26.7	3.9	266 853	20 076	7.5	246 777	25.2	11.2	11.7
District 5	403	25.8	3.9	276 414	15 482	5.6	260 932	29.8	10.5	9.5
PENNSYLVANIA	404	26.1	2.3	5 779 327	344 795	6.0	5 434 532	28.9	11.6	8.3
District 1	404	31.3	7.3	238 775	30 373	12.7	208 402	24.1	9.0	13.0
District 2	479	29.3	4.6	268 681	26 161	9.7	242 520	34.4	6.6	10.3
District 3	472	28.5	3.1	268 148	17 763	6.6	250 385	26.0	11.9	9.4
District 4	332	26.0	1.4	259 398	17 211	6.6	242 187	28.6	12.5	8.7
District 5	334	27.2	2.5	258 701	18 374	7.1	240 327	25.4	11.9	8.2
District 6	367	24.4	2.0	281 279	13 826	4.9	267 453	23.0	13.5	8.0
District 7	568	25.5	1.4	298 825	10 298	3.4	288 527	39.5	10.1	5.8

1. Specified renter-occupied units.   2. Overcrowded or lacking complete plumbing facilities.   3. Percent of total civilian labor force.   4. Persons 16 years old and older.   5. Persons 16 to 64 years of age.

Table E. Congressional Districts 105th Congress — Land Area and Population

STATE District	Land area, 1990[1] (sq km)	Population and population characteristics, 1990										Percent								
		Total persons	Per square kilometer	Race					Hispanic[2]	Foreign born	U.S. citizen	Age						
				White	Black	Am. Indian, Eskimo, Aleut	Asian and Pacific Islander	Other race				Under 5 years	5 to 17 years	18 to 24 years	25 to 34 years	35 to 44 years	45 to 54 years	55 to 64 years
	1	2	3	4	5	6	7	8	9	10	11	12	13	14	15	16	17	18
PENNSYLVANIA—Con.																		
District 8	1 622	565 787	348.9	95.0	2.8	0.1	1.6	0.5	1.6	4.1	98.5	7.4	18.2	9.1	17.8	16.6	11.1	9.0
District 9	17 262	565 803	32.8	98.3	1.2	0.1	0.3	0.1	0.4	0.8	99.7	6.6	18.2	9.8	15.1	14.4	10.7	9.9
District 10	14 406	565 681	39.3	98.1	1.1	0.1	0.5	0.2	0.8	2.0	99.4	6.7	17.5	9.5	15.0	14.3	10.2	9.9
District 11	6 149	565 913	92.0	98.4	0.9	0.1	0.4	0.2	0.7	1.8	99.4	6.0	16.0	10.0	14.5	14.0	10.1	10.6
District 12	10 911	565 794	51.9	98.3	1.3	0.1	0.3	0.1	0.4	0.9	99.7	6.0	17.7	10.3	14.3	14.4	10.1	10.3
District 13	947	565 793	597.4	91.0	6.1	0.1	2.5	0.3	1.2	5.7	97.8	6.7	15.7	8.9	16.8	15.6	11.0	9.9
District 14	501	565 787	1 128.5	80.5	17.8	0.1	1.3	0.2	0.8	3.9	98.2	6.3	14.3	11.9	16.8	14.2	9.2	9.9
District 15	2 046	565 810	276.5	94.0	2.2	0.1	1.1	2.6	4.7	3.8	98.3	6.7	16.4	10.1	16.4	15.3	10.3	9.7
District 16	3 314	565 835	170.7	91.4	5.2	0.1	1.1	2.1	3.8	2.8	98.7	7.8	18.5	10.7	16.6	15.6	10.4	8.3
District 17	3 848	565 742	147.0	91.3	6.7	0.1	1.0	0.9	1.9	1.9	99.2	7.1	17.4	9.5	17.1	15.8	10.4	9.3
District 18	685	565 781	825.9	91.2	7.8	0.1	0.7	0.2	0.6	2.6	99.3	6.2	14.7	8.1	16.1	14.7	10.3	11.4
District 19	4 965	565 831	114.0	95.9	2.6	0.1	0.7	0.6	1.3	1.6	99.4	6.7	17.0	10.9	16.6	15.6	10.7	9.1
District 20	5 534	565 815	102.2	96.2	3.2	0.1	0.5	0.1	0.5	1.7	99.5	6.0	16.8	9.0	14.8	15.3	10.8	10.6
District 21	7 212	565 802	78.5	95.2	3.9	0.1	0.4	0.3	0.8	1.6	99.5	6.8	18.1	11.6	15.0	14.4	10.0	9.4
RHODE ISLAND	2 707	1 003 464	370.8	91.4	3.9	0.4	1.8	2.5	4.6	9.5	94.8	6.7	15.8	12.0	17.3	14.7	9.6	8.9
District 1	838	501 677	598.6	92.8	3.3	0.3	1.3	2.4	3.8	10.4	94.5	6.5	15.2	12.5	17.4	14.2	9.5	9.1
District 2	1 868	501 787	268.6	90.0	4.5	0.5	2.4	2.6	5.3	8.6	95.0	6.8	16.4	11.5	17.2	15.2	9.7	8.7
SOUTH CAROLINA	77 988	3 486 703	44.7	69.0	29.8	0.2	0.6	0.3	0.9	1.4	99.3	7.4	19.0	11.7	17.0	15.0	10.2	8.4
District 1	8 169	581 133	71.1	78.0	20.1	0.3	1.2	0.4	1.4	2.3	99.0	8.0	18.4	12.2	19.6	15.2	9.5	7.7
District 2	12 974	581 099	44.8	73.2	25.1	0.2	1.0	0.5	1.4	2.2	98.8	7.4	18.4	12.4	18.3	15.6	9.8	7.8
District 3	14 508	581 116	40.1	78.3	21.1	0.1	0.4	0.1	0.5	0.9	99.5	6.7	18.4	11.8	15.5	14.6	10.8	9.3
District 4	5 662	581 113	102.6	79.3	19.7	0.1	0.7	0.2	0.8	1.6	99.1	6.9	17.8	10.9	16.6	15.4	11.1	8.9
District 5	17 689	581 131	32.9	68.2	30.8	0.4	0.4	0.2	0.6	0.8	99.6	7.3	19.9	10.7	16.2	15.0	10.5	8.5
District 6	18 986	581 111	30.6	37.2	62.2	0.2	0.3	0.2	0.6	0.7	99.7	7.8	21.3	11.9	15.5	14.2	9.4	8.1
SOUTH DAKOTA	196 571	696 004	3.5	91.6	0.5	7.3	0.4	0.2	0.8	1.1	99.6	7.8	20.7	9.8	15.7	13.7	9.0	8.6
At Large	196 571	696 004	3.5	91.6	0.5	7.3	0.4	0.2	0.8	1.1	99.6	7.8	20.7	9.8	15.7	13.7	9.0	8.6
TENNESSEE	106 758	4 877 185	45.7	83.0	16.0	0.2	0.7	0.2	0.7	1.2	99.3	6.8	18.1	10.8	16.7	15.2	10.8	8.9
District 1	10 924	541 875	49.6	97.5	1.9	0.2	0.3	0.1	0.4	0.7	99.7	5.8	16.9	10.5	15.3	15.1	12.2	10.2
District 2	6 443	541 864	84.1	92.3	6.6	0.2	0.7	0.2	0.6	1.4	99.2	6.4	16.7	11.7	16.6	15.5	11.1	9.1
District 3	11 176	541 866	48.5	87.4	11.6	0.2	0.6	0.2	0.6	1.2	99.4	6.4	17.9	10.1	15.6	15.3	11.3	9.7
District 4	24 191	541 868	22.4	95.8	3.6	0.2	0.2	0.1	0.4	0.5	99.7	6.4	18.7	9.9	14.9	14.3	11.6	9.9
District 5	2 278	541 910	237.9	75.4	22.8	0.2	1.3	0.3	0.9	2.3	98.5	7.1	16.1	11.5	20.2	15.4	9.8	8.3
District 6	13 899	541 977	39.0	93.3	5.7	0.2	0.6	0.1	0.6	1.1	99.3	6.9	19.4	10.7	16.3	16.2	11.3	8.1
District 7	17 117	541 937	31.7	86.2	12.4	0.2	0.9	0.3	1.1	1.6	99.3	7.4	19.3	10.6	17.6	16.3	10.6	7.9
District 8	20 072	541 907	27.0	79.5	19.7	0.2	0.4	0.1	0.7	0.7	99.7	6.9	18.9	11.1	15.4	14.2	10.5	9.0
District 9	657	541 981	825.0	39.7	59.2	0.2	0.7	0.2	0.7	1.3	99.2	8.2	19.0	11.2	18.0	14.3	8.7	8.2
TEXAS	678 358	16 986 510	25.0	75.2	11.9	0.4	1.9	10.6	25.5	9.0	94.1	8.2	20.3	11.1	18.2	14.9	9.6	7.6
District 1	29 959	566 217	18.9	79.5	18.1	0.4	0.3	1.7	3.2	1.9	98.7	6.9	19.5	10.3	14.3	13.5	10.2	9.3
District 2	36 767	566 217	15.4	79.4	16.7	0.4	0.3	3.2	5.6	2.7	98.2	7.0	19.9	10.0	15.3	13.7	10.3	9.6
District 3	945	567 648	600.7	83.4	7.4	0.4	4.5	4.3	8.3	8.4	94.3	8.7	19.8	9.6	22.1	18.5	10.8	5.6
District 4	17 674	566 217	32.0	88.3	8.4	0.6	0.4	2.3	4.3	2.3	98.7	7.3	19.7	9.3	15.8	14.6	10.6	8.9
District 5	17 048	567 457	33.3	74.6	15.8	0.5	1.2	8.0	14.4	7.6	94.4	7.8	17.5	10.3	20.2	14.3	9.2	8.2
District 6	2 158	565 469	262.1	90.0	5.1	0.4	2.3	2.2	5.7	4.3	97.6	8.3	18.9	9.9	21.5	18.0	11.0	6.5
District 7	1 207	564 900	468.0	80.4	6.1	0.3	5.5	7.8	16.4	15.9	89.0	8.5	18.5	9.3	22.4	18.7	10.3	6.4
District 8	7 991	565 090	70.7	89.6	5.1	0.3	1.9	3.0	7.1	5.1	96.7	7.5	20.5	13.6	16.9	16.9	10.9	6.6
District 9	5 317	564 322	106.1	72.4	21.7	0.3	2.1	3.5	9.4	4.7	97.2	7.6	19.8	9.4	17.6	15.4	10.1	8.8
District 10	2 069	566 217	273.7	72.9	11.2	0.4	2.9	12.7	21.4	7.9	94.7	7.7	16.3	16.0	22.4	16.3	8.4	5.7
District 11	29 262	566 217	19.3	76.0	15.9	0.4	1.6	6.0	12.3	4.2	97.9	8.2	18.8	14.2	17.0	12.9	8.6	7.7
District 12	4 463	566 217	126.9	80.1	8.0	0.5	1.9	9.5	16.3	7.4	95.0	8.3	18.8	10.9	18.9	14.2	9.4	7.9
District 13	82 250	566 217	6.9	78.9	8.0	0.6	1.2	11.3	19.4	4.5	97.2	7.7	20.0	11.5	15.7	12.6	9.2	9.0
District 14	39 829	566 217	14.2	77.7	10.6	0.3	0.6	10.7	23.6	4.0	97.5	7.5	20.5	11.0	15.2	14.0	9.5	8.7
District 15	21 886	566 217	25.9	75.5	1.1	0.2	0.3	22.9	74.5	18.0	88.0	8.9	25.8	11.2	14.6	12.8	8.3	7.4
District 16	1 256	566 217	450.7	76.5	3.6	0.4	1.1	18.5	70.4	24.1	83.9	8.9	23.5	12.4	17.0	13.6	8.8	7.5
District 17	72 894	566 217	7.8	85.7	3.5	0.4	0.5	9.8	17.2	3.5	98.0	7.4	19.7	9.8	15.0	13.2	9.7	9.3
District 18	406	567 364	1 395.7	40.2	44.7	0.2	2.7	12.2	23.4	12.7	90.8	8.2	19.1	11.7	19.2	15.0	9.4	7.8
District 19	52 286	566 217	10.8	86.1	2.5	0.4	0.9	10.0	19.6	4.6	97.0	8.1	20.7	11.8	17.3	14.2	9.5	8.2
District 20	753	566 217	751.6	71.8	5.8	0.4	1.3	20.7	60.7	10.0	93.9	8.9	20.6	13.2	19.0	13.4	8.2	7.0
District 21	44 851	566 217	12.6	91.3	2.5	0.4	1.0	4.8	14.1	4.1	97.9	7.1	18.7	8.9	16.5	16.0	10.5	8.8
District 22	4 335	568 160	131.1	71.5	12.7	0.3	6.9	8.5	17.0	12.2	92.7	8.4	21.0	9.2	20.1	18.6	10.5	6.4
District 23	151 286	566 217	3.7	73.9	2.9	0.4	0.7	22.1	62.5	16.4	89.4	9.1	24.7	10.6	15.7	14.1	9.3	7.4
District 24	5 484	567 454	103.5	64.0	20.4	0.6	2.1	12.9	21.0	9.3	93.6	9.1	21.0	11.4	19.0	14.6	9.1	6.7
District 25	749	564 724	754.2	63.3	23.0	0.3	3.8	9.6	18.6	13.0	90.8	8.7	18.8	11.7	21.2	16.3	9.2	6.6
District 26	1 771	564 843	318.9	86.7	5.4	0.4	2.9	4.5	9.5	8.8	94.0	7.7	15.6	10.8	23.8	17.3	10.6	6.6
District 27	10 557	566 217	53.6	78.7	2.4	0.3	0.6	18.0	66.2	13.0	91.8	8.6	24.2	10.6	16.0	13.9	8.8	7.7

1. Dry land or land partially or temporarily covered by water.　2. Hispanic persons may be of any race.

Table E. Congressional Districts 105th Congress — Population, Households, Group Quarters, and Education

STATE District	Population and population characteristics, 1990 (cont'd) Percent (cont'd) Age (cont'd)			Households, 1990			Percent	Persons in mental hospitals, 1990	Persons in nursing homes, 1990	Persons identified as homeless, 1990[2]	Education, 1990 School enrollment	
	65 to 74 years	75 years and over	Percent female	Number	Persons per house-hold	Female family house-holder[1]	One person				Public	Private
	19	20	21	22	23	24	25	26	27	28	29	30
PENNSYLVANIA—Con.												
District 8	6.7	4.2	50.7	199 677	2.79	8.4	19.3	193	4 273	200	102 963	38 849
District 9	8.9	6.4	51.5	212 351	2.60	8.9	23.3	0	5 935	115	108 087	15 583
District 10	9.7	7.1	52.0	212 813	2.58	10.0	24.8	668	4 950	220	105 728	24 191
District 11	10.7	8.0	52.5	218 969	2.50	10.6	27.0	494	6 150	98	101 306	24 342
District 12	10.1	6.9	51.9	213 386	2.57	9.5	24.7	755	5 129	142	117 824	17 040
District 13	8.7	6.7	52.1	211 735	2.58	8.3	24.6	940	6 948	256	83 570	51 078
District 14	10.0	7.5	53.4	231 642	2.34	14.7	33.3	499	4 779	781	100 985	40 274
District 15	8.8	6.2	51.6	213 418	2.57	9.2	23.3	486	5 257	343	99 682	33 141
District 16	6.9	5.1	51.1	197 885	2.76	8.4	20.4	41	6 658	527	107 194	32 987
District 17	7.9	5.6	51.7	216 856	2.55	9.6	24.4	590	6 072	310	104 222	21 221
District 18	11.2	7.4	53.2	232 220	2.41	11.6	28.4	0	4 819	157	95 134	27 001
District 19	7.7	5.6	51.2	212 004	2.58	8.1	22.0	28	5 801	234	104 790	23 425
District 20	10.1	6.7	52.3	217 875	2.54	10.2	24.6	727	4 831	174	108 497	20 511
District 21	8.8	6.0	51.6	209 875	2.59	10.5	24.8	73	5 777	332	116 088	30 634
RHODE ISLAND	8.5	6.5	52.0	377 977	2.55	11.7	26.2	265	10 156	494	191 802	62 833
District 1	8.7	6.9	52.2	191 853	2.50	11.3	27.1	37	6 252	170	86 460	39 128
District 2	8.3	6.1	51.9	186 124	2.60	12.2	25.3	228	3 904	324	105 342	23 705
SOUTH CAROLINA	7.1	4.3	51.6	1 258 044	2.68	14.0	22.4	2 152	18 228	982	807 539	105 471
District 1	6.2	3.1	50.2	210 982	2.67	11.0	21.0	98	1 685	21	129 195	19 405
District 2	6.5	3.7	51.0	210 778	2.62	12.0	22.5	16	2 916	21	136 157	18 888
District 3	7.8	5.1	51.7	215 512	2.61	12.1	22.7	104	3 685	122	135 564	14 899
District 4	7.4	4.9	52.0	220 099	2.57	12.7	23.7	266	3 008	288	117 135	24 754
District 5	7.2	4.6	51.9	205 042	2.76	15.0	21.1	119	3 387	90	136 389	11 887
District 6	7.2	4.6	52.8	195 631	2.86	21.9	23.1	1 549	3 547	440	153 099	15 638
SOUTH DAKOTA	7.8	6.9	50.8	259 034	2.59	8.0	26.4	427	9 356	515	165 993	19 253
At Large	7.8	6.9	50.8	259 034	2.59	8.0	26.4	427	9 356	515	165 993	19 253
TENNESSEE	7.3	5.4	51.8	1 853 725	2.56	12.6	23.9	2 849	35 192	2 151	1 023 651	147 989
District 1	8.3	5.7	51.6	210 363	2.51	10.3	22.7	63	4 727	187	108 560	9 678
District 2	7.7	5.4	52.1	212 752	2.48	11.0	25.1	600	3 077	474	120 208	12 377
District 3	8.0	5.7	52.1	209 558	2.53	12.1	24.4	382	4 305	175	110 709	17 742
District 4	8.3	6.0	51.6	204 747	2.61	10.5	21.1	19	4 748	26	110 283	8 460
District 5	6.6	5.0	52.4	218 369	2.38	14.1	29.6	586	3 684	793	93 390	35 098
District 6	6.3	4.6	51.0	197 185	2.69	9.4	19.3	205	3 245	88	124 211	13 677
District 7	5.8	4.3	50.7	197 446	2.67	9.9	20.6	724	3 583	38	117 616	18 568
District 8	7.9	6.2	51.7	200 919	2.61	12.6	22.6	0	4 661	21	116 347	12 324
District 9	7.1	5.3	53.4	202 386	2.60	22.8	28.6	270	3 162	349	122 327	20 065
TEXAS	5.9	4.2	50.7	6 070 937	2.73	11.6	23.9	5 315	101 005	8 968	4 313 852	492 043
District 1	8.6	7.4	51.9	212 663	2.59	10.9	24.6	0	7 138	81	139 109	9 430
District 2	8.2	6.1	49.9	202 546	2.66	11.0	22.7	143	4 776	101	137 702	9 404
District 3	3.0	1.8	50.6	210 090	2.69	9.2	22.5	51	1 753	6	137 473	21 492
District 4	7.6	6.1	51.5	211 624	2.62	9.3	22.9	448	5 966	63	132 890	13 353
District 5	7.0	5.5	50.0	217 824	2.51	11.5	29.2	44	4 800	114	118 872	15 650
District 6	3.8	2.0	50.3	215 161	2.62	7.5	22.5	43	1 362	0	129 541	23 915
District 7	3.8	2.1	50.4	221 903	2.54	8.3	28.7	7	1 352	109	127 056	24 801
District 8	4.2	2.8	50.1	198 519	2.77	8.1	19.2	82	2 319	0	170 785	16 351
District 9	6.7	4.5	51.1	212 067	2.62	12.7	24.9	100	3 067	391	141 230	14 786
District 10	4.1	2.9	50.0	228 606	2.39	10.6	31.7	597	2 619	471	161 795	18 544
District 11	6.8	5.8	49.8	200 738	2.64	10.6	23.8	223	6 437	148	130 259	21 781
District 12	6.6	5.0	50.6	207 789	2.65	11.2	24.8	258	4 947	928	120 459	19 292
District 13	7.7	6.6	51.4	209 996	2.60	10.0	26.2	868	5 655	372	145 260	9 003
District 14	7.6	5.9	50.6	201 932	2.71	9.9	23.1	136	5 051	21	145 441	12 501
District 15	6.5	4.5	51.5	164 944	3.39	13.7	16.3	0	2 811	179	180 969	8 618
District 16	5.2	3.1	51.4	170 915	3.24	16.0	17.2	209	1 070	434	177 054	13 551
District 17	8.5	7.5	51.2	210 111	2.59	8.7	24.6	380	7 655	274	129 487	15 699
District 18	5.7	3.9	50.2	202 510	2.73	18.7	29.6	213	1 740	1 428	140 552	14 002
District 19	6.0	4.2	51.0	208 449	2.66	8.5	23.5	42	2 464	151	156 876	12 617
District 20	5.6	4.0	51.1	192 134	2.84	16.0	25.1	26	3 205	576	143 916	20 892
District 21	8.0	5.5	51.5	217 836	2.54	8.0	23.9	461	4 574	34	126 397	19 576
District 22	3.7	2.2	49.5	195 058	2.84	9.4	20.1	184	2 347	157	148 588	20 203
District 23	5.5	3.6	51.1	174 390	3.20	12.2	17.5	0	1 871	283	167 218	12 860
District 24	5.1	4.0	50.7	194 480	2.87	14.2	21.7	11	4 087	200	139 409	16 982
District 25	4.6	3.0	51.1	216 809	2.58	13.5	28.3	112	1 932	41	137 616	22 456
District 26	4.4	3.1	50.7	235 193	2.37	7.3	30.9	154	2 112	21	112 179	29 681
District 27	6.2	4.1	51.5	177 612	3.13	14.6	19.3	36	2 419	508	169 692	12 148

1. No spouse present. 2. Persons in emergency shelters and persons visible in street locations.

Table E. Congressional Districts 105th Congress — Education, Money Income, Poverty, and Housing

STATE District	Education, 1990 (cont'd) Attainment[1] (percent) High school graduate or more	Bachelor's degree or more	Money income, 1989 Per capita[2]	Median	Percent with $100,000 or more	Percent below poverty level, 1989 Persons Total	Families Total	Housing units, 1990 Total	Occupied units Total	Owner-occupied Percent	Median value[3] (dollars)	Owner cost as a percent of income With a mortgage	Without a mortgage
	31	32	33	34	35	36	37	38	39	40	41	42	43
PENNSYLVANIA—Con.													
District 8	83.2	25.1	18 374	43 483	7.7	3.9	2.8	209 434	199 677	75.4	140 700	23.1	13.5
District 9	70.2	10.0	11 229	24 309	1.5	12.1	9.1	238 208	212 351	75.2	49 700	18.5	12.7
District 10	75.0	13.9	12 005	25 648	2.1	11.0	8.1	283 288	212 813	71.8	70 600	20.5	13.7
District 11	71.7	12.7	11 937	24 310	1.8	10.7	7.6	248 454	218 969	72.0	58 000	18.9	13.6
District 12	71.6	10.8	10 586	22 024	1.3	14.9	11.6	237 174	213 386	75.0	44 400	19.8	13.1
District 13	84.5	33.5	22 786	44 764	12.0	3.5	2.2	220 507	211 735	73.0	147 500	21.6	13.0
District 14	76.0	22.6	14 255	24 751	3.9	16.3	12.2	252 583	231 642	58.6	52 000	19.6	13.9
District 15	74.1	18.2	15 073	33 049	3.4	7.1	4.8	223 545	213 418	71.6	102 100	21.5	12.7
District 16	76.4	24.3	16 321	37 553	6.2	7.2	4.8	206 629	197 885	70.9	115 800	21.6	12.3
District 17	75.4	16.3	14 434	31 841	2.8	7.7	5.4	229 228	216 856	68.9	76 700	19.8	12.1
District 18	80.0	21.0	15 251	29 003	3.7	9.0	7.2	246 887	232 220	69.9	55 800	19.7	13.7
District 19	74.2	16.0	14 539	32 424	2.7	6.4	4.1	223 078	212 004	73.3	80 600	19.6	11.9
District 20	75.7	17.2	13 349	26 294	3.1	12.8	10.1	232 939	217 875	74.8	56 900	18.6	12.7
District 21	76.5	14.6	11 884	25 845	2.0	12.9	9.7	229 456	209 875	71.8	50 600	17.3	12.6
RHODE ISLAND	72.0	21.3	14 981	32 181	4.1	9.6	6.8	414 572	377 977	59.5	133 500	22.7	13.9
District 1	70.7	21.9	15 224	31 675	4.3	9.2	6.5	206 624	191 853	55.6	137 300	22.6	14.0
District 2	73.3	20.7	14 739	32 729	3.9	10.0	7.2	207 948	186 124	63.4	130 200	22.9	13.8
SOUTH CAROLINA	68.3	16.6	11 897	26 256	2.3	15.4	11.9	1 424 155	1 258 044	69.8	61 100	19.8	13.0
District 1	77.9	19.7	13 112	28 765	2.7	12.4	9.5	266 586	210 982	65.6	75 600	22.0	12.9
District 2	78.4	24.4	13 913	30 693	3.6	12.1	9.2	242 035	210 778	69.3	74 000	20.3	12.6
District 3	64.0	14.0	11 707	25 693	1.8	13.4	9.9	238 600	215 512	74.7	53 900	17.9	12.5
District 4	67.3	17.6	13 011	27 703	2.6	11.3	8.4	235 201	220 099	68.2	59 500	18.1	12.6
District 5	62.9	12.5	11 009	25 215	1.8	16.0	12.4	222 014	205 042	73.5	53 300	18.5	13.1
District 6	59.2	11.5	8 631	19 189	1.2	27.0	22.6	219 719	195 631	67.6	48 500	20.8	14.3
SOUTH DAKOTA	77.1	17.2	10 661	22 503	1.7	15.9	11.6	292 436	259 034	66.1	45 200	19.8	13.3
At Large	77.1	17.2	10 661	22 503	1.7	15.9	11.6	292 436	259 034	66.1	45 200	19.8	13.3
TENNESSEE	67.1	16.0	12 255	24 807	2.6	15.7	12.4	2 026 067	1 853 725	68.0	58 400	20.1	12.6
District 1	61.9	12.7	11 024	21 952	1.7	16.6	12.9	231 024	210 363	74.6	51 200	18.3	12.2
District 2	70.0	19.3	13 118	25 267	2.9	14.1	10.8	229 461	212 752	68.5	59 700	19.0	12.5
District 3	67.5	16.0	12 338	24 687	2.6	15.1	12.0	229 420	209 558	68.7	55 200	18.4	12.6
District 4	56.4	9.0	9 886	20 685	1.2	18.3	15.0	226 325	204 747	75.7	44 600	19.7	12.5
District 5	75.0	23.3	14 874	28 208	3.7	12.9	10.0	240 552	218 369	54.8	74 500	20.9	12.6
District 6	68.2	17.2	13 286	29 234	3.3	11.3	8.6	215 141	197 185	74.2	71 400	21.0	12.6
District 7	72.5	18.6	13 758	29 242	3.9	12.0	9.5	215 917	197 446	70.9	69 600	21.0	12.5
District 8	62.8	10.4	10 712	22 622	1.5	16.8	13.3	219 198	200 919	70.3	47 400	19.5	13.0
District 9	69.5	17.3	11 296	22 117	2.7	24.2	19.8	219 029	202 386	55.5	55 700	20.8	13.5
TEXAS	72.1	20.3	12 904	27 016	3.7	18.1	14.1	7 008 999	6 070 937	60.9	59 600	20.9	13.1
District 1	68.1	13.1	10 785	21 697	1.9	20.1	15.4	247 437	212 663	72.5	44 100	19.0	13.6
District 2	64.9	10.4	10 113	21 216	1.6	20.5	16.2	252 735	202 546	74.2	42 200	19.3	13.8
District 3	88.7	35.9	18 858	41 683	7.6	5.7	4.0	228 860	210 090	60.6	92 400	22.3	12.1
District 4	73.7	16.3	12 724	26 974	2.8	13.7	10.4	243 456	211 624	70.6	57 500	20.8	13.6
District 5	71.1	19.3	13 045	25 817	3.0	17.6	14.0	260 137	217 824	58.4	62 400	20.2	13.5
District 6	90.1	32.6	18 573	40 930	6.4	4.7	3.3	235 118	215 161	63.5	90 900	22.1	12.0
District 7	87.6	40.6	22 666	40 331	11.1	8.6	6.1	249 856	221 903	51.9	92 100	20.9	12.2
District 8	83.0	29.2	16 006	35 809	6.9	10.7	7.0	222 156	198 519	65.1	79 200	20.8	12.8
District 9	76.5	18.9	13 759	29 406	3.3	15.8	12.7	245 527	212 067	63.4	53 400	18.4	13.1
District 10	83.2	34.5	14 978	27 280	4.3	16.2	10.4	257 728	228 606	45.2	77 400	23.0	12.6
District 11	72.6	14.8	10 630	22 283	1.8	18.4	13.7	233 019	200 738	59.4	50 400	20.4	13.2
District 12	70.9	15.3	12 641	27 366	2.5	14.1	10.7	233 681	207 789	61.5	57 800	20.3	12.8
District 13	66.9	13.7	10 344	20 907	1.8	21.3	16.2	249 706	209 996	64.8	38 600	19.3	13.3
District 14	66.1	13.8	11 127	23 812	2.2	20.0	15.1	250 002	201 932	68.9	52 800	20.7	13.2
District 15	50.8	11.5	7 407	17 866	1.7	37.5	31.6	202 513	164 944	69.9	37 200	21.0	12.9
District 16	63.3	15.4	9 195	22 632	2.3	27.0	22.6	179 518	170 915	58.1	57 600	20.5	12.0
District 17	66.2	13.4	10 642	21 532	1.8	19.1	14.5	259 973	210 111	70.6	38 900	20.0	13.4
District 18	62.3	16.0	10 744	22 240	2.1	26.7	22.7	243 275	202 510	49.3	47 600	20.7	14.6
District 19	76.0	20.8	13 184	27 267	3.3	14.7	10.9	235 793	208 449	65.1	55 400	19.5	12.3
District 20	68.4	15.6	9 672	22 372	1.3	24.4	20.4	216 539	192 134	50.1	48 900	20.9	12.7
District 21	83.7	28.0	16 086	32 103	4.8	9.7	7.1	256 664	217 836	66.8	79 400	22.0	12.5
District 22	83.1	29.9	16 291	40 160	5.8	8.4	6.3	215 591	195 058	64.9	70 900	20.4	12.3
District 23	59.7	16.6	9 764	21 555	3.3	29.5	24.2	203 972	174 390	68.1	48 200	22.1	13.1
District 24	68.5	14.7	11 371	27 091	2.0	16.4	12.9	222 698	194 480	58.8	58 800	21.2	13.3
District 25	78.8	25.6	15 056	29 611	4.7	14.8	11.9	248 004	216 809	47.1	63 300	18.5	12.3
District 26	89.4	40.8	23 770	40 269	11.0	6.2	3.9	259 527	235 193	52.4	117 800	22.3	12.5
District 27	60.5	14.8	9 366	21 552	2.2	29.7	24.6	208 727	177 612	61.0	47 700	21.0	12.7

1. Persons 25 years old and older. 2. Based on the population enumerated as of April 1, 1990. 3. Specified owner-occupied units.

Table E. Congressional Districts 105th Congress — **Housing, Labor Force, and Employment**

STATE District	Housing units, 1990 (cont'd) — Occupied units (cont'd) — Renter-occupied			Civilian labor force, 1990			Civilian employment, 1990[4]			Disability, 1990
	Median rent[1] (dollars)	Rent as a percent of income	Substandard units[2] (percent)	Total	Unemployment Total	Unemployment Rate[3]	Total	Percent Professional, managerial, and technical	Percent Precision production, craft, and repair	Work disabled persons[5] (percent)
	44	45	46	47	48	49	50	51	52	53
PENNSYLVANIA—Con.										
District 8	608	25.9	1.4	309 717	11 844	3.8	297 873	33.9	12.2	6.0
District 9	305	24.0	2.7	265 147	17 495	6.6	247 652	20.9	14.0	9.2
District 10	339	25.1	1.9	266 263	15 789	5.9	250 474	24.3	13.2	9.3
District 11	327	25.3	1.6	263 801	16 119	6.1	247 682	23.6	12.8	9.2
District 12	293	26.4	2.3	239 950	21 128	8.8	218 822	22.9	14.1	10.0
District 13	600	25.1	1.2	306 867	9 707	3.2	297 160	40.8	9.1	5.3
District 14	379	27.7	1.8	267 981	20 026	7.5	247 955	34.9	8.1	9.3
District 15	458	25.8	1.9	289 590	12 885	4.4	276 705	28.5	12.2	6.7
District 16	500	24.4	2.6	297 424	9 386	3.2	288 038	30.5	11.8	5.9
District 17	415	23.2	1.9	302 329	11 453	3.8	290 876	27.0	11.9	7.3
District 18	394	25.6	0.9	274 365	16 022	5.8	258 343	33.8	9.7	7.9
District 19	416	23.1	1.7	304 001	11 036	3.6	292 965	25.2	13.0	6.7
District 20	332	26.3	1.8	253 653	19 433	7.7	234 220	29.5	12.4	8.9
District 21	326	25.9	2.0	264 432	18 466	7.0	245 966	25.2	12.7	8.7
RHODE ISLAND	489	27.5	2.6	522 603	34 690	6.6	487 913	30.1	12.0	8.6
District 1	482	26.9	2.3	262 391	17 478	6.7	244 913	30.5	11.3	8.3
District 2	498	28.2	3.0	260 212	17 212	6.6	243 000	29.6	12.6	8.9
SOUTH CAROLINA	376	24.4	5.0	1 698 098	94 673	5.6	1 603 425	25.4	13.8	9.1
District 1	442	24.5	3.9	276 028	12 757	4.6	263 271	29.0	14.6	8.0
District 2	437	23.9	3.9	290 649	12 811	4.4	277 838	32.9	11.5	7.6
District 3	323	23.5	4.1	287 928	15 842	5.5	272 086	23.2	15.8	9.7
District 4	367	23.1	3.3	303 767	14 747	4.9	289 020	26.6	12.9	9.1
District 5	327	24.2	6.3	281 716	17 457	6.2	264 259	20.5	14.9	9.3
District 6	315	28.4	9.0	258 010	21 059	8.2	236 951	19.5	13.3	11.1
SOUTH DAKOTA	306	24.6	3.4	335 874	13 983	4.2	321 891	24.5	10.4	7.8
At Large	306	24.6	3.4	335 874	13 983	4.2	321 891	24.5	10.4	7.8
TENNESSEE	357	25.0	3.8	2 405 077	154 235	6.4	2 250 842	26.1	12.2	9.7
District 1	295	24.3	3.9	264 028	19 158	7.3	244 870	23.0	14.5	11.4
District 2	337	25.0	2.3	274 284	16 495	6.0	257 789	29.4	11.8	9.5
District 3	348	24.7	3.4	262 737	17 177	6.5	245 560	26.8	12.8	10.6
District 4	277	24.1	4.8	253 005	17 298	6.8	235 707	18.0	15.4	12.5
District 5	430	25.3	2.7	293 835	14 595	5.0	279 240	32.4	9.0	7.4
District 6	378	24.7	3.5	281 653	13 889	4.9	267 764	26.0	12.9	8.3
District 7	412	23.5	3.7	267 725	14 231	5.3	253 494	28.5	11.9	8.2
District 8	311	24.4	3.9	251 295	17 570	7.0	233 725	21.4	13.2	10.4
District 9	362	27.7	6.1	256 515	23 822	9.3	232 693	27.4	8.4	9.4
TEXAS	395	24.6	8.5	8 219 028	584 749	7.1	7 634 279	30.0	11.7	7.6
District 1	334	27.3	5.5	248 343	18 426	7.4	229 917	22.6	14.5	10.3
District 2	333	27.1	7.1	231 862	17 989	7.8	213 873	21.9	15.4	11.1
District 3	497	23.4	4.4	335 764	13 097	3.9	322 667	40.3	8.7	4.5
District 4	385	24.7	4.4	274 486	15 980	5.8	258 506	26.7	13.6	8.9
District 5	413	24.8	7.4	280 707	18 708	6.7	261 999	27.8	11.4	8.8
District 6	462	22.6	2.6	330 700	13 134	4.0	317 566	39.5	9.3	4.7
District 7	454	21.9	6.3	325 020	14 092	4.3	310 928	43.3	7.9	4.0
District 8	442	25.4	4.4	289 190	13 473	4.7	275 717	36.8	11.0	5.6
District 9	398	24.4	5.3	272 644	18 696	6.9	253 948	32.2	13.4	8.2
District 10	415	26.8	6.3	316 965	19 172	6.0	297 793	40.2	7.9	5.8
District 11	362	26.1	5.6	230 624	18 035	7.8	212 589	25.9	12.0	9.1
District 12	402	24.8	6.8	280 345	19 321	6.9	261 024	25.2	14.4	8.9
District 13	334	27.2	6.5	253 774	18 172	7.2	235 602	22.6	12.9	9.4
District 14	344	25.4	8.2	259 128	17 480	6.7	241 648	24.0	15.0	8.1
District 15	290	25.7	22.4	217 324	27 532	12.7	189 792	23.1	12.3	8.9
District 16	345	26.0	15.3	233 127	25 066	10.8	208 061	27.8	10.9	7.9
District 17	329	25.5	5.5	247 014	17 941	7.3	229 073	23.4	13.4	9.5
District 18	364	25.1	12.6	277 165	29 987	10.8	247 178	26.0	11.8	9.4
District 19	366	24.6	5.4	278 872	15 098	5.4	263 774	29.1	12.3	6.8
District 20	362	25.6	11.9	250 483	23 567	9.4	226 916	27.3	11.3	9.0
District 21	434	23.5	3.5	282 164	13 371	4.7	268 793	36.6	9.7	6.8
District 22	455	22.2	6.7	304 311	14 399	4.7	289 912	39.3	10.8	5.0
District 23	322	25.1	16.1	236 209	23 453	9.9	212 756	27.6	11.9	7.5
District 24	414	26.1	10.1	284 128	21 079	7.4	263 049	23.1	13.1	7.8
District 25	398	23.3	9.0	303 961	21 051	6.9	282 910	33.0	11.8	6.1
District 26	488	23.1	4.1	342 809	13 625	4.0	329 184	41.8	6.9	4.3
District 27	343	26.5	16.4	238 459	25 238	10.6	213 221	26.7	12.9	8.3

1. Specified renter-occupied units.　2. Overcrowded or lacking complete plumbing facilities.　3. Percent of total civilian labor force.　4. Persons 16 years old and older.　5. Persons 16 to 64 years of age.

STATE District	Land area, 1990[1] (sq km)	Total persons	Per square kilometer	White	Black	Am. Indian, Eskimo, Aleut	Asian and Pacific Islander	Other race	Hispanic[2]	Foreign born	U.S. citizen	Under 5 years	5 to 17 years	18 to 24 years	25 to 34 years	35 to 44 years	45 to 54 years	55 to 64 years
	1	2	3	4	5	6	7	8	9	10	11	12	13	14	15	16	17	18
TEXAS—Con.																		
District 28	31 540	566 217	18.0	68.5	8.5	0.3	0.7	21.9	60.4	9.2	94.3	8.9	23.5	10.6	15.8	13.5	9.2	7.9
District 29	678	568 959	839.1	57.4	15.4	0.3	2.1	24.8	45.1	19.4	85.8	9.7	22.8	12.4	19.2	14.2	8.6	6.3
District 30	685	564 431	823.9	41.8	44.5	0.5	2.1	11.1	18.4	10.2	92.8	8.8	20.1	12.2	20.1	14.3	9.4	7.1
UTAH	212 815	1 722 850	8.1	93.8	0.7	1.4	1.9	2.2	4.9	3.4	98.1	9.8	26.6	11.6	16.0	13.0	8.0	6.2
District 1	88 280	574 286	6.5	94.4	0.9	0.9	1.5	2.3	4.7	2.6	98.6	9.9	27.4	10.8	15.1	12.5	8.2	6.7
District 2	1 187	574 241	483.7	94.4	0.6	0.7	2.3	2.0	4.9	4.4	97.7	9.3	24.6	10.4	17.4	14.6	8.5	6.2
District 3	123 348	574 323	4.7	92.6	0.5	2.6	1.9	2.4	5.1	3.2	98.0	10.3	27.7	13.6	15.3	12.0	7.4	5.8
VERMONT	23 956	562 758	23.5	98.6	0.3	0.3	0.6	0.1	0.7	3.1	98.8	7.3	18.1	11.2	16.9	16.4	10.2	8.0
At Large	23 956	562 758	23.5	98.6	0.3	0.3	0.6	0.1	0.7	3.1	98.8	7.3	18.1	11.2	16.9	16.4	10.2	8.0
VIRGINIA	102 558	6 187 358	60.3	77.4	18.8	0.2	2.6	0.9	2.6	5.0	97.0	7.2	17.2	11.6	18.4	16.0	10.7	8.1
District 1	9 053	562 757	62.2	80.4	17.6	0.3	1.3	0.5	1.5	2.6	99.0	7.3	18.1	10.7	17.4	15.6	10.8	8.6
District 2	735	562 276	765.4	78.1	16.6	0.4	3.8	1.1	3.3	4.9	97.9	8.5	16.9	17.1	22.0	14.5	7.8	6.0
District 3	4 557	562 351	123.4	33.5	64.4	0.4	1.1	0.6	1.4	1.9	98.6	8.4	18.2	12.8	18.6	13.6	8.9	8.1
District 4	14 648	562 466	38.4	66.2	32.1	0.2	1.1	0.3	1.1	1.8	99.4	7.5	18.7	10.0	17.7	15.6	10.6	8.5
District 5	22 860	562 268	24.6	74.4	24.8	0.1	0.6	0.2	0.6	1.2	99.4	6.3	16.6	11.6	15.8	14.4	11.0	9.8
District 6	13 460	562 572	41.8	87.6	11.5	0.1	0.6	0.2	0.7	1.4	99.2	6.2	16.0	12.3	15.6	15.0	10.8	9.6
District 7	6 588	562 643	85.4	87.8	10.0	0.2	1.7	0.3	1.0	3.1	98.5	7.2	17.3	9.3	18.7	17.8	10.7	8.0
District 8	420	562 484	1 340.4	76.0	13.4	0.3	6.7	3.7	8.7	16.7	88.4	6.3	13.1	10.6	22.8	18.6	11.7	7.6
District 9	20 435	562 380	27.5	96.6	2.5	0.1	0.7	0.1	0.5	1.2	99.3	5.7	17.2	13.5	15.0	14.7	11.1	9.4
District 10	9 156	562 664	61.5	90.7	5.8	0.2	2.7	0.7	2.2	5.1	97.2	8.0	18.8	9.4	19.0	17.9	12.2	7.1
District 11	644	562 497	873.0	80.7	8.2	0.3	8.1	2.7	7.4	15.7	90.1	7.4	17.9	10.7	20.3	18.7	12.3	6.8
WASHINGTON	172 445	4 866 692	28.2	88.5	3.1	1.7	4.3	2.4	4.4	6.6	96.4	7.5	18.4	10.0	17.6	16.5	10.3	7.8
District 1	971	540 745	556.8	91.6	1.3	1.0	5.4	0.7	2.3	7.5	96.1	7.6	18.2	8.9	18.6	18.6	11.2	7.4
District 2	16 117	540 739	33.5	93.7	0.9	2.0	2.1	1.3	3.0	5.3	97.3	7.8	19.0	9.8	17.2	16.4	9.8	7.7
District 3	21 827	540 745	24.8	94.8	0.9	1.3	2.1	0.9	2.5	3.6	98.3	7.4	20.1	8.8	15.6	16.5	10.8	8.2
District 4	61 396	540 744	8.8	83.2	1.0	2.8	1.3	11.8	15.9	8.6	93.9	8.3	21.4	9.6	15.3	14.9	9.9	8.2
District 5	45 781	540 744	11.8	93.2	1.2	1.8	1.8	2.0	3.4	3.8	97.9	7.2	19.1	11.8	15.6	15.1	9.8	8.0
District 6	16 188	540 742	33.4	87.3	5.4	2.3	3.9	1.1	3.1	5.1	97.9	7.4	18.0	9.9	16.4	15.4	9.9	8.7
District 7	327	540 747	1 653.1	75.5	10.0	1.4	11.6	1.4	3.5	12.8	92.9	5.8	11.4	11.8	21.5	18.1	9.3	7.4
District 8	7 605	540 742	71.1	92.0	1.6	1.0	4.6	0.7	2.3	6.0	97.0	8.1	20.0	8.3	18.4	18.1	11.9	7.4
District 9	2 233	540 744	242.1	85.5	5.4	1.5	6.1	1.5	3.7	6.8	96.6	8.2	18.3	11.4	19.5	15.6	10.2	7.5
WEST VIRGINIA	62 384	1 793 477	28.7	96.2	3.1	0.1	0.4	0.1	0.5	0.9	99.6	5.9	18.8	10.0	14.6	15.1	10.7	9.9
District 1	15 402	598 056	38.8	97.6	1.6	0.2	0.5	0.1	0.5	1.2	99.5	5.8	17.8	11.1	14.3	14.8	10.7	9.8
District 2	24 490	597 921	24.4	96.0	3.3	0.1	0.4	0.1	0.5	0.8	99.7	6.3	18.6	9.2	15.3	15.4	10.9	9.9
District 3	22 492	597 500	26.6	95.0	4.5	0.1	0.3	0.1	0.4	0.7	99.8	5.7	19.9	9.8	14.2	15.2	10.4	9.9
WISCONSIN	140 672	4 891 769	34.8	92.2	5.0	0.8	1.1	0.9	1.9	2.5	98.8	7.4	19.0	10.5	16.8	14.8	9.8	8.5
District 1	5 718	543 530	95.1	92.0	5.4	0.3	0.6	1.6	3.4	3.0	98.8	7.6	19.3	10.4	16.6	14.8	10.3	8.5
District 2	13 852	543 532	39.2	95.5	2.1	0.3	1.7	0.4	1.2	2.9	98.2	7.1	17.0	13.3	18.5	15.9	9.4	7.4
District 3	27 554	543 533	19.7	98.0	0.2	0.4	1.2	0.1	0.5	1.5	99.1	7.2	19.5	12.6	15.3	14.2	9.3	8.0
District 4	760	543 527	715.5	93.9	0.9	0.8	1.3	3.1	6.3	4.3	98.1	7.2	17.4	9.6	18.4	15.1	9.9	9.1
District 5	261	543 530	2 080.5	61.3	35.2	0.5	1.7	1.3	2.6	4.2	98.1	8.4	18.7	11.8	18.3	14.0	8.3	7.7
District 6	17 398	543 652	31.2	98.1	0.4	0.4	0.7	0.3	0.9	1.5	99.3	7.1	19.3	9.5	16.0	14.4	9.9	9.1
District 7	43 313	543 529	12.5	97.2	0.2	1.5	0.9	0.2	0.5	1.4	99.4	7.1	20.1	9.3	15.5	14.3	9.8	8.8
District 8	25 498	543 404	21.3	96.0	0.3	2.6	0.9	0.2	0.6	1.4	99.3	7.5	19.6	9.3	16.7	14.7	9.9	8.6
District 9	6 318	543 532	86.0	98.1	0.4	0.2	0.9	0.3	1.0	2.2	99.2	7.2	19.9	8.5	15.9	16.0	11.3	8.9
WYOMING	251 501	453 588	1.8	94.2	0.8	2.1	0.6	2.3	5.7	1.7	99.2	7.7	22.2	9.1	16.4	16.4	10.0	7.8
At Large	251 501	453 588	1.8	94.2	0.8	2.1	0.6	2.3	5.7	1.7	99.2	7.7	22.2	9.1	16.4	16.4	10.0	7.8

1. Dry land or land partially or temporarily covered by water.   2. Hispanic persons may be of any race.

Table E. Congressional Districts 105th Congress — Population, Households, Group Quarters, and Education

STATE District	Population and population characteristics, 1990 (cont'd)			Households, 1990				Persons in mental hospitals, 1990	Persons in nursing homes, 1990	Persons identified as homeless, 1990[2]	Education, 1990	
	Percent (cont'd)					Percent					School enrollment	
	Age (cont'd)											
	65 to 74 years	75 years and over	Percent female	Number	Persons per household	Female family householder[1]	One person				Public	Private
	19	20	21	22	23	24	25	26	27	28	29	30
TEXAS—Con.												
District 28	6.3	4.3	51.3	178 888	3.13	15.7	18.0	458	2 375	218	157 245	12 759
District 29	4.3	2.5	49.6	184 101	3.08	14.5	21.6	0	689	211	154 413	11 760
District 30	4.9	3.1	50.9	196 049	2.82	19.5	25.0	29	2 412	1 448	134 369	17 936
UTAH	5.1	3.6	50.3	537 273	3.15	9.1	18.9	462	6 222	912	543 194	67 502
District 1	5.6	3.8	50.1	176 881	3.20	8.7	17.3	69	2 317	325	192 724	9 821
District 2	5.2	3.8	50.5	193 316	2.92	9.4	23.3	72	2 360	410	172 177	18 004
District 3	4.6	3.1	50.4	167 076	3.37	9.3	15.5	321	1 545	177	178 293	39 677
VERMONT	6.6	5.2	51.0	210 650	2.57	9.2	23.4	129	4 809	305	120 725	25 263
At Large	6.6	5.2	51.0	210 650	2.57	9.2	23.4	129	4 809	305	120 725	25 263
VIRGINIA	6.5	4.3	51.0	2 291 830	2.61	11.1	22.9	3 931	37 762	2 814	1 331 800	214 457
District 1	7.1	4.6	50.9	205 434	2.65	9.5	20.8	947	3 955	71	126 100	17 380
District 2	4.6	2.6	47.4	192 765	2.70	9.9	20.2	206	1 705	376	119 067	20 609
District 3	7.0	4.4	53.2	209 435	2.58	23.0	26.9	1 020	3 055	603	131 237	15 601
District 4	7.1	4.4	51.0	199 069	2.73	13.3	19.9	9	3 673	20	122 066	16 907
District 5	8.5	5.9	51.7	212 145	2.56	11.8	23.5	36	4 377	94	121 572	14 065
District 6	8.3	6.3	52.2	215 001	2.47	11.2	25.3	1 197	5 110	342	112 661	24 049
District 7	6.5	4.5	51.9	217 794	2.54	8.7	23.8	6	4 701	116	117 788	20 941
District 8	5.8	3.6	50.6	232 754	2.35	8.5	31.4	1	2 274	765	95 485	30 708
District 9	7.8	5.6	51.3	210 961	2.57	10.0	21.9	407	4 439	42	141 235	8 184
District 10	4.6	2.9	50.0	197 675	2.81	7.7	16.9	83	2 260	73	118 191	20 590
District 11	3.9	2.1	50.4	198 797	2.79	9.0	18.8	19	2 213	312	126 398	25 423
WASHINGTON	6.9	4.9	50.4	1 872 431	2.53	9.4	25.4	2 928	32 840	5 226	1 091 450	160 862
District 1	5.8	3.7	50.7	205 181	2.61	8.4	21.9	89	2 886	137	116 357	21 367
District 2	7.2	5.1	50.0	202 215	2.60	8.6	22.6	143	4 165	460	122 300	14 039
District 3	7.4	5.4	50.8	206 863	2.58	9.6	23.9	33	3 717	406	125 222	12 971
District 4	7.2	5.3	50.1	196 812	2.70	9.7	23.4	47	3 341	376	136 004	10 557
District 5	7.5	5.9	50.8	207 264	2.50	9.9	26.7	601	4 475	547	139 265	20 396
District 6	8.4	5.8	50.4	211 878	2.47	10.2	26.7	1 713	4 350	537	112 644	17 036
District 7	8.0	6.7	51.0	244 606	2.12	9.2	38.9	146	4 366	2 500	100 187	27 234
District 8	5.0	2.9	50.1	195 943	2.74	8.1	18.6	0	1 812	63	123 575	19 386
District 9	5.7	3.5	49.7	201 669	2.60	10.5	23.2	156	3 728	200	115 896	17 876
WEST VIRGINIA	8.7	6.3	52.0	688 557	2.55	10.7	24.5	599	12 591	576	403 602	32 911
District 1	8.9	6.7	52.0	230 990	2.52	10.0	25.4	55	4 787	156	136 269	14 280
District 2	8.4	6.0	51.6	230 330	2.55	10.3	24.0	372	3 929	294	126 081	10 713
District 3	8.7	6.2	52.3	227 237	2.59	11.7	24.1	172	3 875	126	141 252	7 918
WISCONSIN	7.3	6.0	51.1	1 822 118	2.61	9.6	24.3	2 659	50 345	1 471	1 088 366	213 864
District 1	7.0	5.5	51.2	198 940	2.67	10.8	22.7	19	4 527	175	122 994	21 549
District 2	6.3	5.1	50.7	208 577	2.51	7.7	25.6	259	4 531	289	141 960	15 302
District 3	7.4	6.5	50.8	197 728	2.64	7.6	24.1	43	6 905	93	142 442	14 622
District 4	7.8	5.6	51.5	210 102	2.54	10.5	26.3	173	4 348	116	99 448	33 885
District 5	6.7	6.1	53.2	207 859	2.52	19.3	30.1	888	6 819	388	120 632	36 364
District 6	8.1	6.7	50.7	201 139	2.62	7.3	23.5	757	6 854	21	114 170	22 184
District 7	8.2	6.9	50.6	202 076	2.63	7.8	23.9	157	5 845	133	123 503	16 013
District 8	7.6	6.2	50.8	202 772	2.62	7.9	23.5	98	5 442	214	113 855	23 348
District 9	6.9	5.3	50.4	192 925	2.76	6.7	19.0	265	5 074	42	109 362	30 597
WYOMING	6.1	4.3	50.0	168 839	2.63	8.3	24.5	285	2 679	189	127 228	7 511
At Large	6.1	4.3	50.0	168 839	2.63	8.3	24.5	285	2 679	189	127 228	7 511

1. No spouse present. 2. Persons in emergency shelters and persons visible in street locations.

Items 19—30

STATE District	Attainment[1] (percent) High school graduate or more	Bachelor's degree or more	Money income, 1989 Per capita[2]	Median	Percent with $100,000 or more	Percent below poverty level, 1989 Persons Total	Families Total	Housing units, 1990 Total	Occupied units Total	Owner-occupied Percent	Median value[3] (dollars)	Owner cost as a percent of income With a mortgage	Without a mortgage
	31	32	33	34	35	36	37	38	39	40	41	42	43
TEXAS—Con.													
District 28	58.4	8.3	8 050	20 276	0.9	28.2	24.2	204 554	178 888	68.6	40 400	21.1	13.0
District 29	55.6	8.6	9 314	23 808	1.4	21.8	18.3	212 350	184 101	52.0	40 900	19.8	13.0
District 30	65.8	14.2	11 015	24 775	2.0	21.8	18.1	229 883	196 049	47.7	60 200	21.1	13.8
UTAH	85.1	22.3	11 029	29 470	2.5	11.4	8.6	598 388	537 273	68.1	68 900	20.9	12.1
District 1	85.6	20.5	10 856	30 563	1.9	10.1	7.4	196 470	176 881	71.5	69 000	20.3	11.9
District 2	87.4	27.1	12 971	30 960	3.9	8.9	6.7	206 429	193 316	64.9	76 900	21.4	12.1
District 3	82.1	18.6	9 259	26 570	1.6	15.2	11.7	195 489	167 076	68.3	60 100	20.9	12.3
VERMONT	80.8	24.3	13 527	29 792	2.8	9.9	6.9	271 214	210 650	69.0	95 500	21.9	14.7
At Large	80.8	24.3	13 527	29 792	2.8	9.9	6.9	271 214	210 650	69.0	95 500	21.9	14.7
VIRGINIA	75.2	24.5	15 713	33 328	5.2	10.2	7.7	2 496 334	2 291 830	66.3	91 000	21.9	12.5
District 1	77.0	21.3	14 872	33 743	3.7	8.2	5.9	231 932	205 434	71.9	93 600	22.3	12.7
District 2	85.3	23.6	14 492	32 576	3.7	8.1	5.7	210 018	192 765	57.0	93 100	24.5	12.4
District 3	64.2	12.4	10 357	22 351	1.1	21.8	18.8	231 754	209 435	49.1	62 100	22.3	14.5
District 4	69.3	14.1	12 887	30 425	2.3	11.4	8.9	215 276	199 069	71.2	73 200	21.9	13.0
District 5	60.7	13.3	11 675	24 807	1.9	14.1	10.4	237 017	212 145	72.0	56 000	17.4	12.3
District 6	69.8	16.7	13 017	27 155	2.4	11.1	7.8	232 223	215 001	68.1	65 100	17.9	12.2
District 7	81.9	30.5	18 360	38 865	5.9	5.3	3.5	232 273	217 794	70.4	91 800	20.5	12.3
District 8	88.6	48.0	24 799	48 839	11.8	5.4	3.3	249 112	232 754	54.8	209 900	22.3	11.8
District 9	57.6	11.7	10 097	20 857	1.3	19.1	14.7	231 442	210 961	73.9	49 100	18.2	12.1
District 10	81.2	30.3	20 065	46 205	10.3	4.9	3.3	216 181	197 675	74.2	155 400	24.4	12.5
District 11	90.4	44.3	22 202	54 369	12.8	3.9	2.5	209 106	198 797	67.6	191 000	23.6	11.6
WASHINGTON	83.8	22.9	14 923	31 183	3.7	10.9	7.8	2 032 378	1 872 431	62.6	93 400	20.4	11.8
District 1	90.7	31.2	18 687	40 390	6.3	5.1	3.4	214 896	205 181	66.8	148 200	21.7	11.5
District 2	83.4	17.7	14 419	31 305	3.2	9.4	6.6	227 215	202 215	65.7	100 500	21.0	11.9
District 3	81.5	16.9	13 328	29 154	2.4	11.3	8.6	225 971	206 863	64.9	70 400	18.5	11.7
District 4	73.0	16.1	11 578	25 055	2.1	17.6	13.4	221 456	196 812	63.2	60 300	17.3	11.7
District 5	83.0	20.3	12 177	25 107	2.2	15.3	10.7	227 492	207 264	63.8	57 700	18.8	12.0
District 6	82.3	17.8	13 403	27 882	2.4	12.7	9.6	238 327	211 878	61.5	74 700	20.2	12.2
District 7	86.4	37.0	18 021	29 707	4.6	12.2	7.4	257 878	244 606	49.7	133 300	20.9	11.7
District 8	88.7	29.0	18 432	42 379	7.0	5.3	3.8	205 496	195 943	72.1	142 200	21.5	11.5
District 9	84.6	18.2	14 264	32 194	2.7	9.6	7.5	213 647	201 669	58.3	93 300	20.8	11.7
WEST VIRGINIA	66.0	12.3	10 520	20 795	1.5	19.7	16.0	781 295	688 557	74.1	47 900	17.5	12.0
District 1	70.9	13.7	10 920	21 903	1.5	17.3	13.4	258 144	230 990	73.9	46 700	16.9	12.1
District 2	67.3	13.1	11 083	22 253	1.7	17.6	14.2	263 693	230 330	73.9	55 600	17.3	11.8
District 3	59.7	10.2	9 557	18 166	1.4	24.1	20.3	259 458	227 237	74.4	41 900	18.6	12.1
WISCONSIN	78.6	17.7	13 276	29 442	2.6	10.7	7.6	2 055 774	1 822 118	66.7	62 500	20.1	13.4
District 1	77.1	14.8	13 567	31 431	2.4	9.8	7.3	218 877	198 940	68.5	61 700	18.9	12.9
District 2	84.8	26.7	14 319	30 625	3.2	10.1	5.5	221 842	208 577	60.6	70 000	20.8	13.3
District 3	78.1	16.3	11 505	25 758	1.9	13.0	8.3	216 730	197 728	69.7	52 600	19.8	13.8
District 4	78.7	16.6	14 177	32 260	1.9	8.0	6.1	217 561	210 102	60.5	71 800	20.8	13.9
District 5	76.3	23.6	13 277	26 267	3.1	21.0	17.1	219 667	207 859	47.9	63 200	20.6	13.8
District 6	76.4	13.1	12 400	28 038	1.9	8.7	6.1	232 394	201 139	73.2	55 000	19.3	13.0
District 7	75.6	13.2	11 427	25 277	1.7	11.6	8.4	257 014	202 076	74.3	48 600	18.5	13.6
District 8	78.4	14.8	12 628	28 169	2.2	9.9	7.5	269 817	202 772	72.4	58 100	20.1	13.7
District 9	82.1	20.8	16 187	37 579	5.5	4.3	2.9	201 872	192 925	74.7	82 800	20.7	13.1
WYOMING	83.0	18.8	12 311	27 096	2.0	11.9	9.3	203 411	168 839	67.8	61 600	18.8	11.9
At Large	83.0	18.8	12 311	27 096	2.0	11.9	9.3	203 411	168 839	67.8	61 600	18.8	11.9

1. Persons 25 years old and older.   2. Based on the population enumerated as of April 1, 1990.   3. Specified owner-occupied units.

STATE District	Housing units, 1990 (cont'd) Occupied units (cont'd) Renter-occupied Median rent[1] (dollars)	Rent as a percent of income	Substandard units[2] (percent)	Civilian labor force, 1990 Total	Unemployment Total	Rate[3]	Civilian employment, 1990[4] Total	Percent Professional, managerial, and technical	Precision production, craft, and repair	Disability, 1990 Work disabled persons[5] (percent)
	44	45	46	47	48	49	50	51	52	53
TEXAS—Con.										
District 28	328	27.5	14.5	236 118	25 781	10.9	210 337	20.1	14.6	10.0
District 29	357	23.9	17.4	268 722	24 372	9.1	244 350	17.5	17.1	7.7
District 30	413	25.7	12.4	288 610	27 414	9.5	261 196	22.6	10.8	8.9
UTAH	369	23.8	5.4	777 448	41 389	5.3	736 059	30.8	11.4	7.3
District 1	364	22.8	5.1	251 977	13 524	5.4	238 453	30.5	12.0	7.3
District 2	379	23.7	3.8	278 409	12 163	4.4	266 246	34.1	9.6	6.8
District 3	358	24.8	7.7	247 062	15 702	6.4	231 360	27.4	12.8	7.8
VERMONT	446	27.1	2.5	300 746	17 600	5.9	283 146	31.3	12.3	7.9
At Large	446	27.1	2.5	300 746	17 600	5.9	283 146	31.3	12.3	7.9
VIRGINIA	495	25.8	4.1	3 170 410	142 048	4.5	3 028 362	33.8	11.5	7.5
District 1	493	25.1	4.2	278 919	12 261	4.4	266 658	32.1	13.9	7.1
District 2	528	27.3	3.0	244 505	13 336	5.5	231 169	33.7	11.7	6.5
District 3	401	27.6	5.1	256 505	21 111	8.2	235 394	22.1	12.2	10.4
District 4	424	25.8	5.0	270 943	14 187	5.2	256 756	26.2	15.5	8.7
District 5	325	23.0	6.0	283 066	13 267	4.7	269 799	21.8	13.3	9.0
District 6	358	23.6	2.9	284 592	11 948	4.2	272 644	25.8	11.8	8.4
District 7	520	24.5	2.1	314 480	9 016	2.9	305 464	37.2	10.9	5.8
District 8	729	26.1	4.3	338 394	10 174	3.0	328 220	52.5	6.0	4.8
District 9	315	26.8	5.3	250 636	17 841	7.1	232 795	23.1	15.0	12.6
District 10	657	24.9	3.1	317 049	9 985	3.1	307 064	38.5	11.8	5.7
District 11	797	26.3	3.8	331 321	8 922	2.7	322 399	47.9	7.4	4.5
WASHINGTON	445	25.7	4.1	2 433 177	139 216	5.7	2 293 961	31.7	11.6	9.1
District 1	587	25.6	2.5	297 349	10 541	3.5	286 808	37.2	11.3	6.6
District 2	468	25.7	4.1	260 820	13 052	5.0	247 768	25.9	16.0	9.2
District 3	414	24.9	3.5	257 075	17 337	6.7	239 738	27.9	12.2	10.5
District 4	333	24.1	7.4	252 252	21 016	8.3	231 236	25.7	10.2	9.7
District 5	345	26.8	3.3	249 711	18 589	7.4	231 122	30.0	9.8	10.5
District 6	415	26.1	4.2	240 079	17 254	7.2	222 825	29.3	12.6	11.3
District 7	462	26.9	4.3	312 107	15 483	5.0	296 624	40.4	7.3	8.4
District 8	550	24.9	2.8	292 610	11 004	3.8	281 606	36.4	12.0	6.7
District 9	478	24.9	4.4	271 174	14 940	5.5	256 234	28.4	13.6	9.3
WEST VIRGINIA	303	26.8	4.0	742 227	71 142	9.6	671 085	25.4	14.5	12.6
District 1	307	26.8	2.9	259 983	22 313	8.6	237 670	25.8	14.2	9.9
District 2	321	25.0	4.3	262 039	22 157	8.5	239 882	25.4	14.0	11.4
District 3	284	28.9	4.7	220 205	26 672	12.1	193 533	24.9	15.5	16.6
WISCONSIN	399	24.9	2.6	2 517 238	130 799	5.2	2 386 439	26.4	11.5	7.3
District 1	401	24.7	2.4	279 309	16 363	5.9	262 946	24.2	13.6	7.7
District 2	441	25.4	2.4	305 316	11 006	3.6	294 310	32.6	9.2	6.1
District 3	336	25.6	2.7	276 114	14 778	5.4	261 336	23.5	10.4	7.4
District 4	448	24.6	2.7	289 999	13 381	4.6	276 618	27.5	12.3	7.4
District 5	435	28.3	4.0	262 758	21 519	8.2	241 239	32.0	8.3	9.3
District 6	349	23.3	2.0	273 295	13 169	4.8	260 126	21.8	12.8	7.1
District 7	327	24.7	3.0	264 755	16 602	6.3	248 153	22.7	11.4	8.1
District 8	357	23.5	2.4	274 228	14 487	5.3	259 741	24.0	12.4	7.0
District 9	430	22.4	1.5	291 464	9 494	3.3	281 970	28.3	13.0	5.8
WYOMING	333	23.7	3.1	220 980	13 112	5.9	207 868	27.2	13.2	7.3
At Large	333	23.7	3.1	220 980	13 112	5.9	207 868	27.2	13.2	7.3

1. Specified renter-occupied units.   2. Overcrowded or lacking complete plumbing facilities.   3. Percent of total civilian labor force.   4. Persons 16 years old and older.   5. Persons 16 to 64 years of age.

Appendices

Page

A-1   A. Geographic Concepts and Codes

B-1   B. Metropolitan Statistical Areas and Components

C-1   C. Metropolitan Statistical Areas and Components by State

D-1   D. Maps of States and Congressional Districts

E-1   E. Cities by County

F-1   F. Source Notes and Explanations

Appendices

APPENDIX A
GEOGRAPHIC CONCEPTS AND CODES

AREAS FOR WHICH DATA ARE PRESENTED

County and City Extra presents data for States (Table A), States and Counties (Table B), Metropolitan Areas (Table C), Cities (Table D), and Congressional Districts (Table E).

STATES AND COUNTIES

Data are presented for each of the 50 states, the District of Columbia, and the United States as a whole. The states are arranged alphabetically, and in Table B counties are arranged alphabetically within each state.

Data are presented for 3,144 counties and county equivalents. Maps of each state, showing their counties and county equivalents, and their metropolitan areas are contained in Appendix D.

County equivalents

In Louisiana, the primary divisions of the state are known as parishes rather than counties. In Alaska, the county equivalents are the organized boroughs, together with the census areas that were developed for general statistical purposes by the State of Alaska and the U.S. Bureau of the Census. Four states—Maryland, Missouri, Nevada, and Virginia—have one or more incorporated places that are legally independent of any county and thus constitute primary divisions of their states. Similarly, the portion of Yellowstone National Park in Montana was, until 1999, treated as a county equivalent. Within each state, independent cities are listed alphabetically following the list of counties. A list of independent cities is given at the end of this Appendix. The District of Columbia is not divided into counties or county equivalents—data for the entire District are presented as a county equivalent.

For a number of the data series in this volume, separate data are not available for some of the smaller county equivalents. In particular, data for the smaller independent cities in Virginia often are combined with an adjacent county. Where this is known to be the case, it is indicated in the footnotes.

New York City contains five counties—Bronx, Kings, New York, Queens, and Richmond. Where data available for the city as a whole cannot be allocated among the component counties, the data are shown on the line for New York County and a footnote is provided.

Alaska

Two changes in county equivalents in Alaska occurred since 1990.

1) Denali Borough was formed primarily from the Yukon-Koyukuk Census area and a small part of the Southeast Fairbanks Census Area.

2) The Skagway-Yakutat-Angoon Census Area was dissolved and replaced by Yakutat Borough and the Skagway-Hoonah-Angoon Census Area.

METROPOLITAN AREAS

Table C presents data for 335 metropolitan areas comprising 248 metropolitan statistical areas (MSAs), 17 consolidated metropolitan statistical areas (CMSAs), 58 primary metropolitan statistical areas (PMSAs), and 12 New England county metropolitan areas (NECMAs). The left-hand column of each page provides an alphabetical listing of MSAs, CMSAs, and NECMAs—PMSAs are listed alphabetically under the CMSAs of which they are components.

The metropolitan areas used in this edition of *County and City Extra* are those defined by the U.S. government based on 1990 census data. These definitions were first issued by the U.S. Office of Management and Budget in December 1992. Additional revisions were issued in June 1993. One new MSA (Hattiesburg, MS) was added in June 1994 and two others (Flagstaff, AZ and Grand Junction, CO) in June 1995. In 1996, two new MSAs (Jonesboro, AR and Pocatello, ID) were added; and Chester County, TN was added to the Jackson, TN MSA. Missoula, MT was added in 1998. Auburn-Opalika, AL and Corvallis, OR were added in 1999. All definition changes through 1999 have been incorporated into this volume in Table C, Appendix B, and Appendix C. The maps in Appendix D, however, show the metropolitan areas as of 1993.

In general, a metropolitan area is a geographic area consisting of a large population nucleus together with adjacent communities that have a high degree of economic and social integration with that nucleus. The major purpose of defining these areas is to enable all U.S. government agencies to use the same geographic definitions in tabulating and publishing data.

Metropolitan complexes with populations of one million or more may be divided into primary metropolitan statistical areas (PMSAs) with the support of local opinion. When PMSAs are defined, the larger metropolitan area of which they are components is designated a consolidated metropolitan statistical area (CMSA).

For most of the United States, metropolitan areas are defined in terms of counties because counties are the smallest geographical units for which a wide variety of statistical data can be obtained. In New England, however, the metropolitan area definitions are in terms of cities and towns because these subcounty units are of great local significance. An alternative concept for the New England states is the New England County Metropolitan Area (NECMA). NECMAs, rather than MSAs, CMSAs, and PMSAs, are presented for New England in this volume to allow presentation of a variety of data that are available only for counties and groups of counties.

CITIES

Table D presents data for 1,078 cities with 1990 populations of 25,000 or more. Corresponding data for states are also provided. The states are arranged alphabetically, and the cities are arranged alphabetically within each state.

As used in this volume, the term "city" refers to places that have been incorporated as cities, boroughs, towns, or villages under the laws of their respective states. However, towns in the New England states and New York are treated as Minor Civil Divisions (MCDs) and are not included in the cities database. For Hawaii, data for Census Designated Places (CDPs) are included in the Cities table, since the U.S. Bureau of the Census does not recognize any incorporated places in Hawaii. CDPs are delineated by the U.S. Bureau of the Census, in cooperation with states and localities, as statistical counterparts of incorporated places for purposes of the decennial census. CDPs comprise densely settled concentrations of population that are identifiable by name, but are not legally incorporated places.

A consolidated city is an incorporated place that has combined its governmental functions with a county or subcounty entity but contains one or more other semi-independent incorporated places that continue to function as local governments within the consolidated government.

Consolidated cities included in this volume are Milford, CT; Jacksonville, FL; Columbus, GA; Indianapolis, IN; Butte-Silver Bow, MT; and Nashville-Davidson, TN. Two additional consolidated cities in Georgia (Athens-Clarke County and Augusta-Richmond County) were formed since the 1990 Census but this volume continues to include the orginal cities for compatibility with other data sources.

In this volume, the data are for the "consolidated city" where possible. The Census Bureau did not estimate 1999 populations for consolidated cities, so 1999 populations (and 1990 populations to measure change) are for the "remainder" portion: the consolidated city minus any semi-independent places located within the consolidated city. In general, the "remainder" is the primary incorporated place or core city of the consolidated city.

CONGRESSIONAL DISTRICTS

The congressional districts shown in this volume are the districts used for the election of the 105th Congress, which convened in January 1997. These are the districts that were established following the 1990 Census and are based on population data from that census. As a result of litigation, states' Congressional Districts have changed since the 103rd Congress, the original boundaries established after the 1990 Census. Data are shown for the 435 regular districts plus the District of Columbia, which has no voting representative. Corresponding data for each state are also included. States are listed alphabetically and districts numerically within each state. A map showing congressional districts may be found on page D80–D81.

GEOGRAPHIC CODES

Tables A, B, C, and D provide, in one or more columns at the beginning of the table, a geographic code or codes for each area.

In Table B (States and Counties) a five-digit state and county code is given for each state and county. The first two digits indicate the state, the remaining three represent the county. Within each state the counties are numbered in alphabetical order, beginning with 001, with even numbers usually omitted. Independent cities follow the counties and begin with the number 510. In the second column of Table B, a four-digit metropolitan area (MSA, PMSA, or NECMA) code is given for those counties that are within metropolitan areas. In Table A a two-digit state code is provided. The state code is a sequential numbering, with some gaps, of the states and the District of Columbia in alphabetical order from Alabama (01) to Wyoming (56).

These codes have been established by the U.S. government as Federal Information Processing Standards and are often referred to as "FIPS codes." They are used by U.S. government agencies and many other organizations for data presentation. They are provided in this volume for use in matching the data given here with other data sources in which counties may be identified by FIPS code. The metro area codes will also enable the user to identify the metro area of which a county is a component. Table C (Metropolitan Areas) provides the same metro area codes for each metropolitan area.

Table D (Cities) provides, in the first column, a seven-digit state and place code. The first two digits identify the state and are the same as the state FIPS codes described above. The remaining five digits are the place FIPS codes established by the U.S. government.

INDEPENDENT CITIES

Independent cities are not included in any county; data are presented separately in this volume where available.

MARYLAND:
    Baltimore: (Separate from Baltimore County)

MISSOURI:
    St. Louis: (Separate from St. Louis County)

NEVADA:
    Carson City

VIRGINIA:

Alexandria	Manassas
Bedford	Manassas Park
Bristol	Martinsville
Buena Vista	Newport News
Charlottesville	Norfolk
Chesapeake	Norton
Clifton Forge	Petersburg
Colonial Heights	Poquoson
Covington	Portsmouth
Danville	Radford
Emporia	Richmond
Fairfax	Roanoke
Falls Church	Salem
Franklin	South Boston*
Fredericksburg	Staunton
Galax	Suffolk
Hampton	Virginia Beach
Harrisonburg	Waynesboro
Hopewell	Williamsburg
Lexington	Winchester
Lynchburg	

*In 1995, South Boston City became a town within Halifax County.

COUNTY TYPE

Table B (States and Counties) provides, in the third column, a "county type" code which identifies each county by its metropolitan/nonmetropolitan status and its size. These codes were developed by the Economic Research Service (ERS) of the U.S. Department of Agriculture and are commonly referred to as "Beale" codes after their originator, Calvin Beale. The ERS county typology scheme goes beyond the Beale codes to a detailed typology of economic and land use classifications. In this volume, the basic Beale codes are used:

Metropolitan Counties

(0) Central county of a metropolitan area of 1 milion population or more.

(1) Fringe county of a metropolitan area of 1 million population or more.

(2) County in a metropolitan area of 250,000 to 1,000,000 population.

(3) County in a metropolitan area of less than 250,000 population.

Nonmetropolitan Counties

(4) Urban population of 20,000 or more, adjacent to a metropolitan area.

(5) Urban population of 20,000 or more, not adjacent to a metropolitan area.

(6) Urban population of 2,500–19,999, adjacent to a metropolitan area.

(7) Urban population of 2,500–19,999, not adjacent to a metropolitan area.

(8) Completely rural (no places with a population of 2,500 or more), adjacent to a metropolitan area.

(9) Completely rural (no places with a population of 2,500 or more), not adjacent to a metropolitan area.

METROPOLITAN STATISTICAL AREAS AND COMPONENTS

(MSA = metropolitan statistical area; CMSA = consolidated MSA; PMSA = primary MSA; and
NECMA = New England county metropolitan area. For further information, see Appendix A.)

MSA/ CMSA/ PMSA/ NECMA	State and County	Title and geographic components	1990 population	MSA/ CMSA/ PMSA/ NECMA	State and County	Title and geographic components	1990 population
0040		Abilene, TX MSA	119 655	13 057		Cherokee County, GA	90 204
	48 441	Taylor County, TX	119 655	13 063		Clayton County, GA	182 052
0080		Akron, OH PMSA	657 575	13 067		Cobb County, GA............	447 745
		(See Cleveland-Akron, OH CMSA)		13 077		Coweta County, GA	53 853
0120		Albany, GA MSA	112 561	13 089		De Kalb County, GA	545 837
	13 095	Dougherty County, GA	96 311	13 097		Douglas County, GA	71 120
	13 177	Lee County, GA	16 250	13 113		Fayette County, GA	62 415
0160		Albany-Schenectady-Troy, NY MSA	861 424	13 117		Forsyth County, GA	44 083
	36 001	Albany County, NY	292 594	13 121		Fulton County, GA	648 951
	36 057	Montgomery County, NY	51 981	13 135		Gwinnett County, GA	352 910
	36 083	Rensselaer County, NY	154 429	13 151		Henry County, GA	58 741
	36 091	Saratoga County, NY	181 276	13 217		Newton County, GA	41 808
	36 093	Schenectady County, NY	149 285	13 223		Paulding County, GA	41 611
	36 095	Schoharie County, NY	31 859	13 227		Pickens County, GA	14 432
				13 247		Rockdale County, GA	54 091
0200		Albuquerque, NM MSA	589 131	13 255		Spalding County, GA	54 457
	35 001	Bernalillo County, NM	480 577	13 297		Walton County, GA	38 586
	35 043	Sandoval County, NM	63 319	0560		Atlantic-Cape May, NJ PMSA	319 416
	35 061	Valencia County, NM	45 235			(See Philadelphia-Wilmington-Atlantic City, PA-NJ-DE-MD CMSA)	
0220		Alexandria, LA MSA	131 556				
	22 079	Rapides Parish, LA	131 556	0580		Auburn-Opalika, AL	87 146
0240		Allentown-Bethlehem-Easton, PA MSA	59 081		01 081	Lee County, AL	87 146
	42 025	Carbon County, PA	56 846	0600		Augusta-Aiken, GA-SC MSA	415 184
	42 077	Lehigh County, PA	291 130		13 073	Columbia County, GA	66 031
	42 095	Northampton County, PA	247 105		13 189	McDuffie County, GA	20 119
0280		Altoona, PA MSA	130 542		13 245	Richmond County, GA	189 719
	42 013	Blair County, PA	130 542		45 003	Aiken County, SC	120 940
0320		Amarillo, TX MSA	187 547		45 037	Edgefield County, SC	18 375
	48 375	Potter County, TX	97 874	0640		Austin-San Marcos, TX MSA	846 227
	48 381	Randall County, TX	89 673		48 021	Bastrop County, TX	38 263
0380		Anchorage, AK MSA	226 338		48 055	Caldwell County, TX	26 392
	02 020	Anchorage Borough, AK	226 338		48 209	Hays County, TX	65 614
0440		Ann Arbor, MI PMSA	490 058		48 453	Travis County, TX	576 407
		(See Detroit-Ann Arbor-Flint, MI CMSA)			48 491	Williamson County, TX	139 551
0450		Anniston, AL MSA	116 034	0680		Bakersfield, CA MSA	543 477
	01 015	Calhoun County, AL	116 034		06 029	Kern County, CA	543 477
0460		Appleton-Oshkosh-Neenah, WI MSA	315 121	0720		Baltimore, MD PMSA	2 382 172
	55 015	Calumet County, WI	34 291			(See Washington-Baltimore, DC-MD-VA-WV CMSA)	
	55 087	Outagamie County, WI	140 510				
	55 139	Winnebago County, WI	40 320	0733		Bangor, ME NECMA	146 601
					23 019	Penobscot County, ME	146 601
0480		Asheville, NC MSA	191 774	0743		Barnstable-Yarmouth, MA NECMA	186 605
	37 021	Buncombe County, NC	174 821		25 001	Barnstable County, MA	186 605
	37 115	Madison County, NC	16 953	0760		Baton Rouge, LA MSA	528 264
0500		Athens, GA MSA	126 262		22 005	Ascension Parish, LA	58 214
	13 059	Clarke County, GA	87 594		22 033	East Baton Rouge Parish, LA	380 105
	13 195	Madison County, GA	21 050		22 063	Livingston Parish, LA	70 526
	13 219	Oconee County, GA	17 618		22 121	West Baton Rouge Parish, LA	19 419
0520		Atlanta, GA MSA	2 959 950	0840		Beaumont-Port Arthur, TX MSA	361 226
	13 013	Barrow County, GA	29 721		48 199	Hardin County, TX	41 320
	13 015	Bartow County, GA	55 911		48 245	Jefferson County, TX	239 397
	13 045	Carroll County, GA	71 422		48 361	Orange County, TX	80 509
				0860		Bellingham, WA MSA	127 780
					53 073	Whatcom County, WA	127 780

Metropolitan Statistical Areas and Components – Continued

(MSA = metropolitan statistical area; CMSA = consolidated MSA; PMSA = primary MSA; and NECMA = New England county metropolitan area. For further information, see Appendix A.)

MSA/ CMSA/ PMSA/ NECMA	State and County	Title and geographic components	1990 population
0870		Benton Harbor, MI MSA	161 378
	26 021	Berrien County, MI	161 378
0875		Bergen-Passaic, NJ PMSA	1 278 440
		(See New York-Northern New Jersey-Long Island, NY-NJ-CT-PA CMSA)	
0880		Billings, MT MSA	113 419
	30 111	Yellowstone County, MT	113 419
0920		Biloxi-Gulfport-Pascagoula, MS MSA	312 368
	28 045	Hancock County, MS	31 760
	28 047	Harrison County, MS	165 365
	28 059	Jackson County, MS	115 243
0960		Binghamton, NY MSA	264 497
	36 007	Broome County, NY	212 160
	36 107	Tioga County, NY	52 337
1000		Birmingham, AL MSA	840 140
	01 009	Blount County, AL	39 248
	01 073	Jefferson County, AL	651 525
	01 115	St. Clair County, AL	50 009
	01 117	Shelby County, AL	99 358
1010		Bismarck, ND MSA	83 831
	38 015	Burleigh County, ND	60 131
	38 059	Morton County, ND	23 700
1020		Bloomington, IN MSA	108 978
	18 105	Monroe County, IN	108 978
1040		Bloomington-Normal, IL MSA	129 180
	17 113	McLean County, IL	129 180
1080		Boise City, ID MSA	295 851
	16 001	Ada County, ID	205 775
	16 027	Canyon County, ID	90 076
1123		Boston-Worcester-Lawrence-Lowell-Brockton, MA-NH NECMA	5 685 998
	25 005	Bristol County, MA	506 325
	25 009	Essex County, MA	670 080
	25 017	Middlesex County, MA	1 398 468
	25 021	Norfolk County, MA	616 087
	25 023	Plymouth County, MA	435 276
	25 025	Suffolk County, MA	663 906
	25 027	Worcester County, MA	709 705
	33 011	Hillsborough County, NH	336 073
	33 015	Rockingham County, NH	245 845
	33 017	Strafford County, NH	104 233
1125		Boulder-Longmont, CO PMSA	225 339
		(See Denver-Boulder-Greeley, CO CMSA)	
1145		Brazoria, TX PMSA	191 707
		(See Houston-Galveston-Brazoria, TX CMSA)	
1150		Bremerton, WA PMSA	189 731
		(See Seattle-Tacoma-Bremerton, WA CMSA)	
1240		Brownsville-Harlingen-San Benito, TX MSA	260 120
	48 061	Cameron County, TX	260 120
		Bryan-College Station, TX MSA	121 862
1260	48 041	Brazos County, TX	121 862
1280		Buffalo-Niagara Falls, NY MSA	36 029
	36 029	Erie County, NY	968 532
	36 063	Niagara County, NY	220 756
1303		Burlington, VT NECMA	177 059
	50 007	Chittenden County, VT	131 761
	50 011	Franklin County, VT	39 980
	50 013	Grand Isle County, VT	5 318
1320		Canton-Massillon, OH MSA	394 106
	39 019	Carroll County, OH	26 521
	39 151	Stark County, OH	367 585
1350		Casper, WY MSA	61 226
	56 025	Natrona County, WY	61 226
1360		Cedar Rapids, IA MSA	168 767
	19 113	Linn County, IA	168 767
1400		Champaign-Urbana, IL MSA	173 025
	17 019	Champaign County, IL	173 025
1480		Charleston, WV MSA	250 454
	54 039	Kanawha County, WV	207 619
	54 079	Putnam County, WV	42 835
1440		Charleston-North Charleston, SC MSA	506 875
	45 015	Berkeley County, SC	128 776
	45 019	Charleston County, SC	295 039
	45 035	Dorchester County, SC	83 060
1520		Charlotte-Gastonia-Rock Hill, NC-SC MSA	1 162 093
	37 025	Cabarrus County, NC	98 935
	37 071	Gaston County, NC	175 093
	37 109	Lincoln County, NC	50 319
	37 119	Mecklenburg County, NC	511 433
	37 159	Rowan County, NC	110 605
	37 179	Union County, NC	84 211
	45 091	York County, SC	131 497
1540		Charlottesville, VA MSA	131 107
	51 003	Albemarle County, VA	68 040
	51 065	Fluvanna County, VA	12 429
	51 079	Greene County, VA	10 297
	51 540	Charlottesville City, VA	40 341
1560		Chattanooga, TN-GA MSA	424 347
	13 047	Catoosa County, GA	42 464
	13 083	Dade County, GA	13 147
	13 295	Walker County, GA	58 340
	47 065	Hamilton County, TN	285 536
	47 115	Marion County, TN	24 860
1580		Cheyenne, WY MSA	73 142
	56 021	Laramie County, WY	73 142
14		Chicago-Gary-Kenosha, IL-IN-WI CMSA	8 239 820
1600		Chicago, IL PMSA	7 410 858
	17 031	Cook County, IL	5 105 067
	17 037	De Kalb County, IL	77 932
	17 043	Du Page County, IL	781 666

Metropolitan Statistical Areas and Components – Continued

(MSA = metropolitan statistical area; CMSA = consolidated MSA; PMSA = primary MSA; and NECMA = New England county metropolitan area. For further information, see Appendix A.)

Geographic codes — MSA/CMSA/PMSA/NECMA	State and County	Title and geographic components	1990 population
	17 063	Grundy County, IL	32 337
	17 089	Kane County, IL	317 471
	17 093	Kendall County, IL	39 413
	17 097	Lake County, IL	516 418
	17 111	McHenry County, IL	183 241
	17 197	Will County, IL	357 313
2960		Gary, IN PMSA	604 526
	18 089	Lake County, IN	475 594
	18 127	Porter County, IN	128 932
3740		Kankakee, IL PMSA	96 255
	17 091	Kankakee County, IL	96 255
3800		Kenosha , WI PMSA	128 181
	55 059	Kenosha County, WI	128 181
1620		Chico-Paradise, CA MSA	182 120
	06 007	Butte County, CA	182 120
21		Cincinnati-Hamilton, OH-KY-IN CMSA	1 817 571
1640		Cincinnati, OH-KY-IN PMSA	1 526 092
	18 029	Dearborn County, IN	38 835
	18 115	Ohio County, IN	5 315
	21 015	Boone County, KY	57 589
	21 037	Campbell County, KY	83 866
	21 077	Gallatin County, KY	5 393
	21 081	Grant County, KY	15 737
	21 117	Kenton County, KY	142 031
	21 191	Pendleton County, KY	12 036
	39 015	Brown County, OH	34 966
	39 025	Clermont County, OH	150 187
	39 061	Hamilton County, OH	866 228
	39 165	Waren County, OH	113 909
3200		Hamilton-Middletown, OH PMSA	291 479
	39 017	Butler County, OH	291 479
1660		Clarksville-Hopkinsville, TN-KY MSA	169 439
	21 047	Christian County, KY	68 941
	47 125	Montgomery County, TN	100 498
28		Cleveland-Akron, OH CMSA	2 859 644
0080		Akron, OH PMSA	657 575
	39 133	Portage County, OH	142 585
	39 153	Summit County, OH	514 990
1680		Cleveland-Lorain-Elyria, OH PMSA	2 202 069
	39 007	Ashtabula County, OH	99 821
	39 035	Cuyahoga County, OH	1 412 140
	39 055	Geauga County, OH	81 129
	39 085	Lake County, OH	215 499
	39 093	Lorain County, OH	271 126
	39 103	Medina County, OH	122 354
1720		Colorado Springs, CO MSA	397 014
	08 041	El Paso County, CO	397 014
1740		Columbia, MO MSA	112 379
	29 019	Boone County, MO	112 379

Geographic codes — MSA/CMSA/PMSA/NECMA	State and County	Title and geographic components	1990 population
1760		Columbia, SC MSA	453 331
	45 063	Lexington County, SC	167 611
	45 079	Richland County, SC	285 720
1800		Columbus, GA-AL MSA	260 860
	01 113	Russell County, AL	46 860
	13 053	Chattahoochee County, GA	16 934
	13 145	Harris County, GA	17 788
	13 215	Muscogee County, GA	179 278
1840		Columbus, OH MSA	1 345 450
	39 041	Delaware County, OH	66 929
	39 045	Fairfield County, OH	103 461
	39 049	Franklin County, OH	961 437
	39 089	Licking County, OH	128 300
	39 097	Madison County, OH	37 068
	39 129	Pickaway County, OH	48 255
1880		Corpus Christi, TX MSA	349 894
	48 355	Nueces County, TX	291 145
	48 409	San Patricio County, TX	58 749
1890		Corvallis, OR	70 811
	41 003	Benton County, OR	70 811
1900		Cumberland, MD-WV MSA	101 643
	24 001	Allegany County, MD	74 946
	54 057	Mineral County, WV	26 697
31		Dallas-Fort Worth, TX CMSA	4 037 282
1920		Dallas, TX PMSA	2 676 248
	48 085	Collin County, TX	264 036
	48 113	Dallas County, TX	1 852 810
	48 121	Denton County, TX	273 525
	48 139	Ellis County, TX	85 167
	48 213	Henderson County, TX	58 543
	48 231	Hunt County, TX	64 343
	48 257	Kaufman County, TX	52 220
	48 397	Rockwall County, TX	25 604
2800		Fort Worth-Arlington, TX PMSA	1 361 034
	48 221	Hood County, TX	28 981
	48 251	Johnson County, TX	97 165
	48 367	Parker County, TX	64 785
	48 439	Tarrant County, TX	1 170 103
1950		Danville, VA MSA	108 711
	51 143	Pittsylvania County, VA	55 655
	51 590	Danville City, VA	53 056
1960		Davenport-Moline-Rock Island , IA-IL MSA	350 861
	17 073	Henry County, IL	51 159
	17 161	Rock Island County, IL	148 723
	19 163	Scott County, IA	150 979
2000		Dayton-Springfield, OH MSA	951 270
	39 023	Clark County, OH	147 548
	39 057	Greene County, OH	136 731
	39 109	Miami County, OH	93 182
	39 113	Montgomery County, OH	573 809
2020		Daytona Beach, FL MSA	399 413
	12 035	Flagler County, FL	28 701
	12 127	Volusia County, FL	370 712

Metropolitan Statistical Areas and Components – Continued

(MSA = metropolitan statistical area; CMSA = consolidated MSA; PMSA = primary MSA; and
NECMA = New England county metropolitan area. For further information, see Appendix A.)

MSA/CMSA/PMSA/NECMA	State and County	Title and geographic components	1990 population	MSA/CMSA/PMSA/NECMA	State and County	Title and geographic components	1990 population
2030		Decatur, AL MSA	131 556	2290		Eau Claire, WI MSA	137 543
	01 079	Lawrence County, AL	31 513		55 017	Chippewa County, WI	52 360
	01 103	Morgan County, AL	100 043		55 035	Eau Claire County, WI	851 83
2040		Decatur, IL MSA	117 206	2320		El Paso, TX MSA	591 610
	17 115	Macon County, IL	117 206		48 141	El Paso County, TX	591 610
34		Denver-Boulder-Greeley, CO CMSA	1 980 140	2330		Elkhart-Goshen, IN MSA	156 198
					18 039	Elkhart County, IN	156 198
1125		Boulder-Longmont, CO PMSA	225 339				
	08 013	Boulder County, CO	225 339	2335		Elmira, NY MSA	95 195
					36 015	Chemung County, NY	95 195
2080		Denver, CO PMSA	1 622 980				
	08 001	Adams County, CO	265 038	2340		Enid, OK MSA	56 735
	08 005	Arapahoe County, CO	391 511		40 047	Garfield County, OK	56 735
	08 031	Denver County, CO	467 610				
	08 035	Douglas County, CO	60 391	2360		Erie, PA MSA	275 572
	08 059	Jefferson County, CO	438 430		42 049	Erie County, PA	275 572
3060		Greeley, CO PMSA	131 821	2400		Eugene-Springfield, OR MSA	282 912
	08 123	Weld County, CO	131 821		41 039	Lane County, OR	282 912
2120		Des Moines, IA MSA	392 928	2440		Evansville-Henderson, IN-KY MSA	278 990
	19 049	Dallas County, IA	29 755		18 129	Posey County, IN	25 968
	19 153	Polk County, IA	327 140		18 163	Vanderburgh County, IN	165 058
	19 181	Warren County, IA	36 033		18 173	Warrick County, IN	44 920
35		Detroit-Ann Arbor-Flint, MI CMSA	5 187 171		21 101	Henderson County, KY	43 044
				2520		Fargo-Moorehead, ND-MN MSA	153 296
0440		Ann Arbor, MI PMSA	490 058		27 027	Clay County, MN	50 422
	26 091	Lenawee County, MI	91 476		38 017	Cass County, ND	102 874
	26 093	Livingston County, MI	115 645	2560		Fayetteville, NC MSA	274 566
	26 161	Washtenaw County, MI	282 937		37 051	Cumberland County, NC	274 566
2160		Detroit, MI PMSA	4 266 654	2580		Fayetteville-Springdale-Rogers, AR MSA	210 908
	26 087	Lapeer County, MI	74 768		05 007	Benton County, AR	97 499
	26 099	Macomb County, MI	717 400		05 143	Washington County, AR	113 409
	26 115	Monroe County, MI	133 600	2620		Flagstaff, AZ-UT MSA	101 760
	26 125	Oakland County, MI	1 083 592		04 005	Coconino County, AZ	96 591
	26 147	St. Clair County, MI	145 607		49 025	Kane County, UT	5 169
	26 163	Wayne County, MI	2 111 687	2640		Flint, MI PMSA	430 459
2640		Flint, MI PMSA	430 459			(See Detroit-Ann Arbor-Flint, MI CMSA)	
	26 049	Genesee County, MI	430 459				
2180		Dothan, AL MSA	130 964	2650		Florence, AL MSA	131 327
	01 045	Dale County, AL	50 632		01 033	Colbert County, AL	51 666
	01 069	Houston County, AL	81 331		01 077	Lauderdale County, AL	79 661
2190		Dover, DE MSA	110 993	2655		Florence, SC MSA	114 344
	10 001	Kent County, DE	110 993		45 041	Florence County, SC	114 344
2200		Dubuque, IA MSA	86 403	2670		Fort Collins-Loveland, CO MSA	186 136
	19 061	Dubuque County, IA	86 403		08 069	Larimer County, CO	186 136
2240		Duluth-Superior, MN-WI MSA	239 971	2680		Fort Lauderdale, FL PMSA	1 255 488
	27 137	St. Louis County, MN	198 213			(See Miami-Fort Lauderdale, FL CMSA)	
	55 031	Douglas County, WI	41 758				
2281		Dutchess County, NY PMSA	259 462	2700		Fort Myers-Cape Coral, FL MSA	335 113
		(See New York-Northern New Jersey-Long Island, NY-NJ-CT-PA CMSA)			12 071	Lee County, FL	335 113

Metropolitan Statistical Areas and Components – Continued

(MSA = metropolitan statistical area; CMSA = consolidated MSA; PMSA = primary MSA; and
NECMA = New England county metropolitan area. For further information, see Appendix A.)

MSA/ CMSA/ PMSA/ NECMA	State and County	Title and geographic components	1990 population	MSA/ CMSA/ PMSA/ NECMA	State and County	Title and geographic components	1990 population
						(See Denver-Boulder-Greeley, CO CMSA)	
2710		Fort Pierce-Port St. Lucie, FL MSA	251 071				
	12 085	Martin County, FL	100 900	3080		Green Bay, WI MSA	194 594
	12 111	St. Lucie County, FL	150 171		55 009	Brown County, WI	194 594
2720		Fort Smith, AR-OK MSA	175 911	3120		Greensboro-Winston Salem-	
	05 033	Crawford County, AR	42 493			High Point, NC MSA	1 050 304
	05 131	Sebastian County, AR	99 590		37 001	Alamance County, NC	108 213
	40 135	Sequoyah County, OK	33 828		37 057	Davidson County, NC	126 677
					37 059	Davie County, NC	27 859
2750		Fort Walton Beach, FL MSA	143 776		37 067	Forsyth County, NC	265 878
	12 091	Okaloosa County, FL	143 776		37 081	Guilford County, NC	347 420
2760		Fort Wayne, IN MSA	456 281		37 151	Randolph County, NC	106 546
	18 001	Adams County, IN	31 095		37 169	Stokes County, NC	37 223
	18 003	Allen County, IN	300 836		37 197	Yadkin County, NC	30 488
	18 033	De Kalb County, IN	35 324				
	18 069	Huntington County, IN	35 427	3150		Greenville, NC MSA	107 924
	18 179	Wells County, IN	25 948		37 147	Pitt County, NC	107 924
	18 183	Whitley County, IN	27 651	3160		Greenville-Spartanburg-Anderson, SC MSA	830 563
2800		Fort Worth-Arlington, TX PMSA	1 361 034		45 007	Anderson County, SC	145 196
		(See Dallas-Fort Worth, TX CMSA)			45 021	Cherokee County, SC	44 506
					45 045	Greenville County, SC	320 167
2840		Fresno, CA MSA	755 580		45 077	Pickens County, SC	93 894
	06 019	Fresno County, CA	667 490		45 083	Spartanburg County, SC	226 800
	06 039	Madera County, CA	88 090	3180		Hagerstown, MD PMSA	121 393
2880		Gadsden, AL MSA	99 840			(See Washington-Baltimore, DC-MD-VA-WV CMSA)	
	01 055	Etowah County, AL	99 840				
		.		3200		Hamilton-Middletown, OH PMSA	29 479
2900		Gainesville, FL MSA	181 596			(See Cincinnati-Hamilton, OH-KY-IN CMSA)	
	12 001	Alachua County, FL	181 596				
2920		Galveston-Texas City, TX PMSA	217 399	3240		Harrisburg-Lebanon-Carlisle, PA MSA	587 986
		(See Houston-Galveston-			42 041	Cumberland County, PA	195 257
		Brazoria, TX CMSA)			42 043	Dauphin County, PA	237 813
					42 075	Lebanon County, PA	113 744
2960		Gary, IN PMSA	604 526		42 099	Perry County, PA	41 172
		(See Chicago-Gary-Kenosha, IL-IN-WI CMSA)		3283		Hartford, CT NECMA	1 123 678
					09 003	Hartford County, CT	851 783
2975		Glens Falls, NY MSA	118 539		09 007	Middlesex County, CT	143 196
	36 113	Warren County, NY	59 209		09 013	Tolland County, CT	128 699
	36 115	Washington County, NY	59 330	3285		Hattiesburg, MS MSA	98 738
2980		Goldsboro, NC MSA	104 666		28 035	Forrest County, MS	68 314
	37 191	Wayne County, NC	104 666		28 073	Lamar County, MS	30 424
2985		Grand Forks, ND-MN MSA	103 181	3290		Hickory-Morganton-Lenoir, NC MSA	292 409
	27 119	Polk County, MN	32 498		37 003	Alexander County, NC	27 544
	38 035	Grand Forks County, ND	70 683		37 023	Burke County, NC	75 744
2995		Grand Junction, CO MSA	93 145		37 027	Caldwell County, NC	70 709
	08 077	Mesa County, CO	93 145		37 035	Catawba County, NC	118 412
3000		Grand Rapids-Muskegon-Holland, MI MSA	937 891	3320		Honolulu, HI MSA	836 231
	26 005	Allegan County, MI	90 509		15 003	Honolulu County, HI	836 231
	26 081	Kent County, MI	500 631	3350		Houma, LA MSA	182 842
	26 121	Muskegon County, MI	158 983		22 057	Lafourche Parish, LA	85 860
	26 139	Ottawa County, MI	187 768		22 109	Terrebonne Parish, LA	96 982
3040		Great Falls, MT MSA	77 691	42		Houston-Galveston-Brazoria, TX CMSA	3 731 131
	30 013	Cascade County, MT	77 691				
3060		Greeley, CO PMSA	131 821	1145		Brazoria, TX PMSA	191 707

Metropolitan Statistical Areas and Components – Continued

(MSA = metropolitan statistical area; CMSA = consolidated MSA; PMSA = primary MSA; and
NECMA = New England county metropolitan area. For further information, see Appendix A.)

Geographic codes		Title and geographic components	1990 population	Geographic codes		Title and geographic components	1990 population
MSA/ CMSA/ PMSA/ NECMA	State and County			MSA/ CMSA/ PMSA/ NECMA	State and County		
	48 039	Brazoria County, TX	191 707	3640		Jersey City, NJ PMSA	553 099
2920		Galveston-Texas City, TX PMSA	217 399			(See New York-Northern New Jersey-	
	48 167	Galveston County, TX	217 399			Long Island, NY-NJ-CT-PA CMSA)	
3360		Houston, TX PMSA	3 322 025	3660		Johnson City-Kingsport-Bristol, TN-VA MSA	436 047
	48 071	Chambers County, TX	20 088		47 019	Carter County, TN	51 505
	48 157	Fort Bend County, TX	225 421		47 073	Hawkins County, TN	44 565
	48 201	Harris County, TX	2 818 199		47 163	Sullivan County, TN	143 596
	48 291	Liberty County, TX	52 726		47 171	Unicoi County, TN	16 549
	48 339	Montgomery County, TX	182 201		47 179	Washington County, TN	92 315
	48 473	Waller County, TX	23 390		51 169	Scott County, VA	23 204
3400		Huntington-Ashland, WV-KY-OH MSA	312 529		51 191	Washington County, VA	45 887
	21 019	Boyd County, KY	51 150		51 520	Bristol City, VA	18 426
	21 043	Carter County, KY	24 340	3680		Johnstown, PA MSA	241 247
	21 089	Greenup County, KY	36 742		42 021	Cambria County, PA	163 029
	39 087	Lawrence County, OH	61 834		42 111	Somerset County, PA	78 218
	54 011	Cabell County, WV	96 827	3700		Jonesboro, AR MSA	68 956
	54 099	Wayne County, WV	41 636		05 031	Craighead County, AR	68 956
3440		Huntsville, AL MSA	293 047	3710		Joplin, MO MSA	134 910
	01 083	Limestone County, AL	54 135		29 097	Jasper County, MO	90 465
	01 089	Madison County, AL	238 912		29 145	Newton County, MO	44 445
3480		Indianapolis, IN MSA	1 380 491	3720		Kalamazoo-Battle Creek, MI MSA	429 453
	18 011	Boone County, IN	38 147		26 025	Calhoun County, MI	135 982
	18 057	Hamilton County, IN	108 936		26 077	Kalamazoo County, MI	223 411
	18 059	Hancock County, IN	45 527		26 159	Van Buren County, MI	70 060
	18 063	Hendricks County, IN	75 717				
	18 081	Johnson County, IN	88 109	3740		Kankakee, IL PMSA	96 255
	18 095	Madison County, IN	130 669			(See Chicago-Gary-Kenosha, IL-IN-WI CMSA)	
	18 097	Marion County, IN	797 159	3760		Kansas City, MO-KS MSA	1 582 875
	18 109	Morgan County, IN	55 920		20 091	Johnson County, KS	355 054
	18 145	Shelby County, IN	40 307		20 103	Leavenworth County, KS	64 371
3500		Iowa City, IA MSA	96 119		20 121	Miami County, KS	23 466
	19 103	Johnson County, IA	96 119		20 209	Wyandotte County, KS	161 993
3520		Jackson, MI MSA	149 756		29 037	Cass County, MO	63 808
	26 075	Jackson County, MI	149 756		29 047	Clay County, MO	153 411
3560		Jackson, MS MSA	395 396		29 049	Clinton County, MO	16 595
	28 049	Hinds County, MS	254 441		29 095	Jackson County, MO	633 232
	28 089	Madison County, MS	53 794		29 107	Lafayette County, MO	31 107
	28 121	Rankin County, MS	87 161		29 165	Platte County, MO	57 867
					29 177	Ray County, MO	21 971
3580		Jackson, TN MSA	90 801	3800		Kenosha, WI PMSA	128 181
	47 023	Chester County, TN	12 819			(See Chicago-Gary-Kenosha, IL-IN-WI CMSA)	
	47 113	Madison County, TN	77 982	3810		Killeen-Temple, TX MSA	255 301
3600		Jacksonville, FL MSA	906 727		48 027	Bell County, TX	191 088
	12 019	Clay County, FL	105 986		48 099	Coryell County, TX	64 213
	12 031	Duval County, FL	672 971				
	12 089	Nassau County, FL	43 941	3840		Knoxville, TN MSA	585 960
	12 109	St. Johns County, FL	83 829		47 001	Anderson County, TN	68 250
3605		Jacksonville, NC MSA	149 838		47 009	Blount County, TN	85 969
	37 133	Onslow County, NC	149 838		47 093	Knox County, TN	335 749
3610		Jamestown, NY MSA	141 895		47 105	Loudon County, TN	31 255
	36 013	Chautauqua County, NY	141 895		47 155	Sevier County, TN	51 043
3620		Janesville-Beloit, WI MSA	139 510		47 173	Union County, TN	13 694
	55 105	Rock County, WI	139 510	3850		Kokomo, IN MSA	96 946
					18 067	Howard County, IN	80 827
					18 159	Tipton County, IN	16 119

Metropolitan Statistical Areas and Components – Continued

(MSA = metropolitan statistical area; CMSA = consolidated MSA; PMSA = primary MSA; and
NECMA = New England county metropolitan area. For further information, see Appendix A.)

MSA/CMSA/PMSA/NECMA	State and County	Title and geographic components	1990 population	MSA/CMSA/PMSA/NECMA	State and County	Title and geographic components	1990 population
				31 109		Lancaster County, NE	213 641
3870		La Crosse, WI-MN MSA	116 401				
	27 055	Houston County, MN	18 497	4400		Little Rock-North Little Rock, AR MSA	513 117
	55 063	La Crosse County, WI	97 904		05 045	Faulkner County, AR	60 006
3920		Lafayette, IN MSA	161 572		05 085	Lonoke County, AR	39 268
	18 023	Clinton County, IN	30 974		05 119	Pulaski County, AR	349 660
	18 157	Tippecanoe County, IN	130 598		05 125	Saline County, AR	64 183
3880		Lafayette, LA MSA	344 953	4420		Longview-Marshall, TX MSA	193 801
	22 001	Acadia Parish, LA	55 882		48 183	Gregg County, TX	104 948
	22 055	Lafayette Parish, LA	164 762		48 203	Harrison County, TX	57 483
	22 097	St. Landry Parish, LA	80 331		48 459	Upshur County, TX	31 370
	22 099	St. Martin Parish, LA	43 978	49		Los Angeles-Riverside-Orange, CA CMSA	14 531 529
3960		Lake Charles, LA MSA	168 134	4480		Los Angeles-Long Beach, CA PMSA	8 863 164
	22 019	Calcasieu Parish, LA	168 134		06 037	Los Angeles County, CA	8 863 164
3980		Lakeland-Winter Haven, FL MSA	405 382	5945		Orange County, CA PMSA	2 410 556
	12 105	Polk County, FL	405 382		06 059	Orange County, CA	2 410 556
4000		Lancaster, PA MSA	422 822	6780		Riverside-San Bernardino, CA PMSA	2 588 793
	42 071	Lancaster County, PA	422 822		06 065	Riverside County, CA	1 170 413
4040		Lansing-East Lansing, MI MSA	432 674		06 071	San Bernardino County, CA	1 418 380
	26 037	Clinton County, MI	57 883	8735		Ventura, CA PMSA	669 016
	26 045	Eaton County, MI	92 879		06 111	Ventura County, CA	669 016
	26 065	Ingham County, MI	281 912	4520		Louisville, KY-IN MSA	948 829
4080		Laredo, TX MSA	133 239		18 019	Clark County, IN	87 777
	48 479	Webb County, TX	133 239		18 043	Floyd County, IN	64 404
4100		Las Cruces, NM MSA	135 510		18 061	Harrison County, IN	29 890
	35 013	Dona Ana County, NM	135 510		18 143	Scott County, IN	20 991
4120		Las Vegas, NV-AZ MSA	852 737		21 029	Bullitt County, KY	47 567
	04 015	Mohave County, AZ	93 497		21 111	Jefferson County, KY	664 937
	32 003	Clark County, NV	741 459		21 185	Oldham County, KY	33 263
	32 023	Nye County, NV	17 781	4600		Lubbock, TX MSA	222 636
4150		Lawrence, KS MSA	81 798		48 303	Lubbock County, TX	222 636
	20 045	Douglas County, KS	81 798	4640		Lynchburg, VA MSA	193 928
4200		Lawton, OK MSA	111 486		51 009	Amherst County, VA	28 578
	40 031	Comanche County, OK	111 486		51 019	Bedford County, VA	45 656
4243		Lewiston-Auburn, ME NECMA	105 259		51 031	Campbell County, VA	47 572
	23 001	Androscoggin County, ME	105 259		51 515	Bedford City, VA	6 073
4280		Lexington, KY MSA	405 936		51 680	Lynchburg City, VA	66 049
	21 017	Bourbon County, KY	19 236	4680		Macon, GA MSA	290 909
	21 049	Clark County, KY	29 496		13 021	Bibb County, GA	149 967
	21 067	Fayette County, KY	225 366		13 153	Houston County, GA	89 208
	21 113	Jessamine County, KY	30 508		13 169	Jones County, GA	20 739
	21 151	Madison County, KY	57 508		13 225	Peach County, GA	21 189
	21 209	Scott County, KY	23 867		13 289	Twiggs County, GA	9 806
	21 239	Woodford County, KY	19 955	4720		Madison, WI MSA	367 085
4320		Lima, OH MSA	154 340		55 025	Dane County, WI	367 085
	39 003	Allen County, OH	109 755	4800		Mansfield, OH MSA	174 007
	39 011	Auglaize County, OH	44 585		39 033	Crawford County, OH	47 870
					39 139	Richland County, OH	126 137
				4880		McAllen-Edinburg-Mission, TX MSA	383 545
4360		Lincoln, NE MSA	213 641		48 215	Hidalgo County, TX	383 545
				4890		Medford-Ashland, OR MSA	146 389

Metropolitan Statistical Areas and Components – Continued

(MSA = metropolitan statistical area; CMSA = consolidated MSA; PMSA = primary MSA; and
NECMA = New England county metropolitan area. For further information, see Appendix A.)

MSA/ CMSA/ PMSA/ NECMA	State and County	Title and geographic components	1990 population	MSA/ CMSA/ PMSA/ NECMA	State and County	Title and geographic components	1990 population
	41 029	Jackson County, OR	146 389	5240		Montgomery, AL MSA	292 517
4900		Melbourne-Titusville-Palm Bay, FL MSA	398 978		01 001	Autauga County, AL	34 222
	12 009	Brevard County, FL	398 978		01 051	Elmore County, AL	49 210
					01 101	Montgomery County, AL	209 085
4920		Memphis, TN-AR-MS MSA	1 007 306	5280		Muncie, IN MSA	119 659
	05 035	Crittenden County, AR	49 939		18 035	Delaware County, IN	119 659
	28 033	De Soto County, MS	67 910	5330		Myrtle Beach, SC MSA	144 053
	47 047	Fayette County, TN	25 559		45 051	Horry County, SC	144 053
	47 157	Shelby County, TN	826 330	5345		Naples, FL MSA	152 099
	47 167	Tipton County, TN	37 568		12 021	Collier County, FL	152 099
4940		Merced, CA MSA	178 403	5360		Nashville, TN MSA	985 026
	06 047	Merced County, CA	178 403		47 021	Cheatham County, TN	27 140
					47 037	Davidson County, TN	510 784
56		Miami-Fort Lauderdale, FL CMSA	3 192 582		47 043	Dickson County, TN	35 061
					47 147	Robertson County, TN	41 494
2680		Fort Lauderdale, FL PMSA	1 255 488		47 149	Rutherford County, TN	118 570
	12 011	Broward County, FL	1 255 488		47 165	Sumner County, TN	103 281
					47 187	Williamson County, TN	81 021
5000		Miami, FL PMSA	1 937 094		47 189	Wilson County, TN	67 675
	12 025	Dade County, FL	1 937 094				
				5380		Nassau-Suffolk, NY PMSA	2 609 212
63		Milwaukee-Racine, WI CMSA	1 607 183			(See New York-Northern New Jersey-	
						Long Island, NY-NJ-CT-PA CMSA)	
5080		Milwaukee-Waukesha , WI PMSA	1 432 149				
	55 079	Milwaukee County, WI	959 275	5523		New London-Norwich, CT NECMA	254 957
	55 089	Ozaukee County, WI	72 831		09 011	New London County, CT	254 957
	55 131	Washington County, WI	95 328				
	55 133	Waukesha County, WI	304 715	5560		New Orleans, LA MSA	1 285 270
					22 051	Jefferson Parish, LA	448 306
6600		Racine, WI PMSA	175 034		22 071	Orleans Parish, LA	496 938
	55 101	Racine County, WI	175 034		22 075	Plaquemines Parish, LA	25 575
					22 087	St. Bernard Parish, LA	66 631
5120		Minneapolis-St. Paul, MN-WI MSA	2 538 834		22 089	St. Charles Parish, LA	42 437
	27 003	Anoka County, MN	243 641		22 093	St. James Parish, LA	20 879
	27 019	Carver County, MN	47 915		22 095	St. John the Baptist Parish, LA	39 996
	27 025	Chisago County, MN	30 521		22 103	St. Tammany Parish, LA	144 508
	27 037	Dakota County, MN	275 227				
	27 053	Hennepin County, MN	1 032 431	5600		New York, NY PMSA	8 546 846
	27 059	Isanti County, MN	25 921			(See New York-Northern New Jersey-	
	27 123	Ramsey County, MN	485 765			Long Island, NY-NJ-CT-PA CMSA)	
	27 139	Scott County, MN	57 846				
	27 141	Sherburne County, MN	41 945	70		New York-Northern New Jersey-Long Island, NY-NJ-CT-PA CMSA	19 462 450
	27 163	Washington County, MN	145 896				
	27 171	Wright County, MN	68 710	0875		Bergen-Passaic, NJ PMSA	1 278 440
	55 093	Pierce County, WI	32 765		34 003	Bergen County, NJ	825 380
	55 109	St. Croix County, WI	50 251		34 031	Passaic County, NJ	453 060
5140		Missoula, MT MSA	78 687	2281		Dutchess County, NY PMSA	259 462
	30 063	Missoula County, MT	78 687		36 027	Dutchess County, NY	259 462
5160		Mobile, AL MSA	476 923	3640		Jersey City, NJ PMSA	553 099
	01 003	Baldwin County, AL	98 280		34 017	Hudson County, NJ	553 099
	01 097	Mobile County, AL	378 643				
				5015		Middlesex-Somerset-Hunterdon, NJ PMSA	1 019 835
5170		Modesto, CA MSA	370 522		34 019	Hunterdon County, NJ	107 776
	06 099	Stanislaus County, CA	370 522		34 023	Middlesex County, NJ	671 780
					34 035	Somerset County, NJ	240 279
5190		Monmouth-Ocean, NJ PMSA	986 327				
		(See New York-Northern New Jersey-		5190		Monmouth-Ocean, NJ PMSA	986 327
		Long Island, NY-NJ-CT-PA CMSA)			34 025	Monmouth County, NJ	553 124
5200		Monroe, LA MSA	142 191				
	22 073	Ouachita Parish, LA	142 191				

Metropolitan Statistical Areas and Components – Continued

(MSA = metropolitan statistical area; CMSA = consolidated MSA; PMSA = primary MSA; and
NECMA = New England county metropolitan area. For further information, see Appendix A.)

MSA/ CMSA/ PMSA/ NECMA	State and County	Title and geographic components	1990 population	MSA/ CMSA/ PMSA/ NECMA	State and County	Title and geographic components	1990 population
	34 029	Ocean County, NJ	433 203		40 027	Cleveland County, OK	174 253
5380		Nassau-Suffolk, NY PMSA	2 609 212		40 083	Logan County, OK	29 011
	36 059	Nassau County, NY	1 287 348		40 087	McClain County, OK	22 795
	36 103	Suffolk County, NY	1 321 864		40 109	Oklahoma County, OK	599 611
5483		New Haven-Bridgeport-Stamford-Danbury-			40 125	Pottawatomie County, OK	58 760
		Waterbury, CT NECMA	1 631 864	5910		Olympia, WA PMSA	161 238
	09 001	Fairfield County, CT	827 645			(See Seattle-Tacoma-Bremerton, WA CMSA)	
	09 009	New Haven County, CT	804 219				
				5920		Omaha, NE-IA MSA	639 580
5600		New York, NY PMSA	8 546 846		19 155	Pottawattamie County, IA	82 628
	36 005	Bronx County, NY	1 203 789		31 025	Cass County, NE	21 318
	36 047	Kings County, NY	2 300 664		31 055	Douglas County, NE	416 444
	36 061	New York County, NY	1 487 536		31 153	Sarpy County, NE	102 583
	36 079	Putnam County, NY	83 941		31 177	Washington County, NE	16 607
	36 081	Queens County, NY	1 951 598				
	36 085	Richmond County, NY	378 977	5945		Orange County, CA PMSA	2 410 556
	36 087	Rockland County, NY	265 475			(See Los Angeles-Riverside-Orange	
	36 119	Westchester County, NY	874 866			County, CA CMSA)	
5640		Newark, NJ PMSA	1 915 928	5960		Orlando, FL MSA	1 224 852
	34 013	Essex County, NJ	778 206		12 069	Lake County, FL	152 104
	34 027	Morris County, NJ	421 353		12 095	Orange County, FL	677 491
	34 037	Sussex County, NJ	130 943		12 097	Osceola County, FL	107 728
	34 039	Union County, NJ	493 819		12 117	Seminole County, FL	287 529
	34 041	Warren County, NJ	91 607	5990		Owensboro, KY MSA	87 189
5660		Newburgh, NY-PA PMSA	335 613		21 059	Daviess County, KY	87 189
	36 071	Orange County, NY	307 647	6015		Panama City, FL MSA	126 994
	42 103	Pike County, PA	27 966		12 005	Bay County, FL	126 994
8480		Trenton, NJ PMSA	325 824	6020		Parkersburg-Marietta, WV-OH MSA	149 169
	34 021	Mercer County, NJ	325 824		39 167	Washington County, OH	62 254
5720		Norfolk-Virginia Beach-Newport News,			54 107	Wood County, WV	86 915
		VA-NC MSA	1 443 244				
	37 053	Currituck County, NC	13 736	6080		Pensacola, FL MSA	344 406
	51 073	Gloucester County, VA	30 131		12 033	Escambia County, FL	262 798
	51 093	Isle of Wight County, VA	25 053		12 113	Santa Rosa County, FL	81 608
	51 095	James City County, VA	34 859				
	51 115	Mathews County, VA	8 348	6120		Peoria-Pekin, IL MSA	339 172
	51 199	York County, VA	42 422		17 143	Peoria County, IL	182 827
	51 550	Chesapeake City, VA	151 976		17 179	Tazewell County, IL	123 692
	51 650	Hampton City, VA	133 793		17 203	Woodford County, IL	32 653
	51 700	Newport News City, VA	170 045				
	51 710	Norfolk City, VA	261 229	77		Philadelphia-Wilmington-Atlantic City,	
	51 735	Poquoson City, VA	11 005			PA-NJ-DE-MD CMSA	5 892 937
	51 740	Portsmouth City, VA	103 907				
	51 800	Suffolk City, VA	52 141	0560		Atlantic-Cape May, NJ PMSA	319 416
	51 810	Virginia Beach City, VA	393 069		34 001	Atlantic County, NJ	224 327
	51 830	Williamsburg City, VA	11 530		34 009	Cape May County, NJ	95 089
5775		Oakland, CA PMSA	2 082 914	6160		Philadelphia, PA-NJ PMSA	4 922 175
		(See San Francisco-Oakland-			34 005	Burlington County, NJ	395 066
		San Jose, CA CMSA)			34 007	Camden County, NJ	502 824
5790		Ocala, FL MSA	194 833		34 015	Gloucester County, NJ	230 082
	12 083	Marion County, FL	194 833		34 033	Salem County, NJ	65 294
5800		Odessa-Midland, TX MSA	225 545		42 017	Bucks County, PA	541 174
	48 135	Ector County, TX	118 934		42 029	Chester County, PA	376 396
	48 329	Midland County, TX	106 611		42 045	Delaware County, PA	547 651
					42 091	Montgomery County, PA	678 111
					42 101	Philadelphia County, PA	1 585 577
5880		Oklahoma City, OK MSA	958 839	8760		Vineland-Millville-Bridgeton, NJ PMSA	138 053
	40 017	Canadian County, OK	74 409		34 011	Cumberland County, NJ	138 053

(MSA = metropolitan statistical area; CMSA = consolidated MSA; PMSA = primary MSA; and
NECMA = New England county metropolitan area. For further information, see Appendix A.)

MSA/CMSA/PMSA/NECMA	State and County	Title and geographic components	1990 population	MSA/CMSA/PMSA/NECMA	State and County	Title and geographic components	1990 population
				37 101		Johnston County, NC	81 306
9160		Wilmington-Newark, DE-MD PMSA	513 293	37 135		Orange County, NC	93 851
	10 003	New Castle County, DE	441 946	37 183		Wake County, NC	423 380
	24 015	Cecil County, MD	71 347				
6200		Phoenix-Mesa, AZ MSA	2 238 480	6660		Rapid City, SD MSA	81 343
	04 013	Maricopa County, AZ	2 122 101		46 103	Pennington County, SD	81 343
	04 021	Pinal County, AZ	116 379				
				6680		Reading, PA MSA	336 523
6240		Pine Bluff, AR MSA	85 487		42 011	Berks County, PA	336 523
	05 069	Jefferson County, AR	85 487				
				6690		Redding, CA MSA	147 036
6280		Pittsburgh, PA MSA	2 394 811		06 089	Shasta County, CA	147 036
	42 003	Allegheny County, PA	1 336 449				
	42 007	Beaver County, PA	186 093	6720		Reno, NV MSA	254 667
	42 019	Butler County, PA	152 013		32 031	Washoe County, NV	254 667
	42 051	Fayette County, PA	145 351				
	42 125	Washington County, PA	204 584	6740		Richland-Kennewick-Pasco, WA MSA	150 033
	42 129	Westmoreland County, PA	370 321		53 005	Benton County, WA	112 560
					53 021	Franklin County, WA	37 473
6323		Pittsfield, MA NECMA	139 352				
	25 003	Berkshire County, MA	139 352	6760		Richmond-Petersburg, VA MSA	865 640
					51 036	Charles City County, VA	6 282
6340		Pocatello, ID MSA	66 026		51 041	Chesterfield County, VA	209 274
	16 005	Bannock County, ID	66 026		51 053	Dinwiddie County, VA	20 960
					51 075	Goochland County, VA	14 163
6403		Portland, ME NECMA	243 135		51 085	Hanover County, VA	63 306
	23 005	Cumberland County, ME	243 135		51 087	Henrico County, VA	217 881
					51 127	New Kent County, VA	10 445
79		Portland-Salem, OR-WA CMSA	1 793 476		51 145	Powhatan County, VA	15 328
					51 149	Prince George County, VA	27 394
6440		Portland-Vancouver, OR-WA PMSA	1 515 452		51 570	Colonial Heights City, VA	16 064
	41 005	Clackamas County, OR	278 850		51 670	Hopewell City, VA	23 101
	41 009	Columbia County, OR	37 557		51 730	Petersburg City, VA	38 386
	41 051	Multnomah County, OR	583 887		51 760	Richmond City, VA	203 056
	41 067	Washington County, OR	311 554				
	41 071	Yamhill County, OR	65 551	6780		Riverside-San Bernardino, CA PMSA	2 588 793
	53 011	Clark County, WA	238 053			(See Los Angeles-Riverside-Orange County, CA CMSA)	
7080		Salem, OR PMSA	278 024				
	41 047	Marion County, OR	228 483	6800		Roanoke, VA MSA	224 477
	41 053	Polk County, OR	49 541		51 023	Botetourt County, VA	24 992
					51 161	Roanoke County, VA	79 332
6483		Providence-Warwick-Pawtucket, RI NECMA	916 270		51 770	Roanoke City, VA	96 397
	44 001	Bristol County, RI	48 859		51 775	Salem City, VA	23 756
	44 003	Kent County, RI	161 135				
	44 007	Providence County, RI	596 270	6820		Rochester, MN MSA	106 470
	44 009	Washington County, RI	110 006		27 109	Olmsted County, MN	106 470
6520		Provo-Orem, UT MSA	263 590	6840		Rochester, NY MSA	1 062 470
	49 049	Utah County, UT	263 590		36 037	Genesee County, NY	60 060
					36 051	Livingston County, NY	62 372
6560		Pueblo, CO MSA	123 051		36 055	Monroe County, NY	713 968
	08 101	Pueblo County, CO	123 051		36 069	Ontario County, NY	95 101
					36 073	Orleans County, NY	41 846
6580		Punta Gorda, FL MSA	110 975		36 117	Wayne County, NY	89 123
	12 015	Charlotte County, FL	110 975				
				6880		Rockford, IL MSA	329 676
6600		Racine, WI PMSA	175 034		17 007	Boone County, IL	30 806
		(See Milwaukee-Racine, WI CMSA)			17 141	Ogle County, IL	45 957
					17 201	Winnebago County, IL	252 913
6640		Raleigh-Durham-Chapel Hill, NC MSA	855 545				
	37 037	Chatham County, NC	38 759	6895		Rocky Mount, NC MSA	133 235
	37 063	Durham County, NC	181 835		37 065	Edgecombe County, NC	56 558
	37 069	Franklin County, NC	36 414		37 127	Nash County, NC	76 677

Metropolitan Statistical Areas and Components – Continued

(MSA = metropolitan statistical area; CMSA = consolidated MSA; PMSA = primary MSA; and NECMA = New England county metropolitan area. For further information, see Appendix A.)

MSA/CMSA/PMSA/NECMA	State and County	Title and geographic components	1990 population
82		Sacramento-Yolo, CA CMSA	1 481 102
6920		Sacramento, CA PMSA	1 340 010
	06 017	El Dorado County, CA	125 995
	06 061	Placer County, CA	172 796
	06 067	Sacramento County, CA	1 041 219
9270		Yolo, CA PMSA	141 092
	06 113	Yolo County, CA	141 092
6960		Saginaw-Bay City-Midland, MI MSA	399 320
	26 017	Bay County, MI	111 723
	26 111	Midland County, MI	75 651
	26 145	Saginaw County, MI	211 946
6980		St. Cloud, MN MSA	148 976
	27 009	Benton County, MN	30 185
	27 145	Stearns County, MN	118 791
7000		St. Joseph, MO MSA	97 715
	29 003	Andrew County, MO	14 632
	29 021	Buchanan County, MO	83 083
7040		St. Louis, MO-IL MSA	2 492 525
	17 027	Clinton County, IL	33 944
	17 083	Jersey County, IL	20 539
	17 119	Madison County, IL	249 238
	17 133	Monroe County, IL	22 422
	17 163	St. Clair County, IL	262 852
	29 071	Franklin County, MO	80 603
	29 099	Jefferson County, MO	171 380
	29 113	Lincoln County, MO	28 892
	29 183	St. Charles County, MO	212 907
	29 510	St. Louis City, MO	396 685
	29 189	St. Louis County, MO	993 529
	29 219	Warren County, MO	19 534
7080		Salem, OR PMSA	278 024
		(See Portland-Salem, OR-WA CMSA)	
7120		Salinas, CA MSA	355 660
	06 053	Monterey County, CA	355 660
7160		Salt Lake City-Ogden, UT MSA	1 072 227
	49 011	Davis County, UT	187 941
	49 035	Salt Lake County, UT	725 956
	49 057	Weber County, UT	158 330
7200		San Angelo, TX MSA	98 458
	48 451	Tom Green County, TX	98 458
7240		San Antonio, TX MSA	1 324 749
	48 029	Bexar County, TX	1 185 394
	48 091	Comal County, TX	51 832
	48 187	Guadalupe, TX	64 873
	48 493	Wilson County, TX	22 650
7320		San Diego, CA MSA	2 498 016
	06 073	San Diego County, CA	2 498 016
84		San Francisco-Oakland-San Jose, CA CMSA	6 253 311
5775		Oakland, CA PMSA	2 082 914
	06 001	Alameda County, CA	1 279 182
	06 013	Contra Costa County, CA	803 732
7360		San Francisco, CA PMSA	1 603 678
	06 041	Marin County, CA	230 096
	06 075	San Francisco County, CA	723 959
	06 081	San Mateo County, CA	649 623
7400		San Jose, CA PMSA	1 497 577
	06 085	Santa Clara County, CA	1 497 577
7485		Santa Cruz-Watsonville, CA PMSA	229 734
	06 087	Santa Cruz County, CA	229 734
7500		Santa Rosa, CA PMSA	388 222
	06 097	Sonoma County, CA	388 222
8720		Vallejo-Fairfield-Napa, CA PMSA	451 186
	06 055	Napa County, CA	110 765
	06 095	Solano County, CA	340 421
7460		San Luis Obispo-Atascadero-Paso Robles, CA MSA	217 162
	06 079	San Luis Obispo County, CA	217 162
7480		Santa Barbara-Santa Maria-Lompoc, CA MSA	369 608
	06 083	Santa Barbara County, CA	369 608
7490		Santa Fe, NM MSA	117 043
	35 028	Los Alamos County, NM	18 115
	35 049	Santa Fe County, NM	98 928
7510		Sarasota-Bradenton, FL MSA	489 483
	12 081	Manatee County, FL	211 707
	12 115	Sarasota County, FL	277 776
7520		Savannah, GA MSA	258 060
	13 029	Bryan County, GA	15 438
	13 051	Chatham County, GA	216 935
	13 103	Effingham County, GA	25 687
7560		Scranton-Wilkes-Barre-Hazleton, PA MSA	638 466
	42 037	Columbia County, PA	63 202
	42 069	Lackawanna County, PA	219 039
	42 079	Luzerne County, PA	328 149
	42 131	Wyoming County, PA	28 076
91		Seattle-Tacoma-Bremerton, WA CMSA	2 970 328
1150		Bremerton, WA PMSA	189 731
	53 035	Kitsap County, WA	189 731
5910		Olympia, WA PMSA	161 238
	53 067	Thurston County, WA	161 238
7600		Seattle-Bellevue-Everett, WA PMSA	2 033 156
	53 029	Island County, WA	60 195
	53 033	King County, WA	1 507 319
	53 061	Snohomish County, WA	465 642
8200		Tacoma, WA PMSA	586 203
	53 053	Pierce County, WA	586 203
7610		Sharon, PA MSA	121 003
	42 085	Mercer County, PA	121 003
7620		Sheboygan, WI MSA	103 877
	55 117	Sheboygan County, WI	103 877

Metropolitan Statistical Areas and Components – Continued

(MSA = metropolitan statistical area; CMSA = consolidated MSA; PMSA = primary MSA; and
NECMA = New England county metropolitan area. For further information, see Appendix A.)

MSA/CMSA/PMSA/NECMA	State and County	Title and geographic components	1990 population	MSA/CMSA/PMSA/NECMA	State and County	Title and geographic components	1990 population
7640		Sherman-Denison, TX MSA	95 021		12 101	Pasco County, FL	281 131
	48 181	Grayson County, TX	95 021		12 103	Pinellas County, FL	851 659
7680		Shreveport-Bossier City, LA MSA	376 330	8320		Terre Haute, IN MSA	147 585
	22 015	Bossier Parish, LA	86 088		18 021	Clay County, IN	24 705
	22 017	Caddo Parish, LA	248 253		18 165	Vermillion County, IN	16 773
	22 119	Webster Parish, LA	41 989		18 167	Vigo County, IN	106 107
7720		Sioux City, IA-NE MSA	115 018	8360		Texarkana, TX-Texarkana, AR MSA	120 132
	19 193	Woodbury County, IA	98 276		05 091	Miller County, AR	38 467
	31 043	Dakota County, NE	16 742		48 037	Bowie County, TX	81 665
7760		Sioux Falls, SD MSA	139 236	8400		Toledo, OH MSA	614 128
	46 083	Lincoln County, SD	15 427		39 051	Fulton County, OH	38 498
	46 099	Minnehaha County, SD	123 809		39 095	Lucas County, OH	462 361
7800		South Bend, IN MSA	247 052		39 173	Wood County, OH	113 269
	18 141	St. Joseph County, IN	247 052	8440		Topeka, KS MSA	160 976
7840		Spokane, WA MSA	361 364		20 177	Shawnee County, KS	160 976
	53 063	Spokane County, WA	361 364	8480		Trenton, NJ PMSA	325 824
7880		Springfield, IL MSA	189 550			(See New York-Northern New Jersey-Long Island, NY-NJ-CT-PA CMSA)	
	17 129	Menard County, IL	11 164	8520		Tucson, AZ MSA	666 880
	17 167	Sangamon County, IL	178 386		04 019	Pima County, AZ	666 880
8003		Springfield, MA NECMA	602 878	8560		Tulsa, OK MSA	708 954
	25 013	Hampden County, MA	456 310		40 037	Creek County, OK	60 915
	25 015	Hampshire County, MA	146 568		40 113	Osage County, OK	41 645
7920		Springfield, MO MSA	264 346		40 131	Rogers County, OK	55 170
	29 043	Christian County, MO	32 644		40 143	Tulsa County, OK	503 341
	29 077	Greene County, MO	207 949		40 145	Wagoner County, OK	47 883
	29 225	Webster County, MO	23 753	8600		Tuscaloosa, AL MSA	150 522
8050		State College, PA MSA	123 786		01 125	Tuscaloosa County, AL	150 522
	42 027	Centre County, PA	123 786	8640		Tyler, TX MSA	151 309
8080		Steubenville-Weirton, OH-WV MSA	142 523		48 423	Smith County, TX	151 309
	39 081	Jefferson County, OH	80 298	8680		Utica-Rome, NY MSA	316 633
	54 009	Brooke County, WV	26 992		36 043	Herkimer County, NY	65 797
	54 029	Hancock County, WV	35 233		36 065	Oneida County, NY	250 836
8120		Stockton-Lodi, CA MSA	480 628	8720		Vallejo-Fairfield-Napa, CA PMSA	451 186
	06 077	San Joaquin County, CA	480 628			(See San Francisco-Oakland-San Jose, CA CMSA)	
8140		Sumter, SC MSA	102 637	8735		Ventura, CA PMSA	669 016
	45 085	Sumter County, SC	102 637			(See Los Angeles-Riverside-Orange County, CA CMSA)	
8160		Syracuse, NY MSA	742 177				
	36 011	Cayuga County, NY	82 313	8750		Victoria, TX MSA	74 361
	36 053	Madison County, NY	69 120		48 469	Victoria County, TX	74 361
	36 067	Onondaga County, NY	468 973	8760		Vineland-Millville-Bridgeton, NJ PMSA ..	138 053
	36 075	Oswego County, NY	121 771			(See Philadelphia-Wilmington-Atlantic City, PA-NJ-DE-MD CMSA)	
8200		Tacoma, WA PMSA	586 203				
		(See Seattle-Tacoma-Bremerton, WA CMSA)		8780		Visalia-Tulare-Porterville, CA MSA	311 921
8240		Tallahassee, FL MSA	233 598		06 107	Tulare County, CA	311 921
	12 039	Gadsden County, FL	41 105	8800		Waco, TX MSA	189 123
	12 073	Leon County, FL	192 493		48 309	McLennan County, TX	189 123
8280		Tampa-St. Petersburg-Clearwater, FL MSA	2 067 959				
	12 053	Hernando County, FL	101 115				
	12 057	Hillsborough County, FL	834 054				

Metropolitan Statistical Areas and Components – Continued

(MSA = metropolitan statistical area; CMSA = consolidated MSA; PMSA = primary MSA; and NECMA = New England county metropolitan area. For further information, see Appendix A.)

MSA/ CMSA/ PMSA/ NECMA	State and County	Title and geographic components	1990 population	MSA/ CMSA/ PMSA/ NECMA	State and County	Title and geographic components	1990 population
97		Washington-Baltimore, DC-MD-VA-WV CMSA	6 727 050	8960		West Palm Beach-Boca Raton, FL MSA	863 518
					12 099	Palm Beach County, FL	863 518
0720		Baltimore, MD PMSA	2 382 172				
	24 003	Anne Arundel County, MD	427 239	9000		Wheeling, WV-OH MSA	159 301
	24 005	Baltimore County, MD	692 134		39 013	Belmont County, OH	71 074
	24 013	Carroll County, MD	123 372		54 051	Marshall County, WV	37 356
	24 025	Harford County, MD	182 132		54 069	Ohio County, WV	50 871
	24 027	Howard County, MD	187 328				
	24 035	Queen Anne's County, MD	33 953	9080		Wichita Falls, TX MSA	130 351
	24 510	Baltimore City, MD	736 014		48 009	Archer County, TX	7 973
3180		Hagerstown, MD PMSA	121 393		48 485	Wichita County, TX	122 378
	24 043	Washington County, MD	121 393	9040		Wichita, KS MSA	485 270
					20 015	Butler County, KS	50 580
8840		Washington, DC-MD-VA-WV PMSA	4 223 485		20 079	Harvey County, KS	31 028
	11 001	District of Columbia	606 900		20 173	Sedgwick County, KS	403 662
	24 009	Calvert County, MD	51 372				
	24 017	Charles County, MD	101 154	9140		Williamsport, PA MSA	118 710
	24 021	Frederick County, MD	150 208		42 081	Lycoming County, PA	118 710
	24 031	Montgomery County, MD	757 027				
	24 033	Prince George's County, MD	729 268	9200		Wilmington, NC MSA	171 269
	51 013	Arlington County, VA	170 936		37 019	Brunswick County, NC	50 985
	51 043	Clarke County, VA	12 101		37 129	New Hanover County, NC	120 284
	51 047	Culpeper County, VA	27 791				
	51 059	Fairfax County, VA	818 584	9160		Wilmington-Newark, DE-MD PMSA	513 293
	51 061	Fauquier County, VA	48 741			(See Philadelphia-Wilmington-	
	51 099	King George County, VA	13 527			Atlantic City, PA-NJ-DE-MD CMSA)	
	51 107	Loudoun County, VA	86 129				
	51 153	Prince William County, VA	215 686	9260		Yakima, WA MSA	188 823
	51 177	Spotsylvania County, VA	57 403		53 077	Yakima County, WA	188 823
	51 179	Stafford County, VA	61 236				
	51 187	Warren County, VA	26 142	9270		Yolo, CA PMSA...	141 092
	51 510	Alexandria City, VA	111 183			(See Sacramento-Yolo, CA CMSA)	
	51 600	Fairfax City, VA	19 622				
	51 610	Falls Church City, VA	9 578	9280		York, PA MSA	339 574
	51 630	Fredericksburg City, VA	19 027		42 133	York County, PA	339 574
	51 683	Manassas City, VA	27 957				
	51 685	Manassas Park City, VA	6 734	9320		Youngstown-Warren, OH MSA	600 895
	54 003	Berkeley County, WV	59 253		39 029	Columbiana County, OH	108 276
	54 037	Jefferson County, WV	35 926		39 099	Mahoning County, OH	264 806
					39 155	Trumbull County, OH	227 813
8920		Waterloo-Cedar Falls, IA MSA	123 798				
	19 013	Black Hawk County, IA	123 798	9340		Yuba City, CA MSA	122 643
					06 101	Sutter County, CA	64 415
8940		Wausau, WI MSA...	115 400		06 115	Yuba County, CA	58 228
	55 073	Marathon County, WI	115 400				
				9360		Yuma, AZ MSA	106 895
					04 027	Yuma County, AZ	106 895

APPENDIX C
METROPOLITAN STATISTICAL AREAS AND COMPONENTS BY STATE

The following table is arranged alphabetically by state. Under each state heading, all of the metropolitan areas that lie wholly or partly within that state are listed alphabetically along with their component counties, which are also listed alphabetically. For metropolitan areas that cross state lines, only the counties within a particular state are included under that state. However, the metropolitan area names include the two letter abbreviation for each state involved, and the remaining counties can be located under their respective state headings.

For states containing Consolidated Metropolitan Statistical Areas (CMSAs), or parts of such areas, the CMSAs appear first, followed by the Primary Metropolitan Statistical Areas (PMSAs) that make up the CMSA, and their component counties.

(MSA = metropolitan statistical area; CMSA = consolidated MSA; PMSA = primary MSA; and
NECMA = New England county metropolitan area. For further information, see Appendix A.)

Geographic codes MSA/CMSA/ PMSA/ NECMA	Title and geographic components	Geographic codes MSA/CMSA/ PMSA/ NECMA	Title and geographic components
	ALABAMA		Yuma
0450	ANNISTON, AL (MSA)		
	Calhoun		**ARKANSAS**
0580	AUBURN-OPALIKA, AL (MSA)	2580	FAYETTEVILLE-SPRINGDALE-ROGERS, AR (MSA)
	Lee		Benton
1000	BIRMINGHAM, AL (MSA)		Washington
	Blount	2720	FORT SMITH, AR-OK (MSA)
	Jefferson		Crawford
	St. Clair		Sebastian
	Shelby	3700	JONESBORO, AR (MSA)
1800	COLUMBUS, GA-AL (MSA)		Craighead
	Russell	4400	LITTLE ROCK-NORTH LITTLE ROCK, AR (MSA)
2030	DECATUR, AL (MSA)		Faulkner
	Lawrence		Lonoke
	Morgan		Pulaski
2180	DOTHAN, AL (MSA)		Saline
	Dale	4920	MEMPHIS, TN-AR-MS (MSA)
	Houston		Crittenden
2650	FLORENCE, AL (MSA)	6240	PINE BLUFF, AR (MSA)
	Colbert		Jefferson
	Etowah	8360	TEXARKANA, TX-TEXARKANA, AR (MSA)
3440	HUNTSVILLE, AL (MSA)		Miller
	Limestone		
	Madison		**CALIFORNIA**
5160	MOBILE, AL (MSA)	49	LOS ANGELES-RIVERSIDE-ORANGE COUNTY, CA (CMSA)
	Baldwin	4480	LOS ANGELES-LONG BEACH, CA (PMSA)
	Mobile		Los Angeles
5240	MONTGOMERY, AL (MSA)	5945	ORANGE COUNTY, CA (PMSA)
	Autauga		Orange
	Elmore	6780	RIVERSIDE-SAN BERNARDINO, CA (PMSA)
8600	TUSCALOOSA, AL (MSA)		Riverside
	Tuscaloosa		San Bernardino
		8735	VENTURA, CA (PMSA)
	ALASKA		Ventura
0380	ANCHORAGE, AK (MSA)	82	SACRAMENTO-YOLO, CA (CMSA)
	Anchorage	6920	SACRAMENTO, CA (PMSA)
			El Dorado
	ARIZONA		Placer
2620	FLAGSTAFF, AZ-UT (MSA)		Sacramento
	Coconino	9270	YOLO, CA (PMSA)
4120	LAS VEGAS, NV-AZ (MSA)		Yolo
	Mohave	84	SAN FRANCISCO-OAKLAND-SAN JOSE, CA (CMSA)
6200	PHOENIX-MESA, AZ (MSA)	5775	OAKLAND, CA (PMSA)
	Maricopa		Alameda
	Pinal		Contra Costa
8520	TUCSON, AZ (MSA)	7360	SAN FRANCISCO, CA (PMSA)
	Pima		Marin
9360	YUMA, AZ (MSA)		San Francisco
			San Mateo

(MSA = metropolitan statistical area; CMSA = consolidated MSA; PMSA = primary MSA; and
NECMA = New England county metropolitan area. For further information, see Appendix A.)

Geographic codes MSA/CMSA/ PMSA/ NECMA	Title and geographic components	Geographic codes MSA/CMSA/ PMSA/ NECMA	Title and geographic components
7400	SAN JOSE, CA (PMSA)		Fairfield
	Santa Clara		New Haven
7485	SANTA CRUZ-WATSONVILLE, CA (PMSA)	3283	HARTFORD, CT (NECMA)
	Santa Cruz		Hartford
7500	SANTA ROSA, CA (PMSA)		Middlesex
	Sonoma		Tolland
8720	VALLEJO-FAIRFIELD-NAPA, CA (PMSA)	5523	NEW LONDON-NORWICH, CT (NECMA)
	Napa		New London
	Solano		
0680	BAKERSFIELD, CA (MSA)		**DELAWARE**
	Kern	77	PHILADELPHIA-WILMINGTON-ATLANTIC CITY, PA-NJ-DE-MD (CMSA)
1620	CHICO-PARADISE, CA (MSA)	9160	WILMINGTON-NEWARK, DE-MD (PMSA)
	Butte		New Castle
2840	FRESNO, CA (MSA)	2190	DOVER, DE (MSA)
	Fresno		Kent
	Madera		
4940	MERCED, CA (MSA)		**DISTRICT OF COLUMBIA**
	Merced	97	WASHINGTON-BALTIMORE, DC-MD-VA-WV (CMSA)
5170	MODESTO, CA (MSA)	8840	WASHINGTON, DC-MD-VA-WV (PMSA)
	Stanislaus		District of Columbia
6690	REDDING, CA (MSA)		
	Shasta		**FLORIDA**
7120	SALINAS, CA (MSA)	56	MIAMI-FORT LAUDERDALE, FL (CMSA)
	Monterey	2680	FORT LAUDERDALE, FL (PMSA)
7320	SAN DIEGO, CA (MSA)		Broward
	San Diego	5000	MIAMI, FL (PMSA)
7460	SAN LUIS OBISPO-ATASCADERO-PASO ROBLES, CA (MSA)		Dade
	San Luis Obispo	2020	DAYTONA BEACH, FL (MSA)
7480	SANTA BARBARA-SANTA MARIA-LOMPOC, CA (MSA)		Flagler
	Santa Barbara		Volusia
8120	STOCKTON-LODI, CA (MSA)	2700	FORT MYERS-CAPE CORAL, FL (MSA)
	San Joaquin		Lee
8780	VISALIA-TULARE-PORTERVILLE, CA (MSA)	2710	FORT PIERCE-PORT ST. LUCIE, FL (MSA)
	Tulare		Martin
9340	YUBA CITY, CA (MSA)		St. Lucie
	Sutter	2750	FORT WALTON BEACH, FL (MSA)
	Yuba		Okaloosa
		2900	GAINESVILLE, FL (MSA)
	COLORADO		Alachua
34	DENVER-BOULDER-GREELEY, CO (CMSA)	3600	JACKSONVILLE, FL (MSA)
1125	BOULDER-LONGMONT, CO (PMSA)		Clay
	Boulder		Duval
2080	DENVER, CO (PMSA)		Nassau
	Adams		St. Johns
	Arapahoe	3980	LAKELAND-WINTER HAVEN, FL (MSA)
	Denver		Polk
	Douglas	4900	MELBOURNE-TITUSVILLE-PALM BAY,FL (MSA)
	Jefferson		Brevard
3060	GREELEY, CO (PMSA)	5345	NAPLES, FL (MSA)
	Weld		Collier
1720	COLORADO SPRINGS, CO (MSA)	5790	OCALA, FL (MSA)
	El Paso		Marion
2670	FORT COLLINS-LOVELAND, CO (MSA)	5960	ORLANDO, FL (MSA)
	Larimer		Lake
2995	GRAND JUNCTION, CO (MSA)		Orange
	Mesa		Osceola
6560	PUEBLO, CO (MSA)		Seminole
	Pueblo	6015	PANAMA CITY, FL (MSA)
			Bay
	CONNECTICUT	6080	PENSACOLA, FL (MSA)
70	NEW YORK-NORTHERN NEW JERSEY-LONG ISLAND, NY-NJ-CT-PA (CMSA)		Escambia
			Santa Rosa
5483	NEW HAVEN-BRIDGEPORT-STAMFORD-DANBURY-WATERBURY, CT (NECMA)	6580	PUNTA GORDA, FL (MSA)
			Charlotte
		7510	SARASOTA-BRADENTON, FL (MSA)

(MSA = metropolitan statistical area; CMSA = consolidated MSA; PMSA = primary MSA; and
NECMA = New England county metropolitan area. For further information, see Appendix A.)

Geographic codes MSA/CMSA/ PMSA/ NECMA	Title and geographic components	Geographic codes MSA/CMSA/ PMSA/ NECMA	Title and geographic components
	Manatee		Honolulu
	Sarasota		**IDAHO**
8240	TALLAHASSEE, FL (MSA)	1080	BOISE CITY, ID (MSA)
	Gadsden		Ada
	Leon		Canyon
8280	TAMPA-ST PETERSBURG-CLEARWATER, FL (MSA)	6340	POCATELLO, ID (MSA)
	Hernando		Bannock
	Hillsborough		
	Pasco		**ILLINOIS**
	Pinellas	14	CHICAGO-GARY-KENOSHA, IL-IN-WI (CMSA)
8960	WEST PALM BEACH-BOCA RATON, FL (MSA)	1600	CHICAGO, IL (PMSA)
	Palm Beach		Cook
			De Kalb
	GEORGIA		Du Page
0120	ALBANY, GA (MSA)		Grundy
	Dougherty		Kane
	Lee		Kendall
0500	ATHENS, GA (MSA)		Lake
	Clarke		McHenry
	Madison		Will
	Oconee	3740	KANKAKEE, IL (PMSA)
0520	ATLANTA, GA (MSA)		Kankakee
	Barrow	1040	BLOOMINGTON-NORMAL, IL (MSA)
	Bartow		McLean
	Carroll	1400	CHAMPAIGN-URBANA, IL (MSA)
	Cherokee		Champaign
	Clayton	1960	DAVENPORT-MOLINE-ROCK ISLAND, IA-IL (MSA)
	Cobb		Henry
	Coweta		Rock Island
	De Kalb	2040	DECATUR, IL (MSA)
	Douglas		Macon
	Fayette	6120	PEORIA-PEKIN, IL (MSA)
	Forsyth		Peoria
	Fulton		Tazewell
	Gwinnett		Woodford
	Henry	6880	ROCKFORD, IL (MSA)
	Newton		Boone
	Paulding		Ogle
	Pickens		Winnebago
	Rockdale	7040	ST. LOUIS, MO-IL (MSA)
	Spalding		Clinton
	Walton		Jersey
0600	AUGUSTA-AIKEN, GA-SC (MSA)		Madison
	Columbia		Monroe
	McDuffie		St. Clair
	Richmond	7880	SPRINGFIELD, IL (MSA)
1560	CHATTANOOGA, TN-GA (MSA)		Menard
	Catoosa		Sangamon
	Dade		
	Walker		**INDIANA**
1800	COLUMBUS, GA-AL (MSA)	14	CHICAGO-GARY-KENOSHA, IL-IN-WI (CMSA)
	Chattahoochee	2960	GARY, IN (PMSA)
	Harris		Lake
	Muscogee		Porter
4680	MACON, GA (MSA)	21	CINCINNATI-HAMILTON, OH-KY-IN (CMSA)
	Bibb	1640	CINCINNATI, OH-KY-IN (PMSA)
	Houston		Dearborn
	Jones		Ohio
	Peach	1020	BLOOMINGTON, IN (MSA)
	Twiggs		Monroe
7520	SAVANNAH, GA (MSA)	2330	ELKHART-GOSHEN, IN (MSA)
	Bryan		Elkhart
	Chatham	2440	EVANSVILLE-HENDERSON, IN-KY (MSA)
	Effingham		Posey
	HAWAII		
3320	HONOLULU, HI (MSA)		

Geographic codes MSA/CMSA/ PMSA/ NECMA	Title and geographic components	Geographic codes MSA/CMSA/ PMSA/ NECMA	Title and geographic components
	Vanderburgh	8440	TOPEKA, KS (MSA)
	Warrick		Shawnee
2760	FORT WAYNE, IN (MSA)	9040	WICHITA, KS (MSA)
	Adams		Butler
	Allen		Harvey
	De Kalb		Sedgwick
	Huntington		
	Wells		**KENTUCKY**
	Whitley	21	CINCINNATI-HAMILTON, OH-KY-IN (CMSA)
3480	INDIANAPOLIS, IN (MSA)	1640	CINCINNATI, OH-KY-IN (PMSA)
	Boone		Boone
	Hamilton		Campbell
	Hancock		Gallatin
	Hendricks		Grant
	Johnson		Kenton
	Madison		Pendleton
	Marion	1660	CLARKSVILLE-HOPKINSVILLE, TN-KY (MSA)
	Morgan		Christian
	Shelby	2440	EVANSVILLE-HENDERSON, IN-KY (MSA)
3850	KOKOMO, IN (MSA)		Henderson
	Howard	3400	HUNTINGTON-ASHLAND, WV-KY-OH (MSA)
	Tipton		Boyd
3920	LAFAYETTE, IN (MSA)		Carter
	Clinton		Greenup
	Tippecanoe	4280	LEXINGTON, KY (MSA)
4520	LOUISVILLE, KY-IN (MSA)		Bourbon
	Clark		Clark
	Floyd		Fayette
	Harrison		Jessamine
	Scott		Madison
5280	MUNCIE, IN (MSA)		Scott
	Delaware		Woodford
7800	SOUTH BEND, IN (MSA)	4520	LOUISVILLE, KY-IN (MSA)
	St. Joseph		Bullitt
8320	TERRE HAUTE, IN (MSA)		Jefferson
	Clay		Oldham
	Vermillion	5990	OWENSBORO, KY (MSA)
	Vigo		Daviess
	IOWA		**LOUISIANA**
1360	CEDAR RAPIDS, IA (MSA)	0220	ALEXANDRIA, LA (MSA)
	Linn		Rapides
1960	DAVENPORT-MOLINE-ROCK ISLAND, IA-IL (MSA)	0760	BATON ROUGE, LA (MSA)
	Scott		Ascension
2120	DES MOINES, IA (MSA)		East Baton Rouge
	Dallas		Livingston
	Polk		West Baton Rouge
	Warren	3350	HOUMA, LA (MSA)
2200	DUBUQUE, IA (MSA)		Lafourche
	Dubuque		Terrebonne
3500	IOWA CITY, IA (MSA)	3880	LAFAYETTE, LA (MSA)
	Johnson		Acadia
5920	OMAHA, NE-IA (MSA)		Lafayette
	Pottawattamie		St. Landry
7720	SIOUX CITY, IA-NE (MSA)		St. Martin
	Woodbury	3960	LAKE CHARLES, LA (MSA)
8920	WATERLOO-CEDAR FALLS, IA (MSA)		Calcasieu
	Black Hawk	5200	MONROE, LA (MSA)
			Ouachita
	KANSAS	5560	NEW ORLEANS, LA (MSA)
3760	KANSAS CITY, MO-KS (MSA)		Jefferson
	Johnson		Orleans
	Leavenworth		Plaquemines
	Miami		St. Bernard
	Wyandotte		St. Charles
4150	LAWRENCE, KS (MSA)		St. James
	Douglas		

Metropolitan Areas and Components by State – Continued

(MSA = metropolitan statistical area; CMSA = consolidated MSA; PMSA = primary MSA; and NECMA = New England county metropolitan area. For further information, see Appendix A.)

Geographic codes MSA/CMSA/ PMSA/ NECMA	Title and geographic components	Geographic codes MSA/CMSA/ PMSA/ NECMA	Title and geographic components
	St. John the Baptist		Livingston
	St. Tammany		Washtenaw
7680	SHREVEPORT-BOSSIER CITY, LA (MSA)	2160	DETROIT, MI (PMSA)
	Bossier		Lapeer
	Caddo		Macomb
	Webster		Monroe
			Oakland
	MAINE		St. Clair
0733	BANGOR, ME (NECMA)		Wayne
	Penobscot	2640	FLINT, MI (PMSA)
4243	LEWISTON-AUBURN, ME (NECMA)		Genesee
	Androscoggin	0870	BENTON HARBOR, MI (MSA)
6403	PORTLAND, ME (NECMA)		Berrien
	Cumberland	3000	GRAND RAPIDS-MUSKEGON-HOLLAND, MI (MSA)
	MARYLAND		Allegan
77	PHILADELPHIA-WILMINGTON-ATLANTIC CITY, PA-NJ-DE-MD (CMSA)		Kent
			Muskegon
9160	WILMINGTON-NEWARK, DE-MD (PMSA)		Ottawa
	Cecil	3520	JACKSON, MI (MSA)
97	WASHINGTON-BALTIMORE, DC-MD-VA-WV (CMSA)		Jackson
0720	BALTIMORE, MD (PMSA)	3720	KALAMAZOO-BATTLE CREEK, MI (MSA)
	Anne Arundel		Calhoun
	Baltimore		Kalamazoo
	Carroll		Van Buren
	Harford	4040	LANSING-EAST LANSING, MI (MSA)
	Howard		Clinton
	Queen Anne's		Eaton
	Baltimore City		Ingham
3180	HAGERSTOWN, MD (PMSA)	6960	SAGINAW-BAY CITY-MIDLAND, MI (MSA)
	Washington		Bay
8840	WASHINGTON, DC-MD-VA-WV (PMSA)		Midland
	Calvert		Saginaw
	Charles		
	Frederick		**MINNESOTA**
	Montgomery	2240	DULUTH-SUPERIOR, MN-WI (MSA)
	Prince George's		St. Louis
1900	CUMBERLAND, MD-WV (MSA)	2520	FARGO-MOORHEAD, ND-MN (MSA)
	Allegany		Clay
		2985	GRAND FORKS, ND-MN (MSA)
	MASSACHUSETTS		Polk
0743	BARNSTABLE-YARMOUTH, MA (NECMA)	3870	LA CROSSE, WI-MN (MSA)
	Barnstable		Houston
1123	BOSTON-WORCESTER-LAWRENCE-LOWELL-BROCKTON, MA-NH (NECMA)	5120	MINNEAPOLIS-ST. PAUL, MN-WI (MSA)
	Bristol		Anoka
	Essex		Carver
	Middlesex		Chisago
	Norfolk		Dakota
	Plymouth		Hennepin
	Suffolk		Isanti
	Worcester		Ramsey
6323	PITTSFIELD, MA (NECMA)		Scott
	Berkshire		Sherburne
8003	SPRINGFIELD, MA (NECMA)		Washington
	Hampden		Wright
	Hampshire	6820	ROCHESTER, MN (MSA)
			Olmsted
	MICHIGAN	6980	ST. CLOUD, MN (MSA)
35	DETROIT-ANN ARBOR-FLINT, MI (CMSA)		Benton
0440	ANN ARBOR, MI (PMSA)		Stearns
	Lenawee		
			MISSISSIPPI
		0920	BILOXI-GULFPORT-PASCAGOULA, MS (MSA)
			Hancock
			Harrison
			Jackson
		3285	HATTIESBURG, MS (MSA)

(MSA = metropolitan statistical area; CMSA = consolidated MSA; PMSA = primary MSA; and
NECMA = New England county metropolitan area. For further information, see Appendix A.)

Geographic codes MSA/CMSA/ PMSA/ NECMA	Title and geographic components	Geographic codes MSA/CMSA/ PMSA/ NECMA	Title and geographic components
	Forrest		Washoe
	Lamar		**NEW HAMPSHIRE**
3560	JACKSON, MS (MSA)	1123	BOSTON-WORCESTER-LAWRENCE-LOWELL-BROCKTON, MA-NH (NECMA)
	Hinds		Hillsborough
	Madison		Rockingham
	Rankin		Strafford
4920	MEMPHIS, TN-AR-MS (MSA)		
	De Soto		**NEW JERSEY**
	MISSOURI	70	NEW YORK-NORTHERN NEW JERSEY-LONG ISLAND, NY-NJ-CT-PA (CMSA)
1740	COLUMBIA, MO (MSA)	0875	BERGEN-PASSAIC, NJ (PMSA)
	Boone		Bergen
3710	JOPLIN, MO (MSA)		Passaic
	Jasper	3640	JERSEY CITY, NJ (PMSA)
	Newton		Hudson
3760	KANSAS CITY, MO-KS (MSA)	5015	MIDDLESEX-SOMERSET-HUNTERDON, NJ (PMSA)
	Cass		Hunterdon
	Clay		Middlesex
	Clinton		Somerset
	Jackson	5190	MONMOUTH-OCEAN, NJ (PMSA)
	Lafayette		Monmouth
	Platte		Ocean
	Ray	5640	NEWARK, NJ (PMSA)
7000	ST. JOSEPH, MO (MSA)		Essex
	Andrew		Morris
	Buchanan		Sussex
7040	ST. LOUIS, MO-IL (MSA)		Union
	Franklin		Warren
	Jefferson	8480	TRENTON, NJ (PMSA)
	Lincoln		Mercer
	St. Charles	77	PHILADELPHIA-WILMINGTON-ATLANTIC CITY, PA-NJ-DE-MD (CMSA)
	St. Louis	0560	ATLANTIC-CAPE MAY, NJ (PMSA)
	Warren		Atlantic
	St. Louis City		Cape May
7920	SPRINGFIELD, MO (MSA)	6160	PHILADELPHIA, PA-NJ (PMSA)
	Christian		Burlington
	Greene		Camden
	Webster		Gloucester
	MONTANA		Salem
0880	BILLINGS, MT (MSA)	8760	VINELAND-MILLVILLE-BRIDGETON, NJ (PMSA)
	Yellowstone		Cumberland
3040	GREAT FALLS, MT (MSA)		
	Cascade		**NEW MEXICO**
5140	MISSOULA, MT (MSA)	0200	ALBUQUERQUE, NM (MSA)
	Missoula		Bernalillo
			Sandoval
	NEBRASKA		Valencia
4360	LINCOLN, NE (MSA)	4100	LAS CRUCES, NM (MSA)
	Lancaster		Dona Ana
5920	OMAHA, NE-IA (MSA)	7490	SANTA FE, NM (MSA)
	Cass		Los Alamos
	Douglas		Santa Fe
	Sarpy		
	Washington		**NEW YORK**
7720	SIOUX CITY, IA-NE (MSA)	70	NEW YORK-NORTHERN NEW JERSEY-LONG ISLAND, NY-NJ-CT-PA (CMSA)
	Dakota	2281	DUTCHESS COUNTY, NY (PMSA)
	NEVADA		Dutchess
4120	LAS VEGAS, NV-AZ (MSA)	5380	NASSAU-SUFFOLK, NY (PMSA)
	Clark		
	Nye		
6720	RENO, NV (MSA)		

Metropolitan Areas and Components by State – Continued

(MSA = metropolitan statistical area; CMSA = consolidated MSA; PMSA = primary MSA; and
NECMA = New England county metropolitan area. For further information, see Appendix A.)

Geographic codes MSA/CMSA/ PMSA/ NECMA	Title and geographic components	Geographic codes MSA/CMSA/ PMSA/ NECMA	Title and geographic components
	Nassau	2980	GOLDSBORO, NC (MSA)
	Suffolk		Wayne
5600	NEW YORK, NY (PMSA)	3120	GREENSBORO—WINSTON-SALEM—HIGH POINT, NC (MSA)
	Bronx		Alamance
	Kings		Davidson
	New York		Davie
	Putnam		Forsyth
	Queens		Guilford
	Richmond		Randolph
	Rockland		Stokes
	Westchester		Yadkin
5660	NEWBURGH, NY-PA (PMSA)	3150	GREENVILLE, NC (MSA)
	Orange		Pitt
0160	ALBANY-SCHENECTADY-TROY, NY (MSA)	3290	HICKORY-MORGANTON-LENOIR, NC (MSA)
	Albany		Alexander
	Montgomery		Burke
	Rensselaer		Caldwell
	Saratoga		Catawba
	Schenectady	3605	JACKSONVILLE, NC (MSA)
	Schoharie		Onslow
0960	BINGHAMTON, NY (MSA)	5720	NORFOLK-VIRGINIA BEACH-NEWPORT NEWS, VA-NC (MSA)
	Broome		
	Tioga		Currituck
1280	BUFFALO-NIAGARA FALLS, NY (MSA)	6640	RALEIGH-DURHAM-CHAPEL HILL, NC (MSA)
	Erie		Chatham
	Niagara		Durham
2335	ELMIRA, NY (MSA)		Franklin
	Chemung		Johnston
2975	GLENS FALLS, NY (MSA)		Orange
	Warren		Wake
	Washington	6895	ROCKY MOUNT, NC (MSA)
3610	JAMESTOWN, NY (MSA)		Edgecombe
	Chautauqua		Nash
6840	ROCHESTER, NY (MSA)	9200	WILMINGTON, NC (MSA)
	Genesee		Brunswick
	Livingston		New Hanover
	Monroe		
	Ontario		**NORTH DAKOTA**
	Orleans	1010	BISMARCK, ND (MSA)
	Wayne		Burleigh
8160	SYRACUSE, NY (MSA)		Morton
	Cayuga	2520	FARGO-MOORHEAD, ND-MN (MSA)
	Madison		Cass
	Onondaga	2985	GRAND FORKS, ND-MN (MSA)
	Oswego		Grand Forks
8680	UTICA-ROME, NY (MSA)		
	Herkimer		**OHIO**
	Oneida	21	CINCINNATI-HAMILTON, OH-KY-IN (CMSA)
		1640	CINCINNATI, OH-KY-IN (PMSA)
	NORTH CAROLINA		Brown
0480	ASHEVILLE, NC (MSA)		Clermont
	Buncombe		Hamilton
	Madison		Warren
1520	CHARLOTTE-GASTONIA-ROCK HILL, NC-SC (MSA)	3200	HAMILTON-MIDDLETOWN, OH (PMSA)
	Cabarrus		Butler
	Gaston	28	CLEVELAND-AKRON, OH (CMSA)
	Lincoln	0080	AKRON, OH (PMSA)
	Mecklenburg		Portage
	Rowan		Summit
	Union	1680	CLEVELAND-LORAIN-ELYRIA, OH (PMSA)
2560	FAYETTEVILLE, NC (MSA)		Ashtabula
	Cumberland		Cuyahoga
			Geauga
			Lake

(MSA = metropolitan statistical area; CMSA = consolidated MSA; PMSA = primary MSA; and
NECMA = New England county metropolitan area. For further information, see Appendix A.)

Geographic codes MSA/CMSA/ PMSA/ NECMA	Title and geographic components	Geographic codes MSA/CMSA/ PMSA/ NECMA	Title and geographic components
	Lorain		Columbia
	Medina		Multnomah
1320	CANTON-MASSILLON, OH (MSA)		Washington
	Carroll		Yamhill
	Stark	7080	SALEM, OR (PMSA)
1840	COLUMBUS, OH (MSA)		Marion
	Delaware		Polk
	Fairfield	2400	EUGENE-SPRINGFIELD, OR (MSA)
	Franklin		Lane
	Licking	4890	MEDFORD-ASHLAND, OR (MSA)
	Madison		Jackson
	Pickaway		
2000	DAYTON-SPRINGFIELD, OH (MSA)		**PENNSYLVANIA**
	Clark	70	NEW YORK-NORTHERN NEW JERSEY-LONG ISLAND, NY-NJ-CT-PA (CMSA)
	Greene	5660	NEWBURGH, NY-PA (PMSA)
	Miami		Pike
	Montgomery	77	PHILADELPHIA-WILMINGTON-ATLANTIC CITY, PA-NJ-DE-MD (CMSA)
3400	HUNTINGTON-ASHLAND, WV-KY-OH (MSA)	6160	PHILADELPHIA, PA-NJ (PMSA)
	Lawrence		Bucks
4320	LIMA, OH (MSA)		Chester
	Allen		Delaware
	Auglaize		Montgomery
4800	MANSFIELD, OH (MSA)		Philadelphia
	Crawford		
	Richland	0240	ALLENTOWN-BETHLEHEM-EASTON, PA (MSA)
6020	PARKERSBURG-MARIETTA, WV-OH (MSA)		Carbon
	Washington		Lehigh
8080	STEUBENVILLE-WEIRTON, OH-WV (MSA)		Northampton
	Jefferson	0280	ALTOONA, PA (MSA)
8400	TOLEDO, OH (MSA)		Blair
	Fulton	2360	ERIE, PA (MSA)
	Lucas		Erie
	Wood	3240	HARRISBURG-LEBANON-CARLISLE, PA (MSA)
9000	WHEELING, WV-OH (MSA)		Cumberland
	Belmont		Dauphin
9320	YOUNGSTOWN-WARREN, OH (MSA)		Lebanon
	Columbiana		Perry
	Mahoning	3680	JOHNSTOWN, PA (MSA)
	Trumbull		Cambria
			Somerset
	OKLAHOMA	4000	LANCASTER, PA (MSA)
2340	ENID, OK (MSA)		Lancaster
	Garfield	6280	PITTSBURGH, PA (MSA)
2720	FORT SMITH, AR-OK (MSA)		Allegheny
	Sequoyah		Beaver
4200	LAWTON, OK (MSA)		Butler
	Comanche		Fayette
5880	OKLAHOMA CITY, OK (MSA)		Washington
	Canadian		Westmoreland
	Cleveland	6680	READING, PA (MSA)
	Logan		Berks
	McClain	7560	SCRANTON—WILKES-BARRE—HAZLETON, PA (MSA)
	Oklahoma		Columbia
	Pottawatomie		Lackawanna
8560	TULSA, OK (MSA)		Luzerne
	Creek		Wyoming
	Osage	7610	SHARON, PA (MSA)
	Rogers		Mercer
	Tulsa	8050	STATE COLLEGE, PA (MSA)
	Wagoner		Centre
		9140	WILLIAMSPORT, PA (MSA)
	OREGON		Lycoming
1890	CORVALLIS, OR (MSA)		
	Benton		
79	PORTLAND-SALEM, OR-WA (CMSA)		
6440	PORTLAND-VANCOUVER, OR-WA (PMSA)		
	Clackamas		

(MSA = metropolitan statistical area; CMSA = consolidated MSA; PMSA = primary MSA; and
NECMA = New England county metropolitan area. For further information, see Appendix A.)

Geographic codes MSA/CMSA/ PMSA/ NECMA	Title and geographic components	Geographic codes MSA/CMSA/ PMSA/ NECMA	Title and geographic components
9280	YORK, PA (MSA)	4920	MEMPHIS, TN-AR-MS (MSA)
	York		Fayette
			Shelby
	RHODE ISLAND		Tipton
6483	PROVIDENCE-WARWICK-PAWTUCKET, RI (NECMA)	5360	NASHVILLE, TN (MSA)
	Bristol		Cheatham
	Kent		Davidson
	Providence		Dickson
	Washington		Robertson
			Rutherford
	SOUTH CAROLINA		Sumner
0600	AUGUSTA-AIKEN, GA-SC (MSA)		Williamson
	Aiken		Wilson
	Edgefield		
1440	CHARLESTON-NORTH CHARLESTON, SC (MSA)		**TEXAS**
	Berkeley	31	DALLAS-FORT WORTH, TX (CMSA)
	Charleston	1920	DALLAS, TX (PMSA)
	Dorchester		Collin
1520	CHARLOTTE-GASTONIA-ROCK HILL, NC-SC (MSA)		Dallas
	York		Denton
1760	COLUMBIA, SC (MSA)		Ellis
	Lexington		Henderson
	Richland		Hunt
2655	FLORENCE, SC (MSA)		Kaufman
	Florence		Rockwall
3160	GREENVILLE-SPARTANBURG-ANDERSON, SC (MSA)	2800	FORT WORTH-ARLINGTON, TX (PMSA)
	Anderson		Hood
	Cherokee		Johnson
	Greenville		Parker
	Pickens		Tarrant
	Spartanburg	42	HOUSTON-GALVESTON-BRAZORIA, TX (CMSA)
5330	MYRTLE BEACH, SC (MSA)	1145	BRAZORIA, TX (PMSA)
	Horry		Brazoria
8140	SUMTER, SC (MSA)	2920	GALVESTON-TEXAS CITY, TX (PMSA)
	Sumter		Galveston
		3360	HOUSTON, TX (PMSA)
	SOUTH DAKOTA		Chambers
6660	RAPID CITY, SD (MSA)		Fort Bend
	Pennington		Harris
7760	SIOUX FALLS, SD (MSA)		Liberty
	Lincoln		Montgomery
	Minnehaha		Waller
		0040	ABILENE, TX (MSA)
	TENNESSEE		Taylor
1560	CHATTANOOGA, TN-GA (MSA)	0320	AMARILLO, TX (MSA)
	Hamilton		Potter
	Marion		Randall
1660	CLARKSVILLE-HOPKINSVILLE, TN-KY (MSA)	0640	AUSTIN-SAN MARCOS, TX (MSA)
	Montgomery		Bastrop
3580	JACKSON, TN (MSA)		Caldwell
	Chester		Hays
	Madison		Travis
3660	JOHNSON CITY-KINGSPORT-BRISTOL, TN-VA (MSA)		Williamson
	Carter	0840	BEAUMONT-PORT ARTHUR, TX (MSA)
	Hawkins		Hardin
	Sullivan		Jefferson
	Unicoi		Orange
	Washington	1240	BROWNSVILLE-HARLINGEN-SAN BENITO, TX (MSA)
3840	KNOXVILLE, TN (MSA)		Cameron
	Anderson	1260	BRYAN-COLLEGE STATION, TX (MSA)
	Blount		Brazos
	Knox	1880	CORPUS CHRISTI, TX (MSA)
	Loudon		Nueces
	Sevier		San Patricio
	Union	2320	EL PASO, TX (MSA)
			El Paso

(MSA = metropolitan statistical area; CMSA = consolidated MSA; PMSA = primary MSA; and
NECMA = New England county metropolitan area. For further information, see Appendix A.)

Geographic codes MSA/CMSA/ PMSA/ NECMA	Title and geographic components	Geographic codes MSA/CMSA/ PMSA/ NECMA	Title and geographic components
3810	KILLEEN-TEMPLE, TX (MSA)		**VIRGINIA**
	Bell	97	WASHINGTON-BALTIMORE, DC-MD-VA-WV (CMSA)
	Coryell	8840	WASHINGTON, DC-MD-VA-WV (PMSA)
4080	LAREDO, TX (MSA)		Arlington
	Webb		Clarke
4420	LONGVIEW-MARSHALL, TX (MSA)		Culpeper
	Gregg		Fairfax
	Harrison		Fauquier
	Upshur		King George
4600	LUBBOCK, TX (MSA)		Loudoun
	Lubbock		Prince William
4880	MCALLEN-EDINBURG-MISSION, TX (MSA)		Spotsylvania
	Hidalgo		Stafford
5800	ODESSA-MIDLAND, TX (MSA)		Warren
	Ector		Alexandria City
	Midland		Fairfax City
7200	SAN ANGELO, TX (MSA)		Falls Church City
	Tom Green		Fredericksburg City
7240	SAN ANTONIO, TX (MSA)		Manassas City
	Bexar		Manassas Park City
	Comal	1540	CHARLOTTESVILLE, VA (MSA)
	Guadalupe		Albemarle
	Wilson		Fluvanna
7640	SHERMAN-DENISON, TX (MSA)		Greene
	Grayson		Charlottesville City
8360	TEXARKANA, TX-TEXARKANA, AR (MSA)	1950	DANVILLE, VA (MSA)
	Bowie		Pittsylvania
8640	TYLER, TX (MSA)		Danville City
	Smith	3660	JOHNSON CITY-KINGSPORT-BRISTOL, TN-VA (MSA)
8750	VICTORIA, TX (MSA)		Scott
	Victoria		Washington
8800	WACO, TX (MSA)		Bristol City
	McLennan	4640	LYNCHBURG, VA (MSA)
9080	WICHITA FALLS, TX (MSA)		Amherst
	Archer		Bedford
	Wichita		Campbell
			Bedford City
	UTAH		Lynchburg City
2620	FLAGSTAFF, AZ-UT (MSA)	5720	NORFOLK-VIRGINIA BEACH-NEWPORT NEWS, VA-NC (MSA)
	Kane		Gloucester
6520	PROVO-OREM, UT (MSA)		Isle of Wight
	Utah		James City County
7160	SALT LAKE CITY-OGDEN, UT (MSA)		Mathews
	Davis		York
	Salt Lake		Chesapeake City
	Weber		Hampton City
			Newport News City
	VERMONT		Norfolk City
1303	BURLINGTON, VT (NECMA)		Poquoson City
	Chittenden		Portsmouth City
	Franklin		Suffolk City
	Grand Isle		Virginia Beach City
			Williamsburg City
		6760	RICHMOND-PETERSBURG, VA (MSA)
			Charles City County
			Chesterfield
			Dinwiddie
			Goochland
			Hanover
			Henrico
			New Kent
			Powhatan
			Prince George
			Colonial Heights City
			Hopewell City
			Petersburg City
			Richmond City

(MSA = metropolitan statistical area; CMSA = consolidated MSA; PMSA = primary MSA; and NECMA = New England county metropolitan area. For further information, see Appendix A.)

Geographic codes MSA/CMSA/ PMSA/ NECMA	Title and geographic components	Geographic codes MSA/CMSA/ PMSA/ NECMA	Title and geographic components

6800	ROANOKE, VA (MSA)
	    Botetourt
	    Roanoke
	    Roanoke City
	    Salem City
		9000	WHEELING, WV-OH (MSA)
			    Marshall
			    Ohio

	WASHINGTON		**WISCONSIN**
79	PORTLAND-SALEM, OR-WA (CMSA)	14	CHICAGO-GARY-KENOSHA, IL-IN-WI (CMSA)

6440	PORTLAND-VANCOUVER, OR-WA (PMSA)
	    Clark
		3800	KENOSHA, WI (PMSA)
			    Kenosha

91	SEATTLE-TACOMA-BREMERTON, WA (CMSA)	63	MILWAUKEE-RACINE, WI (CMSA)

1150	BREMERTON, WA (PMSA)
	    Kitsap
		5080	MILWAUKEE-WAUKESHA, WI (PMSA)
			    Milwaukee
			    Ozaukee

5910	OLYMPIA, WA (PMSA)
	    Thurston
			Washington
			    Waukesha

7600	SEATTLE-BELLEVUE-EVERETT, WA (PMSA)
	    Island
	    King
	    Snohomish
		6600	RACINE, WI (PMSA)
			    Racine

8200	TACOMA, WA (PMSA)
	    Pierce
		0460	APPLETON-OSHKOSH-NEENAH, WI (MSA)
			    Calumet
			    Outagamie
			    Winnebago

0860	BELLINGHAM, WA (MSA)
	    Whatcom
		2240	DULUTH-SUPERIOR, MN-WI (MSA)
			    Douglas

6740	RICHLAND-KENNEWICK-PASCO, WA (MSA)
	    Benton
	    Franklin
		2290	EAU CLAIRE, WI (MSA)
			    Chippewa
			    Eau Claire

7840	SPOKANE, WA (MSA)
	    Spokane
		3080	GREEN BAY, WI (MSA)
			    Brown

9260	YAKIMA, WA (MSA)
	    Yakima
		3620	JANESVILLE-BELOIT, WI (MSA)
			    Rock

	WEST VIRGINIA	3870	LA CROSSE, WI-MN (MSA) La Crosse
97	WASHINGTON-BALTIMORE, DC-MD-VA-WV (CMSA)	4720	MADISON, WI (MSA) Dane

8840	WASHINGTON, DC-MD-VA-WV (PMSA)
	    Berkeley
	    Jefferson
		5120	MINNEAPOLIS-ST. PAUL, MN-WI (MSA)
			    Pierce
			    St. Croix

1480	CHARLESTON, WV (MSA)
	    Kanawha
	    Putnam
		7620	SHEBOYGAN, WI (MSA)
			    Sheboygan

1900	CUMBERLAND, MD-WV (MSA)
	    Mineral
		8940	WAUSAU, WI (MSA)
			    Marathon

3400	HUNTINGTON-ASHLAND, WV-KY-OH (MSA)
	    Cabell
	    Wayne
			WYOMING

6020	PARKERSBURG-MARIETTA, WV-OH (MSA)
	    Wood
		1350	CASPER, WY (MSA)
			    Natrona

8080	STEUBENVILLE-WEIRTON, OH-WV (MSA)
	    Brooke
	    Hancock
		1580	CHEYENNE, WY (MSA)
			    Laramie

ALABAMA - Metropolitan Areas, Counties, and Selected Places

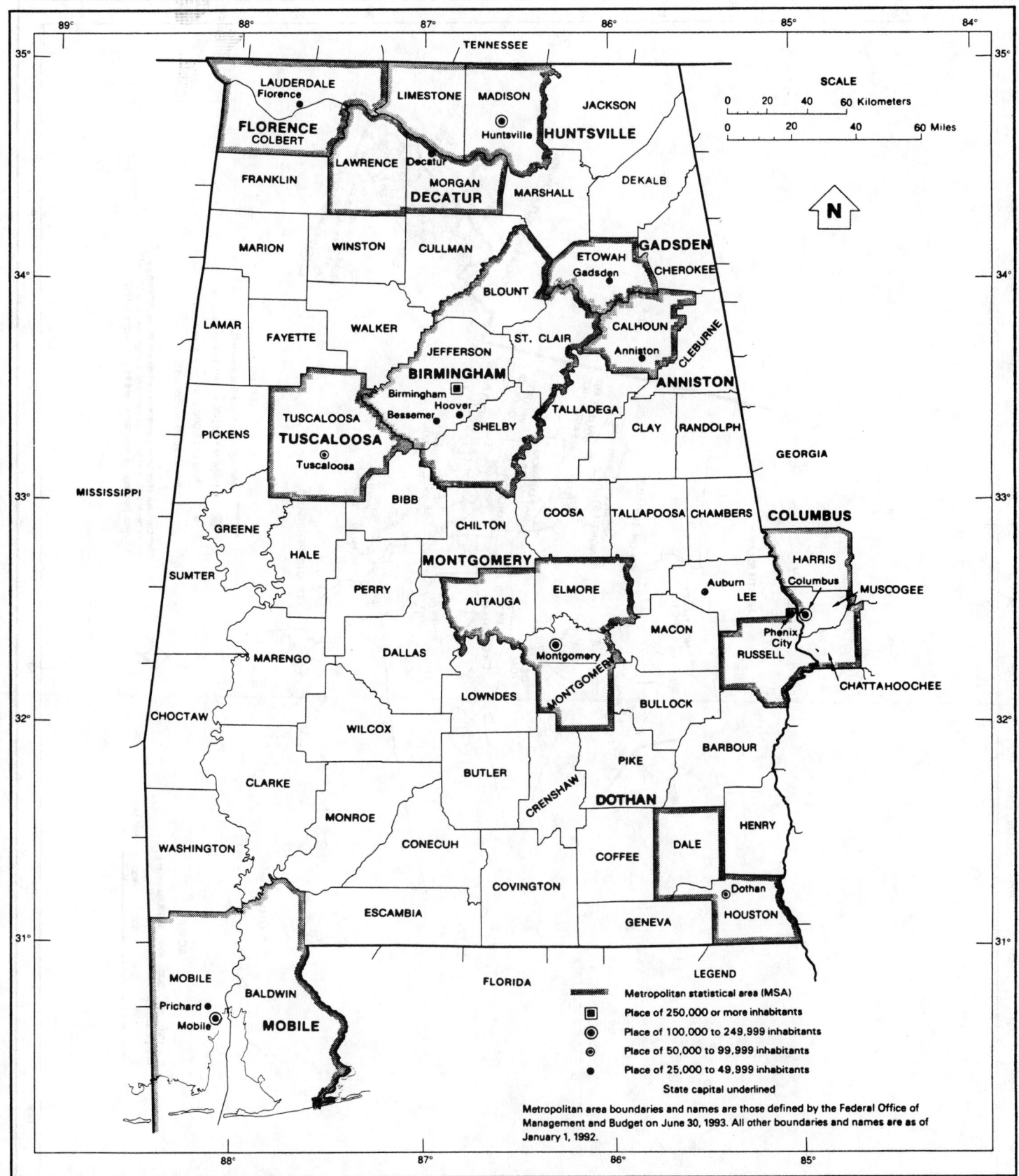

SCALE

0 20 40 60 Kilometers

0 20 40 60 Miles

N

LEGEND

━━━ Metropolitan statistical area (MSA)

▣ Place of 250,000 or more inhabitants

◉ Place of 100,000 to 249,999 inhabitants

◎ Place of 50,000 to 99,999 inhabitants

● Place of 25,000 to 49,999 inhabitants

State capital underlined

Metropolitan area boundaries and names are those defined by the Federal Office of
Management and Budget on June 30, 1993. All other boundaries and names are as of
January 1, 1992.

ALASKA - Metropolitan Area, Boroughs, Census Areas, and Selected Places

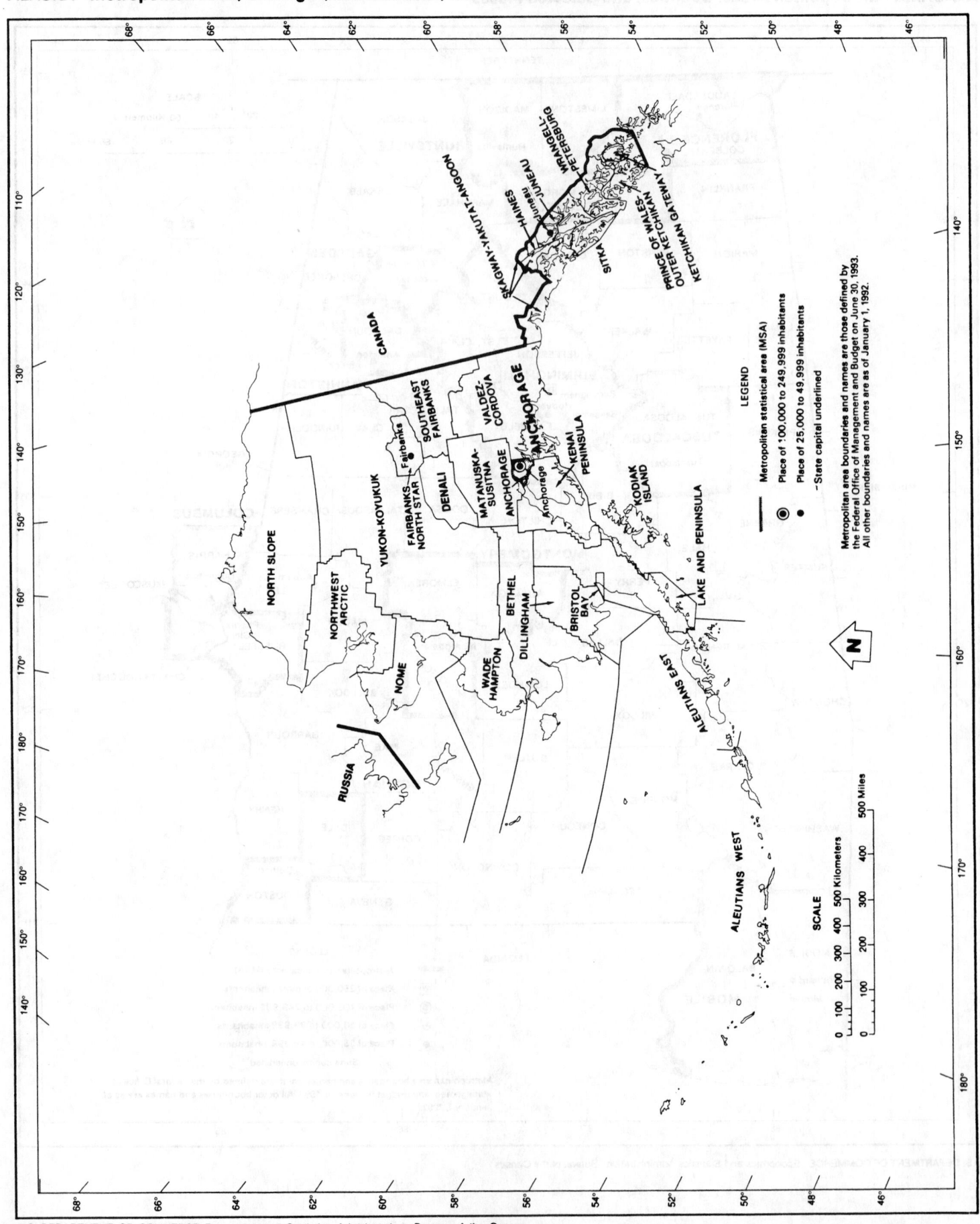

LEGEND

⊙ Metropolitan statistical area (MSA)

◉ Place of 100,000 to 249,999 inhabitants

● Place of 25,000 to 49,999 inhabitants

— State capital underlined

Metropolitan area boundaries and names are those defined by the Federal Office of Management and Budget on June 30, 1993. All other boundaries and names are as of January 1, 1992.

SCALE

0 100 200 300 400 500 Kilometers

0 100 200 300 400 500 Miles

ARIZONA - Metropolitan Areas, Counties, and Selected Places

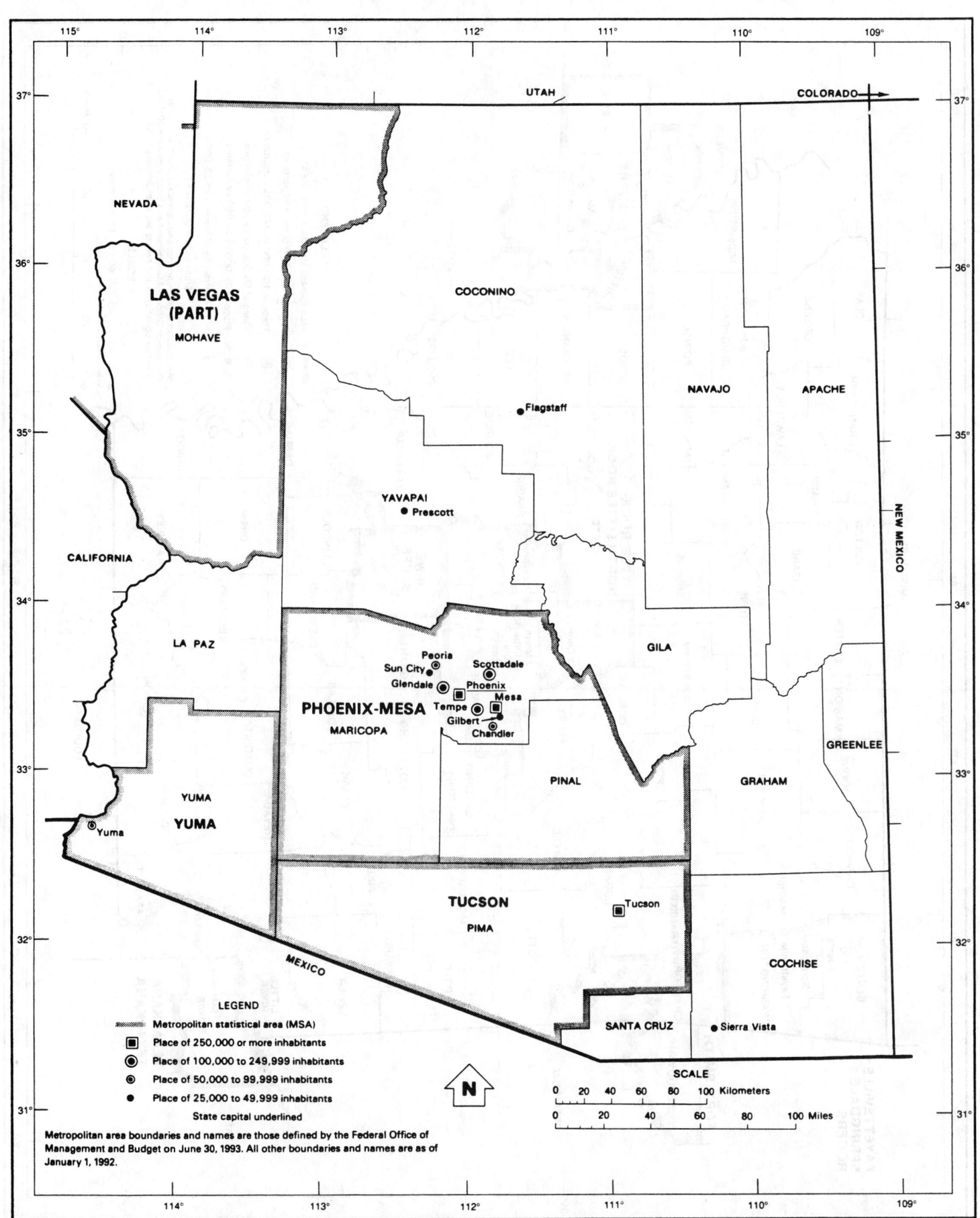

LEGEND

~~~~~ Metropolitan statistical area (MSA)
▪ Place of 250,000 or more inhabitants
◉ Place of 100,000 to 249,999 inhabitants
◉ Place of 50,000 to 99,999 inhabitants
● Place of 25,000 to 49,999 inhabitants
State capital underlined

Metropolitan area boundaries and names are those defined by the Federal Office of
Management and Budget on June 30, 1993. All other boundaries and names are as of
January 1, 1992.

SCALE

0   20   40   60   80   100 Kilometers
0   20   40   60   80   100 Miles

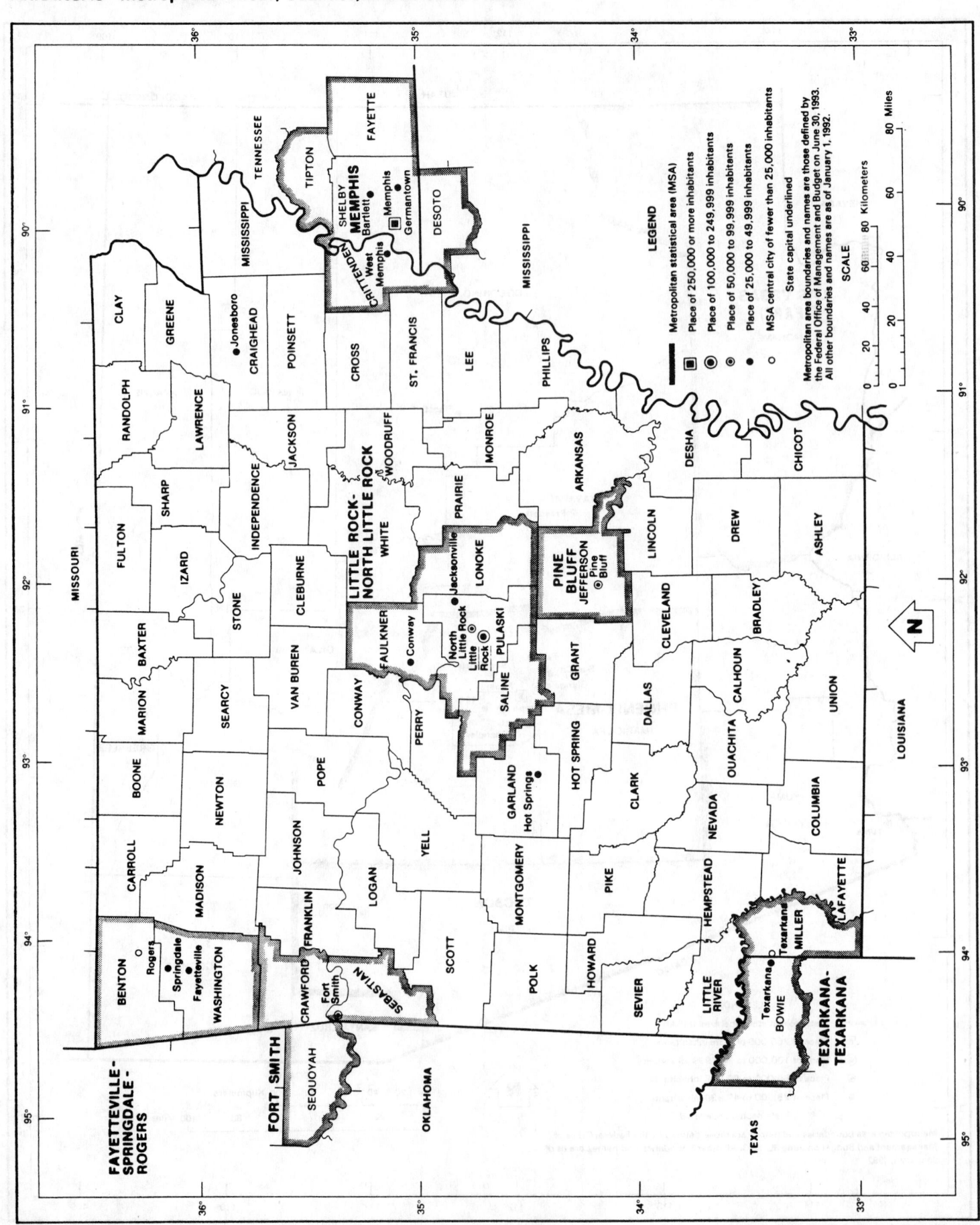

LEGEND

Metropolitan statistical area (MSA)

Place of 250,000 or more inhabitants

Place of 100,000 to 249,999 inhabitants

Place of 50,000 to 99,999 inhabitants

Place of 25,000 to 49,999 inhabitants

Place of fewer than 25,000 inhabitants

MSA central city of fewer than 25,000 inhabitants

State capital underlined

Metropolitan area boundaries and names are those defined by
the Federal Office of Management and Budget on June 30, 1993.
All other boundaries and names are as of January 1, 1992.

SCALE

U.S. DEPARTMENT OF COMMERCE Economics and Statistics Administration Bureau of the Census

CALIFORNIA - Metropolitan Areas, Counties, and Selected Places

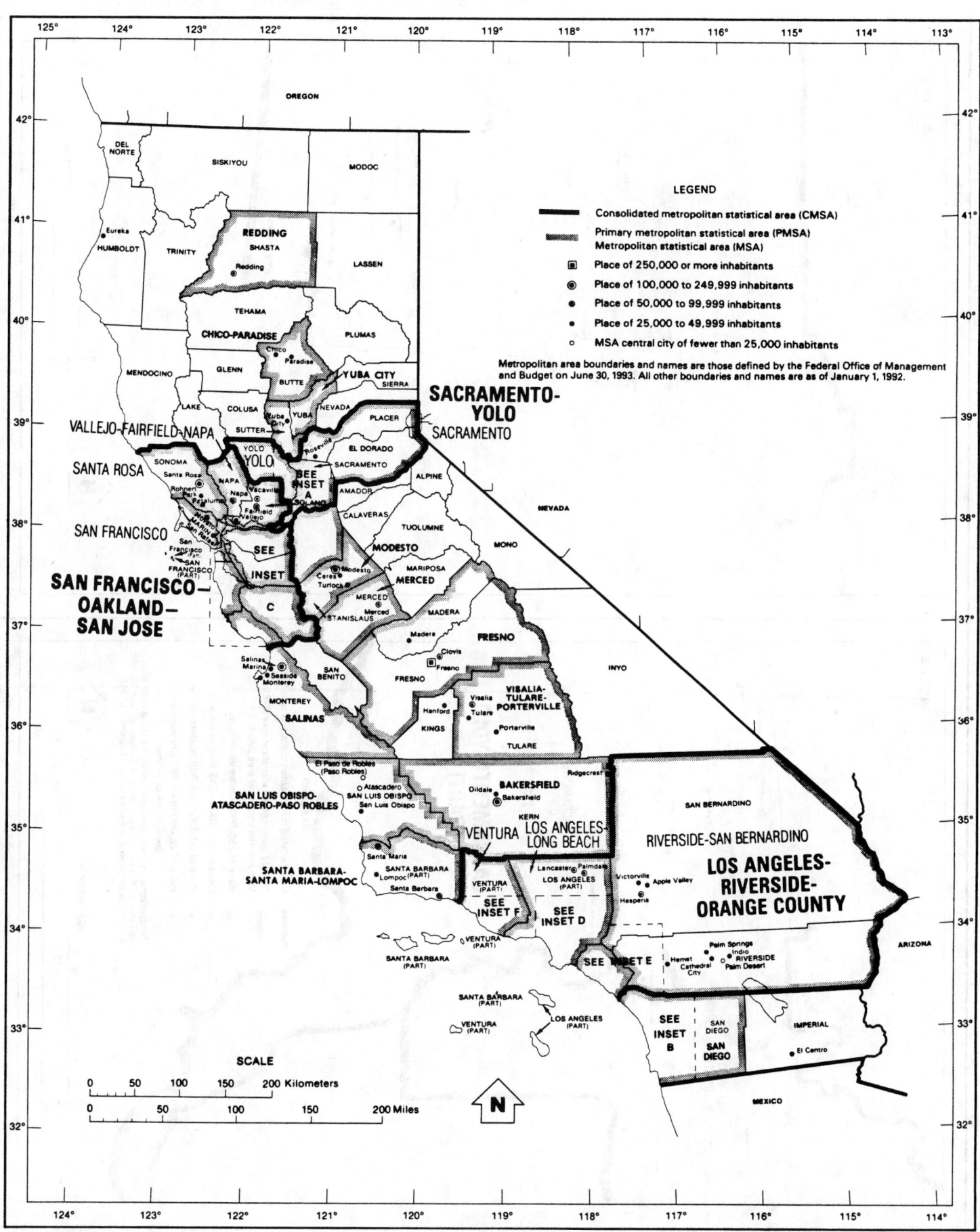

LEGEND

━━━ Consolidated metropolitan statistical area (CMSA)

▓▓▓ Primary metropolitan statistical area (PMSA)
Metropolitan statistical area (MSA)

▣ Place of 250,000 or more inhabitants

◉ Place of 100,000 to 249,999 inhabitants

● Place of 50,000 to 99,999 inhabitants

• Place of 25,000 to 49,999 inhabitants

○ MSA central city of fewer than 25,000 inhabitants

Metropolitan area boundaries and names are those defined by the Federal Office of Management and Budget on June 30, 1993. All other boundaries and names are as of January 1, 1992.

SCALE

0 50 100 150 200 Kilometers

0 50 100 150 200 Miles

N

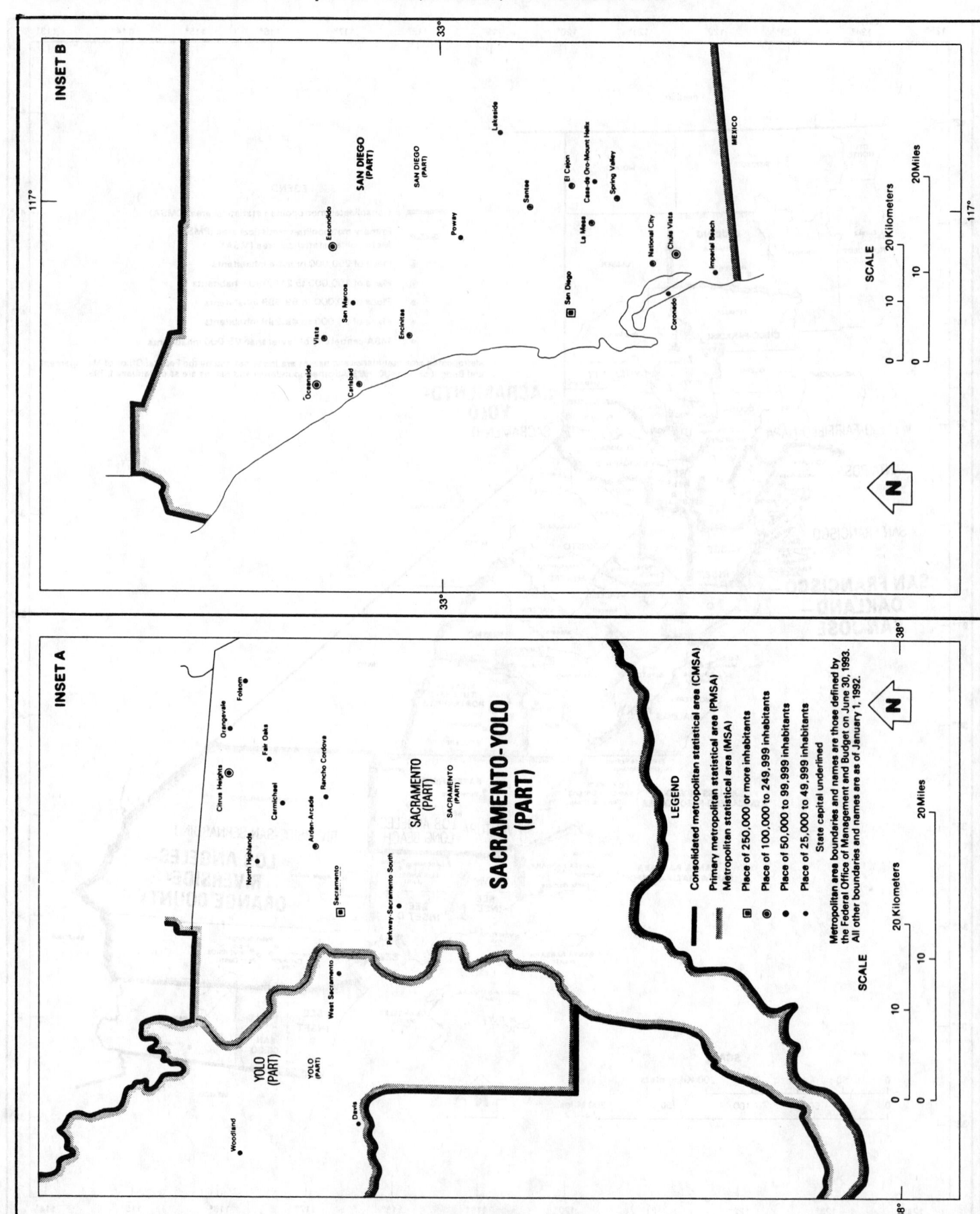

INSET B

SAN DIEGO
(PART)

SAN DIEGO
(PART)

Lakeside

El Cajon

Casa de Oro-Mount Helix

Spring Valley

Escondido

Poway

Santee

La Mesa

San Marcos

Encinitas

Vista

National City

Chula Vista

Oceanside

Carlsbad

San Diego

Coronado

Imperial Beach

MEXICO

N

SCALE

0   10   20 Kilometers

0   10   20 Miles

117°

33°

INSET A

Folsom

Orangevale

Citrus Heights

Fair Oaks

Carmichael

Rancho Cordova

Arden-Arcade

North Highlands

Sacramento

Parkway-Sacramento South

West Sacramento

SACRAMENTO-
YOLO
(PART)

SACRAMENTO
(PART)

SACRAMENTO
(PART)

YOLO
(PART)

YOLO
(PART)

Davis

Woodland

N

SCALE

0   10   20 Kilometers

0   10   20 Miles

38°

LEGEND

▬ Consolidated metropolitan statistical area (CMSA)

▬ Primary metropolitan statistical area (PMSA)

▬ Metropolitan statistical area (MSA)

▣ Place of 250,000 or more inhabitants

◉ Place of 100,000 to 249,999 inhabitants

● Place of 50,000 to 99,999 inhabitants

• Place of 25,000 to 49,999 inhabitants

State capital underlined

Metropolitan area boundaries and names are those defined by
the Federal Office of Management and Budget on June 30, 1993.
All other boundaries and names are as of January 1, 1992.

CALIFORNIA (Inset C) - Metropolitan Areas, Counties, and Selected Places

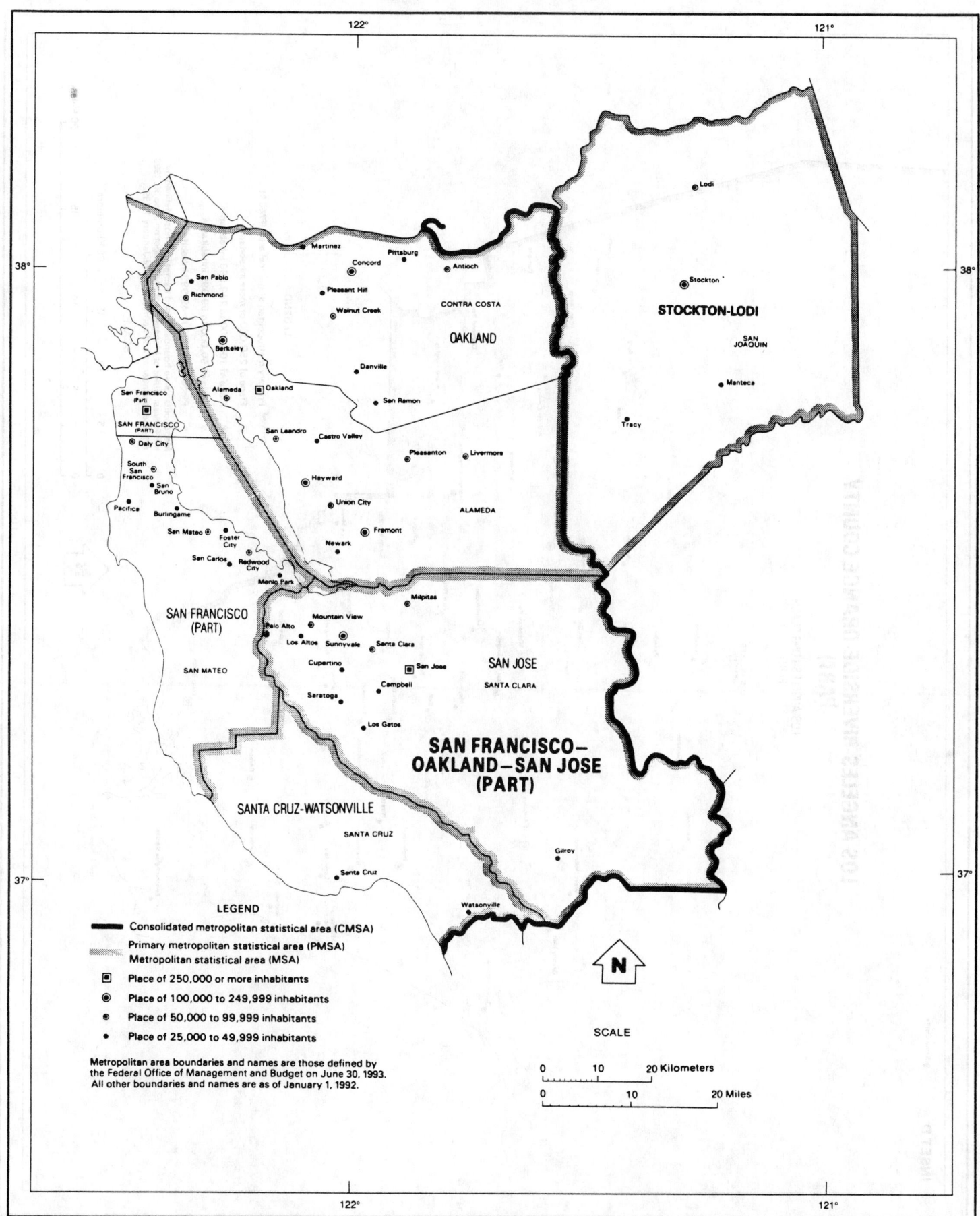

LEGEND

━━━ Consolidated metropolitan statistical area (CMSA)

▒▒▒ Primary metropolitan statistical area (PMSA)
Metropolitan statistical area (MSA)

▣ Place of 250,000 or more inhabitants

◉ Place of 100,000 to 249,999 inhabitants

◍ Place of 50,000 to 99,999 inhabitants

• Place of 25,000 to 49,999 inhabitants

Metropolitan area boundaries and names are those defined by
the Federal Office of Management and Budget on June 30, 1993.
All other boundaries and names are as of January 1, 1992.

N

SCALE

0   10   20 Kilometers

0   10   20 Miles

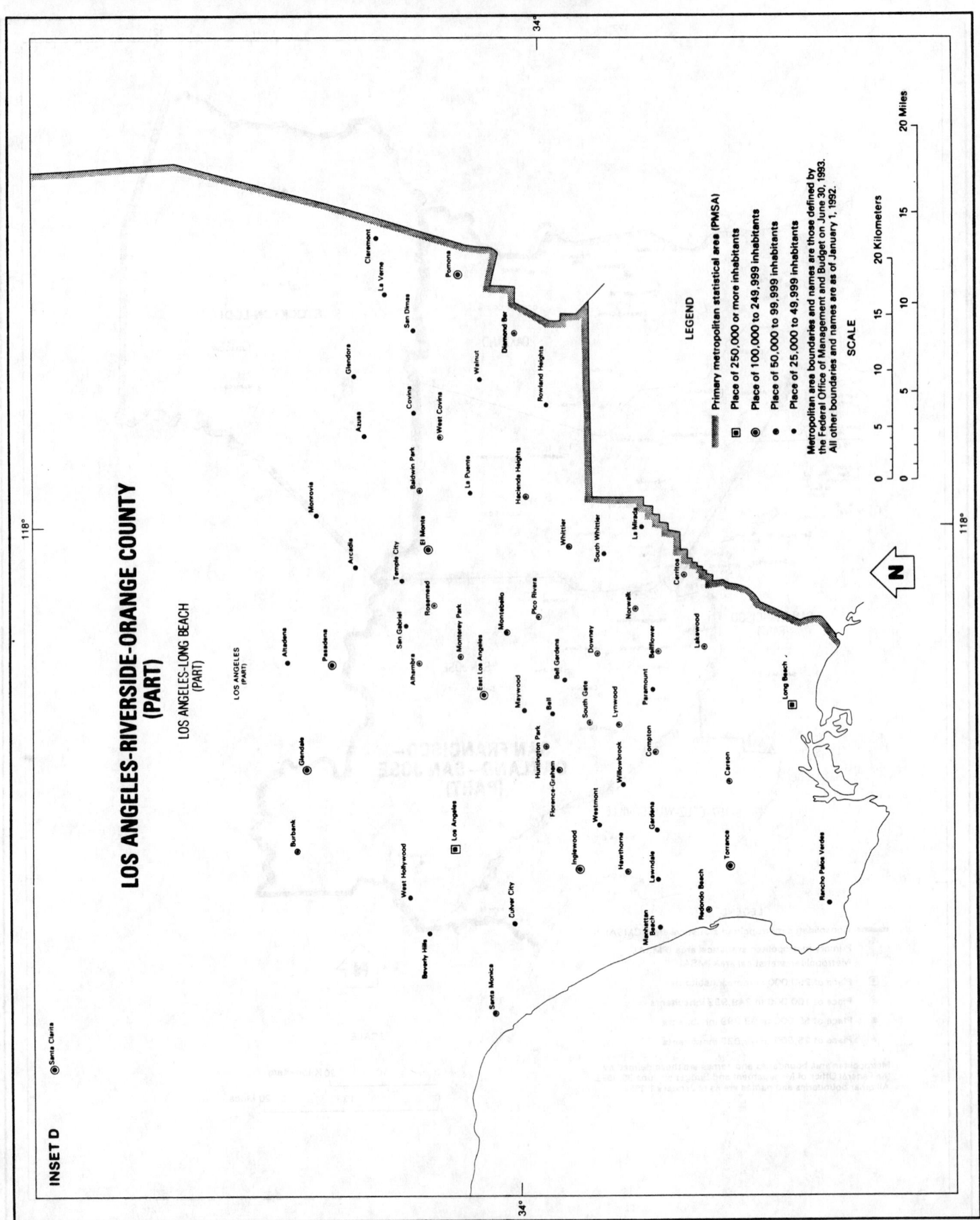

LOS ANGELES-RIVERSIDE-ORANGE COUNTY (PART)

LOS ANGELES-LONG BEACH (PART)

LOS ANGELES (PART)

INSET D

LEGEND

Primary metropolitan statistical area (PMSA)

Place of 250,000 or more inhabitants

Place of 100,000 to 249,999 inhabitants

Place of 50,000 to 99,999 inhabitants

Place of 25,000 to 49,999 inhabitants

Metropolitan area boundaries and names are those defined by the Federal Office of Management and Budget on June 30, 1993. All other boundaries and names are as of January 1, 1992.

SCALE

0   5   10   15   20 Miles

0   5   10   15   20 Kilometers

N

CALIFORNIA (Insets E and F) - Metropolitan Areas, Counties, and Selected Places

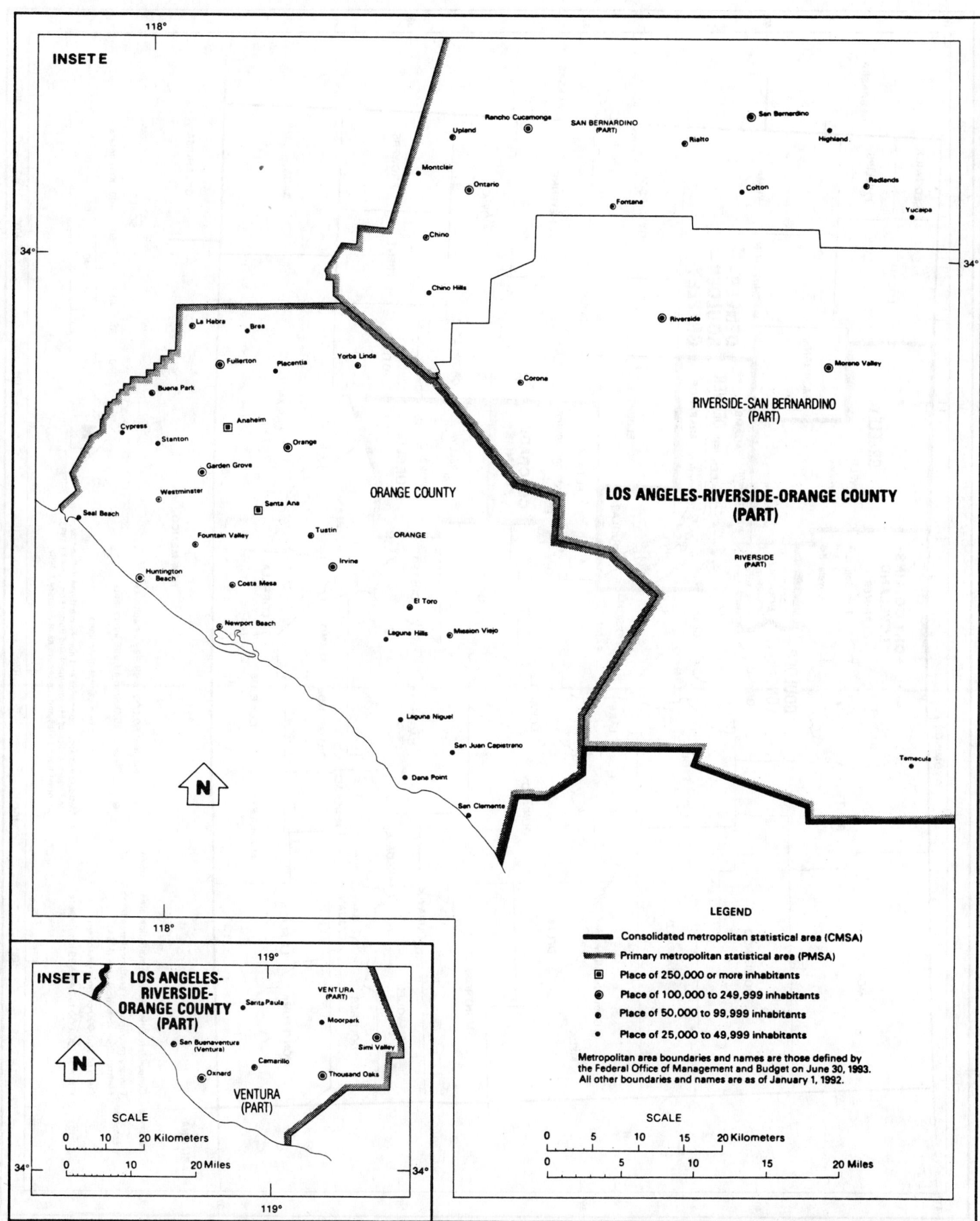

INSET E

118°

34°

Rancho Cucamonga

SAN BERNARDINO (PART)

San Bernardino

Upland

Rialto

Highland

Montclair

Colton

Redlands

Ontario

Fontana

Yucaipa

Chino

34°

Chino Hills

Riverside

La Habra

Brea

Fullerton

Placentia

Yorba Linda

Moreno Valley

Buena Park

RIVERSIDE-SAN BERNARDINO (PART)

Corona

Cypress

Anaheim

Stanton

Orange

Garden Grove

LOS ANGELES-RIVERSIDE-ORANGE COUNTY (PART)

Westminster

ORANGE COUNTY

Seal Beach

Santa Ana

RIVERSIDE (PART)

Fountain Valley

Tustin

ORANGE

Huntington Beach

Irvine

Costa Mesa

El Toro

Newport Beach

Laguna Hills

Mission Viejo

Laguna Niguel

San Juan Capistrano

Temecula

Dana Point

San Clemente

N

118°

LEGEND

━━━━ Consolidated metropolitan statistical area (CMSA)

▨▨▨ Primary metropolitan statistical area (PMSA)

▣ Place of 250,000 or more inhabitants

◉ Place of 100,000 to 249,999 inhabitants

● Place of 50,000 to 99,999 inhabitants

• Place of 25,000 to 49,999 inhabitants

Metropolitan area boundaries and names are those defined by the Federal Office of Management and Budget on June 30, 1993. All other boundaries and names are as of January 1, 1992.

SCALE

0   5   10   15   20 Kilometers

0   5   10   15   20 Miles

INSET F   **LOS ANGELES-RIVERSIDE-ORANGE COUNTY (PART)**

119°

VENTURA (PART)

Santa Paula

Moorpark

N

San Buenaventura (Ventura)

Camarillo

Simi Valley

Oxnard

Thousand Oaks

VENTURA (PART)

SCALE

0   10   20 Kilometers

0   10   20 Miles

34°

119°

U.S. DEPARTMENT OF COMMERCE Economics and Statistics Administration Bureau of the Census

COLORADO - Metropolitan Areas, Counties, and Selected Places

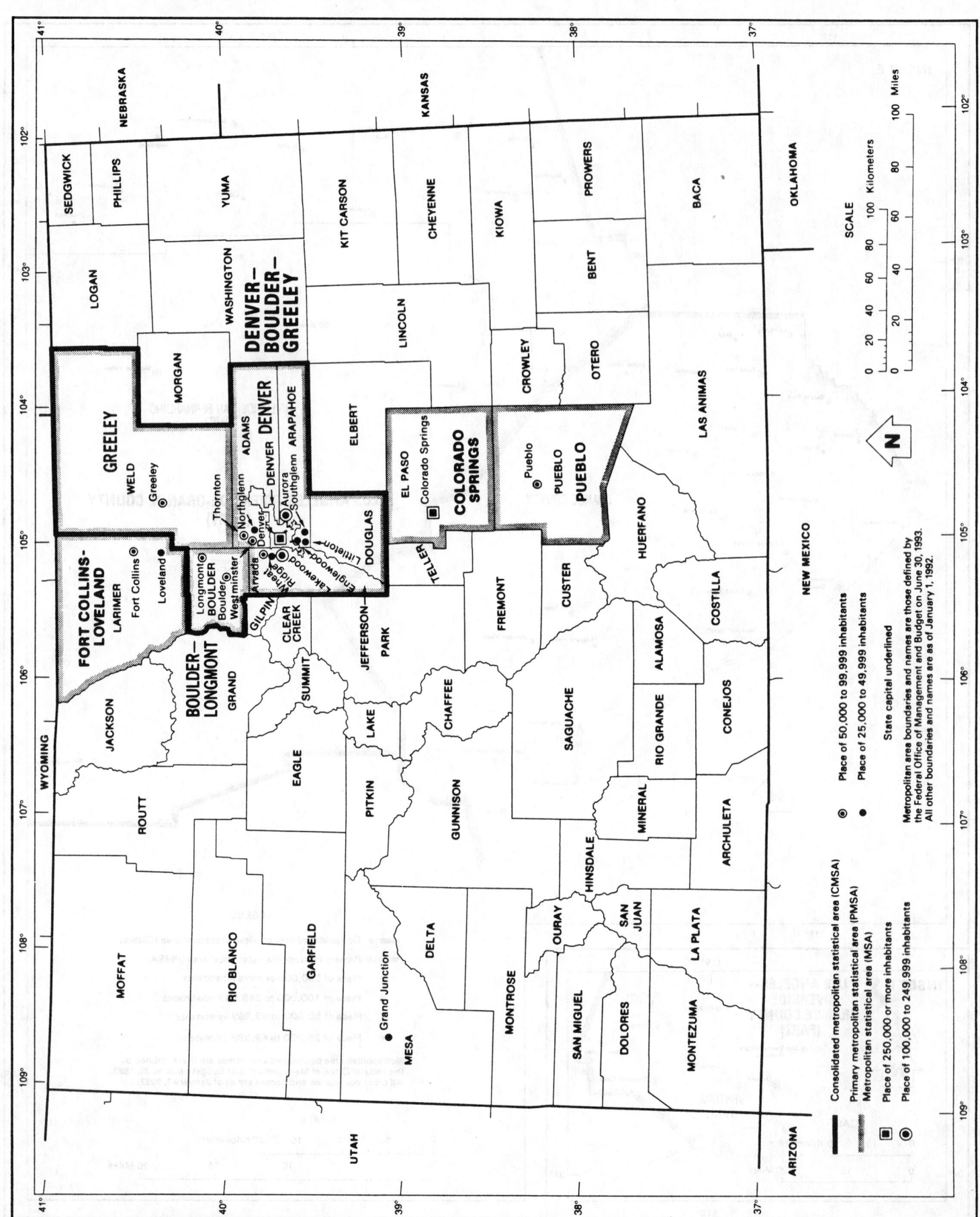

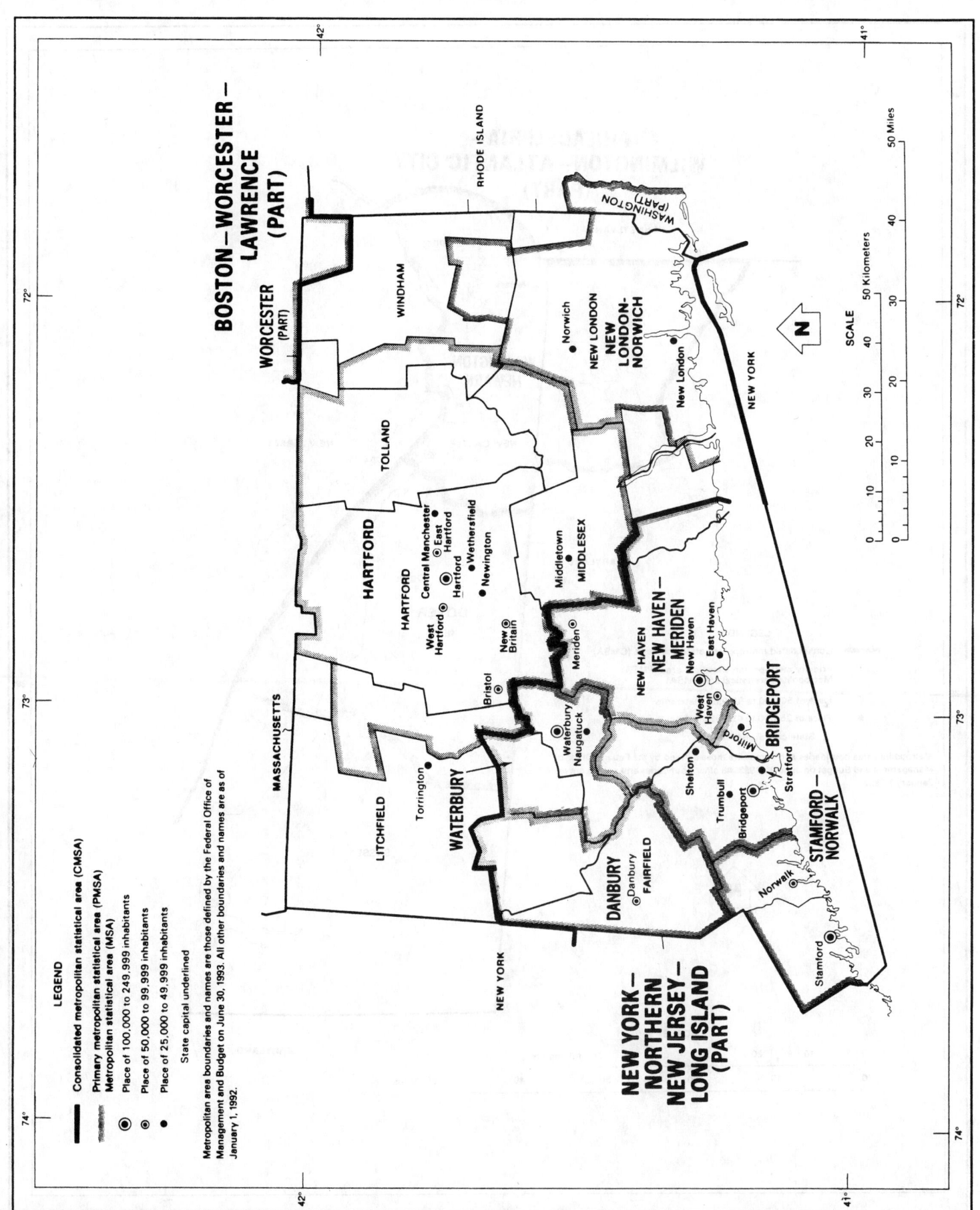

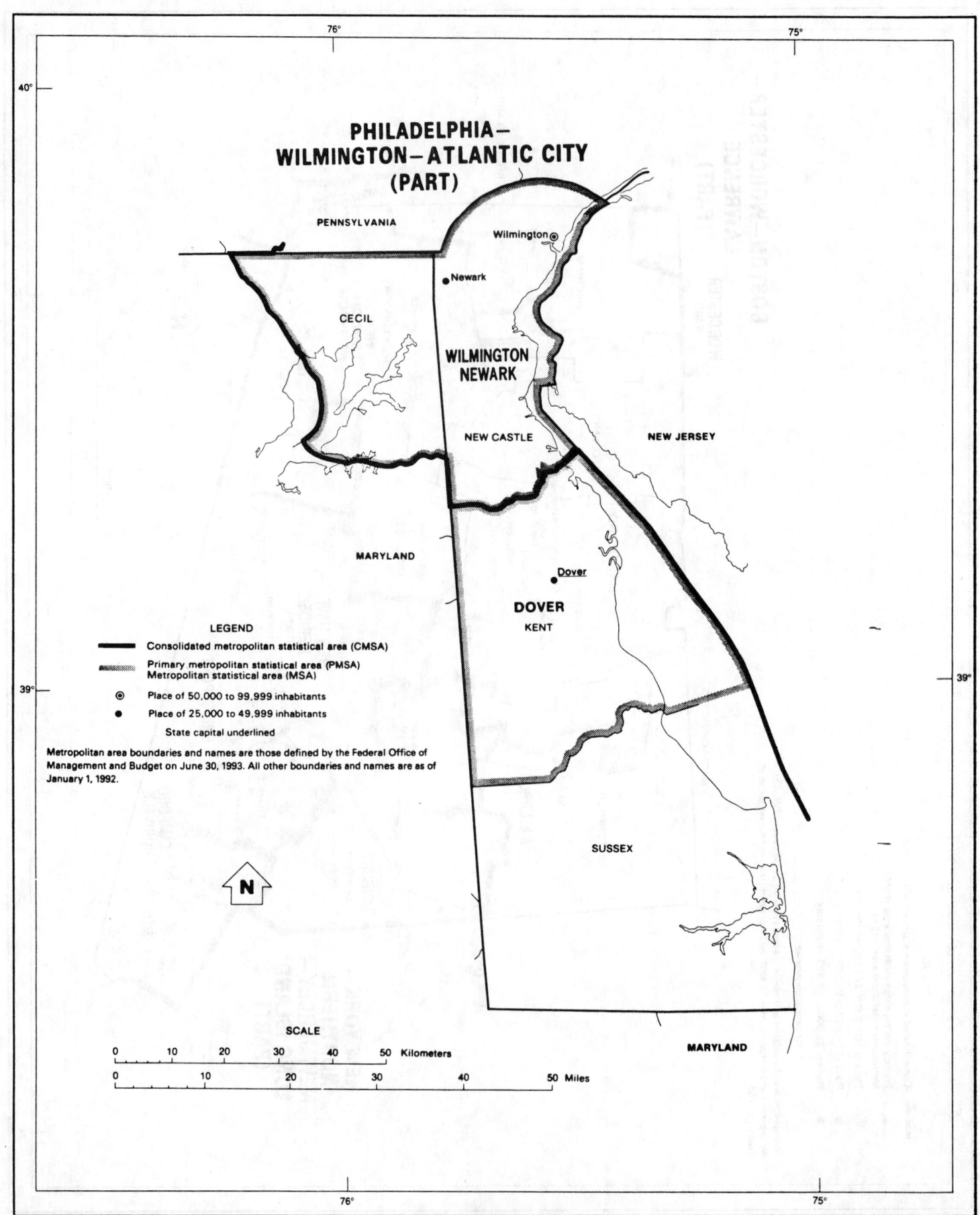

PHILADELPHIA—WILMINGTON—ATLANTIC CITY (PART)

PENNSYLVANIA

Wilmington ⊙

● Newark

CECIL

WILMINGTON
NEWARK

NEW CASTLE

NEW JERSEY

MARYLAND

● Dover

DOVER
KENT

LEGEND

━━━━━ Consolidated metropolitan statistical area (CMSA)

▨▨▨▨ Primary metropolitan statistical area (PMSA)
Metropolitan statistical area (MSA)

⊙ Place of 50,000 to 99,999 inhabitants

● Place of 25,000 to 49,999 inhabitants

State capital underlined

Metropolitan area boundaries and names are those defined by the Federal Office of
Management and Budget on June 30, 1993. All other boundaries and names are as of
January 1, 1992.

SUSSEX

N

SCALE

0 10 20 30 40 50 Kilometers

0 10 20 30 40 50 Miles

MARYLAND

DISTRICT OF COLUMBIA - Metropolitan Area, District of Columbia, Counties, Independent Cities, and Other Selected Places

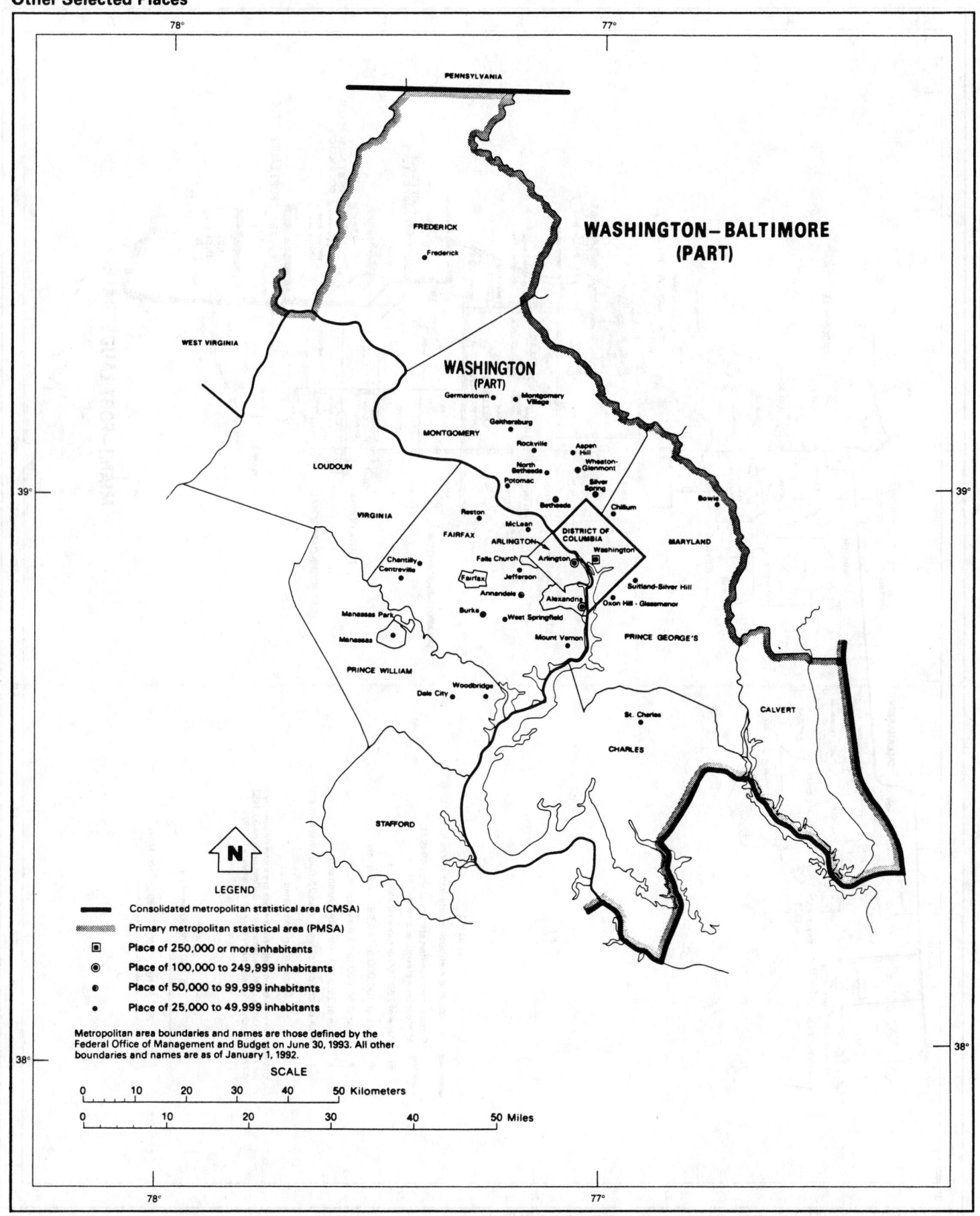

WASHINGTON—BALTIMORE (PART)

WASHINGTON (PART)

PENNSYLVANIA

WEST VIRGINIA

FREDERICK

Frederick

MONTGOMERY

Germantown · Montgomery Village

Gaithersburg

Rockville

North Bethesda · Aspen Hill

Potomac · Wheaton-Glenmont

Silver Spring

Bethesda · Chillum

Bowie

LOUDOUN

VIRGINIA

Reston

McLean

FAIRFAX

ARLINGTON

DISTRICT OF COLUMBIA

Falls Church · Arlington · Washington

Fairfax · Jefferson

Annandale · Alexandria

Suitland-Silver Hill

Oxon Hill - Glassmanor

MARYLAND

Chantilly Centreville

Manassas Park

Burke · West Springfield

Manassas

Mount Vernon

PRINCE GEORGE'S

PRINCE WILLIAM

Dale City · Woodbridge

St. Charles

CALVERT

CHARLES

STAFFORD

LEGEND

▬▬▬	Consolidated metropolitan statistical area (CMSA)
▓▓▓▓	Primary metropolitan statistical area (PMSA)
▣	Place of 250,000 or more inhabitants
◉	Place of 100,000 to 249,999 inhabitants
◎	Place of 50,000 to 99,999 inhabitants
•	Place of 25,000 to 49,999 inhabitants

Metropolitan area boundaries and names are those defined by the Federal Office of Management and Budget on June 30, 1993. All other boundaries and names are as of January 1, 1992.

SCALE

0 10 20 30 40 50 Kilometers

0 10 20 30 40 50 Miles

U.S. DEPARTMENT OF COMMERCE Economics and Statistics Administration Bureau of the Census

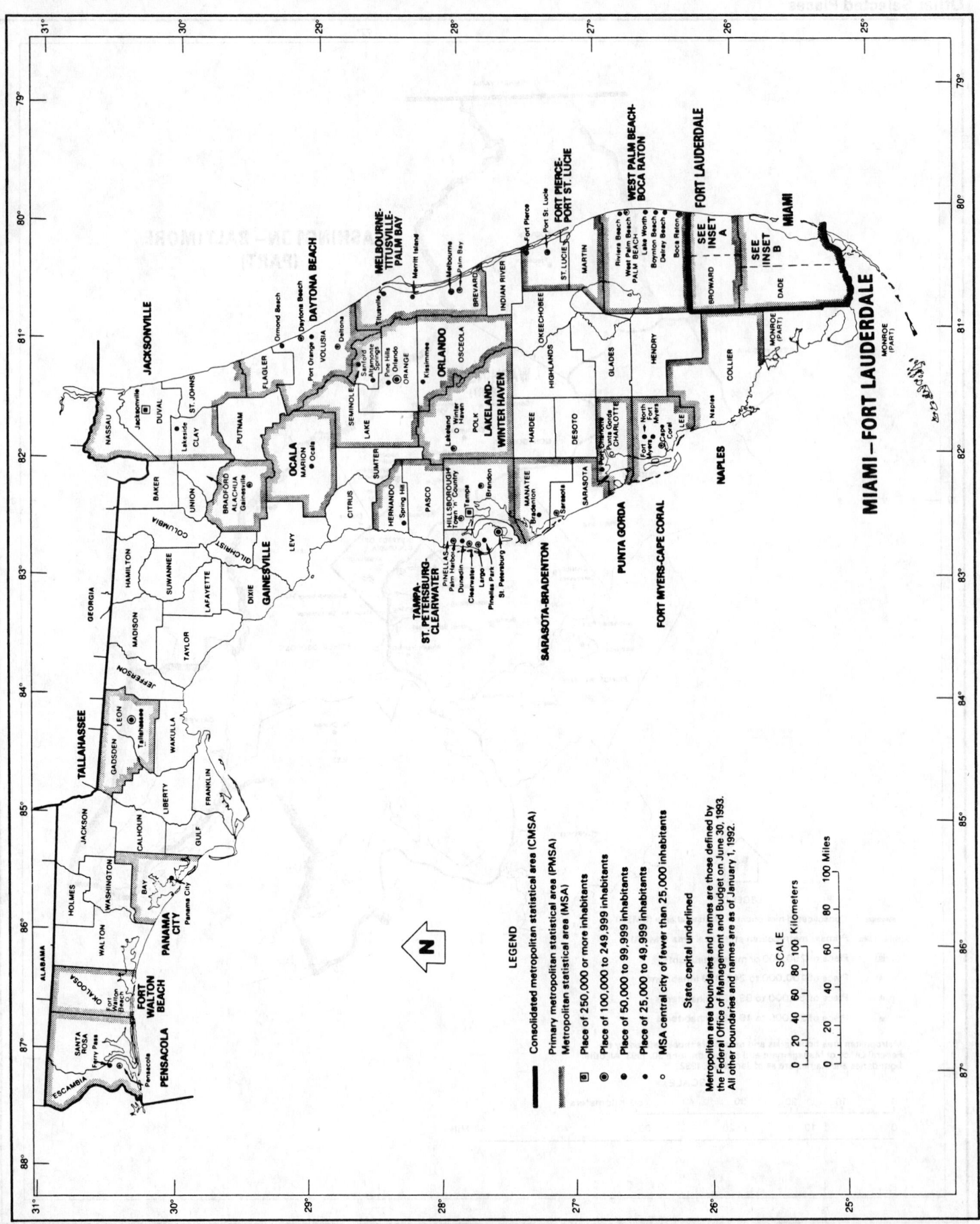

FLORIDA - Metropolitan Areas, Counties, and Selected Places

LEGEND

Consolidated metropolitan statistical area (CMSA)
Primary metropolitan statistical area (PMSA)
Metropolitan statistical area (MSA)

Place of 250,000 or more inhabitants
Place of 100,000 to 249,999 inhabitants
Place of 50,000 to 99,999 inhabitants
Place of 25,000 to 49,999 inhabitants
MSA central city of fewer than 25,000 inhabitants

State capital underlined

Metropolitan area boundaries and names are those defined by the Federal Office of Management and Budget on June 30, 1993. All other boundaries and names are as of January 1, 1992.

SCALE

N

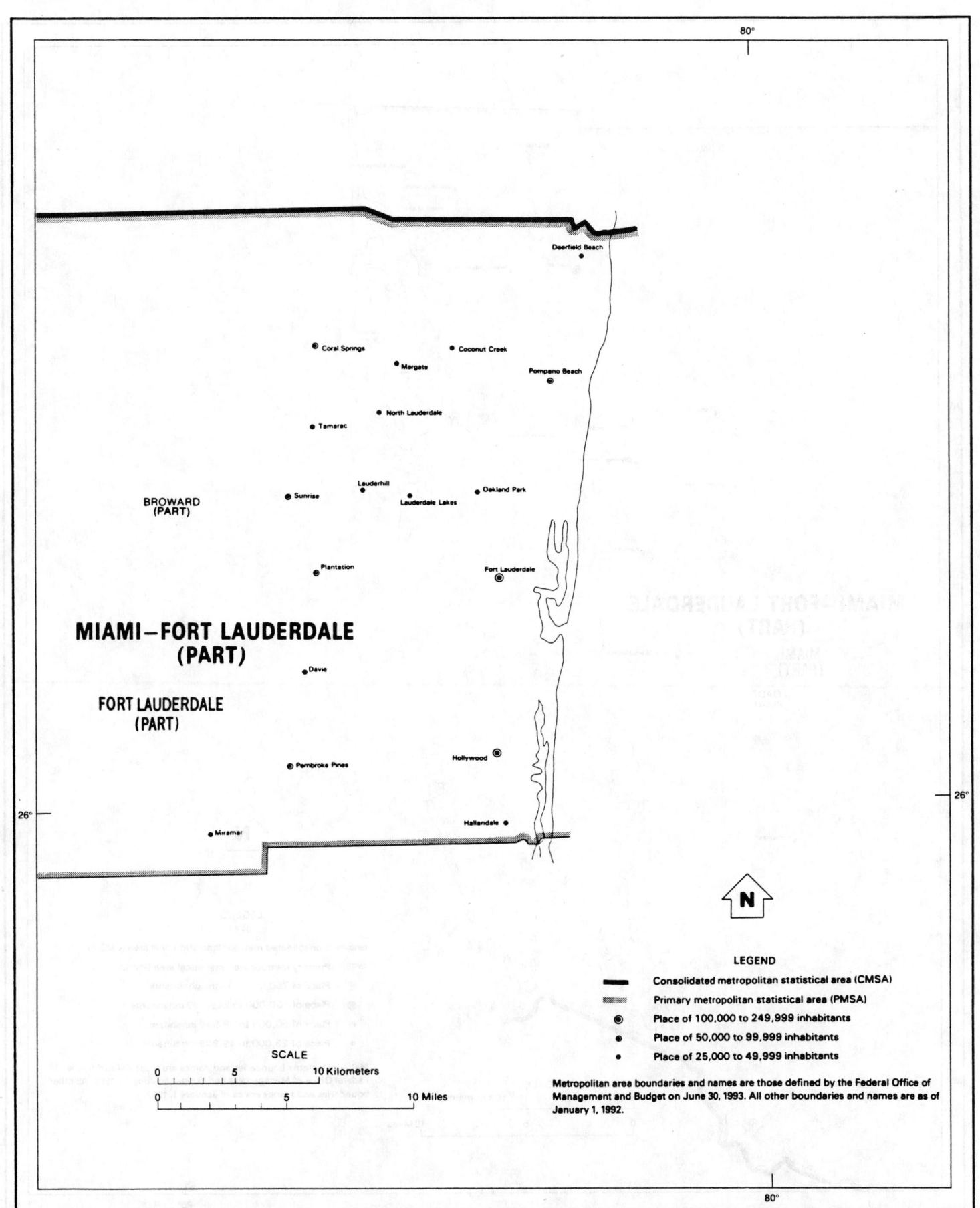

80°

Deerfield Beach

Coral Springs   Coconut Creek

Margate

Pompano Beach

North Lauderdale

Tamarac

BROWARD
(PART)

Lauderhill   Oakland Park
Sunrise   Lauderdale Lakes

Fort Lauderdale

**MIAMI—FORT LAUDERDALE
(PART)**

Plantation

Davie

**FORT LAUDERDALE
(PART)**

Hollywood

26°   26°

Pembroke Pines

Hallandale

Miramar

N

LEGEND

▬▬▬ Consolidated metropolitan statistical area (CMSA)

▨▨▨ Primary metropolitan statistical area (PMSA)

◉ Place of 100,000 to 249,999 inhabitants

● Place of 50,000 to 99,999 inhabitants

• Place of 25,000 to 49,999 inhabitants

Metropolitan area boundaries and names are those defined by the Federal Office of
Management and Budget on June 30, 1993. All other boundaries and names are as of
January 1, 1992.

SCALE

0   5   10 Kilometers

0   5   10 Miles

80°

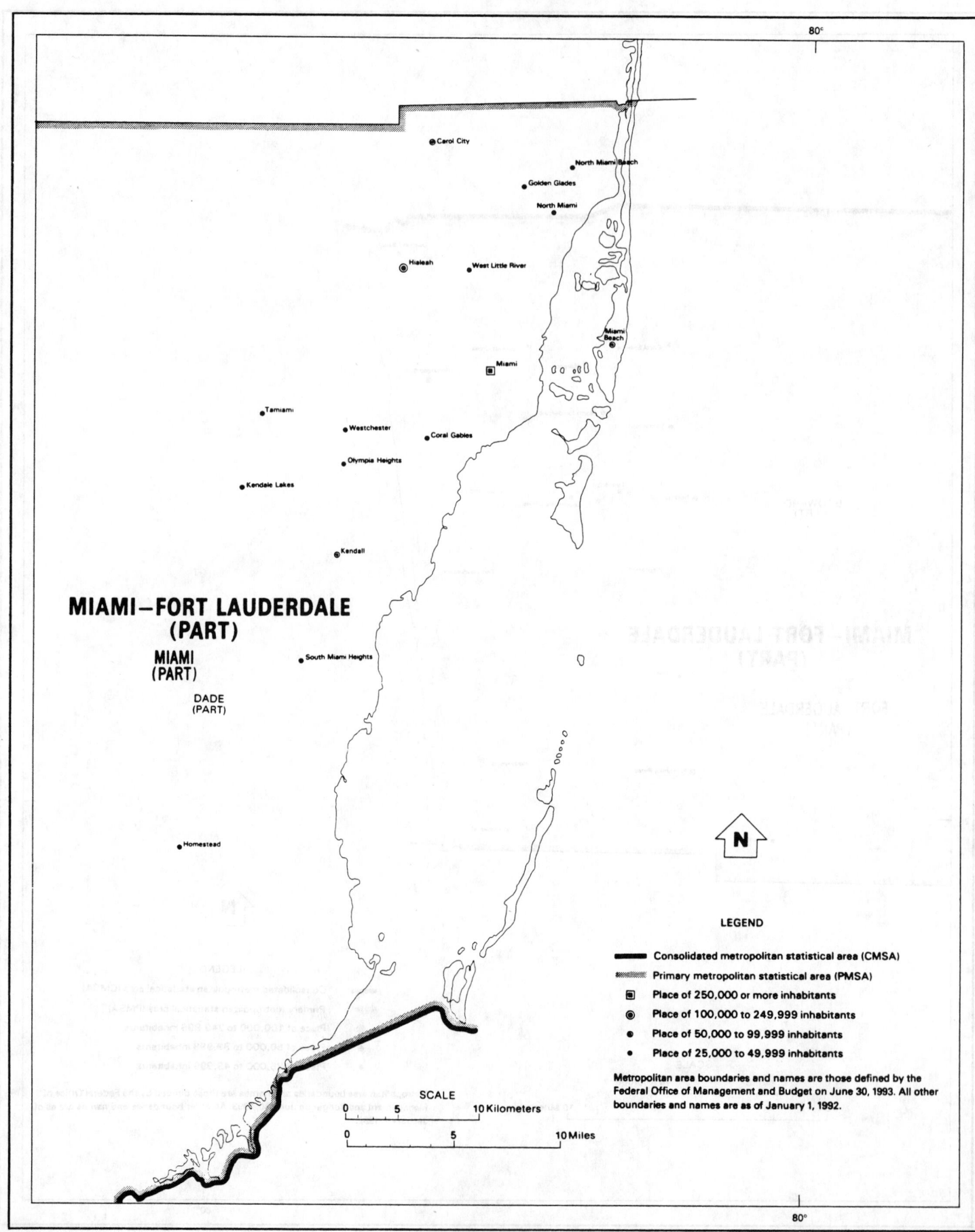

MIAMI–FORT LAUDERDALE
(PART)

MIAMI
(PART)

DADE
(PART)

N

LEGEND

▬▬ Consolidated metropolitan statistical area (CMSA)

▨▨ Primary metropolitan statistical area (PMSA)

▣ Place of 250,000 or more inhabitants

◉ Place of 100,000 to 249,999 inhabitants

● Place of 50,000 to 99,999 inhabitants

• Place of 25,000 to 49,999 inhabitants

Metropolitan area boundaries and names are those defined by the Federal Office of Management and Budget on June 30, 1993. All other boundaries and names are as of January 1, 1992.

SCALE

0   5   10 Kilometers

0   5   10 Miles

Places on map: Carol City, North Miami Beach, Golden Glades, North Miami, Hialeah, West Little River, Miami Beach, Miami, Tamiami, Westchester, Coral Gables, Olympia Heights, Kendale Lakes, Kendall, South Miami Heights, Homestead

GEORGIA - Metropolitan Areas, Counties, and Selected Places

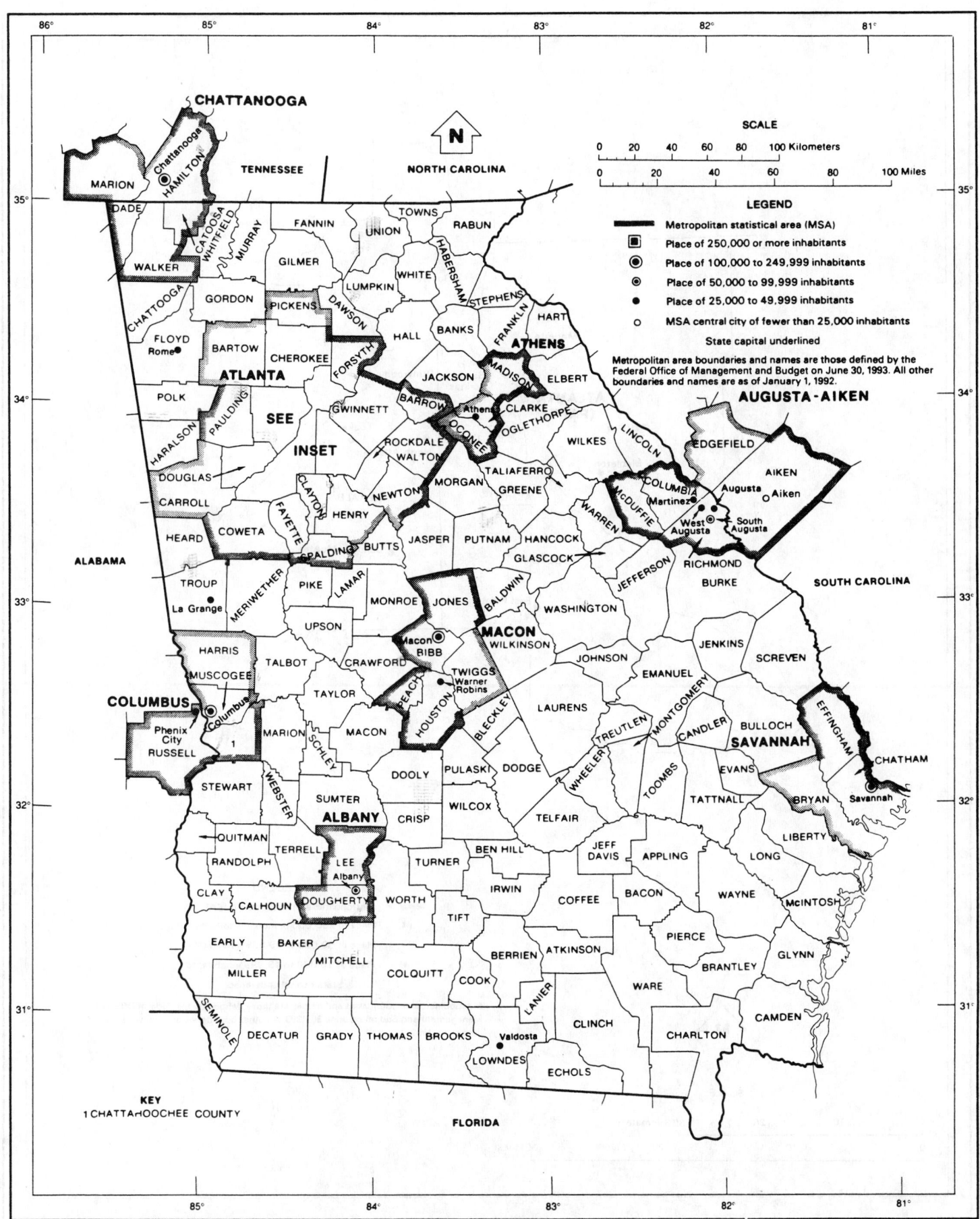

SCALE

| 0 | 20 | 40 | 60 | 80 | 100 Kilometers |

| 0 | 20 | 40 | 60 | 80 | 100 Miles |

LEGEND

— Metropolitan statistical area (MSA)

▪ Place of 250,000 or more inhabitants

◉ Place of 100,000 to 249,999 inhabitants

◎ Place of 50,000 to 99,999 inhabitants

● Place of 25,000 to 49,999 inhabitants

○ MSA central city of fewer than 25,000 inhabitants

State capital underlined

Metropolitan area boundaries and names are those defined by the Federal Office of Management and Budget on June 30, 1993. All other boundaries and names are as of January 1, 1992.

KEY
1 CHATTAHOOCHEE COUNTY

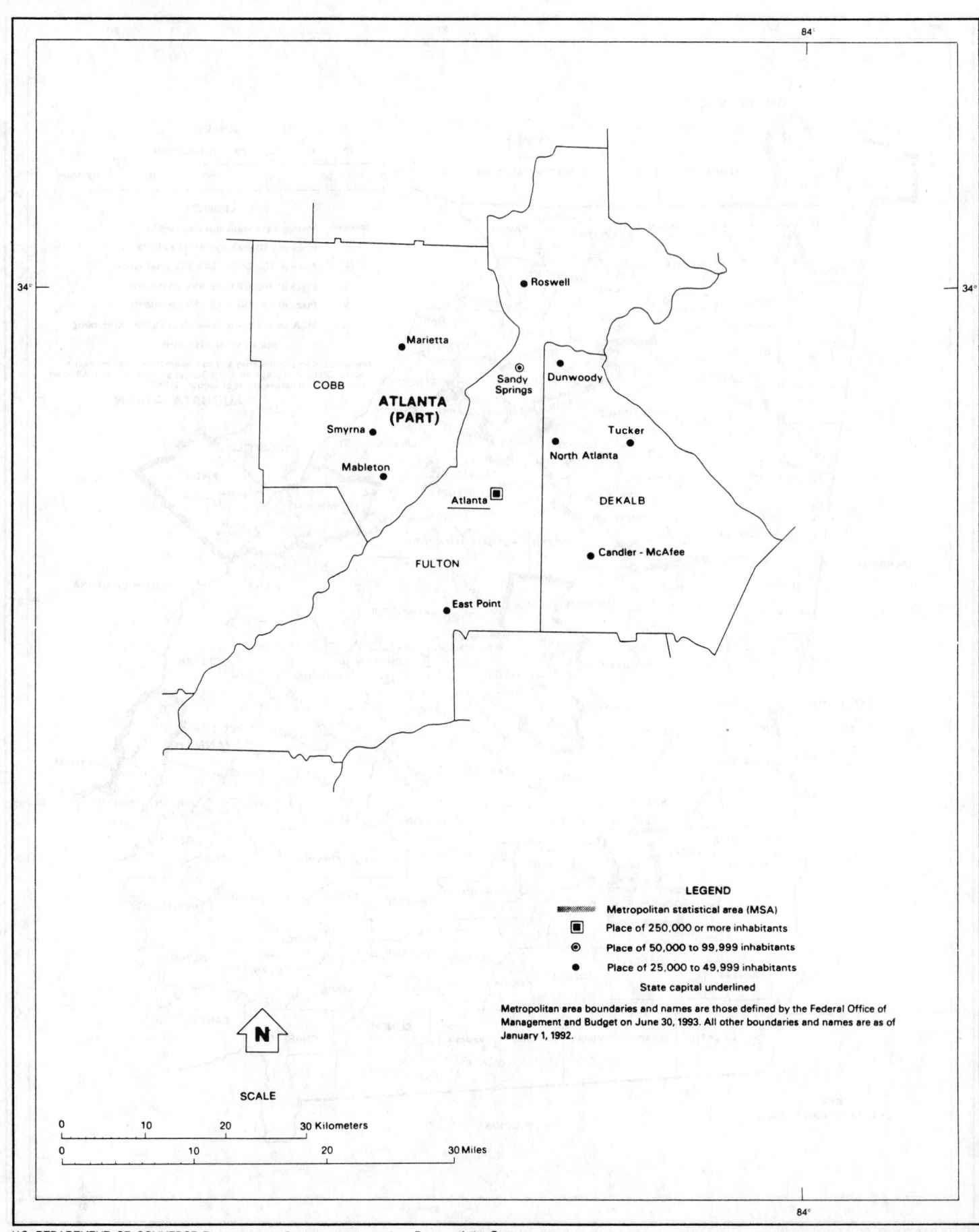

84°

34°   34°

● Roswell

● Marietta

⊙ Sandy   ● Dunwoody
Springs

COBB

**ATLANTA
(PART)**

● Tucker

Smyrna ●

● North Atlanta

Mableton ●

Atlanta ■   **DEKALB**

● Candler - McAfee

FULTON

● East Point

LEGEND

▨▨▨ Metropolitan statistical area (MSA)

■ Place of 250,000 or more inhabitants

⊙ Place of 50,000 to 99,999 inhabitants

● Place of 25,000 to 49,999 inhabitants

State capital underlined

Metropolitan area boundaries and names are those defined by the Federal Office of
Management and Budget on June 30, 1993. All other boundaries and names are as of
January 1, 1992.

N

SCALE

0   10   20   30 Kilometers

0   10   20   30 Miles

84°

HAWAII - Metropolitan Area, Counties, and Selected Places

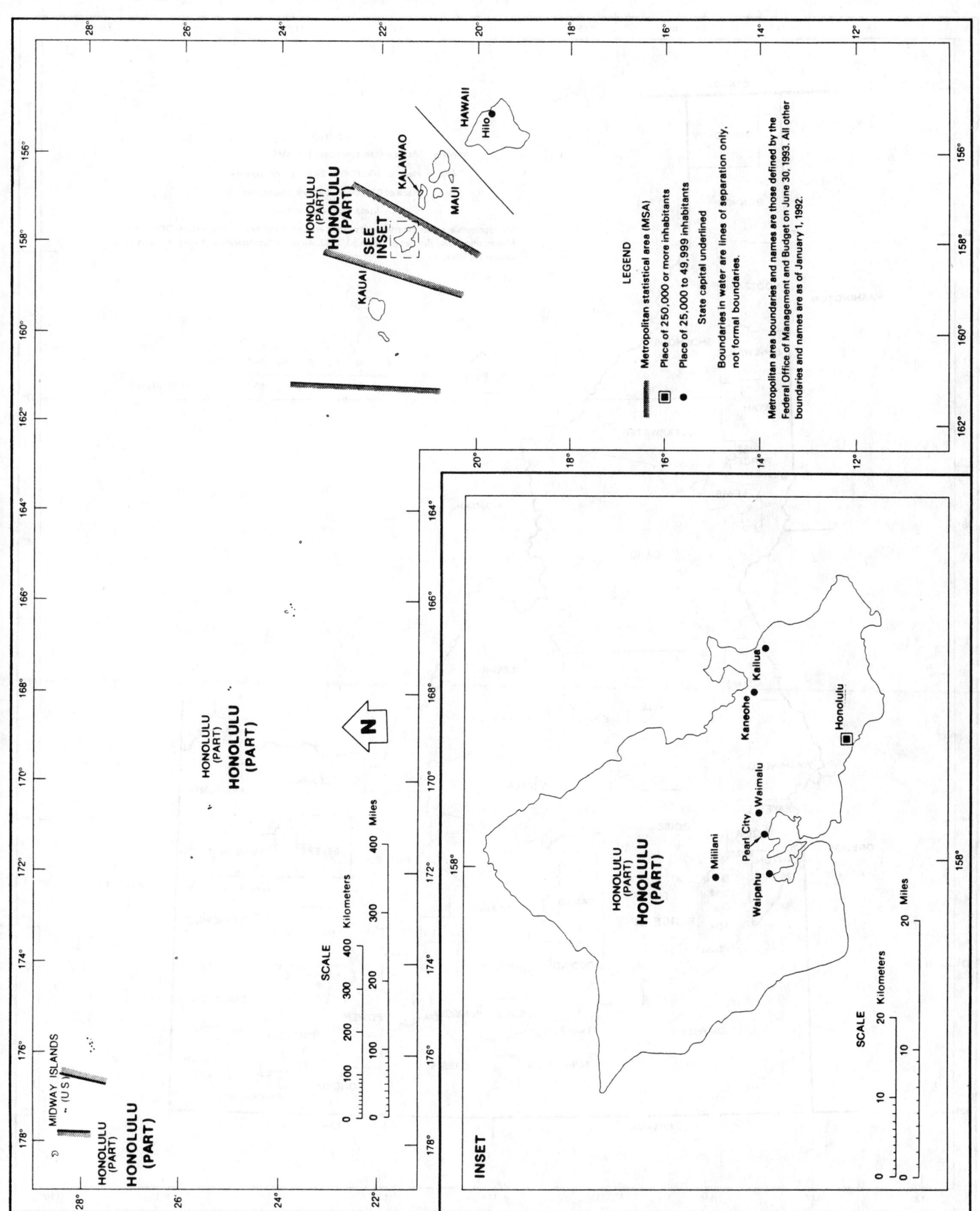

Appendix D

IDAHO - Metropolitan Area, Counties, and Selected Places

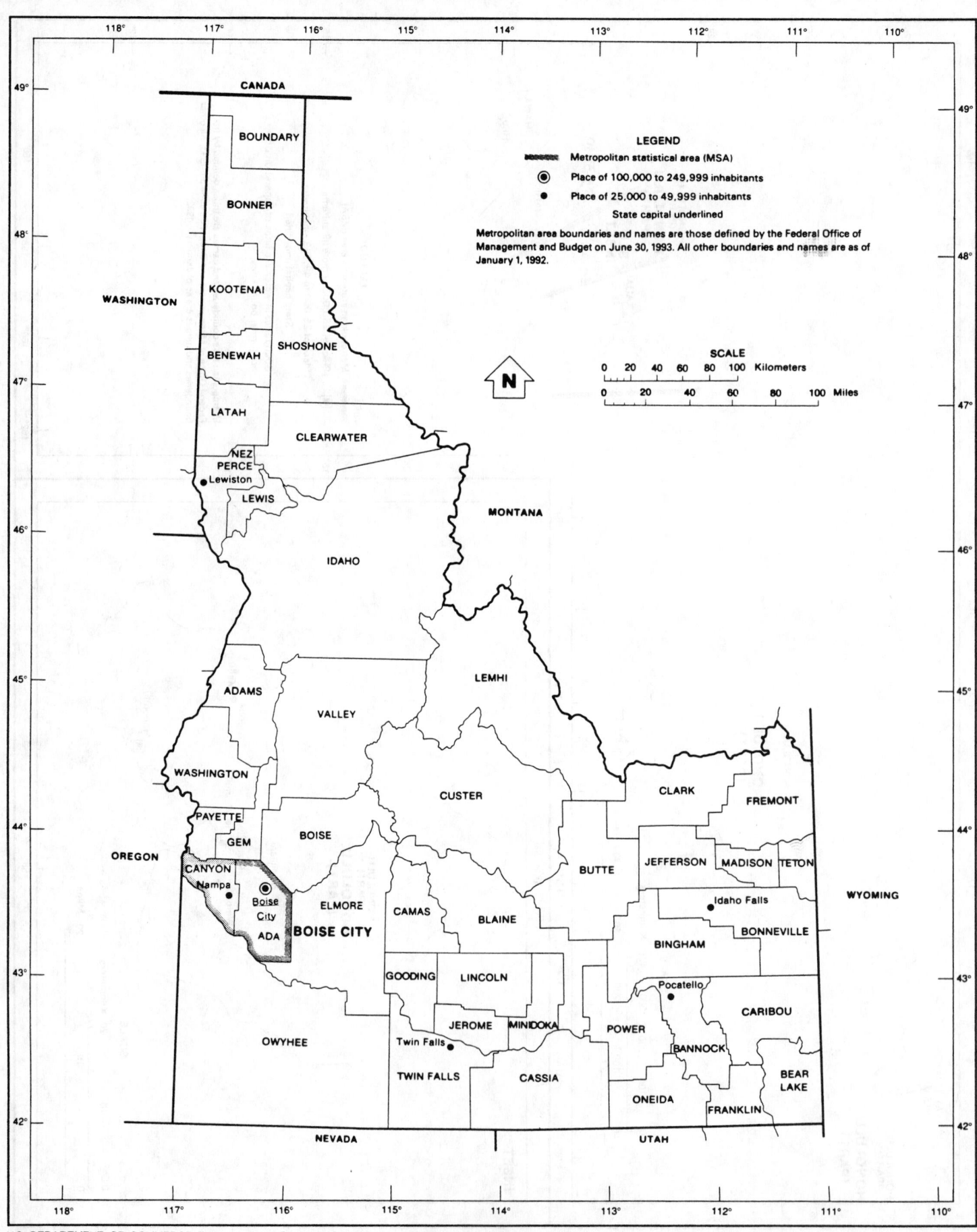

LEGEND

Metropolitan statistical area (MSA)

⦿ Place of 100,000 to 249,999 inhabitants

• Place of 25,000 to 49,999 inhabitants

State capital underlined

Metropolitan area boundaries and names are those defined by the Federal Office of Management and Budget on June 30, 1993. All other boundaries and names are as of January 1, 1992.

U.S. DEPARTMENT OF COMMERCE Economics and Statistics Administration Bureau of the Census

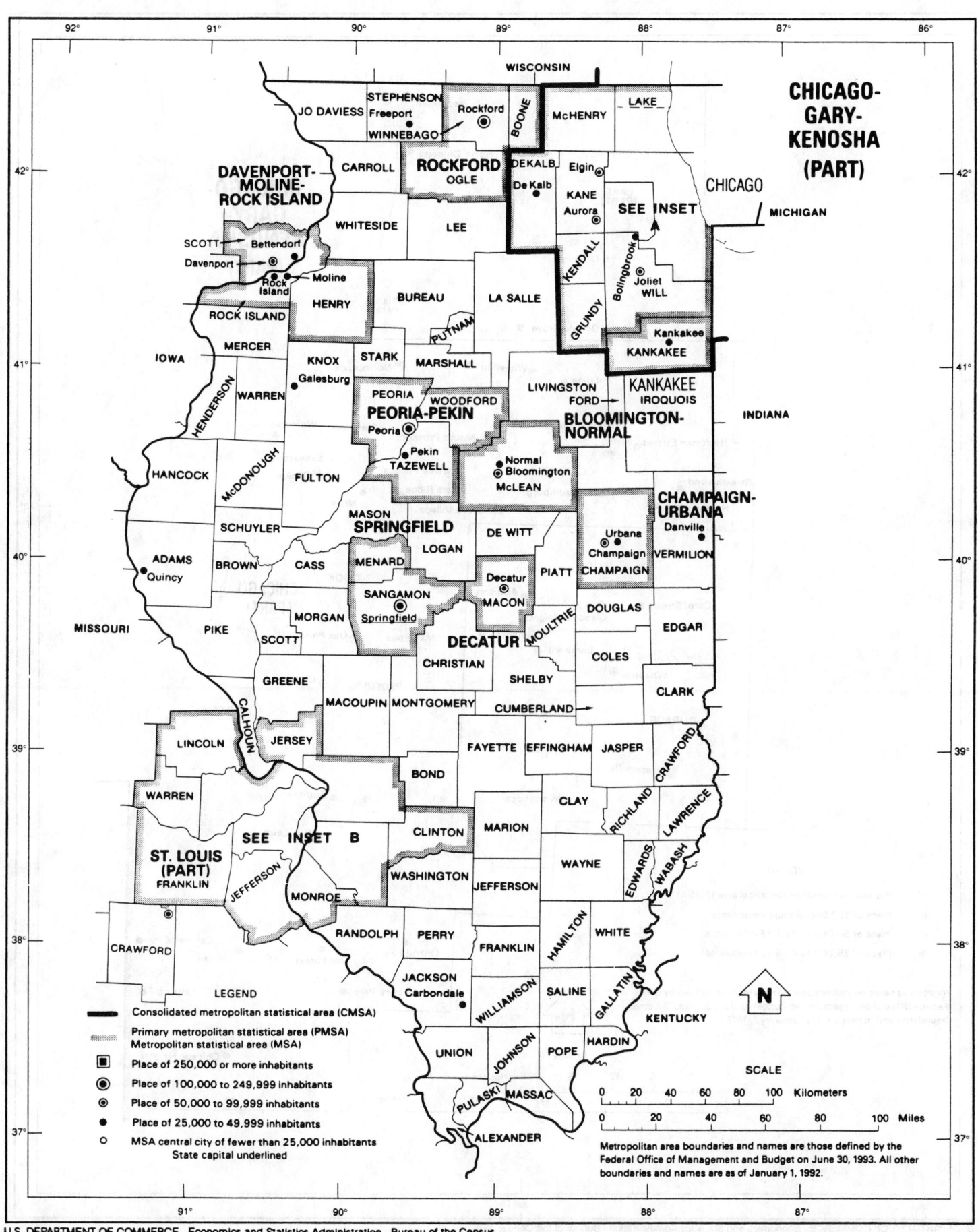

CHICAGO-
GARY-
KENOSHA
(PART)

LEGEND

Consolidated metropolitan statistical area (CMSA)

Primary metropolitan statistical area (PMSA)
Metropolitan statistical area (MSA)

■ Place of 250,000 or more inhabitants

◉ Place of 100,000 to 249,999 inhabitants

⊙ Place of 50,000 to 99,999 inhabitants

● Place of 25,000 to 49,999 inhabitants

○ MSA central city of fewer than 25,000 inhabitants
State capital underlined

SCALE

0   20   40   60   80   100   Kilometers

0   20   40   60   80   100   Miles

Metropolitan area boundaries and names are those defined by the
Federal Office of Management and Budget on June 30, 1993. All other
boundaries and names are as of January 1, 1992.

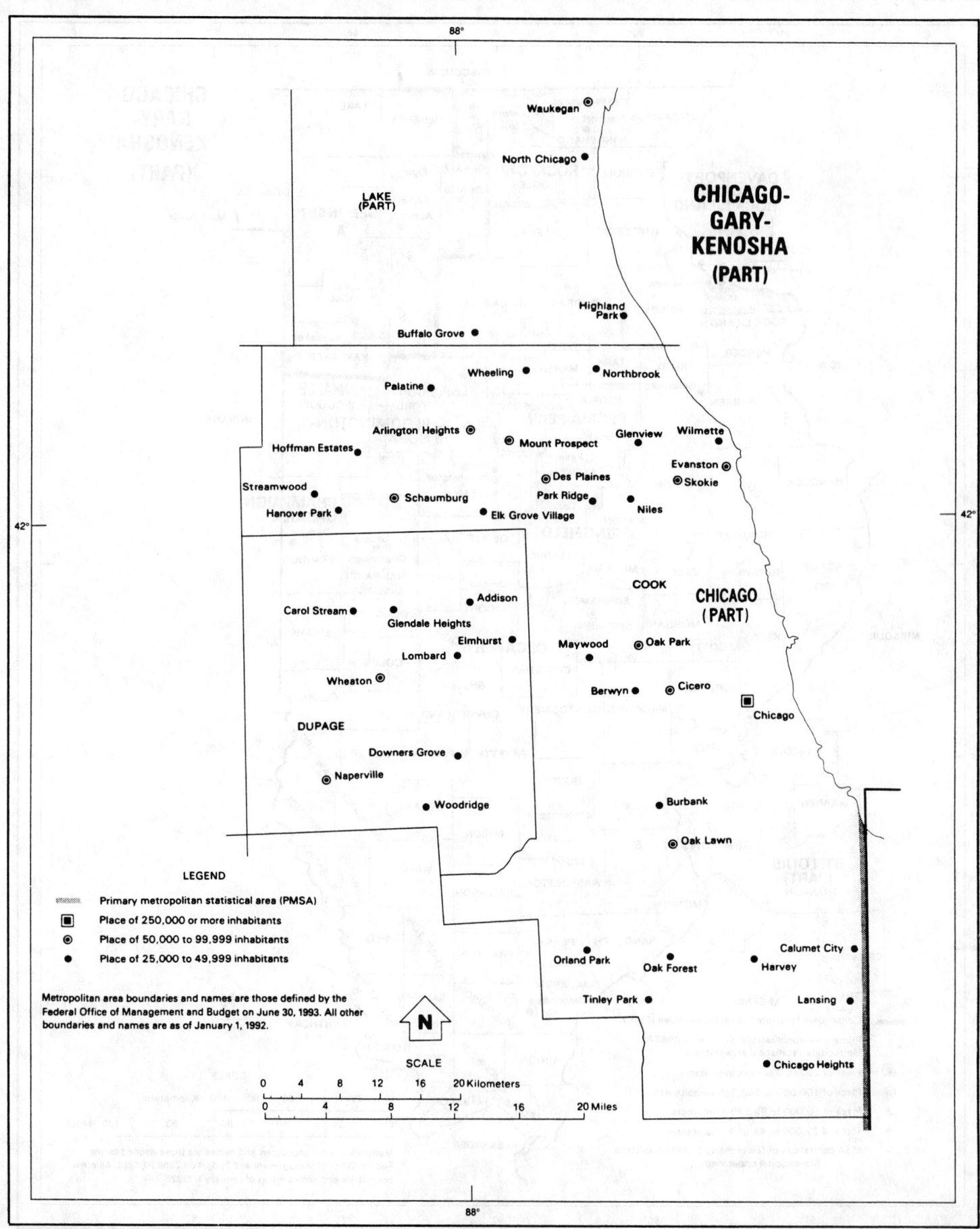

ILLINOIS (Inset A) - Metropolitan Areas, Counties, Independent City, and Other Selected Places

88°

CHICAGO-
GARY-
KENOSHA
(PART)

Waukegan

North Chicago

LAKE
(PART)

Highland
Park

Buffalo Grove

Wheeling   Northbrook

Palatine

Arlington Heights   Mount Prospect   Glenview   Wilmette

Hoffman Estates   Evanston

Des Plaines   Skokie

Streamwood   Schaumburg   Park Ridge

Hanover Park   Elk Grove Village   Niles

42°   42°

COOK   CHICAGO
(PART)

Addison

Carol Stream

Glendale Heights

Elmhurst   Maywood   Oak Park

Lombard

Wheaton   Berwyn   Cicero

Chicago

DUPAGE

Downers Grove

Naperville

Woodridge   Burbank

Oak Lawn

LEGEND

▩ Primary metropolitan statistical area (PMSA)

◼ Place of 250,000 or more inhabitants

◉ Place of 50,000 to 99,999 inhabitants

● Place of 25,000 to 49,999 inhabitants

Metropolitan area boundaries and names are those defined by the
Federal Office of Management and Budget on June 30, 1993. All other
boundaries and names are as of January 1, 1992.

N

Calumet City

Orland Park   Oak Forest   Harvey

Tinley Park   Lansing

SCALE

0   4   8   12   16   20 Kilometers
0   4   8   12   16   20 Miles

Chicago Heights

88°

ILLINOIS (Inset B) - Metropolitan Areas, Counties, Independent City, and Other Selected Places

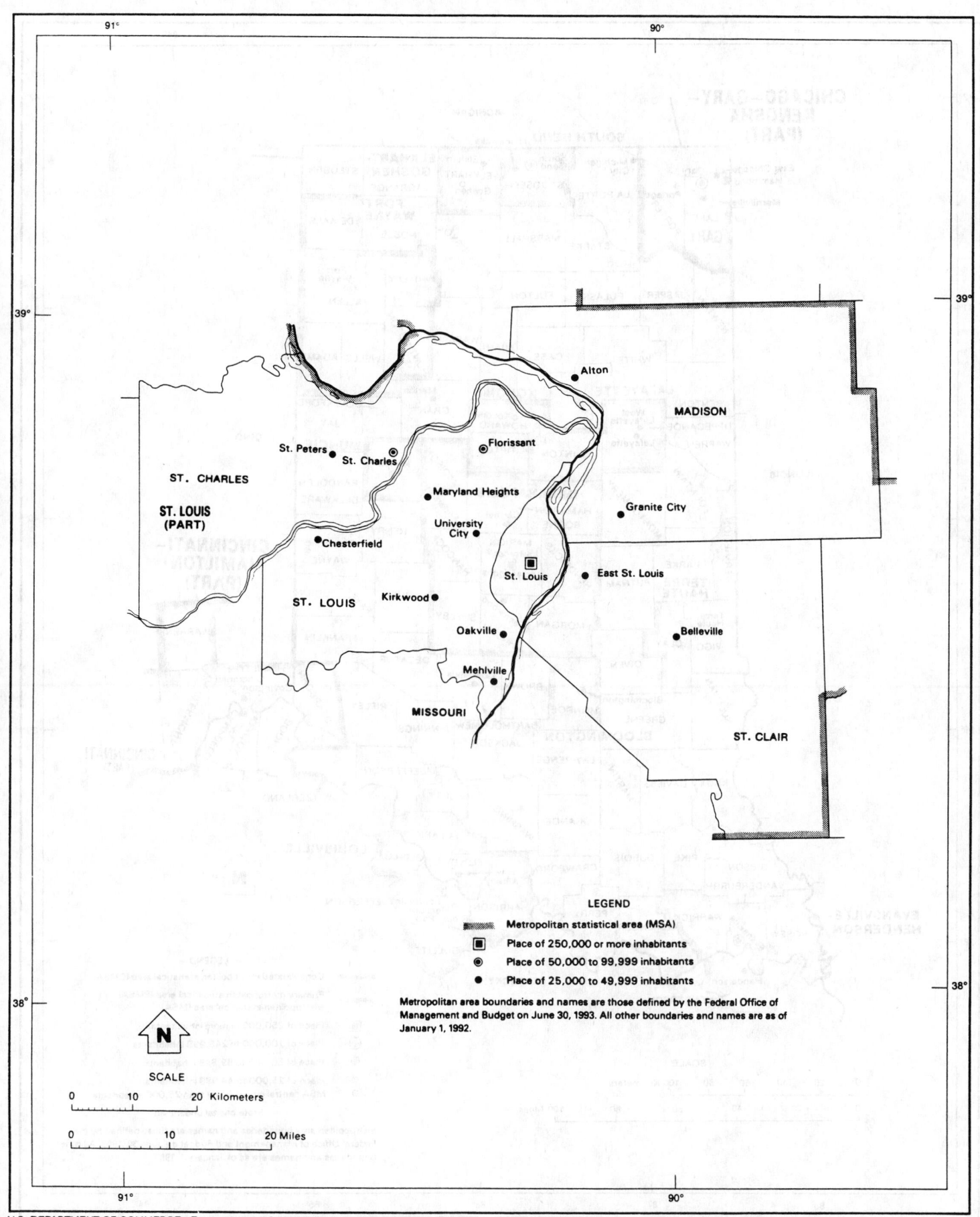

LEGEND

Metropolitan statistical area (MSA)

■ Place of 250,000 or more inhabitants

◉ Place of 50,000 to 99,999 inhabitants

● Place of 25,000 to 49,999 inhabitants

Metropolitan area boundaries and names are those defined by the Federal Office of Management and Budget on June 30, 1993. All other boundaries and names are as of January 1, 1992.

SCALE

0   10   20 Kilometers

0   10   20 Miles

U.S. DEPARTMENT OF COMMERCE   Economics and Statistics Administration   Bureau of the Census

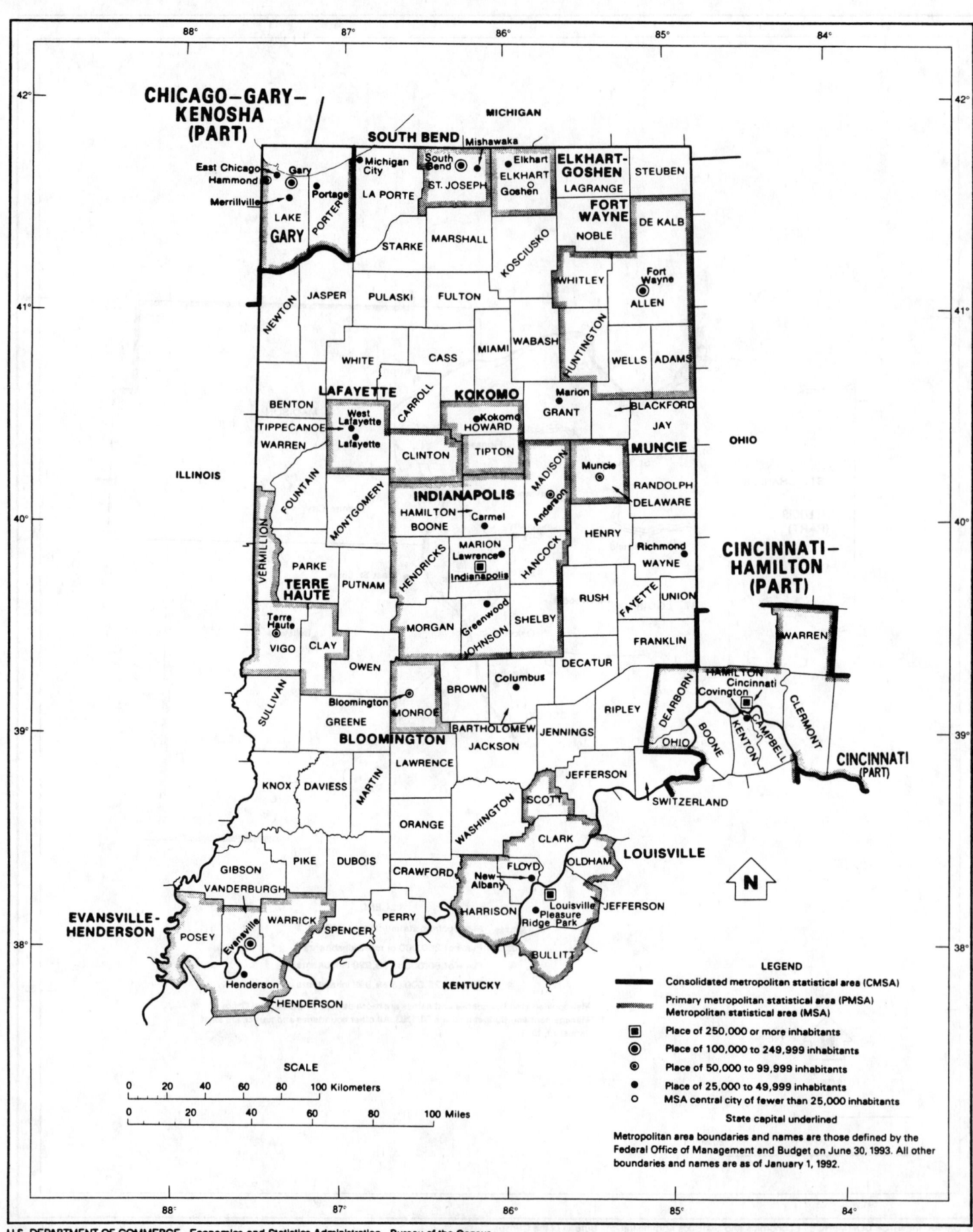

CHICAGO–GARY–
KENOSHA
(PART)

SOUTH BEND

MICHIGAN

ELKHART–
GOSHEN

FORT
WAYNE

LAFAYETTE

KOKOMO

MUNCIE

OHIO

INDIANAPOLIS

ILLINOIS

TERRE
HAUTE

CINCINNATI–
HAMILTON
(PART)

BLOOMINGTON

CINCINNATI
(PART)

LOUISVILLE

EVANSVILLE–
HENDERSON

KENTUCKY

LEGEND

━━━ Consolidated metropolitan statistical area (CMSA)

▬▬▬ Primary metropolitan statistical area (PMSA)
Metropolitan statistical area (MSA)

▣ Place of 250,000 or more inhabitants

◉ Place of 100,000 to 249,999 inhabitants

◉ Place of 50,000 to 99,999 inhabitants

● Place of 25,000 to 49,999 inhabitants

○ MSA central city of fewer than 25,000 inhabitants

State capital underlined

Metropolitan area boundaries and names are those defined by the
Federal Office of Management and Budget on June 30, 1993. All other
boundaries and names are as of January 1, 1992.

SCALE

0 20 40 60 80 100 Kilometers

0 20 40 60 80 100 Miles

N

IOWA - Metropolitan Areas, Counties, and Selected Places

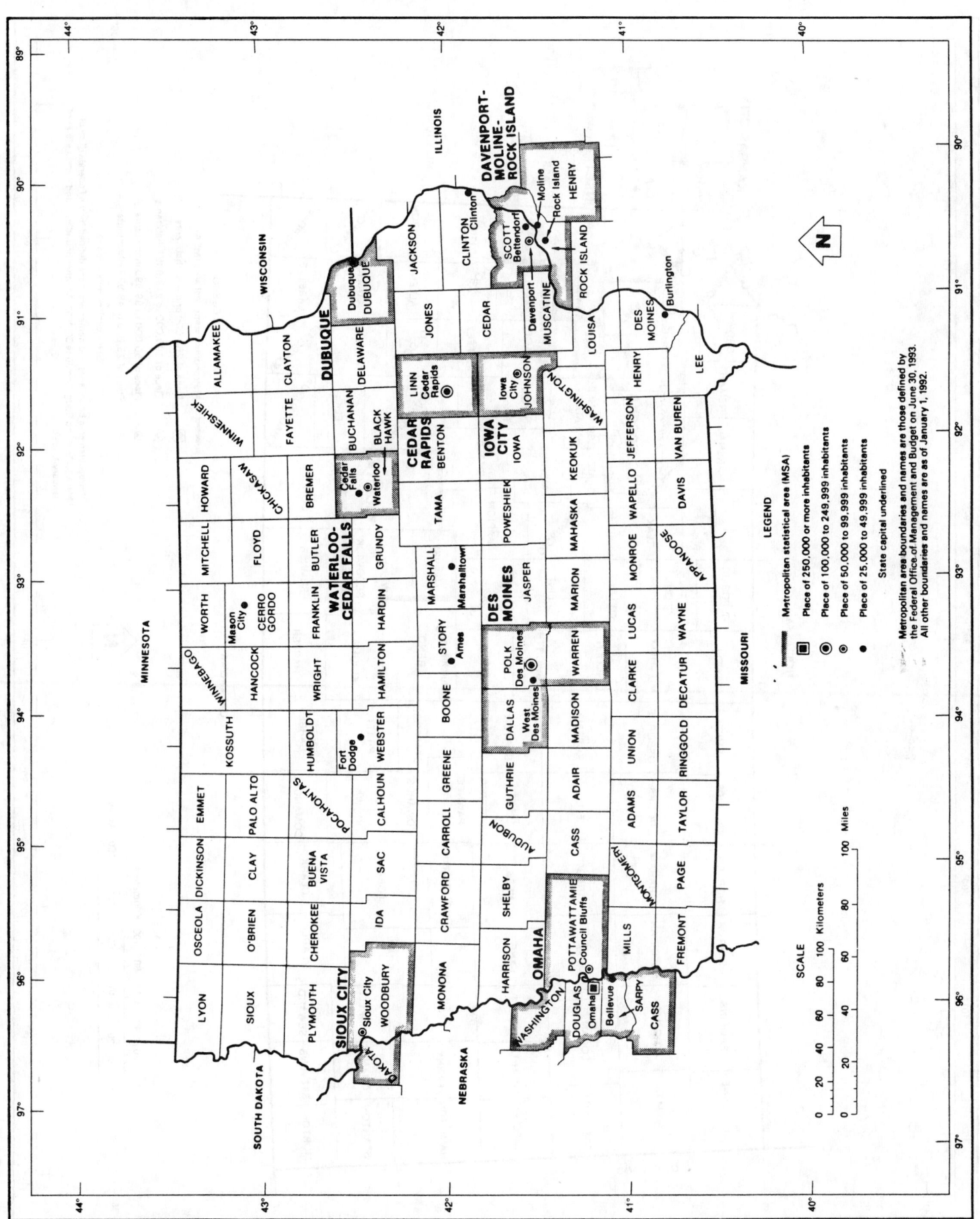

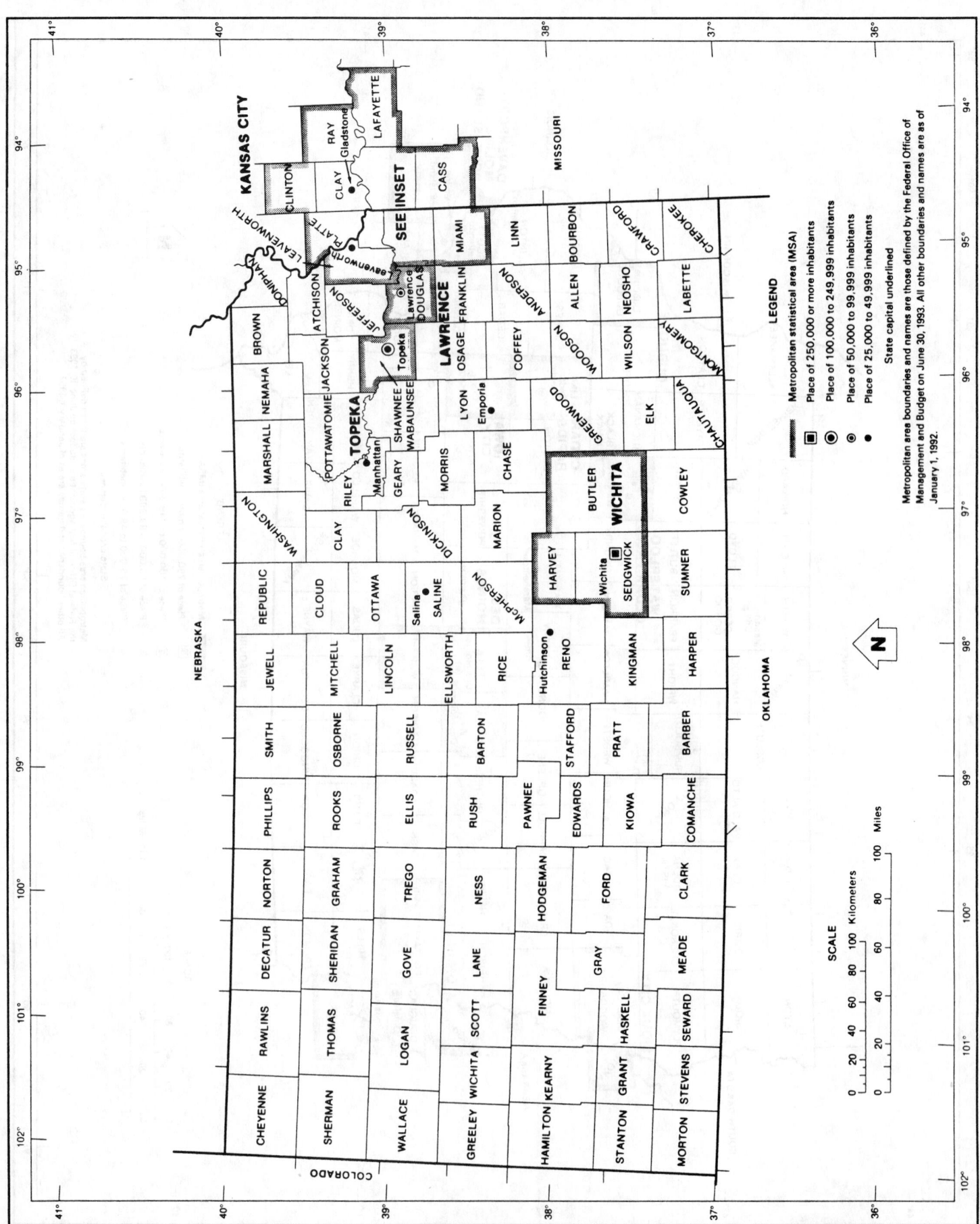

LEGEND

Metropolitan statistical area (MSA)

■ Place of 250,000 or more inhabitants

◉ Place of 100,000 to 249,999 inhabitants

◎ Place of 50,000 to 99,999 inhabitants

● Place of 25,000 to 49,999 inhabitants

State capital underlined

Metropolitan area boundaries and names are those defined by the Federal Office of Management and Budget on June 30, 1993. All other boundaries and names are as of January 1, 1992.

N

SCALE

Kilometers

0   20   40   60   80   100

0   20   40   60   80   100   Miles

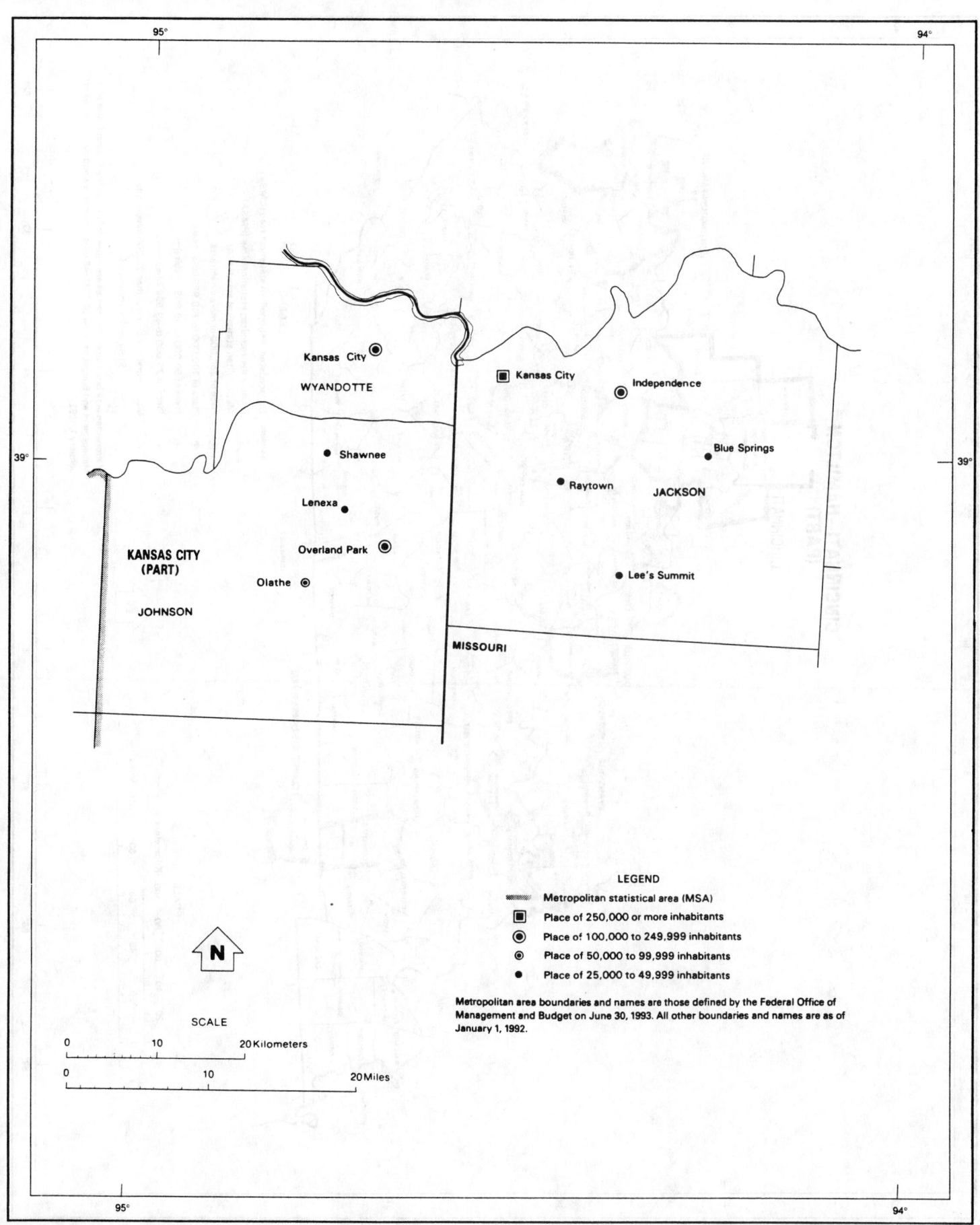

95°   94°

Kansas City ◉

WYANDOTTE

▣ Kansas City   ◉ Independence

39°   ● Shawnee   ● Blue Springs   39°

● Raytown   JACKSON

Lenexa ●

KANSAS CITY (PART)   Overland Park ◉

Olathe ◉

JOHNSON   ● Lee's Summit

MISSOURI

LEGEND

〰️ Metropolitan statistical area (MSA)

▣ Place of 250,000 or more inhabitants

◉ Place of 100,000 to 249,999 inhabitants

◉ Place of 50,000 to 99,999 inhabitants

● Place of 25,000 to 49,999 inhabitants

Metropolitan area boundaries and names are those defined by the Federal Office of Management and Budget on June 30, 1993. All other boundaries and names are as of January 1, 1992.

N

SCALE

0   10   20 Kilometers

0   10   20 Miles

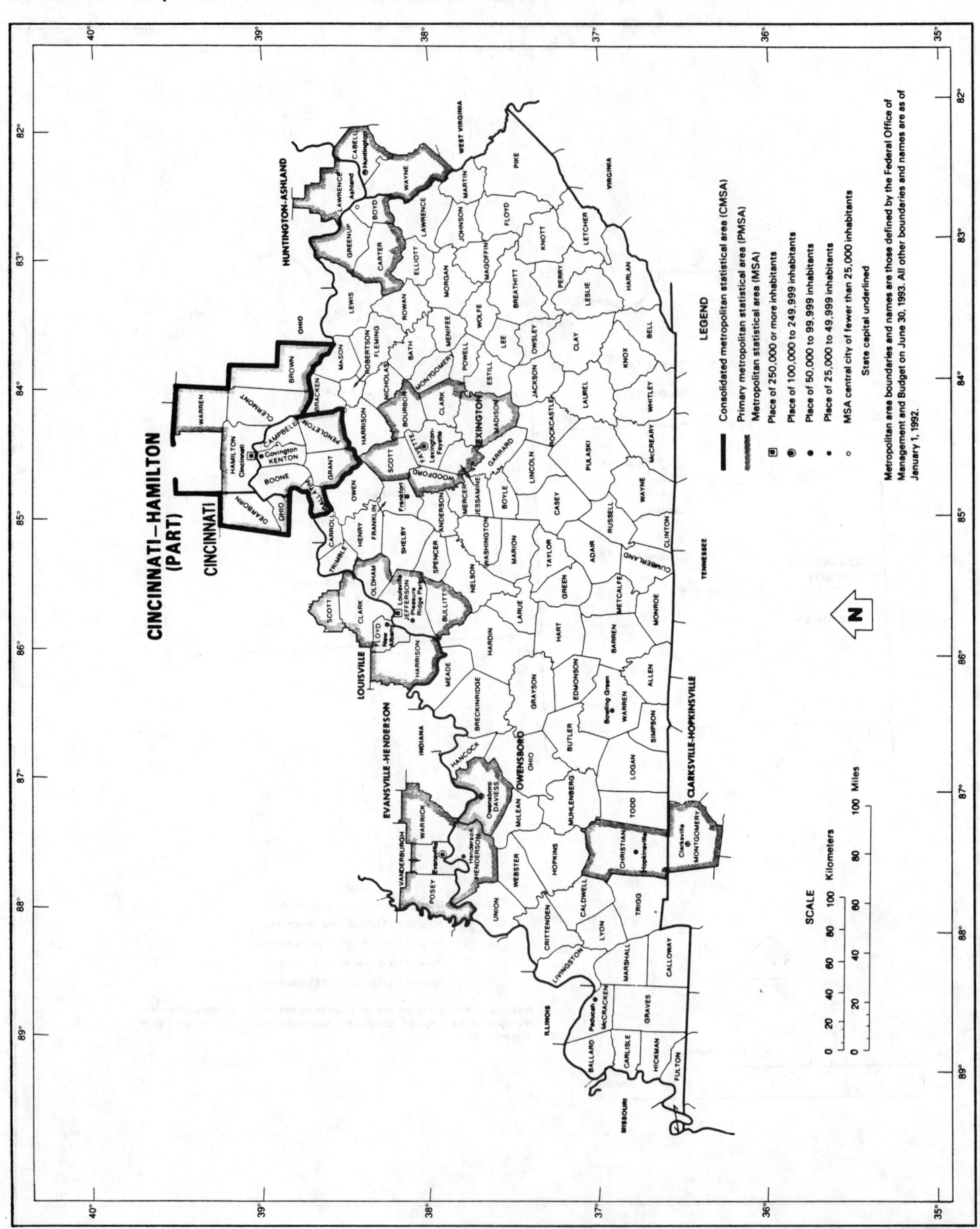

LOUISIANA - Metropolitan Areas, Parishes, and Selected Places

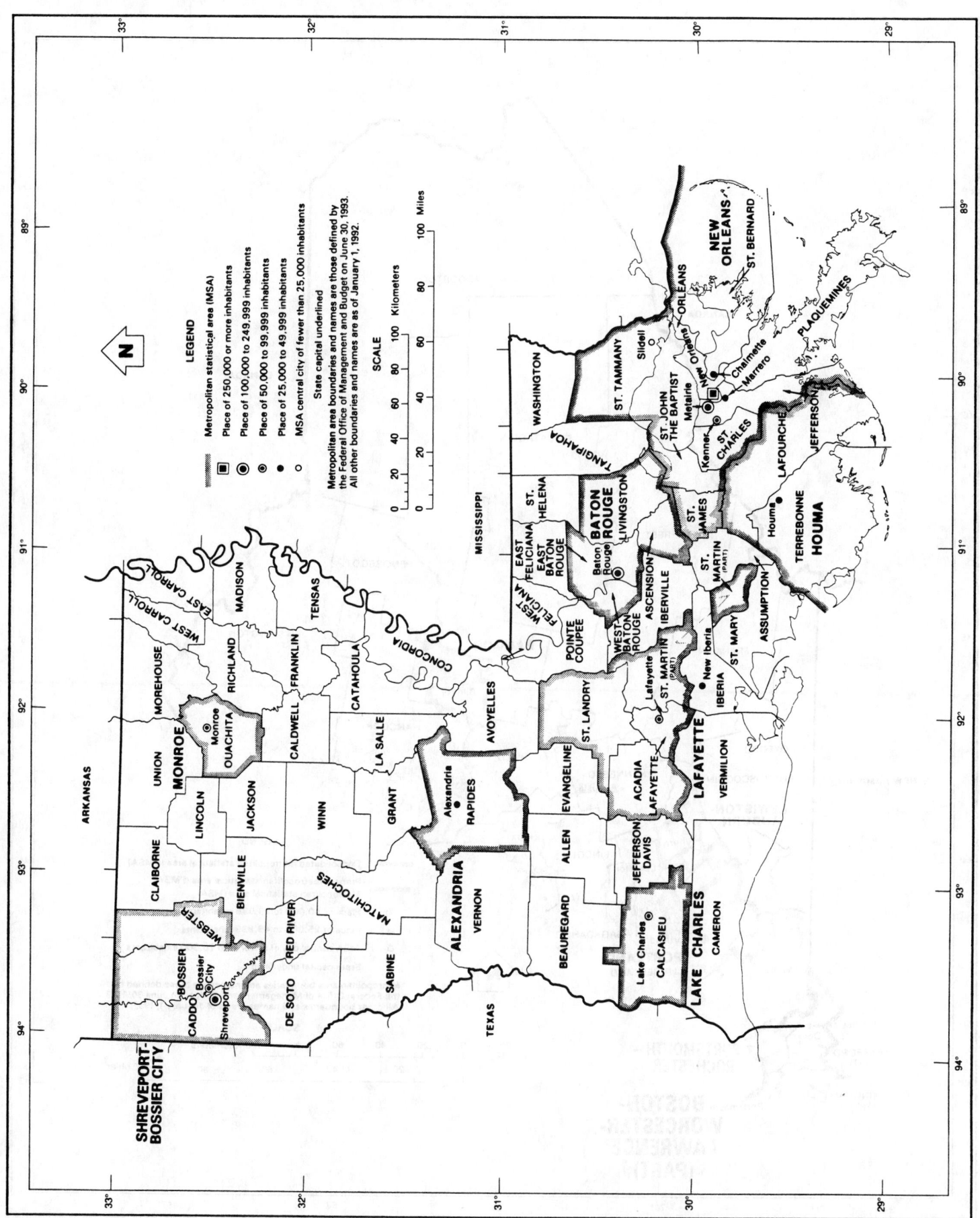

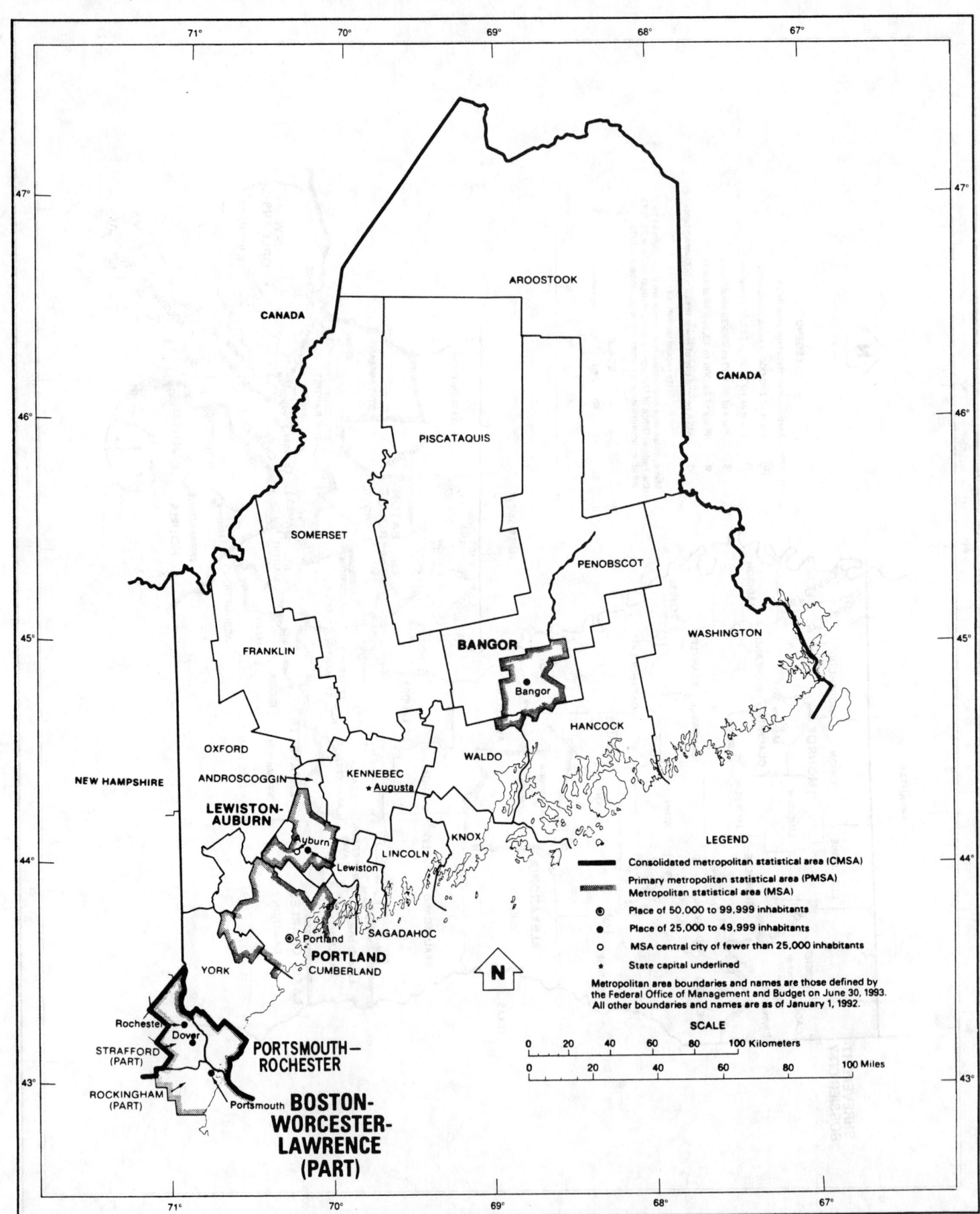

MAINE - Metropolitan Areas, Counties, and Selected Places

CANADA

AROOSTOOK

PISCATAQUIS

SOMERSET

PENOBSCOT

CANADA

BANGOR

● Bangor

WASHINGTON

FRANKLIN

HANCOCK

OXFORD

WALDO

KENNEBEC
★ Augusta

NEW HAMPSHIRE

ANDROSCOGGIN

LEWISTON-
AUBURN

● Auburn

KNOX

LINCOLN

● Lewiston

YORK

SAGADAHOC

◎ Portland

PORTLAND
CUMBERLAND

Rochester

Dover

**PORTSMOUTH—
ROCHESTER**

STRAFFORD
(PART)

ROCKINGHAM
(PART)

Portsmouth

**BOSTON-
WORCESTER-
LAWRENCE
(PART)**

LEGEND

▬▬▬ Consolidated metropolitan statistical area (CMSA)

▬▬▬ Primary metropolitan statistical area (PMSA)
Metropolitan statistical area (MSA)

◉ Place of 50,000 to 99,999 inhabitants

● Place of 25,000 to 49,999 inhabitants

○ MSA central city of fewer than 25,000 inhabitants

★ State capital underlined

Metropolitan area boundaries and names are those defined by
the Federal Office of Management and Budget on June 30, 1993.
All other boundaries and names are as of January 1, 1992.

SCALE

0   20   40   60   80   100 Kilometers

0   20   40   60   80   100 Miles

N

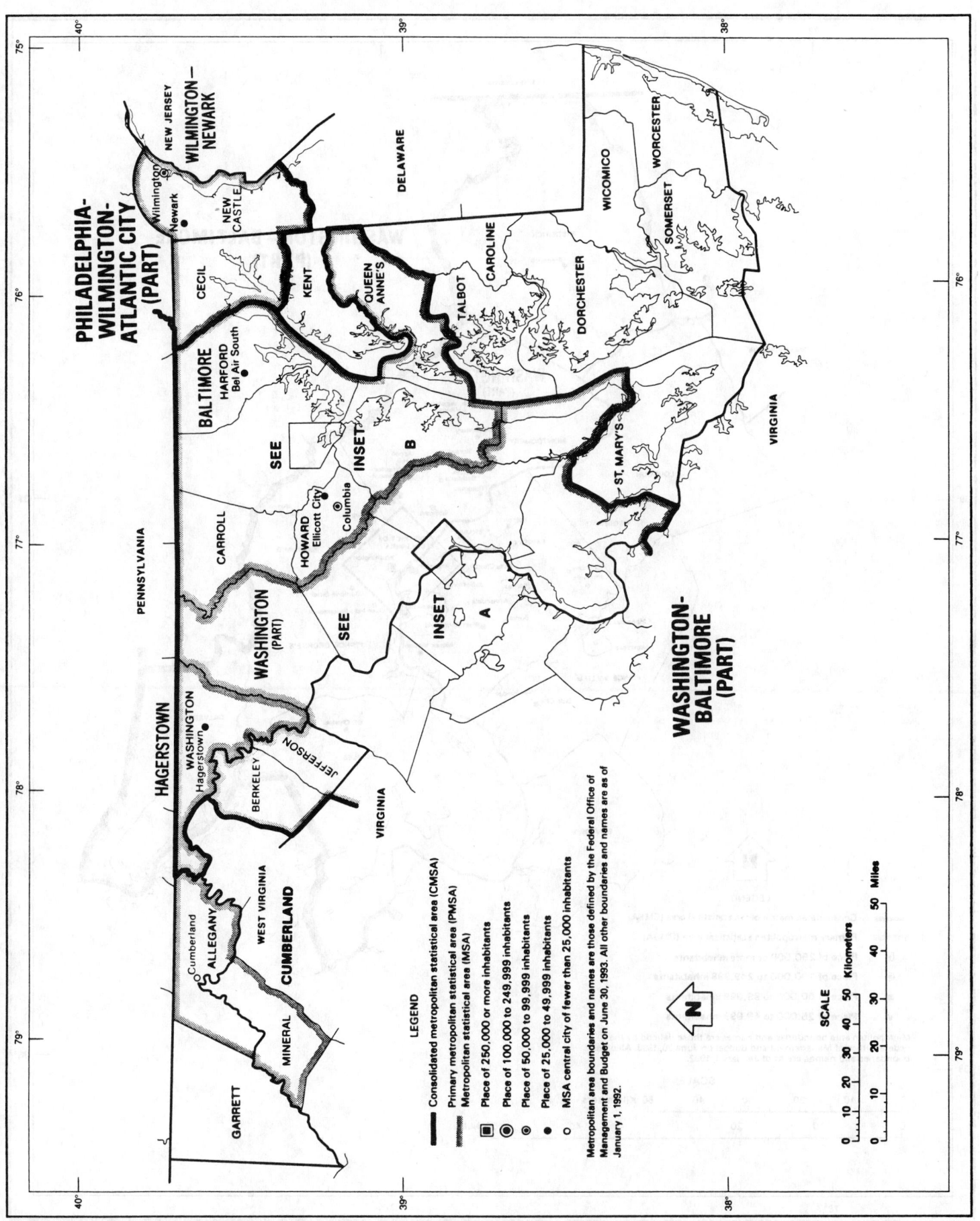

LEGEND

Consolidated metropolitan statistical area (CMSA)
Primary metropolitan statistical area (PMSA)
Metropolitan statistical area (MSA)

Place of 250,000 or more inhabitants
Place of 100,000 to 249,999 inhabitants
Place of 50,000 to 99,999 inhabitants
Place of 25,000 to 49,999 inhabitants
MSA central city of fewer than 25,000 inhabitants

Metropolitan area boundaries and names are those defined by the Federal Office of Management and Budget on June 30, 1993. All other boundaries and names are as of January 1, 1992.

N

SCALE

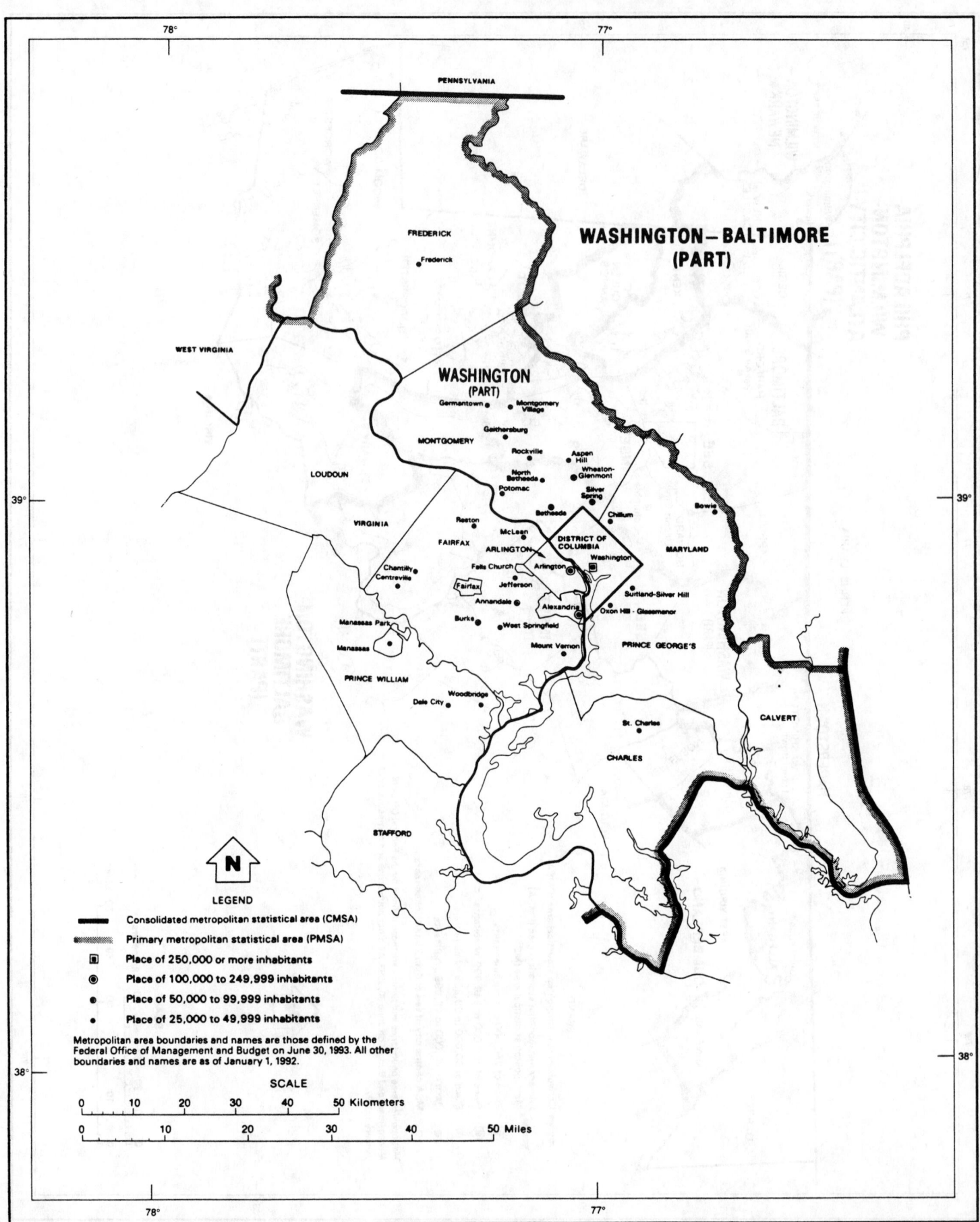

LEGEND

▬	Consolidated metropolitan statistical area (CMSA)
▬	Primary metropolitan statistical area (PMSA)
▣	Place of 250,000 or more inhabitants
◉	Place of 100,000 to 249,999 inhabitants
●	Place of 50,000 to 99,999 inhabitants
•	Place of 25,000 to 49,999 inhabitants

Metropolitan area boundaries and names are those defined by the Federal Office of Management and Budget on June 30, 1993. All other boundaries and names are as of January 1, 1992.

SCALE

0 10 20 30 40 50 Kilometers

0 10 20 30 40 50 Miles

U.S. DEPARTMENT OF COMMERCE Economics and Statistics Administration Bureau of the Census

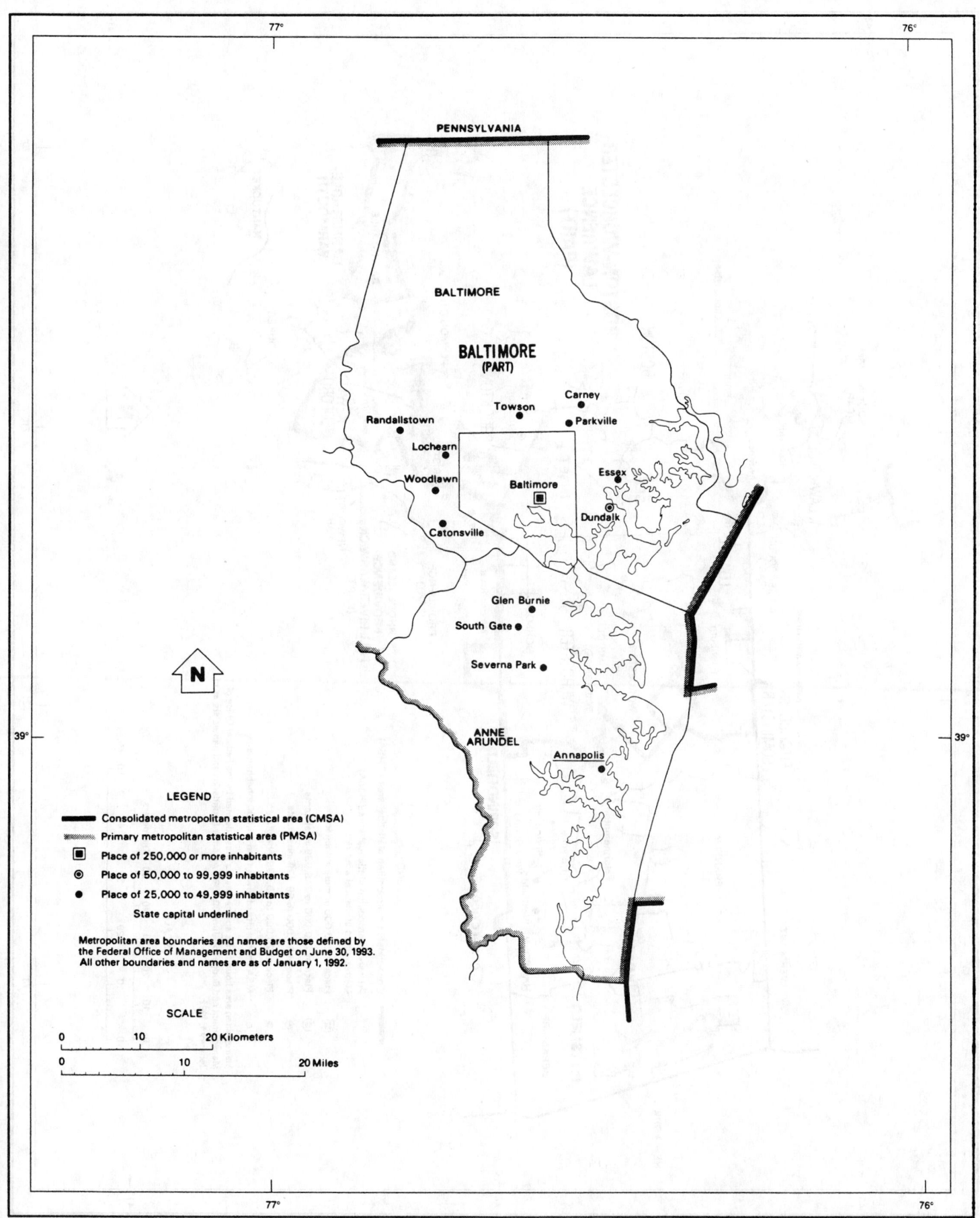

LEGEND

━━━ Consolidated metropolitan statistical area (CMSA)

▨▨▨ Primary metropolitan statistical area (PMSA)

▣ Place of 250,000 or more inhabitants

◉ Place of 50,000 to 99,999 inhabitants

● Place of 25,000 to 49,999 inhabitants

State capital underlined

Metropolitan area boundaries and names are those defined by
the Federal Office of Management and Budget on June 30, 1993.
All other boundaries and names are as of January 1, 1992.

SCALE

0   10   20 Kilometers

0   10   20 Miles

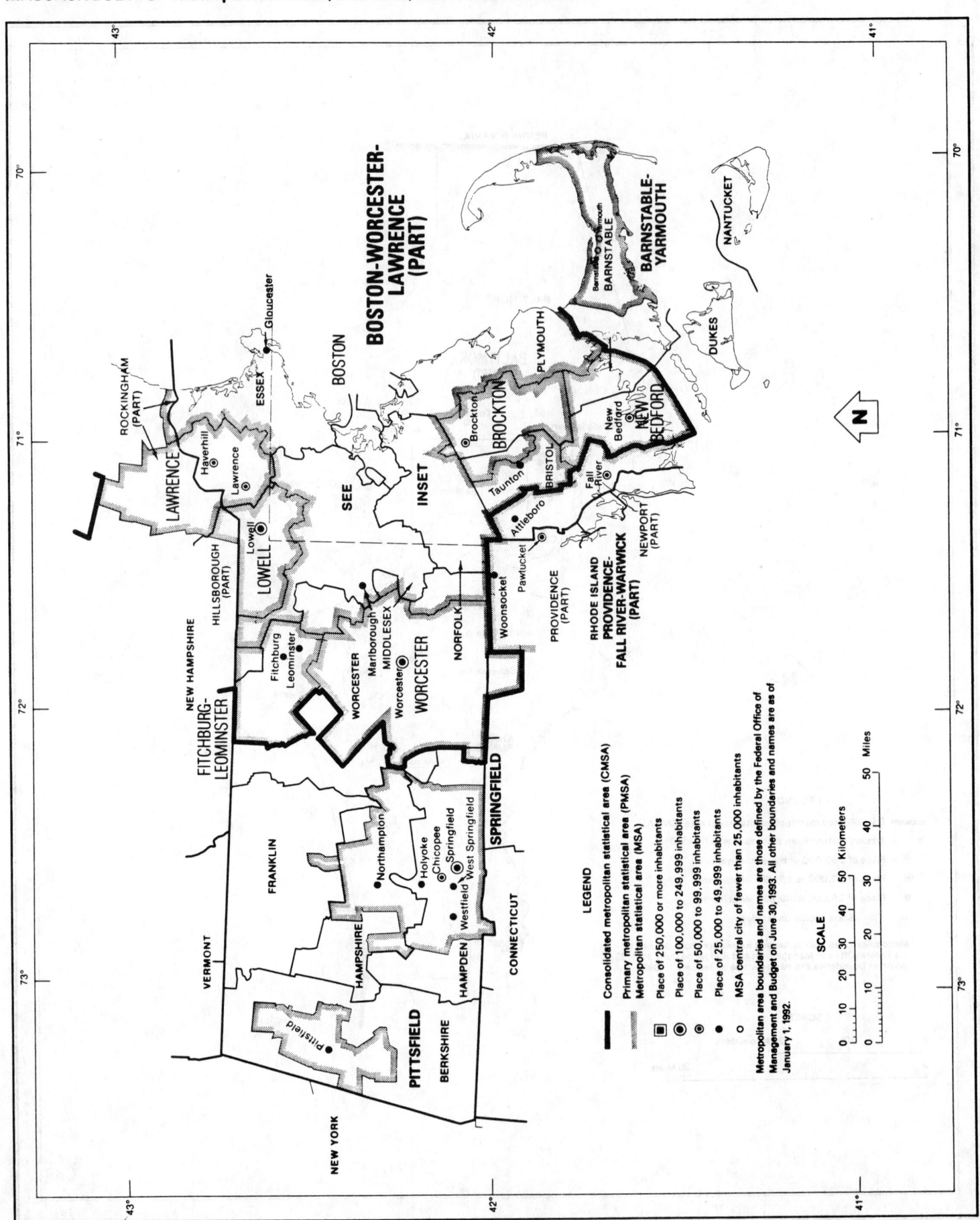

MASSACHUSETTS - Metropolitan Areas, Counties, and Selected Places

BOSTON-WORCESTER-LAWRENCE (PART)

BARNSTABLE-YARMOUTH

SEE BOSTON INSET

LEGEND

▬ Consolidated metropolitan statistical area (CMSA)

▭ Primary metropolitan statistical area (PMSA)
  Metropolitan statistical area (MSA)

◙ Place of 250,000 or more inhabitants

◉ Place of 100,000 to 249,999 inhabitants

◎ Place of 50,000 to 99,999 inhabitants

● Place of 25,000 to 49,999 inhabitants

○ MSA central city of fewer than 25,000 inhabitants

Metropolitan area boundaries and names are those defined by the Federal Office of Management and Budget on June 30, 1993. All other boundaries and names are as of January 1, 1992.

SCALE

Kilometers

Miles

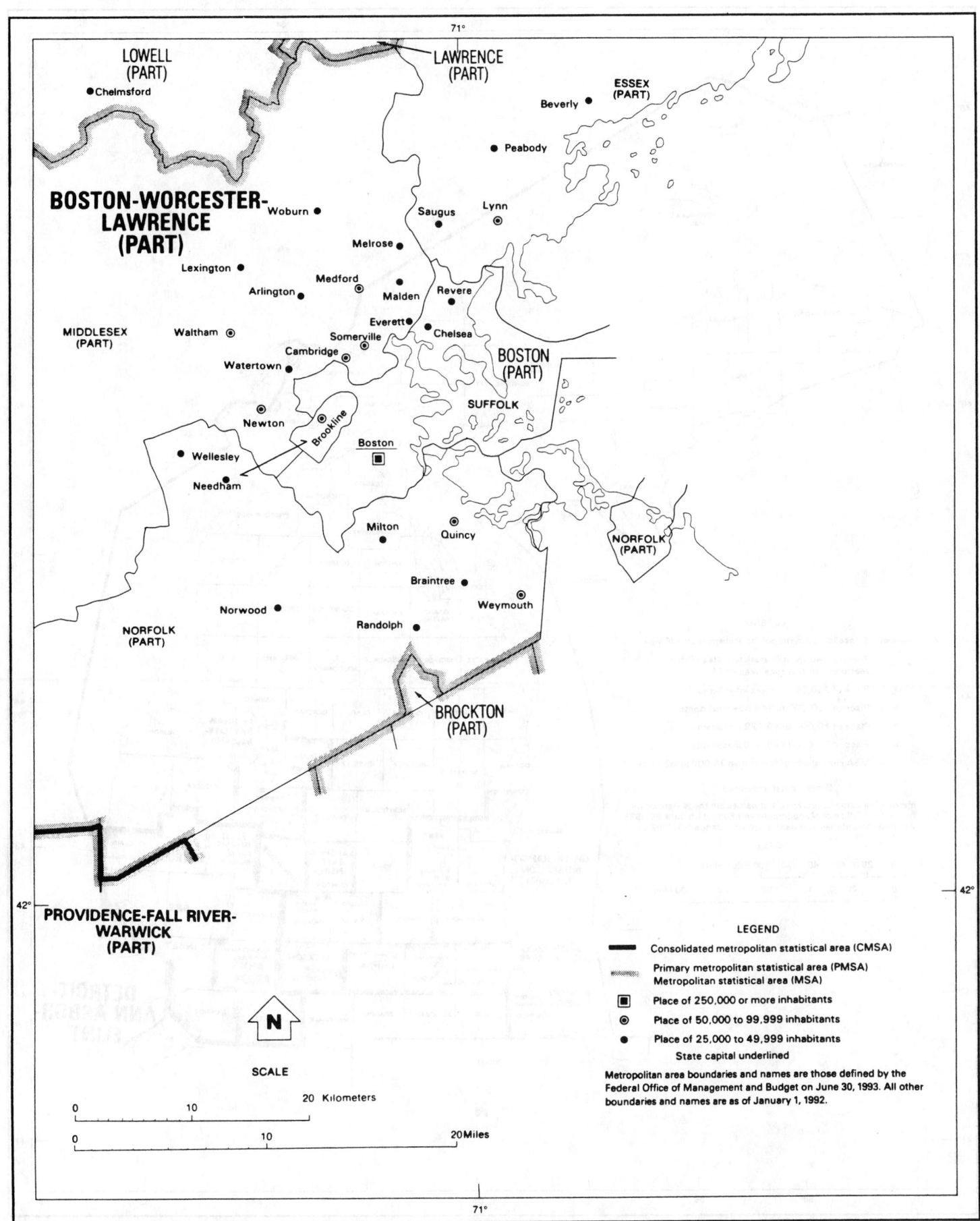

71°

LOWELL
(PART)
● Chelmsford

LAWRENCE
(PART)

ESSEX
(PART)
Beverly ●

● Peabody

**BOSTON-WORCESTER-LAWRENCE
(PART)**

Woburn ●

Saugus ●

Lynn ◉

Melrose ●

Lexington ●

Medford ◉

Malden ●

Revere ●

Arlington ●

MIDDLESEX
(PART)

Waltham ◉

Everett ●

Somerville ◉

Chelsea ●

BOSTON
(PART)

Cambridge ◉

Watertown ●

SUFFOLK

Newton ◉

Brookline ◉

Wellesley ●

Boston ◼

Needham ●

NORFOLK
(PART)

Milton ●

Quincy ◉

Braintree ●

Weymouth ◉

Norwood ●

NORFOLK
(PART)

Randolph ●

BROCKTON
(PART)

42°

**PROVIDENCE-FALL RIVER-
WARWICK
(PART)**

42°

LEGEND

▬▬▬ Consolidated metropolitan statistical area (CMSA)

▨▨▨ Primary metropolitan statistical area (PMSA)
Metropolitan statistical area (MSA)

◼ Place of 250,000 or more inhabitants

◉ Place of 50,000 to 99,999 inhabitants

● Place of 25,000 to 49,999 inhabitants
State capital underlined

Metropolitan area boundaries and names are those defined by the
Federal Office of Management and Budget on June 30, 1993. All other
boundaries and names are as of January 1, 1992.

N

SCALE

0   10   20 Kilometers

0   10   20 Miles

71°

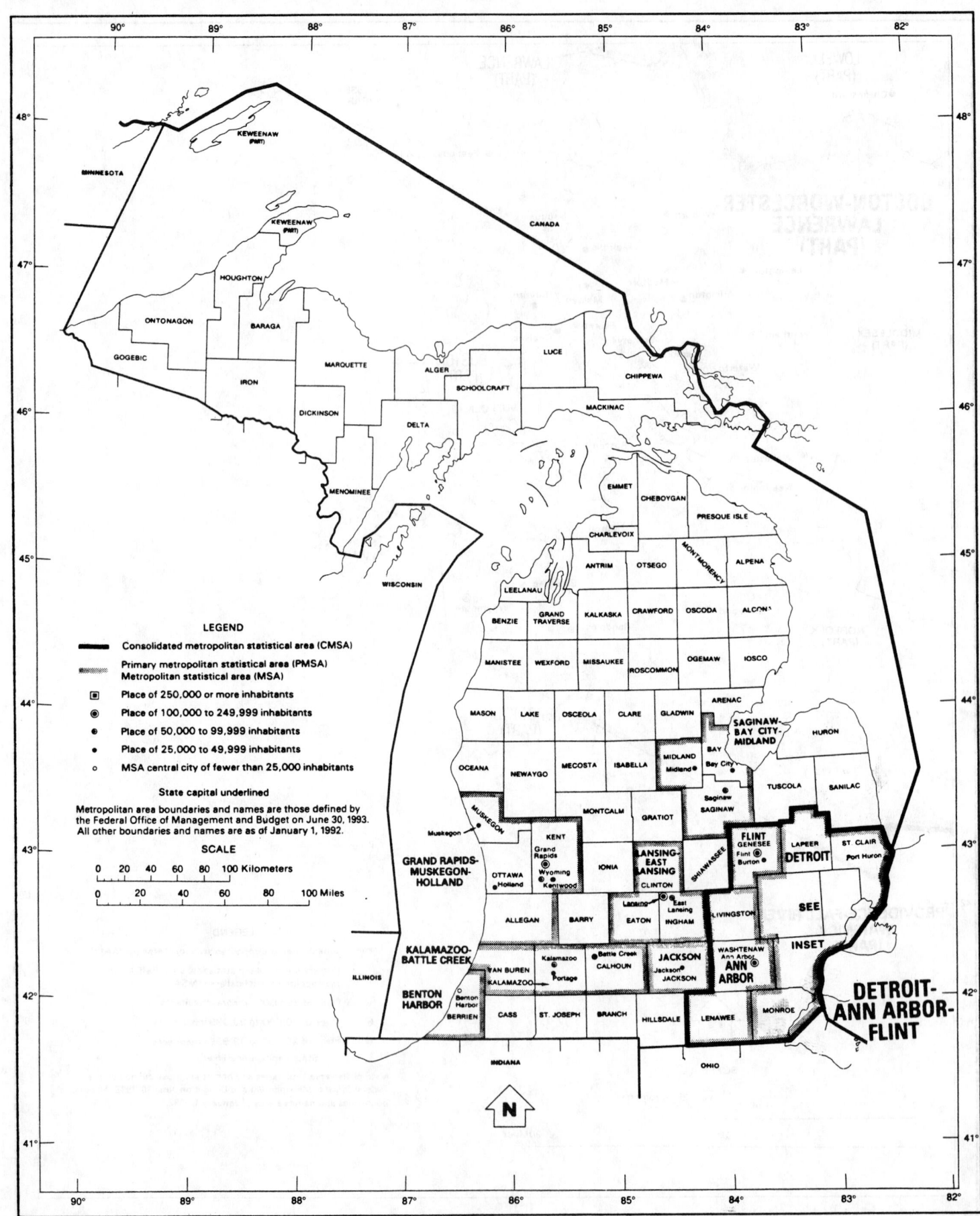

LEGEND

▬▬▬ Consolidated metropolitan statistical area (CMSA)

▬▬▬ Primary metropolitan statistical area (PMSA)
Metropolitan statistical area (MSA)

▣ Place of 250,000 or more inhabitants

◉ Place of 100,000 to 249,999 inhabitants

◕ Place of 50,000 to 99,999 inhabitants

• Place of 25,000 to 49,999 inhabitants

○ MSA central city of fewer than 25,000 inhabitants

State capital underlined

Metropolitan area boundaries and names are those defined by
the Federal Office of Management and Budget on June 30, 1993.
All other boundaries and names are as of January 1, 1992.

SCALE

0   20   40   60   80   100 Kilometers

0   20   40   60   80   100 Miles

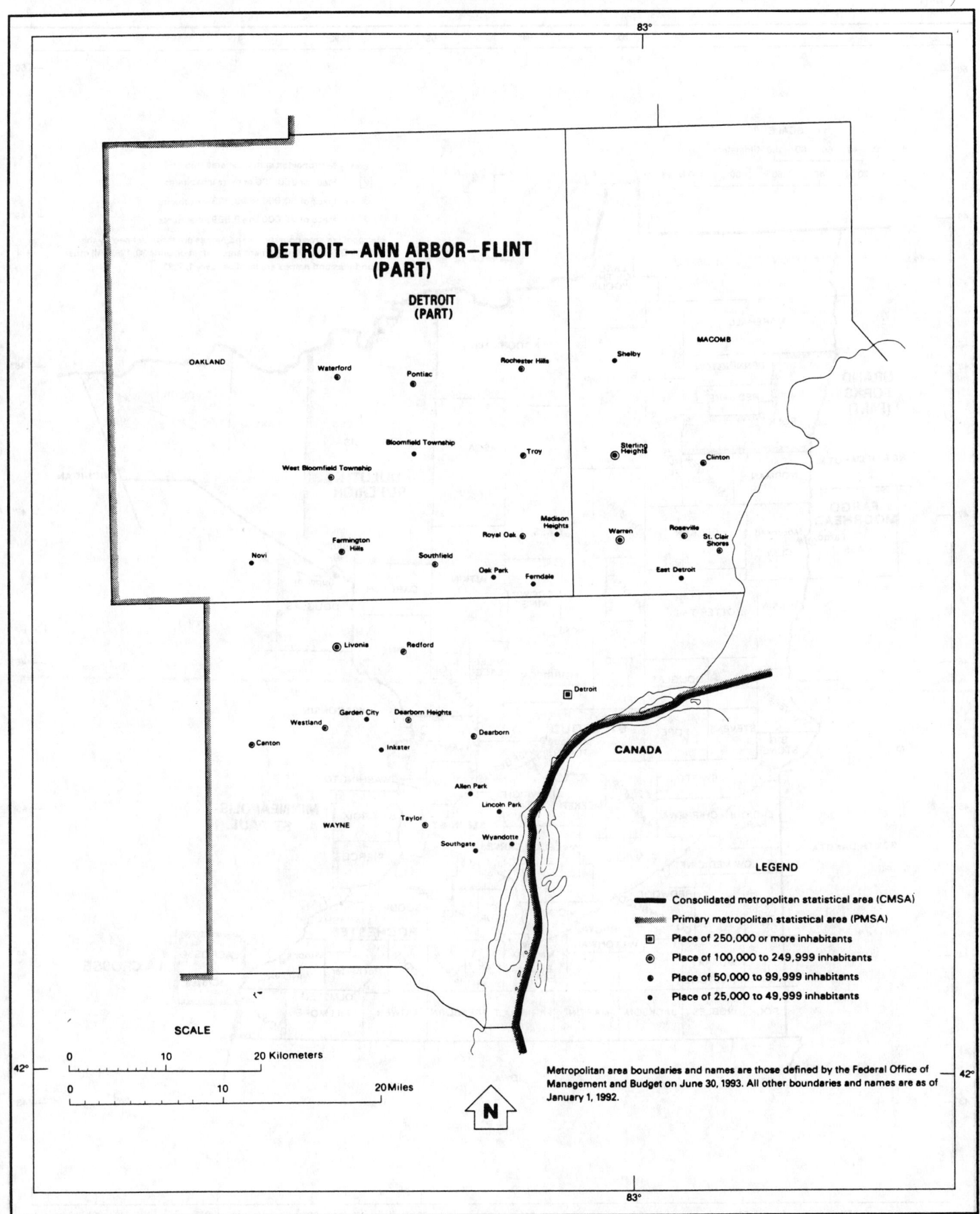

DETROIT—ANN ARBOR—FLINT
(PART)

DETROIT
(PART)

LEGEND

━━━ Consolidated metropolitan statistical area (CMSA)

▨▨▨ Primary metropolitan statistical area (PMSA)

▣ Place of 250,000 or more inhabitants

◉ Place of 100,000 to 249,999 inhabitants

● Place of 50,000 to 99,999 inhabitants

• Place of 25,000 to 49,999 inhabitants

SCALE

Metropolitan area boundaries and names are those defined by the Federal Office of Management and Budget on June 30, 1993. All other boundaries and names are as of January 1, 1992.

N

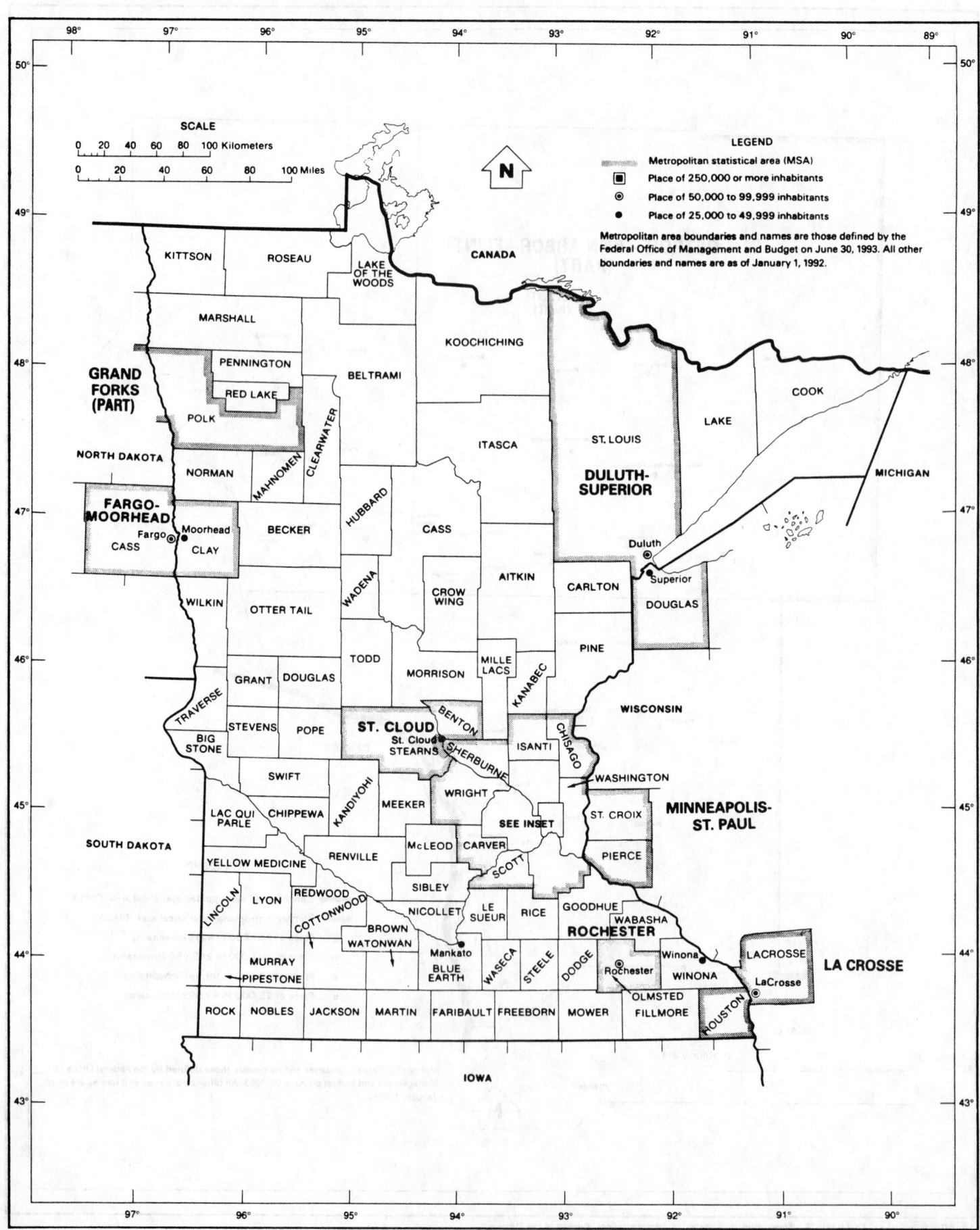

SCALE

0 20 40 60 80 100 Kilometers

0 20 40 60 80 100 Miles

LEGEND

Metropolitan statistical area (MSA)

□ Place of 250,000 or more inhabitants

⊙ Place of 50,000 to 99,999 inhabitants

● Place of 25,000 to 49,999 inhabitants

Metropolitan area boundaries and names are those defined by the Federal Office of Management and Budget on June 30, 1993. All other boundaries and names are as of January 1, 1992.

N

CANADA

KITTSON
ROSEAU
LAKE OF THE WOODS
KOOCHICHING

MARSHALL
PENNINGTON
RED LAKE
POLK
BELTRAMI

GRAND FORKS (PART)

NORTH DAKOTA

NORMAN
MAHNOMEN
CLEARWATER
ITASCA
ST. LOUIS
LAKE
COOK

MICHIGAN

FARGO-MOORHEAD
Moorhead
Fargo
CASS
CLAY
BECKER
HUBBARD
CASS

DULUTH-SUPERIOR

Duluth
Superior

WILKIN
OTTER TAIL
WADENA
CROW WING
AITKIN
CARLTON
DOUGLAS

TRAVERSE
GRANT
DOUGLAS
TODD
MORRISON
MILLE LACS
PINE

KANABEC

WISCONSIN

STEVENS
POPE
ST. CLOUD
St. Cloud
STEARNS
BENTON
SHERBURNE
ISANTI
CHISAGO

BIG STONE

SWIFT
KANDIYOHI
MEEKER
WRIGHT
SEE INSET
WASHINGTON

MINNEAPOLIS-ST. PAUL

LAC QUI PARLE
CHIPPEWA
ST. CROIX
PIERCE

SOUTH DAKOTA

YELLOW MEDICINE
RENVILLE
McLEOD
CARVER
SCOTT

LINCOLN
LYON
REDWOOD
SIBLEY
LE SUEUR
RICE
GOODHUE
WABASHA

COTTONWOOD
BROWN
NICOLLET
ROCHESTER
Winona
WINONA
LACROSSE

LA CROSSE

WATONWAN
Mankato
BLUE EARTH
WASECA
STEELE
DODGE
Rochester
OLMSTED
LaCrosse

MURRAY
PIPESTONE

ROCK
NOBLES
JACKSON
MARTIN
FARIBAULT
FREEBORN
MOWER
FILLMORE
HOUSTON

IOWA

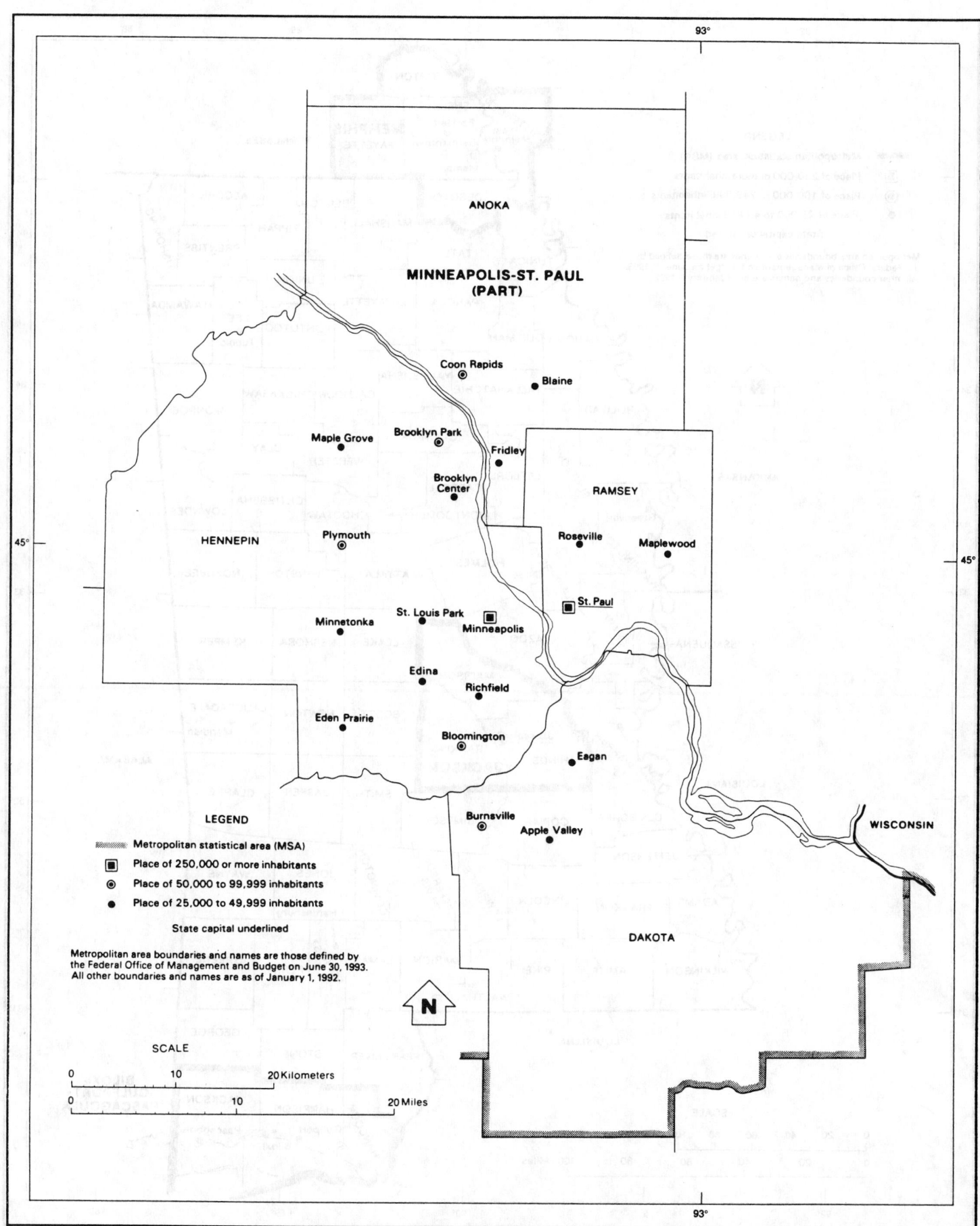

MINNESOTA (Inset) - Metropolitan Areas, Counties, and Selected Places

Appendix D

93°

ANOKA

MINNEAPOLIS-ST. PAUL
(PART)

Coon Rapids

Blaine

Maple Grove

Brooklyn Park

Fridley

Brooklyn
Center

RAMSEY

45°

HENNEPIN

Plymouth

Roseville

Maplewood

St. Louis Park

St. Paul

Minnetonka

Minneapolis

Edina

Richfield

Eden Prairie

Bloomington

Eagan

LEGEND

Metropolitan statistical area (MSA)

Place of 250,000 or more inhabitants

Place of 50,000 to 99,999 inhabitants

Place of 25,000 to 49,999 inhabitants

State capital underlined

Metropolitan area boundaries and names are those defined by
the Federal Office of Management and Budget on June 30, 1993.
All other boundaries and names are as of January 1, 1992.

Burnsville

Apple Valley

WISCONSIN

DAKOTA

N

SCALE

0   10   20 Kilometers

0   10   20 Miles

93°

45°

U.S. DEPARTMENT OF COMMERCE Economics and Statistics Administration Bureau of the Census

MISSISSIPPI - Metropolitan Areas, Counties, and Selected Places

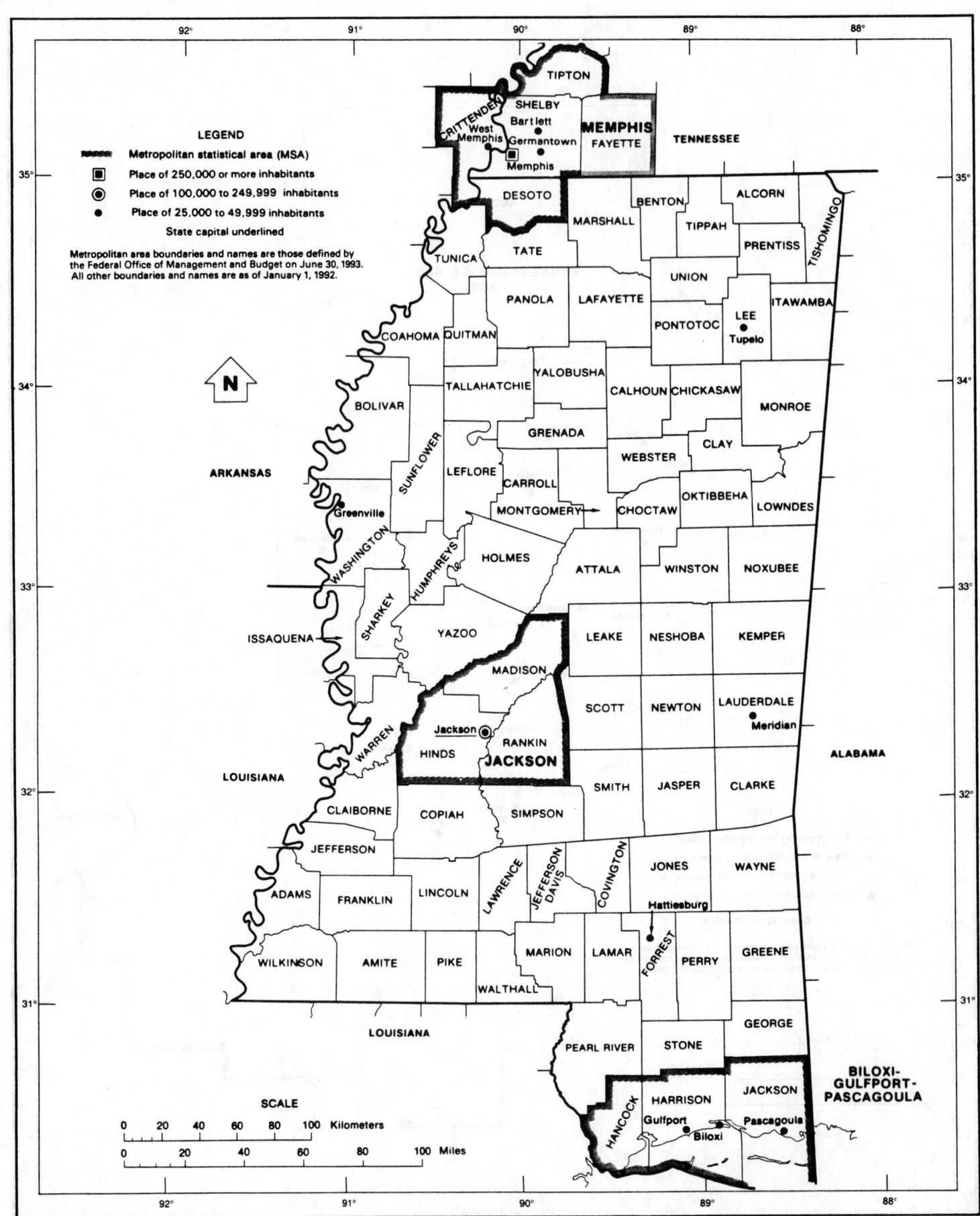

LEGEND

- ~~~ Metropolitan statistical area (MSA)
- ◼ Place of 250,000 or more inhabitants
- ◉ Place of 100,000 to 249,999 inhabitants
- ● Place of 25,000 to 49,999 inhabitants
- State capital underlined

Metropolitan area boundaries and names are those defined by the Federal Office of Management and Budget on June 30, 1993. All other boundaries and names are as of January 1, 1992.

SCALE

```
0   20   40   60   80   100  Kilometers
0        20        40        60        80        100  Miles
```

MISSOURI - Metropolitan Areas, Counties, Independent City, and Other Selected Places

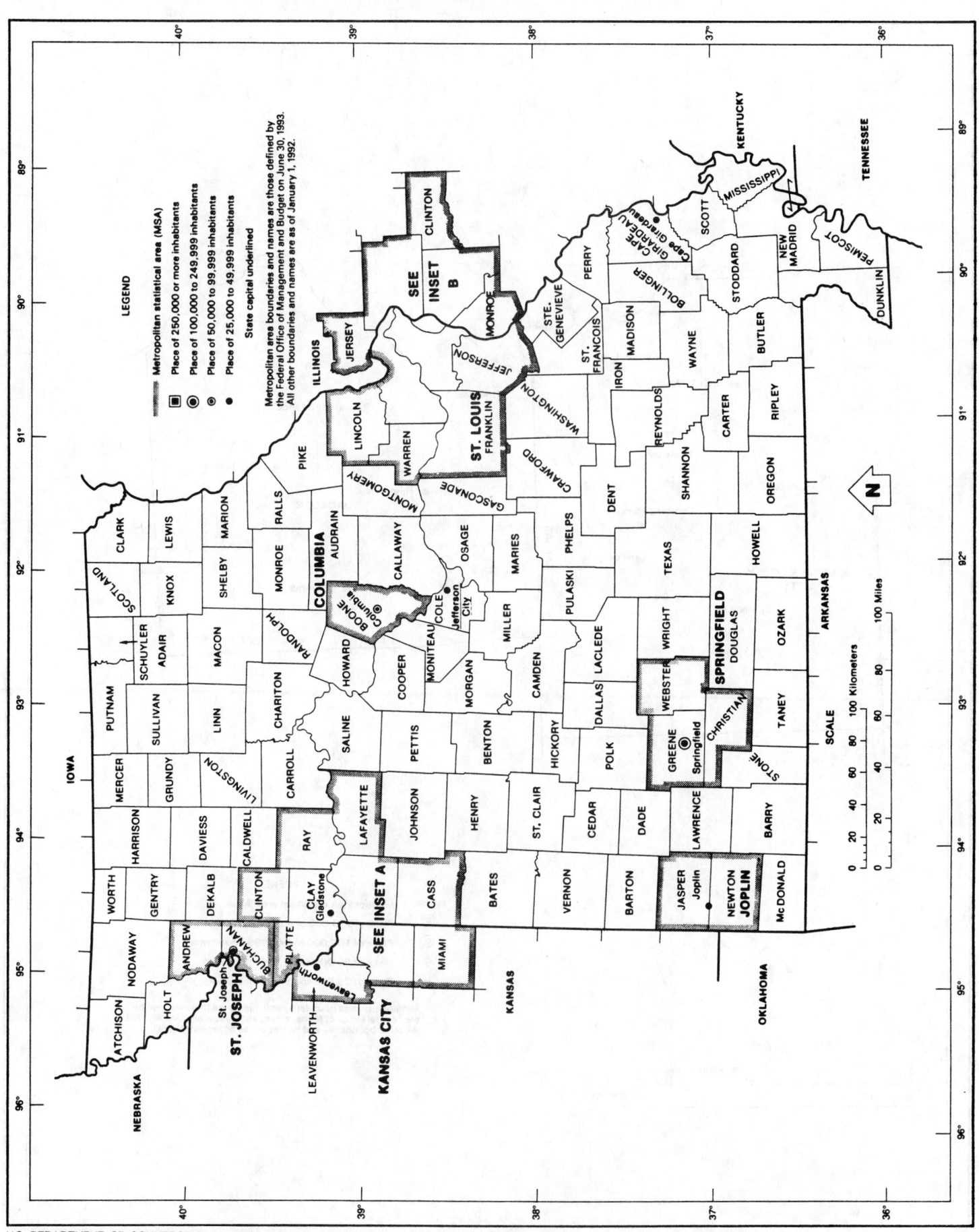

MISSOURI (Inset A) - Metropolitan Areas, Counties, Independent City, and Other Selected Places

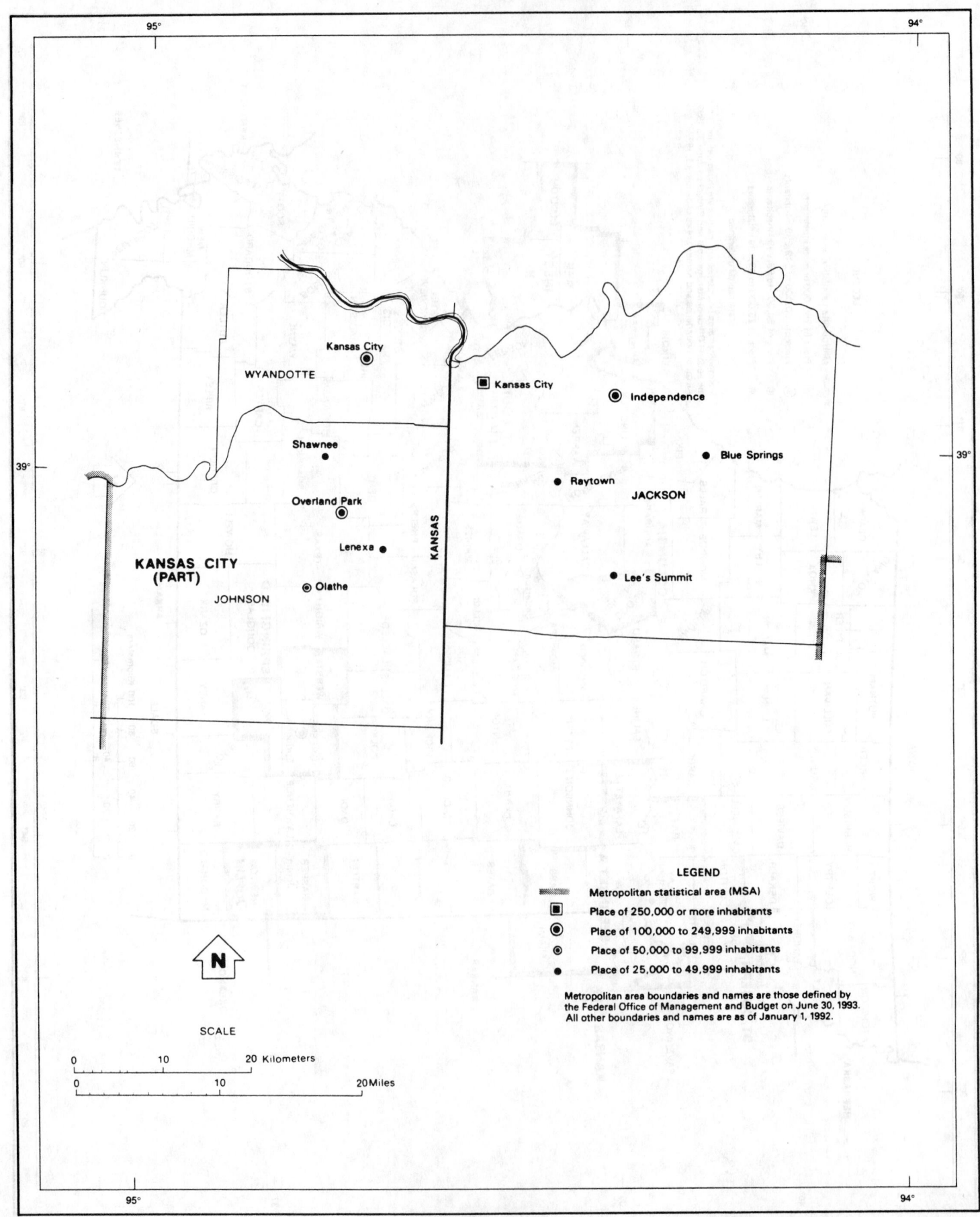

LEGEND

▨ Metropolitan statistical area (MSA)

■ Place of 250,000 or more inhabitants

◉ Place of 100,000 to 249,999 inhabitants

◎ Place of 50,000 to 99,999 inhabitants

● Place of 25,000 to 49,999 inhabitants

Metropolitan area boundaries and names are those defined by the Federal Office of Management and Budget on June 30, 1993. All other boundaries and names are as of January 1, 1992.

SCALE

0   10   20 Kilometers

0   10   20 Miles

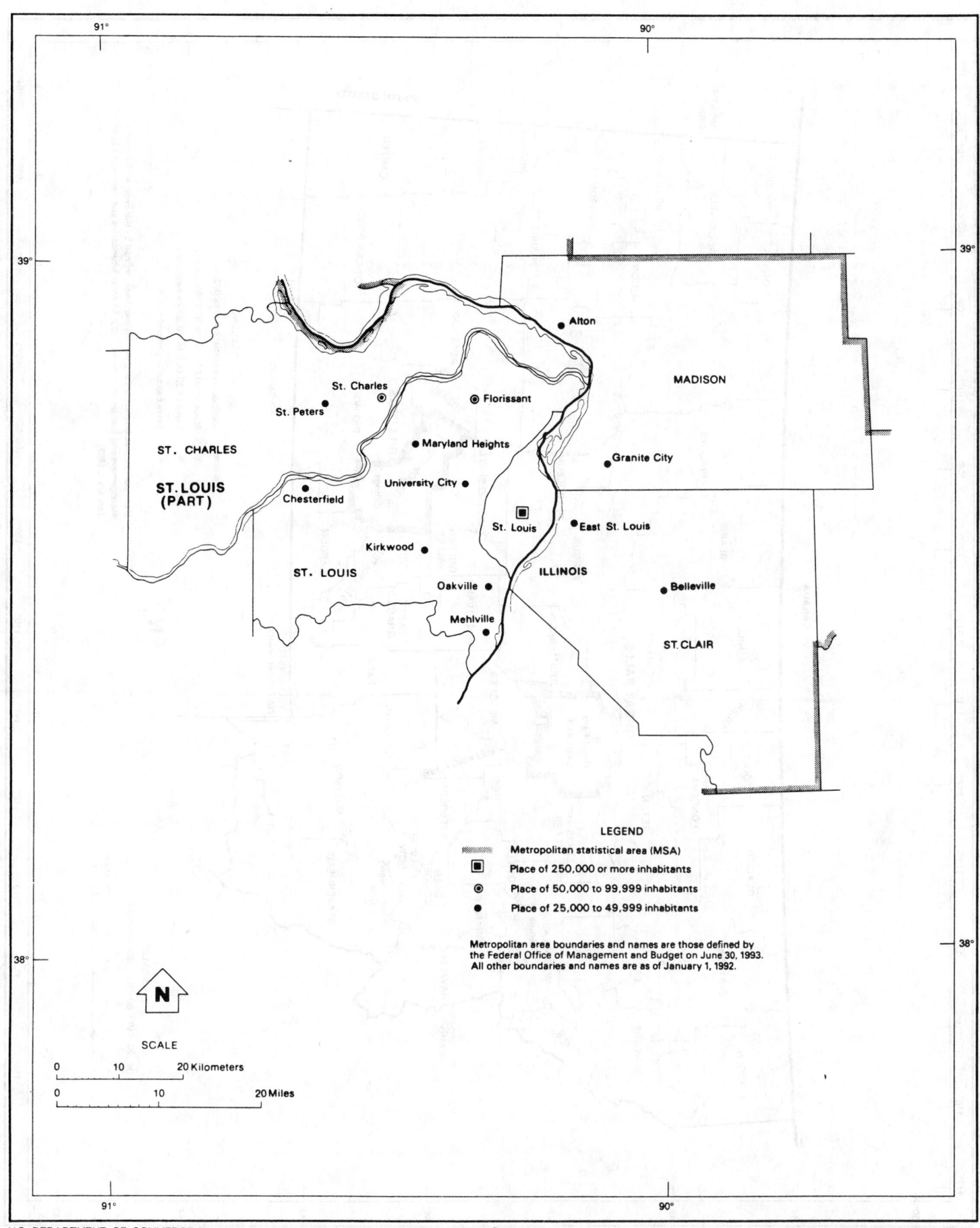

LEGEND

Metropolitan statistical area (MSA)

■ Place of 250,000 or more inhabitants

◉ Place of 50,000 to 99,999 inhabitants

● Place of 25,000 to 49,999 inhabitants

Metropolitan area boundaries and names are those defined by
the Federal Office of Management and Budget on June 30, 1993.
All other boundaries and names are as of January 1, 1992.

SCALE

0   10   20 Kilometers

0   10   20 Miles

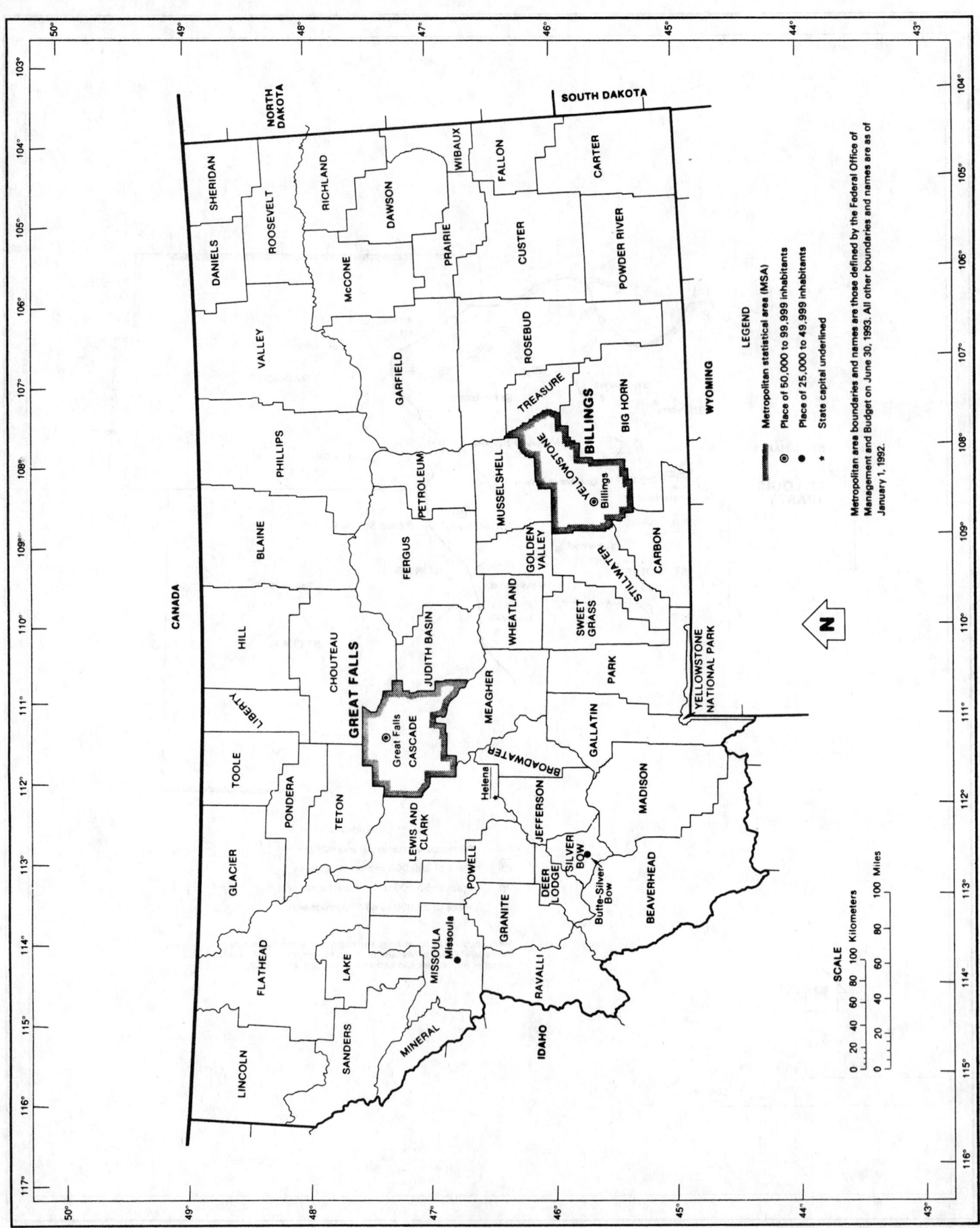

LEGEND

Metropolitan statistical area (MSA)

⊚ Place of 50,000 to 99,999 inhabitants

● Place of 25,000 to 49,999 inhabitants

★ State capital underlined

Metropolitan area boundaries and names are those defined by the Federal Office of Management and Budget on June 30, 1993. All other boundaries and names are as of January 1, 1992.

SCALE

0 20 40 60 80 100 Kilometers

0   20   40   60   80   100 Miles

NEBRASKA - Metropolitan Areas, Counties, and Selected Places

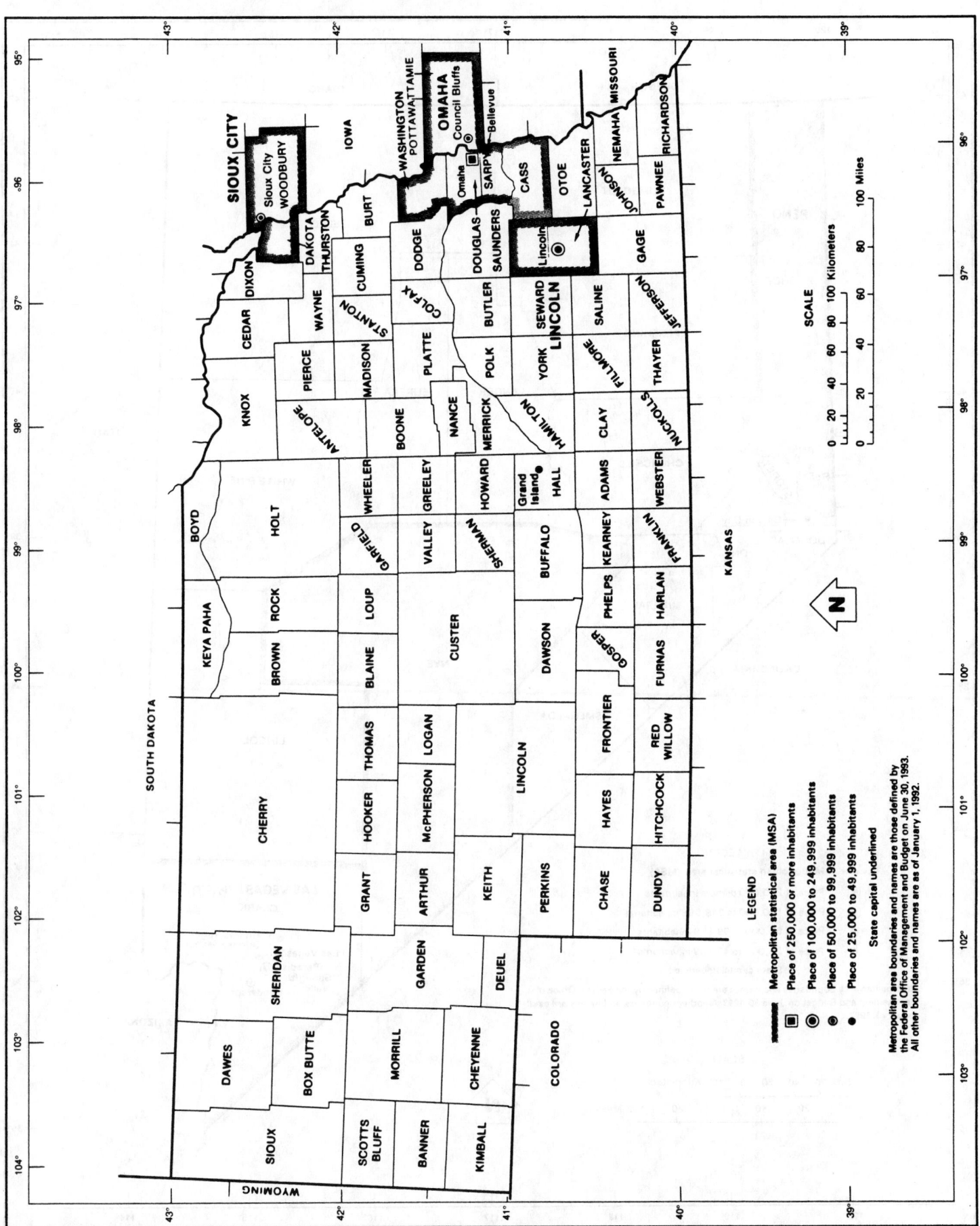

SCALE

LEGEND

Metropolitan statistical area (MSA)

Place of 250,000 or more inhabitants

Place of 100,000 to 249,999 inhabitants

Place of 50,000 to 99,999 inhabitants

Place of 25,000 to 49,999 inhabitants

State capital underlined

Metropolitan area boundaries and names are those defined by
the Federal Office of Management and Budget on June 30, 1993.
All other boundaries and names are as of January 1, 1992.

U.S. DEPARTMENT OF COMMERCE Economics and Statistics Administration Bureau of the Census

NEVADA - Metropolitan Areas, Counties, Independent City, and Other Selected Places

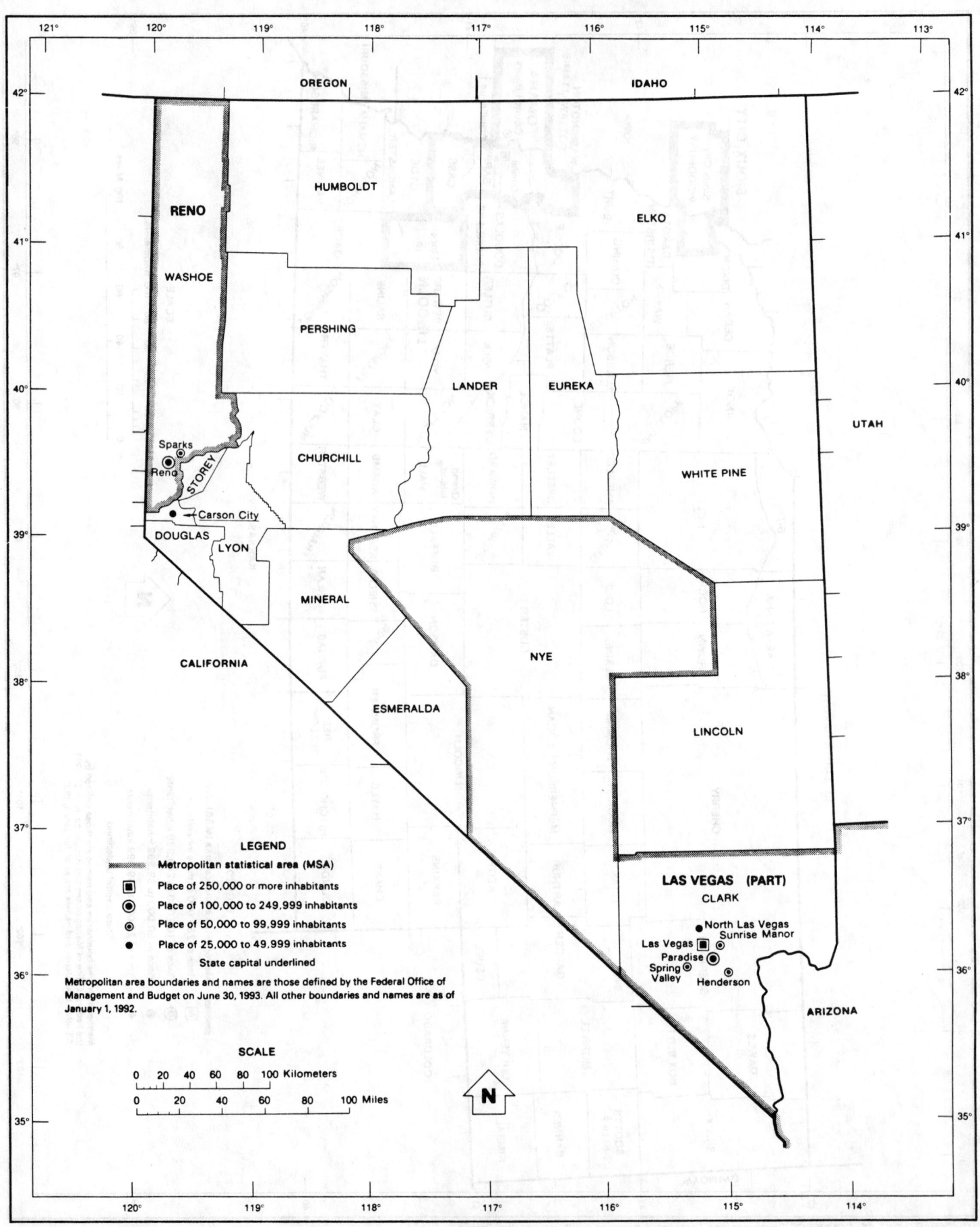

LEGEND

Metropolitan statistical area (MSA)

☐ Place of 250,000 or more inhabitants

◉ Place of 100,000 to 249,999 inhabitants

◉ Place of 50,000 to 99,999 inhabitants

● Place of 25,000 to 49,999 inhabitants

State capital underlined

Metropolitan area boundaries and names are those defined by the Federal Office of Management and Budget on June 30, 1993. All other boundaries and names are as of January 1, 1992.

SCALE

0 20 40 60 80 100 Kilometers

0 20 40 60 80 100 Miles

N

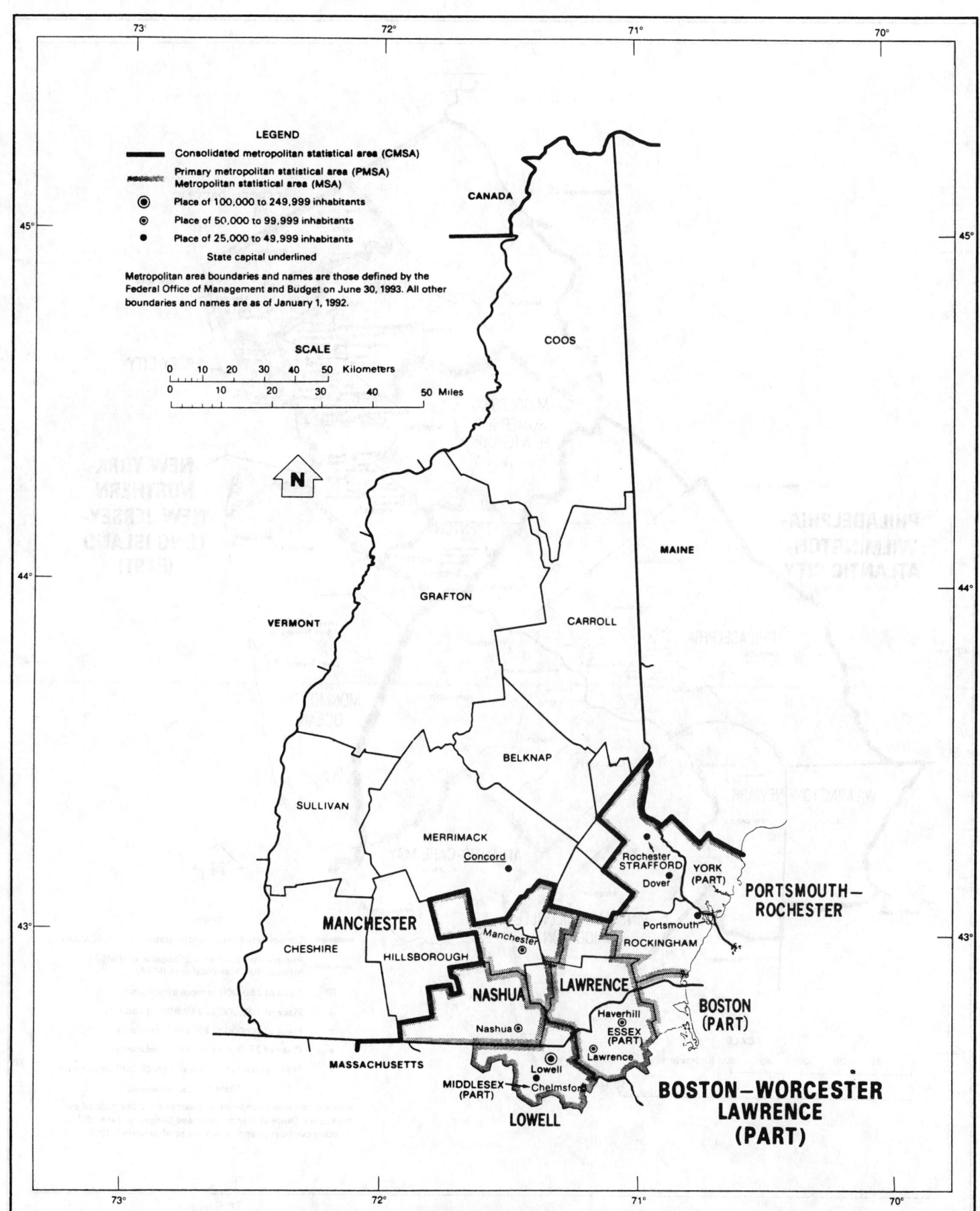

LEGEND

⎯⎯ Consolidated metropolitan statistical area (CMSA)

⎯⎯ Primary metropolitan statistical area (PMSA)
Metropolitan statistical area (MSA)

◉ Place of 100,000 to 249,999 inhabitants

◉ Place of 50,000 to 99,999 inhabitants

● Place of 25,000 to 49,999 inhabitants

State capital underlined

Metropolitan area boundaries and names are those defined by the Federal Office of Management and Budget on June 30, 1993. All other boundaries and names are as of January 1, 1992.

SCALE

```
0   10   20   30   40   50   Kilometers
0        10        20        30        40   50   Miles
```

N

CANADA

COOS

MAINE

VERMONT

GRAFTON

CARROLL

BELKNAP

SULLIVAN

MERRIMACK

<u>Concord</u>

Rochester
STRAFFORD

Dover

YORK
(PART)

PORTSMOUTH—
ROCHESTER

MANCHESTER

CHESHIRE

HILLSBOROUGH

Manchester
◉

Portsmouth

ROCKINGHAM

NASHUA

LAWRENCE

Nashua ◉

BOSTON
(PART)

Haverhill
◉

ESSEX
(PART)

Lawrence

**BOSTON—WORCESTER
LAWRENCE
(PART)**

MASSACHUSETTS

Lowell

MIDDLESEX
(PART)

Chelmsford

LOWELL

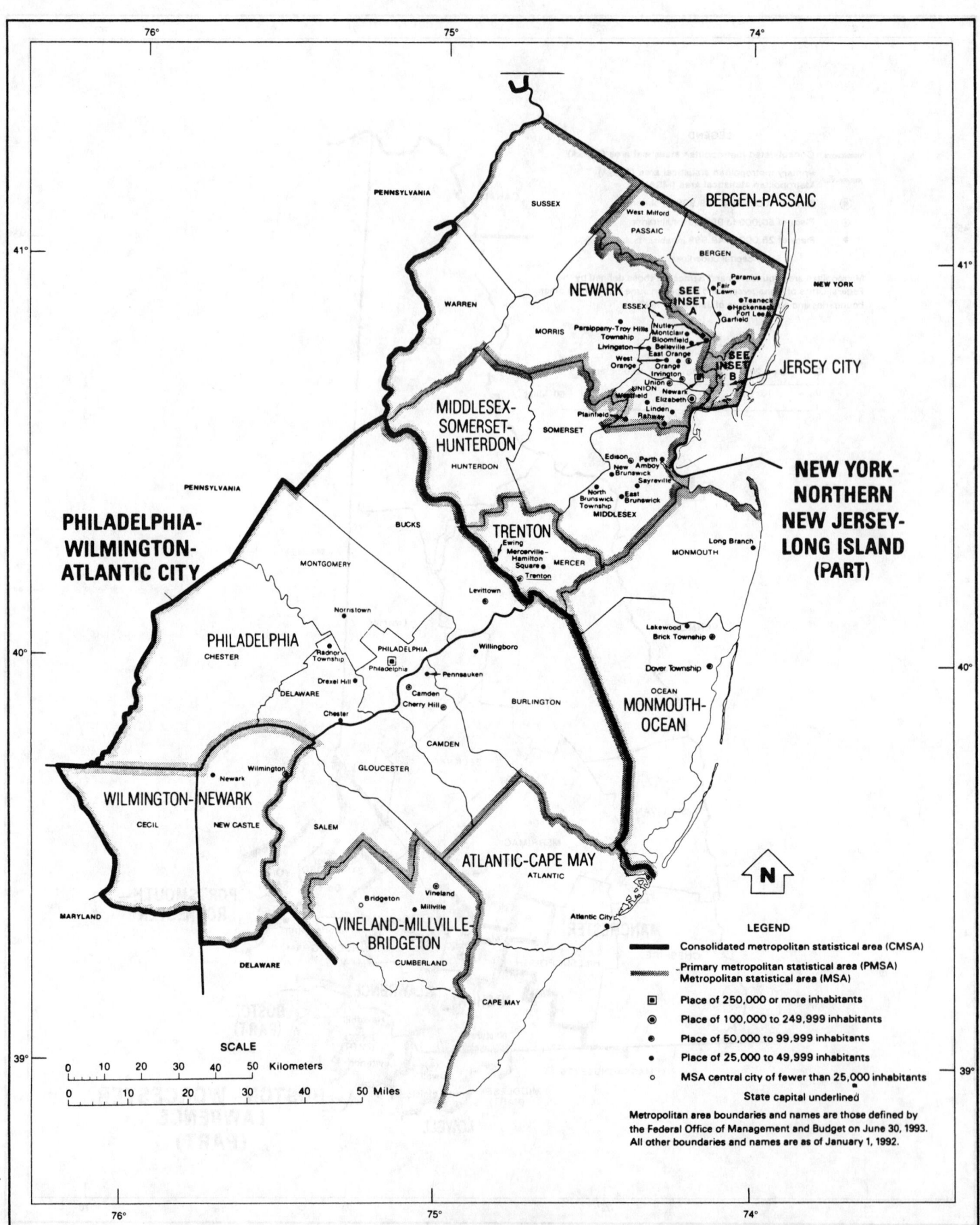

NEW YORK-
NORTHERN
NEW JERSEY-
LONG ISLAND
(PART)

BERGEN-PASSAIC

PHILADELPHIA-
WILMINGTON-
ATLANTIC CITY

MIDDLESEX-
SOMERSET-
HUNTERDON

NEWARK

JERSEY CITY

TRENTON

MONMOUTH-
OCEAN

PHILADELPHIA

WILMINGTON-NEWARK

ATLANTIC-CAPE MAY

VINELAND-MILLVILLE-
BRIDGETON

SCALE

| 0 | 10 | 20 | 30 | 40 | 50 | Kilometers |
| 0 | 10 | 20 | 30 | 40 | 50 | Miles |

LEGEND

——— Consolidated metropolitan statistical area (CMSA)
~~~ Primary metropolitan statistical area (PMSA)
Metropolitan statistical area (MSA)

▣ Place of 250,000 or more inhabitants
◉ Place of 100,000 to 249,999 inhabitants
● Place of 50,000 to 99,999 inhabitants
• Place of 25,000 to 49,999 inhabitants
○ MSA central city of fewer than 25,000 inhabitants
State capital underlined

Metropolitan area boundaries and names are those defined by
the Federal Office of Management and Budget on June 30, 1993.
All other boundaries and names are as of January 1, 1992.

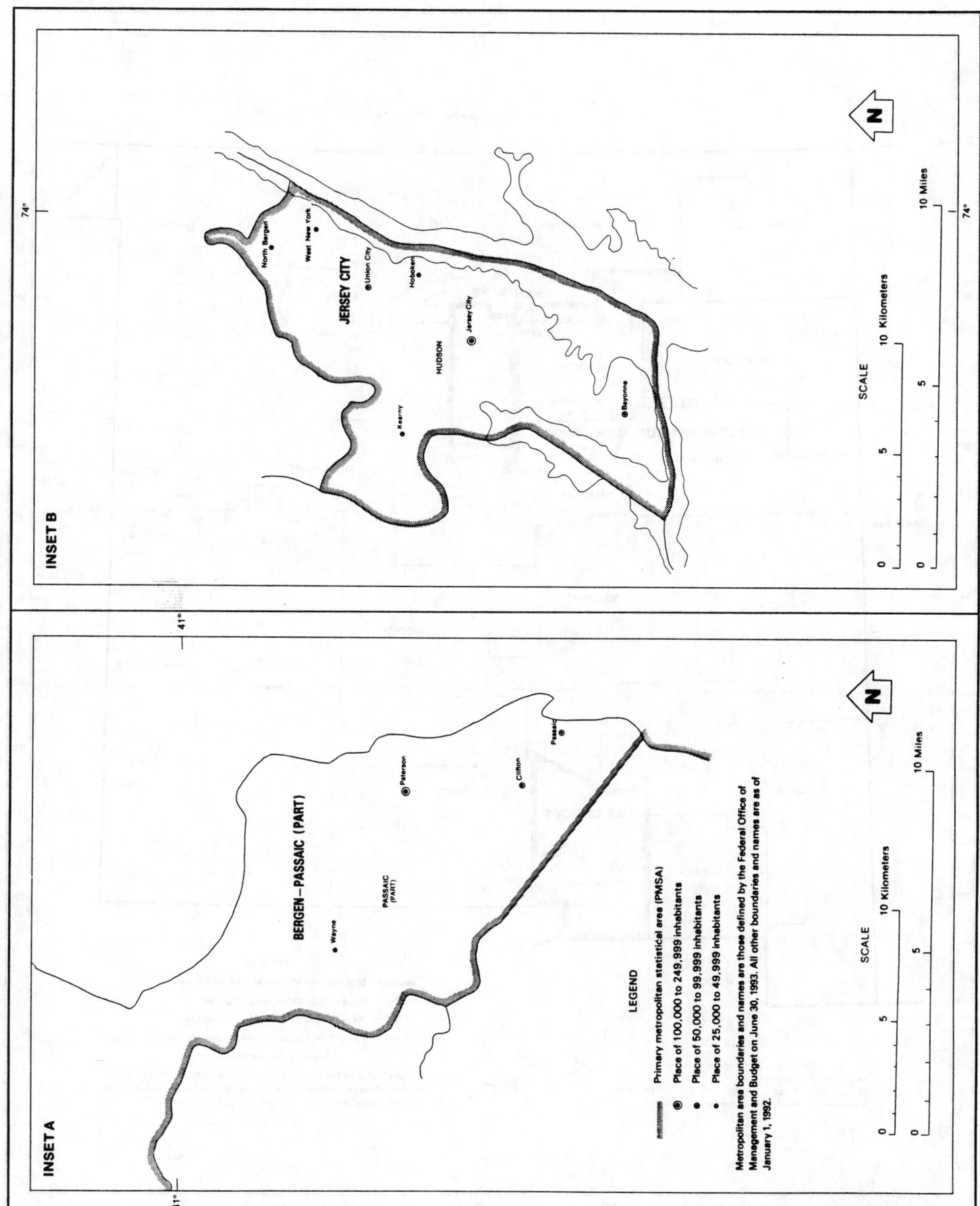

INSET B

North Bergen

West New York

JERSEY CITY

Union City

Hoboken

Kearny

HUDSON

Jersey City

Bayonne

SCALE

0   5   5   10 Kilometers

0   5   10 Miles

INSET A

BERGEN—PASSAIC (PART)

Wayne

PASSAIC
(PART)

Paterson

Clifton

Passaic

LEGEND

Primary metropolitan statistical area (PMSA)

⊙ Place of 100,000 to 249,999 inhabitants

● Place of 50,000 to 99,999 inhabitants

• Place of 25,000 to 49,999 inhabitants

Metropolitan area boundaries and names are those defined by the Federal Office of
Management and Budget on June 30, 1993. All other boundaries and names are as of
January 1, 1992.

SCALE

0   5   5   10 Kilometers

0   5   10 Miles

NEW MEXICO - Metropolitan Areas, Counties, and Selected Places

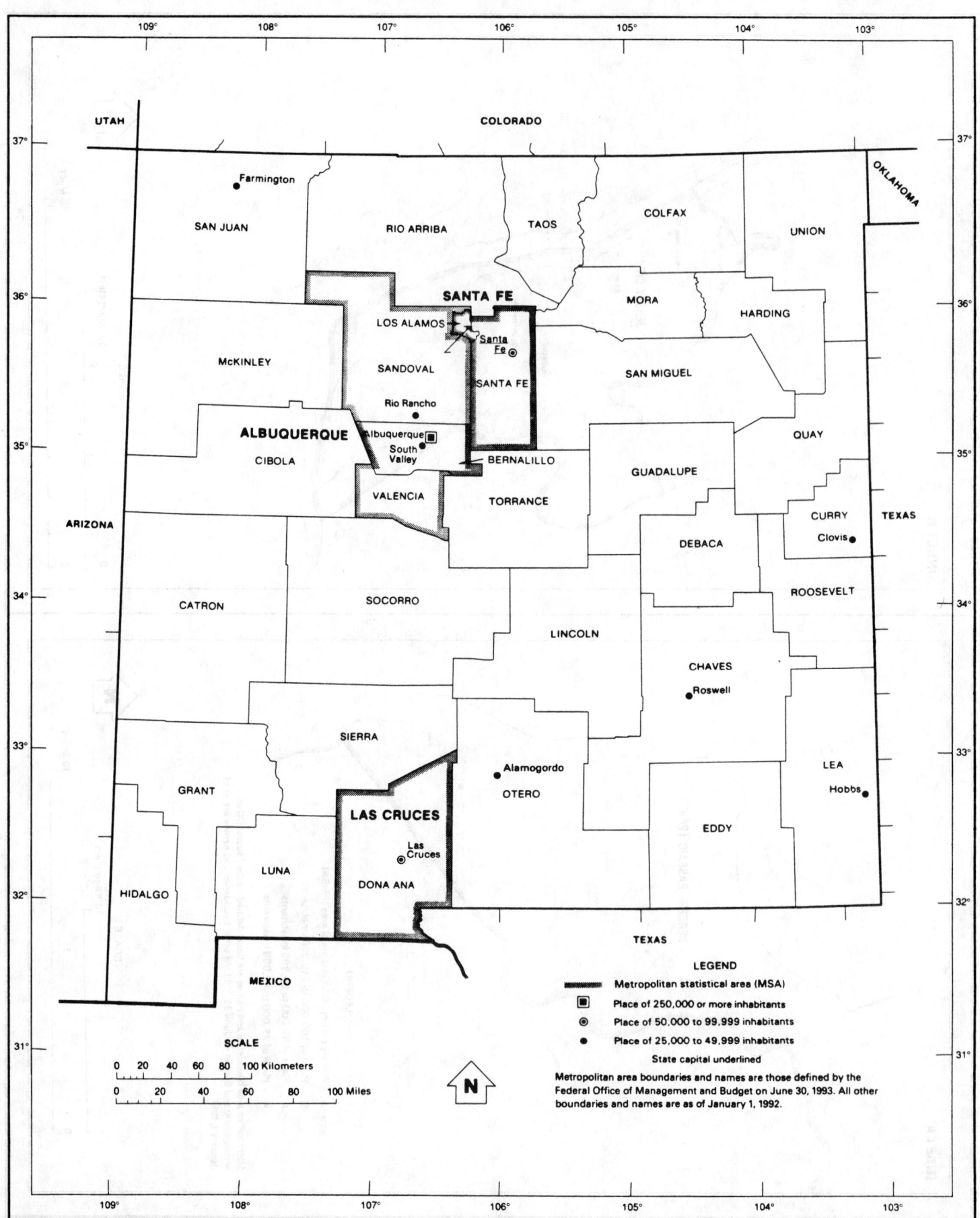

LEGEND

▬ Metropolitan statistical area (MSA)

■ Place of 250,000 or more inhabitants

◉ Place of 50,000 to 99,999 inhabitants

● Place of 25,000 to 49,999 inhabitants

State capital underlined

Metropolitan area boundaries and names are those defined by the Federal Office of Management and Budget on June 30, 1993. All other boundaries and names are as of January 1, 1992.

SCALE

0 20 40 60 80 100 Kilometers

0 20 40 60 80 100 Miles

N

NEW YORK - Metropolitan Areas, Counties, and Selected Places

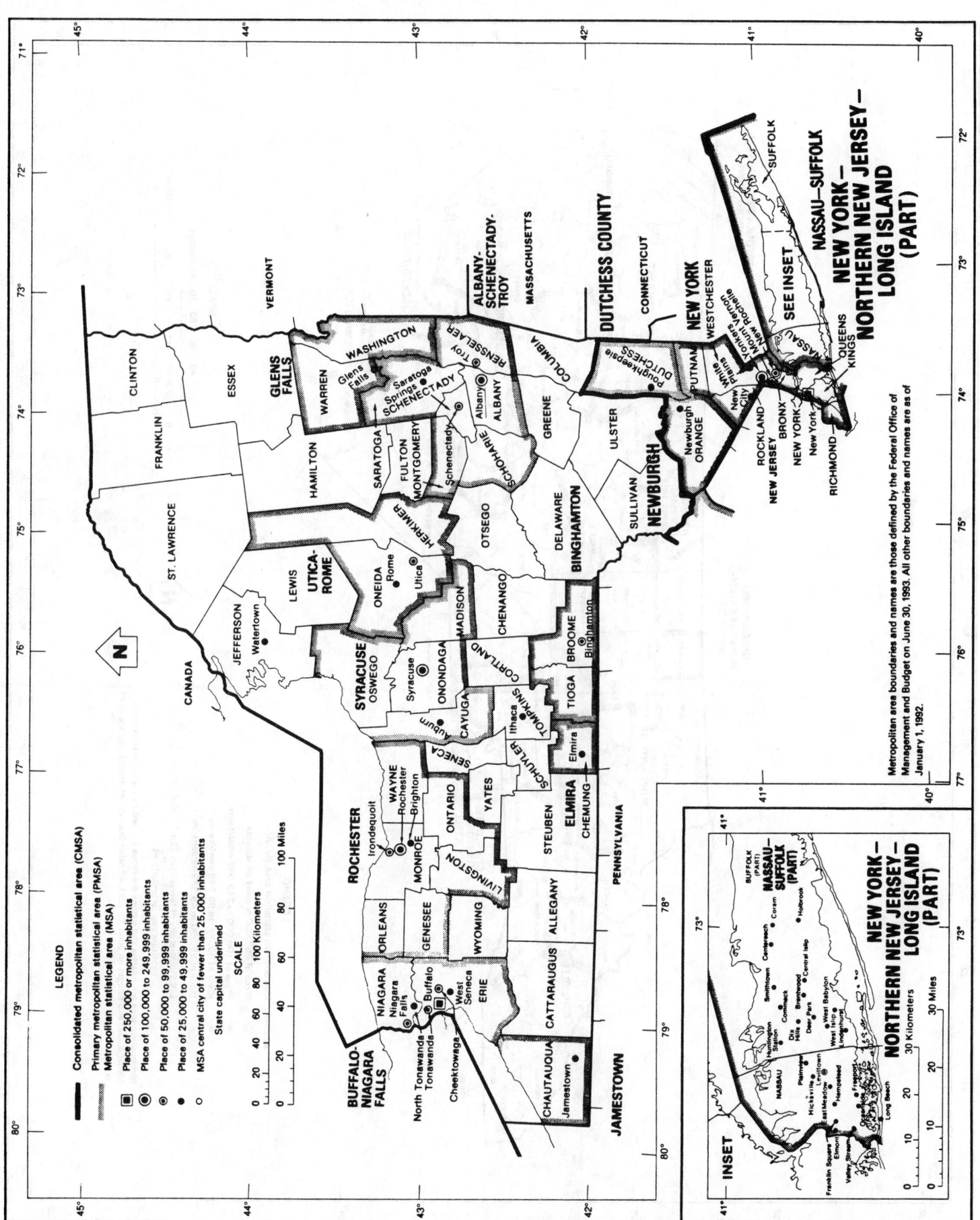

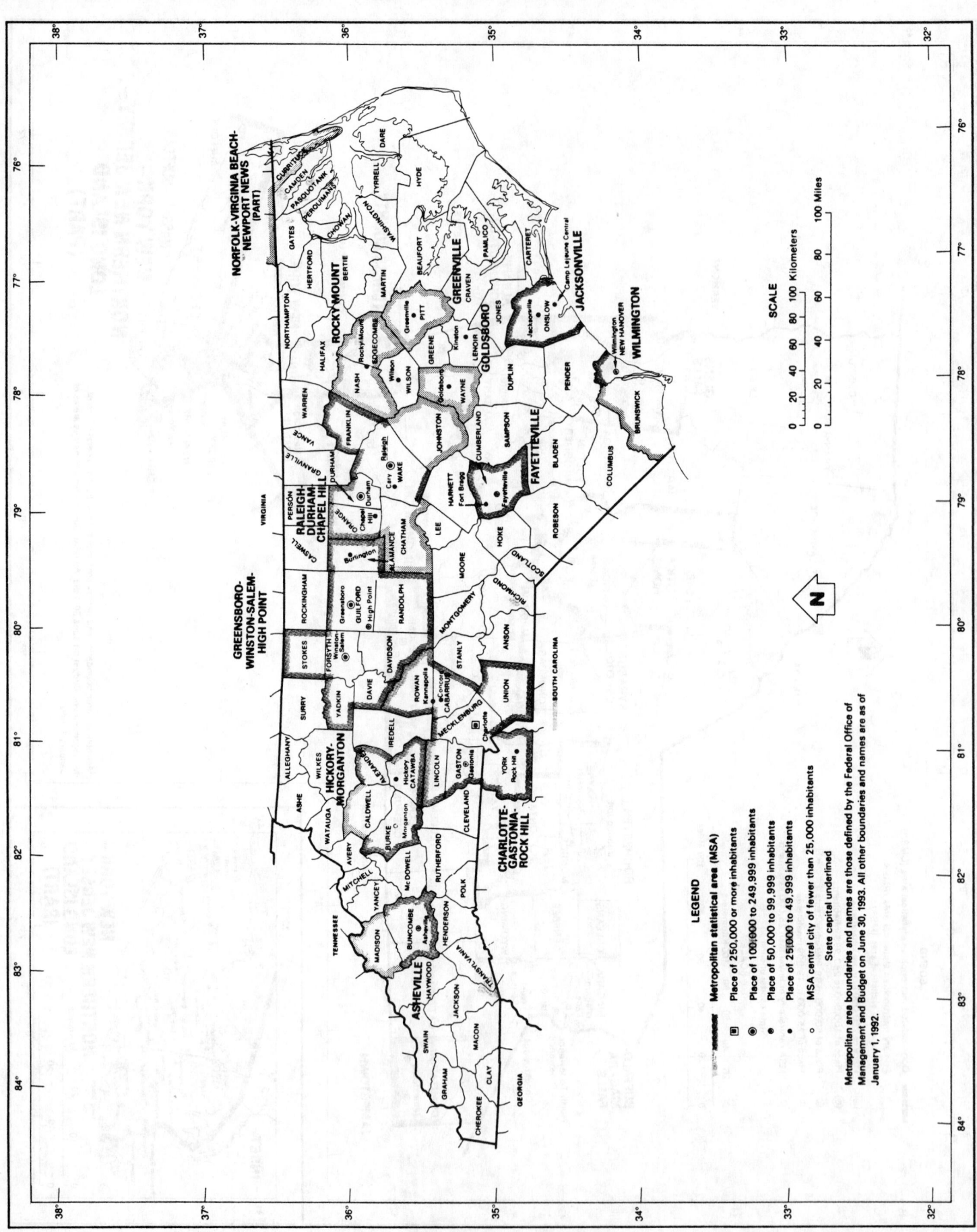

LEGEND

Metropolitan statistical area (MSA)

▣ Place of 250,000 or more inhabitants

◉ Place of 100,000 to 249,999 inhabitants

◍ Place of 50,000 to 99,999 inhabitants

● Place of 25,000 to 49,999 inhabitants

○ Place of fewer than 25,000 inhabitants

MSA central city of fewer than 25,000 inhabitants

State capital underlined

Metropolitan area boundaries and names are those defined by the Federal Office of Management and Budget on June 30, 1993. All other boundaries and names are as of January 1, 1992.

SCALE

N

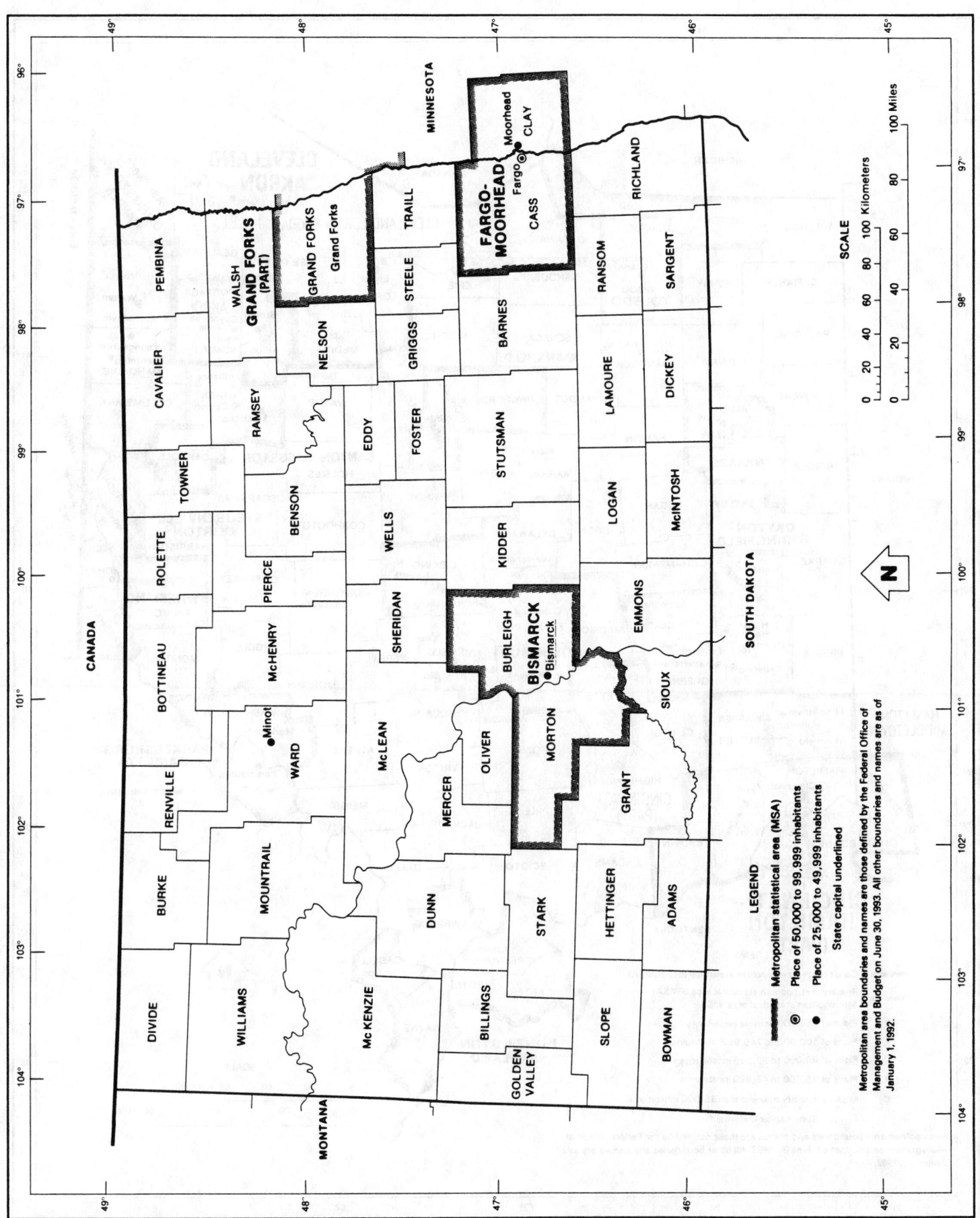

LEGEND

Metropolitan statistical area (MSA)

◉ Place of 50,000 to 99,999 inhabitants

● Place of 25,000 to 49,999 inhabitants

State capital underlined

Metropolitan area boundaries and names are those defined by the Federal Office of Management and Budget on June 30, 1993. All other boundaries and names are as of January 1, 1992.

SCALE

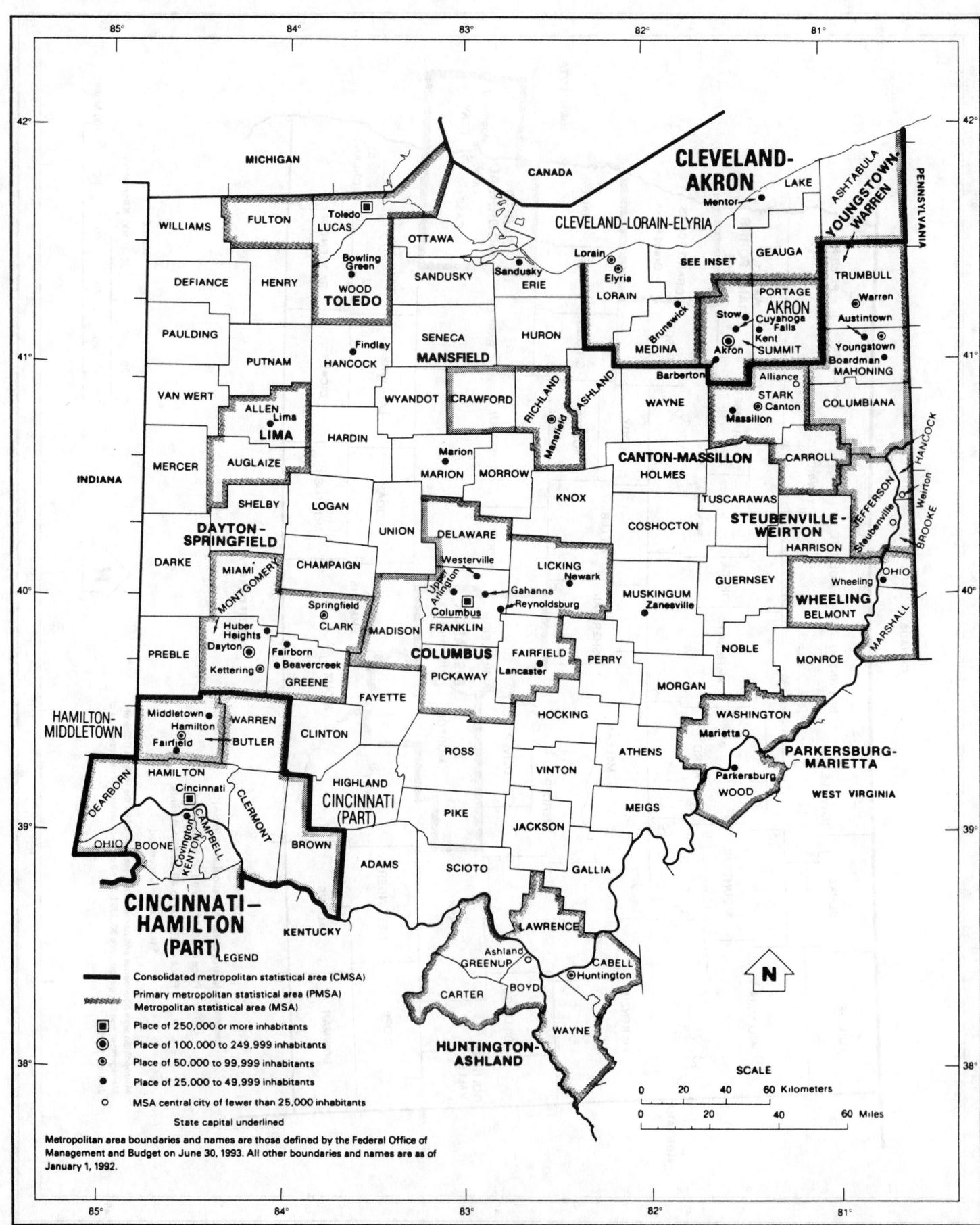

OHIO - Metropolitan Areas, Counties, and Selected Places

LEGEND

— Consolidated metropolitan statistical area (CMSA)

〰 Primary metropolitan statistical area (PMSA)
Metropolitan statistical area (MSA)

▪ Place of 250,000 or more inhabitants

◉ Place of 100,000 to 249,999 inhabitants

⊙ Place of 50,000 to 99,999 inhabitants

● Place of 25,000 to 49,999 inhabitants

○ MSA central city of fewer than 25,000 inhabitants

State capital underlined

Metropolitan area boundaries and names are those defined by the Federal Office of
Management and Budget on June 30, 1993. All other boundaries and names are as of
January 1, 1992.

SCALE

0   20   40   60 Kilometers

0   20   40   60 Miles

N

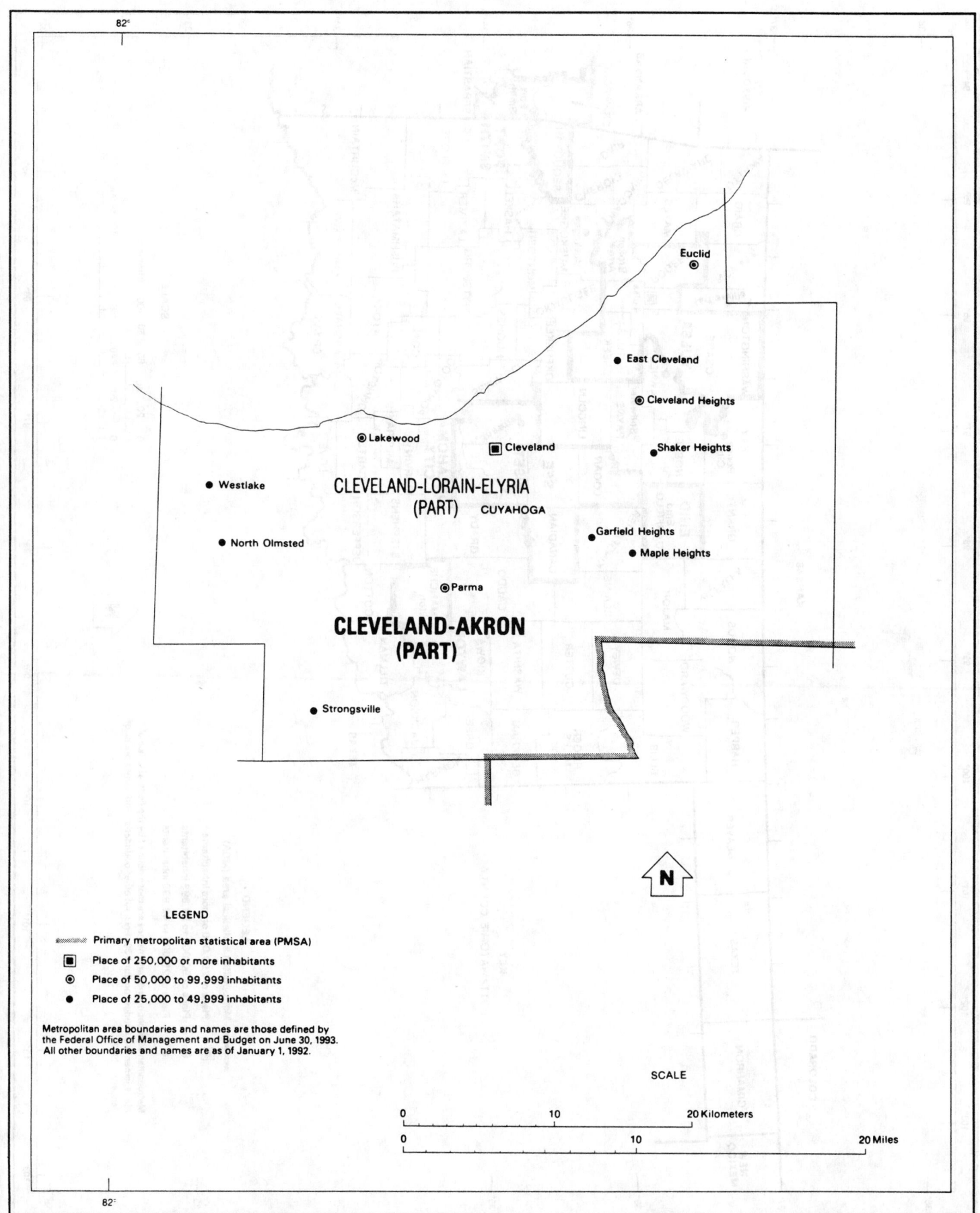

82°

Euclid

● East Cleveland

◎ Cleveland Heights

◎ Lakewood   ■ Cleveland   ● Shaker Heights

CLEVELAND-LORAIN-ELYRIA
(PART)   CUYAHOGA

● Westlake

● North Olmsted   ● Garfield Heights
                     ● Maple Heights

◎ Parma

CLEVELAND-AKRON
(PART)

● Strongsville

N

LEGEND

〰〰〰 Primary metropolitan statistical area (PMSA)

■ Place of 250,000 or more inhabitants

◎ Place of 50,000 to 99,999 inhabitants

● Place of 25,000 to 49,999 inhabitants

Metropolitan area boundaries and names are those defined by
the Federal Office of Management and Budget on June 30, 1993.
All other boundaries and names are as of January 1, 1992.

SCALE

0   10   20 Kilometers

0   10   20 Miles

82°

U.S. DEPARTMENT OF COMMERCE Economics and Statistics Administration Bureau of the Census

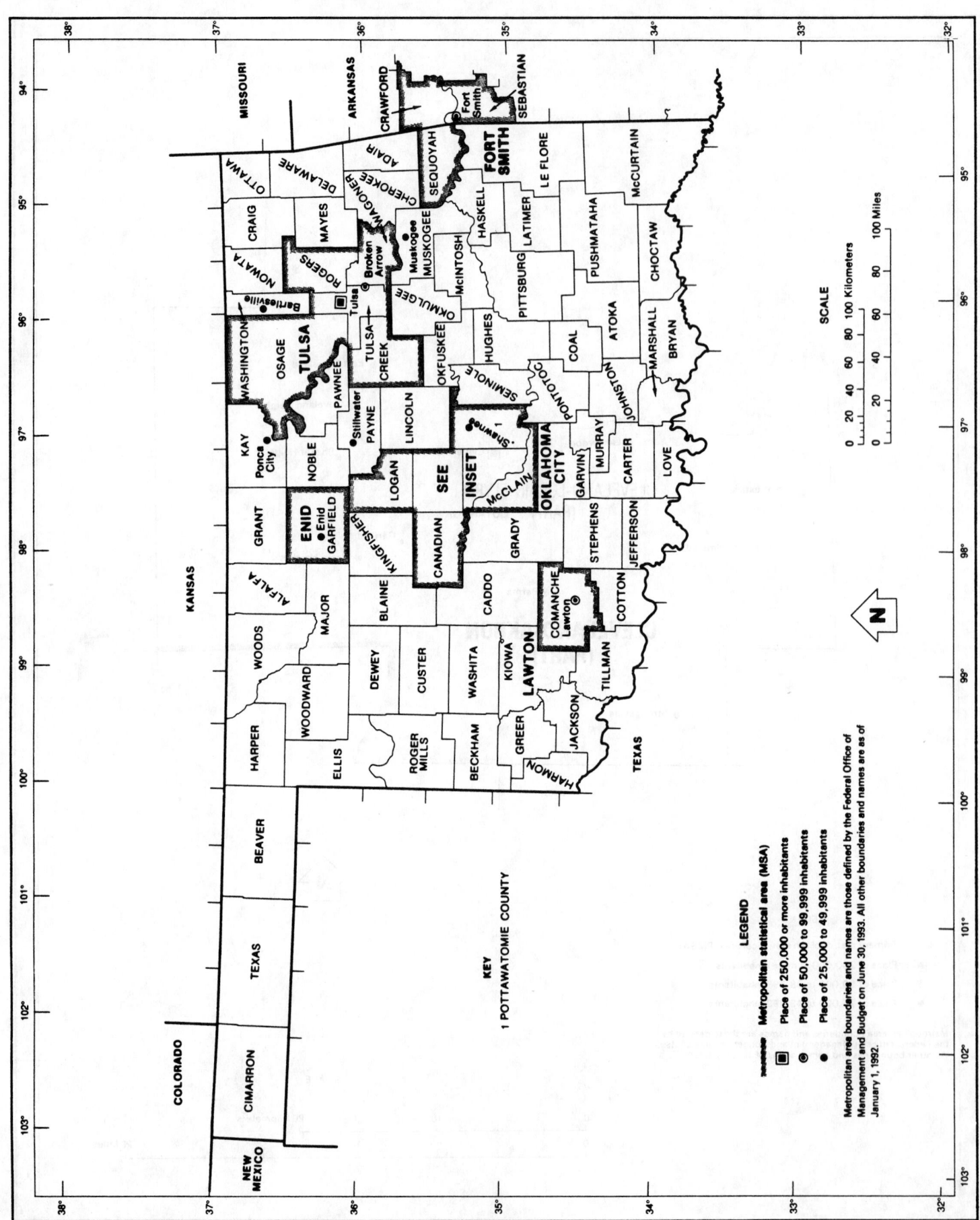

LEGEND

■ Metropolitan statistical area (MSA)

▣ Place of 250,000 or more inhabitants

◉ Place of 50,000 to 99,999 inhabitants

● Place of 25,000 to 49,999 inhabitants

Metropolitan area boundaries and names are those defined by the Federal Office of Management and Budget on June 30, 1993. All other boundaries and names are as of January 1, 1992.

KEY
1 POTTAWATOMIE COUNTY

SCALE

0 20 40 60 80 100 Kilometers

0 20 40 60 80 100 Miles

OKLAHOMA (Inset) - Metropolitan Areas, Counties, and Selected Places

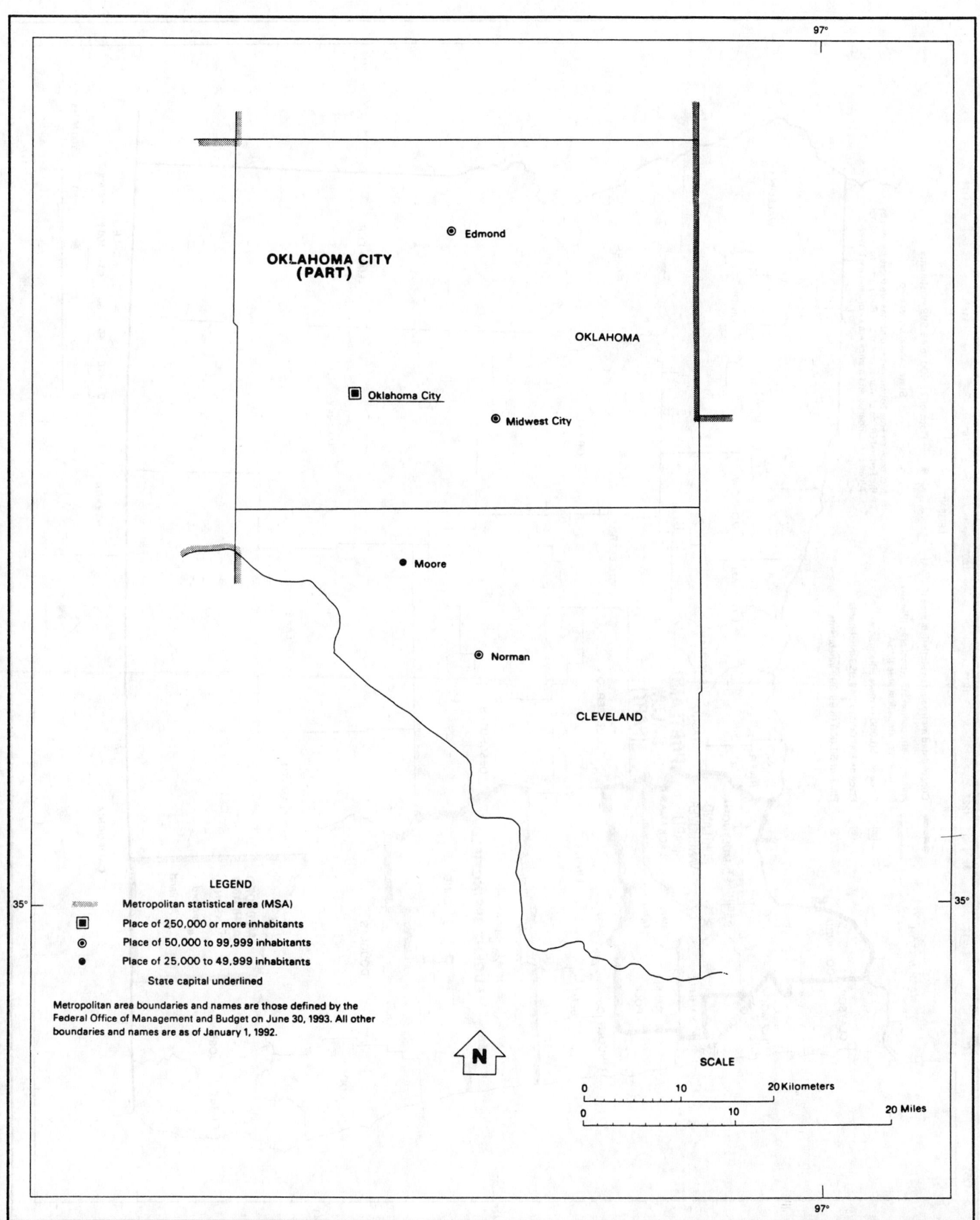

97°

OKLAHOMA CITY
(PART)

◉ Edmond

OKLAHOMA

■ Oklahoma City

◉ Midwest City

● Moore

◉ Norman

CLEVELAND

35°

35°

LEGEND

Metropolitan statistical area (MSA)

■ Place of 250,000 or more inhabitants

◉ Place of 50,000 to 99,999 inhabitants

● Place of 25,000 to 49,999 inhabitants

State capital underlined

Metropolitan area boundaries and names are those defined by the
Federal Office of Management and Budget on June 30, 1993. All other
boundaries and names are as of January 1, 1992.

N

SCALE

0   10   20 Kilometers

0   10   20 Miles

97°

U.S. DEPARTMENT OF COMMERCE Economics and Statistics Administration Bureau of the Census

OREGON - Metropolitan Areas, Counties, and Selected Places

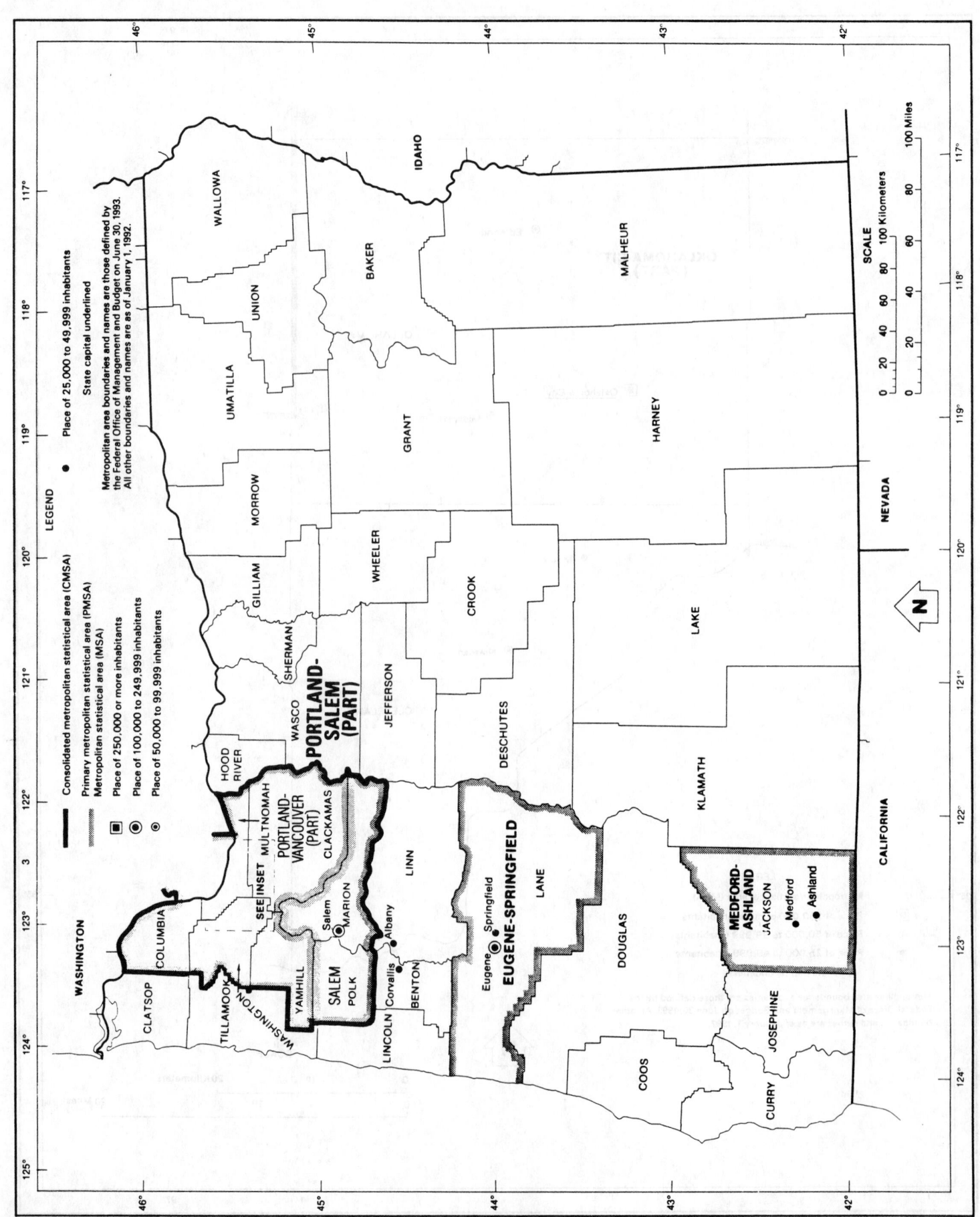

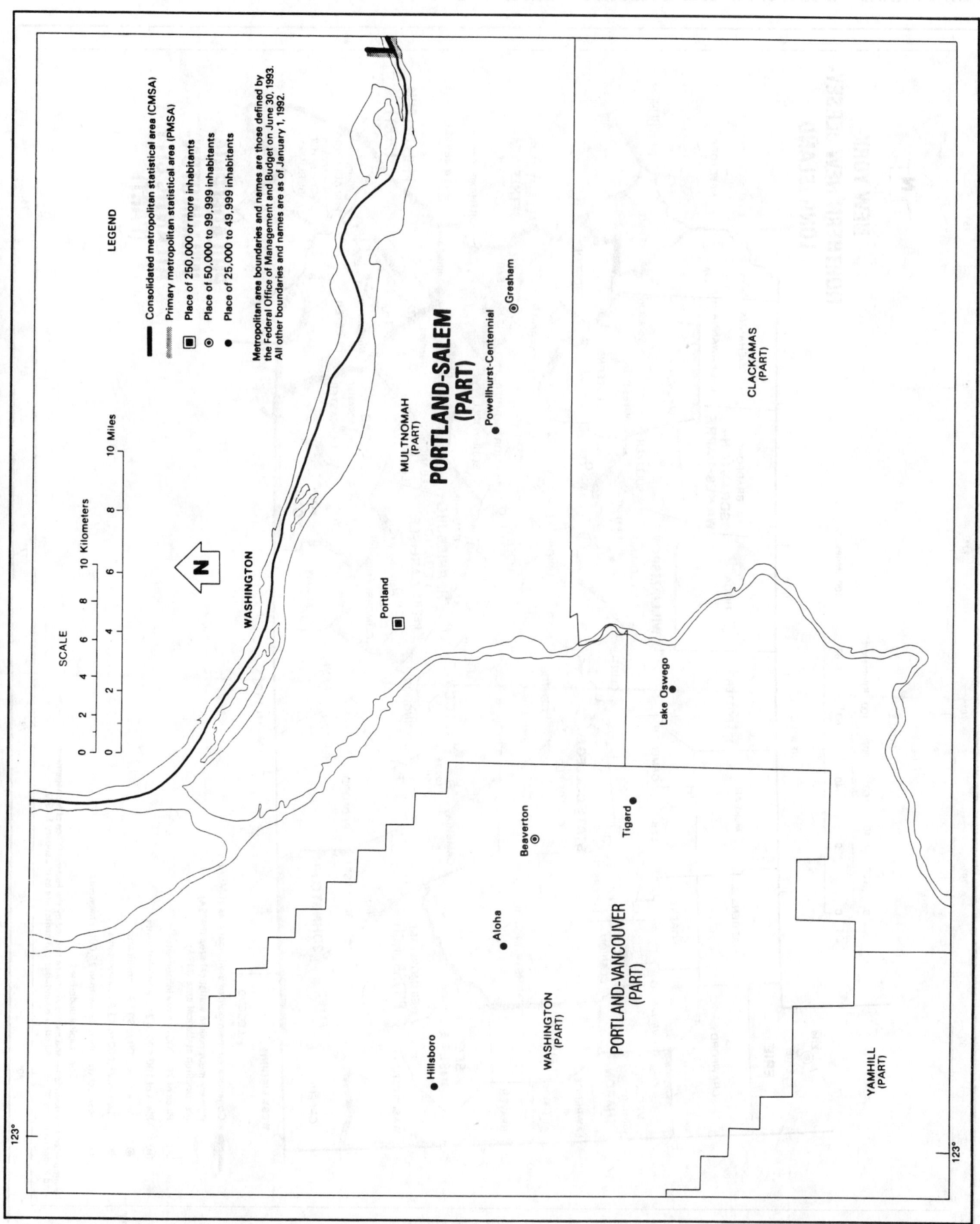

LEGEND

Consolidated metropolitan statistical area (CMSA)

Primary metropolitan statistical area (PMSA)

■ Place of 250,000 or more inhabitants

◉ Place of 50,000 to 99,999 inhabitants

● Place of 25,000 to 49,999 inhabitants

Metropolitan area boundaries and names are those defined by the Federal Office of Management and Budget on June 30, 1993. All other boundaries and names are as of January 1, 1992.

SCALE

N

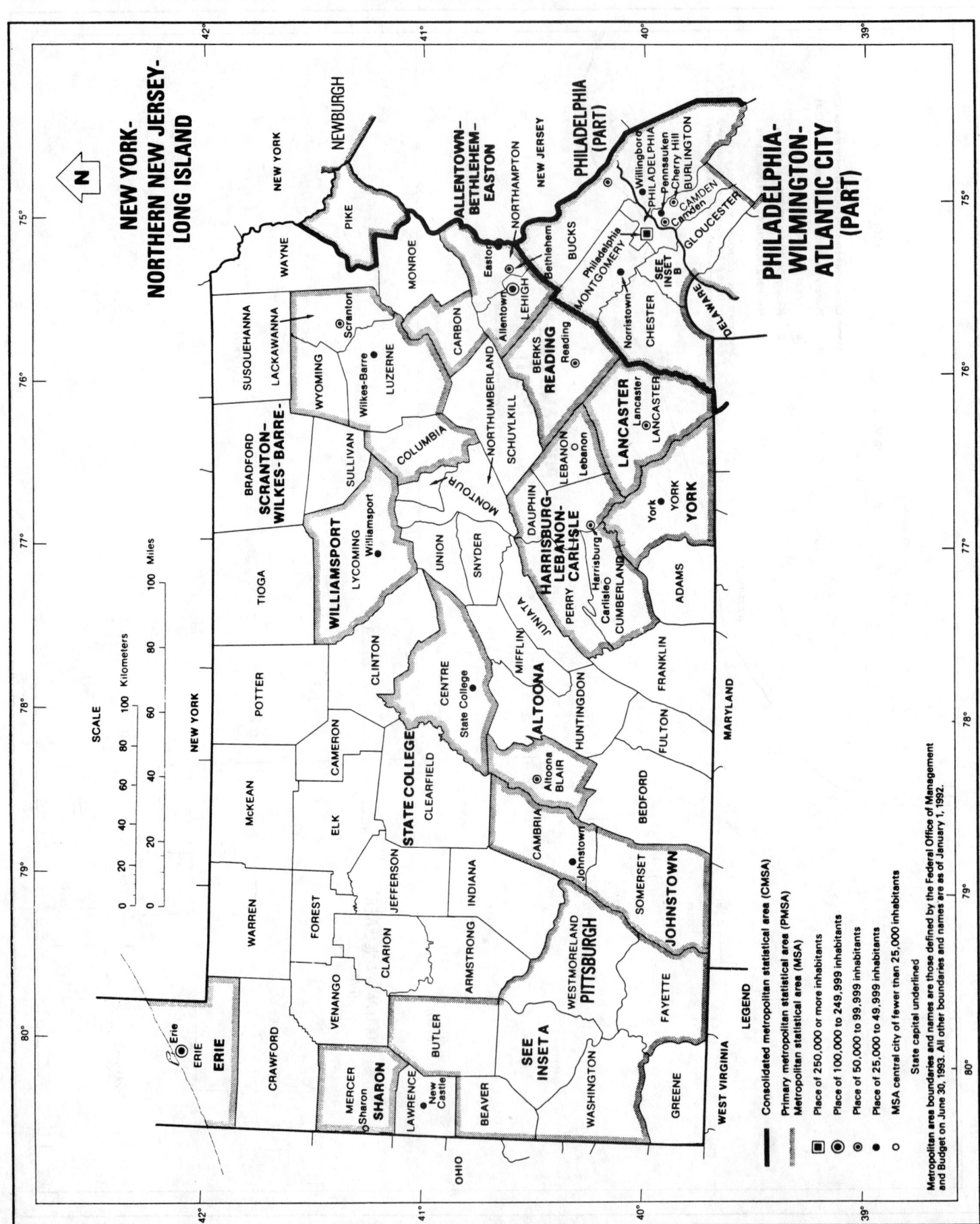

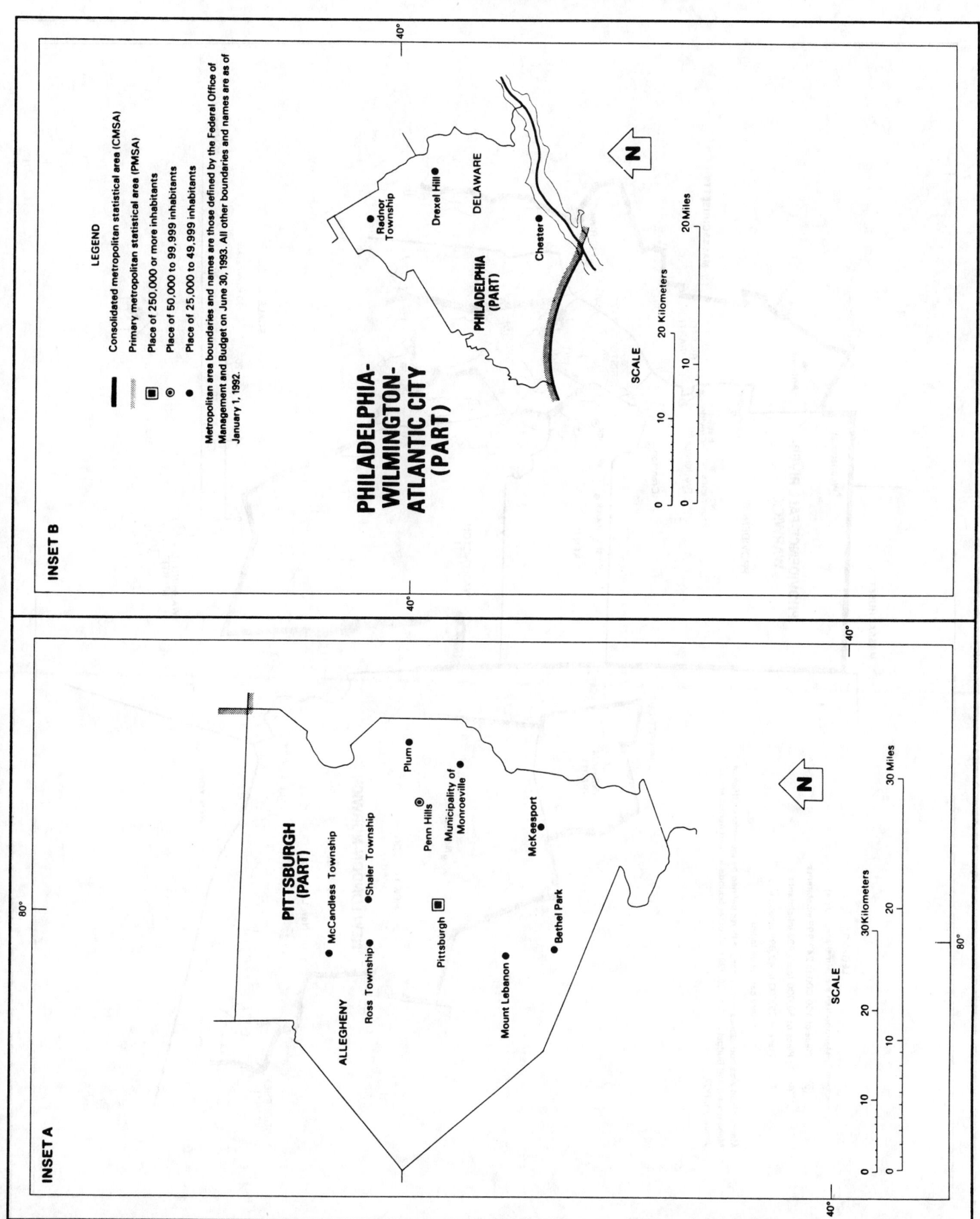

PITTSBURGH (PART)

ALLEGHENY

INSET A

PHILADELPHIA-WILMINGTON-ATLANTIC CITY (PART)

PHILADELPHIA (PART)

DELAWARE

INSET B

LEGEND

Consolidated metropolitan statistical area (CMSA)

Primary metropolitan statistical area (PMSA)

Place of 250,000 or more inhabitants

Place of 50,000 to 99,999 inhabitants

Place of 25,000 to 49,999 inhabitants

Metropolitan area boundaries and names are those defined by the Federal Office of Management and Budget on June 30, 1993. All other boundaries and names are as of January 1, 1992.

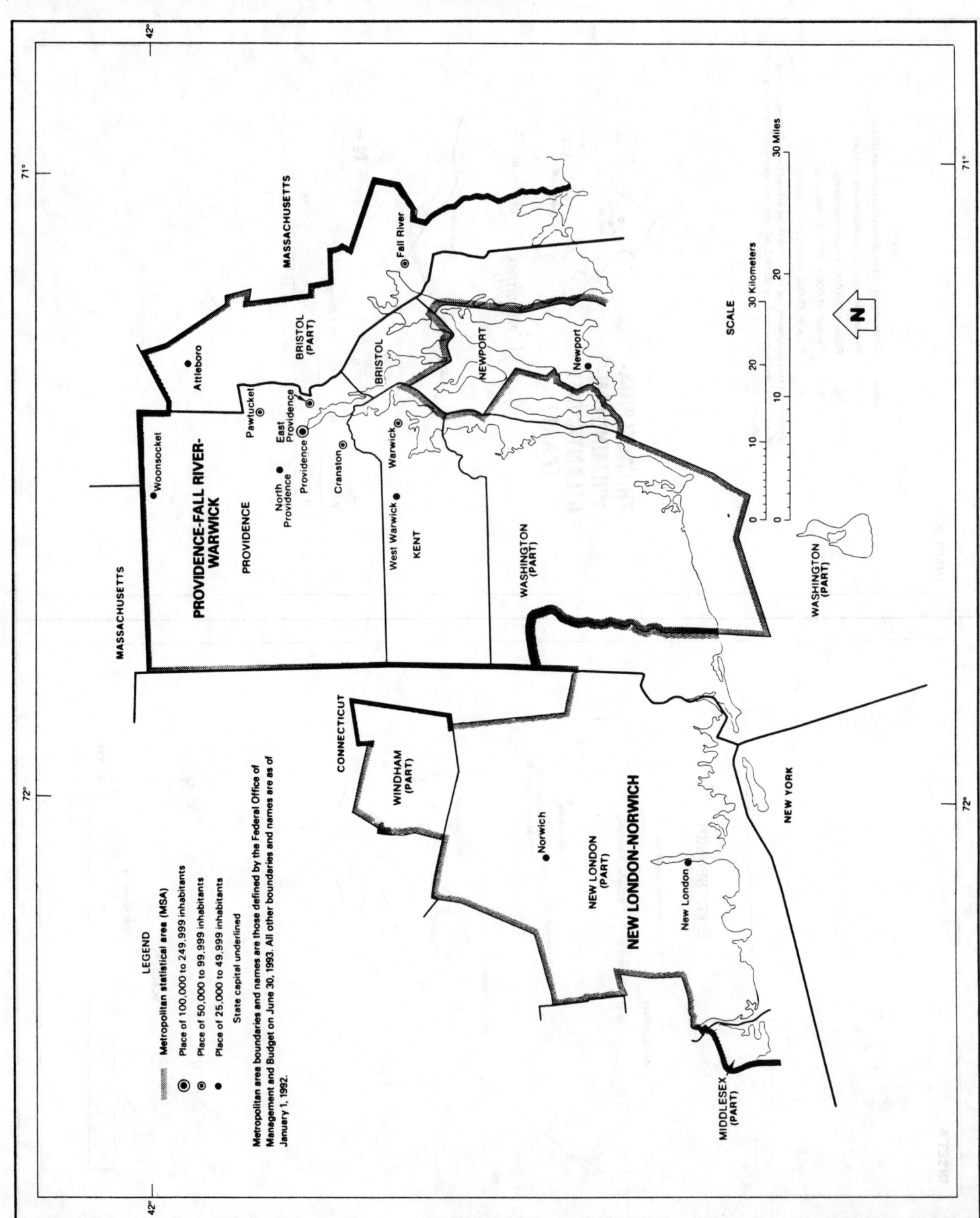

SOUTH CAROLINA - Metropolitan Areas, Counties, and Selected Places

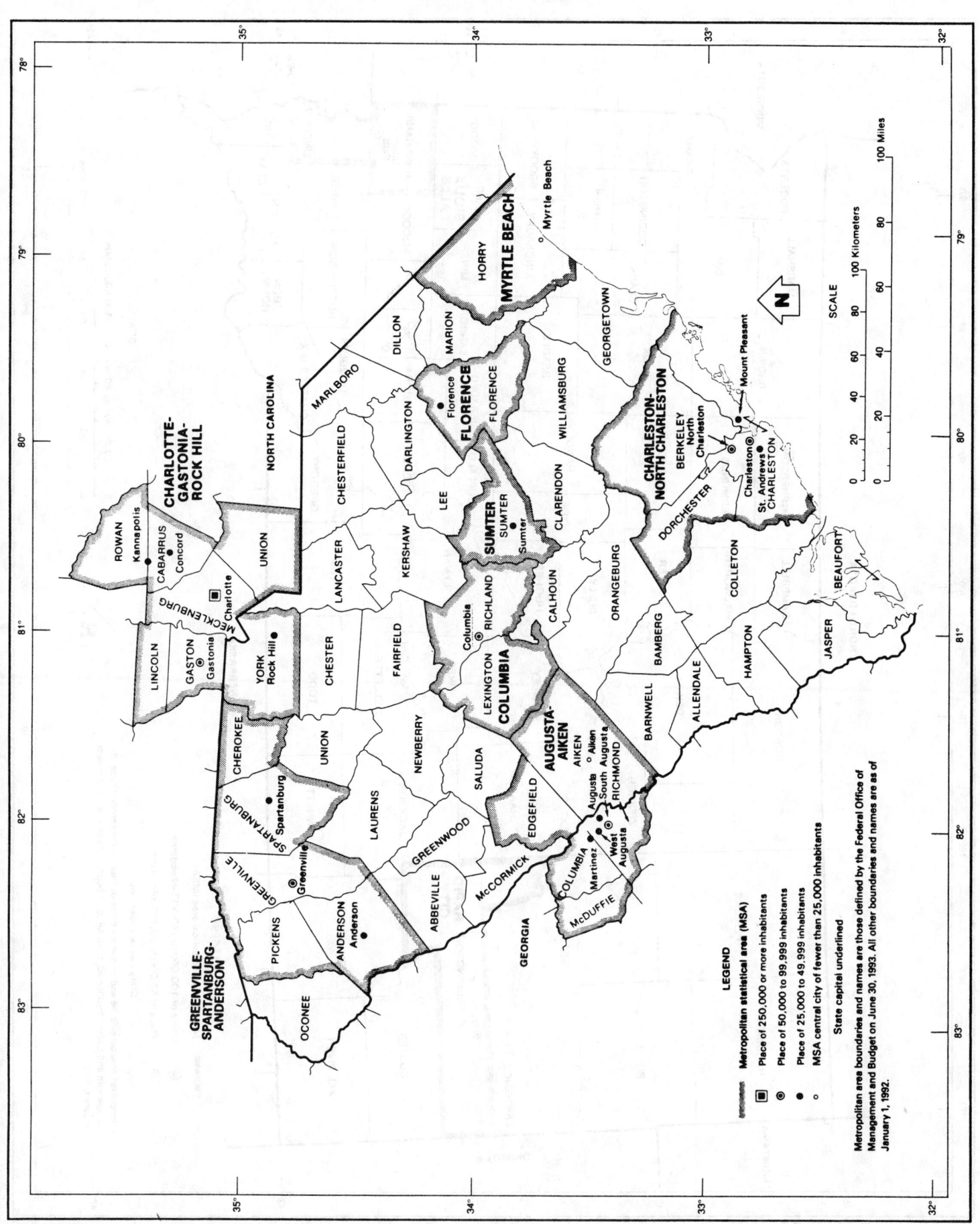

LEGEND

- ▣ Metropolitan statistical area (MSA)
- ◉ Place of 250,000 or more inhabitants
- ● Place of 50,000 to 99,999 inhabitants
- ● Place of 25,000 to 49,999 inhabitants
- ○ MSA central city of fewer than 25,000 inhabitants

State capital underlined

Metropolitan area boundaries and names are those defined by the Federal Office of Management and Budget on June 30, 1993. All other boundaries and names are as of January 1, 1992.

SOUTH DAKOTA - Metropolitan Areas, Counties, and Selected Places

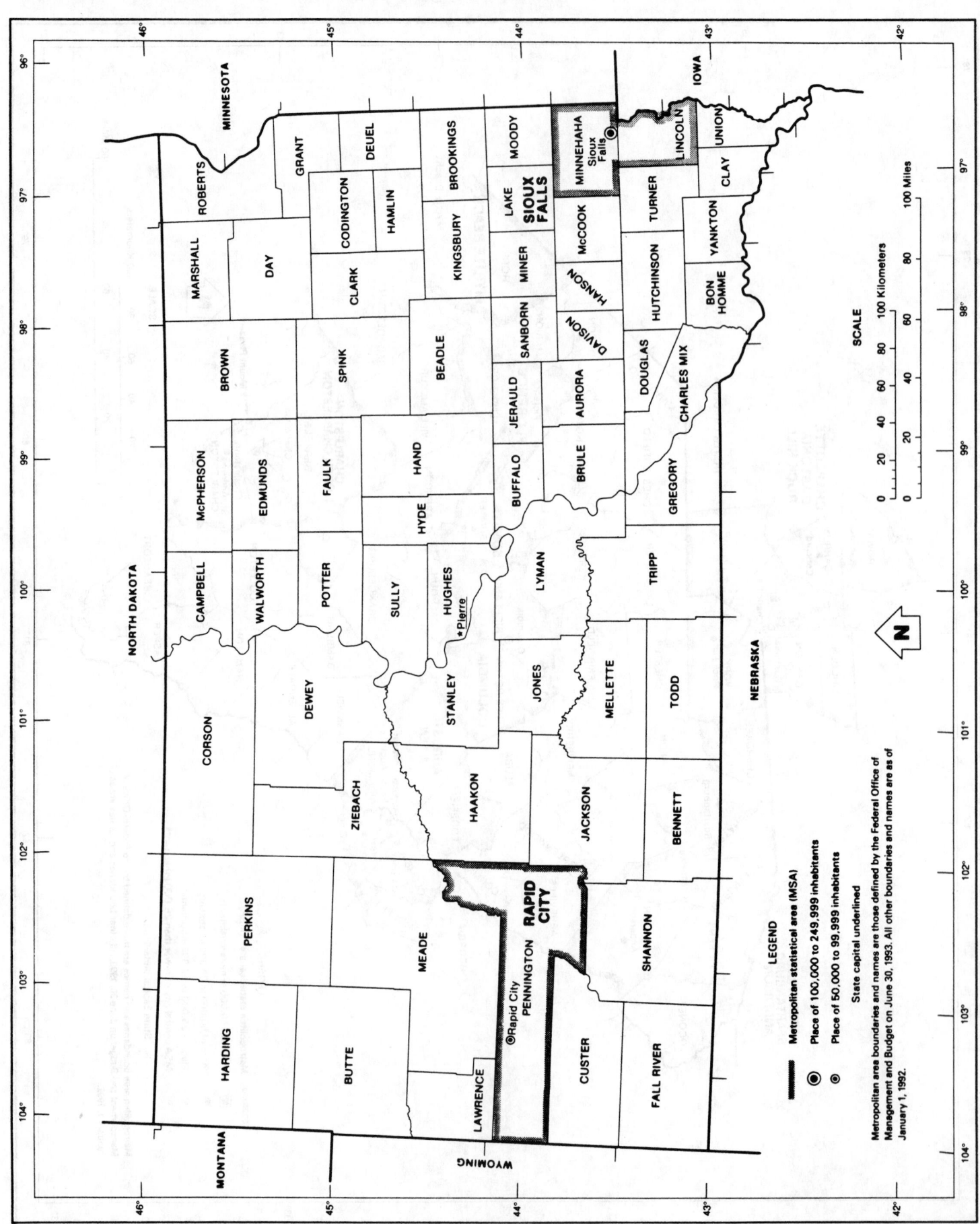

LEGEND

■ Metropolitan statistical area (MSA)

◉ Place of 100,000 to 249,999 inhabitants

◉ Place of 50,000 to 99,999 inhabitants

State capital underlined

Metropolitan area boundaries and names are those defined by the Federal Office of Management and Budget on June 30, 1993. All other boundaries and names are as of January 1, 1992.

SCALE

0   20   40   60   80   100 Miles

0   20   40   60   80   100 Kilometers

TENNESSEE - Metropolitan Areas, Counties, Independent City, and Other Selected Places

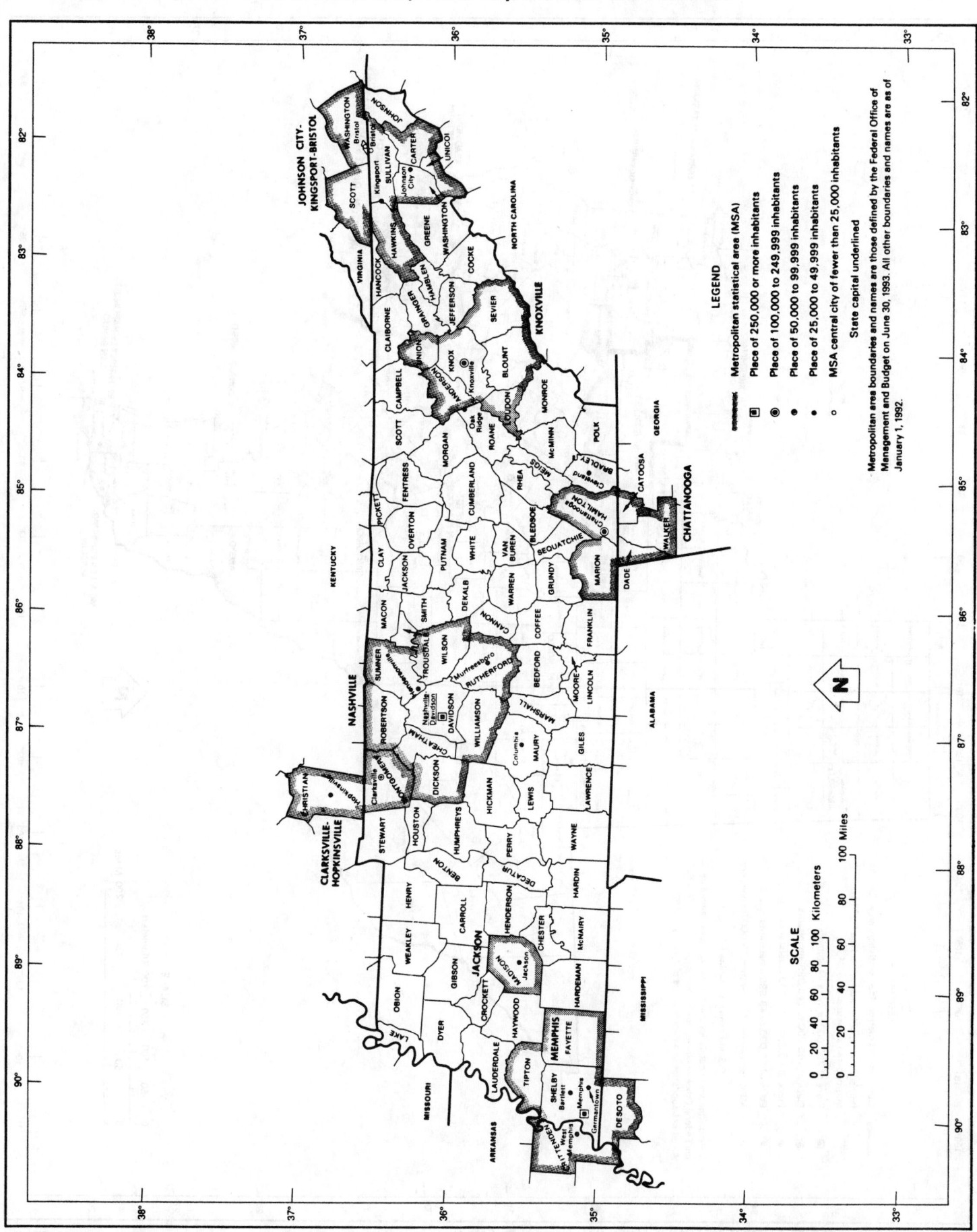

LEGEND

▣ Metropolitan statistical area (MSA)

◉ Place of 250,000 or more inhabitants

◉ Place of 100,000 to 249,999 inhabitants

● Place of 50,000 to 99,999 inhabitants

● Place of 25,000 to 49,999 inhabitants

○ MSA central city of fewer than 25,000 inhabitants

State capital underlined

Metropolitan area boundaries and names are those defined by the Federal Office of Management and Budget on June 30, 1993. All other boundaries and names are as of January 1, 1992.

SCALE

0 20 40 60 80 100 Kilometers

0 20 40 60 80 100 Miles

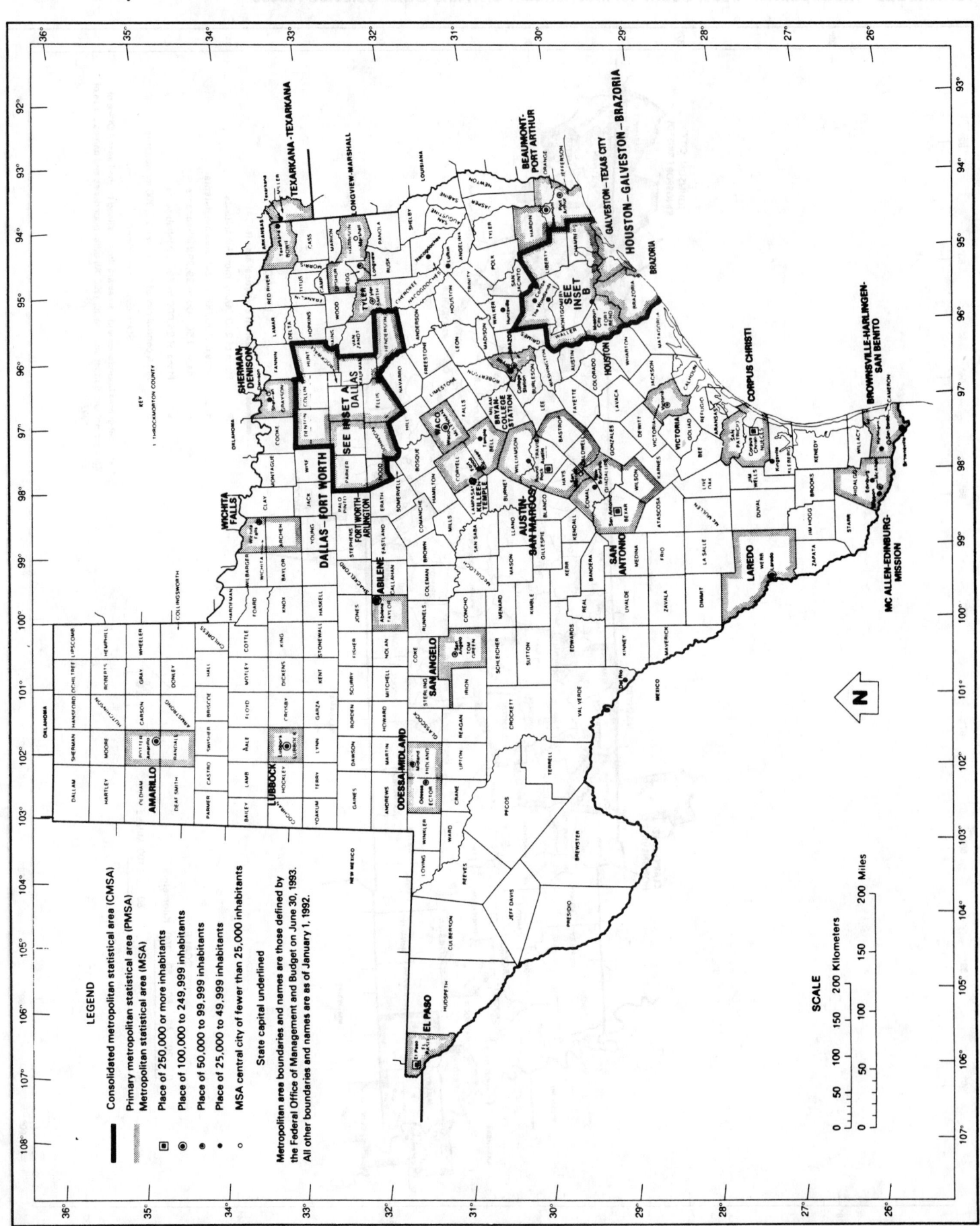

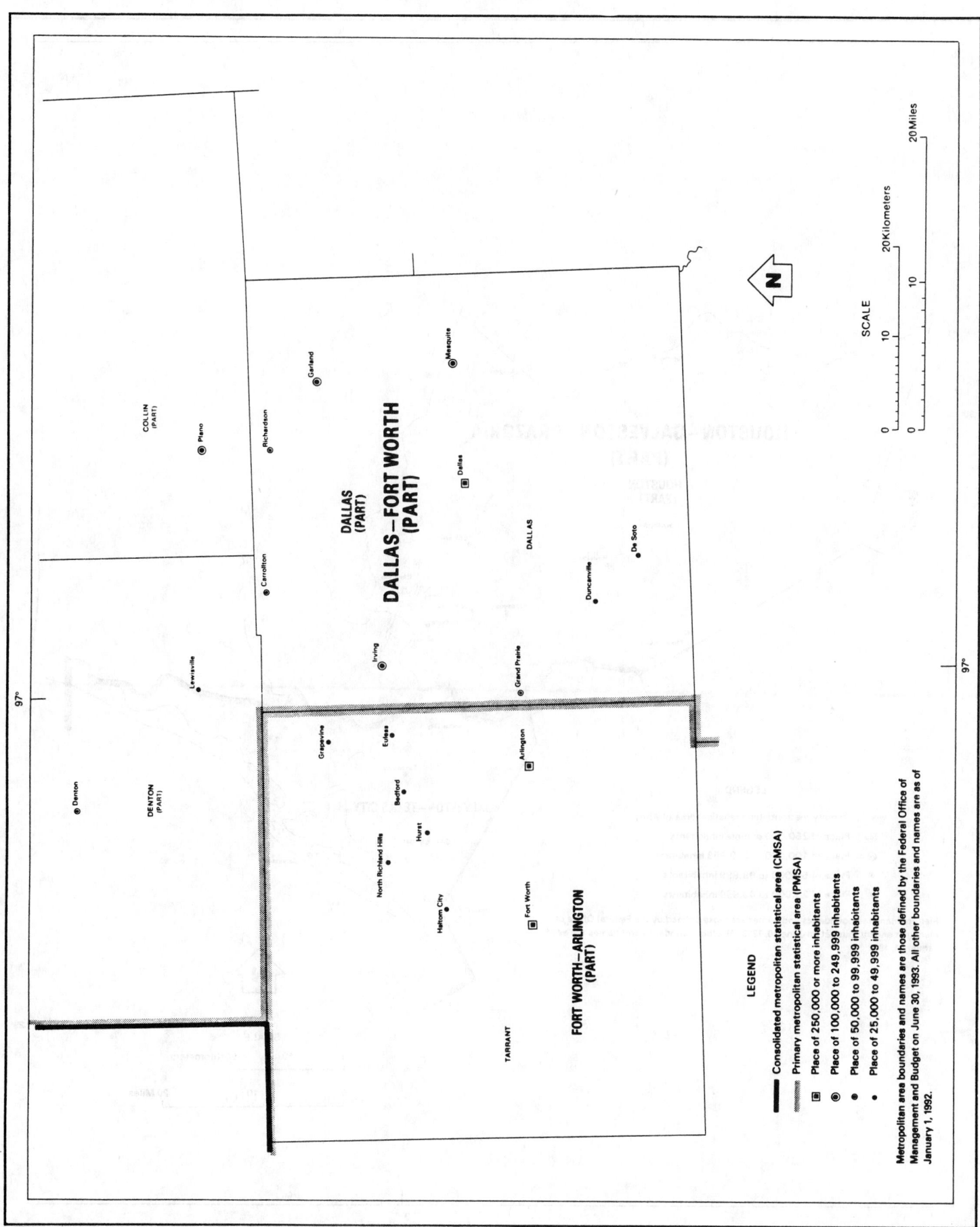

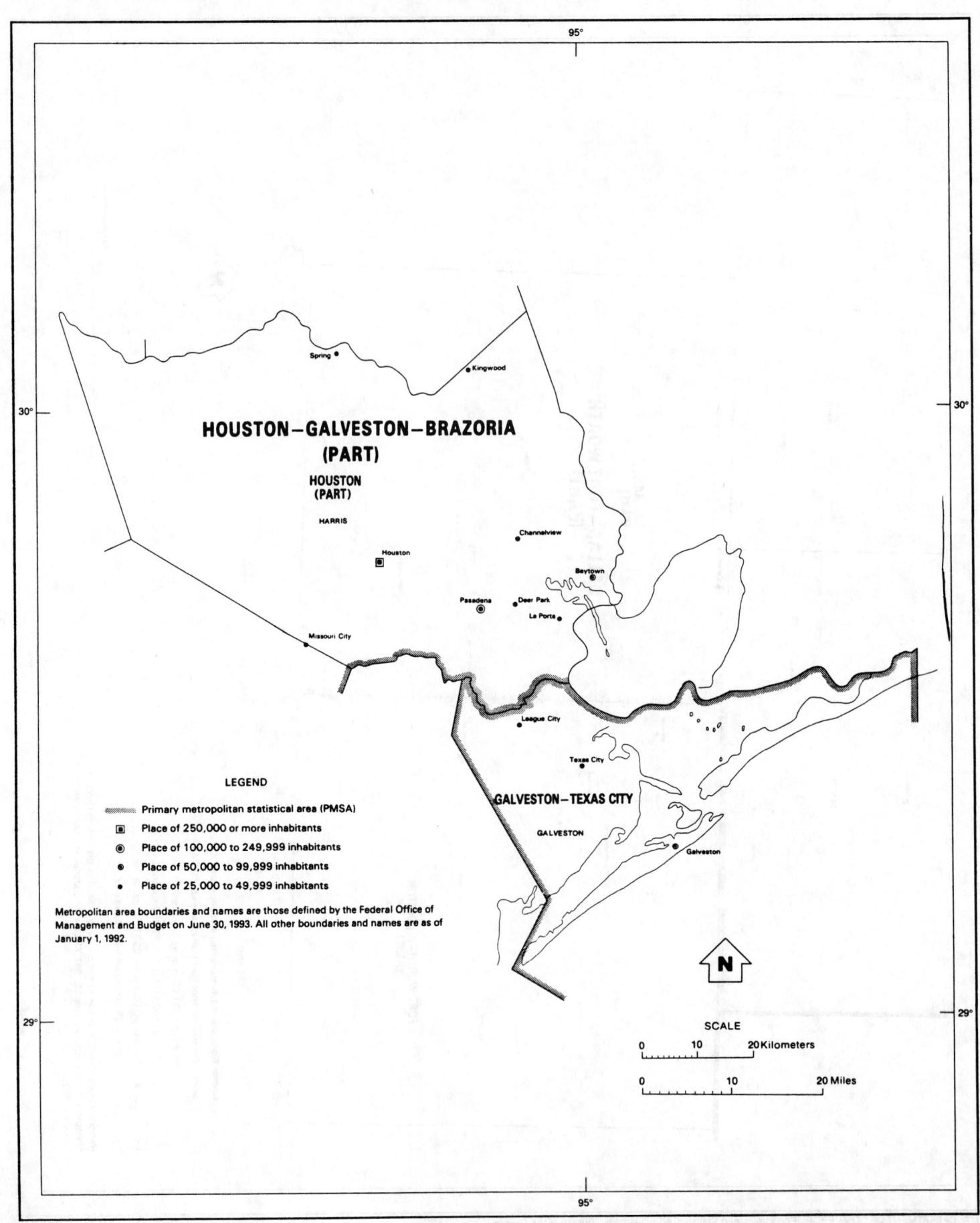

TEXAS (Inset B) - Metropolitan Areas, Counties, and Selected Places

95°

30°   30°

HOUSTON–GALVESTON–BRAZORIA
(PART)

HOUSTON
(PART)

HARRIS

Spring
Kingwood

Channelview
Houston
Baytown
Pasadena   Deer Park
La Porte
Missouri City

League City

Texas City

GALVESTON–TEXAS CITY

GALVESTON

Galveston

LEGEND

Primary metropolitan statistical area (PMSA)

▣ Place of 250,000 or more inhabitants

◉ Place of 100,000 to 249,999 inhabitants

◉ Place of 50,000 to 99,999 inhabitants

• Place of 25,000 to 49,999 inhabitants

Metropolitan area boundaries and names are those defined by the Federal Office of
Management and Budget on June 30, 1993. All other boundaries and names are as of
January 1, 1992.

N

29°   29°

SCALE

0   10   20 Kilometers

0   10   20 Miles

95°

UTAH - Metropolitan Areas, Counties, and Selected Places

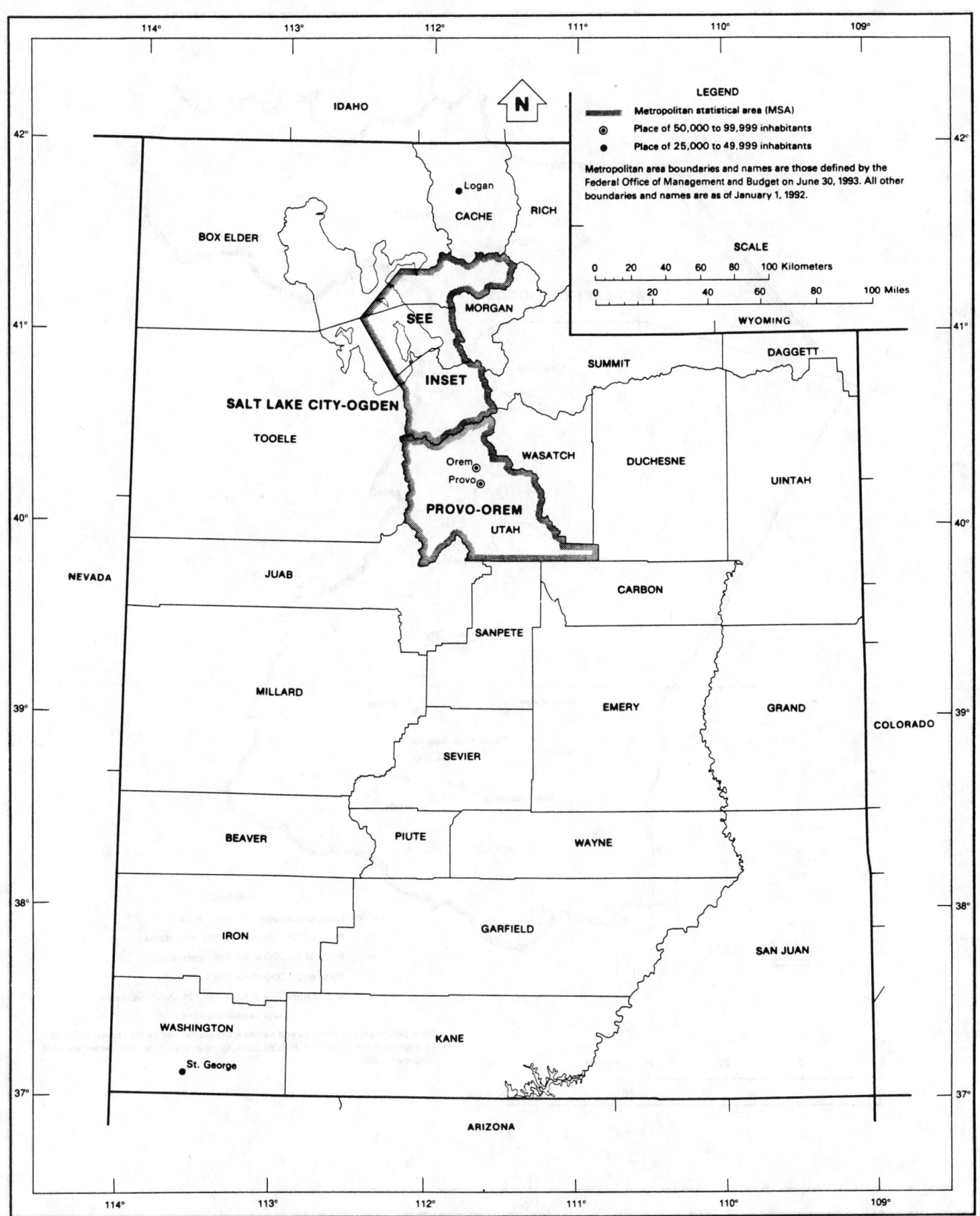

LEGEND

Metropolitan statistical area (MSA)

◉ Place of 50,000 to 99,999 inhabitants

● Place of 25,000 to 49,999 inhabitants

Metropolitan area boundaries and names are those defined by the Federal Office of Management and Budget on June 30, 1993. All other boundaries and names are as of January 1, 1992.

SCALE

0 20 40 60 80 100 Kilometers

0 20 40 60 80 100 Miles

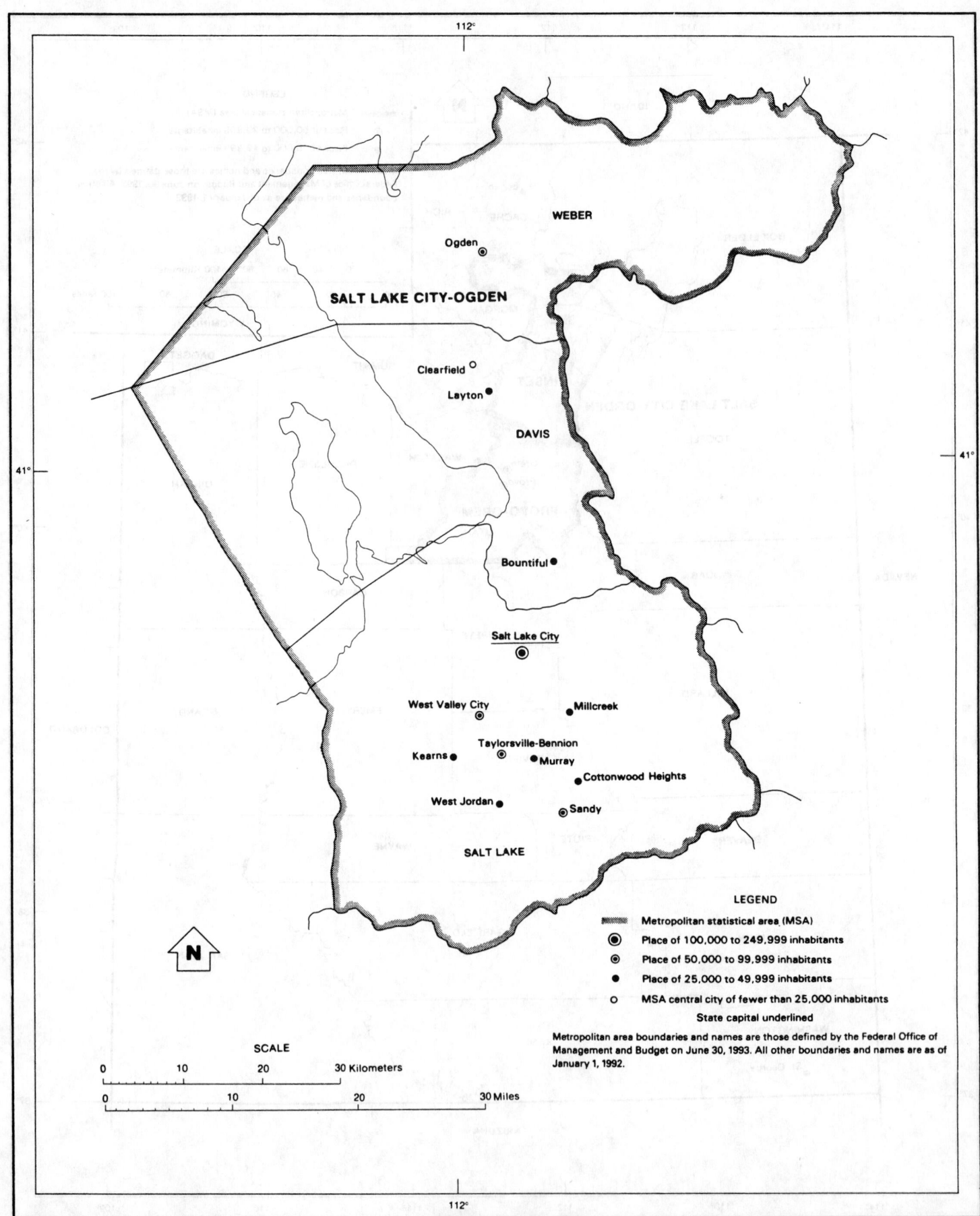

112°

WEBER

Ogden ⊚

SALT LAKE CITY-OGDEN

Clearfield ○

Layton ●

DAVIS

41°

Bountiful ●

Salt Lake City ⊚

West Valley City ⊚   Millcreek ●

Taylorsville-Bennion ⊚

Kearns ●   Murray ●

Cottonwood Heights ●

West Jordan ●   ⊚ Sandy

SALT LAKE

N

LEGEND

▬▬▬ Metropolitan statistical area (MSA)

⊚ Place of 100,000 to 249,999 inhabitants

⊙ Place of 50,000 to 99,999 inhabitants

● Place of 25,000 to 49,999 inhabitants

○ MSA central city of fewer than 25,000 inhabitants

State capital underlined

Metropolitan area boundaries and names are those defined by the Federal Office of Management and Budget on June 30, 1993. All other boundaries and names are as of January 1, 1992.

SCALE

0   10   20   30 Kilometers

0   10   20   30 Miles

112°

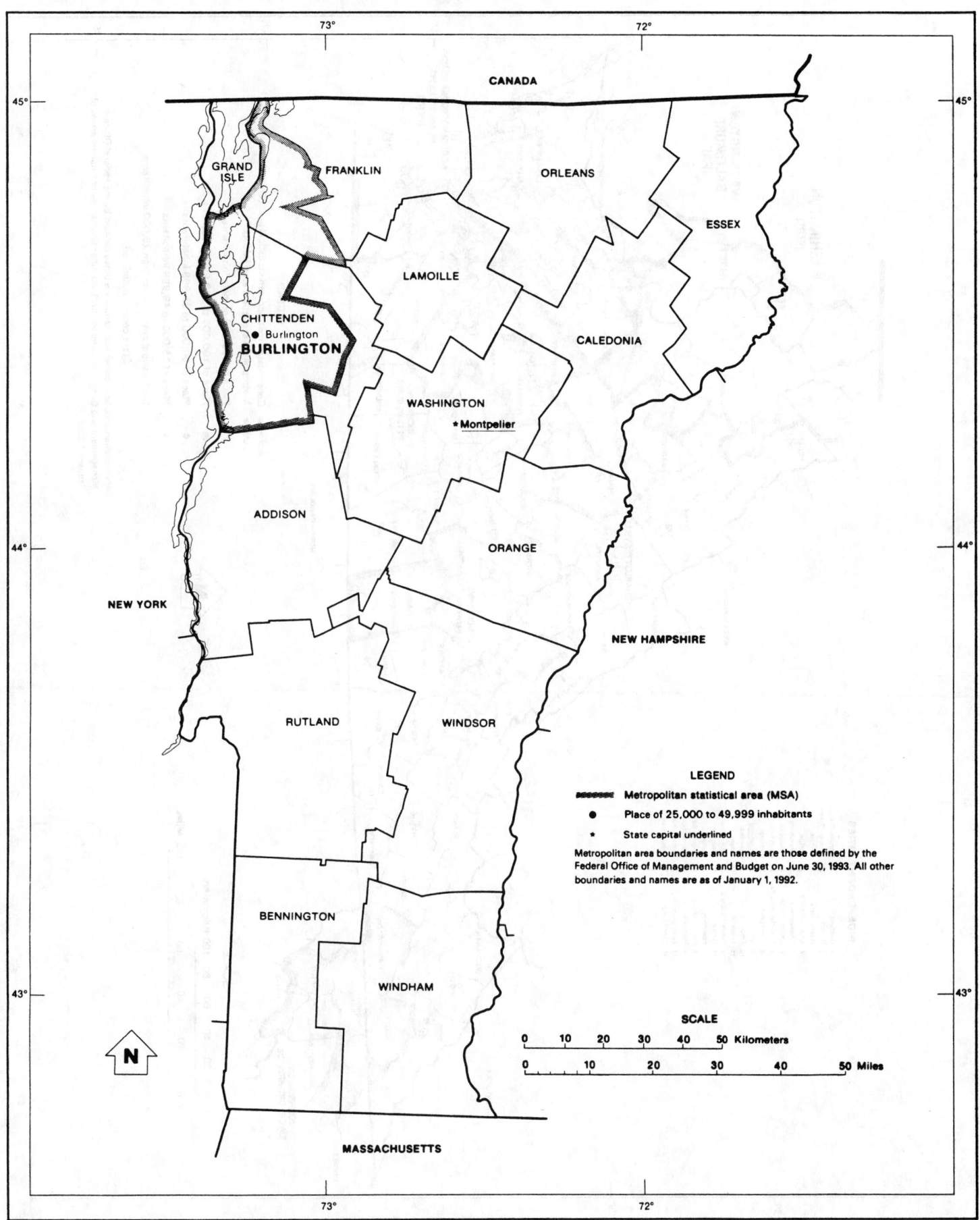

VERMONT - Metropolitan Areas, Counties, and Selected Places

Appendix D

CANADA

GRAND ISLE

FRANKLIN

ORLEANS

ESSEX

LAMOILLE

CHITTENDEN
● Burlington
BURLINGTON

CALEDONIA

WASHINGTON
*Montpelier

ADDISON

ORANGE

NEW YORK

NEW HAMPSHIRE

RUTLAND

WINDSOR

LEGEND

〰〰〰 Metropolitan statistical area (MSA)

● Place of 25,000 to 49,999 inhabitants

* State capital underlined

Metropolitan area boundaries and names are those defined by the
Federal Office of Management and Budget on June 30, 1993. All other
boundaries and names are as of January 1, 1992.

BENNINGTON

WINDHAM

SCALE

0   10   20   30   40   50   Kilometers

0   10   20   30   40   50   Miles

N

MASSACHUSETTS

VIRGINIA - Metropolitan Areas, District of Columbia, Counties, Independent Cities, and Other Selected Places

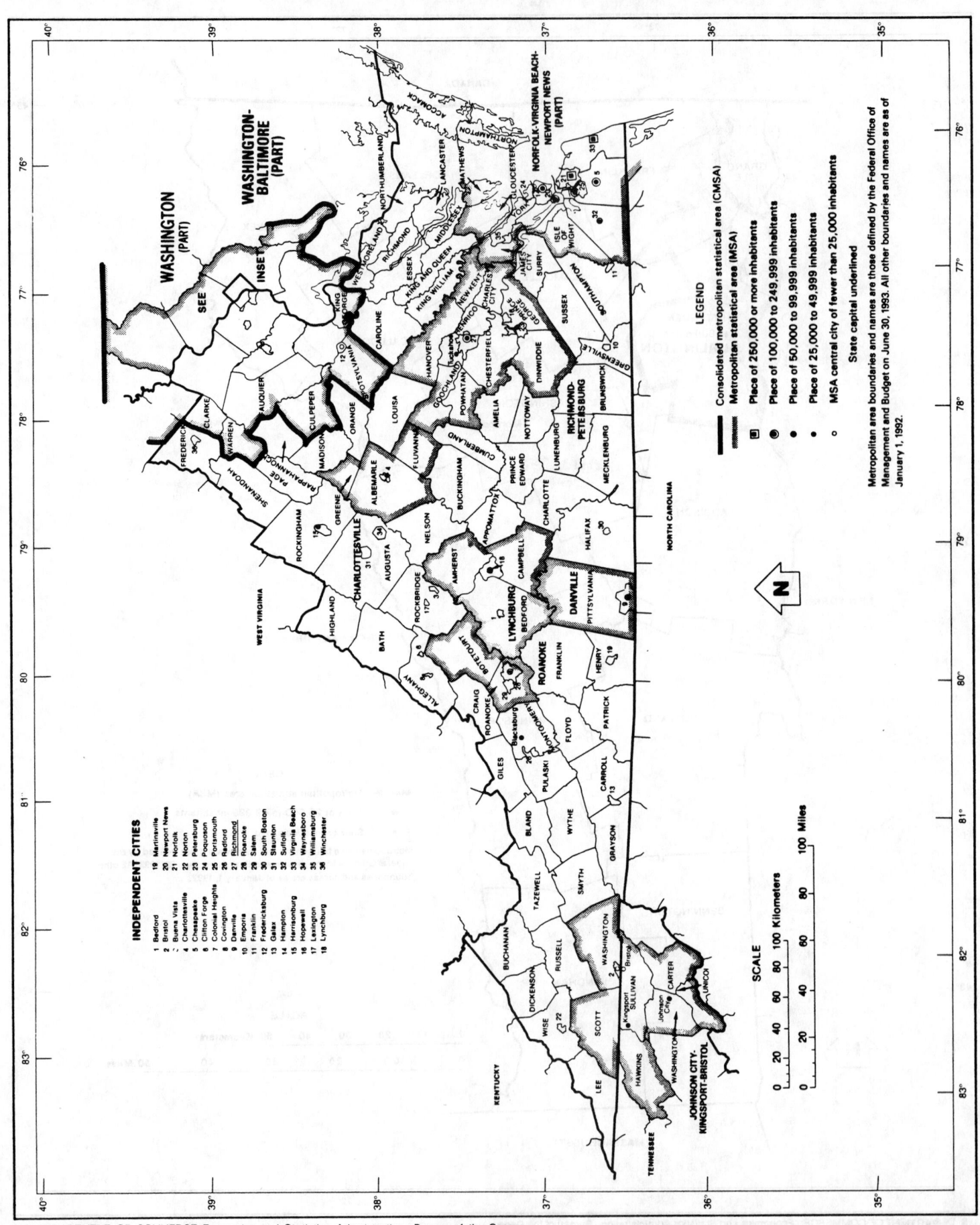

INDEPENDENT CITIES

1 Bedford
2 Bristol
3 Buena Vista
4 Charlottesville
5 Chesapeake
6 Clifton Forge
7 Colonial Heights
8 Covington
9 Danville
10 Emporia
11 Franklin
12 Fredericksburg
13 Galax
14 Hampton
15 Harrisonburg
16 Hopewell
17 Lexington
18 Lynchburg
19 Martinsville
20 Newport News
21 Norfolk
22 Norton
23 Petersburg
24 Poquoson
25 Portsmouth
26 Radford
27 Richmond
28 Roanoke
29 Salem
30 South Boston
31 Staunton
32 Suffolk
33 Virginia Beach
34 Waynesboro
35 Williamsburg
36 Winchester

LEGEND

━━━ Consolidated metropolitan statistical area (CMSA)
━━━ Metropolitan statistical area (MSA)

Place of 250,000 or more inhabitants
Place of 100,000 to 249,999 inhabitants
Place of 50,000 to 99,999 inhabitants
Place of 25,000 to 49,999 inhabitants
Place of fewer than 25,000 inhabitants
MSA central city of fewer than 25,000 inhabitants

State capital underlined

Metropolitan area boundaries and names are those defined by the Federal Office of Management and Budget on June 30, 1993. All other boundaries and names are as of January 1, 1992.

SCALE

0   20   40   60   80   100 Kilometers
0   20   40   60   80   100 Miles

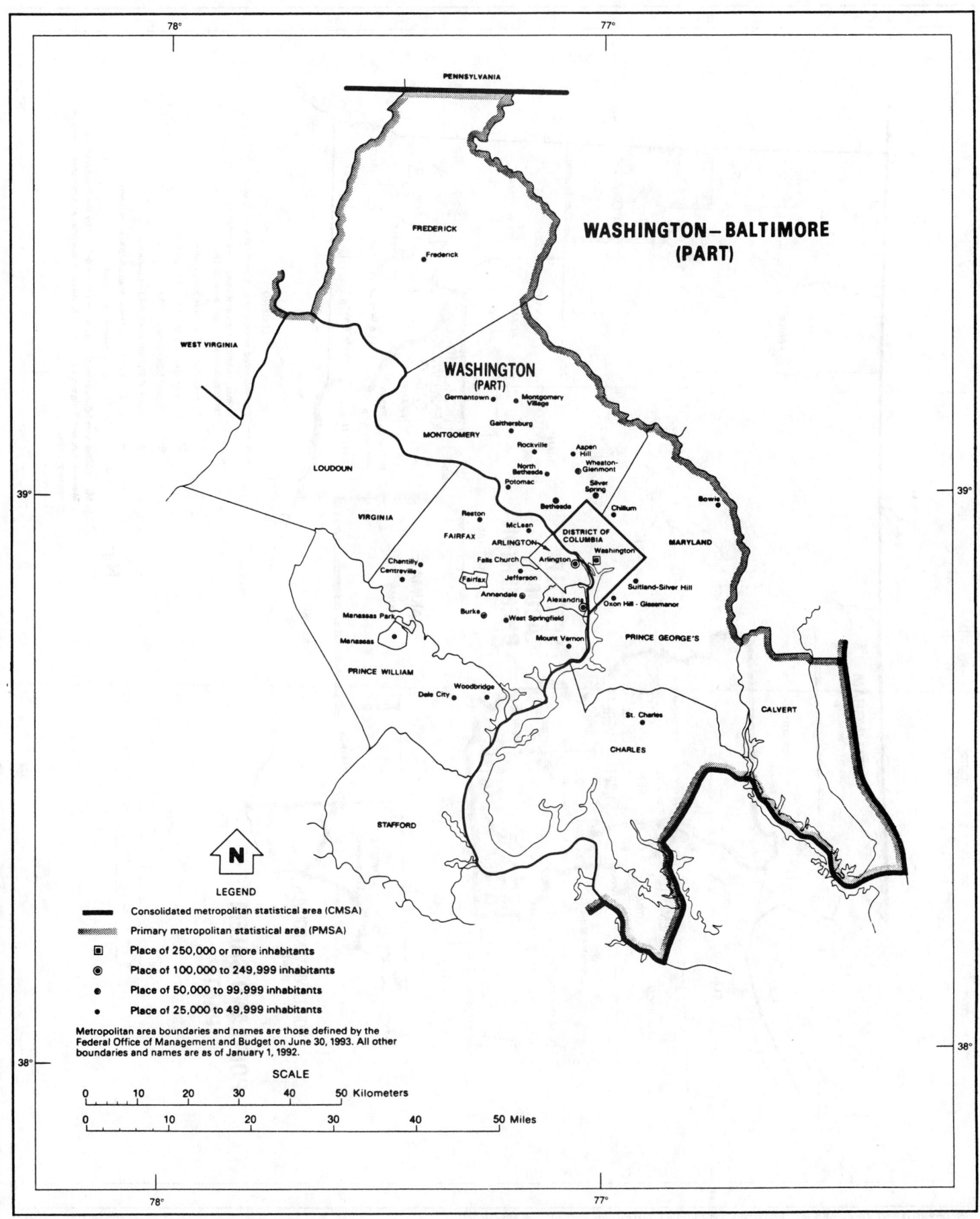

WASHINGTON–BALTIMORE
(PART)

WASHINGTON
(PART)

LEGEND

▬▬▬ Consolidated metropolitan statistical area (CMSA)

▒▒▒▒ Primary metropolitan statistical area (PMSA)

▣ Place of 250,000 or more inhabitants

◉ Place of 100,000 to 249,999 inhabitants

● Place of 50,000 to 99,999 inhabitants

• Place of 25,000 to 49,999 inhabitants

Metropolitan area boundaries and names are those defined by the
Federal Office of Management and Budget on June 30, 1993. All other
boundaries and names are as of January 1, 1992.

SCALE

| 0 | 10 | 20 | 30 | 40 | 50 Kilometers |

| 0 | 10 | 20 | 30 | 40 | 50 Miles |

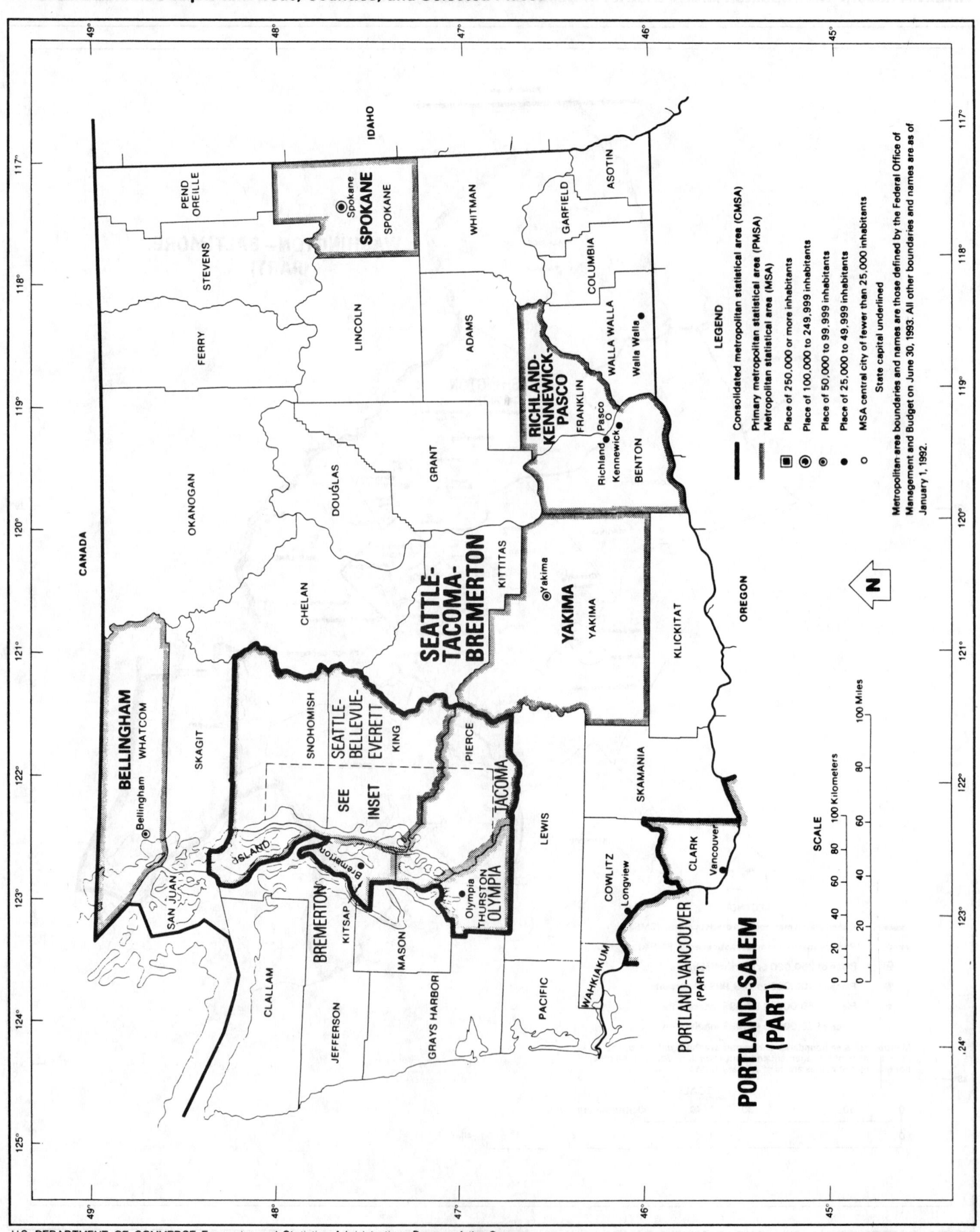

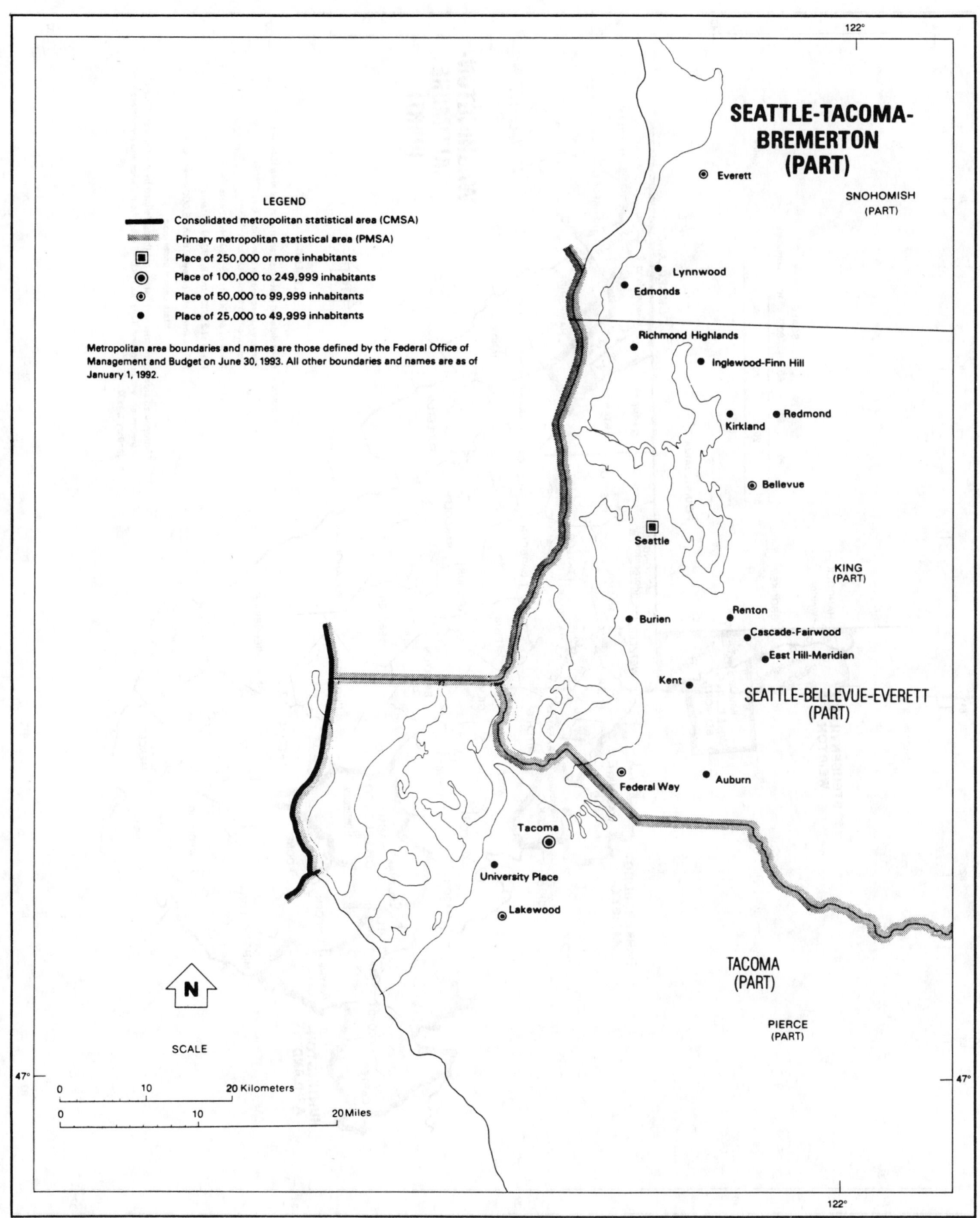

SEATTLE-TACOMA-BREMERTON (PART)

SNOHOMISH (PART)

KING (PART)

SEATTLE-BELLEVUE-EVERETT (PART)

TACOMA (PART)

PIERCE (PART)

LEGEND

— Consolidated metropolitan statistical area (CMSA)

— Primary metropolitan statistical area (PMSA)

▣ Place of 250,000 or more inhabitants

◉ Place of 100,000 to 249,999 inhabitants

⊙ Place of 50,000 to 99,999 inhabitants

● Place of 25,000 to 49,999 inhabitants

Metropolitan area boundaries and names are those defined by the Federal Office of Management and Budget on June 30, 1993. All other boundaries and names are as of January 1, 1992.

Everett
Lynnwood
Edmonds
Richmond Highlands
Inglewood-Finn Hill
Kirkland
Redmond
Bellevue
Seattle
Renton
Burien
Cascade-Fairwood
East Hill-Meridian
Kent
Federal Way
Auburn
Tacoma
University Place
Lakewood

N

SCALE

0   10   20 Kilometers

0   10   20 Miles

122°

47°   47°

122°

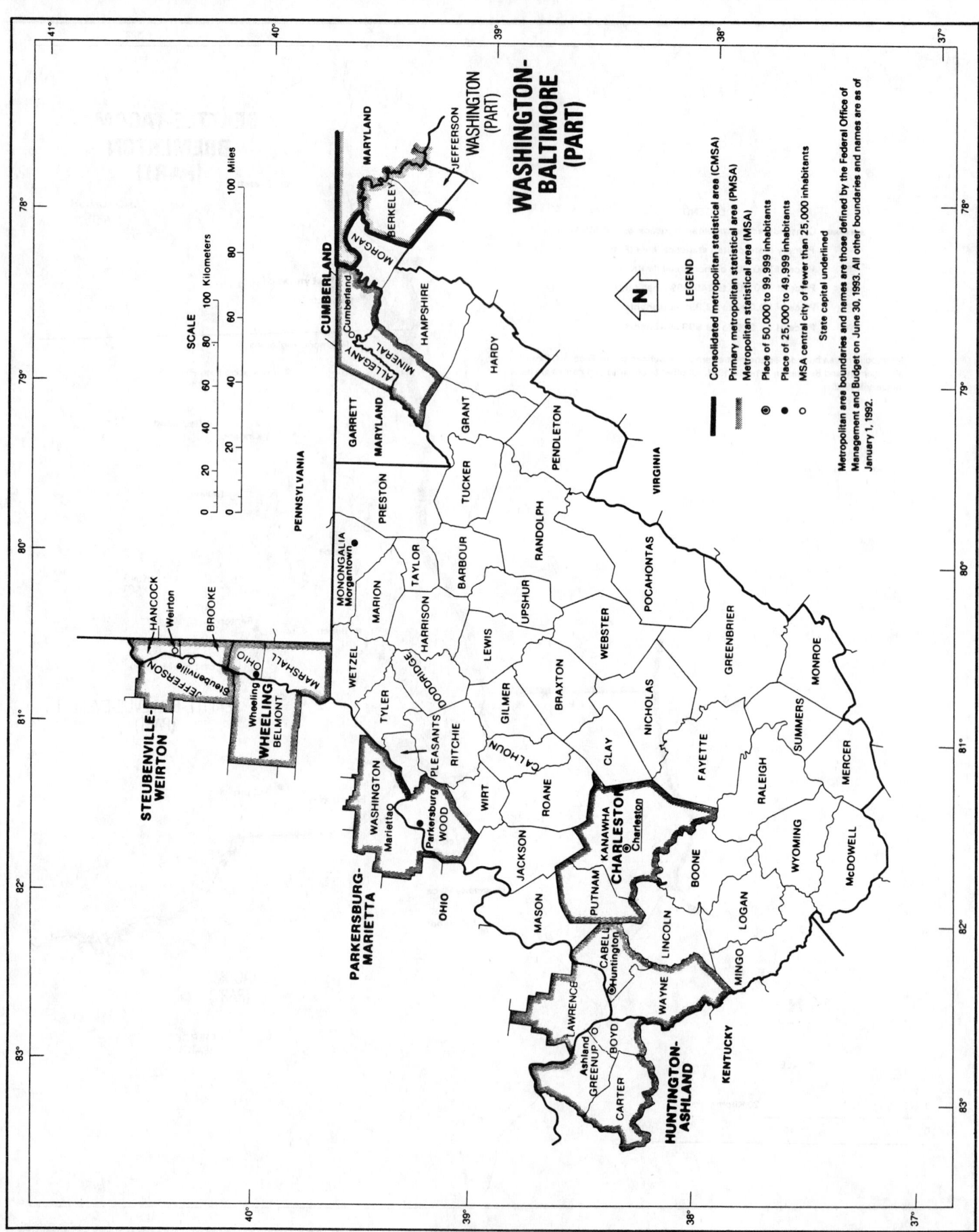

WASHINGTON-BALTIMORE (PART)

WASHINGTON (PART)

CUMBERLAND

STEUBENVILLE-WEIRTON

WHEELING

PARKERSBURG-MARIETTA

CHARLESTON

HUNTINGTON-ASHLAND

MARYLAND

PENNSYLVANIA

VIRGINIA

KENTUCKY

LEGEND

Consolidated metropolitan statistical area (CMSA)

Primary metropolitan statistical area (PMSA)
Metropolitan statistical area (MSA)

⊛ Place of 50,000 to 99,999 inhabitants

● Place of 25,000 to 49,999 inhabitants

○ Place of fewer than 25,000 inhabitants

○ MSA central city of fewer than 25,000 inhabitants

State capital underlined

Metropolitan area boundaries and names are those defined by the Federal Office of
Management and Budget on June 30, 1993. All other boundaries and names are as of
January 1, 1992.

SCALE

Counties: HANCOCK, BROOKE, OHIO, MARSHALL, WETZEL, TYLER, PLEASANTS, WOOD, WIRT, JACKSON, MASON, CABELL, WAYNE, LINCOLN, PUTNAM, KANAWHA, ROANE, CALHOUN, GILMER, RITCHIE, DODDRIDGE, HARRISON, MARION, MONONGALIA, PRESTON, TAYLOR, BARBOUR, TUCKER, GRANT, MINERAL, HAMPSHIRE, HARDY, PENDLETON, RANDOLPH, UPSHUR, LEWIS, BRAXTON, WEBSTER, POCAHONTAS, NICHOLAS, CLAY, BOONE, LOGAN, MINGO, WYOMING, McDOWELL, MERCER, SUMMERS, MONROE, GREENBRIER, FAYETTE, RALEIGH, NICHOLAS

Places: Weirton, Steubenville, Morgantown, Marietta, Parkersburg, Charleston, Huntington, Ashland

WISCONSIN - Metropolitan Areas, Counties, and Selected Places

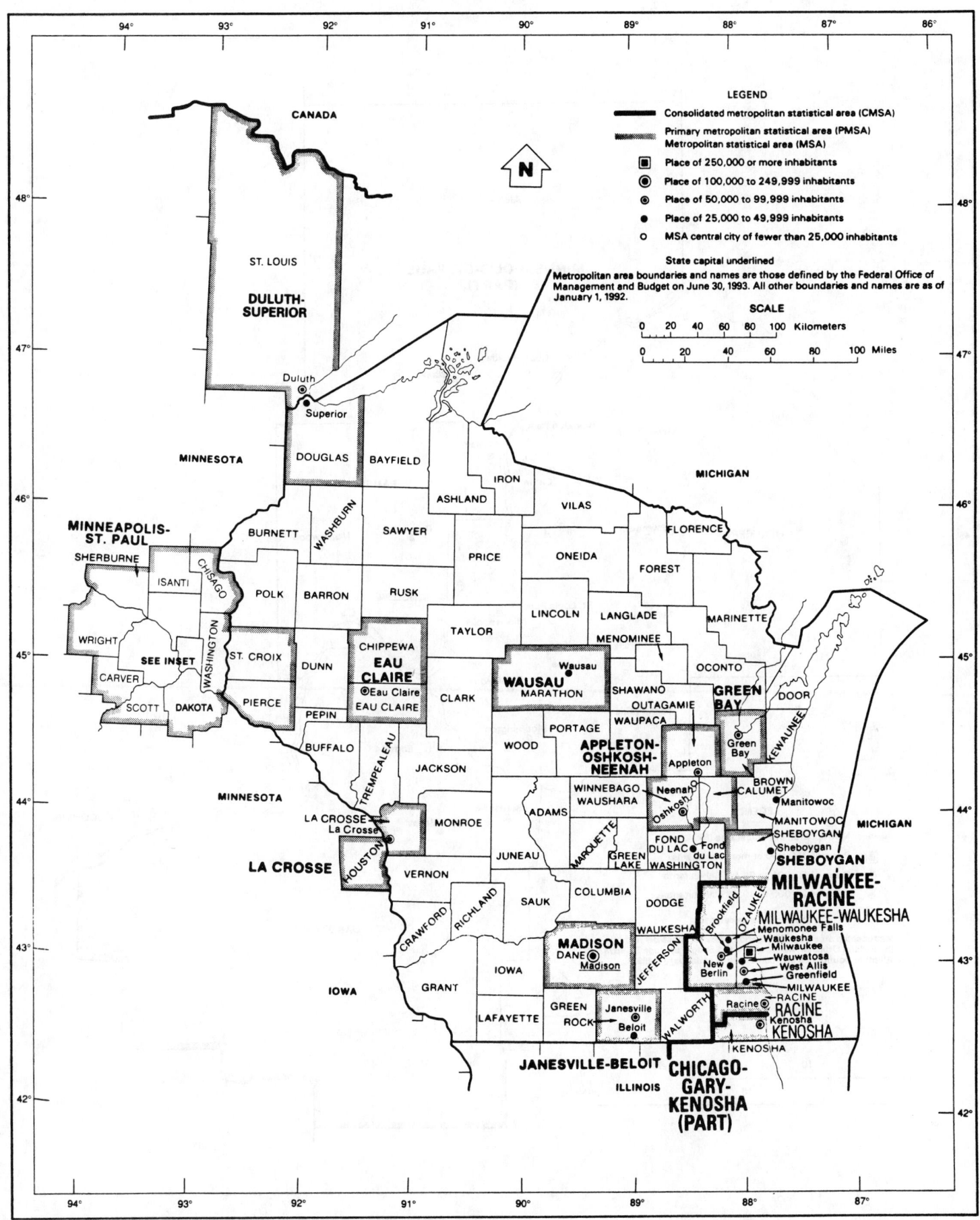

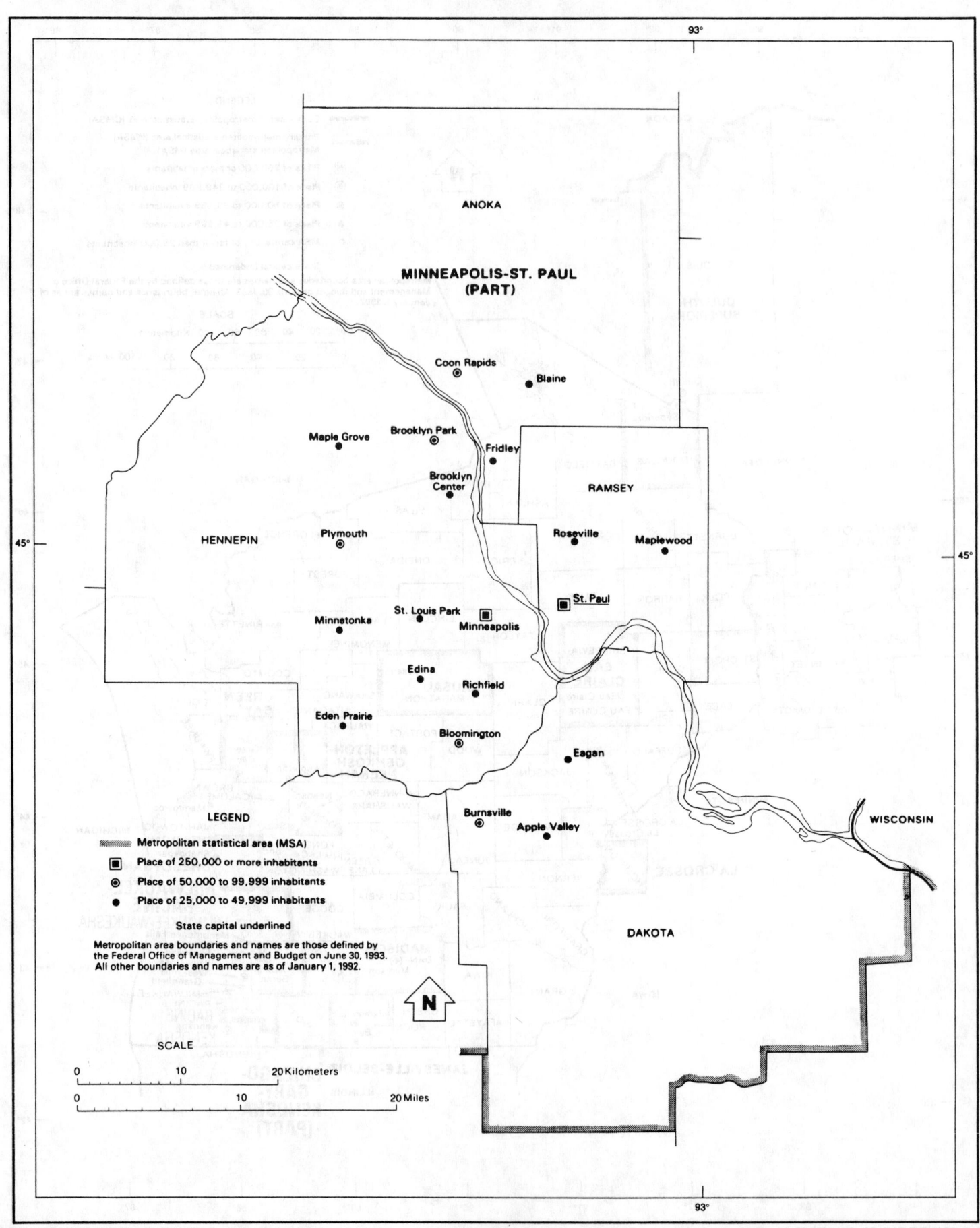

93°

ANOKA

**MINNEAPOLIS-ST. PAUL
(PART)**

Coon Rapids
Blaine

Maple Grove
Brooklyn Park
Fridley

Brooklyn
Center

RAMSEY

HENNEPIN

Plymouth

Roseville
Maplewood

45°   45°

St. Louis Park

Minnetonka
Minneapolis
St. Paul

Edina
Richfield

Eden Prairie
Bloomington

Eagan

WISCONSIN

LEGEND

▨▨▨ Metropolitan statistical area (MSA)

■ Place of 250,000 or more inhabitants

◉ Place of 50,000 to 99,999 inhabitants

● Place of 25,000 to 49,999 inhabitants

State capital underlined

Metropolitan area boundaries and names are those defined by
the Federal Office of Management and Budget on June 30, 1993.
All other boundaries and names are as of January 1, 1992.

Burnsville
Apple Valley

DAKOTA

N

SCALE

0   10   20 Kilometers

0   10   20 Miles

93°

WYOMING - Metropolitan Areas, Counties, and Selected Places

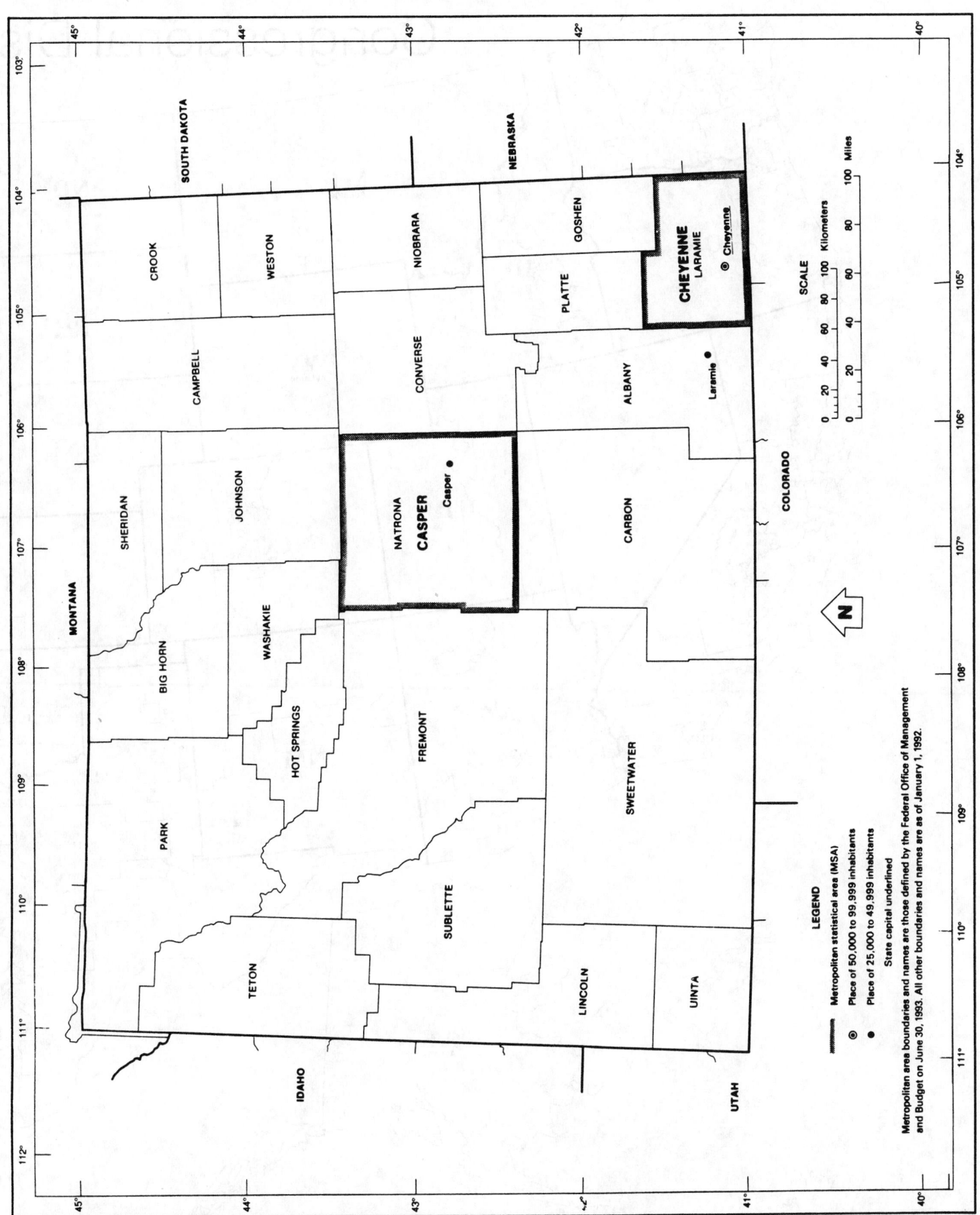

U.S. DEPARTMENT OF COMMERCE Economics and Statistics Administration Bureau of the Census

WYOMING Metropolitan Areas, Counties, and Selected Places

WA

2

6

9 8

4

3

1

5

OR

4

2

2

3

6

11

16

10

18

CA
19

17

20

22

21

23 25

43

48

51

44

52

40

5 MT
At Large

5 ND
At Large

4

SD
At Large

WY
At Large

3 NE

1

ID

1

2

NV
2

1

UT
3

CO

2

3

5

4

1 KS

4

AZ

3

6

3

NM

1

2

5

2

19

6

13

17

TX

23

21

11

10

28

27

HI
2

AK
At Large

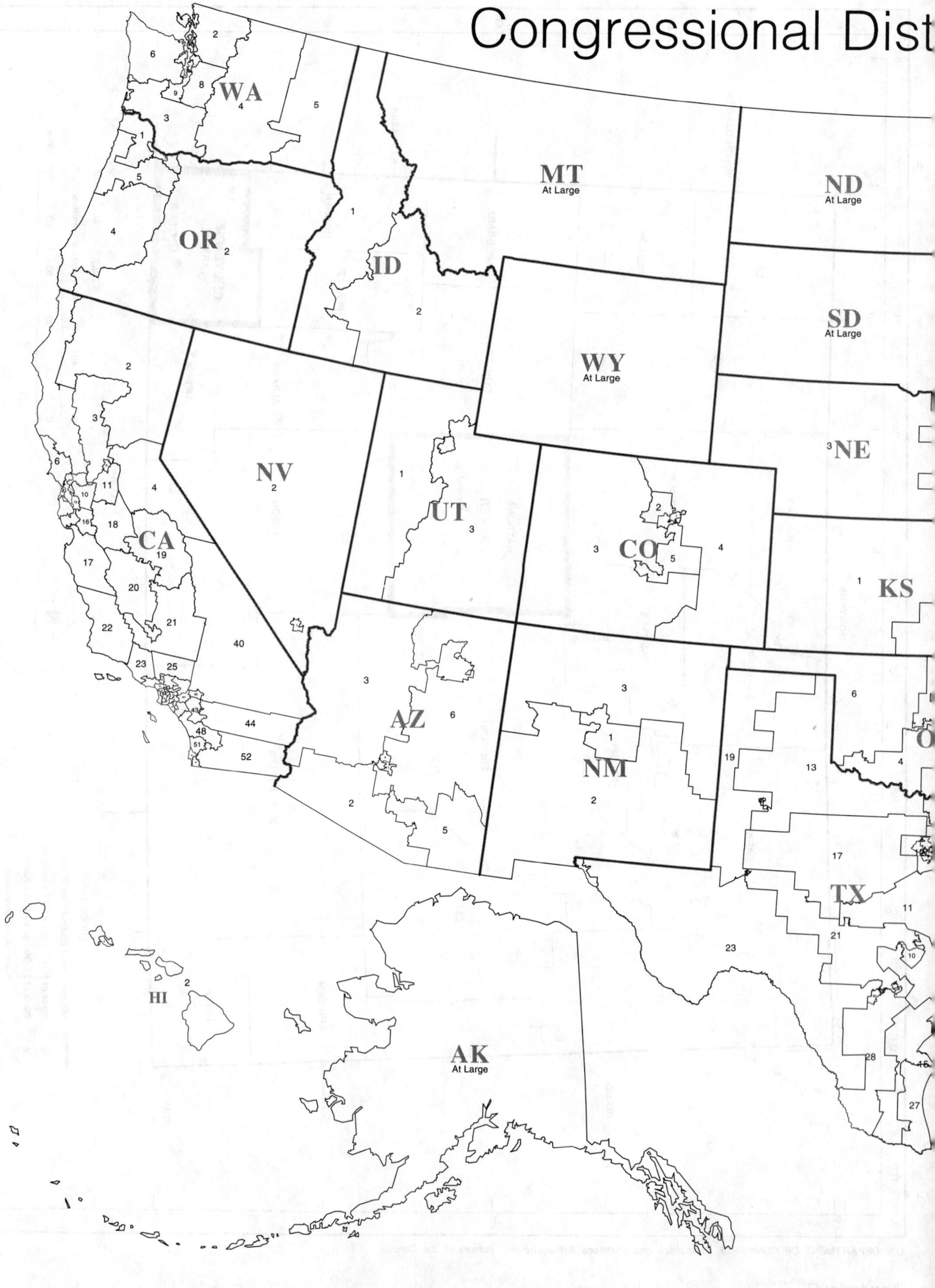

ts 105th Congress

APPENDIX E
CITIES BY COUNTY

The following table is arranged alphabetically by state. Under each state heading are listed all cities with a 1990 Census population over 25,000 along with their component counties and the population in each component.

State Code	Place Code	County Code	Geographic Area Name	1990 population	State Code	Place Code	County Code	Geographic Area Name	1990 population
01			**ALABAMA**		04	23620		Flagstaff city	45 857
01	01852		Anniston city	26 623	04	23620	005	Coconino County	45 857
01	01852	015	Calhoun County	26 623					
					04	27400		Gilbert town	29 188
01	03076		Auburn city	33 830	04	27400	013	Maricopa County	29 188
01	03076	081	Lee County	33 830					
					04	27820		Glendale city	148 134
01	05980		Bessemer city	33 497	04	27820	013	Maricopa County	148 134
01	05980	073	Jefferson County	33 497					
					04	46000		Mesa city	288 091
01	07000		Birmingham city	265 968	04	46000	013	Maricopa County	288 091
01	07000	073	Jefferson County	265 196					
01	07000	117	Shelby County	772	04	54050		Peoria city	50 618
					04	54050	013	Maricopa County	50 618
01	20104		Decatur city	48 761					
01	20104	083	Limestone County	55	04	55000		Phoenix city	983 403
01	20104	103	Morgan County	48 706	04	55000	013	Maricopa County	983 403
01	21184		Dothan city	53 589	04	57380		Prescott city	26 455
01	21184	045	Dale County	259	04	57380	025	Yavapai County	26 455
01	21184	069	Houston County	53 330					
					04	65000		Scottsdale city	130 069
01	26896		Florence city	36 426	04	65000	013	Maricopa County	130 069
01	26896	077	Lauderdale County	36 426					
					04	66820		Sierra Vista city	32 983
01	28696		Gadsden city	42 523	04	66820	003	Cochise County	32 983
01	28696	055	Etowah County	42 523					
					04	73000		Tempe city	141 865
01	35896		Hoover city	39 788	04	73000	013	Maricopa County	141 865
01	35896	073	Jefferson County	33 035					
01	35896	117	Shelby County	6 753	04	77000		Tucson city	405 390
					04	77000	019	Pima County	405 390
01	37000		Huntsville city	159 789					
01	37000	083	Limestone County	339	04	85540		Yuma city	54 923
01	37000	089	Madison County	159 450	04	85540	027	Yuma County	54 923
01	50000		Mobile city	196 278	05			**ARKANSAS**	
01	50000	097	Mobile County	196 278	05	15190		Conway city	26 481
					05	15190	045	Faulkner County	26 481
01	51000		Montgomery city	187 106					
01	51000	101	Montgomery County	187 106	05	23290		Fayetteville city	42 099
					05	23290	143	Washington County	42 099
01	59472		Phenix City city	25 312					
01	59472	081	Lee County	670	05	24550		Fort Smith city	72 798
01	59472	113	Russell County	24 642	05	24550	131	Sebastian County	72 798
01	62496		Prichard city	34 311	05	33460		Hot Springs city	32 462
01	62496	097	Mobile County	34 311	05	33460	051	Garland County	32 462
01	77256		Tuscaloosa city	77 759	05	34750		Jacksonville city	29 101
01	77256	125	Tuscaloosa County	77 759	05	34750	119	Pulaski County	29 101
02			**ALASKA**		05	35710		Jonesboro city	46 535
02	03000		Anchorage city	226 338	05	35710	031	Craighead County	46 535
02	03000	020	Anchorage Borough	226 338					
					05	41000	.	Little Rock city	175 795
02	24230		Fairbanks city	30 843	05	41000	119	Pulaski County	175 795
02	24230	090	Fairbanks North Star Borough ..	30 843					
					05	50450		North Little Rock city	61 741
02	36400		Juneau city	26 751	05	50450	119	Pulaski County	61 741
02	36400	110	Juneau Borough	26 751					
					05	55310		Pine Bluff city	57 140
04			**ARIZONA**		05	55310	069	Jefferson County	57 140
04	12000		Chandler city	90 533					
04	12000	013	Maricopa County	90 533	05	66080		Springdale city	29 941
					05	66080	007	Benton County	907
					05	66080	143	Washington County	29 034

State Code	Place Code	County Code	Geographic Area Name	1990 population	State Code	Place Code	County Code	Geographic Area Name	1990 population
05	74540		West Memphis city	28 259	06	12048		Cathedral City city	30 085
05	74540	035	Crittenden County	28 259	06	12048	065	Riverside County	30 085
06			**CALIFORNIA**		06	12524		Ceres city	26 314
06	00562		Alameda city	76 459	06	12524	099	Stanislaus County	26 314
06	00562	001	Alameda County	76 459					
					06	12552		Cerritos city	53 240
06	00884		Alhambra city	82 106	06	12552	037	Los Angeles County	53 240
06	00884	037	Los Angeles County	82 106					
					06	13014		Chico city	40 079
06	02000		Anaheim city	266 406	06	13014	007	Butte County	40 079
06	02000	059	Orange County	266 406					
					06	13210		Chino city	59 682
06	02252		Antioch city	62 195	06	13210	071	San Bernardino County	59 682
06	02252	013	Contra Costa County	62 195					
					06	13392		Chula Vista city	135 163
06	02364		Apple Valley town	46 079	06	13392	073	San Diego County	135 163
06	02364	071	San Bernardino County	46 079					
					06	13756		Claremont city	32 503
06	02462		Arcadia city	48 290	06	13756	037	Los Angeles County	32 503
06	02462	037	Los Angeles County	48 290					
					06	14218		Clovis city	50 323
06	03386		Azusa city	41 333	06	14218	019	Fresno County	50 323
06	03386	037	Los Angeles County	41 333					
					06	14890		Colton city	40 213
06	03526		Bakersfield city	174 820	06	14890	071	San Bernardino County	40 213
06	03526	029	Kern County	174 820					
					06	15044		Compton city	90 454
06	03666		Baldwin Park city	69 330	06	15044	037	Los Angeles County	90 454
06	03666	037	Los Angeles County	69 330					
					06	16000		Concord city	111 348
06	04870		Bell city	34 365	06	16000	013	Contra Costa County	111 348
06	04870	037	Los Angeles County	34 365					
					06	16350		Corona city	76 095
06	04982		Bellflower city	61 815	06	16350	065	Riverside County	76 095
06	04982	037	Los Angeles County	61 815					
					06	16378		Coronado city	26 540
06	04996		Bell Gardens city	42 355	06	16378	073	San Diego County	26 540
06	04996	037	Los Angeles County	42 355					
					06	16532		Costa Mesa city	96 357
06	06000		Berkeley city	102 724	06	16532	059	Orange County	96 357
06	06000	001	Alameda County	102 724					
					06	16742		Covina city	43 207
06	06308		Beverly Hills city	31 971	06	16742	037	Los Angeles County	43 207
06	06308	037	Los Angeles County	31 971					
					06	17568		Culver City city	38 793
06	08100		Brea city	32 873	06	17568	037	Los Angeles County	38 793
06	08100	059	Orange County	32 873					
					06	17610		Cupertino city	40 263
06	08786		Buena Park city	68 784	06	17610	085	Santa Clara County	40 263
06	08786	059	Orange County	68 784					
					06	17750		Cypress city	42 655
06	08954		Burbank city	93 643	06	17750	059	Orange County	42 655
06	08954	037	Los Angeles County	93 643					
					06	17918		Daly City city	92 311
06	09066		Burlingame city	26 801	06	17918	081	San Mateo County	92 311
06	09066	081	San Mateo County	26 801					
					06	17946		Dana Point city	31 896
06	10046		Camarillo city	52 303	06	17946	059	Orange County	31 896
06	10046	111	Ventura County	52 303					
					06	17988		Danville city	31 306
06	10340		Campbell city	36 048	06	17988	013	Contra Costa County	31 306
06	10340	085	Santa Clara County	36 048					
					06	18100		Davis city	46 209
06	11194		Carlsbad city	63 126	06	18100	113	Yolo County	46 209
06	11194	073	San Diego County	63 126					
					06	19192		Diamond Bar city	53 672
06	11530		Carson city	83 995	06	19192	037	Los Angeles County	53 672
06	11530	037	Los Angeles County	83 995					

State Code	Place Code	County Code	Geographic Area Name	1990 population	State Code	Place Code	County Code	Geographic Area Name	1990 population
06	19766		Downey city	91 444	06	33182		Hemet city	36 094
06	19766	037	Los Angeles County	91 444	06	33182	065	Riverside County	36 094
06	21712		El Cajon city	88 693	06	33434		Hesperia city	50 418
06	21712	073	San Diego County	88 693	06	33434	071	San Bernardino County	50 418
06	21782		El Centro city	31 384	06	33588		Highland city	34 439
06	21782	025	Imperial County	31 384	06	33588	071	San Bernardino County	34 439
06	22230		El Monte city	106 209	06	36000		Huntington Beach city	181 519
06	22230	037	Los Angeles County	106 209	06	36000	059	Orange County	181 519
06	22678		Encinitas city	55 386	06	36056		Huntington Park city	56 065
06	22678	073	San Diego County	55 386	06	36056	037	Los Angeles County	56 065
06	22804		Escondido city	108 635	06	36294		Imperial Beach city	26 512
06	22804	073	San Diego County	108 635	06	36294	073	San Diego County	26 512
06	23042		Eureka city	27 025	06	36448		Indio city	36 793
06	23042	023	Humboldt County	27 025	06	36448	065	Riverside County	36 793
06	23182		Fairfield city	77 211	06	36546		Inglewood city	109 602
06	23182	095	Solano County	77 211	06	36546	037	Los Angeles County	109 602
06	24638		Folsom city	29 802	06	36770		Irvine city	110 330
06	24638	067	Sacramento County	29 802	06	36770	059	Orange County	110 330
06	24680		Fontana city	87 535	06	39248		Laguna Niguel city	44 400
06	24680	071	San Bernardino County	87 535	06	39248	059	Orange County	44 400
06	25338		Foster City city	28 176	06	39290		La Habra city	51 266
06	25338	081	San Mateo County	28 176	06	39290	059	Orange County	51 266
06	25380		Fountain Valley city	53 691	06	39892		Lakewood city	73 557
06	25380	059	Orange County	53 691	06	39892	037	Los Angeles County	73 557
06	26000		Fremont city	173 339	06	40004		La Mesa city	52 931
06	26000	001	Alameda County	173 339	06	40004	073	San Diego County	52 931
06	27000		Fresno city	354 202	06	40032		La Mirada city	40 452
06	27000	019	Fresno County	354 202	06	40032	037	Los Angeles County	40 452
06	28000		Fullerton city	114 144	06	40130		Lancaster city	97 291
06	28000	059	Orange County	114 144	06	40130	037	Los Angeles County	97 291
06	28168		Gardena city	49 847	06	40340		La Puente city	36 955
06	28168	037	Los Angeles County	49 847	06	40340	037	Los Angeles County	36 955
06	29000		Garden Grove city	143 050	06	40830		La Verne city	30 897
06	29000	059	Orange County	143 050	06	40830	037	Los Angeles County	30 897
06	29504		Gilroy city	31 487	06	40886		Lawndale city	27 331
06	29504	085	Santa Clara County	31 487	06	40886	037	Los Angeles County	27 331
06	30000		Glendale city	180 038	06	41992		Livermore city	56 741
06	30000	037	Los Angeles County	180 038	06	41992	001	Alameda County	56 741
06	30014		Glendora city	47 828	06	42202		Lodi city	51 874
06	30014	037	Los Angeles County	47 828	06	42202	077	San Joaquin County	51 874
06	31960		Hanford city	30 897	06	42524		Lompoc city	37 649
06	31960	031	Kings County	30 897	06	42524	083	Santa Barbara County	37 649
06	32548		Hawthorne city	71 349	06	43000		Long Beach city	429 433
06	32548	037	Los Angeles County	71 349	06	43000	037	Los Angeles County	429 433
06	33000		Hayward city	111 498	06	43280		Los Altos city	26 303
06	33000	001	Alameda County	111 498	06	43280	085	Santa Clara County	26 303

State Code	Place Code	County Code	Geographic Area Name	1990 population	State Code	Place Code	County Code	Geographic Area Name	1990 population
06	44000		Los Angeles city	3 485 398	06	50398		National City city	54 249
06	44000	037	Los Angeles County	3 485 398	06	50398	073	San Diego County	54 249
06	44112		Los Gatos town	27 357	06	50916		Newark city	37 861
06	44112	085	Santa Clara County	27 357	06	50916	001	Alameda County	37 861
06	44574		Lynwood city	61 945	06	51182		Newport Beach city	66 643
06	44574	037	Los Angeles County	61 945	06	51182	059	Orange County	66 643
06	45022		Madera city	29 281	06	52526		Norwalk city	94 279
06	45022	039	Madera County	29 281	06	52526	037	Los Angeles County	94 279
06	45400		Manhattan Beach city	32 063	06	52582		Novato city	47 585
06	45400	037	Los Angeles County	32 063	06	52582	041	Marin County	47 585
06	45484		Manteca city	40 773	06	53000		Oakland city	372 242
06	45484	077	San Joaquin County	40 773	06	53000	001	Alameda County	372 242
06	45778		Marina city	26 436	06	53322		Oceanside city	128 398
06	45778	053	Monterey County	26 436	06	53322	073	San Diego County	128 398
06	46114		Martinez city	31 808	06	53896		Ontario city	133 179
06	46114	013	Contra Costa County	31 808	06	53896	071	San Bernardino County	133 179
06	46492		Maywood city	27 850	06	53980		Orange city	110 658
06	46492	037	Los Angeles County	27 850	06	53980	059	Orange County	110 658
06	46870		Menlo Park city	28 040	06	54652		Oxnard city	142 216
06	46870	081	San Mateo County	28 040	06	54652	111	Ventura County	142 216
06	46898		Merced city	56 216	06	54806		Pacifica city	37 670
06	46898	047	Merced County	56 216	06	54806	081	San Mateo County	37 670
06	47766		Milpitas city	50 686	06	55156		Palmdale city	68 842
06	47766	085	Santa Clara County	50 686	06	55156	037	Los Angeles County	68 842
06	48256		Mission Viejo city	72 820	06	55254		Palm Springs city	40 181
06	48256	059	Orange County	72 820	06	55254	065	Riverside County	40 181
06	48354		Modesto city	164 730	06	55282		Palo Alto city	55 900
06	48354	099	Stanislaus County	164 730	06	55282	085	Santa Clara County	55 900
06	48648		Monrovia city	35 761	06	55520		Paradise town	25 408
06	48648	037	Los Angeles County	35 761	06	55520	007	Butte County	25 408
06	48788		Montclair city	28 434	06	55618		Paramount city	47 669
06	48788	071	San Bernardino County	28 434	06	55618	037	Los Angeles County	47 669
06	48816		Montebello city	59 564	06	56000		Pasadena city	131 591
06	48816	037	Los Angeles County	59 564	06	56000	037	Los Angeles County	131 591
06	48872		Monterey city	31 954	06	56784		Petaluma city	43 184
06	48872	053	Monterey County	31 954	06	56784	097	Sonoma County	43 184
06	48914		Monterey Park city	60 738	06	56924		Pico Rivera city	59 177
06	48914	037	Los Angeles County	60 738	06	56924	037	Los Angeles County	59 177
06	49138		Moorpark city	25 494	06	57456		Pittsburg city	47 564
06	49138	111	Ventura County	25 494	06	57456	013	Contra Costa County	47 564
06	49270		Moreno Valley city	118 779	06	57526		Placentia city	41 259
06	49270	065	Riverside County	118 779	06	57526	059	Orange County	41 259
06	49670		Mountain View city	67 460	06	57764		Pleasant Hill city	31 585
06	49670	085	Santa Clara County	67 460	06	57764	013	Contra Costa County	31 585
06	50258		Napa city	61 842	06	57792		Pleasanton city	50 553
06	50258	055	Napa County	61 842	06	57792	001	Alameda County	50 553

State Code	Place Code	County Code	Geographic Area Name	1990 population	State Code	Place Code	County Code	Geographic Area Name	1990 population
06	58072		Pomona city	131 723	06	66000		San Diego city	1 110 549
06	58072	037	Los Angeles County	131 723	06	66000	073	San Diego County	1 110 549
06	58240		Porterville city	29 563	06	66070		San Dimas city	32 397
06	58240	107	Tulare County	29 563	06	66070	037	Los Angeles County	32 397
06	58520		Poway city	43 516	06	67000		San Francisco city	723 959
06	58520	073	San Diego County	43 516	06	67000	075	San Francisco County	723 959
06	59451		Rancho Cucamonga city	101 409	06	67042		San Gabriel city	37 120
06	59451	071	San Bernardino County	101 409	06	67042	037	Los Angeles County	37 120
06	59514		Rancho Palos Verdes city	41 659	06	68000		San Jose city	782 248
06	59514	037	Los Angeles County	41 659	06	68000	085	Santa Clara County	782 248
06	59920		Redding city	66 462	06	68028		San Juan Capistrano city	26 183
06	59920	089	Shasta County	66 462	06	68028	059	Orange County	26 183
06	59962		Redlands city	60 394	06	68084		San Leandro city	68 223
06	59962	071	San Bernardino County	60 394	06	68084	001	Alameda County	68 223
06	60018		Redondo Beach city	60 167	06	68154		San Luis Obispo city	41 958
06	60018	037	Los Angeles County	60 167	06	68154	079	San Luis Obispo County	41 958
06	60102		Redwood City city	66 072	06	68196		San Marcos city	38 974
06	60102	081	San Mateo County	66 072	06	68196	073	San Diego County	38 974
06	60466		Rialto city	72 388	06	68252		San Mateo city	85 486
06	60466	071	San Bernardino County ....:	72 388	06	68252	081	San Mateo County	85 486
06	60620		Richmond city	87 425	06	68294		San Pablo city	25 158
06	60620	013	Contra Costa County	87 425	06	68294	013	Contra Costa County	25 158
06	60704		Ridgecrest city	27 725	06	68364		San Rafael city	48 404
06	60704	029	Kern County	27 725	06	68364	041	Marin County	48 404
06	62000		Riverside city	226 505	06	68378		San Ramon city	35 303
06	62000	065	Riverside County	226 505	06	68378	013	Contra Costa County	35 303
06	62546		Rohnert Park city	36 326	06	69000		Santa Ana city	293 742
06	62546	097	Sonoma County	36 326	06	69000	059	Orange County	293 742
06	62896		Rosemead city	51 638	06	69070		Santa Barbara city	85 571
06	62896	037	Los Angeles County	51 638	06	69070	083	Santa Barbara County	85 571
06	62938		Roseville city	44 685	06	69084		Santa Clara city	93 613
06	62938	061	Placer County	44 685	06	69084	085	Santa Clara County	93 613
06	64000		Sacramento city	369 365	06	69088		Santa Clarita city	110 642
06	64000	067	Sacramento County	369 365	06	69088	037	Los Angeles County	110 642
06	64224		Salinas city	108 777	06	69112		Santa Cruz city	49 040
06	64224	053	Monterey County	108 777	06	69112	087	Santa Cruz County	49 040
06	65000		San Bernardino city	164 164	06	69196		Santa Maria city	61 284
06	65000	071	San Bernardino County	164 164	06	69196	083	Santa Barbara County	61 284
06	65028		San Bruno city	38 961	06	70000		Santa Monica city	86 905
06	65028	081	San Mateo County	38 961	06	70000	037	Los Angeles County	86 905
06	65042		San Buenaventura (Ventura) city .	92 575	06	70042		Santa Paula city	25 062
06	65042	111	Ventura County	92 575	06	70042	111	Ventura County	25 062
06	65070		San Carlos city	26 167	06	70098		Santa Rosa city	113 313
06	65070	081	San Mateo County	26 167	06	70098	097	Sonoma County	113 313
06	65084		San Clemente city	41 100	06	70224		Santee city	52 902
06	65084	059	Orange County	41 100	06	70224	073	San Diego County	52 902

Cities by County — Continued

State Code	Place Code	County Code	Geographic Area Name	1990 population	State Code	Place Code	County Code	Geographic Area Name	1990 population
06	70280		Saratoga city	28 061	06	82996		Vista city	71 872
06	70280	085	Santa Clara County	28 061	06	82996	073	San Diego County	71 872
06	70686		Seal Beach city	25 098	06	83332		Walnut city	29 105
06	70686	059	Orange County	25 098	06	83332	037	Los Angeles County	29 105
06	70742		Seaside city	38 901	06	83346		Walnut Creek city	60 569
06	70742	053	Monterey County	38 901	06	83346	013	Contra Costa County	60 569
06	72016		Simi Valley city	100 217	06	83668		Watsonville city	31 099
06	72016	111	Ventura County	100 217	06	83668	087	Santa Cruz County	31 099
06	73080		South Gate city	86 284	06	84200		West Covina city	96 086
06	73080	037	Los Angeles County	86 284	06	84200	037	Los Angeles County	96 086
06	73262		South San Francisco city	54 312	06	84410		West Hollywood city	36 118
06	73262	081	San Mateo County	54 312	06	84410	037	Los Angeles County	36 118
06	73962		Stanton city	30 491	06	84550		Westminster city	78 118
06	73962	059	Orange County	30 491	06	84550	059	Orange County	78 118
06	75000		Stockton city	210 943	06	84816		West Sacramento city	28 898
06	75000	077	San Joaquin County	210 943	06	84816	113	Yolo County	28 898
06	77000		Sunnyvale city	117 229	06	85292		Whittier city	77 671
06	77000	085	Santa Clara County	117 229	06	85292	037	Los Angeles County	77 671
06	78120		Temecula city	27 099	06	86328		Woodland city	39 802
06	78120	065	Riverside County	27 099	06	86328	113	Yolo County	39 802
06	78148		Temple City city	31 100	06	86832		Yorba Linda city	52 422
06	78148	037	Los Angeles County	31 100	06	86832	059	Orange County	52 422
06	78582		Thousand Oaks city	104 352	06	86972		Yuba City city	27 437
06	78582	111	Ventura County	104 352	06	86972	101	Sutter County	27 437
06	80000		Torrance city	133 107	06	87042		Yucaipa city	32 824
06	80000	037	Los Angeles County	133 107	06	87042	071	San Bernardino County	32 824
06	80238		Tracy city	33 558	08			**COLORADO**	
06	80238	077	San Joaquin County	33 558	08	03455		Arvada city	89 235
06	80644		Tulare city	33 249	08	03455	001	Adams County	2 347
06	80644	107	Tulare County	33 249	08	03455	059	Jefferson County	86 888
06	80812		Turlock city	42 198	08	04000		Aurora city	222 103
06	80812	099	Stanislaus County	42 198	08	04000	001	Adams County	27 747
06	80854		Tustin city	50 689	08	04000	005	Arapahoe County	194 352
06	80854	059	Orange County	50 689	08	04000	035	Douglas County	4
06	81204		Union City city	53 762	08	07850		Boulder city	83 312
06	81204	001	Alameda County	53 762	08	07850	013	Boulder County	83 312
06	81344		Upland city	63 374	08	16000		Colorado Springs city	281 140
06	81344	071	San Bernardino County	63 374	08	16000	041	El Paso County	281 140
06	81554		Vacaville city	71 479	08	20000		Denver city	467 610
06	81554	095	Solano County	71 479	08	20000	031	Denver County	467 610
06	81666		Vallejo city	109 199	08	24785		Englewood city	29 387
06	81666	095	Solano County	109 199	08	24785	005	Arapahoe County	29 387
06	82590		Victorville city	40 674	08	27425		Fort Collins city	87 758
06	82590	071	San Bernardino County	40 674	08	27425	069	Larimer County	87 758
06	82954		Visalia city	75 636	08	31660		Grand Junction city	29 034
06	82954	107	Tulare County	75 636	08	31660	077	Mesa County	29 034
					08	32155		Greeley city	60 536
					08	32155	123	Weld County	60 536

State Code	Place Code	County Code	Geographic Area Name	1990 population	State Code	Place Code	County Code	Geographic Area Name	1990 population
08	43000		Lakewood city	126 481	09	68100		Shelton city	35 418
08	43000	059	Jefferson County	126 481	09	68100	001	Fairfield County	35 418
08	45255		Littleton city	33 685	09	73000		Stamford city	108 056
08	45255	005	Arapahoe County	33 577	09	73000	001	Fairfield County	108 056
08	45255	035	Douglas County	108					
					09	76500		Torrington city	33 687
08	45970		Longmont city	51 555	09	76500	005	Litchfield County	33 687
08	45970	013	Boulder County	51 555					
					09	80000		Waterbury city	108 961
08	46465		Loveland city	37 352	09	80000	009	New Haven County	108 961
08	46465	069	Larimer County	37 352					
					09	82800		West Haven city	54 021
08	54330		Northglenn city	27 195	09	82800	009	New Haven County	54 021
08	54330	001	Adams County	27 195					
08	54330	123	Weld County	0	10			**DELAWARE**	
					10	21200		Dover city	27 630
08	62000		Pueblo city	98 640	10	21200	001	Kent County	27 630
08	62000	101	Pueblo County	98 640					
					10	50670		Newark city	25 098
08	77290		Thornton city	55 031	10	50670	003	New Castle County	25 098
08	77290	001	Adams County	55 031					
					10	77580		Wilmington city	71 529
08	83835		Westminster city	74 625	10	77580	003	New Castle County	71 529
08	83835	001	Adams County	41 639					
08	83835	059	Jefferson County	32 986	11			**DISTRICT OF COLUMBIA**	
					11	50000		Washington city	606 900
08	84440		Wheat Ridge city	29 419	11	50000	001	District of Columbia	606 900
08	84440	059	Jefferson County	29 419					
					12			**FLORIDA**	
09			**CONNECTICUT**		12	00950		Altamonte Springs city	34 879
09	08000		Bridgeport city	141 686	12	00950	117	Seminole County	34 879
09	08000	001	Fairfield County	141 686					
					12	07300		Boca Raton city	61 492
09	08420		Bristol city	60 640	12	07300	099	Palm Beach County	61 492
09	08420	003	Hartford County	60 640					
					12	07875		Boynton Beach city	46 194
09	18430		Danbury city	65 585	12	07875	099	Palm Beach County	46 194
09	18430	001	Fairfield County	65 585					
					12	07950		Bradenton city	43 779
09	37000		Hartford city	139 739	12	07950	081	Manatee County	43 779
09	37000	003	Hartford County	139 739					
					12	10275		Cape Coral city	74 991
09	46450		Meriden city	59 479	12	10275	071	Lee County	74 991
09	46450	009	New Haven County	59 479					
					12	12875		Clearwater city	98 784
09	47290		Middletown city	42 762	12	12875	103	Pinellas County	98 784
09	47290	007	Middlesex County	42 762					
					12	13275		Coconut Creek city	27 485
09	47590		Milford city	48 168	12	13275	011	Broward County	27 485
09	47590	009	New Haven County	48 168					
					12	14250		Coral Gables city	40 091
09	49880		Naugatuck borough	30 625	12	14250	025	Dade County	40 091
09	49880	009	New Haven County	30 625					
					12	14400		Coral Springs city	79 443
09	50370		New Britain city	75 491	12	14400	011	Broward County	79 443
09	50370	003	Hartford County	75 491					
					12	16475		Davie town	47 217
09	52000		New Haven city	130 474	12	16475	011	Broward County	47 217
09	52000	009	New Haven County	130 474					
					12	16525		Daytona Beach city	61 921
09	52280		New London city	28 540	12	16525	127	Volusia County	61 921
09	52280	011	New London County	28 540					
					12	16725		Deerfield Beach city	46 325
09	55990		Norwalk city	78 331	12	16725	011	Broward County	46 325
09	55990	001	Fairfield County	78 331					
					12	17100		Delray Beach city	47 181
09	56200		Norwich city	37 391	12	17100	099	Palm Beach County	47 181
09	56200	011	New London County	37 391					

Cities by County — Continued

State Code	Place Code	County Code	Geographic Area Name	1990 population	State Code	Place Code	County Code	Geographic Area Name	1990 population
12	18575		Dunedin city	34 012	12	49475		North Miami Beach city	35 359
12	18575	103	Pinellas County	34 012	12	49475	025	Dade County	35 359
12	24000		Fort Lauderdale city	149 377	12	50575		Oakland Park city	26 326
12	24000	011	Broward County	149 377	12	50575	011	Broward County	26 326
12	24125		Fort Myers city	45 206	12	50750		Ocala city	42 045
12	24125	071	Lee County	45 206	12	50750	083	Marion County	42 045
12	24300		Fort Pierce city	36 830	12	53000		Orlando city	164 693
12	24300	111	St. Lucie County	36 830	12	53000	095	Orange County	164 693
12	25175		Gainesville city	84 770	12	53150		Ormond Beach city	29 721
12	25175	001	Alachua County	84 770	12	53150	127	Volusia County	29 721
12	28450		Hallandale city	30 996	12	54000		Palm Bay city	62 632
12	28450	011	Broward County	30 996	12	54000	009	Brevard County	62 632
12	30000		Hialeah city	188 004	12	54700		Panama City city	34 378
12	30000	025	Dade County	188 004	12	54700	005	Bay County	34 378
12	32000		Hollywood city	121 697	12	55775		Pembroke Pines city	65 452
12	32000	011	Broward County	121 697	12	55775	011	Broward County	65 452
12	32275		Homestead city	26 866	12	55925		Pensacola city	58 165
12	32275	025	Dade County	26 866	12	55925	033	Escambia County	58 165
12	35160		Jacksonville city	635 230	12	56975		Pinellas Park city	43 426
12	35160	031	Duval County	635 230	12	56975	103	Pinellas County	43 426
12	36950		Kissimmee city	30 050	12	57425		Plantation city	66 692
12	36950	097	Osceola County	30 050	12	57425	011	Broward County	66 692
12	38250		Lakeland city	70 576	12	58050		Pompano Beach city	72 411
12	38250	105	Polk County	70 576	12	58050	011	Broward County	72 411
12	39075		Lake Worth city	28 564	12	58575		Port Orange city	35 317
12	39075	099	Palm Beach County	28 564	12	58575	127	Volusia County	35 317
12	39425		Largo city	65 674	12	58725		Port St. Lucie city	55 866
12	39425	103	Pinellas County	65 674	12	58725	111	St. Lucie County	55 866
12	39525		Lauderdale Lakes city	27 341	12	60975		Riviera Beach city	27 639
12	39525	011	Broward County	27 341	12	60975	099	Palm Beach County	27 639
12	39550		Lauderhill city	49 708	12	63000		St. Petersburg city	238 629
12	39550	011	Broward County	49 708	12	63000	103	Pinellas County	238 629
12	43125		Margate city	42 985	12	63650		Sanford city	32 387
12	43125	011	Broward County	42 985	12	63650	117	Seminole County	32 387
12	43975		Melbourne city	59 646	12	64175		Sarasota city	50 961
12	43975	009	Brevard County	59 646	12	64175	115	Sarasota County	50 961
12	45000		Miami city	358 548	12	69700		Sunrise city	64 407
12	45000	025	Dade County	358 548	12	69700	011	Broward County	64 407
12	45025		Miami Beach city	92 639	12	70600		Tallahassee city	124 773
12	45025	025	Dade County	92 639	12	70600	073	Leon County	124 773
12	45975		Miramar city	40 663	12	70675		Tamarac city	44 822
12	45975	011	Broward County	40 663	12	70675	011	Broward County	44 822
12	49425		North Lauderdale city	26 506	12	71000		Tampa city	280 015
12	49425	011	Broward County	26 506	12	71000	057	Hillsborough County	280 015
12	49450		North Miami city	49 998	12	71900		Titusville city	39 394
12	49450	025	Dade County	49 998	12	71900	009	Brevard County	39 394

State Code	Place Code	County Code	Geographic Area Name	1990 population	State Code	Place Code	County Code	Geographic Area Name	1990 population
12	76600		West Palm Beach city	67 643	15	77750		Waimalu CDP	29 967
12	76600	099	Palm Beach County	67 643	15	77750	003	Honolulu County	29 967
13			**GEORGIA**		15	79700		Waipahu CDP	31 435
13	01052		Albany city	78 122	15	79700	003	Honolulu County	31 435
13	01052	095	Dougherty County	78 122	16			**IDAHO**	
13	03432		Athens city	45 734	16	08830		Boise City city	125 738
13	03432	059	Clarke County	45 734	16	08830	001	Ada County	125 738
13	04000		Atlanta city	394 017	16	39700		Idaho Falls city	43 929
13	04000	089	DeKalb County	33 539	16	39700	019	Bonneville County	43 929
13	04000	121	Fulton County	360 478	16	46540		Lewiston city	28 082
13	04196		Augusta city	44 639	16	46540	069	Nez Perce County	28 082
13	04196	245	Richmond County	44 639	16	56260		Nampa city	28 365
13	19030		Columbus city	178 681	16	56260	027	Canyon County	28 365
13	19030	215	Muscogee County	178 681	16	64090		Pocatello city	46 080
13	25720		East Point city	34 402	16	64090	005	Bannock County	46 027
13	25720	121	Fulton County	34 402	16	64090	077	Power County	53
13	44340		La Grange city	25 597	16	82810		Twin Falls city	27 591
13	44340	285	Troup County	25 597	16	82810	083	Twin Falls County	27 591
13	49000		Macon city	106 612	17			**ILLINOIS**	
13	49000	021	Bibb County	106 210	17	00243		Addison village	32 058
13	49000	169	Jones County	402	17	00243	043	DuPage County	32 058
13	49756		Marietta city	44 129	17	01114		Alton city	32 905
13	49756	067	Cobb County	44 129	17	01114	119	Madison County	32 905
13	66668		Rome city	30 326	17	02154		Arlington Heights village	75 460
13	66668	115	Floyd County	30 326	17	02154	031	Cook County	75 460
13	67284		Roswell city	47 923	17	03012		Aurora city	99 581
13	67284	121	Fulton County	47 923	17	03012	043	DuPage County	14 811
					17	03012	089	Kane County	84 770
13	69000		Savannah city	137 560	17	04845		Belleville city	42 785
13	69000	051	Chatham County	137 560	17	04845	163	St. Clair County	42 785
13	71492		Smyrna city	30 981	17	05573		Berwyn city	45 426
13	71492	067	Cobb County	30 981	17	05573	031	Cook County	45 426
13	78800		Valdosta city	39 806	17	06613		Bloomington city	51 972
13	78800	185	Lowndes County	39 806	17	06613	113	McLean County	51 972
13	80508		Warner Robins city	43 726	17	07133		Bolingbrook village	40 843
13	80508	153	Houston County	43 726	17	07133	043	DuPage County	1 472
15			**HAWAII**		17	07133	197	Will County	39 371
15	14650		Hilo CDP	37 808	17	09447		Buffalo Grove village	36 427
15	14650	001	Hawaii County	37 808	17	09447	031	Cook County	14 497
					17	09447	097	Lake County	21 930
15	17000		Honolulu CDP	365 272	17	09642		Burbank city	27 600
15	17000	003	Honolulu County	365 272	17	09642	031	Cook County	27 600
15	23150		Kailua CDP	36 818	17	10487		Calumet City city	37 840
15	23150	003	Honolulu County	36 818	17	10487	031	Cook County	37 840
15	28250		Kaneohe CDP	35 448	17	11163		Carbondale city	27 033
15	28250	003	Honolulu County	35 448	17	11163	077	Jackson County	27 033
15	51050		Mililani Town CDP	29 359	17	11332		Carol Stream village	31 716
15	51050	003	Honolulu County	29 359	17	11332	043	DuPage County	31 716
15	62600		Pearl City CDP	30 993					
15	62600	003	Honolulu County	30 993					

Cities by County — Continued

State Code	Place Code	County Code	Geographic Area Name	1990 population	State Code	Place Code	County Code	Geographic Area Name	1990 population
17	12385		Champaign city	63 502	17	35411		Hoffman Estates village	46 561
17	12385	019	Champaign County	63 502	17	35411	031	Cook County	46 561
					17	35411	089	Kane County	0
17	14000		Chicago city	2 783 726					
17	14000	031	Cook County	2 783 726	17	38570		Joliet city	76 836
17	14000	043	DuPage County	0	17	38570	197	Will County	76 836
17	14026		Chicago Heights city	33 072	17	38934		Kankakee city	27 575
17	14026	031	Cook County	33 072	17	38934	091	Kankakee County	27 575
17	14351		Cicero town	67 436	17	42028		Lansing village	28 086
17	14351	031	Cook County	67 436	17	42028	031	Cook County	28 086
17	18563		Danville city	33 828	17	44407		Lombard village	39 408
17	18563	183	Vermilion County	33 828	17	44407	043	DuPage County	39 408
17	18823		Decatur city	83 885	17	47774		Maywood village	27 139
17	18823	115	Macon County	83 885	17	47774	031	Cook County	27 139
17	19161		De Kalb city	34 925	17	49867		Moline city	43 202
17	19161	037	DeKalb County	34 925	17	49867	161	Rock Island County	43 202
17	19642		Des Plaines city	53 223	17	51089		Mount Prospect village	53 170
17	19642	031	Cook County	53 223	17	51089	031	Cook County	53 170
17	20591		Downers Grove village	46 858	17	51622		Naperville city	85 351
17	20591	043	DuPage County	46 858	17	51622	043	DuPage County	72 931
					17	51622	197	Will County	12 420
17	22255		East St. Louis city	40 944					
17	22255	163	St. Clair County	40 944	17	53000		Niles village	28 284
					17	53000	031	Cook County	28 284
17	23074		Elgin city	77 010					
17	23074	031	Cook County	15 400	17	53234		Normal town	40 023
17	23074	089	Kane County	61 610	17	53234	113	McLean County	40 023
17	23256		Elk Grove Village village	33 429	17	53481		Northbrook village	32 308
17	23256	031	Cook County	33 429	17	53481	031	Cook County	32 308
17	23256	043	DuPage County	0					
					17	53559		North Chicago city	34 978
17	23620		Elmhurst city	42 029	17	53559	097	Lake County	34 978
17	23620	043	DuPage County	42 029					
					17	54638		Oak Forest city	26 203
17	24582		Evanston city	73 233	17	54638	031	Cook County	26 203
17	24582	031	Cook County	73 233					
					17	54820		Oak Lawn village	56 182
17	27884		Freeport city	25 840	17	54820	031	Cook County	56 182
17	27884	177	Stephenson County	25 840					
					17	54885		Oak Park village	53 648
17	28326		Galesburg city	33 530	17	54885	031	Cook County	53 648
17	28326	095	Knox County	33 530					
					17	56640		Orland Park village	35 720
17	29730		Glendale Heights village	27 973	17	56640	031	Cook County	35 720
17	29730	043	DuPage County	27 973					
					17	57225		Palatine village	39 253
17	29938		Glenview village	37 093	17	57225	031	Cook County	39 253
17	29938	031	Cook County	37 093					
					17	57875		Park Ridge city	36 175
17	30926		Granite City city	32 862	17	57875	031	Cook County	36 175
17	30926	119	Madison County	32 862					
					17	58447		Pekin city	32 254
17	32746		Hanover Park village	32 895	17	58447	143	Peoria County	0
17	32746	031	Cook County	18 662	17	58447	179	Tazewell County	32 254
17	32746	043	DuPage County	14 233					
					17	59000		Peoria city	113 504
17	33383		Harvey city	29 771	17	59000	143	Peoria County	113 504
17	33383	031	Cook County	29 771					
					17	62367		Quincy city	39 681
17	34722		Highland Park city	30 575	17	62367	001	Adams County	39 681
17	34722	097	Lake County	30 575					

State Code	Place Code	County Code	Geographic Area Name	1990 population	State Code	Place Code	County Code	Geographic Area Name	1990 population
17	65000		Rockford city	139 426	18	29898		Greenwood city	26 265
17	65000	201	Winnebago County	139 426	18	29898	081	Johnson County	26 265
17	65078		Rock Island city	40 552	18	31000		Hammond city	84 236
17	65078	161	Rock Island County	40 552	18	31000	089	Lake County	84 236
17	68003		Schaumburg village	68 586	18	36010		Indianapolis city	731 327
17	68003	031	Cook County	68 586	18	36010	097	Marion County	731 327
17	68003	043	DuPage County	0	18	40392		Kokomo city	44 962
17	70122		Skokie village	59 432	18	40392	067	Howard County	44 962
17	70122	031	Cook County	59 432	18	40788		Lafayette city	43 764
17	72000		Springfield city	105 227	18	40788	157	Tippecanoe County	43 764
17	72000	167	Sangamon County	105 227	18	42426		Lawrence city	26 763
17	73157		Streamwood village	30 987	18	42426	097	Marion County	26 763
17	73157	031	Cook County	30 987	18	46908		Marion city	32 618
17	75484		Tinley Park village	37 121	18	46908	053	Grant County	32 618
17	75484	031	Cook County	37 040	18	48528		Merrillville town	27 257
17	75484	197	Will County	81	18	48528	089	Lake County	27 257
17	77005		Urbana city	36 344	18	48798		Michigan City city	33 822
17	77005	019	Champaign County	36 344	18	48798	091	La Porte County	33 822
17	79293		Waukegan city	69 392	18	49932		Mishawaka city	42 608
17	79293	097	Lake County	69 392	18	49932	141	St. Joseph County	42 608
17	81048		Wheaton city	51 464	18	51876		Muncie city	71 035
17	81048	043	DuPage County	51 464	18	51876	035	Delaware County	71 035
17	81087		Wheeling village	29 911	18	52326		New Albany city	36 322
17	81087	031	Cook County	29 911	18	52326	043	Floyd County	36 322
17	81087	097	Lake County	0	18	61092		Portage city	29 060
17	82075		Wilmette village	26 690	18	61092	127	Porter County	29 060
17	82075	031	Cook County	26 690	18	64260		Richmond city	38 705
17	83245		Woodridge village	26 256	18	64260	177	Wayne County	38 705
17	83245	043	DuPage County	26 232	18	71000		South Bend city	105 511
17	83245	197	Will County	24	18	71000	141	St. Joseph County	105 511
18			**INDIANA**		18	75428		Terre Haute city	57 483
18	01468		Anderson city	59 459	18	75428	167	Vigo County	57 483
18	01468	095	Madison County	59 459	18	82862		West Lafayette city	25 907
18	05860		Bloomington city	60 633	18	82862	157	Tippecanoe County	25 907
18	05860	105	Monroe County	60 633	19			**IOWA**	
18	10342		Carmel city	25 380	19	01855		Ames city	47 198
18	10342	057	Hamilton County	25 380	19	01855	169	Story County	47 198
18	14734		Columbus city	31 802	19	06355		Bettendorf city	28 132
18	14734	005	Bartholomew County	31 802	19	06355	163	Scott County	28 132
18	19486		East Chicago city	33 892	19	09550		Burlington city	27 208
18	19486	089	Lake County	33 892	19	09550	057	Des Moines County	27 208
18	20728		Elkhart city	43 627	19	11755		Cedar Falls city	34 298
18	20728	039	Elkhart County	43 627	19	11755	013	Black Hawk County	34 298
18	22000		Evansville city	126 272	19	12000		Cedar Rapids city	108 751
18	22000	163	Vanderburgh County	126 272	19	12000	113	Linn County	108 751
18	25000		Fort Wayne city	173 072	19	14430		Clinton city	29 201
18	25000	003	Allen County	173 072	19	14430	045	Clinton County	29 201
18	27000		Gary city	116 646					
18	27000	089	Lake County	116 646					

State Code	Place Code	County Code	Geographic Area Name	1990 population	State Code	Place Code	County Code	Geographic Area Name	1990 population
19	16860		Council Bluffs city	54 315	20	71000		Topeka city	119 883
19	16860	155	Pottawattamie County	54 315	20	71000	177	Shawnee County	119 883
19	19000		Davenport city	95 333	20	79000		Wichita city	304 011
19	19000	163	Scott County	95 333	20	79000	173	Sedgwick County	304 011
19	21000		Des Moines city	193 187	21			**KENTUCKY**	
19	21000	153	Polk County	193 187	21	08902		Bowling Green city	40 641
					21	08902	227	Warren County	40 641
19	22395		Dubuque city	57 546					
19	22395	061	Dubuque County	57 546	21	17848		Covington city	43 264
					21	17848	117	Kenton County	43 264
19	28515		Fort Dodge city	25 894					
19	28515	187	Webster County	25 894	21	28900		Frankfort city	25 968
					21	28900	073	Franklin County	25 968
19	38595		Iowa City city	59 738					
19	38595	103	Johnson County	59 738	21	35866		Henderson city	25 945
					21	35866	101	Henderson County	25 945
19	49755		Marshalltown city	25 178					
19	49755	127	Marshall County	25 178	21	37918		Hopkinsville city	29 809
					21	37918	047	Christian County	29 809
19	50160		Mason City city	29 040					
19	50160	033	Cerro Gordo County	29 040	21	46000		Lexington-Fayette	225 366
					21	46000	067	Fayette County	225 366
19	73335		Sioux City city	80 505					
19	73335	193	Woodbury County	80 505	21	48000		Louisville city	269 063
					21	48000	111	Jefferson County	269 063
19	82425		Waterloo city	66 467					
19	82425	013	Black Hawk County	66 467	21	58620		Owensboro city	53 549
					21	58620	059	Daviess County	53 549
19	83910		West Des Moines city	31 702					
19	83910	049	Dallas County	7	21	58836		Paducah city	27 256
19	83910	153	Polk County	31 695	21	58836	145	McCracken County	27 256
20			**KANSAS**		22			**LOUISIANA**	
20	21275		Emporia city	25 512	22	00975		Alexandria city	49 188
20	21275	111	Lyon County	25 512	22	00975	079	Rapides Parish	49 188
20	33625		Hutchinson city	39 308	22	05000		Baton Rouge city	219 531
20	33625	155	Reno County	39 308	22	05000	033	East Baton Rouge Parish	219 531
20	36000		Kansas City city	149 767	22	08920		Bossier City city	52 721
20	36000	209	Wyandotte County	149 767	22	08920	015	Bossier Parish	52 721
20	38900		Lawrence city	65 608	22	36255		Houma city	30 495
20	38900	045	Douglas County	65 608	22	36255	109	Terrebonne Parish	30 495
20	39000		Leavenworth city	38 495	22	39475		Kenner city	72 033
20	39000	103	Leavenworth County	38 495	22	39475	051	Jefferson Parish	72 033
20	39350		Lenexa city	34 034	22	40735		Lafayette city	94 440
20	39350	091	Johnson County	34 034	22	40735	055	Lafayette Parish	94 440
20	44250		Manhattan city	37 712	22	41155		Lake Charles city	70 580
20	44250	149	Pottawatomie County	143	22	41155	019	Calcasieu Parish	70 580
20	44250	161	Riley County	37 569					
					22	51410		Monroe city	54 909
20	52575		Olathe city	63 352	22	51410	073	Ouachita Parish	54 909
20	52575	091	Johnson County	63 352					
					22	54035		New Iberia city	31 828
20	53775		Overland Park city	111 790	22	54035	045	Iberia Parish	31 828
20	53775	091	Johnson County	111 790					
					22	55000		New Orleans city	496 938
20	62700		Salina city	42 303	22	55000	071	Orleans Parish	496 938
20	62700	169	Saline County	42 303					
					22	70000		Shreveport city	198 525
20	64500		Shawnee city	37 993	22	70000	015	Bossier Parish	491
20	64500	091	Johnson County	37 993	22	70000	017	Caddo Parish	198 034

Cities by County — Continued

State Code	Place Code	County Code	Geographic Area Name	1990 population	State Code	Place Code	County Code	Geographic Area Name	1990 population
23			**MAINE**		25	30840		Holyoke city	43 704
23	02795		Bangor city	33 181	25	30840	013	Hampden County	43 704
23	02795	019	Penobscot County	33 181					
					25	34550		Lawrence city	70 207
23	38740		Lewiston city	39 757	25	34550	009	Essex County	70 207
23	38740	001	Androscoggin County	39 757					
					25	35075		Leominster city	38 145
23	60545		Portland city	64 358	25	35075	027	Worcester County	38 145
23	60545	005	Cumberland County	64 358					
					25	37000		Lowell city	103 439
24			**MARYLAND**		25	37000	017	Middlesex County	103 439
24	01600		Annapolis city	33 187					
24	01600	003	Anne Arundel County	33 187	25	37490		Lynn city	81 245
					25	37490	009	Essex County	81 245
24	04000		Baltimore city	736 014					
24	04000	510	Baltimore city	736 014	25	37875		Malden city	53 884
					25	37875	017	Middlesex County	53 884
24	08775		Bowie city	37 589					
24	08775	033	Prince George's County	37 589	25	38715		Marlborough city	31 813
					25	38715	017	Middlesex County	31 813
24	30325		Frederick city	40 148					
24	30325	021	Frederick County	40 148	25	39835		Medford city	57 407
					25	39835	017	Middlesex County	57 407
24	31175		Gaithersburg city	39 542					
24	31175	031	Montgomery County	39 542	25	40115		Melrose city	28 150
					25	40115	017	Middlesex County	28 150
24	36075		Hagerstown city	35 445					
24	36075	043	Washington County	35 445	25	45000		New Bedford city	99 922
					25	45000	005	Bristol County	99 922
24	67675		Rockville city	44 835					
24	67675	031	Montgomery County	44 835	25	45560		Newton city	82 585
					25	45560	017	Middlesex County	82 585
25			**MASSACHUSETTS**						
25	02690		Attleboro city	38 383	25	46330		Northampton city	29 289
25	02690	005	Bristol County	38 383	25	46330	015	Hampshire County	29 289
25	05595		Beverly city	38 195	25	52490		Peabody city	47 039
25	05595	009	Essex County	38 195	25	52490	009	Essex County	47 039
25	07000		Boston city	574 283	25	53960		Pittsfield city	48 622
25	07000	025	Suffolk County	574 283	25	53960	003	Berkshire County	48 622
25	09000		Brockton city	92 788	25	55745		Quincy city	84 985
25	09000	023	Plymouth County	92 788	25	55745	021	Norfolk County	84 985
25	11000		Cambridge city	95 802	25	56585		Revere city	42 786
25	11000	017	Middlesex County	95 802	25	56585	025	Suffolk County	42 786
25	13205		Chelsea city	28 710	25	59105		Salem city	38 091
25	13205	025	Suffolk County	28 710	25	59105	009	Essex County	38 091
25	13660		Chicopee city	56 632	25	62535		Somerville city	76 210
25	13660	013	Hampden County	56 632	25	62535	017	Middlesex County	76 210
25	21990		Everett city	35 701	25	67000		Springfield city	156 983
25	21990	017	Middlesex County	35 701	25	67000	013	Hampden County	156 983
25	23000		Fall River city	92 703	25	69170		Taunton city	49 832
25	23000	005	Bristol County	92 703	25	69170	005	Bristol County	49 832
25	23875		Fitchburg city	41 194	25	72600		Waltham city	57 878
25	23875	027	Worcester County	41 194	25	72600	017	Middlesex County	57 878
25	26150		Gloucester city	28 716	25	76030		Westfield city	38 372
25	26150	009	Essex County	28 716	25	76030	013	Hampden County	38 372
25	29405		Haverhill city	51 418	25	81035		Woburn city	35 943
25	29405	009	Essex County	51 418	25	81035	017	Middlesex County	35 943

Cities by County — Continued

State Code	Place Code	County Code	Geographic Area Name	1990 population	State Code	Place Code	County Code	Geographic Area Name	1990 population
25	82000		Worcester city	169 759	26	47800		Lincoln Park city	41 832
25	82000	027	Worcester County	169 759	26	47800	163	Wayne County	41 832
26			**MICHIGAN**		26	49000		Livonia city	100 850
26	01380		Allen Park city	31 092	26	49000	163	Wayne County	100 850
26	01380	163	Wayne County	31 092					
					26	50560		Madison Heights city	32 196
26	03000		Ann Arbor city	109 592	26	50560	125	Oakland County	32 196
26	03000	161	Washtenaw County	109 592					
					26	53780		Midland city	38 053
26	05920		Battle Creek city	53 540	26	53780	017	Bay County	234
26	05920	025	Calhoun County	53 540	26	53780	111	Midland County	37 819
26	06020		Bay City city	38 936	26	56320		Muskegon city	40 283
26	06020	017	Bay County	38 936	26	56320	121	Muskegon County	40 283
26	12060		Burton city	27 617	26	59440		Novi city	32 998
26	12060	049	Genesee County	27 617	26	59440	125	Oakland County	32 998
26	21000		Dearborn city	89 286	26	59920		Oak Park city	30 462
26	21000	163	Wayne County	89 286	26	59920	125	Oakland County	30 462
26	21020		Dearborn Heights city	60 838	26	65440		Pontiac city	71 166
26	21020	163	Wayne County	60 838	26	65440	125	Oakland County	71 166
26	22000		Detroit city	1 027 974	26	65560		Portage city	41 042
26	22000	163	Wayne County	1 027 974	26	65560	077	Kalamazoo County	41 042
26	23920		East Detroit city	35 283	26	65820		Port Huron city	33 694
26	23920	099	Macomb County	35 283	26	65820	147	St. Clair County	33 694
26	24120		East Lansing city	50 677	26	69035		Rochester Hills city	61 766
26	24120	065	Ingham County	50 677	26	69035	125	Oakland County	61 766
26	27440		Farmington Hills city	74 652	26	69800		Roseville city	51 412
26	27440	125	Oakland County	74 652	26	69800	099	Macomb County	51 412
26	27880		Ferndale city	25 084	26	70040		Royal Oak city	65 410
26	27880	125	Oakland County	25 084	26	70040	125	Oakland County	65 410
26	29000		Flint city	140 761	26	70520		Saginaw city	69 512
26	29000	049	Genesee County	140 761	26	70520	145	Saginaw County	69 512
26	31420		Garden City city	31 846	26	70760		St. Clair Shores city	68 107
26	31420	163	Wayne County	31 846	26	70760	099	Macomb County	68 107
26	34000		Grand Rapids city	189 126	26	74900		Southfield city	75 728
26	34000	081	Kent County	189 126	26	74900	125	Oakland County	75 728
26	38640		Holland city	30 745	26	74960		Southgate city	30 771
26	38640	005	Allegan County	5 659	26	74960	163	Wayne County	30 771
26	38640	139	Ottawa County	25 086					
					26	76460		Sterling Heights city	117 810
26	40680		Inkster city	30 772	26	76460	099	Macomb County	117 810
26	40680	163	Wayne County	30 772					
					26	79000		Taylor city	70 811
26	41420		Jackson city	37 446	26	79000	163	Wayne County	70 811
26	41420	075	Jackson County	37 446					
					26	80700		Troy city	72 884
26	42160		Kalamazoo city	80 277	26	80700	125	Oakland County	72 884
26	42160	077	Kalamazoo County	80 277					
					26	84000		Warren city	144 864
26	42820		Kentwood city	37 826	26	84000	099	Macomb County	144 864
26	42820	081	Kent County	37 826					
					26	86000		Westland city	84 724
26	46000		Lansing city	127 321	26	86000	163	Wayne County	84 724
26	46000	045	Eaton County	4 621					
26	46000	065	Ingham County	122 700	26	88900		Wyandotte city	30 938
					26	88900	163	Wayne County	30 938

State Code	Place Code	County Code	Geographic Area Name	1990 population	State Code	Place Code	County Code	Geographic Area Name	1990 population
26	88940		Wyoming city	63 891	27	55852		Roseville city	33 485
26	88940	081	Kent County	63 891	27	55852	123	Ramsey County	33 485
27			**MINNESOTA**		27	56896		St. Cloud city	48 812
27	01900		Apple Valley city	34 598	27	56896	009	Benton County	5 950
27	01900	037	Dakota County	34 598	27	56896	141	Sherburne County	5 246
					27	56896	145	Stearns County	37 616
27	06382		Blaine city	38 975					
27	06382	003	Anoka County	38 975	27	57220		St. Louis Park city	43 787
27	06382	123	Ramsey County	0	27	57220	053	Hennepin County	43 787
27	06616		Bloomington city	86 335	27	58000		St. Paul city	272 235
27	06616	053	Hennepin County	86 335	27	58000	123	Ramsey County	272 235
27	07948		Brooklyn Center city	28 887	27	71032		Winona city	25 399
27	07948	053	Hennepin County	28 887	27	71032	169	Winona County	25 399
27	07966		Brooklyn Park city	56 381	28			**MISSISSIPPI**	
27	07966	053	Hennepin County	56 381	28	06220		Biloxi city	46 319
					28	06220	047	Harrison County	46 319
27	08794		Burnsville city	51 288					
27	08794	037	Dakota County	51 288	28	29180		Greenville city	45 226
					28	29180	151	Washington County	45 226
27	13114		Coon Rapids city	52 978					
27	13114	003	Anoka County	52 978	28	29700		Gulfport city	40 775
					28	29700	047	Harrison County	40 775
27	17000		Duluth city	85 493					
27	17000	137	St. Louis County	85 493	28	31020		Hattiesburg city	41 882
					28	31020	035	Forrest County	39 784
27	17288		Eagan city	47 409	28	31020	073	Lamar County	2 098
27	17288	037	Dakota County	47 409					
					28	36000		Jackson city	196 637
27	18116		Eden Prairie city	39 311	28	36000	049	Hinds County	195 906
27	18116	053	Hennepin County	39 311	28	36000	089	Madison County	727
					28	36000	121	Rankin County	4
27	18188		Edina city	46 070					
27	18188	053	Hennepin County	46 070	28	46640		Meridian city	41 036
					28	46640	075	Lauderdale County	41 036
27	22814		Fridley city	28 335					
27	22814	003	Anoka County	28 335	28	55360		Pascagoula city	25 899
					28	55360	059	Jackson County	25 899
27	39878		Mankato city	31 477					
27	39878	013	Blue Earth County	31 468	28	74840		Tupelo city	30 685
27	39878	103	Nicollet County	9	28	74840	081	Lee County	30 685
27	40166		Maple Grove city	38 736	29			**MISSOURI**	
27	40166	053	Hennepin County	38 736	29	06652		Blue Springs city	40 153
					29	06652	095	Jackson County	40 153
27	40382		Maplewood city	30 954					
27	40382	123	Ramsey County	30 954	29	11242		Cape Girardeau city	34 438
					29	11242	031	Cape Girardeau County	34 438
27	43000		Minneapolis city	368 383	29	11242	201	Scott County	0
27	43000	053	Hennepin County	368 383					
					29	13600		Chesterfield city	37 991
27	43252		Minnetonka city	48 370	29	13600	189	St. Louis County	37 991
27	43252	053	Hennepin County	48 370					
					29	15670		Columbia city	69 101
27	43864		Moorhead city	32 295	29	15670	019	Boone County	69 101
27	43864	027	Clay County	32 295					
					29	24778		Florissant city	51 206
27	51730		Plymouth city	50 889	29	24778	189	St. Louis County	51 206
27	51730	053	Hennepin County	50 889					
					29	27190		Gladstone city	26 243
27	54214		Richfield city	35 710	29	27190	047	Clay County	26 243
27	54214	053	Hennepin County	35 710					
					29	35000		Independence city	112 301
27	54880		Rochester city	70 745	29	35000	047	Clay County	0
27	54880	109	Olmsted County	70 745	29	35000	095	Jackson County	112 301

Cities by County — Continued

State Code	Place Code	County Code	Geographic Area Name	1990 population	State Code	Place Code	County Code	Geographic Area Name	1990 population
29	37000		Jefferson City city	35 481	31	37000		Omaha city	335 795
29	37000	027	Callaway County	306	31	37000	055	Douglas County	335 795
29	37000	051	Cole County	35 175	32			**NEVADA**	
29	37592		Joplin city	40 961	32	09700		Carson City	40 443
29	37592	097	Jasper County	37 032	32	09700	510	Carson City	40 443
29	37592	145	Newton County	3 929	32	31900		Henderson city	64 942
29	38000		Kansas City city	435 146	32	31900	003	Clark County	64 942
29	38000	037	Cass County	42					
29	38000	047	Clay County	69 316	32	40000		Las Vegas city	258 295
29	38000	095	Jackson County	341 179	32	40000	003	Clark County	258 295
29	38000	165	Platte County	24 609	32	51800		North Las Vegas city	47 707
29	39044		Kirkwood city	27 291	32	51800	003	Clark County	47 707
29	39044	189	St. Louis County	27 291	32	60600		Reno city	133 850
29	41348		Lee's Summit city	46 418	32	60600	031	Washoe County	133 850
29	41348	037	Cass County	433	32	68400		Sparks city	53 367
29	41348	095	Jackson County	45 985	32	68400	031	Washoe County	53 367
29	46586		Maryland Heights city	25 407	33			**NEW HAMPSHIRE**	
29	46586	189	St. Louis County	25 407	33	14200		Concord city	36 006
29	60788		Raytown city	30 601	33	14200	013	Merrimack County	36 006
29	60788	095	Jackson County	30 601	33	18820		Dover city	25 042
29	64082		St. Charles city	54 555	33	18820	017	Strafford County	25 042
29	64082	183	St. Charles County	54 555	33	45140		Manchester city	99 567
29	64550		St. Joseph city	71 852	33	45140	011	Hillsborough County	99 567
29	64550	021	Buchanan County	71 852	33	50260		Nashua city	79 662
29	65000		St. Louis city	396 685	33	50260	011	Hillsborough County	79 662
29	65000	510	St. Louis city	396 685	33	62900		Portsmouth city	25 925
29	65126		St. Peters city	45 779	33	62900	015	Rockingham County	25 925
29	65126	183	St. Charles County	45 779	33	65140		Rochester city	26 630
29	70000		Springfield city	140 494	33	65140	017	Strafford County	26 630
29	70000	043	Christian County	0	34			**NEW JERSEY**	
29	70000	077	Greene County	140 494	34	02080		Atlantic City city	37 986
29	75220		University City city	40 087	34	02080	001	Atlantic County	37 986
29	75220	189	St. Louis County	40 087	34	03580		Bayonne city	61 444
30			**MONTANA**		34	03580	017	Hudson County	61 444
30	06550		Billings city	81 151	34	10000		Camden city	87 492
30	06550	111	Yellowstone County	81 151	34	10000	007	Camden County	87 492
30	11397		Butte-Silver Bow	33 336	34	13690		Clifton city	71 742
30	11397	093	Silver Bow County	33 336	34	13690	031	Passaic County	71 742
30	32800		Great Falls city	55 097	34	19390		East Orange city	73 552
30	32800	013	Cascade County	55 097	34	19390	013	Essex County	73 552
30	50200		Missoula city	42 918	34	21000		Elizabeth city	110 002
30	50200	063	Missoula County	42 918	34	21000	039	Union County	110 002
31			**NEBRASKA**		34	22470		Fair Lawn borough	30 548
31	03950		Bellevue city	30 982	34	22470	003	Bergen County	30 548
31	03950	153	Sarpy County	30 982	34	24420		Fort Lee borough	31 997
31	19595		Grand Island city	39 386	34	24420	003	Bergen County	31 997
31	19595	079	Hall County	39 386	34	25770		Garfield city	26 727
31	28000		Lincoln city	191 972	34	25770	003	Bergen County	26 727
31	28000	109	Lancaster County	191 972					

State Code	Place Code	County Code	Geographic Area Name	1990 population	State Code	Place Code	County Code	Geographic Area Name	1990 population
34	28680		Hackensack city	37 049	35	16420		Clovis city	30 954
34	28680	003	Bergen County	37 049	35	16420	009	Curry County	30 954
34	32250		Hoboken city	33 397	35	25800		Farmington city	33 997
34	32250	017	Hudson County	33 397	35	25800	045	San Juan County	33 997
34	36000		Jersey City city	228 537	35	32520		Hobbs city	29 115
34	36000	017	Hudson County	228 537	35	32520	025	Lea County	29 115
34	36510		Kearny town	34 874	35	39380		Las Cruces city	62 126
34	36510	017	Hudson County	34 874	35	39380	013	Dona Ana County	62 126
34	40350		Linden city	36 701	35	63530		Rio Rancho city	32 505
34	40350	039	Union County	36 701	35	63530	043	Sandoval County	32 505
34	41310		Long Branch city	28 658	35	64930		Roswell city	44 654
34	41310	025	Monmouth County	28 658	35	64930	005	Chaves County	44 654
34	46680		Millville city	25 992	35	70500		Santa Fe city	55 859
34	46680	011	Cumberland County	25 992	35	70500	049	Santa Fe County	55 859
34	51000		Newark city	275 221	36			**NEW YORK**	
34	51000	013	Essex County	275 221	36	01000		Albany city	101 082
					36	01000	001	Albany County	101 082
34	51210		New Brunswick city	41 711	36	03078		Auburn city	31 258
34	51210	023	Middlesex County	41 711	36	03078	011	Cayuga County	31 258
34	55950		Paramus borough	25 067	36	06607		Binghamton city	53 008
34	55950	003	Bergen County	25 067	36	06607	007	Broome County	53 008
34	56550		Passaic city	58 041	36	11000		Buffalo city	328 123
34	56550	031	Passaic County	58 041	36	11000	029	Erie County	328 123
34	57000		Paterson city	140 891	36	24229		Elmira city	33 724
34	57000	031	Passaic County	140 891	36	24229	015	Chemung County	33 724
34	58200		Perth Amboy city	41 967	36	27485		Freeport village	39 894
34	58200	023	Middlesex County	41 967	36	27485	059	Nassau County	39 894
34	59190		Plainfield city	46 567	36	33139		Hempstead village	49 453
34	59190	039	Union County	46 567	36	33139	059	Nassau County	49 453
34	61530		Rahway city	25 325	36	38077		Ithaca city	29 541
34	61530	039	Union County	25 325	36	38077	109	Tompkins County	29 541
34	65790		Sayreville borough	34 986	36	38264		Jamestown city	34 681
34	65790	023	Middlesex County	34 986	36	38264	013	Chautauqua County	34 681
34	74000		Trenton city	88 675	36	42554		Lindenhurst village	26 879
34	74000	021	Mercer County	88 675	36	42554	103	Suffolk County	26 879
34	74630		Union City city	58 012	36	43335		Long Beach city	33 510
34	74630	017	Hudson County	58 012	36	43335	059	Nassau County	33 510
34	76070		Vineland city	54 780	36	49121		Mount Vernon city	67 153
34	76070	011	Cumberland County	54 780	36	49121	119	Westchester County	67 153
34	79040		Westfield town	28 870	36	50034		Newburgh city	26 454
34	79040	039	Union County	28 870	36	50034	071	Orange County	26 454
34	79610		West New York town	38 125	36	50617		New Rochelle city	67 265
34	79610	017	Hudson County	38 125	36	50617	119	Westchester County	67 265
35			**NEW MEXICO**		36	51000		New York city	7 322 564
35	01780		Alamogordo city	27 596	36	51000	005	Bronx County	1 203 789
35	01780	035	Otero County	27 596	36	51000	047	Kings County	2 300 664
35	02000		Albuquerque city	384 736	36	51000	061	New York County	1 487 536
35	02000	001	Bernalillo County	384 736	36	51000	081	Queens County	1 951 598
					36	51000	085	Richmond County	378 977

State Code	Place Code	County Code	Geographic Area Name	1990 population	State Code	Place Code	County Code	Geographic Area Name	1990 population
36	51055		Niagara Falls city	61 840	37	25580		Gastonia city	54 732
36	51055	063	Niagara County	61 840	37	25580	071	Gaston County	54 732
36	53682		North Tonawanda city	34 989	37	26880		Goldsboro city	40 709
36	53682	063	Niagara County	34 989	37	26880	191	Wayne County	40 709
36	59641		Poughkeepsie city	28 844	37	28000		Greensboro city	183 521
36	59641	027	Dutchess County	28 844	37	28000	081	Guilford County	183 521
36	63000		Rochester city	231 636	37	28080		Greenville city	44 972
36	63000	055	Monroe County	231 636	37	28080	147	Pitt County	44 972
36	63418		Rome city	44 350	37	31060		Hickory city	28 301
36	63418	065	Oneida County	44 350	37	31060	023	Burke County	79
					37	31060	035	Catawba County	28 222
36	65255		Saratoga Springs city	25 001					
36	65255	091	Saratoga County	25 001	37	31400		High Point city	69 496
					37	31400	057	Davidson County	471
36	65508		Schenectady city	65 566	37	31400	067	Forsyth County	6
36	65508	093	Schenectady County	65 566	37	31400	081	Guilford County	68 982
					37	31400	151	Randolph County	37
36	73000		Syracuse city	163 860					
36	73000	067	Onondaga County	163 860	37	34200		Jacksonville city	30 013
					37	34200	133	Onslow County	30 013
36	75484		Troy city	54 269					
36	75484	083	Rensselaer County	54 269	37	35200		Kannapolis city	29 696
					37	35200	025	Cabarrus County	21 220
36	76540		Utica city	68 637	37	35200	159	Rowan County	8 476
36	76540	065	Oneida County	68 637					
					37	35920		Kinston city	25 295
36	76705		Valley Stream village	33 946	37	35920	107	Lenoir County	25 295
36	76705	059	Nassau County	33 946					
					37	55000		Raleigh city	207 951
36	78608		Watertown city	29 429	37	55000	183	Wake County	207 951
36	78608	045	Jefferson County	29 429					
					37	57500		Rocky Mount city	48 997
36	81677		White Plains city	48 718	37	57500	065	Edgecombe County	17 057
36	81677	119	Westchester County	48 718	37	57500	127	Nash County	31 940
36	84000		Yonkers city	188 082	37	74440		Wilmington city	55 530
36	84000	119	Westchester County	188 082	37	74440	129	New Hanover County	55 530
37			**NORTH CAROLINA**		37	74540		Wilson city	36 930
37	02140		Asheville city	61 607	37	74540	195	Wilson County	36 930
37	02140	021	Buncombe County	61 607					
					37	75000		Winston-Salem city	143 485
37	09060		Burlington city	39 498	37	75000	067	Forsyth County	143 485
37	09060	001	Alamance County	39 498					
					38			**NORTH DAKOTA**	
37	10740		Cary town	43 858	38	07200		Bismarck city	49 256
37	10740	183	Wake County	43 858	38	07200	015	Burleigh County	49 256
37	11800		Chapel Hill town	38 719	38	25700		Fargo city	74 111
37	11800	063	Durham County	1 115	38	25700	017	Cass County	74 111
37	11800	135	Orange County	37 604					
					38	32060		Grand Forks city	49 425
37	12000		Charlotte city	395 934	38	32060	035	Grand Forks County	49 425
37	12000	119	Mecklenburg County	395 934					
					38	53380		Minot city	34 544
37	14100		Concord city	27 347	38	53380	101	Ward County	34 544
37	14100	025	Cabarrus County	27 347					
					39			**OHIO**	
37	19000		Durham city	136 611	39	01000		Akron city	223 019
37	19000	063	Durham County	136 594	39	01000	153	Summit County	223 019
37	19000	135	Orange County	17					
					39	03828		Barberton city	27 623
37	22920		Fayetteville city	75 695	39	03828	153	Summit County	27 623
37	22920	051	Cumberland County	75 695					
					39	04720		Beavercreek city	33 626
					39	04720	057	Greene County	33 626

State Code	Place Code	County Code	Geographic Area Name	1990 population	State Code	Place Code	County Code	Geographic Area Name	1990 population
39	07972		Bowling Green city	28 176	39	41720		Lancaster city	34 507
39	07972	173	Wood County	28 176	39	41720	045	Fairfield County	34 507
39	09680		Brunswick city	28 230	39	43554		Lima city	45 549
39	09680	103	Medina County	28 230	39	43554	003	Allen County	45 549
39	12000		Canton city	84 161	39	44856		Lorain city	71 245
39	12000	151	Stark County	84 161	39	44856	093	Lorain County	71 245
39	15000		Cincinnati city	364 040	39	47138		Mansfield city	50 627
39	15000	061	Hamilton County	364 040	39	47138	139	Richland County	50 627
39	16000		Cleveland city	505 616	39	47306		Maple Heights city	27 089
39	16000	035	Cuyahoga County	505 616	39	47306	035	Cuyahoga County	27 089
39	16014		Cleveland Heights city	54 052	39	47754		Marion city	34 075
39	16014	035	Cuyahoga County	54 052	39	47754	101	Marion County	34 075
39	18000		Columbus city	632 910	39	48244		Massillon city	31 007
39	18000	045	Fairfield County	640	39	48244	151	Stark County	31 007
39	18000	049	Franklin County	632 270	39	49056		Mentor city	47 358
39	19778		Cuyahoga Falls city	48 950	39	49056	085	Lake County	47 358
39	19778	153	Summit County	48 950	39	49840		Middletown city	46 022
39	21000		Dayton city	182 044	39	49840	017	Butler County	45 991
39	21000	113	Montgomery County	182 044	39	49840	165	Warren County	31
39	23380		East Cleveland city	33 096	39	54040		Newark city	44 389
39	23380	035	Cuyahoga County	33 096	39	54040	089	Licking County	44 389
39	25256		Elyria city	56 746	39	56882		North Olmsted city	34 204
39	25256	093	Lorain County	56 746	39	56882	035	Cuyahoga County	34 204
39	25704		Euclid city	54 875	39	61000		Parma city	87 876
39	25704	035	Cuyahoga County	54 875	39	61000	035	Cuyahoga County	87 876
39	25914		Fairborn city	31 300	39	66390		Reynoldsburg city	25 748
39	25914	057	Greene County	31 300	39	66390	045	Fairfield County	0
39	25970		Fairfield city	39 729	39	66390	049	Franklin County	24 483
39	25970	017	Butler County	39 729	39	66390	089	Licking County	1 265
39	25970	061	Hamilton County	0	39	70380		Sandusky city	29 764
39	27048		Findlay city	35 703	39	70380	043	Erie County	29 764
39	27048	063	Hancock County	35 703	39	71682		Shaker Heights city	30 831
39	29106		Gahanna city	27 791	39	71682	035	Cuyahoga County	30 831
39	29106	049	Franklin County	27 791	39	74118		Springfield city	70 487
39	29428		Garfield Heights city	31 739	39	74118	023	Clark County	70 487
39	29428	035	Cuyahoga County	31 739	39	74944		Stow city	27 702
39	33012		Hamilton city	61 368	39	74944	153	Summit County	27 702
39	33012	017	Butler County	61 368	39	75098		Strongsville city	35 308
39	36610		Huber Heights city	38 696	39	75098	035	Cuyahoga County	35 308
39	36610	109	Miami County	10	39	77000		Toledo city	332 943
39	36610	113	Montgomery County	38 686	39	77000	095	Lucas County	332 943
39	39872		Kent city	28 835	39	79002		Upper Arlington city	34 128
39	39872	133	Portage County	28 835	39	79002	049	Franklin County	34 128
39	40040		Kettering city	60 569	39	80892		Warren city	50 793
39	40040	057	Greene County	0	39	80892	155	Trumbull County	50 793
39	40040	113	Montgomery County	60 569	39	83342		Westerville city	30 269
39	41664		Lakewood city	59 718	39	83342	041	Delaware County	1 177
39	41664	035	Cuyahoga County	59 718	39	83342	049	Franklin County	29 092

State Code	Place Code	County Code	Geographic Area Name	1990 population
39	83622		Westlake city	27 018
39	83622	035	Cuyahoga County	27 018
39	88000		Youngstown city	95 732
39	88000	099	Mahoning County	95 706
39	88000	155	Trumbull County	26
39	88084		Zanesville city	26 778
39	88084	119	Muskingum County	26 778
40			**OKLAHOMA**	
40	04450		Bartlesville city	34 256
40	04450	113	Osage County	4
40	04450	147	Washington County	34 252
40	09050		Broken Arrow city	58 043
40	09050	143	Tulsa County	52 642
40	09050	145	Wagoner County	5 401
40	23200		Edmond city	52 315
40	23200	109	Oklahoma County	52 315
40	23950		Enid city	45 309
40	23950	047	Garfield County	45 309
40	41850		Lawton city	80 561
40	41850	031	Comanche County	80 561
40	48350		Midwest City city	52 267
40	48350	109	Oklahoma County	52 267
40	49200		Moore city	40 318
40	49200	027	Cleveland County	40 318
40	50050		Muskogee city	37 708
40	50050	101	Muskogee County	37 708
40	52500		Norman city	80 071
40	52500	027	Cleveland County	80 071
40	55000		Oklahoma City city	444 719
40	55000	017	Canadian County	18 716
40	55000	027	Cleveland County	34 693
40	55000	087	McClain County	109
40	55000	109	Oklahoma County	391 137
40	55000	125	Pottawatomie County	64
40	59850		Ponca City city	26 359
40	59850	071	Kay County	26 359
40	59850	113	Osage County	0
40	66800		Shawnee city	26 017
40	66800	125	Pottawatomie County	26 017
40	70300		Stillwater city	36 676
40	70300	119	Payne County	36 676
40	75000		Tulsa city	367 302
40	75000	113	Osage County	5 674
40	75000	131	Rogers County	0
40	75000	143	Tulsa County	361 628
41			**OREGON**	
41	01000		Albany city	29 462
41	01000	003	Benton County	21
41	01000	043	Linn County	29 441
41	05350		Beaverton city	53 310
41	05350	067	Washington County	53 310
41	15800		Corvallis city	44 757
41	15800	003	Benton County	44 757
41	23850		Eugene city	112 669
41	23850	039	Lane County	112 669
41	31250		Gresham city	68 235
41	31250	051	Multnomah County	68 235
41	34100		Hillsboro city	37 520
41	34100	067	Washington County	37 520
41	40550		Lake Oswego city	30 576
41	40550	005	Clackamas County	28 317
41	40550	051	Multnomah County	2 253
41	40550	067	Washington County	6
41	47000		Medford city	46 951
41	47000	029	Jackson County	46 951
41	59000		Portland city	437 319
41	59000	005	Clackamas County	707
41	59000	051	Multnomah County	435 415
41	59000	067	Washington County	1 197
41	64900		Salem city	107 786
41	64900	047	Marion County	94 983
41	64900	053	Polk County	12 803
41	69600		Springfield city	44 683
41	69600	039	Lane County	44 683
41	73650		Tigard city	29 344
41	73650	067	Washington County	29 344
42			**PENNSYLVANIA**	
42	02000		Allentown city	105 090
42	02000	077	Lehigh County	105 090
42	02184		Altoona city	51 881
42	02184	013	Blair County	51 881
42	06064		Bethel Park borough	33 823
42	06064	003	Allegheny County	33 823
42	06088		Bethlehem city	71 428
42	06088	077	Lehigh County	18 867
42	06088	095	Northampton County	52 561
42	13208		Chester city	41 856
42	13208	045	Delaware County	41 856
42	21648		Easton city	26 276
42	21648	095	Northampton County	26 276
42	24000		Erie city	108 718
42	24000	049	Erie County	108 718
42	32800		Harrisburg city	52 376
42	32800	043	Dauphin County	52 376
42	38288		Johnstown city	28 134
42	38288	021	Cambria County	28 134
42	41216		Lancaster city	55 551
42	41216	071	Lancaster County	55 551
42	46256		McKeesport city	26 016
42	46256	003	Allegheny County	26 016

Cities by County — Continued

State Code	Place Code	County Code	Geographic Area Name	1990 population	State Code	Place Code	County Code	Geographic Area Name	1990 population
42	52330		Monroeville borough	29 169	45	30850		Greenville city	58 282
42	52330	003	Allegheny County	29 169	45	30850	045	Greenville County	58 282
42	53368		New Castle city	28 334	45	48535		Mount Pleasant town	30 108
42	53368	073	Lawrence County	28 334	45	48535	019	Charleston County	30 108
42	54656		Norristown borough	30 749	45	50875		North Charleston city	70 218
42	54656	091	Montgomery County	30 749	45	50875	015	Berkeley County	0
42	60000		Philadelphia city	1 585 577	45	50875	019	Charleston County	69 111
42	60000	101	Philadelphia County	1 585 577	45	50875	035	Dorchester County	1 107
42	61000		Pittsburgh city	369 879	45	61405		Rock Hill city	41 643
42	61000	003	Allegheny County	369 879	45	61405	091	York County	41 643
42	61536		Plum borough	25 609	45	68290		Spartanburg city	43 467
42	61536	003	Allegheny County	25 609	45	68290	083	Spartanburg County	43 467
42	63624		Reading city	78 380	45	70405		Sumter city	41 943
42	63624	011	Berks County	78 380	45	70405	085	Sumter County	41 943
42	69000		Scranton city	81 805	46			**SOUTH DAKOTA**	
42	69000	069	Lackawanna County	81 805	46	52980		Rapid City city	54 523
42	73808		State College borough	38 923	46	52980	103	Pennington County	54 523
42	73808	027	Centre County	38 923	46	59020		Sioux Falls city	100 814
42	85152		Wilkes-Barre city	47 523	46	59020	083	Lincoln County	1 409
42	85152	079	Luzerne County	47 523	46	59020	099	Minnehaha County	99 405
42	85312		Williamsport city	31 933	47			**TENNESSEE**	
42	85312	081	Lycoming County	31 933	47	03440		Bartlett town	26 989
42	87048		York city	42 192	47	03440	157	Shelby County	26 989
42	87048	133	York County	42 192	47	14000		Chattanooga city	152 466
44			**RHODE ISLAND**		47	14000	065	Hamilton County	152 466
44	19180		Cranston city	76 060	47	15160		Clarksville city	75 494
44	19180	007	Providence County	76 060	47	15160	125	Montgomery County	75 494
44	22960		East Providence city	50 380	47	15400		Cleveland city	30 354
44	22960	007	Providence County	50 380	47	15400	011	Bradley County	30 354
44	49960		Newport city	28 227	47	16540		Columbia city	28 583
44	49960	005	Newport County	28 227	47	16540	119	Maury County	28 583
44	54640		Pawtucket city	72 644	47	28960		Germantown city	32 893
44	54640	007	Providence County	72 644	47	28960	157	Shelby County	32 893
44	59000		Providence city	160 728	47	33280		Hendersonville city	32 188
44	59000	007	Providence County	160 728	47	33280	165	Sumner County	32 188
44	74300		Warwick city	85 427	47	37640		Jackson city	48 949
44	74300	003	Kent County	85 427	47	37640	113	Madison County	48 949
44	80780		Woonsocket city	43 877	47	38320		Johnson City city	49 381
44	80780	007	Providence County	43 877	47	38320	019	Carter County	944
45			**SOUTH CAROLINA**		47	38320	163	Sullivan County	96
45	01360		Anderson city	26 184	47	38320	179	Washington County	48 341
45	01360	007	Anderson County	26 184	47	39560		Kingsport city	36 365
45	13330		Charleston city	80 414	47	39560	073	Hawkins County	2 204
45	13330	019	Charleston County	80 414	47	39560	163	Sullivan County	34 161
45	16000		Columbia city	98 052	47	40000		Knoxville city	165 121
45	16000	079	Richland County	98 052	47	40000	093	Knox County	165 121
45	25810		Florence city	29 813	47	48000		Memphis city	610 337
45	25810	041	Florence County	29 813	47	48000	157	Shelby County	610 337
					47	51560		Murfreesboro city	44 922
					47	51560	149	Rutherford County	44 922

Cities by County — Continued

State Code	Place Code	County Code	Geographic Area Name	1990 population
47	52006		Nashville-Davidson	488 374
47	52006	037	Davidson County	488 374
47	55120		Oak Ridge city	27 310
47	55120	001	Anderson County	24 743
47	55120	145	Roane County	2 567
48			**TEXAS**	
48	01000		Abilene city	106 654
48	01000	253	Jones County	797
48	01000	441	Taylor County	105 857
48	03000		Amarillo city	157 615
48	03000	375	Potter County	91 502
48	03000	381	Randall County	66 113
48	04000		Arlington city	261 721
48	04000	439	Tarrant County	261 721
48	05000		Austin city	465 622
48	05000	453	Travis County	463 178
48	05000	491	Williamson County	2 444
48	06128		Baytown city	63 850
48	06128	071	Chambers County	2 724
48	06128	201	Harris County	61 126
48	07000		Beaumont city	114 323
48	07000	245	Jefferson County	114 323
48	07132		Bedford city	43 762
48	07132	439	Tarrant County	43 762
48	10768		Brownsville city	98 962
48	10768	061	Cameron County	98 962
48	10912		Bryan city	55 002
48	10912	041	Brazos County	55 002
48	13024		Carrollton city	82 169
48	13024	085	Collin County	0
48	13024	113	Dallas County	40 024
48	13024	121	Denton County	42 145
48	15976		College Station city	52 456
48	15976	041	Brazos County	52 456
48	16432		Conroe city	27 610
48	16432	339	Montgomery County	27 610
48	17000		Corpus Christi city	257 453
48	17000	273	Kleberg County	0
48	17000	355	Nueces County	257 453
48	17000	409	San Patricio County	0
48	19000		Dallas city	1 006 877
48	19000	085	Collin County	26 325
48	19000	113	Dallas County	966 168
48	19000	121	Denton County	14 338
48	19000	257	Kaufman County	7
48	19000	397	Rockwall County	39
48	19624		Deer Park city	27 652
48	19624	201	Harris County	27 652
48	19792		Del Rio city	30 705
48	19792	465	Val Verde County	30 705
48	19972		Denton city	66 270
48	19972	121	Denton County	66 270
48	20092		DeSoto city	30 544
48	20092	113	Dallas County	30 544
48	21628		Duncanville city	35 748
48	21628	113	Dallas County	35 748
48	22660		Edinburg city	29 885
48	22660	215	Hidalgo County	29 885
48	24000		El Paso city	515 342
48	24000	141	El Paso County	515 342
48	24768		Euless city	38 149
48	24768	439	Tarrant County	38 149
48	26736	099	Coryell County	18 559
48	27000		Fort Worth city	447 619
48	27000	121	Denton County	0
48	27000	439	Tarrant County	447 619
48	28068		Galveston city	59 070
48	28068	167	Galveston County	59 070
48	29000		Garland city	180 650
48	29000	085	Collin County	15
48	29000	113	Dallas County	180 635
48	29000	397	Rockwall County	0
48	30464		Grand Prairie city	99 616
48	30464	113	Dallas County	81 527
48	30464	139	Ellis County	3
48	30464	439	Tarrant County	18 086
48	30644		Grapevine city	29 202
48	30644	113	Dallas County	3
48	30644	121	Denton County	0
48	30644	439	Tarrant County	29 199
48	31928		Haltom City city	32 856
48	31928	439	Tarrant County	32 856
48	32372		Harlingen city	48 735
48	32372	061	Cameron County	48 735
48	35000		Houston city	1 630 553
48	35000	157	Fort Bend County	27 027
48	35000	201	Harris County	1 603 524
48	35000	339	Montgomery County	2
48	35528		Huntsville city	27 925
48	35528	471	Walker County	27 925
48	35576		Hurst city	33 574
48	35576	439	Tarrant County	33 574
48	37000		Irving city	155 037
48	37000	113	Dallas County	155 037
48	39148		Killeen city	63 535
48	39148	027	Bell County	63 535
48	39352		Kingsville city	25 276
48	39352	273	Kleberg County	25 276
48	41440		La Porte city	27 910
48	41440	201	Harris County	27 910
48	41464		Laredo city	122 899
48	41464	479	Webb County	122 899

State Code	Place Code	County Code	Geographic Area Name	1990 population	State Code	Place Code	County Code	Geographic Area Name	1990 population
48	41980		League City city	30 159	48	64472		San Angelo city	84 474
48	41980	167	Galveston County	30 026	48	64472	451	Tom Green County	84 474
48	41980	201	Harris County	133	48	65000		San Antonio city	935 933
48	42508		Lewisville city	46 521	48	65000	029	Bexar County	935 933
48	42508	113	Dallas County	555					
48	42508	121	Denton County	45 966	48	65600		San Marcos city	28 743
					48	65600	055	Caldwell County	0
48	43888		Longview city	70 311	48	65600	209	Hays County	28 743
48	43888	183	Gregg County	68 655					
48	43888	203	Harrison County	1 656	48	67496		Sherman city	31 601
					48	67496	181	Grayson County	31 601
48	45000		Lubbock city	186 206					
48	45000	303	Lubbock County	186 206	48	72176		Temple city	46 109
					48	72176	027	Bell County	46 109
48	45072		Lufkin city	30 206					
48	45072	005	Angelina County	30 206	48	72368		Texarkana city	31 656
					48	72368	037	Bowie County	31 656
48	45384		McAllen city	84 021					
48	45384	215	Hidalgo County	84 021	48	72392		Texas City city	40 822
					48	72392	167	Galveston County	40 822
48	47892		Mesquite city	101 484					
48	47892	113	Dallas County	101 484	48	74144		Tyler city	75 450
					48	74144	423	Smith County	75 450
48	48072		Midland city	89 443					
48	48072	317	Martin County	0	48	75428		Victoria city	55 076
48	48072	329	Midland County	89 443	48	75428	469	Victoria County	55 076
48	48768		Mission city	28 653	48	76000		Waco city	103 590
48	48768	215	Hidalgo County	28 653	48	76000	309	McLennan County	103 590
48	48804		Missouri City city	36 176	48	79000		Wichita Falls city	96 259
48	48804	157	Fort Bend County	32 219	48	79000	009	Archer County	0
48	48804	201	Harris County	3 957	48	79000	485	Wichita County	96 259
48	50256		Nacogdoches city	30 872	49			**UTAH**	
48	50256	347	Nacogdoches County	30 872	49	07690		Bountiful city	36 659
					49	07690	011	Davis County	36 659
48	50820		New Braunfels city	27 334					
48	50820	091	Comal County	27 091	49	43660		Layton city	41 784
48	50820	187	Guadalupe County	243	49	43660	011	Davis County	41 784
48	52356		North Richland Hills city	45 895	49	45860		Logan city	32 762
48	52356	439	Tarrant County	45 895	49	45860	005	Cache County	32 762
48	53388		Odessa city	89 699	49	53230		Murray city	31 282
48	53388	135	Ector County	89 504	49	53230	035	Salt Lake County	31 282
48	53388	329	Midland County	195	49	55980		Ogden city	63 909
48	56000		Pasadena city	119 363	49	55980	057	Weber County	63 909
48	56000	201	Harris County	119 363	49	57300		Orem city	67 561
48	57200		Pharr city	32 921	49	57300	049	Utah County	67 561
48	57200	215	Hidalgo County	32 921	49	62470		Provo city	86 835
48	58016		Plano city	128 713	49	62470	049	Utah County	86 835
48	58016	085	Collin County	128 673	49	65330		St. George city	28 502
48	58016	121	Denton County	40	49	65330	053	Washington County	28 502
48	58820		Port Arthur city	58 724	49	67000		Salt Lake City city	159 936
48	58820	245	Jefferson County	58 724	49	67000	035	Salt Lake County	159 936
48	61796		Richardson city	74 840	49	67550		Sandy city	75 058
48	61796	085	Collin County	9 979	49	67550	035	Salt Lake County	75 058
48	61796	113	Dallas County	64 861					
48	63500		Round Rock city	30 923	49	82950		West Jordan city	42 892
48	63500	453	Travis County	0	49	82950	035	Salt Lake County	42 892
48	63500	491	Williamson County	30 923					

State Code	Place Code	County Code	Geographic Area Name	1990 population	State Code	Place Code	County Code	Geographic Area Name	1990 population
49	83445		West Valley City city	86 976	53	07695		Bremerton city	38 142
49	83445	035	Salt Lake County	86 976	53	07695	035	Kitsap County	38 142
50			**VERMONT**		53	20750		Edmonds city	30 744
50	10675		Burlington city	39 127	53	20750	061	Snohomish County	30 744
50	10675	007	Chittenden County	39 127	53	22640		Everett city	69 961
51			**VIRGINIA**		53	22640	061	Snohomish County	69 961
51	01000		Alexandria city	111 183	53	35275		Kennewick city	42 155
51	01000	510	Alexandria city	111 183	53	35275	005	Benton County	42 155
51	07784		Blacksburg town	34 590	53	35415		Kent city	37 960
51	07784	121	Montgomery County	34 590	53	35415	033	King County	37 960
51	14968		Charlottesville city	40 341	53	35940		Kirkland city	40 052
51	14968	540	Charlottesville city	40 341	53	35940	033	King County	40 052
51	16000		Chesapeake city	151 976	53	40245		Longview city	31 499
51	16000	550	Chesapeake city	151 976	53	40245	015	Cowlitz County	31 499
51	21344		Danville city	53 056	53	40840		Lynnwood city	28 695
51	21344	590	Danville city	53 056	53	40840	061	Snohomish County	28 695
51	35000		Hampton city	133 793	53	51300		Olympia city	33 840
51	35000	650	Hampton city	133 793	53	51300	067	Thurston County	33 840
51	35624		Harrisonburg city	30 707	53	57535		Redmond city	35 800
51	35624	660	Harrisonburg city	30 707	53	57535	033	King County	35 800
51	47672		Lynchburg city	66 049	53	57745		Renton city	41 688
51	47672	680	Lynchburg city	66 049	53	57745	033	King County	41 688
51	48952		Manassas city	27 957	53	58235		Richland city	32 315
51	48952	683	Manassas city	27 957	53	58235	005	Benton County	32 315
51	56000		Newport News city	170 045	53	63000		Seattle city	516 259
51	56000	700	Newport News city	170 045	53	63000	033	King County	516 259
51	57000		Norfolk city	261 229	53	67000		Spokane city	177 196
51	57000	710	Norfolk city	261 229	53	67000	063	Spokane County	177 196
51	61832		Petersburg city	38 386	53	70000		Tacoma city	176 664
51	61832	730	Petersburg city	38 386	53	70000	053	Pierce County	176 664
51	64000		Portsmouth city	103 907	53	74060		Vancouver city	46 380
51	64000	740	Portsmouth city	103 907	53	74060	011	Clark County	46 380
51	67000		Richmond city	203 056	53	75775		Walla Walla city	26 478
51	67000	760	Richmond city	203 056	53	75775	071	Walla Walla County	26 478
51	68000		Roanoke city	96 397	53	80010		Yakima city	54 827
51	68000	770	Roanoke city	96 397	53	80010	077	Yakima County	54 827
51	76432		Suffolk city	52 141	54			**WEST VIRGINIA**	
51	76432	800	Suffolk city	52 141	54	14600		Charleston city	57 287
51	82000		Virginia Beach city	393 069	54	14600	039	Kanawha County	57 287
51	82000	810	Virginia Beach city	393 069	54	39460		Huntington city	54 844
53			**WASHINGTON**		54	39460	011	Cabell County	50 505
53	03180		Auburn city	33 102	54	39460	099	Wayne County	4 339
53	03180	033	King County	33 102	54	55756		Morgantown city	25 879
53	05210		Bellevue city	86 874	54	55756	061	Monongalia County	25 879
53	05210	033	King County	86 874	54	62140		Parkersburg city	33 862
53	05280		Bellingham city	52 179	54	62140	107	Wood County	33 862
53	05280	073	Whatcom County	52 179					

State Code	Place Code	County Code	Geographic Area Name	1990 population	State Code	Place Code	County Code	Geographic Area Name	1990 population
54	86452		Wheeling city	34 882	55	51000		Menomonee Falls village	26 840
54	86452	051	Marshall County	182	55	51000	133	Waukesha County	26 840
54	86452	069	Ohio County	34 700					
					55	53000		Milwaukee city	628 088
55			**WISCONSIN**		55	53000	079	Milwaukee County	628 088
55	02375		Appleton city	65 695	55	53000	131	Washington County	0
55	02375	015	Calumet County	9 075	55	53000	133	Waukesha County	0
55	02375	087	Outagamie County	56 177					
55	02375	139	Winnebago County	443	55	56375		New Berlin city	33 592
					55	56375	133	Waukesha County	33 592
55	06500		Beloit city	35 573					
55	06500	105	Rock County	35 573	55	60500		Oshkosh city	55 006
					55	60500	139	Winnebago County	55 006
55	10025		Brookfield city	35 184					
55	10025	133	Waukesha County	35 184	55	66000		Racine city	84 298
					55	66000	101	Racine County	84 298
55	22300		Eau Claire city	56 856					
55	22300	017	Chippewa County	1 676	55	72975		Sheboygan city	49 676
55	22300	035	Eau Claire County	55 180	55	72975	117	Sheboygan County	49 676
55	26275		Fond du Lac city	37 757	55	78650		Superior city	27 134
55	26275	039	Fond du Lac County	37 757	55	78650	031	Douglas County	27 134
55	31000		Green Bay city	96 466	55	84250		Waukesha city	56 958
55	31000	009	Brown County	96 466	55	84250	133	Waukesha County	56 958
55	31175		Greenfield city	33 403	55	84475		Wausau city	37 060
55	31175	079	Milwaukee County	33 403	55	84475	073	Marathon County	37 060
55	37825		Janesville city	52 133	55	84675		Wauwatosa city	49 366
55	37825	105	Rock County	52 133	55	84675	079	Milwaukee County	49 366
55	39225		Kenosha city	80 352	55	85300		West Allis city	63 221
55	39225	059	Kenosha County	80 352	55	85300	079	Milwaukee County	63 221
55	40775		La Crosse city	51 003	56			**WYOMING**	
55	40775	063	La Crosse County	51 003	56	13150		Casper city	46 742
					56	13150	025	Natrona County	46 742
55	48000		Madison city	191 262					
55	48000	025	Dane County	191 262	56	13900		Cheyenne city	50 008
					56	13900	021	Laramie County	50 008
55	48500		Manitowoc city	32 520					
55	48500	071	Manitowoc County	32 520	56	45050		Laramie city	26 687
					56	45050	001	Albany County	26 687

APPENDIX F
SOURCE NOTES AND EXPLANATIONS

TABLE A—STATES

Table A presents 327 items for the United States as a whole, each state, and the District of Columbia. The states are presented in alphabetical order.

The following documentation is provided in the order in which the items appear in the databases.

LAND AREA, Items 1 and 5
Source: U.S. Bureau of the Census

Land area measurements are shown to the nearest square kilometer. Land area includes dry land and land temporarily or partially covered by water, such as marshlands, swamps, and river floodplains.

POPULATION, Item 2
Source: U.S. Bureau of the Census—2000 Census of Population and Housing.

The 2000 population data are from the decennial census and represent the resident population of the 50 states and the District of Columbia as of April 1, 2000.

POPULATION AND POPULATION CHANGE, Items 3–5; 29–30; and 33–37
Source: U.S. Bureau of the Census

The population data for 1999 are U.S. Bureau of the Census estimates of the resident population as of July 1 of that year.

The population data for 1980 and 1990 are from the decennial censuses and represent the resident population as of April 1, 1980 and 1990, respectively. The change in population between 1990 and 1999 is composed of (a) natural increase—the excess of births over deaths, and (b) net migration—the difference between the number of persons moving into a particular state and the number of persons moving out.

POPULATION PROJECTIONS, Items 31–32
Source: U.S. Bureau of the Census

These projections of the population in the years 2000 and 2025 are based on the 1990 census counts and the 1994 estimates of state population. Separate assumptions about future trends were developed for each component of population change: births; deaths; internal migration; and international migration. The state projections are consistent with the national population projection. The data in this volume are the Bureau of the Census' "preferred series"

(series A). Three alternative projection series are available from the Bureau of the Census.

Detailed data and information on projection methodology may be found in the Bureau of the Census publication *PPL-47, Population Projections for States, by Age, Sex, Race, and Hispanic Origin: 1995 to 2025*, Paul R. Campbell, U.S. Bureau of the Census, Washington, DC, 1996.

POPULATION CHARACTERISTICS, Items 6–20 and 38–54
Source: U.S. Bureau of the Census—1990 Census of Population and Housing for 1990 data and Census Bureau estimates for 1999 data

Population by race as defined by the Census Bureau, reflects self-identification by respondents; it does not denote any clear-cut scientific definition of biological stock.

The White population is defined as persons who indicated their race as white, as well as persons who did not classify themselves in one of the specific race categories listed on the questionnaire but entered a nationality such as Canadian, German, Italian, Lebanese, or Polish.

The Black population includes persons who indicated their race as black or Negro, as well as persons who did not classify themselves in one of the specific race categories but reported entries such as Haitian, Jamaican, Nigerian, or West Indian.

The American Indian, Eskimo, and Aleut population includes persons who indicated their race as Indian (American), Eskimo, or Aleut, as well as persons who did not indicate a specific race category but reported the name of an Indian tribe.

The Asian and Pacific Islander population includes persons who indicated their race as Chinese, Filipino, Japanese, Asian Indian, Korean, Vietnamese, Hawaiian, Samoan, and Guamanian, as well as persons who provided write-in entries of such Asian and Pacific Islander groups as Cambodian, Laotian, Pakistani, and Fiji Islander. Also, persons who wrote in an entry indicating one of the specific categories were classified accordingly.

Other race includes all persons not included in the race categories described above, including write-in entries such as multiracial, multi-ethnic, mixed, or a Hispanic group such as Mexican, Cuban, or Puerto Rican where a specific race was not mentioned.

The Hispanic population is based on a complete-count question that asked respondents to identify whether they were of Spanish/Hispanic origin. Persons marking any one of the four Hispanic categories (i.e., Mexican, Puerto Rican, Cuban, or other Spanish) are collectively referred to as Hispanic. Hispanic is not a race category; Hispanic persons may be of any race.

The foreign-born population is based on birthplace and citizenship questions asked of a sample of persons in the 1990 census.

Foreign-born includes persons not born in the United States, Puerto Rico, or an outlying area of the United States. Persons who were born in a foreign country but who have at least one American parent are not included.

Age is defined as age at last birthday (i.e., number of completed years from birth to April 1, 1990 for the 1990 Census.

The 1998 estimates were developed by the Census Bureau's Population Division using a traditional cohort component method. Starting with a basic population from the 1990 Census, each component of population change—births, deaths, domestic migration, and international migration—is estimated separately for each birth cohort by sex, race, and Hispanic origin.

HOUSEHOLDS, Items 21–27 and 55–59
Source: U.S. Bureau of the Census—1990 Census of Population and Housing for 1990 data and the Census Bureau Estimates for 1998 data

A household consists of persons occupying a single housing unit. A housing unit is a house, an apartment, a group of rooms, or a single room occupied as separate living quarters. The occupants may be a single family, one person living alone, two or more families living together, or any other group of related or unrelated persons who share a housing unit. The number of households is the same as the number of year-round occupied housing units.

A family household consists of two or more persons, including the householder, who are related by birth, marriage, or adoption and who live together as one household; all such persons are considered as members of one family. A married-couple family is one in which the householder and spouse are enumerated as members of the same household.

The measure of persons per household is obtained by dividing the number of persons in households by the number of households or householders. The category **Female family householder** includes only female-headed family households with no spouse present. 1998 estimates of the number of housing units are calculated by updating the number of housing units from the 1990 census with data on subsequent gains and losses to the housing inventory. One person in each household is designated as the householder. In most cases, this is the person, or one of the persons, in whose name the home is owned, being bought, or rented. If there is no such person in the household, any adult household member 15 years old and over could be designated as the householder.

IMMIGRANTS, Item 28
Source: U.S. Department of Justice, Immigration and Naturalization Service

The number of immigrants by their state of intended residence is summarized from the administrative records of the Immigration and Naturalization Service. This information is compiled from immigrant visas and forms granting legal permanent resident status.

An **immigrant** is an alien admitted to the United States as a lawful permanent resident. Immigrants are those persons lawfully accorded the privilege of residing permanently in the United States. They may be newly-arrived individuals who were issued immigrant visas by the Department of State overseas or they may be U.S. residents who were admitted to permanent resident status in 1996 by the Immigration and Naturalization Service in the United States.

BIRTHS AND DEATHS, Items 60–66
Source: U.S. Centers for Disease Control

The registration of births, deaths, and other vital events in the United States is primarily a state and local function. The civil laws of every state provide for a continuous and permanent birth and death registration system. Through the National Vital Statistics System, the National Center for Health Statistics (NCHS) obtains data on births and deaths from the registration offices of each state, New York City, and the District of Columbia.

Birth and death statistics are limited to events occurring during the year. The data are by place of residence and exclude events occurring to nonresidents of the United States. Births or deaths that occur outside the United States are excluded.

Birth and death rates represent the number of births and deaths per 1,000 resident population enumerated as of April 1 for decennial census years and estimated as of July 1 for other years.

Figures for infant deaths include deaths of children under 1 year of age—they exclude fetal deaths. The infant death rate is per 1,000 live births.

The rates of almost all causes of disease, injury, and death vary by age. Age adjustment is a technique for "removing" the effects of age from crude rates, so as to allow meaningful comparisons across populations with different underlying age structures. For example, comparing the crude death rate in Florida to that of California is misleading, since the relatively older population in Florida will lead to a higher crude death rate. For such a comparison, age-adjusted rates would be preferable.

Age-adjusted rates are calculated by applying the age-specific rates of various populations to a single standard population. In this volume, the standard population is 1940. Thus, the age-adjusted rates show what the 1998 death rates would be if the age structure of the population were the same as in 1940.

PHYSICIANS, Items 67–68
Source: Health Market Science, Inc., as published in Bernan's *Health and Healthcare in the United States*, copyright 1999 NationsHealth Corporation, LLC. Reprinted with permission.

Physicians are health practitioners having the degree of M.D. (Doctor of Medicine) or D.O. (Doctor of Osteopathy) primarily engaged in the practice of general or specialized medicine or surgery. The rate of physicians per 100,000 resident population is an indicator of the supply of physicians within a geographic area.

HOSPITALS, Items 69–71
Source: Health Market Science, Inc., as published in Bernan's *Health and Healthcare in the United States*, copyright 1999 NationsHealth Corporation, LLC. Reprinted with permission.

Hospitals are licensed institutions with at least six beds whose primary function is to provide diagnostic and therapeutic patient services for medical conditions by an organized physician staff, and have continuous nursing services under the supervision of registered nurses. Only short term general hospitals are included in these figures.

A hospital bed is any bed that is licensed for use by inpatients. The count of beds in a facility typically represents the count of beds at the end of reporting period (e.g., a year) regardless of whether it is operational or not. The number of hospitals beds per 100,000 population is a measure of the supply of hospitals beds within a geographic area.

MEDICARE ENROLLEES, Item 72
Source: Health Care Financing Administration

The Health Care Financing Administration (HCFA) administers Medicare which provides health insurance to people aged 65 and over and those who have permanent kidney failure and certain people with disabilities. Medicare has two parts: Hospital Insurance and Supplemental Medical Insurance. The numbers in this volume include persons enrolled in either or both parts of the program as of July 1, 1999, by their state of residence.

CRIME, Items 73–76
Source: U.S. Federal Bureau of Investigation—Uniform Crime Reports

Crime data are as reported to the FBI by law enforcement agencies and have not been adjusted for under-reporting. This may affect comparability between geographic areas or over time.

For some states, reporting by jurisdictions within the state is not sufficiently complete to be representative of the state as a whole, and state totals for these states have been estimated by the FBI.

Through the voluntary contribution of crime statistics by law enforcement agencies across the United States, the Uniform Crime Reporting (UCR) Program provides periodic assessments of crime in the nation as measured by offenses coming to the attention of the law enforcement community. The Committee on Uniform Crime Records of the International Association of Chiefs of Police initiated this voluntary national data-collection effort in 1930. UCR Program contributors compile and submit their crime data in 1 of 2 means: either directly to the FBI or through the state UCR Programs.

Seven offenses, because of their seriousness, frequency of occurrence, and likelihood of being reported to police, were initially selected to serve as an index for evaluating fluctuations in the volume of crime. These serious crimes were murder and nonnegligent manslaughter, forcible rape, robbery, aggravated assault, burglary, larceny/theft, and motor vehicle theft. By con-

gressional mandate, arson was added as the eighth index offense in 1979. Arson is not included in the totals given in this volume.

Violent offenses include 4 crime categories: (1) Murder and nonnegligent manslaughter, as defined in the UCR Program, is the willful (nonnegligent) killing of one human being by another. This offense excludes deaths caused by negligence, suicide or accident; justifiable homicides; and attempts to murder or assaults to murder. (2) Forcible rape is the carnal knowledge of a female forcibly and against her will. Assaults or attempts to commit rape by force or threat of force are also included; however, statutory rape (without force) and other sex offenses are excluded. (3) Robbery is the taking or attempting to take anything of value from the care, custody, or control of a person or persons by force or threat of force or violence and/or by putting the victim in fear. (4) Aggravated assault is an unlawful attack by 1 person upon another for the purpose of inflicting severe or aggravated bodily injury. This type of assault is usually accompanied by the use of a weapon or by means likely to produce death or great bodily harm. Attempts are included since an injury does not necessarily have to result when a gun, knife, or other weapon is used, which could and probably would result in a serious personal injury if the crime were successfully completed.

Property crimes include 3 categories: (1) Burglary, or breaking and entering, is the unlawful entry of a structure to commit a felony or theft, even though no force was used to gain entrance. (2) Larceny/theft is the unauthorized taking of the personal property of another, without the use of force. (3) Motor vehicle theft is the unauthorized taking of any motor vehicle.

ELEMENTARY AND SECONDARY SCHOOL ENROLLMENT, Items 77–78
Source: U.S. Department of Education, National Center for Education Statistics; Common Core of Data for public schools, and Private School Survey for private schools.

Data on public school enrollment is from the *Common Core of Data* 1997–1998 survey while that for private elementary and secondary enrollment is from the *Private School Survey* of 1997–1998. The private school figures include grades kindergarten through grade 12, including special education, vocational/technical education and alternative schools. Excluded from private enrollment is prekindergarten enrollment or enrollment in schools that do not offer first grade or above. Public school enrollment includes prekindergarten through grade 12.

EDUCATIONAL ATTAINMENT, Items 79–82
Source: U.S. Bureau of the Census—1990 Census of Population and Housing for 1990 data and the Current Population Survey for 2000 data

The 1990 census data on educational attainment were obtained from a sample of the population.

Statistics for educational attainment are for persons 25 years old and over. The 1990 data were derived from a question on the 1990 census questionnaire that asked respondents for the highest level of school they had completed or the highest degree they had received. The 1998 data were derived from a similar question on the Current Population Survey. Persons who passed a high school equivalency examination were considered high school graduates. Schooling received in foreign schools was to be reported as the equivalent grade or years in the regular American school system.

LOCAL GOVERNMENT EDUCATION EXPENDITURES, Items 83–84
Source: U.S. Department of Education, National Center for Education Statistics, Common Core of Data

These data pertain to expenditures for public elementary and secondary education. Current expenditures includes expenditures for instruction, school administration, operation and maintenance, student transportation, food services, support services, adult education, and community services. Total expenditures also includes capital outlay and interest on debt. Current expenditures per pupil is the current expenditures divided by the number of students in membership as reported in the Common Core of Data Nonfiscal Survey for school year 1997–1998. Student membership is the count of students enrolled on or about October 1.

MONEY INCOME AND POVERTY, Items 85–95
Source: U.S. Bureau of the Census—1990 Census of Population and Housing for 1989 data and the Current Population Survey for 1997–1999 data

The data on income and poverty are derived from the responses of a sample of persons 15 years and older. The data for 1989 are from the 1990 census "long form" sample—a sample large enough to permit publication of data for small geographic areas. The 1997–1999 data were gathered each March from a national sample of about 60,000 households. These data are available for states but not for counties or cities.

Total money income is defined by the Bureau of the Census for statistical purposes as the sum of the following: wage or salary income; nonfarm self-employment income; net farm self-employment income; Social Security and railroad retirement income; public assistance income; and all other regularly received income such as interest, dividends, veterans payments, pensions, unemployment compensation, and alimony. Receipts not counted as income include various "lump sum" payments such as capital gains or inheritances.

The total represents the amount of income received before deductions for personal income taxes, Social Security, bond purchases, union dues, Medicare deductions, etc.

Per capita income for 1989 is based on resident population enumerated as of April 1, 1990.

Household income includes the income of the householder and all other persons 15 years and older in the household. Median household income is usually less than median family income because many households consist of only 1 person. The median divides the income distribution into 2 equal parts, 1 having in-

comes above the median, the other with incomes below.

The constant-dollar figures are based on an annual average Consumer Price Index from the Bureau of Labor Statistics. Constant-dollar figures are estimates representing an effort to remove the effects of price changes from statistical series reported in dollar terms. However, the estimates do not reflect the price and cost-of-living differences that may exist between areas.

Money income differs in definition from personal income (item 98). For example, money income does not include the pension rights, employer provided health insurance, food stamps, or Medicare payments that are included in personal income.

Poverty status is based on the definition prescribed by the U.S. Office of Management and Budget as the standard to be used by federal agencies for statistical purposes. Families and persons are classified as below the poverty level if their total family income or unrelated individual income was less than the poverty threshold specified for the applicable family size, age of householder, and number of related children under 18 present. The poverty threshold for a 4-person family was $12,674 in 1989 and $17,029 in 1999.

In the 1990 census, poverty status was determined for all families (and by implication all family members). For persons not in families, poverty status is determined by their income in relation to the appropriate poverty threshold. Inmates of institutions, persons in military group quarters or college dormitories, and unrelated individuals under age 15 are excluded.

PERSONS LACKING HEALTH INSURANCE, Items 96–97
Source: U.S. Bureau of the Census—Current Population Survey

The data on which these estimates are based were gathered in March 2000 from a national sample of about 60,000 households — the same sample from which the 1999 data on income and poverty were obtained. Data are available for states but not for counties or cities.

Those lacking coverage are the percent of the population of each state who were covered neither by private health plans nor by Medicaid, Medicare, or military health care.

PERSONAL INCOME AND EARNINGS, Items 98–122
Source: U.S. Bureau of Economic Analysis, Regional Economic Information System

Total personal income is the current income received by residents of an area from all sources. It is measured before deductions of income and other personal taxes but after deduction of personal contributions for Social Security, government retirement, and other social insurance programs. It consists of wage and salary disbursements (covering all employee earnings, including executive salaries, bonuses, commissions, payments-in-kind, incentive payments, and tips), various types of supplementary earnings, such as employers' contributions to pension funds, (termed "other labor income"); proprietors' income; rental income of persons; dividends; personal interest income; and government and business transfer payments.

Proprietors' income is the monetary income and income in-kind of proprietorships and partnerships, including the independent professions, and of tax-exempt cooperatives. **Dividends** are cash payments by corporations to stockholders who are U.S. residents. **Interest** is the monetary and imputed interest income of persons from all sources. **Rent** is the monetary income of persons from the rental of real property, except the income of persons primarily engaged in the real estate business, the imputed net rental income of owner-occupants of nonfarm dwellings, and the royalties received by persons.

Transfer payments are income for which services are not currently rendered. They consist of both government and business transfer payments. Government transfer payments include payments under the following programs: Federal Old-age, Survivors, and Disability Insurance ("Social Security"); Medicare and medical vendor payments; unemployment insurance, railroad and government retirement; federal and state government-insured workers' compensation; veterans benefits, including veterans life insurance; food stamps; black lung; Supplemental Security Income; and Aid to Families with Dependent Children. Government payments to nonprofit institutions, other than for work under research and development contracts, are also included. The principal business transfers are corporate gifts to nonprofit institutions and consumer bad debts.

Per capita personal income is based on resident population estimated as of July 1 of the year shown.

Personal tax payments includes taxes paid by individuals to federal, state, and local governments. Personal taxes include individual income taxes, estate and gift taxes, motor vehicle license taxes, and personal property taxes. Personal contributions to social insurance ("social security taxes") are not included, nor are sales taxes.

Disposable personal income equals personal income less personal tax payments. It is a measure of the income available to persons for spending or saving.

Earnings cover wage and salary disbursements, other labor income, and proprietors' income.

Data for earnings obtained from the Bureau of Economic Analysis (BEA) are based on place of work. In computing personal income, BEA makes an "adjustment for residence" to earnings, based on commuting patterns so that personal income is presented on a place of residence basis.

Farm earnings include the income of farm workers (wages and salaries and other labor income) and farm proprietors. Farm proprietors' income includes only the income of sole proprietorships and partnerships.

Farm earning estimates are benchmarked to data collected in the Census of Agriculture and the revised U.S. Department of Agriculture state totals of income and expense items.

Goods related industries include mining, construction, and manufacturing. Service-related and other include private sector earnings in agricultural services, forestry and fisheries; transportation and public utilities; wholesale trade; retail trade; finance, insurance, and real estate; and services. Government earnings include all levels of government.

GROSS STATE PRODUCT, Item 123
Source: Bureau of Economic Analysis, Regional Economic Information System

GSP for a state is derived as the sum of gross state product originating in all industries in the state. In concept, an industry's GSP, referred to as its "value added," is equivalent to its gross output (sales or receipts and other operating income, commodity taxes, and inventory change) minus its intermediate inputs (consumption of goods and services purchased from other industries or imported). As such, it is often referred to as the state counterpart of the nation's gross domestic product (GDP). In practice, GSP estimates are measured as the sum of distributions by industry of the components of gross domestic income—that is, the sum of the costs incurred (such as compensation of employees, net interest, and indirect business taxes) and the profits earned in production.

HOUSING, Items 124–137
Source: U.S. Bureau of the Census—1990 Census of Population and Housing for 1990 data and the Current Population Survey for 1998 data

A **housing unit** is a house, apartment, mobile home or trailer, group of rooms, or single room occupied or, if vacant, intended for occupancy as separate living quarters. Separate living quarters are those in which the occupants do not live and eat with any other persons in the structure and which have direct access from the outside of the building through a common hall.

The occupants of a housing unit may be a single family, 1 person living alone, or 2 or more families living together, or any other group of related or unrelated persons who share living arrangements. Both occupied and vacant housing units are included in the housing inventory, with the exception that recreational vehicles, tents, caves, boats, railroad cars, and the like are included only if they are occupied as a person's usual place of residence.

A housing unit is classified as occupied if it is the usual place of residence of the person or group of persons living in it at the time of enumeration or if the occupants are only temporarily absent (e.g., away on vacation). A household consists of all persons who occupy a housing unit as their usual place of residence.

Median value is the dollar amount that divides the distribution of owner occupied housing units into 2 equal parts, one half of the units falling below this value and the other half exceeding it. Value is defined as the respondent's estimate of what the house would sell for if for sale. Data are presented for 1-family units on less than 10 acres and with no business or medical office on the property.

Median rent divides the distribution of renter-occupied housing units into 2 equal parts. The rent concept used in this volume is gross rent, which includes the amount of cash rent a renter pays (contract rent) plus the estimated average cost of utilities and fuels if paid by the renter. The rent is the amount of rent only for living quarters, not for any business or other space occupied. Single family houses on lots of 10 or more acres are excluded.

Housing cost as a percent of income is shown separately for owners with mortgages, owners without mortgages, and renters. Rent as a percent of income is a computed ratio of gross rent and monthly household income (total household income in 1989 divided by 12). Selected owner costs include utilities and fuels, as well as mortgage payments, insurance, taxes, etc. In each case, the ratio of housing cost to income is computed separately for each housing unit. The ratios for one-half of the units are above the median shown in this book, and one-half are below.

Substandard units are occupied units which are overcrowded or lack complete plumbing facilities. For the purposes of this item, "overcrowded" is defined as having 1.01 persons or more per room. Complete plumbing facilities include hot and cold piped water, a flush toilet, and a bathtub or shower. These facilities must be located inside the housing unit but not necessarily in the same room.

SOCIAL SECURITY AND SUPPLEMENTAL SECURITY INCOME, Items 138–140
Source: U.S. Social Security Administration

Social Security beneficiaries is the number of persons receiving benefits under the Old Age, Survivors, and Disability Insurance Program. These include retired or disabled workers covered by the program, their spouses and dependent children, and the surviving spouses and dependent children of deceased workers.

Supplemental Security Income (SSI) recipients is the number of persons receiving SSI payments. Data are as of December of the year shown.

CIVILIAN EMPLOYMENT, Items 141–143
Source: U.S. Bureau of the Census—
Current Population Survey, March 1999

Total employment includes all civilians 16 years old and older who were either (1) "at work" — those who did any work at all during the reference week as paid employees, worked in their own business or profession, worked on their own farm, or worked 15 hours or more as unpaid workers in a family farm or business; or were (2) "with a job, but not at work" — those who had a job but were not at work that week due to illness, weather, industrial dispute, vacation, or other personal reasons. The "reference week" for these employment questions was during March.

The **occupational categories** shown are consistent with the 1980 edition of the *Standard Occupational Classification Manual (SOC)*, published by the Office of Federal Statistical Policy and Standards, U.S. Department of Commerce. Professional, managerial, and technical occupations include the following categories: executive, administrative, and managerial occupations (000-042); professional specialty occupations (043-202); and technicians and related support occupations (203-242). Precision production, craft, and repair include SOC codes 503-702.

CIVILIAN LABOR FORCE AND UNEMPLOYMENT, Items 144–148
Source: U.S. Bureau of Labor Statistics

Data for the civilian labor force are the product of a federal-state cooperative program in which state employment security agencies prepare labor force and unemployment estimates under concepts, definitions, and technical procedures established by the Bureau of Labor Statistics. The civilian labor force consists of all civilians 16 years and over who are either employed or unemployed.

Unemployment includes all persons who did not work during the survey week, made specific efforts to find a job in the prior 4 weeks, and were available for work during the survey week (except for temporary illness). Persons waiting to be called back to a job from which they had been laid off and those waiting to report to a new job within the next 30 days are included in unemployment figures.

PRIVATE NONFARM EMPLOYMENT AND EARNINGS, Items 149–159
Source: U.S. Bureau of Labor Statistics,
Current Employment Survey

Data for private nonfarm employment and earnings are compiled from payroll information reported monthly on a voluntary basis to the BLS and its cooperating state agencies. More than 350,000 establishments represent all industries except agriculture.

Employment is the annual average of monthly totals of persons who received pay for any part of the pay period including the 12th day of the month. Included are all full-time and part-time workers in nonfarm establishments. Not covered are government employees, proprietors, the self-employed, unpaid volunteers or family workers, farm workers, and domestic workers in households. The data by industry conform to the definitions used in the 1987 Standard Industrial Classification (SIC).

Earnings of production workers in manufacturing industries are derived from reports of gross payrolls and corresponding paid hours. Payroll is reported before deductions of any kind. Total hours during the pay period include all hours worked (including overtime hours) and hours paid for holidays, vacations, and sick leave.

AGRICULTURE, Items 160–177
Source: U.S. Department of Agriculture,
National Agricultural Statistics Service
1997 Census of Agriculture

Data for the 1997 Census of Agriculture were collected in 1998 and pertain to the year 1997.

The Bureau of the Census took a census of agriculture every 10 years from 1840 to 1920 and roughly every 5 years from 1925 to 1992. The 1997 Census of Agriculture was transferred to the National Agricultural Statistics Service of the U.S. Department of Agriculture. Over time, the definition of a farm has varied. For recent censuses, including the 1997 census, a farm has been defined as any place from which $1,000 or more of agricultural products were sold or normally would have been sold during the census year.

The term **operator** refers to a person who operates a farm, either doing the work or making day-to-day decisions about such things as planting, harvesting, feeding, marketing, etc. The operator may be the owner, a member of the owner's household, a salaried manager, a tenant, a renter, or a sharecropper. For partnerships, only 1 partner is counted as an operator. For census purposes, the number of operators is the same as the number of farms.

The acreage designated as **land in farms** consists primarily of agricultural land used for crops, pasture, or grazing. It also includes woodland and wasteland not actually under cultivation or used for pasture or grazing, provided it was part of the farm operator's total operation.

Land in farms is an operating-unit concept and includes land owned and operated, as well as land rented from others. Land used rent free is classified as land rented from others. All land in Indian reservations used for growing crops or grazing livestock is classified as land in farms.

Irrigated land covers any land in farms to which water was artificially applied in the census year. Land irrigated prior to but not in the census year is not included. Irrigation may have been used for producing a harvested crop, for pasture or grazing lands, for cultivated summer fallow, or for land planted with a crop intended for future harvest. Land flooded during high-water periods was included as irrigated only if water was diverted to agricultural lands by dams, canals, or other works.

Cropland consists of land from which crops were harvested and land that could have been used for crops without additional improvements. This includes land in nonbearing orchards and vineyards, land from which any hay was cut, land on which crops failed, idle or fallow land, and land used for grazing purposes.

Respondents were asked to report their estimate of the current market **value of land and buildings** owned, rented, or leased from others, and rented and leased to others. Market value refers to the respondent's estimate of what the land and buildings would sell for under current market conditions.

The **value of machinery and equipment** was estimated by the respondent as the current market value of all cars, trucks, tractors, combines, balers, irrigation equipment, etc., used on the farm. This value is an estimate of what the machinery and equipment would sell for in its present condition and not the replacement or depreciated value. Share interests are reported at full value at the farm where the equipment and machinery are usually kept. Only equipment that was actually used in 1996 and 1997, or newly purchased but not yet used, and physically located at the farm on December 31, 1997 is included.

The **value of farm products sold** by farms represent the gross market value before taxes and production expenses of all agricultural products sold or removed from the place in 1997 regardless of who received the payment. It includes sales by the operator as well as the value of any share received by partners, landlords, contractors, and others associated with the operation. It represents the sum of all crops, including nursery products, sold and livestock and poultry and their products sold.

The value of crops sold in 1997 does not necessarily represent the sales from crops harvested that year. The data include sales from crops produced in earlier years and exclude some crops produced in 1997 but held in storage and not sold in the census year. For crops sold through a co-op that made payments in several installments, only the total value received in the census year was to be reported.

LAND USE, Items 178–179
Source: U.S. Department of Agriculture, Natural Resources Conservation Service, 1997 National Resources Inventory

The National Resources Inventory has been conducted every five years since 1982. The 1997 NRI is based on a sample of about 800,000 locations throughout the United States (excluding Alaska and the District of Columbia.) Federally owned lands include military bases, national forests, wildlife refuges, parks, grassland game preserves, scenic waterways, wilderness areas, monuments, lakeshore, parkways, battlefields, Bureau of Land Management lands, and other federal lands. Developed land includes any built-up area greater than 1/4 acre. Built-up areas include residential, industrial, commercial, and institutional land; construction sites; public administrative sites; railroad yards; cemeteries; airports; golf courses; sanitary landfills; sewage treatment plants; water control structures and spillways; other land used for such purposes; small parks (less than 10 acres) within urban and built-up areas; and highways, railroads, and other transportation facilities if they are surrounded by urban areas. Also included are tracts of less than 10 acres that do not meet the above definition but are completely surrounded by urban and built-up land and all highways, roads, railroads and associated rights-of-way outside urban and built-up areas (including private roads to farmsteads or ranch headquarters, logging roads, and other private roads).

WATER CONSUMPTION, Item 180
Source: U.S. Geological Survey, National Water Use Information Program, 1995 Water Use Data.

Every five years the U.S. Geological Survey compiles national water-use estimates. This volume includes the total freshwater withdrawals expressed as million gallons per day. Estimates of withdrawals of ground and surface water are given for the following categories of use: public water supplies, domestic, commercial, irrigation, livestock, industrial, mining, and thermoelectric power.

MANUFACTURES, Items 181–190
Source: U.S. Bureau of the Census— 1998 Annual Survey of Manufacturers

The Annual Survey of Manufacturers has been conducted every year since 1949.

The **all employees** number is the average number of production workers for the payroll periods including the 12th of March, May, August, and November plus the number of other employees in mid-

March. Included are all persons on paid sick leave, paid holidays, and paid vacations during the pay period. Officers of corporations are included as employees—proprietors and partners of unincorporated firms are excluded.

Payroll figures include the gross annual earnings of all employees on the payroll of operating manufacturing establishments. The definition, which is the same as the one used for calculating the federal withholding tax, includes all forms of compensation, such as salaries, wages, commissions, dismissal pay, all bonuses, vacation and sick leave pay, and compensation-in-kind, prior to such deductions as employees' Social Security contributions, withholding taxes, group insurance, union dues, and savings bonds. The total includes salaries of officers of corporations but excludes payments to proprietors or partners of unincorporated concerns. Also excluded are payments to members of the Armed Forces and to pensioners carried on the active payroll of manufacturing establishments.

Production workers include workers (up through the line-supervisor level) engaged in fabricating; processing; assembling; inspecting; receiving; storing; handling; packing; warehousing; shipping (but not delivering); maintenance; repair; janitorial and guard services; product development; auxiliary production for plant's own use (e.g., power plant); record-keeping; and other services closely associated with these production operations. Employees above the working supervisor level are excluded.

The number of production workers is the average for the payroll periods including the 12th of March, May, August, and November. Not included in this classification are all other employees, defined as non-production employees, including those engaged in factory supervision above the line-supervisor level.

Production worker hours cover hours worked or paid for at the plant, including actual overtime hours (not straight-time-equivalent hours). The data exclude hours paid for vacations, holidays, or sick leave. Production wages represent all compensation paid to production workers.

Value added by manufacture is derived by subtracting the cost of materials, supplies, containers, fuel, purchased electricity, and contract work from the value of shipments (products manufactured plus receipts for services rendered). The result of this calculation is adjusted by the addition of value added by merchandising operations (i.e., the difference between the sales value and cost of merchandise sold without further manufacture, processing, or assembly) plus the net change in finished goods and work in process between the beginning-and end-of-year inventories.

Value of shipments covers the received or receivable net selling values; free on board plant (exclusive freight charges and taxes) of all products shipped, both primary and secondary; as well as miscellaneous receipts, such as receipts for contract work performed for others, installation and repair, sales of scrap, and sales of products bought and resold without further processing. Included are all items made by or for the establishment from materials owned by it, whether sold, transferred to other plants of the same company, or shipped on consignment. The net selling value of products made in 1 plant on a contract basis from materials owned by another was reported by the plant providing the materials.

In the case of multi-unit companies, the manufacturer was requested to report the value of products transferred to other establishments of the same company at full economic or commercial value, including not only the direct costs of production but also a reasonable proportion of "all other costs" (including company overhead) and profit.

The aggregate of the value of shipments figure for industry groups and for all manufacturing industries includes large amounts of duplication since the products of some industries are used as materials by others. Estimates as to the overall extent of this duplication indicate that the value of manufactured products exclusive of such duplication (the value of finished manufactures) tend to approximate two-thirds of the total value of products reported in the census of manufactures.

TOTAL CAPITIAL EXPENDITURES (NEW AND USED)

For establishments in operation and any known plants under construction, manufacturers were asked to report their new and used expenditures for (1) permanent additions and major alterations to manufacturing establishments and (2) machinery and equipment used for replacement and additions to plant capacity if they were of the type for which depreciation accounts were ordinarily maintained.

Totals for expenditures include the costs of assets leased from nonmanufacturing concerns through capital leases. New facilities owned by the federal government but operated under contract by private companies and plant and equipment furnished to the manufacturer by communities and nonprofit organizations are excluded. Also excluded are expenditures for land and cost of maintenance and repairs charged as current operating expenses.

For any equipment or structure transferred for the use of the reporting establishment by the parent company or one of its subsidiaries, the value at which it was transferred to the establishment was to be reported.

If an establishment changed ownership during the year, the cost of the fixed assets (building and equipment) was to be reported.

1997 ECONOMIC CENSUS: OVERVIEW
Items 191–278
Source: U.S. Bureau of the Census

The Economic Census provides a detailed portrait of the nation's economy once every five years, from the national to the local level. The 1997 Economic Census covers nearly all of the U.S. economy in its basic collection of establishment statistics. It is the first major data source to use the new North American Industry Classification System (NAICS) and is therefore not comparable to economic data from prior years which were based on the Standard Industrial Classification (SIC) system.

NAICS, developed in cooperation with Canada and Mexico, classifies North America's economic activities at 2-, 3-, 4-, and 5-digit levels of detail, and the U.S. version of NAICS further defines industries to a sixth digit. The Economic Census takes advantage of this hierarchy to publish data at these successive levels of detail: sector (2-digit); subsector (3-digit); industry group (4-digit); industry(5-digit); and U.S. industry(6-digit.) Information in Table A is at the 2-digit level, with a few 3- and 4-digit items.

Several key statistics are tabulated for all industries included in this volume: number of establishments (or companies); number of employees; payroll; and a measure of output (sales, receipts, revenue, value of shipments, or value of construction work done.)

Number of Establishments. An establishment is a single physical location at which business is conducted. It is not necessarily identical with a company or enterprise, which may consist of one establishment or more. Economic Census figures represent a summary of reports for individual establishments rather than companies. For cases where a census report was received, separate information was obtained for each location where business was conducted. When administrative records of other Federal agencies were used instead of a census report, no information was available on the number of locations operated. Each Economic Census establishment was tabulated according to the physical location at which the business was conducted. The count of establishments represents those in business at any time during 1997.

When two activities or more were carried on at a single location under a single ownership, all activities generally were grouped together as a single establishment. The entire establishment was classified on the basis of its major activity and all data for it were included in that classification. However, when distinct and separate economic activities (for which different industry classification codes were appropriate) were conducted at a single location under a single ownership, separate establishment reports for each of the different activities were obtained in the census.

Number of Employees. Paid employees consist of the full-time and part-time employees, including salaried officers and executives of corporations. Included are employees on paid sick leave, paid holidays, and paid vacations; not included are proprietors and partners of unincorporated businesses. The definition of paid employees is the same as that used on IRS form 941.

Payroll. Payroll includes all forms of compensation such as salaries, wages, commissions, dismissal pay, bonuses, vacation allowances, sick-leave pay, and employee contributions to qualified pension plans paid during the year to all employees. For corporations, payroll includes amounts paid to officers and executives; for unincorporated businesses, it does not include profit or other compensation of proprietors or partners. Payroll is reported before deductions for social security, income tax, insurance, union dues, etc. This definition of payroll is the same as that used by the Internal Revenue Service (IRS) on form 941.

Sales, Shipments, Receipts, Revenue, or Business Done. This measure includes the total sales, shipments, receipts, revenue, or business done by establishments within the scope of the Economic Census. The definition of each of these items is specific to the economic sector measured.

CONSTRUCTION (Items 191–194)
Source: U.S. Bureau of the Census,
1997 Economic Census
(See Overview of 1997 Economic Census prior to
Item 191)

The Construction sector (sector 23) comprises establishments primarily engaged in the construction of buildings and other structures, heavy construction (except buildings), additions, alterations, reconstruction, installation, and maintenance and repairs. Establishments engaged in demolition or wrecking of buildings and other structures, clearing of building sites, and sale of materials from demolished structures are also included. This sector also includes those establishments engaged in blasting, test drilling, landfill, leveling, earthmoving, excavating, land drainage, and other land preparation. The industries within this sector have been defined on the basis of their unique production processes. As with all industries, the production processes are distinguished by their use of specialized human resources and specialized physical capital. Construction activities are generally administered or managed at a relatively fixed place of business, but the actual construction work is performed at one or more different project sites. This sector is divided into three subsectors of construction activities: (1) building construction and land subdivision and land development; (2) heavy construction (except buildings), such as highways, power plants, and pipelines; and (3) construction activity by special trade contractors.

WHOLESALE TRADE, Items 195–198
Source: U.S. Bureau of the Census,
1997 Economic Census
(See Overview of 1997 Economic Census
prior to Item 191)

The Wholesale Trade sector (sector 42) comprises establishments engaged in wholesaling merchandise, generally without transformation, and rendering services incidental to the sale of merchandise. The wholesaling process is an intermediate step in the distribution of merchandise. Wholesalers are organized to sell or arrange the purchase or sale of (a) goods for resale (i.e., goods sold to other wholesalers or retailers), (b) capital or durable nonconsumer goods, and (c) raw and intermediate materials and supplies used in production.

Wholesalers sell merchandise to other businesses and normally operate from a warehouse or office. These warehouses and offices are characterized by having little or no display of merchandise. In addition, neither the design nor the location of the premises is intended to solicit walk-in traffic. Wholesalers do not normally use advertising directed to the general public. Customers are generally reached initially via telephone, in-person marketing, or by specialized advertising that may include Internet and other electronic means. Follow-up orders are either vendor-initiated or client-initiated, generally based on previous sales, and typically exhibit strong ties between sellers and buyers. In fact, transactions are often conducted between wholesalers and clients that have long-standing business relationships.

This sector comprises two main types of wholesalers: those that sell goods on their own account and those that arrange sales and purchases for others for a commission or fee.

(1) Establishments that sell goods on their own account are known as wholesale merchants, distributors, jobbers, drop shippers, import/export merchants, and sales branches. These establishments typically maintain their own warehouse, where they receive and handle goods for their customers. Goods are generally sold without transformation, but may include integral functions, such as sorting, packaging, labeling, and other marketing services.

(2) Establishments arranging for the purchase or sale of goods owned by others or purchasing goods on a commission basis are known as agents and brokers, commission merchants, import/export agents and brokers, auction companies, and manufacturers' representatives. These establishments operate from offices and generally do not own or handle the goods they sell.

Some wholesale establishments may be connected with a single manufacturer and promote and sell the particular manufacturer's products to a wide range of other wholesalers or retailers. Other wholesalers may be connected to a retail chain or a limited number of retail chains and only provide a variety of products needed by that particular retail operation(s). These wholesalers may obtain the products from a wide range of manufacturers. Still other wholesalers may not take title to the goods, but act as agents and brokers for a commission.

Although, in general, wholesaling normally denotes sales in large volumes, durable nonconsumer goods may be sold in single units. Sales of capital or durable nonconsumer goods used in the production of goods and services, such as farm machinery, medium and heavy duty trucks, and industrial machinery, are always included in wholesale trade.

RETAIL TRADE, Items 199–206
Source: U.S. Bureau of the Census,
1997 Economic Census
(See Overview of 1997 Economic Census
prior to Item 191)

The Retail Trade sector (44-45) comprises establishments engaged in retailing merchandise, generally without transformation, and rendering services incidental to the sale of merchandise.

The retailing process is the final step in the distribution of merchandise; retailers are, therefore, organized to sell merchandise in small quantities to the general public. This sector comprises two main types of retailers: store and nonstore retailers.

Store retailers operate fixed point-of-sale locations, located and designed to attract a high volume of walk-in customers. In general, retail stores have extensive displays of merchandise and use mass-media advertising to attract customers. They typically sell merchandise to the general public for personal or household consumption, but some also serve business and institutional clients. These include establishments, such as office supply stores, computer and software stores, building materials dealers, plumbing supply stores, and electrical supply stores. Catalog showrooms, gasoline service stations, automotive dealers, and mobile home dealers are treated as store retailers.

In addition to retailing merchandise, some types of store retailers are also engaged in the provision of after-sales services, such as repair and installation. For example, new automobile dealers, electronic and appliance stores, and musical instrument and supply stores often provide repair services. As a general rule, establishments engaged in retailing merchandise and providing after-sales services are classified in this sector.

Nonstore retailers, like store retailers, are organized to serve the general public, but their retailing methods differ. The establishments of this subsector reach customers and market merchandise with methods, such as the broadcasting of "infomercials," the broadcasting and publishing of direct-response advertising, the publishing of paper and electronic catalogs, door-to-door solicitation, in-home demonstration, selling from portable stalls (street vendors, except food), and distribution through vending machines. Establishments engaged in the direct sale (nonstore) of products, such as home heating oil dealers and home delivery newspaper routes.

The buying of goods for resale is a characteristic of retail trade establishments that particularly distinguishes them from establishments in the agriculture, manufacturing, and construction industries. For example, farms that sell their products at or from the point of production are not classified in retail, but rather in agriculture. Similarly, establishments that both manufacture and sell their products to the general public are not classified in retail, but rather in manufacturing. However, establishments that engage in processing activities incidental to retailing are classified in retail.

Industries in the **Motor Vehicle and Parts Dealers** subsector (441) retail motor vehicle and parts merchandise from fixed point-of-sale locations. Establishments in this subsector typically operate from a showroom and/or an open lot where the vehicles are on display. The display of vehicles and the related parts require little by way of display equipment. The personnel generally include both the sales and sales support staff familiar with the requirements for registering and financing a vehicle as well as a staff of parts experts and mechanics trained to provide repair and maintenance services for the vehicles. Specific industries have been included in this subsector to identify the type of vehicle being retailed. Sales of capital or durable nonconsumer goods, such as medium and heavy-duty trucks, are always included in wholesale trade. These goods are virtually never sold through retail methods.

Industries in the **Food and Beverage Stores** subsector (445) usually retail food and beverage merchandise from fixed point-of-sale locations. Establishments in this subsector have special equipment (e.g., freezers, refrigerated display cases, refrigerators) for displaying food and beverage goods. They have staff trained in the processing of food products to guarantee the proper storage and sanitary conditions required by regulatory authority.

Industries in the **Clothing and Clothing Accessories Stores** subsector (448) retail new clothing and clothing accessories merchandise from fixed point-of-sale locations. Establishments in this subsector have similar display equipment and staff that is knowledgeable regarding fashion trends and the proper match of styles, colors, and combinations of clothing and accessories to the characteristics and tastes of the customer.

Industries in the **General Merchandise Stores** subsector (452) retail new general merchandise from fixed point-of-sale locations. Establishments in this subsector are unique in that they have the equipment and staff capable of retailing a large variety of goods from a single location. This includes a variety of display equipment and staff trained to provide information on many lines of products.

TRANSPORTATION AND WAREHOUSING, Items 207–210
Source: U.S. Bureau of the Census, 1997 Economic Census (See Overview of 1997 Economic Census prior to Item 191)

The Transportation and Warehousing sector (48-49) includes industries providing transportation of passengers and cargo, warehousing and storage for goods, scenic and sightseeing transportation, and support activities related to modes of transportation. Establishments in these industries use transportation equipment or transportation related facilities as a productive asset. The type of equipment depends on the mode of transportation. The modes of transportation are air, rail, water, road, and pipeline.

The Transportation and Warehousing sector distinguishes three basic types of activities: subsectors for each mode of transportation, a subsector for warehousing and storage, and a subsector for establishments providing support activities for transportation. In addition, there are subsectors for establishments that provide passenger transportation for scenic and sightseeing purposes, postal services, and courier services.

FINANCE AND INSURANCE, Items 211–214
Source: U.S. Bureau of the Census, 1997 Economic Census (See Overview of 1997 Economic Census prior to Item 191)

The Finance and Insurance sector (52) comprises establishments primarily engaged in financial transactions (transactions involving the creation, liquidation, or change in ownership of financial assets) and/or in facilitating financial transactions. Three principal types of activities are identified:

(1) Raising funds by taking deposits and/or issuing securities and, in the process, incurring liabilities. Establishments engaged in this activity use raised funds to acquire financial assets by making loans and/or purchasing securities. Putting themselves at risk, they channel funds from lenders to borrowers and transform or repackage the funds with respect to maturity, scale and risk. This activity is known as financial intermediation.

(2) Pooling of risk by underwriting insurance and annuities. Establishments engaged in this activity collect fees, insurance premiums, or annuity considerations; build up reserves; invest those reserves; and make contractual payments. Fees are based on the expected incidence of the insured risk and the expected return on investment.

(3) Providing specialized services facilitating or supporting financial intermediation, insurance, and employee benefit programs.

In addition, monetary authorities charged with monetary control are included in this sector.

REAL ESTATE AND RENTAL AND LEASING, Items 215–218
Source: U.S. Bureau of the Census, 1997 Economic Census (See Overview of 1997 Economic Census prior to Item 191)

The Real Estate and Rental and Leasing sector (53) comprises establishments primarily engaged in renting, leasing, or otherwise allowing the use of tangible or intangible assets, and establishments providing related services. The major portion of this sector comprises establishments that rent, lease, or otherwise allow the use of their own assets by others. The assets may be tangible, as is the case of real estate and equipment, or intangible, as is the case with patents and trademarks.

This sector also includes establishments primarily engaged in managing real estate for others, selling, renting and/or buying real estate for others, and appraising real estate. These activities are closely related to this sector's main activity, and it was felt that from a production basis they would best be included here. In addition, a substantial proportion of property management is self-performed by lessors.

The main components of this sector are the real estate lessors industries; equipment lessors industries (including motor vehicles, computers, and consumer goods); and lessors of nonfinancial intangible assets (except copyrighted works).

INFORMATION, Items 219–226
Source: U.S. Bureau of the Census, 1997 Economic Census (See Overview of 1997 Economic Census prior to Item 191)

The Information sector (51) comprises establishments engaged in the following processes: (a) producing and distributing information and cultural products, (b) providing the means to transmit or distribute these products as well as data or communications, and (c) processing data.

The main components of this sector are the publishing industries, including software publishing, the motion picture and sound recording industries, the broadcasting and telecommunications industries, and the information services and data processing industries.

For the purpose of NAICS, it is the transformation of information into a commodity that is produced and distributed by a number of growing industries that is at issue. The Information sector groups three types of establishments: (1) those engaged in producing and distributing information and cultural products; (2) those that provide the means to transmit or distribute these products as well as data or communications; and (3) those that process data. Cultural products are those that directly express attitudes, opinions, ideas, values, and artistic creativity; provide entertainment; or offer information and analysis concerning the past and present. Included in this definition are popular, mass-produced, products as well as cultural products that normally have a more limited audience, such as poetry books, literary magazines, or classical records. These activities were formerly classified throughout the existing national classifications. Traditional publishing was in manufacturing; broadcasting in communications; software production in business services; film production in amusement services; and so forth.

Industries in the **Publishing Industries** subsector (511) group establishments engaged in the publishing of newspapers, magazines, other periodicals, and books, as well as database and software publishing. In general, these establishments, which are known as publishers, issue copies of works for which they usually possess copyright. Works may be in one or more formats including traditional print form, CD-ROM, or on-line. Publishers may publish works originally created by others for which they have obtained the rights and/or works that they have created in-house. Software publishing is included here because the activity, creation of a copyrighted product and bringing it to market, is equivalent to the creation process for other types of intellectual products.

In NAICS, publishing—the reporting, writing, editing, and other processes that are required to create an edition of a book or a newspaper—is treated as a major economic activity in its own right, rather than as a subsidiary activity to a manufacturing activity, printing. Thus, publishing is classified in the Information sector; whereas, printing remains in the NAICS Manufacturing sector. In part, the NAICS classification reflects the fact that publishing increasingly takes place in establishments that are physically separate from the associated printing establishments. More crucially, the NAICS classification of book and newspaper publishing is intended to portray their roles in a modern economy, in which they do not resemble manufacturing activities.

Music publishers are not included in the Publishing Industries subsector, but are included in the Motion Picture and Sound Recording Industries subsector. Reproduction of prepackaged software is treated in NAICS as a manufacturing activity; on-line distribution of software products is in the Information sector, and custom design of software to client specifications is included in the Professional, Scientific, and Technical Services sector. These distinctions arise because of the different ways that software is created, reproduced, and distributed.

The Information sector does not include products, such as manifold business forms. Information is not the essential component of these items. Establishments producing these items are included in Subsector 323, Printing and Related Support Activities.

Industries in the **Motion Picture and Sound Recording Industries** subsector (512) group establishments involved in the production and distribution of motion pictures and sound recordings. While producers and distributors of motion pictures and sound recordings issue works for sale as traditional publishers do, the processes are sufficiently different to warrant placing establishments engaged in these activities in a separate subsector. Produc-

tion is typically a complex process that involves several distinct types of establishments that are engaged in activities, such as contracting with performers, creating the film or sound content, and providing technical postproduction services. Film distribution is often to exhibitors, such as theaters and broadcasters, rather than through the wholesale and retail distribution chain. When the product is in a mass-produced form, NAICS treats production and distribution as the major economic activity as it does in the Publishing Industries subsector, rather than as a subsidiary activity to the manufacture of such products.

This subsector does not include establishments primarily engaged in the wholesale distribution of video cassettes and sound recordings, such as compact discs and audio tapes; these establishments are included in the Wholesale Trade sector. Reproduction of video cassettes and sound recordings that is carried out separately from establishments engaged in production and distribution is treated in NAICS as a manufacturing activity.

Industries in the **Broadcasting and Telecommunications** subsector (513) include establishments providing point-to-point communications and the services related to that activity. The industry groups (Radio and Television Broadcasting, Cable Networks and Program Distribution, and Telecommunications) are based on differences in the methods of communication and in the nature of services provided. The Radio and Television Broadcasting industry group includes establishments that operate broadcasting studios and facilities for over the air or satellite delivery of radio and television programs of entertainment, news, talk, and the like. These establishments are often engaged in the production and purchase of programs and generating revenues from the sale of air time to advertisers and from donations, subsidies, and/or the sale of programs. The Cable Networks and Program Distribution industry group includes two types of establishments. Those in the Cable Networks industry operate studios and facilities for the broadcasting of programs that are typically narrowcast in nature (limited format, such as news, sports, education, and youth-oriented programming). The services of these establishments are typically sold on a subscription or fee basis. Delivery of the programs to customers is handled by other establishments, in the Cable and Other Program Distribution industry, that operate cable systems, direct-to-home satellite systems, or other similar systems. The Telecommunications industry group is primarily engaged in operating, maintaining, and/or providing access to facilities for the transmission of voice, data, text, sound, and full motion picture video between network termination points. A transmission facility may be based on a single technology or a combination of technologies. Establishments primarily engaged as independent contractors in the maintenance and installation of broadcasting and telecommunications systems are classified in Sector 23, Construction.

Industries in the **Information Services and Data Processing Services** subsector (514) group establishments providing information, storing information, providing access to information, and processing information. The main components of the subsector are news syndicates, libraries, archives, on-line information service providers, and data processors.

UTILITIES, Items 227–230
Source: U.S. Bureau of the Census, 1997 Economic Census
(See Overview of 1997 Economic Census prior to Item 191)

The Utilities sector (22) comprises establishments engaged in the provision of the following utility services: electric power, natural gas, steam supply, water supply, and sewage removal. Within this sector, the specific activities associated with the utility services provided vary by utility: electric power includes generation, transmission, and distribution; natural gas includes distribution; steam supply includes provision and/or distribution; water supply includes treatment and distribution; and sewage removal includes collection, treatment, and disposal of waste through sewer systems and sewage treatment facilities.

Excluded from this sector are establishments primarily engaged in waste management services classified in Subsector 562, Waste Management and Remediation Services, which also collect, treat, and dispose of waste materials; however, they do not use sewer systems or sewage treatment facilities.

PROFESSIONAL, SCIENTIFIC, AND TECHNICAL SERVICES, Items 231–238
Source: U.S. Bureau of the Census, 1997 Economic Census
(See Overview of 1997 Economic Census prior to Item 191)

The Professional, Scientific, and Technical Services sector (54) comprises establishments that specialize in performing professional, scientific, and technical activities for others. These activities require a high degree of expertise and training. The establishments in this sector specialize according to expertise and provide these services to clients in a variety of industries and, in some cases, to households. Activities performed include: legal advice and representation; accounting, bookkeeping, and payroll services; architectural, engineering, and specialized design services; computer services; consulting services; research services; advertising services; photographic services; translation and interpretation services; veterinary services; and other professional, scientific, and technical services.

This volume includes only those establishments subject to federal income tax.

This sector excludes establishments primarily engaged in providing a range of day-to-day office administrative services, such as financial planning, billing and recordkeeping, personnel, and physical distribution and logistics. These establishments are classified in Sector 56, Administrative and Support and Waste Management and Remediation Services.

Legal Services is a NAICS industry group (5411) that includes establishments classified in the following NAICS industries: 54111, Offices of Lawyers; and 54119, Other Legal Services.

Accounting, Tax Preparation, Bookkeeping, and Payroll Services is a NAICS industry group (5412) that comprises establishments primarily engaged in providing services, such as auditing of accounting records, designing accounting systems, preparing financial statements, developing budgets, preparing tax returns, processing payrolls, bookkeeping, and billing.

Architectural, Engineering, and Related Services is a NAICS industry group (5413) that includes establishments classified in the following NAICS industries: 54131, Architectural Services; 54133, Engineering Services; 54134, Drafting Services; 54135, Building Inspection Services; 54136, Geophysical Surveying and Mapping Services; 54137, Surveying and Mapping (Except Geophysical) Services; and 54138, Testing Laboratories.

Computer Systems Design and Related Services is a NAICS industry that comprises establishments primarily engaged in providing expertise in the field of information technologies through one or more of the following activities: (1) writing, modifying, testing, and supporting software to meet the needs of a particular customer; (2) planning and designing computer systems that integrate computer hardware, software, and communication technologies; (3) on-site management and operation of clients' computer systems and/or data processing facilities; and (4) other professional and technical computer-related advice and services.

ARTS, ENTERTAINMENT, AND RECREATION, Items 239–242
Source: U.S. Bureau of the Census, 1997 Economic Census
(See Overview of 1997 Economic Census prior to Item 191)

The Arts, Entertainment, and Recreation sector (71) includes a wide range of establishments that operate facilities or provide services to meet varied cultural, entertainment, and recreational interests of their patrons. This sector comprises (1) establishments that are involved in producing, promoting, or participating in live performances, events, or exhibits intended for public viewing; (2) establishments that preserve and exhibit objects and sites of historical, cultural, or educational interest; and (3) establishments that operate facilities or provide services that enable patrons to participate in recreational activities or pursue amusement, hobby, and leisure time interests.

Some establishments that provide cultural, entertainment, or recreational facilities and services are classified in other sectors. Excluded from this sector are: (1) establishments that provide both accommodations and recreational facilities, such as hunting and fishing camps and resort and casino hotels are classified in Subsector 721, Accommodation; (2) restaurants and night clubs that provide live entertainment in addition to the sale of food and beverages are classified in Subsector 722, Food Services and Drinking Places; (3) motion picture theaters, libraries and archives, and publishers of newspapers, magazines, books, periodicals, and computer software are classified in Sector 51, Information; and (4) establishments using transportation equipment to provide recreational and entertainment services, such as those operating sightseeing buses, dinner cruises, or helicopter rides are classified in Subsector 487, Scenic and Sightseeing Transportation.

HEALTH CARE AND SOCIAL ASSISTANCE, Items 243–254
Source: U.S. Bureau of the Census, 1997 Economic Census
(See Overview of 1997 Economic Census prior to Item 191)

The Health Care and Social Assistance sector (62) comprises establishments providing health care and social assistance for individuals. The sector includes both health care and social assistance because it is sometimes difficult to distinguish between the boundaries of these two activities. The industries in this sector are arranged on a continuum starting with those establishments providing medical care exclusively, continuing with those providing health care and social assistance, and finally finishing with those providing only social assistance. The services provided by establishments in this sector are delivered by trained professionals. All industries in the sector share this commonality of process, namely, labor inputs of health practitioners or social workers with the requisite expertise. Many of the industries in the sector are defined based on the educational degree held by the practitioners included in the industry.

In this volume, taxable and tax-exempt establishments are presented separately.

Excluded from this sector are aerobic classes in Subsector 713, Amusement, Gambling and Recreation Industries and nonmedical diet and weight reducing centers in Subsector 812, Personal and Laundry Services. Although these can be viewed as health services, these services are not typically delivered by health practitioners.

Industries in the **Ambulatory Health Care Services** subsector (621) provide health care services directly or indirectly to ambulatory patients and do not usually provide inpatient services. Health practitioners in this subsector provide outpatient services, with the facilities and equipment not usually being the most significant part of the production process.

Industries in the **Hospitals** subsector (622) provide medical, diagnostic, and treatment services that include physician, nursing, and other health services to inpatients and the specialized accommodation services required by inpatients. Hospitals may also provide outpatient services as a secondary activity. Establishments in the Hospitals subsector provide inpatient health services, many of which can only be provided using the specialized facilities and equipment that form a significant and integral part of the production process.

ACCOMMODATION AND FOOD SERVICES, Items 255–259
Source: U.S. Bureau of the Census, 1997 Economic Census
(See Overview of 1997 Economic Censu prior to Item 191)

The Accommodation and Food Services sector (72) comprises establishments providing customers with lodging and/or preparing meals, snacks, and beverages for immediate consumption. The sector includes both accommodation and food services establishments because the two activities are often combined at the same establishment.

Excluded from this sector are civic and social organizations; amusement and recreation parks; theaters; and other recreation or entertainment facilities providing food and beverage services.

Industries in the **Food Services and Drinking Places** subsector (722) prepare meals, snacks, and beverages to customer order for immediate on-premises and off-premises consumption. There is a wide range of establishments in these industries. Some provide food and drink only; while others provide various combinations of seating space, waiter/waitress services and incidental amenities, such as limited entertainment. The industries in the subsector are grouped based on the type and level of services provided. The industry groups are full-service restaurants; limited-service eating places; special food services, such as food service contractors, caterers, and mobile food services, and drinking places.

Food services and drink activities at hotels and motels; amusement parks, theaters, casinos, country clubs, and similar recreational facilities; and civic and social organizations are included in this subsector only if these services are provided by a separate establishment primarily engaged in providing food and beverage services.

Excluded from this subsector are establishments operating dinner cruises. These establishments are classified in Subsector 487, Scenic and Sightseeing Transportation because those establishments utilize transportation equipment to provide scenic recreational entertainment.

OTHER SERVICES, Items 260–266
Source: U.S. Bureau of the Census, 1997 Economic Census
(See Overview of 1997 Economic Census prior to Item 191)

The Other Services (except Public Administration) sector (81) comprises establishments engaged in providing services not specifically provided for elsewhere in the classification system. Establishments in this sector are primarily engaged in activities, such as equipment and machinery repairing, promoting or administering religious activities, grantmaking, advocacy, and providing drycleaning and laundry services, personal care services, death care services, pet care services, photofinishing services, temporary parking services, and dating services.

Private households that engage in employing workers on or about the premises in activities primarily concerned with the operation of the household are included in this sector.

In this volume, only firms subject to federal tax are included in the categories that include the full "other services" sector, as well as the number of employees in the "Repair and Maintenance" and "Personal and Laundry Services" subsectors. However, the number of employees in the "Religious, Civic, and Similar Services" subsector include only non-taxable establishments.

Excluded from this sector are establishments primarily engaged in retailing new equipment and also performing repairs and general maintenance on equipment. These establishments are classified in Sector 44-45, Retail Trade.

Industries in the **Repair and Maintenance** subsector (811) restore machinery, equipment, and other products to working order. These establishments also typically provide general or routine maintenance (i.e., servicing) on such products to ensure they work efficiently and to prevent breakdown and unnecessary repairs.

The NAICS structure for this subsector brings together most types of repair and maintenance establishments and categorizes them based on production processes (i.e., on the type of repair and maintenance activity performed, and the necessary skills, expertise, and processes that are found in different repair and maintenance establishments). This NAICS classification does not delineate between repair services provided to businesses versus those that serve households. Although some industries primarily serve either businesses or households, separation by class of customer is limited by the fact that many establishments serve both. Establishments repairing computers and consumer electronics products are two examples of such overlap.

The Repair and Maintenance subsector does not include all establishments that do repair and maintenance. For example, a substantial amount of repair is done by establishments that also manufacture machinery, equipment, and other goods. These establishments are included in the Manufacturing sector in NAICS. In addition, repair of transportation equipment is often provided by or based at transportation facilities, such as airports, seaports, and these activities are included in the Transportation and Warehousing sector. A particularly unique situation exists with repair of buildings. Plumbing, electrical installation and repair, painting and decorating, and other construction-related establishments are often involved in performing installation or other work on new construction as well as providing repair services on existing structures. While some specialize in repair, it is difficult to distinguish between the two types and all have been included in the Construction sector.

Excluded from this subsector are establishments primarily engaged in rebuilding or remanufacturing machinery and equipment. These are classified in Sector 31-33, Manufacturing. Also excluded are retail establishments that provide after-sale services and repair. These are classified in Sector 44-45, Retail Trade.

Industries in the **Personal and Laundry Services** subsector (812) group establishments that provide personal and laundry services to individuals, households, and businesses. Services performed include: personal care services; death care services; laundry and drycleaning services; and a wide range of other personal services, such as pet care (except veterinary) services, photofinishing services, temporary parking services, and dating services.

The Personal and Laundry Services subsector is by no means all-inclusive of the services that could be termed personal services (i.e., those provided to individuals rather than businesses). There are many other subsectors, as well as sectors, that provide services to persons. Establishments providing legal, accounting, tax preparation, architectural, portrait photography, and similar professional services are classified in Sector 54, Professional, Scientific, and Technical Services; those providing job placement, travel arrange-

ment, home security, interior and exterior house cleaning, exterminating, lawn and garden care, and similar support services are classified in Sector 56, Administrative and Support, Waste Management and Remediation Services; those providing health and social services are classified in Sector 62, Health Care and Social Assistance; those providing amusement and recreation services are classified in Sector 71, Arts, Entertainment and Recreation; those providing educational instruction are classified in Sector 61, Educational Services; those providing repair services are classified in Subsector 811, Repair and Maintenance; and those providing spiritual, civic, and advocacy services are classified in Subsector 813, Religious, Grantmaking, Civic, Professional, and Similar Organizations.

Industries in the **Religious, Grantmaking, Civic, Professional, and Similar Organizations** subsector (813) group establishments that organize and promote religious activities; support various causes through grantmaking; advocate various social and political causes; and promote and defend the interests of their members. This category includes only tax-exempt establishments.

The industry groups within the subsector are defined in terms of their activities, such as establishments that provide funding for specific causes or for a variety of charitable causes; establishments that advocate and actively promote causes and beliefs for the public good; and establishments that have an active membership structure to promote causes and represent the interests of their members. Establishments in this subsector may publish newsletters, books, and periodicals, for distribution to their membership.

ECONOMIC CENSUS BY SIC CODE
(Items 267–278)
Source: U.S. Bureau of the Census, 1997 Economic Census
(See Overview of 1997 Economic Census prior to Item 191)

Because the 1997 Economic Census used the new North American Industry Classification System (NAICS), it is not directly comparable with Economic Census data from previous years. Because 1997 Economic Census records were assigned both SIC and NAICS codes, the Census Bureau was able to compile comparative statistics in which the 1997 data are compared with 1992 data using the Standard Industrial Classification (SIC) system. This volume includes the number of employees and the percent change from 1992 for six SIC sectors.

While many of the individual SIC industries correspond directly to industries as defined under the NAICS system, most of the higher level groupings do not. Particular care should be taken in comparing data for retail trade, wholesale trade, and manufacturing, which are sector titles used in both NAICS and SIC, but cover somewhat different groups of industries. The industry definitions discuss the relationships between NAICS and SIC industries. Where changes are significant, it will not be possible to construct time series that include data for points both before and after 1997.

For the SIC-based tables from the 1997 Economic Census, all auxiliaries are included in the category titled "Auxiliaries" and are not included in this volume. Note that in published reports from previous censuses for manufacturing and mining, auxiliary establishments were included in, or along with, data for the industries served; for other SIC divisions, auxiliary establishments were excluded from the detailed tables.

Construction. While some changes affecting construction were within the sector, this sector now includes industries that were previously classified in other sectors. Prominent among these industries are construction management and land subdividers and developers. In addition, although the construction sector is enumerated on an establishment basis, statistical information was obtained in the census by a survey which included all large employers and a sample of the smaller ones.

Manufacturing. While most of the changes affecting the manufacturing sector were within the sector, this sector now excludes industries which were previously within the scope of manufacturing and includes others that were not in manufacturing. Prominent among the industries that are excluded from manufacturing are logging and portions of publishing. Prominent among the industries that are now included in manufacturing are bakeries, candy stores where candy is made on the premises, custom tailors, makers of custom draperies, and tire retreading. The Information sector (new) includes publishing establishments that were classified in Manufacturing under the SIC.

Wholesale Trade. This sector includes most of what was classified in Wholesale Trade under the SIC system. Excluded from this sector, however, are establishments with retail selling characteristics; these establishments are now clasified in the Retail Trade sector. Prominent examples of these are auto parts, farm supplies, and building products dealers and lumber yards.

In addition, this sector now includes prerecorded video tape wholesalers; this industry was previously classified in Services Industries under the SIC system.

Retail Trade. This sector includes much of what was classified in Retail Trade under the SIC system. Excluded from this sector, however, are eating and drinking places and mobile foodservices (which are now in the Accommodation and Foodservices sector); pawn shops (which are now in the Finance and Insurance sector); and bakeries (which are now in the Manufacturing sector).

In addition, this sector now includes industries previously classified in Wholesale Trade that sold merchandise using facilities open to the general public. Prominent examples of these are automotive supplies dealers, computer and peripheral equipment merchants, office supplies dealers, farm supplies dealers, and building materials dealers.

Finance, Insurance, and Real Estate. The Finance and Insurance sector and the Real Estate Rental and Leasing sector were created from the SIC Finance, Insurance, and Real Estate sector. While most of the changes affecting finance and insurance were minor at the sector level, some industries left the finance part of this sector and other industries came into this sector. Prominent among those leaving are holding companies and patent owners and lessors. Prominent among the industries coming into the sector are pawnshops. Also, there are conceptual differences in what defines an establishment in this sector, since distinct activities have a less physical/geographical basis than industries in most other sectors. Note that funds, trusts, and other financial vehicles (except for

REITs), although part of this sector, are not in scope of the 1997 Economic Census.

While most of the changes affecting real estate were minor at the sector level, some industries left the real estate part of this sector and other industries came into this sector. Prominent among those leaving are title abstract offices and land subdividers and developers. Prominent among the industries coming into the sector are patent owners and lessors, miniwarehouses, and most of the rental industries previously classified in the Services Division of the SIC, including video tape, motor vehicle, computer, and equipment rental and leasing. Rental of equipment with operators is classified elsewhere, depending on the services provided.

Service Industries. The Professional, Scientific, and Technical Services sector primarily includes professional and other highly specialized technical service establishments that were classified Services under the SIC. The Educational Services sector, the Health Care and Social Assistance sector, the Arts, Entertainment, and Recreation sector, and the Other Services Sector primarily include establishments that were classified as Services under the SIC.

BUILDING PERMITS, Items 279–281
Source: U.S. Bureau of the Census— Building Permits Survey

Figures represent private residential construction authorized by building permits in approximately 19,000 places in the United States. Valuation represents the expected cost of construction as recorded on the building permit. This figure usually excludes the cost of on-site and off-site development and improvements and the cost of heating, plumbing, electrical, and elevator installations.

County, state, and U.S. totals were obtained by adding the data for permit issuing places within each jurisdiction. These totals thus are limited to permits issued in the 19,000 place universe covered by the Census Bureau and may not include all permits issued within the state.

Residential building permits include buildings with any number of housing units. Apartment hotels, hotels, dormitories, fraternity houses, and other non-housekeeping residential buildings are not included.

MANUFACTURED HOUSING UNITS, Item 282
Source: U.S. Bureau of the Census, Survey of New Mobile Home Placements

The Survey of New Mobile Home Placements involves a monthly sample of new mobile homes shipped by manufacturers. The dealer to whom the sampled unit was shipped is contacted by

A mobile home, often referred to as a "manufactured housing unit", is defined as a movable dwelling, 8 feet or more wide and 40 feet or more long, designed to be towed on its own chassis, with transportation gear integral to the unit when it leaves the factory, and without need of a permanent foundation. These mobile homes include multiwides, which are counted as single units, and expandable mobile homes. Excluded are travel trailers, motor homes, and modular housing.

EXPORTS, Items 283–285
Source: U.S. Bureau of the Census

The data on exports of goods by state of origin are based on the location of the exporter, that is, the principal party responsible for effecting export from the United States. Exporters often are intermediaries, so the data do not necessarily represent the states where the goods were actually produced. The total includes reexports of foreign goods.

FEDERAL FUNDS, Items 286–302
Source: U.S. Bureau of the Census—
Consolidated Federal Funds Report

Data on federal expenditures and obligations are obtained from a report prepared by the Bureau of the Census in accordance with the Consolidated Federal Funds Report (CFFR) Act of 1982 (P.L. 97-326). The data are for federal fiscal years beginning on October 1 and ending the following September 30.

Direct payments for individuals include social security benefits, federal government retirement, medicare, supplemental security income, food stamps, educational and housing assistance, and other categories not shown separately. All data represent actual expenditures during the fiscal year.

Direct payments for educational assistance consist primarily of higher education grants and insured loans. Direct housing assistance includes primarily the Low Income Housing Assistance Program.

Grants data represent the federal obligations incurred at the time the grant is awarded. The amounts reported do not represent actual expenditures since obligations in one time period may not result in outlays during the same time period. Moreover, initial amounts obligated may be adjusted at a later date, either through enhancements or de-obligations.

Medicaid and other health-related grants include a variety of grants from the Department of Health and Human Services for health services and research.

Nutrition and family welfare grants include a variety of grants by the Department of Health and Human Services for child welfare, special programs for the aging, and related areas. The school lunch program and other nutritional assistance programs administered by the Department of Agriculture are also included.

Energy and environment grants include grants from the Department of Energy for energy development, energy conservation, and nuclear waste disposal, as well as from the Environmental Protection Agency for a variety of pollution control and waste management activities.

Education grants include a variety of grant programs relating to elementary, secondary, and post-secondary education; adult education; vocational education; faculty training; and related areas.

Housing and community development grants include Community Development Block Grants, housing demonstration programs, rental housing rehabilitation, and other housing programs.

Salaries and wages represent actual federal expenditures during the fiscal year; the geographic distribution of these amounts by state and county was estimated based upon place of employment.

Procurement contract awards cover awards by the United States Postal Service (USPS) as well as all other federal agencies. Amounts provided by the USPS represent actual outlays for contractual commitments, while amounts for other agencies represent the value of obligations for contract actions and do not reflect actual federal government expenditures. In general, only current-year contract actions are included—however, multiple-year obligations may be reported for contract actions of less than 3 years duration.

STATE GOVERNMENT FINANCES,
Items 303–321
Source: U.S. Bureau of the Census

Data are from an annual survey conducted by the Bureau of the Census and pertain to state government fiscal years ending between July 1, 1996 and June 30, 1997.

Total general revenue includes all revenue except utility, liquor stores, and insurance trust revenue. All tax revenue and intergovernmental revenue, even if designated for employee-retirement or local utility purpose, are classified as general revenue.

Intergovernmental revenue covers amounts received from the federal government as fiscal aid, reimbursements for performance of general government functions and specific services for the paying government, or in lieu of taxes. It excludes any amounts received from other governments for sale of property, commodities, and utility services.

Taxes consist of compulsory contributions exacted by governments for public purposes. However, this category excludes employer and employee payments for retirement and social insurance purposes, which are classified as insurance trust revenue, and special assessments, which are classified as non-tax general revenue. Sales and gross receipts taxes, including "licenses" at more than normal rates, are based on volume or value of transfers of goods or services, on gross receipts, or on gross income, and related taxes based on use, storage, production, importation, or consumption of goods. Sales and gross receipts taxes exclude dealer discounts or "commissions" allowed to merchants for collection of taxes from consumers. General sales taxes and selected taxes on sales of motor fuels, tobacco products, and other particular commodities and services are included.

General government expenditure includes capital outlay, of which a major portion is commonly financed by borrowing, while governmental revenue does not include receipts from borrowing. Among other things, this distorts the relationship between totals of revenue and expenditure figures that are presented and renders it useless as a direct measure of the degree of budgetary "balance," as that term is generally applied.

Direct general expenditure comprises all expenditures of the state governments, excluding utility, liquor stores, insurance trust expenditures, and any intergovernmental payments.

State government expenditures for **education** are mainly for provision and support of schools and other educational facilities and services, including those for educational institutions beyond high school. They cover such related services as pupil transportation; school lunch and other cafeteria operations; school health, recreation, and library services; and dormitories, dining halls, and bookstores operated by public institutions of higher education.

Health and hospital expenditures include health research; clinics; nursing; immunization; and other categorical, environmental, and general health services provided by health agencies; establishment and operation of hospital facilities; provision of hospital care; and support of other public and private hospitals.

Highway expenditure is for provision and maintenance of highway facilities, including toll turnpikes, bridges, tunnels, and ferries, as well as regular roads, highways, and streets. Also included are expenditures for street lighting and for snow and ice removal.

Public safety expenditure includes police and correctional institution expenditure.

Public welfare expenditure covers support of and assistance to needy persons contingent upon their needs. Included are cash assistance paid directly to needy persons under categorical (Old Age Assistance, Aid to Families with Dependent Children, Aid to the Blind, and Aid to the Disabled) and other welfare programs; vendor payments made directly to private purveyors for medical care, burials, and other commodities and services provided under welfare programs; welfare institutions; and any intergovernmental or other direct expenditure for welfare purposes. Pensions to former employees and other benefits not contingent on need are excluded.

Debt outstanding includes all long-term debt obligations of the government and its agencies (exclusive of utility debt) and all interest-bearing short-term (i.e., repayable within 1 year) debt

obligations remaining unpaid at the close of the fiscal year. It includes judgments, mortgages, and revenue bonds, as well as general obligation bonds, notes, and interest-bearing warrants. It includes non-interest-bearing short-term obligations; inter-fund obligations; amounts owed in a trust or agency capacity; advances and contingent loans from other governments; and rights of individuals to benefits from government-administered employee retirement funds.

GOVERNMENT EMPLOYMENT, Items 322–324
Source: U.S. Bureau of Economic Analysis

Employment is measured as the average annual number of jobs, full-time plus part-time. The estimates are on a place-of-work basis. The data for federal civilian employment include civilian employees of the Department of Defense. Military employment includes all person on active duty status.

ELECTION STATISTICS, Items 325–327
Source: Federal Election Commission

Election results show the percentage of the total vote cast for the Democratic and Republican candidates, as well as the combined percentage for all other candidates in the 2000 presidential election.

TABLES B AND C—STATES/COUNTIES and METRO AREAS

Table B presents 197 items for the United States as a whole; each state and the District of Columbia; and each county, county equivalent, or independent city. The counties are presented in alphabetical order within states, which are also in alphabetical order. Independent cities, which are found in Maryland, Missouri, Nevada, and Virginia, are placed in alphabetical order at the end of the list of counties for those states. The District of Columbia is included in Table B as both a county and a state (it is also included as a city in Table D).

Table C presents the same data for each of the 335 metropolitan areas.

LAND AREA, Items 1 and 4
Source: U.S. Bureau of the Census

Land area measurements are shown to the nearest square kilometer. Land area includes dry land and land temporarily or partially covered by water, such as marshland, swamps, and river floodplains.

POPULATION, Items 2–4
Source: U.S. Bureau of the Census

The population data are based on the population estimated as of July 1, 1999. The ranks are shown for counties (including independent cities and the District of Columbia) and separately, for metropolitan areas (including MSAs, PMSAs, and NECMAs but excluding CMSAs).

POPULATION BY AGE, RACE, SEX AND HISPANIC ORIGIN, Items 5–19
Source: U.S. Bureau of the Census—Estimates of the population of counties by age, race, sex, and Hispanic origin

County estimates of population characteristics are developed in a two-step procedure. First, a set of state estimates is developed using a cohort-component technique. Then county estimates are derived by applying ratios to an independent estimate of the county population.

Population by race, as defined by the Census Bureau, reflects self-identification by respondents; it does not denote any clear-cut scientific definition of biological stock. In the 1990 census, data were obtained through self-classification.

The White population is defined as persons who indicated their race as white, as well as persons who did not classify themselves in one of the specific race categories listed on the questionnaire but entered a nationality such as Canadian, German, Italian, Lebanese, or Polish.

The Black population includes persons who indicated their race as black or Negro, as well as persons who did not classify themselves in one of the specific race categories but reported entries such as Black Puerto Rican, Haitian, Jamaican, Nigerian, or West Indian.

The American Indian, Eskimo, and Aleut population includes persons who indicated their race as Indian (American), Eskimo, or Aleut, as well as persons who did not indicate a specific race category but reported the name of an Indian tribe.

The Asian and Pacific Islander population includes persons who indicated their race as Chinese, Filipino, Japanese, Asian Indian, Korean, Vietnamese, Hawaiian, Samoan, or Guamanian. Also included are persons who provided write-in entries of such Asian and Pacific Islander groups as Cambodian, Laotian, Pakistani, and Fiji Islander.

The **Hispanic population** is based on a complete-count question that asked respondents to identify whether they were of Spanish/Hispanic origin. Persons marking any one of the 4 Spanish categories (i.e., Mexican, Puerto Rican, Cuban, or Other Spanish) are collectively referred to as "Hispanic." Hispanic is not a race category; Hispanic persons may be of any race.

Age derived from the census (1990) is classified as age at last birthday (i.e., number of completed years from birth to April 1). The percent figures are derived by dividing the number of persons in a specified age group by the total population of a given geographic area. Data on age are based on complete counts of resident population.

The female population of a geographic area is shown as a percent of the total population of the area.

POPULATION—COMPONENTS OF CHANGE, Items 20–26
Source: U.S. Bureau of the Census

Data on components of change cover an area's population for a specified number of years. Net change is the difference between the count of persons in the 1990 census and the Census Bureau's estimate of the population on July 1, 1999. It is equal to natural change (the number of births minus the number of deaths) plus net migration. Natural change shows the total number of births and deaths in a particular area during the decade. Net migration represents the difference between the number of persons moving into a particular area and the number of persons moving away from the area. A positive figure indicates net immigration to the area; a negative figure indicates net out-migration from the area.

Because the 1999 population estimates are based on a model that begins with a national population estimate, the county components of change do not always exactly add up to the difference between the 1990 census population and the 1999 estimates.

HOUSEHOLDS, Items 27–31
Source: U.S. Bureau of the Census— 1990 Census of Population and Housing

A household consists of persons occupying a single housing unit. A housing unit is a house, an apartment, a group of rooms, or a single room occupied as separate living quarters. The occupants may be a single family, one person living alone, 2 or more families living together, or any other group of related or unrelated persons sharing a housing unit. The number of households is the same as the number of year-round occupied housing units.

A family household consists of 2 or more persons, including the householder, who are related by birth, marriage, or adoption and who live together as one household; all such persons are considered as members of 1 family.

The measure of persons per household is obtained by dividing the number of persons in households by the number of households or householders. The category **female family householder** includes only female-headed family households with no spouse present.

BIRTHS AND DEATHS, Items 32–37
Source: U.S. Centers for Disease Control

The registration of births, deaths, and other vital events in the United States is primarily a state and local function. The civil laws of every state provide for a continuous and permanent birth and death registration system. Through the National Vital Statistics System, the National Center for Health Statistics (NCHS) obtains data on births and deaths from the registration offices of each state, New York City, and the District of Columbia.

Birth and death statistics are limited to events occurring during the year. The data are by place of residence and exclude events occurring to nonresidents of the United States. Births or deaths that occur outside the United States are excluded.

Birth and death rates represent the number of births and deaths per 1,000 resident population enumerated as of April 1 for decennial census years and estimated as of July 1 for other years.

Figures for infant deaths include deaths of children under 1 year of age; they exclude fetal deaths. The infant death rate is per 1,000 live births.

In order to protect the privacy of individuals, the Centers for Disease Control does not make county-level data available where the number of individual events falls below a threshold figure. Since a 3-year time span allows time for more events to occur, cumulative data covering 3 years tend to be more complete than data for a single year. Also, an average for a 3-year period may more accurately represent the trend level when the number of events each year is small. For these reasons, the county data in this volume are presented as an average computed from data covering a 3-year time span. State data in this table are presented on the same basis in order to maintain comparability. Even with the 3-year average, death rates based on fewer than 20 deaths should be considered unreliable.

PHYSICIANS, Items 38–39
Source: Health Market Science, Inc., as published in Bernan's *Health and Healthcare in the United States*, copyright 1999 NationsHealth Corporation, LLC. Reprinted with permission.

Physicians are health practitioners having the degree of M.D. (Doctor of Medicine) or D.O. (Doctor of Osteopathy) primarily engaged in the practice of general or specialized medicine or surgery. The rate of physicians per 100,000 resident population is an indicator of the supply of physicians within a geographic area.

HOSPITALS, Items 40–42
Source: Health Market Science, Inc., as published in Bernan's *Health and Healthcare in the United States*, copyright 1999 NationsHealth Corporation, LLC. Reprinted with permission.

Hospitals are licensed institutions with at least six beds whose primary function is to provide diagnostic and therapeutic patient services for medical conditions by an organized physician staff, and have continuous nursing services under the supervision of registered nurses. Only short term general hospitals are included in these figures.

A hospital bed is any bed that is licensed for use by inpatients. The count of beds in a facility typically represents the count of beds at the end of the reporting period (e.g., a year) regardless of whether it is operational or not. The number of hospital beds per 100,000 population is a measure of the supply of hospital beds within a geographic area.

MEDICARE ENROLLEES, Item 43
Source: Health Care Financing Administration

The Health Care Financing Administration (HCFA) administers Medicare which provides health insurance to people aged 65 and over and those who have permanent kidney failure and certain people with disabilities. Medicare has two parts: Hospital Insurance and Supplemental Medical Insurance. The numbers in this volume include persons enrolled in either or both parts of the program as of July 1, 1999, by their state of residence.

CRIME, Items 44–47
Source: U.S. Federal Bureau of Investigation—Uniform Crime Reports

Crime data are as reported to the FBI by law enforcement agencies and have not been adjusted for under-reporting. This may affect comparability between geographic areas or over time.

Through the voluntary contribution of crime statistics by law enforcement agencies across the United States, the Uniform Crime Reporting (UCR) Program provides periodic assessments of crime in the nation as measured by those offenses which come to the attention of the law enforcement community. The Committee on Uniform Crime Records of the International Association of Chiefs of Police initiated this voluntary national data-collection effort in 1930. UCR Program contributors compile and submit their crime data in 1 of 2 manners: either directly to the FBI or through the state UCR Programs.

Seven offenses, because of their seriousness, frequency of occurrence, and likelihood of being reported to police, were initially selected to serve as an index for evaluating fluctuations in the volume of crime. These serious crimes were murder and nonnegligent manslaughter, forcible rape, robbery, aggravated assault, burglary, larceny-theft, and motor vehicle theft. By congressional mandate, arson was added as the eighth index offense in 1979. The totals shown in this volume do not include arson.

Violent offenses include 4 crime categories: (1) Murder and nonnegligent manslaughter, as defined in the UCR Program, is the willful (nonnegligent) killing of 1 human being by another. This offense excludes deaths caused by negligence, suicide or accident; justifiable homicides; and attempts to murder or assaults to murder. (2) Forcible rape is the carnal knowledge of a female forcibly and against her will. Assaults or attempts to commit rape by force or threat of force are also included; however, statutory rape (without force) and other sex offenses are excluded. (3) Robbery is the taking or attempting to take anything of value from the care, custody, or control of a person or persons by force or threat of force or violence and/or by putting the victim in fear. (4) Aggravated assault is an unlawful attack by 1 person upon another for the purpose of inflicting severe or aggravated bodily injury. This type of assault is usually accompanied by the use of a weapon or by means likely to produce death or great bodily harm. Attempts are included since an injury does not necessarily have to result when a gun, knife, or other weapon is used, which could and probably would result in a serious personal injury if the crime were successfully completed.

Property crimes include 3 categories: (1) Burglary, or breaking and entering, is the unlawful entry of a structure to commit a felony or theft, even though no force was used to gain entrance. (2) Larceny/theft is the unauthorized taking of the personal property of another, without the use of force. (3) Motor vehicle theft is the unauthorized taking of any motor vehicle.

Rates are based on population estimates provided by the FBI. The county totals published in this volume were obtained by aggregating individual reporting units within each county. If the population total for the units aggregated was less than 75 percent of the county's population (as estimated by the Bureau of the Census), the total was not considered representative of the county as a whole and is not published. State and US totals include FBI estimates for those areas.

EDUCATION—SCHOOL ENROLLMENT AND EDUCATIONAL ATTAINMENT, Items 48–51
Source: U.S. Bureau of the Census— 1990 Census of Population and Housing

Data on school enrollment and educational attainment were derived from a sample of the population. Persons were classified as enrolled in school if they reported attending a "regular" public or private school (or college) at any time between February 1, 1990 and the time of enumeration. The instructions were to "include only nursery school, kindergarten, elementary school, and schooling which would lead to a high school diploma or a college degree" as regular school. Public school is defined as "any school or college controlled and supported by a local, county, state, or federal government." Schools supported and controlled primarily by religious organizations or other private groups are defined as private.

Statistics for years of school completed are for persons 25 years old and over. The data were derived from a question on the 1990 census questionnaire that asked respondents for the highest level of school they had completed or the highest degree they had received. Persons who passed a high school equivalency examination were considered high school graduates. Schooling received in

foreign schools was to be reported as the equivalent grade or years in the regular American school system.

LOCAL GOVERNMENT EDUCATION EXPENDITURES, Items 52–53
Source: U.S. National Center for Educational Statistics

Total expenditure for education includes provision or support of schools and facilities for elementary and secondary education. It encompasses instructional, support, and auxiliary services (school lunch, student activities, and community services) offered by public school systems. Retirement benefits paid to former education employees and interest payments are not included. Current expenditure includes all components of total expenditure except capital outlay. Expenditure data are obtained by the U.S. Bureau of the Census through its annual surveys of government finances and are supplied by the Bureau of the Census to the National Center for Education Statistics. Current expenditures per pupil is current expenditures divided by the number of students enrolled. The number of students enrolled is based on an annual "membership" count of students on or about October 1.

NCES uses the Common Core of Data (CCD) Survey to acquire and maintain statistical data from each of the 50 states, the District of Columbia, and the outlying areas. The state education agencies compile and submit data for approximately 85,000 schools and 15,000 local school districts. Typically this results in varying interpretation of NCES definitions and different record-keeping systems, leading to large amounts of missing data for several states in this volume. Schools and school districts are included in the county where the school district offices (the Local Education Agency) are located.

MONEY INCOME, Items 54–57
Source: U.S. Bureau of the Census— 1990 Census of Population and Housing

The data on income are derived from the responses of a sample of persons 15 years old and older. **Total money income** is defined by the Bureau of the Census for statistical purposes as the sum of the following: wage or salary income; nonfarm self-employment income; net farm self-employment income; Social Security and railroad retirement income; public assistance income; and all other regularly received income such as interest, dividends, veterans' payments, pensions, unemployment compensation, and alimony. Receipts not counted as income include various "lump sum" payments such as capital gains or inheritances.

The total represents the amount of income received before deductions for personal income taxes, Social Security, bond purchases, union dues, Medicare deductions, etc.

Per capita income is based on resident population enumerated as of April 1, 1990.

Income of households includes the income of the householder and all other persons 15 years old and older in the household. Median household income is usually less than median family income because many households consist of only 1 person. The median divides the income distribution into 2 equal parts, 1 having incomes above the median, the other with incomes below.

The constant-dollar figures are based on an annual average Consumer Price Index from the Bureau of Labor Statistics. Constant-dollar figures are estimates representing an effort to remove the effects of price changes from statistical series reported in dollar terms. However, the estimates do not reflect the price and cost-of-living differences that may exist between areas.

Money income differs in definition from personal income (item 62). For example, money income does not include the pension rights, employer provided health insurance, food stamps, or Medicare payments that are included in personal income.

INCOME AND POVERTY, Items 58–61
Source: U.S. Bureau of the Census—Small Area Income and Poverty Estimates Program

The 1997 income and poverty estimates by county are constructed from statistical models that relate income and poverty to indicators based on summary data from federal income tax returns, data about participation in the Food Stamp program, and the previous Census.

Poverty status is based on the definition prescribed by the Federal Office of Management and Budget as the standard to be used by federal agencies for statistical purposes. Families and persons are classified as being below the poverty level if their total family income or unrelated individual income was less than the poverty threshold specified for the applicable family size, age of householder, and number of related children present under 18. Poverty status is determined for all families (and by implication all family members). For persons not in families, poverty status is determined by their income in relation to the appropriate poverty threshold. Inmates of institutions, persons in military group quarters or college dormitories, and unrelated individuals under 15 are excluded.

The 1997 poverty thresholds are shown in Figure 1.

Figure 1.
Poverty Thresholds in 1997 by Size of Family

Size of Family Unit	Weighted average thresholds
One person (unrelated individual)	$8,183
Under 65 years	8,350
65 years and over	7,698
Two persons	10,473
Householder under 65 years	10,805
Householder 65 years and over	9,712
Three persons	12,802
Four persons	16,400
Five persons	19,380
Six persons	21,886
Seven persons	24,802
Eight persons	27,593
Nine or more persons	32,566

PERSONAL INCOME AND EARNINGS, Items 62–83
Source: U.S. Bureau of Economic Analysis

Total personal income is the current income received by residents of an area from all sources. It is measured before deductions of income and other personal taxes but after deduction of personal contributions for Social Security, government retirement, and other social insurance programs. It consists of **wage and salary disbursements** (covering all employee earnings, including executive salaries, bonuses, commissions, payments-in-kind, incentive payments, and tips), **other labor income** (primarily employer contributions to private pension funds), proprietors' income, rental income of persons, dividends, personal interest income, and government and business transfer payments.

Proprietors' income is the monetary income and income in-kind of proprietorships and partnerships, including the independent professions, and of tax-exempt cooperatives. **Dividends** are cash payments by for-profit corporations to stockholders who are U.S. residents. **Interest** is the monetary and imputed interest income of persons from all sources. **Rent** is the monetary income of persons from the rental of real property except the income of persons primarily engaged in the real estate business, the imputed net rental income of owner-occupants of nonfarm dwellings, and the royalties received by persons.

Transfer payments are income for which services are not currently rendered. They consist of both government and business transfer payments. Government transfer payments include payments under the following programs: Federal Old-age, Survivors, and Disability Insurance ("Social Security"); Medicare and medical vendor payments; unemployment insurance, railroad and government retirement; federal and state government-insured workers' compensation; veterans benefits, including veterans life insurance; food stamps; black lung; Supplemental Security Income; and Aid to Families with Dependent Children. Government payments to nonprofit institutions, other than for work under research and development contracts, are also included. The principal business transfers are corporate gifts to nonprofit institutions and consumer bad debts.

Per capita personal income is based on resident population estimated as of July 1 of the year shown.

Personal income differs in definition from money income (items 54-57). For example, personal income includes pension rights, employer provided health insurance, food stamps, and Medicare. These are not included in the definition of money income.

Earnings cover wage and salary disbursements, other labor income, and proprietors' income.

Data for earnings obtained from the Bureau of Economic Analysis (BEA) are based on place of work. In computing personal income, BEA makes an "adjustment for residence" to earnings based on commuting patterns, so that personal income is presented on a place of residence basis.

Farm earnings include the income of farm workers (wages and salaries and other labor income) and farm proprietors. Farm proprietors' income includes only the income of sole proprietorships and partnerships.

Farm earning estimates are benchmarked to data collected in the Census of Agriculture and the revised U.S. Department of Agriculture State totals of income and expense items.

"Goods-related" industries include mining, construction, and manufacturing. "Service-related and other" includes private sector earnings in agricultural services, forestry and fisheries; transportation and public utilities; wholesale trade; retail trade; finance, insurance, and real estate; and services. Government earnings include all levels of government.

SOCIAL SECURITY AND SUPPLEMENTAL SECURITY INCOME, Items 84–86
Source: U.S. Social Security Administration

Social Security beneficiaries is the number of persons receiving benefits under the Old-age, Survivors, and Disability Insurance Program. These include retired or disabled workers covered by the program, their spouses and dependent children, and the surviving spouses and dependent children of deceased workers.

Supplemental Security Income (SSI) recipients is the number of persons receiving SSI payments. Data are as of December of the year shown.

HOUSING, Items 87–96
Source: U.S. Bureau of the Census— 1990 Census of Population and Housing

A **housing unit** is a house, apartment, mobile home or trailer, group of rooms, or single room occupied or, if vacant, intended for occupancy as separate living quarters. Separate living quarters are those in which the occupants do not live and eat with any other persons in the structure and which have direct access from the outside of the building through a common hall.

The occupants of a housing unit may be a single family, 1 person living alone, 2 or more families living together, or a group of related or unrelated persons who share living arrangements. For vacant units, the criteria of separateness and direct access are applied to the intended occupants whenever possible. If that information cannot be obtained, the criteria are applied to the previous occupants. Both occupied and vacant housing units are included in the housing inventory, except that recreational vehicles, tents, caves, boats, railroad cars, and the like are included only if they are occupied as someone's usual place of residence.

A housing unit is classified as occupied if it is the usual place of residence of the person or group of persons living in it at the time of enumeration, or if the occupants are only temporarily absent (e.g., away on vacation). A household consists of all persons who occupy a housing unit as their usual place of residence.

The percent change represents the difference in the number of total housing units in a specified area over the decade 1980-1990.

Median value is the dollar amount that divides the distribution of owner-occupied housing units into 2 equal parts, with one half of the units falling below this value and the other half exceeding it. Value is defined as the respondent's estimate of what the house would sell for if it were for sale. Data are presented for 1-family units on less than 10 acres and with no business or medical office on the property.

Median rent divides the distribution of renter-occupied housing units into 2 equal parts. Median rent represents the amount of cash rent a renter pays (contract rent) plus the estimated average cost of utilities and fuels if paid by the renter (gross rent). Rent is to be reported only for living quarters, not for any business or other space occupied. Single family houses on lots of 10 or more acres are excluded.

Housing cost as a percent of income is shown separately for owners with mortgages, owners without mortgages, and renters. Rent as a percentage of income is a computed ratio of gross rent and monthly household income (total household income in 1989 divided by 12). Selected owner costs include utilities and fuels, as well as mortgage payments, insurance, taxes, etc. In each case, the ratio of housing cost to income is computed separately for each housing unit. The ratios for one-half of the units are above the median shown in this book, and one-half are below.

Substandard units are occupied units which are overcrowded or lack complete plumbing facilities. For the purposes of this item "overcrowded" is defined as having 1.01 persons or more per room. Complete plumbing facilities include hot and cold piped water, a flush toilet, and a bathtub or shower. These facilities must be located inside the housing unit but not necessarily in the same room.

CIVILIAN LABOR FORCE AND UNEMPLOYMENT, Items 97–100
Source: U.S. Bureau of Labor Statistics

Data for the civilian labor force are the product of a federal-state cooperative program in which state employment security agencies prepare labor force and unemployment estimates under concepts, definitions, and technical procedures established by the Bureau of Labor Statistics. The civilian labor force consists of all civilians 16 years and over who are either employed in a civilian job or unemployed.

Unemployment includes all persons who did not work during the survey week, made specific efforts to find a job in the prior four weeks, and were available for work during the survey week (except for temporary illness). Persons waiting to be called back to a job from which they had been laid off and those waiting to report to a new job within the next 30 days are included in unemployment figures.

CIVILIAN EMPLOYMENT, 1990, Items 101–103
Source: U.S. Bureau of the Census— 1990 Census of Population and Housing

Total employment includes all civilians 16 years old or older who were either (1) "at work" — those who did any work at all during the reference week as paid employees, worked in their own business or profession, worked on their own farm, or worked 15 hours or more as unpaid workers in a family farm or business; or were (2) "with a job, but not at work" — those who had a job but were not at work that week due to illness, weather, industrial dispute, vacation, or other personal reasons.

The **occupation categories** shown are consistent with the 1980 edition of the *Standard Occupational Classification Manual (SOC)*, published by the Office of Federal Statistical Policy and Standards, U.S. Department of Commerce. Professional, managerial, and technical occupations include the following categories: executive, administrative, and managerial occupations (000-042); professional specialty occupations (043-202); and technicians and related support occupations (203-242). Precision production, craft and repair includes SOC codes 503-702.

PRIVATE NONFARM ESTABLISHMENTS AND EMPLOYMENT, Items 104–112
Source: U.S. Bureau of the Census— County Business Patterns

Data for private nonfarm establishments, employment, and payroll are reported in the U.S. Bureau of the Census publication *County Business Patterns*. The estimates are based on surveys conducted by the Bureau of the Census and administrative records from the Internal Revenue Service (IRS).

The following types of employment are excluded from the tables: government employment; self employed persons; farm workers; and domestic service workers. Railroad employment jointly covered by social security and railroad retirement programs, employment on oceanborne vessels, and employment in foreign countries are also excluded.

Annual payroll is the combined amount of wages paid, tips reported, and other compensation (including salaries, vacation allowances, bonuses, commissions, sick leave pay, and the value of payments-in-kind such as free meals and lodging) paid to employees before deductions for Social Security, income tax, insurance, union dues, etc. All forms of compensation are included, whether or not subject to income tax or Federal Insurance Contributions Act tax, with the exception of annuities, third-party sick pay, and supplemental unemployment compensation benefits (even if income tax was withheld). For corporations, total annual payroll includes compensation paid to officers and executives; for unincorporated businesses, it does not include profit or other compensation of proprietors or partners.

AGRICULTURE, Items 113–130
Source: U.S. Department of Agriculture, National Agricultural Statistics Service— 1997 Census of Agriculture

Data for the 1997 Census of Agriculture were collected in 1998 and pertain to the year 1997.

The Bureau of the Census took a census of agriculture every 10 years from 1840 to 1920 and roughly every 5 years from 1925 to 1992. The 1997 Census of Agriculture was transfered to the National Agricultural Statistics Service of the U.S. Department of Agriculture. Over time, the definition of a farm has varied. For recent censuses, including the 1997 census, a farm has been defined as any place from which $1,000 or more of agricultural products were sold or normally would have been sold during the census year.

The term **operator** refers to a person who operates a farm, either doing the work or making day-to-day decisions about such things as planting, harvesting, feeding, marketing, etc. The operator may be the owner, a member of the owner's household, a salaried manager, a tenant, a renter, or a sharecropper. For partnerships, only one partner is counted as an operator. For census purposes, the number of operators is the same as the number of farms.

The acreage designated as **land in farms** consists primarily of agricultural land used for crops, pasture, or grazing. It also includes woodland and wasteland not actually under cultivation or used for pasture or grazing, if it was part of the operator's total operation.

Land in farms is an operating-unit concept and includes land owned and operated, as well as land rented from others. Land used rent free was to be reported as land rented from others. All land in Indian reservations used for growing crops or grazing livestock was to be included as land in farms.

With few exceptions, the land in each farm was tabulated as being in the operator's principal county. The principal county was defined as the one where the largest value of agricultural products were raised or produced; it was usually the county containing all or the largest proportion of the land in the farm. For a limited number of Western states, this procedure resulted in the allocation of more land in farms to a county than the total land area of the county.

Irrigated land covers any land in farms to which water was artificially applied in the census year. Land irrigated prior to, but not in the census year, is not included. Irrigation may have been used for producing a harvested crop, for pasture or grazing lands, for cultivated summer fallow, or for land planted to a crop intended for future harvest. Land flooded during high-water periods was included as irrigated only if water was diverted to agricultural lands by dams, canals, or other works.

Cropland consists of land from which crops were harvested and land that could have been used for crops without additional improvements. This includes land in nonbearing orchards and vineyards, land from which any hay was cut, land on which crops failed, idle or fallow land, and land used for grazing purposes.

Respondents were asked to report their estimate of the current market value of land and buildings owned, rented, or leased from others, and rented and leased to others. Market value refers to the respondent's estimate of what the land and buildings would sell for under current market conditions. If the value of land and buildings was not reported, it was estimated during processing by using the average value of land and buildings from similar farms in the same geographic area.

The **value of machinery and equipment** was estimated by the respondent as the current market value of all cars, trucks, tractors, combines, balers, irrigation equipment, etc., used on the farm. This value is an estimate of what the machinery and equipment would sell for in its present condition and not the replacement or depreciated value. Share interests are reported at full value at the farm where the equipment and machinery are usually kept. Only equipment that was actually used in 1996 and 1997, or newly purchased but not yet used, and physically located at the farm on December 31, 1997 is included

The **value of farm products sold** by farms represents the gross market value before taxes and production expenses of all agricultural products sold or removed from the place in 1997 regardless of who received the payment. It includes sales by the operator as well as the value of any share received by partners, landlords, contractors, and others associated with the operation. It represents the sum of all crops, including nursery products sold and livestock and poultry and their products sold.

The value of crops sold in 1997 does not necessarily represent the sales from crops harvested that year. The data include sales from crops produced in earlier years and exclude some crops produced in 1997 but held in storage and not sold in the census year. For crops sold through a co-op that made payments in several installments, only the total value received in the census year was to be reported.

LAND USE, Item 131
Source: U.S. Department of Agriculture,
Natural Resources Conservation Service,
1997 National Resources Inventory

The National Resources Inventory has been conducted every five years since 1982. The 1997 NRI is based on a sample of about 800,000 locations throughout the United States (excluding Alaska and the District of Columbia.) Federally owned lands include military bases, national forests, wildlife refuges, parks, grassland game preserves, scenic waterways, wilderness areas, monuments, lakeshore, parkways, battlefields, Bureau of Land Management lands, and other federal lands.

WATER CONSUMPTION, Item 132
Source: U.S. Geological Survey, National Water Use Information Program, 1995 Water Use Data.

Every five years the U.S. Geological Survey compiles national water-use estimates. This volume includes the total freshwater withdrawals expressed as million gallons per day. Estimates of withdrawals of ground and surface water are given for the following categories of use: public water supplies, domestic, commercial, irrigation, livestock, industrial, mining, and thermoelectric power.

CONSTRUCTION—BUILDING PERMITS,
Items 133–134
Source: U.S. Bureau of the Census—
Building Permits Survey

Figures represent private residential construction authorized by building permits in approximately 19,000 places in the United States. Valuation represents the cost of construction as recorded on the building permit. This figure usually excludes the cost of on-site and off-site development and improvements and the cost of heating, plumbing, electrical, and elevator installations.

County, state, and U.S. totals were obtained by summing the data for permit-issuing places within each jurisdiction. Thus, these totals are limited to permits issued in the 19,000 place universe covered by the Census Bureau and may not include all permits issued within the county. If a county does not contain permit-issuing places covered by the Census Bureau, an "NA" is shown. Counties with permit-issuing places that issued no permits during the period are represented by a "0."

Residential building permits include buildings with any number of housing units. Hotels, apartment hotels, dormitories, fraternity houses, and other non-housekeeping residential buildings are not included.

1997 ECONOMIC CENSUS: OVERVIEW
Items 135–166
Source: U.S. Bureau of the Census

The Economic Census provides a detailed portrait of the nation's economy once every five years, from the national to the local level. The 1997 Economic Census covers nearly all of the U.S. economy in its basic collection of establishment statistics. It is the first major data source to use the new North American Industry Classification System (NAICS) and is therefore not comparable to economic data from prior years which were based on the Standard Industrial Classification (SIC) system.

NAICS, developed in cooperation with Canada and Mexico, classifies North America's economic activities at 2-, 3-, 4-, and 5-digit levels of detail, and the U.S. version of NAICS further defines industries to a sixth digit. The Economic Census takes advantage of this hierarchy to publish data at these successive levels of detail: sector (2-digit); subsector (3-digit); industry group (4-digit); industry(5-digit); and U.S. industry(6-digit.)

This volume was published during the initial release of the 1997 Economic Census and therefore includes those sectors that were available at the time of publication. The information in Tables B and C is at the 2-digit level.

Several key statistics are tabulated for all industries included in this volume: number of establishments (or companies); number of employees; payroll; and a measure of output (sales, receipts, revenue, value of shipments, or value of construction work done.)

Number of Establishments. An establishment is a single physical location at which business is conducted. It is not necessarily identical with a company or enterprise, which may consist of one establishment or more. Economic Census figures represent a summary of reports for individual establishments rather than companies. For cases where a census report was received, separate information was obtained for each location where business was conducted. When administrative records of other Federal agencies were used instead of a census report, no information was available on the number of locations operated. Each Economic Census establishment was tabulated according to the physical location at which the business was conducted. The count of establishments represents those in business at any time during 1997.

When two activities or more were carried on at a single location under a single ownership, all activities generally were grouped together as a single establishment. The entire establishment was classified on the basis of its major activity and all data for it were included in that classification. However, when distinct and separate economic activities (for which different industry classification codes were appropriate) were conducted at a single location under a single ownership, separate establishment reports for each of the different activities were obtained in the census.

Number of Employees. Paid employees consist of the full-time and part-time employees, including salaried officers and executives of corporations. Included are employees on paid sick leave, paid holidays, and paid vacations; not included are proprietors and partners of unincorporated businesses. The definition of paid employees is the same as that used on IRS form 941.

Payroll. Payroll includes all forms of compensation such as salaries, wages, commissions, dismissal pay, bonuses, vacation allowances, sick-leave pay, and employee contributions to qualified pension plans paid during the year to all employees. For corporations, payroll includes amounts paid to officers and executives; for unincorporated businesses, it does not include profit or other compensation of proprietors or partners. Payroll is reported before deductions for social security, income tax, insurance, union dues, etc. This definition of payroll is the same as that used by the Internal Revenue Service (IRS) on form 941.

Sales, Shipments, Receipts, Revenue, or Business Done. This measure includes the total sales, shipments, receipts, revenue, or business done by establishments within the scope of the Economic Census. The definition of each of these items is specific to the economic sector measured.

WHOLESALE TRADE, Items 135–138
**Source: U.S. Bureau of the Census,
1997 Economic Census
(See Overview of 1997 Economic Census
prior to Item 135)**

The Wholesale Trade sector (sector 42) comprises establishments engaged in wholesaling merchandise, generally without transformation, and rendering services incidental to the sale of merchandise. The wholesaling process is an intermediate step in the distribution of merchandise.

Wholesalers are organized to sell or arrange the purchase or sale of (a) goods for resale (i.e., goods sold to other wholesalers or retailers), (b) capital or durable nonconsumer goods, and (c) raw and intermediate materials and supplies used in production.

Wholesalers sell merchandise to other businesses and normally operate from a warehouse or office. These warehouses and offices are characterized by having little or no display of merchandise. In addition, neither the design nor the location of the premises is intended to solicit walk-in traffic. Wholesalers do not normally use advertising directed to the general public. Customers are generally reached initially via telephone, in-person marketing, or by specialized advertising that may include Internet and other electronic means. Follow-up orders are either vendor-initiated or client-initiated, generally based on previous sales, and typically exhibit strong ties between sellers and buyers. In fact, transactions are often conducted between wholesalers and clients that have long-standing business relationships.

This sector comprises two main types of wholesalers: those that sell goods on their own account and those that arrange sales and purchases for others for a commission or fee.

(1) Establishments that sell goods on their own account are known as wholesale merchants, distributors, jobbers, drop shippers, import/export merchants, and sales branches. These establishments typically maintain their own warehouse, where they receive and handle goods for their customers. Goods are generally sold without transformation, but may include integral functions, such as sorting, packaging, labeling, and other marketing services.

(2) Establishments arranging for the purchase or sale of goods owned by others or purchasing goods on a commission basis are known as agents and brokers, commission merchants, import/export agents and brokers, auction companies, and manufacturers' representatives. These establishments operate from offices and generally do not own or handle the goods they sell.

Some wholesale establishments may be connected with a single manufacturer and promote and sell the particular manufacturer=s products to a wide range of other wholesalers or retailers. Other wholesalers may be connected to a retail chain or a limited number of retail chains and only provide a variety of products needed by that particular retail operation(s). These wholesalers may obtain the products from a wide range of manufacturers. Still other wholesalers may not take title to the goods, but act as agents and brokers for a commission.

Although, in general, wholesaling normally denotes sales in large volumes, durable nonconsumer goods may be sold in single units. Sales of capital or durable nonconsumer goods used in the production of goods and services, such as farm machinery, medium and heavy duty trucks, and industrial machinery, are always included in wholesale trade.

RETAIL TRADE, Items 139–142
**Source: U.S. Bureau of the Census,
1997 Economic Census
(See Overview of 1997 Economic Census
prior to Item 135)**

The Retail Trade sector (44-45) comprises establishments engaged in retailing merchandise, generally without transformation, and rendering services incidental to the sale of merchandise.

The retailing process is the final step in the distribution of merchandise; retailers are, therefore, organized to sell merchandise in small quantities to the general public. This sector comprises two main types of retailers: store and nonstore retailers.

Store retailers operate fixed point-of-sale locations, located and designed to attract a high volume of walk-in customers. In general, retail stores have extensive displays of merchandise and use mass-media advertising to attract customers. They typically sell merchandise to the general public for personal or household consumption, but some also serve business and institutional clients. These include establishments, such as office supply stores, computer and software stores, building materials dealers, plumbing supply stores, and electrical supply stores. Catalog showrooms, gasoline service stations, automotive dealers, and mobile home dealers are treated as store retailers.

In addition to retailing merchandise, some types of store retailers are also engaged in the provision of after-sales services, such as repair and installation. For example, new automobile dealers, electronic and appliance stores, and musical instrument and supply stores often provide repair services. As a general rule, establishments engaged in retailing merchandise and providing after-sales services are classified in this sector.

Nonstore retailers, like store retailers, are organized to serve the general public, but their retailing methods differ. The establishments of this subsector reach customers and market merchandise with methods, such as the broadcasting of "infomercials," the broadcasting and publishing of direct-response advertising, the publishing of paper and electronic catalogs, door-to-door solicitation, in-home demonstration, selling from portable stalls (street vendors, except food), and distribution through vending machines. Establishments engaged in the direct sale (nonstore) of products, such as home heating oil dealers and home delivery newspaper routes.

The buying of goods for resale is a characteristic of retail trade establishments that particularly distinguishes them from establishments in the agriculture, manufacturing, and construction industries. For example, farms that sell their products at or from the point of production are not classified in retail, but rather in agriculture. Similarly, establishments that both manufacture and sell their products to the general public are not classified in retail, but rather in manufacturing. However, establishments that engage in processing activities incidental to retailing are classified in retail.

REAL ESTATE AND RENTAL AND LEASING, Items 143–146
Source: U.S. Bureau of the Census, 1997 Economic Census
(See Overview of 1997 Economic Census prior to Item 135)

The Real Estate and Rental and Leasing sector (53) comprises establishments primarily engaged in renting, leasing, or otherwise allowing the use of tangible or intangible assets, and establishments providing related services. The major portion of this sector comprises establishments that rent, lease, or otherwise allow the use of their own assets by others. The assets may be tangible, as is the case of real estate and equipment, or intangible, as is the case with patents and trademarks.

This sector also includes establishments primarily engaged in managing real estate for others, selling, renting and/or buying real estate for others, and appraising real estate. These activities are closely related to this sector's main activity, and it was felt that from a production basis they would best be included here. In addition, a substantial proportion of property management is self-performed by lessors.

The main components of this sector are the real estate lessors industries; equipment lessors industries (including motor vehicles, computers, and consumer goods); and lessors of nonfinancial intangible assets (except copyrighted works).

PROFESSIONAL, SCIENTIFIC, AND TECHNICAL SERVICES, Items 147–150
Source: U.S. Bureau of the Census, 1997 Economic Census
(See Overview of 1997 Economic Census prior to Item 135)

The Professional, Scientific, and Technical Services sector (54) comprises establishments that specialize in performing professional, scientific, and technical activities for others. These activities require a high degree of expertise and training. The establishments in this sector specialize according to expertise and provide these services to clients in a variety of industries and, in some cases, to households. Activities performed include: legal advice and representation; accounting, bookkeeping, and payroll services; architectural, engineering, and specialized design services; computer services; consulting services; research services; advertising services; photographic services; translation and interpretation services; veterinary services; and other professional, scientific, and technical services.

This volume includes only those establishments subject to federal income tax.

This sector excludes establishments primarily engaged in providing a range of day-to-day office administrative services, such as financial planning, billing and recordkeeping, personnel, and physical distribution and logistics. These establishments are classified in Sector 56, Administrative and Support and Waste Management and Remediation Services.

MANUFACTURING, Items 151–154
Source: U.S. Bureau of the Census, 1997 Economic Census
(See Overview of 1997 Economic Census prior to Item 135)

The Manufacturing sector comprises establishments engaged in the mechanical, physical, or chemical transformation of materials, substances, or components into new products. The assembling of component parts of manufactured products is considered manufacturing, except in cases where the activity is appropriately classified as Construction. Establishments in the Manufacturing sector are often described as plants, factories, or mills and characteristically use power-driven machines and materials-handling equipment. However, establishments that transform materials or substances into new products by hand or in the worker's home and those engaged in selling to the general public products made on the same premises from which they are sold, such as bakeries, candy stores, and custom tailors, may also be included in this sector. Manufacturing establishments may process materials or may contract with other establishments to process their materials for them. Both types of establishments are included in manufacturing. The materials, substances, or components transformed by manufacturing establishments are raw materials that are products of agriculture, forestry, fishing, mining, or quarrying as well as products of other manufacturing establishments. The materials used may be purchased directly from producers, obtained through customary trade channels, or secured without recourse to the market by transferring the product from one establishment to another, under the same ownership. The new product of a manufacturing establishment may be finished in the sense that it is ready for utilization or consumption, or it may be semifinished to become an input for an establishment engaged in further manufacturing. For example, the product of the alumina refinery is the input used in the primary production of aluminum; primary aluminum is the input to an aluminum wire drawing plant; and aluminum wire is the input for a fabricated wire product manufacturing establishment.

Data are included for counties with 500 or more employees in the manufacturing sector.

ACCOMMODATION AND FOOD SERVICES, Items 155–158
Source: U.S. Bureau of the Census, 1997 Economic Census (See Overview of 1997 Economic Census prior to Item 135)

The Accommodation and Food Services sector (72) comprises establishments providing customers with lodging and/or preparing meals, snacks, and beverages for immediate consumption. The sector includes both accommodation and food services establishments because the two activities are often combined at the same establishment.

Excluded from this sector are civic and social organizations; amusement and recreation parks; theaters; and other recreation or entertainment facilities providing food and beverage services.

HEALTH CARE AND SOCIAL ASSISTANCE, Items 159–162
Source: U.S. Bureau of the Census, 1997 Economic Census (See Overview of 1997 Economic Census prior to Item 135)

The Health Care and Social Assistance sector (62) comprises establishments providing health care and social assistance for individuals. The sector includes both health care and social assistance because it is sometimes difficult to distinguish between the boundaries of these two activities. The industries in this sector are arranged on a continuum starting with those establishments providing medical care exclusively, continuing with those providing health care and social assistance, and finally finishing with those providing only social assistance. The services provided by establishments in this sector are delivered by trained professionals. All industries in the sector share this commonality of process, namely, labor inputs of health practitioners or social workers with the requisite expertise. Many of the industries in the sector are defined based on the educational degree held by the practitioners included in the industry.

In this volume, only taxable establishments are included in Table B and Table C.

Excluded from this sector are aerobic classes in Subsector 713, Amusement, Gambling and Recreation Industries and nonmedical diet and weight reducing centers in Subsector 812, Personal and Laundry Services. Although these can be viewed as health services, these services are not typically delivered by health practitioners.

OTHER SERVICES, Items 163–166
Source: U.S. Bureau of the Census, 1997 Economic Census (See Overview of 1997 Economic Census prior to Item 135)

The Other Services (except Public Administration) sector (81) comprises establishments engaged in providing services not specifically provided for elsewhere in the classification system. Establishments in this sector are primarily engaged in activities, such as equipment and machinery repairing, promoting or administering religious activities, grantmaking, advocacy, and providing drycleaning and laundry services, personal care services, death care services, pet care services, photofinishing services, temporary parking services, and dating services.

Private households that engage in employing workers on or about the premises in activities primarily concerned with the operation of the household are included in this sector.

In this volume, only firms subject to federal tax are included.

Excluded from this sector are establishments primarily engaged in retailing new equipment and also performing repairs and general maintenance on equipment. These establishments are classified in Sector 44-45, Retail Trade.

FEDERAL FUNDS, Items 167–177
Source: U.S. Bureau of the Census— Consolidated Federal Funds Report

Data on federal expenditures and obligations are obtained from a report prepared by the Bureau of the Census in accordance with the Consolidated Federal Funds Report (CFFR) Act of 1982 (P.L. 97-326). The data are for federal fiscal years beginning on October 1 and ending the following September 30. Dollar amounts reported can reflect expenditures or obligations. In some cases dollar amounts are negative representing deobligations of financial assistance that had been previously awarded. Such amounts generally appear in the grant categories.

Direct payments for individuals include social security benefits, federal government retirement, medicare, supplemental security income, food stamps, and certain other payments, including educational and housing assistance, not shown separately. All data represent actual expenditures during the fiscal year.

Salaries and wages represent actual federal expenditures during the fiscal year; the geographic distribution of these amounts by state and county was estimated based upon place of employment.

Procurement contract awards cover awards by the United States Postal Service (USPS) as well as all other federal agencies. Amounts provided by the USPS represent actual outlays for contractual commitments, while amounts for other agencies represent the value of obligations for contract actions and do not reflect actual federal government expenditures. In general, only current-year contract actions are included—however, multiple-year obligations may be reported for contract actions of less than 3 years duration.

Grants data represent the federal obligations incurred at the time the grant is awarded. The amounts reported do not represent actual expenditures since obligations in one time period may not result in outlays during the same time period. Moreover, initial amounts obligated may be adjusted at a later date, either through enhancements or de-obligations. All grant awards were reported by state, county, and city of the initial recipient. For many grants, this recipient is the state government even though the grant monies are subsequently distributed to county, municipal, or township governments.

Medicaid and other health-related grants include a variety of grants from the Department of Health and Human Services for health services and research.

Nutrition and family welfare grants include a variety of grants by the Department of Health and Human Services for child welfare, special programs for the aging, and related areas. The school lunch program and other nutritional assistance programs administered by the Department of Agriculture are also included.

Education grants include a variety of grant programs relating to elementary, secondary, and post-secondary education; adult education; vocational education; faculty training; and related areas.

LOCAL GOVERNMENT FINANCES,
Items 178–191
Source: U.S. Bureau of the Census

Data on local government finances are based on results of the 1997 Census of Governments. For each county area, the financial data comprise amounts for all local governments—not only the county government but also any municipalities, townships, school districts, and special districts within the county. Statistics from governmental units located in two or more county areas are assigned to the county area containing the administrative office.

Revenue and expenditure items include all amounts of money received and paid out, respectively, by a government and its agencies (net of correcting transactions such as recoveries of refunds), with the exception of amounts for debt issuance and retirement and for loan and investment, agency, and private transactions.

Payments among the various funds and agencies of a particular government are excluded from revenue and expenditure items as representing internal transfers. Therefore, a government's contribution to a retirement fund that it administers is not counted as expenditure, nor is the receipt of this contribution by the retirement fund counted as revenue.

Total **general revenue** includes all revenue except utility, liquor stores, and insurance trust revenue. All tax revenue and intergovernmental revenue, even if designated for employee-retirement or local utility purpose, are classified as general rev-

enue. However, to avoid duplication, revenue figures are net of reported transactions between local governments.

Intergovernmental revenue covers amounts received from the federal or state government as fiscal aid, reimbursements for performance of general government functions and specific services for the paying government, or amounts received in lieu of taxes. It excludes amounts received from other governments for sale of property, commodities, and utility services.

Taxes consist of compulsory contributions exacted by governments for public purposes. However, this category excludes employer and employee payments for retirement and social insurance purposes, which are classified as insurance trust revenue, and special assessments, which are classified as non-tax general revenue. Property taxes are taxes conditioned on ownership of property and assessed by its value.

Government expenditure includes all capital outlay, of which a major portion is commonly financed by borrowing, while governmental revenue does not include receipts from borrowing. Among other things, this distorts the relationship between totals of revenue and expenditure figures that are presented, and renders this relationship useless as a direct measure of the degree of budgetary "balance," as that term is generally applied.

Direct general expenditure comprises all expenditures of the local governments, excluding utility, liquor stores, insurance trust expenditures, and any intergovernmental payments.

Local government expenditures for **education** are mainly for provision and support of schools and other educational facilities and services, including those for educational institutions beyond the high school level operated by local governments. They cover such related services as pupil transportation; school lunch and other cafeteria operations; school health, recreation, and library services administered by local school systems; and dormitories, dining halls, and bookstores operated by public institutions of higher education.

Health and hospital expenditures include health research, clinics, nursing, immunization, and other categorical, environmental, and general health services provided by health agencies. It also includes establishment and operation of hospital facilities, provision of hospital care, and support of other public and private hospitals.

Police protection expenditure includes police activities such as patrols, communications, custody of persons awaiting trial, and vehicular inspection.

Public welfare expenditure covers support of and assistance to needy persons contingent upon their needs. Included are cash assistance paid directly to needy persons under categorical (Old Age Assistance, Aid to Families with Dependent Children, Aid to the Blind, and Aid to the Disabled) and other welfare programs; vendor payments made directly to private purveyors for medical care, burials, and other commodities and services provided under welfare programs; welfare institutions; and any intergovernmental or other direct expenditure for welfare purposes. Pensions to former employees and other benefits not contingent upon need are excluded.

Highway expenditure is for provision and maintenance of highway facilities, including toll turnpikes, bridges, tunnels, and ferries, as well as regular roads, highways, and streets. Also included are expenditures for street lighting and for snow and ice removal.

Debt outstanding includes all long-term debt obligations of the government and its agencies (exclusive of utility debt) and all interest-bearing short-term (i.e., repayable within one year) debt obligations remaining unpaid at the close of the fiscal year. It includes judgments, mortgages, and revenue bonds, as well as general obligation bonds, notes, and interest-bearing warrants. It includes non-interest-bearing short-term obligations, inter-fund obligations, amounts owed in a trust or agency capacity, advances and contingent loans from other governments, and rights of individuals to benefits from government-administered employee retirement funds.

GOVERNMENT EMPLOYMENT, Items 192–194
Source: U.S. Bureau of Economic Analysis

Employment is measured as the average annual number of jobs, full-time plus part-time. The estimates are on a place-of-work basis. State and local government employment includes employment in all state and local government agencies and enterprises.

Federal civilian employment includes all civilian employees of the federal government, including civilian employees of the Department of Defense. Military employment includes all person on active duty status.

ELECTION STATISTICS, Items 195–197
Source: Federal Election Commission and State Election Offices

Election results show the percentage of the total vote cast for each of the Democratic and Republican candidates, as well as the combined percentage for all other candidates in the 1996 presidential election.

TABLE D—CITIES

Table D presents 147 items of data for cities that had a population of 25,000 or more at the time of the 1990 census.

LAND AREA, Items 1 and 4
Source: U.S. Bureau of the Census

Land area measurements are shown to the nearest square kilometer. Land area includes dry land and land temporarily or partially covered by water, such as marshland, swamps, and river floodplains.

POPULATION, Items 2–4
Source: U.S. Bureau of the Census

The population data are U.S. Bureau of the Census estimates of the resident population as of July 1 of the year shown.

POPULATION AND POPULATION CHANGE, Items 5–8
Source: 1980 and 1990 Census of Population and Housing

These population counts are from the decennial census and represent resident population as of April 1, 1980 and 1990 respectively. Population change 1990-1999 is calculated from 1990 census data and 1999 estimates based on city boundaries as they existed in 1990 and 1999 respectively. No attempt was made to adjust the data to reflect boundary changes.

Population change 1980-1990 is calculated from 1980 and 1990 data based on city boundaries as they existed in 1980 and 1990 respectively. No attempt was made to adjust the data to reflect boundary changes.

Some 1990 census counts were revised in 1999 to reflect corrections. The 1980-1990 change numbers in this volume are based on the new 1990 numbers but the components of change are not.

POPULATION BY RACE AND HISPANIC ORIGIN, Items 9–14
Source: U.S. Bureau of the Census— 1990 Census of Population and Housing

Population by race, as defined by the Census Bureau, reflects self-identification by respondents; it does not denote any clear-cut scientific definition of biological stock. In the 1990 census, data were obtained through self-classification.

The White population is defined as persons who indicated their race as white, as well as persons who did not classify themselves in one of the specific race categories listed on the questionnaire but entered a nationality such as Canadian, German, Italian, Lebanese, or Polish.

The Black population includes persons who indicated their race as black or Negro, as well as persons who did not classify them-

selves in one of the specific race categories but reported entries such as Black Puerto Rican, Haitian, Jamaican, Nigerian, or West Indian.

The American Indian, Eskimo, and Aleut population includes persons who indicated their race as Indian (American), Eskimo, or Aleut, as well as persons who did not indicate a specific race category but reported the name of an Indian tribe.

The Asian and Pacific Islander population includes persons who indicated their race as Chinese, Filipino, Japanese, Asian Indian, Korean, Vietnamese, Hawaiian, Samoan, or Guamanian. As well as persons who provided write-in entries of such Asian and Pacific Islander groups as Cambodian, Laotian, Pakistani, and Fiji Islander.

The **Hispanic population** is based on a complete-count question that asked respondents to identify whether they were of Spanish/Hispanic origin. Persons marking any 1 of the 4 Spanish categories (i.e., Mexican, Puerto Rican, Cuban, or Other Spanish) are collectively referred to as Hispanic. Hispanic is not a race category; Hispanic persons may be of any race.

POPULATION—FOREIGN-BORN, Item 15
Source: U.S. Bureau of the Census— 1990 Census of Population and Housing

The foreign-born population is based on birthplace and citizenship questions asked of a sample of persons in the 1990 census. **Foreign-born** includes persons not born in the United States, Puerto Rico, or an outlying area of the United States. Persons who were born in a foreign country but who have at least 1 American parent are excluded from this category.

POPULATION—AGE, Items 16–24
Source: U.S. Bureau of the Census— 1990 Census of Population and Housing

Age derived from the census (1990) is classified as age at last birthday (i.e., number of completed years from birth to April 1). The percent figures are derived by dividing the number of persons in a specified age group by the total population of a given geographic area. Data on age are based on complete counts of resident population.

POPULATION—PERCENT FEMALE, Item 25
Source: U.S. Bureau of the Census— 1990 Census of Population and Housing

The female population of a geographic area is shown as a percent of the total population of the area.

HOUSEHOLDS, 1990, Items 26–30
Source: U.S. Bureau of the Census— 1990 Census of Population and Housing

A household consists of persons occupying a single housing unit. A housing unit is a house, an apartment, a group of rooms, or a single room occupied as separate living quarters. The occupants may be a single family, 1 person living alone, 2 or more families living together, or any other group of related or unrelated persons who share a housing unit. The number of households is the same as the number of year-round occupied housing units.

A family household consists of 2 or more persons, including the householder, who are related by birth, marriage, or adoption and who live together as 1 household; all such persons are considered as members of one family.

The measure of persons per household is obtained by dividing the number of persons in households by the number of households or householders. The category **female family householder** includes only female-headed family households with no spouse present.

GROUP QUARTERS, Items 31–34
Source: U.S. Bureau of the Census—
1990 Census of Population and Housing

All persons not living in households are classified by the Census Bureau as living in group quarters. This volume includes the total number of persons in group quarters and in selected types of group quarters.

Mental (Psychiatric) hospitals include psychiatric wards of general hospitals and veterans' hospitals and hospitals or wards for the criminally insane not operated by a prison. Patients receive supervised medical/nursing care from formally-trained staff.

Nursing homes comprise a heterogeneous group of places. The majority of patients are elderly, although persons who require nursing care because of chronic physical conditions may be found in these homes regardless of their age. Included in this category are skilled-nursing facilities, intermediate-care facilities, long-term care rooms in wards or buildings on the grounds of hospitals, or long-term care rooms/nursing wings in congregate housing facilities. Also included are nursing, convalescent, and rest homes, such as soldiers', sailors', veterans', and fraternal or religious homes for the aged, with or without nursing care.

Persons identified as **homeless** include persons in emergency shelters for homeless persons (with sleeping facilities) and persons visible in street locations. This includes persons enumerated during the 1990 Census "Shelter-and-Street-Night" operation. Enumerators were instructed not to ask if a person was "homeless." A person at one of these locations was counted as homeless.

Other types of group quarters, not shown separately in this volume, include (among others) correctional institutions, juvenile institutions, college dormitories, and military quarters.

CRIME, Items 35–38
Source: U.S. Federal Bureau of Investigation—
Uniform Crime Reports

Crime data are as reported to the FBI by law enforcement agencies and have not been adjusted for under-reporting. This may affect comparability between geographic areas or over time.

Through the voluntary contribution of crime statistics by law enforcement agencies across the United States, the Uniform Crime Reporting (UCR) Program provides periodic assessments of crime in the nation as measured by those offenses which come to the attention of the law enforcement community. The Committee on Uniform Crime Records of the International Association of Chiefs of Police initiated this voluntary national data-collection effort in 1930. UCR Program contributors compile and submit their crime data in 1 of 2 manners: either directly to the FBI or through the State UCR Programs.

Seven offenses, because of their seriousness, frequency of occurrence, and likelihood of being reported to police, were initially selected to serve as an index for evaluating fluctuations in the volume of crime. These serious crimes were murder and nonnegligent manslaughter, forcible rape, robbery, aggravated assault, burglary, larceny-theft, and motor vehicle theft. By congressional mandate, arson was added as the eighth index offense in 1979. The totals shown in this volume do not include arson.

Violent offenses include 4 crime categories: (1) Murder and nonnegligent manslaughter, as defined in the UCR Program, is the willful (nonnegligent) killing of 1 human being by another. This offense excludes deaths caused by negligence, suicide or accident; justifiable homicides; and attempts to murder or assaults to murder. (2) Forcible rape is the carnal knowledge of a female forcibly and against her will. Assaults or attempts to commit rape by force or threat of force are also included; however, statutory rape (without force) and other sex offenses are excluded. (3) Robbery is the taking or attempting to take anything of value from the care, custody, or control of a person or persons by force or threat of force or violence and/or by putting the victim in fear. (4) Aggravated assault is an unlawful attack by 1 person upon another for the purpose of inflicting severe or aggravated bodily injury. This type of assault is usually accompanied by the use of a weapon or by means likely to produce death or great bodily harm. Attempts are included since an injury does not necessarily have to result when a gun, knife, or other weapon is used, which could and probably would result in a serious personal injury if the crime were successfully completed.

Property crimes include 3 categories: (1) Burglary, or breaking and entering, is the unlawful entry of a structure to commit a felony or theft, even though no force was used to gain entrance. (2) Larceny/theft is the unauthorized taking of the personal property of another, without the use of force. (3) Motor vehicle theft is the unauthorized taking of any motor vehicle.

Rates are based on population estimates provided by the FBI.

EDUCATION—SCHOOL ENROLLMENT AND EDUCATIONAL ATTAINMENT, Items 39–42
Source: U.S. Bureau of the Census—
1990 Census of Population and Housing

Data on school enrollment and educational attainment were derived from a sample of the population. Persons were classified as enrolled in school if they reported attending a "regular" public or private school (or college) at any time between February 1, 1990 and the time of enumeration. The instructions were to "include only nursery school, kindergarten, elementary school, and schooling which would lead to a high school diploma or a college degree" as regular school. Public school is defined as "any school or college controlled and supported by a local, county, state, or federal government." Schools supported and controlled primarily by religious organizations or other private groups are defined as private.

Statistics for years of school completed are for persons 25 years old and over. The data were derived from a question on the 1990 census questionnaire that asked respondents for the highest level of school they had completed or the highest degree they had received. Persons who passed a high school equivalency examination were considered high school graduates. Schooling received in foreign schools was to be reported as the equivalent grade or years in the regular American school system.

MONEY INCOME, Items 43–46
Source: U.S. Bureau of the Census—
1990 Census of Population and Housing

The data on income are derived from the responses of a sample of persons 15 years old and older. **Total money income** is defined by the Bureau of the Census for statistical purposes as the sum of the following: wage or salary income; nonfarm self-employment income; net farm self-employment income; Social Security and railroad retirement income; public assistance income; and all other regularly received income such as interest, dividends, veterans' payments, pensions, unemployment compensation, and alimony. Receipts not counted as income include various "lump sum" payments such as capital gains or inheritances.

The total represents the amount of income received before deductions for personal income taxes, Social Security, bond purchases, union dues, Medicare deductions, etc.

Per capita income is based on resident population enumerated as of April 1, 1990.

Income of households includes the income of the householder and all other persons 15 years old and older in the household. Household income is usually less than family income because many households consist of only 1 person. The median divides the income distribution into 2 equal parts, 1 having incomes above the median, the other with incomes below. The constant-dollar figures are based on an annual average Consumer Price Index from the Bureau of Labor Statistics. Constant-dollar figures are estimates representing an effort to remove the effects of price changes from statistical series reported in dollar terms. However, the estimates do not reflect the price and cost-of-living differences that may exist between areas.

POVERTY, Items 47–49
Source: U.S. Bureau of the Census—
1990 Census of Population and Housing

The data on poverty are derived from the same questions as the data on money income. Poverty status is based on the definition prescribed by the Federal Office of Management and Budget as the standard to be used by federal agencies for statistical purposes. Families and persons are classified as below the poverty level if their total family income or unrelated individual income was less than the poverty threshold specified for the applicable family size, age of householder, and number of related children present under 18. Poverty status is determined for all families (and by implication all family members). For persons not in families, poverty status is determined by their income in relation to the appropriate poverty threshold. Inmates of institutions, persons in military group quarters or college dormitories, and unrelated individuals under 15 are excluded.

The 1989 poverty thresholds are shown in Figure 1.

Figure 1.
Poverty Thresholds in 1989 by Size of Family

Size of Family Unit	Weighted average thresholds
One person (unrelated individual)	$6,310
Under 65 years	6,451
65 years and over	5,947
Two persons	8,076
Householder under 65 years	8,343
Householder 65 years and over	7,501
Three persons	9,885
Four persons	12,674
Five persons	14,990
Six persons	16,921
Seven persons	19,162
Eight persons	21,328
Nine or more persons	25,480

HOUSING, Items 50–60
Source: U.S. Bureau of the Census—
1990 Census of Population and Housing

A **housing unit** is a house, apartment, mobile home or trailer, group of rooms, or single room occupied or, if vacant, intended for occupancy as separate living quarters. Separate living quarters are those in which the occupants do not live and eat with any other persons in the structure and which have direct access from the outside of the building through a common hall.

The occupants of a housing unit may be a single family, 1 person living alone, 2 or more families living together, or a group of related or unrelated persons who share living arrangements. For vacant units, the criteria of separateness and direct access are applied to the intended occupants whenever possible. If that information cannot be obtained, the criteria are applied to the previous occupants. Both occupied and vacant housing units are included in the housing inventory, except that recreational vehicles, tents, caves, boats, railroad cars, and the like are included only if they are occupied as someone's usual place of residence.

A housing unit is classified as occupied if it is the usual place of residence of the person or group of persons living in it at the time of enumeration or if the occupants are only temporarily absent (e.g., away on vacation). A household consists of all persons who occupy a housing unit as their usual place of residence. Vacant units for sale or rent include units rented or sold but not occupied and any other units held off the market.

The percent change represents the difference in the number of total housing units in a specified area over the decade 1980-1990.

Median value is the dollar amount that divides the distribution of owner-occupied housing units into 2 equal parts with one half of the units falling below this value and the other half exceeding it. Value is defined as the respondent's estimate of what the house would sell for if it were for sale. Data are presented for 1-family unit on less than 10 acres and with no business or medical office on the property.

Median rent divides the distribution of renter-occupied housing units into 2 equal parts. Median rent represents the amount of cash rent a renter pays (contract rent) plus the estimated average cost of utilities and fuels if paid by the renter (gross rent). Rent is to be reported only for living quarters, not for any business or other space occupied. Single family houses on lots of 10 or more acres are excluded.

Housing cost as a percent of income is shown separately for owners with mortgages, owners without mortgages, and renters. Rent as a percentage of income is computed as the ratio of gross rent and monthly household income (total household income in 1989 divided by 12). Selected owner costs include utilities and fuels, as well as mortgage payments, insurance, taxes, etc. In each case, the ratio of housing cost to income is computed separately for each housing unit. The ratios for one-half of the units are above the median shown in this book, and one-half are below.

Substandard units are occupied units which are overcrowded or lack complete plumbing facilities. For the purposes of this item "overcrowded" is defined as having 1.01 persons or more per room. Complete plumbing facilities include hot and cold piped water, a flush toilet, and a bathtub or shower. All these facilities must be located inside the housing unit but not necessarily in the same room.

CIVILIAN LABOR FORCE AND UNEMPLOYMENT, Items 61–64
Source: U.S. Bureau of Labor Statistics

Data for the civilian labor force are the product of a federal-state cooperative program in which state employment security agencies prepare labor force and unemployment estimates under concepts, definitions, and technical procedures established by the Bureau of Labor Statistics. The civilian labor force consists of all persons 16 years and over who are either employed in a civilian job or unemployed.

Unemployment includes all persons who did not work during the survey week, made specific efforts to find a job in the prior 4 weeks, and were available for work during the survey week (except for temporary illness). Persons waiting to be called back to a job from which they had been laid off and those waiting to report to a new job within the next 30 days are included in unemployment figures.

CIVILIAN EMPLOYMENT, 1990, Items 65–67
Source: U.S. Bureau of the Census— 1990 Census of Population and Housing

Total employment includes all civilians 16 years old or older who were either (1) "at work" — those who did any work at all during the reference week as paid employees, worked in their own business or profession, worked on their own farm, or worked 15 hours or more as unpaid workers in a family farm or business; or were (2) "with a job, but not at work"—those who had a job but were not at work that week due to illness, weather, industrial dispute, vacation, or other personal reasons.

The **occupation categories** shown are consistent with the 1980 edition of the *Standard Occupational Classification Manual (SOC)* published by the Office of Federal Statistical Policy and Standards, U.S. Department of Commerce. Professional, managerial, and technical occupations include the following categories: executive administrative, and managerial occupations (000-042); professional specialty occupations (043-202); and technicians and related support occupations (203-242). Precision production, craft, and repair includes SOC codes 503-702.

WORK DISABILITY, Item 68
Source: U.S. Bureau of the Census— 1990 Census of Population and Housing

Data are shown for persons 16 to 64 years old in 1990. Persons were identified as having a work disability if they reported a health condition that had lasted 6 months or more and which limited the kind or amount of work they could do at a job or business.

CONSTRUCTION—BUILDING PERMITS, Items 69–71
Source: U.S. Bureau of the Census— Building Permits Survey

Figures represent private residential construction authorized by building permits in approximately 19,000 places in the United States. Valuation represents the cost of construction as recorded on the building permit. This figure usually excludes the cost of on-site and off-site development and improvements and the cost of heating, plumbing, electrical, and elevator installations.

If a city is not a permit-issuing place covered by the Census Bureau, an "NA" is shown. Cities that are permit-issuing places but that issued no permits during the period are represented by a "0." State and U.S. totals were obtained by summing the data for permit issuing places within each jurisdiction.

Residential building permits include buildings with any number of housing units. Hotels, apartment hotels, dormitories, fraternity houses, and other non-housekeeping residential buildings are not included.

1997 ECONOMIC CENSUS: OVERVIEW
Items 72–107
Source: U.S. Bureau of the Census

The Economic Census provides a detailed portrait of the nation's economy once every five years, from the national to the local level. The 1997 Economic Census covers nearly all of the U.S. economy in its basic collection of establishment statistics. It is the first major data source to use the new North American Industry Classification System (NAICS) and is therefore not comparable to economic data from prior years which were based on the Standard Industrial Classification (SIC) system.

NAICS, developed in cooperation with Canada and Mexico, classifies North America's economic activities at 2-, 3-, 4-, and 5-digit levels of detail, and the U.S. version of NAICS further defines industries to a sixth digit. The Economic Census takes advantage of this hierarchy to publish data at these successive levels of detail: sector (2-digit); subsector (3-digit); industry group (4-digit); industry(5-digit); and U.S. industry(6-digit.)

This volume was published during the initial release of the 1997 Economic Census and therefore includes those sectors that were available at the time of publication. The information in Table D is at the 2-digit level.

Several key statistics are tabulated for all industries included in this volume: number of establishments (or companies); number of employees; payroll; and a measure of output (sales, receipts, revenue, value of shipments, or value of construction work done.)

Number of Establishments. An establishment is a single physical location at which business is conducted. It is not necessarily identical with a company or enterprise, which may consist of one establishment or more. Economic Census figures represent a summary of reports for individual establishments rather than companies. For cases where a census report was received, separate information was obtained for each location where business was conducted. When administrative records of other Federal agencies were used instead of a census report, no information was available on the number of locations operated. Each Economic Census establishment was tabulated according to the physical location at which the business was conducted. The count of establishments represents those in business at any time during 1997.

When two activities or more were carried on at a single location under a single ownership, all activities generally were grouped together as a single establishment. The entire establishment was classified on the basis of its major activity and all data for it were included in that classification. However, when distinct and separate economic activities (for which different industry classification codes were appropriate) were conducted at a single location under a single ownership, separate establishment reports for each of the different activities were obtained in the census.

Number of Employees. Paid employees consist of the full-time and part-time employees, including salaried officers and executives of corporations. Included are employees on paid sick leave, paid holidays, and paid vacations; not included are proprietors and partners of unincorporated businesses. The definition of paid employees is the same as that used on IRS form 941.

Payroll. Payroll includes all forms of compensation such as salaries, wages, commissions, dismissal pay, bonuses, vacation allowances, sick-leave pay, and employee contributions to qualified pension plans paid during the year to all employees. For corporations, payroll includes amounts paid to officers and executives; for unincorporated businesses, it does not include profit or other compensation of proprietors or partners. Payroll is reported before deductions for social security, income tax, insurance, union dues, etc. This definition of payroll is the same as that used by the Internal Revenue Service (IRS) on form 941.

Sales, Shipments, Receipts, Revenue, or Business Done. This measure includes the total sales, shipments, receipts, revenue, or business done by establishments within the scope of the Economic Census. The definition of each of these items is specific to the economic sector measured.

WHOLESALE TRADE, Items 72–75
Source: U.S. Bureau of the Census,
1997 Economic Census
(See Overview of 1997 Economic Census
prior to Item 72)

The Wholesale Trade sector (sector 42) comprises establishments engaged in wholesaling merchandise, generally without transformation, and rendering services incidental to the sale of merchandise. The wholesaling process is an intermediate step in the distribution of merchandise.

Wholesalers are organized to sell or arrange the purchase or sale of (a) goods for resale (i.e., goods sold to other wholesalers or retailers), (b) capital or durable nonconsumer goods, and (c) raw and intermediate materials and supplies used in production.

Wholesalers sell merchandise to other businesses and normally operate from a warehouse or office. These warehouses and offices are characterized by having little or no display of merchandise. In addition, neither the design nor the location of the premises is intended to solicit walk-in traffic. Wholesalers do not normally use advertising directed to the general public. Customers are generally reached initially via telephone, in-person marketing, or by specialized advertising that may include Internet and other electronic means. Follow-up orders are either vendor-initiated or client-initiated, generally based on previous sales, and typically exhibit strong ties between sellers and buyers. In fact, transactions are often conducted between wholesalers and clients that have long-standing business relationships.

This sector comprises two main types of wholesalers: those that sell goods on their own account and those that arrange sales and purchases for others for a commission or fee.

(1) Establishments that sell goods on their own account are known as wholesale merchants, distributors, jobbers, drop shippers, import/export merchants, and sales branches. These establishments typically maintain their own warehouse, where they receive and handle goods for their customers. Goods are generally sold without transformation, but may include integral functions, such as sorting, packaging, labeling, and other marketing services.

(2) Establishments arranging for the purchase or sale of goods owned by others or purchasing goods on a commission basis are known as agents and brokers, commission merchants, import/export agents and brokers, auction companies, and manufacturers' representatives. These establishments operate from offices and generally do not own or handle the goods they sell.

Some wholesale establishments may be connected with a single manufacturer and promote and sell the particular manufacturer=s products to a wide range of other wholesalers or retailers. Other wholesalers may be connected to a retail chain or a limited number of retail chains and only provide a variety of products needed by that particular retail operation(s). These wholesalers may obtain the products from a wide range of manufacturers. Still other wholesalers may not take title to the goods, but act as agents and brokers for a commission.

Although, in general, wholesaling normally denotes sales in large volumes, durable nonconsumer goods may be sold in single units. Sales of capital or durable nonconsumer goods used in the production of goods and services, such as farm machinery, medium and heavy duty trucks, and industrial machinery, are always included in wholesale trade.

RETAIL TRADE, Items 76–79
Source: U.S. Bureau of the Census,
1997 Economic Census
(See Overview of 1997 Economic Census
prior to Item 72)

The Retail Trade sector (44-45) comprises establishments engaged in retailing merchandise, generally without transformation, and rendering services incidental to the sale of merchandise.

The retailing process is the final step in the distribution of merchandise; retailers are, therefore, organized to sell merchandise in small quantities to the general public. This sector comprises two main types of retailers: store and nonstore retailers.

Store retailers operate fixed point-of-sale locations, located and designed to attract a high volume of walk-in customers. In general, retail stores have extensive displays of merchandise and use mass-media advertising to attract customers. They typically sell merchandise to the general public for personal or household consumption, but some also serve business and institutional clients. These include establishments, such as office supply stores, computer and software stores, building materials dealers, plumbing supply stores, and electrical supply stores. Catalog showrooms, gasoline service stations, automotive dealers, and mobile home dealers are treated as store retailers.

In addition to retailing merchandise, some types of store retailers are also engaged in the provision of after-sales services, such as repair and installation. For example, new automobile dealers, electronic and appliance stores, and musical instrument and supply stores often provide repair services. As a general rule, establishments engaged in retailing merchandise and providing after-sales services are classified in this sector.

Nonstore retailers, like store retailers, are organized to serve the general public, but their retailing methods differ. The establishments of this subsector reach customers and market merchandise with methods, such as the broadcasting of "infomercials," the broadcasting and publishing of direct-response advertising, the publishing of paper and electronic catalogs, door-to-door solicitation, in-home demonstration, selling from portable stalls (street vendors, except food), and distribution through vending machines.

Establishments engaged in the direct sale (nonstore) of products, such as home heating oil dealers and home delivery newspaper routes.

The buying of goods for resale is a characteristic of retail trade establishments that particularly distinguishes them from establishments in the agriculture, manufacturing, and construction industries. For example, farms that sell their products at or from the point of production are not classified in retail, but rather in agriculture. Similarly, establishments that both manufacture and sell their products to the general public are not classified in retail, but rather in manufacturing. However, establishments that engage in processing activities incidental to retailing are classified in retail.

REAL ESTATE AND RENTAL AND LEASING, Items 80–83
Source: U.S. Bureau of the Census,
1997 Economic Census
(See Overview of 1997 Economic Census
prior to Item 72)

The Real Estate and Rental and Leasing sector (53) comprises establishments primarily engaged in renting, leasing, or otherwise allowing the use of tangible or intangible assets, and establishments providing related services. The major portion of this sector comprises establishments that rent, lease, or otherwise allow the use of their own assets by others. The assets may be tangible, as is the case of real estate and equipment, or intangible, as is the case with patents and trademarks.

This sector also includes establishments primarily engaged in managing real estate for others, selling, renting and/or buying real estate for others, and appraising real estate. These activities are closely related to this sector's main activity, and it was felt that from a production basis they would best be included here. In addition, a substantial proportion of property management is self-performed by lessors.

The main components of this sector are the real estate lessors industries; equipment lessors industries (including motor vehicles, computers, and consumer goods); and lessors of nonfinancial intangible assets (except copyrighted works).

PROFESSIONAL, SCIENTIFIC, AND TECHNICAL SERVICES, Items 84–87
Source: U.S. Bureau of the Census,
1997 Economic Census
(See Overview of 1997 Economic Census
prior to Item 72)

The Professional, Scientific, and Technical Services sector (54) comprises establishments that specialize in performing professional, scientific, and technical activities for others. These activities require a high degree of expertise and training. The establishments in this sector specialize according to expertise and provide these services to clients in a variety of industries and, in some cases, to households. Activities performed include: legal advice and representation; accounting, bookkeeping, and payroll services; architectural, engineering, and specialized design services; computer services; consulting services; research services; advertising services; photographic services; translation and interpretation services; veterinary services; and other professional, scientific, and technical services.

This volume includes only those establishments subject to federal income tax.

This sector excludes establishments primarily engaged in providing a range of day-to-day office administrative services, such as financial planning, billing and recordkeeping, personnel, and physical distribution and logistics. These establishments are classified in Sector 56, Administrative and Support and Waste Management and Remediation Services.

MANUFACTURING, Items 88-91
**Source: U.S. Bureau of the Census,
1997 Economic Census
(See Overview of 1997 Economic Census prior to Item 72)**

The Manufacturing sector comprises establishments engaged in the mechanical, physical, or chemical transformation of materials, substances, or components into new products. The assembling of component parts of manufactured products is considered manufacturing, except in cases where the activity is appropriately classified as Construction. Establishments in the Manufacturing sector are often described as plants, factories, or mills and characteristically use power-driven machines and materials-handling equipment. However, establishments that transform materials or substances into new products by hand or in the worker's home and those engaged in selling to the general public products made on the same premises from which they are sold, such as bakeries, candy stores, and custom tailors, may also be included in this sector. Manufacturing establishments may process materials or may contract with other establishments to process their materials for them. Both types of establishments are included in manufacturing. The materials, substances, or components transformed by manufacturing establishments are raw materials that are products of agriculture, forestry, fishing, mining, or quarrying as well as products of other manufacturing establishments. The materials used may be purchased directly from producers, obtained through customary trade channels, or secured without recourse to the market by transferring the product from one establishment to another, under the same ownership. The new product of a manufacturing establishment may be finished in the sense that it is ready for utilization or consumption, or it may be semifinished to become an input for an establishment engaged in further manufacturing. For example, the product of the alumina refinery is the input used in the primary production of aluminum; primary aluminum is the input to an aluminum wire drawing plant; and aluminum wire is the input for a fabricated wire product manufacturing establishment.

Data are included for cities with 500 or more employees in the manufacturing sector.

ACCOMMODATION AND FOOD SERVICES, Items 92–95
**Source: U.S. Bureau of the Census,
1997 Economic Census
(See Overview of 1997 Economic Census prior to Item 72)**

The Accommodation and Food Services sector (72) comprises establishments providing customers with lodging and/or preparing meals, snacks, and beverages for immediate consumption. The sector includes both accommodation and food services establishments because the two activities are often combined at the same establishment.

Excluded from this sector are civic and social organizations; amusement and recreation parks; theaters; and other recreation or entertainment facilities providing food and beverage services.

ARTS, ENTERTAINMENT, AND RECREATION, Items 96–99
**Source: U.S. Bureau of the Census,
1997 Economic Census
(See Overview of 1997 Economic Census prior to Item 181)**

The Arts, Entertainment, and Recreation sector (71) includes a wide range of establishments that operate facilities or provide services to meet varied cultural, entertainment, and recreational interests of their patrons. This sector comprises (1) establishments that are involved in producing, promoting, or participating in live performances, events, or exhibits intended for public viewing; (2) establishments that preserve and exhibit objects and sites of historical, cultural, or educational interest; and (3) establishments that operate facilities or provide services that enable patrons to participate in recreational activities or pursue amusement, hobby, and leisure time interests.

Some establishments that provide cultural, entertainment, or recreational facilities and services are classified in other sectors. Excluded from this sector are: (1) establishments that provide both accommodations and recreational facilities, such as hunting and fishing camps and resort and casino hotels are classified in Subsector 721, Accommodation; (2) restaurants and night clubs that provide live entertainment in addition to the sale of food and beverages are classified in Subsector 722, Food Services and Drinking Places; (3) motion picture theaters, libraries and archives, and publishers of newspapers, magazines, books, periodicals, and computer software are classified in Sector 51, Information; and (4) establishments using transportation equipment to provide recreational and entertainment services, such as those operating sightseeing buses, dinner cruises, or helicopter rides are classified in Subsector 487, Scenic and Sightseeing Transportation.

HEALTH CARE AND SOCIAL ASSISTANCE, Items 100–103
Source: U.S. Bureau of the Census, 1997 Economic Census
(See Overview of 1997 Economic Census prior to Item 72)

The Health Care and Social Assistance sector (62) comprises establishments providing health care and social assistance for individuals. The sector includes both health care and social assistance because it is sometimes difficult to distinguish between the boundaries of these two activities. The industries in this sector are arranged on a continuum starting with those establishments providing medical care exclusively, continuing with those providing health care and social assistance, and finally finishing with those providing only social assistance. The services provided by establishments in this sector are delivered by trained professionals. All industries in the sector share this commonality of process, namely, labor inputs of health practitioners or social workers with the requisite expertise. Many of the industries in the sector are defined based on the educational degree held by the practitioners included in the industry.

In this volume, only taxable establishments are included in Table D.

Excluded from this sector are aerobic classes in Subsector 713, Amusement, Gambling and Recreation Industries and nonmedical diet and weight reducing centers in Subsector 812, Personal and Laundry Services. Although these can be viewed as health services, these services are not typically delivered by health practitioners.

OTHER SERVICES, Items 104–107
Source: U.S. Bureau of the Census, 1997 Economic Census
(See Overview of 1997 Economic Census prior to Item 72)

The Other Services (except Public Administration) sector (81) comprises establishments engaged in providing services not specifically provided for elsewhere in the classification system. Establishments in this sector are primarily engaged in activities, such as equipment and machinery repairing, promoting or administering religious activities, grantmaking, advocacy, and providing drycleaning and laundry services, personal care services, death care services, pet care services, photofinishing services, temporary parking services, and dating services.

Private households that engage in employing workers on or about the premises in activities primarily concerned with the operation of the household are included in this sector.

In this volume, only firms subject to federal tax are included.

Excluded from this sector are establishments primarily engaged in retailing new equipment and also performing repairs and general maintenance on equipment. These establishments are classified in Sector 44–45, Retail Trade.

FEDERAL FUNDS, Items 108–116
Source: U.S. Bureau of the Census— Consolidated Federal Funds Report

Data on federal expenditures and obligations are obtained from a report prepared by the Bureau of the Census in accordance with the Consolidated Federal Funds Report (CFFR) Act of 1982 (P.L. 97-326). The data are for federal fiscal years beginning on October 1 and ending the following September 30.

Only selected categories of data from the CFFR can be allocated to the city level. The city items shown in this book are "selected" federal funds and do not represent all federal funds received by individuals and entities within the city.

Dollar amounts reported can reflect expenditure or obligations. In some cases, dollar amounts are negative, representing deobligations of financial assistance that had been previously awarded. Such amounts generally appear in the grant categories. Many categories are assigned only to state and county levels and never assigned to cities. Even the District of Columbia has funds assigned to "state undistributed" or "county undistributed," with the resulting "city" total enabling a more accurate comparison with other cities

Direct payments for individuals represent actual expenditures during the fiscal year. Direct payments data at the city level are limited largely to educational and housing assistance payments. Direct payments for educational assistance consist primarily of higher education grants and insured loans. Direct housing assistance includes primarily the Low Income Housing Assistance Program. Data on other types of direct payments, including food stamps, social security, and federal retirement, and data on federal wages and salaries are available for counties but not for cities.

Procurement contract awards cover awards by the United States Postal Service (USPS) as well as all other federal agencies. Amounts provided by the USPS represent actual outlays for contractual commitments, while amounts for other agencies represent the value of obligations for contract actions and do not reflect actual federal government expenditures. In general, only current-year contract actions are included—however, multiple-year obligations may be reported for contract actions of less than 3 years duration. The procurement contract data for cities are relatively complete.

Salaries and wages represent actual federal expenditures during the fiscal year; the geographic distribution of these amounts by state and county was estimated based upon place of employment.

Grants data represent the federal obligations incurred at the time the grant is awarded. The amounts reported do not represent actual expenditures since obligations in one time period may not result in outlays during the same time period. Moreover, initial amounts obligated may be adjusted at a later date, either through enhancements or de-obligations. All grant awards were reported by state, county, and city of the initial recipient. For many grants, this recipient is the state government even though the grant monies are subsequently distributed to county, municipal, or township governments. The grants for cities data exclude a number of large grant categories, such as grants made for the school lunch program.

Health and family welfare grants include a variety of grants by the U.S. Department of Health and Human Services for health research, child welfare, special programs for the aging, and related areas. The school lunch program and other nutritional assistance programs administered by the U.S. Department of Agriculture are also included.

Energy and environment grants include grants from the U.S. Department of Energy for energy development, energy conservation, and nuclear waste disposal, as well as from the Environmental Protection Agency for a variety of pollution control and waste management activities.

Education grants include a variety of grant programs relating to elementary, secondary, and post-secondary education; adult education; vocational education; faculty training; and related areas.

Housing and community development grants include Community Development Block Grants, housing demonstration programs, rental housing rehabilitation, and other housing programs.

CITY GOVERNMENT FINANCES,
Items 117–139
Source: U.S. Bureau of the Census—
1997 Census of Governments

Revenue and expenditure data for the city government only are included in this table. The numbers do not include funds of any special district governments located in the city.

Total **general revenue** includes all government revenue except utility, liquor store, and employee-retirement or other insurance trust revenue. It includes all tax collections and intergovernmental revenue, even if designated for employee-retirement or local utility purposes.

Intergovernmental revenue consists of amounts received from other governments as fiscal aid in the form of shared revenues and grants-in-aid, as reimbursements for performance of general expenditure functions and specific services for the paying government (e.g., care of prisoners or contractual research), or amounts in lieu of taxes. It excludes amounts received from other governments for sale of property, commodities, and utility services. All intergovernmental revenue is classified as general revenue. Intergovernmental revenue from the state government includes amounts originally from the federal government but channeled through the state.

Taxes are compulsory contributions exacted by a government for public purposes, and exclude employee and employer assessments for retirement and social insurance purposes, which are classified as insurance trust revenue. All tax revenue is classified as general revenue and comprises amounts received (including interest and penalties but excluding protested amounts and refunds) from all taxes imposed by a government. Note that local government tax revenue excludes any amounts from shares of state-imposed and collected taxes, which are classified as intergovernmental revenue.

Property taxes are based on ownership of property and measured by its value. They include general property taxes related to property as a whole—real and personal, tangible or intangible—whether taxed at a single rate or at classified rates. Also included are taxes on selected types of property, such as motor vehicles or certain or all intangibles.

Sales and gross receipts taxes include: "licenses" at more than nominal rates, based on volume or value of transfers of goods or services; taxes upon gross receipts, or upon gross income; and related taxes based upon use, storage, production (other than severance of natural resources), importation, or consumption of goods. Dealer discounts of "commissions" allowed to merchants for collection of taxes from consumers are excluded.

Total **general expenditure** includes all city expenditure other than the specifically enumerated kinds of expenditure classified as utility, liquor store, and employee retirement and other insurance trust expenditures.

Capital outlays are direct expenditures for contract or force account construction of buildings, roads, and other improvements, and for purchases of equipment, land, and existing structures. They include amounts for additions, replacements, and major alterations to fixed works and structures. Expenditure for repair to such works and structures, however, is classified as current operation expenditure.

A major portion of capital outlay is commonly financed by borrowing, while governmental revenue does not include receipts from borrowing. Among other things, this distorts the relationship between the totals presented for revenue and expenditure and renders this relationship useless as a direct measure of the degree of budgetary "balance," as that term is generally applied.

Public welfare is defined as support of and assistance to needy persons contingent upon their need. This excludes pensions to former employees and other benefits not contingent upon need. Health and hospital services provided directly by the government through its own hospitals and health agencies, as well as any payments to other governments for such purposes, are classified under those functional headings rather than being included as part of public welfare.

Highways includes construction, maintenance, and operation of highways, streets, and related structures, including toll highways, bridges, tunnels, ferries, street lighting, and snow and ice removal. Not included are highway policing and traffic control, which are considered as part of police protection.

Parking facilities include the construction, purchase, maintenance, and operation of public-use parking lots, garages, parking meters, and other distinctive parking facilities on a commercial basis.

Education includes provision or support of schools and facilities for elementary and secondary, higher, and other education. Elementary and secondary education includes the provision of public kindergarten through high school education by local governments. It encompasses instructional, support, and auxiliary services (school lunch, student activities, and community services) offered by public school systems. Higher education consists of all local institutions of higher education.

Health expenditures include outpatient health services other than hospital care, such as public health administration; research and education; categorical health programs; treatment and immunization clinics; nursing; environmental health activities such as air and water pollution control; ambulance service if provided separately from fire protection services; and other general public health activities such as mosquito abatement. School health services provided by health agencies (rather than school agencies) are included here. Not included are sewage treatment operations, which are classified as part of sewerage and sanitation. Hospital expenditures include financing, construction, acquisition, maintenance and operation of hospital facilities, provision of hospital care, and support of public or private hospitals.

Police protection encompasses expenditures for the preservation of law and order, as well as for traffic safety. It includes police patrols and communications, crime prevention activities, detention and custody of persons awaiting trial, traffic safety, and vehicular inspection.

Sewerage and sanitation includes sanitary and storm sewers, sewage disposal facilities and services, and other government activities for such purposes. Street cleaning and the collection and disposal of garbage and other waste are also included.

Parks and recreation includes cultural and scientific activities such as museums and art galleries; organized recreation, including playgrounds and playing fields, swimming pools, and bathing beaches; and municipal parks and special recreation facilities, such as auditoriums, stadiums, auto camps, recreation piers, and boat harbors.

Housing and community development includes city housing and redevelopment projects and the regulation, promotion, and support of private housing and redevelopment activities. Data from Arizona, Kentucky, Michigan, New Mexico, New York, and Virginia generally include municipal housing authorities. Housing authorities for other cities are usually classified as independent governments, and data for them are not included.

Interest on debt are the amounts paid for the use of borrowed money.

Total **debt** outstanding is the total of all debt obligations remaining unpaid on the date specified.

Utility debt is that portion of outstanding debt originally issued specifically to finance government owned and operated water, electric, gas, or transit utility facilities.

CITY GOVERNMENT EMPLOYMENT, Item 140
Source: U.S. Bureau of the Census— Survey of Governments, 1999: Employment Statistics

The data are from an annual survey conducted by the Bureau of the Census and represent paid employment by city governments during October 1999. Full-time equivalent employment is a computed statistic representing the number of full-time employees that would have been employed if the hours worked by the part-time employees were converted to full-time equivalents.

CLIMATE, Items 141–147
Source: National Oceanic and Atmospheric Administration

All climate data are average values for the 30-year period from 1961-1990.

Mean temperatures for January and July were determined by adding the average daily maximum temperatures and the average daily minimum temperatures and dividing by 2.

Temperature limits represent average daily minimum for January and average daily maximum for July.

Annual precipitation values are the average annual water equivalent of all precipitation for the 30-year period.

Heating and cooling degree days are used as relative measures of the energy required for heating and cooling buildings. One heating degree day is accumulated for each whole degree that the mean daily temperature is below 65 degrees Fahrenheit (i.e., a mean daily temperature of 62 degrees Fahrenheit will produce three heating degree days). Cooling degree days are accumulated in similar fashion for deviations of the mean daily temperature above 65 degrees Fahrenheit.

TABLE E—CONGRESSIONAL DISTRICTS OF THE 105TH CONGRESS

LAND AREA, Items 1–3
Source: U.S. Bureau of the Census

Land area measurements are shown to the nearest square kilometer. Land area includes dry land and land temporarily or partially covered by water, such as marshland, swamps, and river floodplains.

POPULATION, Items 2–3
Source: U.S. Bureau of the Census—
1990 Census of Population and Housing

The population data are based on the 100 percent count from the 1990 census.

POPULATION BY RACE AND HISPANIC ORIGIN, Items 4–9
Source: U.S. Bureau of the Census—
1990 Census of Population and Housing

Population by race, as defined by the Census Bureau, reflects self-identification by respondents; it does not denote any clear-cut scientific definition of biological stock. In the 1990 census, data were obtained through self-classification.

The White population is defined as persons who indicated their race as white, as well as persons who did not classify themselves in one of the specific race categories listed on the questionnaire but entered a nationality such as Canadian, German, Italian, Lebanese, or Polish.

The Black population includes persons who indicated their race as black or Negro, as well as persons who did not classify themselves in one of the specific race categories but reported entries such as Black Puerto Rican, Haitian, Jamaican, Nigerian, or West Indian.

The American Indian, Eskimo, and Aleut population includes persons who indicated their race as Indian (American), Eskimo, or Aleut, as well as persons who did not indicate a specific race category but reported the name of an Indian tribe.

The Asian and Pacific Islander population includes persons who indicated their race as Chinese, Filipino, Japanese, Asian Indian, Korean, Vietnamese, Hawaiian, Samoan, or Guamanian, as well as persons who provided write-in entries of such Asian and Pacific Islander groups as Cambodian, Laotian, Pakistani, and Fiji Islander.

The Hispanic population is based on a complete-count question that asked respondents to identify whether they were of Spanish/Hispanic origin. Persons marking any one of the four Spanish categories (i.e., Mexican, Puerto Rican, Cuban, or Other Spanish) are collectively referred to as Hispanic. Hispanic is not a race category; Hispanic persons may be of any race.

POPULATION—FOREIGN-BORN, Item 10
Source: U.S. Bureau of the Census—
1990 Census of Population and Housing

The foreign-born population is based on birthplace and citizenship questions asked of a sample of persons in the 1990 census. **Foreign-born** includes persons not born in the United States, Puerto Rico, or an outlying area of the United States. Persons who were born in a foreign country but who have at least one American parent are excluded from this category.

POPULATION—CITIZENSHIP, Item 11
Source: U.S. Bureau of the Census—
1990 Census of Population and Housing

Data on citizenship were obtained from a sample of the population. The category U.S. citizen includes native-born persons and foreign-born persons who indicated that they had become naturalized citizens.

POPULATION—AGE, Items 12–20
Source: U.S. Bureau of the Census—
1990 Census of Population and Housing

Age derived from the census (1990) is classified as age at last birthday (i.e., number of completed years from birth to April 1). The percent figures are derived by dividing the number of persons in a specified age group by the total population of a given geographic area.

POPULATION—PERCENT FEMALE, Item 21
Source: U.S. Bureau of the Census—
1990 Census of Population and Housing

The female population of a geographic area is shown as a percent of the total population of the area.

HOUSEHOLDS, Items 22–25
Source: U.S. Bureau of the Census—
1990 Census of Population and Housing

A household consists of persons occupying a single housing unit. A housing unit is a house, an apartment, a group of rooms, or a single room occupied as separate living quarters. The occupants may be a single family, 1 person living alone, 2 or more families living together, or any other group of related or unrelated persons sharing a housing unit. The number of households is the same as the number of year-round occupied housing units.

A family household consists of 2 or more persons, including the householder, who are related by birth, marriage, or adoption and who live together as 1 household; all such persons are considered as members of 1 family.

The measure of persons per household is obtained by dividing the number of persons in households by the number of households or householders. The category **female family householder** includes only female-headed family households with no spouse present.

PERSONS IN MENTAL HOSPITALS, Item 26
**Source: U.S. Bureau of the Census—
1990 Census of Population and Housing**

Mental (Psychiatric) hospitals include psychiatric wards of general hospitals and veterans' hospitals and hospitals or wards for the criminally insane not operated by a prison. Patients receive supervised medical/nursing care from formally-trained staff.

PERSONS IN NURSING HOMES, Item 27
**Source: U.S. Bureau of the Census—
1990 Census of Population and Housing**

Nursing homes comprise a heterogeneous group of places. The majority of patients are elderly, although persons who require nursing care because of chronic physical conditions may be found in these homes regardless of their age. Included in this category are skilled-nursing facilities, intermediate-care facilities, long-term care rooms in wards or buildings on the grounds of hospitals, or long-term care rooms/nursing wings in congregate housing facilities. Also included are nursing, convalescent, and rest homes, such as soldiers', sailors', veterans', and fraternal or religious homes for the aged, with or without nursing care.

PERSONS IDENTIFIED AS HOMELESS, Item 28
**Source: U.S. Bureau of the Census—
1990 Census of Population and Housing**

Persons identified as homeless include persons in emergency shelters for homeless persons (with sleeping facilities) and persons visible in street locations. This includes persons enumerated during the 1990 Census "Shelter-and-Street-Night" operation. Enumerators were instructed not to ask if a person was "homeless." A person at 1 of these locations was counted as homeless.

EDUCATION—SCHOOL ENROLLMENT AND EDUCATIONAL ATTAINMENT, Items 29–32
**Source: U.S. Bureau of the Census—
1990 Census of Population and Housing**

Data on school enrollment and educational attainment were derived from a sample of the population. Persons were classified as enrolled in school if they reported attending a "regular" public or private school (or college) at any time between February 1, 1990 and the time of enumeration. The instructions were to "include only nursery school, kindergarten, elementary school, and schooling which would lead to a high school diploma or a college degree" as regular school. Public school is defined as "any school or college controlled and supported by a local, county, state, or federal government." Schools supported and controlled primarily by religious organizations or other private groups are defined as

private. Statistics for years of school completed are for persons 25 years old and over. The data were derived from a question on the 1990 census questionnaire that asked respondents for the highest level of school they had completed or the highest degree they had received. Persons who passed a high school equivalency examination were considered high school graduates. Schooling received in foreign schools was to be reported as the equivalent grade or years in the regular American school system.

MONEY INCOME, Items 33–35
**Source: U.S. Bureau of the Census—
1990 Census of Population and Housing**

The data on income are derived from the responses of a sample of persons 15 years old and older. **Total money income** is defined by the Bureau of the Census for statistical purposes as the sum of the following: wage or salary income; nonfarm self-employment income; net farm self-employment income; Social Security and railroad retirement income; public assistance income; and all other regularly received income such as interest, dividends, veterans' payments, pensions, unemployment compensation, and alimony. Receipts not counted as income include various "lump sum" payments such as capital gains or inheritances.

The total represents the amount of income received before deductions for personal income taxes, Social Security, bond purchases, union dues, Medicare deductions, etc.

Per capita income is based on resident population enumerated as of April 1, 1990.

Income of households includes the income of the householder and all other persons 15 years old and older in the household. Median household income is usually less than median family income because many households consist of only 1 person. The median divides the income distribution into 2 equal parts, 1 having incomes above the median, the other with incomes below.

The constant-dollar figures are based on an annual average Consumer Price Index from the Bureau of Labor Statistics. Constant-dollar figures are estimates representing an effort to remove the effects of price changes from statistical series reported in dollar terms. However, the estimates do not reflect the price and cost-of-living differences that may exist between areas.

POVERTY, Items 36–37
**Source: U.S. Bureau of the Census—
1990 Census of Population and Housing**

The data on poverty are derived from the same questions as the data on money income. Poverty status is based on the definition prescribed by the Federal Office of Management and Budget as the standard to be used by federal agencies for statistical purposes. Families and persons are classified as being below the poverty level if their total family income or unrelated individual income was less than the poverty threshold specified for the applicable family size, age of householder, and number of related children present under 18. Poverty status is determined for all families (and by implication all family members). For persons not in families, poverty status is determined by their income in relation to the appropriate poverty threshold. Inmates of institutions, persons in military group quarters or college dormitories, and unrelated individuals under 15 are excluded.

The 1989 poverty thresholds are shown in Figure 1.

Figure 1.
Poverty Thresholds in 1989 by Size of Family

Size of Family Unit	Weighted average thresholds
One person (unrelated individual)	$6,310
Under 65 years	6,451
65 years and over	5,947
Two persons	8,076
Householder under 65 years	8,343
Householder 65 years and over	7,501
Three persons	9,885
Four persons	12,674
Five persons	14,990
Six persons	16,921
Seven persons	19,162
Eight persons	21,328
Nine or more persons	25,480

HOUSING, Items 38–46
Source: U.S. Bureau of the Census— 1990 Census of Population and Housing

A **housing unit** is a house, apartment, mobile home or trailer, group of rooms, or single room occupied or, if vacant, intended for occupancy as separate living quarters. Separate living quarters are those in which the occupants do not live and eat with any other persons in the structure and which have direct access from the outside of the building through a common hall.

The occupants of a housing unit may be a single family, 1 person living alone, 2 or more families living together, or any other group of related or unrelated persons who share living arrangements (except as described in the definition for persons "living in group quarters"). For vacant units, the criteria of separateness and direct access are applied to the intended occupants whenever possible. If that information cannot be obtained, the criteria are applied to the previous occupants. Both occupied and vacant housing units are included in the housing inventory, except that recreational vehicles, tents, caves, boats, railroad cars, and the like are included only if they are occupied as someone's usual place of residence.

A housing unit is classified as occupied if it is the usual place of residence of the person or group of persons living in it at the time of enumeration, or if the occupants are only temporarily absent (e.g., away on vacation). A household consists of all persons who occupy a housing unit as their usual place of residence.

The percent change represents the difference in the number of total housing units in a specified area over the decade 1980-1990.

Median value is the dollar amount that divides the distribution of owner occupied housing units into 2 equal parts, with one half of the units falling below this value and the other half exceeding it. Value is defined as the respondent's estimate of what the house would sell for if it were for sale. Data are presented for 1-family units on less than 10 acres and with no business or medical office on the property.

Median rent divides the distribution of renter-occupied housing units into 2 equal parts. Median rent represents the amount of cash rent a renter pays (contract rent) plus the estimated average cost of utilities and fuels if paid by the renter (gross rent). Rent is to be reported only for living quarters, not for any business or other space occupied. Single family houses on lots of 10 or more acres are excluded.

Housing cost as a percent of income is shown separately for owners with mortgages, owners without mortgages, and renters. Rent as a percentage of income is a computed ratio of gross rent and monthly household income (total household income in 1989 divided by 12). Selected owner costs include utilities and fuels, as well as mortgage payments, insurance, taxes, etc. In each case, the ratio of housing cost to income is computed separately for each housing unit. The ratio for one-half of the units is above the median shown in this book, and one-half is below.

Substandard units are occupied units which are overcrowded or lack complete plumbing facilities. For the purposes of this item "overcrowded" is defined as having 1.01 persons or more per room. Complete plumbing facilities include hot and cold piped water, a flush toilet, and a bathtub or shower. These facilities must be located inside the housing unit but not necessarily in the same room.

CIVILIAN LABOR FORCE, UNEMPLOYMENT, EMPLOYMENT, Items 47–52
Source: U.S. Bureau of the Census— 1990 Census of Population and Housing

All data pertain to persons 16 years of age and over. The civilian labor force consists of persons classified as either employed or unemployed in accordance with the criteria described below.

Unemployment data include all persons who did not work during the survey week, made specific efforts to find a job in the prior 4 weeks, and were available for work during the survey week (except for temporary illness). Persons waiting to be called back to a job from which they had been laid off and those waiting to report to a new job within the next 30 days are included in unemployment figures.

Total employment includes all civilians who were either (1) "at work" — those who did any work at all during the reference week as paid employees, worked in their own business or profession, worked on their own farm, or worked 15 hours or more as unpaid workers in a family farm or business; or were (2) "with a job but not at work" — those who had a job but were not at work that week due to illness, weather, industrial dispute, vacation, or other personal reasons.

The occupation categories shown are consistent with the 1980 edition of the *Standard Occupational Classification Manual (SOC)*, published by the Office of Federal Statistical Policy and Standards, U.S. Department of Commerce. Professional, managerial, and technical occupations include the following categories: executive, administrative, and managerial occupations (000-042); professional specialty occupations (043-202); and technicians and related support occupations (203-242). Precision production, craft and repair includes SOC codes 503-702.

WORK DISABILITY, Item 53
Source: U.S. Bureau of the Census—
1990 Census of Population and Housing

Data are shown for persons 16 to 64 years old in 1990. Persons were identified as having a work disability if they reported a health condition that had lasted 6 months or more and which limited the kind or amount of work they could do at a job or business.